THE OFFICIAL ENCYCLOPEDIA OF MAJOR LEAGUE BASEBALL

TOTAL BASEBALL

SIXTH EDITION

EDITED BY

JOHN THORN, PETE PALMER,

MICHAEL GERSHMAN, AND DAVID PIETRUSZA

WITH MATTHEW SILVERMAN AND SEAN LAHMAN

Published by Total Sports, 445 Park Avenue, New York, New York 10022

For information about permission to reproduce selections from this book, please write to: Permissions, Total Sports, 105 Abeel Street, Kingston, New York 12401

Total Sports™ is a trademark of Total Sports, Inc.
Total Baseball™ is a trademark of Total Sports, Inc.

This edition published in 1999 by Total Sports

10 9 8 7 6 5 4 3 2 1

Official Publication—Major League Baseball

ISBN 1-892129-03-5
CIP data available

This book is printed on acid-free paper.

Printed in United States of America
Set in Times Roman
Designed by Marc Cheshire

Contents

PART TWO

The Registers, Leaders, and Rosters

Appendixes

Acknowledgments

This sixth edition of *Total Baseball* could not have been published without legions of writers, researchers, editors, designers, and production people. The principal contributors in these areas are credited in the table of contents; others may be acknowledged within the text or in the separate introductions to the various sections of Part 2.

Since the last edition of *Total Baseball,* we merged with Koz Sports of Raleigh, N.C. to become Total Sports and published the first editions of both *Total Football* and *Total Hockey,* the official encyclopedias of the NFL and NHL. Our warmest thanks to Frank Daniels, George Schlukbier, and the many men and women in Raleigh and Kingston, N.Y. who have helped us realize our dream of becoming publishers. Moreover, this alliance enabled us to augment our web site, totalbaseball.com, with up-to-the-minute news and TotalCasts™ of every Major League Baseball game under the direction of Eric "Zonker" Harris, Gary Bell, Gaylen Duskey, and Gary Gillette as well as our national network of correspondents.

Also new to our lineup this edition are Don Hintze, Director of Publications at Major League Baseball, and rookie editor Sean Lahman. They both added a fresh eye to the book and helped to improve it in numerous ways. We also stocked our bullpen by adding Peter Haugen, Jackie Azoulay, and Connie Neuhauser.

We owe our stylish jacket to Todd Radom with assists from Donna Harris and Chad Lawrence. F-stop Fitzgerald helped with production advice, and Peggy Goddard and Jed Thorn exercised their eagle eyes in post-production. If you picked up this copy of *Total Baseball* at your local bookstore, the credit goes to our newest ally, Publishers Group West, and their able sales force, and Quebecor, which printed the book.

We were fortunate to extend our relationship with Starkey & Henricks, which has been the typographer for every edition of *Total Baseball.* To Peter and Doug Bird, and Peter Compton, George Galgoczi, and Ellen Curcio go our admiration and gratitude.

Marc Cheshire's splendid design for the first edition has stood the test of time, and Gypsy da Silva earned the *croix de guerre* for her production work on the second. Jacquie Roland was important to the third edition, as Ray Shaw was to the fourth, and adding James Charlton's day-by-day history of baseball has informed the Annual Record in both editions five and six.

We will also not forget our friends at Sony and the pioneers at CMC (Creative Multimedia Corporation), both of whom published *Total Baseball* in electronic form way back in 1991, Microsoft, which incorporated much of this work in its *Complete Baseball,* and Franklin Electronic Publishing and Headland Digital Media, which also enlarged our audience.

We are forever indebted to David Reuther, whose contributions to the editorial, production, and business aspects of the first two editions of *Total Baseball* were truly awesome.

For research help, particularly into the years before 1920, we extend heartfelt thanks (alphabetically) to the Society for American Baseball Research colleagues Bill Carle, Bob McConnell, David Neft, Bob Tiemann, and Frank Williams. Bill Carle helped us with biographical data, especially debut dates. Bob McConnell lent his personal expertise and his knowledge of the John Tattersall research collection to clear up a variety of perplexing areas. David Neft supplied us with heretofore unknown RBI data for the National League of 1880-1885 and inspired us by his example, as the man who headed the Information Concepts, Inc., team that produced *The Baseball Encyclopedia* of 1969. Bob Tiemann provided game scores and sites for a host of pre-1900 games that were most helpful in deriving, for the first time, home-road stats for the 19th century; he also headed the SABR research project that yielded new National Association data. And Frank Williams continued his remarkable efforts in correcting pitcher won-lost records before 1920. Since our debut in 1989, an army of readers has taken us up on our invitation to write with their corrections and suggestions, from the mathematical to the typographical; we thank them in the aggregate here and list them by name in the Notes on Contributors near the end of the book.

Deserving of special mention here, however, is Tim Cashion, whose amazingly thorough review of recent editions has made *Total Baseball* as close to error-free as human frailty will permit.

And last, we thank some giants of baseball research whose work informs these pages but who are no longer with us to receive the tribute: in no particular order, Ernie Lanigan, John Tattersall, S.C. Thompson, Alex Haas, Preston D. Orem, Len Gettelson, Lee Allen, and Harold Seymour.

The Editors

This book is dedicated to the home run kings,
who have led all major league players either for a single season,
or, for an entire career:

Hank Aaron

Dan Brouthers

Roger Connor

George Hall

Charley Jones

Roger Maris

Mark McGwire

Babe Ruth

Harry Stovey

Ned Williamson

Honorable Mention—Sammy Sosa

Introduction

When it first appeared, in 1989, *Total Baseball* was the most complete, most authoritative, and most informative—not to mention the biggest—baseball book ever published. It came into being because its creators saw that there was nothing else like it and because its publishers had faith that fans would want such a book—a virtual baseball library in one volume. In fact, it could be said that *Total Baseball* is the first true baseball encyclopedia because it offers not only the game's numbers but also the stories and statistical principles that underlie them.

In this sixth edition, *Total Baseball* builds upon that foundation to provide new stories, new stats, and a thorough review of all the data that went into the first five editions. We welcomed, in a dramatic new development, the endorsement of *Total Baseball* by Major League Baseball as the official encyclopedia of the game in 1995, and we are pleased to continue our partnership in this edition.

This book is divided into two parts. The first consists of prose features on subjects of interest to all baseball fans, from the general reader who wishes to know more about the game's trivia and lore to the advanced fan who wants to know about its humble beginnings in other countries. The origins of the farm system; complete balloting for the Hall of Fame and major awards; ballparks; women in baseball . . . but why tease you with the pleasures that await?

Simply be assured that *Total Baseball* will be totally absorbing. The writers gathered together here are experts in their fields, as befits an encyclopedic reference work, and even the most erudite reader will learn countless new things about our great game.

The same holds true for Part 2, which contains the playing and pitching registers, a variety of rosters, a year-by-year statistical summary of major league play since 1871, and more. The stats will please the devotee of sabermetrics, who can use the Total Player Ranking to compare Mark McGwire's record-shattering 1998 season against Roger Maris' legendary 1961 season—or the reader can add both those performances together and find that it just surpasses Babe Ruth's best season. The traditional computations will appeal to baseball scholars, who know what a tangle of briars the historical record has become over the last two decades, as individual player records have been altered without corresponding changes to other players on the same team. (For more on this, see the essay, "The History of Major League Baseball Statistics.") And the cornucopia of stats old and new of baseball's 15,000 players—for everyone from all-time leaders to cup-of-coffee nonentities—will provide days, months, and years of archaeological delight for baseball fans of all stripes.

Total Baseball joins the game's most knowledgeable writers, most of them members of the Society for American Baseball Research (SABR), with the game's great historical database, the one built up over two decades by Pete Palmer. Benefiting from the painstaking research of hundreds of friends and colleagues in SABR, we have corrected many errors and omissions in other reference works, relying not upon the numbers enshrined by tradition or official edict but upon the evidence. How many hours have been spent scanning the handwritten official records of the early years of the century, or reviewing box scores and scoresheets and game summaries! It would have been easier not to bother, to accept, for example, a game mistakenly entered twice in the record for 1910 so that Ty Cobb could keep his career total of 4,191 hits. But there can be no statute of limitations on historical error; the researcher and historian must go where the evidence leads them.

This book is as good as we know how to make it, but we do want to hear from you about our blunders (we know there will be some, as there were in the previous editions) or about your research (which may be as important to subsequent editions of *Total Baseball* as that of, say, Joe Wayman was for the fourth). We believe that history is process, not product, and our aim has been for *Total Baseball* to reflect the state of the art in baseball research and to convey its editors' love for the game.

## CHAPTER 1

Our Game

John Thorn

Baseball has been, most often for better but occasionally for worse, the American game. It has given our people rest and recreation, myths and memories, heroes and history and hope. It has mirrored our society, sometimes propelling it with models for democracy, community, commerce, and common humanity, sometimes lagging behind with equally instructive models of futility and resistance to change. And as our national game, baseball in no small measure defines us as Americans, connecting us with our countrymen across all barriers of generation, class, race, and creed.

Baseball in the Americas is more than a game, an observation to which the scope of this book is testimony and tribute. But it is first and foremost about *play*, a fact obscured amid today's ferment of free agency, salary caps, and sky boxes. Some 150 years ago, an overly solemn America was first indebted to baseball for the freedom it gave to play. As overture to this volume's chronicle of baseball's history, let's look at how child's play came to be our national pastime.

America Learns to Play

Even when baseball was in its infancy in the 1850s—having just evolved from the boyhood game of rounders and its more formalized derivative, town ball—the sport was already shaping the life of the country. Americans of the previous generation had been blind to the virtue of play, much perplexing our European cousins. We permitted ourselves few amusements that could not be justified in terms of social or business utility, or "seriousness." Nonconformists like the Olympic Town Ball Club of Philadelphia in the 1830s had to put up with a lot of guff, as this contemporary account details:

The first day that the Philadelphia men took the field . . . only four men were found to play, so they started in by playing a game called cat ball. All the players were over twenty-five years of age, and to see them playing a game like this caused much merriment among the friends of the players. It required "sand" in those days to go out on the field and play, as the prejudice against the game was very great. It took nearly a whole season to get men enough together to make a team, owing to the ridicule heaped upon the players for taking part in such childish sports.

What brought scorn upon the heads of these staunch devotees of town ball (also known as "Boston Ball" or the "Massachusetts Game") was that although the game had regularly positioned fielders and demanded a modicum of strategic play, it still bore the childish essence of rounders: the retirement of a baserunner by throwing the ball *at* him, which necessitated a softer, less resilient ball than that used in the manly sport of cricket.

Who was the genius who came up with the idea of retiring a runner by touching him with the ball or securing it "in the hands of an adversary on the base"? Perhaps it was Alexander Cartwright, who is known to many as "the man who invented baseball," though baseball was not invented; it evolved. But it may have been Daniel Lucius Adams or William Wheaton or Lewis F. Wadsworth.

No matter—this was the first step toward making an American game that could challenge boys and men alike, and that could take its place in the life of our nation as cricket had done in England. Henry Chadwick, the English-born cricket reporter who coined the term "national pastime" and became known as the "Father of Baseball," wrote that early on he

. . . was struck with the idea that base ball was just the game for a national sport for Americans and . . . that from this game of ball a powerful lever might be made by which our people could be lifted into a position of more devotion to physical exercise and healthful out-door recreation than they had, hitherto, been noted for. . . . In fact, as is well-known, we were the regular target for the shafts of raillery and even abuse from our outdoor-sport-loving cousins of England, in consequence of our national neglect of sports and pastimes, and our too great devotion to business and the "Almighty Dollar." But thanks to Base Ball . . . we have been transformed into quite another people. . . .

The transformation was from a hard-working but grim citizenry to a nation devoted to fresh air and exercise, not unlike the current rage for jogging, aerobics, and body building. Amateur baseball clubs sprang up like dandelions in the years immediately before the Civil War, but these were formed more for camaraderie and calisthenics than the pursuit of victory or the honing of skills. The demands of the new game on athleticism were few, as the one-bound rule remained in effect (an out was recorded if a ball was caught on a bounce), and a couple of weeks' practice were enough to make a novice of forty a creditable player.

Men viewed baseball as a mild pastime, or relief from the mental strains of work; as a tonic, restorative of the physical energies needed for work; or as a release of the

surplus nervous energy that impedes young men in their pursuit of purposeful work. America in the mid-1850s was learning how to play, but still viewed sport in terms of its salutary effects on commerce; not until the close of the War Between the States would the focus shift to learning how to play well—for its own sake.

The Charm of the Game

Today we think of baseball as an anachronism, a last vestige of America's agrarian paradise—an idyllic game that takes us back to a more innocent time. But baseball originated in New York City, not rural Cooperstown, and in truth it was an exercise in nostalgia from the beginning. Alexander Cartwright and his Knickerbockers began play in Madison Square in 1842, and the city's northward progress soon compelled them to move uptown to Murray Hill.

When the grounds there were also threatened by the march of industry, the Knicks ferried across the Hudson River to the Elysian Fields of Hoboken, a landscaped retreat of picnic grounds and scenic vistas that was designed by its proprietors to relieve New Yorkers of city air and city care. In other words, the purpose of baseball's primal park was the same as that of New York's Central Park or, much later, Boston's Fenway Park—to give an increasingly urban populace a park within the city, a place reminiscent of the idealized farms that had sent all these lads to the metropolis.

Thus the attraction of the game in its earliest days was first the novelty and exhilaration of play; second the opportunity for deskbound city clerks to expend surplus energy in a sylvan setting, freed from the tyranny of the clock; and third, to harmonize with an American golden age that was almost entirely legendary.

Simple charms, simple pleasures. In the late 1860s, advancing skills led to heightened appetites for victory, which led to hot pursuit of the game's gifted players, which inevitably led to *sub rosa* payments and, by 1870, rampant professionalism. (Doesn't that chain reaction put one in mind of college football or basketball?) The gentlemanly players of baseball's first generation retreated from the field, shaking their heads in dismay at how greed had perverted the "grand old game"—now barely 20 years old—and probably ruined it forever.

Sound familiar? It should—the same dire and premature announcements of the demise of the game have been issued ever since, spurred by free-agent signings, long-term contracts, no-trade provisions, strikes and lockouts, integration, night ball, rival leagues, ad infinitum. The only conclusions a calm head might draw from this recurring cycle of disdain for the present and glorification of the past are that (a) things aren't what they used to be and never were; (b) accurate assessment of a present predicament is impossible, for it requires perspective; and (c) no matter what the owners or players or rulesmakers or fans do, they can't kill baseball. All three conclusions are correct. In baseball, the distinction between amateur and professional is not clear-cut: an amateur may play for devotion to the game (*amat* being the Latin for he loves), but a professional does not play for pursuit of gain alone; he plays for love, too.

Oh, don't you remember the game of base-ball we saw twenty years ago played,
When contests were true, and the sight free to all, and home-runs in plenty were made?
When we lay on the grass, and with thrills of delight, watched the ball squarely pitched at the bat,
And easily hit, and then mount out of sight along with our cheers and our hat?
And then, while the fielders raced after the ball, the men on the bases flew round,
And came in together—four batters in all. Ah! That was the old game renowned.
Now salaried pitchers, who throw the ball curved at padded and masked catchers lame
And gate-money music and seats all reserved is all that is left of the game.
Oh, give us the glorious matches of old, when love of true sport made them great,
And not this new-fashioned affair always sold for the boodle they take at the gate.

H. C. Dodge

That doomsday ditty was published in 1886.

The National Pastime

America before the Civil War was still populated by a handful of veterans of the Revolutionary War and many who remembered vividly the War of 1812. The era of Anglo-American amity had not yet dawned; our country's spiritual separation from the Mother Country, though effected by treaty in 1783, was still in process. And having baseball to rival and replace cricket was an important step in that process. Moreover when England, seeking to maintain its supply of cotton from the American South, appeared over-cordial to the Confederate cause, anti-British feeling swept the North. An America long suffering from an inferiority complex toward England now turned against cricket and embraced baseball with increased fervor.

From 1856 on, Henry Chadwick had been eager for baseball to rise to the status in America that cricket held in his native England. He championed the game tirelessly, helping to refine its rules and practices to make it the equal of cricket as a "manly" and "scientific" game. And baseball soon became, in his words, like cricket "a game requiring the mental powers of judgment, calculation and quick perception to excel in it—while in its demands upon the vigor, endurance and courage of manhood, its requirements excel those requisite to become equally expert as a cricketer."

Chadwick invented a method of scorekeeping and statistical compilation patterned on those which were inaugurated in cricket. Baseball was an elemental game—pitch, hit, catch, throw—like other games of ball; but keeping records of the contests and later printing box scores and individual averages elevated it from rounders and placed it on an equal footing with its transatlantic counterpart. (As important, the records served to legitimize men's concern with what had been merely a boys' exercise by making it more systematic, like the numerically annotated world of business.) Today a baseball with-

out records is inconceivable: They are what keep Babe Ruth and Ty Cobb and Walter Johnson alive in our minds in a way that President James K. Polk, Walter Reed, or Admiral Dewey—arguably greater men—are not.

By the end of the Civil War cricket in this country remained a pastime for a shrinking band of Anglophiles, while the New York Game of Baseball (as it was then called to differentiate it from the nearly vanished Massachusetts Game) was spreading across the country, courtesy of returning veterans whose first exposure to baseball might have come in a prisoner-of-war camp. In the press, baseball was typically proclaimed The National Game—the same term Britons used for cricket.

Play for Pay

From its creation in 1871 to its crash five years later, the National Association had a rocky time as America's first professional league. Franchises came and went with dizzying speed, often folding in midseason. Schedules were not played out if a club slated to go on the road saw little prospect of gain. Drinking and gambling and game-fixing were rife. And the Boston Red Stockings of Al Spalding and the Wright brothers dominated play, going 71-8 in the last of their four straight championship seasons; their predictable and one-sided victories crushed the competition and, at last, interest in the entire circuit.

But from the ashes of the National Association emerged the Red Stockings' model of success and the entrepreneurial genius of Chicago's William Hulbert. After raiding Boston to obtain four of the biggest stars in the game—Spalding, Ross Barnes, Deacon White, and Cal McVey—and lining up the services of the Philadelphia Athletics' Adrian "Cap" Anson, the White Stockings were ready to roll in the National League of Professional Base Ball Clubs, founded on Feb. 2, 1876 in New York's Grand Central Hotel.

The first five years of the NL were nearly as unsettled as the final years of the NA, with franchises appearing and then disappearing in such cities as Syracuse, Indianapolis, and Hartford while major cities like New York and Philadelphia were, after the league's inaugural year, unrepresented. In 1878 the fledgling circuit was forced to cut back to six teams: Milwaukee, Indianapolis, Chicago, Providence, Cincinnati, and Boston. *National* League? *National* Game? It seemed Americans had plenty of appetite for playing the game, but not much for watching it.

Yet as the National League suffered with growing pains, it was introducing some elements that were critical to the explosion of interest that came with the 1880s. It created a professional (paid) umpiring crew; insisted that the league schedule be honored; banned pool selling and hard-liquor consumption in the stands; and created a system of management-owned teams as opposed to the player-run cooperatives that had largely characterized the NA. As the public's renewed faith in the integrity of the game coincided with an upswing in the national economy, not only did the National League flourish; along came an interloper, the rival American Association, to offer patrons 25-cent baseball (NL admissions were 50 cents), Sunday games, and beer. With the public's new appetite for the game seeming insatiable, a group of investors led by St. Louis' Henry Lucas launched a *third* major league, the Union Association, for 1884.

As brash stars like Cap Anson, Tim Keefe, Dan Brouthers, and the larger-than-life King Kelly captured the newspaper headlines and the nation's imagination, the age of the baseball idol arrived. Before this decade, men like Jim Creighton, Joe Start, and George Wright had been admired in New York and New England, but now a baseball hero's image could be mass-produced for nationwide sale, or licensed for advertising, or inspire odes and songs. Kelly inspired "Slide, Kelly, Slide," its arcane references now largely forgotten but once the most popular song in the land:

> *Slide, Kelly, slide!*
> *Your running's a disgrace!*
> *Slide, Kelly, slide!*
> *Stay there, hold your base!*
> *If someone doesn't steal ya,*
> *And your batting doesn't fail ya,*
> *They'll take you to Australia!*
> *Slide, Kelly, slide!*

And although Ernest Lawrence Thayer always denied it, Kelly could well have been the model for "Casey at the Bat," the immortal lyric ballad Thayer penned in 1888. ("Casey" was sometimes reprinted in the newspapers of the 1880s as "Kelly at the Bat," changing the locale from Mudville to Beantown.)

Baseball was ascendant in the 1880s, and like the budding nation whose pastime it was, pretty cocksure of itself. In the same year that "Casey" made his debut, Albert Spalding led a contingent of baseball players on a round the world tour, spreading the gospel of bat and ball to such places as Egypt, Italy, England, Hawaii, and the above-mentioned Australia. Baseball, America thought, was too grand a game to be merely a national pastime; it ought to be the international pastime.

At a New York banquet for Spalding's returning "world tourists" in 1889, speaker Mark Twain declared, "Baseball is the very symbol, the outward and visible expression of the drive and push and rush and struggle of the raging, tearing, booming nineteenth century." Spalding himself later wrote:

I claim that Base Ball owes its prestige as our National Game to the fact that as no other form of sport it is the exponent of American Courage, Confidence, Combativeness; American Dash, Discipline, Determination; American Energy, Eagerness, Enthusiasm; American Pluck, Persistency, Performance; American Spirit, Sagacity, Success; American Vim, Vigor, Virility.

In fact baseball had become more than the mere reflection of our rising industrial and political power and its propensity for bluster and hokum: the national game was beginning to *supply* emblems for democracy, industry, and community that would change America and the world—not in the ways that Spalding's Tourists may have envisioned, but indisputably for the better.

A Model Institution

Father Henry Chadwick had been typically prescient when he wrote in 1876, the inaugural year of the National League and the centenary of America's birth:

What Cricket is to an Englishman, Base-Ball has become to an American. . . . On the Cricket-field—and there only—the Peer and the Peasant meet on equal terms; the possession of courage, nerve, judgment, skill, endurance and activity alone giving the palm of superiority. In fact, a more democratic institution does not exist in Europe than this self-same Cricket; and as regards its popularity, the records of the thousands of Commoners, Divines and Lawyers, Legislators and Artisans, and Literateurs as well as Mechanics and Laborers, show how great a hold it has on the people. If this is the characteristic of Cricket in aristocratic and monarchical England, how much more will the same characteristics mark Base-Ball in democratic and republican America.

Chadwick's vision of baseball as a model democratic institution would have to wait for the turn of the century to be fully articulated, and for Jackie Robinson and Branch Rickey to be fully realized. But Chadwick's belief that baseball could be more than a game, could become a model of and for American life, presaged baseball's golden age of 1903-1930.

The tumultuous 1890s witnessed a player revolt against high-handed and monopolistic management, epitomized by a cap on salaries, followed by a nearly ruinous contraction from three major leagues to one 12-team circuit. The national economy suffered a panic in 1893 and a sluggish recovery thereafter; baseball attendance dwindled; and the lack of postseason interleague competition after 1890 (as there had been since 1884) was sorely felt. The game was in a period of consolidation, or hibernation, or stagnation; one's perspective depended upon whether he were an owner, fan, or player.

But then Ban Johnson came along, fired by the same vision of a rival league that had inflamed the Players League and the American and Union Associations before him, and that would beckon to the Federal and Continental Leagues later on. With the declaration by the American League that it would conduct business as a major league in 1901, and the signing of a peace treaty with the Nationals two years later, the World Series was resumed, prosperity returned, and the popularity and influence of the game exploded.

Baseball mania seized America as new heroes like Christy Mathewson, Honus Wagner, Ty Cobb, Walter Johnson, and Nap Lajoie found a public hungry for knowledge of their every action, their every thought. A fan's affiliation with his team could exceed in vigor his attachment to his church, his trade, his political party—all but family and country, and even these were wrapped up in baseball. The national pastime became the great repository of national ideals, the symbol of all that was good in American life: fair play (sportsmanship); the rule of law (objective arbitration of disputes); equal opportunity (each side has its innings); the brotherhood of man (bleacher harmony); and more.

The baseball boom of the early twentieth century built on the game's simple charms of exercise and communal celebration, adding the psychological and social complexities of vicarious play: civic pride, role models, and hero worship. It became routine for the President to throw out the first ball of the season. Supreme Court Justices had inning-by-inning scores from the World Series relayed to their chambers. Business leaders, perhaps disingenuously, praised baseball as a model of competition and fair play. "Baseball," opined a writer for *American Magazine* in 1913, "has given our public a fine lesson in commercial morals. . . . Some day all business will be reorganized and conducted by baseball standards."

Leaders of recent immigrant groups advised their peoples to learn the national game if they wanted to become Americans, and foreign-language newspapers devoted space to educating their readers about America's strange and wonderful game. (New York's *Staats-Zeitung,* for example, applauded *Kraftiges Schlagen*—hard hitting—and cautioned German fans not to kill the *Unparteiischer.*) As historian Harold Seymour wrote, "The argot of baseball supplied a common means of communication and strengthened the bond which the game helped to establish among those sorely in need of it—the mass of urban dwellers and immigrants living in the anonymity and impersonal vortex of large industrial cities. . . . With the loss of the traditional ties known in a rural society, baseball gave to many the feeling of belonging." And rooting for a baseball team permitted city folk, newcomers and native-born, the sense of pride in community that in former times—when they may have lived in small towns—was commonplace.

Thus baseball offered a model of how to be an American, to be part of the team: Baseball was "second only to death as a leveler," wrote essayist Allen Sangree. Even in those horrifically leveling years of 1941-1945, when so many of our bravest and best gave their lives to defend American ideals, baseball's role as a vital enterprise was confirmed by President Franklin Delano Roosevelt's "green light" for continued play. Many of baseball's finest players—Ted Williams, Joe DiMaggio, Hank Greenberg, Bob Feller, to name a few—swapped their baseball gear for Uncle Sam's, and served with military distinction or helped to boost the nation's morale. Even oldtimers like Babe Ruth, Walter Johnson, and Ty Cobb donned uniforms in service of their country—baseball uniforms, as they staged exhibitions on behalf of war bonds. Servicemen overseas looked to letters from home and the box scores in *The Sporting News* to keep them in touch with what they had left behind, and what they were fighting for—an American way of life that was a beacon for a world in which the light of freedom had been nearly extinguished.

I was one of the countless immigrants who from the 1860s on saw baseball as the "open sesame" to the door of their adopted land. A Polish Jew born in occupied Germany to Holocaust survivors, I arrived on these shores at age 2. After checking in at Ellis Island, I happened by chance to spend the first night in my new land in the no-longer-elegant hotel where in 1876 the National League had been founded. I learned to read by studying the backs of Topps baseball cards, and to be an American by attaching myself passionately to the Brooklyn Dodgers (who also taught me about the fickleness of love).

The Brooklyn Dodgers, in the persons particularly of Rickey and Robinson, also taught America a lesson: that baseball's integrative and democratic models, by the 1940s long held to be verities, were hollow at the core. David Halberstam has written:

. . . it was part of our folklore, basic to our national democratic myth, that sports was the great American equalizer, that money and social status did not matter upon the playing fields. Elsewhere life was assumed to be unfair: those who had privilege passed it on to their children, who in turn had easier, softer lives. Those without privilege were doomed to accept the essential injustices of daily life. But according to the American myth, in sports the poor but honest kid from across the tracks could gain (often in competition with richer, snottier kids) recognition and acclaim for his talents.

Until Oct. 23, 1945, when Robinson signed a contract to play for the Montreal Royals, Brooklyn's top farm club, the myth as far as African Americans were concerned was not a sustaining legend but a mere falsehood.

Rickey's rectitude and Robinson's courage have become central parables of baseball and America, exemplars of decency and strength that inspire all of us. Their "great experiment" came too late for such heroes of black ball as Josh Gibson and Oscar Charleston and Ray Dandridge, but its success has been complete. Once the integrative or leveling model of baseball—all America playing and working in harmony—was extended to African Americans, the effect on the nation was profound. Eighty years after the Civil War, America had proved itself unable to practice the values for which it was fought; baseball showed the way. This is what Commissioner Ford Frick said to the St. Louis Cardinals, rumored to be planning a strike in May 1947:

If you do this you will be suspended from the league. You will find that the friends you think you have in the press box will not support you, that you will be outcasts. I do not care if half the league strikes. Those who do it will encounter quick retribution. They will be suspended and I don't care if it wrecks the National League for five years. This is the United States of America, and one citizen has as much right to play as any other. The National League will go down the line with Robinson whatever the consequence.

As Monte Irvin said, "Baseball has done more to move America in the right direction than all the professional patriots with their billions of cheap words." The Supreme Court decision of *Brown v. Topeka Board of Education*; civil rights heroes like Martin Luther King, Jr., James Meredith, Thurgood Marshall, and others; the freedom marches and the voting rights act—all were vital to America's progress toward unity, but the title of one of Jackie Robinson's books may not overstate the case: *Baseball Has Done It*.

A final way in which baseball supplies models for America is one that has been present from the game's beginning: a model for children wishing to be grownups, wrestling with their insecurities and wondering, *What does it mean to be a man? What does a man do?* (Most of

us old boys occasionally wonder this as well.) The answers in baseball, at least, are unequivocal; as Satchel Paige said in his later years, "I loved baseball. There wasn't no 'maybe so' about it."

Baseball gives children a sense of how wide the world is, in its possibilities but also in its geography. Reading the summations of minor league ball in *The Sporting News* each week piqued the curiosity of baseball-mad boys like me: where were Kokomo and Mattoon and Thibodeaux and Nogales? How did people behave in Salinas or Rocky Mount? What did they eat in Artesia? How many exciting, exotic places this enormous country contained! But a note of comfort—they couldn't be all that strange if baseball was played there.

And to that other vast *terra incognita*—the world of adults—baseball also offered a road map. How many boys and girls learned to talk with adults, principally their fathers, by nodding wisely at an assessment of a shortstop's range or a pitcher's heart, and mock-confidently venturing an opinion about the hometown team's chances? Our dads are our first heroes (and, decades later, our last); but in between, baseball players are what we want to be. For heroes are larger than life, and when as adults we have taken the measure of ourselves and found we are no more than life-size, and on our bad days seemingly less than that, baseball can puff us up a bit.

Douglass Wallop put it nicely:

. . . only yesterday the fan was a kid of nine or ten bolting his breakfast on Saturday morning and hurtling from the house with a glove buttoned over his belt and a bat over his shoulder, rushing to the nearest vacant lot, perhaps the nearest alley, where the other guys were gathering, a place where it would always be spring. For him, baseball would always have the sound and look and smell of that morning and of other mornings just like it. Only by an accident of chance would he find himself, in the years to come, up in the grandstand, looking on. But for a quirk of fate, he himself would be down on that field; it would be his likeness on the television screen and his name in the newspaper high on the list of .300 hitters. He was a fan, but a fan only incidentally. He was, first and always, himself a baseball player.

The Fifties

If the America that was survives anywhere as more than a memory, it is in baseball, that strangely pastoral game in no matter what setting—domed stadium or Little League field. As hindsight improves upon foresight, memory improves upon reality, so that the endless monotony and grinding physical labor of small-town life before the Civil War are now thought quite romantic. For all our complaints today, it may likewise be argued that America is better than it ever was.

Today's players *are* better than those in the game's golden age; the strategy of the game and even its execution are more adept (forget all that moaning about how nobody knows the "fundamentals" any more . . . the average player of fifty years ago didn't know them either); and the opportunities to watch baseball, if not to play it, far exceed those of say, the 1950s, today broadly regarded

as the game's halcyon era. (A golden age may be defined flexibly, it seems, so as to coincide with the period of one's youth.) For all its pull toward the good old days, for all its statistical illusions of an Olympian era when titans strode the basepaths, for all its seeming permanence in a world aswirl with change, baseball has in fact moved with America, and improved with it.

The period after World War II was a heady time for the nation and its pastime, both of them buoyed by returning veterans and removed restrictions. But in 1946 the major leagues still represented only the sixteen cities that had participated in the National Agreement of 1903, none west of St. Louis; a handful of African Americans were just entering the minor leagues after a half-century's exclusion; and because television was not yet a staple of the American home, most baseball fans had never seen *even a single big-league game*.

Women had been courted as patrons (even nonpaying patrons) ever since the game's dawn. Baseball management hoped that their presence would lend "tone" to the proceedings and keep a lid on the rowdies, in the stands and on the field. But women's participation in the game's labor force and management was even more limited than their role in the nation's business and industry—Rosie the Riveter and Eleanor Roosevelt as yet had no counterparts in Organized Baseball. The All-American Girls Baseball League made its debut in 1943, the brainchild of Chicago Cubs' owner Philip K. Wrigley. The women's "league of their own" won many admirers over the next decade, but the majors always regarded it as separate and unequal.

On the amateur level, while American Legion Junior Baseball had begun as early as 1928, and Little League in 1939, neither attained their heights until after the War ended. Naysayers will point out that baseball has lost ground as more kids today play football, basketball, soccer, and tennis than fifty years ago—but far more play baseball, too, and not only in America. The annual pursuit of the Little League championship in Williamsport, Pa. (like the Pan-American Games), has become an international affair, an instrument of diplomacy that State Department officials envy. Indeed, baseball may yet hold the key to neighborly relations with all nations in the hemisphere.

Baseball in the colleges, now so vibrant and so fertile with major league talent, was on the path to extinction by the end of the War, only to be brought back from the brink by the G.I. Bill: the explosive growth in enrollment that the returning veterans produced also created a sudden need for expanded athletic programs, and baseball was the prime beneficiary. The NCAA's introduction of the College World Series in 1947 affirmed the game's recovery on campus, and since locating in Omaha three years later it has grown steadily.

In 1951 Major League Baseball, as dated from the inception of the National League in 1876, reached the august age of 75 and proclaimed its "diamond jubilee." Celebratory banquets were held, a plaque was erected at the old hotel where the league was founded, and all NL players wore a commemorative patch on their sleeves. (Coincidentally but less flashily the American League marked its fiftieth birthday as a major circuit.) Let's take a moment to look at where baseball stood at that point.

There was no question it was booming. On the professional level, a whopping 59 leagues contained 448 teams employing about 8,000 players—or 19 minor leaguers competing for each of the then 400 spots in the big show. Little League would soon send its first alumnus to the majors, which had already accepted hundreds of graduates from Legion and other programs. Happy Chandler secured from television a then mind-boggling but now quaint $6 million for broadcast rights to the next six World Series. And with the game's most powerful teams bunched in New York City—the Yankees, the Dodgers, and the Giants—the publicity mills and the turnstiles were spinning as they had never spun before.

But the excitement of the first five postwar years was not confined to New York: even such perennial tailenders as the Boston Braves, the Philadelphia Phillies, and the Cleveland Indians fought their way into the World Series; and staid old Cleveland, under Bill Veeck's carnival-barker aegis, set staggering new attendance records. Many of the newly admitted African-American players had become stars and—satisfyingly, though few but Branch Rickey had predicted it—box-office attractions: Jackie Robinson, Roy Campanella, and Don Newcombe of the Dodgers; Monte Irvin and rookie Willie Mays of the Giants; Sam Jethroe of the Braves; Larry Doby and Satchel Paige of the Indians. Many prewar stars continued to shine, like Bob Feller, Stan Musial, and Ted Williams (though with the Korean War he answered Uncle Sam's call yet again), and new ones like Gotham's center field trio of Duke Snider, Mickey Mantle, and Mays replenished the stock as heroes like Joe DiMaggio hung up their spikes.

But most of these blessings had their downside. Opening the game to African Americans was indubitably right, but it killed the Negro Leagues, ruining owners and abruptly ending many playing careers. The increasing organization of youth baseball, particularly the rise of Little League, heightened the stress of the game at its formative levels and drained much of the fun, as driven parents began to see their Junior as tomorrow's big leaguer, not as just a boy having fun while learning a thing or two. The game on the field was dominated by the home run, making for a brand of ball that some might term dull. League champs registered such stolen-base totals as Dom DiMaggio's 15 or Jackie Jensen's 22; Early Wynn led the AL in ERA one year with a mark of 3.20; and the three-base hit, despite the big old parks still prevalent, went the way of the dodo. And the pennant domination by the three New York teams—principally the Yankees, of course—made the national pastime a rather parochial pleasure; it was hard for fans in Pittsburgh or Detroit to wax rhapsodic over a Subway Series. No, the blessings of the 1950s were not unmitigated, any more than on the national scene the tranquility of the Eisenhower years was without cost.

Take television, for instance: the revenues were great, and so was the publicity value of electronically extending major league play to people in southern and western areas. But the novelty of big-time heroes on the small screen kept those folks at home when formerly they had gone to the local ballpark. The minors began their long decline, one that didn't bottom out until 1964; by then the 59 leagues of 1951 had become 19, and the 8,000-odd professional players had dwindled to fewer than 2,500.

Moreover, television whetted the baseball appetites of Californians and Texans (and Georgians and Washingtonians and more). That demand plus the development of faster passenger planes gave ideas to owners of two of baseball's decaying franchises. Walter O'Malley, owner of the Brooklyn Dodgers, and Giants' owner Horace Stoneham had seen the solidarity of the original 16-city composition broken in 1953, when the venerable Boston Braves (a franchise established in the first year of the National Association, 1871) became the darlings of Milwaukee, and further weakened by the defections in 1954-55 of the St. Louis Browns to Baltimore and the Philadelphia Athletics to Kansas City. Amid weeping and gnashing of teeth that continue to this day, the Dodgers and Giants left for the Golden West in 1958.

In a strange twist, the architect of the move, Walter O'Malley, was (and in the East, still is) widely reviled as the man responsible for ending the grand old game's paradisical age. Yet the placement of franchises in California, as distressing as it was for Brooklyn and Manhattan and as roundly condemned as it was by traditionalists, may now be seen as the best thing to happen to baseball in the decade. And Walter O'Malley, if you will permit your mind a considerable stretch, may be viewed not as the snake offering baseball the mortal apple but as a latter-day Johnny Appleseed (in the footsteps of Alexander Cartwright, who in 1849 also headed for California in pursuit of gold, yet who is remembered not for his venality but for bringing the New York Game to the West).

It was imperative that baseball take the game to where the people were, precisely as it had in 1903. America's population had already begun the westward and southward shift that was to become so pronounced in the 1960s and '70s. The move to Los Angeles and San Francisco, rather than confirming those cities' stature as "big-league," as is so often written, brought baseball into step with America, which had long recognized them as such. Baseball could now call itself the national pastime without apology.

The Sixties

A chaotic decade for our country, the 1960s were worrisome, stormy years for baseball as well, with dramatic changes in league composition, playing styles, competitive balance and, most distressingly, the game's appeal to the American people. Baseball endured its ordeal by fire, and came through not unscathed but strengthened.

The departure of the Dodgers and Giants in 1958 created a vacuum in New York and an increased hunger for baseball in new boomtowns like Houston, Atlanta, and Minneapolis. Enter Branch Rickey, nearly eighty but still possessed of a keen nose for new opportunity. The great innovator who had already brought baseball the farm system and integration now created the Continental League, a paper league with paper franchises. Nonetheless, Rickey's mirage worried Organized Baseball into expansion.

Two of the Continental "franchises"—the future New York Mets and Houston Colt .45s—were admitted for 1962. The American League was authorized to commence its western foray one year earlier with the expansion-draft Los Angeles Angels and the relocated Minnesota Twins (the latter being the transplanted Washington Senators, who were replaced in the nation's capital by an ill-fated expansion team).

Other franchise shifts and startups in the decade saw baseball's original vagabonds, the Milwaukee Braves by way of Boston, move to Atlanta in 1966. Two years later the erstwhile Athletics of Philadelphia, having failed in Kansas City, directed their caravan toward Oakland.

The A's were quickly replaced in KC by the Royals, one of two new teams introduced in each league with the expansion of 1969. This in turn precipitated divisional play and the League Championship Series, both inventions much decried at the time but now generally applauded. And in one of baseball's more forgettable debacles, the expansion Pilots of 1969 lost their course in Seattle after only one year and ran aground in Milwaukee, where they were rechristened as the Brewers. The National League's expansion into San Diego and Montreal proceeded more smoothly, although Padres' attendance lagged expectations and the Expos' Olympic Stadium (replacing the stopgap Jarry Park) took longer to open its dome than Michelangelo took to paint St. Peter's.

On the field, the big-bang game of the 1950s was giving way to a pitching-and-defense formula, at least in the National League, which began to outstrip its long-time tormentor at the box office and in World Series and All Star confrontations. Speed returned to the equation, too, as personified by first Maury Wills and then Lou Brock (though both were preceded, in the AL, by Luis Aparicio). And a revolution in baseball strategy was brewing, as the 1959 success of such relievers as Larry Sherry, Lindy McDaniel, and Roy Face paved the way for the universal adoption of the bullpen stopper in the 1960s.

In the American League expansion year of 1961, the first played to a 162-game schedule, the Bronx Bombers hit a whopping 240 homers. Sluggers Harmon Killebrew, Norm Cash, and Rocky Colavito all hit more than 40 homers; Mickey Mantle hit more than 50. These totals were troubling to Commissioner Ford Frick, but nowhere near as consternating as the 61 homers struck by Roger Maris to top the game's most famous record, the 60 that Babe Ruth had walloped in 1927. After seeing the National League's scoring increase in 1962, its first year of expansion, Frick became concerned that pitchers were becoming an endangered species. He said:

I would even like the spitball to come back. Take a look at the batting, home run, and slugging record for recent seasons, and you become convinced that the pitchers need help urgently.

Disastrously, Frick convinced the owners to widen the strike zone for 1963 to its pre-1950 dimensions: top of the armpit to bottom of the knee. The result was to increase strikeouts, reduce walks, and shrink batting averages within five years to levels unseen since 1908, the nadir of the Dead Ball Era. The once-proud Yankees, who had continued their long domination of the American League to mid-decade, saw their team batting average sink to an incredible .214 in 1968. That year produced an overall AL mark of .230 and a batting champion, Carl Yastrzemski, with an average of .301.

As pitchers vanquished batters, seemingly for all eternity, the bottom line was that the fans stayed away in droves. Attendance in the National League, which in 1966 reached 15 million, fell by 1968 to only 11.7 million. In fact, despite the addition of four new clubs in 1961-62, attendance in 1968 was only 3 million more than it had been in 1960. Critics charged that baseball was a geriatric vestige of an America that had vanished, a game too slow for a nation that was rushing toward the moon; its decline would only steepen, they claimed, as that more with-it national pastime, pro football, extended its mastery of the airwaves.

But the sky was not falling, despite the alarms. The owners acted quickly to redress the game's balance between offense and defense, reducing the strike zone and lowering the pitcher's mound. But the most important change may have been one that was introduced in 1965 and was only beginning to take effect: the amateur free-agent draft. Typically successful teams like the Yankees, Dodgers, Braves, and Cardinals had stayed successful because of their attention to scouting. Consistently they were able to garner more top prospects for their farm systems than clubs with less deep pockets or more volatile management. Now, teams that had fallen on hard times need not look toward a generation of famine before returning to the feast. Now, dynasties—awe-inspiring but not healthy for the game—were suddenly rendered implausible. Now, baseball had a competitive balance that could produce a rotation of electrifying successes among the leagues' cities, like the ascension of the Boston Red Sox from ninth place in 1966 to the pennant the next, and the amazing rise of the New York Mets from the netherworld they had known to World Champions in 1969. The game would still have some hard rows to hoe in the 1970s, but there was no mistaking the reversal of its downturn: in the new age of "relevance," baseball was back.

The Seventies

The 1970s saw a continuation of the trend toward new stadium construction that had marked the 1960s and may well have triggered that decade's batting drought, as hitter's havens like Ebbets Field, the Polo Grounds, and Sportsman's Park fell to the wrecker's ball. The 1960s had brought new ballparks to 11 cities—San Francisco, Los Angeles, Washington, Bloomington (Minn.), New York (NL), Houston, Atlanta, Anaheim, St. Louis, Oakland, and San Diego. In 1970-1971, baseball bade farewell to old friends Crosley Field, Forbes Field, and Shibe Park as new stadiums—artificial-turf clones of each other—sprang up in Cincinnati, Pittsburgh, and Philadelphia. Other new parks were built in Arlington, Kansas City, Montreal, Seattle, and Toronto (the latter two, expansion franchises added to the American League in 1977), and Yankee Stadium underwent a massive facelift.

All this construction activity seemed to bespeak the game's profitability. Indeed, attendance was climbing in almost all major league cities, as heroes like Henry Aaron, Johnny Bench, Reggie Jackson, and Pete Rose, to name but a few, gave the fans plenty to cheer about. And the controversial adoption of the designated hitter innovation by the American League in 1973 gave a further boost

to hitting while giving fans much to argue about, which after all is one of the game's great pleasures.

But the game's financial health was imperiled by rising unrest over labor issues, centered on the reserve clause which bound a player to his team in perpetuity while denying him the opportunity to gauge his worth in the free market. The reformulation of the relationship between players and management became the hallmark of the decade and sorely tested fans' devotion to the game.

It began with the momentous case brought against Organized Baseball by veteran outfielder Curt Flood in 1970, challenging the legality of the reserve clause. The Supreme Court ruled against Flood the following year, but the tenor for the 1970s had been set. A 13-day player strike delayed the opening of the 1972 season, and arbitrator Peter Seitz ruled in 1975 (in what has come to be known as the Messersmith-McNally case) that a player could establish his right of free agency by playing out his option year without a signed contract. The writing on the wall was clear: free agency was the wave of the future.

Big-name players like Jim Hunter, Reggie Jackson, and Rich Gossage migrated to New York and lesser lights like Wayne Garland and Oscar Gamble signed elsewhere for figures that seemed incredible. In the race to sign available talent some owners spun out of control while others like Minnesota's Cal Griffith, without corporate coffers behind them, had no choice but to sit on the sidelines. Player movement among stars jeopardized fan allegiances, pundits alleged, as Gossage and Jackson played for three teams in three years and championship teams like the Oakland A's and Boston Red Sox were broken up through trades that were forced by the specter of impending—and uncompensated—free-agent departures.

(Comfortingly to the historian, all this hubbub had occurred in very much the same way in 1869-1870, before the advent of the reserve clause, when Henry Chadwick was fulminating about the perniciousness of players "revolving" from one team to another simply to advance their fortunes. Also, baseball's first avowedly professional team, Harry Wright's Cincinnati Red Stockings of 1869 and '70, were roundly abused for constructing their powerhouse team with "mercenaries" from other states—thus scorning baseball's core appeal to civic pride.)

What actually compromised fan loyalties in the '70s was not player movement—it took Yankee fans, oh, maybe, ten minutes to regard Reggie as a born pinstriper—but player salaries. When the major league minimum was under $5,000 or so and only a Mantle, Williams, Musial, and DiMaggio made $100,000 a year, fans saw with their heroes as, by and large, working colleagues who had the supreme good fortune to play ball for a living. If a star made a splendiferous salary, that was socially useful as a proof that any worker could make it big if only he had sufficient ability to emerge from the pack. But when stars began routinely to command seven-figure salaries, and, more importantly, the annual wage of the average major leaguer rose to six-figure levels, and eventually seven figures, many adult breadwinners struggled to remain fans.

That they succeeded is testament to their love of the game, for fans have had a difficult assignment in reshaping their views of baseball players along the lines of media stars. The princely compensations of actors and

pop musicians have long been accepted by the public as the verdict of the marketplace. If the movie "The Terminator" makes hundreds of millions of dollars for its studio and distributor, then Arnold Schwarzenegger's multimillion-dollar fee for the film seems not out of line. Analogously, if the Dodgers were fabulously lucrative for ownership, then a lofty salary for Steve Garvey ought not to have given rise in the 1970s to resentment among the fans. This sort of reeducation is by no means complete, but barroom banter about baseball in the 1990s is not as bitterly one-note about "greedy players" as it had been fifteen years previous.

And one didn't hear a peep about pro football replacing baseball as the national game.

The Eighties and Nineties

The game on the field in the 1970s had been marked by an unprecedented commingling of power and speed; the great teams of Cincinnati, Baltimore, and Oakland; the return to prominence of the Yankees; and the historic exploits of Henry Aaron and Pete Rose. The game in the '80s would begin with the Philadelphia Phillies, led by free-agent Rose and future Hall of Famers Mike Schmidt and Steve Carlton, ridding themselves of a historic stain. Until their victory over the Kansas City Royals, the Phils were the only one of the original sixteen major-league franchises never to have won a World Series (the St. Louis Browns had to accept the help of their modern incarnation, the Baltimore Orioles).

The next year brought baseball's darkest moment since the Brotherhood revolt and ensuing Players League of 1890, as major-league players walked off their jobs at the height of the season and didn't return for fifty days. By that time even diehard fans were thoroughly fed up with baseball's seeming inability to resolve its problems fairly and with dispatch. Talk of a fan boycott never amounted to much, but as players and management looked toward their Basic Agreement negotiation in 1989—the centenary of the Brotherhood's break with Organized Baseball—both reflected back on the damage wrought in 1981.

The 1980s brought unprecedented parity on the playing field and misery off it. The drug problem endemic in our society struck baseball, inevitably as well, and Pete Rose's itch for gambling disgraced him and the game. Baseball's victims are highly publicized and their fall from grace is judged more reprehensible for all the advantages that today's players enjoy—but the game is an American institution reflecting what is wrong with our people as well as what is right with them. Let's hope that in this most difficult area of addictive behavior baseball can again—as it did with integration—lead America rather than follow it.

The year of 1989 became a nightmare, with Commissioner Bart Giamatti's expulsion of Rose followed by his own sudden and shocking death days later, a second finding of collusion by owners to undermine the free-agent market, and a Bay Area World Series rudely interrupted by an earthquake. But baseball recovered even from these calamities, as well as a spring training lockout in 1990, to embark upon an era that gave promise of unprecedented prosperity. The attendance of the Toronto Blue Jays exceeded the 4 million mark while the team captured back-to-back World Series, the first such feat since the Cincinnati Reds of 1975-1976. And in 1993 the National League expanded to 14 teams, welcoming franchises in Miami and Colorado that were instantly and wildly prosperous, with the Rockies setting an all-time attendance peak of nearly 4.5 million fans.

And then came 1994, a year of wonderment on the playing fields, as Ken Griffey, Jr., Matt Williams, Frank Thomas, Jeff Bagwell, Tony Gwynn, Greg Maddux, and a host of others appeared to be initiating a new golden age of baseball . . . until play stopped on Aug. 12 and did not resume. The leagues, which had divided into three divisions for the first time, now had no opportunity to try out their new idea of an additional round of postseason play, with the introduction of a Wild Card team that had not been a division winner.

As fans, we were presented with a dilemma: to side with the players, who went on strike hoping to extend their gains of the previous two decades? Or to side with the owners, who stood fast in insisting upon a balance between costs and revenues? As fans, we tried to side with the game of baseball, and wish that its most intense contests would soon reconvene to the field of play.

And they did, with splendid seasons in 1995 and 1996, though some fans continued to withhold their affections, hoping that baseball owners and players would give peace a chance—as at last they did.

Baseball is not a conventional industry. It belongs neither to the players nor management, but to all of us. It is our national pastime, our national symbol, and our national treasure.

The monumental 1998 season enriched that treasure in so many ways, from the excitement of the home run race between Mark McGwire and Sammy Sosa to the awesome victory total of the New York Yankees. Gloriously, baseball's ghosts came back to life, in the daily press and in dinner-table conversations everywhere. Roger Maris, Babe Ruth, Hack Wilson, even Tinker and Evers and Chance, played invisibly alongside our heroes of today.

The Weather of Our Lives

Ever changing in ways that are so small as to preserve the illusion that "nothing changes in baseball," the game has introduced, in the lifetime of many of us: night ball, plane travel, television, integration, bullpen stoppers, expansion, the amateur draft, competitive parity, indoor stadiums, artificial turf, free agency, the designated hitter, Wild Card contestants, interleague contests, international play and expansion to 30 teams in 1998. Not far off, perhaps, are further expansion to 32 teams and intercontinental championships.

For fans accustomed to the game's languorous rhythms and conservative resistance to innovation, the changes of the past twenty years in particular seem positively frenetic. Yet for all its changes, baseball has not strayed far from its origins, and in fact has changed far less than other American institutions of equivalent antiquity. What sustains baseball in the hearts of Americans, finally, is not its responsiveness to changes in society nor its propensity for

novelty, but its myths, its lore, its records, and its essential stability. As historian Bruce Catton noted in 1959:

A gaffer from the era of William McKinley, abruptly brought back to the second half of the twentieth century, would find very little in modern life that would not seem new, strange, and rather bewildering, but put in a good grandstand seat back of first base he would see nothing that was not completely familiar.

It's still a game of bat and ball, played without regard for the clock; a game of 90-foot basepaths, nine innings, nine men in the field; three outs, all out; and three strikes still send you to the bench, no matter whom you know in city hall. It's the national anthem before every game; it's playing catch with your son or daughter; it's learning how to win and how to deal with loss, and how to connect with something larger than our selves.

"Baseball," wrote Thomas Wolfe, "has been not merely 'the great national game' but really a part of the whole weather of our lives, of the thing that is our own, of the whole fabric, the million memories of America." Spring comes in America not on the vernal equinox but on Opening Day; summer sets in with a Memorial Day doubleheader and does not truly end until the last out of the regular season. Winter begins the day after the World Series.

Where were you when Bobby Thomson hit the shot heard 'round the world? Or the night Carlton Fisk hit his homer in the 12th? Or when the Mets, with batter after batter one strike away from their loss in the World Series, staged their famous rally? These are milestones in the lives of America and Americans.

We grow up with baseball; we mark—and, for a moment, stop—the passage of time with it; and we grow old with it. It is our game, for all our days.

## CHAPTER 2

Team Histories

Frederick Ivor-Campbell and Matthew Silverman

When the Tampa Bay Devil Rays and Arizona Diamondbacks began play in 1998 they brought to 112 the number of clubs (plus those of the Negro major leagues) that have played major league ball at one time or another since baseball's first professional league—the National Association—was organized in 1871. Some of the early teams dropped out after only a few games, but several have played for more than a century, and one—the present Atlanta Braves—has played every season from 1871 to the present. The only existing franchise older than Atlanta's (which originated as the Boston Red Stockings, then became the Boston and Milwaukee Braves before moving to Atlanta) is the Chicago Cubs, which organized in 1870, a year before league play began. The White Stockings (as they were first known) missed two seasons (1872-1873) in the aftermath of the great Chicago fire, but have since then continuously represented the same city longer than any other club in baseball history.

Here are brief histories of 30 current big-league clubs, arranged alphabetically by city or state. These are followed by summary histories of the 82 other clubs—now defunct—that at one time also represented their cities in the major leagues.

Anaheim Angels

Of the 10 teams added to the major leagues in the 1960s and '70s, the Angels were quickest to put together a winning season, finishing third in the American League in only their second year of play.

Former cowboy actor and singer Gene Autry brought the club into being as the Los Angeles Angels in December 1960. They played their first season, 1961, in Los Angeles' Wrigley Field, a former minor league park with power alleys only five feet deeper than the foul poles; five Angels hit 20 or more home runs that year. Though the team finished seventh in the standings, they were second in homers only to the mighty Yankees.

What the Angels lost in home runs in 1962 (when they moved out of Wrigley Field into the Dodgers' new stadium), they more than made up in pitching. Paced by rookie Dean Chance, the Angels nearly doubled their wins on the road, and, as late as mid-August, stood in second place, within striking distance of New York. Though they tailed off in September, they finished a respectable third, 10 games back.

The team collapsed to ninth the next year, but in 1964 Chance's pitching and splendid relief by rookie Bob Lee helped lift the team back into the first division. Among Chance's league-leading 11 shutouts were six 1-0 victories.

Los Angeles became the California Angels in 1965 in anticipation of their move south to a new stadium in Anaheim the following year, but neither the name change nor the new location stirred them out of the second division. In 1967 with below-average run production but the league's third-best pitching, the Angels shot up from ninth to third in midseason before leveling off to fifth. After dismal seasons in 1968-1969, career years in 1970 by pitcher Clyde Wright (22 wins, including a no-hitter) and newly acquired left fielder Alex Johnson (202 hits and a league-high .329 batting average) helped the Angels snap back with an 86-76 record that matched their previous best (1962).

The seven losing seasons which followed 1970 were somewhat redeemed by the arrival in 1972 of pitcher Nolan Ryan, who burst into superstardom as an Angel, setting a modern record of 383 strikeouts in 1973 and hurling four no-hitters in three years (1973-1975). Ryan's effectiveness dipped in 1978, but the club as a whole came to life, contending closely for the Western Division title all season until Kansas City shot ahead in September.

In 1979 Don Baylor became the first (and, so far, only) DH to be named league Most Valuable Player, as a renewed offense powered California to its first division title. Baltimore stopped the Angels in the ALCS, though. The team's run production dropped off dramatically the next year, and the club followed up its best season with its worst.

After another losing season in 1981 (during which Jim Fregosi was replaced as manager by 20-year veteran Gene Mauch), California lured free agent Reggie Jackson from the Yankees. With Jackson leading a resurgent offense and Geoff Zahn headlining the league's second-best pitching staff, the Angels rebounded to 93 wins in 1982 and their second division title. They defeated Milwaukee in the first two games of the ALCS, but lost the next three. A disappointed Mauch retired.

Again, in 1983, the Angels followed a championship with a poor season—not quite as bad as 1980, but still their third worst to that point. In 1984 they rebounded to .500, good enough for second in a weak division. Pitcher Mike Witt concluded his rise to staff ace with a perfect game on the season's last day.

Gene Mauch came out of retirement to manage the

Angels again in 1985. With pitching that featured splendid relief from newly acquired Donnie Moore (31 saves; 1.92 ERA), the team led the division much of the season, but lost three of four to Kansas City in the final week to fall a game behind the Royals into second.

With Witt's 18 wins and 2.84 ERA pacing the staff and rookie first baseman Wally Joyner leading the offense, California won the 1986 division crown with ease. In the ALCS against Boston, the Angels took three of the first four games, and were within one pitch of capturing their first pennant in Game 5, but the Red Sox rallied to win.

For the third time the Angels followed up their division championship with a losing season, this time dropping the 1987 season finale to tie for last place in the AL West. Manager Mauch retired again, this time for good. After another losing season brought them home a distant fourth in 1988, the Angels signed Doug Rader to manage the club. They also acquired a veteran pitcher—Bert Blyleven—who led a resurgence that lifted the club to its third best won-lost record ever. Since the West was now the stronger AL division, the team's 91 wins carried them only into third place. In 1990 they dropped just one place in the standings, but finished again below .500, 23 games out of first.

The Angels began strong in 1991, and moved into the division lead on July 3, but seven straight losses plunged them to fifth; although they finished at .500 for the season, just 14 games out of first, they wound up in the division cellar.

After four sub-500 seasons the Angels (paced by Jim Edmonds' 107 RBIs and Mark Langston's 15-7 mark) led the AL West for most of the 1995 season, only to fade and finish in a tie in the division race with the upstart Seattle Mariners. The AL West title was decided by a one-game playoff in which the Mariners' Randy Johnson made the difference. California's improvement made it one of only three major league clubs to register an increase in per-game attendance over 1994.

The Angels fell to last in 1996, resulting in manager Marcel Lachemann's firing. He was replaced by John McNamara on an interim basis, and former Astros pilot Terry Collins took over the post later. At the end of 1996 the Angels changed their name (to Anaheim Angels), owners (the Walt Disney Company purchased the team), and manager (Collins arrived from Houston). In 1998 they changed their stadium (a reconstructed ballpark was renamed Edison Field), but they could not change their luck. In 1997 the Angels chased both the Mariners for the AL West title and the Yankees for the AL Wild Card before coming up short of both. Injuries, which hurt the team's chances in 1997, caught up to them again in '98. The Texas Rangers supplanted the Angels atop the standings in the final week of the season to win the AL West title.

Arizona Diamondbacks

Along with the Tampa Bay Devil Rays, the Arizona Diamondbacks were granted a $130 million NL expansion franchise on March 9, 1995.

The Diamondbacks ownership group is headed by Phoenix Suns owner Jerry Colangelo. Minority investors included Nike chairman Phil Knight and comedian Billy Crystal. Joe Garagiola, Jr., a former player agent, was named the team's first general manager. In November 1995, more than two years before the first scheduled game, the Diamondbacks named former Yankees manager Buck Showalter as the franchise's first field manager.

In Bank One Ballpark, a $335 million retractable-roofed, natural-grass facility in downtown Phoenix, the Diamondbacks drew 3,602,856 fans their first season. After getting off to a rocky start—they lost their first five games—the Diamondbacks finished strong and posted key victories in the closing weeks of the season against the Chicago Cubs, San Francisco Giants, and New York Mets, who were locked in a fight-to-the-finish struggle for the final playoff berth. Mound ace Andy Benes came within two outs of a September no-hitter, and Travis Lee, who had the first hit and home run in club history, was one of the year's top rookies. Devon White was the team's first All-Star.

Atlanta Braves

The Atlanta Braves, who first played in 1871 as Boston's Red Stockings, are the only club to field a team every season of professional league baseball.

When the game's first openly professional club, the Cincinnati Red Stockings, decided to revert to amateur status, manager/outfielder Harry Wright and three of his teammates took their talents and club nickname to Boston, where, with infielders Ross Barnes and Harry Schafer and pitcher Al Spalding, they formed the nucleus of a team that would dominate the five-year history of the first professional league, the National Association. After a close second-place finish in their first year, the Red Stockings won four pennants in convincing fashion, including a 71-8 record in 1875 with an .899 winning percentage that has never since been approached in major league ball.

When the National League replaced the NA in 1876, four of Boston's best players, including Spalding and Barnes, deserted the club for Chicago. After a fourth-place finish in 1876, the Red Stockings lured pitcher Tommy Bond from Hartford and finished at the top in 1877 and '78. Bond dominated NL pitching, winning 80 games (40 each year), 22 more than his nearest rival. Although he won 43 more in 1879, Boston slipped to second.

In 1880 the Red Stockings suffered their first losing season. After a second consecutive sixth-place finish the next year, Wright left to manage Providence, but Boston rebounded to third in 1882 and surprised everyone in 1883 by outplaying favored Chicago and Providence to capture their seventh pennant.

Providence knocked them out of the race late in 1884, and Boston remained out of contention the next four seasons. In 1889, though, with several players signed from the defunct Detroit Wolverines (including batting champ Dan Brouthers), and 49 wins from pitcher John Clarkson, the Beaneaters (as they were now more commonly known) waged a two-team race for the championship with the New York Giants. Boston won as many games as the Giants, but lost two more and finished a

game behind their New York rivals.

Frank Selee, who had managed two straight minor league pennant winners, was hired from Omaha along with his star pitcher, Charles "Kid" Nichols. Their arrival in 1890 ushered in Boston's second golden era. When they left the club 12 years later, the Beaneaters had won five more NL pennants. Nichols won 27 games in his rookie season, but Boston—decimated by defections to the outlaw Players League— finished only fifth. With the return of some of the defectors in 1891, Clarkson won 33 games, Nichols recorded the first of seven 30-win seasons, and the Beaneaters returned to the top.

When the NL expanded in 1892 from eight teams to 12, the schedule was also expanded, and the season divided into two halves. Boston won the first half, and the Cleveland Spiders the second. In a World Series to determine the league champion, the Beaneaters (102-48) defeated the Spiders.

The split season was abandoned and the schedule reduced in 1893—and Boston captured its third straight pennant. Center fielder Hugh Duffy hit .363. The next year Duffy led the way with .440, which is still the major league record. His Beaneaters didn't win the pennant, but they became the first club in a decade (and the last until 1920) to hit over 100 home runs. Five Beaneaters drove in 100 runs or more, and the team set a big league record for runs scored (1,220).

Boston dropped out of contention for a couple of years, but bounced back in 1897 to edge Baltimore for the pennant. In the Temple Cup series, though, played between the first-and second-place teams for the world title, the Orioles overwhelmed Boston, four games to one. The next year Boston won 102 games to lead the league, but the league had abandoned the four-year-old Temple Cup.

After coming in second in 1899, Boston dropped out of pennant contention for 14 years, finishing as far back as 66½ games (in 1906) and losing as many as 108 (in 1909). The Braves (as they were now known) rose to fifth in 1913 under new manager George Stallings. Through the first half of 1914, however, the Braves seemed to be destined for another cellar finish.

In mid-July they stood a last-place eighth in a tight field. Six days and six wins later they were third. By mid-August they had climbed to second; on Aug. 26 they replaced the New York Giants in first. For two weeks they alternated between first and second, then broke out of the park to win the pennant by 10½ games.

Boston's heroes were pitchers Dick Rudolph and Bill James, both in only their second full big league seasons. Rudolph won 26 games in 1914 and James won 26; then they added two more each in the "Miracle" Braves' World Series sweep of the heavily favored Philadelphia Athletics.

A seven-game losing streak in early September dropped them out of a tie for first in 1916. They rallied, but finished third. It was the Braves' last close race for 32 years.

From 1917 through 1945 the Braves finished only as high as fourth three seasons and only once as close as nine games from the top. With four years in the cellar and 11 in seventh place, the team finished near the bottom of the league more than half the time.

In 1946, with dynamic new ownership headed by con-tractor Lou Perini, a new manager—Billy Southworth, who had led the Cardinals to three pennants and two world championships—and the return of war veterans like pitchers Warren Spahn and Johnny Sain, the Braves had their first winning season in eight years. At the end of the season Boston acquired third baseman Bob Elliott from Pittsburgh. He enjoyed a career year in 1947, powering the Braves to third place. Spahn and Sain won 21 games each.

Spahn dropped to 15 wins in 1948, but Sain won 24. Four veterans—plus rookie shortstop Alvin Dark—hit over .300. With the league's best pitching and hitting, the Braves moved out in front in June, and shook off their last challengers with a September spurt. From there on, the Braves' path in Boston was downhill. Cleveland beat them in the World Series, and the club dropped to fourth for the next three years. Southworth resigned part way through the 1951 season. In 1952 the team fell to seventh; home attendance was less than one-fifth what it had been four years earlier. The next spring Perini moved the franchise to Milwaukee in the league's first realignment since 1900.

The move was a spectacular success. Not only did the Braves rebound to second place, but attendance jumped 649 percent over their previous year in Boston to set an NL record of more than 1.8 million. The league's best pitching staff was led by the trio that would anchor Milwaukee's years of greatness: veteran Warren Spahn, sophomore Lew Burdette, and rookie Bob Buhl. In 1953 Eddie Mathews led the league in home runs, a category the Braves would own in the coming years as Hank Aaron joined the team the following year.

The Braves were slightly ahead through much of the 1956 season until five straight losses in early September brought them even with the surging Dodgers. It was not settled until the final day, when a Dodger victory over Pittsburgh left Milwaukee a game back in second.

The acquisition of veteran second baseman Red Schoendienst from St. Louis in June 1957 steadied the infield and gave the team a baserunner for Mathews and Aaron to drive home. In August the Braves drew away from the pack, and recovered from a September slump to win the pennant by eight games over St. Louis. The Yankees took them to seven games in the World Series, but Burdette's shutout in the finale brought the Braves their first world championship since 1914.

Milwaukee repeated as league champions in 1958, but in the Fall Classic, after taking the first two games from the Yankees, they lost the Series in seven. The race was much tighter in 1959 until the Giants moved away from the Dodgers and Braves in August. In September the Giants faltered as the others surged past them, and the season ended with the Braves and Dodgers tied. In a best-of-three playoff, the Dodgers took the pennant in two games—but both by only one run and the second only after 12 innings.

A portent for the Braves' future could be seen in the crowd of under 20,000 that attended the first playoff game in Milwaukee. After setting a third NL record in 1957, Milwaukee attendance had gradually declined, dropping below 2 million in 1958, the club's second pennant year, and even farther in this year of the tight pennant race. When attendance dropped in 1965 to a new Milwaukee

low of just over half a million, the club pulled up stakes again and moved to Atlanta.

The Braves' won-lost records in 1965 and '66 were nearly identical. But in Atlanta attendance improved by almost a million. Aaron was still at the height of his powers, and younger players were beginning to make their mark. Reliever Phil Niekro was converted to a starter in 1967 and responded with the league's best ERA.

After finishing no higher than fifth in their first three seasons in Atlanta, the Braves celebrated 1969, the first year of divisional play, with a late-season drive that carried them to the championship of the West. Veteran Orlando Cepeda, newly acquired from St. Louis, joined Aaron in supplying power, and Niekro won 23 games as the Braves won 10 in a row to clinch the title in their next-to-last game. In the league's first Championship Series, though, the "Miracle" Mets of New York swept Atlanta in three games.

From there it was mostly downhill for the next decade. After breaking Babe Ruth's career home run record in the 1974 home opener, Aaron returned to Milwaukee (to the AL Brewers) in 1975. Attendance in Atlanta dwindled without Aaron. Yachtsman Ted Turner bought the club in 1976 and attendance rose, but the team sank to the bottom of the division for four years.

In 1982, though, with power from outfielder Dale Murphy and third baseman Bob Horner, and exceptional pitching from Niekro (17-4) and reliever Gene Garber (30 saves), Atlanta grabbed the division lead with a season-opening 13-game winning streak and recovered from a midsummer collapse to edge Los Angeles by one game for their second divisional crown. But they were swept by St. Louis in the NLCS.

For the next two seasons Murphy's league-leading slugging carried the Braves to second place. By 1986, though, they had sunk into the division cellar. Murphy boosted them up a notch in 1987 with the most productive season of his career, but as his power at the plate dropped the next year, the Braves sunk to their worst finish in 53 years.

With the first bottom-to-top comeback in NL history, the Braves captured the West in 1991. As Atlanta's home attendance zoomed back above 2 million for the first time since 1983, the Braves won a battle with Los Angeles that saw 11 ties or lead changes in the season's final weeks. The Braves captured the city's first pennant with a victory over Pittsburgh in seven games. Free agent Terry Pendleton (the NL MVP) joined David Justice and Ron Gant to power Atlanta's offense, while a trio of young pitchers—Tom Glavine, Steve Avery, and John Smoltz—anchored one of the league's best staffs.

In the World Series the Braves overcame a two-game deficit to take a Series lead before falling short by one extra-inning run in each of the final two games. The following season was very similar. Once again the Braves won the NL West and edged Pittsburgh for the pennant, although this time it took a come-from-behind win in the final at bat of Game 7 to beat the Pirates. Once again they faltered in the World Series, this time succumbing to Toronto in six games.

For the third season in a row the Braves topped the NL West in 1993, this time charging from 10 games back in July to a four-game lead in mid-September, then holding off resurgent San Francisco to clinch the crown on the season's final day. After building a 2-1 lead in the NLCS, though, they fell to the Phillies in six games.

When the players' strike ended the 1994 season in August, pitcher Greg Maddux, en route to a record third consecutive Cy Young Award, was fashioning one of the greatest seasons in years. Atlanta's 68-46 record ranked second in the NL only to Montreal's 74-40. But a new divisional alignment had moved the Braves from the NL West to the East—Montreal's division—so they finished second, six games behind the Expos.

Behind Maddux (19-2, 1.63 ERA), who won his fourth straight Cy Young, and rookie star Chipper Jones, the Braves bounced back in 1995, romping to a the NL East title. Atlanta also charged past Wild Card Colorado in the first round of the new postseason format and swept the Reds in the NLCS. In the World Series the Braves met the Indians in a rematch of the 1948 Fall Classic. This time the results were far different as Atlanta triumphed in six games.

The Braves won the NL East again in 1996. Atlanta's staff was paced this time by Cy Young Award winner John Smoltz (24-8, 276 strikeouts), Tom Glavine (15-10), and Mark Wohlers (39 saves); its offense was led by Chipper Jones (.309, 30 HR, 110 RBIs), Ryan Klesko (34 HR, 93 RBIs), and Fred McGriff (28 HR, 107 RBIs). In the first round of the postseason Atlanta rolled over Los Angeles. In the NLCS, the club had its back to the wall. Down three games to one, it rallied with 12-1, 3-1, and 15-0 wins over Tony LaRussa's Cards. The Braves kept it up in the first two games of the World Series, stomping Joe Torre's Yankees 12-1 and 4-0. The pundits were about to anoint the Braves as one of history's greatest teams. Then, suddenly, they ran out of gas, losing the next four straight to New York.

The Braves won the NL East again in 1997 and swept Houston in the Division Series. But Florida, the NL Wild Card, knocked the Braves out of the NLCS. The Braves were never challenged in 1998 as they won the East by 18 games and won a club-record 106 times. Atlanta had five pitchers win at least 15 games and Kerry Ligtenberg (30 saves) emerged as the team's new closer. Andres Galarraga, who replaced Fred McGriff at first base, brought more power to an already potent lineup. After the Braves swept the Cubs in the Division Series, however, they scored just three runs in losing the first three games of the NLCS to San Diego. Although Atlanta became the first team in major league history to go down 3-0 and still force a sixth game, the Padres won Game 6 and the NL pennant.

Baltimore Orioles

The history of major league baseball in Baltimore dates back to 1872, to the Lord Baltimores of the National Association, and includes the great National League Orioles of the 1890s. The city was also represented in the American League's first big league seasons, 1901-1902. But when those Orioles moved to New York in 1903 and became the Highlanders (later Yankees), Baltimore was without a big league club for more than half a century, until the transfer of the Browns from St. Louis in 1954.

The current Orioles didn't get their start in St. Louis, though. Their first home was Milwaukee, where they finished in the AL cellar in 1901. When they moved to St. Louis the next year, they lured several valuable players from the city's NL Cardinals—including 1901 batting champ Jesse Burkett, star shortstop Bobby Wallace, and the Cards' three best pitchers. They also took on the Cardinals' discarded nickname: becoming the new St. Louis Browns.

The Browns finished a strong second to the Philadelphia Athletics in their first St. Louis season, but fell to sixth the next year and, except for a fourth-place finish in 1908 (thanks to the pitching of newly acquired veteran Rube Waddell), remained mired in the second division until 1920. Late in the 1913 season a young Branch Rickey was hired to manage the Browns. In his two full seasons he was unable to lift the club out of the second division, but he did sign college star George Sisler (whom he had coached at the University of Michigan).

In 1916, his first full season, Sisler led the Browns in hitting as they caught fire in August to record their first winning season in eight years. Pitcher Urban Shocker was obtained from the Yankees two years later and by 1920 had developed into a 20-game winner. Also in 1920, Sisler connected for what is still a major league record 257 hits and batted .407 to help move the Browns up to fourth, their first finish that high since 1908. The next year Shocker's 27 victories brought them a winning season and third place. And in 1922 the team recorded its finest record ever in St. Louis: 93 wins and a .604 winning percentage.

The 1922 Browns, led by Sisler's sizzling .420 average, hit .313 as a team to lead the league. Left fielder Ken Williams ran away with the RBI title and beat out Babe Ruth and Tilly Walker for the home run crown. (Ruth, to be honest, did miss nearly a third of the season that year.) Sisler and Williams even finished one-two in stolen bases. And though Shocker slipped a bit to 24 wins, he led a pitching staff that recorded the league's lowest ERA. The team led the league in the standings throughout July and into August before the Yankees nudged ahead of them. The Browns never regained the lead, remaining second, a heartbreaking single game back, at season's end.

Falling back to fifth the next year, as Sisler missed the whole season with a sinus infection, the Browns remained out of contention for the next 21 years, dropping to their lowest point in 1939 with 111 losses. They had three winning seasons in the war years 1942-1945. The Browns captured their only pennant in 1944, edging the Detroit Tigers on the final day after trailing them through most of September. The World Series—an all-St. Louis affair—proved anticlimactic for the Browns as they lost to the Cardinals in six games.

The Browns finished third in 1945 before sinking back into the second division. Even the club's purchase by the dynamic Bill Veeck in July 1951 couldn't rouse them. (A month after buying the Browns, Veeck made his best-remembered move; bringing in midget Eddie Gaedel for one plate appearance—he walked.)

Unable to earn either victories or money in St. Louis, Veeck sold the club in September 1953 to a Baltimore group, who relocated and renamed them the Orioles. The new owners hired the brilliant Paul Richards to rebuild

the team as manager. It took him (and Lee MacPhail, who became general manager and president in 1958) several years to move the Orioles above .500. In 1960 young third baseman Brooks Robinson and rookie Jim Gentile led the team as it made its first run for the pennant since 1944. In first place in early September, they finished second when the Yanks won 15 straight.

The next year the O's did even better, winning six more games than they had in 1960. Gentile hit 46 home runs and drove in 141. But the Yankees and Tigers had even better years and the Orioles finished a distant third.

When Hank Bauer was brought in to manage the Orioles in 1964, the team entered its golden decades—20 years which saw them win seven division titles, six pennants, and three world championships, with only two finishes below third. With Robinson driving in runs and left fielder Boog Powell slugging at a league-leading pace, the O's finished with wins in seven of their final eight games. But the White Sox won their last nine and the Yankees put together an 11-game streak near the end to take the pennant and leave Baltimore third, two games back.

After another third-place finish in 1965, the Orioles acquired slugging Frank Robinson from Cincinnati and moved second-year pitcher Jim Palmer into the starting rotation. Palmer won 15 to lead a balanced staff, and Frank Robinson captured the Triple Crown. With both Robinsons and Powell driving in 100 runs or more, the O's romped to their first pennant. They continued the romp in the World Series, holding Los Angeles to a total of just two runs as they swept to their first world title.

A drop in offensive production and the loss of Palmer to injuries for most of the season plunged Baltimore into a tie for sixth in 1967. Palmer was out the next year, too, but pitchers Dave McNally and Jim Hardin burst to the forefront with fine seasons to lift the club back to second.

Baltimore coach Earl Weaver, a pennant-winning manager in the O's farm system, replaced Hank Bauer at the Orioles' helm in mid-1968 to begin what became one of the longest and most successful managerial tenures of recent times. In 14 full seasons Weaver led his club to six Eastern Division titles and six second-place finishes, with one season each in third and fourth. In seven of the 14 years the Orioles compiled the league's lowest ERA, including five consecutive seasons (1969-1973). Baltimore pitchers put together 21 different 20-game seasons in those 14 seasons (eight of them by Jim Palmer), and garnered six Cy Young Awards.

In the first three years of divisional play Baltimore ran away with the East championship and swept the American League Championship Series to capture the pennant each time. The 1969 team (despite an embarrassingly easy loss to the New York Mets in the World Series) is often ranked among the greatest clubs of all time. With overwhelming pitching and fielding, the Orioles took the division crown by 19 games, winning a club-record 109. The Orioles also were tops in fielding and their pitchers gave up nearly a run less per game than the league average.

Baltimore's performance in 1970 was nearly as impressive. Mike Cuellar and Dave McNally won 24 games each, and Jim Palmer contributed 20 more wins to the O's total of 108. This time they won the World Series as well, rolling over Cincinnati in five games behind an unforget-

table performance by Series MVP Brooks Robinson.

In the 1971 World Series, though, Pittsburgh came back from losses in the first two games to defeat the Orioles by a run in Game 7. The O's captured divisional titles in 1973 and '74, but it was 1979 before they again triumphed in the ALCS. Once again, however, they faced the Pirates in the World Series, and once again took the Series lead, only to fall again in the seventh game.

The 1979 pennant was Weaver's last, as late-season Oriole surges in 1980 and '82 fell just short. But in 1983 the O's—paced by the pitching of veteran Scott McGregor and rookie Mike Boddicker, and the hitting and fielding of Cal Ripken, Jr. at short, and Eddie Murray at first—made new manager Joe Altobelli look good. After a comfortable divisional win, they trounced the Chicago White Sox in the ALCS and the Philadelphia Phillies in the World Series.

Despite the return of Earl Weaver in 1985-1986, the Orioles finished last in the East in 1986. Though they rose to sixth in 1987, their .414 winning percentage was their lowest in 32 years. Then in 1988 they hit rock bottom, not only finishing last but also beginning the season with an AL record-setting 21 consecutive defeats.

Baltimore's rebound was even more startling than its plummet. Under manager Frank Robinson (who had been handed the hapless O's early in the 1988 season) the 1989 Orioles took over first place in late April, held the lead through August, and stayed within the reach of the division title until Toronto defeated them in the season's penultimate game to clinch the crown. The newly potent bat of catcher Mickey Tettleton and splendid relief from rookie Gregg Olson highlighted the Baltimore resurgence. Olson remained effective in 1990, but the offense faltered, and an August-September slide dropped the Orioles out of the race.

The O's began slowly in 1991, and manager Robinson was replaced by coach Johnny Oates in May, with the club in last place. But although Cal Ripken put together an MVP season, the O's never caught fire, and finished sixth, 24 games out. In 1992, at festive new Orioles Park at Camden Yards, Baltimore snapped back to challenge Toronto through much of the season before slipping to third.

At a bankruptcy auction in August 1993, a group led by Peter Angelos agreed to purchase the club for a record $173 million. On the field, 1993 was much like 1992. Only half a game out of first as late as Sept. 9, the Orioles finished 10 games back, tied for third with Detroit. They challenged again in 1994, but Baltimore's second-place finish was not good enough to save manager Oates' job.

Cal Ripken, Jr. had twice won AL MVP honors and was a fixture on the All-Star team, but none of these accomplishments could compare to the spectacle at Camden Yards in 1995. He finally broke Lou Gehrig's consecutive game playing streak on Sept. 6 in an uplifting ceremony that highlighted an otherwise disappointing season.

Under new manager Davey Johnson, the Orioles (88-74) underperformed until midseason. Owner Angelos resisted temptations to break up the team and instead acquired veteran Eddie Murray, who hit his 500th home run and helped spark a successful stretch run for a Wild Card berth. Offense was the name of the game for this team as it slammed a major league record 257 homers. Standouts

included Brady Anderson (50 HR, 110 RBIs), Rafael Palmeiro (39 HR, 142 RBIs), Roberto Alomar (22 HR, 94 RBIs), Cal Ripken (26 HR, 102 RBIs), and pitcher Mike Mussina (19-11).

Baltimore's 1996 postseason appearance (its first since 1983) was overshadowed, however, by Alomar's spitting on umpire John Hirschbeck. Baltimore upset the favored Indians in the Division Series, but in the ALCS (aided by a controversial Game 1 home run that should have been ruled fan interference) the O's fell to Joe Torre's Yankees in five games.

The Orioles won the AL East in 1997 and knocked off the Seattle Mariners in the Division Series with surprising ease. Nothing was easy in the ALCS. Mussina's dominating performance—25 strikeouts in 15 innings and a 0.60 ERA—was wasted as the Orioles lost both his starts to Cleveland in extra innings. On the day that Davey Johnson was named AL Manager of the Year he resigned as the result of a dispute with Angelos.

Ray Miller moved from pitching coach to manager in 1998, but the Orioles suffered through an up-and-down season that culminated with Ripken unexpectedly ending his consecutive game streak at 2,632 in Baltimore's final home game.

Boston Red Sox

Since the end of World War II, the Red Sox have won the American League pennant four times, only to lose the World Series each time in the seventh game. It was not always thus. In their first two decades they were the league's most successful club, winners of six pennants and five world championships. (No World Series was played the year of their second pennant.)

Organized in 1901 as one of four new eastern clubs in Ban Johnson's newly-formed American League, Boston's Americans (or Pilgrims, Puritans, Plymouth Rocks, or Somersets, as they were variously called) quickly established themselves as one of the game's strongest teams. Star third baseman Jimmy Collins was lured from Boston's NL club to manage the new Americans, and he assembled a team that included such former NL standouts as slugger Buck Freeman and pitcher Cy Young. Finishing a strong second in the AL's inaugural major league season, the Pilgrims quickly supplanted their mediocre NL counterparts in the hearts and wallets of Boston fans.

After a third-place finish in 1902, the Pilgrims ran away from the rest of the league in 1903 to take their first pennant by 14½ games over Philadelphia. Young led the league in victories for the third straight season, Freeman took titles in home runs, total bases, and RBIs and second-year outfielder Patsy Dougherty finished first in hits and runs scored. In the first modern World Series, Boston overcame Pittsburgh's favored Pirates, thereby confirming the AL's claim to major league status in the public mind.

Boston repeated as pennant winners in 1904, but by a much narrower margin, after a struggle with the New York Highlanders that wasn't settled until the next-to-last game of the season. The NL Giants refused to play Boston in a World Series that year.

Over the next few years, as the Pilgrims dropped into

the league cellar, new owner John I. Taylor (whose father, *Boston Globe* publisher Charles Taylor, was said to have bought the club for his son to give him something useful to do) rid the team of many of the players who had brought it glory. Eventually Taylor was himself maneuvered out of the club presidency, but it turned out he had not been a wanton destroyer. In driving out the old guard he had been making room for new young players: pitcher Joe Wood, for example, and a sprightly outfield of Tris Speaker, Harry Hooper, and Duffy Lewis. The club—now known as the Red Sox—rose out of its depths in the final years of Taylor's presidency, even challenging the league leaders through much of 1909 before dropping away in late August. In 1911, in one of the last acts of his presidency, Taylor had, with his father, purchased land in Boston's Fenway section and built a new ballpark.

Sparked by the spectacular pitching of Wood and Speaker's play at the bat and in center field, the Red Sox of 1912 took the league lead in early June and were never headed, finishing with a club-record 105 victories. In the World Series they edged John McGraw's Giants and Christy Mathewson in one of the most exciting Series ever, four games to three, with one tie. Three years later, with a staff that boasted the AL's four top pitchers in winning percentage (including rookie Babe Ruth), the Sox captured their fourth pennant. After a first-game loss to the Phillies in the World Series, Boston recovered to sweep the next four by one run apiece.

Joe Wood's ailing arm finally gave out, and Tris Speaker was traded to Cleveland at the start of the 1916 season following a salary dispute. But with Ruth winning 23 games to lead the team, the Sox slid past the White Sox and Tigers in mid-September to take their fifth pennant and waltzed over Brooklyn in the Series.

Incipient disaster struck the Red Sox that December when New York theatrical entrepreneurs Hugh Ward and Harry Frazee bought the club. They put little cash into the deal, counting on future profits to pay the bulk of the purchase price. Ward sailed for Australia, leaving Frazee to run the club. For a while the future looked bright. After a second-place finish in 1917, Frazee hired minor league executive Ed Barrow as manager, and when many of the team's regulars left for military service in World War I, Frazee bought and traded for worthy replacements. In a season shortened a month because of the war, the Sox edged Cleveland for their sixth pennant and defeated the Chicago Cubs for their fifth world championship.

Frazee's theater losses put him in a financial bind and gradually forced him to sell off the best of his players— mostly to the Yankees, who had plenty of money, and an office just a short hop from Frazee's New York theater. Though the Sox fell to sixth place in 1919, Babe Ruth kept attention fixed on the team as he went to the outfield and startled the baseball world with a record 29 home runs. But that winter Frazee sold Ruth to the Yankees for $100,000 and a $300,000 mortgage on Fenway Park.

The Red Sox were on a 15-year sojourn in the second division that even a 1923 change in ownership was powerless to end. From 1922 through 1932 the Sox emerged from last place only twice. In 1932 they reached their nadir, losing 111 games and finishing 64 games out of first.

Young and wealthy Tom Yawkey bought the club in 1933 and promptly began what would be a lifetime effort to restore Boston to its former glory. His first efforts to buy success ready-made with such established stars as Lefty Grove, Jimmie Foxx, and Joe Cronin pulled the club out of the cellar but failed to lift it into pennant contention. But as general manager Eddie Collins began turning up young players to join the veterans, the club's fortune rose. The emergence between 1938 and 1942 of players like Bobby Doerr, Ted Williams, and pitcher Tex Hughson brought Boston a level of success not seen since 1918. In four of the five years they finished second to the Yankees, achieving, in 1942, their highest winning percentage since 1915.

The loss of most of these newcomers to military service in World War II delayed further progress. But with the arrival of rookie pitching sensation Dave Ferriss in 1945, and the acquisition of slugging first baseman Rudy York that winter, the club was prepared for its returning war veterans to join in bringing Boston its greatest season since 1912. With 104 victories, the 1946 Sox won their long-delayed seventh pennant by 12 games over second-place Detroit. In the World Series the favored Sox bowed to the Cardinals in Game 7 by one run.

The Yankees ran away from the pack in 1947, but the three years that followed saw the Red Sox three times in the throes of pennant fever. In 1948, after falling back a bit in late September, the Sox won four at the very end to tie Cleveland for first—but lost the one-game playoff. The next year they were 12 games behind the Yankees on July 4 but pulled up gradually to take a one-game lead into the final two-game series in New York. One Sox victory would win the pennant, but the Yankees took both games. In 1950 Boston played the league's best ball through July and August, to pull within a game of the Yankees on Sept. 18 but then lost four in a row and all hope of the pennant.

In 1951 the Sox collapsed at season's end to finish third, 11 games back. They came no closer the next 15 years, finishing with eight consecutive losing seasons from 1959 through 1966.

In 1967 the Sox awakened from their long slumber. A 10-game win streak in mid-July shot them out of mediocrity into the midst of a four-team race for the pennant that was not settled until Boston beat Minnesota and Detroit split a doubleheader on the final day, leaving the Sox on top. Carl Yastrzemski, who had replaced Ted Williams in left field seven years earlier, clinched the Triple Crown with a game-winning home run and six other hits in the final two must-win games. But Boston lost the World Series to St. Louis in seven games.

It was eight years before the Red Sox won another pennant, but they came close in 1972, losing the AL East crown by half a game to Detroit in the season's final series. They led the division two years later from mid-July through early September, then fell apart and finished third. But the next year, 1975, they maintained to the end the lead they first took in May, and swept Oakland in the ALCS for their ninth pennant. Television viewers will long remember Carlton Fisk's home run that won Game 6 of the World Series from Cincinnati, but Red Sox fans also remember that the Sox lost Game 7 the next day, 4-3. Owner Tom Yawkey died the following July without winning the world championship he had sought for more than 40 years.

Boston contended seriously in 1977 in a tight three-way race, pulling ahead for a time in June and again in August, but ultimately falling 2½ games short. The next year, though, the Sox pulled off another amazing finish. After blowing a 7½-game late-August lead, they won their final eight scheduled games to tie the Yankees. But in the one-game playoff, Yankees shortstop Bucky Dent's three-run pop-fly homer over Fenway's cozy left field wall proved Boston's ruin. The Sox rallied in the eighth to draw within a run, but with two out and a man on third in the ninth, Yastrzemski popped up and the season was history.

Yaz retired in 1983, but outfielders Jim Rice and Dwight Evans remained from the 1975 champions. In Wade Boggs, the Red Sox had their most consistent hitter since Ted Williams, and, in Roger Clemens, Boston had its most exciting pitcher since Joe Wood. In 1986 the Red Sox won their 10th pennant, with an amazing comeback over California from a 3-1 deficit in the ALCS. Against the New York Mets in the World Series, the Red Sox were within one pitch of capturing their first world title in 68 years, but they lost the game, and again lost Game 7.

When a pitching decline dropped the Sox to fifth place in 1987, and the All-Star break the next year found them barely above .500, manager John McNamara was replaced by coach Joe Morgan. The Sox responded with 19 wins in their next 20 games and, despite a slump at season's end, took the title in the AL East by one game. In the ALCS, though, Oakland swept to the pennant in four games.

In 1990, with Clemens back in peak form after a season and a half below par, the Sox arrived at midseason in first place. After trading the lead back and forth with Toronto, they captured the crown of the East on the season's final day. But in the ALCS Oakland again swept past them to the pennant.

Roger Clemens won his third Cy Young award in 1991, and the Sox came from 11½ games back in August to within half a game of first-place Toronto in September. But they dropped back and finished in a second-place tie with Detroit. Manager Joe Morgan was replaced by Butch Hobson for 1992, but the downhill slide continued.

Hobson's disappointing tenure was filled with fast starts and sudden collapses. The Sox, who started 1994 with the majors' best record, were one game out of last place the day the players' strike ended the season. Hobson's days in Boston ended shortly thereafter.

His replacement, Kevin Kennedy, constantly juggled lineups to give the Sox the 1995 AL East by the surprisingly comfortable margin of seven games over the Yankees. Key to the club's victory was AL RBI king Mo Vaughn, who captured MVP honors in a tight race over Cleveland's Albert Belle. Boston, however, was no match for the powerful Indians, falling to them, 3-0, in the first round of the postseason, with Vaughn and Jose Canseco particularly ineffective at bat.

In 1996 the Sox got off to a sluggish start, but finished strong—not strong enough, however, to save manager Kennedy's job (he was replaced by longtime Braves coach Jimy Williams). Standouts for the third-place (85-77) Red Sox included Vaughn (44 HR, 143 RBIs, 207 hits) and Clemens (an AL-best 257 strikeouts, including a record-tying 20 in one game against Detroit.)

After a disappointing 78-84 season in 1997—the lone bright spot was AL Rookie of the Year Nomar Garciaparra—the Red Sox put a dramatically retooled team on the field in 1998. The Sox traded for 1997 NL Cy Young Award winner Pedro Martinez and made him the highest-paid player in the game. Mo Vaughn narrowly missed his first batting title in 1998, but more importantly for Red Sox fans, the team held off a late charge by Toronto to win the AL Wild Card. In the Division Series, the Red Sox ended a 13-game losing streak in the postseason (dating back to Game 5 of the 1986 World Series), but the Sox got little other than what their stars could provide: Vaughn and Garciaparra drove in 19 of the team's 20 runs, and Martinez won his only start as Cleveland took the series in four games.

Chicago Cubs

The Cubs have represented the same city in the major leagues longer than any other club. Organized in 1870 to provide a professional challenge to Cincinnati's Red Stockings, the next year the White Stockings (as they were originally known) were one of the founding members of the game's first professional league—the National Association.

Despite the great Chicago fire, which destroyed their ballpark, uniforms, and club business records late in the 1871 season, the White Stockings completed their schedule, finishing third to the Athletics of Philadelphia. But they dropped out of the NA for the next two years because of the fire's devastation. In 1875, in the midst of a second losing season following their return, the club arranged for four of champion Boston's best players to jump to Chicago for the 1876 season. That winter, White Stockings president William A. Hulbert and pitcher/manager Al Spalding (one of the jumpers) led in forming a new league to replace the NA.

Sparked by its Boston players and infielder Adrian "Cap" Anson (lured from the Athletics), the 1876 White Stockings outscored their opponents by more than five runs per game and handily won the first championship of the new National League. The next year, when Spalding (whose pitching had brought Chicago 47 of its 52 victories in 1876) switched over to first base, the club fell to fifth. Spalding retired from the field in 1878 to attend to his young sporting goods firm (though he returned as club president from 1882 through 1891).

In 1879 Anson was named to manage the team. For the next 12 years the White Stockings ranked among baseball's best, garnering five pennants (1880-1882, 1885-1886) and four second-place finishes. Anson's strict discipline did not make him popular with his often rowdy teammates, but his consistency as a player set an example, and his innovative management made the most of his players' abilities. Anson's forcefulness, however, contributed to baseball's most grievous setback: His adamant refusal in the mid-1880s to take the field against black players prevented the racial integration of the major leagues.

After a close finish behind Boston in 1891, the White Stockings' first era as an NL power ended. In each of the next 11 seasons they fell at least 15 games short of the top.

The team's youthful ineptitude was reflected in the nicknames that succeeded "White Stockings": the "Colts," the "Orphans" (in 1898, after Anson—known as "Pop"—was fired after 19 years at the helm), and finally, the "Cubs."

When Frank Selee (who had led Boston to greatness in the 1890s) was hired to manage the Cubs in 1902, he inherited a team that had ended the 1901 season 37 games out. By 1903 he had turned catcher/outfielder Frank Chance into a first baseman, moved Joe Tinker from third to short, and brought Johnny Evers up from Troy to play second. The new double-play combination flourished not only in the field but at the bat. The Cubs finished third in 1903 with their best record since 1898.

That winter Selee traded for pitcher Mordecai "Three Finger" Brown. After leading the Cubs to second place in 1904, Selee signed rookie hurler Ed Reulbach, but, ill with tuberculosis, he took a leave of absence in the middle of the 1905 season. Chance took his place and brought the team to third; Selee never returned, but he had gone a long way toward building a championship team.

Trades for outfielder Jimmy Sheckard and third baseman Harry Steinfeldt, the signing of rookie pitcher Jack Pfiester, and the acquisition during the 1906 season of pitchers Orval Overall and Jack Taylor completed one of the greatest teams of all time. The Cubs passed the Giants to take the lead early in May and kept on rising. New York and Pittsburgh made a race of it through July, but the Cubs won 55 of their final 65 games to finish with a record 116 victories, 20 games ahead of second-place New York.

Brown's 1.04 ERA was the league's best, with Pfiester and Reulbach second and third. The team ERA was a remarkably low 1.76. Overall, Chicago scored 80 more runs than its nearest rival, and yielded 89 fewer. But in the World Series, the crosstown "Hitless Wonder" White Sox matched the Cubs' hitting and pitched twice as effectively to take the crown in six games.

The Cubs' hitting and run production fell off in 1907, but their pitching did not (ERA: 1.73). With 107 wins, they captured their second straight pennant, by 17 games. This time their dominance carried over into the World Series as they swept Detroit after an opening-game tie.

The pennant race of 1908 was one of the tightest in baseball history. On Sept. 22 the Cubs won two from the Giants to pull into a virtual tie for first (with Pittsburgh third, 1½ games back). The next day the Giants appeared to have beaten the Cubs with an RBI single in the last of the ninth. But young Fred Merkle, on first when the hit was made, failed to continue on to second and was forced out by alert Cubs second baseman Johnny Evers for the third out, which negated the Giant run. Because of increasing darkness and the mood of excited fans on the field, the game was called and ruled a tie.

After another week and a half in which all three teams took turns in front, Chicago defeated Pittsburgh to pull ahead by half a game, leaving the Pirates and Giants tied for second. But New York had one more game—and defeated the Boston Braves to pull into a tie with the Cubs. The "Merkle boner" game thus had to be replayed, and, this time, the Cubs won to take their third straight pennant. In the World Series they again beat Detroit in five games. Their second straight world title was also, to date, their last.

The Cubs won 104 games in 1909 as their pitching staff recorded an ERA under 2.00 for the third time in four years. Chicago still finished second to the powerful Pirates, who won 110 and captured the World Series.

In 1910 their 104 wins carried them to another pennant, by a comfortable 13 games. After a World Series loss to the Philadelphia Athletics, and seasons in second and third place, Chance resigned, protesting the unwillingness of owner Charles Murphy to spend money for top players.

The Cubs got a new owner in 1916, and with him a new ballpark. Charles Weeghman, who had owned the Chicago Whales in the short-lived Federal League, purchased the Cubs when the FL went under, and moved them into the park he had built for the Whales.

The team that next carried Chicago to the pennant, in the war-shortened season of 1918, featured only one name familiar to Cubs fans from earlier championship seasons—Fred Merkle. The man whose rookie boner as a Giant had made possible their pennant in 1908 was now their leading run producer. As in earlier pennant-winning seasons, fine pitching predominated, with veteran James "Hippo" Vaughn the league's best pitcher on the league's top staff.

Several years of decline followed the Cubs' World Series loss to the Boston Red Sox. The club hit bottom in 1925 with its first cellar finish in 53 years of league play, but a new era of greatness was at hand. In 1921 wealthy chewing-gum manufacturer William Wrigley had purchased control of the Cubs, with a determination to spend what was needed to produce a winner.

The seeds Wrigley planted eventually bore fruit. In 1926 he hired Joe McCarthy—a successful minor league manager—to lead the club and drafted outfielder Lewis "Hack" Wilson from Toledo. Wilson immediately became one of the league's leading offensive threats, and the Cubs rebounded to the first division. In 1927 they even led the league through August before dropping back to fourth. A postseason trade brought them outfielder Hazen "Kiki" Cuyler and a close third-place finish in 1928. Then the Cubs traded with the Braves for second baseman Rogers Hornsby, and in 1929 returned to the top. Led by Wilson's 159 RBIs and Hornsby's 149, five Cubs drove in more than 90 runs each. After battling Pittsburgh for the lead through mid-July, the Cubs hurtled ahead to take the pennant by 10½ games, despite a late-season slump. The slump continued through the World Series, though, as the Athletics humbled the Cubs in five games.

Just four games from the end of the hot pennant race in 1930 (the year Wilson set the major league RBI record with 190), McCarthy—still smarting from criticism arising from the World Series loss—quit as manager. With Hornsby at the helm, the Cubs preserved a second-place finish. They dropped to third the next year, but returned to the top in 1932. Hornsby, near the end of his playing days, was dropped as manager in August, with the Cubs in second, and replaced by first baseman Charlie Grimm. Pitcher Lon Warneke, in his first full season as a starter, led the league in wins and ERA. The club enjoyed a hot streak in August to move out in front of slumping Pittsburgh and hung on to take the flag by four games. The Yankees provided the World Series humiliation this time, a four-game sweep that provided McCarthy (now the Yankees manager) with sweet revenge for the Chicago

fans' criticism three years earlier.

It had become a pattern: three years, another pennant. In 1935 a balanced offense (led by catcher Gabby Hartnett and second baseman Billy Herman) and the league's best pitching brought the Cubs up from fourth in late June to first in September. They clinched the pennant with three games to go, with their 20th win of a 21-game streak. In the World Series, Detroit stopped the Cubs in six games.

After two seasons in second, it was time for another pennant. Bill Lee, the club's top pitcher in 1935, was now the league's finest, as was the Cubs' staff. With the club languishing six and a half games back in midseason, Grimm quit as manager and was replaced by catcher Hartnett. In September the Cubs came to life, rising to second early in the month. They overtook Pittsburgh with their ninth consecutive win on Hartnett's homer against the Pirates in the growing darkness with two away in the bottom of the ninth, which became known as the "Home Run in the Gloaming." The Cubs clinched the pennant four games later, on the next-to-last day of the season. The Yankees swept Chicago to hand the Cubs their sixth straight World Series loss.

In 1940, after 14 straight winning seasons, the Cubs began a five-year stretch below .500. Jimmie Wilson replaced Hartnett as manager in 1941; then Grimm returned near the start of the 1944 season. The club finished a distant fourth that year, but in 1945, after a middling start, they won 26 of 30 midseason games to take a lead they never relinquished. Balanced pitching (sparked by Hank Borowy, who went 11-2 after coming over from the Yankees in July) and the hitting of veteran first baseman Phil Cavarretta (.355) and center fielder Andy Pafko (110 RBIs) held off the pressing St. Louis Cardinals to preserve a 16th Cubs pennant. Although they battled Detroit through a full seven games in the World Series, they ended up losing again.

For the next 23 years the Cubs remained out of pennant contention. But in 1969, the first year of divisional play, under the lively management of Leo Durocher, they took an early lead in the NL East. With a potent offense led by veteran sluggers Ron Santo, Ernie Banks, and Billy Williams, the team continued rising through early August. But the New York Mets rose even faster and farther; they didn't pause when Chicago leveled off in late August, and while the Cubs were losing eight straight in September the Mets were winning 10 in a row. The Cubs wound up eight games back.

The 1970s were a disappointing decade, with several division leads melting away in the summertime sun at Wrigley. In 1981 the Wrigley family sold the club to the Chicago Tribune Company. Three years later, with a new manager, Jim Frey, and an almost wholly different roster, the new management capped its rebuilding program with the acquisition of pitcher Rick Sutcliffe from Cleveland in mid-June 1984. As Sutcliffe fashioned a 16-1 record for his new club, the Cubs went on to capture their first division title. After winning the first two games of the NLCS against San Diego, the pennant was swept out from under them as the Padres took the final three.

In 1989 the team, now managed by Don Zimmer, bounced back to duplicate its 1984 success. With a balanced offense and pitching vastly improved over the previous season, the Cubs took the NL East lead for good on Aug. 7. Once again, though, they were unable to persevere to the pennant, losing the best-of-seven NLCS to San Francisco in five games.

As they had done in 1989, Andre Dawson, Mark Grace and Ryne Sandberg continued to provide offensive clout over the next three years, and in 1992 Cy Young Award winner Greg Maddux and newly acquired Mike Morgan fashioned sterling seasons on the mound. But the team could not carve out a winning season, finishing tied for fourth in 1990, and fourth by themselves in 1991 and '92. Ownership snarled when baseball commissioner Fay Vincent proposed transferring the club from the NL East to the West in 1993, but the threat passed when Vincent, under pressure from owners dissatisfied with his leadership, resigned before the end of the 1992 season.

Free agents Dawson and Maddux left for greener pastures in 1993, but catcher Rick Wilkins and outfielder Sammy Sosa blossomed into power hitters, and newly acquired closer Randy Myers garnered a league-record 53 saves. While the Cubs once again finished only fourth, they put together their first winning season in four years. The improvement wasn't enough to satisfy management, though, and second-year manager Jim Lefebvre was replaced by coach Tom Treblehorn at the end of the 1993 season.

Ryne Sandberg, claiming to have lost his competitive drive, retired during the 1994 season, and the Cubs followed suit, settling themselves firmly in the cellar of the newly formed Central division.

Chicago, under manager Jim Riggleman, bounced back to third (73-71) in 1995 as Mark Grace led the NL with 51 doubles. And at season's end Sandberg, now 36, announced he was ending his retirement and returning to the Cubs. The 1996 Cubs fell to fourth place and the 1997 team lost a National League-record 14 games to start the season and finished last in the NL Central.

But if 1997 was a nightmare for Chicago, 1998 was a sweet dream. The Cubs bolstered the team through free agent signings (Rod Beck, Henry Rodriguez, and Jeff Blauser), brought up a rookie (Kerry Wood) who tied the major league record with 20 strikeouts in his third start on his way to NL Rookie of the Year, and found a savior on the waiver wire (Gary Gaetti).

Even those contributions paled in comparison to the season put forth by Sammy Sosa. Sosa set a major league record with 20 home runs in June and his longball exploits challenged even those of Mark McGwire. Sosa was at Busch Stadium when McGwire hit his record-breaking 62nd home run off Cubs teammate Steve Trachsel and a few days later Sosa also hit number 62. He finished the season with 66 home runs and became just the fourth player with 50 home runs, 150 RBIs, and 400 total bases. More importantly, the Cubs survived many bullets in the closing days of the season to force a one-game playoff for the NL Wild Card. The Cubs beat the Giants to advance to the NL Division Series against the Braves. But Atlanta, winners of 106 games during the season, swept the Cubs in three games.

Chicago White Sox

When minor league owner Charlie Comiskey transferred

his club from St. Paul to Chicago as part of the move to upgrade the American League to major league status, he called it the White Stockings, after the Chicago team that dominated the National League in its early years. The new Chicago team revived memories of the old White Stockings, winning the AL championship in 1900, and repeating the triumph in 1901, the league's first major league season. Manager Clark Griffith (who had jumped to the White Stockings from Chicago's NL Cubs) was the team's star pitcher in 1901, winning 24 of 31 decisions as his team took the lead in May and held off the threatening Boston Somersets the rest of the way.

Griffith's effectiveness fell off in 1902, as did the team, (now called the White Sox) which took a sizable lead in July, only to slide back to fourth in August. Griffith left the next year and the White Sox sank to seventh. It would take 18 years and baseball's biggest scandal for the Sox to finish that low again.

In 1904, after center fielder Fielder Jones replaced left fielder Nixey Callahan as manager, the Sox rose into first place for a moment in August before settling back to third. The next year they made up a seven-game deficit in September to catch the Philadelphia Athletics, but the loss of two games to the A's stalled their drive and left them in second.

Nothing stalled the White Sox drive in 1906. Although they ranked at the very bottom of the league in hitting and entered June five games below .500, their pitching and hustle pulled them through. "Big Ed" Walsh, who had finally mastered the spitball after two years of trying, won 17 games, including a league-high 10 shutouts. Doc White contributed 18 wins with a league-best 1.52 ERA, and Frank Owen and Nick Altrock won 22 and 20, respectively. The Sox shot to the top in August with a 19-game win streak (including eight shutouts). Early in September, New York's Highlanders passed them, but after the two teams had traded the lead back and forth for a couple of weeks the Sox spurted to take the pennant by three games. If the race was close, so were the individual games: the Sox achieved nearly one-third of their victories by the margin of a single run. The "Hitless Wonders" carried their momentum through the World Series, shocking the mighty crosstown Cubs (who had won a record 116 games that year) in six games.

In 1907, after leading the league much of the first half, the Sox slipped to third. The next year Walsh pitched in the final seven games on his way to a career-high 40 wins. In a tight finish he pulled the Sox to within a half game of first-place Detroit before they dropped back to third with a loss to the Tigers on the final day.

It was 1915 before the Sox (piloted by rookie manager Clarence H. "Pants" Rowland) next finished that high, and 1916 before they again challenged seriously for the pennant. Comiskey, though accused of pinching pennies in his payment of players, was willing to spend what was needed to acquire them. After the 1914 season he purchased star second baseman Eddie Collins from the A's, and promising young Oscar "Happy" Felsch from minor league Milwaukee. The following August he acquired the great "Shoeless" Joe Jackson from Cleveland. Together with the league's best pitching staff, they carried the Sox into the thick of a three-way race and a close second-place finish in 1916. A year later the Sox took the pennant with

the best winning percentage the club has ever compiled. Ten-year veteran pitcher Eddie Cicotte enjoyed his first 20-win season with a league-high 28 victories, and a league-and-career-best 1.53 ERA. After dueling the Boston Red Sox most of the season, Chicago streaked out of reach in late August to finish with 100 wins. In the World Series against the New York Giants they captured their second (and, to date, their last) world title, in six games.

With several key players out much of 1918 for military or civilian war service, the White Sox finished out of the running, a dismal sixth. But in 1919, with the team back at full strength, the race once again went to Chicago. If their pitching didn't have quite the depth of the 1917 squad, its best hurlers were in peak form. Cicotte, after an off-year in 1918, attained a career high with 29 wins, as did Lefty Williams with 23 victories. Collins and Jackson enjoyed their best seasons in several years, and Buck Weaver had never been better. Old-time pitcher/second baseman Kid Gleason was a rookie as a big league manager, but his Sox began strong and, after slipping briefly into second in midseason, pulled ahead in July to stay.

When the Sox lost the World Series to underdog Cincinnati, there were rumors of a fix, but nothing came to light for nearly a year. The White Sox looked better than ever in 1920. Though they fell back in May after a hot April, by mid-August they had risen to the thick of a tight three-team race. Felsch, Collins, and Weaver had never played better, Jackson was enjoying one of his very best seasons, and four pitchers were on their way to more than 20 wins. Chicago might not have caught Cleveland's rampaging Indians, but it didn't help that talk of a White Sox scandal revived late in the season, or that the grand jury convened only eight games from the end, or that eight Sox players were indicted and suspended with just three games to play. The team finished two games back, in second place.

The indicted players—infielders Chick Gandil, Swede Risberg, and Fred McMullin, plus Cicotte, Felsch, Jackson, Weaver, and Williams—were acquitted in court when three crucial confessions disappeared, but they were banned for life from organized baseball by Commissioner Kenesaw Mountain Landis. The White Sox did not soon recover from the loss. In 1921 they began 15 years of wandering in the second division. The Sox finished last three times in that span, plus a seventh-place finish in 1932 that left the Sox a club-worst 56½ games out of first.

Two of the club's greatest and most durable players arrived during these years: pitcher Ted Lyons (who won 260 games for the Sox in 21 years) in 1923, and in 1930 shortstop Luke Appling (who averaged .310 in his 20 years with the club). Owner Comiskey died in 1931, in the midst of his Sox's most dismal era, but Lyons and Appling were around long enough to enjoy a few fourth- and third-place seasons. But neither saw the Sox contend seriously for the pennant. After his playing career was over, Lyons managed the team for a few years—until 1948, when the Sox lost 101 games and finished last.

That year Frank Lane was lured from the presidency of the American Association to take charge as Chicago's general manager. When Lane hired Paul Richards to manage the club in 1951, the Sox began what became a 17-year string of winning seasons.

In 1951, Richards' first season, the Sox spent a month

in first place before drifting down to fourth, and the next year began a five-year run in third place. In 1954 they won 94 games but were out of the race by August—that was the year Cleveland won 111 and the second-place Yankees 103. Richards moved on to Baltimore, but Marty Marion, who replaced him, kept the Sox in third place.

After the Sox fell from first place in early September, Frank Lane left at the end of the 1955 season. Young Chuck Comiskey (one of the grandchildren of Charlie Comiskey who now owned the club) took over the front office. A year later Comiskey replaced Marion with Al Lopez, who had piloted the great Cleveland club of 1954 and whose teams, in his six seasons of managing, had never finished below second. Lopez continued his success in Chicago: the Sox moved up to second (though well behind the Yankees) in 1957 and '58. In March 1959, Bill Veeck (who had in previous years owned the Cleveland Indians and the St. Louis Browns) bought a controlling interest in the White Sox from the Comiskey family and stepped into instant success.

With the Yankees suffering an off-year in 1959, Chicago and Cleveland battled for the lead throughout the summer, until the White Sox pulled away in late August. The same 94-60 record that had given them only a distant third in 1954 now carried them to their first pennant in 40 years. The close and successful pennant race, and the club's dynamic new ownership, pushed Sox home attendance up more than 78 percent to a new club record.

As they had in 1906, pitching and hustle won the Sox their 1959 pennant. The league's best staff was led by veteran Early Wynn (enjoying his last big season with a league high of 22 wins) and young Bob Shaw (with a career high of 18), and featured the league's top relievers in Gerry Staley and Turk Lown. Shortstop Luis Aparicio, in the midst of a nine-year reign as stolen-base leader, set a personal high in runs scored as the club went 35-15 in one-run games. But in the World Series, Los Angeles stopped Chicago in six games.

The next year the Sox remained competitive until September, but finished third. After dropping to fourth and fifth the next two years (in a league now expanded to 10 teams), they returned to second in 1963. The next year the Sox finished a season-long three-way race with nine straight wins, enough to pull them past Baltimore, but a game short of catching the Yankees, whose 11-game streak a week earlier had put them out in front. After a third straight second-place finish in 1965, manager Lopez resigned for health reasons.

Under Eddie Stanky—and with the AL's stingiest pitching staff in 49 years—the Sox competed into the final week of a hot 1967 race, when five straight losses at the end dropped them to fourth. They would rise above .500 only twice in the next 13 years. In 1970 they lost a club-record 106 games to finish at the bottom of the AL West. Two years later they took the division lead briefly in late August before dropping back to second, and in 1977 they held the lead through much of the summer before tailing off to third.

Bill Veeck had sold the club and repurchased it in 1976. But in January 1981, after three losing seasons and troubled by poor health and skyrocketing player salaries, he sold the Sox once again, to a group headed by Jerry

Reinsdorf and Eddie Einhorn. With Reinsdorf heading the club's baseball operations and lawyer Tony LaRussa piloting the team on the field, the Sox briefly became one of the best teams in baseball. With their best record since 1920, the 1983 Sox carried the AL West by 20 games. Rookie slugger Ron Kittle led the attack, backed up by fourth-year outfielder Harold Baines and resurgent old-timers Greg Luzinski and Carlton Fisk. Pitchers LaMarr Hoyt and Rich Dotson attained personal bests to lead the majors in wins (with 24 and 22), and White Sox home attendance for the first time topped 2 million. In the ALCS, though, after a close win over Baltimore in the opener, Chicago lost the next three games and the pennant. Chicago's pitching and offense (except for Baines) collapsed the next season, and the team remained out of serious contention for six years.

Most forecasters predicted another dismal season for the Sox in 1990, but as fans watched a new Comiskey Park arise next door, they also saw their club celebrate its final year in the old yard with an astonishing resurgence. With their best start in decades, the Sox stayed close to mighty Oakland through the first half of the season, and even took over first place for brief periods in June and July before Oakland pulled away. Anchoring a strong bullpen, closer Bobby Thigpen shattered the major league record for saves, passing the old record of 46 with a month to go and finishing with 57.

First baseman Frank Thomas helped keep the Sox competitive through much of 1991, the inaugural season of their new park. Rookie Wilson Alvarez's no-hitter capped a seven-game win streak in August that pulled the team to just a game from the top, but 15 losses in their next 17 games stifled their pennant hopes and they finished second. Thomas continued his awesome offense in 1992, and Jack McDowell showed himself one of the AL's best pitchers, but the team won one game fewer than the year before, and finished third.

McDowell, Alvarez, and Alex Fernandez led the league's stingiest pitching staff in 1993, and Thomas turned in an MVP season as the Sox carried a narrow lead into the All-Star break, held it into late September, then pulled away to an eight-game margin of victory at the finish. In the postseason, though, the Sox came up short, losing the AL pennant to Toronto in six games.

In 1994 Frank Thomas was rising to even greater heights and became the first American Leaguer since Roger Maris in 1960 and 1961 to be named MVP in back-to-back seasons. The Sox were hanging on to a slim first-place lead over Cleveland in the new Central division when the players struck to end the season.

Despite another strong season by Thomas (.308, 40 HR, 111 RBIs) the club slumped to third in 1995, 32 games back of Cleveland. In 1996 the Sox again finished second to the Tribe. After the season they shocked the baseball world by signing Albert Belle to a $10 million per year contract, but the highlight of the 1997 season was the first-ever Cubs-Sox interleague series. Terry Bevington was fired after the season and his replacement, Jerry Manuel, struggled through the first half of 1998 before the White Sox surged to a 45-31 record in the second half to end the season in second place.

Cincinnati Reds

Red Stockings was the nickname of two pioneering Cincinnati ballclubs—the first avowedly professional team, which was undefeated in 1869, and the charter member club in the National League of 1876-1880. After a year on the sidelines, the reformed Reds joined the new American Association and captured the 1882 pennant by 11½ games, with a .688 winning percentage that is still the club record. Seven Reds enjoyed career highs in batting, pitcher Will White led the association with 40 wins, and rookie second baseman John "Bid" McPhee proved himself already one of the game's classiest fielders.

McPhee remained 18 years with the Reds and established himself as the finest second baseman of the 19th century. But the club would go 37 years before it won another pennant. Twice in their seven remaining years in the AA the Reds finished second, and they enjoyed six winning seasons. Transferring from the AA to the NL in 1890, they finished fourth; at 10½ games out of first it was their closest finish in 34 years between 1884 and their next pennant-winning season, 1919.

In 1902 club owner John T. Brush sold out to a group of Cincinnati's political bosses, who in mid-August named August "Garry" Herrmann (formerly head of the water works commission) to run it. Herrmann not only remained president of the Reds for 25 years, but he also chaired the three-man National Commission that oversaw organized baseball, from its establishment in 1903 until 1920 (when his resignation brought about the commission's demise).

A midseason trade in 1916 brought the Reds Christy Mathewson (at the end of his pitching career) to manage the team, plus outfielder Edd Roush. The next year, with Roush leading the league in batting, the Reds edged above .500 and into fourth place. In 1918 an August spurt boosted the Reds into third place, in a season shortened by a month at the end because of World War I. Roush enjoyed another banner year, but Mathewson left for the Army just before the season ended.

First baseman Hal Chase—suspected of throwing games—was traded away after the season and replaced by veteran Jake Daubert. Southpaw Slim Sallee was purchased from the Giants and right-hander Ray Fisher from the Yankees. Pat Moran (who had led the Phillies to a pennant in 1915) was hired to replace Mathewson at the Cincinnati helm. Thus fortified, the Reds in 1919 won their second pennant. Three pitchers—Sallee (21-7), Hod Eller (20-9), and Dutch Ruether (19-7, 1.82 ERA)—reached career peaks, Fisher (14-5) enjoyed one of his best years, Roush won another batting title and finished second in NL RBIs, and three Reds finished in the league's top four in runs scored. The Reds probe quickly from the gate, but faltered in May and didn't pass the Giants for first place until July. They finished nine games in front. Rumors of a White Sox fix to throw the World Series clouded the Reds' Series triumph—and spoiled it entirely when, a year later, the scandal became public and the truth of the rumors was confirmed.

In 1920 Cincinnati led the league entering September, but Brooklyn spurted and the Reds slumped to a third-place finish, 10½ games out. They dropped to sixth in 1921, but recovered for five years in the first division,

including three second-place finishes.

The Reds finished in the second division for 11 years, hitting bottom with four straight cellar finishes from 1931 through 1934. President Herrmann retired after the 1927 season, and within two years a controlling interest in the Reds was sold to a wealthy Cincinnatian, Sidney Weil. But Weil lost his fortune in the stock market crash of 1929. While he continued to run the Reds for four years, his stock in the club was held by the Central Trust Company. In his efforts to turn the club around, Weil acquired catcher Ernie Lombardi from Brooklyn in March 1932 and pitcher Paul Derringer from the St. Louis Cardinals the following May. Derringer lost 25 games in his first season in Cincinnati and 21 the next, but both remained with the club long enough to star in its return to glory. Owner Weil, however, relinquished his control to the bank in 1933, at the depth of the Depression and of the team's fortunes.

The bank hired Larry MacPhail (who had rescued minor league Columbus by introducing night baseball there) to run the Reds. MacPhail in turn hired Frank Lane to develop a minor league farm system, and persuaded Cincinnati industrialist Powel Crosley, Jr., to invest in the club. On May 24, 1935, Crosley and MacPhail brought night ball to the major leagues (the Reds, with Derringer pitching, beat the Phillies, 2-1), and with it a sharp upswing in attendance at Crosley Field. By June 1936, Crosley's increased investment in the Reds had made him the majority owner. The temperamental MacPhail quit suddenly in mid-September 1936, but the Reds replaced him with another successful minor league executive, Warren Giles, who ran the club until his selection in 1952 as president of the NL.

After rising to sixth place in 1935 and fifth the next year, the Reds dropped back into the cellar in 1937. But the following year, under new manager Bill McKechnie, they rose into the first division once again—even holding second place briefly in September before slipping to fourth. Derringer enjoyed the first of three peak seasons, young Johnny Vander Meer contributed 15 wins (including two consecutive no-hitters) and Bucky Walters, after his acquisition from the Phillies in June, compiled his first winning season since converting from third baseman to pitcher in 1935. Lombardi led the NL in batting, and first baseman Frank McCormick, in his first full season, led the league in hits. The stage was set for the club's first back-to-back pennants.

Several Reds reached the apex of their careers in 1939, among them Walters (27-11) and Derringer (25-7), who between them topped most of the league's pitching stats, and McCormick, who led the league in RBIs and hits and finished second in batting. The club pulled out of the pack to the front before the end of May and held the lead to the end, although St. Louis closed the gap with a late-season surge before slipping four and a half games back.

Cincinnati's sweep by the Yankees in the World Series was something of a shock, but the club had recovered its poise by the next spring. Starting strong and—except for a small dip in August—pushing steadily upward throughout the season, the Reds shook off the persistent Dodgers in midseason and finished 12 games in front with their first 100-win season. McCormick and Lombardi powered the offense, and Walters for the second year in a row took

NL crowns in wins and ERA. This time the team's triumph carried through the World Series as Walters and Derringer won two games apiece to edge the Tigers in seven games to win their second world championship.

The Reds' pitching remained strong in 1941, but their hitting and run production fell off and the team struggled to finish third. They remained in the upper division through 1944, but then dropped into an 11-year trough of losing seasons.

Ted Kluszewski was in his ninth season as the Reds' slugging first baseman when Cincinnati next offered a serious run for the pennant in 1956 under manager Birdie Tebbetts. Kluszewski led the club in hitting and RBIs, but his 35 home runs were good enough only for third behind rookie Frank Robinson's 38 and Wally Post's 36 on a team that hammered 221 during the season to tie the then-major league record set nine years earlier by the Giants. The Reds' offense led the league in runs scored and kept them in the thick of a three-team race throughout the season. That same year, for the first time ever they drew more than a million fans at home.

The Reds dropped out of a tight race in August 1957, and suffered losing seasons the next three years. Gabe Paul, who had succeeded Warren Giles as club president and general manager, left to help organize the new Houston club after the 1960 season. Owner Crosley died the following spring. Bill DeWitt, who replaced Paul as president (and ultimately purchased control of the club), acquired pitcher Joey Jay from the Milwaukee Braves and third baseman Gene Freese from the White Sox. Jay in 1961 tied for the league lead with 21 wins, and Freese homered 26 times and drove in 87 runs—both career highs. Most of the team improved on their 1960 stats, and despite a poor start that saw them enter May in last place, the Reds had risen to the top by mid-June. The streaking Dodgers caught them briefly in August, but then fell away. In the World Series, though, it was the Yankees winning in five games.

The Reds next threatened in 1964 when, in a wild three-way finish, they won nine straight in late September to take first place for a day before slipping into a tie for second, one game behind St. Louis. In 1965 a young Pete Rose recorded the first of his 10 seasons with 200 hits as the Reds battled among the leaders much of the summer before dropping off to fourth.

That December, after a decade of standout offense in Cincinnati, Frank Robinson was traded to Baltimore. The next year, while Robinson won the Triple Crown in assisting his new team to the world championship, the Reds suffered their first losing season in six years and sank to seventh place. That winter, owner DeWitt completed the sale of the team to a group led by Cincinnati newspaper publisher Francis Dale and brothers James and William Williams who later acquired a controlling interest in the club.

In 1969, the first year of divisional play, the Reds rose into the thick of a five-way race in the NL West before stumbling as Atlanta and San Francisco surged in the final three weeks. But the season provided a foretaste of the decade to come as the team captured league crowns in slugging and home runs.

At midseason in 1970 the Reds moved out of Crosley Field—their home for 58 years—into the new Riverfront Stadium. Catcher Johnny Bench and third baseman Tony Perez, with the finest seasons of their long careers, paced an overwhelming offense as the team hammered out a new club-high 102 wins to reward rookie manager Sparky Anderson with victory in the NL West by 14½ games, and gain the name "Big Red Machine." In the National League Championship Series the Reds continued their triumph with a three-game sweep of East winner Pittsburgh. But mighty Baltimore humbled the Reds in the World Series, 4-1.

Cincinnati's hitting and run production fell off sharply the next year, and the club dropped to fourth with their only losing season of the decade. But in 1972—spurred on after a slow start by Johnny Bench's recovery of power, Gary Nolan's finest season on the mound, and the all-around mastery of newly acquired second baseman Joe Morgan—the Reds cruised to a division title. Victory in the NLCS came harder, as powerful Pittsburgh carried the series to the full five games before handing the Reds the pennant with a wild pitch in the last of the ninth inning of the final game. Cincinnati's defeat in the World Series was also close: the Reds won three, and Oakland's four wins were each achieved by a margin of just one run.

The Reds repeated in the NL West in 1973 with a second-half surge from fourth place that carried them past front-runner Los Angeles in September. But the much weaker New York Mets ended Cincinnati's pennant hopes in a five-game loss in the NLCS best remembered for Rose's brawl with Bud Harrelson.

In 1974 the Reds finished four games behind the Dodgers in second place. But over the next two years the Big Red Machine flattened all opposition. In 1975, after hovering around .500 through mid-May, the Reds began an ascent that carried them to what are still club records: 108 victories and a winning margin of 20 games. The team featured balanced pitching (six starters won in double figures), an offense in which every regular drove in more than 45 runs (averaging nearly 77 apiece), the best fielding in the majors, and a big NL lead in stolen bases. After a three-game sweep of Pittsburgh in the NLCS, the Reds subdued the stubborn Boston Red Sox in seven games for their first world title in 35 years, and their third overall.

They won their fourth the next year. Joe Morgan, at the peak of his career, led the NL in slugging, finished second to teammate George Foster in RBIs, and stole 60 bases as he won his second consecutive MVP award. Balanced pitching and offense again put the Reds in front to stay in June, carrying the team to 102 wins and a 10-game lead over Los Angeles at the finish. The NLCS produced another sweep—of Philadelphia this time. The World Series was also a sweep as the Reds dispatched the Yankees as the Reds became the first team to go through the Championship Series and World Series without losing a game.

Two years of second-place finishes followed, and the Reds replaced Sparky Anderson at the helm with John McNamara, who led the club back to the top of the NL West in 1979. Pete Rose, after 16 years in Cincinnati, had signed with the Phillies as a free agent, but Ray Knight (who replaced Rose at third base) minimized the loss with a team-high .318 batting average. Houston led the division much of the summer, but a sustained Reds' surge in August brought them even, then pulled them ahead in early September, where they hung on to take the title by

just 1½ games. But that was the end of the Reds' decade of splendor; Pittsburgh swept past them to the pennant in the NLCS.

Joe Morgan left the club after the season, returning as a free agent to Houston, whence he had come eight years earlier. In 1980 the Reds dipped in midseason, recovering to make a race of it in August, only to fade a bit and finish third. The next year, in a season shortened and split in two by a players' strike, the Reds compiled the best overall record in the majors. But they came away empty-handed by finishing half a game behind Los Angeles in the first half-season and 1½ games back of Houston in the second half, losing a chance at postseason play when the owners decided to pit the half-season winners against each other.

As a penurious front office continued to trade away its stars or lose them to free agency, the dispirited Reds dropped to the bottom of the NL West in 1982 with a club-worst 101 losses. Manager McNamara yielded in midseason to coach Russ Nixon, who was himself replaced by Vern Rapp after another last-place finish in 1983. Robert Howsam, Sr., whose shrewd trading as general manager had been instrumental in building the mighty Reds of the 1970s, was called out of semiretirement to restore the club to respectability. Howsam signed free-agent slugger Dave Parker from Pittsburgh, and late in the 1984 season brought Pete Rose back as player-manager. Early in 1985 the NL approved the sale of the Reds to Marge Schott, a Cincinnati automobile dealer. With Parker enjoying his most productive seasons in several years, and the emergence of outfielder Eric Davis and reliever John Franco, owner Schott's public enthusiasm for her team was rewarded with four straight second-place finishes. The highlight of that period came in 1985 when Rose broke Ty Cobb's record for most career hits.

Turmoil ruled the Reds in 1989. Disabling injuries to a dozen players, including such 1988 standouts as pitcher Danny Jackson (whose 23 wins tied for the league high) and infielders Barry Larkin and Chris Sabo, contributed most to the team's drop to fifth place. Baseball's investigation of manager Pete Rose on charges of gambling on baseball games and other offenses—an investigation which resulted in Rose's lifetime banishment from the game in August—did nothing to bolster Cincinnati's play on the field.

The distress of 1989 was all but forgotten in 1990 as the Reds, under new manager Lou Piniella, leaped to a 9-0 start and, surviving threats from San Francisco in August and Los Angeles in September, held on to first place through the entire season. Larkin and Sabo—whole again—anchored a balanced offense, while pitchers Randy Myers (acquired from the Mets in a trade for John Franco), Rob Dibble, and Norm Charlton (nicknamed "The Nasty Boys") provided All-Star relief to a solid core of starters. In the NLCS, the Reds overcame an opening-game loss to capture the pennant from Pittsburgh in six games, then startled Oakland's heavily favored Athletics with a four-game sweep.

The Reds remained in the thick of the 1991 race through mid-season, despite a 10-game losing streak in July. But as Atlanta rose to battle early leader Los Angeles, Cincinnati settled into a long decline that at the end left them 20 games back, in fifth place. Barry Larkin and Bip Roberts sparked the league's strongest offense in

1992, as the Reds rebounded to win 90 games. But they let a six-game midseason lead get away and finished eight games behind repeat champion Atlanta.

Piniella was replaced by Cincinnati hero—but managing novice—Tony Perez for 1993. Perez lasted only until May 24, when veteran manager Davey Johnson took his place. Meanwhile, Marge Schott's fellow NL owners banned her for the season from active participation in club affairs for making racial slurs. With their season further marred by injuries and backbiting, the Reds finished fifth, 31 games out.

With Kevin Mitchell pacing a strong, balanced offense, the Reds turned their fortunes around in 1994 and reached the All-Star break atop the new Central division by 2½ games. They were still clinging to a half-game lead over Houston when the season ended Aug. 12. When play resumed in 1995 the Reds showed they had indeed been for real, winning the division by nine games. Standouts included MVP Barry Larkin (.319, 15 HR, 66 RBIs), Mets discard Pete Schourek (18-7), Ron Gant (29 HR, 88 RBIs), Reggie Sanders (28 HR, 99 RBIs), and Jeff Brantley (28 saves). The Reds swept LA in the first round of playoffs but in turn were swept by the Braves in the NLCS. At season's end manager Davey Johnson left the team for Baltimore and was replaced by Ray Knight. The 1996 season saw owner Schott again embroiled in controversy and the team fall to third place (81-81).

By mid-1997 the Reds were floundering under Knight and Jack McKeon took over as a field manager. Jeff Shaw, whose career high was four saves a year earlier, led the NL with 42 saves. Shaw, along with pitcher Dave Burba, were traded in separate deals in 1998 to bring in young players that the Reds hope will eventually help return the team to its former glory.

Cleveland Indians

The Indians finished in the top half of the league nearly 70 percent of the time through their first 68 years, and wound up in the cellar only once (in 1914). Cleveland then experienced only five winning seasons from 1969 through 1993. The team's greatest period of success has come in just the last four years.

The Indians (who were at first called the Blues because of the color of their uniforms) succeeded Cleveland's National League Spiders, who in 1899, their final season, lost a major league record 134 games. When the NL dropped the Spiders at the end of the season, Ban Johnson, president of the emerging American League, grasped the opportunity to move into this major market. In 1901, when Johnson proclaimed the AL a major league, Cleveland lured several players from NL clubs and played much better than the Spiders had, but still finished next-to-last in their first big league season. The next year the Bronchos (as they decided to call themselves) languished in last place through June. But during the season they acquired several players through trade and purchase—most notably star second baseman Napoleon "Nap" Lajoie and pitcher Bill Bernhard—who turned the Bronchos around in midseason and lifted them above .500 (and into fifth place) by season's end.

With Lajoie sparkling in the field and dominating the

league at the plate, the fans soon settled on another nickname for the club—the Naps—that lasted as long as Lajoie remained in Cleveland. Late in the 1904 season, Lajoie was named manager. After enjoying moderate success in two of the next three seasons, the Naps in 1908 experienced their best year and one of the team's most exciting finishes ever.

With a 10-game winning streak near the end of the season, they moved from fourth to first, only to be surpassed by Detroit's 10-game streak. Both teams won their season finale, but the Tigers, because they had not made up an earlier rainout, took the pennant by half a game. Cleveland protested that if Detroit had played the missed game and lost, Cleveland would have gained a tie, forcing a playoff that might have brought them the championship. The dispute eventually led to a rules change requiring ties or washouts to be replayed if their outcome could determine the pennant winner.

Poor seasons alternated with good the next few years. Lajoie quit as manager but remained as player. Pitching ace Addie Joss pitched a second no-hitter (he had hurled a perfect game at the height of the 1908 race), but before the start of the 1911 season, he was dead of tubercular meningitis. Outfielder Joe Jackson—acquired from the Athletics—hit .408 in his first full big league season. The club reached bottom in 1914 with a last-place finish that found them 18½ games out of seventh place, 48½ out of first. After the season Lajoie went to Philadelphia (the fans then voted to rename the club the Indians), and the next August Jackson was sold to the Chicago White Sox as attendance dropped to its lowest level since 1901.

By the time the 1916 season began, though, new ownership had acquired the great Tris Speaker from Boston and brought up from the minors a pair of promising pitchers, Jim Bagby (Sr.) and Stan Coveleski. Sparked by the three newcomers, the Indians rose to third in 1917, and to close second-place finishes the next two years. In 1920 everything came together. Speaker, who had taken over as manager the previous July, hit .388 enjoyed one of his best years, as did Coveleski with 24 wins. Bagby, in the finest season of his career, led the league with 31 victories, and veteran pitcher Ray Caldwell (picked up from the Boston Red Sox the previous summer) added another 20. Six regulars hit over .300; the club as a whole hit .303.

The team rebounded from the devastating loss of Ray Chapman, who was killed by a pitch from Carl Mays. The Yankees dropped back a bit in mid-September, but the White Sox hung close until the final week, when eight of their players were indicted and suspended as suspects in the Black Sox scandal of 1919. The Sox lost two of their final three games and all hope of tying Cleveland to force a playoff. The Indians defeated Brooklyn in a World Series that is best remembered for second baseman Bill Wambsganss' unassisted triple play in Game 5.

Cleveland led much of the way in 1921 before a late slump and a New York surge gave the Yankees their first pennant. Through the next quarter century the Indians came close to a pennant only twice. In 1926, with two veteran Georges—pitcher Uhle and first baseman Burns—enjoying their finest seasons, the Indians came to life in midseason and drew within three games of the Yankees by season's end. Fourteen years later, in 1940,

behind the 27 wins of 21-year-old Bob Feller and the inspired play (in the field and at the bat) of second-year shortstop Lou Boudreau, Cleveland made an even closer run for the flag. Throughout the summer the Indians were in or near first place, but six losses in nine games with a resurgent Detroit in late August and September left them a game back at the finish.

Two years later Boudreau, at age 24, was named to manage the Tribe. His team stirred little interest through the war years. But in 1946, with Feller back from military service and pitching his best ever, Cleveland fans boosted home attendance above a million for the first time. The next year, their first full season under new president Bill Veeck, the Indians climbed to fourth. More significantly, Veeck hired the league's first black player, Larry Doby, who became a mainstay of the Indians for the next eight years.

In 1948 the Indians began a nine-year era of excellence with a victory in one of the closest pennant races ever. Through June they ran a three-way race with the Yankees and the surprisingly lively Philadelphia Athletics; in July the Red Sox rose out of nowhere to make it a four-way struggle. In September the A's fell behind, but the three remaining clubs stayed close, and on Sept. 24 found themselves in a three-way tie. Cleveland moved ahead with a four-game win streak, but Boston, after a pair of losses, won their final four (including two to eliminate New York). Cleveland's final-day loss to Detroit left them tied with Boston. In a one-game playoff in Boston the next day (the first playoff in AL history), manager-shortstop Boudreau capped his MVP season with two home runs to help give rookie Gene Bearden his 20th win and the Tribe their second pennant. The exciting race drew more than 2.6 million Cleveland fans to Municipal Stadium, a new major league record. The World Series against the Boston Braves was anticlimactic—a Cleveland triumph in six games.

By 1951 both owner Veeck and manager Boudreau had moved on, but under new manager Al Lopez the Indians fashioned a six-year stretch in which they finished second to the Yankees five times, and in 1954 they won their third pennant with 111 victories—the most in AL history. The Lopez years, 1951-1956, were punctuated by the power of players like Doby, Luke Easter, Al Rosen, and Vic Wertz. But it was pitching that gave the team its consistency. Bob Lemon and Early Wynn won between 17 and 23 games in every one of the six years, as did Mike Garcia through 1954. As Garcia and Feller (who won 22 in 1951) faded, Art Houtteman was acquired from Detroit for a couple of good years, and Herb Score came along for his two explosive seasons.

The 1954 season was the Yankees' best season in 18 years from 1943 through 1960, a period in which they won 12 pennants, but it turned out to be the best year in Cleveland history. The Yankees kept the race close until the end of July and finished with 103 wins. But the Indians won an AL-record 111 games to beat New York. Wynn and Lemon tied for the league lead with 23 wins apiece, and Garcia copped the ERA crown. Doby led the league in homers and RBIs, and second baseman Bobby Avila took the batting title. Heavily favored to defeat the Giants in the World Series, the Tribe and their fans were shocked when the NL champs swept them in four games.

After Lopez left to manage the White Sox in 1957, the Indians slipped below .500 for the first time in a decade. Rocky Colavito's power and Cal McLish's pitching brought them back in 1959, when they finished second to Lopez's White Sox. Their next highest post-Lopez finish came nine years later, in 1968, when Luis Tiant and Sam McDowell pitched them into third.

From 1969 through 1989 the Indians completed every season in the bottom half of the AL East, rising above .500 in only four seasons while finishing seven years in the division cellar. In 1990, though, with three straight wins at season's end, they passed Baltimore by half a game to wind up fourth.

The effort proved too much. In July 1991, the Indians dropped into the cellar to stay, and spiraled on-down to a club-record 105 losses. With nowhere to go but up, the 1992 team, spurred by the offense of Carlos Baerga and Albert Belle and the impressive pitching of Charles Nagy, played the best ball in the AL after the All-Star break, lifting themselves out of the cellar into a fourth place-tie with the Yankees.

The tragic preseason deaths of relievers Tim Crews and Steve Olin and severe injury to starter Bob Ojeda in a boating accident cast a pall over the team's final season in Cleveland Stadium. With Nagy also out much of the season, the Indians' pitching was among the league's worst. Offensively, though, they ranked among the better clubs, paced by Baerga, Belle, and sophomore Kenny Lofton, whose league-leading 70 stolen bases set a new club record. The team finished sixth.

The Indians—playing in brand-new Jacobs Field—were up for 1994. Belle, who ranked among AL leaders in almost every offensive category, and Lofton, who added the league lead in hits to another stolen base title, paced a powerful offense that kept the team in the thick of a tight race with Chicago in the league's new Central division. With their best chance in decades to bring Cleveland a winner, the Indians trailed the White Sox by just one game when the season ended prematurely.

The Indians dominated the AL in 1995, rolling to a 100-44 record and capturing the AL Central division by a phenomenal 30 games. Paced by Albert Belle (who despite the shortened season led the AL with 50 homers, 121 runs, 377 total bases, 52 doubles, and a .690 slugging percentage), the Indians batted .291 and slugged 207 homers. Meanwhile Tribe pitchers posted a league-best 3.83 ERA (the only AL ERA under 4.00). Jose Mesa led league relievers with 46 saves.

The Indians swept the Red Sox in the first round of the postseason, then edged the upstart Mariners in the ALCS, before falling to Atlanta, 4-2, in the World Series. The fans appreciated their team's superb effort, however, and in the offseason the club became the first to sell out every seat for the entire upcoming campaign.

Despite discarding Eddie Murray and Carlos Baerga in midseason, the 1996 Indians (99-62, with a league-leading .293 team batting average) repeated as AL Central champions. Team standouts included Albert Belle (48 home runs and an AL-best 148 RBIs), Kenny Lofton (.317 and a league-leading 75 stolen bases), Jim Thome (38 HR), Jose Mesa (39 saves), and Charles Nagy (17-5, 3.41). The Tribe fell, however, to Wild Card Baltimore in the first round of the postseason.

The Indians returned to the World Series in 1997, surprising both the Yankees and the Orioles along the way. Sandy Alomar, Jr., who had been the MVP at the All-Star Game at Jacobs Field in July, continued his heroics in October. His home run off New York's Mariano Rivera in the eighth inning of Game 4 of the Division Series tied the game as the Indians rallied to win the series. The Indians beat the favored Orioles in the ALCS on a series-deciding home run by Tony Fernandez in the top of the 11th inning of Game 6. The World Series went seven games and was also decided in the 11th inning, but the Florida Marlins were the winners. The 1998 Indians won the AL Central Division for the fourth consecutive season. Second-year pitchers Bartolo Colon and Jaret Wright combined to win 26 games and Charles Nagy and newcomer Dave Burba won 15 games apiece. Manny Ramirez led the offense with 45 home runs and 145 RBIs and shortstop Omar Vizquel won his sixth consecutive Gold Glove. The Indians lost the first game of the Division Series to the Red Sox, but won the next three games to take the series. Next came the Yankees, who had bettered Cleveland's AL record with 114 wins in 1998, and the Indians briefly held a 2-1 series lead before New York won in six games. Still, the Indians were the only team to win any postseason games against the eventual world champions.

Colorado Rockies

Denver was one of two cities awarded a National League franchise in June 1991 (Miami was the other), in the league's first expansion since Montreal and San Diego were added in 1969. The new teams took the field for the first time in 1993, their rosters stocked primarily with players selected from the other major league clubs in a special expansion draft. Denver, which chose to call itself the Colorado Rockies, drew nearly 4.5 million fans to cavernous Mile High Stadium, the highest season attendance in the history of sport.

Though their 5.41 ERA was by far the worst in the majors, the Rockies, under rookie manager Don Baylor, not only avoided the NL West cellar, but they also set a new record for wins by a first-year expansion team, with 67. Andres Galarraga, Charlie Hayes, and Dante Bichette headed a solid offense, with Galarraga hitting more than 100 points above his previous major league career average to lead the NL in batting at .370.

Galarraga was in the midst of another fine season in 1994 when a pitch broke his hand on July 28. Despite a 50-54 record, the Rockies stood in second place in the weak NL West, just half a game out of first. By the time the season ended two weeks later, though, they had slipped to third, 6 1/2 games out.

In 1995 the Rockies moved into Coors Field (drawing 3.3 million fans), and Baylor won NL Manager of the Year honors as Colorado finished just one game behind LA in the NL West and earned a wild card playoff slot in the process. Key Rockies were Galarraga (31 HR, 106 RBIs), Vinny Castilla (32 HR, 90 RBIs, .309), Dante Bichette (.340 and a league-leading 40 HR, 128 RBIs, 359 total bases, and a .620 slugging mark), Eric Young (.317 and an NL-leading nine triples), and Larry Walker (36 HR, 101 RBIs). The dream ended in the first round of

the playoffs, however, as Colorado fell to Atlanta, three games to one.

The 1996 Rockies finished third, eight games behind surprising San Diego. Standouts included Galarraga (a league-leading 47 HR and 150 RBIs), Bichette (141 RBIs, 198 hits), Young (a league-leading 53 stolen bases) and Ellis Burks (40 HR,.344, 211 hits, 128 RBIs, and an NL-best 142 runs scored).

The 1997 and 1998 seasons were similar in that the team continued to lead the league in hitting (1998 marked the fourth straight time), but, in the thin air of Colorado, their pitching staff was among the worst in baseball. (Even the 1998 All-Star Game was a typical Mile High slugfest, a 13-8 AL win at Coors Field). After a strong finish in 1997, Galarraga left for Atlanta and Darryl Kile came to Denver as a free agent. Larry Walker, the 1997 NL MVP, won the batting title in 1998, while Dante Bichette finished third in the '98 batting race. First baseman Todd Helton emerged as one of the league's top rookies, and Vinny Castilla had his finest professional season. But all the offense couldn't save the job of the team's first manager, Don Baylor. Jim Leyland, who won the 1997 World Series with the other team born in 1993, the Florida Marlins, was hired to manage the Rockies.

Detroit Tigers

One of the more successful clubs in the American League, the Tigers have enjoyed winning seasons nearly 70 percent of the time. In 18 of their 61 winning seasons, they have remained in contention into the final days, 11 times emerging triumphant as league or division champions.

Detroit was one of the clubs from Ban Johnson's Western League that (renamed the American League) raised itself to major league status in 1901 with a talent raid on the long-established National League. In their first six big league seasons, the Tigers displayed little bite, finishing four times in the second division and never threatening for the league lead.

In 1907 all that changed. Sparked by a young right fielder, Ty Cobb (who in his first full big league season led the league in batting, slugging, hits, RBIs, and stolen bases) and led by a dynamic new manager, Hugh "Eeyah" Jennings (who knew enough not to try to tell Cobb how to play the game), the Tigers clawed their way to the pennant in a four-way race. The outcome might have been different if two late-season games with second-place Philadelphia had not been rained out. (Today's rules would require that the games be made up.)

The 1908 race was even closer, with four teams contending into late September. The race wasn't settled until the final day, when Detroit beat Chicago to edge Cleveland by half a game. Once again the pennant hinged on a rainout that had not been made up. And once again Cobb dominated the league's hitters (though he slipped to fourth in stolen bases).

The Tigers had a slightly easier time of it the next year. It was a three-way race into September, but Detroit then pulled away to finish three and a half games ahead of Philadelphia. Cobb, in his best season yet, took the Triple Crown and returned to the top in stolen bases. But the Tigers were again unable to win a World Series. In 1907, after an opening-game tie, the Chicago Cubs swept the next four. The Cubs lost Game 3 the next year, but won the other four. And in 1909 Pittsburgh and Detroit alternated victories, with the Pirates emerging world champions in seven games.

Jennings managed Detroit for 11 more seasons; then Cobb took the reins for six years before leaving for Philadelphia. But the Tigers won no more pennants in the Cobb era. Cobb himself continued to dominate the league offensively through 1919. In 1911 he achieved career highs in most offensive categories, including a batting average of .420, but the Tigers managed no better than a distant second to the Athletics. In 1915 they started strong and remained in the race throughout the season. Cobb stole what was for 47 years a modern-record 96 bases, and the team's 100 wins proved to be the highest total in their first 33 years. But after running neck and neck with the Red Sox through most of August, the Tigers slumped a bit in early September—just enough for the Sox to take the flag by two and a half games. A close third-place finish the next year marked the Tigers' last serious challenge for 18 years.

In 1934, after six straight years in the second division, and only three years after their most distant finish ever (47 games out), the Tigers turned themselves around to win the pennant with a 101-53 record and a .656 winning percentage, the highest in club history. Two newly acquired veterans—manager/catcher Mickey Cochrane and outfielder Goose Goslin—enjoyed fine seasons at the bat, as did first baseman Hank Greenberg (.339, 139 RBIs) in his first full season, and second baseman Charlie Gehringer (.356, 127 RBIs). The two other infielders, third baseman Marv Owen and shortstop Billy Rogell enjoyed their finest seasons at the plate for a club whose batting average led the league at .300. It took the Tigers a month to get going, but by mid-July they had shot ahead of the Yankees to win by seven games. But once again, victory in the World Series eluded them as the St. Louis Cardinals blew them away, 11-0, in Game 7.

Paced by Greenberg's 170 RBIs in 1935, Detroit—after another slow start—moved up so sharply in July and August that even a September slump gave the Yankees no opportunity to catch them. And finally, in their fifth try, the Tigers won a world championship, overcoming Chicago in six games despite the loss of Greenberg, who broke his wrist in Game 2. Part-owner Frank Navin, who had run the club for three decades, had finally seen his Tigers reach the very top. A month later, after falling from a horse, he suffered a heart attack and died.

Del Baker had replaced Cochrane as manager when Detroit next made a run for the pennant in 1940. In a tight race the Tigers caught up with Cleveland in early September and traded the lead with them for two weeks before pulling ahead to stay with two wins in a three-game series. In the pennant clincher, Detroit's Floyd Giebell outdueled Cleveland great Bob Feller 2-0 for his third—and last—big league victory. In the World Series the Tigers lost once again, as Cincinnati came from behind in Game 7 for a 2-1 win.

Two losing seasons followed, and Steve O'Neill replaced Baker at the helm. In 1944, the wartime Tigers, behind the splendid pitching of workhorses Dizzy Trout

and Hal Newhouser (one-two in ERA and innings pitched, and winners of 27 and 29 games), joined the race in late August and found themselves tied with the St. Louis Browns for first going into the last game of the season. But the Browns beat the Yankees, and Detroit lost to Washington.

Hank Greenberg's release from military service in mid-1945 sparked another run for the pennant. They held the lead from mid-June through August, but in September a surging Washington caught up with them. The race once again went down to the final day, and the final inning, when Greenberg's grand slam overcame a St. Louis lead to give Detroit the flag over the idle Senators. Newhouser, with 25 wins and a 1.81 ERA, was named AL MVP for the second straight year. In the World Series his ERA shot up to 6.10, but he still managed to win two games (including the finale) as the Tigers took the Cubs in seven for their second world title.

In the 23 years that passed before their next pennant, the Tigers came close only twice. In 1950 they led the race through the middle of the season, but were caught by the Yankees late in August. After retaking the lead in early September, the two clubs ran neck-and-neck for a while before Detroit fell away to second.

Two years later the Tigers reached their nadir: their first cellar finish. After a decade in which they finished no higher than fourth, they rebounded in 1961 as first baseman Norm Cash and left fielder Rocky Colavito both enjoyed the most explosive seasons of their careers. Compiling their best season record since 1934, Detroit led the league through parts of June and July. But this was the year of Maris and Mantle and 109 Yankee victories; when the season ended, the Tigers' 101 wins had earned them only second place.

They came much closer six years later in the great four-way race of 1967 that saw three clubs still contending on the final day, when the Tigers split a doubleheader to tie with Minnesota for second. If 1967 was a scramble, 1968 belonged to Detroit. Denny McLain won 31 games (the last major leaguer to win 30) to lead the team to a 103-win finish, 12 games ahead of Baltimore. Down three games to one in the World Series, the pitching of McLain in Game 6 and Mickey Lolich in Games 5 and 7 brought the Tigers back against the Cardinals and gave them their third world championship.

A strike at the start of 1972 contributed to the Tigers' first divisional title, which culminated a four-way race in the AL East. Detroit defeated Boston two games out of three at season's end, to edge the Sox by half a game. But if the strike had not wiped out an unequal number of games, the end of the season could have seen the two clubs tied.

The Tigers lost the pennant to Oakland with a 2-1 loss in the finale of a close American League Championship Series, and dropped out of contention for a decade. In 1974 they finished at the bottom of the division and the next year lost 102 games to post the worst record in the majors.

Finally, after seven seasons in the second division, Detroit put together a strong second half in strike-divided 1981, fading only at the end to tie for second. Three years later the Tigers were back on top with one of their best

years. Opening the season 9-0, they ended April at 18-2, stretched their mark to 35-5 by late May, and were never headed, finishing a team-record 15 games in front with 104 wins, their most ever. Their balanced pitching staff led the league in ERA, even though none of their starters finished among the top ten. Willie Hernandez (who with Aurelio Lopez compiled a 19-4 record from the bullpen, with 46 saves) earned both Cy Young and MVP awards. After sweeping Kansas City in the ALCS, the Tigers took the world championship—their fourth—from San Diego in five games.

In 1987 the Tigers caught the Blue Jays in the season's final series, tying them for the lead in the first game, moving to the front with a 12-inning win in the second game, and clinching the division crown in the finale, 1-0. In the ALCS, though, Minnesota stopped the favored Tigers, four games to one.

Injuries sidelined veteran keystoners Alan Trammell and Lou Whitaker more than a month each and derailed the season of starter Jeff Robinson in August just as he was emerging as ace of Detroit's pitchers. All the same, the Tigers led the AL East much of the 1988 season before falling back and rallied at season's end to finish second, one game behind Boston.

The next year, though, as new waves of injury broke over an aging lineup, the Tigers dropped into the division cellar in June and kept sinking, finishing with 103 losses and the worst record in the majors. But in 1990 Trammell rebounded from one of his worst seasons with one of his best and, with newly acquired first baseman Cecil Fielder, sparked a recovery to third place. Fielder, back in the AL after a season in Japan, topped the majors in home runs (with 51, the most in the AL since 1961), slugging percentage, and runs batted in.

The 1991 Tigers clawed their way back from an eight-game deficit in mid-July into a tie with first-place Toronto seven weeks later; they finished tied for second with Boston. In 1992, for the third year in a row, Detroit led the AL in home runs, but this time their big bats couldn't lift the club above sixth place. Texas edged the Tigers for the home run crown in 1993, but Detroit challenged for their division lead through August and, after a dip in September, surged to tie Baltimore for third place. In strike-shortened 1994 they finished last in the AL East, 18 games out.

On the field in 1995 little of substance changed for the Tigers, as Fielder slammed 31 homers and the team finished a distant fourth (60-84), but momentous changes occurred off it. Sparky Anderson resigned as Tiger manager at season's end, and plans to replace Tiger Stadium with another downtown ballpark accelerated.

The Buddy Bell-led 1996 Tigers compiled baseball's worst record (53-109). The season saw Cecil Fielder leave for the Yankees in midseason and Alan Trammell retire at season's end. The 1997 Tigers, however, were 26 games better than the previous season's club and paced by 100 RBIs from both first baseman Tony Clark and outfielder Bobby Higginson, the team finished third. The Tigers shifted to the AL Central in 1998 and the team foundered. Bell was dismissed late in the season and was replaced by Larry Parrish.

Florida Marlins

One of two new clubs to join the National League in 1993, the Florida Marlins were formed after the selection, in June 1991, of Miami and Denver as cities for the league's first expansion teams since 1969. Headed by entertainment magnate H. Wayne Huizenga, the Marlins played in Joe Robbie Stadium (which Huizenga partially owned). In their first season the Marlins featured one of the game's premier relievers in Bryan Harvey, whose 45 saves ranked third in the NL and contributed to 70 percent of the club's 64 victories. Though the Marlins lost their final six games, they finished ahead of the New York Mets for sixth place in the NL East.

In the strike-shortened seasons of 1994 and 1995 they finished in the division cellar. In 1995, however, Pat Rapp showed signs of promise with a 14-7 mark and rookie second baseman Quilvio Veras led the NL with 56 stolen bases. Even though the Marlins fired manager Rene Lachemann in midseason 1996 (replacing him with interim manager John Boles) they moved up to third place (80-82) with help from Gary Sheffield (42 HR, 120 RBIs, 118 runs scored), Al Leiter (200 strikeouts), Kevin Brown (league-leading 1.89 ERA), and Robb Nen (35 saves).

In the offseason, the Marlins signed manager Jim Leyland and within a few months they had practically a whole new team. In less than three weeks the Marlins signed six free agents—Bobby Bonilla, Moises Alou, Alex Fernandez, Jim Eisenreich, John Cangelosi, and Dennis Cook—and suddenly they were one of the best teams in baseball. The Marlins battled Atlanta for the NL East title (they went 8-4 against the Braves during the season), but failing that, they still managed to hold off the Mets for the Wild Card. The Marlins swept the Giants in the Division Series and then shocked the Braves in six games to win the pennant.

Rookie Livan Hernandez, who was Most Valuable Player of the NLCS, earned MVP honors for the World Series as well. It was second-year shortstop Edgar Rentaria, however, who won the World Series with a single in the bottom of the 11th inning of Game 7 to score Craig Counsell, whose sacrifice fly had tied the game in the ninth. Their victory over Cleveland not only made the Marlins the first Wild Card team to win the World Series, but in only their fifth season of existence, they were also the fastest expansion team to win a world championship.

As quickly as success had come, it disappeared. Quoting huge financial losses on the championship team, owner Huizenga looked to sell the Marlins, and in the meantime, traded away the nucleus of the world champions before they ever got a chance to defend the title. By the end of the year, only everyday players Renteria and Counsel remained (and Renteria was traded to St. Louis during the winter meetings). The Marlins were finally sold to commodities trader John Henry and John Boles was named manager of the team for the second time after the 1998 season, replacing Jim Leyland, who resigned. General manager Dave Dombrowski, who, in Huizenga's "house cleaning" had secured several top prospects from other organizations, signed a five-year contract to remain with the club.

Houston Astros

The Colt .45s (as the Astros were originally known) had hoped to begin their history in the Harris County Domed Stadium. When the start of the vast project was delayed, a temporary outdoor park was built for them next door in time for their 1962 inaugural. Heat, humidity, and giant mosquitoes held Colt home attendance below a million in each of their three outdoor seasons. In 1965, they brought big league baseball indoors for the first time, and the fans arrived—more than 2 million the first year. The original grass under the dome was real, but when the skylight panels were coated over so fielders wouldn't lose sight of high flies, the grass died. In 1966 the club (now known as the Astros) and the stadium (now called the Astrodome) brought to baseball yet another innovation—AstroTurf.

The Houston franchise, conceived as an entry in the abortive Continental League, first took the field instead in the National League. Houston and the New York Mets were part of the league's first expansion since shrinking from 12 teams to eight in 1900. Shrewd player selection by general manager Paul Richards kept the new team from being as bad as the Mets. Although they suffered just as long playing below .500 (seven years), they finished below New York in the standings only once.

When the NL added two more teams in 1969 and split into two divisions, the Astros for the first time made a serious title run. Though they wound up fifth in the West (ahead of only the expansion San Diego Padres), they rose to within two games of the top in August, and again in September before a six-game losing streak dropped them out of contention. With an 81-81 record, they finished out of the ranks of losers for the first time.

After dropping below .500 again in 1970 and '71, the Astros made their second run for the division title in 1972. At the end of June they were battling with Cincinnati for the lead, but the Reds pulled away over the rest of the season while Houston leveled off for an eventual second-place finish 10½ games back. With a record of 84-69, the Astros had fashioned their first winning season.

In 1975 they endured their worst year ever, losing 97 games to finish at the bottom of the West, 43½ games behind the Reds. But the next year pitcher J.R. Richard, with the first of several fine seasons, brought the club up to third with his 20 wins. By 1979 Richard was the NL's most overwhelming pitcher, leading the league with 313 strikeouts and a 2.71 ERA. His 18 wins and teammate Joe Niekro's 21 sparked a team that spent much of the summer in first place before falling to a game and a half behind Cincinnati at the end.

Houston and Los Angeles battled back and forth for the division lead throughout 1980. Richard began strong and seemed headed for his finest year. With a 10-4 record, he was the starting pitcher in the All-Star Game. But shortly after midseason he suffered a stroke that ended his big league career. Led by Joe Niekro, Nolan Ryan, and Vern Ruhle (who replaced Richard in the rotation and finished 12-4), the best pitching staff in baseball kept the Astros in the race to season's end, although three straight losses to the Dodgers had left the clubs tied for first. In a one-game playoff, Houston rebounded with a 7-1 win (Niekro's 20th) to capture the division title. In the National League Championship Series, the Astros took the Phillies to the

10th inning of the final game before bowing three games to two.

When a player strike cut the middle out of the 1981 season, intradivisional playoffs were scheduled between the winners of the two halves. Houston, the second-half champion, defeated first-half victor Los Angeles in the first two games, but lost the next three, and the division title.

After four years in the middle of the division, the Astros stormed back in 1986 with their best season ever, winning 15 of their last 19 games to conquer the West. Pitcher Mike Scott, who had developed a deceptive split-finger fastball, won 18 and led the NL in strikeouts, innings, and ERA. On Sept. 25 he clinched the division crown with a no-hitter. In the NLCS the Astros lost to the Mets in six games, but three of New York's wins came in its final at bat, including a 16-inning victory in Game 6.

In each of the next three seasons the Astros drew within a game and a half of first place in August, only to tumble out of the race in the season's final weeks. Rookie first baseman Jeff Bagwell's strong performance at the plate gave Astros fans one of their few reasons to cheer in 1991 as their team plummeted to last place.

The offense set club records in batting average and home runs in 1993, and the pitching staff compiled the second lowest ERA in the majors, as ace Mark Portugal concluded his brilliant 18-4 season with 12 straight wins. But the Astros couldn't approach powerful Atlanta and San Francisco, and finished third in their division, 19 games out.

Free agent Portugal departed for San Francisco in 1994, but pitcher Doug Drabek rebounded after an off year, and MVP Bagwell's slugging dominated the NL. Playing in the Central division under new manager Terry Collins, the Astros struggled to catch division leader Cincinnati, and had drawn within half a game of the Reds when the season ended. The following year was almost a replay of 1994, as the Astros again finished second to Cincinnati. In 1996 the Astros were bridesmaids again, this time finishing second (82-80), six games behind St. Louis.

At season's end Astros broadcaster Larry Dierker replaced Collins as manager. Dierker, the ace of the Astros pitching staff more than two decades earlier, let developing pitchers like Shane Reynolds, Mike Hampton, and Jose Lima stay in games longer and they quickly learned from their mistakes and gained confidence. After three years of finishing second, the Astros finally won the NL Central in Dierker's rookie season as manager. They were quickly swept by Atlanta in the playoffs.

Even though 1997 ace Darryl Kile (19-7, 2.57 ERA) left for Colorado as a free agent, the Astros repeated as division champs in 1998. A last-minute trade for Randy Johnson of Seattle fortified an already solid pitching staff and helped Houston to a club record 102 wins. The hot Astros ran into an even hotter Padres team and lost in the Division Series, three games to one.

Kansas City Royals

Two years after the Athletics abandoned Kansas City for the West Coast, patent medicine millionaire Ewing Kauffman bankrolled an expansion club for the city. Where the A's had been unable in 13 years to fashion even one winning season, the Royals did it in 1971, their third year. One of the most successful of all expansion clubs, the Royals finished either first or second in their division in 14 of their first 20 years.

In their fifth season, 1973, the year they moved into new Royals Stadium, the Royals also made their first serious run for the division title. A midsummer spurt carried them into first place in August before they leveled off to another second-place finish behind Oakland.

After a third second-place race with Oakland in 1975 (during which manager Jack McKeon was replaced by Whitey Herzog), the Royals won the division crown in 1976, taking the lead two months into the season and holding it to the end. Third baseman George Brett won his first AL batting championship by one point over teammate Hal McRae. The Royals and New York were tied after four games in the American League Championship Series, but the Yankees snatched the pennant on Chris Chambliss' home run in the bottom of the ninth inning of the final game.

For two more years the Royals dominated the AL West but failed to stop the Yankees in the ALCS. In 1977, with a pitching staff that led the league in ERA and a balanced offense that included four players with more than 20 home runs and 80 RBIs, the Royals compiled a record of 102-60—their finest to date. Though they didn't move into the division lead until mid-August, they were nearly unstoppable the rest of the way. In the ALCS they once again battled New York all the way, only to lose the Series and pennant for the second time in the final inning of Game 5.

The American League West divisional race was a bit tighter in 1978, as California hung close to Kansas City through much of August and into September, before the Royals finally pulled away. In the ALCS, the Royals tied the series with a big win in Game 2, but the Yankees came back to take the next two by one run each for their third straight flag.

The Royals slipped to second place in 1979, but the next year (led now by rookie manager Jim Frey) they overwhelmed the rest of a weak division. Despite a month-long decline in September, Kansas City finished the season 14 games ahead of Oakland for their fourth divisional title. This was the year Brett chased .400 (ending at .390, the highest major league average since Ted Williams hit .406 in 1941), reliever Dan Quisenberry enjoyed his first big season (12 wins, 33 saves), and starter Dennis Leonard came back from an off-year to record his third 20-win season in four years. It was also the year the Royals finally beat the Yankees to capture their first pennant—with a three-game sweep in the ALCS. In the World Series, though, it was Philadelphia in six games.

The player strike of 1981 divided the season into two halves. In the first half the Royals finished fifth, but part way through the second half Dick Howser (who had managed the Yankees to the East title the previous year) replaced Frey as Royals manager.

The Royals rallied to finish first, a game ahead of Oakland. But in the special playoffs, the A's (who had won the first-half race) beat Kansas City for the division

title with a three-game sweep.

Two more second-place finishes in 1982 (a close race with California) and 1983 (20 games behind the Chicago White Sox) were followed in 1984 by a fifth division championship in a three-way race with California and Minnesota. But Detroit swept away the Royals' pennant hopes in the ALCS, in the minimum three games.

For Kansas City, 1985 was a season of catching up. Few picked the Royals to win the West, but with starters Charlie Leibrandt (17-9) and Bret Saberhagen (20-6) finishing two-three in the league ERA race, reliever Quisenberry leading the league in saves for the fourth straight year, and veteran George Brett healthy and enjoying one of his best seasons ever, the Royals chased California throughout the summer and caught them in the final week to take their sixth division crown by a single game. In the ALCS against Toronto, the Royals fell behind three games to one, which would have eliminated them in earlier years. Saved by the expansion of the series from five games to seven, they came back with three straight wins for their second pennant. Repeating the suspense in the World Series, the Royals again fell behind 3-1 to St. Louis, before rallying once again to win three straight for their first world championship.

During the 1986 season, manager Howser left the club because of a brain tumor. The Royals dropped below .500 and finished third, their lowest rank in a dozen years. Howser was unable to return to the helm in 1987 as he had hoped and died during the summer.

In 1989 Bret Saberhagen, with his most sparkling season yet (23-6, 2.16 ERA), hurled the Royals to their best record since 1980, but their 92 wins earned them only a ninth second-place finish—although Saberhagen earned his second Cy Young Award. Confounding predictions of another strong season, following free agent acquisitions Mark Davis and Storm Davis, the Royals in 1990 floundered in the division cellar much of the summer. They wound up in sixth place, 27½ games out. George Brett, now 37, rallied from the worst start of his career (a .200 batting average in early May) to hit .329 and capture his third AL batting title.

Slugging outfielder Danny Tartabull enjoyed a peak season in 1991, and helped lift Kansas City back above .500. But in the strong AL West no club suffered a losing season, so the Royals again had to settle for sixth. When Tartabull left for the Yankees in 1992, the Royals faltered again. But as the West was now the weaker division, the club's 72-90 record was good enough for a fifth-place tie.

In the final season of his playing career at Kansas City, George Brett led his team in RBIs in 1993, and Kevin Appier led AL pitchers in ERA, as the Royals returned above .500 to finish third. Ewing Kauffman, the club's founder and owner, died in August, and Royals Stadium was renamed in his honor.

In 1994, after a sluggish first half, the Royals picked up the pace to challenge Chicago and Cleveland in the new American League Central division. At season's end, the Royals were still third but—thanks largely to Cy Young Award winner David Cone's 16-5 season—only four games behind first-place Chicago. Manager Bob Boone's Royals finished second again in 1995—but this time 30 games back of Cleveland. In 1996, playing on natural turf for the first time in Kauffman Stadium's history, the

Royals finished last again (75-86, 24 games out).

The 1997 Royals had an eight-game losing streak heading into the All-Star Game; after the break they had a new manager, Tony Muser, and lost four more before they finally won in 14 innings. The Royals finished last, but Kansas City rebounded to finish third in 1998, despite losing Chili Davis and Jay Bell to free agency and seeing Kevin Appier miss most of the season with injuries.

Los Angeles Dodgers

When the Dodgers left Brooklyn for Los Angeles, an era ended. From baseball's earliest days Brooklyn had been prominent; the city's Atlantics were the nation's best in the mid-1860s, and since 1884 Brooklyn had been home to major league ball. But before the start of the 1958 season, its link to the big time was severed by an owner who saw greener fields to the west.

The club's origins were modest. After winning the championship of the minor Inter-State Association in 1883, Brooklyn moved up to the major league American Association in 1884 and endured three losing seasons in its first four years. But in 1888, after signing three regulars from New York's newly defunct Mets and buying pitching/hitting stars Bob Caruthers and Dave Foutz from the AA champion St. Louis Browns, Brooklyn finished second to St. Louis, and the next year dethroned the Browns for their first big league pennant. In a World Series against the National League champion New York Giants, the Bridegrooms (as the Brooklyns had been nicknamed) won three of the first four games, but lost the next five.

Before the start of the 1890 season, Brooklyn transferred from the AA to the more prestigious NL. Many NL clubs performed below par that year, weakened by the loss of players to the outlaw Players League. But Brooklyn held on to most of its players and swept to its second straight pennant. In postseason play, poor weather and lack of fan support caused the World Series against AA winner Louisville to be called off after each team had won three games and tied one. The next year, with other NL teams renewed by players from the failed PL, Brooklyn finished sixth.

When the AA folded after the 1891 season, Brooklyn picked up slugger Dan Brouthers and pitcher George Haddock from pennant-winning Boston, and rebounded in 1892 to finish second and third in the two halves of a divided season. But for the next five years they finished no higher than fifth, and in 1898 sank to 10th in what was then a 12-team league.

Help was on the way, however. The owners of the Baltimore Orioles—Harry Von der Horst and Ned Hanlon—seeing an opportunity to move into the more lucrative Brooklyn market, purchased a half interest in the Bridegrooms. Hanlon retained his Baltimore presidency, but took over as manager in Brooklyn, bringing along with him the core of the Orioles —shortstop Hughie Jennings and outfielders Joe Kelley and Willie Keeler—plus his two best pitchers, Jim Hughes and Doc McJames.

The infusion of new talent worked wonders, as Brooklyn in 1899 (with a new nickname, the Superbas) took the NL lead in late May, during a 22-game winning streak,

and held it the rest of the way. That winter, when Baltimore was dropped as the NL cut back from 12 teams to eight, Hanlon moved more Orioles to Brooklyn (including pitcher Joe "Iron Man" McGinnity), and once again led the Superbas to the pennant. That year they also won their first world championship in a series played with second-place Pittsburgh for the elegant Chronicle-Telegraph Cup.

Charley Ebbets, who had risen from ticket seller to president, took over majority ownership with the purchase of Von der Horst's stock, thereby quashing Hanlon's proposed move back to Baltimore. Ebbets' clashes with Hanlon hastened the club's decline. In 1903 the team began a 12-year sojourn in the second division, including a last-place finish in 1905 with their worst record ever (48-104, 56½ games out). Perhaps the most memorable events of these years were the change in nickname to Dodgers, and their move to brand-new Ebbets Field in 1913.

Hanlon was fired as manager after the disastrous 1905 season, but it was not until Wilbert Robinson took over in 1914 that the team began to pull out of its doldrums. Pitcher Jack Pfeffer, in his first full big-league season, won 23 games for the fifth-place Dodgers that year, and two years later led them to the pennant with 25 wins on a sparkling 1.92 ERA.

But the Dodgers lost the 1916 World Series to the Boston Red Sox, and in 1917 fell all the way to seventh. After three years in the second division, they bounced back in 1920, turning a three-way race into a rout with 16 wins in their final 18 games. After another World Series loss, to Cleveland, the Dodgers returned to the second division for another three years. In 1924 they began slowly, but leaped from 12 games back to an early-September lead, only to slip 1½ games behind the Giants at the finish.

Charley Ebbets died the following April, and Robinson was named to replace him. In his five years as president the club suffered on the field, finishing sixth each year. Fired as president but retained as manager, "Uncle Robby" saw his Robins (as the Dodgers were now known) lead the league in 1930 most of the time from mid-May to a mid-August decline, then retake the lead for a day in mid-September before tailing off once more to finish fourth. That was Uncle Robby's last hurrah. When the Robins provided no serious challenge in their fourth-place run the next year, he resigned after 18 years at the wheel.

A succession of managers followed, but it was not until the Dodgers brought in the free-spending Larry MacPhail as general manager in 1938 that the club began to pull itself back into contention. The highlight of MacPhail's first year with the Dodgers was not the team's finish (seventh) but the introduction of night baseball to Ebbets Field (on June 15, when Cincinnati's Johnny Vander Meer defeated Brooklyn with his second consecutive no-hitter).

MacPhail's most brilliant move may have been his conversion of shortstop Leo Durocher into manager Leo Durocher. The loud, driven Durocher alienated many (including MacPhail himself), but provided inspired leadership and a will to win that overcame complaints against him. After a third-place finish in 1939 and second place in

1940, the Dodgers battled the St. Louis Cardinals through all of 1941 before pulling ahead to clinch the pennant with just two games remaining. Veteran first baseman Dolf Camilli led the league in home runs and RBIs, sophomore outfielder Pete Reiser led the league in batting, slugging, and runs scored, and pitchers Kirby Higbe and Whitlow Wyatt tied for the league lead with 22 wins apiece, as the Dodgers won 100 games. Only their loss to the Yankees in the World Series marred their finest season in 42 years.

In 1942 they played even better, winning 104 games. But a late-season five-game slump dropped them behind the surging Cardinals. MacPhail and many of his players left for the war, and though the club finished third in 1943 and 1945, it was not until 1946 that the Dodgers again presented a serious challenge. Once again the Cards and Dodgers made a two-team race of it, but this time the race ended in a tie, forcing the first league playoff ever. St. Louis won the pennant with wins in the first two games.

When MacPhail left for the Army, Branch Rickey was hired to run the club. MacPhail had left the club financially sound; Rickey set about to make it a consistent winner. Famed as the developer of the Cardinals farm system, he was determined at Brooklyn to tap the one source of talent that the major leagues had willfully neglected: black players. He signed Jackie Robinson to Montreal (Brooklyn's leading farm team), and after a year there promoted him to the Dodgers for the 1947 season. Thus began the club's golden Brooklyn decade: 10 years in which they won six pennants and—in 1955—a World Series. Two other races went right to the wire; only once did they finish as low as third.

With manager Durocher suspended from baseball for a year for consorting with gamblers, the Dodgers in 1947 were led by grandfatherly Burt Shotton, brought out of his Florida retirement. Robinson's hustle put him at the top of the league in stolen bases and second in runs scored. The team pulled up from fourth in June to first in July, and held the lead to the end. In the World Series they lost to the Yankees in an exciting seven games.

Durocher returned to the helm in 1948, but was replaced by Shotton in midsummer, with the Dodgers in fifth place. Shotton saw the team rise to third that season, then battle back and forth with the Cardinals throughout 1949 before edging them by a game on the final day. Robinson, in his finest season, led the NL in hitting and stolen bases, and finished among the leaders in most other offensive categories. Rookie pitcher Don Newcombe led the team in victories with 17, and Preacher Roe led the league in winning percentage. Again the World Series was a loss to the Yankees, this time in only five games.

In 1950 the Dodgers nearly caught the staggering Phillies, losing out only in the 10th inning of the final game. President Rickey left the club for Pittsburgh and was replaced by Walter O'Malley, who replaced manager Shotton with Charlie Dressen. The slugging of catcher Roy Campanella and first baseman Gil Hodges, and 20-win seasons by Roe (22-3) and Newcombe (20-9) kept the Dodgers in front through most of 1951, but New York's surging Giants closed from 13 games back in August to tie for the lead at the finish. The teams split the first two playoff games. In Game 3 the Dodgers were leading by two runs in the last of the ninth when Bobby Thomson's

three-run homer gave New York the flag.

The next year, though, the Giants fell short and Brooklyn took the pennant with relative ease. But not the World Series. Although Brooklyn held a 3-2 lead after five games, the Yankees came back to take the final two.

The Dodgers repeated as NL champions in 1953 with their best season ever. The Dodgers overwhelmed the league, hitting 19 points and slugging 63 points above the league average, as the team outscored its nearest rival by more than a run per game. With a club-record 105 wins, the Dodgers cruised to the pennant by 13 games. But again the Yankees took the World Series, in six games.

Dressen wanted a three-year contract and was let go when he turned down another for only one year. Minor league manager Walter Alston wasn't so demanding, and signed for 1954 the first of a historic string of 23 one-year Dodger contracts that would see him into the Hall of Fame. After a second-place finish in Alston's rookie season, the Dodgers in 1955 took the lead from the start and—never challenged—walked away with their 11th pennant. Outfielder Duke Snider, with one of his most productive seasons, led the league's most powerful squad; Newcombe (20-5) paced the league's best pitching staff.

Once more in the World Series, Brooklyn faced the Yankees, and once more the Series went seven games. But this time there was joy in Brooklyn—Johnny Podres shut out New York in the finale! In an exciting three-way fight in 1956, the Dodgers repeated as pennant-winners, taking their final three games to edge the Milwaukee Braves. Newcombe, in his greatest year, clinched the flag on the final day with his 27th win. In the World Series, though, it was deja vu time—a sixth Yankee triumph, in seven games. The golden decade was over.

The Dodgers (despite the league's best pitching) vacated the 1957 race in August, finishing third. Before the start of the next season, they had vacated Brooklyn as well, for Los Angeles. Playing in Memorial Coliseum (a converted football stadium) the L.A. Dodgers sank to seventh place in 1958. But the next year the reawakened bats of aging Duke Snider and Gil Hodges, the fiery pitching of young Don Drysdale, and the late-season pitching heroics of Roger Craig (recalled from Spokane) kept the team in the thick of a tight race that found them tied with the Braves at season's end. The Dodgers won the first playoff game in Milwaukee, and captured big league baseball's first West Coast pennant at home the next day, in the 12th inning. Then they defeated the Chicago White Sox to give the West its first World Series winner.

After finishes of fourth and second, the Dodgers produced record-breaking excitement in 1962 as they moved into brand-new Dodger Stadium in the hills above Los Angeles. Between the new ballpark and the excitement generated on the field, more than 2.75 million fans passed through the turnstiles—a new attendance record that would last until the Dodgers themselves broke it 15 years later. As pitcher Don Drysdale and left fielder Tommy Davis ignited the league with career-high seasons, and shortstop Maury Wills became the first major leaguer of the century to steal 100 bases, the team locked into a season-long struggle for first place with archrival San Francisco. But after holding a narrow lead much of the season, the Dodgers dropped their last four games to finish in yet another tie. The playoff must have reminded

fans of 1951. As they had then, the Giants and Dodgers split the first two games, and the Dodgers once again brought a 4-2 lead into the ninth inning of the third game. This time, though, it was not a home run that undid them, but a bases-loaded walk.

Sandy Koufax—who had won 14 games in 1962 (and the first of five straight ERA crowns) despite losing half the year with circulation problems in his fingers—rose to dominate the world of pitching the next four years. For three of those years his Dodgers dominated the NL. In 1963 Koufax's 25-5 season carried Los Angeles into the World Series against the Yankees, where two more wins helped put the New Yorkers away in the minimum four games. The next year Koufax slipped to 19 wins, but the Dodgers fell all the way to a tie for sixth.

They rebounded to the top in 1965. Koufax won 26 and Drysdale 23 in a tight four-team race that saw them fall behind the Giants in early September, only to retake the lead for good later in the month with 13 straight wins. The World Series against Minnesota went to the seventh game before Koufax nailed down another world title with his second shutout in three days.

The race in 1966 was just as close as in '65, with three teams switching leads throughout the season. But the Dodgers, third at the end of August, put together streaks of five and seven wins in September to move to the top, where Koufax clinched the pennant on the final day with his 27th victory. And then it was all over. After a losing effort in Game 2 of the World Series (a Baltimore sweep), Koufax, at age 30, retired because of arthritis in his pitching elbow. The Dodgers sank to eighth the next year and rose only to seventh in 1968.

In 1969, the first season of divisional play, Los Angeles found itself in the thick of a five-team race in the West until eight straight losses in late September dropped them to fourth. No one challenged Cincinnati in 1970, but the next year the Dodgers closed to within a game of the front-running Giants in September before their drive stalled.

A late-season slump let Cincinnati get to the top in 1973, but the Dodgers held their lead to the end in 1974. Newly acquired veteran outfielder Jimmy Wynn and first baseman Steve Garvey, in his first full season, led the club offensively; pitcher Mike Marshall set a modern major league record with 106 appearances in relief of a staff that was the league's best (which earned him the Cy Young Award). The Dodgers beat Pittsburgh handily in the National League Championship Series for their fifth Los Angeles pennant, but lost the World Series to Oakland in five games.

Cincinnati proved untouchable in 1975 and '76, but in 1977 the Dodgers—under new manager Tom Lasorda, who moved up from the coaching staff when Alston retired—jumped to an early lead and held it all the way. Garvey's 33 home runs led a balanced offense in which four players hit 30 or more homers. Again the Dodgers won the NLCS (in four games, against Philadelphia), and again they lost the World Series (to the Yankees, in six games).

Although the divisional race was closer—and the Dodgers broke baseball's 3 million attendance barrier for the first time—1978 was in most respects a replay of 1977. Garvey again led the club offensively, the Dodgers

again beat out Cincinnati in the West and Philadelphia in a four-game NLCS, and the Yankees again defeated the Dodgers in a six-game World Series.

A season-long back-and-forth battle with Houston in 1980 ended in a tie for first—the fifth tie for the Dodgers, three more than any other club. In the playoff (reduced from three games to one to bring the NL into line with AL practice), Houston won easily.

When the players went out on strike part way through 1981, the Dodgers, paced by the spectacular pitching of rookie Fernando Valenzuela, found themselves half a game in front of Cincinnati. In a special playoff with Houston, the winner of the NL West second half of the split season, the Dodgers defeated the Astros in five games for the division title, and also went the distance in beating Montreal for the pennant. Facing the Yankees for the 11th time in World Series play, they lost the first two games, but swept the next four to capture their sixth world title.

In 1982, after a poor start, the Dodgers fought back to take the lead in August and again in September before dropping back to second, a game out. More successful drives in 1983 and '85 led to their fifth and sixth division titles, but culminated in defeat in the NLCS—to Philadelphia in 1983 and St. Louis two years later.

In 1988, with an infusion of talent from the American League—most notably slugger Kirk Gibson and relief ace Jay Howell—and a spectacular season from starter Orel Hershiser (who concluded his 23-8 year with a major-league record 59 consecutive scoreless innings), the Dodgers bounced back to the top of the NL West. It took them the full seven games to down the favored Mets in the NLCS, but in the World Series they humbled Oakland's powerful Athletics in just five games for their seventh world crown. Kirk Gibson's pinch-hit two-run homer in the bottom of the ninth off Dennis Eckersley in Game 1 was the turning point of the series. A panel of local experts later selected the home run by the gimpy Gibson as the greatest moment in Los Angeles sports history.

Led by Hershiser (whose 15-15 record belied another strong season) the Dodgers yielded the fewest runs in the NL in 1989. A lack of offense, however, left the team no better than fourth. Hershiser underwent shoulder surgery in April 1991, but young Ramon Martinez picked up the slack and won 20 games for the second-place Dodgers.

From early May to late August 1991, the Dodgers occupied first place in their division, paced by the majors' stingiest pitching staff and the hot bats of free agent signees Brett Butler and Darryl Strawberry. Seven straight losses after the All-Star break began the team's descent into a great struggle with ascendant Atlanta. From Aug. 21 through season's end the two clubs stayed within two games of each other. With four games to go, Los Angeles held a one-game lead. But they lost their next three games, and all hope of the division crown.

In 1992 everything fell apart. Unable to parry the twin blows of injury and inexperience, the Dodgers stumbled to the worst record in the majors, and finished last for only the second time in their 109 years of major league play. Rookie catcher Mike Piazza burst upon the scene in 1993 to rank among NL leaders in batting, slugging, home runs, and RBIs, as the Dodgers recovered to finish in fourth place. A final-game victory over San Francisco brought their season record to .500, and deprived the Giants of a tie for the division title.

Japanese rookie sensation Hideo Nomo paced the NL with 236 strikeouts in 1995 and led the Dodgers to the NL West title—by just one game over the power-hitting Colorado Rockies. But in the first round of the postseason, Los Angeles fell to Cincinnati in three straight.

In mid-1996 a heart attack felled Lasorda, and he handed over the club's reins to Bill Russell. Mike Piazza (.344, 36 HR, 105 RBIs,), Eric Karros (34 HR, 121 RBIs), and Raul Mondesi (.297, 24 HR) led the offense. Out-fielder Todd Hollandsworth (.291) became the fifth consecutive Dodger to win NL Rookie of the Year honors. Ramon Martinez (15-6), Ismael Valdes (15-7), Hideo Nomo (16-11, 234 strikeouts), and Todd Worrell (44 saves) paced a staff that led the majors with a 3.46 ERA. Los Angeles (90-72) lost the West Division title to San Diego on the final day of the season but achieved a post-season berth via the Wild Card route. The 1996 Dodgers faced Atlanta in the playoffs and met the same fate as the 1995 team had at the hands of the Reds: a humiliating three-game sweep.

The Dodgers, the model of stability in baseball for decades, underwent huge changes over the next two years. First, major league owners grudgingly approved Rupert Murdoch and the Fox Corporation as the new owners of the team. Then, the team traded its biggest star, Mike Piazza, after he turned down a sizeable contract offer from the Dodgers. The trade, which brought Bobby Bonilla, Gary Sheffield, and Charles Johnson from the Marlins, was made by Fox executives and didn't go through general manager Fred Claire. Russell and Claire were both dismissed soon after and were replaced by minor-league manager Glenn Hoffman and Tommy Lasorda, who returned as interim GM. The Dodgers ended the season in third place, their lowest finish since 1993. Kevin Malone was hired as full-time general manager late in 1998 and Davey Johnson became the team's third manager in six months after the franchise had just two managers from 1954 to 1996. To cap off the changes, they signed Kevin Brown to a seven-year, $105 million contract.

Milwaukee Brewers

When in 1969 the new Seattle Pilots played their home opener in the refurbished minor league Sick's Stadium, 7,000 seats and the left field fence were still unfinished. The Pilots may not have needed the seats. Fewer than 700,000 fans came to see them play—the third-worst attendance in the league—as they drifted into the cellar of the American League West with 98 losses. (In fact the most memorable thing about that season was a controversial book, *Ball Four,* by Pilots pitcher Jim Bouton.). That winter the Pilots— renamed the Brewers—moved to Milwaukee, where a genuine big league stadium (vacated by the Braves five years earlier) awaited them.

Attendance improved nearly 38 percent in Milwaukee, although the Brewers of 1970 won only one game more than the Pilots had in Seattle. It would be eight more years before they experienced their first winning season. Meanwhile, in 1972, they switched divisions from West to East,

trading places with the Washington Senators, who moved West to become the Texas Rangers. Hank Aaron came to the Brewers in 1975 to finish his career where it had started in 1954 (with the Milwaukee Braves), but Aaron's presence helped the club at the gate more than in the standings.

The Brewers broke their losing pattern in 1978. One key front-office move leading to the turnaround was the signing of free agent Larry Hisle (who the previous year with Minnesota had led the league in RBIs). Hisle proved his worth in 1978, leading an offense that sprang to life under rookie manager George Bamberger to top the league in hitting, slugging, homers, and runs scored. On the mound Mike Caldwell won 22 games in the best season of his career. Although the Brewers never threatened the Boston Red Sox or the New York Yankees for the lead, they did rise from below .500 in early June to finish a solid third, 24 games above .500.

A shoulder injury the next April marked the beginning of the end of Hisle's career and perhaps cost Milwaukee the division title. Even without him the team compiled what is still their best winning percentage (.590), as outfielder Gorman Thomas (45 home runs, 123 RBIs) and several other hitters attained new career peaks of productivity. While they never seriously threatened front-running Baltimore, they rose past Boston in late August to finish second.

Most of the Milwaukee bats remained hot in 1980, but injuries, ragged pitching, and Bamberger's heart attack (which caused him to miss the first part of the season and retire in early September) contributed to a distant third-place finish. In strike-divided 1981, league-leading performances by two newly acquired pitchers—starter Pete Vuckovich (14-4) and reliever Rollie Fingers (28 saves)—helped give the Brewers the best overall record in the AL East, and the second-half championship. But in the special intradivisional playoffs with first-half winner New York, the Yankees captured the division crown three games to two.

The Brewers started slowly in 1982; at the end of May they were two games below .500, near the bottom of the division. A day later Buck Rodgers, the Milwaukee coach who had replaced Bamberger as manager two years earlier, was himself replaced by coach Harvey Kuenn. By mid-July the team had risen to first place, and they led the West by more than six games as September neared. Baltimore had cut the lead to three games by the time Milwaukee arrived for the season's final four games. One win would give the Brewers their first division championship, but they lost the first three games by five, six, and eight runs. Don Sutton, who had been acquired from Houston a month earlier, faced Oriole Jim Palmer in the season finale: the Brewers took the division title with a 10-2 win.

Milwaukee's offense—"Harvey's Wallbangers"—had been awesome, scoring more than a run per game above the league average. Just about every offensive category featured one or two Brewers among the league's top three: in hits they took all three top spots. Shortstop Robin Yount, who finished first in slugging, hits, total bases, and doubles, was named major league player of the year.

In postseason play California took a 2-0 lead in the ALCS, but Milwaukee came back to take the final three games and the pennant. In the World Series against St. Louis, the Brewers twice took the lead in games, but the Cardinals scored the last five runs of Game 7 to win the Series.

Milwaukee dropped to fifth in 1983, then to a last-place seventh the next year, 36½ games back. It was not until 1987 that they returned to the winning track, finishing third with 91 victories. As veterans Robin Yount and Paul Molitor continued to spark the team's offense, and starter Ted Higuera and reliever Dan Plesac headlined the AL East's best pitching staff, the Brewers in 1988 rose above .500 to stay at the end of August, and finished in a tie for third, just two games behind champion Boston. With Yount and Molitor enjoying even more productive seasons in 1989, and reliever Plesac on a club-record pace for saves, the Brewers drew within half a game of first place in August. But injuries and league-worst fielding took their toll, and the club finished fourth, right at .500. In 1990, as poor fielding led to more than 100 unearned runs, the Brewers dropped to sixth.

Paul Molitor enjoyed a banner season in 1991, and, from the first week in August to the finish, the Brewers played at a torrid .750 clip. But they had begun their comeback 15 games behind, and too late to raise themselves more than one place in the standings. With another sterling season from Molitor in 1992, plus Robin Yount's milestone 3,000th hit, and another strong finish (after a better first half), Milwaukee drew within two games of ultimately victorious Toronto in the season's final week. Still, the Brewers' 92-70 record and second-place finish were their best since their pennant-winning season a decade earlier. In 1993, though, free agent Molitor departed for Toronto, sparking the Blue Jays' run for a second straight world championship as the Brewers fell into the AL East cellar, 26 games behind the Jays.

In 1994 the Brewers were one of five clubs inserted into the AL's new Central Division, thus becoming the only club to play in three different divisions. They finished last once again, dropping behind Minnesota just three days before the season concluded in August. Only marginal improvement occurred in 1995 as manager Phil Garner's Brewers finished fourth (65-79). In 1996, despite slugger Greg Vaughn's midseason departure to San Diego, Milwaukee moved up to third (80-82) thanks to Dave Nilsson (.331) and Mike Fetters (32 saves).

The 1997 Brewers pulled within 2½ games of first-place Cleveland on Sept. 2, but faded to eight games back by season's end. Garner, the Brewers' all-time winningest manager, guided the team to fifth place in the first league switch of the century. Because of the addition of a new team to each league in 1998, it was decided that one existing team had to switch leagues to make both leagues have an even number of teams for scheduling purposes. Milwaukee, which had been home to the Braves from 1953-1965, returned to the National League with a game between the Brewers and, fittingly, the Braves in Atlanta on March 31. Bud Selig, who had been acting commissioners since 1992, put his shares of the Brewers in a trust and handed ownership of the club to his daughter when he was officially named commissioner in 1998.

Minnesota Twins

The Twins' beginnings as the Washington Senators were inauspicious. When American League president Ban Johnson established the Senators as part of his move in 1901 to raise the league to major league status, he staffed it with the manager and many of the players from his disbanded Kansas City franchise. Within a decade, four of the eight teams in the new major league had won two or more pennants, and three others had enjoyed at least one season in second place. But the Senators, after sixth-place finishes in their first two seasons, spent the next nine years in seventh or eighth.

Even the arrival of promising young fireballer Walter Johnson didn't seem to help. By 1909 he was the league's second-best strikeout artist, but he lost 25 games and the Senators finished farther back than ever—56 games from the top. Johnson turned his record around the next two years, winning 25 games in 1910 and in 1911, but the team rose only to seventh.

When Clark Griffith—a 42-year-old former pitching great and one of the founders of the American League— was hired to manage the Senators after the 1911 season, the club's fortunes took an immediate turn for the better. Griffith revamped the lineup—most strikingly in the acquisition of first baseman Chick Gandil from minor league Montreal. The Senators in 1912 won 17 straight games after Gandil was put into the lineup, and found themselves in the midst of a pennant race. The Boston Red Sox eventually ran away from the field, but the Senators held off Philadelphia for second place. Johnson won 33 games, and his 1.39 ERA led the league.

The next season was Johnson's finest. His league-leading 36 wins, 11 shutouts, and 1.14 ERA were also career bests and enabled Washington to overtake Cleveland late in the season for another second-place finish. But while Johnson continued to top 20 wins per season for several years before beginning to fade, his team was unable to stay competitive.

Griffith wanted the Senators to spend more to attract good players; when his demands were rejected, he bought a controlling interest in the club and named himself president. A year later, in 1921, he retired as field manager. Under a succession of veteran player-managers the team showed some improvement over the next three years, but Griffith's surprise appointment of 27-year-old second baseman Bucky Harris to manage the team in 1924 worked wonders. Left fielder Goose Goslin drove in more runs than Babe Ruth, and Walter Johnson put together his best season in years to head the league's best pitching staff. A hot streak in June shot the team from fifth to first, and a strong stretch drive in August and September brought home their first pennant. In the World Series a ground ball's lucky bounce over the head of the Giants' third baseman brought the Senators victory in the last of the 12th inning of the seventh game.

Though the Senators, aided by the acquisition of veteran pitcher Stan Coveleski from Cleveland, fought off the A's to repeat as pennant winners in 1925, they were less successful in postseason play. Once again the Series went the full seven games, but this time Pittsburgh won the world title.

The Senators enjoyed winning seasons in five of the next seven years, as Johnson retired from the mound and replaced Harris as manager. But it was not until 1933, when Johnson was replaced by 26-year-old shortstop Joe Cronin, that the team again pursued the pennant beyond midseason. Two veteran pitchers at the top of their form—Alvin "General" Crowder and Earl Whitehill— and a balanced offense led by Cronin and first baseman Joe Kuhel kept the Senators close to New York through July, and then, as the Yankees leveled off in August, shot the team up out of reach. Although they tailed off a bit at the end, the Senators won the pennant handily, compiling a .651 winning percentage that is still the club record. The New York Giants, though, took Washington's measure in the World Series and overcame them in five games.

The following October a drop from third place in June to a distant seventh at season's end had plunged home attendance nearly 25 percent below the previous year. With finances always a problem in Washington, Griffith traded Joe Cronin, his manager, star shortstop, and (since September) son-in-law, to the Boston Red Sox for a lesser shortstop and $225,000.

Only twice in their remaining quarter century in Washington did the Senators rise higher than fourth or finish closer than 17 games from the top. In 1943 they placed second, 13½ games behind the runaway Yankees. And two years later, after a poor start, they caught up with frontrunner Detroit in September, only to stall and finish one and a half games out. The Senators finished in the cellar in four of their last six seasons in Washington.

Calvin Griffith, Clark's adopted son, assumed the club presidency when his father died in 1955. Within three years he was making plans to move the club to Minneapolis. There were threats from Congress and a plea from President Eisenhower not to move the Senators—and at first the league itself opposed the move. But Washington was not a good baseball town even when the Senators were playing well, and in October 1960 a solution was reached. The league would let Griffith move his club to Minnesota, and Washington would be granted a new expansion team.

Players like outfielders Bob Allison and Harmon Killebrew, and pitcher Camilo Pascual, who had enjoyed productive seasons before the move, were even more productive at Metropolitan Stadium in Minnesota. Other standouts became regulars or joined the club after the move—Zoilo Versalles at shortstop, Rich Rollins at third, Jim Kaat on the mound, and (arriving in 1964) outfielder Tony Oliva and pitcher Jim "Mudcat" Grant. Infielder Rod Carew began a remarkable 12-year stint with the Twins in 1967.

Former outfielder Sam Mele made his major league managerial debut during 1961, and in 1962 saw his Twins come close to catching the Yankees in mid-September, finishing second. The next year they didn't catch fire until August and wound up third. In 1964 they dropped below .500 into a tie for sixth. But after the end of June 1965 no one challenged them as they breezed to their first Minnesota pennant. Oliva led the league in batting for the second straight year, and Versalles (in what was far and away his finest season) led the league in total bases and runs scored. Mudcat Grant led the league with 21 victories (his only 20-win season) and six shutouts, and Kaat's 18 wins were the league's third best. In the World Series it took a

three-hitter by Los Angeles' Sandy Koufax to stop the Twins in the seventh game.

After a poor start in 1966 that saw them enter July deep in fifth place, the Twins played better than anyone else the rest of the season to sneak ahead of Detroit into second. Killebrew, who had been injured much of the previous year, returned with his old power in '66, and Kaat enjoyed a career-high season with 25 wins.

The Twins began 1967 with another poor start. With the team in disarray and in sixth place, the easygoing Mele was replaced in June by hard-driving Cal Ermer, a longtime minor league manager. By mid-July the team had risen to second, and a month later (after dropping back to fourth) moved to the top in one of the greatest pennant races ever. Four clubs battled for the title, with three still in the running on the final day. But Boston defeated Minnesota to win the pennant, and Detroit split a doubleheader to tie the Twins for second. The next year Minnesota finished seventh.

Fiery rookie manager Billy Martin replaced Ermer in 1969 and, in this first season of divisional play, piloted the Twins to the championship of the West. Killebrew exploded for the best season of his career (49 home runs, 140 runs driven in), and Carew won the first of his seven batting titles. The first American League Championship Series, though, was a disaster for the Twins as Baltimore swept to the pennant in three games. Veteran manager Bill Rigney replaced the difficult Martin at the helm, and piloted Minnesota to an almost identical division crown in 1970, again by a nine-game margin. Pitcher Jim Perry, with 24 victories, enjoyed his second straight 20-win season, and the best of his career. The ALCS, though, was another repeat performance—a Baltimore sweep.

For the next 13 years the Twins remained out of contention; it was not until the flowering of a new generation of young players in 1984 that a Minnesota title threat could be taken seriously.

The Twins' decline on the field was matched by a decline in attendance, which even their move indoors to the Hubert H. Humphrey Metrodome in 1982 did not significantly redress. The Griffith family, unwilling to risk the high cost of luring proven talent, decided to give up the club after more than 60 years of family ownership. Early in 1984 a buyer was found in Carl Pohlad, a wealthy Minneapolis banker. By the time Pohlad's purchase was completed at the end of July, the Twins' young team had blossomed into the West's front-runner, paced by pitcher Frank Viola's sudden development into a winner, and by the arrival in May of rookie centerfield sparkplug Kirby Puckett. Although the Twins leveled off in August and lost their final six games, to fall to .500 and a tie for second, they had brought the crowds back to the ballpark. The 1984 team drew more than 1.5 million fans for the first time ever and remained well above a million the next two years despite a pair of losing seasons.

In 1987, under manager Tom Kelly, the Minnesota fans were rewarded for their faithfulness. Although the Twins lost their last five games to finish only eight above .500, their winning record at home was the best in the league, and their title in the West was never in doubt. More surprising was their decisive triumph over favored Detroit in the ALCS, four games to one. In the first World Series

to feature indoor play, the Twins won the four games played in their Metrodome to capture Minnesota's first baseball world championship in seven games.

Although the Twins in 1988 improved on their 1987 won-lost record—and Frank Viola, Kirby Puckett, and relief ace Jeff Reardon enjoyed career peaks—they finished well back of Oakland in the race for the division crown. But their home attendance, which had jumped 66 percent in 1987 to top 2 million for the first time, bounded another 45 percent in 1988 to make the Twins the first AL club ever to attract more than 3 million fans in a season.

As the team suffered a general decline in pitching and hitting in 1989, Viola—in the middle of a disappointing season—was traded to the Mets; and the Twins finished fifth. Reardon, a free agent, left for Boston after the season. The Twins continued their downhill slide in 1990, slipping from fifth place at midseason to their first cellar finish in eight years.

On May 27, 1991, the Twins stood sixth in the AL West. Three weeks later, after winning 18 of 19 games, they were first. There they finished, becoming (like Atlanta in the NL) the first AL team to rise from last place to first in successive seasons. Minnesota's attack featured a balanced offense in which seven players drove in 50 runs or more, and a pitching revival that starred veteran free agent Jack Morris and a pair of young hurlers with their first big seasons, Scott Erickson (who won 12 in a row before the end of June) and Kevin Tapani (16-9, 2.99 ERA). In the ALCS, the Twins overcame Toronto in five games, then came back from a 3-2 World Series deficit to defeat Atlanta with a pair of extra-inning victories, including a 10-inning win in Game 7 as Morris pitched the shutout and Barry Larkin drove in the only run.

After his single starring season in Minnesota, Morris moved on to Toronto to hurl the Blue Jays into the championship. The Twins, meanwhile, arrived at midseason-1992 first in the AL West, where they remained into early August before drifting back into a second-place finish behind Oakland. Veteran superstar Dave Winfield left Toronto for Minnesota in 1993, where in September he passed the 3,000 hit mark. But the Twins slid out of contention early, and finished tied for fifth.

In early August 1994, now playing in the new Central Division, they finished fourth. In 1995 the Twins tied Toronto for the majors' worst record (56-88) and saw attendance drop 38 percent from the previous season. Among the few bright spots were Chuck Knoblauch (.333) and AL Rookie of the Year Marty Cordova (24 HR, 84 RBIs, .277).

Minnesota rebounded back to fourth (78-84) in 1996, helped largely by the efforts of Knoblauch and Paul Molitor (.341 and an AL-best 225 hits). Molitor, a Minnesota native, recorded his 3,000th hit during the season, and became the first player in history to reach the milestone with a triple. The season was also tinged with sadness as Puckett officially retired due to glaucoma.

Brad Radke was the brightest spot for Minnesota in 1997. He tied a club record with wins in 12 consecutive starts and became the team's first 20-game winner since 1991. Solid pitching bolstered the Twins in the first half of 1998, but the club slipped to fourth in the AL Central in the second half.

Montreal Expos

In the spring of 1969, in an unfinished "temporary" ballpark that would be the Expos' home for eight years, major league baseball came to Canada. One of two clubs added to the National League in this first year of divisional play—Montreal in the East and San Diego in the West—the Expos finished 48 games out of first. Although they matched San Diego's 52-110 record and last-place divisional finish, they outdrew the Padres by better than two to one, with a home attendance of more than 1.2 million fans.

After a second last-place (but much improved at 73-89) season in 1970, the Expos moved a notch out of the cellar to fifth in 1971 and '72, and into pennant contention in 1973. Outfielder Ken Singleton became the first Expo to drive in 100 or more runs, rookie pitcher Steve Rogers compiled a sparkling 1.54 ERA, and reliever Mike Marshall set a new major-league record with 92 pitching appearances (winning 14 games and saving a league-high 31). In the tightest race of the century, all six clubs remained in contention into September, when Philadelphia dropped away. In mid-September Montreal won six straight to catch front-running Pittsburgh, but the Expos finished the season in fourth place, three and a half games behind the champion New York Mets.

Center fielder Willie Davis (acquired from Los Angeles in a trade for Mike Marshall) led the Expos' offense in another fourth-place season in 1974. The club sank back to a tie for last in 1975 and sole possession of the cellar a year later, with a 55-107 record nearly as bad as their first season (and a home attendance little more than half that of 1969).

But with the acquisition of heavy-hitting Tony Perez from Cincinnati, a new manager—the controversial Dick Williams—and strong seasons from catcher Gary Carter, sophomore outfielder Ellis Valentine, and rookie Andre Dawson, the club snapped back in 1977 to win 20 more games than the previous year and rise to fifth. And with their move into the new Olympic Stadium (built for the 1976 Olympics), attendance rebounded from a club low to a new high.

After climbing another notch to fourth in 1978 (as the newly acquired Ross Grimsley became their first—and, to date, only—20-game winner), the Expos put on a run for the title that drove attendance in 1979 to over 2 million. Third baseman Larry Parrish, with a career-high season, led the club in batting and home runs in a balanced attack that saw five players drive in more than 70 runs. The pitching too was balanced, with six pitchers winning 10 games or more on a staff that compiled the league's lowest ERA. With a fast start in April, the Expos led the East through much of June and into July, when a surging Pittsburgh caught up with them. Both clubs climbed away from the pack to the end of the season. Montreal fell back a bit in August but caught up with the Pirates in September and carried the race to the final day before dropping off to second.

The 1980 race was just as exciting. A three-way struggle with Philadelphia and Pittsburgh through most of the summer narrowed to two teams in September as the Pirates fell away. In a crucial late-September series, the Expos beat the Phillies two games of three to take a half-game lead, but in the final series a week later Philadelphia won two games to clinch the crown.

In a 1981 season divided by a players' strike, Montreal finished the first part of the season in third place, but held off St. Louis to win the second part by half a game. The Expos then won the division championship in a special playoff with first-half winner Philadelphia—their first title—but lost the National League Championship Series to Los Angeles.

As the Expos declined gradually over the next five years, most of the regulars left through trade, free agency, or retirement. But in 1987, two 1981 rookies who had remained in Montreal—outfielder Tim Raines and third baseman Tim Wallach—helped lead the Expos to third place, just four games back, with 91 wins.

Strong midsummer surges in 1988 and 1989 propelled the Expos into the thick of the race in the NL East, in 1989 lifting them into the lead for six straight weeks following the acquisition from Seattle of mound ace Mark Langston. But in both years, late-season slumps dropped the club to identical 81-81 finishes. In 1990 strong pitching (despite the loss of free agents Langston, Bryn Smith, and Pascual Perez) kept the Expos competitive well into September before they fell out of the race.

The collapse of a huge cement beam at Olympic Stadium in September 1991—which forced the Expos to play all their remaining games on the road—was emblematic of the team's collapse into the cellar with their worst record in 15 years. But the club revived in 1992 under new manager Felipe Alou, who was promoted from coach in late May. The Expos rose from fifth place to second behind the pitching of Ken Hill and veteran ace Dennis Martinez, and the offensive leadership of right fielder Larry Walker. The Expos finished an even closer second in 1993, just three games behind Philadelphia, with a record of 94-68. On Aug. 7, 1994, pitcher Hill moved into the NL lead with his 16th win of the season. Walker and Moises Alou— manager Felipe's son—dueled for the club's offensive leadership. Montreal stood atop the mountain with the best record in the majors. Five days later, the season was over when the players went on strike.

Even though the club fell to last (66-78) in 1995, the club turned a $40,000 profit—a dramatic turnaround from 1994 when due to the strike the club lost an estimated $15.9 million. Helping the Expos balance sheet was the modesty of their payroll—just $10 million. The Expos (88-74) challenged for a postseason berth in 1996 but fell short in the final week despite the efforts of Henry Rodriguez (36 HR, 103 RBIs), Mark Grudzielanek (.306, 201 hits), Jeff Fassero (15-11, 222 strikeouts), and Mel Rojas (36 saves).

Pedro Martinez became the first Expos pitcher to win the NL Cy Young Award in 1997. He was the first pitcher to combine 300 strikeouts and an ERA below 2.00. since Steve Carlton in 1972, but it was a bittersweet year for Montreal. Escalating salaries forced the Expos to trade Martinez as well as second baseman Mike Lansing and to allow first baseman David Segui, catcher Darrin Fletcher, and outfielder Henry Rodriguez leave as free agents.

The 1998 Expos spent most of the season in fourth place, but Vladimir Guerrero established club records in several categories while Ugueth Urbina emerged as one of the league's top closers. General manager Jim Beattie

signed both players to long-term contracts. After the season, just when it seemed like Felipe Alou would reluctantly leave the team, Beattie was able to sign his manager as well.

New York Mets

Branch Rickey's projected Continental League never materialized, but its New York and Houston franchises were admitted to the National League, expanding the league to 10 clubs in 1962. Few major league teams have been as inept as the New York Mets were in their first season. Despite the presence of such New York favorites as manager Casey Stengel, pitcher Roger Craig, and first baseman Gil Hodges, and of players like outfielders Richie Ashburn and Frank Thomas who were still near peak form, the Mets finished at the bottom of the league in batting, fielding, and pitching. They won only one game in four and suffered a 20th-century record 120 losses.

New York fans—deprived of National League baseball since the defection of the Dodgers and Giants to the West Coast four years earlier—found their ineptitude lovable. By their third season, having moved out of the old Polo Grounds into brand-new Shea Stadium, the last-place Mets were regularly outdrawing the pennant-bound Yankees.

Former New York Giants catcher Wes Westrum replaced the aging Stengel as manager part way through the 1965 season, and the next year saw the club rise out of the cellar for the first time. They fell back to 10th in 1967 (despite rookie Tom Seaver's 16 wins), and Westrum was replaced at the helm by Gil Hodges. With Jerry Koosman joining Seaver in the starting rotation and setting a new club record with 19 victories, Hodges led the Mets in 1968 back up to ninth place with their first season of more than 70 victories.

In 1969 the majors inaugurated divisional play, but the Mets got off to their usual indifferent start. At the end of May, however, they began to win consistently. By early June they were second in the NL East, though well back of the explosive Chicago Cubs. By September, though, the Cubs were faltering. The "Miracle Mets" caught and passed them with a 10-game winning streak and continued on to take the division title. In Tom Seaver's Hall of Fame career, it was probably his finest season. He won his last 10 starts, sparking the team's final push to triumph, and finished with a league-high 25 wins that still stands as the club record. After a three-game sweep of West champion Atlanta in the league's first Championship Series, the Mets faced the mighty Baltimore Orioles—regarded by many as one of baseball's all-time greatest teams—for the world championship. The Met miracle continued; after an opening game loss, the New Yorkers humbled the Orioles with four straight wins.

The Mets of 1970 remained competitive into mid-September as they sought to repeat their '69 triumph. But they fell back at the end while Pittsburgh spurted, and finished third. Just before the start of the 1972 season, coach Yogi Berra moved up to manage the club after Hodges suffered a fatal heart attack two days before his 48th birthday.

In 1973 the NL East experienced the tightest major league race of the century. Chicago moved out in front of the pack early in the season, but folded in July and August. So did the Mets, who fell from third to a last-place sixth. Although the Mets were last in late August, they were less than seven games out of first. A series of bursts in September, culminating in a seven-game winning streak, shot the Mets through the division into first place by Sept. 21. Although they finished the season only three games above .500, they topped the division by a game and a half. In the NLCS they held off the favored Cincinnati Reds to take the pennant in the maximum five games, but they lost the World Series in seven when Oakland won the final two games.

The Mets then entered a decade-long decline. Though they won as often in 1975 and '76 as they had in 1973, they didn't come close to winning the East, and dropped into a seven-year trough in 1977 which included five seasons in last place. Seaver was traded to Cincinnati in 1977, and Koosman (after two disastrous seasons) was sent to Minnesota in the fall of 1978 (where he won 20 the next year). The heirs of original owner Joan Whitney Payson sold the club to Nelson Doubleday (of the publishing company) and Fred Wilpon in January 1980. In February the new owners hired Frank Cashen as general manager, hoping he could rebuild the Mets as he had the Baltimore Orioles in the late 1960s.

It took a few years to achieve the right blend, but when outfielder Darryl Strawberry was brought up from the minors early in 1983 and first baseman Keith Hernandez was acquired from St. Louis in June, the mix had nearly all the needed ingredients. In 1984, under new manager Davey Johnson, and with rookie pitchers Dwight Gooden and Ron Darling combining for 29 wins, the Mets rebounded to second place with their second-best season record up till then.

The rise continued in 1985. With catcher Gary Carter (newly acquired from Montreal) leading the club in homers and RBIs, and Gooden cementing his superstardom at age 20 with a phenomenal 24-4, 1.53 ERA season, the Mets won 98 games—eight more than the year before—and came within a game of tying St. Louis late in September before slipping three games back at the finish.

When the Mets acquired pitcher Bob Ojeda from the Boston Red Sox after the season, many predicted an easy division title for them in 1986. For once, the pundits were right. With Carter, Strawberry, and Hernandez powering the offense, and Ojeda, Darling, and Gooden all placing among the league's top five pitchers in ERA, the Mets won two of every three games (108 in all) to capture the division title by 21½ games.

The postseason battles were tougher. The Mets won the pennant from Houston with a 16-inning victory in Game 6 of the NLCS, but came within a strike of elimination by the Red Sox in Game 6 of the World Series before rallying to take that game and the next for their second world crown.

Strawberry enjoyed his finest season yet in 1987, and pitchers Terry Leach and Rick Aguilera put together a combined won-lost record of 22-4. But Ojeda was lost to injury early in the season, and the Mets, though they hung close and posted 92 wins, lost out—as in 1985—to St. Louis by three games.

David Cone (20-3, 2.22 ERA) emerged in 1988 as the

ace of the league's best pitching staff, which, with the power of Darryl Strawberry and Kevin McReynolds behind it, carried the Mets back to the top of the NL East, 15 games ahead of runner-up Pittsburgh. But the favored Mets lost the pennant to underdog Los Angeles in seven games.

With co-captains Carter and Hernandez injured and in decline, the Mets floundered through 1989, salvaging a narrow second-place finish with four wins in the season's final three days. The two captains were released after the season. Early the following season, with the Mets mired almost 10 games out, manager Davey Johnson was replaced by coach Bud Harrelson. In June the team took off, ignited by Strawberry's suddenly hot bat and propelled themselves into first place before the end of the month. Through July and August the Mets and Pittsburgh lobbed the division lead back and forth, until the Pirates consigned the New Yorkers to second place for good with a three-game sweep in early September.

Free agent Strawberry signed with Los Angeles for 1991, but the Mets competed strongly into July before tumbling to fifth place with their first losing season in eight years. Manager Harrelson was fired in the final week of the season. Jeff Torborg was hired to manage and ex-Pirates star Bobby Bonilla signed with the Mets as a free agent in 1992, but injuries plagued the team throughout the season, and the finish found them once again a distant fifth.

Things only got worse in 1993. Dallas Green replaced Torborg in May, and even a six-game win streak at the end of the season couldn't keep them from the worst record in the majors and, with 103 losses, the club's worst season in 28 years.

The Mets crawled to within three games of .500 in 1994, but the club also stumbled out of the gate in 1995. When they rid themselves of such high-priced talent as Bret Saberhagen, Bonilla, and center fielder Brett Butler, it appeared the club might hit a very deep bottom. Instead, new talent such as Bill Pulsipher and Jason Isringhausen lifted manager Dallas Green's young team to a surprising second place finish (69-75).

Adding another highly-rated pitching prospect, Paul Wilson, to the starting rotation gave Mets fans high hopes for 1996 but these were not realized. Despite standout seasons from Bernard Gilkey (.317, 117 RBIs), Lance Johnson (.333, 227 hits, 21 triples), and Todd Hundley (a record 41 home runs for a catcher), the club faltered, and Bobby Valentine replaced Green as manager. New York's 71-91 record was good only for fourth place.

The Mets had their best season in seven years in 1997. They had the most come-from-behind victories in baseball (47) and the Mets won the first-ever regular season game against the Yankees. The Mets were full of surprises, but the biggest was Rick Reed, a former replacement player who finished sixth in the league with a 2.89 ERA. In 1998 the Mets had the same record as the year before (88-74), but the club remained in the hunt for the Wild Card until the final day of the season. Two players acquired from the Marlins, pitcher Al Leiter (17-6, 2.47 ERA) and catcher Mike Piazza (.329, 32 HR, 111 RBIs), teamed with John Olerud (.353) to help put the Mets in a position to reach the postseason for the first time in a decade. The year ended in agonizing fashion as New York lost its last five games of the season and finished one game shy of the Giants and Cubs in what would have been the first three-way playoff in major league history.

New York Yankees

In its first 20 seasons, the club that became the New York Yankees won no league championships and finished second only twice. But for the next 44 years the Yankees dominated the American League, winning nearly two of every three pennants and 20 World Series. After another pennant drought of 12 years, the club in six years won five division titles, four pennants, and two world championships. Their next pennant drought, which ended in 1996, lasted 14 years, and was the second longest in their history. Through 1998 the Yankees had started yet another streak, with two World Series titles in three years.

The Yankees began as the Baltimore Orioles in 1901. But AL president Ban Johnson really wanted a club in New York and, after outmaneuvering the politically influential Giants (who didn't want a competing big league team in their city), Johnson moved the Orioles to the northern end of Manhattan in 1903.

In 1904 the Highlanders (as they were known during their first years in New York because of the high land on which their park was built) chased the Boston Pilgrims through midsummer, catching them in August and trading first place back and forth into October. After Jack Chesbro defeated Boston on Oct. 7 to give New York a half-game lead (his 41st win, a 20th-century major league record), the Pilgrims came back to win the next two. In the fourth game of the series, with Chesbro again pitching and the score tied, 2-2, in the top of the ninth, a wild pitch over the New York catcher's head let in Boston's pennant-clinching run.

The Highlanders again led the league in late September two years later, before tailing off to finish three games behind Chicago. But that was the last time they contended seriously for the title for 14 years. In that span they finished last twice: in 1908 they lost 103 games, and in 1912 the team suffered through its most distant finish ever—55 games behind the Red Sox.

In 1914 Colonel Jake Ruppert and Tillinghast Huston bought the Yankees, and the next year they purchased pitcher Bob Shawkey from the Philadelphia A's. Shawkey's 24 victories in 1916 led the Yankees to their first winning season in six years, and in 1919, on returning from military service, his 20 wins (plus nine by Carl Mays, who came to the club in a controversial mid-season deal with the Red Sox) brought the Yankees to third—their closest finish in 13 years.

That winter, on the recommendation of manager Miller Huggins, the Yankees paid a then-record $125,000 (plus a $300,000 loan) to the Red Sox for Babe Ruth. Ruth, with 54 home runs in 1920, obliterated the record of 29 he had set the year before, and Mays and Shawkey won 46 games in a three-way pennant race that ended with New York a close third.

At season's end Ruppert hired Ed Barrow as general manager. While managing the Red Sox, Barrow had converted Ruth from a pitcher to outfielder. His December trade with Boston that gave the Yankees pitcher Waite

Hoyt and catcher Wally Schang was just the improvement needed to bring the Yankees their first pennant in 1921. Ruth's 59 homers and his career-high 171 RBIs didn't hurt, either.

The prickly Carl Mays, staff ace in 1921 with a 27-9 record, slipped to 13-14 the next year. But the Yankees continued to decimate the Red Sox roster with trades that brought them pitchers "Bullet Joe" Bush and "Sad Sam" Jones, and infielders Everett Scott and Joe Dugan. Bush's 26 wins in 1922 made up for Mays' decline, and the Yankees captured their second straight league championship.

Both races had been tight two-way struggles—with Cleveland in 1921 and the St. Louis Browns in 1922—and both pennants had been followed by a World Series loss to the Giants. But in 1923 the Yankees at last put everything together. After sharing the Giants' Polo Grounds since 1913, they were at home in brand-new Yankee Stadium just across the Harlem River in the Bronx. With the addition of yet another pitcher from the Red Sox—Herb Pennock—and a .393 year from Ruth, they took the lead from the start and built it over the summer to a 16-game margin by the end. For the third time the Yankees faced the Giants in the World Series; this time they beat them, in six games, for their first world championship.

The Yankees lost a close race to Washington in 1924 and collapsed into seventh place in 1925—a year in which Ruth was lost much of the season to surgery and suspension. It wasn't all bad. Center fielder Earle Combs, in his first full season, hit .342 to lead Yankee regulars. Left fielder Bob Meusel filled Ruth's shoes as AL home run and RBI leader, and first baseman Lou Gehrig arrived to stay. With Ruth's return to full strength in 1926 and the establishment of a new middle infield of Tony Lazzeri and Mark Koenig, the Yankees took their fourth pennant. They lost a close World Series to the Cardinals.

Many observers rank the 1927 Yankees as baseball's greatest team ever. Ruth hit his 60 home runs, and Gehrig drove in 175 as the Yankees fashioned a remarkable 110-44 mark. Waite Hoyt led the league in ERA, and rookie Wilcy Moore proved the league's premier reliever. As a team the Yankees led the league in hitting (.307) and slugging (.489); their pitchers compiled a 3.20 ERA (the next best team, the White Sox, had an ERA of 3.91). In the World Series they swept the Pittsburgh Pirates.

The resurgent Athletics made the 1928 race much closer, but New York won three in a row from the A's in mid-September to pull ahead, and held on for their sixth pennant. Another Series sweep (this time against the Cardinals) gave them their third world title.

An ill Huggins yielded the club's reins in September 1929 and died before the season ended. By the time the Yankees returned to the top in 1932, their manager was Joe McCarthy. He had led the Chicago Cubs to the NL pennant in 1929; in 15 seasons at New York he would lead his club to eight more pennants and seven world championships.

A New York pennant and World Series triumph over the Cubs in 1932 was followed by three second-place finishes to Washington (in 1933) and Detroit (in 1934 and 1935). Ruth had retired by the time the Bronx Bombers returned to the top in 1936, but Gehrig was still in top

form, catcher Bill Dickey and outfielder George Selkirk developed into formidable sluggers, and Joe DiMaggio arrived to take over center field. New York finished 19½ games in front and buried the Giants in the World Series.

Three more pennants and three more world titles followed in 1937-1939. Lefty Gomez emerged as the league's premier pitcher in 1937, and DiMaggio picked up the home run and slugging crowns. Again the Giants were vanquished in the World Series. Rookie second baseman Joe Gordon and sophomore outfielder Tommy Henrich joined Dickey, DiMaggio, and a declining Gehrig in leading the slugging Yankees to the 1938 crown and a Series sweep of the Cubs. A balanced attack in 1939 saw seven of the eight starters (including Babe Dahlgren, who replaced the dying Gehrig at first) drive in 80 runs or more as the Yankees won 106 to run away with their 11th pennant—and eighth World Series, another sweep, with Cincinnati the victim. For the fourth straight year the offense topped the league in slugging, and overshadowed the steady—if unspectacular—pitching staff, which compiled the league's stingiest ERA for the sixth consecutive year.

After catching the Tigers with a 19-4 spurt in late summer, the 1940 Yankees fell away to finish a close third. But then came another three convincing pennant wins and a pair of Series triumphs as the nation moved into World War II. Outfielders DiMaggio and Charlie Keller dominated the offense in 1941, and rookie shortstop Phil Rizzuto hit .307. Brooklyn was the loser in a five-game World Series.

Keller, DiMaggio, and Gordon provided the power, and Tiny Bonham (with 21 wins), Spud Chandler, and rookie Hank Borowy headed the league-leading pitching staff that propelled the Yankees to 103 wins and another easy pennant in 1942. But after winning their previous eight World Series, the Yankees were finally stopped, in five games, by the St. Louis Cardinals.

By 1943 many Yankees were in military service. But pitchers Chandler, Bonham, Borowy, and Murphy were not, and they led the charge to the team's seventh pennant in eight years. In the Series the Yankees reversed the results of the previous year, turning back St. Louis in five.

In January 1945, Dan Topping and Del Webb bought the club and installed Larry MacPhail as president, giving him a third of the club and a 10-year contract to run it. The volatile, innovative MacPhail had previously brought life to Cincinnati and Brooklyn. But manager McCarthy, who couldn't get along with MacPhail, quit early in the 1946 season, and the team finished a distant third.

DiMaggio and the others were back from the war by 1946, but it was not until 1947—under new manager Bucky Harris, and with sparkling pitching from Allie Reynolds (acquired from Cleveland), rookie Frank "Spec" Shea, and reliever Joe Page—that the Yankees returned to the top of the heap with an easy pennant win and a narrow World Series triumph over Brooklyn. On the day the Yankees won the Series, though, president MacPhail embarrassed the club and undid himself by brawling in public. Topping and Webb bought out his contract and share of the ownership. Topping took over the presidency, promoting farm director George Weiss to run the club as general manager.

After the Yankees dropped a pair of season-ending

games to the Red Sox to finish third in a tight 1948 race, Weiss replaced manager Harris with Casey Stengel, who in nine years of managing the Braves and Dodgers had only twice seen his club finish as high as fifth. But with Weiss providing a steady stream of talented players via the farm system and canny trades, the Yankees under Stengel proved all but invincible into the '60s.

Stengel's Yankees began by putting together a record string of five world championships. No major league club had ever won five pennants in a row, let alone five World Series, and the Yankees didn't accomplish the feat easily. In 1949, for example, they saw the Red Sox come from 12 games back in midseason to pass them with a three-game series sweep in late September, only to rescue the title with two close must-win victories over the Sox in the season's final games. In the World Series, Brooklyn was again the victim, in five games.

After losing much of 1949 to injury, DiMaggio returned with power in 1950, shortstop Rizzuto and catcher Yogi Berra enjoyed the finest seasons of their careers, and pitcher Whitey Ford broke into the majors, winning all nine of his decisions as a starter (he lost once in relief). Though three of the games in the World Series were decided by just one run, New York took Philadelphia's "Whiz Kids" in four straight.

No Yankee drove in as many as 90 runs in 1951, and Whitey Ford was drafted for two years of military service. But the remaining pitchers doubled their shutout production and lowered the team ERA by more than half a run per game, enough to propel the club ahead of Cleveland in mid-September. In the World Series the Yankees shook the Giants, four games to two. Cleveland challenged once again in 1952, and again fell just short, as did Brooklyn in carrying the World Series to seven games.

Finally, in 1953, Stengel's Yankees won with relative ease. Ford, back from the Army, won 18 to lead the club to a finish eight and a half games in front. Once again it was Brooklyn in the World Series, and once again the Yankees beat them. In 1954 New York won 103 games—the most in Stengel's 12-year tenure. But Cleveland won an AL-record 111 to take the flag by eight games.

In 1955, though, it was back to second place for Cleveland as New York, with Mickey Mantle now established as one of the game's most productive hitters, settled in for another four pennants. As August passed into September, three teams were within a game of each other at the top. But the Chicago White Sox faltered, leaving the Yankees and Indians to fight it out. With two weeks left, New York won eight straight to pass Cleveland for good. Facing the Dodgers in the World Series for the sixth time, the Yankees finally lost, as Johnny Podres shut them out in Game 7 to give Brooklyn its first world title since 1900.

From 1956 through 1958 the Yankees seldom found themselves out of first place. In postseason play, they went the full seven games all three years, winning twice—from the Dodgers for the sixth time in 1956, and from the Milwaukee Braves in 1958, after losing to the Braves the year before.

In 1959 the Yankees started poorly and never did rise much above .500, finishing a distant third with their worst won-lost record in 34 years. After the season, George Weiss sent an aging Hank Bauer to Kansas City in a trade that brought Roger Maris to New York. In 1960 Maris,

with AL titles in slugging and RBIs, won the MVP award. He and Mantle dominated the power stats and led the charge back to the top as the Yankees won their final 15 games to bury the faltering Orioles.

New York's 1960 pennant was the first in another five-flag streak, but it was the last for Stengel. After Pittsburgh toppled the Yankees in the World Series on Bill Mazeroski's famous home run, president Topping retired both the 70-year-old Stengel and general manager Weiss, 65, who had been with the club for 28 years.

With the season lengthened by eight games in 1961, Maris broke Ruth's home-run record and rookie manager Ralph Houk led the club to 109 wins. Ford enjoyed a splendid 25-4 season and celebrated with two more wins in the World Series as the Yankees humbled Cincinnati in five games.

Pitcher Ralph Terry moved out of Ford's shadow in 1962 with 23 wins. Though the Yankees finished just five games ahead of Minnesota, there was little doubt about the outcome from midseason on. In a close World Series with San Francisco, Terry won two, including the clincher with a 1-0 shutout.

Though New York won pennants the next two years, the 1962 world title was to be their last until the Steinbrenner era 15 years later. Despite the loss to injuries of Mantle and Maris for much of 1963, New York dominated the AL, winning by 10½ games with 104 wins. But in postseason play the Yankees were themselves dominated by the Dodgers (now in Los Angeles), who held them to just four runs in a Series sweep.

Yogi Berra replaced Houk as manager for 1964. In a season-long three-way race with the White Sox and Orioles that found the clubs virtually tied in mid-September, only an 11-game win streak gave the Yankees the space they needed for their final one-game margin of victory. Pitcher Jim Bouton won a pair in the World Series, but the Cardinals took the crown in seven. Berra was fired.

During the 1964 season Topping had sold the Yankees to CBS. The next year the club, which had gone 40 years without a losing season, dropped to sixth place, and in 1966 fell to a last-place 10th, their first cellar finish in more than half a century. Even Houk's return as manager in 1967—though it led to some winning seasons—failed to restore the once-proud club to pennant contention, except once, in 1972, when it was mid-September before they fell out of a tight race to finish fourth.

In January 1973 a syndicate headed by Cleveland shipping magnate George Steinbrenner purchased the Yankees from CBS. Although he had vowed not to take a prominent role in running the club, Steinbrenner soon emerged as one of baseball's most active owners. Through a series of shrewd trades, offers of big contracts to free agents, and what became a round robin of managerial changes, Steinbrenner's Yankees became competitive again in 1974 (finishing a close second to Baltimore) and returned to the top with three successive pennants and a pair of world championships.

Manager Billy Martin (a former Yankees second baseman) led the renewed club to a runaway division title in 1976. First baseman Chris Chambliss homered in the last of the ninth of the final game of the American League Championship Series to give the Yankees the pennant over the Kansas City Royals. Cincinnati swept New York

in the World Series, but the Yankees came back the next year to edge Baltimore and Boston in a three-way race that saw the teams shift back and forth in the standings throughout the season. Slugger Reggie Jackson, signed as a free agent the previous autumn, turned the club's power trio of Chambliss, Graig Nettles, and Thurman Munson into a quartet as the Yankees recorded their first 100-win season in 14 years. After another ninth-inning win over Kansas City in the ALCS finale, New York won the World Series in six games over Los Angeles. Jackson became "Mr. October" with five home runs—three of them in successive at-bats in the final game.

The 1978 season provided as exciting a race as baseball is likely to see. In mid-July it looked like a Red Sox romp, but the fourth-place Yankees put on a great surge, catching the faltering Sox with a four-game series sweep in early September. Boston dropped three and a half games back, but won their final eight games to catch New York on the final day. In the one-game tiebreaker, shortstop Bucky Dent lofted a wind-blown three-run homer over Boston's close left field wall in the seventh, and Jackson homered an inning later for New York's final run in the 5-4 win. Again the Royals were the victims in the ALCS, as were the Dodgers in the World Series.

After dropping to fourth in 1979, the Yankees held off Baltimore in 1980 to win their fourth division title—but this time Kansas City swept to the pennant in three games. In 1981 the Yankees found themselves in first place when the players struck in June and were thus admitted to an intradivisional playoff with the season's second-half winner, Milwaukee. Narrowly defeating the Brewers for the division title, New York swept Oakland for the pennant in the ALCS. But after taking the first two games from Los Angeles in the World Series, they were stopped cold as the Dodgers won the next four.

The Yankees fell below .500 the next year, and although they revived to win 91 games in 1983, they failed to frighten the division leaders until 1985. First baseman Don Mattingly drove in more runs than any American leaguer since 1953 and newcomer (from Oakland) Rickey Henderson scored more often than any major leaguer since 1949 to keep the Yankees in the running until Toronto eliminated them with just one game to go.

But constant roster manipulation and managerial rotation (Billy Martin alone was hired and fired five times) at last set in motion a steady drop in effectiveness. While the team remained in the thick of a tight 1988 divisional race until three season-ending losses set them back into fifth place, their won-lost record showed a third straight season of decline. In 1989 the Yankees sank to their worst finish in 22 years and in 1990 they dropped to the floor of the AL East with the club's worst record since 1913.

Before the 1990 season ended, Steinbrenner was gone. As penalty for his dealings with a gambler named Howard Spira in an attempt to gain information damaging to Yankees outfielder Dave Winfield, Steinbrenner relinquished his controlling interest in the club in August. When fans at Yankee Stadium heard the news, they stood and applauded for 90 seconds.

Their string of consecutive losing seasons stretched to four, something that hadn't happened to the Yankees in 76 years. In 1993 the Yankees bounced back and—bolstered by the league's best hitting and a strong season from

newly acquired pitcher Jimmy Key—contended seriously into September, finishing second to Toronto.

They were even better in 1994. With Key in the midst of one of his best seasons ever, and a solid offense paced by right fielder Paul O'Neill (whose .603 slugging average stood 99 points above his previous career high), the Yankees were enjoying the league's best won-lost record and a 6½-game lead in the AL East when the players' strike cut the season short in August.

The 1995 Yankees earned the first-ever AL Wild Card slot. Standouts included Wade Boggs (.324), Paul O'Neill (24 HR), Bernie Williams (.307), David Cone (9-2 with New York after coming over from Toronto), and Jack McDowell (15-10). After taking a tough loss to Seattle in the division series, the Yankees saw the departure of McDowell, veteran Don Mattingly, and manager Buck Showalter (who became manager of the new Arizona Diamondbacks). Joe Torre replaced Showalter, continuing a tradition of managers—Casey Stengel, Yogi Berra, and Dallas Green—who have managed both the Mets and the Yankees.

In 1996, despite a late season swoon, Torre's Yankees (92-70) captured the AL East championship. Standout Yankees included Bernie Williams (.305, 29 HR, 102 RBIs), Paul O'Neill (.302, 19 HR, 91 RBIs), Tino Martinez (.292, 25 HR, 117 RBIs), AL Rookie of the Year Derek Jeter (.314), Andy Pettitte (21-8), and John Wetteland (43 saves). In the first round of the postseason, New York overcame Texas in four games.

In the ALCS, the Yanks rolled over Baltimore in five games. Assisting the Bombers was the "Angel in the Outfield," a 12-year-old boy who caught Jeter's flyball over the right field wall in Game 1. Instead of a fan interference call, Jeter was credited with a pivotal homer.

In the first two games of the World Series against Atlanta the Yankees looked outclassed, losing, 12-1, and 4-0. But New York rebounded to win the next four, including a 10-inning Game 4 comeback from a 6-0 deficit. The victory was particularly sweet for manager Torre, whose brother Frank, received a long-awaited heart transplant the day before Game 6.

In 1997 the Yankees reached the postseason as a Wild Card team and seemed to have the easier assignment in facing Cleveland, but the Indians had the Yankees' number. Cleveland rallied to take the last two games to end New York's season.

The Yankees dominated baseball in 1998. They eclipsed the AL record with 114 wins as they rolled through the regular season. They allowed Texas just one run in three Division Series games, but ran into trouble again with the Indians. A controversial Game 2 loss in the ALCS was followed by another loss in Cleveland as the Yankees trailed 2-1 in the series. From there, New York ran the table, winning the last three games in the ALCS and winning four straight against the Padres. It marked the Yankees' seventh sweep and 24th world championship.

Oakland Athletics

The history of the Athletics is a tale of three cities—a story of the best of teams and of the worst of teams. With

a 13-year sojourn in Kansas City between residence in Philadelphia and Oakland, the A's are the only club to include a stop in Middle America in their trek from the East Coast to West. They have won 15 American League pennants (plus three Western Division championships that didn't lead to a pennant) While the A's are second only to the Yankees in AL championships, they have also finished last in the league or division 27 times, and in 16 seasons have lost 100 games or more—both AL worsts, by far. A club of extremes, they have been either at the top or at the bottom in nearly one season out of two.

When Ban Johnson established four eastern clubs for his American League in 1901, he chose Connie Mack to manage the new Philadelphia Athletics and gave him a quarter ownership of the club. Mack, who had been managing the league's Milwaukee franchise, settled in at Philadelphia and set a record for managerial longevity—50 years—that is unlikely ever to be surpassed.

In his first 14 years the A's dominated the league with six pennants and two close second-place finishes. After finishing fourth in 1901, the club won its first pennant the next year, pulling away from the field with spurts in August and September. Rube Waddell led the team with 24 wins, and six regulars hit over .300. The next two years saw the A's fade in August, but in 1905, after forging ahead in early August and hanging on to the lead with two crucial wins over Chicago's surging White Sox in late September, the A's opened October with a five-game winning streak to clinch their second flag. Waddell, with 26 wins, once again led the club (followed closely by Eddie Plank's 25) and compiled a league-leading 1.48 ERA. In the Athletics' first World Series appearance, though, New York's Christy Mathewson provided most of the pitching heroics, shutting out the A's three times in the Giants' 4-1 Series triumph.

Another August decline in 1906 was followed in 1907 by a comeback struggle from fifth place in late May to a 2½-game lead in mid-September. But the loss of a crucial game to Detroit several days later, and the failure to make up a rainout and a tie, left the A's 1½ games behind the Tigers at the finish.

In 1908 the A's suffered their first losing season, but they rebounded in 1909 to chase the Tigers throughout the summer before tailing off to second. In 1910, with a pitching staff that compiled a stunning 1.79 ERA (paced by Jack Coombs, whose 31 wins included 13 shutouts) and with league-leading fielding and hitting, the A's pulled ahead for good in June, increasing their lead through the rest of the season to finish 14½ games in front. In the World Series they continued to dominate, outscoring the Chicago Cubs 35-15 as they took their first world title, in five games. The A's repeated just as convincingly in 1911. With their "$100,000 infield" of Stuffy McInnis, Eddie Collins, Jack Barry, and Frank "Home Run" Baker averaging .323 at the bat, and Jack Coombs winning 28 games to again lead the club (and the league), the A's overtook Detroit in August to win by 13½ games. In the World Series, Baker homered against the Giants, and the A's defeated Mathewson twice, avenging their 1905 humiliation with a victory in six games.

A third-place finish in 1912 broke the pennant streak, but the Athletics came back for two more in 1913 and '14, in both seasons pulling away in early June for easy wins.

In the 1913 World Series the A's again felled the Giants, this time in just five games, but the next year they were in turn humiliated by the upstart Boston Braves, who stunned Philadelphia with the first sweep since the renewal of World Series play in 1903.

That winter, Mack began to dismantle his championship club, selling second baseman Collins to the White Sox and releasing pitchers Coombs, Eddie Plank, and Chief Bender. Third baseman Baker, homesick for the country life, sat out the 1915 season before moving on to the Yankees. Though Mack received $50,000 for Collins, his unconditional release of the three pitchers suggests that he had another reason than financial need for purging his club. (Suspicion of corrupt play in the 1914 World Series has been hinted.)

Whatever Mack's reasons, the changes did not help the club. The A's sank immediately to last place, where they remained for seven years. In 1915 they lost 109 games and finished 58½ games out. The next year they lost 117 games to set a league record for ineptitude that has never been matched.

It was a decade before Mack was able to restore the club to respectability. In 1924 he brought up Al Simmons, and the next year Jimmie Foxx and pitcher Lefty Grove. Thus renewed, the A's in 1925 battled Washington to the end of August before backing off to second. In 1927 they won 91 games, though their second-place finish was 19 games back of the overwhelming Yankees. In 1928 the A's battled from well back of New York in midseason to overtake them briefly in September, only to lose three of four games in a critical Yankee series and slip back to second.

From 1929 through 1931, though, the A's interrupted New York's domination of the AL with three spectacular seasons. In 1929 sophomore pitcher George Earnshaw blossomed into the league's big winner with 24 victories and Grove led the league's stingiest staff with a league-low 2.81 ERA. Six players drove in 79 runs or more (led by Simmons' league-high 157) in powering the A's to 104 wins and an impressive finish 18 games ahead of the second-place Yankees.

After swamping the Cubs in the World Series (including a record-setting 10-run eighth inning to wipe out an 8-0 deficit in Game 4), the A's repeated as pennant winners in 1930. Simmons led the league in batting (.381), and Grove led its pitchers in just about everything: wins (28), ERA, strikeouts—even saves (nine). Again the World Series was no contest as the A's downed the Cardinals in six.

Earnshaw won more than 20 games for his third successive season in 1931, Simmons repeated as batting leader (.390), and Grove enjoyed what would be the finest season of his career (31-4, 2.06 ERA) in carrying the A's to 107 wins—their best record ever. But in Game 7 the Cardinals ended Philadelphia's championship run.

Following a second-place finish in 1932, Mack began selling off his stars again. This time the reason was primarily economic. Home attendance—never robust—fell off sharply after 1931, as the Great Depression and the A's decline made their impact felt. By 1935 the Athletics were back in the cellar, where they finished in 10 of Mack's final 16 years as manager.

In 1946 Mack, who had been the A's majority stock-

holder since 1940, divided his shares among his three sons, provoking a family squabble over control of the club. In 1950 the two eldest, Roy and Earle, bought out Connie Jr. and pressured their 87-year-old father to retire. But with Connie Sr. gone, attendance (which had risen to new highs in the baseball boom that followed World War II) dropped off again. When the A's finished 60 games behind champion Cleveland and attendance dropped to an 18-year low in 1954, the Macks sold the club to Chicagoan Arnold Johnson, who moved it to Kansas City.

Attendance increased by more than a million the first season in Kansas City and the team rose a couple of places to sixth. But 1955 was the high point of their 13-year stay in the Midwest; the Kansas City A's never again rose above seventh, and they finished last six times.

Owner Johnson died in March 1960, and that December his heirs sold the club to the enterprising but abrasive Charles O. Finley. Finley brought in a succession of new managers over the next few years, and in 1965 outfitted his players in new bright green-and-yellow uniforms. But with the league's expansion to 10 teams in 1961, the A's had two places lower to sink—and did. After finishing 10th in 1967 for the third time in four years, Finley moved the club to California.

In 1968, their first year on the West Coast, they put together their first winning season in 16 years. The next year, with the start of divisional play, the A's took second in the AL West. Reggie Jackson, in only his second full big league season, enjoyed his finest year, with 47 home runs, 118 RBIs, and AL highs in slugging (.608) and runs scored (123).

After another second-place finish in 1970, the A's were ready for a return to glory. In the next five years they won five division titles, winning both the AL pennant and the World Series from 1972 to 1974. In 1971, with a new manager, Dick Williams, and three pitchers (Vida Blue, Catfish Hunter, and reliever Rollie Fingers) who reached their prime all at once, the A's enjoyed their best season in forty years and won the West by 16 games. Baltimore swept them in the American League Championship Series, but they came back to take the West again the next year. Detroit took them to the limit in the ALCS, as did Cincinnati in the World Series, but in both series the A's prevailed in the deciding game by the margin of a single run.

The next year, 1973, Jackson led the league in slugging, homers, and RBIs, Ken Holtzman joined Blue and Hunter in the 20-win column, and home attendance crept over a million for the first time in Oakland as the A's ran their string of Western Division titles to three. Once again they were pushed to the limit in the postseason—by Baltimore in the ALCS and the New York Mets in the World Series—and once again they emerged as world champions.

Manager Williams quit in a dispute with Finley and was replaced by Alvin Dark, but the outcome in 1974 (except for a drop in attendance to under a million) was the same. Hunter bore more of the pitching load and wound up tied for the AL lead with 25 wins. His 2.49 ERA also led the league, as the staff ended Baltimore's five-year hold on the ERA title. The A's toppled the Orioles in the ALCS and (in the first World Series held entirely on the West Coast) won their third consecutive

world title in five closely fought games with Los Angeles.

Catfish Hunter moved to the Yankees as a free agent, and Baltimore regained the ERA crown in 1975, but pitchers Paul Lindblad and newcomer Dick Bosman combined for a 20-5 record to supplement the efforts of Blue, Holtzman, and Fingers and carry Oakland to an unprecedented fifth straight division title. But there the magic stopped, as Boston swept to the pennant in the ALCS.

Finley, with moves reminiscent of Connie Mack, tried to sell off his star players: Blue, Jackson, Fingers, Holtzman, and outfielder/first baseman Joe Rudi, one of the team's steadiest hitters. The proposed sales made some sense: the players planned to leave the club at the end of their 1976 option year, and by disposing of them before they played out their option Finley could at least be compensated for his loss. The Jackson and Holtzman deals were approved, but baseball commissioner Bowie Kuhn blocked the sale of the others, citing the "best interests of baseball."

The weakened A's came back from a poor start to close within two and a half games of the Kansas City Royals in 1976, but they dropped to last place the next year. After another last-place finish in 1979, Finley hired fiery Billy Martin to manage the club. Martin brought the A's in second in 1980 (and his propensity for leaving starters in resulted in an astounding 94 complete games, almost twice as many as Milwaukee's second-best total) . The A's finished first in the first half of strike-divided 1981. They won the Western Division championship by sweeping Kansas City in the special intradivisional playoffs but were swept by the Yankees in the ALCS.

Finley's sale of the club in 1981 to the folks who bring us Levi's jeans signaled a turn toward normalcy and popularity. Despite a losing season in 1982, the club set a home attendance record as over 1.7 million fans came to watch Rickey Henderson's successful assault on the stolen-base record. In 1987 the A's finished right at .500—for the first time in their history a perfectly average team.

The next season they inaugurated a new multiyear reign as the league's best. Starter Dave Stewart and closer Dennis Eckersley anchored the league's strongest pitching staff and "Bash Brothers" Jose Canseco and Mark McGwire headlined an awesome offense. From 1988 through 1990 the team had its second run of three straight pennants since moving to Oakland (and the third three-pennant run in franchise history). In 1988 they built a 13-game margin of victory over runner-up Minnesota, winning 104 games and drawing more than 2 million fans to their home games for the first time. They swept Boston in the ALCS, but faltered in the World Series, losing to underdog Los Angeles in five games.

Injuries to several key players—especially Canseco, who missed the first half of the season with a broken wrist—kept the A's from dominating AL play through most of 1989. But the preseason signing of free agent starter Mike Moore had strengthened the pitching, and a June trade that brought Rickey Henderson back after more than four years with the Yankees gave the A's the push they needed to prevail.

At full strength by season's end, the A's overwhelmed Toronto in five games for their 14th pennant, then swept San Francisco for their world title.

Only the surprising White Sox challenged Oakland in

1990, and they too fell away in the latter half of the season as the A's walked to the division title with 103 wins. The potent offense was made even more formidable by the late-season acquisition of Harold Baines from Texas and Willie McGee from St. Louis. But the key to Oakland's dominance was its pitchers, who for the third year in a row compiled the league's lowest earned run average. Bob Welch led the majors with 27 wins, Dave Stewart put together his fourth straight 20-win season, and Dennis Eckersley rebounded from an injury-hampered 1989 with his finest relief year yet. The A's swept Boston to take their third straight pennant, but—shades of 1988!—floundered in the World Series, succumbing in just four games to Cincinnati's aroused Reds.

In 1991 the A's stayed at or near the top into late June before slipping to fourth. Eckersley remained in top form, however, and in 1992 proved almost invincible, with 51 saves to earn the Cy Young Award. Jose Canseco's trade to Texas during the season severed the Bash Brothers' tandem offense, but Mark McGwire enjoyed a banner season at the bat. Despite a wave of injuries that would have sunk most teams, the A's stayed afloat near the front through the first half season and held steady in the second half to win their fourth division title in five years. In the ALCS the A's fell to Toronto in six games.

With an injury to McGwire that sidelined him more than four months, plus a general decline on the mound and at the bat that saw the team finish with the league's worst batting and earned run averages, the 1993 A's did what only two major league clubs before them (the 1915 Athletics and 1885 St. Louis Maroons) had ever done before: tumble into the cellar after a first-place finish the year before.

The A's weren't winning much more often in 1994 when the players' strike halted play in August, but in the weak AL West their 51-63 record was good enough to land them in second place, just a game out of first. In 1995 their 67-77 mark earned them last place in the AL West. More significant, though, was the sale of the club by the Haas family to Bay Area businessmen Steve Schott and Ken Hofmann and the departure at season's end of manager Tony LaRussa.

The power-hitting 1996 A's (78-84) edged up to third place, largely on the basis of McGwire's 52 homers. The 1997 season was a disappointment all around: the A's failed to have a pitcher win 10 games for the second straight year, third baseman Scott Brosius batted .101 points lower than in 1996, and the team was forced to trade McGwire rather than lose him to free agency. Pitcher Kenny Rogers, who came from the Yankees in a trade for Brosius, was the team's top winner in 1998, and Ben Grieve (the AL Rookie of the Year) gave the A's a young power bat to go along with sluggers Matt Stairs and Jason Giambi.

Philadelphia Phillies

It took the Phillies 32 years to win their first pennant, and 97 years to win their first world championship. They have finished last in their league or division 29 times—one season in four. In the nine years from 1975 through 1983, though, they were one of the most formidable teams in baseball.

Alfred J. Reach, a sporting goods entrepreneur and former player, and Colonel John Rogers, a Philadelphia lawyer and politician, organized the Phillies in 1883 to bring Philadelphia back into the National League after a six-year absence. In their first season, the Phillies won only 17 of 98 decisions to finish last, as far out of seventh as the seventh-place team was from first.

Reach hired the respected Harry Wright to manage the Phillies in 1884, and while Wright failed to lead them to a pennant in a decade at the helm, he did make them respectable. His fourth-place 1886 team, in fact, compiled a winning percentage of .623 that remained the club's best for 90 years. In 1887 the Phillies, with three pitchers winning more than 20 games, finished second, just three and a half games behind Detroit— their closest finish until their first pennant 28 years later.

The Phillies remained in the upper division 12 of the next 14 years. For five years—1891-1895— they fielded an outfield of Ed Delahanty, Billy Hamilton, and Sam Thompson—Hall of Famers who rank among the top hitters of all time. In the three heavy-hitting seasons that followed the lengthening of the pitching distance to its present 60 feet, 6 inches in 1893, Delahanty, Hamilton, and Thompson—with help from players like catcher Jack Clements (.394 in 1895) and utility outfielder Tuck Turner (.416 in 1894)— sparked the Phillies to three team batting titles with batting averages of over .300. In 1894 the big three joined Turner in batting over .400 and the team hit .349—still the major league club record.

In 1899, with Delahanty's .410 leading the way, the Phillies once again topped .300 to lead the league. Though the team finished third, they won 94 games, a club high they would not surpass for 77 years. President Reach sold his interest in the club after a dispute with co-owner Rogers, and Rogers lost star second baseman Larry Lajoie in a salary dispute to the Athletics (Philadelphia's new entry in the rival American League). But the Phillies chased front-runner Pittsburgh through much of 1901. Though they slumped in August, they recovered to finish second.

It was the end of an era. Delahanty deserted to the AL the next season, and the Phillies dropped to seventh. Rogers sold the club to a syndicate. By 1904 the team was in last place, losing 100 games for the first time. They rose into the first division the next season, but didn't mount a serious pennant run until 1911, when the pitching of rookie Grover Cleveland Alexander kept them in the thick of the race into midseason. Two years later the Phillies enjoyed first place through most of June until they faded to a distant second.

In 1915 Alexander brought his ERA down more than a run per game to a league-low and career-best 1.22, with 12 shutouts among his 31 wins. Right fielder Gavvy Cravath and first baseman Fred Luderus finished one-two among NL sluggers, and Cravath won home run and RBI crowns. For half a season all eight clubs were in the thick of a tight race, with the Cubs and Phillies at the top of the heap. But in July the Cubs folded, and in August and September the Phillies took off to outdistance the late-surging Boston Braves for their first pennant.

The World Series was a Phillies' heartbreak. Four of the five games were decided by a single run— but the runs

belonged to the Boston Red Sox, who swept four after the Phillies had taken the opener.

Alexander shut out a record-tying 16 opponents the following year, winning a career-high 33, and teammate Eppa Rixey had his first big year with 22 wins. Through most of the season, the club trailed the leading Dodgers but caught them in September, only to fall away again in the final week.

After Alexander's 30 wins had brought the Phillies another second-place finish in 1917, the club dealt him to Chicago and embarked on 31 years of wandering in the desert. After 14 losing seasons (eight of them in last place), Philadelphia climbed to fourth, two games above .500, in 1932, but dropped back the next year into the second division (including nine last-place finishes) for 16 more years.

Several outstanding players spent time in Philadelphia during these years: Dave Bancroft (a rookie in their pennant season), Cy Williams, Freddy Leach, Chuck Klein, Lefty O'Doul, and Dick Bartell. Of these, only Williams and Klein retired as Phillies. The financially strapped management traded away the others at the height of their careers in deals that included cash as well as players. Even Klein—perhaps the greatest of them all—was sold twice before returning a third time to Philly to end his career.

The Phillies in 1930 produced a season that ranks among the most extraordinary of all time. With Klein and O'Doul leading the way at .386 and .383, every regular hit at least .280, to give the Phillies a team batting average of .315. But Phillies pitchers yielded a record 1199 runs while compiling the worst big league ERA ever—6.71. The club lost 102 games and finished last.

The Phillies' move in 1938 out of tiny, antiquated Baker Bowl into the Athletics' Shibe Park did nothing for attendance—or for performance. The team strung together a club-record five consecutive last-place finishes from 1938 to 1942, in which they averaged 107 losses per season and finished between 43 and 62½ games out of first.

In February 1943 the league took control of the debt-ridden club and sold it to a group headed by New York sportsman William D. Cox. Cox didn't last long; before the year was out he was barred from baseball for betting on the Phillies. His controlling interest was sold to Robert M. Carpenter, who installed his son, Robert Jr., as president. The younger Carpenter hired former pitcher Herb Pennock as general manager with instructions to build a farm system, and a new era began in the club's history.

Outfielder Del Ennis had come up to hit .313 in 1946, but Pennock died (in January 1948) before he could see the full fruits of his labor. First baseman Dick Sisler would be purchased in March; rookie outfielder Richie Ashburn would lead Philadelphia hitters in 1948 with a .333 average. Willie Jones wouldn't nail down third base for another year, and rookie pitchers Robin Roberts and Curt Simmons wouldn't overawe the opposition for a couple of seasons yet. But the team that would be dubbed the "Whiz Kids" was gathering. Triple A manager Eddie Sawyer was brought up in late July.

In 1949 the loss of first baseman Eddie Waitkus (shot in the chest by a crazed young woman) and midseason complacency threatened to strand the Phillies in the second division in 1949. Sawyer fired up his players in a special team meeting, and the Phillies rallied to finish third with the club's best record in 32 years.

With new red-pinstripe uniforms and a recovered Eddie Waitkus, the 1950 Phillies pulled away from a tightly bunched first division in July and August, but late in September they fell to within two games of onrushing Brooklyn. The Dodgers took the first game of a season-ending two-game series to narrow the gap to one. In the finale Ashburn threw out a Dodger at the plate in the ninth to preserve a tie and Sisler gave the Phillies the lead with a three-run homer the next inning. When Brooklyn failed to score in the bottom of the tenth, the Whiz Kids had their pennant.

Curt Simmons, who was called up for military service in September after winning 17 games, missed the World Series. As in 1915, the result for Philadelphia was frustration and heartbreak, as the Phillies were swept by the Yankees—in the first three games by a single run.

Roberts' pitching kept the Phillies in the first division for four of the next five years, but the team made no serious run at another pennant. And when Roberts began to lose his effectiveness the team kept sinking, to fifth for two years, then to four years in the cellar, culminating in 1961 with the longest big league losing streak of the century—23 games.

The club stuck with new manager Gene Mauch, and the 1962 Phillies edged above .500 for the first time in nine years (finishing seventh in a league newly expanded to 10 teams). In 1963 they moved up to fourth with a strong second half. In 1964, with the acquisition of pitcher Jim Bunning from Detroit and infielder Richie (later Dick) Allen's productive rookie season, Mauch's Phillies moved way out in front in August. But they blew their lead with 10 straight losses in late September while Cincinnati was winning nine and St. Louis eight in a row. Only victories in their final two games salvaged a second-place tie.

Pitcher Steve Carlton, acquired from St. Louis in an off-season trade, accounted for nearly half the Phillies' 59 wins in 1972. His 27 victories for the league's worst team gave the club a ray of hope for the future and earned Carlton the Cy Young Award. Carlton lost a league-high 20 games the next year. He regained his form over the next three seasons, and the Phillies gradually rose to the top of the division.

In 1974 sophomore third baseman Mike Schmidt burst to the forefront of the league's power hitters. The Phillies dropped out of contention in August, but wound up third, their best finish since the league split into divisions in 1969. The next year outfielder Greg Luzinski joined Schmidt among the league's top sluggers, and the club rose to second, with their first winning season since 1967.

In 1976 they enjoyed their finest regular season ever. With Schmidt and Luzinski providing the power, Carlton returning to the ranks of 20-game winners and Jim Lonborg climaxing a long comeback with 18 wins, the Phillies took the division lead in May and pulled away, recovering from a late-season dive to finish well ahead of Pittsburgh. Their 101 wins, .624 winning percentage, and nine-game margin of victory remain club records.

The Phillies were swept by Cincinnati in the National League Championship Series, but they came back the next season to duplicate their record 101 wins for another

comfortable first-place finish. Carlton won 23 (and his second Cy Young Award), and Luzinski enjoyed the best season of his career, driving in 130 runs. After defeating Los Angeles in the NLCS opener, though, the Phillies lost the pennant with three straight defeats.

In 1978, even though Schmidt and Carlton had off-years, the Phillies led much of the season and captured the division title a third straight time. But it was a tight race, and they barely survived a late-season Pittsburgh surge to finish a game and a half in front. For the third time, their triumph in the East was followed by defeat in the NLCS—for the second time at the hands of Los Angeles in four games.

Danny Ozark, in his seventh year as Phillies manager, was replaced by Dallas Green late in a disappointing 1979 season that saw the club stumble after a strong start. The club rallied in September to finish fourth. But Schmidt was back in top form, and Pete Rose had arrived via free agency to add his bat and hustle.

In a three-way race in 1980 that remained close through August, the Phillies hung tight without being able to move into the lead. But as Pittsburgh folded in late August and early September, the Phillies edged in front briefly, then battled back and forth with Montreal. Tied with the Expos as the clubs met in Montreal for the season's final three games, Philadelphia took the first, 2-1, then—in 11 innings—the second, to clinch their fourth division title in five years. Schmidt, with perhaps his finest season, drove in 121 runs and was named NL MVP; Carlton, with 24 wins, won his third Cy Young Award; and veteran reliever Tug McGraw enjoyed his best season in years. In an NLCS in which four of the five games went into extra innings, the Phillies prevailed over Houston, capturing their first pennant since the Whiz Kids 30 years earlier. And in the World Series, fortune finally smiled on the team as they overcame Kansas City in six games.

The Phillies won the first half of the strike-divided 1981 season. In the special intradivisional playoff against Montreal, Philadelphia fought back to tie the series after losing the first two games—only to lose the finale. The Carpenter family—citing the prohibitive cost of running a major league club—sold the team. Manager Dallas Green also left and was replaced by Pat Corrales, who kept the club in the thick of the 1982 race until the final month, when the Phillies slipped 3½ games back, to second. And Steve Carlton did it again: his 23 wins earned him the Cy Young trophy, making him the first pitcher to win the award four times.

Mike Schmidt again dominated the Phillies' offense in 1983, but Carlton yielded to John Denny as the team's pitching ace. Newly acquired reliever Al Holland emerged as one of the league's best. After general manager Paul Owens took over for Corrales as manager in midseason, the Phillies came alive and took the division title by six games. Carlton dominated the NLCS with an 0.66 ERA and two wins as the Phillies won their fourth pennant.

But their golden age ended in the World Series, when Baltimore triumphed in five games. The Phillies dropped to .500 and fourth place in 1984, and suffered a losing fifth-place season in 1985. They rebounded to second in 1986 (but 21½ games behind New York), then dropped back below .500 in 1987. Mike Schmidt, the only remain-ing member of the 1980 world champions, continued to power the offense. Despite an impressive lineup of every-day players in 1988, the Phils collapsed, finishing in the division cellar for the first time in 15 years. Unable to recover from a shoulder injury, Schmidt retired in May 1989, and despite several midseason trades the Phillies again finished last in the NL East. The Phillies followed that with a tie for fourth in 1990, a distant third in 1991, and, in 1992, the team's third last place finish in five years.

Strengthened by the signing of several free agents and sustained by solid performances throughout the roster, the Phillies reversed course in 1993. Led by Len Dykstra's peak season at the plate, the team grabbed the division lead at the start of the year and never let go, fending off Montreal's late-season surge to take the NL East title by three games. In the NLCS they won their fifth NL pennant, defeating Atlanta in six games, but in the World Series they blew a pair of late-inning leads and fell in six games to repeat champion Toronto. Plagued by illness and injury, the Phillies never caught fire in 1994, finishing a distant fourth in the NL East. In 1995 they finished tied for second (but 21 games back).

The following year saw the Phillies riddled by injuries and falling to last (67-95), with the worst record in the NL. The club's failure led to manager Jim Fregosi's firing at season's end. Standouts in the futile effort were out-fielder Jim Eisenreich (.361), starter Curt Schilling (3.19 ERA), reliever Ricky Bottalico (34 saves), and catcher Benito Santiago (30 home runs).

Under new manager Terry Francona, the Phillies started from scratch in 1997. At first, the results were disastrous. The Phils were 24-61 in the first half, but had a 44-33 mark after the All-Star break as Scott Rolen earned NL Rookie of the Year honors and Curt Schilling reached 300 strikeouts. Schilling notched 300 strikeouts again in 1998 as the Phillies actually competed for the NL Wild Card until an August slump pushed them out of the running. Still, the team's 75 wins were the most in Philadelphia since the team won the 1993 pennant.

Pittsburgh Pirates

Pittsburgh became a big league city in 1882, when its Allegheny baseball club joined with five other teams to form the American Association. Allegheny president H.D. McKnight was named president of the new league, but Allegheny made little stir until the club hired Horace Phillips to manage it and replaced its team in 1885 with players from the defunct Columbus club, which had fin-ished second in the AA the year before. The new Al-leghenys finished a distant third in 1885, but after purchasing Pud Galvin from Buffalo they improved in 1886 to finish a respectable second behind the invincible St. Louis Browns.

Flushed with success, Allegheny in 1887 became the first club to desert the AA for the older and more highly regarded National League. There they found the competi-tion stiffer and sank back into the second division. In 1890, when most of the team jumped to the rival Pitts-burgh Players' League club, Allegheny (known that year as the Innocents) suffered the worst season in Pittsburgh

major league history, finishing last, 66½ games out of first place (and 23 out of seventh), with a won-lost record of 23-113.

When the Players League folded after just one season, Allegheny merged with its PL counterpart to form the Pittsburgh Athletic Company, thereby retrieving many of its old regulars. The club also hired a second baseman—Lou Bierbauer—whose signing (or theft, as his old club saw it) gave the Innocents a new and more enduring nickname: the Pirates. The renewed club still finished last in 1891, but 36 games closer to the top than the year before, and only fractionally out of seventh place.

In 1893 a rules change moved the pitcher 10½ feet farther back from home plate. Of all the NL clubs, the Pirates benefited most from the change: their batting average jumped 63 points—28 more than that of the league as a whole—while their pitchers suffered less than most. The club finished second, with a .628 winning percentage that was their best of the century. Lefty Frank Killen, acquired from Washington, led the club's resurgence with a league-leading 34 wins.

Although catcher Connie Mack was called upon to manage the club toward the end of the 1894 season and led them to winning seasons the next two years, the Pirates did not make another serious run for the pennant until 1900. With a team transformed yet again by players from a defunct club—this time the Louisville Colonels—the Pirates battled Brooklyn's Superbas almost to the end of the season before dropping four and a half games back, a solid second. Although they lost the postseason Chronicle-Telegraph Cup games (that year's World Series) to the Superbas, the Pirates were embarked on an era of greatness.

In the merger that brought the Louisville players to Pittsburgh, the Colonels' owner Barney Dreyfuss acquired half ownership of the Pirates. A year later he bought the other half. His perennial hope for the club was a first-division finish; the Pirates reached that goal in 26 of his 32 years as owner.

Four of the former Louisville players—outfielder-turned-shortstop Honus Wagner, outfielder/manager Fred Clarke, third baseman/outfielder Tommy Leach, and pitcher Deacon Phillippe—and one carryover from the old Pirates, pitcher Sam Leever, remained with Pittsburgh long enough to help lead them to four pennants and, in 1909, their first world championship. In the 16 years Clarke managed the Pirates, they also finished second five times and slipped out of the first division only in Clarke's final two seasons at the helm.

In contrast to the club's devastation by the Players' League raid of 1890, the Pirates were unaffected in 1901 by raiders from the American League (which that year turned itself into a major league largely by drawing off talent from National League clubs). Only third baseman Jimmy Williams defected to the Americans, and he was ably replaced by Tommy Leach. The Pirates, with the league's best pitching (Jesse Tannehill and Deacon Phillippe finished one-two in ERA, and Jack Chesbro at 21-10 led in winning percentage), captured their first pennant by a comfortable seven and a half games over the Philadelphia Phillies.

The Pirates repeated as pennant winners in 1902 and 1903. The 1902 team was overwhelming. One Pirate or another led the league in nearly every offensive category: Ginger Beaumont in hits and batting; Tommy Leach in home runs; and Honus Wagner in slugging, RBIs, runs scored, doubles, and stolen bases. Pitcher Jack Chesbro's 28 wins led the league, and the top five NL pitchers in winning percentage were all Pirates. The club held the lead the whole season, finishing 27½ games ahead of second-place Brooklyn, still a major league record.

Pitchers Chesbro and Tannehill deserted to the AL's New York Highlanders the next season, but their loss merely made Pittsburgh's pennant-winning margin (6½ games) smaller than it might have been. Wagner beat out teammate Fred Clarke for the NL batting crown and finished second to Clarke in slugging. Beaumont took the titles in hits, runs, and total bases. Pitcher Sam Leever, with his finest season, led the club with 25 wins and the league in ERA and winning percentage. Owner Dreyfuss arranged with the AL champion Boston Pilgrims for a best-of-nine World Series—the first between NL and AL champions—but the Pirates lost it in eight games as their tired pitchers at last succumbed to overwork.

Although the Pirates twice finished second over the next four years, they didn't come close to capturing another pennant until 1908, when, in one of the tightest NL races ever, they were edged out by the Chicago Cubs and finished one game back, tied with the New York Giants for second. The following year, though, they moved in June into the new concrete-and-steel Forbes Field and celebrated by returning to the top of the league with a club record 110 wins—holding off the dogged Cubs throughout the season to win the pennant by six and a half games. And this time they won the World Series, too, although they needed the full seven games to subdue the Detroit Tigers. Honus Wagner remained the league's dominant offensive force. Aging pitchers Leever and Phillippe were overshadowed by a new crop of standouts: Vic Willis, Howie Camnitz, Nick Maddox, and Lefty Leifield—and the astonishing rookie Babe Adams, who after going 12-3 (with a 1.11 ERA) during the season, won three more games in the World Series.

The Series triumph ended an era. Wagner was past his prime and wound down his long career over the next several seasons as the Pirates dropped out of contention for a dozen years. Only Babe Adams remained of the world championship team when Pittsburgh next made a contest of the pennant race in 1921. That season saw the Pirates take an early lead and holding it most of the summer until an August-September decline dropped them to second place.

Former Pittsburgh infielder Bill McKechnie replaced George Gibson as manager during the following season with the club in fifth place, and saw the Pirates spurt to second before fading to third at the finish. Two more third-place seasons—with the Pirates finishing just three games out of first in 1924— paved the way for another pennant in 1925.

The 1925 Pirates fielded several stars: shortstop Glenn Wright, who led the club with 121 RBIs; sophomore right fielder Kiki Cuyler, who led the team in hitting (.357) and the league in runs scored; third baseman Pie Traynor, who shone on the field and at the bat; and Max Carey, who beat out Cuyler for the league stolen base title and enjoyed his finest season (.343) at the plate. The team as a whole hit

.307 to lead the league and ran away with the pennant, spurting to catch the front-running Giants in midseason and pushing ahead to an eight and a half-game lead by season's end. The World Series was tougher, but the Pirates prevailed over the Washington Senators, defeating veteran Walter Johnson in a seventh-game slugfest, 9-7. Babe Adams, hero of the 1909 Series and now, at 43, nearing the end of his long career, pitched one shutout inning in Game 4.

Rookie outfielder Paul Waner arrived the next season and hit .336, but the team, which had led the race going into August, fell into decline late in the month and finished third, four and a half games out. Max Carey sparked an unsuccessful player uprising against the management and was sold to Brooklyn just before the Pirates collapsed in August, and manager McKechnie was replaced after the season by former Washington manager Donie Bush.

In 1927, his first season at the helm, Bush won the pennant, even though Kiki Cuyler was benched for half the season for refusing to bat second in the order. But Paul Waner's younger brother Lloyd arrived to join Paul in the outfield, and the pair tore up the league, finishing one-two in hits (237 and 223) as Paul also took crowns in batting (.380; Lloyd was third at .355), RBIs, and total bases, while Lloyd led in runs scored. In and out of first place throughout the season, the Pirates moved into the lead a final time at the start of September and held on to edge the St. Louis Cardinals by a game and a half. In the World Series, though (played with Cuyler on the bench), the Pirates were swept by the imposing '27 Yankees, a team widely acclaimed as the greatest of all time.

Barney Dreyfuss died in February 1932. Ownership of the Pirates passed to his widow, who named their son-in-law Bill Benswanger president. The team finished a competitive second in 1932 and 1933, but then fell back until 1938. With Pie Traynor now manager, they moved out in front in midseason and held their lead comfortably until late September, when 10 straight Chicago victories (including three against Pittsburgh) dropped the Pirates to second place, where they finished two games back.

The Pirates showcased some great players in their lean years, like shortstop Arky Vaughan in the 1930s and early '40s, and slugger Ralph Kiner, who won or shared the league home run title all seven of his seasons with Pittsburgh in the 1940s and '50s. But after 1938 the club finished no closer than eight games from the top for 21 years.

The Pirates were purchased in 1946 by a four-man syndicate that included singer Bing Crosby and real estate tycoon John W. Galbreath. Galbreath later bought a majority interest in the club and, as president, hired Branch Rickey to rebuild the Pirates into contenders.

Barney Dreyfuss had resisted the development of minor league systems and preferred to scour unaffiliated minor league teams himself in search of young talent. Rickey, who pioneered the farm system in St. Louis and Brooklyn, laid the foundation for Pittsburgh's resurgence. Six of the eight regulars who would lead the Pirates to their next championship in 1960 were already in the 1958 lineup, including Dick Groat, Bill Mazeroski, and Roberto Clemente; and the leading pitchers of 1958—Bob Friend, Vern Law, and reliever Roy Face—topped the 1960 staff, too.

They began strong in 1960 and, shaking off their last challenger in late July, built up a seven-game margin of victory by season's end. League batting champion Groat paced a balanced offense that led the league in hitting, and pitcher Law, with 20 wins, enjoyed the finest season of his career. Facing the Yankees in the World Series, the Pirates were overwhelmed in the three games they lost, but they won the world title with four close wins, capped by Mazeroski's famous home run in the bottom of the ninth inning of the final game.

Pittsburgh again led the league in batting in 1961, with Clemente (whose .351 batting average led the league) and first baseman Dick Stuart (35 home runs, 117 RBIs) enjoying especially fine seasons. But the pitching fell apart, and the club dropped to sixth place.

When the Pirates next made a serious run for the pennant, in 1966, Harry Walker managed the team and center fielder Matty Alou (newly acquired from San Francisco) won the batting crown. (His brother Felipe of Atlanta was runner-up—the only one-two brother finish ever.) In a season-long three-way race, the Pirates took a lead in August but lost it early in September and finished third, three games out. They dropped to sixth again the next season and remained out of the pennant race for three years.

In 1970 John Galbreath's son Daniel was named Pirates' president, and Danny Murtaugh returned a third time to pilot the Pirates. (His second stint was for half a season in 1967.) The team began slowly and entered June with a record under .500. But they were already on their way up, and they moved out of aging Forbes Field into the brand-new Three Rivers Stadium in mid-July. They slipped into a three-way tangle for first in the NL East in mid-September, but shot ahead later in the month to take the division title. The power was now supplied by first baseman Bob Robertson and outfielder Willie Stargell, but Roberto Clemente was still in top form and Bill Mazeroski was still at second base, though nearing the end of his career.

In the 1970 National League Championship Series, the Pirates were swept by Cincinnati. But they came back the next season to overwhelm the East in a race that was no race after June, then defeated San Francisco for their eighth pennant, three games to one. Their slugging—paced by Stargell's league-leading 48 home runs—was tops in the NL, and reliever Dave Giusti saved a league-leading 30 games in support of a balanced pitching staff. Clemente hit .414 in the World Series (with half his hits going for extra bases) as the Pirates overcame a 2-0 deficit to edge Baltimore in seven games for their fourth world title.

In 1972, after a slow start, Pittsburgh (now managed by their former center fielder Bill Virdon) rocketed to their third straight division championship—by 11 games over Chicago. The club lost, narrowly, to Cincinnati in the NLCS, then suffered an even greater loss when Clemente was killed that winter in a plane crash. Clemente, who had collected exactly 3,000 hits with the Pirates, had the usual five-year waiting period waved by the Hall of Fame and was enshrined in Cooperstown in 1973.

The Pirates played poorly the next season, yet even with a losing record finished third in a five-way divisional race. Danny Murtaugh returned as manager a fourth (and

final) time late in the season and piloted the club to two more NL East titles the next two years.

The 1974 championship drive featured a comeback from last place in early July to first by late August, followed by a nip-and-tuck race in September with St. Louis that was settled by a 10th-inning Pittsburgh victory over Chicago in the season's final game. Stargell's bat was joined by those of Al Oliver and Richie Zisk as the Pirates outhit the rest of the league. In the NLCS, though, the Los Angeles Dodgers overcame Pittsburgh handily, three games to one.

The Pirates won the 1975 race more easily, holding the lead from early June as right fielder Dave Parker, in his first full big league season, led the club in home runs and RBIs, and the league in slugging. Rennie Stennett, now the second baseman, tied Wilbert Robinson's 1892 record by going 7-for-7 in a nine-inning game at Wrigley Field. Their regular season success failed to carry over to the postseason as Pittsburgh fell in the NLCS for the fourth time in five tries.

A distant second-place finish in 1976 was followed that December by manager Murtaugh's untimely death. His successor, Chuck Tanner (acquired in a trade with Oakland), kept the Pirates competitive in his first two seasons, steering them to within five games of the champion Phillies in 1977, then—with an amazing August-September spurt from way below .500—to within a game and a half of the Phillies in 1978.

In 1979 the Pirates again started slowly but began to move up in May and pushed to the front, ahead of Montreal, in late July. By mid-September, though, the Expos had caught up, and it was not until the final day that Pittsburgh had its sixth NL East title. Parker and the aging Stargell (now called "Pops") were still the club's big bats. Submariner Kent Tekulve had emerged as the bullpen ace and was one of six Pittsburgh pitchers to win 10 games or more.

In the NLCS the Pirates repaid Cincinnati for their 1975 humiliation, sweeping to the pennant in three games. In the World Series they seemed to have met their match in Baltimore, falling behind, three games to one. But Pops rallied his "family" to victory in the final three must-win contests, and Pittsburgh for a fifth time reigned at the top of the baseball world. Stargell was a three-time MVP that season, winning the honor in the NLCS and World Series, and sharing the regular season MVP trophy with Keith Hernandez of St. Louis.

For seven years the Pirates drifted downhill. The club's family spirit disintegrated, fans deserted the team, and it seemed for a time that the Pirates would leave Pittsburgh. But in 1985 a group of local corporations and individuals purchased the club from the Galbreaths, determined (with the assistance of a loan from the city of Pittsburgh) to keep the Pirates in town. Syd Thrift, a trader of consummate skill, was named general manager, and Chicago White Sox coach Jim Leyland was hired to his first job as a big league pilot. Under the new regime the club improved gradually, until in 1988 it once again proved itself a serious contender in the NL East. Thrift had built a team second only to New York's mighty Mets, one that drew more than 1.8 million fans in Pittsburgh—a club record. Thrift, however, clashed with the team's directors and he was fired at season's end.

Plagued all season by injuries, Pittsburgh plunged to fifth in 1989. But in 1990, as Doug Drabek put together a career season on the mound and the bats of Barry Bonds and Bobby Bonilla boomed, the Pirates arrived at the All-Star break in first place by half a game over New York. With Drabek and Zane Smith (newly acquired from Montreal) all but unbeatable down the stretch, the Pirates, after exchanging the lead with New York several times, swept a series against the Mets in early September to extend a narrow lead. The Bucs clinched the NL East title at the end of the month with eight straight wins.

The Pirates repeated as division champions in 1991 and 1992. Bonds and Bonilla again led the offense in 1991, and pitcher John Smiley won 20 games as the team built an early lead and enlarged it to 14 games by season's end. In 1992, even the departure of Bonilla (who signed with the Mets as a free agent) and Smiley (dealt to Minnesota) didn't hamper the Pirates. Center fielder Andy Van Slyke took up the offensive slack with one of his best seasons, and pitcher Tim Wakefield rose from the minors at the end of July to compile an 8-1 record as the Pirates breezed to the title by nine games. But the three-time division champions could not win a pennant. In the 1990 NLCS they fell to Cincinnati in six games. The next year they built a 3-2 lead over Atlanta, but lost the final two games. And in 1992, down three games to two, the Bucs fought back to within one out of victory in Game 7 before an Atlanta pinch hit cut them down once again.

The departure of free agent Barry Bonds to San Francisco was the most crucial of many roster changes for 1993, which saw more than half the 1992 NL East championship squad replaced. The revamped Pirates fielded near the top of the league and batted near the middle, but their pitching fell apart and the team finished fifth.

When the strike ended the 1994 season, the Pirates' .465 winning percentage was only two points better than the year before, but in the NL's new Central Division, that was good enough for a third-place tie with St. Louis. However, financial problems continued to haunt the team, and the payroll was slashed to the bone in 1995, resulting in the Pirates posting the NL's worst record (58-86). In February 1996 Sacramento newspaper heir Kevin McClatchy, 32, moved to purchase the club for $90 million.

Despite an 11-game winning streak in September, the Pirates (73-89) remained in the basement in 1996, prompting Jim Leyland to resign at season's end. Several of Pittsburgh's best players followed Leyland out of town in cost-cutting trades, but the Pirates turned out to be one of baseball's biggest surprises in 1997. Manager Gene Lamont kept the Pirates alive in the NL Central chase until the final week of the season. The highlight of the year came when Francisco Cordova and Ricardo Rincon combined for a no-hitter against first-place Houston at sold-out Three Rivers Stadium. The 1998 Pirates, however, slid to sixth place in the NL Central as the team lost its last eight games.

St. Louis Cardinals

The club that is now the Cardinals first fielded a team in 1881, and the next season became a charter member of

the American Association, a new major league formed in part to offer fans the beer and Sunday baseball forbidden by the older National League. Chris Von der Ahe, one of the club's founders and its first president, at first saw in baseball simply a source of customers for his St. Louis saloon and beer garden, but he developed a love for the game itself as his Brown Stockings—or Browns—developed into one of the era's greatest teams.

After a losing season in 1882, Von der Ahe hired Ted Sullivan, a noted judge of baseball talent, to manage the Browns. Sullivan brought in third baseman Arlie Latham and pitcher Tony Mullane to strengthen a team that already boasted a fine pitcher in Jumbo McGinnis (25-18 in 1882) and one of the game's premier first baseman in Charlie Comiskey. Although Sullivan quit before the end of his first season because of the continued interference of the volatile Von der Ahe, the Browns finished second in the AA, just a game behind champion Philadelphia.

When Mullane bolted the Browns in 1884, the club slipped to fourth. But help was on the way. In July Von der Ahe purchased the Bay City, Michigan, club to acquire its heavy-hitting pitcher Dave Foutz, and in September added another hitting pitcher, "Parisian Bob" Caruthers, to the roster. In 1885— with Comiskey now the manager, left fielder Tip O'Neill blossoming into one of baseball's best hitters, and Caruthers and Foutz winning 40 and 33 games—the Browns rose to the top, 16 games ahead of second-place Cincinnati. They finished on top four years in a row, tying Chicago's White Stockings (3-3-1) in the 1885 World Series and defeating them, four games to two, the next year for the AA's only Series triumph over their NL rivals.

Pitcher Silver King joined the club in 1887, and outfielder Tommy McCarthy arrived the following year. They helped keep the Browns at the top of the AA through 1888 (although the team lost the World Series both years). But Von der Ahe's sale of Foutz and Caruthers to Brooklyn following the 1887 season boosted Brooklyn to second place in 1888. The next year Brooklyn edged the Browns for the pennant, and the club's first era of greatness was over.

When the AA folded after the 1891 season, the Browns were taken into the NL, but fared poorly there, finishing ninth and then 11th in the divided season of 1892. They rose no higher than ninth in the remaining years of Von der Ahe's ownership, dropping into the cellar (63½ games out) in 1897 and returning to the bottom with a club-worst 111 losses the next season.

New owners Frank and Stanley Robison (who also controlled the Cleveland club) transferred the best Cleveland players and their manager to St. Louis in 1899. Dubbed the Perfectos, the revitalized St. Louis club fell short of perfection, but did rise to a first-division fifth place that year and (now known as the Cardinals) rose to fourth in 1901 before sinking back into the second division for a dozen years.

After Stanley Robison died in 1911 (his brother Frank had died in 1905), the club passed into the possession of Frank's daughter Helene Britton, who ran it behind the scenes until, in 1916, she sold it to a syndicate headed by her attorney James C. Jones. Jones hired Branch Rickey away from the AL Browns to run the club.

Rickey took over a team with two chief assets: manager Miller Huggins and a promising young infielder, Rogers Hornsby. Huggins had managed the Cards to third place in 1914, before Hornsby arrived, and, after a pair of losing seasons brought them up to third again in 1917. Huggins was lost to the New York Yankees the next year, and Rickey left the club temporarily for military service in the Great War. When Rickey returned in 1919, he took over as manager himself. In 1921 and 1922 the team finished third, closer to the leaders than the club had finished since joining the NL in 1891. Led by Hornsby's .397 and .401 batting, the team hit over .300 both seasons.

Sam Breadon increased his investment in the Cardinals until he was majority stockholder and club president in 1920, with Rickey as vice president and general manager. Breadon moved the Cards out of the inadequate wooden Cardinal Park during the 1920 season into the more modern Sportsman's Park, owned by the Browns and built on the site of Von der Ahe's original ground.

Early in the 1925 season, with the Cards in last place, Breadon replaced Rickey as field manager with second baseman Hornsby. The switch worked. In 1925 the Cards rebounded to fourth, and in 1926 they captured their first pennant since the glory days of the old Browns four decades earlier—edging Cincinnati in the final week of the season. The season was made perfect by victory in the World Series over Miller Huggins' Yankees as midseason pickup Grover Cleveland Alexander won Game 6 and saved Game 7 for the Cardinals.

But Breadon and his irascible player-manager had a falling out, and Hornsby was traded that winter to the New York Giants for second baseman Frank Frisch and pitcher Jimmy Ring. The trade enraged fans, but the team finished a close second in 1927, and returned to the top (under new manager Bill McKechnie) in a tight race the following season.

McKechnie, fired after the Yankees swept the Cards in the 1928 World Series and rehired in the midst of a St. Louis slump the next season, left to manage the Boston Braves in 1930. Former catcher Gabby Street, who replaced him, led the Cards back to the top again for successive pennants in 1930 and 1931, and in 1931 to a World Series victory over the Philadelphia Athletics. The 1930 race saw the club shoot from below .500 in mid-June to 30 games over .500 by season's end, overtaking three other teams to clinch the flag just three games from the finish. The 1931 team ran away with the pennant, leading all the way and finishing 13 games in front. Outfielder Chick Hafey and first baseman Jim Bottomley finished first and third in NL batting, and pitcher Bill Hallahan led the league in strikeouts (for the second year in a row) and tied for the lead in wins, with 19. Four of the league's top five base stealers—led by Frank Frisch and including outfielder Pepper Martin in his first full season—were Cardinals.

When the Cards dropped to sixth place in 1932 and showed little improvement the following year, Breadon replaced manager Street with Frisch. Breadon's move paid immediate dividends. Though the club finished fifth that season, their record improved after Frisch took over, and the next year, in a season-long uphill struggle, the Cards won 13 of their final 15 games to pass the front-running New York Giants in the final week.

Writers labeled the 1934 Cardinals the "Gashouse

Gang" for their rowdy and daring play. In addition to team veterans Frisch and Martin (who had been shifted from the outfield to third base), the gang included shortstop Leo Durocher, left fielder Joe "Ducky"Medwick, and the team's leading hitter and slugger, first baseman Rip Collins, who in a career-best season led the league in slugging average and tied for first in home runs.

The pitching staff was headed by the league-leading Jerome "Dizzy" Dean (30-7) and his rookie brother Paul (19-11). Of the team's final nine wins, Diz and Paul accounted for seven. Each won another pair in the Cards' World Series triumph over Detroit.

The next two seasons the Cardinals moved into the lead late in the season only to wind up second. After the team slipped into the second division in 1938, Breadon replaced Frisch as manager with Ray Blades, who led a late-season run for the flag in 1939 but finished second. When the Cards failed to contend in 1940, Breadon brought up Rochester manager Billy Southworth for a second time. Southworth had failed as McKechnie's replacement in 1929, but this time he stuck, becoming one of the club's greatest skippers.

Through all these years Branch Rickey was revolutionizing baseball as he built the game's first and most extensive "farm system" of minor league clubs. The Cardinals' farm teams would—until the other major league clubs caught on and caught up—provide St. Louis with a competitive advantage in the recruitment and development of young players.

In the closing days of the 1941 season, perhaps that system's greatest product arrived at the big club: Stan Musial. Southworth brought the club in a close second that year after a season-long back-and-forth struggle with Brooklyn. The next year—Musial's first full season—the Cardinals enjoyed their winningest season ever: 106 victories. They needed them all, too, for Brooklyn won 104 games, leading the race until mid-September, when the Cardinals passed them and held on to a narrow lead by winning 12 of their final 13 games. St. Louis pitchers Mort Cooper and Johnny Beazley finished one-two in National League wins and ERA, while Enos Slaughter and Musial paced the offense. The club maintained its momentum in the World Series, taking the Yankees in five games.

St. Louis retained its preeminence for two more years as baseball gradually lost players to military service in World War II. Slaughter and Beazley were gone by 1943. But Cooper remained to compile two more 20-plus winning seasons, and Musial was not called until after the 1944 season. With 105 wins in both 1943 and 1944, the Cards ran away with two more pennants, losing to the Yankees in the 1943 World Series, but taking their sixth world title the next year from their St. Louis landlords, the AL champion Browns.

Owner Breadon had fired Branch Rickey in 1942 (objecting to the personal profit Rickey made from selling the club's unneeded farm players) and Southworth left to manage the Boston Braves after the 1945 season. Rickey went to head the Brooklyn Dodgers, building for them a farm system and tapping the large reservoir of black players. In 1946, the last year of all-white major league ball, the Cards (managed now by Eddie Dyer) and the Dodgers waged a two-team pennant race, ending the sea-

son in the first major league tie for first place. St. Louis won the first two games in a best-of-three playoff against Brooklyn and went on to surprise the favored Boston Red Sox in the World Series in seven games.

St. Louis was slow to integrate and the Cards lost ground to teams like Brooklyn, whose black players brought an immediate upswing in the club's success. After the 1947 season Breadon sold the club to Fred Saigh and Robert Hannegan (the U.S. Postmaster General). Musial enjoyed his finest season in 1948, but the club finished second again in a lackluster race. The next year, though, the Cards and Dodgers tangled in a season-long struggle for first place that was not resolved until the season's last day—with Brooklyn on top.

The Cardinals threatened to move to Milwaukee, but beer magnate August Busch, Jr., purchased the club early in 1953 and the same year bought Sportsman's Park from the Browns (who were moving to Baltimore). With Busch's infusion of money and enthusiasm, the club slowly revived. They made runs for the pennant in 1957, 1960, and 1963, but each time tailed off sharply in the final week of the season.

The Cards were playing below .500, in seventh place, in mid-June 1964 when the arrival (via a trade with the Cubs) of speedy young Lou Brock sparked a revival of both the team and player. Brock, who had been hitting .251 in Chicago, with 10 stolen bases, hit .348 the rest of the season and stole 33 more bases as the Cards hurtled into the midst of a four-way race for the pennant that was settled only when they took the flag with an 11-5 win on the final day. After surprising the Yankees in seven games in the World Series, the Cardinals were themselves surprised when manager Johnny Keane left to take the helm of the Yankees. The club slipped into the second division for a couple of years under the management of their great former second baseman Red Schoendienst.

Busch built them a striking new stadium in 1966, and the next season the team rebounded to the top again, running away from the field in the last half of the season behind the heavy hitting of Orlando Cepeda, the bat and speed of Brock, and a pitching staff of remarkable breadth and balance. Bob Gibson's three World Series wins over Boston edged the Cards to a ninth world title and set the stage for Gibson's astonishing season the following year.

With his 22 wins leading the Cards to another pennant in 1968, Gibson hurled 13 shutouts and compiled an ERA of just 1.12—both feats the best in more than half a century, both ranking among the top five big league performances ever. After winning two World Series games, Gibson lost Game 7 as Detroit took the crown.

Red Schoendienst continued as manager through 1976—a club record 12 years—but led the team to no more championships. When divisional play was inaugurated in 1969, geography was ignored as the Cards were installed in the East to add strength to what seemed the weaker division. But it was 14 years before they won their first divisional championship. Four times they finished second, losing twice by only a game and a half in the back-to-back tight races of 1973 and 1974.

In the strike-shortened divided season of 1981, manager Dorrel "Whitey" Herzog's Cards compiled the best overall record in the NL East, but because they had finished the two halves of the season second to Philadelphia

and Montreal they were ineligible for postseason play.

With the defensive wizard shortstop Ozzie Smith (acquired from San Diego) and rookie speedster Willie McGee bolstering an already strong team, the Cardinals of 1982 prevailed against the Phillies in the race for the East. St. Louis then swept West champion Atlanta for the pennant and captured their 10th World Series crown in a seven-game struggle with Milwaukee.

After two seasons out of the running, the Cards in 1985 gained the power of veteran Jack Clark (acquired from San Francisco) and the speed of rookie Vince Coleman. With career-best seasons from Willie McGee and newly acquired pitcher John Tudor, the team edged the New York Mets for the division title and defeated Los Angeles for the pennant but lost the World Series in seven games to Kansas City.

Jack Clark missed two-thirds of the 1986 season to injury, and the Cards finished below .500, but they rebounded to edge the Mets again for the championship of the East in 1987 as Clark and Vince Coleman enjoyed their finest seasons at the bat. The reinjured Clark made only a token appearance as the Cards edged San Francisco for the league championship, and he missed the World Series entirely as St. Louis bowed to Minnesota in seven games. That winter Clark signed as a free agent with the Yankees, and, in 1988, the Cardinals dropped to fifth place, 25 games out.

With solid pitching and hitting, and the league's best fielding, the 1989 Cardinals drew within half a game of the division lead on Sept. 8, then fell out of the race with six straight losses, finishing third. As the season drew to a close, long-time owner August Busch, Jr., died at age 90. The next July, with the club uncharacteristically mired at the bottom of the NL East, manager Whitey Herzog resigned. Under new manager Joe Torre (a former NL MVP in St. Louis) the Cards revived briefly, but then dropped their final seven games to insure their first basement finish in 72 years.

Reliever Lee Smith provided the key to St. Louis' 1991 rebound to second place: his 47 saves—a new NL record—preserved more than half the wins of a team that won 37 games by a single run. Smith saved another 43 games in 1992 and the Cards won nearly as often as they had the previous year, but this time finished third. The defense developed a leak in 1993, and the pitching faltered, but four regulars— Bernard Gilkey, Todd Zeile, and newcomers Gregg Jefferies and Mark Whiten (who became the 12th player to hit four home runs in a game)— scaled new heights offensively to keep the Cardinals competitive through much of the season and give them another third place finish. In 1994 the team—now playing in the NL's new Central Division—performed below .500 for the first time since 1990.

The weak-hitting Cards slipped to fourth in 1995. Manager Joe Torre was fired as the season wound down and was replaced by interim manager Mike Jorgensen and ultimately by former A's pilot Tony LaRussa. The big news of the year, however, came in December when Anheuser-Busch sold the club for $150 million to an investment group headed by St. Louis banker Andrew Baur and William DeWitt Jr., whose father had once owned the Browns and the Reds.

In 1996, Ozzie Smith's last season, the LaRussa-led Cards (88-74) outpaced Houston and Cincinnati for the NL Central championship. Aiding St. Louis's effort were Ron Gant (30 HR, 82 RBIs), Brian Jordan (17 HR, 104 RBIs), Andy Benes (18-10), and Dennis Eckersley (30 saves). In the first round of the postseason the Cards rolled over San Diego in three straight but in the NLCS ran into the Atlanta buzzsaw. Ahead three games to one, the Cards couldn't put away the pennant as the Braves rolled to 12-1, 3-1, and 15-0 victories in the last three games.

The 1997 and 1998 seasons were disappointing in the standings, but the Cardinals nonetheless became a top drawing card at home and on the road. A 1997 trading deadline deal with Oakland for Mark McGwire was worth its weight in gold. McGwire's combined total of 58 homers in 1997 was the most since Roger Maris broke Babe Ruth's mark with 61 home runs in 1961. In 1998 McGwire obliterated that record. As fans packed the left field stands across the country just to see McGwire take batting practice, "Big Mac" became the first player to hit 50 home runs in three straight seasons. Before a national television audience, McGwire hit his record-breaking 62nd home run on Sept. 8. He finished with an astounding 70 home runs, beating out Sammy Sosa, who blasted 66 homers for the Cubs.

San Diego Padres

In their first 15 years the Padres put together only one winning season. In their 16th, they won the National League pennant. Founded in the 1969 expansion that saw the two major leagues divide into East and West divisions, the Padres finished last in the six-team NL West their first six seasons, ending each year from 28½ to 42 games behind the division champion.

Their first season was their worst. With 110 losses, the Padres finished not only 41 games out of first but 29 games out of fifth. First baseman Nate Colbert, with 24 home runs, provided San Diego's brightest ray of hope. He proved to be one of the Padres' standout performers through their last-place years, and in 1972 became the first Padre to drive in more than 100 runs. Colbert also had the greatest day in club history with five home runs and 13 RBIs in a doubleheader against Atlanta on Aug. 1, 1972.

Big league baseball was not an instant hit in San Diego. Home attendance barely topped half a million in the Padres' first year, and, though it rose a little over the next few seasons, the increase was not enough to make the club viable. Owner C. Arnholt Smith decided early in 1974 to sell the franchise to a buyer who planned to move the team to Washington, D.C. New uniforms had been manufactured and the club's files were packed for the move, when the builder of the McDonald's fast-food empire, longtime baseball fan Ray Kroc, stepped in with an offer to buy the Padres for cash and keep them in San Diego.

Though Kroc's 1974 Padres finished last with the same 60-102 record they had posted the year before, his sense of showmanship drew spectators. Home attendance shot up 76 percent, rising above a million for the first time. The Padres then began to draw fans on their own merits as they finally pulled themselves out of the cellar. Pitcher Randy

Jones, who in 1974 had led the league with 22 losses, turned his record around and for two years shone as one of the game's finest pitchers. He halved his 1974 ERA to a league-leading 2.24, winning 20 games as the Padres rose to fourth place in 1975 and posted a winning percentage over .400 for the first time. The next year Jones won a league-high 22 games and earned the Cy Young Award—the first major award to come to a San Diego player.

Outfielder Dave Winfield came up as a rookie in 1973, and the following year became the team RBI leader, a position he held in six of his seven full seasons with the Padres. Reliever Rollie Fingers signed as a free agent. In each of his four seasons in San Diego (1977-1980) he led the team in saves, twice also leading the league. In 1978 the Padres acquired veteran pitcher Gaylord Perry from Texas and installed rookie Ozzie Smith at shortstop. Perry's sparkling 21-6 season gave San Diego its second Cy Young winner, and together with Smith's play in the field, Winfield's bat (.308, 97 RBIs) and Fingers' 37 saves, brought the Padres their first winning season.

All these stars had gone—and owner Kroc had recently died—by the time the Padres recorded a second winning season six years later, and won the division title and NL pennant with a new blend of experience and youth. Sparked by recently acquired veterans Steve Garvey at first, Graig Nettles at third, and Goose Gossage in the bullpen, and by a bevy of younger stars like batting champ Tony Gwynn and hard-hitting outfielder Kevin McReynolds, the Padres moved into first place to stay in early June. From Aug. 3 to the end of the season, they played only .500 ball but still won the championship of the weak Western Division by 12 games. Underdogs in the National League Championship Series, the Padres lost the first two games in Chicago, but pulled themselves together to take the pennant with three come-from-behind wins at home.

Their decline began with their World Series loss to Detroit. The end of 1985 saw them tied for third, and in 1986 they slipped below .500 and into fourth place. In 1987 Gwynn won his second batting title, and rookie catcher Benito Santiago capped the season with a 34-game hitting streak to cop Rookie of the Year honors. But with most of the 1984 standouts faded or traded, the Padres' decline was complete: the club for the ninth time in its 19 years finished last.

In late May 1988, with the team at 16-30, general manager Jack McKeon took over as field manager from Larry Bowa. Under McKeon the Padres went 67-48, with nine wins in their final 10 games, and shot from sixth place to third in the NL West.

In 1989 a trio of veteran pitchers—starters Bruce Hurst (lured from Boston as a free agent) and Ed Whitson and closer Mark Davis—attained new peaks of performance. Slugger Jack Clark (newly acquired from the Yankees) turned on the power after a slow start to complement Tony Gwynn's fourth season as NL batting leader. The Padres stumbled through the first half, arriving at the All-Star break four games below .500, but climbed steadily through the final two months to a second-place finish with their second-best winning percentage ever.

With the loss of free agent Davis in 1990, plus injuries to Clark and catcher Santiago, even the new power of Joe Carter (traded from Cleveland) could not lift the club above a tie for fourth. New owners, headed by TV pro-ducer Tom Werner, took control of the Padres from Ray Kroc's widow Joan in mid-June. Jack McKeon resigned his managerial position, which went to coach Greg Riddoch a month later, and was fired as general manager in September.

Slugger Fred McGriff arrived for 1991 (in a trade that sent Carter and young Roberto Alomar to Toronto) and helped power the Padres into third place. In 1992 he was joined by Gary Sheffield, who revived after an injury-ridden season at Milwaukee to lead the NL in batting and rank with McGriff among the league leaders in home runs and RBIs. The Padres again finished third, but Sheffield and McGriff were traded away during the 1993 season in cost-cutting moves that, combined with poor team pitching and fielding, dumped the Padres into the NL West cellar, a club record 43 games out of first.

Although the Padres had improved their winning percentage somewhat over 1993 by the time the 1994 season was cut short in August by the strike, their 47-70 record was the worst in the majors. One of San Diego's few reasons to cheer in 1994 was the hitting of Tony Gwynn, whose .394 batting average was the best in the NL since Bill Terry's .401 in 1930.

In December 1994 a group led by Larry Lucchino and John Moores acquired the club. GM Randy Smith resigned in midseason 1995, but the club rebounded slightly to a third place finish (70-74) as Gwynn (.368) won his sixth batting title.

The 1996 Padres (91-71) surprised virtually everyone by catching the Dodgers and capturing the NL West title on the last day of the season. Standout Padres included Tony Gwynn (with a league-leading .353 average), NL MVP Ken Caminiti (40 HR, 130 RBIs), Steve Finley (30 HR, 95 RBIs), Rickey Henderson (37 stolen bases), and Trevor Hoffman (42 saves). Their Cinderella season, however, came to an end in the first round of the post-season as they lost in three straight to St. Louis.

Other than Gwynn winning his eighth batting crown (tying Honus Wagner for the most in NL history), the 1997 season was a disappointment in San Diego. The Padres rebounded for a franchise-best 98 wins in 1998. New acquisition Kevin Brown anchored the rotation (18-7, 2.38 ERA, 257 strikeouts), Trevor Hoffman shattered the Padres record with 53 saves, and Greg Vaughn exploded for a club-record 50 home runs. The Padres surprised the favored Astros in the Division Series and then won the pennant in six games against Atlanta. They were tied or held a lead late in three of the four World Series games, but they could not stop the Yankees' march to a sweep. The Padres' biggest victory of the year, however, came on Nov. 3, when voters approved a new stadium for the ballclub.

San Francisco Giants

The expulsion of Troy and Worcester from the National League after the 1882 season cleared the way for the league to reestablish clubs in the major markets of Philadelphia and New York. Manufacturer John B. Day was awarded the New York franchise. Purchasing the defunct Troy club, he divided their players between the new NL Gothams and his other club, the Metropolitans of the

American Association, and set them up on adjoining grounds north of Central Park, on a field once used for polo.

The Mets fared better than the Gothams, finishing fourth in 1883 to the Gothams' sixth, and winning the AA pennant the next year while the Gothams rose only to fifth in the NL. Since the NL, with greater prestige and higher ticket prices, offered potentially greater profit, Day switched some of his Mets to the Gothams in 1885, including ace hurler Tim Keefe and manager Jim Mutrie. The results were immediate: the Mets sank to seventh place while the Gothams (dubbed "my Giants" by an enthusiastic Mutrie) rose to the thick of a pennant race with Chicago. At the finish Chicago was on top by two games, but the Giants had won more than three games out of four for a .759 winning percentage that is not only the club's best ever, but one of the highest in major-league history. Pitchers Keefe and Mickey Welch together won 76 of the team's 85 victories, and first-baseman Roger Connor led the league in batting.

The Giants won their first pennant in 1888 and their second the next year in a one-game squeaker over Boston. Keefe and Welch, still going strong, combined for 61 wins in '88 and 55 in '89. Continuing their winning ways in the World Series, the Giants triumphed easily over St. Louis in 1888, and overcame a three-games-to-one deficit to vanquish Brooklyn the next year.

In 1890, ravaged by the loss of players to the rival Players League, the Giants finished sixth, but they recovered several players when the PL folded at the end of the season. (They also moved into the PL ballpark, named it after their original Polo Grounds, and played there for 67 years). They rose to third in 1891, but Day could no longer afford to maintain the team and sold out to financier Edward Talcott. Talcott brought back former Giants star J.M. Ward to manage the club and in 1894 saw the team rise to a close second-place finish behind Baltimore. Pitchers Amos Rusie and Jouett Meekin tied for the league lead with 36 wins apiece. In postseason Temple Cup play, the Giants swept Baltimore in four games for their third world championship.

That winter Talcott sold control of the club to Tammany Hall politician Andrew Freedman. The club's fortunes sank under Freedman's abrasive and heavy-handed rule. In 1902, his final year of ownership, the Giants suffered their lowest winning percentage—.353—and most distant finish ever—53½ games behind champion Pittsburgh.

In the midst of the 1902 season, though, a skirmish in the war between the NL and the upstart American League led to a Giants turnaround. John T. Brush, owner of the NL Cincinnati Reds, bought the AL Baltimore Orioles, then released Orioles manager John McGraw and several key players to sign with NL clubs. Five joined the Giants, including McGraw, catcher Roger Bresnahan, and pitcher Joe "Iron Man" McGinnity. That winter, Brush sold the Reds and Orioles and bought the Giants.

In 1903, with Bresnahan hitting .350 and McGinnity winning a league-high 31 games (closely followed by third-year phenom Christy Mathewson's 30 wins), manager McGraw saw his Giants win 36 more games than they had in 1902 and finish a solid second in the standings. In McGraw's 29 full seasons at the helm, the team won 10 pennants and finished second 11 times.

Just two years after their worst season ever, McGraw in 1904 led the Giants to one of their best. Their 106 wins and 13-game winning margin remain franchise records. The club led the NL in pitching, hitting, fielding, and base stealing. McGinnity led league pitchers in several categories with a career-best 35-8, 1.61 ERA season. Mathewson, right behind with 33 wins, led the league in strikeouts.

The only disappointment of 1904 was McGraw's refusal to face Boston in a World Series. His rejection of the AL champions as worthy opponents was the last shot fired in a war between the two leagues. By the time the Giants had repeated as NL pennant winners a year later, the World Series was an official and permanent feature of the baseball landscape.

Mathewson led NL pitchers in 1905 with 31 wins and an ERA of 1.27, and outfielder "Turkey Mike" Donlin, acquired from Cincinnati the previous July, erupted with the best season of his career, batting a team-high .356 and scoring a league-high 124 runs. The Giants won only one game less than the year before and held a comfortable lead throughout the season. Matty's three shutouts against the Philadelphia Athletics in the World Series secured the club's fourth world crown.

It was 1911 before the Giants won their next pennant. Despite 96 wins in 1906 they finished a distant second to the Chicago Cubs, who won a record 116 games. In 1908 the Giants came within a disputed play of the pennant. On Sept. 23, playing Chicago (with whom they were tied at the top of a three-way race), Giants baserunner Fred Merkle failed to run to second on a single by Al Bridwell that would have driven in the winning run from third. Merkle was forced at second after the ball (or a second ball—the argument still rages) was recovered amid the horde of fans who overran the field. The force out at second negated the run, and the game was ruled a tie. At season's end, when the two clubs found themselves again tied at the top, the "Merkle boner" game was replayed. The Cubs won the game and flag, leaving the Giants in a second-place tie with Pittsburgh.

In 1911 the Giants pulled away from the Cubs in September for the first of three straight pennants. (Early in the season most of the Polo Grounds was rebuilt in concrete after fire destroyed the wooden stands.) The following year the Giants took the lead in May and held it comfortably the rest of the way. In 1913 they didn't move into first until late June, but then they quickly put the flag out of reach and finished 12½ games ahead of the faltering Phillies. Mathewson led the team in victories over the three years, with 74, followed closely by Rube Marquard, who enjoyed the three best seasons of his career with 73 wins. Matty led the NL in ERA in 1911 and 1913, and rookie Jeff Tesreau took the honors in 1912 (winning 17 games that season and 22 the next). Giants pitching led the league all three seasons, as did their hitting, which featured a balanced offense paced by infielders Larry Doyle and Art Fletcher and catcher John "Chief" Myers.

In the World Series, though, the Giants fell short of the title three times. The Philadelphia Athletics defeated them handily in 1911 and 1913, but the Giants carried the 1912 Series against the Boston Red Sox to the 10th inning of the final game before a pair of fielding lapses by the

Giants enabled Boston to rally for the win.

Boston's "Miracle" Braves, in their 1914 surge from last place to the pennant, passed the front-running Giants for good in early September. The next year, five of the eight NL clubs found themselves bunched within three and a half games of one another at the lower end of the standings as the season ended—with the Giants at the very bottom. The 1916 season was characterized by dips and surges, but even a 26-game winning streak in September couldn't raise the team higher than fourth. In 1917 a balanced pitching staff— paced by Ferdie Schupp's one big season (21-7, 1.95 ERA)—hurled the Giants to the front early in June and kept them there to the finish. Once more, though, the World Series proved to be a disappointment, with a loss to the Chicago White Sox in six games.

Three years of second-place finishes followed, in the midst of which the Giants changed owners. Brush had died in 1912 and was succeeded as president by his son-in-law Harry Hempstead. But in January 1919 Brush's heirs sold the club to financier and racehorse fancier Charles A. Stoneham, with manager McGraw becoming a minority stockholder.

In 1921 McGraw brought home the first of four straight winners for Stoneham. Seven regulars hit over .300 (led by third baseman Frank Frisch's .341); first baseman George Kelly's 23 home runs topped the NL. The club hung close to Pittsburgh through August, then broke into a lead which the fading Pirates could not challenge. In postseason play the Giants lost the first two games to the Yankees, but charged back to win their fifth world title. The next year outfielder Emil "Irish" Meusel celebrated his first full season in New York with a team-high 132 RBIs, as the Giants fended off a midseason challenge from St. Louis to pull away to a comfortable margin at the end. The World Series was especially sweet: a four-game sweep of the Yankees.

Cincinnati and Pittsburgh hung just behind the Giants through much of 1923, but never quite caught up. The Giants' league-leading offense was led by individual NL highs in RBIs (Meusel), runs scored (outfielder Ross Youngs), and hits and total bases (Frisch). But the Yankees finally caught the Giants in the World Series, 4-2.

George Kelly took the NL RBI title in 1924. The club's hitting remained the league's best, and by early August the Giants had taken a 10-game lead. But they then leveled off while Brooklyn and Pittsburgh surged. Brooklyn, in fact, took over the lead for a day in early September, but the Giants emerged triumphant at the end by 1½ games. The World Series, though, was as heartbreaking as the pennant race had been heartstopping: the Giants lost to Washington in the last of the 12th inning of the seventh game when a grounder bounced over the head of Giants rookie third baseman Fred Lindstrom to drive in the Series-ending run.

Close finishes in 1927 and 1928 were the nearest McGraw's Giants came to another pennant. Ill and tired, he quit early in the 1932 season with the team in last place, naming first baseman Bill Terry to replace him. Under Terry the Giants rose only to sixth that season, but McGraw had built a squad fit for a new era of greatness. He had persuaded Terry to leave a career with Standard Oil for one with the Giants; he had saved Mel Ott's unique but effective batting stance from revision by well-meaning minor league managers by keeping Ott out of the minors; and he had rescued pitcher Carl Hubbell from mediocrity by encouraging the screwball pitch other managers had tried to suppress in the minors.

Hubbell and Ott formed the heart of the club that would win a trio of pennants under Terry's management. In 1933 the Giants moved to the front in June and, despite a late-September slump, finished well ahead of runner-up Pittsburgh. Ott, with what was for him an off-year, powered the offense with 23 homers and 103 RBIs, while Hubbell led the league in wins, shutouts, and ERA. Hubbell also hurled two wins against Washington in the World Series, and Ott won it all for New York with a 10th-inning home run in Game 5. McGraw, still the club's vice president, threw a party for "his" Giants after the Series. The following February he died, at age 60.

As they had the previous season, the Giants of 1934 emerged from the crowd to take and hold first place into late September. They rose higher than they had in 1933 and didn't slump as far at the end. But their five end-of-season losses were enough to drop them two games behind the surging Cardinals at the finish. Again in 1935 they led the league much of the season. But they had begun to level off in mid-July and finished the season well back in third. Charles Stoneham died in January 1936, and his son Horace— who at age 33 had already run the club for a year—assumed the club presidency.

In 1936, and again in 1937, the Giants came from behind to take the flag. Hubbell sparked their second-half resurgence in 1936, winning his final 16 decisions of the season as the Giants rose from fourth to first. In the World Series, though, Hubbell, after one win, was stopped by the Yankees in his try for a second. The Yankees took the Series in six games.

Again the next year the Giants hid behind the leaders most of the season until a surge in late August coincided with a Chicago decline and shot the Giants to the front. The Cubs recovered, but New York continued its winning ways and finished ahead by three games. But again the Yankees dominated the World Series, winning in five games.

Hubbell's years of greatness were now over, and while the Giants led the NL through the first half of 1938, they finished five games out in third place. It would be 12 years before they again finished that close to the top. Mel Ott replaced Terry as manager in 1942, but the Giants sank to the cellar in 1943 with their second-worst season ever, and finished last again three years later.

Halfway through the 1948 season the baseball world was startled to learn that Leo Durocher, the fiery manager of the Brooklyn Dodgers, had switched his allegiance to their arch foes, the Giants. Durocher discarded the club's top three home run hitters of 1947 and added agile infielders Alvin Dark and Eddie Stanky to the roster. By 1950, with the blossoming of Sal Maglie into a first-rank pitcher and the timely midseason purchase of hurler Jim Hearn, the Giants were once more a challenger, spurting in the second half from below .500 to within five games of the top.

After losing their first 11 games the next year, the Giants began a long climb. A 16-game August winning streak and a seven-game streak at season's end tied them with Brooklyn and forced a three-game playoff. After a

win and a loss, the Giants entered the last of the ninth inning of Game 3 trailing by a 4-1 score. Two singles and a double cut the deficit by a run and brought on Ralph Branca to face Bobby Thomson. Thomson homered to left and the Giants won the pennant. Their defeat by the Yankees in the World Series dimmed the miracle a bit, but it couldn't detract from the career bests of pitchers Maglie and Larry Jansen, who tied for the NL lead with 23 wins apiece, and of former Negro League great Monte Irvin, who hit .312 and led the league in RBIs.

The next year Irvin was lost until August with a broken ankle, Jansen (with a back problem) fell off to 11-11, and Willie Mays—a promising rookie in 1951—left early in the season for a hitch in the Army. Still, the Giants hung close to Brooklyn for much of the summer and finished second. In 1953, though, they fell apart in midseason and wound up in fifth, 35 games out.

Mays returned in 1954 to enjoy one of his strongest seasons, and pitchers Johnny Antonelli (newly acquired from Milwaukee), sophomore Ruben Gomez, and reliever Marv Grissom all burst forth with the best seasons of their careers. The Giants pulled away from Brooklyn in July and held on with a late-season rush to win by five games. Underdogs to powerful Cleveland in the World Series, they stunned the Indians (and the rest of the baseball world) with a four-game sweep. It was their eighth world title—and, so far, their last.

Manager Durocher retired after a distant third-place finish in 1955, and Bill Rigney, who replaced him (the first of seven straight rookie managers to be hired by the Giants over the next 20 years), presided over a pair of sixth-place seasons in the club's final years in New York. Persuaded by the Dodgers' Walter O'Malley that California was the land of baseball opportunity, Giants owner Stoneham announced in August 1957 his decision to move the club to San Francisco before the next season.

The move succeeded. Home attendance doubled, even though the team had to play in a former minor league park that seated fewer than 23,000 fans. When new Candlestick Park opened in 1960 attendance climbed to nearly 1.8 million, a new club high. Better still, rookie sensations like Orlando Cepeda in 1958 and Willie McCovey in 1959, plus the continuing mastery of Willie Mays, made the Giants competitive once again. In their first 14 San Francisco seasons, they compiled winning records—a longer string than they had ever known in New York.

Candlestick Park, though, proved a cold and windy place to watch baseball, and after its inaugural season fans began to drift away. Attendance picked up some in 1962, however, as the Giants battled for first all summer with the Los Angeles Dodgers. Mays, Cepeda, and Felipe Alou headlined the league's best offense, and a pair of veteran pitchers—Jack Sanford and Billy O'Dell—garnered the most wins of their careers (24 and 19) as part of a balanced staff that also got 16 wins from veteran Billy Pierce and 18 from the emerging great Juan Marichal. Still, the Giants trailed the Dodgers most of the season until the Giants won and the Dodgers lost on the final day to force another playoff. As in 1951, the Giants won the first game and lost the second, and overcame a ninth-inning deficit in the finale to win the pennant. Also as in 1951, they lost the World Series to the Yankees, although this time they held on until the final out of Game 7 before

losing their grip on the crown.

The 1963 Giants offered little challenge to the leaders after June, but the next three years found them locked to the end in tight struggles for the flag. Although they finished fourth in 1964, they were still in contention with just two games to play, in one of the closest four-way races ever. The next year they took the lead from the Dodgers early in September, only to lose it in the final week. And in 1966, in a season-long three-way race with the Dodgers and Pirates, the Giants weren't eliminated until the final day.

The turbulence of these races was reflected in the team itself. Cepeda (until traded to St. Louis in 1966) continually railed against his managers and his low pay. Alvin Dark, after four winning seasons as manager, was fired in 1964 when some of his racist comments ended up in print. And Marichal was fined and suspended for nine days in 1965 for hitting Dodgers catcher John Roseboro over the head with his bat.

After a pair of distant second-place finishes, the Giants in 1969 (with the fine work of Marichal and McCovey augmented by the speed and power of young outfielder Bobby Bonds) found themselves in the thick of a five-way race for the championship of the newly created NL West. The race wasn't settled until the final week, when Atlanta's 10-game winning streak knocked the Giants out of first. Two years later, with Bonds the chief source of offensive power and fine pitching from starters Marichal and Gaylord Perry and reliever Jerry Johnson, the Giants moved out in front at the start of the season and held their lead all the way. In the National League Championship Series, though, they succumbed to Pittsburgh with three losses after an opening-game win.

The NLCS loss signaled the end of an era. McCovey was past his prime and Marichal had enjoyed his last big year. Mays, after 20 seasons as a Giant was sent to the Mets in 1972 so he could close out his career in New York, where it began. That year the Giants suffered their first losing season in San Francisco, and attendance for the first time dropped below what it had been in their final New York season.

Attendance had reached such a low point by the mid-1970s that Stoneham negotiated the club's sale to a Canadian brewery which planned to move it to Toronto. But San Francisco's mayor George Moscone delayed the sale until a buyer could be found who would keep the Giants in the city. San Francisco realtor Robert Lurie stepped forth with half the purchase price, and Arizona cattleman Arthur "Bud" Herseth provided the rest. (Toronto settled for an expansion club, the Blue Jays.)

After six years out of the running, the Giants in 1978 played at the top of the NL West through much of the summer before dropping to third (and home attendance jumped more than a million above the previous year). But they fell below .500 the next two years—making seven losing seasons in the nine that followed their division title of 1971.

In 1982 the Giants—paced by the slugging of Jack Clark and Greg Minton's sparkling relief pitching—made one of the most impressive comebacks since divisional play was instituted in 1969, driving from 10 games below .500 to within two games of champion Atlanta at season's end. But they dropped to fifth the following year, and to a

last-place sixth in 1984 and 1985.

When Roger Craig was called on to manage the final weeks of the 1985 season, there was no stopping the Giants' slide to a club-record 100 losses. But the next year, inspiring a "can do" spirit among the players, Craig turned the club around. Veteran hurler Mike Krukow won a career-high 20 games, eight players contributed more than 40 RBIs each, and the team captured 26 of their 83 wins in their final at bat. In first place at midseason, the Giants slipped (in part because of injuries) to third by season's end, but the fans were back—over 700,000 more than a year earlier.

The club set a new home attendance record of more than 1.9 million in 1987 as it returned to the top of the NL West for the first time in 16 years. Sophomore first baseman Will Clark led a balanced offense, and several shrewd in-season acquisitions by the front office spurred a second-half drive from five games back to a six-game lead at the finish. But after taking a three-games-to-two advantage over St. Louis in the NLCS, the Giants failed to score in the final two games and the Cardinals captured the flag.

Injuries contributed to the Giants' decline to fourth place the next year, but in 1989 Clark enjoyed his strongest season yet, and left fielder Kevin Mitchell erupted with league-high power, pacing the NL in homers (47), RBIs (125), and slugging percentage (.635) to lead a San Francisco assault on the division title. For the first time, the Giants passed the 2 million mark in home attendance. After holding first place from mid-June to the finish, they pushed past the stubborn Cubs in the NLCS to win the first Giants pennant in 27 years and the 19th in franchise history. But the earthquake that delayed Game 3 of the World Series only postponed a sweep by mighty Oakland.

The Giants' downward slide over the next three years—to third place in 1990, fourth in 1991, and fifth in 1992—coincided with futile efforts to persuade Bay area voters to approve public funding for a new stadium to replace unpopular Candlestick Park. In August 1992, owner Bob Lurie arranged to sell the club to a group of investors who planned to move it to St. Petersburg, Florida. In November, though, the sale and move were blocked by the other major league owners.

The signing of free agent Barry Bonds ignited a turnaround in 1993. As Bonds put together another Ruthian season, and Matt Williams rebounded from his worst season to his best, starting pitchers John Burkett and Bill Swift developed into 20-game winners and closer Rod Beck saved the second most games (48) in NL history. The Giants lost their once-big lead to surging Atlanta in September, but revived to tie the Braves with three games to go. Although a final-game loss to Los Angeles cost them the division title, their 103 wins tied for third best in club history.

On Aug. 11, 1994, the Giants stood five games below .500, but only three and a half games out of first place in the weak NL West. Barry Bonds was enjoying another fine season at the bat, but Matt Williams' 43 home runs (within legitimate striking distance of Roger Maris' record of 61) stole the headlines. When the players went out on strike the next day, one of the most exciting offensive seasons ever went down the drain.

In 1995 manager Dusty Baker's Giants fell to last (67-77) despite Barry Bonds' 33 homers and 104 RBIs. The Giants (68-94) remained in the NL basement in 1996 as Bonds (.308, 42 HR, 129 RBIs) again compiled superstar numbers.

The Giants were transformed from "worst to first" in 1997. The additions of second baseman Jeff Kent (28 HR, 118 RBIs) and three pitchers from the White Sox (Wilson Alvarez, Roberto Hernandez, and Danny Darwin) plus the emergence of starter Shawn Estes (19-5, 3.48 ERA) helped push the Giants to the division title. The eventual world champion Florida Marlins beat the Giants twice in their last at bat on the way to a sweep in the Division Series. In 1998 the Giants put together a six-game winning in the final week of the season to come from four games behind to tie the Cubs and force a one-game playoff for the NL Wild Card. Despite a late rally by the Giants in the playoff game, the Cubs held on to win at Wrigley Field.

Seattle Mariners

The Mariners began play in 1977, returning major league baseball to the Pacific Northwest eight years after the Seattle Pilots had moved to Milwaukee after only one season. With a 64-98 inaugural season, the Mariners avoided last place in the American League West only because the Oakland A's had plummeted faster and farther. The hitting of first baseman Dan Meyer, outfielder Leroy Stanton, and rookie center fielder Ruppert Jones—who combined for 73 home runs—and the relief pitching of rookie Enrique Romo, who contributed 16 saves and eight wins, provided most of the high points of that first season.

There was less to cheer about the next year as the production of the first-season heroes fell off and the Mariners took early possession of the cellar and lost a club-record 104 games. They finished 12 games out of sixth place, 35 out of first. Much of the offense that was generated came from outfielder Leon Roberts. Acquired from Houston over the winter, Roberts became the Mariners' first .300 hitter.

The club moved up a notch in 1979, to sixth place (and Seattle also hosted that year's All-Star Game). Meyer and Jones regained much of their earlier power, first baseman Bruce Bochte hit .316 and drove in 100 runs, and DH Willie Horton, near the end of a long career, enjoyed one of his finest seasons, driving in 106 runs and leading the club with 29 homers.

As the Mariners, with the league's weakest hitting, dropped back into the cellar the next season, attendance fell to a new low, and some of the original owners decided to sell out. In January 1981 California real-estate magnate George Argyros purchased control of the club, and later bought out the remaining partners to take sole ownership.

Pitching finally arrived in 1982 in the form of Bill Caudill and rookie Ed Vande Berg. The pair, working in relief, combined for 21 wins and 31 saves. Starter Floyd Bannister led the league in strikeouts while winning 12 games (tying Caudill for the team lead), and veteran Gaylord Perry added 10 victories, including his 300th career win in May. The team finished above .450 for the first time, fourth in the AL West, a new high.

Caudill's 26 saves in 1983 couldn't prevent a slide back

into last place. But the club's farm system was beginning to produce quality talent, and 1984 saw the arrival of two standouts: first baseman Alvin Davis, whose 27 homers and 116 RBIs earned him AL Rookie of the Year honors, and pitcher Mark Langston, a 17-game winner in 1984 and AL strikeout leader in three of his first four seasons. Rookie third baseman Jim Presley hit 10 home runs in 70 games and proceeded to blossom into one of the Seattle club's leading power hitters the next year.

After sixth-place finishes in 1984 and '85, the Mariners fell off to last again in 1986. Langston's 19 wins led the team's 1987 rebound to fourth. Infielder Harold Reynolds stole his 60th base in the final game to give the Mariners their first league leader in an offensive category.

After dropping back into the cellar in 1988 and rising a notch to sixth in 1989, the Mariners revived under new ownership in 1990 to challenge the .500 barrier. Center fielder Ken Griffey, Jr., began to fulfill the promise he had shown as a 19-year-old rookie the previous summer. Sophomore hurler Erik Hanson—with 18 wins and an ERA among the league's best—replaced the traded Mark Langston as ace of a young pitching staff that compiled the league's third lowest ERA. The Mariners entered August third in the strong AL West, with a winning record which they maintained through mid-month before stumbling to fifth place with their 14th straight losing season.

At last, in 1991, Seattle produced its first winning season, rising from an even .500 with six wins in the final eight games. Griffey Jr. overcame a lackluster first half to reach new Mariner heights in batting (.327) and slugging (.527), but the club still finished fifth, and manager Jim Lefebvre was fired. It also continued to lose money, so in June 1992, as the Mariners sailed for the sixth time to the bottom of the AL West, the club was sold. The new ownership group included (for the first time) substantial local representation, but as major financing came from Hiroshi Yamauchi, the Japanese president of computer game giant Nintendo, and his son-in-law, a Washington State resident but Japanese national, the sale was delayed until jingoistic opposition to it subsided—and the deal was restructured to insure American control of the club. On the field Griffey enjoyed another strong season, and third baseman Edgar Martinez hit .343 to give Seattle its first league batting champion.

A torn hamstring sidelined Martinez much of 1993, but Griffey shone brighter than ever at the bat, and pitcher Randy Johnson finished with nine straight wins (for a 19-8 season record) and 308 strikeouts (a 15-year AL high). Their exploits lifted the Mariners into third place for a day in late September before they settled into fourth, with their second winning season ever.

In 1994 the Mariners again enjoyed stellar performances from Griffey and Johnson, but despite six straight wins before the season ended in August, they wound up 14 games below .500. In the weak AL West, though, their ministreak brought them within two games of division leader Texas—and a third place finish, their highest ever.

After a long climb during the 1995 season, the Mariners (paced by Edgar Martinez's league-leading .356 average and Randy Johnson's league-leading 294 strikeouts and 2.48 ERA) caught the Angels in the AL West division race and forced a one-game playoff. Behind Johnson, Seattle took the game and went on to nip the New York Yankees in the first round of the postseason in one of the most exciting series in baseball history. But in the ALCS the powerhouse Indians proved too much for Seattle, defeating them in six games.

Injuries to Johnson and Edgar Martinez hampered the 1996 Mariners and they slipped to second (85-76) despite shortstop Alex Rodriguez's major league-best .358 average and 54 doubles. The Mariners survived a rocky bullpen to stave off the Angels for the AL West title in 1997. Griffey earned AL MVP honors and led the league with 55 home runs, 147 RBIs, 125 runs, .646. slugging, and 393 total bases. Attendance, which topped 1 million just twice in the team's first eight seasons reached 3 million in 1997. The Mariners faltered in the Division Series, however, falling to the Orioles in four games.

Poor pitching buried the Mariners early in 1998 and not even 56 home runs from Griffey could save the Mariners from a distant third-place finish.

Tampa Bay Devil Rays

Along with the Arizona Diamondbacks, the Tampa Bay Devil Rays were granted a $130 million major league expansion franchise on March 9, 1995. The Devil Rays played their first game at the newly-renovated (and renamed) Tropicana Field in St. Petersburg on March 31, 1998. The first pitch in franchise history, by Wilson Alvarez, was a long time in coming to finally bring baseball to the Tampa area.

The White Sox had planned to move to St. Petersburg in the late 1980s and only remained in the Windy City when funding was approved for a new Comiskey Park. The Mariners had considered moving to St. Petersburg in 1991. And in late 1992 a Tampa Bay group led by businessman Vince Naimoli thought it had purchased the San Francisco Giants from Bob Lurie for $115 million, but NL owners voted against moving the club from one Bay Area to another. Naimoli was eventually awarded the Devil Rays franchise and he named Chuck LaMar as the club's first general manager. Shortly after the Florida Marlins won the 1997 World Series, Tampa Bay scooped up Marlins pitching coach Larry Rothschild and made him the team's first manager.

Rookie Rolando Arrojo, the team's first All-Star won 14 games to break the single-season expansion record. By contrast, the rest of the starters won just 25 games between them There were plenty of whiffs at Tropicana Field: Tampa Bay pitchers fanned 1,003 batters and their hitters struck out 1,101 times. Highlights of their first season included Tampa native Wade Boggs hitting the first home run in club history; Quinton McCracken setting the expansion record for hits and outfield assists; and the Devil Rays becoming the first expansion team to be four games over .500 in their first season at 10-6. Their fast start was all that kept the Devil Rays from hitting the century mark in losses as the team finished its inaugural season with the AL's worst record at 63-99.

Texas Rangers

As part of the first American League expansion, a new

Washington club was added to the league in November 1960, to replace the old Senators, who were moving to Minnesota to become the Twins. The old Senators had languished in the second division their final 14 years in Washington, and the new Senators scarcely improved on that record. In each of their first four seasons they lost 100 games or more, tying for last place in 1961 and holding down the bottom all by themselves for two years before rising to ninth in 1964.

Although as an expansion team the new Senators had to make do at first with expendable players from the established clubs, they were not devoid of talent. In their first season, pitcher Dick Donovan led the league with a 2.40 earned run average, though injuries and the lack of offensive support held his won-lost record to 10-10. Perhaps their most promising player, he was traded with two teammates to Cleveland for outfielder Jimmy Piersall. Piersall proved a major disappointment in Washington, batting only .244 while Donovan was winning 20 games for his new club.

Not all the Senators' trades proved disastrous. In late 1964 they sent another promising pitcher— Claude Osteen—to the Dodgers in a deal that brought them five players, including third baseman Ken McMullen and outfielder Frank Howard. Osteen blossomed into a consistent winner in Los Angeles, but at the same time, McMullen brought strength to the Washington infield and Howard became one of the league's offensive stars.

The Senators' blend of youth and experience jelled in 1969 under rookie manager Ted Williams, as several key players—including McMullen and Howard—enjoyed career-best seasons. The club finished above .500 for the first time, driving with a late-season spurt to within a game of third-place Boston in the league's Eastern Division.

But 1969 was a one-year phenomenon. After losing seasons in 1970 and '71 (and the loss of much of their fan support), owner Bob Short pulled up stakes and moved the club to Arlington, Texas (midway between Fort Worth and Dallas), where, as the Texas Rangers, they have been ever since. Their first summer in Texas resembled their first in Washington: they lost 100 games (despite a strike-shortened season) and finished last. Williams was replaced by a new rookie manager—Whitey Herzog—but the club did no better in 1973.

Before the season's end Herzog gave way to Billy Martin. Martin came too late to save the Rangers from another lost season, but the next year he spurred the team to the kind of turnaround Williams had managed five years earlier. Behind the 25-12 pitching of Ferguson Jenkins (acquired in the offseason from the Cubs) and the hitting of league MVP Jeff Burroughs and AL Rookie of the Year Mike Hargrove, the Rangers spurted in the second half of 1974 from a sub-.500 record to second place in the American League West, only five games behind Oakland.

The Rangers rebounded from two losing seasons to their finest season yet in 1977 (94-68, .580) and second place, behind strong pitching and the blooming of Jim Sundberg as a hitter to go along with his league-leading catching. The return of Fergie Jenkins (after two years in Boston), the sparkling 11-5 season of rookie Steve Comer, and a September surge kept the club competitive

in 1978. Jim Kern's brilliant relief work the next season helped the club recover from a nosedive in July and August to edge Minnesota for a strong third-place finish.

After a losing season in 1980, the Rangers bounced back in 1981 to record their second-best winning percentage ever (.543)—and finishes of second and third in the two halves of the strike-divided season. Then they slipped below .500 again for four more years. Pitcher Charlie Hough's knuckleball, and strong seasons at the bat from Pete O'Brien, Larry Parrish, Scott Fletcher, and rookie Pete Incaviglia helped new manager Bobby Valentine guide the Rangers to a second-place finish after last-place seasons in 1984 and '85.

Once more, though, the turnaround was brief: in 1987 losses in their final games of the season dropped the Rangers into a tie at the bottom of the division, and in 1988 they finished only two games out of the cellar, in sixth place.

A group of investors headed by George W. Bush—the President's son—purchased control of the Rangers in March 1989, and strikeout king Nolan Ryan returned to the American League as a Ranger after nine years in Houston. The strong arms of starter Ryan (who recorded his 5,000th career strikeout during the season) and reliever Jeff Russell, the potent bats of outfielder Ruben Sierra and second baseman Julio Franco (newly acquired from Cleveland), and a 10-1 start that put the club in first place for a month (before they settled back to fourth) highlighted a return to the winning side of the ledger. In 1990 Ryan hurled his 300th win and sixth no-hitter, first baseman Rafael Palmeiro peaked at the plate, and pitcher Bobby Witt enjoyed his finest season, with 17 wins. After a slow first half, the Rangers rose from sixth place to third, compiling an 83-79 record identical to that of the year before.

A 14-game win streak in May 1991 boosted the Rangers into first place for several days, although they again finished third. Jose Guzman joined Ryan (who fashioned a seventh no-hitter) among the league's top pitchers, and young slugger Juan Gonzalez formed with Franco, Palmeiro, and Sierra a powerful quartet that made the Rangers the top scoring team in the majors. In 1992 pitcher Kevin Brown won 21 games, and Gonzalez topped the majors in home runs. But an overall decline in offense, and disastrous fielding and relief pitching dropped the team below .500 after a competitive first half as manager Valentine was fired in July. In the year's biggest in-season trade, the club acquired Jose Canseco from Oakland for Sierra, Witt, and Russell.

The Rangers surged to within a game of first place in mid-July 1993 and remained competitive into September, finishing second. Canseco injured his elbow in a relief pitching stint in June and was lost for the season, but Gonzalez again led the league in home runs (with 46), while also leading his team in batting and RBIs. Nolan Ryan retired after an injury-shortened season, and as the Rangers ended their tenure at Texas Stadium, their new home arose on the other side of the parking lot.

In the weak AL West of 1994, it didn't matter that the Rangers played losing ball in the new Ballpark in Arlington. Despite their worst record in six years—a .456 winning percentage that would have consigned them to the cellar of the East or Central divisions—the Rangers were

a game ahead of Oakland, in first place, when the strike ended the season. Texas's won-lost percentage improved to .538 in 1995 but that was only good enough for third.

In 1996 the Rangers (90-72) won their first division title on the heavy hitting of MVP Juan Gonzalez (47 HR, 144 RBIs), Dean Palmer (38 HR, 107 RBIs), Rusty Greer (.321, 100 RBIs), and Kevin Elster (24 HR, 99 RBIs). The Rangers boasted an unusually well-balanced rotation—Ken Hill (16-10), Roger Pavlik (15-8), Bobby Witt (16-12), and Darren Oliver (14-6)—along with reliever Mike Henneman (31 saves) and late season addition John Burkett (5-2). The Yankees, however, rolled over Texas in the first round of the postseason despite five home runs by Gonzalez.

Johnny Oates, who shared AL Manager of the Year honors in 1996, could do little with the Rangers in 1997. The most significant thing that happened in Texas was the first-ever interleague game on June 12; later in the month, Texas starter Bobby Witt became the first AL pitcher to homer in the regular season in 25 years. The Rangers jousted with the Angels for first place in the AL West for much of 1998 before they swept Anaheim in the final week of the season to capture the title. Trades for Royce Clayton and Todd Zeille revitalized the left side of the infield while new acquisition Todd Stottlemyre won several big games down the stretch. Juan Gonzalez, who had 100 RBIs at the All-Star break, drove in 157 runs and won his second AL MVP. Rick Helling became the third 20-game winner in Rangers history and John Wetteland set the club record with 42 saves. Just as in 1996, they ran into the Yankees in the Division Series and the Rangers were quickly dispatched.

Toronto Blue Jays

For a while, in February 1976, it looked as if the National League's San Francisco Giants would move to Toronto, where there were buyers eager for the club. But when the Giants were sold in March to new owners determined to keep them in San Francisco, the American League jumped in to establish Toronto as an American League city, setting up an expansion club, the Blue Jays, who began play the next year.

It took seven years for the Jays to lift themselves out of last place in the seven-team American League East. For five years they had the cellar all to themselves, never finishing closer than 11 games behind the sixth-place club.

In their first season, the Jays' 107 losses left them 45½ games out of first, as the team performed at the bottom of the division in hitting, fielding, and pitching. In 1978 their fielding improved dramatically, but the Jays still lost over 100 games, and there was little doubt after April who would finish last.

The next year was the team's worst ever. While every other Eastern Division club was compiling a winning record, Toronto plunged relentlessly downward and, despite a brief rally in September, finished 28½ games out of sixth place (50½ out of first), with 109 losses.

The club's turnaround began in 1980. It was late June before the Jays began their drop away from the rest of the division, and for the first time they finished with fewer than 100 losses. Pitchers Jim Clancy and Dave Stieb each had an ERA below 4.00 for the first time, and newly acquired second baseman Damaso Garcia combined with shortstop Alfredo Griffin to form the league's best double-play combination. There were still two more seasons in the cellar, but in strike-divided 1981 the Jays played a creditable second half for the first time, and in 1982 they spurted in September to tie the Indians for sixth at season's end. Garcia in 1982 became a .300 hitter and a leading base stealer, Clancy put together his first winning season and Stieb his second, and Stieb's five shutouts led the league.

In 1983, with seven of the Blue Jays' eight principal pitchers enjoying winning seasons, and the Jays' hitters leading the league in team batting and slugging, Toronto recorded its first winning season—in fourth place, only nine games out of first. Their balanced pitching and offense carried them to a repeat 89-73 record in 1984—this time for second place (though they finished a distant 15 games behind Detroit).

In 1985 the Blue Jays topped their division with 99 victories, edging the Yankees by two games. Their pitching was better than ever. Doyle Alexander won 17 games, Jimmy Key and Dave Stieb contributed 14 each, and reliever Dennis Lamp compiled an impressive 11-0 record. Stieb led the league in ERA, with Key fourth. Tony Fernandez, in his first full big league season, sparkled as expected at short, but also proved unexpectedly solid at the bat. Eight Jays drove in more than 50 runs, with outfielders George Bell (95), Jesse Barfield (84), and Lloyd Moseby (71) pacing the club's balanced attack.

In the ALCS the Jays won three of their first four games against Kansas City, but lost the next three—and the pennant. Equally discouraging was their drop to fourth place in 1986. Barfield, Bell, and Fernandez all improved at the plate, but the league-leading pitchers of 1985 dropped back to the middle of the pack in '86 (though rookie Mark Eichorn sparkled in long relief).

Toronto sprang back stronger than ever in 1987. Jim Clancy (15-11, 3.54 ERA) enjoyed his best season yet, as did Jimmy Key (17-8), whose 2.76 ERA led the league. Once again, as in 1985, the team ERA was the league's lowest. And the offense remained strong. (George Bell, league RBI leader with 134, was named the American League MVP at season's end.) The Jays led their division going into the season's final series against second-place Detroit, though four straight losses had reduced the lead to just one game. Needing to win two of the three games to take the AL East title, or one to tie the Tigers and force a playoff, Toronto lost the first two games. In the season finale, Jimmy Key hurled a three-hitter, striking out eight. But one of the hits was a home run—the only run of the game, as it turned out. Toronto's seven-game losing streak had cost them what would have been their second title in three years.

In 1988, a rocky season made worse by George Bell's feud with manager Jimy Williams (who wanted the unwilling outfielder to serve as designated hitter), the Jays surged at the end—with six straight wins—into a tie for third place. Dave Steib pitched two one-hitters in September, both of which were no-hitters through 8⅔ innings.

When Toronto's front office replaced manager Williams with batting coach Cito Gaston in mid-May 1989,

the Jays were drowning near the bottom of the AL East with a record of 12-24. By mid-August they had bobbed above .500 to stay, and on Sept. 1 replaced Baltimore in first place. With a pair of one-run victories over the Orioles at the end of September, the Jays preserved their narrow lead and clinched the division title. But Oakland outplayed them in the ALCS, taking the pennant in five games.

From mid-June 1990 to the final day of the season, the Blue Jays battled Boston for the division lead before settling for second. Dave Stieb (after two more one-hitters in 1989) at last hurled a no-hitter, and third baseman Kelly Gruber earned a place with Bell and McGriff among Toronto's power elite. But the brightest Toronto star of 1989-90 was the new SkyDome, with its 11,000-ton retractable roof and its restaurants and hotel rooms above the outfield wall. After the Jays moved into the Dome on June 5, 1989, attendance zoomed, and by season's end the club set a new American League home attendance record of nearly 3.4 million. In 1990, with a full season in the Dome, the Jays attracted a new major league record of 3,885,284. Attendance surpassed 4 million in 1991 and 1992.

McGriff and Bell had departed by 1991, but an improved Devon White, plus newly acquired slugger Joe Carter and second-baseman Roberto Alomar, led an offense that—together with the league's stingiest pitching staff—brought the Jays through a tight race to their third divisional title. For the third time, though, they crashed in the ALCS, this time trampled by Minnesota in five games. With the addition of a pair of free-agent veterans—pitcher Jack Morris (who went 21-6) and Dave Winfield (108 RBIs)—Toronto in 1992 finally completed the puzzle. The Jays sported a balanced offense (six players drove in 60 runs or more) and outstanding pitching from starter Juan Guzman (16-5; 2.64 ERA) and relievers Tom Henke and Duane Ward. In the ALCS the Jays defeated Oakland in six games to bring Canada its first major league baseball pennant, and then they stopped stubborn Atlanta in six games to carry home the championship of the world.

Nearly half the team was new in 1993, but after a tight battle with several clubs through most of the season, the Blue Jays pulled away to capture their fourth divisional title in five years, by a comfortable seven-game margin. John Olerud hit over .400 through the first half of the season and finished with a league-high .363. Paul Molitor, signed from Milwaukee as a free agent, hit better than anyone else in the league from midseason on, and finished second in the AL. Together with Roberto Alomar, Olerud and Molitor became the first teammates since 1893 to take the top three spots in a major league batting race. In the ALCS the Blue Jays bowled over the Chicago White Sox for the AL pennant in six games. The World Series wasn't necessarily pretty (Toronto beat the Philadelphia Phillies in Game 4 by a dizzying 15-14 score), but it was memorable. Joe Carter's two-out, three-run home run off Mitch Williams in climactic Game 6 made it just the second World Series to end on a home run.

The glory faded fast in 1994. At the July All-Star break the Blue Jays lay at the bottom of the AL East. While they pulled themselves up to third before the players' strike ended the season in August, they remained 16 games out of first, their first losing season in a dozen years. The losing continued in 1995 as the Jays stripped their roster of most of the veterans of its world championship squad. Toronto tied Minnesota for the dubious honor of worst won-lost record (56-88).

Toronto edged up slightly in 1996, to fourth (74-88) in the AL East. Pat Hentgen (20-10, 181 strikeouts) won the 1996 AL Cy Young Award and Roger Clemens—with a league-leading 21 wins, 2.05 ERA, and 292 strikeouts—kept the award in Toronto in 1997. Clemens won it again in 1998 (his record fifth Cy Young), in a season in which he earned his 3,000th strikeout, ended the year with 15 consecutive wins, and copped his second consecutive Triple Crown. Offensively, Jose Canseco socked 46 home runs and Tony Fernandez batted .321 in his third tour of duty with the Blue Jays. Led by new manager Tim Johnson, who replaced Cito Gaston, Toronto made a late run at the Red Sox for the AL Wild Card. The Blue Jays won 11 straight games and 14 of 16 in the closing weeks of the season, but Toronto finished four games behind Boston.

Defunct Clubs

In addition to the many Negro League teams, some 112 ballclubs have played in the major leagues since the first professional association was formed in 1871. The 30 that still do are described above; here are the other 82, listed according to the league and year in which they first played major league ball. Official club names precede the name of the city; nicknames follow.

National Association, 1871-1875

Two of the 23 clubs that played at one time or another in baseball's first professional league still play in the majors: the Atlanta Braves (then the Boston Red Stockings) and the Chicago Cubs (then the White Stockings). The other 21 are:

Athletic of Philadelphia: NA 1871-1875, NL 1876. Organized in 1860 as an amateur club, the Athletics became one of the dominant teams of the decade. As professionals they won the first NA pennant in 1871. After one year in the NL, they were expelled for failing to make the final western trip of the season.

Forest City of Cleveland, NA 1871-1872. In the midst of a second losing season, the club disbanded in August 1872.

Forest City of Rockford, Ill., NA 1871. As an amateur club, Forest City (with its 16-year-old pitcher Al Spalding) was the only team to defeat the famous Washington Nationals on their pioneering midwestern tour of 1867. As professionals, Forest City finished seventh of the nine NA teams in 1871.

Kekionga of Fort Wayne, NA 1871. The Kekiongas won the first NA game ever played but dropped out of the association before the end of the season.

Mutual of New York, NA 1871-1875, NL 1876. Organized as an amateur club in 1857, the Mutuals were said to be backed financially by New York's notorious William M. "Boss" Tweed. Frequently accused of corrupt prac-

tices, the club was one of the leading eastern teams of the late 1860s. They were declared national champions of 1868 and proclaimed themselves national champions of 1870. On the demise of the NA the Mutuals entered the NL, but they were expelled after one season (along with the Athletics) for failing to play their final games in the West.

Olympic of Washington, D.C., NA 1871-1872. Unsuccessful in 1872 after playing well the year before, the Olympics disbanded about midseason.

Union of Troy, N.Y., NA 1871-1872. The Haymakers, as they were popularly known, dropped out of the NA halfway through the 1872 season.

Atlantic of Brooklyn, NA 1872-1875. One of the greatest of the amateur clubs, the Atlantics (organized in 1855) went undefeated in 1864 and 1865 and won three successive national championships, 1864-1866. But in four NA seasons their combined won-lost record was only 49-139, including a dismal 2-42 in 1875.

Eckford of Brooklyn, NA 1872. Another great early amateur club—like the Atlantics, organized in 1855— they won the national championship in 1862 and again (with an undefeated season of 10 games) the next year. The Eckfords actually joined the NA in August 1871, replacing Kekionga, but their 1871 games were later erased from the record because they had failed to enter the association at the start of the season.

Lord Baltimore of Baltimore, NA 1872-1874. After twice finishing third, the Lord Baltimores (or "Canaries," for their yellow silk jerseys) disbanded two games before the end of the 1874 season, while in last place.

Mansfield of Middletown, Conn., NA 1872. Disbanded in late August.

National of Washington, D.C., NA 1872-1873, 1875. Organized as amateurs in 1859, the Nationals were the first eastern club to tour as far west as Chicago and St. Louis. After skipping the 1874 race, the Nationals re-entered the NA in 1875, but dropped out in July.

Maryland of Baltimore, NA 1873. Dropped out after only six games.

Philadelphia, NA 1873-1875. Known successively as the "White Stockings," "Pearls," and "Phillies," the team finished a strong second to Boston in their first season, but slipped to fourth and fifth the next two years.

Resolute of Elizabeth, N.J, NA 1873. Disbanded in August with a 2-21 record.

Hartford Dark Blues, NA 1874-1875, NL 1876-1877. After a weak first season, the Dark Blues finished third in its next three seasons, as standings are presently reckoned. But by the 1876 guidelines (which used the number of games won rather than winning percentage), Hartford that year placed second. In 1877 the club played its home games in Brooklyn, N.Y.

Centennial of Philadelphia, NA 1875. Dropped out in late May.

New Haven Elm Citys, NA 1875. Failed to play out their schedule.

St. Louis Brown Stockings, NA 1875, NL 1876-1877. George Bradley pitched all but five of the Browns' 39 wins in 1875, when they finished fourth, and all 45 victories in 1876, when they finished a strong third in number of victories; they were second in winning percentage. With Bradley lost to Chicago the next year, St. Louis dropped below .500—and out of the league.

St. Louis Red Stockings, NA 1875. A successful amateur club that decided to take a fling at pro ball, the Red Stockings played only a few games in the NA.

Western of Keokuk, Iowa, NA 1875. Disbanded in mid-June.

National League, 1876-

When the NL was founded to replace the ill-organized NA, it included six of the stronger NA clubs plus independent clubs in Cincinnati and Louisville. The league's composition was in continual flux to the end of the century as clubs were dropped and added, shrinking the league to as few as six teams and expanding it to as many as 12. Two clubs that first played major league ball in the NL still do: the Philadelphia Phillies and the San Francisco (originally New York) Giants, both organized in 1883. (The Boston and Chicago franchises—that continue to this day as the Atlanta Braves and Chicago Cubs—had their starts in the National Association.) Those that have not survived:

Cincinnati Red Stockings, NL 1876-1880. From last place in 1876 (and 1877, when their games were not counted because of the club's reorganization and failure to pay its dues), the Reds—with seven new regulars—rose to second in 1878, only to fall back to fifth in 1879 and last again in 1880. That fall, when they refused to accept a new rule abolishing liquor sales and Sunday baseball on club grounds, they were dropped from league membership.

Louisville Grays, NL 1876-1877. The strong Louisville team led the league in mid-August 1877, but seven suspicious losses to chief rivals Boston and Hartford dropped the Grays out of first place. After Boston clinched the pennant, Louisville revived to secure second place, but four players—including pitching ace Jim Devlin—were expelled from baseball for throwing games. Their expulsion showed the NL's determination to wipe out corruption, but it also caused the St. Louis Browns, who had planned to sign three of the four Louisville players for 1878, to resign from the league. Louisville, too, dropped out of the league before the next season, unable to find adequate replacements for the four.

Indianapolis Browns, NL 1878. Finished fifth of six teams.

Milwaukee Grays (or Cream Citys), NL 1878. Finished a last-place sixth, 26 games back of Boston.

Providence Grays, NL 1878-1885. One of the great teams in the NL's early years, Providence won pennants in 1879 and 1884, finishing no lower than third in seven of their eight seasons. In 1884, pitcher Charley "Old Hoss"

Radbourn won a record 59 games, then pitched the Grays to victory in baseball's first World Series with a three-game sweep of the American Association champion New York Mets. But as they dropped to fourth place the next year, finishing for the first time below .500, their fans deserted them. Late that autumn the club was dissolved.

Buffalo Bisons, NL 1879-1885. Buffalo moved up to the majors after winning the International Association pennant in 1878. Jim "Pud" Galvin pitched nearly 70 percent of Buffalo's victories as he led them to four first-division finishes in seven big league seasons. First baseman Dan Brouthers, in his five years with Buffalo, twice won the batting title and led NL sluggers five times.

Cleveland Blues, NL 1879-1884. Cleveland's fortunes rested in large measure with pitcher Jim McCormick (who also managed the club their first two seasons). In 1880, their best season, McCormick won a career-high 45 games to bring the Blues in third. In 1883 Cleveland was in first place when McCormick's injured arm put him out for the season after he had won 23 games. The Blues dropped to fourth. The club folded after a seventh-place finish in 1884, a season that saw McCormick and two other Blues jump to the Union Association.

Stars of Syracuse, NL 1879. After finishing a close second to Buffalo in the International League in 1878, the Stars moved up with the Bisons to the NL, but disbanded after a single unsuccessful season.

Troy, N.Y., Trojans, NL 1879-1882. After four losing seasons the franchise was expelled to make room for a club in New York City.

Worcester, Mass., Brown Stockings, NL 1880-1882. After a pair of losing minor league seasons, Worcester was admitted to the NL to replace the defunct Stars of Syracuse. After finishing a respectable fifth in 1880, Worcester dropped into the cellar for two seasons before being ousted in 1883 for a new Philadelphia club.

Detroit Wolverines, NL 1881-1888. Buffalo's sale of its "big four" (Dan Brouthers, Hardy Richardson, Jack Rowe, and Deacon White) to Detroit late in 1885 transformed a perennial also-ran into a contender. The club finished second in 1886 and won the pennant in 1887. In a World Series played in 10 different cities, the Wolverines trounced St. Louis 10 games to five. In 1888, after finishing fifth, they expired.

Kansas City Cowboys, NL 1886. They finished seventh, 58½ games out.

Washington Senators, NL 1886-1889. In their four seasons, the Senators finished out of the cellar only once: next to last in 1887.

Indianapolis Hoosiers, NL 1887-1889. After dropping below Washington into the cellar in 1887, the Hoosiers and Senators traded places for their final two years.

American Association, 1882-1891

Three of the six clubs that formed the AA in 1882 still represent their cities in the majors today: Allegheny (Pittsburgh), Cincinnati, and St. Louis. Brooklyn, which entered the AA two years later, today represents Los Angeles. The others:

Athletic of Philadelphia, AA 1882-1890. After finishing a distant second in the AA's first season, the Athletics in 1883 took the pennant from St. Louis by a single game. First baseman Harry Stovey, who led AA batters in most offensive categories that year, was even more productive in 1884. The A's dropped to seventh and never challenged for the crown again. Expelled from the AA after the 1890 season for financial reasons, they were replaced by the Philadelphia club from the defunct Players League.

Baltimore Orioles, AA 1882-1889, 1890-1891, NL 1892-1899. After eight seasons out of pennant contention (including four in last place), the Orioles dropped out of the AA to play minor league ball in 1890. Toward the end of the season, when Brooklyn's new franchise went under, the Orioles returned to complete Brooklyn's season (finishing a combined last). After rising to third in 1891, the AA's final year, the Orioles were invited into the expanding NL, where they dropped to a 12th-place last (54½ games out) in 1892.

Ned Hanlon, hired to manage Baltimore early in the 1892 season, set about building a championship club. By 1894, with a lineup that included six future Hall of Famers, Hanlon led his club to a narrow pennant victory over New York, though the Giants swept the Orioles in the first Temple Cup World Series, 4-0.

For five years Hanlon's brand of scrappy, hustling play made the Orioles the terror of the NL. Led by shortstop Hughie Jennings and outfielders Willie Keeler and Joe Kelley, the club repeated as NL champions in 1895 and 1896, and finished second to Boston the next two years. They lost the Temple Cup to Cleveland (four games to one) in 1895, but swept the Spiders the next year, 4-0, and took the cup again in 1897, defeating Boston, 4-1, in what turned out to be the Series swan song.

Baltimore owners Hanlon and Harry Von der Horst purchased a half-interest in the Brooklyn club in 1899 (retaining a half-interest in Baltimore), and switched Jennings, Kelley, and Keeler to Brooklyn. Hanlon also went over as manager, leaving third baseman John McGraw in charge of the Orioles. McGraw hit .391 and rookie pitcher Joe McGinnity won 28 games to bring the team in fourth. But Hanlon's Superbas won the pennant, and, when the NL cut back to eight teams after the season, Baltimore got the ax.

Eclipse of Louisville/Louisville Colonels (or Cyclones), AA 1882-1891, NL 1892-1899. The club, which changed its official name from Eclipse to Louisville after the 1883 season, was one of only two teams to play all 10 seasons of the major league AA. (St. Louis—the present Cardinals—was the other.) Louisville finished above .500 in five of its first six years, but only once in that time closed within 10 games of the top—in 1884, when Guy Hecker's 52 wins brought the team in third. Slugger Pete Browning paced the offense in their early years, winning batting titles in 1882 (his rookie season), 1885, and 1886, and hammering a second-best .402 in 1887. (A bat made for him by woodworker John Hillerich inspired the creation of the Louisville Slugger.)

By 1889, though, the club had sunk to last place, finish-

ing 66½ games out of first, with 111 losses. The next year, although Hecker and Browning defected to the outlaw PL, the club was less affected by deserters than other AA teams. The Colonels (paced by the league's best hitter, William "Chicken" Wolf, and its best pitcher, Scott Stratton) made one of the greatest turnarounds in big league history, winning the pennant by 10 games over second-place Columbus. In the World Series against Brooklyn, poor weather and small crowds ended play after the teams had tied once and won three apiece.

Even though the Colonels finished next to last in 1891, they were one of four clubs taken into the NL after the AA folded. They never finished higher than ninth in the NL, and for three straight years (1894-1896) they occupied the cellar. When the league cut back from 12 teams to eight after the 1899 season, Louisville merged with the Pittsburgh Pirates.

Columbus Colts (or Senators), AA 1883-1884. From sixth place in 1883, Columbus climbed to second in 1884 behind the 34-13 pitching of rookie Ed Morris. But when the AA dropped back from 12 clubs to eight in 1885, Columbus was out.

Metropolitan of New York, AA 1883-1887. After success in minor league and independent play since 1880, the Mets entered the AA in 1883 as the association expanded from six clubs to eight. With 41 victories from pitcher Tim Keefe (who was picked up from disbanded Troy), the Mets finished fourth. The next season, with first baseman Dave Orr hitting .354 in his first full major league season and pitcher Jack Lynch matching Keefe with 37 wins apiece, the Mets won the AA pennant handily. But they lost baseball's first World Series to the Providence Grays. When manager Jim Mutrie, third baseman Dude Esterbrook, and pitcher Keefe were transferred in 1885 to the New York Giants (the two clubs had the same owner), the Mets sank to seventh place, where they finished in their final three seasons.

Indianapolis Blues, AA 1884. Finished 11th of 12 clubs, 46 games behind.

Toledo Blue Stockings, AA 1884. Catcher Fleet Walker (who played in 42 games) and his brother Welday (five games) were the major leagues' first black players and the only blacks until Jackie Robinson broke the color bar for good in 1947.

Washington, D.C., AA 1884. The popularity of the city's Union Association Nationals proved too much for this inept AA club, which went under in early August.

Virginia of Richmond, AA 1884. When Washington disbanded in August, the Wilmington club of the Eastern League was invited to join the AA as its replacement. Wilmington declined (and later jumped to the UA), but Virginia—also a member of the EL—accepted the invitation and took over Washington's remaining games. Washington-Virginia finished a combined 24-81, in last place.

Cleveland Spiders, AA 1887-1888, NL 1889-1899. After two losing seasons in the AA, the Spiders moved to the NL, where they continued below .500 for three more years. But in 1892 Cy Young's league-leading pitching brought them the second-half championship of the league's experimental split season. Cleveland lost the World Series to first-half winner Boston, losing five after tying the first game.

Second-place finishes in 1895 and 1896 qualified the Spiders for the Temple Cup series against champion Baltimore. In 1895 they beat the Orioles for the world title four games to one, but were swept the next year.

In 1899, when owner Frank Robison transferred all the team's best players to St. Louis (which he also owned), Cleveland suffered the worst season in major league history, winning only 20 games while losing a record 134. They finished 35 games behind 11th-place Washington and 84 games out of first. After the season the Spiders died, as the NL cut back from 12 teams to eight.

Kansas City Blues, AA 1888-1889. Finished last in 1888, next to last in 1889.

Columbus Colts (or Solons), AA 1889-1891. In 1890, with the AA weakened by the replacement of half its franchises with new clubs and by defections to the outlaw PL, Columbus (which retained several of its regulars) rose from its 1889 sixth-place finish to second behind Louisville. When the PL folded and the defectors returned in 1891, Columbus dropped back to sixth.

Brooklyn Gladiators, AA 1890. Formed as a replacement for the Brooklyn club that forsook the AA for the NL in 1890, the Gladiators floundered and were replaced by Baltimore late in the season.

Rochesters, AA 1890. Played .500 ball, finishing fifth.

Syracuse Stars, AA 1890. Finished sixth.

Toledo Maumees, AA 1890. Finished fourth.

Cincinnati Porkers, AA 1891. Also known as "Kelly's Killers" for their manager Mike "King" Kelly, the club went bankrupt in August and was replaced by Milwaukee.

Milwaukee Brewers, AA 1891. This Western League club moved up to the AA in August. Taking five players and the 43-57 record from the defunct Cincinnati club, Milwaukee went 21-15 the rest of the way to lift the Cincinnati-Milwaukee combination from seventh to fifth by season's end.

Washington Senators, AA 1891, NL 1892-1899. Despite a cellar finish in the AA's final year, the Senators were taken into the expanding NL. Of its nine losing seasons, the best was a tie for sixth in the 12-team NL of 1897.

Union Association, 1884

Formed in opposition to the reserve rule that governed players in the National League and American Association, the Union Association struggled through one season. The first eight clubs listed here began the season. The other five are listed according to the month they entered the UA as replacement teams. All 13—like the Union Association itself—are long extinct:

Altoona, Pa., Unions, UA 1884. The first of several Union Association clubs to drop out of competition during the season, Altoona disbanded on May 31, but reorganized as an independent club two days later with many of

the same players taking the field.

Baltimore Unions, UA 1884. Bill Sweeney's league-leading 40 wins accounted for 70 percent of third-place Baltimore's victories.

Boston Unions, UA 1884. Outfielder Tom McCarthy, the UA's only Hall of Famer, hit .215 in this, his rookie big league season. Boston finished fourth.

Chicago Browns/Pittsburgh Stogies, UA 1884. Financial woes caused the Chicago Browns to relocate in Pittsburgh in late August, but the club quit altogether less than a month later.

Cincinnati Outlaw Reds, UA 1884. With three 20-game winners—including Jim McCormick, who won 21 after defecting from the NL in midseason—Cincinnati compiled a strong 69-36 record, but still finished 21 games behind champion St. Louis.

Keystone of Philadelphia, UA 1884. In early August Keystone dropped out of the league and reorganized as an independent semipro club.

National of Washington, D.C., UA 1884. Finished sixth, 46½ games back.

St. Louis Maroons, UA 1884, NL 1885-1886. Batting 47 points above the league average, the Maroons scored 184 runs more than the next-best club to run away with the pennant. They were the only UA club to survive 1884 as a major league team. In the NL, where they were dubbed "the black diamonds," because of their previously expelled players, they were unable to fashion a winning season or finish higher than sixth.

Kansas City Unions, UA 1884. Formed to replace Altoona, Kansas City went 16-63 in its partial season.

Wilmington, Del., UA 1884. After Wilmington had gone 51-12 to sew up the Eastern League championship, they jumped to the UA in August to replace Philadelphia's Keystones. But as several players failed to make the jump with them, the move was a disaster on the field (2-16) and financially. They failed in mid-September.

Milwaukee Grays, UA 1884. One of only two teams left in the deteriorating Northwestern League, Milwaukee moved up to the UA in September to complete the schedule of dropout Pittsburgh.

St. Paul White Caps, UA 1884. With the disbanding of the Northwestern League in September, St. Paul joined the UA to take over Wilmington's remaining games.

Players League, 1890

Formed in rebellion against the NL owner John T. Brush's classification plan, a scheme to limit players' pay, the PL drew many of the finest players from the NL and AA, and proved the most popular league with the fans. But when only one club turned a profit, the clubs' financial backers deserted and the league died. Two clubs were admitted to the AA, and many of the rest merged with their National League counterparts:

Boston Red Stockings, PL 1890, AA 1891. Boston won the PL pennant with such stars as Dan Brouthers, Charley Radbourn, Hardy Richardson, and manager Michael "King" Kelly. The only PL club to make money, Boston joined the AA the next year and won another pennant. But when the popular Kelly defected to Boston's NL Beaneaters (who also won a pennant for the city in 1891), the fans defected too, and the Red Stockings died along with the AA at the end of the season.

Brooklyn Wonders, PL 1890. At the end of a season in which they edged New York for second place, the Wonders merged with Brooklyn's NL pennant-winners.

Buffalo Bisons, PL 1890. After a last-place finish 20 games back of their nearest competitor, the Bisons simply went out of business.

Chicago Pirates, PL 1890. Mark Baldwin, with a league-high 34 wins, and Charles "Silver" King, with 30, pitched Chicago into fourth place. Both went to Pittsburgh the next year, although the franchise was absorbed by Chicago's NL Colts.

Cleveland Infants, PL 1890. Like Cleveland's NL Spiders of 1890, the Infants finished next to last. But one of their three managers, infielder Oliver Wendell "Patsy" Tebeau, would go on to lead the Spiders to their finest seasons.

Philadelphia Quakers, PL 1890, Athletic AA 1891. Although they finished sixth in their PL season, the Quakers compiled a winning record. When the Athletics of the AA were expelled following the 1890 season, the Quakers were admitted in their place and awarded the name "Athletic." The team finished fourth in 1891, but was not among the four clubs taken into the NL when the AA folded, because Philadelphia already had an NL team (the Phillies).

New York Giants, PL 1890. Paced by the hitting of first baseman Roger Connor and outfielder Jim O'Rourke, New York's PL Giants finished third. In November the club merged with the city's NL Giants.

Pittsburgh Burghers, PL 1890. After a sixth-place finish, the Pittsburgh PL club and the NL Allegheny Club combined to form the new Pittsburgh Athletic Club, which still represents Pittsburgh in the NL.

American League, 1901-

When Western League president Ban Johnson renamed the circuit in 1900 and proclaimed it a major league the next year, he little knew how stable it would be. For over half a century (1903-1953) the same eight clubs represented the same eight cities. Even today, although the league has expanded and several clubs have moved to new cities, not one franchise has perished.

Federal League, 1914-1915

After an inaugural season as a six-team minor league in 1913, the FL expanded to eight teams and declared war on the NL and AL for their players. After two big league seasons, and despite two of the game's most exciting pennant races ever, the league died for lack of patronage, and with it went its eight franchises:

Baltimore Terrapins, FL 1914-1915. Jack Quinn and George Suggs, with 26 and 25 wins, pitched Baltimore to third place in 1914. But when Quinn and Suggs lost their stuff the next year, the club sank out of sight, 24 games behind seventh-place Brooklyn.

Brooklyn Tip-Tops (or Brookfeds), FL 1914-1915. The Brookfeds finished fifth in 1915 and not even the acquisition of batting and base-stealing champ Benny Kauff could stop Brooklyn from slipping to seventh the next year.

Buffalo Buffeds, FL 1914-1915. Finished fourth in 1914, sixth the next year.

Chicago Chifeds (or Whales), FL 1914-1915. After leading the league through July and much of August in 1914, only to lose out after a late-season struggle with Indianapolis, the Whales came back in 1915 to triumph in an even tighter race that saw the three top teams separated at the finish by only half a game. Owner Charles Weeghman was permitted to buy the NL Cubs in 1916, and many Whales joined the Cubs to play at what was then Weeghman Park and is now known as Wrigley Field.

Indianapolis Federals (or Hoosiers), FL 1914; Newark Peps, FL 1915. Five regulars hit over .300 (paced by Benny Kauff's league-leading .370) in 1914, and the team as a whole hit 22 points above the league average. From fourth place in August the Hoosiers fought back to capture the flag from Chicago by 1½ games, with seven consecutive wins at the end. The only major league pennant winner to move to a new city the next year, the Hoosiers became the Peps in 1915. Though they remained competitive into September, an eight-game losing streak dropped them out of the race and they finished fifth.

Kansas City Packers, FL 1914-1915. After a sixth-place finish in 1914, the Packers competed in a five-way race through much of 1915. But from first place on Aug. 21 they dropped to fifth a week later and finished fourth.

Pittsburgh Rebels, FL 1914-1915. After avoiding last place in 1914 only by St. Louis' late-season nosedive, Pittsburgh turned itself around the next year, luring first baseman Ed Konetchy from their NL rival Pirates, and pitcher Frank Allen from the NL Brooklyn Robins. Both enjoyed the best season of their careers to lead the Rebels into first place in late August, where they remained until they were dropped to third by losing three out of four at the end to the champion Whales.

St. Louis Terriers, FL 1914-1915. After finishing last in 1914, St. Louis added veteran pitcher Eddie Plank to its roster. From a club with two 20-game losers, the Terriers became in 1915 a team with three 20-game winners (including Plank), pulling up from fifth late in August to catch the leaders with a nine-game winning streak. At the finish, though, they ranked second—by less than one percentage point, the narrowest big league pennant margin ever. For 1916, Terriers' owner Phil Ball took over the AL St. Louis Browns.

## CHAPTER 3

Ballparks

Philip J. Lowry

What follows are the vital statistics of each of the current 30 major league baseball parks and a selection of the storied parks of the past. My book, *Green Cathedrals,* from which much of this section is taken, encompasses the whole of major league history, from 1871 to the present, including the extraordinary variety of early playing sites, from cricket grounds and polo fields to agricultural fairgrounds and cow pastures. That book also covers Negro League ballparks in a depth beyond the scope possible here, including the vast array of barnstorming sites, even for official league games, that was characteristic of impoverished ballclubs looking to maximize their gate receipts in any way possible. All the same, despite the space constraints imposed upon this entry, the primary Negro League parks will be covered, as well as classic shrines such as Ebbets Field, Griffith Stadium, Forbes Field, and others.

The focus here is on ballpark geometry and the oddities in play that resulted from the unique configuration of the park. Dimensional changes are catalogued and dated, particularly in outfield fence distances and heights. This subject is crucial to an understanding of the statistical history of baseball, whether or not one is a devotee of the park-adjusted figures on display in this volume.

The following leagues are covered by this study. The accompanying abbreviations may be employed for the 20th century's principal leagues:

NL	National League, 1876–
AL	American League, 1901–
FL	Federal League, 1914–1915
NNL	Negro National League, 1920–1931, 1933–1948
ECL	Eastern Colored League, 1923–1928
NAL	Negro American League, 1929, 1937–1950
NSL	Negro Southern League, 1932
NEWL	Negro East-West League, 1932

Before 1900, most parks were small wooden grandstands hastily constructed around recreation fields that often were not even enclosed by outfield fences. Beginning with the erection of Shibe Park and Forbes Field in 1909, however, concrete-and-steel ballparks became the rule. These palaces signaled the growing prominence of baseball and constituted to my mind the best in ballpark design; the term I have applied to this type of park is "Classic." Beginning in the 1950s, multipurpose stadiums were developed. "Multipurpose" means, for this essay, that a stadium was used for both football and baseball, a marriage not made in heaven. "New Classic"

reflects the return to asymmetrical, baseball-only parks—in Baltimore, Cleveland, Dallas, Denver, and Phoenix.

Using the Outlines

"Style" defines the structural design of the park.

"A.K.A." (Also Known As) lists alternate names and nicknames used for the ballpark.

"Occupant" lists teams using the park in chronological order. Inclusive dates of play within the league follow.

"Event" contains neutral site and All-Star Games.

"Location" lists the surrounding streets. When possible, fields and bases are associated with the streets. Geographical directions, (N) for North, (S) for South, (E) for East, and (W) for West, are provided when available.

Because all older stadiums had grass "surfaces," information concerning carpet or grass is included only for modern ballparks.

Under "Dimensions" the distance is given in feet from home plate to the fences, and to the backstop. Dates, in parentheses, denote the *first* month and/or year when the boundaries stood at the stated distance.

"Fences" lists the heights of the outfield fences in feet. Dates denote the *first* time the fences stood at the stated height.

"Former Use" describes how the site was utilized before stadium construction. Similarly, "Current Use" chronicles the development of the site after a ballpark was demolished or abandoned.

"Phenomena" is a more general category for historical data. Included here will be special features of the park's physical plant, important changes over the years, and events of note throughout the years of operation.

ANAHEIM, CALIFORNIA

EDISON FIELD

STYLE Multipurpose
A.K.A. Big A 1966, Bigger A 1980, Anaheim Stadium 1996-97
OCCUPANT AL Angels April 19, 1966 to date
EVENT All-Star Game 1967, 1989
LOCATION *Left Field (N)* Katella Avenue; *3rd Base (W)* 2000 State College Boulevard, then Interstate 5; *1st Base (S)* Orangewood Avenue, then Santa Ana River; *Center Field (E)* Orange Freeway
SURFACE Bluegrass
DIMENSIONS *Foul Lines:* 333; *Bullpens:* 362; *Power*

Alleys: 375 (1966), 369 (1973), 374 (1974), 370 (1989); *Deep Alleys:* 386; *Center Field:* 406 (1966), 402 (1973), 404 (1974); *Backstop:* 55 (1966), 60.5 (1973)
FENCES *Majority of the Fence:* 10 (wire 1966), 7.86 (wire 1973), 7.86 (padded 1981); *Corners Between Foul Poles and Bullpens:* 4.75 (steel 1966); *Left-center Between 386 and 404 Marks:* 7.5 (padded 1981); *Padded Posts at the Left Sides of Both Left and Right Field; Bullpen Gates:* 9 (padded 1981); *Bullpen Gates:* 9.95 (wire 1966)
FORMER USE Four farms—Camille Allec's 39 acres of orange and eucalyptus trees, Roland Reynolds' 70 acres of alfalfa, John Knutgen's 20 acres of corn, Bill Ross and George Lenney's 19 acres of corn
CAPACITY 40,000
PHENOMENA
• Power hitter's park, the ball carries well.
• Huge 230-foot-high letter "A" stood behind the fence in left as a scoreboard support until 1980, then it was moved to the parking lot. The letter has a gold halo at its top.
• Sections 69 and 70 in center covered by green-canvas batters' background.
• Two thin black TV cables used to run in fair territory on the warning track from the left field corner bullpen gate to the foul pole, and then along the wall in foul territory about 50 feet toward third base, then into the stands.
• Outfield enclosed and triple-decked in 1980; new owner Disney un-enclosed it and ripped out the distant outfield structure in 1997.
• Six doors on ivy-covered wall in deep left-center behind outfield fence labeled: "warning track," "skin material," "screen clay mounds," "raw clay," "sand," "equipment."

ATLANTA, GEORGIA

TURNER FIELD

STYLE New Classic
A.K.A. Olympic Stadium 1996
OCCUPANT NL Braves April 4, 1997 to date
LOCATION (N) Ralph Abernathy Boulevard; (E) Capital Avenue; (S) Love Street; (W) Washington Street
SURFACE Grass
DIMENSIONS *Left Field:* 335; *Left-Center:* 380; *Center Field:* 401; *Right-Center:* 390; *Right Field:* 330; *Backstop:* 53.
FENCES 8
CAPACITY 50,528
PHENOMENA
• Built to host 1996 Summer Olympics.
• A hand-operated scoreboard posts out-of-town scores above the left field stands.
• Upper level seats afford view of downtown Atlanta.
• Atlanta-Fulton County Stadium razed to create parking for Turner Field.
• Monument Grove, a large park-like area at the north entrance, contains statues of Ty Cobb, Hank Aaron and Phil Niekro that had been at Atlanta-Fulton County Stadium. Also contains retired number statues of five players—Aaron, Niekro, Warren Spahn, Eddie Mathews, and Dale Murphy.
• Center field scoreboard is dominated by a 100-foot

image of Hank Aaron hitting his 715th home run.
• Huge Coke bottle in upper deck in left field.

BALTIMORE, MARYLAND

CAMDEN YARDS

STYLE New Classic
A.K.A. Oriole Park
OCCUPANT AL Orioles April 6, 1992 to date
EVENT All-Star Game 1993
LOCATION (N) Camden Street; (W) Russell Street; (E) Howard Street; (S) Martin Luther King Boulevard
SURFACE Maryland Bluegrass ("Prescription Athletic Turf")
DIMENSIONS *Left Field:* 333; *Left-Center:* 364; *Deepest Left-Center:* 410; *Center Field:* 400; *Right-Center:* 373; *Right Field:* 318; *Backstop:* 57.5
FENCES 25 in right, 7 elsewhere
FORMER USE Le Comte de Rochambeau, French general, camped his troops here on the way to Yorktown in 1781; former station of Baltimore & Ohio Railroad
CAPACITY 48,262
PHENOMENA
• Camden Yards complex includes the Baltimore & Ohio Warehouse, longest building on the East Coast (1,016 feet long but only 51 feet wide). Houses Orioles offices as well as a cafeteria, sports bar, and the exclusive Camden Club. Banks of lights are mounted on roof.
• Each aisle seat features an 1890s Orioles logo.
• Unique double-decked bullpens in left-center field.
• Hearing-impaired persons may hook into "hearing assistance channels" at their seats.
• Playing field is 16 feet below street level.
• Located only two blocks from Babe Ruth's birthplace; Babe's father operated Ruth's Cafe at 406 Conway Street, the site of which is now located in center field.
• Designed by HOK Sports Facility Group.
• Site of unique three league triple header on June 6, 1992. Fans could take in a morning Hagerstown game, an afternoon Frederick contest, and end up under the lights at Camden Yards.
• Large Babe Ruth statue has the Bambino incorrectly wearing a right-handed fielder's glove.
• Faced with brick to present a traditional appearance.
• Warehouse is 432 feet from home plate.
• Sportswriter John Steadman's unofficial measurements reveal that LCF is 352 rather than 364, deepest LCF is 397 rather than 410, and RCF is 363 rather than 373.

BOSTON, MASSACHUSETTS

FENWAY PARK

STYLE Classic
OCCUPANT AL Red Sox April 20, 1912 to date
EVENT NL Braves vs. New York April 19, May 30, 1913; Aug. 1 and 8, Sept. 7 to 29, 1914; 1914 World Series; April 14 to July 26, 1915; All-Star Game 1946, 1961
LOCATION *Left Field (N)* Lansdowne Street, Boston & Albany Railroad tracks, and Mass. Turnpike/Interstate 90; *3rd Base (W)* Brookline Avenue and 24 Jersey Street,

renamed 24 Yawkey Way in 1976, also bowling alley building attached to park; *1st Base (S)* Van Ness Street built after park was done; *Right Field (E)* Ipswich Street and Fenway Garage building

SURFACE Bluegrass

DIMENSIONS *Left Field:* 324 (1921), 320.5 (1926), 320 (1930), 318 (1931), 320 (1933), 312 (1934), 315 (1936), 310 (1995); *Left-Center:* 379 (1934); *Deep Left-Center at Flagpole:* 388 (1934); *Flagpole Removed from Field of Play in 1970; Centerfield:* 488 (1922), 468 (1930), 388.67 (1934), 389.67 (1954); *Deepest Corner, Just Right of Center:* 550 (1922), 593 (1931), 420 (1934) [Note: 593 is cited in 1931-33 Bluebooks; this could be a misprint.] *Right-Center, Just Right of Deepest Corner Where the Bullpen Begins:* 380 (1938), 383 (1955); *Right of Right-Center:* 405 (1939), 382 (1940), 381 (1942), 380 (1943); *Right Field:* 313.5 (1921), 358.5 (1926), 358 (1930), 325 (1931) 358 (1933), 334 (1934), 332 (1936), 322 (1938), 332 (1939), 304 (1940), 302 (1942); *Backstop:* 68 (1912), 60 (1934); *Foul Territory:* Very small, smallest in the majors

FENCES *Left Field:* 25 (wood 1912), 37.17 (tin over wood over concrete lower section 1934), 37.17 (hard plastic 1976); *Left Field Wall to Center Bleacher Wall Behind Flagpole:* 18 sloping to 17 (concrete 1934), (padding 1976) crash pad added from 18 inches to 6 feet on left and center field walls (1976); *Center Field to Bullpen Fence:* 8.75 (wood 1940); *Right-Center Bullpen Fence:* 5.25 (wood 1940); *Right Field Wall and Railing:* Bullpen 3.42 sloping to 5.37 at foul pole (steel 1940); *Right Field Belly:* the low railing and wall curve out sharply from the 302 marker at the right field foul pole into deep right field—many a right fielder has run toward the foul line and watched helplessly as a 302-foot pop fly falls over the railing for a home run.

CAPACITY 33,871

PHENOMENA

• Seats made of oak.

• 1976 electronic scoreboard in center field significantly altered the wind currents.

• 43 private rooftop boxes added 1984.

• Duffy's Cliff was a 10-foot-high mound which formed an incline in front of the left field wall from 1912 to 1933, extending from the left field foul pole to the flag pole in center—named after Red Sox left fielder Duffy Lewis, who was the acknowledged master of defensive play on the cliff. It was greatly reduced but not completely eliminated in 1934.

• The Green Monster Wall in left completely dominates the field of play—now all green, it used to be covered with advertisements.

• Ladder starts near upper-left corner of scoreboard, 13 feet above ground, and rises to top of the Green Monster to allow groundskeeper to remove batting practice home run balls from the netting above the Wall.

• Scoreboard numbers—runs and hits: 16 inches by 16 inches, 3 pounds; errors, innings, pitcher's numbers: 12 inches by 16 inches, 2 pounds.

• No ball has ever been hit over the right field roof.

• Balls that hit uprights above the Wall, and should have been homers, have been declared in play by the umpires.

• Wooden bleachers stood down the left field line in foul territory in the 1910s and 1920s, but burned down on May 8, 1926. The charred remains were removed, increasing the size of foul territory. Wooden bleachers were completed in center and right-center by the 1912 World Series.

• Infield grass was transplanted from Huntington Avenue Baseball Grounds to Fenway in 1912.

• During the winter of 1933-34, all the wooden grandstands were replaced with concrete and steel. A big fire on Jan. 5, 1934, destroyed much of what had already been built, but all was finished for the 1934 season opener on April 17.

• In 1936, a 23-foot seven-inch net was placed atop the wall in left to protect windows on Landsdowne Street.

• Wind usually helps the batters. New pressbox built in late 1980s above home plate causes wind swirl which pushes foul balls back into fair territory. This is the park with the tiniest foul territory in the majors.

• When tin covered the two-by-fours on the Wall, balls hitting the tin over two-by-fours had a live bounce, but balls hitting between the two-by-fours were dead and just dropped straight down.

• In 1940, in an effort to help Ted Williams hit home runs, the Red Sox added the right field bullpens, called Williamsburg, which reduced the distance to the fence by 23 feet.

• In 1947 all advertisements were removed from the left field wall, which was painted green.

• Tom A. Yawkey's and his wife Jean R. Yawkey's initials, TAY and JRY, appear in Morse code in two vertical stripes on the scoreboard in left. The 1946 roof boxes were replaced in 1982.

• The screen behind home plate, designed to protect fans and allow foul balls to roll back down onto the field of play, was the first of its kind in the majors.

• Left field scoreboard, installed on the Wall in 1934, was moved 20 feet to the right in 1976. The low concrete base of the left and center field walls was padded after the 1975 World Series, during which Fred Lynn crashed into the concrete wall in center.

• The left field foul line was measured by Art Keefe and George Sullivan, authors of *The Picture History of the Boston Red Sox,* in 1975 as 309 feet 5 inches. On Oct. 19, 1975, the Boston *Globe* used aerial photography and measured it at 304.779 feet. Osborn Engineering Co. blueprints document the distance at 308 feet. The sign was changed from 315 to 310 in 1995.

• Fenway—"where you can sit for hours and feel a security that does not exist anywhere else in the world."

CHICAGO, ILLINOIS

COMISKEY PARK

STYLE Superstructure

A.K.A. New Comiskey Park

OCCUPANT AL White Sox April 18, 1991 to date

LOCATION West 36th Street (South); 333 West 35th Street (North); Dan Ryan Expressway (East); Wentworth Ave. (West)

SURFACE Natural Grass (Bluegrass)

DIMENSIONS *Left field:* 347; *Power Alleys:* 383; (1991), 375 (1992); *Center Field:* 400; *Right Field:* 347; *Backstop:* 60

FENCES 8
FORMER USE Approximately 80 privately owned residential buildings
CAPACITY 44,321
PHENOMENA
• Unlike the Picnic Area at old Comiskey Park, entry to the new Picnic Area's buffet costs $30 over the ticket price.
• Echoing the nickname of Charles Comiskey, food court contains a shop called Old Roman Pizza.
• Management boasts "Ratio of washroom fixtures to fan capacity, one of the best in baseball" but fans complain of long washroom lines.
• During construction the frame of the new Comiskey Park was visible from the old Comiskey Park next door throughout its final season.
• Large scoreboard in center field replicates one designed by Bill Veeck at former Comiskey Park.
• Twenty-two dump trucks brought the 550 tons of infield dirt from old to new Comiskey.
• Built at a cost of $134.9 million; paid for in large part by a new hotel tax.
• Seats in front row of the upper deck are farther from home plate than those in last row at old Comiskey.

WRIGLEY FIELD

STYLE Classic
A.K.A. North Side Ball Park, 1914; Weeghman Park, 1914-15; Cubs' Park, 1916-26; Whales Park, 1915; Eddie Dorr's House
OCCUPANT FL Whales April 23, 1914 to Oct. 3, 1915; NL Cubs April 20, 1916 to date
EVENT All-Star Game 1947, 1962, 1990
LOCATION *Left Field (N)* West Waveland Avenue; *3rd Base (W)* Seminary Avenue; *Home Plate (SW)* North Clark Street; *1st Base (S)* 1060 West Addison Street; *Right Field (E)* North Sheffield Avenue
SURFACE Grass, mixture of Merion Bluegrass and clover; Ivy vines on the outfield walls.
DIMENSIONS *Left Field:* 310 (April 1914), 335 (May 1914), 327 (June 1914), 343 (1921), 325 (1923), 348 (1926), 364 (1928), 355 (1938); *Deepest Left-Center:* 357 (1938); *Power Alleys:* 364 (1914), 368 (1938); *Center Field:* 440 (1914), 447 (1923), 436 (1928), 400 (1938); *Deepest Right-Center:* 363 (1938); *Right Field:* 356 (April 1914), 345 (June 1914), 321 (1915), 298 (1921), 399 (1922), 318 (1923), 321 (1928), 353 (1938); *Backstop:* 62.42 (1930), 60.5 (1957), 62.42 (1982), 60.5 (1993); *Foul Territory:* very small
FENCES *Left Field Corner:* 15.92 (11.33 brick with Boston and Bittersweet Ivy, below 4.59 plywood), 3 wire basket in front 1985 (does not change height of fence); *Transition Between Left Field Corner and Bleachers:* 12.5 (screen and yellow railing on top of brick wall); *Left-Center to Right-Center:* 8 (screen 1914), 11.33 (brick with ivy 1938); in front is wire basket (May 1970); *Left Field Scoreboard:* 40 (wood July 9 to September 3, 1937); *Center Field Screen:* 1933 (8 wire above 11.33 brick June 18, 1963 to October 1964); *Right-Center Triangle:* 17.5 in front of catwalk steps sloping down to 15.5 (screen 1928, plywood 1979, removed 1985); *Right Field Corner:* 15.5 (11.33 brick with ivy, below 4.17 plywood), wire basket in front (1985)

CAPACITY 38,884
PHENOMENA
• Home Run Distance calculation appears on center field scoreboard after a home run.
• The only remaining Federal League ballpark.
• Beautiful ivy vines on the outfield wall.
• After the game, a blue flag with a white W flying from the center field flag pole signifies a win, a white flag with a blue L a Cubs loss.
• Sea breeze off the lake favors pitchers.
• Seats added July 1985 to catwalks near foul pole, in fair territory.
• The center field 400 sign is right of straight-away center.
• The only park where it's more difficult to hit a homer down the foul line than to hit one 50 or so feet out in fair territory because the bleachers protrude into the outfield in what are called "wells".
• In 1923, the foul lines were shifted slightly amidst park renovations.
• From 1923 through 1930s Bobby Dorr, the grounds superintendent, lived in a six-room apartment at the ballpark, adjacent to the left field corner gate; the apartment is still there.
• Eight-foot-high batter's background wire fence, 64 feet wide, stood on top of the center field wall from June 18, 1963 through the end of the 1964 season. Called the Whitlow fence because Cubs Athletic Director Robert Whitlow put it up. The screen prevented 10 homers, by Cubs and by visitors, one each by 500+ homer hitters Ernie Banks and Willie McCovey.
• AstroTurf cover on center field seats used for batters' background, debuted on May 18, 1967; replaced by beautiful vines in 1990s.
• In the winter of 1924-25, the left field bleachers were removed, the grandstand was doubledecked, and the playing area was lowered several feet.
• For the World Series in 1929, 1932, and 1935, extra bleachers were built on the street on Waveland and Sheffield.
• The park was located so it would be easy for fans to get there on the Milwaukee Road train.
• The 27-foot-high, 75-foot-wide scoreboard was built in 1937 by Bill Veeck. Its top is 85 feet above the field. The 10-foot diameter clock was added in 1941.
• In 1937 the bleacher stairstep was created to allow potted plants and eight huge Chinese elm trees to grow, complementing the ivy. The trees were eventually removed.
• Ivy planted on the outfield walls in 1937 by Bill Veeck. Originally 350 Japanese bittersweet plants and 200 Boston ivy plants.
• During the 1937 season, new outfield bleachers were built, and the six gates in the brick wall were installed. They were red, repainted blue in 1981, then green in the mid-1980s.
• The bleachers were expanded to their present state in the 1940s; famous Bleacher Bums formed here in 1966 by 10 bleacher fans.
• Lights were inside the park in the early 1940s ready to be installed, but owner Philip K. Wrigley donated them to the war effort instead on Dec. 8, 1941, thus allowing Wrigley Field to remain dark at night until 1988.

• The right field wall was remodeled in 1950-51.
• On April 14, 1976, Mets slugger Dave "King Kong" Kingman hit a homer 550 feet over Waveland and against a frame house three doors down on the east side of Kenmore Avenue. If the ball had carried three feet higher, it would have crashed through a window and smashed a TV screen on which Naomi Martinez was watching Kingman round the bases.
• Park is affected by wind conditions more than any other major league park, with the possible exception of Candlestick.
• More home runs than normal are caused by high altitude of over 600 feet above sea level, and by the heat.
• William F. Wrigley, Jr. Water Fountain moved to the Cubs Hall of Fame under the first base stands, near the Friendly Confines café dedicated by Tinker-Evers handshake.
• Arched dormers on the roof.
• Outfield wall distances before 1981 were marked on plywood markers screwed into the brick. Since then they have been painted directly on the brick.
• Foul pole screens have distances marked on plywood vertically "355" and "353."
• The most distant outfield measurement sign was on the roof of a house across Sheffield Avenue in right-center, the sign said "495."
• Winds blowing toward the lake take homers with them.

CINCINNATI, OHIO

CINERGY FIELD

STYLE   Multipurpose
OCCUPANT   NL Reds June 30, 1970 to date
A.K.A.   Riverfront Stadium 1970-96
EVENT   All-Star Game 1970
LOCATION   *Left Field (E)* Riverfront Coliseum, Central Bridge and Broadway; *3rd Base (N)* 201 East Second Street, renamed Pete Rose Way on Sept. 10, 1985; *1st Base (W)* Interstate 71 Suspension Bridge Approach Ramp; *Right Field (S)* Mehring Way, railroad tracks, and Ohio River
SURFACE   AstroTurf—hard, balls bounce high off it
DIMENSIONS   *Foul Lines:* 330; *Power Alleys:* 375; *Center Field:* 404; *Backstop:* 51; *Foul Territory:* Small
FENCES   12 (wood, 1970); 8 (wood, 1984)
CAPACITY   52,952
PHENOMENA
• First to paint metric distances on outfield walls: 100.58 down the lines, 114.30 to the alleys, 123.13 to center.
• Uses Crosley Field's home plate.
• Parking garage beneath stadium.
• 4,192 circle in left-center commemorated Pete Rose's 4,192nd hit here on Sept. 10, 1985 vs. the Padres.
• Reds and Pirates played slowest game ever here Aug. 30, 1978—80.6 minutes per inning, called off after 3½ innings and 3½ hours of rain delays at 12:47 a.m.
• Winds help right-handed hitters.
• From 1996 to 1998, the club retired six numbers and put them on display at the stadium: Johnny Bench (No. 5), Fred Hutchinson (No. 1), Jackie Robinson (No. 42), Frank Robinson (No. 20), Joe Morgan (No. 8), and Ted Kluszewski (No. 18).

CLEVELAND, OHIO

JACOBS FIELD

STYLE   New Classic
OCCUPANT   AL Indians, April 4, 1994 to present
EVENT   All-Star Game 1997
A.K.A.   Gateway, The Jake
LOCATION   *Left Field (SW):* Ontario Avenue; *First Base (SE)* Carnegie Avenue; *Right Field (NE)* East 9th Street
SURFACE   Natural Grass
DIMENSIONS   *Left Field:* 325; *Left-Center:* 368; *Deepest Center Field:* 410; *Center Field:* 405; *Right-Center:* 375; *Right Field:* 325; *Backstop:* 59; *Foul Territory:* Small.
FENCES   *Left Field:* 19; *Center and Right Field:* 8; *Right Field corner at the foul line:* 14.
CAPACITY   43,863
PHENOMENA
• Original plan was for a downtown domed stadium but local voters fortunately rejected it.
• Base of exterior facade consists of Atlantic green granite; remainder is Kasota stone, limestone, and buff-colored brick.
• Picnic Plaza located beyond center field fence.
• Executive Offices located in separate building in back of left field stands.
• Adjacent to home of NBA's Cleveland Cavaliers.
• Scoreboard located in left field.
• Indians bullpen in deep right center field; visitors in right field corner; each with three pitching mounds.
• Bullpens elevated above playing field.
• Features "Kidsland" near the family seating area.
• Home plate from Cleveland Stadium transplanted at end of 1993 season.
• Indians have a batting cage under the stands, behind their dugout.

DALLAS, TEXAS

BALLPARK AT ARLINGTON

STYLE   New Classic
OCCUPANT   AL Rangers, April 11, 1994 to present
EVENT   All-Star Game 1995
LOCATION   Northwest corner of Stadium Drive and Randol Road, in suburban Arlington
SURFACE   Natural Grass
DIMENSIONS   *Left Field:* 332; *Left-Center:* 388; *Center Field:* 400; *Deepest Right-Center:* 403; *Right-Center:* 381; *Right Field:* 325; *Backstop:* 60; *Foul Territory:* Small.
FENCES   *Left Field:* 14; *Center and Right Field:* 8
CAPACITY   49,178
PHENOMENA
• Granite and brick facade.
• Covered pavilion porch in right field features pillars reminiscent of Tiger Stadium.
• Playing field is 22 feet below street level.
• Wind helps carry balls hit to right-center.
• Bullpens raised five feet above playing surface so fans can see who is warming up.

- Part of a complex that includes two manmade lakes and a Riverwalk area featuring shops and restaurants.
- Picnic area in front of four-story office building in center field.
- Outfield has many nooks and crannies reminiscent of Ebbets Field in Brooklyn.
- Rangers have a warning track under the stands behind their dugout for players to warm up on.
- Was the site of the first interleague game in major league history on June 12, 1997. Willie Mays threw out the ceremonial first pitch to NL president Leonard Coleman and Nolan Ryan threw one to AL president Leonard Coleman. The Giants won the historic game, 4-3.

DENVER, COLORADO

COORS FIELD

STYLE   New Classic
OCCUPANT   NL Rockies, April 26, 1995 to date
EVENT   All-Star Game 1998
LOCATION   20th and Blake
SURFACE   Bluegrass with strains of rye
DIMENSIONS   *Left field:* 347; *Left-Center:* 390; *Deepest Left-Center:* 420; *Center Field:* 415; *Right-Center:* 375; *Deepest Right-Center:* 424; *Right Field Corner:* 358; *Right Field:* 350; *Backstop:* 56.33
FENCES   *Left Field Corner to Right-Center:* 8; *Right Field (Manual Scoreboard):* 14
FORMER USE   Rail Yard
CAPACITY   50,200
PHENOMENA

- Originally designed for only 43,800 capacity but increased due to huge crowds at temporary Mile High Stadium, where the Rockies drew 4,483,350, and once had a single game crowd of 80,227.
- Club level features 22-inch wide seats and waiter/waitress service.
- Upper deck center field bleachers known as the "Rockpile."
- Ten miles of handrails throughout the park.
- The 21st row of the upper deck is marked in purple to indicate it is 5,280 feet above sea level — mile high.
- Home and visitors bullpens are located back-to-back in center field.
- Warning track is 90 percent crushed lava, 10 red clay.
- Features spectacular view of Rocky Mountains from first base and right field seats.
- Exceptional hitting park because of altitude.

DETROIT, MICHIGAN

TIGER STADIUM

STYLE   Classic
A.K.A.   Bennett Park 1896 to 1911, Navin Field 1912 to 1937, Briggs Stadium 1938 to 1960
OCCUPANT   AL Tigers April 20, 1912 to date, NNL Stars 1920-31, NEWL Wolves 1932, NNL Stars 1933, NAL Stars 1937
EVENT   All-Star Game 1941, 1951, 1971
LOCATION   *Left Field (NW)* Cherry Street, later Kaline Drive, then Interstate 75; *3rd Base (SW)* National Avenue, later Cochrane Avenue; *1st Base (SE)* Michigan Avenue; *Right Field (NE)* 2121 Trumbull Avenue, same site as Bennett Park but turned around 90 degrees, in the Corktown neighborhood
SURFACE   Bluegrass
DIMENSIONS   *Left Field:* 345 (1921), 340.58 (1926), 339 (1930), 367 (1931), 339 (1934), 340 (1938), 342 (1939), 340 (1942); *Left-Center:* 365 (1942); *Center Field:* 467 (1927), 455 (1930), 464 (1931), 459 (1936), 450 (1937), 440 (1938), 450 (1939), 420 (1942), 440 (1944); *Right-Center:* 370 (1942), 375 (1982); *Right Field:* 370 (1921), 370.91 (1926), 372 (1930), 367 (1931), 325 (1936), 315 (1939), 325 (1942), 302 (1954), 325 (1955); *Backstop:* 54.35 (1954), 66 (1955); *Foul Territory:* Small
FENCES   *All Fences:* 5 concrete topped by screen; *Left Field:* 20 (1935), 30 (1937), 10 (1938), 12 (1940), 15 (1946), 12 (1953), 14 (1954), 12 (1955), 11 (1958), 9 (1962); *Center Field:* 9 (1940), 15 (1946), 11 (1950), 9 (1953), 14 (1954), 9 (1955); *Right of Flag Pole:* 7 (1946); *Right Field:* 8 (1940), 30 (1944), 10 (1945), 20 (1950), 8 (1953), 9 (1958), 30 (1961), 9 (1962); *Flag Pole:* 125 in play (5 feet in front of fence in center field, just left of dead center)
FORMER USE   Haymarket in 1890s
CAPACITY   52,416
PHENOMENA

- First named for Frank Navin, Tigers president 1908-1935.
- Right field second deck overhangs the lower deck by 10 feet. Screen in right in 1944 and in 1961 required balls to be hit into the second deck to be home runs.
- Only doubledecked bleachers in the majors—upper deck from left-center to center, lower deck from center to right-center.
- A 125-foot-high flag pole in play in deep center, just to the left of the 440 mark—highest outfield obstacle ever in play in baseball history. The scoreboard now on the left field fence was originally placed at the 440 mark in dead center in 1961 but was moved when Norm Cash, Al Kaline, and Charlie Maxwell complained that it hindered the batters' view of the pitch.
- There is a string of spotlights mounted under the overhang to illuminate the right field warning track which is shadowed from the normal light standards.
- Cobb's Lake—area in front of plate which was always soaked with water by the groundskeepers to slow down Ty Cobb's bunts.
- When slugging teams came to visit, manager Ty Cobb had the groundskeepers put in temporary bleachers in the outfield, turning long drives into ground-rule doubles.
- Sign above entrance to visitors' clubhouse: "Visitors' Clubhouse—No Visitors Allowed."
- Doubledecked in 1923-24 from first to third base.
- Capacity increased in winter of 1935-36 by doubledecking the right field stands, and in the winter of 1937-38 by doubledecking both the left field stands and the center field bleachers.
- In the 1930s and 1940s, there was a 315 marker on the second deck in right field.
- In 1942 and 1943, the center field distance was only 420. The notches just left and right of dead center were closer than 420, at 405.

• Next-to-last classic old ballyard to put in lights. Tiger Stadium hosted its first night game in 1948.

• Saved in 1974 when owner John Fetzer told the Pontiac Silverdome committee, "This franchise belongs to the inner city of Detroit; I'm just the caretaker." Now that mantle of caretaker has been passed on to Frank Rashid's Tiger Stadium Fan Club and the Cochrane Plan, an architectural plan to preserve the ballpark.

• First homer at Navin Field, on May 5, 1912, came on a fluke bounce which hopped through the side door of the left-center scoreboard.

• Home plate and batters' boxes oriented towards right-center rather than straight out to the mound. This tends to give righthanded pitchers more outside corner strike calls and can disorient visiting batters.

HOUSTON, TEXAS

ASTRODOME

STYLE Dome
A.K.A. Harris County Domed Stadium 1965, Eighth Wonder of the World
OCCUPANT NL Astros April 12, 1965 to date
EVENT All-Star Game 1968, 1986
LOCATION *Center Field (E)* Fannin Street; *3rd Base (N)* Old Spanish Trail; *Home Plate (W)* Kirby Drive; *1st Base (S)* South Loop Freeway/Interstate 610; *Above:* Domed roof of 4796 Lucite panels and steel girders
SURFACE *Infield:* Grass (1965) Tifway 419 Bermuda grass specially selected for indoor play—died; AstroTurf on all but the part normally dirt 1966-70; on all the infield except for sliding pits 1971 to date; *Outfield:* Grass April 12, 1965 to July 19, 1966—died too; AstroTurf (July 19, 1966 to date
DIMENSIONS *Foul Lines:* 340 (1965), 330 (1972), 340 (1977), 330 (1985), 325 (1992), 330 (1993), 325 (1994); *Power Alleys:* 375 (1965), 390 (1966), 378 (1972), 390 (1977), 378 (1985), 375 (1992), 380 (1993), 375 (1994); *Center Field:* 406 (1965), 400 (1972), 406 (1977), 400 (1985); *Apex of Dome:* 208; *Backstop:* 60.5 (1965), 67 (1990), 52 (1993)
FENCES *Left and Right Field:* 16 (9 concrete below 3 wire, 2 concrete, and 2 wire plus railing, 1965), 12 (concrete, 1969), 10 (concrete, 1977); 10 (canvas, 1990); 19.5 (concrete, 1991); 10 canvas (1992); Between foul poles and scoreboards: 8 (canvas, 1994), Scoreboards in left and right 16 (steel, 1994); *Center Field* 12 (concrete, 1965), 10 (concrete, 1977), 10 (canvas 1990)
CAPACITY 54,370
PHENOMENA

• The second major league covered stadium, the first being the field under the Queensboro 59th Street Bridge in New York City used by the New York Cubans of the Negro National League in the 1930s.

• Maximum height of the dome is 208 feet, just beyond second base.

• The roof had 4,796 clear panes of glass originally, but they caused a glare that prevented fielders from seeing the ball, thus two of the eight roof sections were painted white. This killed the grass and unfortunately introduced the world to AstroTurf.

• Excepting Yankee Stadium's Death Valley, the most distant power alleys in the majors at 390 feet, until changed in 1985. Few homers are hit here.

• Yellow, orange, and red seats.

• Infielders can catch foul flies in the dugout, either by jumping a fence or by entering the dugout through a gap in the middle of the fence.

• Hard to see through the screen from behind the plate.

• In its inaugural season of 1965, the Astrodome was the scene of a unique groundskeeping argument. The New York Mets claimed that the groundskeepers were roof-keeping as well by manipulating the air conditioning system so that the air currents helped Astro long balls and hindered visitors' long balls.

• Actual backstop distance is less than stated 52 feet.

• Shoeshine stands behind home plate in lower deck.

• On April 28, 1965, Mets announcer Lindsey Nelson broadcast a game from a gondola suspended from the apex of the dome.

• On June 10, 1974, Phillies third baseman Mike Schmidt hit the public address speaker 117 feet up and 329 feet from home—what would have been a 500-plus-foot homer ended up as a single as the ball dropped in center field.

• On June 15, 1976, a game was rained out because of flooding in the streets.

• The old location of Colt Stadium (now rebuilt in Torreon, Mexico) is just northwest of the Astrodome; Astrohall and Astroarena are just south of the Astrodome.

• Flowers planted between seats and fence, all around the outfield between the two scoreboards.

KANSAS CITY, MISSOURI

KAUFFMAN STADIUM

STYLE Superstructure
A.K.A. Harry S. Truman Sports Complex, Royals Stadium 1973 to 1993
OCCUPANT AL Royals April 10, 1973 to date
EVENT All-Star Game 1973
LOCATION *Center Field (N)* Spectacular Drive, then Interstate 70; *3rd Base (W)* Lancer Lane, then Dutton Brookfield Drive; *Home Plate (S)* Royal Way, then Chiefs Way, Arrowhead Stadium, Raytown Road, and CRI&P Railroad tracks; *1st Base (E)* Red Coat Drive, then Blue Ridge Cut-Off
SURFACE AstroTurf—very fast (1973-1994); Grass 1995 to date
DIMENSIONS *Foul Lines:* 330 (1973); 320 (1995); *Power Alleys:* 375 (1973); 385 (1990); 375 (1995); *Center Field:* 405 (1973); 410 (1980); 400 (1995); *Backstop:* 60; *Foul Territory:* Small
FENCES 12 (canvas, 1973), 9 (canvas, 1995)
CAPACITY 40,625
PHENOMENA

• Waterfalls and fountains run for 322 feet on the embankment overlooking right-center.

• Best visibility for hitters in the majors.

• Homers are few here because alleys are deep and the fence cuts away sharply from the foul poles.

• During rain delays, thousands of sawed webworm moths appear.

• A good park for hitting triples.

• Kenny Pippin, in his frogman suit, cleans the pond periodically in right-center.

• Royals 1985 World Series cup and other trophies are on display through the sixth inning of each game at the park's Section 107.

• Upper deck fans near foul poles are in relative darkness.

• Before 1995, when grass replaced the hated carpet, the best groundskeeper in baseball had the ironic job of maintaining an ugly plastic carpet. He kept busy maintaining the Runway and the Baja, the grassy running area and the 125-tree forest beyond the left-center fence.

LOS ANGELES, CALIFORNIA

DODGER STADIUM

STYLE Superstructure

A.K.A. Chavez Ravine during AL use 1962 to 1965 by Los Angeles Angels, Taj O'Malley, O'Malley's Golden Gulch

OCCUPANT NL Dodgers April 10, 1962 to date; AL Angels April 17, 1962 to Sept. 22, 1965

EVENT All-Star Game 1980

LOCATION *Left Field (NW)* Glendale Boulevard; *3rd Base (SW)* Sunset Boulevard; *Home Plate (S)* 1000 Elysian Park Avenue; *1st Base (SE)* Pasadena Freeway; *Right Field (NE)* Los Angeles Police Academy, Elysian Park, and Golden State Freeway/Interstate; in Chavez Ravine, on a hill overlooking downtown Los Angeles

SURFACE Santa Ana Bermuda grass

DIMENSIONS *Foul Lines:* 330; *Power Alleys:* 380 (1962), 370 (1969), 385 (1983); *Center Field:* 410 (1962), 400 (1969); *Back Stop:* 65 (1962), 68.19 (1963), 75 (1969); *Foul Territory:* Large

FENCES *Left-Center to Right-Center:* 10 (wood 1962), 8 (1973); *Foul Poles to Bullpens in Left and Right Field Corners:* 3.75 (steel 1962), 3.83 (1969); *The Dip:* (where low corner steel wall and screen bullpen fence meet) 3.42 (1962), 3.5 (1969)

FORMER USE Used by squatters and goats.

CAPACITY 56,000

PHENOMENA

• A classic pitcher's park.

• Dugout level box seats behind the plate patterned after Tokyo's Korakuen Stadium.

• Designed by architect Emil Praeger to be expandable to 85,000 seats.

• Only major league park where capacity has never changed.

• Painted every offseason, cleanest ballpark, bar none.

• Infield dirt and outfield warning track made of 70 percent crushed red building brick and 30 percent mountain clay and calcium chlorate. Palm trees beyond the fence down the foul lines.

• See-through windows in bullpen fence installed in 1974.

• Although the center field 400 sign came down in 1980, the distance is still 400 to center; the two 395 signs are left and right of dead center. Many references say it is 395 to center; they are incorrect.

• No drinking-water fountains when stadium was first built. Original design had a huge fountain in center field,

like that in right-center at Royals Stadium.

• When foul poles were installed in 1962, they were discovered to be positioned completely foul. Special dispensation was received from National League so they were recognized as fair, but the next year the plate was moved so that poles are now actually fair.

MIAMI, FLORIDA

PRO PLAYER STADIUM

STYLE Multipurpose

OCCUPANT NL Marlins April 5, 1993 to date

A.K.A. Joe Robbie Stadium

LOCATION 2269 N.W. 199th Street

SURFACE Natural Grass "Bermuda 419"

DIMENSIONS *Left Field:* 335; *Power Alleys:* 380; *Center Field:* 410; *Right Field:* 345; *Backstop:* 58

FENCES *Left-Center scoreboard:* 33; *everywhere else:* 8

CAPACITY 41,855

PHENOMENA

• Opening Day for football: Aug. 16, 1987 (Bears vs. Dolphins).

• First baseball game: Los Angeles Dodgers vs. Baltimore Orioles on March 11, 1988, exhibition.

• A helipad site in the parking lot.

• All the second-deck outfield seats are usually covered by canvas and are not used.

• Many fans speak Spanish, with a Cuban-American accent.

• Left field wall is called the "Teal Monster."

MILWAUKEE, WISCONSIN

COUNTY STADIUM

STYLE Multipurpose

OCCUPANT NL Braves April 14, 1953 to Sept. 22, 1965; AL White Sox for nine 1968 games and 11 in 1969; games from May 15, 1968 to Sept. 26, 1969; AL Brewers April 7, 1970 to 1997, NL Brewers 1998 to date

EVENT All-Star Game 1955, 1975

LOCATION *Left Field (E)* Menominee River and South 44th Street, later US-41 Stadium Freeway; *3rd Base (N)* Story Parkway and Interstate 94; *1st Base (W)* General Mitchell Boulevard; *Right Field (S)* West National Avenue and the National Soldiers Home

SURFACE Bluegrass

DIMENSIONS *Left Field:* 320 (1953), 315 (1975); *Power Alleys:* 355 (1953), 362 (1962); *Deep Alleys:* 397 (1953), 392 (1955); *Center Field:* 404 (1953), 410 (1954), 402 (1955); *Right Field:* 320 (1953), 315.37 (1954); *Backstop:* 60

FENCES *Left Field:* 4 (1953), 8 (1955), 8.33 (1959), 10 (1985); *Center Field:* 4 (1953), 8 (1955), 8.33 (1959), 10 (1985); *Right Field:* 4 (1953), 10 (1955)

FORMER USE Stone Quarry

CAPACITY 53,192

PHENOMENA

• Surveyor's mark on right field foul pole: "315.37."

• Before the park was expanded from 1953 to 1973, hospital patients at the National Soldiers Home V.A.

Hospital sat outside their rooms on Mockingbird Hill overlooking right field and watched the game for free.
• Perini's Woods, spruce and fir trees behind center field fence, planted in 1954, replaced by bleachers in 1961.
• Braves Reservation, a picnic area down the left field line, was inaugurated in 1961.
• Bernie Brewer slides into a huge beer stein in right-center whenever a Brewer hits a homer.
• Only homer ever hit over left field roof was hit by Cecil Fielder.
• Scene of Midwest League minor league game on Aug. 27, 1966 between Fox Cities and Wisconsin Rapids.
• Braves hosted both the Reds and the Cards on Sept. 24, 1954. The first game was the finish of a game two days earlier whose conclusion on a disputed double play was successfully protested by the Reds. The Reds tied the game after the protested game's resumption, but the Braves won 4-3 in the bottom of the ninth, and then beat the Cards, 4-2.

MINNEAPOLIS, MINNESOTA

HUBERT H. HUMPHREY METRODOME
STYLE Dome
A.K.A. Minnedome, Bounce Dome, Hump Dome, Homer Dome, Hubie Dome, Sweat Box (before June 28, 1983, when air conditioning arrived), Thunderdome
OCCUPANT AL Twins April 6, 1982 to date
EVENT All-Star Game 1985
LOCATION *Left Field (SW)* Fourth Street South; *3rd Base (NW)* 501 Chicago Avenue South; *1st Base (NE)* Sixth Street South; *Right Field (SE)* Tenth Avenue South; *Above:* Domed roof
SURFACE SporTurf (1982 to 1986—liveliest bounce ever), AstroTurf (1987 to date)
DIMENSIONS *Apex of Dome:* 186; *Left Field:* 344 (1982), 343 (1983); *Left-Center:* 385; *Center Field:* 407 (1982), 408 (1983); *Right-Center:* 367; *Right Field:* 327; *Backstop:* 60; *Foul Territory:* Small
FENCES *Left Field:* 7 (canvas 1982), 13 (6 plexiglass above 7 canvas 1983), 7 (canvas 1994); *Center Field:* 7 (canvas 1982); *Right Field:* 7 (canvas 1982), 13 (canvas early in 1983), 23 (canvas later in 1983)
CAPACITY 48,678
PHENOMENA
• A power hitter's park.
• Right field wall called Hefty Bag, or Trash Bag.
• Almost an exact duplicate of the domed stadiums in Seattle, Pontiac, and Vancouver. All four were built by the same engineering firm.
• Game on May 31, 1998 played with a temporary white 10-foot left field foul pole after a violent rainstorm the previous evening snapped the cable connecting the normal 45-foot pole to the roof, causing it to fall over.
• The white air-supported fabric Teflon roof makes it difficult to see the ball when hit high in the air.
• Playoffs and World Series of 1991 set new decibel records for sound in the Thunderdome.
• The Twins have never lost a World Series game at the Metrodome (8-0) and are 11-1 in postseason games in the Dome.
• Sections 107 to 113 are football seats which in baseball

season are tilted up and back to create a 40-foot wall behind the right field fence.
• The roof collapsed on April 14, 1983 from the weight of heavy snow. That night's game with the Angels had to be rescheduled, the only postponement in the stadium's history.
• Twins batter Randy Bush hit a ball off the roof in 1983. The ball was caught in foul territory for an out by Blue Jays catcher Buck Martinez. Rob Deer hit two such flyball outs to shortstop on consecutive at bats on May 30, 1992.
• On May 4, 1984, in the top of the fourth inning, A's batter Dave Kingman hit a ball through the roof. It should have been a homer, but Kingman got only a double.
• Balls bounced very high off the carpet used from 1982 to 1986.
• More home runs tend to be hit when the air conditioning is turned off.
• Curvature of wall behind plate causes wild pitches and passed balls to bounce directly toward first base.

MONTREAL, QUEBEC

STADE OLYMPIQUE
STYLE Dome
A.K.A. Olympic Stadium, Big O, Big Owe
OCCUPANT NL Expos April 15, 1977 to date
EVENT All-Star Game 1982
LOCATION *Left Field (NW)* rue Sherbrooke; *3rd Base (SW)* boulevard Pie-IX; *1st Base (SE)* 4549, avenue Pierre-de-Coubertin; *Right Field (NE)* boulevard Viau
SURFACE AstroTurf
DIMENSIONS *Foul Lines:* 325 (1977), 330 (1981), 325 (1983); *Power Alleys:* 375; *Center Field:* 404 (1977), 405 (1979), 404 (1980), 400 (1981), 404 (1983); *Apex of Dome:* 171; *Backstop:* 62 (1977), 65 (1983), 53 (1989); *Foul Territory:* Large
FENCES 12 (wood 1977), 12 (foam 1989)
CAPACITY 43,739
PHENOMENA
• Labatt's Noise-Meter high above right field is baseball's answer to the old NBA Sacramento Kings' Arco Arena Noise-Meter.
• Roof improved offense by keeping out extreme cold.
• Built for 1976 Olympics.
• Plaque inside and statue of Jackie Robinson at main entrance. Robinson starred at the Delorimier Downs for the IL Montreal Royals in 1946.
• Huge 623-foot-high umbrella tower in center field from section 766 in left-center to section 767 in right-center stood half finished from 1976 to 1987.
• Became a fixed-dome stadium in 1989. The once retractable dome is silver on top, and orange on the bottom, with 26 white cones which link the roof to the tower. It consists of 60,696 square feet of Kevlar, weighing 50 tons. Retractable roof not actually retractable until 1988 due to generator problems, then became balky and decision was made to keep it closed.
• The stadium became open air again in 1998 when the dilapidated roof was removed in midseason.
• Parts of the concrete upper section of the stadium fell down in 1991, forcing the Expos to reschedule their September home games for the road.

NEW YORK, NEW YORK

YANKEE STADIUM

STYLE Classic
A.K.A. House That Ruth Built
OCCUPANT AL Yankees April 18, 1923 to Sept. 30, 1973; NNL Black Yankees 1946 to 1948; Negro League World Series 3rd game, 1942; 1st game 1947; AL Yankees April 15, 1976 to date
EVENT All-Star Game 1939, 1960, 1977
LOCATION *Left Field (N)* East 161st Street; *3rd Base (W)* Doughty Street, later Ruppert Place; *Home Plate (SW)* Major Degan Expressway/Interstate 87, then Harlem River; *1st Base (S)* East 157th Street; *Right Field (S)* River Avenue and IRT elevated tracks; in the southwest Bronx
SURFACE Grass—Merion Bluegrass
DIMENSIONS *Left Field:* 280.58 (1923), 301 (1928), 312 (1976), 318 (1988); *Left Side of Bullpen Gate in Short Left-Center:* 395 (1923), 402 (1928), 387 (1976), 379 (1985); *Right Side of Bullpen Gate:* 415 (1937); *Deepest Left-Center:* 500 (1923), 490 (1924), 457 (1937), 430 (1976), 411 (1985), 399 (1988); *Left Side of Center Field Screen:* 466 (1937); *Center Field:* 487 (1923), 461 (1937), 463 (1967), 417 (1976), 410 (1985), 408 (1988); *Deepest Right-Center:* 429 (1923), 407 (1937), 385 (1976); *Left Side of Bullpen Gate in Short Right-Center:* 350 (1923), 367 (1937), 353 (1976); *Right Side of Bullpen Gate:* 344 (1937); *Right Field:* 294.75 (1923), 295 (1930), 296 (1939), 310 (1976), 314 (1988); *Backstop:* 82 (1942), 80 (1953), 84 (1976); *Foul Territory:* Large for the catcher behind home plate, but small for fielders down the foul lines
FENCES *Left Field–Foul Line:* 3.92 (3 wire above .92 concrete 1923), 8 (canvas 1976); *Left-Center–Left of Visitors' Bullpen:* 3.58 (3 wire above .58 concrete); *Right of Visitors' Bullpen:* 7.83 (3 wire above 4.83 concrete), 7 (canvas 1976); *Center Field-Left Screen When Up for Hitters' Background:* 20 (1953), 22.25 (1959), 22.42 (1954); *Screen When Down:* 13.83,7 (canvas 1976); *Right-Center-Right of Screen:* 14.5 (3 wire above 11.5 concrete 1923); *Left of Home Bullpen:* 7.83 (3 wire above 4.83 concrete 1923); *Right of Home Bullpen:* 3.58 (3 wire above .58 concrete 1923), 8 (canvas 1976), 9 (canvas 1979); *Right Field-Foul Line:* 3.75 (3 wire above .75 concrete 1923), 10 (canvas 1976)
CAPACITY 57,545
FORMER USE City plot 2106, lot 100, a farm granted to John Lion Gardiner before the Revolutionary War.
PHENOMENA
- Accessible by C, D, and 4 trains; subway tracks just behind the bleachers in right-center.
- Left-center field monuments and plaques before the 1974-75 renovation: Monuments in fair territory, Lou Gehrig on the left, Miller Huggins in the middle, Babe Ruth on the right; now the monuments are beyond the fence same as before plus Mickey Mantle in 1996. Plaques beyond the fence: Ed Barrow, Jacob Ruppert, Joe DiMaggio, Mickey Mantle, Casey Stengel, Joe McCarthy, Pope Paul VI, Thurman Munson, Pope John Paul II, Billy Martin, Whitey Ford, Lefty Gomez, Roger Maris, Allie Reynolds, Elston Howard, Phil Rizzuto, Bill Dickey, Thurman Munson, and Yogi Berra.
- A ball hitting the foul pole in the 1930s was ruled to be in play, not a homer.
- Until Rule 48 was changed by major league baseball in December 1930, with the exception of several months in 1920, balls leaving the field fair but which hooked foul before they landed were foul. Could this have prevented some extra homers by Babe Ruth?
- "Death Valley" in left-center.
- Green curtain in center during the 1940s-1960s was sometimes raised and lowered like a window shade to force visiting batters to face a background of white-shirted bleacher fans but allow Yankee hitters to face a dark green background. Removed in World Series to sell more seats.
- Bleachers in right-center often called Ruthville and Gehrigville.
- Warning track red cinders; later on, red brick dust.
- Extra grass used to be kept near monuments in center, in play.
- Underneath second base in old stadium there was a 15-foot-deep brick-lined vault with electrical, telephone, and telegraphic connections for boxing events.
- As originally constructed, from May 5, 1922, to April 18, 1923, three concrete decks extended from behind home plate to each corner, with a single deck in left-center, and wooden bleachers around the rest of the outfield.
- In the winter of 1927-28, second and third decks were added to left-center, and several rows of box seats were removed in left, extending the foul pole from 281 to 301.
- During the 1936 season, the winter of 1936-37, and continuing through the 1937 season, the wooden bleachers were replaced with concrete ones. During the 1937 season, second and third decks were added in right-center. The bleacher changes shortened straightaway center from 490 to 461 and reduced seating capacity from the 80,000s to the 70,000s.
- As the outfield bench seats were gradually replaced with chair seats, in the 1930s and 1940s, the seating capacity gradually dropped from over 70,000 to about 67,000.
- Bloody Angle—between the bleachers and the right field foul line in 1923 season was very asymmetric and caused crazy bounces.
- Eliminating this in 1924 caused the plate to be moved 13 feet, and the deepest left-center corner changed from 500 to 490.
- Auxiliary scoreboards were built in the late 1940s, which covered up the 367 right-center sign and the 415 left-center sign.
- Minor modifications were made in the winter of 1966-67. During this work, a new 463 sign and a 433 sign appeared in the power alleys, and the exterior was painted blue and white.
- During 1974-75 renovation, iron third deck distinctive facade was removed, and a portion was placed in the bleachers.
- Home dugout switched from third base to first base on April 19, 1946.

SHEA STADIUM

STYLE Multipurpose

A.K.A. Flushing Meadow Stadium 1964

OCCUPANT NL Mets April 17, 1964 to date; AL Yankees, April 6, 1974 to Sept. 28, 1975, April 15, 1998

EVENT All-Star Game 1964

LOCATION *Center Field (NE)* 126th Street; *3rd Base (NW)* Northern Boulevard, then Whitestone Expressway/Interstate 678, then Flushing Bay; *Home Plate (SW)* Grand Central Parkway; *1st Base (SE)* Roosevelt Avenue; in Queens, near Flushing Meadow Park, site of 1939 and 1964 World's Fairs, just southeast of La Guardia Airport, in Queens.

SURFACE Bluegrass

DIMENSIONS *Foul Line:* 330 (marked 1964), 341 (actual 1964), 341 (1965), 338 (1979); *Power Alleys:* 371; *Center Field:* 410; *Backstop:* 80 (1964); *Foul Territory:* Very large

FENCES *Foul Lines:* 16.33 (4 wire and railing above 12.33 brick 1964), 12.33 (brick 1965), 8 (wood 1979); *Power Alleys:* 8 (wood); *Center Field:* Small section 8.75 (wood), most 8 (wood)

CAPACITY 55,601

PHENOMENA

• Designed to be expandable to 90,000 seats.

• Noisiest ballpark; frequent La Guardia Airport air traffic noise overhead.

• Named for attorney William Shea, who obtained the Mets franchise for New York by organizing the Continental League, which never got off the ground.

• Right-center scoreboard is 86 feet high with Bulova clock on top, 25 feet behind the outfield fence, and 175 feet long.

• Practice facilities under the right field stands.

• Behind fence in center, just to the right of the 410 mark, is a Mets Magic Top Hat. When a Met hits a homer, a red Big Apple rises out of the black top hat, which actually looks more like a big kettle.

• Foul lines from 1965 to 1978 had an orange home run line painted at the top of the 12-foot, 4-inch brick wall. Above this was a 4-foot wire screen and railing. A ball was a homer if it hit above the line. Like a similar ground rule at Crosley Field in center field, this caused many controversies, so in 1979 an inner 8-foot wooden fence was installed.

• Worst visibility for hitters in the majors.

• Church-like spire beyond center field fence formerly graced "Serval Zippers" sign.

• Outfield fences also marked as 358 and 396. From 1973 to 1979, there were also distance markers, outside the field of play, on the rear bullpen walls at 428, base of left-center light tower at 442, bottom edge of right-center scoreboard at 405 on right field end and 420 on center field end.

• 1964 Mets Banner Day—"Mongolia Loves The Mets" (in Mongolian) banner carried by the author; other banners included "E=mc2" (or Errors = Mets times customers squared),"Eamus Metropoli" (Let's go Mets in Latin).

• Christened April 16, 1964 with Dodgers Holy Water from the Gowanus Canal in Brooklyn and Giants Holy Water from the Harlem River at the exact location where it passed the old Polo Grounds.

• Fans can watch games for free from a walkway connecting to the 7 train Willets Point subway station.

• After a beam collapsed at Yankee Stadium, the Yankees were forced to play at Shea during the afternoon of April 15, 1998, even though the Mets had a game scheduled that night. It marked the first time in the 20th century that one ballpark housed two games for four different teams. In this odd day-night doubleheader the Yankees defeated the Angels, 6-3, and the Mets beat the Cubs, 2-1.

OAKLAND, CALIFORNIA

OAKLAND-ALAMEDA COUNTY COLISEUM

STYLE Multipurpose

A.K.A. Oakland Coliseum Complex, Oakland Mausoleum, 1970s

OCCUPANT AL Athletics April 17, 1968 to date

EVENT All-Star Game 1987

LOCATION *Center Field (NE)* San Leandro Street, then Southern Pacific Railroad tracks; *3rd Base (NW)* 66th Avenue; *Home Plate (SW)* Oakland-Alameda County Coliseum Arena, Nimitz Freeway, then San Leandro Bay; *1st Base (SE)* Hegenberger Drive

SURFACE Bluegrass

DIMENSIONS *Foul Lines:* 330; *Power Alleys:* 378 (1968), 375 (1969), 372 (1981), 367 (1996); *Center Field:* 410 (1968), 400 (1969), 396 (1981), 397 (1982), 400 (1990); *Backstop:* 90 (1968), 60 (1969); *Foul Territory:* Huge, largest in the majors

FENCES 8 (plywood 1968), 10 (canvas over plywood and plexiglass 1981), 8 (1986), Power Alleys 18 (1996)

CAPACITY 39,875

PHENOMENA

• Surrounded by beautiful green ivy slope.

• Backstop is a notch cut in stands.

• Possible to watch game for free from concourse behind the field seats by peering between wooden slats on cyclone fence.

• Steel shell of pitcher's mound was exposed on Opening Day April 17, 1968 and had to keep being covered between innings.

• Right field scoreboard installed June 1968.

• Finley Fun Board put in for 1969 season—24 feet high and 126 feet long.

• Named the Mausoleum in the late 1970s when the scoreboard didn't work, the entire stadium was gray concrete in color, and the A's were terrible.

• Huge foul area reduces batting by five to seven points, making this the best pitcher's park in the AL.

• Fun picnic atmosphere is the very best in the majors of all new concrete circular ugly ashtray stadia.

• Best food in baseball.

• Winds favor left-handed batters.

• Next door to Jewel Box, home of the NBA Golden State Warriors.

• Scoreboard shows upcoming home stands, with A's annihilating the opposition.

• Fans sitting at the foul poles can catch home run fair balls by reaching in front of the foul pole screens.

• Hand-operated scoreboard showing major league line scores installed in 1986.

• Renovated and expanded for Raiders football during 1996 season.

• UMAX Technologies bought the naming rights to the Coliseum in September 1997. A dispute arose and a 1998 court decision reinstated the original name.

PHILADELPHIA, PENNSYLVANIA

VETERANS STADIUM

STYLE Multipurpose
A.K.A. The Vet
OCCUPANT April 10, 1971 to date
EVENT All-Star Game 1976, 1996
LOCATION *Left Field (NE)* Packer Street and Interstate 76; *3rd Base (NW)* Broad Street, then Philadelphia Naval Hospital; *1st Base (SW)* Pattison Avenue, Spectrum; *Right Field (SE)* Tenth Street
SURFACE AstroTurf—fast, but slower since 1977
DIMENSIONS *Foul Lines:* 330; *Power Alleys:* 371; *Center Field:* 408; *Backstop:* 60; *Foul Territory:* Large
FENCES 6 (wood April 1972); 8 (wood June 1971); 12 (6 plexiglass above 6 wood 1972)
CAPACITY 62,363
PHENOMENA
• The park's rounded rectangular shape is called an octorad by the architects.
• Connie Mack Stadium's home plate was transplanted here.
• Plastic tarp covered unfinished right field wall in April 1971.
• "Liberty Bell" used to hang from center field roof in fourth level—hit only by Greg Luzinski on May 16, 1972.
• First ball dropped from a helicopter on April 10, 1971.
• Smallest hot dogs and loudest boos in baseball.
• Statues of Connie Mack and a sliding runner outside the park.
• Phils downed Padres 6-5 in 10 innings here on July 3, 1993 in the nightcap of a thrice rain-delayed twinbill that ended at 4:40 a.m.

PHOENIX, ARIZONA

BANK ONE BALLPARK

STYLE Retractable Dome
A.K.A. The Bob
OCCUPANT NL Diamondbacks March 31, 1998 to date
LOCATION *(W)* Fourth Street, *(N)* Jefferson Street, *(E)* Seventh Street, *(S)* Southern Pacific railroad tracks.
SURFACE Shade-tolerant DeAnza zoysia natural grass
DIMENSIONS *Left Field:* 330; *Power Alleys:* 374; *Center Field:* 407; *Deepest Left-Center and Right-Center:* 413; *Right Field:* 334; *Apex of Dome:* 200.
FENCES 8
CAPACITY 48,700
PHENOMENA
• Dirt path between pitcher's mound and the plate is first in over five decades.
• Sun Pool Pavilion features a pool and jacuzzi which hold 35 people, 415 feet from home plate, behind the fence in right center field.
• With an approximate elevation of 1,100 feet, Bank One Ballpark is the second highest facility in the majors, trailing only Coors Field.
• A pair of 200-horsepower motors can open or close the roof in slightly less than five minutes, utilizing more than four miles of cable strung through a pulley system.
• Each half of the roof consists of three moveable trusses which telescope over a fixed end truss. The east and west sides of the roof can operate either in unison or independently.
• More than 80 percent of the seats are inside the foul poles, and there is no upper deck around the outfield.

PITTSBURGH, PENNSYLVANIA

THREE RIVERS STADIUM

STYLE Multipurpose
A.K.A. House That Clemente Built
OCCUPANT NL Pirates July 16, 1970 to date
EVENT All-Star Game 1974, 1994
LOCATION *Left Field (E)* Interstate 279 Fort Duquesne Bridge approach ramp; *3rd Base (N)* Reedsdale Street; *1st Base (W)* Allegheny Avenue, Ohio River, and the original point where the Monongahela River joins the Allegheny River to form the Ohio River; *Right Field (S)* North Shore Avenue, Roberto Clemente Memorial Park, Allegheny River; Stadium Circle encircles the park
SURFACE Carpet—Tartanturf 1970 to 1982; AstroTurf to date
DIMENSIONS *Foul Lines:* 340 (1970), 335 (1975); *Power Alleys:* 385 (1970), 375 (1975); *Center Field:* 410 (1970), 400 (1975); *Backstop:* 60; *Foul Territory:* Large
FENCES 10 (wood)
CAPACITY 47,972
PHENOMENA
• Roberto Clemente statue dedicated here in 1994.
• On a site that was an island during the French and Indian Wars. It had been an Indian burial ground, a fact discovered when the Big Flood of 1763 uncovered many graves. Named Kilbuck Island after a friendly Delaware Indian chief. Back channels were filled with silt, and it was no longer an island by 1852.
• Numbers painted on seats in right field upper deck where Willie Stargell's homers landed.
• Without the inner fence, the outfield would be 342 down the lines and 434 to center.
• The Honus Wagner statue, which used to stand outside of Forbes Field, now stands outside of Three Rivers.
• An 8- by 12-foot area of the 406 marker section of the Forbes Field brick wall, 12 Romanesque window frames, and the Babe Ruth plaque showing where his 714th home run landed, are in the Allegheny Club at Three Rivers.
• Original design by Erik Sirko was for a "Stadium Over the Monongahela," with stadium above two parking lot levels, all sitting above the Monongahela River with plenty of room for boats to pass beneath on the river.
• Fan drove his car into the stadium and overturned a 70-gallon jug of cheese dip on Dec. 3, 1987.

ST. LOUIS, MISSOURI

BUSCH STADIUM (II)

STYLE Multipurpose

A.K.A. Civic Center Stadium 1966, Busch Memorial Stadium 1966 to 1983

OCCUPANT NL Cardinals May 12, 1966 to date

EVENT All-Star Game 1966

LOCATION *Left Field (E)* Broadway, then Interstate 70, Gateway Arch and Mississippi River; *3rd Base (N)* Walnut Street; *1st Base (W)* Seventh Street, also named McGwire Way; *Right Field (S)* Spruce Street.

SURFACE Grass 1966 to 1969. Carpet—very fast—1970 to 1995. Grass 1996 to date. From 1970 to 1976, the entire field was carpeted except for the part of the infield that is normally dirt on a grass field. In 1977 this was carpeted except for the sliding pits. This is one of only two instances where there was a full dirt infield, with an otherwise fully carpeted field, the other being Candlestick in 1971.

DIMENSIONS *Foul Lines:* 330; *Power Alleys:* 386 (1966), 376 (1973), 386 (1977), 383 (July 1983), 375 (1992); *Center Field:* 414 (1966), 410 (1971), 414 (1972), 404 (1973), 414 (1977), 402 (1992); *Backstop:* 64 (Vin Scully's unofficial measurement during 1985 World Series showed this to be 50 rather than 64); *Foul Territory:* Large

FENCES *Left and Right Fields:* 10.5 (padded concrete), 8 (padded canvas 1992); *Center Field:* 10.5 (padded concrete 1966), 8 (wood 1973), 10.5 (padded concrete 1977), 8 (padded canvas 1992)

CAPACITY 49,676

PHENOMENA

• A line drive park because of the deep alleys, deep center field and the quick surface.

• Open arches surround the field just below the roof.

• From 1966 to 1982 right field scoreboard lights showed a cardinal in flight when a Cardinal hit a home run; same show was put on each time Lou Brock set a new base-stealing record.

• Home plate transplanted from old Busch Stadium at opener on May 12, 1966.

• Next to the Gateway Arch and the Mississippi River; you can see the Arch from the top deck behind first base.

• Statue of "Stan the Man" Musial outside the stadium was unveiled in 1968.

• Small sections of bleachers in the outfield.

• Chicken wire basket (à la Wrigley Field in Chicago), installed in front of left-center and right-center bleacher sections in July 1983, was 2 feet high and reduced distance to fence by 3 feet (386 to 383 in power alleys). It did not raise the height of the 10½ foot wall.

• At league direction, the site designated for any Cubs playoffs or World Series home games from 1986 until 1988, when Wrigley Field got lights.

• Most fans at the stadium seem to be wearing Cardinal red.

• Seventh inning brings the Clydesdale horses to the scoreboard.

• When Anheuser-Busch owned the Cards, they played "King of Beers" theme song on the organ during the seventh inning stretch instead of "Take Me Out to the Ballgame."

ST. PETERSBURG, FLORIDA

TROPICANA FIELD

STYLE Dome

A.K.A. Thunderdome, Florida Suncoast Dome

OCCUPANT AL Devil Rays March 31, 1998 to date

LOCATION *Left field (N),* Central Avenue; *third base (W),* 16th Street N; *first base (S),* Dunmore Avenue S; *right field (E),* 11th Street S

SURFACE AstroTurf-12 with dirt infield

DIMENSIONS *Left Field:* 315; *Power Alleys:* 371; *Deepest Left-Center:* 415; *Center Field:* 407; *Right Field:* 322; *Apex of Dome:* 225.

FENCES 9½

CAPACITY 45,360

PHENOMENA

• Opened in 1990 in an attempt to lure a major league team. White Sox nearly came in 1990. Giants announced in a September 1992 press conference that they would be moving; the deal later fell through. Several other teams used the threat of a move to St. Petersburg as leverage with their own hometown.

• Patterned after Ebbets Field's outfield dimensions. The main entrance on the east side of stadium features an Ebbets Field style rotunda.

• Scene of only the third full dirt infield on an otherwise fully carpeted field; the others being the Astrodome 1966-70 and Candlestick Park in 1971.

• Scene of furious rhubarbs over ground rules concerning whether balls which hit the four catwalks which hang over the outfield were homers or in play. On May 27, 1998, the league approved a ground rule change making balls hitting the two lower catwalks automatic home runs.

• Restaurant in straightaway center field features a specially designed dark film that gives batters an ideal background for seeing a pitch coming off the mound.

• Translucent roof is illuminated orange on nights when Devil Rays are not playing.

SAN DIEGO, CALIFORNIA

QUALCOMM STADIUM

STYLE Multipurpose

A.K.A. San Diego Stadium 1969 to 1980, Jack Murphy Stadium 1981 to 1996, The Murph

OCCUPANT NL Padres April 8, 1969 to date

EVENT All-Star Games 1978, 1992

LOCATION *Left Field (N)* 9449 Friars Road; *3rd Base (W)* Stadium Way then a quarry; *1st Base (S)* San Diego River, then Camino del Rio North, and Interstate 8; *Right Field (E)* Interstate 15

SURFACE Santa Ana Bermuda grass

DIMENSIONS *Foul Lines:* 330 (1969), fence 327 (1982), foul poles 329 (1982); *Power Alleys:* 375 (1969), 370 (1982); *Center Field:* 420 (1969), 410 (1973), 420 (1978), 405 (1982); *Backstop:* 80 (1969), 75 (1982)

FENCES *Left and Right Fields:* 17.5 (concrete 1969), 9 (line painted on concrete 1973), 18 (concrete 1974), 8.5 (canvas 1982); *Center Field:* 17.5 (concrete 1969), 10 (wood 1973), 18 (concrete 1978), 8.5 (canvas 1982), one section in right center 9 (canvas 1982); *Right field:* 17.5 (scoreboard 1997)

FORMER USE San Diego River ran through the area, which was then a marshy swampland.

CAPACITY 59,772

PHENOMENA

• Was originally named for Jack Murphy, the local sports editor who campaigned to bring major league baseball to San Diego.

• Noticeable lack of Spanish-speaking fans and Spanish language advertisements in the only major league ballpark adjacent to the Mexican border was reversed in the late 1990s.

• Foul poles sit two feet behind the fence, and one foot in front of the wall.

• The right-center scoreboard sits directly behind the right-center seats, and used to be so hot that fans there could feel the heat on their backs.

• Only park where bullpen dirt area touches the foul lines.

• Only park where a foul ball can be caught out of sight of all umpires and most players. Location is in either bullpen near the foul poles.

• After 1981 season, the plate was moved 5 feet back toward the backstop.

• Expanded during 1983 football season by adding seats in right and right-center.

• Ivy put on center field fence in 1980.

• A 20-foot-wide black batter's eye section on both center field wall and fence July-October 1982.

SAN FRANCISCO, CALIFORNIA

3COM PARK

STYLE Multipurpose

OCCUPANT NL Giants April 12, 1960 to date

A.K.A. Candlestick Park 1960 to 1996, The Stick, Maury's Lake, Cave of the Winds, Wind Tunnel, Croix de Candlestick, North Pole

EVENT All-Star Game 1961, 1984

LOCATION *Left Field (NW)* Giants Drive; *3rd Base (SW)* Jamestown Avenue, then Bay View Hill; *1st Base (SE)* Jamestown Avenue, Candlestick Point and San Francisco Bay; *Right Field (NE)* Hunters Point Expressway, then San Francisco Bay; Candlestick Point, with its rock outcroppings, was leveled to fill in the water for the parking lots.

SURFACE Grass (1960), Carpet (1971), Bluegrass (1979)

DIMENSIONS *Left Field:* 330 (1960), 335 (1968); *Left-Center:* 397 (1960), 365 (1961); *Center Field:* 420 (1960), 410 (1961), 400 (1993); *Right-Center:* 397 (1960), 365 (1961); *Right Field:* 330 (1965), 335 (1968), 330 (1991), 328 (1993); *Backstop:* 73 (1960), 70 (1961), 55 (1975), 65 (1982), 66 (1985); *Foul Territory:* Very large

FENCES 10 (wire 1960); 8 (wire 1972); 12 (6 canvas below 6 plexiglass 1975); 9 (6 canvas below 3 plexiglass 1982); 9 (wire 1984), 9.5 (fence posts 1984); 8 (canvas 1993)

CAPACITY 62,000

PHENOMENA

• Named for jagged rocks and trees which rise from the tidelands like giant candlesticks.

• Many fans arrived by boat in 1960s.

• Only hot-water-heated open-air stadium in the majors.

• Bay View Hill overlooks the park from behind third base.

• Before the bleachers were enclosed, so many fans would stream out of the bleachers in right-center when Mays and McCovey batted and crowd up against the flimsy cyclone fence, that a white line was painted on the asphalt 20 feet behind the fence. Fans had to stand behind this line.

• Fifty-nine posts every 20 feet or so on the outfield fence can cause strange bounces—their tips extend 6 inches above the 9 foot wire fence.

• Wind, wind, and more wind! Before the stadium was enclosed, wind blew in from left-center and out toward right-center. Now that it is enclosed, the wind is a swirling monster, just as strong as before.

• Giants retired numbers on white baseballs on the right field fence.

• Maury's Lake—the basepath between first and second was drenched before the game to make it more difficult for Dodger Maury Wills to steal second in the early 1960s.

• Umps protested location of foul poles being completely in fair territory in third inning of opening game on April 12, 1960.

• Stu Miller was blown off the mound by the wind in the 1961 All-Star Game.

• The stadium was enlarged and fully enclosed in the winter of 1971-72 to house the 49ers.

• Architect John Bolles' boomerang-shaped concrete shell baffle behind the upper tier's last row of seats was intended to protect the park from wind; it didn't work.

• In the winter of 1978-79, the Giants ripped up their carpet and replaced it with grass.

• Coldest park in the majors, resulting in fewer home runs.

• Croix de Candlestick pin awarded to fans at conclusion of night extra-inning games because of extreme wind chill conditions.

SEATTLE, WASHINGTON

KINGDOME

STYLE Dome

A.K.A. King County Stadium, The Tomb (1980s), Puget Puke (1980s)

OCCUPANT AL Mariners April 6, 1977 to date

EVENT All-Star Game 1979

LOCATION *Left Field (N)* 201 South King Street; *3rd Base (W)* 589 Occidental Avenue South; *1st Base (S)* South Royal Brougham Way; *Right Field (E)* Fourth Avenue South, then Burlington Northern Railroad tracks; *Above:* Domed roof

SURFACE AstroTurf

DIMENSIONS *Left Field:* 315 (1977), 316 (marked 1978), 314 (actual 1978), 324 (1990), 331 (1991); *Left-Center:* 375 (1977), 365 (1978), 357 (1981), 362 (1990), 376 (1991); *Deep Left-Center:* 385 (1990), 389 (1991); *Center Field:* 405 (1977), 410 (1978), 405 (1981), 410 (1986), 405 (1991); *Deep Right-Center:* 375 (1990), 380 (1991); *Right-Center:* 375 (1977), 365 (1978), 357 (1981), 352 (1990); *Right Field:* 315 (1977), 316 (1978),

314 (1990), 312 (1991); *Speakers in Left (3), Left-Center, and Center:* 110 (1977), 133.5 (1981); *11 other speakers* 130; *Backstop:* 63; *Apex of Dome:* 250; *Foul Territory:* Large

FENCES *Left Field:* 11.5 (wood 1977), 17.5 (6 plexiglass over wood 1988), 11.5 (wood 1990); *Center Field:* 11.5 (wood 1977); *Right Field:* 11.5 (wood 1977), 23.25 (wood 1982), 11.5 (wood 1988)

CAPACITY 59,084

PHENOMENA

• Large American flag flies above the concrete dome.

• A 23-foot Mini-Green Monster in right and right-center is called the Walla Walla.

• Carpet is rolled out by the Rhinoceros machine, and smoothed by the Grasshopper machine after it has been zipped together.

• Baby-changing areas in aisles 111, 113, 201, 203.

• Domed roof looks from below like it's made of thousands of bricks.

• Sick's Stadium home plate on display in Royal Brougham trophy case.

• In the winter of 1980-81, the three speakers above left, left-center, and center were raised from 102 to 133.5 feet to reduce the chance of their being hit again.

• Two foul balls have gone up but never come down: Aug. 4, 1979—Ruppert Jones of Mariners hit a foul ball that stuck in the speaker above the first base dugout, thus disproving the old adage of physics that what goes up must come down. On May 20, 1983, Ricky Nelson of the Brewers did the same. By some arcane logic, both fly balls were ruled strikes.

• Four foul balls have bounced off speakers and been caught for outs: Aug. 3, 1979, caught by A's pitcher Matt Keough; Sept. 3, 1979, caught by Mariners' first baseman; May 19, 1980, caught by Mariners' first baseman; April 25, 1985, caught by Mariners' pitcher Mark Langston.

• Other foul balls have bounced off the Supersonics basketball speakers above first base and the basketball scoreboard above and behind home plate, without being caught.

• One fair ball bounced off a roof support wire and remained in play on April 11, 1985—a ball hit by Dave Kingman of A's was caught for an out in deep left: it would have been a home run. One fair ball has struck the right field speaker—Ken Phelps of the Mariners hit a tape-measure homer on August 13, 1987—the ball landed foul.

• Seven fair balls have bounced off speakers and remained in play.

• Called the Tomb by visiting sportswriters because it was sickeningly gray concrete and quiet in the 1980s.

• Roof's hanging red, white, and blue streamers can tangle up an infield fly and deflect it.

• U.S.S. *Mariner*—a huge yellow sailing ship behind the center-field fence which fires a cannon after every Mariner homer.

• There are 42 air-conditioning units, 16 in fair territory, 26 in foul territory, eight ducts in each unit. These blow air in toward the field which means fewer home runs in what would normally be a "Homer Dome" because of the short 357 foot power alleys.

• Outfield distances marked on fences in both feet and fathoms 1977-80 (1 fathom = 6 feet).

• Third deck highest at third base and in right field. AL East and AL West standings posted on right field third deck facade.

• Plate moved 10 feet toward first base dugout in 1990 in a change that altered outfield distances.

• New classic "in-play" 123-feet by 11½-foot scoreboard placed on right field wall in 1990 in dramatic facelift. It matches the Metrodome's right field wall as the second-highest wall in the major leagues (23 feet) after Boston's "Green Monster" at Fenway Park (37 feet).

• Scene of Funny Nose-Eye Glasses night and Buhner Buzz Night.

• Mariners played home games on the road just before the 1994 strike after tiles fell off roof on July 19.

TORONTO, ONTARIO

SKYDOME

STYLE Retractable Dome

OCCUPANT AL Blue Jays June 5, 1989 to date

EVENT All-Star Game 1991

LOCATION *Center Field (N)* Front Street West; *3rd Base (W)* Spadina Avenue; *Home Plate (S)* Gardiner Expressway; *1st Base (E)* John Street, then CN Tower, the world's largest free-standing structure

SURFACE AstroTurf

DIMENSIONS *Left Field:* 328; *Left-Center:* 375; *Center Field:* 400; *Right-Center:* 375; *Right Field:* 328; *Apex of Dome:* 282

FENCES 10 (canvas)

FORMER USE Water Supply pumping station where second base is now

CAPACITY 51,000

PHENOMENA

• The 400-foot sign in center is actually right of dead center.

• Stands 31 stories high (Astrodome is just 18).

• SkyDome's Jumbotron scoreboard is the world's biggest video display board (115 by 33 feet).

• Hotel inside SkyDome has 348 rooms, 70 with a view of (and by) the stadium.

• SkyDome Fitness Club boasts the world's largest indoor running track (2.2 laps per mile circuit) at the top of the stadium.

• First park to draw over 4 million fans in a season (1991-93).

• SkyDome's retractable four-panel, 11,000-ton roof takes 20 minutes to open or close; uses $500 Canadian in electricity in doing so.

• When roof is opened 91 percent of all seats are exposed to sky.

• Facilities include a Hard Rock Cafe and the 650-seat Windows on SkyDome restaurant.

• Jose Canseco became the first player to hit a home run into the stadium's fifth deck with a memorable blast in Game 4 of the 1989 ALCS.

• Site of first World Series games played outside United States.

• Also home to the Toronto Argonauts of the Canadian Football League.

• Two 30-pound roof tiles fell during a game on June 22, 1995, injuring seven fans.

Storied Parks of the Past

ATLANTA, GEORGIA

ATLANTA-FULTON COUNTY STADIUM
STYLE   Multipurpose
A.K.A.   Atlanta Stadium 1965-74, Launching Pad
OCCUPANT   NL Braves April 12, 1966 to October 24, 1996
EVENT   All-Star Game 1972
LOCATION   *Left Field (NE)* Puliman Street then Interstate 20; *3rd Base (NW)* Washington Street then Interstate 75/85; *1st Base (SW)* 521 Capitol Avenue; *Right Field (SE)* Fulton Street
SURFACE   Grass
DIMENSIONS   *Foul Lines:* 325 (1966), 330 (1967); *Power Alleys:* 385 (1966), 375 (1969), 385 (1974); *Center Field:* 402 (1966), 400 (1969), 402 (1973); *Backstop:* 59.92 (1973); *Foul Territory:* Large (1966), Medium (1977)
FENCES   6 (wire 1966), 10 (4 plexiglass above 6 wire 1983), 10 (plexiglass 1985)
CAPACITY   52,270
PHENOMENA
• Three statues outside the stadium honored Ty Cobb, Hank Aaron, and Phil Niekro.
• Big Victor, a large totem-pole-styled figure, stood in the stadium in 1966. The huge head tilted and the eyes rolled whenever a Brave hit a home run.
• With an altitude of more than 1,000 feet above sea level, it was—until Colorado entered the major leagues—the highest park in the majors, which resulted in many homers.
• Chief Noc-A-Homa's Wigwam replaced Big Victor in 1967. From 1967 to 1971 the teepee stood on a 20-foot-square platform behind the left field fence. In 1972 the teepee was moved to right field. From 1973 to 1977 it returned to left field. From 1978 to August 1982 the teepee was moved to left-center, occupying 235 seats between aisles 128 and 130, rows 18-30. From August to early September 1982, it was removed in anticipation of additional revenue in the playoffs, "causing" a disastrous tailspin for the first-place Braves. Its replacement coincided with the Braves' comeback to win the division crown in 1982. The teepee's removal on Aug. 11, 1983, saw another losing streak which could not be overcome by its return on Sept. 16.
• A 22-foot outfield wall was never in play.
• An 80-year-old calliope organ was installed in 1971.
• Only park to close with a World Series contest.
• Called "The Launching Pad" because hot weather caused many home runs.
• Mets defeated Braves here 16-13 in 19 innings. The game was twice delayed by rain and ended at 3:55 a.m. on July 5, 1985.

PONCE DE LEON PARK
STYLE   Minor League
A.K.A.   Spiller Park 1924 to 1932, Poncey
OCCUPANT   NSL Black Crackers 1932; NAL Black Crackers 1938
LOCATION   *Left Field: (N)* Parking lot; *3rd Base (W)* North Boulevard; *1st Base (S)* 650 Ponce de Leon Boulevard; *Right Field: (E)* Southern Railroad tracks
DIMENSIONS   *Left Field* 365 (1932), 330 (1949); *Left-Center, Left Side of Scoreboard* 525; *Center Field* 462 (1932), 448 (1938), 410 (1949); *Right Field* 321 (1932), 324 (1938)
FENCES   *Left Field:* 2 (hedge, April 1949), 4 (cyclone fence, May 1949); *Left-Center:* 25 (scoreboard); *Center Field* 6; *Right-Center:* Magnolia Tree halfway up very steep embankment, no fence; *Right Field:* 15
CURRENT USE   Parking lot opposite Sears department store since being torn down in 1967
PHENOMENA
• First Ponce de Leon Park, built in 1907, burned down Sept. 9, 1923.
• A 2-foot-high hedge formed the outfield fence from the left field line to the right side of the left-center scoreboard in 1949. It reduced the foul line from 365 to 330 and caused numerous arguments because a left fielder had to stay within the hedge. If he fell over it, the hit was a homer.

BALTIMORE, MARYLAND

MEMORIAL STADIUM
STYLE   Multipurpose
OCCUPANT   AL Orioles April 15, 1954 to Sept. 30, 1991
EVENT   All-Star Game 1958
LOCATION   *Center Field (N)* East 36th Street; *3rd Base (W)* Ellerslie Avenue; *Home Plate (S)* 1000 East 33rd Street, section of 33rd Street near ballpark known as Babe Ruth Plaza; *1st Base (E)* Ednor Road
SURFACE   Bluegrass
DIMENSIONS   *Foul Lines:* 309; where the 7-foot fence meets the 14-foot wall, 360; *Power Alleys:* 446 (1954), 447 (1955), 405 (1956), 380 (1958), 370 (1962), 385 (1970), 375 (1976), 378 (1977), 376 (1980), 378 (1990); *Center Field:* 445 (1954), 450 (1955), 425 (1956), 410 (1958), 400 (1976), 405 (1977), 410 (1978), 405 (1980); *Backstop:* 78 (1954), 58 (1961), 54 (1980), 75 (1987); *Foul Territory:* Large
FENCES   *Foul Line Corners:* 11.33 (concrete 1954), 14 (11 concrete below 3 plywood 1959); these walls bounce balls toward center, reducing triples; *Left-Center to Right-Center:* 10 (hedges April and May, 1954), 8 (wire June 1954), 7 (wire 1955), 6 (wire 1958), 14 (wire 1961), 6 (wire 1963), 7 (canvas 1977)
FORMER USE   Venable Stadium
PHENOMENA
• Beautiful trees on an embankment beyond the fence in center.
• Oriole Landing was a picnic area in the upper deck in the 1960s.
• At the beginning of the 1954 season, hedges served as the center field fence. In June 1954 a wire fence was erected which stood right in front of a row of high hedges. The top 6 feet of the fence were covered with canvas padding in 1958 after Harvey Kuenn cut his face trying to catch a home run ball by climbing the fence. The walls in the left and right field corners were also padded after Curt Blefary injured his hip chasing a Max Alvis fly.

• Fans yell "O" (for Orioles) in unison when "The Star-Spangled Banner" reaches "O say does that star-spangled banner yet wave . . ."
• Wind usually helped hitters.
• Venable Stadium, a football stadium also used for baseball after the July 4, 1944 fire destroyed Oriole Park (V), was torn down to make way for Memorial Stadium. Home plate was moved from where it had been in the north to its current location in the south.
• Home of the best crabcakes in baseball; crab races in the bottom of the sixth on the scoreboard between Wee Willie in orange, Paco in blue, and Mugsy in yellow.
• Inscribed into the concrete facade: "Dedicated as a memorial to all who so valiantly fought in the world wars with eternal gratitude to those who made the supreme sacrifice to preserve equality and freedom throughout the world—time will not dim the glory of their deeds."
• Used for Eastern League Bowie Baysox games in 1993.

BOSTON, MASSACHUSETTS

HUNTINGTON AVENUE BASEBALL GROUNDS
STYLE Wooden
OCCUPANT AL Red Sox May 8, 1901 to Oct. 7, 1911
LOCATION *Left Field (N)* Huntington Avenue; *3rd Base (W)* Rogers Avenue, later Forsyth Street; *1st Base (S)* New York, New Haven and Hartford Railroad Tracks; *Right Field (E)* New Gravely Street and Gainsborough Street; just north of South End Grounds
DIMENSIONS *Left Field:* 440; *Center Field:* 635; *Right Field:* 280; *Backstop:* 60
FORMER USE Circuses and carnivals
CURRENT USE Northeastern University's indoor athletic building, known officially as Godfrey Lowell Cabot Physical Education Center and informally as Cabot Cage. A room there, devoted to mementos of the 1901 to 1911 era, is called the World Series Exhibit Room. A plaque commemorating the former location of the right field foul pole was unveiled in May 1956.
PHENOMENA
• Scene of the first NL-AL World Series in 1903.
• The 635 distance to center is an approximation by Bob Bluthardt, working from a scale drawing.

BRAVES FIELD
STYLE Classic
A.K.A. National League Field, 1936 to 1940; National League Ball Park, 1936 to 1940; Bee Hive, 1936 to 1940; Wigwam, Nickerson Field
OCCUPANT NL Braves August 18, 1915 to Sept. 21, 1952 AL Red Sox 1915 and 1916 World Series, and Sunday games 1929 to June 1932
LOCATION *Left Field (NW)* Boston and Albany R.R. tracks, Storrow Drive, and Charles River; *3rd Base (SW)* Babcock Street; *1st Base (SE)* Commonwealth Avenue; *Right Field (NE)* 34 Gaffney Street
DIMENSIONS *Left Field:* 402.5 (early 1915), 396 (late 1915), 402.42 (1921), 404 (1922), 402.5 (1926), 320 (April 1928), 353.5 (July 1928), 340 (1930), 353.67 (1931), 359 (1933), 353.67 (1934), 368 (1936), 350 (1940), 337 (1941), 334 (1942), 340 (1943), 337 (1944); *Left-Center:* 330 (April, 1928), 359 (July, 1928), 365

(1942); *Center Field:* 520 (1926), 387 (April 1928), 417 (July 1928), 387.17 (1929), 394.5 (1930), 387.25 (1931), 417 (1933), 426 (1936), 407 (1937), 408 (1939), 385 (1940), 401 (1941), 375 (1942), 370 (1943), 390 (1944), 380 (1945), 370 (1946); *Deepest Center Field corner,* just right of straightaway center: 550 (1915), 401 (1942), 390 (1943); *Right-Center:* 362 (1942), 355 (1943); *Right Field:* 402 (early 1915), 375 (late 1915), 365 (1921), 364 (1928), 297.75 (1929), 297.92 (1931), 364 (1933), 297 (1936) 376 (1937), 378 (1938), 350 (1940), 340 (early 1943), 320 (late 1943), 340 (April 1944), 320 (May 1944), 340 (April 1946), 320 (May 1946), 318 (1947), 320 (1948), 319 (1948); *Backstop:* 75 (1915), 60 (1936)
FENCES *Left Field to Right-Center:* 10 (concrete 1915), 8 (wood 1928), 20 (wood 1946), 25 (wood 1948), 19 (wood 1953); *Left Field scoreboard sides:* 64 (1949); *middle arch:* 68 (1949); *Left-Center:* 1 (gravestones July, 1928); *Right-Center:* exit gate 8 (wire); *Right Field:* 10 (6 screen above 4 wood)
FORMER USE Allston Golf Club
CURRENT USE Nickerson Field, a football stadium, home for the B.U. Terriers and 1983 USFL Boston Breakers. Also Myles Standish Dorms, three Boston University dorm towers near 3rd base.
PHENOMENA
• In 1915 there was a ground level scoreboard in left.
• In 1928 plate was turned towards right and inner fences were added.
• The infield grass was transported from the old South End Grounds in 1915, and was kept very long by the groundskeepers.
• Left field bleachers installed April 1928, removed slowly in a process that took from mid-June to the end of the season. Scoreboard moved from top of the left-center wall to the rear of right field in 1928; later moved to Kansas City Municipal Stadium in 1955.
• Jury Box—small bleachers section behind the fence in right with very vocal fans.
• In 1936 home plate was moved 15 feet closer to the backstop.
• In the 1940s fir trees were planted beyond the fence in center in an unsuccessful attempt to hide from the fans the huge clouds of railroad locomotive smoke belching from the Boston and Albany tracks in left and center.
• In 1946 the field was turned again slightly toward right. In 1937, a notch was cut in the right field bleachers, which can still be seen today in the former home of the United States Football League Breakers, Nickerson Field.
• In 1946, 5,000 fans left the home opener with green paint on their clothing because that morning's paint job on the seats had not yet dried—the Braves paid $6,000 in claims to irate fans, and played the rest of their April home games at Fenway.
• In June 1947, the field was lowered by 18 inches.
• Boston University purchased the field in the 1950s, and laid out a football carpet from the first base dugout to right center.
• The right field foul line bleachers, extending from first base to the right field foul pole, still stand.
• The Gaffney Street first base entrance still stands.
• The concrete outer wall in right and center still stands.

BROOKLYN, NEW YORK

EBBETS FIELD

STYLE Classic
OCCUPANT NL Dodgers April 9, 1913 to Sept. 24, 1957, NNL Eagles 1935
EVENT All-Star Game 1949
LOCATION *Left Field (NE)* Montgomery Street; *3rd Base (NW)* Franklin Avenue, later Cedar Place, later Mc-Keever Place; *1st Base (SW)* 55 Sullivan Place; *Right Field (SE)* Bedford Avenue; in the Pigtown/Crown Heights district of Flatbush, near the Gowanus Canal.
DIMENSIONS *Left Field:* 419 (1913), 410 (1914), 418.75 (1921), 383.67 (1926), 382.83 (1930), 384 (1931), 353 (1932), 356.33 (1934), 365 (1938), 357 (1939), 365 (1940), 356 (1942), 357 (1947), 343 (1948), 348 (1953), 343 (1955), 348 (1957). There is some confusion about distances because the left field foul line and grandstand wall were the same near the corner between the 343 and 357 markers. *Left-Center:* 365 (1932), 351 (1948); *Deep Left-Center at Bend in Wall:* 407 (1932), 393 (1948), 395 (1954); *Center Field:* 450 (1914), 466 (1930), 460.79 (early 1931), 447 (late 1931), 399.42 (1932), 399 (1936), 402 (1938), 400 (1939), 399 (1947), 384 (1948), 393 (1955); *Right Side of Center Field Grandstand:* 390 (1932), 376 (1948); *Right-Center's Deepest Corner:* 500 (1913), 476.75 (1926), 415 (1932), 403 (1948), 405 (1950), 403 (1955); *Right Side of Right-Center Field Exit Gate:* 399 (1932); *Right-Center:* 352; *Scoreboard:* left side 344, right side 318; *Right Field:* 301 (1913), 300 (1914), 296.17 (1921), 292 (1922), 301 (1926), 296.08 (1930), 295.92 (1931), 296.5 (1934), 297 (1938); *Backstop:* 64 (1942), 70.5 (1954), 72 (1957)
FENCES *Left Field to Left-Center:* 20 (1913), 3 (wood 1920), 9.87 (concrete 1931); *Center Field:* 20 (1913), 393 marker: 9.87 (concrete 1931) sloping upward; 376 marker: 15 (concrete 1931); *Right-Center:* 9 (concrete 1913), from 376 point to screen: 15 sloping upward to 19, then down to 13; *Right-Center to Right Field:* 38 (top 19 screen, bottom 19 concave concrete wall, bent at 9.5 midpoint, vertical top half, concave angled bottom half); *Screen in Center Field:* 20 (screen above sloping concrete 1920s); *Right Field Before the Screen:* 9 (concrete 1913)
FORMER USE The Pigtown garbage dump
CURRENT USE Scoreboard clock was moved to top of right field scoreboard at McCormick Field, Asheville, N.C. Ebbets Field Apartments housing development built in 1963 and the I.S. 320 Intermediate School is across the road. Apartments renamed Jackie Robinson Apartments at Ebbets Field in 1972; renamed Ebbets Field Apartments in mid-1970s. Jackie Robinson School, previously known as Crown Heights, houses the Brooklyn Dodger Hall of Fame.
PHENOMENA
• Rotunda was 80-foot circle enclosed in Italian marble with floor tiled with stitches of a baseball, a chandelier with 12 baseball-bat arms holding 12 globes shaped like baseballs. There were 12 turnstiles and 12 gilded ticket windows. The domed ceiling was 27 feet high at its center.
• Little kids watched the game through a gap under the metal gate in right-center.
• Cobblestoned Bedford Avenue was a hill, climbing from a low point in right field to higher ground in center field.
• Right field wall and scoreboard had approximately 289 different angles—the scoreboard jutted out 5 feet from the wall at a 45-degree angle. Overhang of the center field second deck hung out over the field. Scoreboard built after 1930.
• Schaefer Beer sign on the top of the right-center scoreboard notified fans of official scorer's decision—the "H" in Schaefer lit up for a hit, an "E" for an error—the sign was erected after World War II.
• Abe Stark sign offered a free suit at 1514 Pitkin Avenue to any batter hitting the 3-foot-by-30-foot sign.
• Opened on April 5, 1913 for an exhibition game vs. the Yankees; it was discovered that the flag, a press box, and the keys to the bleachers had been forgotten. A press box was finally added in 1929.
• In the winter of 1931-32, the double deck was extended from third base to the left field corner and across to center field.
• According to Roger Kahn, the park was "a narrow cockpit of iron and concrete along a steep cobblestone slope."
• In the winter of 1937-38, box seats were added in center field.
• In the winter of 1947-48, more seats were added to left and center.
• Demolition began on Feb. 23, 1960. Same wrecking ball used four years later to demolish Polo Grounds. Eight light towers were moved to Downing Stadium on Randall's Island.
• George Cutshaw of Dodgers hit groundball home run in 1916, which bounced crazily up the concave wall in right and over the fence, to the amazement of Phillies rightfielder Gavvy Cravath.

DEXTER PARK

STYLE Negro League
A.K.A. Sterling Oval
OCCUPANT ECL Royal Giants 1923 to 1927
LOCATION *Left (N)* Simpson Street, now called Park Lane South; *3rd Base (NW)* Cypress Hills Cemetery; *1st Base (W)* Elderta Lane and 75th Street; *Center Field (E)* Lott Avenue, now called 76th Street, in Woodhaven, on Long Island.
PHENOMENA
• Had probably the most creative outfield wall billboard ever. An optician's ad read: "Don't Kill the Umpire—Maybe It's Your Eyes."
• Owners Max and Milt Rosner operated the semipro Brooklyn Bushwicks here.
• Huge incline in right field caused by horse buried under the grass.
• First lights installed on the East Coast, 1930.

CHICAGO, ILLINOIS

COMISKEY PARK

STYLE Classic
A.K.A. White Sox Park (II) 1910 to 1912, Charles A. Comiskey's Baseball Palace 1910, White Sox Park(III) May 1962 to 1975

OCCUPANT AL White Sox July 1, 1910 through September 30, 1990; NL Cubs 1918 World Series; NAL American Giants 1941 to 1950

EVENT First major league All-Star Game, 1933; All-Star Game 1950, 1983; all Negro League East-West All-Star games, 1933 to 1950; Negro League World Series, eighth through tenth games, 1926; third game, 1943; fifth game, 1946; fourth game, 1947

LOCATION *Left Field (N)* West 34th; *3rd Base (W)* Portland Avenue, later called South Shield's Avenue; *1st Base (S)* 324 West 35th Street; *Right Field (E)* South Wentworth Avenue, later Dan Ryan Expressway/I-94

SURFACE *Outfield:* Grass; *Infield:* Grass (1910), Carpet (1969), Grass (1976)

DIMENSIONS *Foul Lines:* 363 (1910), 362 (1911), 365 (1927), 362 (1930), 342 (1934), 353 (1935), 340 (1936), 352 (1937), 332 (April 22, 1949), 352 (May 5, 1949), 335 (1969), 352 (marked 1971), 349 (actual 1971), 341 (1983), 347 (1986); *Power Alleys:* 382 (1910), 375 (1927), 370 (1934), 382 (1942), 362 (April 22, 1949), 375 (May 5, 1949), 382 (1954), 365 (1955), 375 (1956), 365 (1959), 375 (1968), 370 (1969), 375 (marked 1971), 382 (actual 1971), 374 (1983), 382 (1986); *Center Field:* 420 (1910), 450 (1926), 455 (1927), 450 (1930), 436 (1934), 422 (1936), 440 (1937), 420 (April 22, 1949), 415 (May 5, 1949), 410 (1951), 415 (1952), 400 (1969), 440 (1976), 445 (1977), 402 (marked 1981), 409 (actual 1981), 401 (1983), 409 (1986); *Backstop:* 98 (1910), 71 (1933), 85 (1934), 86 (1955); *Foul Territory:* Large

FENCES *Foul Lines and Power Alleys:* 12 (concrete 1955), 9.83 (concrete 1959), 5 (wire 1969), 9.83 (concrete 1971); *Center Field:* 15 (1927), 30 (1948), 17 (1976), 18 (1980); *Left-Center to Right-Center Inner Fences:* 5 (canvas 1949), 6.5 (24-foot section in front of bullpens 1969), 9 (1974), 7 (canvas 1981), 7.5 (1982), 11 (1984), 7.5 (1986)

FORMER USE A truck garden owned by Signor Scavado, and/or a city dump. South Side Park (II) was almost on the same site, across Wentworth Avenue.

PHENOMENA

• Foul lines were old water hoses, painted white and squished flat.

• In 1910, there were bleachers in left and right, but not in center.

• In the winter of 1926-27, wooden bleachers were replaced with concrete and steel, and the pavilions from left around home plate to right were doubledecked. The scoreboard was moved from right-center to two locations on the left field and right field walls.

• Center field bleachers were eliminated in 1947 to improve batter's visibility.

• Section of grandstand collapsed May 17, 1913.

• Special elevator for Lou Comiskey, in use from 1931 to 1982, had an inlaid tile floor.

• In 1950 the bullpens were moved from foul territory down the lines to behind the center field fence.

• Green cornerstone laid on St. Patrick's Day in 1910 stayed green until 1960 when the exterior was painted all white by Bill Veeck.

• In 1960 Bill Veeck installed the first exploding scoreboard in the majors, high above the bleachers in center. In 1982, when the Diamond Vision Board re-

placed the original, the pinwheels were retained.

• Scene of many masterful groundskeeping tricks by Roger, Gene, and Emil Bossard: (a) Camp Swampy in 1967 referred to the area in front of the plate, dug up and soaked with water when White Sox sinkerball pitchers were on the mound, but mixed with clay and gasoline and burned to provide hard soil if a sinkerballer was pitching for the visiting team. (b) Opposing team bullpen mounds were lowered or raised from the standard 10-inch height to upset visiting pitchers' rhythm. (c) Under Eddie Stanky's managerial tenure, the grass in front of shortstop was cut long because the Sox shortstop had limited range, but at second the grass was cut short because the Sox second sacker had very good range. (d) When the Sox had a lousy defensive outfield, the grass was cut long to turn triples into doubles. (e) When the Sox had speedy line drive hitters, the outfield grass was cut long to turn singles into doubles. (f) When the Sox had good bunters, more paint was added to the foul line in order to tilt the ball back fair. Veeck estimated the Bossards were responsible for 12 additional Sox victories a year.

• Nine speaker horns on the center field bleacher wall.

• Clock on wall in center to left of flag pole.

• Picnic areas, including Bullring in left and Bullpens I and II in right and right-center, Bavarian and Mexican restaurants and beer halls under the stands behind the plate.

• Showers in the bleachers in center.

• Foul poles bend back slightly to join the top of the roof.

• The 540 center field listing in 1931-33 *Baseball Guides* must have been a misprint.

• Organist Nancy Faust played "Na-na-na-na, hey-hey, Good bye."

• Open arches between first and second decks.

SOUTH SIDE PARK (III)

STYLE Cricket Ground

A.K.A. 39th Street Grounds (11), White Stocking Park (III) 1901 to 1903, Chicago Cricket Club, White Sox Park (I) 1904 to 1910, American Giants Field 1911 to 1940, Schorling's Park 1920 to 1940

OCCUPANT AL White Sox April 24, 1901 to June 27, 1910; NNL Giants 1920; NNL American Giants 1920 to 1931, 1933 to 1935; NSL American Giants 1932; NAL American Giants 1937 to 1940; Neutral site use by NNL Cleveland Tigers 1928, by NNL Kansas City Monarchs in 1920s, by NNL Cuban Stars West in 1920s

LOCATION *Left Field (N)* West 38th Street; *3rd Base (W)* South Princeton Avenue; *1st Base (S)* West 39th Street, now West Pershing Road; *Right Field (E)* Wentworth Avenue

DIMENSIONS *Left Field:* 355; *Left-Center:* 400; *Center Field:* 450

FORMER USE Home of Wanderers cricket team

CURRENT USE Housing project three blocks from Comiskey Park

PHENOMENA

• Opened in 1900.

• Overhanging roof added in 1902.

• Fence cut back sharply around J. F. Kidwell Greenhouse buildings in right center, making right-center relatively short compared to center and right.

• Used as a dog racing track during the summer of 1933,

forcing the NNL American Giants to move all their home games from May 28 through the end of the 1933 season to Indianapolis.

• Burned down Christmas Day, 1940.

CINCINNATI, OHIO

CROSLEY FIELD

STYLE Classic

A.K.A. Redland Field 1912 to 1933

OCCUPANT NL Reds April 11, 1912 to June 24, 1970; NAL Tigers 1937; NAL Clowns 1942 to 1945

EVENT All-Star Games 1938, 1953

LOCATION *Left Field* (N) York Street; *3rd Base* (W) McLean Avenue; *1st Base* (S) Findlay Street; *Center Field* (NE) Western Avenue

DIMENSIONS *Left field:* 360 (1912), 320 (321), 352 (1926), 339 (1927), 328 (1938); *Scoreboard in Left-Center* 380, 383 feet left to right; *Center Field:* 420 (1912), 417 (1926), 395 (1927), 393 (1930), 407 (1931), 393 (1933), 407 (1936), 387 (1938), 380 (1939), 387 (1940), 390 (1944), 387 (1955); *Right-Center Field:* 383 (1955); *Deepest Corner:* 387 (1944); *Right Field:* 360 (1912), 384 (1921), 400 (1926), 383 (early 1927), 377 (late 1927), 366 (1938), 366 (1938), 342 (1942), 366 (June 30, 1950), 342 (1953), 366 (1958); *Backstop* 38 (1912), 58 (1927), 66 (1943), 78 (1953)

FENCES *Center Field* Canvas shield above fence to protect against street light glare (1935 to June 7, 1940); *Left Field* 18 (1938), 12 (1957), 14 (1962), 18 (1963); *Clock on top of the Scoreboard* 58 (1957), 45 (1967); *Left-Center to Right-Center* 18 (1954), 14 (1962), 13.5 (1963), 23 (9.5 plywood over 13.5 concrete 1965); *Right Field* 7.5 (4.5 wire above 3 concrete 1938), 7.5 (4.5 wire above 3 wood 1942), 10 (7 wire above 3 wood 1949), 12 (9 wire above 3 concrete (June 30, 1950), 10 (7 wire above 3 wood 1953), 10 (7 wire above 3 concrete 1958), 9 (6 wire above 3 concrete 1959); *Flagpole in left center 82, in play*

FORMER USE Brickyard, League Park (1884-1901), Palace of the Fans (1902-1911)

CURRENT USE Reconstructed on farm near Union, Kentucky (a replica has also been constructed at Blue Ash, Ohio). Site used for an industrial park.

PHENOMENA

• Designed by Harry Hake; built at cost of $225,000.

• In the 1920s rented out for movies and dancing, leading to complaints of "immoral dancing" and "vulgar conduct between boys and girls in unlighted portions of the grandstand."

• Steep incline in front of the fence all around the outfield; a pratfall on it by Babe Ruth on May 28, 1935 helped speed his retirement.

• Renamed for Reds owner Powel Crosley, manufacturer of radios, refrigerators and autos.

• Scene of first major league night game vs. Phillies on May 24, 1935.

• In January 1937 the Mill Creek flooded, covering the playing field with 21 feet of water. Pitcher Lee Grissom and Reds traveling secretary John McDonald rowed a boat over the center field fence.

• Pressbox was not erected until 1938. Prior to that

sportswriters sat in the front row of the second deck.

• Both home and visitor clubhouses were located behind left field stands.

• *"Hit this sign and win a Siebler suit"* prominently displayed on Superior Towel & Linen Service Building across street.

• Capacity rose from 20,000 in 1912 to 29,488 in 1970; yet largest crowd was 36,691 for an April 27, 1947 doubleheader.

• A 65 by 50.2 foot scoreboard installed in left center field in 1957.

PALACE OF THE FANS

STYLE Wooden

A.K.A. League Park (III)

OCCUPANT NL Reds April 17, 1902 to October 6, 1911

LOCATION *Left Field* (N) York Street; *3rd Base* (W) McLean Avenue; *1st Base* (S) Findlay Street; *Right Field* (E) Western Avenue; *Center Field* (NE) Western Avenue

PHENOMENA

• Pillars and columns patterned after those of the 1893 Columbian Exposition in Chicago.

• Rooters Row—beer drinkers' area next to the field down both foul lines.

• Burned down in the fall of 1911.

CLEVELAND, OHIO

CLEVELAND STADIUM

STYLE Multipurpose

A.K.A. Lakefront Stadium 1930s, Cleveland Public Municipal Stadium 1930s, Municipal Stadium 1940s and 1950s; Mistake by the Lake

OCCUPANT AL Indians July 31, 1932 to Sept. 24, 1933; Aug. 2, 1936 vs. New York; AL Indians May 30 to Sept. 6, 1937 Sundays and holidays only between Memorial Day and Labor Day; April 1938 to June 1939 Sundays, holidays and selected important games only; AL Indians June 27, 1939 to September 1947 nights, Sundays, holidays, and selected important games (this was a majority of home games in 1940, 1942-46); AL Indians April 15, 1947 to Sept. 26, 1993.

EVENT All-Star Game 1935, 1954, 1963, 1981

LOCATION *Center Field (NE)* East Ninth Street; *3rd Base (NW)* Erieside Avenue, then Donald Gray Lakefront Gardens Port Authority Dock 28 and Lake Erie; *Home Plate (SW)* West Third Street; *1st Base (SE)* Cleveland Memorial Shoreway, Amtrak/Conrail railroad tracks; Boudreau Boulevard encircled the park

SURFACE Bluegrass

DIMENSIONS *Foul Lines:* 322 (1932), 320 (1933), 321 (1948), 320 (1953); *Corners Where Inner Fence Met Stadium Walls:* 362 (1947), 370 (1980); *Power Alleys:* 435 (1932), 365 (1947), 362 (1948), 385 (1949), 380 (1954), 400 (1965), 390 (1967), 395 (1968), 385 (1970), 395 (1991); *Left-Center:* 377 (1980); *Right-Center:* 385 (1980); *Deep Left-Center:* 387 (1980); *Deep Right-Center:* 395 (1980); *Bleacher Corners:* 463 (1932); *Grandstand Corners:* 435 (1932); *Center Field:* 470 (1932), 467 (1938), 450 (1939), 410 (April 27, 1947), 408 (1966), 407 (1967), 410 (1968), 400 (1970), 415 (1990),

404 (1992); *Backstop:* 60; *Foul Territory:* Large
FENCES   *Left and Right Field:* 5.25 (concrete 1932),
5.5 (wire April 27, 1947), 5.25 (concrete June 6, 1947), 6
(1955), 9 (1976), 8 (1977), 8 (canvas 1984)
PHENOMENA
• Architectural style has been called "stripped classi-
cism," and has been compared to later Memorial and
County Stadiums in Baltimore and Milwaukee,
respectively.
• Groundskeepers' tools kept in foul territory in 1930s
and 1940s.
• Before the inner fences were installed on April 27 after
the first two weeks of the 1947 season, there was an
incline in front of the center field bleacher wall; strange
shape in power alleys caused by the end of the doubledecked grandstand, where the fence jumped abruptly
deeper to the bleacher wall in center. The April 27 inner
fence curved all the way to the foul poles. On June 6,
1947, it was changed so the inner fence just stretched
across center field, hitting the permanent wall at 362
mark.
• Teepees erected in 1946 in center.
• Foul poles were 32 feet 8 inches high, 27 inches wide,
and the screen on them is 22 inches wide.
• No one ever hit a ball into the center field bleachers.
• Music bandstand in center field between fence and
bleachers set up in 1953.
• Wind usually blew out toward the lake.
• Center field standing-room area was a garden in 1957.
• Field was lowered 2 feet in 1976.
• Cleveland Stadium/League Park ratio of home games
from 1936 to 1946: 1/77, 15/63, 18/58, 30/47, 49/33, 32/
45, 46/34, 48/29, 44/34, 46/31, 41/36.
• Featured in two movies—*The Kid from Cleveland* in
1949, *Fortune Cookie* in mid-1960s.
• Opened formally on July 1, 1931—13 months before
the Indians' first home game on July 31, 1932.
• Largest regular season crowd ever—86,563 (84,587
paid)—for doubleheader against Yankees, Sept. 12, 1954.
• Torn down in 1996-1997, after the NFL Browns left for
Baltimore to become the Ravens.

LEAGUE PARK
STYLE   Classic
A.K.A.   Dunn Field 1916 to 1927
OCCUPANT   AL Indians April 21, 1910 to July 1932;
April 1934 to Sept. 21, 1946; NAL Bears 1939 to 1940;
NAL Buckeyes 1943 to 1948, 1950; Negro League World
Series 1st game 1945; 2nd and 5th games 1947
LOCATION   *Left Field (E)* East 70th Street; *3rd Base
(N)* Linwood Avenue; *1st Base (W)* Dunham Street, later
East 66th Street; *Right Field (S)* Lexington Avenue
Northeast
DIMENSIONS   *Left Field:* 385 (1910), 376 (1921),
374 (1930), 373 (1934) 374 (1938) 375 (1942); *Left-
Center:* 415 (1942); *Deepest corner, just left of Center
Field:* 505 (1916), 450 (1926), 467 (1930), 465 (1938),
460 (1939); *Center Field:* 420; *Right-Center:* 400 (1942);
Right Field: 290 (1921), 240 (when roped off for overflow
crowds); *Backstop:* 76 (1910), 60 (1942)
FENCES   *Left Field:* 5 (concrete); *Left-Center:* 10 (7
screen above 3 concrete); *Center Field Scoreboard:* 35;
Right-Center Clock: 20 (left and right sides), 22 (center of

clock); *Right Field:* 45 (20 concrete topped by 25 screen
1920), 40 (20 concrete topped by 20 screen 1934)
CURRENT USE   Public park, stands were razed in 1950
PHENOMENA
• Named after owner James Dunn (1916 to 1927).
• Seats added in left and center in August 1920 which
considerably reduced fence distances. Until that time,
center field fence was as distant as center field at Polo
Grounds.
• Steel beams protruded from the wall in right, causing
balls to bounce at crazy angles. Only here did left fielders
handle doubles to right field.
• Large green scoreboard in center field, and a clock just
to the right of the scoreboard.
• Megaphone speakers on left center wall.
• Tepees erected in 1946.
• Ticket booths and part of left field stands remain as
League Park Community Center.

DALLAS, TEXAS

ARLINGTON STADIUM
STYLE   Expanded Minor League
A.K.A.   Turnpike Stadium 1965 to 1971
OCCUPANT   AL Rangers April 21, 1972 to Oct. 3,
1993.
LOCATION   Suburban Arlington, between Dallas and
Fort Worth; *Left Field (E)* Stadium Drive East, then Six
Flags Over Texas Amusement Park; *3rd Base (N)* 1500
South Copeland Road; *1st Base (W)* Stadium Drive West;
Right Field (S) Randol Mill Road
SURFACE   419 Bermuda grass
DIMENSIONS   *Foul Lines:* 330; *Power Alleys:* 380
(1972), 370 (1974), 383 (1981), 380 (1982); *Center
Field:* 400; *Backstop:* 60; *Foul Territory:* Small
FENCES   11 (1972), 12 (1981), 11 (1986)
FORMER USE   Minor league ballpark from 1965 to
1971 called Turnpike Stadium
PHENOMENA
• Like Dodger Stadium, the field was below the sur-
rounding parking lots. Before 1978, when the upper deck
was added, fans would walk in at the top of the stadium.
• Wind blew in directly from the outfield.
• Hottest park in the majors, which increased the number
of home runs hit here since the warm humid air is not as
dense as cooler drier air elsewhere and therefore does not
offer as much resistance to the ball in flight.
• More advertising signs than any other major league
park.
• The Lone Ranger on Diamond Vision scoreboard
rooted for the Rangers.

DENVER, COLORADO

MILE HIGH STADIUM
STYLE   Expanded Minor League
A.K.A.   Bears Stadium 1948-1967
OCCUPANT   NL Rockies, April 9, 1993 to Aug. 11,
1994
LOCATION   *Left Field* Clay Street; *3rd Base* West 20th
Street; *1st Base* Elliot Street; *Right Field* Interstate 25

SURFACE Natural Grass ("Prescription Athletic Turf")
DIMENSIONS *Left Field:* 335; *Left-Center:* 375; *Center Field:* 423; *Right-Center:* 400; *Right Field:* 370
FENCES 10 (padded)
CAPACITY 19,000 (1960), 43,103 (1975), 75,123 (1985), 76,037 (1993)
PHENOMENA
• Home of American Association and Pacific Coast League Denver Bears/Zephyrs from 1948 to 1992.
• Also home of NFL's Denver Broncos; former home of United States Football League's Denver Gold.
• Near McNichols Sports Arena, home of NBA Nuggets.
• Rockies drew largest ever season attendance of 4,483,350 in 1993.
• Entire east stands (built in 1977; capacity 21,000) movable to accommodate both football and baseball; conversion time to football is 10 hours; back to baseball, 12 hours.
• Playing field is heated electrically to prevent surface freezing and to allow year-round growth.
• First "fully distributed sound system" in any major U.S. stadium—delivers "near stereo quality sound."
• Largest NL regular season paid crowd ever—80,227—against Expos on April 9, 1993, with this author present. The only bigger AL regular season paid crowds have been:
84,587—Sept. 12, 1954—Cleveland Stadium
82,871—June 20, 1948—Cleveland Stadium
81,841—May 30, 1938—Yankee Stadium
81,622—Sept. 9, 1928—Yankee Stadium

EAST ORANGE, NEW JERSEY

GROVE STREET OVAL
STYLE Negro League
A.K.A. Grove Street Senior Ball Diamond, Monte Irvin Field, East Orange Oval
OCCUPANT NNL Cubans 1940 to 1948; NAL Cubans 1949 to 1950; also neutral site used by NNL Newark Eagles 1936 to 1948
LOCATION *Left Field (E)* Greenwood Avenue; *3rd Base (N)* Grove Place; *1st Base (W)* Grove Street North; *Right Field (S)* Eaton Place
DIMENSIONS *Left Field:* 240; *Center Field:* 360 to the water fountain; *Right Field:* 280
FENCES Left Field: 25 (garage walls); Center Field: 4 (water fountain); Right Field: None
CURRENT USE Still used as a community ball diamond
PHENOMENA
• No fence in center field where there were some hedges.
• Water fountain in play in deepest center field.
• Trees in right, as well as tennis courts beyond.
• Scoreboard in left, as well as poplar trees.
• Clubhouse down right field line in foul territory.
• "Bujum" Jud Wilson hit longest ball ever hit over water fountain in center.
• Property purchased by city in October 1907 and park dedicated Labor Day 1908 in a game between the New

Jersey State Senate and the New Jersey State General Assembly.
• Fire destroyed the first grandstand at 4 a.m. on May 3, 1925; new grandstand dedicated May 1, 1926. Renamed Monte Irvin Field at June 6, 1986 ceremony in culmination of four years effort initiated by this author and the SABR Negro Leagues Committee, who designed the plaque marking the site.

HONOLULU, HAWAII

ALOHA STADIUM
STYLE Multipurpose
A.K.A. Halawa Stadium 1975
OCCUPANT NL Padres and Cardinals April 19-20, 1997
SURFACE Monsanto AstroTurf
DIMENSIONS *Left Field:* 325; *Power Alleys:* 375; *Center Field:* 400; *Right Field:* 325
CAPACITY 50,000
PHENOMENA
• Site of first major league game in Hawaii. Padres moved three-game series to Aloha Stadium because construction limited capacity at Qualcomm Stadium early in the season.
• Home of Hawaii Islanders, member of the Pacific Coast League from 1961 to 1987. Current home to the University of Hawaii Rainbows and host of the NFL's annual Pro Bowl.
• Replaced old Honolulu Stadium, known as the Termite Palace, in 1975.

HOUSTON, TEXAS

COLT STADIUM
STYLE Temporary
A.K.A. Mosquito Heaven
OCCUPANT NL Colt .45s April 10, 1962 to Sept. 27, 1964
LOCATION *(N)* East/West Utility Road; *(E)* North Stadium Drive; *1st Base (S)* Astrodome—future site; *3rd Base* Loop 610 South, also called South Main Street; *Home Plate* Kirby Drive
DIMENSIONS *Foul Lines:* 360; *Power Alleys:* 395; *Center Field:* 420; *Deepest corners in center just left and right of straightaway center:* 427; *Backstop:* 60
FENCES Left and Right 8; Center Field Screen 30
CURRENT USE Blacktop in northern Astrodome parking lot
PHENOMENA
• Scoreboard in center on both sides of 30-foot-high batters' background.
• Stiff wind blew in from right toward home.
• Power alley measurements not marked on the wall.
• Home of largest and peskiest mosquitoes in major league history. Park was regularly sprayed by the ground crew between innings.
• Lay in decay until early 1970s when it was bought and moved to Torreon, Mexico by a Mexican League team.

JERSEY CITY, NEW JERSEY

ROOSEVELT STADIUM

STYLE Minor League
OCCUPANT Some NNL New York Black Yankees games in 1940s; NL Dodgers for seven 1956 games and eight 1957 games from April 19, 1956 to Sept. 3, 1957
LOCATION *Left Field (NE)* Hackensack River; *3rd Base (NW)* Newark Bay; *1st Base (SW)* Danforth Avenue; *Right Field (SE)* State Highway 440; at Droyers Point
DIMENSIONS *Foul Lines:* 330; *Power Alleys:* 397; *Center Field:* 411; *Backstop:* 60
FENCES: *Foul Line Corners:* 11; *Left Field to Center Field:* 4; *Right-Center to Right Field:* 7
FORMER USE A landfill for dirt excavated from Holland Tunnel
PHENOMENA
• Built as a WPA project in 1937 and named for FDR.
• Newark Bay brought mosquitoes and mist into the outfield.
• Thanksgiving morning football games between St. Peter's and Dickinson were always sold out in the 1940s.
• Torn down in 1984.

KANSAS CITY, MISSOURI

MUNICIPAL STADIUM

STYLE Expanded Minor League
A.K.A. Muehlebach Field 1923 to 1937, Ruppert Stadium 1938 to 1942, Blues Stadium 1943 to 1954
OCCUPANT NAL Monarchs 1923 to 1950; AL Athletics April 12, 1955 to Sept. 27, 1967; AL Royals April 8, 1969 to Oct. 4, 1972; Negro World Series, Games 5-7, 1924; 1-4, 1925; 4, 1942, 3-4, 1946
LOCATION *Left Field (N)* 21st Street; *3rd Base (W)* Euclid Avenue; *1st Base (S)* 22nd Street; *Right Field (E)* 2128 Brooklyn Avenue
DIMENSIONS *Left Field:* 350 (1923), 312 (1955), 330 (1956), 370 (1961), 353 (1962), 331 (1963), 370 (1965), 369 (1967); *Left-Center:* 408 (1923), 382 (1955), 375 (1957), 390 (1961), 364 (1963), 392 (1964), 409 (1965), 408 (1969); *Center Field:* 450 (1923), 432 (1950), 430 (1955), 421 (1956), 410 (1964), 421 (1965); *Right-Center:* 382 (1955), 387 (1957), 364 (1962), 360 (1963), 392 (1964), 360 (1965), 382 (1969); *Right Field:* 350 (1923), 347 (1955), 352 (1956), 353 (1957), 338 (1963), 325 (1965), 338 (1966); *Backstop:* 60 (1955), 70 (1963)
FENCES *Left Field:* 24 (screen 1956), 18.5 (concrete 1958), 38.5 (20 screen over 18.5 concrete 1959), 10 (1961), 13.5 (1962), 10 (1963), 22 (1967), 13 (1969); *Center Field:* 12 (1958), 14 (1959), 12 (1961), 13.5 (1962), 10 (1963), 22 (screen 1966), 40 (screen 1969), 22 (screen 1970); *Right Field:* 12 (1956), 14 (1959), 12 (1961), 13.5 (1962), 10 (1963), 4.5 (plywood 1965), 40 (screen 1966), 13 (1969), 12 (screen 1970)
FORMER USE Swimming hole, frog pond, and ash heap
PHENOMENA
• Opened on July 23, 1923.
• Originally named for owner George Muehlebach.
• When rebuilt for the 1955 American League season,

home plate was moved 25 feet toward the outfield.
• In the spring of 1955, the right-center field scoreboard was put into position. It had previously stood in Boston's Braves Field.
• The bottom of the left-center light tower was in play—the warning track detoured around it.
• Right field embankment zoo—the mule Charlie O., sheep, China golden pheasants, Capuchin monkeys, German checker rabbits, peafowl, and a German shorthaired pointer dog all lived out there.
• Little Blowhard was a subterranean device that blew compressed air through the middle of the plate so that the umpire didn't have to brush it off.
• Harvey the Mechanical Rabbit rose out of the ground to the right of the plate to offer the umpire new baseballs from a basket between his ears.
• Pennant Porch: Charles O. Finley believed that one reason the Yankees won so many pennants was their 296-foot right field porch. In April 1965, he created his own 296-foot pennant porch in Municipal Stadium's right field, but the league forced him to remove it.

LAS VEGAS, NEVADA

CASHMAN FIELD

STYLE Minor League
A.K.A. Cashman Field Center
OCCUPANT AL Athletics April 1-7, 1996
LOCATION Las Vegas Boulevard
DIMENSIONS *Foul Lines:* 328; *Power Alleys:* 364; *Center Field:* 433; *Backstop:* 43
FENCES *Left and Right Field:* 20; *Center Field:* 22
CAPACITY 9,353
PHENOMENA
• A's played two series here because their Coliseum was torn up by construction to accommodate the returning NFL Raiders.
• Grassy embankment on the hill behind left field was filled with picnicking fans.
• Usherettes danced the polka in the aisles between innings.
• Home of Las Vegas PCL franchise.
• Most billboards ever at a major league park—47 in fair territory, nine in foul territory, including Caesar's Palace Magical Empire, Anderson Dairy—Since 1907, Arizona Charlie's—Hit Charlie $ Win Dinner for 2, 92.3 KOMP Rocks Vegas.

LOS ANGELES, CALIFORNIA

LOS ANGELES MEMORIAL COLISEUM

STYLE Football Stadium
A.K.A. O'Malley's Chinese Theatre, O'Malley's Alley
OCCUPANT NL Dodgers April 18, 1958 to Sept. 20, 1961
EVENT All-Star Game 1959
LOCATION *Left Field (N)* Exposition Boulevard; *3rd Base (W)* Merlo Avenue, Los Angeles Olympic Swimming Stadium; *1st Base (S)* Santa Barbara Avenue, now Martin Luther King, Jr. Drive; *Right Field (E)* 3911 South Figueroa Street, Los Angeles Memorial Sports Arena

DIMENSIONS *Left Field:* 250 (1958), 251.6 (1959); *Left-Center:* 320 at end of screen rectangle; *Left-Center Where Fence Met Wall:* 425 (1958), 417 (1959); *Center Field:* 425 (1958), 420 (1959); *Right-Center:* 440 (1958), 375 (1959), 394 (1960), 380 (1961); *Right Field Where Fence Met Wall:* 390 (1958), 333 (1959), 340 (1960); *Right Field:* 301 (1958), 300 (1959); *Back-stop:* 60 (1958), 66 (1959); *Foul Territory:* Large; tremendous area on 3rd base line, but almost none on 1st base line

FENCES *Left Field:* 40 (screen 1958), 42 (screen 1959); 60 (2 support towers for screen 1958); *Left-Center:* 40 (fence (1958); from foul pole 140 feet into left center, 42 sloping to ground at 30 degree angle from 320 mark to 348 mark for a distance of 24 feet (1959 to 1960); 4 steps down from 42 to 8: 1st step left corner 42 sloping to 41, 2nd step 31, 3rd step 20, 4th step 12 (1961); *Right of Screen in Left-Center:* 8 (wire); *Center Field to Right Field Corner:* 6 (wire); *Right Field Corner:* 4 (concrete)

FORMER USE Agriculture Park in 1890s—fairs, livestock shows, amusement park booths, horse-racing track and barns, saloons. Exposition Park—armory, museum, gardens from 1908 to 1921, along with gravel pit.

PHENOMENA

• Wall in left-center jutted out twice, going from chest to thigh level, jutting out to ankle level, jutting out to thigh level, then back again to chest level.

• Concrete wall in the right field corner was the wall surrounding the football field. It sloped sharply away, creating a Fenway-like belly, and allowing a situation where a long drive near the right field foul line would be an out but a short fly down the line would be a home run.

• Huge tunnel behind home plate.

• First used for baseball by USC Trojans, who worked out here before the Dodgers opened the 1958 season.

• O'Malley considered using the Rose Bowl in Pasadena for the first years after the move from Brooklyn and before Dodger Stadium opened. It would have been laid out differently from the Coliseum. Ten rows would have been removed in right and left to deepen the foul lines to 300 feet, and center field would have been 460. The field would have been symmetrical, because home plate would have been in one end zone and center field in the other end zone. Box seats were to have been added behind the plate and between first and third.

• The Coliseum's 42-foot screen in left placed to prevent 251 foot popups from becoming homers.

• Commissioner Ford Frick attempted to order the Dodgers to construct a second screen in left, in the seats at 333 feet.

• A ball clearing both screens would be a home run, but a ball clearing just the shorter screen would be a double. The California Earthquake Law made construction of such a screen illegal.

• It was 700 feet to furthest seats under peristylum.

• Two stones are on exhibit under the peristylum atop the bleachers in right-center at one end of the oval—the one on the left from Altis, Olympia, Greece, and the one on the right from the Colosseum, Rome, Italy.

• Rim of stadium 110 feet above ground level, field 33 feet below ground level.

• Cable, towers and wires above the screen in left field in play.

• Small green light pole in field of play in right field.

• There were 74,000 seats built from 1921 to 1923, expanded to 105,000 seats because of the 1932 Olympic games.

• The right-center fence was shortened in 1959 after 182 homers were hit to left but only three to center and eight to right.

• In 1959, there were 132 homers to left, one to center, 39 to right. In 1960, 155 to left, three to center, 28 to right. In 1961, 147 to left, seven to center, 38 to right.

• Largest World Series crowd ever—92,706 against White Sox on Oct. 6, 1959.

WRIGLEY FIELD

STYLE Expanded Minor League
OCCUPANT AL Angels April 27 to Oct. 1, 1961
LOCATION *Left Field (E)* Avalon Boulevard; *3rd Base (S)* East 42nd Place; *1st Base (W)* San Pedro Street; *Right Field (N)* East 41st Place
DIMENSIONS *Left Field:* 340; *Power Alleys:* 345; *Center Field:* 412; *Right Field:* 338.5; *Backstop:* 56
FENCES *Left Field to Center Field:* 14.5 (concrete); *Center Field to Right Field:* 9 (6 wire above 3 concrete)
CURRENT USE Gilbert Lindsay Park, a public playground, and City Center Community Mental Health Facility
PHENOMENA

• Dedicated on Sept. 27, 1925.

• Named for Cubs owner William Wrigley when Los Angeles was a Cubs farm team.

• In its minor league days, there were two walls and a picnic area in right. A large office tower stood just to the first base side of home plate above the grandstand. The bottom of the light tower in left center was in play.

• Rear wall at foul pole was 346.58 in 1961.

• In 1961, Wrigley Field set the current record for most homers in one park in one season—248. The reason was that the power alleys were only 5 feet more distant than the foul pole in left.

• Demolished in 1966.

BLOOMINGTON, MINNESOTA

METROPOLITAN STADIUM

STYLE Expanded Minor League
A.K.A. Met
OCCUPANT AL Twins April 21, 1961 to Sept. 30, 1981
LOCATION *Left Field (E)* 24th Avenue South, and a cornfield during the 1960s; *3rd Base (N)* Interstate 494; *1st Base (W)* 8001 Cedar Avenue; *Right Field (S)* West 78th Street, later named Killebrew Drive in 1973
SURFACE Grass
DIMENSIONS *Left Field:* 329 (1961), 330 (1962), 344 (1965), 346 (1967), 330 (1975), 343 (1977); *Short Left-Center:* 365 (1961), 360 (1966), 373 (1972), 350 (1975), 346 (1976), 360 (1977); *Deep Left-Center:* 402 (1961), 435 (1965), 430 (1968), 410 (1975), 406 (1976); *Deep Left-Center Corner:* 430 (1965), 406 (1975); *Center Field:* 412 (1961), 430 (1965), 425 (1968), 410 (1975), 402 (1977); *Deep Right-Center Corner:* 430 (1965); *Deep Right-Center:* 402 (1961), 435 (1965), 430 (1968), 410 (1977); *Short Right-Center:* 365 (1961), 373

(1968), 365 (1972), 370 (1977); *Right Field:* 329 (1961), 330 (1962); *Backstop:* 60
FENCES   *Left Field:* 8 (wire 1961), 12 (1964), 7 (1974), 12 (1977); *Center Field:* 8 (wire 1961); *Right Field:* 8 (wire 1961), 12 (1964), 8 (1970)
FORMER USE   Opened on April 24, 1956 by minor league Millers
CURRENT USE   Razed 1984-1985. Future site of Convention Center and amusement park
PHENOMENA
• The 330 foot marker was curiously far away from the foul pole in right, raising the distinct possibility that the distance to right was actually less than 330.
• Most poorly maintained ballpark in the majors. In 1981, broken railings on the third deck overlooking the left field bleachers created a distinct safety hazard.

MONTERREY, NUEVO LEON

ESTADIO MONTERREY

STYLE   Minor League
OCCUPANT   NL Padres vs. Mets Aug. 16-18, 1996
DIMENSIONS   *Center Field:* 400; *Foul Lines:* 310
CAPACITY   27,000
PHENOMENA
• Site of first major league game played outside the United States or Canada.
• Mexico's Fernando Valenzuela pitched and won first game of "La Primera Serie."
• Fireworks after every homer.
• Home of Monterrey's Mexican League franchise.
• Modeled after San Diego's Jack Murphy Stadium.
• Next to Monterrey's soccer stadium.
• Harp music over P.A. after every strikeout.

MONTREAL, QUEBEC

PARC JARRY

STYLE   For Temporary Use
A.K.A.   Jarry Park
OCCUPANT   NL Expos April 14, 1969 to Sept. 26, 1976
LOCATION   *Left Field (NW)* rue Jarry; *3rd Base (SW)* Canadian Pacific Railroad tracks; *1st Base (SE)* 285, ouest rue Faillon; *Right Field (NE)* rue St. Laurent and a public swimming pool
DIMENSIONS   *Left Field:* 340; *Left-Center:* 368; *Center Field:* 415 (1969), 417 (1971), 420 (1974); *Right-Center:* 368; *Right Field:* 340; *Backstop:* 62
FENCES   8 (wire 1969), 5 (wire 1970), 8 (wire 1976)
PHENOMENA
• Still under construction during the first two months of Expos home games in April and May 1969.
• Jet stream wind helped drives to left-center. Homers to right landed in a swimming pool.
• On April 13, 1971, Opening Day, fans stood on snow plowed high in mounds behind the 8½-foot wall that stood behind the 5-foot wire screen fence in right field and viewed the game free.
• Destroyed in 1995; after many years as a tennis stadium.

NASHVILLE, TENNESSEE

SULPHUR DELL (II)

STYLE   Minor League
A.K.A.   Sulphur Springs Bottom, Sulphur Dell Park, Athletic Park, Dump, Suffer Hell
OCCUPANT   NNL Elite Giants 1933 to 1934
LOCATION   *Left Field (N)* Jackson Street; *3rd Base (W)* Summer Street, later 900 Fifth Avenue North; *1st Base (S)* Tennessee Central Railroad tracks; *Right Field (E)* Cherry Street, later Fourth Avenue North
DIMENSIONS   *Left Field:* 334; *Center Field:* 421; *Right Field:* 262 (235 when fans sat behind ropes on the bank)
FENCES   *All Around:* 16 (wood 1927); *Left and Center:* 16 (wood 1931); *Right Field:* 38.5 to 46 (16 wood below 22.5 to 30 screen to a point 186 feet from the right field foul line)
PHENOMENA
• Only one-quarter mile from the Cumberland River, the park was often flooded.
• Nicknamed "the Dump" in honor of the exceptional fragrance that drifted over from the nearby smoldering city dump, and lent unique character to Sulphur Dell hot dogs!
• Sulphur Dell had the craziest right field in history. Right fielders were called mountain goats because they had to go up and down the irregular hills in right-center and right.
• The incline in right rose 25 feet, beginning gradually behind first, then rising sharply at a 45-degree angle, then leveling off at a 10-foot-wide shelf one-third of the way up the incline, and then continuing at a 45-degree angle to the fence.
• Fielders used to play on the shelf, 235 feet from the plate.
• When overflow crowds were attracted to a game, a rope was extended in front of the shelf, and fans sat on the upper two thirds of the incline, reducing right field to 235 rather than 262.
• The stands were very close to the pancake-shaped diamond.
• First base was 42 feet from the seats; third base was 26 feet from the seats.
• Embankments began in left at 301 and in right at 224. Casey Stengel once joked that he hit a bunt home run down the first base line.

NEW YORK, NEW YORK

HILLTOP PARK

STYLE   Wooden
A.K.A.   Highlanders Park, New York American League Ballpark, Rockpile, The Hilltop
OCCUPANT   AL Yankees April 30, 1903 to Oct. 5, 1912; NL Giants April 15 to May 30, 1911
LOCATION   *(N)* West 168th Street; *(W)* Fort Washington Avenue; *(SW)* Deaf and Dumb Asylum; *(S)* West 165th Street; *(E)* Broadway
DIMENSIONS   *Left Field:* 365; *Center Field:* 542; *Right Field:* 400
CURRENT USE   Columbia Presbyterian Hospital

PHENOMENA
- Excellent view of the Hudson River and the New Jersey Palisades from the upper seats behind the plate.
- Scoreboard in left.
- Large exit gate in right from which fans left after the game.
- Bull Durham sign shaped like a bull in right center in 1909, twice the height of the rest of the fence.
- Memorial dedicated at site of home plate in 1993 through cooperation of the Society for American Baseball Research (SABR), the New York Yankees, and Columbia Presbyterian Hospital.

POLO GROUNDS (IV)
STYLE Classic
A.K.A. Brush Stadium 1911 to 1919, Coogan's Bluff, Coogan's Hollow, Matty Schwab's House, Harlem Meadow
OCCUPANT NL Giants June 28, 1911 to Sept. 29, 1957; AL Yankees May 30, 1912 (morning game); April 17, 1913 to Oct. 8, 1922; NL Mets April 13, 1962 to Sept. 18, 1962
EVENT Negro League World Series first game, 1946; All-Star Game 1934, 1942
LOCATION *Center Field (SE)* Eighth Avenue, then IRT elevated tracks, Harlem River and Harlem River Drive; *3rd Base (NE)* West 159th Street and IRT Rail Yards; *Home Plate (NW)* Bridge Park, then Harlem River Speedway, Coogan's Bluff, and Croton Aqueduct; *1st Base (SW)* West 157th Street trace; Same site as Polo Grounds (III); In Coogan's Hollow, 115 feet below Coogan's Bluff, the last remaining portion of a farm granted to Mr. John Lion Gardiner by the King of England in the seventeenth century
DIMENSIONS *Left Field:* 277 (1911), 286.67 (1921), 279.67 (1923), 279 (1930), 280 (1943), 279 (1955); *Left Field, Second Deck:* 250; *Left-Center, Left of Bullpen:* 447; *Left-Center, Right of Bullpen:* 455; *Front Clubhouse Steps:* 460; *Center Field:* 433 (1911), 483 (1923), 484.75 (1927), 505 (1930), 430 (1931), 480 (1934), 430 (1938), 505 (1940), 490 (1943), 505 (1944), 480 (1945), 490 (1946), 484 (1947), 505 (1949), 483 (1952), 480 (1953), 483 (1954), 480 (1955), 475 (1962), 483 (1963); *Bleacher Corners:* 475; *Right-Center, Left of Bullpen:* 449; *Right-Center, Right of Bullpen:* 440; *Right Field:* 256.25 (1921), 257.67 (1923), 257.5 (1931), 257.67 (1942), 259 (1943), 257.67 (1944); *Right Field Photographers Perch:* 249; *Backstop:* 65 (1942), 70 (1943), 65 (1944), 70 (1946), 74 (1949), 65 (1954), 74 (1955), 65 (1962); *Foul Territory:* Very large. There's a lot of confusion here. During the Giants' stay it was 483 to the front of the clubhouse, and probably 505 to the rear clubhouse wall above the overhang. Why the 483 marker sometimes was changed to 480 or 475, is not known but it could have been due to re-measurements or a slight shift of home plate's location. Or it could have been a measurement to the base of the Eddie Grant Memorial. In the Giants' time, reading from left to right, the markers read 315, 360, 414, 447, 455, 483, 455, 449, 395, 338, 294. In the Mets' time, they read 306, 405, 475, 405, 281. The foul lines were never marked. One possibility is that it was 433 feet to the front of the bleachers, 475 to the beginning of the clubhouse overhang, 483 to the rear wall under the overhang,

and 505 to the front of the high wall. The 21-foot overhang of the second deck in left reduced the distance to the second deck from 279 to 250, not 258, because of the angle involved.
FENCES—1911-22 *Left to Center:* 10 (concrete); *Center:* 20 (tarp); *Right-Center:* 10 (concrete); *Right Field:* 12 sloping to 11 at pole (concrete)
FENCES—1923-63 *Left Field:* 16.81 (concrete); *Left-Center:* 18 (concrete); *Where Left-Center Wall Ended at Bleachers:* 12 (concrete); *Center Field Bleachers Wall:* 8.5 (4.25 wire on top of 4.25 concrete) on both sides of clubhouse runway; *Center Field Hitters' Background:* 16.5 on both sides of clubhouse runway; *Center Field Clubhouse:* 60 high and 60 wide—50 high in 1963; *Center Field Top of Longines Clock:* 80; *Center Field Top of Right Side of Scoreboard:* 71; *Center Field Top of Left Side of Scoreboard:* 68; *Center Field Top of Middle of Scoreboard:* 64; *Center Field Top of 5 Right Scoreboard Windows:* 57; *Center Field Top of 4 Left Scoreboard Windows:* 55; *Center Field Bottom of 5 Right Scoreboard Windows:* 53; *Center Field Bottom of 4 Left Scoreboard Windows:* 48; *Center Field Bottom of Clubhouse Scoreboard:* 31; *Center Field Top of Rear Clubhouse Wall:* 28; *Center Field Top of Front Clubhouse Wall:* 19; *Center Field Top of 14 Lower Clubhouse Windows:* 16; *Center Field Bottom of 14 Lower Clubhouse Windows:* 11; *Center Field Clubhouse floor Overhang:* 8; *Center Field Top of Eddie Grant Memorial:* 5; *Center Field Width of Little Office on Top of Lower Clubhouse:* 10; *Right-Center:* 12 (concrete); *Right Field:* 10.64 (concrete)
FORMER USE Underneath the Harlem River until filled in with dirt in the late 1870s.
CURRENT USE Polo Grounds Towers—four 30-story apartment buildings. Willie Mays Field—an asphalt playground with six basketball backboards where center field used to be, a brass historical marker in place.
PHENOMENA
- Originally named for owner John T. Brush.
- Second deck in right had 9-foot photographer's perch overhang 60 feet from foul pole out into right-center.
- Bullpens in fair territory in left-center and right-center.
- There was no line on the 60-foot-high center field clubhouse above which a ball would be a home run.
- The outfield was slightly sunken. A manager, standing in his dugout, could see only the top half of his outfielders. At the wall, the field was 8 feet below the infield.
- The left field second deck overhang meant that a homer to left was easier than a homer to right, even though the wall in left was 279 and the wall in right was 258. The overhang was 21 feet, but it effectively shortened the distance required for a pop-fly homer to the second deck in left to 250 feet because of the angle involved.
- The overhangs here and at Tiger Stadium and Shibe Park have more significance than one might suspect, according to research published by the professional society for physicists, the American Physical Society. The batted ball's trajectory consists of two component vectors, horizontal, and vertical. The vertical deceleration is constant over time due to gravity, but the horizontal deceleration increases over time due to wind resistance and atmospheric drag. Near the end of its flight, the ball is coming down sharply, rather than arcing down as it arched up, as would occur in a vacuum. So many outfielders have

watched helplessly as a ball they could catch dropped into the second deck.

• Hitter's background extended beyond the end of the bleacher wall, several feet into the clubhouse gap.

• The field sloped in a "turtle back" just beyond the infield dirt. It sloped down 1.5 feet to drains about 20 feet into the outfield, then back up again.

• Right-center wall sloped gradually from 11 feet at pole to 12 feet at the bleachers.

• Left-center wall sloped from 16 feet 9.75 inches at the pole to 18 feet in left center, then abruptly fell to 16 feet and then to 14 feet and sloped gradually to 12 feet at the bleachers. When ad signs were removed in the 1940s, the abrupt changes in height in left-center all disappeared.

• After the all-wooden Polo Grounds (III) burned down April 14, 1911, Polo Grounds (IV) was built with temporary stands for 1911. The infield stands were rebuilt with concrete for 1912, and the outfield concrete double deck was finished in 1922. The bleachers in left-center and center were wood remaining from before the fire.

• In 1914 there were two bends in the wall in the Polo Grounds (III) right-center.

• In 1917 the fans exited from the field through gates under the center field bleachers.

• Morris James Mansion sat up on Coogan's Bluff, overlooking the ballpark.

• Brush Stairway led down from Coogan's Bluff to the Speedway and the ticket booths behind home plate.

• Coats of arms of all the teams in the National League on the top of the grandstand. Removed in the 1920s.

• Dedicated on May 30, 1921, to a former Giant killed in World War I, the Eddie Grant Memorial stood in center at the base of the clubhouse wall. It was 5 feet high. The Memorial reads:

In Memory of
Capt. Edward Leslie Grant
307th Infantry - 77th Division
A.E.F.
Soldier - Scholar - Athlete
Killed in action
Argonne Forest
October 5, 1918
Philadelphia Nationals
1907-1908-1909-1910
Cincinnati Reds
1911-1912-1913
New York Giants
1913-1914-1915
Erected by friends in Baseball,
Journalism, and the Service.

• In the winter of 1922-23, the concrete double decks were extended all the way to either side of the new concrete bleachers in center, housing the clubhouse. Unfortunately, the Roman Colosseum facade frescoes were removed during that winter also.

• Bleachers in center remodeled in 1923.

• In 1929, the first attempt was made to wire the umpires for sound and connect them into the PA system. It didn't work too well.

• Speaker placed above Grant Memorial in 1931.

• Field raised 4½ feet in 1949 to help with drainage. In 1609 and 1874 maps, the location is shown to be underneath the Harlem River. The water table was only 2-6 feet below the playing surface, and drainage was complicated by rainwater cascading off the 115-foot-high Coogan's Bluff down onto the site.

• During the 1950s, groundskeeper Matty Schwab and his family lived in an apartment under Section 3 of the left field stands built for him by Horace Stoneham. The apartment was the main bait in Stoneham's successful offer to grab Schwab away from the hated Dodgers in 1950.

• A 2-foot-square section of sod from center field was removed and taken to San Francisco in the fall of 1957.

• Home plate was moved out toward center several feet by the Mets in the winter of 1961-62.

• During the Mets' stay in 1962 and 1963, Johnny McCarthy and his crew of groundskeepers painted Schwab's four rooms pink, installed a shower and plywood on the floor and lockers, and called it their Pink Room.

• In 1962 and 1963, the Howard Clothes sign on the outfield wall promised a boat to any player hitting it.

• Demolition started on April 10, 1964, with same wrecking ball that demolished Ebbets Field.

DYCKMAN OVAL
STYLE Negro League
OCCUPANT NNL Cuban Stars 1922; ECL Cuban Stars East 1923 to 1928; ECL Bachrach Giants many games 1923 to 1928; NAL Cuban Stars East 1929; NNL Cuban House of David 1931; NEWL Cuban Stars 1932
LOCATION Left Field (NE) West 204th Street; 3rd Base (NW) Nagle Avenue; 1st Base (SW) Academy Street; Right Field (SE) Tenth Avenue. In Upper Manhattan, 8 blocks east of the Henry Hudson Parkway, 5 blocks east of Inwood Hill Park, south of the Harlem Ship Canal, 4 blocks north of Dyckman Street, in Dyckman section
PHENOMENA
• The first major league park in New York to have lights for evening games. They were installed in 1930 by Cuban Stars owner Alex Pompez.

CAPITAL TEXTURE
STYLE Negro League
OCCUPANT ECL Lincoln Giants 1928; NAL Lincoln Giants 1929
LOCATION (N) East 138th Street; (W) Fifth Avenue; (S) East 135th Street; (E) Madison Avenue
CURRENT USE Riverton Apartments

CATHOLIC PROTECTORY OVAL
STYLE Negro League
OCCUPANT ECL Lincoln Giants 1923 to 1926; NNL Cubans 1935 to 1936
LOCATION *Left Field (E)* Hoguet Avenue; *3rd Base (N)* East Tremont Avenue; *1st Base (W)* White Plains Road; *Right Field (S)* McGraw Avenue. Bronx, 5 miles northeast of Yankee Stadium
CURRENT USE Parkchester Apartments, built by the Metropolitan Life Insurance Company—Unionport Road now crosses the site from home plate to center field; Metropolitan Avenue now runs from right field in to second base and then curves out to left field.
PHENOMENA
• The Protectory was a Catholic home and school for impoverished boys whose 50-piece marching band was

much in demand. One of their students, Hank Greenberg, is now enshrined in the National Baseball Hall of Fame in Cooperstown, N.Y.

- No grass in the infield.
- Leveled in 1939 so that Parkchester Apartments could be built.

TRIBOROUGH STADIUM
STYLE   Football Stadium
A.K.A.   Randall's Island Stadium, J. J. Downing Memorial Stadium
OCCUPANT   NNL Black Yankees 1938
LOCATION   (N) Bronx Kills and Harlem River, Eastern Parkway and Triborough Bridge; (W) House of Refuge, Vesta Avenue; (S) Little Hell Gate, East River, and Ward's Island, Sutter Avenue; (E) Sunken Meadow, Powell Street, Triborough Bridge
CURRENT USE   Still standing, used for WFL Stars football in 1974 and NASL Cosmos soccer in 1975
PHENOMENA
- A U-shaped stadium, open at the southwest end.
- Eight Ebbets Field light towers were moved here when Ebbets had new lights installed.

PATERSON, NEW JERSEY

HINCHCLIFFE STADIUM
STYLE   Football Stadium
OCCUPANT   NNL Black Yankees 1936 to 1937, 1939 to 1945
LOCATION   *Center Field (SE)* Passaic River; *3rd Base (NE)* Redwood Avenue; *Home Plate (NW)* Liberty Street; *1st Base (SW)* Maple Street
CURRENT USE   Community baseball park, still standing, opened 1932

PHILADELPHIA, PENNSYLVANIA

BAKER BOWL
STYLE   Classic
A.K.A.   Huntingdon Street Baseball Grounds 1895 to July 1913, National League Park (III) 1895 to 1938, Hump, Cigar Box, Band Box, Philadelphia Park
OCCUPANT   NL Phillies April 14, 1904 to May 14, 1927 to June 20, 1938; also neutral use by NL Cleveland vs. Baltimore July 29, July 30, and Aug. 11, 1898; and versus Washington August 5, 6, and 8, 1898
EVENT   Negro League World Series first and second games 1924, fifth and sixth games 1925, fourth and fifth games 1926
LOCATION   *Left Field (N)* West Lehigh Avenue; *3rd Base (W)* North 15th Street; *1st Base (S)* West Huntingdon Street; *Right Field (E)* North Broad Street; *Beneath* Philadelphia and Reading Railroad tracks in a tunnel
DIMENSIONS   *Left Field:* 335 (1921), 341.5 (1926), 341 (1930), 341.5 (1931); *Center Field:* 408; *Right-Center:* 300; *Right Field:* 272 (1921), 279.5 (1924), 280.5 (1925); *Backstop:* 60
FENCES   *Left Field:* 4 (1895), 12 July (1929); *Left-Center Field to Right-Center:* 35 (1895), 47 (with 12 screen on top 1915); *Right Field:* 40 (tin over brick 1895),

60 (40 tin over brick, topped by 20 screen 1915)
CURRENT USE   Parking lot and car wash in right-center, gas station in center, bus garage from home down right field foul line
PHENOMENA
- Named after Phillies owner William F. Baker.
- Named the Hump because it was on an elevated piece of ground that had a railroad tunnel underneath the outfield.
- Swimming pool in the basement of the center field clubhouse prior to World War I.
- Coke and "Health Soap Stops B.O." Lifebuoy signs on the high right field wall.
- Extra seats added in front of the fence in center for the 1915 World Series led directly to the Phillies losing the Series' last game.
- During Prohibition, the outfield wall liquor ads were boarded over with dirty grimy blank boards.
- Home plate moved back a foot in 1925, making the right field foul pole 280.5 rather than 279.5.
- Torn down in 1950.

SHIBE PARK
STYLE   Classic
A.K.A.   Connie Mack Stadium 1953 to 1970
OCCUPANT   AL Athletics April 12, 1909 to Sept. 19, 1954; NL Phillies May 16 to May 28, 1927; NL Phillies July 4, 1938 to Oct. 1, 1970
EVENT   Negro League World Series fifth game 1942; fourth game 1945; third game 1947; All-Star Game 1943, 1952
LOCATION   *Left Field (N)* West Somerset Street; *3rd Base (W)* North 21st Street; *1st Base (S)* West Lehigh Avenue; *Right Field (E)* North 20th Street
DIMENSIONS   *Left Field:* 360 (1909), 378 (late 1909), 380 (1921), 334 (1922), 312 (1926), 334 (1930); *Center:* 515 (1909), 502 (late 1909), 468 (1922), 448 (1950), 440 (1951), 460 (1953), 468 (1954), 447 (1956), 410 (1969); *Right-Center:* 393 (1909), 390 (1969); *Right-Center, Left of Scoreboard:* 400 (1942); *Right Field:* 360 (1909), 340 (late 1909), 380 (1921), 307 (1926), 331 (1931), 331 (to lower 1934), 329 (to upper iron fence 1934); *Backstop:* 90 (1942), 86 (1943), 78 (1956), 64 (1960)
FENCES   *Left Field to Left-Center:* 12 (4 screen above 8 concrete 1949); *Center Field, Small Section:* 20 (1955), 8 (wood 1956), 3 (canvas 1969); *Right-Center Scoreboard:* 50 (top of black scoreboard 1956), 60 (top of Ballantine Beer sign 1956); *Right Field:* 12 (concrete 1909), 34 (22 corrugated iron above 12 concrete 1935), 30 (1943), 50 (1949), 40 (1953), 30 (1954), 40 (1955), 32 (1956)
FORMER USE   City dog pound, also a brickyard in the Swampoodle neighborhood nearby
CURRENT USE   Vacant site. Several hundred of the seats were moved to Duncan Park, former home of the Sally League Phillies in Spartanburg, S.C., and to War Memorial Stadium, Greensboro, N.C.
PHENOMENA
- The first concrete and steel stadium of its kind in the majors.
- Named for Ben Shibe, an A's stockholder and baseball manufacturer.

• French Renaissance church-like dome on exterior roof behind the plate which housed Connie Mack's office.

• Sod transplanted here from Columbia Park.

• Highest pitcher's mound—20 inches high.

• Batting cage sat behind short fence in center when the measurement was only 447.

• Corrugated iron fence in right—balls bounced at crazy angles off it—top 22 feet of 34-foot fence—2-foot-deep frame—was 329 to front of frame, 331 to rear of frame where iron sheets were.

• Right field wall reinforcement in 1934 reduced distance to front of the frame from 331 to 329, but sign wasn't changed until 1956.

• Conduit on right field wall was in play.

• Slopes in front of the outfield fences in early years.

• Ladder in front of left field scoreboard in 1909 went all the way to the top.

• Doubledecked in 1925; left field stands also constructed that season.

• Mezzanine added in 1929.

• Before 1935, 20th Street residents could sit in their front bedroom or on their roof and see the game free over the 12-foot right-field fence. Fans could see the lines of laundry on the roof of 20th Street houses. Connie Mack lost a suit to prevent this, so he built the high right field fence.

• Purported 1948 plans to add 18,000 seats in right field and reduce foul line to 315 feet never materialized. That season the A's drew their highest attendance in Philadelphia (945,076). Two years later they drew one-third that many fans.

• In 1956 the old Yankee Stadium scoreboard was installed in front of the right-center wall; later a clock was added—balls hitting the clock were homers—top of clock was 75 feet high; top of the Ballantine Beer sign was 60 feet high.

• In 1956 the normal screen was replaced by see-through plexiglass, protecting the fans behind the plate from foul balls.

• Last game on Oct. 1, 1970.

• Home plate moved to Veterans Stadium in 1971.

• Fire damaged it on Aug. 20, 1971.

• Torn down in June 1976.

HILLDALE PARK
STYLE High School
A.K.A. Darby Catholic School Stadium
OCCUPANT ECL Hilldales 1923 to 1927; NAL Hilldales 1929; NEWL Hilldales 1932
LOCATION *Left Field (N)* Bunting Lane, later MacDade Boulevard; *3rd Base (W)* Greenhouses and Cedar Avenue; *1st Base (S)* Chester Avenue; *Right Field (E)* Yeadon School In the suburbs of Philadelphia at a Catholic school on the Darby-Yeadon borderline, mostly in Yeardon.
DIMENSIONS *Left Field:* 315; *Right-Center:* 400; *Right Field:* 370
CURRENT USE Acme Super Saver supermarket and drive-in bank
PHENOMENA
• A huge tree sat beyond the fence in right-center; branches hung over the fence and were in play.

PITTSBURGH, PENNSYLVANIA
FORBES FIELD
STYLE Classic
A.K.A. Oakland Orchard, Dreyfuss' Folly
OCCUPANT NL Pirates June 30, 1909 to June 28, 1970; NNL Grays 1939 to 1948
EVENT Negro League World Series second game 1942; fourth and fifth games 1944; second game in 1945; All-Star Game 1944, 1959
LOCATION *Left Field (NE)* Schenley Park, then Bigelow Boulevard; *3rd Base (NW)* Sennott (also mis-spelled "Sonnett" at times) Street, then Cathedral of Learning; *1st Base (SW)* Boquet (also spelled "Bouquet" at times) Street; *Right Field (SE)* Joncaire Street, Pierre Ravine, Junction Hollow, Junction Railroad tracks
DIMENSIONS *Left Field:* 360 (1909), 356.5 (1921), 356 (1922), 360 (1926), 365 (1930), 335 (1947), 365 (1954); *Deepest Corner, Left of Straightaway Center, at the Flag Pole:* 462 (1909), 457 (1930); *Center Field:* 442 (1926), 435 (1930); *Right-Center, Right Side of Exit Gate:* 416 (1955); *Right-Center:* 375 (1942); *Bend at Left End of Screen:* 375; *Right Field:* 376 (1909), 376.5 (1921), 376 (1922), 300 (1925); *Backstop:* 110 (1909), 84 (1938), 80 (1947), 84 (1953), 75 (1959)
FENCES *Left Field Front Fence:* 8 (5 screen above 3 wood 1947), 12 (9 screen on top of 3 wood 1949), 14 (screen 1950); *Left Field Wall:* 12 (1909), 12 (brick and ivy 1946); *Left Field Scoreboard:* 25.42 (steel left and right sides), 27 (middle); *Wooden Marine Sergeant at Parade Rest to Right of Scoreboard:* 32 (June 26, 1943 to end of season); *Side Wall Angling Back to Meet Brick Wall in Left-Center:* 12 (wood, when front fence was up); *Cages Around Light Tower Just Right of Scoreboard and in Power Alleys:* 16.5; *Center Field:* 12 (wood 1909), 12 (brick and ivy 1946); *Right-Center:* 9.5 (concrete 1925); *Screen—Left Side at 375 Mark:* 24 (14.5 wire above 9.5 concrete 1932); *Screen—Right Side at Flag Pole:* 27.67 (18.17 wire above 9.5 concrete 1932)
FORMER USE Part of Schenley Farms, a hothouse and livery stable. Land for grazing cows. Ravine where right field would be. Football site for University of Pennsylvania vs. Carnegie Tech Oct. 31, 1908, game. Penn won on the rocky field.
CURRENT USE Mervis Hall, out in right field, and the University of Pittsburgh's Forbes Quadrangle in the infield. The center field and right-center brick walls still stand, along with the base of the flagpole. Mazeroski Field, a Little League diamond beyond the left field brick wall, still remains. Roberto Clemente Drive now bisects the site, and runs about 10 feet under what used to be the playing surface of the infield.
PHENOMENA
• First base by a misspelled street: Boquet Street was named for General Henry Bouquet, a Swiss soldier who fought for the British in the French and Indian War's decisive battle at Fort Duquesne.

• Named for General John Forbes, a British general in the French and Indian War who captured Fort Duquesne and renamed it Fort Pitt in 1758.

• Ivy-covered brick wall in left and left-center.

• The 14-foot Longines clock and speaker horns on top of the park's left field scoreboard were out of play—a

drive hitting against them was a home run.

• Fans in the upper left corner of the left field bleachers could not see the plate because of the third base grandstand, which stood between them and the plate. Right field roof was 86 feet high.

• During World War II, the right field screen could not be replaced due to the priority given to the war effort. It deteriorated badly.

• No no-hitter was ever pitched here.

• Home plate remains in almost its exact original location, only now it is encased in glass on the first-floor walkway of the University of Pittsburgh's Forbes Quadrangle.

• The bottoms of the light-tower cages in left-center, center, and right-center were in play, as was the bottom of the center field flag pole.

• Just to the left of the flagpole stood the batting cage, also in play. Before being placed in left-center, it stood behind home plate during batting practice.

• Very hard infield surface—ask Tony Kubek!

• Back in the 1910s, there was a small scoreboard on the center field wall.

• In the 1920s cars and trucks were repaired and sold beneath the left field bleachers.

• Right field stands built in 1925, reducing distance to right field foul pole by 76.5 feet. Right field screen added in 1932. It was taken down for a short period once, then put back up.

• Barney Dreyfuss Monument was just to the left of the exit gate in right-center, where fans exited the ballpark into Schenley Park after a game. It was installed on June 30, 1934, on the park's 25th anniversary, and was made of granite with a bronze tablet.

• Greenberg Gardens, also called Kiner's Korner: the area between the scoreboard and a chicken coop wire short fence in left put there to increase home run production from 1947 to 1953. It was called Greenberg Gardens 1947, Kiner's Korner 1948 to 1953.

• When Greenberg Gardens were in place, a Western Union clock stood on top of the scoreboard, to the right of the familiar Gruen Clock.

• In 1938 with the Buccos apparently on their way to the World Series, they built a third deck of seats behind the plate called the Crow's Nest, which had the major leagues' first elevator. Bucs finally made the Series 22 years later.

• During World War II, from June 26 through the end of the 1943 season, a huge U.S. Marine made of wood stood against the left field wall, just to the right of the scoreboard. Standing at parade rest, the Marine sergeant was 32 feet high, 15 feet wide across his feet, and in play.

• Honus Wagner statue in Schenley Park erected 1955. It stood 18 feet high, 1,800 pounds—moved to Three Rivers with Bucs in 1970.

• A plaque today marks the spot where Bill Mazeroski's World Series-winning homer left the park in 1960 and flew into the trees above Yogi Berra's head.

• Green foam rubber crash pads placed on concrete wall in right and right-center, first in majors. Wooden walls installed in left and center in 1909, replaced with brick and ivy in 1946.

• Street deadending into Sennott Street by third base variously called Pennant Place and Forbes Field Avenue.

• Fires damaged Forbes Field on Dec. 24, 1970, and July 17, 1971.

• Destruction began July 28, 1971.

• Site also occupied today by Deliverance Evangelistic Church.

AMMON FIELD

STYLE Negro League
OCCUPANT NNL Keystones 1922
CURRENT USE Ammon Playground
PHENOMENA

• Historical marker, dedicated Sept. 23, 1996, commemorates Josh Gibson's over 800 home runs.

GUS GREEN LEE FIELD

STYLE Negro League
OCCUPANT NEWL Grays 1932; NEWL Crawfords 1932; NNL Grays 1933, 1935 to 1938; NNL Crawfords 1933 to 1938
LOCATION In the hill District *Left Field (N)* Ridgeway Street; *3rd Base (W)* Junilia Street; *1st Base (S)* 2500 Bedford Avenue; *Right Field (E)* Municipal Hospital and Francis Street
FORMER USE Entress Brick Company factory
CURRENT USE Pittsburgh Housing Authority projects
PHENOMENA

• Opened on April 29, 1932.

• Tin fence in outfield.

• Left field foul line was longer than at Forbes Field, where it was 365.

• The structure was torn down on Dec. 10, 1938.

ST. LOUIS, MISSOURI

SPORTSMAN'S PARK (IV)

STYLE Classic
A.K.A. Busch Stadium (I) 1953 to 1966, Bill Veeck's House
OCCUPANT AL Browns April 14, 1909 to Sept. 27, 1953; NL Cardinals July 1, 1920 to May 8, 1966; NAL New Orleans–St. Louis Stars one game 1941
EVENT All-Star Game 1940, 1948, 1957
LOCATION *Left Field (NE)* Sullivan Avenue; *3rd Base (NW)* North Spring Avenue; *1st Base (SW)* 3623 Dodier Street; *Right Field (SE)* 2911 North Grand Avenue, later North Grand Boulevard. Same as earlier Sportsman's Parks, but turned around so that home plate was in the west-southwest corner
DIMENSIONS *Left Field:* 368 (1909), 340 (1921), 356 (1923), 355 (1926), 360 (1930), 351.1 (1931); *Left-Center:* 379; *Center Field:* 430 (1926), 450 (1930), 445 (1931), 420 (1938), 422 (1939); *Deepest Corner Just Left of Dead Center:* 426 (1938); *Deepest Corner Just Right of Dead Center:* 422 (1938); *Right-Center:* 354 (1942); *Right Field:* 335 (1909), 315 (1921), 320 (1926), 310 (1931), 332 (1938), 309.5 (1939); *Backstop:* 75 (1942), 67 (1953)
FENCES *Left to Center:* 11.5 (concrete); *354 Mark in Right-Center to Right:* 11.5 (1909), 33 (11.5 concrete below 21.5 wire July 5, 1929), 11.5 (1955), 36.67 (11.5 concrete below 25.17 wire 1956)

CURRENT USE Herbert Hoover Boys' Club, with a baseball diamond where the major league one used to be
PHENOMENA
• The local newspaper, the *Globe-Democrat*, had an ad on the right-center wall which showed the star of the previous game. Just to the right of this ad, the league standings for both leagues were listed.
• The Busch eagle would flap its wings after a Cardinal home run. It sat on top of the left-center scoreboard. During World War II, there was a War Chest sign there.
• Cards office was at 3623 Dodier, Browns office was at 2911 North Grand.
• Pavilion seats in the power alley in right-center.
• Second deck from first to third added in 1909.
• Second deck expanded to foul poles in 1925.
• Bleachers were added to parts of outfield in 1926.
• Beginning in the 1940s, the outfield signs were 351, 358, 379, 400, 426, 425, 422, 422, 405, 354, 322, and 310. In the mid 1950s, the 426 and the right 422 signs that marked the corners just left and right of straightaway center were removed.
• Flag pole in fair territory until removed in the 1950s.
• Bill Veeck's family lived in an apartment under the stands in the 1950s.
• When he bought the stadium from the Browns in 1953, Cardinals owner Gussie Busch almost named it Budweiser Stadium, but was prevented by league pressure.
• The wire screen in front of the right field pavilion was removed for the entire 1955 season. It had been installed on July 5, 1929.
• A helicopter carried home plate to Busch Memorial Stadium after the last game on May 8, 1966.
• The old grandstand behind home plate from 1902 to 1908 became the left field pavilion in this park from 1909 to 1925 when it was replaced.

SAN FRANCISCO, CALIFORNIA

SEALS STADIUM
STYLE Expanded Minor League
A.K.A. Home Plate Mine
OCCUPANT NL Giants April 15, 1958 to Sept. 20, 1959
LOCATION *Left Field (E)* Potrero Avenue; *3rd Base (N)* Alameda Street; *1st Base (W)* Bryant Street; *Right Field (S)* 16th Street and Franklin Square Park
DIMENSIONS *Left Field:* 365 (1958), 361 (1959); *Left-Center:* 375 (1958), 364 (1959); *Just Left of Straightaway Center in the Corner:* 404; *Center Field:* 410 (1958), 400 (1959); *Just Right of Straightaway Center in the Corner:* 415; *Just Right of the 415 Mark Where the Seats Jutted Out:* 397; *Right Field:* 355 (1958), 350 (1959); *Back Stop:* 55.42
FENCES *Left Field:* 15 (5 concrete below 10 wire); *Center Field Scoreboard:* 30.5; *Right Field:* 16 (5 concrete below 11 wire)
CURRENT USE San Francisco Auto Center
PHENOMENA
• Opened April 7, 1931.
• The original deed for the land under the park was listed as "Home Plate Mine."
• No warning track.

• Stiff San Francisco wind blew from right to left.
• Nearby Hamms Brewery still standing.

SEATTLE, WASHINGTON

SICK'S STADIUM
STYLE Expanded Minor League
A.K.A. Sick's Select Stadium 1940s, Seattle Stadium 1940s
OCCUPANT AL Pilots April 11 to Oct. 2, 1969
LOCATION *Left Field (E)* Empire Way South; *3rd Base (N)* South Bayview Street; *1st Base (W)* 2700 Ranier Avenue South; *Right Field (S)* South McClellan Street
DIMENSIONS *Left Field:* 305; *Power Alleys:* 345; *Corners just right and left of center:* 405; *Center Field:* 402; *Right Field:* 320; *Backstop:* 54
FENCES *Left Field:* 8 (3 concrete below 5 wire); *Center Field:* 12.55 (3 concrete below 9.55 wire); *Right Field:* 8 (3 concrete below 5 wire)
PHENOMENA
• Opened June 15, 1938 for PCL franchise.
• Bleachers down the left field line just as at Forbes Field. Fans could see Mt. Rainier in the distance.
• On April 11, 1969, fans could get a free view of the Pilots' Opening Day game by looking through numerous openings in the unfinished left field fence. Seven thousand seats were unfinished and 700 fans had to wait an hour before they could take their seats while the carpenters finished their work.
• Insufficient water pressure if crowd was large.
• Used by Class A teams in early 1970s.

WASHINGTON, D.C.

GRIFFITH STADIUM
STYLE Classic
A.K.A. National Park (III) 1911 to 1921, Clark Griffith Park 1922
OCCUPANT AL Senators (I) April 12, 1911 to Oct. 2, 1960; ECL Potomacs 1924; NEWL Pilots 1932; NNL Elite Giants 1936 to 1937; NNL Washington-Homestead Grays half of their home games 1937 to 1948; NNL Black Senators 1938; AL Senators (II) April 10 to Sept. 21, 1961; Negro League World Series first game 1942, first and second games 1943; third game 1945
EVENT All-Star Game 1937, 1956
LOCATION *Left Field (E)* Larch Street, later Fifth Street NW; *3rd Base (N)* Howard University, then W Street NW; *1st Base (W)* J. Frank Kelley Lumber and Mill Works, then Georgia Avenue NW, also called Seventh Street NW; *Right Field (S)* Spruce Street, later U Street NW
DIMENSIONS *Left Field:* 407 (1911), 424 (1921), 358 (1926), 407 (1931), 402 (1936), 405 (1942), 375 (Opening Day 1947), 405 (remainder 1947), 402 (1948), 386 (1950), 408 (1951), 405 (1952), 388 (1954), 386 (1956), 350 (1957), 388 (1961); *Left of Left-Center at Corner:* 383 (1931), 366 (1954), 360 (1956); *Right of Left-Center at Bend in Bleachers:* 409 (1942), 398 (1954), 383 (1955), 380 (1956); *Left-Center:* 391 (1911), 380 (1950); *Center Field:* 421; *Center Field Corner to Left of Building Protection Wall:* 423 (1926), 441 (1930), 422 (1931), 426 (1936), 420 (1942), 426 (1948), 420

(1950), 394 (1951), 420 (1952) 421 (1953), 426 (1954), 421 (1955), 426 (1961); *Inner Tip of Building Protection Wall:* 409 (1943), 408 (1953); *Deepest Corner—Right End of Building Protection Wall*; *Right-Center:* 378 (1954), 372 (1955), 373 (1956); *Right Field:* 328 (1909), 326 (1921), 328 (marked 1926), 320 (actual 1926), 320 (1956); *Backstop:* 61

FENCES *Left Field:* 11.25 (foul pole to 408 mark concrete 1953), 12 (from 410 corner near left field foul pole to 408 mark just right of dead center 1954), 8 to 10 (wood in the corner in front of the bullpen at the foul pole 1955), 6.5 (wire and plywood in front of bullpen 1956); *Center Field:* 30 (concrete 408 mark to 457 mark 1953), 31 (concrete 408 mark to 457 mark 1954), 6 (wire and plywood 1956); *Right-Center*: to the left of the scoreboard in front of the bullpen: 4 (wood from 457 mark to 435 mark 1953), 10 (wood 1955), 4 (wood 1959); *Right-Center Scoreboard:* 41 (1946); *National Bohemian Beer Bottle:* 56 (1946); *Right Field:* 30 (concrete 1953), 31 (concrete 1954)

CURRENT USE Howard University Medical Center and Howard University College of Dentistry, 909 seats were moved to Tinker Field in Orlando, Florida

PHENOMENA

- Loudspeaker horn high on the wall in center.
- The center field wall detoured around five houses and a huge tree in center, jutting into the field of play.
- Right field foul line was the grandstand wall for the last 15 or so feet in front of the foul pole, so there was no way to catch a foul ball there.
- It was downhill from the plate to first base, supposedly to help save a step for slow Washington batters.
- Right field clock out of play.
- Ball rolling between top of scoreboard and bottom of the clock was in play: if it didn't come out, it was a homer; if it did, the outfielder could throw it back into play.
- U.S. presidents traditionally opened each season here by throwing out the first ball.
- Memorials honoring Walter Johnson and Clark Griffith stood outside the main entrance to the first base grandstand. The former now stands at Walter Johnson High School in Bethesda, Maryland; the latter at RFK Stadium.
- Height of National Bohemian Beer Bottle, above right-center scoreboard, 50 feet.
- Park rebuilt after March 17, 1911 fire; completed on July 24, 1911.
- Doubledecked in 1920 from the bases down to the foul poles with a roof higher than the original second deck roof behind the plate.
- Temporary seats placed in front of left field bleachers for the 1924 World Series.
- In 1954 the visitor's bullpen was enclosed behind a screen fence in the left field corner in fair territory.
- Clark Calvin Griffith Memorial, dedicated by Vice President Nixon on Aug. 8, 1956, was later moved to R.F.K. Stadium.
- In 1956 all the distances to the outfield fences were re-measured, and it was discovered that right field had lost 8 feet over the years!
- Also in 1956, 10 rows of temporary seats were added in front of the left field bleacher section.
- Park demolished from Jan. 26 to Aug. 14, 1965.

## CHAPTER 4

Major League Attendance
Robert L. Tiemann and Pete Palmer

I f you have the patience to sift through them, the figures on the following pages, dating from 1871 through 1998, tell a remarkable story. Season attendance has approached 4.5 million in Colorado in 1993, and it has been as little as 6,088 in Cleveland in 1899, when the awful Spiders went 20–134. The first club to pass the million mark was the New York Yankees of 1920, featuring a newcomer named Ruth and a ballpark borrowed from the Giants (who did not reach the mark themselves until 1945). In the depths of the Depression, the St. Louis Browns posted annual attendance figures (80,922 in 1935; 88,113 in 1933) below what a weekend set produces in many major league venues today.

Why did attendance stagnate in the 1890s? How much did the entry of the American League into National League strongholds New York, Chicago, Philadelphia, and St. Louis hurt the senior franchises? Were the Dodgers justified in leaving Brooklyn? How did baseball survive in Washington as long as it did, surpassing the million mark only once from 1892 to 1971? Did anyone notice that Atlanta's attendance of 1990 doubled, and then tripled, over the next two years? Or that while major league attendance increased by 25.8 percent from 1992 to 1993, almost all of that gain came from the senior circuit? (The American League rose a modest 5 percent while the National League posted a whopping gain of 53 percent; even if we subtract expansion clubs Florida and Colorado, the NL increase was an impressive 21.8 percent.)

You get the picture. There's stuff here that permits you to chart trends in baseball that you already know about, and if you are eagle-eyed you may pick up a figure that prompts you to rethink what you thought you knew.

A researcher's goldmine, the tables that follow tell an interesting story for the average fan as well. Does winning a pennant correlate with higher attendance? Are first-division teams more profitable than those in the second division? What is the impact on attendance of a new stadium?

By the time the next edition rolls around we may be able to gather figures going back to the dawn of professional baseball. Here are some scattered tidbits:

- In their first year of existence, 1871, the Boston Red Stockings counted 32,600 fans in 18 home games.
- In 1882, the last year of its existence as an NL franchise, the Troy Haymakers drew a whopping 26,000 attendees for its 42 home games, with one late season date posting a recorded crowd of 12 (that's not a typo).
- The 1891 American Association, in its final year of operation, counted 1,296,000 fans, or an average of 162,000 per team, a figure very comparable to the 169,060 of the National League. In 1892, with the AA gone and the NL a 12-team circuit, the average team attendance was less than 152,000. Is there a lesson to be drawn from this?

Yes, and the lesson is plain for magnates no less than for fans and students of the game.

	1871	1872	1873	1874	1875	1876	1877	1878	1879	1880
NATIONAL LEAGUE										
ATH	51,000	61,000	36,000	33,000	45,500					
ATL		10,000	20,000	21,000	11,000					
BAL			40,500	25,000	12,000					
BOS	36,500	38,500	52,000	46,500	50,000	51,000	55,240	48,915	36,501	34,000
BUF									26,000	20,000
CEN					4,500					
CHI	69,000			66,000	60,323	65,441	46,454	58,691	67,687	66,708
CIN						24,000	28,000	41,000	28,000	21,000
CLE	16,000	7,500							25,000	35,000
ECK		4,000								
HAR				30,500	41,000	18,000	22,000			
IND								12,000		
KEK	3,500									
LOU						25,000	24,000			
MAN		5,500								
MAR			1,500							
MIL								17,000		
MUT	40,500	48,500	29,000	37,000	32,000					
NAT		1,500								
NH					17,500					
NY						23,000				
OLY	26,000	3,000								
PHI			50,000	23,000	29,500	24,000				
PRO								46,000	47,595	37,220
RES			3,000							
RS					6,500					
ROK	6,500									
STL					78,500	36,000	29,000			
SYR									9,000	
TRO	17,500	17,000							12,000	18,500
WAS			8,000		7,500					
WES					4,000					
WOR										24,000
TOT	266,500	237,000	224,500	269,000	387,823	266,441	204,694	223,606	251,783	256,428

	1881	1882	1883	1884	1885	1886	1887	1888	1889	1890
NATIONAL LEAGUE										
BOS	34,343	50,971	128,968	146,777	110,290	133,683	261,000	265,015	283,257	147,539
BRO										121,412
BUF	32,173	28,000	32,000	42,000	35,000					
CHI	82,000	125,452	124,880	87,667	117,519	142,438	217,070	228,906	149,175	102,536
CIN										131,980
CLE	34,000	30,000	63,000	38,000					144,425	47,478
DET	53,720	75,000	70,000	32,000	43,000	105,000	95,000	75,000		
IND							84,000	78,000	105,850	
KC						55,000				
NY			75,000	105,000	185,000	189,000	270,945	305,455	201,989	60,667
PHI			55,992	100,475	150,698	175,623	253,671	151,804	281,869	148,366
PIT							140,000	112,000	117,338	16,064
PRO	30,000	57,477	61,314	64,409	49,000					
STL					62,000	99,000				
TRO	18,000	26,488								
WAS						60,000	80,000	57,000	68,652	
WOR	17,000	11,000								
TOT	301,236	404,388	611,154	616,328	752,507	959,744	1,401,686	1,273,180	1,352,555	776,042

	1882	1883	1884	1885	1886	1887	1888	1889	1890	1891
AMERICAN ASSOCIATION										
BAL	36,000	110,000	120,000	60,000	70,000	142,000	38,000	115,000	34,000	150,000
BOS										170,000
BRO			65,000	85,000	185,000	273,000	245,000	353,690	37,000	
CIN	65,000	86,000	110,000	120,000	138,563	185,397	132,606	131,000		63,000
CLE						72,000	60,000			
COL		48,000	66,000					90,000	85,000	105,000
IND			56,000							
KC							50,000	85,000		
LOU	50,000	78,000	111,000	108,000	123,000	128,000	76,000	60,000	206,200	140,000
MIL										45,000
NY		50,000	68,000	64,000	67,000	105,000				
PHI	72,000	305,000	116,000	169,000	179,000	163,000	201,000	220,000	134,000	168,000
PIT	42,000	85,000	60,000	82,000	195,000					
RIC			16,000							
ROC									82,000	
STL	135,000	243,000	212,000	129,000	205,000	244,000	166,000	175,000	105,000	220,000
SYR									50,000	
TOL			55,000						70,000	
WAS			25,000							112,000
TOT	400,000	1,005,000	1,080,000	817,000	1,162,563	1,312,397	968,606	1,229,690	803,200	1,173,000
ML	804,388	1,616,154	1,696,328	1,569,507	2,122,307	2,714,083	2,241,786	2,582,245	1,579,242	2,525,487

	1891	1892	1893	1894	1895	1896	1897	1898	1899	1900
NATIONAL LEAGUE										
BAL		93,589	143,000	328,000	293,000	249,448	273,046	123,416	121,935	
BOS	184,472	146,421	193,300	152,800	242,000	240,000	334,800	229,275	200,384	190,000
BRO	181,477	183,727	235,000	214,000	230,000	201,000	220,831	122,514	269,641	170,000
CHI	201,188	109,067	223,500	239,000	382,300	317,500	327,160	424,352	352,130	248,577
CIN	97,500	196,473	194,250	158,000	281,000	373,000	336,800	336,378	259,536	155,000
CLE	132,000	139,928	130,000	82,000	143,000	152,000	115,250	70,496	6,088	
LOU		131,159	53,683	75,000	92,000	133,000	145,210	128,980	109,319	
NY	210,568	130,566	290,000	387,000	240,000	274,000	390,340	206,700	121,384	175,000
PHI	217,282	193,731	293,019	352,773	474,971	357,025	288,816	265,414	388,933	301,913
PIT	128,000	177,205	184,000	159,000	188,000	197,000	165,950	150,900	251,834	250,000
STL		192,442	195,000	155,000	170,000	184,000	136,400	151,700	373,909	255,000
WAS		128,279	90,000	125,000	153,000	223,000	151,028	103,250	86,392	
TOT	1,352,487	1,822,587	2,224,752	2,427,573	2,889,271	2,900,973	2,885,631	2,313,375	2,541,485	1,745,490
ML	2,525,487	1,822,587	2,224,752	2,427,573	2,889,271	2,900,973	2,885,631	2,313,375	2,541,485	1,745,490

	1901	1902	1903	1904	1905	1906	1907	1908	1909	1910
NATIONAL LEAGUE										
BOS	146,502	116,960	143,155	140,694	150,003	143,280	203,221	253,750	195,188	149,027
BRO	198,200	199,868	224,670	214,600	227,924	277,400	312,500	275,600	321,300	279,321
CHI	205,071	263,700	386,205	439,100	509,900	654,300	422,550	665,325	633,480	526,152
CIN	205,728	217,300	351,680	391,915	313,927	330,056	317,500	399,200	424,643	380,622
NY	297,650	302,875	579,530	609,826	552,700	402,850	538,350	910,000	783,700	511,785
PHI	234,937	112,066	151,729	140,771	317,932	294,680	341,216	420,660	303,177	296,597
PIT	251,955	243,826	326,855	340,615	369,124	394,877	319,506	382,444	534,950	436,586
STL	379,988	226,417	226,538	386,750	292,800	283,770	185,377	205,129	299,982	355,668
TOT	1,920,031	1,683,012	2,390,362	2,664,271	2,734,310	2,781,213	2,640,220	3,512,108	3,496,420	2,935,758
AMERICAN LEAGUE										
BAL	141,952	174,606								
BOS	289,448	348,567	379,338	623,295	468,828	410,209	436,777	473,048	668,965	584,619
CHI	354,350	337,898	286,183	557,123	687,419	585,202	666,307	636,096	478,400	552,084
CLE	131,380	275,395	311,280	264,749	316,306	325,733	382,046	422,262	354,627	293,456
DET	259,430	189,469	224,523	177,796	193,384	174,043	297,079	436,199	490,490	391,288
MIL	139,034									
NY			211,808	438,919	309,100	434,700	350,020	305,500	501,700	355,857
PHI	206,329	420,078	422,473	512,294	554,576	489,129	625,581	455,062	674,915	588,905
STL		272,283	380,405	318,108	339,112	389,157	419,025	618,947	366,274	249,889
WAS	161,661	188,158	128,878	131,744	252,027	129,903	221,929	264,252	205,199	254,591
TOT	1,683,584	2,206,454	2,344,888	3,024,028	3,120,752	2,938,076	3,398,764	3,611,366	3,740,570	3,270,689
ML	3,603,615	3,889,466	4,735,250	5,688,299	5,855,062	5,719,289	6,038,984	7,123,474	7,236,990	6,206,447

	1911	1912	1913	1914	1915	1916	1917	1918	1919	1920
NATIONAL LEAGUE										
BOS	116,000	121,000	208,000	382,913	376,283	313,495	174,253	84,938	167,401	162,483
BRO	269,000	243,000	347,000	122,671	297,766	447,747	221,619	83,831	360,721	808,722
CHI	576,000	514,000	419,000	202,516	217,058	453,685	360,218	337,256	424,430	480,783
CIN	300,000	344,000	258,000	100,791	218,878	255,846	269,056	163,009	532,501	568,107
NY	675,000	638,000	630,000	364,313	391,850	552,056	500,264	256,618	708,857	929,609
PHI	416,000	250,000	470,000	138,474	449,898	515,365	354,428	122,266	240,424	330,998
PIT	432,000	384,000	296,000	139,620	225,743	289,132	192,807	213,610	276,810	429,037
STL	447,768	241,759	203,531	256,099	252,666	224,308	288,491	110,599	167,059	326,836
TOT	3,231,768	2,735,759	2,831,531	1,707,397	2,430,142	3,051,634	2,361,136	1,372,127	2,878,203	4,036,575
AMERICAN LEAGUE										
BOS	503,961	597,096	437,194	481,359	539,885	496,397	387,856	249,513	417,291	402,445
CHI	583,208	602,241	644,501	469,290	539,461	679,923	684,521	195,081	627,186	833,492
CLE	406,296	336,844	541,000	185,997	159,285	492,106	477,298	295,515	538,135	912,832
DET	484,988	402,870	398,502	416,225	476,105	616,772	457,289	203,719	643,805	579,650
NY	302,444	242,194	357,551	359,477	256,035	469,211	330,294	282,047	619,164	1,289,422
PHI	605,749	517,653	571,896	346,641	146,223	184,471	221,432	177,926	225,209	287,888
STL	207,984	214,070	250,330	244,714	150,358	335,740	210,486	122,076	349,350	419,311
WAS	244,884	350,663	325,831	243,888	167,332	177,265	89,682	182,122	234,096	359,260
TOT	3,339,514	3,263,631	3,526,805	2,747,591	2,434,684	3,451,885	2,858,858	1,707,999	3,654,236	5,084,300
ML	6,571,282	5,999,390	6,358,336	4,454,988	4,864,826	6,503,519	5,219,994	3,080,126	6,532,439	9,120,875

	1921	1922	1923	1924	1925	1926	1927	1928	1929	1930
NATIONAL LEAGUE										
BOS	318,627	167,965	227,802	177,478	313,528	303,598	288,685	227,001	372,351	464,835
BRO	613,245	498,865	564,666	818,883	659,435	650,819	637,230	664,863	731,886	1,097,329
CHI	410,107	542,283	703,705	716,922	622,610	885,063	1,159,168	1,143,740	1,485,166	1,463,624
CIN	311,227	493,754	575,063	473,707	464,920	672,987	442,164	490,490	295,040	386,727
NY	973,477	945,809	820,780	844,068	778,993	700,362	858,190	916,191	868,806	868,714
PHI	273,961	232,471	228,168	299,818	304,905	240,600	305,420	182,168	281,200	299,007
PIT	701,567	523,675	611,082	736,883	804,354	798,542	869,720	495,070	491,377	357,795
STL	384,773	536,998	338,551	272,885	404,959	668,428	749,340	761,574	399,887	508,501
TOT	3,986,984	3,941,820	4,069,817	4,340,644	4,353,704	4,920,399	5,309,917	4,881,097	4,925,713	5,446,532

	1921	1922	1923	1924	1925	1926	1927	1928	1929	1930
AMERICAN LEAGUE										
BOS	279,273	259,184	229,688	448,556	267,782	285,155	305,275	396,920	394,620	444,045
CHI	543,650	602,860	573,778	606,658	832,231	710,339	614,423	494,152	426,795	406,123
CLE	748,705	528,145	558,856	481,905	419,005	627,426	373,138	375,907	536,210	528,657
DET	661,527	861,206	911,377	1,015,136	820,766	711,914	773,716	474,323	869,318	649,450
NY	1,230,696	1,026,134	1,007,066	1,053,533	697,267	1,027,675	1,164,015	1,072,132	960,148	1,169,230
PHI	344,430	425,356	534,122	531,992	869,703	714,508	605,529	689,756	839,176	721,663
STL	355,978	712,918	430,296	533,349	462,898	283,986	247,879	339,497	280,697	152,088
WAS	456,069	458,552	357,406	584,310	817,199	551,580	528,976	378,501	355,506	614,474
TOT	4,620,328	4,874,355	4,602,589	5,255,439	5,186,851	4,912,583	4,612,951	4,221,188	4,662,470	4,685,730
ML	8,607,312	8,816,175	8,672,406	9,596,083	9,540,555	9,832,982	9,922,868	9,102,285	9,588,183	10,132,262

	1931	1932	1933	1934	1935	1936	1937	1938	1939	1940
NATIONAL LEAGUE										
BOS	515,005	507,606	517,803	303,205	232,754	340,585	385,339	341,149	285,994	241,616
BRO	753,133	681,827	526,815	434,188	470,517	489,618	482,481	663,087	955,668	975,978
CHI	1,086,422	974,688	594,112	707,525	692,604	699,370	895,020	951,640	726,663	534,878
CIN	263,316	356,950	218,281	206,773	448,247	466,345	411,221	706,756	981,443	850,180
NY	812,163	484,868	604,471	730,851	748,748	837,952	926,887	799,633	702,457	747,852
PHI	284,849	268,914	156,421	169,885	205,470	249,219	212,790	166,111	277,973	207,177
PIT	260,392	287,262	288,747	322,622	352,885	372,524	459,679	641,033	376,734	507,934
STL	608,535	279,219	256,171	325,056	506,084	448,078	430,811	291,418	400,245	324,078
TOT	4,583,815	3,841,334	3,162,821	3,200,105	3,657,309	3,903,691	4,204,228	4,560,827	4,707,177	4,389,693
AMERICAN LEAGUE										
BOS	350,975	182,150	268,715	610,640	558,568	626,895	559,659	646,459	573,070	716,234
CHI	403,550	233,198	397,789	236,559	470,281	440,810	589,245	338,278	594,104	660,336
CLE	483,027	468,953	387,936	391,338	397,615	500,391	564,849	652,006	563,926	902,576
DET	434,056	397,157	320,972	919,161	1,034,929	875,948	1,072,276	799,557	836,279	1,112,693
NY	912,437	962,320	728,014	854,682	657,508	976,913	998,148	970,916	859,785	988,975
PHI	627,464	405,500	297,138	305,847	233,173	285,173	430,738	385,357	395,022	432,145
STL	179,126	112,558	88,113	115,305	80,922	93,267	123,121	130,417	109,159	239,591
WAS	492,657	371,396	437,533	330,074	255,011	379,525	397,799	522,694	339,257	381,241
TOT	3,883,292	3,133,232	2,926,210	3,763,606	3,688,007	4,178,922	4,735,835	4,445,684	4,270,602	5,433,791
ML	8,467,107	6,974,566	6,089,031	6,963,711	7,345,316	8,082,613	8,940,063	9,006,511	8,977,779	9,823,484

	1941	1942	1943	1944	1945	1946	1947	1948	1949	1950
NATIONAL LEAGUE										
BOS	263,680	285,332	271,289	208,691	374,178	969,673	1,277,361	1,455,439	1,081,795	944,391
BRO	1,214,910	1,037,765	661,739	605,905	1,059,220	1,796,824	1,807,526	1,398,967	1,633,747	1,185,896
CHI	545,159	590,972	508,247	640,110	1,036,386	1,342,970	1,364,039	1,237,792	1,143,139	1,165,944
CIN	643,513	427,031	379,122	409,567	290,070	715,751	899,975	823,386	707,782	538,794
NY	763,098	779,621	466,095	674,483	1,016,468	1,219,873	1,600,793	1,459,269	1,218,446	1,008,878
PHI	231,401	230,183	466,975	369,586	285,057	1,045,247	907,332	767,429	819,698	1,217,035
PIT	482,241	448,897	498,740	604,278	604,694	749,962	1,283,531	1,517,021	1,449,435	1,166,267
STL	633,645	553,552	517,135	461,968	594,630	1,061,807	1,247,913	1,111,440	1,430,676	1,093,411
TOT	4,777,647	4,353,353	3,769,342	3,974,588	5,260,703	8,902,107	10,388,470	9,770,743	9,484,718	8,320,616
AMERICAN LEAGUE										
BOS	718,497	730,340	358,275	506,975	603,794	1,416,944	1,427,315	1,558,798	1,596,650	1,344,080
CHI	677,077	425,734	508,962	563,539	657,981	983,403	876,948	777,844	937,151	781,330
CLE	745,948	459,447	438,894	475,272	558,182	1,057,289	1,521,978	2,620,627	2,233,771	1,727,464
DET	684,915	580,087	606,287	923,176	1,280,341	1,722,590	1,398,093	1,743,035	1,821,204	1,951,474
NY	964,722	922,011	618,330	789,995	881,845	2,265,512	2,178,937	2,373,901	2,283,676	2,081,380
PHI	528,894	423,487	376,735	505,322	462,631	621,793	911,566	945,076	816,514	309,805
STL	176,240	255,617	214,392	508,644	482,986	526,435	320,474	335,564	270,936	247,131
WAS	415,663	403,493	574,694	525,235	652,660	1,027,216	850,758	795,254	770,745	699,697
TOT	4,911,956	4,200,216	3,696,569	4,798,158	5,580,420	9,621,182	9,486,069	11,150,099	10,730,647	9,142,361
ML	9,689,603	8,553,569	7,465,911	8,772,746	10,841,123	18,523,288	19,874,540	20,920,842	20,215,364	17,462,976

	1951	1952	1953	1954	1955	1956	1957	1958	1959	1960
NATIONAL LEAGUE										
BOS	487,475	281,278								
BRO	1,282,628	1,088,704	1,163,419	1,020,531	1,033,589	1,213,562	1,028,258			
CHI	894,415	1,024,826	763,658	748,183	875,800	720,118	670,629	979,904	858,255	809,770
CIN	588,268	604,197	548,086	704,167	693,662	1,125,928	1,070,850	788,582	801,298	663,486
LA								1,845,556	2,071,045	2,253,887
MIL			1,826,397	2,131,388	2,005,836	2,046,331	2,215,404	1,971,101	1,749,112	1,497,799
NY	1,059,530	984,940	811,518	1,155,067	824,112	629,179	653,923			
PHI	937,658	755,417	853,644	738,991	922,886	934,798	1,146,230	931,110	802,815	862,205
PIT	980,590	686,673	572,757	475,494	469,397	949,878	850,732	1,311,988	1,359,917	1,705,828
STL	1,013,429	913,113	880,242	1,039,698	849,130	1,029,773	1,183,575	1,063,730	929,953	1,096,632
SF								1,272,625	1,422,130	1,795,356
TOT	7,244,002	6,339,148	7,419,721	8,013,519	7,674,412	8,649,567	8,819,601	10,164,596	9,994,525	10,684,963
AMERICAN LEAGUE										
BAL				1,060,910	852,039	901,201	1,029,581	829,991	891,926	1,187,849
BOS	1,312,282	1,115,750	1,026,133	931,127	1,203,200	1,137,158	1,181,087	1,077,047	984,102	1,129,866
CHI	1,328,234	1,231,675	1,191,353	1,231,629	1,175,684	1,000,090	1,135,668	797,451	1,423,144	1,644,460
CLE	1,704,984	1,444,607	1,069,176	1,335,472	1,221,780	865,467	722,256	663,805	1,497,976	950,985

	1951	1952	1953	1954	1955	1956	1957	1958	1959	1960
DET	1,132,641	1,026,846	884,658	1,079,847	1,181,838	1,051,182	1,272,346	1,098,924	1,221,221	1,167,669
KC					1,393,054	1,015,154	901,067	925,090	963,683	774,944
NY	1,950,107	1,629,665	1,537,811	1,475,171	1,490,138	1,491,784	1,497,134	1,428,438	1,552,030	1,627,349
PHI	465,469	627,100	362,113	304,666						
STL	293,790	518,796	297,238							
WAS	695,167	699,457	595,594	503,542	425,238	431,647	457,079	475,288	615,372	743,404
TOT	8,882,674	8,293,896	6,964,076	7,922,364	8,942,971	7,893,683	8,196,218	7,296,034	9,149,454	9,226,526
ML	16,126,676	14,633,044	14,383,797	15,935,883	16,617,383	16,543,250	17,015,820	17,460,630	19,143,980	19,911,488

	1961	1962	1963	1964	1965	1966	1967	1968	1969	1970
NATIONAL LEAGUE										
ATL						1,539,801	1,389,222	1,126,540	1,458,320	1,078,848
CHI	673,057	609,802	979,551	751,647	641,361	635,891	977,226	1,043,409	1,674,993	1,642,705
CIN	1,117,603	982,095	858,805	862,466	1,047,824	742,958	958,300	733,354	987,991	1,803,568
HOU		924,456	719,502	725,773	2,151,470	1,872,108	1,348,303	1,312,887	1,442,995	1,253,444
LA	1,804,250	2,755,184	2,538,602	2,228,751	2,553,577	2,617,029	1,664,362	1,581,093	1,784,527	1,697,142
MIL	1,101,441	766,921	773,018	910,911	555,584					
MON									1,212,608	1,424,683
NY		922,530	1,080,108	1,732,597	1,768,389	1,932,693	1,565,492	1,781,657	2,175,373	2,697,479
PHI	590,039	762,034	907,141	1,425,891	1,166,376	1,108,201	828,888	664,546	519,414	708,247
PIT	1,199,128	1,090,648	783,648	759,496	909,279	1,196,618	907,012	693,485	769,369	1,341,947
STL	855,305	953,895	1,170,546	1,143,294	1,241,201	1,712,980	2,090,145	2,011,167	1,682,783	1,629,736
SD									512,970	643,679
SF	1,390,679	1,592,594	1,571,306	1,504,364	1,546,075	1,657,192	1,242,480	837,220	873,603	740,720
TOT	8,731,502	11,360,159	11,382,227	12,045,190	13,581,136	15,015,471	12,971,430	11,785,358	15,094,946	16,662,198
AMERICAN LEAGUE										
BAL	951,089	790,254	774,343	1,116,215	781,649	1,203,366	955,053	943,977	1,062,069	1,057,069
BOS	850,589	733,080	942,642	883,276	652,201	811,172	1,727,832	1,940,788	1,833,246	1,595,278
CAL					566,727	1,400,321	1,317,713	1,025,956	758,388	1,077,741
CHI	1,146,019	1,131,562	1,158,848	1,250,053	1,130,519	990,016	985,634	803,775	589,546	495,355
CLE	725,547	716,076	562,507	653,293	934,786	903,359	662,980	857,994	619,970	729,752
DET	1,600,710	1,207,881	821,952	816,139	1,029,645	1,124,293	1,447,143	2,031,847	1,577,481	1,501,293
KC	683,817	635,675	762,364	642,478	528,344	773,929	726,639		902,414	693,047
LA	603,510	1,144,063	821,015	760,439						
MIL										933,690
MIN	1,256,723	1,433,116	1,406,652	1,207,514	1,463,258	1,259,374	1,483,547	1,143,257	1,349,328	1,261,887
NY	1,747,725	1,493,574	1,308,920	1,305,638	1,213,552	1,124,648	1,259,514	1,185,666	1,067,996	1,136,879
OAK								837,466	778,232	778,355
SEA									677,944	
WAS	597,287	729,775	535,604	600,106	560,083	576,260	770,868	546,661	918,106	824,789
TOT	10,163,016	10,015,056	9,094,847	9,235,151	8,860,764	10,166,738	11,336,923	11,317,387	12,134,720	12,085,135
ML	18,894,518	21,375,216	20,477,074	21,280,340	22,441,900	25,182,208	24,308,352	23,102,744	27,229,666	28,747,332

	1971	1972	1973	1974	1975	1976	1977	1978	1979	1980
NATIONAL LEAGUE										
ATL	1,006,320	752,973	800,655	981,085	534,672	818,179	872,464	904,494	769,465	1,048,411
CHI	1,653,007	1,299,163	1,351,705	1,015,378	1,034,819	1,026,217	1,439,834	1,525,311	1,648,587	1,206,776
CIN	1,501,122	1,611,459	2,017,601	2,164,307	2,315,603	2,629,708	2,519,670	2,532,497	2,356,933	2,022,450
HOU	1,261,589	1,469,247	1,394,004	1,090,728	858,002	886,146	1,109,560	1,126,145	1,900,312	2,278,217
LA	2,064,594	1,860,858	2,136,192	2,632,474	2,539,349	2,386,301	2,955,087	3,347,845	2,860,954	3,249,287
MON	1,290,963	1,142,145	1,246,863	1,019,134	908,292	646,704	1,433,757	1,427,007	2,102,173	2,208,175
NY	2,266,680	2,134,185	1,912,390	1,722,209	1,730,566	1,468,754	1,066,825	1,007,328	788,905	1,192,073
PHI	1,511,223	1,343,329	1,475,934	1,808,648	1,909,233	2,480,150	2,700,070	2,583,389	2,775,011	2,651,650
PIT	1,501,132	1,427,460	1,319,913	1,110,552	1,270,018	1,025,945	1,237,349	964,106	1,435,454	1,646,757
STL	1,604,671	1,196,894	1,574,046	1,838,413	1,695,270	1,207,079	1,659,287	1,278,215	1,627,256	1,385,147
SD	557,513	644,273	611,826	1,075,399	1,281,747	1,458,478	1,376,269	1,670,107	1,456,967	1,139,026
SF	1,106,043	647,744	834,193	519,987	522,919	626,868	700,056	1,740,477	1,456,402	1,096,115
TOT	17,324,856	15,529,730	16,675,322	16,978,314	16,600,490	16,660,529	19,070,228	20,106,922	21,178,416	21,124,086
AMERICAN LEAGUE										
BAL	1,023,037	899,950	958,667	962,572	1,002,157	1,058,609	1,195,769	1,051,724	1,681,009	1,797,438
BOS	1,678,732	1,441,718	1,481,002	1,556,411	1,748,587	1,895,846	2,074,549	2,320,643	2,353,114	1,956,092
CAL	926,373	744,190	1,058,206	917,269	1,058,163	1,006,774	1,432,633	1,755,386	2,523,575	2,297,327
CHI	833,891	1,177,318	1,302,527	1,149,596	750,802	914,945	1,657,135	1,491,100	1,280,702	1,200,365
CLE	591,361	626,354	615,107	1,114,262	977,039	948,776	900,365	800,584	1,011,644	1,033,827
DET	1,591,073	1,892,386	1,724,146	1,243,080	1,058,836	1,467,020	1,359,856	1,714,893	1,630,929	1,785,293
KC	910,784	707,656	1,345,341	1,173,292	1,151,836	1,680,265	1,852,603	2,255,493	2,261,845	2,288,714
MIL	731,531	600,440	1,092,158	955,741	1,213,357	1,012,164	1,114,938	1,601,406	1,918,343	1,857,408
MIN	940,858	797,901	907,499	662,401	737,156	715,394	1,162,727	787,878	1,070,521	769,206
NY	1,070,771	966,328	1,262,103	1,273,075	1,288,048	2,012,434	2,103,092	2,335,871	2,537,765	2,627,417
OAK	914,993	921,323	1,000,763	845,693	1,075,518	780,593	495,599	526,999	306,763	842,259
SEA							1,338,511	877,440	844,447	836,204
TEX		662,974	686,085	1,193,902	1,127,924	1,164,982	1,250,722	1,447,963	1,519,671	1,198,175
TOR							1,701,052	1,562,585	1,431,651	1,400,327
WAS	655,156									
TOT	11,868,560	11,438,538	13,433,604	13,047,294	13,189,423	14,657,802	19,639,552	20,529,964	22,371,980	21,890,052
ML	29,193,416	26,968,268	30,108,926	30,025,608	29,789,912	31,318,332	38,709,780	40,636,888	43,550,396	43,014,136

	1981	1982	1983	1984	1985	1986	1987	1988	1989	1990
NATIONAL LEAGUE										
ATL	535,418	1,801,985	2,119,935	1,724,892	1,350,137	1,387,181	1,217,402	848,089	984,930	980,129
CHI	565,637	1,249,278	1,479,717	2,107,655	2,161,534	1,859,102	2,035,130	2,089,034	2,491,942	2,243,791
CIN	1,093,730	1,326,528	1,190,419	1,275,887	1,834,619	1,692,432	2,185,205	2,072,528	1,979,320	2,400,892
HOU	1,321,282	1,558,555	1,351,962	1,229,862	1,184,314	1,734,276	1,909,902	1,933,505	1,834,908	1,310,927
LA	2,381,292	3,608,881	3,510,313	3,134,824	3,264,593	3,023,208	2,797,409	2,980,262	2,944,653	3,002,396
MON	1,534,564	2,318,292	2,320,651	1,606,531	1,502,494	1,128,981	1,850,324	1,478,659	1,783,533	1,373,087
NY	704,244	1,323,036	1,112,774	1,842,695	2,761,601	2,767,601	3,034,129	3,055,445	2,918,710	2,732,745
PHI	1,638,752	2,376,394	2,128,339	2,062,693	1,830,350	1,933,335	2,100,110	1,990,041	1,861,985	1,992,484
PIT	541,789	1,024,106	1,225,916	773,500	735,900	1,000,917	1,161,193	1,866,713	1,374,141	2,049,908
STL	1,010,247	2,111,906	2,317,914	2,037,448	2,637,563	2,471,974	3,072,122	2,892,799	3,080,980	2,573,225
SD	519,161	1,607,516	1,539,815	1,983,904	2,210,352	1,805,716	1,454,061	1,506,896	2,009,031	1,856,396
SF	632,274	1,200,948	1,251,530	1,001,545	818,697	1,528,748	1,917,168	1,785,297	2,059,701	1,975,528
TOT	12,478,390	21,507,424	21,549,284	20,781,436	22,292,156	22,333,472	24,734,156	24,499,268	25,323,834	24,491,508
AMERICAN LEAGUE										
BAL	1,024,247	1,613,031	2,042,071	2,045,784	2,132,387	1,973,176	1,835,692	1,660,738	2,535,208	2,415,189
BOS	1,060,379	1,950,124	1,782,285	1,661,618	1,786,633	2,147,641	2,231,551	2,464,851	2,510,012	2,528,986
CAL	1,441,545	2,807,360	2,555,016	2,402,997	2,567,427	2,655,872	2,696,299	2,340,925	2,647,291	2,555,688
CHI	946,651	1,567,787	2,132,821	2,136,988	1,669,888	1,424,313	1,208,060	1,115,749	1,045,651	2,002,357
CLE	661,395	1,044,021	768,941	734,079	655,181	1,471,805	1,077,898	1,411,610	1,285,542	1,225,240
DET	1,149,144	1,636,058	1,829,636	2,704,794	2,286,609	1,899,437	2,061,830	2,081,162	1,543,656	1,495,785
KC	1,279,403	2,284,464	1,963,875	1,810,018	2,162,717	2,320,794	2,392,471	2,350,181	2,477,700	2,244,956
MIL	874,292	1,978,896	2,397,131	1,608,509	1,360,265	1,265,041	1,909,244	1,923,238	1,970,735	1,752,900
MIN	469,090	921,186	858,939	1,598,692	1,651,814	1,255,453	2,081,976	3,030,672	2,277,438	1,751,584
NY	1,614,353	2,041,219	2,257,976	1,821,815	2,214,587	2,268,030	2,427,672	2,633,701	2,170,485	2,006,436
OAK	1,304,052	1,735,489	1,294,941	1,353,281	1,334,599	1,314,646	1,678,921	2,287,335	2,667,225	2,900,217
SEA	636,276	1,070,404	813,537	870,372	1,128,696	1,029,045	1,134,255	1,022,398	1,298,443	1,509,727
TEX	850,076	1,154,432	1,363,469	1,102,471	1,112,497	1,692,002	1,763,053	1,581,901	2,043,993	2,057,911
TOR	755,083	1,275,978	1,930,415	2,110,009	2,468,925	2,455,477	2,778,429	2,595,175	3,375,883	3,885,284
TOT	14,065,986	23,080,448	23,991,052	23,961,428	24,532,220	25,172,732	27,277,350	28,499,636	29,849,264	30,332,260
ML	26,544,376	44,587,872	45,540,336	44,742,864	46,824,376	47,506,204	52,011,504	52,998,904	55,173,096	54,823,768

	1991	1992	1993	1994	1995	1996	1997	1998
NATIONAL LEAGUE								
ARI								3,602,856
ATL	2,140,217	3,077,400	3,884,725	2,539,240	2,561,831	2,901,242	3,464,488	3,361,350
CHI	2,314,250	2,126,720	2,653,763	1,845,208	1,918,265	2,219,110	2,190,308	2,623,000
CIN	2,372,377	2,315,946	2,453,232	1,897,681	1,837,649	1,861,428	1,785,788	1,793,679
COL			4,483,350	3,281,511	3,390,037	3,891,014	3,888,453	3,789,347
FLA			3,064,847	1,937,467	1,700,466	1,746,767	2,364,387	1,750,395
HOU	1,196,152	1,211,412	2,084,546	1,561,136	1,363,801	1,975,888	2,046,781	2,450,451
LA	3,348,170	2,473,266	3,170,392	2,279,355	2,766,251	3,188,454	3,319,504	3,089,222
MIL								1,811,548
MON	934,742	1,669,077	1,641,437	1,276,250	1,309,618	1,616,709	1,497,609	914,717
NY	2,284,484	1,779,534	1,873,183	1,151,471	1,273,183	1,588,323	1,766,174	2,287,942
PHI	2,050,012	1,927,448	3,137,674	2,290,971	2,043,598	1,801,677	1,490,638	1,715,702
PIT	2,065,302	1,829,395	1,650,593	1,222,520	905,517	1,332,150	1,657,022	1,560,950
STL	2,448,699	2,418,483	2,844,328	1,866,544	1,756,727	2,654,718	2,634,014	3,195,021
SD	1,804,289	1,722,102	1,375,432	953,857	1,041,805	2,187,886	2,089,333	2,555,901
SF	1,737,478	1,561,987	2,606,354	1,704,608	1,241,500	1,413,922	1,690,869	1,925,634
TOT	24,696,174	24,112,770	36,923,856	25,807,820	25,110,248	30,379,288	31,885,364	38,427,716
AMERICAN LEAGUE								
ANA							1,767,330	2,519,210
BAL	2,552,753	3,567,819	3,644,965	2,535,359	3,098,475	3,646,950	3,711,132	3,685,194
BOS	2,562,435	2,468,574	2,422,021	1,775,818	2,164,410	2,315,231	2,226,136	2,314,721
CAL	2,416,236	2,065,444	2,057,460	1,512,622	1,748,680	1,820,521		
CHI	2,934,154	2,681,156	2,581,091	1,697,398	1,609,773	1,676,403	1,864,782	1,391,146
CLE	1,051,863	1,224,274	2,177,908	1,995,174	2,842,745	3,318,174	3,404,750	3,467,299
DET	1,641,661	1,423,963	1,971,421	1,184,783	1,180,979	1,168,610	1,365,157	1,409,391
KC	2,161,537	1,867,689	1,934,578	1,400,494	1,233,530	1,435,997	1,517,638	1,494,875
MIL	1,478,729	1,857,314	1,688,080	1,268,399	1,087,560	1,327,155	1,444,027	
MIN	2,293,842	2,482,428	2,048,673	1,398,565	1,057,667	1,437,352	1,411,064	1,165,980
NY	1,863,733	1,748,733	2,416,965	1,675,556	1,705,263	2,250,877	2,580,325	2,949,734
OAK	2,713,493	2,494,160	2,035,025	1,242,692	1,174,310	1,148,380	1,264,218	1,232,339
SEA	2,147,905	1,651,398	2,051,853	1,104,206	1,643,203	2,723,850	3,192,237	2,644,166
TB								2,506,023
TEX	2,297,720	2,198,231	2,244,616	2,503,198	1,985,910	2,889,020	2,945,228	2,927,409
TOR	4,001,527	4,028,318	4,057,947	2,907,933	2,826,483	2,559,573	2,589,297	2,454,303
TOT	32,117,584	31,759,506	33,332,598	24,202,196	25,358,990	29,718,094	31,283,320	32,161,792
ML	56,813,760	55,872,276	70,256,456	50,010,016	50,469,240	60,097,384	63,168,684	70,589,504

1884 UNION ASSOCIATION

ALT	11,000	KC	54,000	WAS	56,000
BAL	45,000	MIL	10,000	WIL	3,000
BOS	28,000	PHI	19,000	TOT	411,000
CIN	41,000	STL	116,000		
CP	28,000	STP	0		

1890 PLAYERS LEAGUE

BOS	197,346	NY	148,197
BRO	79,272	PHI	170,399
BUF	61,244	PIT	117,123
CHI	148,876	TOT	980,887
CLE	58,430		

## CHAPTER 5

The True Father of Baseball

John Thorn

The history of baseball is a lie from beginning to end, from its creation myth to its rosy models of commerce, community, and fair play. The game's epic feats and revered figures, its pieties about racial harmony and bleacher democracy, its artful blurring of sport and business—all of it is bunk, tossed up with a wink and a nudge. Yet Abner Doubleday, for example, will not be consigned to the dustbin of baseball history no matter how convincingly one argues that he did not invent baseball.

But if the history of baseball is a lie, it is a glorious, vibrant and, in the grand scheme of life, harmless lie, gripping us in a way that good, gray fact seldom can. The bearer of fact cannot hope to annihilate the legends in baseball's Elysian Fields, but simply to play alongside them, occasionally getting a turn at bat.

I believe that the conventional tale of the game's birth is substantially incorrect. By this I refer not to the Doubleday fable, pointless to attack, but to the scarcely less legendary development of the Knickerbocker game, ostensibly sired by Alexander Cartwright.

Let's look at the delicate condition of baseball's paternity. There would have been no need to establish Alexander Cartwright as a baseball deity had the Mills Commission report of 1907—created by Albert Spalding not to explore the origins of the game but to confirm its American roots—*not* named Abner Doubleday the father of the game; however, the absurdity of the Doubleday claim agitated Cartwright's son Bruce so much that he protested to Spalding, and to *Collier's* writer Will Irwin, that baseball did not exist before the advent of Cartwright and the Knickerbocker Base Ball Club of New York City. This claim came at a time when men were still alive who had seen some rural variant of baseball in the 1820s or 1830s or who had even played baseball in an urban setting with one of the several ballclubs that had preceded the formation of the Knicks in 1845, such as the New York Base Ball Club, the Brooklyn Ball Club, the Eagles of New York, or the Olympics of Philadelphia.

Earlier histories of baseball—from those published annually by Henry Chadwick in the Beadle, DeWitt, and Spalding Guides to book-length histories such as Charles Peverelly's *Book of American Pastimes* (1866) and Jacob Morse's *Sphere and Ash* (1888)—gave credit to the Knickerbockers for the eventual ascendance of the New York Game of baseball over the competing Massachusetts Game; however, they did not single out Cartwright as the sole creator. In 1860, in the premier edition of the Beadle *Dime Base Ball Player,* Chadwick acknowledged the existence of the New York Base Ball Club prior to the organization of the Knicks, but stated "we shall not be far wrong if we award to the Knickerbocker the honor of being the pioneers of the present game of base ball." Still, he never swerved from his assertion in that same essay that it was rounders, the English childhood game, "from which base ball is derived." Only in the next century did Cartwright become—no less than Doubleday—a tool of those who wished to establish baseball as the product of an identifiable spark of American ingenuity, without foreign or Darwinian taint.

What *did* Cartwright do? He suggested that the Knickerbockers, who had been playing informally since at least 1842, be organized as a club, with a constitution and playing rules that he did much to formulate (although not alone—three other Knickerbockers were equally involved in drafting the original fourteen playing rules). Notable among these rules—which simply codified the game that the Knicks were already playing—were the laying out of baseball on a "diamond" rather than a square, the concept of foul territory, and the elimination of the rounders and town-ball practice of retiring a runner by throwing the ball *at* him.

These are critical differences from earlier games, sufficient in and of themselves to term the Knickerbocker game a landmark in the evolution of baseball. But what Cartwright assuredly did *not* do was any of the three central things credited to him on his plaque in the Baseball Hall of Fame: "Set bases 90 feet apart. Established 9 innings as a game and 9 players as a team." (More on this in a moment.) He also did not create the 45-foot pitching distance, nor the requirement that a ball be caught on the fly to register an out, nor a system for calling balls and strikes.

The truth of the paternity question? Eighty-year-old Henry Chadwick had it right when he said in 1904, only one year before the formation of the Mills Commission, "Like Topsy, baseball never had no 'fadder'; it jest growed." In fact, until Papa Doubleday was pulled out of the hat, it was Chadwick himself who had most frequently been honored with the sobriquet "Father of Baseball," not for any powers of invention but for his role in popularizing and shaping the game. Others to have been accorded patriarchal honors were Harry Wright, who organized the first openly professional team; Albert Spalding, the tireless player, magnate, and tour promoter; William Hulbert, founder of the National League in 1876; and Daniel L. Adams, whose name today is scarcely known. Allow me to introduce him.

Daniel Lucius Adams was born on November 1, 1814, in Mt. Vernon, N.H., the younger of two sons of Dr.

110

Daniel Adams and Nancy Mulliken Adams. He spent his first two years of college at Amherst, then graduated from Yale in 1835. Afterwards came a medical degree from Harvard in 1838, then a general practice in New York City, coupled with an active involvement with treating the poor at the New York Dispensaries. He resided and practiced at 14 Bond Street.

"Doc" Adams, as he was known to all, began to play baseball in 1839. "I was always interested in athletics while in college and afterward," he told an interviewer at the age of 81, "and soon after going to New York I began to play base ball just for exercise, with a number of other young medical men. Before that there had been a club called the New York Base Ball Club, but it had no very definite organization and did not last long. Some of the younger members of that club got together and formed the Knickerbocker Base Ball Club, September 24, 1845 [actually September 23]. The players included merchants, lawyers, Union Bank clerks [like Cartwright], insurance clerks and others who were at liberty after 3 o'clock in the afternoon. They went into it just for exercise and enjoyment, and I think they used to get a good deal more solid fun out of it than the players in the big games do nowadays.

"About a month after the organization of this club, several of us medical fellows joined it, myself among the number. The following year I was made president and served as long as I was willing to retain the office."

What's new here? Plenty. According to Adams, the New York Base Ball Club not only preceded the Knickerbocker, but formed it; for example, such early New York Base Ball Club members as James Lee, Abraham Tucker, and William Wheaton all became Knickerbockers in 1845–1846. As early as 1840, Adams played a game in New York that he understood to be baseball. It was the same game as that played by the men who would become the Knickerbockers, played on a square, at first with eleven men on a side, as in cricket and perhaps the Massachusetts Game.

This game—called base ball and not rounders or town ball—was played in New York City as early as 1832 by two clubs, one composed of residents of the first ward (the lower part of the city), the other in the upper part of the city (ninth and 15th wards). By 1843, when the Knicks were still playing at their original site in Madison Square, the teams had been reduced to eight—which included a "pitch," a "behind," three basemen and three in the field—and the playing field had been changed from a square to a diamond, as in rounders. According to Alphonse Martin, a prominent pitcher in the 1860s who left an unpublished manuscript "History of Base Ball," it was Cartwright who prompted this move. In later years, when asked how the game of baseball originated, Doc Adams declined to identify a distinct starting point; he believed it grew from rounders.

Actually, baseball as played by the Knicks in the years 1845–1849 (Cartwright left for California in the gold-rush spring of 1849) was almost never a nine-man game; eight, 10, and 11 were all more frequently employed numbers to the side. Play was conducted in accord with Cartwright's model of only three basemen, and on the rare occasions when nine or more fielding positions were created by a surfeit of players, the "extras" were put into the outfield. In a game in late May 1847, for example, when 11 men were available to each side, the Knickerbockers' response was to play with nine, including four outfielders, and hold two men out as substitutes.

The advent of the short fielder, or shortstop, was a crucial break with rounders, and this position was created in 1849 or 1850 by Adams. "I used to play shortstop," he reminisced, "and I believe I was the first one to occupy that place, as it had formerly been left uncovered." But when Adams first went out to short, it was not to bolster the infield but to assist in relays from the outfield. The early Knickerbocker ball was so light that it could not be thrown even 200 feet; thus the need for a short fielder to send the ball in to the pitcher's point.

"We had a great deal of trouble in getting balls made," Adams recalled, "and for six or seven years I made all the balls myself, not only for our club but also for other clubs when they were organized. [He also supervised the turning of the bats during this period.] I went all over New York to find someone who would undertake this work, but no one could be induced to try it for love or money. Finally I found a Scotch saddler who was able to show me a good way to cover the balls with horsehide, such as was used for whip lashes. I used to make the stuffing out of three or four ounces of rubber cuttings, wound with yarn and then covered with the leather. Those balls were, of course, a great deal softer than the balls now in use."

When the ball was wound tighter, gaining more hardness and resilience, it could be hit farther and, crucially, thrown farther. This permitted the shortstop to come into the infield, which Adams did. Even more important, the introduction of the hard ball permitted a change in the dimensions of the playing field. The Knickerbocker rules of 1845 had specified no pitching distance, and no baseline length; all that was indicated was: "from 'home' to second base, 42 paces; from first to third base, 42 paces, equidistant."

It has been presumed by scholars that when a three-foot pace is plugged in, the resulting baselines of eighty-nine feet are close enough to the present ninety so that we can proclaim Cartwright's genius. In fact, the pace in 1845 was either an imprecise and variable measure—to gauge distances by "stepping off"—or precisely two and a half feet, in which case the distance from home to second would have been 105 feet and the Cartwright basepaths would have been 74.25 feet. The pace of 1845 could not have been interpreted as the equivalent of three feet. The alternate definition of a pace as a three-foot measure did not come into practice until much later in the century.

Here is the definition of a pace from *An American Dictionary of the English Language,* by Noah Webster, 1828: Pace: "1. A step. 2. The space between the two feet in walking, estimated at two feet and a half. But the geometrical pace is five feet, or the whole space passed over by the same foot from one step to another." This definition was not changed for Webster's 1853 revised edition.

My research indicates that 75-foot basepaths were the norm well into the mid-1850s—when the basepaths were first prescribed as "42 paces or yards"—and were the standard for youth play well into the next decade.

In 1848 Adams, as Knickerbocker president, headed the Committee to Revise the Constitution and By-Laws;

Alexander Cartwright served under him. Adams' interest in refining the rules of the game, already evident, was further piqued by the formation of additional clubs, beginning with the Washington Base Ball Club in 1850, which was constructed around several former New York Base Ball Club members. In 1852 the Washingtons were renamed the Gothams and took in additional players, and the Eagle Club, which had been organized to play town ball in 1840, reconstituted itself to become the Eagle Base Ball Club.

"The playing rules remained very crude up to this time," Adams said, "but in 1853 the three clubs united in a revision of the rules and regulations. At the close of 1856 there were 12 clubs in existence, and it was decided to hold a convention of delegates from all of these for the purpose of establishing a permanent code of rules by which all should be governed.

"A call was therefore issued, signed by the officers of the Knickerbocker Club as the senior organization, and the result was the assembling of the first convention of base ball players in May, 1857. I was elected presiding officer."

It was at this meeting, eight years after Cartwright's western expedition, that the winner of a game was defined as the team that was ahead at the conclusion of nine innings, rather than the first team to score 21 runs. "In March of the next year the second convention was held, and at this meeting the annual convention was declared a permanent organization, and with the requisite constitution and by-laws became the 'National Association of Ball Players.'

"I was chairman of the Committee on Rules and Regulations from the start and so long as I retained membership. I presented the first draft of rules, prepared after much careful study of the matter, and it was in the main adopted. The distance between bases I fixed at 30 yards—the only previous determination of distance being 'the bases shall be from home to second base 42 paces, from first to third base 42 paces equidistant'—which was rather vague. In every meeting of the National Association while a member, I advocated the fly-game—that is, not to allow first-bound catches—but I was always defeated on the vote. The change was made, however, soon after I left, as I predicted in my last speech on the subject before the convention.

"The distance from home to pitcher's base I made 45 feet. Many of the old rules, such as those defining a foul, remain substantially the same today," he concluded in 1896, "while others are changed and, of course, many new ones added. I resigned in 1862, but not before thousands were present to witness matches, and any number of outside players standing ready to take a hand on regular playing days."

In the 1840s players could not be relied upon to show up for practice. Adams recalled that the Knickerbockers frequently went to Hoboken to find only two or three members present, and were often obliged to take their exercise "in the form of 'old cat,' 'one,' or 'two' as the case might be." But, he summed up in 1896, "we pioneers never expected to see the game so universal as it has now become."

On May 7, 1861, Adams married Cornelia A. Cook. Less than a year later he resigned from the Knickerbocker Base Ball Club, and in 1865 he retired from his practice in New York and moved to Ridgefield, Conn. He played his last formal game of baseball on Sept. 27, 1875, in an oldtimers' contest arranged by longtime Knickerbocker comrade James Whyte Davis.

Adams played backyard ball with his sons even into his eighth decade, when he moved his family to New Haven, where the boys attended Sheffield Scientific School. On Jan. 3, 1899, Daniel Lucius Adams died in his home at 146 Edwards Street.

Success has many fathers, failure none. For his role in making baseball the success it is, Doc Adams may be counted as first among the Fathers of Baseball.

## CHAPTER 6

Casey Stengel in 1949

Robert W. Creamer

Fifty years ago, on March 1, 1949, the first day of spring training, Charles Dillon (Casey) Stengel pulled on his New York Yankees uniform and for the first time walked onto a baseball field to face the Yankees as their manager. It was a shaky, uneasy debut, which may seem surprising to those who know that Stengel went on to manage the Yankees for 12 seasons, and that he won the American League pennant 10 times in those 12 years, the first five in a row. Only one other manager in baseball history, John McGraw, won as many league championships as Casey's 10, and no other manager has ever won five in a row. Stengel also won the World Series seven times (McGraw won three), and only Joe McCarthy won as many World Series. But McCarthy didn't win five World Series in five years, as Casey did, and neither did anyone else. Stengel had an unparalleled record of success as a manager.

Later, after being retired by the Yankees in 1960, Stengel came back to the baseball wars in 1962 to become manager of the brand-new, expansion-team New York Mets. Then in his 70s, the oldest man other than Philadelphia's Connie Mack ever to manage a big league team, Stengel gained added acclaim as the comical leader and brilliant promoter of his woeful but somehow lovable last-place Mets. He was a great manager with the best team in baseball and with the worst. In 1966, a year after he finally retired for good at the age of 75, he was elected to baseball's Hall of Fame. He died in California in 1975 at the age of 85.

Famous? Casey Stengel? You bet. Still remembered today as one of the greatest and most colorful managers in baseball history? Absolutely.

Yet it wasn't that way in St. Petersburg, Fla., that March day in 1949, before Casey won all those pennants and World Series and before his endearing days with the Mets. All that was still tucked away in the future when Casey went out to face his Yankees squad for the first time.

He was already an old man by baseball standards. He had been born in 1890 (in Kansas City, hence his nickname) and was less than a year and a half short of his 60th birthday. He had been in professional baseball since 1910. He had been a run-of-the-mill major league outfielder for a dozen years or so in the early part of the century, and he had been managing off and on in the minors and the majors since 1925. He had won a few pennants in the minor leagues, but in nine seasons managing in the majors he had never had a team finish higher than fifth. And it was six years since he had last managed in the major leagues.

In short, his record was mediocre. He was better known in baseball circles as a joker, a wit, a happy-go-lucky good-time Charlie who had done zany things in his career. As a minor league player during dull moments in batting practice he'd suddenly run several steps and slide, honing his base-running skills. Shagging flies in left field one day he noticed a metal cover in the outfield over a receptacle that held water pipes and valves. When no one was looking Stengel lifted the cover and hid in the receptacle, peeking out. A fly ball was hit his way but to everyone's surprise no one was there, until the nonexistent Casey suddenly reappeared, seemingly rising out of the ground to catch the ball. In Brooklyn's Ebbets Field one Sunday afternoon Stengel came to bat after misplaying a ball in the outfield and was greeted with a shower of boos. Unabashed, Casey turned to the crowd, lifted his cap and a sparrow flew off his head. In the 1923 World Series he hit a home run and cheerfully thumbed his nose at the rival bench as he circled the bases. Perhaps the most famous story about Casey says that in a spring training stunt one year he was supposed to drop a baseball from a small airplane for his manager, Wilbert Robinson, to catch. Instead Casey dropped a grapefruit that splattered the face and chest of the portly, red-faced manager. The fact that it was not Stengel who dropped the grapefruit didn't matter. In baseball lore, told and retold, it was Casey who did it.

His penchant for bizarre behavior carried over into his managing days. He was president and player-manager of a team in a lesser minor league when a chance to manage a high minor team came along. Afraid that the owner of his club would not give him his release so that he could take the new job, Stengel as president of the club released himself as a player and fired himself as manager. Then he resigned as president and went merrily on his way to his new job.

When Casey was signed to manage the Yankees in October 1948 the team had fallen on hard times, comparatively. After finishing first or second 20 times in 23 years, they had been higher than third only once in five seasons. They had gone through four managers in three years. The dignified Colonel Jacob Ruppert, owner of the Yankees since 1915, had died several years before and ownership had moved to a partnership headed by Larry MacPhail, a boisterous, flamboyant operator who in 1941 had lifted the previously moribund Brooklyn Dodgers to their first pennant in 20 years. Edward G. Barrow, who had been the Yankees' *de facto* general manager since 1920, had grown old and retired when the club was taken over by MacPhail, who functioned as his own general manager. George Weiss, who had been in baseball for more than 30

years and who had run the Yankees' minor league farm system under Barrow, became MacPhail's principal assistant. After MacPhail went through three mangers in 1946 and was looking for a new man to take over in 1947, Weiss recommended Stengel. He had seen through Stengel's clownish exterior as far back as 1925, when Casey was a rookie manager in the Eastern League, in which Weiss owned a rival club. He was impressed by Stengel's understanding of the game and he admired the way Casey managed his minor league teams. But Stengel's history got in the way. "That clown?" MacPhail said, and turned to Bucky Harris, a quiet, colorless veteran who had managed in the major leagues for 20 seasons.

Harris seemed to fill the bill because in 1947 he guided the Yankees to the pennant and victory in the World Series. But after the Series MacPhail impulsively sold his share of the club to his partners, Dan Topping and Del Webb, and left the baseball scene. Topping and Webb turned the front office operation over to Weiss, who knew the game inside out. Weiss did not like the way Harris managed and when the Yankees finished third in 1948 he fired him as soon as the season was over.

The man Weiss wanted, as he had two years earlier, was Stengel. He met some reluctance in the Yankees front office when he proposed Stengel for the job, but he prevailed and Casey was hired. The announcement was made at a press conference the day after the 1948 World Series ended and, to put it bluntly, baseball was stunned by the news. Stengel's antic reputation did not fit the image of New York Yankees dignity. My brother, a Yankees fan all his life, was stunned and disappointed by Stengel's appointment, and so were a lot of other people. After the press conference the amiable Casey put on a Yankees shirt and cap and mugged for photographers, looking down at a backlighted baseball as though he were a fortune teller peering into a crystal ball. It was an amusing photo, and it ran in newspapers everywhere. You still see it from time to time in stories and books about Yankees history. But when it first appeared it startled people, even shocked some. A disenchanted member of the Yankees front office muttered, "My god, we *have* hired a clown." In Boston, where Casey had managed without success for several years, a sports columnist wrote, "The Yankees have now been mathematically eliminated from the 1949 pennant race. They eliminated themselves when they engaged Perfesser Casey Stengel to mismanage them for the next two years, and you may be sure that the perfesser will oblige to the best of his unique ability."

The anti-Stengel feeling persisted into spring training. Casey introduced a radical departure in training procedures that didn't sit too well at first. He split the squad into several groups and had different coaches work with each group: an infield specialist with infielders, a catcher with catchers, a first baseman with first basemen, and so on. But a manager didn't have as many coaches on his staff then, and veteran players were called on to work with younger men. Joe DiMaggio, still the club's center fielder and the unquestioned star of the Yankees, worked with outfielders, and so did Tommy Henrich, another veteran of the Yankees outfield. That sort of seminar approach to training is fairly standard today, but it wasn't back then. It bothered traditionalists, and Casey had to defend it to dubious sportswriters.

"I don't see how a player can fail to be helped," he said. "By god, I'd have loved to have had a player like DiMaggio show me how to play the outfield when I was young."

Two years later, in 1951, firmly established as a successful manager, Stengel inaugurated an "instructional school" early in spring training at which promising rookies (Mickey Mantle was one) received specialized training. But in 1949 his methods seemed bizarre.

One day DiMaggio, who had broken in with the Yankees 13 years earlier under the conservative manager Joe McCarthy, asked a sportswriter friend, Arthur Daley of the *New York Times,* "What do you think of our new manager?"

"I never saw such a bewildered guy in my life," Daley said. "He doesn't seem to know what it's all about."

"That's the impression I have," DiMaggio said, "and the rest of the fellows feel the same."

But DiMaggio and the rest of the fellows were wrong. Stengel knew exactly what he was doing, and he did it in the face of adversity. Injuries and illness hounded the Yankees that year. DiMaggio lasted only one day as an instructor because pain flared up in his heel, which had been operated on the previous October. He was sent to Johns Hopkins Hospital in Baltimore for a check-up and soon returned, but the heel continued to hurt badly and before the end of spring training he was back in the hospital, this time for an extended stay. He missed the opening of the season and all of April and May, and there was no clear indication when he'd be able to return to action.

In DiMaggio's absence and with other veterans like outfielder Charlie Keller and second baseman George Sternweiss also ailing Stengel began working younger players and lesser lights into the lineup, shuffling them in and out depending on who was pitching and what the game situation was. At that time second-stringers for the most part got into games only as pinch hitters, or as late-inning substitutes, or as fill-ins when a regular was out with an injury or mired in a slump. But in the minors, particularly when he was managing in the Pacific Coast League, Stengel was forever moving players in and out of games, using all the men on his roster, and he began doing that with the 1949 Yankees. It was not unprecedented, but no manager before him had ever made such total use of his bench as Stengel did.

It came to be called "platooning" and, as the writer Ed Linn observed, "Stengel showed that the bench and the bullpen were just as important as the starting lineup. He demonstrated how games could be won by protecting even good hitters from pitchers who could exploit their one weakness, and by choosing the one best spot to exploit a weaker hitter's strength. It was Stengel who showed that your top pinch hitter should be wheeled in at the first opportunity to break the game open, insisted of being husbanded until the late innings."

But with DiMaggio sidelined and strange faces in and out of the lineup as spring training ended, the Yankees failed to impress. A poll of sportswriters before Opening Day made the Boston Red Sox heavy favorites to win the 1949 American League pennant, with the defending champion Cleveland Indians second and the Yankees no better than third. Red Smith, the famous sports columnist, had them fourth.

However, Stengel's team had strengths he recognized but others overlooked. One was the pitching, led by three unspectacular but very solid starters, all of them past 30—Allie Reynolds, who pitched two no-hit games in the same year a couple of seasons later; Vic Raschi, who averaged 18 wins a year under Casey; and Ed Lopat, a left-hander who had a .689 winning percentage over the next five seasons. He also had a 29-year-old semi-rookie left-hander named Tommy Byrne, who had spent the bulk of his previous time with the Yankees in the bullpen. As a starter Byrne went 15-7 for Casey. And he had a left-handed reliever named Joe Page, who had been sensational in 1947 and so-so in 1948. Page went back to being sensational in 1949, winning 13 games and saving 27.

Stengel also admired a short, stocky 23-year-old catcher-outfielder who could hit but who wasn't much of a fielder and who was considered a buffoon by the sportswriters and some of his veteran teammates. Stengel saw the athletic skill beyond the awkwardness and turned the youngster over to coach Bill Dickey, who had been a Hall of Fame catcher with the Yankees, for tutoring. The youngster had been dividing his time between catching and the outfield, but under Stengel he became a full-time catcher. His name was Lawrence "Yogi" Berra, and in time everyone said admiring things about his skill as a ballplayer (he won the Most Valuable Player award three times playing for Stengel) but, as the renowned sportswriter Frank Graham observed, "Casey said them first."

The season started. Stengel had been in baseball nearly 40 years, but like the brightest rookie in the league he was nothing until he proved himself.

The Yankees won on Opening Day—Berra drove in the tying run, and Henrich, the old reliable outfielder, drove in the winning run. Stengel was very fond of Henrich, who was dependable on the field and off. "He's a fine judge of a flyball," Casey said of Henrich. "He fields grounders like an infielder. He never makes a wrong throw. And if he comes back to the hotel at three in the morning and says he's been sitting up with a sick friend, he's been sitting up with a sick friend."

The Yankees took over first place and kept winning. The Red Sox played poorly in April and May and early June, but then they began to get hot just as Stengel's patchwork lineup, still without DiMaggio, began to cool off. When the Yankees went to Boston late in June to play three games with the Red Sox in Fenway Park, the Bostonians had won 12 of 16 games and were coming on with a rush.

And that's when DiMaggio returned, riding to the rescue like a knight on a white charger. He tested his heel in an exhibition game, and it felt okay. He flew to Boston to join the team, told Casey he was ready, and in the three games in Fenway, the first he had played all season, he hit four homers, batted in nine runs and powered the Yanks to a three-game sweep that knocked Boston sideways. The Red Sox went on to lose eight straight and were 12 games behind the Yankees by July 4.

DiMaggio continued to hit—he batted .346 for the season—and Stengel continued to move players in and out of the lineup like a magician. But in September DiMaggio came down with viral pneumonia, Henrich fractured a couple of ribs and Johnny Mize, the slugging first baseman, separated his shoulder. The Red Sox were coming on again. They had cut New York's lead to eight games by the end of July and to three by the end of August, and late in September, they beat the Yankees three straight times to edge past them by a game with less than a week to go in the pennant race.

The Yankees were behind, and they were still behind by a game when the Red Sox came into New York to play them twice on the final weekend of the season. The Yankees had to win both games to win the pennant. If Boston took only one of the two the Red Sox would have the pennant. "Well," said Stengel, "that puts it up to us to show if we're a good ball club."

Stengel had Reynolds and Raschi ready. DiMaggio, still weak from pneumonia, said he was going to play. In the Saturday game the Red Sox scored early, and Stengel brought in Page, his star reliever, in the third inning. He needed a stopper, and he needed him now. Page was shaky at first but settled in and pitched shutout ball the rest of the way—6⅔ innings of relief. DiMaggio doubled to start one rally and singled to prolong another, and the Yankees rallied to win, 5-4. The two teams were in a flat tie for first place.

On Sunday, the last day of the season, the Yankees scored a run in the first inning and held a slender 1-0 lead into the eighth. They scored four more runs in that inning to open a 5-0 lead, but the Red Sox rallied in the top of the ninth, scored three times and had a man on third base before Henrich caught a foul fly for the last out.

The Yankees had their pennant, and Stengel had vindication. He wasn't a clown. His team went on to whip the Brooklyn Dodgers four games to one in the World Series, and Casey went home to California for the winter, sitting on top of the world. When he ran into his old friend, Babe Herman, he said proudly, "Babe, I won one."

He went on to win again . . . and again . . . and again . . . and again. . . . Yes, despite the criticism, the perfesser knew what he was doing.

## CHAPTER 7

The 400 Greatest

John B. Holway and Bob Carroll

In the following pages you'll find biographical sketches of 400 men, all in one way or another connected to baseball. Two questions naturally arise. First, why 400? And second, why these 400?

To deal with the easier question first, we were limited by space. If we were going to say anything worthwhile, we had to forget about doing 15,000 baseballers and concentrate our attention somewhere in the 350–500 range. We also knew that we would include a number of men for reasons other than how well they played. For example, Earl Weaver never made the majors as a second baseman and Judge Landis played a punk first base, but we knew they belonged on our list.

Once we settled on 400 total, we were ready for the hard part. Who?

We had to have the 237 members of the Hall of Fame. Most of them would have been included under any reasonable criteria anyway. The few arguable enshrinees belong in our 400 just because they are enshrinees, sort of a self-fulfilling immortality.

A few individuals not yet in the Hall of Fame made the cut as managers or contributors. We were ruthless here and probably a little hard on managers. Well, they're used to rejection.

Four other factors weighed heavily in our choices of players.

We wanted a strong sampling of players from all nine positions—nine and a half counting the designated hitter. Pitching may be 75 percent of baseball, as Connie Mack used to say, but we weren't about to present 300 pitchers and 100 position players. Neither did we want 112 slugging left fielders and eight catchers. We decided that we'd include roughly 30 players at each position.

Obviously we had to consider quality. Everyone has an opinion, but most of us could agree on the greatest-of-the-great—maybe even on the great. It was the "darned good's" that gave us trouble. Example: no one would leave out Ted Williams and few would skip Billy Williams. But what about Cy, Dick, Earl or Ken?

Pete Palmer, Bill James, and a few others have done valuable work using statistical analysis in ranking players from different eras of baseball history. We used their various rankings as a starting point, but we couldn't follow them slavishly. They do not always agree in their rankings.

Which brings us to our third consideration—fame. Quite often, as we made our final cuts, we were faced with two or three or more players who seemed virtually interchangeable. When we could find no statistical reason to include one and not the others, we made a judgment as to which player was the best known to a modern reader. If

our estimate was correct, we included the one you would most like to read about.

Two large groups of players were helped by our including fame in our calculations: 19th-century players and players from the Negro Leagues. Both groups are at a disadvantage in that their statistical records are incomplete and those that exist do not always relate well to modern major league baseball's numbers. Was a 30-game winner in 1880 the equivalent of a 15-game winner today? What does a .350 batting average in the Negro National League of 1935 really mean? We must depend on contemporary accounts to rank these players.

Our fourth and final consideration applied to only a few players. These were borderline candidates. They could have been in or out. If one player had a more interesting story than another of apparently equal worthiness, we told the more entertaining tale.

We have to say something about why a few men were not included. Fame was a consideration but not when all other factors said no. Smead Jolley was famous but overrated as a hitter, and in the field he was unsafe at any speed. Alex Rodriguez is famous, but he needs a few more years of excellent play to be included. All of the Black Sox were notorious; we included Eddie Cicotte and Joe Jackson, with some misgivings, because their records prior to their shame were too good to ignore.

We passed on players who had supreme moments of accomplishment but failed to measure up over the long haul. Johnny Vander Meer and Bobby Thomson came awfully close anyway. Bobo Holloman and Pat Seerey didn't.

We did not use any absolute statistical cutoffs. Dave Kingman hit 442 home runs, Riggs Stephenson hit .336, and Tony Mullane won 285 games. We thought some other players were better.

In preparing the biographical sketches, we wanted to show first of all why we included each man in our 400. Much of this involves repeating numbers. For the most part, we tried to rely on traditional categories that nearly everyone understands: batting average, ERA, RBIs, strikeouts, etc. There are often more meaningful statistics, pioneered by Palmer, James, and others, but this does not seem the proper forum to explain them. We refer you to the Introduction to the statistical portion of this book.

We tried to avoid speculation. We don't pretend to know what might have happened if there'd been no war, if the fences had been moved in, if Herb Score had ducked, if Cap Anson had played for the 1927 Yankees. We have our hands full with what did happen; let others worry about might have been.

A few purists may find a note of levity in some of the sketches. Does that mean we do not view the annual pennant struggles as being on a par with, say, the struggle for world peace? Golly, we hope so. We can certainly be accused of enjoying our subjects. When baseball isn't fun anymore, we're all going to be in trouble.

1. Hank Aaron
2. Babe Adams
3. Grover Cleveland Alexander
4. Dick Allen
5. Walter Alston
6. Sparky Anderson
7. Cap Anson
8. Luis Aparicio
9. Luke Appling
10. Richie Ashburn
11. Earl Averill
12. Jeff Bagwell
13. Frank Baker
14. Dave Bancroft
15. Ernie Banks
16. Al Barlick
17. Edward Barrow
18. Dick Bartell
19. Jake Beckley
20. John Beckwith
21. Buddy Bell
22. Cool Papa Bell
23. Albert Belle
24. Johnny Bench
25. Chief Bender
26. Yogi Berra
27. Bert Blyleven
28. Wade Boggs
29. Barry Bonds
30. Bobby Bonds
31. Bob Boone
32. Jim Bottomley
33. Lou Boudreau
34. Ken Boyer
35. Harry Brecheen
36. Roger Bresnahan
37. George Brett
38. Tommy Bridges
39. Lou Brock
40. Dan Brouthers
41. Three Finger Brown
42. Pete Browning
43. Morgan G. Bulkeley
44. Jim Bunning
45. Lew Burdette
46. Jesse Burkett
47. Roy Campanella
48. Rod Carew
49. Max Carey
50. Steve Carlton
51. Gary Carter
52. Alexander Cartwright
53. Bob Caruthers
54. Norm Cash
55. Cesar Cedeno
56. Orlando Cepeda
57. Henry Chadwick
58. Frank Chance
59. Happy Chandler
60. Ray Chapman
61. Oscar Charleston
62. Jack Chesbro
63. Eddie Cicotte
64. Fred Clarke
65. John Clarkson
66. Roger Clemens
67. Roberto Clemente
68. Harlond Clift
69. Ty Cobb
70. Mickey Cochrane
71. Rocky Colavito
72. Eddie Collins
73. Jimmy Collins
74. Earle Combs
75. Charles Comiskey
76. Davey Concepcion
77. Jocko Conlan
78. Tom Connolly
79. Roger Connor
80. Walker Cooper
81. Stan Coveleski
82. Gavvy Cravath
83. Sam Crawford
84. Joe Cronin
85. Candy Cummings
86. Kiki Cuyler
87. Ray Dandridge
88. George Davis
89. Andre Dawson
90. Leon Day
91. Dizzy Dean
92. Ed Delahanty
93. Bill Dickey
94. Martin Dihigo
95. Dom DiMaggio
96. Joe DiMaggio
97. Larry Doby
98. Bobby Doerr
99. Don Drysdale
100. Hugh Duffy

101. Fred Dunlap
102. Leo Durocher
103. Jimmy Dykes
104. Dennis Eckersley
105. Billy Evans
106. Darrell Evans
107. Dwight Evans
108. Johnny Evers
109. Buck Ewing
110. Red Faber
111. Elroy Face
112. Bob Feller
113. Rick Ferrell
114. Wes Ferrell
115. Rollie Fingers
116. Charles O. Finley
117. Carlton Fisk
118. Freddie Fitzsimmons
119. Elmer Flick
120. Curt Flood
121. Whitey Ford
122. Bill Foster
123. George Foster
124. Rube Foster
125. Nellie Fox
126. Jimmie Foxx
127. Bill Freehan
128. Larry French
129. Ford Frick
130. Frankie Frisch
131. Pud Galvin
132. Lou Gehrig
133. Charlie Gehringer
134. Bob Gibson
135. Josh Gibson
136. Warren Giles
137. Tom Glavine
138. Lefty Gomez
139. Joe Gordon
140. Goose Goslin
141. Goose Gossage
142. Hank Greenberg
143. Gus Greenlee
144. Bobby Grich
145. Ken Griffey, Jr.
146. Clark Griffith
147. Burleigh Grimes
148. Heinie Groh
149. Lefty Grove
150. Ron Guidry
151. Tony Gwynn
152. Stan Hack
153. Chick Hafey
154. Jesse Haines
155. Billy Hamilton
156. Ned Hanlon
157. Mel Harder
158. Mike Hargrove
159. Will Harridge
160. Bucky Harris
161. Gabby Hartnett
162. Guy Hecker
163. Harry Heilmann
164. Rickey Henderson
165. Tommy Henrich
166. Babe Herman
167. Billy Herman
168. Keith Hernandez
169. Whitey Herzog
170. Gil Hodges
171. Harry Hooper
172. Rogers Hornsby
173. Frank Howard
174. Waite Hoyt
175. Cal Hubbard
176. Carl Hubbell
177. Miller Huggins
178. William Hulbert
179. Catfish Hunter
180. Monte Irvin
181. Joe Jackson
182. Reggie Jackson
183. Travis Jackson
184. Ferguson Jenkins
185. Hughie Jennings
186. Tommy John
187. "Indian Bob" Johnson
188. Ban Johnson
189. Judy Johnson
190. Randy Johnson
191. Walter Johnson
192. Addie Joss
193. Jim Kaat
194. Al Kaline
195. Willie Kamm
196. Tim Keefe
197. Willie Keeler
198. George Kell
199. Charlie Keller
200. Joe Kelley

201. George Kelly
202. King Kelly
203. Harmon Killebrew
204. Ralph Kiner
205. Chuck Klein
206. Bill Klem
207. Jerry Koosman
208. Sandy Koufax
209. Bowie Kuhn
210. Napoleon Lajoie
211. Kenesaw Mountain Landis
212. Tommy Lasorda
213. Tony Lazzeri
214. Bob Lemon
215. Buck Leonard
216. Freddie Lindstrom
217. Pop Lloyd
218. Sherm Lollar
219. Ernie Lombardi
220. Al Lopez
221. Dick Lundy
222. Dolf Luque
223. Sparky Lyle
224. Fred Lynn
225. Ted Lyons
226. Connie Mack
227. Biz Mackey
228. Larry MacPhail
229. Lee MacPhail
230. Greg Maddux
231. Sherry Magee
232. Sal Maglie
233. Mickey Mantle
234. Heinie Manush
235. Rabbit Maranville
236. Firpo Marberry
237. Juan Marichal
238. Roger Maris
239. Rube Marquard
240. Mike Marshall
241. Billy Martin
242. Eddie Mathews
243. Christy Mathewson
244. Carl Mays
245. Willie Mays
246. Bill Mazeroski
247. Joe McCarthy
248. Tommy McCarthy
249. Jim McCormick
250. Willie McCovey
251. Joe McGinnity
252. Bill McGowan
253. John McGraw
254. Mark McGwire
255. Bill McKechnie
256. Bid McPhee
257. Joe Medwick
258. Jose Mendez
259. Andy Messersmith
260. Marvin Miller
261. Minnie Minoso
262. Johnny Mize
263. Paul Molitor
264. Joe Morgan
265. Thurman Munson
266. Dale Murphy
267. Eddie Murray
268. Stan Musial
269. Graig Nettles
270. Don Newcombe
271. Hal Newhouser
272. Kid Nichols
273. Phil Niekro
274. Tony Oliva
275. James O'Rourke
276. Mel Ott
277. Satchel Paige
278. Jim Palmer
279. Dave Parker
280. Roger Peckinpaugh
281. Herb Pennock
282. Tony Perez
283. Gaylord Perry
284. Deacon Phillippe
285. Mike Piazza
286. Billy Pierce
287. Eddie Plank
288. Cum Posey
289. Boog Powell
290. Del Pratt
291. Jack Quinn
292. Dan Quisenberry
293. Dick Radatz
294. Charles Radbourn
295. Tim Raines
296. Willie Randolph
297. Dick Redding
298. Pee Wee Reese
299. Ed Reulbach
300. Jim Rice

301. Sam Rice
302. Branch Rickey
303. Cal Ripken, Jr.
304. Eppa Rixey
305. Phil Rizzuto
306. Robin Roberts
307. Brooks Robinson
308. Frank Robinson
309. Jackie Robinson
310. Wilbert Robinson
311. Bullet Joe Rogan
312. Eddie Rommel
313. Pete Rose
314. Al Rosen
315. Edd Roush
316. Red Ruffing
317. Amos Rusie
318. Babe Ruth
319. Nolan Ryan
320. Ryne Sandberg
321. Ron Santo
322. Ray Schalk
323. Wally Schang
324. Mike Schmidt
325. Red Schoendienst
326. Tom Seaver
327. Frank Selee
328. Joe Sewell
329. Urban Shocker
330. Al Simmons
331. Ted Simmons
332. George Sisler
333. Enos Slaughter
334. Ozzie Smith
335. Reggie Smith
336. Duke Snider
337. Sammy Sosa
338. Warren Spahn
339. Al Spalding
340. Tris Speaker
341. Willie Stargell
342. Rusty Staub
343. Turkey Stearnes
344. George Steinbrenner
345. Casey Stengel
346. Bruce Sutter
347. Don Sutton
348. Jesse Tannehill
349. Jack Taylor
350. Gene Tenace
351. Bill Terry
352. Frank Thomas
353. Sam Thompson
354. Luis Tiant
355. Joe Tinker
356. Joe Torre
357. Cristobal Torriente
358. Alan Trammell
359. Pie Traynor
360. Dizzy Trout
361. Dazzy Vance
362. Arky Vaughan
363. Hippo Vaughn
364. Bill Veeck
365. Rube Waddell
366. Honus Wagner
367. Larry Walker
368. Bobby Wallace
369. Ed Walsh
370. Bucky Walters
371. Lloyd Waner
372. Paul Waner
373. John Montgomery Ward
374. Lon Warneke
375. Earl Weaver
376. George Weiss
377. Mickey Welch
378. Willie Wells
379. Zack Wheat
380. Deacon White
381. Sol White
382. Hoyt Wilhelm
383. J.L. Wilkinson
384. Billy Williams
385. Ken Williams
386. Smokey Joe Williams
387. Ted Williams
388. Vic Willis
389. Maury Wills
390. Hack Wilson
391. Dave Winfield
392. George Wright
393. Harry Wright
394. Early Wynn
395. Jim Wynn
396. Carl Yastrzemski
397. Tom Yawkey
398. Cy Young
399. Ross Youngs
400. Robin Yount

HANK AARON
Outfielder, Mil (N) 1954-65, Atl (N) 1966-74, Mil (A) 1975-76

If charisma were a baseball stat, Aaron would have been benched. No question he was great, but was he box office? Yearly, while lesser lights adorned magazine covers, the unassuming Alabaman quietly went his Hall of Fame way, winning baseball games with his quick feet, strong arm, and powerful bat. No Rodney Dangerfield, he always got respect; he deserved adulation.

His numbers were terrific: he led the league four times in home runs, four times in RBIs, thrice he scored the most runs, twice he had the most hits, and twice he topped all National Leaguers in batting average. In 1957, when his Braves were world champs, he was MVP, but most fans recognized him as a great player quicker than they'd have recognized him on the street. He made a more exciting stat line than an interview. It didn't help that he played in Milwaukee and Atlanta. Worst of all, he was pleasant, modest, hard-working, and uncontroversial.

Then, as he neared the end of his career, this unpretentious superstar was thrust into the full glare of media hype as he fought the battle of his life—taking on Babe Ruth's ghost. "Hammerin' Hank" finished the 1973 season with 713 career home runs, only one fewer than Ruth's lifetime 714. After enduring a whole winter of "experts" speculating when he would, whether he could, and even if he should break the record, Aaron tied it in his first at bat of 1974. A few days later, on April 8, at 9:07 p.m. EST, before 53,775 Atlanta fans, he elevated Al Downing's pitch into the record books as number 715. Before retiring in 1976, Aaron brought his record total up to 755.

More than two decades later, the "greatest home run hitter" ruckus remains unsettled. Aaronites like to point out that Hank faced some un-Ruthian obstacles in playing most of his career in a "pitcher's park," facing more "good" pitchers and batting under lights. Ah, yes, say the pro-Ruthians, but the Babe had charisma!

Although he was never spectacular, on the basis of consistency Aaron was awesome. Among all players, he ranks third in games and hits, second in at bats, runs, and first in home runs and RBIs—and grounding into double plays. His average season over 23 years was .305, 33 home runs, 100 RBIs. He hit 40 home runs or better eight times, the last when he was 39 years old. Just running out his homers covered over 51 miles. He was named to the Hall of Fame in 1982.

CHARLES "BABE" ADAMS
Pitcher, StL (N) 1906, Pit (N) 1907-26

The 1909 World Series had Detroit's Ty Cobb and Pittsburgh's Honus Wagner, but the star of the classic was Adams, a 27-year-old rookie. The quiet right-hander from Indiana—a creditable 12-3 in 1909 but hardly Pittsburgh's ace—might not have pitched at all had star hurler Howie Camnitz not come down with an attack of quinsy.

Pittsburgh manager Fred Clarke had been tipped that Adams threw with the "same style but faster" than rookie Washington Senators pitcher Dolly Gray, who'd stumped Detroit batters during the season. Playing the hunch, Clarke sent the boy to do a man's job in the Series opener. Adams responded with a six-hitter, then six-hit the Tigers again in the fifth and seventh games to make the Pirates world champs.

Babe's best pitches were a good fastball (which earned him his nickname as a kid) but especially a curveball that could freeze batters in their tracks. His real talent, however, was his control. It took him to 194 Pirates wins over 18 seasons, including 22-12 in 1911 and 21-10 in 1913. In 1914 he pitched a 21-inning game without allowing a single walk. He averaged just 1.29 walks per nine innings over his career, with a pinpoint 0.62 record in 1920 (18 walks in 263 innings), tying with Christy Mathewson (1913) for best of all time.

GROVER CLEVELAND "PETE" ALEXANDER
Pitcher, Phi (N) 1911-17, 1930, Chi (N) 1918-26, StL (N) 1926-29

When Grover Cleveland Alexander retired in 1930, he saw his name at the top of the "Games Won" column in the National League record book. A recount eventually added one more win to Christy Mathewson's lifetime total to leave them tied at 373. That was kind of fitting because one or the other was certainly the best NL right-hander of the first half of the 20th century.

Alexander went into the Hall of Fame in 1938, two years after Mathewson. Military service in World War I cost Alex one-plus years after three straight 30-win seasons, and a shell that burst in his ear may have triggered the epilepsy and led to the alcoholism that plagued him for the rest of his days. A gas attack in a training drill eventually cost Mathewson his life. Matty's out pitch was his fadeaway; Alex had a good fastball and better curve, all delivered with an easy, just-tossin' motion. Both had the kind of control that could carve a roast. Alex won two of the three games in which they faced each other.

Not even Mathewson ever had a moment like Alexander's in the 1926 World Series. The grizzled veteran, nearing 40, won his second Series game for the Cardinals in Game 6 and then celebrated mightily with, shall we say, refreshment stronger than sarsaparilla. The next day groggy Pete was summoned to the mound in the seventh inning of the final game. The Cards led, 3-2, but the Yankees had slugger Tony Lazzeri up with two outs and the bases loaded. Alex worked the count to 1-and-2, including a heart-stopping foul down the left field line, then whooshed strike three past Lazzeri. After two more shutout innings, the Cards were champs and Alexander was a legend. The incident served as the climax of the movie "The Winning Team," with Ronald Reagan portraying Alexander.

The Lazzeri strikeout crowned a career that glittered with three 30-win seasons and six 20-win seasons. His 90 career shutouts are second only to Walter Johnson's 110. His lifetime ERA of 2.56 included seasons of 1.22, 1.55, 1.72, and 1.73.

Alexander's 227 strikeouts in 1911 set the rookie record; Dwight Gooden broke it in 1984. But his 28 wins still stand as the freshman mark; four were consecutive shutouts. In 1915 he led the Phillies to a pennant, winning 31 and clinching the flag with a one-hitter. He won one more in the World Series against Boston—the last Series win for the Phils until 1980.

All this was doubly impressive because he pitched his home games from 1911 to 1917 in little Baker Bowl, with a right field wall just off the second baseman's hip, and,

from 1918 to 1925, at hitter-friendly Wrigley Field. In 1916 Alexander tied a 40-year-old mark with 16 shutouts—and nine of these were registered at Baker Bowl.

As his career closed, Alexander's alcoholism was so bad he couldn't shake hands without taking three stabs at it, and his wife hid her perfume so he wouldn't drink that. He ended up re-enacting the Lazzeri strikeout with a Times Square flea circus. In 1950 he died alone in a rented room.

DICK ALLEN
Third Baseman/First Baseman, Phi (N) 1963-69,
1975-76, StL (N) 1970, LA (N) 1971, Chi (A) 1972-74,
Oak (A) 1977

Dick ("Don't call me Richie!") Allen had baseball talent and opera-star temperament. When his mood was right, he was a one-man offense who could carry a team for a week or a month. When his mood was wrong, he could pout or even disappear for an equal length of time. He found spring training a waste of time and avoided as much of it as possible. He drove enemy pitchers and friendly managers crazy with equal nonchalance.

He came to the Phillies a professed third baseman in 1963, led the league in errors a couple of times, and from 1969 until he retired in 1977 was more or less a first baseman. Allen lived by his bat: seven seasons over .300, 10 seasons with 20 or more homers, and six seasons of 90-plus RBIs.

In 1970 the Phillies traded him to the Cardinals, who kept him a year and then passed him on to the Dodgers. In both cases, the teams improved their records, but decided Allen would never win the Employee of the Month award. In 1972 he was sent to the White Sox and patient manager Chuck Tanner. Allen responded with an MVP year, hitting .308 and leading the AL in homers (37) and RBIs (113). After that, he got bored or sulky or whatever. By 1974, even Tanner was miffed over such Allen foibles as taking the last month of the season off to go tend his prize horses. Always his own man but often his worst enemy (despite heated competition from former teammates), Allen was ever an enigma.

WALTER ALSTON
First base, StL (N) 1936.
Manager, Bkn (N) 1954-57, LA (N) 1958-76

For 23 years—all on one-year contracts—Alston managed the Dodgers, overseeing their migration from Brooklyn to Los Angeles and presiding as they became baseball's most financially successful franchise. The Dodgers topped 2 million in attendance seven times with Walter in the dugout, their prosperity based on consistent wins. Alston brought them to four world championships, seven pennants, and eight second-place finishes. Only John McGraw, who managed 31 years, won more National League games or pennants.

Alston's entire major league playing career consisted of one at bat. Lon Warneke struck him out. But 20 years of playing and managing in the minors taught him to handle a team with patience and straightforward honesty. He was managing Nashua in the Dodgers' system in 1946, when the presence of black players was a hot potato. He volunteered to be the first white manager for a couple of talented black prospects and sent Roy Campanella and Don Newcombe on to stardom.

His Dodgers teams had many stars but were most renowned for their pitchers. Sandy Koufax and Don Drysdale are Hall of Famers, and countless others starred while hurling in the Dodger blue. Some of the credit goes to Alston and his patient handling. Named Major League Manager of the Year by *The Sporting News* in 1955, 1959, and 1963, Alston was elected to the Baseball Hall of Fame in 1983 and died the following year.

GEORGE "SPARKY" ANDERSON
Second base, Phi (N) 1959.
Manager, Cin (N) 1970-78, Det (A) 1979-95

To paraphrase Will Rogers, Anderson never met a man he didn't talk to death. If he could have hit as well as he talks, he'd have been an All-Star player. Instead he batted a mute .218 in his only major league season as a player. Despite his own lack of prowess, the loquacious leader became one of baseball's great managers.

Employing a slow fuse with problem players and a quick hook for pitchers, Anderson is the only man to win a World Series in both leagues, the first to win 100 games in both leagues, and the first to be Manager of the Year in both leagues. In 1970, his first year at the helm, he guided Cincinnati's Big Red Machine to a pennant, then followed with more in 1972, 1973, 1975, and 1976; the latter two years also produced world championships. It was the first time since John McGraw's New York Giants in 1921-1922 that a National League team had won back-to-back championships.

In 1984 he led the Tigers to a 35-5 start on the way to a world title. He guided his teams to seven first-place finishes and five seconds. All told, he managed his teams to seven first-place finishes and five seconds. His postseason record, 34-21 and .619, is the best of any manager.

After leaving the Tigers at the end of the 1995 season, Anderson became a color commentator for the Anaheim Angels.

ADRIAN "CAP" ANSON
First Baseman/Third Baseman, Rock (NA) 1871, Phil
(NA) 1872-75, Chi (N) 1876-97. Manager, Chi (N) 1879-
1897, NY (N) 1898

Anson was the biggest star of the 19th century, one of the men who popularized baseball. During his 27-season career (1871-1897), he had 24 seasons batting .300; he topped .380 three times. He had good power for the Dead Ball Era. In 1884 he slugged five homers in two games, a feat that would not be matched until 1925.

He wasn't much of a fielder, though. His 58 errors in 1884 is still a record for first basemen. Even fielding with bare hands, that's a ton.

Cap managed Chicago's NL team (then called the "White Stockings") to five pennants between 1880 and 1886. He was a pioneer in the use of the hit-and-run, signals, platoons, a pitching rotation, and spring training. A big man—6 feet 2 inches, 220 pounds—he was a stiff-backed martinet who marched his men onto the field in military formation and used his fists to enforce his rules, the least popular being his no-drinking edict. Once he threw Chicago team owner A.G. Spalding off the field for challenging one of his decisions.

When he finally retired, the league tried to award him a

pension. He turned it down. Anson died in 1922, three days after his 70th birthday.

LUIS APARICIO
Shortstop, Chi (A) 1956-62, 1968-70, Bal (A) 1963-67, Bos (A) 1971-73

"Little Looie" played 2,581 games, more than any other shortstop, led the American League in stolen bases nine times (in a row), topped AL shortstops in fielding average eight times, and in 1984 became the first Venezuelan voted into the Hall of Fame. But he wasn't the be-all and end-all of short fielders. His lifetime batting average of .262 embraces nada power, and his .308 on-base average is embarrassing for a guy who almost always used to lead off. Small wonder he never scored 100 runs and rarely led even his own team. What he did on offense was steal bases—506 of them. On the other hand, he was thrown out over 100 times.

He was smooth defensively—he won nine Gold Gloves. After being among the league leaders in total chances early in his career, his putouts and assists declined as his fielding average went up, indicating sure hands but the loss of the kind of range that wins extra ballgames. But no shortstop was ever more durable, and the amiable Aparicio helped win flags for the White Sox in 1959 and for the Orioles in 1966. He was arguably the best player in the AL in 1960 when Roger Maris was named the MVP. That year Luis hit only .277 but stole 51 bases, led all shortstops in assists and fielding average, and knocked in 62 runs as a leadoff man.

LUKE APPLING
Shortstop, Chi (A) 1930-50. Manager, KC (A) 1967

Shortstops who can hit are as rare as Chicago pennants. Luke Appling could hit, and he spent 20 years wearing a White Sox uniform while other teams popped champagne corks at seasons' end. Although he never got into a World Series, he played in seven All-Star Games and averaged .444 there. He led the AL in batting in 1936, hitting .388, still the highest average by a shortstop in this century. He copped another crown in 1943, with .328. His career average of .310 came on 2,749 hits, and while he was never a power hitter (45 homers), he both scored and batted in over 1,000 runs. In 1964, he was elected to the Hall of Fame.

His specialty was fouling off pitches until he got one he wanted. According to legend, he once fouled 12 straight into the stands when the hard-strapped White Sox management refused him a dozen souvenir balls for friends.

Originally a poor fielder, he led AL shortstops in errors six times and finished with a record seven years leading in assists.

Nicknamed "Old Aches and Pains" because he led the league in hypochondria every year, he somehow survived aching ankles, pink eye, perpetual flu, a permanently sore back, headaches, inflamed throats, chills, vertigo, a real broken finger, and a fractured leg to play 20 years and usually top the Sox in games played. Among AL shortstops, only Aparicio and Ripken put in more time at the position. At age 75, he was healthy enough to slug a home run in the first Cracker Jack Old-Timers' Game in Washington, in 1984. Appling died seven years later at the age of 83.

RICHIE ASHBURN
Outfielder, Phi (N) 1948-59, Chi (N) 1960-61, NY (N) 1962

Ashburn was one of the three best defensive center fielders ever. From 1948 through 1958 he led National League outfielders in chances per game every year but 1955 (when he finished second by 0.1). Sure, the other Phillies outfielders never won any dash medals, and ace Robin Roberts threw flyballs like they'd been ordered C.O.D., but Ashburn's gift for covering center made it all work. Willie Mays got the Gold Gloves; Ashburn got the outs—about 50 more each season. According to Pete Palmer's analytical stats, only Tris Speaker and Max Carey rank ahead of Richie as fly chasers, and then by a margin so small you'd get a recount in most states.

Ashburn's arm never got him a blue ribbon, but it got the Phillies a pennant in 1950, when he gunned down the Dodgers' Cal Abrams at the plate to preserve a tie in the season's final game. The Phillies won the game and the flag in the 10th inning.

Richie broke in with the Phillies in 1948, topping the NL in steals and hitting in 23 straight games, the rookie record until Benito Santiago passed it in 1987. He led the league in batting in 1955 and 1958. He hit over .300 in nine seasons. He was a leadoff man who homered rarely, but he led the NL in hits three times and bases on balls four times. His career on-base average was near .400.

He closed out by batting 306 for the expansion Mets, providing some respectability to an otherwise comical outfit. He then went on to become one of the top broadcasters in the game for the Phillies until his death in 1997. In 1995 he was elected to the Hall of Fame.

EARL AVERILL
Outfielder, Cle (A) 1929-39, Det (A) 1939-40, Bos (N) 1941

After three excellent seasons with San Francisco of the Pacific Coast League, Averill was purchased by the Indians in 1929 for $50,000. In his first major league at bat, he homered. He stood only 5 feet 9 inches and weighed just 172, but he generated home run power. For a half dozen years in the 1930s, he was one of the most feared batters in baseball. A back injury and a malformed spine affected his swing in 1937, left him as just an ordinary hitter, and prematurely shortened his career.

When Averill joined the Hall of Fame in 1975, he complained that he had waited 34 years. "Stats alone are enough," he said. His numbers were impressive, all right: .318 career batting average, 238 home runs, 1,164 RBIs, and 1,224 runs scored. During his 10 best seasons, he averaged 23 home runs, 12 triples. 108 RBIs and 115 runs scored. He also led all outfielders in putouts twice. But hitting stats were inflated by an animated baseball during the time Averill was at his peak. Probably a better gauge of his ability is that he was the only outfielder selected to the first six All-Star Games.

The most famous incident in his career came in the 1937 All-Star Game, when a line drive off his bat broke pitcher Dizzy Dean's toe. Dean tried to come back from the injury too soon, altered his pitching motion, and ruined his arm. Ironically it was during that same 1937 season that Averill's back problem began to cut into his career.

JEFF BAGWELL
First Baseman, Hou (N) 1991-

When it's time for Red Sox fans to cry in their beer, the trade of Jeff Bagwell to the Astros doesn't quite rank with sending Babe Ruth to the Yankees, but the 1990 deal that brought middle reliever Larry Anderson to Boston for the power-hitting first baseman can still bring enough tears to dilute a few steins at Cheers. The Astros got an immediate lift when Bagwell won NL Rookie of the Year honors in 1991. In 1994 he was voted the National League's Most Valuable Player when he blasted 39 home runs and drove in 116 runs in the shortened season.

Perhaps part of the Red Sox willingness to trade Bagwell away despite his sterling minor league slugging was fear that his weird batting stance would never work in the majors. Admittedly, it is the opposite of stances used by successful hitters. He stands with his feet planted wide apart, and as the ball approaches, he shortens his foot-spread instead of striding into the pitch. Somehow it works for him. Unfortunately, his habit of crowding the plate has twice produced a broken left hand. He now wears a pillow the size of a brick on his hand when batting.

FRANK "HOME RUN" BAKER
Third Baseman, Phi (A) 1908-14, NY (A) 1916-19, 1921-22

Although he led the American League in homers four straight years (1911-1914) with his 52-ounce bat, Baker's season high was an un-Ruthian 12 in1913. He spent most of his career in the Dead Ball Era. His "Home Run" nickname stemmed from two timely shots off Christy Mathewson and Rube Marquard to win a pair of games in the 1911 World Series.

Later third basemen punched more round-trippers with a bouncier baseball, but few could match Baker's all-around play. Named to the Hall of Fame in 1955, his career Relative Batting Average (batting average adjusted to the league average) of .307 is surpassed only by Wade Boggs and George Brett among third basemen. He was anchor man of the Philadelphia A's "$100,000 infield" (with first baseman Stuffy McInnis, second baseman Eddie Collins, and shortstop Jack Barry), a quartet so adept that Connie Mack's club won four pennants in five years. In World Series play, Baker hit .409 in 1910, .375 in 1911, and .450 in 1913. When he slipped to .250 in 1914, the A's lost the Series four straight.

Baker sat out the 1915 season in a salary dispute. (He also missed the 1920 season due to the death of his wife.) Mack began selling off his stars, and Baker was sold to the Yankees in 1916 for a then-tidy $37,500. He was New York's biggest drawing card until Babe Ruth arrived in 1920 and redefined the job description for "home run hitter."

DAVE "BEAUTY" BANCROFT
Shortstop, Phi (N) 1915-19, NY (N) 1920-23, Bos (N) 1924-27, Bkn (N) 1928-29, NY (N) 1930. Manager, Bos (N) 1924-27

Bancroft is less famous than some, but he's one of the three top fielding shortstops ever, along with Ozzie Smith and Art Fletcher. No shortstop has ever handled more chances than Bancroft did in 1922 with the Giants—984 (Smith's busiest season was 933 in 1980). Of course, strikeouts were fewer in Beauty's day than in Ozzie's, meaning more opportunities for fielders, and the ball is more lively today. But gloves were much smaller in 1922, which explains why Bancroft committed 60 errors or more three times.

Bancroft, who was named to the Hall of Fame in 1971, was a winner. Manager Pat Moran gave him credit for sparking the Phils from sixth place to the pennant as a rookie in 1915. Traded to New York in 1920, Bancroft was made captain right away, and the next year the Giants won their first of four straight flags. He teamed with Frankie Frisch on the double play, and with George Kelly at first base and Heinie Groh at third, to form one of the game's top infields. Bancroft got his nickname from his habit of yelling "Beauty!" whenever his pitcher made a good pitch.

A switch-hitting leadoff man who crowded the plate, Bancroft coaxed plenty of walks but was a light hitter until the lively ball appeared in 1920. That year he hit .299 and followed it up with three consecutive .300 seasons, skipped a year, and then hit .300 twice more.

Bancroft was a sparkplug on the field, a fiery team leader with great instincts for the game who also managed during his four seasons in Boston. When he first joined the Giants, they asked if he wanted to go over their signs. "I don't have to," Beauty said, "I know them already."

ERNIE BANKS
Shortstop/First Baseman, Chi (N) 1953-71

Likable, popular Ernie Banks hit more home runs than any other shortstop, 47 in 1958. He's also the first National Leaguer to win back-to-back MVPs (Hal Newhouser did it first in the AL).

A slim man for a slugger, Banks had fast wrists and swung a light, 31-ounce bat, producing a powerful buggy-whip action. His 44 home runs in 1955 included a National League record five grand slams. He led the NL with 47 homers in 1958 and again with 41 in 1960, to complete four straight years of 40-plus homers. But his homer totals are slightly inflated because he played in "the friendly confines of Wrigley Field" (his words)—he hit 290 home runs at Wrigley, 222 away.

Banks' batting average was modest, and he was a disaster on base. He was thrown out more often than he stole, 53-50. Although he was a solid fielder and set an NL season record for shortstops in fielding average with .985 (only 12 errors) in 1959, Banks did not win many games with his glove. And he could never lead the Cubs to a pennant—they finished fifth in both his MVP years. Banks was at first base, where he had moved in 1962, when the Cubs collapsed in 1969 and lost the pennant to the Mets. But at age 38, Banks still contributed 23 home runs and 106 runs batted in and led NL first basemen in fielding percentage.

His sunny disposition and his chirpy "Let's play two!" made him "Mr. Cub," a favorite of Wrigley's bleacher bums. In 1977 he was elected to the Hall of Fame.

AL BARLICK
Umpire, NL 1940-43, 1946-1955, 1958-71

When a labor strike shut down the coal mine where he worked in Springfield, Ill., young Al Barlick turned to

umpiring local sandlot games for a dollar each. Soon he entered the minor leagues, and in 1940, when famed ump Bill Klem was sidelined with an injury, Al was brought up to the majors. He stayed for 31 years, with time out for military service during World War II and two years off after suffering a heart attack in the mid-1950s.

Barlick worked a record seven All-Star Games and seven World Series. He was universally regarded as strict but fair—unyielding in his demand for respect. Fellow man-in-blue Ed Vargo called him "an umpire's umpire."

In 1990 he became only the sixth umpire to be named to the Hall of Fame.

EDWARD BARROW

Executive, Bos (AL) 1917-20, NY (A) 1921-45. Manager, Det (A) 1903-04, Boston (A) 1918-20

The beetle-browed Barrow discovered Honus Wagner, switched Babe Ruth to the outfield, developed the Yankees' farm system, and masterminded them to 14 pennants and ten world championships.

This former bare-knuckle fighter also pioneered night ball (at Paterson, N.J. in 1896), sanctioned the first woman to pitch in organized baseball (Lizzie Arlington, Eastern League, in 1897), was the first man to paint distances on outfield fences (Yankees, 1923), and the first to put large size numbers on players' uniforms (Yanks, 1929).

After starting as a concession manager in 1894, he managed, operated, and part-owned several minor league teams, including Wheeling, W.V., where author Zane Grey played outfield. Barrow also was a fight promoter, and he sometimes hired heavyweight champs John L. Sullivan, James Corbett, and Jim Jeffries as umpires.

In 1917 Barrow became manager of the Red Sox. He led them to the world championship in 1918, when he began the transition of Ruth from pitcher to everyday player. Sox owner Harry Frazee sold Ruth to New York in 1920, and Barrow followed in 1921 as general manager.

Upon his arrival he told Yankees owner Colonel Jacob Ruppert, "If you ran your brewery the way you run this club, you'd go broke." Babe's 54 homers in 1920 had not been enough to move New York out of third place, but the next year, Barrow's first, the Yanks finally won their first pennant. As he and assistant George Weiss built up a farm system, the Yankees would win six pennants in Barrow's first eight years, another in 1932, and another four between 1936 and 1939.

Barrow became president of the Yankees after the death of Ruppert in 1939 and held that position until the team was sold in 1945. He is memorialized with plaques in Cooperstown and one in center field of Yankee Stadium, the park he did so much to build.

DICK BARTELL

Shortstop, Pit (N) 1927-30, Phi (N) 1931-34, NY (N) 1935-38, Chi (N) 1939, Det (A) 1940-41, NY (N) 1941-43, 1946

In his autobiography, *Rowdy Richard*, Bartell modestly argued that he ought to be in the Hall of Fame. He found few backers outside his immediate family, but the old battler has a better case for the Hall than if he were running for Mr. Congeniality. In Pete Palmer's Linear Weights System, Bartell's 27 Games Won put him ahead

of five shortstops now in the Hall—Ernie Banks, Travis Jackson, Joe Tinker, Pee Wee Reese, and Luis Aparicio.

A pepperpot who usually batted first or second in the order, he hit over .300 six times in his career. In 1933 he tied a record with four doubles in one game. Dick was at the top of his game in 1936 and 1937. In the former year he hit .298 for the Giants and led all shortstops in assists, double plays, and total chances per game. His teammate, Carl Hubbell, was the MVP with 26 victories, but Bartell played every day and may have had more total value. In the World Series Bartell hammered the Yankees at a .381 clip in a losing cause. The Giants won the NL pennant again in 1937 as he hit .306 and again led in total chances per game.

In 1940 Bartell was traded to Detroit in the AL. He hit only .233, but the Tigers won nine games more than they had the year before without him and rose all the way from fifth to first. Bartell was the World Series goat, though. With the Tigers leading the seventh game, 1-0, he took a throw from the outfield with his back to the plate and let Cincinnati's Frank McCormick score the tying run. Detroit eventually lost, 2-1.

Bartell was sent back to the Giants the next year, after a slow start in which he saw little action. He batted .303 for New York over the rest of the season. The Tigers fell back to fifth.

For all his participation on pennant winners, the image that remains (and the one Bartell himself perpetuates in his autobiography) is one of a hot-headed scrapper who enjoyed fighting and baseball in that order. He died in 1985 at the age of 87.

JAKE "EAGLE EYE" BECKLEY

First Baseman, Pit (N) 1888-89, 1891-96, Pit (P) 1890, NY (N) 1896-97, Cin (N) 1897-1903, StL (N) 1904-07

One of the last of the handlebar-mustache players and a big star at the turn of the century, Beckley's 2,377 games at first base ranks second all-time, trailing only Eddie Murray. Jake rapped out 2,930 hits, paving the way to his Hall of Fame election in 1971. He batted over .300 in 13 seasons, and hit three home runs in one game in 1897, a feat that would not be repeated for 25 years (by Ken Williams in 1922).

It was hard to hit homers then. Not only were the baseballs deader than Saturday night in Des Moines, but the fences were deeper because they built ballparks to the shapes of city blocks. The center field fence could be some 550 feet away with an area in front roped off for carriages. Players could sooner mail the ball to the fence than hit it there. Triples were a better indicator of power. Jake hit 243, more than anyone in his day, and fourth best all time, behind Ty Cobb, Sam Crawford, and Honus Wagner. He hit three in one game twice.

When the players revolted against management in 1890 and formed the short-lived Players League, Beckley was one of the many stars who jumped with them. "I'm only in this game for the money," he said candidly.

But he played with verve, too. Sometimes he turned the bat around and bunted with the handle. His favorite stunt was a cute hidden ball trick. Jake liked to hide the ball under first base, and then pull it out and shock the runner. Somehow the naive runners never caught on.

JOHN BECKWITH

Shortstop/ Catcher, Negro Leagues, 1919-38: Chicago Giants, Chicago American Giants, Baltimore Black Sox, Homestead Grays, Harrisburg Giants, Lincoln Giants, Bacharach Giants, New York Black Yankees, Newark Dodgers, Brooklyn Royal Giants

Beckwith was only 19 when he knocked the first ball ever hit over the left field fence at Redland Field, Cincinnati, in 1920. A right-handed pull hitter, he went on to rank as one of the great longball sluggers in the black leagues, clouting a reported 72 and 54 home runs in two of his seasons in Chicago. After he moved East in the late 1920s, he topped all hitters there, including Josh Gibson, in home runs in 1930 and 1931.

John could also hit for average, belting black and white big leaguers equally well—.323 in the black majors and .311 in 29 games against top white big leaguers. His two best seasons were 1924, when he led all hitters with a .452 average, and 1930, when he posted an amazing .546.

A big man at 230 pounds, Beckwith could play any position on the field and would even pitch occasionally. He was a moody, antisocial man whose personality may have kept him on the move from team to team. But it also helped enhance his reputation as one of the most fearsome sluggers of his day.

DAVID "BUDDY" BELL

Third Baseman, Cle (A) 1972-78, Tex (A) 1979-85, 1989 Cin (N) 1986-87, Hou (N) 1988. Manager, Det (A) 1996-1998

Buddy never made it to a World Series or even to the playoffs, so he never got much national publicity, but he was among the top four defensive third basemen, according to Pete Palmer's linear weights. His hard-nosed, give-all-for-the-team style of play made him a crowd favorite at each of his stops and won him six consecutive Gold Gloves. Bell was a 16th-round Cleveland draft pick as an outfielder and wasn't moved to third until his second year with the Indians.

A consistent .280-.290 hitter throughout his career, Bell's best season was 1979, his first in Texas. He played in every game, led the league in at bats, and hit .299, with 200 hits, 42 doubles, 18 home runs, and 101 RBIs. He gave the Rangers two more .290 seasons and two .300 years before being packed off to Cincinnati, where he had his first 20-home run season. Bell left holding the Texas records for doubles, RBIs, extra-base hits, and total bases.

Over his career, Bell amassed more than 2,500 hits, and his 201 homers, when added to his father Gus' 206, give the Bells third place in the father-son home run derby, after Bobby and Barry Bonds and Ken Griffey, Jr. and Sr. The debut of Bell's son David with the Indians in 1995 made the Bells one of only a handful of three-generation major league families.

JAMES "COOL PAPA" BELL

Outfielder, Negro Leagues, 1922-46; St. Louis Stars, Pittsburgh Crawfords, Detroit Wolves, Kansas City Monarchs, Chicago American Giants, Memphis Red Sox, Homestead Grays

That Bell could switch off the light and jump into bed before the room got dark, as Satchel Paige always claimed, may be a slight exaggeration. (Bell says he did it but admits that the light switch had a short in it.) But he was fast enough to score from second on a fly, which he did against Dizzy Dean in Yankee Stadium in 1935, and to score from first on a sacrifice, which he did against Bob Lemon in 1948, when Bell was 45 years old. According to legend at least, Cool Papa was the fastest man in spikes.

Like Ruth, George Sisler, and Stan Musial, Bell started as a pitcher at age 19, with the St. Louis Stars. He threw a knuckleball and won his first three games, calmly sleeping before a big game against Rube Foster's American Giants to earn his nickname, "Cool Papa."

Bell, who stood over six feet, could also hit the long ball right-handed. His manager, Big Bill Gatewood, who taught Satchel Paige the hesitation pitch, converted the rookie Bell into a switch-hitting outfielder and told him to hit the ball on the ground. Infielders like Judy Johnson admit that if the ball took two hops, you might as well put it in your pocket.

Eventually Bell joined two of the most famous teams in Negro League annals, the Crawfords (with Paige, Josh Gibson, Johnson, and Oscar Charleston), and the Grays (with Gibson and Buck Leonard).

Bell's lifetime batting average, though records are still incomplete, is 10th on the Negro League list. Surprisingly he is ninth among home run hitters. In games against white big leaguers Bell hit .392.

Although he never had a chance at the white majors himself, Cool Papa helped some others. He was hitting .411 in 1946, but he sat out the final doubleheader so the batting title would go to young Monte Irvin and help boost him into integrated ball. Bell also counseled Jackie Robinson to give up playing shortstop and concentrate on second, the position he settled on with the Dodgers. He said his greatest thrill was the day Jackie made good in the majors.

In 1974 Cool Papa was named to the Baseball Hall of Fame. He died in 1991 at the age of 87.

ALBERT BELLE

Outfielder, Cle (A) 1989-96, Chi (A) 1997-98

Belle will be voted Mr. Congeniality right after they begin handing out pilot licenses to pigs. One of baseball's foremost sluggers, his career has oscillated between heroic feats on the field and controversy off. Whether beaning a taunting fan with a better throw than he ever made in a game, delivering an linebackerish elbow to a rival second baseman, chasing down fleeing kids with his car, corking his bat, or storming at NBC's Hannah Storm in language no Marine would touch with rubber gloves, Belle has always been consistent—he always readily admitted it was someone else's fault. Yet, fair or not, it's been Belle who sat out the suspensions and paid the fines. If his defense in the field was as quick as his reaction to criticism, he'd be Willie Mays. But, in fairness, he's worked hard to improve his outfielding which has progressed steadily from abysmal to nearly adequate.

The upside is that the man can hit a ton. His thundering bat has won him forgiveness from his teammates, managers, and club owners. On Nov. 20, 1996, the Chicago White Sox forgave him away from the Cleveland Indians with a five-year, $55 million contract. Belle vowed to improve his behavior, then missed his new team's first autograph session. After a sub-par first season in Chicago,

he was back to his normal numbers. Belle, who in 1995 became the first player with 50 home runs and 50 doubles in the same season (doing it in a 144-game schedule), blasted 49 home runs and drove in 152 runs in 1998.

He took advantage of a clause in his contract to become a free agent after the '98 season and signed with Baltimore.

JOHNNY BENCH
Catcher, Cin (N) 1967-83

Bench was all but elected to Cooperstown in 1970 at the age of 22 when he slugged 45 home runs with 148 RBIs and was named MVP. It was a bit of an overreaction. He proved to be an outstanding player and a certain Hall of Famer over the rest of his career, but he never quite matched that 1970 season. His second best season came two years later in 1972, when he hit 40 home runs and won his second MVP.

With 11 seasons of 20-plus home runs, Bench demolished the home run record for catchers with 325 (to Yogi Berra's 313). But his batting average was unimpressive, and even his high RBI totals were dependent on the wealth of opportunities offered anyone batting mid-lineup for Cincinnati's Big Red Machine.

Johnny had a splendid Series in 1976, hitting .529 in his direct competition with Yankee Thurman Munson, the AL's top catcher. Bench's two homers and five RBIs was the coup de grace in Game 4 of the Reds' sweep.

No one, including Bench, could live up to Bench's reputation as a catcher. In his first year, 1968, he led in both assists and passed balls. As esteem for his throwing arm grew, runners tested it less, and his caught-stealing numbers declined. Whether he was the best came second to whether everyone thought he was the best.

He called the pitches as Cincinnati's Big Red Machine rolled to six division titles, four NL pennants, and two World Series. Although he handled only one 20-game winner, none would question Bench's ability behind the plate. In 1989 he was elected to the Hall of Fame.

ALBERT "CHIEF" BENDER
Pitcher, Phi (A) 1903-14, Bal (F) 1915, Phi (N) 1916-17, Chi (A) 1925

This half-Chippewa Indian from the White Earth reservation in Minnesota was the money pitcher on Connie Mack's champion A's of the 1905-1914 era. Of all the great pitchers on those teams, Bender was the man Mack said he'd pick if he had one game he had to win. Connie never spoke with a forked tongue, yet oddly Bender pitched only one must-win game in his life, the final game of the 1905 World Series, and lost it, 2-0. Altogether the Chief won six out of 10 Series games for Philadelphia. In 1910 Eddie Plank was hurt, and Bender and Jack Coombs pitched the entire Series, winning in five games. In 1913, when Coombs was hurt, Mack asked Bender to pitch out of turn and promised to pay the Chief's mortgage of $2,500 if he would do it. Said Connie: "I knew then the Giants were done for." Bender won both his starts.

A product of the Carlisle Indian School, Bender never pitched in the minors and won the first big league game he pitched, a four-hitter, when he was 19. He was a big man (6 feet 2 inches), who pitched with a high kick and an overhand delivery. His out pitch, in those days before

doctoring was illegal, was the "talcum ball," which he rubbed with talcum powder to make it smooth. He claimed it gave the ball a sharp drop.

Although he won 212 games in his 16 seasons, the Chief won 20 games only twice (in 1910 and 1913). But he had some terrific ERA years. Four times he went under 2.00. Even in the Dead Ball Era, that wasn't chopped liver. He was elected to the Hall of Fame in 1953.

LAWRENCE "YOGI" BERRA
Catcher, NY (A) 1946-63, NY (N) 1965. Manager NY (A) 1964, 1984-85, NY (N) 1972-75

Yogi just might have been the best catcher the game has ever seen. Certainly he's the most-seen catcher, having appeared on TV in a record 14 World Series, 10 of them as a member of the world champs. He holds the records for most Series games (75) and most hits (71). Yogi is also the only catcher ever to call a perfect World Series game.

After shuttling between catching and the outfield, Berra was handed the first-string catcher's job by new manager Casey Stengel in 1949, and the Yankees won the first of five straight pennants. The two facts are not a coincidence. Yogi was "the man who holds us together," Stengel said in 1955, when Yogi won his third MVP.

One of the game's great bad-ball hitters, Berra hit only .285, but Orioles manager Paul Richards called him the most dangerous hitter in baseball after the seventh inning. He totaled 358 homers, and his 313 as a catcher are more than any backstop except Johnny Bench. Yogi could field, too, once going 148 straight games and 950 chances without an error. His handling of pitchers always earned good reviews, and the Yankees staff numbers indicate the kudos were deserved.

Berra's best year was 1950, when he hit .322 with 124 RBIs but saw the MVP go to teammate Phil Rizzuto. Berra did win the award in 1951, 1954, and 1955. In 1972 he was elected to the Hall of Fame.

Though an intelligent student of baseball (and an intelligent person), Berra was considered a buffoon by people who think reading the headlines on the sports page makes them experts. Yogi's favorite reading was comic books, he finished out of the money in the Mark Harmon Look-alike Contest, and his natural shyness sometimes makes him seem slow on the uptake. His malaprops have made him the most quoted person in baseball history, although it's getting harder every year to know what he said and what they said he said. Either way, he's moving up fast on Shakespeare in Bartlett's. Some Yogi-isms: "He was a big clog in their machine." "It gets late early there ." "Nobody goes there anymore, it's too crowded." "Take it with a grin of salt." Or the immortal "It's never over till it's over." When Yogi was given a benefit on his retirement, he graciously thanked "all those who made this day necessary."

Thus it came as a surprise when Berra was named to manage the Yankees in 1964. Despite injuries to Mantle, Whitey Ford, and others, they came from six games back to win. But Yogi lost the Series to Johnny Keane's Cards, then was summarily replaced by Keane. He went cross-town to coach the Mets and managed them to a pennant in 1973. His winning percentage as a manager is an impressive .522.

BERT BLYLEVEN

Pitcher, Min (A) 1970-76, Tex (A) 1976-77, Pit (N) 1978-80, Cle (A) 1981-85, Min (A) 1985-88, Cal (A) 1989-90, 1992

One of six foreign-born pitchers to win over 200 games, handsome Bert Blyleven was born in Holland. Had he stayed there, he might have wasted his long fingers plugging dikes instead of throwing the most wicked curves since the Burma Road. Bert's roundhouse was voted best in the league by AL managers, but the hitters knew it before the ballots were passed out. He didn't get to number three on the all-time strikeout list by throwing tulips.

Blyleven was a control pitcher. When his hook wasn't hooking, he spent a lot of time watching the ball sail into the seats. He surrendered an amazing 50 home runs in 1986, although pitching in the Metrodome surely had something to do with that.

He had been one of the top AL pitchers of his generation. Unfortunately he had some of his best years for teams ranging from bad to mediocre, making his 287 wins all the more impressive. In 1973 Blyleven was 20-17 for third-place Minnesota, his only 20-win season. Eleven years later, he almost made it at 19-7 for the tail-end Indians.

In one of his rare sojourns with a strong team, he was 12-5 for the 1979 Pirates and won a playoff game and a World Series contest. His complaints the next year that he was being underutilized by manager Chuck Tanner did not endear him to Pirates fans but won him a ticket back to the American League. His subsequent record would tend to support his argument. He helped the Twins to the AL pennant in 1987 with a pair of ALCS wins and added another in the World Series victory over the Cardinals.

BARRY BONDS

Outfielder, Pit (N) 1986-92, SF (N) 1993-1998

With Most Valuable Player Awards in 1990, 1992, and 1993 as well as a couple of near misses, Bonds is arguably the top player of the decade. Certainly the son of former great Bobby Bonds started with a strong pedigree, but his mixture of power and speed has eclipsed his father and stands comparison with his godfather, Willie Mays. The only man ever to hit over 400 home runs and steal over 400 bases, Bonds bats around .300 every year, handles left field with the best, and, though his arm is only average, it's very accurate. What more could anyone ask?

Perhaps a little humility. Bonds is tremendously self-absorbed —so much so that he sometimes seems to think "baseball" is spelled with an "I". His EGO exceeds his OBA and makes him easier to admire than to like. On the other hand, his self-confidence has helped him find parts in several movies, a career he may pursue after he retires from baseball.

His other bad habit is flopping in the playoffs. In three trips to the NL playoffs with the Pirates, he hit one home run and twice batted under .200. In 1997 with the Giants he batted .250 with two RBIs in three losses to Florida. No Mr. October here.

On the other hand, he's quite good at getting his team to the playoffs. He did it three times with the Pirates, once with the Giants, and led their 1998 comeback to tie for the NL Wild Card, although San Francisco lost to the Cubs in a one-game playoff.

BOBBY BONDS

Outfield, SF (N) 1968-74, NY (A) 1975, Cal (A) 1976-77, Chi (A) 1978, Tex (A) 1978, Cle (A) 1979, StL (N) 1980, Chi (N) 1981

Bonds combined power and speed like no player before him. In 1969 he became only the fourth player to hit 30 home runs and steal 30 bases in a season, and then he went on to repeat that feat four more times, to take permanent possession. He was also the first man to 30-30 in both leagues.

Bobby stole 461 bases and hit 332 homers, 35 of them as leadoff man, 11 of those in one season, both records at the time. He is one of two men to hit a grand slam in his first big league game, and the first to do it since 1898.

Twice he led the league in runs scored and once in total bases, but where he was a real pacesetter was in strikeouts. He set the major league record when he whiffed 187 times in 1969 and then broke it with 189 in 1970. He averaged one strikeout in every four at bats and ranks number six on the all-time strikeout list.

After seven seasons with the Giants, Bonds became a nomad, spending the next seven years with seven teams, all of them looking for his instant offense. In 1979, at age 33, he hit 25 home runs and stole 34 bases for Cleveland, missing a sixth 30-30 season.

With son Barry's 410 home runs, the Bondses top the all-time father-son home run championship.

BOB BOONE

Catcher, Phi (A) 1972-81, Cal (A) 1982-88, KC 1989-90. Manager, KC (A) 1995-1997

Until Carlton Fisk passed him in 1993, Boone had caught more games than any other man in big league history. He surpassed Hall of Famer Al Lopez (1,918 games) in 1987.

As a defensive catcher, Boone was one of the best. He led league catchers in assists in 1973 and 1984. His 89 assists in 1973 were the most for a rookie since Johnny Bench had 108 in 1968. With California from 1982 to 1988, he threw out better than 45 percent of runners attempting to steal, including 58 percent in his first year with the Angels. He won his first Gold Glove in 1978 with a .991 fielding average, breaking Bench's 10-year streak. He won four more over the course of his career.

Boone's record as a handler of pitchers was a mixed bag. The ERAs of both the Phillies and Angels went up after he joined them, and when he left the Phils, the club ERA went down. Nevertheless on his arrival in California, the Angels immediately rose from fifth to first. In all, he guided his staffs to six division flags. And although Tim McCarver was Steve Carlton's personal catcher in Philadelphia in the late 1970s, Steve's wins went up from 18 to 24 when Boone took over in 1980.

Not much of a hitter during the regular season, Boone had a splendid postseason record with the bat—.311, including .400 for the Phils in the 1977 NLCS and .455 for the Angels in the 1986 Championship Series. He appeared in one World Series, with Philadelphia in 1980, and batted .412.

Bob and father Ray, a longtime infielder for Cleveland and Detroit, were the second father-and-son team after the Bells to each have 100 career home runs. Bob's sons Bret and Aaron played together for the Reds in 1997 and 1998.

"SUNNY JIM" BOTTOMLEY

First Baseman, StL (N) 1922-32, Cin (N) 1933-35, StL (A) 1936-37. Manager StL (A) 1937

Swaggering, popular, his hat cocked rakishly on the side of his head, Sunny Jim is in the record books for batting in 12 runs in one game. He did it in 1924 on two homers, a double, and three singles. That game, more than his career record, got him elected to the Hall of Fame in 1974.

In his 16 major league seasons, Bottomley batted .300 eight times and batted in 100 or more runs six years in a row. Certainly not a wimp record but less impressive than it would be if it had occurred at any time in history other than the hit-happy 1920s and 1930s. In those days .300 hitters were as common as hip flasks. Bottomley was not particularly adept defensively, leading NL first basemen in errors four times.

Jim helped the Cardinals win four flags, in 1926, 1928, 1930, and 1931. He was named MVP in 1928 after leading the league in RBIs and triples and tying for homers with Hack Wilson. In 1931 Bottomley figured in the closest batting race in history. Though injured, he hit .3482, losing to Bill Terry with .3486, and to his own roommate, Chick Hafey, who had .3489.

LOU BOUDREAU

Shortstop, Cle (A) 1938-50, Bos (A) 1951-52. Manager, Cle (A) 1942-50, Bos (A) 1952-54, KC (A) 1955-57, Chi (N) 1960

Boudreau got a lot of ink by pulling the "Boudreau Shift" against Ted Williams in 1946, bunching six of his Cleveland players on the right side of second base and daring Williams to take a shot. Actually Boudreau's manager Roger Peckinpaugh had first used the shift against Ted in 1941. But the maneuver earned Lou a reputation as a creative strategist, an attribute unsupported by his record, which, except for one unforgettable year, was a losing one.

Lou Boudreau's greatest asset as a manager was that he could write the name Lou Boudreau in at shortstop every day. His hitting and his fielding combined to make him one of the half-dozen best shortstops in this century.

A fine fielder, he led AL shortstops in fielding average a record-tying eight times, in double plays five times, and in putouts four. His 134 double plays in 1943 was a record, as was his .982 fielding average in 1947. His arm was only so-so, and others had more flat-out range, but Boudreau's knowledge of hitters allowed him to compensate by positioning himself where the action was.

In 1942, at the age of 24, Lou applied for the Cleveland manager's job and got it, becoming the youngest man to manage a full season. The Indians finished fourth, the same spot they had held under Peckinpaugh. The Tribe moved up to third in 1943, then slipped to fifth in 1944, although Boudreau won the batting title with .327.

By 1947, when the Indians finished a ho-hum fourth, new owner Bill Veeck tried to trade Boudreau to the St. Louis Browns, a fate considered only slightly more humane than the guillotine. Angry Cleveland fans cast a newspaper vote 90 percent in favor of keeping Lou and trading Veeck. The owner decided to stick with Lou for one more year.

What a year! "Lou was determined to prove I was a jerk," Veeck wrote. "And he did." In that magical 1948 Boudreau hit .355, with 18 homers and 106 RBIs. He was always—or seemed always—to be at the center of a rally. One day he sat out with a slight injury, then came off the bench to pinch hit for a win. More, he inspired his team; several players had career years. A furious four-way pennant race ended with the Indians and Red Sox tied. In a one-game playoff at Boston, Boudreau daringly named a rookie lefty, Gene Bearden, to start. He himself smacked two home runs to destroy the Sox, 8-3. The Indians then bested the Braves in the Series. Lou was AL MVP with more than 100 votes to spare.

Everything after that was an anticlimax. Boudreau managed four teams, finishing between third and eighth, before becoming a broadcaster for the Cubs and the father-in-law of Denny McLain. In 1970 he was elected to the Hall of Fame.

KEN BOYER

Third Baseman, StL (N) 1955-65, NY (N) 1966-67, Chi (A) 1967-68, LA (N) 1968-69. Manager, StL 1978-80

The best of six brothers who all played professional ball, Ken was a third baseman in the Brooks Robinson mold, diving into the hole to snare hard grounders or running them down backhand behind the bag. Pie Traynor called him the best he ever saw.

Five times Ken led NL third basemen in double plays. He won Gold Gloves six times. He even played center field one season, 1957, and led all NL outfielders in fielding average. His kid brother Clete, a Yankees' third baseman, was perhaps even better afield, but lacked Ken's bat. Ken hit over .300 five times and drove in 90 runs or better seven years in a row.

Boyer sparked the Cards to the flag in 1964, hitting .295 with, 24 home runs and a league-leading 119 RBIs, and won the MVP. It was to be his last big season before a bad back slowed him down.

In the Series that year Ken beat Clete's Yanks in Game 4 with a grand slam to even the Series. Then he helped win Game 7 with a homer and three runs scored. It was the only time brothers hit homers in the same Series game.

HARRY BRECHEEN

Pitcher, StL (N) 1940-52, StL (A) 1953

Brecheen was the Cardinals pitcher in 1946 when Enos Slaughter raced home from first to beat the Red Sox in the seventh game of the World Series. It gave Harry his third win of the Series, making him the first man to notch three since Stan Coveleski 26 years earlier and the only left-hander until Mickey Lolich 22 years later. The moment was a teensy tainted: pitching in relief, Brecheen had just allowed two inherited runners to score, blowing the lead he'd been sent in to hold. But he nailed the win by shutting out the Sox in the ninth.

Two years later, 1948, Brecheen posted a 20-7 mark and the NL's lowest ERA. He won 14 games or better six years in a row for the Cardinals and pitched in three World Series, winning four and losing one. After 11 seasons with the proud Cardinals, he moved over to the humble Browns and discovered where their humility came from. He went 5-13 despite a decent 3.07 ERA. The next year the Browns moved to Baltimore and Harry became the pitching coach.

Nicknamed "the Cat" for the way he would pounce off the mound to field his position, Harry's World Series ERA of 0.83 is the second-best ever.

ROGER BRESNAHAN
Catcher, Was (N) 1897, Chi (N) 1900, Bal (A) 1901-02, NY (N) 1902-08, StL (N) 1909-12, Chi (N) 1913-15. Manager, StL (N) 1910-12, Chi (N) 1915

Bresnahan is best known as the man who introduced shin guards for catchers in 1907, though some insist they had been worn earlier by black infielders. Some white catchers also reportedly wore protection under their socks. But Roger was the first white big leaguer to wear them openly, which brought jeering from fans and other players. He is said to have borrowed the idea from cricket. He also pioneered a crude leather batting helmet as early as 1908, after nearly being killed by a beaning.

Bresnahan caught Christy Mathewson and Joe McGinnity for the Giants. He, McGinnity, and manager John McGraw had arrived from Baltimore, with the Giants in last place. With McGinnity's career reborn and Christy Mathewson showing the promise that led him to 373 wins, the Giants rose to second in 1903 and first in 1904 and 1905. In 1905 Bresnahan achieved a feat that may never be duplicated—he caught four World Series shutouts, three of them by Matty. He also batted .313.

At bat, Bresnahan favored the thick-handled bats popular then. His best season was 1903, when he batted .350 with 42 extra-base hits and 34 stolen bases. He was unusually fast for a catcher, enough to bat first or second in the lineup. He had started out as a pitcher and then played center field, not becoming a regular catcher until 1905. He was a natural leader and, like his boss, McGraw, a fiery umpire baiter with frequent suspensions.

In 1945 Bresnahan became the first catcher elected to the Hall of Fame, two years ahead of Mickey Cochrane, who was a much better hitter and arguably better defensively and as a handler of pitchers. Roger said he was born in Tralee, Ireland, so he was nicknamed "The Duke of Tralee." Actually, he was born (and died) in Toledo, Ohio.

GEORGE BRETT
Third Baseman/First Baseman KC (A) 1973-93

A curly-haired heart throb, Brett was the jewel in batting coach Charlie Lau's crown. He'd never gotten to .300 in the minor leagues, yet hitting off his front foot with the distinctive one-hand follow-through Lau taught, the left-handed hitter went on to win three American League batting titles, the last one in 1990 to become the first to win batting crowns in three decades.

His .390 in 1980 came within a point of John McGraw's 1899 mark for highest batting average by a third baseman and was the closest assault on .400 since Ted Williams' .406 in 1941. Also in 1980, Brett knocked in 118 runs in 117 games to become the first player since Joe DiMaggio in 1948 to drive in over one run per game played.

Three times (in 1975, 1976, and 1979) George led the AL in both hits and triples during the same season, a feat matched only by Ty Cobb. In 1979 he became one of only five players to slug 20 doubles, triples, and home runs in the same season.

Brett thrived in postseason play, leading Kansas City to the playoffs six times, and hitting .349 in postseason competition. His nine homers—three in one 1978 game—are a record in the playoffs. His three-run shot off the Yanks' Goose Gossage, won the 1980 ALCS, ending three years of consecutive playoff losses to New York.

Ironically Brett may be remembered longest for one at bat at Yankee Stadium in 1985 and the homer he did—didn't—did hit. In the ninth inning, Brett put the ball in the stands to give Kansas City the lead. But Yankees manager Billy Martin convinced the umpire to take a homer away from him because there was too much pine tar on the bat handle. The usually calm Brett blew up like the Hindenburg. His frenzied, screaming protest is still among the most popular and amusing TV replays. A couple of days later, AL president Lee MacPhail overruled his umpires and restored the homer on the grounds that they should have called the bat for excess pine tar before Brett batted.

TOMMY BRIDGES
Pitcher, Det (A) 1930-46

In his first major league appearance, Bridges entered the game in relief against the Yankees, got Babe Ruth to ground out, and struck out Lou Gehrig. He went on from there to carve out an outstanding career with the Tigers. The slightly built right-hander's trademark was a hard-breaking, heart-breaking curve that skittered sharply down and away. It helped make him one of the top AL pitchers of the 1930s, a group that included Lefty Grove, Ted Lyons, Red Ruffing, and Lefty Gomez—Hall of Famers all.

Tommy won 20 games three years in a row, 1934-1936, and helped pitch the Tigers to pennants in the first two. He also led the league in strikeouts in 1935 and 1936. But Bridges was also prone to control problems; he walked over 100 batters six times and averaged 3.79 walks per nine innings pitched. Nevertheless his career ERA of 3.57 wasn't bad at all in an era when the league averaged well above 4.00. Bridges missed perfect-game immortality in 1932, when he gave up a single to pinch hitter Dave Harris (.327) with two outs in the ninth.

He pitched in four World Series, winning four games and losing one. The win they all remember came in the 1935 Series, when, leading 4-3 in the ninth inning of Game 6, he gave up a leadoff triple to Stan Hack of the Cubs. Bridges slammed the door with a strikeout, a grounder, and a fly to make the Tigers champs.

LOU BROCK
Outfielder, Chi (N) 1961-64, StL (N) 1964-79

According to traditionalists, the trade that sent Brock from the Cubs to the Cardinals in 1964 for pitcher Ernie Broglio was the greatest steal since Brinks. "Steal," of course, is a significant word when discussing Brock—he once held the season record for stolen bases with his 118 in 1974. Actually the Cards also got a couple of guys named Jack Spring and Paul Toth, and the Cubs received Bobby Shantz and Doug Clemens, but Shantz was near the end of the line and the others never had one to begin with. So when Broglio won only seven games for Chicago in three years before disappearing into a trivia question and Brock played in the Cardinals outfield for 16 years, made over 3,000 hits, and led the Cards to three pennants,

the deal looked pretty darn good for the Redbirds.

But wait! According to some revisionist statisticians, Brock wasn't the bargain he was cracked up to be. They point out that Brock didn't walk enough for a leadoff man, so that his 3,023 career hits and .293 batting average become only a .341 on-base percentage. They also murmur seductively that he struck out way too often—1,730 times. And even though Brock finished up as the all-time base-stealing champ with 938 and led the NL eight times, revisionists ho-hum. They weigh the rally-killing effect of a caught-stealing against the marginal value of a successful theft, and downgrade the whole maneuver as something that just keeps 'em happy in the cheap seats. Finally revisionists point out that Brock was barely adequate in left field and had a weak arm.

Against all that evidence, the traditionalists can only mumble that Lou led the league in runs scored twice and crossed the plate 1,610 times. That he hit 149 homers and drove in 900, both above par for leadoff batters. That he hit .300 in one World Series, .400-plus in two, and twice stole seven bases in a Series, for an all-time record of 14. He also scored 16 runs in 21 World Series games and knocked in 13. And, the traditionalists quibble, for all those seasons he played in St. Louis, opponents thought he was doing things that beat them and had the losses to show for it. Almost as fast as he ran, Brock was voted into the Hall of Fame in 1985.

DENNIS "DAN" BROUTHERS

First Baseman, Troy (N) 1879-80, Buf (N) 1881-85, Det (N) 1886-88, Bos (N) 1889, Bos (P) 1890, Bos (AA) 1891, Bkn (N) 1892-93, Bal (N) 1894-95, Lou (N) 1895, Phi (N) 1896

Brouthers (pronounced "Broothers") was the Mickey Mantle of the 1880s. He hit only 106 home runs—no one hit many in those days—but many of Dan's were tape-measure blows. In 1886 one knocked the fans out of a tower behind the park in Boston. He led the National League in home runs twice (1881 and 1886), not counting a career-high 14 in 1884.

A big man for his era (6-foot-2, 220 pounds), Brouthers possessed a great batting eye and rarely struck out. He is said to have originated the phrase "Keep your eye on the ball." And that he did. His lifetime batting average of .342 is ninth-best all-time. He was the first man to win back-to-back batting titles, in 1882 and 1883; he won five overall. He drove in 100 or more runs five times and led in slugging average six straight seasons (1881-1886); his .519 lifetime slugging average was by far the best in the 19th century.

With Buffalo in the early 1880s, Brouthers played lead assassin in baseball's first Murderers' Row: "the Big Four" that also included Hardy Richardson, Jack Rowe, and Deacon White. All four were sold to Detroit after the 1885 season for a then princely $7,500. They won the pennant in 1887 and beat American Association champ St. Louis in a challenge Series, 10 games to five. "We slugged 'em to death," Dan said. Brouthers moved up to Boston in 1889, where he played in three leagues in three years. His Players League and AA teams won pennants. Finally, at Baltimore in 1894 he teamed with John McGraw to help the Orioles win their first flag. Brouthers ended as a night watchman at the Polo Grounds. He died

in 1932 and was inducted into the Hall of Fame in 1945.

MORDECAI "THREE FINGER" BROWN

Pitcher, StL (N) 1903, Chi (N) 1904-12, 1916, Cin (N) 1913, StL (F) 1914, Bkn (F) 1914, Chi (F) 1915. Manager StL (F) 1914

When Brown was 7 years old, he stuck his right hand in his uncle's corn shredder, cutting off the top two joints of his index finger and paralyzing his little finger. The accident probably put him in the Hall of Fame. The damaged fingers gave Mordecai a natural knuckler, and he used it to star for the Cubs in their great years, 1905-1910. The shredder became a tourist attraction.

His biggest win was one of the most famous games ever played, the 1908 makeup of the Cubs-Giants game suspended when Fred Merkle failed to touch second base. Merkle's "boner" nullified a Giants win and left the teams tied at season's end. The makeup game was in New York in a park loaded with partisan fans, who thought they had been cheated out of victory. Brown and other Cubs received fistfuls of "black hand letters"—death threats—before they took the field. When Chicago starter Jack Pfeister got in trouble in the first inning, manager Frank Chance quickly called in Brown, who walked to the mound amid savage catcalls while a policeman stood guard. Brown was 29-9 in 1908 with a 1.47 ERA, while his mound opponent, Christy Mathewson, was 37-11, 1.43, but Brown had the edge that day, winning 4-2.

It was one of nine straight victories Mordecai scored over Matty going back to 1905. Their lifetime record versus each other: 13-11, Brown.

From 1904 through 1910, Brown had ERAs of 1.87, 2.17, 1.04, 1.39, 1.47, 1.31, and 1.86. That 1.04 is the record and the only time he led the NL. Low ERAs were the norm during those Dead-Ball days, but such consistency was scary. On the subject of consistency, he won 20 or more for six straight seasons from 1906 through 1911. Brown totaled a tidy 239 career wins, with a .648 winning percentage. In addition, he recorded 49 saves. By the modern definition of saves, he led the league four years in a row, topped by 13 in 1910. Of course, he had a first-rate team—the Tinker-to-Evers-to-Chance Cubs—playing behind him. Or maybe they had a great pitcher out front. He three-fingered Chicago to pennants in 1906, 1907, 1908, and 1910, and then took the Chicago Feds to the flag in 1915 with 17-8, 2.10.

LOUIS "PETE" BROWNING

Outfielder, Lou (AA) 1882-89, Cle (P) 1890, Pit (N) 1891, Cin (N) 1891-92, Lou (N) 1892-93, StL (N) 1894, Bkn (N) 1894

The original Louisville Slugger, Browning hit a career .341 back in the 1880s, mostly for Louisville of the AA. Pete, who lived and died in the city by the Ohio River, was the first man to have his bats made to order for him, by John Hillerich, who went on to found the famous bat-making firm, Hillerich and Bradsby.

Although he led the American Association in batting twice and the Players League once, Pete's best year was 1887, when he finished second. He hit .471 under that year's rule which counted walks as hits. With the walks factored out, he dropped to "only" .402. His worst year was .256 in 1889. He blamed it on too much "German

tea," swore off the stuff, and hit .373 the next season.

A pure hitter, Browning was pollution in the field with a lifetime .882 fielding average.

MORGAN G. BULKELEY
Executive

Ever since Bulkeley was elected to the Hall of Fame in 1937, Cooperstown apologists have been hard-pressed to explain the error. They point out that old Bulks was a successful businessman and banker, head of Aetna Life Insurance for years, governor of Connecticut (1889-1893), U.S. senator (1905-1911), and a distinguished citizen of many public and personal virtues all his long life—all of which should get him into the Hall of Fame about as much as wearing a tutu should get you into the Marines.

As to what he did for baseball: well, he was president of the Hartford Dark Blues baseball club in 1874-1875. Remember them? Then, because they needed a figurehead, he let them make him president of the brand-new National League in 1876. He doesn't seem to have done anything during his year in office, but that's pretty much what the real power in the league—founder William Hulbert—wanted. When he didn't show up at the 1877 meeting, the club presidents elected Hulbert president since he'd been doing Bulkeley's job anyway. About 30 years later, Bulkeley's name was on the report of the committee that decided Abner Doubleday invented baseball, but Bulkeley doesn't appear to have been any more active in that than he'd been as NL prexy. At least that's in his favor.

In point of fact, Bulkeley was a fine person who got into the Hall of Fame because the selectors of 1937 didn't know beans about baseball's history and figured the first NL president must have been a pioneer. They were wrong.

JIM BUNNING
Pitcher, Det (A) 1955-63, Phi (N) 1964-67, 1970-71, Pit (N) 1968-69, LA (N) 1969

Bunning not only won 100 games in each league, he pitched a no-hitter in each. His NL effort was a perfect game, one of only 13 in the history of the game, thrown against the last-place Mets on Father's Day in 1964. Jim won 20 only once, 20-8 with the fourth-place Tigers in 1957, but he won 19 in 1962 for the Tigers and three straight times for the Phillies (1964-1966).

Bunning was an intimidating power pitcher. He led the AL twice in strikeouts and the NL once. When he retired, he had 2,855 strikeouts, then second only to Walter Johnson.

With a degree in economics and nine children to support, Bunning went into Republican politics in his home state of Kentucky when he left baseball. He lost a bid to become governor, but later won a seat in the U.S. House of Representatives. In 1998 Bunning was elected to the U.S. Senate. He was elected to the Hall of Fame in 1996.

SELVA "LEW" BURDETTE
Pitcher, NY (A) 1950, Bos (N) 1951-52, Mil (N) 1953-63, StL (N) 1963-64, Chi (N) 1964-65, Phi (N) 1965, Cal (N) 1966-67

Burdette was born in Nitro, W.V., and media types liked to refer to him as "Nitro Lew" during his career because it gave their accounts an excitingly explosive ambiance. Burdette's temper could go off occasionally. And his curve—especially his wet curve—could drop like a bomb. But his career was anything but rocketlike.

He was 27 before he became a journeyman starter with the Braves in 1953, playing a right-handed second banana to Warren Spahn's left-handed lead. He was 30 when he became a very good pitcher in 1956, winning 19 and leading the NL in ERA. He was nearing 32 the next year when, after 17 regular-season wins, he became a great pitcher in the World Series. In that fall of 1957, he defeated the Yankees three times, throwing three complete games. Two of them—including the seventh game—were shutouts. His Series ERA was 0.67 and he allowed just 21 hits (seven in each start).

Having hit his peak, he stayed for a while, winning 60 games in the next three seasons, including a 1-0 no-hit win in 1960. Then came a slow decline into spot starter and reliever, until he closed up shop with 203 career victories in 1967.

JESSE BURKETT
Outfield, NY (N) 1890, Cle (N) 1891-98, StL (N) 1899-1901, StL (A) 1902-04, Bos (A) 1905

Burkett was known as the "Crab." He was argumentative, surly, and unpopular with both opponents and teammates. He once punched a rival manager in the nose and left a game another time under police guard for fomenting a riot. When he wasn't fighting, he was complaining. He griped almost as often as he cracked out base hits.

Burkett hit .400 twice. He hit .409 in 1895, and .410 in 1896. Those two marks led the NL, but his 1899 .396 left him second to Ed Delahanty's .410. How he must have grumbled about that! Two years later, the Crab got his third NL batting title with a solid .376. Those were hitters' years. The pitcher's mound had been moved back to its present position of 60 feet, 6 inches from home plate in 1894, and the batters were able to tee off on those longer throws.

But Jesse would have hit, anyway. With the kind of speed that enabled him to steal 389 bases in his career and beat out many infield hits, Jesse boasted he could bunt .300. He bunted so well, in fact, that he could foul off third strikes indefinitely. His prowess inspired the creation of the present rule calling a bunted foul with two strikes an out.

Jesse started out as a pitcher for the Giants, but he proved a much better hitter and was moved to the outfield by the Cleveland Spiders. But he never seemed to get the hang of the outfield and, also hampered by the small gloves of the day, was perennially among the league leaders in errors. His .338 lifetime batting average made up for his bobbles and made his personality almost tolerable.

ROY CAMPANELLA
Catcher, Negro Leagues, 1937-45, Baltimore Elite Giants, Bkn (N) 1948-57

For a decade with the Brooklyn Dodgers (1948-1957), Campanella was one of the two best catchers in baseball. His only serious rival was the Yankees' Yogi Berra. The Dodgers and Yankees dominated their leagues during that period, and each catcher received three MVP awards. An

auto accident in 1958 left Campy substantially paralyzed and ended his career. In 1969 he was elected to the Hall of Fame.

The squat, powerful Campanella began playing in the Negro Leagues with the Baltimore Elite Giants while still a teenager. He played in All-Star Games in 1941, 1944, and 1945. He was the second black player (after Jackie Robinson) signed by the Dodgers, and he joined Nashua in the Brooklyn farm system in 1946.

In 1948, a month into the season, he was called up to the Dodgers and quickly established himself as the NL's top catcher. Campanella was excellent defensively, an acknowledged master in handling pitchers, and durable. His rookie year was the only one of his ten in the majors in which he didn't catch in over 100 games.

Campy's Dodgers won NL pennants in 1949, 1952, 1953, 1955, and 1956. The 1955 crew defeated the Yankees in the World Series to become the first Brooklyn world champs in this century. Although he was always steady as Gibraltar behind the plate, Campanella's hitting fluctuated wildly. But in his best seasons he was a terror. In 1951 he hit .325 with 33 home runs and 108 RBIs to win his first MVP Award. Two years later, in 1953, he won his second MVP with .312, 41 homers, and a league-leading 142 RBIs. At the time, both the home run and RBI marks were records for catchers. He slipped to his poorest season in 1954, batting only .207. But in the championship year of 1955 he bounced back with .318, 32 homers, and 107 RBIs to gain his third MVP. His career totals were .276, 242 home runs, and 856 RBIs, with the home run total being the most ever hit by a catcher up to that time.

Campanella's autobiography, *It's Good to be Alive*, told the story of his courageous struggle to overcome the effects of his auto accident. It was later made into a movie for television. He died in 1993 at the age of 71.

ROD CAREW
Second Baseman/First Baseman, Min (A) 1967-78, Cal (A) 1979-85

Only Ty Cobb won more AL batting championships than Carew, the moody Panamanian who sprayed 3,053 hits where they ain't. He won seven AL titles for Minnesota, including four in a row from 1972 through 1975. In 1969, when Rod won his first batting crown with .332, he stole home seven times, tying a mark set by Brooklyn's Pete Reiser. In 1972 Rod hit a league-leading .318 without a single homer, the only batting champ ever to do that. Fifteen of his hits were bunts. Carew's high mark was .388 in 1977, like Ted Williams' mark of 1957 the second highest batting average in the majors since 1941. That year he also led in runs scored (128) and triples (16). He was named MVP.

Carew spent his last seven years with the Angels in a poor park for hitters. Although he won no more batting championships in California, he was over .300 in his first five seasons there. He retired with a .328 career average. Carew was elected to the Hall of Fame in 1991.

The main raps against Carew related to his defense. He played second base through 1975, but critics carped that his arm was too weak for the job. Shifted to first base for his remaining 10 seasons, he caught flack as a singles hitter in a power position.

MAX CAREY
Outfielder, Pit (N) 1910-26, Bkn (N) 1926-29.
Manager, Bkn (N) 1932-33

Pittsburgh's Max Carey was probably the best center fielder National League batters ever cursed. The only thing that covered more grass at Forbes Field was smoke from the steel mills. In Palmer's Linear Weights, only Tris Speaker ranks with Max as an outfield bandit.

Born Maximillian Carnerius, the former divinity student led the league in putouts nine times and retired with an NL record of 6,363, a mark later broken by Willie Mays in a longer career. Carey's 339 assists are still the 20th-century NL record.

A good-but-not-great hitter, Carey averaged .285 and led the league twice in triples, more on speed than power. He was a great baserunner—ninth on the all-time stolen base list with 738. He led the league in thefts 10 times and once, in 1922, he stole 51 bases in 53 attempts.

In 1925, his final full year with Pittsburgh, at age 35, he stole second, third, and home in the same inning on two different days in August. Playing in the World Series that year with a broken rib, he batted .458, stole three bases, and in the seventh game clipped Walter Johnson for four hits and scored three times to help win the world championship, 9-7. In 1961 Carey was elected to the Hall of Fame.

STEVE CARLTON
Pitcher, StL (N) 1965-71, Phi (N) 1972-86, SF (N) 1986, Chi (A) 1986, Cle (A) 1987, Min (A) 1987-88

For most of his career Carlton answered a short "——" to questions from the press and refused to grant interviews. He let his pitching do his talking, but as a consequence his training methods remained a mystery. One report had him preparing for a game with meditation while floating weightless in total darkness. However he prepared, it worked.

With Warren Spahn and Sandy Koufax, Carlton was one of the three best NL left-handers of all time. He won 329 games, second only to Spahn among lefties. He had 4,131 strikeouts—19 in one game—more than anyone except Nolan Ryan. (He's also second to Ryan in walks with 1,828.) He won four Cy Youngs, one of them unanimous.

He's the only man to win a Cy Young with a last-place team. That was in 1972, after he'd been swapped from the Cardinals. Steve was an amazing 27-10 with the Phils, who won only 32 without him that year. He was a Triple Crown winner—wins, ERA, and strikeouts (27, 1.97, 310). It earned him a record salary from the Phillies the following year—$167,000. Carlton took special delight during 1972 in whipping his old team, the Cards, who had refused to give him a raise after his 20-9 season helped them take second place in 1971. He beat the Birds four times, allowing a total of only two runs. One of the wins was his 100th. He also got his 300th victory over St. Louis Cardinals.

Steve had four more 20-win seasons as the Phillies moved from being "phutile" in the early 1970s to contenders, finally becoming world champions in 1980. He won two games in the 1980 World Series, including the Game 6 clincher.

Using a fastball, curve, and legendary slider, the 6-

foot-4-inch lefty was a workhorse, leading the NL in innings pitched five times. When he suffered a strained shoulder in 1985, he went on the disabled list for the first time in his career. Carlton was elected to the Hall of Fame in 1994.

GARY CARTER

Catcher, Mon (N) 1974-84,1992, NY (N) 1985-89, SF (N) 1990, LA(N) 1991

Widely regarded as the best catcher of the late 1970s and early 1980s, Gary Carter was also one of the era's most popular players. He was known for his ability to handle pitchers, his excellent throwing arm, and his clutch hitting. His career batting average is in the middling range, but his power stats are excellent: 324 career home runs, with a high of 32 in 1985; four seasons with over 100 RBIs, including a league-leading 106 in 1984.

In the strike-shortened 1981 season, Gary hit only .251 for the Expos but slugged .421 in the divisional series to help get them into the playoff and .438 there, as they lost to the Dodgers. In the 1986 World Series he hit two key home runs for the Mets in the third-game win and ignited the 10th-inning rally in Game 6 that culminated in Bill Buckner's fatal error.

The Mets made a blockbuster trade to acquire Carter from the Expos in order to help stabilize a young but very promising pitching staff. He is given much of the credit for the development of young Dwight Gooden into a star. Other pitchers who emerged under Carter's tutelage include David Cone, Sid Fernandez, and Randy Myers.

ALEXANDER JOY CARTWRIGHT

Pioneer

The first man to formulate baseball's rules, Cartwright may have "invented" baseball in 1845 when he organized the New York Knickerbockers, who played their first match game in Hoboken, N.J., on the June 19 the following year (and lost 23-1).

The Knicks were a company of volunteer firemen, and Cartwright a bank teller, when the historic marriage was made. It was a game for gentlemen, and Cartwright once fined a Knick sixpence for swearing. The rules for the "New York Game" included three strikes per out, and three outs per inning. But balls hit over the fence were fouls, a ball caught on one bounce was an out, and the first team to score 21 runs ("aces") was declared the winner. A committee later provided formally for nine-men teams, for nine innings to the game, and for 90 feet between bases.

Then he went west to California, where he found the '49ers in the big Gold Rush, spreading his new game, like Johnny Appleseed, at every village he stopped. He eventually reached Honolulu, where he found business success and became a respected civic leader. He died in 1892, but the publicity surrounding the Abner Doubleday legend with the foundation of the Hall of Fame at Cooperstown led to an investigation of Cartwright's role in the origin of the game. He was enshrined in the Hall in 1938.

BOB CARUTHERS

Pitcher, StL (AA) 1884-87, Bkn (AA) 1888-89, 1890-91, StL (N) 1892

Twice a 40-game winner, 138-pound Bob Caruthers retired with a 218-99 record for an amazing .688 percentage, the highest of any pitcher with a significant number of decisions. In a nine-year career Caruthers pitched for five championship teams and one runner-up. His only losing team was sixth place Brooklyn in 1891, but he was still 18-14.

As a 21-year-old rookie with the old St. Louis Browns, Bob led the American Association in wins, percentage, and ERA (40-13, .755, 2.07). The next year he was 30-14. In the postseason series against Cap Anson's NL White Stockings, he won a one-hit shutout over Jim McCormick. When he tried to come back the next day, he was blasted for 12 hits. But he won the sixth and final game, 4-3, over Hall of Famer John Clarkson in 10 innings. Parisian Bob—so named for his off-season trip to France—was 29-9 in 1887, as the Browns won their third straight flag.

After a 29-15 season with second-place Brooklyn, he had his best year in 1889, 40-11, as the Brooks won the AA pennant. As the rules governing pitching tightened and the number of balls needed for a base on balls fell, Caruthers' walks increased. His wins dropped to 23, then 18. After starting 1892 at 2-10 for St. Louis, he called it a career.

NORM CASH

First Baseman, Chi (A) 1958-59, Det (A) 1960-74

Cash hit .300 only once, and it was a big one—.361 in 1961, his second year as the Tigers' first baseman. He also slugged 41 home runs and knocked in 132.

The next year Cash fell 118 points to .263, a record fall for a batting champ. He never approached 100 RBIs again or hit higher than .283, but he remained a dangerous batter. He had more RBIs per official at bat than his roommate, Al Kaline, in part because Norm drew 1,043 walks. He finished with 1,046 runs scored, 1,103 RBIs, and 377 homers. Four times he cleared the roof at Tiger Stadium.

The popular and personable first sacker was somewhat immobile in the field, but he had sure hands and twice led AL first basemen in fielding. He hit .385 in the 1968 World Series to help the Tigers win in seven.

A good football player at Sul Ross State in Texas, Cash had been a 13th-round draft choice of the NFL Chicago Bears, but he chose to play baseball. He died in 1986 at the age of 51.

CESAR CEDENO

Outfielder, Hou (N) 1970-81, Cin (N) 1982-85, StL (N) 1985, LA (N) 1986

Leo Durocher once called Cedeno another Willie Mays. Then, in his third and fourth seasons, the young Dominican made the mistake of compiling back-to-back .320 years. From there on, he staggered through the remainder of his career under that back-breaking tonnage of potential. Cedeno might have come closer to imitating Mays if he'd played anywhere but Houston, where his long drives were outs. It didn't help that he got into only two postseason series with Houston and didn't do well in either.

For one brief period he was the player everyone predicted he'd be. In 1985 the Cardinals picked him up in late season. In 28 games, he hit .434 to help St. Louis to

the division title. Again he slumped in postseason play, hitting only .167 in the NLCS and .133 in the World Series.

His career totals of 2,087 hits for a .285 average, 976 RBIs, and 199 home runs would look a lot better if so much hadn't been expected of him. His 550 stolen bases put him in ninth place all-time when he retired, but more than a dozen players had passed him within a few years of his retirement.

ORLANDO CEPEDA

First Baseman, SF (N) 1958-66, StL (N) 1966-68, Atl (N) 1969-72, Oak (A) 1972, Bos (A) 1973, KC (A) 1974

Cepeda's first big league home run was also the first major league homer ever hit on the West Coast. It came in 1958 against Los Angeles. Orlando hit 24 more to win the Rookie of the Year and helped pull the Giants from sixth to third. He was only 20 years old. His father, Perucho, a shortstop, had been hailed as the greatest player in Puerto Rico. Orlando's first seven seasons gave rise to predictions that he would become the greatest Latin player. In those seven seasons, he topped .300 six times, had at least 96 RBIs each year, and totaled 222 home runs. His 46 homers and 142 RBIs led the NL in 1961. Despite his success in San Francisco, his stay was stormy as he fought managers and fans who tagged him as lazy.

A bad knee had begun to limit his play, and surgery in 1965 cost him most of the season. The Cards took a chance on him, and he was named Comeback of the Year in 1966 with 20 homers and 73 RBIs. The next year, as the Cardinals won the pennant, he was a unanimous choice for MVP. He hit a career high .325, with 25 home runs and a league-high 111 RBIs. Cepeda hit a disappointing .103 in the World Series.

Further knee problems pulled down the rest of his career, although he showed occasional flashes of his old power. His career totals of .297, 379 homers, and 1,365 RBIs put him in rarefied atmosphere. However, a 10-month prison sentence for marijuana possession following his retirement has thus far weighed more heavily with Cooperstown selectors.

HENRY CHADWICK

Pioneer

Having played cricket and rounders in his native England, Chadwick came to America with his family in 1837 at age 13. He first played baseball in 1847 and pronounced it a descendant of the earlier English games. When nearly a decade later he first saw games between skilled players, he recognized baseball's potential to become America's national game. His writings and influence helped make that potential a fact.

In the late 1850s, he began covering baseball games as a reporter for several newspapers, most notably the New York Clipper and the Brooklyn Eagle. In connection with this, he developed the box score and devised a system of scoring that is little changed today.

Chadwick continued to write and comment on baseball for more than 50 years. He originated the first guide, *Beadle's Dime Baseball Player*, in 1860, edited *DeWitt's Guide* through the 1870s and *Spalding's Base Ball Guide* from 1881 to 1908. His *The Game of Base Ball* (1868)

was the first hardcover book published on the subject.

Widely influential for his writings, he also had a direct influence in shaping the game by serving on various rules committees, beginning in 1858. He opposed gambling, drunkenness, and rowdiness among players, sometimes to no avail. Chadwick considered himself one of "the intelligent majority" who preferred scientific hitting over slugging and fielding prowess.

Among the honors he received during his lifetime were an honorary membership in the National League in 1894 (though the $600-a-year pension the league granted two years later had more practical value) and a medal awarded at the St. Louis World's Fair.

The "Father of Baseball," as he was called, died from pneumonia in 1908 after attending Opening Day in Brooklyn. Flags around the league flew at half-staff in his honor. In 1938 he was named to the Hall of Fame.

FRANK "HUSK" CHANCE

First Baseman, Chi (N) 1898-1912, NY (A) 1913-14. Manager, Chi (N) 1905-12, NY (A) 1913-14, Bos (A) 1923

Because of the popularity of F.P. Adams's poem bemoaning that his favorites, the Giants, were often victims of double plays by the Cubs' Tinker-to-Evers-to-Chance, there is a tendency to view the trio's election to Cooperstown in 1946 as some sort of P.R. fluke. In point of fact, a strong case can be made for Tinker's and Evers' enshrinements as players. Chance, however, had too short a career as a regular to rank with the game's foremost first basemen. Nevertheless he's the most deserving Hall of Famer of the three. He was called "The Peerless Leader" for good reason.

Chance never played in the minors. He broke in as a catcher before winning the first base job in 1903. By 1904 he was captain of the team, and in 1905 at age 27 he succeeded Frank Selee as manager.

As the Cubs manager he led the Chicago to glory in 1906-1910, when they won four flags in five years. They also won two World Series under Chance, which is two more than they've won since. In his first full year at the helm, the Cubbies won 116 games, a record that still stands, despite the fact that modern teams play more games. The Cubs averaged 106 wins in the five-year span. Of course, he had good players, but so did John McGraw in New York and Fred Clarke in Pittsburgh.

Even counting two seventh-place years with the New York Highlanders (1913-14) and one last-place finish with the Red Sox (1923), Frank's winning percentage of .593 is the sixth best ever.

And he wasn't a bad first baseman, big for his day and very powerful. He played only six full years. The victim of frequent beanings, Frank played his last full season in 1908. He hit .272 and slammed three hits against Christy Mathewson in the unforgettable playoff that gave the Cubs the flag. In the World Series victory over Detroit, he hit .421. He averaged .310 in Series play overall, and his 10 Series stolen bases are topped only by Eddie Collins and Lou Brock. His career batting average was a strong .296 during the most inert days of the Dead Ball Era. He usually batted cleanup, just another indication that he knew what to do with a good player when he had one.

A.B. "HAPPY" CHANDLER
Commissioner

The popular, outgoing Kentucky U.S. senator (and former governor) was a surprise choice to become commissioner of baseball in 1945, filling the office held by Judge Kenesaw Mountain Landis until his death in 1944. Chandler was the choice of the Yankees' Leland "Larry" MacPhail. Other candidates had included Ford Frick, Jim Farley, J. Edgar Hoover, and Tom Dewey.

As commissioner, Chandler proved well liked by fans, press, and even most players. Undoubtedly many of his decisions worked to the benefit of baseball. His downfall was that he made decisions when most baseball owners would have preferred a figurehead.

Early in his tenure, he was confronted with the decision of the Dodgers' Branch Rickey to sign Jackie Robinson and other black players. Chandler was already on record as favoring black entrance to the heretofore all-white major leagues. Over the objections of the other 15 owners, the commissioner stood behind Rickey, making baseball open to all.

Early in 1946 Chandler faced another crisis when 18 major league players jumped to the Mexican League for promises of higher salaries Chandler banned the players from major league baseball for five years. Many believe that this decision more than any other eventually led to his downfall as commissioner because it left baseball's reserve clause open to the courts. The player ban was lifted in 1950, and most of the players returned to their former clubs—some, such as pitcher Sal Maglie, to outstanding success. However, a suit filed by outfielder Danny Gardella shook baseball to its foundations.

One of Chandler's more controversial decisions was a suspension handed out to popular manager Leo Durocher for the 1947 season. The action was apparently precipitated by Durocher's being seen in the company of known gamblers. Chandler was criticized at the time for not taking action against some owners, including MacPhail, who also numbered gamblers among their acquaintances. His defense was that Durocher's suspension was the culmination of a long string of controversial incidents.

In 1951 Chandler received only nine of 16 owner votes for his re-election. A two-thirds endorsement was necessary. Chandler resigned and returned to Kentucky, where he was again elected governor. In 1982 he was named to the Baseball Hall of Fame.

RAY CHAPMAN
Shortstop, Cle (A) 1912-20

Chapman was the only major leaguer ever killed in a game. On Aug. 16, 1920, as his Indians fought toward their first pennant, he froze on a Carl Mays pitch. The ball fractured his skull and he died the next day. He was 29 years old.

At the time Chapman was the AL's leading shortstop. He had hit .300 in three of his last four seasons and was among the leaders each year in stolen bases. A clever hit-and-run man, he led in walks in 1918. In the field he had the best range in the league.

In the furor after his death, most "trick" pitches were banned, among them the spitball. Ironically Mays' pitch had been a fastball. More important, the leagues mandated more frequent disposal of discolored or bruised baseballs; this produced conditions that were safer—and ultimately more advantageous—for batters.

OSCAR CHARLESTON
Outfielder, Negro Leagues, 1915-50, Indianapolis ABCs, Lincoln Stars, Chicago American Giants, St. Louis Giants, Harrisburg Giants, Hilldale, Homestead Grays, Pittsburgh Crawfords, Toledo Crawfords, Indianapolis Crawfords, Philadelphia Stars, Brooklyn Brown Dodgers

Charleston is often cited as the greatest player of the Negro Leagues. Contemporaries lauded him as "the black Tris Speaker" for his center field play, "the black Ty Cobb" for his base running, and "the black Babe Ruth" for his hitting. While such analogies are useful in showing the range of Charleston's abilities, they have a counterfeit aura that is unfair to a unique performer. His combination of speed and strength places him among the foremost players, black or white, of all time. New York Giants' manager John McGraw said Charleston was the best player, period. Then he sighed: "If only I could calcimine him."

As a center fielder, Charleston was able to play unusually shallow because his great speed and judgment allowed him to get back for deep flyballs. He ranged far to his left and right, enabling the other outfielders to play closer to the foul lines. His arm has been reported as "weak", but all sources agree on its accuracy.

Charleston ran bases with speed (he was clocked at 23 seconds for the 220-yard dash) and savagery. He was quick-tempered and possessed legendary strength. Many who saw him remark on his "mean streak," indicating he preferred running over an opponent or spiking him than sliding around him to avoid a tag. On the other hand, some of the same observers indicate that Charleston picked his victims judiciously, always choosing those he knew he could physically bully.

He hit with great power and consistency. While statistics are incomplete, it is known that he batted .366 in the Negro National League in 1920 and followed that with .434 in 1921. He is unofficially credited with a lifetime league average of .353, and he batted .318 with 11 home runs in 53 barnstorming games against white major leaguers. He led the NNL in home runs several times, and many of his homers were of the tape-measure variety.

He started in 1915, became a player-manager in the late 1920s, and was active as a manager until his death in 1954. When Branch Rickey decided to break white baseball's color line, he had Charleston scout the Negro Leagues. Among his recommendations were Jackie Robinson and Roy Campanella. Charleston was elected to the Hall of Fame in 1976.

JACK CHESBRO
Pitcher, Pit (N) 1899-1902, NY (A) 1903-09, Bos (A) 1909

Until Ralph Branca threw the "Shot Heard 'Round the World" to Bobby Thomson in 1951, Chesbro was notorious for tossing the most infamous pitch in history. It was probably a spitter, and it definitely sailed over the head of New York Highlander catcher Red Kleinow, and, according to baseball lore, it absolutely cost New York the 1904 pennant.

It was the final day of the season at old Hilltop Park

(now the site of the Columbia Presbyterian Hospital). The Highlanders were a game and a half behind Boston but could have won the pennant by sweeping a doubleheader against the Red Sox (then called the Puritans). Chesbro pitched the first game for New York. The score was 1-1 with two outs in the Boston ninth. Boston's Lou Criger was on third and the count was 2-0. Then Chesbro threw the pitch. Jack, and later Mrs. Chesbro, always maintained that Kleinow should have caught the ball, but neither was a disinterested observer and there was no instant replay. New York won the second game of the doubleheader (though by then Boston couldn't have cared less).

The New York press elected Chesbro goat and never let him forget it. No one ever seemed to notice that the team could have won by rallying in its half of the ninth (or by scoring two more runs in any of the earlier innings). It was like pulling teeth to get anyone in New York to admit that the Highlanders wouldn't have had a sniff at the pennant had it not been for Chesbro. He'd earlier earned the nickname "Happy Jack" for his pleasant disposition while working in the state mental hospital in Middletown, N.Y. To smile after that pitch no doubt required steel facial muscles.

Ironically, up to that awful pitch the stocky right-hander was enjoying one of the best seasons of any pitcher in the 20th century: it would end up 41-12, with a 1.82 ERA. He started 51 games, completed 48, pitched 455 innings, and whiffed 239—still the Yankees record.

Chesbro won 21 and 28 with Pittsburgh in 1901-02, then jumped to New York. He won 21 in his first year there, but missed pitching in the 1903 World Series with the Pirates. He won 19 in 1905 and 23 in 1906, but people kept asking, "Yeah, but what about that pitch in 1904?"

Chesbro was named to the Hall of Fame in 1946 for what he did on all his other pitches.

EDDIE "KNUCKLES" CICOTTE
Pitcher, Det (A) 1905, Bos (A) 1908-12, Chi (A) 1912-20
Cicotte was a key conspirator in the infamous "Black Sox" scandal over the 1919 World Series. He tearfully confessed: "I did it for the wife and kiddies." Although neither he nor any of the other seven Soiled Sox were ever convicted of their misdeeds in a court of law—the evidence mysteriously disappeared before the trial—they were banned from baseball for life.

Until the revelations of the scandal, Cicotte was one of the AL's most successful pitchers, using trick pitches such as the knuckleball, shine ball, emery ball, and spitball. From 1908 through 1916, he won between 10 and 18 games each season. In 1917, when the Sox won the AL pennant, he was 28-12, leading the league in wins, innings pitched and ERA. After an off-year, he bounced back with his best season in 1919: he led in both wins and percentage with a 29-7 mark. In spite of Cicotte's success, White Sox owner Charles Comiskey paid him considerably less than several lesser pitchers in the league received. Apparently this left him open to entreaties by gamblers that he help throw the 1919 World Series to underdog Cincinnati.

He lost two Series games to the Reds, both under circumstances that appeared more suspicious when the fix conspiracy became public. That did not occur until near the end of the 1920 season, one in which Cicotte had a 21-10 record as one of four Sox pitchers with 20 wins.

After he was barred from baseball, Cicotte lived in Detroit, using a pseudonym to protect the family for whom he claimed to have entered the conspiracy. He died in 1969 at the age of 85.

FRED CLARKE
Outfielder, Lou (N) 1894-99, Pit (N) 1900-1915. Manager, Lou (N) 1897-99, Pit (N) 1900-15
Clarke was a sure-handed, speedy outfielder and an excellent hitter with surprising power for a 160-pounder. He hit .390 in 1897, one of 11 seasons in which he topped .300. He totaled 2,672 hits, scored 1,619 runs, drove in 1,015, batted .312, and stole 506 bases.

But he was an even better manager. He won four pennants at Pittsburgh and finished second five times. He came to Pittsburgh from Louisville in 1900 when the NL pared down from a dozen to eight teams. Honus Wagner, Tommy Leach, Deacon Phillippe, and Claude Ritchey were among the other former Louisville players who joined the Pirates. In his first year as Pirate skipper, 1900, Clarke and the other Louisville imports lifted the Pirates from seventh to the thick of the pennant fight—and they eventually finished second.

He brought the Buccos in first the next three years, 1901-1903. In 1903 he took them to the first World Series, losing to Boston only after eight hard-fought games.

In 1909 the Pirates won 110, a total exceeded only by the 1906 Cubs, the 1954 Indians, and the 1998 Yankees. In the World Series, Fred's three-run homer in the seventh inning of Game 5 broke open a 3-3 tie, as Pittsburgh went on to defeat Ty Cobb's Tigers. Clarke drove in seven runs in the Series.

He was elected to the Hall of Fame in 1951.

JOHN CLARKSON
Pitcher, Wor (N) 1882, Chi (N) 1884-87, Bos (N) 1890-92, Cle (N) 1892-94
One of the greatest pitchers of the 19th century, Clarkson combined a curve and cunning to win 327 games, but his manager in Chicago insisted that he "pitched on praise" and needed continuous ego boosting to be effective. If scolded, the handsome, high-strung right-hander would lose all confidence and sulk. The temperamental pitcher ended his years confined in an insane asylum.

Clarkson joined Chicago in 1884 and the next year led the NL in victories while compiling a 53-16 record. He won 36 in 1886 and 38 in 1887, again leading in victories in the latter year.

By the 1888 season Clarkson and outfielder/catcher King Kelly had been sold to Boston for $10,000 each, an incredible sum at that time. Clarkson justified the price by continuing his outstanding pitching, winning 33 in 1889, 49 in 1890 (when he also led the NL in winning percentage and ERA), 25 in 1891, and 33 in 1892.

Clarkson died of pneumonia in 1909 at the age of 47. In 1963 he was named to the Hall of Fame.

ROGER CLEMENS
Pitcher, 1984-96 Bos (A); Tor (A) 1997-
Clemens has been baseball's foremost power pitcher since Nolan Ryan retired. If he's lost anything off the fastball that earned him the nickname "Rocket" in the

1980s, he's more than made up for it in craftiness. In fact, since abandoning Boston for Toronto via free agency in 1997, he's enjoyed two of his best seasons to become the first pitcher to win five Cy Young Awards.

Clemens won his first Cy Young in 1986 with a spectacular 24-4 season that also earned him the American League's MVP trophy. He followed that by skipping training camp in a contract dispute, limping out of the gate at 4-6 by June, and then smashing through the league to finish 20-9 and earn his second Cy. Despite some shoulder problems, he put together a 21-6 season with a major-league low 1.93 ERA in 1990 yet did not win his third Cy Young until the next season when he had a lesser 18-10 mark.

He won only 50 games from 1993 through 1996 due to a combination of injuries and poor support. Feeling unappreciated by the Red Sox front office, he emigrated to Toronto and rejuvenated his career as well as his bank balance.

Twice Clemens has had major league record 20-strikeout games, and he continues to move up on the all-time "K" list, rocketing past 3,000 in 1998. He won 15 consecutive games to finish the '98 season en route to his second successive pitching Triple Crown.

ROBERTO CLEMENTE
Outfielder, Pit (N) 1955-72
The first Hispanic to be elected to the Hall of Fame and the second ballplayer to be honored on a U.S. stamp, Clemente won four batting titles.

A proud, even vain, man, Clemente was sensitive to prejudice against Latin players and quick to speak out against real or imagined slights. He believed he deserved more MVP Awards than the one that he won in 1966. Whether that was true or not, Roberto was handicapped by playing his entire career in Pittsburgh instead of New York or Los Angeles. Critics also pointed out that he missed many games and labeled him a hypochondriac. Clemente's physical ills were real, the worst being a chronic bad back stemming from a 1956 auto accident. He played in over 100 games in each of his 18 major league seasons, but the criticism remained.

Clemente finished with a .317 career batting average, an even 3,000 base hits, 1,416 runs scored, and 1,305 RBIs. Standing deep in the right-hand batter's box, he put all of his body into an all-or-nothing swing, but though he cracked 240 homers, he was not really a home run hitter. His forte was the line drive, often lashing pitches to the opposite field for extra-base hits.

His arm became legendary. He set the NL record by leading in assists five times. His season high was 27 in 1961. He won 12 straight Gold Gloves.

Roberto led the Pirates to two world championships, hitting .362 in the World Series. His great showcase was in 1971, when he hit .414 and played with an inspiring recklessness in leading the Pirates to a seven-game victory over the Baltimore Orioles. Only then did some of his severest critics admit his greatness.

He died in a plane crash on New Year's Eve, 1973, on a mercy flight carrying supplies to earthquake victims in Nicaragua. The usual five-year waiting period was waived, and Clemente was named to the Hall of Fame in 1973.

HARLOND CLIFT
Third Baseman, StL (A) 1934-43, Was (A) 1943-45
Clift was an outstanding player whose many talents were hidden by his St. Louis Browns teammates. It was difficult for fans in the 1930s to think of anyone with the laughing-stock Browns as a serious talent. Of course, the Browns' attendance was so low in the 1930s—in only two seasons did they draw over 200,000—that there were few in the stands to admire Clift or chuckle at his teammates.

An exceptional fielder, he was the first third baseman to start 50 double plays in a season. And while that record was in part due to a penchant that Brownies' pitchers had for putting runners on base, the rest of Clift's fielding stats support the idea that he had range and reliability beyond most AL third sackers.

He was certainly the most productive hitter among the league's third basemen. He hit .300 a couple of times, but his career batting average was an unexceptional .272. Yet he walked a lot, going over the 100 mark seven times in eight seasons. And he hit with more power than any third baseman ever had. In 1937 he set a record for third basemen with 29 homers. The next year he upped that to 34. In both years he drove in more than 100 runs.

TY COBB
Outfielder, Det (A) 1905-26, Phi (A) 1927-28.
Manager, Det (A) 1921-26
In 1936 Cobb was the first man elected to Cooperstown, mostly by voters who grew up in his era. Babe Ruth was second. The majority of today's critics would reverse the order and maybe drop Cobb a few more pegs besides. The reason, of course, is that the modern game, with its emphasis on home runs, has evolved in a Ruthian rather than a Cobbian direction.

After all these years, he's still first in batting average (.366), second in hits (4,189), fourth in steals (892), and first in runs scored (2,245). He collected 10 AL batting titles, hit over .400 three times, led in steals six times and in runs scored five. In other words, he was the best at the things he tried to be best at.

He was no home run hitter, managing only 118 in 24 seasons. But for most of those seasons, going for homers against the dead ball was a losing proposition. He did lead in slugging average eight times, proving he wasn't just a powder-puff hitter with extra puffs. The ball was invigorated during the last third of Cobb's career, but that was a little late to ask the old dog to learn a new trick. Still, in 1925 he hit three homers in one game, just showing off.

Admittedly, for all his heavy hitting his Tigers won only three pennants and no World Series. The fault, dear Brutus, was not in their star; it was on their pitcher's mound. Cobb was the best player of his time—or at least the first two-thirds of his time.

Considering all that, it's a bit disconcerting to find a few modernists working overtime to chisel Cobb down to a so-so level. Essentially, the argument is that modern players are bigger, faster, better trained, and face more difficult challenges. None of the old-timers could make it big today, they say. Cobb might hit .260.

One critic snickered at Cobb's batting stance; he held his hands apart and then choked up or swung from the end, according to the pitch. Tyrus, the critic insisted, would be tied up by Dwight Gooden or Nolan Ryan. The

critic apparently credits Cobb with the IQ of an ashtray. It would take him about half of one at bat to figure out what he had to do to adjust. Moreover, our "modern" Cobb would have the same advantages in diet, training, and baseball experiences the other moderns have. He'd be bigger, faster, and better trained. He might not hit .366—though we shouldn't bet against it—but he'd be right up there showing other moderns his heels.

Relative comparisons from one era to another work better when they have some statistical reality—like Bill Terry's .401 in 1930, when just about everybody else hit .300, being adjusted down (but we still leave him at the top for that year!). Given Cobb's situation, he excelled all others in batting average.

Now, if the critics want to stomp on Cobb, they can put their clodhoppers on his personality. "The Georgia Peach" was no peach. He was mean, vindictive, selfish, vain, a bully, a racist, paranoid, cruel, and hot-tempered. He spiked infielders just for the hell of it, fought—that is, physically attacked—anyone who crossed him, would do literally anything to be first in literally anything.

But it was just because of those nasty attributes that Cobb would have found a way to win in any age. The Cobb persona made him a great player, gave him a boatload of records, and put him into the Hall of Fame first. And when he died, three baseball people showed up at the funeral, probably only because they were expecting free eats afterward.

GORDON "MICKEY" COCHRANE
Catcher, Phi (A) 1925-33, Det (A) 1934-37.
Manager, Det (A) 1934-38
They used to argue who was the greatest catcher ever, Cochrane or Bill Dickey. Modern statistical techniques have moved Gabby Hartnett into the discussion. Josh Gibson has his backers. And later ages shout the praises of Yogi Berra and Johnny Bench. But the final cut usually comes down to "Cochrane or—."

When Mickey gets the edge, it's usually on "leadership," which is measured as easily as the distance to Oz. Nevertheless, Cochrane played on five AL pennant winners in a seven-year stretch, and that's at least tertiary evidence that he was officer material. As a matter of fact, he managed two of those teams (Detroit in 1934-1935) while taking his regular turn behind the plate.

If Mickey had a fault, it was that his fire burned too bright. He was such an intense, take-charge competitor that he used himself up some seasons. Connie Mack called him the biggest factor in the Athletics' three straight pennants (1929-1931), but there must have been times when nobody wanted to be in the same room with Cochrane.

He was considered an exceptional defender once he underwent intensive instruction from old pro Cy Perkins. So it shocked everyone when Pepper Martin, the "Wild Horse of the Osage," stole five bases on him in the 1931 World Series—"ran wild" is the way it's usually put. Most people blamed the Philadelphia pitchers.

Cochrane got high marks in his day for handling pitchers, and there's not much doubt that he did it well. Of course, having guys like Lefty Grove, George Earnshaw, and Tommy Bridges to work with gave him a leg up.

We can measure what he did at the plate better than what he did behind it. From the time Mack purchased his contract for $50,000 in 1925, through his sale to the Tigers for $100,000 in 1934, until a Bump Hadley pitch ended his career and nearly killed him in 1937, "Black Mike" averaged .320, the best career mark for any catcher. He had good speed for a catcher (64 stolen bases) and usually batted second. He scored 1,041 runs—four times over 100. He was a line drive hitter, but in 1932, when he drove in 112 runs, he also knocked 23 homers. He won Most Valuable Player Awards in 1928 and 1934, although neither year was his best with a bat. He was named to the Hall of Fame in 1947.

ROCCO "ROCKY" COLAVITO
Outfielder, Cle (A) 1955-59, 1965-67, Det (A) 1960-63, KC (A) 1964, Chi (A) 1967, LA (N) 1968, NY (A) 1968
Colavito hit with power—374 career homers, three seasons over 40—and threw like a cannon. He hit four home runs in a row in a 1959 game against Baltimore. And though he was as slow as a tax refund, he was sure-handed. He played in 234 straight games in 1964-1966 before anybody said "E, Colavito." He only led the league in assists once, but that was because runners knew enough not to challenge him. There ought to be a stat for runners who don't tag up and score on a fly; Rocky was responsible for a lot of those.

In 1959, when he led the AL in homers with 42, he was the most adored player in Cleveland, maybe the most popular person. So naturally, the Indians' brain trust traded him to Detroit for singles hitter Harvey Kuenn. And right then and there a lot of Cleveland baseball fans started looking for another kind of summer entertainment. Some of them haven't forgiven the Indians yet.

EDDIE "COCKY" COLLINS
Second Baseman, Phi (A) 1906-14, 1927-30, Chi (A) 1915-26. Manager, Chi (A) 1925-26
Photos of Collins in his prime show a wimpy-looking guy, thin but hippy, with come-fly-with-me ears, a generous nose, and a chin that barely clears his neck. He wasn't a hunk, but he was a real beauty at second base. For a quarter century, 1906-1930, Collins suited up for major league games, and for 19 of those years he was the regular at a position that lends itself to injuries. He was the pivot man in the A's "$100,000 Infield" that helped win four pennants from 1910 through 1914. Then he did the same job for the world champion White Sox of 1917 and the 1919 club, a hose of a different color.

Batting left-handed, he cracked out 3,310 hits for a .333 career batting average. He was a perfect leadoff or number two hitter, drawing five walks for every strikeout, but for much of his career he batted third, where his lack of home run power limited his RBIs. He ended with 1,299, which puts him behind a lot of sluggers. Once on base, though, he got around, scoring 1,819 runs, including seven seasons of 100-plus. He led the American League three years in a row (1912-14).

His 744 steals ranks sixth all-time. And he is the only man since 1900 to steal six bases in one game. He did it on Sept. 11, 1912. Eleven days later he did it again. He set the mark for most World Series steals, with 14, later tied by Brock. However, his stolen base percentage was only 65 percent.

No second baseman has accepted more chances than Collins, nor led the league in fielding as many times—nine. Connie Mack, who managed both Collins and Nap Lajoie, called Eddie the best second baseman he ever saw. Even so, Collins went into the Hall of Fame in 1939, two years after Lajoie.

JIMMY COLLINS
Third Baseman, Lou (N) 1895, Bos (N) 1895-1900, Bos (A) 1901-07, Phi (A) 1907-08. Manager, Bos (A) 1901-06

Back at the turn of the century, Collins revolutionized third base play. Before his time, most third sackers anchored themselves on the basepath. Collins was one of the first men to play in or back depending upon the situation. It allowed him to range over more ground than any other third baseman of his time.

As a brash rookie in 1895, he dared the greatest bunters of a bunting era—Keeler, McGraw, Jennings, Burkett, Hamilton—to test him. When they did, he charged in to bare-hand the ball and whip it to first, S.O.P. for third basemen now but a real marvel in his day.

In 1898 Jimmy played the hot corner on the Boston Beaneaters' great infield of Fred Tenney, Bobby Lowe, and Herman Long, which led Boston to the pennant. He hit .328 with a National League-leading 15 homers. His best year afield was 1900; he handled 601 putouts and assists, which is still the record.

In 1901 Collins jumped to the new Boston Americans, as player/manager, hit .332, and brought the club in second. In 1903 he led them to the pennant and that fall became the first manager to win a World Series. Collins' club had no chance to defend its honors against the NL in 1904; no Series was played that year, but his team won a second consecutive AL pennant. He was elected to the Hall of Fame in 1945, less than two years after his death.

EARLE COMBS
Outfielder, NY (A) 1924-35

Combs (it rhymes with "tombs") was the whippet-fast leadoff man for the Ruth-Gehrig Yankees. Possessing a warm and generous personality, he seemed unruffled that the sluggers got the spotlight; his job was to get on and get home. From 1925 through 1932 he scored at least 100 runs each season. In 1927, when the Babe hit 60 homers, Combs batted .356, scored 137 runs, and led the AL in hits (231) and triples (23). When Gehrig drove in 184 runs in 1931, Combs scored 120. The next year he touched home 143 times. He had a career batting average of .325, led the AL three times in three-base hits, and scored 1,186 runs.

He was at his best in three World Series (1926, 1927, and 1932), hitting a cumulative .350 and scoring 17 runs in 15 games. A broken finger limited him to a single pinch-hitting appearance in the 1928 Series; he drove in a run in the final-game win with a sacrifice fly.

His arm didn't intimidate anyone. Speed was his trademark in center field. He used it well, leading AL outfielders in putouts a couple times. He suffered a fractured skull when he crashed into an outfield fence in 1934 and retired after one more year. He was named to the Hall of Fame in 1970.

CHARLES COMISKEY
First Baseman, StL (AA) 1882-89, 1891, Chi (P) 1890, Cin (N) 1892-94. Manager, StL (AA) 1883-89, Chi (P) 1890, StL (AA) 1891, Cin (N) 1892-94

Comiskey helped Ban Johnson create the American League and was one of its strongest voices until his death in 1931. He founded the White Sox and owned the AL team for its first 31 years. He gave Chicago two world champions, four pennants, and the ballpark that bears his name. He was called the "Old Roman" because of his handsome, John Barrymore profile, and wavy, silver hair.

He was also, to put it charitably, a cheapskate. An example of Comiskey's miserliness: pitcher Dickie Kerr, one of the honest Sox in the 1919 World Series, won twice against the Reds and half his own team, then won 21 in 1920 and 19 in 1921. Comiskey paid him $4,500 and refused to give him a raise. Kerr quit. He could make $5,000 playing semipro!

The fact that Comiskey severely underpaid some of his greatest players coolie wages has been used by some revisionist historians to justify the action of the eight Black Sox players in selling the 1919 World Series down the river. Whether Commie "deserved" what he got, America's baseball fans didn't.

Before owning the White Sox, Comiskey played first base for the old St. Louis Browns of the American Association. He wasn't much as a hitter—lifetime .264—but he's credited with revolutionizing the position by letting the pitcher cover on grounders wide of the bag. As captain and manager, beginning at age 25, he pioneered moving his fielders around for different hitters. He led the Browns to four straight AA flags, 1885-1888.

Some have found it curious that Comiskey could treat his White Sox players like indentured servants yet was one of the players who supported the Players League in 1890. Comiskey died in 1931 at the age of 72. He was elected to the Hall of Fame in 1939.

DAVEY CONCEPCION
Shortstop, Cin (N) 1970-88

Among major league shortstops from Venezuela, Concepcion ranks second in reputation only to Luis Aparicio. Luis may have had a little more range at his best, but, playing on AstroTurf, Concepcion popularized the technique of bouncing long throws from the hole to first to get runners who would have beaten high-arc tosses. With career batting averages in the .260s, neither set any hitting records. Davey had more power—he surprised with 16 homers in 1979—but Luis stole a couple hundred more bases.

Although Concepcion topped .300 only twice (and never in a championship year), he got hot in the October playoffs and Series. He averaged over .400 in the 1975 and 1979 playoffs and over .300 in the 1970, 1972, and 1976 World Series. In the 1975 classic, Concepcion came up in the ninth inning of Game 2 with the Reds losing 2-1, two out, and Johnny Bench on second. He slapped a single to tie the score, stole second, and scored on Ken Griffey's double to win the game.

JOHN "JOCKO" CONLAN
Umpire, AL 1941-1964

A long-time minor league outfielder with two brief shots

at the White Sox, Conlan got into umpiring by accident in 1935 in Chicago. One of the regular umpires was overcome by the heat. Jocko, who was on the bench, was rushed in to pinch-ump and did well.

In Conlan's first year as a real umpire, 1941, he ejected 26 men. His favorite target was Leo Durocher. He gradually mellowed, learned to use psychology and snappy retorts instead of his thumb to keep order. His trademarks were a polka-dot bow tie and a quick grin.

He spent 27 seasons as an NL umpire, worked six World Series, six All-Star Games, and four pennant-deciding playoffs. In 1974, he was elected to the Hall of Fame.

TOM CONNOLLY
Umpire, NL 1898-1900, AL 1901-1931

Connolly was born in England and came to the U.S. with his family at age 15 in 1885. Enamored of baseball, he studied the rule book assiduously and became an NL umpire in 1898. He quit in 1900 because the weak league president wouldn't support his rulings. Hired by the AL, he umpired the first league game, Chicago and Cleveland, on April 24, 1901. He was also chosen to umpire the first World Series in 1903.

In those days umpires worked alone, one to a game (two in the Series), and took the taunts of both players and fans. Connally once rowed out of Boston at midnight under threat from irate fans. Pitcher Joe McGinnity reportedly spit in his face, was fined and suspended, and jumped to the NL. But even the irascible Ty Cobb learned to back off when Tom's neck turned red. Eventually, Connolly was able to go 10 years straight without ejecting a dissenter.

After 33 years behind the mask, Connolly became chief of AL umpires for 23 more, calling it quits in 1954 at the age of 83. He lived to be 91. In 1953, he was named to the Hall of Fame along with Bill Klem, the first two umpires so honored.

ROGER CONNOR
First Baseman, Tro (N) 1880-82, NY (N) 1883-89, 1891, 1893-94, NY (P) 1890, Phi (N) 1892, StL (N) 1894-97. Manager, StL (N) 1896

Whose career home run record did Babe Ruth break? Connor's, of course. Roger hit 137 (some sources say 132) of the old dead balls for four bases. The mark stood until 1921, when Babe broke it on his way to 59.

Oddly, Connor only once led his league in homers (13 in the 1890 Players League), but he got as high as 17 in 1887. Triples were his specialty—he was tops in that department twice, in double figures 12 times, and cracked a personal high of 25 in 1894. He hit 233 altogether, and only four men have topped that mark.

At 6-foot-2-inches and 210 pounds, Connor was a big man for his day. He was one of the men New York manager Jim Mutrie meant when he called his team "Giants. In 1888 and 1889, Connor helped the Giants to two pennants. Connor died in 1931 at the age of 73. He was named to the Hall of Fame in 1976.

WALKER COOPER
Catcher, StL (N) 1940-45, 1956-57, NY (N) 1946-49, Cin (N) 1949-50, Bos (N) 1950-52, Mil (N) 1953, Pit (N)

1954, Chi (N) 1954-55

Lon Warneke, who pitched to him and against him and umpired behind him, called Cooper a better catcher than Bill Dickey or Gabby Hartnett. The 6-foot-3-inch "Coop" gave the Cardinals, Giants, Braves, and nearly every other team in the NL solid catching for years and years. He hit .300 several times and ended with a .285 career average. In three World Series, he averaged .300. When he got too old to do the job behind the plate, he remained an effective pinch hitter.

The Giants wanted him so badly in 1946 they paid the Cardinals $175,000 for him while he was still in the Navy. In 1947 he hit 35 home runs for New York, but that was uncharacteristic. His next highest season total was 20. He wasn't Dickey or Hartnett, but he was a darn sight better than most.

STAN COVELESKI
Pitcher, Phi (A) 1912, Cle (A) 1916-24, Was (A) 1925-27, NY (A) 1928

Baseball got Coveleski out of the Pennsylvania coal mines (five cents an hour, 72 hours a week). "I only saw the sun on Sundays," he cracked. "I would have been great in night baseball." And the spitter got him into the majors with Cleveland in 1916 at the age of 27. In his first year, the introverted right-hander was 15-13 with a sixth-place club. Over the next few years, the Indians moved up in the standings. Coveleski followed a 19-win sophomore season with four straight 20-plus-win years (22, 24, 24, and 23). In 1920, when the Indians won the pennant, Jim Bagby led the staff with 31 wins to Coveleski's 24. But in the World Series against Brooklyn, Coveleski ran up the best performance since Christy Mathewson's three shutouts in the 1905 classic, winning 3-1, 5-1, and 3-0 for an 0.67 ERA.

Only of average build, Covie was a workhorse, three times hurling 300 innings. One reason was the spitter, which is easy on arms. The other was Stan's philosophy: let them hit the first pitch. They seldom hit it far. Stan allowed only one home run per 46 innings, even in tiny League Park with its 290-foot right field fence. He had superb control of the spitter. Supposedly, he once went seven straight innings without throwing a called ball.

After Covie won 23 in 1921, Cleveland slipped in the standings and his victory totals declined. He led the AL in ERA in 1923 but won only 13. Traded to Washington in 1925, he responded with another league-leading ERA and a 20-5 record, as the Senators won the pennant. He'd lost his World Series magic, however, and lost twice to the world champion Pirates.

Stan's older brother Harry was known as the "Giant Killer" when, as a rookie with the Phils in 1908, he beat the Giants three times down the stretch. More than Fred Merkle's "boner," Harry's efforts knocked New York out of pennant contention.

Stan Coveleski was named to the Hall of Fame in 1969. He died in 1984 at the age of 94.

CLIFFORD "GAVVY" CRAVATH
Outfielder, Bos (A) 1908, Chi (A) 1909, Was (A) 1909, Phi (N) 1912-20. Manager, Phi (N) 1919-20

Born a generation too soon, Cravath was the home run king in the years immediately preceding the Babe Ruth

Revolution. In a seven-year span—1913-1919—the Phillies' outfielder led the NL in homers five times and tied once. A short right field target in Philadelphia's Baker Bowl helped quite a bit, but Gavvy, a right-handed batter deserves credit for knowing what to do with it.

He flunked two earlier trials in the AL and didn't get to the Phillies until 1912, when he was 31. A genial practical joker, he kept his teammates loose with his jokes and pitchers up tight with his bat. In 1915 he helped Philadelphia to a pennant with a league-high 115 RBIs and a then-20th-century record of 24 homers.

SAM CRAWFORD
Outfielder, Cin (N) 1899-1902, Det (A) 1903-17
"Wahoo Sam" (he was born in Wahoo, Neb.), played right field beside Ty Cobb on the Tigers, hit behind him—and once even pinch hit for him; however, he was overshadowed by him, much as Lou Gehrig was overshadowed by Babe Ruth.

Cobb disliked Crawford. Supposedly Tyrus Rex was convinced the modest right fielder was jealous of his accomplishments. More likely he resented Crawford for already being a star when Cobb arrived in Detroit. Another possibility was that Cobb envied Crawford for being both a great player and a likable person.

Nevertheless, Cobb campaigned for years to get Crawford into the Hall of Fame. It was an uncharacteristic act on Cobb's part, but Crawford shouldn't have needed any campaign. He was elected to the Hall of Fame in 1957 and deservedly so.

Sam was the greatest triples hitter in history, with 309 to Ty's 297. Only two contemporaries, Honus Wagner and Tris Speaker, were even over 200, and no modern player has hit half as many. Crawford lashed 26 of them in 1914 for an AL record (tied by Joe Jackson), and led the league six times. It's a given, today, to assume that Crawford would have hit tons of home runs with a livelier ball. He did lead the NL in homers with 16 in 1901 and the AL with seven in 1908, but mostly he hit screaming line drives that might have bounced off (or punctured) modern fences.

Sam had six with 100 RBIs or more and led the American League three times in that category. Many of Cobb's record 2,245 runs scored were batted in by Sam.

He left the majors after 1917, just 39 hits shy of 3,000. The figure was no big deal then, or he might have hung around and picked them up. Two years later he still hit .360 in the Pacific Coast League.

JOE CRONIN
Shortstop/Manager, Pit (N) 1926-27, Was (A) 1928-34, Bos (A) 1935-45
Cronin spent 50 years in baseball, rising from All-Star shortstop to pennant-winning manager, to general manager, and finally to AL president. He was even nominated for commissioner. Horatio Alger should have written his bio.

Born in San Francisco just after the 1906 earthquake, Joe joined the Washington Senators in 1928 and was a full-fledged star by 1930, when he hit .346 and drove in 126. He was the AL's MVP. In all, he had eight seasons with over 100 RBIs, 10 full seasons over .300, and 170 homers. Only seven shortstops have ever scored 100 runs

and batted in 100 in the same season. Honus Wagner did it three times, Cronin four. He sure didn't hit like a shortstop. He didn't field like one either, at least not like the best.

In 1933, a near-beardless youth of 26, he was named manager of the Senators. Darned if he didn't win the pennant that year, and no Senators manager ever won another. The next year he married the boss' niece in September. And in October the boss sold him to the Red Sox for $225,000.

He continued as player/manager for the Bosox, although he mainly pinch hit after 1941. In 1943 he pinch hit five homers, an AL record. In 1946, after he'd become strictly a bench manager, his Red Sox won the pennant. Two years later he moved upstairs to become the Boston general manager, and in 1959 he was elected AL president serving until 1973. He was the AL's chairman of the board until his death in 1984.

A hearty, affable man, modest to a fault, Cronin was a great player, an adequate manager (albeit with a tendency to chew up his pitching staff), and a popular executive. He was named to the Hall of Fame in 1956.

ARTHUR "CANDY" CUMMINGS
Pitcher, NY (NA) 1872, Bal (NA) 1873, Phi (NA) 1874, Hartford (NA) 1875, Hartford (NL) 1876, Cin (NL) 1877
Cummings was elected to the Hall of Fame in 1939 as the inventor of the curveball, and historians have been perplexed ever since. Well, he said he came up with the curve in 1866 after seeing a spinning clamshell curve as it was skipped across the water. Clamshell spinning and curveball tossing are unrelated throwing techniques, but let that pass. Cummings apparently used his clam-curve against Harvard the next year, and the scholars were baffled. So was President Andrew Johnson, another early observer. (Johnson was baffled by just about everything while he was in the White House.)

Cummings was a pitcher for the Excelsiors of Brooklyn when the revolutionary discovery was made. Back then pitchers had to throw underhand with both feet on the ground, but they were only 45 feet away from the batter. Cummings discovered that he could make the ball curve with the wind in his face but not with it at his back.

Anyway, the curve brought Cummings success, and in 1870 Henry Chadwick, the most knowledgeable authority of the day, said that he was the best pitcher in the land. Chadwick sometimes agreed with Cummings's clam-curve-creation claims, but at other times talked about seeing curves in the 1850s.

Between 1872 and 1875, Cummings won 124 games in the National Association, the league that preceded the NL. He also picked up his nickname—"candy" meant "best" in 19th-century slang. But he was just a little wisp of a thing, barely 120 pounds, and the overwork caught up with him. By 1878 he was done.

Many others disputed Cummings's claim to being the first curveball pitcher. Among them were Alphonse Martin, Bobby Mathews, Fred Goldsmith, and Joseph Mann. Most likely it was invented independently by many different pitchers over a couple of decades.

HAZEN "KIKI" CUYLER
Outfielder, Pit (N) 1921-27, Chi (N) 1928-35, Cin (N)

1935-37, Bkn (N) 1938
Cuyler broke in with Pittsburgh in 1924, hitting .354, and he was hailed as "another Cobb." The next year he made the prophets look good as he hit .357, with 17 homers, 26 triples, and 45 doubles. He drove in 102 runs and scored 144. He even stole 41 bases. In one span, he had 10 consecutive hits. The Pirates won the pennant. That October, Cuyler homered to win the second Series game against Washington. He came up in the seventh game with the bases loaded against Walter Johnson, crossed himself, and doubled in two for the victory.

After a .321 season in 1926, when he led the NL in runs scored and stolen bases, he ran into l'affaire de Bush in 1927. Manager Donie Bush wanted Cuyler to bat second (which was a little strange because Cuyler was the best home run threat on the club). Kiki was superstitious about the slot, insisting he couldn't and wouldn't hit second. Bush benched Cuyler, accused him of not hustling, and put a lesser player in Cuyler's position. The Pirates still won the pennant but lost the Series four straight. Around Pittsburgh there are fans to this day who'll swear the Bucs, with Cuyler, would have wiped up those 1927 Yankees. After the season, Cuyler was shipped to the Cubs for no one very useful. The Pirates took 33 years to win another pennant.

Meanwhile, Cuyler hit .360 for the pennant-winning Cubs in 1929. In 1930 he slumped all the way to .355. But he had 228 hits, 155 runs scored, and 134 RBIs. In all, he had 10 seasons of .300 or better. He was still around in 1932 to hit a solid .291 when the Cubs won again.

He never became "another Cobb" but, except for that silliness about batting second, it's hard to fault him. He ended with a .321 batting average, scored 1,305 runs, batted in 1,065. He hit line drives, so his homer total was a modest 127, but he had 394 doubles and 157 triples. He led the league in stolen bases four times, used his speed well in the outfield, and had a good arm. He was quiet, never drank or smoked, and only Donie Bush ever accused him of malingering. He was named to the Hall of Fame in 1968.

Some people want to pronounce his nickname "Kee-Kee," as if he was a belly dancer. Actually he got it when other outfielders called for him to take fly balls: "Cuy! Cuy!"

RAY DANDRIDGE
Third Baseman, Negro Leagues, 1933-48, Detroit Stars, Newark Dodgers, Newark Eagles, New York Cubans
Dandridge, old-timers from the Negro Leagues say, could field like Brooks Robinson and hit like Pie Traynor and George Kell. Even allowing for hyperbole, Dandridge was a terrific third baseman—perhaps the best never to play in the white major leagues.

Ray was so bowlegged that "You could drive a freight train through there," Monte Irvin says, "but not a baseball." He was a marvelous fielder, cat-quick, with a powerful arm. Not a power hitter, Dandridge concentrated on hitting the ball where it was pitched. He hit .347 against white big league pitching in barnstorming exhibitions. His best mark in the Negro National League was .370 in 1944.

Much of Ray's career was spent in the Mexican League and in the Cuban winter league. He spurned an offer from Cleveland in 1948 because it didn't carry a bonus. The next year he signed with the New York Giants, who sent him to the Minneapolis Millers of the American Association. He said he was 29; in actuality, he was past 36.

He was AA Rookie of the Year in '49 and the league's MVP the next year when he hit .311 for the champion Millers. The Giants brought other players with lesser records to the majors but—perhaps because of his age—kept Dandridge in the minors, a great disappointment to him. He retired after the 1955 season. In 1987 he was named to the Baseball Hall of Fame.

GEORGE DAVIS
Shortstop, 1890-92 Cle (N); 1893-1901, 1903 NY (N); 1902, 1904-09 Chi (A)
For years baseball historians bemoaned Davis' omission from the Baseball Hall of Fame. Some called him the best player from the Dead Ball Era without a plaque in Cooperstown. Enough of a ruckus was raised that Davis' name became better known among fans with an eye for history than some of the players from that bygone era already in the Hall. Finally, in 1998, the baseball world cheered when Davis was elected. As the event took place 58 years after his death, he had no comment on his tardy admission. But the way these things go, it may be another 58 years before anyone says anything interesting about Davis. The unfortunate tendency seems to be that once the candidate is elected, he is often forgotten in the wake of a campaign for the next overlooked hero.

Forgetting Davis would be a shame. After all, he batted at least .300 for nine consecutive seasons in a career split mostly between the New York Giants and Chicago White Sox, and at one time held the consecutive game hitting streak with 33 games. That would be first-rate hitting for an outfielder, but Davis was a smooth-fielding shortstop. His 2,660 career hits packed a punch, giving him 1,437 RBI and 1,539 runs scored. By 1906, his 17th season, his batting fell off, but he remained the best hitter on the famous "Hitless Wonder" White Sox that upset the Cubs in the 1906 World Series.

ANDRE DAWSON
Outfielder, Mon (N) 1976-86, Chi (N) 1987-92, Bos (A) 1993-94, Fla (N) 1995-96
Rookie of the Year in 1977, Dawson played 10 full seasons in Montreal. He earned a reputation as an excellent fielder and dangerous hitter. In the early 1980s major league players voted him the best all-around player in the NL. He also earned bad knees and several operations on Olympic Stadium's artificial surface.

When he became a free agent in 1987, he sought out the Chicago Cubs, signed a blank contract, and told them to fill in the figure. Despite his uncertain knees, he could have signed with other teams for considerably more money. But Wrigley Field had real grass, reachable walls, and Dawson had hit .346 in Chicago over the preceding 10 years. The Cubs acquired a bargain. Dawson hit only .287, but smashed 49 homers and drove in 137 runs, both NL highs in '87. He was voted the league MVP and signed a new (much more lucrative) contract for 1988.

After he left the "Friendly Confines" of Wrigley in 1992, Dawson was a part-time player on real grass fields in Boston and Florida. He finished his prodigious career

with 2,774 hits, 438 home runs, 1,591 RBIs, and 314 steals.

LEON DAY
Pitcher, Negro Leagues, 1934-50, Bacharach Giants, Brooklyn Eagles, Newark Eagles, Baltimore Elite Giants
The five-seven 140-pound Day was an all-around performer who pitched and played second base and center field. Although many statistics are missing, it is known that he hit over .300 in nearly every season. But his fame rests on his pitching. Day holds the Negro League record with 18 strikeouts in one game in 1940—one of his victims was Roy Campanella (who fanned three times). Day won three of four games he pitched against the legendary Satchel Paige, including victories in the East-West (All-Star) Game and the 1942 Negro World Series.

Day's career was interrupted by World War II service in Europe. In 1945 he defeated Ewell Blackwell for the European Service Championship before 50,000 G.I.'s in Nuremberg. In his first game back home in 1946, he tossed a no-hit game with 17 strikeouts.

He died a week after he was elected to the Hall of Fame in 1995.

JAY HANNA "DIZZY" DEAN
Pitcher, StL (N) 1930-37, Chi (N) 1938-41, StL (A) 1947
After winning 20 games for the 1933 Cardinals, Dizzy was joined on the St. Louis staff by his younger brother. "Me and Paul will probably win 40 games," Dizzy predicted for 1934. He was wrong. They won 49, with Diz winning 30 to lead the Cards to the pennant. "It ain't braggin' if yuh can do it," explained Diz. In the World Series, each brother won two games. Always the headline maker, Dizzy broke up a double play while pinch running in Game 4 by blocking the relay with his forehead. It was feared he might be lost for the remainder of the Series until the next day's headline reported: X-RAY OF DEAN'S HEAD REVEALS NOTHING. At least, that's the way they tell the story, and if it isn't true, it should be.

Dizzy clowned, bragged, and pitched his way to immortality. Even his marvelous work on the mound was sometimes overshadowed by colorful "Dean stories." Supposedly, one day he was interviewed by three different reporters, one after the other. He told each a new "story of Dizzy's life" with different birthdates, birthplaces, and even gave himself three different Christian names. "All those felluhs wanted a exclusive," he explained.

In 1935 Dean won 28 and followed with 24 in 1936. He was in the midst of another fine year in 1937 when a line drive off Earl Averill's bat in the All-Star Game broke his toe. He tried to come back too soon, altered his motion to favor the toe, and ruined his arm. He was 26 and had won 134 games.

Traded to the Cubs in 1938, he used a "nuffin' ball" to sore-arm his way to a 7-1 record for the pennant winners. In a courageous World Series appearance, he held the mighty Yankees at bay for seven innings before the roof fell in. It was his last hurrah.

After retiring, Diz became a colorful national play-by-play announcer who enriched the English language with exciting new grammar, such as "He slud into third." Brief though his career was, it was so brilliant at its height and Dean brought so much more to baseball than his pitching

talent, that he was elected to the Hall of Fame in 1953.

ED DELAHANTY
Outfielder, Phi (N) 1888-89, 1891-01, Cle (P) 1890, Was (A) 1902-03
The Phillies had the trio of Delahanty, Billy Hamilton, and Sam Thompson in the same outfield from 1891 to 1895. They all were magnificent hitters and all three are in the Hall of Fame. Did the Phillies destroy the rest of the league? They did not; they finished fourth four times and third in 1895. Makes you wonder about the rest of the team, doesn't it?

"Big Ed" Delahanty weighed only about 170 pounds, but he went up a couple tons when he had a bat in his hands. His lifetime .346 is the fourth-best of all time. From 1894 to 1896, he hit .407, .404, and .397. That .407 was only fourth-best in the league, and it was a period of high batting averages.

Oldest of four ball-playing brothers, Ed hit with power and speed; his 19 homers in 1893 was one of the highest totals of the 19th century. In 1896 he became the second man to hit four home runs in one game.

A notorious bad-ball hitter, Ed "often" stepped across the plate to smash a fat pitch, according to legend. And try this one. He once reputedly knocked a baseball in half. They sure don't build 'em the way they used to!

Tall tales aside, Delahanty was a magnificent hitter who went into the Hall of Fame in 1945. Unfortunately, he was also a drunk. Beset by drinking, debts, and divorce, he was suspended by Washington in the summer of 1903. He caught a train from Chicago for New York, got boisterously loaded, and was kicked off the team train at Niagara Falls. Still drunk, he staggered onto a bridge, fell into the river, and was swept over the falls. He was 35.

BILL DICKEY
Catcher, NY (A) 1928-43, 1946. Manager, NY (A) 1946
Dickey's reputation appears to have slipped of late, but it's a trick of perception. He was a great catcher, but there have been several great catchers since, and new statistical techniques indicate some of Dickey's contemporaries (and some of those who followed) may have been better than anyone realized at the time. So the question that used to be so popular—who's the greatest catcher, Dickey or Mickey (Cochrane)?—has a few more multiple choices.

Then, too, there's the out-of-sight, out-of-mind philosophy. Dickey caught his last game in 1946. The people who watched him half a century ago figured they were looking at something special in catchers. They could cite several facts to prove their eyes weren't playing tricks.

Dickey caught 100 games or more for 13 straight years, a record. His .362 batting average in 1936 was a record for a catcher. He had a career average of .313, with 202 home runs and 1,209 RBIs. He was on 11 AL All-Star teams, and the first game wasn't played until his fifth year as a regular. He played in eight World Series, hit five homers, and his 24 World Series RBIs are the eighth-highest total ever. Dickey knew how to make 'em count. He had several clutch World Series hits. His ninth-inning single won the Opening Game in 1939. And his two-run homer won the Game 5 in 1943.

Defensive prowess is hard to prove—next to impossible with a catcher—but Dickey got raves when he played

and was called in later to show Yogi Berra the way to do it.

Dickey wasn't the rah-rah type. He led quietly, but the point is, he led. One day in 1932 he took exception to the way a runner slid in at home, so he flattened the guy and broke his jaw. It was out of character for Dickey and got him fined and suspended, but it probably made the next fellow sliding home against the Yankees think twice about how he did it.

If there's an argument against him, it's that Dickey played on so many winning teams that he was bound to look good. How's that for a Catch-22? It's kind of like the Yogi-ism that "Nobody goes there 'cause it's too crowded." Would the Yankees have been good with another catcher? Sure. Would they have been as good? Hah!

Dickey was named to the Hall of Fame in 1954.

MARTIN DIHIGO

Pitcher/Outfielder, Negro Leagues, 1923-45, Cuban Stars (East), New York Cubans, Homestead Grays, Hilldale, Darby Daisies

Dihigo was one of the most versatile athletes in the history of baseball. In a career that lasted from 1923 to 1950, he starred as a pitcher, as a hitter, as an outfielder, and occasionally as an infielder.

As a pitcher, counting several seasons in Mexico, Venezuela, and the Dominican Republic, Dihigo was 256-136. His stock in trade was a blazing fastball.

As a batter, he hit over .400 three times in Cuba and the States. He led the Eastern Colored League in homers in 1926 and the American Negro League in batting with .386 in 1929. Reportedly, his longest home run came in Pittsburgh in 1936, a 500-foot shot that landed on a hospital roof.

In the outfield, he had exceptional range, and his throwing arm was claimed to be among the best ever. Supposedly, a contest was once held in Cuba wherein a jai alai player, using his basket-like cesto, slung a ball from home plate against the center field wall on one bounce. Dihigo threw the ball over the wall.

As a manager, he led the New York Cubans to the Negro National League playoff in 1935 and starred both on the mound and at the plate.

Dihigo was a big man (6 feet 3 inches, 220 pounds), but he was amazingly agile. Friendly, extremely popular, and with a great sense of humor, in 1977 he became the first Cuban ever to be elected to the Baseball Hall of Fame.

DOM DIMAGGIO

Outfielder, Bos (A) 1940-42, 1946-53

Red Sox fans used to sing: "He's better than his brother Joe—Dominick DiMaaaggiiiooooh!" Well, he wasn't. Dom was 5 feet 9 inches, 168 pounds, about 90 percent Joe's size and he was about 90 percent the player Joe was. But 90 percent of Joe DiMaggio is better than 100 percent of most of the guys who've ever drawn major league salaries. Dom wore glasses and because not very many players wore them he was called "The Little Professor," which is a better moniker than "Joe's Kid Brother."

Okay, comparisons are inevitable. Dom didn't have Joe's home run power; he was in double figures for homers only twice (in Fenway!) in his career. Nor did he hit as often; Joe's .325 is 27 points better than Dom's .298. But Dom was a leadoff man, and he did that very well. He led

the AL in runs scored in 1950 and '51. He was more likely to walk than Joe, pulling his .380 OBA to within 14 points of his big brother's. Surprisingly, Dom was more likely to strike out than Joe. He had 571 strikeouts (to Joe's 369) in a lot fewer at bats.

They were both good center fielders. We can give Dom an edge there. He led AL center fielders in chances per game three times when one of the other AL center fielders was Joe. Some would argue that Dom got less help from his left and right fielders and had to accept more chances. The point is, he did it.

In the final game of the 1946 World Series, Dom twisted an ankle while tying the game with a double in the top of the eighth. Enos Slaughter made his famous dash all the way home from first in the bottom of the inning to win the game, but said later he wouldn't have tried it if Dom had still been in center.

JOE DIMAGGIO

Outfielder, NY (A) 1936-42, 1946-51

Jolting Joe, the "Yankee Clipper," sold coffee makers, married Marilyn Monroe, hit in 56 straight games, and was voted baseball's "Greatest Living Player".

Revisionists blame the New York media for the DiMaggio mystique. Like everyone outside the Big Apple thought he was just another ballplayer! Actually, in some cities around the AL where Yankee-hating was a religious test, DiMag received a special dispensation. Fans who would have kicked Tommy Henrich's dog still cheered for DiMaggio.

The revisionists miss the point. Declaring anyone the "greatest" anything may be pretty silly, but when it's done it comes from the heart, not from the stats. DiMaggio warmed more baseball fans' chests than hot-dog heartburn. He was adored, idealized, lionized. The symbol.

As a symbol, he was handsome, quiet, a little aloof. They would have called him a Greek god but he was an Italian. Even that worked because he was a symbol for loyal Italian-Americans at a time when Mussolini's fascists stood for a lot of nasty things.

And did he ever look good on the field! Graceful out there in center, he wasn't slow but it always seemed as if the film had been slowed down a bit so you could catch the nuances. At the plate, he stood with his feet planted wide apart and his bat ready but straight-up, motionless. And when you saw him swing, you never forgot it—no matter where the ball went.

Joe's stats were terrific, maybe not the best ever, but close enough to support the emotions of his fans. He lost three years to the service, but still ended with 2,214 hits, 361 home runs, 1,390 runs scored, 1,537 RBIs, and a .325 career batting average. He led the league in homers twice, RBIs twice, batting average twice. When he batted in 155 runs in 1948, he had more RBIs than games. Only one hitter has done that since. He played 13 years and was named to 13 AL All-Star teams. He was the AL MVP three times, including the 1941 season, in which he hit in a record 56 consecutive games.

Joltin' Joe went into the Hall of Fame in 1955, just a year after he was eligible.

LARRY DOBY

Outfielder, Cle (A) 1947-55, 1958, Chi (A) 1956-57,

1959, Det (A) 1959. Manager, Chi (A) 1978
Doby was the first black to play in the AL, joining Cleveland in 1947 as a second baseman. He was switched to center field the next season, after extensive tutelage by Tris Speaker, and helped the Indians win their first pennant since Speaker played center in 1920. Doby hit .301 for the season; his home run off Johnny Sain won Game 4 of the World Series that year.

Although Doby became an outstanding center fielder, he was more feared for his bat. He is one of the few men to drive one over the distant center field wall at Griffith Stadium in Washington (Ruth, Williams, and Mantle are the others). Larry was the first black player to lead either major league in home runs with his 32 in 1952. He led again with the same total in 1954 and also topped the AL in RBIs with 126, as the Indians won the pennant with an AL record win total of 111. He ended his career with 242 homers, 969 RBIs, and a .283 batting average.

With the black Newark Eagles, Larry teamed with Monte Irvin in 1946 to win the black world championship over Satchel Paige's Kansas City Monarchs. Doby had a brief stint as interim manager of the Chicago White Sox in 1978. He was elected to the Hall of Fame in 1998.

BOBBY DOERR
Second Baseman, Bos (A) 1937-44, 1946-51
The Red Sox of the late 1940s won more games than any team in baseball, but kept coming up just short of a pennant—except in 1946 when they blew the World Series. No one in his right mind ever blamed Doerr for the shortfalls that gave Bosox fans short falls. From the day he took over Boston's second base in 1937 until a chronic bad back forced him to hang up his glove at 33 in 1951, he was a rock—so reliable in the field they should have checked his glove for a 23-jewel movement. In 1948, smack in the middle of a pennant race, Bobby went almost three months—414 chances—without an error. Doerr didn't make spectacular plays. He didn't have to. He anticipated and was already in position. He's still in the all-time top ten second basemen in putouts and double plays, surrounded by guys who played longer.

Bobby was no slouch with a bat either. He adjusted to Fenway's Green Monster early, so that his numbers in Boston are way better than on the road, but that's a way of life for right-handed Red Soxers. Averaging it out, he hit solid .288, with 223 home runs and 1,247 RBIs. In 1944—admittedly a war year—he got his average up to .325 and led the AL in slugging average. Doerr was named MVP that season. During his career, he played in nine All-Star Games.

Doerr had a knack for the clutch, though it sometimes was wasted. He hit .409 in the 1946 Series. In the do-or-die ninth inning of the seventh game, with the Sox down, 4-3, he singled the tying run into scoring position. The next three men made outs. In 1949, in the final game against the Yankees, with the pennant on the line, he slugged a three-run triple against Vic Raschi. The Sox lost anyway.

In 1986 the Veterans Committee put him in the Hall of Fame.

DON DRYSDALE
Pitcher, Bkn (N) 1956-57, LA (N) 1958-69

When Drysdale pitched for the Dodgers, the batters had to be dodgers. The big right-hander could have written "Winning Through Intimidation." At 6-feet 5-inches, he delivered his 90-plus m.p.h. fastball with a big sidearm motion—"all spikes, elbows, and fingernails"—that made right-handed batters think they were under a rocket attack from third base. They say that, halfway through some of his games the groundskeeper had to come out and sprinkle sand in the batter's box. Batter's fears were justified. Big Don hit 154 batters, about 1 every 22 innings. It's the all-time record.

Off the field, Drysdale was always a considerate gentleman; but when he walked onto the field he was all business. He broke one batter's hand and was suspended for throwing beanballs. He threatened to sue and was reinstated. Adding to the terror, Don had a temper and everyone knew it. After giving up one home run, he threw the ball into the stands. He claimed that it "slipped."

Through the 1960s, Drysdale and Sandy Koufax were the Dodgers' one-two mound punch. One year they negotiated their contracts as an entry. Together, they put Los Angeles in three World Series during the decade.

Don compiled a 209-166 record over his 14-year career. His ERA was 2.95 and he totaled 2,486 strikeouts, three times leading the NL. He won the Cy Young Award in 1962 with a 25-9 mark. In 1968 he threw six straight shutouts on his way to a record of 58 consecutive scoreless innings which stood until Orel Hershiser surpassed it in 1988. Drysdale was named to the Baseball Hall of Fame in 1984.

HUGH DUFFY
Outfielder, Chi (N) 1888-89, Chi (P) 1890, Bos (AA) 1891, Bos (N) 1892-1900, Mil (A) 1901, Phi (N) 1904-06. Manager, Mil (A) 1901, Phi (N) 1904-06, Chi (A) 1910-11, Bos (A) 1921-22
Pint-sized Duffy had the biggest batting average ever, .440 (originally thought to be .438) in 1894, the hottest-hitting year ever, when the entire league batted .309. Hugh hit 41 percent better than average, which isn't the record, but is pretty darned good. He also tied for the home run lead with 18 and led in RBIs with 145. It helped put him in the Hall of Fame in 1945.

Rejected by the White Sox in 1889 as too small ("We've got a batboy," Cap Anson said), Duffy was signed by Boston in 1892. There he joined another New England Irishman now in Cooperstown, Tommy McCarthy, to form the best defensive duo of the era. Boston fans called them the "Heavenly Twins." Frustrated batters called them less printable things.

Duffy ended his 17-year career with a .324 batting average, 1,553 runs scored, 1,299 RBIs, and 574 stolen bases.

FRED "SURE SHOT" DUNLAP
Second Baseman, Cle (N) 1880-83, StL (U) 1884, StL (N) 1885-86, Det (N) 1886-87, Pit (N) 1888-90, NY (P) 1890, Was (AA) 1891. Manager, Pit (N) 1889
Dunlap was the biggest star of the one-year Union Association, which is sort of like being the most coveted Cracker Jacks prize. Labeled the "King of Second Basemen" in the 1880s, he was a noble hitter and fielder, but what set him above infield commoners was a powerful

arm, which earned him the nickname "Sure Shot." Reportedly, he didn't so much throw the ball as sling it. He was an established NL star who'd twice hit .300 for Cleveland when Union Association dollars persuaded him to move to that ill-fated league and made him the highest-paid player in baseball.

Dunlap hit .412 in 1884 and led the Union Association in almost everything—batting average, slugging average, hits, runs, home runs, and every second base fielding category but errors—as his St. Louis team won the only ever UA flag.

When the UA folded the next year, Fred folded as a slugger. Back in the NL, his batting average plunged 100 points. He never hit .300 again, but he continued his reign at second for several more seasons.

LEO "THE LIP" DUROCHER
Manager, Bkn (N) 1939-46, 1948, NY (N) 1948-55, Chi (N) 1966-72, Hou (N) 1972-73 Shortstop, NY (A) 1925, 1928-29, Cin (N) 1930-33, StL (N) 1933-37, Bkn (N) 1938-41, 1943, 1945

Loud-mouthed, pugnacious Leo was the Billy Martin of the 1940s. He baited umpires, picked fights, won more games than Stengel, and made his lifelong credo—"Nice guys finish last"—a part of the American language.

He broke in with the 1928 Yankees as a scrappy good-field-no-hit infielder, who delighted in getting Babe Ruth's goat. His gung-ho attitude and gone-south bat earned him the moniker "The All-American Out." By 1934 he was with the Cards, regarded as the best-fielding shortstop in the NL. He reportedly gave them their Gas House Gang nickname and helped spark them to the 1934 pennant.

In 1939 Brooklyn boss Larry MacPhail, a firebrand himself, tapped Durocher to lead the Dodgers. Lippy punched a golf caddy, fought with MacPhail, gambled, was fired, rehired, and raised the Bums from sixth to third, to second, and finally to first in 1941.

In 1946 Leo feuded with MacPhail, then owner of the Yanks, consorted with gangster Bugsy Siegel, married movie star Larraine Day upon her divorce, and finally was suspended for 1947 by Baseball Commissioner Happy Chandler. Leo returned to the helm in Brooklyn the following year, but was let go in midseason. He shocked his fans by moving over to the hated Giants. He had his greatest success in New York. In 1951 he nurtured young Willie Mays through a horrendous career-opening slump and won one of the most thrilling pennant races in history, as Bobby Thomson sank the Dodgers with his "shot heard 'round the world."

Three years later Leo won his third flag, his first World Series—and his third Manager of the Year Award. After the 1955 season, he worked for several years in television.

In 1966 Leo returned to the dugout as manager of the Cubs, where he served until late in the 1972 season. Although he brought the Cubbies into contention, he was unable to get them over the hump. Then he managed Houston at the end of 1972 and all of '73.

Many have written that Durocher was no more than an ordinary manager with a poor team, but that he could ride a winner down a hot pennant race better than any other skipper. Leo's 2,010 victories rank him sixth all-time among managers. His 1,710 losses are seventh. Durocher

was elected to the Hall of Fame in 1994.

JIMMY DYKES
Manager, Chi (A) 1934-46, Phi (A) 1951-53, Bal (A) 1954, Cin (N) 1958, Det (A) 1959-60, Cle (A) 1960-61. Third Baseman, Phi (A) 1918-32, Chi (A) 1933-39

Dykes managed for 21 years in the major leagues and never won a pennant. His teams finished in the first division only eight times and never higher than third. Yet he was regarded as an outstanding manager who got more out of his often-talentless teams than could reasonably be expected. Patient, humorous, knowledgeable, he lost 1,538 games—ninth all-time—but won a creditable 1,407. A quotable, nonstop talker, he said that winning without good players was like trying to steal first base. His best-known statement was to label Yankees' skipper Joe McCarthy a "push-button manager," meaning that McCarthy had only to push the right button to trot out another .300 hitter or quality pitcher. Dykes, of course, had few buttons.

Dykes was an infielder with the Philadelphia A's throughout the 1920s and played on the championship teams of 1929 to 1931. A good and versatile fielder, he performed mostly at third base, but played extensively at second and occasionally at short and first. Initially a poor hitter, he developed into a reliable batsman and finished his career with a .280 batting average, 2,256 hits, and 1,071 RBIs.

DENNIS ECKERSLEY
Pitcher, Cle (A) 1975-77, Bos (A) 1978-84, 1998, Chi (N) 1984-86, Oak (A) 1987-95, StL (N) 1996-97

On the next-to-last day of the 1998 season, Eckersley set the major league record for appearances by a pitcher with 1,071. It only took him two careers to do it.

The Eck's first career as a fine right-handed starting pitcher lasted from 1975 to 1986. His best years were with the Red Sox and included a 20-8 season in 1978, although he pitched a no-hitter at age 22 for the Cleveland Indians in 1977.

In 1987, with 151 wins under his belt, he was traded by the Cubs to Oakland. After an 0-2 beginning and a 6.94 ERA, he was sent to the bullpen by manager Tony LaRussa. Many expected the next step would be retirement. But when the team's regular closer was injured, Eckersley was given the job and his second career began. He still had good stuff for a short spurt, but his greatest skill was his beyond-pinpoint control. In 1989-1990 he walked only seven batters in 131 innings. His 0.61 ERA in '90 was the lowest in history for a pitcher with at least 25 innings.

In 1992, when he had 51 saves to go with his 7-1 record, he was named both Cy Young and MVP winner for the American League. After recording only three saves in his first 13 seasons, he compiled 387 during his "second career" and retired after the 1998 season.

BILLY EVANS
Umpire AL 1906-27

Evans began as a sportswriter and umpired his first minor league game only because the assigned man didn't show up. In 1906 his ability got him promoted all the way from a Class C minor league to the AL. He was only 22.

Billy umpired back when it took guts to wear a blue suit. He once had his skull fractured by a bottle during a riot in a ballpark. Another time he tangled with Ty Cobb under the stands and was nearly choked to death. But Evans learned to substitute diplomacy for belligerence and became one of the great umpires. A friendly, fastidious man, he helped gain respect for all umps.

In Game 2 of the 1909 World Series, Evans and Bill Klem had to ask the bleacherites whether a ball had landed fair or foul because temporary seats jutted out onto the field and hid the deep foul line. The next day four umpires worked the game, a practice that was eventually adopted for all major league games.

After 1927 Evans left umpiring to become the general manager for the Cleveland Indians. He also wrote a sports column, and later served as vice president of the Detroit Tigers. In 1973 Evans was elected to the Baseball Hall of Fame.

DARRELL EVANS
Third Baseman/First Baseman, Atl (N) 1969-76, 1989, SF (N) 1976-83, Det (A) 1983-1988
Evans combined a home run bat and an ability to draw walks into a 21-year major league career. His career batting average hovered around .250.

Evans says his career turned around when he saw a UFO while sitting on his porch in California in 1976. He'd just been traded from Atlanta, where he'd been hitting .173, to San Francisco. He took the sighting as a good omen and began hitting with renewed energy.

In 1985, in friendly Tiger Stadium, Darrell led the AL with 40 homers at the age of 38, to become the oldest home run champ ever, and the first man to hit 40 in both leagues. Two years later he slugged 34, the oldest man to reach that number.

DWIGHT EVANS
Outfielder, Bos (A) 1972-90, Bal (A) 1991
In his first years with the Red Sox, Evans was regarded as a good defensive outfielder but a poor hitter. Slowly he won respect for his bat. His strength was not his batting average, although he finally cracked .300 in his 18th AL season. Evans learned to draw walks, leading the league three times, and at the same time turned into one of the AL's better home run hitters. His 22 in the strike-shortened 1981 season tied for first in the league, but he has also had three seasons with more than 30 homers. Whether making circus World Series catches or driving long shots over or against the Fenway Park's Green Monster, Evans became a darling of Boston fans.

His leaping one-handed catch of Joe Morgan's home run bid in the 11th inning of the Game 6 of the 1975 World Series was one of the most heart-stopping plays ever seen. He then threw to the infield to double off Ken Griffey for the third out, setting the stage for Carlton Fisk's game-winning homer an inning later.

JOHNNY EVERS
Second Baseman, Chi (N) 1902-13, Bos (N) 1914-17, 1929, Phi (N) 1917, Chi (A) 1922. Manager, Chi (N) 1913, 1921; Chi (A) 1924
Rumor to the contrary, Evers did not earn his way into Cooperstown in 1946 by being the middle word in the refrain of F.P. Adams' poem about "Tinker to Evers to Chance." However, like a bowl of chicken soup, it didn't hurt. Except for an un-Evers-like .341 in 1912, his batting averages look sad beside those of AL contemporaries Nap Lajoie and Eddie Collins. Still, at the time Johnny played, what with the dead ball, there weren't many players at any position who hit with Lajoie or Collins. Evers' batting averages were consistently above the league average. Little Johnny was undeniably the top NL second baseman of the 20th century's first two decades.

The double-play combination that set F.P. Adams' pen in motion never led the league in twin killings—and small wonder. The Chicago pitchers kept baserunners to a minimum. What made "T to E to C" exceptional was their timing; on those rare occasions when a DP was crucial, they were the best in the business.

They were the main men in Chicago's four pennants between 1906 and 1910. Of the three, the 140-pound Evers was probably the most valuable player both in the field and at the plate. The hardest to get along with, too. His nickname was "The Crab." Even Tinker didn't like him; except for obligatory "You take it" and "I got it," they didn't speak for years. Grouchy as he was, little Johnny was also skilled, pugnacious, and ingenious.

Evers was the culprit who called for the ball and tagged second base, putting out poor Fred Merkle of the Giants and throwing the 1908 race into a tie. It worked in part because he'd warned the umpire that he would do it if the occasion arose. When Merkle made a beeline for the clubhouse instead of touching second and Johnny put the ball on the bag, the umpire had no choice but to call Fred out. (The game was declared a tie and later replayed with the Cubs winning the pennant.)

Sold to Boston in 1914, Evers joined shortstop Rabbit Maranville and sparked the "Miracle" Braves' unlikely run to the pennant. Evers was voted MVP. Johnny was usually hot in the World Series. He had hit .350 in both 1908 and '09, but he upped that even higher to .438 in this one, and his single drove in the winning run in the fourth and final game.

WILLIAM "BUCK" EWING
Catcher, Tro (N) 1880-82, NY (N) 1883-89, 1891-92, NY (P) 1890, Cle (N) 1893-94, Cin (N) 1895-97. Manager, NY (P) 1890, Cin (N) 1895-99, NY (N) 1900
Ewing was the subject of an early lithograph dramatizing the day he stole second and third, then announced, "And now I'm going to steal home"—and did. In 1919, a quarter-century after he stepped down as a regular, no less authority than the *Reach Guide* linked him with Ty Cobb and Honus Wagner as the three top stars of all time. Very likely, Buck was the greatest all-around player of the 19th century.

He wasn't the greatest with the bat, but he was a strong hitter, averaging .303 over 18 seasons. He led the NL with 10 home runs in 1883 and hit 20 triples the next year. And, as the lithograph showed, he was a daring and dangerous baserunner.

In the field, Ewing was just about as good as it got. He could and did play every position, but he was most famous as a catcher, the most demanding defensive slot. He was quick and had an exceptional arm. In fact, his arm was so strong that he regularly threw out runners without

rising from his catcher's crouch, a feat unheard of before his time.

A field leader par excellence, Ewing captained New York's NL champions of 1888-1889. After he retired as a player, he managed for several years, compiling a 489-395 mark. He was named to the Baseball Hall of Fame in 1939.

Connie Mack, a catcher himself, called Ewing the greatest ever. Buck's teammate, Mickey Welch, called him the greatest player, period. Besides being the first catcher to throw from the crouch, he was one of the first to use the big mitt. His biggest rival was King Kelly of Chicago. Both were consistent—.303 for Ewing, .308 for Kelly. Ewing had power (a league-leading 10 homers in 1883) but Kelly had more (with 13 in '84).

Buck was fast enough to lead off, often stealing over 50 bases a year; but, then again, so did Kelly. In 1893 Ewing played all nine positions. But Kelly played all but pitcher. Kelly and Ewing—what little there was to choose between them was in their handling of pitchers, and in this Ewing had no peer.

URBAN "RED" FABER
Pitcher, Chi (A) 1914-33
The last of the AL's "legal" spitball pitchers, Faber spent his entire career with the White Sox. In 1921 he scored one of the finest pitching feats ever. Playing for the seventh-place White Sox, he was 25-15, with a league-leading ERA of 2.48. To prove it was no fluke, he went 21-17 the next year and again led in ERA, as the White Sox climbed to fifth.

Faber had won 20 earlier with strong teams behind him, but 1921 was the beginning of the post-Black Sox era, when Chicago plunged into the second division for almost two decades. In 15 of Red's 20 seasons, Chicago finished in the second division. Yet, he had only six losing years and finished with 254 victories.

Disdaining strikeouts, Faber wanted batters to hit his pitch—his spitter—right into the dirt. He once pitched a nine-inning game with 67 pitches, or less than three pitches per out.

In the 1917 World Series, Red won three games and lost one. He sat out the 1919 Black Sox Series with an injury, watching eight of his teammates lose on purpose. In 1964 Faber was elected to the Baseball Hall of Fame.

ELROY FACE
Pitcher, Pit (N) 1953, 1955-68, Det (A) 1968, Mon (N) 1969
In 1959 Face and his newfangled forkball set an amazing record, 18-1, in relief for the fourth-place Pirates. Because the practice today is to bring in the "closer" almost exclusively to protect a lead, relief pitchers now accumulate more saves than ever before, but wins are rare. Face often relieved with the score tied or the Pirates a run or two behind. Of course, he "vultured" a few, also—blowing the lead, then getting the victory when the Pirates came from behind to win.

When Pittsburgh reached the World Series the next year, Face saved the first three games, as the Pirates beat the Yankees in the seventh game on Bill Mazeroski's famous homer. With the different utilization of relief pitchers in his day, Face saved 193 games in his 16-year

career. He won 96 games in relief and eight more as a starter. His "out" pitch was the forkball, which he threw as an off-speed pitch. Now it is better known as the split-fingered fastball.

BOB FELLER
Pitcher, Cle (N) 1936-41, 1945-56
Feller came out of Iowa as a phenom—a schoolboy with a legendary fastball. Unlike so many prodigies, Feller made good on his promise. He just may have been the best pitcher ever. Many veterans say Bob was the fastest they ever saw, but Feller had a dangerous curve as well. He set the standard as the strikeout pitcher of his time.

As a 17-year-old kid, just off the farm, in 1936, Bobby whiffed eight Cardinals in three innings in his first big league exhibition. In Bob's AL debut he fanned 15. At the age of 19 in '38 Feller set a record with 18 strikeouts. That year Bob led the league in both strikeouts (240) and walks (208).

In 1939, the 20-year-old Feller had his first big year—24-9, for the third-place Indians. Again he led in K's and walks. At 21 Bob hurled the only Opening Day no-hitter, went on to a 27-11 mark, fanned a league-high 261, and won *The Sporting News*' vote as Player of the Year. His no-hitter was the first of three. He also had a record 12 one-hitters, seven of them spoiled by the scratchiest of hits. Crowds flocked to see him duel Williams or DiMaggio. "It's just me against them," he exulted, "man to man."

Bob was 25-13 in 1941, as the Indians almost won the flag. Then, with his mountaintop years just ahead, he volunteered for combat duty as a naval gunner in the Pacific. He would go on to win eight battle stars. The war took almost four full years out of the very peak of Feller's career, ages 23 through 26. His own estimate, probably conservative, is that it cost him 1,000 strikeouts and 100 wins, enough to give him over 3,500 whiffs and 360 victories.

Instead he ended with 2,581 K's (once third on the all-time list, now farther down) and 266 wins. He also had a then-record 1,764 walks. In his first full season back, in 1946, Feller added a slider and struck out 348, one short of an AL record set by Rube Waddell in 1904. Feller had three more 20-win seasons in the postwar years.

Feller often pitched relief between starts and saved 21 games in addition to his 266 wins. Bob never won a World Series game. In 1948 he lost an opening-game two-hitter, 1-0, when the Braves' Phil Masi was called safe on a pickoff play. Films clearly showed Masi was out, but Masi scored the only run of the game. Feller was elected to the Baseball Hall of Fame in 1962.

RICK FERRELL
Catcher, StL (A) 1929-33, 1941-43, Bos (A) 1933-37, Was (A) 1937-41, 1944-45, 1947
Ferrell was the catcher for the AL in the first All-Star Game and caught all nine innings. Durability was one of his virtues. He held the AL record for most games caught with 1,805 until Carlton Fisk surpassed it in 1988. A fine defensive catcher with a strong arm, he was considered one of the best handlers of pitchers around. Ferrell was a fair hitter, who topped .300 four times, but had little home run power. His brother Wes, a pitcher, hit 10 more career

homers, but Rick seldom struck out and drew more than his share of walks.

From 1934 into 1938, Rick caught his kid brother Wes, one of the more successful brother batteries in history. They were so in tune, it was said, that Rick could catch a whole game without signs. When they were on opposite sides, Rick did well against Wes, once homering off him.

Rick had a rare knack for handling knuckleball pitchers. In 1945 he caught for Washington, a team with four knuckleballers as starters. He was elected to the Baseball Hall of Fame in 1984.

WES FERRELL
Pitcher, Cle (A) 1927-33, Bos (A) 1934-37, Was (A) 1937-38, NY (A) 1939, Bkn (N) 1940, Bos (N) 1941
Ferrell won 20 or more games for the Indians in each of his first four full years, starting in 1929. Possessor of a blazing fastball and a blazing temper, the handsome right-hander was a little wild on the mound. In two of those seasons, his walks outnumbered his strikeouts.

A sore arm in 1933 cost him his fastball and he was traded to Boston the next year, where he joined his catcher brother Rick. Wes became a junkball pitcher and twice won 20 for the Bosox. He had his best season in 1935 when he was 25-14 with the fourth-place Red Sox and led the AL in wins, complete games, and innings pitched. He finished his career with a 193-128 record and .601 percentage. His 4.04 career ERA looks better in the context of his time than it does when compared with earlier and later eras.

Ferrell may have been the best hitting pitcher of all time. He had a career batting average of .280 and his 38 home runs are the most by any pitcher. His best home run year was 1931 when he hit nine. That year he also tossed a no-hitter, a rare feat in the high-hitting 1930s.

An amateur astrologer, Wes guided his career by the stars and said they accurately predicted his ups and downs.

ROLLIE FINGERS
Pitcher, Oak (A) 1968-76, SD (N) 1977-80, Mil (A) 1981-82, 1984-85
In his 17-year career, Fingers saved 341 games. That's more preserving than Grandma used to do at canning time and it's also the all-time record for relief pitchers. His 107 relief wins are fourth on the list.

Rollie was the main man out of the Oakland bullpen in the early 1970s when the A's won five division titles, three pennants, and three world championships. In the 1974 World Series, his one win and two saves earned him the MVP nod. His six saves in three Series is a record.

Fingers pitched for San Diego from 1977 to 1980 and had his two top save seasons there, with 35 in 1977 and 37 the next year. Both marks led the NL. He was named Relief Man of the Year by Rolaids and Fireman of the Year by *The Sporting News* in both seasons.

Returning to the AL with Milwaukee in 1981, he led the AL in saves with 28 in a strike-shortened season and helped the Brewers reach the postseason for the first time. He was named both MVP and Cy Young winner. An arm injury in 1982 kept him out of the World Series and caused him to miss the 1983 season.

Famous for his handlebar mustache, the 6-foot-4-inch right-hander relied on good control of his fastball. Later in his career, Fingers added a slider and increased his effectiveness. He was elected to the Hall of Fame in 1992.

CHARLES O. FINLEY
Owner, KC (A) 1961-67, Oak (A) 1968-80
Only George Steinbrenner, among ballclub owners, has been more controversial than Finley, an insurance tycoon who bought the old Kansas City A's and moved them to Oakland. He feuded with his players, with fans, and with Commissioner Bowie Kuhn. He also built a dynasty around Reggie Jackson, Catfish Hunter, Sal Bando, Rollie Fingers, Vida Blue, and others. His Athletics won five straight division titles from 1971 to 1975, and three consecutive world championships.

Free agency eventually did in his A's. Unwilling to pay the ever-increasing salaries, Finley tried to sell off a few of his stars before they became free agents, but the deals were blocked by the commissioner. Finley went to court but lost. And then he lost the players. Ironically, it was an unpaid insurance policy to Catfish Hunter that inadvertently helped hasten free agency.

Finley hired and fired managers at a pace that seemed breakneck in those pre-Steinbrenner days. He also drew fans with sometimes outrageous promotions. He put a jackass in his bullpen and named it "Charley O." He burst with ideas—many of which were originally laughed at but many of which have also come to pass. He favored night World Series games, colorful uniforms, and designated hitters. He also advocated interleague play, and orange baseballs—we're still waiting on the day-glo baseballs.

Stubborn and volatile, Finley changed baseball in his 20 years with the A's. For the worse, his critics said. For the better, time seems to be saying.

CARLTON FISK
Catcher, Bos (A) 1969-80, Chi (A) 1981-93
The image of Fisk using body English to coax his game-winning homer to stay fair in the 12th inning of Game 6 in the 1975 World Series is locked in the minds of millions of baseball fans who saw it on television. But Fisk was more than a one-hit hero.

He won the Rookie of the Year Award with the Red Sox in 1972, hitting .293 with 22 home runs. Although he topped .300 twice, his batting average was normally well below that of his first year. However, he maintained his long-ball power. In 1985, at age 37, he hit 37 homers. In 1987 he surpassed 300 career home runs. And in 1988 he established a new mark for games caught.

Durable, strong-armed, and an outstanding handler of pitchers, Fisk ranks among the best catchers in the history of the game. In 1981 he left Boston via free agency and signed with the White Sox. He flipped his uniform number from number 27 to 72, when he "changed Sox." The White Sox retired his number in 1997.

FREDDIE FITZSIMMONS
Pitcher, NY (N) 1925-37, Bkn (N) 1937-43. Manager, Phi (N) 1943-45
Fitzsimmons combined with southpaw Carl Hubbell to give the Giants an excellent righty-lefty one-two punch in the late 1920s and early 1930s. Although Hubbell was the Giants' "Meal Ticket," the team also fed on a steady diet

of wins by "Fat Freddie." Fitzsimmons combined a wide assortment of pitches, excellent control, and an odd windup involving a turn toward second base (a la Luis Tiant) to go 20-9 in 1928 and 19-7 in 1930. Twice he won 18.

Traded to Brooklyn in 1937, he was used as a spot starter with great success. His 16-2 mark in 1940 led the NL in winning percentage. In 1941, at the age of 40, Fitzsimmons started Game 3 of the World Series to become the oldest starter in Series history. For seven innings he shut out the mighty Yankees, but a drive off the bat of his mound opponent, Marius Russo, hit him flush on the knee and put him out of the game. The Yankees scored twice in the next inning to win, 2-1.

Fitzsimmons finished his career at 217-146. He then managed the Phillies for parts of three seasons.

ELMER FLICK
Outfielder, Phi (N) 1898-1902; Cle (A) 1902-10
Although he's chiefly famous for winning the 1905 AL batting crown with an average of just .308, Flick was actually one of the top hitters at the turn of the century. In 1905 the league batting average was only .241; Willie Keeler, another pretty good hitter, was the only other regular in the league to get above .300. Elmer's best mark, .367 in 1900, almost won the NL title; he lost to Honus Wagner's .381 on the final day.

For three years straight, 1905 to 1907, Flick led the AL in triples. His career batting average was .313.

Flick was so good, in fact, that when he hit .302 for Cleveland in 1907, Detroit offered to swap their young star outfielder for Elmer even up. Cleveland preferred to stick with Flick and so passed up the offer of Ty Cobb. Unfortunately, injuries all but ended Elmer's career the next year; he played in only 99 more games. Flick was named to the Baseball Hall of Fame in 1963.

CURT FLOOD
Outfielder, Cin (N) 1956-57, StL (N) 1958-69, Was (A) 1971
Flood was one of the most important and influential players in the history of baseball, though his significance was unrelated to his undeniable talent. During the 1960s Flood helped the Cardinals to three pennants as their center fielder. A good hitter (career average .293), Curt excelled in the outfield. He was voted Gold Gloves from 1963 through 1969.

However, when the Cardinals attempted to trade him to the Phillies after the '69 season, he refused. "I do not feel I am a piece of property to be bought and sold irrespective of my wishes," he wrote to Commissioner Bowie Kuhn. He turned down a $100,000 contract with the Phillies to challenge baseball's reserve clause in federal court. The case went all the way to the U.S. Supreme Court, where his plea was rejected, 5-3. Nevertheless, the narrowness of the ruling forced baseball's owners to agree to an arbitration system, which eventually ended the reserve clause.

Flood, a serious, introspective man, briefly attempted a comeback in 1971 and then retired. Though he received none of the benefits of baseball's current free agency, he—more than any other player—is responsible for it. He died in 1997.

ED "WHITEY" FORD
Pitcher, NY (A) 1950, 1953-67
The "Chairman of the Board," Ford ranks as one of the greatest left-handed pitchers of all time. His 236-106 career record yields a winning percentage of .690, second all-time and the best of any 200-game winner in this century. He led the AL in victories three times, ERA and shutouts twice. He won the 1961 Cy Young Award at a time when only one was given to cover both leagues.

But Whitey's fame rests primarily on his ability as a "money pitcher," and pitching for 11 pennant winners gave him ample opportunity to earn his reputation. His World Series performances alone were enough. He started the most games (22), pitched the most innings (146), gave up the most hits (134), struck out the most batters (94), walked the most (34), and won the most (10). He also ranks first with eight losses, but his 2.71 ERA speaks better for the quality of his efforts.

A fun-loving native New Yorker, Whitey first pitched for the Yankees in 1950, when he went 9-1 and added his first Series win after a midseason call-up. He then entered the military for two years, but upon his return, picked up where he'd left off. Yankees manager Casey Stengel used him judiciously throughout the 1950s; in only 1955 did Ford start more than 30 games, limiting the number of wins (and losses) he could earn in a given season. After Stengel was replaced in 1961, the number of Whitey's starts per year increased sharply. He won 25 games in 1961 and 24 in 1963.

Ford pitched with his head more than his arm. He was the master of a variety of pitches, including a few frowned upon in the rulebook. He was moderately wild in his early years, but developed into one of the best control artists in the league. In 1974 Ford was elected to the Baseball Hall of Fame.

BILL FOSTER
Pitcher, Negro Leagues, 1923-37, Memphis Red Sox, Chicago American Giants, Homestead Grays, Kansas City Monarchs, Cole's American Giants
Big Bill, Rube Foster's younger half-brother, was considered one of the two best left-handed pitchers in the black leagues. He ranks first in wins and his 18 victories in 1927 are the third-highest season total.

Foster's two most famous wins came for the Chicago American Giants over "Bullet Joe" Rogan, ace of the rival Kansas City Monarchs, in the 1926 championship playoff. Bill's team was down three games to two, when he beat Rogan, 2-0 and 5-0, in a doubleheader to clinch the pennant.

Foster's best seasons were 1927 (18-3) and '32 (14-6). He was elected to the Hall of Fame in 1996.

ANDREW "RUBE" FOSTER
League President/Owner/ Manager/Pitcher, Negro Leagues, 1902-26, Chicago Union Giants, Cuban-X Giants, Philadelphia Giants, Leland Giants, Chicago American Giants
"The Father of Black Baseball," Rube Foster first attracted attention with his pitching. In 1902 he won four of the Philadelphia Cuban-X Giants' five wins against the Philadelphia Giants in a playoff that was billed as the "Colored Championship of the World." The next year he

switched to the Giants and led them to the title.

In 1910, in partnership with the son-in-law of Charles Comiskey, he formed the Chicago American Giants to play at the White Sox's old South Side Park. Although there was no league, Foster's Giants were generally recognized as the leading black team throughout the decade. As their manager, Foster built his teams on speed and pitching, insisted on disciplined play and initiated several strategies that became standard.

Black baseball was in a chaotic state when Foster and the owners of six Midwestern teams formed the Negro National League. Foster was named president and his Giants won the first three pennants. The NNL raised standards for players, drew fans with pennant races, and, according to many, saved black baseball. As president, Foster worked 15-hour days but drew no regular salary. He did receive a percentage of league-game attendance, but contributed part of that to the league. He preached that if blacks maintained a high level of play, when the whites were ready to open the doors, the blacks would be ready to walk through.

In 1926 Foster suffered a nervous breakdown from overwork. He died four years later, but black baseball had been put on a solid footing. In 1981 Foster was named to the Baseball Hall of Fame.

GEORGE FOSTER
Outfielder, SF (N) 1969-71, Cin (N) 1971-81, NY (N) 1982-86, Chi (A) 1986

Foster earned the nickname "The Destroyer" as well as the NL's 1977 MVP Award for his heavy hitting with Cincinnati's Big Red Machine in the 1970s. A quiet, introspective man with deep religious convictions, he conversely presented one of baseball's most menacing presences when standing at the plate with his black bat and glowering expression. From 1976-78 he led the NL in RBIs, with 121, 149, and 120. He also was home run leader in 1977-1978, with 52 and 40.

Traded to the Mets in 1982, he found himself playing half his games in a poor hitter's park and without the flock of teammates clogging the bases, waiting to be driven home, that he had known in Cincinnati. Although he twice drove in 90 runs, he could never regain the slugging level he'd attained with the Reds, and his fielding—never good—became a major liability. He completed his career with 348 home runs and 1,239 RBIs.

NELLIE FOX
Second Baseman, Phi (A) 1947-49, Chi (A) 1950-63, Hou (N) 1964-65

Little Nellie (5-foot 10 inches, 160 pounds) was a plucky second baseman, known for his choke-up batting grip and huge wad of tobacco. He was the heart of the Go-Go White Sox of the 1950s, teaming first with Chico Carrasquel and then with Luis Aparicio as the AL's premier keystone combo. He led the league's second basemen five times in turning double plays.

Considered a poor hitter when he first arrived in the majors, Fox learned to punch out short drives and led the AL seven straight years (1954-1960) in singles and four years in total hits. He batted .300 or better six times and finished with a .288 career batting average. He struck out about as often as Chicago has an honest election, and ranks as the third-hardest batter to whiff in history.

But more than for his stats, Nellie was known for his all-out hustling play and infectious spirit. When the White Sox won their first pennant in 40 years in 1959, Fox was named Most Valuable Player, though several other players had better statistics. He was elected to the Hall of Fame in 1997.

JIMMIE FOXX
First Baseman, Phi (A) 1925-35, Bos (A) 1936-42, Chi (N) 1942, 1944-45

Foxx, the Maryland strongman discovered appropriately by Home Run Baker, ranks with the greatest sluggers of all time. When he retired, his 534 homers ranked second to Babe Ruth and only four men have hit more in one season than Jimmie's 58 in 1932.

"Double X" loved to show off his bulging biceps by cutting the sleeves off his shirts. "Even his hair has muscles," winced Lefty Gomez, who threw a pitch that Jimmie walloped into the farthest corner of the third deck in Yankee Stadium. "It took 45 minutes to walk up there," Lefty said.

Originally a catcher, Foxx found that way blocked with the A's by Mickey Cochrane. He switched to first base and became one of the key players in Philadelphia's 1929-1931 dynasty. In those three seasons he hit 100 home runs and drove in 343.

In 1932 the good-natured, moon-faced Foxx launched an assault on Babe Ruth's five-year-old mark of 60 homers. Although he fell short with 58, fans noted he had two home runs washed out by rainouts. He also had 169 RBIs, and .364 batting average to win the MVP Award. He won again in 1933 with a Triple Crown year: 48 home runs, 163 RBIs, and a .356 batting average.

Traded to the Red Sox after tying for the home run crown with 36 in 1935, he took advantage of Fenway Park's short left field fence to produce several fine years. In 1938 his league-leading 175 RBIs and .349 batting average earned him his third Most Valuable Player award. Curiously, his 50 homers did not lead the league, but his more modest 35 the next year did.

"The Beast," as he was affectionately known, finished his career with 1,921 RBIs (sixth all-time) and a .325 batting average. His lifetime .609 slugging average ranks fourth behind only Ruth, Williams, and Gehrig. In 1951 Foxx was elected to the Baseball Hall of Fame.

BILL FREEHAN
Catcher, Det (A) 1961, 1963-76

Signed for a $100,000 bonus by the Tigers, Freehan turned out to be an excellent investment. He solved their catching problems for 13 seasons (1963-1975). Freehan was a terrific catcher who won five Gold Gloves and holds the AL record for career fielding percentage (.993) for catchers.

He hit an even .300 in 1964, but most of his batting marks were considerably lower, and he ended with a .262 career average. That was offset by his 200 career home runs. He got high marks as a team leader and helped the Tigers to a world championship in 1968 and an American League East title in 1972.

LARRY FRENCH

Pitcher, Pit (N) 1929-34, Chi (N) 1935-41, Bkn (N) 1942
Four men have broken into the majors with one-hitters. French is the only man who went out with one. He tossed it for the Dodgers in September of 1942 at the age of 34. Then he marched into the Navy for the next 27 years, emerging as a four-stripe captain. His career mark of 197-171 left him just shy of becoming the first pitcher to win 200 without a 20-win season.

A left-handed knuckleballer, French spent the first half of his career with the lowly Pirates, then joined the Cubs in 1935 in time to help them to the pennant with a 17-10 mark.

Chicago won again in 1938, but Larry had his worst season to become the only man ever to lose 19 games with a pennant winner.

FORD FRICK

Commissioner/League President
Starting as a sportswriter (and Ruth's literary "ghost"), Frick spent 43 years in baseball. As NL president (1934-1951), he was pivotal in the Jackie Robinson Revolution. When the Cardinals threatened to strike rather than play against Robinson in 1947, Frick told them bluntly: "I don't care if half the league strikes. Those who do will ... be suspended, and I do not care if it wrecks the NL for five years. This is the United States of America, and one citizen has as much right to play as another."

He was also one of the forces behind the establishment of a Hall of Fame; in 1970 he was elected to the Hall himself.

As commissioner (1951-1968), Frick presided over expansion to Milwaukee, Los Angeles, San Francisco, Minneapolis-St. Paul, Houston, Baltimore, Oakland, and Atlanta. He negotiated a $13-million TV package with NBC, and oversaw the end of the reserve clause and the birth of the free agent draft.

His most controversial ruling was probably his decision that an asterisk be placed beside Roger Maris' 61-homer record, an edict that was never enforced.

FRANKIE FRISCH

Second Baseman, NY (N) 1919-26, StL (N) 1927-37. Manager, StL (N) 1933-38, Pit (N) 1940-46, Chi (N) 1949-51
"The Fordham Flash" stepped straight from the Rams' campus into the major leagues with the Giants in 1919. He was a key man on New York's four straight pennant winners from 1921 through 1924. A slashing switch-hitter, he "never hit a home run when a single would win the game" but cracked plenty of singles, doubles, and triples. He led the NL with 223 hits in 1923, had 13 seasons of batting over .300, scored over 100 seven times, and batted in over 100 three times. His career marks included 1,532 runs scored, 1,244 RBIs, and a .316 batting average.

For several years he was considered the likely heir to John McGraw as manager of the Giants, but the feisty Frisch rebelled at McGraw's dictatorial methods. In 1927 he was traded to St. Louis in exchange for Rogers Hornsby, a swap that shocked and angered Cardinals fans.

Though never the hitter that Hornsby was, Frisch was a better fielder and his equal as a team leader. He played on Cardinals pennant winners in 1928, 1930-1931, and after becoming player-manager, he led the "Gashouse Gang" to a world championship in 1934. All told, he played on eight pennant winners and six runners-up. He was named NL MVP in 1931.

In 16 years as a manager, and despite being saddled with weak Cubs teams during his final seasons, he compiled a .513 winning percentage. He was elected to the Hall of Fame in 1947.

JIM "PUD" GALVIN

Pitcher, StL (NA) 1875, Buf (N) 1879-85, Pit (AA) 1885-86, Pit (N) 1887-89, 1891-92, Pit (P) 1890, StL (N) 1892. Manager, Buf (N) 1885
Supposedly Galvin picked up the nickname "Pud" for making "pudding" out of batters. On the other hand, the 5-foot-8-inch pitcher checked in at 190 pounds at his lightest and once ballooned to 320.

He was the greatest fat pitcher, and the hardest-working. In the early 1880s, when pound-for-pound Galvin was as good as any pitcher around, slabmen threw underhand from a shorter distance. Usually two pitchers worked every other game, and regulars always had high numbers.

One year he pitched 656 innings, the next year 636. He had one 593-inning season and six more over 400. He was effective, too. Although his teams ran from fair to rotten, he had two seasons with 46 wins, one with 37, and seven years with from 20 to 29. He pitched two no-hitters and 57 shutouts. He walked almost no one—1.13 per nine innings. And he had the greatest pickoff move of his day—once nailing three baserunners in the same inning.

In 14 seasons, he won 361 games to rank sixth all-time. His 307 losses are the second-most ever. He's also second all-time in innings pitched (5,941) and complete games (639).

A placid, gentle man, Galvin opened a saloon in Pittsburgh after he retired from baseball. Reportedly the place was always packed, but he went broke anyway. Then the nine bartenders he'd hired each opened a bar.

In 1965 Galvin was named to the Hall of Fame.

LOU GEHRIG

First Baseman, NY (A) 1923-39
Gehrig played in the shadow of Babe Ruth and, later, Joe DiMaggio. He played in an era of great first basemen—Jimmie Foxx, Johnny Mize, Hank Greenberg, and Bill Terry. He also played 2,130 straight games, and became in his quiet way perhaps the best first baseman ever. They called him "The Iron Horse"; he hauled the Yankees to seven pennants.

"I'm not a headline guy," Lou said. When he hit .545 in the 1928 World Series, Ruth hit .625. When Gehrig hit a home run in the 1932 Series, Ruth had just hit his "called shot" homer ahead of him. When Lou slugged four home runs in one game, John McGraw retired the same day to steal the headlines.

When Gehrig was voted MVP in 1927, he was paid $6,000. Ruth got $80,000. That was the year Babe hit 60 homers to 47 for Gehrig. But Lou set some marks even Babe couldn't touch—184 RBIs in 1931. That year Gehrig produced 301 runs (runs scored plus RBIs, minus home runs), the all-time record. His 23 grand slams are

also a record. In the 1932 World Series, Lou was truly Ruthian. In four games he hit three home runs, batted .529, and knocked in a four-game record eight runs.

Before Lou's death at the age of 37, he had hit 493 homers, then the third-highest ever, behind Ruth and Foxx. Some old-timers say Gehrig hit the ball as hard as they did, but he hit it on a line with overspin; they lifted it into the air for greater distance. Gehrig had 1,991 RBIs, third behind Ruth and Hank Aaron. Of course, Babe was on base to score a lot of those runs. On the other hand, Gehrig often came up with the bases empty after Babe had cleared them.

Yankee Stadium didn't help him—he actually hit better on the road. He led the AL in RBIs five times. Gehrig won the Triple Crown in 1934 (.363, 49 homers, 165 RBIs) but finished only fifth in the MVP voting. He won the award in 1936 with 49 home runs, 167 runs scored, and 152 RBIs. In 1939 Gehrig finally took himself out of the lineup. With death approaching, he told 61,000 fans in Yankee Stadium, "I consider myself the luckiest man on the face of the earth." The normal waiting period was waived and he was elected to the Baseball Hall of Fame in 1939.

CHARLIE GEHRINGER
Second Baseman, Det (A) 1924-42
A left-handed hitter, Gehringer slapped hits to all fields. He made 2,839 base hits over 19 years, including 184 home runs, 146 triples, and 574 doubles (13th all-time). He topped .300 in 13 of his 16 full seasons, led the AL with a .371 mark in 1937 to earn MVP honors, drove in 100-plus runs seven times and 1,427 for his career.

In the field his hallmarks were grace and efficiency. He made even the hardest plays look easy. He led AL second basemen in assists seven times, nine times in fielding average. He was tough in World Series play. His home run in the fifth game in 1934 beat Dizzy Dean of the Cardinals. A year later he singled in the ninth against the Cubs and scored the winning run that gave Detroit the championship.

But he hardly ever showed emotion or said anything about anything. They called him the "Mechanical Man." He was as colorful as a glass of water.

He was elected to the Baseball Hall of Fame in 1949.

BOB "HOOT" GIBSON
Pitcher, StL (N) 1959-75
In 1968 Gibson registered the lowest ERA in NL history, 1.12; hurled 13 shutouts, second-best in NL annals; went 22-9; and then fanned a record 35 in the World Series, including 17 in one game to shut out the Tigers and 31-game winner Denny McLain.

A fire-breathing, flame-throwing competitor, Bob was the best right-handed pitcher of the power-pitching 1960s. He won two Cy Youngs and one MVP. In three World Series Bob was 7-2, had a 1.89 ERA, and struck out 92 men in 81 innings. In his first Series, against the Yanks in 1964, he lost the second game, then came back to win Games 5 and 7. Three years later Gibson broke his leg in midseason but threw away his crutches to win three against Boston in the World Series, a six-hitter, a five-hitter, and a three-hitter, in that order.

The broken leg in 1967 came after two 20-win seasons and before three more 20-win years. He also won 19 twice. In 1971 he threw a no-hitter against Pittsburgh, the world champions that year. When Gibson retired, he was the winningest pitcher in St. Louis history (251-174) and second all-time in strikeouts (3,117).

Immensely intimidating on the mound, Bob put every ounce of power into his pitches—primarily a fastball and slider. He had a reputation as a headhunter, but insists he "hardly ever threw at a batter." Nevertheless, he was heard to admit, "When I did, I hit 'em."

He was elected to the Baseball Hall of Fame in 1981.

JOSH GIBSON
Catcher, Negro Leagues, 1930-46, Homestead Grays, Pittsburgh Crawfords
"There is a catcher," said Walter Johnson, the Hall of Fame pitcher, "that any big league club would like to buy for $200,000. His name is Gibson. He can do everything. He hits the ball a mile, catches so easily he might as well be in a rocking chair, throws like a bullet. Bill Dickey isn't as good a catcher. Too bad this Gibson is a colored fellow."

Because black players were barred from the white major leagues during Gibson's time, there is no way to know for certain whether or not he was the best catcher of all time. He may have been only one of the half dozen best. No lower ranking seems possible for the man they called "the Black Babe Ruth."

Actually accounts of his catching skills vary. Some say he was a little weak on pop fouls, but everyone agrees he had a good arm. There's no dispute about his hitting. It was magnificent. The barrel-chested, 215-pound slugger hit home runs of tremendous length. One was measured with a tape at 575 feet, but it may not have been his longest. He also hit them often. One estimate, including barnstorming, Mexican League, Caribbean, and semipro games, puts his total at about 950. In Negro League and semi-pro games he was credited with 75 homers in 1931 and 69 in 1934. His batting average for 17 years with the Homestead Grays and Pittsburgh Crawfords was over .350. He topped .400 at least twice. Combining with Buck Leonard in a "Ruth-Gehrig" tandem, Gibson led the Grays to nine straight pennants (1937-1945).

A warm, fun-loving man, Gibson was popular everywhere he played and, next to Satchel Paige, he was the Negro Leagues' greatest drawing card. For a time, he and Paige were batterymates.

Gibson was 33 years old when Jackie Robinson signed to play for the Dodgers. Reportedly he was bitter at having been passed over. Many believe he would have been signed by a white major league team in 1947, but he died of a brain hemorrhage in January of that year.

In 1972 he became the second Negro League player elected to the Hall of Fame.

WARREN GILES
National League President, 1951-69
Wounded as a lieutenant in World War I, Giles was elected president of the Moline (Ill.) team in the Three-I League in 1919, to start a baseball career that spanned 50 years. He helped Branch Rickey build the Cardinals' farm system into baseball's best. In 1937 he took over as general manager of the last-place Cincinnati Reds. Two

years later he had them in the World Series. In 1940 they were world champions.

As NL president, Giles oversaw league expansion to the West Coast, the attendance boom that followed the Vietnam War, and the battles with the players' union. He was elected to the Hall of Fame in 1979.

TOM GLAVINE
Pitcher, Atl (N) 1987-

Glavine paints the outside edge of the plate like daVinci painted the Mona Lisa—brilliantly! Every batter in the National League knows his game plan but few have been able to do anything about it. Over and over, the lefty brings his 90 mph fastball in low and just nipping the outside edge.

Once he's established the far inch of the plate as his own, he begins to move his pitches further away from frustrated batters. By the late innings, he's getting called strikes on pitches well wide of the strike zone. Should a batter try to adjust by moving closer to the plate, Glavine busts him inside with a strike on his knuckles.

Does Glavine's system work? Four 20-win seasons in the 1990s and two Cy Young Awards (1991 and 1998) would seem to prove it does.

On the mound, Glavine appears unflappably deadpan win or lose. He's got his game plan, walks few, holds runners close to their bases, and fields his position with aplomb. It all adds up to the winningest left-hander of the 1990s.

VERNON "LEFTY" GOMEZ
Pitcher, NY (A) 1930-42, Was (A) 1943

"Goofy" Gomez, inventor of the revolving goldfish bowl for tired goldfish, was one of the wittiest men ever to pitch a baseball. He entertained his teammates with his antics and one-liners. And sometimes—when he wasn't pitching—drew a smile from the opposition. His credo was "I'd rather be lucky than good." Actually he was both.

He was lucky to pitch for powerful Yankees of the 1930s. They gave him baseball's most consistent support with their bats and gloves and enabled him to pitch in five World Series. And he was lucky to pitch half the time in Yankee Stadium, where "Death Valley" in the left field power alley swallowed up long drives from right-handed hitters.

But he was good, too—one of the best left-handers of the century. He won 20 games four times, including a sensational 26-5 year in 1934. He led the AL in strikeouts three times, with a top mark of 194 in 1938. He won 189 and lost 102. And in five World Series, he won six games without a single loss.

He took his pitching seriously, but he had the ability to laugh at himself. He said the secret of his success was "clean living and a fast outfield—I'm the guy who made Joe DiMaggio famous." Gomez was elected to the Hall of Fame in 1972.

JOE GORDON
Second Baseman, NY (A) 1938-43, 1946, Cle (A) 1947-50. Manager, Cle (A) 1958-60, Det (A) 1960, KC (A) 1961, 1969

Anyone with Gordon's surname is likely to be nicknamed "Flash," but Joe lived up to the label with his acrobatic defensive skills. He ranged over the infield, making plays that other second basemen dream about. One game he made 11 assists. He led AL second sackers in assists four times. Of course, the flip side was that in getting to balls others couldn't, he sometimes fumbled them. He led or tied in errors four times too. It was worth the price. In the first six years he cavorted at second base for the Yankees, they went to five World Series.

He seldom hit for average, but he had home run power. The one year he topped .300—.322 in 1942—he was named AL MVP. After he returned from military service, he struggled though a .210 season, and the Yankees, figuring he was washed up, dealt him to Cleveland. There he combined with Lou Boudreau to form what many still consider the most deadly double-play combination ever.

In 1948 he had his greatest season, batting .280, with 32 homers and 124 RBIs, as the Indians won the world championship. He completed his career with 253 home runs and 975 RBIs.

LEON "GOOSE" GOSLIN
Outfield, Was (A) 1921-30, 1933, 1938, StL (A) 1930-32, Det (A) 1934-37

Goslin was the best hitter in Senators history. He was with Washington for all of the 1920s and twice in the 1930s. The Senators were a pretty terrible team through most of their stay in the AL. Everybody knows the line: "Washington: first in war, first in peace, and last in the American League." But actually they weren't so awful when Goslin was with them; they won three pennants, the only ones they'd ever win.

Goslin showed up at the end of the 1921 season, and by the next year he was a fixture in left field. "Fixture" is a little harsh. He was neither the worst nor the slowest outfielder in the AL, just sort of lumbering.

But when he had the lumber in his hands, he was a star. He hit .300 or over in his first seven full years as a Senator. In 1924 he led the AL in RBIs with 129, hit .344 and knocked 12 homers, which was a fair number for anyone playing half his games in cavernous Griffith Stadium. The Senators won their first pennant and only World Series, as Goslin at one point set a record with six consecutive hits. The next year the Senators won their second pennant, as Goslin led the AL in triples, while hitting .334 with 18 homers and 113 RBIs. He hit .354 and .334 in the next two years, then topped the AL in 1928 with a .379 mark in the closest batting race in AL history; Goose singled in his last at bat of the season to edge Heinie Manush by .001.

He hurt his arm horsing around in 1929, and for a time it looked like curtains. The Senators dealt him to the Browns ("St. Louis: Gateway to the West and to the bottom of the American League") and his arm came back. After a couple of good years in St. Louis (the Brownies even finished fifth in 1931), he was sent back to Washington with thanks in 1933. And darned if the Senators didn't win their third and final pennant that year.

Next, it was off to Detroit for Goose and pennants in 1934 and 1935, something they hadn't seen in Detroit since 1909. Goslin finished up with a career batting average of .316 and 248 home runs, but his best thing was batting in runs—1,609. He was elected to the Hall of Fame in 1968.

RICH "GOOSE" GOSSAGE

Pitcher, Chi (A) 1972-76, Pit (N) 1977, NY (A) 1978-83, 1989, SD (N) 1984-87, Chi (N) 1988, SF (N) 1989, Tex (A) 1991, Oak (A) 1992-93, Sea (A) 1994

In his heyday, the big, mustachioed Goose glowered at the hitters, then blew his fastball by them. He didn't have a whole lot more than heat and intimidation, but for an inning or two he was devastating. He led the AL in saves with the fifth-place White Sox in 1975. The next year, desperate for starters, the Sox put him into the rotation. He struggled to 9-17 and was traded to Pittsburgh. Returned to his natural habitat, the bullpen, he saved 26, won 11, and set an NL record for relievers with 151 strikeouts.

In 1978 Goose signed with the Yankees as a free agent. He led the AL with 27 saves and won 10 as New York caught Boston late in the season and then won AL East in a one-playoff that Gossage saved. Gossage spent six seasons in New York, earning a reputation as one of the top relievers in the game.

In 1984 he moved again as a free agent, this time to San Diego, where he helped the Padres to their first pennant. He logged time in the bullpens of six different teams from 1988-1994. Gossage pitched until he was 43, finishing his career as a middle reliever and garnering 310 career saves.

HANK GREENBERG

First Baseman, Det (A) 1930, 1933-41, 1945-46, Pit (N) 1947

One of the most fearsome home run hitters of all time, Greenberg played only nine full seasons, yet amassed 331 homers and 1,276 RBIs. Although he was an impressive 6 feet 4 inches and 210 pounds, his success stemmed more from hard work than natural gifts. Thought too tall and awkward to play baseball, he applied himself with diligence and made himself into an adequate defensive first baseman. In 1940, when the Tigers wanted to get Rudy York's bat into the lineup, Hank went to left field and did the job well enough that the Tigers won the pennant.

In 1934 he led the Tigers to the World Series with 26 homers, 139 RBIs, and a league-leading 63 doubles. In 1935 he was even better, winning his first MVP Award with 36 home runs and 170 RBIs, both leading the AL. The Tigers were world champions.

The following year a broken wrist limited him to 12 games, but in 1937 he came back with 40 home runs and 183 RBIs, the third-highest RBI total ever. Perhaps his 1938 season is his most famous. That year he chased Babe Ruth's record down to the wire, finishing with 58 home runs. He had a knack for hitting more than one in a game, accomplishing that 11 times during the year. Two years later, as the Tigers' new left fielder, he won his second MVP with 41 homers and 150 RBIs, and the Tigers again won the pennant.

Then in 1941, only 19 games into the season, Greenberg was inducted into the Army. He was 31. He did not return to the Tigers until midway through 1945. Fittingly his ninth-inning grand slam on the final day of the season won Detroit another pennant. After once more leading the AL in homers (with 44) and RBIs (with 127) in 1946, he was sold to Pittsburgh before the 1947 season for $75,000. The Pirates shortened the distant left field fence at Forbes Field in his honor by erecting a bullpen, quickly labeled "Greenberg Gardens." Hank hit 25 homers in 1947, then retired, but the Pirates' young slugger, Ralph Kiner, who'd been Greenberg's roommate on the Pirates, credited Greenberg's instruction and example with much of his subsequent success as a home run hitter (and the left field was renamed "Kiner's Korner").

Greenberg was elected to the Hall of Fame in 1956.

GUS GREENLEE

Owner, Negro League

The flamboyant Greenlee, cigar-chomping Pittsburgh racketeer and numbers lord, never would have passed Judge Landis' scrutiny as a white owner. But he may have saved black baseball in the dreary days of the Depression.

Gus owned the Pittsburgh Crawfords, acclaimed by many as the best black team of all time, with Satchel Paige, Josh Gibson, Oscar Charleston, Cool Papa Bell, Judy Johnson, and other greats of black baseball. He waged a spirited war against Homestead Grays' owner Cum Posey for supremacy in Pittsburgh. Cum got his own racketeer to bankroll him, and the two fought both in the park and out.

Greenlee signed Paige from Birmingham and promoted him into the greatest drawing card in black ball. He also publicized Pepper Bassett, who caught Satch sitting in a rocking chair.

In 1933 Gus helped revive the Negro National League after the Depression had put it out for a year. He served as league president from 1933 to 1937. He also provided the inspiration for the East-West or All-Star Game, played in Comiskey Park a month after the first white All-Star Game there. It proved a financial life-saver, with upwards of 50,000 fans some years. The only profit many black clubs made all year was their share of receipts from that one game.

Gus also owned a stable of boxers, including world light-heavyweight champ John Henry Lewis. Like the ball team, the hobby lost money but was a cover for his numbers activities. In 1937 Dominican dictator Rafael Trujillo bought Gus' stars out from under him, the Pittsburgh police finally raided his numbers store, and Gus was on the ropes at last.

BOBBY GRICH

Second Baseman, Bal (A) 1970-76, Cal (A) 1977-86

One of the most underrated players in the game, Grich was an outstanding all-around player who was generally thought of as only a glove man. His fielding, of course, was exceptional. In 1985 he made only two errors all season, to set a new standard for second basemen with a .997 fielding average. In 1973 he had a .995 mark. He won four Gold Gloves.

What was often overlooked was his hitting. He hit .304 in 1981 and got into the .290s a couple of times, but he was more comfortable at .250-.260. Nevertheless his ability to draw walks—twice over 100—kept him on base and allowed him to score 1,033 runs. He had good home run power with 224 career round-trippers. In the strike-shortened 1981 season he tied for the AL homer title with 22. Two years earlier he blasted 30 and drove in 101 runs.

Part of Grich's image problem was his postseason play. With Baltimore and California he appeared in the ALCS five times, always on the losing side. And in 24 ALCS games he hit only .182.

KEN GRIFFEY, JR.
Outfielder, Sea (A) 1989-

After 10 years in the majors and not yet 30 years old, Junior's enshrinement in the Baseball Hall of Fame seems only a matter of waiting until that future date when he'll be five years retired. Many regard him as no worse than the fourth-best center fielder of all time, and some would place him higher on that short list. After finishing close several times, he finally won his first MVP award in 1997 when he cracked 56 homers and knocked in 147. His 1998 figures matched those numbers, and he has won seven Golden Gloves, with countless circus catches decorating highlight films.

The personable son of an outstanding player was marked for stardom when he broke in with Seattle as a 19-year-old in 1989, and he has done nothing to change those predictions. By his third season, he batted in 100 runs; by his fifth, he upped his home run record into the 40s. His batting average is usually around .300. Only injuries have derailed him, limiting him to 72 games in 1995.

At mid-career, he stands at 350 homers, 1,018 RBI, and 940 runs scored. Barring further injuries, he's in line to rewrite the record books.

CLARK GRIFFITH
Pitcher, StL (AA) 1891, Bos (AA) 1891, Chi (N) 1893-1900, Chi (A) 1901-02, NY (A) 1903-07, Cin (N) 1909-10, Was (A) 1912-14. Manager, Chi (A) 1901-02, NY (A) 1903-08, Cin (N) 1909-11, Was (A) 1912-20

"The Old Fox," Griffith was elected to the Hall of Fame in 1946 as one of the game's pioneers. He could just as easily have gone in for his pitching. And he wasn't a bad manager either. Clark was born in a Missouri log cabin. His father was shot and killed when Clark was 2. The boy held Jesse James' horse, was a trapper, cowpuncher, faro dealer, and singer in frontier saloons before taking up baseball.

Standing only 5 feet 8 inches, he learned to use guile from Old Hoss Radbourn, another great little man. He got the hitters out with brains, a primitive slider (Cy Young called it a "dinky-dinky pitch")—and a little scuffing of the ball. He won 20 or more games for Chicago six straight years, from 1894 through 1899. Jumping to the AL in 1901, Griff pitched (24-7) and managed the White Sox to the first flag in the new league's history. He took over as the Yankees (then known as the Highlanders) first manager when the club moved to New York in 1903. It was his last season as a full-time pitcher. His career mark was a sparkling 240-141.

Although the Highlanders nearly won the 1904 American League pennant, and finished second again in 1906, Griff was let go in mid-1908. He always felt he'd been mistreated by the New York owners, fans, and press. It led to his life-long loathing of the Yankees.

After managing Cincinnati for three years, AL president Ban Johnson prevailed upon him to help rescue the failing Washington franchise in 1912. Griffith became manager and mortgaged his ranch to buy 10 percent of the stock. With Walter Johnson pitching and Griffith managing, the Senators finished second two years in a row, then began a slow drift toward the second division as financial problems continued to beset the team.

In 1920 Griffith purchased controlling interest in the Senators, resigned as field manager, and took over as president. Although the team won a world championship in 1924 and pennants in 1925 and 1933, it was always financially strapped. Unable to compete with the richer AL clubs, Griffith was often forced to sell his better players to keep operating. In 1934 he even had to sell his manager-shortstop and son-in-law, Joe Cronin, for $225,000. Griffith was a leader in popularizing night games, the use of on-field entertainers such as Al Schacht, and in the signing of Latin players—all dictated by the constant financial woes of the Senators. Perhaps his greatest achievement was keeping baseball in the nation's capital during his lifetime. He should receive accolades for his off-field friendships with James A. Farley, postmaster general, and President Franklin D. Roosevelt; these friendships were responsible for the famous "green light" to wartime baseball.

BURLEIGH GRIMES
Pitcher, Pit (N) 1916-17, 1928-29, 1934, Bkn (N) 1918-26, NY (N) 1927, Bos (N) 1930, StL (N) 1930-31, 1933-34, Chi (N) 1932-33, NY (A) 1934. Manager, Bkn (N) 1937-38

Grimes threw the last legal spitball in 1934. But "Old Stubblebeard"—a nickname derived from his habit of not shaving on days he pitched—won games as much on willpower as "wetpower." Pitching for the Cardinals in the 1931 World Series, he threw a two-hitter in Game 3 to beat Lefty Grove. Came the final game, he had an inflamed appendix. The trainer put ice packs on his stomach between innings while Grimes shutout Philadelphia for eight innings. He weakened in the ninth, but still got two outs before a reliever nailed down the win.

"Boiley," as they called him in Brooklyn, was a workhorse who led the NL in innings pitched three times and topped 300 innings in five different seasons. A gruff, hard-bitten type he was only too willing to knock down any batter with the temerity to dig in at the plate.

His greatest seasons were with Brooklyn, where he four times won 20 games between 1918 and 1926. In 1920 he helped the Dodgers to a pennant with a 23-11 mark. In the World Series that year, he shut out Cleveland on seven hits in Game 2.

After leaving Brooklyn, Grimes was 19-8 for the Giants in 1927 and 25-14 for Pittsburgh in 1928. He got to St. Louis in 1930 and helped them win two straight pennants.

One of the small group identified as spitballers and allowed to keep throwing the pitch after it was outlawed in 1920, Grimes both lasted longer than the rest and won more games. He finished up in 1934 with a 270-212 mark. His career ERA of 3.53 was acquired in an age of heavy hitting, when any season mark under 4.00 was hot pitching.

He was elected to the Hall of Fame in 1964.

HENRY "HEINIE" GROH
Third Baseman, NY (N) 1912-13, 1922-26, Cin (N) 1913-21, Pit (N) 1927. Manager, Cin (N) 1918

Only 5 feet 8 inches tall five-eight, Heinie was famous for his bat, shaped like a big milk bottle. Its handle ballooned into a thick barrel, which he held high over his right shoulder. He looked sort of like a cartoon. But don't

laugh. In the 1922 World Series, he used it to hit .474. The next year Heinie reportedly drove around with license plate P474.

The Giants picked up Groh in 1922 from Cincinnati, where he'd been an outstanding third baseman for years, and he helped them win pennants for three straight years. A good fielder and dangerous hitter (.292 lifetime), he believed his odd bat gave him better control on bunts.

ROBERT "LEFTY" GROVE
Pitcher, Phi (A) 1925-33, Bos (A) 1934-41
Grove boggles the mind, to say nothing of how he boggled AL batters. The consensus pick as best left-hander in history, Lefty might also have been the best pitcher, period. Some hitters insist he was faster than Johnson or Feller. His ball didn't have a hop at all—but still they couldn't hit it.

He was terrific from the day in 1920 when he first began pitching for Jack Dunn's Baltimore Orioles of the International League. But Dunn wasn't about to sell him to a major league team until he got his price—and the price went up every year. By the close of the 1924 season, Grove had won 108 games for Dunn and had yet to pitch in the majors. Connie Mack finally came up with $100,600, a new record. Grove was 25 when he pitched his first game for the A's.

Although it took him a couple of years to begin rolling up big victory totals, Lefty led the AL in strikeouts as a rookie. He led in walks, too—earning a reputation for wildness that was unmerited after that first season. He was, however, wild after a loss. He set new records for clubhouse tantrums, but it was noted he always punched lockers with his right hand. His theory on kicking water buckets was "Always be sure the bucket is empty."

After leading the league in ERA and strikeouts in 1926, he really got rolling. In the next seven seasons, he won 20 or more seven times, led in wins four times, led in winning percentage four times, in ERA four, in strikeouts five, and in shutouts twice. Death and taxes are less consistent. His 31-4 record in 1931 is his gaudiest season and earned him the MVP.

The A's won pennants from 1929 through 1931, but by 1934 the Depression was killing attendance and Connie Mack needed money. He sold Grove to the Red Sox for $125,000 (a $24,400 capital gain). Lefty's fabled fastball was a memory, and it took him an 8-8 season to change over to a "curves and control" pitcher. Then he won 20 for the eighth time and followed with a couple of 17-win seasons. He also took four more ERA titles. On July 25, 1941, he became the sixth modern pitcher to win 300 games. At 300-141 his .680 career percentage ranks fourth all-time but doesn't include his 55 saves. His lifetime ERA of 3.06, when normalized to the league average and adjusted for home park, was the best ever—even topping Walter Johnson's. In 1947 Grove was named to the Hall of Fame.

RON GUIDRY
Pitcher, NY (A) 1975-88
In 1978 Guidry had one of the most effective years of any pitcher any time any place. The slightly built Louisiana lefthander was 25-3, to lead the AL in both wins and percentage. Also tops were his 1.74 ERA and nine shut-

outs. In 273 innings, he allowed a skimpy 187 hits. He struck out 248 but walked only 72. Led by Guidry, the Yankees moved from 10 games back on July 24 to tie the fading Red Sox on the last day of the season, then won the playoff on Bucky Dent's homer. Naturally it had to be Guidry, on short rest, who started and won the playoff victory. He added two more wins in the postseason.

He won the Cy Young Award hands down and finished second in the MVP voting.

"Louisiana Lightning" was never quite the same world-beater again, though he had several fine seasons, including 21-9 in 1983 and 22-6 in 1985.

TONY GWYNN
Outfielder, SD (N) 1982-
At this late stage of his career, it seems unlikely that Gwynn will hit .400. For years, a staple of preseason predictions was that "this year" Tony would finally become the first .400 hitter since Ted Williams. Age and injuries have taken their toll. His .394 in 1994 may be as close as he'll ever come. In 1998 he could "only" muster a meager .321—low enough to cut into his career average. On the upside, he has hit with more longball power in the past few years.

Often overlooked in the cheers for Gwynn's hitting prowess is the fact that he ranks as one of the National League's best-fielding right fielders.

Few hitters approach their trade as scientifically as Gwynn. Copious notebooks, videotape, and hours and hours of study go into every one of his line drives. The result of his efforts has been eight batting titles. Only Ty Cobb had more.

STAN HACK
Third Baseman, Chi (N) 1932-47. Manager, Chi (N) 1954-56, StL (N) 1958
"Smiling Stan" played on four Cubs pennant winners and hit .348 in the Series (.471 in 1938), though the Cubs lost all four. *The Sporting News* chose him as its all-star third baseman three years in a row, 1940-1942.

A lifetime .301 hitter, he cracked out 2,193 hits in 16 years. He also drew 1,092 walks and scored 1,239 runs. He seldom hit with much power, but he was consistent.

Hack's most famous hit came in the sixth game of the 1935 Series against the Tigers. Down three games to two, and tied in this game, 3-3, Stan led off the ninth inning and smote one of Tommy Bridges' curves over the Tiger center fielder's head for a triple. A sacrifice fly would give the Cubs the lead. But Billy Jurges struck out, Larry French bounced out, and when Augie Galan finally got the fly, it was too late. A half inning later the Tigers won the game and the Series.

CHARLES "CHICK" HAFEY
Outfielder, StL (N) 1924-31, Cin (N) 1932-35, 1937
Hafey had everything you could ask for in a ballplayer except good health. He hit for a good average with fair power. He was fast. He could field. And he had the best throwing arm of any NL outfielder during his time.

The quiet, modest slugger was at the same time known for playing practical jokes on his teammates. He first became a regular with the Cardinals in 1926, as the team fought toward its first pennant. He was beaned several

times during the season, affecting his sight. He was advised to wear glasses, a rarity among players of his day. His sight fluctuated so that he actually used three different pairs, depending on the state of his eyes.

From 1927 through 1931 he hit above .300 each season for the Cards, who won pennants in 1928, 1930, and 1931. He drove in over 100 runs in three of those seasons, and had a career-high 29 home runs in 1929—this despite a chronic sinus infection that required several operations.

In 1931 Hafey won the closest batting race in NL history, nosing out Bill Terry by .0003. Terry hit .3486 to Hafey's .3489. Chick had been a holdout several times before; when he asked for a raise to $17,000 after winning the batting championship, St. Louis traded him to Cincinnati. He had several good seasons with the Reds before retiring in 1935. A comeback attempt in 1937 was unsuccessful. Hafey was elected to the Hall of Fame in 1971.

JESSE "POP" HAINES
Pitcher, Cin (N) 1918, StL (N) 1920-37

Haines was a temperamental workhorse who relied on a good fastball and tricky knuckleball to win 210 games, all with the St. Louis Cardinals. Until Bob Gibson surpassed his mark, he was the Cards' all-time winner. He didn't join the team until he was 26 years old but stayed until he was 45—hence his nickname "Pop."

He won 20 or more three times and pitched a no-hitter in 1924. During his time with the Redbirds, they won five pennants and three world championships. Haines was 3-1 in World Series play.

Haines was 13-4 in 1926, as the Cards won their first pennant. He shut out the Yanks in the World Series, the last time anyone did that to the perennial AL champs for 16 years.

Oddly, Haines was most famous for being relieved in a ball game. In the seventh game of the 1926 Series, he was leading 3-2 when he developed a blister from throwing the knuckler and loaded the bases in the seventh inning with two out and Tony Lazzeri up. Manager Rogers Hornsby waved in Grover Alexander from the bullpen. Alexander's strikeout of Lazzeri is one of the most famous events in baseball history.

Haines was elected to the Hall of Fame in 1970.

BILLY HAMILTON
Outfielder, KC (AA) 1888-89, Phi (N) 1890-95, Bos (N) 1896-1901

"Sliding Billy" epitomized the jackrabbit era of the 1890s. Only 5 feet 6 inches, he stole 912 bases—111 in 1889, 102 in 1890, and 111 in 1891—and led his league in steals in seven of his fourteen seasons. The 111 steals was a record until Lou Brock broke it 85 years later. Of course they were not all what we call stolen bases today. Going from first to third on a single was counted as a "steal."

Hamilton was the most efficient leadoff man ever. He set a record by scoring more runs that he had games played: 1,690 runs in 1,591 games. He also holds the all-time record for runs scored in a single season with 192 in 1894. He led the league four times. He was able to accomplish these things for several reasons in addition to his undeniable speed. In the first place, he was an exceptional hitter, leading the NL twice—.340 in 1891 and .380 in

1893. His career average was .344, eighth best of all time. Second, he walked a lot. He topped the NL in bases on balls five times. Third, he was followed in the batting order through most of his career by other outstanding hitters.

In 1894, his record year for scoring runs, he played center field for the Phillies and hit .404. Left fielder Ed Delahanty hit .407, and right fielder Sam Thompson hit .407. And substitute outfielder Tuck Turner hit .416 in 80 games! Even so, the Phillies finished fourth.

In 1896 the Phillies traded him to Boston for veteran third baseman Billy Nash. He joined Hall of Famer Hugh Duffy in the Beaneaters' outfield and helped his new team win pennants in 1897-1898.

Hamilton was elected to the Hall of Fame in 1961.

NED HANLON
Outfielder, Cle (N) 1880, Det (N) 1881-1888, Pit (N) 1889, 1891, Pit (P) 1890, Bal (N) 1892. Manager, Pit (N) 1889, 1891, Pit (P) 1890, Bal (N) 1892-98, Bkn (N) 1899-1905, Cin (N) 1906-07

Ned Hanlon was the original dirty tricks manager with the old Baltimore Orioles and Brooklyn Superbas of the 1890s. With Willie Keeler, John McGraw, Joe Kelley, Hughie Jennings, and the rest, Hanlon's teams bunted and hit-and-ran their way to five flags.

They also reportedly: raised the foul lines so bunts would stay fair; grabbed runners' belts as they rounded third base; hid extra balls in the outfield grass to throw in on long hits; flashed mirrors in the faces of the other teams' batters and fielders; rolled on the ground and pinched their arms to fake being hit by pitches; and buried cement in front of home plate, then beat balls down on it so they'd bounce high enough to beat out—the famous "Baltimore chop."

After a dozen years as a good field/no hit outfielder, Hanlon took over the Orioles in 1892, when they finished 12th. He picked on young McGraw mercilessly until John offered to "punch his big head"—exactly the reaction Ned wanted.

The next year he had the O's up to eighth, and by 1894 to first. They won three straight flags, then finished second twice. Moving to Brooklyn, he won flags his first two years, 1899-1900, then began a descent to last. But Ned still ended with a .530 winning percentage.

After baseball he went into real estate and made a fortune. He was elected to the Hall of Fame in 1996.

MEL HARDER
Pitcher, Cle (A) 1928-47

Harder won over 223 games in 23 years of pitching for Cleveland, including 20-win seasons in 1934-1935. Only Bob Feller won more for the Tribe. He had the honor of pitching the opening game in Municipal Stadium against Lefty Grove before 82,000 fans. He lost, 1-0. In the 1934 All-Star Game, he hurled five scoreless innings to earn the win.

After retiring from the mound after two decades with the Indians, Mel coached the Cleveland pitchers from 1949 through 1963, the glory years of their magnificent pitching staffs. Harder was credited with helping Feller, Bob Lemon, Early Wynn, Mike Garcia, Herb Score, and others. It was said that "he had a camera in his head"

because of his uncanny ability to spot pitching flaws.

MIKE HARGROVE
First Baseman, Tex (A) 1974-78, SD (N) 1979, Cle (A) 1979-85. Manager, Cle (A) 1991-

Hargrove was called "the Human Rain Delay" because of his long, involved ritual before taking his stance in the batter's box. He'd walk up near the plate and take exactly three deliberate practice swings. Then he would step into the box and meticulously dig in his left foot. Next he'd adjust his helmet. Arrange his uniform. Tug his belt. At last, he was ready. But after the first pitch, he'd go through it all again. He drove pitchers crazy. But it worked. He hit .290 for his 12 seasons, led his league in walks twice, and had four seasons of over 100 walks. His lifetime on-base percentage of .401, when normalized to the league average and adjusted for home park, is among the top 20 of this century.

Hargrove took over as Cleveland's manager midway through the 1991 season. Four years later, he guided the Indians to a 100-44 record and their first postseason appearance in more than 40 years. From 1995-1998 his team won four straight division titles and two American League pennants.

WILL HARRIDGE
American League President, 1931-59

Harridge worked for the Wabash Railroad handling travel arrangements for AL teams and umpires. He had never seen a major league game until he became private secretary to AL president Ban Johnson in 1911. Twenty years later the efficient but colorless, conservative Harridge was promoted to chief and served from 1931 to 1959.

He preferred to stay in the background, but he never hesitated to enforce league rules and decorum. In 1931, shortly after taking office and in the middle of a heated pennant race, he suspended Yankees catcher Bill Dickey for a month for slugging another player. Harridge was a strong advocate of the All-Star Game. He opposed night baseball until he saw that such games made baseball more available to families. He hated gimmicks and showboating, and was not amused when Bill Veeck used a midget as a pinch hitter.

He fined Boston's Ted Williams for spitting at fans. But when Ted won the 1941 All-Star Game with a ninth-inning homer, Harridge lost his reserve. He almost kissed Ted, he said, and would have "if there weren't so many people around." Harridge was named to the Hall of Fame in 1972.

STANLEY "BUCKY" HARRIS
Second Baseman, Was (A) 1919-28, Det (A) 1929, 1931. Manager, Was (A) 1924-28, Det (A) 1929-33, Bos (A) 1934, Was (A) 1935-42, Phi (N) 1943, NY (A) 1947-48, Was (A) 1950-54, Det (A) 1955-56

Harris broke in as a regular second baseman with the Senators in 1920, hitting .300 for the only time in his career. In 1924 "the Boy Manager" became the Senators' skipper at age 27. He took the team to its first pennant and a World Series victory over the Giants. With Washington down three games to two, Harris knocked in both runs to win Game 6 and tie the Series. The next day Bucky drove in three runs to pull his team to a 3-3 tie after nine innings.

They won in the 12th on the famous hit that bounced over third baseman Fred Lindstrom's head. Harris hit .333 for the Series, with seven RBIs, and two homers—he hit only nine other home runs in his career.

Though the Senators repeated as pennant winners in 1925, they lost the Series to the Pirates. In 1929 Harris moved to Detroit as player-manager and began a career as the "Available Man." All told, he managed for 29 years. He had two more sessions in Washington (1935-1942 and 1950-1954), two in Detroit (1929-1933 and 1955-1956), one year in Boston (1934), two-thirds of a season with the Phillies (1943), and two years with the Yankees (1947-1948). Most of the time he was saddled with teams that had little chance to win; 20 of them finished in the second division. But Harris was respected as a manager who got the most out of his limited material.

He won his last pennant and world championship with the Yankees in 1947 but lost a three-way race to Boston and Cleveland in 1948. The Yanks promptly fired Harris and hired Casey Stengel.

Bucky ranks fourth all-time in managerial wins with 2,159 and second in losses with 2,219. He was elected to the Hall of Fame in 1975.

CHARLES "GABBY" HARTNETT
Catcher, Chi (N) 1922-40, NY (N) 1941. Manager, Chi (N) 1938-40

While AL fans argued the merits of Mickey Cochrane and Bill Dickey, NL fans had no problem identifying their circuit's best catcher. Hartnett was the cream of the NL, and to some the best of all. Although he was often described as a "beefy man with a tomato face who talked a lot," his nickname was actually hung on him ironically when as a Cubs rookie in 1922 he said virtually nothing. He developed his communication skills, of course, but for 20 seasons his batting and catching skills spoke louder.

An excellent defensive catcher with a powerful arm and a take-charge handler of pitchers, he caught 1,790 games. In 12 seasons, he played in over 100 games. He led National League catchers in fielding six times.

His lifetime batting average was .297, and at one time he held the record for home runs by a catcher, with 236. He drove in 1,179 runs, with a personal high of 122 in 1930. While he was with them, the Cubs won four pennants. He appeared in five All-Star Games and was NL MVP in 1935.

He was behind the plate in the 1932 World Series when Babe Ruth hit his "called shot" off Charlie Root. Gabby always insisted the Babe didn't point.

In 1934 he caught Carl Hubbell's great All-Star Game feat of striking out Ruth, Lou Gehrig, Jimmie Foxx, Al Simmons, and Joe Cronin. "Just throw them what you throw me," he told Hub, "I can't hit it, and neither will they."

But Hartnett's greatest moment—perhaps the greatest in Chicago baseball history—was his "homer in the gloaming" against Pittsburgh as darkness fell on Wrigley Field, Sept. 28, 1938. Gabby had become Cubs manager in midseason and led the club from six games behind to one behind the Pirates. The teams met in Chicago for a series that would decide the pennant. In the leadoff game, the score was tied after eight innings, and the umps warned that the ninth would be the last. There were two

outs in the bottom of the ninth, 34,465 crazed fans in the stands, and Mace Brown had an 0-2 count against Gabby. Hartnett hit the next ball into the bleachers and the Cubs went on to the flag. He was named to the Hall of Fame in 1955.

GUY HECKER
Pitcher/First Baseman/Manager, Lou (AA) 1882-89, Pit (N) 1890. Manager, Pit (N) 1890
In 1884 Hecker led the old American Association with a 52-20 mark and 1.80 ERA. Two years later he led the league in batting with .342. Guy was surely the best hitting pitcher until Ferrell. He averaged .283 for his career and even stole 48 bases in 1887. On Aug. 15, 1886, he allowed Baltimore four hits in a complete-game victory while registering six hits himself, including three homers and two doubles. He also scored a record of seven runs.

Hecker's pitching was his forte, however. In four years 1883-1886, he averaged 34-22 for a team that finished third, fourth, fifth, and fifth. In his big year, 1884, he also led in complete games, innings pitched, and strikeouts.

HARRY "SLUG" HEILMANN
Outfielder, Det (A) 1914, 1916-29, Cin (N) 1930, 1932
Heilmann was a good hitter who became a great hitter when the lively ball was introduced in 1920. Line drives that fielders had previously reached began whizzing by their gloves before they could react. Harry was a line drive machine. His homer totals were only average; his biggest year was 21 in 1923. But he hit plenty of gappers for doubles and triples. For much of his career he batted behind Ty Cobb, helping him to his all-time record in runs scored. Harry had 1,538 RBIs and topped 100 in eight seasons.

"Slug" didn't help his team in the outfield. He was slow and awkward. For two years the Tigers tried to put him at first base. He led AL first basemen in errors both years, so they sent him back to the outfield, where he had fewer opportunities to be slow and awkward.

But with a bat in his hand, Heilmann rivaled the NL's Rogers Hornsby as the greatest right-handed hitter of the day. He led the AL in hitting four times, oddly—in alternating odd years. In 1921, he led with .394; in 1923 it was .403; in 1925, .393; and in 1927, .398. In his "off-years" between titles, he bided his time with .356, .346, and .367. His career average was .342.

Heilmann was a low-key, articulate man, who told droll stories of his playing days. After retiring, he put those talents to work as a popular play-by-play radio broadcaster for the Tigers. He was named to the Hall of Fame in 1952.

RICKEY HENDERSON
Outfielder, Oak (A) 1979-84, 1989-93, 1994-95, 1998, NY (A) 1985-89, Tor (A) 1993, SD (N) 1996-97, Ana (A) 1997
The greatest thief since Willie Sutton, Henderson demolished the single-season stolen base record in 1982, when he swiped 130 for Oakland. Three times he has gone over 100, and he's led the AL in steals 12 times. He shattered Lou Brock's all-time stolen-base record several years ago and is now hard at work on his second thousand.

An ideal leadoff man, Rickey draws plenty of walks (he's twice led the American League), and scores and scores and scores; he's averaged over 100 runs scored per season for his career.

Henderson also hits with occasional power, setting the record for leadoff home runs. In his later years he's also become adept at collecting uniforms. He signed with the Mets for the 1999 season, his seventh uniform change since 1993.

TOMMY HENRICH
Outfielder, NY (A) 1937-42, 1946-50
"Old Reliable" Henrich played right field on eight champions in 11 years. Tommy was a first-rate player, but his .282 batting average and 183 homers do not quite put him in "best" circles. On the other hand, DiMaggio called him the smartest player in the majors, and nobody gave tests to prove otherwise.

One thing, Tommy was always in the middle of the action. In the 1941 Series, he was at bat when Mickey Owen dropped that third strike. Henrich alertly raced to first, igniting the game-winning rally in Game 4. He got the game-winning hits in three of his team's four victories in the 1947 Series, including the deciding seventh game. He played hurt most of 1949 but was such a clutch hitter that he finished sixth in the MVP voting. He finished the season with a flourish, whipping the home run that beat Boston on the final day to clinch the flag, the first of Casey Stengel's record-breaking five straight pennants. Then, in the opening game of the World Series, Tommy slugged a homer off Don Newcombe in the bottom of the ninth to beat the Dodgers, 1-0.

BILLY HERMAN
Second Baseman, Chi (N) 1931-41, Bkn (N) 1941-43, 1946, Bos (N) 1946, Pit (N) 1947. Manager, Pit (N) 1947, Bos (A) 1964-66
Herman was a great hit-and-run man and smart second baseman, who played on four NL champs with the Cubs and Dodgers, winning every third year—1932, 1935, 1938, and 1941. He succeeded Rogers Hornsby at second base for the Cubs in 1932, hit .314, improved the defense, and helped the team move up from third to the flag. He set an NL record by handling over 900 chances at second for five straight years.

For his first seven seasons in Chicago, Herman teamed with shortstop Billy Jurges in a double-play combination that had even old-time Cubs fans asking "Who-to-who-to-Chance?" Herman's best year was 1935, when he hit .341, cracked 227 hits to lead the NL, and scored 113 runs. His career batting average was .304.

Early in the 1941 season, Billy was sent off to Brooklyn. "I just bought a pennant," Dodgers owner Larry MacPhail crowed. He was right. Herman and his new partner, young Pee Wee Reese, meshed beautifully and the Dodgers won their first flag in 21 years. Herman was elected to the Hall of Fame in 1975.

FLOYD "BABE" HERMAN
Outfielder, Bkn (N) 1926-31, 1945, Cin (N) 1932, 1935-36, Chi (N) 1933-34, Pit (N) 1935, Det (A) 1937
Poor Babe is remembered as the man who hit .393 and couldn't win the batting crown, and as the daffy Dodger

who got hit on the head with a flyball and somehow tripled into a triple play.

True on the first count. Libel on the other two.

Babe hit .393 in 1930, when players were benched for hitting .290 and optioned to Topeka for hitting .280. Bill Terry won the batting championship with .401, the last time a National Leaguer topped the .400 mark.

In 1935 he hit the first night-game home run in big league history. Even after he left Brooklyn, someone was always willing to hire him for his hitting and look the other way while he tried to play the outfield. For his 13 major league seasons, he averaged .324 with his bat and slightly higher with his glove.

Herman was not the naive simpleton that the writers and historians created. He was a thoughtful, intelligent man, and he did not triple into a triple play. He doubled into a double play. It happened like this: With the bases loaded at Ebbets Field, Herman slammed a drive off the wall, and the ball bounced all the way back to second base. One run scored, and someone yelled to throw home. Dazzy Vance, halfway home, turned and scrambled back to third base, where Chick Fewster had already arrived from first base. Herman, running full out but head down, heard the yell and thought Fewster must be scoring, so he raced for third. He slid in safely—even stylishly—to find the other two already there. They called Fewster and Herman out and gave him credit for a double. Ever after, when the Dodgers put three men on base, some wag was sure to ask, "Which base?"

As for getting hit on the head with a fly, Herman stoutly denied it. "How about the shoulder, Babe?" someone asked. "No," he said, "the shoulder don't count."

KEITH HERNANDEZ
First Baseman, StL (N) 1974-83, NY (N) 1983-89, Cle (A) 1990
If Hernandez ever melts down his Gold Gloves, he can fill every cavity in New York. He won 11 and was easily the premier fielding first baseman of his era. The only argument is whether he is the best of all time. The fact that he ranks second in career assists by a first baseman, but is not in the top 10 of games played supports the "Aye" vote.

A consistent .300 hitter with line-drive power, Keith led the NL with a .344 batting average in 1979 and was voted co-MVP with Willie Stargell. In 1982 he hit .299 and drove in 94 runs, as the Cardinals won the world championship. His surprise trade to the Mets the next season is still a sore point with Cardinals fans. Mets fans think of it as akin to Christmas morning.

Hernandez played on his second world champion team with New York in 1986 and led them to a divisional championship in 1988. The handsome left-handed hitter was considered a leader in the clubhouse and on the field. He made as many trips to the mound as most catchers do and helped bail his pitching buddies out of many an inning with 1,654 double plays.

DORREL "WHITEY" HERZOG
Manager, Tex (A) 1973, KC (A) 1975-79, StL (N) 1980-90. Outfielder, Was (A) 1956-58, KC (A) 1958-60, Bal (A) 1961-62, Det (A) 1963
Herzog's playing career was eight years of undistinguished outfielding. His managing career ranks as one of the best and brightest.

He took over at Kansas City in mid-1975 and brought them home second. Three consecutive division titles followed, but the Royals lost the ALCS all three times. When Kansas City finished second in 1979, he was fired.

He crossed the state to St. Louis, where he had his greatest success. His Cardinals won the world championship in 1982 and pennants in 1985 and 1987. In none of those years was St. Louis favored in preseason appraisals. Whitey's best Series may have been 1987. Playing without his top hitter, Jack Clark, and with substitutes in several positions, he still took the Series to seven games against Minnesota.

"Whitey-ball" in the 1980s was tailored to Busch Stadium, with its artificial surface and deep power alleys. Typically his lineup was mostly made up of speedy, good-fielding, line-drive switch-hitters, with at least one strong power hitter to bat cleanup. His pitching staff normally hosted more than the usual number of left-handers.

GIL HODGES
First Baseman, Bkn (N) 1943, 1947-57, LA (N) 1958-61, NY (N) 1962-63. Manager, Was (A) 1963-67, NY (N) 1968-71
Gil was one of the top guns in the Dodgers' glory years of 1948 to 1959. He slugged 370 homers during an 18-year career, drove in 1,274, and was considered a top fielder among National League first basemen. He played on seven Dodgers pennant winners, six in Brooklyn and the last in 1959 for Los Angeles.

Hodges was an even-tempered gentleman of immense strength, both in physique and character. His inner strength helped him persevere during the extended batting slumps that he was prone to as a player. Most fans know Hodges' frustrating 1952 World Series when he went 0-for-21. Dodgers fans were sending him batting tips and lighting candles in church for him. Fewer recall that he hit .364 the next year in the Series or that he drove in both runs of the final game in 1955, as the Dodgers won their first world championship.

As manager of the dreadful Washington Senators (1963-1967), he needed every ounce of his patience. When he brought the team up to sixth in 1967, people said his next project would be parting the Red Sea.

Actually he undertook something more difficult—he became manager of the Mets. Throughout the 1960s the Mets had always been good for a laugh but rarely good for a win. They didn't disappoint the stand-up comics in 1968, Hodges' first year at the helm, finishing ninth. Then, in 1969, with Hodges platooning a lineup of mostly retreads and with a young pitching staff boasting Tom Seaver, Jerry Koosman, and Tug McGraw, the team became the "Amazing" Mets. They won the NL East, brushed aside Atlanta in the first NLCS, and humbled Baltimore in a five-game World Series—"The Miracle of Flushing Meadows." He died shortly before the start of the 1972 season; his number is one of only three retired by the team.

HARRY HOOPER
Outfielder, Bos (A) 1909-20, Chi (A) 1921-25
Hooper was an excellent right fielder with a legendary throwing arm. He played with Tris Speaker and Duffy

Lewis in what old-timers called the best outfield ever. There have been several "best-ever" outfields since, but the trio brought the Red Sox two world titles—in 1912 and 1915. Speaker was the star, of course, but after Spoke moved on to Cleveland, Lewis and Hooper helped the Sox win another World Series in 1916. And then, when Duffy wasn't around in 1918, Hooper was still there for a fourth championship. If you get the idea that Harry was a winner, you're probably running on all cylinders.

In the final game of the 1912 World Series, he went back as far as he could, then leaped, speared Larry Doyle's drive barehanded, and fell backward into the stands. His robbery kept the Sox alive to win in the 10th.

In 1915, after hitting only two home runs all season, he hit two in the final game of the World Series with the last one providing the margin of victory. In the 1916 Series, he hit .333 and scored six runs in five days.

Harry was a leadoff hitter with a modest .281 lifetime batting average, but he drew a lot of walks, which allowed him to score 1,429 runs in his career. Hooper was elected to the Hall of Fame in 1971.

ROGERS HORNSBY
Second Baseman, StL (N) 1915-26, 1933, NY (N) 1927, Bos (N) 1928, Chi (N) 1929-32, StL (A) 1933-37. Manager, StL (N) 1925-26, Bos (N) 1927, Chi (N) 1930-32, StL (A) 1933-37, 1952, Cin (N) 1952-53

Hornsby always said he could have made it to the majors on his fielding even if he'd only been an ordinary hitter. Well, maybe. The question is, how long would he have stayed there? Using his chances-handled-per-game as a gauge, he started out with pretty good range but slowed down fast. By 1920, when he first showed himself to be a great hitter, he was average at best in the field. And throughout the 1920s just about every good team in the NL had a second baseman covering more ground than the Rajah.

Of course, none of them hit as well. Hornsby never had to make a living with his glove; he was a magnificent hitter. Many call him the greatest right-handed hitter of all time. Proving that takes all sorts of adjustments as you try to relate one era to another, so there might have been a righty to rank ahead of Hornsby, but he has to be in the top handful. Take a deep breath and listen:

His career batting average of .358 is second only to Ty Cobb, who batted southpaw. Hornsby is the only right-handed batter to hit .400 three times, and his .424 in 1924 is a record for this century. He won six straight batting titles from 1920 to 1925 and added a seventh in 1928. He made 250 hits in 1922, led the league four times, and cracked over 200 seven times. He led the NL in home runs twice, led in triples once and tied once, led in doubles four times. He led or tied in runs five times and in RBIs four times. He won two Triple Crowns and two MVPs.

In the feet-of-clay department, the Rajah had a royal disdain for the opinions and feelings of everybody he ever met. He was brusque, blunt, hypercritical, dictatorial, moody, and argumentative. He alienated almost everyone sooner or later. St. Louis traded him right after he'd both played and managed them to their first world championship in 1926. The Giants traded him in 1927 after he hit .361. He predicted he'd lead the league again in 1928. He did, and the Braves immediately traded him to the Cubs

for 1929. He wore out his welcome just like he wore out pitchers.

Except for that 1926 pennant in his second year as skipper, he had no success as a major league manager. He never had any other Hornsbys playing for him, and he was satisfied with nothing less.

His only vice—outside of a personality that could sand wood—was betting on horses. He was bad at it. What he was, was a hitter. He never drank, smoked, read, or went to movies because he wanted to protect his batting eye. It worked. Hornsby was elected to the Hall of Fame in 1942.

FRANK HOWARD
Outfielder, LA (N) 1958-64, Was (A) 1965-71, Tex (A) 1972, Det (A) 1972-73. Manager, SD (N) 1981, NY (N) 1983

When 6-foot-7-inch, 255-pound Frank Howard came up to bat, the pitcher must have figured someone had moved the mound closer to the plate. "Hondo" was intimidating and he could deliver. He hit some of the mightiest blasts ever seen and left painted seats in the upper decks all over both leagues as mementos of his homers. Even Ted Williams, his manager at Washington, shook his head in admiration.

Of course Howard struck out a lot, too. But when he connected, the ball flew. Playing for the Dodgers, he walloped a long home run in the 1963 World Series to beat Whitey Ford, 2-1, and complete a four-game sweep of the Yankees. With Washington, he hit 136 home runs from 1968 through 1970. In 1968, the Year of the Pitcher, Howard had a streak of 10 homers in 20 at bats. Number 10, against Mickey Lolich, hit the roof of Tiger Stadium.

He was a bit clumsy in the outfield, but he played hard and was always hustling. He finished with 382 career homers and everyone's respect.

WAITE HOYT
Pitcher, NY (N) 1918, 1932, Bos (A) 1919-20, NY (A) 1921-30, Det (A) 1930-31, Phi (A) 1931, Bkn (N) 1932, 1937-38, Pit (N) 1933-37

"The secret of success," Hoyt once said, "is to pitch for the New York Yankees." This Broadway playboy, vaudeville singer, part-time undertaker, and baseball broadcaster won 237 games, mostly for the great Yankees teams starring Babe Ruth and Lou Gehrig.

Signed by John McGraw when he was only 15, Hoyt pitched only one inning for the Giants before he was sent to the Boston Red Sox in 1919. His record was mediocre over two seasons, except for one brilliant 11-inning perfecto stint sandwiched between hits in a 13-inning game against the Yankees. Impressed, New York acquired him in 1921 and made him a regular starter. Hoyt won 19 as the Yankees won their first pennant. He was sensational in the World Series that fall, pitching three complete games without allowing an earned run. Nevertheless, an error cost him the final game of the Series, 1-0.

He was the ace of the Yankees' staff throughout the 1920s, with his top seasons coming in 1927, when he was 22-7 and led the AL in ERA, and in 1928, when he went 23-7. After leaving the Yankees in 1930, he pitched for many teams with only occasional success as a starter. He was, however, an effective relief pitcher for four seasons with the Pirates in the mid-1930s.

Hoyt, who was elected to the Hall of Fame in 1969, was a popular play-by-play man for Cincinnati for 24 years.

CAL HUBBARD
Umpire, AL 1936-51

Hubbard is the only man in the baseball, college football, and pro football Halls of Fame. A 250-pound behemoth when most football linemen were 200-210 pounds, Big Cal played end and tackle at both Centenary and Geneva Colleges in the mid-1920s, then went on to an all-pro career with the New York Giants and Green Bay Packers of the NFL. A devastating defensive player and road-clearing blocker, he starred on four championship teams.

Cal had taken up umpiring in the summers while still a football player and moved smoothly into his new career. He became an AL umpire in 1936 and served for 16 years. He was known for his intimate knowledge of the rules and for the efficient and authoritative way he ran a game. A hunting accident prematurely ended his active career, but he continued as supervisor of umpires for the AL for another 15 years.

CARL HUBBELL
Pitcher, NY (N) 1928-43

In one of baseball's small ironies, the intelligent, level-headed Hubbell will forever be known as a "screwball" pitcher. The adjective refers, of course, to what he threw, not what he was. The pitch, thrown with a clockwise snap of his left wrist, left Carl with a left arm so twisted that the palm of his hand faced out. It also made him the NL's premier left-hander of the 1930s.

Reportedly, when he was a Tigers farmhand, Detroit manager Ty Cobb discouraged him from throwing "that thing." Fortunately, Carl continued to toss what is, in effect, a reverse curve, and when the Giants bought his contract, he got the chance to use it against major league batters. They hated it!

He had five straight winning seasons under his belt, twice posting 18 wins, when he suddenly blossomed into "Super Pitcher" in 1933. Carl considered his greatest game to be a 1933 18-inning shutout without giving up a base on balls. In July he went 46 straight innings without allowing a run. He pitched 10 shutouts in all that year, had a 23-12 mark for the champion Giants, with the unbelievably low (for those years) ERA of 1.66. He won the MVP.

In the Series that fall, Hub beat Washington in the opener, giving up two unearned runs. In Game 4 he went 11 innings, giving up another unearned run. In the 11th he loaded the bases on a single, a walk, and a bunt that didn't roll foul. Then he calmly ended the game on a double play to win, 2-1. His ERA for the Series was 0.00.

In 1934 he went 21-12, with a league-leading 2.30 ERA. In the All-Star Game that year he struck out Babe Ruth, Lou Gehrig, Jimmie Foxx, Al Simmons, and Joe Cronin in succession.

After a 23-12 year in 1935, "King Carl," the Giants' "Meal Ticket," took them to another pennant in 1936 with his second MVP year, a 26-6 gem that saw him again lead the NL in ERA. That year Hubbell began a 24-game regular-season winning streak that extended into 1937. His 22-8 mark in 1937 gave him five straight 20-win seasons and gave New York one more flag.

Carl became a spot starter for his final six seasons, with

his only losing mark being 11-12 in 1940. He finished with a 253-154 career record, and was elected to the Hall of Fame in 1947. Not bad for a screwball.

MILLER HUGGINS
Second Baseman, Cin (N) 1904-09, StL (N) 1910-16. Manager, StL (N) 1913-17, NY (A) 1918-29

Huggins wasn't a bad little second baseman for 13 years in the NL, but his main claim to fame is as manager of "Murderers Row."

He began as a manager with the Cardinals in 1913. The Redbirds had never won a pennant up till then, and Hug didn't change the status quo. He did, however, twice get them as high as third. That earned him a chance with the Yankees in 1918. New York was another team that had never won a pennant but had some prospects for improvement. Hug got them up to fourth and then third in 1919.

The Yankees bought Babe Ruth in 1920, and when they finished third went out and bought more talent. By 1921 they were ready. Almost as interesting as the yearly pennant races was the relationship between the 5-foot-4-inch, 140-pound Huggins and his overgrown Peck's Bad Boy, Ruth. Hug fought with him, fined him, suspended him, was hung over the rear platform of trains by him, and above all won pennants with him—six of them in eight years, 1921-1928, including three world championships. In 1925 Babe was making $52,000 and hitting .246, when he stayed out three nights in a row. Hug called Babe and all the players into the dugout and slapped a $5,000 fine on him, 10 times the previous record. Ruth complained to owner Jacob Ruppert, who backed Hug. The fine stuck. The Babe apologized.

Many consider Hug's 1927 Yankees the greatest team of all time. Both his 1927 and 1928 teams swept the World Series in four games.

The little guy died suddenly of blood poisoning in 1929. Even Ruth cried at the news. Their monuments now stand side by side in Yankee Stadium's center field. In 1964 Huggins joined Ruth in the Hall of Fame.

WILLIAM HULBERT
National League Founder, President 1877-82

For more than six decades, Hulbert's Hall of Fame plaque was incorrectly identified as "Morgan Bulkeley." The real Bulkeley was a figurehead president in the NL's first year; Hulbert founded the National League. What they did in Cooperstown was sort of like citing that dog that used to listen to "his master's voice" as the inventor of the phonograph. Hulbert was finally recognized when he was elected to the Hall of Fame in 1995.

From 1871 to 1875, the loose, rowdy, gambler-ridden National Association made a stab at being a league. Hulbert, the Chicago team owner, thought it might be nice to have a league with enforced rules, regular schedules, civilized behavior, and scores that weren't known on the mornings of the games. In 1876 he called together some like-minded owners, convinced them there was hope for the future, and formed the National League. The only mistake he made was to get Bulkeley from Hartford to pretend to be president as a sop to the eastern teams. Hulbert had a problem with the east; he'd just lured four of Boston's best players to Chicago.

Well, the next year—after Chicago had won the first

NL pennant—Bulkeley didn't show up at the league meeting, so there was nothing to do but elect Hulbert as president. He did things like kick New York and Philadelphia out of the league for failing to fulfill their schedules, ban four players for life for fixing games, come down hard on drunks and rowdies, and generally run things with a firm hand until his death in 1882.

In the 1800s he was referred to as the "Savior of the Game," which is a bit much, but beats "What's-his-name-from-Hartford" hands down.

JIM "CATFISH" HUNTER
Pitcher, KC (A) 1965-67, Oak (A) 1968-74,
NY (A) 1975-79
Hunter was the ace of the A's great teams in the first half of the 1970s and helped the Yankees win three straight pennants in the second half of the decade. And he started as a batting practice pitcher.

In 1964 A's owner Charles O. Finley signed Hunter to a $50,000 bonus contract. And because Finley thought "Jim Hunter" lacked oomph and because his bonus baby liked to hunt and fish, the owner hung the nickname "Catfish" on him. Considering the possibilities in the animal kingdom, it could have been worse.

In his first season, the 18-year-old right-hander pitched only batting practice for the A's. At one point, Finley had a publicity photo taken with Hunter sitting on the lap of Satchel Paige, who was sitting in a rocker. Maybe you had to be there to appreciate the joke.

In 1965 the 19-year-old Hunter became a regular starter for the A's and went 8-8. The next year he was named to the AL All-Star team; his record was 9-11 with the seventh-place A's. He pitched a perfect game in 1968 but didn't have his first winning season until 1970, when he was 18-14. By then Finley had moved the A's to Oakland, and his young players were becoming stars.

Starting in 1971 Hunter was 21-11, 21-7, and 21-5, and he won the Cy Young Award in 1974 with a 25-12 mark and a league-leading 2.49 ERA. The A's won pennants and world championships from 1972 to 1974. But all was not happy in Oakland. Hunter sued Finley for breach of contract and ended up winning a bigger award than the Cy Young: he was declared a free agent and signed a five-year contract with the Yankees for an estimated $3.75 million.

His best year in New York was his first, 25-14, his fifth straight 20-win season. He slumped after that, but was still a key starter in the three pennant-winning seasons (1976-1978). He retired after the 1979 season with a record of 224-166. In 1987 he was elected to the Hall of Fame.

MONFORD "MONTE" IRVIN
Outfielder, Negro Leagues, 1938-48, Newark Eagles,
NY (N) 1949-55, Chi (N) 1956
Irvin got to the New York Giants after a fine career in the Negro Leagues, where he was credited with two batting titles with the Newark Eagles, .396 in 1941 and .398 in 1946. In the latter year, Irvin played shortstop for Newark, and he and second baseman Larry Doby helped bring the Eagles the black world championship of 1946 over Satchel Paige's Kansas City Monarchs.

Irvin signed with the New York Giants in 1949 and played briefly with the team that year. He was 30 years old, and all agree that his skills had diminished from the level he had shown in the Negro Leagues. The "diminished" Irvin hit .299 in 1950. The next year he upped that to .312, led the NL in RBIs with 121, and knocked out 24 homers. Down the stretch, as the Giants chased the Dodgers to a playoff and ultimate victory, he hit over .400. In the World Series, he hit .458 and even stole home in the opening game.

A broken leg in 1952 almost ended Irvin's career, but he bounced back to hit .323 in 1953. In eight years but only five full seasons, his NL batting average was .293, with 99 homers.

In 1968 Irvin joined the Commissioner's Office. He represented Commissioner Bowie Kuhn at Atlanta when Henry Aaron broke Babe Ruth's home run record. Irvin was elected to the Hall of Fame in 1973.

"SHOELESS JOE" JACKSON
Outfielder, Phi (A) 1908-09, Cle (A) 1910-15, Chi (A)
1915-20
One of the great natural hitters, Shoeless Joe threw his career and his honor away for 30 pieces of silver. Joe averaged .356 for his career, the third best ever, using his favorite bat, "Black Betsy," and a sweet swing that Babe Ruth even copied. Ironically it was Ruth's popularity that helped fans forget the shame that Jackson and his co-conspirators brought to baseball.

An illiterate millhand, Joe hit .408 as a Cleveland rookie in 1911. He finished second to Ty Cobb's .420. The next year Joe hit .395 and finished second again to Cobb (.410). Except for 10 games in 1908-1909, Joe always hit .300. But a trade to the White Sox in 1915 threw him in with the proverbial bad company.

The White Sox were building a great team, but it was a team divided. Joe resented the club's college-educated second baseman Eddie Collins and his cadre of followers. The other side, the ones who griped about the admittedly low salaries owner Charles Comiskey paid, the ones who figured baseball was a stick and they had the wrong end, the ones who hung with the sharpies who looked for an edge, that side accepted Joe. They were his friends. They didn't laugh at his naivete, snicker at his lack of sophistication, or make fun of his southern drawl.

Despite the division on the team, it won the 1917 pennant and World Series. Because 1918 was a war year, Joe took a shipyard job and played in only 17 games. Others were missing. When everyone returned in 1919, the Sox paraded to another pennant and were installed as heavy favorites over Cincinnati in the World Series. But the chiselers on the team had a different idea. They conspired with gamblers to throw the Series for a promised $20,000. In Jackson, who was grossly underpaid at $8,000, the sharpies found a willing conspirator.

The story broke late in the 1920 season, while Jackson was hitting .382. Eight players were indicted in Chicago. Jackson admitted his guilt, but none of the players were convicted in court. There was no doubt of what they'd done, but the carefully assembled evidence suddenly and mysteriously disappeared. No matter, Judge Kenesaw Mountain Landis, the baseball commissioner, banned the "Black Sox" from the game for life.

Jackson, as well as others in the group of "eight men

out," played outlaw ball under an assumed name. Even fat and out of shape he never lost that great swing.

REGGIE JACKSON

Outfielder. KC (A) 1967, Oak (A) 1968-75, 1987, Bal (A) 1976, NY (A) 1977-81, Cal (A) 1982-86

"Mr. October" was perhaps the most electrifying hitter of the 1970s. "I'd like to be able to light the fire a little bit," Jackson said. And he did.

Reggie was at his best in the World Series, hitting .357, ninth best ever. His Series slugging average of .755 is tops all time. He's probably most famous for driving three home runs on three pitches in the final game of the 1977 Series to sink the Dodgers. Reggie was a winner. In 12 years, 1971-1982, his teams—the A's, Yanks, and Angels—won 10 division crowns and five world championships. Jackson won the MVP in 1973, when he led the league with 32 homers and 117 RBIs for Oakland. Perhaps Reggie's longest homer was walloped in the 1971 All-Star Game. It hit a light tower above the roof of Tiger Stadium like a rifle shot.

Jackson is sixth on the all-time home run list with 563 homers. He won four home run crowns and drove in 1,702 runs. He also struck out more than any other man in history, 2,597 times—once in every four at-bats. But he considered the strikeouts a bargain price for the homers.

Intelligent, outspoken, egomaniacal, Reggie fought with his team owners, Charles Finley and George Steinbrenner, and with his managers, especially Billy Martin, who benched him once for loafing.

Jackson wanted to be "the straw that stirs the drink," the highest-paid star, with his own eponymous candy bar. If there were an Ego Hall of Fame, Jackson would be the first one in. But the doors of Cooperstown have opened for him already. He was elected to the Hall of Fame in 1993.

TRAVIS JACKSON

Shortstop, NY (N) 1922-36

Jackson was a member of the Giants' "Hall of Fame Infield" of 1925-27. While Jackson played short and Fred Lindstrom third, they were joined by George Kelly, Bill Terry, Frankie Frisch, and Rogers Hornsby.

However, Jackson and the others had many better years. Travis played on New York pennant winners in 1923, 1924, 1933, and 1936, his final season. He was a reliable shortstop with good range, and inevitably was given the nickname "Stonewall." He led NL shortstops in assists four times, total chances three times, and fielding average twice. Defensively his strongest feature was his powerful throwing arm.

If Jackson had an edge over a half dozen good-fielding shortstops of his day, it was that he hit better. He topped .300 six times and finished with a career mark of .291. That wasn't sensational for the hit-happy time he played in, but it was excellent for a shortstop. He even learned to jerk the ball down the Polo Grounds' short foul lines. One year he hit 21 homers.

FERGUSON JENKINS

Pitcher, Phi (N) 1965-66, Chi (N) 1966-73, 1982-83, Tex (A) 1974-75, 1978-81, Bos (A) 1976-77

Pitching in the hitters' haven, Wrigley Field, Jenkins strung six consecutive 20-win seasons together. In 1971 he was the NL Cy Young winner for the Cubs with a 24-13 mark and 2.77 ERA. He pitched 325 innings that season, one of the five years he topped 300 innings.

Jenkins combined excellent control with a good fastball and curve. Traded to Texas in 1974, he responded with a 25-12 season, leading the AL in wins. In a 19-season career, he never pitched for a pennant winner, yet he compiled a 284-226 mark. Jenkins was elected to the Hall of Fame in 1991.

HUGHIE JENNINGS

Shortstop, Lou (AA) 1891, Lou (N) 1892-93, Bal (N) 1893-99, Bkn (N) 1899-1900, 1903, Phi (N) 1901-02, Det (A) 1907, 1909, 1912, 1918. Manager, Det (A) 1907-20

A law school graduate, Jennings played on the famous rip 'n' run Baltimore Orioles of the 1890s. He was their shortstop and captain, and they won the pennant his first three years, 1894-1896, plus the Temple Cup playoffs the next year. Hugh helped with averages of .335, .386, .401, .355, and .328—the best years he ever had, thanks in part to the new, longer pitching distance, which was inflating everyone's batting stats. In 1895 Hughie scored 159 runs and knocked in 125 more, with only four home runs.

Jennings' specialty was getting hit with the pitch, which he did 49 times in 1896, the record until Ron Hunt broke it in 1971. The Orioles weren't above faking it a bit, by taking a close pitch, then rolling around in supposed pain, while raising a welt by pinching themselves. However, Jennings had his skull fractured by an Amos Rusie pitch in 1897. That one was almost certainly legitimate.

Hughie took over as Detroit manager in 1907 and won pennants in his first three seasons. Only Ralph Houk of the Yankees matched that. In 11 more years of trying, Jennings never won again, but he finished in the first division seven times. His greatest player was, of course, Ty Cobb, whom he disliked but coddled. His other players were treated sternly, often sarcastically.

Jennings' nickname was "Eeyah," because he used to shout it from the coaching box. He said it was Hawaiian for "Watch out!" He was elected to the Hall of Fame in 1945.

TOMMY JOHN

Pitcher, Cle (A) 1963-64, Chi (A) 1965-71, LA (N) 1972-74, 1976-78, NY (A) 1979-82, 1986-89, Cal (A) 1982-85, Oak (A) 1985

John is the bionic man, with two arms and two careers. In July of 1974 he had only a fair 124-106 lifetime mark, but was coming off his best season, a career high of 16 wins for the Dodgers. He was 13-3 for 1974, and seemed headed for a great year when he tore a ligament in his elbow.

Dr. Frank Jobe sewed a new one back in. It was history's first ligament transplant. Tommy said he asked Dr. Jobe to give him Koufax's arm but said he got Mrs. Koufax's by mistake. He could throw again, but he had no fastball—he didn't even have a medium ball. Still, he could throw curves and get them over the plate. And he knew how to pitch.

In 1976 he was 10-10 for the Dodgers and was named the Comeback Player of the Year. That was nice, but he was just beginning his second career. In 1977, he was 20-

7. After joining the New York Yankees as a free agent in 1979, he won 21 and 22. And he pitched on and on: 26 seasons in all and 288 wins, 164 after surgery.

BANCROFT "BAN" JOHNSON
American League President, 1901-27

A former sportswriter, Johnson built the AL from the old Western League, a minor loop which he and Charles Comiskey took over in 1893. In 1900 they changed its name and in 1901 proclaimed it a major league. They raided the NL for star players and managers and built the league into what they claimed it to be.

By 1903 Johnson had forced the NL to make peace, leading to the first modern World Series—won by Ban's AL Boston boys over Pittsburgh. In fact, the AL would win 14 of the first 24 Series.

Johnson ran his league with tunnel vision. A humorless workaholic, his word was law among the original AL team owners. He banned liquor from his ballparks and fined for profanity and rowdyism. He backed his umpires, raising their status. Although nominally the president of the AL, he was called the "Czar of Baseball" because he dominated the three-man commission that governed the game until 1920.

But his power slipped as new owners who resented his dictatorial ways entered the AL. Even his old ally, Comiskey, turned against him. When the Black Sox scandal broke in 1920, Johnson demanded a full investigation, causing a final break with Comiskey, who owned the Sox. One result was that the commission was replaced by one czar, Judge Landis. Ban fought his loss of power for six years before resigning. He was elected to the Hall of Fame in 1937.

"INDIAN BOB" JOHNSON
Outfielder, Phi (A) 1933-42, Was (A) 1943, Bos (A) 1944-45

The lesson of Johnson's career was "Play for a contender or they'll never remember." It was his misfortune to join the Philadelphia A's in 1933, just when Connie Mack was selling off his high-priced stars and the team was heading for the bottom of the AL like a lead submarine. So for 10 years with the awful A's and three more with a couple of other nolo contenderes, Johnson played the outfield, hit a ton, and today is too obscure for a good trivia question.

Even when he'd do things like go 6-for-6 (in 1934) or bat in six runs in one inning (1937), the A's were so far out of contention that their contests were carried on sports pages after "In other games . . ." Of course, fans knew about him then—he was elected to seven All-Star Games—they just forgot quickly because none of his hits ever meant anything in a pennant race.

His numbers were impressive. Five seasons over .300 and a .296 career mark; three years with 30 or better homers among a total of 288; seven straight 100-RBI years (eight altogether) for teams that considered each baserunner a moral victory.

Now, just for a second, close your eyes and picture that record in Yankee pinstripes.

WILLIAM "JUDY" JOHNSON
Third Baseman, Negro League, 1921-38, Hilldale, Homestead Grays, Darby Daisies, Pittsburgh Crawfords

Johnson was one of the three best third baseman during the 1920s and 1930s. A steady defensive player, he was dependable rather than flashy. At bat he was an intelligent, scientific hitter who consistently exceeded .300 and was acclaimed for his ability to come through in the clutch. Known for his quiet, down-to-business manner, Johnson was considered a steadying influence on younger players.

He played on the famous Philadelphia Hilldales (1921-1929), hitting .364 in the 1924 black World Series. His inside-the-park grand slam won Game 4. In 1929 he hit .383 with 22 stolen bases. The next year he joined the Homestead Grays as player-manager. Judy also played on the 1935 Pittsburgh Crawfords, perhaps the best black team of all time, with Satchel Paige, Cool Papa Bell, Oscar Charleston, and Josh Gibson.

In later years, Johnson scouted first for the Philadelphia A's and later found Dick Allen for the Phillies. He was named to the Hall of Fame in 1975.

RANDY JOHNSON
Pitcher, Mon (N) 1988-89; Sea (A) 1889-98; Hou (N) 1998

At 6 foot 10 inches, Johnson is the tallest pitcher in major league history and one of the most intimidating. The "Big Unit" terrorizes left-handed hitters with his 96 mph fastball that seems to come at them from first base. Or the pitch may turn out to be a wicked slider just off the fists. For right-handed batters, Johnson has a big sweeping curve that arcs in from the baseline to nip the plate or a biting curve that sinks like a paper dinghy. He led the American League in strikeouts from 1992 to 1995 and again in 1997.

He won the 1995 AL Cy Young Award as the league leader in ERA and strikeouts while going 18-2 for Seattle, including a victory in a one-game playoff to clinch the Mariners' first postseason berth. Then he won one game as a starter and another in relief in the Division Series. Johnson missed most of the 1996 season with a herniated disk in his back. He came back strong in '97, winning 20 games for the first time.

Rumors of an impending trade were rife before the 1998 season and may have contributed to an up-and-down, un-Johnson-like first half. When he was swapped to Houston at mid-season, the magic returned. He was next to unhittable down the stretch in leading the Astros to the Central Division crown. He signed with the expansion Arizona Diamondbacks as a free agent after the 1998 season.

WALTER JOHNSON
Pitcher, Was (A) 1907-27. Manager, Was (A) 1929-32, Cle (A) 1933-35

Johnson is high up on everyone's list of nominees as the greatest pitcher of all time. His statistics alone are staggering. Working for a Washington team that finished in the second division in 10 of his 21 seasons, he nevertheless won 417 games (second only to Cy Young), pitched in 5,925 innings (third most of all time), threw an all-time record 110 shutouts, and compiled a 2.17 ERA, the seventh-best career mark.

For years his 3,506 strikeouts was considered an unbreakable record, but a more free-swinging age has

changed that; even though he has been surpassed by six latter-day pitchers, Johnson still may be the greatest strikeout artist ever. He won more than 30 games in two seasons, more than 20 in 10 other years. He led the AL in wins six times, in ERA five times, and was the strikeouts leader a dozen times.

He did nearly all of this with a fabled fastball, thrown with an easy side-arm motion. It came in straight as string, but the hitters couldn't get around on it. Only late in his career did Johnson bother to develop a curve. He had good control, and for all his innings pitched only in one season did he walk more than 100 batters.

He won more 1-0 games—and lost more—than any other man. In 1908, Johnson's first full year in the league, he won three shutouts in four days, giving up 12 hits in the three games, yet he had to settle for a 14-14 record for a last-place club. In 1913 he battled for 15 innings to win 1-0; in 1918 he struggled 20 innings for a 1-0 win, giving up only one walk the whole game.

Of all his great seasons, 1913 was no doubt the acme. He was 36-7, to lead in wins and percentage. His ERA was 1.14. In a league-leading 346 innings he gave up only 232 hits, an average of less than six per nine innings. He struck out 243 to lead the league and walked only 38. Oh, yes, he pitched 11 shutouts and had 55⅔ straight shutout innings, a mark which stood until 1968. He even set the record for fielding that year, with no errors in 103 chances. Naturally he was MVP.

Even with a sore arm in 1921 (when he had an 8-10 record), he could still pitch a no-hitter. It was his only one; strangely, he never pitched one in spacious Griffith Stadium.

Johnson finally made it to the World Series in 1924 at the age of 36. The old man was 23-7 and led the league in his usual categories: wins, ERA, strikeouts, and shutouts. The writers gave him another MVP.

As much as batters hated to bat against him, everybody liked "the Big Train." Open, honest, modest, soft-spoken, considerate, shy, he never drank or smoked but didn't condemn those who did. A big evening for him was going to a movie or just talking baseball. If he wasn't the greatest pitcher ever, you'd want him to be. In 1936 he was one of the first five players elected to the Hall of Fame.

ADRIAN "ADDIE" JOSS
Pitcher, Cle (A) 1902-10

Joss' death at age 31 cut off one of baseball's most brilliant pitching careers. He was the hardest man in history to reach base against, just 8.7 runners per nine innings; only 1.4 of them were walks. At 6 feet 3 inches, 185 pounds, the long-armed Joss pitched with an exaggerated pinwheel motion that earned him the nickname of "the Human Hairpin." Addie pivoted away from the hitter before the pitch, then came side-armed with a "jump" ball that—the batters swore—dipped, leveled off, and dipped again, something like Frank Merriwell's fictional curve that broke both ways on the way to the plate. It earned him a lifetime 1.89 ERA, second best ever to Ed Walsh's 1.82.

Joss broke in with Cleveland in 1902. He fanned four of the first six men he faced and ended with a one-hitter, a single by Jesse Burkett. A few days later Addie just missed another no-hitter; with one out in the ninth, an error and two singles spoiled it.

As a rookie, he was 17-13 with fifth-place Cleveland and 18-13 the next year, as the club rose to third. In two years Addie started 60 games and completed 59. For his career he finished 234 out of 260.

Joss won 20 or more each year from 1905 through 1908, with a high of 27 in 1907. His best year came in 1908, when Cleveland made a run for the pennant against Ed Walsh's White Sox and Ty Cobb's Tigers. Addie won seven of his club's first 11 games. The three teams were neck and neck (and neck) on Oct. 2, when Joss faced Walsh. Big Ed was 40-14 at that point. Ed pitched a four-hitter; Addie topped him 1-0 with a perfect game. Though Cleveland lost to Detroit by half a game, Joss was 24-11 with a 1.16 ERA.

Addie was a fine barbershop singer and often harmonized on the sidelines with Walsh.

Joss threw another no-hitter in 1910 but hurt his elbow and ended the season early with a 5-5 record. The next spring he fainted on the trip north; 11 days later he was dead of tubercular meningitis.

Although he played only nine years, his record was so outstanding that the usual 10-year requirement was waived when he was elected to the Hall of Fame in 1978.

JIM KAAT
Pitcher, Was (A) 1959-60, Min (A) 1961-73, Chi (A) 1973-75, Phi (N) 1976-79, NY (A) 1979-80, StL (N) 1980-83

"I've never craved center stage," Kaat said, but only Warren Spahn, Eddie Plank, Steve Carlton, Lefty Grove, and Tommy John won more among lefties than Jim's 283. Three times a 20-game winner, he used a good fastball, guile, and a brutal conditioning program to pitch for 25 seasons in parts four different decades. His best year was 1966 with Minnesota, when he led the league with 25 wins and won The Sporting News Pitcher of the Year Award. His other 20-win seasons came with the White Sox in 1974-1975.

Not only did Kaat put in a lot of years, he put in some workhorse seasons, going over 300 innings twice and over 200 a dozen other times, in spite of several serious injuries.

Kaat helped himself in ways other than with his arm. His .185 career batting average was fair for a pitcher and his 134 career sacrifices is the record for hurlers. He may have been the best-fielding pitcher ever, winning 16 straight Golden Gloves.

AL KALINE
Outfielder, Det (A) 1953-74

Kaline accepted a $30,000 bonus to sign with Detroit in 1953. Two years later, without having spent a day in the minors, the 20-year-old Kaline won the 1955 AL batting title with .a 340 average, the youngest champ ever. Al never hit that high again, but for 22 years he was an outstanding player for Detroit, accumulating 1,622 runs scored and 1,583 RBIs. Kaline finished with 3,007 hits, a .297 batting average, and 399 home runs. He played in 18 All-Star Games.

Kaline was a sensational defensive outfielder, with a powerful, accurate arm. He won 11 Gold Gloves. In 1971 he went through 133 games without an error.

Although Al battled injuries his whole career—he

broke his cheek bone, collar bone, rib, foot, finger, and arm at various times—he set an AL record with 20 years of 100 games or more.

He played in only one World Series. In 1968 he hit .379 with eight RBIs to lead the Tigers to a victory in seven games over the Cardinals. He was elected to the Hall of Fame in 1980.

WILLIE KAMM
Third Baseman, Chi (A) 1923-31, Cle (A) 1931-35
The White Sox bought Kamm from San Francisco of the Pacific Coast League in 1923 for the then sensational price of $100,000 to try to plug the hole at third left by banned Black Soxer Buck Weaver. In a career trapped in the second division, Willie earned a reputation as one of the best-fielding third basemen ever. He led the AL at his position eight times in fielding average and was consistently among the leaders in all fielding categories except errors.

Although he had no home run power, he was a good contact hitter, with a .281 career batting average. His .308 average in 1928 was his single-season best.

TIM KEEFE
Pitcher, Troy (N) 1880-82, NY (AA) 1883-84, NY (N) 1885-89, 1891, NY (P) 1890, Phi (N) 1891-93
Keefe was one of the first great changeup artists. For six straight years, 1883-1888, the unassuming right-hander combined a fair fastball and curve with his changeup to win 32 games or more. Twice he went over 40. He ended his career with 342 victories.

In 1888 he won 19 straight, including one 12-inning effort. That's the year he and fellow Irishman Mickey Welch pitched the Giants to the NL flag. Keefe was top in wins, percentage, ERA, strikeouts, and shutouts. In the championship series against the American Association's St. Louis Browns that October, he won all four of New York's victories.

Tim's finest day came in 1883. He won both ends of a July 4 doubleheader—a one-hitter in the morning and a two-hitter in the afternoon. He was named to the Hall of Fame in 1964.

WILLIE KEELER
Outfielder, NY (N) 1892-93, 1910, Bkn (N) 1893, 1899-1902, Bal (N) 1894-98, NY (A) 1903-09
At 5 feet 4 inches and 140 pounds, "Wee Willie" looked like the batboy. He choked up a foot on his 30-inch bat, the lightest in the league, stood stiff-legged, leaning over the plate, and chopped down on the ball, the famous "Baltimore Chop." The ball bounced into the air, and before it came down, Willie was safe at first. Or if the infielders charged in, he'd bounce it over their heads. His "I hit 'em where they ain't" has been quoted more often than the Gettysburg Address.

He hit .424 in 1897, second best ever, to lead the NL, and followed with a league-topping .385 in 1898. He had four other seasons over .370. His .341 career average ranks him 13th all-time. He had over 200 hits eight years in a row. The ultimate singles hitter, 2,511 of his 2,932 hits were for one base.

Keeler hit in 44 straight games in 1897. No one kept such records then, but in all the years since, only Pete Rose has tied it and only DiMaggio has surpassed it.

Keeler is one of the men responsible for the modern foul-strike rule. He could bunt a pitcher's best offering foul by the hour until they changed the rule and began calling them outs after two strikes.

Known as an outstanding right fielder, he played his first major league games as a left-handed-throwing third baseman. A practical joker in moments of leisure, Keeler was deadly serious on the field. He was elected to the Hall of Fame in 1939.

GEORGE KELL
Third Baseman, Phi (A) 1943-46, Det (A) 1946-52, Bos (A) 1952-54, Chi (A) 1954-56, Bal (A) 1956-57
Kell gave the Tigers and several other AL clubs some steady fielding and .300 hitting after World War II. He led the league in batting average in 1949, just inching out Ted Williams by .0002 with a .3429 mark. Kell was safely in front of Williams as he approached his last at-bat of the season. Teammates urged him to let a pinch hitter bat in his place since an out would lose him the title. He refused and took his place in the on-deck circle, but before he could bat a teammate ended the inning and the season by hitting into a double play. In nine seasons, Kell batted over .300. Never a power hitter, Kell is one of the few modern hitters to have over 100 RBIs with fewer than 10 home runs, a feat he achieved in 1950.

Kell had an excellent throwing arm and was sure-handed. He led AL third basemen in fielding average seven times, in assists four times, and in putouts and double plays twice. In 1983 he was named to the Hall of Fame.

CHARLIE KELLER
Outfielder, NY (A) 1939-43, 1945-49, 1952, Det (A) 1950-51
Until a congenital back problem forced him to the sidelines, Keller seemed destined to take his place as one of the greatest of all the Yankees. "King Kong" played with Joe DiMaggio and Tommy Henrich in the Yankee outfield that helped win four flags in five years, 1939-1943. He used the New York short porch to propel as many as 33 home runs and averaged 98 RBIs a year. Though Keller hit .300 only three times, pitchers respected him and regularly gave him 100 walks. He was a hard man to double up.

Charlie was a great October hitter. In 1939 he hit .438 in the World Series; his two homers and four RBIs won the third game, 7-3, and it was Keller who barreled into the Reds' Ernie Lombardi to score the deciding run in the 10th inning of the final game. In the 1941 Series, Keller hit .389. In the fourth game, after Henrich reached first on Mickey Owen's passed ball, Charlie doubled in the two runs that won the game. Then he scored the run that won the fifth and final game. In 1942 his two-run homer in the second game tied the score in the eighth, though the Cardinals went on to win the game and the Series.

Following another pennant winner in 1943, he went into the Navy. He returned in 1945 and played until 1951, but the back problem limited him to only one more season of more than 83 games. He retired to raise horses on his Maryland farm, Yankeeland.

JOE KELLEY

Outfielder, Bos (N) 1891, 1908, Pit (N) 1891-92, Bal (N) 1892-98, Bkn (N) 1899-01, Bal (A) 1902, Cin (N) 1902-06. Manager, Cin (N) 1902-05, Bos (N) 1908

Kelley was the heavy-hitting left fielder for the famous Baltimore Orioles of the 1890s. Joe played on six pennant winners in seven years, 1894-1900. The final two were with the Brooklyn Superbas, whom he captained.

He hit over .300 for 11 consecutive seasons. In 1894, when he hit .393, he went 9-for-9 in a doubleheader, still the record. Two years later he hit .364. His lifetime average was .317.

Kelley was a speedy outfielder with a powerful arm. He used to come to the park at nine in the morning to practice his bunting and running. A handsome if vain man, he kept a mirror under his cap and liked to sneak looks at himself in the outfield. He was elected to the Hall of Fame in 1971.

GEORGE "HIGHPOCKETS" KELLY

First Baseman, NY (N) 1915-17, 1919-26, Pit (N) 1917, Cin (N) 1927-30, Chi (N) 1930, Bkn (N) 1932

Kelly was the slick-fielding, clutch-hitting first baseman for a Giants team that won four straight NL pennants, 1921-1924. John McGraw, the New York manager, said that Kelly made "more important hits" for him than any player he ever had. He led the NL in RBIs with 94 in 1920, then knocked home over 100 in each of the pennant-winning seasons. In 1924 he led the league again with 136.

A good home run hitter, he led the NL in 1921 with 23 and set a record in 1924 with seven homers in six games.

The lanky "Highpockets" had one of the most powerful arms in the league. His on-the-money throw across the infield completed a brilliant double play to end the 1921 World Series. He consistently ranked high in assists and holds the NL records for most putouts and most chances in a season. He was named to the Hall of Fame in 1973.

MIKE "KING" KELLY

Outfielder/Catcher/Manager, Cin (N) 1878-79, Chi (N) 1880-86, Bos (N) 1887-89, 1891-92, Bos (P) 1890, Cin-Mil (AA) 1891, Bos (AA) 1891, NY (N) 1893

With his dark hair, black mustache, and flashing white smile, the King was a matinee idol and the subject of a popular song, "Slide, Kelly, Slide." ("If your batting doesn't fail ya, they will take ya to Australia / Slide, Kelly, on your belly, slide, slide, slide.")

Mike rode to the park in a silk hat, ascot, and patent leather shoes, in a carriage pulled by two white horses (and sometimes by his "cranks," or fans). He was one of the best-dressed men in America. He went on the stage reciting "Casey at the Bat" and made $3,000 for the use of his picture on advertisements. He was a big gambler and was often seen at the races.

Mike was one of the first hitters to perfect the hit-and-run, one of the first catchers to give finger signals, and one of the first outfielders to play close to back up infield plays. And despite the song, he was one of the first runners to use the hook slide. His most famous slide knocked the ball out of George Wright's hand to clinch the 1882 flag.

He also liked to catch the ump asleep (they had only one then) and cut from first base to third base without going near second. He'd take a similar shortcut from second base to home.

In all, Kelly sparked Anson's White Stockings to five flags in seven years, 1880-1886. He led the NL in hitting with .354 in 1884 and .388 in 1886.

In 1887 Boston bought him for a record price, and he became "the $10,000 Beauty." He reputedly kept $5,000 of his purchase price for the use of his likeness for promotional purposes. Mike hit .322 his first year with them and stole 84 bases.

Kelly also managed and batted the Bostons to the Players League flag in 1890. Mike played all nine positions. Once, while sitting on the bench, a foul fly came back. "Kelly now catching," he shouted and made the catch. They changed the substitute rule after that.

Anson always said, "Mike's only enemy is himself." He died of pneumonia at the age of 36, penniless after giving his only suit of clothes to a tramp while on a boat to Boston to recite "Casey" one more time. The city gave him a grand funeral send-off. He was named to the Hall of Fame in 1945.

HARMON KILLEBREW

First Baseman/Third Baseman/Outfielder, Was (A) 1954-60, Min (A) 1961-74, KC (A) 1975

A few eyebrows went up among the Old School observers when Killebrew was elected to the Hall of Fame in 1984. "The Killer" didn't fit the traditional mold of so many enshrined in Cooperstown.

He didn't hit for breathtaking batting averages; not once in his career did he bat above .288 for a full season, and his career average was a mere .256. Shortstops do better. He was no jackrabbit on the bases, either; he stole 19 in 22 seasons. Catchers do better. He didn't dazzle anyone with his glove; he played three positions without ever winning even a Pyrite Glove, much less real gold. He wasn't even a colorful character, just a modest, nice guy who came to work, did his job, and went home to his wife and children.

Killebrew was a one-dimensional player.

Of course, that one dimension—smashing home runs in gargantuan quantities—produced more runs for his team than all the singles of a half dozen "good" hitters. Killebrew lifted 573 lordly blasts over the fences. Only one AL player hit more—Babe Ruth. In home run frequency, Harmon is fourth behind only Mark McGwire, Babe Ruth and Ralph Kiner. Such slugging helped win the Killer spots on *The Sporting News*' All-Star teams at three different positions—third base, first base, and outfield. Eight times he went over 40 homers; six times he led or tied for the league lead. Harmon was MVP in 1969, when he led the league with 49 homers and 140 RBIs. He had 1,584 RBIs for his career.

And while that .256 batting average draws no raves, he drew 1,559 walks, which puts his on-base percentage up over .375.

RALPH KINER

Outfielder, Pit (N) 1946-53, Chi (N) 1953-54, Cle (A) 1955

Kiner didn't say, "Home run hitters drive Cadillacs," Fritz Ostermueller did. But he was talking about Ralph.

Kiner was, like Harmon Killebrew after him, a "one-dimensional ballplayer," who was worth more than most two- or three-dimensional players who ever lived. Such is the structure of baseball that blasting one three-run home run will help a team more than a leaping one-handed catch, or two or three steals of second. Moaned Warren Spahn: "Kiner can wipe out your lead with one swing."

No one except Babe Ruth ever dominated home run hitting the way Kiner did from 1946 to 1952, as he led or tied for the NL leadership in his first seven major league seasons. Several players hit more, but Ralph averaged 40 every 550 at bats; only Babe Ruth and Mark McGwire did better. In 1947 he hit 51; in 1949 he raised that to 54, the fourth-highest total in NL history.

Like the Babe, Ralph got a lot of walks, going over 100 six times. He was usually found on The Sporting News All-Star team, and by 1951 Ralph was the highest-paid player in the league. But the big difference between them was that the Yankees, with a strong supporting cast, won pennants on Babe's homers; the Pirates were usually last in spite of Ralph's.

Kiner, who was elected to the Hall of Fame in 1975, became a TV commentator for the Mets in the year of their inception, 1962, and remains behind the mike as one of the hardiest of all baseball's voices.

CHUCK KLEIN
Outfielder, Phi (N) 1928-33, 1937-44, Chi (N) 1934-36, Pit (N) 1939
Philadelphia's Baker Bowl, the Phillies' home through the 1930s, had a short right field that was batter-friendly, to say the least. No player ever took better advantage of the situation than Klein, a powerful left-handed hitter whose pokes against and over the Bowl's cozy wall helped him produce a startling five-year record.

In 1929, his first full season, he led the NL with 43 home runs, while hitting .356 and driving in 145 runs. He beat Mel Ott by one for the homer crown when Phillies pitchers walked Mel five straight times on the final day, including once with the bases full.

The next year Klein was awesome: .386, 40 homers, 170 RBIs—but he didn't lead the league in any of those categories in that hit-happy year. He continued his assault in 1931: .337, 31 home runs, and 121 RBIs, the last two figures leading the league.

He was named MVP in 1932, when he led again in homers with 38, while driving in 137 and hitting .348. In 1933 he climaxed his five years of excellence with a Triple Crown: .368, 28, 120.

Traded to the Cubs in 1934, he continued to be a productive hitter, but without his best friend, the short Baker Bowl wall, his great days were over. He finished his career with an even 300 homers and a .320 batting average.

The wall even helped Klein to a defensive record. In 1930 he threw out 44 runners from his up-close and personal right field spot. He was named to the Hall of Fame in 1980.

BILL KLEM
Umpire, NL 1905-40
In a career that stretched for 35 years, Bill Klem was considered the greatest umpire of all time. He's credited by some with being the first umpire to use hand signals and the first to use the smaller chest protector. He also officiated in 18 World Series, a record.

When Bill broke in, there was only one ump per game, and he literally dodged bottles from angry fans. When a player advanced on Klem to argue, he drew a line in the dirt with his shoe and called it "the Rio Grande." One step over, and the player was out.

Bill kind of resembled a catfish, but saying so to his face was another cause for automatic ejection. He once slugged it out with outfielder Goose Goslin in a hotel elevator.

Baseball was "more than a game, it's a religion," Klem said. "I never missed one," he always said of his calls. But after he retired, he would add, "in here," tapping his heart. Klem was elected to the Hall of Fame in 1953.

JERRY KOOSMAN
Pitcher, NY (N) 1967-78, Min (A) 1979-81,
Chi (A) 1981-83, Phi (N) 1984-85
Quietly Koosman emerged as a solid 222-game winner trapped with inferior teams. As a rookie in 1968, Jerry was 19-12, with a 2.08 ERA, tying a rookie record with seven shutouts. (His other record was striking out 62 times in 1968 as a batter.)

Koosman had a sore arm in 1969 but still posted a 17-9 record to join Tom Seaver in sparking the Mets to their dramatic World Series win. Kooz's contribution: a two-hit shutout of the Orioles in Game 2, a 5-3 Series-ending victory in Game 5, and an overall Series ERA of 2.04.

Jerry added another win in the 1973 Series. He won 21 games for the 1976 Mets and 20 for the 1979 Twins. In 1983 he went 11-7 to help the White Sox reach the playoffs.

SANFORD "SANDY" KOUFAX
Pitcher, Bkn (N) 1955-57, LA (N) 1958-66
For five fabulous years, 1962-1966, Sandy Koufax did things with a baseball that no other lefty has done: five ERA titles, four no-hitters, three Cy Youngs, and one MVP. And much of it was achieved pitching while in excruciating pain.

Wild as a youngster, Koufax labored for six years to compile a 36-40 record. Then he found his groove and became a star. In 1965 he struck out 382, breaking Rube Waddell's season record of 349. He also threw a perfect game. In 1966 he won more games, 27, and pitched more shutouts, 11, than any NL lefty in one year in this century.

Then his arm went bad, and he walked away at the age of 30 "while I could still comb my hair." Koufax won only 165 games, but no man who won twice that many ever reached the same heights. In 1972, at 36, he was the youngest man ever elected to Cooperstown. As a fastball hurler, Koufax ranked with Nolan Ryan, Walter Johnson, Bob Feller, and Lefty Grove. Unlike Grove and Johnson, Sandy had a dandy curve, too. He whiffed 18 men in one game twice, in 1959 and 1962.

His World Series ERA was 0.95, although his won-lost record was only 4-3. Four of the 10 runs against him were unearned.

BOWIE KUHN
Commissioner, 1969-84

A Princeton lawyer, Bowie Kuhn replaced "the unknown soldier," General William Eckert, as commissioner for three controversial terms. Considered the owners' commissioner—as indeed every commissioner is—Kuhn resisted players' demands for more money, saying greedy players would bankrupt the teams. Player-negotiator Marvin Miller called it Kuhn's "annual poor-mouth speech."

Ironically many owners also opposed Kuhn, and he was bypassed in the negotiations with Miller. Charles Finley of Oakland led the "dump Bowie movement," which almost succeeded until two owners changed their votes. Kuhn would later void Finley's sales of $3.5 million worth of stars.

One of Kuhn's moves was to sanction playing the World Series at night. He appeared at the first night game on a cold October evening wearing no top coat to dramatize how "mild" the weather was. But he was wearing thermal skivvies underneath.

NAPOLEON "LARRY" LAJOIE
Second Baseman, Phi (N) 1896-1900, Phi (A) 1901-02, 1915-16, Cle (A) 1902-14. Manager, Cle (A) 1905-09.

One of the best second basemen of all time and, by all accounts, the most graceful, Lajoie was also one of the most successful right-handed hitters. An established star with the NL Phillies, where he'd hit .378 in 1899, he jumped to Connie Mack's AL Philadelphia A's in 1901. The presence of Lajoie, Cy Young, and a few others helped legitimize the AL as a major league. Lajoie's .426 is still the highest batting average ever achieved in the American League.

The following year an injunction by the Phillies forced AL president Ban Johnson to shift Lajoie to Cleveland, where he spent the bulk of his career. He led the AL in batting average in 1903 and 1904.

Lajoie's status was such that the team was named after him during his tenure—the Cleveland Naps. He managed the club from 1905 to part of 1909 and got them as high as second in 1908. Late in the 1909 campaign, he gave up the reins because he felt the cares of managing were hurting his play.

Lajoie was a powerful line drive hitter who pulled the ball. In 1910 the popular second baseman was locked in a tight batting race with Ty Cobb, despised by nearly everyone in the AL. The winner of the race was to receive a gift of a new Chalmers automobile. On the final day of the season the St. Louis Browns' manager ordered his young third baseman to play extremely deep on Lajoie during a doubleheader, ostensibly because of Larry's ability to smash the ball. Lajoie went 8-for -8, with seven of the hits being bunts, but lost the title to Cobb by .0007. He was given the auto anyway. In 1981 Paul MacFarlane of *The Sporting News* discovered that Ty got credit for an extra hit that year and Lajoie should have won the title. Commissioner Bowie Kuhn ruled that, damn the facts, the records would remain as they had been.

Lajoie hit over .300 in 16 of his 21 seasons and finished with 3,242 hits for a .338 average. He accumulated 1,599 RBIs and scored 1,504. He led second basemen in fielding six times. In 1937 he was named to the Hall of Fame.

KENESAW MOUNTAIN LANDIS
Commissioner, 1920-44

Baseball's first commissioner and only true czar, Landis demanded and got autocratic power to clean up the Black Sox scandal ruthlessly. By doing so, he restored public confidence in the integrity of baseball. He went on to rule the game with a power never wielded since. Historian David Q. Voigt calls him one of the five most influential men in baseball history.

A shock of white hair, a thin, unsmiling mouth, and a crushed fedora hat—this was the image of Landis, who restored integrity to the game and ruled it for more than two decades.

As a federal judge, Landis had won fame by fining John D. Rockefeller's Standard Oil trust $29 million and for jailing 94 Socialist Labor Party leaders during World War I. But he refused to rule in the Federal League's suit against the NL and AL, saying it "would be a blow against a national institution." It won him the job as commissioner.

Landis banned the eight Black Sox for life, though no court had convicted them. He banned several other players for less publicized fixing charges. He suspended Babe Ruth for barnstorming without permission.

On the other hand, he was zealous in defending player rights. He opposed the farm system, and though he could not stop it, he released 200 farmhands from the Cardinals and Tigers into free agency on the grounds that they were being "covered up" by the teams.

Team owners bridled under his iron rule and never again granted a commissioner such powers. He was elected to the Hall of Fame in 1944, a month after his death.

TOMMY LASORDA
Manager, LA (N) 1977-96

Officially, Lasorda served as the Los Angeles Dodgers' manager for 20 years—a duration at one helm exceeded only by Connie Mack, John McGraw, and Lasorda's predecessor, Walter Alston. Unofficially, Lasorda has been baseball's foremost Good Will Ambassador for even longer. His excellence in both capacities earned him election to the Baseball Hall of Fame in 1997.

As the Dodgers skipper, he won 1,599 games while taking his team to eight National League West championships, four pennants, and two World Series triumphs. The 61 postseason games he managed is second only to Casey Stengel's 63. Perhaps the capstone of Lasorda's career came in the 1988 postseason when his seemingly outmanned team upset the heavily-favored Mets in the NLCS and Oakland in the World Series.

Lasorda's knowledge, energy, amusing stories, unbridled enthusiasm, and unabashed love for baseball have made him a popular after-dinner speaker and a fitting spokesman for the game.

Before becoming a manager, Tommy was a left-handed pitcher who could never quite win a spot with the old Brooklyn Dodgers in the 1950s. His record for parts of two seasons spent in the majors was 0-4. A lesser man might have soured, instead he embraced the game even more.

TONY LAZZERI

Second Baseman, NY (A) 1926-37, Chi (N) 1938, Bkn (N) 1939, NY (N) 1939

Poor Lazzeri. As a 22-year-old rookie, he was the victim of the most famous strikeout in history. He whiffed with the bases loaded against a hung over Grover Alexander in the 1926 World Series. But with a tiny change of wind at Yankee Stadium, Tony could have been the hero; before striking out he hit a long drive to left that faded foul by a few inches. "A few feet more," said Alex, "and he'd have been the hero and I'd have been the bum."

Like his nemesis Alexander, Lazzeri was a victim of epilepsy. And like Alex, he overcame it to have an outstanding career. Ironically Lazzeri hit a World Series grand slam 10 years later in 1936.

Overall he played second base for six pennant winners as a Yankee and helped the Cubs to a flag in 1938. Lazzeri drove in over 100 runs in seven different seasons and finished with a .292 career batting average.

Tony also had one of the greatest minor league years ever—202 runs, 222 RBIs, and 60 home runs for San Francisco of the Pacific Coast League in 1925 (of course, they played a 197-game season).

Lazzeri died in 1946 at the age of 42. He was elected to the Hall of Fame in 1991.

BOB LEMON

Pitcher, Cle (A) 1941-42, 1946-58. Manager, KC (A) 1970-72, Chi (A) 1977-78, NY (A) 1978-82

Lemon was heart and soul of perhaps the finest pitching staff in AL history—the Indians of 1948-1956, with Bob Feller, Early Wynn, Mike Garcia, Herb Score, and others. Lem won 207 games for Cleveland, yet didn't become a pitcher until he was nearly 26 years old.

As a third baseman, he played 10 games with the Tribe before going into military service for World War II. He demonstrated that he was not a good enough hitter to replace Ken Keltner at third for the Indians. Moreover, his arm was erratic. He seemed unable to throw a ball straight.

When he returned to the Tribe in 1946, the decision was made to turn his liability into a virtue by making him a pitcher. He showed promise in 1947 when he won 11. By 1948 he was a star. As the Indians won their first pennant in 28 years, he pitched a no-hitter, 10 shutouts, and won 20 games. He added two more wins in the World Series.

He had seven 20-win seasons from 1948 to 1956. Three times he led the AL in victories. Lem helped himself with his glove and bat. Often used as a pinch hitter, his 37 home runs are second all-time among pitchers.

Lemon, who was elected to the Hall of fame in 1976, had one of his most remarkable seasons two years later. In 1978, after starting the year as manager of the White Sox, Lem took over as manager of the Yankees when they were 10 games behind Boston. With patient handling—plus a raft of Red Sox injuries—Bob achieved one of the unforgettable modern miracles. The Yankees played .706 ball for him down the stretch and beat the Red Sox in a one-game playoff to win the AL East title. Ten games later the Yankees were world champions.

WALTER "BUCK" LEONARD

First Baseman, Negro League, 1933-50, Brooklyn Royal Giants, Homestead Grays

They called Leonard "the black Gehrig." Like Lou, Buck was a durable first baseman with plenty of left-handed power. He teamed with Josh Gibson to give the Homestead Grays a mighty one-two punch as the Grays won nine straight Negro National League flags, 1937-1945. When Gibson left the club for Mexico in 1940, the Grays won on Buck's power alone.

In 1939 Leonard led all black batters with .492. He also slugged seven homers in the short season, hitting them at a rate of 66 for every 550 at bats. Runner-up Gibson hit six (a rate of 59/550). Buck's entire career has not yet been compiled, but one estimate of his Negro League record puts his batting average at .336. He was also one of black baseball's most popular players. Buck was elected to the Hall of Fame in 1972.

FREDDIE LINDSTROM

Third Baseman/Outfielder, NY (N) 1924-32, Pit (N) 1933-34, Chi (N) 1935-36

Lindstrom was a victim of pebbles. It was his bad luck that when he was an 18-year-old Giants rookie in the seventh game of the 1924 World Series against Washington, not one but two balls hit pebbles and bounced over his head. The first, in the eighth inning, let in the tying run. The second, in the 12th, lost the game—and the Series—for the Giants.

Ironically Lindstrom went on to be considered one of the NL's best-fielding third basemen until a foot injury in 1931 forced him to the outfield.

When he became a Giants regular in 1925 and began showing his hitting ability, New York fans called him "the Boy Wonder." A consistent .300 hitter, his top seasons were 1928, when he led the NL with 231 hits and batted .358, and 1930, when he hit .379 and swatted 22 home runs. In 1935 he helped the Cubs to a pennant as an outfielder. He was elected to the Hall of Fame in 1972.

JOHN HENRY "POP" LLOYD

Shortstop, Negro League, 1905-31, Macon Acmes, Cuban-X Giants, Philadelphia Giants, Leland Giants, Lincoln Giants, Chicago American Giants, Brooklyn Royal Giants, Columbus Buckeyes, Bacharach Giants, Hilldale, New York Black Yankees

"You could put Wagner and Lloyd in a bag together," Connie Mack once said, "and whichever you pulled out, you wouldn't go wrong." They called Lloyd "the black Wagner," and Honus said he considered it an honor.

Starting in 1905, Lloyd established himself as the finest shortstop in black baseball and one of the finest ever. He played for independent black teams and in Cuba, where he was adored. They called him Cuchara, which means "scoop" or "shovel." Much like Wagner, he would scoop up a grounder and fire it to first in a hail of dust and pebbles that he'd also shoveled up with the ball.

His finest hour came in 1909 against Ty Cobb and the Tigers in five exhibition games in Havana. Cobb did not steal a base, as Lloyd tagged him out three times. Lloyd hit .500 against the Tigers; Cobb hit .369 against the Cubans. The Georgia Peach was so angry and embarrassed he stomped off the field, vowing never to play

blacks again.

At bat, Lloyd was a scientific hitter, spraying line drives where the ball was pitched. Although he was in his mid-30s when the Negro National League was formed, Lloyd played for a dozen years and compiled a league average of .342. His best season was 1928 when he hit .564 and led the league in home runs at the age of 44.

More than a great shortstop and hitter, Lloyd was the model gentleman of black ball, as Christy Mathewson was the paragon role model of the white game. "Gosh bob it!" was his strongest oath. In 1977 Lloyd was elected to the Hall of Fame.

SHERM LOLLAR
Catcher, Cle (A) 1946, NY (A) 1947-48, StL (A) 1949-51, Chi (A) 1952-63
Lollar put the Stop-Stop in the Go-Go White Sox of the 1950s. The underrated catcher anchored the Sox, a team built on speed, defense, and pitching. On the basepaths, Sherm literally anchored Chicago's running attack as he brought out various allusions to snails, molasses, and Ernie Lombardi. Nevertheless, as one of the few Sox with punch in his bat, he earned his keep on offense. In their pennant year of 1959, he socked 22 homers.

He excelled in defense. He was a rock behind the plate and an excellent handler of pitchers, absolutely crucial in the Sox scheme. And when the opposition tried a little go-going of its own, it was usually gone. In 1954 Sherm played for five months straight without permitting a stolen base.

ERNIE LOMBARDI
Catcher, Bkn (N) 1931, Cin (N) 1932-41, Bos (N) 1942, NY (N) 1943-47
Lombardi was the slowest runner in the Hall of Fame, including executives, pioneers, and exhibits. "Schnozz" was a big, muscular guy, with a banana nose, an easygoing manner, and feet of pure lead. His lack of foot speed was legendary. Infielders played shallow in the outfield and could still throw him out. It was said he had to hit .400 to bat .300.

Nonetheless, Lombardi was one of baseball's greatest catchers. He is the only catcher to ever lead his league in hitting while amassing 400 or more at bats. In 1938 he hit .342 and was voted the MVP. His career average was .306. He hit with tremendous power—he had to because he never got a "leg" hit—but on a line. His home run totals were modest: a high of 20 in 1939 and 190 for his career.

He was considered barely adequate as a defensive catcher in his day, whenever he let a pitch get even a few steps away from him, it was a passed ball for sure. He was on the receiving end of Johnny Vander Meer's two no-hitters and one of the keys to Cincinnati's two straight pennants in 1939-1940.

Lombardi was criticized unfairly for his famous "snooze" in the fourth and final game of the 1939 World Series. What actually happened is this:

With Yankees at the corners and the score tied in the 10th, Joe DiMaggio singled the go-ahead run home. The right fielder misplayed the ball and Charlie Keller, running from first, came charging homeward. He hit Lombardi where the chest protector doesn't cover, and while

Ernie fell to the ground in agony, DiMaggio scored. The play didn't lose the Series, but it probably kept Ernie out of Cooperstown until 1986, nine years after his death.

AL LOPEZ
Catcher, Bkn (N) 1928, 1930-35, Bos (N) 1936-40, Pit (N) 1940-46, Cle (A) 1947. Manager, Cle (A) 1951-56, Chi (A) 1957-65, 1968-69
Until Bob Boone broke it in 1987, Lopez had the record for most games caught. A good take-charge backstop, he played for 19 seasons, mostly with second division clubs, and hit a decent .261. He learned a lot of baseball and a lot more patience. Both helped him become one of baseball's greatest managers.

Taking over the helm at Cleveland in 1951, he chased the Yankees to three straight second-place finishes. The ex-catcher's teams were built on great pitching, with Bob Feller, Bob Lemon, Early Wynn, and Mike Garcia, and home runs. Unfortunately for Cleveland, the Yankees always seemed to have enough pitching and more of everything else. But in 1954 the Indians won 111 games to win the pennant.

Al moved to the White Sox in 1957 and won his second flag two years later. He did it with mirrors, since the Sox had almost no power. Owner Bill Veeck said a typical rally was two bloopers, an error, a passed ball, and two walks. A hit batsman would be "the final crusher." Thirty-five of their wins were by one run.

Lopez was a popular leader. If he had any fault, said Veeck, it was that "he was too decent." From 1949 to 1964 Lopez was the only manager other than a Yankee to win an AL pennant. He also brought his clubs in second 10 times. In 1977 he was elected to the Hall of Fame.

DICK LUNDY
Shortstop, Negro League, 1916-48, Bacharach Giants, Lincoln Giants, Hilldale, Baltimore Black Sox, Philadelphia Stars, Newark Dodgers, New York Cubans, Newark Eagles, Jacksonville Eagles
"King Richard" was one of the top shortstops of blackball history, possessing a strong arm, sure hands, and exceptional range. Although batting records are incomplete, the clever switch-hitter hit in the .330 range over his long career. He hit .400 four times between 1921 and 1930 in the United States and Cuba.

Big, graceful, and a natural leader, Lundy played on several championship teams. In 1925, when he and "Pop" Lloyd, the nonpareil of black shortstops, were both members of the Atlantic City Bacharach Giants, Lloyd moved over to second base because of the younger man's then-superior range. Lundy replaced Lloyd as manager of the Bacharachs and led them from fourth to two straight pennants, while hitting .329 and .306. In 1933-1934 he was a starting shortstop in the first two black All-Star Games.

ADOLFO "DOLF" LUQUE
Pitcher, Bos (N) 1914-15, Cin (N) 1918-29, Bkn (N) 1930-31, NY (N) 1932-35
One of Cuba's first major league pitching stars, Luque was the leading pitcher in the NL in 1923. He was 27-8 for the second-place Reds, with a league-leading 1.93 ERA. Two years later, he led the NL in ERA again with a 2.63

mark. In 20 years of pitching, 12 with the Reds, he won 193 games.

The pride of Havana even found a new career at age 43. He became the bullpen stopper of the New York Giants and led the NL in with eight relief wins. Always hot-tempered, he reportedly stomped into the opposing team's dugout one day in response to some unkind words and popped Casey Stengel on the nose.

ALBERT "SPARKY" LYLE
Pitcher, Bos (A) 1967-71, NY (A) 1972-78, Tex (A) 1979-80, Phi (N) 1980-82, Chi (A) 1982

Lyle won 99 games in relief and saved 238. Every one of his 899 pitching appearances was in relief. The durable left-hander was a big factor in getting the Yankees into the 1976 and 1977 World Series, with 23 saves the first year and 26 the next, when he also won 13 and became the first AL relief pitcher to win the Cy Young Award.

Sparky used his slider to write a fine postseason record in 1977. With New York losing the ALCS two games to one, Lyle pitched five and two thirds shutout innings to beat Kansas City and even the series. The next day he went one and a third more scoreless innings as the Yanks rallied to win. Two days later he pitched three and a third more innings of one-hit ball to beat the Dodgers in the World Series opener.

Then in 1978 his world was shattered when the Yanks paid millions to sign free agent Goose Gossage. Goose pushed Sparky right off the bullpen bench, and he spent the season in mop-up roles. He told of it in his book, *The Bronx Zoo*.

A flake and clubhouse cutup, Sparky once leaped nude onto a birthday cake, only to learn later that it was intended for Yankees manager Ralph Houk.

FRED LYNN
Outfielder, Bos (A) 1974-80, Cal (A) 1981-84, Bal (A) 1985-88, Det (A) 1988-89, SD (N) 1990

Lynn had one of baseball's most remarkable rookie years in 1975; he is the only man to win the MVP his first year in the majors. The Red Sox won the pennant as Lynn, their center fielder, hit .331, led the league in doubles and runs, cracked 21 homers, and batted in 105 runs.

Fred continued to hit with good power, getting up to 39 home runs in 1979, when he won the batting title with .333. In 1982 Lynn helped California win the division title, then walloped .611 in the ALCS. He won four Gold Gloves and was not afraid to run into an infielder or a wall to track down a ball.

Yet Fred's career was a disappointment in view of its brilliant beginning. His batting average fell through the 1980s, as did his RBIs. Many of his problems stemmed from frequent injuries—too frequent, say his critics.

TED LYONS
Pitcher, Chi (A) 1923-42, 1946.
Manager, Chi (A) 1946-48.

Lyons pitched 21 seasons for the White Sox. During those years, the Sox finished in the second division 16 times. Fans in other cities celebrated pennants; in Chicago they celebrated Ted Lyons. Possibly the most popular player ever to take the mound in the Windy City, he earned fans' devotion with his upbeat personality, indomitable spirit,

and by being one of the greatest pitchers of all time.

He came straight out of Baylor University, skipped the minors, and relieved in the first major league game he ever saw. By the next year he was a regular starter. Using a good fastball, curve, and knuckler, he won 20-plus three times with the White Sox in 1925, 1927, and, for the last time, in 1930.

In 1931 a sore arm cost him his fastball and nearly his career. Although he was no longer the dominating pitcher he had been in the 1920s, he used control and guile to remain the Sox stopper through the 1930s. Near the end of the decade, he became a "Sunday" pitcher, always pitching on that day because the biggest crowds showed up then.

Lyons won 260 games for the Sox, many fewer than he might have won for stronger teams, but he never complained. In 1955 he was named to the Hall of Fame.

CONNIE MACK (CORNELIUS McGILLICUDDY)
Catcher, Was (N) 1886-89, Buf (P), 1890, Pit (N) 1891-96. Manager, Pit (N) 1894-96, Phi (A) 1901-50.

For 50 years Mack managed the Philadelphia A's, building and destroying two dynasties. He had some of the greatest and some of the worst teams in history—his 1916 A's lost 117 games. Mack finished first nine times and last 16 times. His lifetime 3,731-3,948 record is first among all managers in both wins and losses.

A lean, sweet-faced man in derby hat and stiff collar, even in the dugout, he was known to everyone as "Mr. Mack." To some he was a skinflint. But lack of money was his lifelong problem. With a modest fortune behind him, he might have dominated the AL, as the Yankees did in the 1920s and 1930s.

Born during the American Civil War, he quit school in the sixth grade to work in a cotton mill. He was a weak-hitting (.245) catcher for a while in the 1880s before sinking his life savings in Buffalo of the Players League. When the league folded after one year, Mack was wiped out.

After three years of managing lackluster Pittsburgh in the 1890s, and a four-year stint with Milwaukee of the Western League, he was given the Philadelphia franchise in the new AL in 1901, with backing from Ben Shibe. Some said the team would be a "White Elephant," a symbol of wasted capital, but Mack brought the A's in first in 1902. The White Elephant became the team's symbol. He developed stars such as Rube Waddell, Eddie Plank, Chief Bender, Eddie Collins, and Home Run Baker and won five flags in 10 years, 1905-1914.

John McGraw's Giants beat him in the 1905 World Series, but Mack got revenge in 1911 and 1913. The "Miracle Braves" of 1914 shocked him in four straight; the Federal League was raiding his stars and bidding salaries up. Mack began selling his best players and the club plunged to the bottom in 1915, and stumbled in last for seven years in a row. Anyone else would have been canned, but Connie was, after all, a stockholder.

Patiently Mack founded another dynasty with Jimmie Foxx, Al Simmons, and Mickey Cochrane, and even shelled out a record $100,600 for Lefty Grove. They brought him three more flags, 1929-1931, before the Depression broke, and he sold his stars to pay the rent.

He was elected to the Hall of Fame in 1937. He was still

managing in 1950 at 87, still looking for that third dynasty. New York gave him a ticker tape parade. He died in 1956 at the age of 93, after his heirs had sold the club to a corporation in Kansas City.

RALEIGH "BIZ" MACKEY
Catcher, Negro League, 1918-47, San Antonio Giants, Indianapolis ABCs, Hilldale, Darby Daisies, Philadelphia Stars, Washington Elite Giants, Baltimore Elite Giants, Newark Eagles

Mackey is usually named as the finest defensive catcher of the Negro Leagues. Josh Gibson hit with much more power, but Mackey was his superior with a glove. "He was the master of defense," his protégé, Roy Campanella, would say. "For real catching skills, I don't think Cochrane was the master that Mackey was."

Pitchers loved to throw to Biz. He built up their confidence, called their game, "stole" borderline strikes for them. A jolly, bubbly man, he "jived" the hitters to take their mind off the game. Infielders loved to cover bases for him. "You didn't have to move your glove six inches," Judy Johnson said. The ball reached second light as a feather.

And he could hit, from either side—.364 in 1923, .363 in 1924, .317 lifetime.

In 1935 Biz met 15-year-old Campanella and shaped him into a Hall of Famer. "You saw Campy catch, you saw Mackey," oldsters say. In 1941 Biz could still outpoll Campy in the balloting for the black All-Star Game by 30,000 votes.

Biz retired as a forklift operator in Los Angeles. When the Dodgers gave Campy a "night" in 1959 before 93,000 fans at the Coliseum, Roy called on Biz to stand and take their applause. He died soon afterwards.

LARRY MACPHAIL
Executive, Owner

Night ball, radio broadcasts, batting helmets, air travel, old-timers' day, fireworks, three championship dynasties, loud feuds with his managers—the chances are that anything that Bill Veeck, Charles Finley, or George Steinbrenner thought up, Larry MacPhail had already done.

Wounded and gassed in World War I, the fiery redhead had even tried to kidnap the German Kaiser in a daring adventure. (All he got was the Kaiser's ashtray.)

Back home Larry took over the Cardinals' Columbus farm team and pioneered night games and air travel by baseball clubs. He also slugged a cop in a hotel lobby and was fired by St. Louis.

As general manager of Cincinnati in 1935, MacPhail brought the first lights to a major league park ("Every night will be a Sunday") and laid the groundwork for the Reds' champs of 1939-1940.

Moving to the moribund Dodgers in 1938, Larry brought Red Barber in to broadcast home games, hired manager Leo Durocher, and built a winner in 1941.

After another tour in the Army as a colonel, MacPhail bought a one-third interest in the Yankees. He installed lights in Yankee Stadium and brought the Yanks to a pennant and world championship in 1947. During the victory celebration, he engaged in a loud public brawl. The next day his partners terminated his contract as club administrator and bought him out.

He was elected to the Hall of Fame in 1978. His legacy lived on in his son, Lee, president of the AL (1974-1983), and grandson, Andy, former general manager of the Minnesota Twins and now president of the Chicago Cubs.

LEE MacPHAIL
Executive

In 1998 when Lee MacPhail joined Larry MacPhail to form the only father-son combination in the Hall of Fame, the temptation was to say "Like father, like son." Both found their way to Cooperstown through their efforts as highly successful baseball executives. Nevertheless, there were marked differences. Son Lee lacked his father's charisma, hair-trigger temper, and knack for innovation. The younger MacPhail was a far steadier entity, and some could argue that in the long run he accomplished more for baseball in his 45-year career than his more meteoric sire.

Lee began as a minor-league exec, then moved up to director of player personnel with the New York Yankees from 1949 to 1958, a period that saw the Bombers win seven world championships. He became general manager of the Baltimore Orioles from 1959 to 1966, laying the groundwork for that clubs later success. He later returned to the Yankees in the same capacity. From 1974 to 1983 he served as American League president before winding up his career as president of the Players Relations Committee. Through it all, he maintained an admirable reputation for integrity and sportsmanship.

GREG MADDUX
Pitcher, Chi (N) 1986-92; Atl (N) 1993-

The "Thinking Man's Pitcher", Maddux never seems to throw the same pitch to a batter in the same place twice. He throws an ordinary major league fastball, then cuts it. He tosses curves, sliders, or changeups at different velocities with varying breaks. And he does it all with unbelievable control—in 1997, he threw only 14 unintentional bases on balls in over 230 innings. By the seventh inning, he still doesn't seem all that impressive to the guy in the stands except for that long string of goose eggs he's put up on the scoreboard.

Maddux broke in with the Cubs in 1986 and hobbled along for a couple of years until he went into high gear with an 18-8 mark in 1988. In 1992 he won his first NL Cy Young. After the season he took the free agent express to Atlanta where he won the next three Cy Youngs. His 1.56 ERA in 1994 was the third best in the majors since 1919.

A good hitter for a pitcher and "fifth infielder" on defense, Maddux cruised past 200 career wins in 1998 with no letup in sight.

SHERRY MAGEE
Outfielder, Phi (N) 1904-14, Bos (N) 1915-17, Cin (N) 1917-19

Magee was an excellent hitter in the Dead Ball Era. He stole a lot of bases (441), hit a lot of doubles (425), and led the league three times in RBIs, twice in slugging average, and once in batting. He finished his career in 1919 with a .291 career average and 1,182 RBIs.

His reputation would be higher today except for two quirks of fate. First, after 11 seasons with the Phillies, he was traded to the Braves in 1915, just before the Phils' first pennant and just after the "Miracle Braves" pennant,

thus depriving him of a World Series showcase. Second, and worse, he is often confused with Lee Magee, a contemporary who was banned from baseball on game-fixing charges.

SAL MAGLIE
Pitcher, NY (N) 1945, 1950-55, Cle (A) 1955-56, Bkn (N) 1956-57, NY (A) 1957-58, StL (N) 1958
Maglie was one of the jumpers who signed with the Mexican League in 1946. It cost him a four-year suspension from the majors. When he returned in 1950 at age 33, he was 18-4.

He had a 23-6 mark in 1951, the year of the "Miracle of Coogan's Bluff". It was Sal who kept the Giants in the race the first half before their other hurlers caught fire. In 1956 the 39-year-old Maglie stunned New York by moving to the Dodgers, where he went 13-5. Sal pitched one crucial September game against fifth-place Philadelphia, when a loss would have put Brooklyn out of the race. He responded with a no-hitter, and the Bums captured the flag.

They called him "the Barber" because he shaved the hitters close with inside pitches (and because he had a permanent five o'clock shadow himself). As a coach, he passed on his philosophy to Jim Bouton: "If you're 2-0 on a guy, go ahead and flatten his ass."

MICKEY MANTLE
Outfielder, NY (A) 1951-68
The most powerful switch hitter ever, Mantle was a magnificent talent who was beset throughout his entire career by injuries. A high school football injury left him with a chronic bone infection in his legs. He had a shoulder operation, a broken foot, a torn hamstring. He taped his legs every day he played; even so, he sometimes took to the field in pants soaked with blood. He compounded his injury problems by refusing to follow exercise programs and partying into the wee hours with his buddies on the team. His attitude was "live now"; no male member of his family had lived past 40.

Joining the Yankees in 1951 as the designated successor to Joe DiMaggio, Mantle had a difficult rookie year, was farmed out, and considered quitting baseball. A visit from his terminally ill father, who had named him Mickey after Mickey Cochrane, convinced the young slugger to go on. He returned to the Yankees but injured a knee in the second game of the World Series that year.

In 1952 he began to show his awesome talent, hitting .311. He quickly became known for his tape measure home runs. Among others during his career, he walloped one to the facade on Yankee Stadium's roof, estimated at 600 feet, hit a 565-footer in Washington, and blasted one in Chicago, which, Yankees manager Casey Stengel said left seats "flyin' around for five minutes."

In 18 seasons he twice topped 50 homers, led the AL in home runs four times, and finished with a total of 536. He scored a Triple Crown in 1956, played in 20 All-Star Games, and earned three MVP Awards (in 1956, 1957, and 1962).

Mantle played in 12 World Series. He hit the most Series homers (18), scored the most runs (42), and batted in the most (40). He was named to the Hall of Fame in 1974.

HEINIE MANUSH
Outfielder, Det (A) 1923-27, StL (A) 1928-30, Was (A) 1930-35, Bos (A) 1936, Bkn (N) 1937-38, Pit (N) 1938-39
Manush was an outstanding hitter during the 1920s and 1930s with several AL teams. He compiled a lifetime batting average of .330. A line drive hitter, he knocked out more triples (160) than home runs (110). As a Detroit rookie in 1923, Heinie played beside Harry Heilmann and Ty Cobb, who gave him batting tips. Three years later he dueled Babe Ruth for the batting title. He went 6-for-9 in the final doubleheader to hit .378 and beat the Babe by six points.

In 1928 he cracked out 241 base hits to again hit .378 but lost the batting crown to Goose Goslin by one point. Two years later the two men would be traded for each other.

WALTER "RABBIT" MARANVILLE
Shortstop, Bos (N) 1912-20, 1929-35, Pit (N) 1921-24, Chi (N) 1925, Bkn (N) 1926, StL (N) 1927-28. Manager, Chi (N) 1925
The real miracle behind the 1914 "Miracle Braves" was a hoppity little 5-foot-5-inch shortstop named Maranville (accent on the "an"). He hit only .246, but he put on a nonpareil show in the field.

Sporting a "vest pocket catch" and a better range than General Electric, Rabbit handled more chances than any shortstop ever had before and teamed with Johnny Evers to lead the league in double plays (far more than Evers had ever made with his Cubs teammates Joe Tinker and Frank Chance).

Maranville was sick for the first few weeks in 1914, as the Braves stumbled in the cellar. Then after July 14 he, and they, stormed to the pennant. In the World Series he even hit .308 as the Braves swept the mighty Philadelphia A's in four straight.

Braves manager George Stallings hailed Maranville as another Ty Cobb, but the only way he might have had Cobb's bat would have been to swipe it from the rack, but the career .258 hitter was an incorrigible prankster, so it's not too far fetched). A free spirit, Maranville was sometimes free with spirits; "there's a lot less alcohol consumed since 1926," he once said, "because that's when I stopped drinking."

He played for 23 seasons and was considered a top glove man to the end. He was elected to the Hall of Fame in 1954.

FRED "FIRPO" MARBERRY
Pitcher, Was (A) 1923-32, 1936, Det (A) 1933-35, NY (N) 1936
One of the earliest relief artists, Marberry was the forerunner of the great relief pitchers of today. Nicknamed for the Argentine fighter Luis Firpo, Marberry had a similar, powerful physique. He both started and relieved, but his reputation was built on relieving as he led the AL in saves five times. He helped Washington to two flags (1924-1925) and Detroit to one (1934).

Marberry had 15 saves in 1924, plus two in the World Series, 15 more in 1925 as the Senators won again, and 22 in 1926. He was 15-5 with three saves for Detroit in 1934 to help them to their first flag in a quarter century, and he ended with a 148-88 won-lost mark and 101 saves.

JUAN MARICHAL
Pitcher, SF (N) 1960-73, Bos (A) 1974, LA (N) 1975
Facing Marichal was like facing a dozen different pitchers. His high leg kick was his trademark, but once the leg came down, the ball could zip toward the batter from any angle—sidearm, three-quarters, over the top—as he delivered fastballs, curves, and sliders in a multiplicity of speeds, yet always with marvelous control. From 1963 through 1969, the brilliant right-hander from the Dominican Republic was the major league's winningest pitcher.

After winning 18 for the Giants in 1962, Marichal won 20 or more in six of the next seven seasons. He was 25-8 in 1963, including a no-hitter, to lead the NL in wins and 25-6 in 1966 to lead in winning percentage. In 1968 he was back on top in wins: 26-9. And the next season he led in ERA.

"Put your club a run ahead in the late innings," manager Alvin Dark said, "and Marichal is the greatest pitcher I ever saw." He completed 244 of his 457 starts and did not have a losing season until 1972. He averaged nearly six strikeouts per nine innings while walking less than two.

Usually easy-going, with a ready, impish grin, Marichal's reputation was tarnished by one out-of-character moment. In 1965, during a game with the Dodgers, he was brushed back by the pitch. Then the return throw from Dodger catcher John Roseboro whizzed close by his ear. Suddenly getting it from in front and behind, Marichal turned and clubbed Roseboro on the head with his bat. He was fined $1,750, an NL record at the time, and suspended for nine days.

In 1983 Marichal was named to the Hall of Fame.

ROGER MARIS
Outfielder, Cle (A) 1957-58, KC (A) 1958-59, NY (A) 1960-66, StL (N) 1967-68
Maris may never be forgiven. He broke the Babe's sacrosanct record of 60 home runs in a season. How dare he! When Hank Aaron passed Ruth's career total, there was anger among the unreasoning, but the 714 never had the magic of 60. And Aaron roared past and added 40 more after he broke it. Maris topped 60 by only one in a season eight games longer than the Babe's. And Aaron was a great player. Maris wasn't.

"I don't want to be Babe Ruth," Maris protested. He needn't have said it. There were too many others anxious to prove that he wasn't. So Maris struck more home runs than any other major league batter had ever hit in a single season and spent the rest of his life hearing what a bum he was. Commissioner Ford Frick even ordered an asterisk placed beside Roger's 61, though he might have preferred a scarlet letter.

Maris was no bum. He was an intelligent, likable man, a bit reserved—a private sort of person—totally unprepared to turn the media blitz that drowned him to his advantage. He was a talented player. All right, not a great player, but a good one. He was sure in the outfield, with a fine arm. He never hit for much of an average, and he ended his 12-year career with only a .260 mark, but he had good home run power. In 11 other seasons he totaled 214 homers.

He was AL MVP the year before his 61-homer season, with 39 home runs and a league-leading 112 RBIs. In 1961, besides the homers, he led in runs (132) and RBIs (142), so his second MVP wasn't just for breaking Ruth's record. In 1962 he had 33 homers and 100 RBIs. He had some injuries after that, and the numbers fell off, but he was the regular right fielder when healthy for five straight Yankees pennant winners (1960-1964). He finished up in 1967-1968, as a regular for two Cardinals teams that won flags.

RICHARD "RUBE" MARQUARD
Pitcher, NY (N) 1908-15, Bkn (N) 1915-20, Cin (N) 1921, Bos (N) 1922-25
The Giants bought Marquard from Indianapolis for a record $11,000 in 1908 and rushed him into the pennant race before he was ready. The result was an "$11,000 Lemon" until careful nurturing by coach Wilbert Robinson turned him into a "beauty" in 1911. Rube was 24-7 to help win the pennant. It was the first of three 20-victory years for the left-hander and three straight flags for the Giants. In the 1911 Series he had a 1.54 ERA but lost his only decision.

In 1912, when he was 26-11, Marquard won his first 19 games to tie Tim Keefe's record. He actually won 20 if modern scoring rules are applied; one "win" was scored a save. In the World Series that year, he had an 0.50 ERA and won two of the Giants' three victories. In 1913 he was 23-10, giving him 73 victories in three years.

Those were his three best years. He had a brief comeback with Brooklyn under Robinson in 1916. He was 13-6, and the Dodgers won the pennant. He upped that to 19-12 the next year, but led the NL in losses in 1918. He helped the Dodgers to another pennant with a 10-7 mark in 1920.

Although nicknamed after another star southpaw, Rube Waddell, Marquard was no Rube. He was sophisticated, a flashy dresser, no drinker (unlike Waddell), and married a Broadway actress. Marquard was elected to the Hall of Fame in 1971.

MIKE MARSHALL
Pitcher, Det (A) 1967, Sea (A) 1969, Hou (N) 1970, Mon (N) 1970-73, LA (N) 1974-76, Atl (N) 1976-77, Tex (A) 1977, Min (A) 1978-80, NY (N) 1981
A doctor of physiology, Marshall jogged four miles a day and set a record pitching in 106 games in 1974. That year he was 15-12 with 21 saves for the Dodgers, all tops in the NL for relievers that year. That performance earned him the Cy Young Award, the first ever won by a reliever. Two other times (1973 and 1979) he went over 90 games.

Mike designed his own conditioning program, but his education intimidated coaches and managers. He fought with Mayo Smith, Sal Maglie, and Harry Walker, with little success, until he joined Montreal under Gene Mauch, who let him do what he wanted. Marshall's saves shot up to 23 in 1971 and 31 in 1973.

In Minnesota in 1979 he used his screwball to save 32 games, his all-time high. He ended his 14-season career with 92 relief wins and 188 saves.

BILLY MARTIN
Second Base, NY (A) 1950-57, KC (A) 1957, Det (A) 1958, Cle (A) 1959, Cin (N) 1960, Mil (N) 1961, Min (A) 1961. Manager, Min (A) 1969, Det (A) 1971-73, Tex (A)

1974-75, NY (A) 1975-78, 1979, 1983, 1985, 1988, Oak (A) 1980-83

"Everybody looks up to Billy Martin," one player said. "That's because he probably just knocked them down."

As a Yankees second baseman in the 1950s, he earned a reputation for light-hitting, heads-up play, and ready fists. He'd once considered becoming a middleweight boxer, and he was only too anxious to demonstrate his prowess. A brawl in the Copacabana night club in 1957 led to a trade to Kansas City and four final nomadic seasons.

He became a major league manager with the Twins in 1969, and the Martin pattern emerged. His clubs invariably improved their record from the previous year—the Twins jumped to the division title. Then Martin would be involved in a well-publicized fight, usually involving alcohol, and would be fired. One season in Minnesota, three in Detroit, two in Texas, and three in Oakland.

His saddest moments came with the Yankees, where he was hired and fired five times. Hired first in 1975, he took them to the pennant in 1976 and a world championship in 1977, only to be fired after 94 games in 1978. He was rehired in 1979 for the final two-thirds of the season, then fired again. After his three years in Oakland, he was back with the Yankees for all of 1983, most of 1985, and part of 1988.

Martin, when sober and with his temper under control, was a bright, articulate man. He had many friends who were intensely loyal, and he showed himself to be a talented manager. Unfortunately his destructive side had one enduring victim—himself. He died on Christmas Day, 1989.

EDDIE MATHEWS

Third Baseman, Bos (N) 1952, Mil (N) 1953-65, Atl (N) 1966, Hou (N) 1967, Det (A) 1967-68. Manager, Atl (N) 1972-74

Mathews was the greatest home run hitter among third basemen until Mike Schmidt. Mathews' 512 homers made him only the seventh man to hit 500, and he had four seasons with over 40, including league-leading marks of 47 in 1953 and 46 in 1959. Although he hit over .300 three times, his career average was only .271; however, he supplemented his 2,315 hits with 1,444 walks, leading the NL four times.

He played 15 of his 27 seasons in a Braves uniform, beginning with the team's last season in Boston and ending with its first year in Atlanta. In between were 13 seasons in Milwaukee. The left-handed slugger combined with Hank Aaron to form perhaps the best one-two punch of all time. Their total of 863 home runs while together ranks ahead of Mays-McCovey (800) and Ruth-Gehrig (772). Mathews usually batted third ahead of Aaron to take advantage of his ability to draw walks. He scored 1,509 runs, often being plated by Aaron. Eddie drove in 1,453 runs himself.

Curiously, with all his outstanding seasons in Milwaukee, two of the most ordinary were the pennant winning years of 1957-1958. The handsome slugger was elected to the Hall of Fame in 1978.

CHRISTY MATHEWSON

Pitcher, NY (N) 1900-16, Cin (N) 1916.

Manager, Cin (N) 1916-18

One of the first five men elected to Cooperstown in 1936, Matty was handsome, intelligent, clean-cut, clean-living, the most popular pitcher of his day and possibly the best. They called Matty "Big Six," after New York's famous fire engine. In an era of roughnecks, Matty was a college man who sang in the Bucknell glee club, belonged to the literary society, was president of his class, and could beat a dozen foes at checkers at the same time. He refused to pitch on Sunday. The childless John McGraw virtually made him his son. Matty was the model for the Frank Merriwell of Yale books and the "Baseball Joe" stories that molded young boys' characters when Great Grandpa was a kid. Christy's own book, *Pitching in a Pinch*, is still a delight to read.

Connie Mack once compared Mathewson with Walter Johnson, who was also one of the first five in the Hall of Fame. "With Johnson, it was brute force," Mack said. "With Mathewson, it was knowledge and judgment, perfect control, and form."

Mathewson was famous for his "fadeaway," a screwball. With it, Matty won 30 three years in a row (1903-1905). He won 37 in 1908 and had nine other seasons with 20 or more wins. He brought the Giants five pennants. Matty's 78 shutouts are surpassed only by Walter Johnson and Grover Cleveland Alexander. In the 1905 World Series, Matty pitched three shutouts in six days, giving up just 14 hits—and only one walk!

Mathewson had great control. In 1908 he had 391 innings pitched, 259 strikeouts, and only 42 walks. In 1913 he averaged only 0.6 walks per nine innings; he went 68 straight innings without a walk. He once won a game with 67 pitches.

Yet he wasn't out for records and always held something in reserve in those pre-relief days.

Before the Perrys and Niekros, Christy and his brother Henry held the record for wins by brothers—373 by Christy, none by Henry, whose big league career produced only one decision. Christy joined the Army in World War I and was the victim of poison gas. He suffered pulmonary tuberculosis brought on by the gas, and died in 1925 at age 45.

DON MATTINGLY

First Baseman, NY (A) 1982-1995

Mattingly won the AL batting title with a .343 mark in 1984, his first full major league season, and he was one of the most consistent hitters in baseball until a 1990 back injury took some of his ability. Up to then perhaps no hitter in the game combined high average with home run power to the same extent. He topped 200 hits three times, 30 homers three times, and 100 RBIs five times. His 145 RBIs in 1985 led the AL. He led in doubles in 1984-1986, and won the AL MVP in 1985.

Mattingly was one of the most popular Yankees of the 1980s. He made headlines in 1988 with his criticism of the atmosphere owner George Steinbrenner produced on the ballclub. The back injury in 1990 robbed him of his power, but Mattingly won nine Gold Glove Awards. After 1,785 career games, Mattingly made his first trip to the postseason in 1995. Two years later he became the 14th Yankee to have his number retired.

CARL MAYS

Pitcher, Bos (A) 1915-19, NY (A) 1919-23, Cin (N) 1924-28, NY (N) 1929

Mays is the man whose submarine pitch killed Cleveland shortstop Ray Chapman in 1920. That tragic incident has obscured the fact that Mays was one of the best pitchers of his day.

Mays had a reputation for throwing at batters—and once he threw at a fan—but he denied intent to hit Chapman, and the game situation—leadoff batter, start of the inning—argues strongly that it was an accident.

Actually, Mays hit only seven batters that year, far from the league high. Still, at least two teams threatened not to play against him after that. But Carl calmly won his next start, 8-0. He was 26-11 for the Yankees that year, and 27-9 the next season when the Yanks won their first pennant.

A morose loner, Mays was unpopular with teammates and extremely so with fans after the Chapman tragedy. Mays "has no friends and doesn't want any," one player said of him.

In addition to his two great years with the Yankees, he earlier won 21 and 22 with the Red Sox, and in the mid-1920s won 20 and 19 for the Reds. He played on six pennant winners in Boston and New York.

WILLIE MAYS

Outfielder, Negro League, 1948-50, Birmingham Black Barons, NY (N) 1951-52, 1954-57, SF (N) 1958-72, NY (N) 1972-73

The most exciting player of the 1960s, Mays hit 660 home runs, raced around the bases or into deepest center field, his hat flying off behind him. "The only man who could have caught that ball," one announcer said, "just hit it."

His catch off Vic Wertz in the 1954 World Series is sometimes cited as the greatest ever—a long sprint, an over-the-shoulder catch near the wall 460 feet away, a spin, and a bullet throw back to the infield. The hat flew off, of course—Willie later admitted he wore hats a size too small to make them do that.

New Yorkers gloried in their three great center fielders, "Willie, Mickey, and the Duke." The most ebullient—and to many the best—was the "Say Hey Kid." He played stickball with the kids in Harlem and hardball in the Polo Grounds at night.

He won 11 straight Gold Gloves and set the record for career putouts by an outfielder and the NL record for total chances.

He also stole 337 bases, led the league four times, and was the first man in the 300/300 club—300 steals, 300 homers. He was one of the few stolen-base kings who wasn't spinning his wheels, with a 77 percent success ratio (anything below 66 percent is a net negative).

Willie came up to the Giants in 1951. He started by going 0-for-22. But manager Leo Durocher stuck with him, pepped him up, and both Willie and the Giants caught fire. The team came from 13 games behind to catch the Dodgers and win the playoff on Bobby Thomson's home run. "The only reason I pitched to Thomson," Dodgers manager Chuck Dressen said, "was because Willie was the next hitter."

After military service in 1953, Mays returned to lead the Giants to the 1954 pennant with an NL-high .345 and 41 homers. He was named MVP. "If he could cook," said Leo, "I'd marry him."

Willie led the league in homers four times, topping 50 twice. Moving to San Francisco in 1958 hurt his home run totals (as Aaron's move to Atlanta helped his). Still, Willie slugged four in one game in 1961. In 1962 he hit 49 with 141 RBIs to lead the Giants to a playoff victory over Los Angeles.

In 1965 he slugged 52 homers, 17 of them in August, to pass 500 and win his second MVP. The Sporting News named him the Player of the 1960s. In 1979 he was elected to the Hall of Fame.

BILL MAZEROSKI

Second Baseman, Pit (N) 1956-72

Possibly the greatest-fielding second baseman who ever lived, Maz's 1,706 double plays is the all-time record for second-sackers. Around Pittsburgh, they called him "no-hands"—the ball seemed to go from the shortstop's shovel pass and ricochet to first with him hardly touching it. He led the league in assists nine times, double plays eight, putouts five, and fielding average three.

Bill also hit as dramatic a home run as any in World Series history, a sayonara blow in the ninth to win the seventh game of the 1960 Series and make the Pirates world champions.

Generally he wasn't too bad at bat, and in a friendlier park he would have been even better. He had a respectable .260 career batting average, with fair home run power. His Series-ending homer in 1960 was his second round-tripper of the Series: his two-run blast provided the margin of victory in Game 1.

JOE McCARTHY

Manager, Chi (N) 1926-30, NY (A) 1931-46, Bos (A) 1948-50

If McCarthy was a "push-button manager," as rival skipper Jimmy Dykes once said, no manager ever pushed them more effectively. In 24 years as a major league manager, his teams won seven world championships, nine pennants, and never finished out of the first division. His .614 winning percentage for nearly 3,500 games is the record, as is his .698 for nine World Series.

A minor league second baseman who never played a game in the majors, McCarthy won American Association pennants at Louisville and was hired by the Cubs in 1926. He instituted discipline on the free-spirited club and in 1929 led them to the NL pennant. They lost the World Series to the A's. The following year McCarthy resigned in September with the Cubs in second place

The Yankees hired him for the 1931 season expressly to bring the team back to the heights it had enjoyed in the 1920s. Despite some resentment by some of the older Yankees, including Babe Ruth, who had expected to be named manager, McCarthy brought the team home second in his first season and won the pennant and his first world championship in 1932.

He kept them in second place for the next three years while retooling the team. By 1936, with the arrival of rookie Joe DiMaggio, he had a dynasty. His Yankees won four straight world championships, slipped to third in 1940, then rebounded for three more pennants and two World Series wins. He resigned in 1945 because of ill health and a personality clash with new Yankees owner

Larry MacPhail.

McCarthy accepted the job as manager of the Red Sox in 1948. The team had an awesome lineup of hitters but lacked pitching. Nevertheless he finished second two years in a row, losing the pennant in a playoff in 1948 and on the last day of the season in 1949. He retired during the 1950 season for health reasons.

Nicknamed "Marse Joe," McCarthy was a strict disciplinarian as a manager, but a warm, friendly man in his off-field moments. He was elected to the Hall of Fame in 1957.

TOMMY McCARTHY
Outfielder, Bos (U) 1884, Bos (N) 1885, 1892-95, Phi (N) 1886-87, StL (AA) 1888-91, Bkn (N) 1896. Manager, StL (AA) 1890

McCarthy broke in with the Union Association in 1884, but did not really establish himself until he joined the American Association's St. Louis Browns in 1888. He helped the Browns win the '88 pennant and gained a reputation as an outstanding defensive player. He stole 93 bases in 1888 and led the AA in stolen bases in 1890.

His greatest years were with Boston's pennant-winning teams of the early 1890s. He and Hugh Duffy became known as the "Heavenly Twins" for their defensive plays in the outfield. Although McCarthy hit .346 in 1893 and .349 the following year, he was not a great hitter; he averaged .292 for his career. His strengths were his speed, his powerful throwing arm, and his scientific approach. He was an excellent bunter, and he and Duffy were brilliant hit-and-run artists and deadly on the double steal. McCarthy also popularized the practice of trapping fly balls and throwing runners out at second, sometimes starting double plays.

He was named to the Hall of Fame in 1946.

JIM McCORMICK
Pitcher, Ind (N) 1878, Cle (N) 1879-84, Cin (U) 1884, Prov (N) 1885, Chi (N) 1885-87. Manager, Cle (N) 1879-80

Way back in 1880, husky, mustachioed McCormick was probably the MVP of the young NL. He won 45, tops in the league, hurled 658 innings, held hitters to a 1.85 ERA—and managed Cleveland to a third-place finish. He was 24 years old.

For much of his career, 1878-1887, Jim suffered with losing clubs—he lost 40 games for sixth-place Cleveland in 1879. Still, he was ERA king twice. Not until 1885-1886 did he land with a flag winner, Anson's White Sox. He rewarded them with seasons of 21-7 and 31-11.

His totals for his 10-year career were 265-214, 2.43 ERA.

WILLIE McCOVEY
First Baseman, SF (N) 1959-73, 1977-80, SD (N) 1974-76, Oak (A) 1976

McCovey slugged 18 grand slams, an NL record, and led the league in homers three times, but according to Willie "the hardest ball I ever hit" was an out. The Giants were losing 1-0 in the ninth inning of the seventh game of the 1962 World Series, but they had the tying run on third and the winning run at second. Willie lined a bullet at Yankees second baseman Bobby Richardson for the final out. A

foot either way and the Giants would have been champs.

In the second game of the Series, McCovey had blasted one against a Candlestick Park light tower off the same pitcher, Ralph Terry.

Although extremely shy in his first years, Willie became a friendly, gregarious team leader. He hit 521 homers and batted in 1,555 runs during his 22 seasons.

His career began with a perfect 4-for-4 against Robin Roberts. He hit .354 that year to win the Rookie of the Year Award. Ten years later he was MVP with 45 homers and 126 RBIs, both league-leading totals, and a .320 batting average.

He was named to the Hall of Fame in 1986.

JOE "IRON MAN" McGINNITY
Pitcher, Bal (N) 1899, Bkn (N) 1900, Bal (A) 1901-02, NY (N) 1902-08

McGinnity got his nickname from working in an iron foundry in his youth, but it just as easily could have come from winning seven games in six days in the minors in 1896, or from pitching five doubleheaders in the majors. Joe also pitched a two-year record for this century of 434 innings in 1903 and 408 the next year, and he was still hurling minor league ball at the age of 54.

Three of those doubleheader victories came in one month—August 1903. Joe won a league-leading 31 games for the second-place Giants that year. He pitched 44 complete games.

McGinnity threw an underhand curveball, with a motion so low his hand almost touched the ground. The fastball broke down, and the curve appeared to break up. Joe called it "Old Sal," and it may have put less strain on his arm than an overhand curve would have. He pitched for 26 years, though only 10 in the majors. After leaving the Giants, Joe could still win 29 and 30 in the International League. He won 246 in the majors, but his total wins, majors and minors, came to 471.

McGinnity won 28 games as a rookie with Baltimore in 1899, but his greatest seasons were with the Giants (1902-1908), for whom he won 31 in 1903 and 35 in 1904.

McGinnity had a reputation for throwing at hitters. He scored one hit batsman for every 19 men he faced—a record. He was named to the Hall of Fame in 1946.

BILL McGOWAN
Umpire, AL 1925-54

McGowan was an American League umpire for 30 years. Although sometimes controversial the universal respect with which he was held in baseball was shown in his nickname: "Number One." He introduced a more dramatic style to umpiring, using vigorous, aggressive, demonstrative gestures.

Often arrogant, blunt, sharp-tongued and irascible, he nevertheless seldom tossed players from games because, in a statement often made of him: "He never ran away but knew when to walk." Despite occasional displays of temper, his fairness was never questioned.

He is credited with not missing an inning in his first 16 seasons—a total of 2,541 games—but in fact he was out for two games in 1931 because of an attack of diabetes. In 1939 he founded a successful umpire's school to teach the AL way of doing things. He umpired four All-Star games and eight World Series.

He was also twice suspended by the league, once for an altercation with a player in 1948 and again in 1952 for "insulting" the press. It is widely believed that lingering animosity among certain sports writers delayed McGowan's election to the Hall of Fame until 1992, 38 years after his death.

JOHN MCGRAW

Third Baseman, Bal (AA) 1891, Bal (N) 1892-99, StL (N) 1900, Bal (A) 1901-02, NY (N) 1902-06. Manager, Bal (N) 1899, Bal (A) 1901-02, NY (N) 1902-32.

A brawling, brilliant bully, McGraw and his Giants won 10 pennants from 1904 to 1924. He dominated the NL for three decades as the Giants manager after nearly a decade as a scrappy third baseman for the old NL Orioles of the 1890s. As a manager, his strategic cleverness and his determination to control every aspect of his team won him the title "Little Napoleon." In 1892 McGraw joined the Baltimore Orioles of Wee Willie Keeler, Hughie Jennings, Ned Hanlon, et al. Mac could trip and spike with the best of them, and he and Keeler are among those who are credited with inventing the hit-and-run. The O's won the flag from 1894 to1896, with McGraw hitting .325 or better each year, the first of nine straight years he would hit .300. The O's won the Temple Cup playoffs in 1896 and 1897.

In 1899 Mac served as player-manager and hit .391; most of the star players had been sent to Brooklyn and the O's team finished fourth. Of all 19th-century players, no one had a higher on-base percentage than McGraw's .460.

He led Baltimore in the new AL in 1901-1902, finishing fifth and seventh. John also fought with umpires and when league president Ban Johnson backed the umps, Mac jumped to New York in the NL, taking fellow Irishmen Joe McGinnity and Roger Bresnahan with him.

The Giants finished last in 1902, but leaped all the way to second in 1903 and first in 1904. McGraw haughtily refused to play a World Series against Johnson's AL. Mac won again in 1905, and this time he played the Series and demolished the AL Athletics in five games.

He lost a pennant narrowly in 1908 after the Merkle "boner," but stoutly defended the young first baseman from criticism. A master psychologist, McGraw played on superstition and in 1911 put a Kansas lunatic, Charlie Faust, in uniform as a good luck mascot; the team charged from third place to the flag, the first of three straight.

By 1911 McGraw was already recognized as a managerial genius, he drove his players hard, called pitches from the bench, and was one of the first managers to grasp the concept of relief pitching, using Claude Elliott, George Ferguson, and Doc Crandall in that role in the first decade of the century. He won another pennant in 1917, though the Giants were upended in the World Series.

McGraw captured an unprecedented four straight pennants in 1921-1924, a record that would stand until Casey Stengel broke it in 1953. Although the Giants stayed in the first division through most of his remaining years, he had won his last flag. Players began to rebel against his vicious, profane tongue lashings. In 1932 the Giants dived to eighth and he resigned after 33 seasons as a manager. His 2,784 career victories rank second only to Connie Mack. He was named to the Hall of Fame in 1937, the same year as Mack.

MARK MCGWIRE

First Baseman, Oak (A) 1986-97, StL (N) 1997-

Perhaps 70 was a bit overkill, but if someone was going to break Roger Maris' home run it would be hard to find a more suitable candidate than McGwire. Back in 1961 Maris was generally unpopular because he was a normal, somewhat introverted guy supplanting the bigger-than-life persona of Babe Ruth. Moreover, he had never hit 40 homers, much less 60. But fans fell in love with the big, friendly, round-faced, Popeye-armed McGwire.

After all, since 1987, his first full season, when he smashed 49 homers, Big Mac had been hitting circuit clouts at a Ruthian clip (and for Ruthian distances). It seemed that only his unusual spate of mid-career injuries kept him from challenging Maris. Then, his health regained, he cracked 52 in 1996, and 58 in 1997. Surely, many fans believed, 1998 would see him go over the top. McGwire didn't disappoint.

He got off to a fast start, focusing early attention on his race for 62. Ken Griffey, Jr. and then Sammy Sosa challenged. Sosa twice drew even only to have Big Mac smash back in front. Number 62 came before the Cardinals had played 154 games, eliminating any talk of a Maris asterisk. Then like a great champion, McGwire showed his finishing kick by knocking out his final five homers in his last three games.

Although the mammoth home run is McGwire's signature, he is a patient hitter, willing to walk or go for a single when the game is on the line. And, despite his size, he is an adept fielder at first base and an intelligent if not speedy baserunner.

BILL MCKECHNIE

Third Baseman, Pit (N) 1907, 1910-12, 1918, 1920, Bos (N) 1913, NY (A) 1913, Ind (F) 1914, Nwk (F) 1915, NY (N) 1916, Cin (N) 1916-17. Manager, Nwk (F) 1915, Pit (N) 1922-26, StL (N) 1928-29, Bos (N) 1930-37, Cin (N) 1938-46

A light-hitting infielder during his playing career, McKechnie became one of baseball's most respected managers, winning pennants with three different NL teams. Known as "the Deacon" because of his years singing in a church choir and his cadaverous "parson" looks, his virtues as a skipper were his deep knowledge of baseball, his likable personality, and his infinite patience.

His first manager's job was with Newark in the short-lived Federal League. In 1922 he took over in Pittsburgh and brought them from the second division to a pennant and world championship in 1925. When the team slipped to third in 1926, he was fired.

He was hired by the Cardinals in 1928 and immediately won the pennant. However, the team lost the World Series in four games. Midway through 1929 he was fired again.

In 1930 he was hired as skipper of the Boston Braves and stayed for eight years. Although Boston was the only NL team he managed that did not win a pennant, he earned wide respect for his efforts in sometimes making "silk purses" out of the material at hand. When he led them to fifth place in 1937, he was named Manager of the Year.

McKechnie moved to Cincinnati in 1938, the scene of

his greatest teams. He won pennants in 1939 and 1940 and the World Series in the latter year. McKechnie was elected to the Hall of Fame in 1962.

JOHN "BID" McPHEE
Second Baseman, Cin (AA) 1882-89, Cin (N) 1890-99. Manager, Cin (N) 1901-02

McPhee was utterly boring. He played 18 seasons before 1900, every one at the same position, second base; every one for the same team, Cincinnati (the team changed leagues in 1890 or McPhee would have stayed in the same one). He played hard but clean. He was never fined and never even thrown out of a game! At a time when rough and rowdy baseballers were providing a wealth of wicked anecdotes, McPhee showed up every day in shape, stayed sober, did his job, and went home to a good night's sleep. The only thing remotely interesting about him was that he refused to wear a glove until 1897, more than a decade after they'd become common.

Oh yes, he was an excellent leadoff man, walked a lot, and scored 1,678 runs on his .271 batting average. He led the American Association in triples in 1887 and totaled 188 for his career. But except for an obvious ability to score runs and an assumption that such an ability might lead to a number of victories, he really wasn't anything special with a bat. See? Boring.

He was at his most monotonous at second base. Game after game, season after season, batters would knock balls his way, and he just kept plucking them from the ground or the air and putting the batters out. He did this with such tedious regularity that he led his league's second basemen in fielding 10 times, finished second four seasons, and was never lower than fourth. He was the leader in double plays 11 years, in putouts eight, and in assists six. He set the record for fielding average with .978 in 1896, the year before he started wearing a glove. That might be slightly interesting except that someone broke his record after a mere 23 years. True, in more than a century, no second baseman has exceeded his 1886 total of 529 putouts. And true, he also holds the career mark in putouts with 6,545, ranks fourth in assists with 6,905, and second in total chances with 14,241.

But what are those things compared to stories of droll nights on the town or a few hundred home runs? What a yawn! No wonder he's not in the Hall of Fame.

JOE MEDWICK
Outfielder, StL (N) 1932-40, 1947-48, Bkn (N) 1940-43, 1946, NY (N) 1943-45, Bos (N) 1945

A rough-house, tough guy from the Cardinals' Gashouse Gang, Medwick was one of the top sluggers of the 1930s. A notorious bad-ball hitter, he led the NL in RBIs three straight years, 1936-38, and won the batting Triple Crown in 1937 (.374, 31, 154). He was named MVP that year.

He picked up the odd nickname "Ducky Wucky" in the minors because of his unusual waddle.

In the seventh game of the 1934 World Series, he slid hard into the Tigers' third baseman—too hard, thought Detroit fans, who pelted him with garbage until Commissioner Landis ordered him out of the game.

Sold to the Dodgers for $125,000 in 1940, he helped them win the 1941 pennant but suffered a near-fatal beaning by former teammate Bob Bowman. Though he recov-

ered and played until 1948, he was never the same hitter he had been. His career totals include a .324 batting average, 202 home runs, and 1,383 RBIs. In 1968 he was elected to the Hall of Fame.

JOSE MENDEZ
Pitcher, Negro League, 1908-26, Cuban Stars, Stars of Cuba, All Nations, Los Angeles White Sox, Chicago American Giants, Detroit Stars, Kansas City Monarchs

Baseball's troubadour of the tropics, Mendez was an outstanding Cuban pitcher in the early 20th century. His success against touring major league clubs made him a national hero. Among others, he won games against Eddie Plank in 1910 and Christy Mathewson in 1911. In 1908 he beat the Cincinnati Reds three times, without allowing a run in 25 innings.

In the summers, Mendez played with the U.S. multiracial All Nations club, the forerunner of the Kansas City Monarchs. Late in his career, as manager of the Monarchs, he put himself in to pitch the final game of the 1924 Black World Series and won, 5-0. Musically talented, Mendez played the cornet for dances after games and later traveled the Caribbean, playing the guitar and teaching baseball.

ANDY MESSERSMITH
Pitcher, Cal (A) 1968-72, LA (N) 1973-75, 1979, Atl (N) 1976-77, NY (A) 1978

Every player today should say a prayer of thanks to Andy Messersmith. It was he, along with Dave McNally, who overturned the sacrosanct reserve clause, leading to the present version of free-agency that has made millionaires of .240 hitters.

He was an excellent pitcher when healthy, winning 20 games for the Angels in 1971. He was traded to the Dodgers after the 1972 season and had a brilliant 20-6 mark in 1974. It was then that he and McNally challenged the reserve clause in their contracts that forced them to re-sign the next year with the same team. Five years earlier Curt Flood had filed suit in an attempt to overturn the clause but had lost in the Supreme Court by a narrow vote. This time the players won on a split decision. The ruling was that by playing the 1975 season without signing contracts, they had fulfilled their "option year." Although McNally chose to retire, Messersmith signed with Atlanta in 1976 for a huge salary increase. Unfortunately a sore arm limited his effectiveness with the Braves, but he had opened the door to free agency for all players.

MARVIN MILLER
Labor Negotiator

Miller, "the players' commissioner," was the enemy of the owners and the real commissioner, but fewer than half a dozen men have turned the baseball world upside down as he did. In 1981 he led the first extended players' strike in history, ushering in a new era in baseball negotiations. A labor economist with the steelworkers' union, Miller was chosen by the players to head their union in 1966, in the most serious challenge to the owners' control since the Players League in 1890.

Miller negotiated five labor contracts with the owners. In the first the owners increased their contribution to the pension fund, increased the minimum major league sal-

ary, and agreed to reconsider the reserve clause. The second recognized the Major League Players Association as the official bargaining agent for players (except with regard to salaries), allowed players to be represented by agents when negotiating salaries, and permitted arbitration in disputes that could not be otherwise settled.

In 1972 Miller led a brief strike to force the negotiation of a third contract. This one extended arbitration and resulted in a further increase in salaries.

In 1975, when Andy Messersmith and Dave McNally were declared free agents by a federal court (by having played out the option years of their contracts), the reserve clause was dead. Miller's fourth contract compromised by limiting free agency to six-year veterans, who would become available through re-entry drafts.

Again salaries soared. Owners demanded compensation for players lost to free agency, and this led to the 1981 strike of 50 days. Again Miller reached a compromise; owners were to receive some compensation in the form of established players from a general pool, but the union had proved its strength. Miller retired in 1984.

MINNIE MINOSO
Third base, Negro League, 1946-48, New York Cubans, outfielder, Cle (A) 1949-51, 1958-59, Chi (A) 1951-57, 1960-61, 1964, 1976, 1980, StL (N) 1962, Was (A) 1963

Minoso didn't have a full season in the majors until he was 28, but when he burst on the scene with the White Sox in 1951, he immediately became one of the most exciting players in the AL. He led in stolen bases, 1951-1953, in triples three times, in doubles once, and once in hits. He compiled a career batting average of .298, lashed out 1,963 hits, and had 1,023 RBIs, most of it crammed into 11 exciting seasons.

Of the 17 seasons he is credited with playing, one was a nine-game "cup of coffee" in 1949, three were as a reserve in the early 1960s, when he was over 40 years old, and two were fan-pleasing, end-of-season returns in 1976 and 1980. When he made his final out in a major league uniform, he was 57.

JOHNNY MIZE
First Baseman, StL (N) 1936-41, NY (N) 1942, 1946-49, NY (A) 1949-53

Mize won four home run crowns, three RBI titles, a batting championship, and finished among the top three in various offensive categories a total of 54 times. His 51 homers with the Giants in 1947 are an NL record for left-handed hitters. The burly first baseman slugged 359 career home runs, hitting three in a game six different times. His .312 batting average and 1,337 RBIs mark him as one of baseball's great sluggers.

In both 1939 and 1940 Mize finished second in the voting for the NL MVP. In 1939 he led in homers (28) and batting average (.349); the next year he topped in homers (43) and RBIs (137).

After a long career with the Cardinals and Giants, "the Big Cat" joined the Yankees in mid-1949 as a part-time first baseman and full-time pinch hitter. In 1952 he became the second man in World Series history to pinch-hit a home run. For the entire Series he batted .400, with three homers and a slugging average of 1.067. Mize was named to the Hall of Fame in 1981.

PAUL MOLITOR
Designated Hitter, Mil (A) 1978-92, Tor (A) 1993-95, Min (A) 1996-98

Molitor quietly moved into eighth place in career hits in 1998, his final major league season. The consummate line drive man, he was a designated hitter for so long one may forget that he actually was the starting second baseman in the 1980 All-Star Game. He played some outfield, third base, and first base, but his real position was hitter. He finished his 21st season with 3,319 base hits, including 605 doubles and, surprisingly, 234 home runs. Surprisingly, in that his 22 homers in 1993 was his only season with more than 20. Still, all those line drives have added up to over 1,300 RBIs and, even more impressive, 1,780 runs scored. He also walked 1,094 times and stole 504 bases.

His numbers could have been even higher had he not been dogged by injuries throughout his career. (Managers found that by writing DH next to his name they stood a better chance of keeping him off the DL.) A ribcage muscle pull in 1980, torn ligaments in his ankle in 1981, ligament damage to his elbow in 1984, various injuries in 1986, a strained hamstring in 1987, two broken fingers in 1990 and assorted other ills cost him nearly 500 games.

Despite playing his career in relatively small markets—Milwaukee, Toronto, and Minnesota—Molitor has seen his share of the national spotlight. He was the first player to have five hits in a World Series game in 1982, his 39-game hitting streak in 1987 was the fourth-longest in AL history, he batted .500 (12-for-24) and earned MVP honors in the 1993 World Series, and that same year he finished behind John Olerud and ahead of Roberto Alomar to make the Blue Jays the first team to have the top three hitters in a batting race.

JOE MORGAN
Second Baseman, Hou (N) 1963-71, 1980, Cin (N) 1972-79, SF (N) 1981-82, Phi (N) 1983, Oak (A) 1984

Little Joe stood only 5 feet 7 inches tall, but he played more games at second base than any man but Eddie Collins and won back-to-back MVPs in 1975 and 1976.

Morgan began his career with Houston, where he twice scored over 100 runs and developed an ability to draw walks. Traded to Cincinnati in 1972, he came into his own as an offensive star with the Big Red Machine. In 1975 he won his first MVP with a .327 batting average, 17 homers, 107 runs scored, 94 RBIs, and 67 stolen bases. The next year he hit .320, with 27 homers, 113 runs scored, 111 RBIs, and 60 stolen bases.

For his career, he hit 268 home runs, scored 1,651 runs, and batted in 1,134. He stole 689 bases and is third all-time in walks with 1,865.

In the field, Morgan won five Gold Gloves with his famously tiny glove, and in 1977-1978 put together a string of 91 straight games without an error. Still, the stubborn fact is that Joe was not a great fielder. Apparently the writers went on form and not substance in voting him those Gold Gloves. For instance, he led the league in assists only once, a sign that he didn't cover a great deal of ground.

But above all, Morgan was a winner. He led the Reds to five division titles and three World Series. After signing with Houston in 1980, he took them to a division title.

And in 1983 he was one of several veterans (they were called "the Wheeze Kids") who brought the Phillies a pennant. Morgan was named to the Hall of Fame in 1990.

THURMAN MUNSON
Catcher, NY (A) 1969-79

A fiery plane crash on Aug. 2, 1979, cut short Munson's career after slightly less than 10 full seasons and knocked the bottom out of the Yankees. The Yankees' captain was an outstanding catcher in the tradition of Bill Dickey, Yogi Berra, and Elston Howard.

He led New York to three straight pennants, 1976-1978, and was voted the AL MVP in 1976, when he batted .302, hit 17 homers, and drove in 105 runs.

A basketball star in college, Munson had good speed (although he was better at throwing out base stealers than he was at stealing bases himself). He packed a home run punch in his bat, but was primarily a line drive hitter.

Munson hit .302 and was AL Rookie of the Year in 1970. He was named to the AL All-Star team in 1971 and then every year from 1973 to 1978. A durable backstop, he played at least 125 games every year except his first season, when he didn't debut until August, and his final season.

His total of 1,423 games exceeds those of several excellent catchers who played far longer. His career batting average was .292.

At the close of the memorable pennant race of 1978, in the ALCS against Kansas City, he trumped George Brett's three homers with a two-run shot of his own in the eighth to win the third game. In the World Series two years earlier, Munson had nearly matched Bench's .533 with a .529 of his own in a battle of super catchers.

He was a proud man with a venomous tongue, and he bridled in 1977, when Reggie Jackson joined the team at a higher salary. The angry energy that flared between the two men nevertheless spurred the dissension-ridden Yanks to two flags.

DALE MURPHY
Outfielder, Atl (N) 1976-90, Phi (N) 1990-92, Col (N) 1993

Nice guys may not always finish last, but Murphy, one of baseball's nicest people, had little luck in NL pennant races. In 11 seasons as a Braves' regular, the best his team has did was one appearance in the 1982 NLCS. No one blamed Murph.

The right-handed slugger came to the Braves as a catcher but was switched to first base in 1978, his first season as a regular. Two years later he was moved again, this time to center field, where he became one of the best.

His strong suit was his powerful bat. He won back-to-back MVP Awards in 1982-1983, leading the NL in RBIs and slugging average both years. In 1984-1985, he led in homers. He paid the price for his 398 homers, striking out over 100 times in ten different seasons.

EDDIE MURRAY
First Baseman, Bal (A) 1977-88,1996, LA (N) 1989-91, NY (N) 1992-93, Cle (A) 1994-96, Ana (A) 1997

One of the better power hitters of the 1980s, Murray averaged over 100 RBIs per season for his first 11 sea-

sons, yet led the AL only once—in the strike-shortened 1981 season. He also tied for the lead in homers that season with 22. Probably the most powerful switch hitter since Mickey Mantle, Murray was the model of consistency for Baltimore until injuries cut into his homer and RBI titles. Fans who had cheered him on with cries of "Ed-dee, Ed-dee!" turned against him and booed. Murray demanded a trade, and generally handled the situation poorly. After a difficult first season in the NL, Murray rebounded to lead the Dodgers with a .330 average in 1990.

Though he played in only two World Series with Baltimore (1979, 1983), he had the Orioles in the thick of six pennant races. His batting average in those Septembers was .318, said baseball analyst Peter Gammons.

During two and a half seasons with the Indians, he set the record for most games played by a first-baseman. He returned to Baltimore to hit his 500th home run in 1996, joining Willie Mays and Hank Aaron as players with 500 home runs and 3,000 hits.

Murray, who commanded a multimillion dollar salary, donated a generous portion of it to provide summer camps for city kids in memory of his mother.

STAN "THE MAN" MUSIAL
Outfielder/First Baseman, StL (N) 1941-44, 1946-63

At one time Musial held almost every NL batting record except homers, and he was close to that, too. He held some 50 major league and NL marks, and his 3,630 career hits were second only to Ty Cobb. Now Pete Rose, Hank Aaron, Willie Mays, and others have passed most of those marks.

Popular with fans and writers alike, Stan was three times MVP, four times coming in second. He used an odd, "peek-a-boo" batting stance—left-handed, curled up, almost as if he was looking around a corner, his bat barrel held back and straight up. It worked for him. Stan led the NL seven times in batting.

Son of a Polish immigrant miner, Stan started as a minor league pitcher until he hurt his arm and switched to the outfield. After playing 12 end-of-season games for the Cardinals in 1941, he led them to the world championship in 1942. He specialized in doubles and triples, and won two batting championships in his first four years (not counting Navy service in 1945). The Cards were NL champs all four of those seasons and world champs three of them.

In 1948 Stan suddenly blossomed as a home run threat. His batting average, doubles, and triples stayed high, too. He was slugging average champion three times before the change and three times after it.

Musial won his last batting title in 1957 at the age of 36 (.351). As a 41-year-old grandfather in 1962, he could still hit .330, third best in the league.

Stan once hit five homers in a doubleheader. His most famous home run won the 1955 All-Star Game in the 12th inning. "I'll get you out of here in a hurry," he told Yogi Berra, the AL catcher, then whacked the first pitch over the wall.

His career totals: .331, 475 home runs, 725 doubles, 177 triples, 1,949 runs, and 1,951 RBIs. He was elected to the Hall of Fame in 1969.

GRAIG NETTLES
Third Baseman, Min (A) 1967-69, Cle (A) 1970-72, NY (A) 1973-83, SD (N) 1984-86, Atl (N) 1987, Mon (N) 1988

One of the best glove men to play third base, Nettles finally began winning Gold Gloves when Brooks Robinson retired, although he'd been an acknowledged master for several years. His eye-popping stops in the 1978 World Series were a big factor in the Yankees victory. And Series watchers saw him pull his spectacular act again in 1981. Only Robinson played more games at third or accepted more fielding chances.

Although his lifetime batting average was below .250, Graig hit with power. His nearly 400 homers put him third among third basemen, after Mike Schmidt and Eddie Mathews. He led the AL in homers with 32 in 1976 and followed with a career-high 37 the next season.

DON NEWCOMBE
Pitcher, Negro League, 1944-45, Newark Eagles; Bkn (N) 1949-51, 1954-57, LA (N) 1958, Cin (N) 1958-60, Cle (A) 1960

Big Don was Rookie of the Year with the Dodgers in 1949, with a 17-8 mark and an NL-leading five shutouts. He jumped to 19-11 in 1950 and 20-9 in '51. Then he lost two years to the Army. It took the 1954 season to get him back to where he'd been, but in the next two seasons, he was brilliant: 20-5 and 27-7 to win the first Cy Young Award.

Suddenly, in 1957, he struggled. The next year he slipped further and was traded to Cincinnati. After a brief comeback to 13-8 with the sixth-place Reds in 1959, he fell off the charts.

After his brilliant beginning, Newk finished his career with a disappointing 149-90 record.

The problem was alcohol. It ruined his career and nearly his life. But, heroically, he pulled himself back and now counsels other baseball alcoholics as a member of the Dodgers' front office.

HAL NEWHOUSER
Pitcher, Det (A) 1939-53, Cle (A) 1954-55

Wrongly stigmatized as a wartime phenom, Newhouser was actually the AL's top left-hander of the 1940s. Ted Williams called him one of the three best hurlers he ever faced. Other stars played part or all of the war years without having their records denigrated. But Newhouser was so dominant in 1944-1945 that it's sometimes forgotten he had two 20-win years and won more than half of his 207 career victories after the war.

In 1944 he overcame the wildness that had plagued him in his first seasons with the Tigers. He was voted AL MVP for his 29-9 record and 2.22 ERA. The next year he was 25-9 and led the AL with eight shutouts and a 1.81 ERA. The Tigers won the AL pennant in 1945, and though he didn't pitch well in the World Series win over the Cubs, he was still credited with two victories. In both 1944 and 1945 he led the AL in strikeouts.

The stars were all back in 1946, but Newhouser kept on sailing. He had the most wins of any pitcher at 26-9 and again led the league in ERA with 1.94 He had his greatest strikeout year at 275, but finished second to Bob Feller's 348. "Prince Hal" was the AL's top winner again in 1948,

with 21. Newhouser was elected to the Hall of Fame in 1992.

CHARLES "KID" NICHOLS
Pitcher, Bos (N) 1890-1901, StL (N) 1904-05, Phi (N) 1905-06. Manager, StL (N) 1904-05

Perhaps the best of the pre-1900 pitching greats, Nichols' seven seasons of 30 or more wins is topped by no one. He won 20 or more games for 10 straight seasons and had a dozen 20-win seasons altogether.

Pitching without a windup, Kid had control and speed but no curve. He took over as ace of Boston in 1890 at the age of 20 and pitched them to five pennants, 1891-1893 and 1897-1898.

His best year was 1892 (35-16). He had three complete-game victories in three days in September, then in the Temple Cup playoff against second-place Cleveland, he dueled Cleveland ace Cy Young (36-11) for 11 scoreless innings before darkness forced a stoppage of play.

Nichols was 30-14 for a fourth-place team in 1896. The next year he beat the Orioles two out of three in September to clinch a flag.

Sixth all-time in wins, with a 362-207 record, Nichols also notched 533 complete games for fourth on the all-time list. In 502 starts with Boston, he was relieved only 25 times. He was elected to the Hall of Fame in 1949.

PHIL NIEKRO
Pitcher, Mil (N) 1964-65, Atl (N) 1966-83, 1987, NY (A) 1984-85, Cle (A) 1986-87, Tor (A) 1987

For 24 years, until the age of 48, Niekro tossed his knuckler, most of the time for weak Atlanta teams in a notorious hitters' park. When he approached win number 300, some experts were surprised; they'd never thought of him as a star. But he was. Hitters knew it long before the writers suspected. Bobby Murcer said hitting Niekro's knuckler was like "eating jelly with chopsticks."

For his 300th win, Phil decided not to throw a single knuckler—until the last batter, when he struck out Jeff Burroughs with three of them. Not only did Phil win 318, he saved 30 others, a rarity for modern starters. Among his 274 losses were 47 shutouts—only Walter Johnson and Cy Young had more.

Niekro wandered seven years in the minors and didn't become a regular starter with the Braves until 1967 when he was 28. He led the NL with a 1.87 ERA that season and was 11-9 with seventh-place Atlanta.

Niekro's club—the Braves—held him down. Atlanta finished last six times with him, and he led the league in defeats four times, a record. He somehow managed to win 20 three times. In 1979 he led the NL in both wins and losses with a 21-20 mark.

Phil's home park also hurt. Atlanta-Fulton County Stadium, otherwise known as "The Launching Pad," was part of the reason he led the league four times in throwing gopher pitches.

Phil was 23-13 in 1969 to lead Atlanta to the division title. He holds the record with 121 wins after the age of 40. He's the second-oldest man (43) to hit a homer.

When he retired in 1987 he had 3,342 strikeouts and was third all-time in bases on balls, fourth in innings pitched, and first in wild pitches, 200. He once threw six wild ones in one game—four in one inning. He was

elected to the Hall of Fame in 1997.

PEDRO "TONY" OLIVA
Outfielder, Min (A) 1962-76
There's no telling what Oliva's batting marks might have been if he'd had a healthy knee. Instead, he had five operations, each one slowing him down a little more. As a Minnesota rookie in 1964, he lined out 217 hits, the AL rookie record. He also tied the rookie mark for total bases and, incidentally, led in batting, .323. Naturally, he was Rookie of the Year.

Tony led the league in batting the next year, too, as the Twins won the pennant and almost won the World Series. He tied Johnny Pesky's mark of leading the league in hits each of his first two seasons.

And then Oliva hurt his knee. Two subpar seasons followed, but by 1969 he was back over .300. In 1971 Oliva was having his best year ever, .375, when he fell and hurt his knee again. His average dropped to .337, and though he hung on to win his third batting title, he was through as an outfielder and as a great hitter. He became exclusively a DH until he finally retired in 1976 with a career average of .304 and 220 home runs.

Incidentally, he was born Pedro Oliva and became Tony when he used his brother's passport to get out of Cuba. A third brother, Juan Carlos, stayed in Havana and became one of Cuba's top pitchers.

JAMES "ORATOR JIM" O'ROURKE
Outfielder, Middletown (NA) 1872, Bos (NA) 1873-75, Bos (N) 1876-78, 1880, Prov (N) 1879, Buf (N) 1881-84, NY (N) 1885-89, 1891-92, 1904, NY (P) 1890, Was (N) 1893. Manager, Buf (N) 1881-84, Was (N) 1893
O'Rourke reportedly had only average speed and a weak arm, but he was a star in the National Association for four seasons before the National League was formed, averaging .317. He helped the Boston Red Stockings to five pennants (three in the National Association), then switched to Providence and helped them win a flag in 1879. Ten years later he was the regular left fielder for the New York Giants, champions of 1888-1889. In between, he spent four seasons as player-manager of Buffalo's NL club.

From 1876 on, he hit over .300 in 11 major league seasons, averaging .310. After retiring he managed and umpired, and at the age of 52 caught a nine-inning game for the Giants, their pennant clincher in 1904. He even got his 2,304th major league hit and scored his 1,446th run. And then he became president of a minor league.

His nickname stemmed from his Yale Law School background and his flowery, bombastic speech. In 1945 he was named to the Baseball Hall of Fame.

MEL OTT
Outfielder, NY (N) 1926-47. Manager, NY (N) 1942-48
With his quick, distinctive leg kick as he stepped into the ball, Ott used to golf high flies into the chummy upper deck of the Polo Grounds, 256 feet away. He hit almost two thirds of his homers at home. When he retired after 22 seasons, he had 511 homers, the third highest total at the time, and a .304 career average. He set new NL career records for runs (1,859), RBIs (1,860), and walks (1,708). The run and RBI marks were first broken by Stan Musial;

the walks by Joe Morgan.

Ott's famous leg kick helped him compensate for his lack of size; he weighed only 165-170 pounds. It was a graceful kick, unlike that of Sadaharu Oh, who lifted his front knee and pulled his foot back with his bat cocked forward. Mel lifted his front foot high, his weight perfectly balanced on the fulcrum of his bat handle at his belt. Babe Ruth, Joe Medwick, Rudy York, and other big men used modified versions of it.

Ott arrived in New York with a straw suitcase at the age of 16 and adopted manager John McGraw as a father. Ott stayed to become one of the Giants' all-time most popular players and six-time home run champ.

Six times Mel led the league in walks and 10 times drew 100 or more. Four times he drew five walks in one game; the first time was on the final day of the 1929 season, when Phillies pitchers gave him five intentional walks, one with the bases loaded, so he couldn't tie Philadelphia's Chuck Klein for the homer title.

Mel hit .389 in the 1933 World Series and won the deciding game with a home run in the 10th inning. It was his eighth season on the Giants, though he was only 25 years old.

Ott became player-manager of the Giants in 1942. It was in reference to Ott that Leo Durocher made his famous pronouncement that "Nice guys finish last." Ott was elected to the Baseball Hall of Fame in 1951.

LEROY "SATCHEL" PAIGE
Pitcher, Negro League, 1926-50, Chattanooga Black Lookouts, Birmingham Black Barons, Cleveland Cubs, Pittsburgh Crawfords, Kansas City Monarchs, New York Black Yankees, Satchel Paige's All-Stars, Philadelphia Stars, Cle (A) 1948-50, StL (A) 1951-53, KC (A) 1965
If Satch wasn't the greatest black pitcher of all time (and many say he was), he was by far the most famous. He began pitching semipro in 1924, and made his professional debut in 1926, age 22; he was 9-6 the next year, and pitched the Birmingham Black Barons into the playoffs. His white major league debut was in 1948 with Cleveland, age 42; he was 6-1, set attendance records, and helped the Indians to the pennant. When they said he should be Rookie of the Year, he asked what year they meant.

Satchel got his name from toting bags at the Mobile railroad station at the age of seven. He got his hesitation pitch from throwing rocks at other kids, fooling them into ducking too soon. After a stretch in reform school for stealing toys, Paige learned his control from Black Baron vets who taught him to throw over a Coke bottle cap until he could "nip frosting off a cake." Satch called it his "be ball", "because it be where I want it to be." He got his fastball from the Lord.

Joining the Pittsburgh Crawfords in 1931, Paige teamed with Josh Gibson in one of the greatest batteries of all time. In 1934 he led all Negro League pitchers with a 16-2 mark and threw a 17-strikeout no-hitter against the Homestead Grays. Barnstorming in the offseason, he dueled many a game against Dizzy Dean and later Bob Feller. Much of his pitching was on tour, traveling packed into a car, knees against chin, to prairie towns, where, "if I didn't pitch, they didn't want the team—in town, let alone the park." From there he sailed to Latin America, where

his fabled bronze arm went dead.

The Kansas City Monarchs took a chance on him, and Paige miraculously pitched his arm back into shape. He usually pitched two or three innings a night to draw a crowd. One of his great moments came when he deliberately walked the bases "drunk" to face his old buddy Gibson, then whiffed Josh. In the 1942 Series against the Grays, he and Hilton Smith held Josh to a .125 average and swept all four games.

Satch loved fast cars and fast women. He was always dallying, then racing to the park, police sirens screaming either in escort or pursuit. Fined $25 dollars for speeding, he peeled off $50 and told the judge, "Here. I'm comin' back tomorrow."

When Satch signed with Cleveland for the 1948 pennant stretch, *The Sporting News* called it a publicity stunt. "Everybody told me he was through," said the Indians' boss, Bill Veeck. "That was understandable. They thought he was human." Satch pitched a shutout in his second start, drew 200,000 fans to his first three starts, plus thousands more who couldn't get in.

In 1951 Veeck took Paige to the St. Louis Browns, where he had his own rocking chair in the bullpen and could still win 12 games and save 10. Finally, in 1965, aged 59, Paige pitched three innings for the Kansas City Athletics to draw a bonus, the oldest man ever to pitch in the majors. He allowed one hit.

Satch's wit has entered the language. His most famous saying is "Never look back. Something may be gaining on you."

Fittingly, Paige was the first man elected to the Hall of Fame by the Committee on Negro Leagues formed in 1971.

JIM PALMER
Pitcher, Bal (A) 1965-67, 1969-84
Winner of three Cy Young Awards, Palmer won 20 games eight times and helped the Orioles win six pennants. The handsome right-hander is the greatest jockey shorts salesman in baseball history, and his seminude posters advertising underwear were almost as famous in Europe and Asia as they were in the United States.

Jim won 268 games despite suffering a sore arm after shutting out the Dodgers as a 20-year-old in the 1966 Series. The injury kept him out of the majors for virtually two years.

When he got back, Palmer won 20 or more four straight seasons, from 1970 to 1973. After an off-year, he put together another four-straight, 20-plus streak, 1975-1978. He won three Cy Young awards, 1973, 1975, and 1976. He led the AL in ERA in 1973 and '75.

Throughout his career, Jim shared a stormy, symbiotic relationship with manager Earl Weaver. They yelled at each other but respected each other and, in the end, helped each other achieve greatness.

As a high fastball pitcher, Palmer gave up a lot of home runs—but never a grand slam. He was also excellent in preventing unearned runs, a neglected side of pitching. He modestly says that's because he gave up few ground balls to make errors on. But his World Series record shows that, even when his mates did kick a ball, Jim slammed the door.

Palmer was elected to the Hall of Fame in 1990.

DAVE PARKER
Outfielder, Pit (N) 1973-83, Cin (N) 1984-87, Oak (A) 1988-89, Mil (A) 1990, Tor (A) 1991
Parker's career divides into three distinct stages.

First, 1975-1979: the superstar. Starting with his first full year, Parker was a .300 hitter, with back-to-back NL batting championships in 1977 and 1978, 30 home runs as NL MVP in 1978, All-Star Game MVP in 1979, and helped lead the Pirates to the world championship that year. He had a reputation as a hustling "complete" player, with speed and the best right field arm in baseball.

Second, 1980-1983: the disappointment. After signing a five-year $5-million contract to become the highest-paid player in baseball, his batting average and power fell off alarmingly, as did his availability. He was constantly injured and obviously overweight. He reacted to criticism by Pittsburgh fans by criticizing the fans. He became arguably the most unpopular player ever to wear a Pirates uniform. One day he was nearly skulled by a battery thrown from the stands. Only later was it learned that he had become deeply involved in drug abuse.

Third, 1984-1991: the aged slugger. Parker signed with Cincinnati as a free agent. Given a new start, he apparently conquered his addiction and produced excellent power stats for the Reds, twice topping 30 homers and leading the NL in RBIs in 1985. No longer an all-around player, he was traded to Oakland for 1988 and became an outstanding DH.

ROGER PECKINPAUGH
Shortstop, Cle (A) 1910-13, NY (A) 1913-21, Was (A) 1922-26, Chi (A) 1927. Manager, NY (A) 1914, Cle (A) 1928-33, 1941
Peckinpaugh was a fine-fielding shortstop with bad luck. In the eight years he played for the Yankees he led AL shortstops in assists three times. In any later age, that sort of range would have had him canonized by the New York media, but Roger did his work in those years when the Giants were the team in New York and the Yankees were a distant "other." The Yanks won the pennant in 1921, his last season with them, but the Giants beat them in the World Series, as Peckinpaugh's error let in the winning run in the final game.

Traded to Washington, he helped the Senators win a pennant and World Series in 1924, but his contributions were overshadowed by those of the "Boy Manager," Bucky Harris, and Walter Johnson, who finally had the chance to pitch for a winner after years with poor teams.

Peckinpaugh was a liability at bat early in his career, but gradually improved to ordinary. He actually hit .305 in 1919. In 1925 he hit a sprightly .294 and fielded brilliantly all season to lead the Senators to another pennant. This time he was named AL MVP just before the World Series.

But the 1925 Series was a nightmare for Roger. By the eighth inning of the final game, he had made seven errors. Suddenly, in the top of the eighth, he became a hero—he hit a home run to put the Senators in the lead. Alas! In the bottom of the eighth, the Pirates tied the game, and poor Roger made his eighth error—a Series record for any position—to keep the inning going. The Pirates scored twice more to become champions.

In Peckinpaugh's greatest season, he became the World

Series' greatest goat.

HERB PENNOCK
Pitcher, Phi (A) 1912-15, Bos (A) 1915-17, 1918-22, 1934, NY (A) 1923-33
Pennock was a smooth left-hander whose effortless style took him to a 240-162 career. Anything but overpowering, he blended curves and excellent control with the excellent bat support he usually received. Although he threw 35 shutouts over his 22 seasons, he was the kind of pitcher who pitched just well enough to win. In World Series competition, he was 5-0.

He came to the big leagues right out of high school, joining the Athletics and winning 11 games for the 1914 team at age 20. When Connie Mack dismantled his team after the loss to the Braves in the 1914 World Series, Pennock was sold to the Red Sox, another strong team. By 1920 the Sox owner began selling his stars. In 1923 Pennock was passed on to the Yankees, with whom he had his best seasons. He was 21-9 in 1924 and 23-11 in 1926, and had two other seasons with 19 wins.

At 160 pounds, Pennock was seldom a staff workhorse. He led the AL with 277 innings pitched in 1925, but he usually threw 50-60 fewer innings. He nearly always gave up more hits than innings pitched, although his low number of walks somewhat compensated for that. He once pitched an 11-hit shutout. His career ERA of 3.61 isn't spectacular. But, while the spectacular pitchers came and went, Pennock and his soft curves prevailed. In 1948 he was elected to the Baseball Hall of Fame.

ATANASIO "TONY" PEREZ
First Baseman/Third Baseman, Cin (N) 1964-76, 1984-86, Mon (N) 1977-79, Bos (A) 1980-82, Phi (N) 1983
One of the biggest cogs in the Big Red Machine of the 1970s, Perez helped put the Reds in four World Series. He knocked in 90 or more runs 11 straight seasons, 1967-1977. His career totals read 1,652 RBIs and 1,272 runs scored. He hit 379 homers, with a high of 40 in 1970. He hit .300 a couple of times and finished with a respectable .279 for 23 seasons. Yet, amazingly, he never led his league in a single important offensive statistic.

But he was consistent. He was also a good enough glove man to play third base for five seasons for Cincinnati so slugger Lee May could play first.

He hit .435 in the 1972 World Series. He went 0-for-15 in the 1975 World Series, then exploded with two homers and four RBIs to win the fifth game, 6-2. He added a two-run homer that tied Game 7; the Reds won the game and the Series, 4-3.

GAYLORD PERRY
Pitcher, SF (N) 1962-71, Cle (A) 1972-75, Tex (A) 1976-77, 1980, SD (N) 1978-79, NY (A) 1980, Atl (N) 1981, Sea (A) 1982-83, KC (A) 1983
The only man to win a Cy Young Award in both leagues, Perry had as much fun outwitting the umpires with his spitter as he did fooling the hitters with it. He even wrote a hilarious book about it, revealing for instance that KY Jelly and Preparation H work as well as the old standbys: spit, sweat, and Vaseline. The trick was to lubricate the fingers enough to squirt the ball out without spin, like squirting a watermelon seed. The ball then behaves like a

knuckleball but is easier to control. Perry was still winning games at the age of 43.

Perry won 20-plus twice for the Giants in the 1960s before he was traded to the AL after the 1971 season. NL umps were glad to see Perry go. Umpire Chris Pelekoudas gave him a giant jar of Vaseline as a going-away present.

His first year in the AL, Perry was 24-16 with the fifth-place Indians. He was the first man to top 20 in both leagues in nearly 50 years.

By 1978 he was back in the NL His 21-6 mark for San Diego earned him his second Cy Young to make him the first pitcher to win the award in both leagues. It was his fifth 20-win season.

In 22 years Perry played on only one division champ. With support like that, a guy needs a little extra edge to win 314 games. Perry was elected to the Hall of Fame in 1991.

CHARLES "DEACON" PHILLIPPE
Pitcher, Lou (N) 1899, Pit (N) 1900-11
Phillippe was the best control pitcher in the 20th century, giving up a stingy 1.25 walks per nine innings.

The Deacon's best year was 25-9 in 1903, his fifth 20-victory year in five years in the league. In the first World Series that fall, Phillippe pitched five complete games in 13 days (a total of 44 innings pitched) and walked only three. He won his first three starts in a period of six days, but he lost Game 6 on ground rule triples into the overflow crowd. The next day he was shut out, 3-0, as Boston took the Series.

The Deacon was still around to pitch six innings in the 1909 Series without allowing an earned run.

MIKE PIAZZA
Catcher, LA (N) 1992-98, Fla (N) 1998, NY (N) 1998-
For a player whom many were ready to concede a Hall of Fame plaque after six seasons, Piazza was passed around like so-so pizza in 1998. At the crux was money. The Dodgers refused to tender him a contract he desired, perhaps believing they could buy several small countries for the same big bucks. After 37 games he was shipped off to the Florida Marlins, an improbable destination in that the Fish were busily conducting a fire sale. Sure enough, after five games, he was traded to the Mets. After an early slump earned him some booing, Piazza came on strong and won over most of the fans. He led the Mets to not quite a Wild Card spot. For the fifth time, he finished with over 100 RBIs.

He is arguably the best hitting catcher ever and his 1997 season (.348, 40 home runs, 124 RBI) is probably the best offensive show ever put up by a catcher. On the other hand, he's less than sparkling behind the plate. He sometimes doesn't block the plate, is ordinary in calling pitches, and his arm—though strong—is erratic. The Mets liked him well enough to sign him to a seven-year contract that briefly made him the highest paid player in history.

BILLY PIERCE
Pitcher, Det (A) 1945, 1948, Chi (A) 1949-61, SF (N) 1962-64
Pierce was the epitome of "stylish lefty," the kind who looks good even when he loses. But Billy didn't lose that

often. The White Sox got him and $10,000 from the Tigers in 1949 for an aging catcher. It was the kind of deal that should have got the Sox four-to-seven at Joliet.

Billy stepped in immediately as the Sox ace; that wasn't any great honor in 1949, but after Chicago added Nellie Fox, Minnie Minoso, and Chico Carrasquel for a few broken bats or bubble gum cards or some other trade imbalance, the White Sox became a consistent first-division team. Billy led the AL in ERA in 1955, won 20 games in 1956 and '57, and totaled 186 wins for his 13 years with the Sox. In 1959 he helped them win their first pennant in 40 years.

In 1962 he joined the Giants and led them to a flag with a record of 16-6 that included a 12-0 mark at Candlestick Park.

EDDIE PLANK

Pitcher, Phi (A) 1901-14, StL (F) 1915, StL (A) 1916-17
Plank came out of Gettysburg College to win 327 games. He held the record for most wins by a left-hander until Warren Spahn surpassed that mark in 1963, 46 years after Eddie retired. He won 20 or more games eight times, seven with the Philadelphia A's and one with St. Louis of the Federal League. He pitched for six AL championship teams with the A's. He was only 2-5 in World Series games, but four of his losses were shutouts. His Series ERA was 1.32. He threw a lot of shutouts himself—69—the most for a lefty and fifth-best of all time.

Plank drove batters crazy before he threw the ball. He'd fuss around the mound, fidgeting with his uniform, talking to the ball ("Only nine more to go," etc.), shaking off signs. By the time he threw the ball, the batter was ready to swing at anything.

Of course, Plank didn't throw just anything. He had a good fastball and curve, which he delivered sidearm with good control. He struck out 2,246 batters and walked fewer than half that many. Despite all his good years, he never led the league in wins, strikeouts, or ERA.

He was named to the Baseball Hall of Fame in 1946.

CUMBERLAND "CUM" POSEY

Outfielder, Owner, Negro League, Homestead Grays, Detroit Wolves
Posey's Homestead Grays wrote a record never approached by any other U.S. pro team in any sport—they won nine straight pennants from 1937 to 1945 with Josh Gibson, Buck Leonard, and Cool Papa Bell generating the power. Only the Tokyo Giants, with nine straight Japanese championships, can match them. Yet they may not have been the greatest Grays teams of all.

The 1926 club, starring Joe Williams, won 43 straight (mostly against white semipro teams). The 1930 Grays, with Williams, Gibson, and Oscar Charleston, won 11 out of 12 from the western champion Monarchs. And the 1931 club boasted a record of 136-17, again mostly against semipros. They even challenged the white major league Pirates to a winner-take-all series, but Pittsburgh simply refused.

Posey's father was a wealthy barge captain, his mother the first black to graduate from Ohio State. At various times Cum attended Penn State, Pitt, and Duquesne universities, but failed to graduate from any of them. He was considered the best colored basketball player in America

in 1913 and also managed the Murdock Grays, a steel mill team. Eventually he founded the Loendi Big Five, which claimed the U.S. basketball championship of 1919. He gained control of the Homestead Grays in the early 1920s, played for the team until 1928, and managed it until 1935.

But when the Depression struck, Posey lost his stars to racketeer Gus Greenlee's well-bankrolled Pittsburgh Crawfords. Cum got his own racketeer, Sonnyman Jackson, and fought back, eventually driving Greenlee out of the league. In 1937 Cum bought Gibson back for $2,500, and the team went 152-11 to embark on their pennant streak.

The Grays shuttled between Pittsburgh and Washington by bus, playing two or three games a day, league and semi-pro. Rain could wipe out all profit for the week, until World War II brought prosperity at last. In 1945 Posey's Grays sometimes drew 30,000 fans to Griffith Stadium hours after the AL Senators had played there before 3,000. But when baseball was at last integrated after the war, the raids of major league clubs soon destroyed Cum's life investment. Luke Easter was snatched up by the Indians for only $10,000. Posey moaned, "It's like coming into a man's store and stealing the merchandise right off the shelves."

JOHN "BOOG" POWELL

First Baseman, Bal (A) 1961-74, Cle (A) 1975-76, LA (N) 1977
Powell drove some long blasts out of parks—469 feet in Baltimore in 1962, over the roof of Tiger Stadium in 1969. He and Frank Robinson provided the power that brought the Orioles four pennants and two world titles between 1966 and 1971. Big Boog (6 feet 4 inches, 230 pounds) crushed 339 home runs, with a high of 39 in 1964. He was named AL MVP in 1970.

Boog hit .357 in the 1966 World Series as Baltimore swept the Dodgers in four straight. In 1969 he hit .385 to help sweep Minnesota in the ALCS and .429 to key the sweep again a year later. In the 1970 Series his home runs won the first two games to get the O's off to a five-game victory over the Big Red Machine.

DEL PRATT

Second Baseman, StL (A) 1912-17, NY (A) 1918-20, Bos (A) 1921-22, Det (A) 1923-24
Pratt had a knack for picking losers. He went from the 1912 Browns to the 1918 Yanks, 1921 Red Sox, and 1923 Tigers, spending most of his 13-year career in the second division.

Del was a fair singles hitter with a high of .324 in 1921. He hit .302 as a rookie, then missed that level for seven straight seasons. But in 1920, with the livelier ball, he suddenly remembered how to do it and batted over .300 in each of his last five seasons, bowing out with .303 in 1924. Pratt played over 100 games in each of his seasons and he quit with 1,996 hits; if he'd been keeping track, he might have tried to hang around for one more year.

He was a good glove man, although he slowed down rapidly near the end. He led AL second basemen in putouts five times.

He was something of a clubhouse lawyer and was traded away from the Yankees following the 1920 season after a dispute over the division of New York's World

Series money for finishing in third place in the AL. The Yankees won the pennant in 1921 and Pratt's new team, Boston, finished fifth, reducing his bonus to nothing. Well, penny wise and pound foolish . . .

The way Pratt got to the Yankees was that he and a teammate sued the Browns owner for calling them "lazy" and intimating they lost games purposely. The players settled out of court and then—surprise!—were traded.

JOHN PICUS "JACK" QUINN
Pitcher, NY (A) 1909-12, 1919-21, Bos (N) 1913, Bal (F) 1914-15, Chi (A) 1918, Bos (A) 1922-25, Phi (A) 1925-30, Bkn (N) 1931-32, Cin (N) 1933
An old spitballer, Quinn pitched almost 1,000 pro games in almost 30 years, 1907-1935. He hit his last home run in the majors at the age of 46 and won his last game when he was 47. Or maybe 47 and 48—there's a disagreement as to when he was born. Anyway, he was old! Spitballers, like knuckleballers, tend to have long careers.

Trapped in a coal mine fire as a youth, Jack had a checkered baseball career. He bounced around the New York Highlanders (before they were the Yankees and when the franchise was down), the minors, the Federal League, the Yanks again when they were rebuilding, 1919-1921, and the Red Sox when they were down, 1922-1924. Finally, he caught on a team on the upswing, the Philadelphia A's. He hurled two Series games in 1930 at the age of 46 (or thereabouts)—the oldest man to do so.

During all that time, he kept his spitball low and usually over the plate. His only 20-win season was with the Feds in 1914, but he won 18 three times in the AL. Well, no one ever said he was great, just good for a long, long time.

DAN QUISENBERRY
Pitcher, KC (A) 1979-88, StL (N) 1988-89, SF (N) 1990
The submarine-throwing Quisenberry was baseball's premier reliever of the 1980s, leading the AL in saves five years out of six, 1980-1985. He was Fireman of the Year four times and was one of the top reasons Kansas City reached the postseason four times in that period.

Calling himself "just a garbage man," Quiz saved 45 in 1983, a record since topped several times. Dan had a dry sense of humor. "I have seen the future," he was fond of saying. "It is much like the present, only longer." As for his underhand style, he shrugged. "I discovered a delivery in my flaw."

He was inducted into the Royals' Hall of Fame in 1998 and died four months later from brain cancer.

DICK RADATZ
Pitcher, Bos (A) 1962-66, Cle (A) 1966-67, Chi (N) 1967, Det (A) 1969, Mon (N) 1969
From 1962 to 1965, Fenway Park's left field wall was only the second-most-fearsome "Monster" in Red Sox land. Number one was the 6-foot-6-inch, 250-pound fastballer who stomped in from the bullpen and turned batters to mush. Radatz won two Fireman of the Year Awards for the Red Sox, 1962 and 1964, when he led the AL in saves. He led in relief wins three straight years, 1962-1964. His 16 relief wins in 1964 set an AL record (since broken).

The Monster intimidated hitters, averaging more than a strikeout an inning, and after every win he'd shove his fist

triumphantly into the air. And just when they didn't think he could get any better, he lost it. As soon as he lost a foot off his fastball, he was done. He didn't have anything else to throw. His final figures: 52-43 and 122 saves—100 in four years.

CHARLES "OL' HOSS" RADBOURN
Pitcher, Buf (N) 1880, Pro (N) 1881-85, Bos (N) 1886-89, Bos (P) 1890, Cin (N) 1891
Radbourn was hardly a "hoss." He stood only 5 feet 9 inches and weighed 168. But he earned his name by winning 60 games in one year, 1884—that's 679 innings, 441 strikeouts, and a 1.38 ERA. He won the NL pennant for Providence. By season's end he was pitching every day until he could barely lift his arm to comb his hair. Then he won three more against the AA champs in the freezing cold in the championship series.

Hoss had a great curveball. He also had an "in-shoot," or screwball. He delivered both underhand, although overhand pitching had been legalized that year. The pitching distance was only 50 feet, but batters could ask for a high or low ball, in effect cutting the strike zone in half.

Charlie had already won 33 in 1882 and 48 in 1883 when the historic 1884 season with Providence began.

The temperamental Radbourn resented young Charlie Sweeney trying to push him out as ace. He was suspended for loafing, but when Sweeney got drunk and jumped the club, they begged Rad to come back. The only pitcher on the roster, he pitched nearly every game until Providence clinched the flag. He pitched 30 of 32 remaining games, won 26 of them—18 in a row, including five shutouts and four one-run games. His winning streak was broken when he lost, 2-0.

Rad had several more good years to bring his career record to 310-195. Then he bought a bar and retired. In 1894 he shot himself hunting, losing one eye and half his face. He ended his days in the back of a pool hall, refusing to come out. He died at age 42. Radbourn was elected to the Baseball Hall of Fame in 1939.

TIM RAINES
Outfielder, Mon (N) 1979-90, Chi (A) 1991-95, NY (A) 1996-
Raines may have been the top player in the NL in the 1980s. A compact switch-hitter, his main weapon was blinding speed, but he also hit with occasional power. As a rookie in 1981, he stole 71 bases in only 88 games. He led the NL in steals in his first four seasons, with a high of 90 in 1983. Entering the 1999 season, he had the second-best base-stealing percentage in history for players with 300 or more steals: 803 out of 948 for 84.7 percent. He led the league in runs scored in 1983 and 1987. In 1986, he topped the NL with a .334 batting average.

He opted for free agency in 1987, but no team made a legitimate offer, an absurd situation that was later ruled to have resulted from collusion on the part of owners. Raines eventually re-signed with Montreal, but he missed spring training and the first month of the season. When he hit .330, he set a lot of people wondering about the need for spring training.

Raines led the Expos to their only postseason appearance in 1981, played for a division-winner with the 1993 White Sox, and was a part-time player on the Yankees

team that won two World Series in three years.

WILLIE RANDOLPH

Second Baseman, Pit (N) 1975, NY (A) 1976-88, LA (N) 1989-1990, Oak (A) 1990, Mil (A) 1991, NY (N) 1992

Randolph was one of the sparkplugs who drove the Yankees to five titles in six years, 1976-1981. Solid defensively and excellent on double plays, he enjoyed his best year at bat in 1980 (.294). His worst was 1981 (.232, two home runs); however, his homer in the ALCS won the third game to clinch the pennant.

Although held back by injuries for a couple of years, he hit .307 in 1987 and a career-high .327 in 1991. One of his strengths was that he walked about twice as often as he struck out.

DICK REDDING

Pitcher, Negro League, 1911-38, Lincoln Giants, Lincoln Stars, Indianapolis ABCs, Chicago American Giants, Brooklyn Royal Giants, Bacharach Giants

"Cannonball Dick" could knock the bat out of a man's hand back in the pre-World War I era. He is credited with 12 no-hitters, though this is unverified and probably mostly against semipro foes.

From 1912 to 1914 Dick teamed with Joe Williams on the Lincoln Giants to form perhaps black baseball's strongest one-two pitching punch ever. Real old-timers insist the two were both faster than the younger and more famous Satchel Paige.

Thereafter Dick and Joe became fierce rivals. In 1920 Redding beat Williams with a no-hitter at Ebbets Field in probably the finest game he ever pitched.

An illiterate Georgian, Redding was credited with 17 straight wins as a rookie in 1911. In 1915 he reportedly won 20 straight. He pitched the Indianapolis ABC's to a championship in 1917, then spent 1918 seeing combat service in France.

No stats were kept until the Eastern League was formed in 1923, when Dick was over the hill and managing the Brooklyn Royals, one of the weakest clubs. He was a losing pitcher then. He often faced Babe Ruth and Lou Gehrig in exhibitions; his job was to groove soft pitches to them to please the customers.

HAROLD "PEE WEE" REESE

Shortstop, Bkn (N) 1940-42, 1946-57, LA (N) 1958

Reese was shortstop on seven pennant-winning Brooklyn teams from 1941 to 1956. An average hitter, he nevertheless led the NL in runs scored in 1949 with 132 and totaled 1,338 for his career. A good baserunner, he played during a time when base stealing was not stressed. His 30 steals led the league in 1952, and his career total of 232 stolen bases is one of the better marks for the era.

He was at his best in the field and in providing leadership as captain of the Dodgers. Reese once faked a splinter in his eye to give his reliever more time to warm up. The performance was so convincing that the hurler dropped the ball and came over to see if he could help. A Southerner, one of Pee Wee's greatest accomplishments was winning Jackie Robinson's acceptance on the team.

His nickname stemmed not from his lack of size (5 feet 10 inches, 160 pounds), but from the fact he was a marbles champion as a lad.

Although he hit .300 only once and never amassed exceptional stats, he finished in the top 10 in MVP voting eight times. Reese was elected to the Baseball Hall of Fame in 1984.

ED REULBACH

Pitcher, Chi (N) 1905-13, Bkn (N) 1913-14, Nwk (F) 1915, Bos (N) 1916-17

Reulbach is the only man ever to pitch a doubleheader shutout, which he did in the stretch of the 1908 pennant race, won by the Cubs in a playoff of the Merkle game. When Chicago's other starters were exhausted after the hectic Giants series (that included the famous Merkle "boner" game), Ed agreed to pitch the doubleheader against the seventh-place Dodgers, whom he had already beaten seven times. He shut them out for 18 innings, and the Cubs went on to win in a playoff.

Reulbach had pitched marathons before—in 1905 he had won an 18-inning game, then went 20 innings to win another.

From 1906 to 1908, Reulbach had a remarkable record—60-15. He led the league in winning percentage all three seasons (only Lefty Grove has matched that)—as the Cubs captured three pennants. In the 1906 World Series against the "Hitless Wonder" White Sox, Ed pitched a one-hitter in Game 2. Reulbach died July 17, 1961, the same day as Ty Cobb.

JIM RICE

Outfielder, Bos (A) 1974-89

Rice was made for Fenway Park and took advantage of it. He and Fred Lynn enjoyed splendid rookie seasons in 1975 to lift the Red Sox to the pennant. An injury kept Rice out of the World Series, which Boston lost to the Reds in seven games.

His best season was the thrilling 1978 pennant race with New York, won by the Yankees in a playoff. Rice led the league in homers (46), RBIs (139), triples (15), and hits (213), with a .315 batting average. He was voted MVP over New York's Ron Guidry in a hotly debated vote.

Rice led in home runs three times and RBIs twice. On the downside, he was also among the all-time leaders in hitting into double plays. But you know who the leader is? Hank Aaron. Not bad company to be in.

EDGAR "SAM" RICE

Outfielder, Was (A) 1915-33, Cle (A) 1934

Rice stopped only 13 hits short of 3,000, hit .322, topped .300 in 14 seasons, stole 351 bases, had good range in the outfield and a strong arm, and played on all three Washington pennant winners. He rarely struck out; in 1929 Sam came to bat 616 times and whiffed only nine times. He had no power; he once hit 182 singles in one season.

A victim of a tragic tornado that killed most of his family, young Sam wandered aimlessly, joining a shipping concern. As a sailor in Mexico, he began to play baseball. Rice joined the Senators as a pitcher in 1915. When Detroit hurler Hooks Dauss tripled off him, Rice became an outfielder.

In 1924 Rice put together a 31-game hit streak, led the AL with 216 hits, and batted .334 as the Senators won their first pennant. In 1925 he hit .350 and cracked 227

hits to lead the Senators into the World Series, then slapped 12 hits in the Series, a record (later broken by Bobby Richardson of the Yankees). In Game 3 he made the most famous play of his life; he chased down Pirate Earl Smith's drive but fell into the stands as he reached the ball. An out or a home run? Rice would never answer directly. "The ump called him out." He would smile mysteriously. He left a letter to be opened at his death. In it, he at last answered the question. He caught the ball.

Rice was elected to the Baseball Hall of Fame in 1963.

BRANCH RICKEY

Catcher/Outfielder, StL(A) 1905-06, 1914, NY(A) 1907. Manager, StL (A) 1913-15, StL (N) 1919-25. Executive.

Rickey invented the farm system and integrated the game. Rickey's decision to sign Jackie Robinson to a Dodgers contract took great courage, but his motives were not completely pure. Robinson, Roy Campanella, and Don Newcombe, and other black stars helped win seven pennants for the Dodgers.

Rickey had powerful fundamentalist religious scruples against playing ball on Sunday. As a player and manager, he was not available on Sundays. He wasn't missed that much as a player. He was a catcher, but he hit only .239 in 120 major league games and once was victimized for 13 stolen bases in a game. He was, however, a brilliant teacher and innovator. After a period as both field manager and business manager of the Browns, he joined the Cardinals as president of the club in 1916. After 1925 he concentrated on his front office job.

In 1919 Rickey conceived the farm system. Unable to outbid the rich clubs for players, he decided to grow his own, and his minor league chain was one reason for the Cardinals' five flags in nine years, 1926-1934. Eventually he had 800 players under contract on 50 teams. Rickey had taken over a team $175,000 in debt and made it a champ. He also instituted Ladies Day, the Knothole Gang (to get kids interested in the game) the batting cage, and the sliding pit.

After the season in 1942, he moved to the Dodgers and laid the groundwork for the champions of 1947 to 1955. He eventually sold his stock in the club for $1 million.

He moved on to Pittsburgh in 1951. There Rickey left a legacy that produced a flag in 1960 after he had gone. His trial balloon of a Continental League pushed baseball to expand in the 1960s.

He was elected to the Baseball Hall of Fame in 1967.

CAL RIPKEN, JR.

Shortstop/Third Baseman, Bal (A) 1981-

Ripken's durability is legend. In fact, he's so well-known for playing every day that some people forget how great a career he has had. Originally a third baseman, Ripken was switched to short in 1982, his first full year with the Orioles. When he slugged 28 home runs and batted in 93 runs, he was named Rookie of the Year. His second season was even better. He led the AL in hits (211), doubles (47), and runs (121), while hitting .318, with 27 homers and 102 RBIs. The Orioles were world champions and Ripken was named MVP.

Although he's been chosen on the AL All-Star team each year since 1983, his batting average and RBIs slipped, until he put together another MVP season in

1991. He surpassed Lou Gehrig's consecutive game streak played in 1995 in a grand celebration at Camden Yards. Ripken took himself out of the lineup for the Orioles' final home game of the 1998 season, ending his streak at 2,632 games. It was the first time he had missed a game in more than 17 years. He moved back to third base in 1997.

EPPA RIXEY

Pitcher, Phi (N) 1912-17, 1919-20, Cin (N) 1921-33

The winningest National League left-hander until Warren Spahn—and still the losingest—Rixey was a control artist who seldom walked anyone and seldom whiffed anyone. If Spahn hadn't broken his record, he said, nobody would have known about him. That's an exaggeration, but he seldom pitched for teams that were likely to make him a household name at World Series time.

Straight off the University of Virginia campus, Rixey began on the 1912 Phillies in the shadow of Grover Cleveland Alexander. He was 11-12 on the 1915 champs and lost his only World Series game.

He was 22-10 for the second-place Phils in 1916, lost 21 for them in 1917, then went into the Army for a year in France. He lost 22 in 1920 as the Phillies finished last.

Switching to the sixth-place Reds, Rixey won 20-plus three times, including a league-leading 25-13 in 1922, when they rose to second. The 6-foot-5-inch stringbean with a big sweeping motion was voted the Reds' all-time left-hander in a 1969 fan vote. He pitched for 21 years, amassing a career record of 266-251. His home run ratio, one per 48 innings, was the best in the Ruthian era. He was named to the Baseball Hall of Fame in 1963.

PHIL "SCOOTER" RIZZUTO

Shortstop, NY (A) 1941-42, 1946-56

Rizzuto played on 10 Yankee pennant winners and in nine World Series. A superior fielder, he led AL shortstops in fielding in 1949 and 1950. Those were his best offensive years, too, as he scored over 100 runs each season. His 1950 season won him the MVP, as he hit .324, some 51 points above his career average.

The 5-foot-6-inch "Scooter" remained highly visible in New York as a Yankees broadcaster. "Holy cow!" became his trademark and he peppered his stories about Yankees legends with mentions of local people.

As a rookie in 1941, he was called to the mound by Lefty Gomez. "Kid, is your mother in the stands?" Lefty asked. "Yes, sir, Mr. Gomez," Phil replied. "Well, stay here and talk to me a little; she'll think you're giving advice to the great Lefty Gomez." That day Phil hit his first home run and circled the bases with his face wreathed in smiles.

After years of hoping, Rizzuto was elected to the Hall of Fame in 1994.

ROBIN ROBERTS

Pitcher, Phi (N) 1948-61, Bal (A) 1962-65, Hou (N) 1965-66, Chi (N) 1966

Roberts had great control and a fastball. He came close to a rare 30 wins with 28 in 1952, and came within 14 of winning 300 games.

His moment supreme came in October 1950, when he hurled the Whiz Kids to their first flag in 35 years. After

pitcher Curt Simmons was drafted into the military, the Phils lost their comfortable lead and went into the final game—against the Dodgers—only one game ahead. Robin, taking up the slack, was making his third start in five days. He battled Don Newcombe into the 10th inning, 1-1, before Dick Sisler's home run finally won it for Robin and the Phils.

In the World Series a weary Roberts started Game 2, but this time he was the loser, 2-1, in the 10th on a home run by Joe DiMaggio. It was his Robin's only World Series. Though he won 20-plus for six years in a row and led the league in five of them, the Phils never got closer than third again.

He was voted MVP in 1952, when he was 28-7 with a fourth-place team. He was 6-0 against the champion Dodgers.

Roberts had excellent control—1.7 walks per game lifetime. In 1953-1954 he had the least walks and most strikeouts per game in the NL. But he gave up more than 500 home runs, including a then-record 46 in 1956, as hitters knew they could dig in on him.

Roberts was a workhorse, leading the league in complete games and innings pitched five times each. It finally cost him the snap in his fastball. Roberts was 10-22 in 1957, 1-10 in 1961. But he learned to pitch with finesse, went to the AL, and won another 52 games. In 1976 he was named to the Baseball Hall of Fame.

BROOKS ROBINSON
Third Baseman, Bal (A) 1955-77
Robbie led AL third basemen in fielding average a record 10 times, he won 16 straight Gold Gloves, and he set the existing career records in assists, putouts, double plays, and fielding average. And he made some plays in the postseason that brought millions of viewers to their feet, cheering.

His best year at bat was 1964, when he hit .317 and led in RBIs and all the fielding categories for his position. Robinson was named AL MVP. In 23 seasons, he had 268 homers, 1,357 RBIs, and a .267 batting average.

The postseason brought out the best in Brooks at bat as well as with the glove. He hit .429 in the 1970 World Series, sparkled in the field, and was named Series MVP. The next year he hit .364 in the ALCS and .318 in the Series.

Personable and extremely popular with fans, he could have been elected King of Baltimore during his playing days. He was elected to the Baseball Hall of Fame in 1983.

FRANK ROBINSON
Outfielder, Cin (N) 1956-65, Bal (A) 1966-71, LA (N) 1972, Cal (A) 1973-74, Cle (A) 1974-76. Manager, Cle (A) 1975-77, SF (N) 1981-84, Bal (A) 1988-91
From 1956, when he blasted 38 home runs to tie the rookie record, until 1976, when he hit his last, Robbie was one of the best-hitting outfielders of all time. His career marks include 586 homers, 1,812 RBIs, 1,829 runs, 2,943 hits, and a .294 batting average. In 1970 he hit two grand slams in a single game.

Frank was also the first black man to lead a white big league team. He managed the Indians to two fourth-place finishes and a fifth from 1975 to 1977, and later managed

San Francisco and Baltimore.

An aggressive, intelligent leader, he's the first man to win MVPs in each league—1961 with the Reds and 1966 with the Orioles. He led them both to pennants, and in the latter year, his first in the AL, won the Triple Crown as well. The two Robinsons, Frank and Brooks, provided the punch for four AL champions: 1966, 1969, 1970, and 1971.

In 1982 he was named to the Baseball Hall of Fame.

JACKIE ROBINSON
Infield, Negro League, 1945, Kansas City Monarchs, Bkn (N) 1947-56
Aggressive, exciting, driven with an inner fire, Jackie Robinson battled his opponents, history, and himself. He made integration succeed, and in doing so helped the Dodgers win six flags. Historian David Q. Voigt calls him one of the five most pivotal men in baseball history—and he ranks right up there in American history as well.

He could drop a bunt, line a homer, or steal a base—whatever was needed to win. "If it wasn't for him," the Cards' Red Schoendienst once remarked, "the Dodgers would be in the second division."

Jackie's story, now taught in schools, is familiar: football star at UCLA, an Army court martial (and acquittal) for refusing to sit in the back of the bus, a year with the Kansas City Monarchs (hitting .345), the surprise announcement that he would be the first black to sign in the white majors, the promise to Branch Rickey to turn the other cheek to insults, the jockeying, the knockdown pitches, the threat of a strike, and the triumphant rookie year of 1947.

Robinson was not the best black prospect, Negro Leaguers agree. But he was college-educated and had played with whites, two intangibles that Rickey sought above sheer talent.

Jackie was 28 before he reached the white majors, his athletic peak behind him. Yet he revolutionized the game with his running, dancing off base to rattle the pitcher, and 19 steals of home—five in one year. It was a new brand of ball in the major leagues, and blacks who followed Robinson's footsteps perfected it.

Jack's best season was 1949. He led the league in batting and stolen bases, knocked in 124 runs, and won the MVP, as the Dodgers captured the pennant by a single game.

In 1951 the Dodgers were fighting to stave off the Giants' amazing drive. On the final day, against the Phils, with the bases loaded, Robinson made a spectacular catch of Eddie Waitkus' drive up the middle to preserve the tie. In the 14th he walloped a homer to win it and end the season all tied up. The Giants, however, won the famous three-game playoff for the pennant, somewhat obscuring one of Robinson's greatest seasons.

Robinson played for only 10 years. He finished with a .311 career batting average, but more important, he led his team to six pennants.

After retiring, Robinson became active in politics and spoke out militantly on civil rights. He was one of the first to denounce the game for not hiring black managers. At last, the tensions took their toll, the fires burned out, and he died at the age of 53, leaving the game unalterably changed.

In 1997 Baseball celebrated the 50th anniversary of his breaking the color line. In an honor unprecedented in sports, all of the teams retired his uniform number, 42.

He was named to the Baseball Hall of Fame in 1962.

WILBERT ROBINSON
Catcher, Phi (AA) 1886-90, Bro-Bal (AA) 1890, Bal (AA) 1891, Bal (N) 1892-99, StL (N) 1900, Bal (A) 1901-02. Manager, Bal (A) 1902, Bkn (N) 1914-31

Wilbert Robinson was chubby and cherubic, a former catching star with the great Orioles, later the lovable manager of Brooklyn's Daffiness Boys and winner of two pennants.

He's one of only two men to get seven hits in a nine-inning game—he drove in 11 runs that same day in 1892. A lifetime .273 hitter, Robinson had three .330-plus years with the Orioles.

In 1911 he joined his old teammate and friend John McGraw as a coach on the Giants. His patient handling helped make an $11,000 beauty out of the former "$11,000 lemon," Rube Marquard.

But the friendship with McGraw broke up in an argument over a missed sign in the 1913 World Series, and Robinson went to manage the crosstown Dodgers. He raised attendance, started a Bonehead Club for stupid plays, and became its first member when he handed the wrong lineup card to the umpire. He agreed to catch a baseball dropped from a plane; the ball turned out to be a grapefruit and splattered all over his chest, and thinking the juice was blood Robinson though he'd been killed. He once benched a player because he couldn't spell his name for the lineup card.

Beloved in Brooklyn, the team was called the Robins during his reign. Uncle Robby won Brooklyn's first 20th-century flag in 1916. He finished fifth in 1919, hired hunchbacked Eddie Bennett as batboy, and finished first in 1920. Robinson left Bennett home and lost the last four games of the World Series in Cleveland. He fired Eddie and fell back to fifth in 1921. He almost won again in 1924 but lost to McGraw by one and a half games.

He was elected to the Baseball Hall of Fame in 1945.

WILBUR "BULLET JOE" ROGAN
Pitcher, Negro League, 1917-46, Los Angeles White Sox, Kansas City Monarchs

Standing just 5 feet 6 inches, Rogan pitched for the Kansas City Monarchs a decade before Satchel Paige, and most black vets who saw them both believe that Joe was the better. Monarch second baseman Newt Allen said, "Satchel had the stuff, but Rogan had the brains."

Joe's 109 wins are second best for the black leagues. Satch is fourth with 100, though several of Paige's seasons have not yet been compiled, and he won 63 more in the white majors and minors. On the other hand, Rogan did not begin pitching in the big time until he was 30.

Satch was languid and loose, Bullet Joe stocky and dour. Paige threw his fastball in a cup, Rogan threw an assortment of curves, sliders, and palmballs all over the plate. Satchel was a comedian at bat, Joe hit cleanup on one of the greatest murderers' rows in blackball annals.

Casey Stengel also called Rogan "one of the best, if not the best, pitchers that ever lived." He discovered Rogan in the Arizona desert with a black cavalry team on the Mexi-can border in 1918. Stengel, a Kansas City native, tipped off the Monarchs' owner, and Joe's pro career was launched at the age of 30.

He pitched and batted the Monarchs to three straight flags, 1923-1925, hitting .426, .450, and .355. On the mound he was 12-9, 19-10, and 12-2 in the 100-game Negro League seasons. He was probably the MVP in 1924 or 1925—if not both. His postseason record was .421 at bat, 8-4 on the mound.

In 15 games against white big leaguers, Joe hit .389. In one 1929 game, Al Simmons went 0-for-5 against Joe, and struck out three times. Rogan was elected to the Hall of Fame in 1998.

EDDIE ROMMEL
Pitcher, Phi (A) 1920-32

In 1922 Rommel had one of the finest seasons of all time—27-13 for the seventh-place A's (they were a last-place team without him), a feat almost as amazing as Steve Carlton's 27-10 with the last-place Phils of 1972.

The next year he led the league in losses, 18-19 with the sixth-place A's. In five roller coaster years, 1921-1925, Ed and his knuckler led the league in victories two times and in losses twice.

By the time the A's dynasty blossomed, Ed was past his prime. Nevertheless, he was 28-11 during the pennant-winning seasons of 1929 to 1931. He later became an outstanding AL umpire.

PETE "CHARLIE HUSTLE" ROSE
Outfielder/First Baseman/Third Baseman/Second Baseman, Cin (N) 1963-78, 1984-86, Phi (N) 1979-83, Mon (N) 1984. Manager, Cin (N) 1984-89

The most exciting player of his age, Charlie Hustle monopolized center stage with his unsuccessful pursuit of Joe DiMaggio's hit streak in 1978 and his successful pursuit of Ty Cobb's lifetime hit record in 1985.

Rose played more games than any other man (3,562), batted more times (14,053), made more hits (4,256), stands second in doubles (746), and fourth in runs (2,165). He had 14 seasons in which he batted .300, 10 seasons of 200 hits (Cobb had only nine), won three batting titles, and made the NL All-Star team 17 times at five positions. He was Rookie of the Year in 1963, MVP in 1973, and played in his last World Series in 1983 at age 42.

He was a hell-for-leather baserunner who wasn't very fast. He was a great hitter who lacked home run power. On any given day in his career there were probably a couple of hundred players in the majors with more talent. None made as much out of his talent as Rose. He didn't drink or smoke and kept himself in perfect shape. He worked and he hustled. In an exhibition game with the lordly Yankees in the early 1960s, he ran out a walk. "Charlie Hustle," they sneered. Rose turned the putdown into a compliment.

He played hard every day. He played wherever he was needed. And he loved every inning. Long after many of those Yankees who sneered had retired, Rose was winning games with head-first dives and key hits.

Above all, Rose was a winner. Pete played on four pennant winners in Cincinnati during the 1970s, then he signed a lucrative contract with the Phillies in 1979 and

helped them to two more pennants in the 1980s. *The Sporting News* voted him Player of the 1970s, then Man of the Year in 1985.

"There are a lot of players better than me," Rose said, "but I do the same thing day in and day out, year in and year out."

Rose's post-playing career has been marked by disappointment, controversy, and personal tragedy. In his first five years as Cincinnati manager, he was unable to lift his team above second place. But there was worse to come. In 1989 Commissioner Bart Giamatti suspended him from baseball for life, after investigating accusations that Rose had bet on baseball games, including those involving the Reds.

And 1990 brought more ugly headlines, as Rose was sentenced to five months in prison for tax evasion. The Hall of Fame clarified their rules for election, stating that players who were banned from baseball were not eligible for induction.

AL ROSEN
Third Baseman, Cle (A) 1947-56
For a few years, Al Rosen was one of the most feared hitters in the American League. He played 35 games for the Indians from 1947 to 1949, but couldn't move Ken Keltner off third base until 1950. That year his 37 homers set an AL rookie record not broken until Mark McGwire in 1987. In 1953 Rosen was AL MVP, narrowly missing the Triple Crown with a .336 batting average, while leading the league with 43 homers (still the record for AL third basemen) and 145 RBIs.

In 1954 he was on his way to an equally impressive season when he suffered a broken finger. The injury permanently affected his grip on the bat. He returned to the lineup and helped the Indians win 111 games and the pennant, but his batting stats fell off badly. He retired two years later. From 1950 to 1954, he averaged .298, 31 home runs, and 114 RBIs.

EDD ROUSH
Outfielder, Chi (A) 1913, Ind (F) 1914, Nwk (F) 1915, NY (N) 1916, 1927-29, Cin (N) 1916-26, 1931
Roush was the Tris Speaker of the NL. He made circus catches and won batting titles—.341 in 1917, his first year as a Cincinnati regular, and .321 in 1919. He just missed the one in between, losing by two points to Brooklyn's Zack Wheat.

Roush's 1919 batting title helped the Reds win the flag, but he hit only .214 in the Series. Not that it mattered; that was the year the Black Sox decided to lose the Series.

Roush swung the heaviest bat in the league, a 48-ounce club, but he wasn't a home run hitter; only 67 of his 2,376 career hits went the distance. He was a singles hitter, but darned consistent. In both 1921 and 1922 he hit .352; then in 1923 he slumped to .351.

Roush was an independent cuss who held out year after year just so he could miss spring training. When he really got into a money dispute in 1930, he held out the entire season. He was named to the Baseball Hall of Fame in 1962.

CHARLES "RED" RUFFING
Pitcher, Bos (A) 1924-30, NY (A) 1930-42, 1945-46, Chi (A) 1947
Mired with the bottom-of-the-barrel Red Sox of the late 1920s, Ruffing seemed to go with the flow, compiling a 39-96 record with appropriate sky-high ERAs. In 1928 he was 10-25; the next year 9-22.

Traded to the Yankees in 1930, he became the new improved version. Buoyed by better defense and far more hitting, Ruffing's pitching "became much better," as though a weight had been lifted. His victories shot up as his ERA dropped. Four straight years (1936-1939), he won 20, and he had eight other seasons of at least 14 wins. His total Yankee record was 231-124. In six World Series he was 7-2, with a 2.63 ERA.

The burly redhead was primarily a fastball pitcher, but though he was often lauded for his "pinpoint" control, he walked more than 100 in three different seasons and finished his career with a total of 1,541 free passes.

Ruffing had hoped for a career as an outfielder, but a childhood accident cost him four toes on his left foot. No longer able to run, he became a pitcher. However, he remained an excellent hitter for a pitcher, averaging .269 with 36 career home runs. He was often used as a pinch hitter. He was named to the Baseball Hall of Fame in 1967.

AMOS RUSIE
Pitcher, Ind (N) 1889, NY (N) 1890-95, 1897-98, Cin (N) 1901
Rusie helped revolutionize the game. The "Hoosier Thunderbolt" was the fastest pitcher of the 1890s. In 1893 they moved the pitching distance back five feet (and six inches) to its present distance because of him and a few others. At the old 50-foot distance (measured from the front of the box, not the back), Rusie had struck out 341, 337, and 288 from 1890 to 1892. After they moved it back, his whiffs dropped to 208—and everyone's batting average jumped up.

Rusie was as wild as he was fast. He whiffed 1,934 batters and walked 1,704. His 289 walks (in 549 innings) in 1890 is the record. In four seasons he led the league in both walks and strikeouts. Amos was a workhorse, often going over 300 innings pitched and twice over 500.

In the eight years he pitched for the Giants, Rusie won 20 or more in each of those eight years. His top year was 1894, 36-13, plus two more wins in the Temple Cup playoff over Baltimore. His ERA that year of 2.78 was awesome compared to the NL average of 5.32.

In 1895 he was 23-23, as the Giants finished 12th. He sat out 1896 in a dispute with his owner, who tried to subtract a fine he had levied from the pitcher's salary for the coming year. Rusie went to court, and the other owners paid the fine and Rusie's 1896 salary rather than see the reserve clause tested.

As the league's top box-office draw he returned in 1897 and went 28-10, lifting the Giants from seventh to second. His wins fell to 20 in 1898, and he blamed it on the wear on his arm. When the club tried to cut his pay again, from $3,000 to $2,000, Rusie sat out for two years. In 1901 he was traded to Cincinnati, but his arm was gone and he retired after three games. The Giants did better on their end of the trade, picking up a kid pitcher named Christy Mathewson.

Rusie, who compiled a 245-174 mark in only nine full

seasons, was named to the Baseball Hall of Fame in 1977.

BABE RUTH
Outfielder, Bos (A) 1914-19, NY (A) 1920-34,
Bos (N) 1935

There has never been another figure in American sports like the Babe. Gargantuan—nay, Rabelaisian—in his appetites, prodigious in his production, he is the most famous athlete this nation has ever produced. Others have topped some of his records, but they can never top him in American mythology.

George Herman Ruth revolutionized the game. Authorities disagree whether his home runs gave birth to the lively ball or vice versa. They also disagree on whether Babe created attendance records with his homers or whether the postwar Roaring '20s prosperity created them. But Babe gave the game a lift after the Black Sox scandal and personified his time as no other American has.

No one has dominated the game as the Babe did.

He began as a left-handed pitcher with the Red Sox. He went 18-8 in his first full season, 23-12 as a sophomore, and 24-13 in 1917, his third year. He led the AL in ERA in 1916. Yet his hitting was so impressive that he became a part-time outfielder in 1918 and won his first home run crown, with 11 in 95 games. In 1919, still batting against the dead ball, he crushed 29 homers, breaking a record that had stood for 35 years.

In 1920 he was sold to the Yankees for an announced figure of $100,000 (in truth it was far more). He arrived in New York the same year the lively ball arrived in baseball. Together, he and the new ball achieved a record 54 homers (in only 458 at bats). He batted .376, and led in RBIs with 137. The next year the Babe had arguably the greatest season any batter ever had: 59 home runs, 171 RBIs, 177 runs, a .378 batting average, and an otherworldly slugging percentage of .846. Only one batter was able to top his 59 homers during the next 40 years—the Babe with 60 in 1927.

All told, he led in home runs 12 times, in RBIs six, in runs scored eight, in walks 11, in slugging percentage 13 times, and in batting average only once (in 1924 with .378).

His career totals: 714 homers, 2,209 RBIs, 2,174 runs, a record 2,056 walks, a record .690 slugging average, and a .342 batting average. Toss on the pile the Bambino's 94-46 pitching record (.671 winning percentage), 2.28 ERA, only 10 home runs allowed in 1,221 innings, and a string of 29⅔ consecutive scoreless inning in the World Series.

Equally important to the Ruthian Mystique was the Public Ruth, the hefty child-man the fans loved. The Private Ruth ate too much, drank too deeply, partied too long, womanized too indiscriminately, cursed like a wounded Marine, held petty grudges, and sometimes bullied lesser mortals. The Public Ruth signed autographs, was naughty but nice, hit home runs for hospitalized boys, grinned on cue, and even "called his shot" before a home run in the 1932 World Series. The "called shot" illustrates how pervasive was the Ruthian Mystique; any other batter would have been merely pointing and yelling at the Cubs' pitcher, as the Chicago players always insisted he did. But the public chose to believe Ruth had pointed to the center field bleachers moments before hitting his 15th and final

World Series home run out there. The fans believed he could do anything, so they let him.

In 1936, a year after he retired, he was named a charter member to the Baseball Hall of Fame.

NOLAN RYAN
Pitcher, NY (N) 1966, 1968-71, Cal (A) 1972-79,
Hou (N) 1980-88, Tex (A) 1989-93

There's no way to know if Ryan threw faster than any of the great fastballers of the past, but no one has ever thrown so fast for so long. In his 27th major league season, at 46, the "Ryan Express" still struck out batters with heat.

As a sheer athlete, he is the greatest pitcher who ever lived. No one else has pitched seven no-hitters. His 383 strikeouts in one year (1973) stands as the record—and that was accomplished in the first year of the DH, so he had no patsies in his opposing lineups. His total strikeouts are 5,386, more than 1,500 past his nearest rival. His 324 wins were accomplished with mostly average or less support. "My job is to give my team a chance to win," he said. "I have no control over how many runs they score."

Actually, Ryan's control was for many years the only flaw in his pitching. He led his league eight times in walks. In 1977 he walked 204 in 299 innings (he also struck out 341). His career total of walks will probably stand as the record as long as his strikeout total. But, as his fastball slowed—relatively—his control improved.

Surprisingly, he never won a Cy Young Award. But consider his 1974 season: most innings pitched, 333; fewest hits per nine innings, 5.97; most strikeouts per nine innings, 9.92; and a 22-16 record with a last-place team.

RYNE SANDBERG
Second Baseman, Phi (N) 1981; Chi (N) 1982-94,
1996-97

Sandberg was the top NL second baseman of the 1980s and arguably one of the best ever. He played third base in 1982, his first season as a Cub, but quickly settled in at second to make it his own. He had an above-average range and arm, and if he lacked the flash of some more acrobatic second-sackers, he was a whole lot steadier. In 1990 he set the second base records for consecutive games and chances without an error. He hustled all the time—not always the easiest thing to do in Chicago where they lose a lot of 10-2 games. He had got home run power—40 in 1990—and a steady bat.

In 1984, when the Cubs went to the postseason for the first time since 1945, Sandberg hit .314, with 19 homers, and he led the league in both triples (19) and in runs scored (114). He was a runaway MVP. He was also, hands-down, the best fielding second baseman in the game. He won nine straight Gold Gloves and played a record 123 consecutive games without an error.

After a poor start in 1994, Sandberg shocked fans by retiring at the age of 34. He returned in 1996 and played two more seasons before hanging them up for good.

RON SANTO
Third Baseman, Chi (N) 1960-73, Chi (A) 1974

The Brooks Robinson of the NL, Santo gave the Cubs some fine third base play in the 1960s. If he wasn't quite the fielder Brooks was, he outhit, outhomered, and out-

RBI'ed Robby. Santo, Billy Williams, and Ernie Banks provided a tremendous power trio for Chicago.

Ron is the fourth highest home run hitter among third basemen, with 342, behind Mike Schmidt, Eddie Mathews, and Graig Nettles. He had 10 seasons of 90 or more RBIs. In his best year, 1969, he drove in 129, as the Cubs made a strongest bid for the postseason, but fell short.

The pitchers feared him; he led in walks four times. In the field Ron was double-play champ five times, putout king six times straight, and assist leader seven straight seasons. Among NL third basemen, only Schmidt rivals him in total chances.

RAY SCHALK
Catcher, Chi (A) 1912-28, NY (A) 1929.
Manager, Chi (A) 1927-28
Schalk was small for a catcher (5 feet 9 inches, 165 pounds), and his nickname "Cracker" reportedly referred to him as viewed from behind; he was said to resemble a cracker box. At any rate he was a cracker jack catcher. He caught 100 or more games in 12 seasons, including 11 in a row. He led AL catchers in fielding eight times.

In 1920 Schalk caught four 20-game winners (Red Faber, Ed Cicotte, Lefty Williams, and Dickie Kerr), a feat matched only by Baltimore's Elrod Hendricks in 1971. Over the years Ray caught four no-hitters (Jim Scott, Joe Benz, Eddie Cicotte, and Charlie Robertson), a feat matched by no one. The last one was a perfect game. Until his death in 1970 Schalk sent telegrams of congratulation to every no-hit catcher.

Schalk caught spitters, shine balls, emery balls, and knucklers. It earned him a fistful of broken fingers. Fast enough to steal 30 bases in 1916, a record for catchers until broken by John Wathan in 1982, Schalk was the first catcher to back up first and third bases. He could make putouts at all four bases and did.

Ray had a strong arm, and he holds the AL record for career assists by a catcher. He had a good record throwing out runners, especially Ty Cobb.

Offensively Schalk wasn't an asset. His career batting average was only .253, and he had no power. He lived by his glove, wits, durability, and honesty. With the White Sox of 1919, that last quality was important, as eight of Schalk's teammates conspired to lose the World Series that year. Schalk was named to the Hall of Fame in 1955.

WALLY SCHANG
Catcher, Phi (A) 1913-17, 1930, Bos (A) 1918-20, NY (A) 1921-25, StL (A) 1926-29, Det (A) 1931
Wally Schang just had a knack for showing up at the right time. In 1913, his rookie year, the Philadelphia A's won the pennant and World Series. They followed with another pennant in his sophomore season. Traded to Boston in 1918, he arrived just in time to enjoy the team's last world championship. Three years later, he was dealt to the Yankees, who had never finished first. But Wally's luck held, and they took the flag in his first three seasons in pinstripes. They even won the world championship in 1923. In 1926 he was traded again—to the St. Louis Browns. Not even Wally and a world of rabbits' feet could help the Brownies, but he did get himself traded back to Philadelphia in 1930. The A's were already world champs

from 1929, but with Schang backing up Mickey Cochrane, they repeated.

All in all, Schang played on seven pennant winners in his 19 years, but it wasn't all serendipity. Schang was an excellent defensive catcher with a deadly arm; in a 1920 game he threw out six runners. He also had a nice sting in his bat. He is the first switch-hitter to hit home runs from both sides of the plate in a single game. He hit over .300 six times and had a career .284 average. On days he wasn't catching, he was sometimes put in the outfield or at third base to keep his bat in the lineup.

MIKE SCHMIDT
Third Baseman, Phi (N) 1972-89
Schmidt is not only the greatest hitter to play third base—everyone knows that—he is also arguably the greatest fielder. His homers are famous; less well known is his 404 assists in 1974, the most ever by an NL third baseman. Three years later his 396 assists were the second highest total in NL history. He won eight Gold Gloves in a row.

Mike also won eight home run crowns, four RBI titles, and three MVPs. His home run to at bat ratio ranks in the top 10 all-time, and he is one of only 14 major leaguers to hit over 500 home runs.

He paid a high price—nearly one strikeout every four at bats, or about three for every home run. But it was indisputably worth it. He put the Phillies into the playoffs six times.

He was amazingly durable. Until his season-ending rotator tear in 1988, he had never been sidelined for an extended period. Schmidt was elected to the Hall of Fame in 1995.

RED SCHOENDIENST
Second Baseman, StL (N) 1945-56, 1961-63, NY (N) 1956-57, Mil (N) 1957-60. Manager, StL (N) 1965-76, 1980, 1989
Schoendienst has spent more than half a century in a baseball uniform, mostly wearing one with a Cardinal on it. He arrived in St. Louis in 1945 as a wartime left fielder, leading the NL in stolen bases with 26 as a rookie. An arm injury caused his switch to second base the next year, as the Cardinals won the world championship.

A smooth fielder—he led league second basemen in fielding seven times—Albert Fred Schoendienst was chosen to 10 All-Star Games. His best seasons were 1952-54, when the red-haired, freckle-faced switch-hitter batted .303, .342, and .315. Redbird fans were shocked when he was traded to the New York Giants in mid-1956. Another trade a year later took him to Milwaukee, where he helped the Braves win two pennants and one world title.

In 1959, he was stricken with tuberculosis and played only five games, but he made a remarkable comeback at age 37 in 1960 to win back his job with the Braves. Schoendienst put in three final seasons as a reserve infielder and pinch-hitter with the Cardinals.

Schoendienst managed the Cardinals for a dozen seasons, winning a world championship in 1967 and a second pennant in 1968. In 1989 he was named to the Hall of Fame.

TOM SEAVER
Pitcher, NY (N) 1967-77, 1983, Cin (N) 1977-82, Chi (A)

1984-86, Bos (A) 1986

Of all the great pitchers since World War II, Seaver may have been the best. He won 311 games, struck out 3,640 batters, compiled a career ERA of 2.86, but most important was the fact that he seemed able to win with both good and losing teams. As Rookie of the Year in 1967, he was 16-13 with the last-place Mets, and he just kept doing that sort of thing. In 20 years of pitching, his winning percentage exceeded his team's in 16 seasons.

He was 25-7 for the "Amazin' Mets" world champs in 1969, when he won his first Cy Young Award. The second came for his 19-10 mark and NL-leading ERA with the 1973 pennant winners. Two years later he was 22-9 with an ERA of 2.38 and won his third Cy Young.

George Thomas Seaver led the NL in strikeouts five times, had 10 seasons with over 200 strikeouts, shares the NL record with 19 whiffs in a nine-inning game, and still holds the major league mark with 10 consecutive strikeouts. But he was never a "thrower." He exhibited excellent control and pitch selection from the start. He just happened to be a heady control pitcher who also threw a 98 mph fastball for most of his career. His power came from tremendous lower body strength and a low pitching motion designed to take full advantage of his leg muscles. When he was throwing correctly, his right knee would drag on the ground with each pitch.

Tom resembled Christy Mathewson—clean-cut, handsome, intelligent, a student of pitching, and a devotee of the *New York Times* crossword puzzle. Ironically, when all votes are in, it may be a toss-up between Matty and Tom Terrific as to who was the best right-hander a New York team ever had. Seaver was elected to the Hall of Fame in 1992.

FRANK SELEE

Manager, Bos (N) 1890-1901, Chi (N) 1902-05

Selee was the number one dynasty builder of the 1890s. Only a so-so minor league outfielder, he turned to managing in the mid-1880s and it was immediately Eureka time. He quickly earned a brace of minor league pennants and a reputation as a judge of talent who could "tell a ball player in his street clothes."

In 1890 the Boston Beaneaters brought him in from Omaha along with star pitcher Kid Nichols. It took Selee only a year to get all the pieces in place. His Beaneaters won pennants from 1891-1893 and then tacked on two more in 1897-1898. The Baltimore Orioles are the team most modern fans remember from that period, but Selee's clubs won more flags. Among his stars: Nichols, Hugh Duffy, Tommy McCarthy, Jimmy Collins, Billy Hamilton, Herman Long, and Bobby Lowe.

When he went three years without a pennant, Boston decided the magic was gone and cut him loose. Sixth-place Chicago snapped him up quicker than you could say Tinker to Evers to Chance—to name only three of the players he discovered and installed as Cubs regulars. Chicago zoomed up in the standings, reaching second by 1904. In mid-1905, tuberculosis forced Selee to take an indefinite leave of absence, which became the cause of his death in 1909. Frank Chance, the "Peerless Leader," won four pennants with the team Selee built.

Mild-mannered and courteous, Selee never had a team finish lower than fifth. Over 16 years, he won at a .598 clip

by identifying talent and putting it on the field where it belonged. Among his most successful moves: turning catchers Chance and Fred Tenney into first basemen and shifting third baseman Joe Tinker to shortstop.

JOE SEWELL

Shortstop, Cle (A) 1920-30, NY (A) 1931-33

Sewell was rushed into the Cleveland infield when shortstop Ray Chapman was killed during the 1920 pennant race. He hit .329 in the stretch to help rally the club back from the tragedy and win a three-way race.

Overshadowed by teammates such as Tris Speaker, and later by Babe Ruth and Lou Gehrig, little Joe quietly made a place among the top shortstops of all time. A good defensive player, he had a career batting average of .312 and both scored and batted in over 1,000 runs.

With his 40-ounce bat, Joe punched the ball where they ain't. Nine times he hit over .300, playing in a hitter's dream era. In 1923 he reached .353 and knocked in 109 runs. In 1925 he hit .336, cracked 204 hits, and batted in 98 runs with only one home run.

Sewell is famous for not striking out—only 114 times in 7,132 at-bats. In 1925 he whiffed an incredible four times in 608 at bats. He also ran up a streak of 1,103 consecutive games.

His brother Luke caught for many years and the two were teammates on the Indians. Joe was named to the Hall of Fame in 1977.

URBAN SHOCKER

Pitcher, NY (A) 1916-17, 1925-28, StL (A) 1918-24

The spitballer Shocker won 20 four years in a row for the Browns, 1920-1923, as St. Louis finished fourth, third, second, and fifth. In 1921 he led the league in wins, going 27-12 with a third-place club. In 1922 he led in strikeouts and went 24-17, almost pitching the Brownies to the pennant over the Yankees—now that would have been a real shocker.

Shocker would be remembered much better today if he had spent his prime years with the Yankees. His first two seasons (1916-1917) were in New York, and he was traded back to them in 1925. That was the year Babe Ruth got his famous bellyache and the team fell to seventh; Shocker would have been better off staying with the Browns. But he won 19 and 18 the next two years, as the Yankees won pennants.

Heart disease took his life in 1928 at the age of 37.

AL SIMMONS

Outfielder, Phi (A) 1924-32, 1940-41, 1944, Chi (A) 1933-35, Det (A) 1936, Was (A) 1937-38, Bos (N) 1939, Cin (A) 1939, Bos (A) 1943

In 1930, when "Bucketfoot Al" was at his best, Connie Mack said he wished he had nine players named Simmons. Actually he didn't have any; Al's real name was Aloys Szymanski.

When he first joined the A's in 1924, everybody hooted. He had a classic "foot-in-the-bucket" batting stance with his left foot pointing at third base, just the way kids are taught not to do it from the time they pick up a bat. Critics said he'd better change or he'd be back in Milwaukee double quick. He hit .308 as a rookie and had the first of 11 straight seasons with 100 RBIs. The next

year he batted .384 and pounded out 253 hits, the second highest total in AL history and the most ever by a right-handed batter.

Al hit .392 in 1927, but his top years were the three A's pennant seasons of 1929-1931. In 1929 he led the league with 157 RBIs, and added 34 homers to go with his .365 average; The Sporting News named him the AL MVP. In 1930 he led in batting with .381, and had 36 homers and 165 RBIs. Then in 1931 he upped his average to .390 and led the league again.

Mack started selling his stars as the Depression hurt him pretty hard. Simmons was sent to the White Sox in 1933, and though he had a few more good years, he great ones were over. He finished with 2,927 hits, 307 home runs, 1,827 RBIs, and a .334 batting average.

In Game 4 of the 1929 World Series, he ignited the famous 10-run seventh inning rally, when the A's came from an 8-0 deficit. Al led off with a blast over the roof against the Cubs' Charlie Root. Before the inning ended, Simmons had not only singled to set up the ninth run but also scored number 10 himself. He was named to the Hall of Fame in 1953.

TED SIMMONS
Catcher, StL (N) 1968-80, Mil (A) 1981-85, Atl (N) 1986-88
Simmons was an outstanding hitter for a catcher. Unfortunately he wasn't an outstanding catcher for a catcher. His receiving, pitcher handling, and throwing were adequate at best. In 1973 he led NL catchers in assists, but much of that may reflect the liberties runners were taking. Ted always seemed like a first baseman waiting to happen. Still, the Cardinals moved Joe Torre to third base to make room for the kid catcher

At bat rather than behind it, Simmons was one of the best, hitting over .300 seven times in his 16 seasons as a regular. Five times he had 20 or more homers, and he had eight seasons of 90 or more RBIs.

GEORGE SISLER
First Baseman, StL (A) 1915-22, 1924-27, Was (A) 1928, Bos (N) 1928-30. Manager, StL (A) 1924-26
The original "Gorgeous George," Sisler was the best first baseman who ever lived until 1923. He was one of the best players ever—until 1923.

Consider: from 1916 to 1919, when the dead ball was still the order of the day, he hit .338 for the Browns. There was another hitter in St. Louis at the time, a fellow named Rogers Hornsby with the Cardinals, Sisler outhit him. He stole 45 bases in 1918 to lead the AL. And the converted pitcher was already regarded as the equal of Hal Chase with a glove, which would make him the best-fielding honest first baseman up till then.

So in 1920 they brought in the lively ball, and everyone's batting average went up—but nobody's more than Sisler's. From 1920 through 1922 he hit .407, .371, and .420. His hit totals were 257 (the all-time record), 216, and 246. He hit 19 homers in 1920, led in stolen bases in 1921 and 1922, batted in over 100 runs, and scored over 125 each season. In 1922 he set the AL record (surpassed only by Joe DiMaggio in 1941) by hitting in 41 straight games. And all the time Sisler kept fielding up a storm. Ty Cobb, who handed out compliments as often as he handed

out $100 bills, said Sisler was "the nearest thing to a perfect ballplayer."

And then came 1923. Sisler missed the whole year with a sinus infection that caused double vision. And when he came back in 1924, he was just a very good ballplayer. He played seven more years, but he never regained the magic. He was elected to the Hall of Fame in 1939.

ENOS "COUNTRY" SLAUGHTER
Outfielder, StL (N) 1938-42, 1946-53, NY (A) 1954-59, KC (A) 1955-56, Mil (N) 1959
In 10 dramatic seconds in the 1946 World Series, Slaughter dashed all the way from first base to immortality. His mad race to score the winning run for the Cardinals in Game 7 was the greatest highlight of his career, but it was certainly not the only highlight.

He had 10 seasons hitting .300 or better, finishing with a career mark right at an even .300. He led the NL in RBIs in 1946, and though he wasn't a big home run hitter (169 in 19 seasons), he led the league in triples twice. He was a fine fielder with a good arm. He played on two world championship teams with the Cardinals in 1942 and 1946; then in the 1950s he helped the Yankees win three pennants.

And until Pete Rose came along, Slaughter was known as the epitome of hustle. When people said "a player like Slaughter," they didn't mean a .300 hitter or a strong-armed outfielder; they meant a smart, aggressive player who never walked anywhere on a ballfield when he could run and who'd cut your throat to win a game.

He was named to the Hall of Fame in 1985.

OSBOURNE "OZZIE" SMITH
Shortstop, SD (N) 1978-81, StL (N) 1982-96
The acrobatic "Wizard of Oz" may be the best defensive shortstop of all time. "He's changed fielding for short-stops," admits Hall of Fame shortstop Lou Boudreau. Smith's famous back flip when he ran to his position at the start of a game was for show, but it illustrated the kind of defensive plays he could make.

His range was exceptional, and while his arm was nothing special, his ability to make accurate, off-balance throws made up for any lack of strength. No shortstop has ever made more assists than Oz in 1980 (621). He helped take the Cards to three World Series, in 1982, 1985, and 1987.

Originally a good field/no hit player, Smith turned himself into a valuable offensive performer. He became adept at drawing walks, held his strikeout totals low, and moved his batting average up. He hit .303 in 1987 and finished his career as a .262 hitter. Although he had no home run power, his ability to steal bases somewhat made up for that. When he hit a rare home run to win Game 5 of the 1985 NLCS, he explained, "I was trying to hit the top half of the ball and hit the bottom by mistake."

At a salary of $2 million a year, Ozzie also changed the old dictum that singles hitters drive Fords.

REGGIE SMITH
Outfielder, Bos (A) 1966-73, StL (N) 1974-76, LA (N) 1976-81, SF (N) 1982
Until injuries wore him down, Smith was one of the best all-around players in baseball. He was also generally un-

recognized as such. He joined the Red Sox in 1967, played a mean center field, contributed 15 homers, and helped the team to the pennant. He got one vote for Rookie of the Year.

Over the next six seasons, he hit .300 three times for the Sox and cracked as many as 30 home runs, yet never finished in the top 20 in MVP voting.

Traded to the NL, he got a little more recognition. With the Cardinals in 1974, he hit .309 and drove in 100 runs. In 1977 he led the Dodgers to a pennant with 32 homers and a .307 batting average. He was fourth in the MVP voting, the only time he ever made the top 10.

Though he may have been overlooked when he played, his career totals mark him as a star: 314 home runs, 2,020 hits, 1,092 RBIs, and a .287 batting average.

EDWIN "DUKE" SNIDER

Outfielder, Bkn (N) 1947-57, LA (N) 1958-62, NY (N) 1963, SF (N) 1964

"Willie, Mickey, and the Duke" gave New Yorkers the game's three hardest hitting center fielders from 1951 to 1957. For the last four of those years the most consistent home run hitter of the three was Snider. He hit 40 or more homers five years in a row, an NL record matched only by Ralph Kiner. Duke was helped by often being the only left-handed batter in the Dodgers' lineup, and Ebbets Field's cozy confines didn't hurt.

Snider was a smooth-fielding center fielder for six Dodgers pennant winners. He was usually at his best in the World Series. His lifetime 11 Series home runs and 26 RBIs are the best marks for any National Leaguer. He hit four homers in both the 1952 Series and in the 1955 Series, when the Dodgers finally defeated the Yankees for the world championship.

The popular, articulate Duke is the all-time Dodgers home run leader. His career totals are 407 homers, 1,333 RBIs, 1,259 runs scored, and a .295 batting average. He was named to the Hall of Fame in 1980.

SAMMY SOSA

Outfielder, Tex (A) 1989, Chi (A) 1989-91, Chi (N) 1992-

Until his breakthrough 1998 season, many baseball fans outside of Chicago would have had trouble identifying Sammy Sosa. In truth, he was a well-kept secret with the Cubs, a team whose usual low finishes made it possible to keep their few good players well hidden from the national limelight.

From the mid-1990s, "Slammin' Sammy" was a good player, hitting 30-40 homers and batting in over 100 runs each year. He showed a cannon arm and good speed. On the other hand, he struck out more often than a guy with B.O. at the big dance, ran bases erratically, and made mistakes in the field. The Cubs expected more.

In 1998, they got it from the personable Dominican. He still struck out too often but became a more patient hitter, raising his batting average and power numbers. He exploded for 20 home runs in June, the most homers every hit in a month. He dueled all season with Mark McGwire for baseball's home run record, and he seemed to delight in McGwire's accomplishments as much as any fan.

Sosa became the second player to surpass Roger Maris' record, but his 66 home runs still left him second in the

league in that department. He did, however, lead the major leagues with 158 RBIs. More important, he became a consummate team player in leading the Cubs to the NL Wild Card. The sum was that in one season he went from obscurely "good" to famous and popular "great." Baseball writers thought so, too, as he was the overwhelming choice for NL MVP.

WARREN SPAHN

Pitcher, Bos (N) 1942, 1946-52, Mil (N) 1953-64, NY (N) 1965, SF (N) 1965

The winningest left-hander of all time, Spahn won 20 or more games 13 times, tying Christy Mathewson's NL record. He needed only 11 more wins to top the NL record of 373 lifetime victories. Yet he didn't win his first major league game until he was 25 years old.

He seemed to get better as he got older. His good control became great; his fastball slipped a little, but he added a screwball and slider to his curve and changeup; and, of course, he got smarter and smarter. His ability to place his pitches and vary the speeds kept batters always off-stride.

He led the NL in strikeouts four straight years (1949-1952), in ERA twice, and in victories eight times, including five straight (1957-1961). His 63 shutouts are the most by an NL lefty.

Spahn had his first 20-win season in 1947; then, curiously, he fell to 15 wins in 1948 when the Boston Braves won the pennant. Nevertheless the Braves' shallow pitching staff was described as "Spahn, Sain, and pray for rain." He was still at the top of his game in 1957-1958, when the Milwaukee Braves won pennants. In 1957 he was voted the Cy Young Award.

In 1960, at the age of 39, he pitched his first no-hitter. The next year, five days past his 40th birthday, he pitched his second.

Spahn was elected to the Hall of Fame in 1973. He would have been elected earlier, but he found it so hard to hang up the spikes that he kept on pitching in the minors in 1966-67, delaying the onset of his eligibility for the Hall.

AL SPALDING

Pitcher, Boston (NA) 1871-75, Chi (N) 1876-78. Manager, Chi (N) 1876-77. Executive

Spalding might have won 300 games if we knew how many he pitched as a teenager in top independent ball. His wins are unknown, but they included one as a 17-year-old in 1867 over George Wright's Washingtons, 29-23.

Al's official record starts when the National Association was founded in 1871. Playing for Boston, his totals were 20-10, 37-8, 41-15, and 52-18. In 1875 he posted an amazing 57-5, including 24 in a row, pitching in every game his team played. He also hit .300 each of the last four years, as the Bostons won four straight flags.

Lured to Chicago with the formation of the National League in 1876, Spalding helped write the new league's constitution. He was that first year's biggest winner at 47-12, as Chicago won the flag. Then his arm finally gave out. He left behind a lifetime W-L percentage of .789. Of course it's the record.

Al opened a sporting goods business and issued the first Spalding Baseball Guide in 1877.

In 1882 he took over as president of the champion Chicago club with stars such as Cap Anson, George Gore, Larry Corcoran, and Fred Goldsmith. He led a world tour of teams in 1888 and was instrumental in the NL's successful war with the Players League in 1890. He helped plan the Chicago World's Fair of 1893. In 1905 he organized a commission to determine where baseball was born: Henry Chadwick had said England; Spalding chauvinistically said America, supporting the Abner Doubleday legend, a claim he repeated in 1911 in his history of baseball, America's National Game.

Spalding ran for the U.S. Senate in 1910 and lost. He died in 1915, but his name remained an essential part of the game, on every official NL ball used until the year 1976.

He was named to the Hall of Fame in 1939.

TRIS SPEAKER
Outfielder, Bos (A) 1907-15, Cle (A) 1916-26, Was (A) 1927, Phi (A) 1928. Manager, Cle (A) 1919-26
Speaker revolutionized center field play, taking advantage of the dead ball to play behind second base almost as a fifth infielder. He made unassisted double plays on short flies (the only man to do it in a World Series), was the pivot man on 4-8-3 plays, and even took pickoff throws from the pitcher. Yet he could still go back to get flies over his head. He is second in lifetime putouts and total chances in the outfield and first in assists—35 of them as a rookie in 1909. He may have been the first outfielder to test the wind by throwing grass in the air.

Speaker won only one batting title, but he topped .375 six times and had a lifetime mark of .344. In 1916 he broke Ty Cobb's streak of five straight batting crowns. His 793 doubles are first on the all-time list, and his 223 triples are sixth. "Spoke" finished with 3,514 hits, knocked in 1,528 runs, and he scored 1,881 times. He almost never struck out. He stole 433 bases.

And he did it all after breaking his right arm as a kid in Texas and learning to throw and hit lefty instead.

Speaker broke in with the Red Sox in 1909 and soon formed, with Harry Hooper and Duffy Lewis, perhaps the best defensive outfield ever. He was MVP in 1912 as the Sox won pennants that year and in 1915. Traded to Cleveland in 1916, he became player-manager in 1919 and led the Indians to their first pennant in 1920. He hit .388.

He was named to the Hall of Fame in 1937.

WILLIE STARGELL
Outfielder/First Baseman, Pit (N) 1962-82
"Pops" could hit the ball a long way. He was the first man to hit a ball clear out of Dodger Stadium—and then he did it a second time. Stargell is also the only man to hit four balls into the upper deck of Three Rivers Stadium. He hit seven over the roof of old Forbes Field (only nine others have done it even once).

Forbes was tough on Willie. In one stretch, 1965-1966, he hit only 19 home runs at home, 41 on the road. His totals took a jump after the Pirates moved to Three Rivers, though even that was a pitchers' park. Willie led the league in homers in 1971 and 1973.

In 1979 Stargell won three MVPs—in the regular season (tying Keith Hernandez), the playoffs, and the World Series. In the World Series against the Orioles, Willie came up in the seventh game with Pittsburgh losing in the sixth. He crashed his third home run of the Series and gave the Pirates the championship.

In 21 years he thumped 475 homers, batted in 1,540 runs, and compiled a .282 batting average. He paid a high price for his homers, striking out once every four at bats.

Not included in Willie's numbers are "intangibles." Much of his 1979 MVP Award was for leadership. As captain of the Pirates, he led with a combination of quiet example and symbols. He passed out "Stargell Star" decals for outstanding plays and developed (and exemplified) the "We are family" slogan which tied the team together.

He was elected to the Hall of Fame in 1988.

DANIEL "RUSTY" STAUB
Outfielder/First Baseman, Hou (N) 1963-68, Mon (N) 1969-71, 1979, NY (N) 1972-75, 1981-85, Det (A) 1976-79, Tex (A) 1980
"Le Grand Orange" (the big redhead), as Montreal fans called him, played well for some undistinguished teams (the Astros, Expos, Mets, and Tigers), usually flirting with .300 and 100 RBIs.

Staub's best year, 1967, he hit .333 in the Hitters' Horror, the Astrodome. He led the league with 44 doubles.

Rusty finally found a winner with the Mets in 1973. He hit only .269 during the season but shone in the World Series, hitting .423. His five RBIs won Game 4 by a score of 6-1.

After he got too "grand" to play the outfield, he became an outstanding DH for the Tigers, twice batting in over 100 runs. Then he finished as a deadly pinch hitter for the Mets. In his final season "Trusty Rusty" became the 11th man to register 100 career pinch hits.

NORMAN "TURKEY" STEARNES
Outfielder, Negro Leagues, 1921-41: Montgomery Grey Sox, Detroit Stars , New York Lincoln Giants, Kansas City Monarchs, Cole's American Giants, Chicago American Giants, Philadelphia Stars, Detroit Black Sox
Stearnes is the all-time home run champ of the Negro Leagues, beating the more famous Josh Gibson, 171-137. (Josh, it is true, had more home runs per at bat). Turkey led or tied the league seven times from 1923-1932; Josh, six. He averaged 30 every 550 at bats. Stearnes led the league in batting average once, with .430 in 1935. His lifetime mark was .341. Against white big leaguers, he hit .313. His fellow Detroiter, Hank Greenberg, heard the stories and asked Cool Papa Bell if they were true. Bell assured him that they were.

Turkey weighed only 168 and swung from an odd left-handed stance, choking up on the bat, with his right toe pointing up. Yet he smashed some long blows, including a 450-footer into the upper deck of Comiskey Park. He played an excellent center field and was fast enough to lead off, which he often did with a home run. In 1935 he and Mule Suttles played together on the Western League champion Chicago American Giants, Stearnes batting leadoff and Suttles cleanup.

Stearnes played his best in the postseason, hitting .474 in nine games, including four home runs. In the 1929 playoff against St. Louis—and Mule Suttles, the black

leagues' number two man in homers—Turkey hit .481 with 11 RBIs and the first homer ever hit over the distant wall 450 feet away at Hamtramck Stadium.

"If they don't put him in the Hall of Fame," said Bell, "they shouldn't put anybody in."

GEORGE STEINBRENNER
Owner

The Yankees' controversial owner was often more newsworthy than his team. He took over in the early 1970s when the once lordly Yankees had wallowed in the depths of the AL for nearly a decade. His stated intention was to return the Yankees to their former glory. He made the moves that brought six pennants to New York, 1976-1978, 1981, 1996, and 1998.

Steinbrenner showed an admirable willingness to spend huge amounts of money in pursuit of excellence. He signed such free agents as Catfish Hunter, Reggie Jackson, Goose Gossage, Dave Winfield, and Jack Clark. His employees were well paid for their efforts.

On the other hand, his constant switching of managers—20 changes after Steinbrenner bought the team—became a national joke. Billy Martin was hired and fired five times. Steinbrenner's verbal battles with his own players, his public second-guessing, and his interference in the daily operation of the team opened him to criticism from those who believed his influence was counterproductive.

He brought back to the Yankees many fans who had switched allegiance to the Mets. At the same time, he sent a large number of former Yankees fans scurrying to Shea Stadium. Volatile, yet often charming, he was forced by the commissioner to give up running the Yankees in 1990 for conduct not in the best interests of baseball.

When the suspension was lifted in 1993, he stayed in the background for the next few seasons, getting a great deal of newspaper ink for not throwing tantrums. Being mellow seemed to work. The Yankees won two World Series and won an AL record 114 games in 1998.

CHARLES "CASEY" STENGEL
Outfielder, Bkn (N) 1912-17, Pit (N) 1918-19, Phi (N) 1920-21, NY (N) 1921-23, Bos (N) 1924-25. Manager, Bkn (N) 1934-36, Bos (N) 1938-43, NY (A) 1949-60, NY (N) 1962-65

Stengel won 10 pennants in 12 years, hid a bird under his hat, and doubled up a Senate hearing with the funniest monologue in the history of the Congressional Record, which, as Will Rogers said, "is goin' some."

Casey put in 14 seasons as a useful NL outfielder, compiling a .284 batting average and a reputation as a prankster. One time he captured a bird in the outfield, then let it escape when he strode to the plate and doffed his cap to the fans.

Stengel embarked on a managerial career in the minors and low majors, frequently getting a pink slip. ("I say fired," he said, "because there is no doubt I had to leave.")

Leading the lowly Dodgers in 1934, he achieved brief fame when Giants manager Bill Terry sneered, "Is Brooklyn still in the league?" The insulted Bums knocked New York out of the pennant.

With the old Boston Braves, 1938-1943, Casey finished seventh four times in a row. When he was hit by a Boston

cab and broke his leg, the city voted the cabbie MVP.

Case went back to the minors, won a flag at Milwaukee and another at Oakland in the Pacific Coast League.

Then fate struck with a surprise call from the Yankees. In Stengel's first year, 1949, the club was hit with a record number of injuries. All summer he juggled his lineup and platooned players, a strategy that would become his trademark. On the last day of the season, the Yankees caught the Red Sox for the pennant. They beat the Dodgers in the World Series to begin a string of five straight world championships, 1949-1953.

In 1954 he won 103 games—and finished second to Cleveland's 111. His Yanks won four pennants in a row (1955-1958) and two more world championships, missed a year, then won Casey's final pennant in 1960. His 10 pennants and seven world titles in 12 years is considered by some the greatest managerial accomplishment of all time.

The Yankees fired him as too old, but he took on the new challenge of wet-nursing the perfectly awful Mets through their first four seasons. Though the team finished a well-deserved last each year, they did show improvement each season.

Casey's warmth, his pixie sense of humor, and his unique, rambling, ungrammatical, nonstop monologues made him perhaps baseball's most loved figure since Babe Ruth.

He was named to the Hall of Fame in 1966.

BRUCE SUTTER
Pitcher, Chi (N) 1976-80, StL (N) 1981-84, Atl (N) 1985-88

Sutter was one of the most effective relief pitchers in history. His split-finger fastball baffled hitters and sent other NL pitchers scrambling to learn how to throw it.

He came to the NL with the Cubs in 1976 and in his second season saved 31 games. His six wins and league-leading 37 saves earned him the Cy Young Award for 1979.

Traded to the Cardinals in 1981, he continued to star. His 36 saves in 1982 helped the team to the world championship in 1982. In 1984 he had a career-high 45 saves, to lead the NL for the fifth time.

He signed with Atlanta as a free agent in 1985, but after a disappointing season, he underwent elbow surgery. He pitched in only 16 games in 1986 and missed all of the 1987 season. Sutter pitched with occasional success in 1988 before retiring at the end of the season.

DON SUTTON
Pitcher, LA (N) 1966-80, 1988, Hou (N) 1981-82, Mil (A) 1982-83, Oak (A) 1985, Cal (A) 1985-87

Sutton won 20 games only once, but he kept plugging away to become one of the big winners of all time. He was probably both hurt and helped by the five-man rotation, which cuts about five starts out of each season but might result in longer careers: Sutton pitched for 23 seasons.

Don was 21-10 for the 1976 Dodgers for his only 20-win year, but he had 11 other seasons with 15 wins or more. One of his best years was 1980 when he was only 13-5, but he led the NL in ERA.

Sutton never pitched a no-hitter, but he has five one-hitters, tying the NL record. His AL career came later, but

he had his share of success. The Brewers picked him up for the pennant drive in 1982 and he won the final game of the season against the Orioles to give Milwaukee the division title. He helped pitch the Angels to the ALCS in 1986.

He was accused of throwing "doctored" pitches, but his long career is evidence of either his legality or his legerdemain. He was elected to the Hall of Fame in 1998.

JESSE TANNEHILL
Pitcher, Cin (N) 1894, 1911, Pit (N) 1897-1902, NY (A) 1903, Bos (A) 1904-08, Was (A) 1908-09

A great control pitcher, left-hander Tannehill won 20 games six times from 1898 to 1905 and had a 197-116 career record. He averaged only 1.6 walks per nine innings. He helped pitch the Pirates to the 1901 and 1902 NL pennants. He won the 1901 ERA title with a 2.18 mark.

The Pirates won the 1903 pennant without Tannehill; he and Jack Chesbro jumped to the New York Highlanders in the AL that year. It cost him a chance to appear in the first World Series.

He was a disappointing 15-15 in New York and was traded to Boston, the winner of the 1903 Series. His 21-11 season helped Boston win the 1904 pennant, but again he lost his World Series chance when the NL's Giants refused to meet the AL champs.

With Cy Young, Bill Dineen, and Tannehill doing most of the pitching, Boston set a team record low of 1.5 walks per nine innings in 1904.

JACK TAYLOR
Pitcher, Chi (N) 1898-1903, 1906-07, StL (N) 1904-06

Taylor won 20 games four times and earned 152 wins during his career, but his claim to fame is an uncanny ability to finish what he started. On June 20, 1901, he pitched a complete game. Through his next 186 starts—more than five years' worth—he would pitch a complete game every time he started. One game went 19 innings; another went 18—he finished them both. On another occasion, he pitched both ends of a doubleheader. Fifteen times he relieved other, less stouthearted hurlers, and each time finished the game.

Taylor wasn't a particularly imposing physical specimen. At 5 feet 10 inches and 170 pounds, he was average or a little less for a pitcher of his day. Finally, on Aug. 9, 1906, he was relieved in a game.

Although he pitched only 10 years in the NL, two of them partial seasons, Taylor had six seasons of over 300 innings and completed 278 of his 286 starts.

GENE TENACE
Catcher, Oak (A) 1969-76, SD (N) 1977-80, StL (N) 1981-82, Pit (N) 1983

Tenace was the steady catcher for the Oakland A's dynasty that won three World Series, 1972-1974. A decent enough defensive catcher, he was actually very dangerous with the bat, despite a dreary .241 batting average. Over his career, he was nearly as likely to get a walk as to get a hit—984 walks to 1,060 hits. He led the AL twice in bases on balls and had a .380 on-base percentage.

When he did get a hit, the odds were five-to-one it would go out of the park. Nearly 20 percent of his hits were homers—201.

Tenace first showed he could be something out of the ordinary in the 1972 World Series. He'd just limped through a .225 season with five homers, followed by an .059 ALCS. He looked like a soft touch to the Reds. So in his first two Series at bats he homered, not only becoming the first to attain that feat but also providing the A's with all the runs they needed in a 3-2 win. For the Series he hit .348 and had four homers and nine RBIs.

BILL TERRY
First Baseman, NY (N) 1923-36.
Manager, NY (N) 1932-41

Terry was the last NL batter to hit .400, but it doesn't impress some modern commentators, who point out that when "Memphis Bill" hit .401 in 1930, the whole blessed league hit .303. Still, anyone who knocks out 254 hits as Terry did in 1930 deserves respect. And it wasn't that he was a one-year wonder. He played 14 seasons and topped .300 in 11 seasons. Besides his .400 year, he had averages of .372, .354, .350, .349, and .341—the last mark also being his career average.

His 154 career homers don't look all that great against Lou Gehrig or Jimmie Foxx, two AL first basemen of the period. There are two answers to that. The first is obvious: Terry wasn't the home run hitter that either of those brawny gentlemen were. He was a line drive hitter who hit to all fields. And that's part of the second answer: he played his home games in the Polo Grounds, which had wonderfully short foul lines for dead pull hitters and horrifyingly deep power alleys for anyone who wasn't. Terry made the decision to go with the percentages, which was considered smart baseball in his day. One tipoff is that in five of the six years from 1927 through 1932, he averaged 20 homers a year. The sixth year was 1930 when he hit only nine. That looks suspiciously as though he cut his swing just a little when he saw a chance to hit .400.

Some old-time sportswriters are kind of happy to see Terry low-rated. He was the kind of player who, if he thought you were a jerk, said so. Some call that "refreshing honesty"; others call it "arrogance."

Once the reputation was set, he couldn't say anything to please some writers. One day in 1934, after he'd become manager of the Giants, a writer asked him what he thought of the Dodgers, at a time when everyone knew the Dodgers were pretty awful. Terry, trying to be one of the guys, made a little joke. "Is Brooklyn still in the league?" he asked. Naturally it got blown all out of proportion, especially when the Dodgers beat the Giants a couple of times at the end of the season to knock them out of the pennant.

One thing about Terry: he was a much better fielder than the home run-hitting first sackers of his time. And he also became a better manager, winning three pennants and a world title in 1933 when he was a player-manager.

FRANK THOMAS
First Baseman, Chi (A) 1990-

Thomas is the only player in history to hit .300 with 20 home runs, 100 RBI, 100 walks, and 100 runs scored in seven consecutive seasons—and two of those seasons were shortened because of the players' strike.

"The Big Hurt" was named American League Most Valuable Player in back-to-back seasons (1993-1994). He has led the league in on-base percentage four times and scored an AL-best 106 runs in 1994. He even hit .353 with an ALCS record 10 walks in his only postseason performance with Chicago in 1993. In 1997 he added his first batting title with a .347 average (although he's hit .353 and .349 in other seasons). He had such a commanding lead in the '97 batting race that he still won the title by 17 points over Edgar Martinez even though Thomas went hitless in his last 10 at bats of the season.

After only 180 minor league games, the White Sox, battling with Oakland for the AL West title in 1993, had no choice but to bring Thomas to the major leagues. He batted .330 in 191 at bats, the highest average by a White Sox hitter with at least 200 plate appearances since 1942. Thomas hasn't stopped hitting since.

SAM THOMPSON
Outfielder, Det (N) 1885-88, Phi (N) 1889-98, Det (A) 1906
"Big Sam" played in two Hall of Fame outfields. In the early 1890s, Thompson, Billy Hamilton, and Ed Delahanty made a heavy-lumber trio for the Phillies. In 1894 Hamilton hit .404, Delahanty .407, and Thompson .407. The second Hall of Fame outfield was in 1906, when the Detroit Tigers had suffered so many injuries that they coaxed Sam out of retirement. For the final eight games of the season, he lined up with Ty Cobb and Sam Crawford. He hit a mere .226, but he was 46 years old at the time.

Thompson started with the old NL Detroit Wolverines in 1885. At first they didn't have a uniform to fit his 6-foot-2-inch, 220-pound frame, and he squeezed into what was available. Running out a double, he split his pants right up the middle.

The modest, good-humored slugger became the most popular player in Detroit. In 1887, when they won the NL pennant, he led the NL with a .372 batting average and 166 RBIs.

Thompson compiled a .331 career batting average. One of the best home run hitters of the 19th century, he led the NL with 20 in 1889 and 18 in 1895. His 127 career homers rank him second only to Roger Connor for the era. And Thompson's ratio of RBIs to games played is the best of all time.

An outstanding fielder, he was renowned for his powerful arm. Reportedly he popularized throwing all the way from the outfield to the catcher on one bounce. In 1974 he was named to the Hall of Fame.

LUIS TIANT
Pitcher, Cle (A) 1964-69, Min (A) 1970, Bos (A) 1971-78, NY (A) 1979-80, Pit (N) 1981, Cal (A) 1982
The herky-jerky Cuban dervish won 20 games four times and finished with a 229-172 record in a career that looked to be over in the middle. After four good years with Cleveland, Tiant was suddenly great in 1968 with a 21-9 mark and a league-leading 1.60 ERA. But the next year he led the AL in losses at 9-20. Traded to Minnesota, he appeared washed up with no arm left.

Boston took a chance on him, but he struggled to 1-7 in 1971. But the next year he was the Comeback of the Year at 15-6 with his second ERA title (1.91). He won 20

games three times for the Red Sox but was at his best in 1975, when his season's record was 18-14. The Sox won the division; then Luis started them on a three-game sweep in the ALCS with a three-hitter over Oakland. He opened the World Series against the powerful Reds with another shutout, threw a 163-pitch, complete game victory in Game 4, and went seven innings in Game 6 before weakening.

After games Luis would entertain writers, puffing his long Cuban cigar and telling stories. Some say he took the cigar with him into the shower.

Tiant's father, Luis Sr., had been a skinny left-handed junk pitcher in the Negro Leagues. Neither had seen the other pitch until the older man got a visa to leave Havana and was given an emotional welcome to Fenway Park.

JOE TINKER
Shortstop, Chi (N) 1902-12, 1916, Cin (N) 1913, Chi (F) 1914-15. Manager, Cin (N) 1913, Chi (F) (1914-15, Chi (N) 1916.
Sometimes the whole is more than the sum of its parts, and that sort of rep seems to forever follow Tinker, Evers, and Chance. Bound together in F.P. Adams' famous bit of doggerel and in their simultaneous election to the Hall of Fame in 1946, the impression persists that they were three ordinary guys who somehow made magic only as a trio. The impression is unfair. Each was an excellent player, and no doubt they could have proved their worth as individuals.

Manager Frank Chance's Cubs depended on pitching, speed, and defense. They won four pennants and two world championships from 1906 to 1910 using that recipe. None of the Cubbies hit much in those dead-ball days; the 1907 world champs didn't have a .300 hitter, their RBI leader had 70, and the Cubs' best home run man had two. Of course, most other NL teams were similar.

In that context, Joe Tinker was a pretty decent hitter for his time. His .262 average ranks right up there with those of shortstops of later, better-hitting eras. He usually knocked in 60-70 runs a season, and he hit six homers in 1908. He was practically a slugger! For some reason, Lord knows why, he always hit Christy Mathewson well, and since the Giants were always trying to nudge the Cubs out of first place, that was a very valuable talent. Once on base, Joe also had the required speed, stealing 336 bases over his career.

But Tinker was paid to field. And that he did very well, leading NL shortstops five times in average, in assists twice, and in putouts twice. He even led once in double plays. Only once, you ask? Isn't that the maneuver T-to-E-to-C were supposedly such whizzes at? Well, they were—everyone who saw them agrees—but the Cubs' pitchers just didn't give them as many chances to get two as some other combinations had. In the case of double plays, it looks as if the sum wasn't always equal to the parts.

JOE TORRE
Catcher/First Baseman/Third Baseman, Mil (N) 1960-65, Atl (N) 1966-68, StL (N) 1969-74, NY (N) 1975-77. Manager, NY (N) 1977-81, Atl (N) 1982-84, StL (N) 1990-1995, NY (A) 1996-
Torre started out with the Braves as a catcher because he

kept getting fat. The idea was that catchers don't have to run much, something fat guys hate to do. Everything went well for a while. Joe didn't have the best arm in the world, but it wasn't embarrassing. He did all the other catching chores OK, and he was a terrific hitter. Torre was selected for the NL All-Star team from 1963 through 1967. The only thing was that catchers need rest every couple of days. In Joe's case, he usually spent his day of rest at first base so they could keep his bat in the lineup.

In 1969 he was traded to the Cardinals, who put him at first base full-time. Along about then, Joe figured he'd better get serious about a diet. It wasn't quite as quick as with the frog who turned into a prince, but in 1971, slim, trim Torre emerged as a third baseman and had the season of his life. He led the NL in batting (.363), hits (230), and RBIs (137). He was named MVP.

Although he never got back to that level, Torre had a lot of good seasons in his 18 years. He finished with a .297 career average, 252 homers, and 1,185 RBIs. Torre spent fifteen seasons toiling as a manager with only moderate success, but that all changed when he went to the Bronx in 1996. He guided the Yankees to a world championship in his first season at the helm (after a record 4,272 games as a player and manager without ever participating in a World Series). Two years later he guided the Yankees to an AL-record 114 wins and a second Series victory.

CRISTOBAL TORRIENTE
Outfielder, Negro League, 1914-32, Cuban Stars, Chicago American Giants, Kansas City Monarchs, Detroit Stars, Gilkerson's Union Giants, Atlanta Black Crackers, Cleveland Cubs
Many authorities pick the big Cuban on the all-time All-Negro League outfield. In 1919 Torriente, Oscar Charleston, and speedster Jimmy Lyons patrolled the outfield for the Chicago American Giants, making perhaps the best trio ever among black teams.

Torriente was called the Ruth of Cuba, and in 1920 the two faced each other in Havana, one on one. Torri got three homers, two off first baseman Highpockets Kelly and one off Ruth himself. The Babe went 0-for-4 against Cuban hurling. Two home runs were usually good enough to lead the league for an entire season in the cavernous parks down there, making Torri's feat the more remarkable.

Cris wore bracelets, which he shook before going to bat, and a red bandana around his neck, for his Cuban club, the Rojos, or Reds.

He was Cuban batting champion three times, stolen base champ four times, and triple and home run champ five times each. In 1919-1920 he led in every batting department. Torriente's highest averages were .401 in Cuba, 1915-1916, and .402 in the U.S. in 1920. He led the Negro League in 1923 with .389.

Torri pitched occasionally and even played a left-handed second base. He was also a notorious playboy, and he died an alcoholic at an early age.

ALAN TRAMMELL
Shortstop, Det (A) 1977-
Trammell was a good glove man who developed an outstanding bat. He and second baseman Lou Whitaker held down the keystone positions for the Tigers for 14 seasons.

A four-time Gold Glove winner, Trammell's home runs climbed from two in 1978, his first full season, to 14 in 1983, to 28 in 1987. His batting average, though its climb was so steady, began in the .260s and peaked with .343 in 1987, as the Tigers won the Eastern Division.

In 1984, when the Tigers won the World Series, Trammell was named Series MVP for his .450 average, including two homers and six RBIs in five games. It capped an outstanding year in which he hit .314 and won his fourth Gold Glove.

HAROLD "PIE" TRAYNOR
Third Baseman, Pit (N) 1920-37.
Manager, Pit (N) 1934-39
Traynor used to be figured as the best-ever third baseman, but his halo has tarnished a little of late, as sluggers like Eddie Mathews, Brooks Robinson, Graig Nettles, and Mike Schmidt have appeared. There even seems to be some effort to show that he wasn't even the best when he was playing, but that's a little harder to swallow.

Traynor, who usually batted fifth for the Pirates, was no home run hitter; he knocked out a mere 58 in his 1,941 games. Of course, half those games were in Forbes Field, where any right-handed batter who swung for the distant left field fence would have been considered a little goofy. Traynor doubled and tripled at a pretty good clip.

He seems to have driven runs home pretty well too, with seven seasons of 100-plus RBIs, but some critics worry that he didn't walk a whole lot. They also point out that batting averages were at an all-time high in the 20 years between the World Wars, making his .320 less impressive. However, it does happen to be the best for any of the third basemen who played during that period.

Traynor was regarded as the top-fielding third baseman of his day. A Pittsburgh sportswriter once wrote: "He doubled down the left field foul line, but Traynor threw him out." He led NL third sackers in putouts seven times, assists three times, and, surprisingly, only once in fielding average. There's no way to really rank him against modern third basemen. His career and single-season marks have been far surpassed by post-World War II players. Fielding stats being what they are, they neither prove nor disprove that he was the best glove man playing third during his time. Most of the fans, teammates, and opponents thought he was, but they could be wrong.

Maybe they gave him extra for personality; Traynor was a genial, articulate man, with more friends than bookkeepers have decimal points. *The Sporting News* named him to its Major League All-Star team seven times between 1925 and 1933. He finished in the top 10 in NL MVP voting six times through the same period. Let's put it this way, the people who looked at third basemen when Pie was playing thought he was Pie a la mode. Traynor was named to the Hall of Fame in 1948.

PAUL "DIZZY" TROUT
Pitcher, Det (A) 1939-52, Bos (A) 1952, Bal (A) 1957
It was a wartime year, but in 1944 Trout was 27-14 and led the AL in ERA, complete games, innings pitched, and shutouts. Dizzy's teammate Hal Newhouser got the headlines with a 29-9 season, but Trout may have been even better. He finished second to "Prince Hal" in the MVP voting, 236-232.

In 1945 Diz was only 18-15 (while Newhouser was 25-9), but in the stretch, he pitched six games in nine days and won four of them, as the Tigers won the pennant on the final day. In the World Series he had an 0.64 ERA but had to split his two decisions. He won the fourth game, 4-1, and lost the sixth game in relief in the 12th inning.

After the war, Trout's record slipped more than Newhouser's, but for two years they were terrific.

Trout's son Steve became a major league pitcher, and their total of more than 250 wins makes them the winningest father-son combo.

ARTHUR "DAZZY" VANCE
Pitcher, Pit (N) 1915, NY (A) 1915, 1918, Bkn (N) 1922-32, 1935, StL (N) 1933-34, Cin (N) 1934
One of the Dodgers' Daffiness Boys, Dazzy didn't win his first big league game until he was 31 in 1922. Vance had pitched five complete games in seven days in the minors, causing a chronic sore arm which almost ended his career. He bounced around the minors for 10 years until manager Wilbert Robinson of the Dodgers tried starting him every fifth day, instead of every fourth, the common practice.

Vance responded magnificently. His high-kick windup and extremely long arms (he had an 83-inch reach) gave him a roaring fastball. Pitching with a tattered sleeve to confuse the hitters, he led the NL in strikeouts seven straight years, a record. He paced the league in ERA three times and twice led in wins.

Dazzy was the best pitcher in the league in 1924, with 28-6, as the Bums almost beat the Giants for the pennant. He won the MVP, even though Rogers Hornsby batted .424 that year.

In 1925 the Bums fell to seventh, but Vance led in wins again, with 22-8. One was a one-hitter, and another, five days later, a rare 1920s no-hitter (against the Phils). In 1928 the Dodgers were sixth, but Vance was 22-10.

Vance was as famous for clowning as for pitching. He liked to party, often staying out until the detectives in the lobby yawned and went to bed. Then he would slip in unnoticed.

He was the key man in the famous play when Babe Herman doubled into a double play. Vance was on second base, but instead of scoring on Herman's drive, he rounded third and then went back to find Herman and one other runner sliding in from the opposite direction.

Vance was named to the Hall of Fame in 1955.

FLOYD "ARKY" VAUGHAN
Shortstop, Pit (N) 1932-41, Bkn (N) 1942-43, 1947-48
Next to Honus Wagner, Vaughan may have been the best-hitting shortstop ever, hitting over .300 a dozen times, including his first 10 years in the NL. His .385 in 1935 is the 20th-century record for shortstops. In 14 seasons he averaged .318 and led the league in runs scored three times. Vaughan had a good eye and rarely whiffed; from 1934 to 1936 he was the top NL hitter in drawing walks.

Though he was not a power hitter, Arky hit 19 homers one season and led the league in triples three different years. He slugged two home runs in the 1941 All-Star Game, the first man to do so.

He fielded his position well and led NL shortstops in putouts and assists three times each.

Vaughan was respected around the league for his honesty and integrity. In 1943, believing Brooklyn manager Leo Durocher had unfairly suspended another player and then lied about him to reporters, he handed in his uniform, threatening to leave the team until Durocher backed down. He retired at the end of the season and didn't return to the Dodgers until 1947, when Durocher was suspended for the season.

Vaughan was named to the Hall of Fame in 1985.

JAMES "HIPPO" VAUGHN
Pitcher, NY (A) 1908, 1910-12, Was (A) 1912, Chi (N) 1913-21
Like Harvey Haddix, left-hander Vaughn is remembered for one outstanding game, somewhat obscuring the fact that he pitched a number of excellent games. Indeed he was one of the best pitchers around during the World War I period. He didn't really settle in until he was 26 years old in 1914. But in seven years with the Cubs, he won 20 or more games five times, 10 once, and 17 once.

In 1918 he was 22-10 to lead the NL in wins, tops in ERA at 1.74, and led in strikeouts and innings pitched. In the World Series that year, he pitched three complete games and gave up only three earned runs, yet he was only 1-2.

Now about "the game." On May 2 in Chicago, he hurled nine no-hit innings against Cincinnati. What made this no-hitter really special was that Fred Toney, pitching for the Reds, also tossed a no-hitter. So they went into the top of the 10th and Hard Luck Hippo gave up a single to light-hitting Larry Kopf. An outfield error followed, putting the runner on third. The next batter, Jim Thorpe, topped a little roller down the third base line. Vaughn was called Hippo because he ran like one, but he was on the ball quickly and shoveled it to the catcher. Too late. The runner slid in with the run. In the bottom of the 10th, Toney retired the Cubs hitless again.

BILL VEECK
Owner, Cle (A), StL (A), Chi (A)
Veeck sent a midget to bat, integrated the AL, invented the exploding scoreboard, put players' names on their uniforms, and gave baseball its first 2 million attendance team, the 1948 Indians. He even tried to field an integrated Phillies club in 1943 until Judge Landis shot down his quest for ownership.

With his open collar, his wooden leg (a souvenir of the Marines), and his extroverted twinkle, Bill was a fans' owner who lounged in the bleachers, chain-drinking beer and listening to gripes. He owned three different AL teams at various times.

He learned the game at the hotdog stand in Wrigley Field, where his father was general manager for the Cubs. Later, Bill himself became general manager of the minor league Milwaukee Brewers.

After the war Veeck brought Cleveland a pennant in 1948. His promotions brought in fans and he brought in the players, including Larry Doby, the AL's first black player and 42-year-old Satchel Paige. In the early 1950s, Veeck tried to save the Browns. Some of his gimmicks were outrageous, such as sending midget Eddie Gaedel to pinch-hit (he walked) and having the fans manage a game by holding up decision cards. As White Sox owner, he gave the team its first flag in 40 years in 1959. He bought

the team again in the 1970s and made ugly uniforms even uglier by making the Sox wear shorts in 1976.

His iconoclastic ways alienated the other owners but enchanted the fans. He wrote about his adventures entertainingly in "Veeck as in Wreck." He even wrote about his sabbatical as a race track owner in a book titled "Thirty Tons a Day." Veeck died in 1986. He was elected to the Hall of Fame in 1991.

GEORGE "RUBE" WADDELL
Pitcher, Lou (N) 1897, 1899, Pit (N) 1900-1901, Chi (N) 1901, Phi (A) 1902-07, StL (N) 1908-10
Left-hander Waddell had a terrific fastball, a biting curve, and exceptional control of his pitches. His life was fast, veered wildly, and had no control whatsoever. He is usually called eccentric, or erratic, or flaky, or unstable, or capricious. He was nutty. Completely uneducated, he fits the old line "If he had a brain, he would be dangerous."

He missed games because he was fishing, or helping the local firemen, or playing marbles, or drunk, or because he just forgot. He missed a World Series because he hurt his arm wrestling. He once dived into a river to save a drowning man—who turned out to be a log.

Everybody liked Rube, even all the managers who fired him, because they never knew if he'd show up or what he'd do if he got there. He was likable—a big, overgrown 6-year-old.

People told all kinds of stories about him. He was so fast he poured ice water on his arm to slow himself down; he hit birds on the wing by throwing stones; he told his fielders to sit down while he struck out the side; and he did cartwheels off the mound after whipping Cy Young in a 20-inning showdown. Actually, he did beat Young, 4-2, in 20 innings, and he may have done the outfield stunt a couple of times in exhibition games.

The only manager ever to have the patience to put up with him for an extended period was Connie Mack, who would have probably called the Mad Hatter "a little odd." Especially if he could pitch.

In truth, Waddell was a heckuva pitcher for Mack for four seasons, and a good pitcher for a couple more years after that. He led in strikeouts for six straight seasons, with 349 in 1904, a record that would stand until 1973. He won 97 games from 1902 through 1905 (but he lost 52 and the A's had strong teams). He got his ERA down to 1.48 in 1905 (but five other pitchers were under 2.00).

Finally, even Mack couldn't take it any longer, and he traded Waddell to the Browns in 1908. The fact that Waddell's pitching was slipping probably made it a little easier. Yet in his first game against the A's, Waddell struck out 16 batters.

By 1910 Rube was back in the minors. A year or so after that, he was visiting in Kentucky when a flood hit. Waddell stood for hours armpit deep in freezing water, passing sandbags to repair a dike. He contracted tuberculosis and died in 1914. He was elected to the Hall of Fame in 1946.

JOHN "HONUS" WAGNER
Shortstop, Lou (N) 1897-99, Pit (N) 1900-17. Manager, Pit (N) 1917
Some say Wagner was the best player of all time. He was voted into Cooperstown in 1936 right behind Ty Cobb and

ahead of Babe Ruth. The argument goes that a great shortstop is inherently more valuable than a great outfielder. Certainly that's true in the field. What might be more to the point is to rank Wagner against Cobb and Ruth as a hitter. Even allowing for the differences in liveliness of the baseballs each batted against in his prime, Cobb and Ruth were probably more dangerous at bat.

Nevertheless Honus hit .300 for 17 consecutive seasons and won eight batting titles in 12 years, 1900-1911. He had a career mark of .327, with 3,415 hits, 640 doubles, 252 triples (third best all-time), 101 homers, 1,736 runs, and 1,732 RBIs. He led the NL in stolen bases five times. He finished with 722 (10th best all-time). He reputedly stole second, third, and home three times in his career.

In Wagner's only showdown against Cobb, in the 1909 World Series, Ty called to him from first base, "Watch out, Krauthead, I'm coming down." The 200-pound Honus knocked Ty's teeth loose with the tag. Wagner batted .333 to Cobb's .200, and stole six bases to Ty's two, as Pittsburgh beat Detroit in seven games. (Wagner's stolen base mark stood until Lou Brock broke it in 1967.)

Wagner was so long-armed and bowlegged, they said he could tie his shoes without bending down. His batting stance, says writer Bob Broeg, resembled a man sitting on a bar stool. He used the hands-apart grip and swung at anything near the plate.

Whether Wagner was the best-fielding shortstop of all time, which you hear sometimes, or just one of the best of his day is hard to tell from fielding stats. He didn't become a full-time shortstop until his seventh NL season. He seems to have been a little rough at first, but he had great range. After he'd been at it for a few years, he led NL shortstops a couple of times in fielding average.

They say that when he fielded a grounder, his big hands scooped up dirt, ball, and all, and that he'd let everything fly, showering the first baseman in pebbles. Honus, who could embroider a story like Aunt Tillie could a seat cushion, said a dog once ran onto the field and snatched the ball; he said he threw both dog and ball to first for the out.

If his stories were incredible, at least you could tell them to your mother, he said. One estimate puts him as the most beloved man in baseball during the time between King Kelly and Babe Ruth. If so, he deserved the adoration. He always had time for a friend; he helped rookies; he had a drink now and then, but he was never a drunk; he was brighter than most but suffered fools with patience; and he never acted the star. He also refused to let a cigarette company put his picture in their packs because he didn't want to encourage kids to smoke. He made them stop distributing one print, making the few in circulation the most valuable baseball cards in the world.

LARRY WALKER
Outfielder, Mtl (N) 1989-94, Col (N) 1995-
Walker was an All-Star before he flew to the Colorado Rockies in 1995. In his first six seasons, all for Montreal, the Canadian-born Walker established himself as a superior defensive outfielder capable of hitting .300 with occasional power. In 1992, he popped 23 home runs, drove in 93, and batted .301. That year, he won his first Gold Glove and played in his first All-Star Game.

Nevertheless, his game went up several notches when

he relocated to the Rocky Mountains as a free agent. In 1995 he set personal highs with 36 homers and 101 RBIs. He missed half the 1996 season with a broken collarbone suffered when he ran into a wall while playing center field. He came back with his best season in '97, batting .366 with 49 home runs and 130 RBIs. Although his power numbers dropped off considerably in 1998, he won his first batting championship with a .363 average.

BOBBY WALLACE
Shortstop, Cle (N) 1894-98, StL (N) 1899-1901, 1917-18, StL (A) 1902-16. Manager, StL (A) 1911-12, Cin (N) 1937
When Bobby Wallace was elected to the Hall of Fame in 1953, a lot of people asked who-in-hell he was. More than 35 years later, when fans file past his plaque at Cooperstown, most of them ask the same question.

To answer: Wallace was the first AL shortstop in the Hall, beating Joe Cronin by three years. He played in the majors for 25 years, although you could only count him as a regular for about 15. He hit .300 twice, but most years he was down around .250 and a couple of years he was lower yet.

He started as a pitcher with the old Cleveland Spiders of the NL, then moved to third base. In 1899 he became a St. Louis Cardinal and switched to shortstop. By 1902 he was so highly regarded that the St. Louis Browns of the new AL paid him a $6,500 advance and signed him to a five-year contract for $32,500, thus making him the highest-paid player in baseball.

He was generally accepted as the best AL shortstop from 1902 until about 1910. The ranking was based almost entirely on his glove. As usual, fielding statistics don't prove a whole lot. Wallace led in fielding percentage and assists three times each. Big deal! His most significant fielding figure is that he averaged 6.1 chances per game; only four shortstops have ever done better.

Naturally, playing for the Browns meant no World Series appearances and mostly losing teams. It's to Wallace's credit that somebody remembered him 40 years later, and it's to the Hall of Fame's credit that they elected a shortstop (in 1953) just because he could field. They've only done that once or twice.

ED WALSH
Pitcher, Chi (A) 1904-16, Bos (N) 1917
The greatest spitballer, Walsh compiled the lowest lifetime ERA in history, 1.82. He was also one of the great iron men of all time, four times leading the league in innings pitched, with an AL record of 464 in 1908. That's the year he won 40 games and almost pitched the White Sox to the flag. From 1907 through 1910, Walsh's ERAs were 1.60, 1.42, 1.41, and 1.26. That last one came in 1910, when he lost 20 games for a sixth-place club that hit .211 with only seven home runs all year. He's the only man to lead the league in both ERA and losses at the same time.

A muscular product of the coal mines, "Big Ed" was square-shouldered and handsome. And he knew it. "He could strut sitting down," someone said.

In 1906 he was 17-13 with a team that hit .230. Ten of his wins were shutouts. In the World Series against the rival Cubs, Walsh whiffed a then-record 12 men to win the third game on a two-hitter.

Walsh's finest season was 1908, when Chicago, Cleveland, and Detroit raced down to the wire. His team hit only three homers all year, one of them by Ed himself. He started 49 games and relieved in 17 more. He threw 11 shutouts and had a 40-15 record; he also had six saves.

Ed pitched seven games in the last nine days of the 1908 season, including a doubleheader win over Boston, in which he allowed one run, one walk, and seven hits. The next day he pitched another nine innings, his third complete game in two days. In a head-to-head showdown against Cleveland ace Addie Joss, Walsh fanned 15 and gave up only four hits—but Joss trumped him with a perfect game.

The next day Walsh was called in to relieve with the bases loaded, two out in the ninth, and Nap Lajoie at bat. He fooled Larry with a fastball instead of a spitter and got him on a called strike three. He would call it the greatest thrill of his career.

Walsh continued to work hard—370 innings in 1910, 369 in 1911, 393 in 1912. He won 27 games in each of the last two years, including a no-hitter. His arm gave out in 1913 and several comeback tries failed. He finished with 195 wins, 57 of them shutouts.

He was named to the Hall of Fame in 1946.

WILLIAM "BUCKY" WALTERS
Pitcher, Bos (N) 1931-34, 1950, Phi (N) 1934-38, Cin (N) 1938-48. Manager, Cin (N) 1948-49
For two magnificent years, 1939-1940, Walters was the premier pitcher in baseball. With Paul Derringer, he led the Reds to their first flags since 1919 after two decades of frustration.

In 1939 Bucky, 27-11, led in wins, ERA, complete games, and strikeouts, easily winning the MVP. In 1940 he led in wins again (22-10), plus ERA and complete games. Walters added two wins in the World Series, holding the Tigers to a 1.50 ERA.

In 1944 Walters had a 23-8 mark for the third-place Reds. He lost a perfect game on a two-out single in the eighth. When the 1948 season began, Bucky needed only two more wins to reach 200 and looked like a dead-bang cinch. But he'd also been named as the Reds' manager that year. He got around to pitching in only seven games and won none of them. Nevertheless, his 198-160 record isn't bad for a fellow who began as a third baseman and never pitched a game until he was in his fifth major league season.

LLOYD WANER
Outfielder, Pit (N) 1927-41, 1944-45, Bos (N) 1941, Cin (N) 1941, Phi (N) 1942, Bkn (N) 1944
A good singles hitter, Lloyd rode to Cooperstown on the coattails of his big brother Paul. The two played next to each other for Pittsburgh from 1927 through 1940.

Lloyd was a steady .300 hitter in an era of steady .300 hitters. As a rookie in 1927, he collected 223 hits, a rookie record; 198 of them were singles, still a record for anyone. He led the NL with 133 runs scored. He hit .355, plus .400 in the World Series, as the Yankees crushed the Pirates in four straight.

He had 221 hits in 1928 and 234 in 1929, when he led the league with 20 triples. An illness cost him most of the 1930 season, but he came back to lead the league with 214

hits in 1931.

Lloyd rarely struck out—only 173 times, an average of once in every 45 at bats. In 1941 he played in 77 games without a single strikeout. The bad news was that he didn't walk very often either, not nearly often enough for a lifetime leadoff man.

His greatest attribute was his speed. It made him an excellent center fielder. Lloyd led the league in putouts four times.

Lloyd was known as "Little Poison" and Paul as "Big Poison," which is Brooklynese for "little person" and "big person." Lloyd didn't drink; Paul was a toper. The two had started out as roomies but later split up. Lloyd "rejoined" Paul in the Hall of Fame in 1967, two years after Paul's death. Certainly the fact that they formed a duo for so many years must have had some influence on the voters, but Lloyd's 2,459 hits, .316 batting average, and excellence in the outfield give him some good credentials on his own.

PAUL WANER
Outfield, Pit (N) 1926-40, Bkn (N) 1941, 1943-44, Bos (N) 1941-42, NY (A) 1944-45

"Big Poison" wasn't a big man, at 5 feet 8 inches, 153 pounds, but he was a big talent. Paul hit over .300 for 12 straight years. He collected 200 hits eight times, tying Willie Keeler's record. Waner won three batting titles in 1927, 1934, and 1936. His .380 in 1927 won him the NL MVP Award.

Paul learned to hit swinging at corncobs in Oklahoma. He stood deep in the box, feet together, and aimed at the top of the ball, swinging down as in a golf shot, a theory he later taught as coach. A line drive hitter, he led in doubles and triples twice each.

Like younger brother Lloyd, Paul wasn't a home run threat, although he hit 15 in 1929. He recognized that approach as a losing game in spacious Forbes Field and became adept at lining the ball down either foul line. The worst that could happen was a foul ball. If the ball hit fair, he had extra bases. In 20 years, Paul had 3,152 hits, including 603 doubles and 190 triples. His batting average was .333, and he scored 1,626 runs and drove in 1,309.

In his prime he was a fine defensive outfielder with the arm to play right field at Forbes. Paul was notorious for his drinking. One year manager Pie Traynor convinced him to lay off the sauce. When Paul's batting average dropped .240, Traynor took him out and bought him a drink.

But despite humorous stories about Paul's hungover hitting, the boozing probably kept him from a couple of batting titles and left him only an ordinary player in the last few years of an otherwise outstanding career.

The story is that Paul beat out a grounder off an infielder's glove one day in 1942 for what could have been his 3,000th hit. However, he signaled the scorer to call it an error, preferring to wait for a clean blow for the big one. The infielder's comment has not survived.

Waner was named to the Hall of Fame in 1952.

JOHN MONTGOMERY WARD
Pitcher/Shortstop, Prov (N) 1878-82, NY (N) 1883-89, 1893-94, Bkn (P) 1890, Bkn (N) 1891-92. Manager, NY (N) 1884, 1893-94, Bkn (P) 1890, Bkn (N) 1891-92.

Executive

When Ward was named to the Hall of Fame in 1964, the only question was whether he should go in as a pitcher, a shortstop, or as an executive. One of the most remarkable figures in baseball history, he excelled at nearly everything he did.

He broke in as an 18-year-old pitcher with Providence in 1878 and led the NL in ERA. The next year he pitched his team to a pennant with a 47-19 mark. In 1880 he pitched the second perfect game in NL history and finished with a 39-24 record. An arm injury ended his pitching career after he'd won 164 games. In 1883 he played center field despite his lame arm—throwing left-handed!

Undaunted, he became the league's top shortstop, hitting .300 three times, and gluing the infield as captain of the 1888-1889 league champion New York Giants. He led the NL twice in stolen bases and finished with 2,105 career hits and 1,408 runs scored.

A handsome society lion, married to an actress, Ward studied law at night at Columbia, graduating with honors. In 1886 he led the formation of the Players' Brotherhood, the first attempt to improve players' rights. When the Brotherhood got no satisfaction, they formed their own league, the Players League, in 1890. One hundred players jumped their teams in support. Ward played for and managed the Brooklyn club in the league. When the owners sought an injunction against the players, Ward argued the case in court and won.

He won the battles but not the war. Even though the new league drew better than either the NL or American Association, the financial backers of the Players League teams became nervous and many pulled out. Ward's league folded after one year, and the players meekly signed new reserve contracts with their old owners.

Ward returned to the Giants, and as player-manager took them to a Temple Cup victory in 1894.

LON WARNEKE
Pitcher, Chi (N) 1930-36, 1942-45, StL (N) 1937-42

"The Arkansas Hummingbird," Warneke was one of the top right-handers of the 1930s, winning 20 games three times and helping the Cubs to two pennants. In 1932 he topped the NL in wins and percentage with a 22-6 mark. He also led in ERA and shutouts. The Cubs won the pennant but lost the World Series to the Yankees. In 1935, when the Cubs won the flag again, Lon went 20-13 and won twice in the World Series.

Although the modest Warneke was one of Chicago's most popular players, he was traded to the Cardinals in 1937. He helped them win the 1942 pennant—after he had been traded back to Chicago. He beat Brooklyn in a crucial September game to give the Cards a slim lead. "Now hold it," he told his old mates, and they did.

Warneke, who finished with a 193-121 career mark, later was a National League umpire from 1949 to 1955.

EARL WEAVER
Manager, Bal (A) 1968-82, 1985-86

Weaver presided over the Orioles' dynasty of the 1970s, leading them to six division titles, four pennants, and one world championship. His winning percentage of .583 ranks in the top 10 all-time. Although it was said his teams relied on "pitching and the three-run homer" to

win, Weaver was actually a highly innovative manager. He schooled his players in fundamentals, pioneered the use of computer charts, extended the use of platooning, and even wrote a training manual used by the entire Orioles organization. Always open to new ideas, his motto became the title of his autobiography: *It's What You Learn After You Know It All That Counts.*

He never got past Double A as a minor league second baseman, but once he moved to managing he found his way to major leagues in 1968. Although one of his hurlers cracked, "The only thing Earl knows about pitching is that he couldn't hit it," he and coach George Bamberger produced 20-game winners 22 times, with six Cy Young Awards mixed in. Several pitchers, including Mike Cuellar, Steve Stone, and Mike Torrez came from other organizations to achieve their best seasons with the Orioles.

Weaver was known for his rages against umpires. He was ejected from 91 games during his career. Once he was booted from both ends of a doubleheader. However, Weaver was so respected as a psychologist that some believe that many of his tantrums were staged to arouse his team. Weaver was elected to the Hall of Fame in 1996.

GEORGE WEISS
Executive

"The last of the empire builders," Weiss, more than any other man, was responsible for the unprecedented success of the New York Yankees from the mid-1930s until the mid-1960s: 22 pennants and 17 world championships.

He began with the Eastern League New Haven franchise in 1919 and advanced to become general manager of Baltimore of the International League in 1929. In 1932 he was made farm director of the Yankees and kept an overpowering fountain of talent flowing to the majors for the next 15 years. Many of the greatest players ever to wear Yankee pinstripes came up through Weiss' farms.

In 1948 he became general manager of the Yankees. One of his first moves was to hire Casey Stengel as manager, despite Stengel's reputation as a clown. With Weiss supplying the players and Stengel managing them, the Yankees won 10 pennants between 1949 and 1960.

Both he and Stengel were let go as "too old" after the 1960 season. Weiss became president of the expansion Mets in 1961, hired Stengel as manager, and together they laid the groundwork for the future success of that team. In the meantime, the Yankees that Weiss had built continued to win pennants through 1964, and then collapsed into the poorest Yankees' decade since before World War I.

Weiss was named to the Hall of Fame in 1971.

MICKEY WELCH
Pitcher, Troy (N) 1880-82, NY (N) 1883-92

"Smiling Mickey" was able to grin 307 times as the winning pitcher in games played between 1880 and 1892. He was the third pitcher to win 300 games, preceded only by Pud Galvin and teammate Tim Keefe. Although Welch was not noted for his speed, he was effective with changes of speed on his curveball and screwball.

Welch led the NL in walks for three straight years, 1884-1886, but averaged over 500 innings pitched for each of those years. In 1885 he won 44 games (including a streak of 17 victories in a row) for the Giants. He finally had a clause written into his contract that he would only pitch every two days.

He and Keefe combined as a one-two pitching punch for the Giants in the late 1880s, helping the team to pennants in 1888 and 1889.

Welch was elected to the Hall of Fame in 1973.

WILLIE "DEVIL" WELLS
Shortstop, Negro League, 1925-49, St. Louis Stars, Detroit Wolves, Kansas City Monarchs, Chicago American Giants, Cole's American Giants, Newark Eagles, Memphis Red Sox, New York Black Yankees, Baltimore Elite Giants

Wells is among the top six Negro League home run hitters of all time. Though not considered a slugger, Wells owns the all-time Negro League home run record, with 27 in 1927, aided by a short left field fence in his St. Louis home park.

In 1930 Willie led the Negro National League with .404. Wells' batting average in the black big leagues was .332. Against white big leaguers, he was even better: .369, with six homers in 31 games.

At shortstop, Wells had sure hands but did not have a strong arm. He compensated with an uncanny ability to play the hitters. He is usually considered the top shortstop in black baseball during the latter 1920s and 1930s. He was chosen to play in the East-West All-Star Game eight times.

A notorious target of beanball pitches, Wells created an early batting helmet by taking a miner's hard-hat and knocking off the gas jet.

He began managing in 1936 with the Newark Eagles and is ranked as one of the finest skippers in Negro League history. His Eagles won the NNL pennant in 1946. Among his players were Ernie Banks, Don Newcombe, Larry Doby, and Monte Irvin. Wells was elected to the Hall of Fame in 1997.

ZACK WHEAT
Outfielder, Bkn (N) 1909-26, Phi (A) 1927

Wheat was a graceful fielder with an amazingly accurate arm and a reliable line drive hitter. For years there was a sign on the Ebbets Field wall: "Zack Wheat caught 345 flies last year; Tanglefoot fly paper caught 10 million." The only thing that had to be repainted from season to season was the appropriate number of putouts by Wheat; he was the Brooklyn left fielder for 18 years.

Although he led the NL in hitting only once—.335 in 1918—Wheat topped .300 in 14 seasons and finished with a .317 career average. He cracked 2,884 hits, scored 1,289 runs, and batted in 1,261. His line drives were usually smoked. Once the lively ball was introduced, drives that had been catchable zoomed past the fielders. Wheat's best batting marks came when he was in his late 30s. In 1924 at the age of 38, he hit .375, with 14 homers and 97 RBIs. The next year he drove in 103 runs, while hitting .359. Noted for his ability to hit curveballs, Wheat had no weaknesses at bat or in the field, but he did have thin, weak ankles that were often injured.

Although he played on Dodgers pennant winners in 1916 and 1920, Wheat always maintained that his favorite game was the 26-inning, 1-1 tie between Brooklyn and Boston in 1920.

He was elected to the Hall of Fame in 1959.

JAMES "DEACON" WHITE

Third Baseman/Catcher, Cle (NA) 1871-72, Bos (NA) 1873-75, Chi (N) 1876, Bos (N) 1877, Cin (N) 1878-80, Buf (N) 1881-85, Det (N) 1886-88, Pit (N) 1889, Buf (P) 1890. Manager Cin (N) 1879

White was one of the most remarkable players of the 19th century. His career was long, productive, and filled with firsts. For example, on May 4, 1871, when the Cleveland Forest Citys played the Fort Wayne Kekiongas in the first game of the spanking new National Association, who strode up to the plate to become the first batter ever in a recognized professional league? White. And a few moments later, who doubled to make the first hit and the first extra-base hit? White. And a short while after that, who became the first to be put out on a double play? White.

After the 1872 campaign, he left Cleveland for the Boston Red Stockings, who then became the first team to win two consecutive pennants, then three consecutive, and then four. And speaking of four, White, Al Spalding, Ross Barnes, and Cal McVey, among Boston's best players, were called "the Big Four" when they deserted for Chicago in 1876. The resulting ruckus brought about the formation of the National League, and Chicago won the NL's first pennant, as White became its first RBI leader.

Back to Boston in 1877, White became Beantown's first batting champion (.387) as the Red Stockings won their first NL pennant. Deacon next formed the catching half of baseball's first brother battery with pitcher Will White, the first player to wear glasses on the field.

In the early 1880s at Buffalo, White became part of the second "Big Four," along with Dan Brouthers, Hardy Richardson, and Jack Rowe. In 1885 all four were sold to Detroit in the first big player deal. And in 1887 they led Detroit to its first (and last) NL pennant. White hit .303 at the age of 40.

White's nickname suited him; he never drank, smoked, or cursed, and he carried his Bible with him when the team was on the road.

SOL WHITE

Second Baseman, Executive, Negro League, 1887-1926, Pittsburgh Keystones, Washington Capital Citys, Wheeling (O.B.), New York Gorhams, York Monarchs (O.B.), Cuban Giants, Genuine Cuban Giants, Fort Wayne (O.B.), Page Fence Giants, Cuban X-Giants, Columbia Giants, Philadelphia Giants, Lincoln Giants, Quaker Giants, Cleveland Browns, Newark Stars

If Rube Foster was the "father of black baseball," White was the grandfather. Born in 1868, he was 19 when major league baseball's bars clanged shut on blacks in 1887, and he lived to see the end of 60 years of baseball apartheid in 1947. White played with white minor league teams in the 1880s (once playing against Ban Johnson); then after baseball segregation, he played for the Cuban Giants, the Page Fence Giants, and the Philadelphia Giants. Finally he joined the Cuban X-Giants, along with black pioneers Charley "Tokahoma" Grant, Rube Foster, Home Run Johnson, Frank Grant, Pop Lloyd, etc.

White managed the 1903 Philadelphia Giants, who beat Newark of the International League four straight but lost the first black World Series to Foster's X-Giants two games to three. He hired Foster and got revenge the following year two-to-one.

In his *History of Colored Baseball*, White wrote of the financial pressures on black teams in 1906 and of walking around towns for hours looking for hotels which would accept them. The average white big leaguer made $2,000 a year, he wrote; the average black, $466.

White took Pop Lloyd, Dick Redding, Louis Santop, and Spotswood Poles to the New York Lincoln Giants in 1911. The Lincolns were perhaps the strongest black team in pre-World War I days.

After retiring, White coached at Wilberforce College and wrote a sports column. In *History of Colored Baseball* he had urged blacks to keep up their skills so they would be ready when the doors were opened again. He was 79 in 1947 when his prophecy came true in Brooklyn.

HOYT WILHELM

Pitcher, NY (N) 1952-56, StL (N) 1957, Cle (A) 1957-58, Bal (A) 1958-62, Chi (A) 1963-68, Cal (A) 1969, Atl (N) 1969-71, Chi (N) 1970, LA (N) 1971-72

The first relief pitcher honored by Cooperstown, Hoyt used his knuckleball to pitch until he was 48. Hoyt's 1,070 games are the second-most by a pitcher (Dennis Eckersley pitched in 1,071). Although he saved 227 games, he never in any season led in saves. He did lead in relief wins twice, and his 123 relief victories are the all-time record.

The way a staff's stopper is used has changed since Wilhelm's day. When he pitched, a top reliever was often brought in when a game was close, no matter which team was leading or what inning it was, a system that led to many wins but reduced the chance for saves. The most common modern practice is to bring in a club's closer primarily in save situations (usually the ninth inning only) with the team ahead. Although saves have increased greatly, a relief win now often means that the reliever must first lose the lead he was sent in to protect.

Wilhelm's top save total was 27 in 1964 with the White Sox. He also had 12 relief wins that year. Yet the only category he led in was relief losses with nine.

An infantryman in World War II, Hoyt was wounded and received the Purple Heart during the Battle of the Bulge. He was 28 before he reached the majors and slugged a home run in his first at bat. He never hit another. (His lifetime batting average was .088.)

Although many pitchers had used the knuckleball before Wilhelm, perhaps no pitcher had ever used it so much to the exclusion of other pitches. Certainly no pitcher popularized it so.

Hoyt baffled the batters—and catchers—with his knuckler. Five of his receivers set records for the most passed balls in an inning, and he gave up a whopping total of unearned runs.

As a rookie with the New York Giants in 1952, Wilhelm led the NL in appearances (71), ERA (2.43), and winning percentage with a 15-3 mark. In late 1958 he was given an infrequent start by the Orioles and responded with a no-hitter over the Yankees. The next year he was used primarily as a starter; he was 15-11 and led the AL in ERA. But after a few starts in 1960, he was returned to the bullpen. He pitched for another dozen years out of the bullpen.

Wilhelm was elected to the Hall of Fame in 1985.

J.L. WILKINSON

Executive, owner, Negro League, 1909-48, All Nations, Kansas City Monarchs

The white owner of the famous Kansas City Monarchs, Wilkinson was one of the pioneers of night baseball who gave Satchel Paige his second chance and Jackie Robinson his first. His lights saved Negro baseball in the Depression and helped to save the white minor league as well.

Wilkinson's first club, the All Nations—a multiracial team of blacks, whites, and orientals, plus a woman—barnstormed the prairies before World War I. He was one of the founders of the Negro National League in 1920. His Monarchs were black world champs in 1924, league champs in 1925, and reached the playoffs in 1926.

When the Depression struck, Wilkie bought portable lights, playing his first night game in Enid, Okla., two weeks before Des Moines opened with its lights and the same night that Independence, Kan. played organized baseball's first night game. Wilkinson took his lights to St. Louis, Detroit, Pittsburgh, and elsewhere, helping spread the idea to countless cities.

In 1937, when Paige's career seemed dead because of a sore arm, Wilkie took a chance on him and the arm magically healed. Satch helped win pennants in 1937, 1939-1942, and 1946, and brought in much needed dollars. Satch got 15 percent off the top.

In 1945 Wilkinson also gave a job to a rookie shortstop named Robinson. When the white big league raids decimated the black leagues, no club lost more than the Monarchs. Wilkinson sold out his interest in 1948.

BILLY WILLIAMS

Outfield, Chi (N) 1959-74, Oak (A) 1975-76

The NL Rookie of the Year in 1961, Williams established himself in left field for the Cubs and remained for 14 seasons. His final two years were spent as a DH with Oakland, where he finally got into a postseason game. Alas, it was the final year of the A's five-year reign as division champ and the team was swept in the ALCS.

Before he left the Cubs, however, Williams set the NL record by playing in 1,117 straight games. It was broken by Steve Garvey in 1982.

Nicknamed "Sweet Swinging" because of his batting swing, the popular Williams slugged 426 home runs and drove in 1,475 runs, while fashioning a .290 career batting average. He, Ernie Banks, and Ron Santo gave the Cubs a terrific power trio throughout the 1960s.

Billy usually hit around 25-30 homers a year, reaching his peak, 42, in 1970. Two years later *The Sporting News* named him Player of the Year, when he led the NL in batting and slugging with .333 and .606.

He was named to the NL All-Star team six times. In 1987 he was elected to the Hall of Fame.

SMOKEY JOE WILLIAMS

Pitcher, Negro League, 1897-1932, San Antonio Bronchos, Leland Giants, Chicago Giants, Lincoln Giants, Chicago American Giants, Bacharach Giants, Brooklyn Royal Giants, Homestead Grays

In a 1952 poll conducted by the *Pittsburgh Courier* a panel of black veterans and sportswriters picked Williams as the best black pitcher of all time. He defeated Satchel

Paige by a single vote. He was considered faster than Paige.

Half-black, half-Comanche, Joe resembled Walter Johnson in age, build, and style—both threw blazing fastballs and little else. In their one head-to-head confrontation, Joe won, 1-0.

It was one of 19 wins (and seven losses) Joe recorded against white big leaguers in exhibition games. He defeated seven Hall of Famers—Johnson, Grover Cleveland Alexander, Chief Bender, Rube Marquard (twice), Waite Hoyt, and Satchel Paige. Two of his losses came after the age of 40; two more were 1-0 decisions.

Joe's best game was a 10-inning, 20-strikeout no-hitter against John McGraw's NL champion Giants in 1917. He lost it 1-0 on an error. Reportedly he gained his nickname after the game when Ross Youngs remarked, "That was a hell of a game, Smokey." Until then Williams had been called Cyclone Joe. In 1930 he fanned 27 Kansas City Monarchs in a 12-inning night game. The primitive lights and tobacco juice on the ball didn't hurt.

Williams and Paige faced each other twice in the early 1930s. They split the two games. "Smokey Joe could throw harder than all of them," Paige declared.

Joe's rival was Cannonball Redding. They started as teammates on the 1911-1914 New York Lincolns, forming one of the best one-two pitching punches in baseball history.

KEN WILLIAMS

Outfield, Cin (N) 1915-16, StL (A) 1918-27, Bos (A) 1928-29

Overshadowed by Babe Ruth and by his own teammate, George Sisler, Williams was a good hitter who in his best season almost batted the Browns to a pennant in 1922. They lost to the Yankees by a single game, and might have won had Sisler not injured his shoulder just before a crucial head-to-head series in the stretch. Ken knocked in 155 runs and won the home run crown with 39. (It should be noted that Ruth missed a quarter of the season that year.) Williams hit 32 of his homers in Sportsman's Park.

Ken played in a fine outfield alongside Jack Tobin and Baby Doll Jacobson. All of them were later picked as outfielders on various Browns all-time teams.

Although he never matched his 1922 numbers, the tall left-handed hitter finished second in the AL in homers in 1921, 1923, and 1925.

TED WILLIAMS

Outfielder, Bos (A) 1939-42, 1946-60.
Manager, Was (A) 1969-71, Tex (A) 1972

Either Williams or Babe Ruth was the greatest hitter of all time, and you could probably cover the difference with an ant's umbrella. Despite losing nearly five seasons in two wars, Williams put together a statistical record that would stand against anyone's. Whether that makes Williams the greatest player of all time is another question altogether.

First the career figures: .344 career batting average, 521 home runs, 1,798 runs, 1,839 RBIs, 2,019 walks, and a .634 slugging average.

And what about individual seasons? He won six AL batting championships, including the famous .406 of 1941; four home run titles, including a personal high of 43 in 1949; six times leading in runs scored; four times in

RBIs; eight times in walks; and nine times in slugging average.

And how about the clutch? Remember Williams' home run with two out in the ninth to win the 1941 All-Star Game? Or the 1946 All-Star homer off Rip Sewell's blooper pitch? Or that he could have sat down the final day in 1941 and finished with a rounded-off .400 (.3995) but insisted on playing and lifted his average to .406? Or that he homered in his last major league at bat?

And remember he won two MVPs, in 1946 and 1949, and his fans never stopped complaining about the ones he didn't win. And remember *The Sporting News* named him Player of the Decade for the 1950s, which raised a few eyebrows among the fans of Stan Musial, Willie Mays, and Mickey Mantle, to name only the M's.

One thing seems certain: Williams will get better every year in our memories as we look at his statistical record. There was never a question that he was the best hitter when he was playing. He was criticized for other things and we tend to forget those. They said he was no better than adequate in the field with a so-so arm, with the footnote that he played Fenway's left field wall very well. They complained that the Red Sox won only a single pennant in all the Williams years, with the footnote that there were some serious pitching problems nearly every year in Boston. They grumbled that he was sometimes boorish, with the footnote that he was often charming.

Most of the gripes were about intangible things. If you were playing a computer baseball game and could pick your roster from players from any era, you'd probably start with Williams if Ruth was already taken. Williams was elected to the Hall of Fame in 1966.

VIC WILLIS
Pitcher, Bos (N) 1898-1905, Pit (N) 1906-09,
StL (N) 1910
Willis holds the NL record for complete games in the 20th century, with 45 in 1902, as well as for losses, with 29 in 1905 for the seventh-place Bostonians. But the curveballer won 20 or more eight times, including four of his first five years, 1898-1902. He finished with a hefty 247-204 record.

As a 22-year-old rookie in 1898, Vic helped pitch Boston to the flag with a 25-13 record. In 1899 he was 27-8 with a no-hitter.

After an off-year in 1900, Willis came back in 1901 to go 18-17 for a fifth-place team. The next year he was 27-19, led in innings pitched and strikeouts, and set a modern record with 45 complete games.

Vic had two big losing years in 1904-1905, when he was 18-25 and 12-29 as Boston stumbled home next-to-last. But a trade to third-place Pittsburgh in 1906 brought him back to a 22-13 record, the first of four straight 20-win years. In the last one, 1909, Willis was 22-11 to lead the Pirates to the world championship.

Willis was elected to the Hall of Fame in 1995.

MAURY WILLS
Shortstop, LA (N) 1959-66, 1969-72, Pit (N) 1967-68,
Mon (N) 1969. Manager, Sea (A) 1980-81
Wills brought the stolen base back into baseball. No NL player had stolen 50 bases since Max Carey in 1923 when Wills grabbed that many in 1960. Two years later he shattered Ty Cobb's 1915 record of 96 and became the first man to break 100 in this century. (Rules in the 19th century counted extra bases taken on others' hits as steals.) Maury's 104 steals lit the way for Lou Brock, Rickey Henderson, and Vince Coleman and changed the nature of the game.

Wills was the shortstop for Los Angeles, a team long on pitching and short on power. His steals were of more value to the Dodgers than they might have been to a team of greater batting proficiency. He led the NL in stolen bases six straight years, 1960-1965, and he finished his 14-year career with 586. In addition to the 104 steals in 1962, which won him the MVP Award, he stole 94 in 1965.

Wills spent eight years in the minors before finally being given a chance with the Dodgers midway through the 1959 season. Although he had no home run power, Wills was more than a one-dimensional player. He had a career batting average of .281, and he twice won Gold Gloves as a shortstop. With Wills at short, the Dodgers won four pennants.

His son, Bump Wills, played six years (1977-1982) in the majors and was also an excellent base stealer. Maury managed against his son briefly as skipper of the Mariners.

LEWIS "HACK" WILSON
Outfield, NY (N) 1923-25, Chi (N) 1926-31, Bkn (N)
1932-34, Phi (N) 1934
It was often said of Wilson that "he was a lowball hitter and a highball drinker." The line could still get a chuckle after his career went down the tube at age 34, but lost its mirth when he died at 48. For five years he was the most fearsome slugger in the NL; then, almost overnight, he became a has-been.

He was one of the strangest-looking men ever to play in the majors. He stood only 5 feet 6 inches tall, but weighed around 210. He had an 18-inch neck and wore a size six shoe. Because someone thought he resembled the famous strongman George Hackenschmidt, Wilson was tagged "Hack," but that probably didn't do him justice. What he really looked like was Barney Rubble with Wilma Flintstone's feet.

After he'd played a couple of years for the Giants and been found wanting, the Cubs picked him up for $5,000 in 1926. Right away he started hitting homers and driving in runs. From 1926 through 1930 he led the NL in homers four times, drove in over 100 runs each year, and hit over .300. The really big seasons were 1929, when he hit .345 and had 159 RBIs to help the Cubs to the pennant, and 1930, which made everything else look like a preamble. In 1930 he hit .356, he scored 146 runs, he hammered out 56 homers—the NL record until broken by Mark McGwire and Sammy Sosa in 1998—and Wilson drove in a grand total of (drum roll) 191 runs! That major league record still stands and has withstood all challengers, including Lou Gehrig (184) in 1931.

Hack was 30 years old and it was "top-of-the-world-ma!" And if you remember what happened next in the James Cagney movie, just about the same thing happened to Hack in 1931. His boozing was at the base. Manager Rogers Hornsby got on his case about the cases he was consuming. Hack sulked and drank more. And when he

hit .261, with 13 homers and 61 RBIs, they exiled him to Brooklyn. By 1934, he was done hitting lowballs.

Wilson was elected to the Hall of Fame in 1979.

DAVE WINFIELD
Outfield, SD (N) 1973-80, NY (A) 1981-88, 1990, Cal (A) 1990-91, Tor (A) 1992, Min (A) 1993-94, Cle (A) 1995
The 6-foot-6-inch, 220-pound Winfield was drafted to play both pro football and pro basketball but opted instead to step directly from the University of Minnesota into a regular job with the Padres in 1973. Although the San Diego park was a poor one for right-handed power hitters and the Padres team was annually awful, he established himself as one of the NL's best players, hitting .300 twice, leading in RBIs in 1979, and earning two Gold Gloves.

Frustrated at playing for a losing team, he signed an estimated $25-million contract as a free agent with the Yankees in 1981. Discounting 1981, the strike year, he batted in at least 100 runs every year as a Yankee except 1987, when he drove home 97. His home run totals were as high as 37 and as low as 19 (in 1984, when he batted .340). He brightened innumerable highlight films with leaping outfield catches and fantastic throws from right field. He was a team leader and has conducted himself as a model citizen, and his Winfield Foundation is known for its charitable work with underprivileged youth.

There's a downside. He was involved in numerous verbal skirmishes and even a lawsuit with Yankees owner George Steinbrenner. The Yankees played in only one World Series (1981) during his tenure in New York, and he hit only .045 in a six-game loss to the Dodgers. And the seagulls of Toronto will never forgive him for his mighty outfield toss that nailed one of their number. Winfield missed the entire 1989 season with a back injury and was traded to California early in 1990.

In 1992 he joined Toronto and helped them win a world championship. In the following year he nailed down his Hall of Fame credentials by surpassing 3,000 hits with his hometown Twins. He finished with 465 home runs.

GEORGE WRIGHT
Shortstop, Bos (NA), 1871-75, Bos (N) 1876-78, 1880-81, Prov (N) 1879, 1882. Manager, Prov (N) 1879
Baseball's Wright brothers weren't related to the airplane inventors, but they got professional baseball off the ground in 1869 with the first completely pro team. George starred at shortstop for older brother Harry's pioneer pro club, the Cincinnati Red Stockings, which went unbeaten that year while playing all comers from East Coast to West. George hit .629, with 49 homers in the Reds' 57 counted games.

George had been named shortstop on pioneer baseball writer Henry Chadwick's first All-Star team in 1868. He was the first shortstop to play out beyond the baselines, thereby increasing his range. He was valued even more for his fielding than his hitting. And small wonder! The Red Stockings won games by scores of 85-7, 40-0, and 103-8. Who needed another hitter?

The Wrights moved to Boston of the new National Association following the 1870 campaign and won four straight flags, 1872-1875. George's batting average ranged from .409 to .336.

When the NL was founded in 1876, George was the first man to come to bat. He hit a grounder to shortstop. His batting began dropping off, however, and with the advent of sidearm and curveball pitching in 1877, it was down to .276, but Boston won the flag and repeated in 1878. In 1879 he moved to Providence as player-manager and beat Harry's Bostonians for the flag, giving him eight pennants in nine years.

George founded a sporting goods company in Boston. An all-around athlete, George had starred at cricket before turning full-time to baseball. After retiring from the diamond, he returned to cricket. He introduced golf to the Boston area and was instrumental in introducing hockey to the United States. He also supported tennis, and his two sons won national championships.

George was named to the Hall of Fame in 1937.

WILLIAM "HARRY" WRIGHT
Outfielder/Pitcher, Bos (NA) 1871-75, Bos (N) 1876-77. Manager, Bos (NA) 1871-75, Bos (N) 1876-81, Pro (N) 1882-83, Phi (N) 1884-93
Henry Chadwick, "the father of baseball," called Harry Wright the "father of pro baseball."

Harry organized the game's first completely professional team, the Cincinnati Red Stockings, paving the way for the first pro league, the National Association. He designed the basic uniform that is still worn today, knee-length knickers instead of pantaloons. And he patented the first scorecard.

A professional cricket player, the British-born Harry decided to try the new American game of baseball in 1858. He joined the New York Knickerbockers as an outfielder. He occasionally pitched in relief, throwing a change-up he called a "dew drop."

In 1867 Harry joined the Cincinnati Red Stockings as a pitcher. Since 1865 he had been a paid bowler for the Cincinnati Union Cricket Club. By 1868, with several pros on the team, the Red Stockings were Midwest champions. The next year his younger brother George, a star shortstop, joined the team, and the Red Stockings took the field as the first fully professional baseball team. The Red Stockings toured the country and won every game in 1869. The winning streak continued until June 14, 1870, when they were finally bested by the Atlantics of Brooklyn in an extra-inning thriller. The publicity the Reds generated stirred public interest in professional baseball and led to the establishment of the National Association, the first pro baseball league, in 1871.

With the formation of the National Association, Harry became manager of the Boston team, called the Red Stockings since the Cincinnati team had disbanded, with George as shortstop. They won four pennants, in 1872-1875. The Red Stockings joined the newly formed National League in 1876, its first year. Harry won pennants in 1877 and 1878.

Harry continued as a manager in the NL until 1893. Although he won no more pennants, several of his teams come close. He was universally respected for his integrity and innovative ideas.

Among the changes he reportedly advocated that were later instituted: the 50-foot and then the 55-foot pitching distance, six balls for a walk instead of nine, pre-game practice, a livelier ball with a cork center, and overhand pitching. One idea that was tried out but did not prevail: a

flat bat. Harry Wright was named to the Hall of Fame in 1953.

EARLY WYNN
Pitcher, Was (A) 1939, 1941-44, 1946-48, Cle (A) 1949-57, 1963, Chi (A) 1958-62

Wynn pitched his first major league game at age 19, but he didn't get any (ahem) early wins. Throwing for the Senators in the 1940s, he was erratic—a burly batch of talent with no clear idea of what to do. He was 18-12 in 1943 and 8-17 the next year, 17-15 in 1947 and 8-19 in 1948, with a 5.82 ERA. The Senators finally said the heck with him and shipped him to Cleveland.

Indians pitching coach Mel Harder taught him the fine art of pitching, sharpened his pitches, and by 1950, the new, improved model was 18-8 with the AL's best ERA. Cleveland had the best pitching in the world in the 1950s, with Bob Feller, Bob Lemon, Mike Garcia, and their equal—sometimes better—Wynn. As an Indian, he won 20 games four times, 18 once, 17 twice.

In a sense, Wynn was a throwback, a 1950s pitcher with the attitude of an old 1890s Oriole. The plate was his. Any batter with the audacity to dig in could expect the next pitch to be aimed at his sinuses. They said Wynn would have brushed back his grandmother. "Only if she dug in," said Early. He didn't so much win games as wrestle for them, earning victory by intimidation, force of will, anger, and downright cussedness.

He walked scads and struck out a ton, eventually leading the AL twice in both departments. In all, he walked 1,775, yet he wasn't really wild; he just refused to give a batter a good pitch.

In 1958, Al Lopez, his former manager in Cleveland, acquired him for the White Sox. His 22-10 record in 1959 helped the Sox win their first pennant in 40 years and earned the 39-year-old Wynn the Cy Young Award.

By 1960 Early needed 29 more victories for 300. He developed a gouty elbow. It took him four years and a lot of pain, but on July 13, 1963, he became baseball's 14th 300-game winner. In 1972 he was elected to the Hall of Fame.

JIM WYNN
Outfielder, Hou (N) 1963-73, LA (N) 1974-75, Atl (N) 1976, NY (A) 1977, Mil (A) 1977

Wynn, at 5 feet 10 inches and 160 pounds, was called "the Toy Cannon" because he generated so much power for his size. For most of his career, he played half his games in the Astrodome, the second worst park to hit a ball out of (the worst is Yellowstone). Nevertheless, he popped 37 homers in 1967 and 33 in 1969. Joe Morgan, a pretty fair hitter, finished second on the team both years with 10 and 15.

Playing for the Astros in the 1960s had other disadvantages. There usually weren't a lot of runners for Jimmy to knock in; he topped 100 RBIs once for Houston but was over 80 three other years. And there was seldom anyone to knock Wynn home when he got on; Wynn walked over 100 times in seven different seasons, four as an Astro. His 148 free passes in 1969 tied the NL record.

In 1974 Wynn was traded to the Dodgers. Chavez Ravine is no hitter's paradise, but finally he was with a winner. He hit 32 homers, scored 108 runs, and batted in

104, to help the Dodgers to a pennant. Wynn finished fifth in the MVP voting, and everyone wondered where he'd been all these years.

CARL YASTRZEMSKI
Outfielder/First Baseman, Bos (A) 1961-83

For one month—September 1967—Ted Williams said, Yaz was the greatest player who ever lived. Almost single-handedly he lifted the Red Sox from ninth in 1966 to the flag. In a final doubleheader victory over pursuing Minnesota, Carl got 7-for-8 to sink the Twins. He won the Triple Crown and played a sensational left field with his glove and arm. Naturally he was MVP. He hit .400 in the World Series against St. Louis, with three homers.

Yaz won three batting titles, including .301 in 1968, the lowest ever to win. But that was the "Year of the Pitcher," when the average American Leaguer hit .230. In a normal year Carl's average would have translated to .331; in the 1930 NL, .388.

Yaz began as a line drive hitter. Then at age 27 he began lifting weights and came out slugging in 1967, the "Impossible Dream" season, with 44 homers. He had two more 40-homer seasons and finished with 452. His career .285 batting average is more impressive in light of his 1,844 RBIs, 1,816 runs scored, and 1,845 walks.

A master at playing Fenway Park's "Green Monster," Yaz led the league in assists six times, more than any other outfielder in AL history. He received 190 intentional walks, more than any other AL hitter since such records were kept (starting in 1955). Yaz was elected to the Hall of Fame in 1989.

TOM YAWKEY
Owner, Bos (A) 1933-77

A wealthy lumberman and mine owner, Yawkey was the adopted son of onetime Detroit owner William Yawkey. He bought the moribund Red Sox in 1933 and set out to buy a pennant by acquiring star players such as Joe Cronin, Lefty Grove, Jimmie Foxx, and Wes Ferrell. It didn't work, mostly because the Yankees were in the league, but he did revive fan interest that had all but disappeared in the years that the Sox spent scraping the bottom of the AL. Yawkey finally won pennants in 1946, 1967, and 1975. He never saw them win a World Series though—they lost in seven games every time.

Generous and popular with his players, Yawkey often worked out with them before games and was interested in their affairs. Critics said that he overpaid and pampered his stars, thus diminishing their desire to win. He was also accused of bucking racial integration; the Sox were the last team to have a black player, and that was not until 1959.

He served as AL vice president from 1956 to 1973. Yawkey was elected to the Hall of Fame in 1980.

DENTON "CY" YOUNG
Pitcher, Cle (N) 1890-98, StL (N) 1899-1900, Bos (A) 1901-08, Cle (A) 1909-11, Bos (N) 1911. Manager, Bos (A) 1907

Young's career record looks like a misprint: 511-313. Surely there must be a typo somewhere! If nothing else, it prepares you to gosh-and-golly through some of the other high points: Young was number one in innings pitched

with 7,357 and in complete games with 749. He had 15 seasons of 20 or more wins, five seasons of winning 30 or more; 76 shutouts; a 2.63 career ERA; three no-hitters, with the one in 1904 a perfect game. Ridiculous!

They called him Cy either because he threw baseballs against a fence until it looked like a cyclone had hit it or because he showed up at the Cleveland Spiders' park in 1890 carrying a cardboard suitcase, wearing a cheap, too-small suit, and looking like what you'd get if you mail-ordered for a hick. But from his first pitch, he was the Spiders' best pitcher, and he continued being the staff ace for whatever team he played for during the next 20 years. His last two seasons he slipped, but there was nothing wrong with his arm; he just got too fat to field bunts.

Young's arm was a wonder. He never had a sore arm, even though he pitched over 400 innings five times and over 300 in 11 other seasons. He'd go home to his Ohio farm in October, do chores all winter, and show up ready for another 400 innings the next spring.

Cy threw a dozen pitches before each game and was ready to go. On the mound he wheeled away from the hitter to hide the ball, then uncorked one of four deliveries, including an overhand curve, a sidearm curve, and a "tobacco ball." Young was a great control pitcher, averaging 1.5 walks per game. Eleven times he led the league in fewest walks and most strikeouts.

If they'd had a Cy Young Award when he pitched, he probably would have won only a couple at most. There was usually somebody having a more phenomenal individual season—Kid Nichols, Amos Rusie, Joe McGinnity, Christy Mathewson, Three-Finger Brown, Addie Joss, or Ed Walsh. A few pitchers in history have been terrific for enough seasons that they might actually rank ahead of Young on the all-time scale. Maybe Lefty Grove, Walter Johnson, Bob Feller, Tom Seaver, Matty, or Grover Cleveland Alexander. Cy had some advantages over most of them. He was almost always on winning teams. He didn't have to fret a lively ball. In its first years, the AL he jumped to in 1901 was definitely weaker than the NL. If you could choose any pitcher who has ever played to pitch for you in a big game, you probably wouldn't pick Young. But if your opponent picked him, he might beat you. After all, Cy won more than anybody ever has—and probably more than anyone ever will.

He was elected to the Hall of Fame in 1937. Fittingly, the award that goes to the best pitcher each year was

named in his honor in 1956.

ROSS YOUNGS
Outfielder, NY (N) 1917-26
Virtually John McGraw's "son"—Mac called him "the greatest outfielder I ever had"—Youngs played on the Giants' four straight pennant winners from 1921 through 1924. When he hit .375 in the 1922 Series to Babe Ruth's .118, Mac said he wouldn't trade him for the Babe. It got a big laugh over at the Yankees office. Hyperbole aside, Youngs was a splendid right fielder—a fast runner, fearless, with excellent judgment and a fine arm. A smart baserunner, too. At bat, the stocky left-handed hitter had double and triple power and hit .300 from the moment he first came to bat in the Polo Grounds.

In 1924 he hit .356. If he wasn't Ruth, he was definitely one of the best players in the NL. Then, in 1925, something was wrong. He struggled at bat all season and finished at .264. In the off-season, he was diagnosed as suffering from Bright's Disease.

He played through 1926 on guts, teaching young Mel Ott everything he knew about playing right field. By will alone he hit .302. By 1927 he was bedridden, and in October he died at the age of 30.

He was elected to the Hall of Fame in 1972.

ROBIN YOUNT
Shortstop/Outfielder, Mil (A) 1974-93
Yount became the Brewers' regular shortstop in 1974 at age 18 and held the job with his glove for a few years until his bat caught up. By the 1980s he was hitting for average and power.

The tousle-headed Yount was the best player in the AL in 1982. Robin smacked two home runs off Jim Palmer to clinch the AL East title for Milwaukee on the final day of the season. He finished with 29 homers, a .331 average, and the best slugging average in the league. He won the MVP by a landslide. Yount stayed hot in the World Series, hitting .414 with a record-setting two four-hit games, as the Brewers lost to the Cardinals in seven games.

After 1,479 games at shortstop, a shoulder injury in 1984 finally sent Yount to center field, where he continued to rank among the AL's best players. A .318 average and 103 RBIs led Yount to a second MVP in 1989. In 1992 he moved into select company with 3,000 career hits.

## CHAPTER 8

Baseball Families

Larry Amman

Just as the Wright brothers were first in flight, so were Wright brothers first in baseball. In the National Association's inaugural season of 1871, the Boston team featured Harry Wright as manager and reserve outfielder, and George at shortstop. Brother Sam joined them on the bench for the 1876 season, after an apprenticeship in New Haven the year before.

Since then there have been 356 brother combinations in the majors. The only season in which there was not at least one such pair was 1899. There were three new ones in 1997 and five in 1998.

The first thing that strikes the eye as one reads the list is the large number who were teammates, however briefly—more than 25 percent.

Another observation one must make is how one-sided the big league performance was between so many of the combinations. For example, there are 25 members of the Hall of Fame who had brothers in the majors—plus the Negro leagues' Foster brothers, Rube and Bill. Yet how many baseball fans have ever heard of the brothers of Bill Dickey, Christy Mathewson, or Honus Wagner? As another example, how many people remember the brothers of Steve Sax, Robin Yount, or Eddie Murray? These big names have brothers who played in the majors briefly.

Of course, being the brother of a major leaguer never guarantees success, nor even a shot at the big leagues. The five Delahantys, the three Boyers, and the two Ferrells all had other brothers who played minor league ball only. Because the combinations in which more than one brother excelled are so rare, we can limit the focus to the more outstanding ones.

In terms of balanced, outstanding achievement no group of three or more brothers can match the DiMaggios. The enduring folk hero status of Joe DiMaggio unfortunately has not done anything to keep alive the memory of his brothers, Vince and Dom. All three were gifted outfielders, good hitters, and fine all-around athletes. Vince, the oldest of these sons of a San Francisco fisherman, played for five different National League teams. In 1941 he had 21 homers and 100 RBIs for Pittsburgh. Four years later he hit four grand slams for the Phillies.

Dom DiMaggio was the youngest and smallest of the three brothers. Although lacking any of the power of the other two, he was the fastest on the bases and yielded nothing to his two brothers in the grace and skill he exhibited in the outfield. His lifetime batting average was just under .300.

In the 1941 All-Star Game, Dom went to right field as a late-inning substitute to play alongside Joe in center. This was a first in the midsummer classic. In the eighth inning, Joe doubled and Dom singled him home. In the 1949 All-Star Game, Joe drove in Dom with what proved to be the margin of victory for the junior circuit.

Dominic, or the "Little Professor" as he was called, started four different All-Star games, including the 1946 contest. That year he was voted to start in center field ahead of his brother. On the season, Dom outhit Joe by 26 points (.316 to .290).

In the 1943 All-Star Game, Vince went 3-for-3, including a ninth-inning home run. While Joe and Dom were away in the military, Vince was "maintaining the family tradition of excellence in All-Star Games."

The first time two brothers played against each other in an All-Star Game was in 1969. Carlos May of the White Sox came to bat as a pinch hitter with brother Lee of the Reds playing first base. In the 1990 midsummer classic, television cameras showed Sandy Alomar, Jr. at bat while Roberto Alomar set himself at second base, ready to field anything his brother might have hit his way. The Alomars have been teammates for the American League five times since then.

For the title of the best brother pitching combination (aside from the Fosters of the Negro Leagues), the competition is very close between the Niekros of Ohio and the Perrys of Williamston, N.C. In 1987 the ancient knuckleballing duo of Phil and Joe Niekro passed Jim and Gaylord Perry in wins. The two families remain very close in most statistical categories.

The Perry brothers had one full season as teammates—1974 with Cleveland, when the two combined for 39 victories, almost half of the team total. A year earlier, when Jim was with Detroit, the two made their only start against each other. Gaylord took the loss for Cleveland. Jim got a no-decision. In the 1970 All-Star Game the National League pitcher in the sixth and seventh innings was Gaylord Perry of the Giants. On the mound for the American League in the seventh and eighth innings was Jim Perry of the Twins. This is the only time two brothers were rival pitchers in the midsummer classic. Both have also won the Cy Young Award.

For Joe and Phil Niekro, pitching against each other was not that uncommon. It happened nine different times. The most noteworthy occasion came on Sept. 26, 1978, in Atlanta. Before this, his last start of the season, Phil was 19–17 for the Braves; Joe was 12–14 for the Astros. Houston won, 2–0, much to the dismay of victor Joe. He

loathed the idea of pitching against his brother in these circumstances.

Harry and Stan Coveleski of the coal-mining country in Pennsylvania were brother hurlers who refused to start games against each other. Stan, the younger, was in his first full season in the majors in 1916 at Cleveland while Harry was winning 20 for the third consecutive year at Detroit. Harry developed arm trouble and did not pitch another full season, but Stan went on to five 20-win seasons and a niche in the Hall of Fame.

Virtually every baseball fan has heard of the game on Sept. 15, 1963, in which Felipe, Matty, and Jesus Alou formed the San Francisco outfield for one inning. A better story about this Dominican family, however, is the race for the 1966 National League batting title.

Going into the season, Felipe, with the Atlanta Braves, had established himself as a hitter of high average and respectable power. Younger brother Matty's career so far had been disappointing. With no power, his lifetime batting average was .260. In the off-season the Giants had traded him to Pittsburgh.

With the Bucs, Matty came under the special tutelage of manager Harry Walker. "Harry the Hat" taught his pupil to chop down on the ball and to hit to left field instead of trying to pull. This, plus over 20 bunt and 30 infield singles, propelled Matty to the top of the league batting race. Second or third to him almost all year was Atlanta leadoff man and first baseman Felipe Alou. Matty won the crown with a .342 average, while Felipe finished second at .327. The elder brother, however, led the circuit in runs, hits, and total bases.

It was only fitting that Harry Walker was the cause of the enormous jump in Matty's batting average. In 1947 Harry Walker the outfielder was traded from the Cardinals to the Phillies early in the season. There he won the batting title with an average 100 points higher than the year before. This was the second batting title in the family. In 1944 older brother Dixie had led the senior circuit with a .357 mark at Brooklyn.

Brother rivalries and brother teammates come into very sharp focus under the media glare of the World Series. The Fall Classics from 1921 to 1923 featured Bob Meusel of the Yankees against older brother Emil or "Irish" of the Giants. These two outfielders were very similar in physical appearance and in capabilities.

Before the 1921 Series one writer summed up the pair:

Bob hits harder than Emil though he is not as consistent in garnering his hits. Bob also excels Emil as a thrower, but Emil is the more finished fielder. Bob is a left field hitter, and Emil often hits to right, so the play of "Meusel flied to Meusel" may be repeated frequently during the Series.

Indeed, it was so in all three Series. In Game 3 of the 1923 World Series, each brother robbed the other of an extra-base hit. Irish emerged superior to Bob in every category—even in extra-base hits. Bob, however, had the last laugh, driving in the go-ahead run in Game 6 of the 1923 World Series to give the Yankees their first world title.

For their entire careers, the Meusels startle the observer with the closeness of all their statistics. Irish averaged .310 to Bob's .309, both for 11 seasons. Bob leads in all other categories, but not by much. If Irish's totals were increased by prorating them based on his 100 fewer games, the two would look like clones. Each man led his league in RBIs one time.

Two brothers whose lifetime batting averages are identical are Bob and Roy Johnson. Both of these Oklahoma Indians hit .296 as American League outfielders in the 1930s. Bob amassed 2,000 hits and almost 300 home runs, playing mostly for Connie Mack. Elder brother Roy was a speedy singles and doubles hitter. He exceeded his brother only in stolen bases in his shorter career.

The 1927 World Series featured Lloyd Waner leading off and playing center field for Pittsburgh while older brother Paul hit third and patrolled right field. In just his second season, Paul had won the batting title. Rookie Lloyd finished second in hits and third in batting average. The two combined for 460 hits during the season and were 11-for-30 in the World Series as the Yankees swept the Pirates in four games.

The Waners played parts of 16 seasons together, much longer than any other pair. Paul hit 17 points higher in batting and almost 70 points higher in slugging. However, "Big Poison" was actually shorter than Lloyd. Paul's moniker came from all the doubles and triples he delivered.

In 1934 Dizzy and Paul Dean had the greatest year any pitching brothers have ever enjoyed. "Me 'n' Paul" together won 49 games during the regular season and all four of the games the Cardinals won from the Tigers in the World Series (as Dizzy had predicted). In 1935 their combined victory total was 47. These two 19-win seasons were Paul's only full years in the majors.

An even more memorable year in St. Louis Cardinals history was 1942. In the last week of August, the Cards were five games behind the defending champion Brooklyn Dodgers. Five weeks later the Cardinals clinched first place with a record September rush. Winning five games in the last month for a total of 22 on the season was Mort Cooper. Catching him was younger brother Walker, in his first season as a regular. Mort won his September games with great flair. He was called the "fashion plate" for wearing the number on his back that equaled the victory he was seeking that day. The Cardinals beat the Yankees in a five-game World Series to shock all of baseball.

Mort also won 20 for the 1943 and 1944 pennant winners and had a victory in each of the World Series. Both brothers were named to *The Sporting News* All-Star team in 1944. Walker hit an even .300 for three Fall Classics.

The Coopers may have been the best of the 15 brother battery combinations, but Wes and Rick Ferrell have to be a close second. Rick caught his younger brother for five straight seasons. Wes won 20 the first two years together.

The next great brother act in the World Series was in 1964, when Ken and Clete Boyer were the opposing third basemen. Elder brother Ken was the National League's Most Valuable Player with a league-leading 119 RBIs for St. Louis. Clete had hit an anemic .219 for the Yankees. Still, this was his chance to show the baseball world he was Ken's equal in the field.

Although neither hit for a high average in the seven games, both did well with the glove. Ken gave his team all its runs in Game 4 with a grand slam as St. Louis won the contest, 4–3. In the seventh game, Ken scored the first run and later homered. Brother Clete helped make the finish

exciting as he hit one of the two solo home runs off Bob Gibson in the ninth inning. Like the Coopers, the Boyers were born and raised in the "Show Me" state. Both parents were in the stands maintaining their strict neutrality and feeling great pride.

The integrity of play when brothers square off against each other has been taken for granted for many years. This wasn't always the case. In 1933 Joe Sewell, playing third base for the Yankees, and Luke Sewell, catching for Washington, found themselves on opposite sides of a hot pennant race. They had been teammates at Cleveland for a number of years.

Reporting on a crucial game in the 1933 AL race, Shirley Povich of the *Washington Post* wrote:

It was brother versus brother in the seventh when Joe Sewell made a whale of a stop and throw to cut down Luke. It's things like that help prove the honesty of baseball.

There have been five brother shortstop–second base combinations in big league history: Granny and Garvin Hamner of the 1945 Phillies, Lou and Dino Chiozza of the 1935 Phillies, Milt and Frank Bolling of the 1958 Tigers, Eddie and Johnny O'Brien of the Pirates in the mid-1950s, and Cal and Bill Ripken of the Orioles from 1987 to 1992 and again in 1996. The O'Briens were one of seven sets of twins in the majors.

Certainly an infield comprised of only two families is something of note. The Cincinnati Reds had just that in a game at the end of the 1998 season. Newcomer Stephen Larkin was playing first. Bret Boone was stationed at the keystone. Barry Larkin was the shortstop and Aaron Boone held down the hot corner.

Josh Clarke with Louisville in the National League in 1898 and George "White Wings" Tebeau of Cleveland in 1894–1895 must have felt some sense of constraint in criticizing their managers. In both cases it was a brother: Fred Clarke and Patsy Tebeau. Both pilots were regular players those seasons as well. Ed Hengle, who never played in the majors, managed his brother Moxie in the Union Association for the entry that began the season in Chicago. By the end of the campaign, both Mengels were gone, and the club had moved to Pittsburgh.

Wes and Rick Ferrell have something in common with Jesse and Lee Tannehill. In each case the pitching brother—Wes and Jesse—had a higher career batting average and more home runs than the brother who played every day.

No, Henry and Tommie Aaron were not the first "soul-brother" brother combination in major-league baseball. The game's first black siblings were Fleet and Welday Walker, who both played for Toledo of the American Association in 1884. That circuit was then considered a major league.

Fathers and Sons

Shortly after breaking into the majors, Dale Berra was asked about similarities between himself and his famous father, Yogi. The younger Berra replied, "Our similarities are different."

Like the many malapropisms of Yogi Berra, this one by his son may appear foolish on the surface, but it contains quite a bit of underlying wisdom. In fact, it can serve as a metaphor for father-son combinations in major league baseball.

Of the 149 combinations, only 50 feature both generations at the same position. There are 23 father-son pitcher combinations, five cases where both father and son caught, one where both played first, three where both played shortstop, and 18 where both father and son were outfielders. Very few fathers and sons at any position have career totals that are at all close. The only Hall of Fame father-son combination is a non-playing one, that of executives Larry and Lee MacPhail.

Another important generalization is the great increase in father-son combinations since World War II, especially in the last 20 years. The first son of a former big leaguer to break into the majors was Jack Doscher in 1903 as a pitcher for the Chicago Cubs—one of the three teams with whom his father, Herm, had toiled as a utility player years earlier. By 1945 the number of father-son combinations was 36. In 1965 the total was 66. Thus almost 40 percent of today's number has been added in the last two decades.

Is the son of a big league ballplayer more apt to develop into a major leaguer than the average boy? Some people think not. In the 1950s Hall of Famer George Sisler was asked this very question. The two-time .400 hitter shook his head over how two of his offspring had made the majors. He pointed out that baseball players are absentee fathers. They don't have much opportunity to teach their boys the fundamentals or to practice with them.

If not their fathers, perhaps other well-qualified professionals have instructed the second generation. A worthwhile study could be conducted to determine how many second-generation players who have broken in during the last two decades attended baseball camps as boys. If the number is significant, this could explain the big increase during this period.

Certainly, the Sisler family deserves special attention. Father George broke into the majors just before World War I as a pitcher for the St. Louis Browns. After being switched to first base, he spent 15 years as one of the greatest performers ever at that position. Accordingly, it is only fitting that he should have one son, Dick, who was a good hitter and another son, Dave, who pitched in the majors briefly. Dick's home run on the last day of the 1950 season, which gave the Philadelphia Whiz Kids the pennant, has given him an identity independent of his father. Also, these two men both managed in the majors for a short time. The Sislers and the Macks are the only families in which both father and son managed in the majors.

Baseball families fall into one of three categories: famous fathers only, famous sons only, and equals.

Let us consider the famous son category first. Another way of describing these men would be to call them "fathers of . . . ." Two families stand out in this category. They are the Muellers and the Walkers.

Walter Mueller was a reserve outfielder for the Pirates for four seasons in the 1920s. His son, Don, hit .296 in 12 seasons as a National League outfielder. In 1954 Mueller and teammate Willie Mays battled all season for the batting title on the pennant-winning Giants. Mays finished

first in hitting by three points, but Mueller led the league in hits with 212.

Dixie Walker was a pitcher for Washington from 1909 through 1912. His lifetime record was 24–30. Both his sons, Fred (or "Dixie") and Harry, won batting titles. These two are the only clear cases of a son of All-Star quality who had a father whose career in the majors was forgettable. Other families with "fathers of . . ." are Coleman, Grimsley, and Smalley.

In contrast, the list of "sons of . . ." is a long one. There are eight playing baseball fathers in the Hall of Fame. Averill, Berra, Collins, Lindstrom, Mack, O'Rourke and Walsh had offspring who fit this category. Four more families—Bagby, Camilli, Trosky, and Wood—had fathers of All-Star quality and sons who are footnotes to their careers. Hegan, Wills, and Trout are families where the sons had respectable careers similar to those of the fathers, but the older generation was clearly superior.

We must consider first whether some of the "sons of..." got to the majors, or second, stayed longer than they merited, because of the family name. Collins, Walsh, and Wood prove the former proposition, and Dale Berra and Marc Sullivan support the latter.

The younger Berra and Sullivan not only had the temerity to go into their father's business, but, like Bill and Cal Ripken, Jr. of Baltimore, and Moises Alou of Montreal, they had dad for their boss. The Ripkens (in 1988) and Dale Berra (in 1985) saw their fathers dismissed as managers early in the season. Moises Alou, on the other hand, voluntarily left his father Felipe's side in Montreal to sign with Florida as a free agent after the 1996 season. Cal Ripken, Sr. was not only the first father to manage two sons at once, but the first without major league playing experience to manage his sons.

Sullivan, whose father owned part of the Red Sox, traded his son to the Houston Astros organization before the 1988 season, where he could commiserate with the Berras on the difficulties of combining a baseball career with family obligations.

By far the most interesting category is that of the fathers and sons whose careers parallel each other.

The two Billy Sullivans caught for both the White Sox and the Tigers. Both played other positions as well as caught in one World Series. Sullivan Senior caught the older Ed Walsh; Junior caught the younger Ed Walsh—both at Chicago.

Jim and Mike Hegan were a father-son combination well known for defensive ability. Father Jim was a great handler of pitchers for Cleveland. Mike played first base and the outfield for several American League teams. Both appeared in two World Series. Mike broke into the majors just four seasons after his father's finale.

The father-son pitching combinations have few parallels. Both Thornton and Don Lee gave up home runs to Ted Williams. Only three families have had both father and son pitch in a World Series. Jim Bagby, Sr. pitched for Cleveland in the 1920 Series and his son for the Red Sox in 1946. Mel Stottlemyre went 1–1 for the Yankees in the 1964 Series. Todd Stottlemyre pitched for Toronto in the 1992 and 1993 World Series. In the 1995 Fall Classic Pedro Borbon, Jr. came in for Atlanta in relief. Pedro Senior pitched for the Reds in four World Series.

Joe Schultz, Jr. received some unwanted publicity in Jim Bouton's book *Ball Four,* for being Bouton's manager. Schultz and his father, Joe Senior, each spent almost a decade in the majors as reserve players. Senior was 46-for-170 as a pinch hitter. Junior went 43-for-160 in that same role.

It is only fitting that Buddy Bell spent a portion of his fine career with the Cincinnati Reds, the team on which his father Gus spent his best years. The two ended their careers with nearly identical batting averages and home run totals.

Ten father-son combinations have played in All-Star Games. Prior to 1990 only the Bell, Boone, Tresh, and Hegan families could have made that boast. Then Barry Bonds, Ken Griffey, Jr., both Alomar sons, Todd Hundley, and Moises Alou made their debuts in the midsummer classic. The senior Tresh and the junior Hegan were named to the All-Star squads but did not play. The Bells and Boones have similar statistics. Gus was 2-for-6, hitting a home run his first time up; Buddy was 1-for-7, hitting a triple in his first plate appearance. Ray Boone went 1-for-5 in All-Star games with a homer; Bob was 2-for-5 in three games.

Both Griffeys have been Most Valuable Player in an All-Star Game: Senior in 1980 and Junior in 1992. Currently the Seattle center fielder is 10-for-21 in the midsummer classic. His father was 5-for-7 in three games. Each has a home run to his credit. Barry Bonds is now 5-for-20 in All-Star competition. His father, Bobby, went 2-for-6 in three contests and was MVP in 1972.

Felipe Alou may have had some feelings of regret mixed with the great pride he felt when his son Moises drove in the winning run in the 1994 All-Star Game. Felipe's one appearance was in 1968. He played one inning in left field and did not have an official time at bat. In the 1996 game Mets catcher Todd Hundley went 0-for-1 to become the 10th combination. His father, Randy, went 0-for-1 in the 1969 game.

In Game 2 of the 1984 World Series, a two-run double by San Diego catcher Terry Kennedy was noted by the television announcers as something significant. This was the first time in the history of the Fall Classic that both a father and son had a World Series RBI. Terry's father, Bob, knocked in a run for Cleveland as an outfielder in the 1948 Series. There have been eight families in which the father and son both played in a World Series. Five have been mentioned already; there is also Ernie and Don Johnson. The father was a substitute infielder for the Yankees in the 1923 Series. Don was the regular second baseman for the Cubs in the 1945 Series. Stan Javier in 1988 and 1989 with Oakland makes seven; his father, Julian, played in four World Series. The latest combination is Felipe and Moises Alou. In 1962, Felipe played all seven games for the Giants, hitting .269. In the '97 Series, Moises hit .321 with three homers and nine RBIs.

Career statistics for the Bonds family deserve special attention. Since the last edition of this book Barry has passed his father in every category except stolen bases. Perhaps Bobby will be remembered as "the father of. . .".

The Bondses are not the first black father-son combination in major league history. That honor goes to the Hairstons. Father Sam played in two games for the Chicago White Sox in 1951. Son Jerry was a respected pinch hitter for that team for over a decade. Grandson Jerry

made his major league debut with the Baltimore Orioles in 1998.

In September 1990 Ken Griffey, Sr. took a place in the Seattle Mariners outfield next to his son. Late in the 1992 season, Bret Boone made his major league debut as the Seattle second baseman to give baseball its first three-generation family. Bret's father was Bob Boone and his grandfather was Ray Boone. In 1995 David Bell, son of Buddy and grandson of Gus, made his major league debut

for the second three-generation family. The Hairston family makes three. Of less significance, but of great sentimental value for Cincinnati Reds fans, was an event that occurred in September 1997. Pete Rose, Jr. played third base for a few games. More than once he threw out hitters at first base to Eduardo Perez. Pete Senior had done that many times with Tony Perez in the city's glory days in the 1970s.

Brothers' Combined Totals (*Still active)

Seasons		Games		Hits		Doubles		Triples	
Alou	47	Alou	5,129	Waner	5,611	DiMaggio	906	Waner	308
Niekro	46	Waner	4,541	Alou	5,094	Waner	884	Delahanty	280
Delahanty	41	DiMaggio	4,245	DiMaggio	4,853	Delahanty	769	Wagner	256
Perry	39	Boyer	3,872	Delahanty	4,211	Alou	765	Clarke	233
Waner	38	Aaron	3,735	Aaron	3,987	Sewell	709	Connor	225
Boyer	36	*Ripken	3,616	Sewell	3,619	Johnson	671	DiMaggio	212
Sewell	35	Delahanty	3,595	*Ripken 3,552 Boyer	3,559	Murray	668	Johnson	178
Brett	35	Sewell	3,532	Wagner	3,489	*Ripken	665	Ewing	178
DiMaggio	34	May	3,236	Murray	3,345	Wagner	658	Wheat	177
Ferrell	33	Cruz	3,077	Johnson	3,343				
Forsch	32	Johnson	3,016	Brett	3,245				
				Meusel	3,214				
				*Gwynn	3,191				

Home Runs		Runs		RBI		Batting Average (10 seasons)		Steals	
Aaron	768	DiMaggio	2,927	DiMaggio	2,739	*Gwynn	.331	Wagner	726
DiMaggio	573	Waner	2,827	Aaron	2,391	Manush	.329	Delahanty	685
Murray	511	Delahanty	2,309	Delahanty	2,153	Wagner	.326	*Nixon	603
Boyer	444	Aaron	2,276	Murray	1,939	Waner	.325	Clarke	557
May	444	Alou	2,213	Waner	1,907	Connor	.314	Milan	501
Nettles	406	Johnson	1,956	Meusel	1,887	Delahanty	.311	Sax	444
*Ripken	404	*Ripken	1,797	Johnson	1,839	Meusel	.309	*Alomar	362
Allen	358	Sewell	1,794	Boyer	1,803	Wheat	.309	Cruz	322
Johnson	346	Wagner	1,762	May	1,780	Clarke	.308	*Gwynn	313
Brett	327	Boyer	1,761	Wagner	1,750	O'Rourke	.308	Alou	294
		Clarke	1,744	*Ripken	1,743	Kell	.304	Yount	271
						Brett	.303	Meusel	253
								Yount	271
								Meusel	253
								Moriarty	250
								Aaron	249

Brother Pitching Totals

Games		Innings		Wins		Losses		Strikeouts		Shutouts		Complete Games	
Niekro	1,566	Niekro	8,988	Niekro	539	Niekro	478	Perry	5,110	Perry	85	Clarkson	571
Perry	1,407	Perry	8,637	Perry	529	Perry	439	Niekro	5,089	Niekro	74	Weyhing	455
Forsch	1,019	Clarkson	5,616	Clarkson	383	Forsch	249	*Martinez	2,536	Coveleski	51	Mathewson	436
McDaniel	1,006	Forsch	4,921	Coveleski	296	Weyhing	239	*Maddux	2,526	Clarkson	43	Perry	412
Maddux	801	Mathewson	4,793	Forsch	282	Clarkson	232	Mathewson	2,504	Forsch	37	Niekro	352
Reuschel	755	Reuschel	3,865					Clarkson	2,326			Coveleski	308
								*Maddux	2,210				

Father-Son Hitters

	Years	Games	Runs	Hits	Homers	RBI	BA	Steals		Years	Games	Runs	Hits	Homers	RBI	BA	Steals
ALOMAR									**BONDS**								
Sandy, Sr.	15	1,481	588	1,168	13	282	.245	227	Bobby	14	1,849	1,258	1,886	332	1,024	.268	461
Roberto	11	1,563	979	1,825	137	709	.301	330	Barry	13	1,898	1,364	1,918	411	1,212	.289	445
Sandy, Jr.	11	853	353	803	80	392	.273	22	**BOONE**								
ALOU									Ray	13	1,373	645	1,260	151	737	.275	21
Felipe	17	2,082	985	2,101	206	852	.286	107	Bob	19	2,264	679	1,838	105	826	.254	38
Moises	8	919	535	966	145	612	.295	73	Bret	7	793	340	727	86	399	.255	25
AVERILL									**CAMILLI**								
Earl, Sr.	13	1,669	1,224	2,020	238	1,165	.318	69	Dolf	12	1,490	936	1,482	239	950	.277	60
Earl, Jr.	9	449	137	249	44	159	.242	3	Doug	9	313	56	153	18	80	.199	0
BELL									**GRIFFEY**								
Gus	15	1,741	865	1,823	206	942	.281	30	Ken, Sr.	19	2,090	1,129	2,143	152	859	.296	200
Buddy	18	2,405	1,150	2,514	201	1,106	.279	55	Ken, Jr.	10	1,375	940	1,596	350	1,018	.300	143
BERRA									**HEGAN**								
Yogi	19	2,120	1,175	2,150	358	1,430	.285	30	Jim	17	1,666	550	1,087	92	525	.228	15
Dale	11	853	236	603	49	278	.236	32	Mike	12	965	281	504	53	229	.242	28

	Years	Games	Runs	Hits	Homers	RBI	BA	Steals
HUNDLEY								
Randy	14	1,061	311	813	82	381	.236	12
Todd	9	829	340	612	124	397	.240	11
KENNEDY								
Bob	16	1,483	514	1,176	63	514	.254	45
Terry	14	1,491	474	1,313	113	628	.264	6
McRAE								
Hal	19	2,084	940	2,091	191	1,097	.290	109
Brian	9	1,220	687	1,248	91	484	.264	194
SCHOFIELD								
Ducky	19	1,321	394	699	21	211	.227	12
Dick	13	1,355	502	985	56	353	.230	119
SISLER								
George	15	2,055	1,283	2,812	99	1,175	.340	375
Dick	8	799	302	720	55	360	.276	6

	Years	Games	Runs	Hits	Homers	RBI	BA	Steals
SMALLEY								
Roy, Jr.	11	872	277	601	61	305	.227	4
Roy, III	13	1,653	745	1,454	163	694	.257	27
SULLIVAN								
Billy, Sr.	16	1,146	363	777	20	378	.212	98
Billy, Jr.	12	962	347	820	29	388	.289	30
TRESH								
Mike	12	1,027	326	788	2	297	.249	19
Tom	9	1,192	595	1,041	153	530	.245	45
WILLS								
Maury	14	1,942	1,067	2,134	20	458	.281	586
Bump	6	831	472	807	36	302	.266	196

Father-Son Pitchers

	Years	Games	W–L	SO	CG	ERA
BAGBY						
Jim, Sr.	9	316	127–89	450	132	3.10
Jim, Jr.	10	303	97–96	431	84	3.96
COLEMAN						
Joe, Sr.	10	223	52–76	444	60	4.38
Joe, Jr.	15	484	142–135	1,728	94	3.69
KRAUSSE						
Lew, Sr.	2	23	5–1	17	3	4.48
Lew, Jr.	12	321	68–91	721	21	4.00
LEE						
Thornton	16	374	117–124	937	155	3.56
Don	9	244	40–44	467	13	3.61
PILLETTE						
Herman	4	107	34–32	148	33	3.45
Duane	8	188	38–66	305	34	4.40

	Years	Games	W–L	SO	CG	ERA
QUEEN						
Mel, Sr.	8	146	27–40	328	15	5.09
Mel, Jr.	9	140	20–17	302	6	3.14
SISLER						
George	7	24	5–6	63	9	2.35
Dave	7	247	38–44	355	12	4.33
STOTTLEMYRE						
Mel, Sr.	11	360	164–139	1,257	152	2.97
Todd	11	332	123–110	1,425	34	4.23
TROUT						
Paul	15	521	170–161	1,256	158	3.23
Steve	12	301	88–92	656	32	4.18
WALSH						
Ed, Sr.	14	430	195–126	2,346	250	1.82
Ed, Jr.	4	79	11–24	107	15	5.57
WRIGHT						
Clyde	10	329	100–111	667	67	3.50
Jaret	2	48	20–13	203	1	4.61

Baseball Families

KEY

tm teammates
F-S father-son

BROTHERS

AARON   Henry & Tommie *tm*
ACOSTA   Jose & Merito
ADAMS   Bobby & Dick *F-S also*
ALLEN   Dick, Hank & Ron *tm*
ALLISON   Art & Doug *tm*
ALOMAR   Roberto & Sandy Jr. *tm*
ALOU   Felipe, Matty & Jesus *tm*
ANDERSON   Kent & Mike
ANDREWS   Rob & Mike
ARMAS   Tony & Marcos
ASPROMONTE   Bob & Ken

BAILEY   Ed & Jim *tm*
BAKER   Dave & Doug
BANDO   Chris & Sal
BANNON   Jimmy & Tom
BARNES   Jesse & Virgil *tm*
BARRETT   Marty & Tom
BAXES   Jim & Mike
BELL   Charlie & Frank
BELL   George & Juan
BENES   Alan & Andy *tm*
BENNETT   Dave & Dennis *tm*
BERGEN   Bill & Marty
BIGBEE   Carson & Lyle *tm*
BLANKENSHIP   Homer & Ted *tm*
BLUEGE   Ossie & Otto
BOLLING   Frank & Milt *tm*
BOONE   Danny & Ike
BOONE   Aaron & Bret *tm*
BOYER   Clete, Ken & Cloyd *tm*
BOYLE   Buzz & Jim
BOYLE   Eddie & Jack
BRASHEAR   Kitty & Roy
BREEDEN   Danny & Hal
BRETT   George & Ken *tm*
BREWER   Mike & Tony
BRINKMAN   Chuck & Ed
BROWN   Dick & Larry
BROWN   Jackie & Paul
BROWN   Oscar & Ollie
BROWN   Curtis & Leon

BULLINGER   Kirk & Jim
BUTLER   Rich & Bob

CAMNITZ   Harry & Howie *tm*
CAMP   Kid & Llewellan *tm*
CAMPBELL   Hugh & Mat *tm*
CANSECO   Jose & Ozzie (twins)
CANTWELL   Mike & Tom
CARLYLE   Cleo & Roy
CASEY   Dan & Dennis *tm*
CEDENO   Andujar & Domingo
CHIOZZA   Dino & Lou *tm*
CHRISTOPHER   Lloyd & Russ
CLAPP   Aaron & John
CLARK   Jerald & Phil
CLARKE   Fred & Josh *tm*
CLARKE   Sumpter & Rufe
CLARKSON   Dad, John & Walter *tm*
CLIBURN   Stan & Stew (twins)
COFFMAN   Dick & Slick
COHEN   Andy & Syd
CONIGLIARO   Billy & Tony
CONNELL   Gene & Joe
CONNOR   Joe & Roger
CONWAY   Jim & Pete
CONWAY   Bill & Dick *tm*
COONEY   Jimmy & Johnny *tm*
         F-S also
COOPER   Mort & Walker *tm*
CORA   Joey & Jose
CORCORAN   Larry & Mike *tm*
COSCARART   Joe & Pete
COVELESKI   Harry & Stan
COVINGTON   Sam & Tex
CROSS   Amos, Frank & Lave *tm*
CRUZ   Hector, Jose & Tommy *tm*
CUCCINELLO   Al & Tony

DAILY   Con & Ed
DALY   Joe & Tom
DANNING   Harry & Ike
DARINGER   Cliff & Rolla
DARWIN   Jeff & Danny
DAVALILLO   Vic & Yo-Yo
DAVENPORT   Claude & Dave
DAVIS   Mark & Mike
DEAN   Dizzy & Paul *tm*
DEASLEY   John & Pat

DELAHANTY   Ed, Frank, Jim, Joe & Tom *tm*
DEMONTREVILLE   Gene & Lee
DICKEY   Bill & George
DILLON   Packy & John *tm*
DIMAGGIO   Vince, Joe & Dom
DONAHUE   Jiggs & Pat
DONNELLY   Pete & John
DONOVAN   Jerry & Tom
DORGAN   Jerry & Mike
DOWNS   Kelly & Dave
DOYLE   Brian & Denny
DRAKE   Sammy & Solly
DUGAN   Bill & Ed *tm*

EDWARDS   Dave, Marshall & Mike (twins)
ENS   Jewel & Mutz
ERAUTT   Eddie & Joe
EVERS   Joe & Johnny
EWING   Buck & John *tm*

FALK   Bibb & Chet
FARMER   Michael & Howard
FERRELL   Rick & Wes *tm*
FERRY   Cy & Jack
FINNEY   Hal & Lou
FISHER   Bob & Newt
FISHER   Chauncey & Tom
FOGARTY   Jim & Joe
FORD   Gene & Russ
FOREMAN   Brownie & Frank *tm*
FORSCH   Bob & Ken
FOUTZ   Dave & Frank
FOWLER   Art & Jesse
FREESE   Gene & George
FRIEL   Bill & Pat
FULLER   Harry & Shorty
FULMER   Chick & Washington

GAGLIANO   Phil & Ralph
GANZEL   Charlie & John *F-S also*
GARBARK   Bob & Mike
GARDELLA   Al & Danny *tm*
GARRETT   Adrian & Wayne
GASTON   Alex & Milt
GEISS   Bill & Emil
GENTRY   Harvey & Rufe
GIAMBI   Jason & Jeremy

GILBERT   Harry & John *tm*
GILBERT   Charlie & Tookie *F-S also*
GLEASON   Bill & Jack *tm*
GLEASON   Harry & Kid
GRABOWSKI   Al & Reggie
GRAVES   Joe & Sid
GREGG   Dave & Vean
GRIMES   Ray & Roy (twins) *F-S also*
GRISSOM   Lee & Marv
GROH   Heine & Lew
GUMBERT   Ad & Billy
GWYNN   Chris & Tony

HACKETT   Mert & Walter *tm*
HAFEY   Bud & Tom
HAIRSTON   Jerry & John *F-S also*
HAMNER   Garvin & Granny *tm*
HAMMOND   Chris & Steve
HANDLEY   Gene & Lee
HARGRAVE   Bubbles & Pinky
HATFIELD   Gil & John
HAYWORTH   Ray & Red
HEMPHILL   Charlie & Frank
HERNANDEZ   Livan & Orlando
HEVING   Joe & Johnnie
HIGH   Andy, Charlie & Hugh
HILL   Hugh & Still Bill
HINCHMAN   Bill & Harry *tm*
HITCHCOCK   Billy & Jim
HOFFMAN   Glenn & Trevor
HOGAN   George & Happy
HOLBERT   Aaron & Ray
HOLMAN   Brian & Brad
HOVLIK   Hick & Joe
HOWARD   Del & Ivon
HUGHES   Jim & Mickey
HUGHES   Ed & Tom
HUNTER   Bill & George (twins)

IGNASIAK   Gary & Mike
IORG   Dane & Garth
IRWIN   Arthur & John

JEFFCOAT   George & Hal
JIMENEZ   Elvio & Manny
JOHNSON   Bob & Roy
JOHNSON   Chet & Earl

JOHNSTON Doc & Jimmy
JONES Darryl & Lynn
JONES Gary & Steve
JONNARD Bubber & Claude (twins)
JORGENS Arndt & Orville

KAPPEL Heinie & Joe
KELL George & Skeeter
KELLER Charlie & Hal
KELLNER Alex & Walt tm
KELLY George & Ren
KENNEDY Jim & Junior
KEOUGH Marty & Joe F-S also
KIEFER Steve & Mark
KILLEFER Bill & Red
KILROY Matt & Mike tm
KLAUS Billy & Bobby
KLING Bill & Johnny
KNODE Mike & Ray
KNOTHE Fritz & George
KOPF Larry & Wally
KRSNICH Mike & Rocky

LACHEMANN Marcel & Rene
LANNING Johnny & Tom
LANSFORD Carney & Joe
LARKIN Barry & Stephen tm
LARY Al & Frank
LAWTON Matt & Mareus
LEITER Al & Mark
LELIVELT Bill & Jack
LILLARD Bill & Gene tm
LOBERT Frank & Hans
LOOK Bruce & Dean
LOWDERMILK Grover & Lou tm
LUSH Billy & Ernie

MACHA Ken & Mike
MACK Quinn & Shane
MADDUX Greg & Mike
MAHLER Mickey & Rick tm
MAISEL Fritz & George
MANCUSO Frank & Gus
MANGUAL Angel & Pepe
MANSELL John, Mike & Tom tm
MANUSH Frank & Heinie
MANZANILLO Josias & Ravelo
MARION Marty & Red
MARTINEZ Pedro & Ramon tm
MASKREY Harry & Leech tm
MATHEWSON Christy & Henry tm
MATTOX Cloy & Jim
MAY Carlos & Lee
MAYER Erskine & Sam
MCDANIEL Lindy & Von tm
MCFARLAN Alex & Dan
MCFARLAND Lamont & Charles
MCGEEHAN Connie & Dan
MCLAUGHLIN Barney & Frank tm
MEUSEL Bob & Irish
MILAN Clyde & Horace tm
MILLER Jake & Russ
MILLER Bing & Ralph tm
MITCHELL John & Charlie
MOFFETT Joe & Sam
MORIARTY Bill & George
MORRISON Johnny & Phil tm
MORRISSEY John & Tom
MOTA Andy & Jose F-S also
MURRAY Eddie & Rich
MYERS Billy & Lynn

NETTLES Graig & Jim
NEWKIRK Floyd & Joel
NIEKRO Joe & Phil tm
NIXON Otis & Donnell
NYMAN Chris & Nyls

O'BRIEN Eddie & Johnny (twins) tm
OGDEN Curley & Jack
OLIVO Chi Chi & Diomedes
O'NEILL Jack, Jim, Mike & Steve tm
ONSLOW Eddie & Jack
O'ROURKE Jim & John F-S also
ORTIZ Baby & Roberto tm
O'TOOLE Denny & Jim
OWEN Dave & Spike

PACIOREK John, Tom & Jim
PARKER Jay & Doc
PARROTT Jiggs & Tom tm
PASCUAL Camilo & Carlos
PATTERSON Ham & Pat
PEITZ Heinie & Joe tm
PENA Ramon & Tony
PEPLOSKI Henry & Pepper

PEREZ Pascual, Melido & Melido
PERRY Gaylord & Jim tm
PFEFFER Big Jeff & Jeff
PIERSON Dave & Dick
PIKE Jay & Lip
PIPGRAS Ed & George
POTTER Dykes & Squire

RAJSICH Dave & Gary
REACH Al & Bob
RECCIUS John & Phil tm
REUSCHEL Paul & Rick tm
REYNOLDS Harold & Don
RICKETTS Dick & Dave
RIDDLE Elmer & Johnny tm
RIPKEN Cal & Billy tm
ROBINSON Bruce & Dave
ROBINSON Fred & Wilbert
ROENICKE Gary & Ron
ROETTGER Oscar & Wally
ROMO Vicente & Romero Enrique
ROOF Gene & Phil
ROSENBERG Harry & Lou
ROTH Braggo & Frank
ROWE Dave & Jack
ROY Charlie & Luther
RUSSELL Allan & Lefty

SADOWSKI Bob, Eddie & Ted
SAUER Ed & Hank
SAX Dave & Steve tm
SAY Jimmie & Lou tm
SCANLAN Doc & Frank
SCHANG Bobby & Wally
SCHAREIN Art & George
SCHMIDT Boss & Walter
SCHULTE Herman & Leonard
SEWELL Luke, Joe & Tommie tm
SHAFFER Orator & Taylor tm
SHANNON Joe & Red (twins) tm
SHANTZ Billy & Bobby
SHERLOCK Monk & Vince
SHERRY Larry & Norm tm
SISLER Dave & Dick F-S also
SMITH Charlie & Fred
SOWDERS Bill, John & Len
STAFFORD John & Jim
STANICEK Steve & Pete
STANLEY Buck & Joe
STOTTLEMYRE Mel, Jr. & Todd
STOVALL George & Jessie
SURHOFF B.J. & Rick
SUTHERLAND Darrell & Gary

TANNEHILL Jesse & Lee
TEBEAU Patsy & White Wings tm
THIELMAN Henry & Jake
THOBE John & Thomas
THOMAS Bill & Roy tm
THOMPSON Homer & Tommy tm
THRONEBERRY Faye & Marv
TOBIN Jim & Johnny
TORRE Frank & Joe tm
TRAFFLEY Bill & John
TREACEY Fred & Pete tm
TREVINO Alex & Bobby
TWOMBLY Babe & George
TYLER Fred & Lefty tm
TYRONE Jim & Wayne

UNDERWOOD Pat & Tom
UPTON Bill & Tom

VALENTIN Jose Antonio & Jose Javier
VAN CUYK Chris & Johnny
WADE Ben & Jake
WAGNER Butts & Honus
WALKER Dixie Sr. & Ernie F-S also
WALKER Dixie Jr. & Harry
WALKER Gee & Hub tm
WALKER Fleet & Welday tm
WANER Lloyd & Paul tm
WATT Al & Frank
WEILAND Bob & Ed
WESTLAKE Jim & Wally
WEYHING Gus & John
WHEAT Mack & Zack
WHITE Deacon & Will tm
WHITNEY Art & Frank
WILLIAMS Gus & Harry
WILTSE Hooks & Snake
WINGO Al & Ivy
WOOD Fred & Pete tm
WORRELL Todd & Tim
WRIGHT George, Harry & Sam tm
YOCHIM Len & Ray

YOUNT Larry & Robin

FATHERS-SONS

ADAMS Bobby-Mike
ALOMAR Sandy-Roberto & Sandy Jr.
ALOU Felipe-Moises
AMARO Ruben-Ruben Jr.
ARAGON Angel-Jack
AVERILL Earl-Earl

BAGBY Jim Sr. & Jr.
BARKLEY Jeff-Brian
BARNHART Clyde-Vic
BEAMON Charlie-Charlie
BELL Buddy-David
BELL Gus-Buddy
BERRA Yogi-Dale
BERRY Charlie-Charlie
BERRY Joe-Joe
BONDS Bobby-Barry
BOONE Ray-Bob
BOONE Bob-Bret & Aaron
BORBON Pedro Sr. & Jr.
BRICKELL Fred-Fritzie
BRUCKER Earle Sr. & Jr.
BRUMLEY Mike-Mike
BUFORD Don-Damon

CAMILLI Dolf-Doug
CAMPANIS Alex-Jim
CARREON Camilo-Mark
COLEMAN Joe-Joe
COLLINS Ed Sr. & Jr.
CONNOLLY Ed Sr. & Jr.
COONEY Jimmy-Jimmy & John
CORRIDEN Red-John
CROUCH Bill-Wilmer
CRUZ Jose Sr. & Jr.

DOSCHER Herm-Jack

ELLSWORTH Dick-Steve
ESCHEN Jim-Larry

FLETCHER Tom-Darrin
FRANCONA Tito-Terry

GABRIELSON Len-Len
GANZEL Charlie-Babe
GILBERT Larry-Charlie & Tookie
GRAHAM Peaches-Jack
GREEN Fred-Gary
GRIEVE Tom-Ben
GRIFFEY Ken Sr. & Jr. tm
GRIMES Ray-Oscar
GRIMSLEY Ross-Ross

HAIRSTON Sam-Jerry & John
HAIRSTON Jerry Sr. & Jr.
HANEY Larry-Chris
HEGAN Jim-Mike
HEINTZELMAN Ken-Tom
HOOD Wally Sr. & Jr.
HOWARD Bruce-David
HUNDLEY Randy-Todd

JAVIER Julian-Stan
JETER Johnny-Shawn
JOHNSON Adam-Adam
JOHNSON Ernie-Don

KENDALL Jason-Fred
KENNEDY Bob-Terry
KEOUGH Marty-Matt
KESSINGER Don-Keith
KRAUSE Lew Sr. & Jr.
KUNKEL Bill-Jeff

LANDRUM Joe-Bill
LANIER Max-Hal
LAW Vern-Vance
LEE Thornton-Don
LERCHEN Dutch-George
LIEBHARDT Glenn-Glenn
LINDSTROM Fred-Charlie
LIVELY Jack-Bud

MACK Connie-Earle
MAGGERT Harl-Harl
MALAY Charlie-Joe
MARTIN Barney-Jerry
MATTHEWS Nelson-T.J.
MATTICK Wally-Bobby
MAY Dave-Derrick
MAY Pinky-Milt
McAndrew Jim-Jamie
McKNIGHT Jim-Jeff
McRAE Hal-Brian

MEINKE Frank-Bob
MILLS Willie-Art
MONTEAGUDO Rene-Aurelio
MOORE Eugene Sr. & Jr.
MORTON Guy Sr. & Jr.
MOTA Manny-Andy & Jose
MUELLER Walter-Don

NARLESKI Bill-Ray
NAVARRO Julio-Jaime
NEN Dick-Robert
NICHOLS Chet Sr. & Jr.
NORTHEY Ron-Scott

O'DONOGHUE John Sr. & Jr.
OKRIE Frank-Len
OLIVARES Ed-Omar
OLIVER Bob-Darren
OLIVO Diomedes-Gilbert Rondon
O'ROURKE Patsy-Joe
O'ROURKE Jim-Queenie
OSBORNE Tiny-Bobo

PARTENHEIMER Steve-Stan
PEREZ Tony-Eduardo
PILLETTE Herman-Duane

QUEEN Mel-Mel

RATH Fred Sr. & Jr.
RIPLEY Walt-Allen
ROSE Pete Sr. & Jr.

SAVIDGE Ralph-Don
SCHOFIELD Ducky-Dick
SCHULTZ Joe Sr. & Jr.
SEGUI Diego-David
SHEELY Earl-Bud
SIEBERT Dick-Paul
SISLER George-Dick & Dave
SKINNER Bob-Joel
SMALLEY Roy Jr.-Roy III
SPEIER Chris-Justin
SPIEZIO Ed-Scott
SPRAGUE Ed Sr. & Jr.
ST. CLAIRE Ebba-Randy
STENHOUSE Dave-Mike
STEPHENSON Joe-Jerry
STILLWELL Ron-Kurt
STOTTLEMYRE Mel-Todd & Mel Jr.
SULLIVAN Billy Sr.-Jr.
SULLIVAN Haywood-Marc
SUSCE George-George

TANNER Chuck-Bruce
TARTABULL Jose-Danny
TORRES Ricardo-Gil
TRESH Mike-Tom
TROSKY Hal Sr. & Jr.
TROUT Paul-Steve

UNSER Al-Del

VIRGIL Ozzie Sr. & Jr.

WAKEFIELD Howard-Dick
WALKER Dixie-Dixie & Harry
WALSH Ed-Ed
WARD Gary-Daryle
WHITE JoJo-Mike
WILLS Maury-Bump
WINE Bobby-Robbie
WOOD Joe-Joe
WRIGHT Clyde-Jaret

YOUNG Del-Del

GREAT GRANDFATHER-GREAT GRANDSON

Jim Bluejacket & Bill Wilkinson

GRANDFATHER-GRANDSON

George Rooks-Lou Possehl
Shano Collins-Bob Gallagher
Bill Brubaker-Dennis Rasmussen
Marty & Ed Herrmann
Ben & Jim Spencer
Lennie & Matt Merullo
Ray & Bret Boone
Bill & Roger Salkeld
Bobby Estalella-Robert Estalella

GRANDFATHER-FATHER-SON

BELL Gus, Buddy & David
BOONE Ray & Bob & Bret, Aaron
HAIRSTON Sam & Jerry & Jerry

## CHAPTER 9

Streaks and Feats

Jack Kavanagh

As every present-day reader knows, 1998 produced a fabulous year of new records and changes to be made in the long-standing text of "Streaks and Feats." Part of the purpose of this collection of epic events is to preserve the feeling of the moment for future readers as the years put space between the event and its later contemplation.

In 1998 a most wonderful moment in baseball history was reached when Mark McGwire crashed out his 70th home run in his last time at bat in the final game of the season. Stride for stride with Sammy Sosa he had overtaken the 37-year-old record, 61, of Roger Maris. Then, in a burst of accomplishment, McGwire hit five home runs in his last 11 times at bat.

Baseball, which had lost its entitlement to be called "The National Pastime," reclaimed the distinction. Fans who had been soured by the churlish behavior of some of its highest achievers, began to follow the daily exploits of McGwire and Sosa and ballparks were packed by the importance of the chase for a new single season home run record. What had been scoffed at in changes intended to expand the defense, the despised and/or lauded designated hitter rule, was not involved. Divisional play did not color the situation. Most importantly, expansion did not significantly weaken the opposition. A new team can now buy respectability by signing free-agent stars. The schedule remained at 162 games. There was no need for an asterisk.

The National League, which has never used the designated hitter on a daily basis (it has used the DH since 1997 in interleague games on the road—about eight games per NL team) provided a pair of genuine, full-time players, both of whom excelled in power hitting: Mark McGwire and Sammy Sosa.

McGwire led the pair all the way, except twice when Sosa went one home run ahead, only to have McGwire catch him less than an hour later. On Aug. 19, Sosa led for 57 minutes; with two and a half games to go, he went ahead—only to have McGwire surge back 46 minutes later. Then came McGwire's extraordinary outburst and the magic number of 70 was posted in the record books.

One never knows about the longevity of the records of a Goliath. They may fall as unexpectedly as they were achieved. Seventy may not stand the test as long as Babe Ruth's 60 endured. McGwire is, as was the Babe, the most logical player to push the mark higher. Ruth set the once unthinkable record at 54 in 1920. He moved it to 59 the next year. Six seasons later he hit a season-ending home run to reach the seemingly permanent mark of 60.

Maris streaked briefly in 1961 to erase Ruth's record.

His achievement came during an expansion season, with an extended schedule and was not a popular achievement. Still, it stood for 37 more years, and Maris' sons were grown men when McGwire embraced them to be part of his own record-breaking celebration.

The genuine good will emanating from McGwire and Sosa toward each other was as rewarding a sight as their home runs that crashed open the gates of posterity. Long after the cheering throngs finally filed out of the stadiums or turned off a TV set, the glow of a special feeling lingered. Kids were experiencing it for the first time and grown-ups were reminded of the dreamy afterglow of a teen's first kiss.

Baseball . . . once again The National Pastime . . . was back!

McGwire's 70-homer season

HR No.	Team Game	Date	Opposing pitcher, Club	Place	On Base
1	1	March 31	Ramon Martinez, Los Angeles	H	3
2	2	April 2	Frank Lankford, Los Angeles	H	2
3	3	April 3	Mark Langston, San Diego	H	1
4	4	April 4	Don Wengert, San Diego	H	2
5	13	April 14	Jeff Suppan, Arizona	H	1
6	13	April 14	Jeff Suppan, Arizona	H	0
7	13	April 14	Barry Manuel, Arizona	H	1
8	16	April 17	Matt Whiteside, Philadelphia	H	1
9	19	April 21	Trey Moore, Montreal	A	1
10	23	April 25	Jerry Spradlin, Philadelphia	A	1
11	27	April 30	Marc Pisciotta, Chicago(N)	A	1
12	28	May 1	Rod Beck, Chicago(N)	A	1
13	34	May 8	Rick Reed, New York(N)	A	1
14	36	May 12	Paul Wagner, Milwaukee	H	2
15	38	May 14	Kevin Millwood, Atlanta	H	0
16	40	May 16	Livan Hernandez, Florida	H	0
17	42	May 18	Jesus Sanchez, Florida	H	0
18	43	May 19	Tyler Green, Philadelphia	A	1
19	43	May 19	Tyler Green, Philadelphia	A	1
20	43	May 19	Wayne Gomes, Philadelphia	A	1
21	46	May 22	Mark Gardner, San Francisco	H	1
22	47	May 23	Rich Rodriguez, San Francisco	H	0
23	47	May 23	John Johnstone, San Francisco	H	2
24	48	May 24	Robb Nen, San Francisco	H	1
25	49	May 25	John Thomson, Colorado	H	0
26	52	May 29	Dan Miceli, San Diego	A	1
27	53	May 30	Andy Ashby, San Diego	A	0
28	59	June 5	Orel Hershiser, San Francisco	H	1
29	62	June 8	Jason Bere, Chicago(A)	A	1
30	64	June 10	Jim Parque, Chicago(A)	A	2
31	65	June 12	Andy Benes, Arizona	A	3
32	69	June 17	Jose Lima, Houston	A	0
33	70	June 18	Shane Reynolds, Houston	A	0
34	76	June 24	Jaret Wright, Cleveland	A	0
35	77	June 25	Dave Burba, Cleveland	A	0
36	79	June 27	Mike Trombley, Minnesota	A	1
37	81	June 30	Glendon Rusch, Kansas City	H	0
38	89	July 11	Billy Wagner, Houston	H	1
39	90	July 12	Sean Bergman, Houston	H	0
40	90	July 12	Scott Elarton, Houston	H	0
41	95	July 17	Brian Bohanon, Los Angeles	H	0
42	95	July 17	Antonio Osuna, Los Angeles	H	0
43	98	July 20	Brian Boehringer, San Diego	A	1
44	104	July 26	John Thomson, Colorado	A	0
45	105	July 28	Mike Myers, Milwaukee	H	0

46	115	Aug. 8	Mark Clark, Chicago(N)	H	0
47	118	Aug. 11	Bobby Jones, New York(N)	H	0
48	124	Aug. 19	Matt Karchner, Chicago(N)	A	0
49	124	Aug. 19	Terry Mulholland, Chicago(N)	A	0
50	125	Aug. *20	Willie Blair, New York(N)	A	0
51	126	Aug. †20	Rick Reed, New York(N)	A	0
52	129	Aug. 22	Francisco Cordova, Pittsburgh	A	0
53	130	Aug. 23	Ricardo Rincon, Pittsburgh	A	0
54	132	Aug. 26	Justin Speier, Florida	H	1
55	136	Aug. 30	Dennis Martinez, Atlanta	H	2
56	138	Sep. 1	Livan Hernandez, Florida	A	0
57	138	Sep. 1	Donn Pall, Florida	A	0
58	139	Sep. 2	Brian Edmondson, Florida	A	1
59	139	Sep. 2	Robby Stanifer, Florida	A	1
60	141	Sep. 5	Dennis Reyes, Cincinnati	H	1
61	143	Sep. 7	Mike Morgan, Chicago(N)	H	0
62	144	Sep. 8	Steve Trachsel, Chicago(N)	H	0
63	151	Sep. *15	Jason Christiansen, Pittsburgh	H	0
64	155	Sep. 18	Rafael Roque, Milwaukee	A	1
65	157	Sep. 20	Scott Karl, Milwaukee	A	1
66	161	Sep. 25	Shayne Bennett, Montreal	H	1
67	162	Sep. 26	Dustin Hermanson, Montreal	H	0
68	162	Sep. 26	Kirk Bullinger, Montreal	H	0
69	163	Sep. 27	Mike Thurman, Montreal	H	0
70	163	Sep. 27	Carl Pavano, Montreal	H	2

*First game of doubleheader. † Second game of doubleheader. St. Louis played 163 games in 1998 (one tie on Aug. 24). McGwire played in 155 games.

Sosa's 66-homer season

HR No.	Team Game	Date	Opposing pitcher, Club	Place	On Base
1	5	April 4	Marc Valdes, Montreal	H	0
2	11	April 11	Anthony Telford, Montreal	A	0
3	14	April 15	Dennis Cook, New York(N)	A	0
4	21	April 23	Dan Miceli, San Diego	H	0
5	22	April 24	Ismael Valdes, Los Angeles	A	0
6	25	April 27	Joey Hamilton, San Diego	A	1
7	30	May 3	Cliff Politte, St. Louis	H	0
8	42	May 16	Scott Sullivan, Cincinnati	A	2
9	47	May 22	Greg Maddux, Atlanta	A	0
10	50	May 25	Kevin Millwood, Atlanta	A	0
11	50	May 25	Mike Cather, Atlanta	A	2
12	51	May 27	Darrin Winston, Philadelphia	H	0
13	51	May 27	Wayne Gomes, Philadelphia	H	1
14	56	June 1	Ryan Dempster, Florida	H	1
15	56	June 1	Oscar Henriquez, Florida	H	2
16	58	June 3	Livan Hernandez, Florida	H	1
17	59	June 5	Jim Parque, Chicago(A)	H	1
18	60	June 6	Carlos Castillo, Chicago(A)	H	0
19	61	June 7	James Baldwin, Chicago(A)	H	2
20	62	June 8	LaTroy Hawkins, Minnesota	A	0
21	66	June 13	Mark Portugal, Philadelphia	A	1
22	68	June 15	Cal Eldred, Milwaukee	H	0
23	68	June 15	Cal Eldred, Milwaukee	H	0
24	68	June 15	Cal Eldred, Milwaukee	H	0
25	70	June 17	Bronswell Patrick, Milwaukee	H	0
26	72	June 19	Carlton Loewer, Philadelphia	H	0
27	72	June 19	Carlton Loewer, Philadelphia	H	1
28	73	June 20	Matt Beech, Philadelphia	H	1
29	73	June 20	Toby Borland, Philadelphia	H	2
30	74	June 21	Tyler Green, Philadelphia	H	0
31	77	June 24	Seth Greisinger, Detroit	A	0
32	78	June 25	Brian Moehler, Detroit	A	0
33	82	June 30	Alan Embree, Arizona	H	0
34	88	July 9	Jeff Juden, Milwaukee	A	1
35	89	July 10	Scott Karl, Milwaukee	A	0
36	95	July 17	Kirt Ojala, Florida	A	1
37	100	July 22	Miguel Batista, Montreal	H	2
38	105	July 26	Rick Reed, New York(N)	H	1
39	106	July 27	Willie Blair, Arizona	H	0
40	106	July 27	Alan Embree, Arizona	H	3
41	107	July 28	Bob Wolcott, Arizona	A	1
42	110	July 31	Jamey Wright, Colorado	H	0
43	115	Aug. 5	Andy Benes, Arizona	H	1
44	117	Aug. 8	Rich Croushore, St. Louis	A	0
45	119	Aug. 10	Russ Ortiz, San Francisco	A	0
46	119	Aug. 10	Chris Brock, San Francisco	A	0
47	124	Aug. 16	Sean Bergman, Houston	A	0
48	126	Aug. 19	Kent Bottenfield, St. Louis	H	1
49	128	Aug. 21	Orel Hershiser, San Francisco	H	1
50	130	Aug. 23	Jose Lima, Houston	H	0
51	130	Aug. 23	Jose Lima, Houston	H	0
52	133	Aug. 26	Brett Tomko, Cincinnati	A	0
53	135	Aug. 28	John Thomson, Colorado	A	1
54	137	Aug. 30	Darryl Kile, Colorado	A	0
55	137	Aug. 31	Brett Tomko, Cincinnati	H	1
56	140	Sept. 2	Jason Bere, Cincinnati	H	0
57	141	Sept. 4	Jason Schmidt, Pittsburgh	A	0
58	142	Sept. 5	Sean Lawrence, Pittsburgh	A	1
59	148	Sept. 11	Bill Pulsipher, Milwaukee	H	0

60	149	Sept. 12	Valerio De Los Santos, Milwaukee	H	2
61	150	Sept. 13	Bronswell Patrick, Milwaukee	H	1
62	150	Sept. 13	Eric Plunk, Milwaukee	H	0
63	153	Sept. 16	Brian Boehringer, San Diego	A	3
64	159	Sept. 23	Rafael Roque, Milwaukee	A	0
65	159	Sept. 23	Rodney Henderson, Milwaukee	A	0
66	160	Sept. 25	Jose Lima, Houston	A	0

*First game of doubleheader. † Second game of doubleheader. Chicago played 163 games in 1998 (one tie-breaker on Sept. 28). Sosa played in 159 games.

Maris' 61-homer season

HR No.	Team Game	Date	Opposing pitcher, Club	Place	On Base
1	11	April 26	Paul Foytack, Detroit	A	5
2	17	May 3	Pedro Ramos, Minnesota	A	7
3	20	May 6	Eli Grba, Los Angeles	A	5
4	29	May 17	Pete Burnside, Washington	H	8
5	30	May 19	Jim Perry, Cleveland	A	1
6	31	May 20	Gary Bell, Cleveland	A	3
7	32	May 21	Chuck Estrada, Baltimore	H	1
8	35	May 24	Gene Conley, Boston	H	4
9	38	May 28	Cal McLish, Chicago	H	2
10	40	May 30	Gene Conley, Boston	A	3
11	40	May 30	Mike Fornieles, Boston	A	8
12	41	May 31	Billy Muffett, Boston	A	3
13	43	June 2	Cal McLish, Chicago	A	3
14	44	June 3	Bob Shaw, Chicago	A	8
15	45	June 4	Russ Kemmerer, Chicago	A	3
16	48	June 6	Ed Palmquist, Minnesota	H	6
17	49	June 7	Pedro Ramos, Minnesota	H	3
18	52	June 9	Ray Herbert, Kansas City	H	7
19	55	June †11	Eli Grba, Los Angeles	H	3
20	55	June †11	Johnny James, Los Angeles	H	7
21	57	June 13	Jim Perry, Cleveland	A	6
22	58	June 14	Gary Bell, Cleveland	A	4
23	61	June 17	Don Mossi, Detroit	A	4
24	62	June 18	Jerry Casale, Detroit	A	8
25	63	June 19	Jim Archer, Kansas City	A	9
26	64	June 20	Joe Nuxhall, Kansas City	A	1
27	66	June 22	Norm Bass, Kansas City	A	2
28	74	July 1	Dave Sisler, Washington	H	9
29	75	July 2	Pete Burnside, Washington	H	3
30	75	July 2	Johnny Klippstein, Washington	H	7
31	77	July 4	Frank Lary, Detroit	H	8
32	78	July 5	Frank Funk, Cleveland	H	7
33	82	July *9	Bill Monbouquette, Boston	H	7
34	84	July 13	Early Wynn, Chicago	A	1
35	86	July 15	Ray Herbert, Chicago	A	3
36	92	July 21	Bill Monbouquette, Boston	A	1
37	95	July *25	Frank Baumann, Chicago	H	4
38	95	July *25	Don Larsen, Chicago	H	8
39	96	July †25	Russ Kemmerer, Chicago	H	4
40	96	July †25	Warren Hacker, Chicago	H	6
41	106	Aug. 4	Camilo Pascual, Minnesota	H	1
42	114	Aug. 11	Pete Burnside, Washington	A	5
43	115	Aug. 12	Dick Donovan, Washington	A	4
44	116	Aug. *13	Bennie Daniels, Washington	A	4
45	117	Aug. †13	Marty Kutyna, Washington	A	1
46	118	Aug. 15	Juan Pizarro, Chicago	H	4
47	119	Aug. 16	Billy Pierce, Chicago	H	1
48	119	Aug. 16	Billy Pierce, Chicago	H	3
49	124	Aug. 20	Jim Perry, Cleveland	A	3
50	125	Aug. 22	Ken McBride, Los Angeles	A	6
51	129	Aug. 26	Jerry Walker, Kansas City	A	6
52	135	Sept. 2	Frank Lary, Detroit	H	6
53	135	Sept. 2	Hank Aguirre, Detroit	H	8
54	140	Sept. 6	Tom Cheney, Washington	H	4
55	141	Sept. 7	Dick Stigman, Cleveland	H	3
56	143	Sept. 9	Mudcat Grant, Cleveland	H	7
57	151	Sept. 16	Frank Lary, Detroit	A	3
58	152	Sept. 17	Terry Fox, Detroit	A 1	2
59	155	Sept. 20	Milt Pappas, Baltimore	A	3
60	159	Sept. 26	Jack Fisher, Baltimore	A	3
61	163	Oct. 1	Tracy Stallard, Boston	H	4

*First game of doubleheader. † Second game of doubleheader. New York played 163 games in 1961 (one tie on April 22). Maris played in 161 games.

Ruth's 60-homer season

HR No.	Team Game	Date	Opposing pitcher, Club	Place	On Base
1	4	April 15	Howard Ehmke, Philadelphia	H	1
2	11	April 23	Rube Walberg, Philadelphia	A	1
3	12	April 24	Sloppy Thurston, Washington	A	6
4	14	April 29	Slim Harriss, Boston	A	5
5	16	May 1	Jack Quinn, Philadelphia	H	1
6	16	May 1	Rube Walberg, Philadelphia	H	8
7	24	May 10	Milt Gaston, St.Louis	A	1

8	25	May 11	Ernie Nevers, St. Louis	A	1
9	29	May 17	Rip Collins, Detroit	A	8
10	33	May 22	Ben Karr, Cleveland	A	6
11	34	May 23	Sloppy Thurston, Washington	A	1
12	37	May *28	Sloppy Thurston, Washington	H	7
13	39	May 29	Danny MacFayden, Boston	H	8
14	40	May 30	Rube Walberg, Philadelphia	A	11
15	42	May *31	Jack Quinn, Philadelphia	A	1
16	43	May 31	Howard Ehmke, Philadelphia	A	5
17	47	June 5	Earl Whitehill, Detroit	H	6
18	48	June 7	Tommy Thomas, Chicago	H	4
19	52	June 11	Garland Buckeye, Cleveland	H	3
20	52	June 11	Garland Buckeye, Cleveland	H	5
21	53	June 12	George Uhle, Cleveland	H	7
22	55	June 16	Tom Zachary, St. Louis	H	1
23	60	June *22	Hal Wiltse, Boston	A	5
24	60	June *22	Hal Wiltse, Boston	A	7
25	70	June 30	Slim Harriss, Boston	H	4
26	73	July 3	Hod Lisenbee, Washington	A	1
27	78	July 8	Don Hankins, Detroit	A	2
28	79	July *9	Ken Holloway, Detroit	A	1
29	79	July *9	Ken Holloway, Detroit	A	4
30	83	July 12	Joe Shaute, Cleveland	A	9
31	94	July 24	Tommy Thomas, Chicago	A	3
32	95	July *26	Milt Gaston, St. Louis	H	1
33	95	July *26	Milt Gaston, St. Louis	H	6
34	98	July 28	Lefty Stewart, St. Louis	H	8
35	106	Aug. 5	George S. Smith, Detroit	H	8
36	110	Aug. 10	Tom Zachary, Washington	A	3
37	114	Aug. 16	Tommy Thomas, Chicago	A	5
38	115	Aug. 17	Sarge Connally, Chicago	A	11
39	118	Aug. 20	Jake Miller, Cleveland	A	1
40	120	Aug. 22	Joe Shaute, Cleveland	A	6
41	124	Aug. 27	Ernie Nevers, St. Louis	A	8
42	125	Aug. 28	Ernie Wingard, St. Louis	A	1
43	127	Aug. 31	Tony Welzer, Boston	H	8
44	128	Sept. 2	Rube Walberg, Philadelphia	A	1
45	132	Sept. *6	Tony Welzer, Boston	A	6
46	132	Sept. *6	Tony Welzer, Boston	A	7
47	133	Sept. 6	Jack Russell, Boston	A	9
48	134	Sept. 7	Danny MacFayden, Boston	A	1
49	134	Sept. 7	Slim Harriss, Boston	A	8
50	138	Sept. 11	Milt Gaston, St. Louis	H	4
51	139	Sept. *13	Willis Hudlin, Cleveland	H	7
52	140	Sept. 13	Joe Shaute, Cleveland	H	4
53	143	Sept. 16	Ted Blankenship, Chicago	H	3
54	147	Sept. 18	Ted Lyons, Chicago	H	5
55	148	Sept. 21	Sam Gibson, Detroit	H	9
56	149	Sept. 22	Ken Holloway, Detroit	H	9
57	152	Sept. 27	Lefty Grove, Philadelphia	H	6
58	153	Sept. 29	Hod Lisenbee, Washington	H	1
59	153	Sept. 29	Paul Hopkins, Washington	H	5
60	154	Sept. 30	Tom Zachary, Washington	H	8

*First game of doubleheader. † Second game of doubleheader. New York played 155 games in 1927 (one tie on April 14). Ruth played in 151 games.

Consecutive Games Played

When the first edition of *Total Baseball* was written, the Streaks section led off with a review of Joe DiMaggio's consecutive game hitting streak. It dismissed the likelihood there would be a plausible challenge to Lou Gehrig's iron man feat of playing in 2,130 consecutive games. It seemed that among the prominent streaks, DiMaggio's was a record likely to be assaulted every season. His 56 consecutive game hitting streak loomed as an annual challenge. DiMaggio's feat had been accomplished in a season which produced largely normal cumulative stats for Jolting Joe. In no offensive category did he have a career high, and, largely due to Ted Williams' phenomonal season, hitting .406, DiMaggio led in only one 1941 category, RBIs, with 125. Surely, someone would be able to string together base hits in more than 56 games. No one has yet come close.

Compared to Gehrig's accomplishment of being in the lineup game after game, DiMaggio seemed much more likely to be challenged by someone on a long hot streak. Gehrig's challengers had already fallen short or were distant blips on the screen. Among those was a young shortstop, Cal Ripken, Jr., off to an impressive early ca-

reer, but not yet a focus for speculation to outlast Lou Gehrig for daily durability. Subsequent editions of *Total Baseball* eventually showed Ripken's name on the list. Finally, he became the only active player on that list and moved relentlessly toward Gehrig's place at the top. He became baseball's antidote to the shaky health of the national pastime.

A good portion of Ripken's charm was his blue collar identity. It takes a talented player to achieve Hall of Fame statistics. It takes a durable and determined one to show up for work every day and play baseball with workman-like technique. Ripken is a rare species in an era in which players limp onto the disabled list in droves.

Beyond Ripken's durability is a viewpoint formed by his baseball-wise father, Cal Ripken, Sr. He managed in the minors, coached, handled special assignments, and became the third base coach of the parent team. When his sons, Billy and Cal, Jr., reached the major league team, they knew most of the older system-developed Orioles. They also knew how to play the game. There are far flashier infielders than Cal Ripken, Jr. There are none whose positioning in anticipation of where a ball will be batted is so expert.

Statistics do not define Cal Ripken, Jr. as they do most players. He will forever be defined by "the streak," his 17 season appearance in the starting lineup. By September 1995 Ripken reached the once unfathomable consecutive-game record of 2,130 held by one of the game's greatest players, Lou Gehrig. The event came a few weeks after the death of the era's most charismatic player, Mickey Mantle. No two men could have approached baseball and life more differently.

In 1995 the most serious threat to his record came when the major leagues prepared to open the season with replacement players. With other members of the players union, Ripken stood firm. He would surrender his opportunity to break Gehrig's record if the American League began the season with a replacement player at shortstop. Orioles owner Peter Angelos added to the complication by refusing to sign replacement players and offering to forfeit games as a result.

When the strike was settled, a 144-game season was finally achieved and baseball's promoters began to set a probable date for Ripken to catch and then pass Gehrig. It happened, to the delight of owner Angelos and the team's stockholders and fans, at Camden Yards.

The record was tied on Sept. 5 and a new one began the next day. Ripken rose to the occasion. It was a national event, covered by worldwide television attention. He batted a combined 5-for-9 with a home run in each game. He accepted the plaudits modestly and shared the moment with the fans by circling the ballpark to shake hands with those who crowded against the railings. He endlessly answered the same questions from reporters. When he had satisfied all demands, he dressed and went home to celebrate with his father, brother Bill, and wife and children. The next day he went to work as usual. By season's end the new record had reached 2,153 games.

As Mark McGwire and Sammy Sosa were scaling new home run heights, Cal Ripken, Jr. quietly ended his own consecutive game playing streak at 2,632. It was an accomplishment comparable to breaking Roger Maris' home run record. Maris and Sosa exploded like volcanos

and Ripken had moved like an unstoppable lava flow season after season. Finally, on Sunday, Sept. 20, the Orioles' last home game, Ripken took himself out of the lineup. By acting as the 1998 season closed, he saved everyone a winter of speculation about continuing the string into 1999. Now Ripken's current ability and degree of personal interest can decide whether to play or not without resorting to subterfuge just to keep his name in the lineup.

Gehrig's Streak

On May 31, 1925, no one thought the young substitute pinch-hitting for the New York Yankees was launching the most extraordinary streak of durability the game had seen. The next day Lou Gehrig took the place of the team's star first baseman, Wally Pipp, and continued his uncertain start toward a goal so distant it was unimaginable.

Gehrig had played for Hartford in the Eastern League after the Yankees signed him off the campus of Columbia University. It was thought he would make the grade, but he had not been handed a starting job. Only when Pipp complained of a headache and was given the day off by manager Miller Huggins did Gehrig get a chance to start a game. So uncertain of the rookie's skills was management that two days later Aaron Ward pinch-hit for Gehrig and Pipp finished the game in the field.

Before June ended, Gehrig had been taken out of games three times for pinch hitters, although he continued to start games. On July 5 he wasn't even the starting first baseman. Fred Merkle, who in 1908, as a rookie himself, had failed to run to second on what appeared to be a game-winning single, started the game.

Of course at the time there was no suspicion that young Lou Gehrig had launched a string of consecutive-game appearances which wouldn't end until 14 years later. He began it as a young giant in the prime of his life and ended it a dying man, forced out of the lineup with a rare disease. From start to finish it became a matter of drama as the survival of the string became a compelling goal which Gehrig sustained despite injury, sickness, accident, and managed to avoid ending inadvertently.

Once Gehrig's penchant for never missing a game was established, just being in the boxscore was the goal. He could have simultaneously set records for consecutive games played at first base, while extending his string of boxscore appearances. However, while in the sixth year of his developing string, in a late-season game, the Yankees promoted a game in which Babe Ruth would pitch while Lou Gehrig took his place in the outfield. Harry Rice, an outfielder who sometimes spelled Gehrig late in one-sided games, played first base.

Gehrig's 2,130-game skein, stretched over 14 seasons, was not simply a matter of having him go out to first base day after day. For one thing, there were times when he could hardly play. When the Iron Horse was no longer a frisky colt, he developed lumbago, and it hobbled him from time to time. In midseason of 1934, Lou was seized by an attack and, immobilized, had to be helped off the field.

There was an acute awareness on the part of the Yankees of the consecutive games Gehrig played, and this was kept alive by the sportswriters who covered the team. Everett Scott had astonished baseball with his consecutive-game appearances at shortstop, ending a string of 1,307 in 1925, the season Gehrig, his rookie roommate, began his string. Scott had started his run of games with the Boston Red Sox, and when he was bought by the Yankees in 1923, he carried on the string without interruption. He slowed down drastically early in 1925 and was first benched, then sold to the Senators. Unlike Scott, Lou Gehrig, the Iron Horse, would never be put out to pasture. However, Scott had left a legend behind, and it served to lead Gehrig toward new standards of durability.

The day after Gehrig had been helped off the field, with his string at 1,426, and Scott's record broken, he made a contrived appearance in the lineup. Hardly able to stand, he was in the lineup of the visiting Yankees in Detroit as the leadoff batter, penciled in to play shortstop. Despite his pain, he lined out a single and, with his appearance established in the boxscore, gave way to pinch runner Red Rolfe, who finished the game at short while Gehrig took his aching back to the hotel. Jack Saltzgaver, a utility infielder who, over the years, replaced Gehrig at first base more often than any other player, filled in at first that day.

Gehrig was back in the regular lineup the next day, collecting four hits, three of them doubles. He was on his way to the only batting title he ever won and the Triple Crown for 1934. But it wasn't a pain-free future ahead for Lou. Lumbago continued to be a problem. He left games early because he was feeling ill, and he had a thumb injury in 1938 which he ignored to keep his string going.

It was during 1938 that the perpetual machine began to show signs of wearing out. For the first time he batted below .300; his stats—a .295 average, 29 home runs, and 107 runs batted in—would have pleased most players. But they were substandard for Lou, and so was his general play. Just age catching up, it was thought, just the way it had slowed Everett Scott in 1925 when Gehrig was starting out.

In spring training the next season, it was evident that something was amiss, but manager Joe McCarthy left it to Gehrig to decide when to call it quits. It was on May 2, 1939, after eight feebly played games had brought his string to 2,130, that Gehrig advised McCarthy to replace him.

The longest streak of its kind, seemingly impossible to ever exceed despite the longer seasons, ended. For 14 seasons Gehrig had played despite a broken thumb, a broken toe, back spasms, frequent colds, and recurring attacks of lumbago. He had been forced from the lineup by something no one could foresee and almost no one had ever heard about. When the tests at Mayo Clinic proved that he had amyotrophic lateral sclerosis, it was so singular an affliction that it was renamed Lou Gehrig's Disease.

He continued to carry the lineup card to home plate during the 1939 pennant-winning season, as the team captain, but soon he had to surrender even that role. On July 4, 1939, a Lou Gehrig Day was arranged at Yankee Stadium. The scene was repeated in the Gary Cooper movie and is seen often in filmed highlights of baseball history.

Babe Ruth, who had broken relations with Gehrig during a 1934 postseason tour to the Pacific and Japan,

embraced his former teammate, and the occasion came to a climax as Gehrig, a man who knew his life was nearly over, stood at a microphone, surrounded by the Yankees who had been his fellow players. He told a choked-up audience, "Today, I consider myself the luckiest man on the face of the earth." He died on June 2, 1941.

Far in the Distance

Everett Scott, whose record Gehrig had eclipsed, now is third on the list, just ahead of Steve Garvey's 1,207 games. For many years, Joe Sewell ranked third behind Scott. Sewell is best remembered for his avoidance of strikeouts. Twice he fanned only four times in a whole season. Once he went 115 games without striking out in 437 times at bat. He set his consecutive-game string with Cleveland, later moving to the Yankees where he played for three years as Lou Gehrig's teammate. He was elected to the Hall of Fame in 1977.

During the 1930s, Gus Suhr, a fine-fielding first baseman for the Pittsburgh Pirates, reached 822 consecutive games played. It was dwarfed, even as he made it, by Gehrig's string in progress, but he far exceeded earlier National League marks.

Gus Suhr's National League record was broken by Stan Musial, who played in 895 straight games, ending in 1957 at age 36. This provided a target for Billy Williams when his career with the Cubs got under way in 1963 and daily appearances were part of his routine. He sailed past Musial to claim the National League record at 1,117. He stopped in 1970, and the occasional rest did him good. He led the National League in batting in 1972 and his career ended with Oakland in 1975. He was elected to the Hall of Fame in 1987.

Williams' new National League record provided an attainable goal for Steve Garvey, who had the stamina and will power required to catch Gehrig. He just didn't get started soon enough. Gehrig was 22 when his streak began; Garvey was 26.

Also, Garvey did not become an everyday regular with the Los Angeles Dodgers until 1975, his sixth season with the team. He had been regarded as erratic at third base but, once moved across the diamond in 1974, he delivered with consistency in the field, at the bat, with power, and refused to budge from the lineup.

He left the Dodgers with his string intact after the 1982 season and took his iron man act to San Diego. A hand injury took him out of the lineup on July 29, 1983. He had broken Billy Williams' record the previous season, and all told he played in 1,207 consecutive games.

A special recognition is due to Pete Rose. Had he not paused to catch his breath during the 1978 season, when he was 37 years old, he would hold the National League record. In 1978 Rose had more realistic aims than Gehrig's too distant goal. During that season he reached the 3,000-hit mark and set aim on Ty Cobb's all-time total. He also captured the headlines with his assault on Joe DiMaggio's 56-game hitting streak.

The year 1978 was also Rose's last season with the Cincinnati Reds and, in a celebrated case of free agency, he moved to Philadelphia. There he not only resumed his climb toward Cobb's hit totals, but played again on a daily

basis. When he sat down for two games in 1978 with the Reds, he snapped a somewhat modest run of 678 games. When he finally left the daily lineup in Philadelphia, in 1983, he had run off an even longer string of 745 games. Add them together and Rose's total is 1,423 games, longer than anyone's stretch except Gehrig's and now Ripken's.

Most Consecutive Games Played

2,632	Cal Ripken, Jr.
2,130	Lou Gehrig
1,307	Everett Scott
1,207	Steve Garvey
1,117	Billy Williams
1,103	Joe Sewell
895	Stan Musial
829	Eddie Yost
822	Gus Suhr
798	Nellie Fox

Longest Hitting Streaks

Joe DiMaggio's streak of hitting safely in 56 games in a row is mind-boggling in its length, yet temptingly attainable by batters capable of hitting for high averages. And any player might get on a hot streak and sustain it long enough to challenge DiMaggio's total. However, those who have set extended streaks did it while accomplishing a high season's average. The trick is to string those games with base hits together. The more games in which a batter has hit safely, the greater the possibility these will come in succession for long stretches.

Until the New York press, wire services, and broadcast industry made Joe DiMaggio's consecutive-game hitting streak a matter of national awareness and interest, this kind of feat was not noted with a daily fanaticism. Streaks drew comment, but this was mostly reserved to be relished during the winter's Hot Stove League sessions among sport-starved fans.

Although Willie Keeler's consecutive-game string became the target for future attempts to exceed it, it might have been only one of the records made under special circumstances. Keeler's 44 consecutive games might only be unusual in retrospect because the string began on Opening Day 1897. Had "Bad Bill" Dahlen not had a most peculiar bad day on Aug. 7, 1894, even Joe DiMaggio's 56-game streak would only be a "modern record" set after 1900. As it is, Bill Dahlen appears high on the list with the 42 games in which he hit safely, but he followed up his "oh-fer" with a 28-game hitting streak.

DiMaggio was stopped by stellar infield play. Bill Dahlen was stopped by his own inability to fatten his record in a game in which almost everyone else did. Dahlen's team, the Chicago Colts, had 17 hits, winning a 10-inning game from Cincinnati, 13–11. Dahlen's blanking was more evident because it was sandwiched between the feats that day of his teammates, Jimmy Ryan and Walter Wilmot. Ryan, the leadoff batter, had five hits, three of them doubles, and Walter Wilmot, who followed Dahlen in the batting order, also had five hits, two of them triples.

Dahlen was at bat a half dozen times, but the Reds' pitchers, Chauncey Fisher and Tom Parrott, found him, uniquely that day, an easy out. Dahlen's feat was obscured when Willie Keeler, a star of greater national awareness, hit safely in 44 games three years later. The eclipsed record was simply noted but not recounted in the detail which was later paid to the strings which exceeded it. Although appearing in 121 games and batting .362, Dahlen was not a regular shortstop at that time, dividing his games between short and third.

It was Keeler's feat which caught the public fancy, particularly as it began on Opening Day, April 22, 1897, and continued for 44 games into the season. He was eventually stopped on June 18. Until then, it seemed he had found an unending series of opportunities to "hit 'em where they ain't"—his simplistic explanation for his hit totals. Keeler's record not only stood the test of time until Joe DiMaggio broke it in 1941, it still stands as the National League record. Pete Rose is the only NL player to tie it, with a highly-publicized streak in 1978.

It wasn't until 1922 that the feat of hitting successfully in successive games became a real target for seekers of new records. Keeler's streak had been regarded more as evidence of his great ability to rap out base hits than as a model of daily consistency. He was a widely admired player, the leadoff batter for the Baltimore Orioles, three times pennant winners prior to the 1897 season.

When Ty Cobb came along, the fact that he nearly equaled Keeler's mark in 1911, when he set an American League record with 40 successive games in which he got at least one hit, was also taken as a sign of his superiority, not necessarily observed as a model event.

But in 1922 the public and press were ready for new records, and they had popular heroes to set them. In 1922 both George Sisler and Rogers Hornsby created new marks in hitting safely in consecutive games. Sisler broke Cobb's American League record and Hornsby notched 33 games in a row in which he had a base hit.

This was hailed as a new record for righthanded batters, at least since 1900. Dahlen's 42 had been made before the turn of the century. While such a demarcation might be a dubious distinction, it serves to create new records. (Eventually those who are insatiable for "new records" will draw a line across some point in the twentieth century and begin proclaiming new records by ignoring those which, like DiMaggio's 56-game streak, seem unbreakable.)

Consider, too, that Ty Cobb, the American League record holder, whose 1911 mark was Sisler's target, was still quite capable of breaking his own record in 1922. Although the hit which raised his final average that year to .401 was argued about, he was still a high-average batter and needed only to string enough games together to set a new mark. Hitting safely in consecutive games was a trademark for Cobb. He hit in 20 or more games in a row seven times during his career.

George Sisler was a very popular player. A college product when the campus was not a direct line to the major leagues, with superlative skills and a gentlemanly manner, he was widely admired. In addition, his team, the St. Louis Browns, was engaged in a hot pennant battle with the New York Yankees.

Sisler began his string on July 27 and continued through August and past Labor Day, getting his base hit in game after game. Then, with his targets in sight—Cobb's American League record and Keeler's major league record, set in the National League—Sisler injured his right shoulder. It was thought at first that not only might he not be able to keep his consecutive string going, but he might not be able to finish the season.

Ironically Sisler found himself at the threshold of Cobb's record while playing against the Detroit Tigers, managed by Cobb, who patrolled center field. Sisler notched games 37 and 38 when the Tigers came to Sportsman's Park in St. Louis. On Sept. 11, struggling to keep his streak alive, Sisler tried for game 39, one short of Cobb's record.

Sisler had been granted a streak-extending single by a generous scorer on a flyball which Bobby Veach had reached but couldn't hold, but in 1922 there were no message boards or public address systems to inform fans of scorer's decisions. So Cobb, playing center field, was too far away from the press box to see the scorer hold up one finger, the traditional sign of a safe hit. He didn't know Veach's muff had been ruled a hit. As far as he knew, Sisler, coming to bat in the bottom of the ninth, with two out, a runner on first, and the score 4–3 in favor of Detroit, was hitless.

Manager Cobb had a choice. He could order Sisler, the Browns' most dangerous hitter, walked. This would move the tying run into scoring position and put the winning run on base. It would have been bad baseball and worse sportsmanship to order an intentional walk. Cobb might have been tempted to deny his rival what he thought was a last chance, but he didn't. He did take the precaution of removing Bob "Fatty" Fothergill, a slow-footed fielder, and replacing him in right with a better defensive player, Ira Flagstead. Then he signaled Howard Ehmke to pitch. He did, and Sisler lined a triple between Cobb and Flagstead. He scored the game-winning run a moment later on a Marty McManus single. Cobb had lost a game he might have won by walking Sisler, and George was within one game of tying Ty's record.

At this point Sisler's shoulder ached so much he couldn't play the next four games, a series against the last-place Boston Red Sox. It was one of those "might have been" situations. He might have set a new American League record then against the Red Sox. However, it was much more dramatically attained when the Yankees, a half game ahead of the Browns in a torrid pennant race's final stages, came to St. Louis for a crucial three-game series.

Sisler's shoulder and right arm were bandaged, and he could only swing his bat with one hand. But, he played and, in a 2–1 loss, he managed a lone hit off Bob Shawkey to tie Cobb's record. The next day, Sept. 17, the Browns evened the series as Babe Ruth's nemesis, Hub Pruett, stopped the Yankees. Ruth did get a home run, but more importantly Sisler managed another one-handed base hit to break Cobb's record.

The final game of the series was won by the Yankees as Joe Bush gained his 25th victory and Sisler went hitless in four plate appearances, never making solid contact. The Yankees left town with an increased lead they nursed to a pennant by a one-game margin. With his team still in contention, Sisler was unable to play. He pinch hit unsuc-

cessfully the next day, as Walter Johnson defeated the Browns, then sat out games until he returned to action with a hit against the Athletics on Sept. 23. He hit safely the next day, and then, in a peculiarity of the 1922 season, the whole league was idle for four days.

When the league resumed for the final Friday, Saturday, and Sunday, the Browns were unable to catch the Yankees, although George Sisler hit safely in the three final games. Leave out the pinch-hit effort against Walter Johnson, a desperate attempt by a player who, if he had been swinging with two hands, would have played the full game. Without an injured shoulder, Sisler arguably might have kept his string alive against Joe Bush. He might not have missed those four games against the pitching-poor Red Sox or the two final games against the Senators. He might have hit safely in all of those games as well as the three he added at the season's end. If he had, he would have finished the season, with no more games to play to extend his streak, with 52 games in which he hit consecutively.

The DiMaggio Streak

Joe DiMaggio was playing poorly when his epochal feat began. He wasn't thinking about hitting in 56 straight games; he was worrying about getting a hit in the game of May 15. In spring training DiMaggio hit safely in every exhibition game, a forecast of the record-setting year ahead. His momentum carried through the first eight games of the 1941 season. Then he was thrown into a slump by a junkball pitcher, Lester McCrabbe of the Philadelphia Athletics.

By mid-May DiMaggio was still floundering, hitting below .300 and without his usual authority. On May 15 he managed a scratch single. It was an unimpressive handle hit off Cotton Ed Smith of the Chicago White Sox. However, it began a streak that wouldn't end until another pitcher named Smith, Al Smith, paired with Jim Bagby, Jr., held Joe hitless in a game against the Cleveland Indians.

The well-known DiMaggio batting eye that had produced batting championships the two preceding seasons, grew sharper, although in most games he made only a single hit. There were 34 games in which the string was kept alive with a lone hit. Not only was this a precarious way to sustain a batting streak, it did not, in its opening stages, draw attention to the feat that was under way. Fans followed Joe's rising batting average but not his successive daily contributions to it. He was thought to be in a contest with Ted Williams, not with the ghosts of recordholders whose feats had been both unchallenged and unnoticed since the 1920s. He never caught Williams, who was enjoying the last season anyone would bat over .400.

As DiMaggio's string lengthened, the days of another Yankee immortal, Lou Gehrig, grew fewer. The Iron Horse, who had set another sort of consecutive streak by appearing in 2,130 games, died on June 2, as DiMaggio's skein reached 19.

As the string stretched into the 20s, reporters began digging into record books. The last time this arcane event excited interest had been in 1922, when George Sisler broke Ty Cobb's American League record but was stopped short of Willie Keeler's total. In 1938 another St. Louis Browns first baseman, George McQuinn, had run off a string of 34 games in which he had hit safely. Since McQuinn was playing in the anonymity of the second division, little attention was paid to his challenge.

Because there are two major leagues, record setters have two targets. DiMaggio was required first to set a league mark at 42 and then proceed to reach 45 and set an all-time mark by breaking Keeler's total set back in 1897.

By regarding DiMaggio first as a right-handed batter, he could challenge the closer record of Rogers Hornsby, who had hit in 33 straight games in 1922. No mention was made of Bill Dahlen's record of 1894. Perhaps the reporters assumed it had been made under different playing conditions and shouldn't count. They were wrong; the pitching distance had been established at 60 feet, 6 inches in 1893, and bunts fouled off counted as strikes from 1894. In any case, Dahlen's 42 games was less than Keeler's total, which became the ultimate target.

When DiMaggio passed Rogers Hornsby's total, the public's attention was heightened. Sisler's American League record was only a week's play away. The hype went into full swing. Les Brown's orchestra hurried a phonograph record onto the market, "Jolting Joe DiMaggio." As banal a tune as ever came from Tin Pan Alley, the song became a pep rally number as the band chanted, "Joe, Joe, DiMaggio, we want you on our side."

Bill "Bojangles" Robinson, who had tap-danced in movies with little Shirley Temple, did routines atop the Yankees dugout while he sprinkled what he called "goofer dust" to enhance DiMaggio's luck.

Despite the distractions of people pressing their attention on the reserved, unemotional DiMaggio, he continued his consistent, game-after-game pursuit of the next milestone, Sisler's league record. At the same time, he was carrying the Yankees toward a pennant. They had lost the title in 1940 after four successive world championships under manager Joe McCarthy. They were out to recapture their league's title.

Interest in Joe DiMaggio's quest went beyond the readers of the sports pages. The wire services carried stories assuring newspaper readers that Joe had extended his string with front page bulletins before they gave the account of the game in which he did it. Radio newscasts began with bulletins about Joe's progress.

Cynics and debunkers, who concentrated their suspicions on anything coming out of New York, particularly if it gave credit to the Yankees, watched closely for scoring decisions which would give DiMaggio a favored ruling.

Rival managers juggled pitching rotations to bring their best to the mound when DiMaggio and the Yankees came to town.

Dan Daniel, a prolific and conscientious sportswriter and editor, was the official scorer for games at Yankee Stadium in 1941, and he covered the team on the road for his paper. He has written extensively about DiMaggio's 56-game hitting streak. He saw every game.

The scorer's circumstances at Yankee Stadium, as described by Daniel, placed him in view of rabid Yankees supporters who gathered behind him to demand a base hit no matter how glaring the error which allowed DiMaggio to reach base.

Daniel wrote afterward that he had to have his home

phone number changed. He also insisted both he and the other scorers around the league became hyperattentive every time DiMaggio came to bat once his string had become established as a potential record breaker.

Daniel also explained that players on the opposing teams were keyed up when DiMaggio batted, none wanting to contribute to extending the string by loafing on a ball and turning it into a hit. DiMaggio's streak lifted the quality of play, umpiring, and press coverage. Everyone, including DiMaggio, wanted him to earn a new record.

Years afterward, DiMaggio looked back on the 56 games and could only find one where he wished the play had not been as judgmental as it was. It came in the 30th game, when he was still short of Hornsby's record. The White Sox came to the Stadium, and Johnny Rigney was the pitcher. He had twice been DiMaggio's victim in earlier games in the streak but on this day had stopped the Yankee Clipper until the seventh inning.

Then DiMaggio hit a routine grounder to Luke Appling. The future Hall of Fame shortstop moved for the ball, but it took a bad bounce, hitting him in the shoulder. In his rush to recover, Appling grabbed at the ball, dropped it, then threw too late. A bad-hop single? Butter-fingered retrieval? The official scorer, Dan Daniel, ruled it a hit. Lucky for Joe and fortunate for legend, too, because on his last time up, in the ninth, Taft Wright made a leaping catch to snatch a home run out of the right field stands. Joe would have been blanked.

The next day DiMaggio got another streak-extending break, almost the same way. This time the ball was hit hard and Appling could only knock it down. He couldn't make a throw. Too hard to handle? Scorer Daniel ruled so and the fans relaxed. A few days later Hornsby's record for right-handed batters would be broken and DiMaggio would be headed for Sisler's mark. However, it took another break for DiMaggio to get there.

Eldon Auker, a St. Louis submarine-ball pitcher, held Joe hitless until the eighth inning at Yankee Stadium. Unless one of the first three batters kept the inning alive, Joe, due up fourth, would not bat again. The Yankees were ahead by two runs, and it did not appear as though there would be a bottom of the ninth.

Johnny Sturm popped up, but Red Rolfe drew a walk. Tommy Henrich, the next batter, had a dilemma. He could still deprive Joe of a chance to bat if he hit into a double play. With manager McCarthy's consent, Henrich bunted and moved Rolfe to second base. Now, with first base open, it was Auker who had a dilemma. He could walk DiMaggio, hit him with a pitch (a strategy as under-handed as his delivery), or pitch to him.

DiMaggio stood at the plate, unruffled. Coolly he smashed the first pitch into left field for a double. It was a close call, but now Sisler's record was in reach.

In a Sunday doubleheader with Washington at Griffith Stadium, on June 29, DiMaggio tied Sisler's record in the first game and broke it in the nightcap. The record-tying hit came off knuckleballer Dutch Leonard and was broken with a last-chance single off the unknown Arnold Anderson. DiMaggio was two games short of tying Willie Keeler's 1897 record.

The only mark left for DiMaggio to eclipse was tied in the second game of a July 1 doubleheader with the Boston Red Sox and broken the next day.

The day DiMaggio claimed the American League record was marked by two extremes of luck. It was fortunate his record-tying hit came early in the game because a downpour deluged Yankee Stadium and the game was called after five innings. It was unfortunate that during the rain delay no one kept an eye on the bat rack. A souvenir hunter reached over the dugout and pulled out a bat. He grabbed DiMaggio's favorite club.

Although he was upset, the man who rarely showed emotion quietly borrowed a bat from teammate Tommy Henrich the next day. It was identical to his own—a 36-inch, 36-ounce bat, and Joe used it to break Keeler's record. His record-smashing hit was a prodigious home run off Dick Newsome, a 19-game winner for the Red Sox. It carried high over the head of his rival, Ted Williams, into the left field stands.

Joe DiMaggio did not rest on his laurels. Actually, with the pressure to produce at least one base hit each game lifted, he began pounding out hits in clusters. He passed the 50-game mark and his luck still held. In the 54th game, he again came up against Johnny Rigney of the White Sox. This time he would have been stopped except for a topped roller. A typical lusty swing sent a dribbler slowly toward third base where Bob Kennedy was playing fearfully deep, a precaution normally taken by rival third baseman against DiMaggio. It worked to Joe's advantage that day as he beat out the slowly hit ball for his only hit. However, it would work to his disadvantage a few days later in Cleveland.

Although Joe DiMaggio said after his streak had ended, "I wish it could have gone on forever," like all good things it had to come to an end. Joe had reached 56 games when the kind of luck which occasionally had sustained him, such as the topped roller against Chicago, turned around. The Yankees came into Cleveland and crowds came, divided between fans' wishes to witness the streak extended and hometeam rooters' hopes that their team could bring the mighty DiMaggio to a halt.

What could only be a matter of time happened. As a minor league star in his native San Francisco, 19-year-old Joe DiMaggio had been stopped after hitting in 61 consecutive games. After the 1941 streak ended, the *San Francisco Chronicle,* which had made daily reports of DiMaggio's record-breaking games, observed that the Pacific Coast League string had been ended by the son of a former major league pitching star, Bob Walsh, whose father, Big Ed Walsh, would be elected to the Hall of Fame. It was pointed out that DiMaggio's major league string was ended, in part, by Jim Bagby, Jr., another son of a successful major leaguer, a 31-game winner for the 1920 world champion Cleveland Indians.

It wasn't so much the pitching of starter Al Smith or reliever Bagby that halted DiMaggio as the glove work on the left side of the Indians' infield. Twice Ken Keltner, playing a very deep third base, took drives down the baseline and turned them into outs. And Joe's last chance found him deserted by luck on a bad bounce. A ball headed up the middle took an erratic hop, and shortstop Lou Boudreau grabbed it and flipped to second to start a double play that closed off DiMaggio's stretch of games in which he had hit safely at 56.

Although the DiMaggio streak had been stopped, he was still a hot hitter, and even his favorite bat was back.

An embarrassed fan from Newark admitted the theft and returned the bat, and Joe used it to continue his torrid hitting. He kept pounding out hits on a daily basis until he had hit safely in 16 more consecutive games. This meant he would have reached an incredible 73 games had not Keltner and Boudreau pulled off outstanding defensive plays after game 56.

As it is, hitting safely in 72 of 73 games is almost unimaginable. Historians had to go back to the overlooked Bad Bill Dahlen to find a comparable feat for DiMaggio to eclipse almost half a century later. Back in 1894, after he had run up a string of 42 games, Dahlen ran off another stretch of 28 games in which he hit safely. He had left a neglected legacy of hitting in 70 of 71 games for DiMaggio to top with 72 in 73.

During his 56-game streak, Joe DiMaggio batted .408. Although he finished the 1941 season with a .357 average, he was second to Ted Williams's league-leading .406. However, DiMaggio had led his team to a championship and this, along with the incredible feat of hitting in 56 straight games, earned him the Most Valuable Player Award by a close margin.

Those whose interest in statistics match, if not exceed, a curiosity about the drama of making them, will want to know that, in hitting .408 during the 56 games, DiMaggio scored 56 runs and batted in 55. He hit 15 home runs, half his season's total, and had 35 extra-base hits among the 91 hits he collected in 223 at bats. He walked 21 times, was hit by a pitch twice, and struck out only seven times.

Joe DiMaggio's 1941 Hitting Streak

Game No.	Date	Club and Pitcher	AB	R	H
1	May 15	White Sox, Smith	4	0	1
2	May 16	White Sox, Lee	4	2	2
3	May 17	White Sox, Rigney	3	1	1
4	May 18	Browns, Harris, Niggeling	3	3	3
5	May 19	Browns, Galehouse	3	0	1
6	May 20	Browns, Auker	5	1	1
7	May 21	Tigers, Rowe, Benton	5	0	2
8	May 22	Tigers, McKain	4	0	1
9	May 23	Red Sox, Newsome	5	0	1
10	May 24	Red Sox, Johnson	4	2	1
11	May 25	Red Sox, Grove	4	0	1
12	May 27	Senators, Chase, Anderson, Carrasquel	5	3	4
13	May 28	Senators, Hudson	4	1	1
14	May 29	Senators, Sundra	3	1	1
15	May 30	Red Sox, Johnson	2	1	1
16	May 30	Red Sox, Harris	3	0	1
17	June 1	Indians, Milnar	4	1	1
18	June 1	Indians, Harder	4	0	1
19	June 2	Indians, Feller	4	2	2
20	June 3	Tigers, Trout	4	1	1
21	June 5	Tigers, Newhouser	5	1	1
22	June 7	Browns, Muncrief, Allen, Caster	5	2	3
23	June 8	Browns, Auker	4	3	2
24	June 8	Browns, Caster, Kramer	4	1	2
25	June 10	White Sox, Rigney	5	1	1
26	June 12	White Sox, Lee	4	1	2
27	June 14	Indians, Feller	2	0	1
28	June 15	Indians, Bagby	3	1	1
29	June 16	Indians, Milnar	5	0	1
30	June 17	White Sox, Rigney	4	1	1
31	June 18	White Sox, Lee	3	0	1
32	June 19	White Sox, Smith, Ross	3	2	3
33	June 20	Tigers, Newsom, McKain	5	3	4
34	June 21	Tigers, Trout	4	0	1
35	June 22	Tigers, Newhouser, Newsom	5	1	1
36	June 24	Browns, Muncrief	4	1	1
37	June 25	Browns, Galehouse	4	1	1
38	June 26	Browns, Auker	4	0	1
39	June 27	Athletics, Dean	3	1	2
40	June 28	Athletics, Babich, Harris	5	1	2
41	June 29	Senators, Leonard	4	1	1
42	June 29	Senators, Anderson	5	1	1
43	July 1	Red Sox, Harris, Ryba	4	0	2
44	July 1	Red Sox, Wilson	3	1	1
45	July 2	Red Sox, Newsome	5	1	1
46	July 5	Athletics, Marchildon	4	2	1
47	July 6	Athletics, Babich, Hadley	5	2	4
48	July 6	Athletics, Knott	4	0	2
49	July 10	Browns, Niggling	2	0	1
50	July 11	Browns, Harris, Kramer	5	1	4
51	July 12	Browns, Auker, Muncrief	5	1	1
52	July 13	White Sox, Lyons, Hallett	4	2	3
53	July 13	White Sox, Lee	4	0	1
54	July 14	White Sox, Rigney	3	0	1
55	July 15	White Sox, Smith	4	1	2
56	July 16	Indians, Milnar, Krakauskas	4	3	3
Totals			223	56	91

The Pete Rose Challenge

The year 1978 was a tremendous one for Pete Rose, whose career with the Cincinnati Reds qualified him as a potential challenger for Joe DiMaggio's record of hitting safely in 56 consecutive games. Although he did not hit for the high averages of the other streakers who had held records—Keeler, Sisler, Hornsby, and DiMaggio—Rose batted leadoff and had amassed 10 seasons with 200 or more hits. Even more, he was the kind of player who would rise to any occasion. He loved a challenge.

Longest Hitting Streaks, NL

Player	Team	Year	G
Willie Keeler	BAL	1897	44
Pete Rose	CIN	1978	44
Bill Dahlen	CHI	1894	42
Tommy Holmes	BOS	1945	37
Billy Hamilton	PHI	1894	36
Fred Clarke	LOU	1895	35
Benito Santiago	SD	1987	34
George Davis	NY	1893	33
Rogers Hornsby	STL	1922	33
Ed Delahanty	PHI	1899	31
Willie Davis	LA	1969	31
Rico Carty	ATL	1970	31
Elmer Smith	CIN	1898	30
Stan Musial	STL	1950	30
Jerome Walton	CHI	1989	30

Longest Hitting Streaks, AL

Player	Team	Year	G
Joe DiMaggio	NY	1941	56
George Sisler	STL	1922	41
Ty Cobb	DET	1911	40
Paul Molitor	MIL	1987	39
Ty Cobb	DET	1917	35
George Sisler	STL	1925	34
George McQuinn	STL	1938	34
Dom DiMaggio	BOS	1949	34
Hal Chase	NY	1907	33
Heinie Manush	WAS	1933	33
Nap Lajoie	CLE	1906	31
Sam Rice	WAS	1924	31
Ken Landreaux	MIN	1980	31
Tris Speaker	BOS	1912	30
Bing Miller	PHI	1929	30
Goose Goslin	DET	1934	30
Ron LeFlore	DET	1976	30
George Brett	KC	1980	30
Sandy Alomar	CLE	1997	30
Nomor Garciaparra	BOS	1997	30
Eric Davis	BAL	1998	30

Before he got around to taking a swing at DiMaggio's record, Rose had, as his first order of business, the matter of making his 3,000th career base hit. He opened the 1978 season needing 34 hits to reach a plateau only 12 others had gained. On May 5 Rose reached 3,000 with a single

off Montreal pitcher Steve Rogers, before a hometown crowd at Riverfront Stadium.

Rose was only batting .267 when he got a pair of hits against the Cubs on June 14. He kept adding hits in the games he played and, eventually, it was decided he had enough in a row to start looking for a record to be broken.

DiMaggio's 56-game streak in 1941 loomed far beyond expectation. However, the record keepers had gerrymandered Willie Keeler, holder of the National League record at 44, out of the books. There was a modern mark of 37, set during the wartime year of 1945, by Tommy Holmes of the Boston Braves.

Pete Rose hustled onward and, as luck would have it, came into Shea Stadium for a series with the Mets on the verge of knocking Holmes out of the record book. Holmes was on hand to root for Rose. He was also the Mets' community relations director.

There was another reward in having Pete Rose break Holmes's record in front of the Mets' fans. In 1973 Pete had been *persona non grata* when he had wrestled on the ground with skinny shortstop Bud Harrelson in a League Championship game after a takeout slide by Rose at second base. The Mets fans remembered Rose calling them "animals" as they threatened to avenge the honor of the team by challenging the wives and children of the Reds' players in field boxes behind the Cincinnati dugout.

On July 24 Pete Rose equaled the record of Tommy Holmes and to chants of "Go, Pete, Go!" broke it the next night against Craig Swan. An appreciative Holmes,

pleased to have been a short-term celebrity, came onto the field to shake the hand of the man who had erased him from the record books. Pete now held the "modern" National League record for hitting safely in consecutive games. In fairness, he would now try to reach Willie Keeler's mark of 44, a feat turned before the century began.

Pete continued his quest. He had the skill, the competitive instincts, and the attitude to do it. He was unruffled by press attention, accustomed to it as the consequence of being the game's most colorful player of his time. Would he break DiMaggio's seemingly unreachable mark? If anyone could, Pete Rose could do it. But first he had to lay the ghost of Willie Keeler and his 81-year-old record to rest.

It was a struggle, as the whole streak had been, but Rose reached Keeler's mark on July 31 in Atlanta. His record-equalling hit came off the knuckleball pitching of Phil Niekro, a man whose own feats as a middle-aged ballplayer also merited recognition.

Keeler had been caught. Would he be passed? No. The next night a rookie left-hander, Larry McWilliams, held Pete Rose hitless through most of the game, and reliever Gene Garber provided the final denial. He struck Rose out.

Pete Rose is joined with Willie Keeler, linked now, regardless of the era when the feat was accomplished, as co-holders of the National League record for hitting safely in consecutive games.

Willie Keeler's 1897 Hitting Streak

Game No.	Date	AB	R	H
1	April 22	5	2	2
2	April 23	4	1	2
3	April 24	4	1	2
4	April 26	4	0	1
5	April 27	5	2	2
6	April 28	5	1	3
7	April 29	4	1	2
8	April 20	4	3	3
9	May 3	4	0	1
10	May 4	4	0	2
11	May 5	4	0	1
12	May 6	5	0	3
13	May 7	6	2	3
14	May 8	3	1	1
15	May 10	4	1	2
16	May 11	5	1	2
17	May 12	5	0	3
18	May 14	5	2	2
19	May 15	6	2	2
20	May 16	6	3	3
21	May 17	4	1	2
22	May 18	6	1	2
23	May 19	4	1	1
24	May 20	4	1	2
25	May 21	3	1	2
26	May 22	4	2	2
27	May 25	5	0	1
28	May 26	5	1	2
29	May 27	5	1	3
30	May 29	6	2	2
31	May 30	4	0	1
32	May 31	4	1	1
33	May 31	5	2	1
34	June 2	5	1	4
35	June 5	5	1	1
36	June 7	4	1	1
37	June 9	5	2	2
38	June 10	4	0	2
39	June 11	5	2	2
40	June 12	5	2	2
41	June 14	5	1	2
42	June 15	3	0	1
43	June 16	5	2	1
44	June 18	4	3	3
Totals		201	49	82

Pete Rose's 1978 Hitting Streak

Game No.	Date	Club and Pitcher	AB	R	H
1	June 14	Cubs, Roberts	4	1	2
2	June 16	Cardinals, Denny	4	1	2
3	June 17	Cardinals, Vuckovich, Schultz	4	2	2
4	June 18	Cardinals, Martinez	4	1	1
5	June 20	Giants, Montefusco	5	2	2
6	June 21	Giants, Halicki	4	0	1
7	June 22	Giants, Knepper	4	0	1
8	June 23	Dodgers, Hooton	4	0	1
9	June 24	Dodgers, Welch	5	1	4
10	June 25	Dodgers, John	3	1	2
11	June 26	Astros, Lemongello	4	1	1
12	June 27	Astros, Niekro	4	1	1
13	June 28	Astros, Dixon	4	0	1
14	June 29	Astros, Bannister	3	0	1
15	June 30	Dodgers, Rautzhan	4	1	1
16	June 30	Dodgers, Welch, Forster, Hough	5	1	3
17	July 1	Dodgers, Rhoden	5	0	1
18	July 2	Dodgers, Rau	4	1	1
19	July 3	Astros, Bannister, McLaughlin	5	1	3
20	July 4	Astros, Richard	4	1	1
21	July 5	Astros, Niekro	4	0	1
22	July 6	Giants, Blue, Curtis	5	1	3
23	July 7	Giants, Barr	4	0	1
24	July 8	Giants, Montefusco	4	1	1
25	July 9	Giants, Halicki, Knepper	4	1	3
26	July 13	Mets, Koosman, Lockwood	5	0	2
27	July 14	Mets, Zachry	5	0	2
28	July 15	Mets, Swan	2	2	1
29	July 16	Mets, Siebert	5	1	1
30	July 17	Expos, Bahnsen	4	0	1
31	July 18	Expos, Dues	4	0	2
32	July 19	Phillies, Reed	4	1	1
33	July 20	Phillies, Kaat	4	0	1
34	July 21	Expos, Grimsley	3	1	1
35	July 22	Expos, Schatzeder	3	0	1
36	July 23	Expos, Rogers, Knowles	4	1	1
37	July 24	Mets, Zachry, Lockwood	5	2	2
38	July 25	Mets, Swan	4	1	3
39	July 26	Mets, Espinosa	3	0	1
40	July 28	Phillies, Lerch	2	1	1
41	July 28	Phillies, Carlton	4	0	1
42	July 29	Phillies, Lonborg, Kaat	3	1	3
43	July 30	Phillies, Christenson	5	0	2
44	July 31	Braves, Niekro	4	0	1
Totals			182	30	70

Successive Pitching Victories

The 1912 baseball season produced a bumper crop of pitchers winning successive victories. Rube Marquard of the New York Giants topped everyone by running up a total of 19. This tied the record set by Tim Keefe, also of New York. Keefe had won his games in 1888, when the pitching distance was only 50 feet between pitcher and batter, but he had won them in a row and that is the measurement of this feat. The present distance of sixty feet, six inches was established in 1893, Keefe's last season.

Marquard's mark remains unmatched within the confines of a single season. The record for consecutive wins beginning in the midst of one season and extending into the next season is held by Carl Hubbell, whose 24 consecutive victories, starting in 1936 and continuing into 1937, tops the list.

However, 1912 produced more than just Marquard's record. It also produced a new American League record and an immediate challenger to it. Even while Rube Marquard was engaged in his run in the National League, Walter Johnson, almost concurrently, was setting the American League record at 16. And by the time he was stopped, another streak was under way, this one by Smokey Joe Wood of the Boston Red Sox.

No one could ask for a better matchup in 1912 than the one which brought Walter Johnson, the record holder, to the mound at Fenway Park to face Joe Wood the challenger. Johnson was the premier pitcher in the American League and its strikeout king. Wood had dazzled the baseball world while en route to a 34–5 season, with 10 shutouts. He won three more games in the 1912 World Series. Then he injured his arm and never returned to his single-season pinnacle.

Walter Johnson, himself a 33-game winner in 1912, had broken the former American League record of 14 straight, set by Jack Chesbro in 1904. By winning his 16th straight game on Aug. 23, he had set a new league mark and had his sights on the brand-new record of Rube Marquard. The New York left-hander had won his 19 by July 3. Johnson never caught Marquard.

Johnson was a victim of both bad luck and a scoring rule which today would not have cost him a loss. He lost a game in relief, taking over in the seventh inning of a tie game. There were two runners on base, and before Johnson could get the side out, one of them scored the winning run. Today the loss would be charged to the starting pitcher, Tom Hughes, who had allowed the runner to get on base. At that time the loss went against whoever was pitching when the winning run scored.

Even so, in 1912 the scorer's decision was denounced by the press and sympathetic fans. However, Ban Johnson, not only president of the American League but its iron-fisted founder, decreed the loss be placed against Walter Johnson's record, and there it remains forever. He had been stopped at 16.

When the 1912 penchant for pitchers winning consecutive victories identified the next challenger as Smokey Joe Wood of the pennant-bound Boston Red Sox, Johnson was called upon to stop him personally. The schedule brought the Washington Senators to Fenway Park to play the Red Sox, and the management was well aware they had a great gate attraction. Both Johnson and Wood had pitched four days earlier.

Whatever the capacity of Fenway Park in 1912, it was far exceeded when, on a weekday, over 30,000 baseball fans crowded the park. The crowd overflowed the stands. In fact, the players could not sit in their dugouts. Instead, they sat on chairs arranged in front of the throngs that stood just outside the baselines. Thousands more people stood in the outfield, behind ropes, reducing the area for the great Red Sox outfield to cover. Tris Speaker, Duffy Lewis, and Harry Hooper would not be able to roam back to catch deep flyballs. These would be automatic doubles if they reached the crowd herded behind the ropes.

Walter Johnson held the American League record, a string of 16 straight victories. Joe Wood had drawn nearer to Johnson's mark in his last start, beating New York on Sept. 2 for his 13th win without a loss during the streak. Today he was after his 14th straight, Chesbro's old mark, and Walter Johnson didn't want him to get it. Unless Johnson himself stopped Wood, his own record, and possibly Marquard's, were in danger.

The game lived up to expectations. Great defensive plays snuffed out rallies, and both pitchers stopped scoring threats with clutch strikeouts. A scoreless tie was broken in the sixth inning, when Tris Speaker hit a flyball that reached the roped-back crowd for a ground-rule double and Duffy Lewis hit an opposite-field double down the right field foul line. It just eluded the grab of Danny Moeller and Speaker scored. And that was it. The game ended, 1–0, as Walter Johnson lost another game in which his team failed to get him any runs. (He lost 65 games during his career when his team was shut out.)

When Wood pitched next, in Chicago, he was not in top form but held a 5–3 lead going into the bottom of the ninth. When the first two White Sox batters reached base with hits, manager Jake Stahl replaced Wood with reliever Charles "Sea Lion" Hall. A sacrifice fly made the final score 5–4, but Hall retired the White Sox without further damage and Joe Wood was within one game of tying Walter Johnson.

The Red Sox rode on to St. Louis in Pullman cars for a game on Sept. 15, and Joe Wood pitched another strong game, a 2–1 victory in eight innings to tie Johnson's record. Darkness caused the game to be called after Wood himself had scored the go-ahead run in the top of the eighth inning.

It all came to an end on Sept. 20 in Detroit. Wood failed to break Walter Johnson's mark. He went the distance but mostly on the sufferance of manager Jake Stahl. Although two of the Tigers' runs were unearned, the 6–4 final score indicated Joe Wood's fastball lacked its usual smoke that day.

The Marquard Inheritance

When Rube Marquard wrote his way into the record books in 1912, with 19 consecutive victories, he established a benchmark which has been approached but never equaled, or excelled, since that time. Although Walter Johnson's American League mark, itself never beaten, took on extra importance because of the affection and awe he inspired in baseball fans, Marquard set the standard for all others to challenge.

Just a kid pitcher, only 18, when the Giants bought him from Indianapolis where he had won 28 games in 1908, Marquard had been a disappointment. He benefited in 1911 when manager John McGraw brought Wilbert Robinson to spring training as a coach to tame the wild-throwing Rube. Robbie produced a 24-game winner. Then in 1912 Marquard began his streak with his first start of the season.

Marquard had shed the label, "The $11,000 Lemon," the year before his record-breaking string, by winning 24 games and leading the league with a .774 winning percentage. Until then he had disappointed Giant fans, who had expected another Mathewson when John McGraw paid the largest amount shelled out for a player to date. The Giant manager had purposely topped the $10,000 price tag paid for Mike "King" Kelly, the leading 19th-century gate attraction. In 1912, Marquard displaced Matty as the leading winner on the staff. While Mathewson won 23 games, Marquard led the league with 26, the first 19 of them in a row. He won his first start on April 11 and did not lose a game until July 8.

Actually, under the present scoring rules, Marquard's record would total 20 consecutive victories. McGraw inserted Rube in the eighth inning of a game at the Polo Grounds, against the Brooklyn Dodgers, which was tied at 3–3. Marquard inherited a bases-loaded situation but stopped Zack Wheat and Jake Daubert, both to become batting champions, and retired George Cutshaw, without a run being scored. The Giants won the game in the bottom of the ninth, but the rules then gave the victory to the starting pitcher.

Streakers Blurred by Time

Although it is convenient to separate the "modern era" of baseball from its ancient past at 1900, the better dividing line would be 1893. That year the pitcher was moved back from fifty feet to the still-prevailing 60 feet, 6 inches. He had been allowed to throw overhand since 1884.

Until the 1890s, teams rarely used more than two principal pitchers. More open dates existed in the schedules, and two strong-armed men could carry the bulk of the work. A third pitcher, or a general substitute, could help out in doubleheaders. However, the regular duo met most occasions and had many more opportunities to reel off long strings of victories.

When Tim Keefe set the mark at 19 straight, he required only seven weeks to do it. Between June 23 and Aug. 10, 1888, he won all his starts, 17 of them complete games. He alternated on the mound with Mickey Welch, himself the owner of an impressive winning streak. In 1885 Smiling Mickey had run off 17 in a row. That had been one less than the record Hoss Radbourn set in 1884. Pitchers in those years were capable of putting together long winning streaks.

Another contemporary, Jim McCormick of Chicago, won 14 in a row in 1885 and 16 straight the next year. When Keefe set his mark in 1888, the public was impressed but not stunned by its magnitude. After all, it only topped the recent mark of Radbourn's by one.

The New York Giants of 1888 were the toast of the town. They were led by Jim Mutrie, who had dubbed them "my Giants," marveling at the magnitude of the star play-ers. Such stalwarts as Roger Connor, Montgomery Ward, and Buck Ewing—all future Hall of Fame members—were in the lineup. Keefe and Welch, pitching in tandem, were also destined for Cooperstown and immortality. The Giants were easy pennant winners over Cap Anson's Chicago team.

Tim Keefe began his 19-game winning streak on June 23. He had lost his previous start to yet another star pitcher, John Clarkson. Also elected to the Hall of Fame, even before Keefe and Welch, Clarkson had won 13 straight in 1885.

Keefe's first win was a squeaker, 7–6, over Philadelphia. Then he marched along, and when he won his 12th in a row, his opponent was Clarkson. During the streak Tim Keefe pitched 17 complete games. The two he failed to finish included one in which he was hit on the arm by a line drive while leading, 8–3, in the sixth inning. A replacement with a name more domineering than the record he left behind, "Cannonball Eddie" Crane, held on for a 9–6 victory credited to Keefe.

The other incomplete game would not have been added to his string by today's scoring rules. On July 16, while leading Chicago, 9–0, Keefe was excused for the day after two innings. The practices of the time gave him the win.

Tim Keefe's string came to an end on Aug. 14, when his defense betrayed him and two unearned runs were the difference in a 4–2 loss. Gus Krock, of the Chicago White Stockings, was a left-handed rookie who soon disappeared from the major leagues, but he had the satisfaction of stopping Keefe at 19.

Considering the winning streaks his contemporaries had run off, it was probably thought that Keefe's record was temporary. Had it not been for the victory gained in that two-inning start, it would have been. He would have been tied with Hoss Radbourn at 18 and eclipsed when Rube Marquard reached 19 in 1912. As it is, more than a century after his feat, Tim Keefe stands beside Marquard with a total no one has surpassed.

American League Record Tied

It wasn't until 1931 that the lesser American League record of 16 consecutive pitching victories was challenged. Lefty Grove came very close to setting a new record in the American League and narrowly missed being the pitcher to break Marquard's mark of 19.

As the season advanced into August, the Athletics were virtually coasting to a pennant. They would win 107 games and distance the runner-up New York Yankees by 13 games. Grove, pitching every fourth game and appearing in relief when needed, was on his personal roll. For the first time in many years, it appeared the American League record for consecutive victories by a pitcher could be broken. It was possible to project that Grove might go on and also catch Marquard's record. There was enough time left.

Grove tied the American League record on Aug. 19 and was expected to break it four days later with his 17th straight win. The day the record co-held by Walter Johnson and Joe Wood since 1912 was to fall was Sunday, Aug. 23.

The St. Louis Browns, a second-division team and perennial victim, would provide only token opposition,

and the unheralded Dick Coffman would be the sacrificial pitching opponent. Grove pitched with close to his usual brilliance, limiting the Browns to six hits, allowing only one run, and striking out six.

However, Dick Coffman, on that particular day, out-pitched Grove and shut out the Athletics with only three hits. Grove's streak came to an end at 16 straight victories. He had only joined Johnson and Wood at the top of the American League's list.

Lefty Grove had never been a gracious, philosophical loser. He refused to accept defeat gracefully. He blamed the loss on the absence of Al Simmons from the lineup. True, Simmons was at home, in Milwaukee, seeing a doctor, and his replacement, Jim Moore, was far from being a sure-handed defensive player. When Moore mis-judged a flyball, which became the game-winning hit, Grove fumed that Simmons would have caught the ball. Further, he complained, Simmons, the league-leading batter, would surely have knocked in a few runs as well as preventing the Browns from scoring a tainted one.

Grove complained every time he was asked about the end of his streak, and the image of Simmons idling away the afternoon, thumbing through *National Geographic*s in a doctor's waiting room, persisted. Actually, Simmons had an infected ankle and had already been out of the lineup for a week.

What made the defeat more bitter in retrospect was that Grove went on to win his next five starts. These victories would have put the record at 21, eclipsing not only the American League record but topping Marquard's all-time total of 19. (Grove won his next two starts, incidentally, with Simmons still missing from the lineup.) He did not lose until the final game of the season, on Sept. 27.

Schoolboy Rowe's Row

It was only a few years later, in 1934, when the next assault was made on the American League record, now held by Lefty Grove as well as by Walter Johnson and Joe Wood. This time it was the colorful Lynwood "School-boy" Rowe, blessed with a rural candor that the press found refreshing and the public fascinating, who made the run.

Rowe had made a slow start, splitting his first eight decisions. His inauspicious beginning offered no portent that when, on June 15, he won his fifth victory, it was the start of a record-equalling skein. During the summer months Rowe shared the spotlight with Dizzy Dean of the National League. However, while Dean was garnering victories which would eventually reach 30 for the season, he did not string them together the way Rowe did.

Rowe won his 16th straight game on Aug. 26 but then ran into the barrier which had blocked other American League pitchers at that point. He joined Grove, Johnson, and Wood at the top of the list but also joined them among the frustrated who could not go past that point.

It was the second game of an Aug. 29 doubleheader, and Rowe was far off form. He was knocked out in the sixth inning. Unlike the contentious Lefty Grove, Rowe blamed no one but himself, saying without rancor that he'd just had an off day. He refused the alibi offered by his manager, Mickey Cochrane, who contended that the de-mands of the press and public on the young pitcher had produced more turmoil than Schoolboy could handle. Rowe scoffed at the idea and went on to finish the season with 24 wins. He didn't face Dizzy Dean in the 1934 World Series, but he split two decisions, as the Cardinals won a seven-game series from Detroit. Another pennant year followed for Detroit, with Rowe winning 19 games. After that a chronic arm problem hindered his career, although he lasted a long while in the major leagues, winning 158 games, with a .610 winning average, over 15 years.

Carl Hubbell's Fabulous Streak

When one adds the start of one season to the end of the preceding one, one finds a 17-game streak for Cleveland's Johnny Allen in 1936–1937 and another for Baltimore's Dave McNally in 1969–1970. But in this area Carl Hub-bell claims all the records.

In the quirky way that records for consecutive victories by pitchers seem to come almost simultaneously, the same two seasons which provided Johnny Allen's 17 straight wins, also produced one of the most fabulous feats of all time. As had been the case with 1912, there was a magic about 1936–1937.

Carl Hubbell, between July 17, 1936, and May 27, 1937, won 24 games in a row. He won his last 16 deci-sions in 1936 and added 8 more victories before losing a game in 1937.

Carl Hubbell, and the team which would support him in his quest for a record, the New York Giants, were at their best in 1936 and 1937. They were the best in the National League at a time when their crosstown rivals, the Yankees, were dominant in the American League and also in the World Series. They beat the Giants both years despite Hubbell's presence.

Carl Hubbell was the ace of the Giants staff and the National League's Most Valuable Player in 1936. He led the league in 1936 with 26 victories, an .813 winning percentage, and a 2.31 ERA. In 1937 he again topped the league in wins with 22 and percentage with .733 and added the strikeout crown with 159, his career high.

It was this kind of consistency that earned Carl Hubbell the nickname "the Meal Ticket." His manager, Bill Terry, knew Hubbell would pitch in rotation and stop any losing streak before it gained momentum.

The Giants were off to a bad start in 1936, although Hubbell was winning two of every three decisions. The day Hubbell's winning streak began, July 17, the Giants were in fifth place, barely over .500 at 42–41 and 10 games behind the defending champion Chicago Cubs. Hubbell had lost his last start, a tough two-hit 1–0 game, to the Cubs' "Big Bill" Lee. Chicago's run was unearned.

Appropriately Hubbell got the Giants back on the win-ning track by shutting out Pittsburgh, 6–0. Oddly, consid-ering the magnitude of Hubbell's record, the streak-starting shutout was the last one he pitched in 1936. He had a season-opening shutout the next year. However, low-run games predominated, and he produced an ERA of 1.95 for the run of 24 games.

Carl Hubbell's great rival was Dizzy Dean, and duels between the two were matchups between two titans. Hub-bell's lefthanded screwball was matched against the fastball of the colorful screwball of the Cardinals. These

confrontations were arranged as often as possible for their gate appeal, and Dean tried to head off Hubbell's march toward glory three times during the string.

Twice he failed gloriously and once ingloriously. During the 1936 portion of the skein, Dean lost, 2–1, in an extra-inning game and lost another 2–1 game in nine innings. These were typical Hubbell-Dean matchups, with both pitchers rising to the occasion. Hubbell, over the years, rose higher more often.

Probably in frustration, when the streak reached 22 on May 19, 1937, Dean lost both the game and his temper when umpire George Barr called a balk against Dizzy for the third time. It gave a reprieve to the batter, Giants shortstop Dick Bartell, who had flied out. He then hit a line drive which Pepper Martin dropped, and a flurry of runs followed.

Dean's retaliation was to throw beanballs at every Giant who dared step to the plate. In this pre-helmet time such tactics were not viewed kindly, and outfielder Jimmy Ripple offered to take Dean on in a one-to-one fistfight. Dean, who spent a career vainly trying to find someone he could lick, accepted the challenge. He was engulfed by Giants, topped by players in Cardinals uniforms, in what turned into one of the best displays of belligerence ever seen on a ballfield. Individual fights ranged all around the diamond. There were no peacemakers among the players. Among the few who chose to be spectators was Carl Hubbell. He had better use for his arm than swinging it at someone. When order was restored, Hubbell finished pitching a one-run, seven-hit game.

Dean protested his subsequent fine and threatened to boycott the upcoming All Star Game. As usual his threat

was unfulfilled. It would have been far better for him if he had stayed away. It was in the 1937 All-Star Game that Dean was hit on the foot by an Earl Averill line drive. He tried to pitch while favoring a broken toe and ruined a great right arm.

The end of Hubbell's streak came on May 31 at the hands of the team which considered any victory over the Giants as compensation for an otherwise dismal season. The Brooklyn Dodgers invaded the Polo Grounds for a doubleheader which drew the second-largest crowd that had ever crammed into the Giants home field.

The Dodgers had always been a tough team for Hubbell. He had beaten them five times during his 24-game streak, twice in relief, but in the opening game of the doubleheader Brooklyn closed the door on Hubbell's feat.

Carl Hubbell took the long walk from the mound to the clubhouse in center field during the third inning. Five runs had scored. There had been seven hits and three walks. In came Dick Coffman, who had been Lefty Grove's nemesis. It would have been fitting if he had stopped the Dodgers in their tracks and the Giants had rallied to save Hubbell's streak so he could extend it the next time. Neither happened; Brooklyn scored five more runs, the Giants only tallied three runs for the whole game.

Baseball records are made to be broken, and some day Carl Hubbell's mark of 26 consecutive wins over two seasons will probably fall. It might fall during the 1999 season. Roger Clemens ended the 1998 with a 15-game winning streak. Hubbell's season ending string stood at 16, and he added his first eight decisions the next year. Clemens had no decision in trying for his 16th straight on the final day of 1998.

Pitchers with 12 or More Straight Victories in Season

National League		
Year	Pitcher	Won
1888	Tim Keefe, N.Y.	19
1912	Rube Marquard, N.Y.	19
1884	Old Hoss Radbourn, Provi.	18
1885	Mikey Welch, N.Y.	17
1890	John Luby, Chi.	17
1959	Elroy Face, Pitts.	17
1886	Jim McCormick, Chi.	16
1936	Carl Hubbell, N.Y.	16
1947	Ewell Blackwell, Cinn.	16
1962	Jack Sanford, S.F.	16
1924	Dazzy Vance, Brook.	15
1968	Bob Gibson, St. L.	15
1972	Steve Carlton, Phila.	15
1998	Roger Clemens, Tor.	15
1885	Jim McCormick, Chi.	14
1886	John Flynn, Chi.	14
1904	Joe McGinnity, N.Y.	14
1909	Ed Reulbach, Chi.	14
1984	Rick Sutcliffe, Chi.	14
1985	Dwight Gooden, N.Y.	14
1996	John Smoltz, Atl.	14
1880	Larry Corcoran, Chi.	13
1884	Charles Buffinton, Bos.	13
1892	Cy Young, Cleve.	13
1893	Frank Killen, Pitts.	13
1896	Frank Dwyer, Cin.	13
1897	Fred Klobedanz, Bos.	13
1898	Ted Lewis, Bos.	13
1909	Christy Mathewson, N.Y.	13
1910	Deacon Phillippe, Pitts.	13
1927	Burleigh Grimes, N.Y.	13
1956	Brooks Lawrence, Cin.	13
1966	Phil Regan, L.A.	13
1971	Dock Ellis, Pitts.	13
1992	Tom Glavine, Atl.	13
1886	Charles Ferguson, Phila.	12
1902	Jack Chesbro, Pitts.	12
1904	Hooks Wiltse, N.Y.	12
1906	Ed Reulbach, Chi.	12
1975	Burt Hooton, L.A.	12
1992	Mark Portugal, Hou.	12

American League		
Year	Pitcher	Won
1912	Walter Johnson, Wash.	16
1912	Joseph Wood, Bos.	16
1931	Robert Grove, Phila.	16
1934	Lynwood Rowe, Det.	16
1932	Alvin Crowder, Wash.	15
1937	John Allen, Cleve.	15
1969	David McNally, Balt.	15
1974	Gaylord Perry, Cleve.	15
1998	Roger Clemens, Tor.	15
1904	John Chesbro, N.Y.	14
1913	Walter Johnson, Wash.	14
1914	Charles Bender, Phila.	14
1928	Robert Grove, Phila.	14
1961	Edward Ford, N.Y.	14
1980	Steven Stone, Balt.	14
1986	Roger Clemens, Bos.	14
1924	Walter Johnson, Wash.	13
1925	Stanley Coveleski, Wash.	13
1930	Wesley Ferrell, Cleve.	13
1940	Louis Newsom, Det.	13
1949	Ellis Kinder, Bos.	13
1971	David McNally, Balt.	13
1973	James Hunter, Oak.	13
1978	Ronald Guidry, N.Y.	13
1983	D. LaMarr Hoyt, Chi.	13
1990	Bobby Witt, Tex.	13
1991	Scott Erickson, Minn.	13
1901	Denton Young, Bos.	12
1910	Russell Ford, N.Y.	12
1914	Hubert Leonard, Bos.	12
1929	Jonathan Zachary, N.Y.	12
1931	George Earnshaw, Phila.	12
1938	John Allen, Cleve.	12
1939	Atley Donald, N.Y.	12
1946	David Ferriss, Bos.	12
1961	Luis Arroyo, N.Y.	12
1963	Edward Ford, N.Y.	12
1968	David McNally, Balt.	12
1971	Patrick Dobson, Balt.	12
1985	Ronald Guidry, N.Y.	12
1991	Scott Erickson, Min.	12
1992	Bobby Witt, Texas	12
1997	Brad Radke, Min.	12

By winning 24 games in a row over two seasons, Carl Hubbell obscured the feat of Elroy Face in 1958 and 1959 when the forkballer won 22 consecutive games, all in relief. That stands as the best achievement for a reliever. Also in 1959, Face equaled Johnny Allen's mark of 17 consecutive wins, doing it all in one season.

Face, only 5 feet 8 inches and weighing just 160 pounds, didn't lose his first decision in 1959 until Sept. 11. He had entered the game in relief and gave up the winning run in the ninth inning of a game at Los Angeles when Charlie Neal hit a single. Until then, it appeared that Roy Face was destined to never lose a game. Even when his forkball wasn't working its usual magic, he won.

A modest man, Face would point to six or seven games when the Pirates' hitters bailed him out. The most extreme of these times came in a June 11 game, when the San Francisco Giants played Pittsburgh. Face came in to protect a 7–5 lead in the eighth inning. The Giants had two men on base and Willie Mays came up as a pinch hitter. He homered and the Giants led, 8–7. In the bottom of the inning, the Pirates erupted with five runs and Face had a win instead of a loss.

During his string, Face won 11 of his games in extra innings.

Consecutive Base Hits

The feat of making a dozen consecutive base hits has been accomplished only twice in all the years major league baseball has been played. The record has rested there for over 40 years and might never see the time when a batter delivers a baker's dozen to provide a new record. The hitter who reaches 13 will cap a slow, gradual climb toward a peak shared by Pinky Higgins and Walt Dropo, both American Leaguers. The National League's record is 10.

The history of consecutive base hits goes back to 1897, when Ed Delahanty, whom you would expect to set such standards, and Jake Gettman, whom you wouldn't, each got 10 hits in a row during the season. Delahanty, one of five major-league-playing brothers, batted .377 for Philadelphia in 129 games. Gettman, who only played one season as a regular, got his 10 straight while appearing in only 36 games for Washington. He hit .315 overall. The National League record is still 10 consecutive hits, and seven others have joined the original pair.

Tris Speaker was the first to top 10, getting 11 straight hits in 1920. Speaker had eclipsed Doc Johnston's American League total of nine, hit in 1919, the same season Brooklyn's Ed Konetchy had joined Delahanty and Gettman with 10.

The next year, when Speaker moved the major league record up a notch, his feat came amid the epic record-setting of Babe Ruth's 54 home runs. This had broken Ruth's own mark of 29 set the season before. It dwarfed Speaker's rattling off 11 straight hits. In fact, Speaker's own accomplishment, leading the Cleveland Indians to a World Series victory despite the loss of shortstop Ray Chapman to a fatal beaning during the pennant chase, overshadowed his own batting feats. This included a run-ner-up .388 to George Sisler's league-leading batting average of .407.

However, Speaker's 11 straight stood the test of time. During the 1920s others made a run at the record but couldn't get beyond 10 straight hits. They included Sisler in 1921 and Harry Heilmann in 1922. Kiki Cuyler in 1925 and Chick Hafey in 1929, all future Hall of Famers, got up to 10 straight in the National League. In 1936 another Hall of Famer to be, Joe Medwick, hit in 10 straight times at bat.

One outsider who edged onto the list with those headed for baseball's Hall of Fame was a reserve catcher, Harry McCurdy. A rookie with the White Sox in 1926, he only played in 33 games, but cracked out 10 straight hits while batting .326. He might have played in more games, but he had a month's vacation in August. He was claimed by the Yankees on waivers, but when New York discovered this included an obligation for the rookie's bonus of $30,000, they refused to complete the deal. The White Sox insisted they were honor-bound. As is usual in baseball, honor lost and McCurdy remained a substitute catcher with Chicago.

Speaker's record finally tumbled in 1938, when Mike "Pinky" Higgins, the Boston Red Sox third baseman, began by going 4-for-4 against the White Sox in Chicago. The next day the Red Sox were in Detroit to play a doubleheader with the Tigers. When Higgins went 4-for-4, with a walk, against Roxie Lawson in the first game, and singled his first time up in the second game, Cal Hubbard, umpiring on the bases, observed, "That makes you 5-for-5 for the day."

Higgins told Hubbard he was 9-for-9, counting the previous day in Chicago. It wasn't enough that Higgins put pressure on himself, but after he got his 10th straight hit, the field announcer at Briggs Field, Ty Tyson, made a public address announcement that Higgins could tie Speaker's record if he got another hit the next time up.

Higgins shook off the hex and got the hit and, with everyone knowing a new record was on the line, ripped a single off Tommy Bridges, the best curveballer in the league, the next time up.

In 1952 the slugging first baseman of the Red Sox, Walt Dropo, tied Higgins' record. He had debuted in 1950 with a sensational season, hitting .322, but he never hit above .300 again. Dropo had begun the season with Boston, but in a multiplayer deal in June, he had been traded to Detroit. Going along with Dropo was Johnny Pesky, long-time shortstop for the Red Sox and, in the way of coincidences in record setting, had reached 11 straight hits, one behind Higgins's record, in 1946. Pesky was at shortstop in the games when Dropo tied him first for runner-up, a spot he now shared with Speaker. He watched as Dropo got his 12th straight.

Like Higgins, Walt Dropo made his run in a doubleheader. He had gone 5-for-5 against the Yankees in a single game on July 14, and the next day, in Griffith Stadium, he had four straight in the first game. All the hits had been singles, but starting off in the first inning of the nightcap, the powerful Dropo hit a triple with the bases loaded.

In the third inning he had his 11th straight hit, another single, and Mickey Vernon, the Washington first baseman, told him he could tie the record with a hit the next

time at bat. He did with a double. And he had another time at bat coming, in the seventh inning. Despite Dropo's hitting, the Tigers trailed, 7–6. He swung from the heels but only lifted a foul fly which catcher Mickey Grasso caught at the edge of the field boxes. The streak was over. Dropo added a single in the ninth inning but had to settle for a shared record which has stood against more recent assaults.

Ken Singleton of Baltimore got 10 in 1981, and Bip Roberts of Cincinnati managed the feat in 1992.

Most Consecutive Hits

American League

Player	Team	Year	H
Pinky Higgins	Bos.	1938	12
Walt Dropo	Det.	1952	12
Tris Speaker	Cleve.	1920	11
Johnny Pesky	Bos.	1946	11
George Sisler	St.L.	1921	10
Harry Heilmann	Det.	1922	10
Harry McCurdy	Chi.	1926	10
Rip Radcliff	Chi.	1938	10
Ken Singleton	Balt.	1981	10
Doc Johnston	Cleve.	1919	9
Ty Cobb	Det.	1925	9
Sam Rice	Wash.	1925	9
Hal Trosky	Cleve.	1936	9
Ted Williams	Bos.	1939	9
Tony Oliva	Minn.	1967	9
Jorge Orta	Cleve.	1980	9
Mickey Hatcher	Minn.	1985	9
Lance Johnson	Chi.	1995	9
Todd Walker	Min.	1998	9

National League

Player	Team	Year	H
Ed Delahanty	Phila.	1897	10
Jake Gettman	Wash.	1897	10
Ed Konetchy	Brook.	1919	10
Kiki Cuyler	Pitts.	1925	10
Chick Hafey	St.L.	1929	10
Joe Medwick	St.L.	1936	10
Buddy Hassett	Bos.	1940	10
Woody Williams	Cin.	1943	10
Bip Roberts	Cin.	1992	10
Joe Kelley	Balt.	1894	9
Rogers Hornsby	St.L.	1924	9
Taylor Douthit	St.L.	1926	9
Babe Herman	Brook.	1926	9
Bill Jurges	N.Y.	1941	9
Terry Moore	St.L.	1947	9
Dick Sisler	Phila.	1950	9
Eddie Waitkus	Phila.	1950	9
Dave Philley	Phila.	1958-59	9
Felipe Alou	S.F.	1962	9
Willie Stargell	Pitts.	1966	9
Rennie Stennett	Pitts.	1975	9
Ron Cey	L.A.	1977	9
Andres Galarraga	Col.	1993	9
Sammy Sosa	Chi.	1991	9
Barry Bonds	S.F.	1998	9
John Olerud	N.Y.	1998	9

Team Winning Streaks

The two longest winning streaks by teams had different outcomes. Twice National League clubs won 21 in a row and the pennant. When the Chicago White Stockings did it, under Cap Anson, in 1880, they were simply running away from the pack. They won the pennant by 15 games.

However, when their descendants, the Chicago Cubs, won 21 in a row in 1935, the drive capped a sensational stretch battle that enabled them to catch and pass their rivals, the St. Louis Cardinals, within a few days of the season's end.

These two 21-game streaks are not the longest on record. The record of 26 games won in a row by the 1916 New York Giants stands as the most perverse record of achievement in baseball. No other team has won so many games so convincingly to such little purpose. The Giants came in fourth, despite having had another win streak the same season of 17 straight. Even more peculiarly, the 26 games in a row were all played at home. Maybe the Giants could only win at the Polo Grounds? No. The 17 straight were all won on the road.

The 1935 Chicago Cubs' 21 straight wins carried them to a pennant, although they faced a task made tougher by the schedule. The St. Louis Cardinals, the Gashouse Gang world champions from 1934, not only led by 2 games, but the indomitable Deans, Dizzy and Paul, headed the staff. Even more comforting for the Cards, the schedule called for the Cubs to play the last five games of the season at Sportsman's Park in St. Louis.

In 1935 the Cubs picked up momentum, and it took them past the Cards in the middle of the streak. They took the lead on Sept. 14 as they won their 11th game and were three games ahead of the crumbling Cards when they reached St. Louis for the final five games. Lon Warneke beat Paul Dean in the opener, 1-0, and Bill Lee won his 20th game of the season, beating Dizzy Dean, 6–3, to clinch the pennant. It was the first game of a doubleheader, and the Cubs reached 21 straight by taking the nightcap.

They lost the next game, a meaningless one in the pennant race, in extra innings on Joe Medwick's second home run of the game. The Cards won the season's finale, 2–1, but it was the Cubs who went on to the World Series.

The next year was also a season of streaks. Again the Cubs got in gear with an impressive run of victories, taking 15 straight before midseason was reached. It did not lead to a pennant. Another 15-game winning streak, by the New York Giants, brought the championship to the Polo Grounds.

It was a streak that started late in the season and ran, in part, concurrently with Carl Hubbell's own string of 16 wins. While the Giants were racking up 15 straight, Hubbell appeared in 10 consecutive games. He never ran out of steam. The season ended with Hubbell experiencing a 16-game streak. He extended it by winning his first eight decisions the next year to reach 24 straight wins over two seasons.

Other very long winning streaks in the National League that added late-season zest to pennant races were those of the 1924 Dodgers and, of course, the 1951 Giants. The Dodgers came up short, unable to catch the leading Giants, who added a fourth straight pennant in 1924, when Brooklyn's 15 straight and Dazzy Vance's MVP season were not enough.

In 1951 the same traditional rivals reversed roles, but not results. It was the Dodgers who were far in front when the Giants, managed by former Dodgers skipper Leo Durocher, began a late-season drive. The Giants had started with the wrong kind of a streak. They lost their first 11 games and spent the season trying to catch the fast-flying Dodgers. They were 13 games behind when they won the first of 16 straight decisions on Aug. 12 and began to close the gap the Dodgers had opened.

The Giants slowly edged closer and into a tie with a

game to play. When both teams won their final games, the Dodgers on Jackie Robinson's extra-inning heroics in Philadelphia, the stage was set for a playoff series. It was won by Bobby Thomson's dramatic home run in the last of the ninth of the third, and decisive, game.

The 1906 American League season produced long strings of wins by two teams locked in a hotly contested pennant race. The Chicago White Sox set a record, since tied by the 1947 Yankees, of 19 straight wins.

Dubbed "the Hitless Wonders" because of a .230 team batting average, the White Sox engaged in a dramatic scenario with the New York team, then called the Highlanders.

In early August the White Sox were in fourth place. Ahead of them were Philadelphia, New York, and Cleveland. Day after day the White Sox chipped away at the lead held by the teams ahead of them. They eventually passed Philadelphia and Cleveland.

The Highlanders benefited from two winning streaks of their own, 11 and 15 in a row. However, in the final surge of the pennant race, it was the White Sox who came home in first place. New York became the first of only two teams (the 1912 Senators being the second) to win 15 in a row and not win a pennant in the American League. In the National League since 1900, four teams have won at least 15 in a row and not won the pennant. The most glaring example, of course, was the 1916 Giants, winners of 26 and 17 straight. The 1936 Cubs won 15 in a row and finished second to the Giants, also winners of 15 straight. The 1907 Giants had the poorest finish. Despite 17 straight wins, they finished fourth, 25 games out of first place.

Team Winning Streaks of 15 or More Games

	Tie	Team		Year	Start End	Manager	Spoiler
21	*2	CHI	NL	1880	6/02 - 7/10	Anson	@CLE(McCormick)
20		STL	UA	1884	4/20 - 5/24	Sullivan	BOS(Bond)
20		PRO	NL	1884	8/07 - 9/09	Bancroft	BUF(Galvin)
16		STL	UA	1884	8/26 - 9/18	Dunlap	@WAS(Wise)
16		BAL	UA	1884	7/14 - 8/16	Henderson	@BOS(Shaw)
17		STL	AA	1885	5/5 - 6/2	Comiskey	@BAL(Henderson)
18		CHI	NL	1885	6/01 - 6/25	Anson	PHI(Daily)
15		DET	NL	1886	5/10 - 5/31	Watkins	@NY(Keefe)
15		STL	AA	1887	4/24 - 5/17	Comiskey	PHI(Seward)
16	*16	PHI	NL	1887	9/15 - 10/8	Wright	BOS(Clarkson) '88
16		PHI	NL	1890	7/08 - 7/28	Allen	@CHI(Hutchison)
18	*2	BOS	NL	1891	9/16 - 10/3	Selee	@PHI(Keefe)
16		PHI	NL	1892	6/10 - 6/29	Wright	BOS(Nichols)
18		BAL	NL	1894	8/24 - 9/16	Hanlon	@CIN(Parrott)
17		BOS	NL	1897	5/31 - 6/22	Selee	@BKN(Kennedy)
15		PIT	NL	1903	6/02 - 6/25	Clarke	@PHI(Mitchell)
18		NY	AL	1904	6/16 - 7/05	McGraw	@PHI(Fraser)
19	*12	CHI	AL	1906	8/02 - 8/25	Jones	@WAS(C.Smith)
15		NY	AL	1906	8/29 - 9/10	Griffith	BOS(Winter)
17		NY	NL	1907	4/25 - 5/20	McGraw	STL(C. Brown)
16		PIT	NL	1909	9/09 - 9/27	Clarke	NY(Wiltse)
17		WS	AL	1912	5/30 - 6/19	Griffith	@PHI(Coombs)
16		NY	NL	1912	6/19 - 7/04	McGraw	BKN(Ragan)
15		PHI	AL	1913	5/27 - 6/11	Mack	STL(Stone)
15		IND	FL	1914	6/11 - 6/25	Phillips	KC(Harris)
17		NY	NL	1916	5/09 - 5/30	McGraw	@PHI(Demaree)
26	*13	NY	NL	1916	9/07 - 9/30	McGraw	BOS(Tyler)
15		BKN	NL	1924	8/25 - 9/06	Robinson	@BOS(Genewich)
16		NY	AL	1926	5/10 - 5/28	Huggins	PHI(Grove)
17		PHI	AL	1931	5/05 - 5/26	Mack	NY(Gomez)
21		CHI	NL	1935	9/04 - 9/28	Grimm	@STL(Walker)
15		CHI	NL	1936	6/04 - 6/21	Grimm	@BKN(Mungo)
15		NY	NL	1936	8/11 - 8/29	Terry	@PIT(Lucas)
15		BOS	AL	1946	4/25 - 5/11	Cronin	@NY(Bonham)
19		NY	AL	1947	6/29 - 7/18	Harris	@DET(Hutchinson)
16		NY	AL	1951	8/12 - 8/28	Durocher	PIT(Pollet)
18		NY	AL	1953	5/27 - 6/16	Stengel	STL(Pillette)
15		NY	AL	1960	9/15 - 10/2	Stengel	End of Season
16		KC	AL	1977	8/31 - 9/16	Herzog	SEA(Medich)
15		MIN	AL	1991	6/01 - 6/17	Kelly	@BAL(Williamson)

(Chart Courtesy of Frank Vaccaro)
*Indicates tie in game number noted.

The Feats

What follows is a celebration of three of baseball's most rare and heroic feats: the Triple Crowns of batting and pitching, and the triple putout by one player, better known as the unassisted triple play. These feats do not rank with the central records of the game: Henry Aaron's 755 homers, Cy Young's 511 wins, Pete Rose's 4,256 hits, and Ty Cobb's lifetime batting average of .366. They are not as distant in memory as a .400 hitter or a 40-game winner. But they are remarkable achievements and—unlike those mentioned above—are not evident from a perusal of the leaders tables found later in this book.

Triple Crown Winners—Batting

Baseball's first Triple Crown winner, Paul Hines, waited 90 years to be enthroned. The crown consists of three jewels: the batting, home run, and runs-batted-in titles must be won in a single season. The RBI count was a late starter among baseball stats and had to be reconstructed for earlier seasons. However, it was not for lack of the RBI distinction that Hines, of the Providence Grays, waited for belated recognition. His feat went unacknowledged until researchers turned up information which made him the true 1878 batting champion.

A special Baseball Records Committee met in 1968 and put a stamp of approval on statistics which had been in dispute or unverified from baseball's past. The new information appeared the next year when Macmillan published the first edition of *The Baseball Encyclopedia*.

Abner Dalrymple had gone to his grave in 1939, the year the Baseball Hall of Fame Museum opened in Cooperstown, N.Y., with one baseball honor to his name. He had won the National League batting championship in 1878. Paul Hines, who died in 1935, was remembered only as the winner of the 1879 title. But new data—coming from the two tie games he played and the one for Dalrymple—have revealed that Hines ought to have been a repeat batting champion, too, for under modern scoring rules, his batting average of .358 was higher than Dalrymple's .356.

Paul Hines enjoyed that distinction from 1969 through 1994, then lost it as Major League Baseball and *Total Baseball* adopted a new stance, acknowledging that the individual marks amassed in tie games were not counted in the NL of 1878, *by the practices of the day*—and thus the championship should return to Dalrymple, despite his lower average under modern reconstruction. Thus with hindsight, we can award Hines 1879 batting-average supremacy (though not the championship), the RBI leadership which resulted from reconstructed stats, and the small but clearly superior total of four home runs. Thus Paul Hines can be said to have attained the first Triple Crown. In addition, when he won the batting title again in 1879, also awarded through later research efforts, he became the first to repeat as hitting leader.

Another 19th-century player, Hugh Duffy, had—since 1969, when his RBI data first were published—been considered the first to wear the Triple Crown. In 1894 he had won the three necessary titles but had almost obscured his own feat by batting .438, later corrected upward to .440.

This remains the highest batting average of all time and in Duffy's later years had always interested interviewers more than the Triple Crown. Duffy's 18 home runs and 145 runs batted in led the league in these departments in 1894, but the idea of linking them as a trio had not yet been formed. No one knew Paul Hines had done it and few cared that Hugh Duffy had. Although the RBI was known as a baseball stat as early as 1879, it was not commonly used until the 1910s, and it did not become an official measure until 1920.

The player who placed the stamp of the superstar most firmly on the concept of the Triple Crown was Nap Lajoie, who was the dominant player in the game when the American League was formed and ushered in 20th-century baseball. The great Napoleon Lajoie had become the star of the Philadelphia Phillies as the 19th century closed. He was the prize recruit for the new league, remaining in Philadelphia where Connie Mack was establishing a new franchise. Lajoie put the team and the American League on the baseball map in 1901, when he provided the league-leading totals in the three prize categories. He batted .426, hit 14 home runs in the Dead Ball Era of the time, and, as later research showed, batted in 145 runs. It was the greatest season the immortal would ever have. He would win two more batting titles and again lead the league in RBIs, however, home runs were not his specialty.

Still, his Triple Crown brought instant respect to the new league and, together with other stars who had switched leagues, forced acceptance that the American League was a full-fledged major league and would be part of the basis of baseball's structure from then on.

Lajoie was succeeded as the American League's superstar by Ty Cobb, who also laid claim to the Triple Crown in 1909. As with Lajoie, hitting home runs was not Cobb's dominant ability, and despite 10 batting championships and four RBI titles, he wore the Triple Crown but once. He came close two other times, in 1907 and 1911, finishing second in home runs each of those years.

Cobb's great rival was the National League's Honus Wagner, who never wore the Triple Crown, although he too missed it by a close margin. In 1908 he was second in home runs, the most difficult final jewel for the superstars of the dead-ball era to achieve. Wagner's eight batting titles and four RBI championships were never accompanied by a home run leadership.

While the list of those who have won the Triple Crown is short, it is a quality list. All but one Triple Crown holder in this century—the gambling suspect Heinie Zimmerman—are in the Hall of Fame.

In 1912 Heinie Zimmerman, one of the best major league third basemen, put together the greatest season he would ever have. Honus Wagner failed to repeat as batting champion, and his 102 RBI total was one less than Zimmerman's, according to the tabulations of Ernie Lanigan. The 14 home runs Zimmerman hit edged teammate Wildfire Schulte, who had led the league in four-baggers the two previous seasons, by one. Only in batting average, where Zimmerman's .372 far distanced the field, did he have a clear superiority, but a Triple Crown by any measure is a rare treasure and it was Heinie's without dispute, that is until the researchers of Information Concepts, Inc., the group that compiled The Baseball Encyclopedia,

downgraded his RBI total to 99. Later, an editor of The Baseball Encyclopedia fudged Zim's RBI count back up to 103 to restore his Triple Crown, but we cannot subscribe to such an arbitrary change.

It was 1922 before the Triple Crown would again rest on a player's head, but when it did, it landed on the brow of the royally nicknamed "Rajah" Hornsby and just eluded Babe Ruth.

Rogers Hornsby strung together six successive batting titles, from 1920 through 1925, and added another in 1928. Although he had home run power to go with his high averages, the title escaped him in 1921, when George Kelly outhomered him by two. It would have been the first Triple Crown for the Rajah and would have given him an eventual three, a total no one has ever achieved.

Babe Ruth, who got two legs up on the Triple Crown seven times without ever winning one, had many home run titles and frequently topped the league in RBIs. However, the competition for batting championships in the 1920s, when Cobb, Sisler, and Heilmann topped .400 and Heilmann alone accounted for four batting titles, was tough. Ruth managed one hitting title but lost the RBI leg that year, 1924, to Goose Goslin.

In the 1930s a quartet of superstars and future Hall of Fame members competed for the Triple Crown during most of the decade, and each took a turn wearing it.

The American League had two great first baseman, Jimmie Foxx and Lou Gehrig. Each was a threat to claim the Crown every year, but when Foxx narrowly failed on two occasions, it was not Gehrig who stymied him. In 1932 Jimmie came frustratingly close. He was edged out of the batting title by the clumsy-fielding Dale Alexander in 1932. Called "Moose," Alexander split the season between Detroit and Boston, the first player to win a batting title while appearing with two teams. Alexander barely qualified for the championship, but his .367 topped the .364 by Foxx. The following year, 1933, Foxx won his lone Triple Crown.

Foxx had his second near-miss of the Triple Crown in 1938. This time it was the home run lead that eluded him. Although Foxx hit 50 home runs in 1938, while winning the batting and RBI honors, Hank Greenberg hit 58 homers to almost equal Babe Ruth's record of 60.

While Gehrig and Foxx were dominating in the American League, two sluggers in the National League were sharing domination of their league. Chuck Klein was the league's outstanding batter during the early 1930s, and Joe Medwick took over for the final half of the decade. Both wore the Triple Crown, Klein getting his in 1933 when Jimmie Foxx was doing likewise. It was the only year that each league produced a Triple Crown winner and, did it in the same city—Philadelphia. Medwick won his in 1937.

The next to claim the Triple Crown was Ted Williams. A brash rookie when he reported to the Boston Red Sox in 1939, he had little to learn from the old guy hitting fungos in practice. Hugh Duffy took one look at Williams' swing and knew the only part he could play was as a role model. Williams had his eye on hitting .400. When he did it, in 1941, his .406 was far short of Duffy's .440, the all-time record.

Williams was also one leg short of the Triple Crown in 1941. He added the home run title to his batting champi-

onship, but his main rival, Joe DiMaggio, had topped the RBI column. DiMaggio had piled up his RBI totals largely during his 56-game hitting streak that season.

Ted Williams won all three titles for the Triple Crown the next season, 1942, and then went off to serve in World War II. Several wartime players won two legs of the Triple Crown: Rudy York, with the Detroit Tigers in 1943, and Bill Nicholson, a Chicago Cubs outfielder in 1943 and 1944. Both hit home runs and batted in runs at league-leading levels, but they were far outdistanced for the batting-average honors.

Williams returned from the war in 1946 and finished second in each of the Triple Crown categories. Mickey Vernon beat him out for the batting title, and Hank Greenberg, who had blocked Jimmie Foxx in 1938, had his last hurrah with the Tigers, topping Williams in both home runs and runs batted in.

The next year, with Greenberg gone to the National League, Ted Williams claimed his second Triple Crown. No one was close to him in any of the three prize categories, and despite three prime seasons lost to wartime service, the Red Sox star seemed most likely to be the first to wear the Triple Crown three times. He had won in 1942 and 1947.

In 1948 his old nemesis, Joe DiMaggio, who was never to win a Triple Crown, picked off two of the crown jewels, leading the American League in home runs with 39 and in runs batted in with 155. Ted Williams was far ahead of the pack as batting champion with a .369 average.

It was 1949 that proved the greatest disappointment to Williams. DiMaggio was injured much of the season and did not compete for individual honors. However, the pennant race was tightly contested between the Yankees and Red Sox, and more interest was focused on that than on the seemingly assured third Triple Crown to be worn by Ted Williams.

As the season reached the final weekend, Boston came to New York for two games between the Red Sox and Yankees. Boston was a game ahead and needed to win only one to gain the pennant. They lost on Saturday, and the teams were tied when Sunday's game began.

The biggest threat to Ted Williams' third Triple Crown came from teammate Vern Stephens, a slugging shortstop who was tied with Ted for RBIs. Williams held a small but probably secure batting lead over George Kell of the Detroit Tigers.

However, Williams and the Red Sox were in a slump, and it cost both the team and the individual their honors. The final game of the season between the Yankees and Red Sox was one of the most exciting of all time. The Yankees staved off a three-run Red Sox rally to win, 5–3.

Williams had gone hitless and ended up not only missing a World Series appearance but his third Triple Crown. While Williams had sputtered in the final games, George Kell, who had missed two stretches of games with injuries, got back in the lineup for Detroit's final three games. With only a batting title at stake, Kell had two hits in his final game. When the final statistics were known, George Kell had batted .3429 and Ted Williams .3427. It was the closest any player ever came to a Triple Crown without actually winning it and the closest anyone has come to earning the honor three times.

The year before, in the National League, Stan Musial

had narrowly missed his bid for a Triple Crown, when he was one behind Johnny Mize and Ralph Kiner, who tied for the home run title with 40.

In 1953 Al Rosen had a near-miss almost as tight as Ted Williams had had in 1949. Rosen won the home run and RBI titles but was edged out, .337 to .336, for the batting championship by Mickey Vernon, of the Washington Senators, who had blocked Williams's bid in that category in 1946.

Mickey Mantle hit his peak in 1956 when he put the necessary ingredients together to win a Triple Crown. He hit .353 for the only batting title he would win, had top totals in home runs with 52, and piled up a leading 130 runs batted in.

Ten years later, in 1966, Frank Robinson reacted to being traded out of the National League by winning the Triple Crown in the American League. His .316 batting average was one of only two above .300 that year in the American League.

In 1967, the year of the Red Sox "Impossible Dream," the team was driven to a surprise championship by the captain, Carl Yastrzemski, who had an astounding year. Yaz won the only home run title of his career and also the lone RBI championship he would record. He joined these with one of his three batting crowns and ended the season with what was to become an elusive honor, the Triple Crown.

He is the last player to wear the title, although a number of players have gained two legs, including Yaz's teammate, Jim Rice, who did this twice. In the American League the inability of power hitters to achieve a high batting average has resulted in a parade of sluggers leading in home runs and runs batted in but falling short in base-hit percentage.

Harmon Killebrew, who tied with Yaz for home runs in Yastrzemski's crown-winning season, Frank Howard, Dick Allen, Reggie Jackson, George Scott, Eddie Murray, Tony Armas, and Jose Canseco have won two legs but failed to capture the batting title.

Since Yaz won the last Triple Crown, two National Leaguers have won batting titles and the RBI championship, but failed in home runs. Joe Torre in 1971 and Al Oliver in 1982 earned two legs one way, and Johnny Bench, Willie Stargell, George Foster, Andre Dawson, and Mike Schmidt have done it with the home run and RBI crowns. Foster did it twice and Schmidt four times.

Carl Yastrzemski might not have been just part of a vanishing breed. He might have been the last example of a breed that has already vanished.

Triple Crown Hitters

American League

Player	Team	Year	HR	RBI	BA
Nap Lajoie	Phila.	1901	14	125	.422
Ty Cobb	Det.	1909	9	115	.377
Jimmie Foxx	Phila.	1933	48	163	.356
Lou Gehrig	N.Y.	1934	49	165	.363
Ted Williams	Bos.	1942	36	137	.356
	Bos.	1947	32	114	.343
Mickey Mantle	N.Y.	1956	52	130	.353
Frank Robinson	Bal.	1966	49	122	.316
Carl Yastrzemski	Bos.	1967	44	121	.326

National League

Player	Team	Year	HR	RBI	BA
Paul Hines*	Prov.	1878	4	50	.358
Hugh Duffy	Bos.	1894	18	145	.438
Heinie Zimmerman**	Chi.	1912	14	103	.372
Rogers Hornsby	St.L.	1922	42	152	.401
	St. L.	1925	39	143	.403
Chuck Klein	Phila.	1933	28	120	.368
Joe Medwick	St.L.	1937	31	154	.374

American Association

Player	Team	Year	HR	RBI	BA
Tip O'Neill	St.L.	1887	14	123	.435

*Hines' batting average was the highest in the NL, but Abner Dalrymple retains his title.

**Zimmerman ranked first in RBIs as calculated by Ernie Lanigan, but only third as calculated by ICI research in 1969.

Triple Crown Winners—Pitching

Tommy Bond, the only 19th-century pitcher on the list of Triple Crown Winners who is not in the Hall of Fame, has, at least, the honor of turning the feat first. When the National League was formed in 1876, Bond was an established star in the National Association. The others who eventually won the pitchers' Triple Crown, for the most wins and strikeouts and the lowest ERA in a single season, began their careers in the National League.

Although he was only 21 when he won the Triple Crown in 1877, Bond had been pitching for prominent teams since he had been 16 and joined the Athletics of Brooklyn. He entered the National League with Hartford but moved to Boston for his best seasons. He was Boston's only pitcher during 1877 and 1878 and pitched the great majority of games in 1879. He won 123 of the 204 games Boston played in those early years of short schedules.

Bond, who later coached baseball at Harvard, was celebrated for his victories and strikeouts. The measurement of earned runs was done retroactively.

As Bond's career lapsed, the next to claim the Triple Crown of pitching emerged. Old Hoss Radbourn reached the peak year that gave him his nickname for durability in 1884. He pitched the Providence Grays to the National League pennant, almost singlehandedly, after Charlie Sweeney's departure had left only Radbourn as the team's pitcher.

His 59 victories is the most ever won by a pitcher in a season. It shines brightest among all such jewels in the Triple Crowns worn by those who came after him. Radbourn won 309 games in his big league career, but the 59 he totaled in his 1884 season—including a streak of 26 wins in 27 decisions—gave him a celebrity which was recognized when he was named to the Hall of Fame in its opening year, 1939.

A Triple Crown is an exacting measurement of a pitcher's superiority at any time. However, because of the circumstance that he started so many games for the league's best team, Radbourn's win totals and strikeout numbers can largely be attributed to opportunity. However, it is his 1.38 ERA at a time when the league mark was 2.98 that stamps Old Hoss as truly remarkable.

Tim Keefe, the next pitcher to annex a Triple Crown, wore his for a season that has kept his name in the active files of modern baseball writers. Whenever a pitcher runs off a string of victories, this prompts a review of the

record book, and Keefe's 19 in a row is remembered as the highest total, shared with Rube Marquard's 1912 season total of 19 straight. In all, Tim Keefe won 35 games for the New York Giants in 1888, just edging out the man who would take the Triple Crown the next year.

John Clarkson pitched Boston to a pennant in 1889, winning the Triple Crown as the workhorse of a staff which included the worn Old Hoss Radbourn. Clarkson won 49 games and Radbourn 20.

Clarkson's career was overlapped by that of Amos Rusie, the most awesome pitcher of the 1890s. A burly farm boy, "the Hoosier Thunderbolt" was the principal reason the distance of the pitcher's box was pushed back in 1893. Rusie responded the following year by continuing to dominate the league in strikeouts, while topping all pitchers with 36 wins and an ERA of 2.78.

Probably because of the increased pitching distance, the league ERA ballooned to 5.32 and batters averaged .309 in 1894. This was the year Hugh Duffy won the batter's Triple Crown and set a still-unexcelled .440 batting record.

Rusie's career peaked in 1894. The next season one of the most oppressive men to own a big league team, Andrew Freedman, bought the Giants and began a blood feud with Rusie. Rusie sat out the 1896 season, but returned as a reluctant star for two more 20-game-winning seasons. Then he tore his arm muscles. After missing two more seasons his reputation was such that Cincinnati traded a future Triple Crown pitcher, Christy Mathewson, for him. Rusie pitched just three games for the Reds before retiring for good.

Just as Nap Lajoie marked the American League's inaugural in 1901 by winning a Triple Crown for batters, another established star, Cy Young, did the same for the pitchers' version. Young, in midcareer as a big league pitcher, won 33 games, a total almost dwarfed among the 511 he won in his career. This latter is one mark certain to stand permanently.

With two major leagues now offering the potential of a Triple Crown winner each year, it took only until 1905 to have both the American and National Leagues produce such winners. Christy Mathewson won the first of the two Triple Crowns he would win for the New York Giants, and the eccentric Rube Waddell had his last great year with the Philadelphia Athletics.

Matty won 31 games, struck out 206, and had an ERA of 1.43. The Rube produced 26 wins, 287 strikeouts, and an ERA of 1.48. The World Series, inaugurated in 1903 but boycotted by the Giants in 1904, was resumed in 1905. It would have provided marvelous theater for the two Triple Crown winners. The confrontation would have been the only one of its kind. Alas, the colorful Rube Waddell injured his arm while wrestling a teammate just before the Series began.

Without Waddell to oppose him, Christy Mathewson won three games, all shutouts, and the Giants took the Series in five games. Matty won the Triple Crown again in 1908 but lost his last start when the Chicago Cubs won the playoff game in a season which had ended in a tie.

Walter Johnson, the next to sport a Triple Crown, won three at widely spaced intervals in his long career. The first came in 1913, the next in 1918, and the last in 1924 when, in his 18th season, Johnson once more topped the

American League in the three prize categories. This time it also brought a pennant to the Senators, the first in their history. The World Series came close to being a disappointing anticlimax for Johnson. He lost the opener to the Giants in extra innings, then lost again, but salvaged glory by winning the seventh game in relief.

Earlier, during Walter Johnson's widely spaced crown jewels, Grover Cleveland Alexander produced the most impressive reign ever enjoyed by a Triple Crown winner. Pitching for the Philadelphia Phillies, he had three successive seasons with 30 or more victories, starting with the pennant-winning 1915 season; each time he led the NL in ERA and K's as well.

While Pete was in the Army, another pitcher claimed the Triple Crown. Jim "Hippo" Vaughn in 1917 had achieved immortality by engaging in a double no-hit game, losing in the 10th inning. In 1918, with Alexander away, Vaughn won the Triple Crown pitching for the Cubs.

Ironically Alexander had served his Army hitch as a new member of the Cubs. With his battery mate, "Reindeer Bill" Killefer, Alexander had been sold to Chicago after winning his third Triple Crown, in 1917. He pitched only three games in 1918 while Vaughn was in the star's role, and in 1919 the two teammates competed for the Triple Crown. Alexander led the league in ERA and Vaughn in strikeouts. Between them they won 37 games, but neither came close to topping the league.

However, in 1920 Alexander again emerged as the Triple Crown winner. It was his fourth, the most ever won by a pitcher. He continued to star, despite personal and physical problems, during the 1920s without again leading in any of the categories which make up the Triple Crown.

Next to wear the Triple Crown of pitchers was Dazzy Vance. Like Rusie, Waddell, and Johnson, Vance began with expectation of finishing each season with a league-leading total in strikeouts. In 1924 he won the Most Valuable Player Award, even though the Brooklyn Dodgers as a team could not win the pennant. To his strikeout superiority, the Dazzler added leadership in wins with 24 and an ERA of 2.16. His domination of the league can best be measured by comparing his ERA to a league total of 3.87 as the lively ball bounded off hitters' bats.

Lefty Grove of the Philadelphia Athletics won back to back Triple Crowns in 1930 and 1931, having missed one of the three legs in 1929. The A's won pennants all three of those years, and Grove was their leading pitcher. In 1929 teammate George Earnshaw topped him in wins, 24 to 20, as Grove missed getting decisions in an unusual number of games.

Another southpaw ace, Lefty Gomez, succeeded Lefty Grove as a Triple Crown winner. Like Grove, he wore the title twice, but not consecutively. He won his first Triple Crown, oddly, in a season when his team, the New York Yankees, didn't win a pennant, 1934. His next came in 1937 as the Yankees were in the midst of a run of four straight pennants.

Gomez was only a spot starter in 1939, when the Yankees met the Reds in the World Series, but Cincinnati had a converted third baseman, Bucky Walters heading

their staff, the first National Leaguer to win the Triple Crown in 15 years.

During World War II Hal Newhouser emerged as a superlative pitcher who might have been equally impressive against peacetime competition. He missed the Triple Crown in 1944, winning two legs but coming in second to Detroit Tiger teammate Dizzy Trout for ERA honors. In 1945, the final wartime year, Newhouser topped the American League in the three prize categories, and winning the Triple Crown went into a long hiatus when the 1946 season resumed with the star pitchers back from service.

Despite leading the league in victories six times and in strikeouts seven, Bob Feller never won an official ERA title to match up with the other components of the Triple Crown. Although Feller's ERA in 1940 is today regarded as the lowest for that year, at that time Ernie Bonham won the title despite pitching only 99 innings.

Warren Spahn topped the National League in victories eight times, led in strikeouts four times, and even took ERA honors three times, but he could never link them up in a single season.

Robin Roberts, like Feller, never won an ERA title, so despite leading in victories four times and strikeouts twice, the singular honor of the Triple Crown eluded him, as it did all other pitchers once baseball had returned to the normalcy of peacetime play.

It wasn't until Sandy Koufax reached stardom and notched three Triple Crown titles that the distinction was again achieved. Koufax topped the three needed categories in 1963, 1965, and 1966. Unlike any other winner of the Triple Crown, Koufax retired with the honor. An aching arthritic arm caused his early retirement, leaving a final season of 27 victories, 317 strikeouts, and an ERA of 1.73. He threw his last pitch for the Dodgers in the World Series.

A Triple Crown-winning pitcher has not always meant a pennant for his team, although the two have gone together more often than not. However, in 1972 Steve Carlton took the honor despite pitching for a last-place team. There has never been such a contrast in the success of a team's best pitcher and the rest of its staff. The Phillies won 59 games, and Carlton was responsible for 27 of them. He also led, for the only time, in ERA, with 1.97, and struck out 310.

Again a drought followed, despite the presence of such star pitchers as Tom Seaver, Fergie Jenkins, Juan Marichal, Jim Palmer, Gaylord Perry, and others who led in some of the prize-earning stats. Then in 1985 the New York Mets' Dwight Gooden took up the challenge and claimed the Triple Crown with a remarkable record: 24-4, 1.53, and 268 strikeouts. Gooden faltered the next year, but Roger Clemens came forward to just miss the honor by finishing second in strikeouts while winning the other two legs.

Clemens would claim the honor twice more a decade later. He was Triple Crown winner in 1997 and again in 1998, winning his final 15 decisions in '98 to tie Rick Helling of Texas and Daniel Cone of the Yankees with 20 victories.

Triple Crown Pitchers

American League

Player	Team	Year	W	L	SO	ERA
Cy Young	Bos.	1901	33	10	158	1.62
Rube Waddell	Phila.	1905	26	11	287	1.48
Walter Johnson	Wash.	1913	36	7	303	1.09
	Wash.	1918	23	13	162	1.27
	Wash.	1924	23	7	158	2.72
Lefty Grove	Phila.	1930	28	5	209	2.54
	Phila.	1931	31	4	175	2.06
Lefty Gomez	N.Y.	1934	26	5	158	2.33
	N.Y.	1937	21	11	194	2.33
Hal Newhouser	Det.	1945	25	9	212	1.81
Roger Clemens	Tor.	1997	21	7	292	2.05
	Tor.	1998	20	6	271	2.65

National League

Player	Team	Year	W	L	SO	ERA
Tommy Bond	Bos.	1877	40	17	170	2.11
Old Hoss Radbourn	Prov.	1884	59	12	441	1.38
Tim Keefe	N.Y.	1888	35	12	333	1.74
John Clarkson	Bos.	1889	49	19	284	2.73
Amos Rusie	N.Y.	1894	36	13	195	2.78
Christy Mathewson	N.Y.	1905	31	8	206	1.27
	N.Y.	1908	37	11	259	1.43
Grover Alexander	Phila.	1915	31	10	241	1.22
	Phila.	1916	33	12	167	1.55
	Phila.	1917	30	13	201	1.86
Hippo Vaughn	Chi.	1918	22	10	148	1.74
Grover Alexander	Chi.	1920	27	14	173	1.91
Dazzy Vance	Brook	1924	28	6	262	2.16
Bucky Walters	Cin.	1939	27	11	137	2.29
Sandy Koufax	L.A.	1963	25	5	306	1.88
	L.A.	1965	26	8	382	2.04
	L.A.	1966	27	9	317	1.73
Steve Carlton	Phila.	1972	27	10	310	1.97
Dwight Gooden	N.Y.	1985	24	4	268	1.53

The Unassisted Triple Play

The unassisted triple play has been turned in regular season major league play only 10 times in this century and just one questionable time in the 19th. (It also happened once in World Series play.)

On May 30, 1987, family and friends of 93-year-old Jimmy Cooney gathered at his home to celebrate the 60th anniversary of his unassisted triple play. Rare? It was the last one made in the NL at that time.

Cooney was no stranger to unassisted triple plays. Two seasons earlier, when he was shortstop for the St. Louis Cardinals, he was doubled off second by Pirates shortstop Glenn Wright, who next tagged out Rogers Hornsby coming from first base. Wright had snared a line drive off the bat of Jim Bottomley to start his triple play. He watched from the Pirates' bench the day Cooney emulated his feat in much the same manner.

Paul Waner provided the line drive to make the first out, with Cooney snaring it as he ran toward second base. Clyde Barnhart had broken for second on the pitch, and Lloyd Waner, the runner on second, had dashed for third as his brother, Paul, swung. Lloyd was doubled off second, and Cooncy simply tagged the startled Barnhart, who thought the ball had gone into center field for a base hit.

There are certain similarities among 10 of the 11 unassisted triple plays which have been recorded. These have occurred with runners on first and second, have been made by infielders, and have required the complicity of baserunners either attempting a double steal or were running on a hit-and-run play. The 11th was by an outfielder, with runners on second and third.

Even the most celebrated unassisted triple play had an explanation that almost absolved the victims, the Brooklyn Dodgers, of bonehead base running. This was the only such event to happen in a World Series, and it was turned in by Bill Wambsganss, the Cleveland Indian second baseman in 1920. Those who have examined the boxscore have questioned the tactics of Wilbert Robinson, the Brooklyn manager whose strategies often were charitably called "unusual." It was the fifth inning, and Brooklyn, behind, 7–0, had the first two runners on base.

Despite being shut out, the Dodgers had been hitting the Cleveland pitcher, Jim Bagby, hard. It was a game in which they made 13 hits and scored a lone run. Bill Wambsganss, who told the story hundreds of times, explained that he chose to play very deep when Clarence Mitchell, a very good-hitting pitcher came to bat in the fifth inning. He didn't think a seven-run lead was too secure the way the Dodgers had been hitting.

When Mitchell cracked the ball on a line, the batters took off, not thinking that Wamby was where the ball was going. He was and ran over and doubled Kilduff off second and turned and found a dumbfounded Otto Miller standing in the baseline. He tagged him out and, as has been the case after every unassisted triple play, trotted off the field in silence. It always takes the crowd a minute or more to realize what has happened.

In the early years of baseball, outfielder Paul Hines of the Providence Grays, had been credited with making an unassisted triple play. Later-day research indicated Hines had made an unassisted double play but had thrown to a base for the third out. But, according to the rules of 1878, Hines did indeed register an unassisted triple play.

Johnny Neun had read in the morning paper of May 31, 1927, about Jimmy Cooney's unassisted triple play in the National League. As first baseman for the Detroit Tigers, known for his fielding and base stealing, Neun was alert to all possibilities when Homer Summa's line drive landed in his glove. Charlie Jamieson was a dead duck, caught off first and easily tagged for the second out. Shortstop Jackie Tavener was jumping up and down at second base calling for the ball. Slow-footed Glen Myatt was lumbering back from third base. Neun waved his shortstop out of the way and raced toward second base, implausibly shouting, "I'm running into the Hall of Fame."

On July 30, 1968, Ron Hansen, playing shortstop for the Washington Senators, made an unassisted triple play, following the process all other shortstops have used. He grabbed a line drive off the bat of Joe Azcue, stepped on second to retire Dave Nelson, and tagged Russ Snyder coming from first. It was the first time the feat had been pulled since 1927.

It was the most memorable event of Hansen's week, which was an unusual one in other ways as well. Following his play, he struck out six consecutive times, perhaps still stunned by the event. Then he regained his batting eye to hit a grand slam. His unassisted triple play had been made on a road trip. He could expect applause when he came to bat the first time before hometown Washington fans when the team returned home. But he didn't get this. Instead, he was traded to the White Sox.

The first unassisted triple play of the 20th century was made on July 19, 1909, by Cleveland shortstop Neal Ball.

Overall Cleveland has been involved in five of the 11 unassisted triple plays in the major leagues. Three times the event has taken place there, twice executed by Cleveland players, and in all a Cleveland player has been involved somewhere five times. It all began with Neal Ball, who snagged a liner hit by Boston's Amby McConnell and retired Charley Wagner and Jake Stahl on the basepaths.

George Burns, playing for the Boston Red Sox between stints as a member of the Indians, turned the tables for Boston and made Cleveland the victim in 1923. He caught Frank Brower's liner, tagged Rube Lutzke off first, and ran to second to get Riggs Stephenson before he could return.

Burns made his play on Sept. 14, and, on Oct. 6, another unassisted triple play occurred, making the feat which had been so rare appear almost commonplace, for a while. This time Ernie Padgett, a red-headed shortstop for the Boston Braves, turned the trick. Again the play was made in typical fashion—a line drive, a runner doubled off second base, and a surprised baserunner from first being tagged out.

Jimmy Cooney's claim on the last NL unassisted triple play ended late in the 1992 season. Rookie second baseman Mickey Morandini of the Philadelphia Phillies made a diving catch of a line drive off the bat of Pittsburgh's Jeff King. Morandini scrambled to second base to double off Andy Van Slyke. Then Barry Bonds, running from first base, bumbled into the surprised second baseman, who pushed him away with a climaxing third-out tag. Unaware of the rarity of his sudden feat, the rookie infielder rolled the ball toward the mound. The ball that was used to make the first play of its kind in the big leagues in 24 seasons was put into play the next inning.

In 1994 Boston's John Valentin replaced Ron Hansen as the last American Leaguer to perform the three-ply putout singlehandedly. On July 15 the Red Sox shortstop had an extraordinary day in an exceptionally well-played game. In the top of the sixth inning, after the Minnesota Twins had put the first two runners on base, Valentin speared Marc Newfield's line drive with the runners moving. He stepped on second to erase Mike Blowers, then noticed Keith Mitchell was about to run past him. It appeared as if the shortstop felt he had done enough to make an unassisted double play and only tagged the runner just in case the inning wasn't really over. As Morandini had done, Valentin nonchalantly dropped the ball on the mound and trotted off the field. Unlike Morandini, whose ball had negligently been put back into play, Valentin retrieved the ball and took it home as a souvenir.

Valentin homered to lead off the bottom of the sixth. The game ended with three game-saving defensive plays. Scott Cooper made a diving stop at third, and Tim Naehring sprawled to dig his throw out of the dirt. Lee Tinsley then made a Game of the Week super catch, grabbing a low line drive in right center, and, finally Wes Chamberlain went to the bullpen fence, leaped high in the air, and came down with a home run ball in the webbing of his glove. Sox fans left Fenway wondering if they would ever see the home team make so many defensive gems in one game again. Not likely.

Unassisted Triple Plays

Player/Team	Date	Pos.	Opp.	Opp. Batter
Paul Hines, Prov.	May 8, 1878	OF	Bos.	Jack Burdock
Neal Ball, Cleve.	July 19, 1909	SS	Bos.	Amby McConnell
Bill Wambsganss, Cleve.	Oct. 10, 1920	2B	Brook.	Clarence Mitchell
George Burns, Bos. (A)	Sept. 14, 1923	1B	Cleve.	Frank Brower
Ernie Padgett, Bos. (N)	Oct. 6, 1923	SS	Phila.	Walter Holke
Glenn Wright, Pitts.	May 7, 1925	SS	St.L.	Jim Bottomley
Jimmy Cooney, Chi. (N)	May 30, 1927	SS	Pitts.	Paul Waner
Johnny Neun, Det.	May 31, 1927	1B	Cleve.	Homer Summa
Ron Hansen, Wash.	July 29, 1968	SS	Cleve.	Joe Azcue
Mickey Morandini, Phi.	Sept. 23, 1992	2B	Pitt.	Jeff King
John Valentin, Bos.	July 15, 1994	SS	Minn.	Marc Newfield

The No-Hitters

What follows is the traditional honor roll of the 200-plus pitchers who have attained the no-hit heights including those 36 games in which a pitcher retired 27 or more batters in succession.

No-hit games, nine or more innings.

(Number to left is career total if greater than one)
(Home team is that of pitcher, unless team is in italics)

Joe Borden, Phi vs. Chi NA, 4-0; July 28, 1875.
George Bradley, StL vs. Har NL, 2-0; July 15, 1876.
Lee Richmond, Wor vs. Cle NL, 1-0; June 12, 1880 (perfect game).
John Ward, Pro vs. Buf NL, 5-0; June 17, 1880.
Larry Corcoran, Chi vs. Bos NL, 6-0; August 19, 1880.
Jim Galvin, Buf vs. *Wor* NL, 1-0; August 20, 1880.
Tony Mullane, Lou vs. *Cin* AA, 2-0; September 11, 1882.
Guy Hecker, Lou vs. *Pit* AA, 3-1; September 19, 1882
2 Larry Corcoran, Chi vs. Wor NL, 5-0; September 20, 1882
Hoss Radbourn, Pro vs. Cle NL, 8-0; July 25, 1883.
Hugh (One Arm). Daily, Cle vs. *Phi* NL, 1-0; September 13, 1883.
Al Atkisson, Phi vs. Pit AA, 10-1; May 24, 1884.
Ed Morris, Col vs. *Pit* AA, 5-0; May 29, 1884.
Frank Mountain, Col vs. *Was* AA, 12-0; June 5, 1884.
3 Larry Corcoran, Chi vs. Pro NL, 6-0; June 27, 1884.
2 Jim Galvin, Buf vs. *Det* NL, 18-0; August 4, 1884.
Dick Burns, Cin vs. *KC* UA, 3-1; August 26, 1884.
Ed Cushman, Mil vs. Was UA, 5-0; September 28, 1884.
Sam Kimber, Bro vs. Tol AA, 0-0; October 4, 1884 (10 innings, tie).
John Clarkson, Chi vs. *Pro* NL, 4-0; July 27, 1885.
Charlie Ferguson, Phi vs. *Pro* NL, 1-0; August 29, 1885.
2 Al Atkisson, Phi vs. NY AA, 3-2; May 1, 1886.
Adonis Terry, Bro vs. StL AA, 1-0; July 24, 1886.
Matt Kilroy, Bal vs. *Pit* AA, 6-0; October 6, 1886.
2 Adonis Terry, Bro vs. Lou AA, 4-0; May 27, 1888.
Henry Porter, KC vs. *Bal* AA, 4-0; June 6, 1888.
Ed Seward, Phi vs. Cin AA, 12-2; July 26, 1888.
Gus Weyhing, Phi vs. KC AA, 4-0; July 31, 1888.
* Silver King, eight innings, Chi vs. Bro PL, 0-1; June 21, 1890.
Cannonball Titcomb, Roch vs. Syr AA, 7-0; September 15, 1890.
Tom Lovett, Bro vs. NY NL, 4-0; June 22, 1891.
Amos Rusie, NY vs. Bro NL, 6-0; July 31, 1891.
Ted Breitenstein, StL vs. Lou AA, 8-0; October 4, 1891 (1st game). (first start in the major leagues).
Jack Stivetts, Bos vs. Bro NL, 11-0; August 6, 1892.
Ben Sanders, Lou vs. Bal NL, 6-2; August 22, 1892.
Bumpus Jones, Cin vs. Pit NL, 7-1; October 15, 1892. (first game in the major leagues).
Bill Hawke, Bal vs. Was NL, 5-0; August 16, 1893.
Cy Young, Cle vs. Cin NL, 6-0; September 18, 1897 (1st game).
2 Ted Breitenstein, Cin vs. Pit NL, 11-0; April 22, 1898.
Jim Hughes, Bal vs. Bos NL, 8-0; April 22, 1898.
Red Donahue, Phi vs. Bos NL, 5-0; July 8, 1898.
Walter Thornton, Chi vs. Bro NL, 2-0; August 21, 1898 (2nd game).
Deacon Phillippe, Lou vs. NY NL, 7-0; May 25, 1899.
Noodles Hahn, Cin vs. Phi NL, 4-0; July 12, 1900.
* Earl Moore, Cle vs. Chi AL, 2-4; May 9, 1901 (lost on two hits in 10th).
Christy Mathewson, NY vs. *StL* NL, 5-0; July 15, 1901.
Jim Callahan, Chi vs. Det AL, 3-0; September 20, 1902 (1st game).
Chick Fraser, Phi vs. *Chi* NL, 10-0; September 18, 1903 (2nd game).
2 Cy Young, Bos vs. Phi AL, 3-0; May 5, 1904 (perfect game).
* Bob Wicker, Chi vs. *NY* NL, 1-0; June 11, 1904. (won in 12 innings after allowing one hit in the 10th).

Jesse Tannehill, Bos vs. *Chi* AL, 6-0; August 17, 1904.
2 Christy Mathewson, NY vs. *Chi* NL, 1-0; June 13, 1905.
Weldon Henley, Phi vs. *StL* AL, 6-0; July 22, 1905 (1st game).
Frank Smith, Chi vs. *Det* AL, 15-0; September 6, 1905 (2nd game).
Bill Dinneen, Bos vs. Chi AL, 2-0; September 27, 1905 (1st game).
Johnny Lush, Phi vs. *Bro* NL, 6-0; May 1, 1906.
Mal Eason, Bro vs. *StL* NL, 2-0; July 20, 1906.
* Harry McIntyre, Bro vs. Pit NL, 0-1; August 1, 1906. (lost on four hits in 13 innings after allowing first hit in 11th).
Frank (Jeff). Pfeffer, Bos vs. Cin NL, 6-0; May 8, 1907.
Nick Maddox, Pit vs. Bro NL, 2-1; September 20, 1907.
3 Cy Young, Bos vs. *NY* AL, 8-0; June 30, 1908.
Hooks Wiltse, NY vs. Phi NL, 1-0; July 4, 1908 (first game, ten innings).
Nap Rucker, Bro vs. Bos NL, 6-0; September 5, 1908 (2nd game).
Dusty Rhoades, Cle vs. Bos AL, 2-1; September 18, 1908.
2 Frank Smith, Chi vs. Phi AL, 1-0; September 20, 1908.
Addie Joss, Cle vs. *Chi AL,* 1-0; October 2, 1908 (perfect game).
* Red Ames, NY vs, Bro NL, 0-3; April 15, 1909. (lost on seven hits in 13 innings after allowing first hit in 10th).
2 Addie Joss, Cle vs. Chi AL, 1-0; April 20, 1910.
Chief Bender, Phi vs. Cle AL, 4-0; May 12, 1910.
* Tom L. Hughes, NY vs. Cle AL, 0-5; August 30, 1910 (2nd game). (lost on seven hits in 11 innings after allowing first hit in 10th).
Joe Wood, Bos vs StL AL, 5-0; July 29, 1911 (1st game).
Ed Walsh, Chi vs. Bos AL, 5-0; August 27, 1911.
George Mullin, Det vs. StL AL, 7-0; July 4, 1912 (2nd game).
Earl Hamilton, StL vs. *Det* AL, 5-1; August 30, 1912.
Jeff Tesreau, NY vs. *Phi* AL, 3-0; September 6, 1912 (1st game).
* Jim Scott, Chi vs. *Was* AL, 0-1; May 14, 1914 (lost on 2 two hits in 10th).
Joe Benz, Chi vs. Cle Al, 6-1; May 31, 1914.
George Davis, Bos vs. Phi NL, 7-0; September 9, 1914 (2nd game).
Ed Lafitte, Bro vs. KC FL, 6-2; September 19, 1914.
Rube Marquard, NY vs. Bro NL, 2-0; April 15, 1915.
Frank Allen, Pit vs. *StL* FL, 2-0; April 24, 1915.
Claude Hendrix, Chi vs. *Pit* FL, 10-0; May 15, 1915.
Alex Main, KC vs *Buf* FL, 5-0; August 16, 1915.
Jimmy Lavender, Chi vs. *NY* NL, 2-0; August 31, 1915 (1st game).
Dave Davenport, StL vs. Chi FL, 3-0; September 7, 1915.
2 Tom L. Hughes, Bos vs. Pit NL, 2-0; June 16, 1916.
Rube Foster, Bos vs. NY AL, 2-0; June 16, 1916.
Joe Bush, Phi vs. Cle AL, 5-0; August 26, 1916.
Hubert (Dutch) Leonard, Bos vs. StL AL, 4-0; August 30, 1916
Eddie Cicotte, Chi vs. *StL* AL, 11-0; April 14, 1917.
George Mogridge, NY vs. *Bos* AL, 2-1; April 24, 1917.
Fred Toney, Cin vs. *Chi* NL, 1-0; May 2, 1917 (10 innings).
* Hippo Vaughn, Chi vs. Cin NL, 0-1; May 2, 1917. (lost on two hits in 10th; Toney pitched a no-hitter in this game).
Ernie Koob, StL vs. Chi AL, 1-0; May 5, 1917.
Bob Groom, StL vs. Chi AL, 3-0; May 6, 1917 (2nd game).
* Ernie Shore, Bos vs. Was AL, 4-0; June 23, 1917 (1st game). (perfect game). (Shore relieved Babe Ruth in the first inning after Ruth had been thrown out of the game for protesting a walk to the first batter. The runner was caught stealing and Shore retired the remaining 26 batters in order).
2 Hubert (Dutch). Leonard, Bos vs. *Det* AL, 5-0; June 3, 1918.
Hod Eller, Cin vs. StL NL, 6-0; May 11, 1919.
Ray Caldwell, Cle vs. *NY* AL, 3-0; September 10, 1919 (1st game).
Walter Johnson, Was vs. *Bos* AL, 1-0; July 1, 1920.
Charlie Robertson, Chi vs. *Det* AL, 2-0; April 30, 1922 (perfect game).
Jesse Barnes, NY vs. Phi NL, 6-0; May 7, 1922.
Sam Jones, NY vs. *Phi* AL, 2-0; September 4, 1923.
Howard Ehmke, Bos vs. *Phi* AL, 4-0; September 7, 1923.
Jesse Haines, StL vs Bos NL, 5-0; July 17, 1924.
Dazzy Vance, Bro vs. Phi NL, 10-1; September 13, 1925 (1st game).
Ted Lyons, Chi vs. *Bos* AL, 6-0; August 21, 1926.
Carl Hubbell, NY vs. Pit NL, 11-0; May 8, 1929.
Wes Ferrell, Cle vs. StL AL, 9-0; April 29, 1931.
Bobby Burke, Was vs. Bos AL, 5-0; August 8, 1931.
* Bobo Newsom, StL vs Bos AL, 1-2; September 18, 1934 (lost on one hit in 10th).
Paul Dean, StL vs. *Bro* NL, 3-0; September 21, 1934 (2nd game).
Vern Kennedy, Chi vs. Cle AL, 5-0; August 31, 1935.
Bill Dietrich, Chi vs. StL AL, 8-0; June 1, 1937.
Johnny Vander Meer, Cin vs. Bos NL, 3-0; June 11, 1938.
2 Johnny Vander Meer, Cin vs. *Bro* NL, 6-0; June 15, 1938 (next start after June 11).
Monte Pearson, NY vs. Cle AL, 13-0; August 27, 1938 (2nd game).
Bob Feller, Cle vs. *Chi* AL, 1-0; April 16, 1940 (opening day).
Tex Carleton, Bro vs. Cin NL, 3-0; April 30, 1940.
Lon Warneke, StL vs. Cin NL, 2-0; August 30, 1941.
Jim Tobin, Bos vs. Bro NL, 2-0; April 27, 1944.
Clyde Shoun, Cin vs. Bos NL, 1-0; May 15, 1944.
Dick Fowler, Phi vs. StL AL, 1-0; September 9, 1945 (2nd game).
Ed Head, Bro vs. Bos NL, 5-0; April 23, 1946.
2 Bob Feller, Cle vs. *NY* AL, 1-0; April 30, 1946.
Ewell Blackwell, Cin vs. Bos NL, 6-0; June 18, 1947.
Don Black, Cle vs. Phi AL, 3-0; July 10, 1947 (1st game).
Bill McCahan, Phi vs. Was AL, 3-0; September 3, 1947.
Bob Lemon, Cle vs. *Det* AL, 2-0; June 30, 1948.
Rex Barney, Bro vs. *NY* NL, 2-0; September 9, 1948.
Vern Bickford, Bos vs. Bro NL, 7-0; August 11, 1950.
Cliff Chambers, Pit vs. *Bos* NL, 3-0; May 6, 1951 (2nd game).
3 Bob Feller, Cle vs. Det AL, 2-1; July 1, 1951 (1st game).

Allie Reynolds, NY vs. *Cle* AL, 1-0; July 12, 1951.
2 Allie Reynolds, NY vs. Bos AL, 8-0; September 28, 1951 (1st game).
Virgil Trucks, Det vs. Was AL, 1-0; May 15, 1952.
Carl Erskine, Bro vs. Chi NL, 5-0; June 19, 1952.
2 Virgil Trucks, Det vs. *NY* AL, 1-0; August 25, 1952.
Bobo Holloman, StL vs. Phi AL, 6-0; May 6, 1953 (first start in the major leagues).
Jim Wilson, Mil vs. Phi NL, 2-0; June 12, 1954.
Sam Jones, Chi vs Pit NL, 4-0; May 12, 1955.
2 Carl Erskine, Bro vs. NY NL, 3-0; May 12, 1956.
* Johnny Klippstein (7 innings), Hershell Freeman (1 inning) and Joe Black (3 innings)., Cin vs. *Mil* NL, 1-2; May 26, 1956. (lost on three hits in 11 innings after allowing first hit in 10th).
Mel Parnell, Bos vs. Chi AL, 4-0; July 14, 1956.
Sal Maglie, Bro vs. Phi NL, 5-0; September 25, 1956.
Don Larsen, NY AL vs. Bro NL, 2-0; October 8, 1956. (World Series). (perfect game).
Bob Keegan, Chi vs. Was AL, 6-0; August 20, 1957 (2nd game).
Jim Bunning, Det vs. *Bos* AL, 3-0; July 20, 1958 (1st game).
Hoyt Wilhelm, Bal vs. NY AL, 1-0; September 20, 1958.
* Harvey Haddix, Pit vs. *Mil* NL, 0-1; May 26, 1959 (lost on one hit in 13 innings after pitching 12 perfect innings).
Don Cardwell, Chi vs. StL NL, 4-0; May 15, 1960 (2nd game).
Lew Burdette, Mil vs. Phi NL, 1-0; August 18, 1960.
Warren Spahn, Mil vs. Phi NL, 4-0; September 16, 1960.
2 Warren Spahn, Mil vs. SF NL, 1-0; April 28, 1961.
Bo Belinsky, LA vs. Bal AL, 2-0; May 5, 1962.
Earl Wilson, Bos vs. LA AL, 2-0; June 26, 1962.
Sandy Koufax, LA vs. NY NL, 5-0; June 30, 1962.
Bill Monbouquette, Bos vs. *Chi* AL, 1-0; August 1, 1962.
Jack Kralick, Min vs. KC AL, 1-0; August 26, 1962.
2 Sandy Koufax, LA vs. SF NL, 8-0; May 11, 1963.
Don Nottebart, Hou vs. Phi NL, 4-1; May 17, 1963.
Juan Marichal, SF vs. Hou NL, 1-0; June 15, 1963.
Ken T. Johnson, Hou vs. Cin NL, 0-1; April 23, 1964 (lost game).
3 Sandy Koufax, LA vs. Phi NL, 3-0; June 4, 1964.
2 Jim Bunning, Phi vs. *NY* NL, 6-0; June 21, 1964 (1st game; perfect game).
* Jim Maloney, Cin vs. NY NL, 0-1; June 14, 1965 (lost on two hits in 11 innings after pitching 10 hitless innings).
Jim Maloney, Cin vs. *Chi* NL, 1-0; August 19, 1965 (1st game; 10 innings).
4 Sandy Koufax, LA vs. Chi NL, 1-0; September 9, 1965 (perfect game).
Dave Morehead, Bos vs. Cle AL, 2-0; September 16, 1965.
Sonny Siebert, Cle vs. Was AL, 2-0; June 10, 1966.
Steve D. Barber (8⅔ innings). and Stu Miller (⅓ inning) Bal vs. Det AL, 1-2; April 30, 1967 (1st game; lost game).
Don Wilson, Hou vs. Atl NL, 2-0; June 18, 1967.
Dean Chance, Min vs. *Cle* AL, 2-1; August 25, 1967 (2nd game).
Joe Horlen, Chi vs. Det AL, 6-0; September 10, 1967 (1st game).
Tom Phoebus, Bal vs. Bos AL, 6-0; April 27, 1968.
Catfish Hunter, Oak vs. Min AL, 4-0; May 8, 1968 (perfect game).
George Culver, Cin vs. *Phi* NL, 6-1; July 29, 1968 (2nd game).
Gaylord Perry, SF vs. StL NL, 1-0; Sept. 17, 1968.
Ray Washburn, StL vs. *SF* NL, 2-0; September 18, 1968.
Bill Stoneman, Mon vs. *Phi* NL, 7-0; April 17, 1969.
3 Jim Maloney, Cin vs. Hou NL, 10-0; April 30, 1969.
2 Don Wilson, Hou vs. *Cin* NL, 4-0; May 1, 1969.
Jim Palmer, Bal vs. Oak AL, 8-0; August 13, 1969.
Ken Holtzman, Chi vs. Atl NL, 3-0; August 19, 1969.
Bob Moose, Pit vs. *NY* NL, 4-0; September 20, 1969.
Dock Ellis, Pit vs. *SD* NL, 2-0; June 12, 1970 (1st game).
Clyde Wright, Cal vs. Oak AL, 4-0; July 3, 1970.
Bill Singer, LA vs Phi NL, 5-0; July 20, 1970.
Vida Blue, Oak vs. Min AL, 6-0; September 21, 1970.
2 Ken Holtzman, Chi vs. Cin NL, 1-0; June 3, 1971.
Rick Wise, Phi vs. *Cin* NL, 4-0; June 23, 1971.
Bob Gibson, StL vs. *Pit* NL, 11-0; August 14, 1971.
Burt Hooton, Chi vs. Phi NL, 4-0; April 16, 1972.
Milt Pappas, Chi vs. SD NL, 8-0; September 2, 1972.
2 Bill Stoneman, Mon vs. NY NL, 7-0; October 2, 1972 (1st game).
Steve Busby, KC vs. *Det* AL, 3-0; April 27, 1973.
Nolan Ryan, Cal vs. *KC* AL, 3-0; May 15, 1973.
2 Nolan Ryan, Cal vs. Det AL, 6-0; July 15, 1973.
Jim Bibby, Tex vs. *Oak* AL, 6-0; July 20, 1973.
Phil Niekro, Atl vs. SD NL, 9-0; August 5, 1973.
2 Steve Busby, KC vs. *Mil* AL, 2-0; June 19, 1974.
Dick Bosman, Cle vs. Oak AL, 4-0; July 19, 1974.
3 Nolan Ryan, Cal vs. Min AL, 4-0; September 28, 1974
4 Nolan Ryan, Cal vs. Bal AL, 1-0; June 1, 1975.
Ed Halicki, SF vs. NY NL, 6-0; August 24, 1975 (2nd game).
Vida Blue (5 innings), Glenn Abbott (1 inning), Paul Lindblad (1 inning), and Rollie Fingers (2 innings), Oak vs. Cal AL, 5-0; September 28, 1975.
Larry Dierker, Hou vs. Mon NL, 6-0; July 9, 1976.
Blue Moon Odom (5 innings) and Francisco Barrios (4 innings), Chi vs. *Oak* AL, 6-0; July 28, 1976.
John Candelaria, Pit vs. LA NL, 2-0; August 9, 1976.
John Montefusco, SF vs. *Atl* NL, 9-0; September 29, 1976.
Jim Colborn, KC vs. Tex AL, 6-0; May 14, 1977.
Dennis Eckersley, Cle vs. Cal AL, 1-0; May 30, 1977.
Bert Blyleven, Tex vs. *Cal* AL, 6-0; September 22, 1977.
Bob Forsch, StL vs. Phi NL, 5-0; April 16, 1978.
Tom Seaver, Cin vs. StL NL, 4-0; June 16, 1978.
Ken Forsch, Hou vs. Atl NL, 6-0; April 7, 1979.

Jerry Reuss, LA vs. *SF* NL, 8-0; June 27, 1980.
Charlie Lea, Mon vs. SF NL, 4-0; May 10, 1981 (2nd game).
Len Barker, Cle vs. Tor AL, 3-0; May 15, 1981 (perfect game).
5 Nolan Ryan, Hou vs. LA NL, 5-0; September 26, 1981.
Dave Righetti, NY vs. Bos AL, 4-0; July 4, 1983.
2 Bob Forsch, StL vs. Mon NL, 3-0; September 26, 1983.
Mike Warren, Oak vs. Chi AL, 3-0; September 29, 1983.
Jack Morris, Det vs. Chi AL, 4-0; April 7, 1984.
Mike Witt, Cal vs. *Tex* AL, 1-0; September 30, 1984 (perfect game).
Joe Cowley, Chi vs. *Cal* AL, 7-1; September 19, 1986.
Mike Scott, Hou vs. SF NL, 2-0; September 25, 1986.
Juan Nieves, Mil vs. Bal AL, 7-0; April 15, 1987.
Tom Browning, Cin vs. LA NL, 1-0; September 16, 1988 (perfect game).
Mark Langston (7 innings) and Mike Witt (2 innings), Cal vs Sea AL, 1-0; April 11, 1990.
Randy Johnson, Sea vs. Det AL, 2-0; June 2, 1990.
6 Nolan Ryan, Tex vs. *Oak* AL, 5-0; June 11, 1990.
Dave Stewart, Oak vs. *Tor* AL, 5-0; June 29, 1990.
Fernando Valenzuela, LA vs. StL NL, 6-0; June 29, 1990.
* Andy Hawkins, NY vs. *Chi* AL, 0-4; July 1, 1990 (8 innings, lost the game).
Terry Mulholland, Phi vs. SF NL, 6-0; August 15, 1990.
Dave Stieb, Tor vs. *Det* AL, 3-0; September 2, 1990.
7 Nolan Ryan, Tex vs. *Tor* AL, 3-0; May 1, 1991.
Tommy Greene, Phi vs. *Mon* NL, 2-0; May 23, 1991.
Bob Milacki, Bal (6 innings), Mike Flanagan (1 inning), Mark Williamson (1 inning), Gregg Olson (1 inning) vs. *Oak* AL, 2-0; July 13, 1991.

* Mark Gardner, Mon vs. *LA* NL, 0-1; July 26, 1991 (9 innings, lost game in 10th).
Dennis Martinez, Mon vs. *LA* NL, 2-0; July 28, 1991 (perfect game).
Wilson Alvarez, Chi vs. *Bal* AL, 7-0; August 11, 1991.
Bret Saberhagen, KC vs. *Chi* AL, 7-0; August 26, 1991.
Kent Mercker (6 innings), Mark Wohlers (2 innings), Alejandro Pena (1 inning), Atl vs. SD NL, 1-0; September 11, 1991.
* Matt Young, Bos vs. *Cle* AL, 1-2; April 12, 1992 (8 innings, lost game).
Kevin Gross, LA vs. *SF* NL, 2-0; August 17, 1992.
Chris Bosio, Sea vs. Bos AL, 7-0; April 22, 1993.
Jim Abbott, NY vs. Cle AL, 4-0; September 4, 1993.
Darryl Kile, Hou vs. NY NL, 7-1; September 8, 1993.
Kent Mercker, Atl vs. *LA*, NL, 6-0; April 8, 1994.
Scott Erickson, Minn vs. Mil AL, 6-0; April 27, 1994.
Kenny Rogers, Tex vs. Cal AL, 4-0; July 29, 1994 (perfect game).
* Pedro Martinez (9 innings) and Mel Rojas (1 inning), Mon. vs. S.D. NL; 1-0; June 3, 1995 (Martinez pitched 9 perfect innings, but allowed a hit in the 10th, Rojas relieved and finished the game).
Ramon Martinez, L.A. vs. Fla. NL, 7-0, July 14, 1995.
Al Leiter, Fla. vs. Col. NL, 11-0; May 11, 1996.
Dwight Gooden, NY vs. Sea. AL, 2-0; May 14, 1996.
Hideo Nomo, L.A. vs. Col. NL, 9-0, September 17, 1996.
Kevin Brown, Fla. vs. *SF* NL, 9-0; June 10, 1997.
Francisco Cordova (9 innings) and Ricardo Rincon (1 inning), Pit. vs. Hou. NL, 30; July 12, 1997
David Wells, NY vs. Min. AL, 4-0; May 17, 1998 (perfect game)

Perfection Plus

Year	Pitcher	Batters	Opponent	Notes
1959	Harvey Haddix	36	Milwaukee	(12 innings)
1919	Waite Hoyt	34	Yanks	(2nd-13th inning)
1880	Pud Galvin	33	Worcester	(6 errors)
1884	Charlie Buffinton	32	Providence	(5 errors)
1971	Rick Wise	32	Chicago	(2nd-12th inning)
1908	Nap Rucker	30	Braves	(3 errors)
1885	John Clarkson	29	Providence	(3 errors, 1 DP)
1883	Hoss Radbourn	28	Cleveland	(1 error)
1884	Pud Galvin	28	Detroit	(1 error)
1905	Christy Mathewson	28	Cubs	(2 errors, one DP)
1910	Tom Hughes	28	Cleveland	(1 error)
1919	Walter Johnson	28**	New York	
1920	Walter Johnson	28	Red Sox	(1 error)
1947	Bill McCahan	28	Washington	(1 error)
1974	Dick Bosman	28	Oakland	(1 error, his own)
1980	Jerry Reuss	28	San Francisco	(1 error)
1880	J. L. Richmond	27	Cleveland	
1880	J. M. Ward	27	Buffalo	
1904	Cy Young	27	Philadelphia	
1906	Lefty Leifield	27	Cubs	(8 innings, 3 errors)
1908	Addie Joss	27	White Sox	

Year	Pitcher	Batters	Opponent	Notes
1919	Walter Johnson	28**	New York	
1922	Charlie Robertson	27	Detroit	
1953	Curt Simmons	27*	Milwaukee	
1956	Don Larsen	27	Brooklyn	
1964	Jim Bunning	27	Mets	
1965	Sandy Koufax	27	Cubs	
1968	Catfish Hunter	27	Minnesota	
1981	Len Barker	27	Toronto	
1984	Mike Witt	27	Texas	
1988	Tom Browning	27	Los Angeles	
1991	Dennis Martinez	27	Los Angeles	
1994	Kenny Rogers	27	California	
1954	Robin Roberts	27*	Cincinnati	
1981	Jim Bibby	27*	Atlanta	
1990	Terry Mulholland	27	San Francisco	(1 error, 1 DP)
1995	Pedro J. Martinez	27	San Diego	
1998	David Wells	27	Minnesota	
1917	Ernie Shore	26†	Washington	

*Retired last twenty-seven batters in a row after giving up a hit to leadoff man.
**Retired twenty-eight batters in a row after allowing a one-out single in the first inning, then allowed a two-out single in the tenth.
†Starter Babe Ruth walked the first man and promptly slugged the umpire in the jaw and was banished. Ernie Shore rushed in from the bull pen, got the runner on a steal attempt, and retired the next twenty-six.
Note: Hooks Wiltse in 1908 and Lew Burdette in 1960 missed perfection because each hit a batter, with Wiltse hitting the *last* batter—the opposing pitcher—with an 0–2 count.

## CHAPTER 10

Awards and Honors

Bill Deane

This chapter presents the history and voting results of baseball's most prestigious awards and honors, including the complete balloting and current constituency of the Baseball Hall of Fame. This material will be of interest to the fan who wonders how a player of the past was viewed by his contemporaries. I have ventured an additional section of "what if" awards: what if the Cy Young Award had been instituted long before its actual inception in 1956, or the Rookie of the Year before its real debut in 1947, and so on. What follows is divided into nine sections:

MVP Award: history and balloting.
Rookie of the Year Award: history and balloting.
Cy Young Award: history and balloting.
Hypothetical Awards: explanation and selections.
Gold Glove Award: history, discussion, and list of winners.
Special MVP Awards: All-Star Game, League Championship Series, World Series.
Periodic Awards: Player and Pitcher of the Month
Off the Field Awards: AP Athlete of the Year, Roberto Clemente, Ford C. Frick, Lou Gehrig, S. Rae Hickok, Fred Hutchinson, Sid Mercer, and J. G. Taylor Spink Awards, and the *Sports Illustrated* Sportsman of the Year.
Hall of Fame: history of elections and balloting.

Balloting tables and lists of winners include each player's first initial, last name, and club city abbreviation (and point total, if applicable).

Most Valuable Player Award: History

The concept of most valuable player awards dates back more than a century. The first documented MVP-type honor in pro ball was bestowed upon James "Deacon" White of the 1875 Boston Red Stockings in the National Association. Catcher White sparked Boston to a remarkable 71-8 record that year, scoring 77 runs in 80 games and batting .355. An ardent Red Stockings' admirer presented Deacon with a silver tray, water pitcher, and loving cup inscribed with the words: WON BY JIM WHITE AS MOST VALUABLE PLAYER TO BOSTON TEAM, 1875.

The first official MVP honor was initiated some 35 years later. Prior to the 1910 season, baseball fan Hugh Chalmers, president and general manager of the Chalmers Motor Company, announced that he would present one of his company's automobiles—a Chalmers "30"—to the major league player who compiled the highest batting average. What appeared to be a harmless promotional gimmick was to soon turn into a public relations disaster.

The rules specified that players must accumulate a specific minimum number of times at bat, depending on position, to qualify for the award. For infielders and outfielders, it was a minimum of 350 at bats; for catchers, 250 at bats; and for pitchers, 100 at bats. Interest in the award was tremendous from the outset. Ty Cobb, who already owned a Chalmers "30" roadster, wrote: "I am glad that something besides medals and trophies is offered for the championship in batting. I think the offer of a Chalmers "30" is simply great and I hope to be lucky enough to own a new Chalmers next fall."

It developed into a two-man race, with Detroit's Cobb and Cleveland's Napoleon Lajoie, both American Leaguers, the only serious challengers for the coveted prize. Throughout the season there were charges and countercharges of favoritism by scorers in various cities. Furthermore, the general consensus of the press was that Cobb's selfish pursuit of this individual honor had cost his team the pennant. The controversy was capped by scandalous circumstances on the final day of the season.

Through games of Sept. 16, Cobb held a solid lead over Lajoie, .368 to .357 (although, because of the era's sloppy record keeping, few actually knew the official figures at the time). From then through Oct. 8, Cobb batted a torrid .532 (25-for-47) to seemingly lock up the crown with a .383 average. But Lajoie refused to surrender, going 30-for-54 (.556) in that same span to enter the final day, Oct. 9, with a .376 mark. Cobb chose to sit out his final game, while Lajoie played the infamous doubleheader with the St. Louis Browns in which he went 8-for-8, including seven bunt hits—remarkable for a slow-footed slugger—to apparently edge out Cobb in the batting race. Browns' manager Jack O'Connor had instructed his rookie third baseman, Red Corriden, to play deep on Lajoie, advice with which Corriden complied. Lajoie took advantage of the strange defensive arrangement with the repeated safe bunts. Although neither Lajoie nor Corriden were implicated, there were charges of a Browns' frame-up to give the coveted batting title (and car) to the respected Lajoie over the disliked Cobb.

O'Connor lost his job due to his role in the alleged fix. Subsequently, AL president Ban Johnson announced that a "discrepancy" had been found in the official records, and that Cobb had actually won the batting crown after all (although this point is challenged by many current researchers, who have evidence that Cobb was credited wrongly for a 2-for-3 game). Meanwhile, Hugh Chalmers, attempting to divorce himself from the controversy, presented autos to both Cobb and Lajoie. It was generally acknowledged that this fiasco doomed the future of indi-

vidual awards of any kind.

Hoping to salvage some goodwill out of the whole idea, Chalmers came up with a new proposal for the 1911 season. This time he would award an auto to one player in each league who "should prove himself as the most important and useful player to his club and to the league at large in point of deportment and value of services rendered." The decision for this honor was to be made by a committee of baseball writers, one writer from each club city in each league. Each writer was to make eight selections, with a first-place ballot scoring eight points, on down to an eighth-place vote counting one point. Thus was born the short-lived Chalmers Award, with Ty Cobb and Frank Schulte earning recognition in 1911. Both Cobb and Schulte voluntarily withdrew from the competition in 1912, although the former received 17 points anyway.

Interest in the award diminished within a few years. By 1914 the public was distracted by baseball's battles with the new Federal League and the escalation of the World War in Europe. The timing was right for the Chalmers Award to quietly disappear; it was noted that Mr. Chalmers had agreed to present vehicles for five years and that the 1914 awards marked the fifth presentations.

On July 15, 1922, the newly formed American League Trophy Committee adopted a set of rules governing the selection of an annual award-winner. The rules specified that "the purpose of the American League Trophy is to honor the baseball player who is of greatest all-round service to his club and credit to the sport during each season; to recognize and reward uncommon skill and ability when exercised by a player for the best interests of his team, and to perpetuate his memory." The rules further instructed voters to seek out the "winning ball player," reminding them that "combined offensive and defensive ability is not always indicated by any system of records."

Eight baseball writers, one from each AL city, were enfranchised, with each required to select exactly one player from each team, for a total of eight selections. Player-managers and previous winners were to be excluded from consideration. Points were distributed the same as in the Chalmers Award: eight for first place, down to one for eighth.

The intention of Ban Johnson was to have a monument to baseball erected in East Potomac Park, Washington, D.C., engraved with the names of winners of the AL Award. This proposal was introduced as a congressional resolution in 1924, and passed in the House of Representatives before dying on the Senate Floor.

The AL voting rules led to growing criticism for several reasons, one of which was the limitation on the number of vote-getters from each team. For example, when the Browns' George Sisler won the first AL Award in 1922, he was named on all eight ballots—thus disqualifying his teammates from receiving any votes. As a result, fellow Brownie Ken Williams, who led the league in home runs (39), RBIs (155), and total bases (367) and became the first player ever to have 30 homers and 30 stolen bases in the same season, was shut out in the voting. Secondly, the rule prohibiting player-managers from eligibility drew fire. In 1925, when this rule eliminated five solid candidates from consideration, The *New York Times* wrote, "to say that it is impossible or impractical to divorce a man's managerial skill from his talents purely as a player is to reflect on the intelligence of the committee that awards the prize."

The *Times* further editorialized on the fallacy of assuming that no player can be the "most valuable" more than one year: "the purpose, of course, is to pass the honor around, but the effect is to pass an empty honor around." This rule became increasingly ridiculous when it eliminated Babe Ruth (and his 60 home runs) from consideration in 1927; by the following year, both Ruth and teammate Lou Gehrig, who were in the process of finishing one-two in the AL home run derby in five consecutive seasons, were ineligible for the League Award.

In 1924 the National League instituted its own award, with radical differences in the selection method: each writer voted for 10 players rather than eight (with 10 points for first place, and so on); he was not bound to vote for a certain number of players from each team; he was free to select a player-manager; and, later, he was allowed to consider previous winners of the award. Additionally, the NL offered a cash "present" of $1,000 to the award-winner.

At various times between 1925 and 1951, writers were permitted to name "honorable mention" candidates, whose vote totals were listed but not counted in the balloting. Another feature of early voting reports was the listing of "cumulative vote leaders"—a forerunner to Bill James's "award shares"—over a period of years.

A number of factors led to the demise of the AL Award, including the award's loss of credibility due to the previously mentioned shortsighted voting rules. Secondly, Ban Johnson, having failed to secure the erection of his proposed monument, felt the award had fallen short of its aim. Finally, management was concerned with the efforts of award-winners to parlay their honors into substantial pay raises. The AL Award was officially voted out at a special league meeting on May 6, 1929.

The National League followed suit with the AL's decision, but agreed to continue its award through the 1929 season.

In October 1929 the Baseball Writers' Association of America (BBWAA) announced the results of an "unofficial" AL most valuable player poll, whose winner was Lew Fonseca of Cleveland.

Two months later, *The Sporting News* (TSN) conducted a poll of the eight writers who had previously voted on the League Award, thereby reporting Al Simmons as the "unofficial" AL Award-winner. Combining the results of these two unofficial polls gives Fonseca 77 points, followed by Heinie Manush (57), Simmons (56), Tony Lazzeri (55) and Charlie Gehringer (44).

The Sporting News announced that, thereafter, they would take it upon themselves to conduct an annual poll to substitute for the defunct league awards. However, they retained the stipulation that each voter must select just one player on each team. In 1930, TSN chose Joe Cronin in the AL and Bill Terry in the NL. Earlier, the Associated Press also had a special committee of writers make an unofficial AL selection for 1930, while the BBWAA did the same for the NL (adding a check for $1,000 for the winner). The respective selections here were Cronin in the AL and Hack Wilson in the NL. Again combining the two

sets of polls, the AL leaders were Cronin (100), Al Simmons (85), Lou Gehrig (68), Charlie Gehringer (67), and Ted Lyons (56). The NL pace-setters were Hack Wilson (111), Frankie Frisch (107), Bill Terry (105), Chuck Klein (57), and Floyd "Babe" Herman (52).

In an effort to standardize MVP voting, the BBWAA, in its annual winter meeting in New York on Dec. 11, 1930, decided to appoint two committees (one in each league) to elect Most Valuable Players, with the association to "award suitable emblems to the players selected." Thus was born what is considered the modern MVP Award, with most of the flaws of its forerunners eliminated.

TSN, however, continued to make its own selections in bitter competition with the BBWAA. Finally, beginning in 1938, TSN agreed to unify the award by abiding with BBWAA balloting, and presenting *The Sporting News* Trophy to the winner. Among the various prizes awarded to the winners were wristwatches and shotguns.

At a meeting during the 1944 World Series, the BBWAA decided to begin issuing its own trophy, the Kenesaw Mountain Landis Award, in honor of the ailing commissioner. Landis died a month later and the official MVP Award has born his name ever since. A plaque engraved with the names of the winners hangs in the National Baseball Library in Cooperstown, N.Y.

The Sporting News went back to naming its own MVPs in 1944 and '45. Then, at the request of the new commissioner, Happy Chandler, TSN "withdrew from the field to cooperate in making the Landis Awards, provided by the major leagues, the official designations of the year." In 1948, however, TSN went back to its own awards, selecting a Player of the Year and Pitcher of the Year in each league, as they have done ever since. For whatever reason, TSN awards have never received the public recognition that the BBWAA honors have.

Two major changes in the MVP voting began in 1938. The BBWAA began polling three writers in each major league city, rather than just one, which remained in effect until it was reduced to two writers per city, starting in 1961. Also in 1938, the process was initiated to award 14 points for each first-place vote, rather than 10.

"Split votes," which have since infiltrated all the major awards, first appeared in MVP Awards in 1959. The American League MVP race that year, by consensus, was between second baseman Nellie Fox and shortstop Luis Aparicio of the champion Chicago White Sox. Late in the season, the suggestion often arose that the two ought to share the award. When the votes were in, Fox had received 14 first-place votes, Aparicio had gotten six, and four writers had split their votes between the two. Tickled with the idea of a split vote, one NL writer also resorted to this option, dividing his first-place nomination between Ernie Banks and Eddie Mathews. The "cop-out vote" having been allowed in '59, has since surfaced in 16 more MVP Awards, 10 Rookie of the Year, and six Cy Young Award elections. The ultimate folly of this practice was best exemplified in 1979. One NL writer split his fourth-place vote between pitching brothers Phil and Joe Niekro, evidently convinced that the two were identical twins. But the writer was still permitted to make six more selections.

That meant that his fifth-, sixth-, and seventh-place selections received more points (six, five and four, respectively) than his fourth-place co-selections, who were credited with just three and a half points apiece! The 1979 NL vote, incidentally, resulted in the only actual split MVP as sentimental favorite Willie Stargell of the Pittsburgh Pirates and batting champion Keith Hernandez of the St. Louis Cardinals each received 216 votes and were declared "co-MVP."

There has long been debate about the consideration of pitchers for the MVP Award, the theory (by some) that a man who plays every fourth game cannot be as valuable as a man who plays every day. The debate escalated after the inception of the Cy Young Award in 1956, giving pitchers their own exclusive honor, and the increasing practice of five-man rotations in the 1970s, giving starting pitchers even less of a chance to contribute.

As far as Jack Lang, assistant secretary of the BBWAA, is concerned, there is no room for controversy. "The rules that are sent out to the voters on the [MVP] committee state: 'Keep in mind that all players are eligible. That includes pitchers, starters and relievers,'" says Lang. "Anybody on the committee that feels they cannot vote for a pitcher, we replace them. In my 24 years running the elections, only two writers have said that to me." Since 1931 pitchers have won the award 10 times in the AL and nine times in the NL.

There have been 16 occasions in which one player received all of the available first-place MVP votes in his league. The AL players so honored are Ty Cobb (1911), Babe Ruth (1923), Hank Greenberg (1935), Al Rosen (1953), Mickey Mantle (1956), Frank Robinson (1966), Denny McLain (1968), Reggie Jackson (1973), Jose Canseco (1988), Frank Thomas (1993), and Ken Griffey, Jr. (1997). The five unanimous NL selections are Carl Hubbell (1936), Orlando Cepeda (1967), Mike Schmidt (1980), Jeff Bagwell (1994), and Ken Caminiti (1996). Hubbell's distinction is disputable, as two of the eight writers did not submit ballots that year and were not replaced on the selection committee.

Following are the maximum possible point totals that could have been earned by an individual receiving the first-place nomination of every writer polled:

NATIONAL LEAGUE		AMERICAN LEAGUE	
1911–14	64	1911–14	64
1924–29	80	1922–28	64
1931–37	80	1931–37	80
1938–60	336	1938–60	336
1961	224	1961–68	280
1962–68	280	1969–76	336
1969–1992	336	1977–present	392
1993–1997	392		
1998	448		

There have been numerous cases in which the MVP vote point totals did not add up to the correct figure. Reasons for this include inaccuracies in tabulation, inaccuracies in reporting, and writers who failed to vote or to complete their ballots. However, the total impact of all these errors is a small fraction of 1 percent of the total voting over the years.

Following is a complete tabulation of all the recognized MVP elections since 1911:

MVP Award:
Chalmers Award, 1911–14

1911 NATIONAL
F. Schulte, CHI 29
C. Mathewson, NY ... 25
L. Doyle, NY 23
H. Wagner, PIT 23
G. Alexander, PHI 23
M. Huggins, SL 21
F. Merkle, NY 19
R. Marquard, NY 19
J. Daubert, BRO 16
J. Tinker, CHI 11
C. Meyers, NY 11
J. Sheckard, CHI 9
M. Mitchell, CIN 9
M. Doolan, PHI 6
B. Harmon, SL........ 6
J. Archer, CHI 5
H. Lobert, PHI 4
G. Gibson, PIT 4
M. Brown, CHI 4
B. Bescher, CIN 4
B. Sweeney, BOS 3
O. Knabe, PHI 2
E. Konetchy, SL 2
D. Hoblitzell, CIN ... 2
J. Walsh, PHI 2
J. Devore, NY 2
F. Luderus, PHI 1
J. Kling, BOS 1
B. Adams, PIT 1
N. Rucker, BRO 1

1911 AMERICAN
T. Cobb, DET 64
E. Walsh, CHI 35
E. Collins, PHI 32
J. Jackson, CLE 28

W. Johnson, WAS ... 19
B. Cree, NY 16
T. Speaker, BOS..... 16
I. Thomas, PHI 12
C. Milan, WAS 10
V. Gregg, CLE 9
F. Baker, PHI 8
J. Coombs, PHI....... 6
N. Lajoie, CLE 5
J. Knight, NY 4
S. Crawford, DET 4
B. Lord, PHI 4
D. Bush, DET 4
R. Ford, NY 3
J. Barry, PHI 3
J. Austin, SL........ 2
F. LaPorte, SL 2
S. McInnis, PHI 1
G. McBride, WAS ... 1

1912 NATIONAL
L. Doyle, NY 48
H. Wagner, PIT 43
C. Meyers, NY 25
J. Tinker, CHI 22
B. Bescher, CIN 17
B. Sweeney, BOS ... 16
H. Zimmerman, CHI . 16
R. Marquard, NY 13
O. Wilson, PIT 13
J. Daubert, BRO 13
O. Knabe, PHI 10
E. Konetchy, SL 8
C. Mathewson, NY ... 8
D. Paskert, PHI 6
J. Tesreau, NY 6
R. Murray, NY 5

M. Huggins, SL ... 5
A. Marsans, CIN 4
F. Merkle, NY 4
J. Evers, CHI 2
C. Hendrix, PIT 2
J. Archer, CHI 1
G. Alexander, PHI ... 1

1912 AMERICAN
T. Speaker, BOS..... 59
E. Walsh, CHI 30
W. Johnson, WAS ... 28
C. Milan, WAS ... 23
J. Wood, BOS 22
E. Collins, PHI 18
F. Baker, PHI 17
T. Cobb, DET 17
J. Jackson, CLE 16
H. Wagner, PIT 12
C. Gandil, WAS 7
B. Shotton, SL...... 6
D. Pratt, SL 5
E. Foster, WAS 4
L. Gardner, BOS 4
S. Crawford, DET 4
J. Barry, PHI 4
B. Carrigan, BOS 3
G. Moriarty, DET 2
J. Birmingham, CLE .. 2
D. Moeller, WAS 2
G. McBride, WAS 2
S. McInnis, PHI 1
B. Daniels, NY 1

1913 AMERICAN
W. Johnson, WAS ... 54
J. Jackson, CLE 43
E. Collins, PHI 30
T. Speaker, BOS..... 26
F. Baker, PHI 21
C. Gandil, WAS 14
S. McInnis, PHI 12

R. Maranville, BOS.. 23
C. Mathewson, NY ... 21
C. Meyers, NY 20
V. Saier, CHI 15
L. Cheney, CHI 12
D. Miller, PIT 11
H. Wagner, PIT 11
J. Evers, CHI 10
T. Seaton, PHI 9
A. Fletcher, NY 7
J. Archer, CHI 6
M. Doolan, PHI 6
B. Sweeney, BOS 6
J. Viox, PIT 6
L. Doyle, NY 5
T. Shafer, NY 5
R. Murray, NY 4
H. Zimmerman, CHI .. 4
O. Knabe, PHI 4
B. Adams, PIT 3
G. Cutshaw, BRO 3
G. Burns, NY 2
A. Marsans, CIN 2
B. Humphries, CHI ... 2
M. Brown, CIN 1

1913 NATIONAL
J. Daubert, BRO 50
G. Cravath, PHI 40

N. Lajoie, CLE 7
D. Bush, DET 6
H. Wagner, BOS 6
R. Russell, CHI 5
B. Shotton, SL....... 5
G. McBride, WAS 5
J. Scott, CHI 5
G. Stovall, SL...... 5
S. Crawford, DET 5
T. Cobb, DET 3
R. Schalk, CHI 3
C. Bender, PHI 2
T. Turner, CLE 2
S. O'Neill, CLE 1
H. Hooper, BOS 1

1914 NATIONAL
J. Evers, BOS 50
R. Maranville, BOS.. 44
B. James, BOS 33
G. Burns, NY 31
J. Miller, SL 18
J. Tesreau, NY 15
D. Rudolph, BOS 14
S. Magee, PHI 14
Z. Wheat, BRO 10
G. Alexander, PHI ... 9
R. Bresnahan, CHI .. 6
L. Magee, SL 6
B. Doak, SL 6
J. Viox, PIT 5
A. Fletcher, NY 5
C. Mathewson, NY ... 4
V. Saier, CHI 4
B. Schmidt, BOS 4
J. Daubert, BRO 4
L. McCarty, BRO 3

H. Groh, CIN........... 2
T. Clarke, CIN 1
G. Cravath, PHI 1

1914 AMERICAN
E. Collins, PHI 63
S. Crawford, DET 35
D. Bush, DET 17
F. Baker, PHI 17
J. Jackson, CLE 15
R. Schalk, CHI 13
E. Foster, WAS 11
B. Weaver, CHI 11
S. McInnis, PHI 11
D. Pratt, SL 10
W. Schang, PHI..... 10
T. Speaker, BOS 9
T. Walker, SL 8
T. Cobb, DET 7
E. Scott, BOS 7
J. Barry, PHI 6
D. Leonard, BOS ... 6
E. Plank, PHI 5
G. McBride, WAS 5
G. Lewis, BOS 4
H. Hooper, BOS 4
F. Maisel, NY 3
R. Peckinpaugh, NY .. 2
C. Milan, WAS 2
S. Agnew, SL 2
R. Hartzell, NY 2
C. Cicotte, CHI 1
G. Moriarty, DET 1

(No official awards, 1915–21)

MVP Award:
League Awards, 1922–29

1922 AMERICAN
G. Sisler, SL 59
E. Rommel, PHI...... 31
R. Schalk, CHI 26
L. Bush, NY 19
E. Collins, CHI 18
J. Bassler, DET 13
S. O'Neill, CLE 13
J. Judge, WAS 12

W. Pipp, NY 12
L. Blue, DET 11
C. Galloway, PHI 10
H. Heilmann, DET..... 8
D. Pratt, BOS 7
W. Schang, NY 7
B. Meusel, NY 6
E. Scott, NY 6
W. Johnson, WAS 5

U. Shocker, SL...... 5
C. Jamieson, CLE ... 4
J. Sewell, CLE 4
G. Burns, BOS...... 2
J. Dykes, PHI 2
J. Harris, WAS 2
R. Peckinpaugh, WAS 2
B. Wambsganss, CLE 2
G. Cutshaw, DET 1

1923 AMERICAN
B. Ruth, NY.......... 64
E. Collins, CHI 37
H. Heilmann, DET..... 31
W. Gerber, SL 20
J. Sewell, CLE 20
C. Jamieson, CLE ... 19

C. Perkins, PHI 1

J. Bassler, DET 17
C. Galloway, PHI 13
G. Uhle, CLE 13
G. Burns, BOS...... 8
H. Ehmke, BOS...... 7
M. Ruel, WAS 7
R. Peckinpaugh, WAS 6
U. Shocker, SL 5
J. Judge, WAS...... 4

M. McManus, SL 4
K. Williams, SL 3
J. Harris, BOS 3
B. Harris, WAS 3
J. Hauser, PHI 1
W. Johnson, WAS ... 1
C. Perkins, PHI 1

(No National League awards, 1922–23)

1924 NATIONAL
D. Vance, BRO 74
R. Hornsby, SL 62
F. Frisch, NY 40
Z. Wheat, BRO 40
R. Youngs, NY 35
G. Kelly, NY 34
R. Maranville, PIT 33
K. Cuyler, PIT 25
J. Fournier, BRO 21
E. Roush, CIN 12
G. Wright, PIT 10
A. High, BRO 9
B. Pinelli, CIN 7
R. Bressler, CIN ... 6
G. Hartnett, CHI 5
B. Grimes, BRO 5
J. Bottomley, SL..... 4
J. Johnston, BRO 4
M. Carey, PIT 3
T. Jackson, NY 3
E. Yde, PIT 2
C. Williams, PHI 1
E. Rixey, CIN 1
G. Alexander, CHI ... 1
H. DeBerry, BRO 1

1924 AMERICAN
W. Johnson, WAS ... 55
E. Collins, CHI 49
C. Jamieson, CLE ... 25
H. Pennock, NY 24

J. Bassler, DET 22
H. Severeid, SL...... 17
J. Hauser, PHI 13
W. Jacobson, SL 11
H. Heilmann, DET 9
J. Sewell, CLE 9
M. Ruel, WAS 7
W. Schang, NY 7
A. Simmons, PHI 7
W. Pipp, NY 6
H. Ehmke, BOS...... 5
I. Flagstead, BOS..... 5
W. Gerber, SL 4
E. Whitehill, DET 4
L. Blue, DET 3
I. Boone, BOS 2
J. Harris, BOS 2
C. Galloway, PHI 1
K. Williams, SL 1

1925 NATIONAL
R. Hornsby, SL 73
K. Cuyler, PIT 61
G. Kelly, NY 52
G. Wright, PIT 43
D. Vance, BRO 42
D. Bancroft, BOS 41
J. Bottomley, SL..... 28
P. Traynor, PIT 27
F. Frisch, NY 13
E. Roush, CIN 12
M. Carey, PIT 11

I. Meusel, NY 6
D. Luque, CIN 5
C. Grimm, CHI 5
Z. Wheat, BRO 5
P. Donohue, CIN..... 4
A. Hargrave, CIN ... 4
G. Harper, PHI 3
J. Sand, PHI 3
W. Gautreau, BOS 2
V. Aldridge, PIT 1

1925 AMERICAN
R. Peckinpaugh,
WAS 45
A. Simmons, PHI ... 41
J. Sewell, CLE 21
H. Heilmann, DET.... 20
L. Rice, SL 18
E. Sheely, CHI 17
I. Flagstead, BOS..... 10
W. Jacobson, SL 10
J. Mostil, CHI 10
J. Rice, SL 8
E. Rommel, PHI...... 7
R. Schalk, CHI 7
A. Wingo, DET 7
N. Combs, NY 6
B. Meusel, NY 6

T. Lyons, CHI 5
G. Burns, CLE 4
M. McManus, SL 4
H. Pennock, NY 4
B. Bengough, NY 2
H. Ehmke, BOS...... 2
L. Gehrig, NY 2
I. Boone, BOS 1
J. Dugan, NY 1
P. Todt, BOS 1

1926 NATIONAL
B. O'Farrell, SL 79
H. Critz, CIN 60
R. Kremer, PIT.... 32
T. Thevenow, SL..... 30
H. Wilson, CHI 25
L. Bell, SL 24
B. Hargrave, CIN ... 24
F. Rhem, SL 20
T. Lindstrom, NY 17
D. Bancroft, BOS 17
H. Carlson, PHI 16
P. Waner, PIT..... 15
P. Traynor, PIT 14
W. Pipp, CIN 12
J. Butler, BRO 10
B. Southworth, NY-SL 5

G. Alexander, CHI-SL. 5
C. Mays, CIN 4
G. Kelly, NY 2
C. Walker, CIN...... 1

1926 AMERICAN
G. Burns, CLE 63
J. Mostil, CHI 33
H. Pennock, NY 32
S. Rice, WAS 18
H. Heilmann, DET.... 16
H. Manush, DET 16
A. Simmons, PHI ... 16
L. Grove, PHI 12
L. Goslin, WAS 9
L. Gehrig, NY 7
T. Lazzeri, NY....... 7
B. Falk, CHI 6
F. Fothergill, DET ... 6
O. Melillo, SL 6
H. Rice, SL 6
O. Bluege, WAS 5
P. Todt, BOS 5
M. Cochrane, PHI ... 4
J. Judge, WAS...... 4
M. McManus, SL 4
B. Meusel, NY 3
E. Rigney, BOS 3

I. Flagstead, BOS..... 2
W. Gerber, SL 2
T. Zachary, SL 2
W. Jacobson, SL-BOS 1

1927 NATIONAL
P. Waner, PIT......... 72
F. Frisch, SL...... 66
R. Hornsby, NY 54
C. Root, CHI 46
T. Jackson, NY 42
L. Waner, PIT...... 25
P. Traynor, PIT 18
J. Haines, SL 16
R. Kremer, PIT 14
G. Hartnett, CHI 12
R. Lucas, CIN 10
H. Wilson, CHI 9
B. Terry, NY 6
J. Bottomley, SL..... 6
B. Hargrave, CIN ... 6
F. May, CIN.......... 6
C. Williams, PHI ... 6
E. Farrell, NY-BOS ... 4
B. Grimes, NY 4
M. Carey, BRO 3
R. Stephenson, CHI 3
G. Alexander, SL ... 3
C. Hill, PIT 2
J. Petty, BRO 2
F. Ulrich, PHI 2
C. Hafey, SL 1

1927 AMERICAN
L. Gehrig, NY 56
H. Heilmann, DET.... 35
T. Lyons, CHI 34

M. Cochrane, PHI ... 18
A. Simmons, PHI 18
G. Goslin, WAS 15
M. Ruel, WAS 15
J. Dykes, PHI 14
L. Sewell, CLE 13
J. Sewell, CLE 9
T. Lazzeri, NY 8
R. Reeves, WAS 7
F. O'Rourke, SL 6
J. Tavener, DET 6
H. Lisenbee, WAS ... 5
E. Miller, SL 5
A. Metzler, CHI 4
I. Flagstead, BOS.... 3
C. Jamieson, CLE ... 3
W. Schang, SL 3

F. Schulte, SL 3
W. Hudlin, CLE 2
W. Regan, BOS 2
J. Rothrock, BOS 2
B. Harriss, BOS 1
P. Todt, BOS 1

1928 NATIONAL
J. Bottomley, SL 76
F. Lindstrom, NY ... 70
B. Grimes, PIT 53
L. Benton, NY 37
H. Critz, CIN 37
P. Traynor, PIT 28
H. Wilson, CHI 21
S. Hogan, NY 17
T. Jackson, NY 16

R. Maranville, SL 14
D. Vance, BRO 13
C. Hafey, SL 11
H. Hornsby, BOS ... 10
G. Hartnett, CHI 6
P. Waner, PIT 5
L. Richbourg, BOS... 5
T. Douthit, SL....... 5
D. Bissonette, BRO .. 3
D. Flowers, BRO 3
J. Wilson, PHI-SL ... 3
A. Whitney, PHI 3
H. Ford, CIN 2
L. Thompson, PHI ... 1

1928 AMERICAN
M. Cochrane, PHI .. 53

H. Manush, SL...... 51
J. Judge, WAS...... 27
T. Lazzeri, NY...... 27
W. Kamm, CHI 15
G. Goslin, WAS 13
E. Combs, NY 13
C. Gehringer, DET ... 12
C. Myer, BOS...... 11
W. Hoyt, NY 8
J. Foxx, PHI 7
J. Sewell, CLE 6
L. Sewell, CLE 6
I. Flagstead, BOS.... 5
E. Morris, BOS 5
H. Heilmann, DET... 4
C. Lind, CLE 4
W. Cissell, CHI 4

A. Thomas, CHI...... 4
O. Carroll, DET 3
H. Rice, DET 3
L. Fonseca, CLE 2
T. Lyons, CHI 2
J. Hodapp, CLE 2
A. Metzler, CHI 1
W. Regan, BOS 1

1929 NATIONAL
R. Hornsby, CHI 60
L. O'Doul, PHI 54
B. Terry, NY 48
B. Grimes, PIT 35
L. Waner, PIT 30
R. Lucas, CIN 29
P. Traynor, PIT 27

H. Wilson, CHI 24
F. Herman, BRO 24
G. Bush, CHI 16
C. Klein, PHI 15
M. Ott, NY 15
T. Douthit, SL...... 14
C. Grimm, CHI 13
T. Jackson, NY 8
R. Maranville, BOS ... 5
H. Critz, CIN 5
B. Friberg, PHI 4
P. Malone, CHI 3
F. Frisch, SL 2
P. Whitney, PHI 2
J. Frederick, BRO.... 2
R. Stephenson, CHI 1
Z. Taylor, BOS-CHI ... 1

(There were no official selections for the American League in 1929 or for either league in 1930.)

MVP Award:
Baseball Writers' Association of America Awards, 1931–Present

1931 NATIONAL
F. Frisch, SL 65
C. Klein, PHI 55
B. Terry, NY 53
W. English, CHI 30
C. Hafey, SL 29
J. Wilson, SL 28
T. Jackson, NY 24
C. Grimm, CHI 21
E. Adams, SL 18
E. Brandt, BOS 15
R. Maranville, BOS ... 15
K. Cuyler, CHI 14
P. Traynor, PIT 12
R. Lucas, CIN 10
L. Waner, PIT 8
J. Bottomley, SL 8
J. Elliott, PHI 6
J. Quinn, BRO 6
N. Finn, BRO 5
W. Clark, BRO 3
P. Derringer, SL 3
C. Root, CHI 3
D. Bartell, PHI 2
J. Vergez, NY 2
F. Fitzsimmons, NY .. 1
L. O'Doul, BRO 1
G. Wright, BRO 1
T. Cuccinello, CIN ... 1
C. Gelbert, SL 1

1931 AMERICAN
L. Grove, PHI 78
L. Gehrig, NY 59
A. Simmons, PHI ... 51
E. Averill, CLE 43
B. Ruth, NY 40
E. Webb, BOS 22
J. Cronin, WAS 18
O. Melillo, SL 17
S. West, WAS....... 16
M. Cochrane, PHI ... 16
G. Earnshaw, PHI ... 12
W. Ferrell, CLE 12
F. Marberry, WAS.... 11
H. Rhyne, BOS 10
B. Chapman, NY 7
J. Stone, DET 6
C. Gehringer, DET ... 4
L. Blue, CHI 4
R. Kress, SL 3
C. Reynolds, CHI 2
W. Stewart, SL 2
G. Goslin, SL 2
D. MacFayden, BOS.. 2
T. Oliver, BOS 2
J. Foxx, PHI 1

1932 NATIONAL
C. Klein, PHI........ 78
L. Warneke, CHI 68
L. O'Doul, BRO 58
P. Waner, PIT 37
R. Stephenson, CHI 32
B. Terry, NY 25
D. Hurst, PHI 24
P. Traynor, PIT 17
H. Berman, CHI..... 16
M. Ott, NY 15
R. Brown, BOS 10

F. Herman, CIN 8
L. Waner, PIT 6
W. Berger, BOS 6
H. Wilson, BRO 6
E. Orsatti, SL 6
R. Maranville, BOS ... 5
J. Wilson, SL 5
T. Cuccinello, BRO ... 4
J. Dean, SL 4
F. Frisch, SL 3
R. Collins, SL 3
A. Vaughan, PIT 1
G. Bush, CHI 1

1932 AMERICAN
J. Foxx, PHI 75
L. Gehrig, NY 55
H. Manush, WAS.... 41
E. Averill, CLE 37
L. Gomez, NY 27
J. Cronin, WAS 26
B. Ruth, NY 26
T. Lazzeri, NY...... 21
A. Simmons, PHI ... 13
C. Gehringer, DET ... 13
D. Alexander,
    DET-BOS 10
W. Cissell, CHI-CLE . 10
R. Ferrell, SL......... 8
L. Grove, PHI 8
J. Allen, NY 8
B. Dickey, NY...... 8
G. Goslin, SL 7
M. Weaver, WAS..... 6
H. Davis, DET...... 5
D. Harris, WAS 5
W. Ferrell, CLE 5
J. Levey, SL 5
T. Lyons, CHI 5
B. Sullivan, CHI 3
E. McNair, PHI...... 3
S. Jolley, CHI-BOS .. 3
G. Crowder, WAS.... 2
M. McManus, BOS ... 2
G. Walker, DET 1
J. Sewell, NY 1

1933 NATIONAL
C. Hubbell, NY 77
C. Klein, PHI 48
W. Berger, BOS 44
B. Terry, NY 35
P. Martin, SL 31
G. Mancuso, NY 24
J. Dean, SL 23
P. Traynor, PIT 20
B. Ryan, NY 19
A. Lopez, BRO...... 18
B. Cantwell, BOS ... 18
H. Schumacher, NY .. 11
R. Maranville, BOS .. 11
G. Bush, CHI 11
L. French, PIT 10
F. Frisch, SL 7
J. Bottomley, CIN ... 5
J. Medwick, SL 5
G. Hartnett, CHI 5
L. Warneke, CHI 4
R. Lucas, CIN 3
D. Bartell, PHI 3

A. Vaughan, PIT 2
R. Moore, BOS 2
V. Davis, PHI 1
C. Hafey, CIN....... 1
D. Luque, NY 1

1933 AMERICAN
J. Foxx, PHI 74
J. Cronin, WAS 62
H. Manush, WAS ... 54
L. Gehrig, NY 39
L. Grove, PHI 35
C. Gehringer, DET ... 32
G. Crowder, WAS... 28
A. Simmons, CHI ... 19
E. Whitehill, WAS ... 18
O. Melillo, SL 12
S. West, SL 11
R. Ferrell, SL-BOS ... 9
B. Dickey, NY...... 9
T. Lazzeri, NY...... 6
J. Kuhel, WAS 5
E. Averill, CLE 5
C. Myer, WAS 5
M. Cochrane, PHI ... 5
B. Johnson, PHI 5
B. Chapman, NY 4
M. Bishop, PHI 1
L. Appling, CHI 1
W. Kamm, CLE 1

1934 NATIONAL
J. Dean, SL 78
P. Waner, PIT 50
J. Moore, NY 42
T. Jackson, NY 39
M. Ott, NY 37
R. Collins, SL 32
B. Terry, NY 30
C. Davis, PHI 18
P. Dean, SL 16
H. Schumacher, NY . 16
C. Hubbell, NY 16
W. Berger, BOS 13
L. Warneke, CHI 10
G. Hartnett, CHI 9
G. Slade, CIN 5
K. Cuyler, CHI 4
B. Frey, CIN 4
F. Frankhouse, BOS .. 4
R. Boyle, BRO 4
B. Herman, CHI..... 4
F. Frisch, SL 4
W. Hoyt, PIT 2
A. Lopez, BRO 1
V. Mungo, BRO 1
A. Vaughan, PIT 1

1934 AMERICAN
M. Cochrane, DET ... 67
C. Gehringer, DET ... 65
L. Gomez, NY 60
S. Rowe, DET 59
L. Gehrig, NY 54
H. Greenberg, DET .. 29
H. Trosky, CLE..... 18
W. Ferrell, BOS 16
M. Owen, DET 16
J. Foxx, PHI 11
A. Simmons, CHI ... 9

W. Werber, BOS 8
R. Johnson, BOS 8
G. Goslin, DET 6
S. West, SL 5
M. Harder, CLE 4
F. Higgins, PHI 3
E. Averill, CLE 3
B. Knickerbocker,
    CLE 2

1935 NATIONAL
G. Hartnett, CHI 75
J. Dean, SL 66
A. Vaughan, PIT 45
B. Herman, CHI 38
J. Medwick, SL 37
C. Hubbell, NY 20
W. Berger, BOS 20
B. Terry, NY 20
A. Galan, CHI 18
P. Martin, SL 16
E. Leiber, NY 11
L. Warneke, CHI 9
E. Lombardi, CIN ... 8
F. Schulte, SL 7
P. Blanton, PIT 5
J. Moore, PHI...... 5
E. Allen, PHI 4
G. Mancuso, NY 4
P. Derringer, CIN ... 4
M. Ott, NY 3
P. Dean, SL....... 2
R. Collins, SL 2
C. Davis, PHI 2
P. Waner, PIT 1
B. Lee, CHI 1
T. Jackson, NY 1
D. Camilli, PHI 1

1935 AMERICAN
H. Greenberg, DET .. 80
W. Ferrell, BOS 62
J. Vosmik, CLE 39
C. Myer, WAS 36
L. Gehrig, NY 29
C. Gehringer, DET .. 26
M. Cochrane, DET ... 24
R. Cramer, PHI 18
M. Solters, BOS-SL.. 16
R. Hemsley, SL 16
J. Foxx, PHI 11
T. Bridges, DET..... 11
T. Lyons, CHI 10
L. Grove, BOS 8
Z. Bonura, CHI 7
L. Appling, CHI 7
L. Sewell, CHI 7
J. Allen, NY 5
J. Whitehead, CHI .. 4
F. Higgins, PHI 3
J. Marcum, PHI 3
E. Auker, DET 2
M. Harder, CLE 2
L. Lary, WAS-SL ... 1

1936 NATIONAL
C. Hubbell, NY 60
J. Dean, SL....... 53
B. Herman, CHI..... 37
J. Medwick, SL 30

P. Waner, PIT 29
M. Ott, NY 28
F. Demaree, CHI.... 17
G. Mancuso, NY..... 13
D. MacFayden, BOS . 12
L. Durocher, SL..... 8
P. Derringer, CIN 6
G. Hartnett, CHI 6
B. Whitehead, NY.... 6
A. Lopez, BOS....... 5
V. Mungo, BRO 5
W. Berger, BOS 4
D. Camilli, PHI 4
G. Phelps, BRO 3
D. Bartell, NY 2
E. Lombardi, CIN ... 1
T. Moore, SL........ 1

1936 AMERICAN
L. Gehrig, NY 73
L. Appling, CHI 65
E. Averill, CLE 48
C. Gehringer, DET ... 39
B. Dickey, NY 29
V. Kennedy, CHI 27
J. Kuhel, WAS 27
J. DiMaggio, NY 26
T. Bridges, DET..... 25
H. Trosky, CLE..... 19
J. Foxx, BOS 16
G. Walker, DET 14
B. Bell, SL 10
W. Moses, PHI 7
L. Grove, BOS 5
J. Dykes, CHI 3
R. Radcliff, CHI 3
S. West, SL 2
Z. Bonura, CHI 1
E. McNair, BOS 1

1937 NATIONAL
J. Medwick, SL 70
G. Hartnett, CHI .. 68
C. Hubbell, NY 52
J. Turner, BOS 30
L. Fette, BOS 29
D. Bartell, NY 26
M. Ott, NY 24
P. Waner, PIT 21
B. Herman, CHI ... 19
J. Mize, SL 18
C. Melton, NY 17
C. Root, CHI 15
P. Whitney, PHI ... 13
H. Danning, NY ... 10
F. Demaree, CHI ... 9
B. Myers, CIN 2
S. Grissom, CIN ... 2
H. Manush, BRO ... 1

1937 AMERICAN
C. Gehringer, DET ... 78
J. DiMaggio, NY ... 74
H. Greenberg, DET .. 48
L. Gehrig, NY 42
L. Sewell, CHI 22
B. Dickey, NY..... 22

J. Cronin, BOS 19
R. Ruffing, NY 18
L. Gomez, NY 14
M. Kreevich, CHI 13
C. Travis, WAS...... 12
W. Moses, PHI 12
J. Allen, CLE........ 11
H. Clift, SL 11
R. Radcliff, CHI 10
B. Lewis, WAS 7
L. Appling, CHI 5
B. Bell, SL 5
E. Averill, CLE 4
L. Lary, CLE 4
R. Lawson, DET 4
G. Walker, DET 3
R. York, DET 1
P. Fox, DET 1

1938 NATIONAL
E. Lombardi, CIN ... 229
B. Lee, CHI 166
A. Vaughan, PIT ... 163
M. Ott, NY 132
F. McCormick, CIN 130
J. Rizzo, PIT 96
S. Hack, CHI 87
P. Derringer, CIN ... 70
M. Brown, PIT 62
G. Hartnett, CHI ... 61
J. Medwick, SL 55
J. Mize, SL 28
T. Cuccinello, BOS .. 23
P. Young, PIT 19
C. Bryant, CHI 16
H. Danning, NY 13
I. Goodman, CIN..... 11
J. VanderMeer, CIN .. 6
L. Durocher, BRO.... 6
D. Coffman, NY..... 6
A. Lopez, BOS...... 5
L. Waner, PIT 5
D. Garms, BOS 5
D. Camilli, BRO 5
C. Root, CHI 4
J. Moore, NY 3
J. Hudson, BRO 3
J. Mulcahy, PHI 3
L. Handley, PIT 2
L. Warneke, SL 1
F. Fitzsimmons, BRO 1
H. Martin, PHI 1

1938 AMERICAN
J. Foxx, BOS 305
B. Dickey, NY..... 196
H. Greenberg, DET . 162
R. Ruffing, NY 146
B. Newsom, SL..... 111
J. DiMaggio, NY ... 106
J. Cronin, BOS 92
E. Averill, CLE 34
C. Travis, WAS.... 33
C. Gehringer, DET ... 27
J. Heath, CLE...... 24
J. Gordon, NY 23
H. Trosky, CLE..... 22
K. Keltner, CLE 16
M. Stratton, CHI ... 15
M. Harder, CLE.... 14

B. Johnson, PHI 13
H. Clift, SL 11
L. Gehrig, NY 10
P. Fox, DET 9
J. Vosmik, BOS 7
G. McQuinn, SL 7
L. Grove, BOS 7
B. Lewis, WAS 5
R. Rolfe, NY 5
C. Myer, WAS 5
E. Brucker, PHI 5
J. Allen, CLE 3
F. Crosetti, NY 2
L. Gomez, NY 1
D. Cramer, BOS 1

1939 NATIONAL
B. Walters, CIN 303
J. Mize, SL 178
P. Derringer, CIN 174
F. McCormick, CIN 159
C. Davis, SL 106
J. Brown, SL 99
J. Medwick, SL 81
L. Durocher, BRO 52
H. Danning, NY 33
L. Hamlin, BRO 32
M. Ott, NY 21
B. Jurges, NY 20
D. Camilli, BRO 20
W. Myers, CIN 18
S. Hack, CHI 17
A. Galan, CHI 15
T. Moore, SL 15
M. Arnovich, PHI 10
L. Frey, CIN 8
B. Lee, CHI 8
E. Slaughter, SL 8
W. Werber, CIN 6
M. West, BOS 5
G. Hartnett, CHI 5
I. Goodman, CIN 4
B. Hassett, BOS 4
P. Coscarart, BRO 4
E. Fletcher, BOS-PIT 4
C. Lavagetto, BRO 3
R. Bowman, SL 2
E. Miller, BOS 1
B. Herman, CHI 1

1939 AMERICAN
J. DiMaggio, NY 280
J. Foxx, BOS 170
B. Feller, CLE 155
T. Williams, BOS 126
R. Ruffing, NY 116
B. Dickey, NY 110
E. Leonard, WAS 71
B. Johnson, PHI 52
J. Gordon, NY 43
M. Kreevich, CHI 38
C. Brown, CHI 34
K. Keltner, CLE 26
G. McQuinn, SL 24
C. Gehringer, DET 21
L. Grove, BOS 17
J. Cronin, BOS 15
T. Lyons, CHI 13
H. Greenberg, DET 12
B. Newsom, SL-DET 11
J. Rigney, CHI 9
J. Kuhel, CHI 8
C. Keller, NY 7
J. Heath, CLE 7
G. Walker, CHI 7
F. Hayes, PHI 7
T. Bridges, DET 7
R. Rolfe, NY 6
B. McCosky, DET 6
E. McNair, CHI 5
H. Trosky, CLE 4
G. Case, WAS 3
M. Hoag, SL 3
R. York, DET 1
L. Appling, CHI 1

1940 NATIONAL
F. McCormick, CIN 274
J. Mize, SL 209
B. Walters, CIN 146
P. Derringer, CIN 121
F. Fitzsimmons, BRO 84
D. Walker, BRO 71
H. Danning, NY 64
S. Hack, CHI 61
E. Lombardi, CIN 38
W. Werber, CIN 36
J. Cooney, BOS 31
D. Camilli, BRO 30
E. Miller, BOS 28
D. Garms, PIT 28
A. Vaughan, PIT 27
C. Passeau, CHI 26
J. Beggs, CIN 19
T. Moore, SL 18
E. Fletcher, PIT 16
B. Nicholson, CHI 12
K. Higbe, PHI 10
C. Rowell, BOS 10
A. Lopez, BOS-PIT 9
M. Van Robays, PIT 8
R. Sewell, PIT 7
P. Reese, BRO 6
M. West, BOS 6
B. Young, NY 6
W. Wyatt, BRO 3
J. Rizzo, PHI 3
P. May, PHI 3
H. Mulcahy, PHI 3
J. Martin, SL 2
F. Gustine, PIT 1

1940 AMERICAN
H. Greenberg, DET 292
B. Feller, CLE 222
J. DiMaggio, NY 151
B. Newsom, DET 120
L. Boudreau, CLE 119
J. Foxx, BOS 110
S. Rowe, DET 62
R. York, DET 61
R. Radcliff, SL 55
L. Appling, CHI 54
R. Weatherly, CLE 34
D. Bartell, DET 26
J. Kuhel, CHI 18
S. Hudson, WAS 16
T. Williams, BOS 16
B. McCosky, DET 11
E. Bonham, NY 8
W. Judnich, SL 6
J. Babich, PHI 5
M. Tresh, CHI 4
F. Hayes, PHI 4
R. Mack, CLE 4
J. Gordon, NY 3
C. Travis, WAS 3
B. Kennedy, CHI 3
C. Gehringer, DET 3
R. Hemsley, CLE 2
T. Lyons, CHI 2
L. Finney, BOS 1
E. Auker, SL 1

1941 NATIONAL
D. Camilli, BRO 300
P. Reiser, BRO 183
W. Wyatt, BRO 151
J. Brown, SL 107
E. Riddle, CIN 98
E. White, SL 77
K. Higbe, BRO 64
J. Hopp, SL 61
J. Mize, SL 48
D. Walker, BRO 34
B. Herman, CHI-BRO 27
T. Moore, SL 26
S. Hack, CHI 26
E. Fletcher, PIT 22
J. Cooney, BOS 20
B. Nicholson, CHI 16
G. Mancuso, SL 14
F. Crespi, SL 13
M. Ott, NY 12
E. Slaughter, SL 12
B. Young, NY 10
V. DiMaggio, PIT 10
J. Tobin, BOS 10
A. Lopez, PIT 8
M. Marion, SL 8
M. Cooper, SL 8
L. Warneke, SL 7
N. Etten, PHI 6
B. Walters, CIN 6
B. Dahlgren, BOS-CHI 6
W. Werber, CIN 6
E. Crabtree, SL 5
J. Rucker, NY 4
D. Litwhiler, PHI 3
H. Danning, NY 2
C. Hubbell, NY 2
C. Lavagetto, BRO 2
A. Vaughan, PIT 2

1941 AMERICAN
J. DiMaggio, NY 291
T. Williams, BOS 254
B. Feller, CLE 174
T. Lee, CHI 144
C. Keller, NY 126
C. Travis, WAS 101
J. Gordon, NY 60
J. Heath, CLE 37
H. Newsome, BOS 32
R. Cullenbine, SL 29
J. Cronin, BOS 26
S. Chapman, PHI 25
B. Dickey, NY 18
T. Henrich, NY 16
B. McCosky, DET 12
T. Lyons, CHI 12
D. Siebert, PHI 10
L. Boudreau, CLE 10
A. Benton, DET 8
P. Rizzuto, NY 7
E. Leonard, WAS 7
B. Campbell, DET 4
R. York, DET 3
F. Hayes, PHI 3
T. Wright, CHI 2
R. Ruffing, NY 2
E. Auker, SL 1
F. Higgins, DET 1
D. DiMaggio, BOS 1

1942 NATIONAL
M. Cooper, SL 263
E. Slaughter, SL 200
M. Ott, NY 190
A. Owen, BRO 103
J. Mize, NY 97
P. Reiser, BRO 91
M. Marion, SL 81
D. Camilli, BRO 42
R. Elliott, PIT 39
C. Passeau, CHI 33
W. Cooper, SL 28
S. Musial, SL 26
E. Lombardi, BOS 24
J. Beazley, SL 24
J. Brown, SL 24
W. Wyatt, BRO 22
J. Medwick, BRO 20
T. Moore, SL 15
B. Nicholson, CHI 14
S. Hack, CHI 11
J. VanderMeer, CIN 11
T. Hughes, PHI 10
R. Starr, CIN 9
L. French, BRO 7
P. Reese, BRO 6
W. Kurowski, SL 6
R. Lamanno, CIN 4
M. West, BOS 4
L. Frey, CIN 4
F. McCormick, CIN 4
A. Javery, BOS 3
E. Miller, BOS 1

1942 AMERICAN
J. Gordon, NY 270
T. Williams, BOS 249
J. Pesky, BOS 143
V. Stephens, SL 140
E. Bonham, NY 102
T. Hughson, BOS 92
J. DiMaggio, NY 86
S. Spence, WAS 65
P. Marchildon, PHI 39
L. Boudreau, CLE 34
B. Doerr, BOS 24
T. Lyons, CHI 23
G. Case, WAS 17
K. Keltner, CLE 15
C. Keller, NY 15
W. Judnich, SL 14
B. Dickey, NY 12
D. Gutteridge, SL 12
P. Rizzuto, NY 9
C. Laabs, SL 9
R. Ferrell, SL 8
H. Borowy, NY 8
J. Bagby, CLE 6
T. Wright, CHI 6
T. Lupien BOS 4
L. Fleming, CLE 4
S. Chandler, NY 3
R. York, DET 3
B. McCosky, DET 1

1943 NATIONAL
S. Musial, SL 267
W. Cooper, SL 192
B. Nicholson, CHI 181
B. Herman, BRO 140
M. Cooper, SL 130
R. Sewell, PIT 127
E. Riddle, CIN 68
R. Elliott, PIT 52
F. McCormick, CIN 26
C. Shoun, CIN 24
E. Miller, CIN 24
M. Witek, NY 21
M. Marion, SL 20
S. Rowe, PHI 18
W. Wyatt, BRO 15
A. Vaughan, BRO 15
R. Mueller, CIN 12
A. Javery, BOS 12
S. Hack, CHI 10
M. Ott, NY 9
E. Fletcher, PIT 7
A. Adams, NY 7
L. Klein, SL 6
A. Galan, BRO 5
D. Walker, BRO 5
J. Tobin, BOS 5
D. Bartell, NY 5
P. Cavaretta, CHI 4
T. Holmes, BOS 2
R. Northey, PHI 2
B. Dahlgren, PHI 2
H. Bithorn, CHI 1
B. Walters, CIN 1
L. Frey, CIN 1

1943 AMERICAN
S. Chandler, NY 246
L. Appling, CHI 215
R. York, DET 152
W. Johnson, NY 135
B. Johnson, WAS 116
D. Wakefield, DET 72
N. Etten, NY 61
B. Dickey, NY 58
V. Stephens, SL 49
L. Boudreau, CLE 40
D. Trout, DET 38
G. Case, WAS 37
C. Keller, NY 31
B. Doerr, BOS 21
A. Smith, CLE 19
G. Priddy, WAS 17
O. Hockett, CLE 14
D. Gutteridge, SL 13
E. Wynn, WAS 13
J. Bagby, CLE 11
R. Cramer, DET 8
F. Higgins, DET 8
C. Laabs, SL 6
J. Early, WAS 6
J. Gordon, NY 4
R. Wolff, PHI 4
L. Newsome, BOS 3
J. Cronin, BOS 3
J. Flores, PHI 3
G. Maltzberger, CHI 3
F. Crosetti, NY 2
K. Keltner, CLE 2
P. Fox, BOS 1
R. Hodgin, CHI 1
J. Murphy, NY 1
D. Siebert, PHI 1
J. Tabor, BOS 1
H. Wagner, PHI 1

1944 NATIONAL
M. Marion, SL 190
B. Nicholson, CHI 189
D. Walker, BRO 145
S. Musial, SL 136
B. Walters, CIN 107
B. Voiselle, NY 107
R. Mueller, CIN 85
W. Cooper, SL 72
M. Cooper, SL 63
R. Elliott, PIT 57
R. Sewell, PIT 49
B. Dahlgren, PIT 33
F. McCormick, CIN 32
P. Cavaretta, CHI 27
R. Sanders, SL 25
M. Ott, NY 20
J. Tobin, BOS 13
J. Hopp, SL 10
R. Northey, PHI 10
J. Medwick, NY 9
J. Barrett, PIT 8
E. Miller, CIN 7
T. Holmes, BOS 6
T. Wilks, SL 4
T. Lupien, PHI 3
S. Hack, CHI 2
M. Lanier, SL 2
C. Ryan, BOS 2
A. Galan, BRO 1
W. Kurowski, SL 1
J. Russell, PIT 1

1944 AMERICAN
H. Newhouser, DET 236
D. Trout, DET 232
V. Stephens, SL 193
S. Stirnweiss, NY 129
D. Wakefield, DET 128
L. Boudreau, CLE 84
B. Doerr, BOS 75
S. Spence, WAS 56
N. Potter, SL 52
B. Johnson, BOS 51
M. Christman, SL 27
T. Hughson, BOS 22
D. Cramer, DET 14
F. Hayes, PHI 13
P. Fox, BOS 12
J. Kramer, SL 9
J. Lindell, NY 8
P. Richards, DET 8
D. Gutteridge, SL 7
F. Higgins, DET 7
G. McQuinn, SL 7
G. Kell, PHI 6
R. Cullenbine, CLE 5
N. Etten, NY 5
R. York, DET 5
R. Hemsley, NY 4
M. Kreevich, SL 4
W. Moses, CHI 4
E. Mayo, DET 3
D. Siebert, PHI 3
H. Borowy, NY 2
F. Crosetti, NY 2
R. Hodgin, CHI 2
B. Muncrief, SL 1

1945 NATIONAL
P. Cavaretta, CHI 279
T. Holmes, BOS 175
C. Barrett, BOS-SL 151
A. Pafko, CHI 131
W. Kurowski, SL 90
H. Borowy, CHI 84
H. Wyse, CHI 72
M. Marion, SL 69
D. Walker, BRO 66
G. Rosen, BRO 56
S. Hack, CHI 42
H. Brecheen, SL 31
M. Ott, NY 22
A. Galan, BRO 18
J. Hopp, SL 17
R. Elliott, PIT 15
L. Olmo, BRO 13
B. Adams, PHI-SL 12
C. Passeau, CHI 9
J. Barrett, PIT 8
E. Heusser, CIN 7
D. Johnson, CHI 7
B. Kerr, NY 7
F. McCormick, CIN 6
B. Salkeld, PIT 6
P. Lowrey, CHI 5
A. Adams, NY 4
A. Karl, PHI 4
H. Gregg, BRO 2
A. Lopez, PIT 2
P. Masi, BOS 2
E. Miller, CIN 2
V. DiMaggio, PHI 1
E. Stanky, BRO 1

1945 AMERICAN
H. Newhouser, DET 236
E. Mayo, DET 164
S. Stirnweiss, NY 161
B. Ferriss, BOS 148
G. Myatt, WAS 98
V. Stephens, SL 94
R. Wolff, WAS 78
L. Boudreau, CLE 70
G. Case, WAS 60
P. Richards, DET 35
M. Tresh, CHI 33
J. Kuhel, WAS 29
R. Cullenbine, DET 26
H. Greenberg, DET 25
N. Etten, NY 21
T. Cuccinello, CHI 18
D. Trout, DET 17
E. Leonard, WAS 16
R. Schalk, CHI 13
J. Heath, CLE 10
G. Binks, WAS 9
B. Muncrief, SL 8
A. Benton, DET 6
R. Ferrell, WAS 6
B. Johnson, BOS 6
M. Christman, SL 5
B. Estalella, PHI 5
F. Hayes, PHI-CLE 5
D. Cramer, DET 4
W. Moses, CHI 4
E. Lake, BOS 2
R. Christopher, PHI 1
L. Newsome, BOS 1
R. York, DET 1

1946 NATIONAL
S. Musial, SL 319
D. Walker, BRO 159
E. Slaughter, SL 144
H. Pollet, SL 116
J. Sain, BOS 95
P. Reese, BRO 79
E. Stanky, BRO 67
D. Ennis, PHI 61
P. Reiser, BRO 58
P. Cavaretta, CHI 49
B. Kerr, NY 37
J. Hopp, BOS 34
E. Waitkus, CHI 21
B. Edwards, BRO 20
K. Higbe, BRO 18
H. Brecheen, SL 14
J. Mize, NY 14
G. Hatton, CIN 12
T. Holmes, BOS 11
J. Tabor, PHI 10
E. Verban, SL-PHI 10
H. Walker, SL 9
L. Rowe, PHI 8
P. Masi, BOS 7
J. VanderMeer, CIN 7
R. Schoendienst, SL 6
B. Cox, PIT 5
F. Gustine, PIT 4
M. Marion, SL 4
R. Kiner, PIT 3
W. Kurowski, SL 3
R. Mueller, CIN 3
J. Schmitz, CHI 3
P. Lowrey, CHI 2
F. McCormick, PHI 2
C. Furillo, BRO 1
O. Judd, PHI 1

1946 AMERICAN
T. Williams, BOS 224
H. Newhouser, DET 197
B. Doerr, BOS 158
J. Pesky, BOS 141
M. Vernon, WAS 134
B. Feller, CLE 105
B. Ferriss, BOS 94
H. Greenberg, DET 91
D. DiMaggio, BOS 56
L. Boudreau, CLE 37
R. York, BOS 28
L. Appling, CHI 26
T. Hughson, BOS 19
E. Caldwell, CHI 18
C. Keller, NY 17
G. Kell, PHI-DET 12
S. Chandler, NY 12
A. Robinson, NY 12
J. DiMaggio, NY 6
B. Newsom, PHI-WAS 6
V. Stephens, SL 6
P. Marchildon, PHI 5
B. Rosar, PHI 4

S. Spence, WAS 4
J. Berardino, SL 2
T. Henrich, NY 1
H. Wagner, BOS 1

1947 NATIONAL
R. Elliott, BOS 205
E. Blackwell, CIN 175
J. Mize, NY 144
B. Edwards, BRO 140
J. Robinson, BRO 106
R. Kiner, PIT 101
L. Jansen, NY 91
P. Reese, BRO 80
W. Kurowski, SL 45
H. Walker, SL-PHI 45
R. Branca, BRO 40
H. Casey, BRO 37
E. Leonard, PHI 32
E. Stanky, BRO 32
W. Spahn, BOS 26
W. Marshall, NY 22
J. Sain, BOS 20
W. Cooper, NY 19
D. Walker, BRO 14
E. Slaughter, SL 12
S. Musial, SL 12
E. Verban, PHI 9
P. Cavaretta, CHI 6
P. Lowrey, CHI 2
E. Miller, CIN 2
A. Pafko, CHI 1

1947 AMERICAN
J. DiMaggio, NY 202
T. Williams, BOS 201
L. Boudreau, CLE 168
J. Page, NY 167
G. Kell, DET 132
G. McQuinn, NY 77
J. Gordon, CLE 59
B. Feller, CLE 58
P. Marchildon, PHI 47
L. Appling, CHI 43
E. Joost, PHI 35
B. McCosky, PHI 35
T. Henrich, NY 33
F. Shea, NY 23
Y. Berra, NY 18
A. Reynolds, NY 18
B. Dillinger, SL 13
J. Pesky, BOS 11
F. Fain, PHI 9
W. Johnson, NY 9
S. Spence, WAS 9
F. Hutchison, DET 8
E. Wynn, WAS 7
B. Doerr, BOS 6
B. Rosar, PHI 6
M. Christman, WAS 4
B. McCahan, PHI 4
D. Mitchell, CLE 4
R. Cullenbine, DET 3
J. Dobson, BOS 3
J. Heath, SL 1
E. Lopat, CHI 1
V. Stephens, SL 1
T. Wright, CHI 1

1948 NATIONAL
S. Musial, SL 303
J. Sain, BOS 223
A. Dark, BOS 174
S. Gordon, NY 72
H. Brecheen, SL 61
P. Reese, BRO 60
R. Kiner, PIT 55
E. Slaughter, SL 55
D. Murtaugh, PIT 52
S. Rojek, PIT 51
R. Ashburn, PHI 48
J. Schmitz, CHI 37
R. Elliott, BOS 33
W. Spahn, BOS 31
J. Robinson, BRO 30
A. Pafko, CHI 25
J. Mize, NY 22
R. Barney, BRO 15
J. VanderMeer, CIN 13
J. Wyrostek, CIN 9
R. Branca, BRO 8
R. Campanella, BRO 8
B. Chesnes, PIT 8
P. Cavaretta, CHI 6
E. Miller, PHI 4
D. Ennis, PHI 3
G. Hatton, CIN 3
L. Jansen, NY 2
D. Walker, PIT 2
G. Hodges, BRO 1
W. Lockman, NY 1
H. Sauer, CIN 1

1948 AMERICAN
L. Boudreau, CLE 324
J. DiMaggio, NY 213
T. Williams, BOS 171
V. Stephens, BOS 121
B. Lemon, CLE 101
J. Gordon, CLE 63
T. Henrich, NY 63
G. Bearden, CLE 52
H. Newhouser, DET 48
E. Joost, PHI 39
H. Majeski, PHI 23
B. Tebbetts, BOS 23
V. Raschi, NY 23
K. Keltner, CLE 18
J. Priddy, SL 16
G. Kell, DET 14
W. Evers, DET 13
A. Zarilla, SL 11
B. Doerr, BOS 10
B. Dillinger, SL 10
J. Hegan, CLE 10
L. Appling, CHI 8
B. Feller, CLE 6
L. Brissie, PHI 5
F. Fain, PHI 5
J. Dobson, BOS 5
B. Goodman, BOS 4
B. McCosky, PHI 4
Y. Berra, NY 3
D. DiMaggio, BOS 3
L. Doby, CLE 3
C. Fannin, SL 2
P. Mullin, DET 1
P. Rizzuto, NY 1

1949 NATIONAL
J. Robinson, BRO 264
S. Musial, SL 226
E. Slaughter, SL 181
R. Kiner, PIT 133
P. Reese, BRO 118
C. Furillo, BRO 68
W. Spahn, BOS 60
D. Newcombe, BRO 55
K. Heintzelman, PHI 48
R. Schoendienst, SL 30
G. Hodges, BRO 29
H. Pollet, SL 29
D. Ennis, PHI 28
B. Thomson, NY 25
R. Campanella, BRO 22
P. Roe, BRO 21
G. Hamner, PHI 9
W. Lockman, NY 9
R. Meyer, PHI 8
K. Raffensberger, CIN 8
H. Sauer, CIN-CHI 8
T. Wilks, SL 8
R. Ashburn, PHI 6
J. Schmitz, CHI 6
A. Dark, BOS 3
M. Marion, SL 3
W. Jones, PHI 2
W. Marshall, NY 2
E. Torgeson, BOS 2
S. Gordon, NY 1
D. Sisler, PHI 1

1949 AMERICAN
T. Williams, BOS 272
P. Rizzuto, NY 175
J. Page, NY 166
M. Parnell, BOS 151
E. Kinder, BOS 122
T. Henrich, NY 121
V. Stephens, BOS 100
G. Kell, DET 80
B. Lemon, CLE 57
V. Wertz, DET 51
V. Raschi, NY 19
J. DiMaggio, NY 18
E. Joost, PHI 11
L. Boudreau, CLE 10
Y. Berra, NY 9
D. DiMaggio, BOS 7
B. Doerr, BOS 7
A. Kellner, PHI 6
E. Robinson, WAS 6
R. Sievers, SL 6
B. Tebbetts, BOS 6
L. Appling, CHI 3
A. Houtteman, DET 3
J. Priddy, SL 3
V. Trucks, DET 3
D. Mitchell, CLE 2
A. Reynolds, NY 2

1950 NATIONAL
J. Konstanty, PHI 286
S. Musial, SL 158
E. Stanky, NY 144
D. Ennis, PHI 104
R. Kiner, PIT 91
G. Hamner, PHI 79
R. Roberts, PHI 68
G. Hodges, BRO 55
D. Snider, BRO 53
S. Maglie, NY 51
E. Blackwell, CIN 41
A. Pafko, CHI 38
R. Campanella, BRO 29
A. Seminick, PHI 25
J. Robinson, BRO 23
C. Simmons, PHI 22
P. Roe, BRO 15
T. Kluszewski, CIN 14
W. Spahn, BOS 14
D. Newcombe, BRO 14
J. Sain, BOS 12
S. Gordon, BOS 11
J. Hearn, SL-NY 10
P. Reese, BRO 8
E. Waitkus, PHI 8
R. Elliott, BOS 8
E. Torgeson, BOS 6
S. Jethroe, BOS 6
H. Sauer, CHI 5
V. Bickford, BOS 4
C. Furillo, BRO 4
W. Westrum, NY 3
D. Sisler, PHI 2
H. Thompson, NY 2
L. Jansen, NY 2
W. Jones, PHI 1

1950 AMERICAN
P. Rizzuto, NY 284
B. Goodman, BOS 180
Y. Berra, NY 146
G. Kell, DET 127
B. Lemon, CLE 102
W. Dropo, BOS 75
V. Raschi, NY 63
L. Doby, CLE 57
J. DiMaggio, NY 54
V. Wertz, DET 50
W. Evers, DET 38
C. Carrasquel, CHI 21
D. Trout, DET 21
D. DiMaggio, BOS 17
I. Noren, WAS 16
B. Doerr, BOS 15
J. Mize, NY 11
J. Priddy, DET 11
A. Rosen, CLE 11
E. Yost, WAS 8
M. Parnell, BOS 7
W. Ford, NY 7
T. Williams, BOS 7
N. Garver, SL 6
V. Stephens, BOS 6
A. Houtteman, DET 6
S. Lollar, SL 4
E. Lopat, NY 3
K. Wood, SL 2
S. Dente, WAS 1
D. Philley, CHI 1

1951 NATIONAL
R. Campanella, BRO 243
S. Musial, SL 191
M. Irvin, NY 166
S. Maglie, NY 153
P. Roe, BRO 138
J. Robinson, BRO 92
R. Ashburn, PHI 69
B. Thomson, NY 62
M. Dickson, PIT 59
R. Kiner, PIT 49
W. Spahn, BOS 45
A. Dark, NY 30
R. Roberts, PHI 27
L. Jansen, NY 26
P. Reese, BRO 15
G. Hodges, BRO 10
S. Gordon, BOS 10
K. Raffensberger, CIN 8
J. Wyrostek, CIN 6
E. Blackwell, CIN 6
C. Furillo, BRO 6
D. Newcombe, BRO 3
P. Cavaretta, CHI 1
H. Sauer, CHI 1

1951 AMERICAN
Y. Berra, NY 184
N. Garver, SL 157
A. Reynolds, NY 125
M. Minoso, CLE-CHI 120
B. Feller, CLE 118
F. Fain, PHI 103
E. Kinder, BOS 66
V. Raschi, NY 64
G. McDougald, NY 63
B. Avila, CLE 49
P. Rizzuto, NY 47
E. Lopat, NY 44
T. Williams, BOS 35
E. Joost, PHI 32
G. Kell, DET 30
E. Wynn, CLE 29
N. Fox, CHI 25
B. Goodman, BOS 21
D. DiMaggio, BOS 16
G. Zernial, CHI-PHI 15
B. Shantz, PHI 14
M. Garcia, CLE 11
G. Coan, WAS 8
M. Parnell, BOS 7
E. Robinson, CHI 7
G. Woodling, NY 5
J. Pesky, BOS 5
I. Noren, WAS 4
D. Mitchell, CLE 4
V. Trucks, DET 2
E. Yost, WAS 2
J. Busby, CHI 2
J. Mize, NY 2

1952 NATIONAL
H. Sauer, CHI 226
R. Roberts, PHI 211
J. Black, BRO 208
H. Wilhelm, NY 133
S. Musial, SL 127
E. Slaughter, SL 92
J. Robinson, BRO 31
P. Reese, BRO 29
D. Snider, BRO 29
R. Campanella, BRO 25
R. Schoendienst, SL 25
A. Dark, NY 24
M. Dickson, PIT 22
D. Ennis, PHI 18
W. Lockman, NY 18
B. Thomson, NY 17
F. Baumholtz, CHI 16
T. Kluszewski, CIN 16
G. Hodges, BRO 15
R. McMillan, CIN 15
E. Mathews, BOS 13
B. Adams, CIN 9
B. Cox, BRO 8
W. Hacker, CHI 8
R. Kiner, PIT 8
S. Maglie, NY 8
K. Raffensberger, CIN 8
W. Spahn, BOS 8
P. Roe, BRO 7
S. Gordon, BOS 6
G. Hamner, PHI 5
S. Hemus, SL 5
M. Irvin, NY 5
G. Shuba, BRO 5
E. Yuhas, SL 5
A. Brazle, SL 3
J. Logan, BOS 3
T. Atwell, CHI 2
C. Metkovich, PIT 2
W. Cooper, BOS 1

1952 AMERICAN
B. Shantz, PHI 280
A. Reynolds, NY 183
M. Mantle, NY 143
Y. Berra, NY 104
E. Wynn, CLE 99
F. Fain, PHI 66
N. Fox, CHI 59
B. Lemon, CLE 58
M. Garcia, CLE 52
A. Rosen, CLE 51
E. Robinson, CHI 47
L. Doby, CLE 46
L. Easter, CLE 40
P. Rizzuto, NY 33
E. Joost, PHI 20
B. Goodman, BOS 18
J. Jensen, NY-WAS 12
S. Paige, SL 12
V. Raschi, NY 12
D. Mitchell, CLE 11
H. Bauer, NY 10
G. Woodling, NY 10
P. Runnels, WAS 8
C. Courtney, SL 7
D. Gernert, BOS 6
W. Dropo, BOS-DET 5
S. Rogovin, CHI 4
S. White, BOS 4
B. Avila, CLE 3
B. Pierce, CHI 3
J. Sain, NY 3
B. Young, SL 3
J. Collins, NY 2
C. Marrero, WAS 1
B. Porterfield, WAS 1

1953 NATIONAL
R. Campanella, BRO 297
E. Mathews, MIL 216
D. Snider, BRO 157
R. Schoendienst, SL 155
W. Spahn, MIL 120
R. Roberts, PHI 106
T. Kluszewski, CIN 69
S. Musial, SL 62
C. Erskine, BRO 54
C. Furillo, BRO 54
P. Reese, BRO 27
J. Robinson, BRO 19
D. Ennis, PHI 14
G. Hodges, BRO 13
M. Irvin, NY 11
D. O'Connell, PIT 10
H. Haddix, SL 9
F. Thomas, PIT 6
R. Ashburn, PHI 5
G. Bell, CIN 3
J. Logan, MIL 3
R. Gomez, NY 2
G. Hamner, PHI 2
D. Crandall, MIL 1
H. Thompson, NY 1

1953 AMERICAN
A. Rosen, CLE 336
Y. Berra, NY 167
M. Vernon, WAS 162
M. Minoso, CHI 100
V. Trucks, SL-CHI 81
P. Rizzuto, NY 76
B. Porterfield, WAS 64
R. Boone, CLE-DET 59
J. Piersall, BOS 56
B. Pierce, CHI 55
E. Kinder, BOS 41
H. Bauer, NY 37
A. Reynolds, NY 33
M. Parnell, BOS 27
H. Kuenn, DET 23
B. Lemon, CLE 22
E. Lopat, NY 18
G. Zernial, PHI 16
D. Philley, PHI 11
W. Ford, NY 8
B. Goodman, BOS 5
M. Mantle, NY 4
G. Woodling, NY 3
E. Yost, WAS 3
B. Martin, NY 2
C. Carrasquel, CHI 1
G. Kell, BOS 1
T. Williams, BOS 1

1954 NATIONAL
W. Mays, NY 283
T. Kluszewski, CIN 217
J. Antonelli, NY 154
D. Snider, BRO 135
A. Dark, NY 110
S. Musial, SL 97
R. Roberts, PHI 70
J. Adcock, MIL 60
P. Reese, BRO 53
G. Hodges, BRO 40
W. Spahn, MIL 38
D. Mueller, NY 30
R. Schoendienst, SL 24
F. Thomas, PIT 24
H. Wilhelm, NY 17
E. Banks, CHI 14
D. Crandall, MIL 13
J. Logan, MIL 9
E. Mathews, MIL 5
G. Hamner, PHI 5
R. Ashburn, PHI 5
S. Maglie, NY 4
G. Conley, MIL 3
M. Grissom, NY 2
R. McMillan, CIN 2
D. Rhodes, NY 1
H. Sauer, CHI 1

1954 AMERICAN
Y. Berra, NY 230
L. Doby, CLE 210
B. Avila, CLE 203
M. Minoso, CHI 186
B. Lemon, CLE 179
E. Wynn, CLE 72
T. Williams, BOS 65
H. Kuenn, DET 37
M. Vernon, WAS 30
N. Fox, CHI 30
B. Grim, NY 25
J. Finigan, PHI 19
V. Trucks, CHI 19
J. Jensen, BOS 17
M. Mantle, NY 16
I. Noren, NY 16
A. Rosen, CLE 16
J. Busby, WAS 7
J. Coleman, NY 6
B. Goodman, BOS 6
M. Garcia, CLE 6
J. Hegan, CLE 5
H. Bauer, NY 4
A. Kaline, DET 4
B. Turley, BAL 4
S. Gromek, DET 1
C. Abrams, BAL 1
R. Boone, DET 1
R. Sievers, WAS 1

1955 NATIONAL
R. Campanella, BRO 226
D. Snider, BRO 221
E. Banks, CHI 195
W. Mays, NY 165
R. Roberts, PHI 159
T. Kluszewski, CIN 111
D. Newcombe, BRO 89
S. Musial, SL 46
H. Aaron, MIL 36
P. Reese, BRO 36
J. Logan, MIL 24
W. Post, CIN 23
D. Ennis, PHI 21
R. Ashburn, PHI 17
C. Labine, BRO 11
B. Friend, PIT 10
D. Crandall, MIL 8
E. Mathews, MIL 6
D. Long, PIT 3
J. Meyer, PHI 3
G. Baker, CHI 2
C. Furillo, BRO 2
V. Law, PIT 1
F. Thomas, PIT 1

1955 AMERICAN
Y. Berra, NY 218
A. Kaline, DET 201
A. Smith, CLE 200
T. Williams, BOS 143
M. Mantle, NY 113
R. Narleski, CLE 90
N. Fox, CHI 84

H. Bauer, NY 64
V. Power, KC 53
J. Jensen, BOS 39
S. Lollar, CHI 37
G. McDougald, NY .. 34
B. Klaus, BOS 27
T. Byrne, NY 24
W. Ford, NY 21
R. Boone, DET 16
R. Sievers, WAS 9
H. Kuenn, DET 8
B. Pierce, CHI 8
D. Philley, CLE-BAL .. 6
E. Wynn, CLE 6
E. Valo, KC 5
M. Vernon, WAS 4
B. Hoeft, DET 1
D. Mossi, CLE 1
F. Sullivan, BOS 1
G. Triandos, BAL 1
J. Valdivielso, WAS ... 1
S. White, BOS 1

1956 NATIONAL
D. Newcombe, BRO 223
S. Maglie, BRO 183
H. Aaron, MIL 146
W. Spahn, MIL 126
J. Gilliam, BRO 103
R. McMillan, CIN 96
F. Robinson, CIN 79
P. Reese, BRO 71
S. Musial, SL 62
D. Snider, BRO 55
J. Adcock, MIL 54
B. Friend, PIT 38
H. Freeman, CIN 25
J. Antonelli, NY 18
T. Kluszewski, CIN ... 18
J. Robinson, BRO 17
W. Mays, NY 14
E. Bailey, CIN 13
B. Virdon, SL-PIT 13
S. Lopata, PHI 11
C. Furillo, BRO 9
L. Burdette, MIL 8
B. Buhl, MIL 7
R. Roberts, PHI 7
B. Lawrence, CIN 6
D. Long, PIT 4
W. Moon, SL 3
E. Banks, CHI 2
K. Boyer, SL 2
C. Labine, BRO 1
J. Logan, MIL 1
R. Ashburn, PHI 1

1956 AMERICAN
M. Mantle, NY 336
Y. Berra, NY 186
A. Kaline, DET 142
H. Kuenn, DET 80
B. Pierce, CHI 75
T. Williams, BOS 70
B. Nieman, CHI-BAL . 55
G. McDougald, NY .. 55
V. Wertz, CLE 45
B. Lemon, CLE 40
H. Simpson, KC 37
W. Ford, NY 33
E. Wynn, CLE 32
J. Piersall, BOS 28
N. Fox, CHI 28
S. Lollar, CHI 27
F. Lary, DET 24
P. Runnels, WAS 24
H. Score, CLE 18
J. Jensen, BOS 15
M. Vernon, BOS 14
T. Brewer, BOS 11
H. Bauer, NY 8
C. Maxwell, DET 8
L. Aparicio, CHI 7
G. Triandos, BAL 6
F. Bolling, DET 3
M. Minoso, CHI 3
V. Power, KC 3
J. Kucks, NY 2
R. Sievers, WAS 1

1957 NATIONAL
H. Aaron, MIL 239
S. Musial, SL 230
R. Schoendienst,
NY-MIL 221
W. Mays, NY 174
W. Spahn, MIL 131
E. Banks, CHI 60
G. Hodges, BRO 54
E. Mathews, MIL 45
F. Robinson, CIN 42
J. Sanford, PHI 39
D. Hoak, CIN 31
D. Blasingame, SL ... 26
E. Bouchee, PHI 26
B. Buhl, MIL 15
D. Ennis, SL 13
D. Groat, PIT 13
A. Dark, SL 12
D. Snider, BRO 10
F. Thomas, PIT 8
D. Drysdale, BRO 8
R. McMillan, CIN 6
D. Drott, CHI 6
G. Hamner, PHI 3
L. Burdette, MIL 2
J. Logan, MIL 1
H. Anderson, PHI 1

1957 AMERICAN
M. Mantle, NY 233
T. Williams, BOS 209
R. Sievers, WAS 205
N. Fox, CHI 193
G. McDougald, NY . 165
V. Wertz, CLE 61
F. Malzone, BOS 58
M. Minoso, CHI 55
J. Bunning, DET 46
A. Kaline, DET 40
B. Pierce, CHI 35
B. Gardner, BAL 22
D. Donovan, CHI 19
Y. Berra, NY 18
G. Woodling, CLE 13
B. Grim, NY 9
B. Boyd, BAL 9
C. Maxwell, DET 5
W. Held, NY-KC 4
W. Ford, NY 4
V. Power, KC 3
J. Piersall, BOS 2
B. Skowron, NY 2
H. Kuenn, DET 2
S. Lollar, CHI 2
T. Kubek, NY 1
B. Shantz, NY 1

1958 NATIONAL
E. Banks, CHI 283
W. Mays, SF 185
H. Aaron, MIL 166
F. Thomas, PIT 143
W. Spahn, MIL 108
B. Friend, PIT 98
R. Ashburn, PHI 62
B. Mazeroski, PIT 61
O. Cepeda, SF 57
D. Crandall, MIL 48
L. Burdette, MIL 47
S. Musial, SL 39
K. Boyer, SL 31
J. Temple, CIN 26
B. Skinner, PIT 18
W. Covington, MIL ... 16
E. Face, PIT 8
H. Anderson, PHI 5
J. Gilliam, LA 4
B. Purkey, CIN 4
F. Robinson, CIN 4
J. Adcock, MIL 2
C. Furillo, LA 1

1958 AMERICAN
J. Jensen, BOS 233
B. Turley, NY 191
R. Colavito, CLE 181
B. Cerv, KC 164
M. Mantle, NY 127
R. Sievers, WAS 95
T. Williams, BOS 89
N. Fox, CHI 88
S. Lollar, CHI 57
P. Runnels, BOS 29
G. Triandos, BAL 27
D. Hyde, WAS 26
H. Kuenn, DET 24
C. McLish, CLE 18
V. Power, KC-CLE ... 15
F. Bolling, DET 10
E. Howard, NY 9
Y. Berra, NY 6
M. Minoso, CLE 6
A. Kaline, DET 5
G. McDougald, NY 5
R. Duren, NY 4
F. Lary, DET 3
J. Harshman, BAL 2
D. Donovan, CHI 1
F. Malzone, BOS 1

1959 NATIONAL
E. Banks, CHI 232½
E. Mathews, MIL .. 189½
H. Aaron, MIL 174
W. Moon, LA 161
S. Jones, SF 130
W. Mays, SF 85
E. Face, PIT 67
C. Neal, LA 64
F. Robinson, CIN 52
K. Boyer, SL 37
D. Crandall, MIL 27
L. Burdette, MIL 14
R. Craig, LA 12
J. Cunningham, SL .. 12
V. Pinson, CIN 11
J. Temple, CIN 8
D. Hoak, PIT 6
G. Hodges, LA 4
O. Cepeda, SF 3
V. Law, PIT 3
W. Spahn, MIL 3
G. Conley, PHI 1
W. McCovey, SF 1
D. Snider, LA 1

1959 AMERICAN
N. Fox, CHI 295
L. Aparicio, CHI 255
E. Wynn, CHI 123
R. Colavito, CLE 117
T. Francona, CLE ... 102
A. Kaline, DET 84
J. Landis, CHI 66
H. Kuenn, DET 64
S. Lollar, CHI 44
J. Jensen, BOS 40
C. McLish, CLE 35
Y. Berra, NY 26
M. Minoso, CLE 26
F. Malzone, BOS 24
H. Killebrew, WAS ... 21
G. Woodling, BAL ... 18
M. Mantle, NY 13
B. Richardson, NY ... 11
C. Pascual, WAS 9
B. Shaw, CHI 8
G. Triandos, BAL 8
B. Daley, KC 7
V. Power, CLE 5
B. Tuttle, KC 5
J. Lemon, WAS 4
P. Runnels, BOS 2
T. Williams, BOS 2
B. Allison, WAS 1
G. Staley, CHI 1

1960 NATIONAL
D. Groat, PIT 276
D. Hoak, PIT 162
W. Mays, SF 155
E. Banks, CHI 100
L. McDaniel, SL 95
K. Boyer, SL 80
V. Law, PIT 80
R. Clemente, PIT 62
E. Broglio, SL 58
E. Mathews, MIL 52
H. Aaron, MIL 49
E. Face, PIT 47
D. Crandall, MIL 31
W. Spahn, MIL 27
N. Larker, LA 21
S. Musial, SL 18
M. Wills, LA 7
V. Pinson, CIN 6
J. Adcock, MIL 5
S. Burgess, PIT 2
F. Robinson, CIN 2
L. Sherry, LA 2
P. Herrera, PHI 1

1960 AMERICAN
R. Maris, NY 225
M. Mantle, NY 222
B. Robinson, BAL ... 211
M. Minoso, CHI 141
R. Hansen, BAL 110
A. Smith, CHI 73
R. Sievers, CHI 58
E. Battey, WAS 57
B. Skowron, NY 56
J. Lemon, WAS 36
T. Kubek, NY 29
C. Estrada, BAL 28
T. Williams, BOS 25
V. Wertz, BOS 22
Y. Berra, NY 21
J. Gentile, BAL 21
P. Runnels, BOS 18
N. Fox, CHI 11
V. Power, CLE 11
S. Barber, BAL 7
L. Aparicio, CHI 6
J. Perry, CLE 6
G. Staley, CHI 4
J. Bunning, DET 3
G. Woodling, BAL 3
H. Kuenn, CLE 3
B. Daley, KC 3
M. Fornieles, BOS 2
C. Maxwell, DET 2
J. Piersall, CLE 2

1961 NATIONAL
F. Robinson, CIN ... 219
O. Cepeda, SF 117
V. Pinson, CIN 104
R. Clemente, PIT 81
J. Jay, CIN 74
W. Mays, SF 70
K. Boyer, SL 43
H. Aaron, MIL 39
M. Wills, LA 36
J. O'Toole, CIN 31
W. Spahn, MIL 31
S. Miller, SF 26
W. Moon, LA 22
G. Altman, CHI 9
J. Podres, LA 9
R. McMillan, MIL 8
E. Mathews, MIL 7
S. Koufax, LA 5
J. Roseboro, LA 4
J. Brosnan, CIN 3
J. Torre, MIL 2
L. Jackson, SL 1
J. Lynch, CIN 1
B. Malkmus, PHI 1
D. Stuart, PIT 1

1961 AMERICAN
R. Maris, NY 202
M. Mantle, NY 198
J. Gentile, BAL 157
N. Cash, DET 151
W. Ford, NY 102
L. Arroyo, NY 95
F. Lary, DET 53
R. Colavito, DET 51
A. Kaline, DET 35
E. Howard, NY 30
H. Killebrew, MIN 29
L. Aparicio, CHI 16
J. Piersall, CLE 10
S. Barber, BAL 7
D. Schwall, BOS 7
N. Siebern, KC 7
D. Donovan, WAS 5
B. Phillips, CLE 5
B. Robinson, BAL 4
C. Schilling, BOS 4
T. Morgan, LA 3
A. Smith, CHI 3
Y. Berra, NY 2
B. Richardson, NY 1
J. Romano, CLE 1
L. Thomas, NY-LA 1
H. Wilhelm, BAL 1

1962 NATIONAL
M. Wills, LA 209
W. Mays, SF 202
T. Davis, LA 175
F. Robinson, CIN ... 164
D. Drysdale, LA 85
H. Aaron, MIL 72
J. Sanford, SF 62
B. Purkey, CIN 33
F. Howard, LA 32
S. Musial, SL 19
J. Pagan, SF 13
D. Demeter, PHI 12
F. Alou, SF 10
B. White, SL 10
O. Cepeda, SF 9
D. Groat, PIT 7
R. Clemente, PIT 6
E. Banks, CHI 5
K. Boyer, SL 5
J. Callison, PHI 5
H. Kuenn, SF 5
J. Marichal, SF 4
B. Skinner, PIT 4
J. Davenport, SF 3
S. Koufax, LA 3
D. Crandall, MIL 2
A. Mahaffey, PHI 2
E. Roebuck, LA 2
E. Kasko, CIN 1
E. Mathews, MIL 1

1962 AMERICAN
M. Mantle, NY 234
B. Richardson, NY .. 152
H. Killebrew, MIN 99
L. Wagner, LA 85
D. Donovan, CLE 64
A. Kaline, DET 58
N. Siebern, KC 53
R. Rollins, MIN 47
B. Robinson, BAL 41
F. Robinson, CHI 33
L. Thomas, LA 32
T. Tresh, NY 30
B. Moran, LA 28
R. Terry, NY 19
C. Pascual, MIN 14
R. Colavito, DET 13
H. Aguirre, DET 10
J. Cunningham, CHI .. 9
P. Runnels, BOS 9
C. Yastrzemski, BOS 9
V. Power, MIN 8
D. Radatz, BOS 8
J. Bunning, DET 8
Z. Versalles, MIN 8
J. Lumpe, KC 7
E. Bressoud, BOS 6
B. Rodgers, LA 6
W. Ford, NY 6
R. Herbert, CHI 5
C. Hinton, WAS 5
F. Malzone, BOS 3
N. Cash, DET 3
A. Smith, CHI 1

1963 NATIONAL
S. Koufax, LA 237
D. Groat, SL 190
H. Aaron, MIL 135
R. Perranoski, LA ... 130
W. Mays, SF 102
J. Gilliam, LA 62
B. White, SL 56
T. Davis, LA 41
R. Santo, CHI 41
V. Pinson, CIN 32
J. Marichal, SF 31
W. Spahn, MIL 30
K. Boyer, SL 19
R. Clemente, PIT 12
J. Callison, PHI 11
T. Taylor, PHI 10
W. McCovey, SF 9
M. Wills, LA 9
D. Ellsworth, CHI 7
J. Maloney, CIN 7
D. Demeter, PHI 3
D. Drysdale, LA 3
T. Gonzalez, PHI 2
C. Flood, SL 1

1963 AMERICAN
E. Howard, NY 248
A. Kaline, DET 148
W. Ford, NY 125
H. Killebrew, MIN 85
D. Radatz, BOS 84
C. Yastrzemski, BOS 81
E. Battey, MIN 57
G. Peters, CHI 55
P. Ward, CHI 52
B. Richardson, NY ... 43
T. Tresh, NY 38
C. Pascual, MIN 29
D. Stuart, BOS 25
A. Pearson, LA 22
B. Allison, MIN 15
J. Bouton, NY 11
M. Alvis, CLE 10
J. Pepitone, NY 10
L. Wagner, LA 9
S. Miller, BAL 9
W. Causey, KC 5
R. Rollins, MIN 5
L. Aparicio, BAL 3
B. Dailey, MIN 3
J. Fregosi, LA 3
N. Fox, CHI 2
T. Kubek, NY 1
F. Robinson, CHI 1
N. Siebern, KC 1

1964 NATIONAL
K. Boyer, SL 243
J. Callison, PHI 187
B. White, SL 106½
F. Robinson, CIN 98
J. Torre, MIL 85
W. Mays, SF 66
R. Allen, PHI 63
R. Santo, CHI 59
R. Clemente, PIT 56
L. Brock, CHI-SL 40
C. Flood, SL 38
L. Jackson, CHI 26
J. Bunning, PHI 23
H. Aaron, MIL 22
J. Marichal, SF 14
S. Ellis, CIN 13
S. Koufax, LA 7½
V. Pinson, CIN 6
J. Hart, SF 6
B. Williams, CHI 6
R. Amaro, PHI 5
T. Davis, LA 4
B. Gibson, SL 2
C. Short, PHI 2
R. Hunt, NY 1
B. Schultz, SL 1

1964 AMERICAN
B. Robinson, BAL .. 269
M. Mantle, NY 171
E. Howard, NY 124
T. Oliva, MIN 99
D. Chance, LA 97
P. Ward, CHI 67½
B. Freehan, DET 44
G. Peters, CHI 44
D. Radatz, BOS 37
H. Killebrew, MIN 31
B. Powell, BAL 28
W. Bunker, BAL 23
J. Fregosi, LA 21
A. Kaline, DET 17
F. Robinson, CHI 14
R. Hansen, CHI 10
B. Richardson, NY 9
L. Wagner, CLE 9
J. Pizarro, CHI 8
H. Wilhelm, CHI 8
J. Horlen, CHI 7
W. Ford, NY 7
B. Allison, MIN 5
R. Colavito, KC 5
M. Stottlemyre, NY ... 4
R. Maris, NY 4
W. Causey, KC 4
L. Aparicio, BAL 3½
D. Stuart, BOS 3
E. Bressoud, BOS 2
C. Osteen, WAS 2
D. Wickersham, DET .. 2
D. Lock, WAS 1

1965 NATIONAL
W. Mays, SF 224
S. Koufax, LA 177
M. Wills, LA 164
D. Johnson, CIN 108
D. Drysdale, LA 77
P. Rose, CIN 67
H. Aaron, MIL 58
R. Clemente, PIT 56
J. Marichal, SF 26
W. McCovey, SF 25
J. Torre, MIL 23

B. Williams, CHI 21
F. Linzy, SF 16
W. Stargell, PIT 15
C. Flood, SL 13
J. Hart, SF 13
V. Law, PIT 12
F. Robinson, CIN 11
R. Santo, CHI 11
E. Mathews, MIL 8
L. Cardenas, CIN 7
J. Maloney, CIN 7
L. Lefebvre, LA 7
J. Callison, PHI 6
L. Johnson, LA 6
C. Rojas, PHI 5
J. Roseboro, LA 5
R. Allen, PHI 4
T. Cloninger, MIL 4
J. Gilliam, LA 3
J. Morgan, HOU 1

1965 AMERICAN

Z. Versalles, MIN 275
T. Oliva, MIN 174
B. Robinson, BAL 150
E. Fisher, CHI 122
R. Colavito, CLE 89
J. Grant, MIN 74
S. Miller, BAL 45
W. Horton, DET 24
T. Tresh, NY 23
E. Battey, MIN 22
D. Wert, DET 22
C. Yastrzemski, BOS 22
J. Hall, MIN 19
M. Stottlemyre, NY 17
H. Killebrew, MIN 15
A. Kaline, DET 9
J. Adair, BAL 7
R. Hansen, CHI 7
S. McDowell, CLE 7
B. Richardson, NY 6
V. Davalillo, CLE 5
J. Fregosi, CAL 5
F. Whitfield, CLE 5
B. Knoop, CAL 4
D. Buford, CHI 3
M. Mantle, NY 3
P. Richert, WAS 3
F. Robinson, CHI 3
B. Campaneris, KC 2
F. Howard, WAS 2
R. Kline, WAS 2
F. Mantilla, BOS 2
N. Cash, DET 1
T. Conigliaro, BOS 1

1966 NATIONAL

R. Clemente, PIT 218
S. Koufax, LA 208
W. Mays, SF 111
R. Allen, PHI 107
F. Alou, ATL 83
J. Marichal, SF 74
P. Regan, LA 66
H. Aaron, ATL 57
M. Alou, PIT 36
P. Rose, CIN 31
G. Alley, PIT 24
R. Santo, CHI 23
J. Roseboro, LA 22
O. Cepeda, SF-SL 22
W. Stargell, PIT 19
J. Torre, ATL 18
W. McCovey, SF 12
J. Lefebvre, LA 8
G. Perry, SF 8
C. Flood, SL 7
M. Wills, LA 5
R. Staub, HOU 4
B. Mazeroski, PIT 3
G. Beckert, CHI 3
J. Maloney, CIN 3
B. White, PHI 3
L. Brock, SL 2
B. Shaw, SF-NY 1
C. Short, PHI 1
W. Davis, LA 1

1966 AMERICAN

F. Robinson, BAL 280
B. Robinson, BAL 153
B. Powell, BAL 122
H. Killebrew, MIN 96
J. Kaat, MIN 84
T. Oliva, MIN 71
A. Kaline, DET 66
T. Agee, CHI 63
L. Aparicio, BAL 51
B. Campaneris, KC 36
S. Miller, BAL 27
N. Cash, DET 23
J. Aker, KC 22
E. Wilson, BOS-DET 13
D. McLain, DET 12
B. Freehan, DET 9
A. Etchebarren, BAL 7
B. Knoop, CAL 6
M. Mantle, NY 5
T. Tresh, NY 5
J. Sanford, CAL 4
R. Reichardt, CAL 4
F. Valentine, WAS 4
W. Horton, DET 4
L. Wagner, CLE 4
P. Richert, WAS 3
J. Pepitone, NY 2
T. Conigliaro, BOS 1
S. Siebert, CLE 1
C. Yastrzemski, BOS 1
J. Fregosi, CAL 1

1967 NATIONAL

O. Cepeda, SL 280
T. McCarver, SL 136
R. Clemente, PIT 129
R. Santo, CHI 103
H. Aaron, ATL 79
M. McCormick, SF 73
L. Brock, SL 49
T. Perez, CIN 43
J. Javier, SL 41
P. Rose, CIN 40
J. Wynn, HOU 29
F. Jenkins, CHI 26
C. Flood, SL 24
E. Banks, CHI 22
N. Briles, SL 20
R. Staub, HOU 12
D. Hughes, SL 10
J. Hart, SF 10
R. Allen, PHI 9
T. Abernathy, CIN 8
C. Boyer, ATL 6
B. Gibson, SL 5
R. Hundley, CHI 5
J. Bunning, PHI 5
T. Seaver, NY 5
T. Davis, NY 3
G. Alley, PIT 3
T. Gonzalez, PHI 3
W. McCovey, SF 2

1967 AMERICAN

C. Yastrzemski, BOS 275
H. Killebrew, MIN 161
B. Freehan, DET 137
J. Horlen, CHI 91
A. Kaline, DET 88
J. Lonborg, BOS 82
C. Tovar, MIN 70
J. Fregosi, CAL 70
G. Peters, CHI 37
G. Scott, BOS 33
F. Robinson, BAL 31
E. Wilson, DET 20
D. Chance, MIN 19
R. Hansen, CHI 13
J. Adair, CHI-BOS 11
P. Blair, BAL 9
R. Petrocelli, BOS 7
E. Howard, NY-BOS 7
T. Oliva, MIN 6
J. Kaat, MIN 4
P. Casanova, WAS 3
D. Mincher, CAL 3
M. Lolich, DET 2
M. Rojas, CAL 1

1968 NATIONAL

B. Gibson, SL 242
P. Rose, CIN 205
W. McCovey, SF 135
C. Flood, SL 116
J. Marichal, SF 93
L. Brock, SL 73
M. Shannon, SL 55
B. Williams, CHI 48
G. Beckert, CHI 40
F. Alou, ATL 33
M. Alou, PIT 32
H. Aaron, ATL 19
W. Mays, SF 14
E. Banks, CHI 14
J. Koosman, NY 14
J. Bench, CIN 11
P. Regan, LA-CHI 7
F. Jenkins, CHI 6
T. Perez, CIN 5
N. Briles, SL 4
D. Maxvill, SL 4
S. Blass, PIT 3
T. Haller, LA 3
R. Santo, CHI 2
C. Carroll, ATL-CIN 1
T. Helms, CIN 1

1968 AMERICAN

D. McLain, DET 280
B. Freehan, DET 161
K. Harrelson, BOS 103
W. Horton, DET 102
D. McNally, BAL 78
L. Tiant, CLE 78
D. McAuliffe, DET 71
F. Howard, WAS 63
C. Yastrzemski, BOS 50
M. Stottlemyre, NY 43
B. Campaneris, OAK. 39
R. White, NY 17
J. Northrup, DET 15
L. Aparicio, CHI 13
J. Fregosi, CAL 11
D. Buford, BAL 11
B. Robinson, BAL 8
R. Jackson, OAK 8
T. Oliva, MIN 5
D. Cater, OAK 5
M. Andrews, BOS 4
B. Powell, BAL 4
N. Cash, DET 3
C. Tovar, MIN 3
M. Stanley, DET 2
W. Wood, CHI 2
T. Uhlaender, MIN 1

1969 NATIONAL

W. McCovey, SF 265
T. Seaver, NY 243
H. Aaron, ATL 188
P. Rose, CIN 127
R. Santo, CHI 124
T. Agee, NY 89
C. Jones, NY 82
R. Clemente, PIT 51
P. Niekro, ATL 47
T. Perez, CIN 28
M. Wills, MON-LA 17
E. Banks, CHI 15
R. Carty, ATL 12
J. Bench, CIN 12
D. Kessinger, CHI 8
T. Gonzalez, SD-ATL 8
R. Hunt, SF 8
D. Menke, HOU 8
W. Granger, CIN 8
J. Wynn, HOU 8
W. Davis, LA 7
W. Stargell, PIT 7
J. Marichal, SF 6
B. Williams, CHI 6
J. Koosman, NY 6
J. Torre, SL 6
M. Alou, PIT 6
L. Dierker, HOU 6
T. Haller, LA 3
B. Gibson, SL 2
B. Bonds, SF 2
R. Hundley, CHI 2
L. May, CIN 2
T. Sizemore, LA 2
W. Parker, LA 2
J. Edwards, HOU 1
R. Staub, MON 1
O. Cepeda, ATL 1

1969 AMERICAN

H. Killebrew, MIN 294
B. Powell, BAL 227
F. Robinson, BAL 162
F. Howard, WAS 115
R. Jackson, OAK 110
D. McLain, DET 85
R. Petrocelli, BOS 71
M. Cuellar, BAL 55
J. Perry, MIN 40
R. Carew, MIN 30
P. Blair, BAL 28
L. Cardenas, MIN 27
R. Perranoski, MIN 25
D. McNally, BAL 25
T. Oliva, MIN 21
S. Bando, OAK 18
C. Tovar, MIN 9
M. Stottlemyre, NY 8
C. Yastrzemski, BOS 8
E. Brinkman, WAS 7
J. Fregosi, CAL 7
R. Smith, BOS 6
D. Unser, WAS 5
B. Robinson, BAL 5
M. Epstein, WAS 4
M. Andrews, BOS 3
D. Bosman, WAS 3
B. Freehan, DET 3
T. Harper, SEA 2
A. Messersmith, CAL 2
R. Reese, MIN 2
K. Tatum, CAL 2
R. White, NY 2
M. Belanger, BAL 2
D. Green, OAK 1
J. Northrup, DET 1
L. Piniella, KC 1

1970 NATIONAL

J. Bench, CIN 326
B. Williams, CHI 218
T. Perez, CIN 149
B. Gibson, SL 110
W. Parker, LA 91
D. Giusti, PIT 72
P. Rose, CIN 54
J. Hickman, CHI 52
W. McCovey, SF 47
R. Carty, ATL 43
M. Sanguillen, PIT 36
R. Clemente, PIT 33
D. Clendenon, NY 26
G. Perry, SF 24
W. Stargell, PIT 20
B. Tolan, CIN 17
H. Aaron, ATL 16
J. Torre, SL 15
T. Agee, NY 13
B. Harrelson, NY 10
F. Jenkins, CHI 8
J. Merritt, CIN 8
D. Kessinger, CHI 6
C. Gaston, SD 5
D. Johnson, PHI 4
L. Walker, PIT 4
C. Morton, MON 3
B. Robertson, PIT 3
T. Seaver, NY 2
W. Granger, CIN 1

1970 AMERICAN

B. Powell, BAL 234
T. Oliva, MIN 157
H. Killebrew, MIN 152
C. Yastrzemski, BOS 136
F. Howard, WAS 91
T. Harper, MIL 78
B. Robinson, BAL 75
A. Johnson, CAL 70
J. Perry, MIN 63
F. Robinson, BAL 60
M. Cuellar, BAL 45
R. Perranoski, MIN 35
J. Fregosi, CAL 35
L. Aparicio, CHI 35
R. White, NY 25
D. McNally, BAL 22
S. McDowell, CLE 22
C. Tovar, MIN 16
T. Munson, NY 15
D. Buford, BAL 13
C. Wright, CAL 8
L. McDaniel, NY 8
R. Fosse, CLE 7
B. Campaneris, OAK 5
J. Palmer, BAL 4
R. Smith, BOS 3
S. Bando, OAK 1
T. Horton, CLE 1
B. Oliver, KC 1

1971 NATIONAL

J. Torre, SL 318
W. Stargell, PIT 222
H. Aaron, ATL 180
B. Bonds, SF 139
R. Clemente, PIT 87
M. Wills, LA 74
F. Jenkins, CHI 71
M. Sanguillen, PIT 49
T. Seaver, NY 46
A. Downing, LA 36
G. Beckert, CHI 35
L. May, CIN 28
L. Brock, SL 20
D. Giusti, PIT 16
W. McCovey, SF 15
T. Simmons, SL 13
W. Davis, LA 13
J. Johnson, SF 12
W. Mays, SF 11
R. Staub, MON 11
B. Williams, CHI 10
B. Harrelson, NY 4
B. Gibson, SL 3
R. Garr, ATL 1
D. Roberts, SD 1
P. Rose, CIN 1

1971 AMERICAN

V. Blue, OAK 268
S. Bando, OAK 182
F. Robinson, BAL 170
B. Robinson, BAL 163
M. Lolich, DET 155
F. Patek, KC 77
B. Murcer, NY 72
A. Otis, KC 67
W. Wood, CHI 54
T. Oliva, MIN 36
D. McNally, BAL 26
N. Cash, DET 21
B. Melton, CHI 18
R. Jackson, OAK 15
C. Rojas, KC 15
K. Sanders, MIL 13
P. Dobson, BAL 9
R. Smith, BOS 9
D. Johnson, BAL 8
M. Rettenmund, BAL . 8
H. Killebrew, MIN 5
J. Palmer, BAL 5
L. Cardenas, MIN 5
M. Cuellar, BAL 4
C. Tovar, MIN 4
G. Scott, BOS 3
D. Buford, BAL 2
J. Hunter, OAK 1
G. Nettles, CLE 1

1972 NATIONAL

J. Bench, CIN 263
B. Williams, CHI 211
W. Stargell, PIT 201
J. Morgan, CIN 197
S. Carlton, PHI 124
C. Cedeno, HOU 112
A. Oliver, PIT 52
N. Colbert, SD 45
L. May, HOU 30
T. Simmons, SL 22
M. Marshall, MON 22
P. Rose, CIN 19
R. Clemente, PIT 16
C. Carroll, CIN 16
L. Brock, SL 13
H. Aaron, ATL 12
M. Sanguillen, PIT 12
S. Blass, PIT 9
R. Garr, ATL 7
G. Clines, PIT 6
B. Tolan, CIN 6
D. Baker, ATL 5
M. Mota, LA 4
D. Kingman, SF 3
T. McGraw, NY 2
R. Staub, NY 2
T. Seaver, NY 2
J. Cardenal, CHI 1
F. Jenkins, CHI 1
C. Speier, SF 1

1972 AMERICAN

R. Allen, CHI 321
J. Rudi, OAK 164
S. Lyle, NY 158
C. Fisk, BOS 96
B. Murcer, NY 89
G. Perry, CLE 88
W. Wood, CHI 78
L. Tiant, BOS 70½
E. Brinkman, DET 62
M. Lolich, DET 60
J. Hunter, OAK 57
J. Mayberry, KC 27
J. Palmer, BAL 21
B. Grich, BAL 16
R. Carew, MIN 16
B. Campaneris, OAK. 11
M. Epstein, OAK 11
L. Aparicio, BOS 9½
R. Petrocelli, BOS 9
R. Jackson, OAK 9
C. May, CHI 6
G. Scott, MIL 6
D. Thompson, MIN 5
T. Harper, BOS 4
A. Kaline, DET 4
B. Freehan, DET 3
K. McMullen, CAL 3
B. Robinson, BAL 3
R. Smith, BOS 3
S. Bando, OAK 2
N. Ryan, CAL 2
A. Otis, KC 1
L. Piniella, KC 1

1973 NATIONAL

P. Rose, CIN 274
W. Stargell, PIT 250
B. Bonds, SF 174
J. Morgan, CIN 102
M. Marshall, MON 93
L. Brock, SL 65
T. Perez, CIN 59
T. Seaver, NY 57
K. Singleton, MON 52
J. Bench, CIN 41
C. Cedeno, HOU 39
H. Aaron, ATL 35
D. Johnson, ATL 34
T. Simmons, SL 20
T. McGraw, NY 17
F. Millan, NY 12
W. Davis, LA 12
D. Evans, ATL 11
L. May, HOU 9
T. Fuentes, SF 8
B. Watson, HOU 7
J. Ferguson LA 7
J. Cardenal, CHI 6
J. Billingham, CIN 6
A. Oliver, PIT 6
R. Hunt, MON 5
R. Bryant, SF 5
G. Maddox, SF 3
B. Harrelson, NY 2
B. Williams, CHI 2
G. Luzinski, PHI 2
B. Russell, LA 1

1973 AMERICAN

R. Jackson, OAK 336
J. Palmer, BAL 172
A. Otis, KC 112
R. Carew, MIN 83
J. Hiller, DET 83
S. Bando, OAK 83
J. Mayberry, KC 76
D. May, MIL 65
B. Murcer, NY 53
T. Davis, BAL 47
J. Hunter, OAK 47
T. Munson, NY 43
T. Harper, BOS 33
G. Scott, MIL 25
O. Cepeda, BOS 21
F. Robinson, CAL 21
N. Ryan, CAL 20
C. Fisk, BOS 16
B. Grich, BAL 9
C. Yastrzemski, BOS . 9
M. Belanger, BAL 8
D. Johnson, OAK 8
J. Briggs, MIL 6
J. Coleman, DET 6
C. Rojas, KC 5
B. Blyleven, MIN 4
G. Perry, CLE 4
B. Campaneris, OAK.. 4
V. Blue, OAK 3

C. May, CHI 3
W. Horton, DET 3
B. North, OAK 3
P. Blair, BAL 2
D. Nelson, TEX 2
R. Allen, CHI 1

1974 NATIONAL

S. Garvey, LA 270
L. Brock, SL 233
M. Marshall, LA 146
J. Bench, CIN 141
J. Wynn, LA 137
M. Schmidt, PHI 136
A. Oliver, PIT 87
J. Morgan, CIN 72
R. Zisk, PIT 54
W. Stargell, PIT 43
R. Smith, SL 39
R. Garr, ATL 11
T. Simmons, SL 7
D. Cash, PHI 6
D. Concepcion, CIN 5
J. Billingham, CIN 4
C. Cedeno, HOU 4
A. Hrabosky, SL 4
A. Messersmith, LA 4
B. Capra, ATL 3
L. McGlothen, SL 2
B. McBride, SL 2
R. Hebner, PIT 2
R. Stennett, PIT 2
B. Buckner, LA 1
R. Cey, LA 1

1974 AMERICAN

J. Burroughs, TEX 248
J. Rudi, OAK 161½
S. Bando, OAK 143½
R. Jackson, OAK 119
F. Jenkins, TEX 118
J. Hunter, OAK 107
R. Carew, MIN 70
E. Maddox, NY 59
B. Grich, BAL 49
M. Cuellar, BAL 42
L. Tiant, BOS 41
B. Robinson, BAL 30
P. Blair, BAL 27
N. Ryan, CAL 24
B. Campaneris, OAK 23
R. Fingers, OAK 21
G. Perry, CLE 18
C. Yastrzemski, BOS 14
K. Henderson, CHI 12
J. Hiller, DET 11
L. Randle, TEX 10
B. Murcer, NY 10
L. Piniella, NY 8
R. Allen, CHI 8
S. Lyle, NY 7
T. Munson, NY 6
T. Davis, BAL 6
M. Belanger, BAL 6
D. Money, MIL 5
T. Murphy, MIL 3
H. McRae, KC 3
S. Busby, KC 3
G. Scott, MIL 2
P. Dobson, NY 1

1975 NATIONAL

J. Morgan, CIN 321½
G. Luzinski, PHI 154
D. Parker, PIT 120
J. Bench, CIN 117
P. Rose, CIN 114
T. Simmons, SL 103
W. Stargell, PIT 69
A. Hrabosky, SL 66
T. Seaver, NY 65
R. Jones, SD 54
S. Garvey, LA 50
B. Madlock, CHI 45
D. Cash, PHI 26
R. Staub, NY 20
T. Perez, CIN 18
M. Schmidt, PHI 16
M. Sanguillen, PIT 16
R. Cey, LA 11½
D. Kingman, NY 9
B. Watson, HOU 8
L. Brock, SL 6
L. Bowa, PHI 3
J. Reuss, PIT 2

A. Messersmith, LA 1
W. Montanez, PHI-SF 1

1975 AMERICAN

F. Lynn, BOS 326
J. Mayberry, KC 157
J. Rice, BOS 154
R. Fingers, OAK 129
R. Jackson, OAK 118
J. Palmer, BAL 82
T. Munson, NY 69
G. Scott, MIL 64½
R. Carew, MIN 54½
K. Singleton, BAL 44
G. Brett, KC 37½
J. Hunter, NY 31
R. Burleson, BOS 28
C. Washington, OAK 22
T. Harrah, TEX 16
M. Torrez, BAL 12
R. Gossage, CHI 11
P. Lindblad, OAK 7
G. Tenace, OAK 7
B. Powell, CLE 6½
D. Baylor, BAL 6
B. Campaneris, OAK 6
B. Lee, BOS 5
J. Todd, OAK 5
D. Doyle, CAL-BOS 5
R. Wise, BOS 4
J. Rudi, OAK 3
J. Kaat, CHI 2
L. May, BAL 2
B. Bonds, NY 1
C. Yastrzemski, BOS 1

1976 NATIONAL

J. Morgan, CIN 311
G. Foster, CIN 221
M. Schmidt, PHI 179
P. Rose, CIN 131
G. Maddox, PHI 98
B. Madlock, CHI 51
S. Garvey, LA 51
G. Luzinski, PHI 49
K. Griffey, CIN 49
R. Jones, SD 48
B. Watson, HOU 38
A. Oliver, PIT 30
R. Eastwick, CIN 26
J. Koosman, NY 20
S. Carlton, PHI 16
D. Cash, PHI 15
J. Richard, HOU 12
R. Monday, CHI 11
D. Kingman, NY 11
D. Parker, PIT 10
B. Robinson, PIT 9
D. Sutton, LA 7
R. Cey, LA 6
W. Montanez, SF-ATL 4
L. Brock, SL 3
C. Cedeno, HOU 3
C. Geronimo, CIN 3
R. Zisk, PIT 3
L. Bowa, PHI 1

1976 AMERICAN

T. Munson, NY 304
G. Brett, KC 217
M. Rivers, NY 179½
H. McRae, KC 99
C. Chambliss, NY 71½
R. Carew, MIN 71
A. Otis, KC 58
B. Campbell, MIN 56
L. May, BAL 51
J. Palmer, BAL 47
M. Fidrych, DET 41
J. Rudi, OAK 35
S. Bando, OAK 31
C. Yastrzemski, BOS 26
F. Tanana, CAL 19
R. Jackson, BAL 17
G. Nettles, NY 17
G. Tenace, OAK 13
R. Fingers, OAK 12
V. Blue, OAK 10
E. Figueroa, NY 9
S. Lyle, NY 8
R. LeFlore, DET 6
M. Littell, KC 5
R. Carty, CLE 5
R. White, NY 3
L. Tiant, BOS 3

J. Mayberry, KC 1
B. Wynegar, MIN 1

1977 NATIONAL

G. Foster, CIN 291
G. Luzinski, PHI 255
D. Parker, PIT 156
R. Smith, LA 112
S. Carlton, PHI 100
S. Garvey, LA 98
B. Sutter, CHI 68
R. Cey, LA 60
T. Simmons, SL 58
M. Schmidt, PHI 48
B. Robinson, PIT 34
T. John, LA 33
G. Templeton, SL 20
R. Fingers, SD 17
P. Rose, CIN 15
J. Burroughs, ATL 9
A. Oliver, PIT 9
J. Candelaria, PIT 8
R. Stennett, PIT 7
W. McCovey, SF 5
J. Bench, CIN 3
R. Reuschel, CHI 3
E. Valentine, MON 3
T. McGraw, PHI 2
L. Bowa, PHI 1
T. Seaver, NY-CIN 1

1977 AMERICAN

R. Carew, MIN 273
A. Cowens, KC 217
K. Singleton, BAL 200
J. Rice, BOS 163
G. Nettles, NY 112
S. Lyle, NY 79
T. Munson, NY 70
R. Jackson, NY 67
C. Fisk, BOS 67
B. Campbell, BOS 65
M. Rivers, NY 59
L. Hisle, MIN 54
G. Brett, KC 51
R. Zisk, CHI 34
J. Sundberg, TEX 30
B. Bonds, CAL 28
C. Yastrzemski, BOS 25
R. Guidry, NY 11
J. Palmer, BAL 9
R. LeFlore, DET 7
J. Thompson, DET 6
R. Burleson, BOS 5
B. Hobson, BOS 4
N. Ryan, CAL 3
G. Scott, BOS 3
H. McRae, KC 3
L. Bostock, MIN 2
T. Johnson, MIN 2
C. Chambliss, NY 1
O. Gamble, CHI 1
D. Leonard, KC 1

1978 NATIONAL

D. Parker, PIT 320
S. Garvey, LA 194
L. Bowa, PHI 189
R. Smith, LA 164
J. Clark, SF 107
G. Foster, CIN 104
G. Luzinski, PHI 48
G. Perry, SD 45
W. Stargell, PIT 39
D. Winfield, SD 37
P. Rose, CIN 35
V. Blue, SF 33
K. Tekulve, PIT 23
R. Fingers, SD 16
B. Hooton, LA 15
D. Lopes, LA 12
P. Niekro, ATL 8
B. Buckner, CHI 8
J. Burroughs, ATL 7
B. Sutter, CHI 5
G. Maddox, PHI 4
E. Cabell, HOU 2
B. Boone, PHI 1

1978 AMERICAN

J. Rice, BOS 352
R. Guidry, NY 291
L. Hisle, MIL 201
A. Otis, KC 90
R. Staub, DET 88

G. Nettles, NY 86
D. Baylor, CAL 51
E. Murray, BAL 50
C. Fisk, BOS 49
D. Porter, KC 48
R. Carew, MIN 46
M. Caldwell, MIL 41
R. Gossage, NY 39
A. Oliver, TEX 26½
J. Sundberg, TEX 24
R. LeFlore, DET 21
R. Jackson, NY 18
C. Yastrzemski, BOS 17
G. Brett, KC 14
A. Thornton, CLE 12½
L. Piniella, NY 11
T. Munson, NY 9
L. Bostock, CAL 8
L. Gura, KC 8
F. Lynn, BOS 6
M. Rivers, NY 6
B. Stanley, BOS 6
D. LaRoche, CAL 6
D. Money, MIL 5
W. Randolph, NY 5
D. Eckersley, BOS 4
H. McRae, KC 4
L. Roberts, SEA 3
R. Gale, KC 2
K. Singleton, BAL 2
R. Burleson, BOS 1
F. Tanana, CAL 1

1979 NATIONAL

W. Stargell, PIT 216
K. Hernandez, SL 216
D. Winfield, SD 155
L. Parrish, MON 128
R. Knight, CIN 82
J. Niekro, HOU 75½
B. Sutter, CHI 69
K. Tekulve, PIT 64
D. Concepcion, CIN 63
D. Parker, PIT 56
D. Kingman, CHI 53
G. Foster, CIN 34
M. Schmidt, PHI 32
S. Garvey, LA 30
O. Moreno, PIT 23
P. Rose, PHI 23
G. Carter, MON 15
B. Madlock, SF-PIT 14
J. Richard, HOU 12
P. Niekro, ATL 11½
J. Sambito, HOU 9
T. Seaver, CIN 9
J. Bench, CIN 7
A. Dawson, MON 6
G. Templeton, SL 5
G. Matthews, ATL 4
D. Collins, CIN 3
B. Horner, ATL 1

1979 AMERICAN

D. Baylor, CAL 347
K. Singleton, BAL 241
G. Brett, KC 226
F. Lynn, BOS 160½
J. Rice, BOS 124
M. Flanagan, BAL 100
G. Thomas, MIL 87
B. Grich, CAL 58
D. Porter, KC 52
B. Bell, TEX 48
E. Murray, BAL 25½
J. Kern, TEX 25
M. Marshall, MIN 25
B. Downing, CAL 24
S. Lezcano, MIL 18
R. Smalley, MIN 16
W. Wilson, KC 15
S. Kemp, DET 15
M. Clear, CAL 12
P. Molitor, MIL 8
R. Burleson, BOS 7
T. John, NY 5
C. Cooper, MIL 4
R. Jackson, NY 3
W. Horton, SEA 3
D. Ford, CAL 1
R. Guidry, NY 1
M. Hargrove, CLE 1

1980 NATIONAL

M. Schmidt, PHI 336

G. Carter, MON 193
J. Cruz, HOU 166
D. Baker, LA 138
S. Carlton, PHI 134
S. Garvey, LA 131
A. Dawson, MON 72
G. Hendrick, SL 50
B. Horner, ATL 42
B. McBride, PHI 32
K. Hernandez, SL 29
D. Murphy, ATL 23
C. Cedeno, HOU 14
J. Bibby, PIT 11
B. Buckner, CHI 11
T. McGraw, PHI 10
J. Bench, CIN 7
J. Clark, SF 6
J. Niekro, HOU 3
M. Easler, PIT 2
J. Reuss, LA 2
K. Griffey, CIN 1
R. LeFlore, MON 1
G. Richards, SD 1
R. Scott, MON 1

1980 AMERICAN

G. Brett, KC 335
R. Jackson, NY 234
R. Gossage, NY 218
W. Wilson, KC 169
C. Cooper, MIL 160
E. Murray, BAL 106
R. Cerone, NY 77
D. Quisenberry, KC 76½
S. Stone, BAL 53
R. Henderson, OAK 51
A. Oliver, TEX 31½
T. Armas, OAK 29
A. Bumbry, BAL 27
B. Oglivie, MIL 27
W. Randolph, NY 10
M. Norris, OAK 10
R. Yount, MIL 8
M. Rivers, TEX 7
B. Bell, TEX 7
A. Trammell, DET 6
K. Singleton, BAL 4
T. Perez, BOS 2
M. Dilone, CLE 2
F. Lynn, BOS 1
J. Wathan, KC 1

1981 NATIONAL

M. Schmidt, PHI 321
A. Dawson, MON 215
G. Foster, CIN 146
D. Concepcion, CIN 108
F. Valenzuela, LA 90
G. Carter, MON 77
D. Baker, LA 65
B. Sutter, SL 59
S. Carlton, PHI 41
T. Seaver, CIN 35
P. Rose, PHI 35
B. Buckner, CHI 35
G. Matthews, PHI 31
J. Cruz, HOU 25
G. Hendrick, SL 25
N. Ryan, HOU 23
B. Madlock, PIT 20
A. Howe, HOU 16
T. Raines, MON 15
R. Camp, ATL 9
K. Hernandez, SL 9
T. Herr, SL 7
G. Minton, SF 4
W. Cromartie, MON 3
S. Garvey, LA 1
M. May, SF 1

1981 AMERICAN

R. Fingers, MIL 319
R. Henderson, OAK 308
D. Evans, BOS 140
T. Armas, OAK 139
E. Murray, BAL 137
C. Lansford, BOS 109
D. Winfield, NY 98
C. Cooper, MIL 96
R. Gossage, NY 62
T. Paciorek, SEA 46
D. Murphy, OAK 45
K. Gibson, DET 40
S. McCatty, OAK 22
B. Grich, CAL 19

J. Morris, DET 17
A. Oliver, TEX 8
R. Yount, MIL 7
B. Bell, TEX 7
B. Almon, CHI 6
J. Mumphrey, NY 5
M. Hargrove, CLE 4
A. Trammell, DET 4
K. Singleton, BAL 3
S. Kemp, DET 3
D. Martinez, BAL 3
G. Luzinski, CHI 3
D. Stieb, TOR 1
G. Brett, KC 1

1982 NATIONAL

D. Murphy, ATL 283
L. Smith, SL 218
P. Guerrero, LA 175
A. Oliver, MON 175
B. Sutter, SL 134
M. Schmidt, PHI 54
J. Clark, SF 53
G. Minton, SF 44
S. Carlton, PHI 41
B. Buckner, CHI 38
B. Madlock, PIT 37
G. Carter, MON 35
O. Smith, SL 25
G. Hendrick, SL 20
T. Kennedy, SD 20
J. Morgan, SF 17
K. Hernandez, SL 12
J. Thompson, PIT 12
G. Garber, ATL 6
J. Andujar, SL 6
F. Valenzuela, LA 3
A. Dawson, MON 3
C. Chambliss, ATL 2
G. Matthews, PHI 2
R. Knight, HOU 1

1982 AMERICAN

R. Yount, MIL 385
E. Murray, BAL 228
D. DeCinces, CAL 178
H. McRae, KC 175
C. Cooper, MIL 152
R. Jackson, CAL 107
D. Evans, BOS 57
G. Thomas, MIL 44½
D. Quisenberry, KC 39
R. Henderson, OAK 38
D. Winfield, NY 33
P. Molitor, MIL 29½
L. Parrish, DET 26
B. Downing, CAL 22
W. Wilson, KC 16
R. Fingers, MIL 12
B. Boone, CAL 12
P. Vuckovich, MIL 11
J. Rice, BOS 10
T. Harrah, CLE 9
H. Baines, CHI 9
G. Brett, KC 9
D. Baylor, CAL 8
A. Thornton, CLE 8
B. Stanley, BOS 6
J. Palmer, BAL 5
D. Garcia, TOR 5
R. Carew, CAL 5
B. Caudill, SEA 4
B. Bell, TEX 3
C. Ripken, BAL 3
C. Lansford, BOS 1
R. Sutcliffe, CLE 1
G. Ward, MIN 1

1983 NATIONAL

D. Murphy, ATL 318
A. Dawson, MON 213
M. Schmidt, PHI 191
P. Guerrero, LA 182
T. Raines, MON 83
J. Cruz, HOU 76
D. Thon, HOU 67
B. Madlock, PIT 45
A. Holland, PHI 42
T. Kennedy, SD 37
G. Hendrick, SL 33
T. Pena, PIT 25
J. Denny, PHI 24
M. Soto, CIN 16
D. Evans, SF 16
R. Ramirez, ATL 15

- J. Orosco, NY 14
- L. Smith, CHI 8½
- A. Oliver, MON 3
- J. Leonard, SF 2
- L. Smith, SL 1½
- J. Davis, CHI 1
- K. Hernandez, SL-NY 1
- B. Horner, ATL 1
- O. Smith, SL 1

1983 AMERICAN

- C. Ripken, BAL 322
- E. Murray, BAL 290
- C. Fisk, CHI 209
- J. Rice, BOS 150
- C. Cooper, MIL 123
- D. Quisenberry, KC 107½
- D. Winfield, NY 85
- L. Whitaker, DET 84
- L. Parrish, DET 66
- H. Baines, CHI 49
- W. Upshaw, TOR 41½
- W. Boggs, BOS 25
- L. Hoyt, CHI 24½
- L. Moseby, TOR 21
- B. Stanley, BOS 11½
- A. Trammell, DET 11
- G. Luzinski, CHI 9
- R. Yount, MIL 6
- T. Simmons, MIL 4
- R. Dotson, CHI 3½
- R. Law, CHI 2
- R. Guidry, NY 2
- J. Morris, DET 2
- J. Cruz, SEA-CHI 1
- R. Henderson, OAK 1
- G. Wright, TEX 1
- T. Martinez, BAL ½

1984 NATIONAL

- R. Sandberg, CHI 326
- K. Hernadez, NY 195
- T. Gwynn, SD 184
- R. Sutcliffe, CHI 151
- G. Matthews, CHI 70
- B. Sutter, SL 67
- M. Schmidt, PHI 55½
- J. Cruz, HOU 53
- D. Murphy, ATL 52½
- J. Davis, CHI 49
- T. Raines, MON 41
- L. Durham, CHI 38
- R. Gossage, SD 34
- G. Carter, MON 32
- D. Gooden, NY 28
- A. Wiggins, SD 14
- R. Cey, CHI 6
- K. McReynolds, SD 6
- B. Dernier, CHI 6
- S. Garvey, SD 5
- B. Brenly, SF 1
- J. Samuel, PHI 1
- J. Leonard, SF 1

1984 AMERICAN

- W. Hernandez, DET 306
- K. Hrbek, MIN 247
- D. Quisenberry, KC 235
- E. Murray, BAL 197
- D. Mattingly, NY 113
- K. Gibson, DET 96
- T. Armas, BOS 87½
- D. Winfield, NY 83
- A. Trammell, DET 76½
- W. Wilson, KC 61
- D. Evans, BOS 39
- A. Davis, SEA 26
- J. Rice, BOS 10
- H. Baines, CHI 10
- D. Kingman, OAK 10
- L. Parrish, DET 8
- W. Upshaw, TOR 8
- B. Downing, CAL 6
- S. Balboni, KC 5
- A. Thornton, CLE 5
- J. Bell, TOR 5
- B. Bell, TEX 4
- D. Stieb, TOR 4
- L. Moseby, TOR 4
- J. Beniquez, CAL 2
- M. Boddicker, BAL 2
- D. Alexander, TOR 1
- C. Ripken, BAL 1

1985 NATIONAL

- W. McGee, SL 280
- D. Parker, CIN 220
- P. Guerrero, LA 208
- D. Gooden, NY 162
- T. Herr, SL 119
- G. Carter, NY 116
- D. Murphy, ATL 63
- K. Hernandez, NY 61
- J. Tudor, SL 61
- J. Clark, SL 20
- V. Coleman, SL 16
- T. Raines, MON 15
- R. Sandberg, CHI 14
- M. Marshall, LA 11
- H. Brooks, MON 11
- O. Hershiser, LA 9
- K. Moreland, CHI 8
- O. Smith, SL 5
- M. Scioscia, LA 5
- J. Reardon, MON 4
- J. Cruz, HOU 2
- B. Doran, HOU 2
- M. Duncan, LA 1
- T. Gwynn, SD 1
- F. Valenzuela, LA 1
- G. Wilson, PHI 1

1985 AMERICAN

- D. Mattingly, NY 367
- G. Brett, KC 274
- R. Henderson, NY 174
- W. Boggs, BOS 159
- E. Murray, BAL 130
- D. Moore, CAL 96
- J. Barfield, TOR 88
- J. Bell, TOR 84
- H. Baines, CHI 49
- B. Saberhagen, KC 45
- D. Quisenberry, KC 39
- D. Winfield, NY 35
- C. Fisk, CHI 29
- Da. Evans, DET 17
- R. Guidry, NY 15
- P. Bradley, SEA 12
- C. Ripken, BAL 9
- K. Gibson, DET 7
- S. Balboni, KC 6
- T. Henke, TOR 5
- D. Lamp, TOR 3
- K. Puckett, MIN 3
- D. Alexander, TOR 3
- D. Garcia, TOR 2
- R. Gedman, BOS 1

1986 NATIONAL

- M. Schmidt, PHI 287
- G. Davis, HOU 231
- G. Carter, NY 181
- K. Hernandez, NY 179
- D. Parker, CIN 144
- T. Raines, MON 99
- K. Bass, HOU 73
- V. Hayes, PHI 41
- T. Gwynn, SD 34
- M. Scott, HOU 33
- B. Doran, HOU 32
- E. Davis, CIN 21
- S. Sax, LA 13
- R. Knight, NY 9
- M. Krukow, SF 8
- T. Worrell, SL 8
- R. McDowell, NY 5
- D. Smith, HOU 5
- F. Valenzuela, LA 4
- L. Dykstra, NY 3
- B. Ojeda, NY 2
- D. Murphy, ATL 2
- C. Maldonado, SF 2

1986 AMERICAN

- R. Clemens, BOS 339
- D. Mattingly, NY 258
- J. Rice, BOS 241
- J. Bell, TOR 125
- J. Barfield, TOR 107
- K. Puckett, MIN 105
- W. Boggs, BOS 87
- W. Joyner, CAL 74
- J. Carter, CLE 72
- D. Righetti, NY 71
- D. DeCinces, CAL 56
- M. Witt, CAL 34
- D. Baylor, BOS 32
- T. Fernandez, TOR 17
- T. Higuera, MIL 7
- G. Gaetti, MIN 6
- P. O'Brien, TEX 5
- S. Fletcher, TEX 5
- M. Barrett, BOS 5
- J. Canseco, OAK 3
- J. Presley, SEA 2
- D. Schofield, CAL 1

1987 NATIONAL

- A. Dawson, CHI 269
- O. Smith, SL 193
- J. Clark, SL 186
- T. Wallach, MON 165
- W. Clark, SF 128
- D. Strawberry, NY 95
- T. Raines, MON 80
- T. Gwynn, SD 75
- E. Davis, CIN 73
- H. Johnson, NY 42
- D. Murphy, ATL 34
- V. Coleman, SL 20
- J. Samuel, PHI 19
- M. Schmidt, PHI 13
- P. Guerrero, LA 12
- S. Bedrosian, PHI 6
- M. Thompson, PHI 4
- B. Doran, HOU 1
- T. Pendleton, SL 1

1987 AMERICAN

- J. Bell, TOR 332
- A. Trammell, DET 311
- K. Puckett, MIN 201
- Dw. Evans, BOS 127
- P. Molitor, MIL 125
- M. McGwire, OAK 109
- D. Mattingly, NY 92
- T. Fernandez, TOR 79
- W. Boggs, BOS 64
- G. Gaetti, MIN 47
- J. Reardon, MIN 37
- Da. Evans, DET 21
- D. Alexander, DET 17
- T. Henke, TOR 17
- W. Joyner, CAL 17
- K. Hrbek, MIN 11
- D. Tartabull, KC 10
- R. Yount, MIL 8
- R. Clemens, BOS 7
- J. Morris, DET 5
- K. Seitzer, KC 5
- R. Sierra, TEX 5
- J. Canseco, OAK 4
- M. Nokes, DET 1

1988 NATIONAL

- K. Gibson, LA 272
- D. Strawberry, NY 236
- K. McReynolds, NY 162
- A. Van Slyke, PIT 160
- W. Clark, SF 135
- O. Hershiser, LA 111
- A. Galarraga, MON 105
- G. Davis, HOU 72
- D. Jackson, CIN 41
- D. Cone, NY 37
- T. Gwynn, SD 29
- J. Franco, CIN 23
- E. Davis, CIN 14
- B. Bonilla, PIT 7
- A. Dawson, CHI 6
- R. Myers, NY 3
- B. Butler, SF 2
- S. Sax, LA 1

1988 AMERICAN

- J. Canseco, OAK 392
- M. Greenwell, BOS 242
- K. Puckett, MIN 219
- D. Winfield, NY 164
- D. Eckersley, OAK 156
- W. Boggs, BOS 107
- A. Trammell, DET 62
- P. Molitor, MIL 50
- Dw. Evans, BOS 49
- F. Viola, MIN 39
- R. Yount, MIL 34
- G. Brett, KC 29
- D. Henderson, OAK 28
- B. Hurst, BOS 15
- D. Jones, CLE 11
- J. Reardon, MIN 11
- F. McGriff, TOR 9
- R. Henderson, NY 8
- M. McGwire, OAK 6
- J. Carter, CLE 5
- L. Smith, BOS 4
- G. Gaetti, MIN 3
- D. Plesac, MIL 3
- D. Stewart, OAK 3
- J. Franco, CLE 2
- T. Fernandez, TOR 1

1989 NATIONAL

- K. Mitchell, SF 314
- W. Clark, SF 225
- P. Guerrero, SL 190
- R. Sandberg, CHI 157
- H. Johnson, NY 153
- M. Davis, SD 76
- G. Davis, HOU 64
- T. Gwynn, SD 57
- E. Davis, CIN 44
- M. Williams, CHI 41
- L. Smith, ATL 34
- J. Clark, SD 16
- J. Walton, CHI 14
- M. Grace, CHI 9
- M. Scott, HOU 6
- B. Bonilla, PIT 5
- B. Butler, SF 3
- T. Raines, MON 3
- M. Thompson, SL 3
- S. Garrelts, SF 2

1989 AMERICAN

- R. Yount, MIL 256
- R. Sierra, TEX 228
- C. Ripken, BAL 216
- J. Bell, TOR 205
- D. Eckersley, OAK 116
- F. McGriff, TOR 96
- K. Puckett, MIN 84
- B. Saberhagen, KC 82
- R. Henderson, NY-OAK 67
- B. Jackson, KC 46
- D. Parker, OAK 44
- G. Olson, BAL 35
- B. Blyleven, CAL 32
- D. Stewart, OAK 30
- D. Mattingly, NY 25
- J. Carter, CLE 23
- C. Lansford, OAK 20
- N. Esasky, BOS 19
- T. Fernandez, TOR 9
- M. Moore, OAK 6
- W. Boggs, BOS 3
- S. Sax, NY 3
- A. Davis, SEA 2
- N. Ryan, TEX 2
- C. Davis, CAL 1
- M. McGwire, OAK 1
- M. Wilson, TOR 1

1990 NATIONAL

- B. Bonds, PIT 331
- B. Bonilla, PIT 212
- D. Strawberry, NY 167
- R. Sandberg, CHI 151
- E. Murray, LA 123
- M. Williams, SF 95
- B. Larkin, CIN 82
- D. Drabek, PIT 59
- L. Dykstra, PHI 41
- T. Wallach, MON 36
- K. Mitchell, SF 20
- E. Davis, CIN 12
- C. Sabo, CIN 11
- R. Gant, ATL 10
- D. Gooden, NY 10
- R. Martinez, LA 9
- J. Carter, SD 7
- R. Myers, CIN 7
- P. O'Neill, CIN 6
- J. Rijo, CIN 6
- A. Dawson, CHI 6
- D. Magadan, NY 4
- B. Santiago, SD 3
- B. Butler, SF 2
- D. Justice, ATL 2
- P. Guerrero, SL 2
- K. Daniels, LA 1
- A. Van Slyke, PIT 1

1990 AMERICAN

- R. Henderson, OAK 317
- C. Fielder, DET 286
- R. Clemens, BOS 212
- K. Gruber, TOR 175
- B. Thigpen, CHI 170
- D. Eckersley, OAK 112
- G. Brett, KC 60
- D. Stewart, OAK 56
- B. Welch, OAK 54
- F. McGriff, TOR 30
- M. McGwire, OAK 29
- J. Canseco, OAK 26
- E. Burks, BOS 25
- R. Palmeiro, TEX 22
- C. Fisk, CHI 16
- D. Parker, MIL 11
- O. Guillen, CHI 10
- J. Reed, BOS 9
- K. Griffey, Jr., SEA 7
- A. Trammell, DET 7
- T. Pena, BOS 6
- W. Boggs, BOS 5
- D. Jones, CLE 3
- C. Ripken, BAL 2
- N. Ryan, TEX 1
- D. Stieb, TOR 1

1991 NATIONAL

- T. Pendleton, ATL 274
- B. Bonds, PIT 259
- B. Bonilla, PIT 191
- W. Clark, SF 118
- H. Johnson, NY 112
- R. Gant, ATL 110
- B. Butler, LA 103
- L. Smith, SL 89
- D. Strawberry, LA 76
- F. McGriff, SD 23
- T. Glavine, ATL 16
- D. Justice, ATL 11
- J. Bell, PIT 11
- A. Dawson, CHI 5
- J. Smiley, PIT 5
- T. Gwynn, SD 4
- J. Kruk, PHI 2
- R. Sandberg, CHI 2
- B. Larkin, CIN 2
- D. Martinez, MON 1
- C. Sabo, CIN 1
- O. Smith, SL 1

1991 AMERICAN

- C. Ripken, BAL 318
- C. Fielder, DET 286
- F. Thomas, CHI 181
- J. Canseco, OAK 145
- J. Carter, TOR 136
- R. Alomar, TOR 128
- K. Puckett, MIN 78
- R. Sierra, TEX 63
- K. Griffey, Jr., SEA 62
- R. Clemens, BOS 57
- P. Molitor, MIL 51
- D. Tartabull, KC 32
- J. Morris, MIN 29
- C. Davis, MIN 21
- J. Franco, TEX 17
- D. White, TOR 15
- S. Erickson, MIN 15
- R. Aguilera, MIN 11
- R. Palmeiro, TEX 6
- R. Ventura, CHI 3
- D. Henderson, OAK 1

1992 NATIONAL

- B. Bonds, PIT 304
- T. Pendleton, ATL 232
- G. Sheffield, SD 204
- A. Van Slyke, PIT 145
- L. Walker, MON 111
- D. Daulton, PHI 100
- F. McGriff, SD 100
- B. Roberts, CIN 64
- M. Grissom, MON 54
- T. Glavine, ATL 18
- G. Maddux, CHI 14
- R. Sandberg, CHI 12
- B. Larkin, CIN 12
- D. Jones, HOU 8
- J. Kruk, PHI 8
- M. Grace, PHI 6
- D. DeShields, MON 6
- R. Lankford, SL 5
- J. Bagwell, HOU 4
- D. Hollins, PHI 3
- B. Butler, LA 2
- O. Smith, SL 2
- O. Nixon, ATL 1
- J. Wetteland, MON 1

1992 AMERICAN

- D. Eckersley, OAK 306
- K. Puckett, MIN 209
- J. Carter, TOR 201
- M. McGwire, OAK 155
- D. Winfield, TOR 141
- R. Alomar, TOR 118
- M. Devereaux, BAL 109
- F. Thomas, CHI 108
- C. Fielder, DET 83
- P. Molitor, MIL 63
- C. Baerga, CLE 31
- E. Martinez, SEA 29
- J. Morris, TOR 18
- R. Clemens, BOS 16
- B. Anderson, BAL 16
- J. Gonzalez, TEX 15
- K. Griffey, Jr., SEA 13
- P. Listach, MIL 8
- J. McDowell, CHI 5
- J. Bell, CHI 3
- M. Bordick, OAK 2
- M. Mussina, BAL 2
- A. Belle, CLE 1

1993 NATIONAL

- B. Bonds, SF 372
- L. Dykstra, PHI 267
- D. Justice, ATL 183
- F. McGriff, SD-ATL 177
- R. Gant, ATL 176
- M. Williams, SF 103
- D. Daulton, PHI 79
- M. Grissom, MON 66
- M. Piazza, LA 49
- A. Galarraga, COL 45
- G. Jefferies, STL 28
- R. Beck, SF 23
- G. Maddux, ATL 17
- B. Harvey, FLA 14
- R. Thompson, SF 11
- J. Blauser, ATL 9
- J. Kruk, PHI 9
- M. Grace, CHI 8
- J. Bell, PIT 4
- J. Bagwell, HOU 3
- T. Gwynn, SD 2
- R. Myers, CHI 2
- J. Rijo, CIN 2
- J. Burkett, SF 1
- T. Glavine, ATL 1
- J. Wetteland, MON 1

1993 AMERICAN

- F. Thomas, CHI 392
- P. Molitor, TOR 209
- J. Olerud, TOR 198
- J. Gonzalez, TEX 185
- K. Griffey, Jr., SEA 182
- R. Alomar, TOR 102
- A. Belle, CLE 81
- R. Palmeiro, TEX 52
- J. McDowell, CHI 51
- C. Baerga, CLE 50
- J. Key, NY 29
- J. Carter, TOR 25
- M. Stanley, NY 15
- J. Montgomery, KC 15
- K. Lofton, CLE 11
- T. Phillips, DET 10
- C. Hoiles, BAL 10
- M. Vaughn, BOS 8
- D. Mattingly, NY 7
- C. Ripken, BAL 7
- A. Fernandez, CHI 4
- D. Ward, TOR 3
- G. Gagne, KC 3
- K. Appier, KC 1
- C. Fielder, DET 1
- R. Johnson, SEA 1

1994 NATIONAL

- J. Bagwell, Hou 392
- M. Williams, SF 201
- M. Alou, Mtl 183
- B. Bonds, SF 144
- G. Maddux, Atl 133
- M. Piazza, LA 121
- T. Gwynn, SD 112
- F. McGriff, Atl 96
- K. Mitchell, Cin 86
- A. Galarraga, Col 42
- L. Walker, Mtl 23

K. Hill, Mtl 22
M. Grissom, Mtl 22
D. Bichette, Col 19
H. Morris, Cin 18
C. Biggio, Hou 17
G. Jefferies, StL 5
J. Conine, Fla 4
T. Wallach, LA 4
J. Franco, NY 3
B. Boone, Cin 2
A. Benes, SD 1
B. Butler, LA 1
B. Saberhagen, NY ... 1

1994 AMERICAN
F. Thomas, Chi 372
K. Griffey, Jr., Sea ..233
A. Belle, Cle 225
K. Lofton, Cle 181
P. O'Neill, NY 150
J. Key, NY 102
K. Puckett, Min 100
J. Franco, Chi 49
D. Cone, KC 40
J. Carter, Tor 35
J. Canseco, Tex 27
C. Ripken, Bal 24
W. Boggs, NY 19
L. Smith, Bal 18
W. Clark, Tex 17
R. Palmeiro, Bal 11
M. Vaughn, Bos 10
D. Mattingly, NY 9
P. Molitor, Tor 9
C. Knoblauch, Min 8
M. Mussina, Bal 8
C. Davis, Cal 3
J. Bere, Chi 1
R. Sierra, Oak 1

1995 NATIONAL
B. Larkin, Cin 281

D. Bichette, Col 251
G. Maddux, Atl 249
M. Piazza, LA 214
E. Karros, LA 135
R. Sanders, Cin 120
L. Walker, Col 88
S. Sosa, Chi 81
T. Gwynn, SD 72
C. Biggio, Hou 58
R. Gant, Cin 31
B. Bonds, SF 21
M. Grace, Chi 14
D. Bell, Hou 12
J. Bagwell, Hou 5
C. Hayes, Phi 4
A. Galarraga, Col 4
C. Jones, Atl 3
V. Castilla, Col 3
F. McGriff, Atl 2
P. Schourek, Cin 2
J. Conine, Fla 1
T. Henke, StL 1

1995 AMERICAN
M. Vaughn, Bos 308
A. Belle, Cle 300
E. Martinez, Sea 244
J. Mesa, Cle 130
J. Buhner, Sea 120
R. Johnson, Sea 111
T. Salmon, Cal 110
F. Thomas, Chi 86
J. Valentin, Bos 57
G. Gaetti, KC 45
R. Palmeiro, Bal 34
M. Ramirez, Cle 30
T. Wakefield, Bos 20
J. Edmonds, Cal 18
P. O'Neill, NY 14
M. McGwire, Oak 7
C. Knoblauch, Min ... 5
W. Boggs, NY 5

G. DiSarcina, Cal 3
C. Ripken, Bal 3
K. Puckett, Min 2

1996 NATIONAL
K. Caminiti, SD 392
M. Piazza, LA 237
E. Burks, Col 186
C. Jones, Atl 158
B. Bonds, SF 132
A. Galarraga, Col ...112
G. Sheffield, Fla 112
B. Jordan, StL 69
J. Bagwell, Hou 59
S. Finley, SD 38
J. Smoltz, Atl 33
B. Larkin, Cin 29
M. Grissom, Atl 23
B. Gilkey, NY 13
S. Sosa, Chi 12
E. Karros, LA 10
H. Rodriguez, Mon.... 9
T. Hundley, NY 7
L. Johnson, NY 7
D. Bichette, Col 6
T. Worrell, LA 3
K. Brown, Fla 2
T. Hoffman, SD 2
M. Alou, Mon 1

1996 AMERICAN
J. Gonzalez, Tex 290
A. Rodriguez, Sea ..228
A. Belle, Cle 228
K. Griffey, Sea 188
M. Vaughn, Bos 124
R. Palmeiro, Bal 104
M. McGwire, Oak ...100
F. Thomas, Chi 88
B. Anderson, Bal 53
I. Rodriguez, Tex 52
K. Lofton, Cle 34

M. Duncan, NY 27
P. Molitor, Min 19
A. Pettite, NY 11
J. Thome, Cle 9
C. Knoblauch, Min ... 8
J. Buhner, Sea 6
B. Williams, NY 4
J. Wetteland, NY 4
R. Alomar............. 3
T. Steinbach, Oak ... 1

1997 NATIONAL
L. Walker, COL 359
M. Piazza, LA 263
J. Bagwell, HOU 233
C. Biggio, HOU 157
B. Bonds, SF 123
T. Gwynn, SD 113
A. Galarraga, COL ... 85
J. Kent, SF 80
C. Jones, ATL 70
M. Alou, FLA......... 60
C. Johnson, FLA..... 22
G. Maddux, ATL 16
E. Alfonzo, NY 10
C. Schilling, PHI 9
R. Mondesi, LA 8
R. Lankford, STL..... 6
P. Martinez, MON ... 6
M. McGwire, STL 6
S. Sosa, CHI........ 6
K. Young, PIT 5
J. Blauser, ATL 4
V. Castilla, COL....... 3
D. Kile, HOU 3
R. Beck, SF.......... 2
T. Womack, PIT 2
K. Lofton, ATL 1
J. Snow, SF 1

1997 AMERICAN
K. Griffey, Jr., SEA ..392
T. Martinez, NY 248

F. Thomas, CHI 172
R. Myers, BAL 128
D. Justice, CLE 90
J. Thome, CLE 89
T. Salmon, ANA 84
N. Garciaparra, BOS . 83
J. Gonzalez, TEX 66
R. Clemens, TOR 56
R. Johnson, SEA 42
P. O'Neill, NY 37
R. Palmeiro, BAL 36
S. Alomar, CLE 22
E. Martinez, SEA 22
I. Rodriguez, TEX 16
B. Williams, NY 14
T. Clark, DET 13
J. Buhner, SEA 12
D. Jones, MIL 5
A. Rhodes, BAL 5
R. Alomar, BAL 4
R. Greer, TEX 4
D. Jeter, NY 3
D. Cruz, DET 2
B. Radke, MIN 2
M. Rivera, NY 2
M. Vaughn, BOS 2
J. Burnitz, MIL 1

1998 NATIONAL
S. Sosa, CHI 438
M. McGwire, SL ...272
M. Alou, HOU 215
G. Vaughn, SD 185
C. Biggio, HOU 163
A. Galarraga, ATL ...147
T. Hoffman, SD 117
B. Bonds, SF 66
C. Jones, ATL 56
J. Kent, SF 56
V. Castilla, COL...... 49
J. Olerud, NY 38
V. Guerrero, MON ... 25

M. Piazza,
  LA-FLA-NY 15
T. Gwynn, SD ... 11
K. Brown, SD 8
L. Walker, COL 7
R. Beck, CHI 5
J. Burnitz, MIL 4
S. Rolen, PHI 3
T. Glavine, ATL 2
R. Johnson, HOU 2
D. Bichette, COL 2
J. Lopez, ATL 1
M. Morandini, CHI ... 1

1998 AMERICAN
J. Gonzalez, TEX ...357
N. Garciaparra,
  BOS 232
D. Jeter, NY 180
M. Vaughn, BOS ...135
K. Griffey, Jr., SEA ...135
M. Ramirez, CLE....127
B. Williams, NY 103
A. Belle, CHI 98
A. Rodriguez, SEA ... 92
I. Rodriguez, TEX 50
R. Clemens, TOR 49
P. O'Neill, NY 36
T. Gordon, BOS 27
D. Erstad, ANA 7
T. Salmon, ANA 7
D. Wells, NY 3
J. Wetteland, TEX ... 3
E. Davis, BAL 2
T. Fryman, CLE 2
R. Palmeiro, BAL 2
C. Delgado, TOR 1
R. Helling, TEX 1
M. Jackson, CLE 1
P. Martinez, BOS 1
J. Thome, CLE........ 1

Rookie of the Year Award: History

The Chicago chapter of the Baseball Writers' Association of America (BBWAA) established an award recognizing the major leagues' top rookie following the 1940 season, selecting Lou Boudreau for the honor. This procedure continued for six more years before going national. The subsequent winners of the Chicago chapter's award were Pete Reiser (1941), Johnny Beazley (1942), Bill Johnson (1943), Bill Voiselle (1944), Boo Ferriss (1945), and Eddie Waitkus (1946).

The Sporting News began naming its own Rookie of the Year in 1946, with the selection of Del Ennis of the Philadelphia Phillies. Their award has competed with that of the BBWAA ever since. In 1949 they began recognizing a winner from each league and in 1957 they started selecting both a rookie player and a rookie pitcher of the year for each league.

In 1947 a group of 39 baseball writers were asked to name five rookies in order of preference, with votes distributed on a 5-4-3-2-1 basis. Thus, Jackie Robinson became the first nationally recognized winner of the BBWAA Rookie of the Year Award, or the J. Louis Comiskey Memorial Award, as it was called. During the 1987 Hall of Fame induction ceremony, Commissioner Peter Ueberroth announced that, hereafter, the Rookie of the Year Award would be officially known as the Jackie Robinson Award.

In 1948 there were 48 writers taking part in the award, this time naming only a single candidate on each ballot. In 1949 the BBWAA began the process of choosing a top rookie in each league. Three writers from each league city, the same men who decided on the MVP Awards, participated in the voting. Voters were free to use their individual judgments as to the eligibility of rookie candidates, which created some problems, especially in 1950 when Al Rosen, and his league-leading 37 homers, was ignored by Rookie of the Year voters. Apparently they felt that Rosen's 58 previous major league at bats were tantamount to veteran status, while winner Walt Dropo's 41 previous at bats were not.

In 1957 formal guidelines were finally established for determining rookie status. A player could not have accumulated more than 75 at bats, 45 innings pitched, or have been on a major league roster between May 15 and Sept. 1 of any previous season. Shortly after, the guidelines were changed to 90 at bats, 45 innings pitched or 45 days on a major league roster before Sept. 1. Finally, in 1971, the guidelines were set at 130 at bats, 50 innings, or 45 days on a roster.

There were several instances, especially in the early days of the award, in which some Rookie of the Year voters didn't bother to exercise their franchise. In 1961, as with the MVP Award, the number of voters was reduced from three to two writers from each league city.

Following two tie votes in four years (1976 NL, 1979 AL), the writers adopted the system used in Cy Young Award balloting: naming three rookies on each ballot, in order of preference, with votes distributed on a 5-3-1 basis. This system began in 1980, although it had been scheduled to start a decade earlier.

The maximum possible point total available to Rookie of the Year Award candidates was 165 in 1947, 48 in 1948, and 24 in each league in 1949-1960. In the National League it was 16 in 1961, 20 in 1962-1968, 24 in 1969-1979, 120 in 1980-1992, 140 from 1993 to 1997, 160 from 1998 to the present. In the American League the maximum point total was 20 in 1961-1968, 24 in 1969-

1976, 28 in 1977-1979, and 140 from 1980 to the present. There have been 14 unanimous Rookie of the Year selections since 1947: Frank Robinson (NL, 1956), Orlando Cepeda (NL, 1958), Willie McCovey (NL, 1959), Carlton Fisk (AL, 1972), Vince Coleman (NL, 1985), Benito Santiago (NL, 1987), Mark McGwire (AL, 1987), Sandy Alomar (AL, 1990), Mike Piazza (NL, 1993), Tim Salmon (AL, 1993), Raul Mondesi (NL, 1994), Derek Jeter (AL, 1996), Scott Rolen (NL, 1997), and Nomar Garciaparra (AL, 1997). Technically, Tony Kubek's 1957 AL selection was also unanimous, as the lone dissenting vote went to an ineligible player.

Rookie of the Year Award

1947
J. Robinson, BRO (NL) 129
L. Jansen, NY (NL) .. 105
F. Shea, NY (AL) 67
F. Fain, PHI (AL) 43
F. Baumholtz, CIN (NL) 42
(Rest of voting unknown)

1948
A. Dark, BOS (NL) ... 27
G. Bearden, CLE (AL) . 8
R. Ashburn, PHI (NL).. 7
L. Brissie, PHI (AL) 3
B. Goodman, BOS (AL) 3

1949 NATIONAL
D. Newcombe, BRO . 21
D. Crandall, BOS 3

1949 AMERICAN
R. Sievers, SL 10
A. Kellner, PHI 5
G. Coleman, NY 4
B. Kuzava, CHI 1
J. Groth, DET 1
M. Garcia, CLE 1

1950 NATIONAL
S. Jethroe, BOS 11
B. Miller, PHI 5
D. O'Connell, PIT 4
E. Church, PHI 2
B. Serena, CHI 1

1950 AMERICAN
W. Dropo, BOS 15
W. Ford, NY 6
C. Carrasquel, CHI ... 2

1951 NATIONAL
W. Mays, NY 18
C. Nichols, BOS 4
C. Labine, BRO 2

1951 AMERICAN
G. McDougald, NY ... 13
M. Minoso, CLE-CHI. 11

1952 NATIONAL
J. Black, BRO 19
H. Wilhelm, NY 3
D. Groat, PIT 2
E. Mathews, BOS 1

1952 AMERICAN
H. Byrd, PHI 9
C. Courtney, SL 8
S. White, BOS 7

1953 NATIONAL
J. Gilliam, BRO 11
H. Haddix, SL 4
R. Jablonski, SL 3
R. Repulski, SL 2
B. Bruton, MIL 2
F. Baczewski, CIN 1
J. Greengrass, CIN 1

1953 AMERICAN
H. Kuenn, DET 23
T. Umphlett, BOS 1

1954 NATIONAL
W. Moon, SL 17
E. Banks, CHI 4
G. Conley, MIL 3
H. Aaron, MIL 1

1954 AMERICAN
B. Grim, NY 15
J. Finigan, PHI 8
A. Kaline, DET 1

1955 NATIONAL
B. Virdon, SL 15
J. Meyer, PHI 7
D. Bessent, BRO 2

1955 AMERICAN
H. Score, CLE 18
B. Klaus, BOS 5
N. Zauchin, BOS 1

1956 NATIONAL
F. Robinson, CIN 24

1956 AMERICAN
L. Aparicio, CHI 22
T. Francona, BAL 1
R. Colavito, CLE 1

1957 NATIONAL
J. Sanford, PHI 16
E. Bouchee, PHI 4
D. Drott, CHI 3
B. Hazle, MIL 1

1957 AMERICAN
T. Kubek, NY 23
F. Malzone, BOS 1

1958 NATIONAL
O. Cepeda, SF 21

1958 AMERICAN
A. Pearson, WAS 14
R. Duren, NY 7
G. Bell, CLE 3

1959 NATIONAL
W. McCovey, SF 24

1959 AMERICAN
B. Allison, WAS 18
J. Perry, CLE 5
R. Snyder, KC 1

1960 NATIONAL
F. Howard, LA 12
P. Herrera, PHI 4
A. Mahaffey, PHI..... 3
R. Santo, CHI 2
T. Davis, LA 1

1960 AMERICAN
R. Hansen, BAL 22
C. Estrada, BAL 1
J. Gentile, BAL 1

1961 NATIONAL
B. Williams, CHI 10
J. Torre, MIL 5
J. Curtis, CHI 1

1961 AMERICAN
D. Schwall, BOS 7
D. Howser, KC........ 6
Fl. Robinson, CHI 2
C. Schilling, BOS 2
L. Thomas, LA 2
J. Wood, DET 1

1962 NATIONAL
K. Hubbs, CHI 19
D. Clendenon, PIT ... 1

1962 AMERICAN
T. Tresh, NY 13
B. Rodgers, LA 4
B. Allen, MIN 1

D. Chance, LA 1
D. Radatz, BOS 1

1963 NATIONAL
P. Rose, CIN......... 17
R. Hunt, NY.......... 2
R. Culp, PHI 1

1963 AMERICAN
G. Peters, CHI 10
P. Ward, DET 6
J. Hall, MIN 4

1964 NATIONAL
R. Allen, PHI 18
R. Carty, MIL 1
J. Hart, SF 1

1964 AMERICAN
T. Oliva, MIN 19
W. Bunker, BAL 1

1965 NATIONAL
J. Lefebvre, LA 13
J. Morgan, HOU 4
F. Linzy, SF 3

1965 AMERICAN
C. Blefary, BAL 12
M. Lopez, CAL 8

1966 NATIONAL
T. Helms, CIN 12
S. Jackson, HOU 3
T. Fuentes, SF 2
R. Hundley, CHI 1
C. Jones, NY 1
L. Jaster, SL 1

1966 AMERICAN
T. Agee, CHI 16
J. Nash, KC 2
D. Johnson, BAL 1
G. Scott, BOS 1

1967 NATIONAL
T. Seaver, NY........ 11
D. Hughes, SL 6
G. Nolan, CIN........ 3

1967 AMERICAN
R. Carew, MIN 19
R. Smith, BOS 1

1968 NATIONAL
J. Bench, CIN 10½
J. Koosman, NY 9½

1968 AMERICAN
S. Bahnsen, NY...... 17
D. Unser, WAS 3

1969 NATIONAL
T. Sizemore, LA...... 14
C. Laboy, MON 3
A. Oliver, PIT 3
B. Didier, ATL 3
L. Hisle, PHI 1

1969 AMERICAN
L. Piniella, KC 9
M. Nagy, BOS 6
C. May, CHI 5
K. Tatum, CAL 4

1970 NATIONAL
C. Morton, MON 11
B. Carbo, CIN 8
L. Bowa, PHI 3
W. Simpson, CIN 1
C. Cedeno, HOU 1

1970 AMERICAN
T. Munson, NY 23
R. Foster, CLE 1

1971 NATIONAL
E. Williams, ATL 18
W. Montanez, PHI ... 6

1971 AMERICAN
C. Chambliss, CLE .. 11
B. Parsons, MIL 5
A. Mangual, OAK ... 4
D. Griffin, BOS 3
P. Splittorff, KC 1

1972 NATIONAL
J. Matlack, NY 19
Dv. Rader, SF 4
J. Milner, NY 1

1972 AMERICAN
C. Fisk, BOS......... 24

1973 NATIONAL
G. Matthews, SF ... 11
S. Rogers, MON 3½
B. Boone, PHI 2
E. Sosa, SF 2
D. Driessen, CIN 2
R. Cey, LA 1
D. Lopes, LA 1
J. Grubb, SD 1
R. Zisk, PIT .... ½

1973 AMERICAN
A. Bumbry, BAL ... 13½
P. Garcia, MIL 3
D. Porter, MIL 2
S. Busby, KC 2
D. Medich, NY 2
R. Coggins, BAL 1½

1974 NATIONAL
B. McBride, SL 16
G. Gross, HOU 7
B. Madlock CHI....... 1

1974 AMERICAN
M. Hargrove, TEX .. 16½
B. Dent, CHI 3
G. Brett, KC 2
R. Burleson, BOS ... 1½
J. Sundberg, TEX ... 1

1975 NATIONAL
J. Montefusco, SF ... 12
G. Carter, MON 9
Lr. Parrish, MON 1
R. Eastwick, CIN 1
M. Trillo, CHI 1

1975 AMERICAN
F. Lynn, BOS 23½
J. Rice, BOS......... ½

1976 NATIONAL
B. Metzger, SD 11
P. Zachry, CIN 11
H. Cruz, SL 2

1976 AMERICAN
M. Fidrych, DET 22
B. Wynegar, MIN ... 2

1977 NATIONAL
A. Dawson, MON ... 10
S. Henderson, NY ... 9
G. Richards, SD 4
F. Bannister, HOU ... 1

1977 AMERICAN
E. Murray, BAL 12½

M. Page, OAK 9½
B. Wills, TEX 4
D. Rozema, DET 2

1978 NATIONAL
B. Horner, ATL 12½
O. Smith, SD 8½
D. Robinson, PIT 3

1978 AMERICAN
L. Whitaker, DET 21
P. Molitor, MIL 3
C. Lansford, CAL 2
R. Gale, KC 1
A. Trammell, DET 1

1979 NATIONAL
R. Sutcliffe, LA....... 20
J. Leonard, HOU 3
S. Thompson, CHI ... 1

1979 AMERICAN
J. Castino, MIN 7
A. Griffin, TOR 7
M. Clear, CAL 5
R. Davis, NY 3
R. Baumgarten, CHI .. 3
P. Putnam, TEX 3

1980 NATIONAL
S. Howe, LA 80
B. Gullickson, MON.. 53
L. Smith, PHI 49
R. Oester, CIN 16
D. Smith, HOU 13

1980 AMERICAN
J. Charboneau, CLE 102
D. Stapleton, BOS ... 40
D. Corbett, MIN 38
D. Garcia, TOR 35
B. Burns, CHI 33
R. Peters, DET 3
R. Dotson, CHI 1

1981 NATIONAL
F. Valenzuela, LA .. 107
T. Raines, MON..... 85
H. Brooks, NY 8½
B. Berenyi, CIN 5
J. Bonilla, SD 5
T. Pena, PIT 4
M. Wilson, NY 1½

1981 AMERICAN
D. Righetti, NY...... 127
R. Gedman, BOS ... 64
B. Ojeda, BOS 36
M. Jones, KC 8
D. Engle, MIN 4½
M. Witt, CAL........ 4
S. Babitt, OAK 4
J. Bell, TOR 2
G. Ward, MIN 1½
B. Havens, MIN 1

1982 NATIONAL
S. Sax, LA 63
J. Ray, PIT.......... 57
W. McGee, SL 39
C. Davis, SF 32
L. DeLeon, SD 10
R. Sandberg, CHI ... 9
R. Bedrosian, ATL ... 3
D. LaPoint, SL 1
E. Show, SD 1

1982 AMERICAN
C. Ripken, BAL 132
K. Hrbek, MIN 90
W. Boggs, BOS 10½
E. Vande Berg, SEA... 9
G. Gaetti, MIN 4
D. Hostetler, TEX ... 3
V. Hayes, CLE 2
J. Barfield, TOR..... 1½

1983 NATIONAL
D. Strawberry, NY .. 106
C. McMurtry, ATL ... 49
M. Hall, CHI 32
G. Redus, CIN 8
B. Doran, HOU 7
F. DiPino, HOU 6
G. Brock, LA......... 3
J. DeLeon, PIT 3
M. Thurmond, SD ... 1
L. Tunnell, PIT 1

1983 AMERICAN
R. Kittle, CHI 104
J. Franco, CLE 78
M. Boddicker, BAL .. 70

1984 NATIONAL
D. Gooden, NY 118
J. Samuel, PHI 67
O. Hershiser, LA 15
D. Gladden, SF 9
R. Darling, NY 3
C. Martinez, SD 2
J. Stone, PHI 1
T. Pendleton, SL..... 1

1984 AMERICAN
A. Davis, SEA....... 134
M. Langston, SEA ... 82
K. Puckett, MIN 23
T. Teufel, MIN........ 5
M. Young, BAL 3
R. Clemens, BOS ... 2
M. Gubicza, KC 1
A. Nipper, BOS 1
R. Romanick, CAL ... 1

1985 NATIONAL
V. Coleman, SL 120
T. Browning, CIN ... 72
M. Duncan, LA........ 9
C. Brown, SF 7
G. Davis, HOU 3
R. McDowell, NY ... 2
J. Orsulak, PIT 2
J. Hesketh, MON ... 1

1985 AMERICAN
O. Guillen, CHI 101
T. Higuera, MIL 67
E. Riles, MIL 29
M. Odowell, TEX ... 25
S. Cliburn, CAL 16
B. Fisher, NY 7
T. Henke, TOR 5
M. Salas, MIN 1

1986 NATIONAL
T. Worrell, SL 118
R. Thompson, SF ... 46
K. Mitchell, NY..... 22
C. Kerfeld, HOU 17
W. Clark, SF 5
B. Bonds, PIT 4
J. Deshaies, HOU.... 1
B. Larkin, CIN 1
B. Ruffin, PHI 1
J. Kruk, SD 1

1986 AMERICAN
J. Canseco, OAK ... 110

W. Joyner, CAL 98
M. Eichhorn, TOR ... 23
C. Snyder, CLE 16
D. Tartabull, SEA..... 4
R. Sierra, TEX......... 1

1987 NATIONAL
B. Santiago, SD ... 120
M. Dunne, PIT 66
J. Magrane, SL 10
C. Candaele, MON .. 9
G. Young, HOU 7
C. James, PHI 1
L. Lancaster, CHI 1
G. Mathews, SL 1
R. Myers, NY 1

1987 AMERICAN
M. McGwire, OAK ..140
K. Seitzer, KC 64
M. Nokes, DET 32
M. Greenwell, BOS ... 9
D. White, CAL 5
M. Henneman, DET .. 1
N. Liriano, TOR 1

1988 NATIONAL
C. Sabo, CIN 79
M. Grace, CHI 61
T. Belcher, LA 35
R. Gant, ATL 22
R. Alomar, SD 11
D. Berryhill, CHI 3
G. Jefferies, NY 3
R. Jordan, PHI 2

1988 AMERICAN
W. Weiss, OAK 103
B. Harvey, CAL 49
J. Reed, BOS 48
D. August, MIL 22
D. Gallagher, CHI ... 18
M. Perez, CHI 9
M. Schooler, SEA..... 2

C. Espy, TEX 1

1989 NATIONAL
J. Walton, CHI 116
D. Smith, CHI 68
G. Jefferies, NY 18
D. Lilliquist, ATL 6
A. Benes, SD 3
C. Hayes, PHI 3
G. Harris, SD 2

1989 AMERICAN
G. Olson, BAL 136
T. Gordon, KC 67
K. Griffey, SEA 21
C. Worthington, BAL.. 16
J. Abbott, CAL 10
K. Brown, TEX 2

1990 NATIONAL
D. Justice, ATL 118
D. DeShields, MON .. 60
H. Morris, CIN 13
J. Burkett, SF 12
M. Harkey, CHI 7
T. Zeile, SL 4
M. Grissom, MON 1
L. Walker, MON 1

1990 AMERICAN
S. Alomar, CLE 140
K. Maas, NY 47
K. Appier, KC 31
J. Olerud, TOR 13
K. Tapani, MIN 9
T. Fryman, DET 5
R. Ventura, CHI 3
B. McDonald, BAL ... 2
A. Cole, CLE 1
S. Radinsky, CHI 1

1991 NATIONAL
J. Bagwell, HOU 118
O. Merced, PIT 53

R. Lankford, SL 28
B. Hunter, ATL 7
B. Barberie, MON 3
W. Chamberlain, PHI . 3
C. McElroy, CHI 3
M. Stanton, ATL 1

1991 AMERICAN
C. Knoblauch, MIN 136
J. Guzman, TOR 68
M. Cuyler, DET 22
I. Rodriguez, TEX 10
B. DeLucia, SEA 7
M. Timlin, TOR 2
M. Whiten, TOR-CLE . 2
L. Gomez, BAL 1
D. Henry, MIL 1
B. Mayne, KC 1
C. Nagy, CLE 1
P. Plantier, BOS 1

1992 NATIONAL
E. Karros, LA 116
M. Alou, MON 30
T. Wakefield, PIT 29
R. Sanders, CIN 23
D. Osborne, SL 12
M. Perez, SL......... 2
B. Rivera, PHI 1
F. Seminara, SD 1
B. Williams, HOU 1
M. Wohlers, ATL 1

1992 AMERICAN
P. Listach, MIL 122
K. Lofton, CLE 85
D. Fleming, SEA 23
C. Eldred, MIL 22

1993 NATIONAL
M. Piazza, LA 140
G. McMicheal, ATL .. 40
J. Conine, FLA 31
C. Carr, FLA 18

A. Martin, PIT 6
K. Stocker, PHI 4
W. Cordero, MON 3
K. Rueter, MON 3
C. Garcia, PIT 2
P. Martinez, LA 2
S. Cooke, PIT........ 1
R. Guttierez, SD...... 1
A. Reynoso, COL 1

1993 AMERICAN
T. Salmon, CAL 140
J. Bere, CHI 59
A. Sele, BOS 19
W. Kirby, CLE 12
A. Amaral, SEA 8
B. Gates, OAK 7
T. Neel, OAK 5
J. DiPoto, CLE...... 1
D. Hulse, TEX........ 1

1994 NATIONAL
R. Mondesi, LA 140
J. Hudek, HOU 27
R. Klesko, ATL 25
T. Trachsel, CHI 22
C. Floyd, MON 10
J. Hamilton, SD...... 10
W. Van Landingham,
   SF 9
H. Carrasco, CIN 3
B. Jones, NY 3
J. Lopez, ATL 2
S. Reynolds, HOU 1

1994 AMERICAN
B. Hamelin, KC 134
M. Ramirez, CLE..... 44
R. Greer, TEX........ 42
D. Hall, TOR 9
C. Gomez, DET 6
B. Risley, SEA 6
B. Anderson, CAL 4
J. Edmonds, CAL 3

J. Valentin, MIL 1

1995 NATIONAL
H. Nomo, LA 118
C. Jones, ATL 104
Q. Veras, FLA 14
J. Isringhausen, NY ... 4
J. Mabry, STL 4
C. Perez, MON 4
C. Fonville, LA 1
B. Hunter, HOU 1
O. Johnson, FLA 1
I. Valdes, LA 1

1995 AMERICAN
M. Cordova, MIN 105
G. Anderson, CAL ... 99
A. Pettite, NY 16
T. Percival, CAL 13
S. Green, TOR 8
R. Durham, CHI 3
J. Tavarez, CLE 3
J. Nunnaly, KC 2
T. Goodwin, KC 1
B. Radke, MIN 1
S. Sparks, MIL....... 1

1996 NATIONAL
Hollandsworth, LA .. 105
E. Renteria, FLA 84
J. Kendall, PIT 30
F. P. Santangelo,
   MON 15
R. Ordonez, NY 7
J. Dye, ATL 6
A. Benes, STL 5

1996 AMERICAN
D. Jeter, NY 140
J. Baldwin, CHI 64
T. Clark, DET 30
R. Cloppinger, BAL .. 6
J. Rosado, KC 6
D. Erstad, CAL....... 3

1997 NATIONAL
S. Rolen, PHI 140
L. Hernandez, FLA .. 25
M. Morris, STL 25
R. Loiselle, PIT 22
A. Jones, ATL 15
V. Guerrero, MON ... 9
J. Guillen, PIT 4
B. Tomko, CIN 4
J. Gonzalez, CHI...... 3
T. Womack, PIT 3
K. Orie, CHI 1
N. Perez, COL 1

1997 AMERICAN
N. Garciaparra,
   BOS 140
J. Cruz, SEA-TOR ... 61
J. Dickson, ANA ... 27
D. Cruz, DET 12
J. Wright, CLE 7
M. Cameron, CHI 5

1998 NATIONAL
K. Wood, CHI 128
T. Helton, COL 119
T. Lee, ARI 21
K. Ligtenberg, ATL ... 18
B. Fullmer, MON 2

1998 AMERICAN
B. Grieve, OAK 130
R. Arrojo, TB 61
M. Caruso, CHI 34
O. Hernandez, NY ... 25
M. Ordoñez, CHI..... 1
S. Ponson, BAL...... 1

Cy Young Award: History

Commissioner Ford Frick, troubled by pitchers' lack of representation in MVP voting, spearheaded the 1956 effort to initiate a "most valuable pitcher" award. Cy Young, baseball's winningest pitcher, who had died the previous November, was the logical choice to name the honor after. At a special meeting on July 9, 1956, the Baseball Writers' Association of America approved, by the slim margin of 14-12, the establishment of the Cy Young Memorial Award, designed to honor the major leagues' outstanding pitcher each year beginning in '56. Ironically, the first winner, Brooklyn's Don Newcombe, also won his league's MVP Award.

One writer from each major league city participated in the balloting. In case of a tie vote, a second balloting was to be taken between the deadlocked pitchers. Hurlers were not to be eligible to win the award more than once, a rule which was evidently scrapped within two years.

Frick was adamantly opposed to the commonly voiced idea to recognize a Cy Young winner in each league but, not long after his December 1965 retirement, the idea became a reality. On March 1, 1967, Frick's successor William Eckert approved the plan for dual awards, with two writers from each league city to select.

The system of having each writer make only one selection prevailed until 1969, when Detroit's Denny McLain and Baltimore's Mike Cuellar tied for the American League Cy Young Award. Thereafter, writers were instructed to name three pitchers in each league, with five points for each first-place vote, three points for second, and one point for third.

The maximum number of points available for one pitcher was 16 from 1956-60, 18 in 1961, 20 in 1962-68, 24 in 1969, 120 in 1970-76 (AL), 1970- 92 (NL), 140 in 1977-present (AL), and 1993-1997, and 160 in 1998-present (NL). As with every other major award, there have been a few instances in Cy Young voting where at least one writer failed to return a ballot.

Unanimous winners of the Cy Young Award are Sandy Koufax (NL, 1963, '65, and '66), Bob Gibson (NL, 1968), Denny McLain (AL, 1968), Steve Carlton (NL, 1972), Ron Guidry (AL, 1978), Rick Sutcliffe (NL, 1984), Dwight Gooden (NL, 1985), Roger Clemens (AL, 1986, 1998), Orel Hershiser (NL, 1988), and Greg Maddux (NL, 1994-1995).

Relief pitchers, once overlooked in Cy Young balloting, have become strong candidates in recent years. Until 1970 only one reliever—Lindy McDaniel in 1960—had received even a single vote. The new voting system helped open opportunities for bullpen aces and in 1974 the Dodgers' Mike Marshall became the first reliever to win the Cy Young Award. He has been followed in that distinction by Sparky Lyle (AL, 1977), Bruce Sutter (NL, 1979), Rollie Fingers (AL, 1981), Willie Hernandez (AL, 1984), Steve Bedrosian (NL, 1987), Mark Davis (NL, 1989), and Dennis Eckersley (AL, 1992).

Cy Young Award

1956
D. Newcombe, BRO
(NL) 10
S. Maglie, BRO (NL) .. 4
W. Spahn, MIL (NL) ... 1
W. Ford, NY (AL) 1

1957
W. Spahn, MIL (NL) .. 15
D. Donovan, CHI (AL) . 1

1958
B. Turley, NY (AL) 5
W. Spahn, MIL (NL) ... 4
B. Friend, PIT (NL) ... 3
L. Burdette, MIL (NL).. 3

1959
E. Wynn, CHI (AL) 13
S. Jones, SF (NL) 2
B. Shaw, CHI (AL) 1

1960
V. Law, PIT (NL) 8
W. Spahn, MIL (NL) ... 4
E. Broglio, SL (NL) 1
L. McDaniel, SL (NL) .. 1

1961
W. Ford, NY (AL) 9
W. Spahn, MIL (NL) ... 6
F. Lary, DET (AL) 2

1962
D. Drysdale, LA (NL) . 14
J. Sanford, SF (NL) ... 4
B. Purkey, CIN (NL) ... 1
B. Pierce, SF (NL) 1

1963
S. Koufax, LA (NL) ... 20

1964
D. Chance, LA (AL) .. 17
L. Jackson, CHI (NL) .. 2
S. Koufax, LA (NL) 1

1965
S. Koufax, LA (NL) ... 20

1966
S. Koufax, LA (NL) ... 20

1967 NATIONAL
M. Mc Cormick, SF .. 18
F. Jenkins, CHI 1
J. Bunning, PHI 1

1967 AMERICAN
J. Lonborg, BOS 18
J. Horlen, CHI 2

1968 NATIONAL
B. Gibson, SL 20

1968 AMERICAN
D. McLain, DET 20

1969 NATIONAL
T. Seaver, NY 23
P. Niekro, ATL 1

1969 AMERICAN
M. Cuellar, BAL 10
D. McLain, DET 10
J. Perry, MIN 3
D. McNally, BAL 1

1970 NATIONAL
B. Gibson, SL 118
G. Perry, SF 51
F. Jenkins CHI 16
D. Giusti, PIT 8
J. Merritt, CIN 8
G. Nolan, CIN 5
T. Seaver, NY 4
W. Granger, CIN 3
C. Morton, MON 2
L. Walker, PIT 1

1970 AMERICAN
J. Perry, MIN 55
D. McNally, BAL 47

S. McDowell, CLE ... 45
M. Cuellar, BAL 44
J. Palmer, BAL 11
C. Wright, CAL 9
R. Perranoski, MIN ... 5

1971 NATIONAL
F. Jenkins, CHI 97
T. Seaver, NY 61
A. Downing, LA 40
D. Ellis, PIT 9
B. Gibson, SL 3
J. Johnson, SF 2
D. Roberts, SD 2
J. Marichal, SF 1
B. Stoneman, MON ... 1

1971 AMERICAN
V. Blue, OAK 98
M. Lolich, DET 85
W. Wood, CHI 23
D. McNally, BAL 8
D. Drago, KC 1
A. Messersmith, CAL . 1

1972 NATIONAL
S. Carlton, PHI 120
S. Blass, PIT 35
F. Jenkins, CHI 23
M. Marshall, MON ... 8
G. Nolan, CIN 6
T. Seaver, NY 6
C. Carroll, CIN 6
D. Sutton, LA 6
B. Gibson, SL 3
M. Pappas, CHI 3

1972 AMERICAN
G. Perry, CLE 64
W. Wood, CHI 58
M. Lolich, DET 27
J. Hunter, OAK 26
J. Palmer, BAL 20
L. Tiant, BOS 16
S. Lyle, NY 3
N. Ryan, CAL 2

1973 NATIONAL
T. Seaver, NY 71
M. Marshall, MON ... 54
R. Bryant, SF 50
J. Billingham, CIN ... 30
D. Sutton, LA 7
F. Norman, SD-CIN ... 3
D. Giusti, PIT 1

1973 AMERICAN
J. Palmer, BAL 88
N. Ryan, CAL 62
J. Hunter, OAK 52
J. Hiller, DET 6
W. Wood, CHI 3
J. Colborn, MIL 2
V. Blue, OAK 1
B. Blyleven, MIN 1
G. Perry, CLE 1

1974 NATIONAL
M. Marshall, LA 96
A. Messersmith, LA .. 66
P. Niekro, ATL 15
D. Sutton, LA 12
A. Hrabosky, SL 9
J. Billingham, CIN 8
G. Gullett, CIN 5
C. Carroll, CIN 2
D. Giusti, PIT 1
B. Capra, ATL 1
I. McGlothen, SL 1

1974 AMERICAN
J. Hunter, OAK 90
F. Jenkins, TEX 75
N. Ryan, CAL 28
G. Perry, CLE 8
L. Tiant, BOS 8
M. Cuellar, BAL 6
J. Hiller, DET 1

1975 NATIONAL
T. Seaver, NY 98
R. Jones, SD 80
A. Hrabosky, SL 33

J. Montefusco, SF 2
D. Gullett, CIN 1
A. Messersmith, LA .. 1
D. Sutton, LA 1

1975 AMERICAN
J. Palmer, BAL 98
J. Hunter, NY 74
R. Fingers, OAK 25
F. Tanana, CAL 7
J. Kaat, CHI 7
V. Blue, OAK 2
R. Gossage, CHI..... 2
R. Wise, BOS 1

1976 NATIONAL
R. Jones, SD 96
J. Koosman, NY ... 69½
D. Sutton, LA 25½
S. Carlton, PHI 11
R. Eastwick, CIN 6
J. Matlack, NY 5
J. Richard, HOU 2
T. Seaver, NY 1

1976 AMERICAN
J. Palmer, BAL 108
M. Fidrych, DET 51
F. Tanana, CAL 18
E. Figueroa, NY 12
L. Tiant, BOS 10
V. Blue, OAK 8
B. Campbell, MIN 7
R. Fingers, OAK 1
W. Garland, BAL 1

1977 NATIONAL
S. Carlton, PHI 104
T. John, LA 54
T. Seaver, NY-CIN ... 18
R. Reuschel, CHI 18
J. Candelaria, PIT ... 17
B. Sutter, CHI 5

1977 AMERICAN
S. Lyle, NY 56½
J. Palmer, BAL 48
N. Ryan, CAL 46
D. Leonard, KC 45
B. Campbell, BOS . 25½
D. Goltz, MIN 19
R. Guidry, NY 5
D. Rozema, DET 4
F. Tanana, CAL 3

1978 NATIONAL
G. Perry, SD 116
B. Hooton, LA 38
V. Blue, SF 17
J. Richard, HOU 13
K. Tekulve, PIT 12
P. Niekro, ATL 10
R. Grimsley, MON ... 7
R. Fingers, SD 5
T. John, LA 1
D. Robinson, PIT 1

1978 AMERICAN
R. Guidry, NY 140
M. Caldwell, MIL.... 76
J. Palmer, BAL 14
D. Eckersley, BOS .. 10
R. Gossage, NY 4
F. Jenkins, TEX 2
E. Figueroa, NY 1
L. Gura, KC 1
D. Leonard, KC 1
M. Marshall, MIN 1
P. Splittorff, KC 1
B. Stanley, BOS 1

1979 NATIONAL
B. Sutter, CHI....... 72
J. Niekro, HOU 66
J. Richard, HOU 41
T. Seaver, CIN 20
K. Tekulve, PIT 14
P. Niekro, ATL 3

1979 AMERICAN
M. Flanagan, BAL . 136
T. John, NY 51
R. Guidry, NY 26

J. Kern, TEX 25
M. Marshall, MIN 7
J. Koosman, MIN 5
D. Eckersley, BOS ... 1
A. Lopez, DET 1

1980 NATIONAL
S. Carlton, PHI 118
J. Reuss, LA 55
J. Bibby, PIT 28
J. Niekro, HOU 11
T. McGraw, PHI 1
S. Rogers, MON 1
J. Sambito, HOU 1
M. Soto, CIN 1

1980 AMERICAN
S. Stone, BAL 100
M. Norris, OAK 91
R. Gossage, NY ... 37½
T. John, NY 14
D. Quisenberry, KC . 7½
L. Gura, KC 1
S. McGregor, BAL ... 1

1981 NATIONAL
F. Valenzuela, LA ... 70
T. Seaver, CIN 67
S. Carlton, PHI 50
N. Ryan, HOU 28
B. Sutter, SL......... 1

1981 AMERICAN
R. Fingers, MIL 126
S. McCatty, OAK .. 84½
J. Morris, DET 21
P. Vuckovich, MIL ... 8½
D. Martinez, BAL ... 3½
R. Gossage, NY 3
R. Guidry, NY 2½
B. Burns, CHI 2
L. Gura, KC 1

1982 NATIONAL
S. Carlton, PHI 112
S. Rogers, MON 29
F. Valenzuela, LA .. 25½
B. Sutter, SL........ 25
P. Niekro, ATL 18
G. Minton, SF....... 4
J. Andujar, SL 1
G. Garber, ATL 1
M. Soto, CIN .... ½

1982 AMERICAN
P. Vuckovich, MIL .. 87
J. Palmer, BAL 59
D. Quisenberry, KC .. 40
D. Stieb, TOR....... 36
R. Sutcliffe, CLE 14
G. Zahn, CAL 3
B. Stanley, BOS 4
B. Caudill, SEA 4
D. Petry, DET 1

1983 NATIONAL
J. Denny, PHI 103
M. Soto, CIN 61
J. Orosco, NY 19
S. Rogers, MON 15
L. McWilliams, PIT ... 7
A. Holland, PHI 4
C. McMurtry, ATL 3
B. Welch, LA......... 2
N. Ryan, HOU 1
L. Smith, CHI 1

1983 AMERICAN
L. Hoyt, CHI 116
D. Quisenberry, KC .. 81
J. Morris, DET 38
R. Dotson, CHI 9
R. Guidry, NY........ 5
S. McGregor, BAL ... 3

1984 NATIONAL
R. Sutcliffe, CHI 120
D. Gooden, NY 45
B. Sutter, SL........ 33½
J. Andujar, SL 12½
R. Gossage, SD 3
M. Soto, CIN 2

1984 AMERICAN
W. Hernandez, DET .. 88
D. Quisenberry, KC .. 71
B. Blyleven, CLE..... 45
M. Boddicker, BAL .. 41
D. Petry, DET 3
F. Viola, MIN 2
J. Morris, DET 1
D. Stieb, TOR 1

1985 NATIONAL
D. Gooden, NY 120
J. Tudor, SL 65
O. Hershiser, LA 17
J. Andujar, SL 6
F. Valenzuela, LA 4
T. Browning, CIN 3
J. Reardon, MON 1

1985 AMERICAN
B. Saberhagen, KC .127
R. Guidry, NY 88
B. Blyleven, MIN 9
D. Quisenberry, KC .. 9
C. Leibrandt, KC 7
D. Alexander, TOR ... 5
B. Burns, CHI 2
D. Moore, CAL....... 2
D. Stieb, TOR........ 2
M. Moore, SEA 1

1986 NATIONAL
M. Scott, HOU 98
F. Valenzuela, LA ... 88
M. Krukow, SF 15
B. Ojeda, NY 9
R. Darling, NY 2
R. Rhoden, PIT 2
D. Gooden, NY 1
S. Fernandez, NY 1

1986 AMERICAN
R. Clemens, BOS ...140
T. Higuera, MIL 42
M. Witt, CAL 35
D. Righetti, NY....... 20
J. Morris, DET 13
M. Eichhorn, TOR ... 2

1987 NATIONAL
S. Bedrosian, PHI ... 57
R. Sutcliffe, CHI 55
R. Reuschel, SF 54
O. Hershiser, LA 14
D. Gooden, NY 12
N. Ryan, HOU 12
M. Scott, HOU 9
B. Welch, LA......... 3

1987 AMERICAN
R. Clemens, BOS ...124
J. Key, TOR 64
D. Stewart, OAK 32
D. Alexander, DET ... 8
M. Langston, SEA ... 7
T. Higuera, MIL 5
F. Viola, MIN 5
J. Reardon, MIN 4
J. Morris, DET 3

1988 NATIONAL
O. Hershisher, LA ...120
D. Jackson, CIN 54
D. Cone, NY 42

1988 AMERICAN
F. Viola, MIN 138
D. Eckersley, OAK .. 52
M. Gubicza, KC..... 26
D. Stewart, OAK 16
B. Hurst, BOS 12
R. Clemens, BOS ... 8

1989 NATIONAL
M. Davis, SD 107
M. Scott, HOU 65
G. Maddux, CHI 17
O. Hershiser, LA 7
J. Magrane, SL 7
T. Belcher, LA 4
S. Garrelts, SF 4
R. Reuschel, SF 3
M. Bielecki, CHI 1

M. Williams, CHI 1

1989 AMERICAN
B. Saberhagen, KC .138
D. Stewart, OAK 80
M. Moore, OAK......10
B. Blyleven, CAL 9
N. Ryan, TEX 5
J. Ballard, BAL...... 3
D. Eckersley, OAK ... 3
G. Olson, BAL 3
J. Russell, TEX 1

1990 NATIONAL
D. Drabek, PIT 118
R. Martinez, LA 70
F. Viola, NY 19
D. Gooden, NY 8
R. Myers, CIN 1

1990 AMERICAN
B. Welch, OAK......107
R. Clemens, BOS 77
D. Stewart, OAK 43
B. Thigpen, CHI 20
D. Eckersley, OAK ... 2
D. Stieb, TOR........ 2
C. Finley, CAL 1

1991 NATIONAL
T. Glavine, ATL 110
L. Smith, SL 60
J. Smiley, PIT 26
J. Rijo, CIN 13
D. Martinez, MON ... 4
S. Avery, ATL 1
A. Benes, SD 1
M. Williams, PHI 1

1991 AMERICAN
R. Clemens, BOS ...119
S. Erickson, MIN..... 56
J. Abbott, CAL....... 26
J. Morris, MIN 17
B. Harvey, CAL 10
M. Langston, CAL ... 7
K. Tapani, MIN 6
B. Gullickson, DET ... 5
J. McDowell, CHI 3
D. Ward, TOR........ 3

1992 NATIONAL
G. Maddux, CHI 112
T. Glavine, ATL 78
B. Tewksbury, SL ... 22
L. Smith, SL 3
D. Drabek, PIT 1

1992 AMERICAN
D. Eckersley, OAK ..107
J. McDowell, CHI.... 51
R. Clemens, BOS ... 48
M. Mussina, BAL ... 26
J. Morris, TOR 10
K. Brown, TEX 9
C. Nagy, CLE 1

1993 NATIONAL
G. Maddux, ATL 119
B. Swift, SF 61
T. Glavine, ATL 49
J. Burkett, SF....... 9
J. Rijo, CIN 8
T. Greene, PHI 2
M. Portugal, HOU.... 2
B. Harvey, FLA 1
R. Myers, CHI 1

1993 AMERICAN
J. McDowell, CHI ...124
R. Johnson SEA 75
K. Appier, KC 30
J. Key, NY 14
D. Ward, TOR....... 5
P. Hentgen, TOR ... 3
J. Guzman, TOR 1

1994 NATIONAL
G. Maddux, ATL 140
K. Hill, MON 56
B. Saberhagen, NY .. 42
M. Freeman, COL.... 4
D. Drabek, HOU 4

D. Jackson, PHI 3	P. Schourek, CIN 55	**1996 NATIONAL**
J. Franco, NY 2	T. Glavine, ATL 30	J. Smoltz, ATL 136
R. Beck, SF 1	H. Nomo, LA 18	K. Brown, FLA 88
	R. Martinez, LA 8	A. Benes, STL 9
1994 AMERICAN		H. Nomo, LA 5
D. Cone, KC 108	**1995 AMERICAN**	T. Hoffman, SD 3
J. Key, NY 96	R. Johnson, SEA ... 136	G. Maddux, ATL 3
R. Johnson, SEA 24	J. Mesa, CLE 54	T. Worrell, LA 3
M. Mussina, BAL 23	D. Cone, TOR-NY ... 18	
L. Smith, BAL 1	M. Mussina, BAL 14	**1996 AMERICAN**
	C. Nagy, CLE 1	P. Hentgen, TOR ... 110
1995 NATIONAL		A. Pettite, NY 104
G. Maddux, ATL 140		M. Rivera, NY 18

C. Nagy, CLE 12	**1997 AMERICAN**	J. Smoltz, ATL 10
M. Mussina, BAL 5	R. Clemens, TOR ... 134	A. Leiter, NY 3
A. Fernandez, CHI 1	R. Johnson, SEA ... 77	R. Johnson, HOU 2
R. Fernandez, CHI 1	B. Radke, MIN 17	
K. Hill, TEX 1	R. Myers, BAL 14	**1998 AMERICAN**
	A. Pettitte, NY 9	R. Clemens, TOR ... 140
1997 NATIONAL	M. Mussina, BAL 1	P. Martinez, BOS 65
P. Martinez, MON .. 134		D. Wells, NY 31
G. Maddux, ATL ... 75	**1998 NATIONAL**	D. Cone, NY 16
D. Neagle, ATL 24	T. Glavine, ATL 99	
C. Schilling, PHI 12	T. Hoffman, SD 88	
D. Kile, HOU 7	K. Brown, SD 76	
	G. Maddux, ATL 10	

Hypothetical Awards

As the "expert" in baseball award-voting, I have been asked to make a set of hypothetical award selections for the years no official honors were given; i.e., pre-1956 Cy Young, pre-1947 Rookie of the Year, and pre-1911 MVP Awards, along with awards for any other "missing" years.

While this assignment gave me unusual freedom, I felt a certain responsibility to make my selections consistent with the perceptions and voting trends of a particular era. For example, although there were better NL players than Cincinnati's Edd Roush in 1919, he did two things which, combined, would have virtually guaranteed him the MVP Award: he won the batting crown, which was *the* individual title in the Dead Ball Era, and he played on a pennant-winner, which has always been a key factor in MVP voting.

Besides my own opinions and intuitions, several sources were instrumental in my selection process, including:

1. Society for American Baseball Research retroactive award surveys, which have been done for pre-1949 Rookie of the Year and pre-1967 Cy Young Awards. The ballots were tremendously helpful in screening candidates and the voting results were carefully compared to my own choices.

2. Linear Weights, an overall player rating system devised by Pete Palmer, first used in *The Hidden Game of Baseball* (Doubleday, 1984, 1985), and continued in *Total Baseball*.

3. MVP voting results, for comparing Cy Young and Rookie candidates. If rookie "A" receives 75 points in the MVP election, while comparable rookie "B" receives just 10, I am forced to conclude that the on-the-spot observers discerned some important difference that we can't see in

the statistics and that "A" is probably the better choice.

4. Unofficial awards, including 1940-46 Rookie and 1929-30 MVP selections.

5. Cy Young (1956-66) and Rookie of the Year (1947-48) balloting, for years in which one league had no official winner.

The resulting selections are not necessarily ones the average reader will agree with, nor even that the writer agrees with; rather, they are the ones which can be best justified with the available evidence.

In comparison with the Palmer system, my selections concurred 54 percent with top player selections and 59 percent with top pitcher nominations. In comparison with the SABR surveys, my selections agreed 84 percent in the Rookie of the Year Award and 79 percent in the Cy Young Award.

The big winner in the hypothetical awards is Christy Mathewson, who picks up a Rookie of the Year, two MVPs, and eight Cy Young Awards. Other pitchers capturing at least three Cy Youngs are Walter Johnson (seven); Lefty Grove (six, consecutively); Warren Spahn (four, to add to the one he actually did win); Grover Cleveland Alexander (four); Burleigh Grimes, Carl Hubbell, Bob Feller, Bucky Walters, Bob Lemon, and appropriately, Cy Young himself (three each).

Notable Rookies of the Year include Grover Cleveland Alexander, Babe Ruth, Rogers Hornsby, Dizzy Dean, Joe DiMaggio, and Ted Williams.

Honus Wagner cops six MVP Awards, including four in succession. Three-time MVPs are Nap Lajoie, Alexander, Ruth, and Hornsby. Ruth (once) and Hornsby (twice) also won official MVP Awards.

The following pages contain my hypothetical Cy Young (124), Rookie of the Year (97), and MVP (42) selections for this century.

Hypothetical Cy Young Award

American League Pitcher/Club	Year	American League Pitcher/Club	Year	American League Pitcher/Club	Year	National League Pitcher/Club	Year	National League Pitcher/Club	Year	National League Pitcher/Club	Year
C. Young, BOS ...	1901	E. Rommel, PHI...	1922	S. Chandler, NY ..	1943	J. Kaat, MIN	1966	G. Alexander, CHI	1920	W. Wyatt, BRO ...	1941
C. Young, BOS ...	1902	G. Uhle, CLE	1923	D. Trout, DET	1944	J. McGinnity, BRO	1900	B. Grimes, BRO ..	1921	M. Cooper, SL....	1942
C. Young, BOS ...	1903	W. Johnson, WAS	1924	H. Newhouser, DET	1945	N. Hahn, CIN	1901	W. Cooper, PIT ...	1922	M. Cooper, SL....	1943
J. Chesbro, NY ...	1904	S. Coveleski, WAS	1925			J. Taylor, CHI	1902	D. Luque, CIN ...	1923	B. Walters, CIN ...	1944
R. Waddell, PHI ...	1905	G. Uhle, CLE	1926	H. Newhouser, DET	1946	C. Mathewson, NY	1903	D. Vance, BRO ...	1924	C. Barrett, BOS-SL	1945
A. Orth, NY	1906	W. Moore, NY	1927	J. Page, NY	1947	J. McGinnity, NY .	1904	D. Vance, BRO ...	1925	H. Pollet, SL.......	1946
E. Walsh, CHI	1907	L. Grove, PHI	1928	B. Lemon, CLE ...	1948	Mathewson, NY ...	1905	R. Kremer, PIT ...	1926	E. Blackwell, CIN .	1947
E. Walsh, CHI	1908	L. Grove, PHI	1929	M. Parnell, BOS ..	1949	M. Brown, CHI....	1906	C. Root, CHI	1927	J. Sain, BOS	1948
F. Smith, CHI	1909	L. Grove, PHI	1930	B. Lemon, CLE ...	1950	Mathewson, NY ...	1907	B. Grimes, PIT ...	1928	W. Spahn, BOS ...	1949
J. Coombs, PHI...	1910	L. Grove, PHI	1931	N. Garver, SL	1951	Mathewson, NY ...	1908	B. Grimes, PIT ...	1929	J. Konstanty, PHI .	1950
W. Johnson, WAS	1911	L. Grove, PHI	1932	B. Shantz, PHI	1952	Mathewson, NY ..	1909	P. Malone, CHI ...	1930	S. Maglie, NY	1951
J. Wood, BOS	1912	L. Grove, PHI	1933	B. Pierce, CHI	1953	Mathewson, NY ..	1910	E. Brandt, BOS ...	1931	R. Roberts, PHI ...	1952
W. Johnson, WAS	1913	L. Gomez, NY	1934	B. Lemon, CLE ...	1954	Mathewson, NY ..	1911	L. Warneke, CHI ..	1932	W. Spahn, MIL....	1953
W. Johnson, WAS	1914	W. Ferrell, BOS ...	1935	R. Narleski, CLE ..	1955	R. Marquard, NY..	1912	C. Hubbell, NY ...	1933	J. Antonelli, NY ...	1954
W. Johnson, WAS	1915	T. Bridges, DET...	1936	B. Pierce, CHI	1956	Mathewson, NY ..	1913	D. Dean, SL	1934	R. Roberts, PHI ...	1955
B. Ruth, BOS	1916	L. Gomez, NY	1937	J. Bunning, DET ..	1957	J. Vaughn, CHI ...	1918	D. Dean, SL	1935	W. Spahn, MIL....	1958
E. Cicotte, CHI ...	1917	R. Ruffing, NY	1938	C. Estrada, BAL ..	1960	J. Vaughn, CHI ...	1919	C. Hubbell, NY ...	1936	S. Jones, SF	1959
W. Johnson, WAS	1918	B. Feller, CLE	1939	D. Donovan, CLE .	1962	G. Alexander, PHI	1915	C. Hubbell, NY ...	1937	W. Spahn, MIL....	1961
W. Johnson, WAS	1919	B. Feller, CLE	1940	W. Ford, NY	1963	G. Alexander, PHI	1916	B. Lee, CHI	1938	L. Jackson, CHI ...	1964
J. Bagby, CLE	1920	B. Feller, CLE	1941	E. Fisher, CHI....	1965	G. Alexander, PHI	1917	B. Walters, CIN ...	1939		
R. Faber, CHI	1921	T. Hughson, BOS .	1942			J. Vaughn, CHI ...	1918	B. Walters, CIN ...	1940		

Hypothetical Federal League Awards

	1914	1915
Most Valuable Player	B. Kauff, IND	D. Zwilling, CHI
Cy Young	C. Hendrix, CHI	G. McConnell, CHI
Rookie of the Year	B. Kauff, IND	E. Johnson, SL

Hypothetical Rookie of the Year Award

American League Player/Club	Year	American League Player/Club	Year	American League Player/Club	Year	National League Player/Club	Year	National League Player/Club	Year	National League Player/Club	Year
S. Seybold, PHI...	1901	A. Sothoron, SL...	1917	B. Johnson, PHI ..	1933	E. Scott, CIN	1900	R. Hornsby, SL ...	1916	P. Derringer, SL ..	1931
A. Joss, CLE......	1902	S. Perry, PHI......	1918	H. Trosky, CLE....	1934	C. Mathewson, NY	1901	L. Cadore, BRO...	1917	D. Dean, SL	1932
C. Bender, PHI ...	1903	D. Kerr, CHI	1919	J. Powell, WAS ...	1935	H. Smoot, SL	1902	C. Hollocher, CHI .	1918	F. Demaree, CHI ..	1933
F. Glade, SL	1904	B. Meusel, NY	1920	J. DiMaggio, NY ..	1936	J. Weimer, CHI ...	1903	O. Tuero, SL	1919	C. Davis, PHI	1934
G. Stone, SL......	1905	J. Sewell, CLE ...	1921	R. York, DET	1937	H. Lumley, BRO ...	1904	J. Haines, SL	1920	C. Blanton, PIT ...	1935
C. Rossman, CLE.	1906	H. Pillette, DET ..	1922	K. Keltner, DET ...	1938	E. Reulbach, CHI .	1905	R. Grimes, CHI ...	1921	J. Mize, SL	1936
S. Nicholls, PHI ..	1907	H. Summa, CLE ..	1923	T. Williams, BOS ..	1939	J. Pfiester, CHI ...	1906	H. Miller, CHI	1922	J. Turner, BOS....	1937
E. Summers, DET.	1908	A. Simmons, PHI .	1924	W. Judnich, SL ...	1940	N. Rucker, BRO ...	1907	G. Grantham, CHI	1923	J. Rizzo, PIT	1938
F. Baker, PHI	1909	E. Combs, NY	1925	P. Rizzuto, NY	1941	G. McQuillan, PHI	1908	K. Cuyler, PIT	1924	H. Casey, BRO ...	1939
R. Ford, NY.......	1910	T. Lazzeri, NY....	1926	J. Pesky, BOS ...	1942	D. Miller, PIT	1909	J. Welsh, BOS	1925	B. Young, NY	1940
V. Gregg, CLE	1911	W. Moore, NY	1927	B. Johnson, NY...	1943	K. Cole, CHI	1910	P. Waner, PIT.....	1926	E. Riddle, CIN	1941
D. Pratt, SL	1912	E. Morris, BOS ...	1928	J. Berry, PHI......	1944	G. Alexander, PHI	1911	L. Waner, PIT.....	1927	J. Beazley, SL	1942
R. Russell, CHI ...	1913	D. Alexander, DET	1929	B. Ferriss, BOS ...	1945	L. Cheney, CHI ...	1912	D. Bissonette,		L. Klein, SL	1943
R. Bressler, PHI ..	1914	S. Jolley, CHI	1930	B. Lemon, CLE ...	1946	J. Viox, PIT	1913	BRO	1928	B. Voiselle, NY....	1944
B. Ruth, BOS	1915	J. Vosmik, CLE ...	1931	F. Shea, NY	1947	J. Pfeffer, BRO ...	1914	J. Frederick, BRO.	1929	K. Burkhart, SL ...	1945
J. Bagby, CLE	1916	J. Allen, NY	1932	G. Bearden, CLE..	1948	T. Long, SL	1915	W. Berger, BOS ..	1930	D. Ennis, PHI	1946

Hypothetical Most Valuable Player Award

American League Player/Club	Year	American League Player/Club	Year	American League Player/Club	Year	National League Player/Club	Year	National League Player/Club	Year	National League Player/Club	Year
N. Lajoie, PHI.....	1901	E. Walsh, CHI.....	1908	B. Ruth, BOS	1918	H. Wagner, PIT ...	1900	H. Wagner, PIT ...	1907	J. Vaughn, CHI ...	1918
C. Young, BOS ...	1902	T. Cobb, DET	1909	J. Jackson, CHI...	1919	H. Wagner, PIT ...	1901	C. Mathewson, NY	1908	E. Roush, CIN	1919
N. Lajoie, CLE ...	1903	J. Coombs, PHI...	1910	B. Ruth, NY	1920	H. Wagner, PIT ...	1902	H. Wagner, PIT ...	1909	R. Hornsby, SL ...	1920
J. Chesbro, NY ...	1904	E. Collins, CHI ...	1915	B. Ruth, NY.......	1921	H. Wagner, PIT ...	1903	S. Magee, PHI	1910	R. Hornsby, SL ...	1921
R. Waddell, PHI ..	1905	T. Speaker, CLE ..	1916	L. Fonseca, CLE ..	1929	J. McGinnity, NY .	1904	G. Alexander, PHI	1915	R. Hornsby, SL ...	1922
N. Lajoie, CLE ...	1906	E. Cicotte, CHI ...	1917	J. Cronin, WAS ...	1930	C. Mathewson, NY	1905	G. Alexander, PHI	1916	D. Luque, CIN	1923
T. Cobb, DET	1907					F. Chance, CHI ...	1906	G. Alexander, PHI	1917	H. Wilson, CHI....	1930

Gold Glove Award: History

In a 1956 spring training survey, Elmer A. Blasco—employed by Rawlings Sporting Goods as advertising, public relations and sales manager—found that 83 percent of the active regular major league players wore Rawlings gloves or mitts. Noting that Hillerich & Bradsby (the major leagues' leading baseball bat supplier) awarded Silver Bats to the leagues' top hitters, Blasco reasoned that Rawlings ought to sponsor some sort of fielding award. After his idea was accepted by Rawlings' management, Blasco contacted the Brown Shoe Company of St. Louis and obtained from them a hide of gold lame-tanned leather used to make ladies' formal slippers. A glove was crafted from this hide, laced and stamped as a regular fielders glove, and attached to a metal fixture on a walnut base with an appropriate engraved plate.

Thus was born the Gold Glove Award.

The Oct. 2, 1957, edition of *The Sporting News* featured a full-page advertisement/announcement: "Recognizing the importance of superior individual fielding performance to the advancement of baseball as America's national game, Rawlings (Sporting Goods Company) has established Annual Gold Glove Awards beginning with the 1957 season.

"Each of the nine Major League players chosen for *The Sporting News* All-Star Fielding Team will be honored with a Rawlings Gold Glove Award. Selections will be made by a Committee named by *The Sporting News*. Awards will be Rawlings custom-built gloves or mitts hand-crafted of special metallic gold-finished leather, each mounted on a suitable hardwood stand bearing an engraved plate."

TSN publisher J.G. Taylor Spink appointed 19 noted sportswriters for the selection task. They included Shirley Povich, Edgar Munzel, Hy Hurwitz, Earl Lawson, Bob Broeg, Allen Lewis, and Hal Lebowitz. A contest to predict the winners, open to baseball-playing boys, was sponsored by Rawlings.

The first Gold Glove winners were announced with great pomp and circumstance in the Dec. 18, 1957, issue of TSN. "Too long neglected, the magicians of the defense have had no real recognition," the article explained, adding that the selections were made "solely on the basis of their defensive ability."

Rawlings and TSN also joined forces that year in the establishment of the Silver Glove Award, given to the top minor league fielder at each position—based entirely on fielding averages.

In 1958 the Gold Glove selection privilege was turned over to the major league players and an All-Star Fielding Team was selected for each league (as it still is). In 1961 the method for selecting outfielders was changed. Rather than choosing a left fielder, center fielder, and right fielder for each league, each voter was instructed to name three outfielders regardless of position (still the practice today).

In 1965 the managers and coaches of each team took over the voting responsibility, which they have retained ever since. Voters are not permitted to select players on their own teams. In 1987, 139 different managers and coaches took part in the balloting.

Perhaps because of its originality, the Gold Glove is the one *Sporting News* award that has gained universal acceptance and prestige in the baseball world. However, as with any award, the selections often draw criticism. One complaint is that too much importance is given to fielding average. Most of us realize that fielding average is not always a reliable indicator of defensive ability, but how much does it influence the Gold Glove voters?

Of the 366 fielding average leaders at the various posi-

tions between 1957 and 1987 (discounting pitchers and counting only one outfielder per league each year), 118 (32 percent) also won their respective Gold Glove Awards (see Table 1). We can say, then, that if a player leads his league in fielding average he has about a one-in-three chance of winning the Gold Glove—not an overwhelming correlation, but about four times better than random chance.

This raises some interesting questions. Since official fielding statistics are not published until months after Gold Gloves (although unofficial stats are readily available) are voted on, any voter relying on fielding stats would probably have to consult (or remember) the previous year's data. Therefore, if fielding average itself really does impress voters, we should expect to see many players winning a Gold Glove the year after they lead in fielding average. Do they? Well, no (see Table 2). The percentage here is 25 percent or one-in-four—again, considerably better than chance, but less of a factor than leading in fielding average in the current year.

And what about the influence of Gold Gloves on fielding averages? Is an official scorer less likely to charge an error against a player simply because he won a Gold Glove the previous year? Apparently not (see Table 3). The percentage of Gold Glove recipients leading in fielding average the following year is 23 percent.

"It is my belief that a lot more is considered than fielding percentage," said TSN editor Tom Barnidge, citing "range, throwing arm, the headiness of the ballplayer." Pete Rose, a two-time Gold Glove winner and later a voter, concurred: "There are a lot of intangibles involved in voting for the Gold Glove. Take an outfielder. The coaches and managers watch these guys all the time. How they play the hitters, how strong their arms are, how often they hit the cutoff man, and all that is taken into consideration—things that do not show up in the statistics."

Another criticism of the Gold Glove is that batting performance plays a role in the selections, contrary to the award's philosophy. As USA Today baseball editor Hal Bodley put it, "A player who is outstanding on defense and respectable on offense has a much better chance of getting a Gold Glove than a counterpart whose forte is fielding alone."

Other factors can be distractions to the voters: flashiness, reputations, and the selection process itself. For insight on some of these and their effects, I consulted an expert on the Gold Glove: Wes Parker, a six-time winner of the award at first base. Parker, it should be noted, would seem to have no reason to gripe about the award. He grasped the honor from a seven-time winner; he won it even when he batted as low as .239; and he became one of only two nonpitchers (Roberto Clemente is the other) to win the award in his final major league season.

"I would say many, if not most, coaches and managers fail to take their voting responsibility seriously," said Parker. "They don't treat it as a vital act. They are usually much more concerned with their team and the pennant race and, as a result, tend to zip through the ballots (distributed in September). So they wind up voting for the most recognizable names."

Parker brought out another rarely discussed procedural problem: "Since players [when they were voting] and coaches are forbidden to vote for anyone on their own team, they often won't vote for the guy who is contending with their team's leading candidate for the same award. That increases their teammate's chances."

On the subject of reputation, Parker asserted that it "has a lot to do with it, absolutely. In 1966, Bill White won the award (for the seventh consecutive time), although even White admitted that I probably deserved it. It takes a couple of years for your reputation to catch up with you, but that can work to your advantage at the end of your career."

"Flashiness is a factor too," continued Parker. "It puts the player's name in the forefront of the voter's minds." Wes also concurred with the theory that a player's bat can be the difference in winning this "fielding' award.

"[Four-time Gold Glove winner Steve] Garvey is a good example of someone who won it with his bat and notoriety, a perfect example, in fact," opines Parker. "Garvey was vastly overrated defensively . . . he had no range, no arm, and no aggressiveness. He would hold the ball and allow opposing runners to take extra bases to avoid throwing errors. That's how he compiled his high averages at first base. Remember, he was a terrible third baseman, worst I ever saw." (In 1972, Garvey's last season as a third-sacker, he led the NL with 28 errors in just 85 games, posting a woeful .902 percentage.)

"Amazingly, despite these prejudices," Parker concluded, "I think the Gold Glove choices have been excellent. At first base I think they have been perfect, with the exception of Garvey."

While the Gold Glove Award has adequately filled the need for a subjective fielding award, there is still something to be said about fielding statistics. It is fashionable to say that fielding stats are meaningless, but, as analyst Bill James said, "If a baseball statistic is meaningless to you, that is simply because you don't know what it means."

With the understanding of which fielding statistics are meaningful for each position, it is possible to make a pretty reliable judgment of a player's defensive skills based on stats alone. In recent years, several analysts have attempted to measure individual fielding performance on the basis of numbers.

One newer method is Linear Weights, Pete Palmer's translation of individual batting, pitching, and fielding statistics into runs gained and thus games won. The fielding portion of the system, Fielding or Defensive Wins, incorporates data (variously weighted according to position) on putouts, assists, errors, and double plays, comparing a player's totals against the league averages.

The formula first determines how many runs a player saves (or costs) his team as compared to an "average" player at the same position. Runs are then translated into wins, based on the league average of runs per win. For example, second baseman Glenn Hubbard was computed to have won about three and a half games for the Braves with his glove in 1986, the top Defensive Wins total in the majors.

Of the 60 players identified by the Palmer system as the best fielders in their leagues between 1957 and 1986, 28 also won their respective Gold Glove Awards.

Palmer has drawn criticism for comparing players with average, rather than replacement-level, players; for over-

emphasizing the double play; and for the use of arbitrary weighting schemes. It is particularly—and admittedly—inadequate in evaluating catchers.

Bill James has also presented a fielding measurement system, Defensive Won/Lost Percentage (DW/L%), although he hasn't used it since 1984. The formula varies from position to position, using four arbitrarily weighted components at each. These components range from readily available statistics (fielding average, assists per game, and so on) to abstruse estimations and calculations, using some data unavailable to the average researcher. The formula is not designed for cross-era comparisons.

The results of these calculations produce the DW/L%, which in turn is translated into defensive wins and losses, based on still more arbitrary assignments of defensive games at each position (ranging from three at first base to 11 at shortstop). Of the 32 players identified by DW/L% as the best at their positions and leagues for the 1983-84 seasons, 12 (38 percent) also won their respective Gold Gloves. The use of a series of arbitrary values is the glaring flaw of DW/L%. Criticism is also due for the complexity and lack of adaptability of the system(s).

The Elias Sports Bureau has demonstrated a simple and generally effective system for evaluating fielders: comparing the number of runs scored per nine innings while a player is on the field to the number scored when he isn't. For example, Elias calculated that the 1982-86 Cardinals averaged allowing 3.85 runs per nine innings with Ozzie Smith at shortstop, as compared to 4.04 per game with other shortstops.

There is nothing new or brilliant about this concept; the difference is that Elias has the data available to make this type of measurement, right down to thirds of an inning, at least since 1975. Since they generally choose not to share this data with the public, however, it is of no value at present.

So, when all is said and done about modern statistical fielding measurements, a subjective measurement—the Gold Glove—is probably still the best tool we have available to rate fielders.

The following pages list the winners of the Gold Glove at each position since 1957. Complete balloting for Gold Glove elections is, unfortunately, neither available nor researchable.

TABLE 1. Fielding Average Leaders Winning Gold Glove, 1957-87 (Maximum 61 Each Position).

POS.	NL	AL	TOT.	PCT.
C	7	7	14	23
1B	13	13	26	43
2B	14	5	19	31
3B	4	15	19	31
SS	14	12	26	43
OF	6	8	14	23
TOT.	58	60	118	32

TABLE 2. Fielding Average Leaders Winning Gold Glove in Following Season, 1956-86 (Maximum 61 Each Position).

POS.	NL	AL	TOT.	PCT.
C	7	7	14	23
1B	8	11	19	31
2B	9	6	15	25
3B	3	13	16	26
SS	11	9	20	33
OF	2	5	7	11
TOT.	40	51	91	25

TABLE 3. Fielding Average Leaders Who Won Gold Glove in Previous Season, 1958-87 (Maximum 59 Each Position).

POS.	NL	AL	TOT.	PCT.
C	3	7	10	17
1B	11	8	19	32
2B	8	2	10	17
3B	2	12	14	24
SS	10	9	19	32
OF	6	5	11	19
TOT.	40	43	83	23

Gold Glove Award

Pitchers

Year	National League	American League
1957	(No selection)	B. Shantz, NY
1958	H. Haddix, CIN	B. Shantz, NY
1959	H. Haddix, PIT	B. Shantz, NY
1960	H. Haddix, PIT	B. Shantz, NY
1961	B. Shantz, PIT	F. Lary, DET
1962	B. Shantz, SL	J. Kaat, MIN
1963	B. Shantz, SL	J. Kaat, MIN
1964	B. Shantz, PHI	J. Kaat, MIN
1965	B. Gibson, SL	J. Kaat, MIN
1966	B. Gibson, SL	J. Kaat, MIN
1967	B. Gibson, SL	J. Kaat, MIN
1968	B. Gibson, SL	J. Kaat, MIN
1969	B. Gibson, SL	J. Kaat, MIN
1970	B. Gibson, SL	J. Kaat, MIN
1971	B. Gibson, SL	J. Kaat, MIN
1972	B. Gibson, SL	J. Kaat, MIN
1973	B. Gibson, SL	J. Kaat, MIN
1974	A. Messersmith, LA	J. Kaat, CHI
1975	A. Messersmith, LA	J. Kaat, CHI
1976	J. Kaat, PHI	J. Palmer, BAL
1977	J. Kaat, PHI	J. Palmer, BAL
1978	P. Niekro, ATL	J. Palmer, BAL
1979	P. Niekro, ATL	J. Palmer, BAL
1980	P. Niekro, ATL	M. Norris, OAK
1981	S. Carlton, PHI	M. Norris, OAK
1982	P. Niekro, ATL	R. Guidry, NY
1983	P. Niekro, ATL	R. Guidry, NY
1984	J. Andujar, SL	R. Guidry, NY
1985	R. Reuschel, PIT	R. Guidry, NY
1986	F. Valenzuela, LA	R. Guidry, NY
1987	R. Reuschel, SF	M. Langston, SEA
1988	O. Hershiser, LA	M. Langston, SEA
1989	R. Darling, NY	B. Saberhagen, KC
1990	G. Maddux, CHI	M. Boddicker, BOS
1991	G. Maddux, CHI	M. Langston, CAL
1992	G. Maddux, CHI	M. Langston, CAL
1993	G. Maddux, ATL	M. Langston, CAL
1994	G. Maddux, ATL	M. Langston, CAL
1995	G. Maddux, ATL	M. Langston, CAL
1996	G. Maddux, ATL	M. Mussina, BAL
1997	G. Maddux, ATL	M. Mussina, BAL
1998	G. Maddux, ATL	M. Mussina, BAL

Catchers

Year	National League	American League
1957	(No selection)	S. Lollar, CHI
1958	D. Crandall, MIL	S. Lollar, CHI
1959	D. Crandall, MIL	S. Lollar, CHI
1960	D. Crandall, MIL	E. Battey, WAS
1961	J. Roseboro, LA	E. Battey, MIN
1962	D. Crandall, MIL	E. Battey, MIN
1963	J. Edwards, CIN	E. Howard, NY
1964	J. Edwards, CIN	E. Howard, NY
1965	J. Torre, MIL	B. Freehan, DET
1966	J. Roseboro, LA	B. Freehan, DET
1967	R. Hundley, CHI	B. Freehan, DET
1968	J. Bench, CIN	B. Freehan, DET
1969	J. Bench, CIN	B. Freehan, DET
1970	J. Bench, CIN	R. Fosse, CLE
1971	J. Bench, CIN	R. Fosse, CLE
1972	J. Bench, CIN	C. Fisk, BOS
1973	J. Bench, CIN	T. Munson, NY
1974	J. Bench, CIN	T. Munson, NY
1975	J. Bench, CIN	T. Munson, NY
1976	J. Bench, CIN	J. Sundberg, TEX
1977	J. Bench, CIN	J. Sundberg, TEX
1978	B. Boone, PHI	J. Sundberg, TEX
1979	B. Boone, PHI	J. Sundberg, TEX
1980	G. Carter, MON	J. Sundberg, TEX
1981	G. Carter, MON	J. Sundberg, TEX
1982	G. Carter, MON	B. Boone, CAL
1983	T. Pena, PIT	Lc. Parrish, DET
1984	T. Pena, PIT	Lo. Parrish, DET
1985	T. Pena, PIT	Lc. Parrish, DET
1986	J. Davis, CHI	B. Boone, CAL
1987	M. LaValliere, PIT	B. Boone, CAL
1988	B. Santiago, SD	B. Boone, CAL
1989	B. Santiago, SD	B. Boone, KC
1990	B. Santiago, SD	S. Alomar, CLE
1991	T. Pagnozzi, SL	T. Pena, BOS
1992	T. Pagnozzi, SL	I. Rodriguez, TEX
1993	K. Manwaring, SF	I. Rodriguez, TEX
1994	T. Pagnozzi, SL	I. Rodriguez, TEX
1995	C. Johnson, FLA	I. Rodriguez, TEX
1996	C. Johnson, FLA	I. Rodriguez, TEX
1997	C. Johnson, FLA	I. Rodriguez, TEX
1998	C. Johnson, FLA-LA	I. Rodriguez, TEX

First Basemen

Year	National League	American League
1957	G. Hodges, BRO	(No selection)
1958	G. Hodges, LA	V. Power, CLE
1959	G. Hodges, LA	V. Power, CLE
1960	B. White, SL	V. Power, CLE
1961	B. White, SL	V. Power, CLE
1962	B. White, SL	V. Power, MIN
1963	B. White, SL	V. Power, MIN
1964	B. White, SL	V. Power, LA
1965	B. White, SL	J. Pepitone, NY
1966	B. White, PHI	J. Pepitone, NY
1967	W. Parker, LA	G. Scott, BOS
1968	W. Parker, LA	G. Scott, BOS
1969	W. Parker, LA	J. Pepitone, NY
1970	W. Parker, LA	J. Spencer, CAL
1971	W. Parker, LA	G. Scott, BOS
1972	W. Parker, LA	G. Scott, MIL
1973	M. Jorgensen, MON	G. Scott, MIL
1974	S. Garvey, LA	G. Scott, MIL
1975	S. Garvey, LA	G. Scott, MIL
1976	S. Garvey, LA	G. Scott, MIL
1977	S. Garvey, LA	J. Spencer, CHI
1978	K. Hernandez, SL	C. Chambliss, NY
1979	K. Hernandez, SL	C. Cooper, MIL
1980	K. Hernandez, SL	C. Cooper, MIL
1981	K. Hernandez, SL	M. Squires, CHI
1982	K. Hernandez, SL	E. Murray, BAL
1983	K. Hernandez, SL-NY	E. Murray, BAL
1984	K. Hernandez, NY	E. Murray, BAL
1985	K. Hernandez, NY	D. Mattingly, NY
1986	K. Hernandez, NY	D. Mattingly, NY
1987	K. Hernandez, NY	D. Mattingly, NY
1988	K. Hernandez, NY	D. Mattingly, NY
1989	A. Galarraga, MON	D. Mattingly, NY
1990	A. Galarraga, MON	M. McGwire, OAK
1991	W. Clark, SF	D. Mattingly, NY
1992	M. Grace, CHI	D. Mattingly, NY
1993	M. Grace, CHI	D. Mattingly, NY
1994	J. Bagwell, HOU	D. Mattingly, NY
1995	M. Grace, CHI	J. Snow, CAL
1996	M. Grace, CHI	J. Snow, CAL
1997	J. Snow, SF	R. Palmeiro, BAL
1998	J. Snow, SF	R. Palmeiro, BAL

Second Basemen

Year	National League	American League
1957	(No selection)	N. Fox, CHI
1958	B. Mazeroski, PIT	F. Bolling, DET
1959	C. Neal, LA	N. Fox, CHI
1960	B. Mazeroski, PIT	N. Fox, CHI
1961	B. Mazeroski, PIT	B. Richardson, NY
1962	K. Hubbs, CHI	B. Richardson, NY
1963	B. Mazeroski, PIT	B. Richardson, NY
1964	B. Mazeroski, PIT	B. Richardson, NY
1965	B. Mazeroski, PIT	B. Richardson, NY
1966	B. Mazeroski, PIT	B. Knoop, CAL
1967	B. Mazeroski, PIT	B. Knoop, CAL
1968	G. Beckert, CHI	B. Knoop, CAL
1969	F. Millan, ATL	D. Johnson, BAL
1970	T. Helms, CIN	D. Johnson, BAL
1971	T. Helms, CIN	D. Johnson, BAL
1972	F. Millan, ATL	D. Griffin, BOS
1973	J. Morgan, CIN	B. Grich, BAL
1974	J. Morgan, CIN	B. Grich, BAL
1975	J. Morgan, CIN	B. Grich, BAL
1976	J. Morgan, CIN	B. Grich, BAL
1977	J. Morgan, CIN	F. White, KC
1978	D. Lopes, LA	F. White, KC
1979	M. Trillo, PHI	F. White, KC
1980	D. Flynn, NY	F. White, KC
1981	M. Trillo, PHI	F. White, KC
1982	M. Trillo, PHI	F. White, KC
1983	R. Sandberg, CHI	L. Whitaker, DET
1984	R. Sandberg, CHI	L. Whitaker, DET
1985	R. Sandberg, CHI	L. Whitaker, DET
1986	R. Sandberg, CHI	F. White, KC
1987	R. Sandberg, CHI	F. White, KC
1988	R. Sandberg, CHI	H. Reynolds, SEA
1989	R. Sandberg, CHI	H. Reynolds, SEA
1990	R. Sandberg, CHI	H. Reynolds, SEA
1991	R. Sandberg, CHI	R. Alomar, TOR
1992	J. Lind, PIT	R. Alomar, TOR
1993	R. Thompson, SF	R. Alomar, TOR
1994	C. Biggio, HOU	R. Alomar, TOR
1995	C. Biggio, HOU	R. Alomar, TOR
1996	C. Biggio, HOU	R. Alomar, TOR
1997	C. Biggio, HOU	C. Knoblauch, MIN
1998	B. Boone, CIN	R. Alomar, BAL

Third Basemen

Year	National League	American League
1957	(No selection)	F. Malzone, BOS
1958	K. Boyer, SL	F. Malzone, BOS
1959	K. Boyer, SL	F. Malzone, BOS
1960	K. Boyer, SL	B. Robinson, BAL
1961	K. Boyer, SL	B. Robinson, BAL
1962	J. Davenport, SF	B. Robinson, BAL
1963	K. Boyer, SL	B. Robinson, BAL
1964	R. Santo, CHI	B. Robinson, BAL
1965	R. Santo, CHI	B. Robinson, BAL
1966	R. Santo, CHI	B. Robinson, BAL
1967	R. Santo, CHI	B. Robinson, BAL
1968	R. Santo, CHI	B. Robinson, BAL
1969	C. Boyer, ATL	B. Robinson, BAL
1970	D. Rader, HOU	B. Robinson, BAL
1971	D. Rader, HOU	B. Robinson, BAL
1972	D. Rader, HOU	B. Robinson, BAL
1973	D. Rader, HOU	B. Robinson, BAL
1974	D. Rader, HOU	B. Robinson, BAL
1975	K. Reitz, SL	B. Robinson, BAL
1976	M. Schmidt, PHI	A. Rodriguez, DET
1977	M. Schmidt, PHI	G. Nettles, NY
1978	M. Schmidt, PHI	G. Nettles, NY
1979	M. Schmidt, PHI	B. Bell, TEX
1980	M. Schmidt, PHI	B. Bell, TEX
1981	M. Schmidt, PHI	B. Bell, TEX
1982	M. Schmidt, PHI	B. Bell, TEX
1983	M. Schmidt, PHI	B. Bell, TEX
1984	M. Schmidt, PHI	B. Bell, TEX
1985	T. Wallach, MON	G. Brett, KC
1986	M. Schmidt, PHI	G. Gaetti, MIN
1987	T. Pendleton, SL	G. Gaetti, MIN
1988	T. Wallach, MON	G. Gaetti, MIN
1989	T. Pendleton, SL	G. Gaetti, MIN
1990	T. Wallach, MON	K. Gruber, TOR
1991	M. Williams, SF	R. Ventura, CHI
1992	T. Pendleton, ATL	R. Ventura, CHI
1993	M. Williams, SF	R. Ventura, CHI
1994	M. Williams, SF	W. Boggs, NY
1995	K. Caminiti, SD	W. Boggs, NY
1996	K. Caminiti, SD	R. Ventura, CHI
1997	K. Caminiti, SD	M. Williams, CLE
1998	S. Rolen, PHI	R. Ventura, CHI

Shortstops

Year	National League	American League
1957	R. McMillan, CIN	(No selection)
1958	R. McMillan, CIN	L. Aparicio, CHI
1959	R. McMillan, CIN	L. Aparicio, CHI
1960	E. Banks, CHI	L. Aparicio, CHI
1961	M. Wills, LA	L. Aparicio, CHI
1962	M. Wills, LA	L. Aparicio, CHI
1963	B. Wine, PHI	Z. Versalles, MIN
1964	R. Amaro, PHI	L. Aparicio, BAL
1965	L. Cardenas, CIN	Z. Versalles, MIN
1966	G. Alley, PIT	L. Aparicio, BAL
1967	G. Alley, PIT	J. Fregosi, CAL
1968	D. Maxvill, SL	L. Aparicio, CHI
1969	D. Kessinger, CHI	M. Belanger, BAL
1970	D. Kessinger, CHI	L. Aparicio, CHI
1971	B. Harrelson, NY	M. Belanger, BAL
1972	L. Bowa, PHI	E. Brinkman, DET
1973	R. Metzger, HOU	M. Belanger, BAL
1974	D. Concepcion, CIN	M. Belanger, BAL
1975	D. Concepcion, CIN	M. Belanger, BAL
1976	D. Concepcion, CIN	M. Belanger, BAL
1977	D. Concepcion, CIN	M. Belanger, BAL
1978	L. Bowa, PHI	M. Belanger, BAL
1979	D. Concepcion, CIN	R. Burleson, BOS
1980	O. Smith, SD	A. Trammell, DET
1981	O. Smith, SD	A. Trammell, DET
1982	O. Smith, SL	R. Yount, MIL
1983	O. Smith, SL	A. Trammell, DET
1984	O. Smith, SL	A. Trammell, DET
1985	O. Smith, SL	A. Griffin, OAK
1986	O. Smith, SL	T. Fernandez, TOR
1987	O. Smith, SL	T. Fernandez, TOR
1988	O. Smith, SL	T. Fernandez, TOR
1989	O. Smith, SL	T. Fernandez, TOR
1990	O. Smith, SL	O. Guillen, CHI
1991	O. Smith, SL	C. Ripken, BAL
1992	O. Smith, SL	C. Ripken, BAL
1993	J. Bell, PIT	O. Vizquel, SEA
1994	B. Larkin, CIN	O. Vizquel, SEA
1995	B. Larkin, CIN	O. Vizquel, CLE
1996	B. Larkin, CIN	O. Vizquel, CLE
1997	R. Ordoñez, NY	O. Vizquel, CLE
1998	R. Ordoñez, NY	O. Vizquel, CLE

National League Outfielders

YEAR	PLAYERS		
1957	W. Mays, NY (CF)	(No other selections)	
1958	F. Robinson, CIN (LF)	W. Mays, SF (CF)	H. Aaron, MIL (RF)
1959	J. Brandt, SF (LF)	W. Mays, SF (CF)	H. Aaron, MIL (RF)
1960	W. Moon, LA (LF)	W. Mays, SF (CF)	H. Aaron, MIL (RF)
1961	W. Mays, SF	R. Clemente, PIT	V. Pinson, CIN
1962	W. Mays, SF	R. Clemente, PIT	B. Virdon, PIT
1963	W. Mays, SF	R. Clemente, PIT	C. Flood, SL
1964	W. Mays, SF	R. Clemente, PIT	C. Flood, SL
1965	W. Mays, SF	R. Clemente, PIT	C. Flood, SL
1966	W. Mays, SF	C. Flood, SL	R. Clemente, PIT
1967	R. Clemente, PIT	C. Flood, SL	W. Mays, SF
1968	W. Mays, SF	R. Clemente, PIT	C. Flood, SL
1969	R. Clemente, PIT	C. Flood, SL	P. Rose, CIN
1970	R. Clemente, PIT	T. Agee, NY	P. Rose, CIN
1971	R. Clemente, PIT	B. Bonds, SF	W. Davis, LA
1972	R. Clemente, PIT	C. Cedeno, HOU	W. Davis, LA
1973	B. Bonds, SF	C. Cedeno, HOU	W. Davis, LA
1974	C. Cedeno, HOU	C. Geronimo, CIN	B. Bonds, SF
1975	C. Cedeno, HOU	C. Geronimo, CIN	G. Maddox, PHI
1976	C. Cedeno, HOU	C. Geronimo, CIN	G. Maddox, PHI
1977	C. Geronimo, CIN	G. Maddox, PHI	D. Parker, PIT
1978	G. Maddox, PHI	D. Parker, PIT	E. Valentine, MON
1979	G. Maddox, PHI	D. Parker, PIT	D. Winfield, SD
1980	A. Dawson, MON	G. Maddox, PHI	D. Winfield, SD
1981	A. Dawson, MON	G. Maddox, PHI	D. Baker, LA
1982	A. Dawson, MON	D. Murphy, ATL	G. Maddox, PHI
1983	A. Dawson, MON	D. Murphy, ATL	W. McGee, SL
1984	D. Murphy, ATL	B. Dernier, CHI	A. Dawson, MON
1985	W. McGee, SL	D. Murphy, ATL	A. Dawson, MON
1986	T. Gwynn, SD	D. Murphy, ATL	W. McGee, SL
1987	E. Davis, CIN	T. Gwynn, SD	A. Dawson, CHI
1988	A. Van Slyke, PIT	E. Davis, CIN	A. Dawson, CHI
1989	A. Van Slyke, PIT	E. Davis, CIN	T. Gwynn, SD
1990	A. Van Slyke, PIT	T. Gwynn, SD	B. Bonds, PIT
1991	A. Van Slyke, PIT	T. Gwynn, SD	B. Bonds, PIT
1992	A. Van Slyke, PIT	L. Walker, MON	B. Bonds, PIT
1993	B. Bonds, SF	L. Walker, MON	M. Grissom, MON
1994	B. Bonds, SF	D. Lewis, SF	M. Grissom, MON
1995	R. Mondesi, LA	M. Grissom, ATL	S. Finley, SD
1996	B. Bonds, SF	M. Grissom, ATL	S. Finley, SD
1997	B. Bonds, SF	R. Mondesi, LA	L.Walker, COL
1998	B. Bonds, SF	A. Jones, ATL	L.Walker, COL

American League Outfielders

YEAR	PLAYERS		
1957	M. Minoso, CHI (LF)	A. Kaline, DET (RF)	(No other selection)
1958	N. Siebern, NY (LF)	J. Piersall, BOS (CF)	A. Kaline, DET (RF)
1959	M. Minoso, CLE (LF)	A. Kaline, DET (CF)	J. Jensen, BOS (RF)
1960	M. Minoso, CHI (LF)	J. Landis, CHI (CF)	R. Maris, NY (RF)
1961	A. Kaline, DET	J. Piersall, CLE	J. Landis, CHI
1962	J. Landis, CHI	M. Mantle, NY	A. Kaline, DET
1963	A. Kaline, DET	C. Yastrzemski, BOS	J. Landis, CHI
1964	A. Kaline, DET	J. Landis, CHI	V. Davalillo, CLE
1965	A. Kaline, DET	T. Tresh, NY	C. Yastrzemski, BOS
1966	A. Kaline, DET	T. Agee, CHI	T. Oliva, MIN
1967	C. Yastrzemski, BOS	P. Blair, BAL	A. Kaline, DET
1968	M. Stanley, DET	C. Yastrzemski, BOS	R. Smith, BOS
1969	P. Blair, BAL	M. Stanley, DET	C. Yastrzemski, BOS
1970	M. Stanley, DET	P. Blair, BAL	K. Berry, CHI
1971	P. Blair, BAL	A. Otis, KC	C. Yastrzemski, BOS
1972	P. Blair, BAL	B. Murcer, NY	K. Berry, CAL
1973	P. Blair, BAL	A. Otis, KC	M. Stanley, DET
1974	P. Blair, BAL	A. Otis, KC	J. Rudi, OAK
1975	P. Blair, BAL	J. Rudi, OAK	F. Lynn, BOS
1976	J. Rudi, OAK	Dw. Evans, BOS	R. Manning, CLE
1977	J. Beniquez, TEX	C. Yastrzemski, BOS	A. Cowens, KC
1978	F. Lynn, BOS	Dw. Evans, BOS	R. Miller, CAL
1979	Dw. Evans, BOS	S. Lezcano, MIL	F. Lynn, BOS
1980	F. Lynn, BOS	D. Murphy, OAK	W. Wilson, KC
1981	D. Murphy, OAK	Dw. Evans, BOS	R. Henderson, OAK
1982	Dw. Evans, BOS	D. Winfield, NY	D. Murphy, OAK
1983	Dw. Evans, BOS	D. Winfield, NY	D. Murphy, OAK
1984	Dw. Evans, BOS	D. Winfield, NY	D. Murphy, OAK
1985	G. Pettis, CAL	D. Winfield, NY	Dw. Evans, BOS & D. Murphy, OAK
1986	G. Pettis, CAL	J. Barfield, TOR	K. Puckett, MIN
1987	J. Barfield, TOR	K. Puckett, MIN	D. Winfield, NY
1988	K. Puckett, MIN	D. White, CAL	G. Pettis, DET
1989	D. White, CAL	G. Pettis, DET	K. Puckett, MIN
1990	G. Pettis, TEX	K. Griffey, Jr., SEA	E. Burks, BOS
1991	K. Puckett, MIN	K. Griffey, Jr., SEA	D. White, TOR
1992	K. Puckett, MIN	K. Griffey, Jr., SEA	D. White, TOR
1993	K. Griffey, Jr., SEA	D. White, TOR	K. Lofton, CLE
1994	K. Griffey, Jr., SEA	D. White, TOR	K. Lofton, CLE
1995	K. Griffey, Jr., SEA	K. Lofton, CLE	D. White, TOR
1996	K. Griffey, Jr., SEA	K. Lofton, CLE	J. Buhner, SEA
1997	J. Edmonds, ANA	K. Griffey, Jr., SEA	B. Williams, NY
1998	J. Edmonds, ANA	K. Griffey, Jr., SEA	B. Williams, NY

Special MVP Awards
The All-Star Game

The All-Star Game MVP Award began in 1962, the last year in which two All-Star Games were played. It was called the Arch Ward Memorial Award, in honor of the late Chicago newspaper writer credited with conceiving the Mid-Summer Classic. Under Bowie Kuhn's regime (1970-84) the award was called the Commissioner's Trophy.

A committee of writers and executives in attendance votes on the recipient of the game's award. Only twice—Brooks Robinson in 1966 and Carl Yastrzemski in 1970—has a member of the losing team been honored. Two-time winners are Willie Mays, Steve Garvey, and Gary Carter.

Following are the winners of the All-Star Game MVP Awards. Complete voting breakdowns for the award are not available.

1962	Maury Wills, LA (NL) [Game 1]	1971	Frank Robinson, BAL (AL)
	Leon Wagner, LA (AL) [Game 2]	1972	Joe Morgan, CIN (NL)
1963	Willie Mays, SF (NL)	1973	Bobby Bonds, SF (NL)
1964	Johnny Callison, PHI (NL)	1974	Steve Garvey, LA (NL)
1965	Juan Marichal, SF (NL)	1975	Bill Madlock, CHI (NL)
1966	Brooks Robinson, BAL (AL)		Jon Matlack, NY (NL)
1967	Tony Perez, CIN (NL)	1976	George Foster, CIN (NL)
1968	Willie Mays, SF (NL)	1977	Don Sutton, LA (NL)
1969	Willie McCovey, SF (NL)	1978	Steve Garvey, LA (NL)
1970	Carl Yastrzemski, BOS (AL)	1979	Dave Parker, PIT (NL)

1980	Ken Griffey, CIN (NL)	1990	Julio Franco, TEX (AL)
1981	Gary Carter, MON (NL)	1991	Cal Ripken, BAL (AL)
1982	Dave Concepcion, CIN (NL)	1992	Ken Griffey, Jr., SEA (AL)
1983	Fred Lynn, CAL (AL)	1993	Kirby Puckett, MIN (AL)
1984	Gary Carter, MON (NL)	1994	Fred McGriff, ATL (NL)
1985	LaMarr Hoyt, SD (NL)	1995	Jeff Conine, FLA (NL)
1986	Roger Clemens, BOS (AL)	1996	Mike Piazza, LA (NL)
1987	Tim Raines, MON (NL)	1997	Sandy Alomar, Jr., CLE (AL)
1988	Terry Steinbach, OAK (AL)	1998	Roberto Alomar, BAL (AL)
1989	Bo Jackson, KC (AL)		

League Championship Series

MVP Awards for the League Championship Series were instituted by the National League in 1977, and in the American League three years later. A committee of writers and executives in attendance does the voting, which is announced at the conclusion of each series. Steve Garvey and Dave Stewart are the only two-time winners thus far. Winners from losing teams are Fred Lynn (1982), Mike Scott (1986), and Jeffrey Leonard (1987).

Following are the winners of LCS MVP Awards. Complete voting breakdowns are not available.

Year	National League	American League
1977	Dusty Baker, LA	
1978	Steve Garvey, LA	
1979	Willie Stargell, PIT	
1980	Manny Trillo, PHI	Frank White, KC
1981	Burt Hooton, LA	Graig Nettles, NY
1982	Darrell Porter, SL	Fred Lynn, CAL

Year	National League	American League
1983	Gary Matthews, PHI	Mike Boddicker, BAL
1984	Steve Garvey, SD	Kirk Gibson, DET
1985	Ozzie Smith, SL	George Brett, KC
1986	Mike Scott, HOU	Marty Barrett, BOS
1987	Jeffrey Leonard, SF	Gary Gaetti, MIN
1988	Orel Hershiser, LA	Dennis Eckersley, OAK

Year	National League	American League
1989	Will Clark, SF	Rickey Henderson, OAK
1990	Rob Dibble, CIN	Dave Stewart, OAK
	Randy Myers, CIN	
1991	Steve Avery, ATL	Kirby Puckett, MIN
1992	John Smoltz, ATL	Roberto Alomar, TOR
1993	Curt Schilling, PHI	Dave Stewart, TOR

Year	National League	American League
1994	(No Series)	(No Series)
1995	Mike Devereaux, ATL	Orel Hershiser, CLE
1996	Javier Lopez, ATL	Bernie Williams, NY
1997	Livan Hernandez, FLA	Marquis Grissom, CLE
1998	Sterling Hitchcock, SD	David Wells, NY

World Series

There are two major World Series MVP Awards. The New York chapter of the Baseball Writers' Association of America established one in memory of Babe Ruth in 1949, the year after the Bambino's death. Six years later, *Sport* magazine introduced its version, presented in cooperation with the Chevrolet Motor Company (which typically presented a Corvette to the winner).

The winner of the *Sport* award was originally chosen by the magazine's editors, but the voting process eventually went to a committee of sports reporters and officials. The award is now sanctioned by Major League Baseball, and has eclipsed the Babe Ruth Award in prestige and public

recognition. The *Sport* award is voted on during the final game of the Series and is presented immediately following its conclusion, whereas the Ruth Award is voted on during a local chapter meeting some time after the Series has concluded.

Following are the winners of the two World Series MVP Awards. Two-time winners of the *Sport* award are Sandy Koufax, Bob Gibson, and Reggie Jackson; double-winners of the Ruth award are Koufax and Jack Morris. Winners from losing teams are Bobby Richardson (*Sport*, 1960), and Luis Tiant (Ruth, 1975). Complete voting breakdowns on either award are not available.

Year	Babe Ruth Award	Sport Magazine Award
1949	Joe Page, NY (AL)	
1950	Jerry Coleman, NY (AL)	
1951	Phil Rizzuto, NY (AL)	
1952	Johnny Mize, NY (AL)	
1953	Billy Martin, NY (AL)	
1954	Dusty Rhodes, NY (NL)	
1955	Johnny Podres, BRO (NL)	Johnny Podres, BRO (NL)
1956	Don Larsen, NY (AL)	Don Larsen, NY (AL)
1957	Lew Burdette, MIL (NL)	Lew Burdette, MIL (NL)
1958	Elston Howard, NY (AL)	Bob Turley, NY (AL)
1959	Larry Sherry, LA (NL)	Larry Sherry, LA (NL)
1960	Bill Mazeroski, PIT (NL)	Bobby Richardson, NY (AL)
1961	Whitey Ford, NY (AL)	Whitey Ford, NY (AL)
1962	Ralph Terry, NY (AL)	Ralph Terry, NY (AL)
1963	Sandy Koufax, LA (NL)	Sandy Koufax, LA (NL)
1964	Bob Gibson, SL (NL)	Bob Gibson, SL (NL)
1965	Sandy Koufax, LA (NL)	Sandy Koufax, LA (NL)
1966	Frank Robinson, BAL (AL)	Frank Robinson, BAL (AL)
1967	Lou Brock, SL (NL)	Bob Gibson, SL (NL)
1968	Mickey Lolich, DET (AL)	Mickey Lolich, DET (AL)
1969	Al Weis, NY (NL)	Donn Clendenon, NY (NL)
1970	Brooks Robinson, BAL (AL)	Brooks Robinson, BAL (AL)
1971	Roberto Clemente, PIT (NL)	Roberto Clemente, PIT (NL)
1972	Gene Tenace, OAK (AL)	Gene Tenace, OAK (AL)
1973	Bert Campaneris, OAK (AL)	Reggie Jackson, OAK (AL)
1974	Dick Green, OAK (AL)	Rollie Fingers, OAK (AL)

Year	Babe Ruth Award	Sport Magazine Award
1975	Luis Tiant, BOS (AL)	Pete Rose, CIN (NL)
1976	Johnny Bench, CIN (NL)	Johnny Bench, CIN (NL)
1977	Reggie Jackson, NY (AL)	Reggie Jackson, NY (AL)
1978	Bucky Dent, NY (AL)	Bucky Dent, NY (AL)
1979	Willie Stargell, PIT (NL)	Willie Stargell, PIT (NL)
1980	Tug McGraw, PHI (NL)	Mike Schmidt, PHI (NL)
1981	Ron Cey, LA (NL)	Ron Cey, LA (NL)
		Pedro Guerrero, LA (NL)
		Steve Yeager, LA (NL)
1982	Bruce Sutter, SL (NL)	Darrell Porter, SL (NL)
1983	Rick Dempsey, BAL (AL)	Rick Dempsey, BAL (AL)
1984	Jack Morris, DET (AL)	Alan Trammell, DET (AL)
1985	Bret Saberhagen, KC (AL)	Bret Saberhagen, KC (AL)
1986	Ray Knight, NY (NL)	Ray Knight, NY (NL)
1987	Frank Viola, MIN (AL)	Frank Viola, MIN (AL)
1988	Orel Hershiser, LA (NL)	Orel Hershiser, LA (NL)
1989	Dave Stewart, OAK (AL)	Dave Stewart, OAK (AL)
1990	Billy Hatcher, CIN (NL)	Jose Rijo, CIN (NL)
1991	Jack Morris, MIN (AL)	Jack Morris, MIN (AL)
1992	Dave Winfield, TOR (AL)	Pat Borders, TOR (AL)
1993	Paul Molitor, TOR (AL)	Paul Molitor, TOR (AL)
1994	(No Series)	(No Series)
1995	Tom Glavine, ATL (NL)	Tom Glavine, ATL (NL)
1996	Cecil Fielder, NY (AL)	John Wetteland, NY (AL)
1997	Moises Alou, FLA (AL)	Livan Hernandez, FLA (AL)
1998	Scott Brosius, NY (AL)	Scott Brosius, NY (AL)

The Player and Pitcher of the Month Awards

On June 4, 1958, NL president Warren Giles announced the very first winners of the Player of the Month Award: future Hall of Famers Stan Musial and Willie Mays, in a tie. Forty baseball writers and broadcasters—five from each NL city—had been polled to select the winners. Among the original voters were Bob Broeg, Harry Caray, Joe Garagiola, and Vin Scully.

Most winners have received a "handsome engraved desk set,"with timepieces and framed portrait photos also serving as trophies. In the early years of the award, none was given for April. The first month was considered too short a trial, featuring only about a dozen games per team in the days of a 154-game schedule. A September nomination was often bypassed, too, perhaps because the league and voters were too consumed by the pennant races and season-long awards. Since 1975, every month has been represented, except during the strike-shortened seasons of 1981, '94 and '95.

There was talk of establishing dual awards—one for everyday players, one for pitchers—as early as July 1958. Pitchers had been practically ignored in the first two POM

polls (amassing just 13 of 79 votes), and there was a feeling that a hurler could not win the nomination. Joey Jay quieted the discussion by capturing the prize for that month, and Lew Burdette ended it by earning the August citation. The two Braves' pitchers unwittingly set back dual awards nearly two decades; it would be 1975 before the NL began separate awards for Players and Pitchers of the Month.

The American League waited until 1974 to establish its version of the Player of the Month Award, and until 1979 to add the Pitcher of the Month. Through 1997, the two leagues had presented a total of 633 Player and Pitcher of the Month Awards, with 367 different winners (including 18 who won in both leagues). The most POM Awards received by any player is 12, by Roger Clemens. Frank Thomas leads non-pitchers with eight citations, while Barry Bonds is the NL leader with seven.

The most POM Awards in one season is three, by Mark McGwire in 1998; dozens of others have won two. Tom Seaver won with two different teams in 1977: the Mets in April, the Reds (to whom he was traded June 15) in

August. Not to be outdone, Fred McGriff won in July 1993 while splitting the month between two teams: he was swapped from the Padres to the Braves on the 18th of that month.

Winners have ranged in age from 19-year-old Robin Yount (April 1975), to 40-year-old Warren Spahn (August 1961). Eighteen rookies have won the award, including Marty Bystrom, the only man to win it in his very first month in the majors (September 1980). At the other end of the spectrum, Al Kaline won the award in his *last* month (September 1974) in the bigs.

A POM winner is typically either a great player having a good month, or a good player having a great month. Occasionally, it is a mediocre player—Jim Hughes and Otto Velez, to name two—who has stumbled into and out of "the zone" just long enough to be honored. On the other hand, winning a POM sometimes signals a player's transformation from mediocrity to superstardom. Two cases in point are Sandy Koufax (June 1962) and Ryne Sandberg (June 1984). Several all-time greats *never* won a POM Award during their careers. Examples include Ernie Banks, Johnny Bench, Bert Blyleven, Dennis Eckersley, Rollie Fingers, Carlton Fisk, Phil Niekro, and Ozzie Smith.

Following is a chart listing all of the Players and Pitchers of the Month since 1958:

NATIONAL LEAGUE PLAYER & PITCHER of the MONTH AWARDS

YEAR	APRIL	MAY	JUNE	JULY	AUGUST	SEPTEMBER
1958		S. Musial/W. Mays	Frank Thomas	Joey Jay	Lew Burdette	Willie Mays
		Hank Aaron			Willie McCovey	
1959		Harvey Haddix	Elroy Face	Don Drysdale	Vern Law	Eddie Mathews
1960		Roberto Clemente	Lindy McDaniel	Don Drysdale	Warren Spahn	Ken Boyer
1961		Joey Jay	George Altman	Frank Robinson	Warren Spahn	Jim O'Toole
1962		Bob Purkey	Sandy Koufax	Frank Howard	Jack Sanford	
1963		Dick Ellsworth	Ron Santo	Willie McCovey	Willie Mays	
1964		Billy Williams	Jim Bunning	Ron Santo	Frank Robinson	Bob Gibson
			Willie Stargell			
1965		Joe Torre	Vern Law	Pete Rose	Willie Mays	
1966		Juan Marichal	Gaylord Perry	Mike Shannon	Pete Rose	
1967		Roberto Clemente	Hank Aaron	Jim Ray Hart	Orlando Cepeda	
1968		Don Drysdale	Bob Gibson	Bob Gibson	Pete Rose	Steve Blass
1969	Willie McCovey	Ken Holtzman	Ron Santo	Roberto Clemente	Willie Davis	
1970		Rico Carty	Tommie Agee	Bill Singer	Bob Gibson	
1971	Willie Stargell	Lou Brock	Willie Stargell	Fergie Jenkins	Joe Torre	
1972	Don Sutton	Bob Watson	Cesar Cedeño	Billy Williams	Ken Henderson	
1973	Jerry Koosman	Willie Crawford	Greg Luzinski	Pete Rose	Dave Johnson	
1974	Tommy John	Ralph Garr	Buzz Capra	Don Gullett	Lou Brock	
	Joe Morgan	Bob Watson	Joe Morgan	Dave Kingman	Tony Perez	Andre Thornton
1975	Don Sutton	Don Sutton	Tom Seaver	Al Hrabosky	Burt Hooton	Burt Hooton
	Mike Schmidt	George Foster	Al Oliver	George Foster	Joe Morgan	Steve Garvey
1976	Randy Jones	Randy Jones	Andy Messersmith	Jerry Koosman	Ray Burris	Don Sutton
	Ron Cey	Ken Reitz	George Foster	Greg Luzinski	George Foster	Cesar Cedeño
1977	Tom Seaver	Bruce Sutter	Rick Reuschel	Rick Reuschel	Tom Seaver	Larry Christenson
	Rick Monday	Jack Clark	Dave Winfield	Pete Rose	Dave Parker	Dave Parker
1978	Ross Grimsley	Bob Knepper	Vida Blue	J. R. Richard	Kent Tekulve	Gaylord Perry
	George Foster	Lou Brock	George Foster	Mike Schmidt	Keith Hernandez	
1979	Ken Forsch	Joe Niekro	Joaquin Andujar	Dick Tidrow	Rick Reuschel	Pete Rose
	Dave Kingman	Mike Schmidt	Rusty Baker	Bob Horner	Dale Murphy	Gary Carter
1980	J. R. Richard	Steve Carlton	Jerry Reuss	Pat Zachry	Rick Reuschel	Marty Bystrom
	Dave Concepcion	Art Howe			Mike Schmidt	Gary Matthews
1981	F. Valenzuela	Charlie Lea			R.Camp/E.Whitson	Tom Seaver
	Dale Murphy	Tim Wallach	Al Oliver	Mike Schmidt	Bill Buckner	C. Washington
1982	Steve Rogers	Dick Ruthven	Steve Howe	John Candelaria	Nolan Ryan	Joaquin Andujar
	Terry Kennedy	Darrell Evans	Andre Dawson	Dusty Baker	Mel Hall	Dale Murphy
1983	Pascual Perez	Bill Laskey	Burt Hooton	Joe Price	Jesse Orosco	John Denny
	Tony Gwynn	Leon Durham	Ryne Sandberg	Jose Cruz	Keith Moreland	Dale Murphy
1984	Rick Honeycutt	Nolan Ryan	Ron Darling	Orel Hershiser	Rick Sutcliffe	Dwight Gooden
	Dale Murphy	Dave Parker	Pedro Guerrero	Keith Hernandez	Willie McGee	Gary Carter
1985	F. Valenzuela	Andy Hawkins	John Tudor	F. Valenzuela	Shane Rawley	Dwight Gooden
	Johnny Ray	Hubie Brooks	Kevin Bass	Eric Davis	Dale Murphy	Steve Sax
1986	Dwight Gooden	Jeff Reardon	Rick Rhoden	Todd Worrell	Bill Gullickson	Mike Krukow
	Eric Davis	Eric Davis	Tony Gwynn	Bo Diaz	Andre Dawson	Darryl Strawberry
1987	Sid Fernandez	Steve Bedrosian	Orel Hershiser	Floyd Youmans	Doug Drabek	Pascual Perez
	Bobby Bonilla	Bobby Bonilla	Will Clark	Tony Gwynn	Eric Davis	Kevin McReynolds
1988	Orel Hershiser	David Cone	Greg Maddux	John Franco	Danny Jackson	Orel Hershiser
	Von Hayes	Will Clark	Howard Johnson	Mark Grace	Pedro Guerrero	Bobby Bonilla
1989	Mark Davis	Rick Reuschel	Mike Scott	Mark Langston	Tom Browning	Tim Belcher
	Bobby Bonilla	Andre Dawson	Ryne Sandberg	Barry Bonds	David Justice	Kal Daniels
1990	John Tudor	Jack Armstrong	Ramon Martinez	D.Darwin/D.Drabek	Doug Drabek	Dwight Gooden
	Felix Jose	David Justice	Barry Larkin	Barry Bonds	Will Clark	Howard Johnson
1991	Lee Smith	Tom Glavine	Rob Dibble	Dennis Martinez	Mitch Williams	Chris Nabholz
	Barry Bonds	Felix Jose	Cory Snyder	Brett Butler	Gary Sheffield	Barry Bonds
1992	Billy Swift	Mike Morgan	Randy Tomlin	Tom Glavine	Dennis Martinez	Jose Rijo
	Barry Bonds	Jeff Bagwell	Andres Galarraga	Fred McGriff	Tony Gwynn	Andres Galarraga
1993	Ken Hill	Tommy Greene	D.Kile/C.Hammond	Billy Swift	Greg Maddux	John Wetteland
	Ellis Burks	L.Dykstra/M.Piazza	Jeff Bagwell	Jeff Bagwell		
1994	Bob Tewksbury	Doug Drabek	Bobby Muñoz	Bret Saberhagen		
		Matt Williams	Jeff Conine	Dante Bichette	Mike Piazza	Dante Bichette
1995		Heathcliff Slocumb	Hideo Nomo	Greg Maddux	Sid Fernandez	Greg Maddux
	Barry Bonds	Jeff Bagwell	Dante Bichette	Sammy Sosa	Ken Caminiti	Ken Caminiti
1996	John Smoltz	John Smoltz	Jeff Fassero	Jeff Fassero	Kevin Brown	Hideo Nomo
	Larry Walker	Tony Gwynn	Mike Piazza	Barry Bonds	Mike Piazza	Mark McGwire
1997	Tom Glavine	Bobby Jones	Kent Mercker	Darryl Kile	Pedro Martinez	Jeff Shaw
	Mark McGwire	Mark McGwire	Sammy Sosa	Vladimir Guerrero	Jeff Kent	Mark McGwire
1998	Tom Glavine	Orel Hershiser	Greg Maddux	Chan Ho Park	Randy Johnson	Randy Johnson

AMERICAN LEAGUE PLAYER & PITCHER of the MONTH AWARDS

YEAR	APRIL	MAY	JUNE	JULY	AUGUST	SEPTEMBER
1974	Graig Nettles	Rod Carew	Gaylord Perry	Doc Medich	Nolan Ryan	Al Kaline
1975	Robin Yount	Jim Hughes	Fred Lynn	John Mayberry	Jim Palmer	Gene Tenace
1976	Willie Horton	Ron LeFlore	Mark Fidrych	Reggie Jackson	Luis Tiant	N.Ryan/F.Tanana
1977	Otto Velez	Frank Tanana	Rod Carew	Jim Rice	Graig Nettles	Rod Carew
1978	Frank Tanana	Jim Rice	Ron Guidry	Doug DeCinces	Jim Rice	Ron Guidry
	Cecil Cooper	Don Baylor	Dan Meyer	Don Baylor	Fred Lynn	Alfredo Griffin
1979	Tommy John	Jim Kern	Mark Clear	Sid Monge	Rick Langford	Goose Gossage
	Lamar Johnson	Ben Oglivie	Rod Carew	G.Brett/R.Jackson	Cecil Cooper	E.Murray/J.Rice
1980	Dave Stieb	Chuck Rainey	Steve Stone	Larry Gura	Bob Stanley	Tim Stoddard
	Ken Singleton	Dwight Evans			Cecil Cooper	E.Murray/W.Wilson
1981	Matt Keough	Mark Clear			Ron Guidry	L.Gura/D.Martinez
	Eddie Murray	Hal McRae	George Brett	Robin Yount	Doug DeCinces	Dave Winfield
1982	Geoff Zahn	LaMarr Hoyt	Jim Beattie	Tippy Martinez	Jim Palmer	Rick Sutcliffe
	George Brett	Rod Carew	Lou Whitaker	Cecil Cooper	Lloyd Moseby	Cal Ripken
1983	Rick Honeycutt	Dave Stieb	Charlie Hough	Scott McGregor	Jack Morris	Rich Dotson
	Alan Trammell	Eddie Murray	Tony Armas	Kent Hrbek	Gary Ward	Greg Walker
1984	Jack Morris	Mike Boddicker	Charlie Hough	Willie Hernandez	Roger Clemens	Doyle Alexander
	Mike Davis	George Brett	Rickey Henderson	George Brett		Don Mattingly
1985	Charlie Leibrandt	Dave Stieb	Jay Howell	Bret Saberhagen	Dave Righetti	Charlie Leibrandt
	Kirby Puckett	Wade Boggs	Kent Hrbek	Scott Fletcher	Doug DeCinces	Don Mattingly
1986	Roger Clemens	Don Aase	Roger Clemens	Jack Morris	Mike Witt	Bruce Hurst
	Brian Downing	Larry Parrish	Wade Boggs	Don Mattingly	Dwight Evans	Alan Trammell
1987	Bret Saberhagen	Jim Clancy	Steve Ontiveros	Frank Viola	Mark Langston	Doyle Alexander
	Dave Winfield	Carney Lansford	Mike Greenwell	Chili Davis	Kent Hrbek	Jose Canseco
1988	Dave Stewart	Frank Viola	Mark Gubicza	Roger Clemens	Bruce Hurst	Mark Langston
	Fred McGriff	Ron Kittle	Ruben Sierra	Robin Yount	G.Bell/N.Esasky	Paul Molitor
1989	Jeff Ballard	Chuck Finley	Mark Gubicza	Mike Moore	Bret Saberhagen	Bret Saberhagen
	Ken Griffey, Jr.	Jose Canseco	Brook Jacoby	George Brett	Cecil Fielder	Kelly Gruber
1990	Dave Stewart	Bobby Thigpen	Randy Johnson	C.Finley/B.Witt	Roger Clemens	Dave Stewart
	Dave Henderson	Ruben Sierra	Joe Carter	Robin Ventura	Frank Thomas	Cal Ripken
1991	Roger Clemens	Scott Erickson	Jack Morris	Bill Krueger	Kevin Tapani	Roger Clemens
	Roberto Alomar	Kirby Puckett	Kirby Puckett	Edgar Martinez	Edgar Martinez	Frank Thomas
1992	Bill Krueger	Roger Clemens	John Smiley	Kevin Appier	Roger Clemens	Cal Eldred
	John Olerud	Paul Molitor	John Olerud	Rafael Palmeiro	Frank Thomas	Chris Hoiles
1993	Jimmy Key	Danny Darwin	Rick Aguilera	F. Valenzuela	Bill Gullickson	Wilson Alvarez
	Joe Carter	Frank Thomas	Albert Belle	Frank Thomas		
1994	Ben McDonald	David Cone	Cal Eldred	Alex Fernandez		
		Manny Ramirez	Edgar Martinez	Garret Anderson	Albert Belle	Albert Belle
1995		Kenny Rogers	Kevin Appier	Tim Wakefield	Erik Hanson	Norm Charlton
	Frank Thomas	Mo Vaughn	Mark McGwire	Juan Gonzalez	Alex Rodriguez	Frank Thomas
1996	Jose Guzman	Charles Nagy	Orel Hershiser	Pat Hentgen	Pat Hentgen	Charles Nagy
	Ken Griffey, Jr.	Frank Thomas	Jeff King	Tim Salmon	Bernie Williams	Juan Gonzalez
1997	Andy Pettitte	Roger Clemens	Randy Johnson	C.Finley/B. Radke	Roger Clemens	Jeff Fassero
	Ivan Rodriguez	Bernie Williams	Rafael Palmeiro	Albert Belle	Derek Jeter	Albert Belle
1998	Chuck Finley	Hideki Irabu	Bartolo Colon	David Cone	Roger Clemens	Rick Helling

Off the Field Awards
The Associated Press Athlete of the Year Award

Associated Press sports editors have been naming male and female athletes of the year since 1931. Following are the baseball honorees, including two-time winner Sandy Koufax:

1931 Pepper Martin	1954 Willie Mays	1965 Sandy Koufax	1978 Ron Guidry
1933 Carl Hubbell	1956 Mickey Mantle	1966 Frank Robinson	1979 Willie Stargell
1934 Dizzy Dean	1957 Ted Williams	1967 Carl Yastrzemski	1985 Dwight Gooden
1941 Joe DiMaggio	1961 Roger Maris	1968 Denny McLain	1988 Orel Hershiser
1948 Lou Boudreau	1962 Maury Wills	1969 Tom Seaver	1995 Cal Ripken, Jr.
1950 Jim Konstanty	1963 Sandy Koufax	1975 Fred Lynn	

The Roberto Clemente Award

Under newcomer Bowie Kuhn in 1971, the Commissioner's Office created a new annual award—simply called the Commissioner's Award—honoring the player who best exemplified baseball on and off the field. Consideration was given to a player's sportsmanship, community involvement, and contribution to his team and baseball.

On March 12, 1973, the award was renamed for Roberto Clemente, the Pittsburgh star who had died 10 weeks earlier during a mercy mission.

This award is not to be confused with a host of others bearing the Hall of Famer's name, all of which appeared soon after his death. The Pittsburgh chapter of the BBWAA instituted the Roberto Clemente Memorial Award, given to the outstanding Pirate each year. The city of Hialeah, Fla. created the Roberto Clemente Humanitarian Award, given to a private citizen in that community who best exemplified Clemente's humanitarian virtues. A third Clemente Award honored the top Latin-American player in the majors.

The Clemente Award given by the Commissioner's Office is selected by a panel of baseball executives and media personnel. It is currently sponsored by True Value, which presents some $175,000 to charities each year in conjunction with the award. Following is a list of the winners:

1971 Willie Mays	1978 Greg Luzinski	1985 Don Baylor	1992 Cal Ripken
1972 Brooks Robinson	1979 Andre Thornton	1986 Garry Maddox	1993 Barry Larkin
1973 Al Kaline	1980 Phil Niekro	1987 Rick Sutcliffe	1994 Dave Winfield
1974 Willie Stargell	1981 Steve Garvey	1988 Dale Murphy	1995 Ozzie Smith
1975 Lou Brock	1982 Ken Singleton	1989 Gary Carter	1996 Kirby Puckett
1976 Pete Rose	1983 Cecil Cooper	1990 Dave Stewart	1997 Eric Davis
1977 Rod Carew	1984 Ron Guidry	1991 Harold Reynolds	1998 Sammy Sosa

The Ford C. Frick Award

The Ford C. Frick Award was established in 1978, and goes to a broadcaster for "major contributions to Baseball." Frick, who died on April 8 of that year, had done some broadcasting early in his career, though he was better-known for his roles as NL president and baseball commissioner.

Winners of the Frick Award are selected by a panel of baseball executives and media personnel, and honored during the annual Hall of Fame induction ceremonies. Contrary to popular belief, however, the award-winners are *not* members of the Baseball Hall of Fame; there is no "Broadcasters' Wing" at the Hall. As with the Spink Award, a list of the Frick honorees is displayed in the Cooperstown museum's "Scribes and Mike-Men" exhibit.

Following are the winners of the Ford C. Frick Award:

1978 Mel Allen, Red Barber	1984 Curt Gowdy	1990 By Saam	1996 Herb Carneal
1979 Bob Elson	1985 Buck Canel	1991 Joe Garagiola	1997 Jimmy Dudley
1980 Russ Hodges	1986 Bob Prince	1992 Milo Hamilton	1998 Jaime Jarrin
1981 Ernie Harwell	1987 Jack Buck	1993 Chuck Thompson	
1982 Vin Scully	1988 Lindsey Nelson	1994 Bob Murphy	
1983 Jack Brickhouse	1989 Harry Caray	1995 Bob Wolff	

The Lou Gehrig Memorial Award

The Lou Gehrig Memorial Award was established by Gehrig's college fraternity in 1955. It is administered by the fraternity's national headquarters in Oxford, Ohio. Its plaque, which resides at the Baseball Hall of Fame in Cooperstown, N.Y., describes the award as follows:

"Presented annually to the major league baseball player who both on and off the field best exemplifies the character of Lou Gehrig, Columbia University '25, who played in 2,164 games as a member of the New York American League Baseball Club. Dedicated by his brothers of Phi Delta Theta." The award is announced each spring.

Following are the winners of the Lou Gehrig Award:

1955 Alvin Dark	1966 Brooks Robinson	1977 Lou Brock	1988 Buddy Bell
1956 Pee Wee Reese	1967 Ernie Banks	1978 Don Kessinger	1989 Ozzie Smith
1957 Stan Musial	1968 Al Kaline	1979 Phil Niekro	1990 Glenn Davis
1958 Gil McDougald	1969 Pete Rose	1980 Tony Perez	1991 Kent Hrbek
1959 Gil Hodges	1970 Hank Aaron	1981 Tommy John	1992 Cal Ripken, Jr.
1960 Dick Groat	1971 Harmon Killebrew	1982 Ron Cey	1993 Don Mattingly
1961 Warren Spahn	1972 Wes Parker	1983 Mike Schmidt	1994 Barry Larkin
1962 Robin Roberts	1973 Ron Santo	1984 Steve Garvey	1995 Curt Schilling
1963 Bobby Richardson	1974 Willie Stargell	1985 Dale Murphy	1996 Brett Butler
1964 Ken Boyer	1975 Johnny Bench	1986 George Brett	1997 Paul Molitor
1965 Vernon Law	1976 Don Sutton	1987 Rick Sutcliffe	

The S. Rae Hickok Professional Athlete of the Year Award

The S. Rae Hickok Professional Athlete of the Year Award—better-known as the Hickok belt—was presented by the Kickik Manufacturing Company of Arlington, Texas, beginning in 1950. The trophy was a large belt of gold and jewelry, reportedly worth $30,000 in 1976, the last year the award was given.

Voting was done each month by several hundred newspaper sports editors nationwide. The 12 monthly winners then competed for the annual prize. Of the 27 annual winners, 15—including two-time winner Sandy Koufax—were from major league baseball. A list of those players follows:

1950 Phil Rizzuto	1958 Bob Turley	1965 Sandy Koufax	1970 Brooks Robinson
1951 Allie Reynolds	1961 Roger Maris	1966 Frank Robinson	1972 Steve Carlton
1954 Willie Mays	1962 Maury Wills	1967 Carl Yastrzemski	1975 Pete Rose
1956 Mickey Mantle	1963 Sandy Koufax	1969 Tom Seaver	

The Fred Hutchinson Memorial Award

Reds' manager Fred Hutchinson died Nov. 12, 1964, at age 45. He had been a well-respected major league pitcher and manager for most of a quarter-century, before losing a courageous battle with cancer (diagnosed by his brother, Dr. William B. Hutchinson). Five of Fred's friends in the media—Ritter Collett, Jim Enright, Joe McGuff, Ernie Harwell, and Bob Prince—sought to keep his name alive by creating the Fred Hutchinson Memorial Award. They raised money from various celebrities, mostly baseball executives and media personnel, and incorporated the project.

The Hutch Award is presented annually to a major leaguer who "best exemplifies the character, dedication and competitive spirit" of the late manager. Consideration is given to players who overcome major physical adversity, and show dedication to their team, community, and family. Winners receive a bronzed engraving of Hutchinson encased in a glass frame. Concurrent with this presentation, a sister award is given—in the way of a scholarship—to a young medical student involved in cancer research. This selection was coordinated by Dr. Hutchinson from the Fred Hutchinson Cancer Center (established in 1975) in Seattle.

Ritter Collett ran the award's business operations from his home address in Dayton, Ohio, until 1994, by which time only three of its five founders were still alive. That year, the award's administration was turned over to the Seattle Mariners in conjunction with the *Seattle Post-Intelligencer* and the Hutchinson Cancer Center.

Voting for the prestigious Hutch Award is done by a panel of baseball writers and broadcasters. Following is a list of the winners:

1965 Mickey Mantle	1974 Danny Thompson	1983 Ray Knight	1992 Carney Lansford
1966 Sandy Koufax	1975 Gary Nolan	1984 Don Robinson	1993 John Olerud
1967 Carl Yastrzemski	1976 Tommy John	1985 Rick Reuschel	1994 Andre Dawson
1968 Pete Rose	1977 Willie McCovey	1986 Dennis Leonard	1995 Jim Abbott
1969 Al Kaline	1978 Willie Stargell	1987 Paul Molitor	1996 Omar Vizquel
1970 Tony Conigliaro	1979 Lou Brock	1988 Ron Oester	1997 Eric Davis
1971 Joe Torre	1980 George Brett	1989 Dave Dravecky	1998 David Cone
1972 Bobby Tolan	1981 Johnny Bench	1990 Sid Bream	
1973 John Hiller	1982 Andre Thornton	1991 Bill Wegman	

The Sid Mercer Memorial Award

Sid Mercer was a talented and beloved sportswriter in St. Louis and New York during the first half of the 20th century. He suggested and arranged for an "Outstanding Player of the Year" award to be presented at the New York BBWAA chapter's awards dinner each January, beginning in 1931. After Mercer's death in 1945, the award was renamed in his memory. The Sid Mercer Memorial Award honors "outstanding achievement and high contribution to (major league) baseball."

Don Mattingly won the Sid Mercer Award three times, while Joe DiMaggio, Ted Williams, Mickey Mantle, Sandy Koufax, George Brett, and Barry Bonds were honored twice each. Following are the annual winners of the award:

1930 Bill Terry	1948 Lou Boudreau	1966 Frank Robinson	1984 Don Mattingly
1931 Lou Gehrig	1949 Phil Rizzuto	1967 Carl Yastrzemski	1985 D. Gooden/D. Mattingly
1932 Herb Pennock	1950 Eddie Stanky	1968 Denny McLain	1986 Don Mattingly
1933 Carl Hubbell	1951 Allie Reynolds	1969 Tom Seaver	1987 Andre Dawson
1934 Dizzy Dean	1952 Pee Wee Reese	1970 Johnny Bench	1988 Jose Canseco
1935 Hank Greenberg	1953 Roy Campanella	1971 Joe Torre	1989 Nolan Ryan
1936 Tony Lazzeri	1954 Willie Mays	1972 Steve Carlton	1990 Cecil Fielder
1937 Joe DiMaggio	1955 Duke Snider	1973 Reggie Jackson	1991 Cal Ripken, Jr.
1938 Jimmie Foxx	1956 Mickey Mantle	1974 Lou Brock	1992 Barry Bonds
1939 Bucky Walters	1957 Ted Williams	1975 Joe Morgan	1993 Barry Bonds
1940 Bob Feller	1958 Bob Turley	1976 Mark Fidrych	1994 Jeff Bagwell
1941 Joe DiMaggio	1959 Nellie Fox	1977 R. Carew/G. Foster	1995 Randy Johnson
1942 Ted Williams	1960 Warren Spahn	1978 Ron Guidry	1996 Alex Rodriguez
1943 Bill Dickey	1961 M. Mantle/R. Maris	1979 George Brett	1997 Larry Walker
1944 Dixie Walker	1962 Maury Wills	1980 George Brett	1998 M. McGwire/S. Sosa
1945 Snuffy Stirnweiss	1963 Sandy Koufax	1981 Mike Schmidt	
1946 Stan Musial	1964 Brooks Robinson	1982 Robin Yount	
1947 Johnny Mize	1965 Sandy Koufax	1983 Dan Quisenberry	

The J.G. Taylor Spink Award

As early as 1944, the Baseball Hall of Fame's administrators suggested that some sort of "Roll of Honor," distinct from actual Hall of Fame induction, be established for distinguished baseball writers. Following the Dec. 7, 1962 death of *The Sporting News*'s long-time publisher, J. G. Taylor Spink, such an award was created. Spink was the first winner of the award bearing his name.

The Spink Award is given "for meritorious contributions to baseball writing." It is voted on by a committee of BBWAA members, and presented during the following year's Hall of Fame induction ceremony. Although the winners are often erroneously said to be "inducted into the Writers' Wing of the Hall of Fame," there is no such wing and these writers are not in fact members of the Hall. The museum's library does have an exhibit, called "Scribes and Mike-Men," which—among other things—lists winners of this award.

Following are winners of the Spink Award:

1962 J. G. Taylor Spink	Dan Daniel	Joe Reichler	Leonard Koppett
1963 Ring Lardner	Fred Lieb	1980 Milton Richman	1992 Bus Saidt
1964 Hugh Fullerton	1972 J. Roy Stockton	Bob Addie	1993 John Wendell Smith
1965 Charles Dryden	Gordon Cobbledick	1981 Allen Lewis	1994 (No honoree)
1966 Grantland Rice	1977 Edgar Munzel	1982 Si Burick	1995 Joseph Durso
1967 Damon Runyon	Tim Murnane	1983 Ken Smith	1996 Charlie Feeney
1968 H. G. Salsinger	1978 Dick Young	1984 Joe McGuff	1997 Sam Lacy
1969 Sid Mercer	Bob Broeg	1985 Earl Lawson	1998 Bob Stevens
1970 Heywood C. Broun	1979 Tommy Holmes	1986 Jack Lang	
1971 Frank Graham		1987 Jim Murray	

The Sports Illustrated Sportsman of the Year Award

The editors of *Sports Illustrated* have honored a "Sportsman of the Year" since 1954, the year the magazine started. Following are baseball's representatives:

1955 Johnny Podres	1967 Carl Yastrzemski	1979 Willie Stargell (co-winner)	1995 Cal Ripken, Jr.
1957 Stan Musial	1969 Tom Seaver	1987 Dale Murphy (co-winner)	1996 Joe Torre
1965 Sandy Koufax	1975 Pete Rose	1988 Orel Hershiser	1998 M. McGwire/S. Sosa

Hall of Fame Elections: History

In the 1930s plans were being made to celebrate baseball's 100th anniversary, based on the ill-advised findings of the Mills Commission three decades earlier: "The first scheme for playing baseball, according to the best evidence obtainable to date, was devised by Abner Double-day at Cooperstown, New York, in 1839." A small-scale baseball museum was established in Cooperstown, and a Centennial Committee composed of six baseball bigwigs ordered the first Hall of Fame election. On Jan. 29, 1936, the results of this election were announced, with five

immortals qualifying for enshrinement (although actual induction was delayed until formal opening of the Hall on June 12, 1939).

Actually, there were two elections in 1936: one a poll of 226 members of the Baseball Writers' Association of America (BBWAA), and the other held by a special veterans' committee of 78 designed to choose from among "old-timers." No specific guidelines were set as to who was eligible for consideration (several active players received strong support), nor to which committee would consider whom (resulting in Cy Young's split vote: 49 percent in the writers' election, 41 percent in the veterans'). A 75 percent majority was necessary for election by either committee, a voting feature which survives.

Elections were held by both the BBWAA and an old-timers' committee for each of the next three years, resulting in a total of 26 inductees in 1939. After that, BBWAA elections were scheduled at three-year intervals, with only one player elected in 1942 and none in 1945. A decision was made to hold annual elections beginning in 1946. This continued through 1956, when it was decided to hold elections only every other year. Annual elections were resumed a decade later and continue to this day.

A nominating system was installed after the 1945 election, providing for the top 20 vote-getters in a preliminary balloting to be listed alphabetically on a second and final ballot. The preliminary election's vote totals were not to be divulged until after the final balloting (so as not to influence voters), nor would they assure anyone of automatic election. However, this system proved an utter failure in 1946 and was amended in December of that year. Thereafter, anyone receiving 75 percent of the votes on the nominating ballot would be automatically elected, eliminating the runoff election.

No runoff was required until 1949, when Charlie Gehringer was elected on the second ballot. The nominating system was discontinued after that year but revived from 1960-68 (providing for reconsideration of the top 30 vote-getters), being put into practice in 1964-67.

Currently, an eligible candidate must have played at least 10 seasons in the majors and been active at some point during a period beginning 20 years and ending five years before a given election (the former rule has been ignored in some recent cases). The five-year wait rule was first implemented in 1954 (excepting candidates who had already received 100 or more votes in a previous election); a one-year wait had been in effect from 1946–53, and no wait was specified before then (due to World War II, it was sometimes unclear who was still "active"). At the other end of the span, the 20-year rule has been in effect since 1962; the cutoff was 30 years in 1956-62, and 25 years in 1946-56.

Following Roberto Clemente's tragic death, a rule was passed in 1973 providing for the immediate consideration of an eligible candidate who dies while still active, or before the five-year waiting period has elapsed. Clemente was inducted overwhelmingly (393 of 424 votes) in a special election held that March. A few months later, the new rule was amended to allow consideration at least six months after a player's death (or five years after his retirement, whichever is less).

The "Pete Rose Rule" was added to the regulations in February 1991: "Any player on Baseball's ineligible list shall not be an eligible candidate."

Ten-year active and honorary members of the BBWAA are eligible to vote in the annual election (the 10-year restriction was installed in 1947). About 450 writers submit ballots each year, voting for up to 10 eligible candidates apiece. At various times over the past three decades, it has been suggested that the enfranchisement be limited to a few dozen of the top baseball writers.

A candidate Screening Committee was first employed in 1968, limiting the ballot to forty candidates. Standards were relaxed somewhat after former pitcher Milt Pappas vociferously objected to his elimination by this committee (Pappas was allowed on the ballot in 1979, receiving five of 432 votes). Nomination by two of the six members of the Screening Committee now ensures a candidate at least one try on the BBWAA ballot; however, if he receives less than 5 percent of the vote, he is eliminated from future consideration. (Fortunately for many, this rule has not always been existent; more than seventy current Hall of Famers received less than 5 percent of the vote in their first tries!)

The Baseball Hall of Fame Committee on Baseball Veterans was established in July 1953. Previously, special old-timers' committees had elected new members in 1936–39, 1944–46, and 1949.

The new committee was composed of 11 members. This number was increased to twelve in 1960, eighteen in 1979, and twenty in 1987; then it was reduced to 18 in 1988 and 15 in 1996. Elections were held every other year at first, but have been held annually since 1961.

In most years the committee has been limited to naming no more than two new inductees per election. Exceptions occurred in the elections of 1953 (six), 1963 (four), 1964 (six), 1970 (three), 1971 (seven), and 1972–77 (three each). Two additional slots opened for 1995-99, one for pre-1920 players, the other for Negro Leaguers. Voting details are not released to the public.

Individuals considered by the Veterans Committee include managers, umpires, executives, and certain players no longer eligible through the BBWAA (except members of the committee). For eligibility under the former three groups, a person must have been retired five years, or six months if he has reached the age of 65 (a rule tailor-made for Casey Stengel's election in 1966). For players, the minimum wait is 23 years; previously, it was 25 years (1953–56, 1974–84), 30 years (1957–62), or 20 years (1963–73).

On June 10, 1971, a nine-member Baseball Hall of Fame Committee on Negro Baseball Leagues was established. Candidates were to have totaled at least ten years of service in the pre-1946 Negro Leagues and/or the major leagues, without being eligible for BBWAA election. A rule specified that the "Committee shall serve until it shall dissolve itself of its own motion or until further notice from the Board of Directors" of the Hall.

At least one new member was inducted by this committee in each year between 1971 and 1977, after which the committee dissolved and was absorbed into the Veterans Committee. Only two Negro League representatives were enshrined between 1978-94.

As far back as 1944, it was suggested that a special "Roll of Honor," distinct from actual Hall of Fame induction, be established for distinguished baseball writers and similar contributors to the baseball world. In 1962 the J. G. Taylor Spink Award was initiated to honor individuals

"for meritorious contributions to baseball writing." In 1978 the Ford C. Frick Award was established to dignify broadcasters "for major contributions to the game of Baseball." The awards are presented annually during the Hall of Fame induction ceremonies and the winners' names are engraved on a plaque hanging in the National Baseball Library (explaining references to a writers' or broadcasters' "wing" at the Hall of Fame). Through 1998 there had been 49 winners of the Spink Award, and 22 recipients of the Frick trophy. But, contrary to what you hear and read elsewhere, these men are not members of the Hall of Fame.

There have been a total of 237 men inducted into the National Baseball Hall of Fame and Museum through 1998, including 237 major league players, 23 classified as pioneers or executives, 15 Negro Leaguers, 14 managers, and seven umpires. (Many of the latter four groups also played in the majors or minors.)

What follows is, first, a roster of the 228 members of the Hall of Fame named between 1936 and early 1996; second, an index of every man who ever received so much as a single vote for the Hall of Fame, detailing each man's total for each year he received support; and third, the top ten finishers in the voting for each year of balloting since 1936. Men named to the Hall of Fame by special commit-

tee action, such as Alexander Cartwright or Josh Gibson, may not have received votes in an election, but they are included in this index as well. (There have been four such committee groupings: the Centennial Commission of 1937–1938, the Old Timers' Committee of 1939–1949, the Veterans Committee of 1953–present, and the Negro Leagues Committee of 1971–1977.)

Of special interest are some prominent players who were not elected or named to the Hall: Gil Hodges, who received the most votes for the Hall of Fame but remains outside it; Herman Long, who finished among the top ten vote-getters in the Veterans Ballot of 1936, which during later years produced twenty-nine future Hall of Famers; Hank Gowdy, who in the 1950s experienced a fate similar to Long's; and Marty Marion and Allie Reynolds, other long-term vote-getters who were not able to bunch their support in a given year.

And don't get Chicago White Sox fans talking about Nellie Fox and the election of 1985, when, in his final year of eligibility for the Baseball Writers Election, Fox fell only two votes short of the 297 that would have granted him enshrinement—the closest any man has ever come without making it.

The Hall of Fame balloting results were researched and compiled by Pete Palmer.

Hall of Fame Roster

FIRST BASEMEN
Anson, Cap
Beckley, Jake
Bottomley, Jim
Brouthers, Dan
Chance, Frank
Connor, Roger
Foxx, Jimmie
Gehrig, Lou
Greenberg, Hank
Kelly, George
Killebrew, Harmon
McCovey, Willie
Mize, Johnny
Sisler, George
Terry, Bill

SECOND BASEMEN
Carew, Rod
Collins, Eddie
Doerr, Bobby
Evers, Johnny
Fox, Nellie
Frisch, Frankie
Gehringer, Charlie
Herman, Billy
Hornsby, Rogers
Lajoie, Nap
Lazzeri, Tony
Morgan, Joe
Robinson, Jackie
Schoendienst, Red

SHORTSTOPS
Aparicio, Luis
Appling, Luke
Bancroft, Dave
Banks, Ernie
Boudreau, Lou
Cronin, Joe
Davis, George
Jackson, Travis
Jennings, Hugh
Maranville, Rabbit

Reese, Pee Wee
Rizzuto, Phil
Sewell, Joe
Tinker, Joe
Vaughan, Arky
Wagner, Honus
Wallace, Bobby
Ward, Monte

THIRD BASEMEN
Baker, Frank
Collins, Jimmy
Kell, George
Lindstrom, Fred
Mathews, Eddie
Robinson, Brooks
Schmidt, Mike
Traynor, Pie

LEFT FIELDERS
Brock, Lou
Burkett, Jesse
Clarke, Fred
Delahanty, Ed
Goslin, Goose
Hafey, Chick
Kelley, Joe
Kiner, Ralph
Manush, Heinie
Medwick, Joe
Musial, Stan
O'Rourke, Jim
Simmons, Al
Stargell, Willie
Wheat, Zack
Williams, Billy
Williams, Ted
Yastrzemski, Carl

CENTER FIELDERS
Ashburn, Richie
Averill, Earl
Carey, Max
Cobb, Ty

Combs, Earle
DiMaggio, Joe
Doby, Larry
Duffy, Hugh
Hamilton, Billy
Mantle, Mickey
Mays, Willie
Roush, Edd
Snider, Duke
Speaker, Tris
Waner, Lloyd
Wilson, Hack

RIGHT FIELDERS
Aaron, Hank
Clemente, Roberto
Crawford, Sam
Cuyler, Kiki
Flick, Elmer
Heilmann, Harry
Hooper, Harry
Kaline, Al
Keeler, Willie
Kelly, King
Klein, Chuck
McCarthy, Tommy
Ott, Mel
Rice, Sam
Robinson, Frank
Ruth, Babe
Slaughter, Enos
Thompson, Sam
Waner, Paul
Youngs, Ross

CATCHERS
Bench, Johnny
Berra, Yogi
Bresnahan, Roger
Campanella, Roy
Cochrane, Mickey
Dickey, Bill
Ewing, Buck
Ferrell, Rick

Hartnett, Gabby
Lombardi, Ernie
Schalk, Ray

PITCHERS
Alexander, Grover
Bender, Chief
Brown, Mordecai
Bunning, Jim
Carlton, Steve
Chesbro, Jack
Clarkson, John
Coveleski, Stan
Dean, Dizzy
Drysdale, Don
Faber, Red
Feller, Bob
Fingers, Rollie
Ford, Whitey
Galvin, Pud
Gibson, Bob
Gomez, Lefty
Grimes, Burleigh
Grove, Lefty
Haines, Jess
Hoyt, Waite
Hubbell, Carl
Hunter, Catfish
Jenkins, Fergie
Johnson, Walter
Joss, Addie
Keefe, Tim
Koufax, Sandy
Lemon, Bob
Lyons, Ted
Marichal, Juan
Marquard, Rube
Mathewson, Christy
McGinnity, Joe
Newhouser, Hal
Nichols, Kid
Niekro, Phil
Palmer, Jim

Pennock, Herb
Perry, Gaylord
Plank, Eddie
Radbourn, Charles
Rixey, Eppa
Roberts, Robin
Ruffing, Red
Rusie, Amos
Seaver, Tom
Spahn, Warren
Sutton, Don
Vance, Dazzy
Waddell, Rube
Walsh, Ed
Welch, Mickey
Wilhelm, Hoyt
Willis, Vic
Wynn, Early
Young, Cy

FROM NEGRO LEAGUES
Bell, Cool Papa
Charleston, Oscar
Dandridge, Ray
Day, Leon
Dihigo, Martin
Foster, Bill
Foster, Rube
Gibson, Josh
Irvin, Monte
Johnson, Judy
Leonard, Buck
Lloyd, John
Paige, Satchel
Rogan, Bullet Joe
Wells, Willie

MANAGERS
Alston, Walter
Durocher, Leo
Hanlon, Ned
Harris, Bucky
Huggins, Miller

Lasorda, Tommy
Lopez, Al
Mack, Connie
McCarthy, Joe
McGraw, John
McKechnie, Bill
Robinson, Wilbert
Stengel, Casey
Weaver, Earl

UMPIRES
Barlick, Al
Conlan, Jocko
Connolly, Tom
Evans, Billy
Hubbard, Cal
Klem, Bill
McGowan, Bill

PIONEERS AND EXECUTIVES
Barrow, Ed
Bulkeley, Morgan
Cartwright, Alexander
Chadwick, Henry
Chandler, Albert
Comiskey, Charles
Cummings, Candy
Frick, Ford
Giles, Warren
Griffith, Clark
Harridge, Will
Hulbert, William
Johnson, Ban
Landis, Kenesaw
MacPhail, Larry
MacPhail, Lee
Rickey, Branch
Spalding, Al
Veeck, Bill
Weiss, George
Wright, George
Wright, Harry
Yawkey, Tom

Hall of Fame Balloting: Vote Totals of All Candidates

Hank Aaron
Inducted in 1982

1982 406

Babe Adams

1937 8
1938 11
1939 11
1942 11

1945 7
1946 NOM......... 6
1947 22
1948 4
1949 5

1950 6
1951 12
1952 9
1953 17
1954 13

1955 24

Sparky Adams

1958 1
1960 1

Bobby Adams

1966 1

Grover Alexander
Inducted in 1938

1936	55
1937	125
1938	212

Dick Allen

1983	14
1985	28
1986	41
1987	55
1988	52
1989	35
1990	58
1991	59
1992	69
1993	70
1994	66
1995	72
1996	89
1997	79

Johnny Allen

1955	1

Felipe Alou

1980	3

Jesus Alou

1985	1

Matty Alou

1980	5

Walt Alston
Inducted in 1983
Manager

1983	Vet. Com.

Nick Altrock

1937	3
1938	7
1939	6
1953	1
1954	2
1958	20
1960	18

Cap Anson
Inducted in 1939

1936 V	40
1939	O/T Com.

Luis Aparicio
Inducted in 1984

1979	120
1980	124
1981	48
1982	174
1983	252
1984	341

Luke Appling
Inducted in 1964

1953	2
1955	3
1956	14
1958	77
1960	72
1962	48
1964	142
1964 RO	189

Jimmy Archer

1937	6
1938	7
1939	3

Richie Ashburn
Inducted in 1996

1968	6
1969	10
1970	11
1971	10
1972	11
1973	25
1974	56
1975	76
1976	85
1977	139
1978	158
1979	130
1980	134
1981	142
1982	126
1995	Vet. Comm.

Jimmy Austin

1958	1

Earl Averill
Inducted in 1975

1949	1
1952	2
1955	2
1956	3
1958	14
1960	11
1962	3
1975	Vet. Com.

Bob Bailey

1984	1

Frank Baker
Inducted in 1955

1936	1
1937	13
1938	32
1939	30
1942	39
1945	26
1946 NOM	39
1946	36
1947	49
1948	4
1950	4
1951	8
1955	Vet. Com.

Dusty Baker

1992	4

Dave Bancroft
Inducted in 1971

1937	3
1938	2
1939	1
1946 NOM	1
1948	4
1949	5
1950	9
1951	9
1952	11
1953	10
1954	10
1955	19
1956	15
1958	43
1960	30
1971	Vet. Com.

Sal Bando

1987	3

Ernie Banks
Inducted in 1977

1977	321

Al Barlick
Inducted in 1989
Umpire

1989	Vet. Com.

Ross Barnes

1936 V	3

Ed Barrow
Inducted in 1953
Executive

1953	Vet. Com.

Jack Barry

1938	3
1939	1

Dick Bartell

1948	1
1951	1
1958	1
1960	1

Joe Battin

1936 V	1

Hank Bauer

1967	23
1967 RO	9

Don Baylor

1994	12
1995	12

Ginger Beaumont

1938	1
1942	1
1945	1
1946 NOM	1

Glenn Beckert

1981	1

Jake Beckley
Inducted in 1971

1936 V	1
1942	1
1971	Vet. Com.

Mark Belanger

1988	16

Buddy Bell

1995	8

Cool Papa Bell
Inducted in 1974

1974	Neg. Com.

Johnny Bench
Inducted in 1989

1989	431

Chief Bender
Inducted in 1953

1936	2
1937	17
1938	33
1939	40
1942	55
1945	40
1946 NOM	39
1946	35
1947	72
1948	5
1949	2
1950	6
1951	35
1952	70
1953	104
1953	Vet. Com.

Charlie Bennett

1936 V	3

Larry Benton

1958	1

Moe Berg

1958	3
1960	5

Marty Bergen

1937	2
1938	1
1939	1

Wally Berger

1956	1
1958	2

Yogi Berra
Inducted in 1972

1971	242
1972	339

Charlie Berry

1955	1
1958	3

Jim Bibby

1990	1

Carson Bigbee

1948	1

Jack Billingham

1986	1

Max Bishop

1955	1
1956	1
1958	4
1960	5

Ewell Blackwell

1968	5
1969	11
1970	14

Ray Blades

1958	1
1960	1

Paul Blair

1986	8

Steve Blass

1980	2

Lu Blue

1954	1

Vida Blue

1992	23
1993	37
1994	14
1995	26

Ossie Bluege

1948	2
1949	1
1954	1
1956	2
1958	2
1960	3

Ping Bodie

1937	2
1949	1

Joe Boley

1942	1

Tommy Bond

1936 V	1

Bobby Bonds

1987	24
1988	27
1989	29
1990	30
1991	39
1992	40
1993	45
1994	37
1995	35
1996	24
1997	20

Bob Boone

1996	36
1997	28
1998	26

Jim Bottomley
Inducted in 1974

1948	4
1949	8
1950	8
1951	6
1952	7
1953	10
1954	16
1955	26
1956	42
1958	57
1960	89
1962	20
1974	Vet. Com.

Lou Boudreau
Inducted in 1970

1956	2
1958	64
1960	35
1962	12
1964	68
1964 RO	43
1966	115
1967	143
1967 RO	68
1968	146
1969	218
1970	232

Jim Bouton

1984	3

Larry Bowa

1991	11

Clete Boyer

1978	1
1979	3

Ken Boyer

1975	9
1976	15
1977	14
1978	18
1979	20
1985	68
1986	95
1987	96
1988	109
1989	62
1990	78
1991	58
1992	71
1993	69
1994	56

Bill Bradley

1936	1
1937	5
1938	2
1939	1
1942	1
1946 NOM	1

Harry Brecheen

1960	7
1968	3
1969	2
1970	3
1971	7
1972	5
1973	3

Ted Breitenstein

1937	1

Roger Bresnahan
Inducted in 1945

1936	47
1937	43
1938	67
1939	67
1942	57
1945	133
1945	O/T Com.

Jim Brewer

1982	2

Tommy Bridges

1956	3
1958	11
1960	4
1962	1
1964	15
1964 RO	1
1966	16

Lou Brock
Inducted in 1985

1985	315

Dan Brouthers
Inducted in 1945

1936 V	2
1945	O/T Com.

Gates Brown

1981	1

Mordecai Brown
Inducted in 1949

1936	6
1937	31
1938	54
1939	54
1942	63
1945	46
1946 NOM	56
1946	48
1949	O/T Com.

Bill Bruton

1971	1

Bill Buckner

1996	10

Morgan Bulkeley
Inducted in 1937
Executive

1937	Cen. Com.

Jim Bunning
Inducted in 1996

1977	146
1978	181
1979	147
1980	177
1981	164
1982	138
1983	138
1984	201
1985	214
1986	279
1987	289
1988	317
1989	283
1990	257
1991	282
1996	Vet. Comm.

Lew Burdette

1973	12
1974	7
1975	11
1976	21
1977	85
1978	76
1979	53
1980	66
1981	48
1982	43
1983	43
1984	97
1985	82
1986	96
1987	96

Smoky Burgess

1973	1
1974	2

Jesse Burkett
Inducted in 1946

1936 V	1
1937	1
1938	2
1942	4
1945	2
1946 NOM	2
1946	O/T Com.

George J. Burns

1937	3
1938	3
1939	1
1949	1
1950	2

Jeff Burroughs

1991	1

Guy Bush
1956 2

Joe Bush
1958 5

Donie Bush
1937 1
1939 2
1942 2
1945 1
1946 NOM 2
1953 1

Leon Cadore
1948 1

Johnny Callison
1979 1

Dolf Camilli
1948 1
1956 1
1958 4
1960 3

Howie Camnitz
1945 1

Roy Campanella
Inducted in 1969
1964 115
1964 RO 138
1966 197
1967 204
1967 RO 170
1968 205
1969 270

Bert Campaneris
1989 14

Bill Campbell
1993 1

Jose Cardenal
1986 1

Leo Cardenas
1981 1
1982 1

Rod Carew
Inducted in 1991
1991 401

Max Carey
Inducted in 1961
1937 6
1938 6
1939 7
1945 1
1948 9
1949 12
1950 14
1951 27
1952 36
1953 55
1954 55
1955 119
1956 65
1958 136
1961 .... Vet. Com.

Steve Carlton
Inducted in 1994
1994 436

Chico Carrasquel
1966 1

Bill Carrigan
1937 5
1938 4
1939 2
1945 3

Clay Carroll
1984 1

Gary Carter
1998 200

Rico Carty
1985 1

Alex Cartwright
Inducted in 1938
Pioneer
1938 .... Cen. Com.

George Case
1958 1
1960 1
1962 1
1964 2

Dave Cash
1986 2

Norm Cash
1980 6

Phil Cavaretta
1962 2
1964 22
1964 RO 1
1966 9
1967 15
1967 RO 4
1968 23
1969 37
1970 51
1971 83
1972 61
1973 73
1974 61
1975 129

Cesar Cedeno
1992 2

Orlando Cepeda
1980 48
1981 77
1982 42
1983 59
1984 124
1985 114
1986 152
1987 179
1988 199
1989 176
1990 211
1991 192
1992 246
1993 252
1994 335

Ron Cey
1993 8

Henry Chadwick
Inducted in 1938
Pioneer
1938 .... Cen. Com.

Frank Chance
Inducted in 1946
1936 5
1937 49
1938 133
1939 158
1942 136
1945 179
1946 NOM 144
1946 150
1946 .... O/T Com.

Happy Chandler
Inducted in 1982
Executive
1982 .... Vet. Com.

Spud Chandler
1950 2

1951 1
1956 1
1962 2
1964 6

Ben Chapman
1949 1
1952 1

Ray Chapman
1938 1

Sam Chapman
1958 1

Oscar Charleston
Inducted in 1976
1976 .... Neg. Com.

Hal Chase
1936 11
1937 18

Jack Chesbro
Inducted in 1946
1937 1
1938 2
1939 6
1946 NOM 1
1946 .... O/T Com.

Bill Cissell
1937 1

Jack Clark
1998 7

Watty Clark
1958 1

Fred Clarke
Inducted in 1945
1936 V 9
1936 1
1937 22
1938 63
1939 59
1942 58
1945 53
1945 .... O/T Com.

John Clarkson
Inducted in 1963
1936 V 5
1946 NOM 1
1963 .... Vet. Com.

Roberto Clemente
Inducted in 1973
1973 .... Spec. El.

Andy Coakley
1938 1

Ty Cobb
Inducted in 1936
1936 222

Mickey Cochrane
Inducted in 1947
1936 80
1939 28
1942 88
1945 125
1946 NOM 80
1946 65
1947 128

Rocky Colavito
1974 2
1975 1

Eddie Collins
Inducted in 1939
1936 60
1937 115
1938 175
1939 213

Jimmy Collins
Inducted in 1945
1936 V 8
1936 58
1937 66
1938 79
1939 72
1942 68
1945 121
1945 .... O/T Com.

Shano Collins
1937 1

Earle Combs
Inducted in 1970
1937 4
1938 7
1939 3
1945 1
1948 6
1949 6
1950 3
1952 1
1953 3
1955 1
1956 14
1958 34
1960 43
1962 6
1970 .... Vet. Com.

Charlie Comiskey
Inducted in 1939
Executive
1936 V 6
1939 .... O/T Com.

Dave Concepcion
1994 31
1995 43
1996 63
1997 60
1998 80

Jocko Conlan
Inducted in 1974
Umpire
1974 .... Vet. Com.

Tommy Connolly
Inducted in 1953
Umpire
1953 .... Vet. Com.

Roger Connor
Inducted in 1976
1976 .... Vet. Com.

Wid Conroy
1945 1

Jack Coombs
1937 2
1938 2
1946 NOM 2
1948 2
1951 1

Mort Cooper
1956 2
1958 3
1960 1
1969 3

Walker Cooper
1968 8
1969 5
1970 9
1971 7
1972 8
1973 8
1974 9
1975 13
1976 56
1977 45

Wilbur Cooper
1938 1

1939 1
1948 2
1949 4
1951 1
1952 2
1953 9
1954 7
1955 11

Clint Courtney
1967 1

Stan Coveleski
Inducted in 1969
1938 1
1948 2
1949 3
1950 1
1958 34
1969 .... Vet. Com.

Billy Cox
1962 1

Doc Cramer
1956 4
1958 2
1960 1
1962 1
1964 12

Del Crandall
1976 15
1977 8
1978 6
1979 9

Doc Crandall
1938 1

Gavvy Cravath
1937 2
1938 2
1939 2
1946 NOM 1
1947 2

Sam Crawford
Inducted in 1957
1936 1
1937 5
1938 11
1939 6
1942 2
1945 4
1946 NOM 9
1957 .... Vet. Com.

Lou Criger
1936 V 1
1936 7
1937 16
1938 11
1939 2
1946 NOM 6

Hughie Critz
1956 2

Joe Cronin
Inducted in 1956
1947 6
1948 25
1949 33
1949 RO 16
1950 33
1951 44
1952 48
1953 69
1954 85
1955 135
1956 152

Frank Crosetti
1950 1
1952 1
1956 1
1958 5
1960 8
1968 15

Lave Cross
1939 1
1942 1

Al Crowder
1958 1
1960 1

Walt Cruise
1938 1

Jose Cruz
1994 2

Tony Cuccinello
1956 1
1958 3

Candy Cummings
Inducted in 1939
Pioneer
1939 .... O/T Com.

Kiki Cuyler
Inducted in 1968
1948 3
1949 4
1950 11
1951 8
1952 10
1953 18
1954 20
1955 35
1956 55
1958 90
1960 72
1962 31
1968 .... Vet. Com.

Bill Dahlen
1936 V 1
1938 1

Ray Dandridge
Inducted in 1987
1987 .... Vet. Com.

Harry Danning
1958 1
1960 1

Alvin Dark
1966 17
1967 38
1967 RO 7
1968 36
1969 48
1970 55
1971 54
1972 55
1973 53
1974 54
1975 48
1976 62
1977 66
1978 60
1979 80
1980 43

Jake Daubert
1936 V 1
1937 2
1938 1
1939 1
1951 1
1955 1

Curt Davis
1958 1

George Davis
Inducted in 1998
1998 .... Vet. Com.

Harry Davis
1945 1
1946 NOM 2

Tommy Davis
1982 5

Spud Davis
1948 1
1949 1

Leon Day
Inducted in 1995
1995 .... Vet. Comm.

Dizzy Dean
Inducted in 1953
1945 NOM 17
1946 NOM 40
1946 45
1947 88
1948 40
1949 88
1949 RO 81
1950 85
1951 145
1952 152
1953 209

Doug DeCinces
1993 2

Ed Delahanty
Inducted in 1945
1936 V 22
1936 17
1937 70
1938 132
1939 145
1942 104
1945 111
1945 ...... O/T Com.

Jerry Denny
1936 V 6

Bucky Dent
1990 3

Paul Derringer
1948 1
1950 1
1951 1
1955 1
1956 12
1958 15
1960 8

Bill Dickey
Inducted in 1954
1945 17
1946 NOM........... 40
1946 32
1948 39
1949 65
1949 RO 39
1950 78
1951 118
1952 139
1953 179
1954 202

Martin Dihigo
Inducted in 1977
1977 .... Neg. Com.

Dom DiMaggio
1960 4
1962 2
1964 12
1968 8
1969 13
1970 15
1971 15
1972 36
1973 43

Joe DiMaggio
Inducted in 1955
1945 1
1953 117
1954 175
1955 223

Bill Dinneen
1938 4
1939 7
1942 1
1945 1
1946 NOM...........1

Bill Doak
1958 3

Larry Doby
Inducted in 1998
1966 7
1967 10
1967 RO 1
1998 .... Vet. Com

Bobby Doerr
Inducted in 1986
1953 2
1956 5
1958 25
1960 15
1962 10
1964 24
1964 RO 5
1966 30
1967 35
1967 RO 15
1968 48
1969 62
1970 75
1971 78
1986 .... Vet. Com.

Mike Donlin
1937 6
1938 5
1939 5
1945 1

Bill Donovan
1937 3
1938 1
1939 2
1945 3
1946 NOM...........4

Red Dooin
1937 1
1938 1

Brian Downing
1998 2

Jack Doyle
1936 V 1

Larry Doyle
1937 2
1938 4
1939 1

Walt Dropo
1967 1

Don Drysdale
Inducted in 1984
1975 76
1976 114
1977 197
1978 219
1979 233
1980 238
1981 243
1982 233
1983 242
1984 316

Hugh Duffy
Inducted in 1945
1936 V 4
1937 7
1938 24
1939 34
1942 77
1945 64
1945 ...... O/T Com.

Joe Dugan
1937 1
1938 1
1948 3
1949 1
1956 1
1958 5
1960 8

Fred Dunlap
1936 V 2

Jack Dunn
1942 1
1945 1
1946 NOM...........1

Leo Durocher
Inducted in 1994
Manager
1948 1
1949 1
1952 1
1956 1
1958 28
1960 10
1962 1
1964 15
1964 RO 2
1994 .... Vet. Com.

Eddie Dyer
1947 1

Jimmy Dykes
1948 5
1949 7
1950 2
1951 3
1952 5
1953 5
1955 1
1956 1
1958 26
1960 27
1962 6

George Earnshaw
1948 3
1949 2
1950 2
1955 2
1956 3

Hank Edwards
1960 2

Howard Ehmke
1938 1
1949 1
1951 1
1952 1
1953 3
1954 4
1955 8
1956 8
1958 7
1960 12

Kid Elberfeld
1936 1
1937 1
1938 2
1942 1
1945 2

Jumbo Elliott
1958 1

Bob Elliott
1960 2
1962 1
1964 4

Dock Ellis
1985 1

Del Ennis
1966 3
1967 2

Jewel Ens
1950 1

Carl Erskine
1966 6
1968 9
1969 4
1970 2
1971 3
1972 4
1973 4
1974 11

Billy Evans
Inducted in 1973
Umpire
1973 .... Vet. Com.

Darrell Evans
1995 8

Dwight Evans
1997 28
1998 49

Johnny Evers
Inducted in 1946
1936 6
1937 44
1938 91
1939 107
1942 91
1945 134
1946 NOM......... 130
1946 110
1946 .... O/T Com.

Buck Ewing
Inducted in 1939
1936 V 40
1939 2
1939 ...... O/T Com.

Red Faber
Inducted in 1964
1937 3
1938 1
1939 3
1942 1
1948 3
1949 6
1950 9
1951 8
1952 9
1953 9
1954 12
1955 27
1956 34
1958 68
1960 83
1962 30
1964 .... Vet. Com.

Elroy Face
1976 23
1977 33
1978 27
1979 35
1980 21
1981 23
1982 22
1983 32
1984 65
1985 62
1986 74
1987 78
1988 79
1989 47
1990 50

Ron Fairly
1985 3

Cy Falkenberg
1937 1

Bob Feller
Inducted in 1962
1962 150

Rick Ferrell
Inducted in 1984
1956 1
1958 1
1960 1
1984 .... Vet. Com.

Wes Ferrell
1948 1
1949 1
1956 7
1960 8
1962 1

Rollie Fingers
Inducted in 1992
1991 291
1992 349

Fred Fitzsimmons
1948 2
1949 2
1950 1
1956 3
1958 16
1960 13
1962 1

Mike Flanagan
1998 2

Art Fletcher
1937 2
1938 3
1939 1
1947 3
1948 3
1949 1
1950 1
1951 4

Elmer Flick
Inducted in 1963
1938 1
1963 .... Vet. Com.

Curt Flood
1977 16
1978 8
1979 14
1985 28
1986 45
1987 50
1988 48
1989 27
1990 35
1991 23
1992 42
1993 36
1994 40
1995 59
1996 71

Lew Fonseca
1948 1
1950 2
1956 2
1958 3
1960 3

Whitey Ford
Inducted in 1974
1973 255
1974 284

Bob Forsch
1995 2

Bill Foster
1996 .... Vet. Com.

Eddie Foster
1938 2

George Foster
1992 24
1993 29
1994 16
1995 19

Rube Foster
Inducted in 1981
Manager
1981 .... Vet. Com.

Nellie Fox
1971 39
1972 64
1973 73
1974 79
1975 76
1976 174
1977 152
1978 149
1979 174
1980 161
1981 168
1982 127
1983 173
1984 246
1985 295
1997 .... Vet. Com

Jimmie Foxx
Inducted in 1951
1936 21
1946 NOM 26
1947 10
1948 50
1949 85
1949 RO 89
1950 103
1951 179

Chick Fraser
1939 1

Bill Freehan
1982 2

Jim Fregosi
1984 4

Ford Frick
Inducted in 1970
Executive
1970 .... Vet. Com.

Frankie Frisch
Inducted in 1947
1936 14
1939 26
1942 84
1945 101
1946 NOM 104
1946 67
1947 136

Carl Furillo
1966 2
1967 2
1970 2
1971 5
1972 2

Augie Galan
1968 2
1970 3

Jim Galvin
Inducted in 1965
1965 .... Vet. Com.

Phil Garner
1994 2

Ned Garver
1967 1

Steve Garvey
1993 176
1994 166
1995 196
1996 175
1997 167
1998 195

Lou Gehrig
Inducted in 1939
1936 51
1939 .... Spec. El.

Charlie Gehringer
Inducted in 1949
1945 10
1946 NOM 43
1946 23
1947 105
1948 52
1949 102
1949 RO 159

Charlie Gelbert
1947 1
1949 2
1950 1
1951 1

Josh Gibson
Inducted in 1972
1972 .... Neg. Com.

Bob Gibson
Inducted in 1981
1981 337

Warren Giles
Inducted in 1979
Executive
1979 .... Vet. Com.

Dave Giusti
1983 1

Jack Glasscock
1936 V 2

Kid Gleason
1937 1
1938 1
1939 1
1945 1

Lefty Gomez
Inducted in 1972
1945 7
1946 NOM 4
1947 1
1948 16
1949 17
1950 18
1951 23
1952 29
1953 35
1954 38
1955 71
1956 89
1958 76
1960 51
1962 20
1972 .... Vet. Com.

Mike Gonzales
1950 1
1952 1
1953 1
1958 3
1960 2

Joe Gordon
1945 1
1955 1
1956 4
1958 11
1960 11
1962 4
1964 30
1964 RO 1
1966 31
1967 66
1967 RO 13
1968 77
1969 97
1970 79

Goose Goslin
Inducted in 1968
1948 1
1949 4
1950 2
1954 1
1955 7
1956 26
1958 26
1960 30
1962 14
1968 .... Vet. Com.

Hank Gowdy
1937 2
1938 8
1939 4
1942 8
1945 3
1947 1
1948 3
1949 10
1950 6
1951 26
1952 34
1953 58
1954 51
1955 90
1956 49
1958 45
1960 38

Eddie Grant
1938 1
1939 2
1942 3
1945 2
1946 NOM 1

George Grantham
1958 1

Hank Greenberg
Inducted in 1956
1945 3
1949 67
1949 RO 44
1950 64
1951 67
1952 75
1953 80
1954 97
1955 157
1956 164

Bobby Grich
1992 11

Ken Griffey, Sr.
1997 22

Clark Griffith
Inducted in 1946
Executive
1937 4
1938 10
1939 20
1942 71
1945 108
1946 NOM 73
1946 82
1946 .... O/T Com.

Burleigh Grimes
Inducted in 1964
1937 1
1938 1
1939 1
1948 7
1949 8
1950 6
1951 5
1952 9
1953 9
1955 3
1956 25
1958 71
1960 92
1962 43
1964 .... Vet. Com.

Charlie Grimm
1939 1
1945 1
1946 NOM 1
1948 6
1949 10
1950 13
1951 9
1952 6
1953 9
1958 26
1960 13
1962 2

Marv Grissom
1966 2

Dick Groat
1973 7
1974 4
1975 4
1976 7
1977 4
1978 3

Heinie Groh
1937 1
1938 3
1945 1
1948 1
1950 2
1954 1
1955 5
1960 1

Steve Gromek
1964 1

Orval Grove
1958 5
1960 7

Lefty Grove
Inducted in 1947
1936 12
1945 28
1946 NOM 71
1946 61
1947 123

Ron Guidry
1994 24
1995 25
1996 37
1997 31
1998 37

Frank Gustine
1958 3

Mule Haas
1955 1
1956 1
1958 1
1960 1

Stan Hack
1948 2
1949 4
1950 8
1951 3
1956 1
1958 6
1960 6

Harvey Haddix
1971 10
1972 9
1973 1
1974 8
1975 8
1976 8
1977 7
1978 7
1979 8
1985 15

Chick Hafey
Inducted in 1971
1948 1

1949 2
1950 4
1951 1
1952 1
1953 2
1954 2
1955 4
1956 16
1958 12
1960 29
1962 7
1971 .... Vet. Com.

Noodles Hahn
1939 1

Jesse Haines
Inducted in 1970
1939 1
1947 1
1948 2
1949 2
1950 11
1953 4
1954 6
1955 10
1956 14
1958 22
1960 20
1962 3
1970 .... Vet. Com.

Bill Hallahan
1948 1
1956 1
1958 1
1960 2

Billy Hamilton
Inducted in 1961
1936 V 2
1942 1
1961 .... Vet. Com.

Ned Hanlon
Inducted in 1996
1996 .... Vet. Com.

Mel Harder
1949 4
1950 2
1951 1
1952 10
1953 8
1958 6
1960 12
1962 7
1964 51
1964 RO 14
1966 34
1967 52
1967 RO 14

Bubbles Hargrave
1947 1
1958 1
1960 1

Mike Hargrove
1991 1

Toby Harrah
1992 1

Bud Harrelson
1986 1

Will Harridge
Inducted in 1972
Executive
1972 .... Vet. Com.

Bucky Harris
Inducted in 1975
Manager
1938 1
1939 1
1948 3
1949 11
1950 4
1951 9

1952 12
1953 21
1958 45
1960 31
1975 .... Vet. Com.

Gabby Hartnett
Inducted in 1955
1945 2
1946 NOM 2
1947 2
1948 33
1949 35
1949 RO 7
1950 54
1951 57
1952 77
1953 104
1954 151
1955 195

Grady Hatton
1966 4
1967 1

Jim Hearn
1966 1
1967 1

Richie Hebner
1991 1

Jim Hegan
1966 5
1967 2

Harry Heilmann
Inducted in 1952
1937 10
1938 14
1939 8
1942 4
1945 5
1946 NOM 23
1947 65
1948 40
1949 59
1949 RO 52
1950 87
1951 153
1952 203

Tommy Helms
1983 1

Solly Hemus
1966 1

Tommy Henrich
1952 4
1953 10
1956 2
1958 11
1960 10
1962 3
1964 13
1968 22
1969 50
1970 62

Babe Herman
1942 1
1948 2
1949 5
1950 2
1951 1
1952 3
1953 1
1954 1
1955 5
1956 11
1958 13
1960 7

Billy Herman
Inducted in 1975
1948 1
1956 2
1958 7
1962 4
1964 26

1964 RO 9
1966 28
1967 59
1967 RO 14
1975 .... Vet. Com.

Keith Hernandez
1996 24

Willie Hernandez
1995 2

Buck Herzog
1938 1

Jim Hickman
1980 1

Mike Higgins
1950 2
1951 1
1958 6
1960 3

John Hiller
1986 11

Bill Hinchman
1937 1

Gil Hodges
1969 82
1970 145
1971 180
1972 161
1973 218
1974 198
1975 188
1976 233
1977 224
1978 226
1979 242
1980 230
1981 241
1982 205
1983 237

Tommy Holmes
1958 2
1960 2

Ken Holtzman
1985 4
1986 5

Harry Hooper
Inducted in 1971
1937 6
1938 4
1939 5
1948 2
1950 2
1951 3
1971 .... Vet. Com.

Burt Hooton
1991 1

Rogers Hornsby
Inducted in 1942
1936 105
1937 53
1938 46
1939 176
1942 182

Willie Horton
1986 4

Art Houtteman
1964 2

Elston Howard
1974 19
1975 23
1976 55
1977 43
1978 41
1979 30

1980 29
1981 83
1982 40
1983 32
1984 45
1985 54
1986 51
1987 44
1988 53

Frank Howard

1979 6

Waite Hoyt
Inducted in 1969

1939 1
1942 1
1946 NOM 1
1948 7
1949 7
1950 11
1951 13
1952 12
1953 14
1954 14
1955 33
1956 37
1958 37
1960 29
1962 18
1969 Vet. Com.

Al Hrabosky

1988 1

Cal Hubbard
Inducted in 1976
Umpire

1976 Vet. Com.

Carl Hubbell
Inducted in 1947

1945 24
1946 NOM 101
1946 75
1947 140

Miller Huggins
Inducted in 1964
Manager

1937 5
1938 48
1939 97
1942 111
1945 133
1946 NOM 129
1946 106
1948 4
1950 2
1964 Vet. Com.

William Hulbert
Inducted in 1995

1995 Vet. Com.

Catfish Hunter
Inducted in 1987

1985 212
1986 289
1987 315

Fred Hutchinson

1962 1
1964 10

Monte Irvin
Inducted in 1973

1973 Neg. Com.

Charlie Irwin

1938 1
1939 1

Joe Jackson

1936 2
1946 NOM 2

Reggie Jackson
Inducted in 1993

1993 396

Sonny Jackson

1980 1

Travis Jackson
Inducted in 1982

1948 5
1949 6
1950 6
1951 4
1952 1
1953 2
1954 1
1955 5
1956 14
1958 11
1960 11
1962 1
1982 Vet. Com.

Fergie Jenkins
Inducted in 1991

1989 234
1990 296
1991 334

Hughie Jennings
Inducted in 1945

1936 V 11
1937 4
1938 23
1939 33
1942 64
1945 92
1945 O/T Com.

Jackie Jensen

1967 3
1968 3
1969 1
1970 1
1971 2
1972 1

Tommy John

1995 98
1996 102

Ban Johnson
Inducted in 1937
Executive

1937 Cen. Com.

Dave Johnson

1984 3

Judy Johnson
Inducted in 1975

1975 Neg. Com.

Bob Johnson

1948 1
1956 1

Walter Johnson
Inducted in 1936

1936 189

Fielder Jones

1946 NOM 1

Sam P. Jones

1939 1
1955 1
1956 1

Tim Jordan

1951 1

Mike Jorgensen

1991 1

Addie Joss
Inducted in 1978

1937 11
1938 18
1939 28
1942 33
1945 23
1946 NOM 14
1960 1
1978 Vet. Com.

Joe Judge

1937 1
1938 2
1949 1
1955 2
1956 2
1958 9
1960 15

Billy Jurges

1949 2
1958 1

Jim Kaat

1989 87
1990 79
1991 62
1992 114
1993 125
1994 98
1995 100
1996 91

Al Kaline
Inducted in 1980

1980 340

Willie Kamm

1958 3
1960 1

Tim Keefe
Inducted in 1964

1936 V 1
1964 Vet. Com.

Willie Keeler
Inducted in 1939

1936 V 33
1936 40
1937 115
1938 177
1939 207

George Kell
Inducted in 1983

1964 33
1964 RO 8
1966 29
1967 40
1967 RO 11
1968 47
1969 60
1970 90
1971 105
1972 115
1973 114
1974 94
1975 114
1976 129
1977 141
1983 Vet. Com.

Charlie Keller

1953 1
1956 2
1958 9
1960 7
1962 1
1964 12
1968 11
1969 14
1970 7
1971 14
1972 24

Joe Kelley
Inducted in 1971

1939 1
1942 1
1971 Vet. Com.

George Kelly
Inducted in 1973

1947 1
1948 2
1949 1
1956 2
1958 2
1960 5
1962 1
1973 Vet. Com.

Mike Kelly
Inducted in 1945

1936 V 15
1945 O/T Com.

Ken Keltner

1958 1
1960 1

Dickie Kerr

1937 1
1938 3
1939 5
1942 1
1945 1
1949 1
1951 3
1952 9
1953 13
1954 13
1955 25

Don Kessinger

1985 2

Harmon Killebrew
Inducted in 1984

1981 239
1982 246
1983 269
1984 335

Bill Killefer

1946 NOM 1

Matt Kilroy

1936 V 1

Ellis Kinder

1964 3

Ralph Kiner
Inducted in 1975

1962 5
1964 31
1964 RO 3
1966 74
1967 124
1967 RO 41
1968 118
1969 137
1970 167
1971 212
1972 235
1973 235
1974 215
1975 273

Dave Kingman

1992 3

Chuck Klein
Inducted in 1980

1948 3
1949 9
1950 14
1951 15
1952 19
1954 11
1955 25
1956 44
1958 36
1960 37
1962 18
1964 56
1964 RO 18
1980 Vet. Com.

Bill Klem
Inducted in 1953
Umpire

1953 Vet. Com.

Johnny Kling

1936 8
1937 20
1938 26
1939 14
1942 15
1945 12
1946 NOM 20
1948 2
1953 1

Ted Kluszewski

1967 9
1968 14
1969 11
1970 8
1971 9
1972 10
1973 14
1974 28
1975 33
1976 50
1977 55
1978 51
1979 58
1980 50
1981 56

Otto Knabe

1939 1
1946 NOM 1

Ray Knight

1994 1

Jerry Koosman

1991 4

Sandy Koufax
Inducted in 1972

1972 344

Ray Kremer

1948 1
1958 2

Red Kress

1958 1
1960 3

Mike Krukow

1995 1

Harvey Kuenn

1977 57
1978 58
1979 63
1980 83
1981 93
1982 62
1983 77
1984 106
1985 125
1986 144
1987 144
1988 168
1989 115
1990 107
1991 100

Joe Kuhel

1956 1

Bob Kuzava

1964 1

Nap Lajoie
Inducted in 1937

1936 V 2
1936 146
1937 168

Judge Landis
Inducted in 1944
Executive

1944 O/T Com.

Bill Lange

1936 V 6
1953 1

Hal Lanier

1979 1

Don Larsen

1974 29
1975 23
1976 47
1977 39
1978 32
1979 53
1980 31
1981 33
1982 32
1983 22
1984 25
1985 32
1986 33
1987 30
1988 31

Arlie Latham

1936 V 1
1938 1
1942 1

Cookie Lavagetto

1958 4
1960 2

Vern Law

1973 9
1974 5
1975 6
1976 9
1977 5
1978 6
1979 9

Tony Lazzeri
Inducted in 1991

1945 1
1947 1
1948 21
1949 20
1949 RO 6
1950 21
1951 27
1952 29
1953 28
1954 30
1955 66
1956 64
1958 80
1960 59
1962 8
1991 Vet. Com.

Fred Leach

1958 2
1960 1

Tommy Leach

1937 1
1939 1

Bill Lee

1988 3

Sam Leever

1937 1

Bob Lemon
Inducted in 1976

1964 24
1964 RO 3
1966 21
1067 35
1967 RO 7
1968 47
1969 56
1970 70
1971 90
1972 117
1973 177
1974 190
1975 233
1976 305

Chet Lemon

1996 1

Buck Leonard
Inducted in 1972

1972 .... Neg. Com.

Dennis Leonard

1992 1

Emil Leonard

1960 2
1968 5
1969 4
1970 5
1971 3
1972 5
1973 6

Duffy Lewis

1937 3
1938 5
1939 6
1945 1
1951 2
1952 11
1953 20
1954 20
1955 34

Fred Lindstrom
Inducted in 1976

1949 1
1956 3
1958 5
1960 6
1962 7
1976 ..... Vet. Com.

John Henry Lloyd
Inducted in 1977

1977 .... Neg. Com.

Hans Lobert

1937 2
1938 1
1939 2
1960 1

Whitey Lockman

1966 4

Mickey Lolich

1985 78
1986 86
1987 84
1988 109
1989 47
1990 27
1991 33
1992 45
1993 43
1994 23
1995 26
1996 33

Ernie Lombardi
Inducted in 1986

1950 3
1951 3
1956 8
1958 4
1960 6
1962 5
1964 33
1964 RO.............9
1966 34
1967 43
1967 RO............25
1986 .... Vet. Com.

Jim Lonborg

1985 3
1986 3

Herman Long

1936 V 16
1937 1
1938 1
1939 1
1945 1
1946 NOM...........1

Ed Lopat

1968 2
1969 2
1970 1
1971 4
1972 2

Davey Lopes

1993 2

Al Lopez
Inducted in 1977
Manager

1949 1
1952 2
1953 2
1956 1
1958 34
1960 26
1962 11
1964 57
1964 RO.............34
1966 109
1967 114
1967 RO............50
1977 .... Vet. Com.

Bobby Lowe

1936 V 2
1942 1
1945 2

John Lowenstein

1991 1

Red Lucas

1949 1
1950 1
1958 1

Dolph Luque

1937 1
1938 1
1939 1
1950 1
1952 1
1953 1
1956 1
1958 15
1960 4

Greg Luzinski

1990 1

Sparky Lyle

1988 56
1989 25
1990 25
1991 15

Fred Lynn

1996 26

Ted Lyons
Inducted in 1955

1945 4
1946 NOM...........3
1948 15
1949 29
1949 RO............14
1950 42
1951 71
1952 101
1953 139
1954 170
1955 217

Connie Mack
Inducted in 1937
Manager

1936 1
1937 .... Cen. Com.

Larry MacPhail
Inducted in 1978
Executive

1978 .... Vet. Com.

Bill Madlock

1993 19

Sherry Magee

1937 2
1938 2
1939 1
1942 1
1945 1
1946 NOM...........1
1950 1
1951 2

Sal Maglie

1964 13
1968 11

Jim Maloney

1978 2
1979 2

Gus Mancuso

1958 1

Mickey Mantle
Inducted in 1974

1974 322

Heinie Manush
Inducted in 1964

1948 1
1949 1
1956 13
1958 22
1960 20
1962 15
1964 .... Vet. Com.

Rabbit Maranville
Inducted in 1954

1937 25
1938 73
1939 82
1942 66
1945 51
1946 NOM.........50
1946 29
1947 91
1948 38
1949 58
1949 RO............39
1950 66
1951 110
1952 133
1953 164
1954 209

Firpo Marberry

1938 1
1950 1
1958 5
1960 2
1962 2

Juan Marichal
Inducted in 1983

1981 233
1982 305
1983 313

Marty Marion

1956 1
1960 37
1962 16
1964 50
1964 RO............17
1966 86
1967 90
1967 RO............22
1968 89
1969 112
1970 120
1971 123
1972 120
1973 127

Roger Maris

1974 78
1975 70
1976 87
1977 72
1978 83
1979 127
1980 111

1981 94
1982 69
1983 69
1984 107
1985 128
1986 177
1987 176
1988 184

Rube Marquard
Inducted in 1971

1936 1
1937 13
1938 10
1939 4
1946 NOM...........6
1947 18
1948 6
1949 4
1951 3
1952 9
1953 19
1954 15
1955 35
1971 .... Vet. Com.

Mike Marshall

1987 6

Billy Martin

1967 1

Pepper Martin

1942 2
1945 1
1946 NOM...........1
1948 7
1949 16
1950 7
1951 19
1952 31
1953 43
1956 7
1958 46
1960 29
1962 6
1964 19
1964 RO.............5

Morrie Martin

1966 2

Eddie Mathews
Inducted in 1978

1974 118
1975 148
1976 189
1977 239
1978 301

Christy Mathewson
Inducted in 1936

1936 205

Lee May

1988 2

Carl Mays

1958 6

Willie Mays
Inducted in 1979

1979 409

Bill Mazeroski

1978 23
1979 36
1980 33
1981 38
1982 28
1983 48
1984 74
1985 87
1986 100
1987 125
1988 143
1989 134
1990 131
1991 142
1992 182

Jim McAleer

1936 V 1

Joe McCarthy
Inducted in 1957
Manager

1939 3
1947 2
1951 1
1953 1
1958 2
1957 .... Vet. Com.

Tommy McCarthy
Inducted in 1946

1936 V 1
1946 .... O/T Com.

Tim McCarver

1986 16

Frank McCormick

1956 3
1962 1
1964 6
1968 3

Willie McCovey
Inducted in 1986

1986 346

Lindy McDaniel

1981 1
1982 3

Gil McDougald

1966 5
1967 4
1968 4
1969 3
1970 1
1971 4
1972 4
1973 2
1974 3

Joe McGinnity
Inducted in 1946

1937 12
1938 36
1939 32
1942 59
1945 44
1946 NOM.........53
1946 47
1946 .... O/T Com.

Bill McGowan
Inducted in 1992
Umpire

1992 .... Vet. Com.

John McGraw
Inducted in 1937
Manager

1936 V 17
1936 4
1937 35
1937 .... Cen. Com.

Tug McGraw

1990 6

Stuffy McInnis

1937 1
1938 4
1939 4
1948 5
1949 8
1950 1
1951 3

Bill McKechnie
Inducted in 1962
Manager

1945 2
1946 NOM...........2
1950 1
1951 8
1962 .... Vet. Com.

Denny McLain

1978 1
1979 3
1985 2

Larry McLean

1937 1

Don McMahon

1980 1

Marty McManus

1958 2
1960 2

Roy McMillan

1972 9
1973 5
1974 4

Dave McNally

1981 5
1982 5
1985 7
1986 12

Cal McVey

1936 V 1

Lee Meadows

1958 2

Ducky Medwick
Inducted in 1968

1948 1
1956 31
1958 50
1960 38
1962 34
1964 108
1964 RO...........130
1966 187
1967 212
1967 RO...........248
1968 240

Andy Messersmith

1985 3
1986 3

Bob Meusel

1937 1
1938 1
1945 1
1948 6
1949 3
1950 2
1952 1
1955 2
1956 1
1958 5
1960 10

Eddie Miksis

1964 1

Clyde Milan

1938 1
1950 1
1951 1
1952 1
1953 1
1954 3
1955 6

Felix Millan

1983 1

Bing Miller

1958 1
1960 6

Dots Miller

1948 1

Hack Miller

1937 1

Minnie Minoso

1969	6
1986	89
1987	82
1988	90
1989	59
1990	51
1991	38
1992	69
1993	67
1994	45
1995	66
1996	62
1997	84
1998	76

Johnny Mize
Inducted in 1981

1960	45
1962	14
1964	54
1964 RO	12
1966	81
1967	89
1967 RO	14
1968	103
1969	116
1970	126
1971	157
1972	157
1973	157
1981	Vet. Com.

Rick Monday

1990	2

Don Money

1989	1

Wally Moon

1971	2

Jo-Jo Moore

1950	1

Terry Moore

1950	1
1953	1
1958	12
1960	7
1962	1
1964	14
1967	3
1968	33

Pat Moran

1937	1
1938	1
1939	1
1945	1

Joe Morgan
Inducted in 1990

1990	363

Wally Moses

1958	1
1960	1
1968	4
1969	4
1970	5
1971	7

Johnny Mostil

1956	1
1958	1

Manny Mota

1988	18
1989	9

Hugh Mulcahy

1948	1

Van Mungo

1945	1
1948	1
1958	2
1960	2

Thurman Munson

1981	62
1982	26
1983	18
1984	29
1985	32
1986	35
1987	28
1988	32
1989	31
1990	33
1991	28
1992	32
1993	40
1994	31
1995	30

Bobby Murcer

1989	3

Danny Murphy

1937	1
1945	1

Red Murray

1937	1
1938	1

Stan Musial
Inducted in 1969

1969	317

Buddy Myer

1949	1

Art Nehf

1937	3
1938	5
1939	1
1949	1
1950	2
1951	4
1952	3
1953	4
1954	7
1955	7
1958	13

Graig Nettles

1994	38
1995	28
1996	37
1997	22

Don Newcombe

1966	7
1967	18
1967 RO	2
1968	9
1969	3
1970	5
1971	8
1972	7
1973	11
1974	7
1975	11
1976	21
1977	43
1978	48
1979	52
1980	59

Hal Newhouser
Inducted in 1992

1962	4
1964	26
1964 RO	3
1966	32
1967	62
1967 RO	13
1968	67
1969	82
1970	80
1971	94
1972	92
1973	79
1974	73
1975	155
1992	Vet. Com.

Bobo Newsom

1960	6
1962	3
1964	17
1964 RO	1
1966	25
1967	19
1967 RO	6
1968	22
1969	32
1970	12
1971	17
1972	31
1973	33

Kid Nichols
Inducted in 1949

1936 V	3
1938	3
1939	7
1942	5
1945	5
1946 NOM	1
1949	O/T Com.

Bill Nicholson

1960	1

Joe Niekro

1994	6

Phil Niekro

1993	278
1994	273
1995	286
1996	321
1997	380

Ron Northey

1964	1

Jim Northrup

1981	1

Lefty O'Doul

1948	4
1949	4
1950	9
1951	13
1952	19
1953	11
1956	5
1958	27
1960	45
1962	13

Joe Oeschger

1948	1

Bob O'Farrell

1950	4
1958	3
1960	3

Charlie O'Leary

1953	1
1958	1
1960	1

Tony Oliva

1982	63
1983	75
1984	124
1985	114
1986	154
1987	160
1988	202
1989	135
1990	142
1991	160
1992	175
1993	157
1994	158
1995	149
1996	170

Al Oliver

1991	19

Steve O'Neill

1948	2
1949	6
1950	1
1951	3
1952	10
1953	13
1958	10

Jim O'Rourke
Inducted in 1945

1945	O/T Com.

Claude Osteen

1981	2

Mel Ott
Inducted in 1951

1949	94
1949 RO	128
1950	115
1951	197

Charlie Pabor

1936 V	1

Andy Pafko

1966	2
1967	1

Satchel Paige
Inducted in 1971

1951	1
1971	Neg. Com.

Jim Palmer
Inducted in 1990

1990	411

Milt Pappas

1979	5

Dave Parker

1997	116
1998	83

Larry Parrish

1994	2

Camilo Pascual

1977	3
1978	1

Dode Paskert

1937	1

Monte Pearson

1958	1

Roger Peckinpaugh

1937	3
1938	2
1939	1
1942	2
1949	1
1952	2
1953	2
1954	1
1955	1

Heinie Peitz

1939	1

Herb Pennock
Inducted in 1948

1937	15
1938	37
1939	40
1942	72
1945	45
1946 NOM	41
1946	16
1947	86
1948	94

Hub Perdue

1938	1
1939	1

Tony Perez

1992	215
1993	233
1994	263
1995	259
1996	309
1997	312
1998	321

Cy Perkins

1958	2

Ron Perranoski

1979	6

Gaylord Perry
Inducted in 1991

1989	304
1990	320
1991	342

Jim Perry

1981	6
1983	7

Johnny Pesky

1960	1

Rico Petrocelli

1982	3

Deacon Phillippe

1939	1
1942	1
1945	1
1946 NOM	1

Billy Pierce

1970	5
1971	7
1972	4
1973	4
1974	4

Lip Pike

1936 V	1

Lou Piniella

1990	2

Vada Pinson

1981	18
1982	6
1983	12
1985	19
1986	43
1987	48
1988	67
1989	33
1990	36
1991	30
1992	36
1993	38
1994	46
1995	32
1996	51

Wally Pipp

1958	1

Eddie Plank
Inducted in 1946

1937	23
1938	38
1939	28
1942	63
1945	33
1946 NOM	34
1946	O/T Com.

Johnny Podres

1975	3
1976	1
1977	3

Bob Porterfield

1966	1

Boog Powell

1983	5

Vic Power

1971	2
1972	3

Herb Pruett

1949	1
1950	1
1951	1
1952	1
1953	1

Terry Puhl

1997	1

Jack Quinn

1948	2
1958	9
1960	2

Dan Quisenberry

1996	18

Charlie Radbourn
Inducted in 1939

1936 V	16
1939	O/T Com.

Willie Randolph

1998	5

Vic Raschi

1962	1
1964	8
1968	1
1969	3
1971	2
1972	4
1973	7
1974	3
1975	37

Bugs Raymond

1937	1

Pee Wee Reese
Inducted in 1984

1964	73
1964 RO	47
1966	95
1967	89
1967 RO	16
1968	81
1969	89
1970	97
1971	127
1972	129
1973	126
1974	141
1975	154
1976	186
1977	163
1978	169
1984	Vet. Com.

Pete Reiser

1958	6
1960	8

Jack Remsen

1936 V	1

Jerry Remy

1990	1

Rick Reuschel

1997	2

Jerry Reuss

1996	2

Allie Reynolds

1956	1
1960	24
1962	15
1964	35

(continued)

1964 RO......6
1966......60
1967......77
1967 RO......19
1968......95
1969......98
1970......89
1971......110
1972......105
1973......93
1974......101

Del Rice
1966......2

Jim Rice
1995......137
1996......166
1997......178
1998......203

Sam Rice
Inducted in 1963
1938......1
1948......1
1949......3
1950......1
1951......1
1952......1
1953......3
1954......9
1955......28
1956......45
1958......90
1960......143
1962......81
1963......Vet. Com.

J. R. Richard
1986......7

Hardy Richardson
1936 V......1

Bobby Richardson
1972......8
1973......2
1974......5

Branch Rickey
Inducted in 1967
Executive
1942......3
1945......2
1967......Vet. Com.

Jimmy Ring
1949......1

Claude Ritchey
1945......1

Mickey Rivers
1990......2

Eppa Rixey
Inducted in 1963
1937......1
1938......2
1945......1
1947......2
1948......5
1949......4
1950......6
1951......5
1952......3
1953......3
1954......5
1955......8
1956......27
1958......32
1960......142
1962......49
1963......Vet. Com.

Phil Rizzuto
Inducted in 1994
1956......1
1962......44
1964......45
1964 RO......11

1966......54
1967......71
1967 RO......14
1968......74
1969......78
1970......79
1971......92
1972......103
1973......111
1974......111
1975......117
1976......149
1994......Vet. Com.

Robin Roberts
Inducted in 1976
1973......213
1974......224
1975......263
1976......337

Dave Robertson
1953......1

Brooks Robinson
Inducted in 1983
1983......344

Frank Robinson
Inducted in 1982
1982......370

Jackie Robinson
Inducted in 1962
1962......124

Wilbert Robinson
Inducted in 1945
Manager
1936 V......6
1937......5
1938......17
1939......46
1942......89
1945......81
1945......O/T Com.

Preacher Roe
1960......1
1962......1
1968......2
1970......1
1971......3
1972......2

Red Rolfe
1950......7
1951......6
1952......4
1953......5
1956......3
1958......13
1960......10
1962......1

Eddie Rommel
1948......3
1949......2
1950......1
1951......1
1952......2
1953......1
1958......7
1960......12

Charlie Root
1945......1
1948......3
1949......1
1950......1
1958......6
1960......2

Pete Rose
1992......41
1993......14
1994......19

Edd Roush
Inducted in 1962
1936......2

1937......10
1938......9
1939......8
1942......1
1945......5
1946 NOM......11
1947......25
1948......17
1949......14
1950......16
1951......21
1952......24
1953......32
1954......52
1955......97
1956......91
1958......112
1960......146
1962......Vet. Com.

Schoolboy Rowe
1958......12
1960......3
1968......6
1969......17

Nap Rucker
1936......1
1937......11
1938......12
1939......13
1942......15
1945......10
1946 NOM......13

Dick Rudolph
1937......1
1951......1

Muddy Ruel
1946 NOM......1
1950......4
1951......1
1952......1
1953......8
1954......5
1955......11
1956......16
1958......10
1960......9

Red Ruffing
Inducted in 1967
1948......4
1949......22
1949 RO......4
1950......12
1951......9
1952......10
1953......24
1954......29
1955......60
1956......97
1958......99
1960......86
1962......72
1964......141
1964 RO......184
1966......208
1967......212
1967 RO......266

Amos Rusie
Inducted in 1977
1936 V......12
1937......1
1938......8
1939......6
1942......1
1945......1
1977......Vet. Com.

Bill Russell
1992......3

Babe Ruth
Inducted in 1936
1936......215

Ray Sadecki
1983......2

Johnny Sain
1962......1
1964......3
1968......7
1969......8
1970......9
1971......11
1972......21
1973......47
1974......51
1975......123

Manny Sanguillen
1986......2

Ron Santo
1980......15
1985......53
1986......64
1987......78
1988......108
1989......75
1990......96
1991......116
1992......136
1993......155
1994......150
1995......139
1996......174
1997......186
1998......204

Hank Sauer
1966......4

Al Schacht
1939......1
1948......2
1951......4
1956......1

Germany Schaefer
1942......1
1953......1

Ray Schalk
Inducted in 1955
1936......4
1937......24
1938......45
1939......35
1942......53
1945......33
1946 NOM......36
1947......50
1948......22
1949......24
1949 RO......17
1950......16
1951......37
1952......44
1953......52
1954......54
1955......113
1955......Vet. Com.

Wally Schang
1948......1
1950......1
1956......1
1958......8
1960......11

Mike Schmidt
Inducted in 1995
1995......444

Red Schoendienst
Inducted in 1989
1969......65
1970......97
1971......123
1972......104
1973......96
1974......110
1975......94
1976......129
1977......105
1978......130
1979......159
1980......164

1981......166
1982......135
1983......146
1989......Vet. Com.

Ossie Schreckengost
1937......2
1938......2
1939......2

Frank Schulte
1937......1

Hal Schumacher
1948......1
1955......1
1956......2
1958......1
1960......11
1962......1
1964......10

Everett Scott
1937......2
1938......2
1939......1
1942......1
1947......1
1948......3
1949......3
1950......3
1951......2
1952......4
1953......5
1954......4
1955......8
1956......1

George Scott
1986......1

Jack Scott
1958......1

Mike Scott
1997......2

Tom Seaver
Inducted in 1992
1992......425

George Selkirk
1948......1
1949......1
1950......1
1951......2
1952......1
1953......1

Hank Severeid
1948......1

Joe Sewell
Inducted in 1977
1937......1
1948......1
1954......1
1955......1
1956......3
1958......1
1960......23
1977......Vet. Com.

Luke Sewell
1948......1
1958......3
1960......3
1962......1

Rip Sewell
1958......1
1962......1
1964......1

Cy Seymour
1945......1

Bobby Shantz
1970......7

1971......5
1972......9
1973......5
1974......3

Jim Sheckard
1938......1
1945......1
1946 NOM......1

Bill Sherdel
1948......1
1949......1
1950......1
1951......1
1953......1
1955......1
1956......1
1958......2
1960......2

Urban Shocker
1938......1
1939......1
1948......1
1949......2
1958......4

Chris Short
1979......1

Sonny Siebert
1981......1

Roy Sievers
1971......4
1972......3

Al Simmons
Inducted in 1953
1936......4
1946 NOM......1
1947......6
1948......60
1949......89
1949 RO......76
1950......90
1951......116
1952......141
1953......199

Curt Simmons
1973......5
1974......3

Ted Simmons
1994......17

George Sisler
Inducted in 1939
1936......77
1937......106
1938......179
1939......235

Sibby Sisti
1960......1

Enos Slaughter
Inducted in 1985
1966......100
1967......123
1967 RO......48
1968......129
1969......128
1970......133
1971......165
1972......149
1973......145
1974......145
1975......177
1976......197
1977......222
1978......261
1979......297
1985......Vet. Com.

Roy Smalley
1964......1

Earl Smith

1948 1
1956 1

Reggie Smith

1988 3

Sherry Smith

1948 1

Duke Snider
Inducted in 1980

1970 51
1971 89
1972 84
1973 101
1974 111
1975 129
1976 159
1977 212
1978 254
1979 308
1980 333

Billy Southworth

1945 1
1946 NOM.............1
1949 7
1950 1
1951 4
1952 1
1953 2
1958 18

Warren Spahn
Inducted in 1973

1973 316

Al Spalding
Inducted in 1939
Pioneer

1936 V 4
1939 .... O/T Com.

Tully Sparks

1946 NOM.............1

Tris Speaker
Inducted in 1937

1936 133
1937 165

Chris Speier

1995 1

Jake Stahl

1938 1
1939 1

Eddie Stanky

1960 3

Mickey Stanley

1984 2

Willie Stargell
Inducted in 1988

1988 352

Rusty Staub

1991 28
1992 26
1993 32
1994 36
1995 23
1996 24
1997 18

Harry Steinfeldt

1937 1
1939 1
1942 1

Casey Stengel
Inducted in 1966
Manager

1938 2
1939 6

1945 2
1948 1
1949 3
1950 3
1951 8
1952 27
1953 61
1966 .... Vet. Com.

Riggs Stephenson

1956 2
1958 1
1960 4
1962 1

Mel Stottlemyre

1980 3

Harry Stovey

1936 V 6

Gabby Street

1937 1
1938 1
1953 1

Gus Suhr

1956 1
1958 1
1960 1

Clyde Sukeforth

1958 1

Billy Sullivan

1937 1
1946 NOM.............1

Jim Sundberg

1995 1

Bruce Sutter

1994 109
1995 137
1996 137
1997 130
1998 147

Don Sutton

1994 259
1995 264
1996 300
1997 346
1998 386

Bill Sweeney

1945 1

Jess Tannehill

1946 NOM.............1

Birdie Tebbetts

1958 8
1960 1

Kent Tekulve

1995 6

Garry Templeton

1997 2

Gene Tenace

1989 1

Fred Tenney

1936 V 1
1937 5
1938 8
1939 3
1942 1
1946 NOM.............1

Bill Terry
Inducted in 1954

1936 9
1938 7
1939 16
1942 36

1945 32
1946 NOM.......... 31
1947 46
1948 52
1949 81
1949 RO........... 48
1950 105
1951 148
1952 155
1953 191
1954 195

Tommy Thevenow

1950 2

Ira Thomas

1938 1

Sam Thompson
Inducted in 1974

1974 .... Vet. Com.

Bobby Thomson

1966 12
1967 10
1967 RO............1
1968 13
1969 6
1970 4
1971 4
1972 10
1973 3
1974 6
1975 10
1976 9
1977 10
1978 5
1979 11

Andre Thornton

1993 2

Luis Tiant

1988 132
1989 47
1990 42
1991 32
1992 50
1993 62
1994 42
1995 45
1996 64
1997 53
1998 62

Joe Tinker
Inducted in 1946

1937 15
1938 16
1939 12
1942 36
1945 49
1946 NOM.......... 55
1946 45
1946 .... O/T Com.

Jim Tobin

1956 2

Fred Toney

1949 1

Earl Torgeson

1967 2

Joe Torre

1983 20
1984 45
1985 44
1986 60
1987 47
1988 60
1989 40
1990 55
1991 41
1992 62
1993 63
1994 53
1995 50
1996 50
1997 105

Mike Torrez

1990 1

Pie Traynor
Inducted in 1948

1936 16
1938 3
1939 10
1942 45
1945 81
1946 NOM.......... 65
1946 53
1947 119
1948 93

Dizzy Trout

1964 1

Virgil Trucks

1964 4

John Tudor

1996 2

Jim Turner

1956 1

Terry Turner

1947 2

George Uhle

1956 1
1958 4
1960 4

Ellis Valentine

1991 1

Elmer Valo

1967 2

Dazzy Vance
Inducted in 1955

1936 1
1937 10
1938 10
1939 15
1942 37
1945 18
1946 NOM.......... 31
1947 50
1948 23
1949 33
1949 RO........... 15
1950 52
1951 70
1952 105
1953 150
1954 158
1955 205

Johnny Vander Meer

1945 1
1956 3
1958 35
1960 31
1962 5
1964 51
1964 RO........... 20
1966 72
1967 87
1967 RO........... 35
1968 79
1969 95
1970 88
1971 98

George Van Haltren

1936 V 1

Arky Vaughan
Inducted in 1985

1953 1
1954 2
1955 4
1956 9
1958 6
1960 10
1962 6
1964 17

1964 RO..............6
1966 36
1967 46
1967 RO........... 19
1968 82
1985 .... Vet. Com.

Bobby Veach

1937 1

Bill Veeck
Inducted in 1991
Executive

1991 .... Vet. Com.

Mickey Vernon

1966 20
1967 14
1967 RO.............2
1968 22
1969 21
1970 10
1971 12
1972 12
1973 23
1974 27
1975 22
1976 52
1977 52
1978 66
1979 88
1980 96

Bill Virdon

1974 3
1975 1

Rube Waddell
Inducted in 1946

1936 33
1937 67
1938 148
1939 179
1942 126
1945 154
1946 NOM......... 122
1946 87
1946 .... O/T Com.

Honus Wagner
Inducted in 1936

1936 V 5
1936 215

Rube Walberg

1958 1
1960 1

Dixie Walker

1962 1
1964 6
1968 6
1969 9

Harry Walker

1958 1

Bobby Wallace
Inducted in 1953

1936 V 1
1937 1
1938 7
1939 5
1942 2
1945 3
1953 .... Vet. Com.

Ed Walsh
Inducted in 1946

1936 20
1937 56
1938 110
1939 132
1942 113
1945 137
1946 NOM......... 115
1946 106
1946 .... O/T Com.

Bucky Walters

1950 4

1952 3
1953 10
1956 5
1958 33
1960 19
1962 5
1964 35
1964 RO..............8
1966 56
1967 65
1967 RO........... 24
1968 67
1969 20
1970 29

Bill Wambsganss

1942 1
1950 1
1953 1
1954 4
1955 5
1956 1

Lloyd Waner
Inducted in 1967

1949 3
1950 1
1951 1
1952 2
1956 18
1958 39
1960 22
1962 5
1964 47
1964 RO.......... 12
1967 .... Vet. Com.

Paul Waner
Inducted in 1952

1946 NOM.............4
1948 51
1949 73
1949 RO........... 63
1950 95
1951 162
1952 195

Monte Ward
Inducted in 1964

1936 V 3
1964 .... Vet. Com.

Lon Warneke

1949 2
1958 2
1960 4
1962 2
1964 13

Bob Watson

1990 3

Earl Weaver
Inducted in 1996

1996 .... Vet. Com.

George Weiss
Inducted in 1971
Executive

1971 .... Vet. Com.

Mickey Welch
Inducted in 1973

1973 .... Vet. Com.

Willie Wells
Inducted in 1973

1973 .... Vet. Com.

Billy Werber

1949 1
1950 1
1952 1
1958 3

Vic Wertz

1970 2
1971 2
1972 4
1973 2
1974 2

1975 5
1976 5
1977 4
1978 4

Sam West
1948 1

Wes Westrum
1964 2

Zach Wheat
Inducted in 1959
1937 5
1938 7
1939 4
1942 3
1945 2
1946 NOM...........6
1947 37
1948 15
1949 15
1950 17
1951 19
1952 30
1953 32
1954 33
1955 51
1956 26
1959 ....Vet. Com.

Deacon White
1936 V 1

Frank White
1996 18

Will White
1975 7
1976 7
1977 4

Burgess Whitehead
1956 1

Earl Whitehill
1956 1
1958 2
1960 3

Hoyt Wilhelm
Inducted in 1985
1978 158
1979 168
1980 209
1981 238
1982 236
1983 243
1984 290
1985 331

Billy Williams
Inducted in 1987
1982 97
1983 153
1984 202
1985 252
1986 315
1987 354

Fred Williams
1938 1
1945 1
1948 1
1949 2
1950 9
1951 7
1952 4
1953 4
1954 4
1955 3
1956 11
1958 6
1960 11

Ken Williams
1956 1
1958 1

Ted Williams
Inducted in 1966
1966 282

Ned Williamson
1936 V 2

Vic Willis
Inducted in 1995
1995 ....Vet. Com.

Maury Wills
1978 115
1979 166
1980 146
1981 163
1982 91
1983 77
1984 104
1985 93
1986 124
1987 113
1988 127
1989 95
1990 95
1991 61
1992 110

Jimmie Wilson
1948 8
1949 6
1950 4
1951 2
1952 7
1953 10
1954 8
1955 13
1956 17
1958 3
1960 6
1962 4

Jim Wilson
1964 2

Hack Wilson
Inducted in 1979
1937 1
1939 1
1942 1
1948 2
1949 24
1949 RO 12
1950 16
1951 21
1952 21
1953 43
1954 48
1955 81
1956 74
1958 94
1960 72
1962 39
1979 ....Vet. Com.

Whitey Witt
1949 1

Joe Wood
1937 13
1938 6
1939 2
1942 1
1946 NOM...........5
1947 29
1948 5
1950 1
1951 5

Wilbur Wood
1984 14
1985 16
1986 23
1987 26
1988 30
1989 14

Glenn Wright
1948 2

1949 1
1950 2
1951 1
1952 1
1953 3
1954 1
1955 4
1956 3
1958 8
1960 18
1962 1

George Wright
Inducted in 1937
Pioneer
1936 V 6
1937 ....Cen. Com.

Harry Wright
Inducted in 1953
Pioneer
1953 ....Vet. Com.

Whit Wyatt
1958 1

Early Wynn
Inducted in 1972
1969 95
1970 140
1971 240
1972 301

Tom Yawkey
Inducted in 1980
Executive
1980 ....Vet. Com.

Carl Yastrzemski
Inducted in 1989
1989 423

Steve Yeager
1992 2

Steve Yerkes
1945 1

Rudy York
1962 1
1964 10

Cy Young
Inducted in 1937
1936 V 32
1936 111
1937 153

Pep Young
1958 1

Ross Youngs
Inducted in 1972
1936 10
1937 16
1938 40
1939 34
1942 44
1945 22
1946 NOM...........25
1947 36
1948 19
1949 20
1949 RO 11
1950 17
1951 34
1952 34
1953 31
1954 34
1955 48
1956 19
1972 ....Vet. Com.

Tom Zachary
1958 1
1960 1

Chief Zimmer
1938 1

Hall of Fame Balloting: Top 10 Candidates in Each Election

1936 Veterans
Needed to Elect: 59

Cap Anson 40
Buck Ewing.......... 40
Willie Keeler 33
Cy Young 32
Ed Delahanty 22
John McGraw 17
Herman Long 16
Charlie Radbourn ... 16
Mike Kelly 15
Amos Rusie 12

1936
Needed to Elect: 170

Ty Cobb 222
Babe Ruth 215
Honus Wagner 215
Christy Mathewson . 205
Walter Johnson 189
Nap Lajoie 146
Tris Speaker 133
Cy Young 111
Rogers Hornsby ... 105
Mickey Cochrane 80

1937
Needed to Elect: 151

Nap Lajoie 168
Tris Speaker 165
Cy Young 153
Pete Alexander 125
Eddie Collins 115
Willie Keeler 115
George Sisler 106
Ed Delahanty 70
Rube Waddell 67

Jimmy Collins 66

1938
Needed to Elect: 197

Pete Alexander 212
George Sisler 179
Willie Keeler 177
Eddie Collins 175
Rube Waddell 148
Frank Chance 133
Ed Delahanty 132
Ed Walsh 110
Johnny Evers 91
Jimmy Collins 79

1939
Needed to Elect: 206

George Sisler 235
Eddie Collins 213
Willie Keeler 207
Rube Waddell 179
Rogers Hornsby ... 176
Frank Chance 158
Ed Delahanty 145
Ed Walsh 132
Johnny Evers 107
Miller Huggins 97

1942
Needed to Elect: 175

Rogers Hornsby ... 182
Frank Chance 136
Rube Waddell 126
Ed Walsh 113
Miller Huggins 111
Ed Delahanty 104
Johnny Evers 91

Wilbert Robinson 89
Mickey Cochrane 88
Frankie Frisch 84

1945
Needed to Elect: 186

Frank Chance 179
Rube Waddell 154
Ed Walsh 137
Johnny Evers 134
Roger Bresnahan ... 133
Miller Huggins 133
Mickey Cochrane ... 125
Jimmy Collins 121
Ed Delahanty 111
Clark Griffith 108

1946 Nominating Total Voting: 202

Frank Chance 144
Johnny Evers 130
Miller Huggins 129
Rube Waddell 122
Ed Walsh 115
Frankie Frisch 104
Carl Hubbell 101
Mickey Cochrane 80
Clark Griffith 73
Lefty Grove 71

1946
Needed to Elect: 198

Frank Chance 150
Johnny Evers 110
Miller Huggins 106
Ed Walsh 106
Rube Waddell 87

Clark Griffith 82
Carl Hubbell 75
Frankie Frisch 67
Mickey Cochrane 65
Lefty Grove 61

1947
Needed to Elect: 121

Carl Hubbell 140
Frankie Frisch 136
Mickey Cochrane ... 128
Lefty Grove 123
Pie Traynor 119
Charlie Gehringer ... 105
Rabbit Maranville ... 91
Dizzy Dean 88
Herb Pennock 86
Chief Bender 72

1948
Needed to Elect: 91

Herb Pennock 94
Pie Traynor 93
Al Simmons 60
Charlie Gehringer ... 52
Bill Terry 52
Paul Waner 51
Jimmie Foxx 50
Dizzy Dean 40
Harry Heilmann 40
Bill Dickey 39

1949
Needed to Elect: 115

Charlie Gehringer ... 102
Mel Ott 94
Al Simmons 89

Dizzy Dean 88
Jimmie Foxx......... 85
Bill Terry 81
Paul Waner 73
Hank Greenberg 67
Bill Dickey 65
Harry Heilmann 59

1949 Run Off
Needed to Elect: 141
One Player Maximum

Charlie Gehringer ... 159
Mel Ott 128
Jimmie Foxx......... 89
Dizzy Dean 81
Al Simmons 76
Paul Waner 63
Harry Heilmann 52
Bill Terry 48
Hank Greenberg 44
Bill Dickey 39
Rabbit Maranville ... 39

1950
Needed to Elect: 126

Mel Ott 115
Bill Terry 105
Jimmie Foxx......... 103
Paul Waner 95
Al Simmons 90
Harry Heilmann 87
Dizzy Dean 85
Bill Dickey 78
Rabbit Maranville ... 66
Hank Greenberg 64

1951
Needed to Elect: 170

Mel Ott 197
Jimmie Foxx........ 179
Paul Waner 162
Harry Heilmann 153
Bill Terry 148
Dizzy Dean 145
Bill Dickey 118
Al Simmons 116
Rabbit Maranville ... 110
Ted Lyons 71

1952
Needed to Elect: 176

Harry Heilmann 203
Paul Waner 195
Bill Terry 155
Dizzy Dean 152
Al Simmons 141
Bill Dickey 139
Rabbit Maranville ... 133
Dazzy Vance 105
Ted Lyons 101
Gabby Hartnett 77

1953
Needed to Elect: 198

Dizzy Dean 209
Al Simmons 199
Bill Terry 191
Bill Dickey 179
Rabbit Maranville ... 164
Dazzy Vance 150
Ted Lyons 139
Joe DiMaggio 117
Chief Bender 104

Gabby Hartnett 104

1954
Needed to Elect: 189

Rabbit Maranville ... 209
Bill Dickey 202
Bill Terry 195
Joe DiMaggio 175
Ted Lyons 170
Dazzy Vance 158
Gabby Hartnett 151
Hank Greenberg 97
Joe Cronin 85
Max Carey 55

1955
Needed to Elect: 189

Joe DiMaggio 223
Ted Lyons 217
Dazzy Vance 205
Gabby Hartnett 195
Hank Greenberg 157
Joe Cronin 135
Max Carey 119
Ray Schalk 113
Edd Roush 97
Hank Gowdy 90

1956
Needed to Elect: 145

Hank Greenberg 164
Joe Cronin 152
Red Ruffing 97
Edd Roush 91
Lefty Gomez 89
Hack Wilson 74
Max Carey 65
Tony Lazzeri 64
Kiki Cuyler 55
Hank Gowdy 49

1958
Needed to Elect: 200

Max Carey 136
Edd Roush 112
Red Ruffing 99
Hack Wilson 94
Kiki Cuyler 90
Sam Rice 90
Tony Lazzeri 80
Luke Appling 77
Lefty Gomez 76
Burleigh Grimes 71

1960
Needed to Elect: 202

Edd Roush 146
Sam Rice 143
Eppa Rixey 142
Burleigh Grimes 92
Jim Bottomley 89
Red Ruffing 86
Red Faber 83
Luke Appling 72
Kiki Cuyler 72
Hack Wilson 72

1962
Needed to Elect: 120

Bob Feller 150
Jackie Robinson 124
Sam Rice 81
Red Ruffing 72
Eppa Rixey 49
Luke Appling 48
Phil Rizzuto 44
Burleigh Grimes 43
Hack Wilson 39
Ducky Medwick 34

1964
Needed to Elect: 151

Luke Appling 142
Red Ruffing 141
Roy Campanella 115
Ducky Medwick 108
Pee Wee Reese 73
Lou Boudreau 68
Al Lopez 57
Chuck Klein 56
Johnny Mize 54
Mel Harder 51
Johnny Vander Meer . 51

1964 Run Off
Needed to Elect: 170
One Player Maximum

Luke Appling 189
Red Ruffing 184
Roy Campanella 138
Ducky Medwick 130
Pee Wee Reese 47
Lou Boudreau 43
Al Lopez 34
Johnny Vander Meer . 20
Chuck Klein 18
Marty Marion 17

1966
Needed to Elect: 227

Ted Williams 282
Red Ruffing 208
Roy Campanella 197
Ducky Medwick 187
Lou Boudreau 115
Al Lopez 109
Enos Slaughter 100
Pee Wee Reese 95
Marty Marion 86
Johnny Mize 81

1967
Needed to Elect: 219

Ducky Medwick 212
Red Ruffing 212
Roy Campanella 204
Lou Boudreau 143
Ralph Kiner 124
Enos Slaughter 123
Al Lopez 114
Marty Marion 90
Johnny Mize 89
Pee Wee Reese 89

1967 Run Off
Needed to Elect: 230
One Player Maximum

Red Ruffing 266
Ducky Medwick 248
Roy Campanella 170
Lou Boudreau 68
Al Lopez 50
Enos Slaughter 48
Ralph Kiner 41
Johnny Vander Meer . 35
Ernie Lombardi 25
Bucky Walters 24

1968
Needed to Elect: 213

Ducky Medwick 240
Roy Campanella 205
Lou Boudreau 146
Enos Slaughter 129
Ralph Kiner 118
Johnny Mize 103
Allie Reynolds 95
Marty Marion 89
Arky Vaughan 82

Pee Wee Reese 81

1969
Needed to Elect: 255

Stan Musial 317
Roy Campanella 270
Lou Boudreau 218
Ralph Kiner 137
Enos Slaughter 128
Johnny Mize 116
Marty Marion 112
Allie Reynolds 98
Joe Gordon 97
Johnny Vander Meer . 95
Early Wynn 95

1970
Needed to Elect: 225

Lou Boudreau 232
Ralph Kiner 167
Gil Hodges 145
Early Wynn 140
Enos Slaughter 133
Johnny Mize 126
Marty Marion 120
Pee Wee Reese 97
Red Schoendienst ... 97
George Kell 90

1971
Needed to Elect: 270

Yogi Berra 242
Early Wynn 240
Ralph Kiner 212
Gil Hodges 180
Enos Slaughter 165
Johnny Mize 157
Pee Wee Reese 127
Marty Marion 123
Red Schoendienst .. 123
Allie Reynolds 110

1972
Needed to Elect: 297

Sandy Koufax 344
Yogi Berra 339
Early Wynn 301
Ralph Kiner 235
Gil Hodges 161
Johnny Mize 157
Enos Slaughter 149
Pee Wee Reese 129
Marty Marion 120
Bob Lemon 117

1973
Needed to Elect: 285

Warren Spahn 316
Whitey Ford 255
Ralph Kiner 235
Gil Hodges 218
Robin Roberts 213
Bob Lemon 177
Johnny Mize 157
Enos Slaughter 145
Marty Marion 127
Pee Wee Reese 126

1974
Needed to Elect: 274

Mickey Mantle 322
Whitey Ford 284
Robin Roberts 224
Ralph Kiner 215
Gil Hodges 198
Bob Lemon 190
Enos Slaughter 145
Pee Wee Reese 141
Eddie Mathews 118

Phil Rizzuto 111
Duke Snider 111

1975
Needed to Elect: 272

Ralph Kiner 273
Robin Roberts 263
Bob Lemon 233
Gil Hodges 188
Enos Slaughter 177
Hal Newhouser 155
Pee Wee Reese 154
Eddie Mathews 148
Phil Cavaretta 129
Duke Snider 129

1976
Needed to Elect: 291

Robin Roberts 337
Bob Lemon 305
Gil Hodges 233
Enos Slaughter 197
Eddie Mathews 189
Pee Wee Reese 186
Nellie Fox 174
Duke Snider 159
Phil Rizzuto 149
George Kell 129
Red Schoendienst .. 129

1977
Needed to Elect: 288

Ernie Banks 321
Eddie Mathews 239
Gil Hodges 224
Enos Slaughter 222
Duke Snider 212
Don Drysdale 197
Pee Wee Reese 163
Nellie Fox 152
Jim Bunning 146
George Kell 141

1978
Needed to Elect: 285

Eddie Mathews 301
Enos Slaughter 261
Duke Snider 254
Gil Hodges 226
Don Drysdale 219
Jim Bunning 181
Pee Wee Reese 169
Richie Ashburn 158
Hoyt Wilhelm 158
Nellie Fox 149

1979
Needed to Elect: 324

Willie Mays 409
Duke Snider 308
Enos Slaughter 297
Gil Hodges 242
Don Drysdale 233
Nellie Fox 174
Hoyt Wilhelm 168
Maury Wills 166
Red Schoendienst .. 159
Jim Bunning 147

1980
Needed to Elect: 289

Al Kaline 340
Duke Snider 333
Don Drysdale 238
Gil Hodges 230
Hoyt Wilhelm 209
Jim Bunning 177
Red Schoendienst . 164
Nellie Fox 161
Maury Wills 146

Richie Ashburn 134

1981
Needed to Elect: 301

Bob Gibson 337
Don Drysdale 243
Gil Hodges 241
Harmon Killebrew ... 239
Hoyt Wilhelm 238
Juan Marichal 233
Nellie Fox 168
Red Schoendienst .. 166
Jim Bunning 164
Maury Wills 163

1982
Needed to Elect: 312

Hank Aaron 406
Frank Robinson 370
Juan Marichal 305
Harmon Killebrew ... 246
Hoyt Wilhelm 236
Don Drysdale 233
Gil Hodges 205
Luis Aparicio 174
Jim Bunning 138
Red Schoendienst .. 135

1983
Needed to Elect: 281

Brooks Robinson ... 344
Juan Marichal 313
Harmon Killebrew ... 269
Luis Aparicio 252
Hoyt Wilhelm 243
Don Drysdale 242
Gil Hodges 237
Nellie Fox 173
Billy Williams 153
Red Schoendienst .. 146

1984
Needed to Elect: 303

Luis Aparicio 341
Harmon Killebrew ... 335
Don Drysdale 316
Hoyt Wilhelm 290
Nellie Fox 246
Billy Williams 202
Jim Bunning 201
Orlando Cepeda 124
Tony Oliva 124
Roger Maris 107

1985
Needed to Elect: 297

Hoyt Wilhelm 331
Lou Brock 315
Nellie Fox 295
Billy Williams 252
Jim Bunning 214
Catfish Hunter 212
Roger Maris 128
Harvey Kuenn 125
Orlando Cepeda 114
Tony Oliva 114

1986
Needed to Elect: 319

Willie McCovey 346
Billy Williams 315
Catfish Hunter 289
Jim Bunning 279
Roger Maris 177
Tony Oliva 154
Orlando Cepeda ... 152
Harvey Kuenn 144
Maury Wills 124
Bill Mazeroski 100

1987
Needed to Elect: 310

Billy Williams 354
Catfish Hunter 315
Jim Bunning 289
Orlando Cepeda ... 179
Roger Maris 176
Tony Oliva 160
Harvey Kuenn 144
Bill Mazeroski 125
Maury Wills 113
Ken Boyer 96
Lew Burdette 96

1988
Needed to Elect: 321

Willie Stargell 352
Jim Bunning 317
Tony Oliva 202
Orlando Cepeda ... 199
Roger Maris 184
Harvey Kuenn 168
Bill Mazeroski 143
Luis Tiant 132
Maury Wills 127
Ken Boyer 109
Mickey Lolich 109

1989
Needed to Elect: 336

Johnny Bench 431
Carl Yastrzemski 423
Gaylord Perry 304
Jim Bunning 283
Fergie Jenkins 234
Orlando Cepeda ... 176
Tony Oliva 135
Bill Mazeroski 134
Harvey Kuenn 115
Maury Wills 95

1990
Needed to Elect: 333

Jim Palmer 411
Joe Morgan 363
Gaylord Perry 320
Fergie Jenkins 296
Jim Bunning 257
Orlando Cepeda ... 211
Tony Oliva 142
Bill Mazeroski 131
Harvey Kuenn 107
Ron Santo 96

1991
Needed to Elect: 333

Rod Carew 401
Gaylord Perry 342
Fergie Jenkins 334
Rollie Fingers 291
Jim Bunning 282
Orlando Cepeda 192
Tony Oliva 160
Bill Mazeroski 142
Ron Santo 116
Harvey Kuenn 100

1992
Needed to Elect: 323

Tom Seaver 425
Rollie Fingers 349
Orlando Cepeda ... 246
Tony Perez 215
Bill Mazeroski 182
Tony Oliva 175
Ron Santo 136
Jim Kaat 114
Maury Wills 110
Ken Boyer 71

1993
Needed to Elect: 318

Reggie Jackson	396
Phil Niekro	278
Orlando Cepeda	252
Tony Perez	233
Steve Garvey	176
Tony Oliva	157
Ron Santo	155
Jim Kaat	125
Dick Allen	70
Ken Boyer	69

1994
Needed to Elect: 342

Steve Carlton	436
Orlando Cepeda	335
Phil Niekro	273
Tony Perez	263
Don Sutton	259
Steve Garvey	166
Tony Oliva	158
Ron Santo	150
Bruce Sutter	109
Jim Kaat	98

1995
Needed to Elect: 345

Mike Schmidt	444
Phil Niekro	286
Don Sutton	264
Tony Perez	259
Steve Garvey	196
Tony Oliva	149
Ron Santo	139
Jim Rice	137
Bruce Sutter	137
Jim Kaat	100

1996
Needed to Elect: 353

Phil Niekro	321
Tony Perez	309
Don Sutton	300
Steve Garvey	175
Ron Santo	174
Tony Oliva	170
Jim Rice	166
Bruce Sutter	137
Tommy John	102
Jim Kaat	91

1997
Needed to Elect: 355

Phil Niekro	380
Don Sutton	346
Tony Perez	312
Ron Santo	186
Jim Rice	178
Steve Garvey	167
Bruce Sutter	130
Jim Kaat	107
Joe Torre	105
Tommy John	97

1998
Needed to Elect: 355

Don Sutton	386
Tony Perez	321
Ron Santo	204
Jim Rice	203
Gary Carter	200
Steve Garvey	195
Bruce Sutter	147
Tommy John	129
Jim Kaat	129
Dave Parker	116

CHAPTER 11

The All-Star Game

Frederick Ivor-Campbell

Although the tradition of All-Star Games in baseball dates back to an 1858 series between teams of stars from Brooklyn and New York (they were called "picked nines" in those days), the current All-Star series began when Arch Ward, sports editor of the *Chicago Tribune*, persuaded hesitant league owners to go along with his proposal for a game between stars from the American League and National League, to be played in Chicago during that city's Century of Progress Exposition in 1933.

All-Star managers (who, except for the first game, have been the pilots of the previous year's pennant winners) shared with fans the selection of players for the first two games. From 1935 through 1946 the manager selected his whole squad. Since 1947, he has chosen his pitchers and all other players except the eight members of the starting lineup. The fans chose the starters from 1947 to 1957; after an incident of ballot-box stuffing by Cincinnati partisans in 1957, the major league players, coaches, and managers made the choice from 1958 to 1969; in 1970 the selection of starting lineups was returned to the fans.

The American League dominated the early years of the series, winning the first three games, and extending their winning margin to eight games (12–4) by 1949. The National League cut the lead in half with four straight wins, and by 1964 had drawn even in the series as the two leagues stood at 17 wins apiece, plus one tie. From 1965 through 1985 the National Leaguers continued their drive, winning 19 All-Star Games while losing only two, to build a commanding 36–19 lead in the series. In recent years, though, the American Leaguers have started to come back, winning in 1993 their seventh game in eight years, and their sixth in a row. The National League won in 1994, though it took extra innings to break the American League streak. The National League won the next two All-Star Games, but the American League won in 1997 and again in 1998 to cut the National's overall advantage to 40–28.

GAME 1
Comiskey Park, Chicago
July 6, 1933
AL, 4–2

```
NL   000 002 000    2 8 0
AL   012 001 00X    4 9 1
```
Pitchers: HALLAHAN, Warneke (3), Hubbell (7) vs GOMEZ, Crowder (4), Grove (7)
Home Runs: Ruth-A, Frisch-N
Attendance: 49,200

Baseball's two grand old managers—Connie Mack and John McGraw—were chosen to lead the American and National League squads in the first All-Star Game, and American League starting pitcher Lefty Gomez of the Yankees took home honors both as the first All-Star winning pitcher and as the first player to drive in an All-Star run (singling in Jimmie Dykes in the second inning). But it was another "grand old man"—Babe Ruth—who made the game's headlines. At 38, in his next-to-last season as a Yankee, he lined a two-run homer in the third to make the score 3–0. In right field he robbed Chick Hafey of a hit with a remarkable running catch of Hafey's line drive in the eighth inning.

Frank Frisch homered for the Nationals, following up Pepper Martin's RBI with a solo shot in the National League's two-run sixth. But the American stars countered with an insurance run in the bottom of the sixth, as Earl Averill singled in Joe Cronin to end the scoring. Carl Hubbell for the Nationals and Lefty Grove for the Americans blanked the opposition through the final innings.

GAME 2
Polo Grounds, New York
July 10, 1934
AL, 9–7

```
AL   000 261 000    9 14 1
NL   103 030 000    7  8 1
```
Pitchers: Gomez, Ruffing (4), HARDER (5) vs Hubbell, Warneke (4), MUNGO (5), J.Dean (6), Frankhouse (9)
Home Runs: Frisch-N, Medwick-N
Attendance: 48,363

This was the game in which Carl Hubbell struck out Babe Ruth, Lou Gehrig, Jimmie Foxx, Al Simmons, and Joe Cronin in order in the first two innings. Hubbell also walked two and gave up two hits in his three innings of work, but allowed no run to score as his Nationals took a 4–0 lead on homers by Frank Frisch in the first and Joe Medwick (for three runs) in the third off American starter (and first-game winner) Lefty Gomez.

But with Hubbell gone, the Americans pounced on Lon Warneke and Van Lingle Mungo for four runs each in the fourth and fifth innings. The Nationals battled back for three off Red Ruffing in their half of the fifth, to come within a run of tying the game. But Mel Harder relieved Ruffing with none out and put out the fire, one-hitting the National stars over the final five innings. The Americans picked up an insurance run in the sixth off Dizzy Dean before Dean and Fred Frankhouse shut them down, too, through the final three frames.

GAME 3
Municipal Stadium, Cleveland
July 8, 1935
AL, 4–1

```
NL   000 100 000    1 4 1
AL   210 010 00X    4 8 0
```
Pitchers: WALKER, Schumacher (3), Derringer (7), J.Dean (8) vs GOMEZ, Harder (7)
Home Runs: Foxx-A
Attendance: 69,812

Lefty Gomez started his third All-Star Game, and pitched a record six innings to pick up his second All-Star win. For three innings he shut out the Nationals as the Americans built a lead behind him on Jimmie Foxx's two-run homer in the first, and Rollie Hemsley's triple and Joe Cronin's run-scoring fly in the second.

The National Leaguers tried to catch up in the fourth, when they put together two of their three hits off Gomez—a double by Arky Vaughan and a single by Bill Terry—and scored a run. But an inning later Foxx nullified the National run, singling Joe Vosmik home for his third RBI.

Gomez blanked the National stars through two more innings before yielding to Mel Harder, who came in to close his second All-Star Game. Harder had created an All-Star record the previous year with his five consecutive scoreless innings pitched, and extended the record to eight, with three more shutout innings to end the game.

GAME 4
Braves Field, Boston
July 7, 1936
NL, 4–3

```
AL   000 000 300    3 7 1
NL   020 020 00X    4 9 0
```
Pitchers: GROVE, Rowe (4), Harder (7) vs J.DEAN, Hubbell (4), C.Davis (7), Warneke (7)
Home Runs: Galan-N, Gehrig-A
Attendance: 25,534

The National League, which had not yet won an All-Star Game, scored first in the second when Gabby Hartnett tripled in a run off Lefty Grove—rookie Joe DiMaggio missing his try for a shoe-top catch of Hartnett's drive to right field. Pinky Whitney then singled in Hartnett. Augie Galan homered off Schoolboy Rowe (and the right field foul pole) in the fifth, and DiMaggio's bobble of Billy Herman's single a batter later put Herman in position to score an unearned fourth run, on Joe Medwick's single, that proved to be the margin of victory.

The Americans, shut out through six by Dizzy Dean and Carl Hubbell, nearly tied the game in the seventh off Curt Davis as Lou Gehrig homered and Luke Appling singled in two more. But Lon Warneke took over and, after loading the bases with a walk, escaped disaster as shortstop Leo Durocher snared DiMaggio's vicious line drive to his right for the third out. Warneke shut the Americans out over the final two innings to preserve the one-run lead and the National League's first All-Star win.

GAME 5
Griffith Stadium, Washington
July 7, 1937
AL, 8–3

```
NL   000 111 000    3 13 0
AL   002 312 00X    8 13 2
```

Pitchers: J.DEAN, Hubbell (4), Blanton (4), Grissom (5), Mungo (6), Walters (8) vs GOMEZ, Bridges (4), Harder (7)
Home Runs: Gehrig-A
Attendance: 31,391

President Franklin Roosevelt attended the game and saw the AL capture its fourth win in five tries. Lou Gehrig homered and doubled to drive in half the American League's eight runs in an easy American win. Lefty Gomez started his fourth All-Star Game in five years and earned his third win. And AL reliever Mel Harder pitched the final innings for the fourth All-Star Game in a row, pushing his record for consecutive All-Star shutout innings to 13. Yet the game is remembered not for any of these things, but for Earl Averill's line drive in the third inning which fractured Dizzy Dean's toe and led to the premature end of his spectacular career. (Dean recovered from the broken toe, but tried to resume his pitching too soon. In favoring the toe, he changed his delivery and irreparably injured his pitching arm.)

The Americans began their scoring when Gehrig, who preceded Averill in the batting order, homered off Dean in the third, with one aboard. They added to their score in each of the next three innings, so that although the Nationals countered with single runs in the three middle innings, they only fell farther behind.

GAME 6
Crosley Field, Cincinnati
July 6, 1938
NL, 4–1

```
AL   000 000 001    1 7 4
NL   100 100 20X    4 8 0
```

Pitchers: GOMEZ, Allen (4), Grove (7) vs VANDER MEER, Lee (4), Brown (7)
Attendance: 27,607

For the fifth (and final) time, Lefty Gomez started for the American League, and although he gave up only two hits and no earned runs in his three innings, he was saddled with the loss when an error by shortstop Joe Cronin paved the way for a National League run in the first.

The Nationals scored their only earned run in the fourth when Mel Ott tripled and Ernie Lombardi singled him home. But in the seventh they recorded two more unearned runs when Leo Durocher bunted to move Frank McCormick to second. Both McCormick and Durocher scored as third baseman Jimmie Foxx threw wildly to first and right fielder Joe DiMaggio (who chased the ball down) missed home plate with his throw.

In the ninth DiMaggio singled and Cronin doubled him home in partial atonement for their errors. But as Johnny Vander Meer and "Big Bill" Lee had each blanked the American stars on one hit in their three-inning stints, and some fine outfield catches had kept them from scoring more than this one run off Mace Brown, the Americans' errors cost them the game.

GAME 7
Yankee Stadium, New York
July 11, 1939
AL, 3–1

```
NL   001 000 000    1 7 1
AL   000 210 00X    3 6 1
```

Pitchers: Derringer, LEE (4), Fette (7) vs Ruffing, BRIDGES (4), Feller (6)
Home Runs: J.DiMaggio-A
Attendance: 62,892

Six Yankees started for the American League, and one of them—Joe DiMaggio—hit the game's only home run. But it was a young Cleveland pitcher—28-year-old Bob Feller, playing in his first All-Star Game—who turned in the most memorable performance.

The Nationals scored first, with a run in the third on three hits off the American League starter, Red Ruffing. But the Americans came back with two runs in the fourth on a walk, two singles, and a bobbled grounder by shortstop Arky Vaughan. DiMaggio hit his insurance homer an inning later.

In the top of the sixth, after two singles and an error had loaded the bases with National stars, with only one out, Feller replaced Tommy Bridges to face Vaughan (who had earlier singled and scored his team's only run). One pitch got Feller out of the inning as Vaughan grounded into a 4–6–3 double play. Feller shut out the National stars over the final three innings, striking out Johnny Mize and Stan Hack in the ninth to end the game and give the Americans their fifth All-Star victory.

GAME 8
Sportsman's Park, St. Louis
July 9, 1940
NL, 4–0

```
AL   000 000 000    0 3 1
NL   300 000 01X    4 7 0
```

Pitchers: RUFFING, Newsom (4), Feller (7) vs DERRINGER, Walters (3), Wyatt (5), French (7), Hubbell (9)
Home Runs: West-N
Attendance: 32,373

The National Leaguers made short work of the Americans, scoring three times in the first inning and holding the opposing stars to three hits for the All-Star Game's first shutout. Before American League starter Red Ruffing retired a single National batter in the bottom of the first inning, three of the game's four runs had been scored, on singles by Arky Vaughan and Billy Herman and Max West's home run to right center.

Ruffing then settled down, and he and Buck Newsom held the Nationals to just three additional hits through the seventh. Bob Feller gave up the Nationals' fourth run in the eighth, on a walk, a sacrifice, and Harry Danning's single.

Five National League pitchers combined for the shutout, permitting only five batters to reach base while striking out seven. Starter Paul Derringer, who struck out three men in his two innings, was awarded the win.

GAME 9
Briggs Stadium, Detroit
July 8, 1941
AL, 7–5

NL	000	001	220	5	10	2
AL	000	101	014	7	11	3

Pitchers: Wyatt, Derringer (3), Walters (5), PASSEAU (7) vs Feller, Lee (4), Hudson (7), SMITH (8)
Home Runs: Vaughan-N (2), Williams-A
Attendance: 54,674

The National Leaguers entered the last of the ninth with a 5–3 lead and hopes of nailing down their first back-to-back All-Star victories. The American stars had scored their first run in the fourth. The Nationals tied the score in the top of the sixth, but the Americans countered with a run later in the inning. The Nationals' Arky Vaughan then made a bid to be the game's hero, homering in the seventh off Sid Hudson with a man aboard to restore the National lead, and homering again an inning later off Edgar Smith for two more runs.

A double and single by the DiMaggio brothers Joe and Dom brought the Americans a run closer in the eighth, but they still needed two to tie as they faced Claude Passeau in the bottom of the ninth. Two one-out singles and a walk loaded the bases, and a force play at second (that just missed being a game-ending double play) scored Ken Keltner from third. With two men now out and the Americans still down a run, Ted Williams homered on a letter-high fastball against the upper parapet in right for three more runs and another American League victory.

GAME 10
Polo Grounds, New York
July 6, 1942
AL, 3–1

AL	300	000	000	3	7	0
NL	000	000	010	1	6	1

Pitchers: CHANDLER, Benton (5) vs M.COOPER, Vander Meer (4), Passeau (7), Walters (9)
Home Runs: Boudreau-A, York-A, Owen-N
Attendance: 33,694

Home runs accounted for all the scoring as the American League, in something of a reverse of the 1940 game, scored three times in the top of the first to defeat the Nationals. Lou Boudreau, leading off, hit the game winner off Mort Cooper's second pitch, into the upper deck in left field. A double and two outs later, Rudy York put one over the fence near the short right field foul line for two more runs.

The Americans hit safely only four more times, and scored no more runs, but they already had more than enough, as Spud Chandler and Al Benton combined to shut out the National League stars for seven innings, until Mickey Owen, pinch-hitting for pitcher Claude Passeau in the eighth, hit his only home run of the summer.

This was the second All-Star Game played in the Polo Grounds. It had been Brooklyn's turn to host the game at Ebbets Field, but because the proceeds were destined for the war effort, the site was shifted to the larger stadium. The game might as well have been held in Brooklyn, though, as a pregame rain held attendance to well below the Polo Grounds' capacity.

GAME 11
Shibe Park, Philadelphia
July 13, 1943
AL, 5–3

NL	100	000	101	3	10	3
AL	031	010	00X	5	8	1

Pitchers: M.COOPER, Vander Meer (3), Sewell (6), Javery (7) vs LEONARD, Newhouser (4), Hughson (7)
Home Runs: Doerr-A, V.DiMaggio-N
Attendance: 31,938

For the first time, the All-Star Game was played at night. And for the only time in All-Star history, no Yankee played—although six had been named to the American League squad. But Yankee Joe McCarthy (serving for the sixth time as American manager) was piqued by criticism that he favored his own players, and retaliated by keeping them all on the bench.

The only DiMaggio in this wartime game was Pittsburgh's Vince, and he provided most of the National League power—going 3-for-3 with eight total bases and two of his team's three runs. But after the Nationals had jumped to a one-run lead in the first, Bobby Doerr of the Americans homered off Mort Cooper with two aboard in the second to put the American stars ahead. They added to their lead with a run in the third and another in the fifth. DiMaggio scored in the seventh after tripling off Tex Hughson and added a homer against Hughson in the ninth, but his heroics were not enough to overcome the American League's march to its third win in a row, and its eighth in 11 tries.

GAME 12
Forbes Field, Pittsburgh
July 11, 1944
NL, 7–1

AL	010	000	000	1	6	3
NL	000	040	21X	7	12	1

Pitchers: Borowy, HUGHSON (4), Muncrief (5), Newhouser (7), Newsom (8) vs Walters, RAFFENSBERGER (4), Sewell (6), Tobin (9)
Attendance: 29,589

For the second time the game was played at night, and for the seventh time Joe McCarthy managed the American League team. But this time—unlike Game 11—he let his Yankees play. He started Yankees pitcher Hank Borowy, who not only shut out the Nationals in his three innings, but drove in a run in the second to give his team the lead.

That was all the American stars got. For the first four innings it was enough, but in the fifth a double, four singles, a walk, an error, and a stolen base brought in four National League runs. In the seventh, Whitey Kurowski doubled in two more National runs, and in the eighth a missed third strike, two walks, and a flyball produced a seventh and final tally.

No home runs were hit in the game, only the second time that had happened in All-Star play. But Phil Cavarretta of the Nationals tripled—and reached base four additional times on a single and three walks for a new All-Star on-base record.

GAME 13
Fenway Park, Boston
July 9, 1946
AL, 12–0

NL	000 000 000	0	3	0
AL	200 130 24X	12	14	1

Pitchers: PASSEAU, Higbe (4),
Blackwell (5), Sewell (8) vs FELLER,
Newhouser (4), Kramer (7)
Home Runs: Keller-A, Williams-A (2)
Attendance: 34,906

No All-Star Game was played in 1945 because of restrictions on wartime travel, but when the classic resumed in 1946 the American stars avenged their 1944 loss with the most decisive All-Star victory to date: 12–0. American pitchers Bob Feller, Hal Newhouser, and Jack Kramer combined to hold the National stars to three singles and a walk, as their teammates pounded National pitching for 14 hits, including two doubles and three home runs.

But the game belonged to Ted Williams. Back after three years at war, and playing before his hometown fans, he equaled Phil Cavarretta's 1944 on-base record in spectacular fashion, with one walk, two singles, and two home runs: one a drive into the center field bleachers and the other the first homer ever hit off Rip Sewell's looping "eephus" pitch. He scored the game's first run in the first inning as Charlie Keller followed his walk with a homer, and went on to break an All-Star record by scoring three more times, while driving in a record five runs.

GAME 14
Wrigley Field, Chicago
July 8, 1947
AL, 2–1

AL	000 001 100	2	8	0
NL	000 100 000	1	5	1

Pitchers: Newhouser, SHEA (4),
Masterson (7), Page (8) vs Blackwell,
Brecheen (4), SAIN (7), Spahn (8)
Home Runs: Mize-N
Attendance: 41,123

Johnny Mize homered for the National League off rookie Spec Shea in the fourth inning for the game's first run, following three one-hit innings by the two lanky starters, Ewell Blackwell of the Nationals and Hal Newhouser of the Americans. Mize's run remained the only score until the sixth inning, when the American Leaguers tied the game on two singles and a double-play grounder.

Sharp baserunning by Bobby Doerr—plus a little luck—led to the Americans' second run an inning later. Doerr singled, then stole second. He took third when pitcher Johnny Sain's pickoff throw bounced off Doerr's back into the outfield. Pinch hitter Stan Spence then singled Doerr home with what proved to be the game's final—and winning—run. The Nationals put men on first and third in the eighth, but shortstop Lou Boudreau's spectacular stop of a hot grounder and sharp throw to first retired the side and ended the threat.

GAME 15
Sportsman's Park, St. Louis
July 13, 1948
AL, 5–2

NL	200 000 000	2	8	0
AL	011 300 00X	5	6	0

Pitchers: Branca, SCHMITZ (4),
Sain (4), Blackwell (6) vs Masterson,
RASCHI (4), Coleman (7)
Home Runs: Musial-N, Evers-A
Attendance: 34,009

Vic Raschi pitched three shutout innings for the American stars and drove in two go-ahead runs with a fourth-inning single. The 5-2 win marked the third time since the All-Star Game originated in 1933—won its third classic in a row that the American League had three straight wins.

The Nationals scored first on Stan Musial's two-run homer in the top of the first. But that was all they got, as starter Walt Masterson settled down and shut out the Nationals through the second and third innings. Raschi then came on for his shutout stint, and Joe Coleman stopped the Nationals without even a hit over the final three innings.

Meanwhile, the Americans scored a run in the second on Hoot Evers' homer, and tied the game with another run in the third on two walks, a double steal, and an outfield fly. Then in the fourth, when two walks and a single had loaded the bases, pitcher Raschi singled in the third and fourth American runs. Joe DiMaggio's pinch-hit sacrifice fly scored a fifth run. Johnny Sain and Ewell Blackwell shut out the Americans the rest of the way, but the damage had been done.

GAME 16
Ebbets Field, Brooklyn
July 12, 1949
AL, 11–7

AL	400 202 300	11	13	1
NL	212 002 000	7	12	5

Pitchers: Parnell, TRUCKS (2),
Brissie (4), Raschi (7) vs Spahn,
NEWCOMBE (2), Munger (5),
Bickford (6), Pollet (7), Blackwell (8),
Roe (9)
Home Runs: Musial-N, Kiner-N
Attendance: 32,577

Each team scored seven earned runs in this game which saw a total of 25 hits, including seven doubles and two home runs. But two first-inning National League errors let in four unearned American runs to provide the margin for the American League's fourth consecutive All-Star win. Stan Musial and Ralph Kiner each drove in two National runs with homers, but Eddie Joost singled in two runs for the Americans and Joe DiMaggio singled and doubled in three more to lead the American attack. For the second year in a row, Vic Raschi shut out the National stars for three innings, this time holding the American lead over the final third of the game.

The game was notable as the first to include black players: three Dodgers (Jackie Robinson, Roy Campanella, and Don Newcombe) for the National League, and Larry Doby for the American. With the Americans now ahead 12-4 in the series, it also marked the farthest extent of American League domination of the midsummer classic.

GAME 17
Comiskey Park, Chicago
July 11, 1950
NL, 4–3

```
NL   020 000 001 000 01   4 10 0
AL   001 020 000 000 00   3  8 1
```

Pitchers: Roberts, Newcombe (4), Konstanty (6), Jansen (7), BLACKWELL (12) vs Raschi, Lemon (4), Houtteman (7), Reynolds (10), GRAY (13), Feller (14)
Home Runs: Kiner-N, Schoendienst-N
Attendance: 46,127

For the first time, the All-Star Game went into extra innings, and for the first time the National League won a game as the visiting team. Three pitchers each hurled three innings of shutout ball: Bob Lemon and Allie Reynolds for the American League and Ewell Blackwell (who finished the game and got the win) for the Nationals. But top pitching honors were earned by National Leaguer Larry Jansen, who struck out six and gave up only one hit over five shutout innings.

The National stars scored first with two runs in the second. The Americans came back with one in the third, and tied and took the lead in the fifth on George Kell's run-scoring fly and an RBI single by Ted Williams (who, it was later learned, had broken his left elbow making an off-the-wall catch in the first inning). But in the top of the ninth, Ralph Kiner of the Nationals hit a game-tying homer, and 4½ scoreless innings later Red Schoendienst—on the first pitch of the 14th inning—homered off American Leaguer Ted Gray with what proved to be the game winner.

GAME 18
Briggs Stadium, Detroit
July 10, 1951
NL, 8–3

```
NL   100 302 110   8 12 1
AL   010 110 000   3 10 2
```

Pitchers: Roberts, MAGLIE (3), Newcombe (6), Blackwell (9) vs Garver, LOPAT (4), Hutchinson (5), Parnell (8), Lemon (9)
Home Runs: Musial-N, Elliott-N, Wertz-A, Kell-A, Hodges-N, Kiner-N
Attendance: 52,075

In a game moved from Philadelphia to help Detroit celebrate its 250th birthday, hometowners Vic Wertz and George Kell of the Tigers hit solo homers in the fourth and fifth innings to bring the American stars within a run of the Nationals. But they came no closer, as the National Leaguers pulled away for a convincing 8-3 victory.

The Nationals, aided by six innings of shutout pitching (including three by Don Newcombe), produced four home runs of their own to drive in six of their eight runs. With the score tied 1-1 going into the fourth inning, Stan Musial greeted Ed Lopat's first pitch with a shot to the right field upper deck. Bob Elliott added two more runs later in the inning with a homer to left. Gil Hodges increased the National League lead to 6–3 with a two-run homer in the sixth, and Ralph Kiner concluded the Nationals' scoring with a solo upper-deck shot to left center in the eighth. For the first time in All-Star play, the National League had won two games in a row.

GAME 19
Shibe Park, Philadelphia
July 8, 1952
NL, 3–2

```
AL   000 20   2 5 0
NL   100 20   3 3 0
```

Pitchers: Raschi, LEMON (3), Shantz (5) vs Simmons, RUSH (4)
Home Runs: J.Robinson-N, Sauer-N
Attendance: 32,785

No sun shone for this rain-shortened game, but two hometown pitchers did. Curt Simmons of the Phillies held the American stars to one hit as he shut them out over the first three innings. And the Athletics' Bobby Shantz—in the midst of an MVP season—struck out the side in the fifth for the Americans.

But home runs and rain determined the final outcome. Jackie Robinson opened the scoring with a homer off Vic Raschi in the bottom of the first to give the Nationals a 1–0 lead. In the fourth the Americans came back to take the lead briefly with two runs on a double, a walk, and two singles off eventual winner Bob Rush. In the bottom of the inning, Hank Sauer's home run off Bob Lemon with one aboard returned the lead to the National League. And there it stayed through a scoreless fifth, when the rain, which had fallen throughout the game, at last brought the soggy festivities to the All-Star series' first premature conclusion.

GAME 20
Crosley Field, Cincinnati
July 14, 1953
NL, 5–1

```
AL   000 000 001   1  5 0
NL   000 020 12X   5 10 0
```

Pitchers: Pierce, REYNOLDS (4), Garcia (6) Paige (8) vs Roberts, SPAHN (4), Simmons (6), Dickson (8)
Attendance: 30,846

For the first 4½ innings, pitchers for both sides held the opposition scoreless, with one hit each. Then the National Leaguers got to Allie Reynolds for two runs in the bottom of the fifth on a hit batsman, a walk, and two singles.

This proved margin enough for the National League's fourth consecutive victory, as four National pitchers held the Americans to just two hits through eight innings before three singles in the ninth gave the American Leaguers their only run. For good measure, though, the National stars added a run in the seventh, and two more in the eighth (with three singles and a walk off Satchel Paige in his only All-Star appearance).

Enos Slaughter of the Nationals provided much of the game's excitement. With two singles, a walk, and a stolen base, he drove in one run and scored two others, and defensively made a spectacular diving catch in right field. Pee Wee Reese's double in the seventh (scoring Slaughter) was the game's only extra-base hit.

GAME 21
Municipal Stadium, Cleveland
July 13, 1954
AL, 11–9

NL	000 520 020	9 14 0
AL	004 121 03X	11 17 1

Pitchers: Roberts, Antonelli (4), Spahn (6), Grissom (6), CONLEY (8), Erskine (8) vs Ford, Consuegra (4), Lemon (4), Porterfield (5), Keegan (8), STONE (8), Trucks (9)
Home Runs: Rosen-A (2), Boone-A, Kluszewski-N, Bell-N, Doby-A
Attendance: 68,751

American starter Whitey Ford gave up only one hit in three shutout innings, and National starter Robin Roberts shut out the American stars through two. But in the bottom of the third Al Rosen tagged Roberts for a three-run homer, and Ray Boone followed with a solo shot. By the end of the game new All-Star records had been set for hits (31), runs (20), and pitchers used (13), and the record of 6 home runs had been equaled.

The Nationals topped the American four-run third with five straight hits off Sandy Consuegra in the fourth, for five runs. The Americans tied the game with a run in their half of the fourth, but Ted Kluszewski homered in the fifth for two more National League runs. In the bottom of the fifth, Rosen homered again, for two, to bring the Americans even again.

A run in the sixth put the Americans ahead, but Gus Bell's two-run blast in the eighth returned the Nationals to the top by one. They were threatening to lengthen that lead when Dean Stone entered the contest in relief of Bob Keegan with two out and Red Schoendienst on third. Before Stone's first delivery, Schoendienst broke for home and was tagged out, setting the stage for Stone to become the winning pitcher without making a pitch. Larry Doby tied it up for the American League later in the eighth with a home run, and Nellie Fox drove in the game's final two runs a few batters later with a bases-loaded single.

In the ninth, the Nationals' Stan Musial blasted two over the fence—both foul—with a man aboard. But Virgil Trucks retired him and Gil Hodges to preserve the American League's first victory in five games.

GAME 22
County Stadium, Milwaukee
July 12, 1955
NL, 6–5

AL	400 001 000 000	5 10 2
NL	000 000 230 001	6 13 1

Pitchers: Pierce, Wynn (4), Ford (7), SULLIVAN (8) vs Roberts, Haddix (4), Newcombe (7), Jones (8), Nuxhall (8), CONLEY (12)
Home Runs: Mantle-A, Musial-N
Attendance: 45,314

Down 5–0 in the seventh inning, the National Leaguers came back to tie the game and send it into extra innings. The Americans attacked early, scoring four runs off Robin Roberts (three of them on Mickey Mantle's home run to center) before the game's first out had been recorded. They added a fifth run in the sixth inning. Meanwhile, pitchers Billy Pierce and Early Wynn were shutting the Nationals down on four hits.

In the seventh, though, two singles, a walk, and an American error gave the Nationals two runs. In the eighth, four two-out singles and another error tied the game. Joe Nuxhall for the Nationals and the Americans' Frank Sullivan prevented further scoring through the 11th. In the top of the 12th, Gene Conley replaced Nuxhall and struck out the side: Al Kaline, Mickey Vernon, and Al Rosen. Sullivan returned for the Americans to face Stan Musial in the bottom of the 12th. Musial hit the first pitch—a fastball—over the screen in right and the game was over.

GAME 23
Griffith Stadium, Washington
July 10, 1956
NL, 7–3

NL	001 211 200	7 11 0
AL	000 003 000	3 11 0

Pitchers: FRIEND, Spahn (4), Antonelli (6) vs PIERCE, Ford (4), Wilson (5), Brewer (6), Score (8), Wynn (9)
Home Runs: Mays-N, Williams-A, Mantle-A, Musial-N
Attendance: 28,843

Four of the game's greatest sluggers—Willie Mays, Stan Musial, Ted Williams, and Mickey Mantle—hit home runs, three of them off two of the game's greatest pitchers—Whitey Ford and Warren Spahn. But the star of the game was National League third baseman Ken Boyer, who went 3-for-5, scoring one run and driving in another, while making three spectacular diving and leaping plays in the field.

The National stars scored five times—including twice in the fourth on Mays's homer off Ford—before the Americans put a run on the board. But in the bottom of the sixth, Williams homered for two runs off Spahn, and Mantle followed with another homer to bring the Americans within two. But that was the end of their scoring, as Johnny Antonelli relieved Spahn to stop the American stars the rest of the way. The Nationals scored twice more in the seventh—one of the runs coming on Musial's homer—ensuring them a comfortable 7–3 victory.

GAME 24
Sportsman's Park, St. Louis
July 9, 1957
AL, 6–5

AL	020 001 003	6 10 0
NL	000 000 203	5 9 1

Pitchers: BUNNING, Loes (4), Wynn (7), Pierce (7), Mossi (9), Grim (9) vs SIMMONS, Burdette (2), Sanford (6), Jackson (7), Labine (9)
Attendance: 30,693

Cincinnati fans stuffed the ballot boxes and elected Reds to start everywhere but first base. Commissioner Ford Frick removed two elected starters, but left five Reds in the lineup. They could not bring the National League the victory, though.

The Americans scored twice in the second on singles and walks to take a lead they held to the finish. Although reliever Lew Burdette—after walking in the second run—stopped the American stars through the fifth, Jim Bunning and Billy Loes were combining to keep the Nationals from scoring through the first six innings. The Americans, meanwhile, added a third run in the top of the sixth on a double, a wild pitch, and a single.

The Nationals scored their first two in the seventh, on two singles and a double, to draw within one of a tie. But in the top of the ninth the Americans combined two singles, an error, a sacrifice bunt, and Minnie Minoso's pinch double for three more runs. They needed them all because the Nationals responded in their half of the ninth with three runs of their own on a blend of walks, hits (including Willie Mays's triple), and a wild pitch. With two out and a runner at second, Gil Hodges lined one deep to left-center. But Minoso, now in left field, snared the drive on the run to end the game.

GAME 25
Memorial Stadium, Baltimore
July 8, 1958
AL, 4–3

NL	210 000 000	3 4 2
AL	110 011 00X	4 9 2

Pitchers: Spahn, FRIEND (4), Jackson (6), Farrell (7) vs Turley, Narleski (2), WYNN (6), O'Dell (7)
Attendance: 48,829

Although American League pitchers held the National Leaguers to only four hits (all singles), the Nationals took a quick lead, and held it for half the game before they were overtaken. Willie Mays and Stan Musial singled in the top of the first, both scoring as American starter Bob Turley proceeded to give up a sacrifice fly, hit a batter, walk a man, and unload a wild pitch.

The Americans came back with one run in their half of the first, but the Nationals drove Turley out with their third run as Mays (who had reached on a fielder's choice) worked his way around the bases on a steal, an error, and Bob Skinner's single. Once again the Americans answered with a run, but they didn't tie the game until Mickey Vernon scored on a bases-loaded ground out in the fifth. An inning later they took the lead when pinch hitter Gil McDougald singled home Frank Malzone.

Billy O'Dell set down the Nationals in order over the final three innings to preserve the lead and give the American Leaguers their second consecutive victory. It would take more than 30 years before the American League could again claim consecutive All-Star victories.

GAME 26
Forbes Field, Pittsburgh
July 7, 1959
NL, 5–4

AL	000 100 030	4 8 0
NL	100 000 22X	5 9 1

Pitchers: Wynn, Duren (4), Bunning (7), FORD (8), Daley (8) vs Drysdale, Burdette (4), Face (7), ANTONELLI (8), Elston (9)
Home Runs: Mathews-N, Kaline-A
Attendance: 35,277

For the third year in a row, the game was decided by one run, with the National League celebrating the city of Pittsburgh's bicentennial by breaking the American League's win streak at two.

Eddie Mathews homered for the Nationals in the bottom of the first for the only run in the first three innings, as Don Drysdale stopped the Americans without a hit or walk, fanning four. Al Kaline tied the game in the top of the fourth with an American home run for the only score of the middle three innings, as Ryne Duren one-hit the Nationals. Like Drysdale, Duren fanned four.

In the last of the seventh, though, a double and two singles off Jim Bunning put the Nationals ahead by two runs. The NL lead lasted only briefly, however, as the Americans moved back into the lead with three runs in the eighth off Roy Face, with two singles, a walk, and a double after Face had retired the first two men. But in their half of the eighth the Nationals hit Whitey Ford, tying the game with a single-sacrifice-single, and scoring the game winner on Willie Mays' triple to center.

GAME 27
Memorial Coliseum, Los Angeles
August 3, 1959
AL, 5–3

AL	012 000 110	5 6 0
NL	100 010 100	3 6 3

Pitchers: WALKER, Wynn (4), Wilhelm, (6), O'Dell (7), McLish (8) vs DRYSDALE, Conley (4), Jones (6), Face (8)
Home Runs: Malzone-A, Berra-A, F. Robinson-N, Gilliam-N, Colavito-A
Attendance: 55,105

To raise extra money for the players' pension fund and other causes, a second All-Star Game was scheduled for 1959, the first ever to be played in August, and the first on the West Coast. The American stars avenged their earlier defeat with a 5–3 win, out-homering the Nationals three to two.

The National Leaguers scored first on a first-inning double and sacrifice fly, but Frank Malzone tied the score with the game's first home run. Yogi Berra homered an inning later with one on for a 3–1 American lead, but Frank Robinson brought the Nationals back to within one with his homer in the fifth. The Americans replaced that run in the top of the seventh on a walk, two errors, and a single, but Junior Gilliam countered with a home run in the last of the inning. Rocky Colavito scored the game's final run for the Americans in the eighth with the game's final homer.

Don Drysdale, the pitching standout of the July game, struck out five this time, but also walked three and gave up three runs on homers to take the loss.

GAME 28
Municipal Stadium, Kansas City
July 11, 1960
NL, 5–3

NL	311 000 000	5 12 4
AL	000 001 020	3 6 1

Pitchers: FRIEND, McCormick (4), Face (6), Buhl (8), Law (9) vs MONBOUQUETTE, Estrada (3), Coates (4), Bell (6), Lary (8), Daley (9)
Home Runs: Banks-N, Crandall-N, Kaline-A
Attendance: 30,619

The day was hot—the temperature broke 100—and so were the National League bats. Willie Mays had three hits, including a leadoff triple and a double; Ernie Banks homered and doubled; Del Crandall homered and singled; and Joe Adcock doubled and singled for three-fourths of the Nationals' 12 hits. The National League scored five unanswered runs in the first three innings to take an unbeatable lead. Starter Bob Friend, meanwhile, blanked the Americans on one hit through three innings and Mike McCormick held them scoreless for two more before yielding the first American run in the sixth on Nellie Fox's bases-loaded single. Roy Face then came on to douse the fire, getting Luis Aparicio to ground into a double play.

Four American League pitchers stopped the National stars after the third inning, and Al Kaline homered for two more American runs in the eighth. In the ninth the Americans put men on first and second with one away. But their comeback fell short, as Vern Law came on to retire Brooks Robinson and Harvey Kuenn and preserve the National victory.

GAME 29
Yankee Stadium, New York
July 13, 1960
NL, 6–0

NL	021 000 102	6 10 0
AL	000 000 000	0 8 0

Pitchers: LAW, Podres (3), S.Williams (5), Jackson (7), Henry (8), McDaniel (9) vs FORD, Wynn (4), Staley (6), Lary (8), Bell (9)
Home Runs: Mathews-N, Mays-N, Musial-N, Boyer-N
Attendance: 38,362

Only two days after the first All-Star Game, the squads met a second time before fewer than 39,000 fans in capacious Yankee Stadium. It was no contest. Vern Law, who had completed and saved the first game, started and won this one. His two shutout innings set the pace for the five National pitchers who followed him to fashion the first National League shutout in 20 years. The American stars got only two fewer hits than the Nationals, but only one was for extra bases, whereas four of the National League hits were home runs.

Eddie Mathews began the scoring with a two-run homer in the second, and Willie Mays (on his way to a second straight 3-for-4 game) homered for the third National run an inning later. No one scored through the three middle innings, but in the seventh Stan Musial broke his own record with his sixth All-Star homer—a mighty shot three tiers up in right—and in the ninth Ken Boyer completed the rout with a two-run shot to left.

GAME 30
Candlestick Park, San Francisco
July 11, 1961
NL, 5–4

AL	000 001 002 1	4 4 2
NL	010 100 010 2	5 11 5

Pitchers: Ford, Lary (4), Donovan (4), Bunning (6), Fornieles (8), WILHELM (8) vs Spahn, Purkey (4), McCormick (6), Face (9), Koufax (9), MILLER (9)
Home Runs: Killebrew-A, Altman-N
Attendance: 44,115

National League pitchers began the game where they had left off the year before. For five innings Warren Spahn and Bob Purkey shut out the American stars without a hit or base on balls. In the sixth, Harmon Killebrew homered off Mike McCormick to end the American drought, but it was the only hit McCormick yielded through the eighth.

Meanwhile, the Nationals had taken a 3–1 lead with runs in the second and fourth innings and George Altman's homer in the eighth. But in the top of the ninth, Candlestick's notorious winds helped put the Americans back in the game. Their second and third hits of the game brought in one run, and their fourth (and last) hit put another man on base. The tying run came in when the wind blew pitcher Stu Miller off the mound for a balk to advance the runners, and then twisted a grounder out of third baseman Ken Boyer's grasp for a run-scoring error. In the 10th, the wind may have contributed to the Americans' go-ahead run as Boyer's throw to first sailed into the outfield, allowing Nellie Fox (who had walked) to score from first.

But in the last of the 10th the wind finally came to the aid of the Nationals, rendering useless the famous knuckleball of American reliever Hoyt Wilhelm, who gave up the tying run on hits by Hank Aaron and Willie Mays and lost the game when Roberto Clemente singled in Mays from second.

GAME 31
Fenway Park, Boston
July 31, 1961
Tie, 1–1

NL	000 001 000	1 5 1
AL	100 000 000	1 4 0

Pitchers: Purkey, Mahaffey (3), Koufax (5), Miller (7) vs Bunning, Schwall (4), Pascual (7)
Home Runs: Colavito-A
Attendance: 31,851

In the second All-Star Game of 1961, the weather again played a crucial role, as heavy rain at the end of the ninth inning forced the first (and, so far, only) All-Star tie.

Rocky Colavito's home run for the Americans in the first inning turned out to be his squad's only run, as four National League pitchers combined to shut out the American stars on only three singles the rest of the way. The American League pitching was just as effective, with starter Jim Bunning and finisher Camilo Pascual each pitching three no-hit innings. Don Schwall, who pitched the middle three innings, gave up all five National League hits and the Nationals' one run. But even that might have been prevented.

In the sixth, with two on and two out, American League shortstop Luis Aparicio waited for a slow grounder, failing to get the ball in time to throw the batter out and end the inning. The Nationals scored when Bill White followed with a hot ground single up the middle. Aparicio made a brilliant stop on White's ball to prevent more than one run from scoring, but it did drive in the game's tying—and final—run.

GAME 32
D.C. Stadium, Washington
July 10, 1962
NL, 3–1

NL	000 002 010	3 8 0
AL	000 001 000	1 4 0

MVP: Willis-N
Pitchers: Drysdale, MARICHAL (4), Purkey (6), Shaw (8) vs Bunning, PASCUAL (4), Donovan (7), Pappas (9)
Attendance: 45,480

The stadium was new, President John F. Kennedy threw out the first ball, and starters Don Drysdale of the Nationals and Jim Bunning of the Americans both pitched three innings of one-hit shutout ball. But Maury Wills stole the show. Entering the game in the sixth inning to run for 41-year-old Stan Musial, who had singled, Wills stole second, then scored on Dick Groat's single up the middle for the game's first run. Another single, a long fly out, and a ground out scored Groat with the second (and, as it turned out, winning) run.

Two singles and a fly out by Roger Maris brought in an American run in the bottom of the sixth off Bob Purkey. But that was all they got, as Purkey and Bob Shaw one-hit the American stars through the final three innings.

In the eighth inning Wills manufactured an insurance run for the Nationals. On first with a leadoff single, he somehow reached third on Jim Davenport's single to short left, racing from second to third as left fielder Rocky Colavito threw in to second. He scored after tagging on a foul out to right. Wills earned All-Star Most Valuable Player honors in the first year it was awarded.

GAME 33
Wrigley Field, Chicago
July 30, 1962
AL, 9–4

AL	001 201 302	9 10 0
NL	010 000 111	4 10 4

MVP: Wagner-A
Pitchers: Stenhouse, HERBERT (3),
  Aguirre (6), Pappas (9) vs Podres,
  MAHAFFEY (3), Gibson (5),
  Farrell (7), Marichal (8)
Home Runs: Runnels-A, Wagner-A,
  Colavito-A, Roseboro-N.
Attendance: 38,359

With this second game of 1962, the
leagues ended their four-year experiment of playing two All-Star
games a year. The Americans
out-homered the Nationals to spoil
the National League's attempt to
even the series at 16 wins apiece.
But no matter—the American stars
would win only once again in the
next twenty years.

The National stars scored first on
a double and single in the second,
but Pete Runnels evened the score
in the third with a solo homer, and
Leon Wagner put the Americans
ahead with a two-run shot an inning later. After Tom Tresh doubled home a fourth American run
in the sixth, Rocky Colavito put the
game out of reach with a three-run
blast in the seventh.

The Nationals tried to come
back with runs in the seventh and
eighth, but the Americans neutralized them with two more of their
own in the ninth (on two errors, two
Juan Marichal wild pitches, a
double, and a long fly out). With
the score now 9-3, John
Roseboro's solo homer in the last
of the ninth put the Nationals in the
home-run column, but that was all.

GAME 34
Municipal Stadium,
Cleveland
July 9, 1963
NL, 5–3

NL	012 010 010	5 6 0
AL	012 000 000	3 11 1

MVP: Mays-N
Pitchers: O'Toole, JACKSON (3),
  Culp (5), Woodeshick (6),
  Drysdale (8) vs McBride,
  BUNNING (4), Bouton (6), Pizarro (7),
  Radatz (8)
Attendance: 44,160

Willie Mays sparked the National
League to victory with his baserunning and timely hitting. Although
he had only one hit—a single—he
scored two runs and drove in two
others in the Nationals' 5–3 win.

The National stars scored first
when Mays walked in the second
inning, stole second, and came in
on a single by Dick Groat. The
Americans tied the game in the last
of the second, but in the top of the
third Mays singled in one run, stole
second again, and scored his second run on Ed Bailey's single.

Once again the Americans came
back in the bottom of the third to tie
the game on Albie Pearson's
double, followed by two singles
sandwiched around an infield out.
But these were their last runs, as
four National pitchers shut them
out on four singles the rest of the
way. Meanwhile, Mays drove in
what proved to be the winning run
with a ground out in the fifth. In the
eighth the Nationals scored a final
run when Ron Santo singled home
Bill White, who had singled and
stolen second.

GAME 35
Shea Stadium, New York
July 7, 1964
NL, 7–4

AL	100 002 100	4 9 1
NL	000 210 004	7 8 0

MVP: Callison-N
Pitchers: Chance, Wyatt (4),
  Pascual (5), RADATZ (7) vs Drysdale,
  Bunning (4), Short (6), Farrell (7),
  MARICHAL (9)
Home Runs: B.Williams-N, Boyer-N,
  Callison-N
Attendance: 50,850

A new stadium in the midst of a
World's Fair was the venue for this
game in which the National League
at last drew even with the American
at 17 wins apiece.

The American stars jumped into
the lead with an unearned run in the
first, but the Nationals (after Dean
Chance had shut them out through
three innings) overtook the Americans in the fourth, on home runs by
Billy Williams and Ken Boyer, and
Dick Groat doubled in a third run in
the fifth. In the top of the sixth the
Americans tied the score when
Brooks Robinson tripled in a pair,
and took the lead again an inning
later on a sacrifice fly that barely
scored Elston Howard ahead of
Willie Mays's throw from center.

The Americans held their slim
lead into the bottom of the ninth.
But Mays walked (after fouling off
five third strikes), stole second, and
scored the tying run on a single to
short right and an errant throw
home. One intentional walk and
two outs later, Johnny Callison hit
Dick Radatz's fastball over the
fence in right to win the game.

GAME 36
Metropolitan Stadium,
Bloomington, Minnesota
July 13, 1965
NL, 6–5

NL	320 000 100	6 11 0
AL	000 140 000	5 8 0

MVP: Marichal-N
Pitchers: Marichal, Maloney (4),
  Drysdale (5), KOUFAX (6), Farrell (7),
  Gibson (8) vs Pappas, Grant (2),
  Richert (4), McDOWELL (6),
  Fisher (8)
Home Runs: Mays-N, Torre-N,
  Stargell-N, McAuliffe-A, Killebrew-A.
Attendance: 46,706

For a while it looked as though the
Nationals would run away with the
game. Willie Mays led off with a
home run in the first, and Joe Torre
added two runs with a homer later
in the inning. In the second Willie
Stargell homered for two more runs
to make the score 5-0. National
starter Juan Marichal stopped the
Americans on one hit through three
innings.

But the American stars battled
back. A single, a walk, and another
single off Marichal's replacement,
Jim Maloney, brought in one run in
the fourth. Maloney retired the first
two men in the fifth, but then he
gave up a walk followed by a home
run to Dick McAuliffe, and a
scratch single followed by a Harmon Killebrew homer—and the
score was tied at 5-5.

Only one more run was scored.
In the seventh, Willie Mays, who
had walked and gone to third on
Hank Aaron's single, scored on
Ron Santo's infield hit to short.
The Nationals held off American
threats in the eighth and ninth to
take the All-Star series lead for the
first time.

GAME 37
Busch Memorial Stadium, St. Louis
July 12, 1966
NL, 2–1

AL	010 000 000 0	1 6 0
NL	000 100 000 1	2 6 0

MVP: B. Robinson-A
Pitchers: McLain, Kaat (4), Stottlemyre (6), Siebert (8), RICHERT (10) vs Koufax, Bunning (4), Marichal (6), G.PERRY (9)
Attendance: 49,936

The celebration of another new stadium and the city's bicentennial—and a temperature of 106 degrees Fahrenheit—greeted participants in the 1966 classic. Pitching dominated: seven pitchers hurled two or more each of shutout ball. American starter Denny McLain threw three perfect innings, but the National League's Sandy Koufax gave the Americans a run in the second when he let loose a wild pitch after Brooks Robinson had tripled.

The Nationals tied the score in the fourth with three singles off Jim Kaat, but that ended the scoring for both sides through the regulation nine innings. Gaylord Perry stopped the American stars in the top of the 10th, but in the last half of the inning, National Leaguer Tim McCarver singled off Pete Richert, was sacrificed to second, and came across with the winning run on Maury Wills's single to right.

GAME 38
Anaheim Stadium, Anaheim, California
July 11, 1967
NL, 2–1

NL	010 000 000 000 001	2 9 0
AL	000 001 000 000 000	1 8 0

MVP: Perez-N
Pitchers: Marichal, Jenkins (4), Gibson (7), Short (9), Cuellar (11), DRYSDALE (13), Seaver (15) vs Chance, McGlothlin (4), Peters (6), Downing (9), HUNTER (11)
Home Runs: Allen-N, B.Robinson-A, Perez-N
Attendance: 46,309

This was a game of strikeouts, home runs, and extra innings. Every one of the dozen pitchers used in the game struck out at least one batter. American Leaguers Gary Peters (who pitched three perfect middle innings) and Catfish Hunter struck out four apiece, while Ferguson Jenkins of the Nationals tied the All-Star record with six. The game total of 30 strikeouts shattered the previous record of 20 set in 1955.

Apart from the splendid pitching, three home runs provided the only excitement—and the only scoring—in this longest All-Star Game. Richie Allen of the Nationals scored first, homering to center off Dean Chance in the second inning. The Americans' Brooks Robinson tied the score in the sixth with a shot off Jenkins. And 8½ innings later, in the top of the 15th, National Leaguer Tony Perez homered off Hunter for the game's third and final run. Tom Seaver set down the Americans in the bottom of the inning, and the game—after a record three hours and 41 minutes—was history.

GAME 39
Astrodome, Houston
July 9, 1968
NL, 1–0

AL	000 000 000	0 3 1
NL	100 000 00X	1 5 0

MVP: Mays-N
Pitchers: TIANT, Odom (3), McLain (5), McDowell (7), Stottlemyre (8), John (8) vs DRYSDALE, Marichal (4), Carlton (6), Seaver (7), Reed (9), Koosman (9)
Attendance: 48,321

This game could be described by what was missing: fresh air and real grass (it was the first All-Star Game held indoors), hitting (the eight hits were a new low for a nine-inning All-Star Game), and earned runs (the game's only run came with the help of an error). In fact, if it weren't for 37-year-old Willie Mays, the game might not have had any runs at all. Starting only because of an injury to Pete Rose, National Leaguer Mays led off the bottom of the first with a single, and took second when first baseman Harmon Killebrew mishandled pitcher Luis Tiant's pick-off throw for an error. Mays took third as the rattled Tiant threw a wild pitch to walk Curt Flood, and scored when Willie McCovey grounded into a double play. Mays became the first two-time All-Star MVP, having also won the award in 1963.

The pitching on both sides was superb, but the National Leaguers shone especially bright. Tom Seaver gave up two of the Americans' three hits (all of which were doubles), but struck out five in his two innings. Juan Marichal hurled two perfect innings, fanning three. And none of the six National pitchers walked a man. One American, Killebrew, couldn't walk. Stretching for a throw at first, the slugger tore a hamstring and missed the next two months, the most serious All-Star Game casualty since Ted Williams's broken elbow 18 years earlier.

GAME 40
R.F.K. Memorial Stadium, Washington, D.C.
July 23, 1969
NL, 9–3

NL	125 100 000	9 11 0
AL	011 100 000	3 6 2

MVP: McCovey-N
Pitchers: CARLTON, Gibson (4), Singer (5), Koosman (7), Dierker (8), P.Niekro (9) vs STOTTLEMYRE, Odom (3), Knowles (3), McLain (4), McNally (5), McDowell (7), Culp (9)
Home Runs: Bench-N, Howard-A, McCovey-N (2), Freehan-A
Attendance: 45,259

After four one-run victories in a row, the National Leaguers finally broke loose, massing 10 of their 11 hits in the first four innings for nine runs and a crushing win. Scoring an unearned run in the first on a dropped outfield fly, and two in the second on Johnny Bench's home run, the Nationals erupted in the third for five runs off Blue Moon Odom before two outs had been recorded. Willie McCovey's two-run homer began the third-inning scoring, and an error, single, and two doubles added three more runs before Odom was mercifully relieved. McCovey homered again in the fourth for the Nationals' final tally.

The American bats were not wholly silent, but the solo homers by Frank Howard and Bill Freehan in the second and third, and a third run in the fourth, couldn't counter the Nationals' attack.

The final five innings of the game were as quiet as the opening four had been noisy. No runs scored, and the two teams together managed only three hits.

GAME 41
Riverfront Stadium, Cincinnati
July 14, 1970
NL, 5–4

```
AL  000 001 120 000   4 12  0
NL  000 000 103 001   5 10  0
```

MVP: Yastrzemski-A
Pitchers: Palmer, McDowell (4), J.Perry (7), Hunter (9), Peterson (9), Stottlemyre (9), WRIGHT (11) vs Seaver, Merritt (4), G.Perry (6), Gibson (8), OSTEEN (10)
Home Runs: Dietz-N
Attendance: 51,838

In a new stadium opened only two weeks earlier, no one scored for the first five innings, as Jim Palmer and Sam McDowell of the Americans and Tom Seaver and Jim Merritt of the Nationals held the opposition to two hits per team. The Americans finally scored a run in the sixth, and another in the seventh. The Nationals got one back in the last of the seventh, but the Americans increased their lead to 4–1 in the eighth when Brooks Robinson tripled home two baserunners.

Fans had already begun to leave the park when the Nationals' Dick Dietz homered off Catfish Hunter to lead off the last of the ninth. Two pitchers, three singles, and a sacrifice fly later, the game was tied and headed for extra innings. Claude Osteen held the Americans scoreless from the 10th through the 12th, and the Nationals also failed to score in the 10th and 11th. But in the last of the 12th, with two out, Pete Rose, Billy Grabarkewitz, and Jim Hickman singled. Hometowner Rose, racing home from second on Hickman's hit, crashed into catcher Ray Fosse with a force that injured both players and still provokes controversy—but which also gave the National League its eighth straight victory.

GAME 42
Tiger Stadium, Detroit
July 13, 1971
AL, 6–4

```
NL  021 000 010   4 5  0
AL  004 002 00X   6 7  0
```

MVP: F. Robinson-A
Pitchers: ELLIS, Marichal (4), Jenkins (6), Wilson (7) vs BLUE, Palmer (4), Cuellar (6), Lolich (8)
Home Runs: Bench-N, Aaron-N, Jackson-A, F.Robinson-A, Killebrew-A, Clemente-N
Attendance: 53,559

With an assist from a favorable wind, six all-time greats homered to account for all the scoring as the American League broke its eight-game All-Star drought with a 6-4 victory. Johnny Bench put the Nationals in front with a two-run homer in the second inning off Vida Blue, and Hank Aaron—with his first All-Star home run—added a third run off Blue an inning later. But the Americans, shut out by Dock Ellis through the first two innings, rocked him in the bottom of the third as Reggie Jackson and Frank Robinson wrested the lead from the Nationals with a pair of two-run homers. Robinson's blast made him the first player to hit an All-Star home run for both leagues and Jackson's memorable homer hit the light tower atop the second deck of the stadium in right-center.

Ferguson Jenkins yielded the game's fifth homer, Harmon Killebrew's two-run shot for the Americans in the sixth. Roberto Clemente brought the Nationals a run closer with his solo homer off Mickey Lolich in the eighth, but that ended the team's scoring, and (for a year, anyway) the National League's All-Star stranglehold.

GAME 43
Atlanta-Fulton County Stadium, Atlanta
July 25, 1972
NL, 4–3

```
AL  001 000 020 0   3 6  0
NL  000 002 001 1   4 8  0
```

MVP: Morgan-N
Pitchers: Palmer, Lolich (4), G.Perry (6), Wood (8), McNALLY (10) vs Gibson, Blass (3), Sutton (4), Carlton (6), Stoneman (7), McGRAW (9)
Home Runs: Aaron-N, Rojas-A
Attendance: 53,107

The American Leaguers tried to extend their All-Star win streak to two games, and for a time it looked as though they might do it. In the third, they scored the only run of the first half of the game as Jim Palmer and Mickey Lolich held the Nationals to two hits through the first five innings. In the sixth Hank Aaron thrilled the hometown crowd with a two-run homer deep to left to shift the lead to the National League. But Cookie Rojas restored the American lead with his own two-run shot in the eighth.

The Americans held their lead into the bottom of the ninth, but after two singles and a force out, the score was tied. Tug McGraw set down the American stars in order in the 10th, but American reliever Dave McNally was not so fortunate. He walked leadoff batter Nate Colbert, who was sacrificed to second. Joe Morgan then sent the American Leaguers back into the ranks of losers with a sharp RBI single to right center. His single also gave the Nationals their seventh win in seven extra-inning games.

GAME 44
Royals Stadium, Kansas City
July 24, 1973
NL, 7–1

```
NL  002 122 000   7 10  0
AL  010 000 000   1 5  0
```

MVP: Bonds-N
Pitchers: WISE, Osteen (3), Sutton (5), Twitchell (6), Giusti (7), Seaver (8), Brewer (9) vs Hunter, Holtzman (2), BLYLEVEN (3), Singer (4), Ryan (6), Lyle (8), Fingers (9)
Home Runs: Bench-N, Bonds-N, W.Davis-N
Attendance: 40,849

Once again a new stadium was chosen to host the All-Star Game, and once again the National League emerged victorious. The Americans scored first, with a run in the second when Reggie Jackson scored from second on a single after doubling off the center field wall. But that was the beginning and end of their offense, as six National pitchers shut them out on three hits the rest of the way.

Meanwhile the National League hitters came to life, producing seven runs in four innings. Two walks and two singles in the third brought in two runs, and Johnny Bench's homer in the fourth made the score 3–1. In the fifth, Bobby Bonds—in the midst of his finest season—homered for two more National runs. And in the sixth, Willie Davis' home run completed the game's scoring, bringing in the Nationals' sixth and seventh runs.

The final third of the game was anticlimactic, as only two hits were made after the sixth inning. But Bonds brought the crowd to life briefly in the seventh, stretching one of those hits into a double with some audacious baserunning (ensuring his selection as the game's MVP).

GAME 45
Three Rivers Stadium, Pittsburgh
July 23, 1974
NL, 7–2

```
AL   002 000 000    2  4 1
NL   010 210 12X    7 10 1
```
MVP: Garvey-N
Pitchers: G.Perry, TIANT (4), Hunter (6), Fingers (8) vs Messersmith, BRETT (4), Matlack (6), McGlothen (7), Marshall (8)
Home Runs: R.Smith-N
Attendance: 50,706

Steve Garvey, who was elected to the National League starting lineup on write-in votes (his name was omitted from the fans' All-Star ballot), sparked the Nationals to yet another convincing win over the hapless American stars. After singling in the second inning, Garvey scored the game's first run on Ron Cey's double.

The Americans took the lead with two runs in the top of the third, capitalizing on two walks and an error sandwiched between Thurman Munson's leadoff double and Dick Allen's single. They might have scored more had not Garvey snared Bobby Murcer's hot grounder for an assist on the third out.

Garvey doubled in the tying run in the fourth, and Cey's RBI groundout restored the Nationals' lead. Lou Brock added a run in the fifth with a single and some inspired baserunning, and Reggie Smith homered in the seventh. Don Kessinger's triple and a wild pitch by Rollie Fingers in the eighth contributed to two final National League runs.

GAME 46
County Stadium, Milwaukee
July 15, 1975
NL, 6–3

```
NL   021 000 003    6 13 1
AL   000 003 000    3 10 1
```
MVP: Matlack-N, Madlock-N
Pitchers: Reuss, Sutton (4), Seaver (6), MATLACK (7), R.Jones (9) vs Blue, Busby (3), Kaat (5), HUNTER (7), Gossage (9)
Home Runs: Garvey-N, Wynn-N, Yastrzemski-A
Attendance: 51,480

When National stars Steve Garvey and Jim Wynn led off the second with back-to-back homers and their teammates added another run in the third, it looked as if the National League might be on its way to another easy win. But the American pitchers shut down the National League offense for the next five innings, and Carl Yastrzemski made a contest of it with a three-run homer in the sixth off Tom Seaver to tie the score.

In the top of the ninth, though, the Americans all but gave the game away. Left fielder Claudell Washington dropped a fly on the run (it was scored a hit) and misplayed a line drive that went for a double. Goose Gossage came in to relieve Catfish Hunter on the mound and hit the next batter to load the bases. Bill Madlock then drove in two of the baserunners with a single through the drawn-in infield, and Pete Rose knocked in the third run of the inning with a sacrifice fly.

Randy Jones set the Americans down in order in the bottom of the ninth, and—voilà!—the National League had won again.

GAME 47
Veterans Stadium, Philadelphia
July 13, 1976
NL, 7–1

```
AL   000 100 000    1  5 0
NL   202 000 03X    7 10 0
```
MVP: Foster-N
Pitchers: FIDRYCH, Hunter (3), Tiant (5), Tanana (7) vs R.JONES, Seaver (4), Montefusco (6), Rhoden (8), K.Forsch (9)
Home Runs: Foster-N, Lynn-A, Cedeno-N
Attendance: 63,974

Tom Seaver gave up a home run to Fred Lynn in the fourth inning, but that was the Americans' only score as the Nationals held the American stars to five hits while celebrating the nation's bicentennial with 10 hits and seven runs.

Rookie standout Mark Fidrych was chosen to start for the Americans and was promptly rapped for two runs. Pete Rose led off with a single and was tripled home by Steve Garvey, who scored himself on a groundout. The Nationals doubled their score in the third inning as George Foster tagged Catfish Hunter for two runs with a mighty home run to left center, and capped their assault with three more in the eighth off Frank Tanana, including a two-run homer by Cesar Cedeno.

The fans had elected five members of Cincinnati's "Big Red Machine" to the National League starting lineup, and Sparky Anderson, the Reds' and National squad's manager, added two more. They provided the bulk of the Nationals' offense, with seven hits, four RBIs, and four runs scored.

GAME 48
Yankee Stadium, New York
July 19, 1977
NL, 7–5

```
NL   401 000 020    7  9 1
AL   000 002 102    5  8 0
```
MVP: Sutton-N
Pitchers: SUTTON, Lavelle (4), Seaver (6), R.Reuschel (8), Gossage (9) vs PALMER, Kern (3), Eckersley (4), LaRoche (6), Campbell (7), Lyle (8)
Home Runs: Morgan-N, Luzinski-N, Garvey-N, Scott-A
Attendance: 56,683

The Nationals' Joe Morgan homered off Jim Palmer to open the game, and before Palmer escaped the first inning three more National Leaguers had crossed the plate on a single, double, and Greg Luzinski's homer. Palmer got through the second inning without further damage, but before he was relieved in the third, Steve Garvey had homered to give the Nationals a 5–0 lead.

The Americans fought back against Tom Seaver in the sixth and seventh. Seaver retired two in the sixth, but then gave up two singles, and two runs as Richie Zisk doubled the runners home. Two more singles in the seventh produced a third American run.

But the Nationals—assisted by pitcher Sparky Lyle's wild pitch and hit batsman—put a sixth and seventh run on the board in the eighth with a double and single. The Americans added two final runs of their own in the bottom of the ninth on George Scott's homer off Goose Gossage, but fell short of victory once again.

GAME 49
San Diego Stadium,
July 11, 1978
NL, 7–3

AL	201	000	000	3	8	1
NL	003	000	04X	7	10	0

MVP: Garvey-N
Pitchers: Palmer, Keough (3),
    Sorensen (4), Kern (7), Guidry (7),
    GOSSAGE (8) vs Blue, Rogers (4),
    Fingers (6), SUTTER (8), P. Niekro (9)
Attendance: 51,549

Rod Carew led off both the first and third innings with triples—an All-Star record—scoring both times as the Americans took a 3–0 lead into the bottom of the third. But then Jim Palmer, who had shut the Nationals out on one hit through the first two innings, lost his touch. After yielding a leadoff single, he retired two batters, but then issued three walks to force in a run, and when Steve Garvey singled past the shortstop two more runs scored to tie the game.

No one scored through the next 4½ innings, with Larry Sorensen turning in the game's top pitching performance as he shut the Nationals out on one hit through the three middle innings. But in the last of the eighth, Goose Gossage (the National League's closer the previous year) took the mound this year for the Americans. Garvey greeted him with a leadoff triple and scored what proved to be the winning run on a wild pitch. A walk and three singles added three insurance runs before the inning ended. Bruce Sutter and Phil Niekro blanked the Americans in the ninth, and the Nationals had extended their current win streak to seven.

GAME 50
Kingdome, Seattle
July 17, 1979
NL, 7–6

NL	211	001	011	7	10	0
AL	302	001	000	6	10	0

MVP: Parker-N
Pitchers: Carlton, Andujar (2),
    Rogers (4), G. Perry (6), Sambito (6),
    LaCoss (6), SUTTER (8) vs Ryan,
    Stanley (3), Clear (5), KERN (7),
    Guidry (9)
Home Runs: Lynn-A, Mazzilli-N
Attendance: 58,905

Mike Schmidt tripled and George Foster doubled to drive in the game's first runs as the Nationals began their scoring in the top of the first. The Americans fought back to take the lead later in the inning as Don Baylor doubled home one run and Fred Lynn homered for two more. The Nationals tied the score with a run in the second and went ahead again in the third when Schmidt scored after doubling. But the Americans recaptured the lead in the bottom of the third, scoring twice on a single, wild pitch, ground out, hit batsman, single, and error.

Three innings later the Nationals again tied the game, but the Americans went ahead for the third time with a run in their half of the sixth. Outstanding throws by right fielder Dave Parker, who notched two assists, helped to keep the Americans from pulling away. In the eighth the Nationals' Lee Mazzilli homered for yet another tie, and an inning later Ron Guidry walked Mazzilli with the bases loaded to force in the Nationals' go-ahead seventh run. When Bruce Sutter kept the Americans from scoring in the bottom of the ninth, the National Leaguers had for the second time defeated the Americans eight years in a row.

GAME 51
Dodger Stadium,
Los Angeles
July 8, 1980
NL, 4–2

AL	000	020	000	2	7	1
NL	000	012	10X	4	7	0

MVP: Griffey-N
Pitchers: Stone, JOHN (4), Farmer (6),
    Stieb (7), Gossage (8) vs Richard,
    Welch (3), REUSS (6), Bibby (7),
    Sutter (8)
Home Runs: Lynn-A, Griffey-N
Attendance: 56,088

For 4⅔ innings J.R. Richard and Bob Welch held the American stars scoreless. But then Rod Carew singled and Fred Lynn drove in the game's first runs with his third All-Star homer.

The Americans' Steve Stone and Tommy John pitched even better, setting the Nationals down in order through four innings. John continued the perfect streak through the first two outs of the fifth, but then Ken Griffey homered, and the Americans' spell on the National Leaguers was broken.

While three National pitchers limited the Americans to a single and a walk over the final four innings, three singles and an error sent the Nationals into the lead in the sixth. A passed ball surrounded by two wild pitches moved Dave Concepcion around the bases in the seventh (he had reached on a fielder's choice) for the Nationals' fourth run. They didn't really need it, though, as Bruce Sutter—the winning pitcher in the two previous All-Star games—saved this one with two final innings of no-hit ball for the Nationals' ninth successive win.

GAME 52
Municipal Stadium,
Cleveland
August 9, 1981
NL, 5–4

NL	000	011	120	5	9	1
AL	010	003	000	4	11	1

MVP: Carter
Pitchers: Valenzuela, Seaver (2),
    Knepper (3), Hooton (5), Ruthven (6),
    BLUE (7), Ryan (8), Sutter (9) vs
    Morris, Barker (3), K.Forsch (5),
    Norris (6), Davis (7), FINGERS (8),
    Stieb (8)
Home Runs: Singleton-A, Carter-N (2),
    Parker-N, Schmidt-N
Attendance: 72,086

The game, delayed until August by the midseason players' strike, drew an All-Star record crowd of more than 72,000 fans, and the managers set a new record by using 56 players. But the game itself followed a familiar pattern.

The Americans scored first in the second inning on Ken Singleton's home run off Tom Seaver, and held their slim lead into the fifth on Len Barker's two innings of perfect pitching. But Ken Forsch replaced Barker in the fifth and Gary Carter homered off his first pitch to tie the score. Dave Parker's homer off Mike Norris an inning later put the Nationals ahead for the first time, but the Americans came right back in the bottom of the inning, putting together four singles and a sacrifice fly for three runs and a two-run advantage.

Gary Carter's second home run of the game—this time off Ron Davis's first pitch—brought the Nationals within one in the seventh, and Mike Schmidt's two-run blast off Rollie Fingers in the eighth restored their lead. Three National pitchers shut out the Americans without a hit over the final three innings as closer Bruce Sutter picked up his second consecutive All-Star save and the National Leaguers had their 10th consecutive victory.

GAME 53
Olympic Stadium, Montreal
July 13, 1982
NL, 4–1

```
AL   100  000  000     1  8  2
NL   021  001  00X     4  8  1
```

MVP: Concepcion-N
Pitchers: ECKERSLEY, Clancy (4), Bannister (5), Quisenberry (6), Fingers (8) vs ROGERS, Carlton (4), Soto (6), Valenzuela (8), Minton (8), Howe (9), Hume (9)
Home Runs: Concepcion-N
Attendance: 59,057

In the first All-Star Game held outside the United States, the American League for the third year in a row put the first run on the board, but for the 11th year in a row the final score showed the National League the winner. Two singles, a wild pitch, and a sacrifice fly gave the Americans a run in the top of the first. But starter Steve Rogers of the host Expos held the Americans scoreless for the remainder of his three innings while the Nationals struck back for two runs in the second on Dave Concepcion's home run, and added another in the third when Ruppert Jones—who had tripled to open the inning—scored on a sacrifice fly.

Six National League pitchers (and shortstop Ozzie Smith's spectacular stop and throw to first with two on in the eighth) joined Rogers in holding the American stars scoreless after the first inning. Two hometowners put together the Nationals' final run in the sixth. Al Oliver, leading off, doubled down the line in left and took third as the ball got by left fielder Rickey Henderson. Two outs later Gary Carter lined a pitch to center, scoring Oliver as Willie Wilson's dive for the ball came up short.

GAME 54
Comiskey Park, Chicago
July 6, 1983
AL, 13–3

```
NL   100  110  000      3  8  3
AL   117  000  22X    13 15  2
```

MVP: Lynn-A
Pitchers: SOTO, Hammaker (3), Dawley (3), Dravecky (5), Perez (7), Orosco (7), L.Smith (8) vs STIEB, Honeycutt (4), Stanley (6), Young (8), Quisenberry (9)
Home Runs: Rice-A, Lynn-A
Attendance: 43,801

The game returned to the park where it had originated 50 years earlier, and the American League, after 11 years of All-Star losses, unleashed its pent-up fury to produce the greatest margin of victory in 37 years. The game began, though, as an embarrassment of errors. American starter Dave Stieb struck out the side in the first, but along the way two errors (one of them Stieb's) let in a run. An unearned run in the bottom of the first tied the score and another in the second put the American League ahead for good (making a loser out of the unfortunate National starter Mario Soto).

The hitting began in earnest in the last of the third as the Americans scored seven times for a new one-inning record. Among their six hits (also a record for an All-Star inning) were a homer by Jim Rice, a triple by George Brett, and a bases-loaded blast by Fred Lynn—his fourth All-Star home run and the first grand slam in All-Star history. With the score now 9–1, the National League's single runs in the fourth and fifth were exercises in futility, and the Americans' two each in the seventh and eighth served chiefly to boost the winning total to 13—another All-Star high.

GAME 55
Candlestick Park,
San Francisco
July 10, 1984
NL, 3–1

```
AL   010  000  000     1  7  2
NL   110  000  01X     3  8  0
```

MVP: Carter-N
Pitchers: STIEB, Morris (3), Dotson (5), Caudill (7), Hernandez (8) vs LEA, Valenzuela (3), Gooden (5), Soto (7), Gossage (9)
Home Runs: Brett-A, Carter-N, Murphy-N
Attendance: 57,756

Only four times in the previous 54 All-Star Games had a pitcher struck out the side in order. In this game, three more pitchers did it. And, on this 50th anniversary of Carl Hubbell's five consecutive strikeouts, two of those pitchers combined to break Hubbell's record with six back-to-back whiffs. Hubbell, who threw out the first ball, also saw an All-Star nine-inning record set with 21 total Ks (11 by National League pitchers, 10 by American).

In the fourth inning, National star Fernando Valenzuela mowed down three of the game's premier sluggers: Dave Winfield, Reggie Jackson, and George Brett. The three men Dwight Gooden retired on strikes an inning later (Lance Parrish, Chet Lemon, and rookie Alvin Davis) were slightly less formidable, still, it was an impressive performance for a 19-year-old rookie (the youngest player in All-Star history). The three that American Leaguer Bill Caudill struck out in the seventh were no slouches either: Tim Raines, Ryne Sandberg (in the midst of an MVP season), and Keith Hernandez.

Three of the four runs scored in the game were homers. The National League's run in the first was unearned, but the Americans' George Brett homered to center to tie the game in the second, and the Nationals' go-ahead run later in the inning came on Gary Carter's blast to left. In the eighth, National Leaguer Dale Murphy also put one over the left field fence to end the scoring.

GAME 56
H. Humphrey Metrodome,
Minneapolis
July 16, 1985
NL, 6–1

```
NL   011  020  002     6  9  1
AL   100  000  000     1  5  0
```

MVP: Hoyt-N
Pitchers: HOYT, Ryan (4), Valenzuela (7), Reardon (8), Gossage (9) vs MORRIS, Key (3), Blyleven (4), Stieb (6), Moore (7), Petry (9), W.Hernandez (9)
Attendance: 54,960

The American Leaguers scored first, as Rickey Henderson led off the bottom of the first with a single and circled the bases on a steal, error, and sacrifice fly. But the five National pitchers blanked the Americans the rest of the way on only four more singles.

Meanwhile, the National stars methodically dismantled the Americans for their 36th All-Star victory. In the top of the second, after Darryl Strawberry singled and stole second, Terry Kennedy, whose error had led to the American League run, redeemed himself by singling Strawberry home. An inning later, with two out, Tom Herr doubled and scored the go-ahead (and winning) run on Steve Garvey's single.

In the fifth the Nationals scored two more runs on a hit batsman, Tim Wallach's ground-rule double, and Ozzie Virgil's single, and finished their scoring in the ninth with another pair on three walks and Willie McGee's double—another ground-rule bounce out of play off the lively Metrodome surface. Goose Gossage struck out the final two American batters in the bottom of the ninth, and the Nationals had increased their winning margin in the series to a new high of 17 games.

GAME 57
Astrodome, Houston
July 15, 1986
AL, 3–2

AL	020 000 100	3 5 0
NL	000 000 020	2 5 1

MVP: Clemens-A
Pitchers: CLEMENS, Higuera (4), Hough (7), Righetti (8), Aase (9) vs GOODEN, Valenzuela (4), Scott (7), Fernandez (8), Krukow (9)
Home Runs: Whitaker-A, White-A
Attendance: 45,774

National League pitchers struck out 12 Americans, led by Fernando Valenzuela's five in a row, which matched the mark set by Carl Hubbell in 1934. (Two years earlier Valenzuela had helped set a multi-pitcher All-Star record of six consecutive strikeouts.) In the eighth inning Sid Fernandez, after walking two, struck out the next three.

Though the American Leaguers struck out fewer men, their pitching was more effective on the whole. Starter Roger Clemens hurled three perfect innings (three balls and 21 strikes), and Teddy Higuera one-hit the Nationals over the next three. Charlie Hough struck out three in the eighth after yielding the Nationals' only extra-base hit (a double) to Chris Brown. But catcher Rich Gedman couldn't handle Hough's knuckleball, and Brown advanced to third on the first strikeout (ruled a wild pitch) and scored on the second, a passed ball which also enabled batter Hubie Brooks to reach first safely. Brooks moved up on a balk and scored the Nationals' second run on Steve Sax's single.

But home runs had already undone the Nationals. With two gone in the second, Dave Winfield doubled off starter Dwight Gooden, and Lou Whitaker clubbed an 0–2 pitch over the fence in right. And in the seventh, Frank White (hitting for Whitaker) knocked Mike Scott's 0–2 pitch over the fence in left-center for what proved the margin of American League victory.

GAME 58
Oakland-Alameda County Coliseum, Oakland
July 14, 1987
NL, 2–0

NL	000 000 000 000 2	2 8 2
AL	000 000 000 000 0	0 6 1

MVP: Raines-N
Pitchers: Scott, Sutcliffe (3), Hershiser (5), R.Reuschel (7), Jo.Franco (8), Bedrosian (9), L.SMITH (10), S. Fernandez (13) vs Saberhagen, Morris (4), Langston (6), Plesac (8), Righetti (9), Henke (9), J.HOWELL (12)
Attendance: 49,671

None of the previous 57 All-Star Games had gone more than five innings without at least one run crossing the plate. But this game went more than twice that before National Leaguer Tim Raines tripled in two runs in the top of the 13th for the game's only scoring. It was the National League's eighth win in eight extra-inning All-Star games.

Both teams missed scoring opportunities in the ninth inning. Raines singled for the Nationals with only one out, and became the game's first runner to reach third when a throw from first on his attempted steal went into center field. But a fly to short right and a foul out left him stranded. In the bottom of the ninth, the Americans came close to winning the game as Dave Winfield headed for home from second on a missed 4-6-1 double play. But National pitcher Steve Bedrosian, covering first, snared the off-center throw from short and fired it home to catch Winfield for the third out.

The Americans again reached third in the 11th as Larry Parrish singled and moved around on a sacrifice and ground out. But pitcher Lee Smith (whose three shutout innings earned him the win) struck out Tony Fernandez to end the threat.

GAME 59
Riverfront Stadium, Cincinnati
July 12, 1988
AL, 2–1

AL	001 100 000	2 6 2
NL	000 100 000	1 5 0

MVP: Steinbach-A
Pitchers: VIOLA, Clemens (3), Gubicza (4), Stieb (6), Russell (7), Jones (8), Plesac (8), Eckersley (9) vs GOODEN, Knepper (4), Cone (5), Gross (6), Davis (7), Walk (7), Hershiser (8), Worrell (9)
Home Run: Steinbach-A
Attendance: 55,837

Oakland's Terry Steinbach was not among the 10 top American League catchers in batting; because of time lost to injuries, he was not even his club's leading catcher in games played. But the fans voted him to start in the All-Star Game, and he won it for the American Leaguers with a home run in his first trip to the plate and a sacrifice fly his next time up. Steinbach's homer—a drive off Dwight Gooden that led off the third inning—caromed off the glove of a leaping Darryl Strawberry over the wall in right for the game's first score. His sacrifice fly—high and deep to left in the fourth inning—scored Dave Winfield (aboard with his record seventh All-Star double) to give the American League a 2–0 lead.

Steinbach also contributed to the National League run later in the fourth. His throwing error on Vince Coleman's steal of second enabled Coleman to advance to third, whence he scored on a wild pitch by Mark Gubicza.

American starter Frank Viola, the midseason league leader in wins, was awarded the victory for his two perfect innings pitched. Dennis Eckersley, the majors' top reliever, preserved the win for the Americans with a perfect ninth inning.

GAME 60
Anaheim Stadium, Anaheim
July 11, 1989
AL, 5–3

NL	200 000 010	3 9 1
AL	212 000 00X	5 12 0

MVP: Jackson-A
Pitchers: Reuschel, SMOLTZ (2), Sutcliffe (3), Burke (4), M. Davis (6), Howell (7), Williams (8) vs Stewart, RYAN (2), Gubicza (4), Moore (5), Swindell (6), Russell (7), Plesac (8), Jones (8)
Home Runs: Jackson-A, Boggs-A
Attendance: 64,036

The National stars struck early with a pair of two-out runs in the top of the first inning, and a double steal put two more runners in scoring position. But left fielder Bo Jackson stifled the assault with a fine running catch, then opened the American half of the first with a massive home run to center field off Rick Reuschel. Wade Boggs, the next man up, added insult to the 40-year-old Reuschel's first All-Star start, tying the game with another homer.

In the second inning Jackson drove in the American League's go-ahead run with a slow grounder off young John Smoltz, and an inning later four American singles produced two more runs. A quartet of National League pitchers held the Americans scoreless on just three hits over the final six innings, and their teammates rallied for a third National run in the eighth. But Doug Jones (the majors' top reliever in 1989) came on to get the final out of the eighth, and in the ninth preserved the American lead to give the American Leaguers their first repeat All-Star victory in 31 years.

National League hurler Smoltz, at age 22 the youngest player in the lineup, took the loss. Nolan Ryan, back in the American League after nine National League seasons, earned the win with two shutout innings. Not only was he the oldest player on either side, he was the oldest All-Star winning pitcher ever.

GAME 61
Wrigley Field, Chicago
July 10, 1990
AL, 2–0

AL	000	000	200	2 7 0
NL	000	000	000	0 2 1

MVP: Ju. Franco-A
Pitchers: Welch, Stieb (3), SABERHAGEN (5), Thigpen (7), Finley (8), Eckersley (9) vs Armstrong, R. Martinez (3), D. Martinez (4), Viola (5), D. Smith (6), BRANTLEY (6), Dibble (7), Myers (8), Jo. Franco (9)
Attendance: 39,071

Back-to-back American League singles off Jeff Brantley had put men on third and first and brought Julio Franco to the plate in the seventh inning, when heavy rain halted the game for more than an hour. During the delay Brantley's side stiffened, so when Franco finally got his turn at bat he faced a new National pitcher, Rob Dibble. Franco lined Dibble's third pitch into the gap in right center for a double—the only extra-base hit of the game—driving in what proved to be the game's only runs.

Damp air and a stiff breeze in from left field helped tame the offense. American League batters managed to accumulate seven hits, but the Nationals were held to two—an All-Star all-time low. No runner advanced as far as third base until the sixth inning, when American stars Kelly Gruber and Jose Canseco pulled a double steal. No National Leaguer reached that far, and if it weren't for Barry Larkin's third-inning steal, no National runner would even have stood on second base.

American League hurler Bret Saberhagen's two perfect middle innings earned him the win, and Dennis Eckersley, after yielding a leadoff hit in the ninth, retired the final three batters to record his second All-Star save in three years. The victory was the third in a row for the American Leaguers, the first time they had put together such a string of triumphs in 41 years.

GAME 62
SkyDome, Toronto
July 9, 1991
AL, 4–2

NL	100	100	000	2 10 1
AL	003	000	10X	4 8 0

MVP: Ripken-A
Pitchers: Glavine, MARTINEZ (3), Viola (5), Harnisch (6), Smiley (7), Dibble (7), Morgan (8) vs Morris, KEY (3), Clemens (4), McDowell (5), Reardon (7), Aguilera (7), Eckersley (9)
Home Runs: Ripken-A, Dawson-N
Attendance: 52,383

The National League took an early 1–0 lead on singles by Tony Gwynn, Will Clark, and Bobby Bonilla in the top of the first, and held it for two innings on Tom Glavine's strong pitching, which included three strikeouts. But Dennis Martinez yielded successive singles to Rickey Henderson and Wade Boggs in the third inning, and the next batter, Cal Ripken, Jr., homered to center to give the Americans all the runs they would need for victory.

National Leaguer Andre Dawson led off the fourth inning with a massive home run to center off Roger Clemens. This brought the Nationals within a run of tying the game, but they scored no more, as a succession of American League pitchers shut them down on a walk and four singles the rest of the way. In the seventh inning the Americans added an insurance run when Joe Carter singled and moved around the bases on a call of catcher interference (the first in All-Star history), a sacrifice bunt, and Harold Baines' sacrifice liner to right.

Jimmy Key, the pitcher of record when Ripken's three-run homer put the American League ahead, was awarded the win. Dennis Eckersley, who pitched a perfect ninth, earned a record third All-Star save.

It was only the second time in All-Star history that the American League had won four games in a row.

GAME 63
Jack Murphy Stadium, San Diego
July 14, 1992
AL, 13–6

AL	411	004	030	13 19 1
NL	000	001	032	6 12 1

MVP: Griffey-A
Pitchers: BROWN, McDowell (2), Guzman (3), Clemens (4), Mussina (5), Langston (6), Nagy (7), Montgomery (8), Aguilera (8), Eckersley (9) vs GLAVINE, Maddux (2), Cone (3), Tewksbury (5), Smoltz (6), Martinez (7), Jones (8), Charlton (9)
Home Runs: Sierra-A, Griffey-A, Clark-N
Attendance: 59,372

By the time the National Leaguers pushed across their first run in the sixth inning, the Americans had already scored 10 times, and although National bats caught fire for five more runs in the eighth and ninth, they were powerless to prevent the American League from stretching its All-Star win streak to five games. National League starting pitcher Tom Glavine could not repeat his strong 1991 start: before his relief after 1⅔ innings in 1992, he was tagged for nine singles and five runs. In the third inning, Ken Griffey, Jr., who had driven in one of the first-inning runs, added the sixth American score with a homer off Greg Maddux. When he came up again to lead off the sixth inning, Griffey doubled to initiate a new American scoring spree, which included two-out doubles by Carlos Baerga and Robin Ventura, capped by Ruben Sierra's home run—all off Bob Tewksbury, who had set down the Americans 1–2–3 an inning earlier. Travis Fryman's RBI single and Roberto Kelly's two-run double in the eighth closed out the American League scoring.

Will Clark's two-out blast off Rick Aguilera in the last of the eighth was the National League's first three-run homer since 1964, but it was too little to make more than a dent in the American lead. With two men out in the ninth, a pair of singles off Dennis Eckersley loaded the bases, and Bip Roberts' single drove in two of the baserunners to bring the NL run total to six (enough to have defeated the AL in the seven previous All-Star Games).

Starter Kevin Brown was awarded the win; Glavine took the loss.

GAME 64
Oriole Park at Camden Yards, Baltimore
July 13, 1993
AL, 9–3

AL	011	033	10X	9 10
NL	200	001	000	3 7 2

MVP: Puckett-A
Pitchers: Mulholland, Benes (3), BURKETT, Avery (5), Smoltz (6), Beck (7), Harvey (8) vs Langston, Johnson (3), McDOWELL (5), Key (6), Montgomery (7), Aguilera (8), Ward (9)
Home Runs: Sheffield-N, Alomar-A, Puckett-A
Attendance: 48,147

Barry Bonds doubled off Mark Langston with one out in the first inning and Gary Sheffield followed with a home run to left that gave the National League two runs before the American Leaguers came to bat. In the bottom of the second inning, though, Kirby Puckett's solo shot over the center field wall off Terry Mulholland narrowed the gap, and an inning later Roberto Alomar led off with a homer to right off Andy Benes that evened the score.

The Americans pushed ahead in the last of the fifth when, with John Burkett pitching, Ivan Rodriguez lined a ground rule double to left and Albert Belle singled him home. Belle took second on an error, and scored on Ken Griffey Jr.'s single; Griffey scored on Puckett's double into the gap at left center. A half inning later, Barry Larkin drove Bonds home with a sacrifice fly to narrow the score to 5–3, but the Americans blew the game open in the sixth with a trio of unearned runs. After shortstop Jeff Blauser failed to field a grounder by Carlos Baerga—depriving pitcher Steve Avery of a 1–2–3 inning—Avery walked Belle and Devon White doubled, sending Baerga home and Bell to third. John Smoltz, who relieved Avery, unloaded a pair of wild pitches that enabled Belle and White to score.

In the bottom of the seventh inning, Terry Steinbach tagged Rod Beck for a double high off the wall in right to drive in the ninth—and final—AL run. The Nationals got runners to second and third in the eighth with just one out, but failed to score. Duane Ward retired the National Leaguers in order in the ninth to give the American League its sixth straight All-Star victory.

GAME 65
Three Rivers Stadium, Pittsburgh
July 12, 1994
NL, 8–7

```
AL   100 003 300 0    7 15 0
NL   103 001 002 1    8 12 1
```

MVP: McGriff-N
Pitchers: Key, Cone (3), Mussina (5), Johnson (6) Hentgen (7), Alvarez (8), L.Smith (9), BERE (10) vs Maddux, Hill (4), Drabek (6), Hudek (6), Jackson (7), Beck (7), Myers (9), JONES (10)
Home Runs: Grissom-N, McGriff-N
Attendance: 59,568

A blend of youth and experience enabled the National League to snap the American Leaguers' six-game winning streak with one of the tightest finishes in All-Star history. In the bottom of the 10th inning, with the score tied, 7–7, Tony Gwynn, a veteran of 10 All-Star games, led off by chopping a single to center off Jason Bere. He took off when novice All-Star Moises Alou drove Bere's second pitch to the base of the wall in left center. AL catcher Ivan Rodriguez received the ball—relayed sharply from the outfield—just as Gwynn slipped between the catcher's legs with the winning run.

It was a close game all the way. The teams traded single runs in the first inning. In the third, the National Leaguers grabbed the biggest lead of the evening when they sandwiched a hit batsman and Gwynn's double between a pair of singles to knock David Cone for three runs. In the top of the sixth the Americans evened the score again with a trio of runs off Doug Drabek. Then Marquis Grissom hit a home run off Randy Johnson a half inning later.

Once again the Americans knotted the game when Scott Cooper doubled home Ivan Rodriguez in the seventh and took their first (and, as it turned out, only) lead when Ken Lofton singled to score Chuck Knoblauch and Cooper. A fourth run would have scored in the seventh, however, if shortstop Ozzie Smith—39 years old and playing in his 13th All-Star contest—had not made a spectacular diving stop of Knoblauch's drive and recovered to force Mickey Tettleton at second.

The Americans maintained their 7–5 advantage into the last of the ninth. Pinch hitter Fred McGriff, after fouling off a third strike, brought National League fans to their feet with a game-tying home run. Doug Jones held the Americans scoreless in the top of the 10th, and the stage was set for the Gwynn–Alou finish.

GAME 66
The Ballpark at Arlington, Texas
July 11, 1995
NL, 3–2

```
NL   000 001 110    3 3 0
AL   000 200 000    2 8 0
```

MVP: Conine-N
Pitchers: Nomo, Smiley (3), Green (5), Neagle (6), Perez (7), SLOCUMB (7), Henke (8), Myers (9) vs Johnson, Appier (3), Martinez (5), Rogers (7), ONTIVEROS (8), Wells (8), Mesa (9)
Home Runs: Thomas-A, Biggio-N, Piazza-N, Conine-N
Attendance: 50,920

On a 96-degree evening at The Ballpark in Arlington, Texas, the National League made the most of just three hits (the lowest for a winning squad since 1952) in defeating the AL, 3-2. The key: all three hits were home runs.

After 5⅔ innings it certainly didn't appear the NL would triumph. AL pitchers Randy Johnson, Kevin Appier, and Dennis Martinez combined to no-hit senior circuit batters. Not until Craig Biggio homered off Martinez did the National Leaguers collect their first hit. That cut the AL's margin to 2-1, since Frank Thomas had delivered a monster two-run homer off John Smiley in the fourth. The ball landed in a left field luxury box and was eventually retrieved by Donald Fehr's 9-year-old nephew.

Mike Piazza tied the game an inning later by homering off Kenny Rogers. In the eighth inning Jeff Conine pinch-hit for Ron Gant. Facing Steve Ontiveros, who had also just entered the game, the 29-year-old Conine delivered a 410-foot homer to the lower deck in left. That was all the National League needed to win—and it earned Conine All-Star MVP honors.

Pregame excitement centered about the figure of Dodgers rookie Hideo Nomo. Nomo, the first Japanese national to appear in an All-Star Game, was also the first rookie to start since Fernando Valenzuela in 1981. Much of his native land stopped work (it was 9 a.m. in Japan) to watch—and cheer—Nomo's performance as he allowed just one hit in two innings and struck out Kenny Lofton, Edgar Martinez, and Albert Belle.

GAME 67
Veterans Stadium, Philadelphia
July 9, 1996
NL, 6–0

```
AL   000 000 000    0  7 0
NL   121 002 00X    6 12 1
```

MVP: Piazza-N
Pitchers: NAGY, Finley (3), Pavlik (5), Percival (7), Hernandez (8) vs. SMOLTZ, Brown (3), Glavine (4), Bottalico (5), Martinez (6), Trachsel (7), Worrell (8), Wohlers (9), Leiter (9)
Home Runs: Piazza-N, Caminiti-N
Attendance: 62,670

Mike Piazza a native of nearby Norristown, Pa., homered his first time up, doubled in his next at bat, and called the signals behind the plate as nine pitchers combined to shut out the potent AL lineup. Indians manager Mike Hargrove's power-packed AL lineup, which had Baltimore's Brady Anderson (who finished the year with 50 homers) batting eighth, managed only seven singles against the NL's parade of pitchers.

John Smoltz, like his counterpart Charles Nagy, was making his first All-Star start. Smoltz allowed only two hits and a walk in two innings to get the win. Nagy, on the other hand, was touched for four hits and three runs, including a 445-foot home run by Piazza leading off the second.

Center fielder Lance Johnson, who started and played the entire game in place of injured Tony Gwynn, had three hits and a stolen base. He set the tone for the game by legging out a double on the first pitch from Nagy, taking third on a groundout by Barry Larkin and scoring on a groundout by Barry Bonds. Following Piazza's homer, Chipper Jones singled and went to second on a groundout by Craig Biggio. Jones scored on a single by Henry Rodriguez. Piazza brought home the NL's fourth run with a double off Chuck Finley to score Larkin. Ken Caminiti homered to right off Roger Pavlik in the sixth and Craig Biggio delivered the final run later in the inning.

Ozzie Smith, playing his 15th and final All-Star Game, stole the show in the latter innings. Smith, who earlier announced that 1996 was his final season, received a long standing ovation when he came to bat in the seventh. He also started a double play at shortstop in the ninth.

GAME 68
Jacobs Field, Cleveland
July 8, 1997
AL, 3-1

```
NL   000 000 100    1 3 0
AL   010 000 20X    3 7 0
```

MVP: S. Alomar-A
Pitchers: Maddux, Schilling (3), Brown (5), Martinez (6), ESTES (7), B.Jones (8) vs. Johnson, Clemens (3), Cone (4), Thompson (5), Hentgen (6), ROSADO (7), Myers (8), Rivera (9)
Home Runs: E. Martinez-A, Lopez-N, S. Alomar-A

Sandy Alomar, Jr. broke a seventh-inning tie and sent the Cleveland crowd into a frenzy with a two-out, two-run home run off Shawn Estes. Although there were three home runs hit at Jacobs Field, pitching was the name of the game. Eight American League pitchers limited the National League to just three hits to halt a three-year losing streak.

The most lasting image of game occurred in the top of the second inning with the long-awaited showdown between Randy Johnson and Larry Walker. The lefty-lefty matchup began with Johnson's first pitch sailing over the head of Walker—reminiscent of Johnson's memorable meeting with John Kruk in the 1993 All-Star Game—but Walker surprised everyone, by turning his helmet around and then stepping across the plate to bat right-handed. He took a pitch (another ball) before returning to bat from the left side and drawing a walk without taking the bat off his shoulder.

Edgar Martinez, the first designated hitter ever voted by the fans to start at the position in the All-Star Game, drilled a line drive over the fence in left field for a 1-0 American League lead in the second inning off Greg Maddux. Outstanding defensive plays by Roberto Alomar, Joey Cora, and Cal Ripken, who made his 14th consecutive All-Star start, but his first at third base, helped four American League pitchers nurse the 1-0 lead until the seventh inning. Javier Lopez, in his first All-Star at bat, pulled a pitch from Luis Rosado off the foul pole in left field to tie the game at 1-1. In the bottom of the seventh inning, Shawn Estes issued the only NL walk of the evening to Bernie Williams and Sandy Alomar, who entered the game having hit in his last 30 games of the first half of the season, homered to make it a 3-1 game. Randy Myers and Mariano Rivera each pitched perfect innings to give the AL its first win since 1993.

GAME 69
Coors Field, Denver
July 7, 1998
AL, 13-8

AL	000	413	113	13	19	2
NL	002	130	020	8	12	1

MVP: R. Alomar-A
Pitchers: Wells, Clemens (3), Radke (4),
  COLON (5), Arrojo (6), Wetteland (7),
  Gordon (8), Percival (9) vs. Maddux,
  Glavine (3), Brown (4), Ashby (5),
  URBINA (6), Hoffman (7), Shaw (8),
  Nen (9)
Home Runs: A. Rodriguez-A, Bonds-N,
  R. Alomar-A
Attendance: 51,267

This Rocky Mountain version of the
All-Star Game featured the most
runs (21), but it was a defensive
play that was the pivotal play of the
game. With the National League
having closed the gap to 10-8 with
runners on first and second and
none out in the eighth, Devon White
singled to left and Fernando Vina
was thrown out at the plate by Paul
O'Neill. Had Vina held up, the bases would have been loaded with
nobody out for Andres Galarraga,
the NL RBI leader the past two
years who had 72 RBI at the
All-Star break, but his smash up the
middle was turned into an inning-ending double play by Omar
Vizquel.

Roberto Alomar was one of
seven All-Stars to have a multi-
ple-hit game, but the second baseman, who also had a walk, a stolen
base, and a home run, was chosen as
the game's Most Valuable Player a
year after his brother, Sandy, was
named MVP in the 1997 game. Roberto Alomar was one of just three
players to homer in a game where
longballs were expected to be plentiful in the thin air of Denver's high
elevation. (The expectations were
further heightened when 83 home
runs were hit in the previous day's
annual Home Run Derby, which
was won by reluctant participant
Ken Griffey.) The furthest ball hit in
the All-Star Game came off the bat
of Barry Bonds, a three-run shot
that gave the NL a short-lived 6-5
lead after five innings.

A rocky sixth inning by both
pitcher Ugueth Urbina and catcher
Javier Lopez included three stolen
bases, a wild pitch, a passed ball,
and a run scoring single by Ivan
Rodriguez that gave the AL a lead it
did not relinquish. The AL scored at
least one run in every inning after
the fourth. One of those runs came
off Jeff Shaw, who spent the first
half of the season pitching for the
Reds, but he was traded to the
Dodgers shortly before the All-Star
break and became the first player to
debut in a new uniform in the
All-Star Game.

## CHAPTER 12

Postseason Play

Frederick Ivor-Campbell and David Pietrusza

When Major League Baseball and the striking players were unable to work out a settlement of their dispute in 1994, they interrupted a tradition of major league postseason play that traced back to 1871, the first year there was a professional league. National Association teams in the 1870s typically followed the conclusion of their championship (regularly scheduled) season with exhibition games against amateur clubs. In the 1880s nearly every major league club played a couple of weeks of postseason games, generally against major and minor league teams they hadn't faced during the regular season. In the 20th century there had been a World Series every year for 90 years, prefaced since 1969 by League Championship Series to determine the American and National League pennant winners.

Before there was a World Series there were city and regional series. In 1882 Cleveland defeated Cincinnati for the championship of Ohio, and the next year teams in Philadelphia and New York played for the championships of those cities. These were informal series, arranged by the clubs themselves without official league sanction, and varied in the number of games scheduled according to the desires of the clubs involved.

The same held true for the early World Series, which had their beginnings in 1884. Two years earlier, the champions of the National League and the brand-new American Association played a pair of postseason contests (in which each team recorded a shutout against the other). Some would like to call these games the first World Series, but no one in 1882 saw them as more than exhibition games. In fact, because the NL didn't yet recognize the legitimacy of the AA and forbade its clubs to play those of the new league, the NL champion Chicago White Stockings had to release their players from their season contracts so they could face AA champion Cincinnati as technically independent players.

That winter the two major leagues made their peace, and although a proposed series between the 1883 NL and AA titlists was called off, the 1884 champion Providence Grays (NL) and the Metropolitan Club of New York (AA) played three games "for the championship of the United States." The winning Grays were acclaimed in the press as "champions of the world," and the World Series was born.

The brief 1884 Series set the stage for more elaborate World Series to follow. From 1885 through 1890 the NL and AA pennant-winners met in Series that ranged in length from six games to fifteen.

The demise of the AA after the 1891 season caused a one-year gap in World Series play. When the National League expanded from eight clubs to 12 the next year (by absorbing four teams from the defunct AA), it divided the regular season into two halves, with the first-half winner playing the winner of the second half for the world title. Boston defeated Cleveland in the first official World Series, but the unpopular divided season was not repeated (that is, until the strike year of 1981).

Two years later a new World Series scheme was devised when one William C. Temple offered a prize cup to the winner of a postseason series between the first- and second-place finishers in the NL. For four years these best-of-seven Temple Cup games served as the officially recognized world championship. But by the end of four lopsided Series (only one of which was won by the pennant-winning club), fan interest—never robust—had declined so much that the trophy was returned to its donor and the series abandoned.

In 1900, partisans of second-place Pittsburgh felt that their Pirates were the equal of pennant-winning Brooklyn, and a Pittsburgh newspaper, the *Chronicle-Telegraph*, offered a silver trophy cup to the winner of a best-of-five series between the clubs, to be played entirely in Pittsburgh. Described in the press as the "world's championship series," the games confirmed the superiority of Brooklyn's Superbas, who needed only four games to subdue the hometown Pirates.

The upgrading of the American League from minor to major league status in 1901 made a return to interleague World Series play theoretically possible, but it was not until after the NL and AL had made peace in 1903 that the first modern Series was contested. The owners of NL champion Pittsburgh and AL champion Boston arranged a best-of-nine postseason Series in 1903, which proved both popular and financially successful—a firm foundation for future Series. When the NL pennant-winning Giants refused to meet repeating AL titlist Boston in 1904, press and fan disappointment led baseball's National Commission to establish the World Series officially in 1905.

The end of the 1903 season saw not only the first modern World Series, but also a revival of city and regional series (which had lapsed when the AA folded) in Chicago, Philadelphia, St. Louis, and Ohio. In 1905 the National Commission offered to oversee these series, too, and give them the stability of official sanction. Until the manpower needs of the World War halted the 1918 season a month early (discouraging postseason play apart from

the World Series), most of the city and regional series—and occasional series between other clubs, like Cleveland and Pittsburgh, and the Boston Red Sox and New York Giants—were played under National Commission auspices.

After the war's end, only Chicago's Cubs and White Sox resumed a city series; they played 16 series between 1921 and 1942, when World War II intervened. For 26 years thereafter the World Series alone remained of the once multifaceted major-league postseason—until the AL and NL split into two divisions each in 1969 and ushered in a new layer of playoffs: the League Championship Series. (In 1981, to recoup some of the money and fan interest lost during a midseason players' strike that split the season in half, a one-time third layer of postseason playoffs was added, pitting the first-half and second-half winners in each division against each other for the division titles—an aberration that made the divisional races even more surreal than the strike itself had done.) From 1969 through 1984 the LCS were played as best-of-five series, but in 1985 they were expanded to match the best-of-seven World Series.

In 1993, the club owners voted to realign each league into three divisions—East, Central, and West—and to install a preliminary layer of playoffs for each league. The three divisional champions and the second-place team with the best record would determine, through a pair of best-of-five series, which two teams would compete for the pennant in the League Championship Series. When the 1994 postseason was cancelled, however, the introduction of the new playoffs was among the casualties.

Key to the Statistics

The statistics in this section of *Total Baseball* are standard—there is little point in applying newer analytical measures to performances that run to seven games or fewer. We do offer, however, stats that were not standard at the time, such as earned run averages for years before

1912 and runs batted in before 1920 (which were determined from box scores and play-by-plays) and saves before 1969. Beyond our powers of reconstruction were the following: runs batted in, stolen bases, and batter strikeouts for the World Series of 1885.

Ignoring the odd 1887 custom of counting walks as base hits, we present the cumulative box score for that year's World Series in accordance with modern practice. Other curiosities of early postseason play include the use of neutral sites for some games in 1885 and 1888 and for the majority of games in 1887, and the use of players who did not appear in so much as an inning for that team during the regular season (Tom Forster, New York Mets, 1884; Bug Holliday, Chicago, 1885; Sy Sutcliffe, Detroit, 1887; Jumbo Davis, Brooklyn 1889).

The length of the World Series varied from three games in 1884 all the way up to 15 in 1887 and 10 the following year. The best-of-seven format came in with the Temple Cup Series of 1894 and has been the norm for World Series ever since (excepting 1900, 1903, and 1919–1921). In recent years this format has become the norm for League Championship Series as well.

If a player appeared at more than one position during the Series, the number of games he played at each is noted (for example, a man who divided seven games at shortstop and third base would carry the notation *ss-4, 3b-3*). Other abbreviations are as follows:

POS	Position	SB	Stolen Bases
AVG	Batting average	W	Wins
G	Games	L	Losses
AB	At bats	ERA	Earned run average
R	Runs	GS	Games started
H	Hits	CG	Complete games
2B	Doubles	SHO	Shutouts
3B	Triples	SV	Saves
HR	Home runs	IP	Innings pitched
RB	Runs batted in	ER	Earned runs
BB	Bases on Balls	SO	Strikeouts

After a flurry of boasts and challenges, Mets manager Jim Mutrie and the Grays' Frank Bancroft arranged a three-game series in New York to determine which team was the nation's best. These were not the first games between NL and AA pennant winners. In 1882, the AA's first season, champion Cincinnati met NL titlist Chicago twice as part of its postseason schedule, in games viewed simply as exhibition contests. (Each team won one). The next year a postseason series was proposed between champions Boston (NL) and the Athletics of Philadelphia (AA), but the Athletics fared so poorly in exhibitions against lesser NL teams that they refused to face Boston.

The 1884 Series was touted as "for the championship of the United States," but the influential weekly *Sporting Life* established precedent for future Series hype by naming victorious Providence "Champions of the World." The weather turned cold and windy as the Series got under way. A hardy opening game crowd of 2,500 saw the Grays' great Charlie "Old Hoss" Radbourn blank the Mets on two singles. Mets pitcher Tim Keefe, wild at the start, paved the way for two first-inning Providence runs by hitting the first two men to face him and assisted them around the bases with a pair of wild pitches. Paul Hines singled in the third for the Grays' first hit and scored as a passed ball and two more wild pitches brought him home. Keefe yielded only four other hits, but they came back to back in the seventh to produce the Grays' final three runs.

The 1,000 spectators at Game 2 witnessed the Series' closest contest. Keefe and Radbourn overwhelmed their opposition for four innings, but in the top of the fifth the Grays bunched three of their five hits for three two-out runs as Jerry Denny homered over the center field fence. The Mets responded with a run in the last of the fifth, but scored no more before darkness ended the game after seven innings.

The Grays had clinched the championship with their second win, and when they saw only a few hundred diehards in the stands for Game 3, they wanted to go home. The Mets must have regretted their insistence on playing the game. Although darkness halted it after only six innings, rookie New York pitcher Buck Becannon (replacing Keefe, who umpired) and awful Mets fielding gave Providence 11 or 12 runs (scorers disagreed), while Radbourn held the New Yorkers to a pair of unearned tallies.

Providence Grays (NL), 3; New York Mets (AA), 0

PRO (N)

PLAYER/POS	AVG	G	AB	R	H	2B	3B	HR	RB	BB	SO	SB
Cliff Carroll, of	.100	3	10	2	1	0	0	0	1	1	1	0
Jerry Denny, 3b	.444	3	9	3	4	0	1	1	2	0	3	0
Jack Farrell, 2b	.444	3	9	3	4	2	0	0	0	0	0	1
Barney Gilligan, c	.444	3	9	3	4	2	0	0	2	0	1	0
Paul Hines, of	.250	3	8	5	2	0	0	0	1	3	0	2
Arthur Irwin, ss	.222	3	9	2	2	0	1	0	2	0	2	0
Charlie Radbourn, p	.100	3	10	1	1	0	0	0	2	1	3	0
Paul Radford, of	.000	3	7	1	0	0	0	0	0	1	0	0
Joe Start, 1b	.100	3	10	0	1	0	0	0	1	0	2	0
TOTAL	.235		81	20	19	4	2	1	12	5	13	3

PITCHER	W	L	ERA	G	GS	CG	SV	SHO	IP	H	ER	BB	SO
Charlie Radbourn	3	0	0.00	3	3	3	0	1	22.0	11	0	0	16
TOTAL	3	0	0.00	3	3	3	0	1	22.0	11	0	0	16

NY (A)

PLAYER/POS	AVG	G	AB	R	H	2B	3B	HR	RB	BB	SO	SB
Buck Becannon, p	.500	1	2	0	1	0	0	0	0	0	0	0
Steve Brady, of	.000	3	10	1	0	0	0	0	0	0	1	0
Dude Esterbrook, 3b	.300	3	10	0	3	1	0	0	0	0	3	1
Tom Forster, 2b	.000	1	3	0	0	0	0	0	0	0	1	0
Bill Holbert, c	.000	1	2	0	0	0	0	0	0	0	1	0
Tim Keefe, p	.200	2	5	0	1	0	0	0	0	0	4	0
Ed Kennedy, of	.000	3	7	0	0	0	0	0	0	2	2	0
Candy Nelson, ss	.100	3	10	0	1	0	0	0	0	0	1	0
Dave Orr, 1b	.111	3	9	0	1	0	0	0	0	0	0	0
Charlie Reipschlager, c	.000	2	5	1	0	0	0	0	0	0	1	0
Chief Roseman, of	.333	3	9	1	3	0	0	0	0	0	1	0
Dasher Troy, 2b	.200	2	5	0	1	0	0	0	1	0	1	0
TOTAL	.143		77	3	11	1	0	0	2	0	16	1

PITCHER	W	L	ERA	G	GS	CG	SV	SHO	IP	H	ER	BB	SO
Buck Becannon	0	1	10.50	1	1	1	0	0	6.0	9	7	2	1
Tim Keefe	0	2	3.60	2	2	2	0	0	15.0	10	6	3	12
TOTAL	0	3	5.57	3	3	3	0	0	21.0	19	13	5	13

GAME 1 AT NY OCT 23

NY	000 000 000	0 2 0
PRO	201 000 30X	6 5 2

Pitchers: KEEFE vs RADBOURN
Attendance: 2,500

GAME 2 AT NY OCT 24

PRO	000 030 0	3 5 4
NY	000 010 0	1 3 1

Pitchers: RADBOURN vs KEEFE
Home Runs: Denny-PRO
Attendance: 1,000
(Game called at end of seventh, darkness)

GAME 3 AT NY OCT 25

PRO	120 144	12 9 3
NY	000 011	2 6 9

Pitchers: RADBOURN vs BECANNON
Attendance: 300
(Game called at end of sixth, darkness)

Before the start of the final game, the two clubs agreed to throw out Game 2, which had been forfeited to Chicago, leaving the Series tied at two wins apiece, plus the one tie. But after the Browns won the seventh game for their third victory, Chicago manager Cap Anson decided his club should retain its forfeit win after all, and a select committee agreed, leaving the Series in a tie instead of a White Stockings defeat.

Game 1, in Chicago, was called for darkness after eight innings, with the score tied 5–5. The Browns scored first with a run in the second and added four more in the top of the fourth. But Chicago came back with a run in the last of the fourth, and in the bottom of the eighth scored four more on a walk, two singles, and Fred Pfeffer's game-tying three-run homer.

The Series moved to St. Louis for the next three games. Chicago was leading 5–4 in the sixth inning of Game 2 when Browns manager Charlie Comiskey pulled his team off the field, objecting to the umpiring of David Sullivan. Umpire Sullivan later forfeited the game to the White Stockings; he worked no more in the Series. The Browns won Game 3, scoring five unearned runs with two out in the top of the first, and holding on for a 7–4 win. Chicago lost again the next day in a much closer game. The Browns scored first with a run in the third inning, but Abner Dalrymple's two-run homer in the fifth gave the White Stockings a 2–1 lead. In the bottom of the eighth, however, St. Louis scored twice and held on for the 3–2 win.

The Series took to the road for its final three games. In Pittsburgh for Game 5, Chicago overwhelmed the Browns 9–2, scoring four runs in the first inning, and their final three just before darkness ended the game after seven innings.

Game 6 and 7 were played in Cincinnati. The White Stockings won the sixth game by the same 9–2 score as Game 5. The Browns' two runs were unearned, as Chicago's Jim McCormick stopped St. Louis on just two hits, both singles. The Browns' victory in the finale was a runaway 13–4, called in the eighth for darkness. St. Louis' six-run fourth inning typified the game's sloppy play, the runs scoring on five hits, four errors, and two passed balls.

Chicago White Stockings (NL), 3; St. Louis Browns (AA), 3; tie, 1

CHI (N)

PLAYER/POS	AVG	G	AB	R	H	2B	3B	HR	RB	BB	SO	SB
Cap Anson, 1b	.423	7	26	8	11	1	1	0		2		
Tom Burns, ss-4,3b-3	.080	7	25	3	2	0	1	0		0		
John Clarkson, p-2,of-2	.154	4	13	1	2	1	0	0		0		
Abner Dalrymple, of	.269	7	26	4	7	2	0	1		2		
Silver Flint, c	.143	4	14	0	2	0	0	0		0		
George Gore, of	.000	1	3	1	0	0	0	0		1		
Bug Holliday, of	.000	1	4	0	0	0	0	0		0		
King Kelly, of-4,c-3	.346	7	26	9	9	3	1	0		2		
Jim McCormick, p	.176	5	17	1	3	0	0	0		0		
Fred Pfeffer, 2b	.407	7	27	5	11	2	0	1		0		
Billy Sunday, of	.273	6	22	5	6	2	0	0		2		
N. Williamson, 3b-4,ss-3	.087	7	23	1	2	0	0	0		4		
TOTAL	.243		226	38	55	11	3	2		13		

PITCHER	W	L	ERA	G	GS	CG	SV	SHO	IP	H	ER	BB	SO
John Clarkson	0	1	1.13	2	2	2	0	0	16.0	15	2	1	15
Jim McCormick	3	2	2.00	5	5	5	0	0	36.0	27	8	6	19
TOTAL	3	3	1.73	7	7	7	0	0	52.0	42	10	7	34

STL (A)

PLAYER/POS	AVG	G	AB	R	H	2B	3B	HR	RB	BB	SO	SB
Sam Barkley, 2b	.087	7	23	3	2	0	0	0		2		
Doc Bushong, c	.154	4	13	1	2	0	0	0		0		
Bob Caruthers, p-3,of-2	.200	5	15	1	3	0	1	0		1		
Charlie Comiskey, 1b	.292	7	24	6	7	0	0	0		0		
Dave Foutz, p	.167	4	12	1	2	0	0	0		0		
Bill Gleason, ss	.231	7	26	5	6	2	0	0		1		
Arlie Latham, 3b	.318	7	22	5	7	3	0	0		2		
Hugh Nicol, of	.000	1	2	0	0	0	0	0		0		
Tip O'Neill, of	.208	7	24	4	5	0	0	0		0		
Yank Robinson, of-4,c-3	.174	7	23	5	4	0	1	0		1		
Curt Welch, of	.148	7	27	5	4	1	1	0		0		
TOTAL	.199		211	36	42	6	3	0		7		

PITCHER	W	L	ERA	G	GS	CG	SV	SHO	IP	H	ER	BB	SO
Bob Caruthers	1	1	2.42	3	3	3	0	0	26.0	25	7	4	16
Dave Foutz	2	2	0.61	4	4	4	0	0	29.1	30	2	9	14
TOTAL	3	3	1.46	7	7	7	0	0	55.1	55	9	13	30

It was a winner-take-all Series, with the club that won four games pocketing the entire proceeds. Attendance, very good for those days, averaged over 7,000 per game and brought the victorious Browns about $14,000.

The first three games were played in Chicago. The White Stockings won the opener on a sparkling five-hit shutout by their ace John Clarkson. But St. Louis's Bob Caruthers improved on Clarkson's performance the next day, blanking Chicago on just two singles as his Browns turned 13 hits and 13 Chicago errors into 12 runs (in a game shortened by darkness to eight innings). The White Stockings improved their fielding in the next game (which was also called after eight innings), and this time their bats came alive. With 11 hits (including home runs by Mike "King" Kelly and George Gore) combining with seven St. Louis errors, they regained the Series advantage with an easy 11–4 win.

When the venue shifted to St. Louis, though, the Browns battled back. In a back-and-forth battle in Game 4, Chicago tied the game at 5–5 with a pair of runs in the sixth, but St. Louis scored three final runs a half inning later, winning when darkness ended play in the middle of the seventh.

Game 5 repeated an innovation from the second game: two umpires (instead of the usual one), plus a "referee" who stood between the pitcher and second base. The umpiring satisfied everyone, but Chicago, handicapped by their scheduled pitcher's sore arm, lost when they sent shortstop Ned Williamson and right fielder Jimmy Ryan into the box. St. Louis got to Williamson and Ryan for 11 hits and 10 runs as their Nat Hudson held Chicago batters to three hits and three runs.

The finale proved to be the Series' best-played and closest game. Chicago's Clarkson shut out the Browns through seven innings as his mates built a three-run lead—one of them scored on Fred's Pfeffer's homer in the fourth. Rain (and a rowdy crowd which poured onto the field) halted play for a while in the fifth. But the game resumed and the rain subsided. In the last of the eighth, Charlie Comiskey scored the Browns' first run on a single, errant throw and run-scoring fly out, and Arlie Latham tripled home two more runners later in the inning to tie the game. The score remained 3–3 into the last of the tenth, when the Browns' Curt Welch singled (for only the fourth St. Louis hit),

St. Louis Browns (AA), 4; Chicago White Stockings (NL), 2

STL (A)

PLAYER/POS	AVG	G	AB	R	H	2B	3B	HR	RB	BB	SO	SB
Doc Bushong, c	.188	6	16	4	3	1	0	0	2	4	5	0
Bob Caruthers, p-3,of-3	.250	6	24	6	6	1	2	0	5	1	4	1
Charlie Comiskey, 1b	.292	6	24	2	7	1	0	0	2	0	4	0
Dave Foutz, p-2,of-2	.200	4	15	2	3	1	1	0	3	0	3	0
Bill Gleason, ss	.208	6	24	3	5	0	0	0	5	1	3	0
Nat Hudson, p-1,of-1	.167	2	6	1	1	0	1	0	0	1	3	0
Arlie Latham, 3b-6,c-1	.174	6	23	4	4	0	1	0	3	3	4	2
Tip O'Neill, of	.400	6	20	4	8	0	2	2	5	4	5	2
Yank Robinson, 2b	.316	6	19	5	6	1	1	0	3	2	3	0
Curt Welch, of	.350	6	20	7	7	0	0	0	1	3	4	2
TOTAL	.262		191	38	50	7	8	2	29	19	38	9

PITCHER	W	L	ERA	G	GS	CG	SV	SHO	IP	H	ER	BB	SO
Bob Caruthers	2	1	2.42	3	3	3	0	1	26.0	18	7	6	12
Dave Foutz	1	1	3.60	2	2	2	0	0	15.0	16	6	6	7
Nat Hudson	1	0	2.57	1	1	1	0	0	7.0	3	2	3	3
TOTAL	4	2	2.81	6	6	6	0	1	48.0	37	15	15	22

CHI (N)

PLAYER/POS	AVG	G	AB	R	H	2B	3B	HR	RB	BB	SO	SB
Cap Anson, 1b-6,c-2	.238	6	21	3	5	1	0	0	1	4	0	1
Tom Burns, 3b-6,of-1	.286	6	21	2	6	2	1	0	1	0	2	0
John Clarkson, p-4,of-1	.067	4	15	0	1	0	0	0	1	0	2	1
Abner Dalrymple, of	.190	6	21	2	4	1	1	0	2	0	5	1
Silver Flint, c	.000	1	3	0	0	0	0	0	1	0	1	0
George Gore, of	.174	6	23	4	4	0	1	1	2	3	3	0
King Kelly, c-5,ss-2,1b-1,3b-1	.208	6	24	4	5	0	1	1	1	2	1	1
Jim McCormick, p	.000	1	3	0	0	0	0	0	0	0	0	0
Fred Pfeffer, 2b	.286	6	21	7	6	0	0	1	4	2	6	2
Jimmy Ryan, of-6,p-1,ss-1	.250	6	20	4	5	1	0	0	0	1	1	1
Ned Williamson, ss-6,p-2,c-1,of-1	.056	6	18	2	1	0	1	0	3	4	5	1
TOTAL	.195		190	28	37	5	3	3	18	15	22	8

PITCHER	W	L	ERA	G	GS	CG	SV	SHO	IP	H	ER	BB	SO
John Clarkson	2	2	2.01	4	4	3	0	1	31.1	25	7	12	28
Jim McCormick	0	1	6.75	1	1	1	0	0	8.0	13	6	2	4
Jimmy Ryan	0	0	9.00	1	0	0	0	0	5.0	8	5	4	4
Ned Williamson	0	1	4.50	2	1	0	0	0	2.0	4	1	1	2
TOTAL	2	4	3.69	8	6	4	0	1	46.1	50	19	19	38

went to second on an infield hit, and took third on a sacrifice. Welch then attempted to steal home but catcher Kelly had smelled out the play and called for a pitchout. Clarkson's delivery was poor and bobbled by Kelly, allowing Welch to steal home with a "$15,000 slide" for the Browns' triumph.

GAME 1 AT CHI OCT 18

STL	000	000	000	0	5 3
CHI	200	001	03X	6	10 4

Pitchers: FOUTZ vs CLARKSON
Attendance: 6,000

GAME 2 AT CHI OCT 19

STL	200	230	50	12	13 2
CHI	000	000	00	0	2 10

Pitchers: CARUTHERS vs McCORMICK
Home Runs: O'Neill-STL (2)
Attendance: 8,000
(Game called at end of eighth, darkness)

GAME 3 AT CHI OCT 20

CHI	200	112	32	11	11 2
STL	010	002	01	4	9 7

Pitchers: CLARKSON, Williamson (8) vs CARUTHERS
Home Runs: Kelly-CHI, Gore-CHI
Attendance: 6,000
(Game called at end of eighth, darkness)

GAME 4 AT STL OCT 21

CHI	300	002	0	5 6 4
STL	011	033	X	8 7 4

Pitchers: CLARKSON vs FOUTZ
Attendance: 8,000
(Game called in seventh, darkness)

GAME 5 AT STL OCT 22

CHI	011	100	00	3 3 3
STL	214	003	0X	10 11 3

Pitchers: WILLIAMSON, Ryan (2) vs HUDSON
Attendance: 10,000
(Game called in eighth, darkness)

GAME 6 AT STL OCT 23

CHI	010	101	000	0	3 6 2
STL	000	000	030	1	4 5 3

Pitchers: CLARKSON vs CARUTHERS
Home Runs: Pfeffer-CHI
Attendance: 8,000

Even though their star slugger Dan Brouthers was sidelined for all but one game by a sprained ankle, the Wolverines—in baseball's longest World Series, played in ten different cities—followed up their only pennant with an easy triumph over repeating AA champion St. Louis. The Browns won the opener at home, though, 6–1. They played errorless ball (rare in that era) as pitcher Bob Caruthers held Detroit scoreless until the ninth inning, and drove in the Browns' second run himself with a first-inning single.

The Wolverines came back to win the next three games. They took an early lead in Game 2 and held on for a 5–3 win in St. Louis to even the Series. Then, in the Series' tightest game (played in Detroit) the Wolverines defeated Caruthers 2–1 in the last of the thirteenth when their pitcher Charlie Getzien led off with a single, advanced to second and third on ground outs, and scored on an infield error. In Game 4 (in Pittsburgh) Detroit's Charles "Lady" Baldwin stopped the Browns on two hits.

Caruthers hurled a seven-hitter in Brooklyn for St. Louis's second win, but Detroit took the next four. Getzien contributed a two-hit shutout in New York, and Baldwin overcame Caruthers 3–1 in Philadelphia the next day. Getzien yielded eight hits the day after that in Boston, but Caruthers gave up thirteen, including two home runs to Sam Thompson, and Detroit took the game 9–2. Back in Philadelphia for Game 9, St. Louis broke a 1–1 tie with a run in the top of the sixth. But the Wolverines scored two in the seventh and a final run in the eighth. The win gave Detroit a 7–2 Series advantage.

Game 10, scheduled for the next day in Washington, was postponed because of rain until the following morning. Detroit's Hardy Richardson opened the game with a home run, but the Wolverines lost an opportunity to clinch the Series as the Browns overwhelmed Getzien with 16 hits for an 11–4 victory featuring a triple play. But that afternoon, in Baltimore, Detroit took the deciding game as decisively as they had lost in the morning, knocking the Browns' Dave Foutz for 14 hits (including four by Richardson and three—including a home run—by Larry Twitchell) as Baldwin held St. Louis to two hits in a 13–3 win.

The Browns and Wolverines split the final four meaningless games, played in Brooklyn, Detroit, Chicago, and St. Louis.

Detroit Wolverines (NL), 10; St. Louis Browns (AA), 5

DET (N)

PLAYER/POS	AVG	G	AB	R	H	2B	3B	HR	RB	BB	SO	SB
Lady Baldwin, p	.235	5	17	1	4	1	0	0	1	2	2	1
Charlie Bennett, c-10,1b-3	.262	11	42	6	11	2	1	0	9	3	5	5
Dan Brouthers, 1b	.667	1	3	0	2	0	0	0	0	0	0	0
Pete Conway, p	.000	4	12	0	0	0	0	0	0	0	2	0
Fred Dunlap, 2b	.150	11	40	5	6	0	1	0	1	0	4	4
Charlie Ganzel, 1b-10,c-7	.224	14	58	5	13	1	0	0	2	1	2	3
Charlie Getzien, p	.300	6	20	5	6	2	0	0	2	3	6	1
Ned Hanlon, of	.220	15	50	5	11	1	1	0	4	5	1	7
Hardy Richardson, of-10,2b-5,3b-1	.197	15	66	12	13	5	2	1	4	1	9	7
Jack Rowe, ss	.333	15	63	12	21	1	1	0	7	2	1	5
Cy Sutcliffe, 1b-3,c-1	.091	4	11	1	1	0	0	0	0	1	1	1
Sam Thompson, of	.362	15	58	8	21	3	0	2	7	3	5	5
Larry Twitchell, of	.250	6	20	5	5	1	0	1	3	0	1	1
Deacon White, 3b-14,1b-1	.207	15	58	8	12	1	1	0	3	2	0	2
TOTAL	.243		518	73	126	17	7	4	43	23	37	42

PITCHER	W	L	ERA	G	GS	CG	SV	SHO	IP	H	ER	BB	SO
Lady Baldwin	4	1	1.50	5	5	5	0	1	42.0	28	7	10	4
Pete Conway	2	2	3.00	4	4	4	0	0	33.0	31	11	6	10
Charlie Getzien	4	2	2.48	6	6	6	0	1	58.0	61	16	15	17
TOTAL	10	5	2.30	15	15	15	0	2	133.0	120	34	31	31

STL (A)

PLAYER/POS	AVG	G	AB	R	H	2B	3B	HR	RB	BB	SO	SB
Jack Boyle, c	.208	6	24	1	5	0	0	0	1	0	4	0
Doc Bushong, c	.241	9	29	3	7	0	0	0	1	4	1	0
Bob Caruthers, p-8,of-3	.239	10	46	2	11	0	0	0	3	1	1	3
Charlie Comiskey, 1b-14,of-1	.306	15	62	8	19	2	0	0	2	1	1	4
Dave Foutz, of-11,p-3,1b-1	.169	15	59	4	10	2	1	0	1	2	3	0
Bill Gleason, ss	.163	13	49	3	8	0	0	1	3	2	1	1
Silver King, p	.071	4	14	0	1	0	0	0	0	0	3	0
Arlie Latham, 3b	.293	15	58	12	17	1	0	1	9	2	15	15
Harry Lyons, ss	.286	2	7	3	2	0	0	0	0	1	0	0
Tip O'Neill, of	.200	15	65	7	13	2	1	1	5	0	2	0
Yank Robinson, 2b	.326	15	46	5	15	5	1	0	4	10	6	4
Curt Welch, of	.207	15	58	6	12	3	1	1	6	0	2	1
TOTAL	.232		517	54	120	15	4	2	25	31	27	28

PITCHER	W	L	ERA	G	GS	CG	SV	SHO	IP	H	ER	BB	SO
Bob Caruthers	4	4	2.13	8	8	8	0	0	71.2	64	17	12	19
Dave Foutz	0	3	3.46	3	3	3	0	0	26.0	36	10	9	6
Silver King	1	3	2.03	4	4	4	0	0	31.0	26	7	2	21
TOTAL	5	10	2.38	15	15	15	0	0	128.2	126	34	23	46

GAME 1 AT STL OCT 10

STL	200 040 000	6	12	0
DET	000 000 001	1	4	5

Pitchers: CARUTHERS vs GETZIEN
Attendance: 4,208

GAME 2 AT STL OCT 11

DET	022 000 100	5	10	2
STL	000 000 120	3	8	7

Pitchers: CONWAY vs FOUTZ
Attendance: 6,408

GAME 3 AT DET OCT 12

STL	010 000 000 000 0	1	13	7
DET	000 000 010 000 1	2	6	1

Pitchers: CARUTHERS vs GETZIEN
Attendance: 4,509

GAME 4 AT PIT OCT 13

DET	410 012 000	8	11	1
STL	000 000 000	0	2	6

Pitchers: BALDWIN vs KING
Attendance: 2,447

GAME 5 AT BRO OCT 14

STL	200 002 100	5	5	4
DET	000 020 000	2	7	5

Pitchers: CARUTHERS vs CONWAY
Attendance: 6,796

GAME 6 AT NY OCT 15

DET	330 000 003	9	12	1
STL	000 000 000	0	2	8

Pitchers: GETZIEN vs FOUTZ
Attendance: 5,797

GAME 7 AT PHI OCT 17

STL	000 000 001	1	8	1
DET	030 000 00X	3	6	1

Pitchers: CARUTHERS vs BALDWIN
Home Runs: O'Neill-STL
Attendance: 6,478

GAME 8 AT BOS OCT 18

DET	031 003 200	9	13	2
STL	100 001 000	2	8	5

Pitchers: GETZIEN vs CARUTHERS
Home Runs: Thompson-DET (2)
Attendance: 2,891

GAME 9 AT PHI OCT 19

STL	000 101 000	2	9	2
DET	000 100 21X	4	6	3

Pitchers: KING vs CONWAY
Attendance: 2,389

GAME 10 AT WAS OCT 21 (AM)

DET	200 010 001	4	8	3
STL	200 031 41X	11	16	5

Pitchers: GETZIEN vs CARUTHERS
Home Runs: Latham-STL, Welch-STL, Richardson-DET
Attendance: 1,261

GAME 11 AT BAL OCT 21 (PM)

STL	110 010 000	3	2	7
DET	100 344 10X	13	14	7

Pitchers: FOUTZ vs BALDWIN
Home Runs: Twitchell-DET
Attendance: 2,707
(Detroit wins best of 15 series 8 to 3)

GAME 12 AT BRO OCT 22

DET	000 100 0	1	5	3
STL	410 000 X	5	10	2

Pitchers: CONWAY vs KING
Attendance: 1,138
(Game called in seventh, darkness)

GAME 13 AT DET OCT 24

DET	020 100 120	6	12	3
STL	100 010 001	3	4	5

Pitchers: BALDWIN vs CARUTHERS
Attendance: 3,389

GAME 14 AT CHI OCT 25

STL	000 002 100	3	10	5
DET	300 010 00X	4	4	4

Pitchers: KING vs GETZIEN
Attendance: 378

GAME 15 AT STL OCT 26

STL	340 110	9	11	5
DET	011 000	2	8	7

Pitchers: CARUTHERS vs BALDWIN
Attendance: 659
(Game called after sixth, cold)

St. Louis, AA champions for the fourth straight year, battled the Giants closely through several games, but blowout losses in Games 6 and 8 undid them. The first three games were played in New York. In a splendidly pitched opener, Brown ace Charles "Silver" King held New York to two hits and a walk while Giants ace Tim Keefe limited the Browns to three hits and a walk, striking out nine on his way to a narrow 2–1 win. St. Louis evened the Series in Game 2 behind the shutout pitching of Elton "Icebox" Chamberlain. Tommy McCarthy scored the Browns' first run in the second inning when, after singling, he moved around to third on two passed balls by Giants catcher Buck Ewing and came home on Ewing's failed attempt to throw out a runner stealing second. Two more runs in the ninth gave St. Louis more than enough insurance for the win.

The Giants scored twice in the first inning of Game 3, and increased their lead to 4–0 before allowing St. Louis a pair of harmless runs in the final innings. They also scored first and led all the way in Game 4 (played in Brooklyn). The Browns took a 4–1 lead into the bottom of the eighth in Game 5 (in New York), but a five-run Giants rally reversed the lead—and the outcome—as the game was called for darkness with St. Louis at bat in the ninth.

Mickey Welch hurled a three-hitter (in Philadelphia) two days later, but St. Louis, capitalizing on walks and a questionable "safe" call at home, carried a 4–1 lead into the sixth inning. New York exploded in the late innings for 11 runs, however, and when darkness ended the game after eight the Giants were just one win away from the title.

The final four games were played in St. Louis. The Browns spoiled New York's hope of quick victory in Game 7, coming from behind to tie the score with three runs in the fourth, and—after New York had scored twice in the sixth—recovering again with a four-run eighth for a 7–5 lead before darkness again halted play after eight innings. But the Browns' win only delayed the inevitable. The Giants hammered Icebox Chamberlain for 12 hits in Game 8 (including home runs by Buck Ewing and Mike Tiernan) to clinch their first world championship with an 11–3 win.

New York Giants (NL), 6;
St. Louis Browns (AA), 4

NY (N)

PLAYER/POS	AVG	G	AB	R	H	2B	3B	HR	RB	BB	SO	SB
Willard Brown, c	.375	2	8	1	3	1	0	0	0	0	0	0
Roger Connor, 1b	.304	7	23	7	7	1	2	0	3	4	0	4
Ed Crane, p	.143	2	7	1	1	0	0	0	2	0	1	0
Buck Ewing, c-6,1b-1	.346	7	26	5	9	0	2	1	6	1	3	5
Bill George, p-1,1b-1	.333	2	9	2	3	1	0	1	4	0	2	0
George Gore, of-2,3b-1	.455	3	11	5	5	0	0	0	2	2	2	2
Gil Hatfield, p-1,2b-1,ss-1	.250	2	8	2	2	0	0	0	1	1	2	1
Tim Keefe, p	.091	4	11	2	1	0	0	0	0	2	2	1
Pat Murphy, c	.100	3	10	1	1	1	0	0	0	1	0	0
Jim O'Rourke, of-7,1b-2,ss-1	.222	10	36	4	8	0	0	0	1	4	2	3
Danny Richardson, 2b	.167	9	36	6	6	2	0	0	6	3	5	3
Mike Slattery, of-10,2b-1	.205	10	39	6	8	2	0	0	5	0	5	6
Mike Tiernan, of	.342	10	38	8	13	0	0	1	6	8	2	5
Ledell Titcomb, p-1,of-1	.500	1	4	1	2	1	0	0	1	0	0	0
Monte Ward, ss	.379	8	29	4	11	1	0	0	6	1	0	6
Mickey Welch, p	.286	2	7	2	2	0	0	0	1	0	0	0
Art Whitney, 3b-9,of-1	.324	10	37	7	12	0	1	0	12	1	4	2
TOTAL	.277		339	64	94	10	5	3	55	27	30	38

PITCHER	W	L	ERA	G	GS	CG	SV	SHO	IP	H	ER	BB	SO
Ed Crane	1	1	2.12	2	2	2	0	0	17.0	15	4	6	12
Bill George	0	1	7.20	1	1	1	0	0	10.0	15	8	3	4
Gil Hatfield	0	0	12.60	1	0	0	0	0	5.0	12	7	3	2
Tim Keefe	4	0	0.51	4	4	4	0	0	35.0	18	2	9	30
Ledell Titcomb	0	1	6.75	1	1	0	0	0	4.0	5	3	2	2
Mickey Welch	1	1	2.65	2	2	2	0	0	17.0	10	5	9	2
TOTAL	6	4	2.97	11	10	9	0	0	88.0	75	29	32	52

STL (A)

PLAYER/POS	AVG	G	AB	R	H	2B	3B	HR	RB	BB	SO	SB
Jack Boyle, c-4,of-1	.438	4	16	4	7	0	1	0	4	2	2	3
Icebox Chamberlain, p	.000	5	13	3	0	0	0	0	0	4	3	1
Charlie Comiskey, 1b-10,of-1	.268	10	41	6	11	1	1	0	3	1	1	4
Jim Devlin, p	.000	1	3	0	0	0	0	0	0	0	0	0
Ed Herr, of	.091	3	11	2	1	0	0	0	0	0	5	1
Silver King, p	.067	5	15	1	1	0	0	0	0	1	6	0
Arlie Latham, 3b	.250	10	40	10	10	0	0	0	3	5	6	11
Harry Lyons, of	.118	5	17	0	2	0	0	0	1	1	5	0
Tommy McCarthy, of	.244	10	41	10	10	1	0	1	9	0	0	6
Jocko Milligan, c-8,1b-1	.400	8	25	5	10	2	1	0	4	3	3	0
Tip O'Neill, of	.243	10	37	8	9	1	0	2	11	6	3	0
Yank Robinson, 2b	.250	10	36	7	9	2	1	0	7	6	12	2
Bill White, ss	.143	10	35	4	5	1	0	0	4	3	6	1
TOTAL	.227		330	60	75	8	4	3	46	32	52	29

PITCHER	W	L	ERA	G	GS	CG	SV	SHO	IP	H	ER	BB	SO
Icebox Chamberlain	2	3	5.32	5	5	5	0	1	44.0	52	26	16	13
Jim Devlin	1	0	2.57	1	0	0	0	0	7.0	5	2	2	5
Silver King	1	3	2.31	5	5	4	0	0	35.0	37	9	9	12
TOTAL	4	6	3.87	11	10	9	0	1	86.0	94	37	27	30

The final two games meant nothing to the outcome, and both clubs used reserve pitchers in Game 9. But St. Louis rewarded the small crowd with a two-run rally in the ninth to tie the game at 11-all and scored three more runs in the tenth to win it. The finale the next day again featured heavy hitting on both hitting on both sides, including a trio of home runs (one of them Tip O'Neill's second in two days) and an 18–7 St. Louis romp.

Six wins was the magic number this year, and it was agreed that—unlike most previous Series—play would not continue beyond the deciding game. At first it seemed Brooklyn might prevail, with an assist from the dark of night. The Giants wanted the opening game called for darkness after the seventh inning, when they led, 10–8. But the umpires held off until Brooklyn, in the deepening gloom, had scored four runs in the last of the eighth to go ahead, 12–10.

The next day, in Brooklyn before more than 16,000 spectators (by far the largest World Series crowd to that time), Ed "Cannonball" Crane held the Grooms to four hits as New York evened the Series. But Brooklyn won the next two for a 3–1 Series advantage. In Game 3, ahead 8–7 in the sixth inning, the Grooms began stalling, waiting for darkness to fall. The score was still 8–7 when the game was finally halted in the top of the ninth with one out and three Giants on base.

Darkness for a third time gave Brooklyn the victory in Game 4. New York overcame a 7–2 Bridegroom lead to tie the score with five runs in the top of the sixth, but in the bottom of the inning Brooklyn's Tom "Oyster" Burns homered in the dark for three runs. The umpires then halted the game.

The five remaining contests went the distance, and the Giants won them all. Crane in Game 5 gave up eight hits, but homered in his own behalf, driving in two runs in his Giants' 11–3 rout. Game 6 was a pitching duel between New York's Hank O'Day and Brooklyn's William "Adonis" Terry. The Grooms scored a run in the second inning, but New York tied the game with two outs in the last of the ninth (when Monte Ward singled, stole second and third, and scored on Roger Connor's single), and won it with two away in the eleventh as Ward drove in a speedy Mike Slattery from second with an infield hit.

Back-to-back homers by Giants Dan Richardson and Jim O'Rourke highlighted an eight-run second inning in Game 7. The Giants' eventual 11–7 win gave them their first Series advantage. In Game 8, two of Brooklyn's five hits were home runs. But the Giants outscored the Grooms 12–2 over the first four innings and beat them, 16–7.

With their backs to the wall, the Bridegrooms scored first in Game 9 and held a 2–1 lead after five innings. But New York tied the

score in the sixth and went ahead 3–2 on a passed ball in the seventh. Meanwhile pitcher Hank O'Day (although he walked five batters)

blanked the Grooms on just two hits after the first inning to bring New York its second straight world championship.

New York Giants (NL), 6; Brooklyn Bridegrooms (AA), 3

NY (N)

PLAYER/POS	AVG	G	AB	R	H	2B	3B	HR	RB	BB	SO	SB
Willard Brown, c	.600	1	5	3	3	0	0	1	2	0	0	0
Roger Connor, 1b	.343	9	35	9	12	2	2	0	12	3	2	8
Ed Crane, p	.278	5	18	3	5	1	1	1	5	1	2	0
Buck Ewing, c	.250	8	36	5	9	4	0	0	7	2	5	1
George Gore, of	.333	5	21	5	7	1	1	0	1	3	0	2
Tim Keefe, p	.500	2	4	1	2	1	0	0	0	1	1	0
Hank O'Day, p	.167	3	6	0	1	0	0	0	0	2	2	0
Jim O'Rourke, of	.389	9	36	7	14	2	2	2	7	2	2	3
Danny Richardson, 2b	.314	9	35	8	11	1	1	3	8	3	5	3
Mike Slattery, of	.188	4	16	6	3	0	0	0	1	3	1	1
Mike Tiernan, of	.289	9	38	12	11	1	1	1	5	5	3	3
Monte Ward, ss	.417	9	36	10	15	0	1	0	7	5	2	10
Mickey Welch, p	.333	1	3	0	1	1	0	0	0	0	1	0
Art Whitney, 3b	.229	9	35	4	8	2	1	0	3	1	0	0
TOTAL	.315		324	73	102	16	10	8	58	31	26	31

PITCHER	W	L	ERA	G	GS	CG	SV	SHO	IP	H	ER	BB	SO
Ed Crane	4	1	3.72	5	5	4	0	0	38.2	29	16	32	19
Tim Keefe	0	1	8.18	2	1	1	1	0	11.0	17	10	2	4
Hank O'Day	2	0	1.17	3	2	2	0	0	23.0	10	3	14	12
Mickey Welch	0	1	9.00	1	1	0	0	0	5.0	11	5	3	1
TOTAL	6	3	3.94	11	9	7	1	0	77.2	67	34	51	36

BRO (A)

PLAYER/POS	AVG	G	AB	R	H	2B	3B	HR	RB	BB	SO	SB
Oyster Burns, of	.229	9	35	8	8	3	0	2	11	5	6	0
Doc Bushong, c	.000	3	8	0	0	0	0	0	0	1	0	0
Bob Caruthers, p	.250	4	8	1	2	0	0	0	1	3	3	0
Bob Clark, c	.417	4	12	3	5	2	0	0	3	2	2	0
Hub Collins, 2b	.371	9	35	13	13	3	0	1	2	7	5	6
Pop Corkhill, of	.208	9	24	4	5	1	0	1	5	6	2	1
Jumbo Davis, ss	.000	1	4	0	0	0	0	0	0	0	0	0
Dave Foutz, 1b-9,p-1	.286	9	35	7	10	2	0	1	9	4	2	3
Mickey Hughes, p	.333	1	3	1	1	1	0	0	0	1	2	0
Tom Lovett, p	.000	1	1	0	0	0	0	0	0	0	0	0
Darby O'Brien, of	.161	9	31	8	5	0	1	0	4	12	6	6
George Pinckney, 3b	.258	9	31	2	8	0	0	0	3	4	2	2
Germany Smith, ss	.172	8	29	2	5	2	1	0	2	3	2	2
Adonis Terry, p-5,1b-1	.167	5	18	1	3	0	0	0	1	1	1	1
Joe Visner, c-3,of-2	.125	5	16	2	2	1	0	0	0	2	3	0
TOTAL	.231		290	52	67	17	2	5	41	51	36	21

PITCHER	W	L	ERA	G	GS	CG	SV	SHO	IP	H	ER	BB	SO
Bob Caruthers	0	2	3.75	4	2	2	1	0	24.0	28	10	6	6
Dave Foutz	0	0	7.20	1	0	0	0	0	5.0	5	4	2	2
Mickey Hughes	1	0	7.71	1	1	0	0	0	7.0	14	6	3	3
Tom Lovett	0	1	24.00	1	1	0	0	0	3.0	8	8	2	1
Adonis Terry	2	3	5.97	5	5	4	0	0	37.2	47	25	18	14
TOTAL	3	6	6.22	12	9	6	1	0	76.2	102	53	31	26

GAME 1 AT NY OCT 18

NY	020 210 50	10 12 2
BRO	510 000 24	12 16 3

Pitchers: KEEFE vs TERRY
Home Runs: Collins-BRO, Richardson-NY
Attendance: 8,848
(Game called at end of eighth, darkness)

GAME 2 AT BRO OCT 19

NY	111 120 000	6 10 4
BRO	110 000 000	2 4 8

Pitchers: CRANE vs CARUTHERS
Attendance: 16,172

GAME 3 AT NY OCT 22

NY	200 032 00	7 15 2
BRO	023 120 00	8 12 3

Pitchers: WELCH, O'Day (6) vs HUGHES, Caruthers (8)
Home Runs: Corkhill-BRO, O'Rourke-NY
Attendance: 5,181
(Game called at end of eighth, darkness)

GAME 4 AT BRO OCT 23

NY	001 105	7 9 8
BRO	202 033	10 7 1

Pitchers: CRANE vs TERRY
Home Runs: Burns-BRO
Attendance: 3,045
(Game called at end of sixth, darkness)

GAME 5 AT BRO OCT 24

NY	004 040 021	11 12 2
BRO	000 111 000	3 8 2

Pitchers: CRANE vs CARUTHERS
Home Runs: Brown-NY, Richardson-NY, Crane-NY
Attendance: 2,901

GAME 6 AT NY OCT 25

BRO	010 000 000 00	1 6 4
NY	000 000 001 01	2 7 1

Pitchers: TERRY vs O'DAY
Attendance: 2,556

GAME 7 AT NY OCT 26

BRO	004 030 000	7 5 3
NY	180 001 10X	11 14 4

Pitchers: LOVETT, Caruthers (4) vs CRANE, Keefe (5)
Home Runs: Richardson-NY, O'Rourke-NY
Attendance: 3,312

GAME 8 AT BRO OCT 28

NY	541 203 001	16 15 4
BRO	200 000 023	7 5 4

Pitchers: CRANE vs TERRY, Foutz (5)
Home Runs: Foutz-BRO, Tiernan-NY, Burns-BRO
Attendance: 2,584

GAME 9 AT NY OCT 29

BRO	200 000 000	2 4 2
NY	100 001 10X	3 8 5

Pitchers: TERRY vs O'DAY
Attendance: 3,067

The Bridegrooms, AA pennant winners in 1889, switched to the NL and returned to World Series play as champions of their new league. Louisville, meanwhile, rose from a last-place finish in 1889 to replace Brooklyn at the top of the AA. The Series, though, seemed meaningless to many who believed that pennant-winning Boston of the outlaw Players League (which had drawn off many of the best NL and AA players) could beat both Louisville and Brooklyn if given the opportunity.

The first four games of the Series were played in Louisville before an ever decreasing number of spectators. The largest crowd—5,600—saw the Cyclones humiliated in the opener 9–0 as Brooklyn's Adonis Terry stopped them on two singles. The Grooms won the second game, too, breaking a 2–2 tie with a pair of runs in the fourth and holding on for a 5–3 win.

Louisville played catch-up throughout Game 3 and entered the last of the eighth still behind 7–4. But a walk, three hits, a sacrifice fly, and a passed ball tied the score before darkness ended the game. Only 1,050 spectators attended the final contest in Louisville, but they saw the first Louisville win. The Cyclones scored three runs in the first inning, but Brooklyn countered with three an inning later, and both teams scored single runs in the third. Louisville's Red Ehret blanked the Grooms the rest of the way, but Brooklyn's Tom Lovett yielded the Cyclones a winning run in the seventh when Tim Shinnick tripled and was sacrificed home.

Rain postponed the first game in Brooklyn for two days, but when it was played—on a cold, muddy day before a small crowd of 1,000—the Grooms took the lead on Oyster Burns's two-run homer in the first inning and held it all the way for their third win. As the weather grew colder, the crowds declined for the final two games. Louisville captured its second win by a 9–8 margin when a three-run Brooklyn rally in the eighth inning of Game 6 stalled one run short of a tie. Only abut 300 diehards saw the Cyclones even the Series in the finale, 6–2 behind Red Ehret's four-hitter. A tie-breaking eighth game seemed called for, but there was not enough interest in playing any further in the bitter cold.

Brooklyn Bridegrooms (NL), 3; Louisville Cyclones (AA), 3; tie, 1

BRO (N)

PLAYER/POS	AVG	G	AB	R	H	2B	3B	HR	RB	BB	SO	SB
Oyster Burns, of-4,3b-3	.222	7	27	6	6	2	0	1	5	3	4	0
Doc Bushong, c	.000	2	6	0	0	0	0	0	0	0	1	0
Bob Caruthers, of	.000	2	6	0	0	0	0	0	0	2	0	1
Bob Clark, c	.667	1	3	2	2	0	1	0	1	0	0	0
Hub Collins, 2b	.310	7	29	7	9	0	1	0	1	3	0	2
Tom Daly, c-6,1b-1	.182	6	22	1	4	2	0	0	3	0	4	2
Patsy Donovan, of	.471	5	17	5	8	1	0	0	3	2	1	3
Dave Foutz, 1b-7,of-1	.300	7	30	6	9	2	1	0	4	0	1	1
Tom Lovett, p-4,of-1	.067	5	15	0	1	0	0	0	0	0	4	0
Darby O'Brien, of	.125	6	24	3	3	0	1	0	3	1	5	3
George Pinckney, 3b	.357	4	14	4	5	0	2	0	3	2	1	1
Germany Smith, ss	.276	7	29	3	8	0	2	0	7	0	3	1
Adonis Terry, p-3,of-3	.050	6	20	5	1	1	0	0	0	6	3	1
TOTAL	.231		242	42	56	8	8	1	30	19	27	14

PITCHER	W	L	ERA	G	GS	CG	SV	SHO	IP	H	ER	BB	SO
Tom Lovett	2	2	2.83	4	4	4	0	0	35.0	29	11	6	14
Adonis Terry	1	1	3.60	3	3	3	0	1	25.0	25	10	10	8
TOTAL	3	3	3.15	7	7	7	0	1	60.0	54	21	16	22

LOU (A)

PLAYER/POS	AVG	G	AB	R	H	2B	3B	HR	RB	BB	SO	SB
Ned Bligh, c	.000	2	3	0	0	0	0	0	0	0	1	0
Ed Daily, of-4,p-2	.136	6	22	1	3	1	1	0	3	1	2	2
Red Ehret, p	.429	3	7	1	3	0	1	0	0	0	0	0
Charlie Hamburg, of	.269	7	26	3	7	1	0	0	2	0	3	0
George Meakim, p	.500	1	2	0	1	0	0	0	0	0	0	0
Harry Raymond, ss-5,ss-3	.148	7	27	5	4	1	1	0	1	2	5	1
John Ryan, c	.053	6	19	0	1	0	0	0	2	0	1	1
Tim Shinnick, 2b	.292	7	24	3	7	1	1	0	3	2	2	2
Scott Stratton, p-3,of-1	.222	4	9	4	2	1	0	0	0	2	1	3
Harry Taylor, 1b	.300	7	30	6	9	1	0	0	2	2	3	3
Phil Tomney, ss	.200	3	5	1	1	0	0	0	0	3	1	0
Farmer Weaver, of	.259	7	27	4	7	1	0	0	4	1	2	5
Pete Weckbecker, c	.000	1	4	0	0	0	0	0	0	0	1	0
Chicken Wolf, 3b-5,of-3	.360	7	25	4	9	3	1	0	8	3	0	2
TOTAL	.235		230	32	54	10	5	0	25	16	22	19

PITCHER	W	L	ERA	G	GS	CG	SV	SHO	IP	H	ER	BB	SO
Ed Daily	0	2	2.65	2	2	2	0	0	17.0	12	5	8	5
Red Ehret	2	0	1.35	3	2	2	1	0	20.0	12	3	6	13
George Meakim	0	0	0.00	1	0	0	0	0	4.0	6	0	1	1
Scott Stratton	1	1	2.37	3	3	1	0	0	19.0	26	5	4	8
TOTAL	3	3	1.95	9	7	5	1	0	60.0	56	13	19	27

GAME 1 AT LOU OCT 17

BRO	300 030 30	9	11	1
LOU	000 000 00	0	2	6

Pitchers: TERRY vs STRATTON
Attendance: 5,600

GAME 2 AT LOU OCT 18

BRO	020 201 000	5	5	3
LOU	101 000 001	3	6	5

Pitchers: LOVETT vs DAILY
Attendance: 2,860

GAME 3 AT LOU OCT 20

BRO	020 130 10	7	10	2
LOU	001 012 03	7	11	3

Pitchers: Terry vs Stratton, Meakim (4)
Attendance: 2,500
(Game called at end of eighth, darkness)

GAME 4 AT LOU OCT 21

BRO	031 000 000	4	7	2
LOU	301 000 10X	5	9	2

Pitchers: LOVETT vs EHRET
Attendance: 1,050

GAME 5 AT BRO OCT 25

LOU	010 010 000	2	5	6
BRO	210 200 20X	7	7	0

Pitchers: DAILY vs LOVETT
Home Runs: Burns-BRO
Attendance: 1,000

GAME 6 AT BRO OCT 27

LOU	012 101 220	9	13	3
BRO	100 004 030	8	12	3

Pitchers: STRATTON, Ehret (7) vs TERRY
Attendance: 600

GAME 7 AT BRO OCT 28

LOU	103 000 020	6	8	3
BRO	200 000 000	2	4	1

Pitchers: EHRET vs LOVETT
Attendance: 300

Interleague squabbling prevented a World Series in 1891, and the AA folded before the next season. Four AA clubs were taken into the NL, expanding the NL to 12 teams. To create a postseason championship series, the regular season was divided in half, with first-half winner Boston meeting second-half victor Cleveland for both the league and world titles.

The first game, in Cleveland, was a pitching and fielding classic. Boston's Jack Stivetts and Cleveland's Cy Young blanked the opposition for eleven innings before darkness halted the game. Young yielded just six hits and Stivetts four—all singles. Just as remarkable in an era when errors were commonplace, Cleveland committed only one and Boston none; several outstanding plays were made in the field.

Boston center fielder Hugh Duffy was the offensive and defensive star of Game 2. He drove in three of the Beaneaters' four runs (with a fly out, a triple, and a double), and scored the fourth himself after tripling a second time. And in the bottom of the ninth he snared a leadoff liner with a great running catch. As it was, Cleveland scored once in the inning to pull within a run of a tie; Duffy's catch prevented a certain tie and a possible Cleveland win. Game 3 was just as close. Pitchers Stivetts and Young each gave up two early runs, but then blanked their foes until the seventh inning, when Boston's Tommy McCarthy singled in Stivetts (who had doubled) with what proved the winning run.

The Series moved to Boston for the next three games. In Game 4, Boston ace Kid Nichols shut out the Spiders, scattering seven hits and fanning eight. Cleveland's Nig Cuppy yielded only six hits, but one was a home run ball to Hugh Duffy for two runs in the third inning, and another was a two-run single to Joe Quinn in the sixth. Cleveland pitcher John Clarkson helped his own cause the next day with a three-run homer in the Spider's six-run second inning. But Boston pitcher Jack Stivetts—with the score now 7–5 Cleveland in the sixth—tripled in a run and scored the tying run. In the seventh, Stivetts scored Boston's twelfth (and final) run after singling, while holding Cleveland scoreless through the final four innings.

Two days later the Beaneaters brought the Series to an end with their fifth straight win. The Spiders scored first, with a three-run third, but pitcher Kid Nichols held them

scoreless after that and singled home Boston's tying and go-ahead runs himself as the Beaneaters tagged Cy Young for eight runs over the final six innings.

Boston Beaneaters, 5; Cleveland Spiders, 0; tie, 1

BOS (N)

PLAYER/POS	AVG	G	AB	R	H	2B	3B	HR	RB	BB	SO	SB
Charlie Bennett, c	.286	2	7	2	2	0	0	1	1	0	2	1
Hugh Duffy, of	.462	6	26	3	12	3	2	1	9	1	0	3
Charlie Ganzel, c	.500	2	8	1	4	0	0	0	2	1	0	0
King Kelly, c	.000	2	8	0	0	0	0	0	0	0	2	1
Herman Long, ss	.222	6	27	4	6	0	0	0	1	0	0	2
Bobby Lowe, of	.130	6	23	8	3	0	0	0	0	1	2	1
Tommy McCarthy, of	.381	6	21	2	8	2	0	0	2	6	1	3
Billy Nash, 3b	.167	6	24	3	4	0	0	0	4	2	3	2
Kid Nichols, p	.286	2	7	1	2	0	0	0	2	0	1	1
Joe Quinn, 2b	.286	6	21	2	6	1	0	0	4	1	2	0
Harry Staley, p	.000	1	4	0	0	0	0	0	0	0	3	0
Jack Stivetts, p	.250	3	12	3	3	1	1	0	1	0	2	0
Tommy Tucker, 1b	.261	6	23	2	6	0	0	1	2	0	1	0
TOTAL	.265		211	31	56	7	4	3	28	12	19	14

PITCHER	W	L	ERA	G	GS	CG	SV	SHO	IP	H	ER	BB	SO
Kid Nichols	2	0	1.00	2	2	2	0	1	18.0	17	2	4	13
Harry Staley	1	0	3.00	1	1	1	0	0	9.0	10	3	1	0
Jack Stivetts	2	0	0.93	3	3	3	0	1	29.0	21	3	7	17
TOTAL	5	0	1.29	6	6	6	0	2	56.0	48	8	12	30

CLE (N)

PLAYER/POS	AVG	G	AB	R	H	2B	3B	HR	RB	BB	SO	SB
Jesse Burkett, of	.320	6	25	3	8	1	0	0	1	0	2	4
Cupid Childs, 2b	.409	6	22	3	9	0	2	0	0	5	1	0
John Clarkson, p	.250	2	8	1	2	0	0	1	3	0	1	0
Nig Cuppy, p	.000	1	3	0	0	0	0	0	0	0	0	0
George Davis, 3b-2	.167	3	6	0	1	0	0	0	0	0	1	0
Jimmy McAleer, of	.182	6	22	0	4	0	0	0	1	2	2	1
Ed McKean, ss	.440	6	25	2	11	0	0	0	6	1	3	0
Jack O'Connor, of	.136	6	22	1	3	0	0	0	0	2	3	0
Patsy Tebeau, 3b	.000	5	18	1	0	0	0	0	0	0	2	1
Jake Virtue, 1b	.125	6	24	1	3	0	0	0	0	2	5	1
Cy Young, p	.091	3	11	1	1	0	0	0	0	0	5	0
Chief Zimmer, c	.261	6	23	2	6	1	1	0	2	0	3	0
TOTAL	.230		209	15	48	2	3	1	13	12	30	7

PITCHER	W	L	ERA	G	GS	CG	SV	SHO	IP	H	ER	BB	SO
John Clarkson	0	2	5.29	2	2	2	0	0	17.0	24	10	5	9
Nig Cuppy	0	1	1.13	1	1	1	0	0	8.0	6	1	4	1
Cy Young	0	2	3.00	3	3	3	0	1	27.0	26	9	3	9
TOTAL	0	5	3.46	6	6	6	0	1	52.0	56	20	12	19

GAME 1 AT CLE OCT 17

CLE	000 000 000 00	0	4	1
BOS	000 000 000 00	0	6	0

Pitchers: YOUNG vs STIVETTS
Attendance: 6,000
(Game called at end of eleventh, darkness)

GAME 2 AT CLE OCT 18

BOS	101 010 010	4	10	2
CLE	001 100 001	3	10	2

Pitchers: STALEY vs CLARKSON
Attendance: 6,700

GAME 3 AT CLE OCT 19

CLE	200 000 000	2	8	0
BOS	110 000 10X	3	9	2

Pitchers: YOUNG vs STIVETTS
Attendance: 5,000

GAME 4 AT BOS OCT 21

CLE	000 000 000	0	7	3
BOS	002 002 00X	4	6	0

Pitchers: CUPPY vs NICHOLS
Home Runs: Duffy-BOS
Attendance: 6,547

GAME 5 AT BOS OCT 22

CLE	060 010 000	7	9	4
BOS	000 324 30X	12	14	3

Pitchers: CLARKSON vs STIVETTS
Home Runs: Clarkson-CLE, Tucker-BOS
Attendance: 3,466

GAME 6 AT BOS OCT 24

CLE	003 000 000	3	10	5
BOS	002 211 11X	8	11	5

Pitchers: YOUNG vs NICHOLS
Home Runs: Bennett-BOS
Attendance: 2,300

As the divided season of 1892 was not repeated, no postseason championship games were held in 1893. But in 1894 Pittsburgh sportsman William C. Temple offered an elegant trophy to the winner of a series between the NL's first- and second-place finishers. For four years the Temple Cup games determined the world championship. In this first matchup, second-place New York swept the feisty pennant-winning Orioles.

Game 1, in Baltimore, was a shutout through four innings as New York's Amos Rusie and Baltimore's Duke Esper held their opponents at bay. But New York's George Van Haltren tripled in the fifth inning and scored the game's first run on a fly to left. The Giants also scored single runs in the sixth, seventh, and eighth innings, while Rusie continued his shutout pitching through the eighth. In the ninth John McGraw singled, and he came around on a sacrifice, stolen base, and single to spoil the shutout. But the effort was too little to deprive Rusie of his win.

Some 200 policemen patrolled the second game the next day to protect the umpires and New York's players and fans from the abusive Orioles and the crowd. Baltimore scored first with two runs in the second and, after losing and regaining the lead, completed the eighth inning tied 5–5. But in the top of the ninth, the Giants put together their second four-run inning of the game. Once again the Orioles came up with a run in the last of the ninth, but once again came up short.

More than 22,000 spectators showed up for Game 3 as the Series shifted to New York—a huge crowd for that era, even for a Saturday. As in the first game, the Giants' Amos Rusie hurled a 4–1 victory. New York broke a 1–1 tie with a run in the fifth on a throwing error and a ground out, and scored the game's final runs an inning later. Threatening weather held down attendance at Game 4 to about 12,000. Baltimore jumped to a quick lead with two runs in the top of the first, but New York pitcher Jouett Meekin held the Orioles to just one run after that as the Giants piled up runs for a 16–3 advantage by the time darkness forced an end to play after eight innings. Meekin, in winning his second game of the Series, connected for three hits himself—half as many as he permitted the whole Baltimore team.

New York Giants, 4; Baltimore Orioles, 0

NY (N)

PLAYER/POS	AVG	G	AB	R	H	2B	3B	HR	RB	BB	SO	SB
Eddie Burke, of	.389	4	18	3	7	1	0	0	2	1	0	1
George Davis, 3b	.313	4	16	5	5	2	2	0	5	2	0	2
Jack Doyle, 1b	.588	4	17	4	10	1	1	0	6	1	1	6
Duke Farrell, c	.400	4	15	5	6	0	0	0	2	1	1	1
Shorty Fuller, ss	.286	4	14	4	4	0	0	0	2	2	0	1
Jouett Meekin, p	.556	2	9	2	5	0	0	0	3	0	1	0
Yale Murphy, of	.000	1	1	0	0	0	0	0	0	0	0	0
Amos Rusie, p	.429	2	7	1	3	1	0	0	1	0	1	0
Mike Tiernan, of	.294	4	17	5	5	0	1	0	3	2	2	0
George Van Haltren, of	.500	4	14	3	7	1	1	0	0	2	2	2
Monte Ward, 2b	.294	4	17	1	5	0	0	0	6	0	0	0
TOTAL	.393		145	33	57	6	5	0	30	11	8	13

PITCHER	W	L	ERA	G	GS	CG	SV	SHO	IP	H	ER	BB	SO
Jouett Meekin	2	0	1.59	2	2	2	0	0	17.0	13	3	8	6
Amos Rusie	2	0	0.50	2	2	2	0	0	18.0	14	1	3	9
TOTAL	4	0	1.03	4	4	4	0	0	35.0	27	4	11	15

BAL (N)

PLAYER/POS	AVG	G	AB	R	H	2B	3B	HR	RB	BB	SO	SB
Frank Bonner, ss-1,of-1	.000	2	5	0	0	0	0	0	0	0	2	0
Steve Brodie, of	.000	4	15	2	0	0	0	0	0	2	1	1
Dan Brouthers, 1b	.188	4	16	2	3	0	0	0	0	1	0	3
Duke Esper, p	.000	1	2	0	0	0	0	0	0	1	1	0
Kid Gleason, p	.200	2	5	0	1	0	1	0	1	0	1	0
Bill Hawke, p	.000	1	2	0	0	0	0	0	0	0	1	0
George Hemming, p	.000	1	3	0	0	0	0	0	0	1	1	0
Hughie Jennings, ss	.143	4	14	0	2	0	0	0	1	0	2	0
Willie Keeler, of	.250	3	12	1	3	0	0	0	1	1	0	0
Joe Kelley, of	.333	4	15	2	5	1	1	0	3	2	1	1
John McGraw, 3b	.250	4	16	2	4	0	0	0	2	0	0	1
Heinie Reitz, 2b	.333	4	15	1	5	0	0	0	4	1	3	1
Wilbert Robinson, c	.267	4	15	1	4	0	0	0	1	1	1	1
TOTAL	.200		135	11	27	1	2	0	10	11	15	8

PITCHER	W	L	ERA	G	GS	CG	SV	SHO	IP	H	ER	BB	SO
Duke Esper	0	1	4.00	1	1	1	0	0	9.0	13	4	1	3
Kid Gleason	0	1	9.69	2	1	1	0	0	13.0	25	14	6	3
Bill Hawke	0	1	9.00	1	1	0	0	0	4.0	9	4	1	0
George Hemming	0	1	1.13	1	1	1	0	0	8.0	10	1	3	2
TOTAL	0	4	6.09	5	4	3	0	0	34.0	57	23	11	8

GAME 1 AT BAL OCT 4

NY	000	011	110	4	13	2
BAL	000	000	001	1	7	1

Pitchers: RUSIE vs ESPER
Attendance: 9,000

GAME 2 AT BAL OCT 5

NY	004	000	014	9	14	3
BAL	022	000	101	6	7	2

Pitchers: MEEKIN vs GLEASON
Attendance: 11,000

GAME 3 AT NY OCT 6

BAL	000	100	000	1	7	4
NY	100	012	00X	4	10	4

Pitchers: HEMMING vs RUSIE
Attendance: 22,000

GAME 4 AT NY OCT 8

BAL	201	000	00	3	6	3
NY	101	351	50	16	20	4

Pitchers: HAWKE, Gleason (5) vs MEEKIN
Attendance: 12,000
(Game called at end of eighth, darkness)

Baltimore, repeating as NL pennant winner, returned to Temple Cup play against new runner-up Cleveland. The first half of the opener—played in Cleveland—featured a scoreless duel between Baltimore veteran John "Sadie" McMahon and the Spiders' great Cy Young. After Cleveland scored the game's first run in the last of the fifth, the teams traded runs and the lead, completing the eighth inning tied 3–3. In the top of the ninth, doubles by Wilbert Robinson and John McGraw restored the edge to Baltimore. But in the bottom of the inning, four straight Cleveland hits pushed across the tying run and filled the bases. One runner was forced at home for the first out, but a grounder that just missed being a double-play ball drove in the winning Cleveland run.

The next three games were not so closely contested. A large and enthusiastic Cleveland crowd watched its Spiders jump on Baltimore for three runs in the bottom of the first inning of Game 2 and coast to a 7–2 win behind the strong pitching of Nig Cuppy, who held the Orioles to five singles. Cleveland repeated itself in Game 3, again exploding for three runs in the bottom of the first on the way to a seven-run total. Cy Young was just as effective in the box as Cuppy had been, scattering four hits over seven shutout innings before Baltimore put together three singles in the eighth for their only run.

When the teams shifted to Baltimore for Game 4, the Orioles came to life. While their pitcher Duke Esper strangled the Spiders on just five singles—only two Cleveland runners advanced as far as second base—Baltimore batters tagged Nig Cuppy for five runs and their first Temple Cup win in two years of trying.

It proved to be their only win of the Series. The next day, in the first close struggle since the opener, Cy Young and Baltimore's rookie ace Bill Hoffer dueled scorelessly through six innings. But in the top of the seventh, Young doubled to start what became a three-run rally, and an inning later the Spiders scored twice more. Baltimore scored a single run in the last of the seventh, and, with two out in the ninth, loaded the bases on two walks and a hit batsman. A Cleveland error brought in the Orioles' second run as the bases remained full for Steve Brodie. But despite the pleas of Baltimore partisans to hit a homer or triple, Brodie didn't deliver and Cleveland copped the cup.

Cleveland Spiders, 4;
Baltimore Orioles, 1

CLE (N)

PLAYER/POS	AVG	G	AB	R	H	2B	3B	HR	RB	BB	SO	SB
Harry Blake, of	.250	5	20	1	5	3	0	0	2	0	2	0
Jesse Burkett, of	.450	5	20	3	9	2	0	0	2	0	0	1
Cupid Childs, 2b	.190	5	21	4	4	1	0	0	2	1	0	1
Nig Cuppy, p	.167	2	6	1	1	0	0	0	1	0	0	0
Jimmy McAleer, of	.286	5	21	2	6	0	0	0	2	0	0	1
Chippy McGarr, 3b	.368	5	19	3	7	2	0	0	1	1	0	2
Ed McKean, ss	.300	5	20	2	6	1	1	0	4	3	0	1
Patsy Tebeau, 1b	.286	5	21	3	6	1	0	0	3	1	1	0
Cy Young, p	.250	3	12	3	3	1	0	0	1	0	1	0
Chief Zimmer, c	.333	4	18	2	6	2	0	0	3	3	4	0
TOTAL	.298		178	24	53	14	1	0	21	9	9*	6

PITCHER	W	L	ERA	G	GS	CG	SV	SHO	IP	H	ER	BB	SO
Nig Cuppy	1	1	3.18	2	2	2	0	0	17.0	14	6	4	6
Cy Young	3	0	2.33	3	3	3	0	0	27.0	28	7	4	2
TOTAL	4	1	2.66	5	5	5	0	0	44.0	42	13	8	8

BAL (N)

PLAYER/POS	AVG	G	AB	R	H	2B	3B	HR	RB	BB	SO	SB
Steve Brodie, of	.200	5	20	1	4	0	0	0	2	0	0	0
Scoops Carey, 1b	.263	5	19	0	5	1	0	0	1	0	0	0
Boileryard Clarke, c	.286	2	7	1	2	0	0	0	0	0	0	2
Duke Esper, p	.000	1	3	0	0	0	0	0	0	1	2	0
Kid Gleason, 2b	.105	5	19	0	2	0	0	0	0	0	1	0
Bill Hoffer, p	.000	2	7	0	0	0	0	0	0	0	2	0
Hughie Jennings, ss	.368	5	19	3	7	2	0	0	2	1	0	1
Willie Keeler, of	.235	5	17	3	4	0	0	0	1	3	1	0
Joe Kelley, of	.368	5	19	1	7	0	0	0	5	1	1	1
John McGraw, 3b	.400	5	20	4	8	2	0	0	1	2	0	2
Sadie McMahon, p	.000	2	7	0	0	0	0	0	0	0	0	0
Wilbert Robinson, c	.250	3	12	1	3	1	0	0	0	0	1	0
TOTAL	.249		169	14	42	6	0	0	12	8	8	6

PITCHER	W	L	ERA	G	GS	CG	SV	SHO	IP	H	ER	BB	SO
Duke Esper	1	0	0.00	1	1	1	0	1	9.0	5	0	0	3
Bill Hoffer	0	2	4.24	2	2	2	0	0	17.0	21	8	6	4
Sadie McMahon	0	2	5.94	2	2	2	0	0	16.2	27	11	3	2
TOTAL	1	4	4.01	5	5	5	0	1	42.2	53	19	9	9

* While the total strikeouts for the team have been confirmed as nine, research has failed, to this point, to identify the missing batter strikeout.

GAME 1 AT CLE OCT 2

BAL	000 001 021	4	12	0
CLE	000 011 012	5	14	3

Pitchers: McMAHON vs YOUNG
Attendance: 8,000

GAME 2 AT CLE OCT 3

BAL	010 001 000	2	5	4
CLE	300 012 10X	7	10	5

Pitchers: HOFFER vs CUPPY
Attendance: 10,000

GAME 3 AT CLE OCT 5

BAL	000 000 010	1	7	1
CLE	300 000 31X	7	13	1

Pitchers: McMAHON vs YOUNG
Attendance: 12,000

GAME 4 AT BAL OCT 7

CLE	000 000 000	0	5	1
BAL	012 000 20X	5	9	1

Pitchers: CUPPY vs ESPER
Attendance: 9,100

GAME 5 AT BAL OCT 8

CLE	000 000 320	5	11	3
BAL	000 000 101	2	9	5

Pitchers: YOUNG vs HOFFER
Attendance: 5,000

Baltimore captured its third consecutive pennant and for the second year in a row faced runner-up Cleveland in the Temple Cup games. But this time the Orioles emerged triumphant—with a sweep in which their margin of victory was never less than four runs.

Aces Bill Hoffer of Baltimore and the Spiders' Cy Young faced each other in the opener, in Baltimore. Hoffer walked four men, but gave up only five hits while the Orioles bombarded Young for 13. When the game ended, Hoffer and Baltimore had a 7–1 win.

Bobby Wallace (who had not yet discovered his role at shortstop that would propel him into the Hall of Fame) pitched for Cleveland in Game 2. He lost the game in the first inning when two Spider errors, a hit batsman, three hits, and a steal of home put four Baltimore runs on the board. The Orioles added two runs in the third and another in the fifth, while their promising 20-year-old pitcher Joe Corbett held the Spiders to two runs on seven hits.

The Orioles' Hoffer gave up 10 hits to Cleveland in Game 3—two more than the Birds made off Nig Cuppy. But all the hits off Hoffer were singles, and he walked only one. Half of Cleveland's hits went toward producing just two runs. Their second run tied the score in the fifth inning, but in the sixth Baltimore regained the lead as John McGraw singled, stole second, took third on an error, and came home on an outfield fly. In the eighth the Orioles bunched four of their eight hits for three insurance runs.

The Series moved to Cleveland for the fourth game. Young Joe Corbett was again sent into the box for Baltimore, this time to face Nig Cuppy. For six innings the game was a scoreless duel. Baltimore hit safely in every inning but the second, but failed to score until the seventh, when Joe Kelley's double and Jack Doyle's single scored the only run they would need. But the Orioles added a second run in that inning and three more in the eighth. Two of the four Cleveland hits against Corbett put men on base in the eighth inning, and Corbett walked two in the ninth to raise Cleveland's hopes. But no Spider scored, and with the 5–0 win the Orioles were world champions at last.

Baltimore Orioles, 4; Cleveland Spiders, 0

BAL (N)

PLAYER/POS	AVG	G	AB	R	H	2B	3B	HR	RB	BB	SO	SB
Steve Brodie, of	.067	4	15	1	1	0	0	0	3	0	0	1
Joe Corbett, p	.500	2	6	1	3	1	0	0	0	1	1	0
Jack Doyle, 1b	.294	4	17	3	5	1	0	0	4	0	0	2
Bill Hoffer, p	.286	2	7	1	2	0	2	0	0	0	1	0
Hughie Jennings, ss	.333	4	15	5	5	2	0	0	3	1	2	1
Willie Keeler, of	.471	4	17	4	8	1	2	0	4	0	0	1
Joe Kelley, of	.471	4	17	3	8	1	0	0	4	0	1	2
John McGraw, 3b	.267	4	15	4	4	0	0	0	1	0	0	4
Joe Quinn, 3b	.000	1	3	1	0	0	0	0	0	0	0	0
Heinie Reitz, 2b	.133	4	15	1	2	0	0	0	2	1	0	0
Wilbert Robinson, c	.267	4	15	1	4	1	0	0	2	0	3	0
TOTAL	.296		142	25	42	7	4	0	23	3	8	11

PITCHER	W	L	ERA	G	GS	CG	SV	SHO	IP	H	ER	BB	SO
Joe Corbett	2	0	0.50	2	2	2	0	1	18.0	11	1	7	10
Bill Hoffer	2	0	1.50	2	2	2	0	0	18.0	15	3	5	10
TOTAL	4	0	1.00	4	4	4	0	1	36.0	26	4	12	20

CLE (N)

PLAYER/POS	AVG	G	AB	R	H	2B	3B	HR	RB	BB	SO	SB
Harry Blake, of	.071	4	14	1	1	0	0	0	0	1	1	1
Jesse Burkett, of	.333	4	15	1	5	0	0	0	0	2	3	0
Cupid Childs, 2b	.231	4	13	2	3	0	0	0	0	4	0	1
Nig Cuppy, p	.143	2	7	0	1	0	0	0	0	0	1	0
Jimmy McAleer, of	.133	4	15	0	2	0	0	0	1	1	2	1
Chippy McGarr, 3b	.063	4	16	1	1	0	0	0	0	0	3	2
Ed McKean, ss	.313	4	16	0	5	1	1	0	1	1	1	1
Jack O'Connor, 1b	.286	4	14	1	4	0	0	0	1	1	2	0
Patsy Tebeau, 1b	.000	1	1	0	0	0	0	0	0	0	0	0
Bobby Wallace, p-1	.200	3	5	0	1	0	0	0	0	0	0	0
Cy Young, p	.000	1	3	0	0	0	0	0	0	0	0	0
Chief Zimmer, c	.214	4	14	0	3	1	0	0	1	2	6	0
TOTAL	.195		133	5	26	2	1	0	4	12	20	6

PITCHER	W	L	ERA	G	GS	CG	SV	SHO	IP	H	ER	BB	SO
Nig Cuppy	0	2	4.76	2	2	2	0	0	17.0	19	9	0	4
Bobby Wallace	0	1	4.50	1	1	1	0	0	8.0	10	4	2	4
Cy Young	0	1	6.00	1	1	1	0	0	9.0	13	6	1	0
TOTAL	0	4	5.03	4	4	4	0	0	34.0	42	19	3	8

GAME 1 AT BAL OCT 2

BAL	002	001	310	7 13 1
CLE	000	001	000	1 5 4

Pitchers: HOFFER vs YOUNG
Attendance: 4,000

GAME 2 AT BAL OCT 3

BAL	402	010	00	7 10 3
CLE	001	001	00	2 7 3

Pitchers: CORBETT vs WALLACE
Attendance: 3,100
(Game called at end of eighth, darkness)

GAME 3 AT BAL OCT 5

BAL	011	001	030	6 8 2
CLE	001	010	000	2 10 2

Pitchers: HOFFER vs CUPPY
Attendance: 2,000

GAME 4 AT CLE OCT 8

CLE	000	000	000	0 4 2
BAL	000	000	23X	5 11 1

Pitchers: CUPPY vs CORBETT
Attendance: 1,500

Boston had edged Baltimore in a close race for the NL pennant, but the Orioles turned the tables on the Beaneaters in Temple Cup play. The Series was a high-scoring affair with an average score of 11-8 for each game.

The opener, in Boston, set the tone for the games. Baltimore sent four runners across the plate in the top of the first inning, and Boston followed in its half with three. The Beaneaters recorded only 12 hits in the game to the Orioles' 20, but they also received seven walks from Baltimore hurler Jerry Nops, and five of those runners scored. The lead switched back and forth in the middle innings, but Boston scored two final runs in the eighth and hung on for a 13–12 win.

Baltimore's Joe Corbett gave up 16 hits (one a home run) and four walks in Game 2 as Boston scored 11 times. But Boston's two pitchers, Fred Klobedanz and Jack Stivetts, were even more generous, handing out seventeen hits (including three homers—one of them to opposing pitcher Corbett, who also hit a double and two singles) and five walks as the Orioles evened the Series with their thirteen-run attack.

Game 3 was the Series' lowest in run production, with Baltimore scoring four in the second inning and another four in the third for an 8–3 win. But rain ended the game before Boston could complete its time at bat in the last of the eighth, which erased from the record four more Orioles runs scored earlier in the inning. Rather than waste the two free days before the Series resumed in Baltimore, the two clubs stayed in Massachusetts and played a pair of exhibition games in Worcester and Springfield. Baltimore won them both, 11–10, and 8–6.

The Orioles continued their roll in Series Game 4, with another close but high-scoring victory, 12–11. It looked at first like a blowout as Baltimore scored six runs in the first inning and five more in the second. But Ted Lewis relieved Boston starter Jack Stivetts and held Baltimore to just one further run as the Beaneaters fought back to within one run of a tie before faltering in the ninth.

Boston batters hit Bill Hoffer safely 15 times in Game Five, but only three Beaneaters scored. Baltimore, with two fewer hits, garnered six more runs than Boston and, with their fourth win, the right to hold the cup for another year. But attendance at the final game

was so small the embarrassed Baltimore management refused to release the figures, and the league gave the cup back to Mr. Temple rather than sponsor another unprofitable Series. There was no postseason championship contest in 1898 or 1899.

Baltimore Orioles, 4; Boston Beaneaters, 1

BAL (N)

PLAYER/POS	AVG	G	AB	R	H	2B	3B	HR	RB	BB	SO	SB
Frank Bowerman, c-1,1b-1	.500	2	8	2	4	0	1	0	4	0	0	0
Boileryard Clarke, c	.563	4	16	5	9	1	1	1	4	1	0	0
Joe Corbett, p	.667	2	6	2	4	1	0	1	2	0	1	0
Jack Doyle, 1b	.526	5	19	7	10	2	0	0	9	0	1	2
Bill Hoffer, p	.250	2	8	2	2	1	0	0	0	0	0	0
Hughie Jennings, ss	.318	5	22	5	7	2	0	0	3	4	0	0
Willie Keeler, of	.391	5	23	5	9	2	0	0	2	4	0	0
Joe Kelley, of	.313	4	16	7	5	3	0	0	5	5	0	0
John McGraw, 3b	.300	5	20	6	6	1	1	0	6	7	0	0
Jerry Nops, p	.286	2	7	0	2	0	0	0	1	1	5	0
Tom O'Brien, of	.400	1	5	2	2	1	0	0	0	0	0	0
Heinie Reitz, 2b	.250	5	20	4	5	1	0	1	4	2	0	0
Jake Stenzel, of	.381	5	21	7	8	1	1	0	3	2	0	2
TOTAL	.382		191	54	73	16	4	3	43	26	7	4

PITCHER	W	L	ERA	G	GS	CG	SV	SHO	IP	H	ER	BB	SO
Joe Corbett	1	0	9.00	2	1	1	0	0	12.0	21	12	8	5
Bill Hoffer	2	0	3.38	2	2	2	0	0	16.0	25	6	4	2
Jerry Nops	1	1	12.86	2	2	1	0	0	14.0	23	20	9	3
TOTAL	4	1	8.14	6	5	4	0	0	42.0	69	38	21	10

BOS (N)

PLAYER/POS	AVG	G	AB	R	H	2B	3B	HR	RB	BB	SO	SB
Marty Bergen, c	.500	1	4	0	2	0	0	0	1	0	1	1
Jimmy Collins, 3b	.182	5	22	4	4	0	0	4	1	0	0
Hugh Duffy, of	.524	5	21	6	11	2	0	0	7	1	0	0
Billy Hamilton, of	.500	4	16	6	8	1	0	0	2	5	3	2
Charlie Hickman, p-1,of-1	.250	1	4	0	1	1	0	0	1	0	0	0
Fred Klobedanz, p	1.000	2	5	3	5	0	0	0	0	0	0	0
Fred Lake, c	.000	1	3	0	0	0	0	0	0	0	1	0
Ted Lewis, p	.500	3	6	1	3	1	0	0	1	1	0	0
Herman Long, ss	.286	5	21	4	6	1	1	1	5	2	2	1
Bobby Lowe, 2b	.391	5	23	6	9	2	0	0	6	1	0	1
Kid Nichols, p	.000	1	3	0	0	0	0	0	1	0	0	0
Chick Stahl, of	.381	5	21	6	8	1	0	0	6	3	2	2
Jack Stivetts, p-2,of-1	.000	3	7	1	0	0	0	0	0	1	0	1
Jim Sullivan, p	.000	1	1	0	0	0	0	0	0	0	0	0
Fred Tenney, 1b	.286	5	21	4	6	0	0	0	2	4	1	2
George Yeager, c	.500	3	12	2	6	1	1	0	2	2	0	0
TOTAL	.365		189	41	69	10	2	1	38	21	10	10

PITCHER	W	L	ERA	G	GS	CG	SV	SHO	IP	H	ER	BB	SO
Charlie Hickman	0	1	3.60	1	1	0	0	0	5.0	7	2	2	0
Fred Klobedanz	0	1	9.35	2	1	0	0	0	8.2	12	9	8	0
Ted Lewis	1	1	6.00	3	1	0	0	0	12	18	8	9	4
Kid Nichols	0	0	12.00	1	1	0	0	0	6.0	14	8	0	3
Jack Stivetts	0	1	18.47	2	1	0	0	0	6.1	16	13	7	0
Jim Sullivan	0	0	3.00	1	0	0	0	0	3.0	6	1	0	0
TOTAL	1	4	9.00	10	5	0	0	0	41.0	73	41	26	7

GAME 1 AT BOS OCT 4

BAL	401	023	200	12 20 4
BOS	300	125	02X	13 12 4

Pitchers: NOPS vs Nichols, LEWIS (7)
Attendance: 9,600

GAME 2 AT BOS OCT 5

BAL	130	160	110	13 17 2
BOS	002	620	100	11 16 3

Pitchers: CORBETT vs KLOBEDANZ, Stivetts (5)
Home Runs: Reitz-BAL, Clarke-BAL, Corbett-BAL, Long-BOS
Attendance: 6,500

GAME 3 AT BOS OCT 6

BAL	044	000	0	8 9 2
BOS	003	000	0	3 10 2

Pitchers: HOFFER vs LEWIS, Klobedanz (3)
Attendance: 5,000
(Game called in eighth, rain)

GAME 4 AT BAL OCT 9

BOS	000	024	320	11 16 3
BAL	650	001	00X	12 14 3

Pitchers: STIVETTS, Lewis (2) vs NOPS, Corbett (7)
Attendance: 2,500

GAME 5 AT BAL OCT 11

BOS	020	000	001	3 15 3
BAL	023	000	22X	9 13 2

Pitchers: HICKMAN, Sullivan (7) vs HOFFER
Attendance: 700

Pennant-winning Brooklyn led the NL in hitting, but runner-up Pittsburgh claimed the best pitching. Honus Wagner was the only Pittsburgh regular to hit over .300, but he enjoyed what turned out to be his finest season offensively, leading the league with a .381 batting average. Pittsburghers believed their club superior to Brooklyn and a best-of-five "world championship" series was arranged, with all the games to be played in Pittsburgh for a silver cup donated by the *Pittsburgh Chronicle-Telegraph*. Brooklyn, however, proved that its pennant was no fluke.

Two of the game's best pitchers faced off in the opener: Pittsburgh's Rube Waddell, who had led the league in ERA, and Joe "Iron Man" McGinnity, whose 28 regular-season wins totaled eight more than those of the league's runners-up. McGinnity prevailed, shutting out the Pirates until two unearned runs came across in the top of the ninth. Pirates errors also gave Brooklyn a pair of unearned runs, but Waddell lost the game on hits—13 in all, including six in the Superbas' three-run third inning.

In Game 2, Brooklyn's Frank Kitson held Pittsburgh to four hits, and although his Superbas scored only one earned run, six Pirate errors gave them their second win, 4–2.

The Pirates staved off a Series sweep with sharp pitching and heavy hitting in Game 3. Deacon Phillippe shut out Brooklyn on six hits as the Pirates jumped on Harry Howell for 13. All Pittsburgh's hits were singles, but combined with Brooklyn errors they were good for ten runs, seven of them unearned.

Three Brooklyn singles and a fumble by Pirates pitcher Sam Leever in the fourth inning of Game 4 gave the Superbas three runs and a 4–0 lead the Pirates could not overcome. Brooklyn hurler McGinnity scattered nine hits and, supported by flawless fielding, held Pittsburgh to a single run to bring Brooklyn its first World Series triumph in three tries—and its last until 1955. The Brooklyn players voted to award their trophy to McGinnity for his fine pitching. The cup may be seen today—along with the Temple Cup and the current World Series trophy—at the Baseball Hall of Fame in Cooperstown.

Brooklyn Superbas, 3; Pittsburgh Pirates, 1

BRO (N)

PLAYER/POS	AVG	G	AB	R	H	2B	3B	HR	RB	BB	SO	SB
Lave Cross, 3b	.278	4	18	2	5	0	1	0	1	0	0	1
Bill Dahlen, ss	.176	4	17	3	3	0	1	0	2	0	3	1
Tom Daly, 2b	.154	4	13	2	2	1	0	0	1	3	1	0
Duke Farrell, c	.375	2	8	0	3	0	0	0	1	0	0	1
Harry Howell, p	.000	1	3	0	0	0	0	0	0	0	2	0
Hughie Jennings, 1b	.167	4	18	1	3	1	0	0	2	1	1	0
Fielder Jones, of	.278	4	18	3	5	0	0	0	4	1	1	1
Willie Keeler, of	.353	4	17	0	6	0	0	0	0	1	0	0
Joe Kelley, of	.176	4	17	2	3	0	0	0	1	2	3	0
Frank Kitson, p	.000	1	3	0	0	0	0	0	0	1	2	0
Joe McGinnity, p	.143	2	7	1	1	0	0	0	0	0	2	0
Deacon McGuire, c	.375	2	8	1	3	1	0	0	0	0	1	0
TOTAL	.231		147	15	34	3	2	0	13	9	16	4

PITCHER	W	L	ERA	G	GS	CG	SV	SHO	IP	H	ER	BB	SO
Harry Howell	0	1	3.38	1	1	1	0	0	8.0	13	3	2	3
Frank Kitson	1	0	1.00	1	1	1	0	0	9.0	4	1	1	2
Joe McGinnity	2	0	0.00	2	2	2	0	0	18.0	14	0	3	5
TOTAL	3	1	1.03	4	4	4	0	0	35.0	31	4	6	10

PIT (N)

PLAYER/POS	AVG	G	AB	R	H	2B	3B	HR	RB	BB	SO	SB
Ginger Beaumont, of	.267	4	15	2	4	0	0	0	1	1	0	1
Fred Ely, ss	.286	4	14	1	4	1	0	0	0	1	1	2
Tommy Leach, of	.176	4	17	4	3	0	0	0	1	1	2	0
Sam Leever, p	.250	2	4	0	1	0	0	0	0	0	1	1
Tom O'Brien, 1b	.125	4	16	1	2	1	0	0	2	0	1	0
Jack O'Connor, c	.250	2	4	0	1	0	0	0	1	1	0	0
Deacon Phillippe, p	.000	1	4	1	0	0	0	0	0	0	1	0
Claude Ritchey, 2b	.333	4	15	3	5	1	0	0	1	1	0	0
Pop Schriver, ph	.000	1	1	0	0	0	0	0	0	0	0	0
Rube Waddell, p	.200	2	5	0	1	0	0	0	0	0	0	0
Honus Wagner, of	.400	4	15	2	6	1	0	0	3	0	1	2
Jimmy Williams, 3b	.214	4	14	0	3	0	0	0	0	1	0	0
Chief Zimmer, c	.111	3	9	1	1	0	0	0	1	0	2	1
TOTAL	.233		133	15	31	4	0	0	10	6	10	7

PITCHER	W	L	ERA	G	GS	CG	SV	SHO	IP	H	ER	BB	SO
Sam Leever	0	2	1.38	2	2	1	0	0	13.0	13	2	4	4
Deacon Phillippe	1	0	0.00	1	1	1	0	1	9.0	6	0	2	5
Rube Waddell	0	1	1.93	2	1	1	0	0	14.0	15	3	3	7
TOTAL	1	3	1.25	5	4	3	0	1	36.0	34	5	9	16

GAME 1 AT PIT OCT 15

BRO	003	101	000	5 13 1
PIT	000	000	002	2 5 4

Pitchers: McGINNITY vs WADDELL
Attendance: 4,000

GAME 2 AT PIT OCT 16

BRO	010	003	000	4 7 0
PIT	000	100	100	2 4 6

Pitchers: KITSON vs LEEVER
Attendance: 1,800

GAME 3 AT PIT OCT 17

BRO	000	000	000	0 6 3
PIT	310	020	13X	10 13 1

Pitchers: HOWELL vs PHILLIPPE
Attendance: 2,500

GAME 4 AT PIT OCT 18

BRO	100	311	000	6 8 0
PIT	000	001	000	1 9 3

Pitchers: McGINNITY vs LEEVER, Waddell (5)
Attendance: 2,335

When the Boston Pilgrims of the young American League accepted a challenge from owner Barney Dreyfuss of the National League Pirates, the modern World Series was born. (In 1901 and 1902, the National and American Leagues were warring, and did not stage a postseason series.) Pittsburgh was favored to win but entered the Series weakened by injuries to pitching ace Sam Leever and shortstop Honus Wagner, and by the loss of pitcher Ed Doheny to mental illness.

Deacon Phillippe, the Pirates' one healthy starter, faced Cy Young in the opener, winning handily as the Pirates, with two out in the top of the first, jumped on Young (and a porous defense) for four runs. Right fielder Jimmy Sebring starred offensively for the Pirates, with four RBIs and the Series's first home run. Boston came back in Game 2 as Bill Dinneen shut out the Pirates on three hits. His teammates scored three runs off the sore-armed Leever and reliever Bucky Veil, two coming on homers by Patsy Dougherty. (They were the last World Series home runs for five years.)

Phillippe, with only a day's rest, started Game 3 and again pitched Pittsburgh into the Series lead, holding Boston to four hits. After a Sunday travel day to Pittsburgh and a day of rain, Phillippe defeated Boston a third time, though he yielded three ninth-inning runs before emerging with a 5–4 win.

The tide began to turn against the Pirates the next day, as Boston knocked five ground-rule triples into the overflow crowd, scoring 10 runs in the sixth and seventh innings to give Young an 11–2 victory. Dinneen bested Leever for a second time in Game 6, holding the Pirates scoreless in eight of their nine innings for a 6–3 win. And in Game 7, Phillippe finally lost and Young won.

After another travel Sunday and another rainout, Phillippe faced the Pilgrims for the fifth time. He pitched well, giving up three runs (only two of them earned). But Bill Dinneen pitched better, holding the Pirates to four hits as he shut them out for the second time to give Boston the Series.

Boston Pilgrims (AL), 5; Pittsburgh Pirates (NL), 3

BOS (A)

PLAYER/POS	AVG	G	AB	R	H	2B	3B	HR	RB	BB	SO	SB
Jimmy Collins, 3b	.250	8	36	5	9	1	2	0	1	1	1	3
Lou Criger, c	.231	8	26	1	6	0	0	0	4	2	3	0
Bill Dinneen, p	.250	4	12	1	3	0	0	0	0	2	2	0
Patsy Dougherty, of	.235	8	34	3	8	0	2	2	5	2	6	0
Duke Farrell, ph	.000	2	2	0	0	0	0	0	1	0	0	0
Hobe Ferris, 2b	.290	8	31	3	9	0	1	0	5	0	6	0
Buck Freeman, of	.281	8	32	6	9	3	0	0	4	2	2	0
Tom Hughes, p	.000	1	0	0	0	0	0	0	0	0	0	0
Candy La Chance, 1b	.222	8	27	5	6	2	1	0	4	3	2	0
Jack O'Ben, ph	.000	2	2	0	0	0	0	0	0	0	1	0
Freddy Parent, ss	.281	8	32	8	9	0	3	0	4	1	1	0
Chick Stahl, of	.303	8	33	6	10	1	3	0	3	1	2	2
Cy Young, p	.133	4	15	1	2	0	1	0	3	0	3	0
TOTAL	.252		282	39	71	4	16	2	34	14	29	5

PITCHER	W	L	ERA	G	GS	CG	SV	SHO	IP	H	ER	BB	SO
Bill Dinneen	3	1	2.06	4	4	4	0	2	35.0	29	8	8	28
Tom Hughes	0	1	9.00	1	1	0	0	0	2.0	4	2	2	0
Cy Young	2	1	1.85	4	3	3	0	0	34.0	31	7	4	17
TOTAL	5	3	2.15	9	8	7	0	2	71.0	64	17	14	45

PIT (N)

PLAYER/POS	AVG	G	AB	R	H	2B	3B	HR	RB	BB	SO	SB
Ginger Beaumont, of	.265	8	34	6	9	0	1	0	1	2	4	2
Kitty Bransfield, 1b	.207	8	29	3	6	0	2	0	1	1	6	1
Fred Clarke, of	.265	8	34	3	9	2	1	0	2	1	5	1
Brickyard Kennedy, p	.500	1	2	0	1	1	0	0	0	0	0	0
Tommy Leach, 3b	.273	8	33	3	9	0	4	0	7	1	4	1
Sam Leever, p	.000	2	4	0	0	0	0	0	0	0	0	0
Ed Phelps, c-7	.231	8	26	1	6	2	0	0	1	1	6	0
Deacon Phillippe, p	.222	5	18	1	4	0	0	0	1	0	3	0
Claude Ritchey, 2b	.111	8	27	2	3	1	0	0	2	4	7	1
Jimmy Sebring, of	.367	8	30	3	11	0	1	1	3	1	4	0
Harry Smith, c	.000	1	3	0	0	0	0	0	0	0	0	0
Gus Thompson, p	.000	1	1	0	0	0	0	0	0	0	0	0
Bucky Veil, p	.000	1	2	0	0	0	0	0	0	0	2	0
Honus Wagner, ss	.222	8	27	2	6	1	0	0	3	3	4	3
TOTAL	.237		270	24	64	7	9	1	21	14	45	9

PITCHER	W	L	ERA	G	GS	CG	SV	SHO	IP	H	ER	BB	SO
Brickyard Kennedy	0	1	5.14	1	1	0	0	0	7.0	11	4	3	3
Sam Leever	0	2	5.40	2	2	1	0	0	10.0	13	6	3	2
Deacon Phillippe	3	2	2.86	5	5	5	0	0	44.0	38	14	3	22
Gus Thompson	0	0	4.50	1	0	0	0	0	2.0	3	1	0	1
Bucky Veil	0	0	1.29	1	0	0	0	0	7.0	6	1	5	1
TOTAL	3	5	3.34	10	8	6	0	0	70.0	71	26	14	29

GAME 1 AT BOS OCT 1

PIT	401	100	100	7	12	2
BOS	000	000	201	3	6	4

Pitchers: PHILLIPPE vs YOUNG
Home Runs: Sebring-PIT
Attendance: 16,242

GAME 2 AT BOS OCT 2

PIT	000	000	000	0	3	2
BOS	200	001	00X	3	9	0

Pitchers: LEEVER, Vail (2) vs DINNEEN
Home Runs: Dougherty-BOS (2)
Attendance: 9,415

GAME 3 AT BOS OCT 3

PIT	012	000	010	4	7	0
BOS	000	100	010	2	4	2

Pitchers: PHILLIPPE vs HUGHES, Young (3)
Attendance: 18,801

GAME 4 AT PIT OCT 6

BOS	000	010	003	4	9	1
PIT	100	010	30X	5	12	1

Pitchers: DINNEEN vs PHILLIPPE
Attendance: 7,600

GAME 5 AT PIT OCT 7

BOS	000	006	410	11	14	2
PIT	000	000	020	2	6	4

Pitchers: YOUNG vs KENNEDY, Thompson (8)
Attendance: 12,322

GAME 6 AT PIT OCT 8

BOS	003	020	100	6	10	1
PIT	000	000	300	3	10	3

Pitchers: DINNEEN vs LEEVER
Attendance: 11,556

GAME 7 AT PIT OCT 10

BOS	200	202	010	7	11	4
PIT	000	101	001	3	10	3

Pitchers: YOUNG vs PHILLIPPE
Attendance: 17,038

GAME 8 AT BOS OCT 13

PIT	000	000	000	0	4	3
BOS	000	201	00X	3	8	0

Pitchers: PHILLIPPE vs DINNEEN
Attendance: 7,455

After a year's gap caused by the Giants' refusal to play the American League champion Boston Pilgrims, the World Series—now established on an official and permanent basis (and reduced to a best-of-seven format)—resumed with a pitching classic. Even though ERA league leader Rube Waddell had ostensibly injured his shoulder and could not pitch in the Series for the A's—rumor had it that gamblers had reached him—the Philadelphia staff recorded a Series ERA of only 1.47. But the Giants' staff—led by Christy Mathewson's three shutouts—registered a matchless ERA of 0.00, permitting only three unearned runs to score in their only Series loss. Every victory in the Series was a shutout.

Mathewson, a 31-game winner in the regular season, continued his winning ways in the Series opener. Though three of the four hits he yielded were doubles, he permitted no more than one hit in any inning, and stopped the only scoring threat, fielding a squeeze bunt to throw out the runner at the plate in the sixth inning.

The A's came back to tie the Series the next day. This time it was Chief Bender's turn to hurl a four-hit shutout. Joe McGinnity also pitched well for the Giants, but New York errors in the third and eighth innings let in three unearned runs—the only runs, as it turned out, to be scored against the Giants in the Series.

Mathewson, pitching with only two days' rest in Game 3, once again permitted only four hits (all singles this time), and Philadelphia's flawed fielding let in seven unearned runs to help give Matty an easy 9–0 win. In Game 4, McGinnity, the hard-luck loser of Game 2, tried again. This time the Giants supported him almost flawlessly, while he gave up only five singles on his way to victory in the Series' tightest game. An A's error led to a single Giants run, and a loss for Eddie Plank, who had pitched even better than McGinnity, giving up only four hits while fanning six.

Chief Bender, the A's winner in Game 2, pitched a five-hitter in Game 6, but he also yielded three walks, all of which contributed to the two New York runs. Mathewson, though he gave up six hits, walked none, retiring the final ten batters to conclude his record third shutout—and the Series.

New York Giants (NL), 4; Philadelphia Athletics (AL), 1

NY (N)

PLAYER/POS	AVG	G	AB	R	H	2B	3B	HR	RB	BB	SO	SB
Red Ames, p	.000	1	0	0	0	0	0	0	0	0	0	0
Roger Bresnahan, c	.313	5	16	3	5	2	0	0	1	4	0	1
George Browne, of	.182	5	22	4	4	0	0	0	1	0	2	2
Bill Dahlen, ss	.000	5	15	1	0	0	0	0	1	3	2	3
Art Devlin, 3b	.250	5	16	0	4	1	0	0	1	1	3	3
Mike Donlin, of	.263	5	19	4	5	1	0	0	1	2	1	2
Billy Gilbert, 2b	.235	5	17	1	4	0	0	0	2	0	2	1
Christy Mathewson, p	.250	3	8	1	2	0	0	0	0	1	1	0
Dan McGann, 1b	.235	5	17	1	4	2	0	0	4	2	7	0
Joe McGinnity, p	.000	2	5	0	0	0	0	0	0	0	2	0
Sam Mertes, of	.176	5	17	2	3	1	0	0	2	2	5	0
Sammy Strang, ph	.000	1	1	0	0	0	0	0	0	0	1	0
TOTAL	.203		153	15	31	7	0	0	13	15	26	12

PITCHER	W	L	ERA	G	GS	CG	SV	SHO	IP	H	ER	BB	SO
Red Ames	0	0	0.00	1	0	0	0	0	1.0	1	0	1	1
Christy Mathewson	3	0	0.00	3	3	3	0	3	27.0	14	0	1	18
Joe McGinnity	1	1	0.00	2	2	1	0	1	17.0	10	0	3	6
TOTAL	4	1	0.00	6	5	4	0	4	45.0	25	0	5	25

PHI (A)

PLAYER/POS	AVG	G	AB	R	H	2B	3B	HR	RB	BB	SO	SB
Chief Bender, p	.000	2	5	0	0	0	0	0	0	0	1	0
Andy Coakley, p	.000	1	3	0	0	0	0	0	0	0	1	0
Lave Cross, 3b	.105	5	19	0	2	0	0	0	0	1	1	0
Monte Cross, ss	.176	5	17	0	3	0	0	0	0	0	7	0
Harry Davis, 1b	.200	5	20	0	4	1	0	0	0	1	0	0
Topsy Hartsel, of	.294	5	17	1	5	1	0	0	0	2	1	2
Danny Hoffman, ph	.000	1	1	0	0	0	0	0	0	0	1	0
Bris Lord, of	.100	5	20	0	2	0	0	0	2	0	5	0
Danny Murphy, 2b	.188	5	16	0	3	0	0	0	0	0	2	0
Eddie Plank, p	.167	2	6	0	1	0	0	0	0	0	2	0
Mike Powers, c	.143	3	7	0	1	1	0	0	0	0	0	0
Ossee Schreckengost, c	.222	3	9	2	2	1	0	0	0	0	0	0
Socks Seybold, of	.125	5	16	0	2	0	0	0	0	0	3	0
TOTAL	.161		155	3	25	5	0	0	2	5	25	2

PITCHER	W	L	ERA	G	GS	CG	SV	SHO	IP	H	ER	BB	SO
Chief Bender	1	1	1.06	2	2	2	0	1	17.0	9	2	6	13
Andy Coakley	0	1	2.00	1	1	1	0	0	9.0	8	2	5	2
Eddie Plank	0	2	1.59	2	2	2	0	0	17.0	14	3	4	11
TOTAL	1	4	1.47	5	5	5	0	1	43.0	31	7	15	26

GAME 1 AT PHI OCT 9

NY	000	020	001	3	10	1
PHI	000	000	000	0	4	0

Pitchers: MATHEWSON vs PLANK
Attendance: 17,955

GAME 2 AT NY OCT 10

PHI	001	000	020	3	6	2
NY	000	000	000	0	4	2

Pitchers: BENDER vs McGINNITY, Ames (9)
Attendance: 24,992

GAME 3 AT PHI OCT 12

NY	200	050	002	9	9	1
PHI	000	000	000	0	4	5

Pitchers: MATHEWSON vs COAKLEY
Attendance: 10,991

GAME 4 AT NY OCT 13

PHI	000	000	000	0	5	2
NY	000	100	00X	1	4	1

Pitchers: PLANK vs McGINNITY
Attendance: 13,598

GAME 5 AT NY OCT 14

PHI	000	000	000	0	6	0
NY	000	010	01X	2	5	1

Pitchers: BENDER vs MATHEWSON
Attendance: 24,187

The Cubs and White Sox have played more postseason City Series than any other clubs, but this was their only all-Chicago World Series. The Cubs were the clear favorites: league leaders in batting, fielding, and pitching (with a team ERA of only 1.76). They were one of baseball's greatest teams ever, with a still-record 116 wins, finishing 20 games ahead of the second-place Giants. The White Sox, by contrast, although their pitching and fielding were good enough to rank second in the American League, were the junior circuit's weakest hitters, batting as a team only .230, 32 points below the Cubs. But in the Series the "hitless wonders" prevailed. Though they hit only .198 and yielded eight unearned runs, the Sox bunched their hits for 20 earned runs—double the Cubs' total. Meanwhile, Sox pitchers held the Cubs to a .196 BA, and produced a team ERA less than half that of Cub pitchers.

Game 1 was a pitcher's duel as the Cubs' Mordecai "Three Finger" Brown and Nick Altrock traded four-hitters and one earned run apiece. But Brown lost the game when his error in the seventh led to the second run for the Sox. The Cubs snapped back to take Game 2 on Ed Reulbach's one-hit 7–1 win. Although Reulbach issued six walks, he didn't really need the five unearned runs handed his club by Sox errors.

In Game 3 the Sox regained the Series lead as Ed Walsh two-hit the Cubs, fanning 12 for the Series' first shutout. The Cubs' Jack Pfiester also pitched shutout ball in eight of his nine innings, but George Rohe's bases-loaded triple in the sixth gave the Sox more than enough to defeat him. Brown brought the Cubs back the next day, evening the Series with a two-hit shutout of his own, winning when Altrock yielded his only run on pairs of singles and sacrifice bunts in the seventh.

The rest of the Series belonged to the hitless wonders, who rocked three Cub pitchers for 12 hits and eight runs to take Game 5, and buried Brown and Orval Overall under 14 hits and another eight runs in Game 6 to capture their first world championship.

Chicago White Sox (AL), 4; Chicago Cubs (NL), 2

CHI (A)

PLAYER/POS	AVG	G	AB	R	H	2B	3B	HR	RB	BB	SO	SB
Nick Altrock, p	.250	2	4	0	1	0	0	0	0	1	1	0
George Davis, ss	.308	3	13	4	4	3	0	0	6	0	1	1
Jiggs Donahue, 1b	.333	6	18	0	6	2	1	0	4	3	3	0
Patsy Dougherty, of	.100	6	20	1	2	0	0	0	1	3	4	2
Eddie Hahn, of	.273	6	22	4	6	0	0	0	0	1	1	0
Frank Isbell, 2b	.308	6	26	4	8	4	0	0	4	0	6	1
Fielder Jones, of	.095	6	21	4	2	0	0	0	0	3	3	0
Ed McFarland, ph	.000	1	1	0	0	0	0	0	0	0	0	0
Bill O'Neill, of	.000	1	1	1	0	0	0	0	0	0	0	0
Frank Owen, p	.000	1	2	0	0	0	0	0	0	0	1	0
George Rohe, 3b	.333	6	21	2	7	1	2	0	4	3	1	2
Billy Sullivan, c	.000	6	21	0	0	0	0	0	0	0	9	0
Lee Tannehill, ss	.111	3	9	1	1	0	0	0	0	0	2	0
Babe Towne, ph	.000	1	1	0	0	0	0	0	0	0	0	0
Ed Walsh, p	.000	2	4	1	0	0	0	0	0	3	3	0
Doc White, p	.000	3	3	0	0	0	0	0	0	1	0	0
TOTAL	.198		187	22	37	10	3	0	19	18	35	6

PITCHER	W	L	ERA	G	GS	CG	SV	SHO	IP	H	ER	BB	SO
Nick Altrock	1	1	1.00	2	2	2	0	0	18.0	11	2	2	5
Frank Owen	0	0	3.00	1	0	0	0	0	6.0	6	2	3	2
Ed Walsh	2	0	1.20	2	2	1	0	1	15.0	7	2	6	17
Doc White	1	1	1.80	3	2	1	1	0	15.0	12	3	7	4
TOTAL	4	2	1.50	8	6	4	1	1	54.0	36	9	18	28

CHI (N)

PLAYER/POS	AVG	G	AB	R	H	2B	3B	HR	RB	BB	SO	SB
Mordecai Brown, p	.333	3	6	0	2	0	0	0	0	0	4	0
Frank Chance, 1b	.238	6	21	3	5	1	0	0	0	2	1	2
Johnny Evers, 2b	.150	6	20	2	3	1	0	0	1	1	3	2
Doc Gessler, ph	.000	2	1	0	0	0	0	0	0	1	0	0
Solly Hofman, of	.304	6	23	3	7	1	0	0	2	3	5	1
Johnny Kling, c	.176	6	17	2	3	1	0	0	0	4	3	0
Pat Moran, ph	.000	2	2	0	0	0	0	0	0	0	0	0
Orval Overall, p	.250	2	4	1	1	1	0	0	0	1	1	0
Jack Pfiester, p	.000	2	2	0	0	0	0	0	0	0	1	0
Ed Reulbach, p	.000	2	3	0	0	0	0	0	0	1	0	0
Frank Schulte, of	.269	6	26	1	7	3	0	0	3	1	3	0
Jimmy Sheckard, of	.000	6	21	0	0	0	0	0	1	2	4	1
Harry Steinfeldt, 3b	.250	6	20	2	5	1	0	0	2	1	0	0
Joe Tinker, ss	.167	6	18	4	3	0	0	0	1	2	2	3
TOTAL	.196		184	18	36	9	0	0	11	18	28	9

PITCHER	W	L	ERA	G	GS	CG	SV	SHO	IP	H	ER	BB	SO
Mordecai Brown	1	2	3.20	3	3	2	0	1	19.2	14	7	4	12
Orval Overall	0	0	2.25	2	0	0	0	0	12.0	10	3	3	8
Jack Pfiester	0	2	6.10	2	1	1	0	0	10.1	7	7	3	11
Ed Reulbach	1	0	2.45	2	2	1	0	0	11.0	6	3	8	4
TOTAL	2	4	3.40	9	6	4	0	1	53.0	37	20	18	35

The two-run lead that Detroit took into the bottom of the ninth inning of Game 1 proved to be its biggest of the Series. And it was short-lived, as Chicago—after Frank Chance's leadoff single—took advantage of a hit batsman, a fumble at third base, and a dropped third strike to even the score. Three scoreless extra innings later, darkness ended the game in a 3–3 tie.

The Tigers pitched well enough in the Series. Wild Bill Donovan and George Mullin, who provided more than 80 percent of Detroit's pitching, allowed only four earned runs each for a combined 1.89 ERA. But Cubs pitchers gave up only four earned runs *as a team,* suffocating the Tigers with a team ERA of 0.75. And while Tiger fielders made one less error than the Cubs, their misplays proved more costly, permitting eight unearned runs to the Cubs' two.

Detroit's three-run eighth in the opener provided half of their Series scoring. Nine Detroit hits in Game 2 produced only one run, while the Cubs bunched six of their nine hits into two innings for three runs and the Series' first win. In Games 3 and 4, while the Tigers were twice again limited to a single run, the Cubs increased their run production to five and six, clustering 40 percent of their hits into two three-run innings, one in each game. Mordecai "Three Finger" Brown wrapped up the Series for Chicago with a shutout, as his Cubs blended a hit in each of the first two innings with three stolen bases and a Detroit error for the game's only two runs.

Detroit's 20-year-old Ty Cobb, the American League batting, RBI, and stolen base leader in his first full big league season, hit an anemic .200 in the World Series, stealing no bases and driving in no runs. If there was an offensive hero, it was Cubs centerfielder Jimmy Slagle. At age 34, nearing the end of a 10-year major league career, he led both clubs with four RBIs (nearly quadruple his season's per-game output) and six stolen bases.

Chicago Cubs (NL), 4;
Detroit Tigers (AL), 0; tie, 1

CHI (N)

PLAYER/POS	AVG	G	AB	R	H	2B	3B	HR	RB	BB	SO	SB
Mordecai Brown, p	.000	1	3	0	0	0	0	0	0	1	0	0
Frank Chance, 1b	.214	4	14	3	3	1	0	0	0	3	2	3
Johnny Evers, 2b-5,ss-1	.350	5	20	2	7	2	0	0	1	0	1	3
Del Howard, 1b-1	.200	2	5	0	1	0	0	0	0	0	2	1
Johnny Kling, c	.211	5	19	2	4	0	0	0	1	1	4	0
Pat Moran, ph	.000	1	0	0	0	0	0	0	0	0	0	0
Orval Overall, p	.200	2	5	0	1	0	0	0	2	0	1	0
Jack Pfiester, p	.000	1	2	0	0	0	0	0	0	0	0	0
Ed Reulbach, p	.200	2	5	0	1	0	0	0	1	0	0	0
Frank Schulte, of	.250	5	20	3	5	0	0	0	2	1	2	0
Jimmy Sheckard, of	.238	5	21	0	5	2	0	0	2	0	4	1
Jimmy Slagle, of	.273	5	22	3	6	0	0	0	4	2	3	6
Harry Steinfeldt, 3b	.471	5	17	2	8	1	1	0	2	1	2	1
Joe Tinker, ss	.154	5	13	4	2	0	0	0	1	3	3	1
Heinie Zimmerman, 2b	.000	1	1	0	0	0	0	0	0	0	1	0
TOTAL	.257		167	19	43	6	1	0	16	12	26	16

PITCHER	W	L	ERA	G	GS	CG	SV	SHO	IP	H	ER	BB	SO
Mordecai Brown	1	0	0.00	1	1	1	0	1	9.0	7	0	1	4
Orval Overall	1	0	1.00	2	2	1	0	0	18.0	14	2	4	11
Jack Pfiester	1	0	1.00	1	1	1	0	0	9.0	9	1	1	3
Ed Reulbach	1	0	0.75	2	1	0	0	0	12.0	6	1	3	4
TOTAL	4	0	0.75	6	5	4	0	1	48.0	36	4	9	22

DET (A)

PLAYER/POS	AVG	G	AB	R	H	2B	3B	HR	RB	BB	SO	SB
Jimmy Archer, c	.000	1	3	0	0	0	0	0	0	0	1	0
Ty Cobb, of	.200	5	20	1	4	0	1	0	0	0	3	0
Bill Coughlin, 3b	.250	5	20	0	5	0	0	0	0	1	4	1
Sam Crawford, of	.238	5	21	1	5	1	0	0	3	0	3	0
Bill Donovan, p	.000	2	8	0	0	0	0	0	0	0	3	0
Davy Jones, of	.353	5	17	1	6	0	0	0	0	4	0	3
Ed Killian, p	.500	1	2	1	1	0	1	0	0	0	0	0
George Mullin, p	.000	2	6	0	0	0	0	0	0	0	1	0
Charley O'Leary, ss	.059	5	17	0	1	0	0	0	0	1	3	0
Fred Payne, c-1	.250	2	4	0	1	0	0	0	1	0	0	1
Claude Rossman, 1b	.400	5	20	1	8	0	1	0	2	1	0	1
Germany Schaefer, 2b	.143	5	21	1	3	0	0	0	0	0	3	0
Boss Schmidt, c-3	.167	4	12	0	2	0	0	0	0	2	1	0
Ed Siever, p	.000	1	1	0	0	0	0	0	0	0	0	0
TOTAL	.209		172	6	36	1	2	0	6	9	22	6

PITCHER	W	L	ERA	G	GS	CG	SV	SHO	IP	H	ER	BB	SO
Bill Donovan	0	1	1.71	2	2	2	0	0	21.0	17	4	5	16
Ed Killian	0	0	2.25	1	0	0	0	0	4.0	3	1	1	1
George Mullin	0	2	2.12	2	2	2	0	0	17.0	16	4	6	8
Ed Siever	0	1	4.50	1	1	0	0	0	4.0	7	2	0	1
TOTAL	0	4	2.15	6	5	4	0	0	46.0	43	11	12	26

The Tigers won their final game of the season to take their second straight pennant, and the Cubs won their third pennant in a row by defeating the Giants in a replay of an earlier tie. Ty Cobb and Detroit improved on their 1907 Series performance, as Cobb led his club in batting, hits, and RBIs, and the Tigers won a game. But the Cubs as a team hit 90 percentage points higher than Detroit, and outscored them 24–15, to take the Series with relative ease.

In Game 1, the Tigers took advantage of the Cubs' ragged fielding to score two runs in the eighth for a 6–5 lead. But in the top of the ninth the Cubs erupted for five runs on six consecutive singles and a double steal to win the game. The next day Chicago's Orval Overall held Detroit to four hits and one ninth-inning run. The Tigers' Wild Bill Donovan pitched even better for seven innings, holding Chicago to a single in the sixth. But in the eighth, Joe Tinker's two-run homer—the first in a World Series since 1903—began an assault that ended only after six Cubs had crossed the plate.

Detroit finally manufactured a Series win, pummeling Jack Pfiester in Game 3 for 10 hits (six of them in the sixth inning) and an 8–3 victory. But that was their last burst. As the Series moved to Detroit for Games 4 and 5, the Tiger offense collapsed. Three Finger Brown, the winner as a reliever in Game 1, won Game 4 as a starter, shutting out the Tigers on four hits. The Cubs needed only three of their 10 hits, combining them with a couple of walks and stolen bases, and a muffed fly ball, to score twice in the third inning and once in the ninth.

Only 6,210 spectators—the smallest World Series crowd of the century—saw Overall strike out four Tigers in the first inning of Game 5 (one reached first on a wild pitch) in what became a three-hit shutout. Meanwhile, his Cubs unloaded for 10 hits, defeating Donovan a second time, scoring runs in the first and fifth innings. Overall—after yielding a leadoff walk to Cobb in the fifth—retired Cobb on a force play and set down the final 11 men to face him.

Chicago Cubs (NL), 4;
Detroit Tigers (AL), 1

CHI (N)

PLAYER/POS	AVG	G	AB	R	H	2B	3B	HR	RB	BB	SO	SB
Mordecai Brown, p	.000	2	4	0	0	0	0	0	0	0	2	0
Frank Chance, 1b	.421	5	19	4	8	0	0	0	2	3	1	5
Johnny Evers, 2b	.350	5	20	5	7	1	0	0	2	1	2	2
Solly Hofman, of	.316	5	19	2	6	0	1	0	4	1	4	2
Del Howard, ph	.000	1	1	0	0	0	0	0	0	0	0	0
Johnny Kling, c	.250	5	16	2	4	1	0	0	2	2	2	0
Orval Overall, p	.333	3	6	0	2	0	0	0	0	0	1	0
Jack Pfiester, p	.000	1	2	0	0	0	0	0	0	0	0	0
Ed Reulbach, p	.000	2	3	0	0	0	0	0	0	0	1	0
Frank Schulte, of	.389	5	18	4	7	0	1	0	2	2	1	2
Jimmy Sheckard, of	.238	5	21	2	5	2	0	0	1	2	3	1
Harry Steinfeldt, 3b	.250	5	16	3	4	0	0	0	3	2	5	1
Joe Tinker, ss	.263	5	19	2	5	0	0	1	4	0	2	2
TOTAL	.293		164	24	48	4	2	1	20	13	26	15

PITCHER	W	L	ERA	G	GS	CG	SV	SHO	IP	H	ER	BB	SO
Mordecai Brown	2	0	0.00	2	1	1	0	1	11.0	6	0	1	5
Orval Overall	2	0	0.98	3	2	2	0	1	18.1	7	2	7	15
Jack Pfiester	0	1	7.87	1	1	0	0	0	8.0	10	7	3	1
Ed Reulbach	0	0	4.70	2	1	0	0	0	7.2	9	4	1	5
TOTAL	4	1	2.60	8	5	3	0	2	45.0	32	13	12	26

DET (A)

PLAYER/POS	AVG	G	AB	R	H	2B	3B	HR	RB	BB	SO	SB
Ty Cobb, of	.368	5	19	3	7	1	0	0	4	1	2	2
Bill Coughlin, 3b	.125	3	8	0	1	0	0	0	1	0	1	0
Sam Crawford, of	.238	5	21	2	5	1	0	0	1	1	2	0
Bill Donovan, p	.000	2	4	0	0	0	0	0	0	1	1	0
Red Downs, 2b	.167	2	6	1	1	1	0	0	1	1	2	0
Davy Jones, ph	.000	3	2	1	0	0	0	0	0	1	1	0
Ed Killian, p	.000	1	0	0	0	0	0	0	0	0	0	0
Matty McIntyre, of	.222	5	18	2	4	1	0	0	0	3	2	1
George Mullin, p	.333	1	3	1	1	0	0	0	1	0	1	0
Charley O'Leary, ss	.158	5	19	2	3	0	0	0	0	0	3	0
Claude Rossman, 1b	.211	5	19	3	4	0	0	0	3	1	4	1
Germany Schaefer, 2b-3,3b-2	.125	5	16	0	2	0	0	0	0	1	4	1
Boss Schmidt, c	.071	4	14	0	1	0	0	0	1	0	2	0
Ed Summers, p	.200	2	5	0	1	0	0	0	1	0	2	0
Ira Thomas, c-1	.500	2	4	0	2	1	0	0	1	1	0	0
George Winter, p-1	.000	2	0	0	0	0	0	0	0	0	0	0
TOTAL	.203		158	15	32	5	0	0	14	12	26	6

PITCHER	W	L	ERA	G	GS	CG	SV	SHO	IP	H	ER	BB	SO
Bill Donovan	0	2	4.24	2	2	2	0	0	17.0	17	8	4	10
Ed Killian	0	0	11.57	1	1	0	0	0	2.1	5	3	3	1
George Mullin	1	0	0.00	1	1	1	0	0	9.0	7	0	1	8
Ed Summers	0	2	4.30	2	1	0	0	0	14.2	18	7	4	7
George Winter	0	0	0.00	1	0	0	0	0	1.0	1	0	1	0
TOTAL	1	4	3.68	7	5	3	0	0	44.0	48	18	13	26

GAME 1 AT DET OCT 10

CHI	004 000 105	10	14	2
DET	100 000 320	6	10	4

Pitchers: Reulbach, Overall (7), BROWN (8) vs Killian, SUMMERS (3)
Attendance: 10,812

GAME 2 AT CHI OCT 11

DET	000 000 001	1	4	1
CHI	000 000 06X	6	7	1

Pitchers: DONOVAN vs OVERALL
Home Runs: Tinker-CHI
Attendance: 17,760

GAME 3 AT CHI OCT 12

DET	100 005 020	8	11	4
CHI	000 300 000	3	7	2

Pitchers: MULLIN vs PFIESTER, Reulbach (9)
Attendance: 14,543

GAME 4 AT DET OCT 13

CHI	002 000 001	3	10	0
DET	000 000 000	0	4	1

Pitchers: BROWN vs SUMMERS, Winter (9)
Attendance: 12,907

GAME 5 AT DET OCT 14

CHI	100 010 000	2	10	0
DET	000 000 000	0	3	0

Pitchers: OVERALL vs DONOVAN
Attendance: 6,210

Babe Adams, a 27-year-old rookie pitcher, was only the fifth biggest winner on the Pittsburgh staff. But his fine 12–3 record was supported by a team-best 1.11 ERA, and manager Fred Clarke started him in the Series opener against Detroit's ace George Mullin (who had led the American League with a career-high 29 wins). Mullin pitched well, giving up only one earned run—manager/outfielder Clarke's homer in the fourth inning. But four Tiger errors led to three Pittsburgh runs in the fifth and sixth. Meanwhile, Adams, after yielding a run in the first, pitched shutout ball the rest of the way for the win.

Detroit came back in Game 2 with seven runs (including Ty Cobb's theft of home) as Wild Bill Donovan held the Pirates to two runs on five hits. In Game 3 the Pirates took an early lead, which Detroit, despite rallies in the seventh and ninth innings, was unable to overcome. Errors determined most of the scoring, as only one of Detroit's six runs and two of Pittsburgh's eight were earned.

Mullin shut out the Pirates on five hits in Game 4, striking out 10 men as Detroit scored five runs (all earned, despite Pittsburgh's six errors) to drive out starter Lefty Leifield after four innings. The seesaw Series continued in Game 5, with Babe Adams winning his second game behind his Pirates' 10-hit, eight-run attack. Adams gave up leadoff homers to Davy Jones in the first and Sam Crawford in the eighth. But Pittsburgh's Clarke more than countered these with his three-run shot in the seventh. (All three homers were hit into temporary seats in center field.)

Back in Detroit for Game 6, the Tigers evened the Series for the third time, Mullin winning his second game in a close contest that saw Pittsburgh pull within a run of tying the game in the ninth before a runner thrown out at home and a game-ending double play cut their rally dead.

In the finale it was Babe Adams once again, scattering six hits for an easy 8–0 win, his third of the Series. Detroit had done better than ever, but still lost their third World Series in three consecutive attempts. A quarter century would pass before they would have a chance to try again.

Pittsburgh Pirates (NL), 4;
Detroit Tigers (AL), 3

PIT (N)

PLAYER/POS	AVG	G	AB	R	H	2B	3B	HR	RB	BB	SO	SB
Ed Abbaticchio, ph	.000	1	1	0	0	0	0	0	0	0	0	0
Bill Abstein, 1b	.231	7	26	3	6	2	0	0	2	3	10	1
Babe Adams, p	.000	3	9	0	0	0	0	0	0	1	1	0
Bobby Byrne, 3b	.250	7	24	5	6	1	0	0	0	1	4	1
Howie Camnitz, p	.000	2	1	0	0	0	0	0	0	0	0	0
Fred Clarke, of	.211	7	19	7	4	0	0	2	7	5	3	3
George Gibson, c	.240	7	25	2	6	2	0	0	2	1	1	2
Ham Hyatt, of-1	.000	2	4	1	0	0	0	0	1	1	0	0
Tommy Leach, of-7,3b-1	.360	7	25	8	9	4	0	0	2	2	1	1
Lefty Leifield, p	.000	1	1	0	0	0	0	0	0	0	1	0
Nick Maddox, p	.000	1	4	0	0	0	0	0	0	0	1	0
Dots Miller, 2b	.250	7	28	2	7	1	0	0	4	2	5	3
Paddy O'Connor, ph	.000	1	1	0	0	0	0	0	0	0	1	0
Deacon Phillippe, p	.000	2	1	0	0	0	0	0	0	0	1	0
Honus Wagner, ss	.333	7	24	4	8	2	1	0	6	4	2	6
Vic Willis, p	.000	2	4	0	0	0	0	0	0	0	1	0
Chief Wilson, of	.154	7	26	2	4	1	0	0	1	0	2	1
TOTAL	.224		223	34	50	13	1	2	25	20	34	18

PITCHER	W	L	ERA	G	GS	CG	SV	SHO	IP	H	ER	BB	SO
Babe Adams	3	0	1.33	3	3	3	0	1	27.0	18	4	6	11
Howie Camnitz	0	1	9.82	2	1	0	0	0	3.2	8	4	2	2
Lefty Leifield	0	1	11.25	1	1	0	0	0	4.0	7	5	1	0
Nick Maddox	1	0	1.00	1	1	1	0	0	9.0	10	1	2	4
Deacon Phillippe	0	0	0.00	2	0	0	0	0	6.0	2	0	1	2
Vic Willis	0	1	3.97	2	1	0	0	0	11.1	10	5	8	3
TOTAL	4	3	2.80	11	7	4	0	1	61.0	55	19	20	22

DET (A)

PLAYER/POS	AVG	G	AB	R	H	2B	3B	HR	RB	BB	SO	SB
Donie Bush, ss	.261	7	23	5	6	1	0	0	3	5	3	1
Ty Cobb, of	.231	7	26	3	6	3	0	0	5	2	2	2
Sam Crawford, of-7,1b-1	.250	7	28	4	7	3	0	1	4	1	1	1
Jim Delahanty, 2b	.346	7	26	2	9	4	0	0	4	2	5	0
Bill Donovan, p	.000	2	4	0	0	0	0	0	0	0	1	0
Davy Jones, of	.233	7	30	6	7	0	0	1	1	1	2	1
Tom Jones, 1b	.250	7	24	3	6	1	0	0	2	2	0	1
Matty McIntyre, of-1	.000	4	3	0	0	0	0	0	0	0	1	0
George Moriarty, 3b	.273	7	22	4	6	1	0	0	1	3	1	0
George Mullin, p-4	.188	6	16	1	3	1	0	0	1	0	3	0
Charley O'Leary, 3b	.000	1	3	0	0	0	0	0	0	0	0	0
Boss Schmidt, c	.222	6	18	0	4	2	0	0	4	2	0	0
Oscar Stanage, c	.200	2	5	0	1	0	0	0	2	0	2	0
Ed Summers, p	.000	2	3	0	0	0	0	0	0	0	2	0
Ed Willett, p	.000	2	2	0	0	0	0	0	0	0	0	0
Ralph Works, p	.000	1	0	0	0	0	0	0	0	0	0	0
TOTAL	.236		233	28	55	16	0	2	26	20	22	6

PITCHER	W	L	ERA	G	GS	CG	SV	SHO	IP	H	ER	BB	SO
Bill Donovan	1	1	3.00	2	2	1	0	0	12.0	7	4	8	7
George Mullin	2	1	2.25	4	3	3	0	1	32.0	23	8	8	20
Ed Summers	0	2	8.59	2	2	0	0	0	7.1	13	7	4	4
Ed Willett	0	0	0.00	2	0	0	0	0	7.2	3	0	0	1
Ralph Works	0	0	9.00	1	0	0	0	0	2.0	4	2	0	2
TOTAL	3	4	3.10	11	7	4	0	1	61.0	50	21	20	34

GAME 1 AT PIT OCT 8

DET	100	000	000	1	6 4
PIT	000	121	00X	4	5 0

Pitchers: MULLIN vs ADAMS
Home Runs: Clarke-PIT
Attendance: 29,264

GAME 2 AT PIT OCT 9

DET	023	020	000	7	9 3
PIT	200	000	000	2	5 1

Pitchers: DONOVAN vs CAMNITZ, Willis (3)
Attendance: 30,915

GAME 3 AT DET OCT 11

PIT	510	000	002	8	10 3
DET	000	000	402	6	10 5

Pitchers: MADDOX vs SUMMERS, Willett (1), Works (8)
Attendance: 18,277

GAME 4 AT DET OCT 12

PIT	000	000	000	0	5 6
DET	020	300	00X	5	8 0

Pitchers: LEIFIELD, Phillippe (5) vs MULLIN
Attendance: 17,036

GAME 5 AT PIT OCT 13

DET	100	002	010	4	6 1
PIT	111	000	41X	8	10 2

Pitchers: SUMMERS, Willett (8) vs ADAMS
Home Runs: D.Jones-DET, Crawford-DET, Clarke-PIT
Attendance: 21,706

GAME 6 AT DET OCT 14

PIT	300	000	001	4	7 3
DET	100	211	00X	5	10 3

Pitchers: WILLIS, Camnitz (6), Phillippe (7) vs MULLIN
Attendance: 10,535

GAME 7 AT DET OCT 16

PIT	020	203	010	8	7 0
DET	000	000	000	0	6 3

Pitchers: ADAMS vs DONOVAN, Mullin (4)
Attendance: 17,562

Pitcher Jack Coombs burst into stardom in 1910, emerging as the ace of a Philadelphia pitching staff which dominated the American League with an ERA of only 1.79. Coombs himself led league pitchers with 31 wins and 13 shutouts, and finished second to Chicago's Ed Walsh with an ERA of 1.30—all career bests. He continued his domination into the World Series, pitching three complete-game victories in the Athletics' surprisingly easy triumph over the Cubs.

The Series' finest pitching performance, though, was turned in by the A's Chief Bender in the opener. Only two batters reached base over the first eight innings—on a single and walk—and both of them were cut down trying to steal second. In the ninth, two Cubs singles and two A's errors produced an unearned run, but as the A's had scored four runs (Bender himself providing the margin of victory with the game's second RBI in the second inning), the Cubs' run did no damage.

Coombs started Game 2 and gave up a run in the top of the first inning. But Philadelphia bats were hot in the Series (their team .316 batting average stood as a Series record for 50 years), and their 14 hits in this game (including four doubles and six runs in the seventh) sank Three Finger Brown and gave Coombs an easy win. Connie Mack also started Coombs in Game 3, two days later, and again the result was a lopsided win. Coombs himself drove in three of his team's 12 runs, and right fielder Danny Murphy added three more with the Series' only home run.

Bender pitched Game 4 and suffered the A's only loss, as the Cubs tied the game at 3–3 with a run in the bottom of the ninth, and won it for reliever Three Finger Brown with a two-out RBI single an inning later.

Coombs faced Brown a second time in Game 5. Both clubs made nine hits, but the A's put four of them together with a walk, a wild pitch, and two stolen bases for five runs in the eighth to sink Brown as they had in Game 2, breaking a tight game wide open for Coombs's third win and the Athletics' first world championship.

Philadelphia Athletics (AL), 4; Chicago Cubs (NL), 1

PHI (A)

PLAYER/POS	AVG	G	AB	R	H	2B	3B	HR	RBI	BB	SO	SB
Frank Baker, 3b	.409	5	22	6	9	3	0	0	4	2	1	0
Jack Barry, ss	.235	5	17	3	4	2	0	0	3	1	3	0
Chief Bender, p	.333	2	6	1	2	0	0	0	1	1	1	0
Eddie Collins, 2b	.429	5	21	5	9	4	0	0	3	2	0	4
Jack Coombs, p	.385	3	13	0	5	1	0	0	3	0	3	0
Harry Davis, 1b	.353	5	17	5	6	3	0	0	2	3	4	0
Topsy Hartsel, of	.200	1	5	2	1	0	0	0	0	0	1	2
Jack Lapp, c	.250	1	4	0	1	0	0	0	1	0	2	0
Bris Lord, of	.182	5	22	3	4	2	0	0	1	1	3	0
Danny Murphy, of	.350	5	20	6	7	3	0	1	9	1	0	1
Amos Strunk, of	.278	4	18	2	5	1	1	0	2	2	5	0
Ira Thomas, c	.250	4	12	2	3	0	0	0	1	4	1	0
TOTAL	.316		177	35	56	19	1	1	30	17	24	7

PITCHER	W	L	ERA	G	GS	CG	SV	SHO	IP	H	ER	BB	SO
Chief Bender	1	1	1.93	2	2	2	0	0	18.2	12	4	4	14
Jack Coombs	3	0	3.33	3	3	3	0	0	27.0	23	10	14	17
TOTAL	4	1	2.76	5	5	5	0	0	45.2	35	14	18	31

CHI (N)

PLAYER/POS	AVG	G	AB	R	H	2B	3B	HR	RBI	BB	SO	SB
Jimmy Archer, c-2,1b-1	.182	3	11	1	2	1	0	0	0	0	3	0
Ginger Beaumont, ph	.000	3	2	1	0	0	0	0	0	1	1	0
Mordecai Brown, p	.000	3	7	0	0	0	0	0	0	0	1	0
Frank Chance, 1b	.353	5	17	1	6	1	1	0	4	0	3	0
King Cole, p	.000	1	2	0	0	0	0	0	0	0	2	0
Solly Hofman, of	.267	5	15	2	4	0	0	0	2	4	3	0
Johnny Kane, pr	.000	1	0	0	0	0	0	0	0	0	0	0
Johnny Kling, c-3	.077	5	13	0	1	0	0	0	1	1	2	0
Harry McIntire, p	.000	2	1	0	0	0	0	0	0	0	1	0
Tom Needham, ph	.000	1	1	0	0	0	0	0	0	0	0	0
Orval Ovall, p	.000	1	1	0	0	0	0	0	0	0	0	0
Jack Pfiester, p	.000	2	2	0	0	0	0	0	0	0	1	0
Ed Reulbach, p	.000	1	0	0	0	0	0	0	0	0	0	0
Lew Richie, p	.000	1	0	0	0	0	0	0	0	0	0	0
Frank Schulte, of	.353	5	17	3	6	3	0	0	2	2	3	0
Jimmy Sheckard, of	.286	5	14	5	4	2	0	0	1	7	2	1
Harry Steinfeldt, 3b	.100	5	20	0	2	1	0	0	1	0	4	0
Joe Tinker, ss	.333	5	18	2	6	3	0	0	0	2	2	1
Heinie Zimmerman, 2b	.235	5	17	0	4	1	0	0	2	1	3	1
TOTAL	.222		158	15	35	11	1	0	13	18	31	3

PITCHER	W	L	ERA	G	GS	CG	SV	SHO	IP	H	ER	BB	SO
Mordecai Brown	1	2	5.50	3	2	1	0	0	18.0	23	11	7	14
King Cole	0	0	3.38	1	1	0	0	0	8.0	10	3	3	5
Harry McIntire	0	1	6.75	2	0	0	0	0	5.1	4	4	3	3
Orval Overall	0	1	9.00	1	1	0	0	0	3.0	6	3	1	1
Jack Pfiester	0	0	0.00	1	0	0	0	0	6.2	9	0	1	1
Ed Reulbach	0	0	9.00	1	1	0	0	0	2.0	3	2	2	0
Lew Richie	0	0	0.00	1	0	0	0	0	1.0	1	0	0	0
TOTAL	1	4	4.70	10	5	1	0	0	44.0	56	23	17	24

GAME 1 AT PHI OCT 17

CHI	000	000	001	1	3	1
PHI	021	000	01X	4	7	2

Pitchers: OVERALL, McIntire (4) vs BENDER
Attendance: 26,891

GAME 2 AT PHI OCT 18

CHI	100	000	101	3	8	3
PHI	002	010	60X	9	14	4

Pitchers: BROWN, Richie (8) vs COOMBS
Attendance: 24,597

GAME 3 AT CHI OCT 20

PHI	125	000	400	12	15	1
CHI	120	000	020	5	6	5

Pitchers: COOMBS vs Reulbach, McINTIRE (3), Pfiester (3)
Home Runs: Murphy-PHI
Attendance: 26,210

GAME 4 AT CHI OCT 22

PHI	001	200	000 0	3	11	3
CHI	100	100	001 1	4	9	1

Pitchers: BENDER vs Cole, BROWN (9)
Attendance: 19,150

GAME 5 AT CHI OCT 23

PHI	100	010	050	7	9	1
CHI	010	000	010	2	9	2

Pitchers: COOMBS vs BROWN
Attendance: 27,374

Connie Mack's pitching aces out-dueled Christy Mathewson, and Frank Baker hit two crucial home runs to become "Home Run" Baker forever more, as the A's avenged their 1905 Series loss to the Giants. Game 1, though, belonged to Matty and New York. Philadelphia scored first, but the Giants tied the game with an unearned run in the fourth inning, and won it with two doubles in the seventh, setting at naught Chief Bender's otherwise splendid 11-strikeout performance.

The A's came back to take three in a row. In Game 2 Eddie Plank held the Giants to one run and Baker hit the first of his homers, breaking a tie in the sixth with a two-run blast off Rube Marquard. The next day, the A's and Jack Coombs handed Mathewson his first World Series loss. Both pitchers went the distance in an 11-inning duel that saw Matty hold the A's scoreless through eight, only to give up a game-tying home run to Baker in the ninth, and two unearned runs in the 11th. Coombs, meanwhile, pitched two-hit, one-run ball through 10 innings. In the last of the 11th, a third Giants hit and an A's error let in a second run, but the rally died when Beals Becker was cut down for the final out trying to steal second.

After a week of rain, Mathewson and Bender squared off in Game 4. The Giants jumped on Bender for two runs in the first, and held the lead until the fourth. But in the last of the fourth, three successive A's doubles and a run-scoring fly put the A's in front to stay as Bender held New York scoreless over the final eight innings.

In Game 5, a three-run homer by the A's Rube Oldring off Rube Marquard in the third provided the only scoring through 6½ innings. But the Giants crept back with one run in the seventh, and two more in the last of the ninth tied the score. Plank replaced Coombs for the A's in the 10th and took the loss as Larry Doyle led off with a double, took third on a missed force play, and scored on Fred Merkle's fly to deep right.

After five closely contested games, Game Six was a laugher. It, too, was close at first—tied 1–1 after 3½ innings. But the A's scored four runs in the fourth on singles and errors, once in the sixth, and seven times in the seventh on a barrage of hits, an error, and a two-run wild pitch. Chief Bender, who gave up only four hits and two unearned runs, was the beneficiary of this largesse, taking his second win of the Series and giving the A's their second consecutive world title.

Philadelphia Athletics (AL), 4; New York Giants (NL), 2

PHI (A)

PLAYER/POS	AVG	G	AB	R	H	2B	3B	HR	RB	BB	SO	SB
Frank Baker, 3b	.375	6	24	7	9	2	0	2	5	1	5	0
Jack Barry, ss	.368	6	19	2	7	4	0	0	2	0	2	2
Chief Bender, p	.091	3	11	0	1	0	0	0	0	0	1	0
Eddie Collins, 2b	.286	6	21	4	6	1	0	0	1	2	2	2
Jack Coombs, p	.250	2	8	1	2	0	0	0	0	0	0	0
Harry Davis, 1b	.208	6	24	3	5	1	0	0	5	0	3	0
Jack Lapp, c	.250	2	8	1	2	0	0	0	0	0	1	0
Bris Lord, of	.185	6	27	2	5	2	0	0	1	0	5	0
Stuffy McInnis, 1b	.000	1	0	0	0	0	0	0	0	0	0	0
Danny Murphy, of	.304	6	23	4	7	3	0	0	3	0	3	0
Rube Oldring, of	.200	6	25	2	5	2	0	1	3	0	5	0
Eddie Plank, p	.000	2	3	0	0	0	0	0	0	0	2	0
Amos Strunk, pr	.000	1	0	0	0	0	0	0	0	0	0	0
Ira Thomas, c	.083	4	12	1	1	0	0	0	1	1	2	0
TOTAL	.244		205	27	50	15	0	3	21	4	31	4

PITCHER	W	L	ERA	G	GS	CG	SV	SHO	IP	H	ER	BB	SO
Chief Bender	2	1	1.04	3	3	3	0	0	26.0	16	3	8	20
Jack Coombs	1	0	1.35	2	2	1	0	0	20.0	11	3	6	16
Eddie Plank	1	1	1.86	2	1	1	0	0	9.2	6	2	0	8
TOTAL	4	2	1.29	7	6	5	0	0	55.2	33	8	14	44

NY (N)

PLAYER/POS	AVG	G	AB	R	H	2B	3B	HR	RB	BB	SO	SB
Red Ames, p	.500	2	2	0	1	0	0	0	0	0	1	0
Beals Becker, ph	.000	3	3	0	0	0	0	0	0	0	0	0
Doc Crandall, p-2	.500	3	2	1	1	1	0	0	1	2	0	0
Josh Devore, of	.167	6	24	1	4	1	0	0	3	1	8	0
Larry Doyle, 2b	.304	6	23	3	7	3	1	0	1	2	1	2
Art Fletcher, ss	.130	6	23	1	3	1	0	0	1	0	4	0
Buck Herzog, 3b	.190	6	21	3	4	2	0	0	0	2	3	2
Rube Marquard, p	.000	3	2	0	0	0	0	0	0	0	2	0
Christy Mathewson, p	.286	3	7	0	2	0	0	0	0	1	3	0
Fred Merkle, 1b	.150	6	20	1	3	1	0	0	1	2	6	0
Chief Meyers, c	.300	6	20	2	6	2	0	0	2	0	3	0
Red Murray, of	.000	6	21	0	0	0	0	0	0	2	5	0
Fred Snodgrass, of	.105	6	19	1	2	0	0	0	1	2	7	0
Art Wilson, c	.000	1	1	0	0	0	0	0	0	0	0	0
Hooks Wiltse, p	.000	2	1	0	0	0	0	0	0	0	1	0
TOTAL	.175		189	13	33	11	1	0	10	14	44	4

PITCHER	W	L	ERA	G	GS	CG	SV	SHO	IP	H	ER	BB	SO
Red Ames	0	1	2.25	2	1	0	0	0	8.0	6	2	1	6
Doc Crandall	1	0	0.00	2	0	0	0	0	4.0	2	0	0	2
Rube Marquard	0	1	1.54	3	2	0	0	0	11.2	9	2	1	8
Christy Mathewson	1	2	2.00	3	3	2	0	0	27.0	25	6	2	13
Hooks Wiltse	0	0	18.90	2	0	0	0	0	3.1	8	7	0	2
TOTAL	2	4	2.83	12	6	2	0	0	54.0	50	17	4	31

GAME 1 AT NY OCT 14

PHI	010 000 000	1	6	2
NY	000 100 10X	2	5	0

Pitchers: BENDER vs MATHEWSON
Attendance: 38,281

GAME 2 AT PHI OCT 16

NY	010 000 000	1	5	3
PHI	100 002 00X	3	4	0

Pitchers: MARQUARD, Crandall (8) vs PLANK
Home Runs: Baker-PHI
Attendance: 26,286

GAME 3 AT NY OCT 17

PHI	000 000 001 02	3	9	2
NY	001 000 000 01	2	3	5

Pitchers: COOMBS vs MATHEWSON
Home Runs: Baker-PHI
Attendance: 37,216

GAME 4 AT PHI OCT 24

NY	200 000 000	2	7	3
PHI	000 310 00X	4	11	1

Pitchers: MATHEWSON, Wiltse (8) vs BENDER
Attendance: 24,355

GAME 5 AT NY OCT 25

PHI	003 000 000 0	3	7	1
NY	000 000 102 1	4	9	2

Pitchers: Coombs, PLANK (10) vs Marquard, Ames (4), CRANDALL (8)
Home Runs: Oldring-PHI
Attendance: 33,228

GAME 6 AT PHI OCT 26

NY	100 000 001	2	4	3
PHI	001 401 70X	13	13	5

Pitchers: AMES, Wiltse (5), Marquard (7) vs BENDER
Attendance: 20,485

The Giants outhit the Red Sox by 50 percentage points, and their pitchers let in one less earned run per game. But this was the Series in which Snodgrass' famous muff of a routine fly to center in the 10th inning of the final game helped turn a slim Giants lead into a Red Sox world championship. In all fairness, it must be admitted that Snodgrass followed his muff with a brilliant catch off the next batter, and indecision by the catcher and first baseman permitted a pop foul to drop, keeping the Sox alive to score the tying and winning runs. For that matter, this final game might not have been needed at all if Snodgrass and Beals Becker hadn't both been cut down trying to steal second in the 11th inning of Game 2, which ended in a tie because of darkness. If either had gone on to score, the Giants would have won the Series in seven games.

Boston's Smokey Joe Wood followed up his spectacular 34–5 regular season with Series wins in Games 1 and 4, before being rocked for six runs in the first inning of Game 7 for a loss. Relieving in the eighth inning of the finale, he stopped the Giants for two innings, but gave up what would have been the losing run in the 10th had not the Giants' fielding in the last of the inning turned the game around, giving Wood the win and the Sox the Series.

Although Wood won three games, the best pitching of the Series was turned in by the Giants' Rube Marquard and Boston's Hugh Bedient. Marquard (who in the regular season had tied a major league record with 19 consecutive wins) won two of his club's three victories (Games 3 and 6), allowing three runs—only one of them earned. Bedient, in two starts and two relief appearances, matched Marquard's 0.50 earned run average, winning a duel with Christy Mathewson in Game 5, and hurling seven effective innings against Matty in the finale.

Mathewson was the Series' hard-luck pitcher: his one tie and two losses were all decided by unearned runs.

Boston Red Sox (AL), 4;
New York Giants (NL), 3; tie, 1

BOS (A)

PLAYER/POS	AVG	G	AB	R	H	2B	3B	HR	RB	BB	SO	SB
Neal Ball, ph	.000	1	1	0	0	0	0	0	0	0	1	0
Hugh Bedient, p	.000	4	6	0	0	0	0	0	0	0	0	0
Hick Cady, c	.136	7	22	1	3	0	0	0	1	0	3	0
Bill Carrigan, c	.000	2	7	0	0	0	0	0	0	0	0	0
Ray Collins, p	.000	2	5	0	0	0	0	0	0	0	2	0
Clyde Engle, ph	.333	3	3	1	1	1	0	0	2	0	0	0
Larry Gardner, 3b	.179	8	28	4	5	2	1	1	5	2	5	0
Charley Hall, p	.750	2	4	0	3	1	0	0	0	1	0	0
Olaf Henricksen, ph	1.000	2	1	0	1	1	0	0	1	0	0	0
Harry Hooper, of	.290	8	31	3	9	2	1	0	1	4	4	2
Duffy Lewis, of	.156	8	32	4	5	3	0	0	2	2	2	0
Buck O'Brien, p	.000	2	2	0	0	0	0	0	0	0	2	0
Tris Speaker, of	.300	8	30	4	9	1	2	0	2	4	2	1
Jake Stahl, 1b	.281	8	32	3	9	2	0	0	2	0	6	2
Heinie Wagner, ss	.167	8	30	1	5	1	0	0	0	3	6	1
Joe Wood, p	.286	4	7	1	2	0	0	0	1	1	0	0
Steve Yerkes, 2b	.250	8	32	3	8	0	2	0	4	2	3	0
TOTAL	.220		273	25	60	14	6	1	21	19	36	6

PITCHER	W	L	ERA	G	GS	CG	SV	SHO	IP	H	ER	BB	SO
Hugh Bedient	1	0	0.50	4	2	1	0	0	18.0	10	1	7	7
Ray Collins	0	0	1.26	2	1	0	0	0	14.1	14	2	0	6
Charley Hall	0	0	3.38	2	0	0	0	0	10.2	11	4	9	1
Buck O'Brien	0	2	5.00	2	2	0	0	0	9.0	12	5	3	4
Joe Wood	3	1	3.68	4	3	2	0	0	22.0	27	9	3	21
TOTAL	4	3	2.55	14	8	3	0	0	74.0	74	21	22	39

NY (N)

PLAYER/POS	AVG	G	AB	R	H	2B	3B	HR	RB	BB	SO	SB
Red Ames, p	.000	1	0	0	0	0	0	0	0	0	0	0
Beals Becker, of-1	.000	2	4	1	0	0	0	0	0	2	0	0
Doc Crandall, p	.000	1	1	0	0	0	0	0	0	0	1	0
Josh Devore, of	.250	7	24	4	6	0	0	0	0	7	5	4
Larry Doyle, 2b	.242	8	33	5	8	1	0	1	2	3	2	2
Art Fletcher, ss	.179	8	28	1	5	1	0	0	3	1	4	1
Buck Herzog, 3b	.400	8	30	6	12	4	1	0	5	1	3	2
Rube Marquard, p	.000	2	4	0	0	0	0	0	0	0	1	0
Christy Mathewson, p	.167	3	12	0	2	0	0	0	0	0	4	0
Moose McCormick, ph	.250	5	4	0	1	0	0	0	1	0	0	0
Fred Merkle, 1b	.273	8	33	5	9	2	1	0	3	0	7	1
Chief Meyers, c	.357	8	28	2	10	0	1	0	3	2	3	1
Red Murray, of	.323	8	31	5	10	4	1	0	4	2	2	0
Tillie Shafer, ss	.000	3	0	0	0	0	0	0	0	0	0	0
Fred Snodgrass, of	.212	8	33	2	7	2	0	0	2	2	5	1
Jeff Tesreau, p	.375	3	8	0	3	0	0	0	2	1	3	0
Art Wilson, c	1.000	2	1	0	1	0	0	0	0	0	0	0
TOTAL	.270		274	31	74	14	4	1	25	22	39	12

PITCHER	W	L	ERA	G	GS	CG	SV	SHO	IP	H	ER	BB	SO
Red Ames	0	0	4.50	1	0	0	0	0	2.0	3	1	1	0
Doc Crandall	0	0	0.00	1	0	0	0	0	2.0	1	0	0	2
Rube Marquard	2	0	0.50	2	2	2	0	0	18.0	14	1	2	9
Christy Mathewson	0	2	1.26	3	3	3	0	0	28.2	23	4	5	10
Jeff Tesreau	1	2	3.13	3	3	1	0	0	23.0	19	8	11	15
TOTAL	3	4	1.71	10	8	6	0	0	73.2	60	14	19	36

Third baseman Frank Baker and catcher Wally Schang drove in more than 60 percent of the Athletics' runs, as Philadelphia dispatched the Giants in five games. Chief Bender led A's pitchers with two wins, and rookie Bullet Joe Bush hurled a nifty five-hitter in Game 3, but the Series highlights were two duels between the A's Eddie Plank and Christy Mathewson of the Giants. The A's heavy hitting made Bender's wins possible and Bush's win easy, but pitching dominated the Plank-Matty games.

Bender yielded 11 hits in the opener, as did the Giants' pitchers. But five of the game's six extra-base hits belonged to the A's—including Baker's two-run homer and triples by Schang and Eddie Collins—and Bender emerged victorious. In Game 2, Plank and Mathewson pitched shutout ball through nine innings, but in the top of the 10th Matty himself singled in the game's first run and scored the second. Taking a 3–0 lead into the bottom of the inning, he set the A's down in order for New York's only Series win.

In Game 3, Schang's solo homer and Collins's three hits (including his second Series triple) and three RBIs led a 12-hit A's attack which, with Bush's fine pitching, put Philadelphia back into the Series lead. Bender won again in Game 4, shutting out the Giants through six innings as his A's scored six runs. But in the seventh, New York's Fred Merkle homered for three runs, and a single, double, and triple in the eighth brought in two more runs. With his lead cut to a single run, Bender bore down in the ninth and retired the side in order.

Plank avenged his earlier loss with a brilliant two-hitter in Game 5, facing the minimum three batters in eight of the nine innings. (His own error in the fifth—a dropped pop-up—led to the Giants' only run.) Mathewson pitched well, too, yielding only six singles. But four of them came in the first and third innings, combining with two sacrifice flies and an error for three runs. Only one Philadelphia batter reached base in the final six innings, but with Plank pitching as he was, the game and the title were in Philadelphia's pocket.

Philadelphia Athletics (AL), 4; New York Giants (NL), 1

PHI (A)

PLAYER/POS	AVG	G	AB	R	H	2B	3B	HR	RB	BB	SO	SB
Frank Baker, 3b	.450	5	20	2	9	0	0	1	7	0	2	1
Jack Barry, ss	.300	5	20	3	6	3	0	0	1	0	0	0
Chief Bender, p	.000	2	8	0	0	0	0	0	1	0	1	0
Joe Bush, p	.250	1	4	0	1	0	0	0	0	0	1	0
Eddie Collins, 2b	.421	5	19	5	8	0	2	0	3	1	2	3
Jack Lapp, c	.250	1	4	0	1	0	0	0	0	0	1	0
Stuffy McInnis, 1b	.118	5	17	1	2	1	0	0	2	0	2	0
Eddie Murphy, of	.227	5	22	2	5	0	0	0	0	2	0	0
Rube Oldring, of	.273	5	22	5	6	0	1	0	0	0	1	1
Eddie Plank, p	.143	2	7	0	1	0	0	0	0	0	0	0
Wally Schang, c	.357	4	14	2	5	0	1	1	7	2	4	0
Amos Strunk, of	.118	5	17	3	2	0	0	0	0	2	2	0
TOTAL	.264		174	23	46	4	4	2	21	7	16	5

PITCHER	W	L	ERA	G	GS	CG	SV	SHO	IP	H	ER	BB	SO
Chief Bender	2	0	4.00	2	2	2	0	0	18.0	19	8	1	9
Joe Bush	1	0	1.00	1	1	1	0	0	9.0	5	1	4	3
Eddie Plank	1	1	0.95	2	2	2	0	0	19.0	9	2	3	7
TOTAL	4	1	2.15	5	5	5	0	0	46.0	33	11	8	19

NY (N)

PLAYER/POS	AVG	G	AB	R	H	2B	3B	HR	RB	BB	SO	SB
George Burns, of	.158	5	19	2	3	2	0	0	2	1	5	1
Claude Cooper, pr	.000	2	0	0	0	0	0	0	0	0	0	1
Doc Crandall, p-2	.000	4	4	0	0	0	0	0	0	0	0	0
Al Demaree, p	.000	1	1	0	0	0	0	0	0	0	0	0
Larry Doyle, 2b	.150	5	20	1	3	0	0	0	2	0	1	0
Art Fletcher, ss	.278	5	18	1	5	0	0	0	3	1	1	1
Eddie Grant, ph	.000	2	1	1	0	0	0	0	0	0	0	0
Buck Herzog, 3b	.053	5	19	1	1	0	0	0	0	0	1	0
Rube Marquard, p	.000	2	1	0	0	0	0	0	0	0	0	0
Christy Mathewson, p	.600	2	5	1	3	0	0	0	1	1	0	0
Moose McCormick, ph	.500	2	2	1	1	0	0	0	0	0	0	0
Larry McLean, c-4	.500	5	12	0	6	0	0	0	2	0	0	0
Fred Merkle, 1b	.231	4	13	3	3	0	0	1	3	1	2	0
Chief Meyers, c	.000	1	4	0	0	0	0	0	0	0	0	0
Red Murray, of	.250	5	16	2	4	0	0	0	1	2	2	2
Tillie Shafer, of-5,3b-1	.158	5	19	2	3	1	1	0	1	2	3	0
Fred Snodgrass, 1b-1,of-1	.333	2	3	0	1	0	0	0	0	0	0	0
Jeff Tesreau, p	.000	2	2	0	0	0	0	0	0	0	1	0
Art Wilson, c	.000	3	3	0	0	0	0	0	0	0	2	0
Hooks Wiltse, 1b	.000	2	2	0	0	0	0	0	0	0	1	0
TOTAL	.201		164	15	33	3	1	1	15	8	19	5

PITCHER	W	L	ERA	G	GS	CG	SV	SHO	IP	H	ER	BB	SO
Doc Crandall	0	0	3.86	2	0	0	0	0	4.2	4	2	0	2
Al Demaree	0	1	4.50	1	1	0	0	0	4.0	7	2	1	0
Rube Marquard	0	1	7.00	2	1	0	0	0	9.0	10	7	3	3
Christy Mathewson	1	1	0.95	2	2	2	0	1	19.0	14	2	2	7
Jeff Tesreau	0	1	6.48	2	1	0	0	0	8.1	11	6	1	4
TOTAL	1	4	3.80	9	5	2	0	1	45.0	46	19	7	16

GAME 1 AT NY OCT 7

PHI	000	320	010	6	11	1
NY	001	030	000	4	11	0

Pitchers: BENDER vs MARQUARD, Crandall (6), Tesreau (8)
Home Runs: Baker-PHI
Attendance: 36,291

GAME 2 AT PHI OCT 8

NY	000	000	000 3	3	7	2
PHI	000	000	000 0	0	8	2

Pitchers: MATHEWSON vs PLANK
Attendance: 20,563

GAME 3 AT NY OCT 9

PHI	320	000	210	8	12	1
NY	000	010	100	2	5	1

Pitchers: BUSH vs TESREAU, Crandall (7)
Home Runs: Schang-PHI
Attendance: 36,896

GAME 4 AT PHI OCT 10

NY	000	000	320	5	8	2
PHI	010	320	00X	6	9	0

Pitchers: DEMAREE, Marquard (5) vs BENDER
Home Runs: Merkle-NY
Attendance: 20,568

GAME 5 AT NY OCT 11

PHI	102	000	000	3	6	1
NY	000	010	000	1	2	2

Pitchers: PLANK vs MATHEWSON
Attendance: 36,682

The Athletics, easy winners of their fourth pennant in five years, were clear favorites over Boston. But the "Miracle Braves"—who moved from last place to first between July 18 and Aug. 25 and kept going to take the pennant by 10½ games—had the momentum and swept the Series.

Boston pitcher Dick Rudolph (who won 27 games during the season) limited the A's to five hits and an unearned run, to take the opener behind the Braves' heavy hitting, 7–1. But the rest of the games were not won so easily. Philadelphia's Eddie Plank held the Braves scoreless through eight innings of Game 2, and gave up only one run in the ninth. But the Braves' Bill James (26–7 during the season) allowed only two hits and no runs at all.

Game 3 was a seesaw affair not settled until the 12th inning. Through 10 innings, starters Lefty Tyler of Boston and Joe Bush of the A's traded runs. Philadelphia scored one in the top of the first, but Braves' catcher Hank Gowdy doubled in the tying run in the second. The teams traded runs again in the fourth, but no one else crossed the plate until the 10th, when Frank Baker's bases-loaded single drove in two. For the third time, the Braves came back to tie it up. Gowdy opened the last of the 10th with the Series' only home run, and after a walk and single, a sacrifice fly knotted the score. Bill James came on to pitch no-hit ball through the 11th and 12th. Bush remained in for the A's, retiring the side in the 11th. But an inning later Gowdy opened with his third crucial hit of the game, a double. Les Mann replaced him as runner, and after a walk, bunt, and wild throw to third, Mann scampered home with the winning run.

Two of Connie Mack's most promising young pitchers, Bob Shawkey and Herb Pennock (who would later find stardom as New York Yankees), shared the A's pitching in Game 4, and gave up only six hits between them. But a walk and an error led to a Boston run in the fourth, and although Shawkey himself doubled in the tying run a half inning later, two more Braves scored in the last of the fifth on Johnny Evers's single. Pennock came on to pitch three innings of shutout relief, but Rudolph held the A's hitless over the final four innings to preserve his second win and the Braves' crown.

Boston Braves (NL), 4; Philadelphia Athletics (AL), 0

BOS (N)

PLAYER/POS	AVG	G	AB	R	H	2B	3B	HR	RB	BB	SO	SB
Ted Cather, of	.000	1	5	0	0	0	0	0	0	0	1	0
Joe Connolly, of	.111	3	9	1	1	0	0	0	1	1	1	0
Charlie Deal, 3b	.125	4	16	1	2	2	0	0	0	0	0	2
Josh Devore, ph	.000	1	1	0	0	0	0	0	0	0	1	0
Johnny Evers, 2b	.438	4	16	2	7	0	0	0	2	2	2	1
Larry Gilbert, ph	.000	1	0	0	0	0	0	0	0	1	0	0
Hank Gowdy, c	.545	4	11	3	6	3	1	1	3	5	1	1
Bill James, p	.000	2	4	0	0	0	0	0	0	0	4	0
Les Mann, of-2	.286	3	7	1	2	0	0	0	1	0	1	0
Rabbit Maranville, ss	.308	4	13	1	4	0	0	0	3	1	1	2
Herbie Moran, of	.077	3	13	2	1	1	0	0	0	1	1	1
Dick Rudolph, p	.333	2	6	1	2	0	0	0	0	1	1	0
Butch Schmidt, 1b	.294	4	17	2	5	0	0	0	2	0	2	1
Lefty Tyler, p	.000	1	3	0	0	0	0	0	0	0	1	0
Possum Whitted, of	.214	4	14	2	3	0	1	0	2	3	1	1
TOTAL	.244		135	16	33	6	2	1	14	15	18	9

PITCHER	W	L	ERA	G	GS	CG	SV	SHO	IP	H	ER	BB	SO
Bill James	2	0	0.00	2	1	1	0	1	11.0	2	0	6	9
Dick Rudolph	2	0	0.50	2	2	2	0	0	18.0	12	1	4	15
Lefty Tyler	0	0	3.60	1	1	0	0	0	10.0	8	4	3	4
TOTAL	4	0	1.15	5	4	3	0	1	39.0	22	5	13	28

PHI (A)

PLAYER/POS	AVG	G	AB	R	H	2B	3B	HR	RB	BB	SO	SB
Frank Baker, 3b	.250	4	16	0	4	2	0	0	2	1	3	0
Jack Barry, ss	.071	4	14	1	1	0	0	0	0	1	3	1
Chief Bender, p	.000	1	2	0	0	0	0	0	0	0	0	0
Joe Bush, p	.000	1	5	0	0	0	0	0	0	0	2	0
Eddie Collins, 2b	.214	4	14	0	3	0	0	0	1	2	1	1
Jack Lapp, c	.000	1	1	0	0	0	0	0	0	0	0	0
Stuffy McInnis, 1b	.143	4	14	2	2	1	0	0	0	3	3	0
Eddie Murphy, of	.188	4	16	3	3	2	0	0	0	2	2	0
Rube Oldring, of	.067	4	15	0	1	0	0	0	0	0	5	0
Herb Pennock, p	.000	1	1	0	0	0	0	0	0	0	0	0
Eddie Plank, p	.000	1	2	0	0	0	0	0	0	0	1	0
Wally Schang, c	.167	4	12	1	2	1	0	0	0	1	4	0
Bob Shawkey, p	.500	1	2	0	1	1	0	0	1	0	1	0
Amos Strunk, of	.286	2	7	0	2	0	0	0	0	0	2	0
Jimmy Walsh, of-2	.333	3	6	0	2	1	0	0	1	3	1	0
Weldon Wyckoff, p	1.000	1	1	0	1	1	0	0	0	0	0	0
TOTAL	.172		128	6	22	9	0	0	5	13	28	2

PITCHER	W	L	ERA	G	GS	CG	SV	SHO	IP	H	ER	BB	SO
Chief Bender	0	1	10.13	1	1	0	0	0	5.1	8	6	2	3
Joe Bush	0	1	3.27	1	1	1	0	0	11.0	9	4	4	4
Herb Pennock	0	0	0.00	1	0	0	0	0	3.0	2	0	2	3
Eddie Plank	0	1	1.00	1	1	1	0	0	9.0	7	1	4	6
Bob Shawkey	0	1	3.60	1	1	0	0	0	5.0	4	2	2	0
Weldon Wyckoff	0	0	2.45	1	0	0	0	0	3.2	3	1	1	2
TOTAL	0	4	3.41	6	4	2	0	0	37.0	33	14	15	18

GAME 1 AT PHI OCT 9

BOS	020 013 010	7	11	2
PHI	010 000 000	1	5	0

Pitchers: RUDOLPH vs BENDER, Wyckoff (6)
Attendance: 20,562

GAME 2 AT PHI OCT 10

BOS	000 000 001	1	7	1
PHI	000 000 000	0	2	1

Pitchers: JAMES vs PLANK
Attendance: 20,562

GAME 3 AT BOS OCT 12

PHI	100 100 000 200	4	8	2
BOS	010 100 000 201	5	9	1

Pitchers: BUSH vs Tyler, JAMES (11)
Home Runs: Gowdy-BOS
Attendance: 35,520

GAME 4 AT BOS OCT 13

PHI	000 010 000	1	7	0
BOS	000 120 00X	3	6	0

Pitchers: SHAWKEY, Pennock (6) vs RUDOLPH
Attendance: 34,365

In a Series characterized by outstanding pitching, Boston's five runs in Game 5 were the most scored by either team. It was also one of the most closely contested Series: the deciding run was not scored until the ninth inning in three of the games, and only in Game 1 was the margin of victory as much as two runs.

Grover Cleveland Alexander pitched the opener for the Phillies, and while the Red Sox tagged him for eight hits, they were all singles, and not until the eighth inning did one manage to drive a runner home. Boston's Ernie Shore pitched just as well, giving up only five singles and four walks. But two Philadelphia hits produced a run in the fourth, and an alternating pair of walks and infield hits in the eighth broke the tie with two runs for the Phillies' only win.

The next three games were 2–1 Boston victories. Rube Foster held the Phillies to three hits in Game 2, and led his team at the bat, going 3-for-4, including a double in the fifth. But it was his single in the ninth with a man on second that produced what proved to be the winning run as he retired the side in the bottom of the ninth to preserve his win. Dutch Leonard duplicated Foster's three-hit pitching two days later as the Series moved to Boston's spacious new Braves Field for Game 3. Before a new Series record crowd of 42,300, Leonard defeated the great Alexander, as Boston's Duffy Lewis—with his third hit of the game—singled over second base to score Harry Hooper from third with two out in the bottom of the ninth.

Ernie Shore returned to the mound for Boston in Game 4, and although he gave up more hits (seven) than he had in Game 1, his Sox had scored their two runs before the Phillies put across their one in the eighth.

Rube Foster was not as effective in Game 5 as he had been in Game 2, twice giving the Phillies a two-run lead as Phillie first baseman Fred Luderus drove in three runs with a double and a home run. But from the fifth inning on, Foster held Philadelphia scoreless on two hits, while Duffy Lewis evened the score with a two-run homer in the eighth, and Harry Hooper (who had tied the score earlier with a home run in the third) won the game and the Series with a second homer in the top of the ninth.

Boston Red Sox (AL), 4;
Philadelphia Phillies (NL), 1

BOS (A)

PLAYER/POS	AVG	G	AB	R	H	2B	3B	HR	RB	BB	SO	SB
Jack Barry, 2b	.176	5	17	1	3	0	0	0	1	1	2	0
Hick Cady, c	.333	4	6	0	2	0	0	0	0	1	2	0
Bill Carrigan, c	.000	1	2	0	0	0	0	0	0	1	1	0
Rube Foster, p	.500	2	8	0	4	1	0	0	1	0	2	0
Del Gainer, 1b	.333	1	3	1	1	0	0	0	0	0	0	0
Larry Gardner, 3b	.235	5	17	2	4	0	1	0	0	1	0	0
Olaf Henricksen, ph	.000	2	2	0	0	0	0	0	0	0	0	0
Dick Hoblitzel, 1b	.313	5	16	1	5	0	0	0	1	0	1	1
Harry Hooper, of	.350	5	20	4	7	0	0	2	3	2	4	0
Hal Janvrin, ss	.000	1	1	0	0	0	0	0	0	0	0	0
Dutch Leonard, p	.000	1	3	0	0	0	0	0	0	0	2	0
Duffy Lewis, of	.444	5	18	1	8	1	0	1	5	1	4	0
Babe Ruth, ph	.000	1	1	0	0	0	0	0	0	0	0	0
Everett Scott, ss	.056	5	18	0	1	0	0	0	0	0	3	0
Ernie Shore, p	.200	2	5	0	1	0	0	0	0	0	3	0
Tris Speaker, of	.294	5	17	2	5	0	1	0	0	4	1	0
Pinch Thomas, c	.200	2	5	0	1	0	0	0	0	0	0	0
TOTAL	.264		159	12	42	2	2	3	11	11	25	1

PITCHER	W	L	ERA	G	GS	CG	SV	SHO	IP	H	ER	BB	SO
Rube Foster	2	0	2.00	2	2	2	0	0	18.0	12	4	2	13
Dutch Leonard	1	0	1.00	1	1	1	0	0	9.0	3	1	0	6
Ernie Shore	1	1	2.12	2	2	2	0	0	17.0	12	4	8	6
TOTAL	4	1	1.84	5	5	5	0	0	44.0	27	9	10	25

PHI (N)

PLAYER/POS	AVG	G	AB	R	H	2B	3B	HR	RB	BB	SO	SB
Pete Alexander, p	.200	2	5	0	1	0	0	0	0	0	1	0
Dave Bancroft, ss	.294	5	17	2	5	0	0	0	1	2	2	0
Beals Becker, of	.000	2	0	0	0	0	0	0	0	0	0	0
Ed Burns, c	.188	5	16	1	3	0	0	0	1	2	0	0
Bobby Byrne, ph	.000	1	1	0	0	0	0	0	0	0	0	0
George Chalmers, p	.333	1	3	0	1	0	0	0	0	0	1	0
Gavvy Cravath, of	.125	5	16	2	2	1	1	0	1	2	6	0
Oscar Dugey, pr	.000	2	0	0	0	0	0	0	0	0	0	1
Bill Killefer, ph	.000	1	1	0	0	0	0	0	0	0	0	0
Fred Luderus, 1b	.438	5	16	1	7	2	0	1	6	1	4	0
Erskine Mayer, p	.000	2	4	0	0	0	0	0	0	0	2	0
Bert Niehoff, 2b	.063	5	16	1	1	0	0	0	0	1	5	0
Dode Paskert, of	.158	5	19	2	3	0	0	0	0	1	2	0
Eppa Rixey, p	.500	1	2	0	1	0	0	0	0	0	0	0
Milt Stock, 3b	.118	5	17	1	2	1	0	0	0	1	0	0
Possum Whitted, of-5,1b-1	.067	5	15	0	1	0	0	0	1	1	0	1
TOTAL	.182		148	10	27	4	1	1	9	10	25	2

PITCHER	W	L	ERA	G	GS	CG	SV	SHO	IP	H	ER	BB	SO
Pete Alexander	1	1	1.53	2	2	2	0	0	17.2	14	3	4	10
George Chalmers	0	1	2.25	1	1	1	0	0	8.0	8	2	3	6
Erskine Mayer	0	1	2.38	2	2	1	0	0	11.1	16	3	2	7
Eppa Rixey	0	1	4.05	1	0	0	0	0	6.2	4	3	2	2
TOTAL	1	4	2.27	6	5	4	0	0	43.2	42	11	11	25

GAME 1 AT PHI OCT 8

BOS	000	000	010	1	8	1
PHI	000	100	02X	3	5	1

Pitchers: SHORE vs ALEXANDER
Attendance: 19,343

GAME 2 AT PHI OCT 9

BOS	100	000	001	2	10	0
PHI	000	010	000	1	3	1

Pitchers: FOSTER vs MAYER
Attendance: 20,306

GAME 3 AT BOS OCT 11

PHI	001	000	000	1	3	0
BOS	000	100	001	2	6	1

Pitchers: ALEXANDER vs LEONARD
Attendance: 42,300

GAME 4 AT BOS OCT 12

PHI	000	000	010	1	7	0
BOS	001	001	00X	2	8	1

Pitchers: CHALMERS vs SHORE
Attendance: 41,096

GAME 5 AT PHI OCT 13

BOS	011	000	021	5	10	1
PHI	200	200	000	4	9	1

Pitchers: FOSTER vs Mayer, RIXEY (3)
Home Runs: Hooper-BOS (2), Lewis-BOS, Luderus-PHI
Attendance: 20,306

In close pennant races, the Red Sox repeated as league champions and Brooklyn won its first pennant since 1900. The first three games of the Series were tightly contested, and the outcomes were determined by only one run apiece. For 6½ innings in the opener, Brooklyn's Rube Marquard dueled Boston's Ernie Shore about equally. But in the last of the seventh the Sox capitalized on a double, some sloppy Brooklyn fielding, and a couple of sacrifice hits for three runs, adding another off reliever Jeff Pfeffer in the eighth for a 6–1 lead. The Robins fought back in the ninth, driving out Shore and drawing within one run of a tie before reliever Carl Mays retired the final man with the bases loaded.

Game 2 was even tighter. Boston starter Babe Ruth gave up a first-inning inside-the-park homer to Hy Myers, but in the third he drove in Everett Scott (who had tripled) to tie the game at 1–1. Then for the next 10 innings he and Robins pitcher Sherry Smith shut off all scoring. Ruth continued to blank Brooklyn in the 14th, and in the last of the inning a walk, sacrifice, and single over the head of the third baseman gave Boston and Ruth the victory.

Brooklyn veteran Jack Coombs took a 4–0 lead into the sixth inning of Game 3 before weakening. But after giving up a third Boston run on Larry Gardner's one-out homer in the seventh, he was relieved by Jeff Pfeffer, who set the Sox down in order the rest of the way. In saving what proved to be Coombs's last World Series appearance (as well as the Robins' only Series win), Pfeffer preserved Coombs's perfect Series won-lost record at 5–0.

Games 4 and 5 proved anti-climactic. In Game 4, Gardner's second homer of the Series—inside-the-park for three runs in the second inning—overcame the Robins' two runs in the first. The Sox added a run here and there to increase their lead, while Sox starter Dutch Leonard shut Brooklyn out through the final eight innings for a comfortable 6–2 win. And in what became the Series finale, Ernie Shore held the Robins to three singles and one unearned run as his Sox took advantage of a bad-hop triple in the second and two third-inning errors by Robin shortstop Ivy Olson to take the lead—and their fourth world championship.

Boston Red Sox (AL), 4; Brooklyn Robins (NL), 1

BOS (A)

PLAYER/POS	AVG	G	AB	R	H	2B	3B	HR	RB	BB	SO	SB
Hick Cady, c	.250	2	4	1	1	0	0	0	0	3	0	0
Bill Carrigan, c	.667	1	3	0	2	0	0	0	1	0	1	0
Rube Foster, p	.000	1	1	0	0	0	0	0	0	0	1	0
Del Gainer, ph	1.000	1	1	0	1	0	0	0	1	0	0	0
Larry Gardner, 3b	.176	5	17	2	3	0	0	2	6	0	2	0
Olaf Henricksen, ph	.000	1	0	1	0	0	0	0	0	1	0	0
Dick Hoblitzel, 1b	.235	5	17	3	4	1	0	0	2	6	0	0
Harry Hooper, of	.333	5	21	6	7	1	1	0	1	3	1	1
Hal Janvrin, 2b	.217	5	23	2	5	3	0	0	1	0	6	0
Dutch Leonard, p	.000	1	3	0	0	0	0	0	0	1	3	0
Duffy Lewis, of	.353	5	17	3	6	2	1	0	1	2	1	0
Carl Mays, p	.000	2	1	0	0	0	0	0	0	0	0	0
Mike McNally, pr	.000	1	0	1	0	0	0	0	0	0	0	0
Babe Ruth, p	.000	1	5	0	0	0	0	0	1	0	2	0
Everett Scott, ss	.125	5	16	1	2	0	1	0	1	1	1	0
Ernie Shore, p	.000	2	7	0	0	0	0	0	0	0	2	0
Chick Shorten, of	.571	2	7	4	4	0	0	0	2	0	1	0
Pinch Thomas, c	.143	3	7	0	1	0	1	0	0	0	1	0
Tilly Walker, of	.273	3	11	1	3	0	1	0	1	1	2	0
Jimmy Walsh, of	.000	1	3	0	0	0	0	0	0	0	0	0
TOTAL	.238		164	21	39	7	6	2	18	18	25	1

PITCHER	W	L	ERA	G	GS	CG	SV	SHO	IP	H	ER	BB	SO
Rube Foster	0	0	0.00	1	0	0	0	0	3.0	3	0	0	1
Dutch Leonard	1	0	1.00	1	1	1	0	0	9.0	5	1	4	3
Carl Mays	0	1	5.06	2	1	0	1	0	5.1	8	3	3	2
Babe Ruth	1	0	0.64	1	1	1	0	0	14.0	6	1	3	4
Ernie Shore	2	0	1.53	2	2	1	0	0	17.2	12	3	4	9
TOTAL	4	1	1.47	7	5	3	1	0	49.0	34	8	14	19

BRO (N)

PLAYER/POS	AVG	G	AB	R	H	2B	3B	HR	RB	BB	SO	SB
Larry Cheney, p	.000	1	0	0	0	0	0	0	0	0	0	0
Jack Coombs, p	.333	1	3	0	1	0	0	0	1	0	0	0
George Cutshaw, 2b	.105	5	19	2	2	1	0	0	2	1	1	0
Jake Daubert, 1b	.176	4	17	1	3	0	1	0	0	2	3	0
Wheezer Dell, p	.000	1	0	0	0	0	0	0	0	0	0	0
Gus Getz, ph	.000	1	1	0	0	0	0	0	0	0	0	0
Jimmy Johnston, of-2	.300	3	10	1	3	0	1	0	0	1	0	0
Rube Marquard, p	.000	2	3	0	0	0	0	0	0	0	1	0
Fred Merkle, 1b-1	.250	3	4	0	1	0	0	0	1	2	0	0
Chief Meyers, c	.200	3	10	0	2	0	1	0	0	1	0	0
Otto Miller, c	.125	2	8	0	1	0	0	0	0	0	1	0
Harry Mowery, 3b	.176	5	17	2	3	0	0	0	1	3	2	0
Hy Myers, of	.182	5	22	2	4	0	1	1	3	0	3	0
Ivy Olson, ss	.250	5	16	1	4	0	1	0	2	2	2	0
Ollie O'Mara, ph	.000	1	1	0	0	0	0	0	0	0	1	0
Jeff Pfeffer, p-3	.250	4	4	0	1	0	0	0	0	0	2	0
Nap Rucker, p	.000	1	0	0	0	0	0	0	0	0	0	0
Sherry Smith, p	.200	1	5	0	1	0	1	0	0	0	0	0
Casey Stengel, of-3	.364	4	11	2	4	0	0	0	0	0	1	0
Zack Wheat, of	.211	5	19	2	4	0	1	0	1	2	2	1
TOTAL	.200		170	13	34	2	5	1	11	14	19	1

PITCHER	W	L	ERA	G	GS	CG	SV	SHO	IP	H	ER	BB	SO
Larry Cheney	0	0	3.00	1	0	0	0	0	3.0	4	1	1	5
Jack Coombs	1	0	4.26	1	1	0	0	0	6.1	7	3	1	1
Wheezer Dell	0	0	0.00	1	0	0	0	0	1.0	1	0	0	0
Rube Marquard	0	2	5.73	2	2	0	0	0	11.0	12	7	6	9
Jeff Pfeffer	0	1	1.69	3	1	0	1	0	10.2	7	2	4	5
Nap Rucker	0	0	0.00	1	0	0	0	0	2.0	1	0	0	3
Sherry Smith	0	1	1.35	1	1	1	0	0	13.1	7	2	6	2
TOTAL	1	4	2.85	10	5	1	1	0	47.1	39	15	18	25

GAME 1 AT BOS OCT 7

BRO	000 100 004	5	10	4
BOS	001 010 31X	6	8	1

Pitchers: MARQUARD, Pfeffer (8) vs SHORE, Mays (9)
Attendance: 36,117

GAME 2 AT BOS OCT 9

BRO	100 000 000 000 00	1	6	2
BOS	001 000 000 000 01	2	7	1

Pitchers: SMITH vs RUTH
Home Runs: H.Myers-BRO
Attendance: 41,373

GAME 3 AT BRO OCT 10

BOS	000 002 100	3	7	1
BRO	001 120 00X	4	10	0

Pitchers: MAYS, Foster (6) vs COOMBS, Pfeffer (7)
Home Runs: Gardner-BOS
Attendance: 21,087

GAME 4 AT BRO OCT 11

BOS	030 110 100	6	10	1
BRO	200 000 000	2	5	4

Pitchers: LEONARD vs MARQUARD, Cheney (5), Rucker (8)
Home Runs: Gardner-BOS
Attendance: 21,662

GAME 5 AT BOS OCT 12

BRO	010 000 000	1	3	3
BOS	012 010 00X	4	7	2

Pitchers: PFEFFER, Dell (8) vs SHORE
Attendance: 42,620

Easy winners in their pennant races, the White Sox and Giants traded pairs of victories in the Series before the Sox came up with a second pair to take the title in six games. In the opener, Happy Felsch's solo homer in the fourth inning gave Sox starter Eddie Cicotte the margin he needed to defeat Slim Sallee, 2–1, and in Game 2 Red Faber went all the way, as his Sox broke a 2–2 tie in the fourth inning with five runs on six singles for Chicago's second win.

The clubs traveled to New York for Games 3 and 4, and Giants pitchers rewarded their fans with a pair of shutouts to even the Series. In Game 3, a triple, double, and single against the Sox' Cicotte in the fourth inning produced the only scoring, as Giant Rube Benton blanked the Sox on five hits, walking none. Giant ace Ferdie Schupp (a 21-game winner during the season) did the honors in Game 4, scattering seven hits, as teammate Benny Kauff, with his first Series hit in the fourth inning, homered inside the park to deep center against Red Faber for the deciding run. Two later runs against Faber and two more in the eighth (on Kauff's second homer) against reliever Dave Danforth made Schupp's win easy.

But Faber, the loser in Game 4, came in to pitch two innings of perfect relief two days later in Chicago for his second win, as the Sox rebounded from a 5–2 deficit with three runs in the bottom of the seventh to tie the game and three more an inning later to win it.

After a day of rest and a return to New York, Faber was given his third start. He pitched well enough, but his third win and the Series clincher was really the gift of some infamous Giants fielding. In the fourth inning, the first two Sox batters—Eddie Collins and Joe Jackson—reached on a high throw to first and a dropped fly. Happy Felsch, the third man up, reached on a fielder's choice as Giants third baseman Heinie Zimmerman chased Collins across the plate in a botched rundown. Jackson and Felsch scored the second and third unearned runs as Chick Gandil singled off the hapless Rube Benton. The Giants recovered to score two runs an inning later, but Faber shut them out the rest of the way to give his Sox the Series.

Chicago White Sox (AL), 4; New York Giants (NL), 2

CHI (A)

PLAYER/POS	AVG	G	AB	R	H	2B	3B	HR	RB	BB	SO	SB
Eddie Cicotte, p	.143	3	7	0	1	0	0	0	0	1	2	0
Eddie Collins, 2b	.409	6	22	4	9	1	0	0	2	2	3	3
Shano Collins, of	.286	6	21	2	6	1	0	0	0	0	2	0
Dave Danforth, p	.000	1	0	0	0	0	0	0	0	0	0	0
Red Faber, p	.143	4	7	0	1	0	0	0	0	2	3	0
Happy Felsch, of	.273	6	22	4	6	1	0	1	3	1	5	0
Chick Gandil, 1b	.261	6	23	1	6	1	0	0	5	0	2	1
Joe Jackson, of	.304	6	23	4	7	0	0	0	2	1	0	1
Nemo Leibold, of	.400	2	5	1	2	0	0	0	1	1	1	0
Byrd Lynn, ph	.000	1	1	0	0	0	0	0	0	0	1	0
Fred McMullin, 3b	.125	6	24	1	3	1	0	0	2	1	6	0
Swede Risberg, ph	.500	2	2	0	1	0	0	0	1	0	0	0
Reb Russell, p	.000	1	0	0	0	0	0	0	0	0	0	0
Ray Schalk, c	.263	6	19	1	5	0	0	0	0	2	1	1
Buck Weaver, ss	.333	6	21	3	7	1	0	0	1	0	2	0
Lefty Williams, p	.000	1	0	0	0	0	0	0	0	0	0	0
TOTAL	.274		197	21	54	6	0	1	17	11	28	6

PITCHER	W	L	ERA	G	GS	CG	SV	SHO	IP	H	ER	BB	SO
Eddie Cicotte	1	1	1.96	3	2	2	0	0	23.0	23	5	2	13
Dave Danforth	0	0	18.00	1	0	0	0	0	1.0	3	2	0	2
Red Faber	3	1	2.33	4	3	2	0	0	27.0	21	7	3	9
Reb Russell	0	0	∞	1	1	0	0	0	0.0	2	1	1	0
Lefty Williams	0	0	9.00	1	0	0	0	0	1.0	2	1	0	3
TOTAL	4	2	2.77	10	6	4	0	0	52.0	51	16	6	27

NY (N)

PLAYER/POS	AVG	G	AB	R	H	2B	3B	HR	RB	BB	SO	SB
Fred Anderson, p	.000	1	0	0	0	0	0	0	0	0	0	0
Rube Benton, p	.000	2	4	0	0	0	0	0	0	0	3	0
George Burns, of	.227	6	22	3	5	0	0	0	2	3	6	1
Art Fletcher, ss	.200	6	25	2	5	1	0	0	0	0	2	0
Buck Herzog, 2b	.250	6	24	1	6	0	1	0	2	0	4	0
Walter Holke, 1b	.286	6	21	2	6	2	0	0	1	0	6	0
Benny Kauff, of	.160	6	25	2	4	1	0	2	5	0	2	1
Lew McCarty, c-2	.400	3	5	1	2	0	1	0	1	0	0	0
Pol Perritt, p	1.000	3	2	0	2	0	0	0	0	0	0	0
Bill Rariden, c	.385	5	13	2	5	0	0	0	2	2	1	0
Dave Robertson, of	.500	6	22	3	11	1	1	0	1	0	0	2
Slim Sallee, p	.167	2	6	0	1	0	0	0	0	0	2	0
Ferdie Schupp, p	.250	2	4	0	1	0	0	0	0	1	0	0
Jeff Tesreau, p	.000	1	0	0	0	0	0	0	0	0	0	0
Jim Thorpe, of	.000	1	0	0	0	0	0	0	0	0	0	0
Joe Wilhoit, ph	.000	2	1	0	0	0	0	0	0	1	0	0
Heinie Zimmerman, 3b	.120	6	25	1	3	0	1	0	0	0	5	0
TOTAL	.256		199	17	51	5	4	2	16	6	27	4

PITCHER	W	L	ERA	G	GS	CG	SV	SHO	IP	H	ER	BB	SO
Fred Anderson	0	1	18.00	1	0	0	0	0	2.0	5	4	0	3
Rube Benton	1	1	0.00	2	2	1	0	1	14.0	9	0	1	8
Pol Perritt	0	0	1.08	3	0	0	0	0	8.1	9	1	3	3
Slim Sallee	0	2	5.28	2	2	1	0	0	15.1	20	9	4	4
Ferdie Schupp	1	0	1.74	2	2	1	0	1	10.1	11	2	2	9
Jeff Tesreau	0	0	0.00	1	0	0	0	0	1.0	0	0	1	1
TOTAL	2	4	2.82	11	6	3	0	2	51.0	54	16	11	28

GAME 1 AT CHI OCT 6

NY	000 010 000	1	7	1
CHI	001 100 00X	2	7	1

Pitchers: SALLEE vs CICOTTE
Home Runs: Felsch-CHI
Attendance: 32,000

GAME 2 AT CHI OCT 7

NY	020 000 000	2	8	1
CHI	020 500 00X	7	14	1

Pitchers: Schupp, ANDERSON (2), Perritt (4), Tesreau (8) vs FABER
Attendance: 32,000

GAME 3 AT NY OCT 10

CHI	000 000 000	0	5	3
NY	000 200 00X	2	8	2

Pitchers: CICOTTE vs BENTON
Attendance: 33,616

GAME 4 AT NY OCT 11

CHI	000 000 000	0	7	0
NY	000 110 12X	5	10	1

Pitchers: FABER, Danforth (8) vs SCHUPP
Home Runs: Kauff-NY (2)
Attendance: 27,746

GAME 5 AT CHI OCT 13

NY	200 200 100	5	12	3
CHI	001 001 33X	8	14	6

Pitchers: SALLEE, Perritt (8) vs Russell, Cicotte (1), Williams (7), FABER (8)
Attendance: 27,323

GAME 6 AT NY OCT 15

CHI	000 300 001	4	7	1
NY	000 020 000	2	6	3

Pitchers: FABER vs BENTON, Perritt (6)
Attendance: 33,969

Although both clubs had lost key players to military service, so had other major league teams, and after a season shortened by a month because of the war, the Red Sox and Cubs found themselves opponents in an early-September World Series.

In the opener, Babe Ruth pushed his string of consecutive scoreless World Series innings to 22, holding the Cubs to six singles as he went the distance. The Cubs' Hippo Vaughn pitched just as well, but two of the five singles he yielded followed a leadoff walk in the fourth and produced the game's only run. Chicago evened the Series in Game 2, bunching four of their seven hits after a walk in the second inning to take a 3–0 lead. Successive triples in Boston's ninth spoiled Lefty Tyler's shutout but not his victory.

Hippo Vaughn lost another close one in Game 3 when he gave up two runs in the fourth inning on a hit batsman and a succession of singles. The Cubs got him one run back in the fifth, but Boston's Carl Mays held Chicago to that one run as he hurled Boston back into the Series lead. Ruth pushed the Sox farther ahead in another squeaker in Game 4. As he continued his mastery over Cubs hitters, he drove Boston into the lead with a two-run triple in the fourth inning (his only Series hit). But in the eighth a run-scoring ground out ended his record setting string of scoreless innings at 29⅔, and a single drove in another run to tie the game. The Sox, though, scored a third run on a Chicago error in the last of the eighth, and reliever Bullet Joe Bush shut down a threat in the ninth to save Ruth's win.

Vaughn, in his third start, finally found what was needed for victory—a shutout, on five hits, as the Cubs added hits to walks from Boston's Sad Sam Jones in the third and eighth to push across their three runs. But in Game 6 the Sox scored two unearned runs on a dropped line drive to right in the third inning. It was their only scoring off Lefty Tyler, but Boston's Carl Mays was on his way to a one-run three-hitter that brought the Red Sox their fifth world championship in five tries. To date, although they have tried four more times, they have not won a sixth.

Boston Red Sox (AL), 4;
Chicago Cubs (NL), 2

BOS (A)

PLAYER/POS	AVG	G	AB	R	H	2B	3B	HR	RB	BB	SO	SB
Sam Agnew, c	.000	4	9	0	0	0	0	0	0	0	0	0
Joe Bush, p	.000	2	2	0	0	0	0	0	0	1	0	0
Jean Dubuc, ph	.000	1	1	0	0	0	0	0	0	0	1	0
Harry Hooper, of	.200	6	20	0	4	0	0	0	0	2	2	0
Sam Jones, p	.000	1	1	0	0	0	0	0	0	0	1	0
Carl Mays, p	.200	2	5	1	1	0	0	0	0	0	1	0
Stuffy McInnis, 1b	.250	6	20	2	5	0	0	0	1	1	1	0
Hack Miller, ph	.000	1	1	0	0	0	0	0	0	0	0	0
Babe Ruth, p-2,of-2	.200	3	5	0	1	0	1	0	2	0	2	0
Wally Schang, c	.444	5	9	1	4	0	0	0	1	2	3	1
Everett Scott, ss	.100	6	20	0	2	0	0	0	1	1	1	0
Dave Shean, 2b	.211	6	19	2	4	1	0	0	0	4	3	1
Amos Strunk, of	.174	6	23	1	4	1	1	0	0	0	5	0
Fred Thomas, 3b	.118	6	17	0	2	0	0	0	0	1	2	0
George Whiteman, of	.250	6	20	2	5	0	1	0	1	2	1	1
TOTAL	.186		172	9	32	2	3	0	6	16	21	3

PITCHER	W	L	ERA	G	GS	CG	SV	SHO	IP	H	ER	BB	SO
Joe Bush	0	1	3.00	2	1	1	1	0	9.0	7	3	3	0
Sam Jones	0	1	3.00	1	1	1	0	0	9.0	7	3	5	5
Carl Mays	2	0	1.00	2	2	2	0	0	18.0	10	2	3	5
Babe Ruth	2	0	1.06	2	2	1	0	1	17.0	13	2	7	4
TOTAL	4	2	1.70	7	6	5	1	1	53.0	37	10	18	14

CHI (N)

PLAYER/POS	AVG	G	AB	R	H	2B	3B	HR	RB	BB	SO	SB
Turner Barber, ph	.000	3	2	0	0	0	0	0	0	0	0	0
Charlie Deal, 3b	.176	6	17	0	3	0	0	0	0	0	1	0
Phil Douglas, p	.000	1	0	0	0	0	0	0	0	0	0	0
Max Flack, of	.263	6	19	2	5	0	0	0	0	4	1	1
Claude Hendrix, p-1	1.000	2	1	0	1	0	0	0	0	0	0	0
Charlie Hollocher, ss	.190	6	21	2	4	0	1	0	1	1	1	1
Bill Killefer, c	.118	6	17	2	2	1	0	0	2	2	0	0
Les Mann, of	.227	6	22	0	5	2	0	0	2	0	0	0
Bill McCabe, ph	.000	3	1	1	0	0	0	0	0	0	0	0
Fred Merkle, 1b	.278	6	18	1	5	0	0	0	1	4	3	0
Bob O'Farrell, c-1	.000	3	3	0	0	0	0	0	0	0	0	0
Dode Paskert, of	.190	6	21	0	4	1	0	0	2	2	2	0
Charlie Pick, 2b	.389	6	18	2	7	1	0	0	0	1	1	1
Lefty Tyler, p	.200	3	5	0	1	0	0	0	2	2	0	0
Hippo Vaughn, p	.000	3	10	0	0	0	0	0	0	0	5	0
Chuck Wortman, 2b	.000	1	1	0	0	0	0	0	0	0	0	0
Rollie Zeider, 3b	.000	2	0	0	0	0	0	0	0	2	0	0
TOTAL	.210		176	10	37	5	1	0	10	18	14	3

PITCHER	W	L	ERA	G	GS	CG	SV	SHO	IP	H	ER	BB	SO
Phil Douglas	0	1	0.00	1	0	0	0	0	1.0	1	0	0	0
Claude Hendrix	0	0	0.00	1	0	0	0	0	1.0	0	0	0	0
Lefty Tyler	1	1	1.17	3	3	1	0	0	23.0	14	3	11	4
Hippo Vaughn	1	2	1.00	3	3	3	0	1	27.0	17	3	5	17
TOTAL	2	4	1.04	8	6	4	0	1	52.0	32	6	16	21

GAME 1 AT CHI SEPT 5

BOS	000 100 000	1	5	0
CHI	000 000 000	0	6	0

Pitchers: RUTH vs VAUGHN
Attendance: 19,274

GAME 2 AT CHI SEPT 6

BOS	000 000 001	1	6	1
CHI	030 000 00X	3	7	1

Pitchers: BUSH vs TYLER
Attendance: 20,040

GAME 3 AT CHI SEPT 7

BOS	000 200 000	2	7	0
CHI	000 010 000	1	7	1

Pitchers: MAYS vs VAUGHN
Attendance: 27,054

GAME 4 AT BOS SEPT 9

CHI	000 000 020	2	7	1
BOS	000 200 01X	3	4	0

Pitchers: Tyler, DOUGLAS (8) vs RUTH, Bush (9)
Attendance: 22,183

GAME 5 AT BOS SEPT 10

CHI	001 000 002	3	7	0
BOS	000 000 000	0	5	0

Pitchers: VAUGHN vs JONES
Attendance: 24,694

GAME 6 AT BOS SEPT 11

CHI	000 100 000	1	3	2
BOS	002 000 00X	2	5	0

Pitchers: TYLER, Hendrix (8) vs MAYS
Attendance: 15,238

In the bottom of the first inning of Game 1, White Sox pitcher Eddie Cicotte hit the first batter to face him, a prearranged signal to gamblers that "the fix was on"—that the Sox would throw the Series. The eight Chicago conspirators—pitching aces Cicotte and Lefty Williams, outfielders Joe Jackson and Happy Felsch, and infielders Chick Gandil, Buck Weaver, Fred McMullin and Swede Risberg—received no more than a fraction of the $100,000 promised them but "honored" their end of the deal. Cicotte (winner of 29 regular-season games, with a 1.82 ERA) gave up seven hits and six runs in the opening innings of Game 1 en route to a 9–1 loss. Williams, though he held the Reds to four hits in Game 2, uncharacteristically walked six and fanned only one, a performance bad enough for a 4–2 loss.

Dickie Kerr, Chicago's third-best pitcher and not in on the fix, won Game 3 with a three-hit shutout. But although Cicotte pitched well in Game 4, Chicago lost a third time as the Reds' Jimmy Ring hurled a three-hit shutout of his own (all three hits coming, ironically, off the bats of conspirators Jackson, Felsch, and Gandil).

Cincinnati's Hod Eller beat Chicago in Game 5 with the Series' third successive three-hit shutout. Loser Lefty Williams once again yielded only four hits, but three came in a four-run sixth inning which also saw a walk and a throwing error by Felsch. (The win, the Reds' fourth, did not decide the Series, which had been expanded to the best five of nine in the exuberance which followed the end of the Great War.)

Chicago exerted itself to win the next two games. In Game 6, Kerr's second win depended on crucial hits by Jackson and Gandil in the tenth inning; and in Game 7 Cicotte held the Reds to one run as Jackson and Felsch drove in all of Chicago's four runs.

But in Game 8, Williams gave up two singles and two doubles before being pulled with only one away in the first. Jackson homered in the third. And he doubled and Gandil tripled to drive in three Chicago runs in the eighth. But by then the Reds had scored 10 runs on their way to an easy win and their tainted world title.

Cincinnati Reds (NL), 5;
Chicago White Sox (AL), 3

CIN (N)

PLAYER/POS	AVG	G	AB	R	H	2B	3B	HR	RB	BB	SO	SB
Jake Daubert, 1b	.241	8	29	4	7	0	1	0	1	1	2	1
Pat Duncan, of	.269	8	26	3	7	2	0	0	8	2	2	0
Hod Eller, p	.286	2	7	2	2	1	0	0	0	0	2	0
Ray Fisher, p	.500	2	2	0	1	0	0	0	0	0	0	0
Heinie Groh, 3b	.172	8	29	6	5	2	0	0	2	6	4	0
Larry Kopf, ss	.222	8	27	3	6	0	2	0	2	3	2	0
Dolf Luque, p	.000	2	1	0	0	0	0	0	0	0	1	0
Sherry Magee, ph	.500	2	2	0	1	0	0	0	0	0	0	0
Greasy Neale, of	.357	8	28	3	10	1	1	0	4	2	5	1
Bill Rariden, c	.211	5	19	0	4	0	0	0	2	0	0	1
Morrie Rath, 2b	.226	8	31	5	7	1	0	0	2	4	1	2
Jimmy Ring, p	.000	2	5	0	0	0	0	0	0	0	2	0
Edd Roush, of	.214	8	28	6	6	2	1	0	7	3	0	2
Dutch Ruether, p-2	.667	3	6	2	4	1	2	0	4	1	0	0
Slim Sallee, p	.000	2	4	0	0	0	0	0	0	0	0	0
Jimmy Smith, pr	.000	1	0	0	0	0	0	0	0	0	0	0
Ivey Wingo, c	.571	3	7	1	4	0	0	0	1	3	1	0
TOTAL	.255		251	35	64	10	7	0	33	25	22	7

PITCHER	W	L	ERA	G	GS	CG	SV	SHO	IP	H	ER	BB	SO
Hod Eller	2	0	2.00	2	2	2	0	1	18.0	13	4	2	15
Ray Fisher	0	1	2.35	2	1	0	0	0	7.2	7	2	2	2
Dolf Luque	0	0	0.00	2	0	0	0	0	5.0	1	0	0	6
Jimmy Ring	1	1	0.64	2	1	1	0	1	14.0	7	1	6	4
Dutch Ruether	1	0	2.57	2	2	1	0	0	14.0	12	4	4	1
Slim Sallee	1	1	1.35	2	2	1	0	0	13.1	19	2	1	2
TOTAL	5	3	1.63	12	8	5	0	2	72.0	59	13	15	30

CHI (A)

PLAYER/POS	AVG	G	AB	R	H	2B	3B	HR	RB	BB	SO	SB
Eddie Cicotte, p	.000	3	8	0	0	0	0	0	0	0	3	0
Eddie Collins, 2b	.226	8	31	2	7	1	0	0	1	1	2	1
Shano Collins, of	.250	4	16	2	4	1	0	0	0	0	0	0
Happy Felsch, of	.192	8	26	2	5	1	0	0	3	1	4	0
Chick Gandil, 1b	.233	8	30	1	7	0	1	0	5	1	3	1
Joe Jackson, of	.375	8	32	5	12	3	0	1	6	1	2	0
Bill James, p	.000	1	2	0	0	0	0	0	0	0	1	0
Dickie Kerr, p	.167	2	6	0	1	0	0	0	0	0	0	0
Nemo Leibold, of	.056	5	18	0	1	0	0	0	0	2	3	1
Grover Lowdermilk, p	.000	1	0	0	0	0	0	0	0	0	0	0
Byrd Lynn, c	.000	1	1	0	0	0	0	0	0	0	0	0
Erskine Mayer, p	.000	1	0	0	0	0	0	0	0	0	0	0
Fred McMullin, ph	.500	2	2	0	1	0	0	0	0	0	0	0
Eddie Murphy, ph	.000	2	2	0	0	0	0	0	0	0	1	0
Swede Risberg, ss	.080	8	25	3	2	0	1	0	0	5	3	1
Ray Schalk, c	.304	8	23	1	7	0	0	0	2	4	2	1
Buck Weaver, 3b	.324	8	34	4	11	4	1	0	0	0	2	0
Roy Wilkinson, p	.000	2	2	0	0	0	0	0	0	0	1	0
Lefty Williams, p	.200	3	5	0	1	0	0	0	0	0	3	0
TOTAL	.224		263	20	59	10	3	1	17	15	30	5

PITCHER	W	L	ERA	G	GS	CG	SV	SHO	IP	H	ER	BB	SO
Eddie Cicotte	1	2	2.91	3	3	2	0	0	21.2	19	7	5	7
Bill James	0	0	5.79	1	0	0	0	0	4.2	8	3	3	2
Dickie Kerr	2	0	1.42	2	2	2	0	0	19.0	14	3	3	6
Grover Lowdermilk	0	0	9.00	1	0	0	0	0	1.0	2	1	1	0
Erskine Mayer	0	0	0.00	1	0	0	0	0	1.0	0	0	1	0
Roy Wilkinson	0	0	1.23	2	0	0	0	0	7.1	9	1	4	3
Lefty Williams	0	3	6.61	3	3	1	0	0	16.1	12	12	8	4
TOTAL	3	5	3.42	13	8	5	0	1	71.0	64	27	25	22

GAME 1 AT CIN OCT 1

CHI   010 000 000   1 6 1
CIN   100 500 21X   9 14 1
Pitchers: CICOTTE, Wilkinson (4),
   Lowdermilk (8) vs RUETHER
Attendance: 30,511

GAME 2 AT CIN OCT 2

CHI   000 000 200   2 10 1
CIN   000 301 00X   4 4 2
Pitchers: WILLIAMS vs SALLEE
Attendance: 29,690

GAME 3 AT CHI OCT 3

CIN   000 000 000   0 3 1
CHI   020 100 00X   3 7 0
Pitchers: FISHER, Luque (8) vs KERR
Attendance: 29,126

GAME 4 AT CHI OCT 4

CIN   000 020 000   2 5 2
CHI   000 000 000   0 3 2
Pitchers: RING vs CICOTTE
Attendance: 34,363

GAME 5 AT CHI OCT 6

CIN   000 004 001   5 4 0
CHI   000 000 000   0 3 3
Pitchers: ELLER vs WILLIAMS,
   Mayer (9)
Attendance: 34,379

GAME 6 AT CIN OCT 7

CHI   000 013 000 1   5 10 3
CIN   002 200 000 0   4 11 0
Pitchers: KERR vs Ruether, RING (6)
Attendance: 32,006

GAME 7 AT CIN OCT 8

CHI   101 020 000   4 10 1
CIN   000 001 000   1 7 4
Pitchers: CICOTTE vs SALLEE,
   Fisher (5), Luque (6)
Attendance: 13,923

GAME 8 AT CHI OCT 9

CIN   410 013 010   10 16 2
CHI   001 000 040   5 10 1
Pitchers: ELLER vs WILLIAMS,
   James (1), Wilkinson (6)
Home Runs: Jackson-CHI
Attendance: 32,930

The Indians outscored the Robins in the Series, 21-8. Yet after losing the opener in Brooklyn, the Robins fought back to take the next two, and held the Series lead as the teams traveled to Cleveland for the next four games.

Both clubs garnered five hits in Game 1, but an error, walk, single, and double gave the Indians two runs in the second and a lead they never yielded, as Stan Coveleski outlasted Rube Marquard for the win. In Game 2, both clubs increased their hit totals to seven, but the Robins bunched six of theirs into three innings for three runs, while Burleigh Grimes, only once yielding two hits in an inning, shut the Indians out. The two runs Brooklyn scored in the first inning of Game 3 were all Sherry Smith needed to give the Robins their second win behind his three-hit pitching. But Brooklyn scored only twice more in the Series as the Indians swept to the championship with four wins in Cleveland.

With the Indians scoring four runs in Game 4 before Brooklyn put its one run on the board, Coveleski breezed to his second five-hit Series run. Jim Bagby had it even easier the next day. The Robins tagged him for 13 hits, but not until the ninth inning were they able to put them together for a run. Meanwhile Bagby and his teammates were registering a couple of Series firsts as they moved to an eight-run lead. Right fielder Elmer Smith opened the scoring in the first inning with the first World Series grand slam, and Bagby himself homered for three more in the fourth—the first pitcher to hit a Series home run.

But the 1920 Series is best remembered for second baseman Bill Wambsganss' unassisted triple play in the fifth inning. With runners on first and second going on pitcher Clarence Mitchell's liner, Wambsganss snared the ball for the first out, stepped on second to force one runner, and tagged the runner coming in from first to retire the side.

In Game 6 Duster Mails, a late-season addition to the team, shut out Brooklyn on three hits in a 1–0 squeaker over Sherry Smith. Coveleski won the clincher the next day, also via the shutout, with his third five-hitter of the Series and his third Series win.

Cleveland Indians (AL), 5; Brooklyn Robins (NL), 2

CLE (A)

PLAYER/POS	AVG	G	AB	R	H	2B	3B	HR	RB	BB	SO	SB
Jim Bagby, p	.333	2	6	1	2	0	0	1	3	0	0	0
George Burns, 1b-4	.300	5	10	1	3	1	0	0	3	3	3	0
Ray Caldwell, p	.000	1	0	0	0	0	0	0	0	0	0	0
Stan Coveleski, p	.100	3	10	2	1	0	0	0	0	0	4	0
Joe Evans, of	.308	4	13	0	4	0	0	0	0	1	0	0
Larry Gardner, 3b	.208	7	24	1	5	1	0	0	2	1	1	0
Jack Graney, of-2	.000	3	3	0	0	0	0	0	0	0	2	0
Charlie Jamieson, of-5	.333	6	15	2	5	1	0	0	1	1	0	1
Doc Johnston, 1b	.273	5	11	1	3	0	0	0	0	2	1	1
Harry Lunte, 2b	.000	1	0	0	0	0	0	0	0	0	0	0
Duster Mails, p	.000	2	5	0	0	0	0	0	0	0	1	0
Les Nunamaker, c-1	.500	2	2	0	1	0	0	0	0	0	0	0
Steve O'Neill, c	.333	7	21	1	7	3	0	0	2	4	3	0
Joe Sewell, ss	.174	7	23	0	4	0	0	0	0	2	1	0
Elmer Smith, of	.308	5	13	1	4	0	1	1	5	1	1	0
Tris Speaker, of	.320	7	25	6	8	2	1	0	1	3	1	0
Pinch Thomas, c	.000	1	0	0	0	0	0	0	0	0	0	0
George Uhle, p	.000	2	0	0	0	0	0	0	0	0	0	0
Bill Wambgsanss, 2b	.154	7	26	3	4	0	0	0	1	2	1	0
Joe Wood, of	.200	4	10	2	2	1	0	0	0	1	2	0
TOTAL	.244		217	21	53	9	2	2	18	21	21	2

PITCHER	W	L	ERA	G	GS	CG	SV	SHO	IP	H	ER	BB	SO
Jim Bagby	1	1	1.80	2	2	1	0	0	15.0	20	3	1	3
Ray Caldwell	0	1	27.00	1	1	0	0	0	0.1	2	1	1	0
Stan Coveleski	3	0	0.67	3	3	3	0	1	27.0	15	2	2	8
Duster Mails	1	0	0.00	2	1	1	0	1	15.2	6	0	6	6
George Uhle	0	0	0.00	2	0	0	0	0	3.0	1	0	0	3
TOTAL	5	2	0.89	10	7	5	0	2	61.0	44	6	10	20

BRO (N)

PLAYER/POS	AVG	G	AB	R	H	2B	3B	HR	RB	BB	SO	SB
Leon Cadore, p	.000	2	0	0	0	0	0	0	0	0	0	0
Tommy Griffith, of	.190	7	21	1	4	2	0	0	3	0	2	0
Burleigh Grimes, p	.333	3	6	1	2	0	0	0	0	0	0	0
Jimmy Johnston, 3b	.214	4	14	2	3	0	0	0	0	0	2	1
Pete Kilduff, 2b	.095	7	21	0	2	0	0	0	0	1	4	0
Ed Konetchy, 1b	.174	7	23	0	4	0	1	0	2	3	2	0
Ernie Krueger, c-3	.167	4	6	0	1	0	0	0	0	0	0	0
Bill Lamar, ph	.000	3	3	0	0	0	0	0	0	0	0	0
Al Mamaux, p	.000	3	1	0	0	0	0	0	0	0	1	0
Rube Marquard, p	.000	2	1	0	0	0	0	0	0	0	0	0
Bill McCabe, pr	.000	1	0	0	0	0	0	0	0	0	0	0
Otto Miller, c	.143	6	14	0	2	0	0	0	0	1	2	0
Clarence Mitchell, p-1	.333	2	3	0	1	0	0	0	0	0	0	0
Hy Myers, of	.231	7	26	0	6	0	0	0	1	0	1	0
Bernie Neis, of-2	.000	4	5	0	0	0	0	0	0	1	0	0
Ivy Olson, ss	.320	7	25	2	8	1	0	0	0	3	1	0
Jeff Pfeffer, p	.000	1	1	0	0	0	0	0	0	0	0	0
Ray Schmandt, ph	.000	1	1	0	0	0	0	0	0	0	0	0
Jack Sheehan, 3b	.182	3	11	0	2	0	0	0	0	0	1	0
Sherry Smith, p	.000	2	6	0	0	0	0	0	0	0	2	0
Zack Wheat, of	.333	7	27	2	9	2	0	0	2	1	2	0
TOTAL	.205		215	8	44	5	1	0	8	10	20	1

PITCHER	W	L	ERA	G	GS	CG	SV	SHO	IP	H	ER	BB	SO
Leon Cadore	0	1	9.00	2	1	0	0	0	2.0	4	2	1	1
Burleigh Grimes	1	2	4.19	3	3	1	0	1	19.1	23	9	9	4
Al Mamaux	0	0	4.50	3	0	0	0	0	4.0	2	2	0	5
Rube Marquard	0	1	3.00	2	1	0	0	0	9.0	7	3	3	6
Clarence Mitchell	0	0	0.00	1	0	0	0	0	4.2	3	0	3	1
Jeff Pfeffer	0	0	3.00	1	0	0	0	0	3.0	4	1	2	1
Sherry Smith	1	1	0.53	2	2	2	0	1	17.0	10	1	3	3
TOTAL	2	5	2.75	14	7	3	0	1	59.0	53	18	21	21

GAME 1 AT BRO OCT 5

CLE	020	100	000	3 5 0
BRO	000	000	100	1 5 1

Pitchers: COVELESKI vs MARQUARD, Mamaux (7), Cadore (9)
Attendance: 23,753

GAME 2 AT BRO OCT 6

CLE	000	000	000	0 7 1
BRO	101	010	00X	3 7 0

Pitchers: BAGBY, Uhle (7) vs GRIMES
Attendance: 22,559

GAME 3 AT BRO OCT 7

CLE	000	100	000	1 3 1
BRO	200	000	00X	2 6 1

Pitchers: CALDWELL, Mails (1), Uhle (8) vs SMITH
Attendance: 25,088

GAME 4 AT CLE OCT 9

BRO	000	100	000	1 5 1
CLE	202	001	00X	5 12 2

Pitchers: CADORE, Mamaux (2), Marquard (3), Pfeffer (6) vs COVELESKI
Attendance: 25,734

GAME 5 AT CLE OCT 10

BRO	000	000	001	1 13 1
CLE	400	310	00X	8 12 2

Pitchers: GRIMES, Mitchell (4) vs BAGBY
Home Runs: E.Smith-CLE, Bagby-CLE
Attendance: 26,884

GAME 6 AT CLE OCT 11

BRO	000	000	000	0 3 0
CLE	000	001	00X	1 7 3

Pitchers: SMITH vs MAILS
Attendance: 27,194

GAME 7 AT CLE OCT 12

BRO	000	000	000	0 5 2
CLE	000	110	10X	3 7 3

Pitchers: GRIMES, Mamaux (8) vs COVELESKI
Attendance: 27,525

Since both the Giants and Yankees called the Polo Grounds home, all eight games were played there, with the two clubs alternating from game to game as the home team. Pitching dominated the first two games—especially Yankees pitching. In Game 1, Giant third baseman Frank Frisch went 4-for-4 against Carl Mays. But Mays gave up only one other hit and walked no one, to fashion a shutout. The next day Art Nehf of the Giants allowed the Yankees only three singles. But the Yankees capitalized on two of them, together with one of Nehf's seven walks, a couple of Giants errors, and Bob Meusel's steal of home to score three times, as pitcher Waite Hoyt shut out the Giants on two singles to put the Yanks two up in the Series.

In Game 3 the hitters finally came alive. With the score tied 4–4 in the last of the seventh, the Giants unloaded for eight hits which, with two walks and a sacrifice fly, produced eight runs and the first Giants win. They evened the Series the next day, scoring three runs in the eighth to take a 3–1 lead, adding another in the ninth. Babe Ruth's first World Series home run, a solo shot in the bottom of the ninth, thrilled the fans but had no effect on the game's outcome.

The Yankees regained the Series lead in Game 5. Waite Hoyt was not as sharp as he had been in the opener, yielding ten hits. But the only run scored against him came as the result of a first-inning error, a deficit his Yankees teammates overcame for a 3–1 win. In Game 6 the Yankees took a quick 3–0 lead in the first. The Giants tied it in the top of the second on home runs by Irish Meusel and Frank Snyder, but Chick Fewster hit a two-run shot a half inning later to restore the Yankees lead. In the fourth inning, though, the Giants parlayed four singles and an error into four runs and a lead that held up for a Series-tying win.

The Yankees scored only one run the rest of the way as the Giants took the final two games on unearned runs. In Game 7, Mays and the Giants' Phil Douglas dueled into the seventh tied 1–1. But in the last of the seventh, Frank Snyder's double drove in Johnny Rawlings, who had reached on an error, for the game's deciding run. In Game 8, Hoyt held the Giants to four hits and completed his third game without giving up an earned run. But a Giants runner had scored in the first inning when a grounder shot through the legs of shortstop Roger Peckinpaugh. It turned out to be the game's only run, as Art Nehf and his Giants' flawless fielding blanked the Yankees to give manager John Mc-Graw his first world championship since 1905.

New York Giants (NL), 5; New York Yankees (AL), 3

NY (N)

PLAYER/POS	AVG	G	AB	R	H	2B	3B	HR	RB	BB	SO	SB
Dave Bancroft, ss	.152	8	33	3	5	1	0	0	3	1	5	0
Jesse Barnes, p	.444	3	9	3	4	0	0	0	0	0	0	0
George Burns, of	.333	8	33	4	11	4	1	0	2	3	5	1
Phil Douglas, p	.000	3	7	0	0	0	0	0	0	0	2	0
Frankie Frisch, 3b	.300	8	30	5	9	0	1	0	1	4	3	3
George Kelly, 1b	.233	8	30	3	7	1	0	0	4	3	10	0
Irish Meusel, of	.345	8	29	4	10	2	1	1	7	2	3	1
Art Nehf, p	.000	3	9	0	0	0	0	0	0	1	3	0
Johnny Rawlings, 2b	.333	8	30	2	10	3	0	0	4	0	3	0
Earl Smith, c-2	.000	3	7	0	0	0	0	0	0	1	0	0
Frank Snyder, c-6	.364	7	22	4	8	1	0	1	3	0	2	0
Fred Toney, p	.000	2	0	0	0	0	0	0	0	0	0	0
Ross Youngs, of	.280	8	25	3	7	1	1	0	4	7	2	2
TOTAL	.269		264	29	71	13	4	2	28	22	38	7

PITCHER	W	L	ERA	G	GS	CG	SV	SHO	IP	H	ER	BB	SO
Jesse Barnes	2	0	1.65	3	0	0	0	0	16.1	10	3	6	18
Phil Douglas	2	1	2.08	3	3	2	0	0	26.0	20	6	5	17
Art Nehf	1	2	1.38	3	3	3	0	1	26.0	13	4	13	8
Fred Toney	0	0	23.63	2	2	0	0	0	2.2	7	7	3	1
TOTAL	5	3	2.54	11	8	5	0	1	71.0	50	20	27	44

NY (A)

PLAYER/POS	AVG	G	AB	R	H	2B	3B	HR	RB	BB	SO	SB
Frank Baker, 3b-2	.250	4	8	0	2	0	0	0	0	1	0	0
Rip Collins, p	.000	1	0	0	0	0	0	0	0	0	0	0
Al DeVormer, c-1	.000	2	1	0	0	0	0	0	0	0	0	0
Chick Fewster, of	.200	4	10	3	2	0	0	1	2	3	3	0
Harry Harper, p	.000	1	0	0	0	0	0	0	0	0	0	0
Waite Hoyt, p	.222	3	9	0	2	0	0	0	1	0	1	0
Carl Mays, p	.111	3	9	0	1	0	0	0	0	0	1	0
Mike McNally, 3b	.200	7	20	3	4	1	0	0	1	3	2	2
Bob Meusel, of	.200	8	30	3	6	2	0	0	3	2	5	1
Elmer Miller, of	.161	8	31	3	5	1	0	0	2	2	5	0
Roger Peckinpaugh, ss	.179	8	28	2	5	1	0	0	0	4	3	0
Bill Piercy, p	.000	1	0	0	0	0	0	0	0	0	0	0
Wally Pipp, 1b	.154	8	26	1	4	1	0	0	2	2	3	1
Jack Quinn, p	.000	1	2	0	0	0	0	0	0	0	1	0
Tom Rogers, p	.000	1	0	0	0	0	0	0	0	0	0	0
Babe Ruth, of	.313	5	16	3	5	0	0	1	4	5	8	2
Wally Schang, c	.286	8	21	6	6	1	0	1	1	5	4	0
Bob Shawkey, p	.500	2	4	2	2	0	0	0	0	0	1	0
Aaron Ward, 2b	.231	8	26	1	6	0	0	0	4	2	6	0
TOTAL	.207		241	22	50	7	1	2	20	27	44	6

PITCHER	W	L	ERA	G	GS	CG	SV	SHO	IP	H	ER	BB	SO
Rip Collins	0	0	54.00	1	0	0	0	0	0.2	4	4	1	0
Harry Harper	0	0	20.25	1	1	0	0	0	1.1	3	3	2	1
Waite Hoyt	2	1	0.00	3	3	3	0	1	27.0	18	0	11	18
Carl Mays	1	2	1.73	3	3	3	0	1	26.0	20	5	0	9
Bill Piercy	0	0	0.00	1	0	0	0	0	1.0	2	0	0	2
Jack Quinn	0	1	9.82	1	0	0	0	0	3.2	8	4	2	2
Tom Rogers	0	0	6.75	1	0	0	0	0	1.1	3	1	0	1
Bob Shawkey	0	1	7.00	2	1	0	0	0	9.0	13	7	6	5
TOTAL	3	5	3.09	13	8	6	0	2	70.0	71	24	22	38

GAME 1 AT NY -N OCT 5

NY-A	100	011	000	3	7	0
NY-N	000	000	000	0	5	0

Pitchers: MAYS vs DOUGLAS, Barnes (9)
Attendance: 30,202

GAME 2 AT NY -A OCT 6

NY-N	000	000	000	0	2	3
NY-A	000	100	02X	3	3	0

Pitchers: NEHF vs HOYT
Attendance: 34,939

GAME 3 AT NY -N OCT 7

NY-A	004	000	010	5	8	0
NY-N	004	000	81X	13	20	0

Pitchers: Shawkey, QUINN (3), Collins (7), Rogers (8) vs Toney, BARNES (3)
Attendance: 36,509

GAME 4 AT NY -A OCT 9

NY-N	000	000	031	4	9	1
NY-A	000	010	001	2	7	1

Pitchers: DOUGLAS vs MAYS
Home Runs: Ruth-NY(A)
Attendance: 36,372

GAME 5 AT NY -N OCT 10

NY-A	001	200	000	3	6	1
NY-N	100	000	000	1	10	1

Pitchers: HOYT vs NEHF
Attendance: 35,758

GAME 6 AT NY -A OCT 11

NY-N	030	401	000	8	13	0
NY-A	320	000	000	5	7	2

Pitchers: Toney, BARNES (1) vs Harper, SHAWKEY (2), Piercy (9)
Home Runs: E.Meusel-NY(N), Snyder-NY(N), Fewster-NY(A)
Attendance: 34,283

GAME 7 AT NY -N OCT 12

NY-A	010	000	000	1	8	1
NY-N	000	100	10X	2	6	0

Pitchers: MAYS vs DOUGLAS
Attendance: 36,503

GAME 8 AT NY -A OCT 13

NY-N	100	000	000	1	6	0
NY-A	000	000	000	0	4	1

Pitchers: NEHF vs HOYT
Attendance: 25,410

The Giants didn't quite sweep the Series—a tie in Game 2 interrupted their string of victories—but they shut down the Yankees offense, holding Yankees to three runs or less per game, and Babe Ruth to two hits and a .118 batting average. This Series restored the best-of-seven-games format after three years of best-of-nine.

The Giants had to come from behind to take Game 1. Bullet Joe Bush and Art Nehf hurled shutout ball through five innings before the Yankees scored single runs in the sixth and seventh innings (Ruth driving in the Series' first run for the second year in a row with his single in the sixth). But in the eighth, Bush gave up four straight singles and two runs before Waite Hoyt relieved him with the score tied and men on first and third. Hoyt set down all three men he faced, but the first out—Ross Youngs' fly to center—drove in what proved to be the Giants' winning run.

The Giants led off Game 2 with three first-inning runs on Irish Meusel's home run, but scored no more as Bob Shawkey stopped them for nine innings while his Yankees picked up runs in the first, fourth (on Aaron Ward's homer), and eighth to tie it all up. At the end of the 10th, with 45 minutes left before sundown, the umpires called the game for darkness and provoked a storm of seat cushions and bottles from the stands.

The Giants resumed their winning ways in Game 3 behind Jack Scott's shutout. Scott—picked up by the Giants in midseason—gave up only four hits, walking one, in the Series' top pitching performance. In Game 4 the Yankees scored twice in the first inning, but in the fifth the Giants pounced on Carl Mays for four hits and two runs before the first out was recorded. Before the inning ended, a ground out and another hit had brought two more Giants across the plate, enough to survive Aaron Ward's second Series home run for a 4–3 win.

Game 5, the clincher, showed Nehf the winner by two runs at game's end, but the game went back and forth before the outcome was decided. Nehf gave up only five hits—all singles—but all of them contributed toward scoring Yankees runs in the first, fifth, and seventh innings. The Giants took the lead in the second with a pair of runs, but again fell behind until four hits and a walk in the eighth undid pitcher Joe Bush's fine effort, giving the Giants three additional runs and John McGraw his third world title.

New York Giants (NL), 4;
New York Yankees (AL), 0; tie, 1

NY (N)

PLAYER/POS	AVG	G	AB	R	H	2B	3B	HR	RB	BB	SO	SB
Dave Bancroft, ss	.211	5	19	4	4	0	0	0	2	2	1	0
Jesse Barnes, p	.000	1	4	0	0	0	0	0	0	0	1	0
Bill Cunningham, of	.200	4	10	0	2	0	0	0	2	2	1	0
Frankie Frisch, 2b	.471	5	17	3	8	1	0	0	2	1	0	1
Heinie Groh, 3b	.474	5	19	4	9	0	1	0	0	2	1	0
George Kelly, 1b	.278	5	18	0	5	0	0	0	2	0	3	0
Lee King, of	1.000	2	1	0	1	0	0	0	1	0	0	0
Hugh McQuillan, p	.250	1	4	1	1	1	0	0	0	0	1	0
Irish Meusel, of	.250	5	20	3	5	0	0	1	7	0	1	0
Art Nehf, p	.000	2	3	0	0	0	0	0	0	2	0	0
Rosy Ryan, p	.000	1	0	0	0	0	0	0	0	0	0	0
Jack Scott, p	.250	1	4	0	1	0	0	0	0	0	1	0
Earl Smith, c-1	.143	4	7	0	1	0	0	0	0	0	2	0
Frank Snyder, c	.333	4	15	1	5	0	0	0	0	0	1	0
Casey Stengel, of	.400	2	5	0	2	0	0	0	0	0	1	0
Ross Youngs, of	.375	5	16	2	6	0	0	0	2	3	1	0
TOTAL	.309		162	18	50	2	1	1	18	12	15	1

PITCHER	W	L	ERA	G	GS	CG	SV	SHO	IP	H	ER	BB	SO
Jesse Barnes	0	0	1.80	1	1	1	0	0	10.0	8	2	2	6
Hugh McQuillan	1	0	3.00	1	1	1	0	0	9.0	8	3	2	4
Art Nehf	1	0	2.25	2	2	1	0	0	16.0	11	4	3	6
Rosy Ryan	1	0	0.00	1	0	0	0	0	2.0	1	0	0	2
Jack Scott	1	0	0.00	1	1	1	0	1	9.0	4	0	1	2
TOTAL	4	0	1.76	6	5	4	0	1	46.0	32	9	8	20

NY (A)

PLAYER/POS	AVG	G	AB	R	H	2B	3B	HR	RB	BB	SO	SB
Frank Baker, ph	.000	1	1	0	0	0	0	0	0	0	0	0
Joe Bush, p	.167	2	6	0	1	0	0	0	1	0	0	0
Joe Dugan, 3b	.250	5	20	4	5	1	0	0	0	0	1	0
Waite Hoyt, p	.500	2	2	0	1	0	0	0	0	0	0	0
Sam Jones, p	.000	2	0	0	0	0	0	0	0	0	0	0
Carl Mays, p	.000	1	2	0	0	0	0	0	0	0	0	0
Norm McMillan, of	.000	1	2	0	0	0	0	0	0	0	0	0
Mike McNally, 2b	.000	1	1	0	0	0	0	0	0	0	0	0
Bob Meusel, of	.300	5	20	2	6	1	0	0	2	1	3	1
Wally Pipp, 1b	.286	5	21	0	6	1	0	0	3	0	2	1
Babe Ruth, of	.118	5	17	1	2	1	0	0	1	2	3	0
Wally Schang, c	.188	5	16	0	3	1	0	0	0	0	3	0
Everett Scott, ss	.143	5	14	0	2	0	0	0	1	1	0	0
Bob Shawkey, p	.000	1	4	0	0	0	0	0	0	0	1	0
Elmer Smith, ph	.000	2	2	0	0	0	0	0	0	0	2	0
Aaron Ward, 2b	.154	5	13	3	2	0	0	2	3	3	3	0
Whitey Witt, of	.222	5	18	1	4	1	1	0	0	1	2	0
TOTAL	.203		158	11	32	6	1	2	11	8	20	2

PITCHER	W	L	ERA	G	GS	CG	SV	SHO	IP	H	ER	BB	SO
Joe Bush	0	2	4.80	2	2	1	0	0	15.0	21	8	5	6
Waite Hoyt	0	1	1.13	2	1	0	0	0	8.0	11	1	2	4
Sam Jones	0	0	0.00	2	0	0	0	0	2.0	1	0	1	0
Carl Mays	0	1	4.50	1	1	0	0	0	8.0	9	4	2	1
Bob Shawkey	0	0	2.70	1	1	1	0	0	10.0	8	3	2	4
TOTAL	0	4	3.35	8	5	2	0	0	43.0	50	16	12	15

GAME 1 AT NY -N OCT 4

NY-A	000 001 100	2	7	0
NY-N	000 000 03X	3	11	3

Pitchers: BUSH, Hoyt (8) vs Nehf, RYAN (8)
Attendance: 36,514

GAME 2 AT NY -A OCT 5

NY-N	300 000 000 0	3	8	1
NY-A	100 100 010 0	3	8	0

Pitchers: Barnes vs Shawkey
Home Runs: E.Meusel-NY(N), Ward-NY(A)
Attendance: 37,020

GAME 3 AT NY -N OCT 6

NY-A	000 000 000	0	4	1
NY-N	002 000 10X	3	12	1

Pitchers: HOYT, Jones (8) vs J.SCOTT
Attendance: 37,620

GAME 4 AT NY -A OCT 7

NY-N	000 040 000	4	9	1
NY-A	200 000 100	3	8	0

Pitchers: McQUILLAN vs MAYS, Jones (9)
Home Runs: Ward-NY(A)
Attendance: 36,242

GAME 5 AT NY -N OCT 8

NY-A	100 010 100	3	5	0
NY-N	020 000 03X	5	10	0

Pitchers: BUSH vs NEHF
Attendance: 38,551

After two Series played entirely in the Polo Grounds, the Giants and Yankees in 1923 had Yankee Stadium across the river to play alternate games in. Celebrating the opener in the new "house that Ruth built," the Yankees took an early three-run lead. In the third inning, though, the Giants drove out starter Waite Hoyt, emerging with four runs. Reliever Joe Bush prevented further scoring for several innings as the Yankees picked up a tying run in the seventh. But with the game still knotted in the top of the ninth, Casey Stengel legged out an inside-the-park homer to win it for the Giants.

Babe Ruth gave Herb Pennock his first World Series win with a pair of homers in Game 2. The first, a solo blast over the roof in right, broke a 1–1 tie in the fourth, and the second, an inning later, concluded the Yankees scoring in their 4–2 win that evened the Series. Stengel sent the Giants ahead in the seventh inning of Game 3, lifting a home run over the fence for the game's only score. The run gave Art Nehf the win in his duel with Sad Sam Jones, and again gave the Giants the Series lead.

Ross Youngs's fourth hit of Game 4, an inside-the-park homer into the Polo Grounds' deep outfield, gave the Giants a fourth run to lead off the bottom of the ninth, but as a rally it fell short; the Yankees, took the game to even the Series. In Game 5 Joe Bush gave up only three Giant hits—a single, double, and triple to Irish Meusel. Irish scored the only Giant run, but his Yankee brother Bob drove in three runs with his three hits—sharing RBI honors with Joe Dugan, whose four hits included the Series' third inside-the-park home run, a three-run shot in the second inning. Final score: 8–1.

In Game 6 Yankees starter Herb Pennock yielded four runs in his seven innings on the mound and seemed on the edge of defeat. But in the top of the eighth, Art Nehf (who had pitched one-hit ball since Ruth homered in the first) lost his stuff. With one out, two singles followed by two walks (on eight pitches) forced in a run. Rosy Ryan replaced Nehf and walked in another run. Ruth struck out, but Bob Meusel's single and a wild throw from center cleared the bases to put the Yankees ahead 6–4, where they remained to game's end for the first of their 24 world championships.

New York Yankees (AL), 4;
New York Giants (NL), 2

NY (A)

PLAYER/POS	AVG	G	AB	R	H	2B	3B	HR	RB	BB	SO	SB
Joe Bush, p-3	.429	4	7	2	3	1	0	0	1	1	1	0
Joe Dugan, 3b	.280	6	25	5	7	2	1	1	5	3	0	0
Hinky Haines, of	.000	2	1	1	0	0	0	0	0	0	0	0
Harvey Hendrick, ph	.000	1	1	0	0	0	0	0	0	0	0	0
Fred Hofmann, ph	.000	2	1	0	0	0	0	0	0	1	0	0
Waite Hoyt, p	.000	1	1	0	0	0	0	0	0	0	1	0
Ernie Johnson, ss-1	.000	2	0	1	0	0	0	0	0	0	0	0
Sam Jones, p	.000	2	2	0	0	0	0	0	0	0	1	0
Bob Meusel, of	.269	6	26	1	7	1	2	0	8	0	3	0
Wally Pipp, 1b	.250	6	20	2	5	0	0	0	2	4	1	0
Babe Ruth, of-6,1b-1	.368	6	19	8	7	1	1	3	3	8	6	0
Wally Schang, c	.318	6	22	3	7	1	0	0	0	1	2	0
Everett Scott, ss	.318	6	22	2	7	0	0	0	3	0	1	0
Bob Shawkey, p	.333	1	3	0	1	0	0	0	1	0	0	0
Aaron Ward, 2b	.417	6	24	4	10	0	0	1	2	1	3	1
Whitey Witt, of	.240	6	25	1	6	2	0	0	0	4	1	0
TOTAL	.293		205	30	60	8	4	5	29	20	22	1

PITCHER	W	L	ERA	G	GS	CG	SV	SHO	IP	H	ER	BB	SO
Joe Bush	1	1	1.08	3	1	1	0	0	16.2	7	2	4	5
Waite Hoyt	0	0	15.43	1	1	0	0	0	2.1	4	4	1	0
Sam Jones	0	1	0.90	2	1	0	1	0	10.0	5	1	2	3
Herb Pennock	2	0	3.63	3	2	1	1	0	17.1	19	7	1	8
Bob Shawkey	1	0	3.52	1	1	0	0	0	7.2	12	3	4	2
TOTAL	4	2	2.83	10	6	2	2	0	54.0	47	17	12	18

NY (N)

PLAYER/POS	AVG	G	AB	R	H	2B	3B	HR	RB	BB	SO	SB
Dave Bancroft, ss	.083	6	24	1	2	0	0	0	0	1	1	2	1
Virgil Barnes, p	.000	2	1	0	0	0	0	0	0	0	1	0
Jack Bentley, p-2	.600	5	5	0	3	1	0	0	4	0	0	0
Bill Cunningham, of-3	.143	4	7	0	1	0	0	0	1	0	1	0
Frankie Frisch, 2b	.400	6	25	2	10	0	1	0	1	0	0	0
Dinty Gearin, p	.000	1	0	0	0	0	0	0	0	0	0	0
Hank Gowdy, c-2	.000	3	4	0	0	0	0	0	0	0	0	0
Heinie Groh, 3b	.182	6	22	3	4	0	1	0	2	3	1	0
Travis Jackson, ph	.000	1	1	0	0	0	0	0	0	0	0	0
Claude Jonnard, p	.000	2	0	0	0	0	0	0	0	0	0	0
George Kelly, 1b	.182	6	22	1	4	0	0	0	1	1	2	0
Freddie Maguire, pr	.000	2	0	1	0	0	0	0	0	0	0	0
Hugh McQuillan, p	.000	2	3	0	0	0	0	0	0	0	0	0
Irish Meusel, of	.280	6	25	3	7	1	1	1	2	0	0	0
Art Nehf, p	.167	2	6	0	1	0	0	0	0	0	4	0
Jimmy O'Connell, ph	.000	2	1	0	0	0	0	0	0	0	0	0
Rosy Ryan, p	.000	3	2	0	0	0	0	0	0	0	1	0
Jack Scott, p	.000	2	1	0	0	0	0	0	0	0	0	0
Frank Snyder, c	.118	5	17	1	2	0	0	1	2	0	2	0
Casey Stengel, of	.417	6	12	3	5	0	0	2	4	4	0	0
Mule Watson, p	.000	1	0	0	0	0	0	0	0	0	0	0
Ross Youngs, of	.348	6	23	2	8	0	0	1	3	2	0	1
TOTAL	.234		201	17	47	2	3	5	17	12	18	1

PITCHER	W	L	ERA	G	GS	CG	SV	SHO	IP	H	ER	BB	SO
Virgil Barnes	0	0	0.00	2	0	0	0	0	4.2	4	0	0	4
Jack Bentley	0	1	9.45	2	1	0	0	0	6.2	10	7	4	1
Claude Jonnard	0	0	0.00	2	0	0	0	0	2.0	1	0	1	1
Hugh McQuillan	0	1	5.00	2	1	0	0	0	9.0	11	5	4	3
Art Nehf	1	1	2.76	2	2	1	0	1	16.1	10	5	6	7
Rosy Ryan	1	0	0.96	3	0	0	0	0	9.1	11	1	3	3
Jack Scott	0	1	12.00	2	1	0	0	0	3.0	9	4	1	2
Mule Watson	0	0	13.50	1	1	0	0	0	2.0	4	3	1	1
TOTAL	2	4	4.25	16	6	1	0	1	53.0	60	25	20	22

GAME 1 AT NY -A OCT 10

NY-N	004 000 001	5 8 0
NY-A	120 000 100	4 12 1

Pitchers: Watson, RYAN (3) vs Hoyt, BUSH (3)
Home Runs: Stengel-NY(N)
Attendance: 55,307

GAME 2 AT NY -N OCT 11

NY-A	010 210 000	4 10 0
NY-N	010 001 000	2 9 2

Pitchers: PENNOCK vs McQUILLAN, Bentley (4)
Home Runs: Ward-NY(A),
E.Meusel-NY(N), Ruth-NY(A) (2)
Attendance: 40,402

GAME 3 AT NY -A OCT 12

NY-N	000 000 100	1 4 0
NY-A	000 000 000	0 6 1

Pitchers: NEHF vs JONES, Bush (9)
Home Runs: Stengel-NY(N)
Attendance: 62,430

GAME 4 AT NY -N OCT 13

NY-A	061 100 000	8 13 1
NY-N	000 000 031	4 13 1

Pitchers: SHAWKEY, Pennock (8) vs J.SCOTT, Ryan (2), McQuillan (2), Jonnard (8), Barnes (9)
Home Runs: Youngs-NY(N)
Attendance: 46,302

GAME 5 AT NY -A OCT 14

NY-N	010 000 000	1 3 2
NY-A	340 100 00X	8 14 0

Pitchers: BENTLEY, J.Scott (2), Barnes (4), Jonnard (8) vs BUSH
Home Runs: Dugan-NY(A)
Attendance: 62,817

GAME 6 AT NY -N OCT 15

NY-A	100 000 050	6 5 0
NY-N	100 111 000	4 10 1

Pitchers: PENNOCK, Jones (8) vs NEHF, Ryan (8)
Home Runs: Ruth-NY(A), Snyder-NY(N)
Attendance: 34,172

Four of the seven games in this exciting Series were decided by one run—two of them after 12 innings. Pitcher Walter Johnson, in his first World Series after 18 big-league seasons and 376 victories, opened for Washington against the Giants' Art Nehf. Although 14 Giants reached base on hits or walks in the first nine innings, only two scored—George Kelly and Bill Terry, both of whom homered. In the bottom of the ninth, the Senators scored their second run to send the game into extra innings. Johnson shut out the Giants for two more frames, but in the top of the 12th, two walks and three singles put New York ahead by two. Washington came back with a run and had a man on third. But Kelly, making his only appearance at second base, stopped Goose Goslin's grounder with his bare hand, and Nehf had the Giants' first win.

Goslin and manager/second baseman Bucky Harris homered in Game 2 to give the Senators a 3–0 lead through six innings. The Giants scored once in the seventh and drove out starter Tom Zachary with two more in the ninth to tie the game, but in the last of the ninth Roger Peckinpaugh doubled in the tie breaker to even the Series.

The Giants took an early lead in Game 3 and held it to retake the Series lead, but Washington (led by Goslin's three-run homer in the third) unleashed a 13-hit, seven-run attack the next day to even the Series once more. In Game 5, though, New York pulled ahead again, defeating Johnson a second time as winning pitcher Jack Bentley put the Giants into the lead for good with a two-run homer in the fifth. In Game 6, Washington's two runs in the fifth inning overcame a first-inning Giant run and gave Tom Zachary all he needed for the Senators' third win, which set the stage for one of the most memorable games in Series history.

Washington scored first in Game 7 on manager Harris' homer in the fourth inning, but the Giants scored three runs in the sixth (two of them on Senator errors) to go ahead, 3–1. In the last of the eighth, though, Harris's grounder to third bounced over the head of rookie Freddie Lindstrom for two more Senator runs and a 3–3 tie. Walter Johnson came in to face the Giants in the ninth, and shut them out through the twelfth, fanning five. Then, in the bottom of the 12th, with one out, Muddy Ruel (given a second chance after Giants catcher Hank Gowdy caught his foot in his mask and missed Ruel's pop foul) doubled to left. Pitcher Johnson then reached first when shortstop Travis Jackson bobbled what should have been a third-out grounder. With men on second and first, Earl McNeely bounced to

Lindstrom at third. But again the ball bounded over Lindstrom's head, and Ruel raced home with Johnson's first Series win and Washington's only world championship.

Washington Senators (AL), 4; New York Giants (NL), 3

WAS (A)

PLAYER/POS	AVG	G	AB	R	H	2B	3B	HR	RB	BB	SO	SB
Ossie Bluege, ss-5,3b-4	.192	7	26	2	5	0	0	0	3	3	4	1
Goose Goslin, of	.344	7	32	4	11	1	0	3	7	0	7	0
Bucky Harris, 2b	.333	7	33	5	11	0	0	2	7	1	4	0
Walter Johnson, p	.111	3	9	0	1	0	0	0	0	0	0	0
Joe Judge, 1b	.385	7	26	4	10	1	0	0	0	5	2	0
Nemo Leibold, of-1	.167	3	6	1	1	1	0	0	0	1	0	0
Firpo Marberry, p	.000	4	2	0	0	0	0	0	0	0	0	0
Joe Martina, p	.000	1	0	0	0	0	0	0	0	0	0	0
Earl McNeely, of	.222	7	27	4	6	3	0	0	1	4	4	1
Ralph Miller, 3b	.182	4	11	0	2	0	0	0	2	1	0	0
George Mogridge, p	.000	2	5	0	0	0	0	0	0	0	5	0
Curly Ogden, p	.000	1	0	0	0	0	0	0	0	0	0	0
Roger Peckinpaugh, ss	.417	4	12	1	5	2	0	0	2	1	0	1
Sam Rice, of	.207	7	29	2	6	0	0	0	1	3	2	2
Muddy Ruel, c	.095	7	21	2	2	1	0	0	0	0	6	1
Allan Russell, p	.000	1	0	0	0	0	0	0	0	0	0	0
Mule Shirley, ph	.500	3	2	1	1	0	0	0	0	1	0	0
Bennie Tate, ph	.000	3	0	0	0	0	0	0	0	1	3	0
Tommy Taylor, 3b	.000	3	2	0	0	0	0	0	0	0	2	0
Tom Zachary, p	.000	2	5	0	0	0	0	0	0	0	1	3	0
TOTAL	.246		248	26	61	9	0	5	25	29	34	5

PITCHER	W	L	ERA	G	GS	CG	SV	SHO	IP	H	ER	BB	SO
Walter Johnson	1	2	2.25	3	3	2	0	0	24.0	30	6	11	20
Firpo Marberry	0	1	1.13	4	1	0	2	0	8.0	9	1	4	10
Joe Martina	0	0	0.00	1	0	0	0	0	1.0	0	0	0	1
George Mogridge	1	0	2.25	2	1	0	0	0	12.0	7	3	6	5
Curly Ogden	0	0	0.00	1	1	0	0	0	0.1	0	0	1	1
Allan Russell	0	0	3.00	1	0	0	0	0	3.0	4	1	0	0
By Speece	0	0	9.00	1	0	0	0	0	1.0	3	1	0	0
Tom Zachary	2	0	2.04	2	2	1	0	0	17.2	13	4	3	3
TOTAL	4	3	2.15	15	7	3	2	0	67.0	66	16	25	40

NY (N)

PLAYER/POS	AVG	G	AB	R	H	2B	3B	HR	RB	BB	SO	SB
Harry Baldwin, p	.000	1	0	0	0	0	0	0	0	0	0	0
Virgil Barnes, p	.000	2	4	0	0	0	0	0	0	1	2	0
Jack Bentley, p-3	.286	5	7	1	2	0	0	1	2	1	1	0
Wayland Dean, p	.000	1	0	0	0	0	0	0	0	0	0	0
Frankie Frisch, 2b-7,3b-1	.333	7	30	1	10	4	1	0	0	4	1	1
Hank Gowdy, c	.259	7	27	4	7	0	0	0	1	2	2	0
Heinie Groh, ph	1.000	1	1	0	1	0	0	0	0	0	0	0
Travis Jackson, ss	.074	7	27	3	2	0	0	0	1	1	4	1
Claude Jonnard, p	.000	1	0	0	0	0	0	0	0	0	0	0
George Kelly, 1b-4,of-4,2b-1	.290	7	31	7	9	1	0	1	4	1	8	0
Fred Lindstrom, 3b	.333	7	30	1	10	2	0	0	4	3	6	0
Hugh McQuillan, p	1.000	3	1	0	1	0	0	0	1	1	0	0
Irish Meusel, of	.154	4	13	0	2	0	0	0	1	2	0	0
Art Nehf, p	.429	3	7	1	3	0	0	0	0	0	0	0
Rosy Ryan, p	.500	2	2	1	1	0	0	1	2	0	0	0
Frank Snyder, ph	.000	1	1	0	0	0	0	0	0	0	0	0
Billy Southworth, of-2	.000	5	1	1	0	0	0	0	0	0	0	0
Bill Terry, 1b-4	.429	5	14	3	6	0	1	1	1	3	1	0
Mule Watson, p	.000	1	0	0	0	0	0	0	0	0	0	0
Hack Wilson, of	.233	7	30	1	7	1	0	0	3	1	9	0
Ross Youngs, of	.185	7	27	3	5	1	0	0	1	5	6	1
TOTAL	.261		253	27	66	9	2	4	21	25	40	3

PITCHER	W	L	ERA	G	GS	CG	SV	SHO	IP	H	ER	BB	SO
Harry Baldwin	0	0	0.00	1	0	0	0	0	2.0	1	0	0	1
Virgil Barnes	0	1	5.68	2	2	0	0	0	12.2	15	8	1	9
Jack Bentley	1	2	3.18	3	2	1	0	0	17.0	18	6	8	10
Wayland Dean	0	0	4.50	1	0	0	0	0	2.0	3	1	0	2
Claude Jonnard	0	0	–	1	0	0	0	0	0.0	0	0	1	0
Hugh McQuillan	0	1	2.57	3	1	0	1	0	7.0	2	2	6	2
Art Nehf	1	1	1.83	3	2	1	0	0	19.2	15	4	9	7
Rosy Ryan	0	0	3.18	2	0	0	0	0	5.2	7	2	4	3
Mule Watson	0	0	0.00	1	0	0	1	0	0.2	0	0	0	0
TOTAL	3	4	3.10	17	7	2	2	0	66.2	61	23	29	34

Johnson pitched the winning day, this time with a strong seventh. In the Game...

GAME 1 AT WAS OCT 4

```
NY   010 100 000 002   4 14 1
WAS  000 001 001 001   3 10 1
```

Pitchers: NEHF vs JOHNSON
Home Runs: Kelly-NY, Terry-NY
Attendance: 35,760

GAME 2 AT WAS OCT 5

```
NY   000 000 102   3 6 0
WAS  200 010 001   4 6 1
```

Pitchers: BENTLEY vs ZACHARY, Marberry (9)
Home Runs: Goslin-WAS, Harris-WAS
Attendance: 35,922

GAME 3 AT NY OCT 6

```
WAS  000 200 011   4 9 2
NY   021 101 01X   6 12 0
```

Pitchers: MARBERRY, Russell (4), Martina (7), Speece (8) vs McQUILLAN, Ryan (4), Jonnard (9), Watson (9)
Home Runs: Ryan-NY
Attendance: 47,608

GAME 4 AT NY OCT 7

```
WAS  003 020 020   7 13 3
NY   100 001 011   4 6 1
```

Pitchers: MOGRIDGE, Marberry (8) vs BARNES, Baldwin (6), Dean (8)
Home Runs: Goslin-WAS
Attendance: 49,243

GAME 5 AT NY OCT 8

```
WAS  000 100 010   2 9 1
NY   001 020 03X   6 13 0
```

Pitchers: JOHNSON vs BENTLEY, McQuillan (8)
Home Runs: Bentley-NY, Goslin-WAS
Attendance: 49,211

GAME 6 AT WAS OCT 9

```
NY   100 000 000   1 7 1
WAS  000 020 00X   2 4 0
```

Pitchers: NEHF, Ryan (8) vs ZACHARY
Attendance: 34,254

GAME 7 AT WAS OCT 10

```
NY   000 003 000 000   3 8 3
WAS  000 100 020 001   4 10 4
```

Pitchers: Barnes, McQuillan (8), Nehf (10), BENTLEY (11) vs Ogden, Mogridge (1), Marberry (6), JOHNSON (9)
Home Runs: Harris-WAS
Attendance: 31,667

Repeating as pennant winners, the Senators found themselves again locked in a tight Series, this time with the Pirates, who hadn't won a pennant since 1909. Again Walter Johnson pitched the Series opener, winning this time with a strong five-hit, 10-strikeout performance, giving up only one run on Pie Traynor's homer in the fifth. Home runs by Pirates Kiki Cuyler and Glenn Wright and Senator Joe Judge accounted for four of the five runs scored in Game 2, in which Vic Aldridge dueled Stan Coveleski to a narrow 3–2 Pittsburgh win, evening the Series.

Washington took Games 3 and 4, though, for a 3–1 Series advantage, Goose Goslin's solo homer in the sixth inning providing the margin of victory in Game 3, and homers by Goslin (for three runs) and Joe Harris the next day providing all the scoring as Johnson shut the Pirates out.

Harris hit his third Series homer in Game 5, but Pittsburgh overwhelmed Coveleski as he lost to Aldridge for a second time. And although Goslin's third homer gave the Senators an early lead in Game 6, Pittsburgh's Ray Kremer shut Washington out from the third inning on as his teammates pulled even with two runs in the bottom of the third, and Eddie Moore's homer in the fifth gave him the run he needed for a win that sent the Series into a seventh game.

Both clubs went with their best in the finale as Johnson, winner of Games 1 and 4, faced Aldridge, victor in Games 2 and 5. But Aldridge was wild, issuing three walks and two wild pitches in addition to two hits before being yanked with only one out in the top of the first. Johnson was hardly more effective: although he lasted the whole game, he gave up 15 hits and five earned runs. But if there was a Series goat, it would have to be Washington shortstop Roger Peckinpaugh, the American League MVP. Though he drove in a run in the first and homered for another in the eighth, his dropped pop fly in the seventh and wild throw in the eighth (his seventh and eighth errors of the Series) opened the way to four unearned runs and Pittsburgh's 9–7 triumph.

Pittsburgh Pirates (NL), 4;
Washington Senators (AL), 3

PIT (N)

PLAYER/POS	AVG	G	AB	R	H	2B	3B	HR	RB	BB	SO	SB
Babe Adams, p	.000	1	0	0	0	0	0	0	0	0	0	0
Vic Aldridge, p	.000	3	7	0	0	0	0	0	0	0	0	0
Clyde Barnhart, of	.250	7	28	1	7	1	0	0	5	3	5	1
Carson Bigbee, of-1	.333	4	3	1	1	1	0	0	1	0	0	1
Max Carey, of	.458	7	24	6	11	4	0	0	2	2	3	3
Kiki Cuyler, of	.269	7	26	3	7	3	0	1	6	1	4	0
Johnny Gooch, c	.000	3	3	0	0	0	0	0	0	0	0	0
George Grantham, 1b-4	.133	5	15	0	2	0	0	0	0	0	3	1
Ray Kremer, p	.143	3	7	0	1	0	0	0	0	1	5	0
Stuffy McInnis, 1b-3	.286	4	14	0	4	0	0	0	1	0	2	0
Lee Meadows, p	.000	1	1	0	0	0	0	0	0	0	1	0
Eddie Moore, 2b	.231	7	26	7	6	1	0	1	2	5	2	0
Johnny Morrison, p	.500	3	2	1	1	0	0	0	0	0	0	0
Red Oldham, p	.000	1	0	0	0	0	0	0	0	0	0	0
Earl Smith, c	.350	6	20	0	7	1	0	0	0	1	2	0
Pie Traynor, 3b	.346	7	26	2	9	0	2	1	4	3	1	1
Glenn Wright, ss	.185	7	27	3	5	1	0	1	3	1	4	0
Emil Yde, p-1	.000	2	1	1	0	0	0	0	0	0	0	0
TOTAL	.265		230	25	61	12	2	4	25	17	32	7

PITCHER	W	L	ERA	G	GS	CG	SV	SHO	IP	H	ER	BB	SO
Babe Adams	0	0	0.00	1	0	0	0	0	1.0	2	0	0	0
Vic Aldridge	2	0	4.42	3	3	2	0	0	18.1	18	9	9	9
Ray Kremer	2	1	3.00	3	2	2	0	0	21.0	17	7	4	9
Lee Meadows	0	1	3.38	1	1	0	0	0	8.0	6	3	0	4
Johnny Morrison	0	0	2.89	3	0	0	0	0	9.1	11	3	1	7
Red Oldham	0	0	0.00	1	0	0	1	0	1.0	0	0	0	2
Emil Yde	0	1	11.57	1	1	0	0	0	2.1	5	3	3	1
TOTAL	4	1	3.69	13	7	4	1	0	61.0	59	25	17	32

WAS (A)

PLAYER/POS	AVG	G	AB	R	H	2B	3B	HR	RB	BB	SO	SB
Spencer Adams, 2b-1	.000	2	1	0	0	0	0	0	0	0	0	0
Win Ballou, p	.000	2	0	0	0	0	0	0	0	0	0	0
Ossie Bluege, 3b	.278	5	18	2	5	1	0	0	2	0	4	0
Stan Coveleski, p	.000	2	3	0	0	0	0	0	0	1	2	0
Alex Ferguson, p	.000	2	4	0	0	0	0	0	0	0	3	0
Goose Goslin, of	.308	7	26	6	8	1	0	3	6	3	3	0
Joe Harris, of	.440	7	25	5	11	2	0	3	6	3	4	0
Bucky Harris, 2b	.087	7	23	2	2	0	0	0	0	1	3	0
Walter Johnson, p	.091	3	11	0	1	0	0	0	0	0	3	0
Joe Judge, 1b	.174	7	23	2	4	1	0	1	4	3	2	0
Nemo Leibold, ph	.500	3	2	1	1	1	0	0	0	1	0	0
Firpo Marberry, p	.000	2	0	0	0	0	0	0	0	0	0	0
Earl McNeely, of-2	.000	4	2	0	0	0	0	0	0	0	0	1
Buddy Myer, 3b	.250	3	8	0	2	0	0	0	0	1	2	0
Roger Peckinpaugh, ss	.250	7	24	1	6	1	0	1	3	1	2	1
Sam Rice, of	.364	7	33	5	12	0	0	0	3	0	1	0
Muddy Ruel, c	.316	7	19	0	6	1	0	0	1	3	2	0
Dutch Ruether, ph	.000	1	1	0	0	0	0	0	0	0	1	0
Hank Severeid, c	.333	1	3	0	1	0	0	0	0	0	0	0
Bobby Veach, ph	.000	2	1	0	0	0	0	0	0	1	0	0
Tom Zachary, p	.000	1	0	0	0	0	0	0	0	0	0	0
TOTAL	.262		225	26	59	8	0	8	26	17	32	2

PITCHER	W	L	ERA	G	GS	CG	SV	SHO	IP	H	ER	BB	SO
Win Ballou	0	0	0.00	2	0	0	0	0	1.2	0	0	1	1
Stan Coveleski	0	2	3.77	2	2	1	0	0	14.1	16	6	5	3
Alex Ferguson	1	1	3.21	2	2	1	0	0	14.0	13	5	6	11
Walter Johnson	2	1	2.08	3	3	3	0	1	26.0	26	6	4	15
Firpo Marberry	0	0	0.00	2	0	0	1	0	2.1	3	0	0	2
Tom Zachary	0	0	10.80	1	0	0	0	0	1.2	3	2	1	0
TOTAL	3	4	2.85	12	7	4	1	1	60.0	61	19	17	32

GAME 1 AT PIT OCT 7

WAS	010 020 001	4	8	1
PIT	000 010 000	1	5	0

Pitchers: JOHNSON vs MEADOWS, Morrison (9)
Home Runs: J.Harris-WAS, Traynor-PIT
Attendance: 41,723

GAME 2 AT PIT OCT 8

WAS	010 000 001	2	8	2
PIT	000 100 02X	3	7	0

Pitchers: COVELESKI vs ALDRIDGE
Home Runs: Judge-WAS, Wright-PIT, Cuyler-PIT
Attendance: 43,364

GAME 3 AT WAS OCT 10

PIT	010 101 000	3	8	3
WAS	001 001 20X	4	10	1

Pitchers: KREMER vs FERGUSON, Marberry (8)
Home Runs: Goslin-WAS
Attendance: 36,495

GAME 4 AT WAS OCT 11

PIT	000 000 000	0	6	1
WAS	004 000 00X	4	12	0

Pitchers: YDE, Morrison (3), Adams (8) vs JOHNSON
Home Runs: Goslin-WAS, J.Harris-WAS
Attendance: 38,701

GAME 5 AT WAS OCT 12

PIT	002 000 211	6	13	0
WAS	100 100 100	3	8	1

Pitchers: ALDRIDGE vs COVELESKI, Ballou (7), Zachary (8), Marberry (9)
Home Runs: J.Harris-WAS
Attendance: 35,899

GAME 6 AT PIT OCT 13

WAS	110 000 000	2	6	2
PIT	002 010 00X	3	7	1

Pitchers: FERGUSON, Ballou (8) vs KREMER
Home Runs: Goslin-WAS, Moore-PIT
Attendance: 43,810

GAME 7 AT PIT OCT 15

WAS	400 200 010	7	7	2
PIT	003 010 23X	9	15	2

Pitchers: JOHNSON vs Aldridge, Morrison (1), KREMER (5), Oldham (9)
Home Runs: Peckinpaugh-WAS
Attendance: 42,856

The Yankees, returning to the World Series after a two-year absence, faced the Cardinals, who had won their first pennant since joining the National League in 1892. Both clubs led their league in slugging and runs scored; this power erupted occasionally in the Series, but over all, pitching dominated as each staff bettered its regular-season earned run average by nearly a run per game.

Herb Pennock of the Yankees pitched a splendid three-hitter in the opener. After yielding two hits and a run in the first inning, he shut out the Cards the rest of the way, holding them hitless until the ninth. St. Louis starter Bill Sherdel also pitched effectively, but three walks in the first and a hit-sacrifice-hit sandwich in the sixth brought in enough runs to beat him.

In Game 2, the veteran Grover Cleveland Alexander evened the Series, striking out 10 and holding the Yankees to four singles (three of them in the two-run second) as Billy Southworth and Tommy Thevenow homered for four of St. Louis's six runs. Two days later Jesse Haines put the Cards into the lead, winning the game both ways with a five-hit shutout and a two-run homer.

New York's big bats finally awoke in Game 4. Five Yankees doubled, and Babe Ruth hit three home runs (a World Series record) in a 14-hit, 10-run assault. Yankees pitcher Waite Hoyt also gave up 14 hits, but 12 were singles and only five runs scored. In contrast, Game 5 was a pitchers' duel. Pennock and Sherdel again faced each other and held the opposition to two runs apiece through nine innings. But in the tenth, rookie Tony Lazzeri's sacrifice fly gave New York a 3–2 lead, which Pennock held in the last of the tenth for his second win.

With St. Louis down three games to two, the Series moved to hostile New York for the final games. This didn't seem to trouble the Cardinals, who erupted in Game 6 for their own 10-run game, four of them driven in by Les Bell's first-inning single and seventh-inning home run. Alexander pitched a complete game for his second Series win, and came back the next day to relieve Haines in the seventh with a 3–2 lead and the bases full. He struck out Lazzeri to end the inning and kept the Yankees off the bases until he issued Babe Ruth his 11th Series walk with two away in the ninth. But Ruth, trying to steal second, was caught, and the Cards were world champions.

St. Louis Cardinals (NL), 4; New York Yankees (AL), 3

STL (N)

PLAYER/POS	AVG	G	AB	R	H	2B	3B	HR	RB	BB	SO	SB
Pete Alexander, p	.000	3	7	1	0	0	0	0	0	0	2	0
Hi Bell, p	.000	1	0	0	0	0	0	0	0	0	0	0
Les Bell, 3b	.259	7	27	4	7	1	0	1	6	2	5	0
Jim Bottomley, 1b	.345	7	29	4	10	3	0	0	5	1	2	0
Taylor Douthit, of	.267	4	15	3	4	2	0	0	1	3	2	0
Jake Flowers, ph	.000	3	3	0	0	0	0	0	0	0	1	0
Chick Hafey, of	.185	7	27	2	5	2	0	0	0	0	7	0
Jesse Haines, p	.600	3	5	1	3	0	0	1	2	0	1	0
Bill Hallahan, p	.000	1	0	0	0	0	0	0	0	0	0	0
Wattie Holm, of-4	.125	5	16	1	2	0	0	0	1	1	2	0
Rogers Hornsby, 2b	.250	7	28	2	7	1	0	0	4	2	2	1
Vic Keen, p	.000	1	0	0	0	0	0	0	0	0	0	0
Bob O'Farrell, c	.304	7	23	2	7	1	0	0	2	2	2	0
Art Reinhart, p	.000	1	0	0	0	0	0	0	0	0	0	0
Flint Rhem, p	.000	1	1	0	0	0	0	0	0	0	1	0
Bill Sherdel, p	.000	2	5	0	0	0	0	0	0	0	2	0
Billy Southworth, of	.345	7	29	6	10	1	1	1	4	0	0	1
Tommy Thevenow, ss	.417	7	24	5	10	1	0	1	4	0	1	0
Specs Toporcer, ph	.000	1	0	0	0	0	0	0	0	1	0	0
TOTAL	.272		239	31	65	12	1	4	30	11	30	2

PITCHER	W	L	ERA	G	GS	CG	SV	SHO	IP	H	ER	BB	SO
Pete Alexander	2	0	1.33	3	2	2	1	0	20.1	12	3	4	17
Hi Bell	0	0	9.00	1	0	0	0	0	2.0	4	2	1	1
Jesse Haines	2	0	1.08	3	2	1	0	1	16.2	13	2	9	5
Bill Hallahan	0	0	4.50	1	0	0	0	0	2.0	2	1	3	1
Vic Keen	0	0	0.00	1	0	0	0	0	1.0	0	0	0	0
Art Reinhart	0	1	∞	1	0	0	0	0	0.0	1	4	4	0
Flint Rhem	0	0	6.75	1	1	0	0	0	4.0	7	3	2	4
Bill Sherdel	0	2	2.12	2	2	1	0	0	17.0	15	4	8	3
TOTAL	4	3	2.71	13	7	4	1	1	63.0	54	19	31	31

NY (A)

PLAYER/POS	AVG	G	AB	R	H	2B	3B	HR	RB	BB	SO	SB
Spencer Adams, ph	.000	2	0	0	0	0	0	0	0	0	0	0
Pat Collins, c	.000	3	2	0	0	0	0	0	0	0	1	0
Earle Combs, of	.357	7	28	3	10	2	0	0	2	5	2	0
Joe Dugan, 3b	.333	7	24	2	8	1	0	0	2	1	1	0
Mike Gazella, 3b	.000	1	0	0	0	0	0	0	0	0	0	0
Lou Gehrig, 1b	.348	7	23	1	8	2	0	0	4	5	4	0
Waite Hoyt, p	.000	2	6	0	0	0	0	0	0	0	1	0
Sam Jones, p	.000	1	0	0	0	0	0	0	0	0	0	0
Mark Koenig, ss	.125	7	32	2	4	1	0	0	2	0	6	0
Tony Lazzeri, 2b	.192	7	26	2	5	1	0	0	3	1	6	0
Bob Meusel, of	.238	7	21	3	5	1	0	1	0	6	1	0
Ben Paschal, ph	.250	5	4	0	1	0	0	0	1	1	2	0
Herb Pennock, p	.143	3	7	1	1	1	0	0	0	0	0	0
Dutch Ruether, p-1	.000	3	4	0	0	0	0	0	0	0	0	0
Babe Ruth, of	.300	7	20	6	6	0	0	4	5	11	2	1
Hank Severeid, c	.273	7	22	1	6	1	0	0	1	1	2	0
Bob Shawkey, p	.000	3	2	0	0	0	0	0	0	0	1	0
Urban Shocker, p	.000	2	2	0	0	0	0	0	0	0	2	0
Myles Thomas, p	.000	2	0	0	0	0	0	0	0	0	0	0
TOTAL	.242		223	21	54	10	1	4	20	31	31	1

PITCHER	W	L	ERA	G	GS	CG	SV	SHO	IP	H	ER	BB	SO
Waite Hoyt	1	1	1.20	2	2	1	0	0	15.0	19	2	1	10
Sam Jones	0	0	9.00	1	0	0	0	0	1.0	2	1	2	1
Herb Pennock	2	0	1.23	3	2	2	0	0	22.0	13	3	4	8
Dutch Ruether	0	1	8.31	1	1	0	0	0	4.1	7	4	2	1
Bob Shawkey	0	1	5.40	3	1	0	0	0	10.0	8	6	2	7
Urban Shocker	0	1	5.87	2	1	0	0	0	7.2	13	5	0	3
Myles Thomas	0	0	3.00	2	0	0	0	0	3.0	3	1	0	0
TOTAL	3	4	3.14	14	7	3	0	0	63.0	65	22	11	30

GAME 1 AT NY OCT 2

STL	100 000 000	1	3	1
NY	100 001 00X	2	6	0

Pitchers: SHERDEL, Haines (8) vs PENNOCK
Attendance: 61,658

GAME 2 AT NY OCT 3

STL	002 000 301	6	12	1
NY	020 000 000	2	4	0

Pitchers: ALEXANDER vs SHOCKER, Shawkey (8), Jones (9)
Home Runs: Southworth-STL, Thevenow-STL
Attendance: 63,600

GAME 3 AT STL OCT 5

NY	000 000 000	0	5	1
STL	000 310 00X	4	8	0

Pitchers: RUETHER, Shawkey (5), Thomas (8) vs HAINES
Home Runs: Haines-STL
Attendance: 37,708

GAME 4 AT STL OCT 6

NY	101 142 100	10	14	1
STL	100 300 001	5	14	0

Pitchers: HOYT vs Rhem, REINHART (5), H.Bell (5), Hallahan (7), Keen (9)
Home Runs: Ruth-NY (3)
Attendance: 38,825

GAME 5 AT STL OCT 7

NY	000 001 001 1	3	9	1
STL	000 100 100 0	2	7	1

Pitchers: PENNOCK vs SHERDEL
Attendance: 39,552

GAME 6 AT NY OCT 9

STL	300 010 501	10	13	2
NY	000 100 100	2	8	1

Pitchers: ALEXANDER vs SHAWKEY, Shocker (7), Thomas (8)
Home Runs: L.Bell-STL
Attendance: 48,615

GAME 7 AT NY OCT 10

STL	000 300 000	3	8	0
NY	001 001 000	2	8	3

Pitchers: HAINES, Alexander (7) vs HOYT, Pennock (7)
Home Runs: Ruth-NY
Attendance: 38,093

The Pirates, who struggled to a narrow pennant win in a four-team race, were no slouches at the bat. Their team batting average of .305 led the National League, and in the Waner brothers—Paul and Lloyd—and Pie Traynor they had three of the league's five top hitters. But in the World Series they came up against a Yankees team that is still widely regarded as the game's greatest ever. With 110 season victories and a 19-game margin over second-place Philadelphia, the Yankees led the American League in nearly every offensive category. Three Yankees—Earle Combs, Lou Gehrig, and Babe Ruth—hit over .350, and divided among them league crowns in runs, hits, doubles, triples, home runs (Ruth's 60), RBIs, and slugging average. The Yankees not only hit, but their pitching staff boasted the league's lowest earned run average.

In the Series, though, it was Pittsburgh's erratic play that brought about the first American League sweep. The Pirates scored four times off Waite Hoyt in Game 1, and might have won the game. But Paul Waner misplayed a Gehrig fly for a run-scoring triple in the first, and in the third, two Pirates errors led to three more runs. A final run in the fifth was all New York needed to win, 5–4.

The Yankees won the next two games more convincingly, with strong pitching and timely hitting. George Pipgras held Pittsburgh to two runs in Game 2 as his Yankees bunched seven of their 11 hits into the third and eighth innings (also taking advantage of two walks and a hit batsman in the eighth) for their six runs. And in Game 3—as Herb Pennock pitched perfectly into the eighth inning before yielding two hits and a run—the Yankees again bunched most of their hits into two innings, scoring two runs on Gehrig's first-inning triple and six more in the seventh, climaxed by Ruth's three-run homer.

Pittsburgh took advantage of two Yankees errors in the seventh inning of Game 4 to score two runs and tie the game at three-all. But in the last of the ninth, after the Pirates' Johnny Miljus had struck out Gehrig and Bob Meusel with the bases loaded, his second wild pitch of the inning undid him— Combs scored from third with the Series' winning run.

New York Yankees (AL), 4; Pittsburgh Pirates (NL), 0

NY (A)

PLAYER/POS	AVG	G	AB	R	H	2B	3B	HR	RB	BB	SO	SB
Benny Bengough, c	.000	2	4	1	0	0	0	0	0	1	0	0
Pat Collins, c	.600	2	5	0	3	1	0	0	0	3	0	0
Earle Combs, of	.313	4	16	6	5	0	0	0	2	1	2	0
Joe Dugan, 3b	.200	4	15	2	3	0	0	0	0	0	0	0
Cedric Durst, ph	.000	1	1	0	0	0	0	0	0	0	0	0
Lou Gehrig, 1b	.308	4	13	2	4	2	2	0	4	3	3	0
Johnny Grabowski, c	.000	1	2	0	0	0	0	0	0	0	0	0
Waite Hoyt, p	.000	1	3	0	0	0	0	0	0	0	0	0
Mark Koenig, ss	.500	4	18	5	9	2	0	0	2	0	2	0
Tony Lazzeri, 2b	.267	4	15	1	4	1	0	0	2	1	4	0
Bob Meusel, of	.118	4	17	1	2	0	0	0	1	1	7	1
Wilcy Moore, p	.200	2	5	0	1	0	0	0	0	0	3	0
Herb Pennock, p	.000	1	4	0	0	0	0	0	0	1	0	0
George Pipgras, p	.333	1	3	0	1	0	0	0	0	0	1	0
Babe Ruth, of	.400	4	15	4	6	0	0	2	7	2	2	1
TOTAL	.279		136	23	38	6	2	2	19	13	25	2

PITCHER	W	L	ERA	G	GS	CG	SV	SHO	IP	H	ER	BB	SO
Waite Hoyt	1	0	4.91	1	1	0	0	0	7.1	8	4	1	2
Wilcy Moore	1	0	0.84	2	1	1	1	0	10.2	11	1	2	2
Herb Pennock	1	0	1.00	1	1	1	0	0	9.0	3	1	0	1
George Pipgras	1	0	2.00	1	1	1	0	0	9.0	7	2	1	2
TOTAL	4	0	2.00	5	4	3	1	0	36.0	29	8	4	7

PIT (N)

PLAYER/POS	AVG	G	AB	R	H	2B	3B	HR	RB	BB	SO	SB
Vic Aldridge, p	.000	1	2	0	0	0	0	0	0	0	0	0
Clyde Barnhart, of	.313	4	16	0	5	1	0	0	4	0	0	0
Fred Brickell, ph	.000	2	2	1	0	0	0	0	0	0	0	0
Mike Cvengros, p	.000	2	0	0	0	0	0	0	0	0	0	0
Joe Dawson, p	.000	1	0	0	0	0	0	0	0	0	0	0
Johnny Gooch, c	.000	3	5	0	0	0	0	0	0	1	1	0
George Grantham, 2b	.364	3	11	0	4	1	0	0	0	1	1	0
Heinie Groh, ph	.000	1	1	0	0	0	0	0	0	0	0	0
Joe Harris, 1b	.200	4	15	0	3	0	0	0	1	0	0	0
Carmen Hill, p	.000	1	1	0	0	0	0	0	0	1	0	0
Ray Kremer, p	.500	1	2	1	1	1	0	0	0	0	1	0
Lee Meadows, p	.000	1	2	0	0	0	0	0	0	0	0	0
Johnny Miljus, p	.000	2	0	0	0	0	0	0	0	0	2	0
Hal Rhyne, 2b	.000	1	4	0	0	0	0	0	0	0	0	0
Earl Smith, c-2	.000	3	8	0	0	0	0	0	0	0	0	0
Roy Spencer, c	.000	1	1	0	0	0	0	0	0	0	0	0
Pie Traynor, 3b	.200	4	15	1	3	1	0	0	0	0	1	0
Lloyd Waner, of	.400	4	15	5	6	1	1	0	0	1	0	0
Paul Waner, of	.333	4	15	0	5	1	0	0	3	0	1	0
Glenn Wright, ss	.154	4	13	1	2	0	0	0	2	0	0	0
Emil Yde, pr	.000	1	0	1	0	0	0	0	0	0	0	0
TOTAL	.223		130	10	29	6	1	0	10	4	7	0

PITCHER	W	L	ERA	G	GS	CG	SV	SHO	IP	H	ER	BB	SO
Vic Aldridge	0	1	7.36	1	1	0	0	0	7.1	10	6	4	4
Mike Cvengros	0	0	3.86	2	0	0	0	0	2.1	3	1	0	2
Joe Dawson	0	0	0.00	1	0	0	0	0	1.0	0	0	0	0
Carmen Hill	0	0	4.50	1	1	0	0	0	6.0	9	3	1	6
Ray Kremer	0	1	3.60	1	1	0	0	0	5.0	5	2	3	1
Lee Meadows	0	1	9.95	1	1	0	0	0	6.1	7	7	1	6
Johnny Miljus	0	1	1.35	2	0	0	0	0	6.2	4	1	4	6
TOTAL	0	4	5.19	9	4	0	0	0	34.2	38	20	13	25

GAME 1 AT PIT OCT 5

| NY | 103 010 000 | 5 6 1 |
| PIT | 101 010 010 | 4 9 2 |

Pitchers: HOYT, Moore (8) vs KREMER, Miljus (6)
Attendance: 41,467

GAME 2 AT PIT OCT 6

| NY | 003 000 030 | 6 11 0 |
| PIT | 100 000 010 | 2 7 2 |

Pitchers: PIPGRAS vs ALDRIDGE, Cvengros (8), Dawson (9)
Attendance: 41,634

GAME 3 AT NY OCT 7

| PIT | 000 000 010 | 1 3 1 |
| NY | 200 000 60X | 8 9 0 |

Pitchers: MEADOWS, Cvengros (7) vs PENNOCK
Home Runs: Ruth-NY
Attendance: 60,695

GAME 4 AT NY OCT 8

| PIT | 100 000 200 | 3 10 1 |
| NY | 100 020 001 | 4 12 2 |

Pitchers: Hill, MILJUS (7) vs MOORE
Home Runs: Ruth-NY
Attendance: 57,909

After squandering a 13½-game lead and falling briefly behind the Athletics in early September, the Yankees recovered to meet the Cardinals—winners of another tight National League race—in the Series. With Herb Pennock lost to arm trouble, the Yankees made do with just three pitchers in extending their Series win streak to eight games.

The four games offered little suspense, but for Yankees fans there were thrills aplenty. The Bronx Bombers' nine home runs (including four by Lou Gehrig and three by Babe Ruth) nearly equalled St. Louis' total scoring (10 runs), and Gehrig himself drove in as many runs (nine) as the entire Cardinals offense. Ruth and Gehrig started things off with successive doubles and a run in the first inning of the opener, and when Bob Meusel followed Ruth's second double with a home run in the fourth, the Yanks had more than they would need to support Waite Hoyt's three-hitter. The Cardinals' Jim Bottomley homered off Hoyt in the seventh, but successive singles by Mark Koenig, Ruth, and Gehrig produced a fourth Yankee run and concluded the scoring.

Gehrig homered in the first inning of Game 2 to get New York off to a 3–0 lead against 41-year-old Grover Cleveland Alexander. The Cards snapped back to tie the game, but the Yankees retook the lead with a run in the last of the second and put together four hits, two walks, and a hit batsman for four more in the third. A final Yankees run in the seventh capped a 9–3 four-hit win for pitcher George Pipgras.

Jim Bottomley gave St. Louis its first lead of the Series with a two-run triple in the first inning of Game 3. But Tom Zachary gave up only one more run, taking the third Yankees win as Gehrig drove in three runs with homers in the second and fourth, and his teammates scored three more in the sixth (thanks in large part to two Cardinals errors and Meusel's steal of home) and a final (unearned) run an inning later.

New York completed its second straight Series sweep with another 7–3 win two days later. Waite Hoyt gained his second victory, mostly on the strength of five solo Yankees homers, including three by Babe Ruth.

New York Yankees (AL), 4; St. Louis Cardinals (NL), 0

NY (A)

PLAYER/POS	AVG	G	AB	R	H	2B	3B	HR	RBI	BB	SO	SB
Benny Bengough, c	.231	4	13	1	3	0	0	0	1	1	1	0
Pat Collins, c	1.000	1	1	0	1	1	0	0	0	0	0	0
Earle Combs, ph	.000	1	0	0	0	0	0	0	1	0	0	0
Joe Dugan, 3b	.167	3	6	0	1	0	0	0	1	0	0	0
Leo Durocher, 2b	.000	4	2	0	0	0	0	0	0	0	1	0
Cedric Durst, of	.375	4	8	3	3	0	0	1	2	0	1	0
Lou Gehrig, 1b	.545	4	11	5	6	1	0	4	9	6	0	0
Waite Hoyt, p	.143	2	7	0	1	0	0	0	0	0	0	0
Mark Koenig, ss	.158	4	19	1	3	0	0	0	0	0	1	0
Tony Lazzeri, 2b	.250	4	12	2	3	1	0	0	0	1	0	2
Bob Meusel, of	.200	4	15	5	3	1	0	1	3	2	5	2
Ben Paschal, of	.200	3	10	0	2	0	0	0	1	0	0	0
George Pipgras, p	.000	1	2	0	0	0	0	0	1	0	1	0
Gene Robertson, 3b	.125	3	8	1	1	0	0	0	2	1	0	0
Babe Ruth, of	.625	4	16	9	10	3	0	3	4	1	2	0
Tom Zachary, p	.000	1	4	0	0	0	0	0	0	0	1	0
TOTAL	.276		134	27	37	7	0	9	25	13	13	4

PITCHER	W	L	ERA	G	GS	CG	SV	SHO	IP	H	ER	BB	SO
Waite Hoyt	2	0	1.50	2	2	2	0	0	18.0	14	3	6	14
George Pipgras	1	0	2.00	1	1	1	0	0	9.0	4	2	4	8
Tom Zachary	1	0	3.00	1	1	1	0	0	9.0	9	3	1	7
TOTAL	4	0	2.00	4	4	4	0	0	36.0	27	8	11	29

STL (N)

PLAYER/POS	AVG	G	AB	R	H	2B	3B	HR	RBI	BB	SO	SB
Pete Alexander, p	.000	2	1	0	0	0	0	0	1	0	0	0
Ray Blades, ph	.000	1	1	0	0	0	0	0	0	0	1	0
Jim Bottomley, 1b	.214	4	14	1	3	0	1	1	3	2	6	0
Taylor Douthit, of	.091	3	11	1	1	0	0	0	1	1	1	0
Frankie Frisch, 2b	.231	4	13	1	3	0	0	0	1	2	2	2
Chick Hafey, of	.200	4	15	0	3	0	0	0	0	1	4	0
Jesse Haines, p	.000	1	2	0	0	0	0	0	0	0	0	0
George Harper, of	.111	3	9	1	1	0	0	0	0	2	2	0
Andy High, 3b	.294	4	17	1	5	2	0	0	1	1	3	0
Wattie Holm, of-1	.167	3	6	1	1	0	0	0	0	1	0	0
Syl Johnson, p	.000	2	0	0	0	0	0	0	0	0	0	0
Rabbit Maranville, ss	.308	4	13	2	4	1	0	0	0	1	1	1
Pepper Martin, pr	.000	1	0	1	0	0	0	0	0	0	0	0
Clarence Mitchell, p	.000	1	2	0	0	0	0	0	0	0	0	0
Ernie Orsatti, of-1	.286	4	7	1	2	1	0	0	0	1	3	0
Flint Rhem, p	.000	1	0	0	0	0	0	0	0	0	0	0
Bill Sherdel, p	.000	2	5	0	0	0	0	0	0	0	2	0
Earl Smith, c	.750	2	4	0	3	0	0	0	0	0	0	0
Tommy Thevenow, ss	.000	1	0	0	0	0	0	0	0	0	0	0
Jimmie Wilson, c	.091	3	11	1	1	1	0	0	1	0	3	0
TOTAL	.206		131	10	27	5	1	1	9	11	29	3

PITCHER	W	L	ERA	G	GS	CG	SV	SHO	IP	H	ER	BB	SO
Pete Alexander	0	1	19.80	2	1	0	0	0	5.0	10	11	4	2
Jesse Haines	0	1	4.50	1	1	0	0	0	6.0	6	3	3	3
Syl Johnson	0	0	4.50	2	0	0	0	0	2.0	4	1	1	1
Clarence Mitchell	0	0	1.59	1	0	0	0	0	5.2	2	1	2	3
Flint Rhem	0	0	0.00	1	0	0	0	0	2.0	0	0	0	1
Bill Sherdel	0	2	4.72	2	2	0	0	0	13.1	15	7	3	3
TOTAL	0	4	6.09	9	4	0	0	0	34.0	37	23	13	13

GAME 1 AT NY OCT 4

STL	000 000 100	1	3	1
NY	100 200 01X	4	7	0

Pitchers: SHERDEL, Johnson (8) vs HOYT
Home Runs: Meusel-NY, Bottomley-STL
Attendance: 61,425

GAME 2 AT NY OCT 5

STL	030 000 000	3	4	1
NY	314 000 10X	9	8	2

Pitchers: ALEXANDER, Mitchell (3) vs PIPGRAS
Home Runs: Gehrig-NY
Attendance: 60,714

GAME 3 AT STL OCT 7

NY	010 203 100	7	7	2
STL	200 010 000	3	9	3

Pitchers: ZACHARY vs HAINES, Johnson (7), Rhem (8)
Home Runs: Gehrig-NY (2)
Attendance: 39,602

GAME 4 AT STL OCT 9

NY	000 100 420	7	15	2
STL	001 100 001	3	11	0

Pitchers: HOYT vs SHERDEL, Alexander (7)
Home Runs: Ruth-NY (3), Durst-NY, Gehrig-NY
Attendance: 37,331

The surprising success of a surprise starter and the ultimate in big innings highlighted the return of the Athletics to World Series play after a gap of 15 years. In the opener, A's manager Connie Mack passed over the aces of his pitching staff in favor of Howard Ehmke, an aging journeyman who that season had started only eight times and pitched under 55 innings. But Ehmke, who (per Mack's instructions) had studied the Cubs' hitters in a series of late-season games, held the Cubs scoreless through the first eight innings of Game 1 (yielding an unearned run in the last of the ninth) while fanning 13 batters for a new Series record. Chicago's Charlie Root also pitched effectively until Jimmie Foxx's solo homer in the seventh gave the A's the game's first score. A pair of errors by Cubs shortstop Woody English in the ninth set up two unearned runs against reliever Guy Bush and gave Ehmke and the A's all the lead they needed.

Home runs by Foxx and Al Simmons drove in five of the A's nine runs in Game 2 as Philadelphia took a 2–0 Series lead. But Guy Bush held Mack's sluggers to nine singles and one run in Game 3 as his Cubs scored three runs in the sixth to take their first win.

The Cubs seemed well on their way to tying the Series in Game 4 as they entered the last of the seventh with an 8–0 lead. But Simmons led off with a homer to erase Charlie Root's shutout, and five of the next six batters singled. Art Nehf relieved Root, but the first batter to face him—Mule Haas—lofted a fly to center which Hack Wilson lost in the sun for a three-run inside-the-park homer, and the score was 8–7. After walking Mickey Cochrane, Nehf was replaced by Sheriff Blake, who gave up two singles and saw the tying run come home before Pat Malone took the mound with two men still on base and only one away. Malone struck out two in a row to end the inning—but not until he first hit a batter and gave up a double by Jimmy Dykes for the two runs that gave the A's a 10–8 win and a 3–1 Series advantage.

Game 5, although inevitably anticlimactic, was not decided until the final at bat. Chicago scored twice off Ehmke in the fourth as Malone shut out the A's with only two hits through eight. But in the last of the ninth a single and Haas' home run tied the score, and—with two men out—Simmons doubled, Foxx was walked intentionally, Bing Miller doubled, and the Series was history.

Philadelphia Athletics (AL), 4; Chicago Cubs (NL), 1

PHI (A)

PLAYER/POS	AVG	G	AB	R	H	2B	3B	HR	RB	BB	SO	SB
Max Bishop, 2b	.190	5	21	2	4	0	0	0	1	2	3	0
Joe Boley, ss	.235	5	17	1	4	0	0	0	1	0	3	0
George Burns, ph	.000	1	2	0	0	0	0	0	0	0	1	0
Mickey Cochrane, c	.400	5	15	5	6	1	0	0	0	7	0	0
Jimmy Dykes, 3b	.421	5	19	2	8	1	0	0	4	1	1	0
George Earnshaw, p	.000	2	5	1	0	0	0	0	0	0	4	0
Howard Ehmke, p	.200	2	5	0	1	0	0	0	0	0	0	0
Jimmie Foxx, 1b	.350	5	20	5	7	1	0	2	5	1	1	0
Walter French, ph	.000	1	1	0	0	0	0	0	0	0	1	0
Lefty Grove, p	.000	2	2	0	0	0	0	0	0	0	1	0
Mule Haas, of	.238	5	21	3	5	0	0	2	6	1	3	0
Bing Miller, of	.368	5	19	1	7	1	0	0	4	0	2	0
Jack Quinn, p	.000	1	2	0	0	0	0	0	0	0	2	0
Eddie Rommel, p	.000	1	0	0	0	0	0	0	0	0	0	0
Al Simmons, of	.300	5	20	6	6	1	0	2	5	1	4	0
Homer Summa, ph	.000	1	1	0	0	0	0	0	0	0	1	0
Rube Walberg, p	.000	2	1	0	0	0	0	0	0	0	0	0
TOTAL	.281		171	26	48	5	0	6	26	13	27	0

PITCHER	W	L	ERA	G	GS	CG	SV	SHO	IP	H	ER	BB	SO
George Earnshaw	1	1	2.63	2	2	1	0	0	13.2	14	4	6	17
Howard Ehmke	1	0	1.42	2	2	1	0	0	12.2	14	2	3	13
Lefty Grove	0	0	0.00	2	0	0	2	0	6.1	3	0	1	10
Jack Quinn	0	0	9.00	1	1	0	0	0	5.0	7	5	2	2
Eddie Rommel	1	0	9.00	1	0	0	0	0	1.0	2	1	1	0
Rube Walberg	1	0	0.00	2	0	0	0	0	6.1	3	0	0	8
TOTAL	4	1	2.40	10	5	2	2	0	45.0	43	12	13	50

CHI (N)

PLAYER/POS	AVG	G	AB	R	H	2B	3B	HR	RB	BB	SO	SB
Footsie Blair, ph	.000	1	1	0	0	0	0	0	0	0	0	0
Sheriff Blake, p	1.000	2	1	0	1	0	0	0	0	0	0	0
Guy Bush, p	.000	2	3	1	0	0	0	0	0	1	3	0
Hal Carlson, p	.000	2	0	0	0	0	0	0	0	0	0	0
Kiki Cuyler, of	.300	5	20	4	6	1	0	0	4	1	7	0
Woody English, ss	.190	5	21	1	4	2	0	0	0	1	6	0
Mike Gonzalez, c-1	.000	2	1	0	0	0	0	0	0	0	1	0
Charlie Grimm, 1b	.389	5	18	2	7	0	0	1	4	1	2	0
Gabby Hartnett, ph	.000	2	3	0	0	0	0	0	0	0	3	0
Cliff Heathcote, ph	.000	2	1	0	0	0	0	0	0	0	0	0
Rogers Hornsby, 2b	.238	5	21	4	5	1	1	0	1	1	8	0
Pat Malone, p	.250	3	4	1	1	1	0	0	0	0	2	0
Norm McMillan, 3b	.100	5	20	0	2	0	0	0	0	2	6	1
Art Nehf, p	.000	2	0	0	0	0	0	0	0	0	0	0
Charlie Root, p	.000	2	5	0	0	0	0	0	0	0	3	0
Riggs Stephenson, of	.316	5	19	3	6	1	0	0	3	2	2	0
Zack Taylor, c	.176	5	17	0	3	0	0	0	0	3	3	0
Chick Tolson, ph	.000	1	1	0	0	0	0	0	0	0	1	0
Hack Wilson, of	.471	5	17	2	8	0	1	0	0	4	3	0
TOTAL	.249		173	17	43	6	2	1	15	13	50	1

PITCHER	W	L	ERA	G	GS	CG	SV	SHO	IP	H	ER	BB	SO
Sheriff Blake	0	1	13.50	2	0	0	0	0	1.1	4	2	0	1
Guy Bush	1	0	0.82	2	1	1	0	0	11.0	12	1	2	4
Hal Carlson	0	0	6.75	2	0	0	0	0	4.0	7	3	1	3
Pat Malone	0	2	4.15	3	2	1	0	0	13.0	12	6	7	11
Art Nehf	0	0	18.00	2	0	0	0	0	1.0	1	2	1	0
Charlie Root	0	1	4.72	2	2	0	0	0	13.1	12	7	2	8
TOTAL	1	4	4.33	13	5	2	0	0	43.2	48	21	13	27

GAME 1 AT CHI OCT 8

PHI	000	000	102	3	6	1
CHI	000	000	001	1	8	2

Pitchers: EHMKE vs ROOT, Bush (8)
Home Runs: Foxx-PHI
Attendance: 50,740

GAME 2 AT CHI OCT 9

PHI	003	300	120	9	12	0
CHI	000	030	000	3	11	1

Pitchers: EARNSHAW, Grove (5) vs MALONE, Blake (4), Carlson (6), Nehf (9)
Home Runs: Simmons-PHI, Foxx-PHI
Attendance: 49,987

GAME 3 AT PHI OCT 11

CHI	000	003	000	3	6	1
PHI	000	010	000	1	9	1

Pitchers: BUSH vs EARNSHAW
Attendance: 29,921

GAME 4 AT PHI OCT 12

CHI	000	205	100	8	10	2
PHI	000	000	100 X	10	15	2

Pitchers: Root, Nehf (7), BLAKE (7), Malone (7), Carlson (8) vs Quinn, Walberg (6), ROMMEL (7), Grove (8)
Home Runs: Grimm-CHI, Haas-PHI, Simmons-PHI
Attendance: 29,921

GAME 5 AT PHI OCT 14

CHI	002	000	000	2	8	1
PHI	000	000	003	3	6	0

Pitchers: MALONE vs Ehmke, WALBERG (4)
Home Runs: Haas-PHI
Attendance: 29,921

Pitching 85 percent of the Series with a combined ERA of 1.02, Philadelphia aces George Earnshaw and Lefty Grove chilled the hot Cardinals, who had hit .314 and averaged more than six runs per game during the season. The A's hit only .197 themselves in the Series, but more than half their hits went for extra bases as they outscored St. Louis 21–12 and took their second consecutive world championship in six games.

Grove faced Cardinals spitballer Burleigh Grimes in the opener, giving up nine hits, including four singles in the Cards' two-run third. The Athletics, for their part, touched Grimes for only five hits, all in separate innings. But every hit—a double, two triples, and home runs by Al Simmons and Mike Cochrane—resulted in a run, and Grove and the A's emerged 5–2 victors. In the first inning of Game 2, Cochrane again homered, sending Earnshaw on his way to Philadelphia's second win, 6–1.

When the Series moved to St. Louis, though, the Cards came alive. Wild Bill Hallahan (their leading winner during the season, with 15) spaced seven hits for a shutout. Taylor Douthit's fourth-inning home run off Rube Walberg was the first St. Louis hit, but the Cards knocked out nine more for four more runs before they were finished. A pair of unearned runs evened the Series the next day when A's third baseman Jimmy Dykes's wild throw to first in the fourth inning let in a tie-breaking run and led to a third against the ultimate loser Lefty Grove. Meanwhile, Cardinals veteran Jesse Haines, after yielding three Philadelphia hits and a run in the first inning, shut out the A's on one hit the rest of the way.

Earnshaw and Grove combined to restore the Series lead to the Athletics in Game 5 with a three-hit shutout. Grove, who took over when Earnshaw left for a pinch hitter in the eighth, garnered his second Series win as Jimmie Foxx homered off Grimes in the top of the ninth for the game's only runs. After a travel day to Philadelphia, Earnshaw pitched again for the A's in Game 6, and pushed the Cardinals' scoreless streak to 21 innings before allowing them a token run in the ninth. But by then seven A's had crossed the plate and the Series was theirs.

Philadelphia Athletics (AL), 4; St. Louis Cardinals (NL), 2

PHI (A)

PLAYER/POS	AVG	G	AB	R	H	2B	3B	HR	RB	BB	SO	SB
Max Bishop, 2b	.222	6	18	5	4	0	0	0	0	7	3	0
Joe Boley, ss	.095	6	21	1	2	0	0	0	1	0	1	0
Mickey Cochrane, c	.222	6	18	5	4	1	0	2	4	5	2	0
Jimmy Dykes, 3b	.222	6	18	2	4	3	0	1	5	5	5	0
George Earnshaw, p	.000	3	9	0	0	0	0	0	0	0	5	0
Jimmie Foxx, 1b	.333	6	21	3	7	2	1	1	3	2	4	0
Lefty Grove, p	.000	3	6	0	0	0	0	0	0	0	3	0
Mule Haas, of	.111	6	18	1	2	0	1	0	1	1	3	0
Eric McNair, ph	.000	1	1	0	0	0	0	0	0	0	0	0
Bing Miller, of	.143	6	21	0	3	2	0	0	3	0	4	0
Jim Moore, of-1	.333	3	3	0	1	0	0	0	0	1	1	0
Jack Quinn, p	.000	1	0	0	0	0	0	0	0	0	0	0
Bill Shores, p	.000	1	0	0	0	0	0	0	0	0	1	0
Al Simmons, of	.364	6	22	4	8	2	0	2	4	2	2	0
Rube Walberg, p	.000	1	2	0	0	0	0	0	0	0	1	0
TOTAL	.197		178	21	35	10	2	6	21	24	32	0

PITCHER	W	L	ERA	G	GS	CG	SV	SHO	IP	H	ER	BB	SO
George Earnshaw	2	0	0.72	3	3	2	0	0	25.0	13	2	7	19
Lefty Grove	2	1	1.42	3	2	2	0	0	19.0	15	3	3	10
Jack Quinn	0	0	4.50	1	0	0	0	0	2.0	3	1	0	1
Bill Shores	0	0	13.50	1	0	0	0	0	1.1	3	2	0	0
Rube Walberg	0	1	3.86	1	1	0	0	0	4.2	4	2	1	3
TOTAL	4	2	1.73	9	6	4	0	0	52.0	38	10	11	33

STL (N)

PLAYER/POS	AVG	G	AB	R	H	2B	3B	HR	RB	BB	SO	SB
Sparky Adams, 3b	.143	6	21	0	3	0	0	0	0	1	4	0
Hi Bell, p	.000	1	0	0	0	0	0	0	0	0	0	0
Ray Blades, of-3	.111	5	9	2	1	0	0	0	0	2	2	0
Jim Bottomley, 1b	.045	6	22	1	1	1	0	0	0	2	9	0
Taylor Douthit, of	.083	6	24	1	2	0	0	1	2	0	2	0
George Fisher, ph	.500	2	2	0	1	1	0	0	0	0	1	0
Frankie Frisch, 2b	.208	6	24	0	5	2	0	0	0	0	0	1
Charlie Gelbert, ss	.353	6	17	2	6	0	1	0	2	3	3	0
Burleigh Grimes, p	.400	2	5	0	2	0	0	0	0	0	1	0
Chick Hafey, of	.273	6	22	2	6	5	0	0	2	1	3	0
Jesse Haines, p	.500	1	2	0	1	0	0	0	0	1	0	0
Bill Hallahan, p	.000	2	2	0	0	0	0	0	0	1	1	0
Andy High, 3b	.500	1	2	1	1	0	0	0	0	0	0	0
Syl Johnson, p	.000	2	0	0	0	0	0	0	0	0	0	0
Jim Lindsey, p	1.000	2	1	0	1	0	0	0	0	0	0	0
Gus Mancuso, c	.286	2	7	1	2	0	0	0	0	1	2	0
Ernie Orsatti, of	.000	1	1	0	0	0	0	0	0	0	0	0
George Puccinelli, ph	.000	1	1	0	0	0	0	0	0	0	0	0
Flint Rhem, p	.000	1	1	0	0	0	0	0	0	0	1	0
George Watkins, of	.167	4	12	2	2	0	0	1	1	1	3	0
Jimmie Wilson, c	.267	4	15	0	4	1	0	0	2	0	1	0
TOTAL	.200		190	12	38	10	1	2	11	11	33	1

PITCHER	W	L	ERA	G	GS	CG	SV	SHO	IP	H	ER	BB	SO
Hi Bell	0	0	0.00	1	0	0	0	0	1.0	0	0	0	0
Burleigh Grimes	0	2	3.71	2	2	2	0	0	17.0	10	7	6	13
Jesse Haines	1	0	1.00	1	1	1	0	0	9.0	4	1	4	2
Bill Hallahan	1	1	1.64	2	2	1	0	1	11.0	9	2	8	8
Syl Johnson	0	0	7.20	2	0	0	0	0	5.0	4	4	3	4
Jim Lindsey	0	0	1.93	2	0	0	0	0	4.2	1	1	1	2
Flint Rhem	0	1	10.80	1	1	0	0	0	3.1	7	4	2	3
TOTAL	2	4	3.35	11	6	4	0	1	51.0	35	19	24	32

For the second year in a row, the A's met the Cardinals in the Series, and once again pitchers Lefty Grove and George Earnshaw provided more than 80 percent of the Athletics' pitching, performing splendidly and winning three games between them. But this time Cardinals pitchers Wild Bill Hallahan and Burleigh Grimes outshone them, winning two games apiece to bring St. Louis the world championship.

Grove gave up four hits and two runs in the first inning of the opener, but shut out the Cards the rest of the way as the A's scored six off Paul Derringer to take the Series lead. Earnshaw also held St. Louis to two runs the next day—both manufactured by Pepper Martin's daring baserunning. But they were more than enough for Hallahan, who shut out the A's on three singles.

The Cardinals took their first Series lead in Game 3, scoring five times off Grove and reliever Roy Mahaffey while Grimes held the A's hitless through seven innings and scoreless through eight before giving up a harmless two-run homer to Al Simmons in the bottom of the ninth. But the A's came back to even the Series the next day on Earnshaw's two-hit shutout.

Pepper Martin, hero of Game 2, homered for two runs in Game 5, and drove in two more of St. Louis' five runs with a sacrifice fly and a single. Meanwhile pitcher Hallahan held Philadelphia to a lone run, returning the Series lead to the Cardinals with his second win.

Game 6 pitted Grove and Derringer against each other again as in the opener, and again Grove emerged the victor, holding the Cardinals to one run and five hits. The Athletics scored four unearned runs in the fifth off the unfortunate Derringer. After an error put a runner on base to open the inning, he allowed two singles and walked four, including two with the bases full, before leaving the game. Four more Philadelphia runs in the seventh (two of them scoring on a dropped fly ball) gave the A's the Series' only lopsided win.

In the finale, Grimes once again held the A's scoreless through eight before giving up two runs in the ninth. And once again the runs proved harmless against an early Cardinals lead, as Hallahan came on to retire Max Bishop for the final out.

St. Louis Cardinals (NL), 4; Philadelphia Athletics (AL), 3

STL (N)

PLAYER/POS	AVG	G	AB	R	H	2B	3B	HR	RB	BB	SO	SB
Sparky Adams, 3b	.250	2	4	0	1	0	0	0	0	0	1	0
Ray Blades, ph	.000	2	2	0	0	0	0	0	0	0	2	0
Jim Bottomley, 1b	.160	7	25	2	4	1	0	0	2	2	5	0
Ripper Collins, ph	.000	2	2	0	0	0	0	0	0	0	1	0
Paul Derringer, p	.000	3	2	0	0	0	0	0	0	0	1	0
Jake Flowers, 3b-4	.091	5	11	1	1	1	0	0	0	1	0	0
Frankie Frisch, 2b	.259	7	27	2	7	2	0	0	1	1	2	1
Charlie Gelbert, ss	.261	7	23	0	6	1	0	0	3	0	4	0
Burleigh Grimes, p	.286	2	7	0	2	0	0	0	2	0	2	0
Chick Hafey, of	.167	6	24	1	4	0	0	0	0	0	5	1
Bill Hallahan, p	.000	3	6	0	0	0	0	0	0	0	3	0
Andy High, 3b	.267	4	15	3	4	0	0	0	0	0	0	0
Syl Johnson, p	.000	3	2	0	0	0	0	0	0	0	2	0
Jim Lindsey, p	.000	2	0	0	0	0	0	0	0	0	0	0
Gus Mancuso, c-1	.000	2	1	0	0	0	0	0	0	0	0	0
Pepper Martin, of	.500	7	24	5	12	4	0	1	5	2	3	5
Ernie Orsatti, of	.000	1	3	0	0	0	0	0	0	0	3	0
Flint Rhem, p	.000	1	0	0	0	0	0	0	0	0	0	0
Wally Roettger, of	.286	3	14	1	4	1	0	0	0	0	3	0
George Watkins, of	.286	5	14	4	4	1	0	1	2	2	1	1
Jimmie Wilson, c	.217	7	23	0	5	0	0	0	2	1	1	0
TOTAL	.236		229	19	54	11	0	2	17	9	41	8

PITCHER	W	L	ERA	G	GS	CG	SV	SHO	IP	H	ER	BB	SO
Paul Derringer	0	2	4.26	3	2	0	0	0	12.2	14	6	7	14
Burleigh Grimes	2	0	2.04	2	2	1	0	0	17.2	9	4	9	11
Bill Hallahan	2	0	0.49	3	2	2	1	1	18.1	12	1	8	12
Syl Johnson	0	1	3.00	3	1	0	0	0	9.0	10	3	1	6
Jim Lindsey	0	0	5.40	2	0	0	0	0	3.1	4	2	3	2
Flint Rhem	0	0	0.00	1	0	0	0	0	1.0	1	0	0	1
TOTAL	4	3	2.32	14	7	3	1	1	62.0	50	16	28	46

PHI (A)

PLAYER/POS	AVG	G	AB	R	H	2B	3B	HR	RB	BB	SO	SB
Max Bishop, 2b	.148	7	27	4	4	0	0	0	0	3	5	0
Joe Boley, ph	.000	1	1	0	0	0	0	0	0	0	1	0
Mickey Cochrane, c	.160	7	25	2	4	0	0	0	1	5	2	0
Doc Cramer, ph	.500	2	2	0	1	0	0	0	0	2	0	0
Jimmy Dykes, 3b	.227	7	22	2	5	0	0	0	2	5	1	0
George Earnshaw, p	.000	3	8	0	0	0	0	0	0	0	2	0
Jimmie Foxx, 1b	.348	7	23	3	8	0	0	1	3	6	5	0
Lefty Grove, p	.000	3	10	0	0	0	0	0	0	0	7	0
Mule Haas, of	.130	7	23	1	3	1	0	0	2	3	5	0
Johnnie Heving, ph	.000	1	1	0	0	0	0	0	0	0	0	0
Waite Hoyt, p	.000	1	1	0	0	0	0	0	0	0	0	0
Roy Mahaffey, p	.000	1	0	0	0	0	0	0	0	0	0	0
Eric McNair, 2b-1	.000	2	2	1	0	0	0	0	0	0	1	0
Bing Miller, of	.269	7	26	3	7	1	0	0	1	0	4	0
Jim Moore, of-1	.333	2	3	0	1	0	0	0	0	0	1	0
Eddie Rommel, p	.000	1	0	0	0	0	0	0	0	0	0	0
Al Simmons, of	.333	7	27	4	9	2	0	2	8	3	3	0
Phil Todt, ph	.000	1	0	0	0	0	0	0	0	1	0	0
Rube Walberg, p	.000	2	0	0	0	0	0	0	0	0	0	0
Dib Williams, ss	.320	7	25	2	8	1	0	0	1	2	9	0
TOTAL	.220		227	22	50	5	0	3	20	28	46	0

PITCHER	W	L	ERA	G	GS	CG	SV	SHO	IP	H	ER	BB	SO
George Earnshaw	1	2	1.88	3	3	2	0	1	24.0	12	5	4	20
Lefty Grove	2	1	2.42	3	3	2	0	0	26.0	28	7	2	16
Waite Hoyt	0	1	4.50	1	1	0	0	0	6.0	7	3	0	1
Roy Mahaffey	0	0	9.00	1	0	0	0	0	1.0	1	1	1	0
Eddie Rommel	0	0	9.00	1	0	0	0	0	1.0	3	1	0	0
Rube Walberg	0	0	3.00	2	0	0	0	0	3.0	3	1	2	4
TOTAL	3	4	2.66	11	7	4	0	1	61.0	54	18	9	41

GAME 1 AT STL OCT 1

PHI	004 000 200	6	11	0
STL	200 000 000	2	12	0

Pitchers: GROVE vs DERRINGER, Johnson (8)
Home Runs: Simmons-PHI
Attendance: 38,529

GAME 2 AT STL OCT 2

PHI	000 000 000	0	3	0
STL	010 000 10X	2	6	1

Pitchers: EARNSHAW vs HALLAHAN
Attendance: 35,947

GAME 3 AT PHI OCT 5

STL	020 200 001	5	12	0
PHI	000 000 002	2	2	0

Pitchers: GRIMES vs GROVE, Mahaffey (9)
Home Runs: Simmons-PHI
Attendance: 32,295

GAME 4 AT PHI OCT 6

STL	000 000 000	0	2	1
PHI	100 002 00X	3	10	0

Pitchers: JOHNSON, Lindsey (6), Derringer (8) vs EARNSHAW
Home Runs: Foxx-PHI
Attendance: 32,295

GAME 5 AT PHI OCT 7

STL	100 002 011	5	12	0
PHI	000 000 100	1	9	0

Pitchers: HALLAHAN vs HOYT, Walberg (7), Rommel (9)
Home Runs: Martin-STL, Watkins-STL
Attendance: 32,295

GAME 6 AT STL OCT 9

PHI	000 040 400	8	8	1
STL	000 001 000	1	5	2

Pitchers: GROVE vs DERRINGER, Johnson (5), Lindsey (7), Rhem (9)
Attendance: 39,401

GAME 7 AT STL OCT 10

PHI	000 000 002	2	7	1
STL	202 000 00X	4	5	0

Pitchers: EARNSHAW, Walberg (8) vs GRIMES, Hallahan (9)
Attendance: 20,805

Lou Gehrig, who hit .529 and scored nearly a quarter of New York's runs, led both clubs in batting, slugging, hits, runs, and RBIs as the Yankees crushed the Cubs in four games. But the Series is best remembered for Babe Ruth's "called" shot in Game 3, when he pointed his bat at pitcher Charlie Root in the fifth inning and broke the game's 4–4 tie a moment later with a massive home run into the center field bleachers. Debate has raged ever since about whether Ruth intended his gesture as a home run prediction. Whether intended or not, it erased from public memory Gehrig's home run that followed Ruth's (and the homers both men had hit earlier in the game), and made memorable an otherwise undistinguished Series.

Chicago scored in the first inning of each game, taking early leads in three of the four, but held no lead beyond the sixth inning. In the opener the Cubs connected for ten hits to the Yankees' eight, but managed to score only half as many runs as the New Yorkers, who put what had been a close game out of reach with five runs in the sixth (on four walks, two singles, and a ground out) and three more in the seventh (a walk, two singles, a hit batsman, a sacrifice fly, and a wild pitch).

Chicago's Lon Warneke walked four batters in Game 2, and three of them went on to score as the Yankees countered single Chicago runs in the first and third with pairs of their own on two walks and two singles in each frame. (A fifth Yankees run—on two singles without bases on balls—concluded the scoring for the game.)

Game 3 featured not only the two homers each by Ruth and Gehrig, but home runs by the Cubs' Kiki Cuyler and Gabby Hartnett. Hartnett's solo shot in the last of the ninth brought Chicago to within two runs of New York for the Series' closest finish.

Four first-inning singles, Frank Demaree's three-run homer, and a Yankees error gave the Cubs a 4–1 advantage early in Game 4—their biggest lead of the Series. But by game's end, 19 Yankees hits (including two home runs by Tony Lazzeri and one by Earle Combs) had created 13 runs, and the world title belonged to the Yankees.

New York Yankees (AL), 4;
Chicago Cubs (NL), 0

NY (A)

PLAYER/POS	AVG	G	AB	R	H	2B	3B	HR	RB	BB	SO	SB
Johnny Allen, p	.000	1	0	0	0	0	0	0	0	0	0	0
Sammy Byrd, of	.000	1	0	0	0	0	0	0	0	0	0	0
Ben Chapman, of	.294	4	17	1	5	2	0	0	6	2	4	0
Earle Combs, of	.375	4	16	8	6	1	0	1	4	4	3	0
Frankie Crosetti, ss	.133	4	15	2	2	1	0	0	0	2	3	0
Bill Dickey, c	.438	4	16	2	7	0	0	0	4	2	1	0
Lou Gehrig, 1b	.529	4	17	9	9	1	0	3	8	2	1	0
Lefty Gomez, p	.000	1	3	0	0	0	0	0	0	0	2	0
Myril Hoag, pr	.000	1	0	1	0	0	0	0	0	0	0	0
Tony Lazzeri, 2b	.294	4	17	4	5	0	0	2	5	2	1	0
Wilcy Moore, p	.333	1	3	0	1	0	0	0	0	0	2	0
Herb Pennock, p	.000	2	1	0	0	0	0	0	0	0	0	0
George Pipgras, p	.000	1	5	0	0	0	0	0	0	0	5	0
Red Ruffing, p-1	.000	4	4	0	0	0	0	0	0	1	1	0
Babe Ruth, of	.333	4	15	6	5	0	0	2	6	4	3	0
Joe Sewell, 3b	.333	4	15	4	5	1	0	0	3	4	0	0
TOTAL	.313		144	37	45	6	0	8	36	23	26	0

PITCHER	W	L	ERA	G	GS	CG	SV	SHO	IP	H	ER	BB	SO
Johnny Allen	0	0	40.50	1	1	0	0	0	0.2	5	3	0	0
Lefty Gomez	1	0	1.00	1	1	1	0	0	9.0	9	1	1	8
Wilcy Moore	1	0	0.00	1	0	0	0	0	5.1	2	0	0	1
Herb Pennock	0	0	2.25	2	0	0	2	0	4.0	2	1	1	4
George Pipgras	1	0	4.50	1	1	0	0	0	8.0	9	4	3	1
Red Ruffing	1	0	3.00	1	1	1	0	0	9.0	10	3	6	10
TOTAL	4	0	3.00	7	4	2	2	0	36.0	37	12	11	24

CHI (N)

PLAYER/POS	AVG	G	AB	R	H	2B	3B	HR	RB	BB	SO	SB
Guy Bush, p	.000	2	1	0	0	0	0	0	0	1	0	0
Kiki Cuyler, of	.278	4	18	2	5	1	1	1	2	0	3	1
Frank Demaree, of	.286	2	7	1	2	0	0	1	4	1	0	0
Woody English, 3b	.176	4	17	2	3	0	0	0	1	2	2	0
Burleigh Grimes, p	.000	2	1	0	0	0	0	0	0	0	1	0
Charlie Grimm, 1b	.333	4	15	2	5	2	0	0	1	2	2	0
Marv Gudat, ph	.000	2	2	0	0	0	0	0	0	0	1	0
Stan Hack, ph	.000	1	0	0	0	0	0	0	0	0	0	0
Gabby Hartnett, c	.313	4	16	2	5	2	0	1	1	1	3	0
Rollie Hemsley, c-1	.000	3	3	0	0	0	0	0	0	0	3	0
Billy Herman, 2b	.222	4	18	5	4	1	0	0	1	1	3	0
Billy Jurges, ss	.364	3	11	1	4	1	0	0	1	0	1	2
Mark Koenig, ss-1	.250	2	4	1	1	0	1	0	1	1	0	0
Pat Malone, p	.000	1	0	0	0	0	0	0	0	0	0	0
Jakie May, p	.000	2	2	0	0	0	0	0	0	0	0	0
Johnny Moore, of	.000	2	7	1	0	0	0	0	0	2	1	0
Charlie Root, p	.000	1	2	0	0	0	0	0	0	0	1	0
Bob Smith, p	.000	1	0	0	0	0	0	0	0	0	0	0
Riggs Stephenson, of	.444	4	18	2	8	1	0	0	4	0	0	0
Bud Tinning, p	.000	2	0	0	0	0	0	0	0	0	0	0
Lon Warneke, p	.000	2	4	0	0	0	0	0	0	0	3	0
TOTAL	.253		146	19	37	8	2	3	16	11	24	3

PITCHER	W	L	ERA	G	GS	CG	SV	SHO	IP	H	ER	BB	SO
Guy Bush	0	1	14.29	2	2	0	0	0	5.2	5	9	6	2
Burleigh Grimes	0	0	23.63	2	0	0	0	0	2.2	7	7	2	0
Pat Malone	0	0	0.00	1	0	0	0	0	2.2	1	0	4	4
Jakie May	0	1	11.57	2	0	0	0	0	4.2	9	6	3	4
Charlie Root	0	1	10.38	1	1	0	0	0	4.1	6	5	3	4
Bob Smith	0	0	9.00	1	0	0	0	0	1.0	2	1	0	1
Bud Tinning	0	0	0.00	2	0	0	0	0	2.1	0	0	3	3
Lon Warneke	0	1	5.91	2	1	1	0	0	10.2	15	7	5	8
TOTAL	0	4	9.26	13	4	1	0	0	34.0	45	35	23	26

GAME 1 AT NY SEPT 28

CHI	200 000 220	6	10	1
NY	000 305 31X	12	8	2

Pitchers: BUSH, Grimes (6), Smith (8) vs RUFFING
Home Runs: Gehrig-NY
Attendance: 41,459

GAME 2 AT NY SEPT 29

CHI	101 000 000	2	9	0
NY	202 010 00X	5	10	1

Pitchers: WARNEKE vs GOMEZ
Attendance: 50,709

GAME 3 AT CHI OCT 1

NY	301 020 001	7	8	1
CHI	102 100 001	5	9	4

Pitchers: PIPGRAS, Pennock (9) vs ROOT, Malone (5), May (7), Tinning (9)
Home Runs: Ruth-NY (2), Gehrig-NY (2), Cuyler-CHI, Hartnett-CHI
Attendance: 49,986

GAME 4 AT CHI OCT 2

NY	102 002 404	13	19	4
CHI	400 001 001	6	9	1

Pitchers: Allen, MOORE (1), Pennock (7) vs Bush, Warneke (1), MAY (4), Tinning (7), Grimes (9)
Home Runs: Demaree-CHI, Lazzeri-NY (2), Combs-NY
Attendance: 49,844

Although John McGraw had retired from managing the Giants in 1932, he continued to regard them as "his" team. Led now by first baseman Bill Terry, the Giants faced a club also led by an active player, shortstop Joe Cronin in his rookie managerial season.

Giants ace Carl Hubbell dominated the first game, striking out 10 while limiting the Senators to five singles and a pair of unearned runs. Mel Ott set the tone for New York with a two-out two-run homer in the first inning, and singled home a third run in the third to build a lead Washington would not overcome. The next day the Senators scored first, on Goose Goslin's solo homer in the third. But that was the only run scored off Hal Schumacher, and when the Giants drove out Senators starter Alvin Crowder with six runs in the sixth they had their second win well in hand.

The Senators revived when the Series moved to Washington for Game 3. Each of second baseman Buddy Myer's three hits scored or drove in a run, providing a growing cushion for pitcher Earl Whitehill, who recorded the Series' only shutout.

Games 4 and 5 went to New York, but not without a struggle. In the fourth game, manager Terry's home run broke the ice in the fourth inning, but Hubbell muffed a bunt in the seventh which led to the tying run. Hubbell and Senators starter Monty Weaver dueled without further scoring until shortstop Blondy Ryan's single in the top of the 11th put New York up by one. Hubbell let men reach second and third with one out in the last of the 11th, but an intentional walk set up the hoped-for double play to end the game.

New York had built a three-run lead in Game 5 when Fred Schulte evened the score in the last of the sixth with a three-run homer. Relievers Jack Russell and Dolf Luque then dueled scorelessly into the 10th, when Mel Ott (whose homer had begun the Series' scoring in the first inning of Game One) homered once again for what proved the Series' final run. Luque shut down the Senators in their half of the 10th, and "McGraw's Giants" were for the fourth time the world's finest. But before the advent of another spring, McGraw was dead.

New York Giants (NL), 4;
Washington Senators (AL), 1

NY (N)

PLAYER/POS	AVG	G	AB	R	H	2B	3B	HR	RB	BB	SO	SB
Hi Bell, p	.000	1	0	0	0	0	0	0	0	0	0	0
Hughie Critz, 2b	.136	5	22	2	3	0	0	0	0	1	0	0
Kiddo Davis, of	.368	5	19	1	7	1	0	0	0	0	3	0
Freddie Fitzsimmons, p	.500	1	2	0	1	0	0	0	0	0	0	0
Carl Hubbell, p	.286	2	7	0	2	0	0	0	0	0	0	0
Travis Jackson, 3b	.222	5	18	3	4	1	0	0	2	1	3	0
Dolf Luque, p	1.000	1	1	0	1	0	0	0	0	0	0	0
Gus Mancuso, c	.118	5	17	2	2	1	0	0	2	3	0	0
Jo-Jo Moore, of	.227	5	22	1	5	1	0	0	1	1	3	0
Lefty O'Doul, ph	1.000	1	1	1	1	0	0	0	2	0	0	0
Mel Ott, of	.389	5	18	3	7	0	0	2	4	4	4	0
Homer Peel, of-1	.500	2	2	0	1	0	0	0	0	0	0	0
Blondy Ryan, ss	.278	5	18	0	5	0	0	0	1	1	5	0
Hal Schumacher, p	.286	2	7	0	2	0	0	0	0	0	3	0
Bill Terry, 1b	.273	5	22	3	6	1	0	1	1	0	0	0
TOTAL	.267		176	16	47	5	0	3	16	11	21	0

PITCHER	W	L	ERA	G	GS	CG	SV	SHO	IP	H	ER	BB	SO
Hi Bell	0	0	0.00	1	0	0	0	0	1.0	0	0	0	0
Freddie Fitzsimmons	0	1	5.14	1	1	0	0	0	7.0	9	4	0	2
Carl Hubbell	2	0	0.00	2	2	2	0	0	20.0	13	0	6	15
Dolf Luque	1	0	0.00	1	0	0	0	0	4.1	2	0	2	5
Hal Schumacher	1	0	2.45	2	2	1	0	0	14.2	13	4	5	3
TOTAL	4	1	1.53	7	5	3	0	0	47.0	37	8	13	25

WAS (A)

PLAYER/POS	AVG	G	AB	R	H	2B	3B	HR	RB	BB	SO	SB
Ossie Bluege, 3b	.125	5	16	1	2	1	0	0	0	1	6	0
Cliff Bolton, ph	.000	2	2	0	0	0	0	0	0	0	0	0
Joe Cronin, ss	.318	5	22	1	7	0	0	0	2	0	2	0
General Crowder, p	.250	2	4	0	1	0	0	0	0	0	0	0
Goose Goslin, of	.250	5	20	2	5	1	0	1	1	1	3	0
Dave Harris, of-1	.000	3	2	0	0	0	0	0	0	2	0	0
John Kerr, pr	.000	1	0	0	0	0	0	0	0	0	0	0
Joe Kuhel, 1b	.150	5	20	1	3	0	0	0	1	1	4	0
Heinie Manush, of	.111	5	18	2	2	0	0	0	0	2	1	0
Alex McColl, p	.000	1	0	0	0	0	0	0	0	0	0	0
Buddy Myer, 2b	.300	5	20	2	6	1	0	0	2	2	3	0
Sam Rice, ph	1.000	1	1	0	1	0	0	0	0	0	0	0
Jack Russell, p	.000	3	2	0	0	0	0	0	0	1	2	0
Fred Schulte, of	.333	5	21	1	7	1	0	1	4	1	1	0
Luke Sewell, c	.176	5	17	1	3	0	0	0	1	2	0	1
Lefty Stewart, p	.000	1	1	0	0	0	0	0	0	0	1	0
Tommy Thomas, p	.000	2	0	0	0	0	0	0	0	0	0	0
Monte Weaver, p	.000	1	4	0	0	0	0	0	0	0	0	0
Earl Whitehill, p	.000	1	3	0	0	0	0	0	0	0	0	0
TOTAL	.214		173	11	37	4	0	2	11	13	25	1

PITCHER	W	L	ERA	G	GS	CG	SV	SHO	IP	H	ER	BB	SO
General Crowder	0	1	7.36	2	2	0	0	0	11.0	16	9	5	7
Alex McColl	0	0	0.00	1	0	0	0	0	2.0	0	0	0	0
Jack Russell	0	1	0.87	3	0	0	0	0	10.1	8	1	0	7
Lefty Stewart	0	1	9.00	1	1	0	0	0	2.0	6	2	0	0
Tommy Thomas	0	0	0.00	2	0	0	0	0	1.1	1	0	0	2
Monte Weaver	0	1	1.74	1	1	0	0	0	10.1	11	2	4	3
Earl Whitehill	1	0	0.00	1	1	1	0	1	9.0	5	0	2	2
TOTAL	1	4	2.74	11	5	1	0	1	46.0	47	14	11	21

GAME 1 AT NY OCT 3

WAS	000 100 001	2 5 3
NY	202 000 00X	4 10 2

Pitchers: STEWART, Russell (3), Thomas (8) vs HUBBELL
Home Runs: Ott-NY
Attendance: 46,672

GAME 2 AT NY OCT 4

WAS	001 000 000	1 5 0
NY	000 006 00X	6 10 0

Pitchers: CROWDER, Thomas (6), McColl (7) vs SCHUMACHER
Home Runs: Goslin-WAS
Attendance: 35,461

GAME 3 AT WAS OCT 5

NY	000 000 000	0 5 0
WAS	210 000 10X	4 9 1

Pitchers: FITZSIMMONS, Bell (8) vs WHITEHILL
Attendance: 25,727

GAME 4 AT WAS OCT 6

NY	000 100 000 01	2 11 1
WAS	000 000 100 00	1 8 0

Pitchers: HUBBELL vs WEAVER, Russell (11)
Home Runs: Terry-NY
Attendance: 26,762

GAME 5 AT WAS OCT 7

NY	020 001 000 1	4 11 1
WAS	000 003 000 0	3 10 0

Pitchers: Schumacher, LUQUE (6) vs Crowder, RUSSELL (6)
Home Runs: Schulte-WAS, Ott-NY
Attendance: 28,454

Pitching brothers Dizzy and Paul Dean won seven games in 10 days to give the Cardinals the pennant on the final day of the season. In the Series they continued their winning ways, chalking up all four Cardinals victories. Dizzy pitched the opener in Detroit. Given a 3–0 lead, thanks to five Detroit errors in the first three innings, he breezed to an 8–3 win.

Detroit's Schoolboy Rowe brought the Tigers back with a pitching masterpiece in Game 2. After giving up single runs in the second and third innings, he allowed only one runner to reach base over the next nine as his Tigers tied the score in the ninth, and won it on two walks and a single in the 12th.

Paul Dean nearly pitched a shutout in Game 3, yielding a harmless run with two out in the ninth after the Cards had built him a 4–0 lead. Brother Diz figured in a curious and painful play in Game 4. Pinch-running in the fourth inning, he was beaned by a would-be double-play throw as he ran to second. The tying run scored from third on the play, but Detroit's pitcher Eldon Auker shut out the Cards through the final five innings, and his teammates scored six more runs to bury St. Louis 10–4, evening the Series at two apiece. Diz was rushed to the hospital, but as no damage was found he started Game 5 the next day. He pitched well enough, but Detroit's Tommy Bridges pitched better, giving the Cardinals only one run to the Tigers' three.

Paul Dean evened the Series again with a win against Rowe in a closely contested sixth game. A grounder through Dean's legs allowed the Tigers to tie the game in the sixth inning, but Paul redeemed his error in the seventh when he singled in the tie-breaking run. Dizzy came back after only a day's rest to hurl a six-hit shutout in the finale. He also scored the game's first run and drove in the sixth with a double and single in his team's seven-run third. Three innings later, frustrated Tigers fans, angered by Joe Medwick's rough slide into their third baseman, pelted Medwick with food and bottles, halting the game for 20 minutes until Commissioner Landis ordered St. Louis from the game. The delay only forestalled Detroit's defeat, as the Cards took the title game, 11–0.

St. Louis Cardinals (NL), 4;
Detroit Tigers (AL), 3

STL (N)

PLAYER/POS	AVG	G	AB	R	H	2B	3B	HR	RBI	BB	SO	SB
Tex Carleton, p	.000	2	1	0	0	0	0	0	0	0	0	0
Ripper Collins, 1b	.367	7	30	4	11	1	0	0	3	1	2	0
Pat Crawford, ph	.000	2	2	0	0	0	0	0	0	0	0	0
Spud Davis, ph	1.000	2	2	0	2	0	0	0	1	0	0	0
Dizzy Dean, p-3	.250	4	12	3	3	2	0	0	1	0	3	0
Paul Dean, p	.167	2	6	0	1	0	0	0	2	0	1	0
Bill DeLancey, c	.172	7	29	3	5	3	0	1	4	2	8	0
Leo Durocher, ss	.259	7	27	4	7	1	1	0	0	0	0	0
Frankie Frisch, 2b	.194	7	31	2	6	1	0	0	4	0	1	0
Chick Fullis, of	.400	3	5	0	2	0	0	0	0	0	0	0
Jesse Haines, p	.000	1	0	0	0	0	0	0	0	0	0	0
Bill Hallahan, p	.000	1	3	0	0	0	0	0	0	0	1	0
Pepper Martin, 3b	.355	7	31	8	11	3	1	0	4	3	3	2
Joe Medwick, of	.379	7	29	4	11	0	1	1	5	1	7	0
Jim Mooney, p	.000	1	0	0	0	0	0	0	0	0	0	0
Ernie Orsatti, of	.318	7	22	3	7	0	1	0	2	3	1	0
Jack Rothrock, of	.233	7	30	3	7	3	1	0	6	1	2	0
Dazzy Vance, p	.000	1	0	0	0	0	0	0	0	0	0	0
Bill Walker, p	.000	2	2	0	0	0	0	0	0	0	2	0
Burgess Whitehead, ss	.000	1	0	0	0	0	0	0	0	0	0	0
TOTAL	.279		262	34	73	14	5	2	32	11	31	2

PITCHER	W	L	ERA	G	GS	CG	SV	SHO	IP	H	ER	BB	SO
Tex Carleton	0	0	7.36	2	1	0	0	0	3.2	5	3	2	2
Dizzy Dean	2	1	1.73	3	3	2	0	1	26.0	20	5	5	17
Paul Dean	2	0	1.00	2	2	2	0	0	18.0	15	2	7	11
Jesse Haines	0	0	0.00	1	0	0	0	0	0.2	1	0	0	2
Bill Hallahan	0	0	2.16	1	1	0	0	0	8.1	6	2	4	6
Jim Mooney	0	0	0.00	1	0	0	0	0	1.0	1	0	0	0
Dazzy Vance	0	0	0.00	1	0	0	0	0	1.1	2	0	1	3
Bill Walker	0	2	7.11	2	0	0	0	0	6.1	6	5	6	2
TOTAL	4	3	2.34	13	7	4	0	1	65.1	56	17	25	43

DET (A)

PLAYER/POS	AVG	G	AB	R	H	2B	3B	HR	RBI	BB	SO	SB
Eldon Auker, p	.000	2	4	0	0	0	0	0	0	0	2	0
Tommy Bridges, p	.143	3	7	0	1	0	0	0	0	1	4	0
Mickey Cochrane, c	.214	7	28	2	6	1	0	0	1	4	3	0
General Crowder, p	.000	2	1	0	0	0	0	0	0	0	0	0
Frank Doljack, of-1	.000	2	2	0	0	0	0	0	0	0	0	0
Pete Fox, of	.286	7	28	1	8	6	0	0	2	1	4	0
Charlie Gehringer, 2b	.379	7	29	5	11	1	0	1	2	3	0	1
Goose Goslin, of	.241	7	29	2	7	1	0	0	2	3	1	0
Hank Greenberg, 1b	.321	7	28	4	9	2	1	1	7	4	9	1
Ray Hayworth, c	.000	1	0	0	0	0	0	0	0	0	0	0
Chief Hogsett, p	.000	3	3	0	0	0	0	0	0	0	1	0
Firpo Marberry, p	.000	2	0	0	0	0	0	0	0	0	0	0
Marv Owen, 3b	.069	7	29	0	2	0	0	0	1	0	5	1
Billy Rogell, ss	.276	7	29	3	8	1	0	0	4	1	4	1
Schoolboy Rowe, p	.000	3	7	0	0	0	0	0	0	0	5	0
Gee Walker, ph	.333	3	3	0	1	0	0	0	1	0	1	0
Jo-Jo White, of	.130	7	23	6	3	0	0	0	0	8	4	1
TOTAL	.224		250	23	56	12	1	2	20	25	43	5

PITCHER	W	L	ERA	G	GS	CG	SV	SHO	IP	H	ER	BB	SO
Eldon Auker	1	1	5.56	2	2	1	0	0	11.1	16	7	5	2
Tommy Bridges	1	1	3.63	3	2	1	0	0	17.1	21	7	1	12
General Crowder	0	1	1.50	2	1	0	0	0	6.0	6	1	2	2
Chief Hogsett	0	0	1.23	3	0	0	0	0	7.1	6	1	3	3
Firpo Marberry	0	0	21.60	2	0	0	0	0	1.2	5	4	1	0
Schoolboy Rowe	1	1	2.95	3	2	2	0	0	21.1	19	7	0	12
TOTAL	3	4	3.74	15	7	4	0	0	65.0	73	27	11	31

With a 21-game September winning streak, the Cubs vaulted over the Giants and Cardinals to face Detroit in the Series, and for a moment it seemed as if their momentum might carry them past the Tigers as well. Chicago scored two runs off Schoolboy Rowe in the top of the first in the opener, and right fielder Frank Demaree homered to open the ninth as Lon Warneke blanked the Tigers on four hits. But Detroit retaliated quickly in Game 2, driving out starter Charlie Root in the first inning with four runs (including Hank Greenberg's two-run homer) before Root had had a chance to record even one out. Tigers pitcher Rocky Bridges gained an easy 8–3 win, but Greenberg broke a wrist and was finished for the Series.

In Game 3 the Cubs scored three times before Detroit countered with their first run in the sixth. But a walk and four Tiger hits in the eighth put the Bengals ahead, 4–3. Billy Rogell turned a foiled steal into a rundown to allow a fifth Tiger to cross the plate. Two Cubs runs in the last of the ninth tied the score, but Detroit pulled out the victory in the 11th as a pair of singles sandwiched Fred Lindstrom's error at third to give them an unearned run.

Detroit's Alvin "General" Crowder followed up the Tigers' advantage the next day with a neat five-hit 2–1 win. Once again the Cubs bobbled away the game, this time with two sixth-inning errors that enabled Detroit to score the winning run without a hit. Chuck Klein's two-run homer saved Chicago from elimination in Game Five as Lon Warneke and Bill Lee shut out the Tigers through eight before letting in a harmless run in the ninth.

Chicago's Larry French and Tiger Rocky Bridges yielded 12 hits apiece in Game 6. Cubs second baseman Billy Herman singled in a run in the third to tie the score, and homered for two more runs in the fifth to put the Cubs ahead. But the Tigers tied it up an inning later, and took their first world title ever when Goose Goslin singled in Mickey Cochrane with two out in the bottom of the ninth.

Detroit Tigers (AL), 4; Chicago Cubs (NL), 2

DET (A)

PLAYER/POS	AVG	G	AB	R	H	2B	3B	HR	RB	BB	SO	SB
Eldon Auker, p	.000	1	2	0	0	0	0	0	0	0	1	0
Tommy Bridges, p	.125	2	8	1	1	0	0	0	1	0	3	0
Flea Clifton, 3b	.000	4	16	1	0	0	0	0	0	2	4	0
Mickey Cochrane, c	.292	6	24	3	7	1	0	0	1	4	1	0
General Crowder, p	.333	1	3	1	1	0	0	0	0	1	0	0
Pete Fox, of	.385	6	26	1	10	3	1	0	4	0	1	0
Charlie Gehringer, 2b	.375	6	24	4	9	3	0	0	4	2	1	1
Goose Goslin, of	.273	6	22	2	6	1	0	0	3	5	0	0
Hank Greenberg, 1b	.167	2	6	1	1	0	0	1	2	1	0	0
Chief Hogsett, p	.000	1	0	0	0	0	0	0	0	0	0	0
Marv Owen, 1b-4,3b-2	.050	6	20	2	1	0	0	0	1	2	3	0
Billy Rogell, ss	.292	6	24	1	7	2	0	0	1	2	5	0
Schoolboy Rowe, p	.250	3	8	0	2	1	0	0	0	0	1	0
Gee Walker, of-1	.250	3	4	1	1	0	0	0	0	0	1	0
Jo-Jo White, of	.263	6	19	3	5	0	0	0	1	5	7	0
TOTAL	.248		206	21	51	11	1	1	18	25	27	1

PITCHER	W	L	ERA	G	GS	CG	SV	SHO	IP	H	ER	BB	SO
Eldon Auker	0	0	3.00	1	1	0	0	0	6.0	6	2	2	1
Tommy Bridges	2	0	2.50	2	2	2	0	0	18.0	18	5	4	9
General Crowder	1	0	1.00	1	1	1	0	0	9.0	5	1	3	5
Chief Hogsett	0	0	0.00	1	0	0	0	0	1.0	0	0	1	0
Schoolboy Rowe	1	2	2.57	3	2	2	0	0	21.0	19	6	1	14
TOTAL	4	2	2.29	8	6	5	0	0	55.0	48	14	11	29

CHI (N)

PLAYER/POS	AVG	G	AB	R	H	2B	3B	HR	RB	BB	SO	SB
Tex Carleton, p	.000	1	1	0	0	0	0	0	0	0	1	0
Phil Cavarretta, 1b	.125	6	24	1	3	0	0	0	0	0	5	0
Frank Demaree, of	.250	6	24	2	6	1	0	2	2	1	4	0
Larry French, p	.250	2	4	1	1	0	0	0	0	0	2	0
Augie Galan, of	.160	6	25	2	4	1	0	0	2	2	2	0
Stan Hack, 3b-6,ss-1	.227	6	22	2	5	1	1	0	0	2	1	1
Gabby Hartnett, c	.292	6	24	1	7	0	0	1	2	0	3	0
Roy Henshaw, p	.000	1	0	0	0	0	0	0	0	0	0	0
Billy Herman, 2b	.333	6	24	3	8	2	1	1	6	0	2	0
Billy Jurges, ss	.250	6	16	3	4	0	0	0	1	4	4	0
Chuck Klein, of-3	.333	5	12	2	4	0	0	1	2	0	2	0
Fabian Kowalik, p	.500	1	2	1	1	0	0	0	0	0	0	0
Bill Lee, p	.000	2	1	0	0	0	0	0	1	0	0	0
Fred Lindstrom, of-4,3b-1	.200	4	15	0	3	1	0	0	0	1	1	0
Ken O'Dea, ph	1.000	1	1	0	1	0	0	0	1	0	0	0
Charlie Root, p	.000	2	0	0	0	0	0	0	0	0	0	0
Walter Stephenson, ph	.000	1	1	0	0	0	0	0	0	0	1	0
Lon Warneke, p	.200	3	5	0	1	0	0	0	0	0	0	0
TOTAL	.238		202	18	48	6	2	5	17	11	29	1

PITCHER	W	L	ERA	G	GS	CG	SV	SHO	IP	H	ER	BB	SO
Tex Carleton	0	1	1.29	1	1	0	0	0	7.0	6	1	7	4
Larry French	0	2	3.38	2	1	1	0	0	10.2	15	4	2	8
Roy Henshaw	0	0	7.36	1	0	0	0	0	3.2	2	3	5	2
Fabian Kowalik	0	0	2.08	1	0	0	0	0	4.1	3	1	1	0
Bill Lee	0	0	4.35	2	1	0	1	0	10.1	11	5	5	5
Charlie Root	0	1	18.00	2	1	0	0	0	2.0	5	4	1	2
Lon Warneke	2	0	0.54	3	2	1	0	1	16.2	9	1	4	5
TOTAL	2	4	3.13	12	6	2	1	1	54.2	51	19	25	27

GAME 1 AT DET OCT 2

CHI	200	000	001	3	7	0
DET	000	000	000	0	4	3

Pitchers: WARNEKE vs ROWE
Home Runs: Demaree-CHI
Attendance: 47,391

GAME 2 AT DET OCT 3

CHI	000	010	200	3	6	1
DET	400	300	10X	8	9	2

Pitchers: ROOT, Henshaw (1), Kowalik (4) vs BRIDGES
Home Runs: Greenberg-DET
Attendance: 46,742

GAME 3 AT CHI OCT 4

DET	000 001 040 01	6	12	2
CHI	020 010 002 00	5	10	3

Pitchers: Auker, Hogsett (7), ROWE (8) vs Lee, Warneke (8), FRENCH (10)
Home Runs: Demaree-CHI
Attendance: 45,532

GAME 4 AT CHI OCT 5

DET	001	001	000	2	7	0
CHI	010	000	000	1	5	2

Pitchers: CROWDER vs CARLETON, Root (8)
Home Runs: Hartnett-CHI
Attendance: 49,350

GAME 5 AT CHI OCT 6

DET	000	000	001	1	7	1
CHI	002	000	10X	3	8	0

Pitchers: ROWE vs WARNEKE, Lee (7)
Home Runs: Klein-CHI
Attendance: 49,237

GAME 6 AT DET OCT 7

CHI	001	020	000	3	12	0
DET	100	101	001	4	12	1

Pitchers: FRENCH vs BRIDGES
Home Runs: Herman-CHI
Attendance: 48,420

The Giants managed to win two games, but this first Series between the cross-river rivals in 13 years was really no contest. Babe Ruth was gone, but Lou Gehrig was still there, and Joe DiMaggio had arrived. The Yankees outhit the Giants by 56 percentage points and outscored them by 20 runs.

Giants ace Carl Hubbell, who had won his final 16 decisions of the regular season, continued his streak in the Series opener. The Yankees scored first on George Selkirk's third-inning homer, but Giants shortstop Dick Bartell homered to even things in the fifth. Hubbell held the Yankees to that one run, but the Giants roughed up Red Ruffing for five more runs, to give the Polo Grounders a brief Series advantage.

Game 2 was a blowout, as the Yankees hammered five Giants pitchers for 18 runs—four of them on Tony Lazzeri's grand slam in the third—to give Lefty Gomez an easy win. By contrast, Game 3 was a pitchers' duel. Although the Giants touched Bump Hadley and Pat Malone for 11 hits, only Jimmy Ripple's fifth-inning homer produced a run. Freddie Fitzsimmons was much more stingy with hits, yielding only four. But one was Gehrig's home run in the second inning, and another was Frank Crosetti's game-winning RBI single in the eighth.

Gehrig homered again in the third inning of Game 4 to give the Yankees an insurmountable lead—and Hubbell his first loss in months. Down three games to one, the Giants struggled back in Game 5. They took a first-inning 3–0 lead, but the Yankees clawed their way back, and by the end of six the score was 4–4. There it stayed until the 10th, when a double, sacrifice, and fly to center put the Giants ahead by a run. Hal Schumacher, who had pitched the whole game, held the Yankees scoreless one more time for the win.

Fitzsimmons, who had pitched so well in his third-game loss, didn't last four innings in Game 6. Though the Giants scored first, Jake Powell (who led all Series hitters at .455) tied the game with a two-run homer in the top of the second for the Yankees. Two more runs in the fourth drove out Fitzsimmons, but the game stayed close until the top of the ninth, when five Yankees singles and three walks produced seven runs and a Series-ending 13–5 rout.

New York Yankees (AL), 4; New York Giants (NL), 2

NY (A)

PLAYER/POS	AVG	G	AB	R	H	2B	3B	HR	RB	BB	SO	SB
Frankie Crosetti, ss	.269	6	26	5	7	2	0	0	3	3	5	0
Bill Dickey, c	.120	6	25	5	3	0	0	1	5	3	4	0
Joe DiMaggio, of	.346	6	26	3	9	3	0	0	3	1	3	0
Lou Gehrig, 1b	.292	6	24	5	7	1	0	2	7	3	2	0
Lefty Gomez, p	.250	2	8	1	2	0	0	0	3	0	3	0
Bump Hadley, p	.000	1	2	0	0	0	0	0	0	0	1	0
Roy Johnson, ph	.000	2	1	0	0	0	0	0	0	1	0	0
Tony Lazzeri, 2b	.250	6	20	4	5	0	0	1	7	4	4	0
Pat Malone, p	1.000	2	1	0	1	0	0	0	0	0	0	0
Johnny Murphy, p	.500	1	2	1	1	0	0	0	1	0	1	0
Monte Pearson, p	.500	1	4	0	2	1	0	0	0	0	0	0
Jake Powell, of	.455	6	22	8	10	1	0	1	5	4	4	1
Red Rolfe, 3b	.400	6	25	5	10	0	0	0	4	3	1	0
Red Ruffing, p-2	.000	3	5	0	0	0	0	0	0	1	2	0
Bob Seeds, pr	.000	1	0	0	0	0	0	0	0	0	0	0
George Selkirk, of	.333	6	24	6	8	0	1	2	3	4	4	0
TOTAL	.302		215	43	65	8	1	7	41	26	35	1

PITCHER	W	L	ERA	G	GS	CG	SV	SHO	IP	H	ER	BB	SO
Lefty Gomez	2	0	4.70	2	2	1	0	0	15.1	14	8	11	9
Bump Hadley	1	0	1.13	1	1	0	0	0	8.0	10	1	1	2
Pat Malone	0	1	1.80	2	0	0	1	0	5.0	2	1	1	2
Johnny Murphy	0	0	3.38	1	0	0	1	0	2.2	1	1	1	1
Monte Pearson	1	0	2.00	1	1	1	0	0	9.0	7	2	2	7
Red Ruffing	0	1	5.14	2	2	1	0	0	14.0	16	8	5	12
TOTAL	4	2	3.50	9	6	3	2	0	54.0	50	21	21	33

NY (N)

PLAYER/POS	AVG	G	AB	R	H	2B	3B	HR	RB	BB	SO	SB
Dick Bartell, ss	.381	6	21	5	8	3	0	1	3	4	4	0
Slick Castleman, p	.500	1	2	1	1	0	0	0	0	0	0	0
Dick Coffman, p	.000	2	0	0	0	0	0	0	0	0	0	0
Harry Danning, c-1	.000	2	2	0	0	0	0	0	0	0	1	0
Kiddo Davis, ph	.500	4	2	1	1	0	0	0	0	0	0	0
Freddie Fitzsimmons, p	.500	2	4	0	2	0	0	0	0	0	1	0
Frank Gabler, p	.000	2	0	0	0	0	0	0	0	1	0	0
Harry Gumbert, p	.000	2	0	0	0	0	0	0	0	0	0	0
Carl Hubbell, p	.333	2	6	0	2	0	0	0	1	0	0	0
Travis Jackson, 3b	.190	6	21	1	4	0	0	0	1	1	3	0
Mark Koenig, 2b-1	.333	3	3	0	1	0	0	0	0	0	1	0
Hank Leiber, of	.000	2	6	0	0	0	0	0	0	2	2	0
Sam Leslie, ph	.667	3	3	0	2	0	0	0	0	0	0	0
Gus Mancuso, c	.263	6	19	3	5	2	0	0	1	3	3	0
Eddie Mayo, 3b	.000	1	1	0	0	0	0	0	0	0	0	0
Jo-Jo Moore, of	.214	6	28	4	6	2	0	1	1	1	4	0
Mel Ott, of	.304	6	23	4	7	2	0	1	3	3	1	0
Jimmy Ripple, of	.333	5	12	2	4	0	0	1	3	3	3	0
Hal Schumacher, p	.000	2	4	0	0	0	0	0	0	1	3	0
Al Smith, p	.000	1	0	0	0	0	0	0	0	0	0	0
Bill Terry, 1b	.240	6	25	1	6	0	0	0	5	1	4	0
Burgess Whitehead, 2b	.048	6	21	1	1	0	0	0	0	2	1	0
TOTAL	.246		203	23	50	9	0	4	20	21	33	0

PITCHER	W	L	ERA	G	GS	CG	SV	SHO	IP	H	ER	BB	SO
Slick Castleman	0	0	2.08	1	0	0	0	0	4.1	3	1	2	5
Dick Coffman	0	0	32.40	2	0	0	0	0	1.2	5	6	1	1
Freddie Fitzsimmons	0	2	5.40	2	2	1	0	0	11.2	13	7	2	6
Frank Gabler	0	0	7.20	2	0	0	0	0	5.0	7	4	4	0
Harry Gumbert	0	0	36.00	2	0	0	0	0	2.0	7	8	4	2
Carl Hubbell	1	1	2.25	2	2	1	0	0	16.0	15	4	2	10
Hal Schumacher	1	1	5.25	2	2	1	0	0	12.0	13	7	10	11
Al Smith	0	0	81.00	1	0	0	0	0	0.1	2	3	1	0
TOTAL	2	4	6.79	14	6	3	0	0	53.0	65	40	26	35

For the second year in a row, the Yankees overwhelmed the Giants, this time in just five games. Giants ace Carl Hubbell, who took the opener in 1936, was unable to repeat this time. For five innings he held the Yankees to one hit. But in the sixth everything fell apart. Before Hubbell was taken out, two walks, five singles, and an error had led in five runs. And the two runners Hubbell left on base scored later on a second Giants error and two walks by reliever Dick Coffman. The Yankees' Lefty Gomez also yielded six hits, but wider spacing and better field support held the Giants to one run in the fifth. Tony Lazzeri's homer in the eighth made the final score 8–1.

The Yankees spread their runs a bit more evenly in Game 2. For the second time the Giants gained a 1–0 lead. Rookie phenom Cliff Melton held the Yankees scoreless through four, but four straight hits for two runs at the start of the fifth drove him out. Reliever Ad Gumbert stopped the Yankees in the rest of the inning but gave up four more hits—and four more runs—in the sixth before Coffman stepped in to stop the assault. But Coffman gave up two final Yankees runs in the seventh, to complete a second straight 8–1 win, as Red Ruffing held the Giants scoreless through the final eight innings.

The Yankees had scored five times off Hal Schumacher in Game 3 before the Giants got their one run in the seventh. But Yankees starter Monte Pearson made the game tighter as he yielded a single and two walks to load the bases in the ninth before Johnny Murphy came on to record the final out.

The Giants' bats finally came alive in the second inning of Game 4. Seven singles, plus a walk and a missed play at the plate gave the club a 6–1 lead, which starter Hubbell protected for the only Giants win of the Series.

Solo homers by Myril Hoag in the second and Joe DiMaggio in the third gave the Yankees a 2–0 lead early in Game 5, but Giants slugger Mel Ott tied it up with a two-run shot off Lefty Gomez in the last of the third. But Gomez shut the Giants down the rest of the way, and singled in Lazzeri in the fifth with what proved the game winner (scoring himself on Lou Gehrig's double for the final run of the Series).

New York Yankees (AL), 4;
New York Giants (NL), 1

NY (A)

PLAYER/POS	AVG	G	AB	R	H	2B	3B	HR	RB	BB	SO	SB
Ivy Andrews, p	.000	1	2	0	0	0	0	0	0	0	1	0
Frankie Crosetti, ss	.048	5	21	2	1	0	0	0	0	3	2	0
Bill Dickey, c	.211	5	19	3	4	0	1	0	3	2	2	0
Joe DiMaggio, of	.273	5	22	2	6	0	0	1	4	0	3	0
Lou Gehrig, 1b	.294	5	17	4	5	1	1	1	3	5	4	0
Lefty Gomez, p	.167	2	6	2	1	0	0	0	1	2	1	0
Bump Hadley, p	.000	1	0	0	0	0	0	0	0	0	0	0
Myril Hoag, of	.300	5	20	4	6	1	0	1	2	0	1	0
Tony Lazzeri, 2b	.400	5	15	3	6	0	1	1	2	3	3	0
Johnny Murphy, p	.000	1	0	0	0	0	0	0	0	0	0	0
Monte Pearson, p	.000	1	3	0	0	0	0	0	0	1	1	0
Jake Powell, ph	.000	1	1	0	0	0	0	0	0	0	1	0
Red Rolfe, 3b	.300	5	20	3	6	2	1	0	1	3	2	0
Red Ruffing, p	.500	1	4	2	2	1	0	0	3	0	0	0
George Selkirk, of	.263	5	19	5	5	1	0	0	6	2	0	0
Kemp Wicker, p	.000	1	0	0	0	0	0	0	0	0	0	0
TOTAL	.249		169	28	42	6	4	4	25	21	21	0

PITCHER	W	L	ERA	G	GS	CG	SV	SHO	IP	H	ER	BB	SO
Ivy Andrews	0	0	3.18	1	0	0	0	0	5.2	6	2	4	1
Lefty Gomez	2	0	1.50	2	2	2	0	0	18.0	16	3	2	8
Bump Hadley	0	1	33.75	1	1	0	0	0	1.1	6	5	0	0
Johnny Murphy	0	0	0.00	1	0	0	1	0	0.1	0	0	0	0
Monte Pearson	1	0	1.04	1	1	0	0	0	8.2	5	1	2	4
Red Ruffing	1	0	1.00	1	1	1	0	0	9.0	7	1	3	8
Kemp Wicker	0	0	0.00	1	0	0	0	0	1.0	0	0	0	0
TOTAL	4	1	2.45	8	5	3	1	0	44.0	40	12	11	21

NY (N)

PLAYER/POS	AVG	G	AB	R	H	2B	3B	HR	RB	BB	SO	SB
Dick Bartell, ss	.238	5	21	3	5	1	0	0	1	0	3	0
Wally Berger, ph	.000	3	3	0	0	0	0	0	0	0	1	0
Don Brennan, p	.000	2	0	0	0	0	0	0	0	0	0	0
Lou Chiozza, of	.286	2	7	0	2	0	0	0	0	1	1	0
Dick Coffman, p	.000	2	1	0	0	0	0	0	0	0	1	0
Harry Danning, c	.250	3	12	0	3	1	0	0	2	0	2	0
Harry Gumbert, p	.000	2	0	0	0	0	0	0	0	0	0	0
Carl Hubbell, p	.000	2	6	1	0	0	0	0	1	0	0	0
Hank Leiber, of	.364	3	11	2	4	0	0	0	2	1	1	0
Sam Leslie, ph	.000	2	1	0	0	0	0	0	0	1	0	0
Gus Mancuso, c-2	.000	3	8	0	0	0	0	0	0	1	1	0
Johnny McCarthy, 1b	.211	5	19	1	4	1	0	0	1	1	2	0
Cliff Melton, p	.000	3	2	0	0	0	0	0	0	0	1	0
Jo-Jo Moore, of	.391	5	23	1	9	1	0	0	1	0	1	0
Mel Ott, 3b	.200	5	20	1	4	0	0	1	3	1	4	0
Jimmy Ripple, of	.294	5	17	2	5	0	0	0	0	3	1	0
Blondy Ryan, ph	.000	1	1	0	0	0	0	0	0	0	0	0
Hal Schumacher, p	.000	1	1	0	0	0	0	0	0	0	1	0
Al Smith, p	.000	2	0	0	0	0	0	0	0	0	0	0
Burgess Whitehead, 2b	.250	5	16	1	4	2	0	0	0	2	0	1
TOTAL	.237		169	12	40	6	0	1	12	11	21	1

PITCHER	W	L	ERA	G	GS	CG	SV	SHO	IP	H	ER	BB	SO
Don Brennan	0	0	0.00	2	0	0	0	0	3.0	1	0	1	1
Dick Coffman	0	0	4.15	2	0	0	0	0	4.1	2	2	5	1
Harry Gumbert	0	0	27.00	2	0	0	0	0	1.1	4	4	1	1
Carl Hubbell	1	1	3.77	2	2	1	0	0	14.1	12	6	4	7
Cliff Melton	0	2	4.91	3	2	0	0	0	11.0	12	6	6	7
Hal Schumacher	0	1	6.00	1	1	0	0	0	6.0	9	4	4	3
Al Smith	0	0	3.00	2	0	0	0	0	3.0	2	1	0	1
TOTAL	1	4	4.81	14	5	1	0	0	43.0	42	23	21	21

GAME 1 AT NY-A OCT 6

NY-N	000 010 000	1	6	2
NY-A	000 007 01X	8	7	0

Pitchers: HUBBELL, Gumbert (6), Coffman (6), Smith (8) vs GOMEZ
Home Runs: Lazzeri-NY(A)
Attendance: 60,573

GAME 2 AT NY-A OCT 7

NY-N	100 000 000	1	7	0
NY-A	000 024 20X	8	12	0

Pitchers: MELTON, Gumbert (5), Coffman (6) vs RUFFING
Attendance: 57,675

GAME 3 AT NY-N OCT 8

NY-A	012 110 000	5	9	0
NY-N	000 000 100	1	5	4

Pitchers: PEARSON, Murphy (9) vs SCHUMACHER, Melton (7), Brennan (9)
Attendance: 37,385

GAME 4 AT NY-N OCT 9

NY-A	101 000 001	3	6	0
NY-N	060 000 10X	7	12	3

Pitchers: HADLEY, Andrews (2), Wicker (8) vs HUBBELL
Home Runs: Gehrig-NY(A)
Attendance: 44,293

GAME 5 AT NY-N OCT 10

NY-A	011 020 000	4	8	0
NY-N	002 000 000	2	10	0

Pitchers: GOMEZ vs MELTON, Smith (6), Brennan (8)
Home Runs: DiMaggio-NY(A), Hoag-NY(A), Ott-NY(N)
Attendance: 38,216

As they had six years earlier, the Cubs faced the Yankees in the World Series, and as they had six years earlier, New York swept the Series in four games. Although Cubs batters made nearly as many hits as the Yankees, they did much less damage, driving in 13 fewer runs. In Game 1, Yankees ace Red Ruffing scattered nine hits, holding Chicago to a single run. The Cubs' Bill Lee was nearly as effective in scattering hits, but a base on balls in the second (the game's only walk) followed by a pair of singles sandwiched around an error accounted for two runs—all the Yankees would need for the win (though they scored once more in the sixth).

In Game 2 the Cubs outhit the Yankees 11 to 7, but scored only half as many runs as the New Yorkers. Chicago's Dizzy Dean, pitching on craft and guile with his fastball gone, managed to keep the game close until the final innings. With a 3–2 lead going into the eighth, though, he gave up a two-run homer to Frank Crosetti, and the same to Joe DiMaggio in the ninth before being relieved. Yankees fireman Johnny Murphy, meanwhile, held Chicago scoreless over the final two innings to preserve Lefty Gomez's win.

Utility outfielder Joe Marty drove in both Chicago runs in Game 3 with a grounder to third in the fifth and a homer in the eighth. (His .500 batting average was tops for both teams, and he drove in five of the Cubs' nine Series runs.) But again the Cubs fell short, as rookie second baseman Joe Gordon homered to tie the score in the bottom of the fifth with the first of what would be five Yankees runs by the time Bill Dickey's homer in the eighth ended the scoring for the day.

Cubs second baseman Billy Herman's wild throw with two out in the second inning of Game 4 led to three unearned runs, and a lead the Yankees would not relinquish. Though their lead was cut to one run (4–3) when Chicago scored twice in the top of the eighth, the Yankees took advantage of two wild pitches and two walks to turn their four hits into four runs that crushed Chicago hopes and gave the New Yorkers a record third consecutive world championship.

New York Yankees (AL), 4; Chicago Cubs (NL), 0

NY (A)

PLAYER/POS	AVG	G	AB	R	H	2B	3B	HR	RB	BB	SO	SB
Frankie Crosetti, ss	.250	4	16	1	4	2	1	1	6	2	4	0
Bill Dickey, c	.400	4	15	2	6	0	0	1	2	1	0	1
Joe DiMaggio, of	.267	4	15	4	4	0	0	1	2	1	1	0
Lou Gehrig, 1b	.286	4	14	4	4	0	0	0	0	2	3	0
Lefty Gomez, p	.000	1	2	0	0	0	0	0	0	0	0	0
Joe Gordon, 2b	.400	4	15	3	6	2	0	1	6	1	3	1
Tommy Henrich, of	.250	4	16	3	4	1	0	1	1	0	1	0
Myril Hoag, of-1	.400	2	5	3	2	1	0	0	1	0	0	0
Johnny Murphy, p	.000	1	0	0	0	0	0	0	0	0	0	0
Monte Pearson, p	.333	1	3	1	1	0	0	0	0	1	0	0
Jake Powell, of	.000	1	0	0	0	0	0	0	0	0	0	0
Red Rolfe, 3b	.167	4	18	0	3	0	0	0	1	0	3	1
Red Ruffing, p	.167	2	6	1	1	0	0	0	1	1	0	0
George Selkirk, of	.200	3	10	0	2	0	0	0	1	2	1	0
TOTAL	.274		135	22	37	6	1	5	21	11	16	3

PITCHER	W	L	ERA	G	GS	CG	SV	SHO	IP	H	ER	BB	SO
Lefty Gomez	1	0	3.86	1	1	0	0	0	7.0	9	3	1	5
Johnny Murphy	0	0	0.00	1	0	0	1	0	2.0	2	0	1	1
Monte Pearson	1	0	1.00	1	1	1	0	0	9.0	5	1	2	9
Red Ruffing	2	0	1.50	2	2	2	0	0	18.0	17	3	2	11
TOTAL	4	0	1.75	5	4	3	1	0	36.0	33	7	6	26

CHI (N)

PLAYER/POS	AVG	G	AB	R	H	2B	3B	HR	RB	BB	SO	SB
Clay Bryant, p	.000	1	2	0	0	0	0	0	0	0	1	0
Tex Carleton, p	.000	1	0	0	0	0	0	0	0	0	0	0
Phil Cavaretta, of-3	.462	4	13	1	6	1	0	0	0	0	1	0
Ripper Collins, 1b	.133	4	15	1	2	0	0	0	0	0	3	0
Dizzy Dean, p	.667	2	3	0	2	0	0	0	0	0	0	0
Frank Demaree, of	.100	3	10	1	1	0	0	0	0	1	2	0
Larry French, p	.000	3	0	0	0	0	0	0	0	0	0	0
Augie Galan, ph	.000	2	2	0	0	0	0	0	0	0	1	0
Stan Hack, 3b	.471	4	17	3	8	1	0	0	1	1	2	0
Gabby Hartnett, c	.091	3	11	0	1	0	1	0	0	0	2	0
Billy Herman, 2b	.188	4	16	1	3	0	0	0	0	1	4	0
Billy Jurges, ss	.231	4	13	0	3	1	0	0	0	1	3	0
Tony Lazzeri, ph	.000	2	2	0	0	0	0	0	0	0	1	0
Bill Lee, p	.000	2	3	0	0	0	0	0	0	0	1	0
Joe Marty, of	.500	3	12	1	6	1	0	1	5	0	2	0
Ken O'Dea, c-1	.200	3	5	1	1	0	0	1	2	1	0	0
Vance Page, p	.000	1	0	0	0	0	0	0	0	0	0	0
Carl Reynolds, of-3	.000	4	12	0	0	0	0	0	0	1	3	0
Charlie Root, p	.000	1	0	0	0	0	0	0	0	0	0	0
Jack Russell, p	.000	2	0	0	0	0	0	0	0	0	0	0
TOTAL	.243		136	9	33	4	1	2	8	6	26	0

PITCHER	W	L	ERA	G	GS	CG	SV	SHO	IP	H	ER	BB	SO
Clay Bryant	0	1	6.75	1	1	0	0	0	5.1	6	4	5	3
Tex Carleton	0	0	∞	1	0	0	0	0	0.0	1	2	2	0
Dizzy Dean	0	1	6.48	2	1	0	0	0	8.1	8	6	1	2
Larry French	0	0	2.70	3	0	0	0	0	3.1	1	1	1	2
Bill Lee	0	2	2.45	2	2	0	0	0	11.0	15	3	1	8
Vance Page	0	0	13.50	1	0	0	0	0	1.1	2	2	0	0
Charlie Root	0	0	3.00	1	0	0	0	0	3.0	3	1	0	1
Jack Russell	0	0	0.00	2	0	0	0	0	1.2	1	0	1	0
TOTAL	0	4	5.03	13	4	0	0	0	34.0	37	19	11	16

GAME 1 AT CHI OCT 5

NY	020 000 100	3	12	1
CHI	001 000 000	1	9	1

Pitchers: RUFFING vs LEE, Russell (9)
Attendance: 43,642

GAME 2 AT CHI OCT 6

NY	020 000 022	6	7	2
CHI	102 000 000	3	11	0

Pitchers: GOMEZ, Murphy (8) vs J.DEAN, French (9)
Home Runs: Crosetti-NY, DiMaggio-NY
Attendance: 42,108

GAME 3 AT NY OCT 8

CHI	000 010 010	2	5	1
NY	000 022 01X	5	7	2

Pitchers: BRYANT, Russell (6), French (7) vs PEARSON
Home Runs: Dickey-NY, Gordon-NY, Marty-CHI
Attendance: 55,236

GAME 4 AT NY OCT 9

CHI	000 100 020	3	8	1
NY	030 001 04X	8	11	1

Pitchers: LEE, Root (4), Page (7), French (8), Carleton (8), J.Dean (8) vs RUFFING
Home Runs: Henrich-NY, O'Dea-CHI
Attendance: 59,847

The Yankees won their fourth consecutive World Series with their second sweep in a row. This time the victim was Cincinnati, in the Series for the first time since their tainted triumph over the Black Sox two decades earlier. New York had lost the power of Lou Gehrig (whose illness forced his retirement early in the season), but in the Series rookie outfielder Charlie Keller took up the slack. He led both clubs in batting, slugging, home runs, RBIs, hits, and runs, and hit one of the Series' two triples. His eight runs scored equalled those of the whole Cincinnati team.

The Yankees' Red Ruffing and Cincinnati's Paul Derringer hurled matching four-hitters through eight innings of Game 1. With the score tied 1–1, Ruffing set the Reds down in order in the ninth. But in the bottom of the ninth Keller tripled off Derringer with one away, and scored the deciding run on catcher Bill Dickey's single.

Babe Dahlgren, Gehrig's replacement at first base, doubled in the third and later scored the Yankees' first run in Game 2, and homered in the next inning for New York's fourth and final run of the game. Reds starter Bucky Walters stopped the Yankees after that, but they had more than enough runs for the win, as Monte Pearson held the Reds hitless through seven and wound up with a two-hit shutout.

Keller provided the margin of victory with a pair of two-run homers in the first and fifth innings of Game 3. Joe DiMaggio's two-run homer in the third and Bill Dickey's solo shot that followed Keller's homer in the fifth accounted for the rest of New York's runs in their 7–3 win.

No one scored through six innings of Game 4. Keller and Dickey then homered in the top of the seventh, but Red Rolfe's error at third in the last of the inning opened the way for the Reds to go ahead with three unearned runs. They earned a fourth run an inning later, but the Yankees tied it up with two in the ninth (one unearned) and took the lead in the 10th with three more runs (two unearned) on a walk, a single, and three more Reds errors. Reliever Johnny Murphy held off a Cincinnati threat in the last of the 10th and the Series was over.

New York Yankees (AL), 4;
Cincinnati Reds (NL), 0

NY (A)

PLAYER/POS	AVG	G	AB	R	H	2B	3B	HR	RB	BB	SO	SB
Frankie Crosetti, ss	.063	4	16	2	1	0	0	0	1	2	2	0
Babe Dahlgren, 1b	.214	4	14	2	3	2	0	1	2	0	4	0
Bill Dickey, c	.267	4	15	2	4	0	0	2	5	1	2	0
Joe DiMaggio, of	.313	4	16	3	5	0	0	1	3	1	1	0
Lefty Gomez, p	.000	1	1	0	0	0	0	0	0	0	1	0
Joe Gordon, 2b	.143	4	14	1	2	0	0	0	1	0	2	0
Bump Hadley, p	.000	1	3	0	0	0	0	0	0	0	0	0
Oral Hildebrand, p	.000	1	1	0	0	0	0	0	0	0	1	0
Charlie Keller, of	.438	4	16	8	7	1	1	3	6	1	2	0
Johnny Murphy, p	.000	1	2	0	0	0	0	0	0	0	1	0
Monte Pearson, p	.000	1	2	0	0	0	0	0	0	0	0	0
Red Rolfe, 3b	.125	4	16	2	2	0	0	0	0	0	0	0
Red Ruffing, p	.333	1	3	0	1	0	0	0	0	0	1	0
George Selkirk, of	.167	4	12	0	2	1	0	0	0	3	2	0
Steve Sundra, p	.000	1	0	0	0	0	0	0	0	0	1	0
TOTAL	.206		131	20	27	4	1	7	18	9	20	0

PITCHER	W	L	ERA	G	GS	CG	SV	SHO	IP	H	ER	BB	SO
Lefty Gomez	0	0	9.00	1	1	0	0	0	1.0	3	1	0	1
Bump Hadley	1	0	2.25	1	0	0	0	0	8.0	7	2	3	2
Oral Hildebrand	0	0	0.00	1	1	0	0	0	4.0	2	0	0	3
Johnny Murphy	1	0	2.70	1	0	0	0	0	3.1	5	1	0	2
Monte Pearson	1	0	0.00	1	1	1	0	1	9.0	2	0	1	8
Red Ruffing	1	0	1.00	1	1	1	0	0	9.0	4	1	1	4
Steve Sundra	0	0	0.00	1	0	0	0	0	2.2	4	0	1	2
TOTAL	4	0	1.22	7	4	2	0	1	37.0	27	5	6	22

CIN (N)

PLAYER/POS	AVG	G	AB	R	H	2B	3B	HR	RB	BB	SO	SB
Wally Berger, of	.000	4	15	0	0	0	0	0	1	0	4	0
Nino Bongiovanni, ph	.000	1	1	0	0	0	0	0	0	0	0	0
Frenchy Bordagaray, pr	.000	2	0	0	0	0	0	0	0	0	0	0
Harry Craft, of	.091	4	11	0	1	0	0	0	0	0	6	0
Paul Derringer, p	.200	2	5	0	1	0	0	0	0	0	0	0
Lonny Frey, 2b	.000	4	17	0	0	0	0	0	0	1	4	0
Lee Gamble, ph	.000	1	1	0	0	0	0	0	0	0	1	0
Ival Goodman, of	.333	4	15	3	5	1	0	0	1	1	2	1
Lee Grissom, p	.000	1	0	0	0	0	0	0	0	0	0	0
Willard Hershberger, c-2	.500	3	2	0	1	0	0	0	1	0	0	0
Ernie Lombardi, c	.214	4	14	0	3	0	0	0	2	0	1	0
Frank McCormick, 1b	.400	4	15	1	6	1	0	0	1	0	1	0
Whitey Moore, p	.000	1	1	0	0	0	0	0	0	0	0	0
Billy Myers, ss	.333	4	12	2	4	0	1	0	2	3	0	0
Al Simmons, of	.250	2	4	1	1	1	0	0	0	0	0	0
Junior Thompson, p	1.000	1	1	0	1	0	0	0	0	0	0	0
Bucky Walters, p	.000	2	3	0	0	0	0	0	0	0	0	0
Billy Werber, 3b	.250	4	16	1	4	0	0	0	2	2	0	0
TOTAL	.203		133	8	27	3	1	0	8	6	22	1

PITCHER	W	L	ERA	G	GS	CG	SV	SHO	IP	H	ER	BB	SO
Paul Derringer	0	1	2.35	2	2	1	0	0	15.1	9	4	3	9
Lee Grissom	0	0	0.00	1	0	0	0	0	1.1	0	0	1	0
Whitey Moore	0	0	0.00	1	0	0	0	0	3.0	0	0	0	2
Junior Thompson	0	1	13.50	1	1	0	0	0	4.2	5	7	4	3
Bucky Walters	0	2	4.91	2	1	1	0	0	11.0	13	6	1	6
TOTAL	0	4	4.33	7	4	2	0	0	35.1	27	17	9	20

GAME 1 AT NY OCT 4

CIN	000	100	000	1	4	0
NY	000	010	001	2	6	0

Pitchers: DERRINGER vs RUFFING
Attendance: 58,541

GAME 2 AT NY OCT 5

CIN	000	000	000	0	2	0
NY	003	100	00X	4	9	0

Pitchers: WALTERS vs PEARSON
Home Runs: Dahlgren-NY
Attendance: 59,791

GAME 3 AT CIN OCT 7

NY	202	030	000	7	5	1
CIN	120	000	000	3	10	0

Pitchers: Gomez, HADLEY (2) vs THOMPSON, Grissom (5), Moore (7)
Home Runs: Keller-NY (2), DiMaggio-NY, Dickey-NY
Attendance: 32,723

GAME 4 AT CIN OCT 8

NY	000	000	202	3	7	1
CIN	000	000	310	0	4	11	4

Pitchers: Hildebrand, Sundra (5), MURPHY (7) vs Derringer, WALTERS (8)
Home Runs: Keller-NY, Dickey-NY
Attendance: 32,794

The Tigers outpitched and out-slugged the Reds, and scored six more runs than the Reds did. What they failed to do was win the Series.

Tigers ace Bobo Newsom, who had enjoyed what would be his finest season in a long career, carried his mastery into the Series opener. Detroit gave him an early lead, driving out Reds starter Paul Derringer with five runs in the second inning, and added a pair of runs in the fifth on Bruce Campbell's home run. Newsom, meanwhile, held the Reds to single runs in the fourth and eighth.

Cincinnati's Bucky Walters walked the first two Tigers he faced in Game 2, and both scored. But two Reds runs in the second tied the game, Jimmy Ripple's two-run homer an inning later gave them the lead, and pitcher Walters scored an insurance run in the fourth after doubling. Another Tigers walk in the sixth led to their third run, but Walters retired the remaining Tigers in order.

Detroit's Rocky Bridges yielded 10 hits and four runs in Game 3, but his teammates responded with 13 hits and seven runs, including a pair of two-run homers by Rudy York and Pinky Higgins in the seventh. Cincinnati again evened the Series the next day, though, with five runs to support Derringer's five-hit, two-run pitching. Although Newsom's father had suffered a fatal heart attack the day after seeing his son win the opener, the son pitched Game 5, and improved on his previous performance with a three-hit shutout. Hank Greenberg's homer in the third inning accounted for the first three of the Tigers' eight runs in their lopsided win.

The Reds returned home needing to win the final two games. Like Newsom, Bucky Walters bettered his earlier win with a shutout in Game 6, and drove in two of the Reds' four runs, one with a solo homer in the eighth. In the Series finale, Newsom and Derringer found themselves evenly matched. The Tigers scored a run in the third, while Newsom held Cincinnati scoreless through six. But in the seventh, leadoff doubles by Frank McCormick and Jimmy Ripple, plus a successful bunt and a fly to deep center, gave the Reds two runs—all they needed as Derringer stopped the Tigers through the final six innings for the victory.

Cincinnati Reds (NL), 4;
Detroit Tigers (AL), 3

CIN (N)

PLAYER/POS	AVG	G	AB	R	H	2B	3B	HR	RB	BB	SO	SB
Morrie Arnovich, of	.000	1	1	0	0	0	0	0	0	0	0	0
Bill Baker, c	.250	3	4	1	1	0	0	0	0	0	1	0
Joe Beggs, p	.000	1	0	0	0	0	0	0	0	0	0	0
Harry Craft, ph	.000	1	1	0	0	0	0	0	0	0	0	0
Paul Derringer, p	.000	3	7	0	0	0	0	0	0	0	1	0
Lonny Frey, ph	.000	3	2	0	0	0	0	0	0	0	0	0
Ival Goodman, of	.276	7	29	5	8	2	0	0	5	0	3	0
Johnny Hutchings, p	.000	1	0	0	0	0	0	0	0	0	0	0
Eddie Joost, 2b	.200	7	25	0	5	0	0	0	2	1	2	0
Ernie Lombardi, c-1	.333	2	3	0	1	1	0	0	0	1	0	0
Frank McCormick, 1b	.214	7	28	2	6	1	0	0	0	1	1	0
Mike McCormick, of	.310	7	29	1	9	3	0	0	2	1	6	0
Whitey Moore, p	.000	3	2	0	0	0	0	0	0	0	1	0
Billy Myers, ss	.130	7	23	0	3	0	0	0	2	2	5	0
Elmer Riddle, p	.000	1	0	0	0	0	0	0	0	0	0	0
Lew Riggs, ph	.000	3	3	1	0	0	0	0	0	0	2	0
Jimmy Ripple, of	.333	7	21	3	7	2	0	1	6	4	2	0
Junior Thompson, p	.000	1	1	0	0	0	0	0	0	0	1	0
Jim Turner, p	.000	1	2	0	0	0	0	0	0	0	0	0
Johnny Vander Meer, p	.000	1	0	0	0	0	0	0	0	0	0	0
Bucky Walters, p	.286	2	7	2	2	1	0	1	2	0	1	0
Billy Werber, 3b	.370	7	27	5	10	4	0	0	2	4	2	0
Jimmie Wilson, c	.353	6	17	2	6	0	0	0	0	1	2	1
TOTAL	.250		232	22	58	14	0	2	21	15	30	1

PITCHER	W	L	ERA	G	GS	CG	SV	SHO	IP	H	ER	BB	SO
Joe Beggs	0	0	9.00	1	0	0	0	0	1.0	3	1	0	1
Paul Derringer	2	1	2.79	3	3	2	0	0	19.1	17	6	10	6
Johnny Hutchings	0	0	9.00	1	0	0	0	0	1.0	2	1	1	0
Whitey Moore	0	0	3.24	3	0	0	0	0	8.1	8	3	6	7
Elmer Riddle	0	0	0.00	1	0	0	0	0	1.0	0	0	0	2
Junior Thompson	0	1	16.20	1	1	0	0	0	3.1	8	6	4	2
Jim Turner	0	1	7.50	1	1	0	0	0	6.0	8	5	0	4
Johnny Vander Meer	0	0	0.00	1	0	0	0	0	3.0	2	0	3	2
Bucky Walters	2	0	1.50	2	2	2	0	1	18.0	8	3	6	6
TOTAL	4	3	3.69	14	7	4	0	1	61.0	56	25	30	30

DET (A)

PLAYER/POS	AVG	G	AB	R	H	2B	3B	HR	RB	BB	SO	SB
Earl Averill, ph	.000	3	3	0	0	0	0	0	0	0	0	0
Dick Bartell, ss	.269	7	26	2	7	2	0	0	3	3	3	0
Tommy Bridges, p	.000	1	3	0	0	0	0	0	0	0	1	0
Bruce Campbell, of	.360	7	25	4	9	1	0	1	5	4	4	0
Frank Croucher, ss	.000	1	0	0	0	0	0	0	0	0	0	0
Pete Fox, ph	.000	1	1	0	0	0	0	0	0	0	0	0
Charlie Gehringer, 2b	.214	7	28	3	6	0	0	0	1	2	0	0
Johnny Gorsica, p	.000	2	4	0	0	0	0	0	0	0	2	0
Hank Greenberg, of	.357	7	28	5	10	2	1	1	6	2	5	0
Pinky Higgins, 3b	.333	7	24	2	8	3	1	1	6	3	3	0
Fred Hutchinson, p	.000	1	0	0	0	0	0	0	0	0	0	0
Barney McCosky, of	.304	7	23	5	7	1	0	0	1	7	0	0
Archie McKain, p	.000	1	0	0	0	0	0	0	0	0	0	0
Bobo Newsom, p	.100	3	10	1	1	0	0	0	0	0	1	0
Schoolboy Rowe, p	.000	2	1	0	0	0	0	0	0	0	1	0
Clay Smith, p	.000	1	1	0	0	0	0	0	0	0	1	0
Billy Sullivan, c-4	.154	5	13	3	2	0	0	0	0	5	2	0
Birdie Tebbetts, c-3	.000	4	11	0	0	0	0	0	0	0	0	0
Dizzy Trout, p	.000	1	1	0	0	0	0	0	0	0	0	0
Rudy York, 1b	.231	7	26	3	6	0	1	1	4	2	4	0
TOTAL	.246		228	28	56	9	3	4	24	30	30	0

PITCHER	W	L	ERA	G	GS	CG	SV	SHO	IP	H	ER	BB	SO
Tommy Bridges	1	0	3.00	1	1	1	0	0	9.0	10	3	1	5
Johnny Gorsica	0	0	0.79	2	0	0	0	0	11.1	6	1	4	4
Fred Hutchinson	0	0	9.00	1	0	0	0	0	1.0	1	1	1	1
Archie McKain	0	0	3.00	1	0	0	0	0	3.0	4	1	0	0
Bobo Newsom	2	1	1.38	3	3	3	0	1	26.0	18	4	4	17
Schoolboy Rowe	0	2	17.18	2	2	0	0	0	3.2	12	7	1	1
Clay Smith	0	0	2.25	1	0	0	0	0	4.0	1	1	3	1
Dizzy Trout	0	1	9.00	1	1	0	0	0	2.0	6	2	1	1
TOTAL	3	4	3.00	12	7	4	0	1	60.0	58	20	15	30

GAME 1 AT CIN OCT 2

DET	050	020	000	7	10	1
CIN	000	100	010	2	8	3

Pitchers: NEWSOM vs DERRINGER, Moore (2), Riddle (9)
Home Runs: Campbell-DET
Attendance: 31,793

GAME 2 AT CIN OCT 3

DET	200	001	000	3	3	1
CIN	022	100	00X	5	9	0

Pitchers: ROWE, Gorsica (4) vs WALTERS
Home Runs: Ripple-CIN
Attendance: 30,640

GAME 3 AT DET OCT 4

CIN	100	000	012	4	10	1
DET	000	100	42X	7	13	1

Pitchers: TURNER, Moore (7), Beggs (8) vs BRIDGES
Home Runs: York-DET, Higgins-DET
Attendance: 52,877

GAME 4 AT DET OCT 5

CIN	201	100	010	5	11	1
DET	001	001	000	2	5	1

Pitchers: DERRINGER vs TROUT, Smith (3), McKain (7)
Attendance: 54,093

GAME 5 AT DET OCT 6

CIN	000	000	000	0	3	0
DET	003	400	01X	8	13	0

Pitchers: THOMPSON, Moore (4), Vander Meer (5), Hutchings (8) vs NEWSOM
Home Runs: Greenberg-DET
Attendance: 55,189

GAME 6 AT CIN OCT 7

DET	000	000	000	0	5	0
CIN	200	001	01X	4	10	2

Pitchers: ROWE, Gorsica (1), Hutchinson (8) vs WALTERS
Home Runs: Walters-CIN
Attendance: 30,481

GAME 7 AT CIN OCT 8

DET	001	000	000	1	7	0
CIN	000	000	20X	2	7	1

Pitchers: NEWSOM vs DERRINGER
Attendance: 26,854

Dodgers catcher Mickey Owen's dropped third strike in Game 4 was the Series' memorable boner, but it was not the chief cause of Brooklyn's downfall. Yankees pitching was. Three Yankees hurled complete-game wins, with each giving the Dodgers only one earned run. And relief ace Johnny Murphy hurled two-hit shutout ball in six innings over two games, winning one.

Joe Gordon opened the Series scoring with a solo homer in the second inning for the Yankees in Game 1, and the Yankees added runs in the fourth and sixth. Owen tripled in the Dodgers' first run in the fifth, and pinch hitter Lew Riggs singled in an unearned run in the seventh. But Yankees starter Red Ruffing held on to his slim lead through the final two innings for the win.

Dodgers ace Whitlow Wyatt gave the Yankees single runs in the second and third innings of Game 2, but held them scoreless the rest of the way. Meanwhile, the Dodgers tied the game in the fifth, and scored an unearned run in the sixth to finish the scoring and give Brooklyn its only win of the Series.

Freddie Fitzsimmons, with the Dodgers' best pitching of the Series, dueled Marius Russo through seven scoreless innings in Game 3. But Fitzsimmons's final out of the seventh—a line drive by Russo that bounced off Fitzsimmons's leg into the glove of shortstop Pee Wee Reese—broke his kneecap. Hugh Casey, who replaced Fitzsimmons in the eighth, retired the first batter, but then gave up four straight singles for two runs before being removed. The Yankees scored no more, and Brooklyn came up with a run in the last of the eighth. But Russo stopped the Dodgers in order in the ninth to preserve his lead for the Yankees' second win.

In Game 4, for the first time in the Series, the margin of victory was more than one run, thanks to catcher Owen's famous boner. Brooklyn held the lead 4–3 with two out in the top of the ninth. Dodgers reliever Casey, who had shut out the Yankees since coming on in the fifth inning, then struck out Tommy Henrich for what should have been the game-ending out. But Owen let the ball get by him, and before the third out was recorded Casey had given up a single, two doubles, and two walks—and four runs, for Brooklyn's third loss.

The Yankees scored twice off Wyatt in the second inning of Game 5, and once more in the fifth (on Henrich's home run), as Tiny Bonham held Brooklyn to four hits and a single run to clinch the ninth Yankees world title.

New York Yankees (AL), 4; Brooklyn Dodgers (NL), 1

NY (A)

PLAYER/POS	AVG	G	AB	R	H	2B	3B	HR	RB	BB	SO	SB
Tiny Bonham, p	.000	1	4	0	0	0	0	0	0	0	4	0
Frenchy Bordagaray, pr	.000	1	0	0	0	0	0	0	0	0	0	0
Marv Breuer, p	.000	1	1	0	0	0	0	0	0	0	0	0
Spud Chandler, p	.500	1	2	0	1	0	0	0	1	0	0	0
Bill Dickey, c	.167	5	18	3	3	1	0	0	1	3	1	0
Joe DiMaggio, of	.263	5	19	1	5	0	0	0	1	2	2	0
Atley Donald, p	.000	1	2	0	0	0	0	0	0	0	1	0
Joe Gordon, 2b	.500	5	14	2	7	1	1	1	5	7	0	0
Tommy Henrich, of	.167	5	18	4	3	1	0	1	1	3	3	0
Charlie Keller, of	.389	5	18	5	7	2	0	0	5	3	1	0
Johnny Murphy, p	.000	2	2	0	0	0	0	0	0	0	0	0
Phil Rizzuto, ss	.111	5	18	0	2	0	0	0	0	3	1	1
Red Rolfe, 3b	.300	5	20	2	6	0	0	0	0	2	1	0
Buddy Rosar, c	.000	1	0	0	0	0	0	0	0	0	0	0
Red Ruffing, p	.000	1	3	0	0	0	0	0	0	0	0	0
Marius Russo, p	.000	1	4	0	0	0	0	0	0	0	1	0
George Selkirk, ph	.500	2	2	0	1	0	0	0	0	0	0	0
Johnny Sturm, 1b	.286	5	21	0	6	0	0	0	0	2	2	1
TOTAL	.247		166	17	41	5	1	2	16	23	18	2

PITCHER	W	L	ERA	G	GS	CG	SV	SHO	IP	H	ER	BB	SO
Tiny Bonham	1	0	1.00	1	1	1	0	0	9.0	4	1	2	2
Marv Breuer	0	0	0.00	1	0	0	0	0	3.0	3	0	1	2
Spud Chandler	0	1	3.60	1	1	0	0	0	5.0	4	2	2	2
Atley Donald	0	0	9.00	1	1	0	0	0	4.0	6	4	3	2
Johnny Murphy	1	0	0.00	2	0	0	0	0	6.0	2	0	1	3
Red Ruffing	1	0	1.00	1	1	1	0	0	9.0	6	1	3	5
Marius Russo	1	0	1.00	1	1	1	0	0	9.0	4	1	2	5
TOTAL	4	1	1.80	8	5	3	0	0	45.0	29	9	14	21

BRO (N)

PLAYER/POS	AVG	G	AB	R	H	2B	3B	HR	RB	BB	SO	SB
Johnny Allen, p	.000	3	0	0	0	0	0	0	0	0	0	0
Dolph Camilli, 1b	.167	5	18	1	3	1	0	0	1	1	6	0
Hugh Casey, p	.500	3	2	0	1	0	0	0	0	0	1	0
Pete Coscarart, 2b	.000	3	7	0	0	0	0	0	0	1	2	0
Curt Davis, p	.000	1	2	0	0	0	0	0	0	0	0	0
Freddie Fitzsimmons, p	.000	1	2	0	0	0	0	0	0	0	0	0
Herman Franks, c	.000	1	1	0	0	0	0	0	0	0	0	0
Larry French, p	.000	2	0	0	0	0	0	0	0	0	0	0
Augie Galan, ph	.000	2	2	0	0	0	0	0	0	0	1	0
Billy Herman, 2b	.125	4	8	0	1	0	0	0	0	2	0	0
Kirby Higbe, p	1.000	1	1	0	1	0	0	0	0	0	0	0
Cookie Lavagetto, 3b	.100	3	10	1	1	0	0	0	0	2	0	0
Joe Medwick, of	.235	5	17	1	4	1	0	0	0	1	2	0
Mickey Owen, c	.167	5	12	1	2	0	1	0	2	3	0	0
Pee Wee Reese, ss	.200	5	20	1	4	0	0	0	0	2	0	0
Pete Reiser, of	.200	5	20	1	4	1	1	1	3	1	6	0
Lew Riggs, 3b-2	.250	3	8	0	2	0	0	0	1	1	1	0
Dixie Walker, of	.222	5	18	3	4	2	0	0	0	2	1	0
Jimmy Wasdell, of-1	.200	3	5	0	1	1	0	0	2	0	0	0
Whit Wyatt, p	.167	2	6	1	1	0	0	0	0	0	1	0
TOTAL	.182		159	11	29	7	2	1	11	14	21	0

PITCHER	W	L	ERA	G	GS	CG	SV	SHO	IP	H	ER	BB	SO
Johnny Allen	0	0	0.00	3	0	0	0	0	3.2	1	0	3	0
Hugh Casey	0	2	3.38	3	0	0	0	0	5.1	9	2	2	1
Curt Davis	0	1	5.06	1	1	0	0	0	5.1	6	3	3	1
Freddie Fitzsimmons	0	0	0.00	1	1	0	0	0	7.0	4	0	3	1
Larry French	0	0	0.00	2	0	0	0	0	1.0	0	0	0	0
Kirby Higbe	0	0	7.36	1	1	0	0	0	3.2	6	3	2	1
Whit Wyatt	1	1	2.50	2	2	2	0	0	18.0	15	5	10	14
TOTAL	1	4	2.66	13	5	2	0	0	44.0	41	13	23	18

GAME 1 AT NY OCT 1

BRO	000	010	100	2	6	0
NY	010	101	00X	3	6	1

Pitchers: DAVIS, Casey (6), Allen (7) vs RUFFING
Home Runs: Gordon-NY
Attendance: 68,540

GAME 2 AT NY OCT 2

BRO	000	021	000	3	6	2
NY	011	000	000	2	9	1

Pitchers: WYATT vs CHANDLER, Murphy (6)
Attendance: 66,248

GAME 3 AT BRO OCT 4

NY	000	000	020	2	8	0
BRO	000	000	010	1	4	0

Pitchers: RUSSO vs Fitzsimmons, CASEY (8), French (8), Allen (9)
Attendance: 33,100

GAME 4 AT BRO OCT 5

NY	100	200	004	7	12	0
BRO	000	220	000	4	9	1

Pitchers: Donald, Breuer (5), MURPHY (8) vs Higbe, French (4), Allen (5), CASEY (5)
Home Runs: Reiser-BRO
Attendance: 33,813

GAME 5 AT BRO OCT 6

NY	020	010	000	3	6	0
BRO	001	000	000	1	4	1

Pitchers: BONHAM vs WYATT
Home Runs: Henrich-NY
Attendance: 34,072

Rookies Stan Musial and Whitey Kurowski drove in game-winning runs for rookie-pitcher Johnny Beazley in Games 2 and 5 as the major leagues' youngest team upset the Yankees. New York won only the opener, building a seven-run lead for starter Red Ruffing, who shut out St. Louis on one hit through 8⅓ innings before giving up four hits and four harmless runs in the last of the ninth.

The Cardinals scored first in Game 2 on catcher Walker Cooper's two-run double in the first inning. Kurowski tripled in a third run in the seventh, but pitcher Beazley, after holding the Yankees scoreless through seven innings, gave up three runs in the eighth on two singles and Charlie Keller's two-run homer. St. Louis regained the lead a half inning later when Musial singled home Enos Slaughter (who had doubled), and stifled a threat in the ninth as Slaughter's great throw from right field nailed a runner at third.

Second-year Cardinals pitcher Ernie White turned in the Series' top mound performance with a six-single, no-walk shutout in Game 3 (aided by outfielders Musial and Slaughter, who hauled in a pair of potential home run blasts in the seventh inning). The Cards managed only five singles themselves, but they combined one with a walk, sacrifice, and ground out for a run in the third, and sandwiched a Yankees error with two hits in the ninth for an unearned insurance run.

Game 4 saw the Series' heaviest hitting. New York scored once in the first, but the Cards exploded in the fourth for six runs on six hits and two walks. The Yankees tied it up two innings later, with Keller's three-run homer the feature of the five-run inning. St. Louis took the lead for good with two runs in the seventh, and added a ninth run in the ninth.

Beazley and Ruffing tangled in Game 5. Phil Rizzuto's solo homer put New York ahead in the first inning. Slaughter's fourth-inning home run tied the score, but the Yankees regained the lead with a run later in the inning. The Cards tied the game again in the sixth, and took the final lead when Kurowski homered for two runs in the top of the ninth. The Yankees threatened in the last of the ninth, putting their first two men on with a single and error. But catcher Cooper picked a runner off second, second baseman Jimmy Brown redeemed his earlier error with a sparkling catch, then fielded a routine grounder for the final out.

St. Louis Cardinals (NL), 4;
New York Yankees (AL), 1

STL (N)

PLAYER/POS	AVG	G	AB	R	H	2B	3B	HR	RB	BB	SO	SB
Johnny Beazley, p	.143	2	7	0	1	0	0	0	0	0	5	0
Jimmy Brown, 2b	.300	5	20	2	6	0	0	0	1	3	0	0
Mort Cooper, p	.200	2	5	1	1	0	0	0	2	0	1	0
Walker Cooper, c	.286	5	21	3	6	1	0	0	4	0	1	0
Creepy Crespi, pr	.000	1	0	1	0	0	0	0	0	0	0	0
Harry Gumbert, p	.000	2	0	0	0	0	0	0	0	0	0	0
Johnny Hopp, 1b	.176	5	17	3	3	0	0	0	0	1	1	0
Whitey Kurowski, 3b	.267	5	15	3	4	0	1	1	5	2	3	0
Max Lanier, p	1.000	2	1	0	1	0	0	0	1	0	0	0
Marty Marion, ss	.111	5	18	2	2	0	1	0	3	1	2	0
Terry Moore, of	.294	5	17	2	5	1	0	0	2	2	3	0
Stan Musial, of	.222	5	18	2	4	1	0	0	2	4	0	0
Ken O'Dea, ph	1.000	1	1	0	1	0	0	0	1	0	0	0
Howie Pollet, p	.000	1	0	0	0	0	0	0	0	0	0	0
Ray Sanders, ph	.000	2	1	1	0	0	0	0	0	0	1	0
Enos Slaughter, of	.263	5	19	3	5	1	0	1	2	3	2	0
Harry Walker, ph	.000	1	1	0	0	0	0	0	0	0	1	0
Ernie White, p	.000	1	2	0	0	0	0	0	0	0	0	0
TOTAL	.239		163	23	39	4	2	2	23	17	19	0

PITCHER	W	L	ERA	G	GS	CG	SV	SHO	IP	H	ER	BB	SO
Johnny Beazley	2	0	2.50	2	2	2	0	0	18.0	17	5	3	6
Mort Cooper	0	1	5.54	2	2	0	0	0	13.0	17	8	4	9
Harry Gumbert	0	0	0.00	2	0	0	0	0	0.2	1	0	0	0
Max Lanier	1	0	0.00	2	0	0	0	0	4.0	3	0	1	1
Howie Pollet	0	0	0.00	1	0	0	0	0	0.1	0	0	0	0
Ernie White	1	0	0.00	1	1	1	0	1	9.0	6	0	0	6
TOTAL	4	1	2.60	10	5	3	0	1	45.0	44	13	8	22

NY (A)

PLAYER/POS	AVG	G	AB	R	H	2B	3B	HR	RB	BB	SO	SB
Tiny Bonham, p	.000	2	2	0	0	0	0	0	0	0	1	0
Hank Borowy, p	.000	1	1	0	0	0	0	0	0	0	1	0
Marv Breuer, p	.000	1	0	0	0	0	0	0	0	0	0	0
Spud Chandler, p	.000	2	2	0	0	0	0	0	0	0	1	0
Frankie Crosetti, 3b	.000	1	3	0	0	0	0	0	0	0	1	0
Roy Cullenbine, of	.263	5	19	3	5	1	0	0	2	1	2	1
Bill Dickey, c	.263	5	19	1	5	0	0	0	0	1	0	0
Joe DiMaggio, of	.333	5	21	3	7	0	0	0	3	0	1	0
Atley Donald, p	.000	1	2	0	0	0	0	0	0	0	0	0
Joe Gordon, 2b	.095	5	21	1	2	1	0	0	0	0	7	0
Buddy Hassett, 1b	.333	3	9	1	3	1	0	0	2	0	1	0
Charlie Keller, of	.200	5	20	2	4	0	0	2	5	1	3	0
Jerry Priddy, 1b-3,3b-1	.100	3	10	0	1	1	0	0	1	1	0	0
Phil Rizzuto, ss	.381	5	21	2	8	0	0	1	1	2	1	2
Red Rolfe, 3b	.353	4	17	5	6	2	0	0	0	1	2	0
Buddy Rosar, ph	1.000	1	1	0	1	0	0	0	0	0	0	0
Red Ruffing, p-2	.222	4	9	0	2	0	0	0	0	0	2	0
George Selkirk, ph	.000	1	1	0	0	0	0	0	0	0	0	0
Tuck Stainback, pr	.000	2	0	0	0	0	0	0	0	0	0	0
Jim Turner, p	.000	1	0	0	0	0	0	0	0	0	0	0
TOTAL	.247		178	18	44	6	0	3	14	8	22	3

PITCHER	W	L	ERA	G	GS	CG	SV	SHO	IP	H	ER	BB	SO
Tiny Bonham	0	1	4.09	2	1	1	0	0	11.0	9	5	3	3
Hank Borowy	0	0	18.00	1	1	0	0	0	3.0	6	6	3	1
Marv Breuer	0	0	—	1	0	0	0	0	0.0	2	0	0	0
Spud Chandler	0	1	1.08	2	1	0	1	0	8.1	5	1	1	3
Atley Donald	0	1	6.00	1	0	0	0	0	3.0	3	2	2	1
Red Ruffing	1	1	4.08	2	2	1	0	0	17.2	14	8	7	11
Jim Turner	0	0	0.00	1	0	0	0	0	1.0	0	0	1	0
TOTAL	1	4	4.50	10	5	2	1	0	44.0	39	22	17	19

GAME 1 AT STL SEPT 30

NY	000 110 032	7 11 0
STL	000 000 004	4 7 4

Pitchers: RUFFING, Chandler (9) vs M.COOPER, Gumbert (8), Lanier (9)
Attendance: 34,769

GAME 2 AT STL OCT 1

NY	000 000 030	3 10 2
STL	200 000 11X	4 6 0

Pitchers: BONHAM vs BEAZLEY
Home Runs: Keller-NY
Attendance: 34,255

GAME 3 AT NY OCT 2

STL	001 000 001	2 5 1
NY	000 000 000	0 6 1

Pitchers: WHITE vs CHANDLER, Breuer (9), Turner (9)
Attendance: 69,123

GAME 4 AT NY OCT 4

STL	000 600 201	9 12 1
NY	100 005 000	6 10 1

Pitchers: M.Cooper, Gumbert (6), Pollet (6), LANIER (7) vs Borowy, DONALD (4), Bonham (7)
Home Runs: Keller-NY
Attendance: 69,902

GAME 5 AT NY OCT 5

STL	000 101 002	4 9 4
NY	100 100 000	2 7 1

Pitchers: BEAZLEY vs RUFFING
Home Runs: Rizzuto-NY, Slaughter-STL, Kurowski-STL
Attendance: 69,052

Although both clubs had lost players to military service since the previous World Series, history seemed to be repeating itself. The Cardinals lost to the Yankees in the opener and won the second game, as they had the previous year. But this year it was the Yankees who took the next three games and the Series, as fine Cardinal pitching gave way to even finer mound work by New York.

Yankees pitcher Spurgeon (Spud) Chandler, coming off his finest season (20–4, 1.64 ERA), continued to overwhelm the opposition in the Series. He held the Cards to two runs (only one earned) in Game 1, and the Yankees took advantage of a wild pitch to score two runs of their own in the sixth inning, breaking a 2–2 tie for a 4–2 win. Cardinals shortstop Marty Marion homered in the third inning for the first run the next day, and first baseman Ray Sanders homered for two more runs in a three-run fourth. Cardinals ace Mort Cooper held New York to one run on four hits through eight innings, but he weakened in the last of the ninth, giving up a double and triple to the first two batters. But only two runs scored as he retired the next three men for St. Louis' only victory.

The Cardinals carried a 2–1 lead into the last of the eighth inning of Game 3, when a pair of errors, two walks, and five hits (including Billy Johnson's three-run triple) undid them. Yankees fireman Johnny Murphy retired the Cards in order in the ninth to save Hank Borowy's win. Max Lanier and Harry Brecheen held New York to just two runs (and six hits) in Game 4, but Yankees pitcher Marius Russo gave up only one run—and that was scored only because of two Yankees errors in the seventh inning.

In the fifth and (as it turned out) final game, St. Louis couldn't score, although they knocked Spud Chandler for 10 hits. But they were all singles and were spaced harmlessly over eight of the nine innings. Three St. Louis pitchers held the Yankees to just seven hits, six of them singles. But in the sixth inning Bill Dickey followed one of the singles with the game's only extra-base hit—a home run—to produce the game's only scoring, and bring the Yankees yet another world championship, their 10th.

New York Yankees (AL), 4;
St. Louis Cardinals (NL), 1

NY (A)

PLAYER/POS	AVG	G	AB	R	H	2B	3B	HR	RB	BB	SO	SB
Tiny Bonham, p	.000	1	2	0	0	0	0	0	0	0	0	0
Hank Borowy, p	.500	1	2	1	1	0	0	0	0	0	1	0
Spud Chandler, p	.167	2	6	0	1	0	0	0	0	0	2	0
Frankie Crosetti, ss	.278	5	18	4	5	0	0	0	1	2	3	1
Bill Dickey, c	.278	5	18	1	5	0	0	1	4	2	2	0
Nick Etten, 1b	.105	5	19	0	2	0	0	0	2	1	2	0
Joe Gordon, 2b	.235	5	17	2	4	1	0	1	2	3	3	0
Billy Johnson, 3b	.300	5	20	3	6	1	1	0	3	0	3	0
Charlie Keller, of	.222	5	18	3	4	0	1	0	2	2	5	1
Johnny Lindell, of	.111	4	9	1	1	0	0	0	0	1	4	0
Bud Metheny, of	.125	2	8	0	1	0	0	0	0	0	2	0
Johnny Murphy, p	.000	2	0	0	0	0	0	0	0	0	0	0
Marius Russo, p	.667	1	3	1	2	2	0	0	0	1	1	0
Tuck Stainback, of	.176	5	17	0	3	0	0	0	0	0	2	0
Snuffy Stirnweiss, ph	.000	1	1	1	0	0	0	0	0	0	0	0
Roy Weatherly, ph	.000	1	1	0	0	0	0	0	0	0	0	0
TOTAL	.220		159	17	35	5	2	2	14	12	30	2

PITCHER	W	L	ERA	G	GS	CG	SV	SHO	IP	H	ER	BB	SO
Tiny Bonham	0	1	4.50	1	1	0	0	0	8.0	6	4	3	9
Hank Borowy	1	0	2.25	1	1	0	0	0	8.0	6	2	3	4
Spud Chandler	2	0	0.50	2	2	2	0	1	18.0	17	1	3	10
Johnny Murphy	0	0	0.00	2	0	0	1	0	2.0	1	0	1	1
Marius Russo	1	0	0.00	1	1	1	0	0	9.0	7	0	1	2
TOTAL	4	1	1.40	7	5	3	1	1	45.0	37	7	11	26

STL (N)

PLAYER/POS	AVG	G	AB	R	H	2B	3B	HR	RB	BB	SO	SB
Al Brazle, p	.000	1	3	0	0	0	0	0	0	0	1	0
Harry Brecheen, p	.000	3	0	0	0	0	0	0	0	0	0	0
Mort Cooper, p	.000	2	5	0	0	0	0	0	0	0	3	0
Walker Cooper, c	.294	5	17	1	5	0	0	0	0	0	1	0
Frank Demaree, ph	.000	1	1	0	0	0	0	0	0	0	0	0
Murry Dickson, p	.000	1	0	0	0	0	0	0	0	0	0	0
Debs Garms, of-1	.000	2	5	0	0	0	0	0	0	0	2	0
Johnny Hopp, of	.000	1	4	0	0	0	0	0	0	0	1	0
Lou Klein, 2b	.136	5	22	0	3	0	0	0	0	1	2	0
Howie Krist, p	.000	1	0	0	0	0	0	0	0	0	0	0
Whitey Kurowski, 3b	.222	5	18	2	4	1	0	0	1	0	3	0
Max Lanier, p	.250	3	4	0	1	0	0	0	1	0	0	0
Danny Litwhiler, of-4	.267	5	15	0	4	1	0	0	2	2	4	0
Marty Marion, ss	.357	5	14	1	5	2	0	1	2	3	1	1
Stan Musial, of	.278	5	18	2	5	0	0	0	0	2	2	0
Sam Narron, ph	.000	1	1	0	0	0	0	0	0	0	0	0
Ken O'Dea, c-1	.667	2	3	0	2	0	0	0	0	0	0	0
Ray Sanders, 1b	.294	5	17	3	5	0	0	1	2	3	4	0
Harry Walker, of	.167	5	18	0	3	1	0	0	0	0	2	0
Ernie White, pr	.000	1	0	0	0	0	0	0	0	0	0	0
TOTAL	.224		165	9	37	5	0	2	8	11	26	1

PITCHER	W	L	ERA	G	GS	CG	SV	SHO	IP	H	ER	BB	SO
Al Brazle	0	1	3.68	1	1	0	0	0	7.1	5	3	2	4
Harry Brecheen	0	1	2.45	3	0	0	0	0	3.2	5	1	3	3
Mort Cooper	1	1	2.81	2	2	1	0	0	16.0	11	5	3	10
Murry Dickson	0	0	0.00	1	0	0	0	0	0.2	0	0	1	0
Howie Krist	0	0	—	1	0	0	0	0	0.0	1	0	0	0
Max Lanier	0	1	1.76	3	2	0	0	0	15.1	13	3	3	13
TOTAL	1	4	2.51	11	5	1	0	0	43.0	35	12	12	30

The Cardinals entered the World Series as clear favorites against their landlord Browns (who owned Sportsman's Park, where both teams played). They won the Series in six games, but if the Browns' fielding had been as good as their pitching the outcome might have been different.

The Browns won the opener on Denny Galehouse's strong pitching. Galehouse gave up seven hits and four walks, but held the Cards scoreless before yielding a run in the ninth. Cardinals ace Mort Cooper also pitched well in six of his seven innings. He allowed the Browns only two hits, but they came back to back in the fourth inning—a single followed by George McQuinn's home run—to give the Browns all the scoring they needed.

Browns pitcher Nelson Potter's two errors (a fumble and a wild throw) on a bunt in the third inning of Game 2 led to an unearned run, and third baseman Mark Christman's bobble an inning later set up a second unearned run. The Browns tied the score with a pair of runs on three two-out hits in the seventh—enough to have won an error-free game—but lost when the Cardinals singled a run across in the last of the eleventh.

Two errors by the Browns led to a pair of unearned runs in Game 3, but Jack Kramer held the Cards scoreless apart from that, striking out 10. Meanwhile, the Browns tied together five singles with two out in the third inning for three runs, adding a fourth run on a wild pitch before the inning ended. In the seventh the Browns tacked on two more runs for a comfortable win and a 2–1 Series advantage.

The Cardinals came back to earn victory in Games 4 and 5, knocking three Browns pitchers for 12 hits in Game 4 (including Stan Musial's two-run homer in the first) and a 5–1 win for pitcher Harry Brecheen, then rapping Denny Galehouse for two solo homers in Game 5 (by Danny Litwhiler and Ray Sanders) for the game's only scoring as Mort Cooper fanned 12 Browns while shutting them out.

Two of the Cardinals' three runs in the fourth inning of Game 6 were made possible by Browns shortstop Vern Stephens's throwing error. They provided the margin of victory, as Cardinals pitchers Max Lanier and Ted Wilks held the Browns to three hits and a single run, and brought the Cards their second world title in three years.

St. Louis Cardinals (NL), 4; St. Louis Browns (AL), 2

STL (N)

PLAYER/POS	AVG	G	AB	R	H	2B	3B	HR	RB	BB	SO	SB
Augie Bergamo, of-2	.000	3	6	0	0	0	0	0	0	1	2	3	0
Harry Brecheen, p	.000	1	4	0	0	0	0	0	0	0	1	0
Bud Byerly, p	.000	1	0	0	0	0	0	0	0	0	0	0
Mort Cooper, p	.000	2	4	0	0	0	0	0	0	0	2	0
Walker Cooper, c	.318	6	22	1	7	2	1	0	2	3	2	0
Blix Donnelly, p	.000	2	1	0	0	0	0	0	0	0	1	0
George Fallon, 2b	.000	2	2	0	0	0	0	0	0	0	1	0
Debs Garms, ph	.000	2	2	0	0	0	0	0	0	0	0	0
Johnny Hopp, of	.185	6	27	2	5	0	0	0	0	0	8	0
Al Jurisich, p	.000	1	0	0	0	0	0	0	0	0	0	0
Whitey Kurowski, 3b	.217	6	23	2	5	1	0	0	1	1	4	0
Max Lanier, p	.500	2	4	0	2	0	0	0	1	0	0	0
Danny Litwhiler, of	.200	5	20	2	4	1	0	1	1	2	7	0
Marty Marion, ss	.227	6	22	1	5	3	0	0	2	2	3	0
Stan Musial, of	.304	6	23	2	7	2	0	1	2	2	0	0
Ken O'Dea, ph	.333	3	3	0	1	0	0	0	2	0	0	0
Ray Sanders, 1b	.286	6	21	5	6	0	0	1	1	5	8	0
Freddy Schmidt, p	.000	1	1	0	0	0	0	0	0	0	1	0
Emil Verban, 2b	.412	6	17	1	7	0	0	0	2	2	0	0
Ted Wilks, p	.000	2	2	0	0	0	0	0	0	0	2	0
TOTAL	.240		204	16	49	9	1	3	15	19	43	0

PITCHER	W	L	ERA	G	GS	CG	SV	SHO	IP	H	ER	BB	SO
Harry Brecheen	1	0	1.00	1	1	1	0	0	9.0	9	1	4	4
Bud Byerly	0	0	0.00	1	0	0	0	0	1.1	0	0	1	0
Mort Cooper	1	1	1.13	2	2	1	0	1	16.0	9	2	0	16
Blix Donnelly	1	0	0.00	2	0	0	0	0	6.0	2	0	1	9
Al Jurisich	0	0	27.00	1	0	0	0	0	0.2	2	2	1	0
Max Lanier	1	0	2.19	2	2	0	0	0	12.1	8	3	8	11
Freddy Schmidt	0	0	0.00	1	0	0	0	0	3.1	1	0	1	1
Ted Wilks	0	1	5.68	2	1	0	1	0	6.1	5	4	3	7
TOTAL	4	2	1.96	12	6	2	1	1	55.0	36	12	23	49

STL (A)

PLAYER/POS	AVG	G	AB	R	H	2B	3B	HR	RB	BB	SO	SB
Floyd Baker, 2b	.000	2	2	0	0	0	0	0	0	0	2	0
Milt Byrnes, ph	.000	3	2	0	0	0	0	0	0	1	2	0
Mike Chartak, ph	.000	2	2	0	0	0	0	0	0	0	2	0
Mark Christman, 3b	.091	6	22	0	2	0	0	0	1	0	6	0
Ellis Clary, ph	.000	1	1	0	0	0	0	0	0	0	0	0
Denny Galehouse, p	.200	2	5	0	1	0	0	0	0	1	1	0
Don Gutteridge, 2b	.143	6	21	1	3	1	0	0	0	3	5	0
Red Hayworth, c	.118	6	17	1	2	1	0	0	1	3	1	0
Al Hollingsworth, p	.000	1	1	0	0	0	0	0	0	0	0	0
Sig Jakucki, p	.000	1	0	0	0	0	0	0	0	0	0	0
Jack Kramer, p	.000	2	4	0	0	0	0	0	0	0	2	0
Mike Kreevich, of	.231	6	26	0	6	3	0	0	0	0	5	0
Chet Laabs, of-4	.200	5	15	1	3	1	1	0	0	4	2	0
Frank Mancuso, c-1	.667	2	3	0	2	0	0	0	1	0	0	0
George McQuinn, 1b	.438	6	16	2	7	2	0	1	5	7	2	0
Gene Moore, of	.182	6	22	4	4	0	0	0	0	3	6	0
Bob Muncrief, p	.000	2	1	0	0	0	0	0	0	0	1	0
Nelson Potter, p	.000	2	4	0	0	0	0	0	0	0	1	0
Tex Shirley, p	.000	2	0	0	0	0	0	0	0	0	0	0
Vern Stephens, ss	.227	6	22	2	5	1	0	0	0	3	3	0
Tom Turner, ph	.000	1	1	0	0	0	0	0	0	0	0	0
Al Zarilla, of-3	.100	4	10	1	1	0	0	0	1	0	4	0
TOTAL	.183		197	12	36	9	1	1	9	23	49	0

PITCHER	W	L	ERA	G	GS	CG	SV	SHO	IP	H	ER	BB	SO
Denny Galehouse	1	1	1.50	2	2	2	0	0	18.0	13	3	5	15
Al Hollingsworth	0	0	2.25	1	0	0	0	0	4.0	5	1	2	1
Sig Jakucki	0	1	9.00	1	1	0	0	0	3.0	5	3	0	4
Jack Kramer	1	0	0.00	2	1	1	0	0	11.0	9	0	4	12
Bob Muncrief	0	1	1.35	2	0	0	0	0	6.2	5	1	4	4
Nelson Potter	0	1	0.93	2	2	0	0	0	9.2	10	1	3	6
Tex Shirley	0	0	0.00	1	0	0	0	0	2.0	2	0	1	1
TOTAL	2	4	1.49	11	6	3	0	0	54.1	49	9	19	43

GAME 1 AT STL-N OCT 4

STL-A	000 200 000	2	2	0
STL-N	000 000 001	1	7	0

Pitchers: GALEHOUSE vs M.COOPER, Donnelly (8)
Home Runs: McQuinn-STL(A)
Attendance: 33,242

GAME 2 AT STL-N OCT 5

STL-A	000 000 200 00	2	7	4
STL-N	001 100 000 01	3	7	0

Pitchers: Potter, MUNCRIEF (7) vs Lanier, DONNELLY (8)
Attendance: 35,076

GAME 3 AT STL-A OCT 6

STL-N	100 000 100	2	7	0
STL-A	004 000 20X	6	8	2

Pitchers: WILKS, Schmidt (3), Jurisich (7), Byerly (7) vs KRAMER
Attendance: 34,737

GAME 4 AT STL-A OCT 7

STL-N	202 001 000	5	12	0
STL-A	000 000 010	1	9	1

Pitchers: BRECHEEN vs JAKUCKI, Hollingsworth (4), Shirley (8)
Home Runs: Musial-STL(N)
Attendance: 35,455

GAME 5 AT STL-A OCT 8

STL-N	000 001 010	2	6	1
STL-A	000 000 000	0	7	1

Pitchers: M.COOPER vs GALEHOUSE
Home Runs: Sanders-STL(N), Litwhiler-STL(N)
Attendance: 36,568

GAME 6 AT STL-N OCT 9

STL-A	010 000 000	1	3	2
STL-N	000 300 00X	3	10	1

Pitchers: POTTER, Kramer (7) vs LANIER, Wilks (6)
Attendance: 31,630

As World War II ended during the summer, military major leaguers began returning to their clubs. Hank Greenberg's return in July provided the spark needed for Detroit's narrow pennant victory, and his three-run homer in Game 2 of the World Series proved to be the decisive blow in the Tigers' successful struggle for the world title.

Chicago started strong as Cubs ace Hank Borowy shut out the Tigers on six singles while his teammates drove out Hal Newhouser with seven runs in the first three innings and won. Chicago continued its assault the next day with a run in the top of the fourth, but in the fifth inning Doc Cramer—with two out and two on—singled in the tying run, and Greenberg followed with his tie-breaking homer for three additional runs. Detroit pitcher Virgil Trucks (who had returned from the Navy in time to pitch in the regular-season finale) held the Cubs scoreless after the fourth inning for the win.

Chicago's Claude Passeau moved the Cubs back into the Series lead with a one-hit shutout in Game 3, but Dizzy Trout's five-hitter in Game 4 again evened the Series. The Tigers bunched four of their seven hits in the fourth inning for all four of their runs.

Detroit took the Series lead for the first time with an 8–4 win in Game 5. Borowy and Newhouser faced each other as they had in the opener, but this time Borowy was hit hard. Driven out when four Tigers opened the sixth inning with safe hits, he took the loss as Newhouser went the distance for the win.

In Game 6, Chicago concluded the seventh inning of a heavy-hitting game with a 7–3 lead. Detroit tied the score with four runs in the top of the eighth (capped by Greenberg's home run), but in the last of the 12th the Cubs' Stan Hack doubled home the winning run to keep Chicago's hopes alive.

Two days later in the finale, Cubs manager Charlie Grimm started Borowy, who had relieved for four shutout innings to win Game 6. But this third appearance in four days proved too much. Removed after the first three batters to face him singled, he took the loss, as the Tigers went on to score nine runs to win the World Series for the second time.

Detroit Tigers (AL), 4;
Chicago Cubs (NL), 3

DET (A)

PLAYER/POS	AVG	G	AB	R	H	2B	3B	HR	RBI	BB	SO	SB
Al Benton, p	.000	3	0	0	0	0	0	0	0	0	0	0
Red Borom, ph	.000	2	1	0	0	0	0	0	0	0	0	0
Tommy Bridges, p	.000	1	0	0	0	0	0	0	0	0	0	0
George Caster, p	.000	1	0	0	0	0	0	0	0	0	0	0
Doc Cramer, of	.379	7	29	7	11	0	0	0	4	1	0	1
Roy Cullenbine, of	.227	7	22	5	5	2	0	0	4	8	2	1
Zeb Eaton, ph	.000	1	1	0	0	0	0	0	0	0	1	0
Hank Greenberg, of	.304	7	23	7	7	3	0	2	7	6	5	0
Joe Hoover, ss	.333	1	3	1	1	0	0	0	0	1	0	0
Chuck Hostetler, ph	.000	3	3	0	0	0	0	0	0	0	0	0
Bob Maier, ph	1.000	1	1	0	1	0	0	0	0	0	0	0
Eddie Mayo, 2b	.250	7	28	4	7	1	0	0	2	3	2	0
John McHale, ph	.000	3	3	0	0	0	0	0	0	0	1	0
Ed Mierkowicz, of	.000	1	0	0	0	0	0	0	0	0	0	0
Les Mueller, p	.000	1	0	0	0	0	0	0	0	0	0	0
Hal Newhouser, p	.000	3	8	0	0	0	0	0	1	1	1	0
Jimmy Outlaw, 3b	.179	7	28	1	5	0	0	0	3	2	1	1
Stubby Overmire, p	.000	1	1	0	0	0	0	0	0	0	0	0
Paul Richards, c	.211	7	19	0	4	2	0	0	6	4	3	0
Bob Swift, c	.250	3	4	1	1	0	0	0	0	2	0	0
Jim Tobin, p	.000	1	1	0	0	0	0	0	0	0	0	0
Dizzy Trout, p	.167	2	6	0	1	0	0	0	0	0	0	0
Virgil Trucks, p	.000	2	4	0	0	0	0	0	0	1	1	0
Hub Walker, ph	.500	2	2	1	1	1	0	0	0	0	0	0
Skeeter Webb, ss	.185	7	27	4	5	0	0	0	1	2	1	0
Rudy York, 1b	.179	7	28	1	5	1	0	0	3	3	4	0
TOTAL	.223		242	32	54	10	0	2	32	33	22	3

PITCHER	W	L	ERA	G	GS	CG	SV	SHO	IP	H	ER	BB	SO
Al Benton	0	0	1.93	3	0	0	0	0	4.2	6	1	0	5
Tommy Bridges	0	0	16.20	1	0	0	0	0	1.2	3	3	3	1
George Caster	0	0	0.00	1	0	0	0	0	0.2	0	0	0	1
Les Mueller	0	0	0.00	1	0	0	0	0	2.0	0	0	1	1
Hal Newhouser	2	1	6.10	3	3	2	0	0	20.2	25	14	4	22
Stubby Overmire	0	1	3.00	1	1	0	0	0	6.0	4	2	2	2
Jim Tobin	0	0	6.00	1	0	0	0	0	3.0	4	2	1	0
Dizzy Trout	1	1	0.66	2	1	1	0	0	13.2	9	1	3	9
Virgil Trucks	1	0	3.38	2	2	1	0	0	13.1	14	5	5	7
TOTAL	4	3	3.84	15	7	4	0	0	65.2	65	28	19	48

CHI (N)

PLAYER/POS	AVG	G	AB	R	H	2B	3B	HR	RBI	BB	SO	SB
Heinz Becker, ph	.500	3	2	0	1	0	0	0	0	1	1	0
Cy Block, pr	.000	1	0	0	0	0	0	0	0	0	0	0
Hank Borowy, p	.167	4	6	1	1	1	0	0	0	0	3	0
Phil Cavaretta, 1b	.423	7	26	7	11	2	0	1	5	4	3	0
Bob Chipman, p	.000	1	0	0	0	0	0	0	0	0	0	0
Paul Derringer, p	.000	3	0	0	0	0	0	0	0	0	0	0
Paul Erickson, p	.000	4	0	0	0	0	0	0	0	0	0	0
Paul Gillespie, c-1	.000	5	6	0	0	0	0	0	0	0	0	0
Stan Hack, 3b	.367	7	30	1	11	3	0	0	4	4	2	0
Roy Hughes, ss	.294	6	17	1	5	1	0	0	3	4	5	0
Don Johnson, 2b	.172	7	29	4	5	2	1	0	0	0	8	1
Mickey Livingston, c	.364	6	22	3	8	3	0	0	4	1	1	0
Peanuts Lowrey, of	.310	7	29	4	9	1	0	0	0	1	2	0
Clyde McCullough, ph	.000	1	1	0	0	0	0	0	0	0	1	0
Lennie Merullo, ss	.000	3	2	0	0	0	0	0	0	0	1	0
Bill Nicholson, of	.214	7	28	1	6	1	1	0	8	2	5	0
Andy Pafko, of	.214	7	28	5	6	2	1	0	2	2	5	1
Claude Passeau, p	.000	3	7	1	0	0	0	0	1	0	4	0
Ray Prim, p	.000	2	2	0	0	0	0	0	0	0	0	0
Ed Sauer, ph	.000	2	2	0	0	0	0	0	0	0	2	0
Bill Schuster, ss-1	.000	2	1	1	0	0	0	0	0	0	0	0
Frank Secory, ph	.200	5	5	0	1	0	0	0	0	0	2	0
Hy Vandenberg, p	.000	3	1	0	0	0	0	0	0	0	0	0
Dewey Williams, c-1	.000	2	2	0	0	0	0	0	0	0	0	0
Hank Wyse, p	.000	3	3	0	0	0	0	0	0	0	2	0
TOTAL	.259		247	29	64	16	3	1	27	19	48	2

PITCHER	W	L	ERA	G	GS	CG	SV	SHO	IP	H	ER	BB	SO
Hank Borowy	2	2	4.00	4	3	1	0	1	18.0	21	8	6	8
Bob Chipman	0	0	0.00	1	0	0	0	0	0.1	0	0	1	0
Paul Derringer	0	0	6.75	3	0	0	0	0	5.1	5	4	7	1
Paul Erickson	0	0	3.86	4	0	0	0	0	7.0	8	3	5	5
Claude Passeau	1	0	2.70	3	2	1	0	1	16.2	7	5	8	3
Ray Prim	0	1	9.00	2	1	0	0	0	4.0	4	4	1	1
Hy Vandenberg	0	0	0.00	3	0	0	0	0	6.0	1	0	3	3
Hank Wyse	0	1	7.04	3	1	0	0	0	7.2	8	6	4	1
TOTAL	3	4	4.15	23	7	2	0	2	65.0	54	30	33	22

GAME 1 AT DET OCT 3

CHI	403	000	200	9	13	0
DET	000	000	000	0	6	0

Pitchers: BOROWY vs NEWHOUSER, Benton (3), Tobin (5), Mueller (8)
Home Runs: Cavaretta-CHI
Attendance: 54,637

GAME 2 AT DET OCT 4

CHI	000	100	000	1	7	0
DET	000	040	00X	4	7	0

Pitchers: WYSE, Erickson (7) vs TRUCKS
Home Runs: Greenberg-DET
Attendance: 53,636

GAME 3 AT DET OCT 5

CHI	000	200	100	3	8	0
DET	000	000	000	0	1	2

Pitchers: PASSEAU vs OVERMIRE, Benton (7)
Attendance: 55,500

GAME 4 AT CHI OCT 6

DET	000	400	000	4	7	1
CHI	000	001	000	1	5	1

Pitchers: TROUT vs PRIM, Derringer (4), Vandenberg (6), Erickson (8)
Attendance: 42,923

GAME 5 AT CHI OCT 7

DET	001	004	102	8	11	0
CHI	001	000	201	4	7	2

Pitchers: NEWHOUSER vs BOROWY, Vandenberg (6), Chipman (6), Derringer (7), Erickson (9)
Attendance: 43,463

GAME 6 AT CHI OCT 8

DET	010	000	240	000	7	13	1
CHI	000	041	200	001	8	15	3

Pitchers: Trucks, Caster (5), Bridges (6), Benton (7), TROUT (8) vs Passeau, Wyse (7), Prim (8), BOROWY (9)
Home Runs: Greenberg-DET
Attendance: 41,708

GAME 7 AT CHI OCT 10

DET	510	000	120	9	9	1
CHI	100	100	010	3	10	0

Pitchers: NEWHOUSER vs BOROWY, Derringer (1), Vandenberg (2), Erickson (6), Passeau (8), Wyse (9)
Attendance: 41,590

With World War II over, the majors were at full strength for the first time in five years. Boston's big bats were back, and the Sox ran away with the American League pennant. St. Louis had Stan Musial back, but they struggled to their pennant, finishing the regular schedule tied with Brooklyn, and defeating them in the first major league tie-breaker playoff, two games to none.

Favored Boston edged St. Louis in the opener, but it took a home run by Rudy York in the top of the 10th to spoil Howie Pollet's strong showing. Harry Brecheen brought the Cards back the next day with the first of his three Series wins—a four-hit shutout.

Boston regained the lead in Game 3. Sox ace Dave Ferriss spaced six hits and a walk, one per inning, in shutting out the Cardinals, and Rudy York hit his second game-winning homer, this time a three-run shot in the first inning. The next day, though, St. Louis exploded for a record-tying 20 hits—four apiece by Enos Slaughter, Joe Garagiola, and Whitey Kurowski—to give pitcher George Munger (who had completed only two of his seven regular-season starts) an easy complete-game 12–3 victory.

For the third time the Red Sox took the Series lead, winning Game 5 behind Joe Dobson's four-hit pitching (the Cards' three runs in the 6–3 loss were unearned), but St. Louis tied the Series for the third time with a win in Game 6. Brecheen, in his second start, again pitched splendidly, holding Boston to a single run in the seventh inning, long after the Cards had driven out Sox starter Mickey Harris with three runs in the third.

The final game, like the Series itself, was a seesaw battle. Boston scored the first run in the top of the first, but St. Louis tied the score an inning later. The Cards took a two-run lead on three hits in the fifth, but the Sox came back in the eighth to tie it up as Dom DiMaggio doubled off reliever Brecheen to drive in a pair of pinch hitters who had singled and doubled off starter Murry Dickson. The Series' final run came a half inning later. Slaughter opened with a single, but moved no farther as the next two batters were retired. Then Harry Walker hit a liner over short. Slaughter, off with the crack of the bat, never paused and beat the relay to the plate with what proved the winning run, as Brecheen held the Sox in the ninth for his third win of the Series to give the Cardinals their third world title in five seasons.

St. Louis Cardinals (NL), 4; Boston Red Sox (AL), 3

STL (N)

PLAYER/POS	AVG	G	AB	R	H	2B	3B	HR	RB	BB	SO	SB
Johnny Beazley, p	.000	1	0	0	0	0	0	0	0	0	0	0
Al Brazle, p	.000	2	0	0	0	0	0	0	0	0	0	0
Harry Brecheen, p	.125	3	8	2	1	0	0	0	1	0	1	0
Murry Dickson, p	.400	2	5	1	2	2	0	0	1	0	1	0
Erv Dusak, of	.250	4	4	0	1	1	0	0	0	2	2	0
Joe Garagiola, c	.316	5	19	2	6	2	0	0	4	0	3	0
Nippy Jones, ph	.000	1	1	0	0	0	0	0	0	0	1	0
Whitey Kurowski, 3b	.296	7	27	5	8	3	0	0	2	0	3	0
Marty Marion, ss	.250	7	24	1	6	2	0	0	4	1	1	0
Terry Moore, of	.148	7	27	1	4	0	0	0	2	2	6	0
Red Munger, p	.250	1	4	0	1	0	0	0	0	0	1	0
Stan Musial, 1b	.222	7	27	3	6	4	1	0	4	4	2	1
Howie Pollet, p	.000	2	4	0	0	0	0	0	0	0	1	0
Del Rice, c	.500	3	6	2	3	1	0	0	0	0	2	0
Red Schoendienst, 2b	.233	7	30	3	7	1	0	0	1	0	2	1
Dick Sisler, ph	.000	2	2	0	0	0	0	0	0	0	0	0
Enos Slaughter, of	.320	7	25	5	8	1	1	1	2	4	3	1
Harry Walker, of	.412	7	17	3	7	2	0	0	6	4	2	0
Ted Wilks, p	.000	1	0	0	0	0	0	0	0	0	0	0
TOTAL	.259		232	28	60	19	2	1	27	19	30	3

PITCHER	W	L	ERA	G	GS	CG	SV	SHO	IP	H	ER	BB	SO
Johnny Beazley	0	0	0.00	1	0	0	0	0	1.0	1	0	0	1
Al Brazle	0	1	5.40	2	0	0	0	0	6.2	7	4	6	4
Harry Brecheen	3	0	0.45	3	2	2	0	1	20.0	14	1	5	11
Murry Dickson	0	1	3.86	2	2	0	0	0	14.0	11	6	4	7
Red Munger	1	0	1.00	1	1	1	0	0	9.0	9	1	3	2
Howie Pollet	0	1	3.48	2	2	1	0	0	10.1	12	4	4	3
Ted Wilks	0	0	0.00	1	0	0	0	0	1.0	2	0	0	0
TOTAL	4	3	2.32	11	7	4	0	1	62.0	56	16	22	28

BOS (A)

PLAYER/POS	AVG	G	AB	R	H	2B	3B	HR	RB	BB	SO	SB
Jim Bagby, p	.000	1	1	0	0	0	0	0	0	0	0	0
Mace Brown, p	.000	1	0	0	0	0	0	0	0	0	0	0
Paul Campbell, pr	.000	1	0	0	0	0	0	0	0	0	0	0
Leon Culberson, of-3	.222	5	9	1	2	0	0	1	1	1	2	1
Dom DiMaggio, of	.259	7	27	2	7	3	0	0	3	2	2	0
Joe Dobson, p	.000	3	3	0	0	0	0	0	0	0	2	0
Bobby Doerr, 2b	.409	6	22	1	9	1	0	1	3	2	2	0
Clem Dreiseward, p	.000	1	0	0	0	0	0	0	0	0	0	0
Dave Ferriss, p	.000	2	6	0	0	0	0	0	0	0	1	0
Don Gutteridge, 2b-2	.400	3	5	1	2	0	0	0	1	0	0	0
Mickey Harris, p	.333	2	3	0	1	0	0	0	0	0	1	0
Pinky Higgins, 3b	.208	7	24	1	5	1	0	0	2	2	0	0
Tex Hughson, p	.333	3	3	0	1	0	0	0	0	1	0	0
Earl Johnson, p	.000	3	1	0	0	0	0	0	0	0	0	0
Bob Klinger, p	.000	1	0	0	0	0	0	0	0	0	0	0
Tom McBride, of-2	.167	5	12	0	2	0	0	0	1	0	1	0
Catfish Metkovich, ph	.500	2	2	1	1	1	0	0	0	0	0	0
Wally Moses, of	.417	4	12	1	5	0	0	0	0	1	2	0
Roy Partee, c	.100	5	10	1	1	0	0	0	1	1	1	0
Johnny Pesky, ss	.233	7	30	2	7	0	0	0	0	1	3	1
Rip Russell, 3b-1	1.000	2	2	1	2	0	0	0	0	0	0	0
Mike Ryba, p	.000	1	0	0	0	0	0	0	0	0	0	0
Hal Wagner, c	.000	5	13	0	0	0	0	0	0	0	1	0
Ted Williams, of	.200	7	25	2	5	0	0	0	1	5	5	0
Rudy York, 1b	.261	7	23	6	6	1	1	2	5	6	4	0
Bill Zuber, p	.000	1	0	0	0	0	0	0	0	0	0	0
TOTAL	.240		233	20	56	7	1	4	18	22	28	2

PITCHER	W	L	ERA	G	GS	CG	SV	SHO	IP	H	ER	BB	SO
Jim Bagby	0	0	3.00	1	0	0	0	0	3.0	6	1	1	1
Mace Brown	0	0	27.00	1	0	0	0	0	1.0	4	3	1	0
Joe Dobson	1	0	0.00	3	1	1	0	0	12.2	4	0	3	10
Clem Dreiseward	0	0	0.00	1	0	0	0	0	0.1	0	0	0	0
Dave Ferriss	1	0	2.03	2	2	1	0	1	13.1	13	3	2	4
Mickey Harris	0	2	3.72	2	2	0	0	0	9.2	11	4	4	5
Tex Hughson	0	1	3.14	3	2	0	0	0	14.1	14	5	3	8
Earl Johnson	1	0	2.70	3	0	0	0	0	3.1	1	1	2	1
Bob Klinger	0	1	13.50	1	0	0	0	0	0.2	2	1	1	0
Mike Ryba	0	0	13.50	1	0	0	0	0	0.2	2	1	1	0
Bill Zuber	0	0	4.50	1	0	0	0	0	2.0	3	1	1	1
TOTAL	3	4	2.95	19	7	2	0	1	61.0	60	20	19	30

GAME 1 AT STL OCT 6

BOS	010	000	001	1	3 9 2
STL	000	001	010	0	2 7 0

Pitchers: Hughson, JOHNSON (9) vs POLLET
Home Runs: York-BOS
Attendance: 36,218

GAME 2 AT STL OCT 7

BOS	000	000	000	0	4 1
STL	001	020	00X	3	6 0

Pitchers: HARRIS, Dobson (8) vs BRECHEEN
Attendance: 35,815

GAME 3 AT BOS OCT 9

STL	000	000	000	0	6 1
BOS	300	000	01X	4	8 0

Pitchers: DICKSON, Wilks (8) vs FERRISS
Home Runs: York-BOS
Attendance: 34,500

GAME 4 AT BOS OCT 10

STL	033	010	104	12	20 1
BOS	000	100	020	3	9 4

Pitchers: MUNGER vs HUGHSON, Bagby (3), Zuber (6), Brown (8), Ryba (9), Dreiseword (9)
Home Runs: Slaughter-STL, Doerr-BOS
Attendance: 35,645

GAME 5 AT BOS OCT 11

STL	010	000	002	3	4 1
BOS	110	001	30X	6	11 3

Pitchers: Pollet, BRAZLE (1), Beazley (8) vs DOBSON
Home Runs: Culberson-BOS
Attendance: 35,982

GAME 6 AT STL OCT 13

BOS	000	000	100	1	7 0
STL	003	000	01X	4	8 0

Pitchers: HARRIS, Hughson (3), Johnson (8) vs BRECHEEN
Attendance: 35,768

GAME 7 AT STL OCT 15

BOS	100	000	020	3	8 0
STL	010	020	01X	4	9 1

Pitchers: Ferriss, Dobson (5), KLINGER (8), Johnson (8) vs Dickson, BRECHEEN (8)
Attendance: 36,143

Two of the most memorable plays in World Series history brought Brooklyn victory in Games 4 and 6, but when the Series had ended the Yankees were world champions for the 11th time. Dodgers ace Ralph Branca set New York down in order through the first four innings of Game 1, but the first five batters to face him in the fifth inning reached base. Branca was lifted, but before the inning was over five Yankees had crossed the plate—more than enough for their first win.

The Yankees won again the next day, rocking four Brooklyn pitchers for 15 hits and an easy 10–3 win. Brooklyn finally made its presence felt in Game 3, another heavy-hitting affair, scoring six times in the second inning to establish a lead the Yankees could not overcome. Both teams recorded 13 hits, but Dodgers fireman Hugh Casey extinguished the last flame in the seventh inning, and preserved a narrow 9–8 Brooklyn lead the rest of the way.

Shortstop Pee Wee Reese's error and a bases-loaded walk gave the Yankees an unearned run in the first inning of Game 4, and they earned a second run in the fourth. Meanwhile, Yankees pitcher Bill Bevens, although he had averaged a walk an inning, had allowed no hits and only one run as the game entered the last of the ninth. Bevens retired two in the ninth, but walked his ninth and 10th batters (one intentionally), then lost both his no-hitter and the game as Dodgers pinch hitter Cookie Lavagetto doubled home the two baserunners to even the Series.

Spec Shea (the winning pitcher in Game 1) held Brooklyn to four hits and one run in Game 5. Joe DiMaggio homered in the fifth inning for New York's second run, enough to put the Yankees back in the Series lead. The Dodgers rebounded in Game 6 to build an early 4–0 lead, but the Yankees tied the score in the last of the third and took a lead in the fourth. Brooklyn regained the lead in the sixth with four runs, but when DiMaggio hit a long fly to left with two on in the bottom half of the inning, it looked as if the score would be tied. But substitute left fielder Al Gionfriddo (in what turned out to be his last big league game) raced to the bullpen fence 415 feet out to rob DiMag of the home run. New York scored a run in the ninth, but thanks to Gionfriddo's catch it was not enough.

Brooklyn scored first in the finale with a pair of second-inning runs, but relievers Bill Bevens and Joe Page shut them out through the final seven innings as their teammates gradually built a Series-clinching 5–2 victory.

New York Yankees (AL), 4;
Brooklyn Dodgers (NL), 3

NY (A)

PLAYER/POS	AVG	G	AB	R	H	2B	3B	HR	RB	BB	SO	SB
Yogi Berra, c-4,of-2	.158	6	19	2	3	0	0	1	2	1	2	0
Bill Bevens, p	.000	2	4	0	0	0	0	0	0	0	2	0
Bobby Brown, ph	1.000	4	3	2	3	2	0	0	3	1	0	0
Spud Chandler, p	.000	1	0	0	0	0	0	0	0	0	0	0
Allie Clark, of-1	.500	3	2	1	1	0	0	0	1	1	0	0
Joe DiMaggio, of	.231	7	26	4	6	0	0	2	5	6	2	0
Karl Drews, p	.000	2	2	0	0	0	0	0	0	0	0	0
Lonny Frey, ph	.000	1	1	0	0	0	0	0	0	1	0	0
Tommy Henrich, of	.323	7	31	2	10	2	0	1	5	2	3	0
Ralph Houk, ph	1.000	1	1	0	1	0	0	0	0	0	0	0
Billy Johnson, 3b	.269	7	26	8	7	0	3	0	2	3	4	0
Johnny Lindell, of	.500	6	18	3	9	3	1	0	7	5	2	0
Sherm Lollar, c	.750	2	4	3	3	2	0	0	1	0	0	0
George McQuinn, 1b	.130	7	23	3	0	0	0	0	1	5	8	0
Bobo Newsom, p	.000	2	0	0	0	0	0	0	0	0	0	0
Joe Page, p	.000	4	4	0	0	0	0	0	0	0	1	0
Jack Phillips, 1b-1	.000	2	2	0	0	0	0	0	0	0	0	0
Vic Raschi, p	.000	2	0	0	0	0	0	0	0	0	0	0
Allie Reynolds, p	.500	2	4	2	2	0	0	0	1	0	0	0
Phil Rizzuto, ss	.308	7	26	3	8	1	0	0	2	4	0	2
Aaron Robinson, c	.200	3	10	2	2	0	0	0	1	2	1	0
Spec Shea, p	.400	3	5	0	2	1	0	0	1	0	2	0
Snuffy Stirnweiss, 2b	.259	7	27	3	7	0	1	0	3	8	8	0
Butch Wensloff, p	.000	1	0	0	0	0	0	0	0	0	0	0
TOTAL	.282		238	38	67	11	5	4	36	38	37	2

PITCHER	W	L	ERA	G	GS	CG	SV	SHO	IP	H	ER	BB	SO
Bill Bevens	0	1	2.38	2	1	1	0	0	11.1	3	3	11	7
Spud Chandler	0	0	9.00	1	0	0	0	0	2.0	2	2	3	1
Karl Drews	0	0	3.00	2	0	0	0	0	3.0	2	1	1	0
Bobo Newsom	0	1	19.29	2	1	0	0	0	2.1	6	5	2	0
Joe Page	1	1	4.15	4	0	0	1	0	13.0	12	6	2	7
Vic Raschi	0	0	6.75	2	0	0	0	0	1.1	2	1	0	1
Allie Reynolds	1	0	4.76	2	2	1	0	0	11.1	15	6	3	6
Spec Shea	2	0	2.35	3	3	1	0	0	15.1	10	4	8	10
Butch Wensloff	0	0	0.00	1	0	0	0	0	2.0	0	0	0	0
TOTAL	4	3	4.09	19	7	3	1	0	61.2	52	28	30	32

BRO (N)

PLAYER/POS	AVG	G	AB	R	H	2B	3B	HR	RB	BB	SO	SB
Dan Bankhead, pr	.000	1	0	1	0	0	0	0	0	0	0	0
Rex Barney, p	.000	3	1	0	0	0	0	0	0	0	0	0
Hank Behrman, p	.000	5	0	0	0	0	0	0	0	0	0	0
Bobby Bragan, ph	1.000	1	1	0	1	1	0	0	1	0	0	0
Ralph Branca, p	.000	3	4	0	0	0	0	0	0	0	1	0
Hugh Casey, p	.000	6	1	0	0	0	0	0	0	0	1	0
Bruce Edwards, c	.222	7	27	3	6	1	0	0	2	2	7	0
Carl Furillo, of	.353	6	17	2	6	2	0	0	3	3	0	0
Al Gionfriddo, of-1	.000	4	3	2	0	0	0	0	0	1	0	1
Hal Gregg, p	.000	3	3	0	0	0	0	0	0	1	1	0
Joe Hatten, p	.333	4	3	1	1	0	0	0	0	1	0	0
Gene Hermanski, of	.158	7	19	4	3	0	1	0	1	3	3	0
Gil Hodges, ph	.000	1	1	0	0	0	0	0	0	0	1	0
Spider Jorgensen, 3b	.200	7	20	1	4	2	0	0	3	2	4	0
Cookie Lavagetto, 3b-3	.143	5	7	0	1	1	0	0	3	0	2	0
Vic Lombardi, p-2	.000	3	3	0	0	0	0	0	0	0	0	0
Eddie Miksis, 2b-1,of-1	.250	5	4	1	1	0	0	0	0	1	0	0
Pee Wee Reese, ss	.304	7	23	5	7	1	0	0	4	6	3	3
Pete Reiser, of-3	.250	5	8	1	2	0	0	0	3	1	0	0
Jackie Robinson, 1b	.259	7	27	3	7	2	0	0	3	2	4	2
Eddie Stanky, 2b	.240	7	25	4	6	1	0	0	2	3	2	0
Harry Taylor, p	.000	1	0	0	0	0	0	0	0	0	0	0
Arky Vaughan, ph	.500	2	2	0	1	1	0	0	0	1	0	0
Dixie Walker, of	.222	7	27	1	6	1	0	1	4	3	1	1
TOTAL	.230		226	29	52	13	1	1	26	30	32	7

PITCHER	W	L	ERA	G	GS	CG	SV	SHO	IP	H	ER	BB	SO
Rex Barney	0	1	2.70	3	1	0	0	0	6.2	4	2	10	3
Hank Behrman	0	0	7.11	5	0	0	0	0	6.1	9	5	5	3
Ralph Branca	1	1	8.64	3	1	0	0	0	8.1	12	8	5	8
Hugh Casey	2	0	0.87	6	0	0	1	0	10.1	5	1	1	3
Hal Gregg	0	1	3.55	3	1	0	0	0	12.2	9	5	8	10
Joe Hatten	0	0	7.00	4	1	0	0	0	9.0	12	7	7	5
Vic Lombardi	0	1	12.15	2	2	0	0	0	6.2	14	9	1	5
Harry Taylor	0	0	—	1	1	0	0	0	0.0	2	0	1	0
TOTAL	3	4	5.55	27	7	0	1	0	60.0	67	37	38	37

Boston outpitched and outhit Cleveland, and the clubs tied in runs scored. But the Braves scored most of their runs in one game, and the Indians, spreading theirs more evenly, took the Series. Boston ace Johnny Sain dueled Bob Feller in the opener. Feller gave up only two singles, but one of them followed a walk and a sacrifice (and a controversial pickoff play at second, in which the Boston runner was ruled safe although photos later showed him clearly out). Both teams registered eight hits in Game 2, but Cleveland's led to four runs, while Indians hurler Bob Lemon held Boston to just one—and that was unearned.

Cleveland's rookie sensation Gene Bearden shut out the Braves on five hits in Game 3 as the Series moved to Cleveland's huge Municipal Stadium. Bearden himself, after doubling in the third, scored on a Boston error what proved to be the winning run. A record 81,897 fans saw Sain face Steve Gromek in Game 4. Only five Indians hit Sain safely, but a first-inning single and double put Cleveland on the board, and Larry Doby's home run two innings later made the score 2–0. Boston's Marv Rickert homered in the seventh to narrow Cleveland's lead, but that ended the scoring.

Another attendance record was set at Game 5 as 86,288 fans gathered to watch Bob Feller sew up the title for Cleveland. They went home disappointed. In a game that featured five of the Series' eight home runs, Boston jumped ahead on Bob Elliott's three-run blast in the first. Dale Mitchell opened Cleveland's half of the inning with a home run, but Elliott neutralized it in the third with his second homer. The Indians drove out Boston starter Nelson Potter with four runs in the fourth inning (three coming on Jim Hegan's homer). But Warren Spahn (who had lost Game 2) hurled one-hit shutout relief over the final five frames as his Braves tied the game on Bill Salkeld's homer in the sixth, and blew out Feller and two relievers with six runs in the seventh. The fourth Indians pitcher, Satchel Paige (in his only World Series appearance), retired two batters to end the inning, but the damage had been done.

A day later though, back in Boston, Cleveland edged the Braves 4–3 for the title. Gene Bearden's relief pitching allowed two inherited baserunners to score in the eighth, but halted Boston's rally one run short of a tie.

Cleveland Indians (AL), 4; Boston Braves (NL), 2

CLE (A)

PLAYER/POS	AVG	G	AB	R	H	2B	3B	HR	RB	BB	SO	SB
Gene Bearden, p	.500	2	4	1	2	1	0	0	0	0	1	0
Ray Boone, ph	.000	1	1	0	0	0	0	0	0	0	0	0
Lou Boudreau, ss	.273	6	22	1	6	4	0	0	3	1	1	0
Russ Christopher, p	.000	1	0	0	0	0	0	0	0	0	0	0
Allie Clark, of	.000	1	3	0	0	0	0	0	0	0	1	0
Larry Doby, of	.318	6	22	1	7	1	0	1	2	2	4	0
Bob Feller, p	.000	2	4	0	0	0	0	0	0	0	2	0
Joe Gordon, 2b	.182	6	22	3	4	0	0	1	2	1	2	1
Steve Gromek, p	.000	1	3	0	0	0	0	0	0	0	1	0
Jim Hegan, c	.211	6	19	2	4	0	0	1	5	1	4	1
Wally Judnich, of	.077	4	13	1	1	0	0	0	1	1	4	0
Ken Keltner, 3b	.095	6	21	3	2	0	0	0	2	3	0	0
Bob Kennedy, of	.500	3	2	0	1	0	0	0	1	0	1	0
Ed Klieman, p	.000	1	0	0	0	0	0	0	0	0	0	0
Bob Lemon, p	.000	2	7	0	0	0	0	0	0	0	0	0
Dale Mitchell, of	.174	6	23	4	4	1	0	1	1	2	0	0
Bob Muncrief, p	.000	1	0	0	0	0	0	0	0	0	0	0
Satchel Paige, p	.000	1	0	0	0	0	0	0	0	0	0	0
Hal Peck, of	.000	1	0	0	0	0	0	0	0	0	0	0
Eddie Robinson, 1b	.300	6	20	0	6	0	0	0	1	1	0	0
Al Rosen, ph	.000	1	1	0	0	0	0	0	0	0	0	0
Joe Tipton, ph	.000	1	1	0	0	0	0	0	0	0	1	0
Thurman Tucker, of	.333	1	3	1	1	0	0	0	0	0	0	0
TOTAL	.199		191	17	38	7	0	4	16	12	26	2

PITCHER	W	L	ERA	G	GS	CG	SV	SHO	IP	H	ER	BB	SO
Gene Bearden	1	0	0.00	2	1	1	1	1	10.2	6	0	1	4
Russ Christopher	0	0	∞	1	0	0	0	0	0.0	2	1	0	0
Bob Feller	0	2	5.02	2	2	1	0	0	14.1	10	8	5	7
Steve Gromek	1	0	1.00	1	1	1	0	0	9.0	7	1	1	2
Ed Klieman	0	0	∞	1	0	0	0	0	0.0	1	3	2	0
Bob Lemon	2	0	1.65	2	2	1	0	0	16.1	16	3	7	6
Bob Muncrief	0	0	0.00	1	0	0	0	0	2.0	1	0	0	0
Satchel Paige	0	0	0.00	1	0	0	0	0	0.2	0	0	0	0
TOTAL	4	2	2.72	11	6	4	1	1	53.0	43	16	16	19

BOS (N)

PLAYER/POS	AVG	G	AB	R	H	2B	3B	HR	RB	BB	SO	SB
Red Barrett, p	.000	2	0	0	0	0	0	0	0	0	0	0
Vern Bickford, p	.000	1	0	0	0	0	0	0	0	0	0	0
Clint Conatser, of	.000	2	4	0	0	0	0	0	1	1	0	0
Alvin Dark, ss	.167	6	24	2	4	1	0	0	0	0	2	0
Bob Elliott, 3b	.333	6	21	4	7	0	0	2	5	2	2	0
Tommy Holmes, of	.192	6	26	3	5	0	0	0	1	0	0	0
Phil Masi, c	.125	5	8	1	1	1	0	0	1	0	0	0
Frank McCormick, 1b-1	.200	3	5	0	1	0	0	0	0	0	2	0
Mike McCormick, of	.261	6	23	1	6	0	0	0	2	0	4	0
Nelson Potter, p	.500	2	2	0	1	0	0	0	0	0	0	0
Marv Rickert, of	.211	5	19	2	4	0	0	1	2	0	4	0
Connie Ryan, ph	.000	2	1	0	0	0	0	0	0	0	1	0
Johnny Sain, p	.200	2	5	0	1	0	0	0	0	0	0	0
Bill Salkeld, c	.222	5	9	2	2	0	0	1	1	5	1	0
Ray Sanders, ph	.000	1	1	0	0	0	0	0	0	1	0	0
Sibby Sisti, 2b	.000	2	1	0	0	0	0	0	0	0	0	0
Warren Spahn, p	.000	3	4	0	0	0	0	0	1	0	1	0
Eddie Stanky, 2b	.286	6	14	4	4	1	0	0	1	7	0	0
Earl Torgeson, 1b	.389	5	18	2	7	3	0	0	1	2	1	1
Bill Voiselle, p	.000	2	2	0	0	0	0	0	0	0	0	0
TOTAL	.230		187	17	43	6	0	4	16	16	19	1

PITCHER	W	L	ERA	G	GS	CG	SV	SHO	IP	H	ER	BB	SO
Red Barrett	0	0	0.00	2	0	0	0	0	3.2	1	0	0	1
Vern Bickford	0	1	2.70	1	1	0	0	0	3.1	4	1	5	1
Nelson Potter	0	0	8.44	2	1	0	0	0	5.1	6	5	2	1
Johnny Sain	1	1	1.06	2	2	2	0	1	17.0	9	2	0	9
Warren Spahn	1	1	3.00	3	1	0	0	0	12.0	10	4	3	12
Bill Voiselle	0	1	2.53	2	1	0	0	0	10.2	8	3	2	2
TOTAL	2	4	2.60	12	6	2	0	1	52.0	38	15	12	26

GAME 1 AT BOS OCT 6

CLE	000 000 000	0 4 0
BOS	000 000 01X	1 2 2

Pitchers: FELLER vs SAIN
Attendance: 40,135

GAME 2 AT BOS OCT 7

CLE	000 210 001	4 8 1
BOS	100 000 000	1 8 3

Pitchers: LEMON vs SPAHN, Barrett (5), Potter (8)
Attendance: 39,633

GAME 3 AT CLE OCT 8

BOS	000 000 000	0 5 1
CLE	001 100 00X	2 5 0

Pitchers: BICKFORD, Voiselle (4), Barrett (8) vs BEARDEN
Attendance: 70,306

GAME 4 AT CLE OCT 9

BOS	000 000 100	1 7 0
CLE	101 000 00X	2 5 0

Pitchers: SAIN vs GROMEK
Home Runs: Doby-CLE, Rickert-BOS
Attendance: 81,897

GAME 5 AT CLE OCT 10

BOS	301 001 600	11 12 0
CLE	100 400 000	5 6 2

Pitchers: Potter, SPAHN (4) vs FELLER, Klieman (7), Christopher (7), Paige (7), Muncrief (8)
Home Runs: Elliott-BOS (2), Mitchell-CLE, Hegan-CLE, Salkeld-BOS
Attendance: 86,288

GAME 6 AT BOS OCT 11

CLE	001 002 010	4 10 0
BOS	000 100 020	3 9 0

Pitchers: LEMON, Bearden (8) vs VOISELLE, Spahn (8)
Home Runs: Gordon-CLE
Attendance: 40,103

Casey Stengel, in the first of his 12 years as Yankees manager, edged his team past the Boston Red Sox for his first of 10 American League pennants, then past the Dodgers for his first of seven world championships. New York and Brooklyn traded 1–0 wins to begin the Series. In Game 1 Allie Reynolds dueled rookie Don Newcombe scorelessly through 8½ innings—until Tommy Henrich led off the last of the ninth with a home run to win the game for the Yankees. Jackie Robinson scored after doubling off Vic Raschi in the second inning of Game 2 for that game's only score, while Dodgers ace Preacher Roe permitted just six scattered hits—never more than one per inning.

The teams entered the ninth inning of Game 3 tied 1–1. But in the top of the ninth, Dodgers starter Ralph Branca, after loading the bases on two walks and a single, gave up another single to pinch hitter Johnny Mize for two runs. Jerry Coleman's single off reliever Jack Banta drove in another run before the third out was made. In the last of the ninth, Yankees fireman Joe Page (who had held Brooklyn scoreless since coming on with the bases loaded in the fourth) finally weakened. But after yielding solo homers to Luis Olmo and Roy Campanella, he struck out pinch hitter Bruce Edwards for New York's second win.

The Yankees' victory in Game 4 came a little easier. They scored first, driving out starter Don Newcombe with three runs in the fourth, and rapping reliever Joe Hatten for three more runs an inning later. Brooklyn retaliated in the sixth, sending Yankees starter Ed Lopat to the showers with seven singles for four runs. But Allie Reynolds came on for 3⅓ innings of no-hit relief to preserve the Yankees lead—and his Series 0.00 earned run average.

After four closely contested games, the Yankees erupted in Game 5 for 10 runs in the first six innings as Brooklyn was held to just two. In the last of the seventh, the Dodgers came back, driving out starter Vic Raschi with a four-run rally, capped by Gil Hodges' three-run homer. But Joe Page came on to get the final out of the seventh, and held the Dodgers scoreless over the final two innings to bring the Yankees' world titles to an even dozen.

New York Yankees (AL), 4; Brooklyn Dodgers (NL), 1

NY (A)

PLAYER/POS	AVG	G	AB	R	H	2B	3B	HR	RB	BB	SO	SB
Hank Bauer, of	.167	3	6	0	1	0	0	0	0	0	0	0
Yogi Berra, c	.063	4	16	2	1	0	0	0	1	1	3	0
Bobby Brown, 3b-3	.500	4	12	4	6	1	2	0	5	2	2	0
Tommy Byrne, p	1.000	1	1	0	1	0	0	0	0	0	0	0
Gerry Coleman, 2b	.250	5	20	0	5	3	0	0	4	0	4	0
Joe DiMaggio, of	.111	5	18	2	2	0	0	1	2	3	5	0
Tommy Henrich, 1b	.263	5	19	4	5	0	0	1	1	3	0	0
Billy Johnson, 3b	.143	2	7	0	1	0	0	0	0	0	2	1
Johnny Lindell, of	.143	2	7	0	1	0	0	0	0	0	2	0
Ed Lopat, p	.333	1	3	0	1	1	0	0	1	0	0	0
Cliff Mapes, of	.100	4	10	3	1	1	0	0	2	4	4	0
Johnny Mize, ph	1.000	2	2	0	2	0	0	0	2	0	0	0
Gus Niarhos, c	.000	1	0	0	0	0	0	0	0	0	0	0
Joe Page, p	.000	3	4	0	0	0	0	0	0	0	2	0
Vic Raschi, p	.200	2	5	0	1	0	0	0	1	1	1	0
Allie Reynolds, p	.500	2	4	0	2	1	0	0	0	0	1	0
Phil Rizzuto, ss	.167	5	18	2	3	0	0	0	1	3	1	1
Charlie Silvera, c	.000	1	2	0	0	0	0	0	0	0	0	0
Snuffy Stirnweiss, ph	.000	1	0	0	0	0	0	0	0	0	0	0
Gene Woodling, of	.400	3	10	4	4	3	0	0	0	3	0	0
TOTAL	.226		164	21	37	10	2	2	20	18	27	2

PITCHER	W	L	ERA	G	GS	CG	SV	SHO	IP	H	ER	BB	SO
Tommy Byrne	0	0	2.70	1	1	0	0	0	3.1	2	1	2	1
Ed Lopat	1	0	6.35	1	1	0	0	0	5.2	9	4	1	4
Joe Page	1	0	2.00	3	0	0	1	0	9.0	6	2	3	8
Vic Raschi	1	1	4.30	2	2	0	0	0	14.2	15	7	5	11
Allie Reynolds	1	0	0.00	2	1	1	1	1	12.1	2	0	4	14
TOTAL	4	1	2.80	9	5	1	2	1	45.0	34	14	15	38

BRO (N)

PLAYER/POS	AVG	G	AB	R	H	2B	3B	HR	RB	BB	SO	SB
Jack Banta, p	.000	3	1	0	0	0	0	0	0	0	0	0
Rex Barney, p	.000	1	0	0	0	0	0	0	0	0	0	0
Ralph Branca, p	.000	1	3	0	0	0	0	0	0	0	3	0
Tommy Brown, ph	.000	2	2	0	0	0	0	0	0	0	1	0
Roy Campanella, c	.267	5	15	2	4	1	0	1	2	3	1	0
Billy Cox, 3b-1	.333	2	3	0	1	0	0	0	0	0	1	0
Bruce Edwards, ph	.500	2	2	0	1	0	0	0	0	0	1	0
Carl Erskine, p	.000	2	0	0	0	0	0	0	0	0	0	0
Carl Furillo, of-2	.125	3	8	0	1	0	0	0	0	1	0	0
Joe Hatten, p	.000	2	0	0	0	0	0	0	0	0	0	0
Gene Hermanski, of	.308	4	13	1	4	0	1	0	2	3	3	0
Gil Hodges, 1b	.235	5	17	2	4	0	0	1	4	1	4	0
Spider Jorgensen, 3b-3	.182	4	11	1	2	2	0	0	0	2	2	0
Mike McCormick, of	.000	1	0	0	0	0	0	0	0	0	0	0
Eddie Miksis, 3b-2	.286	3	7	0	2	1	0	0	0	0	1	0
Paul Minner, p	.000	1	0	0	0	0	0	0	0	0	0	0
Don Newcombe, p	.000	2	4	0	0	0	0	0	0	0	3	0
Luis Olmo, of	.273	4	11	2	3	0	0	1	2	0	2	0
Erv Palica, p	.000	1	0	0	0	0	0	0	0	0	0	0
Marv Rackley, of	.000	2	5	0	0	0	0	0	0	0	2	0
Pee Wee Reese, ss	.316	5	19	2	6	1	0	1	2	1	0	1
Jackie Robinson, 2b	.188	5	16	2	3	1	0	0	2	4	2	0
Preacher Roe, p	.000	1	3	0	0	0	0	0	0	0	3	0
Duke Snider, of	.143	5	21	2	3	1	0	0	0	0	8	0
Dick Whitman, ph	.000	1	1	0	0	0	0	0	0	0	1	0
TOTAL	.210		162	14	34	7	1	4	14	15	38	1

PITCHER	W	L	ERA	G	GS	CG	SV	SHO	IP	H	ER	BB	SO
Jack Banta	0	0	3.18	3	0	0	0	0	5.2	5	2	1	4
Rex Barney	0	1	16.88	1	1	0	0	0	2.2	3	5	6	2
Ralph Branca	0	1	4.15	1	1	0	0	0	8.2	4	4	4	6
Carl Erskine	0	0	16.20	2	0	0	0	0	1.2	3	3	1	0
Joe Hatten	0	0	16.20	2	0	0	0	0	1.2	4	3	2	0
Paul Minner	0	0	0.00	1	0	0	0	0	1.0	1	0	0	0
Don Newcombe	0	2	3.09	2	2	1	0	0	11.2	10	4	3	11
Erv Palica	0	0	0.00	1	0	0	0	0	2.0	1	0	1	1
Preacher Roe	1	0	0.00	1	1	1	0	1	9.0	6	0	0	3
TOTAL	1	4	4.30	14	5	2	0	1	44.0	37	21	18	27

GAME 1 AT NY OCT 5

BRO	000	000	000	0	2	0
NY	000	000	001	1	5	1

Pitchers: NEWCOMBE vs REYNOLDS
Home Runs: Henrich-NY
Attendance: 66,224

GAME 2 AT NY OCT 6

BRO	010	000	000	1	7	2
NY	000	000	000	0	6	1

Pitchers: ROE vs RASCHI, Page (9)
Attendance: 70,053

GAME 3 AT BRO OCT 7

NY	001	000	003	4	5	0
BRO	000	100	002	3	5	0

Pitchers: Byrne, PAGE (4) vs BRANCA, Banta (9)
Home Runs: Reese-BRO, Olmo-BRO, Campanella-BRO
Attendance: 32,788

GAME 4 AT BRO OCT 8

NY	000	330	000	6	10	0
BRO	000	004	000	4	9	1

Pitchers: LOPAT, Reynolds (6) vs NEWCOMBE, Hatten (4), Erskine (6), Banta (7)
Attendance: 33,934

GAME 5 AT BRO OCT 9

NY	203	113	000	10	11	1
BRO	001	001	400	6	11	2

Pitchers: RASCHI, Page (7) vs BARNEY, Banta (3), Erskine (6), Hatten (6), Palica (7), Minner (9)
Home Runs: DiMaggio-NY, Hodges-BRO
Attendance: 33,711

Philadelphia's Whiz Kids, who had capped an exciting pennant race with the Phillies' first flag in 35 years, carried the excitement into the World Series but couldn't quite catch up with the Yankees. New York scored only one run in the opener; Philadelphia didn't score any. The Phillies did score a run in the second game, but the Yankees scored two. In Game 3 the Phillies scored two runs, the Yankees three.

Jim Konstanty, the National League's ace reliever (and MVP), started his first major league game in four years to lead off the Series, and held the Yankees to just four hits in eight innings of work. But Bobby Brown's double in the fourth was followed by two long flies which moved Brown around to the plate—all the scoring New York needed as Vic Raschi held the Phillies to two singles and a walk.

Robin Roberts and Allie Reynolds dueled in Game 2. New York scored first with a run on a walk and two singles in the second inning, but two Philadelphia singles and a fly to left tied the game in the last of the fifth. There matters stood until the top of the tenth, when Joe DiMaggio led off with a home run to the upper deck in left. Reynolds held the Phillies in the bottom of the tenth for the second Yankees win.

The Phillies took a lead for the only time in the Series when they broke a 1–1 tie with a run in the seventh inning of Game 3. But New York scored on a Phillies error to tie the game again in the eighth, and in the last of the ninth—with two outs—Yankees Gene Woodling, Phil Rizzuto, and Jerry Coleman singled to produce the winning run.

Rookie sensation Whitey Ford started Game 4 and held Philadelphia scoreless into the ninth inning as his Yankees scored twice in the first and three more in the sixth. He was taken out with two away in the ninth after two singles, a hit batsman, and a Yankee error had permitted two Phillies to score. But reliever Allie Reynolds struck out the final batter to secure a Series sweep for the Yankees.

New York Yankees (AL), 4; Philadelphia Phillies (NL), 0

NY (A)

PLAYER/POS	AVG	G	AB	R	H	2B	3B	HR	RB	BB	SO	SB
Hank Bauer, of	.133	4	15	0	2	0	0	0	1	0	0	0
Yogi Berra, c	.200	4	15	2	3	0	0	1	2	2	1	0
Bobby Brown, 3b	.333	4	12	2	4	1	1	0	1	0	0	0
Gerry Coleman, 2b	.286	4	14	2	4	1	0	0	3	2	0	0
Joe Collins, 1b	.000	1	0	0	0	0	0	0	0	0	0	0
Joe DiMaggio, of	.308	4	13	2	4	1	0	1	2	3	1	0
Tom Ferrick, p	.000	1	0	0	0	0	0	0	0	0	0	0
Whitey Ford, p	.000	1	3	0	0	0	0	0	0	0	2	0
Johnny Hopp, 1b	.000	3	2	0	0	0	0	0	0	0	0	0
Jackie Jensen, pr	.000	1	0	0	0	0	0	0	0	0	0	0
Billy Johnson, 3b	.000	4	6	0	0	0	0	0	0	0	3	0
Ed Lopat, p	.500	1	2	0	1	0	0	0	0	0	1	0
Cliff Mapes, of	.000	1	4	0	0	0	0	0	0	0	0	0
Johnny Mize, 1b	.133	4	15	0	2	0	0	0	0	0	1	0
Vic Raschi, p	.333	1	3	0	1	0	0	0	0	0	0	0
Allie Reynolds, p	.333	2	3	0	1	0	0	0	0	1	2	0
Phil Rizzuto, ss	.143	4	14	1	2	0	0	0	0	3	1	1
Gene Woodling, of	.429	4	14	2	6	0	0	0	1	2	0	0
TOTAL	.222		135	11	30	3	1	2	10	13	12	1

PITCHER	W	L	ERA	G	GS	CG	SV	SHO	IP	H	ER	BB	SO
Tom Ferrick	1	0	0.00	1	0	0	0	0	1.0	1	0	1	0
Whitey Ford	1	0	0.00	1	1	0	0	0	8.2	7	0	1	7
Ed Lopat	0	0	2.25	1	1	0	0	0	8.0	9	2	0	5
Vic Raschi	1	0	0.00	1	1	1	0	1	9.0	2	0	1	5
Allie Reynolds	1	0	0.87	2	1	1	1	0	10.1	7	1	4	7
TOTAL	4	0	0.73	6	4	2	1	1	37.0	26	3	7	24

PHI (N)

PLAYER/POS	AVG	G	AB	R	H	2B	3B	HR	RB	BB	SO	SB
Richie Ashburn, of	.176	4	17	0	3	1	0	0	1	0	4	0
Jimmy Bloodworth, 2b	.000	1	0	0	0	0	0	0	0	0	0	0
Putsy Caballero, ph	.000	3	1	0	0	0	0	0	0	0	1	0
Del Ennis, of	.143	4	14	1	2	1	0	0	0	0	1	0
Mike Goliat, 2b	.214	4	14	1	3	0	0	0	1	1	2	0
Granny Hamner, ss	.429	4	14	1	6	2	1	0	0	1	2	1
Ken Heintzelman, p	.000	1	2	0	0	0	0	0	0	0	0	0
Ken Johnson, pr	.000	1	0	1	0	0	0	0	0	0	0	0
Willie Jones, 3b	.286	4	14	1	4	1	0	0	0	0	3	0
Jim Konstanty, p	.250	3	4	0	1	0	0	0	0	0	1	0
Stan Lopata, c-1	.000	2	1	0	0	0	0	0	0	0	1	0
Jackie Mayo, of-1	.000	3	0	0	0	0	0	0	0	1	0	0
Russ Meyer, p	.000	2	0	0	0	0	0	0	0	0	0	0
Bob Miller, p	.000	1	0	0	0	0	0	0	0	0	0	0
Robin Roberts, p	.000	2	2	0	0	0	0	0	0	0	1	0
Andy Seminick, c	.182	4	11	0	2	0	0	0	0	1	3	0
Ken Silvestri, c	.000	1	0	0	0	0	0	0	0	0	0	0
Dick Sisler, of	.059	4	17	0	1	0	0	0	1	0	5	0
Eddie Waitkus, 1b	.267	4	15	0	4	1	0	0	0	2	0	0
Dick Whitman, ph	.000	3	2	0	0	0	0	0	0	1	0	0
TOTAL	.203		128	5	26	6	1	0	3	7	24	1

PITCHER	W	L	ERA	G	GS	CG	SV	SHO	IP	H	ER	BB	SO
Ken Heintzelman	0	0	1.17	1	1	0	0	0	7.2	4	1	6	3
Jim Konstanty	0	1	2.40	3	1	0	0	0	15.0	9	4	4	3
Russ Meyer	0	1	5.40	2	0	0	0	0	1.2	4	1	0	1
Bob Miller	0	1	27.00	1	1	0	0	0	0.1	2	1	0	0
Robin Roberts	0	1	1.64	2	1	1	0	0	11.0	11	2	3	5
TOTAL	0	4	2.27	9	4	1	0	0	35.2	30	9	13	12

GAME 1 AT PHI OCT 4

NY	000 100 000	1	5	0
PHI	000 000 000	0	2	1

Pitchers: RASCHI vs KONSTANTY, Meyer (9)
Attendance: 30,746

GAME 2 AT PHI OCT 5

NY	010 000 000 1	2	10	0
PHI	000 010 000 0	1	7	0

Pitchers: REYNOLDS vs ROBERTS
Home Runs: DiMaggio-NY
Attendance: 32,660

GAME 3 AT NY OCT 6

PHI	000 001 100	2	10	2
NY	001 000 011	3	7	0

Pitchers: Heintzelman, Konstanty (8), MEYER (9) vs Lopat, FERRICK (9)
Attendance: 64,505

GAME 4 AT NY OCT 7

PHI	000 000 002	2	7	1
NY	200 003 00X	5	8	2

Pitchers: MILLER, Konstanty (1), Roberts (8) vs FORD, Reynolds (9)
Home Runs: Berra-NY
Attendance: 68,098

The Giants—who caught Brooklyn with a tremendous late-season drive, then defeated them for the pennant on Bobby Thomson's ninth-inning home run in Game 3 of the tie-breaker playoff series—carried their momentum through Game 3 of the World Series before bowing to the Yankees. Dave Koslo (the only Giants starter not to see action in the playoff) pitched the Series opener and held the Yankees to one run. Monte Irvin's steal of home for the Giants' second run in the top of the first was enough for the win, but Alvin Dark made Koslo's lead more secure with a three-run homer in the sixth.

The Yankees evened the Series in Game 2, scoring two early runs (one of them Joe Collins' home run) off Larry Jansen, and holding on for the win behind Ed Lopat's five-hit pitching. But the Giants regained the lead in Game 3 with five unearned runs (three of them on Whitey Lockman's homer) in a fifth inning prolonged by two Yankees errors, as pitchers Jim Hearn and Sheldon Jones combined to hold the Bronx Bombers to five hits and a pair of runs (though Hearn issued eight walks).

But that was the end of the Giants' drive. Although they scored first in both Games 4 and 5 with first-inning runs, they couldn't hold the lead either time. In Game 4 Allie Reynolds held the Giants to two runs as his Yankees scored six—including a two-run homer by Joe DiMaggio in the fifth inning that proved to be the last home run of his career. DiMag drove in three more runs in Game 5, as did Phil Rizzuto, and rookie infielder Gil McDougald contributed a grand slam as the Bombers earned their nickname in obliterating Giants pitching with 13 runs. Ed Lopat, meanwhile, hurled his second five-hitter in four days to give the Yanks the Series lead.

Hank Bauer tripled with the bases full in the sixth inning of Game 6 to break a tie and give the Yankees a 4–1 lead. The Giants loaded the bases with three straight singles to open the top of the ninth, and scored two runners on successive flies to left, to come within one run of a tie. But pinch hitter Sal Yvars (in his only Series at bat) lined out to right and the Yankees had their 14th world title.

New York Yankees (AL), 4; New York Giants (NL), 2

NY (A)

PLAYER/POS	AVG	G	AB	R	H	2B	3B	HR	RB	BB	SO	SB
Hank Bauer, of	.167	6	18	0	3	0	1	0	3	1	1	0
Yogi Berra, c	.261	6	23	4	6	1	0	0	0	2	1	0
Bobby Brown, 3b-4	.357	5	14	1	5	1	0	0	0	2	1	0
Gerry Coleman, 2b	.250	5	8	2	2	0	0	0	0	1	2	0
Joe Collins, 1b-6,of-1	.222	6	18	2	4	0	0	1	3	2	1	0
Joe DiMaggio, of	.261	6	23	3	6	2	0	1	5	2	4	0
Bobby Hogue, p	.000	2	0	0	0	0	0	0	0	0	0	0
Johnny Hopp, ph	.000	1	0	0	0	0	0	0	0	1	0	0
Bob Kuzava, p	.000	1	0	0	0	0	0	0	0	0	0	0
Ed Lopat, p	.125	2	8	0	1	0	0	0	0	0	2	0
Mickey Mantle, of	.200	2	5	1	1	0	0	0	0	2	1	0
Billy Martin, pr	.000	1	0	1	0	0	0	0	0	0	0	0
Gil McDougald, 3b-5,2b-4	.261	6	23	2	6	1	0	1	7	2	2	0
Johnny Mize, 1b-2	.286	4	7	2	2	1	0	0	1	2	0	0
Tom Morgan, p	.000	1	0	0	0	0	0	0	0	0	0	0
Joe Ostrowski, p	.000	1	0	0	0	0	0	0	0	0	0	0
Vic Raschi, p	.000	2	2	0	0	0	0	0	0	0	1	0
Allie Reynolds, p	.333	2	6	0	2	0	0	0	1	0	1	0
Phil Rizzuto, ss	.320	6	25	5	8	0	0	1	3	2	3	0
Johnny Sain, p	.000	1	1	0	0	0	0	0	0	0	0	0
Gene Woodling, of-5	.167	6	18	6	3	1	1	1	1	5	3	0
TOTAL	.246		199	29	49	7	2	5	25	26	23	0

PITCHER	W	L	ERA	G	GS	CG	SV	SHO	IP	H	ER	BB	SO
Bobby Hogue	0	0	0.00	2	0	0	0	0	2.2	1	0	0	0
Bob Kuzava	0	0	0.00	1	0	0	1	0	1.0	0	0	0	0
Ed Lopat	2	0	0.50	2	2	2	0	0	18.0	10	1	3	4
Tom Morgan	0	0	0.00	1	0	0	0	0	2.0	2	0	1	3
Joe Ostrowski	0	0	0.00	1	0	0	0	0	2.0	1	0	0	1
Vic Raschi	1	1	0.87	2	2	0	0	0	10.1	12	1	8	4
Allie Reynolds	1	1	4.20	2	2	1	0	0	15.0	16	7	11	8
Johnny Sain	0	0	9.00	1	0	0	0	0	2.0	4	2	2	2
TOTAL	4	2	1.87	12	6	3	1	0	53.0	46	11	25	22

NY (N)

PLAYER/POS	AVG	G	AB	R	H	2B	3B	HR	RB	BB	SO	SB
Al Corwin, p	.000	1	0	0	0	0	0	0	0	0	0	0
Alvin Dark, ss	.417	6	24	5	10	3	0	1	4	2	3	0
Clint Hartung, of	.000	2	4	0	0	0	0	0	0	0	0	0
Jim Hearn, p	.000	2	3	0	0	0	0	0	0	0	1	0
Monte Irvin, of	.458	6	24	3	11	0	1	0	2	2	1	2
Larry Jansen, p	.000	3	2	0	0	0	0	0	0	0	0	0
Sheldon Jones, p	.000	2	0	0	0	0	0	0	0	0	0	0
Monte Kennedy, p	.000	2	0	0	0	0	0	0	0	0	0	0
Alex Konikowski, p	.000	1	0	0	0	0	0	0	0	0	0	0
Dave Koslo, p	.000	2	5	0	0	0	0	0	0	0	2	0
Whitey Lockman, 1b	.240	6	25	1	6	2	0	1	4	1	2	0
Jack Lohrke, ph	.000	2	2	0	0	0	0	0	0	0	1	0
Sal Maglie, p	.000	1	1	0	0	0	0	0	0	0	1	0
Willie Mays, of	.182	6	22	1	4	0	0	0	1	2	2	0
Ray Noble, c	.000	2	2	0	0	0	0	0	0	0	1	0
Bill Rigney, ph	.250	4	4	0	1	0	0	0	0	1	0	0
Hank Schenz, pr	.000	1	0	0	0	0	0	0	0	0	0	0
George Spencer, p	.000	2	0	0	0	0	0	0	0	0	0	0
Eddie Stanky, 2b	.136	6	22	3	3	0	0	0	1	3	2	0
Hank Thompson, of	.143	5	14	3	2	0	0	0	0	5	2	0
Bobby Thomson, 3b	.238	6	21	1	5	1	0	0	2	5	0	0
Wes Westrum, c	.235	6	17	1	4	1	0	0	0	5	3	0
Davey Williams, ph	.000	2	1	0	0	0	0	0	0	0	0	0
Sal Yvars, ph	.000	1	1	0	0	0	0	0	0	0	0	0
TOTAL	.237		194	18	46	7	1	2	15	25	22	2

PITCHER	W	L	ERA	G	GS	CG	SV	SHO	IP	H	ER	BB	SO
Al Corwin	0	0	0.00	1	0	0	0	0	1.2	1	0	0	1
Jim Hearn	1	0	1.04	2	1	0	0	0	8.2	5	1	8	1
Larry Jansen	0	2	6.30	3	2	0	0	0	10.0	8	7	4	6
Sheldon Jones	0	0	2.08	2	0	0	1	0	4.1	5	1	1	2
Monte Kennedy	0	0	6.00	2	0	0	0	0	3.0	3	2	1	4
Alex Konikowski	0	0	0.00	1	0	0	0	0	1.0	1	0	0	0
Dave Koslo	1	1	3.00	2	2	1	0	0	15.0	12	5	7	6
Sal Maglie	0	1	7.20	1	1	0	0	0	5.0	8	4	2	3
George Spencer	0	0	18.90	2	0	0	0	0	3.1	6	7	3	0
TOTAL	2	4	4.67	16	6	1	1	0	52.0	49	27	26	23

GAME 1 AT NY-A OCT 4

NY-N 200 003 000   5 10 1
NY-A 000 000 000   1 7 1

Pitchers: KOSLO vs REYNOLDS, Hogue (7), Morgan (8)
Home Runs: Dark-NY(N)
Attendance: 65,673

GAME 2 AT NY-A OCT 5

NY-N 000 000 100   1 5 1
NY-A 110 000 01X   3 6 0

Pitchers: JANSEN, Spencer (7) vs LOPAT
Home Runs: Collins-NY(A)
Attendance: 66,018

GAME 3 AT NY-N OCT 6

NY-A 000 000 011   2 5 2
NY-N 010 050 00X   6 7 2

Pitchers: RASCHI, Hogue (5), Ostrowski (7) vs HEARN, Jones (8)
Home Runs: Lockman-NY(N), Woodling-NY(A)
Attendance: 52,035

GAME 4 AT NY-N OCT 8

NY-A 010 120 200   6 12 0
NY-N 100 000 001   2 8 2

Pitchers: REYNOLDS vs MAGLIE, Jones (6), Kennedy (9)
Home Runs: DiMaggio-NY(A)
Attendance: 49,010

GAME 5 AT NY-N OCT 9

NY-A 005 202 400   13 12 1
NY-N 100 000 000   1 5 3

Pitchers: LOPAT vs JANSEN, Kennedy (4), Spencer (6), Corwin (7), Konikowski (9)
Home Runs: McDougald-NY(A), Rizzuto-NY(A)
Attendance: 47,530

GAME 6 AT NY-A OCT 10

NY-N 000 010 002   3 11 1
NY-A 100 003 00X   4 7 0

Pitchers: KOSLO, Hearn (7), Jansen (8) vs RASCHI, Sain (7), Kuzava (9)
Attendance: 61,711

In four of the seven games, home runs provided the margin of victory. Homers accounted for five of the six runs scored in the opener, with Duke Snider's two-run blast in the sixth putting Brooklyn ahead to stay. Star Dodgers reliever Joe Black, in only his third start of the year, held New York to six hits and two runs in defeating Yankees ace Allie Reynolds.

In Game 2 Billy Martin's three-run shot was the centerpiece. Vic Raschi tossed a three-hitter. Brooklyn needed no homers to regain the Series advantage in Game 3. In the top of the ninth, with the Dodgers leading by a run, Pee Wee Reese and Jackie Robinson singled (driving out starter Ed Lopat) and pulled a double steal. Both then scored on a passed ball. Yankees pinch hitter Johnny Mize homered in the last of the ninth, but Preacher Roe escaped without further scoring for a complete-game 5–3 win.

Black opposed Reynolds again in Game 4 and bettered his earlier performance, holding New York to three hits and one run (a Mize homer) in seven innings. But Reynolds improved even more, fanning 10 as he shut the Dodgers out.

Snider hit his second homer of the Series and Mize his third in the fifth inning of Game 5. Mize's shot put New York ahead, but Brooklyn tied the game in the seventh and took a 6–5 lead when Snider doubled home a run in the 11th. Right fielder Carl Furillo's leaping catch in the last of the 11th robbed Mize of another home run, and starter Carl Erskine held on for the win, giving Brooklyn a 3–2 Series lead.

Snider's home run in the last of the sixth ended Vic Raschi's shutout in Game 6, but Yogi Berra, the first Yankee up in the seventh, tied the game and spoiled Billy Loes's shutout with his home run, and pitcher Raschi singled home the go-ahead run two outs later. Mickey Mantle's blast in the eighth (the first of his record 18 World Series home runs) made the score 3–1. Snider's fourth homer of the Series gave the Dodgers a second run in the eighth, but Allie Reynolds relieved Raschi and prevented further scoring, sending the Series to a seventh game.

Joe Black traded three shutout innings with Ed Lopat in the finale before both clubs scored single runs in the fourth and fifth innings. Mantle homered off Black in the sixth for a third run that proved the Series winner, as three Yankees relievers held Brooklyn scoreless through the final four frames.

New York Yankees (AL), 4; Brooklyn Dodgers (NL), 3

NY (A)

PLAYER/POS	AVG	G	AB	R	H	2B	3B	HR	RB	BB	SO	SB
Hank Bauer, of	.056	7	18	2	1	0	0	0	1	4	3	0
Yogi Berra, c	.214	7	28	2	6	1	0	2	3	2	4	0
Ewell Blackwell, p	.000	1	1	0	0	0	0	0	0	0	0	0
Joe Collins, 1b	.000	6	12	1	0	0	0	0	0	1	3	0
Tom Gorman, p	.000	1	0	0	0	0	0	0	0	0	0	0
Ralph Houk, ph	.000	1	1	0	0	0	0	0	0	0	0	0
Bob Kuzava, p	.000	1	1	0	0	0	0	0	0	0	0	0
Ed Lopat, p	.333	2	3	0	1	0	0	0	0	1	1	0
Mickey Mantle, of	.345	7	29	5	10	1	1	2	3	3	4	0
Billy Martin, 2b	.217	7	23	2	5	0	0	1	4	2	2	0
Gil McDougald, 3b	.200	7	25	5	5	0	0	1	3	5	2	1
Johnny Mize, 1b-4	.400	5	15	3	6	1	0	3	6	3	1	0
Irv Noren, of-3	.300	4	10	0	3	0	0	0	1	1	3	0
Vic Raschi, p	.167	3	6	0	1	0	0	0	1	1	2	0
Allie Reynolds, p	.000	4	7	0	0	0	0	0	0	0	2	0
Phil Rizzuto, ss	.148	7	27	2	4	1	0	0	0	5	2	0
Johnny Sain, p-1	.000	2	3	0	0	0	0	0	0	0	0	0
Ray Scarborough, p	.000	1	0	0	0	0	0	0	0	0	0	0
Gene Woodling, of-6	.348	7	23	4	8	1	1	1	1	3	3	0
TOTAL	.216		232	26	50	5	2	10	24	31	32	1

PITCHER	W	L	ERA	G	GS	CG	SV	SHO	IP	H	ER	BB	SO
Ewell Blackwell	0	0	7.20	1	1	0	0	0	5.0	4	4	3	4
Tom Gorman	0	0	0.00	1	0	0	0	0	0.2	1	0	0	0
Bob Kuzava	0	0	0.00	1	0	0	1	0	2.2	0	0	0	2
Ed Lopat	0	1	4.76	2	2	0	0	0	11.1	14	6	4	3
Vic Raschi	2	0	1.59	3	2	1	0	0	17.0	12	3	8	18
Allie Reynolds	2	1	1.77	4	2	1	1	1	20.1	12	4	6	18
Johnny Sain	0	1	3.00	1	0	0	0	0	6.0	6	2	3	3
Ray Scarborough	0	0	9.00	1	0	0	0	0	1.0	1	1	0	1
TOTAL	4	3	2.81	14	7	2	2	1	64.0	50	20	24	49

BRO (N)

PLAYER/POS	AVG	G	AB	R	H	2B	3B	HR	RB	BB	SO	SB
Sandy Amoros, ph	.000	1	0	0	0	0	0	0	0	0	0	0
Joe Black, p	.000	3	6	0	0	0	0	0	0	1	6	0
Roy Campanella, c	.214	7	28	0	6	0	0	0	1	1	6	0
Billy Cox, 3b	.296	7	27	4	8	2	0	0	0	3	4	0
Carl Erskine, p	.000	3	6	1	0	0	0	0	0	0	1	0
Carl Furillo, of	.174	7	23	1	4	2	0	0	0	3	3	0
Gil Hodges, 1b	.000	7	21	1	0	0	0	0	1	5	6	0
Tommy Holmes, of	.000	3	1	0	0	0	0	0	0	0	0	0
Ken Lehman, p	.000	1	0	0	0	0	0	0	0	0	0	0
Billy Loes, p	.333	2	3	0	1	0	0	0	0	0	1	1
Bobby Morgan, 3b	.000	2	1	0	0	0	0	0	0	0	1	0
Rocky Nelson, ph	.000	4	3	0	0	0	0	0	0	1	2	0
Andy Pafko, of-5	.190	7	21	0	4	0	0	0	2	0	4	0
Pee Wee Reese, ss	.345	7	29	4	10	0	0	1	4	2	2	1
Jackie Robinson, 2b	.174	7	23	4	4	0	0	1	2	7	5	2
Preacher Roe, p	.000	3	2	0	0	0	0	0	0	0	0	0
Johnny Rutherford, p	.000	1	0	0	0	0	0	0	0	0	0	0
George Shuba, of-3	.300	4	10	3	3	1	0	0	0	0	4	0
Duke Snider, of	.345	7	29	5	10	2	0	4	8	1	5	1
TOTAL	.215		233	20	50	7	0	6	18	24	49	5

PITCHER	W	L	ERA	G	GS	CG	SV	SHO	IP	H	ER	BB	SO
Joe Black	1	2	2.53	3	3	1	0	0	21.1	15	6	8	9
Carl Erskine	1	1	4.50	3	2	1	0	0	18.0	12	9	10	10
Ken Lehman	0	0	0.00	1	0	0	0	0	2.0	2	0	1	0
Billy Loes	0	1	4.35	2	1	0	0	0	10.1	11	5	5	5
Preacher Roe	1	0	3.18	3	1	1	0	0	11.1	9	4	6	7
Johnny Rutherford	0	0	9.00	1	0	0	0	0	1.0	1	1	1	1
TOTAL	3	4	3.52	13	7	3	0	0	64.0	50	25	31	32

GAME 1 AT BRO OCT 1

NY	010	000	010	2	6	2
BRO	010	002	01X	4	6	0

Pitchers: REYNOLDS, Scarborough (8) vs BLACK
Home Runs: Robinson-BRO, Snider-BRO, Reese-BRO, McDougald-NY
Attendance: 34,861

GAME 2 AT BRO OCT 2

NY	000	115	000	7	10	0
BRO	001	000	000	1	3	1

Pitchers: RASCHI vs ERSKINE, Loes (6), Lehman (8)
Home Runs: Martin-NY
Attendance: 33,792

GAME 3 AT NY OCT 3

BRO	001	010	012	5	11	0
NY	010	000	011	3	6	2

Pitchers: ROE vs LOPAT, Gorman (9)
Home Runs: Berra-NY, Mize-NY
Attendance: 66,698

GAME 4 AT NY OCT 4

BRO	000	000	000	0	4	1
NY	000	100	01X	2	4	1

Pitchers: BLACK, Rutherford (8) vs REYNOLDS
Home Runs: Mize-NY
Attendance: 71,787

GAME 5 AT NY OCT 5

BRO	010	030	100	01	6	10	0
NY	000	050	000	00	5	5	1

Pitchers: ERSKINE vs Blackwell, SAIN (6)
Home Runs: Snider-BRO, Mize-NY
Attendance: 70,536

GAME 6 AT BRO OCT 6

NY	000	000	210	3	9	0
BRO	000	001	010	2	8	1

Pitchers: RASCHI, LOES (8) vs LOES, Roe (9)
Home Runs: Snider-BRO (2), Berra-NY, Mantle-NY
Attendance: 30,037

GAME 7 AT BRO OCT 7

NY	000	111	100	4	10	4
BRO	000	110	000	2	8	1

Pitchers: Lopat, REYNOLDS (4), Raschi (7), Kuzava (7) vs BLACK, Roe (6), Erskine (8)
Home Runs: Woodling-NY, Mantle-NY
Attendance: 33,195

Although the Yankees easily won the American League pennant, the Dodgers seemed even more overwhelming, with a team batting average of .285 and a club-record 105 wins. But when the Series was over, the Yankees had added a record fifth straight world championship to their record fifth straight pennant.

Dodgers ace Carl Erskine lasted only one inning of the Series opener, giving up three walks and two triples for four runs. By the middle of the seventh inning, the Dodgers had tied the score at 5–5. But Joe Collins homered for the Yanks to break the tie in the last of the seventh, and reliever Johnny Sain ensured his own win with a two-run double an inning later. The Dodgers outhit New York in Game 2, and held a 2–1 lead entering the bottom of the seventh. Billy Martin (who hit .500 and slugged .958 in the Series) tied the game with a leadoff homer in the seventh, and Mickey Mantle won it with a two-run blast in the eighth.

Brooklyn evened the Series at home with victories in Games 3 and 4. Erskine redeemed his poor start in Game 1 with a record-setting 14-strikeout performance in Game 3. But it was a narrow win, settled only when Roy Campanella homered in the last of the eighth to break a 2–2 tie. In Game 4, Duke Snider made Billy Loes's three-run pitching a winning performance, driving in four of the Dodgers' seven runs with two doubles and a homer.

But Brooklyn never held the lead in the final two games. Four home runs (including a Mantle grand slam) rocked Dodgers pitching in Game 5 as the Bombers built a lead which Dodger home runs in the eighth and ninth were unable to overcome. In Game 6 the Yankees built a 3–0 lead over Erskine in the first two innings. Brooklyn fought back with a run in the sixth, and tied the game on Carl Furillo's two-run homer in the top of the ninth. But with men on first and second in the last of the ninth, Billy Martin singled in the game-ending, Series-winning run. It was Martin's 12th hit, a new record for a six-game Series.

New York Yankees (AL), 4; Brooklyn Dodgers (NL), 2

NY (A)

PLAYER/POS	AVG	G	AB	R	H	2B	3B	HR	RB	BB	SO	SB
Hank Bauer, of	.261	6	23	6	6	0	1	0	1	2	4	0
Yogi Berra, c	.429	6	21	3	9	1	0	1	4	3	3	0
Don Bollweg, 1b-1	.000	3	2	0	0	0	0	0	0	0	2	0
Joe Collins, 1b	.167	6	24	4	4	1	0	1	2	3	8	0
Whitey Ford, p	.333	2	3	0	1	0	0	0	0	0	0	0
Tom Gorman, p	.000	1	1	0	0	0	0	0	0	0	1	0
Bob Kuzava, p	.000	1	1	0	0	0	0	0	0	0	1	0
Ed Lopat, p	.000	1	3	0	0	0	0	0	0	0	2	0
Mickey Mantle, of	.208	6	24	3	5	0	0	2	7	3	8	0
Billy Martin, 2b	.500	6	24	5	12	1	2	2	8	1	2	1
Jim McDonald, p	.500	1	2	0	1	1	0	0	1	1	1	0
Gil McDougald, 3b	.167	6	24	2	4	0	1	2	4	1	3	0
Johnny Mize, ph	.000	3	3	0	0	0	0	0	0	0	1	0
Irv Noren, of	.000	2	1	0	0	0	0	0	0	1	0	0
Vic Raschi, p	.000	1	2	0	0	0	0	0	0	0	1	0
Allie Reynolds, p	.500	3	2	0	1	0	0	0	0	1	1	0
Phil Rizzuto, ss	.316	6	19	4	6	1	0	0	0	3	2	1
Johnny Sain, p	.500	2	2	1	1	1	0	0	2	0	1	0
Art Schallock, p	.000	1	0	0	0	0	0	0	0	0	0	0
Gene Woodling, of	.300	6	20	5	6	0	0	1	3	6	2	0
TOTAL	.279		201	33	56	6	4	9	32	25	43	2

PITCHER	W	L	ERA	G	GS	CG	SV	SHO	IP	H	ER	BB	SO
Whitey Ford	0	1	4.50	2	2	0	0	0	8.0	9	4	2	7
Tom Gorman	0	0	3.00	1	0	0	0	0	3.0	4	1	0	1
Bob Kuzava	0	0	13.50	1	0	0	0	0	0.2	2	1	0	1
Ed Lopat	1	0	2.00	1	1	1	0	0	9.0	9	2	4	3
Jim McDonald	1	0	5.87	1	1	0	0	0	7.2	12	5	0	3
Vic Raschi	0	1	3.38	1	1	1	0	0	8.0	8	3	3	4
Allie Reynolds	1	0	6.75	3	1	0	1	0	8.0	9	6	4	9
Johnny Sain	1	0	4.76	2	0	0	0	0	5.2	8	3	1	1
Art Schallock	0	0	4.50	1	0	0	0	0	2.0	2	1	1	1
TOTAL	4	2	4.50	13	6	2	1	0	52.0	64	26	15	30

BRO (N)

PLAYER/POS	AVG	G	AB	R	H	2B	3B	HR	RB	BB	SO	SB
Wayne Belardi, ph	.000	2	2	0	0	0	0	0	0	0	1	0
Joe Black, p	.000	1	0	0	0	0	0	0	0	0	0	0
Roy Campanella, c	.273	6	22	6	6	0	0	1	2	2	3	0
Billy Cox, 3b	.304	6	23	3	7	3	0	1	6	1	4	0
Carl Erskine, p	.250	3	4	0	1	0	0	0	0	0	1	0
Carl Furillo, of	.333	6	24	4	8	2	0	1	4	1	3	0
Jim Gilliam, 2b	.296	6	27	4	8	3	0	2	4	0	2	0
Gil Hodges, 1b	.364	6	22	3	8	0	0	1	1	3	3	1
Jim Hughes, p	.000	1	0	0	0	0	0	0	0	0	0	0
Clem Labine, p	.000	3	2	0	0	0	0	0	0	0	1	0
Billy Loes, p	.667	1	3	0	2	0	0	0	0	0	0	0
Russ Meyer, p	.000	1	1	0	0	0	0	0	0	0	1	0
Bob Milliken, p	.000	1	0	0	0	0	0	0	0	0	0	0
Bobby Morgan, ph	.000	1	1	0	0	0	0	0	0	0	0	0
Johnny Podres, p	1.000	1	1	0	1	0	0	0	0	0	0	0
Pee Wee Reese, ss	.208	6	24	0	5	0	1	0	0	4	1	0
Jackie Robinson, of	.320	6	25	3	8	2	0	0	2	1	0	1
Preacher Roe, p	.000	1	3	0	0	0	0	0	0	0	2	0
George Shuba, ph	1.000	2	1	1	1	0	0	1	2	0	0	0
Duke Snider, of	.320	6	25	3	8	3	0	1	5	2	6	0
Don Thompson, of	.000	2	0	0	0	0	0	0	0	0	0	0
Ben Wade, p	.000	2	0	0	0	0	0	0	0	0	0	0
Dick Williams, ph	.500	3	2	0	1	0	0	0	0	1	1	0
TOTAL	.300		213	27	64	13	1	8	26	15	30	2

PITCHER	W	L	ERA	G	GS	CG	SV	SHO	IP	H	ER	BB	SO
Joe Black	0	0	9.00	1	0	0	0	0	1.0	1	1	0	2
Carl Erskine	1	0	5.79	3	3	1	0	0	14.0	14	9	9	16
Jim Hughes	0	0	2.25	1	0	0	0	0	4.0	3	1	1	3
Clem Labine	0	2	3.60	3	0	0	1	0	5.0	10	2	1	3
Billy Loes	1	0	3.38	1	1	0	0	0	8.0	8	3	2	8
Russ Meyer	0	0	6.23	1	0	0	0	0	4.1	8	3	4	5
Bob Milliken	0	0	0.00	1	0	0	0	0	2.0	1	0	1	0
Johnny Podres	0	1	3.38	1	1	0	0	0	2.2	1	1	2	0
Preacher Roe	0	1	4.50	1	1	1	0	0	8.0	5	4	4	4
Ben Wade	0	0	15.43	2	0	0	0	0	2.1	4	4	1	2
TOTAL	2	4	4.91	15	6	2	1	0	51.1	56	28	25	43

GAME 1 AT NY SEPT 30

BRO	000	013	100	5	12 2
NY	400	010	13X	9	12 0

Pitchers: Erskine, Hughes (2), LABINE (6), Wade (8) vs Reynolds, SAIN (6)
Home Runs: Gilliam-BRO, Hodges-BRO, Shuba-BRO, Berra-NY, Collins-NY
Attendance: 69,374

GAME 2 AT NY OCT 1

BRO	000	200	000	2	9 1
NY	100	000	12X	4	5 0

Pitchers: ROE vs LOPAT
Home Runs: Martin-NY, Mantle-NY
Attendance: 66,786

GAME 3 AT BRO OCT 2

NY	000	010	010	2	6 0
BRO	000	011	01X	3	9 0

Pitchers: RASCHI vs ERSKINE
Home Runs: Campanella-BRO
Attendance: 35,270

GAME 4 AT BRO OCT 3

NY	000	020	001	3	9 0
BRO	300	102	10X	7	12 0

Pitchers: FORD, Gorman (2), Sain (5), Schallock (7) vs LOES, Labine (9)
Home Runs: McDougald-NY, Snider-BRO
Attendance: 36,775

GAME 5 AT BRO OCT 4

NY	105	000	311	11	11 1
BRO	010	010	041	7	14 1

Pitchers: McDONALD, Kuzava (8), Reynolds (9) vs PODRES, Meyer (3), Wade (8), Black (9)
Home Runs: Woodling-NY, Mantle-NY, Martin-NY, McDougald-NY, Cox-BRO, Gilliam-BRO
Attendance: 36,775

GAME 6 AT NY OCT 5

BRO	000	001	002	3	8 3
NY	210	000	001	4	13 0

Pitchers: Erskine, Milliken (5), LABINE (7) vs Ford, REYNOLDS (8)
Home Runs: Furillo-BRO
Attendance: 62,370

The Indians, who had won a league-record 111 games to break the American League domination of the New York Yankees, entered the World Series as strong favorites to humble the Giants. It was not to be.

Cleveland would have won the opener had it not been played in New York's Polo Grounds, with their short foul lines and deep center field. Most of the game was a pitchers' duel. Vic Wertz (the only Indian to hit safely in all four games) tripled off Sal Maglie to give Cleveland a two-run lead in the top of the first, but three singles and a walk in the third off Bob Lemon tied the score. Lemon then settled down to hold New York scoreless through the ninth. Cleveland threatened in the eighth when the first two batters reached base, bringing Wertz to the plate. As Wertz had already hit Maglie safely three times, Don Liddle was brought in to pitch to him. Wertz responded with a fly to deep center that would have been a home run in Cleveland, but in New York turned into the most famous catch in World Series history as Willie Mays raced out and tracked down the ball about 425 feet from the plate. Marv Grissom replaced Liddle on the mound and issued a walk to load the bases, but he retired the next two batters and (despite Wertz's double in the top of the 10th) held Cleveland scoreless the rest of the way. In the last of the 10th, Lemon retired the first batter, but Mays walked and stole second, and Hank Thompson was walked intentionally to set up the double play. Pinch hitter Dusty Rhodes then entered the hall of heroes with a short fly to right that—though it would have been an out in Cleveland—fell into the Polo Grounds stands for three runs and a Giants victory.

The rest of the Series was anticlimax. In the second game Rhodes, with half the Giants' four hits, drove in two runs on a single and another homer, providing the margin of victory for ace Johnny Antonelli, who allowed only one of Cleveland's 14 baserunners to score. Game 3 was no contest. New York had scored all six of its runs before the Indians managed to come up with single runs in both the seventh and eighth. Pinch hitter Hank Majeski's three-run homer put Cleveland on the board in the fifth inning of Game 4. But as New York had already scored seven times, even a fourth Cleveland run in the seventh proved too little to prevent a shocking sweep by the Giants.

New York Giants (NL), 4; Cleveland Indians (AL), 0

NY (N)

PLAYER/POS	AVG	G	AB	R	H	2B	3B	HR	RB	BB	SO	SB
Johnny Antonelli, p	.000	2	3	0	0	0	0	0	1	0	0	0
Alvin Dark, ss	.412	4	17	2	7	0	0	0	0	1	1	0
Ruben Gomez, p	.000	1	4	0	0	0	0	0	0	0	2	0
Marv Grissom, p	.000	1	1	0	0	0	0	0	0	0	1	0
Monte Irvin, of	.222	4	9	1	2	1	0	0	2	0	3	0
Don Liddle, p	.000	2	3	0	0	0	0	0	0	0	2	0
Whitey Lockman, 1b	.111	4	18	2	2	0	0	0	0	1	2	0
Sal Maglie, p	.000	1	3	0	0	0	0	0	0	0	2	0
Willie Mays, of	.286	4	14	4	4	1	0	0	3	4	1	1
Don Mueller, of	.389	4	18	4	7	0	0	0	1	0	1	0
Dusty Rhodes, of-2	.667	3	6	2	4	0	0	2	7	1	2	0
Hank Thompson, 3b	.364	4	11	6	4	1	0	0	2	7	1	0
Wes Westrum, c	.273	4	11	0	3	0	0	0	3	1	3	0
Hoyt Wilhelm, p	.000	2	1	0	0	0	0	0	0	0	1	0
Davey Williams, 2b	.000	4	11	0	0	0	0	0	1	2	2	0
TOTAL	.254		130	21	33	3	0	2	20	17	24	1

PITCHER	W	L	ERA	G	GS	CG	SV	SHO	IP	H	ER	BB	SO
Johnny Antonelli	1	0	0.84	2	1	1	1	0	10.2	8	1	7	12
Ruben Gomez	1	0	2.45	1	1	0	0	0	7.1	4	2	3	2
Marv Grissom	1	0	0.00	1	0	0	0	0	2.2	1	0	3	2
Don Liddle	1	0	1.29	2	1	0	0	0	7.0	5	1	1	2
Sal Maglie	0	0	2.57	1	1	0	0	0	7.0	7	2	2	2
Hoyt Wilhelm	0	0	0.00	2	0	0	1	0	2.1	1	0	0	3
TOTAL	4	0	1.46	9	4	1	2	0	37.0	26	6	16	23

CLE (A)

PLAYER/POS	AVG	G	AB	R	H	2B	3B	HR	RB	BB	SO	SB
Bobby Avila, 2b	.133	4	15	1	2	0	0	0	0	2	1	0
Sam Dente, ss	.000	3	3	1	0	0	0	0	0	1	0	0
Larry Doby, of	.125	4	16	0	2	0	0	0	0	2	4	0
Mike Garcia, p	.000	2	0	0	0	0	0	0	0	0	0	0
Bill Glynn, 1b-1	.500	2	2	1	1	1	0	0	0	0	1	0
Mickey Grasso, c	.000	1	0	0	0	0	0	0	0	0	0	0
Jim Hegan, c	.154	4	13	1	2	1	0	0	0	1	1	0
Art Houtteman, p	.000	1	0	0	0	0	0	0	0	0	0	0
Bob Lemon, p-2	.000	3	6	0	0	0	0	0	0	1	1	0
Hank Majeski, 3b-1	.167	4	6	1	1	0	0	1	3	0	1	0
Dale Mitchell, ph	.000	3	2	0	0	0	0	0	0	1	0	0
Don Mossi, p	.000	3	0	0	0	0	0	0	0	0	0	0
Hal Naragon, c	.000	1	0	0	0	0	0	0	0	0	0	0
Ray Narleski, p	.000	2	0	0	0	0	0	0	0	0	0	0
Hal Newhouser, p	.000	1	0	0	0	0	0	0	0	0	0	0
Dave Philley, of-2	.125	4	8	0	1	0	0	0	0	1	3	0
Dave Pope, of-2	.000	3	3	0	0	0	0	0	0	1	1	0
Rudy Regalado, 3b-1	.333	4	3	0	1	0	0	0	1	0	0	0
Al Rosen, 3b	.250	3	12	0	3	0	0	0	0	1	0	0
Al Smith, of	.214	4	14	2	3	0	0	1	2	2	2	0
George Strickland, ss	.000	3	9	0	0	0	0	0	0	0	2	0
Vic Wertz, 1b	.500	4	16	2	8	2	1	1	3	2	2	0
Wally Westlake, of	.143	2	7	0	1	0	0	0	0	0	1	0
Early Wynn, p	.500	1	2	0	1	0	1	0	0	0	0	0
TOTAL	.190		137	9	26	5	1	3	9	16	23	0

PITCHER	W	L	ERA	G	GS	CG	SV	SHO	IP	H	ER	BB	SO
Mike Garcia	0	1	5.40	2	1	0	0	0	5.0	6	3	4	4
Art Houtteman	0	0	4.50	1	0	0	0	0	2.0	2	1	1	1
Bob Lemon	0	2	6.75	2	2	1	0	0	13.1	16	10	8	11
Don Mossi	0	0	0.00	3	0	0	0	0	4.0	3	0	0	1
Ray Narleski	0	0	2.25	2	0	0	0	0	4.0	1	1	1	2
Hal Newhouser	0	0	∞	1	0	0	0	0	0.0	1	1	1	0
Early Wynn	0	1	3.86	1	1	0	0	0	7.0	4	3	2	5
TOTAL	0	4	4.84	12	4	1	0	0	35.1	33	19	17	24

GAME 1 AT NY SEPT 29

CLE	200 000 000 0	2	8	0
NY	002 000 000 3	5	9	3

Pitchers: LEMON vs Maglie, Liddle (8), GRISSOM (8)
Home Runs: Rhodes-NY
Attendance: 52,751

GAME 2 AT NY SEPT 30

CLE	100 000 000	1	8	0
NY	000 020 10X	3	4	0

Pitchers: WYNN, Mossi (8) vs ANTONELLI
Home Runs: Smith-CLE, Rhodes-NY
Attendance: 49,099

GAME 3 AT CLE OCT 1

NY	103 011 000	6	10	1
CLE	000 000 110	2	4	2

Pitchers: GOMEZ, Wilhelm (7) vs GARCIA, Houtteman (4), Narleski (6), Mossi (9)
Home Runs: Wertz-CLE
Attendance: 71,555

GAME 4 AT CLE OCT 2

NY	021 040 000	7	10	3
CLE	000 030 100	4	6	2

Pitchers: LIDDLE, Wilhelm (7), Antonelli (8) vs LEMON, Newhouser (5), Narleski (5), Mossi (6), Garcia (8)
Home Runs: Majeski-CLE
Attendance: 78,102

The Dodgers and Yankees, after a year's absence, faced each other again in the World Series—their sixth Series confrontation in 15 years. And after Brooklyn had lost the first two games it began to look as though 1955 might also mark the Yankees' sixth Series triumph over the Dodgers. But this was Brooklyn's year.

The opener was a hitters' game, but closely contested. Both teams scored twice in the second inning and once in the third, but first baseman Joe Collins' leadoff homer in the last of the fourth gave New York its first lead of the game, and his two-run blast in the sixth made the score 6–3. Brooklyn clawed back in the eighth for two runs—including Jackie Robinson's steal of home—to pull within one run of a tie, but they came no closer. In Game 2, Tommy Byrne held the Dodgers to five hits and two runs, and won his own game at the bat with a two-run single that capped the Yankees' four-run fourth.

The Series turned around as the Dodgers captured the next three games in Brooklyn. Roy Campanella's two-run homer in the first inning of Game 3 gave Brooklyn a quick lead. New York tied the game with a pair of runs in the second (one of them a homer by Mickey Mantle, who appeared in only three Series games because of a leg injury). But two more runs in the last of the second drove out New York starter Bob Turley and put them ahead to stay as Dodgers hurler Johnny Podres held the Yankees to three runs. Home runs by Campanella, Gil Hodges, and Duke Snider accounted for six of Brooklyn's eight runs in Game 4 as the Dodgers evened the Series. Sandy Amoros' second-inning homer initiated the scoring in Game 5, and Snider's blasts in the third and fifth (which made him the first player to hit four home runs in two different Series) gave Brooklyn a 4–1 lead, which even late-inning Yankees homers by Bob Cerv and Yogi Berra could not overcome.

New York bounced back in Game 6, scoring all five of their runs in the first inning (including three on Bill Skowron's homer) to give Whitey Ford a comfortable lead, which he held with a one-run four-hitter. But in the finale, Gil Hodges drove in both Brooklyn runs with a single in the fourth and a sacrifice fly in the sixth. They were all Brooklyn got, but they proved more than enough to carry the Dodgers to their first world title in 55 years, as left fielder Sandy Amoros stifled New York's only real scoring threat with a spectacular running catch in the sixth that started a double play and preserved Johnny Podres' second Series win.

Brooklyn Dodgers (NL), 4;
New York Yankees (AL), 3

BRO (N)

PLAYER/POS	AVG	G	AB	R	H	2B	3B	HR	RBI	BB	SO	SB
Sandy Amoros, of	.333	5	12	3	4	0	0	1	3	4	4	0
Don Bessent, p	.000	3	1	0	0	0	0	0	0	0	1	0
Roy Campanella, c	.259	7	27	4	7	3	0	2	4	3	3	0
Roger Craig, p	.000	1	0	0	0	0	0	0	0	1	0	0
Carl Erskine, p	.000	1	1	0	0	0	0	0	0	0	0	0
Carl Furillo, of	.296	7	27	4	8	1	0	1	3	3	5	0
Jim Gilliam, 2b-5,of-4	.292	7	24	2	7	1	0	0	3	8	1	1
Don Hoak, 3b-1	.333	3	3	0	1	0	0	0	0	2	0	0
Gil Hodges, 1b	.292	7	24	2	7	0	0	1	5	3	2	0
Frank Kellert, ph	.333	3	3	0	1	0	0	0	0	0	0	0
Clem Labine, p	.000	4	4	0	0	0	0	0	0	0	3	0
Billy Loes, p	.000	1	1	0	0	0	0	0	0	0	0	0
Russ Meyer, p	.000	1	0	0	0	0	0	0	0	0	1	0
Don Newcombe, p	.000	1	3	0	0	0	0	0	0	0	0	0
Johnny Podres, p	.143	2	7	1	1	0	0	0	0	0	1	0
Pee Wee Reese, ss	.296	7	27	5	8	1	0	0	2	3	5	0
Jackie Robinson, 3b	.182	6	22	5	4	1	1	0	1	2	1	1
Ed Roebuck, p	.000	1	0	0	0	0	0	0	0	0	0	0
George Shuba, ph	.000	1	1	0	0	0	0	0	0	0	0	0
Duke Snider, of	.320	7	25	5	8	1	0	4	7	2	6	0
Karl Spooner, p	.000	2	0	0	0	0	0	0	0	0	0	0
Don Zimmer, 2b	.222	4	9	0	2	0	0	0	2	2	5	0
TOTAL	.260		223	31	58	8	1	9	30	33	38	2

PITCHER	W	L	ERA	G	GS	CG	SV	SHO	IP	H	ER	BB	SO
Don Bessent	0	0	0.00	3	0	0	0	0	3.1	3	0	1	1
Roger Craig	1	0	3.00	1	1	0	0	0	6.0	4	2	5	4
Carl Erskine	0	0	9.00	1	1	0	0	0	3.0	3	3	2	3
Clem Labine	1	0	2.89	4	0	0	1	0	9.1	6	3	2	2
Billy Loes	0	1	9.82	1	1	0	0	0	3.2	7	4	1	5
Russ Meyer	0	0	0.00	1	0	0	0	0	5.2	4	0	2	4
Don Newcombe	0	1	9.53	1	1	0	0	0	5.2	8	6	2	4
Johnny Podres	2	0	1.00	2	2	2	0	1	18.0	15	2	4	10
Ed Roebuck	0	0	0.00	1	0	0	0	0	2.0	1	0	0	0
Karl Spooner	0	1	13.50	2	1	0	0	0	3.1	4	5	3	6
TOTAL	4	3	3.75	17	7	2	1	1	60.0	55	25	22	39

NY (A)

PLAYER/POS	AVG	G	AB	R	H	2B	3B	HR	RBI	BB	SO	SB
Hank Bauer, of-5	.429	6	14	1	6	0	0	0	1	0	1	0
Yogi Berra, c	.417	7	24	5	10	1	0	1	2	3	1	0
Tommy Byrne, p-2	.167	3	6	0	1	0	0	0	2	0	2	0
Andy Carey, ph	.500	2	2	0	1	0	1	0	1	0	0	0
Tom Carroll, pr	.000	2	0	0	0	0	0	0	0	0	0	0
Bob Cerv, of-4	.125	5	16	1	2	0	0	1	1	0	4	0
Gerry Coleman, ss	.000	3	3	0	0	0	0	0	0	0	1	0
Rip Coleman, p	.000	1	0	0	0	0	0	0	0	0	0	0
Joe Collins, 1b-5,of-1	.167	5	12	6	2	0	0	2	3	6	4	1
Whitey Ford, p	.000	2	6	1	0	0	0	0	0	1	1	0
Bob Grim, p	.000	3	2	0	0	0	0	0	0	0	0	0
Elston Howard, of	.192	7	26	3	5	0	0	1	3	1	8	0
Johnny Kucks, p	.000	2	0	0	0	0	0	0	0	0	0	0
Don Larsen, p	.000	1	2	0	0	0	0	0	0	0	0	0
Mickey Mantle, of-2	.200	3	10	1	2	0	0	1	1	0	2	0
Billy Martin, 2b	.320	7	25	2	8	1	1	0	4	1	5	0
Gil McDougald, 3b	.259	7	27	2	7	0	0	1	1	2	6	0
Tom Morgan, p	.000	2	0	0	0	0	0	0	0	0	0	0
Irv Noren, of	.063	5	16	0	1	0	0	0	1	1	1	0
Phil Rizzuto, ss	.267	7	15	2	4	0	0	0	1	5	1	2
Eddie Robinson, 1b-1	.667	4	3	0	2	0	0	0	1	2	1	0
Bill Skowron, 1b-3	.333	5	12	4	4	2	0	1	3	0	1	0
Tom Sturdivant, p	.000	2	0	0	0	0	0	0	0	0	0	0
Bob Turley, p	.000	3	1	0	0	0	0	0	0	0	0	0
TOTAL	.248		222	26	55	4	2	8	25	22	39	3

PITCHER	W	L	ERA	G	GS	CG	SV	SHO	IP	H	ER	BB	SO
Tommy Byrne	1	1	1.88	2	2	1	0	0	14.1	8	3	8	8
Rip Coleman	0	0	9.00	1	0	0	0	0	1.0	5	1	0	1
Whitey Ford	2	0	2.12	2	2	1	0	0	17.0	13	4	8	10
Bob Grim	0	1	4.15	3	1	0	1	0	8.2	8	4	5	2
Johnny Kucks	0	0	6.00	2	0	0	0	0	3.0	4	2	1	1
Don Larsen	0	1	11.25	1	1	0	0	0	4.0	5	5	2	2
Tom Morgan	0	0	4.91	2	0	0	0	0	3.2	3	2	1	1
Tom Sturdivant	0	0	6.00	2	0	0	0	0	3.0	5	2	2	0
Bob Turley	0	1	8.44	3	1	0	0	0	5.1	7	5	4	7
TOTAL	3	4	4.20	18	7	2	1	0	60.0	58	28	33	38

GAME 1 AT NY SEPT 28

BRO	021 000 020	5 10 0
NY	021 102 00X	6 9 1

Pitchers: NEWCOMBE, Bessent (6), Labine (8) vs FORD, Grim (9)
Home Runs: Furillo-BRO, Snider-BRO, Howard-NY, Collins-NY (2)
Attendance: 63,869

GAME 2 AT NY SEPT 29

BRO	000 110 000	2 5 2
NY	000 400 00X	4 8 0

Pitchers: LOES, Bessent (4), Spooner (5), Labine (8) vs BYRNE
Attendance: 64,707

GAME 3 AT BRO SEPT 30

NY	020 000 100	3 7 0
BRO	220 200 20X	8 11 1

Pitchers: TURLEY, Morgan (2), Kucks (5), Sturdivant (7) vs PODRES
Home Runs: Campanella-BRO, Mantle-NY
Attendance: 34,209

GAME 4 AT BRO OCT 1

NY	110 102 000	5 9 0
BRO	001 330 10X	8 14 0

Pitchers: LARSEN, Kucks (5), R.Coleman (6), Morgan (7), Sturdivant (8) vs Erskine, Bessent (4), LABINE (5)
Home Runs: McDougald-NY, Campanella-BRO, Hodges-BRO, Snider-BRO
Attendance: 36,242

GAME 5 AT BRO OCT 2

NY	000 100 110	3 6 0
BRO	021 010 01X	5 9 2

Pitchers: GRIM, Turley (7) vs CRAIG, Labine (7)
Home Runs: Cerv-NY, Berra-NY, Amoros-BRO, Snider-BRO (2)
Attendance: 36,796

GAME 6 AT NY OCT 3

BRO	000 100 000	1 4 1
NY	500 000 00X	5 8 0

Pitchers: SPOONER, Meyer (1), Roebuck (7) vs FORD
Home Runs: Skowron-NY
Attendance: 64,022

GAME 7 AT NY OCT 4

BRO	000 101 000	2 5 0
NY	000 000 000	0 8 1

Pitchers: PODRES vs BYRNE, Grim (6), Turley (8)
Attendance: 62,465

With both teams repeaters as league champions, the Yankees followed Brooklyn's winning pattern of the previous Series: losing the first two games, winning the next three, then splitting the final pair.

Sal Maglie outlasted Yankees ace Whitey Ford in the opener. Maglie gave up nine hits and three runs (on homers by Mickey Mantle and Billy Martin), but struck out 10 and took the win as Jackie Robinson and Gil Hodges contributed homers for four of Brooklyn's six runs. Dodgers ace Don Newcombe was blown out by six Yankees runs (capped by Yogi Berra's grand slam) in the first two innings of Game 2. But Brooklyn came back with six unearned runs in their half of the second (three of them on Duke Snider's homer) and proceeded to run through seven Yankees pitchers for a 13–8 win and a two-game Series edge.

Whitey Ford tried again in Game 3, and this time held on for a complete-game 5–3 win, supported by Billy Martin's game-tying solo homer in the second and 40-year-old Enos Slaughter's go-ahead three-run shot in the sixth. Tom Sturdivant duplicated Ford's effectiveness and success the next day with a six-hit 6–2 win to even the Series.

Sal Maglie pitched Game 5 for Brooklyn and improved on his winning performance of Game 1, yielding only two runs and holding New York hitless until Mantle's two-out homer in the fourth inning. But no one was a match for Yankees pitcher Don Larsen that day. There was a close out on a deflected Dodger liner in the second inning, and center fielder Mantle made a fine running catch to prevent a hit in the fifth. But Larsen retired the rest routinely, and when Dale Mitchell fanned in the ninth Larsen had his perfect game—a feat still unique in World Series history.

Brooklyn reliever Clem Labine started in Game 6 against Bob Turley. No runner scored for either side until the last of the 10th inning when, with two out, Jackie Robinson lined a Turley pitch over the head of the left fielder, scoring Jim Gilliam from second and forcing New York into a seventh game.

The finale proved an anticlimactic disaster for Brooklyn. Once again Newcombe was driven out—this time by Yogi Berra's two two-run homers and Elston Howard's solo shot. By the time it was over, Bill Skowron had increased the Yankee run total to nine with a grand slam, and Johnny Kucks had shut Brooklyn out on three singles. For New York it was world title number 17.

New York Yankees (AL), 4; Brooklyn Dodgers (NL), 3

NY (A)

PLAYER/POS	AVG	G	AB	R	H	2B	3B	HR	RB	BB	SO	SB
Hank Bauer, of	.281	7	32	3	9	0	0	1	3	0	5	1
Yogi Berra, c	.360	7	25	5	9	2	0	3	10	4	1	0
Tommy Byrne, p-1	.000	2	1	0	0	0	0	0	0	0	0	0
Andy Carey, 3b	.158	7	19	2	3	0	0	0	0	1	6	0
Bob Cerv, ph	1.000	1	1	0	1	0	0	0	0	0	0	0
Gerry Coleman, 2b	.000	2	2	0	0	0	0	0	0	0	0	0
Joe Collins, 1b-5	.238	6	21	2	5	2	0	0	2	2	3	0
Whitey Ford, p	.000	2	4	0	0	0	0	0	0	0	3	0
Elston Howard, of	.400	1	5	1	2	1	0	1	1	0	0	0
Johnny Kucks, p	.000	3	3	0	0	0	0	0	0	0	1	0
Don Larsen, p	.333	2	3	1	1	0	0	0	1	0	1	0
Mickey Mantle, of	.250	7	24	6	6	1	0	3	4	6	5	1
Billy Martin, 2b-7,3b-1	.296	7	27	5	8	0	0	2	3	1	6	0
Maury McDermott, p	1.000	1	1	0	1	0	0	0	0	0	0	0
Gil McDougald, ss	.143	7	21	0	3	0	0	0	0	1	3	0
Tom Morgan, p	1.000	2	1	1	1	0	0	0	0	0	0	0
Norm Siebern, ph	.000	1	1	0	0	0	0	0	0	0	0	0
Bill Skowron, 1b-2	.100	3	10	1	1	0	0	1	4	0	3	0
Enos Slaughter, of	.350	6	20	6	7	0	0	1	4	4	0	0
Tom Sturdivant, p	.333	2	3	0	1	0	0	0	0	0	1	0
Bob Turley, p	.000	3	4	0	0	0	0	0	0	0	1	0
George Wilson, ph	.000	1	1	0	0	0	0	0	0	0	1	0
TOTAL	.253		229	33	58	6	0	12	33	21	43	2

PITCHER	W	L	ERA	G	GS	CG	SV	SHO	IP	H	ER	BB	SO
Tommy Byrne	0	0	0.00	1	0	0	0	0	0.1	1	0	0	1
Whitey Ford	1	1	5.25	2	2	1	0	0	12.0	14	7	2	8
Johnny Kucks	1	0	0.82	3	1	1	0	1	11.0	6	1	3	2
Don Larsen	1	0	0.00	2	2	1	0	1	10.2	1	0	4	7
Maury McDermott	0	0	3.00	1	0	0	0	0	3.0	2	1	3	3
Tom Morgan	0	1	9.00	2	0	0	0	0	4.0	6	4	4	3
Tom Sturdivant	1	0	2.79	2	1	1	0	0	9.2	8	3	8	9
Bob Turley	0	1	0.82	3	1	1	0	0	11.0	4	1	8	14
TOTAL	4	3	2.48	16	7	5	0	2	61.2	42	17	32	47

BRO (N)

PLAYER/POS	AVG	G	AB	R	H	2B	3B	HR	RB	BB	SO	SB
Sandy Amoros, of	.053	6	19	1	1	0	0	0	1	2	4	0
Don Bessent, p	.500	2	2	0	1	0	0	0	1	1	1	0
Roy Campanella, c	.182	7	22	2	4	1	0	0	3	3	7	0
Gino Cimoli, of	.000	1	0	0	0	0	0	0	0	0	0	0
Roger Craig, p	.500	2	2	0	1	0	0	0	0	0	0	0
Don Drysdale, p	.000	1	0	0	0	0	0	0	0	0	0	0
Carl Erskine, p	.000	2	1	0	0	0	0	0	0	0	1	0
Carl Furillo, of	.240	7	25	2	6	2	0	0	1	2	3	0
Jim Gilliam, 2b-6,of-1	.083	7	24	2	2	0	0	0	2	7	3	1
Gil Hodges, 1b	.304	7	23	5	7	2	0	1	8	4	4	0
Ransom Jackson, ph	.000	3	3	0	0	0	0	0	0	0	2	0
Clem Labine, p	.250	2	4	0	1	1	0	0	0	0	2	0
Sal Maglie, p	.000	2	5	0	0	0	0	0	0	0	2	0
Dale Mitchell, ph	.000	4	4	0	0	0	0	0	0	0	1	0
Charlie Neal, 2b	.000	1	4	0	0	0	0	0	0	0	1	0
Don Newcombe, p	.000	2	1	0	0	0	0	0	0	0	0	0
Pee Wee Reese, ss	.222	7	27	3	6	0	0	1	2	2	6	0
Jackie Robinson, 3b	.250	7	24	5	6	1	0	1	2	5	2	0
Ed Roebuck, p	.000	3	0	0	0	0	0	0	0	0	0	0
Duke Snider, of	.304	7	23	5	7	1	0	1	4	6	8	0
Rube Walker, ph	.000	2	2	0	0	0	0	0	0	0	0	0
TOTAL	.195		215	25	42	8	1	3	24	32	47	1

PITCHER	W	L	ERA	G	GS	CG	SV	SHO	IP	H	ER	BB	SO
Don Bessent	1	0	1.80	2	0	0	0	0	10.0	8	2	3	5
Roger Craig	0	1	12.00	2	1	0	0	0	6.0	10	8	3	4
Don Drysdale	0	0	9.00	1	0	0	0	0	2.0	2	2	1	1
Carl Erskine	0	1	5.40	2	1	0	0	0	5.0	4	3	2	2
Clem Labine	1	0	0.00	2	1	1	0	1	12.0	8	0	3	7
Sal Maglie	1	1	2.65	2	2	2	0	0	17.0	14	5	6	15
Don Newcombe	0	1	21.21	2	2	0	0	0	4.2	11	11	3	4
Ed Roebuck	0	0	2.08	3	0	0	0	0	4.1	1	1	0	5
TOTAL	3	4	4.72	16	7	3	0	1	61.0	58	32	21	43

GAME 1 AT BRO OCT 3

NY	200	100	000	3	9	1
BRO	023	100	00X	6	9	0

Pitchers: FORD, Kucks (4), Morgan (6), Turley (8) vs MAGLIE
Home Runs: Mantle-NY, Robinson-BRO, Hodges-BRO, Martin-NY
Attendance: 34,479

GAME 2 AT BRO OCT 5

NY	150	100	001	8	12	2
BRO	061	220	02X	13	12	0

Pitchers: Larsen, Kucks (2), Byrne (2), Sturdivant (3), MORGAN (3), Turley (5), McDermott (6) vs Newcombe, Roebuck (2), BESSENT (3)
Home Runs: Berra-NY, Snider-BRO
Attendance: 36,217

GAME 3 AT NY OCT 6

BRO	010	001	100	3	8	1
NY	010	003	01X	5	8	1

Pitchers: CRAIG, Labine (7) vs FORD
Home Runs: Martin-NY, Slaughter-NY
Attendance: 73,977

GAME 4 AT NY OCT 7

BRO	000	100	001	2	6	0
NY	100	201	20X	6	7	2

Pitchers: ERSKINE, Roebuck (5), Drysdale (7) vs STURDIVANT
Home Runs: Mantle-NY, Bauer-NY
Attendance: 69,705

GAME 5 AT NY OCT 8

BRO	000	000	000	0	0	0
NY	000	101	00X	2	5	0

Pitchers: MAGLIE vs LARSEN
Home Runs: Mantle-NY
Attendance: 64,519

GAME 6 AT BRO OCT 9

NY	000	000	000 0	0	7	0
BRO	000	000	000 1	1	4	0

Pitchers: TURLEY vs LABINE
Attendance: 33,224

GAME 7 AT BRO OCT 10

NY	202	100	400	9	10	0
BRO	000	000	000	0	3	1

Pitchers: KUCKS vs NEWCOMBE, Bessent (4), Craig (7), Roebuck (7), Erskine (9)
Home Runs: Berra-NY (2), Howard-NY, Skowron-NY
Attendance: 33,782

Overall, the Yankees played better than the Yankees, but the Braves had Lew Burdette, who was better than anybody in the Series.

The opener pitted the Braves' established great Warren Spahn against New York's Whitey Ford. Ford prevailed, with a five-hit 3–1 win as Spahn was chased in the sixth. Burdette, winner of 17 regular-season games, started Game 2 against veteran Bobby Shantz, the American League ERA leader. After a scoreless first inning, both pitchers gave up a run in the second and another in the third. Two go-ahead runs in the top of the fourth ended the Braves' scoring, but they were enough, as Burdette blanked New York through the final six innings to even the Series. Before he was finished, Burdette would stretch his consecutive scoreless innings streak to 24.

The Yankees exploded in Game 3, in Milwaukee, running through six Braves pitchers in a 12–3 rout. Braves fans even ended up cheering Yankees rookie Tony Kubek—a Milwaukee native—who opened the scoring with a solo homer in the first, scored again after singling in the fourth (on Mickey Mantle's home run), and concluded the Yankee scoring in the seventh with his second homer, with two aboard.

Warren Spahn carried a 4–1 Braves lead into the ninth inning of Game 4, but after retiring the first two batters in the ninth, he gave up singles to Yogi Berra and Gil McDougald, and a game-tying home run to Elston Howard. In the top of the 10th, Hank Bauer tripled in a go-ahead run, but Milwaukee's Johnny Logan doubled to tie it up in the last of the 10th, and Eddie Mathews homered to give Spahn a shaky victory.

Burdette faced Ford in Game 5. In the sixth inning the Braves put half their hits—three singles—back to back for a run. It was all they needed as Burdette spaced seven singles for the shutout. Back in New York two days later, all the scoring came on home runs. Each club hit a pair, but Berra's in the third was the only one with a man aboard. Braves blasts in the fifth (Frank Torre) and seventh (Hank Aaron) tied the score, but Bauer answered Aaron's homer in the last of the seventh with what proved the winning shot. Bob Turley, who yielded just four hits while fanning eight (the Series high) claimed the victory.

In the finale, Burdette, with only two days' rest, scattered four hits over the first eight innings as the Braves gave him a 5–0 lead. In the bottom of the ninth, though, three Yankees singles loaded the bases with two out. But third baseman Eddie Mathews snared Bill Skowron's sharp grounder and stepped on the bag for a force out that pre-

served Burdette's second shutout and gave Milwaukee its first world championship.

Milwaukee Braves (NL), 4;
New York Yankees (AL), 3

MIL (N)

PLAYER/POS	AVG	G	AB	R	H	2B	3B	HR	RB	BB	SO	SB
Hank Aaron, of	.393	7	28	5	11	0	1	3	7	1	6	0
Joe Adcock, 1b	.200	5	15	1	3	0	0	0	2	0	2	0
Bob Buhl, p	.000	2	1	0	0	0	0	0	0	0	1	0
Lew Burdette, p	.000	3	8	0	0	0	0	0	0	1	2	0
Gene Conley, p	.000	1	0	0	0	0	0	0	0	0	0	0
Wes Covington, of	.208	7	24	1	5	1	0	0	1	2	6	1
Del Crandall, c	.211	6	19	1	4	0	0	1	1	1	1	0
John DeMerit, pr	.000	1	0	0	0	0	0	0	0	0	0	0
Bob Hazle, of	.154	4	13	2	2	0	0	0	0	1	2	0
Ernie Johnson, p	.000	3	1	0	0	0	0	0	0	0	1	0
Nippy Jones, ph	.000	3	2	0	0	0	0	0	0	0	0	0
Johnny Logan, ss	.185	7	27	5	5	1	0	1	2	3	6	0
Felix Mantilla, 2b-3	.000	4	10	1	0	0	0	0	0	1	0	0
Eddie Mathews, 3b	.227	7	22	4	5	3	0	1	4	8	5	0
Don McMahon, p	.000	3	0	0	0	0	0	0	0	0	0	0
Andy Pafko, of-5	.214	6	14	1	3	0	0	0	0	0	1	0
Juan Pizarro, p	.000	1	1	0	0	0	0	0	0	0	0	0
Del Rice, c	.167	2	6	0	1	0	0	0	0	1	2	0
Carl Sawatski, ph	.000	2	2	0	0	0	0	0	0	0	0	0
Red Schoendienst, 2b	.278	5	18	0	5	1	0	0	0	1	0	0
Warren Spahn, p	.000	2	4	0	0	0	0	0	0	1	2	0
Frank Torre, 1b	.300	7	10	2	3	0	0	2	3	2	0	0
Bob Trowbridge, p	.000	1	0	0	0	0	0	0	0	0	0	0
TOTAL	.209		225	23	47	6	1	8	22	22	40	1

PITCHER	W	L	ERA	G	GS	CG	SV	SHO	IP	H	ER	BB	SO
Bob Buhl	0	1	10.80	2	2	0	0	0	3.1	6	4	6	4
Lew Burdette	3	0	0.67	3	3	3	0	2	27.0	21	2	4	13
Gene Conley	0	0	10.80	1	0	0	0	0	1.2	2	2	1	0
Ernie Johnson	0	1	1.29	3	0	0	0	0	7.0	2	1	1	8
Don McMahon	0	0	0.00	3	0	0	0	0	5.0	3	0	3	5
Juan Pizarro	0	0	10.80	1	0	0	0	0	1.2	3	2	2	1
Warren Spahn	1	1	4.70	2	2	1	0	0	15.1	18	8	2	2
Bob Trowbridge	0	0	45.00	1	0	0	0	0	1.0	2	5	3	1
TOTAL	4	3	3.48	16	7	4	0	2	62.0	57	24	22	34

NY (A)

PLAYER/POS	AVG	G	AB	R	H	2B	3B	HR	RB	BB	SO	SB
Hank Bauer, of	.258	7	31	3	8	2	1	2	6	1	6	0
Yogi Berra, c	.320	7	25	5	8	1	0	1	2	4	0	0
Tommy Byrne, p	.500	2	2	0	1	0	0	0	0	0	1	0
Andy Carey, 3b	.286	2	7	0	2	1	0	0	1	1	0	0
Gerry Coleman, 2b	.364	7	22	8	8	2	0	0	2	3	1	0
Joe Collins, 1b-5	.000	6	5	0	0	0	0	0	0	0	3	0
Art Ditmar, p	.000	2	1	0	0	0	0	0	0	0	0	0
Whitey Ford, p	.000	2	5	0	0	0	0	0	0	0	1	0
Bob Grim, p	.000	2	0	0	0	0	0	0	0	0	0	0
Elston Howard, 1b-3	.273	6	11	2	3	0	0	1	3	1	3	0
Tony Kubek, of-5,3b-2	.286	7	28	4	8	0	0	2	4	0	4	0
Johnny Kucks, p	.000	1	0	0	0	0	0	0	0	0	0	0
Don Larsen, p	.000	2	2	1	0	0	0	0	0	2	1	0
Jerry Lumpe, 3b-3	.286	6	14	0	4	0	0	0	0	2	1	0
Mickey Mantle, of-5	.263	6	19	3	5	0	0	1	2	3	1	0
Gil McDougald, ss	.250	7	24	3	6	0	0	0	2	3	3	1
Bobby Richardson, 2b-1	.000	2	0	0	0	0	0	0	0	0	0	0
Bobby Shantz, p	.000	3	1	0	0	0	0	0	0	0	0	0
Harry Simpson, 1b-4	.083	5	12	0	1	0	0	0	1	0	4	0
Bill Skowron, 1b	.000	2	4	0	0	0	0	0	0	0	0	0
Enos Slaughter, of	.250	5	12	2	3	1	0	0	0	3	2	0
Tom Sturdivant, p	.000	2	1	0	0	0	0	0	0	0	0	0
Bob Turley, p	.000	3	4	0	0	0	0	0	0	0	2	0
TOTAL	.248		230	25	57	7	1	7	25	22	34	1

PITCHER	W	L	ERA	G	GS	CG	SV	SHO	IP	H	ER	BB	SO
Tommy Byrne	0	0	5.40	2	0	0	0	0	3.1	1	2	2	1
Art Ditmar	0	0	0.00	2	0	0	0	0	6.0	2	0	0	2
Whitey Ford	1	1	1.13	2	2	1	0	0	16.0	11	2	5	7
Bob Grim	0	1	7.71	2	0	0	0	0	2.1	3	2	0	2
Johnny Kucks	0	0	0.00	1	0	0	0	0	0.2	1	0	1	1
Don Larsen	1	1	3.72	2	1	0	0	0	9.2	8	4	5	6
Bobby Shantz	0	1	4.05	3	1	0	0	0	6.2	8	3	2	7
Tom Sturdivant	0	0	6.00	2	1	0	0	0	6.0	6	4	1	2
Bob Turley	1	0	2.31	3	2	1	0	0	11.2	7	3	6	12
TOTAL	3	4	2.89	19	7	2	0	0	62.1	47	20	22	40

GAME 1 AT NY OCT 2

MIL	000	000	100	1	5	0
NY	000	012	00X	3	9	1

Pitchers: SPAHN, Johnson (6), McMahon (7) vs FORD
Attendance: 69,476

GAME 2 AT NY OCT 3

MIL	011	200	000	4	8	0
NY	011	000	000	2	7	2

Pitchers: BURDETTE vs SHANTZ, Ditmar (4), Grim (8)
Home Runs: Logan-MIL, Bauer-NY
Attendance: 65,202

GAME 3 AT MIL OCT 5

NY	302	200	500	12	9	0
MIL	010	020	000	3	8	1

Pitchers: Turley, LARSEN (2) vs BUHL, Pizarro (1), Conley (3), Johnson (5), Trowbridge (7), McMahon (8)
Home Runs: Kubek-NY (2), Mantle-NY, Aaron-MIL
Attendance: 45,804

GAME 4 AT MIL OCT 6

NY	100	000	003	1	5	11	0
MIL	000	400	000	3	7	7	0

Pitchers: Sturdivant, Shantz (5), Kucks (8), Byrne (8), GRIM (10) vs SPAHN
Home Runs: Aaron-MIL, Torre-MIL, Howard-NY, Mathews-MIL
Attendance: 45,804

GAME 5 AT MIL OCT 7

NY	000	000	000	0	7	0
MIL	000	001	00X	1	6	1

Pitchers: FORD, Turley (8) vs BURDETTE
Attendance: 45,811

GAME 6 AT NY OCT 9

MIL	000	010	100	2	4	0
NY	002	000	10X	3	7	0

Pitchers: Buhl, JOHNSON (3), McMahon (8) vs TURLEY
Home Runs: Berra-NY, Torre-MIL, Aaron-MIL, Bauer-NY
Attendance: 61,408

GAME 7 AT NY OCT 10

MIL	004	000	010	5	9	1
NY	000	000	000	0	7	3

Pitchers: BURDETTE vs LARSEN, Shantz (3), Ditmar (4), Sturdivant (6), Byrne (8)
Home Runs: Crandall-MIL
Attendance: 61,207

After four games, Milwaukee held a 3–1 Series advantage, but New York rebounded to take the final three games and avenge their loss to the Braves the year before. As in the previous series, Warren Spahn faced Whitey Ford in the opener. The durable Spahn emerged the victor when Bill Bruton singled home the Braves' winning run off reliever Ryne Duren in the last of the 10th. In Game 2, home runs by Bruton and pitcher Lew Burdette (for three runs) helped the Braves take a 7–1 lead in the first inning. Milwaukee scored off five Yankees hurlers in their eventual 13–5 win.

Don Larsen and Ryne Duren combined for a shutout in Game 3 to give New York its first victory. Hank Bauer drove in all four runs with a two-run single in the fifth and his third home run in three games in the seventh. Warren Spahn held Bauer hitless in Game 4, blanking New York on two hits to defeat Whitey Ford and bring Milwaukee within a win of the championship.

Bob Turley came up with a shutout of his own the next day, though, fanning 10 men along the way. Gil McDougald's solo homer in the third inning was all the offense Turley needed, but as insurance the Yankees bunched six of their 10 hits into the sixth inning for six more runs.

Spahn and Ford, with only two days' rest, confronted each other a third time in Game 6. Ford lasted less than two innings, but Spahn (despite Hank Bauer's fourth Series home run in the first inning) endured into extra innings, when McDougald put New York ahead with a leadoff homer in the 10th. Two outs and two hits later, Spahn was removed, and Bill Skowron's single off reliever Don McMahon drove home another Yankees run. Milwaukee scored once in the last of the 10th and threatened further damage with men on first and third. But Bob Turley came on to retire the final batter and send the Series to a seventh game.

In the sixth inning of the finale, the Braves' Del Crandall homered against Turley (who had relieved Don Larsen in the third) to tie the game 2–2. But four runs off starter Lew Burdette in the top of the eighth (including Skowron's three-run homer) made the score 6–2, where it remained, as Turley held on to bring Casey Stengel his seventh (and last) Series triumph—and the Yankees their 18th world title.

New York Yankees (AL), 4; Milwaukee Braves (NL), 3

NY (A)

PLAYER/POS	AVG	G	AB	R	H	2B	3B	HR	RB	BB	SO	SB
Hank Bauer, of	.323	7	31	6	10	0	0	4	8	0	5	0
Yogi Berra, c	.222	7	27	3	6	3	0	0	2	1	0	0
Andy Carey, 3b	.083	5	12	1	1	0	0	0	0	0	3	0
Murry Dickson, p	.000	2	0	0	0	0	0	0	0	0	0	0
Art Ditmar, p	.000	1	1	0	0	0	0	0	0	0	0	0
Ryne Duren, p	.000	3	3	0	0	0	0	0	0	0	2	0
Whitey Ford, p	.000	3	4	1	0	0	0	0	0	0	2	0
Elston Howard, of	.222	6	18	4	4	0	0	0	2	1	4	1
Tony Kubek, ss	.048	7	21	0	1	0	0	0	0	1	7	0
Johnny Kucks, p	1.000	2	1	0	1	0	0	0	0	0	0	0
Don Larsen, p	.000	2	2	0	0	0	0	0	0	0	1	0
Jerry Lumpe, 3b-3,ss-2	.167	6	12	0	2	0	0	0	0	1	2	0
Duke Maas, p	.000	1	0	0	0	0	0	0	0	0	0	0
Mickey Mantle, of	.250	7	24	4	6	0	1	2	3	7	4	0
Gil McDougald, 2b	.321	7	28	5	9	2	0	2	4	2	4	0
Zach Monroe, p	.000	1	0	0	0	0	0	0	0	0	0	0
Bobby Richardson, 3b	.000	4	5	0	0	0	0	0	0	0	0	0
Norm Siebern, of	.125	3	8	1	1	0	0	0	0	0	3	0
Bill Skowron, 1b	.259	7	27	3	7	0	0	2	7	1	4	0
Enos Slaughter, ph	.000	4	3	1	0	0	0	0	0	1	1	0
Marv Throneberry, ph	.000	1	1	0	0	0	0	0	0	0	1	0
Bob Turley, p	.200	4	5	0	1	0	0	0	0	0	2	0
TOTAL	.210		233	29	49	5	1	10	29	21	42	1

PITCHER	W	L	ERA	G	GS	CG	SV	SHO	IP	H	ER	BB	SO
Murry Dickson	0	0	4.50	2	0	0	0	0	4.0	4	2	0	1
Art Ditmar	0	0	0.00	1	0	0	0	0	3.2	2	0	0	2
Ryne Duren	1	1	1.93	3	0	0	0	1	9.1	7	2	6	14
Whitey Ford	0	1	4.11	3	3	0	0	0	15.1	19	7	5	16
Johnny Kucks	0	0	2.08	2	0	0	0	0	4.1	4	1	1	0
Don Larsen	1	0	0.96	2	2	0	0	0	9.1	9	1	6	9
Duke Maas	0	0	81.00	1	0	0	0	0	0.1	2	3	1	0
Zach Monroe	0	0	27.00	1	0	0	0	0	1.0	3	3	1	1
Bob Turley	2	1	2.76	4	2	1	1	1	16.1	10	5	7	13
TOTAL	4	3	3.39	19	7	1	2	1	63.2	60	24	27	56

MIL (N)

PLAYER/POS	AVG	G	AB	R	H	2B	3B	HR	RB	BB	SO	SB
Hank Aaron, of	.333	7	27	3	9	2	0	0	2	4	6	0
Joe Adcock, 1b	.308	4	13	1	4	0	0	0	0	1	3	0
Billy Bruton, of	.412	7	17	2	7	0	0	1	2	5	5	0
Lew Burdette, p	.111	3	9	1	1	0	0	1	3	0	3	0
Wes Covington, of	.269	7	26	2	7	0	0	0	4	2	4	0
Del Crandall, c	.240	7	25	4	6	0	0	1	3	3	10	0
Harry Hanebrink, ph	.000	2	2	0	0	0	0	0	0	0	0	0
Johnny Logan, ss	.120	7	25	3	3	2	0	0	2	2	4	0
Felix Mantilla, ss-1	.000	4	0	1	0	0	0	0	0	0	0	0
Eddie Mathews, 3b	.160	7	25	3	4	2	0	0	3	6	11	1
Don McMahon, p	.000	3	0	0	0	0	0	0	0	0	0	0
Andy Pafko, of	.333	4	9	0	3	1	0	0	1	0	0	0
Juan Pizarro, p	.000	1	0	0	0	0	0	0	0	0	0	0
Bob Rush, p	.000	1	2	0	0	0	0	0	0	0	2	0
Red Schoendienst, 2b	.300	7	30	5	9	3	1	0	2	0	1	0
Warren Spahn, p	.333	3	12	0	4	0	0	0	3	0	6	0
Frank Torre, 1b	.176	7	17	0	3	0	0	0	1	2	0	0
Carl Willey, p	.000	1	0	0	0	0	0	0	0	0	0	0
Casey Wise, ph	.000	2	1	0	0	0	0	0	0	0	1	0
TOTAL	.250		240	25	60	10	1	3	24	27	56	1

PITCHER	W	L	ERA	G	GS	CG	SV	SHO	IP	H	ER	BB	SO
Lew Burdette	1	2	5.64	3	3	1	0	0	22.1	22	14	4	12
Don McMahon	0	0	5.40	3	0	0	0	0	3.1	3	2	3	5
Juan Pizarro	0	0	5.40	1	0	0	0	0	1.2	2	1	1	3
Bob Rush	0	1	3.00	1	1	0	0	0	6.0	3	2	5	2
Warren Spahn	2	1	2.20	3	3	2	0	1	28.2	19	7	8	18
Carl Willey	0	0	0.00	1	0	0	0	0	1.0	0	0	0	2
TOTAL	3	4	3.71	12	7	3	0	1	63.0	49	26	21	42

GAME 1 AT MIL OCT 1

NY	000 120 000 0	3	8	1
MIL	000 200 010 1	4	10	0

Pitchers: Ford, DUREN (8) vs SPAHN
Home Runs: Skowron-NY, Bauer-NY
Attendance: 46,367

GAME 2 AT MIL OCT 2

NY	100 100 003	5	7	0
MIL	710 000 23X	13	15	1

Pitchers: TURLEY, Maas (1), Kucks (1), Dickson (5), Monroe (8) vs BURDETTE
Home Runs: Bruton-MIL, Burdette-MIL, Mantle-NY (2), Bauer-NY
Attendance: 46,367

GAME 3 AT NY OCT 4

MIL	000 000 000	0	6	0
NY	000 020 20X	4	4	0

Pitchers: RUSH, McMahon (7) vs LARSEN, Duren (8)
Home Runs: Bauer-NY
Attendance: 71,599

GAME 4 AT NY OCT 5

MIL	000 001 110	3	9	0
NY	000 000 000	0	2	1

Pitchers: SPAHN vs FORD, Kucks (8), Dickson (9)
Attendance: 71,563

GAME 5 AT NY OCT 6

MIL	000 000 000	0	5	0
NY	001 006 00X	7	10	0

Pitchers: BURDETTE, Pizarro (6), Willey (8) vs TURLEY
Home Runs: McDougald-NY
Attendance: 65,279

GAME 6 AT MIL OCT 8

NY	100 001 000 2	4	10	1
MIL	110 000 000 1	3	10	4

Pitchers: Ford, Ditmar (2), DUREN (6), Turley (10) vs SPAHN, McMahon (10)
Home Runs: Bauer-NY, McDougald-NY
Attendance: 46,367

GAME 7 AT MIL OCT 9

NY	020 000 040	6	8	0
MIL	100 001 000	2	5	2

Pitchers: Larsen, TURLEY (3) vs BURDETTE, McMahon (8)
Home Runs: Crandall-MIL, Skowron-NY
Attendance: 46,367

It took a nosedive from first to third by San Francisco and a Dodgers playoff victory over Milwaukee (who had finished the season tied with the Dodgers), to bring Los Angeles the city's first major league pennant. But once they had made it to the Series, the Dodgers dispatched the White Sox in six games.

The opener, though, belonged to Chicago. In their first World Series in 40 years, the White Sox overwhelmed Los Angeles with 11 runs in the first four innings as pitchers Early Wynn and Gerry Staley combined to blank the Dodgers. Chicago's big gun was veteran slugger Ted Kluszewski (acquired from Pittsburgh in late August), whose single and two homers drove in five runs. Chicago scored twice in the first inning the next day, but Dodgers starter Johnny Podres settled down to blank the Sox over the next five innings as home runs by Charlie Neal in the fifth and pinch hitter Chuck Essegian and Neal (again) in the seventh put the Dodgers ahead by two. Rookie reliever Larry Sherry gave up a third Chicago run in the eighth on Al Smith's double, but a second runner was nailed at the plate, and Sherry set down the side in the ninth to save Podres's win.

When the Series moved to Los Angeles' cavernous Coliseum for the West Coast's first World Series games ever, fans turned out in record numbers, setting a new Series mark in each of the next three games. Dodgers starter Don Drysdale yielded 11 hits and four walks in Game 3, but the only run scored against him came on a double play after Larry Sherry had relieved him with two men on in the eighth. As Los Angeles had already scored twice, and added a third run in their half of the eighth, Drysdale emerged with the win and Sherry with his second save. In Game 4, the Sox's Sherm Lollar's three-run homer had tied the score by the time Sherry relieved Dodgers starter Roger Craig in the eighth, so Gil Hodges' solo homer in the last of the eighth gave Sherry the win this time—and Los Angeles a 3–1 Series advantage.

Chicago's Bob Shaw dueled Dodger Sandy Koufax through seven innings of Game 5 before 92,706 spectators (still a Series high). The Sox scored only once off Koufax, but one run was enough for their second win as a pair of Sox relievers continued Shaw's shutout through the final two innings.

Back in Chicago for Game 6, the Dodgers unloaded on Early Wynn and Dick Donovan for eight runs in the third and fourth innings. Ted Kluszewski's three-run homer in the last of the fourth led to Larry Sherry's fourth relief appear-

Los Angeles Dodgers (NL), 4; Chicago White Sox (AL), 2

LA (N)

PLAYER/POS	AVG	G	AB	R	H	2B	3B	HR	RB	BB	SO	SB
Chuck Churn, p	.000	1	0	0	0	0	0	0	0	0	0	0
Roger Craig, p	.000	2	3	0	0	0	0	0	0	0	2	0
Don Demeter, of	.250	6	12	2	3	0	0	0	0	1	3	0
Don Drysdale, p	.000	1	2	0	0	0	0	0	0	0	0	0
Chuck Essegian, ph	.667	4	3	2	2	0	0	2	2	1	1	0
Ron Fairly, of-4	.000	6	3	0	0	0	0	0	0	0	1	0
Carl Furillo, of-1	.250	4	4	0	1	0	0	0	2	0	1	0
Jim Gilliam, 3b	.240	6	25	2	6	0	0	0	0	2	2	2
Gil Hodges, 1b	.391	6	23	2	9	0	1	1	2	1	2	0
Johnny Klippstein, p	.000	1	0	0	0	0	0	0	0	0	0	0
Sandy Koufax, p	.000	2	2	0	0	0	0	0	0	0	1	0
Clem Labine, p	.000	1	0	0	0	0	0	0	0	0	0	0
Norm Larker, of	.188	6	16	2	3	0	0	0	0	2	3	0
Wally Moon, of	.261	6	23	3	6	0	0	1	2	2	2	1
Charlie Neal, 2b	.370	6	27	4	10	2	0	2	6	0	1	1
Joe Pignatano, c	.000	1	0	0	0	0	0	0	0	0	0	0
Johnny Podres, p-2	.500	3	4	1	2	1	0	0	1	0	0	0
Rip Repulski, of	.000	1	0	0	0	0	0	0	0	0	0	0
Johnny Roseboro, c	.095	6	21	0	2	0	0	0	1	0	2	0
Larry Sherry, p-4	.500	5	4	0	2	0	0	0	0	0	1	0
Duke Snider, of-3	.200	4	10	1	2	0	0	1	2	2	0	0
Stan Williams, p	.000	1	0	0	0	0	0	0	0	0	0	0
Maury Wills, ss	.250	6	20	2	5	0	0	0	1	0	3	1
Don Zimmer, ss	.000	1	1	0	0	0	0	0	0	0	0	0
TOTAL	.261		203	21	53	3	1	7	19	12	27	5

PITCHER	W	L	ERA	G	GS	CG	SV	SHO	IP	H	ER	BB	SO
Chuck Churn	0	0	27.00	1	0	0	0	0	0.2	5	2	0	0
Roger Craig	0	1	8.68	2	2	0	0	0	9.1	15	9	5	8
Don Drysdale	1	0	1.29	1	1	0	0	0	7.0	11	1	4	5
Johnny Klippstein	0	0	0.00	1	0	0	0	0	2.0	1	0	0	2
Sandy Koufax	0	1	1.00	2	1	0	0	0	9.0	5	1	1	7
Clem Labine	0	0	0.00	1	0	0	0	0	1.0	0	0	0	1
Johnny Podres	1	0	4.82	2	2	0	0	0	9.1	7	5	6	4
Larry Sherry	2	0	0.71	4	0	0	2	0	12.2	8	1	2	5
Stan Williams	0	0	0.00	1	0	0	0	0	2.0	0	0	2	1
TOTAL	4	2	3.23	15	6	0	2	0	53.0	52	19	20	33

CHI (A)

PLAYER/POS	AVG	G	AB	R	H	2B	3B	HR	RB	BB	SO	SB
Luis Aparicio, ss	.308	6	26	1	8	1	0	0	0	2	3	1
Norm Cash, ph	.000	4	4	0	0	0	0	0	0	0	2	0
Dick Donovan, p	.333	3	3	0	1	0	0	0	0	0	1	0
Sammy Esposito, 3b	.000	2	2	0	0	0	0	0	0	0	1	0
Nellie Fox, 2b	.375	6	24	4	9	3	0	0	0	4	1	0
Billy Goodman, 3b	.231	5	13	1	3	0	0	0	1	0	5	0
Ted Kluszewski, 1b	.391	6	23	5	9	1	0	3	10	2	0	0
Jim Landis, of	.292	6	24	6	7	0	0	0	1	1	7	1
Sherm Lollar, c	.227	6	22	3	5	0	0	1	5	1	3	0
Turk Lown, p	.000	3	0	0	0	0	0	0	0	0	0	0
Jim McAnany, of	.000	3	5	0	0	0	0	0	0	0	0	0
Ray Moore, p	.000	1	0	0	0	0	0	0	0	0	0	0
Bubba Phillips, 3b-3,of-1	.300	3	10	0	3	1	0	0	0	0	0	0
Billy Pierce, p	.000	3	0	0	0	0	0	0	0	0	0	0
Jim Rivera, of	.000	5	11	1	0	0	0	0	0	3	1	0
Johnny Romano, ph	.000	1	1	0	0	0	0	0	0	0	0	0
Bob Shaw, p	.250	2	4	0	1	0	0	0	0	0	2	0
Al Smith, of	.250	6	20	1	5	3	0	0	1	4	4	0
Gerry Staley, p	.000	4	1	0	0	0	0	0	0	1	1	0
Earl Torgeson, 1b-1	.000	3	1	1	0	0	0	0	0	1	0	0
Early Wynn, p	.200	3	5	0	1	1	0	0	1	0	2	0
TOTAL	.261		199	23	52	10	0	4	19	20	33	2

PITCHER	W	L	ERA	G	GS	CG	SV	SHO	IP	H	ER	BB	SO
Dick Donovan	0	1	5.40	3	1	0	1	0	8.1	4	5	3	5
Turk Lown	0	0	0.00	3	0	0	0	0	3.1	2	0	1	3
Ray Moore	0	0	9.00	1	0	0	0	0	1.0	1	1	0	1
Billy Pierce	0	0	0.00	3	0	0	0	0	4.0	2	0	2	3
Bob Shaw	1	1	2.57	2	2	0	0	0	14.0	17	4	2	2
Gerry Staley	0	1	2.16	4	0	0	1	0	8.1	8	2	0	3
Early Wynn	1	1	5.54	3	3	0	0	0	13.0	19	8	4	10
TOTAL	2	4	3.46	19	6	0	2	0	52.0	53	20	12	27

ance—and his second Series win, as he held the Sox scoreless the rest of the game to bring the world championship to the West Coast for the first time.

GAME 1 AT CHI OCT 1

LA	000	000	000	0	8 3
CHI	207	200	00X	11	11 0

Pitchers: CRAIG, Churn (3), Labine (4), Koufax (5), Klippstein (7) vs WYNN, Staley (8)
Home Runs: Kluszewski-CHI (2)
Attendance: 48,013

GAME 2 AT CHI OCT 2

LA	000	010	300	4	9 1
CHI	200	000	010	3	8 0

Pitchers: PODRES, Sherry (7) vs SHAW, Lown (7)
Home Runs: Neal-LA (2), Essegian-LA
Attendance: 47,368

GAME 3 AT LA OCT 4

CHI	000	000	010	1	12 0
LA	000	000	21X	3	5 0

Pitchers: DONOVAN, Staley (7) vs DRYSDALE, Sherry (8)
Attendance: 92,394

GAME 4 AT LA OCT 5

CHI	000	000	400	4	10 3
LA	004	000	01X	5	9 0

Pitchers: Wynn, Lown (3), Pierce (4), STALEY (7) vs Craig, SHERRY (8)
Home Runs: Lollar-CHI, Hodges-LA
Attendance: 92,650

GAME 5 AT LA OCT 6

CHI	000	100	000	1	5 0
LA	000	000	000	0	9 0

Pitchers: SHAW, Pierce (7), Donovan (8) vs KOUFAX, Williams (8)
Attendance: 92,706

GAME 6 AT CHI OCT 8

LA	002	600	001	9	13 0
CHI	000	300	000	3	6 1

Pitchers: Podres, SHERRY (4) vs WYNN, Donovan (4), Staley (5), Pierce (8), Moore (9)
Home Runs: Snider-LA, Moon-LA, Kluszewski-CHI, Essegian-LA
Attendance: 47,653

Through six games and 8½ innings of the seventh, the Yankees had outscored the Pirates by 29 runs. But as Pirates second baseman Bill Mazeroski stepped to the plate to open the last of the ninth, the Series was even at three games apiece, and Game 7 was tied 9–9. The stage was set for Mazeroski to fulfill that ultimate baseball fantasy, and he did, on pitcher Ralph Terry's second pitch.

Roger Maris opened the Series scoring with a solo homer in the first inning of Game 1, and Elston Howard added two more runs with a homer in the ninth for the Yankees. But between the home runs New York scored only one run to the Pirates' six (including a two-run homer by Mazeroski in the fourth).

The Yankees avenged their first-game loss with a blowout in Game 2. Pittsburgh hit safely 13 times, but scored only three runs. New York, though, turned 19 hits (and a Pirates error) into 16 runs—five of them driven in by Mickey Mantle's two home runs. Continuing their assault in New York the next day, the Bronx Bombers scored six runs in the first inning and four in the fourth as Whitey Ford blanked the Pirates on four hits. Mantle homered again, and second baseman Bobby Richardson drove in a Series single-game record six runs with a grand slam and a single.

Pirates ace Vernon Law—the winner of Game 1—started Game 4 and, with relief help once again from Roy Face, held the Yankees to two runs to even the Series. Law's bat proved crucial, too, as he doubled in Pittsburgh's first run and scored the third in a three-run fifth that provided all the Pirate scoring. In Game 5, the Pirates' Mazeroski doubled in what proved the two decisive runs in a three-run second as Harvey Haddix and Roy Face (who recorded his third save of the Series) duplicated the previous day's achievement of limiting New York to two runs.

But once again the Yankees came back. Bobby Richardson drove in three of New York's 12 runs with two triples to establish a new Series record of 12 RBIs as the Yankees, behind Whitey Ford's second shutout, sent the Series into a seventh game.

Home runs dominated the finale. Rocky Nelson's two-run shot in the first opened the scoring, and homers by Bill Skowron in the fifth and Yogi Berra in the sixth contributed four of the five runs that put New York ahead 5–4. Hal Smith's three-run homer in the bottom of the eighth restored the lead to Pittsburgh, 9–7, and after the Yankees had tied the game in the top of the ninth (on three singles and a ground out), Mazeroski's immortal shot over the wall in left gave

Pittsburgh its first world championship in 35 years.

Pittsburgh Pirates (NL), 4; New York Yankees (AL), 3

PIT (N)

PLAYER/POS	AVG	G	AB	R	H	2B	3B	HR	RB	BB	SO	SB
Gene Baker, ph	.000	3	3	0	0	0	0	0	0	0	1	0
Smoky Burgess, c	.333	5	18	2	6	1	0	0	0	2	1	0
Tom Cheney, p	.000	3	0	0	0	0	0	0	0	0	0	0
Joe Christopher, ph	.000	3	0	2	0	0	0	0	0	0	0	0
Gino Cimoli, of-6	.250	7	20	4	5	0	0	0	1	2	4	0
Roberto Clemente, of	.310	7	29	1	9	0	0	0	3	0	2	0
Roy Face, p	.000	4	3	0	0	0	0	0	0	0	0	0
Bob Friend, p	.000	3	1	0	0	0	0	0	0	0	0	0
Joe Gibbon, p	.000	2	0	0	0	0	0	0	0	0	0	0
Fred Green, p	.000	3	1	0	0	0	0	0	0	0	0	0
Dick Groat, ss	.214	7	28	3	6	2	0	0	2	0	1	0
Harvey Haddix, p	.333	2	3	0	1	0	0	0	0	0	1	0
Don Hoak, 3b	.217	7	23	3	5	2	0	0	3	4	1	0
Clem Labine, p	.000	3	0	0	0	0	0	0	0	0	0	0
Vern Law, p	.333	3	6	1	2	1	0	0	1	0	1	0
Bill Mazeroski, 2b	.320	7	25	4	8	2	0	2	5	0	3	0
Vinegar Bend Mizell, p	.000	2	0	0	0	0	0	0	0	0	0	0
Rocky Nelson, 1b-3	.333	4	9	2	3	0	0	1	2	1	1	0
Bob Oldis, c	.000	2	0	0	0	0	0	0	0	0	0	0
Dick Schofield, ss-2	.333	3	3	0	1	0	0	0	0	1	0	0
Bob Skinner, of	.200	2	5	2	1	0	0	0	0	1	1	1
Hal Smith, c	.375	3	8	1	3	0	0	1	3	0	0	0
Dick Stuart, 1b	.150	5	20	0	3	0	0	0	0	0	3	0
Bill Virdon, of	.241	7	29	2	7	3	0	0	5	1	3	1
George Witt, p	.000	3	0	0	0	0	0	0	0	0	0	0
TOTAL	.256		234	27	60	11	0	4	26	12	26	2

PITCHER	W	L	ERA	G	GS	CG	SV	SHO	IP	H	ER	BB	SO
Tom Cheney	0	0	4.50	3	0	0	0	0	4.0	4	2	1	6
Roy Face	0	0	5.23	4	0	0	3	0	10.1	9	6	2	4
Bob Friend	0	2	13.50	3	2	0	0	0	6.0	13	9	3	7
Joe Gibbon	0	0	9.00	2	0	0	0	0	3.0	4	3	1	2
Fred Green	0	0	22.50	3	0	0	0	0	4.0	11	10	1	3
Harvey Haddix	2	0	2.45	2	1	0	0	0	7.1	6	2	2	6
Clem Labine	0	0	13.50	3	0	0	0	0	4.0	13	6	1	2
Vern Law	2	0	3.44	3	3	0	0	0	18.1	22	7	3	8
Vinegar Bend Mizell	0	1	15.43	2	1	0	0	0	2.1	4	4	2	1
George Witt	0	0	0.00	3	0	0	0	0	2.2	5	0	2	1
TOTAL	4	3	7.11	28	7	0	3	0	62.0	91	49	18	40

NY (A)

PLAYER/POS	AVG	G	AB	R	H	2B	3B	HR	RB	BB	SO	SB
Luis Arroyo, p	.000	1	1	0	0	0	0	0	0	0	0	0
Yogi Berra, of-4,c-3	.318	7	22	6	7	0	0	1	8	2	0	0
Johnny Blanchard, c-2	.455	5	11	2	5	2	0	0	2	0	1	0
Clete Boyer, 3b-4,ss-1	.250	4	12	1	3	2	1	0	1	0	1	0
Bob Cerv, of-3	.357	4	14	1	5	0	0	0	0	0	3	0
Jim Coates, p	.000	3	1	0	0	0	0	0	0	0	1	0
Joe De Maestri, ss-3	.500	4	2	1	1	0	0	0	0	0	1	0
Art Ditmar, p	.000	2	0	0	0	0	0	0	0	0	0	0
Ryne Duren, p	.000	2	0	0	0	0	0	0	0	0	0	0
Whitey Ford, p	.250	2	8	1	2	0	0	0	0	0	2	0
Eli Grba, pr	.000	1	0	0	0	0	0	0	0	0	0	0
Elston Howard, c-4	.462	5	13	4	6	1	1	1	4	1	4	0
Tony Kubek, ss-7,of-2	.333	7	30	6	10	1	0	0	3	2	2	0
Dale Long, ph	.333	3	3	0	1	0	0	0	0	0	0	0
Hector Lopez, of-1	.429	3	7	0	3	0	0	0	0	0	0	0
Duke Maas, p	.000	1	0	0	0	0	0	0	0	0	0	0
Mickey Mantle, of	.400	7	25	8	10	1	0	3	11	8	9	0
Roger Maris, of	.267	7	30	6	8	1	0	2	2	2	4	0
Gil McDougald, 3b	.278	6	18	4	5	1	0	0	2	2	3	0
Bobby Richardson, 2b	.367	7	30	8	11	2	2	1	12	1	1	0
Bobby Shantz, p	.333	3	3	0	1	0	0	0	0	0	0	0
Bill Skowron, 1b	.375	7	32	7	12	2	0	2	6	0	6	0
Bill Stafford, p	.000	2	1	0	0	0	0	0	0	0	1	0
Ralph Terry, p	.000	2	2	0	0	0	0	0	0	0	0	0
Bob Turley, p	.250	2	4	0	1	0	0	0	0	1	1	0
TOTAL	.338		269	55	91	13	4	10	54	18	40	0

PITCHER	W	L	ERA	G	GS	CG	SV	SHO	IP	H	ER	BB	SO
Luis Arroyo	0	0	13.50	1	0	0	0	0	0.2	2	1	0	1
Jim Coates	0	0	5.68	3	0	0	0	0	6.1	6	4	1	3
Art Ditmar	0	2	21.60	2	2	0	0	0	1.2	6	4	1	0
Ryne Duren	0	0	2.25	2	0	0	0	0	4.0	2	1	1	5
Whitey Ford	2	0	0.00	2	2	2	0	2	18.0	11	0	2	8
Duke Maas	0	0	4.50	1	0	0	0	0	2.0	2	1	0	1
Bobby Shantz	0	0	4.26	3	0	0	1	0	6.1	4	3	1	1
Bill Stafford	0	0	1.50	2	0	0	0	0	6.0	5	1	1	2
Ralph Terry	0	1	5.40	4	1	0	0	0	6.2	7	4	1	5
Bob Turley	1	0	4.82	2	2	0	0	0	9.1	15	5	4	0
TOTAL	3	4	3.54	20	7	2	1	2	61.0	60	24	12	26

GAME 1 AT PIT OCT 5

NY	100 100 002	4 13 2
PIT	300 201 00X	6 8 0

Pitchers: DITMAR, Coates (1), Maas (5), Duren (7) vs LAW, Face (8)
Home Runs: Maris-NY, Mazeroski-PIT, Howard-NY
Attendance: 36,676

GAME 2 AT PIT OCT 6

NY	002 127 301	16 19 1
PIT	000 100 002	3 13 1

Pitchers: TURLEY, Shantz (9) vs FRIEND, Green (5), Labine (5), Witt (6), Gibbon (7), Cheney (9)
Home Runs: Mantle-NY (2)
Attendance: 37,308

GAME 3 AT NY OCT 8

PIT	000 000 000	0 4 0
NY	600 400 00X	10 16 1

Pitchers: MIZELL, Labine (1), Green (1), Witt (4), Cheney (6), Gibbon (8) vs FORD
Home Runs: Richardson-NY, Mantle-NY
Attendance: 70,001

GAME 4 AT NY OCT 9

PIT	000 030 000	3 7 0
NY	000 100 100	2 8 0

Pitchers: LAW, Face (7) vs TERRY, Shantz (7), Coates (8)
Home Runs: Skowron-NY
Attendance: 67,812

GAME 5 AT NY OCT 10

PIT	031 000 001	5 10 2
NY	011 000 000	2 5 2

Pitchers: HADDIX, Face (7) vs DITMAR, Arroyo (2), Stafford (3), Duren (8)
Home Runs: Maris-NY
Attendance: 62,753

GAME 6 AT PIT OCT 12

NY	015 002 220	12 17 1
PIT	000 000 000	0 7 1

Pitchers: FORD vs FRIEND, Cheney (3), Mizell (4), Green (6), Labine (6), Witt (9)
Attendance: 38,580

GAME 7 AT PIT OCT 13

NY	000 014 022	9 13 1
PIT	220 000 051	10 11 0

Pitchers: Turley, Stafford (2), Shantz (3), Coates (8), TERRY (8) vs Law, Face (6), Friend (9), HADDIX (9)
Home Runs: Nelson-PIT, Skowron-NY, Berra-NY, Smith-PIT, Mazeroski-PIT
Attendance: 36,683

Slugger Mickey Mantle sat out most of the Series with a thigh infection, but rookie manager Ralph Houk enjoyed an otherwise splendid finish to a splendid season as his Yankees mauled the Reds, 27 runs to 13. Yankees ace Whitey Ford, coming off one of his finest seasons (25–4), carried his mound mastery into the Series opener, holding Cincinnati to two singles and a walk as he hurled his third straight World Series shutout. New York recorded only six hits, but two of them were home runs by Elston Howard and Bill Skowron.

Gordy Coleman's two-run homer the next day in the top of the fourth inning broke Cincinnati's scoring drought and gave the Reds a 2–0 lead. Yogi Berra tied the score half an inning later with a two-run blast for New York, but that was all they would get. Reds starter Joey Jay blanked the Yankees the rest of the way as his teammates put across four more runs to even the Series. Bob Purkey pitched for the Reds in Game 3 and blanked New York on one hit through the first six innings, taking a 1–0 lead into the top of the seventh. A pair of singles sandwiched around a passed ball evened the score, but the Reds regained the lead with a run in the last of the seventh. But pinch hitter Johnny Blanchard homered to retie the game in the eighth and—while Yankees relief ace Luis Arroyo stopped the Reds through the final two innings—Roger Maris, who set the major league record with 61 home runs during the season, added another to win the game and regain the Series lead for New York.

Cincinnati never again threatened. In Game 4, Whitey Ford held the Reds to four harmless singles until he was removed in the sixth because of an ankle injury. (In the third inning he passed Babe Ruth's World Series record of 29⅔ consecutive scoreless innings.) Reliever Jim Coates continued Ford's shutout as the Yankees scored seven runs for the decisive win. The fifth and final game also was no contest. Cincinnati did score five runs—three on Frank Robinson's third-inning home run and two on Wally Post's shot in the fifth. But the Yankees ran through eight Cincinnati pitchers, scoring 13 times. Seven of their 15 hits went for extra bases, including Johnny Blanchard's second home run of the Series, and a triple and homer by utility outfielder Hector Lopez.

New York Yankees (AL), 4; Cincinnati Reds (NL), 1

NY (A)

PLAYER/POS	AVG	G	AB	R	H	2B	3B	HR	RB	BB	SO	SB
Luis Arroyo, p	.000	2	0	0	0	0	0	0	0	0	0	0
Yogi Berra, of	.273	4	11	2	3	0	0	1	3	5	1	0
Johnny Blanchard, of-2	.400	4	10	4	4	1	0	2	3	2	0	0
Clete Boyer, 3b	.267	5	15	0	4	2	0	0	3	4	0	0
Jim Coates, p	.000	1	1	0	0	0	0	0	0	0	1	0
Buddy Daley, p	.000	2	1	0	0	0	0	0	0	1	0	0
Whitey Ford, p	.000	2	5	1	0	0	0	0	0	0	1	0
Billy Gardner, ph	.000	1	1	0	0	0	0	0	0	0	0	0
Elston Howard, c	.250	5	20	5	5	3	0	1	1	2	3	0
Tony Kubek, ss	.227	5	22	3	5	0	0	0	1	1	4	0
Hector Lopez, of-3	.333	4	9	3	3	0	1	1	7	2	3	0
Mickey Mantle, of	.167	2	6	0	1	0	0	0	0	0	2	0
Roger Maris, of	.105	5	19	4	2	1	0	1	2	4	6	0
Jack Reed, of	.000	3	0	0	0	0	0	0	0	0	0	0
Bobby Richardson, 2b	.391	5	23	2	9	1	0	0	0	0	0	1
Bill Skowron, 1b	.353	5	17	3	6	0	0	1	5	3	4	0
Bill Stafford, p	.000	1	2	0	0	0	0	0	0	0	0	0
Ralph Terry, p	.000	2	3	0	0	0	0	0	0	0	1	0
TOTAL	.255		165	27	42	8	1	7	26	24	25	1

PITCHER	W	L	ERA	G	GS	CG	SV	SHO	IP	H	ER	BB	SO
Luis Arroyo	1	0	2.25	2	0	0	0	0	4.0	4	1	2	3
Jim Coates	0	0	0.00	1	0	0	1	0	4.0	1	0	1	2
Buddy Daley	1	0	0.00	2	0	0	0	0	7.0	5	0	0	3
Whitey Ford	2	0	0.00	2	2	1	0	1	14.0	6	0	1	7
Bill Stafford	0	0	2.70	1	1	0	0	0	6.2	7	2	2	5
Ralph Terry	0	1	4.82	2	2	0	0	0	9.1	12	5	2	7
TOTAL	4	1	1.60	10	5	1	1	1	45.0	35	8	8	27

CIN (N)

PLAYER/POS	AVG	G	AB	R	H	2B	3B	HR	RB	BB	SO	SB
Gus Bell, ph	.000	3	3	0	0	0	0	0	0	0	0	0
Don Blasingame, 2b	.143	3	7	1	1	0	0	0	0	0	3	0
Jim Brosnan, p	.000	3	0	0	0	0	0	0	0	0	0	0
Leo Cardenas, ph	.333	3	3	0	1	1	0	0	0	0	1	0
Elio Chacon, 2b-3	.250	4	12	2	3	0	0	0	0	1	2	0
Gordie Coleman, 1b	.250	5	20	2	5	0	0	1	2	0	1	0
Johnny Edwards, c	.364	3	11	1	4	2	0	0	2	0	0	0
Gene Freese, 3b	.063	5	16	0	1	1	0	0	0	3	4	0
Dick Gernert, ph	.000	4	4	0	0	0	0	0	0	0	1	0
Bill Henry, p	.000	2	0	0	0	0	0	0	0	0	0	0
Ken Hunt, p	.000	1	0	0	0	0	0	0	0	0	0	0
Joey Jay, p	.000	2	4	0	0	0	0	0	0	0	2	0
Darrell Johnson, c	.500	2	4	0	2	0	0	0	0	0	0	0
Ken Johnson, p	.000	1	0	0	0	0	0	0	0	0	0	0
Sherman Jones, p	.000	1	0	0	0	0	0	0	0	0	0	0
Eddie Kasko, ss	.318	5	22	1	7	0	0	0	1	0	1	0
Jerry Lynch, ph	.000	4	3	0	0	0	0	0	0	1	1	0
Jim Maloney, p	.000	1	0	0	0	0	0	0	0	0	0	0
Jim O'Toole, p	.000	2	3	0	0	0	0	0	0	0	1	0
Vada Pinson, of	.091	5	22	0	2	1	0	0	0	0	1	0
Wally Post, of	.333	5	18	3	6	1	0	1	2	0	1	0
Bob Purkey, p	.000	2	3	0	0	0	0	0	0	0	3	0
Frank Robinson, of	.200	5	15	3	3	2	0	1	4	3	4	0
Jerry Zimmerman, c	.000	2	0	0	0	0	0	0	0	0	0	0
TOTAL	.206		170	13	35	8	0	3	11	8	27	0

PITCHER	W	L	ERA	G	GS	CG	SV	SHO	IP	H	ER	BB	SO
Jim Brosnan	0	0	7.50	3	0	0	0	0	6.0	9	5	4	5
Bill Henry	0	0	19.29	2	0	0	0	0	2.1	4	5	2	3
Ken Hunt	0	0	0.00	1	0	0	0	0	1.0	0	0	1	1
Joey Jay	1	1	5.59	2	2	1	0	0	9.2	8	6	6	6
Ken Johnson	0	0	0.00	1	0	0	0	0	0.2	0	0	0	0
Sherman Jones	0	0	0.00	1	0	0	0	0	0.2	0	0	0	0
Jim Maloney	0	0	27.00	1	0	0	0	0	0.2	4	2	1	1
Jim O'Toole	0	2	3.00	2	2	0	0	0	12.0	11	4	7	4
Bob Purkey	0	1	1.64	2	1	1	0	0	11.0	6	2	3	5
TOTAL	1	4	4.91	15	5	2	0	0	44.0	42	24	24	25

GAME 1 AT NY OCT 4

CIN	000 000 000	0	2	0
NY	000 101 00X	2	6	0

Pitchers: O'TOOLE, Brosnan (8) vs FORD
Home Runs: Howard-NY, Skowron-NY
Attendance: 62,397

GAME 2 AT NY OCT 5

CIN	000 211 020	6	9	0
NY	000 200 000	2	4	3

Pitchers: JAY vs TERRY, Arroyo (8)
Home Runs: Coleman-CIN, Berra-NY
Attendance: 63,083

GAME 3 AT CIN OCT 7

NY	000 000 111	3	6	1
CIN	001 000 100	2	8	0

Pitchers: Stafford, Daley (7), ARROYO (8) vs PURKEY
Home Runs: Blanchard-NY, Maris-NY
Attendance: 32,589

GAME 4 AT CIN OCT 8

NY	000 112 300	7	11	0
CIN	000 000 000	0	5	1

Pitchers: FORD, Coates (6) vs O'TOOLE, Brosnan (6), Henry (9)
Attendance: 32,589

GAME 5 AT CIN OCT 9

NY	510 502 000	13	15	1
CIN	003 020 000	5	11	3

Pitchers: Terry, DALEY (3) vs JAY, Maloney (1), K.Johnson (2), Henry (3), Jones (4), Purkey (5), Brosnan (7), Hunt (9)
Home Runs: Blanchard-NY, Robinson-CIN, Lopez-NY, Post-CIN
Attendance: 32,589

After edging Los Angeles for the pennant in a three-game playoff to break a regular-season tie, San Francisco battled to the final out of Game 7 before falling to New York in the World Series. The teams alternated wins throughout the Series. In the opener Roger Maris doubled two runs home for a quick lead. Whitey Ford gave up a run in the second (ending his record streak for consecutive scoreless World Series innings pitched at 33⅔) and a tying run an inning later. But he blanked the Giants after that, and won the game on Clete Boyer's homer in the seventh.

Jack Sanford blanked the Yankees on three hits in Game 2, but in Game 3 Bill Stafford restored the Series edge to New York with a four-hit 3–2 win (a shutout until Ed Bailey's ninth-inning home run). Both clubs hit safely nine times in Game 4. But one of the Giants' hits was Chuck Hiller's tie-breaking grand slam in the seventh—more than enough for a Giants win and another Series tie. In Game 5 Sanford brought a three-hit 2–2 tie into the last of the eighth. But after he had notched his 10th strikeout, two singles and Tom Tresh's home run drove him out and gave Ralph Terry all the margin he needed to avenge his second-game loss to Sanford, and put the Yankees ahead in the Series for the third time.

When play resumed in San Francisco after several days of rain, Billy Pierce held New York to just three hits. One was Roger Maris' solo homer in the fifth, but Pierce's Giants unloaded on Whitey Ford for five runs, driving Ford out and keeping Giant hopes alive.

The finale pitted Terry against Sanford for the third time. Both pitched effectively, but Terry carried a 1–0 lead into the last of the ninth. Pinch hitter Matty Alou led off with a bunt single, but Terry fanned the next two batters. Then Willie Mays doubled to right, but Maris' slick fielding stopped Alou at third. As Terry faced Willie McCovey (who had homered off him in Game 2), he pondered the home run he had given up to Bill Mazeroski two years earlier to lose the 1960 World Series to Pittsburgh. McCovey lined Terry's third pitch toward right—but right at second baseman Bobby Richardson, who grabbed it for the Yankees' 20th world title. It would be 15 years before they saw another.

New York Yankees (AL), 4;
San Francisco Giants (NL), 3

NY (A)

PLAYER/POS	AVG	G	AB	R	H	2B	3B	HR	RB	BB	SO	SB
Yogi Berra, c-1	.000	2	2	0	0	0	0	0	0	2	0	0
Johnny Blanchard, ph	.000	1	1	0	0	0	0	0	0	0	1	0
Clete Boyer, 3b	.318	7	22	2	7	1	0	1	4	1	3	0
Marshall Bridges, p	.000	2	0	0	0	0	0	0	0	0	0	0
Jim Coates, p	.000	2	0	0	0	0	0	0	0	0	0	0
Buddy Daley, p	.000	1	0	0	0	0	0	0	0	0	0	0
Whitey Ford, p	.000	3	7	0	0	0	0	0	0	0	1	3	0
Elston Howard, c	.143	6	21	1	3	1	0	0	1	1	4	0
Tony Kubek, ss	.276	7	29	2	8	1	0	0	1	1	3	0
Dale Long, 1b	.200	2	5	0	1	0	0	0	1	0	1	0
Hector Lopez, ph	.000	2	2	0	0	0	0	0	0	0	0	0
Mickey Mantle, of	.120	7	25	2	3	1	0	0	0	4	5	2
Roger Maris, of	.174	7	23	4	4	1	0	1	5	5	2	0
Bobby Richardson, 2b	.148	7	27	3	4	0	0	0	0	3	1	0
Bill Skowron, 1b	.222	6	18	1	4	0	1	0	1	1	5	0
Bill Stafford, p	.000	1	3	0	0	0	0	0	0	0	1	0
Ralph Terry, p	.125	3	8	0	1	0	0	0	0	1	6	0
Tom Tresh, of	.321	7	28	5	9	1	0	1	4	1	4	2
TOTAL	.199		221	20	44	6	1	3	17	21	39	4

PITCHER	W	L	ERA	G	GS	CG	SV	SHO	IP	H	ER	BB	SO
Marshall Bridges	0	0	4.91	2	0	0	0	0	3.2	4	2	2	3
Jim Coates	0	1	6.75	2	0	0	0	0	2.2	1	2	1	3
Buddy Daley	0	0	0.00	1	0	0	0	0	1.0	1	0	1	0
Whitey Ford	1	1	4.12	3	3	1	0	0	19.2	24	9	4	12
Bill Stafford	1	0	2.00	1	1	1	0	0	9.0	4	2	2	5
Ralph Terry	2	1	1.80	3	3	2	0	1	25.0	17	5	2	16
TOTAL	4	3	2.95	12	7	4	0	1	61.0	51	20	12	39

SF (N)

PLAYER/POS	AVG	G	AB	R	H	2B	3B	HR	RB	BB	SO	SB
Felipe Alou, of	.269	7	26	2	7	1	1	0	1	1	4	0
Matty Alou, of-4	.333	6	12	2	4	1	0	0	1	0	1	0
Ed Bailey, c-3	.071	6	14	1	1	0	0	1	2	0	3	0
Bobby Bolin, p	.000	2	0	0	0	0	0	0	0	0	0	0
Ernie Bowman, ss-1	.000	2	1	1	0	0	0	0	0	0	0	0
Orlando Cepeda, 1b	.158	5	19	1	3	1	0	0	2	0	4	0
Jim Davenport, 3b	.136	7	22	1	3	1	0	0	1	4	7	0
Tom Haller, c	.286	4	14	1	4	1	0	1	3	0	2	0
Chuck Hiller, 2b	.269	7	26	4	7	3	0	1	5	3	4	0
Harvey Kuenn, of	.083	3	12	1	1	0	0	0	0	1	1	0
Don Larsen, p	.000	3	0	0	0	0	0	0	0	0	0	0
Juan Marichal, p	.000	1	2	0	0	0	0	0	0	0	1	0
Willie Mays, of	.250	7	28	3	7	2	0	0	1	1	5	1
Willie McCovey, 1b-2,of-2	.200	4	15	2	3	0	1	1	1	1	3	0
Stu Miller, p	.000	2	0	0	0	0	0	0	0	0	0	0
Bob Nieman, ph	.000	1	0	0	0	0	0	0	0	1	0	0
Billy O'Dell, p	.333	3	3	0	1	0	0	0	0	0	0	0
John Orsino, c	.000	1	1	0	0	0	0	0	0	0	0	0
Jose Pagan, ss	.368	7	19	2	7	0	0	1	2	0	1	0
Billy Pierce, p	.000	2	5	0	0	0	0	0	0	0	1	0
Jack Sanford, p	.429	3	7	0	3	0	0	0	0	0	2	0
TOTAL	.226		226	21	51	10	2	5	19	12	39	1

PITCHER	W	L	ERA	G	GS	CG	SV	SHO	IP	H	ER	BB	SO
Bobby Bolin	0	0	6.75	2	0	0	0	0	2.2	4	2	2	2
Don Larsen	1	0	3.86	3	0	0	0	0	2.1	1	1	2	0
Juan Marichal	0	0	0.00	1	1	0	0	0	4.0	2	0	2	4
Stu Miller	0	0	0.00	2	0	0	0	0	1.1	1	0	2	0
Billy O'Dell	0	1	4.38	3	1	0	1	0	12.1	12	6	3	9
Billy Pierce	1	1	2.40	2	2	1	0	0	15.0	8	4	2	5
Jack Sanford	1	2	1.93	3	3	1	0	1	23.1	16	5	8	19
TOTAL	3	4	2.66	16	7	2	1	1	61.0	44	18	21	39

GAME 1 AT SF OCT 4

NY	200	000	121	6	11 0
SF	011	000	000	2	10 0

Pitchers: FORD vs O'DELL, Larsen (7), Miller (9)
Home Runs: Boyer-NY
Attendance: 43,852

GAME 2 AT SF OCT 5

NY	000	000	000	0	3 1
SF	100	000	10X	2	6 0

Pitchers: TERRY, Daley (8) vs SANFORD
Home Runs: McCovey-SF
Attendance: 43,910

GAME 3 AT NY OCT 7

SF	000	000	002	2	4 3
NY	000	000	30X	3	5 1

Pitchers: PIERCE, Larsen (7), Bolin (8) vs STAFFORD
Home Runs: Bailey-SF
Attendance: 71,434

GAME 4 AT NY OCT 8

SF	020	000	401	7	9 1
NY	000	002	001	3	9 1

Pitchers: Marichal, Bolin (5), LARSEN (6), O'Dell (7) vs Ford, COATES (7), Bridges (7)
Home Runs: Haller-SF, Hiller-SF
Attendance: 66,607

GAME 5 AT NY OCT 10

SF	001	010	001	3	8 2
NY	000	101	03X	5	6 0

Pitchers: SANFORD, Miller (8) vs TERRY
Home Runs: Pagan-SF, Tresh-NY
Attendance: 63,165

GAME 6 AT SF OCT 15

NY	000	010	010	2	3 2
SF	000	320	00X	5	10 1

Pitchers: FORD, Coates (5), Bridges (8) vs PIERCE
Home Runs: Maris-NY
Attendance: 43,948

GAME 7 AT SF OCT 16

NY	000	100	000	1	7 0
SF	000	000	000	0	4 1

Pitchers: TERRY vs SANFORD, O'Dell (8)
Attendance: 43,948

The Yankees won the American League pennant by 10½ games, but in the Series they were overwhelmed by Dodgers pitching. The opener pitted two all-time greats against each other: Whitey Ford (24–7 that season) and Sandy Koufax (25–5). For an inning it was close. Ford fanned two of the first three batters to face him, and Koufax struck out the side. But in the top of the second the Dodgers' Frank Howard doubled with one out, and before Ford could record the second out, two singles and John Roseboro's home run had put four Dodgers across home plate. Koufax ran his consecutive Ks to five and had tied the Series single-game record of 14 by the time Tom Tresh tagged him for a two-run homer in the eighth. That was New York's only scoring, and Koufax ended the game with a new-record 15th strikeout an inning later.

Veteran Johnny Podres pitched shutout ball through 8⅓ innings of Game 2 as his Dodgers built him a four-run lead (one of the runs a homer by ex-Yankee Bill Skowron). New York scored a run in the last of the ninth, but it was not enough to keep the Dodgers from returning to Los Angeles with a 2–0 Series advantage.

A first-inning walk, a wild pitch, and a single moved Dodger Jim Gilliam around the bases for the only scoring in Game 3 as Jim Bouton hooked up in a duel with Don Drysdale. Bouton left after seven innings for Yankees relief ace Hal Reniff, who held Los Angeles hitless through the final frames. When Drysdale completed his shutout, only three singles had been hit against him, and he had struck out nine.

Ford and Koufax tangled again in the fourth game. Ford pitched much more impressively than he had in the opener, walking just one and yielding only two hits in seven innings. One of the hits was Frank Howard's solo homer in the fifth inning, but Mickey Mantle evened the score with a home run off Koufax in the seventh. In the last of the seventh, Yankee first baseman Joe Pepitone lost sight of a throw from the third baseman for an error that sent batter Jim Gilliam all the way to third, and Willie Davis followed with a fly to center that scored Gilliam with the go-ahead run. No one else scored against Ford (or Reniff, who relieved him in the eighth), but no other Yankee scored against Koufax either, and the Dodgers, with just two hits, captured the game and the Series.

Los Angeles Dodgers (NL), 4; New York Yankees (AL), 0

LA (N)

PLAYER/POS	AVG	G	AB	R	H	2B	3B	HR	RB	BB	SO	SB
Tommy Davis, of	.400	4	15	0	6	0	2	0	2	0	2	1
Willie Davis, of	.167	4	12	2	2	2	0	0	3	0	6	0
Don Drysdale, p	.000	1	1	0	0	0	0	0	0	2	0	0
Ron Fairly, of	.000	4	1	0	0	0	0	0	0	3	0	0
Jim Gilliam, 3b	.154	4	13	3	2	0	0	0	0	3	1	0
Frank Howard, of	.300	3	10	2	3	1	0	1	1	0	2	0
Sandy Koufax, p	.000	2	6	0	0	0	0	0	0	0	2	0
Ron Perranoski, p	.000	1	0	0	0	0	0	0	0	0	0	0
Johnny Podres, p	.250	1	4	0	1	0	0	0	0	0	0	0
Johnny Roseboro, c	.143	4	14	1	2	0	0	1	3	0	4	0
Bill Skowron, 1b	.385	4	13	2	5	0	0	1	3	1	3	0
Dick Tracewski, 2b	.154	4	13	1	2	0	0	0		1	2	0
Maury Wills, ss	.133	4	15	1	2	0	0	0	0	1	3	1
TOTAL	.214		117	12	25	3	2	3	12	11	25	2

PITCHER	W	L	ERA	G	GS	CG	SV	SHO	IP	H	ER	BB	SO
Don Drysdale	1	0	0.00	1	1	1	0	1	9.0	3	0	1	9
Sandy Koufax	2	0	1.50	2	2	2	0	0	18.0	12	3	3	23
Ron Perranoski	0	0	0.00	1	0	0	1	0	0.2	1	0	0	1
Johnny Podres	1	0	1.08	1	1	0	0	0	8.1	6	1	1	4
TOTAL	4	0	1.00	5	4	3	1	1	36.0	22	4	5	37

NY (A)

PLAYER/POS	AVG	G	AB	R	H	2B	3B	HR	RB	BB	SO	SB
Yogi Berra, ph	.000	1	1	0	0	0	0	0	0	0	0	0
Johnny Blanchard, of-1	.000	1	3	0	0	0	0	0	0	0	0	0
Jim Bouton, p	.000	1	2	0	0	0	0	0	0	0	2	0
Clete Boyer, 3b	.077	4	13	0	1	0	0	0	0	1	6	0
Harry Bright, ph	.000	2	2	0	0	0	0	0	0	0	2	0
Al Downing, p	.000	1	1	0	0	0	0	0	0	0	1	0
Whitey Ford, p	.000	2	3	0	0	0	0	0	0	0	0	0
Steve Hamilton, p	.000	1	0	0	0	0	0	0	0	0	0	0
Elston Howard, c	.333	4	15	0	5	0	0	0	1	0	3	0
Tony Kubek, ss	.188	4	16	1	3	0	0	0	0	0	3	0
Phil Linz, ph	.333	3	3	0	1	0	0	0	0	0	1	0
Hector Lopez, of-2	.250	3	8	1	2	2	0	0	0	0	1	0
Mickey Mantle, of	.133	4	15	1	2	0	0	1	1	1	5	0
Roger Maris, of	.000	2	5	0	0	0	0	0	0	0	1	0
Joe Pepitone, 1b	.154	4	13	0	2	0	0	0	0	1	3	0
Hal Reniff, p	.000	3	0	0	0	0	0	0	0	0	0	0
Bobby Richardson, 2b	.214	4	14	0	3	1	0	0	0	1	3	0
Ralph Terry, p	.000	1	0	0	0	0	0	0	0	0	0	0
Tom Tresh, of	.200	4	15	1	3	0	0	1	2	1	6	0
Stan Williams, p	.000	1	0	0	0	0	0	0	0	0	0	0
TOTAL	.171		129	4	22	3	0	2	4	5	37	0

PITCHER	W	L	ERA	G	GS	CG	SV	SHO	IP	H	ER	BB	SO
Jim Bouton	0	1	1.29	1	1	0	0	0	7.0	4	1	5	4
Al Downing	0	1	5.40	1	1	0	0	0	5.0	7	3	1	6
Whitey Ford	0	2	4.50	2	2	0	0	0	12.0	10	6	3	8
Steve Hamilton	0	0	0.00	1	0	0	0	0	1.0	0	0	0	1
Hal Reniff	0	0	0.00	3	0	0	0	0	3.0	0	0	1	1
Ralph Terry	0	0	3.00	1	0	0	0	0	3.0	3	1	1	0
Stan Williams	0	0	0.00	1	0	0	0	0	3.0	1	0	0	5
TOTAL	0	4	2.91	10	4	0	0	0	34.0	25	11	11	25

GAME 1 AT NY OCT 2

LA	041	000	000	5	9	0
NY	000	000	020	2	6	0

Pitchers: KOUFAX vs FORD, Williams (6), Hamilton (9)
Home Runs: Roseboro-LA, Tresh-NY
Attendance: 69,000

GAME 2 AT NY OCT 3

LA	200	100	010	4	10	1
NY	000	000	001	1	7	0

Pitchers: PODRES, Perranoski (9) vs DOWNING, Terry (6), Reniff (9)
Home Runs: Skowron-LA
Attendance: 66,455

GAME 3 AT LA OCT 5

NY	000	000	000	0	3	0
LA	100	000	00X	1	4	1

Pitchers: BOUTON, Reniff (8) vs DRYSDALE
Attendance: 55,912

GAME 4 AT LA OCT 6

NY	000	000	100	1	6	1
LA	000	010	10X	2	2	1

Pitchers: FORD, Reniff (8) vs KOUFAX
Home Runs: F.Howard-LA, Mantle-NY
Attendance: 55,912

With late-season spurts the Cardinals edged the Reds and Phillies for their first pennant in 18 years and the Yankees overtook the White Sox and Orioles for their 15th in 18 years and their 29th over all. But when the Series was over, the long era of Yankee dominance had come to an end.

St. Louis won the opener, a 24-hit slugfest in which Curt Flood's RBI triple in the sixth proved the decisive blow. But New York came back to take the next two games. Rookie Mel Stottlemyre won Game 2, holding the Cards to three runs as his Yankees scored eight. (Loser Bob Gibson struck out nine Yankees, though, on his way to a new Series record of 31.) Game 3, by contrast, featured a pitchers' duel between Jim Bouton and veteran Curt Simmons. Cardinals reliever Barney Schultz, who replaced Simmons for the last of the ninth with the score 1–1, lost the game on his first pitch when Mickey Mantle homered to deep right (his 16th World Series home run, which moved him ahead of Babe Ruth into the all-time Series lead).

Ray Sadecki (the winner in Game One) left with one out in the first inning of Game 4 after four Yankees hit safely, but relievers Roger Craig and Ron Taylor stopped New York on just two singles the rest of the way. The Cards were also held to six hits, but one was Ken Boyer's grand slam in the sixth, which erased a 3–0 Yankees lead and gave St. Louis enough runs to even the Series at two games apiece.

Gibson and Stottlemyre faced off a second time in Game 5. Gibson carried a 2–0 lead into the last of the ninth, when with two out Tom Tresh tagged him for a game-tying home run. In the top of the 10th, though, the Cards regained the lead on Tim McCarver's three-run homer and held on for the win as Gibson notched his 13th K of the game.

Bouton and Simmons tangled again in Game 6. Another 1–1 duel was shattered, this time in the top of the sixth when Roger Maris and Mantle tagged Simmons for back-to-back home runs. New York put the game away in the eighth with five runs off Cardinals relievers—four of them on Joe Pepitone's grand slam.

With the series tied 3–3, Gibson and Stottlemyre were called upon to settle the title. Gibson pitched the whole game, striking out nine. Mantle touched him for a three-run homer in the sixth inning, and Clete Boyer and Phil Linz hit solo shots in the ninth. But as St. Louis had scored six times off Stottlemyre and his replacement Al Downing before the Yankees scored their first runs, the game

ended with the Cards victors and world champions. Yogi Berra, New York's rookie manager, was fired the next day. The following season the Yankees finished sixth.

St. Louis Cardinals (NL), 4; New York Yankees (AL), 3

STL (N)

PLAYER/POS	AVG	G	AB	R	H	2B	3B	HR	RB	BB	SO	SB
Ken Boyer, 3b	.222	7	27	5	6	1	0	2	6	1	5	0
Lou Brock, of	.300	7	30	2	9	2	0	1	5	0	3	0
Gerry Buchek, 2b	1.000	4	1	1	1	0	0	0	0	0	0	0
Roger Craig, p	.000	2	1	0	0	0	0	0	0	0	0	0
Curt Flood, of	.200	7	30	5	6	0	1	0	3	3	1	0
Bob Gibson, p	.222	3	9	1	2	0	0	0	0	0	3	0
Dick Groat, ss	.192	7	26	3	5	1	1	0	1	4	3	0
Bob Humphreys, p	.000	1	0	0	0	0	0	0	0	0	0	0
Charlie James, ph	.000	3	3	0	0	0	0	0	0	0	1	0
Julian Javier, 2b	.000	1	0	1	0	0	0	0	0	0	0	0
Dal Maxvill, 2b	.200	7	20	0	4	1	0	0	1	1	4	0
Tim McCarver, c	.478	7	23	4	11	1	1	1	5	5	1	1
Gordie Richardson, p	.000	2	0	0	0	0	0	0	0	0	0	0
Ray Sadecki, p	.500	2	2	0	1	0	0	0	0	1	0	1
Barney Schultz, p	.000	4	1	0	0	0	0	0	0	0	0	0
Mike Shannon, of	.214	7	28	6	6	0	0	1	2	0	9	1
Curt Simmons, p	.500	2	4	0	2	0	0	0	1	0	1	0
Bob Skinner, ph	.667	4	3	0	2	1	0	0	1	1	0	0
Ron Taylor, p	.000	2	1	0	0	0	0	0	0	0	1	0
Carl Warwick, ph	.750	5	4	2	3	0	0	0	1	1	0	0
Bill White, 1b	.111	7	27	2	3	1	0	0	2	2	6	1
TOTAL	.254		240	32	61	8	3	5	29	18	39	3

PITCHER	W	L	ERA	G	GS	CG	SV	SHO	IP	H	ER	BB	SO
Roger Craig	1	0	0.00	2	0	0	0	0	5.0	2	0	3	9
Bob Gibson	2	1	3.00	3	3	2	0	0	27.0	23	9	8	31
Bob Humphreys	0	0	0.00	1	0	0	0	0	1.0	0	0	0	1
Gordie Richardson	0	0	40.50	2	0	0	0	0	0.2	3	3	2	0
Ray Sadecki	1	0	8.53	2	2	0	0	0	6.1	12	6	5	2
Barney Schultz	0	1	18.00	4	0	0	1	0	4.0	9	8	3	1
Curt Simmons	0	1	2.51	2	2	0	0	0	14.1	11	4	3	8
Ron Taylor	0	0	0.00	2	0	0	1	0	4.2	0	0	1	2
TOTAL	4	3	4.29	18	7	2	2	0	63.0	60	30	25	54

NY (A)

PLAYER/POS	AVG	G	AB	R	H	2B	3B	HR	RB	BB	SO	SB
Johnny Blanchard, ph	.250	4	4	0	1	1	0	0	0	0	1	0
Jim Bouton, p	.143	2	7	0	1	0	0	0	1	0	2	0
Clete Boyer, 3b	.208	7	24	2	5	1	0	1	3	1	5	1
Al Downing, p	.000	3	2	0	0	0	0	0	0	0	2	0
Whitey Ford, p	1.000	1	1	0	1	0	0	0	1	2	0	0
Pedro Gonzalez, 3b	.000	1	1	0	0	0	0	0	0	0	0	0
Steve Hamilton, p	.000	2	0	0	0	0	0	0	0	0	0	0
Mike Hegan, ph	.000	3	1	1	0	0	0	0	0	1	1	0
Elston Howard, c	.292	7	24	5	7	1	0	0	2	4	6	0
Phil Linz, ss	.226	7	31	5	7	1	0	2	2	2	5	0
Hector Lopez, of-1	.000	3	2	0	0	0	0	0	0	0	2	0
Mickey Mantle, of	.333	7	24	8	8	2	0	3	8	6	8	0
Roger Maris, of	.200	7	30	4	6	0	0	1	1	1	4	0
Pete Mikkelsen, p	.000	4	0	0	0	0	0	0	0	0	0	0
Joe Pepitone, 1b	.154	7	26	1	4	1	0	1	5	2	3	0
Hal Reniff, p	.000	1	0	0	0	0	0	0	0	0	0	0
Bobby Richardson, 2b	.406	7	32	3	13	2	0	0	3	0	2	1
Rollie Sheldon, p	.000	2	0	0	0	0	0	0	0	0	0	0
Mel Stottlemyre, p	.125	3	8	0	1	0	0	0	0	0	6	0
Ralph Terry, p	.000	1	0	0	0	0	0	0	0	0	0	0
Tom Tresh, of	.273	7	22	4	6	2	0	2	7	6	7	0
TOTAL	.251		239	33	60	11	0	10	33	25	54	2

PITCHER	W	L	ERA	G	GS	CG	SV	SHO	IP	H	ER	BB	SO
Jim Bouton	2	0	1.56	2	2	1	0	0	17.1	15	3	5	7
Al Downing	0	1	8.22	3	1	0	0	0	7.2	9	7	2	5
Whitey Ford	0	1	8.44	1	1	0	0	0	5.1	8	5	1	4
Steve Hamilton	0	0	4.50	2	0	0	1	0	2.0	3	1	0	2
Pete Mikkelsen	0	1	5.79	4	0	0	0	0	4.2	4	3	2	4
Hal Reniff	0	0	0.00	1	0	0	0	0	0.1	2	0	0	0
Rollie Sheldon	0	0	0.00	2	0	0	0	0	2.2	0	0	2	2
Mel Stottlemyre	1	1	3.15	3	3	1	0	0	20.0	18	7	6	12
Ralph Terry	0	0	0.00	1	0	0	0	0	2.0	2	0	3	3
TOTAL	3	4	3.77	19	7	2	1	0	62.0	61	26	18	39

GAME 1 AT STL OCT 7

NY	030 010 010	5	12	2
STL	110 004 03X	9	12	0

Pitchers: FORD, Downing (6), Sheldon (8), Mikkelsen (9) vs SADECKI, Schultz (7)
Home Runs: Tresh-NY, Shannon-STL
Attendance: 30,805

GAME 2 AT STL OCT 8

NY	000 101 204	8	12	0
STL	001 000 011	3	7	0

Pitchers: STOTTLEMYRE vs GIBSON, Schultz (9), Craig (9), Richardson (9)
Home Runs: Linz-NY
Attendance: 30,805

GAME 3 AT NY OCT 10

STL	000 010 000	1	6	0
NY	010 000 001	2	5	2

Pitchers: Simmons, SCHULTZ (9) vs BOUTON
Home Runs: Mantle-NY
Attendance: 67,101

GAME 4 AT NY OCT 11

STL	000 004 000	4	6	1
NY	300 000 000	3	6	1

Pitchers: Sadecki, CRAIG (1), Taylor (6) vs DOWNING, Mikkelsen (7), Terry (8)
Home Runs: K.Boyer-STL
Attendance: 66,312

GAME 5 AT NY OCT 12

STL	000 020 000 3	5	10	1
NY	000 000 002 0	2	6	2

Pitchers: GIBSON vs Stottlemyre, Reniff (8), MIKKELSEN (8)
Home Runs: Tresh-NY, McCarver-STL
Attendance: 65,633

GAME 6 AT STL OCT 14

NY	000 012 050	8	10	0
STL	100 000 011	3	10	1

Pitchers: BOUTON, Hamilton (9) vs SIMMONS, Taylor (7), Schultz (8), Richardson (8), Humphreys (9)
Home Runs: Maris-NY, Mantle-NY, Pepitone-NY
Attendance: 30,805

GAME 7 AT STL OCT 15

NY	000 003 002	5	9	2
STL	000 330 10X	7	10	1

Pitchers: STOTTLEMYRE, Downing (5), Sheldon (5), Hamilton (7), Mikkelsen (8) vs GIBSON
Home Runs: Brock-STL, Mantle-NY, K.Boyer-STL, C.Boyer-NY, Linz-NY
Attendance: 30,346

The Twins (bringing the World Series to Minnesota for the first time ever) featured heavy hitting, while Dodgers hopes rested on great pitching and speed on the bases. For a while it looked as if power would triumph as the Twins took the first two games at home. They drove out starter Don Drysdale with seven runs in the first three innings of the opener—including home runs by Don Mincher and Zoilo Versalles—on the way to a convincing 8–2 win, and followed up with a 5–1 triumph the next day over Dodgers ace Sandy Koufax (who had declined to pitch Game 1 on Yom Kippur, the holiest day of the Jewish year) and star reliever Ron Perranoski, who was tagged for three of the Twins' runs.

But when the Series moved to Los Angeles, Dodgers pitching began to assert itself. Claude Osteen held Minnesota to five hits and no runs, while Los Angeles bunched seven of their 10 hits in the middle three innings for four runs. Drysdale evened the Series in Game 4, avenging his first-game pounding with a five-hitter. Twins Harmon Killebrew and Tony Oliva tagged him for a pair of solo homers, but that was Minnesota's only scoring—more than balanced by seven Dodgers runs, including homers by Wes Parker and Lou Johnson. In Game 5 the next day, Koufax avenged his earlier loss, carrying Los Angeles to its first Series lead with a shutout in which he allowed only four singles and a walk, while fanning 10 Twins. Speedster Willie Davis stole three bases and Maury Wills stole another as the Dodgers parlayed 14 hits into a 7–0 victory.

Back in Minnesota for Game 6, the Twins rallied, using the long ball to even the Series again with a 5–1 win. Bob Allison opened the scoring with a two-run shot off Claude Osteen in the fourth, and Minnesota pitcher Mudcat Grant insured his own win with a three-run blast two innings later.

In the finale, though, the visiting team won for the only time in the Series. Koufax again struck out 10, stopping the Twins on three hits for his second shutout. Lou Johnson's second Series homer (a fourth-inning solo shot to left off Twins starter Jim Kaat that was barely fair) was all the Dodgers needed for their fifth world championship, but Ron Fairly followed Johnson with a double and Wes Parker singled home an insurance run that drove Kaat from the game and concluded the Series scoring.

Los Angeles Dodgers (NL), 4; Minnesota Twins (AL), 3

LA (N)

PLAYER/POS	AVG	G	AB	R	H	2B	3B	HR	RBI	BB	SO	SB
Jim Brewer, p	.000	1	0	0	0	0	0	0	0	0	0	0
Willie Crawford, ph	.500	2	2	0	1	0	0	0	0	0	1	0
Willie Davis, of	.231	7	26	3	6	0	0	0	0	0	2	3
Don Drysdale, p-2	.000	3	5	0	0	0	0	0	0	0	4	0
Ron Fairly, of	.379	7	29	7	11	3	0	2	6	0	1	0
Jim Gilliam, 3b	.214	7	28	2	6	1	0	0	2	1	0	0
Lou Johnson, of	.296	7	27	3	8	2	0	2	4	1	3	0
John Kennedy, 3b	.000	4	1	0	0	0	0	0	0	0	0	0
Sandy Koufax, p	.111	3	9	0	1	0	0	0	1	1	5	0
Jim Lefebvre, 2b	.400	3	10	2	4	0	0	0	0	0	0	0
Don LeJohn, ph	.000	1	1	0	0	0	0	0	0	0	1	0
Bob Miller, p	.000	2	0	0	0	0	0	0	0	0	0	0
Wally Moon, ph	.000	2	2	0	0	0	0	0	0	0	1	0
Claude Osteen, p	.333	2	3	0	1	0	0	0	0	0	0	0
Wes Parker, 1b	.304	7	23	3	7	0	0	1	1	2	3	2
Ron Perranoski, p	.000	2	0	0	0	0	0	0	0	0	0	0
Howie Reed, p	.000	2	0	0	0	0	0	0	0	0	0	0
Johnny Roseboro, c	.286	7	21	1	6	1	0	0	3	5	3	1
Dick Tracewski, 2b	.118	6	17	0	2	0	0	0	0	1	5	0
Maury Wills, ss	.367	7	30	3	11	3	0	0	3	1	3	3
TOTAL	.274		234	24	64	10	1	5	21	13	31	9

PITCHER	W	L	ERA	G	GS	CG	SV	SHO	IP	H	ER	BB	SO
Jim Brewer	0	0	4.50	1	0	0	0	0	2.0	3	1	0	1
Don Drysdale	1	1	3.86	2	2	1	0	0	11.2	12	5	3	15
Sandy Koufax	2	1	0.38	3	3	2	0	2	24.0	13	1	5	29
Bob Miller	0	0	0.00	2	0	0	0	0	1.1	0	0	0	0
Claude Osteen	1	1	0.64	2	2	1	0	1	14.0	9	1	5	4
Ron Perranoski	0	0	7.36	2	0	0	0	0	3.2	3	3	4	1
Howie Reed	0	0	8.10	2	0	0	0	0	3.1	2	3	2	4
TOTAL	4	3	2.10	14	7	4	0	3	60.0	42	14	19	54

MIN (A)

PLAYER/POS	AVG	G	AB	R	H	2B	3B	HR	RBI	BB	SO	SB
Bob Allison, of	.125	5	16	3	2	1	0	1	2	2	9	1
Earl Battey, c	.120	7	25	1	3	0	1	0	2	0	5	0
Dave Boswell, p	.000	1	0	0	0	0	0	0	0	0	0	0
Mudcat Grant, p	.250	3	8	3	2	1	0	1	3	0	1	0
Jimmie Hall, of	.143	2	7	0	1	0	0	0	0	1	5	0
Jim Kaat, p	.167	3	6	0	1	0	0	0	0	2	5	0
Harmon Killebrew, 3b	.286	7	21	2	6	0	0	1	2	6	4	0
Johnny Klippstein, p	.000	2	0	0	0	0	0	0	0	0	0	0
Jim Merritt, p	.000	2	0	0	0	0	0	0	0	0	0	0
Don Mincher, 1b	.130	7	23	3	3	0	0	1	1	2	7	0
Joe Nossek, of-5	.200	6	20	0	4	0	0	0	0	0	1	0
Tony Oliva, of	.192	7	26	2	5	1	0	1	2	1	6	0
Camilo Pascual, p	.000	1	1	0	0	0	0	0	0	0	0	0
Jim Perry, p	.000	2	0	0	0	0	0	0	0	0	0	0
Bill Pleis, p	.000	1	0	0	0	0	0	0	0	0	0	0
Frank Quilici, 2b	.200	7	20	2	4	2	0	0	1	4	3	0
Rich Rollins, ph	.000	3	2	0	0	0	0	0	0	0	0	0
Sandy Valdespino, of-2	.273	5	11	1	3	1	0	0	0	0	1	0
Zoilo Versalles, ss	.286	7	28	3	8	1	1	1	4	2	7	1
Al Worthington, p	.000	2	0	0	0	0	0	0	0	0	0	0
Jerry Zimmerman, c	.000	2	1	0	0	0	0	0	0	0	1	0
TOTAL	.195		215	20	42	7	2	6	19	19	54	2

PITCHER	W	L	ERA	G	GS	CG	SV	SHO	IP	H	ER	BB	SO
Dave Boswell	0	0	3.38	1	0	0	0	0	2.2	3	1	2	3
Mudcat Grant	2	1	2.74	3	3	2	0	0	23.0	22	7	2	12
Jim Kaat	1	2	3.77	3	3	1	0	0	14.1	18	6	2	6
Johnny Klippstein	0	0	0.00	2	0	0	0	0	2.2	2	0	2	3
Jim Merritt	0	0	2.70	2	0	0	0	0	3.1	2	1	0	1
Camilo Pascual	0	1	5.40	1	1	0	0	0	5.0	8	3	1	0
Jim Perry	0	0	4.50	2	0	0	0	0	4.0	5	2	2	4
Bill Pleis	0	0	9.00	1	0	0	0	0	1.0	2	1	0	0
Al Worthington	0	0	0.00	2	0	0	0	0	4.0	2	0	2	2
TOTAL	3	4	3.15	17	7	3	0	0	60.0	64	21	13	31

GAME 1 AT MIN OCT 6

LA	010 000 001	2 10 1
MIN	016 001 00X	8 10 0

Pitchers: DRYSDALE, Reed (3), Brewer (5), Perranoski (7) vs GRANT
Home Runs: Fairly-LA, Mincher-MIN, Versalles-MIN
Attendance: 47,797

GAME 2 AT MIN OCT 7

LA	000 000 100	1 7 3
MIN	000 002 12X	5 9 0

Pitchers: KOUFAX, Perranoski (7), Miller (8) vs KAAT
Attendance: 48,700

GAME 3 AT LA OCT 9

MIN	000 000 000	0 5 0
LA	000 211 00X	4 10 1

Pitchers: PASCUAL, Merritt (6), Klippstein (8) vs OSTEEN
Attendance: 55,934

GAME 4 AT LA OCT 10

MIN	000 101 000	2 5 2
LA	110 103 01X	7 10 0

Pitchers: GRANT, Worthington (6), Pleis (8) vs DRYSDALE
Home Runs: Killebrew-MIN, Parker-LA, Oliva-MIN, Johnson-LA
Attendance: 55,920

GAME 5 AT LA OCT 11

MIN	000 000 000	0 4 1
LA	202 100 20X	7 14 0

Pitchers: KAAT, Boswell (3), Perry (6) vs KOUFAX
Attendance: 55,801

GAME 6 AT MIN OCT 13

LA	000 000 100	1 6 1
MIN	000 203 00X	5 6 1

Pitchers: OSTEEN, Reed (6), Miller (8) vs GRANT
Home Runs: Allison-MIN, Grant-MIN, Fairly-LA
Attendance: 49,578

GAME 7 AT MIN OCT 14

LA	000 200 000	2 7 0
MIN	000 000 000	0 3 1

Pitchers: KOUFAX vs KAAT, Worthington (4), Klippstein (6), Merritt (7), Perry (9)
Home Runs: Johnson-LA
Attendance: 50,596

The Orioles, with their first pennant since moving from St. Louis in 1954, won the franchise's first World Series ever, crushing NL repeater Los Angeles in four games. Back-to-back home runs by Frank and Brooks Robinson in the top of the first inning of the opener gave Baltimore a quick three-run lead, and the O's added a fourth run an inning later before the Dodgers attempted to come back with single runs in the second and third innings. But by then Orioles reliever Moe Drabowsky had come on to pitch, and he stopped the Dodgers on one hit the rest of the way, striking out 11 (including six in a row in the fourth and fifth innings). The Dodgers would not score again in the Series.

Sophomore Jim Palmer (a week shy of his 21st birthday) hurled a four-hit shutout at Los Angeles in Game 2, defeating the great—but critically sore-armed—Sandy Koufax, who, though only 30 years old, was pitching the final game of his career. Three errors by center fielder Willie Davis in the fifth (including a pair of flies lost in the sun) led to three unearned runs—the first scoring against Koufax. Frank Robinson's leadoff triple in the sixth and Boog Powell's single gave the Orioles an earned run before a double play ended the inning. Koufax was replaced after the inning by a succession of Dodgers relievers as Baltimore went on to win, 6–0.

Wally Bunker did the honors for the Orioles in Game 3, emerging the victor of a pitching duel with Claude Osteen on the strength of a fifth-inning home run by Paul Blair, a tremendous 430-foot shot to left. Osteen yielded only two other Orioles hits—both singles—in his seven innings, and Dodger reliever Phil Regan retired the side in the eighth. But one run was all Bunker needed for his shutout win.

Dave McNally, who had given up the Dodgers' only Series runs in Game 1, mended his ways with a four-hit shutout in Game 4. He needed the shutout for the sweep, for Don Drysdale was also in top form. Drysdale, too, gave up only four hits. But one of them was Frank Robinson's second home run of the Series, a fourth-inning solo shot to left for the game's only scoring.

Baltimore Orioles (AL), 4; Los Angeles Dodgers (NL), 0

BAL (A)

PLAYER/POS	AVG	G	AB	R	H	2B	3B	HR	RB	BB	SO	SB
Luis Aparicio, ss	.250	4	16	0	4	1	0	0	2	0	0	0
Paul Blair, of	.167	4	6	2	1	0	0	1	1	1	0	0
Curt Blefary, of	.077	4	13	0	1	0	0	0	0	2	3	0
Wally Bunker, p	.000	1	2	0	0	0	0	0	0	0	1	0
Moe Drabowsky, p	.000	1	2	0	0	0	0	0	0	1	1	0
Andy Etchebarren, c	.083	4	12	2	1	0	0	0	0	2	4	0
Davey Johnson, 2b	.286	4	14	1	4	1	0	0	1	0	1	0
Dave McNally, p	.000	2	3	0	0	0	0	0	0	0	1	0
Jim Palmer, p	.000	1	4	0	0	0	0	0	0	0	2	0
Boog Powell, 1b	.357	4	14	1	5	1	0	0	1	0	1	0
Brooks Robinson, 3b	.214	4	14	2	3	0	0	1	1	1	0	0
Frank Robinson, of	.286	4	14	4	4	0	1	2	3	2	3	0
Russ Snyder, of	.167	3	6	1	1	0	0	0	1	2	0	0
TOTAL	.200		120	13	24	3	1	4	10	11	17	0

PITCHER	W	L	ERA	G	GS	CG	SV	SHO	IP	H	ER	BB	SO
Wally Bunker	1	0	0.00	1	1	1	0	1	9.0	6	0	1	6
Moe Drabowsky	1	0	0.00	1	0	0	0	0	6.2	1	0	2	11
Dave McNally	1	0	1.59	2	2	1	0	1	11.1	6	2	7	5
Jim Palmer	1	0	0.00	1	1	1	0	1	9.0	4	0	3	6
TOTAL	4	0	0.50	5	4	3	0	3	36.0	17	2	13	28

LA (N)

PLAYER/POS	AVG	G	AB	R	H	2B	3B	HR	RB	BB	SO	SB
Jim Barbieri, ph	.000	1	1	0	0	0	0	0	0	0	1	0
Jim Brewer, p	.000	1	0	0	0	0	0	0	0	0	0	0
Wes Covington, ph	.000	1	1	0	0	0	0	0	0	0	1	0
Tommy Davis, of-3	.250	4	8	0	2	0	0	0	0	1	1	0
Willie Davis, of	.063	4	16	0	1	0	0	0	0	0	4	0
Don Drysdale, p	.000	2	2	0	0	0	0	0	0	0	1	0
Ron Fairly, of-2,1b-1	.143	3	7	0	1	0	0	0	0	2	4	0
Al Ferrara, ph	1.000	1	1	0	1	0	0	0	0	0	0	0
Jim Gilliam, 3b	.000	2	6	0	0	0	0	0	1	2	0	0
Lou Johnson, of	.267	4	15	1	4	1	0	0	0	1	1	0
John Kennedy, 3b	.200	2	5	0	1	0	0	0	0	0	0	0
Sandy Koufax, p	.000	1	2	0	0	0	0	0	0	0	0	0
Jim Lefebvre, 2b	.167	4	12	1	2	0	0	1	1	3	4	0
Bob Miller, p	.000	1	0	0	0	0	0	0	0	0	0	0
Joe Moeller, p	.000	1	0	0	0	0	0	0	0	0	0	0
Nate Oliver, pr	.000	1	0	0	0	0	0	0	0	0	0	0
Claude Osteen, p	.000	1	2	0	0	0	0	0	0	0	1	0
Wes Parker, 1b	.231	4	13	0	3	2	0	0	0	1	3	0
Ron Perranoski, p	.000	2	0	0	0	0	0	0	0	0	0	0
Phil Regan, p	.000	2	0	0	0	0	0	0	0	0	0	0
Johnny Roseboro, c	.071	4	14	0	1	0	0	0	0	0	3	0
Dick Stuart, ph	.000	2	2	0	0	0	0	0	0	0	1	0
Maury Wills, ss	.077	4	13	0	1	0	0	0	0	3	3	1
TOTAL	.142		120	2	17	3	0	1	2	13	28	1

PITCHER	W	L	ERA	G	GS	CG	SV	SHO	IP	H	ER	BB	SO
Jim Brewer	0	0	0.00	1	0	0	0	0	1.0	0	0	0	1
Don Drysdale	0	2	4.50	2	2	1	0	0	10.0	8	5	3	6
Sandy Koufax	0	1	1.50	1	1	0	0	0	6.0	6	1	2	2
Bob Miller	0	0	0.00	1	0	0	0	0	3.0	2	0	2	1
Joe Moeller	0	0	4.50	1	0	0	0	0	2.0	1	1	1	0
Claude Osteen	0	1	1.29	1	1	0	0	0	7.0	3	1	1	3
Ron Perranoski	0	0	5.40	2	0	0	0	0	3.1	4	2	1	2
Phil Regan	0	0	0.00	2	0	0	0	0	1.2	0	0	1	2
TOTAL	0	4	2.65	11	4	1	0	0	34.0	24	10	11	17

GAME 1 AT LA OCT 5

BAL	310 100 000	5	9	0
LA	011 000 000	2	3	0

Pitchers: McNally, DRABOWSKY (3) vs DRYSDALE, Moeller (3), Miller (5), Perranoski (8)
Home Runs: F.Robinson-BAL, B.Robinson-BAL, Lefebvre-LA
Attendance: 55,941

GAME 2 AT LA OCT 6

BAL	000 031 020	6	8	0
LA	000 000 000	0	4	6

Pitchers: PALMER vs KOUFAX, Perranoski (7), Regan (8), Brewer (9)
Attendance: 55,947

GAME 3 AT BAL OCT 8

LA	000 000 000	0	6	0
BAL	000 010 00X	1	3	0

Pitchers: OSTEEN, Regan (8) vs BUNKER
Home Runs: Blair-BAL
Attendance: 54,445

GAME 4 AT BAL OCT 9

LA	000 000 000	0	4	0
BAL	000 100 00X	1	4	0

Pitchers: DRYSDALE vs McNALLY
Home Runs: F.Robinson-BAL
Attendance: 54,458

The Cardinals cruised into the Series leading by 10½ games, whereas the Red Sox eked out their pennant over Minnesota and Detroit only by a dramatic win at season's end. The Sox continued to claw their way through six games of the Series before finally falling to superior pitching and hitting in the seventh game. Cardinals hurler Bob Gibson (who had missed a third of the season with a broken leg) edged Boston in the opener 2–1 with a six-hitter that included 10 strikeouts. The only run against him came on a solo homer by opposing pitcher Jose Santiago in the third that tied the game. But Santiago was undone when Lou Brock singled off him to open the seventh, then stole second, and moved around to score on a pair of ground outs.

Boston ace Jim Lonborg evened the Series the next day with a brilliant one-hit shutout. Triple Crown winner Carl Yastrzemski accounted for four of Boston's five runs with homers in the fourth and seventh innings. Cardinal Nelson Briles outlasted a succession of Boston pitchers for a go-ahead 5–2 win in Game 3, and Gibson, with a five-hit shutout in Game 4, put St. Louis up three games to one.

But Boston's Lonborg kept Red Sox hopes alive with another pitching gem—a three-hitter in which the only extra-base hit was Roger Maris' harmless home run in the last of the ninth, after the Sox had already scored three runs (two of them unearned). Boston's bats came alive as the Series moved to Boston for Game 6, and the Sox evened the Series with an 8–4 win. The Cards used eight pitchers in a futile effort to hold off the Boston assault. Boston's score would have been greater had not all four Boston homers (including three in the fourth inning by Yastrzemski, Reggie Smith, and Rico Petrocelli—his second of the game) been solo shots.

With the Series tied, the Series' two-game winners, Gibson and Lonborg, faced off in Game 7. It turned out to be no contest. Lonborg gave up 10 hits and seven runs (including a homer by pitcher Gibson in the fifth and a three-run blast by Julian Javier an inning later) in six innings. Four Boston relievers held the Cards scoreless the rest of the game, but it was too late. Gibson's three-hitter included 10 strikeouts and, as he had in 1964, Gibson walked off the mound a winner in the seventh game.

St. Louis Cardinals (NL), 4;
Boston Red Sox (AL), 3

STL (N)

PLAYER/POS	AVG	G	AB	R	H	2B	3B	HR	RB	BB	SO	SB
Eddie Bressoud, ss	.000	2	0	0	0	0	0	0	0	0	0	0
Nelson Briles, p	.000	2	3	0	0	0	0	0	0	0	0	0
Lou Brock, of	.414	7	29	8	12	2	1	1	3	2	3	7
Steve Carlton, p	.000	1	1	0	0	0	0	0	0	0	0	0
Orlando Cepeda, 1b	.103	7	29	1	3	2	0	0	1	0	4	0
Curt Flood, of	.179	7	28	2	5	1	0	0	3	3	3	0
Phil Gagliano, ph	.000	1	1	0	0	0	0	0	0	0	0	0
Bob Gibson, p	.091	3	11	1	1	0	0	1	1	1	2	0
Joe Hoerner, p	.000	2	0	0	0	0	0	0	0	0	0	0
Dick Hughes, p	.000	2	3	0	0	0	0	0	0	0	3	0
Larry Jaster, p	.000	1	0	0	0	0	0	0	0	0	0	0
Julian Javier, 2b	.360	7	25	2	9	3	0	1	4	0	6	0
Jack Lamabe, p	.000	3	0	0	0	0	0	0	0	0	0	0
Roger Maris, of	.385	7	26	3	10	1	0	1	7	3	1	0
Dal Maxvill, ss	.158	7	19	1	3	0	1	0	1	4	1	0
Tim McCarver, c	.125	7	24	3	3	1	0	0	2	2	2	0
Dave Ricketts, ph	.000	3	3	0	0	0	0	0	0	0	0	0
Mike Shannon, 3b	.208	7	24	3	5	1	0	1	2	1	4	0
Ed Spiezio, ph	.000	1	1	0	0	0	0	0	0	0	0	0
Bobby Tolan, ph	.000	3	2	1	0	0	0	0	0	1	1	0
Ray Washburn, p	.000	2	0	0	0	0	0	0	0	0	0	0
Ron Willis, p	.000	3	0	0	0	0	0	0	0	0	0	0
Hal Woodeshick, p	.000	1	0	0	0	0	0	0	0	0	0	0
TOTAL	.223		229	25	51	11	2	5	24	17	30	7

PITCHER	W	L	ERA	G	GS	CG	SV	SHO	IP	H	ER	BB	SO
Nelson Briles	1	0	1.64	2	1	1	0	0	11.0	7	2	1	4
Steve Carlton	0	1	0.00	1	1	0	0	0	6.0	3	0	2	5
Bob Gibson	3	0	1.00	3	3	3	0	1	27.0	14	3	5	26
Joe Hoerner	0	0	40.50	2	0	0	0	0	0.2	4	3	1	0
Dick Hughes	0	1	5.00	2	2	0	0	0	9.0	9	5	3	7
Larry Jaster	0	0	0.00	1	0	0	0	0	0.1	2	0	0	0
Jack Lamabe	0	1	6.75	3	0	0	0	0	2.2	5	2	0	4
Ray Washburn	0	0	0.00	2	0	0	0	0	2.1	1	0	1	2
Ron Willis	0	0	27.00	3	0	0	0	0	1.0	2	3	4	1
Hal Woodeshick	0	0	0.00	1	0	0	0	0	1.0	1	0	0	0
TOTAL	4	3	2.66	20	7	4	0	1	61.0	48	18	17	49

BOS (A)

PLAYER/POS	AVG	G	AB	R	H	2B	3B	HR	RB	BB	SO	SB
Jerry Adair, 2b-4	.125	5	16	0	2	0	0	0	1	0	3	1
Mike Andrews, 2b-3	.308	5	13	2	4	0	0	0	1	0	1	0
Gary Bell, p	.000	3	0	0	0	0	0	0	0	0	0	0
Ken Brett, p	.000	2	0	0	0	0	0	0	0	0	0	0
Joe Foy, 3b-3	.133	6	15	2	2	1	0	0	1	1	5	0
Russ Gibson, c	.000	2	2	0	0	0	0	0	0	0	2	0
Ken Harrelson, of	.077	4	13	0	1	0	0	0	1	1	3	0
Elston Howard, c	.111	7	18	0	2	0	0	0	1	1	2	0
Dalton Jones, 3b-4	.389	6	18	2	7	0	0	0	1	1	3	0
Jim Lonborg, p	.000	3	9	0	0	0	0	0	0	0	7	0
Dave Morehead, p	.000	2	0	0	0	0	0	0	0	0	0	0
Dan Osinski, p	.000	2	0	0	0	0	0	0	0	0	0	0
Rico Petrocelli, ss	.200	7	20	3	4	1	0	2	3	3	8	0
Mike Ryan, c	.000	1	2	0	0	0	0	0	0	0	1	0
Jose Santiago, p	.500	3	2	1	1	0	0	1	1	0	1	0
George Scott, 1b	.231	7	26	3	6	1	1	0	0	3	6	0
Norm Siebern, of-1	.333	3	3	0	1	0	0	0	1	0	0	0
Reggie Smith, of	.250	7	24	3	6	1	0	2	3	2	2	0
Lee Stange, p	.000	1	0	0	0	0	0	0	0	0	0	0
Jerry Stephenson, p	.000	1	0	0	0	0	0	0	0	0	0	0
Jose Tartabull, of-6	.154	7	13	1	2	0	0	0	0	1	2	0
George Thomas, of-1	.000	2	2	0	0	0	0	0	0	0	1	0
Gary Waslewski, p	.000	2	1	0	0	0	0	0	0	0	1	0
John Wyatt, p	.000	2	0	0	0	0	0	0	0	0	0	0
Carl Yastrzemski, of	.400	7	25	4	10	2	0	3	5	4	1	0
TOTAL	.216		222	21	48	6	1	8	19	17	49	1

PITCHER	W	L	ERA	G	GS	CG	SV	SHO	IP	H	ER	BB	SO
Gary Bell	0	1	5.06	3	1	0	0	0	5.1	8	3	1	1
Ken Brett	0	0	0.00	2	0	0	0	0	1.1	0	0	1	1
Jim Lonborg	2	1	2.63	3	3	2	0	1	24.0	14	7	2	11
Dave Morehead	0	0	0.00	2	0	0	0	0	3.1	0	0	4	3
Dan Osinski	0	0	6.75	2	0	0	0	0	1.1	2	1	0	0
Jose Santiago	0	2	5.59	3	2	0	0	0	9.2	16	6	3	6
Lee Stange	0	0	0.00	1	0	0	0	0	2.0	3	0	0	0
Jerry Stephenson	0	0	9.00	1	0	0	0	0	2.0	3	2	1	0
Gary Waslewski	0	0	2.16	2	1	0	0	0	8.1	4	2	2	7
John Wyatt	1	0	4.91	2	0	0	0	0	3.2	1	2	3	1
TOTAL	3	4	3.39	21	7	2	1	1	61.0	51	23	17	30

GAME 1 AT BOS OCT 4

STL	001 000 100	2	10	0
BOS	001 000 000	1	6	0

Pitchers: GIBSON vs SANTIAGO, Wyatt (8)
Home Runs: Santiago-BOS
Attendance: 34,796

GAME 2 AT BOS OCT 5

STL	000 000 000	0	1	1
BOS	000 101 30X	5	9	0

Pitchers: HUGHES, Willis (6), Hoerner (7), Lamabe (7) vs LONBORG
Home Runs: Yastrzemski-BOS (2)
Attendance: 35,188

GAME 3 AT STL OCT 7

BOS	000 001 100	2	7	1
STL	120 001 01X	5	10	0

Pitchers: BELL, Waslewski (3), Stange (6), Osinski (8) vs BRILES
Home Runs: Shannon-STL, Smith-BOS
Attendance: 54,575

GAME 4 AT STL OCT 8

BOS	000 000 000	0	5	0
STL	402 000 00X	6	9	0

Pitchers: SANTIAGO, Bell (1), Stephenson (3), Morehead (5), Brett (8) vs GIBSON
Attendance: 54,575

GAME 5 AT STL OCT 9

BOS	001 000 002	3	6	1
STL	000 000 001	1	3	2

Pitchers: LONBORG vs CARLTON, Washburn (7), Willis (9), Lamabe (9)
Home Runs: Maris-STL
Attendance: 54,575

GAME 6 AT BOS OCT 11

STL	002 000 200	4	8	0
BOS	010 300 40X	8	12	1

Pitchers: Hughes, Willis (4), Briles (5), LAMABE (7), Hoerner (7), Jaster (7), Washburn (7), Woodeshick (8) vs Waslewski, WYATT (6), Bell (8)
Home Runs: Petrocelli-BOS (2), Yastrzemski-BOS, Smith-BOS, Brock-STL
Attendance: 35,188

GAME 7 AT BOS OCT 12

STL	002 023 000	7	10	1
BOS	000 010 010	2	3	1

Pitchers: GIBSON vs LONBORG, Santiago (7), Morehead (9), Osinski (9), Brett (9)
Home Runs: Gibson-STL, Javier-STL
Attendance: 35,188

In this "year of the pitcher," Tiger Denny McLain's 31 wins were the most for a major leaguer in thirty-seven years. Cardinal Bob Gibson's 1.12 ERA was the majors' best since Dutch Leonard's 1.01 in 1914, and his 13 season shutouts tied for third best of all time. In the Series, though, it was Detroit's second-best pitcher—Mickey Lolich—who emerged as the hero.

McLain came off second-best against Gibson in the opener. He yielded only three hits in his five innings, but two singles in the fourth combined with a pair of walks and a Tigers error for three runs. Gibson, meanwhile, was in the process of striking out a Series-record 17 batters on the way to a five-hit shutout. But Lolich brought Detroit back in Game 2. He struck out nine, and his third-inning home run (the only one of his major league career) for the second run provided all the scoring needed for a Detroit victory, although the Tigers kept putting runs across for an eventual 8–1 win.

Home runs accounted for most of the scoring in Game 3. Veteran Al Kaline's two-run shot in the third opened the scoring, but Tim McCarver's three-run blast in the fifth put St. Louis ahead. Dick McAuliffe's solo shot later in the inning brought Detroit within one run of a tie, but the Cardinals put the game away on Orlando Cepeda's three-run homer in the seventh.

McLain faced Gibson again in Game 4, and again came off second-best. Lou Brock led off the game with a home run, and before the end of the third inning McLain was gone. Gibson gave up a solo homer to Jim Northrup in the fourth, but that was the only Detroit run he allowed. Gibson homered himself and struck out ten in an easy 10–1 win.

Down three games to one, the Tigers were saved from elimination by Lolich's arm. Although three hits in the top of the first (including Orlando Cepeda's second homer of the Series) gave St. Louis a quick three runs, Lolich held the Cards scoreless the rest of the game as his Tigers fought back with two runs in the fourth and three more in the seventh (with a rally started by Lolich's single). McLain finally came through in Game 6, evening the Series with an easy 13–1 victory, in which Jim Northrup's grand slam provided the big blow of a 10-run third inning.

Lolich and Gibson—both 2–0 in the Series—faced off in the finale. Gibson broke his own World Series strikeout record in the third inning (finishing with 8 for the game and 35 for the Series), and both pitchers hurled shutout ball through six innings. But four two-out Tigers

Detroit Tigers (AL), 4; St. Louis Cardinals (NL), 3

DET (A)

PLAYER/POS	AVG	G	AB	R	H	2B	3B	HR	RB	BB	SO	SB
Gates Brown, ph	.000	1	1	0	0	0	0	0	0	0	0	0
Norm Cash, 1b	.385	7	26	5	10	0	0	1	5	3	5	0
Wayne Comer, ph	1.000	1	1	0	1	0	0	0	0	0	0	0
Pat Dobson, p	.000	3	0	0	0	0	0	0	0	0	0	0
Bill Freehan, c	.083	7	24	0	2	1	0	0	2	4	8	0
John Hiller, p	.000	2	0	0	0	0	0	0	0	0	0	0
Willie Horton, of	.304	7	23	6	7	1	1	1	3	5	6	0
Al Kaline, of	.379	7	29	6	11	2	0	2	8	0	7	0
Fred Lasher, p	.000	1	0	0	0	0	0	0	0	0	0	0
Mickey Lolich, p	.250	3	12	2	3	0	0	1	2	1	5	0
Tom Matchick, ph	.000	3	3	0	0	0	0	0	0	0	0	0
Eddie Mathews, 3b-1	.333	2	3	0	1	0	0	0	0	1	1	0
Dick McAuliffe, 2b	.222	7	27	5	6	0	0	1	3	4	6	0
Denny McLain, p	.000	3	6	0	0	0	0	0	0	0	4	0
Don McMahon, p	.000	2	0	0	0	0	0	0	0	0	0	0
Jim Northrup, of	.250	7	28	4	7	0	1	2	8	1	5	0
Ray Oyler, ss	.000	4	0	0	0	0	0	0	0	0	0	0
Daryl Patterson, p	.000	2	0	0	0	0	0	0	0	0	0	0
Jim Price, ph	.000	2	2	0	0	0	0	0	0	0	1	0
Joe Sparma, p	.000	1	0	0	0	0	0	0	0	0	0	0
Mickey Stanley, ss-7,of-4	.214	7	28	4	6	0	1	0	0	2	4	0
Dick Tracewski, 3b-1	.000	2	0	1	0	0	0	0	0	0	0	0
Don Wert, 3b	.118	6	17	1	2	0	0	0	2	6	5	0
Earl Wilson, p	.000	1	1	0	0	0	0	0	0	0	1	0
TOTAL	.242		231	34	56	4	3	8	33	27	59	0

PITCHER	W	L	ERA	G	GS	CG	SV	SHO	IP	H	ER	BB	SO
Pat Dobson	0	0	3.86	3	0	0	0	0	4.2	5	2	1	0
John Hiller	0	0	13.50	2	0	0	0	0	2.0	6	3	3	1
Fred Lasher	0	0	0.00	1	0	0	0	0	2.0	1	0	0	1
Mickey Lolich	3	0	1.67	3	3	3	0	0	27.0	20	5	6	21
Denny McLain	1	2	3.24	3	3	1	0	0	16.2	18	6	4	13
Don McMahon	0	0	13.50	2	0	0	0	0	2.0	4	3	0	1
Daryl Patterson	0	0	0.00	2	0	0	0	0	3.0	1	0	1	0
Joe Sparma	0	0	54.00	1	0	0	0	0	0.1	2	2	0	0
Earl Wilson	0	1	6.23	1	1	0	0	0	4.1	4	3	6	3
TOTAL	4	3	3.48	18	7	4	0	0	62.0	61	24	21	40

STL (N)

PLAYER/POS	AVG	G	AB	R	H	2B	3B	HR	RB	BB	SO	SB
Nelson Briles, p	.000	2	0	0	0	0	0	0	0	0	4	0
Lou Brock, of	.464	7	28	6	13	3	1	2	5	3	4	7
Steve Carlton, p	.000	2	0	0	0	0	0	0	0	0	0	0
Orlando Cepeda, 1b	.250	7	28	2	7	0	0	2	6	2	3	0
Ron Davis, of	.000	2	7	0	0	0	0	0	0	0	2	0
Johnny Edwards, ph	.000	1	1	0	0	0	0	0	0	0	1	0
Curt Flood, of	.286	7	28	4	8	1	0	0	2	2	2	3
Phil Gagliano, ph	.000	3	3	0	0	0	0	0	0	0	0	0
Bob Gibson, p	.125	3	8	2	1	0	0	1	2	1	2	0
Wayne Granger, p	.000	1	0	0	0	0	0	0	0	0	0	0
Joe Hoerner, p	.500	3	2	0	1	0	0	0	0	0	1	0
Dick Hughes, p	.000	1	0	0	0	0	0	0	0	0	0	0
Larry Jaster, p	.000	1	0	0	0	0	0	0	0	0	0	0
Julian Javier, 2b	.333	7	27	1	9	1	0	0	3	3	4	1
Roger Maris, of-5	.158	6	19	5	3	1	0	0	1	3	3	0
Dal Maxvill, ss	.000	7	22	1	0	0	0	0	0	4	3	0
Tim McCarver, c	.333	7	27	3	9	0	2	1	4	3	2	0
Mel Nelson, p	.000	1	0	0	0	0	0	0	0	0	0	0
Dave Ricketts, ph	1.000	1	1	0	1	0	0	0	0	0	0	0
Dick Schofield, ss-1	.000	2	2	0	0	0	0	0	0	0	0	0
Mike Shannon, 3b	.276	7	29	3	8	1	0	1	4	1	5	0
Ed Spiezio, ph	1.000	1	1	0	1	0	0	0	0	0	0	0
Bobby Tolan, ph	.000	1	1	0	0	0	0	0	0	0	1	0
Ray Washburn, p	.000	2	3	0	0	0	0	0	0	0	0	0
Ron Willis, p	.000	3	0	0	0	0	0	0	0	0	0	0
TOTAL	.255		239	27	61	7	3	7	27	21	40	11

PITCHER	W	L	ERA	G	GS	CG	SV	SHO	IP	H	ER	BB	SO
Nelson Briles	0	1	5.56	2	2	0	0	0	11.1	13	7	4	7
Steve Carlton	0	0	6.75	2	0	0	0	0	4.0	7	3	1	3
Bob Gibson	2	1	1.67	3	3	3	0	1	27.0	18	5	4	35
Wayne Granger	0	0	0.00	1	0	0	0	0	2.0	0	0	1	1
Joe Hoerner	0	1	3.86	3	0	0	1	0	4.2	5	2	5	3
Dick Hughes	0	0	0.00	1	0	0	0	0	0.1	0	0	0	0
Larry Jaster	0	0	∞	1	0	0	0	0	0.0	2	3	1	0
Mel Nelson	0	0	0.00	1	0	0	0	0	1.0	0	0	1	0
Ray Washburn	1	1	9.82	2	2	0	0	0	7.1	8	8	7	6
Ron Willis	0	0	8.31	5	0	0	0	0	4.1	2	4	4	3
TOTAL	3	4	4.65	19	7	3	1	1	62.0	56	32	27	59

hits in the top of the seventh—including a misplayed flyball in center field—put three runs on the board, and another run in the ninth made the score 4–0. In the last of the ninth, Mike Shannon's solo homer spoiled Lolich's shutout, but not his third Series win—or the Tigers' comeback world title.

GAME 1 AT STL OCT 2

DET	000	000	000	0	5	3
STL	000	300	10X	4	6	0

Pitchers: McLAIN, Dobson (6), McMahon (8) vs GIBSON
Home Runs: Brock-STL
Attendance: 54,692

GAME 2 AT STL OCT 3

DET	011	003	102	8	13	1
STL	000	001	000	1	6	1

Pitchers: LOLICH vs BRILES, Carlton (6), Willis (7), Hoerner (9)
Home Runs: Horton-DET, Lolich-DET, Cash-DET
Attendance: 54,692

GAME 3 AT DET OCT 5

STL	000	040	300	7	13	0
DET	002	010	000	3	4	0

Pitchers: WASHBURN, Hoerner (6) vs WILSON, Dobson (5), McMahon (6), Patterson (7), Hiller (8)
Home Runs: Kaline-DET, McCarver-STL, McAuliffe-DET, Cepeda-STL
Attendance: 53,634

GAME 4 AT DET OCT 6

STL	202	200	040	10	13	0
DET	000	100	000	1	5	4

Pitchers: GIBSON vs McLAIN, Sparma (3), Patterson (4), Lasher (6), Hiller (8), Dobson (8)
Home Runs: Brock-STL, Gibson-STL, Northrup-DET
Attendance: 53,634

GAME 5 AT DET OCT 7

STL	300	000	000	3	9	0
DET	000	200	30X	5	9	1

Pitchers: Briles, HOERNER (7), Willis (7) vs LOLICH
Home Runs: Cepeda-STL
Attendance: 53,634

GAME 6 AT STL OCT 9

DET	021	010	000	13	12	1
STL	000	000	001	1	9	1

Pitchers: McLAIN vs WASHBURN, Jaster (3), Willis (3), Hughes (3), Carlton (4), Granger (7), Nelson (9)
Home Runs: Northrup-DET, Kaline-DET
Attendance: 54,692

GAME 7 AT STL OCT 10

DET	000	000	301	4	8	1
STL	000	000	001	1	5	0

Pitchers: LOLICH vs GIBSON
Home Runs: Shannon-STL
Attendance: 54,692

Atlanta's Hank Aaron homered in each game and drove in a series-high seven runs. But the "Miracle Mets" as a team outhomered the Braves six to five, outhit them by 72 percentage points, and scored nearly twice as many runs.

Twice in the first game the Braves came from behind to lead by a run, but in the top of the eighth, five New York hits and poor Atlanta fielding buried starter Phil Niekro under five runs. In Game 2, home runs by Tommie Agee and Ken Boswell helped New York take an early 8–0 lead that even Aaron's three-run homer in the fifth couldn't threaten.

In the third game the lead changed hands three times on home runs. Aaron began the barrage with a two-run shot in the first inning. Agee's homer in the third followed by Boswell's for two runs in the fourth put the Mets ahead— until Orlando Cepeda's two-run homer in the fifth gave Atlanta another lead. But in the bottom of the fifth, Mets rookie Wayne Garrett's two-run blast reversed the lead one last time and, after four final shutout innings by 22-year-old reliever Nolan Ryan, the Mets had swept to their first pennant.

New York Mets (East), 3;
Atlanta Braves (West), 0

NY (E)

PLAYER/POS	AVG	G	AB	R	H	2B	3B	HR	RB	BB	SO	SB
Tommie Agee, of	.357	3	14	4	5	1	0	2	4	2	5	2
Ken Boswell, 2b	.333	3	12	4	4	0	0	2	5	1	2	0
Wayne Garrett, 3b	.385	3	13	3	5	2	0	1	3	2	2	1
Rod Gaspar, of	.000	3	0	0	0	0	0	0	0	0	0	0
Gary Gentry, p	.000	1	0	0	0	0	0	0	0	0	0	0
Jerry Grote, c	.167	3	12	3	2	1	0	0	1	1	4	0
Bud Harrelson, ss	.182	3	11	2	2	1	1	0	3	1	2	0
Cleon Jones, of	.429	3	14	4	6	2	0	1	4	1	2	2
Jerry Koosman, p	.000	1	2	1	0	0	0	0	0	1	2	0
Ed Kranepool, 1b	.250	3	12	2	3	1	0	0	1	1	2	0
J. C. Martin, ph	.500	2	2	0	1	0	0	0	2	0	0	0
Tug McGraw, p	.000	1	0	0	0	0	0	0	0	0	0	0
Nolan Ryan, p	.500	1	4	1	2	0	0	0	0	0	1	0
Tom Seaver, p	.000	1	3	0	0	0	0	0	0	0	0	0
Art Shamsky, of	.538	3	13	3	7	0	0	0	1	0	3	0
Ron Taylor, p	.000	2	0	0	0	0	0	0	0	0	0	0
Al Weis, 2b	.000	3	1	0	0	0	0	0	0	0	0	0
TOTAL	.327		113	27	37	8	1	6	24	10	25	5

PITCHER	W	L	ERA	G	GS	CG	SV	SHO	IP	H	ER	BB	SO
Gary Gentry	0	0	9.00	1	1	0	0	0	2.0	5	2	1	1
Jerry Koosman	0	0	11.57	1	1	0	0	0	4.2	7	6	4	5
Tug McGraw	0	0	0.00	1	0	0	1	0	3.0	1	0	1	1
Nolan Ryan	1	0	2.57	1	0	0	0	0	7.0	3	2	2	7
Tom Seaver	1	0	6.43	1	1	0	0	0	7.0	8	5	3	2
Ron Taylor	1	0	0.00	2	0	0	1	0	3.1	3	0	0	4
TOTAL	3	0	5.00	7	3	0	2	0	27.0	27	15	11	20

ATL (W)

PLAYER/POS	AVG	G	AB	R	H	2B	3B	HR	RB	BB	SO	SB
Hank Aaron, of	.357	3	14	3	5	2	0	3	7	0	1	0
Tommie Aaron, ph	.000	1	1	0	0	0	0	0	0	0	0	0
Felipe Alou, ph	.000	1	1	0	0	0	0	0	0	0	0	0
Bob Aspromonte, ph	.000	3	3	0	0	0	0	0	0	0	0	0
Clete Boyer, 3b	.111	3	9	0	1	0	0	0	3	2	3	0
Jim Britton, p	.000	1	0	0	0	0	0	0	0	0	0	0
Rico Carty, of	.300	3	10	4	3	2	0	0	3	1	0
Orlando Cepeda, 1b	.455	3	11	2	5	2	0	1	3	1	2	1
Bob Didier, c	.000	3	11	0	0	0	0	0	0	0	2	0
Paul Doyle, p	.000	1	0	0	0	0	0	0	0	0	0	0
Gil Garrido, ss	.200	3	10	0	2	0	0	0	0	1	1	0
Tony Gonzalez, of	.357	3	14	4	5	1	0	1	2	1	4	0
Sonny Jackson, ss	.000	1	0	0	0	0	0	0	0	0	0	0
Pat Jarvis, p	.000	1	2	0	0	0	0	0	0	0	2	0
Mike Lum, of-1	1.000	2	2	0	2	1	0	0	0	0	0	0
Felix Millan, 2b	.333	3	12	2	4	1	0	0	0	3	0	0
Gary Neibauer, p	.000	1	0	0	0	0	0	0	0	0	0	0
Phil Niekro, p	.000	1	3	0	0	0	0	0	0	0	1	0
Milt Pappas, p	.000	1	1	0	0	0	0	0	0	0	1	0
Ron Reed, p	.000	1	0	0	0	0	0	0	0	0	0	0
George Stone, p	.000	1	1	0	0	0	0	0	0	0	1	0
Bob Tillman, c	.000	1	0	0	0	0	0	0	0	0	0	0
Cecil Upshaw, p	.000	3	1	0	0	0	0	0	0	0	1	0
TOTAL	.255		106	15	27	9	0	5	15	11	20	1

PITCHER	W	L	ERA	G	GS	CG	SV	SHO	IP	H	ER	BB	SO
Jim Britton	0	0	0.00	1	0	0	0	0	0.1	0	0	1	0
Paul Doyle	0	0	0.00	1	0	0	0	0	1.0	2	0	1	3
Pat Jarvis	0	1	12.46	1	1	0	0	0	4.1	10	6	0	6
Gary Neibauer	0	0	0.00	1	0	0	0	0	1.0	0	0	0	1
Phil Niekro	0	1	4.50	1	1	0	0	0	8.0	9	4	4	4
Milt Pappas	0	0	11.57	1	0	0	0	0	2.1	4	3	0	4
Ron Reed	0	1	21.60	1	1	0	0	0	1.2	5	4	3	3
George Stone	0	0	9.00	1	0	0	0	0	1.0	2	1	0	0
Cecil Upshaw	0	0	2.84	3	0	0	0	0	6.1	5	2	1	4
TOTAL	0	3	6.92	11	3	0	0	0	26.0	37	20	10	25

GAME 1 AT ATL OCT 4

NY	020	200	050	9 10 1
ATL	012	010	100	5 10 2

Pitchers: SEAVER, Taylor (8) vs NIEKRO, Upshaw (9)
Home Runs: Gonzalez-ATL, H.Aaron-ATL
Attendance: 50,122

GAME 2 AT ATL OCT 5

NY	132	210	200	11 13 1
ATL	000	150	000	6 9 3

Pitchers: Koosman, TAYLOR (5), McGraw (7) vs REED, Doyle (2), Pappas (3), Britton (6), Upshaw (6), Neibauer (9)
Home Runs: Agee-NY, Boswell-NY, H.Aaron-ATL, Jones-NY
Attendance: 50,270

GAME 3 AT NY OCT 6

ATL	200	020	000	4 8 1
NY	001	231	00X	7 14 0

Pitchers: JARVIS, Stone (5), Upshaw (6) vs Gentry, RYAN (3)
Home Runs: H.Aaron-ATL, Agee-NY, Boswell-NY, Cepeda-ATL, Garrett-NY
Attendance: 53,195

Minnesota led the league in batting, Baltimore in pitching. In the ALCS, pitching prevailed as the Twins were held to a series batting average 113 points below their season mark.

Still, Minnesota nearly won the first game with three runs on only four hits. But the Orioles tied the score on Boog Powell's homer in the bottom of the ninth and won the game three innings later on Paul Blair's suicide squeeze bunt with two away. In Game 2, Minnesota's Dave Boswell scattered seven Baltimore hits over 10⅔ scoreless innings before giving way to Ron Perranoski in the 11th. But Orioles pitcher Dave McNally was more than a match for Boswell. He gave up only three hits—none in the final 7⅔ innings of the 11 he pitched—and took the win when Baltimore pinch hitter Curt Motton lined a single off Perranoski to score Powell from second with the game's only run.

In the third game, the Twins fell apart as the Orioles battered seven Minnesota pitchers for 18 hits. Baltimore's Jim Palmer gave up more than a hit an inning himself, but coasted to the pennant 11–2.

Baltimore Orioles (East), 3;
Minnesota Twins (West), 0

BAL (E)

PLAYER/POS	AVG	G	AB	R	H	2B	3B	HR	RB	BB	SO	SB
Mark Belanger, ss	.267	3	15	4	4	0	1	1	1	1	0	0
Paul Blair, of	.400	3	15	1	6	2	0	1	6	2	2	0
Don Buford, of	.286	3	14	3	4	1	0	0	1	3	0	0
Mike Cuellar, p	.000	1	2	0	0	0	0	0	0	0	1	0
Andy Etchebarren, c	.000	2	4	0	0	0	0	0	0	0	0	0
Dick Hall, p	.000	1	0	0	0	0	0	0	0	0	0	0
Elrod Hendricks, c	.250	3	8	2	2	2	0	0	3	1	2	0
Davey Johnson, 2b	.231	3	13	2	3	0	0	0	0	2	1	0
Marcelino Lopez, p	.000	1	0	0	0	0	0	0	0	0	0	0
Dave May, ph	.000	1	1	0	0	0	0	0	0	0	0	0
Dave McNally, p	.000	1	4	0	0	0	0	0	0	0	2	0
Curt Motton, ph	.500	2	2	0	1	0	0	0	1	0	0	0
Jim Palmer, p	.000	1	5	0	0	0	0	0	0	0	3	0
Boog Powell, 1b	.385	3	13	2	5	0	0	1	1	2	0	0
Merv Rettenmund, ph	.000	1	0	0	0	0	0	0	0	0	0	0
Pete Richert, p	.000	1	0	0	0	0	0	0	0	0	0	0
Brooks Robinson, 3b	.500	3	14	1	7	1	0	0	0	0	0	0
Frank Robinson, of	.333	3	12	1	4	2	0	1	2	3	3	0
Chico Salmon, ph	.000	1	1	0	0	0	0	0	0	0	0	0
Eddie Watt, p	.000	1	0	0	0	0	0	0	0	0	0	0
TOTAL	.293		123	16	36	8	1	4	15	13	14	0

PITCHER	W	L	ERA	G	GS	CG	SV	SHO	IP	H	ER	BB	SO
Mike Cuellar	0	0	2.25	1	1	0	0	0	8.0	3	2	1	7
Dick Hall	1	0	0.00	1	0	0	0	0	0.2	0	0	0	1
Marcelino Lopez	0	0	0.00	1	0	0	0	0	0.1	1	0	2	0
Dave McNally	1	0	0.00	1	1	1	0	1	11.0	3	0	5	11
Jim Palmer	1	0	2.00	1	1	1	0	0	9.0	10	2	4	4
Pete Richert	0	0	0.00	1	0	0	0	0	1.0	0	0	2	0
Eddie Watt	0	0	0.00	1	0	0	0	0	2.0	0	0	0	2
TOTAL	3	0	1.13	7	3	2	0	1	32.0	17	4	12	27

MIN (W)

PLAYER/POS	AVG	G	AB	R	H	2B	3B	HR	RB	BB	SO	SB
Bob Allison, of	.000	2	8	0	0	0	0	0	0	1	0	0
Dave Boswell, p	.000	1	4	0	0	0	0	0	0	0	4	0
Leo Cardenas, ss	.154	3	13	0	2	0	1	0	0	0	7	0
Rod Carew, 2b	.071	3	14	0	1	0	0	0	0	1	4	0
Dean Chance, p	.000	1	0	0	0	0	0	0	0	0	0	0
Joe Grzenda, p	.000	1	0	0	0	0	0	0	0	0	0	0
Tom Hall, p	.000	1	0	0	0	0	0	0	0	0	0	0
Harmon Killebrew, 3b	.125	3	8	2	1	1	0	0	0	6	2	0
Chuck Manuel, ph	.000	1	0	0	0	0	0	0	0	1	0	0
Bob Miller, p	.000	1	0	0	0	0	0	0	0	0	0	0
George Mitterwald, c	.143	2	7	0	1	0	0	0	0	1	3	0
Graig Nettles, ph	1.000	1	1	0	1	0	0	0	0	0	0	0
Tony Oliva, of	.385	3	13	3	5	0	0	1	2	1	3	1
Ron Perranoski, p	.000	3	1	0	0	0	0	0	0	0	1	0
Jim Perry, p	.000	1	3	0	0	0	0	0	0	0	0	0
Rich Reese, 1b	.167	3	12	0	2	0	0	0	2	1	1	0
Rich Renick, ph	.000	1	1	0	0	0	0	0	0	0	0	0
John Roseboro, c	.200	2	5	0	1	0	0	0	0	0	0	0
Cesar Tovar, of	.077	3	13	0	1	0	0	0	0	0	2	1
Ted Uhlaender, of	.167	2	6	0	1	0	0	0	0	0	0	0
Dick Woodson, p	1.000	1	1	0	1	0	0	0	0	0	0	0
Al Worthington, p	.000	1	0	0	0	0	0	0	0	0	0	0
TOTAL	.155		110	5	17	3	1	1	5	12	27	2

PITCHER	W	L	ERA	G	GS	CG	SV	SHO	IP	H	ER	BB	SO
Dave Boswell	0	1	0.84	1	1	0	0	0	10.2	7	1	7	4
Dean Chance	0	0	13.50	1	0	0	0	0	2.0	4	3	0	2
Joe Grzenda	0	0	0.00	1	0	0	0	0	0.2	0	0	0	0
Tom Hall	0	0	0.00	1	0	0	0	0	0.2	0	0	1	0
Bob Miller	0	1	5.40	1	1	0	0	0	1.2	5	1	0	0
Ron Perranoski	0	1	5.79	3	0	0	0	0	4.2	8	3	0	2
Jim Perry	0	0	3.38	1	1	0	0	0	8.0	6	3	3	3
Dick Woodson	0	0	10.80	1	0	0	0	0	1.2	3	2	3	2
Al Worthington	0	0	6.75	1	0	0	0	0	1.1	3	1	0	1
TOTAL	0	3	4.02	11	3	0	0	0	31.1	36	14	13	14

GAME 1 AT BAL OCT 4

MIN	000	010	200	000	3	4	2
BAL	000	110	001	001	4	10	1

Pitchers: Perry, PERRANOSKI (9) vs Cuellar, Richert (9), Watt (10), Lopez (12), HALL (12)
Home Runs: F.Robinson-BAL, Belanger-BAL, Oliva-MIN, Powell-BAL
Attendance: 39,324

GAME 2 AT BAL OCT 5

MIN	000	000	000	00	0	3	1
BAL	000	000	000	01	1	8	0

Pitchers: BOSWELL, Perranoski (11) vs McNALLY
Attendance: 41,704

GAME 3 AT MIN OCT 6

BAL	030	201	023	11	18	0
MIN	100	010	000	2	10	2

Pitchers: PALMER vs MILLER, Woodson (2), Hall (4), Worthington (5), Grzenda (6), Chance (7), Perranoski (9)
Home Runs: Blair-BAL
Attendance: 32,735

The heavy-hitting, slick-fielding Orioles, who also boasted the majors' top pitching staff, entered the Series clear favorites against the upstart Mets. But the "Miracle Mets," after losing the opener, polished off Baltimore with four straight wins.

Tom Seaver (25–7) and Mike Cuellar (23–11) faced each other in the opener. Baltimore's leadoff batter, Don Buford, greeted Seaver with a home run, and a three-run rally with two out in the fourth made the score 4–0 before the Mets scored their first Series run in the seventh. Cuellar held New York to that one run for the victory.

No one scored for three innings of Game 2 off Oriole Dave McNally or even hit Met Jerry Koosman safely. But Donn Clendenon led off the fourth with a home run for the Mets as Koosman continued to no-hit Baltimore for three more innings. In the seventh, though, Baltimore's Paul Blair spoiled Koosman's no-hitter with a leadoff single, and after stealing second, scored the tying run on Brooks Robinson's single. But those were the only hits the O's would get, and in the top of the ninth three successive two-out singles produced what proved to be the winning run.

Mets pitchers Gary Gentry and Nolan Ryan (with the assist of two spectacular catches by center fielder Tommie Agee that saved a total of five runs) combined for a shutout in Game 3. Agee's leadoff homer against Jim Palmer in the first was all the scoring the Mets would need, but they added four more runs before the game ended. Game 4 was the Series' tightest. Seaver went the distance for the win, holding a 1–0 lead until a sacrifice fly scored the tying Baltimore run in the top of the ninth (Ron Swoboda's diving catch kept it from being an extra base hit). In the bottom of the 10th, the Mets finally won it as a bunt thrown to first hit the runner and bounded away, allowing pinch runner Rod Gaspar to score all the way from second.

Dave McNally and Jerry Koosman tangled a second time in Game 5, and again Koosman and the Mets emerged victorious. McNally's two-run homer in the third gave him a lead which Frank Robinson expanded with a solo shot. But in an eerie sixth inning reprise of Game 4 of the 1957 World Series featuring Nippy Jones, the Mets' Cleon Jones was struck by a pitch on the foot and awarded first base after inspection by the home plate umpire revealed tell-tale shoe polish on the ball. And just like Nippy Jones 12 years earlier, Cleon Jones scored a key run on Donn Clendenon's home run which followed immediately.

New York Mets (NL), 4; Baltimore Orioles (AL), 1

NY (N)

PLAYER/POS	AVG	G	AB	R	H	2B	3B	HR	RB	BB	SO	SB
Tommie Agee, of	.167	5	18	1	3	0	0	1	1	2	5	1
Ken Boswell, 2b	.333	1	3	1	1	0	0	0	0	0	0	0
Don Cardwell, p	.000	1	0	0	0	0	0	0	0	0	0	0
Ed Charles, 3b	.133	4	15	1	2	1	0	0	0	0	2	0
Donn Clendenon, 1b	.357	4	14	4	5	1	0	3	4	2	6	0
Duffy Dyer, ph	.000	1	1	0	0	0	0	0	0	0	0	0
Wayne Garrett, 3b	.000	2	1	0	0	0	0	0	0	2	1	0
Rod Gaspar, of-1	.000	3	2	1	0	0	0	0	0	0	0	0
Gary Gentry, p	.333	1	3	0	1	1	0	0	2	0	2	0
Jerry Grote, c	.211	5	19	1	4	2	0	0	1	1	3	0
Bud Harrelson, ss	.176	5	17	1	3	0	0	0	0	3	4	0
Cleon Jones, of	.158	5	19	2	3	1	0	0	0	0	1	0
Jerry Koosman, p	.143	2	7	0	1	1	0	0	0	0	4	0
Ed Kranepool, 1b	.250	1	4	1	1	0	0	1	1	0	0	0
J.C. Martin, ph	.000	1	0	0	0	0	0	0	0	0	0	0
Nolan Ryan, p	.000	1	0	0	0	0	0	0	0	0	0	0
Tom Seaver, p	.000	2	4	0	0	0	0	0	0	0	2	0
Art Shamsky, of-1	.000	3	6	0	0	0	0	0	0	0	0	0
Ron Swoboda, of	.400	4	15	1	6	1	0	0	1	1	3	0
Ron Taylor, p	.000	2	0	0	0	0	0	0	0	0	0	0
Al Weis, 2b	.455	5	11	1	5	0	0	1	3	4	2	0
TOTAL	.220		159	15	35	8	0	6	13	15	35	1

PITCHER	W	L	ERA	G	GS	CG	SV	SHO	IP	H	ER	BB	SO
Don Cardwell	0	0	0.00	1	0	0	0	0	1.0	0	0	0	0
Gary Gentry	1	0	0.00	1	1	0	0	0	6.2	3	0	5	4
Jerry Koosman	2	0	2.04	2	2	1	0	0	17.2	7	4	4	9
Nolan Ryan	0	0	0.00	1	0	0	1	0	2.1	1	0	2	3
Tom Seaver	1	1	3.00	2	2	1	0	0	15.0	12	5	3	9
Ron Taylor	0	0	0.00	2	0	0	1	0	2.1	0	0	1	3
TOTAL	4	1	1.80	9	5	2	2	0	45.0	23	9	15	28

BAL (A)

PLAYER/POS	AVG	G	AB	R	H	2B	3B	HR	RB	BB	SO	SB
Mark Belanger, ss	.200	5	15	2	3	0	0	0	1	2	1	0
Paul Blair, of	.100	5	20	1	2	0	0	0	0	2	5	1
Don Buford, of	.100	5	20	1	2	1	0	1	2	2	4	0
Mike Cuellar, p	.400	2	5	0	2	0	0	0	1	0	3	0
Clay Dalrymple, ph	1.000	2	2	0	2	0	0	0	0	0	0	0
Andy Etchebarren, c	.000	2	6	0	0	0	0	0	0	0	1	0
Dick Hall, p	.000	1	0	0	0	0	0	0	0	0	0	0
Elrod Hendricks, c	.100	3	10	1	1	0	0	0	0	1	0	0
Davey Johnson, 2b	.063	5	16	1	1	0	0	0	0	2	1	0
Dave Leonhard, p	.000	1	0	0	0	0	0	0	0	0	0	0
Dave May, ph	.000	2	1	0	0	0	0	0	0	1	1	0
Dave McNally, p	.200	2	5	1	1	0	0	1	2	0	2	0
Curt Motton, ph	.000	1	1	0	0	0	0	0	0	0	0	0
Jim Palmer, p	.000	1	2	0	0	0	0	0	0	0	0	0
Boog Powell, 1b	.263	5	19	0	5	0	0	0	0	1	4	0
Merv Rettenmund, pr	.000	1	0	0	0	0	0	0	0	0	0	0
Pete Richert, p	.000	1	0	0	0	0	0	0	0	0	0	0
Brooks Robinson, 3b	.053	5	19	0	1	0	0	0	2	0	3	0
Frank Robinson, of	.188	5	16	2	3	0	0	1	1	4	3	0
Chico Salmon, pr	.000	2	0	0	0	0	0	0	0	0	0	0
Eddie Watt, p	.000	2	0	0	0	0	0	0	0	0	0	0
TOTAL	.146		157	9	23	1	0	3	9	15	28	1

PITCHER	W	L	ERA	G	GS	CG	SV	SHO	IP	H	ER	BB	SO
Mike Cuellar	1	0	1.13	2	2	1	0	0	16.0	13	2	4	13
Dick Hall	0	1	-	1	0	0	0	0	0.0	1	0	1	0
Dave Leonhard	0	0	4.50	1	0	0	0	0	2.0	1	1	1	1
Dave McNally	0	1	2.81	2	2	1	0	0	16.0	11	5	5	13
Jim Palmer	0	1	6.00	1	1	0	0	0	6.0	5	4	4	5
Pete Richert	0	0	-	1	0	0	0	0	0.0	0	0	0	0
Eddie Watt	0	1	3.00	2	0	0	0	0	3.0	4	1	0	3
TOTAL	1	4	2.72	10	5	2	0	0	43.0	35	13	15	35

Al Weis homered in the seventh for a 3–3 tie. With McNally now gone, two doubles off Eddie Watt in the eighth brought in the go-ahead run, and a pair of errors let in a run for insurance. Koosman held Baltimore scoreless in the ninth and the Mets miracle was complete.

GAME 1 AT BAL OCT 11

NY	000 000 100		1	6	1
BAL	100 300 00X		4	6	0

Pitchers: SEAVER, Cardwell (6), Taylor (7) vs CUELLAR
Home Runs: Buford-BAL
Attendance: 50,429

GAME 2 AT BAL OCT 12

NY	000 100 001		2	6	0
BAL	000 000 100		1	2	0

Pitchers: KOOSMAN, Taylor (9) vs McNALLY
Home Runs: Clendenon-NY
Attendance: 50,850

GAME 3 AT NY OCT 14

BAL	000 000 000		0	4	1
NY	120 001 01X		5	6	0

Pitchers: PALMER, Leonhard (7) vs GENTRY, Ryan (7)
Home Runs: Agee-NY, Kranepool-NY
Attendance: 56,335

GAME 4 AT NY OCT 15

BAL	000 000 001 0		1	6	1
NY	010 000 000 1		2	10	1

Pitchers: Cuellar, Watt (8), HALL (10), Richert (10) vs SEAVER
Home Runs: Clendenon-NY
Attendance: 57,367

GAME 5 AT NY OCT 16

BAL	003 000 000		3	5	2
NY	000 002 12X		5	7	0

Pitchers: McNally, WATT (8) vs KOOSMAN
Home Runs: McNally-BAL, F.Robinson-BAL, Clendenon-NY, Weis-NY
Attendance: 57,397

Pitching was the name of the game and three the magic number, as Cincinnati swept Pittsburgh, scoring three runs in each game while holding the Pirates to just three runs for the whole series.

Pirates pitcher Dock Ellis matched the Reds' Gary Nolan for nine scoreless innings in Game 1 before a pinch-hit triple, a single, and a double undid him for three runs in the top of the 10th. In Game Two Pittsburgh scored its first series run, but Red center fielder Bobby Tolan scored three for Baltimore—including a home run—to give Cincinnati its second win.

The Pirates took a lead for the only time in the series with a run in the top of the first inning of Game 3. But Tony Perez and Johnny Bench homered in the bottom of the inning to put the Reds up 2–1. The Pirates tied the score in the fifth, but three Cincinnati relievers combined to shut them out over the final four innings. Tolan sank the Pirates ship with his second game-winner in two days: a single in the eighth that drove in Cincinnati's third—and final—run.

Cincinnati Reds (West), 3; Pittsburgh Pirates (East), 0

CIN (W)

PLAYER/POS	AVG	G	AB	R	H	2B	3B	HR	RB	BB	SO	SB
Johnny Bench, c	.222	3	9	2	2	0	0	1	1	3	1	0
Angel Bravo, ph	.000	1	1	0	0	0	0	0	0	0	0	0
Bernie Carbo, of	.000	2	6	0	0	0	0	0	0	1	2	0
Clay Carroll, p	.000	2	0	0	0	0	0	0	0	0	0	0
Ty Cline, of-1	1.000	2	1	2	1	0	1	0	0	1	0	0
Tony Cloninger, p	.000	1	1	0	0	0	0	0	0	0	0	0
Dave Concepcion, ss	.000	3	0	0	0	0	0	0	0	0	0	0
Wayne Granger, p	.000	1	0	0	0	0	0	0	0	0	0	0
Don Gullett, p	.000	2	1	0	0	0	0	0	0	0	1	0
Tommy Helms, 2b	.273	3	11	0	3	0	0	0	0	0	1	0
Lee May, 1b	.167	3	12	0	2	1	0	0	2	0	2	0
Hal McRae, of-1	.000	2	4	0	0	0	0	0	0	0	2	0
Jim Merritt, p	.000	1	2	0	0	0	0	0	0	0	2	0
Gary Nolan, p	.333	1	3	0	1	0	0	0	0	0	0	0
Tony Perez, 3b-3,1b-1	.333	3	12	1	4	2	0	1	2	1	1	0
Pete Rose, of	.231	3	13	1	3	0	0	0	1	0	0	0
Jimmy Stewart, of	.000	1	2	0	0	0	0	0	0	0	0	0
Bobby Tolan, of	.417	3	12	3	5	0	0	1	2	1	1	1
Milt Wilcox, p	.000	1	0	0	0	0	0	0	0	0	0	0
Woody Woodward, ss-3,3b-3	.100	3	10	0	1	0	0	0	0	1	0	0
TOTAL	.220		100	9	22	3	1	3	8	8	12	1

PITCHER	W	L	ERA	G	GS	CG	SV	SHO	IP	H	ER	BB	SO
Clay Carroll	0	0	0.00	2	0	0	1	0	1.1	2	0	0	2
Tony Cloninger	0	0	3.60	1	1	0	0	0	5.0	7	2	4	1
Wayne Granger	0	0	0.00	1	0	0	0	0	0.2	1	0	0	0
Don Gullett	0	0	0.00	2	0	0	2	0	3.2	1	0	2	3
Jim Merritt	1	0	1.69	1	1	0	0	0	5.1	3	1	0	2
Gary Nolan	1	0	0.00	1	1	0	0	0	9.0	8	0	4	6
Milt Wilcox	1	0	0.00	1	0	0	0	0	3.0	1	0	2	5
TOTAL	3	0	0.96	9	3	0	3	0	28.0	23	3	12	19

PIT (E)

PLAYER, POS	AVG	G	AB	R	H	2B	3B	HR	RB	BB	SO	SB
Gene Alley, ss	.000	2	7	0	0	0	0	0	0	1	2	0
Matty Alou, of	.250	3	12	1	3	1	0	0	0	2	1	0
Dave Cash, 2b	.125	2	8	1	1	1	0	0	0	1	1	0
Roberto Clemente, of	.214	3	14	1	3	0	0	0	1	0	4	0
Dock Ellis, p	.000	1	2	0	0	0	0	0	0	0	1	0
Joe Gibbon, p	.000	2	0	0	0	0	0	0	0	0	0	0
Dave Giusti, p	.000	2	0	0	0	0	0	0	0	0	0	0
Richie Hebner, 3b	.667	2	6	0	4	2	0	0	0	2	1	0
Johnny Jeter, of-1	.000	3	2	0	0	0	0	0	0	0	2	0
Bill Mazeroski, 2b	.000	1	2	0	0	0	0	0	0	2	0	0
Bob Moose, p	.000	1	4	0	0	0	0	0	0	0	1	0
Al Oliver, 1b	.250	2	8	0	2	0	0	0	1	1	0	0
Jose Pagan, 3b	.333	1	3	0	1	0	0	0	0	1	1	0
Freddie Patek, ss	.000	1	3	0	0	0	0	0	0	1	2	0
Bob Robertson, 1b-1	.200	2	5	0	1	1	0	0	0	0	0	0
Manny Sanguillen, c	.167	3	12	0	2	0	0	0	0	0	1	0
Willie Stargell, of	.500	3	12	0	6	1	0	0	1	1	1	0
Luke Walker, p	.000	1	2	0	0	0	0	0	0	0	1	0
TOTAL	.225		102	3	23	6	0	0	3	12	19	0

PITCHER	W	L	ERA	G	GS	CG	SV	SHO	IP	H	ER	BB	SO
Dock Ellis	0	1	2.79	1	1	0	0	0	9.2	9	3	4	1
Joe Gibbon	0	0	0.00	2	0	0	0	0	0.1	1	0	0	1
Dave Giusti	0	0	3.86	2	0	0	0	0	2.1	3	1	1	1
Bob Moose	0	1	3.52	1	1	0	0	0	7.2	4	3	2	4
Luke Walker	0	1	1.29	1	1	0	0	0	7.0	5	1	1	5
TOTAL	0	3	2.67	7	3	0	0	0	27.0	22	8	8	12

GAME 1 AT PIT OCT 3

CIN	000 000 000 3	3	9	0
PIT	000 000 000 0	0	8	0

Pitchers: NOLAN, Carroll (10) vs ELLIS, Gibbon (10)
Attendance: 33,088

GAME 2 AT PIT OCT 4

CIN	001 010 010	3	8	1
PIT	000 001 000	1	5	2

Pitchers: MERRITT, Carroll (6), Gullett (6) vs WALKER, Giusti (8)
Home Runs: Tolan-CIN
Attendance: 39,317

GAME 3 AT CIN OCT 5

PIT	100 010 000	2	10	0
CIN	200 000 01X	3	5	0

Pitchers: MOOSE, Gibbon (8), Giusti (8) vs Cloninger, WILCOX (6), Granger (9), Gullett (9)
Home Runs: Perez-CIN, Bench-CIN
Attendance: 40,538

For the second year in a row, Baltimore swept Minnesota in the ALCS. In the first two games the Orioles' attack featured the big inning. The score was tied 2–2 in the first game as the Orioles came to bat in the top of the fourth. But by the time the Twins came to bat in the inning, they were seven runs behind—thanks in part to a grand slam by Baltimore pitcher Mike Cuellar. Harmon Killebrew's two-run homer in the fifth helped bring the Twins within three, but they came no closer.

Except for home runs to Killebrew and Tony Oliva in the fourth inning, Orioles pitcher Dave Mc-Nally stopped the Twins in Game 2, and Baltimore held a close 4–3 lead after eight. If they had been playing at home, they wouldn't have needed to bat at all in the ninth. But they did come to bat in the top of the ninth, and they once again buried Minnesota under a seven-run inning.

In the third game, for the second year in a row, pitcher Jim Palmer breezed through the series clincher. Baltimore scored five runs for him in the first three innings, and another in the eighth—four more than he needed to carry his club to another pennant.

Baltimore Orioles (East), 3;
Minnesota Twins (West), 0

BAL (E)

PLAYER/POS	AVG	G	AB	R	H	2B	3B	HR	RB	BB	SO	SB
Mark Belanger, ss	.333	3	12	5	4	0	0	0	1	1	0	0
Paul Blair, of	.077	3	13	0	1	0	0	0	0	1	4	0
Don Buford, of	.429	2	7	2	3	1	0	1	3	2	0	0
Mike Cuellar, p	.500	1	2	1	1	0	0	1	4	0	1	0
Andy Etchebarren, c	.111	2	9	1	1	0	0	0	0	0	3	0
Dick Hall, p	.500	1	2	1	1	0	0	0	0	0	1	0
Elrod Hendricks, c	.400	1	5	2	2	0	0	0	0	0	1	0
Davey Johnson, 2b	.364	3	11	4	4	0	0	2	4	1	1	0
Dave McNally, p	.400	1	5	1	2	1	0	0	1	0	1	0
Jim Palmer, p	.250	1	4	1	1	1	0	0	1	0	0	0
Boog Powell, 1b	.429	3	14	2	6	2	0	1	6	0	3	0
Merv Rettenmund, of	.333	1	3	1	1	0	0	0	1	2	1	1
Brooks Robinson, 3b	.583	3	12	3	7	2	0	0	1	0	1	0
Frank Robinson, of	.200	3	10	3	2	0	0	1	2	5	2	0
TOTAL	.330		109	27	36	7	0	6	24	12	19	1

PITCHER	W	L	ERA	G	GS	CG	SV	SHO	IP	H	ER	BB	SO
Mike Cuellar	0	0	12.46	1	1	0	0	0	4.1	10	6	1	2
Dick Hall	1	0	0.00	1	0	0	0	0	4.2	1	0	0	3
Dave McNally	1	0	3.00	1	1	1	0	0	9.0	6	3	5	5
Jim Palmer	1	0	1.00	1	1	1	0	0	9.0	7	1	3	12
TOTAL	3	0	3.33	4	3	2	0	0	27.0	24	10	9	22

MIN (W)

PLAYER/POS	AVG	G	AB	R	H	2B	3B	HR	RB	BB	SO	SB
Bob Allison, ph	.000	3	2	0	0	0	0	0	0	1	1	0
Brant Alyea, of-2	.000	3	7	1	0	0	0	0	0	2	3	0
Bert Blyleven, p	.000	1	0	0	0	0	0	0	0	0	0	0
Leo Cardenas, ss	.182	3	11	1	2	0	0	0	1	1	1	0
Rod Carew, ph	.000	2	2	0	0	0	0	0	0	0	1	0
Tom Hall, p	.000	2	1	0	0	0	0	0	0	0	1	0
Jim Holt, of	.000	3	5	0	0	0	0	0	0	0	2	0
Jim Kaat, p	.000	1	1	0	0	0	0	0	0	0	1	0
Harmon Killebrew, 3b-2,1b-1	.273	3	11	2	3	0	0	2	4	2	4	0
Chuck Manuel, ph	.000	1	1	0	0	0	0	0	0	0	1	0
George Mitterwald, c	.500	2	8	2	4	1	0	0	2	0	2	0
Tony Oliva, of	.500	3	12	2	6	2	0	1	1	0	1	0
Ron Perranoski, p	.000	2	0	0	0	0	0	0	0	0	0	0
Jim Perry, p	.000	2	1	0	0	0	0	0	1	0	0	0
Frank Quilici, 2b-2	.000	3	2	0	0	0	0	0	0	0	1	0
Paul Ratliff, c	.250	1	4	0	1	0	0	0	0	0	1	0
Rich Reese, 1b	.143	2	7	0	1	0	0	0	0	1	1	0
Rich Renick, 3b-1	.200	2	5	0	1	0	0	0	0	0	1	0
Danny Thompson, 2b	.125	3	8	0	1	1	0	0	0	1	0	0
Luis Tiant, p-1, pr-1	.000	2	0	0	0	0	0	0	0	0	0	0
Cesar Tovar, of-3,2b-1	.385	3	13	2	5	0	1	0	1	0	0	0
Stan Williams, p	.000	2	0	0	0	0	0	0	0	1	0	0
Dick Woodson, p	.000	1	0	0	0	0	0	0	0	0	0	0
Bill Zepp, p	.000	2	0	0	0	0	0	0	0	0	0	0
TOTAL	.238		101	10	24	4	1	3	10	9	22	0

PITCHER	W	L	ERA	G	GS	CG	SV	SHO	IP	H	ER	BB	SO
Bert Blyleven	0	0	0.00	1	0	0	0	0	2.0	2	0	0	2
Tom Hall	0	1	6.75	2	1	0	0	0	5.1	6	4	4	6
Jim Kaat	0	1	9.00	1	1	0	0	0	2.0	6	2	2	1
Ron Perranoski	0	0	19.29	2	0	0	0	0	2.1	5	5	1	3
Jim Perry	0	1	13.50	2	2	0	0	0	5.1	10	8	1	3
Luis Tiant	0	0	13.50	1	0	0	0	0	0.2	1	1	0	0
Stan Williams	0	0	0.00	2	0	0	0	0	6.0	2	0	1	2
Dick Woodson	0	0	9.00	1	0	0	0	0	1.0	2	1	1	0
Bill Zepp	0	0	6.75	2	0	0	0	0	1.1	2	1	2	2
TOTAL	0	3	7.62	14	3	0	0	0	26.0	36	22	12	19

GAME 1 AT MIN OCT 3

BAL	020	701	000	10	13	0
MIN	110	130	000	6	11	2

Pitchers: Cuellar, HALL (5) vs PERRY, Zepp (4), Woodson (5), Williams (6), Perranoski (9)
Home Runs: Cuellar-BAL, Buford-BAL, Powell-BAL, Killebrew-MIN
Attendance: 26,847

GAME 2 AT MIN OCT 4

BAL	102	100	007	11	13	0
MIN	000	300	000	3	6	2

Pitchers: McNALLY vs HALL, Zepp (4), Williams (5), Perranoski (8), Tiant (9)
Home Runs: F.Robinson-BAL, Killebrew-MIN, Oliva-MIN, Johnson-BAL
Attendance: 27,490

GAME 3 AT BAL OCT 5

MIN	000	010	000	1	7	2
BAL	113	000	10X	6	10	0

Pitchers: KAAT, Blyleven (3), Hall (5), Perry (7) vs PALMER
Home Runs: Johnson-BAL
Attendance: 27,608

With a near-sweep of Cincinnati, the Orioles helped Baltimore fans forget their 1969 Series humiliation by the New York Mets. Baltimore's first two wins, though, were closely contested. In the opener in Cincinnati (the first World Series game played on artificial grass), a run in the first inning and Lee May's third-inning two-run homer off Orioles starter Jim Palmer gave Cincinnati a 3–0 lead. But Orioles Boog Powell and Elrod Hendricks tagged Gary Nolan for home runs in the fourth and fifth that evened the score, and Brooks Robinson—whose other-worldly defense at third gave Reds righthanded hitters nightmares throughout the Series—homered in the seventh for a one-run Baltimore lead that held up as Palmer settled down to pitch one-hit ball from the fourth inning until he was relieved for the final out of the ninth.

Game 2 was just as close. The Reds scored four runs in the first three innings, but Baltimore came back with six in the fourth and fifth. Johnny Bench's leadoff homer in the last of the sixth brought the Reds within one, but that was the end of the scoring for either side. In Game 3 Dave McNally gave up nine hits and three runs. But he himself hit a grand slam in the sixth inning to cement what became a 9–3 Baltimore victory.

On the verge of a Series sweep, the Orioles scored three runs in the last of the third inning of Game 4 to take a 4–2 lead. But the Reds' Pete Rose homered in the fifth, and although Baltimore got the run back in the sixth, Lee May's three-run blast in the eighth overcame the Orioles lead and gave the Reds a narrow 6–5 win as Reds reliever Clay Carroll permitted only one Oriole to hit safely over the final 3⅔ innings.

Mike Cuellar, driven out of Game 2 in the third inning, hurled the complete game for Baltimore in Game 5, even though Cincinnati hammered him for four hits (three of them doubles) and three runs in the top of the first inning. But as Orioles home runs by Frank Robinson and Merv Rettenmund highlighted a Baltimore onslaught that produced 15 hits and nine runs, Cuellar settled down, holding Cincinnati to a walk and a pair of harmless singles over the final eight innings to bring Baltimore its second world title in five years.

Baltimore Orioles (AL), 4; Cincinnati Reds (NL), 1

BAL (A)

PLAYER/POS	AVG	G	AB	R	H	2B	3B	HR	RB	BB	SO	SB
Mark Belanger, ss	.105	5	19	0	2	0	0	0	0	1	2	0
Paul Blair, of	.474	5	19	5	9	1	0	0	3	2	4	0
Don Buford, of	.267	4	15	3	4	0	0	1	1	3	2	0
Terry Crowley, ph	.000	1	1	0	0	0	0	0	0	0	0	0
Mike Cuellar, p	.000	2	4	0	0	0	0	0	0	0	2	0
Moe Drabowsky, p	.000	2	1	0	0	0	0	0	0	0	1	0
Andy Etchebarren, c	.143	2	7	1	1	0	0	0	0	2	3	0
Dick Hall, p	.000	1	1	0	0	0	0	0	0	0	1	0
Elrod Hendricks, c	.364	3	11	1	4	1	0	1	4	1	2	0
Davey Johnson, 2b	.313	5	16	2	5	2	0	0	2	5	2	0
Marcelino Lopez, p	.000	1	0	0	0	0	0	0	0	0	0	0
Dave McNally, p	.250	1	4	1	1	0	0	1	4	0	2	0
Jim Palmer, p	.143	2	7	1	1	0	0	0	0	0	3	0
Tom Phoebus, p	.000	1	0	0	0	0	0	0	0	0	0	0
Boog Powell, 1b	.294	5	17	6	5	1	0	2	5	5	2	0
Merv Rettenmund, of-1	.400	2	5	2	2	0	0	1	2	1	0	0
Pete Richert, p	.000	1	0	0	0	0	0	0	0	0	0	0
Brooks Robinson, 3b	.429	5	21	5	9	2	0	2	6	0	2	0
Frank Robinson, of	.273	5	22	5	6	0	0	2	4	0	5	0
Chico Salmon, ph	1.000	1	1	1	1	0	0	0	0	0	0	0
Eddie Watt, p	.000	1	0	0	0	0	0	0	0	0	0	0
TOTAL	.292		171	33	50	7	0	10	32	20	33	0

PITCHER	W	L	ERA	G	GS	CG	SV	SHO	IP	H	ER	BB	SO
Mike Cuellar	1	0	3.18	2	2	1	0	0	11.1	10	4	2	5
Moe Drabowsky	0	0	2.70	2	0	0	0	0	3.1	2	1	1	1
Dick Hall	0	0	0.00	1	0	0	1	0	2.1	0	0	0	0
Marcelino Lopez	0	0	0.00	1	0	0	0	0	0.1	0	0	0	0
Dave McNally	1	0	3.00	1	1	1	0	0	9.0	9	3	2	5
Jim Palmer	1	0	4.60	2	2	0	0	0	15.2	11	8	9	9
Tom Phoebus	1	0	0.00	1	0	0	0	0	1.2	1	0	0	0
Pete Richert	0	0	0.00	1	0	0	1	0	0.1	0	0	0	0
Eddie Watt	0	1	9.00	1	0	0	0	0	1.0	2	1	1	3
TOTAL	4	1	3.40	12	5	2	2	0	45.0	35	17	15	23

CIN (N)

PLAYER/POS	AVG	G	AB	R	H	2B	3B	HR	RB	BB	SO	SB
Johnny Bench, c	.211	5	19	3	4	0	0	1	3	1	2	0
Angel Bravo, ph	.000	4	2	0	0	0	0	0	0	1	1	0
Bernie Carbo, of-2	.000	4	8	0	0	0	0	0	0	2	3	0
Clay Carroll, p	.000	4	1	0	0	0	0	0	0	0	1	0
Darrel Chaney, ss	.000	3	1	0	0	0	0	0	0	0	1	0
Ty Cline, ph	.333	3	3	0	1	0	0	0	0	0	0	0
Tony Cloninger, p	.000	2	2	0	0	0	0	0	0	0	1	0
Dave Concepcion, ss	.333	3	9	0	3	0	1	0	3	0	0	0
Pat Corrales, ph	.000	1	1	0	0	0	0	0	0	0	0	0
Wayne Granger, p	.000	2	0	0	0	0	0	0	0	0	0	0
Don Gullett, p	.000	3	1	0	0	0	0	0	0	0	1	0
Tommy Helms, 2b	.222	5	18	1	4	0	0	0	0	1	1	0
Lee May, 1b	.389	5	18	6	7	2	0	2	8	2	2	0
Jim McGlothlin, p	.000	1	2	0	0	0	0	0	0	0	1	0
Hal McRae, of	.455	3	11	1	5	2	0	0	3	0	1	0
Jim Merritt, p	.000	1	1	0	0	0	0	0	0	0	1	0
Gary Nolan, p	.000	2	3	0	0	0	0	0	0	0	0	0
Tony Perez, 3b	.056	5	18	2	1	0	0	0	0	3	4	0
Pete Rose, of	.250	5	20	2	5	1	0	1	2	2	0	0
Jimmy Stewart, ph	.000	2	2	0	0	0	0	0	0	0	1	0
Bobby Tolan, of	.211	5	19	5	4	1	0	1	3	2	1	1
Ray Washburn, p	.000	1	0	0	0	0	0	0	0	0	0	0
Milt Wilcox, p	.000	2	0	0	0	0	0	0	0	0	0	0
Woody Woodward, ss-3	.200	4	5	0	1	0	0	0	0	0	0	0
TOTAL	.213		164	20	35	6	1	5	20	15	23	1

PITCHER	W	L	ERA	G	GS	CG	SV	SHO	IP	H	ER	BB	SO
Clay Carroll	1	0	0.00	4	0	0	0	0	9.0	5	0	2	11
Tony Cloninger	0	1	7.36	2	2	0	0	0	7.1	10	6	5	4
Wayne Granger	0	0	33.75	2	0	0	0	0	1.1	7	5	1	1
Don Gullett	0	0	1.35	3	0	0	0	0	6.2	5	1	4	4
Jim McGlothlin	0	0	8.31	1	1	0	0	0	4.1	6	4	2	2
Jim Merritt	0	1	21.60	1	1	0	0	0	1.2	3	4	1	0
Gary Nolan	0	1	7.71	2	2	0	0	0	9.1	9	8	3	9
Ray Washburn	0	0	13.50	1	0	0	0	0	1.1	2	2	2	0
Milt Wilcox	0	1	9.00	2	0	0	0	0	2.0	3	2	2	2
TOTAL	1	4	6.70	18	5	0	0	0	43.0	50	32	20	33

GAME 1 AT CIN OCT 10

BAL	000 210 100	4 7 2
CIN	102 000 000	3 5 0

Pitchers: PALMER, Richert (9) vs NOLAN, Carroll (7)
Home Runs: May-CIN, Powell-BAL, Hendricks-BAL, B.Robinson-BAL
Attendance: 51,531

GAME 2 AT CIN OCT 11

BAL	000 150 000	6 10 2
CIN	301 001 000	5 7 0

Pitchers: Cuellar, PHOEBUS (3), Drabowsky (5), Lopez (7), Hall (7) vs McGlothlin, WILCOX (5), Carroll (5), Gullett (8)
Home Runs: Tolan-CIN, Powell-BAL, Bench-CIN
Attendance: 51,531

GAME 3 AT BAL OCT 13

CIN	010 000 200	3 9 0
BAL	201 014 10X	9 10 1

Pitchers: CLONINGER, Granger (6), Gullett (7) vs McNALLY
Home Runs: F.Robinson-BAL, Buford-BAL, McNally-BAL
Attendance: 51,773

GAME 4 AT BAL OCT 14

CIN	011 010 030	6 8 3
BAL	013 001 000	5 8 0

Pitchers: Nolan, Gullett (3), CARROLL (6) vs Palmer, WATT (8), Drabowsky (9)
Home Runs: B.Robinson-BAL, Rose-CIN, May-CIN
Attendance: 53,007

GAME 5 AT BAL OCT 15

CIN	300 000 000	3 6 0
BAL	222 010 02X	9 15 0

Pitchers: MERRITT, Granger (2), Wilcox (3), Cloninger (5), Washburn (7), Carroll (8) vs CUELLAR
Home Runs: F.Robinson-BAL, Rettenmund-BAL
Attendance: 45,341

For the first time, an LCS went more than the minimum three games, as Pittsburgh rebounded from a loss in the opener to take the next three from San Francisco.

The Pirates scored first, with two runs in the third inning of Game 1, but the Giants came back with a run in the bottom of the inning and put the game away in the fifth as Tito Fuentes and Willie McCovey both hit two-out two-run homers. Pirates first baseman Bob Robertson avenged his club's opening-game defeat the next day, battering four of the Giants' six pitchers for three home runs and a double—and five RBIs—in the Pirates' 9–5 win. Robertson continued his assault in Game 3, homering off Juan Marichal in the second. The Giants came back with a run in the sixth, but third baseman Richie Hebner put the game away with a second Pirates home run off Marichal in the eighth.

Both clubs scored five times in the first two innings of Game 4. But Pirates relievers Bruce Kison and Dave Giusti then pinned the Giants down for the final seven innings, while Roberto Clemente and Al Oliver combined for four RBIs in the sixth to capture the flag.

Pittsburgh Pirates (East), 3;
San Francisco Giants (West), 1

PIT (E)

PLAYER/POS	AVG	G	AB	R	H	2B	3B	HR	RB	BB	SO	SB
Gene Alley, ss	.500	1	2	1	1	0	0	0	0	0	0	0
Steve Blass, p	.000	2	1	0	0	0	0	0	0	0	1	0
Dave Cash, 2b	.421	4	19	5	8	2	0	0	1	0	1	1
Roberto Clemente, of	.333	4	18	2	6	0	0	0	4	1	6	0
Gene Clines, of	.333	1	3	1	1	0	0	1	1	0	1	0
Vic Davalillo, ph	.000	2	2	0	0	0	0	0	0	0	1	0
Dock Ellis, p	.000	1	3	0	0	0	0	0	0	0	2	0
Dave Giusti, p	.000	4	1	0	0	0	0	0	0	0	0	0
Richie Hebner, 3b	.294	4	17	3	5	1	0	2	4	0	4	0
Jackie Hernandez, ss	.231	4	13	2	3	0	0	0	1	0	4	0
Bob Johnson, p	.000	1	2	0	0	0	0	0	0	0	1	0
Bruce Kison, p	.000	1	2	0	0	0	0	0	0	0	0	0
Milt May, ph	.000	1	1	0	0	0	0	0	0	0	0	0
Bill Mazeroski, ph	1.000	1	1	1	1	0	0	0	0	0	0	0
Bob Miller, p	.000	1	1	0	0	0	0	0	0	0	0	0
Bob Moose, p	.000	1	0	0	0	0	0	0	0	0	0	0
Al Oliver, of	.250	4	12	2	3	0	0	1	5	1	3	0
Jose Pagan, 3b	.000	1	1	0	0	0	0	0	0	0	0	0
Bob Robertson, 1b	.438	4	16	5	7	1	0	4	6	0	2	0
Manny Sanguillen, c	.267	4	15	1	4	0	0	0	1	1	1	1
Willie Stargell, of	.000	4	14	1	0	0	0	0	0	2	6	0
TOTAL	.271		144	24	39	4	0	8	23	5	33	2

PITCHER	W	L	ERA	G	GS	CG	SV	SHO	IP	H	ER	BB	SO
Steve Blass	0	1	11.57	2	2	0	0	0	7.0	14	9	2	11
Dock Ellis	1	0	3.60	1	1	0	0	0	5.0	6	2	4	1
Dave Giusti	0	0	0.00	4	0	0	3	0	5.1	1	0	2	3
Bob Johnson	1	0	0.00	1	1	0	0	0	8.0	5	0	3	7
Bruce Kison	1	0	0.00	1	0	0	0	0	4.2	2	0	2	3
Bob Miller	0	0	6.00	1	0	0	0	0	3.0	3	2	3	3
Bob Moose	0	0	0.00	1	0	0	0	0	2.0	0	0	0	0
TOTAL	3	1	3.34	11	4	0	3	0	35.0	31	13	16	28

SF (W)

PLAYER/POS	AVG	G	AB	R	H	2B	3B	HR	RB	BB	SO	SB
Jim Barr, p	.000	1	1	0	0	0	0	0	0	0	0	0
Bobby Bonds, of	.250	3	8	0	2	0	0	0	0	2	4	0
Ron Bryant, p	.000	1	0	0	0	0	0	0	0	0	0	0
Don Carrithers, p	.000	1	0	0	0	0	0	0	0	0	0	0
John Cumberland, p	.000	1	0	0	0	0	0	0	0	0	0	0
Dick Dietz, c	.067	4	15	0	1	0	0	0	0	2	5	0
Frank Duffy, ph	.000	1	1	0	0	0	0	0	0	0	1	0
Tito Fuentes, 2b	.313	4	16	4	5	1	0	1	2	1	3	0
Alan Gallagher, 3b	.100	4	10	0	1	0	0	0	0	0	2	0
Steve Hamilton, p	.000	1	0	0	0	0	0	0	0	0	0	0
Jim Ray Hart, 3b-1	.000	3	5	0	0	0	0	0	0	0	2	0
Ken Henderson, of	.313	4	16	3	5	1	0	0	2	2	1	1
Jerry Johnson, p	.000	1	0	0	0	0	0	0	0	0	0	0
Dave Kingman, of-2	.111	4	9	0	1	0	0	0	0	1	3	0
Hal Lanier, 3b	.000	1	1	0	0	0	0	0	0	0	0	0
Juan Marichal, p	.000	1	3	0	0	0	0	0	0	0	1	0
Willie Mays, of	.267	4	15	2	4	2	0	1	3	3	3	1
Willie McCovey, 1b	.429	4	14	2	6	0	0	2	6	4	2	0
Don McMahon, p	.000	2	0	0	0	0	0	0	0	0	0	0
Gaylord Perry, p	.250	2	4	0	1	0	0	0	0	0	0	0
Jimmy Rosario, pr	.000	1	0	0	0	0	0	0	0	0	0	0
Chris Speier, ss	.357	4	14	4	5	0	0	1	1	1	1	0
TOTAL	.235		132	15	31	5	0	5	14	16	28	2

PITCHER	W	L	ERA	G	GS	CG	SV	SHO	IP	H	ER	BB	SO
Jim Barr	0	0	9.00	1	0	0	0	0	1.0	3	1	0	2
Ron Bryant	0	0	4.50	1	0	0	0	0	2.0	1	1	1	2
Don Carrithers	0	0	∞	1	0	0	0	0	0.0	3	3	0	0
John Cumberland	0	1	9.00	1	0	0	0	0	3.0	7	3	0	4
Steve Hamilton	0	0	9.00	1	0	0	0	0	1.0	1	1	0	3
Jerry Johnson	0	0	13.50	1	0	0	0	0	1.1	1	2	1	2
Juan Marichal	0	1	2.25	1	1	1	0	0	8.0	4	2	0	6
Don McMahon	0	0	0.00	2	0	0	0	0	3.0	0	0	0	3
Gaylord Perry	1	1	6.14	2	2	1	0	0	14.2	19	10	3	11
TOTAL	1	3	6.09	11	4	2	0	0	34.0	39	23	5	33

Baltimore, dividing its 15 runs evenly among the three games, swept the ALCS for the third year in a row.

Oakland's Vida Blue took a 3–1 lead into the seventh inning of Game 1, but with two away and men on first and third, a single and two doubles pushed across four runs to beat him, 5–3. Orioles starter Dave McNally and reliever Eddie Watt held the A's scoreless from the fifth inning on. In the second game Oakland managed only one run off Mike Cuellar, while the Orioles hammered Catfish Hunter for five runs on four homers—two of them by Boog Powell, including one in the eighth with a man aboard.

Reggie Jackson retaliated for the A's in Game 3 with two home runs off Jim Palmer, and Sal Bando added a third. But Palmer permitted no other A's to score, and—supported by a Baltimore run in the first and two each in the fifth and seventh—preserved the lead throughout the game. For the third year in a row Palmer clinched the pennant for Baltimore with a complete-game victory.

Baltimore Orioles (East), 3;
Oakland A's (West), 0

BAL (E)

PLAYER/POS	AVG	G	AB	R	H	2B	3B	HR	RB	BB	SO	SB
Mark Belanger, ss	.250	3	8	1	2	0	0	0	1	3	2	0
Paul Blair, of	.333	3	9	1	3	1	0	0	2	0	3	0
Don Buford, of	.429	2	7	1	3	0	1	0	0	2	1	0
Mike Cuellar, p	.333	1	3	0	1	0	0	0	0	0	2	0
Andy Etchebarren, c	.000	2	5	0	0	0	0	0	0	0	0	0
Elrod Hendricks, c	.500	2	4	1	2	0	0	1	2	1	1	0
Davey Johnson, 2b	.300	3	10	2	3	2	0	0	0	3	1	0
Dave McNally, p	.000	1	2	0	0	0	0	0	0	0	0	0
Curt Motton, ph	1.000	1	1	0	1	1	0	0	1	0	0	0
Jim Palmer, p-1	.200	2	5	1	1	0	0	0	0	0	1	0
Boog Powell, 1b	.300	3	10	4	3	0	0	2	3	3	3	0
Merv Rettenmund, of	.250	3	8	0	2	1	0	0	1	0	3	0
Brooks Robinson, 3b	.364	3	11	2	4	1	0	1	3	0	1	0
Frank Robinson, of	.083	3	12	2	1	1	0	0	1	1	4	0
Eddie Watt, p	.000	1	0	0	0	0	0	0	0	0	0	0
TOTAL	.274		95	15	26	7	1	4	14	13	22	0

PITCHER	W	L	ERA	G	GS	CG	SV	SHO	IP	H	ER	BB	SO
Mike Cuellar	1	0	1.00	1	1	1	0	0	9.0	6	1	1	2
Dave McNally	1	0	3.86	1	1	0	0	0	7.0	7	3	1	5
Jim Palmer	1	0	3.00	1	1	1	0	0	9.0	7	3	3	8
Eddie Watt	0	0	0.00	1	0	0	1	0	2.0	2	0	0	1
TOTAL	3	0	2.33	4	3	2	1	0	27.0	22	7	5	16

OAK (W)

PLAYER/POS	AVG	G	AB	R	H	2B	3B	HR	RB	BB	SO	SB
Sal Bando, 3b	.364	3	11	3	4	2	0	1	1	1	0	0
Curt Blefary, ph	.000	1	1	0	0	0	0	0	0	0	1	0
Vida Blue, p	.000	1	3	0	0	0	0	0	0	0	3	0
Bert Campaneris, ss	.167	3	12	0	2	1	0	0	0	0	1	0
Tommy Davis, 1b-2	.375	3	8	1	3	1	0	0	0	0	0	0
Dave Duncan, c	.500	2	6	0	3	1	0	0	2	0	0	0
Mike Epstein, 1b-1	.200	2	5	0	1	0	0	0	0	0	3	0
Rollie Fingers, p	.000	2	0	0	0	0	0	0	0	0	0	0
Mudcat Grant, p	.000	1	0	0	0	0	0	0	0	0	0	0
Dick Green, 2b	.286	3	7	0	2	0	0	0	0	1	1	0
Mike Hegan, ph	.000	1	1	0	0	0	0	0	0	0	1	0
Catfish Hunter, p	.000	1	3	0	0	0	0	0	0	0	1	0
Reggie Jackson, of	.333	3	12	2	4	1	0	2	2	0	1	0
Darold Knowles, p	.000	1	0	0	0	0	0	0	0	0	0	0
Bob Locker, p	.000	1	0	0	0	0	0	0	0	0	0	0
Angel Mangual, of	.167	3	12	1	2	1	1	0	2	0	1	0
Rick Monday, of	.000	3	3	0	0	0	0	0	0	1	2	0
Joe Rudi, of	.143	2	7	0	1	1	0	0	0	0	0	0
Diego Segui, p	.000	1	2	0	0	0	0	0	0	0	0	0
Gene Tenace, c	.000	1	3	0	0	0	0	0	0	1	1	0
TOTAL	.229		96	7	22	8	1	3	7	5	16	0

PITCHER	W	L	ERA	G	GS	CG	SV	SHO	IP	H	ER	BB	SO
Vida Blue	0	1	6.43	1	1	0	0	0	7.0	7	5	2	8
Rollie Fingers	0	0	7.71	2	0	0	0	0	2.1	2	2	1	2
Mudcat Grant	0	0	0.00	1	0	0	0	0	2.0	3	0	0	2
Catfish Hunter	0	1	5.63	1	1	1	0	0	8.0	7	5	2	6
Darold Knowles	0	0	0.00	1	0	0	0	0	0.1	1	0	0	0
Bob Locker	0	0	0.00	1	0	0	0	0	0.2	0	0	2	0
Diego Segui	0	1	5.79	1	1	0	0	0	4.2	6	3	6	4
TOTAL	0	3	5.40	8	3	1	0	0	25.0	26	15	13	22

GAME 1 AT BAL OCT 3

OAK	020	100	000	3	9	0
BAL	000	100	40X	5	7	1

Pitchers: BLUE, Fingers (8) vs
 McNALLY, Watt (8)
Attendance: 42,621

GAME 2 AT BAL OCT 4

OAK	000	100	000	1	6	0
BAL	011	000	12X	5	7	0

Pitchers: HUNTER vs CUELLAR
Home Runs: B.Robinson-BAL,
 Powell-BAL (2), Hendricks-BAL
Attendance: 35,003

GAME 3 AT OAK OCT 5

BAL	100	020	200	5	12	0
OAK	001	001	010	3	7	0

Pitchers: PALMER vs SEGUI,
 Fingers (5), Knowles (7), Locker (7),
 Grant (8)
Home Runs: Jackson-OAK (2),
 Bando-OAK
Attendance: 33,176

In its third successive Series, Baltimore faced its third different opponent and beat the Pirates in the first two games. A walk, a wild pitch, two Baltimore errors, and a single in the second inning of the opener gave Pittsburgh an early 3–0 lead. But Dave McNally shut out the Pirates on two hits the rest of the game as Frank Robinson, Merv Rettenmund, and Don Buford homered to give Baltimore a 5–3 victory. Jim Palmer took the win in Game 2 as Baltimore hammered Pirates pitching for 14 hits and 11 runs before Palmer issued Richie Hebner a three-run homer—Pittsburgh's only scoring—in the eighth.

The Pirates overtook the Orioles when the Series moved to Pittsburgh. Steve Blass pitched a three-hitter in Game 3, and while Frank Robinson's solo homer in the seventh ended Blass' shutout, a three-run shot by Bob Robertson in the last of the inning cemented a 5–1 Pittsburgh win. The next evening (in the first World Series night game ever), Baltimore scored three times in the top of the first inning, but two Pirates runs later in the inning and another run in the third tied the game. It remained tied until Pirates pinch hitter Milt May singled home the game winner with two away in the seventh.

With the Series now even at two wins apiece, Pittsburgh's Nelson Briles stopped the Orioles in Game 5 on a pair of singles. Bob Robertson's leadoff homer in the second proved all the Pirates needed for the win, but Briles himself drove in an insurance run later in the inning and Pittsburgh went on to win, 4–0.

The Pirates tried to win it all in Game 6, scoring single runs against the O's Jim Palmer in the second inning and the third (Roberto Clemente's home run). But Pirates starter Bob Moose was replaced after giving up a solo homer to Don Buford in the sixth, and a tying Baltimore run came home an inning later. A ninth-inning pinch hitter for Palmer produced nothing, but Baltimore won in the last of the 10th, when Frank Robinson scored on Brooks Robinson's sacrifice fly to shallow center.

Steve Blass, who had defeated Mike Cuellar in Game 3, faced him again in the finale and again emerged the victor of a pitching duel. Clemente's two-out homer in the fourth inning provided the game's only run until the eighth, when both teams scored single runs. Blass retired Baltimore in order in the ninth and the Pirates were world champions.

Pittsburgh Pirates (NL), 4;
Baltimore Orioles (AL), 3

PIT (N)

PLAYER/POS	AVG	G	AB	R	H	2B	3B	HR	RB	BB	SO	SB
Gene Alley, ss	.000	2	2	0	0	0	0	0	0	1	0	0
Steve Blass, p	.000	2	7	0	0	0	0	0	0	0	1	0
Nelson Briles, p	.500	1	2	0	1	0	0	0	1	0	1	0
Dave Cash, 2b	.133	7	30	2	4	1	0	0	1	3	1	1
Roberto Clemente, of	.414	7	29	3	12	2	1	2	4	2	2	0
Gene Clines, of	.091	3	11	2	1	0	1	0	0	1	1	1
Vic Davalillo, of-2	.333	3	3	1	1	0	0	0	0	0	0	0
Dock Ellis, p	.000	1	1	0	0	0	0	0	0	0	1	0
Dave Giusti, p	.000	3	0	0	0	0	0	0	0	0	0	0
Richie Hebner, 3b	.167	3	12	2	2	0	0	1	3	3	3	0
Jackie Hernandez, ss	.222	7	18	2	4	0	0	0	1	2	5	1
Bob Johnson, p	.000	2	3	0	0	0	0	0	0	0	2	0
Bruce Kison, p	.000	2	2	0	0	0	0	0	0	1	2	0
Milt May, ph	.500	2	2	0	1	0	0	0	1	0	0	0
Bill Mazeroski, ph	.000	1	1	0	0	0	0	0	0	0	0	0
Bob Miller, p	.000	3	0	0	0	0	0	0	0	0	0	0
Bob Moose, p	.000	3	2	0	0	0	0	0	0	0	1	0
Al Oliver, of-4	.211	5	19	1	4	2	0	0	2	2	5	0
Jose Pagan, 3b	.267	4	15	0	4	2	0	0	2	0	1	0
Bob Robertson, 1b	.240	7	25	4	6	0	0	2	5	4	8	0
Charlie Sands, ph	.000	1	1	0	0	0	0	0	0	0	1	0
Manny Sanguillen, c	.379	7	29	3	11	1	0	0	0	0	3	2
Willie Stargell, of	.208	7	24	3	5	1	0	0	1	7	9	0
Bob Veale, p	.000	1	0	0	0	0	0	0	0	0	0	0
Luke Walker, p	.000	1	0	0	0	0	0	0	0	0	0	0
TOTAL	.235		238	23	56	9	2	5	21	26	47	5

PITCHER	W	L	ERA	G	GS	CG	SV	SHO	IP	H	ER	BB	SO
Steve Blass	2	0	1.00	2	2	2	0	0	18.0	7	2	4	13
Nelson Briles	1	0	0.00	1	1	1	0	1	9.0	2	0	2	2
Dock Ellis	0	1	15.43	1	1	0	0	0	2.1	4	4	1	1
Dave Giusti	0	0	0.00	3	0	0	1	0	5.1	3	0	2	4
Bob Johnson	0	1	9.00	2	1	0	0	0	5.0	5	5	3	3
Bruce Kison	1	0	0.00	2	0	0	0	0	6.1	1	0	2	3
Bob Miller	0	1	3.86	3	0	0	0	0	4.2	7	2	1	2
Bob Moose	0	0	6.52	3	1	0	0	0	9.2	12	7	2	7
Bob Veale	0	0	13.50	1	0	0	0	0	0.2	1	1	2	0
Luke Walker	0	0	40.50	1	1	0	0	0	0.2	3	3	1	0
TOTAL	4	3	3.50	19	7	3	1	1	61.2	45	24	20	35

BAL (A)

PLAYER/POS	AVG	G	AB	R	H	2B	3B	HR	RB	BB	SO	SB
Mark Belanger, ss	.238	7	21	4	5	0	1	0	0	5	2	1
Paul Blair, of-3	.333	4	9	2	3	1	0	0	0	0	1	0
Don Buford, of	.261	6	23	3	6	1	0	2	4	3	3	0
Mike Cuellar, p	.000	2	3	0	0	0	0	0	0	1	2	0
Pat Dobson, p	.000	3	2	0	0	0	0	0	0	0	2	0
Tom Dukes, p	.000	2	0	0	0	0	0	0	0	0	0	0
Andy Etchebarren, c	.000	1	2	0	0	0	0	0	0	0	0	0
Dick Hall, p	.000	1	0	0	0	0	0	0	0	0	0	0
Elrod Hendricks, c	.263	6	19	3	5	1	0	0	1	3	3	0
Grant Jackson, p	.000	1	0	0	0	0	0	0	0	0	0	0
Davy Johnson, 2b	.148	7	27	1	4	0	0	0	3	0	1	0
Dave Leonhard, p	.000	1	0	0	0	0	0	0	0	0	0	0
Dave McNally, p	.000	4	4	0	0	0	0	0	0	0	3	0
Jim Palmer, p	.000	2	4	0	0	0	0	0	2	2	2	0
Boog Powell, 1b	.111	7	27	1	3	0	0	0	1	1	3	0
Merv Rettenmund, of-6	.185	7	27	3	5	0	0	1	4	0	4	0
Pete Richert, p	.000	1	0	0	0	0	0	0	0	0	0	0
Brooks Robinson, 3b	.318	7	22	2	7	0	0	0	5	3	1	0
Frank Robinson, of	.280	7	25	5	7	0	0	2	2	2	8	0
Tom Shopay, ph	.000	5	4	0	0	0	0	0	0	0	0	0
Eddie Watt, p	.000	2	0	0	0	0	0	0	0	0	0	0
TOTAL	.205		219	24	45	3	1	5	22	20	35	1

PITCHER	W	L	ERA	G	GS	CG	SV	SHO	IP	H	ER	BB	SO
Mike Cuellar	0	2	3.86	2	2	0	0	0	14.0	11	6	6	10
Pat Dobson	0	0	4.05	3	1	0	0	0	6.2	13	3	4	6
Tom Dukes	0	0	0.00	2	0	0	0	0	4.0	2	0	0	1
Dick Hall	0	0	0.00	1	0	0	1	0	1.0	1	0	0	0
Grant Jackson	0	0	0.00	1	0	0	0	0	0.2	0	0	1	0
Dave Leonhard	0	0	0.00	1	0	0	0	0	1.0	0	0	1	0
Dave McNally	2	1	1.98	4	2	1	0	0	13.2	10	3	5	12
Jim Palmer	1	0	2.65	2	2	0	0	0	17.0	15	5	9	15
Pete Richert	0	0	0.00	1	0	0	0	0	0.2	0	0	0	0
Eddie Watt	0	1	3.86	2	0	0	0	0	2.1	4	1	0	2
TOTAL	3	4	2.66	19	7	1	1	0	61.0	56	18	26	47

GAME 1 AT BAL OCT 9

PIT	030	000	000	3	3	0
BAL	013	010	00X	5	10	3

Pitchers: ELLIS, Moose (3), Miller (7) vs McNALLY
Home Runs: F.Robinson-BAL, Rettenmund-BAL, Buford-BAL
Attendance: 53,229

GAME 2 AT BAL OCT 11

PIT	000	000	030	3	8	1
BAL	010	361	00X	11	14	1

Pitchers: R.JOHNSON, Kison (4), Moose (4), Veale (5), Miller (6), Giusti (8) vs PALMER, Hall (9)
Home Runs: Hebner-PIT
Attendance: 53,239

GAME 3 AT PIT OCT 12

BAL	000	000	100	1	3	3
PIT	100	001	30X	5	7	0

Pitchers: CUELLAR, Dukes (7), Watt (8) vs BLASS
Home Runs: F.Robinson-BAL, Robertson-PIT
Attendance: 50,403

GAME 4 AT PIT OCT 13

BAL	300	000	000	3	4	1
PIT	201	000	10X	4	14	0

Pitchers: Dobson, Jackson (6), WATT (7), Richert (8) vs Walker, KISON (1), Giusti (8)
Attendance: 51,378

GAME 5 AT PIT OCT 14

BAL	000	000	000	0	2	1
PIT	021	010	00X	4	9	0

Pitchers: McNALLY, Leonhard (5), Dukes (6) vs BRILES
Home Runs: Robertson-PIT
Attendance: 51,377

GAME 6 AT BAL OCT 16

PIT	011	000	000	0	2	9	1
BAL	000	001	100	1	3	8	0

Pitchers: Moose, R.Johnson (6), Giusti (7), MILLER (10) vs Palmer, Dobson (10), McNally (10)
Home Runs: Clemente-PIT, Buford-BAL
Attendance: 44,174

GAME 7 AT BAL OCT 17

PIT	000	100	010	2	6	1
BAL	000	000	010	1	4	0

Pitchers: BLASS vs CUELLAR, Dobson (9), McNally (9)
Home Runs: Clemente-PIT
Attendance: 47,291

Pittsburgh traded wins with Cincinnati through the first four games—winning the first and third—and took a lead into the ninth inning of the fifth game before a home run and a wild pitch undid them.

Cincinnati got eight hits in each of the first two games. In the first game, though, only Joe Morgan's first-inning homer produced a run, and the Reds lost, 5–1. But the next day, five first-inning hits gave the Reds four runs and a lead the Pirates could not overcome.

Pirates catcher Manny Sanguillen brought Pittsburgh back in Game 3 with a home run in the fifth and the game-winning RBI in the eighth. But Reds pitcher Ross Grimsley evened the series for Cincinnati the next day with a two-hitter, in the series' only complete-game performance.

Game 5 was Pittsburgh's for 8½ innings. The Pirates scored first, and held the lead into the bottom of the ninth. But Johnny Bench opened the Reds' half of the ninth with a game-tying home run, and Tony Perez and Denis Menke followed him with singles. Bob Moose came in and retired the next two men, though George Foster (running for Perez) took third on a fly to right. Moose then threw away the pennant with a run-scoring, series-ending wild pitch.

Cincinnati Reds (West), 3; Pittsburgh Pirates (East), 2

CIN (W)

PLAYER/POS	AVG	G	AB	R	H	2B	3B	HR	RB	BB	SO	SB
Johnny Bench, c	.333	5	18	3	6	1	1	1	2	1	3	2
Jack Billingham, p	.000	1	2	0	0	0	0	0	0	0	1	0
Pedro Borbon, p	.000	3	0	0	0	0	0	0	0	0	0	0
Clay Carroll, p	.000	2	0	0	0	0	0	0	0	0	0	0
Darrel Chaney, ss	.188	5	16	3	3	0	0	0	1	1	1	1
Dave Concepcion, ss-1	.000	3	2	0	0	0	0	0	0	0	0	0
George Foster, pr	.000	1	0	1	0	0	0	0	0	0	0	0
Cesar Geronimo, of	.100	5	20	2	2	0	0	1	1	0	2	0
Ross Grimsley, p	.500	1	4	0	2	1	0	0	1	0	1	0
Don Gullett, p	.500	2	2	0	1	0	0	0	0	0	0	0
Joe Hague, ph	.000	3	1	0	0	0	0	0	0	2	1	0
Tom Hall, p	.000	2	1	0	0	0	0	0	0	0	0	0
Jim McGlothlin, p	.000	1	0	0	0	0	0	0	0	0	0	0
Hal McRae, ph	.000	1	0	0	0	0	0	0	0	0	0	0
Denis Menke, 3b	.250	5	16	1	4	1	0	0	4	3	0
Joe Morgan, 2b	.263	5	19	5	5	0	0	2	3	1	2	1
Gary Nolan, p	.000	1	2	0	0	0	0	0	0	0	1	0
Tony Perez, 1b	.200	5	20	0	4	1	0	0	2	0	7	0
Pete Rose, of	.450	5	20	1	9	4	0	0	2	1	2	0
Bobby Tolan, of	.238	5	21	3	5	1	1	0	4	0	4	0
Ted Uhlaender, ph	.500	2	2	0	1	0	0	0	0	0	0	0
TOTAL	.253		166	19	42	9	2	4	16	10	28	4

PITCHER	W	L	ERA	G	GS	CG	SV	SHO	IP	H	ER	BB	SO
Jack Billingham	0	0	3.86	1	1	0	0	0	4.2	5	2	2	4
Pedro Borbon	0	0	2.08	3	0	0	0	0	4.1	2	1	0	1
Clay Carroll	1	1	3.38	2	0	0	0	0	2.2	2	1	3	0
Ross Grimsley	1	0	1.00	1	1	1	0	0	9.0	2	1	0	5
Don Gullett	0	1	8.00	2	2	0	0	0	9.0	12	8	0	5
Tom Hall	1	0	1.23	2	0	0	0	0	7.1	3	1	3	8
Jim McGlothlin	0	0	0.00	1	0	0	0	0	1.0	0	0	0	0
Gary Nolan	0	0	1.50	1	1	0	0	0	6.0	4	1	1	4
TOTAL	3	2	3.07	13	5	1	0	0	44.0	30	15	9	27

PIT (E)

PLAYER/POS	AVG	G	AB	R	H	2B	3B	HR	RB	BB	SO	SB
Gene Alley, ss	.000	5	16	1	0	0	0	0	0	0	3	0
Steve Blass, p	.000	2	6	0	0	0	0	0	0	0	3	0
Nelson Briles, p	.000	1	2	0	0	0	0	0	0	0	1	0
Dave Cash, 2b	.211	5	19	0	4	0	0	0	3	0	0	0
Roberto Clemente, of	.235	5	17	1	4	1	0	1	2	3	5	0
Gene Clines, ph	.000	3	2	1	0	0	0	0	0	0	1	0
Vic Davalillo, ph	.000	1	0	0	0	0	0	0	0	1	0	0
Dock Ellis, p-1	.000	2	1	0	0	0	0	0	0	0	0	0
Dave Giusti, p	.000	3	1	0	0	0	0	0	0	0	0	0
Richie Hebner, 3b	.188	5	16	2	3	1	0	0	1	1	3	0
Ramon Hernandez, p	.000	3	0	0	0	0	0	0	0	0	0	0
Bob Johnson, p	.000	2	1	0	0	0	0	0	0	0	1	0
Bruce Kison, p	.000	2	2	0	0	0	0	0	0	0	0	0
Milt May, c	.500	1	2	0	1	0	0	0	1	0	0	0
Bill Mazeroski, ph	.500	2	2	0	1	0	0	0	0	0	1	0
Bob Miller, p	.000	1	0	0	0	0	0	0	0	0	0	0
Bob Moose, p	.000	2	0	0	0	0	0	0	0	0	0	0
Al Oliver, of	.250	5	20	3	5	2	1	1	3	0	4	0
Bob Robertson, 1b	.000	4	0	0	0	0	0	0	0	1	0	0
Manny Sanguillen, c	.313	5	16	4	5	1	0	1	2	0	0	0
Willie Stargell, 1b-5,of-1	.063	5	16	1	1	1	0	0	1	2	5	0
Rennie Stennett, of-5,2b-1	.286	5	21	2	6	0	0	0	0	1	1	0
Luke Walker, p	.000	1	0	0	0	0	0	0	0	0	0	0
TOTAL	.190		158	15	30	6	1	3	14	9	27	0

PITCHER	W	L	ERA	G	GS	CG	SV	SHO	IP	H	ER	BB	SO
Steve Blass	1	0	1.72	2	2	0	0	0	15.2	12	3	6	5
Nelson Briles	0	0	3.00	1	1	0	0	0	6.0	6	2	1	3
Dock Ellis	0	1	3.00	1	1	0	0	0	5.0	5	0	1	3
Dave Giusti	0	1	6.75	3	0	0	1	0	2.2	5	2	0	3
Ramon Hernandez	0	0	2.70	3	0	0	1	0	3.1	1	1	0	3
Bob Johnson	0	0	3.00	2	0	0	0	0	6.0	4	2	2	7
Bruce Kison	1	0	0.00	2	0	0	0	0	2.1	1	0	0	3
Bob Miller	0	0	0.00	1	0	0	0	0	1.0	0	0	0	1
Bob Moose	0	1	54.00	2	1	0	0	0	0.2	5	4	0	0
Luke Walker	0	0	18.00	1	0	0	0	0	1.0	3	2	0	0
TOTAL	2	3	3.30	18	5	0	2	0	43.2	42	16	10	28

GAME 1 AT PIT OCT 7

CIN	100	000	000	1	8	0
PIT	300	020	00X	5	6	0

Pitchers: GULLETT, Borbon (7) vs BLASS, R.Hernandez (9)
Home Runs: Morgan-CIN, Oliver-PIT
Attendance: 50,476

GAME 2 AT PIT OCT 8

CIN	400	000	010	5	8	1
PIT	000	000	000	3	7	1

Pitchers: Billingham, HALL (5) vs MOOSE, Johnson (1), Kison (6), R.Hernandez (7), Giusti (9)
Home Runs: Morgan-CIN
Attendance: 50,584

GAME 3 AT CIN OCT 9

PIT	000	010	110	3	7	0
CIN	002	000	000	2	8	1

Pitchers: Briles, KISON (7), Giusti (8) vs Nolan, Borbon (7), CARROLL (7), McGlothlin (9)
Home Runs: Sanguillen-PIT
Attendance: 52,420

GAME 4 AT CIN OCT 10

PIT	000	000	100	1	2	3
CIN	100	202	20X	7	11	1

Pitchers: ELLIS, Johnson (6), Walker (7), Miller (8) vs GRIMSLEY
Home Runs: Clemente-PIT
Attendance: 39,447

GAME 5 AT CIN OCT 11

PIT	020	100	000	3	8	0
CIN	001	010	002	4	7	1

Pitchers: Blass, R.Hernandez (8), GIUSTI (9), Moose (9) vs Gullett, Borbon (4), Hall (6), CARROLL (9)
Home Runs: Geronimo-CIN, Bench-CIN
Attendance: 41,887

Oakland turned back the Tigers in the first two games, but Detroit evened the series before succumbing in the fifth game.

In Game 1 Al Kaline homered off Rollie Fingers in the eleventh to give Detroit starter Mickey Lolich a 2–1 lead. But in the last of the inning, pinch hitter Gonzalo Marquez singled off Tigers reliever Chuck Seelbach with two on to drive in the tying run, and Gene Tenace scored to win it on the same play as right fielder Kaline threw the ball away. Blue Moon Odom increased the A's series lead with a three-hit shutout in Game 2, but Detroit's Joe Coleman retaliated with 14 strikeouts and a shutout of his own to save the Tigers from elimination in Game 3.

In Game 4 the A's pulled out of a 1–1 tie with two runs in the top of the 10th. But Detroit in its half of the inning went through three Oakland relievers for three runs and the win. In the finale, after Odom, the A's starter, had given Detroit a run and a brief lead in the first, he and Vida Blue divided eight shutout innings between them as the A's scored twice to capture their first pennant since Connie Mack won his last in Philadelphia 41 years earlier.

Oakland A's (West), 3;
Detroit Tigers (East), 2

OAK (W)

PLAYER/POS	AVG	G	AB	R	H	2B	3B	HR	RB	BB	SO	SB
Matty Alou, of	.381	5	21	2	8	4	0	0	2	0	2	1
Sal Bando, 3b	.200	5	20	0	4	0	0	0	0	0	3	0
Vida Blue, p	.000	4	1	0	0	0	0	0	0	0	0	0
Bert Campaneris, ss	.429	2	7	3	3	0	0	0	0	1	0	2
Tim Cullen, ss	.000	2	1	0	0	0	0	0	0	0	0	0
Dave Duncan, c	.000	2	2	0	0	0	0	0	0	1	1	0
Mike Epstein, 1b	.188	5	16	1	3	0	0	1	1	4	5	1
Rollie Fingers, p	.000	3	1	0	0	0	0	0	0	0	0	0
Dick Green, 2b	.125	5	8	0	1	1	0	0	0	0	0	0
Dave Hamilton, p	.000	1	0	0	0	0	0	0	0	0	0	0
Mike Hegan, 1b-1	.000	3	1	1	0	0	0	0	0	0	0	0
George Hendrick, of-1	.143	5	7	2	1	0	0	0	0	0	1	0
Ken Holtzman, p	.000	1	1	0	0	0	0	0	0	0	1	0
Joe Horlen, p	.000	1	0	0	0	0	0	0	0	0	0	0
Catfish Hunter, p	.167	2	6	0	1	0	0	0	0	0	2	0
Reggie Jackson, of	.278	5	18	1	5	1	0	0	2	1	6	2
Ted Kubiak, 2b-3,ss-1	.500	4	4	0	2	0	0	0	1	0	0	0
Bob Locker, p	.000	2	0	0	0	0	0	0	0	0	0	0
Angel Mangual, ph	.000	3	3	0	0	0	0	0	0	0	0	0
Gonzalo Marquez, ph	.667	3	3	1	2	0	0	0	1	0	0	0
Dal Maxvill, ss-4,2b-1	.125	5	8	0	1	0	0	0	0	1	2	1
Don Mincher, ph	.000	1	1	0	0	0	0	0	0	0	1	0
Blue Moon Odom, p-2	.250	3	4	0	1	1	0	0	0	0	1	0
Joe Rudi, of	.250	5	20	1	5	1	0	0	2	1	4	0
Gene Tenace, c-5,2b-2	.059	5	17	1	1	0	0	0	1	3	5	0
TOTAL	.224		170	13	38	8	0	1	10	12	35	7

PITCHER	W	L	ERA	G	GS	CG	SV	SHO	IP	H	ER	BB	SO
Vida Blue	0	0	0.00	4	0	0	1	0	5.1	4	0	1	5
Rollie Fingers	1	0	1.69	3	0	0	0	0	5.1	4	1	1	3
Dave Hamilton	0	0	∞	1	0	0	0	0	0.0	1	0	1	0
Ken Holtzman	0	1	4.50	1	1	0	0	0	4.0	4	2	2	2
Joe Horlen	0	1	∞	1	0	0	0	0	0.0	0	1	1	0
Catfish Hunter	0	0	1.17	2	2	0	0	0	15.1	10	2	5	9
Bob Locker	0	0	13.50	2	0	0	0	0	2.0	4	3	0	1
Blue Moon Odom	2	0	0.00	2	2	1	0	1	14.0	5	0	2	5
TOTAL	3	2	1.76	16	5	1	1	1	46.0	32	9	13	25

DET (E)

PLAYER/POS	AVG	G	AB	R	H	2B	3B	HR	RB	BB	SO	SB
Ed Brinkman, ss	.250	1	4	0	1	1	0	0	0	0	0	0
Ike Brown, 1b	.500	1	2	0	1	0	0	0	2	0	1	0
Gates Brown, ph	.000	3	2	1	0	0	0	0	0	1	0	0
Norm Cash, 1b	.267	5	15	1	4	0	0	1	2	2	3	0
Joe Coleman, p	.500	1	2	0	1	0	0	0	0	0	0	0
Bill Freehan, c	.250	3	12	2	3	1	0	1	3	0	1	0
Woody Fryman, p	.000	2	3	0	0	0	0	0	0	0	0	0
Tom Haller, ph	.000	1	1	0	0	0	0	0	0	0	0	0
John Hiller, p	.000	3	0	0	0	0	0	0	0	0	0	0
Willie Horton, of-3	.100	5	10	0	1	0	0	0	0	1	3	0
Al Kaline, of	.263	5	19	3	5	0	0	1	1	2	2	0
John Knox, pr	.000	1	0	0	0	0	0	0	0	0	0	0
Lerrin LaGrow, p	.000	1	0	0	0	0	0	0	0	0	0	0
Mickey Lolich, p	.000	2	7	0	0	0	0	0	0	0	2	0
Dick McAuliffe, ss-4,2b-1	.200	5	20	3	4	0	0	1	1	1	4	0
Joe Niekro, pr	.000	0	0	0	0	0	0	0	0	0	0	0
Jim Northrup, of	.357	5	14	0	5	0	0	0	1	2	3	0
Aurelio Rodriguez, 3b	.000	5	16	0	0	0	0	0	0	2	2	0
Fred Scherman, p	.000	1	0	0	0	0	0	0	0	0	0	0
Chuck Seelbach, p	.000	2	0	0	0	0	0	0	0	0	0	0
Duke Sims, c-2,of-2	.214	4	14	0	3	2	1	0	0	1	2	0
Mickey Stanley, of-3	.333	4	6	0	2	0	0	0	0	0	0	0
Tony Taylor, 2b	.133	4	15	0	2	2	0	0	0	0	2	0
Chris Zachary, p	.000	1	0	0	0	0	0	0	0	0	0	0
TOTAL	.198		162	10	32	6	1	4	10	13	25	0

PITCHER	W	L	ERA	G	GS	CG	SV	SHO	IP	H	ER	BB	SO
Joe Coleman	1	0	0.00	1	1	1	0	1	9.0	7	0	3	14
Woody Fryman	0	2	3.65	2	2	0	0	0	12.1	11	5	2	8
John Hiller	0	0	0.00	3	0	0	0	0	3.1	1	0	1	1
Lerrin La Grow	0	0	0.00	1	0	0	0	0	1.0	0	0	0	1
Mickey Lolich	0	1	1.42	2	2	0	0	0	19.0	14	3	5	10
Fred Scherman	0	0	0.00	1	0	0	0	0	0.2	1	0	0	1
Chuck Seelbach	0	0	18.00	1	0	0	0	0	1.0	4	2	0	0
Chris Zachary	0	0	∞	1	0	0	0	0	0.0	0	1	1	0
TOTAL	2	3	2.14	13	5	1	0	1	46.1	38	11	12	35

GAME 1 AT OAK OCT 7

```
DET   010 000 000 01   2  6  2
OAK   001 000 000 02   3 10  1
```
Pitchers: LOLICH, Seelbach (11) vs Hunter, Blue (9), FINGERS (9)
Home Runs: Cash-DET, Kaline-DET
Attendance: 29,536

GAME 2 AT OAK OCT 8

```
DET   000 000 000   0  3  1
OAK   100 040 00X   5  8  0
```
Pitchers: FRYMAN, Zachary (5), Scherman (5), LaGrow (6), Hiller (7) vs ODOM
Attendance: 31,088

GAME 3 AT DET OCT 10

```
OAK   000 000 000   0  7  0
DET   000 200 01X   3  8  1
```
Pitchers: HOLTZMAN, Fingers (5), Blue (6), Locker (7) vs COLEMAN
Home Runs: Freehan-DET
Attendance: 41,156

GAME 4 AT DET OCT 11

```
OAK   000 000 100 2   3  9  2
DET   001 000 000 3   4 10  1
```
Pitchers: Hunter, Fingers (8), Blue (9), Locker (10), HORLEN (10), Hamilton (10), Seelbach (10), HILLER (10)
Home Runs: McAuliffe-DET, Epstein-OAK
Attendance: 37,615

GAME 5 AT DET OCT 12

```
OAK   010 100 000   2  4  0
DET   100 000 000   1  5  2
```
Pitchers: ODOM, Blue (6) vs FRYMAN, Hiller (9)
Attendance: 50,276

Oakland slugger Reggie Jackson missed the Series with a pulled hamstring, but Gene Tenace (the A's backup catcher during the season) took up the slack, hitting four of the club's five homers and driving in nine of their 16 runs.

Six of the seven games were decided by a single run. Oakland won the first two in Cincinnati, 3–2, and 2–1. Tenace made the difference in the opener, driving in all the A's runs with a two-run homer in the second inning and a solo shot in the fifth. In the second game, A's starting pitcher Catfish Hunter singled in a run in the second inning which proved the margin of his victory. His 8⅔-inning performance was the longest mound outing in a Series which saw the two clubs together use nearly seven pitchers per game.

Cincinnati took the first game in Oakland, 1–0. Blue Moon Odom dueled the Reds' Jack Billingham scorelessly on one hit through six innings before giving up the game's only run on a single-sacrifice-single in the seventh. Billingham, too, yielded only three hits in eight-plus innings before yielding to ace reliever Clay Carroll, who retired the side in the ninth.

Game 4 went to Oakland, 3–2. Tenace opened the scoring with a solo homer in the fifth. The Reds' Bobby Tolan doubled in a pair in the eighth to put Cincinnati ahead, but in the last of the ninth four successive A's singles scored two runs, with Tenace scoring the game winner on pinch hitter Angel Mangual's hit. Tenace homered again in Game 5 for three runs, but it wasn't enough as the Reds tied the score in the eighth and won on Pete Rose's RBI single in the ninth.

The Reds produced the Series' only blowout with five runs in the seventh inning of Game 6 to make the score, 8–1. The finale saw Tenace drive in a run in the top of the first for a narrow Oakland lead which held until the Reds tied the game in the fifth. In the sixth the A's scored twice—Tenace doubling in the go-ahead run. Cincinnati scored once more in the eighth as a runner inherited by A's reliever Rollie Fingers came home on a sacrifice fly. But Fingers permitted no other runs to score, and the A's took the crown with their fourth one-run victory.

Oakland Athletics (AL), 4; Cincinnati Reds (NL), 3

OAK (A)

PLAYER/POS	AVG	G	AB	R	H	2B	3B	HR	RB	BB	SO	SB
Matty Alou, of	.042	7	24	0	1	0	0	0	0	3	0	1
Sal Bando, 3b	.269	7	26	2	7	1	0	0	1	2	5	0
Vida Blue, p	.000	4	1	0	0	0	0	0	0	2	1	0
Bert Campaneris, ss	.179	7	28	1	5	0	0	0	0	1	4	0
Dave Duncan, c-1	.200	3	5	0	1	0	0	0	0	1	3	0
Mike Epstein, 1b	.000	6	16	1	0	0	0	0	0	5	3	0
Rollie Fingers, p	.000	6	1	0	0	0	0	0	0	0	0	0
Dick Green, 2b	.333	7	18	0	6	2	0	0	1	0	4	0
Dave Hamilton, p	.000	2	0	0	0	0	0	0	0	0	0	0
Mike Hegan, 1b-5	.200	6	5	0	1	0	0	0	0	0	2	0
George Hendrick, of	.133	5	15	3	2	0	0	0	0	1	2	0
Ken Holtzman, p	.000	3	5	0	0	0	0	0	0	0	0	0
Joe Horlen, p	.000	1	0	0	0	0	0	0	0	0	0	0
Catfish Hunter, p	.200	3	5	0	1	0	0	0	1	2	1	0
Ted Kubiak, 2b	.333	4	3	0	1	0	0	0	0	0	0	0
Allan Lewis, pr	.000	6	0	2	0	0	0	0	0	0	0	0
Bob Locker, p	.000	1	0	0	0	0	0	0	0	0	0	0
Angel Mangual, of-2	.300	4	10	1	3	0	0	0	1	0	0	0
Gonzalo Marquez, ph	.600	5	5	0	3	0	0	0	1	0	0	0
Don Mincher, ph	1.000	3	1	0	1	0	0	0	1	0	0	0
Blue Moon Odom, p-2	.000	4	4	0	0	0	0	0	0	0	3	0
Joe Rudi, of	.240	7	25	1	6	0	0	1	1	2	5	0
Gene Tenace, c-6,1b-1	.348	7	23	5	8	1	0	4	9	4	0	0
TOTAL	.209		220	16	46	4	0	5	16	21	37	1

PITCHER	W	L	ERA	G	GS	CG	SV	SHO	IP	H	ER	BB	SO
Vida Blue	0	1	4.15	4	1	0	1	0	8.2	8	4	5	5
Rollie Fingers	1	1	1.74	6	0	0	2	0	10.1	4	2	4	11
Dave Hamilton	0	0	27.00	2	0	0	0	0	1.1	3	4	1	1
Ken Holtzman	1	0	2.13	3	2	0	0	0	12.2	11	3	3	4
Joe Horlen	0	0	6.75	1	0	0	0	0	1.1	2	1	2	1
Catfish Hunter	2	0	2.81	3	2	0	0	0	16.0	12	5	6	11
Bob Locker	0	0	0.00	1	0	0	0	0	0.1	1	0	0	0
Blue Moon Odom	0	1	1.59	2	2	0	0	0	11.1	5	2	6	13
TOTAL	4	3	3.05	22	7	0	3	0	62.0	46	21	27	46

CIN (N)

PLAYER/POS	AVG	G	AB	R	H	2B	3B	HR	RB	BB	SO	SB
Johnny Bench, c	.261	7	23	4	6	1	0	1	1	5	5	2
Jack Billingham, p	.000	3	5	0	0	0	0	0	0	0	4	0
Pedro Borbon, p	.000	6	0	0	0	0	0	0	0	0	0	0
Clay Carroll, p	.000	5	0	0	0	0	0	0	0	0	0	0
Darrel Chaney, ss-3	.000	4	7	0	0	0	0	0	0	2	2	0
Dave Concepcion, ss-5	.308	6	13	2	4	0	1	0	2	2	2	1
George Foster, of-1	.000	2	0	0	0	0	0	0	0	0	0	0
Cesar Geronimo, of	.158	7	19	1	3	0	0	0	3	1	4	1
Ross Grimsley, p	.000	4	2	0	0	0	0	0	0	0	2	0
Don Gullett, p	.000	1	2	0	0	0	0	0	0	0	0	0
Joe Hague, of-1	.000	3	3	0	0	0	0	0	0	0	0	0
Tom Hall, p	.000	4	2	0	0	0	0	0	0	0	1	0
Julian Javier, ph	.000	4	2	0	0	0	0	0	0	0	0	0
Jim McGlothlin, p	.000	1	1	0	0	0	0	0	0	0	0	0
Hal McRae, of-2	.444	5	9	1	4	1	0	0	2	0	1	0
Denis Menke, 3b	.083	7	24	1	2	0	0	1	2	2	6	0
Joe Morgan, 2b	.125	7	24	4	3	2	0	0	1	6	3	1
Gary Nolan, p	.000	2	3	0	0	0	0	0	0	0	3	0
Tony Perez, 1b	.435	7	23	3	10	2	0	0	2	4	4	0
Pete Rose, of	.214	7	28	3	6	0	0	1	2	4	4	1
Bobby Tolan, of	.269	7	26	2	7	1	0	0	6	1	4	5
Ted Uhlaender, ph	.250	4	4	0	1	1	0	0	0	0	1	0
TOTAL	.209		220	21	46	8	1	3	21	27	46	12

PITCHER	W	L	ERA	G	GS	CG	SV	SHO	IP	H	ER	BB	SO
Jack Billingham	1	0	0.00	3	2	0	1	0	13.2	6	0	4	11
Pedro Borbon	0	1	3.86	6	0	0	0	0	7.0	7	3	2	4
Clay Carroll	0	1	1.59	5	0	0	1	0	5.2	6	1	4	3
Ross Grimsley	2	1	2.57	4	1	0	0	0	7.0	7	2	3	2
Don Gullett	0	0	1.29	1	1	0	0	0	7.0	5	1	2	4
Tom Hall	0	0	0.00	4	0	0	1	0	8.1	6	0	2	7
Jim McGlothlin	0	0	12.00	1	1	0	0	0	3.0	4	4	2	3
Gary Nolan	0	1	3.38	2	2	0	0	0	10.2	7	4	2	3
TOTAL	3	2	2.17	26	7	0	3	0	62.1	46	15	21	37

GAME 1 AT CIN OCT 14

OAK	020 010 000	3	4	0
CIN	010 100 000	2	7	0

Pitchers: HOLTZMAN, Fingers (7), Blue (7) vs NOLAN, Borbon (7), Carroll (8)
Home Runs: Tenace-OAK (2)
Attendance: 52,918

GAME 2 AT CIN OCT 15

OAK	011 000 000	2	9	2
CIN	000 000 001	1	6	0

Pitchers: HUNTER, Fingers (9) vs GRIMSLEY, Borbon (6), Hall (8)
Home Runs: Rudi-OAK
Attendance: 53,224

GAME 3 AT OAK OCT 18

CIN	000 000 100	1	4	2
OAK	000 000 000	0	3	2

Pitchers: BILLINGHAM, Carroll (9) vs ODOM, Blue (8), Fingers (8)
Attendance: 49,410

GAME 4 AT OAK OCT 19

CIN	000 000 020	2	7	1
OAK	000 010 002	3	10	1

Pitchers: Gullett, Borbon (8), CARROLL (9) vs Holtzman, Blue (8), FINGERS (9)
Home Runs: Tenace-OAK
Attendance: 49,410

GAME 5 AT OAK OCT 20

CIN	100 110 011	5	8	0
OAK	030 100 000	4	7	2

Pitchers: McGlothlin, Borbon (4), Hall (5), Carroll (7), GRIMSLEY (8), Billingham (9) vs Hunter, FINGERS (5), Hamilton (9)
Home Runs: Rose-CIN, Tenace-OAK, Menke-CIN
Attendance: 49,410

GAME 6 AT CIN OCT 21

OAK	000 010 000	1	7	1
CIN	000 111 50X	8	10	0

Pitchers: BLUE, Locker (6), Hamilton (7), Horlen (7) vs Nolan, GRIMSLEY (5), Borbon (6), Hall (7)
Home Runs: Bench-CIN
Attendance: 52,737

GAME 7 AT CIN OCT 22

OAK	100 002 000	3	6	1
CIN	000 010 010	2	4	2

Pitchers: Odom, HUNTER (5), Holtzman (8), Fingers (8) vs Billingham, BORBON (6), Carroll (6), Grimsley (7), Hall (8)
Attendance: 56,040

The Mets received strong pitching throughout the series, and their offense came through just often enough to defeat Cincinnati in five games.

Though three Reds pitchers held New York to three hits in Game 1, the single Mets run in the second seemed for a time enough for a win. But Tom Seaver gave up a home run to Pete Rose in the eighth and lost the game in the ninth when Johnny Bench homered. Not wanting another last-inning loss in Game 2, the Mets unloaded for four runs in the top of the ninth to add to their one in the fourth. But this time one would have been enough as Jon Matlack blanked the Reds on two hits.

The Mets made it easy for Jerry Koosman in Game 3 in New York, scoring nine times in the first four innings. Things were more difficult for shortstop Bud Harrelson, who exchanged blows with Pete Rose following Rose's hard slide in the fifth inning. A bench-clearing melee ensued, and fans in the left field stands showered Rose with debris until a delegation of Tom Seaver, Willie Mays, and Rusty Staub visited the area to calm nerves and eliminate the threat of a forfeit. In Game 4, though, Mets bats were stifled once again as four Reds pitchers combined for a 12-inning three-hitter. The Reds won the game and tied the series on Rose's sweetly vengeful 12th-inning homer.

In the finale the Mets took a quick two-run lead. Cincinnati tied the game in the top of the fifth, but New York retaliated with four more in the bottom of the fifth. Seaver—and Tug McGraw in the ninth—held the Reds scoreless the rest of the way.

New York Mets (East), 3; Cincinnati Reds (West), 2

NY (E)

PLAYER/POS	AVG	G	AB	R	H	2B	3B	HR	RB	BB	SO	SB
Ken Boswell, ph	.000	1	1	0	0	0	0	0	0	0	0	0
Wayne Garrett, 3b	.087	5	23	1	2	1	0	0	1	0	5	0
Jerry Grote, c	.211	5	19	2	4	0	0	0	2	1	3	0
Don Hahn, of	.235	5	17	2	4	0	0	0	1	2	4	0
Bud Harrelson, ss	.167	5	18	1	3	0	0	0	2	1	1	0
Cleon Jones, of	.300	5	20	3	6	2	0	0	3	2	4	0
Jerry Koosman, p	.500	1	4	1	2	0	0	0	1	0	0	0
Ed Kranepool, of	.500	1	2	0	1	0	0	0	2	0	0	0
Jon Matlack, p	.000	1	2	0	0	0	0	0	0	1	2	0
Willie Mays, of	.333	1	3	1	1	0	0	0	1	0	0	0
Tug McGraw, p	.000	2	1	0	0	0	0	0	0	0	1	0
Felix Millan, 2b	.316	5	19	5	6	0	0	0	2	2	1	0
John Milner, 1b	.176	5	17	2	3	0	0	0	1	5	3	0
Harry Parker, p	.000	1	0	0	0	0	0	0	0	0	0	0
Tom Seaver, p	.333	2	6	1	2	2	0	0	1	1	1	0
Rusty Staub, of	.200	4	15	4	3	0	0	3	5	3	2	0
George Stone, p	.000	1	1	0	0	0	0	0	0	1	1	0
TOTAL	.220		168	23	37	5	0	3	22	19	28	0

PITCHER	W	L	ERA	G	GS	CG	SV	SHO	IP	H	ER	BB	SO
Jerry Koosman	1	0	2.00	1	1	1	0	0	9.0	8	2	0	9
Jon Matlack	1	0	0.00	1	1	1	0	1	9.0	2	0	3	9
Tug McGraw	0	0	0.00	2	0	0	1	0	5.0	4	0	3	3
Harry Parker	0	1	9.00	1	0	0	0	0	1.0	1	1	0	0
Tom Seaver	1	1	1.62	2	2	1	0	0	16.2	13	3	5	17
George Stone	0	0	1.35	1	1	0	0	0	6.2	3	1	2	4
TOTAL	3	2	1.33	8	5	3	1	1	47.1	31	7	13	42

CIN (W)

PLAYER/POS	AVG	G	AB	R	H	2B	3B	HR	RB	BB	SO	SB
Ed Armbrister, of-1	.167	3	6	0	1	0	0	0	0	0	5	0
Johnny Bench, c	.263	5	19	1	5	2	0	1	1	2	3	0
Jack Billingham, p	.000	2	3	0	0	0	0	0	0	0	1	0
Pedro Borbon, p	.000	4	0	0	0	0	0	0	0	0	0	0
Clay Carroll, p	.000	3	0	0	0	0	0	0	0	0	0	0
Darrel Chaney, ph	.000	5	9	0	0	0	0	0	0	3	4	0
Ed Crosby, ss-2	.500	3	2	0	1	0	0	0	0	0	1	0
Dan Driessen, 3b	.167	4	12	0	2	1	0	0	1	0	2	0
Phil Gagliano, ph	.000	3	3	0	0	0	0	0	0	0	1	0
Cesar Geronimo, of	.067	4	15	0	1	0	0	0	0	0	7	0
Ken Griffey, of-2	.143	3	7	0	1	1	0	0	0	0	1	0
Ross Grimsley, p	.000	2	0	0	0	0	0	0	0	0	0	0
Don Gullett, p	.000	3	1	0	0	0	0	0	0	0	0	0
Tom Hall, p	.000	3	0	0	0	0	0	0	0	0	0	0
Hal King, ph	.500	3	2	0	1	0	0	0	0	1	1	0
Andy Kosco, of	.300	3	10	0	3	0	0	0	0	2	3	0
Denis Menke, ss-2,3b-2	.222	3	9	1	2	0	0	1	1	1	2	0
Joe Morgan, 2b	.100	5	20	1	2	1	0	0	1	2	2	0
Roger Nelson, p	.000	1	1	0	0	0	0	0	0	0	1	0
Fred Norman, p	.000	1	1	0	0	0	0	0	0	0	1	0
Tony Perez, 1b	.091	5	22	1	2	0	0	1	2	0	4	0
Pete Rose, of	.381	5	21	3	8	1	0	2	2	2	2	0
Larry Stahl, ph	.500	4	4	1	2	0	0	0	0	0	1	0
Dave Tomlin, p	.000	1	0	0	0	0	0	0	0	0	0	0
TOTAL	.186		167	8	31	6	0	5	8	13	42	0

PITCHER	W	L	ERA	G	GS	CG	SV	SHO	IP	H	ER	BB	SO
Jack Billingham	0	1	4.50	2	2	0	0	0	12.0	9	6	4	9
Pedro Borbon	1	0	0.00	4	0	0	1	0	4.2	3	0	0	3
Clay Carroll	1	0	1.29	3	0	0	0	0	7.0	5	1	1	2
Ross Grimsley	0	1	12.27	2	1	0	0	0	3.2	7	5	2	3
Don Gullett	0	1	2.00	3	1	0	0	0	9.0	4	2	3	6
Tom Hall	0	0	67.50	3	0	0	0	0	0.2	3	5	4	1
Roger Nelson	0	0	0.00	1	0	0	0	0	2.1	0	0	1	0
Fred Norman	0	0	1.80	1	1	0	0	0	5.0	1	1	3	3
Dave Tomlin	0	0	16.20	1	0	0	0	0	1.2	5	3	1	1
TOTAL	2	3	4.50	20	5	0	1	0	46.0	37	23	19	28

GAME 1 AT CIN OCT 6

NY	010	000	000	1	3 0
CIN	000	000	011	2	6 0

Pitchers: SEAVER vs Billingham, Hall (9), BORBON (9)
Home Runs: Rose-CIN, Bench-CIN
Attendance: 53,431

GAME 2 AT CIN OCT 7

NY	000	100	004	5	7 0
CIN	000	000	000	0	2 0

Pitchers: MATLACK vs GULLETT, Carroll (6), Hall (9), Borbon (9)
Home Runs: Staub-NY
Attendance: 54,041

GAME 3 AT NY OCT 8

CIN	002	000	000	2	8 1
NY	151	200	00X	9	11 1

Pitchers: GRIMSLEY, Hall (2), Tomlin (3), Nelson (4), Borbon (7) vs KOOSMAN
Home Runs: Staub-NY (2), Menke-CIN
Attendance: 53,967

GAME 4 AT NY OCT 9

CIN	000	000	100	001	2 8 0
NY	001	000	000	000	1 3 2

Pitchers: Norman, Gullett (6), CARROLL (10), Borbon (12) vs Stone, McGraw (7), PARKER (12)
Home Runs: Perez-CIN, Rose-CIN
Attendance: 50,786

GAME 5 AT NY OCT 10

CIN	001	010	000	2	7 1
NY	200	041	00X	7	13 1

Pitchers: BILLINGHAM, Gullett (5), Carroll (5), Grimsley (7) vs SEAVER, McGraw (9)
Attendance: 50,323

The Orioles finally met their match in an ALCS as Oakland took its second consecutive pennant. Baltimore started strong, chasing A's starter Vida Blue with four runs in the first inning as Jim Palmer—pitching the series opener for a change—blanked the A's on five hits. But Oakland snapped back in Game 2, with five of their six runs coming on homers by Sal Bando (two, for three runs), Joe Rudi, and Bert Campaneris.

Oriole Mike Cuellar and the A's Ken Holtzman cut down opposing batters for 10½ innings in Game 3 before Oakland's Campaneris broke the 1–1 tie in the bottom of the 11th with a leadoff home run. The next day Palmer was driven out in the second inning by three Oakland runs, and the A's added to their lead with another run in the sixth. But Andy Etchebarren led a four-run Orioles comeback in the seventh with a three-run homer, and Bobby Grich's solo shot in the next inning gave the Orioles the margin they needed to win the game and tie the series.

The A's took it all in the finale, though, needing only one of their three runs as Catfish Hunter stopped Baltimore cold on five scattered hits.

Oakland A's (West), 3;
Baltimore Orioles (East), 2

OAK (W)

PLAYER/POS	AVG	G	AB	R	H	2B	3B	HR	RB	BB	SO	SB
Jesus Alou, dh-1	.333	4	6	0	2	0	0	0	1	0	1	0
Mike Andrews, 1b-1,dh-1	.000	2	1	0	0	0	0	0	0	0	0	0
Sal Bando, 3b	.167	5	18	2	3	0	0	2	3	3	6	0
Vida Blue, p	.000	2	0	0	0	0	0	0	0	0	0	0
Pat Bourque, dh	.000	2	1	0	0	0	0	0	0	2	1	0
Bert Campaneris, ss	.333	5	21	3	7	1	0	2	3	2	2	3
Billy Conigliaro, of	.000	1	4	0	0	0	0	0	0	0	2	0
Vic Davalillo, 1b-2,of-2	.625	4	8	2	5	1	1	0	1	1	0	0
Rollie Fingers, p	.000	3	0	0	0	0	0	0	0	0	0	0
Ray Fosse, c	.091	5	11	2	1	1	0	0	3	2	2	0
Dick Green, 2b	.077	5	13	0	1	1	0	0	1	0	4	0
Ken Holtzman, p	.000	1	0	0	0	0	0	0	0	0	0	0
Catfish Hunter, p	.000	2	0	0	0	0	0	0	0	0	0	0
Reggie Jackson, of	.143	5	21	0	3	0	0	0	0	0	6	0
Deron Johnson, dh	.100	4	10	0	1	0	0	0	0	2	6	0
Ted Kubiak, 2b	.000	3	2	0	0	0	0	0	0	0	1	0
Allan Lewis, pr	.000	2	0	1	0	0	0	0	0	0	0	0
Angel Mangual, of	.111	3	9	1	1	0	0	0	0	0	0	0
Blue Moon Odom, p	.000	1	0	0	0	0	0	0	0	0	0	0
Horacio Pina, p	.000	1	0	0	0	0	0	0	0	0	0	0
Joe Rudi, of	.222	5	18	1	4	0	0	1	3	3	1	0
Gene Tenace, 1b-5,c-3	.235	5	17	3	4	1	0	0	0	2	4	0
TOTAL	.200		160	15	32	5	1	5	15	17	39	3

PITCHER	W	L	ERA	G	GS	CG	SV	SHO	IP	H	ER	BB	SO
Vida Blue	0	1	10.29	2	2	0	0	0	7.0	8	8	5	3
Rollie Fingers	0	1	1.93	3	0	0	1	0	4.2	4	1	2	4
Ken Holtzman	1	0	0.82	1	1	0	0	0	11.0	3	1	1	7
Catfish Hunter	2	0	1.65	2	2	1	0	0	16.1	12	3	5	6
Blue Moon Odom	0	0	1.80	1	0	0	0	0	5.0	6	1	2	4
Horacio Pina	0	0	0.00	1	0	0	0	0	2.0	3	0	1	1
TOTAL	3	2	2.74	10	5	2	1	0	46.0	36	14	16	25

BAL (E)

PLAYER/POS	AVG	G	AB	R	H	2B	3B	HR	RB	BB	SO	SB
Doyle Alexander, p	.000	1	0	0	0	0	0	0	0	0	0	0
Frank Baker, ss	.000	2	0	0	0	0	0	0	0	0	0	0
Don Baylor, of-3	.273	4	11	3	3	0	0	0	1	3	5	0
Mark Belanger, ss	.125	5	16	0	2	0	0	0	1	1	1	0
Paul Blair, of	.167	5	18	2	3	0	0	0	0	1	5	0
Larry Brown, 3b	.000	1	0	0	0	0	0	0	0	0	0	0
Al Bumbry, of	.000	2	7	1	0	0	0	0	0	2	2	1
Rich Coggins, of	.444	2	9	1	4	1	0	0	0	0	0	0
Terry Crowley, of-1	.000	2	2	0	0	0	0	0	0	0	0	0
Mike Cuellar, p	.000	1	0	0	0	0	0	0	0	0	0	0
Tommy Davis, dh	.286	5	21	1	6	0	0	0	2	1	0	0
Andy Etchebarren, c	.357	4	14	1	5	1	0	1	4	0	1	0
Bobby Grich, 2b	.100	5	20	1	2	0	0	1	1	2	5	0
Don Hood, pr	.000	0	0	0	0	0	0	0	0	0	0	0
Grant Jackson, p	.000	2	0	0	0	0	0	0	0	0	0	0
Dave McNally, p	.000	1	0	0	0	0	0	0	0	0	0	0
Jim Palmer, p	.000	3	0	0	0	0	0	0	0	0	0	0
Boog Powell, 1b	.000	1	4	1	0	0	0	0	0	0	1	0
Merv Rettenmund, of	.091	3	11	1	1	0	0	0	0	3	2	0
Bob Reynolds, p	.000	2	0	0	0	0	0	0	0	0	0	0
Brooks Robinson, 3b	.250	5	20	1	5	2	0	0	2	1	1	0
Eddie Watt, p	.000	1	0	0	0	0	0	0	0	0	0	0
Earl Williams, 1b-4,c-1	.278	5	18	2	5	2	0	1	4	2	2	0
TOTAL	.211		171	15	36	7	0	3	15	16	25	1

PITCHER	W	L	ERA	G	GS	CG	SV	SHO	IP	H	ER	BB	SO
Doyle Alexander	0	1	4.91	1	1	0	0	0	3.2	5	2	0	1
Mike Cuellar	0	1	1.80	1	1	1	0	0	10.0	4	2	3	11
Grant Jackson	1	0	0.00	2	0	0	0	0	3.0	0	0	1	0
Dave McNally	0	1	5.87	1	1	0	0	0	7.2	7	5	2	7
Jim Palmer	1	0	1.84	3	2	1	0	1	14.2	11	3	8	15
Bob Reynolds	0	0	3.18	2	0	0	0	0	5.2	5	2	3	5
Eddie Watt	0	0	0.00	1	0	0	0	0	0.1	0	0	0	0
TOTAL	2	3	2.80	11	5	2	0	1	45.0	32	14	17	39

GAME 1 AT BAL OCT 6

OAK	000	000	000	0	5	1
BAL	400	000	11X	6	12	0

Pitchers: BLUE, Pina (1), Odom (3), Fingers (8) vs PALMER
Attendance: 41,279

GAME 2 AT BAL OCT 7

OAK	100	002	021	6	9	0
BAL	100	001	010	3	8	0

Pitchers: HUNTER, Fingers (8) vs McNALLY, Reynolds (8), G.Jackson (9)
Home Runs: Campaneris-OAK, Rudi-OAK, Bando-OAK (2)
Attendance: 48,425

GAME 3 AT OAK OCT 9

BAL	010	000	000	00	1	3	0
OAK	000	000	010	01	2	4	3

Pitchers: CUELLAR vs HOLTZMAN
Home Runs: Williams-BAL, Campaneris-OAK
Attendance: 34,367

GAME 4 AT OAK OCT 10

BAL	000	000	410	5	8	0
OAK	030	001	000	4	7	0

Pitchers: Palmer, Reynolds (2), Watt (7), G.JACKSON (7) vs Blue, FINGERS (7)
Home Runs: Etchebarren-BAL, Grich-BAL
Attendance: 27,497

GAME 5 AT OAK OCT 11

BAL	000	000	000	0	5	2
OAK	001	200	00X	3	7	0

Pitchers: ALEXANDER, Palmer (4) vs HUNTER
Attendance: 24,265

For the second year in a row, the A's were outpitched and outscored by their Series opposition, and this time they were outhit as well. But again, when the dust of Game 7 had settled, they still wore the crown. A's starter Ken Holtzman, who because of the American League's new designated hitter rule had not batted all season, doubled for the A's first hit in the third inning of Game 1 and scored the first Oakland run on an error. The A's scored again in the inning, enough for the win as Holtzman and two relievers held New York to a single run.

The Mets evened things in a Game 2 that lasted a then-record 4 hours 13 minutes. New York scored four runs with two out in the top of the 12th inning for a lead the A's were not able to overcome. (Three of the runs scored on a pair of errors by second baseman Mike Andrews, prompting a flap that rocked the baseball world as A's owner Charlie Finley tried—unsuccessfully—to "fire" Andrews by declaring him injured.) Final score of the slugfest: 10–7.

In a somewhat more normal third game, the Mets grabbed an early lead on Wayne Garrett's lead-off homer in the bottom of the first and scored a second run on two singles and wild pitch for a 2–0 lead that held up until Oakland tied the game in the eighth. In the 11th, the A's Ted Kubiak worked his way around the bases on a walk, passed ball, and single for a lead that reliever Rollie Fingers held in the bottom of the inning.

New York evened the Series on Rusty Staub's three-run homer in the first inning of Game 4 (scoring three more times later for a 6–1 win). The Mets moved in front on a sparkling 2–0 three-hitter by Jerry Koosman and Tug McGraw in Game 5, but lost their edge as the Series returned to Oakland for Game 6, losing when Reggie Jackson's doubles in the first and third drove in two runs to give the A's a lead New York was unable to overtake.

Oakland made the finale look easy. Bert Campaneris and Jackson both hit two-run homers in the third inning, and Campaneris scored a fifth run two innings later before New York finally got on the board in the sixth. In the ninth inning the Mets scored a second run with two outs, but reliever Darold Knowles came on for a record seventh pitching appearance and retired the final batter for his second Series save.

Oakland Athletics (AL), 4;
New York Mets (NL), 3

OAK (A)

PLAYER/POS	AVG	G	AB	R	H	2B	3B	HR	RB	BB	SO	SB
Jesus Alou, of-6	.158	7	19	0	3	1	0	0	3	0	0	0
Mike Andrews, 2b-1	.000	2	3	0	0	0	0	0	0	1	1	0
Sal Bando, 3b	.231	7	26	5	6	1	1	0	1	4	7	0
Vida Blue, p	.000	2	4	0	0	0	0	0	0	0	4	0
Pat Bourque, 1b	.500	2	2	0	1	0	0	0	0	0	0	0
Bert Campaneris, ss	.290	7	31	6	9	0	1	1	3	1	7	3
Billy Conigliaro, ph	.000	3	3	0	0	0	0	0	0	0	1	0
Vic Davalillo, of-4,1b-1	.091	6	11	0	1	0	0	0	0	2	1	0
Rollie Fingers, p	.333	6	3	0	1	0	0	0	0	0	1	0
Ray Fosse, c	.158	7	19	0	3	1	0	0	0	1	4	0
Dick Green, 2b	.063	7	16	0	1	0	0	0	0	1	6	0
Ken Holtzman, p	.667	3	3	2	2	2	0	0	0	0	0	0
Catfish Hunter, p	.000	2	5	0	0	0	0	0	0	0	3	0
Reggie Jackson, of	.310	7	29	3	9	3	1	1	6	2	7	0
Deron Johnson, 1b-2	.300	6	10	0	3	1	0	0	0	1	4	0
Darold Knowles, p	.000	7	0	0	0	0	0	0	0	0	0	0
Ted Kubiak, 2b	.000	4	3	1	0	0	0	0	0	1	1	0
Allan Lewis, pr	.000	3	0	1	0	0	0	0	0	0	0	0
Paul Lindblad, p	.000	3	1	0	0	0	0	0	0	0	0	0
Angel Mangual, of-1	.000	5	6	0	0	0	0	0	0	0	3	0
Blue Moon Odom, p-2	.000	3	1	0	0	0	0	0	0	0	1	0
Horacio Pina, p	.000	2	0	0	0	0	0	0	0	0	0	0
Joe Rudi, of	.333	7	27	3	9	2	0	0	4	3	4	0
Gene Tenace, 1b-7,c-3	.158	7	19	3	3	1	0	0	3	11	7	0
TOTAL	.212		241	21	51	12	3	2	20	28	62	3

PITCHER	W	L	ERA	G	GS	CG	SV	SHO	IP	H	ER	BB	SO
Vida Blue	0	1	4.91	2	2	0	0	0	11.0	10	6	3	8
Rollie Fingers	0	1	0.66	6	0	0	2	0	13.2	13	1	4	8
Ken Holtzman	2	1	4.22	3	3	0	0	0	10.2	13	5	5	6
Catfish Hunter	1	0	2.03	2	2	0	0	0	13.1	11	3	4	6
Darold Knowles	0	0	0.00	7	0	0	2	0	6.1	4	0	5	5
Paul Lindblad	1	0	0.00	3	0	0	0	0	3.1	4	0	1	1
Blue Moon Odom	0	0	3.86	2	0	0	0	0	4.2	5	2	2	2
Horacio Pina	0	0	0.00	2	0	0	0	0	3.0	6	0	2	0
TOTAL	4	3	2.32	27	7	0	4	0	66.0	66	17	26	36

NY (N)

PLAYER/POS	AVG	G	AB	R	H	2B	3B	HR	RB	BB	SO	SB
Jim Beauchamp, ph	.000	4	4	0	0	0	0	0	0	0	1	0
Ken Boswell, ph	1.000	3	3	1	3	0	0	0	0	0	0	0
Wayne Garrett, 3b	.167	7	30	4	5	0	0	2	2	5	11	0
Jerry Grote, c	.267	7	30	2	8	0	0	0	0	0	1	0
Don Hahn, of	.241	7	29	2	7	1	1	0	2	1	6	0
Bud Harrelson, ss	.250	7	24	2	6	1	0	0	1	5	3	0
Ron Hodges, ph	.000	1	0	0	0	0	0	0	0	1	0	0
Cleon Jones, of	.286	7	28	5	8	2	0	1	1	4	2	0
Jerry Koosman, p	.000	2	4	0	0	0	0	0	0	0	3	0
Ed Kranepool, ph	.000	4	3	0	0	0	0	0	0	0	0	0
Ted Martinez, pr	.000	2	0	0	0	0	0	0	0	0	0	0
Jon Matlack, p	.250	3	4	0	1	0	0	0	0	2	1	0
Willie Mays, of-2	.286	3	7	1	2	0	0	0	1	0	1	0
Tug McGraw, p	.333	5	3	1	1	0	0	0	0	0	0	0
Felix Millan, 2b	.188	7	32	3	6	1	1	0	1	1	1	0
John Milner, 1b	.296	7	27	2	8	0	0	0	2	5	1	0
Harry Parker, p	.000	3	0	0	0	0	0	0	0	0	0	0
Ray Sadecki, p	.000	4	0	0	0	0	0	0	0	0	0	0
Tom Seaver, p	.000	2	5	0	0	0	0	0	0	0	2	0
Rusty Staub, of	.423	7	26	1	11	2	0	1	6	2	2	0
George Stone, p	.000	2	0	0	0	0	0	0	0	0	0	0
George Theodore, of-1	.000	2	2	0	0	0	0	0	0	0	0	0
TOTAL	.253		261	24	66	7	2	4	16	26	36	0

PITCHER	W	L	ERA	G	GS	CG	SV	SHO	IP	H	ER	BB	SO
Jerry Koosman	1	0	3.12	2	2	0	0	0	8.2	9	3	7	8
Jon Matlack	1	2	2.16	3	3	0	0	0	16.2	10	4	5	11
Tug McGraw	1	0	2.63	5	0	0	1	0	13.2	8	4	9	14
Harry Parker	0	1	0.00	3	0	0	0	0	3.1	2	0	2	2
Ray Sadecki	0	0	1.93	4	0	0	1	0	4.2	5	1	1	6
Tom Seaver	0	1	2.40	2	2	0	0	0	15.0	13	4	3	18
George Stone	0	0	0.00	2	0	0	1	0	3.0	4	0	1	3
TOTAL	3	4	2.22	21	7	0	3	0	65.0	51	16	28	62

GAME 1 AT OAK OCT 13

NY	000 100 000	1 7 2
OAK	002 000 00X	2 4 0

Pitchers: MATLACK, McGraw (7) vs HOLTZMAN, Fingers (6), Knowles (9)
Attendance: 46,021

GAME 2 AT OAK OCT 14

NY	011 004 000 004	10 15 1
OAK	210 000 102 001	7 13 5

Pitchers: Koosman, Sadecki (3), Parker (5), McGraw (6), Stone (12) vs Blue, Pina (6), Knowles (6), Odom (8), FINGERS (10), Lindblad (12)
Home Runs: Jones-NY, Garrett-NY
Attendance: 49,151

GAME 3 AT NY OCT 16

OAK	000 001 010 01	3 10 1
NY	200 000 000 00	2 10 2

Pitchers: Hunter, Knowles (7), LINDBLAD (9), Fingers (11) vs Seaver, Sadecki (9), McGraw (9), PARKER (11)
Home Runs: Garrett-NY
Attendance: 54,817

GAME 4 AT NY OCT 17

OAK	000 100 000	1 5 1
NY	300 300 00X	6 13 1

Pitchers: HOLTZMAN, Odom (1), Knowles (4), Pina (5), MATLACK, Sadecki (9)
Home Runs: Staub-NY
Attendance: 54,817

GAME 5 AT NY OCT 18

OAK	000 000 000	0 3 1
NY	010 001 00X	2 7 1

Pitchers: BLUE, Knowles (6), Fingers (7) vs KOOSMAN, McGraw (7)
Attendance: 54,817

GAME 6 AT OAK OCT 20

NY	000 000 010	1 6 2
OAK	101 000 01X	3 7 0

Pitchers: SEAVER, McGraw (8) vs HUNTER, Knowles (8), Fingers (8)
Attendance: 49,333

GAME 7 AT OAK OCT 21

NY	000 001 001	2 8 1
OAK	004 010 00X	5 9 1

Pitchers: MATLACK, Parker (3), Sadecki (5), Stone (7) vs HOLTZMAN, Fingers (6), Knowles (9)
Home Runs: Campaneris-OAK, Jackson-OAK
Attendance: 49,333

Dodgers pitcher Don Sutton—who had brought his won-lost record from 10–9 to 19–9 with a nine-game winning streak in the regular season—continued his winning ways in the NLCS, surrendering only seven hits and one run in 17 innings and taking both the opener and clincher of the four-game series. Los Angeles' Andy Messersmith followed up Sutton's opening-game shutout with six shutout innings of his own in Game 2 before Pittsburgh scored its first two runs of the series in the seventh. They tied the score, but the Dodgers countered with three more in the top of the eighth to assure their second win.

The Pirates captured their only victory in Game 3, as Richie Hebner and Willie Stargell homered for five of the Bucs' seven runs, while Bruce Kison and Ramon Hernandez shut out the Dodgers on four hits.

Pittsburgh finally got to Sutton for a run when Stargell homered in the seventh inning of Game 4. But it was too little, and too late to stem a 12-run attack led by Steve Garvey's four hits (two of them home runs) and four RBIs for the Dodgers.

Los Angeles Dodgers (West), 3; Pittsburgh Pirates (East), 1

LA (W)

PLAYER/POS	AVG	G	AB	R	H	2B	3B	HR	RB	BB	SO	SB
Rick Auerbach, ph	1.000	1	1	0	1	1	0	0	0	0	0	0
Bill Buckner, of	.167	4	18	0	3	1	0	0	0	0	2	0
Ron Cey, 3b	.313	4	16	2	5	3	0	1	1	3	2	0
Willie Crawford, of	.250	2	4	1	1	0	0	0	1	1	1	0
Al Downing, p	.000	1	1	0	0	0	0	0	0	0	0	0
Joe Ferguson, of-3,c-2	.231	4	13	3	3	0	0	0	2	5	1	0
Steve Garvey, 1b	.389	4	18	4	7	1	0	2	5	1	1	0
Charlie Hough, p	.000	1	0	0	0	0	0	0	0	0	0	0
Von Joshua, ph	.000	1	0	0	0	0	0	0	0	1	0	0
Lee Lacy, pr	.000	1	0	0	0	0	0	0	0	0	0	0
Davey Lopes, 2b	.267	4	15	4	4	1	0	3	5	1	3
Mike Marshall, p	.000	2	0	0	0	0	0	0	0	0	0	0
Ken McMullen, ph	.000	1	1	0	0	0	0	0	0	0	1	0
Andy Messersmith, p	.000	1	3	0	0	0	0	0	0	0	1	0
Manny Mota, of-1	.333	3	3	0	1	0	0	0	1	0	0	0
Tom Paciorek, of	1.000	1	1	0	1	0	0	0	0	0	0	0
Doug Rau, p	.000	1	0	0	0	0	0	0	0	0	0	0
Bill Russell, ss	.389	4	18	1	7	0	0	0	3	1	0
Eddie Solomon, p	.000	1	0	0	0	0	0	0	0	0	0	0
Don Sutton, p	.286	2	7	0	2	0	0	0	1	2	0
Jimmy Wynn, of	.200	4	10	4	2	2	0	0	2	9	1	1
Steve Yeager, c	.000	3	9	1	0	0	0	0	0	3	3	1
TOTAL	.268		138	20	37	8	1	3	19	30	16	5

PITCHER	W	L	ERA	G	GS	CG	SV	SHO	IP	H	ER	BB	SO
Al Downing	0	0	0.00	1	0	0	0	0	4.0	1	0	1	0
Charlie Hough	0	0	7.71	1	0	0	0	0	2.1	4	2	0	2
Mike Marshall	0	0	0.00	2	0	0	0	0	3.0	0	0	0	1
Andy Messersmith	1	0	2.57	1	1	0	0	0	7.0	8	2	3	0
Doug Rau	0	1	40.50	1	1	0	0	0	0.2	3	3	1	0
Eddie Solomon	0	0	0.00	1	0	0	0	0	2.0	2	0	1	1
Don Sutton	2	0	0.53	2	2	1	0	1	17.0	7	1	2	13
TOTAL	3	1	2.00	9	4	1	0	1	36.0	25	8	8	17

PIT (E)

PLAYER/POS	AVG	G	AB	R	H	2B	3B	HR	RB	BB	SO	SB
Ken Brett, p	.000	1	1	0	0	0	0	0	0	0	1	0
Gene Clines, of	.000	2	1	1	0	0	0	0	0	0	0	0
Larry Demery, p	.000	2	0	0	0	0	0	0	0	0	0	0
Dave Giusti, p	.000	3	0	0	0	0	0	0	0	0	0	0
Richie Hebner, 3b	.231	4	13	1	3	0	0	1	4	1	4	0
Ramon Hernandez, p	.000	2	1	0	0	0	0	0	0	0	1	0
Art Howe, ph	.000	1	1	0	0	0	0	0	0	0	0	0
Ed Kirkpatrick, 1b	.000	3	9	0	0	0	0	0	0	2	0	0
Bruce Kison, p	.000	1	0	0	0	0	0	0	0	0	2	0
Mario Mendoza, ss	.200	3	5	0	1	0	0	0	1	1	0	0
Al Oliver, of	.143	4	14	1	2	0	0	0	1	2	2	0
Dave Parker, of-2	.125	3	8	0	1	0	0	0	0	0	1	0
Juan Pizarro, p	.000	1	0	0	0	0	0	0	0	0	0	0
Paul Popovich, ss	.600	3	5	1	3	0	0	0	0	0	0	0
Jerry Reuss, p	.000	2	2	0	0	0	0	0	0	0	0	0
Bob Robertson, 1b	.000	1	5	1	0	0	0	0	0	0	0	0
Jim Rooker, p	.500	1	2	0	1	0	0	0	0	0	0	0
Manny Sanguillen, c	.250	4	16	0	4	1	0	0	0	0	0	0
Willie Stargell, of	.400	4	15	3	6	0	0	2	4	1	2	0
Rennie Stennett, 2b	.063	4	16	1	1	0	0	0	0	1	1	0
Frank Taveras, ss	.000	2	2	0	0	0	0	0	0	0	0	1
Richie Zisk, of-2	.300	3	10	1	3	0	0	0	0	0	3	0
TOTAL	.194		129	10	25	1	0	3	10	8	17	1

PITCHER	W	L	ERA	G	GS	CG	SV	SHO	IP	H	ER	BB	SO
Ken Brett	0	0	7.71	1	0	0	0	0	2.1	3	2	2	1
Larry Demery	0	0	36.00	2	0	0	0	0	1.0	3	4	2	0
Dave Giusti	0	1	21.60	3	0	0	0	0	3.1	13	8	5	1
Ramon Hernandez	0	0	0.00	2	0	0	0	0	4.1	3	0	1	2
Bruce Kison	1	0	0.00	1	1	0	0	0	6.2	2	0	6	5
Juan Pizarro	0	0	0.00	1	0	0	0	0	0.2	0	0	1	0
Jerry Reuss	0	2	3.72	2	2	0	0	0	9.2	7	4	8	3
Jim Rooker	0	0	2.57	1	1	0	0	0	7.0	6	2	5	4
TOTAL	1	3	5.14	13	4	0	0	0	35.0	37	20	30	16

GAME 1 AT PIT OCT 5

LA	010	000	002	3	9 2
PIT	000	000	000	0	4 0

Pitchers: SUTTON vs REUSS, Giusti (8)
Attendance: 40,638

GAME 2 AT PIT OCT 6

LA	100	100	030	5	12 0
PIT	000	000	200	2	8 3

Pitchers: MESSERSMITH, Marshall (8) vs Rooker, GIUSTI (8), Demery (8), Hernandez (8)
Home Runs: Cey-LA
Attendance: 49,247

GAME 3 AT LA OCT 8

PIT	502	000	000	7	10 0
LA	000	000	000	0	4 5

Pitchers: KISON, Hernandez (7) vs RAU, Hough (1), Downing (4), Solomon (8)
Home Runs: Stargell-PIT, Hebner-PIT
Attendance: 55,953

GAME 4 AT LA OCT 9

PIT	000	000	100	1	3 1
LA	102	022	23X	12	12 0

Pitchers: REUSS, Brett (3), Demery (6), Giusti (7), Pizarro (8) vs SUTTON, Marshall (9)
Home Runs: Garvey-LA (2), Stargell-PIT
Attendance: 54,424

After spotting Baltimore a win in the opener, Oakland took the next three games and their third consecutive pennant. Although the A's got nine hits in Game One—their series high—the Orioles hit harder, burying Oakland under home runs by Paul Blair, Brooks Robinson, and Bobby Grich. In Game 2, though, Ken Holtzman shut out Baltimore on five hits as Sal Bando and Ray Fosse homered. Bando homered again in the third game for the only Oakland run as Jim Palmer limited the A's to four hits. But one run was enough to defeat Baltimore, for Vida Blue shut them out on a masterful two-hitter.

Orioles starter Mike Cuellar walked nine men in 4⅔ innings of Game 4, including four in the fifth to force in Oakland's first run. Two innings later Reggie Jackson's double (the only Oakland hit of the game) off reliever Ross Grimsley drove in Oakland's second run, while starter Catfish Hunter was blanking the O's through seven-plus innings. After failing to score for 30 consecutive innings, the Orioles got to reliever Rollie Fingers for a run with two out in the bottom of the ninth. But Fingers then struck out Don Baylor, and the A's had their pennant.

Oakland A's (West), 3; Baltimore Orioles (East), 1

OAK (W)

PLAYER/POS	AVG	G	AB	R	H	2B	3B	HR	RB	BB	SO	SB
Jesus Alou, ph	1.000	1	1	0	1	0	0	0	0	0	0	0
Sal Bando, 3b	.231	4	13	4	3	0	0	2	2	4	0	0
Vida Blue, p	.000	1	0	0	0	0	0	0	0	0	0	0
Bert Campaneris, ss	.176	4	17	0	3	0	0	0	3	0	3	1
Rollie Fingers, p	.000	2	0	0	0	0	0	0	0	0	0	0
Ray Fosse, c	.333	4	12	1	4	1	0	1	3	1	2	0
Dick Green, 2b	.222	4	9	0	2	0	0	0	0	2	1	0
Jim Holt, 1b-1	.000	2	0	0	0	0	0	0	0	1	0	0
Ken Holtzman, p	.000	1	0	0	0	0	0	0	0	0	0	0
Catfish Hunter, p	.000	2	0	0	0	0	0	0	0	0	0	0
Reggie Jackson, dh-3,of-1	.167	4	12	0	2	1	0	0	1	5	2	0
Angel Mangual, dh	.250	1	4	0	1	0	0	0	0	0	0	0
Dal Maxvill, 2b	.000	1	1	0	0	0	0	0	0	0	1	0
Billy North, of	.063	4	16	3	1	1	0	0	0	2	1	1
Blue Moon Odom, p-1	.000	3	0	0	0	0	0	0	0	0	0	0
Joe Rudi, of	.154	4	13	0	2	0	1	0	1	3	2	0
Gene Tenace, 1b	.000	4	11	1	0	0	0	0	1	4	4	1
Manny Trillo, pr	.000	1	0	1	0	0	0	0	0	0	0	0
Claudell Washington, of-3	.273	4	11	1	3	1	0	0	0	0	0	0
Herb Washington, pr	.000	2	0	0	0	0	0	0	0	0	0	0
TOTAL	.183		120	11	22	4	1	3	11	22	16	3

PITCHER	W	L	ERA	G	GS	CG	SV	SHO	IP	H	ER	BB	SO
Vida Blue	1	0	0.00	1	1	1	0	1	9.0	2	0	0	7
Rollie Fingers	0	0	3.00	2	0	0	1	0	3.0	3	1	1	3
Ken Holtzman	1	0	0.00	1	1	1	0	1	9.0	5	0	2	3
Catfish Hunter	1	1	4.63	2	2	0	0	0	11.2	11	6	2	6
Blue Moon Odom	0	0	0.00	1	0	0	0	0	3.1	1	0	0	1
TOTAL	3	1	1.75	7	4	2	1	2	36.0	22	7	5	20

BAL (E)

PLAYER/POS	AVG	G	AB	R	H	2B	3B	HR	RB	BB	SO	SB
Frank Baker, ss	.000	2	0	0	0	0	0	0	0	0	0	0
Don Baylor, of	.267	4	15	0	4	0	0	0	0	0	2	0
Mark Belanger, ss	.000	4	9	0	0	0	0	0	0	1	3	0
Paul Blair, of	.286	4	14	3	4	0	0	1	2	2	2	0
Al Bumbry, ph	.000	2	1	0	0	0	0	0	0	0	1	0
Enos Cabell, of-1	.250	3	4	0	1	0	0	0	0	0	2	0
Rich Coggins, of	.000	3	11	0	0	0	0	0	0	0	3	0
Mike Cuellar, p	.000	2	0	0	0	0	0	0	0	0	0	0
Tommy Davis, dh	.267	4	15	0	4	0	0	0	1	0	1	0
Andy Etchebarren, c	.333	2	6	0	2	0	0	0	0	0	0	0
Wayne Garland, p	.000	1	0	0	0	0	0	0	0	0	0	0
Bobby Grich, 2b	.250	4	16	2	4	1	0	1	2	0	1	0
Ross Grimsley, p	.000	2	0	0	0	0	0	0	0	0	0	0
Elrod Hendricks, c	.167	3	6	1	1	0	0	0	0	1	3	0
Grant Jackson, p	.000	1	0	0	0	0	0	0	0	0	0	0
Dave McNally, p	.000	1	0	0	0	0	0	0	0	0	0	0
Curt Motton, ph	.000	1	1	0	0	0	0	0	0	0	0	0
Jim Palmer, p-1	.000	2	0	0	0	0	0	0	0	0	0	0
Boog Powell, 1b	.125	2	8	0	1	0	0	0	1	0	0	0
Bob Reynolds, p	.000	1	0	0	0	0	0	0	0	0	0	0
Brooks Robinson, 3b	.083	4	12	1	1	0	0	1	1	1	0	0
Earl Williams, 1b	.000	2	6	0	0	0	0	0	0	0	2	0
TOTAL	.177		124	7	22	1	0	3	7	5	20	0

PITCHER	W	L	ERA	G	GS	CG	SV	SHO	IP	H	ER	BB	SO
Mike Cuellar	1	1	2.84	2	2	0	0	0	12.2	9	4	13	6
Wayne Garland	0	0	0.00	1	0	0	0	0	0.2	1	0	1	0
Ross Grimsley	0	0	1.69	2	0	0	0	0	5.1	1	1	2	2
Grant Jackson	0	0	0.00	1	0	0	0	0	0.1	1	0	0	1
Dave McNally	0	1	1.59	1	1	0	0	0	5.2	6	1	2	2
Jim Palmer	0	1	1.00	1	1	1	0	0	9.0	4	1	1	4
Bob Reynolds	0	0	0.00	1	0	0	0	0	1.1	0	0	3	1
TOTAL	1	3	1.80	9	4	1	0	0	35.0	22	7	22	16

GAME 1 AT OAK OCT 5

BAL	100 140 000	6 10 0
OAK	001 010 001	3 9 0

Pitchers: CUELLAR, Grimsley (9) vs HUNTER, Odom (5), Fingers (9)
Home Runs: Blair-BAL, Robinson-BAL, Grich-BAL
Attendance: 41,609

GAME 2 AT OAK OCT 6

BAL	000 000 000	0 5 2
OAK	000 101 03X	5 8 0

Pitchers: McNALLY, Garland (6), Reynolds (7), G.Jackson (8) vs HOLTZMAN
Home Runs: Bando-OAK, Fosse-OAK
Attendance: 42,810

GAME 3 AT BAL OCT 8

OAK	000 100 000	1 4 2
BAL	000 000 000	0 2 1

Pitchers: BLUE vs PALMER
Home Runs: Bando-OAK
Attendance: 32,060

GAME 4 AT BAL OCT 9

OAK	000 010 100	2 1 0
BAL	000 000 001	1 5 1

Pitchers: HUNTER, Fingers (8) vs CUELLAR, Grimsley (5)
Attendance: 28,136

Although the A's were in a turmoil of dislike for owner Charlie Finley—and for each other—they played well enough together to take their third consecutive world championship in just five games. Still, victory didn't come easily, as three of Oakland's wins came by identical 3–2 scores (as did the Dodgers' one victory), and their biggest winning margin was three runs in Game 4. It was the first World Series held entirely on the West Coast.

The A's and Dodgers split the first two games in Los Angeles. Oakland won the opener on the strength of Reggie Jackson's home run in the second inning, pitcher Ken Holtzman's double in the fifth (he moved around on a wild pitch and squeeze bunt), and a Dodgers throwing error in the eighth. The Dodgers evened the Series on Joe Ferguson's two-run homer in the sixth inning of the second game, which gave Los Angeles a 3–0 lead that an Oakland rally in the ninth failed to catch.

Los Angeles outhit Oakland in Game 3, but two of the A's runs were unearned, coming after Dodgers catcher Ferguson bobbled what should have been a third-out play in the third inning.

Pitcher Ken Holtzman, who had now gone two regular seasons without a time at bat, produced in Game 4 his second hit of the Series, this one a homer in the third inning for the game's first run. The Dodgers' Bill Russell tripled off him for two runs a half inning later, but in the last of the sixth inning Oakland regained the lead on three walks interspersed with a pair of singles and an RBI grounder to short. Four runs scored—more in this one inning than either team scored in any of the other four games.

Oakland took an early 2–0 lead in Game 5, with single runs in the first and second innings (the latter a Ray Fosse home run). The Dodgers put together a pinch-hit double, a walk, a pair of sacrifices (bunt and fly), and a single to tie the score in the sixth. But Joe Rudi hit the first pitch of Oakland's half of the seventh into the stands in left for the run that decided the game and the Series.

Oakland Athletics (AL), 4;
Los Angeles Dodgers (NL), 1

OAK (A)

PLAYER/POS	AVG	G	AB	R	H	2B	3B	HR	RB	BB	SO	SB
Jesus Alou, ph	.000	1	1	0	0	0	0	0	0	0	1	0
Sal Bando, 3b	.063	5	16	3	1	0	0	0	2	2	5	0
Vida Blue, p	.000	2	4	0	0	0	0	0	0	0	4	0
Bert Campaneris, ss	.353	5	17	1	6	2	0	0	2	0	2	1
Rollie Fingers, p	.000	4	2	0	0	0	0	0	0	0	1	0
Ray Fosse, c	.143	5	14	1	2	0	0	1	1	1	5	0
Dick Green, 2b	.000	5	13	1	0	0	0	0	0	1	4	0
Larry Haney, c	.000	2	0	0	0	0	0	0	0	0	0	0
Jim Holt, 1b-1	.667	4	3	0	2	0	0	0	2	0	0	0
Ken Holtzman, p	.500	2	4	2	2	1	0	1	1	1	1	0
Catfish Hunter, p	.000	2	2	0	0	0	0	0	0	0	2	0
Reggie Jackson, of	.286	5	14	3	4	1	0	1	1	1	5	1
Angel Mangual, ph	.000	1	1	0	0	0	0	0	0	0	1	0
Dal Maxvill, 2b	.000	2	0	0	0	0	0	0	0	0	0	0
Billy North, of	.059	5	17	3	1	0	0	0	0	2	5	1
Blue Moon Odom, p	.000	2	0	0	0	0	0	0	0	0	0	0
Joe Rudi, of-5,1b-2	.333	5	18	1	6	0	0	1	4	0	3	0
Gene Tenace, 1b	.222	5	9	0	2	0	0	0	0	3	4	0
Claudell Washington, of	.571	5	7	1	4	0	0	0	0	0	1	0
Herb Washington, pr	.000	3	0	0	0	0	0	0	0	0	0	0
TOTAL	.211		142	16	30	4	0	4	14	16	42	3

PITCHER	W	L	ERA	G	GS	CG	SV	SHO	IP	H	ER	BB	SO
Vida Blue	0	1	3.29	2	2	0	0	0	13.2	10	5	7	9
Rollie Fingers	1	0	1.93	4	0	0	2	0	9.1	8	2	2	6
Ken Holtzman	1	0	1.50	2	2	0	0	0	12.0	13	2	4	10
Catfish Hunter	1	0	1.17	2	1	0	1	0	7.2	5	1	2	5
Blue Moon Odom	1	0	0.00	2	0	0	0	0	1.1	0	0	1	2
TOTAL	4	1	2.05	12	5	0	3		44.0	36	10	16	32

LA (N)

PLAYER/POS	AVG	G	AB	R	H	2B	3B	HR	RB	BB	SO	SB
Rick Auerbach, pr	.000	1	0	0	0	0	0	0	0	0	0	0
Jim Brewer, p	.000	1	0	0	0	0	0	0	0	0	0	0
Bill Buckner, of	.250	5	20	1	5	1	0	1	1	0	1	0
Ron Cey, 3b	.176	5	17	1	3	0	0	0	0	3	3	0
Willie Crawford, of-2	.333	3	6	1	2	0	0	1	1	0	0	0
Al Downing, p	.000	1	1	0	0	0	0	0	0	0	0	0
Joe Ferguson, of-4,c-2	.125	5	16	2	2	0	0	1	2	4	6	1
Steve Garvey, 1b	.381	5	21	2	8	0	0	0	1	0	3	0
Charlie Hough, p	.000	1	0	0	0	0	0	0	0	0	0	0
Von Joshua, ph	.000	4	4	0	0	0	0	0	0	0	0	0
Lee Lacy, ph	.000	1	1	0	0	0	0	0	0	0	1	0
Davey Lopes, 2b	.111	5	18	2	2	0	0	0	0	3	4	2
Mike Marshall, p	.000	5	0	0	0	0	0	0	0	1	0	0
Andy Messersmith, p	.500	2	4	0	2	0	0	0	0	0	2	0
Tom Paciorek, ph	.500	3	2	1	1	1	0	0	0	0	0	0
Bill Russell, ss	.222	5	18	0	4	0	1	0	2	0	2	0
Don Sutton, p	.000	2	3	0	0	0	0	0	0	0	2	0
Jimmy Wynn, of	.188	5	16	1	3	1	0	1	2	4	4	0
Steve Yeager, c	.364	4	11	0	4	1	0	0	1	1	4	0
TOTAL	.228		158	11	36	4	1	4	10	16	32	3

PITCHER	W	L	ERA	G	GS	CG	SV	SHO	IP	H	ER	BB	SO
Jim Brewer	0	0	0.00	1	0	0	0	0	0.1	0	0	0	1
Al Downing	0	1	2.45	1	1	0	0	0	3.2	4	1	4	3
Charlie Hough	0	0	0.00	1	0	0	0	0	2.0	0	0	1	4
Mike Marshall	0	1	1.00	5	0	0	1	0	9.0	6	1	1	10
Andy Messersmith	0	2	4.50	2	2	0	0	0	14.0	11	7	7	12
Don Sutton	1	0	2.77	2	2	0	0	0	13.0	9	4	3	12
TOTAL	1	4	2.79	12	5	0	1	0	42.0	30	13	16	42

The Reds, who had steamrolled the National League during the season, continued their roll in the NLCS. Reds pitcher Don Gullett gave up three Pirate runs in the first game, but he drove in three himself with a home run and a single. Pitching the series' only complete game, he won easily behind his club's 12-hit, eight-run attack. The Reds won just as handily in Game 2, with Fred Norman and reliever Rawley Eastwick holding the Pirates to one run as Tony Perez drove in half the Reds' six runs—two of them with a first-inning homer.

In Game 3 the Pirates struggled gamely against elimination. Cincinnati scored first in the second, but in the sixth Al Oliver put Pittsburgh ahead with a two-run homer. In the eighth, though, Pete Rose restored the Reds' lead (and nullified rookie John Candelaria's 14-strikeout effort over 7⅔ innings) with his two-run shot. The Pirates were granted a brief reprieve when Reds reliever Eastwick walked in the tying run in the bottom of the ninth. But in the 10th the Reds scored twice on three hits, and when Eastwick's replacement Pedro Borbon shut the Pirates down in the bottom of the tenth, Cincinnati had its series sweep.

Cincinnati Reds (West), 3; Pittsburgh Pirates (East), 0

CIN (W)

PLAYER/POS	AVG	G	AB	R	H	2B	3B	HR	RB	BB	SO	SB
Ed Armbrister, ph	.000	2	0	0	0	0	0	0	0	1	0	0
Johnny Bench, c	.077	3	13	1	1	0	0	0	0	1	6	1
Pedro Borbon, p	.000	1	0	0	0	0	0	0	0	0	0	0
Clay Carroll, p	.000	1	0	0	0	0	0	0	0	0	0	0
Dave Concepcion, ss	.455	3	11	2	5	0	0	1	1	1	2	2
Terry Crowley, ph	.000	1	0	0	0	0	0	0	0	0	0	0
Rawly Eastwick, p	.000	2	0	0	0	0	0	0	0	0	0	0
George Foster, of	.364	3	11	3	4	0	0	0	0	1	2	1
Cesar Geronimo, of	.000	3	10	0	0	0	0	0	1	1	7	0
Ken Griffey, of	.333	3	12	3	4	1	0	0	4	0	3	3
Don Gullett, p	.500	1	4	1	2	0	0	1	3	0	0	0
Will McEnaney, p	.000	1	0	0	0	0	0	0	0	0	0	0
Joe Morgan, 2b	.273	3	11	2	3	3	0	0	1	3	2	4
Gary Nolan, p	.000	1	2	0	0	0	0	0	0	0	2	0
Fred Norman, p	.000	1	1	0	0	0	0	0	1	0	0	0
Tony Perez, 1b	.417	3	12	3	5	0	0	1	4	1	2	0
Merv Rettenmund, ph	.000	2	1	1	0	0	0	0	0	1	0	0
Pete Rose, 3b	.357	3	14	3	5	0	0	1	2	0	2	0
TOTAL	.284		102	19	29	4	0	4	18	9	28	11

PITCHER	W	L	ERA	G	GS	CG	SV	SHO	IP	H	ER	BB	SO
Pedro Borbon	0	0	0.00	1	0	0	1	0	1.0	0	0	0	1
Clay Carroll	0	0	0.00	1	0	0	0	0	1.0	0	0	1	1
Rawly Eastwick	1	0	0.00	2	0	0	1	0	3.2	2	0	2	1
Don Gullett	1	0	3.00	1	1	1	0	0	9.0	8	3	2	5
Will McEnaney	0	0	6.75	1	0	0	0	0	1.1	1	1	0	1
Gary Nolan	0	0	3.00	1	1	0	0	0	6.0	5	2	0	5
Fred Norman	1	0	1.50	1	1	0	0	0	6.0	4	1	5	4
TOTAL	3	0	2.25	8	3	1	2	0	28.0	20	7	10	18

PIT (E)

PLAYER/POS	AVG	G	AB	R	H	2B	3B	HR	RB	BB	SO	SB
Ken Brett, p	.000	2	0	0	0	0	0	0	0	0	0	0
John Candelaria, p	.000	1	3	0	0	0	0	0	0	0	3	0
Larry Demery, p	.000	1	0	0	0	0	0	0	0	0	0	0
Duffy Dyer, ph	.000	1	0	0	0	0	0	0	0	1	0	0
Dock Ellis, p	.000	1	0	0	0	0	0	0	0	0	0	0
Dave Giusti, p	.000	1	0	0	0	0	0	0	0	0	0	0
Richie Hebner, 3b	.333	3	12	2	4	1	0	0	2	1	1	0
Ramon Hernandez, p	.000	1	0	0	0	0	0	0	0	0	0	0
Ed Kirkpatrick, ph	.000	2	2	0	0	0	0	0	0	0	0	0
Bruce Kison, p	.000	1	0	0	0	0	0	0	0	0	0	0
Al Oliver, of	.182	3	11	1	2	0	0	1	2	2	0	0
Dave Parker, of	.000	3	10	2	0	0	0	0	0	1	3	0
Willie Randolph, 2b-1	.000	2	2	1	0	0	0	0	0	0	1	0
Jerry Reuss, p	.000	1	1	0	0	0	0	0	0	0	0	0
Craig Reynolds, ss-1	.000	2	2	0	0	0	0	0	0	0	0	0
Bob Robertson, 1b-1	.500	3	2	0	1	0	0	0	1	1	0	0
Bill Robinson, ph	.000	2	2	0	0	0	0	0	0	0	0	0
Jim Rooker, p	.000	1	1	0	0	0	0	0	0	0	1	0
Manny Sanguillen, c	.167	3	12	0	2	0	0	0	0	0	0	0
Willie Stargell, 1b	.182	3	11	1	2	1	0	0	0	1	3	0
Rennie Stennett, 2b-3,ss-1	.214	3	14	0	3	0	0	0	0	0	1	0
Frank Taveras, ss	.143	3	7	0	1	0	0	0	1	1	2	0
Kent Tekulve, p	.000	2	0	0	0	0	0	0	0	0	0	0
Richie Zisk, of	.500	3	10	0	5	1	0	0	0	2	2	0
TOTAL	.198		101	7	20	3	0	1	7	10	18	0

PITCHER	W	L	ERA	G	GS	CG	SV	SHO	IP	H	ER	BB	SO
Ken Brett	0	0	0.00	2	0	0	0	0	2.1	1	0	0	1
John Candelaria	0	0	3.52	1	1	0	0	0	7.2	3	3	2	14
Larry Demery	0	0	18.00	1	0	0	0	0	2.0	4	4	1	1
Dock Ellis	0	0	0.00	1	0	0	0	0	2.0	2	0	0	2
Dave Giusti	0	0	0.00	1	0	0	0	0	1.1	0	0	0	1
Ramon Hernandez	0	1	27.00	1	0	0	0	0	0.2	3	2	0	0
Bruce Kison	0	0	4.50	1	0	0	0	0	2.0	2	1	1	1
Jerry Reuss	0	1	13.50	1	1	0	0	0	2.2	4	4	4	1
Jim Rooker	0	1	9.00	1	1	0	0	0	4.0	7	4	0	5
Kent Tekulve	0	0	6.75	2	0	0	0	0	1.1	3	1	1	2
TOTAL	0	3	6.58	12	3	0	0	0	26.0	29	19	9	28

GAME 1 AT CIN OCT 4

PIT	020 000 001	3	8	0
CIN	013 040 00X	8	11	0

Pitchers: REUSS, Brett (3), Demery (5), Ellis (7) vs GULLETT
Home Runs: Gullett-CIN
Attendance: 54,633

GAME 2 AT CIN OCT 5

PIT	000 100 000	1	5	0
CIN	200 201 10X	6	12	1

Pitchers: ROOKER, Tekulve (5), Brett (6), Kison (7) vs NORMAN, Eastwick (7)
Home Runs: Perez-CIN
Attendance: 54,752

GAME 3 AT PIT OCT 7

CIN	010 000 020 2	5	6	0
PIT	000 002 001 0	3	7	2

Pitchers: NOLAN, C.Carroll (7), McEnaney (8), EASTWICK (9), Borbon (10) vs Candelaria, Giusti (8), HERNANDEZ (10), Tekulve (10)
Home Runs: Concepcion-CIN, Oliver-PIT, Rose-CIN
Attendance: 46,355

The Oakland A's ran their domination of the American League West to five years, but an aroused Boston team stifled their try for a fourth straight pennant.

In the first game Luis Tiant held Oakland to three hits as his teammates—aided by four Oakland errors—scored seven times before giving the A's an unearned run in the eighth. Oakland scored first in Game 2 on Reggie Jackson's two-run homer in the first inning and added a run in the fourth. But Carl Yastrzemski's two-run shot in the last of the fourth, followed by a Carlton Fisk double and a Fred Lynn single, drove out A's starter Vida Blue, and the tying run scored on a double play. Single Boston runs in the sixth, seventh, and eighth put the game away.

The A's started Ken Holtzman for the second time in Game 3, after only two days of rest. He held the Sox scoreless for three innings, but was driven from the game in the fifth. Boston scored four times before Oakland put a run on the board, and retained the lead to the game's conclusion.

Boston Red Sox (East), 3; Oakland A's (West), 0

BOS (E)

PLAYER/POS	AVG	G	AB	R	H	2B	3B	HR	RB	BB	SO	SB
Juan Beniquez, dh	.250	3	12	2	3	0	0	0	1	0	1	2
Rick Burleson, ss	.444	3	9	2	4	2	0	0	1	1	0	0
Reggie Cleveland, p	.000	1	0	0	0	0	0	0	0	0	0	0
Cecil Cooper, 1b	.400	3	10	0	4	2	0	0	1	0	2	0
Denny Doyle, 2b	.273	3	11	3	3	0	0	0	1	0	1	0
Dick Drago, p	.000	2	0	0	0	0	0	0	0	0	0	0
Dwight Evans, of	.100	3	10	1	1	1	0	0	1	1	2	0
Carlton Fisk, c	.417	3	12	4	5	1	0	0	2	0	2	1
Fred Lynn, of	.364	3	11	1	4	1	0	0	3	0	0	0
Roger Moret, p	.000	1	0	0	0	0	0	0	0	0	0	0
Rico Petrocelli, 3b	.167	3	12	1	2	0	0	1	2	0	3	0
Luis Tiant, p	.000	1	0	0	0	0	0	0	0	0	0	0
Rick Wise, p	.000	1	0	0	0	0	0	0	0	0	0	0
Carl Yastrzemski, of	.455	3	11	4	5	1	0	1	2	1	1	0
TOTAL	.316		98	18	31	8	0	2	14	3	12	3

PITCHER	W	L	ERA	G	GS	CG	SV	SHO	IP	H	ER	BB	SO
Reggie Cleveland	0	0	5.40	1	1	0	0	0	5.0	7	3	1	2
Dick Drago	0	0	0.00	2	0	0	2	0	4.2	2	0	1	2
Roger Moret	1	0	0.00	1	0	0	0	0	1.0	1	0	1	0
Luis Tiant	1	0	0.00	1	1	1	0	0	9.0	3	0	3	8
Rick Wise	1	0	2.45	1	1	0	0	0	7.1	6	2	3	2
TOTAL	3	0	1.67	6	3	1	2		27.0	19	5	9	14

OAK (W)

PLAYER/POS	AVG	G	AB	R	H	2B	3B	HR	RB	BB	SO	SB
Glenn Abbott, p	.000	1	0	0	0	0	0	0	0	0	0	0
Sal Bando, 3b	.500	3	12	1	6	2	0	0	2	0	3	0
Vida Blue, p	.000	1	0	0	0	0	0	0	0	0	0	0
Dick Bosman, p	.000	1	0	0	0	0	0	0	0	0	0	0
Bert Campaneris, ss	.000	3	11	1	0	0	0	0	0	1	1	0
Rollie Fingers, p	.000	1	0	0	0	0	0	0	0	0	0	0
Ray Fosse, c	.000	1	2	0	0	0	0	0	0	0	1	0
Phil Garner, 2b	.000	3	5	0	0	0	0	0	0	0	1	0
Tommy Harper, ph	.000	1	1	0	0	0	0	0	0	1	0	0
Jim Holt, 1b-1	.333	3	3	0	1	1	0	0	0	0	0	0
Ken Holtzman, p	.000	2	0	0	0	0	0	0	0	0	0	0
Don Hopkins, dh	.000	1	0	0	0	0	0	0	0	0	0	0
Reggie Jackson, of	.417	3	12	1	5	0	0	1	3	0	2	0
Paul Lindblad, p	.000	2	0	0	0	0	0	0	0	0	0	0
Ted Martinez, 2b	.000	3	0	0	0	0	0	0	0	0	0	0
Billy North, of	.000	3	10	0	0	0	0	0	1	2	0	0
Joe Rudi, 1b-2,of-1	.250	3	12	1	3	2	0	0	0	0	1	0
Gene Tenace, c-3,1b-1	.000	3	9	0	0	0	0	0	0	3	2	0
Jim Todd, p	.000	3	0	0	0	0	0	0	0	0	0	0
Cesar Tovar, 2b-1	.500	2	2	2	1	0	0	0	0	1	0	0
Claudell Washington, of-2,dh-1	.250	3	12	1	3	1	0	0	1	0	2	0
Billy Williams, dh-2	.000	3	8	0	0	0	0	0	0	1	1	0
TOTAL	.194		98	7	19	6	0	1	7	9	14	0

PITCHER	W	L	ERA	G	GS	CG	SV	SHO	IP	H	ER	BB	SO
Glenn Abbott	0	0	0.00	1	0	0	0	0	1.0	0	0	0	0
Vida Blue	0	0	9.00	1	1	0	0	0	3.0	6	3	0	2
Dick Bosman	0	0	0.00	1	0	0	0	0	0.1	0	0	0	0
Rollie Fingers	0	1	6.75	1	0	0	0	0	4.0	5	3	1	3
Ken Holtzman	0	2	4.09	2	2	0	0	0	11.0	12	5	1	7
Paul Lindblad	0	0	0.00	2	0	0	0	0	4.2	5	0	1	0
Jim Todd	0	0	9.00	3	0	0	0	0	1.0	3	1	0	0
TOTAL	0	3	4.32	11	3	0	0		25.0	31	12	3	12

GAME 1 AT BOS OCT 4

OAK	000 000 010	1	3	4
BOS	200 000 50X	7	8	3

Pitchers: HOLTZMAN, Todd (7), Lindblad (7), Bosman (7), Abbott (8) vs TIANT
Attendance: 35,578

GAME 2 AT BOS OCT 5

OAK	200 100 000	3	10	0
BOS	000 301 11X	6	12	0

Pitchers: Blue, Todd (4), FINGERS (5) vs Cleveland, MORET (6), Drago (7)
Home Runs: Jackson-OAK, Yastrzemski-BOS, Petrocelli-BOS
Attendance: 35,578

GAME 3 AT OAK OCT 7

BOS	000 130 010	5	11	1
OAK	000 001 020	3	6	2

Pitchers: WISE, Drago (8) vs HOLTZMAN, Todd (5), Lindblad (5)
Attendance: 49,358

The Red Sox entered the Series as underdogs to the mighty Reds, who had won 108 regular-season games. In the opening game, though, the Reds were surprised by veteran Sox starter Luis Tiant, who shut them out on five hits with the Series' first complete-game pitching effort in four years. Tiant also opened the Boston seventh with a single, starting a rally that ended only when he fouled out to end the inning after six runs had scored.

Boston took a 2–1 lead into the ninth inning of Game 2 before Johnny Bench doubled to drive out starter Bill Lee, and Dave Concepcion and Ken Griffey drove in runs off reliever Dick Drago to turn the tide for Cincinnati. The Reds moved ahead in the Series with a 10-inning victory in Game 3, a slugfest in which each club hit three home runs and used five pitchers. Boston tied the score on Dwight Evans's two-run homer in the ninth, but in the last of the 10th, the Reds' Joe Morgan drove one over the center fielder's head with the bases full to end the game.

Tiant pitched Game 4 for Boston. Four of the nine hits against him went for extra bases, and each drove in a run. But the Sox bunched six of their 11 hits in the fourth inning for five runs—their only scoring, but enough for the win. Tiant himself scored the fifth run after singling. The Reds moved nearer the title in Game 5, though, as Tony Perez homered twice for four runs in a 6–2 win for a 3–2 Series advantage.

A day of travel to Boston and three days of rain between Games 5 and 6 brought Tiant back to the mound for a third time. Rookie standout Fred Lynn gave Tiant a three-run lead with a first-inning homer, but Ken Griffey's triple and Johnny Bench's long single drove in the tying runs in the fifth. Two more runs in the seventh and Cesar Geronimo's leadoff homer in the eighth drove out Tiant, but Boston pinch hitter Bernie Carbo homered to center in the last of the eighth for three runs that tied the score again. After a trio of Boston relievers had held Cincinnati in check through the top of the 12th inning, the Sox leadoff hitter in the last of the 12th, Carlton Fisk, ended the game dramatically with a home run to left on the first pitch that came within inches of being foul.

After the pyrotechnics of Game 6 (ranked by some as the greatest World Series game ever), the seventh game, close as it was, came as an anticlimax. Boston scored three runs in the third inning, but the Reds began their comeback with Tony Perez's two-run homer in the sixth, tied the game an inning later,

Cincinnati Reds (NL), 4;
Boston Red Sox (AL), 3

CIN (N)

PLAYER/POS	AVG	G	AB	R	H	2B	3B	HR	RB	BB	SO	SB
Ed Armbrister, ph	.000	4	1	1	0	0	0	0	0	2	0	0
Johnny Bench, c	.207	7	29	5	6	2	0	1	4	2	4	0
Jack Billingham, p	.000	3	2	0	0	0	0	0	0	0	0	0
Pedro Borbon, p	.000	3	1	0	0	0	0	0	0	0	0	0
Clay Carroll, p	.000	5	0	0	0	0	0	0	0	0	0	0
Darrel Chaney, ph	.000	2	2	0	0	0	0	0	0	0	1	0
Dave Concepcion, ss	.179	7	28	3	5	1	0	1	4	0	1	3
Terry Crowley, ph	.500	2	2	0	1	0	0	0	0	1	0	0
Pat Darcy, p	.000	2	1	0	0	0	0	0	0	0	1	0
Dan Driessen, ph	.000	2	2	0	0	0	0	0	0	0	0	0
Rawly Eastwick, p	.000	5	1	0	0	0	0	0	0	0	0	0
George Foster, of	.276	7	29	1	8	1	0	0	2	1	1	1
Cesar Geronimo, of	.280	7	25	3	7	0	1	2	3	3	5	0
Ken Griffey, of	.269	7	26	4	7	3	1	0	4	4	2	2
Don Gullett, p	.286	3	7	1	2	0	0	0	0	0	2	0
Will McEnaney, p	1.000	5	1	0	1	0	0	0	0	0	0	0
Joe Morgan, 2b	.259	7	27	4	7	1	0	0	3	5	1	2
Gary Nolan, p	.000	2	1	0	0	0	0	0	0	0	0	0
Fred Norman, p	.000	2	1	0	0	0	0	0	0	0	0	0
Tony Perez, 1b	.179	7	28	4	5	0	0	3	7	3	9	1
Merv Rettenmund, ph	.000	3	3	0	0	0	0	0	0	0	1	0
Pete Rose, 3b	.370	7	27	3	10	1	1	0	2	5	1	0
TOTAL	.242		244	29	59	9	3	7	29	25	30	9

PITCHER	W	L	ERA	G	GS	CG	SV	SHO	IP	H	ER	BB	SO
Jack Billingham	0	0	1.00	3	1	0	0	0	9.0	8	1	5	7
Pedro Borbon	0	0	6.00	3	0	0	0	0	3.0	3	2	2	1
Clay Carroll	1	0	3.18	5	0	0	0	0	5.2	4	2	2	3
Pat Darcy	0	1	4.50	2	0	0	0	0	4.0	3	2	2	1
Rawly Eastwick	2	0	2.25	5	0	0	1	0	8.0	6	2	3	4
Don Gullett	1	1	4.34	3	3	0	0	0	18.2	19	9	10	15
Will McEnaney	0	0	2.70	5	0	0	1	0	6.2	3	2	2	5
Gary Nolan	0	0	6.00	2	2	0	0	0	6.0	6	4	1	2
Fred Norman	0	1	9.00	2	1	0	0	0	4.0	8	4	3	2
TOTAL	4	3	3.88	30	7	0	2	0	65.0	60	28	30	40

BOS (A)

PLAYER/POS	AVG	G	AB	R	H	2B	3B	HR	RB	BB	SO	SB
Juan Beniquez, of-2	.125	3	8	0	1	0	0	0	0	1	1	0
Rick Burleson, ss	.292	7	24	1	7	1	0	0	2	4	2	0
Jim Burton, p	.000	2	0	0	0	0	0	0	0	0	0	0
Bernie Carbo, of-2	.429	4	7	3	3	1	0	2	4	1	1	0
Reggie Cleveland, p	.000	3	2	0	0	0	0	0	0	0	2	0
Cecil Cooper, 1b	.053	5	19	0	1	1	0	0	1	0	3	0
Denny Doyle, 2b	.267	7	30	3	8	1	0	0	0	2	1	0
Dick Drago, p	.000	2	0	0	0	0	0	0	0	0	0	0
Dwight Evans, of	.292	7	24	3	7	1	1	1	5	3	4	0
Carlton Fisk, c	.240	7	25	5	6	0	0	2	4	7	7	0
Doug Griffin, ph	.000	1	1	0	0	0	0	0	0	0	0	0
Bill Lee, p	.167	2	6	0	1	0	0	0	0	0	3	0
Fred Lynn, of	.280	7	25	3	7	1	0	1	5	3	5	0
Rick Miller, of-2	.000	3	2	0	0	0	0	0	0	0	0	0
Bob Montgomery, ph	.000	1	1	0	0	0	0	0	0	0	0	0
Roger Moret, p	.000	3	0	0	0	0	0	0	0	0	0	0
Rico Petrocelli, 3b	.308	7	26	3	8	1	0	0	4	3	6	0
Dick Pole, p	.000	1	0	0	0	0	0	0	0	0	0	0
Diego Segui, p	.000	1	0	0	0	0	0	0	0	0	0	0
Luis Tiant, p	.250	3	8	2	2	0	0	0	0	2	4	0
Jim Willoughby, p	.000	3	0	0	0	0	0	0	0	0	0	0
Rick Wise, p	.000	2	0	0	0	0	0	0	0	0	0	0
Carl Yastrzemski, 1b-4,of-4	.310	7	29	7	9	0	0	0	4	4	1	0
TOTAL	.251		239	30	60	7	2	6	30	30	40	0

PITCHER	W	L	ERA	G	GS	CG	SV	SHO	IP	H	ER	BB	SO
Jim Burton	0	1	9.00	2	0	0	0	0	1.0	1	1	3	0
Reggie Cleveland	0	1	6.75	3	1	0	0	0	6.2	7	5	3	5
Dick Drago	0	1	2.25	2	0	0	0	0	4.0	3	1	1	1
Bill Lee	0	0	3.14	2	2	0	0	0	14.1	12	5	3	7
Roger Moret	0	0	0.00	3	0	0	0	0	1.2	2	0	3	1
Dick Pole	0	0	INF	1	0	0	0	0	0.0	0	1	2	0
Diego Segui	0	0	0.00	1	0	0	0	0	2.0	0	0	4	0
Luis Tiant	2	0	3.60	3	3	2	0	1	25.0	25	10	8	12
Jim Willoughby	0	1	0.00	3	0	0	0	0	6.1	3	0	0	2
Rick Wise	1	0	8.44	2	1	0	0	0	5.1	6	5	2	2
TOTAL	3	4	3.86	22	7	2	0	1	65.1	59	28	25	30

and took a 4–3 lead on Joe Morgan's bloop RBI single in the ninth. Reliever Will McEnaney came on to set the Sox down in order in the last of the ninth, and the Reds went home with their first world title in 35 years.

GAME 1 AT BOS OCT 11

CIN	000 000 000	0	5	0
BOS	000 000 60X	6	12	0

Pitchers: GULLETT, Carroll (7), McEnaney (7) vs TIANT
Attendance: 35,205

GAME 2 AT BOS OCT 12

CIN	000 100 002	3	7	1
BOS	100 001 000	2	7	0

Pitchers: Billingham, Borbon (6), McEnaney (7), EASTWICK (8) vs Lee, Drago (9)
Attendance: 35,205

GAME 3 AT CIN OCT 14

BOS	010 001 102 0	5	10	2
CIN	000 230 000 1	6	7	0

Pitchers: Wise, Burton (5), Cleveland (5), WILLOUGHBY (7), Moret (10) vs Nolan, Darcy (5), Carroll (7), McEnaney (7), EASTWICK (9)
Home Runs: Fisk-BOS, Bench-CIN, Concepcion-CIN, Geronimo-CIN, Carbo-BOS, Evans-BOS
Attendance: 55,392

GAME 4 AT CIN OCT 15

BOS	000 500 000	5	11	1
CIN	200 200 000	4	9	1

Pitchers: TIANT vs NORMAN, Borbon (4), Carroll (5), Eastwick (7)
Attendance: 55,667

GAME 5 AT CIN OCT 16

BOS	100 000 001	2	5	0
CIN	000 113 01X	6	8	0

Pitchers: CLEVELAND, Willoughby (6), Pole (8), Segui (8) vs GULLETT, Eastwick (9)
Home Runs: Perez-CIN (2)
Attendance: 56,393

GAME 6 AT BOS OCT 21

CIN	000 030 210 000	6	14	0
BOS	300 000 030 001	7	10	1

Pitchers: Nolan, Norman (3), Billingham (5), Carroll (5), Borbon (6), Eastwick (8), McEnaney (9), DARCY (10) vs Tiant, Moret (8), Drago (9), WISE (12)
Home Runs: Lynn-BOS, Geronimo-CIN, Carbo-BOS, Fisk-BOS
Attendance: 35,205

GAME 7 AT BOS OCT 22

CIN	000 002 101	4	9	0
BOS	003 000 000	3	5	2

Pitchers: Gullett, Billingham (5), CARROLL (7), McEnaney (9) vs Lee, Moret (7), Willoughby (7), BURTON (9), Cleveland (9)
Home Runs: Perez-CIN
Attendance: 35,205

Philadelphia outhit Cincinnati in two of the three games, but couldn't turn enough hits into runs, as the Reds for the second year in a row swept the NLCS. The Phillies scored first in Game 1 with a run in the first inning. But pitcher Don Gullett held them scoreless for the next seven innings as his Reds caught up in the third, moved ahead in the sixth, and took a five-run lead into the last of the ninth. The Phillies scored twice in their half of the inning, but the rally fell short.

In the second game the Phillies outhit the Reds (10-6), scoring the game's first two runs while their starter Jim Lonborg threw a no-hitter for five innings. But in the sixth a walk and two singles drove Lonborg out and set the Reds off on a two-inning six-run spree for their second win.

Again in Game 3 the Phillies outhit the Reds, this time going into the last of the ninth ahead by two runs. But George Foster and Johnny Bench hit back-to-back homers off Ron Reed to tie the score, and two relievers (and a single and two walks) later, the Reds brought home another pennant as Ken Griffey's high-bouncing chop glanced off first baseman Bobby Tolan's outstretched glove.

Cincinnati Reds (West), 3; Philadelphia Phillies (East), 0

CIN (W)

PLAYER/POS	AVG	G	AB	R	H	2B	3B	HR	RB	BB	SO	SB
Ed Armbrister, ph	.000	1	0	0	0	0	0	0	0	0	0	0
Johnny Bench, c	.333	3	12	3	4	1	0	1	1	1	2	1
Pedro Borbon, p	.000	2	2	1	0	0	0	0	0	0	2	0
Dave Concepcion, ss	.200	3	10	4	2	1	0	0	0	2	1	0
Dan Driessen, ph	.000	1	1	0	0	0	0	0	0	0	0	0
Rawly Eastwick, p	.000	2	0	0	0	0	0	0	0	0	0	0
Doug Flynn, 2b	.000	1	0	0	0	0	0	0	0	0	0	0
George Foster, of	.167	3	12	2	2	0	0	2	4	0	4	0
Cesar Geronimo, of	.182	3	11	0	2	0	1	0	2	1	3	0
Ken Griffey, of	.385	3	13	2	5	0	1	0	2	2	1	2
Don Gullett, p	.500	1	4	1	2	1	0	0	3	0	0	0
Mike Lum, ph	.000	1	1	0	0	0	0	0	0	0	0	0
Joe Morgan, 2b	.000	3	7	2	0	0	0	0	0	6	1	2
Gary Nolan, p	.000	1	0	0	0	0	0	0	0	0	1	0
Tony Perez, 1b	.200	3	10	1	2	0	0	0	3	1	2	0
Pete Rose, 3b	.429	3	14	3	6	2	1	0	2	1	0	0
Manny Sarmiento, p	.000	1	1	0	0	0	0	0	0	0	0	0
Pat Zachry, p	.000	1	1	0	0	0	0	0	0	0	0	0
TOTAL	.253		99	19	25	5	3	3	17	15	16	5

PITCHER	W	L	ERA	G	GS	CG	SV	SHO	IP	H	ER	BB	SO
Pedro Borbon	0	0	0.00	2	0	0	1	0	4.1	4	0	1	0
Rawly Eastwick	1	0	12.00	2	0	0	0	0	3.0	7	4	2	1
Don Gullett	1	0	1.13	1	1	0	0	0	8.0	2	1	3	4
Gary Nolan	0	0	1.59	1	1	0	0	0	5.2	6	1	2	1
Manny Sarmiento	0	0	18.00	1	0	0	0	0	1.0	2	2	1	0
Pat Zachry	1	0	3.60	1	1	0	0	0	5.0	6	2	3	3
TOTAL	3	0	3.33	8	3	0	1	0	27.0	27	10	12	9

PHI (E)

PLAYER/POS	AVG	G	AB	R	H	2B	3B	HR	RB	BB	SO	SB
Richie Allen, 1b	.222	3	9	1	2	0	0	0	0	3	2	0
Bob Boone, c	.286	3	7	0	2	0	0	0	1	1	0	0
Larry Bowa, ss	.125	3	8	1	1	1	0	0	1	3	0	0
Ollie Brown, of	.000	1	2	0	0	0	0	0	0	1	1	0
Steve Carlton, p	.000	1	2	0	0	0	0	0	0	0	0	0
Dave Cash, 2b	.308	3	13	1	4	1	0	0	1	0	0	0
Gene Garber, p	.000	2	0	0	0	0	0	0	0	0	0	0
Terry Harmon, pr	.000	1	0	1	0	0	0	0	0	0	0	0
Tom Hutton, ph	.000	1	1	0	0	0	0	0	0	0	0	0
Jay Johnstone, of-2	.778	3	9	1	7	1	1	0	2	1	0	0
Jim Kaat, p	.500	1	2	0	1	0	0	0	0	0	0	0
Jim Lonborg, p	.000	1	2	0	0	0	0	0	0	0	0	0
Greg Luzinski, of	.273	3	11	2	3	2	0	1	2	1	4	0
Garry Maddox, of	.231	3	13	2	3	1	0	0	2	1	0	0
Jerry Martin, of	.000	1	1	1	0	0	0	0	0	0	0	0
Tim McCarver, c-1	.000	2	4	0	0	0	0	0	0	0	1	0
Tug McGraw, p	.000	2	0	0	0	0	0	0	0	0	0	0
Johnny Oates, c	.000	1	1	0	0	0	0	0	0	0	0	0
Ron Reed, p	.000	2	1	0	0	0	0	0	0	0	0	0
Mike Schmidt, 3b	.308	3	13	1	4	2	0	0	2	0	1	0
Bobby Tolan, 1b-1,of-1	.000	3	2	0	0	0	0	0	0	1	0	0
Tom Underwood, p	.000	1	0	0	0	0	0	0	0	0	0	0
TOTAL	.270		100	11	27	8	1	1	11	12	9	0

PITCHER	W	L	ERA	G	GS	CG	SV	SHO	IP	H	ER	BB	SO
Steve Carlton	0	1	5.14	1	1	0	0	0	7.0	8	4	5	6
Gene Garber	0	1	13.50	2	0	0	0	0	0.2	2	1	1	0
Jim Kaat	0	0	3.00	1	1	0	0	0	6.0	2	2	2	1
Jim Lonborg	0	1	1.69	1	1	0	0	0	5.1	2	1	2	2
Tug McGraw	0	0	11.57	2	0	0	0	0	2.1	4	3	1	5
Ron Reed	0	0	7.71	2	0	0	0	0	4.2	6	4	2	2
Tom Underwood	0	0	0.00	1	0	0	0	0	0.1	1	0	2	0
TOTAL	0	3	5.13	10	3	0	0	0	26.1	25	15	15	16

GAME 1 AT PHI OCT 9

CIN	001 002 030	6	10	0
PHI	100 000 002	3	6	1

Pitchers: GULLETT, Eastwick (9) vs CARLTON, McGraw (8)
Home Runs: Foster-CIN
Attendance: 62,640

GAME 2 AT PHI OCT 10

CIN	000 004 200	6	6	0
PHI	010 010 000	2	10	1

Pitchers: ZACHRY, Borbon (6) vs LONBORG, Garber (6), McGraw (7), Reed (7)
Home Runs: Luzinski-PHI
Attendance: 62,651

GAME 3 AT CIN OCT 12

PHI	000 100 221	6	11	0
CIN	000 000 403	7	9	2

Pitchers: Kaat, Reed (7), GARBER (9), Underwood (9) vs Nolan, Sarmiento (6), Borbon (7), EASTWICK (8)
Home Runs: Foster-CIN, Bench-CIN
Attendance: 55,047

Returning to postseason play after a dozen years' absence, the Yankees found themselves evenly matched with the first-time-champion Royals. They didn't really need their two ninth-inning runs in the first game: the two they scored in the first inning proved cushion enough for Catfish Hunter's five-hitter. But Kansas City came back the next day, scoring first, losing the lead in the third, then regaining it for good in the sixth to gain a split in Kansas City.

The Royals again took a first-inning lead in Game 3, but this time the Yankees, once they went ahead in the sixth, didn't let go. Kansas City held on to its early lead in Game 4, building on it throughout the game for a second win, despite Graig Nettles' two home runs for New York.

But Game 5—like the series itself—was a seesaw affair. For the fourth time the Royals scored first, with a pair in the first on John Mayberry's home run. But the Yankees tied the game when they came to bat, and K.C. retook the lead in the second. New York went ahead again in the third and increased its lead to 6–3 in the sixth. But in the top of the eighth, George Brett's three-run homer tied the score once again, setting the stage for Chris Chambliss to win the 30th American League pennant for the Yankees with his first-pitch home run in the bottom of the ninth.

New York Yankees (East), 3; Kansas City Royals (West), 2

NY (E)

PLAYER/POS	AVG	G	AB	R	H	2B	3B	HR	RB	BB	SO	SB
Sandy Alomar, dh-1	.000	2	1	0	0	0	0	0	0	0	0	0
Chris Chambliss, 1b	.524	5	21	5	11	1	1	2	8	0	1	2
Dock Ellis, p	.000	1	0	0	0	0	0	0	0	0	0	0
Ed Figueroa, p	.000	2	0	0	0	0	0	0	0	0	0	0
Oscar Gamble, of	.250	3	8	1	2	1	0	0	1	1	1	0
Ron Guidry, pr	.000	1	0	0	0	0	0	0	0	0	0	0
Elrod Hendricks, ph	1.000	1	1	0	1	0	0	0	0	0	0	0
Catfish Hunter, p	.000	2	0	0	0	0	0	0	0	0	0	0
Grant Jackson, p	.000	2	0	0	0	0	0	0	0	0	0	0
Sparky Lyle, p	.000	1	0	0	0	0	0	0	0	0	0	0
Elliott Maddox, of	.222	3	9	0	2	1	0	0	1	0	1	0
Jim Mason, ss	.000	2	0	0	0	0	0	0	0	0	0	0
Carlos May, dh	.200	3	10	1	2	1	0	0	0	1	4	0
Thurman Munson, c	.435	5	23	3	10	2	0	0	3	0	1	0
Graig Nettles, 3b	.235	5	17	2	4	1	0	2	4	3	3	0
Lou Piniella, dh-3	.273	4	11	1	3	1	0	0	0	0	1	0
Willie Randolph, 2b	.118	5	17	0	2	0	0	0	1	3	1	1
Mickey Rivers, of	.348	5	23	5	8	0	1	0	0	1	1	0
Fred Stanley, ss	.333	5	15	1	5	2	0	0	2	0	2	0
Dick Tidrow, p	.000	3	0	0	0	0	0	0	0	0	0	0
Otto Velez, ph	.000	1	1	0	0	0	0	0	0	0	0	0
Roy White, of	.294	5	17	4	5	3	0	0	3	5	1	1
TOTAL	.316		174	23	55	13	2	4	21	16	15	4

PITCHER	W	L	ERA	G	GS	CG	SV	SHO	IP	H	ER	BB	SO
Dock Ellis	1	0	3.38	1	1	0	0	0	8.0	6	3	2	5
Ed Figueroa	0	1	5.84	2	2	0	0	0	12.1	14	8	2	5
Catfish Hunter	1	1	4.50	2	2	1	0	0	12.0	10	6	1	5
Grant Jackson	0	0	8.10	2	0	0	0	0	3.1	4	3	1	3
Sparky Lyle	0	0	0.00	1	0	0	1	0	1.0	0	0	1	0
Dick Tidrow	1	0	3.68	3	0	0	0	0	7.1	6	3	4	0
TOTAL	3	2	4.70	11	5	1	1	0	44.0	40	23	11	18

KC (W)

PLAYER/POS	AVG	G	AB	R	H	2B	3B	HR	RB	BB	SO	SB
Doug Bird, p	.000	1	0	0	0	0	0	0	0	0	0	0
George Brett, 3b	.444	5	18	4	8	1	1	1	5	2	1	0
Al Cowens, of	.190	5	21	3	4	0	1	0	0	1	1	2
Larry Gura, p	.000	2	0	0	0	0	0	0	0	0	0	0
Tom Hall, p	.000	1	0	0	0	0	0	0	0	0	0	0
Andy Hassler, p	.000	2	0	0	0	0	0	0	0	0	0	0
Dennis Leonard, p	.000	2	0	0	0	0	0	0	0	0	0	0
Mark Littell, p	.000	3	0	0	0	0	0	0	0	0	0	0
Buck Martinez, c	.333	5	15	0	5	0	0	0	4	1	3	0
John Mayberry, 1b	.222	5	18	4	4	0	0	1	3	1	0	0
Hal McRae, dh-3,of-2	.118	5	17	2	2	1	1	0	1	1	4	0
Steve Mingori, p	.000	3	0	0	0	0	0	0	0	0	0	0
Dave Nelson, dh-1	.000	2	2	0	0	0	0	0	0	0	1	0
Amos Otis, of	.000	1	1	0	0	0	0	0	0	0	0	0
Freddie Patek, ss	.389	5	18	2	7	2	0	0	4	0	1	0
Marty Pattin, p	.000	2	0	0	0	0	0	0	0	0	0	0
Tom Poquette, of	.188	5	16	1	3	2	0	0	4	2	3	0
Jamie Quirk, dh-2	.143	4	7	1	1	0	1	0	2	0	2	0
Cookie Rojas, 2b	.333	4	9	2	3	0	0	0	1	0	0	1
Paul Splittorff, p	.000	2	0	0	0	0	0	0	0	0	0	0
Bob Stinson, c-1	.000	2	1	0	0	0	0	0	0	0	0	0
John Wathan, c	.000	1	0	0	0	0	0	0	0	0	0	0
Frank White, 2b	.125	4	8	2	1	0	0	0	0	0	1	0
Jim Wohlford, of	.182	5	11	3	2	0	0	0	0	3	1	2
TOTAL	.247		162	24	40	6	4	2	24	11	18	5

PITCHER	W	L	ERA	G	GS	CG	SV	SHO	IP	H	ER	BB	SO
Doug Bird	1	0	1.93	1	0	0	0	0	4.2	4	1	0	1
Larry Gura	0	1	4.22	2	2	0	0	0	10.2	18	5	1	4
Tom Hall	0	0	0.00	1	0	0	0	0	0.1	1	0	0	0
Andy Hassler	0	1	6.14	2	1	0	0	0	7.1	8	5	6	4
Dennis Leonard	0	0	19.29	2	2	0	0	0	2.1	9	5	2	0
Mark Littell	0	1	1.93	3	0	0	0	0	4.2	4	1	1	3
Steve Mingori	0	0	2.70	3	0	0	1	0	3.1	4	1	0	1
Marty Pattin	0	0	27.00	2	0	0	0	0	0.1	0	1	1	0
Paul Splittorff	1	0	1.93	2	0	0	0	0	9.1	7	2	5	2
TOTAL	2	3	4.40	18	5	0	1	0	43.0	55	21	16	15

GAME 1 AT KC OCT 9

NY	200	000	002	4	12	0
KC	000	000	010	1	5	2

Pitchers: HUNTER vs GURA, Littell (9)
Attendance: 41,077

GAME 2 AT KC OCT 10

NY	012	000	000	3	12	5
KC	200	002	03X	7	9	0

Pitchers: FIGUEROA, Tidrow (6) vs Leonard, SPLITTORFF (3), Mingori (9)
Attendance: 41,091

GAME 3 AT NY OCT 12

KC	300	000	000	3	6	0
NY	000	203	00X	5	9	0

Pitchers: HASSLER, Pattin (6), Hall (6), Mingori (6), Littell (6) vs ELLIS, Lyle (9)
Home Runs: Chambliss-NY
Attendance: 56,808

GAME 4 AT NY OCT 13

KC	030	201	010	7	9	1
NY	020	000	101	4	11	0

Pitchers: Gura, BIRD (3), Mingori (7) vs HUNTER, Tidrow (7), Jackson (7)
Home Runs: Nettles-NY (2)
Attendance: 56,355

GAME 5 AT NY OCT 14

KC	210	000	030	6	11	1
NY	202	002	001	7	11	1

Pitchers: Leonard, Splittorff (1), Pattin (4), Hassler (5), LITTELL (7) vs Figueroa, Jackson (8), TIDROW (9)
Home Runs: Mayberry-KC, Brett-KC, Chambliss-NY
Attendance: 56,821

The Reds led the National League in virtually every offensive category and in fielding as well. In the Series (which, incidentally, was the first to employ the designated hitter), the Big Red Machine continued its roll over the Yankees to become the first National League club in 54 years to repeat as world champions, as well as the first team to sweep both a League Championship and World Series. Reds catcher Johnny Bench led the attack with eight hits, half of them for extra bases, for a batting average of .533 and a 1.133 average in slugging.

Joe Morgan's home run for Cincinnati in the first inning of Game 1 was the first hit of the Series, but New York pushed across a tying run half an inning later on a sacrifice fly. Pitchers Don Gullett and Pedro Borbon held the Yankees scoreless after that as the Reds regained the lead with a run in the third and extended it in the sixth and seventh for a 5–1 win.

Game 2 turned out to be the Reds' only narrow victory. They scored first, with three runs in the second inning. In the fourth the Yankees scored their first run, and they tied the score with two more runs in the seventh. But with two men out in the last of the ninth, a throwing error by Yankee shortstop Fred Stanley allowed Ken Griffey to reach second. Griffey then scored the winning run on Tony Perez's line single to left.

In Game 3, four hits and a pair of stolen bases put Cincinnati ahead 3–0 in the second inning, and Dan Driessen homered in the fourth to make it 4–0 before the Yankees scored their first run. Another quartet of hits in the eighth gave the Reds two more runs and a 6–2 win.

New York took the lead for the only time in the Series when Chris Chambliss doubled in Thurman Munson in the first inning of Game 4. (Munson had singled with the third of what became six straight hits.) But the Reds' George Foster drove in a tying run in the fourth, and Johnny Bench followed him with a two-run homer. New York scored again an inning later to come close, but Bench's second home run, a three-run blast in the ninth, put the game out of reach, and a pair of ground-rule doubles touched by New York fans put a lid on Cincinnati's sweep.

Cincinnati Reds (NL), 4;
New York Yankees (AL), 0

CIN (N)

PLAYER/POS	AVG	G	AB	R	H	2B	3B	HR	RB	BB	SO	SB
Johnny Bench, c	.533	4	15	4	8	1	1	2	6	0	1	0
Jack Billingham, p	.000	1	0	0	0	0	0	0	0	0	0	0
Pedro Borbon, p	.000	1	0	0	0	0	0	0	0	0	0	0
Dave Concepcion, ss	.357	4	14	1	5	1	1	0	3	1	3	1
Dan Driessen, dh	.357	4	14	4	5	2	0	1	1	2	0	1
George Foster, of	.429	4	14	3	6	1	0	0	4	2	3	0
Cesar Geronimo, of	.308	4	13	3	4	2	0	0	1	2	2	2
Ken Griffey, of	.059	4	17	2	1	0	0	0	1	0	1	1
Don Gullett, p	.000	1	0	0	0	0	0	0	0	0	0	0
Will McEnaney, p	.000	2	0	0	0	0	0	0	0	0	0	0
Joe Morgan, 2b	.333	4	15	3	5	1	1	1	2	2	2	2
Gary Nolan, p	.000	1	0	0	0	0	0	0	0	0	0	0
Fred Norman, p	.000	1	0	0	0	0	0	0	0	0	0	0
Tony Perez, 1b	.313	4	16	1	5	1	0	0	2	1	2	0
Pete Rose, 3b	.188	4	16	1	3	1	0	0	1	2	2	0
Pat Zachry, p	.000	1	0	0	0	0	0	0	0	0	0	0
TOTAL	.313		134	22	42	10	3	4	21	12	16	7

PITCHER	W	L	ERA	G	GS	CG	SV	SHO	IP	H	ER	BB	SO
Jack Billingham	1	0	0.00	1	0	0	0	0	2.2	0	0	0	1
Pedro Borbon	0	0	0.00	1	0	0	0	0	1.2	0	0	0	0
Don Gullett	1	0	1.23	1	1	0	0	0	7.1	5	1	3	4
Will McEnaney	0	0	0.00	2	0	0	2	0	4.2	2	0	1	2
Gary Nolan	1	0	2.70	1	1	0	0	0	6.2	8	2	1	1
Fred Norman	0	0	4.26	1	1	0	0	0	6.1	9	3	2	2
Pat Zachry	1	0	2.70	1	1	0	0	0	6.2	6	2	5	6
TOTAL	4	0	2.00	8	4	0	2	0	36.0	30	8	12	16

NY (A)

PLAYER/POS	AVG	G	AB	R	H	2B	3B	HR	RB	BB	SO	SB
Doyle Alexander, p	.000	1	0	0	0	0	0	0	0	0	0	0
Chris Chambliss, 1b	.313	4	16	1	5	1	0	0	1	0	2	0
Dock Ellis, p	.000	1	0	0	0	0	0	0	0	0	0	0
Ed Figueroa, p	.000	1	0	0	0	0	0	0	0	0	0	0
Oscar Gamble, of-2	.125	2	8	0	1	0	0	0	1	0	0	0
Elrod Hendricks, ph	.000	2	2	0	0	0	0	0	0	0	0	0
Catfish Hunter, p	.000	1	0	0	0	0	0	0	0	0	0	0
Grant Jackson, p	.000	1	0	0	0	0	0	0	0	0	0	0
Sparky Lyle, p	.000	2	0	0	0	0	0	0	0	0	0	0
Elliott Maddox, of-1,dh-1	.200	2	5	0	1	0	1	0	0	1	2	0
Jim Mason, ss	1.000	3	1	1	1	0	0	1	1	0	0	0
Carlos May, dh	.000	4	9	0	0	0	0	0	0	0	1	0
Thurman Munson, c	.529	4	17	2	9	0	0	0	2	0	1	0
Graig Nettles, 3b	.250	4	12	0	3	0	0	0	1	2	3	1
Lou Piniella, of-2,dh-2	.333	4	9	1	3	1	0	0	0	0	0	0
Willie Randolph, 2b	.071	4	14	1	1	0	0	0	0	1	3	0
Mickey Rivers, of	.167	4	18	1	3	0	0	0	0	1	2	1
Fred Stanley, ss	.167	4	6	1	1	1	0	0	1	3	1	0
Dick Tidrow, p	.000	2	0	0	0	0	0	0	0	0	0	0
Otto Velez, ph	.000	3	3	0	0	0	0	0	0	0	3	0
Roy White, of	.133	4	15	0	2	0	0	0	0	3	0	0
TOTAL	.222		135	8	30	3	1	1	8	12	16	1

PITCHER	W	L	ERA	G	GS	CG	SV	SHO	IP	H	ER	BB	SO
Doyle Alexander	0	1	7.50	1	1	0	0	0	6.0	9	5	2	1
Dock Ellis	0	1	10.80	1	1	0	0	0	3.1	7	4	0	1
Ed Figueroa	0	1	5.63	1	1	0	0	0	8.0	6	5	5	2
Catfish Hunter	0	1	3.12	1	1	1	0	0	8.2	10	3	4	5
Grant Jackson	0	0	4.91	1	0	0	0	0	3.2	4	2	0	3
Sparky Lyle	0	0	0.00	2	0	0	0	0	2.2	1	0	0	3
Dick Tidrow	0	0	7.71	2	0	0	0	0	2.1	5	2	1	1
TOTAL	0	4	5.45	9	4	1	0	0	34.2	42	21	12	16

GAME 1 AT CIN OCT 16

NY	010 000 000	1	5	1
CIN	101 001 20X	5	10	1

Pitchers: ALEXANDER, Lyle (7) vs GULLETT, Borbon (8)
Home Runs: Morgan-CIN
Attendance: 54,826

GAME 2 AT CIN OCT 17

NY	000 100 200	3	9	1
CIN	030 000 001	4	10	0

Pitchers: HUNTER vs Norman, BILLINGHAM (7)
Attendance: 54,816

GAME 3 AT NY OCT 19

CIN	030 100 020	6	13	2
NY	000 100 100	2	8	0

Pitchers: ZACHRY, McEnaney (7) vs ELLIS, Jackson (4), Tidrow (8)
Home Runs: Driessen-CIN, Mason-NY
Attendance: 56,667

GAME 4 AT NY OCT 21

CIN	000 300 004	7	9	2
NY	100 010 000	2	8	0

Pitchers: NOLAN, McEnaney (7) vs FIGUEROA, Tidrow (9), Lyle (9)
Home Runs: Bench-CIN (2)
Attendance: 56,700

The Phillies took the first game, but the Dodgers proved better at turning hits into runs and swept the next three. Philadelphia jumped ahead in the first inning of Game 1, and had built a 5–1 lead by the seventh, when Ron Cey tied the score with a grand slam. But the Phillies came back with two runs on three singles in the top of the ninth and held on for the win. As in Game 1, both clubs again got nine hits apiece in Game 2, but this time Dodgers pitcher Don Sutton scattered the Phillies' hits for a single run over nine innings, while Phillies starter Jim Lonborg—in the four innings he pitched—yielded five runs, including a grand slam to Dusty Baker.

In Game 3 Los Angeles outhit the Phillies, but the Dodgers were nearly undone when starter Burt Hooton walked in three Philadelphia runs in the second inning. The Phillies took a two-run lead into the ninth, but after two men were out the Dodgers rebounded, thanks largely to a couple of old pros. Pinch hitter Vic Davalillo, age 38, beat out a drag bunt on a disputed call, and 39-year-old Manny Mota doubled to deep left. Two more singles scored three runs that proved enough for the win.

The Dodgers didn't even need all of their five hits to take the final game behind Tommy John's one-run seven-hitter, for one of those hits was another Dusty Baker home run with a man aboard.

Los Angeles Dodgers (West), 3; Philadelphia Phillies (East), 1

LA (W)

PLAYER/POS	AVG	G	AB	R	H	2B	3B	HR	RB	BB	SO	SB
Dusty Baker, of	.357	4	14	4	5	1	0	2	8	2	3	0
Glenn Burke, of	.000	4	7	0	0	0	0	0	0	0	3	0
Ron Cey, 3b	.308	4	13	4	4	1	0	1	4	2	4	1
Vic Davalillo, ph	1.000	1	1	1	1	0	0	0	0	0	0	0
Mike Garman, p	.000	2	0	0	0	0	0	0	0	0	0	0
Steve Garvey, 1b	.308	4	13	2	4	0	0	0	2	1	1	1
Ed Goodson, ph	.000	1	1	0	0	0	0	0	0	0	0	0
Jerry Grote, c-1	.000	2	0	0	0	0	0	0	0	1	0	0
Burt Hooton, p	1.000	1	1	0	1	1	0	0	0	0	0	0
Charlie Hough, p	.000	1	0	0	0	0	0	0	0	0	0	0
Tommy John, p	.200	2	5	0	1	0	0	0	0	0	2	0
Lee Lacy, ph	1.000	1	1	1	1	1	0	0	0	0	0	0
Davey Lopes, 2b	.235	4	17	2	4	0	0	0	3	2	0	0
Rick Monday, of	.286	3	7	1	2	1	0	0	0	2	1	0
Manny Mota, ph	1.000	1	1	1	1	1	0	0	0	0	0	0
Doug Rau, p	.000	1	0	0	0	0	0	0	0	0	0	0
Lance Rautzhan, p	.000	1	0	0	0	0	0	0	0	0	0	0
Rick Rhoden, p	.000	1	1	0	0	0	0	0	0	0	0	0
Bill Russell, ss	.278	4	18	3	5	1	0	0	2	0	0	0
Reggie Smith, of	.188	4	16	2	3	0	1	0	1	2	5	1
Elias Sosa, p	.000	2	0	0	0	0	0	0	0	0	0	0
Don Sutton, p	.000	1	3	0	0	0	0	0	0	0	0	0
Steve Yeager, c	.231	4	13	1	3	0	0	0	2	1	3	0
TOTAL	.263		133	22	35	6	1	3	20	14	22	3

PITCHER	W	L	ERA	G	GS	CG	SV	SHO	IP	H	ER	BB	SO
Mike Garman	0	0	0.00	2	0	0	1	0	1.1	0	0	0	1
Burt Hooton	0	0	16.20	1	1	0	0	0	1.2	2	3	4	1
Charlie Hough	0	0	4.50	1	0	0	0	0	2.0	2	1	0	3
Tommy John	1	0	0.66	2	2	1	0	0	13.2	11	1	5	11
Doug Rau	0	0	0.00	1	0	0	0	0	1.0	0	0	0	1
Lance Rautzhan	1	0	0.00	1	0	0	0	0	0.1	0	0	0	0
Rick Rhoden	0	0	0.00	1	0	0	0	0	4.1	2	0	2	0
Elias Sosa	0	1	10.13	2	0	0	0	0	2.2	5	3	0	0
Don Sutton	1	0	1.00	1	1	1	0	0	9.0	9	1	0	4
TOTAL	3	1	2.25	12	4	2	1	0	36.0	31	9	11	21

PHI (E)

PLAYER/POS	AVG	G	AB	R	H	2B	3B	HR	RB	BB	SO	SB
Bob Boone, c	.400	4	10	1	4	0	0	0	0	0	0	0
Larry Bowa, ss	.118	4	17	2	2	0	0	0	1	1	0	0
Ollie Brown, ph	.000	2	2	0	0	0	0	0	0	0	1	0
Warren Brusstar, p	.000	2	0	0	0	0	0	0	0	0	0	0
Steve Carlton, p	.500	2	4	0	2	0	0	0	1	0	2	0
Larry Christenson, p	.000	1	0	0	0	0	0	0	0	1	1	0
Gene Garber, p	.000	3	0	0	0	0	0	0	0	0	0	0
Richie Hebner, 1b-3	.357	4	14	2	5	2	0	0	0	0	1	0
Tom Hutton, 1b-1	.000	3	3	0	0	0	0	0	0	0	0	0
Davey Johnson, 1b	.250	1	4	0	1	0	0	0	2	0	1	0
Jay Johnstone, of	.200	2	5	0	1	0	0	0	0	0	1	0
Jim Lonborg, p	.000	1	1	0	0	0	0	0	0	0	1	0
Greg Luzinski, of	.286	4	14	2	4	1	0	1	2	3	3	1
Garry Maddox, of	.429	2	7	1	3	0	0	0	2	0	1	0
Jerry Martin, of-1	.000	3	4	0	0	0	0	0	0	0	2	0
Bake McBride, of	.222	4	18	2	4	0	0	1	2	1	2	0
Tim McCarver, c-2	.167	3	6	1	1	0	0	0	0	1	3	0
Tug McGraw, p	.000	2	0	0	0	0	0	0	0	0	0	0
Ron Reed, p	.000	3	0	0	0	0	0	0	0	0	0	0
Mike Schmidt, 3b	.063	4	16	2	1	0	0	0	1	2	3	0
Ted Sizemore, 2b	.231	4	13	1	3	0	0	0	0	2	0	0
TOTAL	.225		138	14	31	3	0	2	12	11	21	1

PITCHER	W	L	ERA	G	GS	CG	SV	SHO	IP	H	ER	BB	SO
Warren Brusstar	0	0	3.38	2	0	0	0	0	2.2	2	1	1	2
Steve Carlton	0	1	6.94	2	2	0	0	0	11.2	13	9	8	6
Larry Christenson	0	0	8.10	1	1	0	0	0	3.1	7	3	0	2
Gene Garber	1	1	3.38	3	0	0	0	0	5.1	4	2	0	3
Jim Lonborg	0	1	11.25	1	1	0	0	0	4.0	5	5	1	1
Tug McGraw	0	0	0.00	2	0	0	1	0	3.0	1	0	2	3
Ron Reed	0	0	1.80	3	0	0	0	0	5.0	3	1	2	5
TOTAL	1	3	5.40	14	4	0	1	0	35.0	35	21	14	22

GAME 1 AT LA OCT 4

PHI	200	021	002	7	9	0
LA	000	010	400	5	9	2

Pitchers: Carlton, GARBER (7), McGraw (9) vs John, Garman (5), Hough (6), SOSA (8)
Home Runs: Luzinski-PHI, Cey-LA
Attendance: 55,968

GAME 2 AT LA OCT 5

PHI	001	000	000	1	9	1
LA	001	401	10X	7	9	1

Pitchers: LONBORG, Reed (5), Brusstar (7) vs SUTTON
Home Runs: McBride-PHI, Baker-LA
Attendance: 55,973

GAME 3 AT PHI OCT 7

LA	020	100	003	6	12	2
PHI	030	000	020	5	6	2

Pitchers: Hooton, Rhoden (2), Rau (7), Sosa (8), RAUTZHAN (8), Garman (9) vs Christensen, Brusstar (4), Reed (5), GARBER (7)
Attendance: 63,719

GAME 4 AT PHI OCT 8

LA	020	020	000	4	5	0
PHI	000	100	000	1	7	0

Pitchers: JOHN vs CARLTON, Reed (6), McGraw (7), Garber (9)
Home Runs: Baker-LA
Attendance: 64,924

As in 1976 the Royals met the Yankees in the ALCS, and as in 1976 the series went five games, with the Royals outscoring New York by a single run. But this time Kansas City won the first game, and as the teams traded victories through the first four games and K.C. took a lead into the ninth inning of Game 5, it began to look as though this year the Royals might take the pennant.

Royals hitters began things with a bang, scoring six of their seven runs in Game 1 in the first three innings for an insurmountable lead. New York came back to take the second game 6–2 behind Ron Guidry's three-hitter, but the Royals reversed the score the next day as Dennis Leonard limited the Yankees to four hits. Yankees reliever Sparky Lyle shut K.C. down over the final five innings of Game 4 after the Royals had drawn within a run of New York in the fourth inning, and the series was tied.

In the finale, Kansas City drew first blood with two runs in the bottom of the first and led by one run after eight. But with the pennant in sight, the Royals gave up three runs in the top of the ninth, scoring nothing themselves as reliever Lyle held them off to give the Yankees their thirty-first flag.

New York Yankees (East), 3; Kansas City Royals (West), 2

NY (E)

PLAYER/POS	AVG	G	AB	R	H	2B	3B	HR	RB	BB	SO	SB
Paul Blair, of	.400	3	5	1	2	0	0	0	0	0	0	0
Chris Chambliss, 1b	.059	5	17	0	1	0	0	0	0	3	4	0
Bucky Dent, ss	.214	5	14	1	3	1	0	0	2	1	0	0
Ed Figueroa, p	.000	1	0	0	0	0	0	0	0	0	0	0
Ron Guidry, p	.000	2	0	0	0	0	0	0	0	0	0	0
Don Gullett, p	.000	1	0	0	0	0	0	0	0	0	0	0
Reggie Jackson, of-4,dh-1	.125	5	16	1	2	0	0	0	1	2	2	1
Cliff Johnson, dh-4	.400	5	15	2	6	2	0	1	2	1	2	0
Sparky Lyle, p	.000	4	0	0	0	0	0	0	0	0	0	0
Thurman Munson, c	.286	5	21	3	6	1	0	1	5	0	2	0
Graig Nettles, 3b	.150	5	20	1	3	0	0	0	1	0	3	0
Lou Piniella, of-4,dh-1	.333	5	21	1	7	3	0	0	2	0	1	0
Willie Randolph, 2b	.278	5	18	4	5	1	0	0	2	1	0	0
Mickey Rivers, of	.391	5	23	5	9	2	0	0	2	0	2	1
Fred Stanley, ss	.000	2	0	0	0	0	0	0	0	0	0	0
Dick Tidrow, p	.000	2	0	0	0	0	0	0	0	0	0	0
Mike Torrez, p	.000	2	0	0	0	0	0	0	0	0	0	0
Roy White, of-1,dh-1	.400	4	5	2	2	2	0	0	0	1	0	0
TOTAL	.263		175	21	46	12	0	2	17	9	16	2

PITCHER	W	L	ERA	G	GS	CG	SV	SHO	IP	H	ER	BB	SO
Ed Figueroa	0	0	10.80	1	1	0	0	0	3.1	5	4	2	3
Ron Guidry	1	0	3.97	2	2	1	0	0	11.1	9	5	3	8
Don Gullett	0	1	18.00	1	1	0	0	0	2.0	4	4	2	0
Sparky Lyle	2	0	0.96	4	0	0	0	0	9.1	7	1	0	3
Dick Tidrow	0	0	3.86	2	0	0	0	0	7.0	6	3	3	3
Mike Torrez	0	1	4.09	2	1	0	0	0	11.0	11	5	5	5
TOTAL	3	2	4.50	12	5	1	0	0	44.0	42	22	15	22

KC (W)

PLAYER/POS	AVG	G	AB	R	H	2B	3B	HR	RB	BB	SO	SB
Doug Bird, p	.000	3	0	0	0	0	0	0	0	0	0	0
George Brett, 3b	.300	5	20	2	6	0	2	0	2	1	0	0
Al Cowens, of	.263	5	19	2	5	0	0	1	5	1	3	0
Larry Gura, p	.000	2	0	0	0	0	0	0	0	0	0	0
Andy Hassler, p	.000	1	0	0	0	0	0	0	0	0	0	0
Pete LaCock, 1b	.000	1	1	0	0	0	0	0	0	1	1	0
Joe Lahoud, dh	.000	1	1	2	0	0	0	0	0	2	0	0
Dennis Leonard, p	.000	2	0	0	0	0	0	0	0	0	0	0
Mark Littell, p	.000	2	0	0	0	0	0	0	0	0	0	0
John Mayberry, 1b	.167	4	12	1	2	1	0	1	3	1	2	0
Hal McRae, dh-3,of-2	.444	5	18	6	8	3	0	1	2	3	1	0
Steve Mingori, p	.000	3	0	0	0	0	0	0	0	0	0	0
Amos Otis, of	.125	5	16	1	2	1	0	0	2	2	3	2
Freddie Patek, ss	.389	5	18	4	7	3	1	0	5	1	2	0
Marty Pattin, p	.000	1	0	0	0	0	0	0	0	0	0	0
Tom Poquette, of	.167	2	6	0	1	0	0	0	0	0	0	0
Darrell Porter, c	.333	5	15	3	5	0	0	0	3	0	0	0
Cookie Rojas, dh	.250	1	4	0	1	0	0	0	0	0	1	1
Paul Splittorff, p	.000	2	0	0	0	0	0	0	0	0	0	0
John Wathan, 1b-2,c-1,dh-1	.000	4	6	0	0	0	0	0	0	0	3	0
Frank White, 2b	.278	5	18	1	5	1	0	0	2	0	4	1
Joe Zdeb, of	.000	4	9	0	0	0	0	0	0	0	2	1
TOTAL	.258		163	22	42	9	3	3	21	15	22	5

PITCHER	W	L	ERA	G	GS	CG	SV	SHO	IP	H	ER	BB	SO
Doug Bird	0	0	0.00	3	0	0	0	0	2.0	4	0	0	1
Larry Gura	0	1	18.00	2	1	0	0	0	2.0	7	4	1	2
Andy Hassler	0	1	4.76	1	1	0	0	0	5.2	5	3	0	3
Dennis Leonard	1	1	3.00	2	1	1	0	0	9.0	5	3	2	4
Mark Littell	0	0	3.00	2	0	0	0	0	3.0	5	1	3	1
Steve Mingori	0	0	0.00	3	0	0	0	0	1.1	0	0	0	1
Marty Pattin	0	0	1.50	1	0	0	0	0	6.0	6	1	0	0
Paul Splittorff	1	0	2.40	2	2	0	0	0	15.0	14	4	3	4
TOTAL	2	3	3.27	16	5	1	0	0	44.0	46	16	9	16

GAME 1 AT NY OCT 5

KC	222 000 010	7	9	0
NY	002 000 000	2	9	0

Pitchers: SPLITTORFF, Bird (9) vs GULLETT. Tidrow (3), Lyle (9)
Home Runs: McRae-KC, Mayberry-KC, Munson-NY, Cowens-KC
Attendance: 54,930

GAME 2 AT NY OCT 6

KC	001 001 000	2	3	1
NY	000 023 01X	6	10	1

Pitchers: HASSLER, Littell (6), Mingori (8) VS GUIDRY
Home Runs: Johnson-NY
Attendance: 56,230

GAME 3 AT KC OCT 7

NY	000 010 001	2	4	1
KC	011 012 10X	6	12	1

Pitchers: TORREZ, Lyle (6) vs LEONARD
Attendance: 41,285

GAME 4 AT KC OCT 8

NY	121 100 001	6	13	0
KC	002 200 000	4	8	2

Pitchers: Figueroa, Tidrow (4), LYLE (4) vs GURA, Pattin (3), Mingori (9), Bird (9)
Attendance: 41,135

GAME 5 AT KC OCT 9

NY	001 000 013	5	10	0
KC	201 000 000	3	10	1

Pitchers: Guidry, Torrez (3), LYLE (8) vs Splittorff, Bird (8), Mingori (8), LEONARD (9), Gura (9), Littell (9)
Attendance: 41,133

This was the Series in which Reggie Jackson established his reputation as "Mr. October" with a record five home runs, including three in successive at bats in the final game, and the Yankees showed that after a decade or so of decline they were once again the world's best. Los Angeles scored first in the opening game with a pair of first-inning runs. But New York gained back half the ground in the bottom of the first and tied the game on Willie Randolph's leadoff homer in the sixth. The clubs traded runs in the eighth and ninth to take the game into extra innings. The impasse was not breached until the last of the 12th, when Randolph doubled and Paul Blair singled him home.

Game 2, by contrast, was a run-away Dodgers victory. Home runs in the first three innings by Ron Cey, Steve Yeager, and Reggie Smith made the score 5–0 before New York scored its lone run in the fourth. Burt Hooton got the win with a five-hitter, and for good measure, Steve Garvey homered in the ninth inning. The Yankees returned to form two days later in Los Angeles, though, scoring three runs in the top of the first on pairs of doubles and singles (and a Dodgers error). Dusty Baker's three-run homer tied the game in the third, but single runs in the next two innings provided Yankees pitcher Mike Torrez with runs enough for the win.

Two of the four hits yielded by emerging Yankees ace Ron Guidry in Game 4 were pitcher Rick Rhoden's double followed by Davey Lopes' home run in the third inning. But the Yankees had already scored three times in the second, and Reggie Jackson homered in the sixth as Guidry held Los Angeles scoreless after the third for a 4–2 win. New York's assault against pitcher Don Sutton in Game 5 included back-to-back home runs by Thurman Munson and Jackson in the eighth inning. But Los Angeles rocked Yankees pitching even harder, with homers by Steve Yeager and Reggie Smith producing five of the Dodgers' 10 runs as the club evaded elimination with its second win.

The Dodgers scored first in the sixth game when Steve Garvey's first-inning triple drove in two runners. Chris Chambliss matched that an inning later for the Yankees with a two-run homer. Smith restored the lead to Los Angeles with a solo shot in the third inning, but Jackson put the Yankees back in front with the first of his three home runs, a two-run blast in the fourth. By the time he had homered again for two in the fifth and for the third time in the eighth, the Yankees' 21st world title was well in hand.

New York Yankees (AL), 4;
Los Angeles Dodgers (NL), 2

NY (A)

PLAYER/POS	AVG	G	AB	R	H	2B	3B	HR	RB	BB	SO	SB
Paul Blair, of-3	.250	4	4	0	1	0	0	0	0	1	0	0
Chris Chambliss, 1b	.292	6	24	4	7	2	0	1	4	0	2	0
Ken Clay, p	.000	2	0	0	0	0	0	0	0	0	0	0
Bucky Dent, ss	.263	6	19	0	5	0	0	0	2	2	1	0
Ron Guidry, p	.000	1	2	0	0	0	0	0	0	0	1	0
Don Gullett, p	.000	2	0	0	0	0	0	0	0	0	2	0
Catfish Hunter, p	.000	2	0	0	0	0	0	0	0	0	0	0
Reggie Jackson, of	.450	6	20	10	9	1	0	5	8	3	4	0
Cliff Johnson, c-1	.000	2	1	0	0	0	0	0	0	0	0	0
Sparky Lyle, p	.000	2	2	0	0	0	0	0	0	0	0	0
Thurman Munson, c	.320	6	25	4	8	2	0	1	3	2	8	0
Graig Nettles, 3b	.190	6	21	1	4	1	0	0	2	2	3	0
Lou Piniella, of	.273	6	22	1	6	0	0	0	3	0	3	0
Willie Randolph, 2b	.160	6	25	5	4	2	0	1	1	1	2	0
Mickey Rivers, of	.222	6	27	1	6	2	0	0	1	0	2	1
Fred Stanley, ss	.000	1	0	0	0	0	0	0	0	0	0	0
Dick Tidrow, p	.000	2	1	0	0	0	0	0	0	0	1	0
Mike Torrez, p	.000	2	6	0	0	0	0	0	0	0	4	0
Roy White, ph	.000	2	2	0	0	0	0	0	0	0	0	0
George Zeber, ph	.000	2	2	0	0	0	0	0	0	0	2	0
TOTAL	.244		205	26	50	10	0	8	25	11	37	1

PITCHER	W	L	ERA	G	GS	CG	SV	SHO	IP	H	ER	BB	SO
Ken Clay	0	0	2.45	2	0	0	0	0	3.2	2	1	1	0
Ron Guidry	1	0	2.00	1	1	1	0	0	9.0	4	2	3	7
Don Gullett	0	1	6.39	2	2	0	0	0	12.2	13	9	7	10
Catfish Hunter	0	1	10.38	2	1	0	0	0	4.1	6	5	0	1
Sparky Lyle	1	0	1.93	2	0	0	0	0	4.2	2	1	0	2
Dick Tidrow	0	0	4.91	2	0	0	0	0	3.2	5	2	0	1
Mike Torrez	2	0	2.50	2	2	2	0	0	18.0	16	5	5	15
TOTAL	4	2	4.02	13	6	3	0	0	56.0	48	25	16	36

LA (N)

PLAYER/POS	AVG	G	AB	R	H	2B	3B	HR	RB	BB	SO	SB
Dusty Baker, of	.292	6	24	4	7	0	0	1	5	0	2	0
Glenn Burke, of	.200	3	5	0	1	0	0	0	0	0	1	0
Ron Cey, 3b	.190	6	21	2	4	1	0	1	3	3	5	0
Vic Davalillo, ph	.333	3	3	0	1	0	0	0	1	0	0	0
Mike Garman, p	.000	2	0	0	0	0	0	0	0	0	0	0
Steve Garvey, 1b	.375	6	24	5	9	1	1	1	3	1	4	0
Ed Goodson, ph	.000	1	1	0	0	0	0	0	0	0	1	0
Jerry Grote, c	.000	1	1	0	0	0	0	0	0	0	0	0
Burt Hooton, p	.000	2	5	0	0	0	0	0	0	0	2	0
Charlie Hough, p	.000	2	0	0	0	0	0	0	0	0	0	0
Tommy John, p	.000	1	2	0	0	0	0	0	0	0	2	0
Lee Lacy, of-2	.429	4	7	1	3	0	0	0	2	1	1	0
Rafael Landestoy, pr	.000	1	0	0	0	0	0	0	0	0	0	0
Davey Lopes, 2b	.167	6	24	3	4	0	1	1	2	4	3	2
Rick Monday, of	.167	4	12	0	2	0	0	0	0	0	3	0
Manny Mota, ph	.000	3	3	0	0	0	0	0	0	0	1	0
Johnny Oates, c	.000	1	1	0	0	0	0	0	0	0	0	0
Doug Rau, p	.000	2	0	0	0	0	0	0	0	0	0	0
Lance Rautzhan, p	.000	1	0	0	0	0	0	0	0	0	0	0
Rick Rhoden, p	.500	2	2	1	1	1	0	0	0	0	0	0
Bill Russell, ss	.154	6	26	3	4	0	1	0	2	1	3	0
Reggie Smith, of	.273	6	22	7	6	1	0	3	5	4	3	0
Elias Sosa, p	.000	2	0	0	0	0	0	0	0	0	0	0
Don Sutton, p	.000	2	6	0	0	0	0	0	0	1	4	0
Steve Yeager, c	.316	6	19	2	6	1	0	2	5	1	1	0
TOTAL	.231		208	28	48	5	3	9	28	16	36	2

PITCHER	W	L	ERA	G	GS	CG	SV	SHO	IP	H	ER	BB	SO
Mike Garman	0	0	0.00	2	0	0	0	0	4.0	2	0	1	3
Burt Hooton	1	1	3.75	2	2	1	0	0	12.0	8	5	2	9
Charlie Hough	0	0	1.80	2	0	0	0	0	5.0	3	1	0	5
Tommy John	0	1	6.00	1	1	0	0	0	6.0	9	4	3	7
Doug Rau	0	1	11.57	2	1	0	0	0	2.1	4	3	0	1
Lance Rautzhan	0	0	0.00	1	0	0	0	0	0.1	0	0	2	0
Rick Rhoden	0	1	2.57	2	0	0	0	0	7.0	4	2	1	5
Elias Sosa	0	0	11.57	2	0	0	0	0	2.1	3	3	1	1
Don Sutton	1	0	3.94	2	2	1	0	0	16.0	17	7	1	6
TOTAL	2	4	4.09	16	6	2	0	0	55.0	50	25	11	37

GAME 1 AT NY OCT 11

LA	200 000 001 000	3	6	0
NY	100 001 010 001	4	11	0

Pitchers: Sutton, Rautzhan (8), Sosa (8), Garman (9), RHODEN (12) vs Gullett, LYLE (9)
Home Runs: Randolph-NY
Attendance: 56,668

GAME 2 AT NY OCT 12

LA	212 000 001	6	9	0
NY	000 100 000	1	5	0

Pitchers: HOOTON vs HUNTER, Tidrow (3), Clay (6), Lyle (9)
Home Runs: Cey-LA, Yeager-LA, Smith-LA, Garvey-LA
Attendance: 56,691

GAME 3 AT LA OCT 14

NY	300 110 000	5	10	0
LA	003 000 000	3	7	1

Pitchers: TORREZ vs JOHN, Hough (7)
Home Runs: Baker-LA
Attendance: 55,992

GAME 4 AT LA OCT 15

NY	030 001 000	4	7	0
LA	002 000 000	2	4	0

Pitchers: GUIDRY vs RAU, Rhoden (2), Garman (9)
Home Runs: Lopes-LA, Jackson-NY
Attendance: 55,995

GAME 5 AT LA OCT 16

NY	000 000 220	4	9	2
LA	100 432 00X	10	13	0

Pitchers: GULLETT, Clay (5), Tidrow (6), Hunter (7) vs SUTTON
Home Runs: Yeager-LA, Smith-LA, Munson-NY, Jackson-NY
Attendance: 55,955

GAME 6 AT NY OCT 18

LA	201 000 001	4	9	0
NY	020 320 01X	8	8	1

Pitchers: HOOTON, Sosa (4), Rau (5), Hough (7) vs TORREZ
Home Runs: Chambliss-NY, Smith-LA, Jackson-NY (3)
Attendance: 56,407

Steve Garvey hit half the Dodgers' eight home runs and Tommy John hurled the first LCS shutout in four years as Los Angeles, for the second year in a row, defeated the Phillies for the pennant in four games. Philadelphia's five runs in Game 1 would have been enough to win any of the other games, but not this one as the Dodgers outhomered the Phillies four to one (including two by Garvey) and scored nine times. Dodger Davey Lopes hit the game's only home run the next day (with a man aboard), but it was more than enough support for John's four-hit shutout.

The series' most decisive win went to the Phillies in Game 3. Steve Carlton allowed four runs to score, but he made up for it by driving four runs of his own on a homer and sacrifice fly. His teammates added five more, rendering futile Garvey's third series home run.

But Garvey's fourth homer, in Game 4, helped carry the Dodgers into the 10th inning, when Bill Russell—capitalizing on Gary Maddox's muff of Ron Cey's fly to center—singled home Cey with the Dodgers' unearned pennant winner.

Los Angeles Dodgers (West), 3;
Philadelphia Phillies (East), 1

LA (W)

PLAYER/POS	AVG	G	AB	R	H	2B	3B	HR	RB	BB	SO	SB
Dusty Baker, of	.467	4	15	1	7	2	0	0	1	3	0	0
Ron Cey, 3b	.313	4	16	4	5	1	0	1	3	2	4	0
Joe Ferguson, ph	.000	2	2	0	0	0	0	0	0	0	1	0
Terry Forster, p	.000	1	0	0	0	0	0	0	0	0	0	0
Steve Garvey, 1b	.389	4	18	6	7	1	1	4	7	0	1	0
Jerry Grote, c	.000	1	0	0	0	0	0	0	0	0	0	0
Burt Hooton, p	.000	1	2	0	0	0	0	0	0	0	1	0
Charlie Hough, p	.000	1	0	0	0	0	0	0	0	0	0	0
Tommy John, p	.000	1	3	0	0	0	0	0	0	0	0	0
Lee Lacy, ph	.000	2	2	0	0	0	0	0	0	0	0	0
Davey Lopes, 2b	.389	4	18	3	7	1	1	2	5	0	1	1
Rick Monday, of	.200	3	10	2	2	0	1	0	0	1	5	0
Manny Mota, ph	1.000	2	1	0	1	1	0	0	0	0	0	0
Billy North, of	.000	4	8	0	0	0	0	0	0	0	1	0
Doug Rau, p	.000	1	1	0	0	0	0	0	0	0	0	0
Lance Rautzhan, p	.000	1	0	0	0	0	0	0	0	0	0	0
Rick Rhoden, p	.000	1	1	0	0	0	0	0	0	0	0	0
Bill Russell, ss	.412	4	17	1	7	1	0	0	2	1	1	0
Reggie Smith, of	.188	4	16	2	3	1	0	0	1	0	2	0
Don Sutton, p	.000	1	0	0	0	0	0	0	0	0	0	0
Bob Welch, p	.000	1	2	0	0	0	0	0	0	0	1	0
Steve Yeager, c	.231	4	13	2	3	0	0	1	2	2	2	1
TOTAL	.286		147	21	42	8	3	8	21	9	22	2

PITCHER	W	L	ERA	G	GS	CG	SV	SHO	IP	H	ER	BB	SO
Terry Forster	1	0	0.00	1	0	0	0	0	1.0	1	0	0	2
Burt Hooton	0	0	7.71	1	1	0	0	0	4.2	10	4	0	5
Charlie Hough	0	0	4.50	1	0	0	0	0	2.0	1	1	0	1
Tommy John	1	0	0.00	1	1	1	0	1	9.0	4	0	2	4
Doug Rau	0	0	3.60	1	1	0	0	0	5.0	5	2	2	1
Lance Rautzhan	0	0	6.75	1	0	0	0	0	1.1	3	1	2	0
Rick Rhoden	0	0	2.25	1	0	0	0	0	4.0	2	1	1	3
Don Sutton	0	1	6.35	1	1	0	0	0	5.2	7	4	2	0
Bob Welch	1	0	2.08	1	0	0	0	0	4.1	2	1	0	5
TOTAL	3	1	3.41	9	4	1	0	1	37.0	35	14	9	21

PHI (E)

PLAYER/POS	AVG	G	AB	R	H	2B	3B	HR	RB	BB	SO	SB
Bob Boone, c	.182	3	11	0	2	0	0	0	0	0	1	0
Larry Bowa, ss	.333	4	18	2	6	0	0	0	0	1	2	0
Warren Brusstar, p	.000	3	0	0	0	0	0	0	0	0	0	0
Jose Cardenal, 1b	.167	2	6	0	1	0	0	0	0	1	1	0
Steve Carlton, p	.500	1	4	2	2	0	0	1	4	0	0	0
Larry Christenson, p	.000	1	1	0	0	0	0	0	0	0	1	0
Rawly Eastwick, p	.000	1	0	0	0	0	0	0	0	0	0	0
Barry Foote, ph	.000	1	1	0	0	0	0	0	0	0	1	0
Orlando Gonzalez, ph	.000	1	1	0	0	0	0	0	0	0	1	0
Richie Hebner, 1b-2	.111	3	9	0	1	0	0	0	1	0	0	0
Randy Lerch, p	.000	1	2	0	0	0	0	0	0	0	0	0
Greg Luzinski, of	.375	4	16	3	6	0	1	2	3	1	2	0
Garry Maddox, of	.263	4	19	1	5	0	0	0	2	0	3	0
Jerry Martin, of-3	.222	4	9	1	2	1	0	1	2	1	3	0
Bake McBride, of-2	.222	3	9	2	2	0	0	1	1	0	2	0
Tim McCarver, c-1	.000	2	4	2	0	0	0	0	0	1	2	0
Tug McGraw, p	.000	3	0	0	0	0	0	0	0	0	0	0
Jim Morrison, ph	.000	1	1	0	0	0	0	0	0	0	1	0
Ron Reed, p	.000	2	0	0	0	0	0	0	0	0	0	0
Dick Ruthven, p	.000	1	1	0	0	0	0	0	0	0	1	0
Mike Schmidt, 3b	.200	4	15	1	3	2	0	0	1	2	2	0
Ted Sizemore, 2b	.385	4	13	3	5	0	1	0	1	1	0	0
TOTAL	.250		140	17	35	3	2	5	16	9	21	0

PITCHER	W	L	ERA	G	GS	CG	SV	SHO	IP	H	ER	BB	SO
Warren Brusstar	0	0	0.00	3	0	0	0	0	2.2	2	0	1	0
Steve Carlton	1	0	4.00	1	1	1	0	0	9.0	8	4	2	8
Larry Christenson	0	1	12.46	1	1	0	0	0	4.1	7	6	1	3
Rawly Eastwick	0	0	9.00	1	0	0	0	0	1.0	3	1	0	1
Randy Lerch	0	0	5.06	1	1	0	0	0	5.1	7	3	0	0
Tug McGraw	0	1	1.59	3	0	0	0	0	5.2	3	1	5	5
Ron Reed	0	0	2.25	2	0	0	0	0	4.0	6	1	0	2
Dick Ruthven	0	1	5.79	1	1	0	0	0	4.2	6	3	0	3
TOTAL	1	3	4.66	13	4	1	0	0	36.2	42	19	9	22

GAME 1 AT PHI OCT 4

LA	004	211	001	9	13	1
PHI	010	030	001	5	12	1

Pitchers: Hooton, WELCH (5) vs CHRISTENSEN, Brusstar (5), Eastwick (6), McGraw (7)
Home Runs: Garvey-LA (2), Lopes-LA, Yeager-LA, Martin-PHI
Attendance: 63,460

GAME 2 AT PHI OCT 5

LA	000	120	100	4	8	0
PHI	000	000	000	0	4	0

Pitchers: JOHN vs RUTHVEN, Brusstar (5), Reed (7), McGraw (9)
Home Runs: Lopes-LA
Attendance: 60,642

GAME 3 AT LA OCT 6

PHI	040	003	101	9	11	1
LA	012	000	010	4	8	2

Pitchers: CARLTON vs SUTTON, Rautzhan (6), Hough (8)
Home Runs: Carlton-PHI, Luzinski-PHI, Garvey-LA
Attendance: 55,043

GAME 4 AT LA OCT 7

PHI	002	000	100	0	3	8	2
LA	010	101	000	1	4	13	0

Pitchers: Lerch, Brusstar (6), Reed (7), McGRAW (9) vs Rau, Rhoden (6), FORSTER (10)
Home Runs: Luzinski-PHI, Cey-LA, Garvey-LA, McBride-PHI
Attendance: 55,124

It took Bucky Dent's pop-fly home run against Boston in an Eastern Division tiebreaker to carry the Yankees into the ALCS. But once there they took the pennant, downing the Royals for the third year in a row. Reggie Jackson's three-run homer in the eighth inning of Game 1 capped a 16-hit attack that scored seven runs as pitchers Jim Beattie and Ken Clay combined to limit Kansas City to two hits and a single run. The Royals, though, made it look just as easy the next day as their own 16 hits and ten runs evened the series.

Twice in Game 3 George Brett gave the Royals a lead with a home run, and he tied the game with a third homer in the fifth. But Jackson's two-run homer in the fourth brought the Yankees back, and Thurman Munson's two-run shot in the eighth gave New York a close win. Game 4 was just as close, but more of a pitcher's duel. Dennis Leonard, who went the distance, gave up only four hits, but two of them were home runs to Graig Nettles and Roy White. Yankees starter Ron Guidry allowed a run in the first, but shut out the Royals for the next seven innings. Goose Gossage preserved Guidry's good work—and the pennant—in the ninth.

New York Yankees (East), 3; Kansas City Royals (West), 1

NY (E)

PLAYER/POS	AVG	G	AB	R	H	2B	3B	HR	RB	BB	SO	SB
Jim Beattie, p	.000	1	0	0	0	0	0	0	0	0	0	0
Paul Blair, of-3,2b-1	.000	4	6	1	0	0	0	0	0	0	1	0
Chris Chambliss, 1b	.400	4	15	1	6	0	0	0	2	0	4	0
Ken Clay, p	.000	1	0	0	0	0	0	0	0	0	0	0
Bucky Dent, ss	.200	4	15	0	3	0	0	0	4	0	0	0
Brian Doyle, 2b	.286	3	7	0	2	0	0	0	1	1	1	0
Ed Figueroa, p	.000	1	0	0	0	0	0	0	0	0	0	0
Rich Gossage, p	.000	2	0	0	0	0	0	0	0	0	0	0
Ron Guidry, p	.000	1	0	0	0	0	0	0	0	0	0	0
Catfish Hunter, p	.000	1	0	0	0	0	0	0	0	0	0	0
Reggie Jackson, dh-3,of-1	.462	4	13	5	6	1	0	2	6	3	4	0
Cliff Johnson, ph	.000	1	1	0	0	0	0	0	0	0	0	0
Sparky Lyle, p	.000	1	0	0	0	0	0	0	0	0	0	0
Thurman Munson, c	.278	4	18	2	5	1	0	1	2	0	0	0
Graig Nettles, 3b	.333	4	15	3	5	0	1	1	2	0	1	0
Lou Piniella, of	.235	4	17	2	4	0	0	0	0	0	3	0
Mickey Rivers, of	.455	4	11	0	5	0	0	0	0	2	0	0
Fred Stanley, 2b	.200	2	5	0	1	0	0	0	0	0	2	0
Gary Thomasson, of	.000	3	1	0	0	0	0	0	0	0	0	0
Dick Tidrow, p	.000	1	0	0	0	0	0	0	0	0	0	0
Roy White, of-3,dh-1	.313	4	16	5	5	1	0	1	1	1	2	0
TOTAL	.300		140	19	42	3	1	5	18	7	18	0

PITCHER	W	L	ERA	G	GS	CG	SV	SHO	IP	H	ER	BB	SO
Jim Beattie	1	0	1.69	1	1	0	0	0	5.1	2	1	5	3
Ken Clay	0	0	0.00	1	0	0	1	0	3.2	0	0	3	2
Ed Figueroa	0	1	27.00	1	1	0	0	0	1.0	5	3	0	0
Rich Gossage	1	0	4.50	2	0	0	1	0	4.0	3	2	0	3
Ron Guidry	1	0	1.13	1	1	0	0	0	8.0	7	1	1	7
Catfish Hunter	0	0	4.50	1	1	0	0	0	6.0	7	3	3	5
Sparky Lyle	0	0	13.50	1	0	0	0	0	1.1	3	2	0	0
Dick Tidrow	0	0	4.76	1	0	0	0	0	5.2	8	3	2	1
TOTAL	3	1	3.86	9	4	0	2	0	35.0	35	15	14	21

KC (W)

PLAYER/POS	AVG	G	AB	R	H	2B	3B	HR	RB	BB	SO	SB
Doug Bird, p	.000	2	0	0	0	0	0	0	0	0	0	0
Steve Braun, of-1	.000	2	5	0	0	0	0	0	0	1	1	0
George Brett, 3b	.389	4	18	7	7	1	1	3	3	0	1	0
Al Cowens, of	.133	4	15	2	2	0	0	0	1	0	2	0
Larry Gura, p	.000	1	0	0	0	0	0	0	0	0	0	0
Al Hrabosky, p	.000	3	0	0	0	0	0	0	0	0	0	0
Clint Hurdle, of-2	.375	4	8	1	3	0	1	0	1	2	3	0
Pete LaCock, 1b-3	.364	4	11	1	4	2	1	0	1	3	1	1
Dennis Leonard, p	.000	2	0	0	0	0	0	0	0	0	0	0
Hal McRae, dh	.214	4	14	0	3	0	0	0	2	2	2	1
Steve Mingori, p	.000	2	0	0	0	0	0	0	0	0	0	0
Amos Otis, of	.429	4	14	2	6	2	0	0	1	3	5	4
Freddie Patek, ss	.077	4	13	2	1	0	0	1	2	1	4	0
Marty Pattin, p	.000	1	0	0	0	0	0	0	0	0	0	0
Tom Poquette, ph	.000	1	1	0	0	0	0	0	0	0	0	0
Darrell Porter, c	.357	4	14	1	5	1	0	0	3	2	0	0
Paul Splittorff, p	.000	1	0	0	0	0	0	0	0	0	0	0
John Wathan, 1b	.000	3	3	0	0	0	0	0	0	0	0	0
Frank White, 2b	.231	4	13	1	3	0	0	0	0	0	2	0
Willie Wilson, of	.250	3	4	0	1	0	0	0	0	0	0	0
TOTAL	.263		133	17	35	6	3	4	16	14	21	6

PITCHER	W	L	ERA	G	GS	CG	SV	SHO	IP	H	ER	BB	SO
Doug Bird	0	1	9.00	2	0	0	0	0	1.0	2	1	0	1
Larry Gura	1	0	2.84	1	1	0	0	0	6.1	8	2	2	2
Al Hrabosky	0	0	3.00	3	0	0	0	0	3.0	3	1	0	2
Dennis Leonard	0	2	3.75	2	2	1	0	0	12.0	13	5	2	11
Steve Mingori	0	0	7.36	1	0	0	0	0	3.2	5	3	3	0
Marty Pattin	0	0	27.00	1	0	0	0	0	0.2	2	2	0	0
Paul Splittorff	0	0	4.91	1	1	0	0	0	7.1	9	4	0	2
TOTAL	1	3	4.76	11	4	1	0	0	34.0	42	18	7	18

The outcome was the same as in 1977: the Yankees over the Dodgers in six games. But this year New York overcame a two-game deficit by sweeping the next four, a feat never before achieved in a World Series.

Los Angeles overwhelmed New York in the opener. Home runs in the second and fourth innings by Dusty Baker and Davey Lopes (who had two homers and five RBIs) and another run in the fifth, gave the Dodgers a 7–0 lead before Reggie Jackson's leadoff homer in the seventh gave New York its first score. The Yankees scored four more times, but so did the Dodgers for an 11–5 win. Game 2 was closer. The Yankees scored first and held a lead through the top of the sixth, but Ron Cey's three-run homer in the bottom of the inning gave Los Angeles the runs they needed to win 4–3.

Ron Guidry, coming off a spectacular 25–3 regular season, gave up eight hits and issued seven walks. But only one baserunner scored, thanks in large part to several memorable stops and throws by third baseman Graig Nettles. Meanwhile, Roy White's home run in the first inning began the scoring in what would become a 5–1 Yankees' win.

It took 10 innings for New York to win Game 4. Starters Tommy John and Ed Figueroa hurled shutout ball until Reggie Smith tagged Figueroa for a three-run homer in the top of the fifth. The Yankees clawed back in the sixth. Reggie Jackson singled in one run, then—in a play that stirred great controversy—got in the way (the Dodgers claimed intentionally) of a throw from second on an attempted double play, deflecting the ball to the outfield and permitting a second run to score. In the eighth, Thurman Munson doubled home the tying run, and in the last of the 10th Lou Piniella's two-out drive to center scored baserunner Roy White with the game winner.

Game 5 was a blowout. No one hit home runs, but the Yankees hit 16 singles (a Series record) and two doubles for 12 runs (five of them driven in by Munson's three hits) to give Jim Beattie (nine hits, two runs) an easy win. Back in Los Angeles for the sixth game, the Yankees won the crown on the hitting of two men at the bottom of the batting order: Denny Doyle and Bucky Dent. With three hits each, they combined for five RBIs in the 7–2 win. For good measure, Reggie Jackson concluded the Series scoring with a mighty two-run homer in the seventh.

New York Yankees (AL), 4; Los Angeles Dodgers (NL), 2

NY (A)

PLAYER/POS	AVG	G	AB	R	H	2B	3B	HR	RBI	BB	SO	SB
Jim Beattie, p	.000	1	0	0	0	0	0	0	0	0	0	0
Paul Blair, of	.375	6	8	2	3	1	0	0	0	1	4	0
Chris Chambliss, 1b	.182	3	11	1	2	0	0	0	0	1	1	0
Ken Clay, p	.000	1	0	0	0	0	0	0	0	0	0	0
Bucky Dent, ss	.417	6	24	3	10	1	0	0	7	1	2	0
Brian Doyle, 2b	.438	6	16	4	7	1	0	0	2	0	0	0
Ed Figueroa, p	.000	2	0	0	0	0	0	0	0	0	0	0
Rich Gossage, p	.000	3	0	0	0	0	0	0	0	0	0	0
Ron Guidry, p	.000	1	0	0	0	0	0	0	0	0	0	0
Mike Heath, c	.000	1	0	0	0	0	0	0	0	0	0	0
Catfish Hunter, p	.000	2	0	0	0	0	0	0	0	0	0	0
Reggie Jackson, dh	.391	6	23	2	9	1	0	2	8	3	7	0
Cliff Johnson, ph	.000	2	2	0	0	0	0	0	0	0	1	0
Jay Johnstone, of	.000	2	0	0	0	0	0	0	0	0	0	0
Paul Lindblad, p	.000	1	0	0	0	0	0	0	0	0	0	0
Thurman Munson, c	.320	6	25	5	8	3	0	0	7	3	7	1
Graig Nettles, 3b	.160	6	25	2	4	0	0	0	1	0	6	0
Lou Piniella, of	.280	6	25	3	7	0	0	0	4	0	1	0
Mickey Rivers, of-4	.333	5	18	2	6	0	0	0	1	0	2	1
Jim Spencer, 1b-3	.167	4	12	3	2	0	0	0	0	2	4	0
Fred Stanley, 2b	.200	3	5	0	1	1	0	0	0	1	0	0
Gary Thomasson, of	.250	3	4	0	1	0	0	0	0	0	1	0
Dick Tidrow, p	.000	2	0	0	0	0	0	0	0	0	0	0
Roy White, of	.333	6	24	9	8	0	0	1	4	4	5	2
TOTAL	.306		222	36	68	8	0	3	34	16	40	5

PITCHER	W	L	ERA	G	GS	CG	SV	SHO	IP	H	ER	BB	SO
Jim Beattie	1	0	2.00	1	1	1	0	0	9.0	9	2	4	8
Ken Clay	0	0	11.57	1	0	0	0	0	2.1	4	3	2	2
Ed Figueroa	0	1	8.10	2	2	0	0	0	6.2	9	6	5	2
Rich Gossage	1	0	0.00	3	0	0	0	0	6.0	1	0	1	4
Ron Guidry	1	0	1.00	1	1	1	0	0	9.0	8	1	7	4
Catfish Hunter	1	1	4.15	2	2	0	0	0	13.0	13	6	1	5
Paul Lindblad	0	0	11.57	1	0	0	0	0	2.1	4	3	0	1
Dick Tidrow	0	0	1.93	2	0	0	0	0	4.2	4	1	0	5
TOTAL	4	2	3.74	13	6	2	0	0	53.0	52	22	20	31

LA (N)

PLAYER/POS	AVG	G	AB	R	H	2B	3B	HR	RBI	BB	SO	SB
Dusty Baker, of	.238	6	21	2	5	0	0	1	1	1	3	0
Ron Cey, 3b	.286	6	21	2	6	0	0	1	4	3	3	0
Vic Davalillo, dh-1	.333	2	3	0	1	0	0	0	0	0	0	0
Joe Ferguson, c	.500	2	4	1	2	2	0	0	0	0	1	0
Terry Forster, p	.000	3	0	0	0	0	0	0	0	0	0	0
Steve Garvey, 1b	.208	6	24	1	5	1	0	0	0	1	7	1
Jerry Grote, c	.000	2	0	0	0	0	0	0	0	0	0	0
Burt Hooton, p	.000	2	0	0	0	0	0	0	0	0	0	0
Charlie Hough, p	.000	2	0	0	0	0	0	0	0	0	0	0
Tommy John, p	.000	2	0	0	0	0	0	0	0	0	0	0
Lee Lacy, dh	.143	4	14	0	2	0	0	0	1	1	3	0
Davey Lopes, 2b	.308	6	26	7	8	0	0	3	7	2	1	2
Rick Monday, of-4,dh-1	.154	5	13	2	2	1	0	0	0	4	3	0
Manny Mota, ph	.000	1	0	0	0	0	0	0	0	1	0	0
Billy North, of	.125	4	8	2	1	1	0	0	0	2	1	1
Johnny Oates, c	1.000	1	1	0	1	0	0	0	0	1	0	0
Doug Rau, p	.000	1	0	0	0	0	0	0	0	0	0	0
Lance Rautzhan, p	.000	2	0	0	0	0	0	0	0	0	0	0
Bill Russell, ss	.423	6	26	1	11	2	0	0	2	2	2	1
Reggie Smith, of	.200	6	25	3	5	0	0	1	5	2	6	0
Don Sutton, p	.000	2	0	0	0	0	0	0	0	0	0	0
Bob Welch, p	.000	3	0	0	0	0	0	0	0	0	0	0
Steve Yeager, c	.231	5	13	2	3	1	0	0	0	1	2	0
TOTAL	.261		199	23	52	8	0	6	22	20	31	5

PITCHER	W	L	ERA	G	GS	CG	SV	SHO	IP	H	ER	BB	SO
Terry Forster	0	0	0.00	3	0	0	0	0	4.0	5	0	1	6
Burt Hooton	1	1	6.48	2	2	0	0	0	8.1	13	6	3	6
Charlie Hough	0	0	8.44	2	0	0	0	0	5.1	10	5	2	5
Tommy John	1	0	3.07	2	2	0	0	0	14.2	14	5	4	6
Doug Rau	0	0	0.00	1	0	0	0	0	2.0	1	0	0	3
Lance Rautzhan	0	0	13.50	2	0	0	0	0	2.0	4	3	0	0
Don Sutton	0	2	7.50	2	2	0	0	0	12.0	17	10	4	8
Bob Welch	0	1	6.23	3	0	0	1	0	4.1	4	3	2	6
TOTAL	2	4	5.47	17	6	0	1	0	52.2	68	32	16	40

GAME 1 AT LA OCT 10

NY	000	000	320	5	9 1
LA	030	310	31X	11	15 2

Pitchers: FIGUEROA, Clay (2), Lindblad (5), Tidrow (7) vs JOHN, Forster (8)
Home Runs: Baker-LA, Lopes-LA (2), Jackson-NY
Attendance: 55,997

GAME 2 AT LA OCT 11

NY	002	000	100	3	11 0
LA	000	103	00X	4	7 0

Pitchers: HUNTER, Gossage (7) vs HOOTON, Forster (7), Welch (9)
Home Runs: Cey-LA
Attendance: 55,982

GAME 3 AT NY OCT 13

LA	001	000	000	1	8 0
NY	110	000	30X	5	10 1

Pitchers: SUTTON, Rautzhan (7), Hough (8) vs GUIDRY
Home Runs: White-NY
Attendance: 56,447

GAME 4 AT NY OCT 14

LA	000	030	000 0	3	6 1
NY	000	002	010 1	4	9 0

Pitchers: John, Forster (8), WELCH (8) vs Figueroa, Tidrow (6), GOSSAGE (9)
Home Runs: Smith-LA
Attendance: 56,445

GAME 5 AT NY OCT 15

LA	101	000	000	2	9 3
NY	004	300	41X	12	18 0

Pitchers: HOOTON, Rautzhan (3), Hough (4) vs BEATTIE
Attendance: 56,448

GAME 6 AT LA OCT 17

NY	030	002	200	7	11 0
LA	101	000	000	2	7 1

Pitchers: HUNTER, Gossage (8) vs SUTTON, Welch (7), Rau (8)
Home Runs: Lopes-LA, Jackson-NY
Attendance: 55,985

The Pirates—with a better season's record than Cincinnati and stronger hitting and pitching—proved their superiority in the NLCS as well, dominating the statistics and sweeping the series. Yet the games were closer than the stats alone would suggest. Pittsburgh won the first game by three runs—but they didn't come until Willie Stargell's homer in the 11th inning broke a 2–2 tie.

In Game 2, Cincinnati scored first. The Pirates tied the game with a run in the fourth and took a narrow lead with another in the fifth. But the Reds came back on a game-tying pair of doubles in the ninth, and it wasn't until the 10th that Pittsburgh eked out its victory with a run on two singles and Don Robinson's shutout relief.

Only in the third game did the Pirates take a commanding lead, with six runs in the first four innings (two of them on home runs by Stargell and Bill Madlock). The Reds outhit Pittsburgh, but only Johnny Bench's homer brought them a run, as Bert Blyleven overcame them in the series' only complete-game pitching performance. The Pirates, who had lost to the Reds twice in the NLCS in the 1970s, ended the decade by overcoming Cincinnati for the pennant.

Pittsburgh Pirates (East), 3;
Cincinnati Reds (West), 0

PIT (E)

PLAYER/POS	AVG	G	AB	R	H	2B	3B	HR	RB	BB	SO	SB
Matt Alexander, pr	.000	1	0	1	0	0	0	0	0	0	0	0
Jim Bibby, p	.000	1	0	0	0	0	0	0	0	1	0	0
Bert Blyleven, p	.333	1	3	1	1	0	0	0	0	0	1	0
John Candelaria, p	.000	1	3	0	0	0	0	0	0	0	2	0
Mike Easler, ph	.000	1	1	0	0	0	0	0	0	0	0	0
Tim Foli, ss	.333	3	12	1	4	1	0	0	3	0	0	0
Phil Garner, 2b-3,ss-1	.417	3	12	4	5	0	1	1	1	1	0	0
Grant Jackson, p	.000	2	1	0	0	0	0	0	0	0	0	0
Bill Madlock, 3b	.250	3	12	1	3	0	0	1	2	2	0	2
John Milner, of	.000	3	9	0	0	0	0	0	0	2	0	0
Omar Moreno, of	.250	3	12	3	3	0	1	0	0	2	2	1
Ed Ott, c	.231	3	13	0	3	0	0	0	0	0	2	0
Dave Parker, of	.333	3	12	2	4	0	0	0	2	2	3	1
Dave Roberts, p	.000	1	0	0	0	0	0	0	0	0	0	0
Don Robinson, p	.000	2	0	0	0	0	0	0	0	0	0	0
Bill Robinson, of	.000	3	3	0	0	0	0	0	0	0	0	0
Enrique Romo, p	.000	2	0	0	0	0	0	0	0	0	0	0
Willie Stargell, 1b	.455	3	11	2	5	2	0	2	6	3	2	0
Rennie Stennett, 2b	.000	1	0	0	0	0	0	0	0	0	0	0
Kent Tekulve, p	.000	2	1	0	0	0	0	0	0	0	1	0
TOTAL	.267		105	15	28	3	2	4	14	13	13	4

PITCHER	W	L	ERA	G	GS	CG	SV	SHO	IP	H	ER	BB	SO
Jim Bibby	0	0	1.29	1	1	0	0	0	7.0	4	1	4	5
Bert Blyleven	1	0	1.00	1	1	1	0	0	9.0	8	1	0	9
John Candelaria	0	0	2.57	1	1	0	0	0	7.0	5	2	1	4
Grant Jackson	1	0	0.00	2	0	0	0	0	2.0	1	0	1	2
Dave Roberts	0	0	∞	1	0	0	0	0	0.0	0	0	1	0
Don Robinson	1	0	0.00	2	0	0	1	0	2.0	0	0	1	3
Enrique Romo	0	0	0.00	2	0	0	0	0	0.1	3	0	1	1
Kent Tekulve	0	0	3.38	2	0	0	0	0	2.2	2	1	2	2
TOTAL	3	0	1.50	12	3	1	1	0	30	23	5	11	26

CIN (W)

PLAYER/POS	AVG	G	AB	R	H	2B	3B	HR	RB	BB	SO	SB
Rick Auerbach, ph	.000	2	2	0	0	0	0	0	0	0	1	0
Doug Bair, p	.000	1	0	0	0	0	0	0	0	0	0	0
Johnny Bench, c	.250	3	12	1	3	0	1	1	1	2	2	0
Dave Collins, of	.357	3	14	0	5	1	0	0	1	0	2	2
Dave Concepcion, ss	.429	3	14	1	6	1	0	0	0	0	3	0
Hector Cruz, of-1	.200	2	5	1	1	1	0	0	0	0	1	0
Dan Driessen, 1b	.083	3	12	1	1	0	0	0	0	1	3	0
George Foster, of	.200	3	10	1	2	0	0	1	2	4	3	0
Cesar Geronimo, of	.143	2	7	0	1	0	0	0	0	0	5	0
Tom Hume, p	.000	3	1	0	0	0	0	0	0	0	1	0
Ray Knight, 3b	.286	3	14	0	4	1	0	0	0	0	2	1
Mike LaCoss, p	.000	1	0	0	0	0	0	0	0	0	0	0
Charlie Leibrandt, p	.000	1	0	0	0	0	0	0	0	0	0	0
Joe Morgan, 2b	.000	3	11	0	0	0	0	0	0	3	1	1
Fred Norman, p	.000	1	1	0	0	0	0	0	0	0	1	0
Frank Pastore, p	.000	1	0	0	0	0	0	0	1	1	0	0
Tom Seaver, p	.000	1	2	0	0	0	0	0	0	0	1	0
Mario Soto, p	.000	1	0	0	0	0	0	0	0	0	0	0
Harry Spilman, ph	.000	2	2	0	0	0	0	0	0	0	0	0
Dave Tomlin, p	.000	3	0	0	0	0	0	0	0	0	0	0
TOTAL	.215		107	5	23	4	1	2	5	11	26	4

PITCHER	W	L	ERA	G	GS	CG	SV	SHO	IP	H	ER	BB	SO
Doug Bair	0	1	9.00	1	0	0	0	0	1.0	2	1	1	0
Tom Hume	0	1	6.75	3	0	0	0	0	4.0	6	3	0	2
Mike LaCoss	0	1	10.80	1	1	0	0	0	1.2	1	2	4	0
Charlie Leibrandt	0	0	0.00	1	0	0	0	0	0.1	0	0	0	0
Fred Norman	0	0	18.00	1	0	0	0	0	2.0	4	4	1	1
Frank Pastore	0	0	2.57	1	1	0	0	0	7.0	7	2	3	1
Tom Seaver	0	0	2.25	1	1	0	0	0	8.0	5	2	2	5
Mario Soto	0	0	0.00	1	0	0	0	0	2.0	0	0	0	1
Dave Tomlin	0	0	0.00	3	0	0	0	0	3.0	3	0	2	3
TOTAL	0	3	4.34	13	3	0	0	0	29.0	28	14	13	13

GAME 1 AT CIN OCT 2

PIT	002 000 000 03	5	10	0
CIN	000 200 000 00	2	7	0

Pitchers: Candelaria, Romo (8), Tekulve (8), JACKSON (10), D.Robinson (11) vs Seaver, HUME (9), Tomlin (11)
Home Runs: Garner-PIT, Foster-CIN, Stargell-PIT
Attendance: 55,006

GAME 2 AT CIN OCT 3

PIT	000 110 000 1	3	11	0
CIN	010 000 001 0	2	8	0

Pitchers: Bibby, Jackson (8), Romo (8), Tekulve (8), Roberts (9), D.ROBINSON (9) vs Pastore, Tomlin (8), Hume (8), BAIR (10)
Attendance: 55,000

GAME 3 AT PIT OCT 5

CIN	000 001 000	1	8	1
PIT	112 200 01X	7	7	0

Pitchers: LaCOSS, Norman (2), Leibrandt (4), Soto (5), Tomlin (7), Hume (8) vs BLYLEVEN
Home Runs: Stargell-PIT, Madlock-PIT, Bench-CIN
Attendance: 42,240

Baltimore, returning to postseason play after a four-year absence, struggled with first-timer California through three games before blowing them away in the fourth. Game 1 went into the last of the 10th tied 3–3, when Oriole pinch hitter John Lowenstein, up with two men on, ended it with a two-out, two-strike shot that just cleared the left field wall.

Game 2 looked like a blowout for Baltimore. Eddie Murray drove in four runs, and the rest of the team added five more to give the O's a 9–1 lead by the end of three. But California chipped away at the lead in the latter half of the game and drew within one in the ninth, before Brian Downing hit into a forceout with the bases full to end their scoring.

The Angels' late rally in Game 3 was more successful. Down by a run in the bottom of the ninth, they scored twice, on a walk, a dropped outfield fly, and Larry Harlow's game-winning double. The final game, though, was all Baltimore's, as Scott McGregor—pitching the series' only complete game—blanked the Angels on six hits. The Orioles scored two in the third and another in the fourth, before Pat Kelly put California pennant hopes out of reach with a three-run homer in the O's five-run seventh.

Baltimore Orioles (East), 3; California Angels (West), 1

BAL (E)

PLAYER/POS	AVG	G	AB	R	H	2B	3B	HR	RB	BB	SO	SB
Mark Belanger, ss	.200	3	5	0	1	0	0	0	0	1	0	2	0
Al Bumbry, of	.250	4	16	5	4	0	1	0	0	4	3	2
Terry Crowley, ph	.500	2	2	0	1	0	0	0	1	0	0	0
Rich Dauer, 2b	.182	4	11	0	2	0	0	0	0	0	1	0
Doug DeCinces, 3b	.308	4	13	4	4	1	0	0	3	1	1	0
Rick Dempsey, c	.400	3	10	3	4	2	0	0	2	1	0	1
Mike Flanagan, p	.000	1	0	0	0	0	0	0	0	0	0	0
Kiko Garcia, ss	.273	3	11	1	3	0	0	0	2	2	4	0
Pat Kelly, dh-2,of-1	.364	3	11	3	4	0	0	1	4	1	3	2
John Lowenstein, of-3	.167	4	6	2	1	0	0	1	3	2	2	0
Dennis Martinez, p	.000	1	0	0	0	0	0	0	0	0	0	0
Lee May, dh	.143	2	7	0	1	0	0	0	1	1	3	0
Scott McGregor, p	.000	1	0	0	0	0	0	0	0	0	0	0
Eddie Murray, 1b	.417	4	12	3	5	0	0	1	5	5	2	0
Jim Palmer, p	.000	1	0	0	0	0	0	0	0	0	0	0
Gary Roenicke, of	.200	2	5	1	1	0	0	0	1	0	0	0
Ken Singleton, of	.375	4	16	4	6	2	0	0	2	1	2	0
Dave Skaggs, c	.000	1	4	0	0	0	0	0	0	0	0	0
Billy Smith, 2b	.000	1	4	0	0	0	0	0	0	0	1	0
Don Stanhouse, p	.000	3	0	0	0	0	0	0	0	0	0	0
TOTAL	.278		133	26	37	5	1	3	25	18	24	5

PITCHER	W	L	ERA	G	GS	CG	SV	SHO	IP	H	ER	BB	SO
Mike Flanagan	1	0	5.14	1	1	0	0	0	7.0	6	4	1	2
Dennis Martinez	0	0	3.24	1	1	0	0	0	8.1	8	3	0	4
Scott McGregor	1	0	0.00	1	1	1	0	1	9.0	6	0	1	4
Jim Palmer	0	0	3.00	1	1	0	0	0	9.0	7	3	2	3
Don Stanhouse	1	1	6.00	3	0	0	0	0	3.0	5	2	3	0
TOTAL	3	1	2.97	7	4	1	0	1	36.1	32	12	7	13

CAL (W)

PLAYER/POS	AVG	G	AB	R	H	2B	3B	HR	RB	BB	SO	SB
Don Aase, p	.000	2	0	0	0	0	0	0	0	0	0	0
Jim Anderson, ss	.091	4	11	0	1	0	0	0	0	0	1	0
Mike Barlow, p	.000	1	0	0	0	0	0	0	0	0	0	0
Don Baylor, dh-3,of-1	.188	4	16	2	3	0	0	1	2	1	2	0
Bert Campaneris, ss	.000	1	0	0	0	0	0	0	0	0	0	0
Rod Carew, 1b	.412	4	17	4	7	3	0	0	1	0	0	1
Bobby Clark, of	.000	1	3	0	0	0	0	0	0	0	2	0
Mark Clear, p	.000	1	0	0	0	0	0	0	0	0	0	0
Willie Davis, ph	.500	2	2	1	1	1	0	0	0	0	0	0
Brian Downing, c	.200	4	15	1	3	0	0	0	1	1	1	0
Dan Ford, of	.294	4	17	2	5	1	0	2	4	0	0	0
Dave Frost, p	.000	2	0	0	0	0	0	0	0	0	0	0
Bobby Grich, 2b	.154	4	13	0	2	1	0	0	2	1	1	0
Larry Harlow, of-2	.125	3	8	0	1	1	0	0	1	1	2	0
Chris Knapp, p	.000	1	0	0	0	0	0	0	0	0	0	0
Carney Lansford, 3b	.294	4	17	2	5	0	0	0	3	1	2	1
Dave LaRoche, p	.000	1	0	0	0	0	0	0	0	0	0	0
Rick Miller, of	.250	4	16	2	4	0	0	0	0	0	1	0
John Montague, p	.000	2	0	0	0	0	0	0	0	0	0	0
Merv Rettenmund, dh	.000	2	2	0	0	0	0	0	0	2	1	0
Nolan Ryan, p	.000	1	0	0	0	0	0	0	0	0	0	0
Frank Tanana, p	.000	1	0	0	0	0	0	0	0	0	0	0
Dickie Thon, ss	.000	1	0	1	0	0	0	0	0	0	0	0
TOTAL	.234		137	15	32	7	0	3	14	7	13	2

PITCHER	W	L	ERA	G	GS	CG	SV	SHO	IP	H	ER	BB	SO
Don Aase	1	0	1.80	2	0	0	0	0	5.0	4	1	2	6
Mike Barlow	0	0	0.00	1	0	0	0	0	1.0	0	0	0	0
Mark Clear	0	0	4.76	1	0	0	0	0	5.2	4	3	2	3
Dave Frost	0	1	18.69	2	1	0	0	0	4.1	8	9	5	1
Chris Knapp	0	1	7.71	1	1	0	0	0	2.1	5	2	1	0
Dave LaRoche	0	0	6.75	1	0	0	0	0	1.1	2	1	1	1
John Montague	0	1	9.00	2	0	0	0	0	4.0	4	4	2	2
Nolan Ryan	0	0	1.29	1	1	0	0	0	7.0	4	1	3	8
Frank Tanana	0	0	3.60	1	1	0	0	0	5.0	6	2	2	3
TOTAL	1	3	5.80	12	4	0	0	0	35.2	37	23	18	24

GAME 1 AT BAL OCT 3

CAL	101 001 000 0	3	7	1
BAL	002 100 000 1	6	6	0

Pitchers: Ryan, MONTAGUE (8) vs Palmer, STANHOUSE (10)
Home Runs: Ford-CAL, Lowenstein-BAL
Attendance: 52,787

GAME 2 AT BAL OCT 4

CAL	100 001 132	8	10	1
BAL	441 000 00X	9	11	1

Pitchers: FROST, Clear (2), Aase (8) vs FLANAGAN, Stanhouse (8)
Home Runs: Ford-CAL, Murray-BAL
Attendance: 52,108

GAME 3 AT CAL OCT 5

BAL	000 101 100	3	8	3
CAL	100 100 002	4	9	0

Pitchers: D.Martinez, STANHOUSE (9) vs Tanana, AASE (6)
Home Runs: Baylor-CAL
Attendance: 43,199

GAME 4 AT CAL OCT 6

BAL	002 100 500	8	12	1
CAL	000 000 000	0	6	0

Pitchers: McGREGOR vs KNAPP, LaRoche (3), Frost (4), Montague (7), Barlow (9)
Home Runs: Kelly-BAL
Attendance: 43,199

Veteran Willie Stargell was "Pops," and in the Series he showed his Pirate "family" the way. Seven of his 12 hits went for extra bases, and he drove in a Series-high seven runs. What Stargell began, submarine reliever Kent Tekulve finished, appearing in five of the seven games and recording a record-tying three saves.

Stargell drove in a pair of runs in the opener—one of them with an eighth-inning homer—but Pittsburgh's four runs fell short of the five Baltimore had scored in the first inning. The only extra-base hits in Game 2 came from the bat of Eddie Murray, who homered and doubled to drive in both Baltimore runs. But three singles and a sacrifice fly had already given Pittsburgh two runs in the second inning, and two more singles and a walk in the top of the ninth made the score 3–2. Tekulve came on in the last of the ninth to preserve the lead, fanning two as he retired the side in order.

Baltimore bounced back, though, to take the next two games in convincing fashion. The score favored the Orioles 8–4 when Tekulve came on to set the O's down in order over the final two innings. But Baltimore starter Scott McGregor had by then settled into his groove, retiring the final 11 Pirates with relative ease to preserve his lead and the win. It took four Orioles pitchers to hold the Pirates in Game 4. Stargell led the Bucs' 17-hit attack with a homer, double, and single, and the Pirates led 6–3 entering the eighth inning. But Baltimore loaded the bases in the top of the eighth, prompting Pirates manager Chuck Tanner to bring Tekulve in again. This one time the strategy failed, as Tekulve saw six runs score before he retired his first batter.

Down three games to one, the Pirates rebounded in Game 5, scoring seven times in the final three innings for a 7–1 victory. Baltimore starter Jim Palmer matched John Candelaria's shutout pitching through six innings of Game 6 before the Pirates tagged him for pairs of runs in the seventh and eighth. Tekulve, meanwhile, continued Candelaria's shutout through the final three innings, retiring the last seven men in order, four by strikeout. Baltimore scored first in the finale on Rich Dauer's leadoff home run in the third inning, but Stargell put the Pirates ahead with a two-run homer in the sixth. Tekulve came in with two Orioles on base in the eighth to stifle the threat, and (after the Pirates had scored a pair of insurance runs in the top of the ninth) set Baltimore down in order to complete the Pittsburgh's comeback.

Pittsburgh Pirates (NL), 4;
Baltimore Orioles (AL), 3

PIT (N)

PLAYER/POS	AVG	G	AB	R	H	2B	3B	HR	RB	BB	SO	SB
Matt Alexander, of	.000	1	0	0	0	0	0	0	0	0	0	0
Jim Bibby, p	.000	2	4	0	0	0	0	0	0	0	1	0
Bert Blyleven, p	.000	2	3	0	0	0	0	0	0	0	0	0
John Candelaria, p	.333	2	3	0	1	0	0	0	0	0	2	0
Mike Easler, ph	.000	2	1	0	0	0	0	0	0	1	0	0
Tim Foli, ss	.333	7	30	6	10	1	1	0	3	2	0	0
Phil Garner, 2b	.500	7	24	4	12	4	0	0	5	3	1	0
Grant Jackson, p	.000	4	1	0	0	0	0	0	0	0	0	0
Bruce Kison, p	.000	1	0	0	0	0	0	0	0	0	0	0
Lee Lacy, ph	.250	4	4	0	1	0	0	0	0	0	1	0
Bill Madlock, 3b	.375	7	24	2	9	1	0	0	3	5	1	0
John Milner, of	.333	3	9	2	3	1	0	0	1	2	0	0
Omar Moreno, of	.333	7	33	4	11	2	0	0	3	1	7	0
Steve Nicosia, c	.063	4	16	1	1	0	0	0	0	0	2	0
Ed Ott, c	.333	3	12	2	4	1	0	0	3	0	2	0
Dave Parker, of	.345	7	29	2	10	3	0	0	4	2	7	0
Don Robinson, p	.000	4	0	0	0	0	0	0	0	0	0	0
Bill Robinson, of-6	.263	7	19	2	5	1	0	0	2	0	4	0
Enrique Romo, p	.000	2	1	0	0	0	0	0	0	0	0	0
Jim Rooker, p	.000	2	2	0	0	0	0	0	0	0	1	0
Manny Sanguillen, ph	.333	3	3	0	1	0	0	0	1	0	0	0
Willie Stargell, 1b	.400	7	30	7	12	4	0	3	7	0	6	0
Rennie Stennett, ph	1.000	1	1	0	1	0	0	0	0	0	0	0
Kent Tekulve, p	.000	5	2	0	0	0	0	0	0	0	0	0
TOTAL	.323		251	32	81	18	1	3	32	16	35	0

PITCHER	W	L	ERA	G	GS	CG	SV	SHO	IP	H	ER	BB	SO
Jim Bibby	0	0	2.61	2	2	0	0	0	10.1	10	3	2	10
Bert Blyleven	1	0	1.80	2	1	0	0	0	10.0	8	2	3	4
John Candelaria	1	1	5.00	2	2	0	0	0	9.0	14	5	2	4
Grant Jackson	1	0	0.00	4	0	0	0	0	4.2	1	0	2	2
Bruce Kison	0	1	108.00	1	1	0	0	0	0.1	3	4	2	0
Don Robinson	1	0	5.40	4	0	0	0	0	5.0	4	3	6	3
Enrique Romo	0	0	3.86	2	0	0	0	0	4.2	5	2	3	4
Jim Rooker	0	0	1.04	2	1	0	0	0	8.2	5	1	3	4
Kent Tekulve	0	1	2.89	5	0	0	3	0	9.1	4	3	3	10
TOTAL	4	3	3.34	24	7	0	3	0	62.0	54	23	26	41

BAL (A)

PLAYER/POS	AVG	G	AB	R	H	2B	3B	HR	RB	BB	SO	SB
Benny Ayala, of-3	.333	4	6	1	2	0	0	1	2	1	0	0
Mark Belanger, ss-4	.000	5	6	1	0	0	0	0	0	1	1	0
Al Bumbry, of	.143	7	21	3	3	0	0	0	1	2	1	0
Terry Crowley, ph	.250	5	4	0	1	1	0	0	2	1	0	0
Rich Dauer, 2b-5	.294	6	17	2	5	1	0	1	1	0	1	0
Doug DeCinces, 3b	.200	7	25	2	5	0	0	1	3	5	5	1
Rick Dempsey, c-6	.286	7	21	3	6	2	0	0	1	3	0	0
Mike Flanagan, p	.000	3	5	0	0	0	0	0	0	1	2	0
Kiko Garcia, ss	.400	6	20	4	8	2	1	0	6	1	3	0
Pat Kelly, ph	.250	5	4	0	1	0	0	0	0	1	1	0
John Lowenstein, of-3	.231	6	13	2	3	1	0	0	3	1	3	0
Tippy Martinez, p	.000	3	0	0	0	0	0	0	0	0	0	0
Dennis Martinez, p	.000	2	0	0	0	0	0	0	0	0	0	0
Lee May, ph	.000	2	1	0	0	0	0	0	0	1	1	0
Scott McGregor, p	.000	2	4	1	0	0	0	0	0	0	0	0
Eddie Murray, 1b	.154	7	26	3	4	0	0	1	2	4	4	1
Jim Palmer, p	.000	2	4	0	0	0	0	0	0	0	3	0
Gary Roenicke, of-5	.125	6	16	1	2	1	0	0	0	0	6	0
Ken Singleton, of	.357	7	28	1	10	1	0	0	2	2	5	0
Dave Skaggs, c	.333	1	3	1	1	0	0	0	0	0	0	0
Billy Smith, 2b-2	.286	4	7	1	2	0	0	0	0	2	0	0
Don Stanhouse, p	.000	3	0	0	0	0	0	0	0	0	0	0
Sammy Stewart, p	.000	1	1	0	0	0	0	0	0	0	1	0
Tim Stoddard, p	1.000	4	1	0	1	0	0	0	1	0	0	0
Steve Stone, p	.000	1	0	0	0	0	0	0	0	0	0	0
TOTAL	.232		233	26	54	10	1	4	23	26	41	2

PITCHER	W	L	ERA	G	GS	CG	SV	SHO	IP	H	ER	BB	SO
Mike Flanagan	1	1	3.00	3	2	1	0	0	15.0	18	5	2	13
Tippy Martinez	0	0	6.75	3	0	0	0	0	1.1	3	1	0	1
Dennis Martinez	0	0	18.00	2	1	0	0	0	2.0	6	4	0	0
Scott McGregor	1	1	3.18	2	2	1	0	0	17.0	16	6	2	8
Jim Palmer	0	1	3.60	2	2	0	0	0	15.0	18	6	5	8
Don Stanhouse	0	1	13.50	3	0	0	0	0	2.0	6	3	3	0
Sammy Stewart	0	0	0.00	1	0	0	0	0	2.2	4	0	1	0
Tim Stoddard	1	0	5.40	4	0	0	0	0	5.0	6	3	1	3
Steve Stone	0	0	9.00	1	0	0	0	0	2.0	4	2	2	2
TOTAL	3	4	4.35	21	7	2	0	0	62.0	81	30	16	35

GAME 1 AT BAL OCT 10

```
PIT   000 102 010    4 11 3
BAL   500 000 000    5  6 3
```
Pitchers: KISON, Rooker (1), Romo (5), D.Robinson (6), Jackson (8) vs FLANAGAN
Home Runs: Stargell-PIT, DeCinces-BAL
Attendance: 53,735

GAME 2 AT BAL OCT 11

```
PIT   020 000 001    3 11 2
BAL   010 001 000    2  6 1
```
Pitchers: Blyleven, D.ROBINSON (7), Tekulve (9) vs PALMER, T.Martinez (8), Stanhouse (9)
Home Runs: Murray-BAL
Attendance: 53,739

GAME 3 AT PIT OCT 12

```
BAL   002 500 100    8 13 0
PIT   120 001 000    4  9 2
```
Pitchers: McGREGOR vs CANDELARIA, Romo (4), Jackson (7), Tekulve (8)
Home Runs: Ayala-BAL
Attendance: 50,848

GAME 4 AT PIT OCT 13

```
BAL   003 000 060    9 12 0
PIT   040 011 000    6 17 1
```
Pitchers: D.Martinez, Stewart (2), Stone (5), STODDARD (7) vs Bibby, Jackson (6), D.Robinson (8), TEKULVE (8)
Home Runs: Stargell-PIT
Attendance: 50,883

GAME 5 AT PIT OCT 14

```
BAL   000 010 000    1  6 2
PIT   000 002 23X    7 13 1
```
Pitchers: FLANAGAN, Stoddard (7), T.Martinez (8) vs Rooker, BLYLEVEN (6)
Attendance: 50,920

GAME 6 AT BAL OCT 16

```
PIT   000 000 220    4 10 0
BAL   000 000 000    0  7 1
```
Pitchers: CANDELARIA, Tekulve (7) vs PALMER, Stoddard (9)
Attendance: 53,739

GAME 7 AT BAL OCT 17

```
PIT   000 002 002    4 10 0
BAL   001 000 000    1  4 2
```
Pitchers: Bibby, D.Robinson (5), JACKSON (5), Tekulve (8) vs McGREGOR, Stoddard (9), Flanagan (9), Stanhouse (9), T.Martinez (9), D.Martinez (9)
Home Runs: Stargell-PIT, Dauer-BAL
Attendance: 53,733

In the tightest LCS yet, the Phillies took the opener 3–1 on the series' only home run—Greg Luzinski's two-run blast in the sixth inning. It was the only game not to go into extra innings.

The Astros evened the series in Game 2—demolishing a 3–3 tie with four runs in the 10th—and took the series lead in a Game 3 pitchers' duel that saw Joe Niekro hurl ten scoreless innings for Houston. Reliever Dave Smith continued the shutout and took the win as Joe Morgan's triple and Denny Walling's sacrifice fly off Phillies reliever Tug McGraw scored the game's only run in the bottom of the 11th.

The Phillies rebounded, though, with their own set of extra-inning victories. In Game 4, a single and two doubles pushed across two go-ahead runs in the top of the tenth, and McGraw preserved the edge for his second series save. And in the finale—which saw the lead change hands three times—after Del Unser scored on Gary Maddox's 10th-inning double, Dick Ruthven held off Houston to bring the Phillies their first pennant in 30 years.

Philadelphia Phillies (East), 3; Houston Astros (West), 2

PHI (E)

PLAYER/POS	AVG	G	AB	R	H	2B	3B	HR	RB	BB	SO	SB
Ramon Aviles, pr	.000	1	0	1	0	0	0	0	0	0	0	0
Bob Boone, c	.222	5	18	1	4	0	0	0	2	1	2	0
Larry Bowa, ss	.316	5	19	2	6	0	0	0	0	3	3	1
Warren Brusstar, p	.000	2	1	0	0	0	0	0	0	0	0	0
Marty Bystrom, p	.000	1	2	0	0	0	0	0	0	0	1	0
Steve Carlton, p	.000	2	4	0	0	0	0	0	0	0	1	0
Larry Christenson, p	.000	1	2	0	0	0	0	0	0	0	1	0
Greg Gross, of-1	.750	4	4	2	3	0	0	0	1	0	0	0
Greg Luzinski, of	.294	5	17	3	5	2	0	1	4	0	6	0
Garry Maddox, of	.300	5	20	2	6	2	0	0	3	2	2	0
Bake McBride, of	.238	5	21	0	5	0	0	0	0	1	5	2
Tug McGraw, p	.000	5	1	0	0	0	0	0	0	0	0	0
Keith Moreland, c-1	.000	2	1	0	0	0	0	0	1	0	0	0
Dickie Noles, p	.000	2	0	0	0	0	0	0	0	0	0	0
Ron Reed, p	.000	3	0	0	0	0	0	0	0	0	0	0
Pete Rose, 1b	.400	5	20	3	8	0	0	0	2	5	3	0
Dick Ruthven, p	.000	2	2	0	0	0	0	0	0	0	2	0
Kevin Saucier, p	.000	2	0	0	0	0	0	0	0	0	0	0
Mike Schmidt, 3b	.208	5	24	1	5	1	0	0	1	1	6	1
Lonnie Smith, of-2	.600	3	5	2	3	0	0	0	0	0	0	1
Manny Trillo, 2b	.381	5	21	1	8	2	1	0	4	0	2	0
Del Unser, of-2	.400	5	5	2	2	1	0	0	1	0	2	0
George Vukovich, of-1	.000	4	3	0	0	0	0	0	0	0	0	0
TOTAL	.289		190	20	55	8	1	1	19	13	37	7

PITCHER	W	L	ERA	G	GS	CG	SV	SHO	IP	H	ER	BB	SO
Warren Brusstar	1	0	3.38	2	0	0	0	0	2.2	1	1	1	0
Marty Bystrom	0	0	1.69	1	1	0	0	0	5.1	7	1	2	1
Steve Carlton	1	0	2.19	2	2	0	0	0	12.1	11	3	8	6
Larry Christenson	0	0	4.05	1	1	0	0	0	6.2	5	3	5	2
Tug McGraw	0	1	4.50	5	0	0	2	0	8.0	8	4	4	5
Dickie Noles	0	0	0.00	2	0	0	0	0	2.2	1	0	3	0
Ron Reed	0	1	18.00	3	0	0	0	0	2.0	3	4	1	1
Dick Ruthven	1	0	2.00	2	1	0	0	0	9.0	3	2	5	4
Kevin Saucier	0	0	0.00	2	0	0	0	0	0.2	1	0	2	0
TOTAL	3	2	3.28	20	5	0	2	0	49.1	40	18	31	19

HOU (W)

PLAYER/POS	AVG	G	AB	R	H	2B	3B	HR	RB	BB	SO	SB
Joaquin Andujar, p	.000	1	0	0	0	0	0	0	0	0	0	0
Alan Ashby, c	.125	2	8	0	1	0	0	0	1	0	0	0
Dave Bergman, 1b	.333	4	3	0	1	0	1	0	2	0	0	0
Bruce Bochy, c	.000	1	1	0	0	0	0	0	0	0	0	0
Enos Cabell, 3b	.238	5	21	1	5	1	0	0	0	1	3	0
Cesar Cedeno, of	.182	3	11	1	2	0	0	0	1	1	0	0
Jose Cruz, of	.400	5	15	3	6	1	1	0	4	8	1	0
Ken Forsch, p	1.000	2	2	0	2	0	0	0	0	0	0	0
Danny Heep, ph	.000	1	1	0	0	0	0	0	0	0	0	0
Art Howe, 1b-4	.200	5	15	0	3	1	1	0	2	2	2	0
Frank LaCorte, p	.000	2	1	0	0	0	0	0	0	0	0	0
Rafael Landestoy, 2b-3,ss-1	.222	5	9	3	2	0	0	0	2	1	0	1
Jeffrey Leonard, of-1	.000	3	3	0	0	0	0	0	0	0	2	0
Joe Morgan, 2b	.154	4	13	1	2	1	1	0	0	6	1	0
Joe Niekro, p	.000	1	3	0	0	0	0	0	0	0	1	0
Terry Puhl, of-4	.526	5	19	4	10	2	0	0	3	3	2	2
Luis Pujols, c	.100	4	10	1	1	0	1	0	0	3	0	0
Craig Reynolds, ss	.154	4	13	2	2	1	0	0	0	3	1	0
Vern Ruhle, p	.000	1	3	0	0	0	0	0	0	0	1	0
Nolan Ryan, p	.000	2	4	1	0	0	0	0	0	1	2	0
Joe Sambito, p	.000	3	0	0	0	0	0	0	0	0	0	0
Dave Smith, p	.000	3	0	0	0	0	0	0	0	0	0	0
Denny Walling, of-2,1b-1	.111	3	9	2	1	0	0	0	2	1	0	0
Gary Woods, of-3	.250	4	8	0	2	0	0	0	1	1	3	1
TOTAL	.233		172	19	40	7	5	0	18	31	19	4

PITCHER	W	L	ERA	G	GS	CG	SV	SHO	IP	H	ER	BB	SO
Joaquin Andujar	0	0	0.00	1	0	0	1	0	1.0	0	0	1	0
Ken Forsch	0	1	4.15	2	1	1	0	0	8.2	10	4	1	6
Frank LaCorte	1	1	3.00	2	0	0	0	0	3.0	7	1	2	2
Joe Niekro	0	0	0.00	1	1	0	0	0	10.0	6	0	1	2
Vern Ruhle	0	0	3.86	1	1	0	0	0	7.0	8	3	1	3
Nolan Ryan	0	0	5.40	2	2	0	0	0	13.1	16	8	3	14
Joe Sambito	0	1	4.91	3	0	0	0	0	3.2	4	2	2	6
Dave Smith	1	0	3.86	3	0	0	0	0	2.1	4	1	2	4
TOTAL	2	3	3.49	15	5	1	1	0	49.0	55	19	13	37

GAME 1 AT PHI OCT 7

HOU	001	000	000		1	7	0
PHI	000	002	10X		3	8	1

Pitchers: FORSCH vs CARLTON, McGraw (8)
Home Runs: Luzinski-PHI
Attendance: 65,277

GAME 2 AT PHI OCT 8

HOU	001	000	110	4	7	8	1
PHI	000	200	010	1	4	14	2

Pitchers: Ryan, Sambito (7), D.Smith (7), LaCORTE (9), Andujar (10) vs Ruthven, McGraw (8), REED (9), Saucier (10)
Attendance: 65,476

GAME 3 AT HOU OCT 10

PHI	000	000	000	00	0	7	1
HOU	000	000	000	01	1	6	1

Pitchers: Christensen, Noles (7), McGraw (8) vs Niekro, D.SMITH (11)
Attendance: 44,443

GAME 4 AT HOU OCT 11

PHI	000	000	030	2	5	13	0
HOU	000	110	000	0	3	5	1

Pitchers: Carlton, Noles (6), Saucier (7), Reed (7), BRUSSTAR (8), McGraw (10) vs Ruhle, D.Smith (8), SAMBITO (8)
Attendance: 44,952

GAME 5 AT HOU OCT 12

PHI	020	000	050	1	8	13	2
HOU	100	001	320	0	7	14	0

Pitchers: Bystrom, Brusstar (6), Christensen (7), Reed (7), McGraw (8), RUTHVEN (9) vs Ryan, Sambito (8), Forsch (8), LaCORTE (9)
Attendance: 44,802

Kansas City and New York met for the fourth time in the ALCS, and this time the Royals swept to their first pennant. In the first game the Yankees scored first, with second-inning home runs by Rick Cerone and Lou Piniella, but the Royals' Frank White doubled in a pair later in the inning to tie it, and Willie Aikens's hit in the third gave K.C. the lead. They held it to the end as Larry Gura shut out New York the rest of the way.

The Royals scored three runs in the third inning of Game 2, on Willie Wilson's two-run triple and an RBI double by U. L. Washington. Yankees starter Rudy May stopped K.C. after that, but the Royals already had enough for the win as Dennis Leonard held New York to two runs in eight innings. Dan Quisenberry kept the lid on in the ninth for the save.

Game 3 was decided by home runs. White scored first for the Royals with a solo shot in the fifth. New York took the lead briefly with a two-run sixth, but lost it— and the pennant—in the top of the seventh when Goose Gossage, relieving starter Tommy John with two outs and a man on, gave up an infield single to Washington and a home run to George Brett.

Kansas City Royals (West), 3; New York Yankees (East), 0

KC (W)

PLAYER/POS	AVG	G	AB	R	H	2B	3B	HR	RB	BB	SO	SB
Willie Aikens, 1b	.364	3	11	0	4	0	0	0	2	0	1	0
George Brett, 3b	.273	3	11	3	3	1	0	2	4	1	0	0
Larry Gura, p	.000	1	0	0	0	0	0	0	0	0	0	0
Clint Hurdle, of	.000	3	2	0	0	0	0	0	0	0	1	0
Pete LaCock, 1b	.000	1	0	0	0	0	0	0	0	0	0	0
Dennis Leonard, p	.000	1	0	0	0	0	0	0	0	0	0	0
Hal McRae, dh	.200	3	10	0	2	0	0	0	0	1	3	0
Amos Otis, of	.333	3	12	2	4	1	0	0	0	0	3	2
Darrell Porter, c	.100	3	10	2	1	0	0	0	0	1	0	0
Dan Quisenberry, p	.000	2	0	0	0	0	0	0	0	0	0	0
Paul Splittorff, p	.000	1	0	0	0	0	0	0	0	0	0	0
U. L. Washington, ss	.364	3	11	1	4	1	0	0	1	2	3	0
John Wathan, of	.000	3	6	1	0	0	0	0	0	3	1	0
Frank White, 2b	.545	3	11	3	6	1	0	1	3	0	1	1
Willie Wilson, of	.308	3	13	2	4	2	1	0	4	1	2	0
TOTAL	.289		97	14	28	6	1	3	14	9	15	3

PITCHER	W	L	ERA	G	GS	CG	SV	SHO	IP	H	ER	BB	SO
Larry Gura	1	0	2.00	1	1	1	0	0	9.0	10	2	1	4
Dennis Leonard	1	0	2.25	1	1	0	0	0	8.0	7	2	1	8
Dan Quisenberry	1	0	0.00	2	0	0	1	0	4.2	4	0	2	1
Paul Splittorff	0	0	1.69	1	1	0	0	0	5.1	5	1	2	3
TOTAL	3	0	1.67	5	3	1	1	0	27.0	26	5	6	16

NY (E)

PLAYER/POS	AVG	G	AB	R	H	2B	3B	HR	RB	BB	SO	SB
Bobby Brown, of	.000	3	10	1	0	0	0	0	0	1	2	0
Rick Cerone, c	.333	3	12	1	4	0	0	1	2	0	1	0
Ron Davis, p	.000	1	0	0	0	0	0	0	0	0	0	0
Bucky Dent, ss	.182	3	11	0	2	0	0	0	0	0	1	0
Oscar Gamble, of-1,dh-1	.200	2	5	1	1	0	0	0	0	1	1	0
Rich Gossage, p	.000	1	0	0	0	0	0	0	0	0	0	0
Ron Guidry, p	.000	1	0	0	0	0	0	0	0	0	0	0
Reggie Jackson, of	.273	3	11	1	3	1	0	0	0	1	4	0
Tommy John, p	.000	1	0	0	0	0	0	0	0	0	0	0
Joe Lefebvre, of	.000	1	0	0	0	0	0	0	0	0	0	0
Rudy May, p	.000	1	0	0	0	0	0	0	0	0	0	0
Bobby Murcer, dh	.000	1	4	0	0	0	0	0	0	0	2	0
Graig Nettles, 3b	.167	2	6	1	1	0	0	1	1	0	1	0
Lou Piniella, of	.200	2	5	1	1	0	0	1	1	1	2	0
Willie Randolph, 2b	.385	3	13	0	5	2	0	0	1	1	3	0
Aurelio Rodriguez, 3b	.333	2	6	0	2	1	0	0	0	0	0	0
Eric Soderholm, dh	.167	2	6	0	1	0	0	0	0	0	0	0
Jim Spencer, ph	.000	1	0	0	0	0	0	0	0	0	0	0
Tom Underwood, p	.000	2	0	0	0	0	0	0	0	0	0	0
Bob Watson, 1b	.500	3	12	0	6	3	1	0	0	0	0	0
TOTAL	.255		102	6	26	7	1	3	5	6	16	0

PITCHER	W	L	ERA	G	GS	CG	SV	SHO	IP	H	ER	BB	SO
Ron Davis	0	0	2.25	1	0	0	0	0	4.0	3	1	1	3
Rich Gossage	0	1	54.00	1	0	0	0	0	0.1	3	2	0	0
Ron Guidry	0	1	12.00	1	1	0	0	0	3.0	5	4	4	2
Tommy John	0	0	2.70	1	1	0	0	0	6.2	8	2	1	3
Rudy May	0	1	3.38	1	1	1	0	0	8.0	6	3	3	4
Tom Underwood	0	0	0.00	2	0	0	0	0	3.0	3	0	0	3
TOTAL	0	3	4.32	7	3	1	0	0	25.0	28	12	9	15

GAME 1 AT KC OCT 8

NY	020 000 000	2 10 1
KC	022 000 12X	7 10 0

Pitchers: GUIDRY, Davis (4), Underwood (8) vs GURA
Home Runs: Cerone-NY, Piniella-NY, G.Brett-KC
Attendance: 42,598

GAME 2 AT KC OCT 9

NY	000 020 000	2 8 0
KC	003 000 00X	3 6 0

Pitchers: MAY vs LEONARD, Quisenberry (9)
Home Runs: Nettles-NY
Attendance: 42,633

GAME 3 AT NY OCT 10

KC	000 010 300	4 12 1
NY	000 002 000	2 8 0

Pitchers: Splittorff, QUISENBERRY (6) vs John, GOSSAGE (7), Underwood (8)
Home Runs: White-KC, G.Brett-KC
Attendance: 56,588

Both clubs had won divisional ti-tles three years in a row—1976–1978—only to lose the League Championship Series. But both overcame the jinx in 1980 to face off in the World Series—the Phillies for the first time in 30 years, the Royals for the first time ever. Kansas City began with a rush in the opener, scoring two runs on Amos Otis' homer in the second inning and two more on Willie Aikens' blast an inning later. But the Phillies came back to take the lead in their half of the third with a five-run rally capped by Bake McBride's three-run homer. Single runs in each of the next two innings kept the Phillies out of reach of Aikens' second two-run shot in the eighth for a narrow 7–6 win. The Phillies ex-tended their Series advantage with a 6–4 win in the second game, re-bounding from a two-run deficit with four runs in the eighth inning.

The two clubs traded single runs throughout Game 3. George Brett's first-inning homer began the scoring. The Phillies got the run back in the second inning, the Royals took the lead back in the fourth, Mike Schmidt homered to tie it again in the fifth, Amos Otis countered with a homer in the seventh, and Pete Rose singled in another tying run for Philadelphia in the eighth. Phillies reliever Tug McGraw (who had a save in the opening game) came on to pitch the last of the 10th inning, but couldn't hold the tie, though two men were out before Aikens sin-gled in the Royals' winning run. The Royals evened the Series with their second victory the next day, scoring four times in the first in-ning and once in the second (with Aikens for the second time in the Series hitting two home runs in a game), then holding on for a 5–3 win.

But the Phillies recovered to win the next two, and their first world crown. Mike Schmidt's fourth-in-ning two-run homer began the Phillies' scoring in Game 5. The Royals replied with one run in the fifth, and Amos Otis' home run an inning later tied the game. A sec-ond K.C. run in the inning put the Royals ahead until the top of the ninth, when pinch hitter Del Unser doubled home Schmidt to tie the game, and Manny Trillo drove home Unser with the go-ahead run. Tug McGraw, who had held K.C. scoreless through two innings of relief, loaded the bases in the last of the ninth with three walks, but at last fanned Jose Cardenal for the final out. In Game 6, with the Phil-lies ahead 4–0 in the eighth inning, McGraw relieved starter Steve Carlton with two men on, and loaded the bases with a walk. One Royal scored on a sacrifice fly be-fore McGraw got his third out. In

the ninth, another McGraw walk and two singles again loaded the bases with only one away, but Frank White popped up in foul ter-ritory, the ball bouncing off Bob Boone's catcher's mitt into Pete Rose's hand. Willie Wilson then struck out for the 12th time to end the Series and give the Phillies their first world championship.

Philadelphia Phillies (NL), 4; Kansas City Royals (AL), 2

PHI (N)

PLAYER/POS	AVG	G	AB	R	H	2B	3B	HR	RB	BB	SO	SB
Bob Boone, c	.412	6	17	3	7	2	0	0	4	4	0	0
Larry Bowa, ss	.375	6	24	3	9	1	0	0	2	0	0	3
Warren Brusstar, p	.000	1	0	0	0	0	0	0	0	0	0	0
Marty Bystrom, p	.000	1	0	0	0	0	0	0	0	0	0	0
Steve Carlton, p	.000	2	0	0	0	0	0	0	0	0	0	0
Larry Christenson, p	.000	1	0	0	0	0	0	0	0	0	0	0
Greg Gross, of-3	.000	4	0	0	0	0	0	0	0	0	0	0
Greg Luzinski, dh-2,of-1	.000	3	9	0	0	0	0	0	0	1	5	0
Garry Maddox, of	.227	6	22	1	5	2	0	0	1	1	3	0
Bake McBride, of	.304	6	23	3	7	1	0	1	5	2	1	0
Tug McGraw, p	.000	4	0	0	0	0	0	0	0	0	0	0
Keith Moreland, dh	.333	3	12	1	4	0	0	0	1	0	1	0
Dickie Noles, p	.000	1	0	0	0	0	0	0	0	0	0	0
Ron Reed, p	.000	2	0	0	0	0	0	0	0	0	0	0
Pete Rose, 1b	.261	6	23	2	6	1	0	0	1	2	2	0
Dick Ruthven, p	.000	1	0	0	0	0	0	0	0	0	0	0
Kevin Saucier, p	.000	1	0	0	0	0	0	0	0	0	0	0
Mike Schmidt, 3b	.381	6	21	6	8	1	0	2	7	4	3	0
Lonnie Smith, of-5,dh-1	.263	6	19	2	5	1	0	0	1	1	1	0
Manny Trillo, 2b	.217	6	23	4	5	2	0	0	2	0	0	0
Del Unser, of	.500	3	6	2	3	2	0	0	2	0	1	0
Bob Walk, p	.000	1	0	0	0	0	0	0	0	0	0	0
TOTAL	.294		201	27	59	13	0	3	26	15	17	3

PITCHER	W	L	ERA	G	GS	CG	SV	SHO	IP	H	ER	BB	SO
Warren Brusstar	0	0	0.00	1	0	0	0	0	2.1	0	0	1	0
Marty Bystrom	0	0	5.40	1	1	0	0	0	5.0	10	3	1	4
Steve Carlton	2	0	2.40	2	2	0	0	0	15.0	14	4	9	17
Larry Christenson	0	1	108.00	1	1	0	0	0	0.1	5	4	1	0
Tug McGraw	1	1	1.17	4	0	0	2	0	7.2	7	1	8	10
Dickie Noles	0	0	1.93	1	0	0	0	0	4.2	5	1	2	6
Ron Reed	0	0	0.00	2	0	0	1	0	2.0	2	0	0	2
Dick Ruthven	0	0	3.00	1	1	0	0	0	9.0	9	3	0	7
Kevin Saucier	0	0	0.00	1	0	0	0	0	0.2	0	0	2	0
Bob Walk	1	0	7.71	1	1	0	0	0	7.0	8	6	3	3
TOTAL	4	2	3.69	15	6	0	3	0	53.2	60	22	27	49

KC (A)

PLAYER/POS	AVG	G	AB	R	H	2B	3B	HR	RB	BB	SO	SB
Willie Aikens, 1b	.400	6	20	5	8	0	1	4	8	6	8	0
George Brett, 3b	.375	6	24	3	9	2	1	1	3	2	4	1
Jose Cardenal, of	.200	4	10	0	2	0	0	0	0	0	3	0
Dave Chalk, 3b	.000	1	0	1	0	0	0	0	0	1	0	1
Onix Concepcion, pr	.000	3	0	0	0	0	0	0	0	0	0	0
Rich Gale, p	.000	2	0	0	0	0	0	0	0	0	0	0
Larry Gura, p	.000	2	0	0	0	0	0	0	0	0	0	0
Clint Hurdle, of	.417	4	12	1	5	1	0	0	2	1	1	1
Pete LaCock, 1b	.000	1	0	0	0	0	0	0	0	0	0	0
Dennis Leonard, p	.000	2	0	0	0	0	0	0	0	0	0	0
Renie Martin, p	.000	3	0	0	0	0	0	0	0	0	0	0
Hal McRae, dh	.375	6	24	3	9	3	0	0	1	2	2	0
Amos Otis, of	.478	6	23	4	11	2	0	3	7	3	3	0
Marty Pattin, p	.000	1	0	0	0	0	0	0	0	0	0	0
Darrell Porter, c-4	.143	5	14	1	2	0	0	0	0	3	4	0
Dan Quisenberry, p	.000	6	0	0	0	0	0	0	0	0	0	0
Paul Splittorff, p	.000	1	0	0	0	0	0	0	0	0	0	0
U L Washington, ss	.273	6	22	1	6	0	0	0	2	0	6	0
John Wathan, c-2,of-1	.286	3	7	1	2	0	0	0	1	2	1	0
Frank White, 2b	.080	6	25	0	2	0	0	0	0	1	5	1
Willie Wilson, of	.154	6	26	3	4	1	0	0	4	4	12	2
TOTAL	.290		207	23	60	9	2	8	22	26	49	6

PITCHER	W	L	ERA	G	GS	CG	SV	SHO	IP	H	ER	BB	SO
Rich Gale	0	1	4.26	2	2	0	0	0	6.1	11	3	4	4
Larry Gura	0	0	2.19	2	2	0	0	0	12.1	8	3	4	4
Dennis Leonard	1	1	6.75	2	2	0	0	0	10.2	15	8	2	5
Renie Martin	0	0	2.79	3	0	0	0	0	9.2	11	3	3	2
Marty Pattin	0	0	0.00	1	0	0	0	0	1.0	0	0	0	2
Dan Quisenberry	1	2	5.23	6	0	0	1	0	10.1	10	6	3	0
Paul Splittorff	0	0	5.40	1	0	0	0	0	1.2	4	1	0	0
TOTAL	2	4	4.15	17	6	0	1	0	52.0	59	24	15	17

GAME 1 AT PHI OCT 14

```
KC    022 000 020    6 9 1
PHI   005 110 00X    7 11 0
```

Pitchers: LEONARD, Martin (4), Quisenberry (8) vs WALK, McGraw (8)
Home Runs: Otis-KC, Aikens-KC (2), McBride-PHI
Attendance: 65,791

GAME 2 AT PHI OCT 15

```
KC    000 001 300    4 11 0
PHI   000 020 04X    6 8 1
```

Pitchers: Gura, QUISENBERRY (7) vs CARLTON, Reed (9)
Attendance: 65,775

GAME 3 AT KC OCT 17

```
PHI   010 010 010 0    3 14 0
KC    100 100 100 1    4 11 1
```

Pitchers: Ruthven, McGRAW (10) vs Gale, Martin (5), QUISENBERRY (8)
Home Runs: Schmidt-PHI, G.Brett-KC, Otis-KC
Attendance: 42,380

GAME 4 AT KC OCT 18

```
PHI   010 000 110    3 10 1
KC    410 000 00X    5 10 2
```

Pitchers: CHRISTENSEN, Noles (1), Saucier (6), Brusstar (6) vs LEONARD, Quisenberry (8)
Home Runs: Aikens-KC (2)
Attendance: 42,363

GAME 5 AT KC OCT 19

```
PHI   000 200 002    4 7 0
KC    000 012 000    3 12 2
```

Pitchers: Bystrom, Reed (6), McGRAW (7) vs Gura, QUISENBERRY (7)
Home Runs: Schmidt-PHI, Otis-KC
Attendance: 42,369

GAME 6 AT PHI OCT 21

```
KC    000 000 010    1 7 2
PHI   002 011 00X    4 9 0
```

Pitchers: GALE, Martin (3), Splittorff (5), Pattin (7), Quisenberry (8) vs CARLTON, McGraw (8)
Attendance: 65,838

The Expos, who triumphed over the NL East in the second half of the season, won the first two playoff games at home by identical 3–1 scores over the first-half champion Phillies. In the first postseason game played in Canada the Phillies rapped Expos ace Steve Rogers for 10 hits in Game 1, but Keith Moreland's solo home run in the second was the only hit to produce a run. The homer tied the score briefly, but the Expos regained the lead in the last of the second inning on Chris Speier's double and increased it to 3–1 two innings later. The Expos scored their three runs early in Game 2 on Speier's second-inning single and Gary Carter's two-run homer an inning later. Expos starter Bill Gullickson blanked the Phillies on three hits through 7⅔ innings, but three two-out hits in the eighth scored a run and brought on reliever Jeff Reardon, who ended the threat for his second save in as many days.

When the Series moved to Philadelphia, the Phillies recovered to even things with a pair of wins. After an easy 13-hit 6–2 victory in Game 3, they took a 4–0 lead into the fourth inning of Game 4. Montreal fought back to tie the game, fell behind again, then re-tied the score at 5–5 in the top of the seventh. The final innings featured a duel between relievers Tug McGraw and Jeff Reardon. McGraw stopped the Expos on one hit through three innings, and took the win when Reardon, after retiring eight Phillies in a row, gave up a leadoff homer to pinch hitter George Vukovich in the bottom of the 10th.

Steve Rogers won the division title for Montreal in the finale, hurling a six-hit shutout against the Phillies and driving in the first two of Montreal's three runs with a bases-loaded single through the box in the fifth inning.

Montreal Expos, 3; Philadelphia Phillies, 2

MON (E)

PLAYER/POS	AVG	G	AB	R	H	2B	3B	HR	RB	BB	SO	SB
Stan Bahnsen, p	.000	1	0	0	0	0	0	0	0	0	0	0
Ray Burris, p	.000	1	2	0	0	0	0	0	0	0	2	0
Gary Carter, c	.421	5	19	3	8	3	0	2	6	1	1	0
Warren Cromartie, 1b	.227	5	22	1	5	2	0	0	1	0	9	0
Andre Dawson, of	.300	5	20	1	6	0	1	0	0	1	6	2
Terry Francona, of	.333	5	12	0	4	0	0	0	0	2	2	2
Woody Fryman, p	.000	1	0	0	0	0	0	0	0	0	0	0
Bill Gullickson, p	.000	1	3	0	0	0	0	0	0	0	1	0
Wallace Johnson, ph	.500	2	2	0	1	0	0	0	1	0	0	0
Bill Lee, p	.000	1	0	0	0	0	0	0	0	0	0	0
Jerry Manuel, 2b	.071	5	14	0	1	0	0	0	0	2	5	0
Brad Mills, ph	.000	1	0	0	0	0	0	0	0	1	0	0
John Milner, ph	.500	2	2	0	1	0	0	0	1	0	0	0
Larry Parrish, 3b	.150	5	20	3	3	1	0	0	1	1	3	0
Mike Phillips, 2b	.000	1	1	0	0	0	0	0	0	0	0	0
Jeff Reardon, p	.000	3	0	0	0	0	0	0	0	0	1	0
Steve Rogers, p	.400	2	5	0	2	0	0	0	2	0	1	0
Scott Sanderson, p	.000	1	1	0	0	0	0	0	0	0	1	0
Elias Sosa, p	.000	2	0	0	0	0	0	0	0	0	0	0
Chris Speier, ss	.400	5	15	4	6	2	0	0	3	4	2	0
Tim Wallach, of-3	.250	4	4	1	1	1	0	0	0	4	0	0
Jerry White, of	.167	5	18	3	3	1	0	0	1	2	2	3
TOTAL	.255		161	16	41	10	1	2	16	18	36	7

PITCHER	W	L	ERA	G	GS	CG	SV	SHO	IP	H	ER	BB	SO
Stan Bahnsen	0	0	0.00	1	0	0	0	0	1.1	1	0	1	1
Ray Burris	0	1	5.06	1	1	0	0	0	5.1	7	3	4	4
Woody Fryman	0	0	6.75	1	0	0	0	0	1.1	3	1	1	0
Bill Gullickson	1	0	1.17	1	1	0	0	0	7.2	6	1	1	3
Bill Lee	0	0	0.00	1	0	0	0	0	0.2	0	0	0	1
Jeff Reardon	0	1	2.08	3	0	0	2	0	4.1	1	1	1	2
Steve Rogers	2	0	0.51	2	2	1	0	1	17.2	16	1	3	5
Scott Sanderson	0	0	6.75	1	1	0	0	0	2.2	4	2	2	2
Elias Sosa	0	0	3.00	2	0	0	0	0	3.0	4	1	0	1
TOTAL	3	2	2.05	13	5	1	2	1	44.0	44	10	13	19

PHI (E)

PLAYER/POS	AVG	G	AB	R	H	2B	3B	HR	RB	BB	SO	SB
Luis Aguayo, pr	.000	2	0	1	0	0	0	0	0	0	0	0
Ramon Aviles, ph	.000	1	0	0	0	0	0	0	0	1	0	0
Bob Boone, c	.000	3	5	0	0	0	0	0	0	0	0	0
Larry Bowa, ss	.176	5	17	0	3	1	0	0	1	0	0	0
Warren Brusstar, p	.000	2	0	0	0	0	0	0	0	0	0	0
Steve Carlton, p	.250	2	4	0	1	0	0	0	0	0	0	0
Larry Christenson, p	.000	1	2	0	0	0	0	0	0	0	1	0
Dick Davis, of	.000	1	2	0	0	0	0	0	0	0	1	0
Greg Gross, of-2	.000	4	4	0	0	0	0	0	0	0	0	0
Sparky Lyle, p	.000	3	0	0	0	0	0	0	0	0	0	0
Garry Maddox, of	.333	5	3	2	0	1	1	0	0	0	0	0
Gary Matthews, of	.400	5	20	3	8	0	0	1	1	1	0	2	0
Bake McBride, of	.200	4	15	1	3	1	0	0	0	0	5	0
Tug McGraw, p	.000	5	0	0	0	0	0	0	0	0	0	0
Keith Moreland, c	.462	4	13	2	6	0	0	1	3	1	1	0
Dickie Noles, p	.000	1	0	0	0	0	0	0	0	1	0	0
Ron Reed, p	.000	4	0	0	0	0	0	0	0	0	0	0
Pete Rose, 1b	.300	5	20	1	6	1	0	0	0	2	2	0
Dick Ruthven, p	.000	1	1	0	0	0	0	0	0	0	0	0
Mike Schmidt, 3b	.250	5	16	3	4	1	0	1	2	4	2	0
Lonnie Smith, of	.263	5	19	1	5	1	0	0	0	0	4	0
Manny Trillo, 2b	.188	5	16	1	3	0	0	0	1	4	0	0
George Vukovich, of-3	.444	5	9	1	4	0	0	1	2	0	3	0
TOTAL	.265		166	14	44	6	1	4	12	13	19	0

PITCHER	W	L	ERA	G	GS	CG	SV	SHO	IP	H	ER	BB	SO
Warren Brusstar	0	0	4.91	2	0	0	0	0	3.2	5	2	1	3
Steve Carlton	0	2	3.86	2	2	0	0	0	14.0	14	6	8	13
Larry Christenson	1	0	1.50	1	1	0	0	0	6.0	4	1	1	8
Sparky Lyle	0	0	0.00	3	0	0	0	0	2.1	4	0	2	1
Tug McGraw	1	0	0.00	2	0	0	0	0	4.0	2	0	0	2
Dickie Noles	0	0	4.50	1	1	0	0	0	4.0	4	2	2	5
Ron Reed	0	0	3.00	4	0	0	0	0	6.0	5	2	3	4
Dick Ruthven	0	1	4.50	1	1	0	0	0	4.0	3	2	1	0
TOTAL	2	3	3.07	16	5	0	0	0	44.0	41	15	18	36

GAME 1 AT MON OCT 7

```
PHI   010 000 000    1 10 1
MON   110 100 00X    3  8 0
```
Pitchers: CARLTON, R.Reed (7) vs ROGERS, Reardon (9)
Home Runs: Moreland-PHI
Attendance: 34,327

GAME 2 AT MON OCT 8

```
PHI   000 000 010    1  6 2
MON   012 000 00X    3  7 0
```
Pitchers: RUTHVEN, Brusstar (5), Lyle (7), McGraw (8) vs GULLICKSON, Reardon (8)
Home Runs: Carter-MON
Attendance: 45,896

GAME 3 AT PHI OCT 9

```
MON   010 000 010    2  8 4
PHI   020 002 20X    6 13 0
```
Pitchers: BURRIS, Lee (6), Sosa (7) vs CHRISTENSON, Lyle (7), R.Reed (8)
Attendance: 36,835

GAME 4 AT PHI OCT 10

```
MON   000 112 100 0    5 10 1
PHI   202 001 000 1    6  9 0
```
Pitchers: Sanderson, Bahnsen (3), Sosa (5), Fryman (6), REARDON (7) vs Noles, Brusstar (5), Lyle (6), R.Reed (7), McGRAW (8)
Home Runs: Carter-MON, Schmidt-PHI, Matthews-PHI, G.Vukovich-PHI
Attendance: 38,818

GAME 5 AT PHI OCT 11

```
MON   000 021 000    3  8 1
PHI   000 000 000    0  6 0
```
Pitchers: ROGERS vs CARLTON, R.Reed (9)
Attendance: 47,384

Cincinnati, with the league's best overall season record, failed to win either half season in the NL West, and watched from the sidelines as first-half winner Los Angeles, down two games to none, recovered to win the final three games—and the division title—from second-half victor Houston. In the opener, Alan Ashby's two-run homer in the last of the ninth broke a 1–1 tie and gave Nolan Ryan a two-hit victory. The next day, Denny Walling's two-out bases-loaded single in the last of the 11th scored Phil Garner with the game's only run.

When the clubs shifted to Los Angeles for the remainder of the series, the Dodgers came alive. In Game 3, a first-inning double by Dusty Baker and home run by Steve Garvey drove in three runs. Pitcher Burt Hooton and two relievers held Houston to three hits in what became a 6–1 Dodgers victory. The next day, Fernando Valenzuela and Vern Ruhle hurled matching four-hitters. But Pedro Guerrero's home run in the fifth inning and a pair of singles sandwiched around a sacrifice and intentional walk in the seventh gave Los Angeles two runs, while Valenzuela held Houston to a single run in the ninth. In the finale, Jerry Reuss blanked the Astros on five hits while his Dodgers blended three of their seven hits with a walk and an Astros error for three runs in the sixth. Two more hits produced a final run an inning later.

Los Angeles Dodgers, 3; Houston Astros, 2

LA (W)

PLAYER/POS	AVG	G	AB	R	H	2B	3B	HR	RB	BB	SO	SB
Dusty Baker, of	.167	5	18	2	3	1	0	0	1	2	0	0
Terry Forster, p	.000	1	0	0	0	0	0	0	0	0	0	0
Steve Garvey, 1b	.368	5	19	4	7	0	1	2	4	0	2	0
Pedro Guerrero, 3b	.176	5	17	1	3	1	0	1	1	2	4	1
Burt Hooton, p	.000	1	3	0	0	0	0	0	0	0	0	0
Steve Howe, p	.000	2	0	0	0	0	0	0	0	0	0	0
Jay Johnstone, ph	.000	1	1	0	0	0	0	0	0	0	0	0
Ken Landreaux, of	.200	5	20	1	4	1	0	0	1	0	1	0
Davey Lopes, 2b	.200	5	20	1	4	1	0	0	0	3	7	1
Mike Marshall, ph	.000	1	1	0	0	0	0	0	0	0	1	0
Rick Monday, of	.214	5	14	1	3	0	0	0	1	2	4	0
Tom Niedenfuer, p	.000	1	0	0	0	0	0	0	0	0	0	0
Jerry Reuss, p	.000	2	8	0	0	0	0	0	0	0	8	0
Bill Russell, ss	.250	5	16	1	4	1	0	0	2	3	1	0
Steve Sax, 2b	.000	1	0	0	0	0	0	0	0	0	0	0
Mike Scioscia, c	.154	4	13	0	2	0	0	0	1	1	2	0
Reggie Smith, ph	.000	2	1	0	0	0	0	0	0	1	0	0
Dave Stewart, p	.000	2	0	0	0	0	0	0	0	0	0	0
Derrel Thomas, of	.000	4	2	1	0	0	0	0	0	0	1	0
Fernando Valenzuela, p	.000	2	4	0	0	0	0	0	0	0	1	0
Bob Welch, p	.000	1	0	0	0	0	0	0	0	0	0	0
Steve Yeager, c	.400	2	5	1	2	1	0	0	0	0	1	0
TOTAL	.198		162	13	32	6	1	3	12	13	34	2

PITCHER	W	L	ERA	G	GS	CG	SV	SHO	IP	H	ER	BB	SO
Terry Forster	0	0	0.00	1	0	0	0	0	0.1	0	0	0	0
Burt Hooton	1	0	1.29	1	1	0	0	0	7.0	3	1	3	2
Steve Howe	0	0	0.00	2	0	0	0	0	2.0	1	0	0	2
Tom Niedenfuer	0	0	0.00	1	0	0	0	0	0.1	1	0	1	1
Jerry Reuss	1	0	0.00	2	2	1	0	1	18.0	10	0	5	7
Dave Stewart	0	2	40.50	2	0	0	0	0	0.2	4	3	0	1
Fernando Valenzuela	1	0	1.06	2	2	1	0	0	17.0	10	2	3	10
Bob Welch	0	0	0.00	1	0	0	0	0	1.0	0	0	1	1
TOTAL	3	2	1.17	12	5	2	0		46.1	29	6	13	24

HOU (W)

PLAYER/POS	AVG	G	AB	R	H	2B	3B	HR	RB	BB	SO	SB
Alan Ashby, c	.111	3	9	1	1	0	0	1	2	2	0	0
Cesar Cedeno, 1b	.231	4	13	0	3	1	0	0	0	2	2	2
Jose Cruz, of	.300	5	20	0	6	1	0	0	0	1	1	1
Kiko Garcia, ss-1	.000	2	4	0	0	0	0	0	0	0	1	0
Phil Garner, 2b	.111	5	18	1	2	0	0	0	0	3	3	0
Art Howe, 3b	.235	5	17	1	4	0	0	1	1	2	1	0
Bob Knepper, p	.000	1	1	0	0	0	0	0	0	0	0	0
Frank LaCorte, p	.000	2	0	0	0	0	0	0	0	0	0	0
Joe Niekro, p	.000	1	2	0	0	0	0	0	0	0	0	0
Joe Pittman, ph	.000	2	2	0	0	0	0	0	0	0	0	0
Terry Puhl, of	.190	5	21	2	4	1	0	0	0	0	1	1
Luis Pujols, c	.000	2	6	0	0	0	0	0	0	0	1	0
Craig Reynolds, ss-1	.333	2	3	1	1	0	0	0	0	0	1	0
Dave Roberts, ph	.000	1	1	0	0	0	0	0	0	0	1	0
Vern Ruhle, p	.000	1	1	0	0	0	0	0	0	0	1	0
Nolan Ryan, p	.250	2	4	0	1	0	0	0	0	0	1	0
Joe Sambito, p	.000	2	0	0	0	0	0	0	0	0	0	0
Tony Scott, of	.150	5	20	0	3	0	0	0	2	1	6	0
Billy Smith, p	.000	1	0	0	0	0	0	0	0	0	0	0
Dave Smith, p	.000	2	0	0	0	0	0	0	0	0	0	0
Harry Spilman, ph	.000	1	1	0	0	0	0	0	0	0	0	0
Dickie Thon, ss	.182	4	11	0	2	0	0	0	0	1	0	0
Denny Walling, 1b-2	.333	3	6	0	2	0	0	0	1	0	1	0
Gary Woods, ph	.000	2	2	0	0	0	0	0	0	0	1	0
TOTAL	.179		162	6	29	3	0	2	6	13	24	4

PITCHER	W	L	ERA	G	GS	CG	SV	SHO	IP	H	ER	BB	SO
Bob Knepper	0	1	5.40	1	1	0	0	0	5.0	6	3	2	4
Frank LaCorte	0	0	0.00	2	0	0	0	0	3.2	2	0	1	5
Joe Niekro	0	0	0.00	1	1	0	0	0	8.0	7	0	3	4
Vern Ruhle	0	1	2.25	1	1	1	0	0	8.0	4	2	2	1
Nolan Ryan	1	1	1.80	2	2	1	0	0	15.0	6	3	3	14
Joe Sambito	1	0	16.20	2	0	0	0	0	1.2	5	3	2	2
Billy Smith	0	0	0.00	1	0	0	0	0	0.1	0	0	0	0
Dave Smith	0	0	3.86	2	0	0	0	0	2.1	2	1	0	4
TOTAL	2	3	2.45	12	5	2	0	0	44.0	32	12	13	34

GAME 1 AT HOU OCT 6

LA	000	000	100	1	2 0
HOU	000	001	002	3	8 0

Pitchers: Valenzuela, STEWART (9) vs RYAN
Home Runs: Garvey-LA, Ashby-HOU
Attendance: 44,836

GAME 2 AT HOU OCT 7

LA	000	000	000 00	0	9 1
HOU	000	000	000 01	1	9 0

Pitchers: Reuss, S.Howe (10), STEWART (11), Forster (11), Niedenfuer (11) vs Niekro, D.Smith (9), SAMBITO (11)
Attendance: 42,398

GAME 3 AT LA OCT 9

HOU	001	000	000	1	3 2
LA	300	000	03X	6	10 0

Pitchers: KNEPPER, LaCorte (6), Sambito (8), B.Smith (8) vs HOOTON, S.Howe (9), Welch (9)
Home Runs: Garvey-LA, A.Howe-HOU
Attendance: 46,820

GAME 4 AT LA OCT 10

HOU	000	000	001	1	4 0
LA	000	010	10X	2	4 0

Pitchers: RUHLE vs VALENZUELA
Home Runs: Guerrero-LA
Attendance: 55,983

GAME 5 AT LA OCT 11

HOU	000	000	000	0	5 3
LA	000	003	10X	4	7 2

Pitchers: RYAN, D.Smith (7), LaCorte (7) vs REUSS
Attendance: 55,979

The home field didn't seem to offer any advantage. First-half winner New York captured both games played in Milwaukee, but when the Series moved to Yankee Stadium for the final three games, the second-half champion Brewers evened the series.

Milwaukee took a 2–0 lead early in the opener, but New York erupted for four runs in the fourth on Oscar Gamble's two-run homer and Rick Cerone's double, and held on to win, 5–3. In Game 2 rookie starter Dave Righetti fanned ten Brewers in his six innings and Goose Gossage's brilliant relief earned him his second save in two days as the Yankees took a 3–0 win on homers by Lou Piniella and Reggie Jackson.

Milwaukee, struggling against elimination, took the lead in the seventh inning of Game 3 on Ted Simmons' two-run homer. New York tied the score at 3–3 in their half of the inning, but Paul Molitor broke the tie in the eighth with a solo homer. Simmons doubled home an insurance run later in the inning for a 5–3 Brewers win. The Brewers managed only four hits in Game 4, but three of them came in the fourth inning and combined with a sacrifice fly to produce the Brewers' two runs. New York scored once in the sixth, but base-running errors an inning later ended their only other scoring threat.

In the finale Milwaukee scored two early runs, but the Yankees (as they had done in the opener) took the lead with a four-run fourth—this time on home runs by Reggie Jackson and Oscar Gamble, and Rick Cerone's single. Cerone later hit an insurance homer, as the home team finally won a game—and captured the division crown.

New York Yankees, 3; Milwaukee Brewers, 2

NY (E)

PLAYER/POS	AVG	G	AB	R	H	2B	3B	HR	RB	BB	SO	SB
Bobby Brown, pr	.000	1	0	0	0	0	0	0	0	0	0	0
Rick Cerone, c	.333	5	18	1	6	2	0	1	5	0	2	0
Ron Davis, p	.000	3	0	0	0	0	0	0	0	0	0	0
Barry Foote, ph	.000	1	0	0	0	0	0	0	0	0	0	0
Oscar Gamble, dh	.556	4	9	2	5	1	0	2	3	1	2	0
Rich Gossage, p	.000	3	0	0	0	0	0	0	0	0	0	0
Ron Guidry, p	.000	2	0	0	0	0	0	0	0	0	0	0
Reggie Jackson, of	.300	5	20	4	6	0	0	2	4	1	5	0
Tommy John, p	.000	1	0	0	0	0	0	0	0	0	0	0
Rudy May, p	.000	1	0	0	0	0	0	0	0	0	0	0
Larry Milbourne, ss	.316	5	19	4	6	1	0	0	0	0	1	0
Jerry Mumphrey, of	.095	5	21	2	2	0	0	0	0	0	1	1
Bobby Murcer, ph	.000	2	1	0	0	0	0	0	0	1	0	0
Graig Nettles, 3b	.059	5	17	1	1	0	0	0	1	3	1	0
Lou Piniella, dh	.200	4	10	1	2	1	0	1	3	0	0	0
Willie Randolph, 2b	.200	5	20	0	4	0	0	0	1	1	4	0
Rick Reuschel, p	.000	1	0	0	0	0	0	0	0	0	0	0
Dave Revering, 1b	.000	2	0	0	0	0	0	0	0	0	0	0
Dave Righetti, p	.000	2	0	0	0	0	0	0	0	0	0	0
Bob Watson, 1b	.438	5	16	2	7	0	0	0	1	1	1	0
Dave Winfield, of	.350	5	20	2	7	3	0	0	0	1	5	0
TOTAL	.269		171	19	46	8	0	6	18	9	22	1

PITCHER	W	L	ERA	G	GS	CG	SV	SHO	IP	H	ER	BB	SO
Ron Davis	1	0	0.00	3	0	0	0	0	6.0	1	0	2	6
Rich Gossage	0	0	0.00	3	0	0	3	0	6.2	3	0	2	8
Ron Guidry	0	0	5.40	2	2	0	0	0	8.1	11	5	3	8
Tommy John	0	1	6.43	1	1	0	0	0	7.0	8	5	2	0
Rudy May	0	0	0.00	1	0	0	0	0	2.0	1	0	0	1
Rick Reuschel	0	1	3.00	1	1	0	0	0	6.0	4	2	1	3
Dave Righetti	2	0	1.00	2	1	0	0	0	9.0	8	1	3	13
TOTAL	3	2	2.60	13	5	0	3	0	45.0	36	13	13	39

MIL (E)

PLAYER/POS	AVG	G	AB	R	H	2B	3B	HR	RB	BB	SO	SB
Sal Bando, 3b	.294	5	17	1	5	3	0	0	1	2	3	0
Dwight Bernard, p	.000	2	0	0	0	0	0	0	0	0	0	0
Thad Bosley, dh	.000	1	0	0	0	0	0	0	0	0	0	0
Mike Caldwell, p	.000	2	0	0	0	0	0	0	0	0	0	0
Cecil Cooper, 1b	.222	5	18	1	4	0	0	0	3	1	3	0
Jamie Easterly, p	.000	2	0	0	0	0	0	0	0	0	0	0
Marshall Edwards, of	.000	2	1	0	0	0	0	0	0	0	1	0
Rollie Fingers, p	.000	3	0	0	0	0	0	0	0	0	0	0
Jim Gantner, 2b	.143	4	14	1	2	1	0	0	0	0	2	0
Moose Haas, p	.000	2	0	0	0	0	0	0	0	0	0	0
Roy Howell, dh-3	.400	4	5	0	2	0	0	0	0	2	2	0
Randy Lerch, p	.000	1	0	0	0	0	0	0	0	0	0	0
Bob McClure, p	.000	3	0	0	0	0	0	0	0	0	0	0
Paul Molitor, of	.250	5	20	2	5	0	0	1	1	2	5	0
Don Money, 2b-1,dh-1	.000	2	3	0	0	0	0	0	0	0	0	0
Charlie Moore, of-2,dh-2	.222	4	9	0	2	0	0	0	1	1	2	0
Ben Oglivie, of	.167	5	18	0	3	1	0	0	1	0	7	0
Ed Romero, 2b	.500	1	2	1	1	0	0	0	0	0	1	0
Ted Simmons, c	.222	5	18	1	4	1	0	1	4	2	2	0
Jim Slaton, p	.000	4	0	0	0	0	0	0	0	0	0	0
Gorman Thomas, of-3,dh-2	.111	5	18	2	2	0	0	1	1	1	9	0
Pete Vuckovich, p	.000	2	0	0	0	0	0	0	0	0	0	0
Robin Yount, ss	.316	5	19	4	6	0	1	0	1	2	2	1
TOTAL	.222		162	13	36	6	1	3	13	13	39	1

PITCHER	W	L	ERA	G	GS	CG	SV	SHO	IP	H	ER	BB	SO
Dwight Bernard	0	0	0.00	2	0	0	0	0	2.1	0	0	0	0
Mike Caldwell	0	1	4.32	2	1	0	0	0	8.1	9	4	0	4
Jamie Easterly	0	0	6.75	2	0	0	0	0	1.1	2	1	0	1
Rollie Fingers	1	0	3.86	3	0	0	1	0	4.2	7	2	1	5
Moose Haas	0	2	9.45	2	2	0	0	0	6.2	13	7	1	1
Randy Lerch	0	0	1.50	1	1	0	0	0	6.0	3	1	4	3
Bob McClure	0	0	0.00	3	0	0	0	0	3.1	4	0	0	2
Jim Slaton	0	0	3.00	4	0	0	0	0	6.0	6	2	0	2
Pete Vuckovich	1	0	3.52	2	1	0	0	0	5.1	2	0	3	4
TOTAL	2	3	3.48	21	5	0	1	0	44.0	46	17	9	22

GAME 1 AT MIL OCT 7

NY   000 400 001   5 13 1
MIL   011 010 000   3 8 3

Pitchers: Guidry, DAVIS (5), Gossage (8) vs HAAS, Bernard (4), McClure (5), Slaton (6), Fingers (8)
Home Runs: Gamble-NY
Attendance: 35,064

GAME 2 AT MIL OCT 8

NY   000 100 002   3 7 0
MIL   000 000 000   0 7 0

Pitchers: RIGHETTI, Davis (7), Gossage (7) vs CALDWELL, Slaton (9)
Home Runs: Piniella-NY, Jackson-NY
Attendance: 26,395

GAME 3 AT NY OCT 9

MIL   000 000 320   5 9 0
NY   000 100 200   3 8 2

Pitchers: Lerch, FINGERS (7) vs JOHN, May (8)
Home Runs: Simmons-MIL, Molitor-MIL
Attendance: 56,411

GAME 4 AT NY OCT 10

MIL   000 200 000   2 4 2
NY   000 001 000   1 5 0

Pitchers: VUCKOVICH, Easterly (6), Slaton (7), McClure (8), Fingers (9) vs REUSCHEL, Davis (7)
Attendance: 52,077

GAME 5 AT NY OCT 11

MIL   011 000 100   3 8 0
NY   000 400 12X   7 13 0

Pitchers: HAAS, Caldwell (4), Bernard (4), McClure (6), Slaton (7), Easterly (8) vs Guidry, RIGHETTI (5), Gossage (8)
Home Runs: Thomas-MIL, Jackson-NY, Gamble-NY, Cerone-NY
Attendance: 47,505

First-half winner Oakland, with the league's best win-loss record over the full season, swept the division title from second-half champ Kansas City (who, with a full-season record of 50–53, had become the only club in major-league history to qualify for postseason play with a losing record). Twice in the opener the Royals loaded the bases against Mike Norris with fewer than two outs, but both times failed to score. Meanwhile, after a Royals error had prolonged the A's fourth inning, Wayne Gross homered for three unearned Oakland runs. Dwayne Murphy's eighth-inning solo shot gave the A's a fourth run. The game ended with Norris possessor of a four-hit shutout.

Game 2 was closer. Oakland's Tony Armas doubled in a run in the top of the first, and doubled home another in the eighth (his fourth hit of the game) to break a 1–1 tie and provide the margin needed for pitcher Steve McCatty's six-hit win. Oakland's Rick Langford yielded 10 hits in Game 3 (including Kansas City's only extra-base hit of the series, a double), but only one Royal scored. The A's, meanwhile, were sending four runs across the plate—three of them by Rickey Henderson, who reached base four times on pairs of hits and walks.

Oakland Athletics, 3;
Kansas City Royals, 0

KC (W)

PLAYER/POS	AVG	G	AB	R	H	2B	3B	HR	RB	BB	SO	SB
Willie Aikens, 1b	.333	3	9	0	3	0	0	0	0	3	2	0
George Brett, 3b	.167	3	12	0	2	0	0	0	0	0	0	0
Cesar Geronimo, pr	.000	1	0	0	0	0	0	0	0	0	0	0
Larry Gura, p	.000	1	0	0	0	0	0	0	0	0	0	0
Clint Hurdle, of	.273	3	11	0	3	0	0	0	0	1	1	0
Mike Jones, p	.000	1	0	0	0	0	0	0	0	0	0	0
Dennis Leonard, p	.000	1	0	0	0	0	0	0	0	0	0	0
Renie Martin, p	.000	2	0	0	0	0	0	0	0	0	0	0
Lee May, 1b	.000	1	0	0	0	0	0	0	0	0	0	0
Hal McRae, dh	.091	3	11	0	1	1	0	0	0	1	1	0
Amos Otis, of	.000	3	12	0	0	0	0	0	1	0	4	0
Dan Quisenberry, p	.000	1	0	0	0	0	0	0	0	0	0	0
U. L. Washington, ss	.222	3	9	0	2	0	0	0	0	0	1	0
John Wathan, c	.300	3	10	1	3	0	0	0	0	1	1	0
Frank White, 2b	.182	3	11	1	2	0	0	0	0	1	1	0
Willie Wilson, of	.308	3	13	0	4	0	0	0	1	0	0	0
TOTAL	.204		98	2	20	1	0	0	2	7	11	0

PITCHER	W	L	ERA	G	GS	CG	SV	SHO	IP	H	ER	BB	SO
Larry Gura	0	1	7.36	1	1	0	0	0	3.2	7	3	3	3
Mike Jones	0	1	2.25	1	1	0	0	0	8.0	9	2	0	2
Dennis Leonard	0	1	1.13	1	1	0	0	0	8.0	7	1	1	3
Renie Martin	0	0	0.00	2	0	0	0	0	5.1	1	0	2	2
Dan Quisenberry	0	0	0.00	1	0	0	0	0	1.0	1	0	0	0
TOTAL	0	3	2.08	6	3	0	0	0	26.0	25	6	6	10

OAK (W)

PLAYER/POS	AVG	G	AB	R	H	2B	3B	HR	RB	BB	SO	SB
Tony Armas, of	.545	3	11	1	6	2	0	0	3	1	1	0
Dave Beard, p	.000	1	0	0	0	0	0	0	0	0	0	0
Rick Bosetti, of	.000	1	0	0	0	0	0	0	0	0	0	0
Keith Drumright, dh	.250	1	4	0	1	0	0	0	0	0	0	0
Wayne Gross, 3b-1	.400	2	5	1	2	0	0	1	3	0	0	0
Mike Heath, c	.000	2	8	0	0	0	0	0	0	0	1	0
Rickey Henderson, of	.182	3	11	3	2	0	0	0	0	2	0	2
Cliff Johnson, dh	.286	2	7	0	2	1	0	0	0	0	1	0
Mickey Klutts, 3b	.143	2	7	0	1	0	0	0	0	0	1	0
Rick Langford, p	.000	1	0	0	0	0	0	0	0	0	0	0
Steve McCatty, p	.000	1	0	0	0	0	0	0	0	0	0	0
Dave McKay, 2b	.273	3	11	1	3	0	0	1	1	1	1	0
Kelvin Moore, 1b	.000	2	8	0	0	0	0	0	0	0	2	0
Dwayne Murphy, of	.545	3	11	4	6	1	0	1	2	1	1	0
Jeff Newman, c	.000	1	3	0	0	0	0	0	0	0	1	0
Mike Norris, p	.000	1	0	0	0	0	0	0	0	0	0	0
Rob Picciolo, ss	.333	1	3	0	1	0	0	0	0	0	0	0
Jim Spencer, 1b	.250	1	4	0	1	1	0	0	0	0	0	0
Fred Stanley, ss	.000	3	6	0	0	0	0	0	0	1	1	0
Tom Underwood, p	.000	1	0	0	0	0	0	0	0	0	0	0
TOTAL	.253		99	10	25	5	0	3	9	6	10	2

PITCHER	W	L	ERA	G	GS	CG	SV	SHO	IP	H	ER	BB	SO
Dave Beard	0	0	0.00	1	0	0	1	0	1.1	0	0	0	2
Rick Langford	1	0	1.23	1	1	0	0	0	7.1	10	1	0	3
Steve McCatty	1	0	1.00	1	1	1	0	0	9.0	6	1	4	3
Mike Norris	1	0	0.00	1	1	1	0	1	9.0	4	0	3	2
Tom Underwood	0	0	0.00	1	0	0	0	0	0.1	0	0	0	1
TOTAL	3	0	0.67	5	3	2	1	1	27.0	20	2	7	11

GAME 1 AT KC OCT 6

						R	H	E
OAK	000	300	010			4	8	2
KC	000	000	000			0	4	1

Pitchers: NORRIS vs LEONARD, Martin (9)
Home Runs: Gross-OAK, Murphy-OAK
Attendance: 40,592

GAME 2 AT KC OCT 7

						R	H	E
OAK	100	000	010			2	10	1
KC	000	010	000			1	6	0

Pitchers: McCATTY vs JONES, Quisenberry (9)
Attendance: 40,274

GAME 3 AT OAK OCT 9

						R	H	E
KC	000	100	000			1	10	3
OAK	101	200	00X			4	7	0

Pitchers: GURA, Martin (4) vs LANGFORD, Underwood (8), Beard (8)
Home Runs: McKay-OAK
Attendance: 40,002

Fine pitching characterized the series, with the losing team held to one run in four of the five games. In the exception Ray Burris hurled a shutout for the Expos.

Montreal put men on base in each inning of the opener. But the pitching of Burt Hooton and Bob Welch—plus some fine Dodgers fielding—kept the Expos from scoring until the ninth, when their one run was too little to overcome the Dodger's four-run cushion. Burris' shutout evened the series in Game 2 as the Expos scored three times against rookie sensation Fernando Valenzuela. The Expos took the series lead in Game 3, overcoming a 1–0 deficit with a two-out four-run burst in the sixth (capped by Jerry White's three-run homer).

In the end, though, the Dodgers prevailed. Through seven innings of Game 4, Hooton and the Expos' Bill Gullickson dueled at 1–1. But in the top of the eighth, Steve Garvey homered with a man aboard, and four more Dodger runs in the ninth put the game away. The finale—Burris vs. Valenzuela again—featured another 1–1 duel, this one reaching into the top of the ninth when, with two out, Rick Monday homered off Steve Rogers, who came on in relief of Burris. In the bottom of the ninth, Valenzuela walked two batters after retiring two, but Welch came on to save the game and the pennant.

Los Angeles Dodgers (West), 3; Montreal Expos (East), 2

LA (W)

PLAYER/POS	AVG	G	AB	R	H	2B	3B	HR	RB	BB	SO	SB
Dusty Baker, of	.316	5	19	3	6	1	0	0	3	1	0	0
Bobby Castillo, p	.000	1	0	0	0	0	0	0	0	0	0	0
Ron Cey, 3b	.278	5	18	1	5	1	0	0	3	3	2	0
Terry Forster, p	.000	1	0	0	0	0	0	0	0	0	0	0
Steve Garvey, 1b	.286	5	21	2	6	0	0	1	2	0	4	0
Pedro Guerrero, of	.105	5	19	1	2	0	0	1	2	1	4	0
Burt Hooton, p	.000	2	5	0	0	0	0	0	0	0	2	0
Steve Howe, p	.000	2	0	0	0	0	0	0	0	0	0	0
Jay Johnstone, ph	.000	2	2	0	0	0	0	0	0	0	0	0
Ken Landreaux, of-3	.100	5	10	0	1	1	0	0	0	3	2	0
Davey Lopes, 2b	.278	5	18	0	5	0	0	0	0	1	3	5
Rick Monday, of-2	.333	3	9	2	3	0	0	1	1	0	4	0
Tom Niedenfuer, p	.000	1	0	0	0	0	0	0	0	0	0	0
Alejandro Pena, p	.000	2	0	0	0	0	0	0	0	0	0	0
Jerry Reuss, p	.000	1	2	0	0	0	0	0	0	0	0	0
Bill Russell, ss	.313	5	16	2	5	0	1	0	1	1	1	0
Steve Sax, 2b	.000	1	0	0	0	0	0	0	0	0	0	0
Mike Scioscia, c	.133	5	15	1	2	0	0	1	1	2	1	0
Reggie Smith, ph	1.000	1	1	0	1	0	0	0	1	0	0	0
Derrel Thomas, 3b-1,of-1	1.000	2	1	2	1	0	0	0	0	0	0	0
Fernando Valenzuela, p	.000	2	5	0	0	0	0	0	1	0	0	0
Bob Welch, p	.000	3	0	0	0	0	0	0	0	0	0	0
Steve Yeager, c	.500	1	2	1	1	0	0	0	0	0	0	0
TOTAL	.233		163	15	38	3	1	4	15	12	23	5

PITCHER	W	L	ERA	G	GS	CG	SV	SHO	IP	H	ER	BB	SO
Bobby Castillo	0	0	0.00	1	0	0	0	0	1.0	0	0	0	1
Terry Forster	0	0	0.00	1	0	0	0	0	0.1	0	0	0	1
Burt Hooton	2	0	0.00	2	2	0	0	0	14.2	11	0	6	7
Steve Howe	0	0	0.00	2	0	0	0	0	2.0	1	0	0	2
Tom Niedenfuer	0	0	0.00	1	0	0	0	0	0.1	2	0	0	0
Alejandro Pena	0	0	0.00	2	0	0	0	0	2.1	1	0	0	0
Jerry Reuss	0	1	5.14	1	1	0	0	0	7.0	7	4	1	2
Fernando Valenzuela	1	1	2.45	2	2	0	0	0	14.2	10	4	5	10
Bob Welch	0	0	5.40	3	0	0	1	0	1.2	2	1	0	2
TOTAL	3	2	1.84	15	5	0	1	0	44.0	34	9	12	25

MON (E)

PLAYER/POS	AVG	G	AB	R	H	2B	3B	HR	RB	BB	SO	SB
Ray Burris, p	.000	2	6	0	0	0	0	0	0	0	4	0
Gary Carter, c	.438	5	16	3	7	1	0	0	0	4	2	0
Warren Cromartie, 1b	.167	5	18	0	3	1	0	0	2	0	2	0
Andre Dawson, of	.150	5	20	2	3	0	0	0	0	0	4	0
Terry Francona, of-1	.000	2	1	0	0	0	0	0	0	0	1	0
Woody Fryman, p	.000	1	0	0	0	0	0	0	0	0	0	0
Bill Gullickson, p	.000	2	3	0	0	0	0	0	0	1	2	0
Bill Lee, p	.000	1	0	0	0	0	0	0	0	0	0	0
Jerry Manuel, pr	.000	1	0	0	0	0	0	0	0	0	0	0
John Milner, ph	.000	1	1	0	0	0	0	0	0	0	1	0
Larry Parrish, 3b	.263	5	19	2	5	2	0	0	2	1	1	0
Tim Raines, of	.238	5	21	1	5	2	0	0	1	0	3	0
Jeff Reardon, p	.000	1	0	0	0	0	0	0	0	0	0	0
Steve Rogers, p	.000	2	2	0	0	0	0	0	0	0	1	0
Rodney Scott, 2b	.167	5	18	0	3	0	0	0	0	1	3	1
Elias Sosa, p	.000	1	0	0	0	0	0	0	0	0	0	0
Chris Speier, ss	.188	5	16	0	3	0	0	0	2	0	0	0
Tim Wallach, ph	.000	1	1	0	0	0	0	0	0	0	0	0
Jerry White, of	.313	5	16	2	5	1	0	1	3	3	1	1
TOTAL	.215		158	10	34	7	0	1	8	12	25	2

PITCHER	W	L	ERA	G	GS	CG	SV	SHO	IP	H	ER	BB	SO
Ray Burris	1	0	0.53	2	2	1	0	1	17.0	10	1	3	4
Woody Fryman	0	0	36.00	1	0	0	0	0	1.0	3	4	1	1
Bill Gullickson	0	2	2.51	2	2	0	0	0	14.1	12	4	6	12
Bill Lee	0	0	0.00	1	0	0	0	0	0.1	1	0	0	0
Jeff Reardon	0	0	27.00	1	0	0	0	0	1.0	3	3	0	0
Steve Rogers	1	1	1.80	2	1	1	0	0	10.0	8	2	1	6
Elias Sosa	0	0	0.00	1	0	0	0	0	0.1	1	0	1	0
TOTAL	2	3	2.86	10	5	2	0	1	44.0	38	14	12	23

GAME 1 AT LA OCT 13

MON	000	000	001	1	9	0
LA	020	000	03X	5	8	0

Pitchers: GULLICKSON, Reardon (8) vs HOOTON, Welch (8), Howe (9)
Home Runs: Guerrero-LA, Scioscia-LA
Attendance: 51,273

GAME 2 AT LA OCT 14

MON	020	001	000	3	10	1
LA	000	000	000	0	5	1

Pitchers: BURRIS vs VALENZUELA, Niedenfuer (7), Forster (7), Pena (7), Castillo (9)
Attendance: 53,463

GAME 3 AT MON OCT 16

LA	000	100	000	1	7	0
MON	000	004	00X	4	7	1

Pitchers: REUSS, Pena (8) vs ROGERS
Home Runs: White-MON
Attendance: 54,372

GAME 4 AT MON OCT 17

LA	001	000	024	7	12	1
MON	000	100	000	1	5	1

Pitchers: HOOTON, Welch (8), Howe (9) vs GULLICKSON, Fryman (8), Sosa (9), Lee (9)
Home Runs: Garvey-LA
Attendance: 54,499

GAME 5 AT MON OCT 19

LA	000	010	001	2	6	0
MON	100	000	000	1	3	1

Pitchers: VALENZUELA, Welch (9) vs Burris, ROGERS (9)
Home Runs: Monday-LA
Attendance: 36,491

The A's scored only four runs to their opponents' 20 as the Yankees swept the series. And only two of New York's six pitchers permitted an Oakland runner to score, while not one of Oakland's eight pitchers held New York scoreless. Even so, two of the three games were closely contested.

Oakland's Mike Norris gave up a bases-loaded double to Graig Nettles in the first inning of Game 1 before settling down to pitch shutout ball. But the three runs Nettles drove in were more than enough, as Tommy John and two relievers held the A's to a single run.

Game 2 was the series' only blowout, and even it remained close for three innings. But, led by a pair of three-run homers from Nettles and Lou Piniella, the Yankees parlayed 19 hits into 13 runs as Yankee reliever George Frazier held the A's scoreless over the final five frames.

Game 3 remained tight until the ninth. Through eight innings the only run came on Willie Randolph's homer off Oakland starter Matt Keough. But in the top of the ninth, Graig Nettles tagged reliever Tom Underwood for his second bases-clearing double of the series. The three runs weren't really needed, as Dave Righetti, Ron Davis, and Goose Gossage combined to shut out the A's for the full nine.

New York Yankees (East), 3; Oakland A's (West), 0

NY (E)

PLAYER/POS	AVG	G	AB	R	H	2B	3B	HR	RB	BB	SO	SB
Bobby Brown, of-2	1.000	3	1	2	1	0	0	0	0	0	0	0
Rick Cerone, c	.100	3	10	1	1	0	0	0	0	0	0	0
Ron Davis, p	.000	2	0	0	0	0	0	0	0	0	0	0
Barry Foote, c-1	1.000	2	1	0	1	0	0	0	0	0	0	0
George Frazier, p	.000	1	0	0	0	0	0	0	0	0	0	0
Oscar Gamble, dh-2,of-1	.167	3	6	2	1	0	0	0	1	5	3	0
Rich Gossage, p	.000	2	0	0	0	0	0	0	0	0	0	0
Reggie Jackson, of	.000	2	4	1	0	0	0	0	1	1	0	1
Tommy John, p	.000	1	0	0	0	0	0	0	0	0	0	0
Rudy May, p	.000	1	0	0	0	0	0	0	0	0	0	0
Larry Milbourne, ss	.462	3	13	4	6	0	0	0	1	0	0	0
Jerry Mumphrey, of	.500	3	12	2	6	1	0	0	3	2	0
Bobby Murcer, dh	.333	1	3	0	1	0	0	0	0	1	1	0
Graig Nettles, 3b	.500	3	12	2	6	2	0	1	9	1	0	0
Lou Piniella, dh-2,of-1	.600	3	5	2	3	0	0	1	3	0	0	0
Willie Randolph, 2b	.333	3	12	2	4	0	0	1	2	0	1	0
Dave Revering, 1b	.500	2	2	0	1	0	0	0	0	0	0	0
Dave Righetti, p	.000	1	0	0	0	0	0	0	0	0	0	0
Andre Robertson, ss	.000	1	1	0	0	0	0	0	0	0	0	0
Aurelio Rodriguez, 3b	.000	1	0	0	0	0	0	0	0	0	0	0
Bob Watson, 1b	.250	3	12	0	3	0	0	0	1	0	1	0
Dave Winfield, of	.154	3	13	2	2	1	0	0	2	2	2	1
TOTAL	.336		107	20	36	4	0	3	20	13	10	2

PITCHER	W	L	ERA	G	GS	CG	SV	SHO	IP	H	ER	BB	SO
Ron Davis	0	0	0.00	2	0	0	0	0	3.1	0	0	2	4
George Frazier	1	0	0.00	1	0	0	0	0	5.2	5	0	1	5
Rich Gossage	0	0	0.00	2	0	0	1	0	2.2	1	0	0	2
Tommy John	1	0	1.50	1	1	0	0	0	6.0	6	1	1	3
Rudy May	0	0	8.10	1	0	0	0	0	3.1	6	3	0	5
Dave Righetti	1	0	0.00	1	1	0	0	0	6.0	4	0	2	4
TOTAL	3	0	1.33	8	2	0	1	0	27.0	22	4	6	23

OAK (W)

PLAYER/POS	AVG	G	AB	R	H	2B	3B	HR	RB	BB	SO	SB
Tony Armas, of	.167	3	12	0	2	0	0	0	0	0	5	0
Dave Beard, p	.000	1	0	0	0	0	0	0	0	0	0	0
Rick Bosetti, of-1,dh-1	.250	2	4	1	1	1	0	0	0	0	1	0
Mike Davis, ph	1.000	1	1	0	1	0	0	0	0	0	0	0
Keith Drumright, dh-1	.000	3	4	0	0	0	0	0	0	1	0	0
Wayne Gross, 3b	.000	3	5	0	0	0	0	0	0	0	0	0
Mike Heath, c-2,of-1	.333	3	6	1	2	0	0	0	0	0	1	0
Rickey Henderson, of	.364	3	11	0	4	2	1	0	1	1	2	2
Cliff Johnson, dh	.000	2	6	0	0	0	0	0	0	2	2	0
Jeff Jones, p	.000	1	0	0	0	0	0	0	0	0	0	0
Matt Keough, p	.000	1	0	0	0	0	0	0	0	0	0	0
Brian Kingman, p	.000	1	0	0	0	0	0	0	0	0	0	0
Mickey Klutts, 3b	.429	3	7	1	3	0	0	0	0	0	1	0
Steve McCatty, p	.000	1	0	0	0	0	0	0	0	0	0	0
Dave McKay, 2b	.273	3	11	0	3	0	0	0	1	0	2	0
Kelvin Moore, 1b	.250	3	8	0	2	0	0	0	0	0	1	0
Dwayne Murphy, of	.250	3	8	0	2	1	0	0	1	2	3	0
Jeff Newman, c	.000	2	5	0	0	0	0	0	0	0	0	0
Mike Norris, p	.000	1	0	0	0	0	0	0	0	0	0	0
Bob Owchinko, p	.000	1	0	0	0	0	0	0	0	0	0	0
Rob Picciolo, ss	.200	2	5	1	1	0	0	0	0	0	2	0
Jim Spencer, 1b	.000	2	3	0	0	0	0	0	0	0	0	0
Fred Stanley, ss	.333	2	3	0	1	0	0	0	0	1	1	0
Tom Underwood, p	.000	2	0	0	0	0	0	0	0	0	0	0
TOTAL	.222		99	4	22	4	1	0	4	6	23	2

PITCHER	W	L	ERA	G	GS	CG	SV	SHO	IP	H	ER	BB	SO
Dave Beard	0	0	40.50	1	0	0	0	0	0.2	5	3	0	0
Jeff Jones	0	0	4.50	1	0	0	0	0	2.0	2	1	1	0
Matt Keough	0	1	1.08	1	1	0	0	0	8.1	7	1	6	4
Brian Kingman	0	0	81.00	1	0	0	0	0	0.1	3	3	0	0
Steve McCatty	0	1	13.50	1	1	0	0	0	3.1	6	5	2	2
Mike Norris	0	1	3.68	1	1	0	0	0	7.1	6	3	2	4
Bob Owchinko	0	0	5.40	1	0	0	0	0	1.2	3	1	0	0
Tom Underwood	0	0	13.50	2	0	0	0	0	1.1	4	2	2	0
TOTAL	0	3	6.84	9	3	0	0	0	25.0	36	19	13	10

GAME 1 AT NY OCT 13

OAK	000	010	000	1	6	1
NY	300	000	00X	3	7	1

Pitchers: NORRIS, Underwood (8) vs JOHN, Davis (7), Gossage (8)
Attendance: 55,740

GAME 2 AT NY OCT 14

OAK	001	200	000	3	11	1
NY	100	701	40X	13	19	0

Pitchers: McCATTY, Beard (4), Jones (5), Kingman (7), Owchinko (7) vs MAY, FRAZIER (4)
Home Runs: Piniella-NY, Nettles-NY
Attendance: 48,497

GAME 3 AT OAK OCT 15

NY	000	001	003	4	10	0
OAK	000	000	000	0	5	2

Pitchers: RIGHETTI, Davis (7), Gossage (9) vs KEOUGH, Underwood (9)
Home Runs: Randolph-NY
Attendance: 47,302

What the Yankees had done to the Dodgers three years earlier, the Dodgers now did to the Yankees in this, their 11th meeting in the Series: they took the crown with four straight wins after losing the first two games. In the opener Bob Watson's first-inning three-run homer gave New York an insurmountable lead. Yankees starter Ron Guidry pitched seven strong innings, yielding just one run on a Steve Yeager homer, but two eighth-inning Dodgers runs charged to reliever Ron Davis made things exciting until Yankees third baseman Graig Nettles dampened the rally with a splendid diving catch of Steve Garvey's line drive. In Game 2, Tommy John (now a Yankee) shut out his old teammates on three hits for seven innings. Reliever Goose Gossage completed the shutout, earning his second save in two days in the 3–0 Yankees victory.

But as the Series moved to Los Angeles, the Dodgers took the upper hand. Rookie ace Fernando Valenzuela experienced rocky going in the early innings of Game 3, yielding six hits (including home runs to Bob Watson and Rick Cerone) and four runs in the second and third innings. But Ron Cey's first-inning home run had given Los Angeles three early runs, and the Dodgers added two more in the fifth as Valenzuela settled down to blank New York on three hits over the final six innings. The next day the Dodgers evened the Series with another close win. New York scored four times before the Dodgers got their first runs, but L.A. tied the game at 6–6 in the sixth and took an 8–6 lead an inning later. Reggie Jackson homered in the eighth to bring New York within one run of a tie, but they came no closer.

In Game 5, for the third day in a row, the Dodgers overcame a Yankees lead to claim a one-run victory. Jerry Reuss gave the Yankees a run on two hits in the second inning, but shut them out on just three additional hits the rest of the way. Yankees starter Ron Guidry, meanwhile, stopped the Dodgers on two hits through the first six innings, but then gave up back-to-back homers to Pedro Guerrero and Steve Yeager in the seventh—runs enough for a 2–1 Dodgers win. The final game was close for four innings, but in the fifth and sixth the Dodgers broke it open with seven runs and coasted in on Steve Howe's 3⅔ innings of shutout relief to a 9–2 win and, including 1900, their sixth world championship.

Los Angeles Dodgers (NL), 4; New York Yankees (AL), 2

LA (N)

PLAYER/POS	AVG	G	AB	R	H	2B	3B	HR	RB	BB	SO	SB
Dusty Baker, of	.167	6	24	3	4	0	0	0	1	1	6	0
Bobby Castillo, p	.000	1	0	0	0	0	0	0	0	0	0	0
Ron Cey, 3b	.350	6	20	3	7	0	0	1	6	3	3	0
Terry Forster, p	.000	2	0	0	0	0	0	0	0	0	0	0
Steve Garvey, 1b	.417	6	24	3	10	1	0	0	0	2	5	0
Dave Goltz, p	.000	2	0	0	0	0	0	0	0	0	0	0
Pedro Guerrero, of	.333	6	21	2	7	1	1	2	7	2	6	0
Burt Hooton, p	.000	2	4	1	0	0	0	0	0	1	3	0
Steve Howe, p	.000	3	2	0	0	0	0	0	0	0	2	0
Jay Johnstone, ph	.667	3	3	1	2	0	0	1	3	0	0	0
Ken Landreaux, of-3	.167	5	6	1	1	1	0	0	0	0	2	1
Davey Lopes, 2b	.227	6	22	6	5	1	0	0	2	4	3	4
Rick Monday, of-4	.231	5	13	3	3	1	0	0	0	3	6	0
Tom Niedenfuer, p	.000	2	0	0	0	0	0	0	0	0	0	0
Jerry Reuss, p	.000	2	3	0	0	0	0	0	0	1	2	0
Bill Russell, ss	.240	6	25	1	6	0	0	0	2	0	1	1
Steve Sax, 2b-1	.000	2	1	0	0	0	0	0	0	0	0	0
Mike Scioscia, c	.250	3	4	1	1	0	0	0	0	1	0	0
Reggie Smith, ph	.500	2	2	0	1	0	0	0	0	0	1	0
Dave Stewart, p	.000	2	0	0	0	0	0	0	0	0	0	0
Derrel Thomas, of-3,3b-2,ss-1	.000	5	7	2	0	0	0	0	1	1	2	0
Fernando Valenzuela, p	.000	1	3	0	0	0	0	0	0	1	0	0
Bob Welch, p	.000	1	0	0	0	0	0	0	0	0	0	0
Steve Yeager, c	.286	6	14	2	4	1	0	2	4	0	2	0
TOTAL	.258		198	27	51	6	1	6	26	20	44	6

PITCHER	W	L	ERA	G	GS	CG	SV	SHO	IP	H	ER	BB	SO
Bobby Castillo	0	0	9.00	1	0	0	0	0	1.0	0	1	5	0
Terry Forster	0	0	0.00	2	0	0	0	0	2.0	1	0	3	0
Dave Goltz	0	0	5.40	2	0	0	0	0	3.1	4	2	1	2
Burt Hooton	1	1	1.59	2	2	0	0	0	11.1	8	2	9	3
Steve Howe	1	0	3.86	3	0	0	1	0	7.0	7	3	1	4
Tom Niedenfuer	0	0	0.00	3	0	0	0	0	5.0	3	0	1	0
Jerry Reuss	1	1	3.86	2	2	1	0	0	11.2	10	5	3	8
Dave Stewart	0	0	0.00	2	0	0	0	0	1.2	1	0	2	1
Fernando Valenzuela	1	0	4.00	1	1	1	0	0	9.0	9	4	7	6
Bob Welch	0	0	∞	1	0	0	0	0	0.0	3	2	1	0
TOTAL	4	2	3.29	18	6	2	1	0	52.0	46	19	33	24

NY (A)

PLAYER/POS	AVG	G	AB	R	H	2B	3B	HR	RB	BB	SO	SB
Bobby Brown, of-2	.000	4	1	1	0	0	0	0	0	0	1	0
Rick Cerone, c	.190	6	21	2	4	1	0	1	3	4	2	0
Ron Davis, p	.000	4	0	0	0	0	0	0	0	0	0	0
Barry Foote, ph	.000	1	1	0	0	0	0	0	0	0	1	0
George Frazier, p	.000	3	2	0	0	0	0	0	0	0	1	0
Oscar Gamble, of-2	.333	3	6	1	2	0	0	0	1	1	0	0
Rich Gossage, p	.000	3	1	0	0	0	0	0	0	0	1	0
Ron Guidry, p	.000	2	5	0	0	0	0	0	0	0	3	0
Reggie Jackson, of	.333	3	12	3	4	1	0	1	1	2	3	0
Tommy John, p	.000	3	2	0	0	0	0	0	0	0	0	0
Dave LaRoche, p	.000	1	0	0	0	0	0	0	0	0	0	0
Rudy May, p	.000	3	1	0	0	0	0	0	0	0	0	0
Larry Milbourne, ss	.250	6	20	2	5	2	0	0	3	4	0	0
Jerry Mumphrey, of	.200	5	15	2	3	0	0	0	0	3	2	1
Bobby Murcer, ph	.000	4	3	0	0	0	0	0	0	0	0	0
Graig Nettles, 3b	.400	3	10	1	4	1	0	0	0	1	1	0
Lou Piniella, of-3	.438	6	16	2	7	1	0	0	3	0	1	1
Willie Randolph, 2b	.222	6	18	5	4	1	1	2	3	9	0	1
Rick Reuschel, p	.000	2	2	0	0	0	0	0	0	0	1	0
Dave Righetti, p	.000	1	1	0	0	0	0	0	0	0	0	0
Andre Robertson, pr	.000	2	0	0	0	0	0	0	0	0	0	0
Aurelio Rodriguez, 3b-3	.417	4	12	1	5	0	0	0	0	1	2	0
Bob Watson, 1b	.318	6	22	2	7	1	0	2	7	3	0	0
Dave Winfield, of	.045	6	22	0	1	0	0	0	1	5	4	1
TOTAL	.238		193	22	46	8	1	6	22	33	24	4

PITCHER	W	L	ERA	G	GS	CG	SV	SHO	IP	H	ER	BB	SO
Ron Davis	0	0	23.14	4	0	0	0	0	2.1	4	6	5	4
George Frazier	0	3	17.18	3	0	0	0	0	3.2	9	7	3	2
Rich Gossage	0	0	0.00	3	0	0	2	0	5.0	2	0	2	5
Ron Guidry	1	1	1.93	2	2	0	0	0	14.0	8	3	4	15
Tommy John	1	0	0.69	3	2	0	0	0	13.0	11	1	0	8
Dave LaRoche	0	0	0.00	1	0	0	0	0	1.0	0	0	0	1
Rudy May	0	0	2.84	3	0	0	0	0	6.1	5	2	1	5
Rick Reuschel	0	0	4.91	2	1	0	0	0	3.2	7	2	3	2
Dave Righetti	0	0	13.50	1	0	0	0	0	2.0	5	3	2	1
TOTAL	2	4	4.24	22	6	0	2	0	51.0	51	24	20	44

GAME 1 AT NY OCT 20

LA	000	010	020	3	5	0
NY	301	100	00X	5	6	0

Pitchers: REUSS, Castillo (3), Goltz (4), Niedenfuer (5), Stewart (8) vs GUIDRY, Davis (8), Gossage (8)
Home Runs: Watson-NY, Yeager-LA
Attendance: 56,470

GAME 2 AT NY OCT 21

LA	000	000	000	0	4	2
NY	000	010	02X	3	6	1

Pitchers: HOOTON, Forster (7), Howe (8), Stewart (8) vs JOHN, Gossage (8)
Attendance: 56,505

GAME 3 AT LA OCT 23

NY	022	000	000	4	9	0
LA	300	020	00X	5	11	1

Pitchers: Righetti, FRAZIER (3), May (5), Davis (8) vs VALENZUELA
Home Runs: Cey-LA, Watson-NY, Cerone-NY
Attendance: 56,236

GAME 4 AT LA OCT 24

NY	211	002	010	7	13	1
LA	002	013	20X	8	14	2

Pitchers: Reuschel, May (4), Davis (5), FRAZIER (5), John (7) vs Welch, Goltz (1), Forster (4), Niedenfuer (5), HOWE (7)
Home Runs: Johnstone-LA, Randolph-NY, Jackson-NY
Attendance: 56,242

GAME 5 AT LA OCT 25

NY	010	000	000	1	5	0
LA	000	000	20X	2	4	3

Pitchers: GUIDRY, Gossage (8) vs REUSS
Home Runs: Guerrero-LA, Yeager-LA
Attendance: 56,115

GAME 6 AT NY OCT 28

LA	000	134	010	9	13	1
NY	001	001	000	2	7	2

Pitchers: HOOTON, Howe (6) vs John, FRAZIER (5), Davis (6), Reuschel (6), May (7), LaRoche (9)
Home Runs: Guerrero-LA, Randolph-NY
Attendance: 56,513

The official records show Atlanta ahead only once in a three-game series swept by the Cardinals. But in the original Game 1, Phil Niekro held a slim 1–0 Atlanta lead in the fifth inning when rain wiped out the game just before it could become official.

In the first official game, the Braves scored nothing at all as Bob Forsch held them to three hits. Atlanta's Pascual Perez gave up only one run through the first five innings, but the Cardinals exploded for five runs in the sixth to put the game away. Following another rainout, Niekro tried again in Game 2. He gave up a run in the first, but Atlanta came back with three before he yielded a second run in the sixth. Gene Garber, who relieved Niekro, gave up the tying run in the eighth and lost the game in the bottom of the ninth on Ken Oberkfell's RBI liner over the center fielder's head.

Joaquin Andujar shut out the Braves through six innings of Game Three before giving up two runs in the seventh. But by then St. Louis had scored five times. Bruce Sutter retired the last seven Braves in relief of Andujar, and the Cardinals had their pennant.

St. Louis Cardinals (East), 3; Atlanta Braves (West), 0

STL (E)

PLAYER/POS	AVG	G	AB	R	H	2B	3B	HR	RB	BB	SO	SB
Joaquin Andujar, p	.000	1	1	0	0	0	0	0	0	0	1	0
Doug Bair, p	.000	1	0	0	0	0	0	0	0	0	0	0
Steve Braun, ph	.000	1	1	0	0	0	0	0	0	0	0	0
Bob Forsch, p	.667	1	3	1	2	0	0	0	1	0	0	0
David Green, of	1.000	2	1	1	1	0	0	0	0	0	0	0
George Hendrick, of	.308	3	13	2	4	0	0	0	2	1	2	0
Keith Hernandez, 1b	.333	3	12	3	4	0	0	0	1	2	3	0
Tommy Herr, 2b	.231	3	13	1	3	1	0	0	0	1	2	0
Willie McGee, of	.308	3	13	4	4	0	2	1	5	0	5	0
Ken Oberkfell, 3b	.200	3	15	1	3	0	0	0	2	0	0	0
Darrell Porter, c	.556	3	9	3	5	3	0	0	1	5	2	0
Lonnie Smith, of	.273	3	11	1	3	0	0	0	0	1	0	1
Ozzie Smith, ss	.556	3	9	0	5	0	0	0	3	3	0	0
John Stuper, p	.000	1	1	0	0	0	0	0	0	0	0	0
Bruce Sutter, p	.000	2	1	0	0	0	0	0	0	0	0	0
TOTAL	.330		103	17	34	4	2	1	16	12	16	1

PITCHER	W	L	ERA	G	GS	CG	SV	SHO	IP	H	ER	BB	SO
Joaquin Andujar	1	0	2.70	1	1	0	0	0	6.2	6	2	2	4
Doug Bair	0	0	0.00	1	0	0	0	0	1.0	2	0	3	0
Bob Forsch	1	0	0.00	1	1	1	0	1	9.0	3	0	0	6
John Stuper	0	0	3.00	1	1	0	0	0	6.0	4	2	1	4
Bruce Sutter	1	0	0.00	2	0	0	1	0	4.1	0	0	0	1
TOTAL	3	0	1.33	6	3	1	1	1	27.0	15	4	6	15

ATL (W)

PLAYER/POS	AVG	G	AB	R	H	2B	3B	HR	RB	BB	SO	SB
Steve Bedrosian, p	.000	2	0	0	0	0	0	0	0	0	0	0
Bruce Benedict, c	.250	3	8	1	2	1	0	0	0	2	1	0
Brett Butler, of-1	.000	2	1	0	0	0	0	0	0	0	0	0
Rick Camp, p	.000	1	0	0	0	0	0	0	0	0	0	0
Chris Chambliss, 1b	.000	3	10	0	0	0	0	0	0	1	0	0
Gene Garber, p	.000	2	1	0	0	0	0	0	0	0	0	0
Terry Harper, of	.000	1	1	1	0	0	0	0	0	0	0	0
Bob Horner, 3b	.091	3	11	0	1	0	0	0	0	0	2	0
Glenn Hubbard, 2b	.222	3	9	1	2	0	0	0	1	0	3	0
Rick Mahler, p	.000	1	0	0	0	0	0	0	0	0	0	0
Donnie Moore, p	.000	2	0	0	0	0	0	0	0	0	0	0
Dale Murphy, of	.273	3	11	1	3	0	0	0	0	0	2	1
Phil Niekro, p	.000	1	0	0	0	0	0	0	0	1	0	0
Pascual Perez, p	.000	2	3	0	0	0	0	0	0	0	1	0
Biff Pocoroba, ph	.000	1	1	0	0	0	0	0	0	0	0	0
Rafael Ramirez, ss	.182	3	11	1	2	0	0	0	1	1	1	0
Jerry Royster, of-3,3b-1	.182	3	11	0	2	0	0	0	0	0	2	0
Bob Walk, p	.000	1	0	0	0	0	0	0	0	0	0	0
Claudell Washington, of	.333	3	9	0	3	0	0	0	0	2	2	0
Larry Whisenton, ph	.000	2	2	0	0	0	0	0	0	0	1	0
TOTAL	.169		89	5	15	1	0	0	3	6	15	1

PITCHER	W	L	ERA	G	GS	CG	SV	SHO	IP	H	ER	BB	SO
Steve Bedrosian	0	0	18.00	2	0	0	0	0	1.0	3	2	1	2
Rick Camp	0	1	36.00	1	1	0	0	0	1.0	4	4	1	0
Gene Garber	0	1	8.10	2	0	0	0	0	3.1	4	3	1	3
Rick Mahler	0	0	0.00	1	0	0	0	0	1.2	3	0	2	0
Donnie Moore	0	0	0.00	2	0	0	0	0	2.2	2	0	0	1
Phil Niekro	0	0	3.00	1	1	0	0	0	6.0	6	2	4	5
Pascual Perez	0	1	5.19	2	1	0	0	0	8.2	10	5	2	4
Bob Walk	0	0	9.00	1	0	0	0	0	1.0	2	1	1	1
TOTAL	0	3	6.04	12	3	0	0	0	25.1	34	17	12	16

GAME 1 AT STL OCT 7

ATL	000	000	000	0	3	0
STL	001	005	01X	7	13	1

Pitchers: PEREZ, Bedrosian (6), Moore (6), Walk (8) vs FORSCH
Attendance: 53,008

GAME 2 AT STL OCT 9

ATL	002	010	000	3	6	0
STL	100	001	011	4	9	1

Pitchers: Niekro, GARBER (7) vs Stuper, Bair (7), SUTTER (8)
Attendance: 53,408

GAME 3 AT ATL OCT 10

STL	040	010	001	6	12	0
ATL	000	000	200	2	6	1

Pitchers: ANDUJAR, Sutter (7) vs CAMP, Perez (2), Moore (5), Mahler (7), Bedrosian (8), Garber (9)
Home Runs: McGee-STL
Attendance: 52,173

For the first time in LCS play, a club won the first two games but lost the series. The Angels overcame a 3–1 deficit to take Game 1, with four runs in the third and three more later, while starter Tommy John settled down to stop the Brewers through the final six innings. In Game 2 Bruce Kison prevailed, as the Angels built a 4–0 lead over Milwaukee and Pete Vuckovich before Kison gave up what proved to be a harmless two-run homer to Paul Molitor in the fifth.

With three chances to clinch the pennant, California three times fell short. In the third game, their three eighth-inning runs couldn't catch the Brewers, who already had five. In Game 4, Don Baylor's eighth-inning grand slam completed California scoring at five runs, but Milwaukee had already scored seven, and they added two more. In the finale, Kison held a 3–2 lead when he was relieved after five innings. But Cecil Cooper singled off Luis Sanchez in the seventh (with two out and the bases loaded) for two runs and a Brewers lead. Bob McClure and Pete Ladd held off the Angels through the final two innings, and the Brewers were on their way to their first World Series.

Milwaukee Brewers (East), 3;
California Angels (West), 2

MIL (E)

PLAYER/POS	AVG	G	AB	R	H	2B	3B	HR	RB	BB	SO	SB
Dwight Bernard, p	.000	1	0	0	0	0	0	0	0	0	0	0
Mark Brouhard, of	.750	1	4	4	3	1	0	1	3	0	0	0
Mike Caldwell, p	.000	1	0	0	0	0	0	0	0	0	0	0
Cecil Cooper, 1b	.150	5	20	1	3	2	0	0	4	0	6	0
Marshall Edwards, dh-2,of-1	.000	3	1	2	0	0	0	0	0	0	0	1
Jim Gantner, 2b	.188	5	16	1	3	0	0	0	2	1	1	0
Moose Haas, p	.000	1	0	0	0	0	0	0	0	0	0	0
Roy Howell, dh	.000	1	3	0	0	0	0	0	0	0	1	0
Pete Ladd, p	.000	3	0	0	0	0	0	0	0	0	0	0
Bob McClure, p	.000	1	0	0	0	0	0	0	0	0	0	0
Paul Molitor, 3b	.316	5	19	4	6	1	0	2	5	2	3	1
Don Money, dh	.182	4	11	2	2	0	0	0	1	3	1	0
Charlie Moore, of	.462	5	13	3	6	0	0	0	0	1	2	0
Ben Oglivie, of	.133	4	15	1	2	0	0	1	1	0	3	0
Ted Simmons, c	.167	5	18	3	3	0	0	0	1	1	4	0
Jim Slaton, p	.000	2	0	0	0	0	0	0	0	0	0	0
Don Sutton, p	.000	1	0	0	0	0	0	0	0	0	0	0
Gorman Thomas, of	.067	5	15	1	1	0	0	1	3	2	7	0
Pete Vuckovich, p	.000	2	0	0	0	0	0	0	0	0	0	0
Robin Yount, ss	.250	5	16	1	4	0	0	0	0	5	0	0
TOTAL	.219		151	23	33	4	0	5	20	15	28	2

PITCHER	W	L	ERA	G	GS	CG	SV	SHO	IP	H	ER	BB	SO
Dwight Bernard	0	0	0.00	1	0	0	0	0	1.0	0	0	0	0
Mike Caldwell	0	1	15.00	1	1	0	0	0	3.0	7	5	1	2
Moose Haas	1	0	4.91	1	1	0	0	0	7.1	5	4	5	7
Pete Ladd	0	0	0.00	3	0	0	2	0	3.1	0	0	0	5
Bob McClure	1	0	0.00	1	0	0	0	0	1.2	2	0	0	0
Jim Slaton	0	0	1.93	2	0	0	1	0	4.2	3	1	1	3
Don Sutton	1	0	3.52	1	1	0	0	0	7.2	8	3	2	9
Pete Vuckovich	0	1	4.40	2	2	1	0	0	14.1	15	7	7	8
TOTAL	3	2	4.19	12	5	1	3	0	43.0	40	20	16	34

CAL (W)

PLAYER/POS	AVG	G	AB	R	H	2B	3B	HR	RB	BB	SO	SB
Don Baylor, dh	.294	5	17	2	5	1	1	1	10	2	0	0
Juan Beniquez, of	.000	2	0	0	0	0	0	0	0	0	0	0
Bob Boone, c	.250	5	16	3	4	0	0	1	4	0	2	0
Rod Carew, 1b	.176	5	17	2	3	1	0	0	0	4	4	1
Bobby Clark, of	.000	2	0	0	0	0	0	0	0	0	0	0
Doug De Cinces, 3b	.316	5	19	5	6	2	0	0	0	1	5	0
Brian Downing, of	.158	5	19	4	3	1	0	0	0	3	2	0
Tim Foli, ss	.125	5	16	2	2	0	0	0	1	0	3	0
Dave Goltz, p	.000	1	0	0	0	0	0	0	0	0	0	0
Bobby Grich, 2b	.200	5	15	1	3	1	0	0	1	2	7	0
Andy Hassler, p	.000	2	0	0	0	0	0	0	0	0	0	0
Reggie Jackson, of	.111	5	18	2	2	0	0	1	2	2	7	0
Ron Jackson, ph	1.000	1	1	0	1	0	0	0	0	0	0	0
Tommy John, p	.000	2	0	0	0	0	0	0	0	0	0	0
Bruce Kison, p	.000	2	0	0	0	0	0	0	0	0	0	0
Fred Lynn, of	.611	5	18	4	11	2	0	1	5	2	3	0
Luis Sanchez, p	.000	2	0	0	0	0	0	0	0	0	0	0
Rob Wilfong, ph	.000	2	1	0	0	0	0	0	0	0	1	0
Mike Witt, p	.000	1	0	0	0	0	0	0	0	0	0	0
Geoff Zahn, p	.000	1	0	0	0	0	0	0	0	0	0	0
TOTAL	.255		157	23	40	8	1	4	23	16	34	1

PITCHER	W	L	ERA	G	GS	CG	SV	SHO	IP	H	ER	BB	SO
Dave Goltz	0	0	7.36	1	0	0	0	0	3.2	4	3	2	2
Andy Hassler	0	0	0.00	2	0	0	0	0	2.2	0	0	0	2
Tommy John	1	1	5.11	2	2	1	0	0	12.1	11	7	6	6
Bruce Kison	1	0	1.93	2	2	1	0	0	14.0	8	3	3	12
Luis Sanchez	0	1	6.75	2	0	0	0	0	2.2	4	2	1	1
Mike Witt	0	0	6.00	1	0	0	0	0	3.0	2	2	2	3
Geoff Zahn	0	1	7.36	1	1	0	0	0	3.2	4	3	1	2
TOTAL	2	3	4.29	11	5	2	0	0	42.0	33	20	15	28

GAME 1 AT CAL OCT 5

MIL	021	000	000	3	7	2
CAL	104	210	00X	8	10	0

Pitchers: CALDWELL, Slaton (4), Ladd (7), Bernard (8) vs JOHN
Home Runs: Thomas-MIL, Lynn-CAL
Attendance: 64,406

GAME 2 AT CAL OCT 6

MIL	000	020	000	2	5	0
CAL	021	100	00X	4	6	0

Pitchers: VUCKOVICH vs KISON
Home Runs: Re.Jackson-CAL, Molitor-MIL
Attendance: 64,179

GAME 3 AT MIL OCT 8

CAL	000	000	030	3	8	0
MIL	000	300	20X	5	6	0

Pitchers: ZAHN, Witt (4), Hassler (7) vs SUTTON, Ladd (8)
Home Runs: Molitor-MIL, Boone-CAL
Attendance: 50,135

GAME 4 AT MIL OCT 9

CAL	000	001	040	5	5	3
MIL	030	301	02X	9	9	2

Pitchers: JOHN, Goltz (4), Sanchez (8) vs HAAS, Slaton (8)
Home Runs: Baylor-CAL, Brouhard-MIL
Attendance: 51,003

GAME 5 AT MIL OCT 10

CAL	101	100	000	3	11	1
MIL	100	100	20X	4	6	4

Pitchers: Kison, SANCHEZ (6), Hassler (7) vs Vuckovich, McCLURE (7), Ladd (9)
Home Runs: Oglivie-MIL
Attendance: 54,968

The Series was anticipated as a matchup of Cardinals speed and Brewers power. In the event, though, St. Louis outslugged the Brewers and wound up as world champions.

The Brewers, in their first World Series, looked unstoppable in the opening game. Hammering four Cardinals pitchers for 17 hits (including a record five for Paul Molitor), they scored 10 runs while pitcher Mike Caldwell was shutting out the Cards on three hits. In the second game Milwaukee continued the onslaught, building an early 3–0 lead. But St. Louis finally got on the scoreboard with two runs in the last of the third, and tied the game at 4–4 in the sixth on Darrell Porter's two-run double. And the Cards won the game on a bases-loaded walk in the eighth as relievers Doug Bair and Bruce Sutter held the Brewers scoreless over the final four innings.

St. Louis pushed into the Series lead in Game 3, thanks mostly to the 6⅓ shutout innings of starter Joaquin Andujar and the fielding and batting of center fielder Willie McGee. McGee drove in four of the six Cardinal runs with a pair of homers and prevented an extra-base hit and a two-run Brewers homer with leaping catches in the first and final innings. The Cards pressed their advantage in Game 4 with four early runs. But in the last of the seventh (with the score now 5–1), an error by Cardinals pitcher Dave LaPoint opened the way for Milwaukee to win the game with six two-out runs on a barrage of hits (and the added assistance of a pair of walks and a wild pitch).

Mike Caldwell wasn't as effective in Game 5 as he had been in the opener, yielding 14 hits and four runs in 8⅓ innings of work. But he was never behind in the game as his teammates, with 11 hits of their own (four of them by Robin Yount, including a home run) and several fielding gems put Milwaukee ahead again in the Series with a 6–4 win.

The Cards had their backs to the wall as the Series moved to St. Louis for the final games. But in Game 6 the Cards responded to their opening-game humiliation with a laugher of their own, 13–1, on John Stuper's four-hitter. And in the finale they rocked Brewers ace Pete Vuckovich and three relievers for 15 hits and a 6–3 victory that gave starter Joaquin Andujar his second Series win and reliever Bruce Sutter his second save.

St. Louis Cardinals (NL), 4; Milwaukee Brewers (AL), 3

STL (N)

PLAYER/POS	AVG	G	AB	R	H	2B	3B	HR	RB	BB	SO	SB
Joaquin Andujar, p	.000	2	0	0	0	0	0	0	0	0	0	0
Doug Bair, p	.000	3	0	0	0	0	0	0	0	0	0	0
Steve Braun, dh	.500	2	2	0	1	0	0	0	2	1	0	0
Glenn Brummer, c	.000	1	0	0	0	0	0	0	0	0	0	0
Bob Forsch, p	.000	2	0	0	0	0	0	0	0	0	0	0
David Green, of-4,dh-3	.200	7	10	3	2	1	1	0	0	1	3	0
George Hendrick, of	.321	7	28	5	9	0	0	0	5	2	2	0
Keith Hernandez, 1b	.259	7	27	4	7	2	0	1	8	4	2	0
Tommy Herr, 2b	.160	7	25	2	4	2	0	0	5	3	3	0
Dane Iorg, dh	.529	5	17	4	9	4	1	0	1	0	0	0
Jim Kaat, p	.000	4	0	0	0	0	0	0	0	0	0	0
Jeff Lahti, p	.000	2	0	0	0	0	0	0	0	0	0	0
Dave LaPoint, p	.000	2	0	0	0	0	0	0	0	0	0	0
Willie McGee, of	.240	6	25	6	6	0	0	2	5	1	3	2
Ken Oberkfell, 3b	.292	7	24	4	7	1	0	0	1	2	1	2
Darrell Porter, c	.286	7	28	1	8	2	0	1	5	1	4	0
Mike Ramsey, 3b-2	.000	3	1	1	0	0	0	0	0	0	1	0
Lonnie Smith, of-6,dh-1	.321	7	28	6	9	4	1	0	1	1	5	2
Ozzie Smith, ss	.208	7	24	3	5	0	0	0	1	3	0	1
John Stuper, p	.000	2	0	0	0	0	0	0	0	0	0	0
Bruce Sutter, p	.000	4	0	0	0	0	0	0	0	0	0	0
Gene Tenace, dh-1	.000	5	6	0	0	0	0	0	0	1	2	0
TOTAL	.273		245	39	67	16	3	4	34	20	26	7

PITCHER	W	L	ERA	G	GS	CG	SV	SHO	IP	H	ER	BB	SO
Joaquin Andujar	2	0	1.35	2	2	0	0	0	13.1	10	2	1	4
Doug Bair	0	1	9.00	3	0	0	0	0	2.0	2	2	2	3
Bob Forsch	0	2	4.97	2	2	0	0	0	12.2	18	7	3	4
Jim Kaat	0	0	3.86	4	0	0	0	0	2.1	4	1	2	2
Jeff Lahti	0	0	10.80	2	0	0	0	0	1.2	4	2	1	1
Dave LaPoint	0	0	3.24	2	1	0	0	0	8.1	10	3	2	3
John Stuper	1	0	3.46	2	2	1	0	0	13.0	10	5	5	5
Bruce Sutter	1	0	4.70	4	0	0	2	0	7.2	6	4	3	6
TOTAL	4	3	3.84	21	7	1	2	0	61.0	64	26	19	28

MIL (A)

PLAYER/POS	AVG	G	AB	R	H	2B	3B	HR	RB	BB	SO	SB
Dwight Bernard, p	.000	1	0	0	0	0	0	0	0	0	0	0
Mike Caldwell, p	.000	3	0	0	0	0	0	0	0	0	0	0
Cecil Cooper, 1b	.286	7	28	3	8	1	0	1	6	1	1	0
Marshall Edwards, of	.000	1	0	0	0	0	0	0	0	0	0	0
Jim Gantner, 2b	.333	7	24	5	8	4	1	0	4	1	1	0
Moose Haas, p	.000	2	0	0	0	0	0	0	0	0	0	0
Roy Howell, dh	.000	4	11	1	0	0	0	0	0	0	3	0
Pete Ladd, p	.000	1	0	0	0	0	0	0	0	0	0	0
Bob McClure, p	.000	5	0	0	0	0	0	0	0	0	0	0
Doc Medich, p	.000	1	0	0	0	0	0	0	0	0	0	0
Paul Molitor, 3b	.355	7	31	5	11	0	0	0	3	2	4	1
Don Money, dh-4	.231	5	13	4	3	1	0	0	1	2	3	0
Charlie Moore, of	.346	7	26	3	9	3	0	0	2	1	0	0
Ben Oglivie, of	.222	7	27	4	6	0	1	1	1	2	4	0
Ted Simmons, c	.174	7	23	2	4	0	0	2	3	5	3	0
Jim Slaton, p	.000	2	0	0	0	0	0	0	0	0	0	0
Don Sutton, p	.000	2	0	0	0	0	0	0	0	0	0	0
Gorman Thomas, of	.115	7	26	0	3	0	0	0	3	2	7	0
Pete Vuckovich, p	.000	2	0	0	0	0	0	0	0	0	0	0
Ned Yost, c	.000	1	0	0	0	0	0	0	0	1	0	0
Robin Yount, ss	.414	7	29	6	12	3	0	1	6	2	2	0
TOTAL	.269		238	33	64	12	2	5	29	19	28	1

PITCHER	W	L	ERA	G	GS	CG	SV	SHO	IP	H	ER	BB	SO
Dwight Bernard	0	0	0.00	1	0	0	0	0	1.0	0	0	0	1
Mike Caldwell	2	0	2.04	3	2	1	0	1	17.2	19	4	3	6
Moose Haas	0	0	7.36	2	1	0	0	0	7.1	8	6	3	4
Pete Ladd	0	0	0.00	1	0	0	0	0	0.2	1	0	2	0
Bob McClure	0	2	4.15	5	0	0	2	0	4.1	5	2	3	5
Doc Medich	0	0	18.00	1	0	0	0	0	2.0	5	4	1	0
Jim Slaton	1	0	0.00	2	0	0	0	0	2.2	1	0	2	1
Don Sutton	0	1	7.84	2	2	0	0	0	10.1	12	9	1	5
Pete Vuckovich	0	1	4.50	2	2	0	0	0	14.0	16	7	5	4
TOTAL	3	4	4.80	19	7	1	2	1	60.0	67	32	20	26

GAME 1 AT STL OCT 12

MIL	200	112	004	10	17 0
STL	000	000	000	0	3 1

Pitchers: CALDWELL vs FORSCH, Kaat (6), LaPoint (8), Lahti (9)
Home Runs: Simmons-MIL
Attendance: 53,723

GAME 2 AT STL OCT 13

MIL	012	010	000	4	10 1
STL	002	002	01X	5	8 0

Pitchers: Sutton, McCLURE (7), Ladd (8) vs Stuper, Kaat (5), Bair (5), SUTTER (7)
Home Runs: Simmons-MIL
Attendance: 53,723

GAME 3 AT MIL OCT 15

STL	000	030	201	6	6 1
MIL	000	000	020	2	5 3

Pitchers: ANDUJAR, Kaat (7), Bair (7), Sutter (7) vs VUCKOVICH, McClure (9)
Home Runs: McGee-STL (2), Cooper-MIL
Attendance: 56,556

GAME 4 AT MIL OCT 16

STL	130	001	000	5	8 1
MIL	000	010	60X	7	10 2

Pitchers: LaPoint, BAIR (7), Kaat (7), Lahti (7) vs Haas, SLATON (6), McClure (8)
Attendance: 56,560

GAME 5 AT MIL OCT 17

STL	001	000	102	4	15 2
MIL	101	010	12X	6	11 1

Pitchers: FORSCH, Sutter (8) vs CALDWELL, McClure (9)
Home Runs: Yount-MIL
Attendance: 56,562

GAME 6 AT STL OCT 19

MIL	000	000	001	1	4 4
STL	020	326	00X	13	12 1

Pitchers: SUTTON, Slaton (5), Medich (6), Bernard (8) vs STUPER
Home Runs: Porter-STL, Hernandez-STL
Attendance: 53,723

GAME 7 AT STL OCT 20

MIL	000	012	000	3	7 0
STL	000	103	02X	6	15 1

Pitchers: Vuckovich, McCLURE (6), Haas (6), Caldwell (8) vs ANDUJAR, Sutter (8)
Home Runs: Oglivie-MIL
Attendance: 53,723

The Dodgers earned only four runs off Philadelphia pitching, and even though they doubled their run total to eight on unearned runs, the Phillies scored twice that number to take the pennant in four games.

Mike Schmidt homered off Jerry Reuss in the first inning of the opener for the game's only run. Phillies starter Steve Carlton loaded the bases in the eighth, but Al Holland came on to get the third out and preserve the shutout. The Phillies also scored only one run in the second game, on Gary Matthews' homer off Fernando Valenzuela in the second. But this time the run only tied the score, and in the fifth Pedro Guerrero tripled in two unearned runs to give Valenzuela the Dodgers' only win.

The Phillies' Charlie Hudson hurled the series' only complete game—a four-hitter—to win Game 3. Gary Matthews' four hits in Game 3 and 4 included his second and third series homers, and drove in half the Phillies' 14 runs as they took the two games by identical 7–2 scores.

Philadelphia Phillies (East), 3;
Los Angeles Dodgers (West), 1

PHI (E)

PLAYER/POS	AVG	G	AB	R	H	2B	3B	HR	RB	BB	SO	SB
Steve Carlton, p	.200	2	5	0	1	0	0	0	0	0	3	0
Ivan DeJesus, ss	.250	4	12	0	3	0	0	0	1	3	3	0
John Denny, p	.000	1	1	0	0	0	0	0	0	0	0	0
Bob Dernier, of	.000	1	0	0	0	0	0	0	0	0	0	0
Bo Diaz, c	.154	4	13	0	2	1	0	0	0	2	1	0
Greg Gross, of-3	.000	4	5	1	0	0	0	0	0	2	2	0
Von Hayes, of-1	.000	2	2	0	0	0	0	0	0	0	0	0
Al Holland, p	.000	2	0	0	0	0	0	0	0	0	0	0
Charles Hudson, p	.000	1	4	0	0	0	0	0	0	0	3	0
Joe Lefebvre, of-1	.000	2	2	0	0	0	0	0	0	1	1	0
Sixto Lezcano, of	.308	4	13	2	4	0	0	1	2	1	1	0
Garry Maddox, of	.273	3	11	0	3	1	0	0	1	0	1	0
Gary Matthews, of	.429	4	14	4	6	0	0	3	8	2	1	1
Joe Morgan, 2b	.067	4	15	1	1	0	0	0	0	2	1	0
Tony Perez, ph	1.000	1	1	0	1	0	0	0	0	0	0	0
Ron Reed, p	.000	2	0	0	0	0	0	0	0	0	0	0
Pete Rose, 1b	.375	4	16	3	6	0	0	0	1	1	1	1
Juan Samuel, pr	.000	1	0	0	0	0	0	0	0	0	0	0
Mike Schmidt, 3b	.467	4	15	5	7	2	0	1	2	2	3	0
Ossie Virgil, ph	.000	1	1	0	0	0	0	0	0	0	1	0
TOTAL	.262		130	16	34	4	0	5	15	15	22	2

PITCHER	W	L	ERA	G	GS	CG	SV	SHO	IP	H	ER	BB	SO
Steve Carlton	2	0	0.66	2	2	0	0	0	13.2	13	1	5	13
John Denny	0	1	0.00	1	1	0	0	0	6.0	5	0	3	3
Al Holland	0	0	0.00	2	0	0	1	0	3.0	1	0	0	3
Charles Hudson	1	0	2.00	1	1	1	0	0	9.0	4	2	2	9
Ron Reed	0	0	2.70	2	0	0	0	0	3.1	4	1	1	3
TOTAL	3	1	1.03	8	4	1	1	0	35.0	27	4	11	31

LA (W)

PLAYER/POS	AVG	G	AB	R	H	2B	3B	HR	RB	BB	SO	SB
Dusty Baker, of	.357	4	14	4	5	1	0	1	1	2	0	0
Joe Beckwith, p	.000	2	0	0	0	0	0	0	0	0	0	0
Greg Brock, 1b	.000	3	9	1	0	0	0	0	0	0	3	0
Jack Fimple, c	.143	3	7	0	1	0	0	0	1	0	3	0
Pedro Guerrero, 3b	.250	4	12	1	3	1	1	0	2	3	3	0
Rick Honeycutt, p	.000	2	0	0	0	0	0	0	0	0	0	0
Rafael Landestoy, ph	.000	2	2	0	0	0	0	0	0	0	1	0
Ken Landreaux, of	.143	4	14	0	2	0	0	0	1	1	3	0
Candy Maldonado, ph	.000	2	2	0	0	0	0	0	0	0	1	0
Mike Marshall, 1b-3,of-2	.133	4	15	1	2	1	0	1	2	1	6	0
Rick Monday, ph	.000	1	0	0	0	0	0	0	0	0	0	0
Jose Morales, ph	.000	2	2	0	0	0	0	0	0	0	1	0
Tom Niedenfuer, p	.000	2	0	0	0	0	0	0	0	0	0	0
Alejandro Pena, p	1.000	1	1	0	1	0	0	0	0	0	0	0
Jerry Reuss, p	.000	2	3	0	0	0	0	0	0	0	3	0
Bill Russell, ss	.286	4	14	1	4	0	0	0	0	2	4	1
Steve Sax, 2b	.250	4	16	0	4	0	0	0	0	1	0	1
Derrel Thomas, of	.444	4	9	4	4	1	0	0	0	3	1	1
Fernando Valenzuela, p	.000	1	3	0	0	0	0	0	0	1	0	0
Bob Welch, p	.000	1	0	0	0	0	0	0	0	0	0	0
Steve Yeager, c	.167	2	6	0	1	1	0	0	0	0	0	0
Pat Zachry, p	.000	2	0	0	0	0	0	0	0	0	0	0
TOTAL	.209		129	8	27	5	1	2	7	11	31	3

PITCHER	W	L	ERA	G	GS	CG	SV	SHO	IP	H	ER	BB	SO
Joe Beckwith	0	0	0.00	2	0	0	0	0	2.1	1	0	2	3
Rick Honeycutt	0	0	21.60	2	0	0	0	0	1.2	4	4	0	2
Tom Niedenfuer	0	0	0.00	2	0	0	1	0	2.0	0	0	1	3
Alejandro Pena	0	0	6.75	1	0	0	0	0	2.2	4	2	1	3
Jerry Reuss	0	2	4.50	2	2	0	0	0	12.0	14	6	3	4
Fernando Valenzuela	1	0	1.13	1	1	0	0	0	8.0	7	1	4	5
Bob Welch	0	1	6.75	1	1	0	0	0	1.1	0	1	2	0
Pat Zachry	0	0	2.25	2	0	0	0	0	4.0	4	1	2	2
TOTAL	1	3	3.97	13	4	0	1	0	34.0	34	15	15	22

The White Sox and Orioles entered the ALCS evenly matched, with similar season's records and stats. But Baltimore all but shut down Chicago's run production in this quick four-game meeting. Both teams had 28 hits, but the Sox, held to four for extra bases, found themselves outslugged by 116 percentage points and outscored by 16 runs.

Chicago won the first game, scoring two of their three series runs as LaMarr Hoyt shut out Baltimore for eight innings before letting in a run in the ninth. But the White Sox had concluded their effective scoring. In Game 2, Orioles rookie Mike Boddicker shut them out on five hits, striking out 14. In Game 3 the Sox scored their final run. The Orioles got only two more hits than Chicago but blended them with nine walks, a hit batsman, and a Sox error to score 11 runs.

In the fourth game, Orioles pitchers Storm Davis and Tippy Martinez saw to it that ten Chicago hits scored no runs. Britt Burns held Baltimore scoreless, too, through nine innings. But Tito Landrum's solo homer in the top of the 10th drove Burns out, and two more Orioles runs provided more than enough scoring to win Baltimore the flag.

Baltimore Orioles (East), 3; Chicago White Sox (West), 1

BAL (E)

PLAYER/POS	AVG	G	AB	R	H	2B	3B	HR	RB	BB	SO	SB
Benny Ayala, dh	.000	1	0	0	0	0	0	0	0	1	0	0
Mike Boddicker, p	.000	1	0	0	0	0	0	0	0	0	0	0
Al Bumbry, of	.125	3	8	0	1	1	0	0	1	0	2	0
Todd Cruz, 3b	.133	4	15	0	2	0	0	0	1	0	5	0
Rich Dauer, 2b	.000	4	14	0	0	0	0	0	0	1	0	0
Storm Davis, p	.000	1	0	0	0	0	0	0	0	0	0	0
Rick Dempsey, c	.167	4	12	1	2	0	0	0	0	1	1	0
Jim Dwyer, of-1	.250	2	4	1	1	1	0	0	0	1	0	0
Mike Flanagan, p	.000	1	0	0	0	0	0	0	0	0	0	0
Dan Ford, of-1	.200	4	5	0	1	1	0	0	0	0	1	0
Tito Landrum, of-3	.200	4	10	2	2	0	0	1	1	0	2	0
John Lowenstein, of-2	.167	3	6	0	1	1	0	0	2	1	2	0
Tippy Martinez, p	.000	2	0	0	0	0	0	0	0	0	0	0
Scott McGregor, p	.000	1	0	0	0	0	0	0	0	0	0	0
Eddie Murray, 1b	.267	4	15	5	4	0	0	1	3	3	3	1
Joe Nolan, ph	.000	1	0	0	0	0	0	0	1	0	0	0
Jim Palmer, pr	.000	1	0	0	0	0	0	0	0	0	0	0
Cal Ripken, ss	.400	4	15	5	6	2	0	0	1	2	3	0
Gary Roenicke, of	.750	3	4	4	3	1	0	1	4	5	0	0
John Shelby, of-2	.222	4	9	1	2	0	0	0	0	1	3	1
Ken Singleton, dh	.250	4	12	0	3	2	0	0	1	2	2	0
Sammy Stewart, p	.000	2	0	0	0	0	0	0	0	0	0	0
TOTAL	.217		129	19	28	9	0	3	17	16	24	2

PITCHER	W	L	ERA	G	GS	CG	SV	SHO	IP	H	ER	BB	SO
Mike Boddicker	1	0	0.00	1	1	1	0	1	9.0	5	0	3	14
Storm Davis	0	0	0.00	1	1	0	0	0	6.0	5	0	2	2
Mike Flanagan	1	0	1.80	1	1	0	0	0	5.0	5	1	0	1
Tippy Martinez	1	0	0.00	2	0	0	0	0	6.0	5	0	3	5
Scott McGregor	0	1	1.35	1	1	0	0	0	6.2	6	1	3	2
Sammy Stewart	0	0	0.00	2	0	0	1	0	4.1	2	0	1	2
TOTAL	3	1	0.49	8	4	1	1	1	37.0	28	2	12	26

CHI (W)

PLAYER/POS	AVG	G	AB	R	H	2B	3B	HR	RB	BB	SO	SB
Juan Agosto, p	.000	1	0	0	0	0	0	0	0	0	0	0
Harold Baines, of	.125	4	16	0	2	0	0	0	0	1	3	0
Floyd Bannister, p	.000	1	0	0	0	0	0	0	0	0	0	0
Salome Barojas, p	.000	2	0	0	0	0	0	0	0	0	0	0
Britt Burns, p	.000	1	0	0	0	0	0	0	0	0	0	0
Julio Cruz, 2b	.333	4	12	0	4	0	0	0	0	3	4	2
Richard Dotson, p	.000	1	0	0	0	0	0	0	0	0	0	0
Jerry Dybzinski, ss	.250	2	4	0	1	0	0	0	0	0	0	0
Carlton Fisk, c	.176	4	17	0	3	1	0	0	0	0	3	0
Scott Fletcher, ss	.000	3	7	0	0	0	0	0	0	1	0	0
Jerry Hairston, of	.000	2	3	0	0	0	0	0	0	1	1	0
LaMarr Hoyt, p	.000	1	0	0	0	0	0	0	0	0	0	0
Ron Kittle, of	.286	3	7	1	2	1	0	0	0	1	2	0
Jerry Koosman, p	.000	1	0	0	0	0	0	0	0	0	0	0
Dennis Lamp, p	.000	3	0	0	0	0	0	0	0	0	0	0
Rudy Law, of	.389	4	18	1	7	1	0	0	0	0	1	2
Vance Law, 3b	.182	4	11	0	2	0	0	0	1	1	3	0
Greg Luzinski, dh	.133	4	15	0	2	1	0	0	1	1	5	0
Tom Paciorek, 1b-3,of-2	.250	4	16	1	4	0	0	0	1	1	2	0
Aurelio Rodriguez, 3b	.000	2	0	0	0	0	0	0	0	0	0	0
Mike Squires, 1b-3	.000	4	4	0	0	0	0	0	0	0	0	0
Dick Tidrow, p	.000	1	0	0	0	0	0	0	0	0	0	0
Greg Walker, 1b-1	.333	2	3	0	1	0	0	0	0	1	2	0
TOTAL	.211		133	3	28	4	0	0	2	12	26	4

PITCHER	W	L	ERA	G	GS	CG	SV	SHO	IP	H	ER	BB	SO
Juan Agosto	0	0	0.00	1	0	0	0	0	0.1	0	0	0	0
Floyd Bannister	0	1	4.50	1	1	0	0	0	6.0	5	3	1	5
Salome Barojas	0	0	18.00	2	0	0	0	0	1.0	4	2	0	0
Britt Burns	0	1	0.96	1	1	0	0	0	9.1	6	1	5	8
Richard Dotson	0	1	10.80	1	1	0	0	0	5.0	6	6	3	3
LaMarr Hoyt	1	0	1.00	1	1	1	0	0	9.0	5	1	0	4
Jerry Koosman	0	0	54.00	1	0	0	0	0	0.1	1	2	2	0
Dennis Lamp	0	0	0.00	3	0	0	0	0	2.0	0	0	2	1
Dick Tidrow	0	0	3.00	1	0	0	0	0	3.0	1	1	3	3
TOTAL	1	3	4.00	12	4	1	0	0	36.0	28	16	16	24

GAME 1 AT BAL OCT 5

CHI	001	001	000	2	7	0
BAL	000	000	001	1	5	1

Pitchers: HOYT vs McGREGOR, Stewart (7), T.Martinez (8)
Attendance: 51,289

GAME 2 AT BAL OCT 6

CHI	000	000	000	0	5	2
BAL	010	102	00X	4	6	0

Pitchers: BANNISTER, Barojas (7), Lamp (8) vs BODDICKER
Home Runs: Roenicke-BAL
Attendance: 52,347

GAME 3 AT CHI OCT 7

BAL	310	020	014	11	8	1
CHI	010	000	000	1	6	1

Pitchers: FLANAGAN, Stewart (6) vs DOTSON, Tidrow (6), Koosman (9), Lamp (9)
Home Runs: Murray-BAL
Attendance: 46,635

GAME 4 AT CHI OCT 8

BAL	000	000	000	3	3	9	0
CHI	000	000	000	0	0	10	0

Pitchers: Davis, T.MARTINEZ (7) vs BURNS, Barojas (10), Agosto (10), Lamp (10)
Home Runs: Landrum-BAL
Attendance: 45,477

Near neighbors Baltimore and Philadelphia met in a World Series for the first time. Both clubs were led by new managers: Baltimore by Joe Altobelli, who inherited a team built under longtime Orioles manager Earl Weaver, and the Phillies by general manager Paul Owens, who replaced Pat Corrales with himself in midseason.

Both started their top winners in the opener, and the result was a pitchers' duel, with all three runs scored on solo homers. John Denny gave up the first to Jim Dwyer in the first inning, but after that (with late-inning help from Al Holland) he blanked the Orioles, while Baltimore's Scott McGregor, after five and two thirds scoreless innings gave up home runs to Joe Morgan and (the deciding blast two innings later) to Garry Maddox.

The Orioles swept the next four games. In Game 2, Mike Boddicker yielded just three singles (and no walks) to Philadelphia. Though one of the singles led to a run in the fourth inning, giving the Phillies a 1–0 lead, John Lowenstein tied the score with a home run in the fifth. Three more hits in the inning and a sacrifice fly gave the Orioles the lead, 3–1, and three two-out singles in the seventh inning brought in a fourth Baltimore run.

Philadelphia again scored first in Game 3, on leadoff home runs in the second and third innings by Gary Matthews and Joe Morgan. But the Orioles finally got to veteran starter Steve Carlton in the sixth for one run and drove him out after a second run scored an inning later. Carlton suffered the loss when the baserunner he left scored the tie-breaking run from second on an error by shortstop Ivan DeJesus.

The Phillies also lost Game 4 by a single run. Baltimore scored first with two runs in the top of the fourth, but Philadelphia recovered with one run in the fourth and two an inning later. They would not lead again in the Series. Baltimore scored twice in the sixth to go ahead again, and once more in the seventh. The Phillies scored once more with two down in the last of the ninth to draw within one run of a tie, but Joe Morgan lined out to second to end the game.

Home runs by Rick Dempsey and Eddie Murray (who hit two) accounted for four of Baltimore's five runs in the final game—more than enough to support Scott McGregor's five-hit shutout pitching.

Baltimore Orioles (AL), 4; Philadelphia Phillies (NL), 1

BAL (A)

PLAYER/POS	AVG	G	AB	R	H	2B	3B	HR	RB	BB	SO	SB
Benny Ayala, ph	1.000	1	1	1	1	0	0	0	1	0	0	0
Mike Boddicker, p	.000	1	3	0	0	0	0	0	0	1	0	0
Al Bumbry, of	.091	4	11	0	1	1	0	0	1	0	1	0
Todd Cruz, 3b	.125	5	16	1	2	0	0	0	0	1	3	0
Rich Dauer, 2b	.211	5	19	2	4	1	0	0	3	0	3	0
Storm Davis, p	.000	1	2	0	0	0	0	0	0	0	2	0
Rick Dempsey, c	.385	5	13	3	5	4	0	1	2	2	2	0
Jim Dwyer, of	.375	2	8	3	3	1	0	1	1	0	0	0
Mike Flanagan, p	.000	1	1	0	0	0	0	0	0	0	1	0
Dan Ford, of-4	.167	5	12	1	2	0	0	1	1	1	5	0
Tito Landrum, of	.000	3	0	0	0	0	0	0	0	0	0	1
John Lowenstein, of	.385	4	13	2	5	1	0	1	1	0	3	0
Tippy Martinez, p	.000	3	0	0	0	0	0	0	0	0	0	0
Scott McGregor, p	.000	2	5	0	0	0	0	0	0	0	0	0
Eddie Murray, 1b	.250	5	20	2	5	0	0	2	3	1	4	0
Joe Nolan, c	.000	2	2	0	0	0	0	0	0	1	0	0
Jim Palmer, p	.000	1	0	0	0	0	0	0	0	0	0	0
Cal Ripken, ss	.167	5	18	2	3	0	0	0	1	3	4	0
Gary Roenicke, of-2	.000	3	7	0	0	0	0	0	0	2	0	0
Len Sakata, 2b	.000	1	1	0	0	0	0	0	0	0	0	0
John Shelby, of	.444	5	9	1	4	0	0	0	1	0	4	0
Ken Singleton, ph	.000	2	1	0	0	0	0	0	0	1	1	0
Sammy Stewart, p	.000	3	2	0	0	0	0	0	0	0	1	0
TOTAL	.213		164	18	35	8	0	6	17	10	37	1

PITCHER	W	L	ERA	G	GS	CG	SV	SHO	IP	H	ER	BB	SO
Mike Boddicker	1	0	0.00	1	1	1	0	0	9.0	3	0	0	6
Storm Davis	1	0	5.40	1	1	0	0	0	5.0	6	3	1	3
Mike Flanagan	0	0	4.50	1	1	0	0	0	4.0	6	2	1	1
Tippy Martinez	0	0	3.00	3	0	0	2	0	3.0	3	1	0	0
Scott McGregor	1	1	1.06	2	2	1	0	1	17.0	9	2	2	12
Jim Palmer	1	0	0.00	1	0	0	0	0	2.0	2	0	1	1
Sammy Stewart	0	0	0.00	3	0	0	0	0	5.0	2	0	2	6
TOTAL	4	1	1.60	12	5	2	2	1	45.0	31	8	7	29

PHI (N)

PLAYER/POS	AVG	G	AB	R	H	2B	3B	HR	RB	BB	SO	SB
Larry Andersen, p	.000	2	0	0	0	0	0	0	0	0	0	0
Marty Bystrom, p	.000	1	0	0	0	0	0	0	0	0	0	0
Steve Carlton, p	.000	1	3	0	0	0	0	0	0	0	1	0
Ivan DeJesus, ss	.125	5	16	0	2	0	0	0	0	1	2	0
John Denny, p	.200	2	5	1	1	0	0	0	1	0	1	0
Bob Dernier, pr	.000	1	0	1	0	0	0	0	0	0	0	0
Bo Diaz, c	.333	5	15	1	5	1	0	0	0	1	2	0
Greg Gross, of	.000	2	6	0	0	0	0	0	0	0	0	0
Von Hayes, of-1	.000	4	3	0	0	0	0	0	0	0	0	0
Willie Hernandez, p	.000	3	0	0	0	0	0	0	0	0	0	0
Al Holland, p	.000	2	0	0	0	0	0	0	0	0	0	0
Charles Hudson, p	.000	2	2	0	0	0	0	0	0	0	1	0
Joe Lefebvre, of-2	.200	3	5	0	1	1	0	0	0	2	1	0
Sixto Lezcano, of-3	.125	4	8	0	1	0	0	0	0	0	2	0
Garry Maddox, of-3	.250	4	12	1	3	1	0	1	1	0	2	0
Gary Matthews, of	.250	5	16	1	4	0	0	1	1	2	2	0
Joe Morgan, 2b	.263	5	19	3	5	0	1	2	2	2	3	1
Tony Perez, 1b-2	.200	4	10	0	2	0	0	0	0	0	2	0
Ron Reed, p	.000	3	0	0	0	0	0	0	0	0	0	0
Pete Rose, 1b-3,of-1	.313	5	16	1	5	1	0	0	1	1	3	0
Juan Samuel, ph	.000	3	1	0	0	0	0	0	0	0	0	0
Mike Schmidt, 3b	.050	5	20	0	1	0	0	0	0	0	6	0
Ossie Virgil, c-1	.500	3	2	0	1	0	0	0	0	1	0	0
TOTAL	.195		159	9	31	4	1	4	9	7	29	1

PITCHER	W	L	ERA	G	GS	CG	SV	SHO	IP	H	ER	BB	SO
Larry Andersen	0	0	2.25	2	0	0	0	0	4.0	4	1	0	1
Marty Bystrom	0	0	0.00	1	0	0	0	0	1.0	0	0	0	1
Steve Carlton	0	1	2.70	1	1	0	0	0	6.2	5	2	3	7
John Denny	1	1	3.46	2	2	0	0	0	13.0	12	5	3	9
Willie Hernandez	0	0	0.00	3	0	0	0	0	4.0	0	0	1	4
Al Holland	0	0	0.00	2	0	0	1	0	3.2	1	0	0	5
Charles Hudson	0	2	8.64	2	2	0	0	0	8.1	9	8	1	6
Ron Reed	0	0	2.70	3	0	0	0	0	3.1	4	1	2	4
TOTAL	1	4	3.48	16	5	0	1	0	44.0	35	17	10	37

After two games in Chicago, the Cubs appeared headed for their first pennant in 39 years. Rick Sutcliffe and Warren Brusstar shut out the Padres, 13–0, in an opener enlivened by five Cubs home runs, including two homers by Gary Matthews and one by Sutcliffe. In a quieter second game, the Cubs built a 4–1 lead over the first four innings and held on for the win.

When the series moved to San Diego, though, the Padres came to life. In the fifth and sixth innings of Game 3, they obliterated a 1–0 Cubs lead with seven runs, as Ed Whitson and Goose Gossage held the Cubs scoreless after the second inning for what turned into an easy Padres win.

Game 4 was not so easy. San Diego scored first in the third inning, lost their lead in the fourth, tied it in the fifth, went ahead in the seventh, and fell back into a 5–5 tie in the eighth. But in the bottom of the ninth, Steve Garvey's two-run homer sent the series into a fifth game.

Leon Durham put the Cubs ahead with a two-run homer in the first inning of the finale, and Jody Davis added to the lead with a solo shot in the second. Rick Sutcliffe, meanwhile, was setting down Padres as he added five shutout innings to his seven from Game 1. But he gave up two runs in the sixth, and after first baseman Durham allowed a grounder go through his legs to let in the tying run in the seventh, the Cubs watched the pennant slip away as Tony Gwynn's double and Garvey's single drove in the game's final three runs.

San Diego Padres (West), 3; Chicago Cubs (East), 2

SD (W)

PLAYER/POS	AVG	G	AB	R	H	2B	3B	HR	RB	BB	SO	SB
Kurt Bevacqua, ph	.000	2	2	0	0	0	0	0	0	0	0	0
Greg Booker, p	.000	1	0	0	0	0	0	0	0	0	0	0
Bobby Brown, of	.000	3	4	1	0	0	0	0	0	1	2	1
Dave Dravecky, p	.000	3	0	0	0	0	0	0	0	0	0	0
Tim Flannery, ph	.500	3	2	1	1	0	0	0	0	0	0	0
Steve Garvey, 1b	.400	5	20	1	8	1	0	1	7	1	2	0
Rich Gossage, p	.000	3	0	0	0	0	0	0	0	0	0	0
Tony Gwynn, of	.368	5	19	6	7	3	0	0	3	1	2	0
Greg Harris, p	.000	1	0	0	0	0	0	0	0	0	0	0
Andy Hawkins, p	.000	3	0	0	0	0	0	0	0	0	0	0
Terry Kennedy, c	.222	5	18	2	4	0	0	0	1	1	3	0
Craig Lefferts, p	.000	3	0	0	0	0	0	0	0	0	0	0
Tim Lollar, p	.000	1	1	0	0	0	0	0	0	0	1	0
Carmelo Martinez, of	.176	5	17	1	3	0	0	0	0	2	4	0
Kevin McReynolds, of	.300	4	10	2	3	0	0	1	4	3	1	0
Graig Nettles, 3b	.143	4	14	1	2	0	0	0	2	1	1	0
Mario Ramirez, ph	.000	2	2	0	0	0	0	0	0	0	0	0
Luis Salazar, of-2,3b-1	.200	3	5	0	1	0	1	0	0	0	1	0
Eric Show, p	.000	2	1	0	0	0	0	0	0	0	1	0
Champ Summers, ph	.000	2	2	0	0	0	0	0	0	0	1	0
Garry Templeton, ss	.333	5	15	2	5	1	0	0	2	2	0	1
Mark Thurmond, p	1.000	1	1	0	1	0	0	0	0	0	0	0
Ed Whitson, p	.000	3	3	0	0	0	0	0	0	0	1	0
Alan Wiggins, 2b	.316	5	19	4	6	0	0	0	1	2	2	0
TOTAL	.265		155	22	41	5	1	2	20	14	22	2

PITCHER	W	L	ERA	G	GS	CG	SV	SHO	IP	H	ER	BB	SO
Greg Booker	0	0	0.00	1	0	0	0	0	2.0	2	0	1	2
Dave Dravecky	0	0	0.00	3	0	0	0	0	6.0	2	0	0	5
Rich Gossage	0	0	4.50	3	0	0	1	0	4.0	5	2	1	5
Greg Harris	0	0	31.50	1	0	0	0	0	2.0	9	7	3	2
Andy Hawkins	0	0	0.00	3	0	0	0	0	3.2	4	0	2	1
Craig Lefferts	2	0	0.00	3	0	0	0	0	4.0	1	0	1	1
Tim Lollar	0	0	6.23	1	1	0	0	0	4.1	3	3	4	3
Eric Show	0	1	13.50	2	2	0	0	0	5.1	8	8	4	2
Mark Thurmond	0	1	9.82	1	1	0	0	0	3.2	7	4	2	1
Ed Whitson	1	0	1.13	1	1	0	0	0	8.0	5	1	2	6
TOTAL	3	2	5.23	19	5	0	1	0	43.0	42	25	20	28

CHI (E)

PLAYER/POS	AVG	G	AB	R	H	2B	3B	HR	RB	BB	SO	SB
Thad Bosley, ph	.000	2	2	0	0	0	0	0	0	0	2	0
Larry Bowa, ss	.200	5	15	1	3	1	0	0	1	1	0	0
Warren Brusstar, p	.000	3	1	0	0	0	0	0	0	0	0	0
Ron Cey, 3b	.158	5	19	3	3	1	0	1	3	3	3	0
Henry Cotto, of	1.000	3	1	1	1	0	0	0	0	0	0	0
Jody Davis, c	.389	5	18	3	7	0	0	2	6	0	3	0
Bob Dernier, of	.235	5	17	5	4	2	0	1	1	5	4	2
Leon Durham, 1b	.150	5	20	2	3	0	0	2	4	1	4	0
Dennis Eckersley, p	.000	1	2	0	0	0	0	0	0	0	1	0
George Frazier, p	.000	1	0	0	0	0	0	0	0	0	0	0
Richie Hebner, ph	.000	2	1	0	0	0	0	0	0	0	0	0
Steve Lake, c	1.000	1	1	0	1	1	0	0	0	0	0	0
Davey Lopes, of-1	.000	2	1	0	0	0	0	0	0	0	0	0
Gary Matthews, of	.200	5	15	4	3	0	0	2	5	6	4	1
Keith Moreland, of	.333	5	18	3	6	2	0	0	2	1	1	0
Ryne Sandberg, 2b	.368	5	19	3	7	2	0	0	2	3	2	3
Scott Sanderson, p	.000	1	2	0	0	0	0	0	0	0	1	0
Lee Smith, p	.000	2	0	0	0	0	0	0	0	0	0	0
Tim Stoddard, p	.000	2	0	0	0	0	0	0	0	0	0	0
Rick Sutcliffe, p	.500	2	6	1	3	0	0	1	1	0	2	0
Steve Trout, p	.500	2	2	0	1	0	0	0	0	0	0	0
Tom Veryzer, ss-2,3b-1	.000	3	1	0	0	0	0	0	0	0	0	0
Gary Woods, of	.000	1	1	0	0	0	0	0	0	0	1	0
TOTAL	.259		162	26	42	11	0	9	25	20	28	6

PITCHER	W	L	ERA	G	GS	CG	SV	SHO	IP	H	ER	BB	SO
Warren Brusstar	0	0	0.00	3	0	0	0	0	4.1	6	0	0	1
Dennis Eckersley	0	1	8.44	1	1	0	0	0	5.1	9	5	0	0
George Frazier	0	0	10.80	1	0	0	0	0	1.2	2	2	0	1
Scott Sanderson	0	0	5.79	1	1	0	0	0	4.2	6	3	1	2
Lee Smith	0	1	9.00	2	0	0	1	0	2.0	3	2	0	3
Tim Stoddard	0	0	4.50	2	0	0	0	0	2.0	1	1	2	2
Rick Sutcliffe	1	1	3.38	2	2	0	0	0	13.1	9	5	8	10
Steve Trout	1	0	2.00	2	1	0	0	0	9.0	5	2	3	3
TOTAL	2	3	4.25	14	5	0	1	0	42.1	41	20	14	22

GAME 1 AT CHI OCT 2

SD	000	000	000	0	6	1
CHI	203	062	00X	13	16	0

Pitchers: SHOW, Harris (5), Booker (7) vs SUTCLIFFE, Brusstar (8)
Home Runs: Dernier-CHI, Matthews-CHI (2), Sutcliffe-CHI, Cey-CHI
Attendance: 36,282

GAME 2 AT CHI OCT 3

SD	000	101	000	2	5	0
CHI	102	100	00X	4	8	1

Pitchers: THURMOND, Hawkins (4), Dravecky (6), Lefferts (8) vs TROUT, Smith (9)
Attendance: 36,282

GAME 3 AT SD OCT 4

CHI	010	000	000	1	5	0
SD	000	034	00X	7	11	0

Pitchers: ECKERSLEY, Frazier (6), Stoddard (8) vs WHITSON, Gossage (9)
Home Runs: McReynolds-SD
Attendance: 58,346

GAME 4 AT SD OCT 6

CHI	000	300	020	5	8	1
SD	002	010	202	7	11	0

Pitchers: Sanderson, Brusstar (5), Stoddard (7), SMITH (8) vs Lollar, Hawkins (5), Dravecky (6), Gossage (8), LEFFERTS (9)
Home Runs: Davis-CHI, Durham-CHI, Garvey-SD
Attendance: 58,354

GAME 5 AT SD OCT 7

CHI	210	000	000	3	5	1
SD	000	002	40X	6	8	0

Pitchers: SUTCLIFFE, Trout (7), Brusstar (8) vs Show, Hawkins (2), Dravecky (4), LEFFERTS (6), Gossage (8)
Home Runs: Durham-CHI, Davis-CHI
Attendance: 58,359

The heavily favored Tigers swept the series, but not without difficulty, despite a 14-hit, three-homer, 8–1 romp in the opener.

Games 2 and 3 were much tighter. In the second game, after Detroit had built a 3–0 lead over the first three innings, rookie starter Bret Saberhagen settled down and blanked the Tigers for the next five innings as K.C. inched its way to a tie with runs in the fourth, seventh, and eighth. Through the ninth and 10th innings, Tigers reliever Aurelio Lopez and Dan Quisenberry of the Royals dueled scorelessly, but in the top of the 11th Johnny Grubb doubled home two Tigers runs. Lopez struggled but held the Royals scoreless in the last of the 11th for the win.

In Game 3 the Royals' Charlie Leibrandt and Tigers' Milt Wilcox and Willie Hernandez hurled matching three-hitters. But the Tigers secured the game—and the pennant—when Chet Lemon scored on a broken double play in the second inning for the game's only run.

Detroit Tigers (East), 3;
Kansas City Royals (West), 0

DET (E)

PLAYER/POS	AVG	G	AB	R	H	2B	3B	HR	RB	BB	SO	SB
Doug Baker, ss	.000	1	0	0	0	0	0	0	0	0	0	0
Dave Bergman, 1b-1	1.000	2	1	1	1	0	0	0	0	0	0	1
Tom Brookens, 2b-1,3b-1	.000	2	2	0	0	0	0	0	0	0	1	0
Marty Castillo, 3b	.250	3	8	0	2	0	0	0	2	0	3	1
Darrell Evans, 1b-3,3b-1	.300	3	10	1	3	1	0	0	1	1	0	1
Barbaro Garbey, dh-2	.333	3	9	1	3	0	0	0	0	0	1	0
Kirk Gibson, of	.417	3	12	2	5	1	0	1	2	2	1	1
Johnny Grubb, dh	.250	1	4	0	1	1	0	0	2	0	0	0
Willie Hernandez, p	.000	3	0	0	0	0	0	0	0	0	0	0
Larry Herndon, of	.200	2	5	1	1	0	0	1	1	1	2	0
Ruppert Jones, of	.000	2	5	1	0	0	0	0	0	1	1	0
Rusty Kuntz, of	.000	1	1	0	0	0	0	0	0	0	0	0
Chet Lemon, of	.000	3	13	1	0	0	0	0	0	0	1	0
Aurelio Lopez, p	.000	1	0	0	0	0	0	0	0	0	0	0
Jack Morris, p	.000	1	0	0	0	0	0	0	0	0	0	0
Lance Parrish, c	.250	3	12	1	3	1	0	1	3	0	3	0
Dan Petry, p	.000	1	0	0	0	0	0	0	0	0	0	0
Alan Trammell, ss	.364	3	11	2	4	0	1	1	3	3	1	0
Lou Whitaker, 2b	.143	3	14	3	2	0	0	0	0	0	3	0
Milt Wilcox, p	.000	1	0	0	0	0	0	0	0	0	0	0
TOTAL	.234		107	14	25	4	1	4	14	8	17	4

PITCHER	W	L	ERA	G	GS	CG	SV	SHO	IP	H	ER	BB	SO
Willie Hernandez	0	0	2.25	3	0	0	1	0	4.0	3	1	1	3
Aurelio Lopez	1	0	0.00	1	0	0	0	0	3.0	4	0	1	2
Jack Morris	1	0	1.29	1	1	0	0	0	7.0	5	1	1	4
Dan Petry	0	0	2.57	1	1	0	0	0	7.0	4	2	1	4
Milt Wilcox	1	0	0.00	1	1	0	0	0	8.0	2	0	2	8
TOTAL	3	0	1.24	7	3	0	1	0	29.0	18	4	6	21

KC (W)

PLAYER/POS	AVG	G	AB	R	H	2B	3B	HR	RB	BB	SO	SB
Steve Balboni, 1b	.091	3	11	0	1	0	0	0	0	1	4	0
Buddy Biancalana, ss	.000	2	1	0	0	0	0	0	0	0	1	0
Bud Black, p	.000	1	0	0	0	0	0	0	0	0	0	0
George Brett, 3b	.231	3	13	0	3	0	0	0	0	0	2	0
Onix Concepcion, ss	.000	3	7	0	0	0	0	0	0	0	0	0
Mark Huismann, p	.000	1	0	0	0	0	0	0	0	0	0	0
Dane Iorg, ph	.500	2	2	0	1	0	0	0	1	0	0	0
Lynn Jones, of-2	.200	3	5	1	1	0	0	0	0	0	0	0
Mike Jones, p	.000	1	0	0	0	0	0	0	0	0	0	0
Charlie Leibrandt, p	.000	1	0	0	0	0	0	0	0	0	0	0
Hal McRae, ph	1.000	2	2	0	2	1	0	0	1	0	0	0
Darryl Motley, of	.167	3	12	0	2	0	0	0	1	1	3	0
Jorge Orta, dh	.100	3	10	1	1	0	1	0	1	0	2	0
Greg Pryor, 3b	.000	1	0	0	0	0	0	0	0	0	0	0
Dan Quisenberry, p	.000	1	0	0	0	0	0	0	0	0	0	0
Bret Saberhagen, p	.000	1	0	0	0	0	0	0	0	0	0	0
Pat Sheridan, of	.000	3	6	1	0	0	0	0	0	3	3	0
Don Slaught, c	.364	3	11	0	4	0	0	0	0	0	0	0
U. L. Washington, ph	.000	2	1	0	0	0	0	0	0	0	1	0
John Wathan, dh	.000	1	1	0	0	0	0	0	0	0	0	0
Frank White, 2b	.091	3	11	1	1	0	0	0	0	0	3	0
Willie Wilson, of	.154	3	13	0	2	0	0	0	0	1	2	0
TOTAL	.170		106	4	18	1	1	0	4	6	21	0

PITCHER	W	L	ERA	G	GS	CG	SV	SHO	IP	H	ER	BB	SO
Bud Black	0	1	7.20	1	1	0	0	0	5.0	7	4	1	3
Mark Huismann	0	0	6.75	1	0	0	0	0	2.2	6	2	1	2
Mike Jones	0	0	6.75	1	0	0	0	0	1.1	1	1	0	0
Charlie Leibrandt	0	1	1.13	1	1	1	0	0	8.0	3	1	4	6
Dan Quisenberry	0	1	3.00	1	0	0	0	0	3.0	2	1	1	1
Bret Saberhagen	0	0	2.25	1	1	0	0	0	8.0	6	2	1	5
TOTAL	0	3	3.54	6	3	1	0	0	28.0	25	11	8	17

GAME 1 AT KC OCT 2

DET	200 110 121	8 14 0
KC	000 000 100	1 5 0

Pitchers: MORRIS, Hernandez (8) vs BLACK, Huismann (6), M.Jones (8)
Home Runs: Herndon-DET, Trammell-DET, Parrish-DET
Attendance: 41,973

GAME 2 AT KC OCT 3

DET	201 000 000 02	5 8 1
KC	000 100 110 00	3 10 3

Pitchers: Petry, Hernandez (8), LOPEZ (9) vs Saberhagen, QUISENBERRY (9)
Home Runs: Gibson-DET
Attendance: 42,019

GAME 3 AT DET OCT 5

KC	000 000 000	0 3 3
DET	010 000 00X	1 3 0

Pitchers: LEIBRANDT vs WILCOX, Hernandez (9)
Attendance: 52,168

Few objective observers expected the Padres (playing in their first World Series) to best the mighty Tigers—and they didn't. Detroit's first two batters in Game 1 hit safely to produce the Series' first scoring before an out had been recorded. San Diego countered with three two-out hits in their half of the first to go ahead, 2–1. But Detroit starter Jack Morris settled down to shut out the Padres over the final eight innings, and his Tigers scored the tying and winning runs in the fifth on Larry Herndon's two-run homer.

The Tigers scored again in Game 2 before the first out was recorded and drove out Ed Whitson with three first-inning runs on five singles. But this time Detroit was shut out (by relievers Andy Hawkins and Craig Lefferts) over the final eight, while San Diego scored single runs in the first and fourth and the winning runs in the fifth on a three-run homer by the normally light-hitting Kurt Bevacqua.

The Tigers won Game 3 on walks—a Series-record 11—as the Series moved to Detroit. After scoring their first two runs in the second on a single and Marty Castillo's home run, they put across two more in the inning on a pair of hits alternated with three walks (the last with the bases full). Three more walks an inning later, followed by a hit batsman, gave Detroit its final run in what became a 5–2 win.

Alan Trammell's two-run homer in the first inning of Game 4 put the Tigers ahead to stay. Jack Morris gave up a solo home run to Terry Kennedy in the second, but Trammell swatted a second two-run shot an inning later for a 4–1 lead. Morris let a second run score on a wild pitch in the ninth, but then retired Kennedy for the third out and his second Series win.

Kirk Gibson's two home runs framed Detroit's scoring in the final game. His two-run shot in the first inning opened the game's scoring. San Diego tied it up with runs in the third and fourth, but Detroit took a 5–3 lead with runs in the fifth and seventh (the latter on Lance Parrish's homer). The unlikely Kurt Bevacqua brought the Padres within a run of tying the game with his second Series homer in the eighth (doubling his regular-season total), but Gibson ended the scoring—and Padres hopes—with a three-run blast half an inning later.

Detroit Tigers (AL), 4; San Diego Padres (NL), 1

DET (A)

PLAYER/POS	AVG	G	AB	R	H	2B	3B	HR	RB	BB	SO	SB
Doug Bair, p	.000	1	0	0	0	0	0	0	0	0	0	0
Dave Bergman, 1b	.000	5	5	0	0	0	0	0	0	0	1	0
Tom Brookens, 3b	.000	3	3	0	0	0	0	0	0	0	1	0
Marty Castillo, 3b	.333	3	9	2	3	0	0	1	2	2	1	0
Darrell Evans, 1b-4,3b-2	.067	5	15	1	1	0	0	0	1	4	4	0
Barbaro Garbey, dh-3	.000	4	12	0	0	0	0	0	0	0	2	0
Kirk Gibson, of	.333	5	18	4	6	0	0	2	7	4	4	3
Johnny Grubb, dh-2	.333	4	3	0	1	0	0	0	0	0	0	0
Willie Hernandez, p	.000	3	0	0	0	0	0	0	0	0	0	0
Larry Herndon, of	.333	5	15	1	5	0	0	1	3	3	2	0
Howard Johnson, ph	.000	1	1	0	0	0	0	0	0	0	0	0
Ruppert Jones, of	.000	2	3	0	0	0	0	0	0	0	1	0
Rusty Kuntz, ph	.000	2	1	0	0	0	0	0	0	1	1	0
Chet Lemon, of	.294	5	17	1	5	0	0	0	1	2	2	2
Aurelio Lopez, p	.000	2	0	0	0	0	0	0	0	0	0	0
Jack Morris, p	.000	2	0	0	0	0	0	0	0	0	0	0
Lance Parrish, c	.278	5	18	3	5	1	0	1	2	3	2	1
Dan Petry, p	.000	2	0	0	0	0	0	0	0	0	0	0
Bill Scherrer, p	.000	3	0	0	0	0	0	0	0	0	0	0
Alan Trammell, ss	.450	5	20	5	9	1	0	2	6	2	2	1
Lou Whitaker, 2b	.278	5	18	6	5	2	0	0	0	4	4	0
Milt Wilcox, p	.000	1	0	0	0	0	0	0	0	0	0	0
TOTAL	.253		158	23	40	4	0	7	23	24	27	7

PITCHER	W	L	ERA	G	GS	CG	SV	SHO	IP	H	ER	BB	SO
Doug Bair	0	0	0.00	1	0	0	0	0	0.2	0	0	0	1
Willie Hernandez	0	0	1.69	3	0	0	2	0	5.1	4	1	0	0
Aurelio Lopez	1	0	0.00	2	0	0	0	0	3.0	1	0	1	4
Jack Morris	2	0	2.00	2	2	2	0	0	18.0	13	4	3	13
Dan Petry	0	1	9.00	2	2	0	0	0	8.0	14	8	5	4
Bill Scherrer	0	0	3.00	3	0	0	0	0	3.0	5	1	0	0
Milt Wilcox	1	0	1.50	1	1	0	0	0	6.0	7	1	2	4
TOTAL	4	1	3.07	14	5	2	2	0	44.0	44	15	11	26

SD (N)

PLAYER/POS	AVG	G	AB	R	H	2B	3B	HR	RB	BB	SO	SB
Kurt Bevacqua, dh	.412	5	17	4	7	2	0	2	4	1	2	0
Bruce Bochy, ph	1.000	1	1	0	1	0	0	0	0	0	0	0
Greg Booker, p	.000	1	0	0	0	0	0	0	0	0	0	0
Bobby Brown, of	.067	5	15	1	1	0	0	0	2	0	4	0
Dave Dravecky, p	.000	2	0	0	0	0	0	0	0	0	0	0
Tim Flannery, 2b	1.000	1	1	0	1	0	0	0	0	0	0	0
Steve Garvey, 1b	.200	5	20	2	4	2	0	0	2	0	2	0
Rich Gossage, p	.000	2	0	0	0	0	0	0	0	0	0	0
Tony Gwynn, of	.263	5	19	1	5	0	0	0	0	3	2	1
Greg Harris, p	.000	1	0	0	0	0	0	0	0	0	0	0
Terry Kennedy, c	.211	5	19	2	4	1	0	1	3	1	1	0
Craig Lefferts, p	.000	3	0	0	0	0	0	0	0	0	0	0
Tim Lollar, p	.000	1	0	0	0	0	0	0	0	0	0	0
Carmelo Martinez, of	.176	5	17	0	3	0	0	0	0	1	9	0
Graig Nettles, 3b	.250	5	12	2	3	0	0	0	2	5	0	0
Ron Roenicke, of-1	.000	2	0	0	0	0	0	0	0	0	0	0
Luis Salazar, of-2,3b-1	.333	4	3	0	1	0	0	0	0	0	0	0
Eric Show, p	.000	1	0	0	0	0	0	0	0	0	0	0
Champ Summers, ph	.000	1	1	0	0	0	0	0	0	0	1	0
Garry Templeton, ss	.316	5	19	1	6	1	0	0	0	0	3	0
Mark Thurmond, p	.000	2	0	0	0	0	0	0	0	0	0	0
Ed Whitson, p	.000	1	0	0	0	0	0	0	0	0	0	0
Alan Wiggins, 2b	.364	5	22	2	8	1	0	0	1	0	2	1
TOTAL	.265		166	15	44	7	0	3	14	11	26	2

PITCHER	W	L	ERA	G	GS	CG	SV	SHO	IP	H	ER	BB	SO
Greg Booker	0	0	9.00	1	0	0	0	0	1.0	0	1	4	0
Dave Dravecky	0	0	0.00	2	0	0	0	0	4.2	3	0	1	5
Rich Gossage	0	0	13.50	2	0	0	0	0	2.2	3	4	1	2
Greg Harris	0	0	0.00	1	0	0	0	0	5.1	3	0	5	5
Andy Hawkins	1	1	0.75	3	0	0	0	0	12.0	4	1	6	4
Craig Lefferts	0	0	0.00	3	0	0	1	0	6.0	2	0	1	7
Tim Lollar	0	1	21.60	1	1	0	0	0	1.2	4	4	4	0
Eric Show	0	1	10.13	1	1	0	0	0	2.2	4	3	1	2
Mark Thurmond	0	1	10.13	2	2	0	0	0	5.1	12	6	3	2
Ed Whitson	0	0	40.50	1	1	0	0	0	0.2	5	3	0	0
TOTAL	1	4	4.71	17	5	0	1	0	42.0	40	22	24	27

GAME 1 AT SD OCT 9

DET	100	020	000	3	8	0
SD	200	000	000	2	8	1

Pitchers: MORRIS vs THURMOND, Hawkins (6), Dravecky (8)
Home Runs: Herndon-DET
Attendance: 57,908

GAME 2 AT SD OCT 10

DET	300	000	000	3	7	3
SD	100	130	00X	5	11	0

Pitchers: PETRY, Lopez (5), Scherrer (6), Bair (7), Hernandez (8) vs Whitson, HAWKINS (1), Lefferts (7)
Home Runs: Bevacqua-SD
Attendance: 57,911

GAME 3 AT DET OCT 12

SD	001	000	100	2	5	0
DET	041	000	00X	5	7	0

Pitchers: LOLLAR, Booker (2), Harris (3) vs WILCOX, Scherrer (7), Hernandez (7)
Home Runs: Castillo-DET
Attendance: 51,970

GAME 4 AT DET OCT 13

SD	010	000	001	2	10	2
DET	202	000	00X	4	7	0

Pitchers: SHOW, Dravecky (3), Lefferts (7), Gossage (8) vs MORRIS
Home Runs: Trammell-DET (2), Kennedy-SD
Attendance: 52,130

GAME 5 AT DET OCT 14

SD	001	200	010	4	10	1
DET	300	010	13X	8	11	1

Pitchers: Thurmond, HAWKINS (1), Lefferts (5), Gossage (7) vs Petry, Scherrer (4), LOPEZ (5), Hernandez (8)
Home Runs: Gibson-DET (2), Parrish-DET, Bevacqua-SD
Attendance: 51,901

The Dodgers' league-leading pitchers held St. Louis to three runs over the first two games, even though the Cardinals recorded eight hits per game. But the Cards' league-leading hitters put their blows to better advantage in the next four games of the expanded NLCS, scoring 26 times for four wins and the pennant.

Fernando Valenzuela captured Game 1 for the Dodgers, thanks in part to some ragged fielding by the usually sharp Cardinals infield. And as Orel Hershiser was holding St. Louis to two runs in Game 2, an errant Cardinals pickoff throw and heavy Dodgers hitting gave him an increasingly comfortable lead.

When the series shifted to St. Louis for Game 3, the Cardinals revived, scoring twice in each of the first two innings for a quick lead, which they held for their first win. In Game 4 they unloaded for nine runs in the second inning, and in Game 5—with the game and series tied in the bottom of the ninth—Ozzie Smith hit his first left-handed home run ever to give St. Louis the series lead.

Back in Los Angeles, the Dodgers scored first in Game 6, and held a 4–1 lead after six innings. But three Cardinals scored on four hits in the seventh, and though Mike Marshall's eighth-inning home run restored the lead to Los Angeles, Jack Clark settled things for St. Louis with a three-run homer in the ninth.

St. Louis Cardinals (East), 4;
Los Angeles Dodgers (West), 2

STL (E)

PLAYER/POS	AVG	G	AB	R	H	2B	3B	HR	RB	BB	SO	SB
Joaquin Andujar, p	.250	2	4	1	1	1	0	0	0	0	1	0
Steve Braun, ph	.000	2	2	0	0	0	0	0	0	0	0	0
Bill Campbell, p	.000	3	0	0	0	0	0	0	0	0	0	0
Cesar Cedeno, of-4	.167	5	12	2	2	1	0	0	0	2	3	0
Jack Clark, 1b	.381	6	21	4	8	0	0	1	4	5	5	0
Vince Coleman, of	.286	3	14	2	4	0	0	0	1	0	2	1
Danny Cox, p	.000	1	2	0	0	0	0	0	0	1	1	0
Ken Dayley, p	.500	5	2	0	1	0	0	0	0	0	0	0
Bob Forsch, p	.000	2	0	0	0	0	0	0	0	0	0	0
Brian Harper, ph	.000	1	1	0	0	0	0	0	0	0	0	0
Tommy Herr, 2b	.333	6	21	2	7	4	0	1	6	5	2	1
Rick Horton, p	.000	3	0	0	0	0	0	0	0	0	0	0
Mike Jorgensen, ph	.000	2	2	0	0	0	0	0	0	0	1	0
Jeff Lahti, p	.000	2	0	0	0	0	0	0	0	0	0	0
Tito Landrum, of-4	.429	5	14	2	6	0	0	0	4	1	1	1
Willie McGee, of	.269	6	26	6	7	1	0	0	3	3	6	2
Tom Nieto, c	.000	1	3	1	0	0	0	0	0	0	2	0
Terry Pendleton, 3b	.208	6	24	2	5	1	0	0	4	1	3	0
Darrell Porter, c	.267	5	15	1	4	1	0	0	0	5	4	0
Ozzie Smith, ss	.435	6	23	4	10	1	1	1	3	3	1	1
John Tudor, p	.000	2	4	1	0	0	0	0	0	0	1	0
Andy Van Slyke, of	.091	5	11	1	1	0	0	0	1	2	1	0
Todd Worrell, p	.000	4	0	0	0	0	0	0	0	0	0	0
TOTAL	.279		201	29	56	10	1	3	26	30	34	6

PITCHER	W	L	ERA	G	GS	CG	SV	SHO	IP	H	ER	BB	SO
Joaquin Andujar	0	1	6.97	2	2	0	0	0	10.1	14	8	4	9
Bill Campbell	0	0	0.00	3	0	0	0	0	2.1	3	0	0	2
Danny Cox	1	0	3.00	1	1	0	0	0	6.0	4	2	5	4
Ken Dayley	0	0	0.00	5	0	0	0	0	6.0	2	0	1	3
Bob Forsch	0	0	5.40	1	1	0	0	0	3.1	3	2	2	0
Rick Horton	0	0	9.00	3	0	0	0	0	3.0	4	3	2	1
Jeff Lahti	1	0	0.00	2	0	0	0	0	2.0	2	0	0	1
John Tudor	1	1	2.84	2	2	0	0	0	12.2	10	4	3	8
Todd Worrell	1	0	1.42	4	0	0	0	0	6.1	4	1	2	3
TOTAL	4	2	3.46	23	6	0	2	0	52.0	46	20	19	31

LA (W)

PLAYER/POS	AVG	G	AB	R	H	2B	3B	HR	RB	BB	SO	SB
Dave Anderson, ss-3,3b-1	.000	4	5	1	0	0	0	0	0	3	1	0
Bob Bailor, 3b	.000	2	1	0	0	0	0	0	0	0	0	0
Greg Brock, 1b-4	.083	5	12	2	1	0	0	1	2	2	2	0
Enos Cabell, 1b-3	.077	5	13	1	1	0	0	0	0	0	3	0
Bobby Castillo, p	.000	1	2	0	0	0	0	0	0	0	1	0
Carlos Diaz, p	.000	2	0	0	0	0	0	0	0	0	0	0
Mariano Duncan, ss	.222	5	18	2	4	2	1	0	1	1	3	1
Pedro Guerrero, of	.250	6	20	2	5	1	0	0	4	5	2	2
Orel Hershiser, p	.286	2	7	1	2	0	0	0	1	0	2	0
Rick Honeycutt, p	.000	2	0	0	0	0	0	0	0	0	0	0
Ken Howell, p	.000	1	0	0	0	0	0	0	0	0	0	0
Jay Johnstone, ph	.000	1	1	0	0	0	0	0	0	0	0	0
Ken Landreaux, of	.389	5	18	4	7	3	0	0	2	1	1	0
Bill Madlock, 3b	.333	6	24	5	8	1	0	3	7	0	2	1
Candy Maldonado, of-3	.143	4	7	0	1	0	0	0	1	0	3	0
Mike Marshall, of	.217	6	23	1	5	2	0	1	3	1	3	0
Len Matuszek, 1b-1,of-1	1.000	3	1	1	1	0	0	0	0	0	0	0
Tom Niedenfuer, p	.000	3	1	0	0	0	0	0	0	0	1	0
Jerry Reuss, p	.000	1	0	0	0	0	0	0	0	0	0	0
Steve Sax, 2b	.300	6	20	1	6	0	0	0	1	1	5	0
Mike Scioscia, c	.250	6	16	2	4	0	0	0	1	4	0	0
Fernando Valenzuela, p	.200	2	5	0	1	0	0	0	0	0	0	0
Bob Welch, p	.000	1	0	0	0	0	0	0	0	0	1	0
Terry Whitfield, ph	.000	1	0	0	0	0	0	0	0	0	0	0
Steve Yeager, c	.000	1	2	0	0	0	0	0	0	0	1	0
TOTAL	.234		197	23	46	12	1	5	23	19	31	4

PITCHER	W	L	ERA	G	GS	CG	SV	SHO	IP	H	ER	BB	SO
Bobby Castillo	0	0	3.38	1	0	0	0	0	5.1	4	2	2	4
Carlos Diaz	0	0	3.00	2	0	0	0	0	3.0	5	1	1	2
Orel Hershiser	1	0	3.52	2	2	1	0	0	15.1	17	6	6	5
Rick Honeycutt	0	0	13.50	2	0	0	0	0	1.1	4	2	1	1
Ken Howell	0	0	0.00	1	0	0	0	0	2.0	0	0	0	2
Tom Niedenfuer	0	2	6.35	3	0	0	1	0	5.2	5	4	2	5
Jerry Reuss	0	1	10.80	1	1	0	0	0	1.2	5	2	1	0
F. Valenzuela	1	0	1.88	2	2	0	0	0	14.1	11	3	10	13
Bob Welch	0	1	6.75	1	1	0	0	0	2.2	5	2	6	2
TOTAL	2	4	3.86	15	6	1	1	0	51.1	56	22	30	34

GAME 1 AT LA OCT 9

STL   000 000 100   1 8 1
LA   000 103 00X   4 8 0

Pitchers: TUDOR, Dayley (6), Campbell (7), Worrell (8) vs VALENZUELA, Niedenfuer (7)
Attendance: 55,270

GAME 2 AT LA OCT 10

STL   001 000 001   2 8 1
LA   003 212 00X   8 13 1

Pitchers: ANDUJAR, Horton (5), Campbell (6), Dayley (7), Lahti (8) vs HERSHISER
Home Runs: Brock-LA
Attendance: 55,222

GAME 3 AT STL OCT 12

LA   000 100 100   2 7 2
STL   220 000 00X   4 8 0

Pitchers: WELCH, Honeycutt (3), Diaz (5), Howell (7) vs COX, Horton (7), Worrell (7), Dayley (9)
Home Runs: Herr-STL
Attendance: 53,708

GAME 4 AT STL OCT 13

LA   000 000 110   2 5 2
STL   090 110 01X   12 15 0

Pitchers: REUSS, Honeycutt (2), Castillo (2), Diaz (8) vs TUDOR, Horton (8), Campbell (9)
Home Runs: Madlock-LA
Attendance: 53,708

GAME 5 AT STL OCT 14

LA   000 200 000   2 5 1
STL   200 000 001   3 5 1

Pitchers: Valenzuela, NIEDENFUER (9) vs Forsch, Dayley (4), Worrell (7), LAHTI (9)
Home Runs: Madlock-LA, Smith-STL
Attendance: 53,708

GAME 6 AT LA OCT 16

STL   001 000 303   7 12 1
LA   110 020 010   5 8 0

Pitchers: Andujar, WORRELL (7), Dayley (9) vs Hershiser, NIEDENFUER (7)
Home Runs: Madlock-LA, Marshall-LA, Clark-STL
Attendance: 55,208

Were it not for the expansion of the ALCS to a best-of-seven series, the Blue Jays would have won the pennant. But after winning three of the first four games, the Jays lost their steam, and K.C. swept to their second pennant.

The pitching of Toronto ace Dave Stieb proved a key to the club's fortunes. Three times he started for the Jays. In the opener he threw eight shutout innings as the Jays won easily. In Game 4 he continued to dominate batters, though three walks in the sixth helped the Royals score a go-ahead run before Toronto pulled it out (for reliever Tom Henke) with a three-run ninth.

Had the series ended there, Stieb would have been a hero. But it didn't, and he was called upon again for Game 7—perhaps with inadequate rest. This time he faltered. After giving up single runs in the second and fourth innings, he loaded the bases in the sixth with two walks and a hit batsman. Jim Sundberg unloaded them with a wind-blown triple, later scoring himself, and the Royals were on the road to victory.

George Brett keyed Kansas City's triumph. His four hits in Game 3 (including two home runs) gave the club its first victory, and his RBI ground out in Game 5 and go-ahead homer in Game 6 proved game-winners in contests the Royals had to win.

Kansas City Royals (West), 4; Toronto Blue Jays (East), 3

KC (W)

PLAYER/POS	AVG	G	AB	R	H	2B	3B	HR	RBI	BB	SO	SB
Steve Balboni, 1b	.120	7	25	1	3	0	0	0	1	2	8	0
Buddy Biancalana, ss	.222	7	18	2	4	1	0	0	1	1	6	0
Bud Black, p	.000	3	0	0	0	0	0	0	0	0	0	0
George Brett, 3b	.348	7	23	6	8	2	0	3	5	7	5	0
Onix Concepcion, ss	.000	4	1	0	0	0	0	0	0	0	0	0
Steve Farr, p	.000	2	0	0	0	0	0	0	0	0	0	0
Mark Gubicza, p	.000	2	0	0	0	0	0	0	0	0	0	0
Dane Iorg, ph	.500	4	2	0	1	1	0	0	0	2	0	0
Danny Jackson, p	.000	2	0	0	0	0	0	0	0	0	0	0
Lynn Jones, of	.000	5	0	0	0	0	0	0	0	0	0	0
Charlie Leibrandt, p	.000	3	0	0	0	0	0	0	0	0	0	0
Hal McRae, dh	.261	6	23	1	6	2	0	0	3	1	6	0
Darryl Motley, of	.333	2	3	1	1	0	0	0	1	1	2	0
Jorge Orta, dh-1	.000	2	5	0	0	0	0	0	0	0	1	0
Jamie Quirk, ph	.000	1	1	0	0	0	0	0	0	0	0	0
Dan Quisenberry, p	.000	4	0	0	0	0	0	0	0	0	0	0
Bret Saberhagen, p	.000	2	0	0	0	0	0	0	0	0	0	0
Pat Sheridan, of	.150	7	20	4	3	0	0	2	3	2	3	0
Lonnie Smith, of	.250	7	28	2	7	2	0	0	1	3	6	1
Jim Sundberg, c	.167	7	24	3	4	1	1	1	6	1	7	0
Frank White, 2b	.200	7	25	1	5	0	0	0	3	1	2	0
Willie Wilson, of	.310	7	29	5	9	0	1	0	1	2	1	5	1
TOTAL	.225		227	26	51	9	1	7	26	22	51	2

PITCHER	W	L	ERA	G	GS	CG	SV	SHO	IP	H	ER	BB	SO
Bud Black	0	0	1.69	3	1	0	0	0	10.2	11	2	4	8
Steve Farr	1	0	1.42	2	0	0	0	0	6.1	4	1	1	3
Mark Gubicza	1	0	3.24	2	1	0	0	0	8.1	4	3	4	4
Danny Jackson	1	0	0.00	2	1	1	0	1	10.0	10	0	1	7
Charlie Leibrandt	1	2	5.28	3	2	0	0	0	15.1	17	9	4	6
Dan Quisenberry	0	1	3.86	4	0	0	1	0	4.2	7	2	0	3
Bret Saberhagen	0	0	6.14	2	2	0	0	0	7.1	12	5	2	6
TOTAL	4	3	3.16	18	7	1	1	1	62.2	65	22	16	37

TOR (E)

PLAYER/POS	AVG	G	AB	R	H	2B	3B	HR	RBI	BB	SO	SB
Jim Acker, p	.000	2	0	0	0	0	0	0	0	0	0	0
Doyle Alexander, p	.000	2	0	0	0	0	0	0	0	0	0	0
Jesse Barfield, of	.280	7	25	3	7	1	0	1	4	3	7	1
George Bell, of	.321	7	28	4	9	3	0	0	1	0	4	0
Jeff Burroughs, ph	.000	1	1	0	0	0	0	0	0	0	0	0
Jim Clancy, p	.000	1	0	0	0	0	0	0	0	0	0	0
Tony Fernandez, ss	.333	7	24	2	8	2	0	0	2	1	2	0
Cecil Fielder, dh	.333	3	3	0	1	1	0	0	0	0	1	0
Damaso Garcia, 2b	.233	7	30	4	7	4	0	0	1	3	3	0
Jeff Hearron, c	.000	2	0	0	0	0	0	0	0	0	0	0
Tom Henke, p	.000	3	0	0	0	0	0	0	0	0	0	0
Garth Iorg, 3b	.133	6	15	1	2	0	0	0	1	0	3	0
Cliff Johnson, dh	.368	7	19	1	7	2	0	0	2	1	4	0
Jimmy Key, p	.000	2	0	0	0	0	0	0	0	0	0	0
Dennis Lamp, p	.000	3	0	0	0	0	0	0	0	0	0	0
Gary Lavelle, p	.000	1	0	0	0	0	0	0	0	0	0	0
Manny Lee, 2b	.000	1	0	0	0	0	0	0	0	0	0	0
Lloyd Moseby, of	.226	7	31	5	7	1	0	0	4	2	3	1
Rance Mulliniks, 3b	.364	5	11	1	4	1	0	1	3	2	2	0
Al Oliver, dh	.375	5	8	0	3	1	0	0	3	0	0	0
Dave Stieb, p	.000	3	0	0	0	0	0	0	0	0	0	0
Lou Thornton, pr	.000	2	0	1	0	0	0	0	0	0	0	0
Willie Upshaw, 1b	.231	7	26	2	6	2	0	0	1	1	4	0
Ernie Whitt, c	.190	7	21	1	4	1	0	0	2	2	4	0
TOTAL	.269		242	25	65	19	0	2	23	16	37	2

PITCHER	W	L	ERA	G	GS	CG	SV	SHO	IP	H	ER	BB	SO
Jim Acker	0	0	0.00	2	0	0	0	0	6.0	2	0	0	5
Doyle Alexander	0	1	8.71	2	2	0	0	0	10.1	14	10	3	9
Jim Clancy	0	1	9.00	1	0	0	0	0	1.0	2	1	1	0
Tom Henke	2	0	4.26	3	0	0	0	0	6.1	5	3	4	4
Jimmy Key	0	1	5.19	2	2	0	0	0	8.2	15	5	2	5
Dennis Lamp	0	0	0.00	3	0	0	0	0	9.1	2	0	1	10
Gary Lavelle	0	0	—	1	0	0	0	0	0.0	0	0	1	0
Dave Stieb	1	1	3.10	3	3	0	0	0	20.1	11	7	10	18
TOTAL	3	4	3.77	17	7	0	0	0	62.0	51	26	22	51

GAME 1 AT TOR OCT 8

```
KC    000 000 001    1  5  1
TOR   023 100 00X    6 11  0
```
Pitchers: LEIBRANDT, Farr (3), Gubicza (5), Jackson (8) vs STIEB, Henke (9)
Attendance: 39,115

GAME 2 AT TOR OCT 9

```
KC    002 100 001    1  5 10  3
TOR   000 102 010    2  6 10  0
```
Pitchers: Black, QUISENBERRY (8) vs Key, Lamp (4), Lavelle (8), HENKE (8)
Home Runs: Wilson-KC, Sheridan-KC
Attendance: 34,029

GAME 3 AT KC OCT 11

```
TOR   000 050 000    5 13  1
KC    100 112 01X    6 10  1
```
Pitchers: Alexander, Lamp (6), CLANCY (8) vs Saberhagen, Black (5), FARR (5)
Home Runs: Brett-KC (2), Barfield-TOR, Mulliniks-TOR, Sundberg-KC
Attendance: 40,224

GAME 4 AT KC OCT 12

```
TOR   000 000 003    3  7  0
KC    000 001 000    1  2  0
```
Pitchers: Stieb, HENKE (7) vs LEIBRANDT, Quisenberry (9)
Attendance: 41,112

GAME 5 AT KC OCT 13

```
TOR   000 000 000    0  8  0
KC    110 000 00X    2  8  0
```
Pitchers: KEY, Acker (6) vs JACKSON
Attendance: 40,046

GAME 6 AT TOR OCT 15

```
KC    101 012 000    5  8  1
TOR   101 001 000    3  8  2
```
Pitchers: GUBICZA, Black (6), Quisenberry (9) vs ALEXANDER, Lamp (6)
Home Runs: Brett-KC
Attendance: 37,557

GAME 7 AT TOR OCT 16

```
KC    010 104 000    6  8  0
TOR   000 010 001    2  8  1
```
Pitchers: Saberhagen, LEIBRANDT (4), Quisenberry (9) vs STIEB, Acker (6)
Home Runs: Sheridan-KC
Attendance: 32,084

The underdog Royals surprised St. Louis with superior hitting and pitching and even outstole the speedy Cards, six bases to two. Still, had an umpire not muffed a call at first base in Game 6, St. Louis might have emerged from the game wearing the world crown.

The Cardinals broke a 1–1 tie in the fourth inning of the opener with back-to-back doubles off Danny Jackson and held on behind the strong pitching of John Tudor and reliever Todd Worrell for a 3–1 win. In Game 2, except for the fourth inning, when he yielded a single and two doubles (for two runs) before retiring his first batter, Cardinals starter Danny Cox held the Royals in check. Royals starter Charlie Leibrandt hurled even more effectively, holding St. Louis to two hits—until the ninth inning, when four hits (three of them doubles) produced four runs and a second Card victory.

Kansas City finally demonstrated its punch in Game 3. Frank White hit a two-run homer in the fifth, and the Royals scored four more times to win behind the six-hit hurling of sophomore sensation Bret Saberhagen. The next day, though, Royals bats died again against John Tudor, who shut them out on five hits. Three Royals pitchers yielded only six hits, but two were home runs to Tito Landrum and Willie McGee, and one was a triple to Terry Pendleton, who scored on a squeeze play.

Down three games to one, the Royals hammered 11 hits in Game 5 for six runs to win behind Danny Jackson's five-hitter. Seven hits in the first eight innings of Game 6, though, scored no runs against Cardinals starter Danny Cox and reliever Ken Dayley. But in the last of the ninth, with the Cards ahead, 1–0, and Todd Worrell now pitching, Royals pinch hitter Jorge Orta was ruled safe at first on what the cameras showed clearly as an out. This miscall, followed by a pop foul that first baseman Jack Clark should have caught but didn't, opened the door to disintegration by St. Louis. A single and passed ball put Royals at second and third, and, after an intentional walk to set up the double play, pinch hitter Dane Iorg singled home the tying and winning runs for the Royals.

The Cardinals threw seven pitchers at Kansas City in the finale in a vain attempt to halt the Royals' 14-hit, 11-run attack, while Bret Saberhagen stopped the Cards cold on five hits to bring the Royals their first world title.

Kansas City Royals (AL), 4; St. Louis Cardinals (NL), 3

KC (A)

PLAYER/POS	AVG	G	AB	R	H	2B	3B	HR	RB	BB	SO	SB
Steve Balboni, 1b	.320	7	25	2	8	0	0	0	3	5	4	0
Joe Beckwith, p	.000	1	0	0	0	0	0	0	0	0	0	0
Buddy Biancalana, ss	.278	7	18	2	5	0	0	0	2	5	4	0
Bud Black, p	.000	2	1	0	0	0	0	0	0	0	1	0
George Brett, 3b	.370	7	27	5	10	1	0	0	1	4	7	1
Onix Concepcion, ss-2	.000	3	0	1	0	0	0	0	0	0	0	0
Dane Iorg, ph	.500	2	2	0	1	0	0	0	2	0	0	0
Danny Jackson, p	.000	2	6	0	0	0	0	0	0	0	5	0
Lynn Jones, of-4	.667	6	3	0	2	1	1	0	0	0	0	0
Charlie Leibrandt, p	.000	2	4	0	0	0	0	0	0	0	2	0
Hal McRae, ph	.000	3	1	0	0	0	0	0	0	1	0	0
Darryl Motley, of-4	.364	5	11	1	4	0	0	1	3	0	1	0
Jorge Orta, ph	.333	3	3	0	1	0	0	0	0	0	0	0
Greg Pryor, 3b	.000	1	0	0	0	0	0	0	0	0	0	0
Dan Quisenberry, p	.000	4	0	0	0	0	0	0	0	0	0	0
Bret Saberhagen, p	.000	2	7	1	0	0	0	0	0	0	4	0
Pat Sheridan, of-4	.222	5	18	0	4	2	0	0	1	0	7	0
Lonnie Smith, of	.333	7	27	4	9	3	0	0	4	3	8	2
Jim Sundberg, c	.250	7	24	6	6	2	0	0	1	6	4	0
John Wathan, ph	.000	2	1	0	0	0	0	0	0	0	1	0
Frank White, 2b	.250	7	28	4	7	3	0	1	6	3	4	1
Willie Wilson, of	.367	7	30	2	11	0	1	0	3	1	4	3
TOTAL	.288		236	28	68	12	2	2	26	28	56	7

PITCHER	W	L	ERA	G	GS	CG	SV	SHO	IP	H	ER	BB	SO
Joe Beckwith	0	0	0.00	1	0	0	0	0	2.0	1	0	0	3
Bud Black	0	1	5.06	2	1	0	0	0	5.1	4	3	5	4
Danny Jackson	1	1	1.69	2	2	1	0	0	16.0	9	3	5	12
Charlie Leibrandt	0	1	2.76	2	2	0	0	0	16.1	10	5	4	10
Dan Quisenberry	1	0	2.08	4	0	0	0	0	4.1	5	1	3	3
Bret Saberhagen	2	0	0.50	2	2	2	0	1	18.0	11	1	1	10
TOTAL	4	3	1.89	13	7	3	0	1	62.0	40	13	18	42

STL (N)

PLAYER/POS	AVG	G	AB	R	H	2B	3B	HR	RB	BB	SO	SB
Joaquin Andujar, p	.000	2	1	0	0	0	0	0	0	0	1	0
Steve Braun, ph	.000	1	1	0	0	0	0	0	0	0	0	0
Bill Campbell, p	.000	3	0	0	0	0	0	0	0	0	0	0
Cesar Cedeno, of	.133	5	15	1	2	1	0	0	1	2	2	0
Jack Clark, 1b	.240	7	25	1	6	2	0	0	4	3	9	0
Danny Cox, p	.000	2	4	0	0	0	0	0	0	0	2	0
Ken Dayley, p	.000	4	0	0	0	0	0	0	0	0	0	0
Ivan DeJesus, ph	.000	1	1	0	0	0	0	0	0	0	0	0
Bob Forsch, p	.000	2	0	0	0	0	0	0	0	0	0	0
Brian Harper, ph	.250	4	4	0	1	0	0	0	1	0	1	0
Tommy Herr, 2b	.154	7	26	2	4	2	0	0	0	2	2	0
Rick Horton, p	.000	3	1	0	0	0	0	0	0	0	0	0
Mike Jorgensen, of-1	.000	2	3	0	0	0	0	0	0	1	0	0
Jeff Lahti, p	.000	3	0	0	0	0	0	0	0	0	0	0
Tito Landrum, of	.360	7	25	3	9	2	0	1	1	0	2	0
Tom Lawless, pr	.000	1	0	0	0	0	0	0	0	0	0	0
Willie McGee, of	.259	7	27	2	7	2	0	1	2	1	3	1
Tom Nieto, c	.000	2	5	0	0	0	0	0	1	1	2	0
Terry Pendleton, 3b	.261	7	23	3	6	1	1	0	3	3	2	0
Darrell Porter, c	.133	5	15	0	2	0	0	0	0	2	5	0
Ozzie Smith, ss	.087	7	23	1	2	0	0	0	0	4	0	1
John Tudor, p	.000	3	5	0	0	0	0	0	0	0	4	0
Andy Van Slyke, of	.091	6	11	0	1	0	0	0	0	0	5	0
Todd Worrell, p	.000	3	1	0	0	0	0	0	0	0	1	0
TOTAL	.185		216	13	40	10	1	2	13	18	42	2

PITCHER	W	L	ERA	G	GS	CG	SV	SHO	IP	H	ER	BB	SO
Joaquin Andujar	0	1	9.00	2	1	0	0	0	4.0	10	4	4	3
Bill Campbell	0	0	2.25	3	0	0	0	0	4.0	4	1	2	5
Danny Cox	0	0	1.29	2	2	0	0	0	14.0	14	2	4	13
Ken Dayley	1	0	0.00	4	0	0	0	0	6.0	1	0	3	5
Bob Forsch	0	1	12.00	2	1	0	0	0	3.0	6	4	1	3
Rick Horton	0	0	6.75	3	0	0	0	0	4.0	4	3	5	5
Jeff Lahti	0	0	12.27	3	0	0	1	0	3.2	10	5	0	2
John Tudor	2	1	3.00	3	3	1	0	1	18.0	15	6	7	14
Todd Worrell	0	1	3.86	3	0	0	1	0	4.2	4	2	2	6
TOTAL	3	4	3.96	25	7	1	2	1	61.1	68	27	28	56

GAME 1 AT KC OCT 19

STL	001	100	001	3	7	1
KC	010	000	000	1	8	0

Pitchers: TUDOR, Worrell (7) vs JACKSON, Quisenberry (8), Black (9)
Attendance: 41,650

GAME 2 AT KC OCT 20

STL	000	000	004	4	6	0
KC	000	200	000	2	9	0

Pitchers: Cox, DAYLEY (8), Lahti (9) vs LEIBRANDT, Quisenberry (9)
Attendance: 41,656

GAME 3 AT STL OCT 22

KC	000	220	200	6	11	0
STL	000	001	000	1	6	0

Pitchers: SABERHAGEN vs ANDUJAR, Campbell (5), Horton (6), Dayley (8)
Home Runs: White-KC
Attendance: 53,634

GAME 4 AT STL OCT 23

KC	000	000	000	0	5	1
STL	011	010	00X	3	6	0

Pitchers: BLACK, Beckwith (6), Quisenberry (8) vs TUDOR
Home Runs: Landrum-STL, McGee-STL
Attendance: 53,634

GAME 5 AT STL OCT 24

KC	130	000	011	6	11	2
STL	100	000	000	1	5	1

Pitchers: JACKSON vs FORSCH, Horton (2), Campbell (4), Worrell (6), Lahti (8)
Attendance: 53,634

GAME 6 AT KC OCT 26

STL	000	000	010	1	5	0
KC	000	000	002	2	10	0

Pitchers: Cox, Dayley (8), WORRELL (9) vs Leibrandt, QUISENBERRY (8)
Attendance: 41,628

GAME 7 AT KC OCT 27

STL	000	000	000	0	5	0
KC	023	060	00X	11	14	0

Pitchers: TUDOR, Campbell (3), Lahti (5), Horton (5), Andujar (5), Forsch (5), Dayley (7) vs SABERHAGEN
Home Runs: Motley-KC
Attendance: 41,658

Houston pitcher Mike Scott overwhelmed the Mets in Games 1 and 4, and would have faced them a third time in Game 7 if the Astros had won Game 6. They tried, scoring three runs in the first as Bob Knepper shut out the Mets on two hits through eight innings of the sixth game. But in the top of the ninth New York tied the game and held on into extra innings. No one scored again until the Mets put a run across in the 14th. Billy Hatcher tied it up again later in the 14th with a home run just inside the left field foul pole. Two innings later the Mets (aided by a pair of wild pitches) scored three runs. Again the Astros came back, scoring twice, but fell just short as Jesse Orosco struck out Kevin Bass with two men on base to win his third game of the series and give New York the pennant.

In the series opener Houston scored just one run off Dwight Gooden, but it was enough, as Mike Scott, fanning 14, shut out the Mets on five hits. New York came back with five runs in Game 2 to win behind Bob Ojeda, who gave up 10 hits but only one run. In Game 3 the Astros held the lead into the last of the sixth, when New York tied the score with four runs. Houston retook the lead in the seventh with a run, but Len Dykstra won it for New York with a two-run homer in the bottom of the ninth.

The Astros' win in Game 4 evened the series. Houston had scored three runs by the time Scott (on his way to a three-hitter) gave the Mets their only run in the eighth. Houston's Nolan Ryan gave up only two hits in the first nine innings of Game 5 (one of them Darryl Strawberry's game-tying solo homer in the fifth), striking out 12. But New York's Gooden also yielded only one run in 10 innings of work. Charlie Kerfeld shut out the Mets in the 10th and 11th, and the Mets' Orosco stopped Houston in the 11th and 12th. But in the last of the 12th, Gary Carter singled home a run off Kerfeld to end the game (and his series-long batting slump)—setting the stage for the 16-inning marathon the next day.

New York Mets (East), 4; Houston Astros (West), 2

NY (E)

PLAYER/POS	AVG	G	AB	R	H	2B	3B	HR	RB	BB	SO	SB
Rick Aguilera, p	.000	2	0	0	0	0	0	0	0	0	0	0
Wally Backman, 2b	.238	6	21	5	5	0	0	0	2	2	4	1
Gary Carter, c	.148	6	27	1	4	1	0	0	2	2	5	0
Ron Darling, p	.000	1	1	0	0	0	0	0	0	0	0	0
Lenny Dykstra, of	.304	6	23	3	7	1	1	1	3	2	4	1
Kevin Elster, ss	.000	4	3	0	0	0	0	0	0	0	1	0
Sid Fernandez, p	.000	1	1	0	0	0	0	0	0	0	0	0
Dwight Gooden, p	.000	2	5	0	0	0	0	0	0	0	2	0
Danny Heep, of-1	.250	5	4	0	1	0	0	0	1	0	2	0
Keith Hernandez, 1b	.269	6	26	3	7	1	1	0	3	3	6	0
Howard Johnson, ph	.000	2	2	0	0	0	0	0	0	0	0	0
Ray Knight, 3b	.167	6	24	1	4	0	0	0	2	1	5	0
Lee Mazzilli, ph	.200	5	5	0	1	0	0	0	0	0	3	0
Roger McDowell, p	.000	2	1	0	0	0	0	0	0	0	0	0
Kevin Mitchell, of	.250	2	8	1	2	0	0	0	0	0	1	0
Bob Ojeda, p	.000	2	5	1	0	0	0	0	0	0	2	0
Jesse Orosco, p	.000	4	0	0	0	0	0	0	0	0	0	0
Rafael Santana, ss	.176	6	17	0	3	0	0	0	0	0	3	0
Doug Sisk, p	.000	1	0	0	0	0	0	0	0	0	0	0
Darryl Strawberry, of	.227	6	22	4	5	1	0	2	5	3	12	1
Tim Teufel, 2b	.167	2	6	0	1	0	0	0	0	0	0	0
Mookie Wilson, of	.115	6	26	2	3	0	0	0	1	1	7	1
TOTAL	.189		227	21	43	4	2	3	19	14	57	4

PITCHER	W	L	ERA	G	GS	CG	SV	SHO	IP	H	ER	BB	SO
Rick Aguilera	0	0	0.00	2	0	0	0	0	5.0	2	0	2	2
Ron Darling	0	0	7.20	1	1	0	0	0	5.0	6	4	2	5
Sid Fernandez	0	1	4.50	1	1	0	0	0	6.0	3	3	1	5
Dwight Gooden	0	1	1.06	2	2	0	0	0	17.0	16	2	5	9
Roger McDowell	0	0	0.00	2	0	0	0	0	7.0	1	0	0	3
Bob Ojeda	1	0	2.57	2	2	1	0	0	14.0	15	4	4	6
Jesse Orosco	3	0	3.38	4	0	0	0	0	8.0	5	3	2	10
Doug Sisk	0	0	0.00	1	0	0	0	0	1.0	1	0	1	0
TOTAL	4	2	2.29	15	6	1	0	0	63.0	49	16	17	40

HOU (W)

PLAYER/POS	AVG	G	AB	R	H	2B	3B	HR	RB	BB	SO	SB
Larry Andersen, p	.000	2	0	0	0	0	0	0	0	0	0	0
Alan Ashby, c	.130	6	23	2	3	1	0	1	2	2	1	0
Kevin Bass, of	.292	6	24	0	7	2	0	0	4	4	2	2
Jeff Calhoun, p	.000	1	0	0	0	0	0	0	0	0	0	0
Jose Cruz, of	.192	6	26	0	5	0	0	0	2	1	8	0
Glenn Davis, 1b	.269	6	26	3	7	1	0	1	3	1	3	0
Bill Doran, 2b	.222	6	27	3	6	0	0	1	3	2	2	2
Phil Garner, 3b	.222	3	9	1	2	1	0	0	2	1	2	0
Billy Hatcher, of	.280	6	25	4	7	0	0	1	2	3	2	3
Charlie Kerfeld, p	.000	3	0	0	0	0	0	0	0	0	0	0
Bob Knepper, p	.000	2	5	0	0	0	0	0	0	1	2	0
Davey Lopes, ph	.000	3	2	1	0	0	0	0	0	1	0	0
Aurelio Lopez, p	.000	2	0	0	0	0	0	0	0	0	0	0
Jim Pankovits, ph	.000	2	2	0	0	0	0	0	0	0	1	0
Terry Puhl, ph	.667	3	3	0	2	0	0	0	0	0	0	1
Craig Reynolds, ss	.333	4	12	1	4	0	0	0	0	1	3	0
Nolan Ryan, p	.000	2	4	0	0	0	0	0	0	0	2	0
Mike Scott, p	.000	2	6	0	0	0	0	0	0	0	5	0
Dave Smith, p	.000	2	0	0	0	0	0	0	0	0	0	0
Dickie Thon, ss	.250	6	12	1	3	0	0	1	1	0	1	0
Denny Walling, 3b	.158	5	19	1	3	1	0	0	2	0	4	0
TOTAL	.218		225	17	49	6	0	5	17	17	40	8

PITCHER	W	L	ERA	G	GS	CG	SV	SHO	IP	H	ER	BB	SO
Larry Andersen	0	0	0.00	2	0	0	0	0	5.0	1	0	2	3
Jeff Calhoun	0	0	9.00	1	0	0	0	0	1.0	1	1	1	0
Charlie Kerfeld	0	1	2.25	3	0	0	0	0	4.0	2	1	1	4
Bob Knepper	0	0	3.52	2	2	0	0	0	15.1	13	6	1	9
Aurelio Lopez	0	1	8.10	2	0	0	0	0	3.1	7	3	4	3
Nolan Ryan	0	1	3.86	2	2	0	0	0	14.0	9	6	1	17
Mike Scott	2	0	0.50	2	2	2	0	1	18.0	8	1	1	19
Dave Smith	0	1	9.00	2	0	0	0	0	2.0	2	2	3	2
TOTAL	2	4	2.87	16	6	2	0	1	62.2	43	20	14	57

For the second time in the two years of the expanded ALCS, a club that would have been eliminated in a five-game series came back to take the pennant in seven games. The first two games were one-sided. California scored five early runs off Roger Clemens and breezed to an easy 8–1 win in the opener. Boston retaliated in Game 2 with nine runs, breaking the game open with six unanswered runs in the seventh and eighth innings.

Game 3 was close until the Angels homered twice for three runs with two out in the seventh to break a 1–1 tie. In Game 4, the Angels were handed a tie in the last of the ninth when Boston reliever Calvin Schiraldi hit a batter with the bases loaded and won in the 11th on Bobby Grich's RBI single.

The Red Sox, down three games to one, were on the brink of elimination in Game Five, with two outs in the ninth, when Dave Henderson, after fouling off one third-strike pitch, hit the next for a two-run homer that gave Boston a one-run lead. The Angels tied the game in the last of the ninth, but Henderson's sacrifice fly in the 11th put the Sox ahead for good.

Boston needed two more wins and got them with surprising ease, 10–4 and 8–1, as Oil Can Boyd and Clemens redeemed their earlier losses.

Boston Red Sox (East), 4; California Angels (West), 3

BOS (E)

PLAYER/POS	AVG	G	AB	R	H	2B	3B	HR	RB	BB	SO	SB
Tony Armas, of	.125	5	16	1	2	1	0	0	0	0	2	0
Marty Barrett, 2b	.367	7	30	4	11	2	0	0	5	2	2	0
Don Baylor, dh	.346	7	26	6	9	3	0	1	4	2	5	0
Wade Boggs, 3b	.233	7	30	3	7	1	1	0	2	4	1	0
Oil Can Boyd, p	.000	2	0	0	0	0	0	0	0	0	0	0
Bill Buckner, 1b	.214	7	28	3	6	1	0	0	3	0	2	0
Roger Clemens, p	.000	3	0	0	0	0	0	0	0	0	0	0
Steve Crawford, p	.000	1	0	0	0	0	0	0	0	0	0	0
Dwight Evans, of	.214	7	28	2	6	1	0	1	4	3	3	0
Rich Gedman, c	.357	7	28	4	10	1	0	1	6	0	4	0
Mike Greenwell, ph	.500	2	2	0	1	0	0	0	0	0	0	0
Dave Henderson, of	.111	5	9	3	1	0	0	1	4	2	2	0
Bruce Hurst, p	.000	2	0	0	0	0	0	0	0	0	0	0
Spike Owen, ss	.429	7	21	5	9	0	1	0	3	2	1	1
Jim Rice, of	.161	7	31	8	5	1	0	2	6	1	8	0
Ed Romero, ss	.000	1	2	0	0	0	0	0	0	0	0	0
Joe Sambito, p	.000	3	0	0	0	0	0	0	0	0	0	0
Calvin Schiraldi, p	.000	4	0	0	0	0	0	0	0	0	0	0
Bob Stanley, p	.000	3	0	0	0	0	0	0	0	0	0	0
Dave Stapleton, 1b	.667	4	3	2	2	0	0	0	0	1	0	0
TOTAL	.272		254	41	69	11	2	6	35	19	31	1

PITCHER	W	L	ERA	G	GS	CG	SV	SHO	IP	H	ER	BB	SO
Oil Can Boyd	1	1	4.61	2	2	0	0	0	13.2	17	7	3	8
Roger Clemens	1	1	4.37	3	3	0	0	0	22.2	22	11	7	17
Steve Crawford	1	0	0.00	1	0	0	0	0	1.2	1	0	2	1
Bruce Hurst	1	0	2.40	2	2	1	0	0	15.0	18	4	1	8
Joe Sambito	0	0	0.00	3	0	0	0	0	0.2	1	0	1	0
Calvin Schiraldi	0	1	1.50	4	0	0	1	0	6.0	5	1	3	9
Bob Stanley	0	0	4.76	3	0	0	0	0	5.2	7	3	3	1
TOTAL	4	3	3.58	18	7	1	1	0	65.1	71	26	20	44

CAL (W)

PLAYER/POS	AVG	G	AB	R	H	2B	3B	HR	RB	BB	SO	SB
Bob Boone, c	.455	7	22	4	10	0	0	1	2	1	3	0
Rick Burleson, 2b-2,dh-1	.273	4	11	0	3	0	0	0	0	0	0	0
John Candelaria, p	.000	2	0	0	0	0	0	0	0	0	0	0
Doug Corbett, p	.000	3	0	0	0	0	0	0	0	0	0	0
Doug DeCinces, 3b	.281	7	32	2	9	3	0	1	3	0	2	0
Brian Downing, of	.222	7	27	2	6	0	0	1	7	4	5	0
Chuck Finley, p	.000	3	0	0	0	0	0	0	0	0	0	0
Bobby Grich, 2b-3,1b-3	.208	6	24	1	5	0	0	1	3	0	8	0
George Hendrick, of-2,1b-1	.083	3	12	0	1	0	0	0	0	0	2	0
Jack Howell, ph	.000	2	1	0	0	0	0	0	0	1	1	0
Reggie Jackson, dh	.192	6	26	2	5	2	0	0	2	2	7	0
Ruppert Jones, of-5	.176	6	17	4	3	1	0	0	2	5	2	0
Wally Joyner, 1b	.455	3	11	3	5	2	0	1	2	2	0	0
Gary Lucas, p	.000	4	0	0	0	0	0	0	0	0	0	0
Kirk McCaskill, p	.000	2	0	0	0	0	0	0	0	0	0	0
Donnie Moore, p	.000	3	0	0	0	0	0	0	0	0	0	0
Jerry Narron, c-3	.500	4	2	1	1	0	0	0	0	1	1	0
Gary Pettis, of	.346	7	26	4	9	1	0	1	4	3	5	0
Vern Ruhle, p	.000	1	0	0	0	0	0	0	0	0	0	0
Dick Schofield, ss	.300	7	30	4	9	1	0	1	2	1	5	1
Don Sutton, p	.000	2	0	0	0	0	0	0	0	0	0	0
Devon White, of-3	.500	4	2	2	1	0	0	0	0	0	1	0
Rob Wilfong, 2b	.308	4	13	1	4	1	0	0	2	0	2	0
Mike Witt, p	.000	2	0	0	0	0	0	0	0	0	2	0
TOTAL	.277		256	30	71	11	0	7	29	20	44	1

PITCHER	W	L	ERA	G	GS	CG	SV	SHO	IP	H	ER	BB	SO
John Candelaria	1	1	0.84	2	2	0	0	0	10.2	11	1	6	7
Doug Corbett	1	0	5.40	3	0	0	0	0	6.2	9	4	2	2
Chuck Finley	0	0	0.00	3	0	0	0	0	2.0	1	0	0	1
Gary Lucas	0	0	11.57	4	0	0	0	0	2.1	3	3	1	2
Kirk McCaskill	0	2	7.71	2	2	0	0	0	9.1	16	8	5	7
Donnie Moore	0	1	7.20	3	0	0	1	0	5.0	8	4	2	0
Vern Ruhle	0	0	13.50	1	0	0	0	0	0.2	1	1	0	0
Don Sutton	0	0	1.86	2	1	0	0	0	9.2	6	2	1	4
Mike Witt	1	0	2.55	2	2	1	0	0	17.2	13	5	2	8
TOTAL	3	4	3.94	22	7	1	1	0	64.0	69	28	19	31

GAME 1 AT BOS OCT 7

CAL	041	000	030	8	11	0
BOS	000	000	001	1	5	1

Pitchers: WITT vs CLEMENS, Sambito (8), Stanley (8)
Attendance: 32,993

GAME 2 AT BOS OCT 8

CAL	000	110	000	2	11	3
BOS	110	010	33X	9	13	2

Pitchers: McCASKILL, Lucas (8), Corbett (8) vs HURST
Home Runs: Joyner-CAL, Rice-BOS
Attendance: 32,786

GAME 3 AT CAL OCT 10

BOS	010	000	020	3	9	1
CAL	000	001	31X	5	8	0

Pitchers: BOYD, Sambito (7), Schiraldi (8) vs CANDELARIA, Moore (8)
Home Runs: Schofield-CAL, Pettis-CAL
Attendance: 64,206

GAME 4 AT CAL OCT 11

BOS	000	001	020	00	3	6	1
CAL	000	000	003	01	4	11	2

Pitchers: Clemens, SCHIRALDI (9) vs Sutton, Lucas (7), Ruhle (7), Finley (8), CORBETT (8)
Home Runs: DeCinces-CAL
Attendance: 64,223

GAME 5 AT CAL OCT 12

BOS	020	000	004	01	7	12	0
CAL	001	002	201	00	6	13	0

Pitchers: Hurst, Stanley (7), Sambito (9), CRAWFORD (9), Schiraldi (11) vs Witt, Lucas (9), MOORE (9), Finley (11)
Home Runs: Gedman-BOS, Boone-CAL, Grich-CAL, Baylor-BOS, Henderson-BOS
Attendance: 64,223

GAME 6 AT BOS OCT 14

CAL	200	000	110	4	11	1
BOS	205	010	20X	10	16	1

Pitchers: McCASKILL, Lucas (3), Corbett (4), Finley (7) vs BOYD, Stanley (8)
Home Runs: Downing-CAL
Attendance: 32,998

GAME 7 AT BOS OCT 15

CAL	000	000	010	1	6	2
BOS	030	400	10X	8	8	1

Pitchers: CANDELARIA, Sutton (4), Moore (8) vs CLEMENS, Schiraldi (8)
Home Runs: Rice-BOS, Evans-BOS
Attendance: 33,001

In their three most recent Series appearances—1946, 1967, and 1975—the Red Sox had battled to a seventh game, only to lose. This time they came within one strike of winning the crown in the sixth game—but wound up losing again in Game 7.

Boston surprised the favored Mets by taking the first two games in New York. Bruce Hurst (with relief from Calvin Schiraldi in the ninth) pitched a four-hitter. New York's Ron Darling hurled just as well but lost when a seventh-inning walk, a wild pitch, and an error by second baseman Tim Teufel moved Jim Rice around the bases with the game's only run. Game 2, close for three innings, turned into a 9–3 Boston blowout as the Sox racked New York pitching for 18 hits, including home runs by Dave Henderson and Dwight Evans.

When the Series moved to Boston, though, the Mets revived to rap Sox starter Oil Can Boyd and two relievers for 13 hits and seven runs (starting with Len Dykstra's lead-off home run in the first inning) as former Sox pitcher Bob Ojeda subdued his old teammates, giving up just one run on five hits in his seven innings of work. The next day Ron Darling redeemed his first-game loss with seven shutout innings as his teammates built him a 6–0 lead (five of the runs scoring on homers by Dykstra and a pair by Gary Carter). The game ended at 6–2, with the Series even at two wins apiece.

Boston recovered in its final home appearance, taking a 4–0 lead and holding it until Teufel spoiled Bruce Hurst's try for a second shutout by homering in the eighth inning. Hurst yielded a second run with two outs in the ninth, but struck out Len Dykstra on three pitches to seal his second win.

The ninth inning of Game 6 ended with the score tied, 3–3. Boston's Dave Henderson led off the 10th with a home run and two more Sox hits made the score, 5–3. Boston reliever Calvin Schiraldi retired the first two Mets in the last of the 10th on long flies, but then three Mets singled, driving in one run and driving out Schiraldi. Bob Stanley, his replacement, had two strikes on Mookie Wilson when a wild pitch let in the tying run, and then Wilson's grounder went through first baseman Bill Buckner's legs as the winning run bounded across the plate for the Mets.

The Red Sox nearly recovered in Game 7. Second-inning home runs by Dwight Evans and Rich Gedman, a walk, sacrifice, and single gave Boston a 3–0 lead which they held into the sixth inning. But then starter Bruce Hurst lost his touch: four hits and a walk later the

New York Mets (NL), 4;
Boston Red Sox (AL), 3

NY (N)

PLAYER/POS	AVG	G	AB	R	H	2B	3B	HR	RB	BB	SO	SB
Rick Aguilera, p	.000	1	0	0	0	0	0	0	0	0	0	0
Wally Backman, 2b	.333	6	18	4	6	0	0	0	1	3	2	1
Gary Carter, c	.276	7	29	4	8	2	0	2	9	0	4	0
Ron Darling, p	.000	3	3	0	0	0	0	0	0	0	1	0
Lenny Dykstra, of	.296	7	27	4	8	0	0	2	3	2	7	0
Kevin Elster, ss	.000	1	1	0	0	0	0	0	0	0	0	0
Sid Fernandez, p	.000	3	0	0	0	0	0	0	0	0	0	0
Dwight Gooden, p	.500	2	2	1	1	0	0	0	0	0	0	0
Danny Heep, dh-2,of-1	.091	5	11	0	1	0	0	0	2	1	1	0
Keith Hernandez, 1b	.231	7	26	1	6	0	0	0	4	5	1	0
Howard Johnson, 3b-1,ss-1	.000	2	5	0	0	0	0	0	0	0	2	0
Ray Knight, 3b	.391	6	23	4	9	1	0	1	5	2	2	0
Lee Mazzilli, of-1	.400	4	5	2	2	0	0	0	0	0	0	0
Roger McDowell, p	.000	5	0	0	0	0	0	0	0	0	0	0
Kevin Mitchell, of-2,dh-1	.250	5	8	1	2	0	0	0	0	0	3	0
Bob Ojeda, p	.000	2	2	0	0	0	0	0	0	0	1	0
Jesse Orosco, p	1.000	4	1	0	1	0	0	0	1	0	0	0
Rafael Santana, ss	.250	7	20	3	5	0	0	0	2	2	5	0
Doug Sisk, p	.000	1	0	0	0	0	0	0	0	0	0	0
Darryl Strawberry, of	.208	7	24	4	5	1	0	1	1	4	6	3
Tim Teufel, 2b	.444	3	9	1	4	1	0	1	1	1	2	0
Mookie Wilson, of	.269	7	26	3	7	1	0	0	0	1	6	3
TOTAL	.271		240	32	65	6	0	7	29	21	43	7

PITCHER	W	L	ERA	G	GS	CG	SV	SHO	IP	H	ER	BB	SO
Rick Aguilera	1	0	12.00	1	0	0	0	0	3.0	8	4	1	4
Ron Darling	1	1	1.53	3	3	0	0	0	17.2	13	3	10	12
Sid Fernandez	0	0	1.35	3	0	0	0	0	6.2	6	1	4	10
Dwight Gooden	0	2	8.00	2	2	0	0	0	9.0	17	8	4	9
Roger McDowell	1	0	4.91	5	0	0	0	0	7.1	10	4	6	2
Bob Ojeda	1	0	2.08	2	2	0	0	0	13.0	13	3	5	9
Jesse Orosco	0	0	0.00	4	0	0	2	0	5.2	2	0	0	6
Doug Sisk	0	0	0.00	1	0	0	0	0	0.2	0	0	1	1
TOTAL	4	3	3.29	21	7	0	2	0	63.0	69	23	28	53

BOS (A)

PLAYER/POS	AVG	G	AB	R	H	2B	3B	HR	RB	BB	SO	SB
Tony Armas, ph	.000	1	1	0	0	0	0	0	0	0	1	0
Marty Barrett, 2b	.433	7	30	1	13	2	0	0	4	5	2	0
Don Baylor, dh-3	.182	4	11	1	2	1	0	0	1	1	3	0
Wade Boggs, 3b	.290	7	31	3	9	3	0	0	3	4	2	0
Oil Can Boyd, p	.000	1	0	0	0	0	0	0	0	0	0	0
Bill Buckner, 1b	.188	7	32	2	6	0	0	0	1	0	3	0
Roger Clemens, p	.000	2	4	1	0	0	0	0	0	0	1	0
Steve Crawford, p	.000	3	1	0	0	0	0	0	0	0	0	0
Dwight Evans, of	.308	7	26	4	8	2	0	2	9	4	3	0
Rich Gedman, c	.200	7	30	1	6	1	0	1	1	0	10	0
Mike Greenwell, ph	.000	4	3	0	0	0	0	0	0	1	2	0
Dave Henderson, of	.400	7	25	6	10	1	1	2	5	2	6	0
Bruce Hurst, p	.000	3	3	0	0	0	0	0	0	0	3	0
Al Nipper, p	.000	2	0	0	0	0	0	0	0	0	0	0
Spike Owen, ss	.300	7	20	2	6	0	0	0	2	5	6	0
Jim Rice, of	.333	7	27	6	9	1	1	0	0	6	9	0
Ed Romero, ss	.000	3	1	0	0	0	0	0	0	0	0	0
Joe Sambito, p	.000	2	0	0	0	0	0	0	0	0	0	0
Calvin Schiraldi, p	.000	3	1	0	0	0	0	0	0	0	1	0
Bob Stanley, p	.000	5	1	0	0	0	0	0	0	0	1	0
Dave Stapleton, 1b	.000	3	1	0	0	0	0	0	0	0	0	0
TOTAL	.278		248	27	69	11	2	5	26	28	53	0

PITCHER	W	L	ERA	G	GS	CG	SV	SHO	IP	H	ER	BB	SO
Oil Can Boyd	0	1	7.71	1	1	0	0	0	7.0	9	6	1	4
Roger Clemens	0	0	3.18	2	2	0	0	0	11.1	9	4	6	11
Steve Crawford	1	0	6.23	3	0	0	0	0	4.1	5	3	0	4
Bruce Hurst	2	0	1.96	3	3	1	0	0	23.0	18	5	6	17
Al Nipper	0	1	7.11	2	1	0	0	0	6.1	10	5	2	2
Joe Sambito	0	0	27.00	2	0	0	0	0	0.1	2	1	2	0
Calvin Schiraldi	0	2	13.50	3	0	0	1	0	4.0	7	6	3	2
Bob Stanley	0	0	0.00	5	0	0	1	0	6.1	5	0	1	4
TOTAL	3	4	4.31	21	7	1	2	0	62.2	65	30	21	43

score was tied. A succession of five Sox relievers tried to hold the line, but the Mets scored five runs to Boston's two in the final innings for an 8–5 triumph.

GAME 1 AT NY OCT 18

BOS	000	000	100	1	5 0
NY	000	000	000	0	4 1

Pitchers: HURST, Schiraldi (9) vs DARLING, McDowell (8)
Attendance: 55,076

GAME 2 AT NY OCT 19

BOS	003	120	201	9	18 0
NY	002	010	000	3	8 1

Pitchers: Clemens, CRAWFORD (7), Stanley (7) vs GOODEN, Aguilera (6), Orosco (7), Fernandez (9), Sisk (9)
Home Runs: Henderson-BOS, Evans-BOS
Attendance: 55,063

GAME 3 AT BOS OCT 21

NY	400	000	210	7	13 0
BOS	001	000	000	1	5 0

Pitchers: OJEDA, McDowell (8) vs BOYD, Sambito (8), Stanley (8)
Home Runs: Dykstra-NY
Attendance: 33,595

GAME 4 AT BOS OCT 22

NY	000	300	210	6	12 0
BOS	000	000	020	2	7 1

Pitchers: DARLING, McDowell (7), Orosco (7) vs NIPPER, Crawford (7), Stanley (9)
Home Runs: Dykstra-NY, Carter-NY (2)
Attendance: 33,920

GAME 5 AT BOS OCT 23

NY	000	000	011	2	10 1
BOS	011	020	00X	4	12 0

Pitchers: GOODEN, Fernandez (5) vs HURST
Home Runs: Teufel-NY
Attendance: 34,010

GAME 6 AT NY OCT 25

BOS	110	000	100	2	5 13 3
NY	000	020	010	3	6 8 2

Pitchers: Clemens, SCHIRALDI (8), Stanley (10) vs Ojeda, McDowell (7), Orosco (8), AGUILERA (9)
Home Runs: Henderson-BOS
Attendance: 55,078

GAME 7 AT NY OCT 27

BOS	030	000	020	5	9 0
NY	000	003	32X	8	10 0

Pitchers: Hurst, SCHIRALDI (7), Sambito (7), Stanley (7), Nipper (8), Crawford (8) vs Darling, Fernandez (4), McDOWELL (8), Orosco (9)
Home Runs: Evans-BOS, Gedman-BOS, Knight-NY, Strawberry-NY
Attendance: 55,032

The Giants scored four times in the fourth inning of Game 5, winning the game and taking a 3–2 series advantage. But Cardinals pitchers shut them out the rest of the series (an NLCS record 22 innings) to capture the flag.

St. Louis won the opener, 5–3, with pitcher Greg Mathews's two-run single in the sixth providing his margin of victory. The Giants came back in Game 2, supporting Dave Dravecky's two-hit shutout with home runs by Will Clark and Jeffrey Leonard. But the Cards retook the series lead in Game 3, overcoming a 4–0 deficit with two runs on Jim Lindeman's homer in the sixth and four more in the seventh (capped by Lindeman's sacrifice fly) for an eventual 6–5 win.

The Giants snapped back with a pair of wins, scoring four runs on three homers in Game 4 (including Leonard's fourth in successive games—an LCS record), and six runs in Game 5. But Dravecky and the Giants lost a heartbreaker in Game 6 when right fielder Candy Maldonado lost Tony Pena's fly in the lights for a triple. Pena scored on a sacrifice fly for the game's only run, as John Tudor and two late-inning relievers blanked the Giants. Danny Cox pitched an easier shutout in the finale as his Cardinals hammered seven San Francisco pitchers for 12 hits and six runs.

St. Louis Cardinals (East), 4; San Francisco Giants (West), 3

STL (E)

PLAYER/POS	AVG	G	AB	R	H	2B	3B	HR	RB	BB	SO	SB
Jack Clark, ph	.000	1	1	0	0	0	0	0	0	0	1	0
Vince Coleman, of	.269	7	26	3	7	1	0	0	4	4	6	1
Danny Cox, p	.333	2	6	0	2	0	0	0	1	0	2	0
Ken Dayley, p	.000	3	0	0	0	0	0	0	0	0	0	0
Dan Driessen, 1b-4	.250	5	12	1	3	2	0	0	1	1	1	0
Curt Ford, of	.333	4	9	2	3	0	0	0	0	1	1	0
Bob Forsch, p	.000	3	0	0	0	0	0	0	0	0	0	0
Tommy Herr, 2b	.222	7	27	0	6	0	0	0	3	0	1	1
Rick Horton, p	.000	1	0	0	0	0	0	0	0	0	0	1
Lance Johnson, pr	.000	1	0	1	0	0	0	0	0	0	0	1
Tom Lawless, 3b-2,of-1	.333	3	6	0	2	0	0	0	0	1	1	0
Jim Lindeman, 1b	.308	5	13	1	4	0	0	1	3	0	3	0
Joe Magrane, p	.000	1	1	0	0	0	0	0	0	0	0	0
Greg Mathews, p	1.000	2	2	0	2	0	0	0	2	0	0	0
Willie McGee, of	.308	7	26	2	8	1	1	0	2	0	5	0
John Morris, of	.000	3	3	0	0	0	0	0	0	0	0	0
Jose Oquendo, of-5,3b-1	.167	5	12	3	2	0	0	1	4	3	2	0
Tom Pagnozzi, ph	.000	1	1	0	0	0	0	0	0	0	0	0
Tony Pena, c	.381	7	21	5	8	1	0	0	3	4	1	0
Terry Pendleton, 3b	.211	6	19	3	4	1	0	1	1	0	6	0
Ozzie Smith, ss	.200	7	25	2	5	0	1	0	1	3	4	0
John Tudor, p	.000	2	4	0	0	0	0	0	0	0	0	0
Todd Worrell, p-3,of-1	.000	3	1	0	0	0	0	0	0	0	1	0
TOTAL	.260		215	23	56	4	4	2	22	16	42	4

PITCHER	W	L	ERA	G	GS	CG	SV	SHO	IP	H	ER	BB	SO
Danny Cox	1	1	2.12	2	2	2	0	1	17.0	17	4	3	11
Ken Dayley	0	0	0.00	3	0	0	2	0	4.0	1	0	2	4
Bob Forsch	1	1	12.00	3	0	0	0	0	3.0	4	4	1	3
Rick Horton	0	0	0.00	1	0	0	0	0	3.0	2	0	0	2
Joe Magrane	0	0	9.00	1	1	0	0	0	4.0	4	4	2	3
Greg Mathews	1	0	3.48	2	2	0	0	0	10.1	6	4	3	10
John Tudor	1	1	1.76	2	2	0	0	0	15.1	16	3	5	12
Todd Worrell	0	0	2.08	3	0	0	1	0	4.1	4	1	1	6
TOTAL	4	3	2.95	17	7	2	3	1	61.0	54	20	17	51

SF (W)

PLAYER/POS	AVG	G	AB	R	H	2B	3B	HR	RB	BB	SO	SB
Mike Aldrete, of-3	.100	5	10	0	1	0	0	0	1	0	2	0
Bob Brenly, c	.235	6	17	3	4	1	0	1	2	3	7	0
Will Clark, 1b	.360	7	25	3	9	2	0	1	3	3	6	1
Chili Davis, of	.150	6	20	2	3	1	0	0	1	4	0	0
Kelly Downs, p	.000	1	0	0	0	0	0	0	0	0	0	0
Dave Dravecky, p	.167	2	6	0	1	0	0	0	0	0	1	0
Scott Garrelts, p	.000	2	0	0	0	0	0	0	0	0	0	0
Atlee Hammaker, p	.000	2	3	0	0	0	0	0	0	0	2	0
Mike Krukow, p	.000	1	1	0	0	0	0	0	0	1	0	0
Mike LaCoss, p	.000	2	0	0	0	0	0	0	0	0	0	0
Craig Lefferts, p	.000	3	0	0	0	0	0	0	0	0	0	0
Jeffrey Leonard, of	.417	7	24	5	10	0	0	4	5	3	4	0
Candy Maldonado, of	.211	5	19	2	4	1	0	0	2	0	3	0
Bob Melvin, c-2	.429	3	7	0	3	0	0	0	0	1	1	0
Eddie Milner, of-4	.143	6	7	0	1	0	0	0	0	3	0	0
Kevin Mitchell, 3b	.267	7	30	2	8	1	0	1	2	0	3	1
Joe Price, p	.000	2	1	0	0	0	0	0	0	0	1	0
Rick Reuschel, p	.000	2	2	0	0	0	0	0	0	0	1	0
Don Robinson, p	.000	3	0	0	0	0	0	0	0	0	0	0
Chris Speier, 2b-1	.000	3	5	0	0	0	0	0	0	0	2	0
Harry Spilman, ph	.500	3	2	1	1	0	0	1	1	0	0	0
Rob Thompson, 2b-6	.100	7	20	4	2	0	2	1	2	5	7	2
Jose Uribe, ss	.269	7	26	1	7	1	0	0	2	0	4	1
TOTAL	.239		226	23	54	7	1	9	20	17	51	5

PITCHER	W	L	ERA	G	GS	CG	SV	SHO	IP	H	ER	BB	SO
Kelly Downs	0	0	0.00	1	0	0	0	0	1.1	1	0	0	0
Dave Dravecky	1	1	0.60	2	2	1	0	1	15.0	7	1	4	14
Scott Garrelts	0	0	6.75	2	0	0	0	0	2.2	2	2	4	4
Atlee Hammaker	0	1	7.87	2	2	0	0	0	8.0	12	7	0	7
Mike Krukow	1	0	2.00	1	1	1	0	0	9.0	9	2	1	3
Mike LaCoss	0	0	0.00	2	0	0	0	0	3.1	0	0	3	2
Craig Lefferts	0	0	0.00	3	0	0	0	0	2.0	3	0	1	0
Joe Price	1	0	0.00	2	0	0	0	0	5.2	3	0	1	7
Rick Reuschel	0	1	6.30	2	2	0	0	0	10.0	15	7	2	2
Don Robinson	0	1	9.00	3	0	0	0	0	3.0	3	3	0	3
TOTAL	3	4	3.30	20	7	3	0	1	60.0	56	22	16	42

GAME 1 AT STL OCT 6

SF	100	100	010		3	7	1
STL	001	103	00X		5	10	1

Pitchers: REUSCHEL, Lefferts (7), Garrelts (8) vs MATHEWS, Worrell (8), Dayley (8)
Home Runs: Leonard-SF
Attendance: 55,331

GAME 2 AT STL OCT 7

SF	020	100	020		5	10	0
STL	000	000	000		0	2	1

Pitchers: DRAVECKY vs TUDOR, Forsch (9)
Home Runs: Clark-SF, Leonard-SF
Attendance: 55,331

GAME 3 AT SF OCT 9

STL	000	002	400		6	11	1
SF	031	000	001		5	7	1

Pitchers: Magrane, FORSCH (5), Worrell (7) vs Hammaker, D.ROBINSON (7), Lefferts (7), LaCoss (8)
Home Runs: Lindeman-STL, Leonard-SF, Spilman-SF
Attendance: 57,913

GAME 4 AT SF OCT 10

STL	020	000	000		2	9	0
SF	000	120	01X		4	9	2

Pitchers: COX vs KRUKOW
Home Runs: Thompson-SF, Leonard-SF, Brenly-SF
Attendance: 57,997

GAME 5 AT SF OCT 11

STL	101	100	000		3	7	0
SF	101	400	00X		6	7	1

Pitchers: Mathews, FORSCH (4), Horton (4), Dayley (7) vs Reuschel, PRICE (5)
Home Runs: Mitchell-SF
Attendance: 59,363

GAME 6 AT STL OCT 13

SF	000	000	000		0	6	0
STL	010	000	00X		1	5	0

Pitchers: DRAVECKY, D.Robinson (7) vs TUDOR, Worrell (8), Dayley (9)
Attendance: 55,331

GAME 7 AT STL OCT 14

SF	000	000	000		0	8	1
STL	040	002	00X		6	12	0

Pitchers: HAMMAKER, Price (3), Downs (3), Garrelts (5), Lefferts (6), LaCoss (6), D.Robinson (8) vs COX
Home Runs: Oquendo-STL
Attendance: 55,331

The Tigers, with the best overall won-lost record in the majors, were favored to defeat the Twins, whose record was the ninth best in baseball. Minnesota, however, held the home field advantage and the major leagues' best record at home. Tigers pitcher Doyle Alexander—he had been 9–0 since joining Detroit in mid-August—took a 5–4 lead into the last of the eighth in Game 1. But a single and double drove him out, and before the inning was over three more Twins had scored to sew up their first win. Detroit scored twice in the second inning the next day, but the Twins responded later in the inning with three runs, two on Tim Laudner's double off Tigers ace Jack Morris, and increased their lead in the fourth and fifth to seal Morris' first loss in Minnesota after 11 wins.

The Tigers won a game after the series moved to Detroit, when Pat Sheridan's two-run homer in the eighth inning of Game 3 restored a lead they had squandered in the middle innings. But that was it for Detroit, as the Twins surprised everyone by subduing the Tigers in their den. In Game 4 they took the lead for good on Greg Gagne's fourth-inning home run. And in Game 5, after initiating the scoring with four runs in the second, Minnesota pushed on to a 9–5 win and their first pennant in 22 years.

Minnesota Twins (West) 4; Detroit Tigers (East), 1

MIN (W)

PLAYER/POS	AVG	G	AB	R	H	2B	3B	HR	RB	BB	SO	SB
Keith Atherton, p	.000	1	0	0	0	0	0	0	0	0	0	0
Don Baylor, dh	.400	2	5	0	2	0	0	0	1	0	0	0
Juan Berenguer, p	.000	4	0	0	0	0	0	0	0	0	0	0
Bert Blyleven, p	.000	2	0	0	0	0	0	0	0	0	0	0
Tom Brunansky, of	.412	5	17	5	7	4	0	2	9	4	3	0
Randy Bush, dh	.250	4	12	4	3	0	1	0	2	3	2	3
Sal Butera, c	.667	1	3	0	2	0	0	0	0	0	0	0
Mark Davidson, pr	.000	1	0	0	0	0	0	0	0	0	0	0
Gary Gaetti, 3b	.300	5	20	5	6	1	0	2	5	1	3	0
Greg Gagne, ss	.278	5	18	5	5	3	0	2	3	3	4	0
Dan Gladden, of	.350	5	20	5	7	2	0	0	5	2	1	0
Kent Hrbek, 1b	.150	5	20	4	3	0	0	1	1	3	0	0
Gene Larkin, ph	1.000	1	1	0	1	1	0	0	1	0	0	0
Tim Laudner, c	.071	5	14	1	1	1	0	0	2	2	5	0
Steve Lombardozzi, 2b	.267	5	15	2	4	0	0	0	1	2	2	0
Al Newman, 2b	.000	1	2	0	0	0	0	0	0	0	0	0
Kirby Puckett, of	.208	5	24	3	5	1	0	1	3	0	5	1
Jeff Reardon, p	.000	4	0	0	0	0	0	0	0	0	0	0
Dan Schatzeder, p	.000	2	0	0	0	0	0	0	0	0	0	0
Les Straker, p	.000	1	0	0	0	0	0	0	0	0	0	0
Frank Viola, p	.000	2	0	0	0	0	0	0	0	0	0	0
TOTAL	.269		171	34	46	13	1	8	33	20	25	4

PITCHER	W	L	ERA	G	GS	CG	SV	SHO	IP	H	ER	BB	SO
Keith Atherton	0	0	0.00	1	0	0	0	0	0.1	1	0	0	0
Juan Berenguer	0	0	1.50	4	0	0	1	0	6.0	1	1	3	6
Bert Blyleven	2	0	4.05	2	2	0	0	0	13.1	12	6	3	9
Jeff Reardon	1	1	5.06	4	0	0	2	0	5.1	7	3	3	5
Dan Schatzeder	0	0	0.00	2	0	0	0	0	4.1	2	0	0	5
Les Straker	0	0	16.88	1	1	0	0	0	2.2	3	5	4	1
Frank Viola	1	0	5.25	2	2	0	0	0	12.0	14	7	5	9
TOTAL	4	1	4.50	16	5	0	3	0	44.0	40	22	18	35

DET (E)

PLAYER/POS	AVG	G	AB	R	H	2B	3B	HR	RB	BB	SO	SB
Doyle Alexander, p	.000	2	0	0	0	0	0	0	0	0	0	0
Dave Bergman, 1b-1,dh-1	.250	4	4	0	1	0	0	0	0	2	1	0
Tom Brookens, 3b	.000	5	13	0	0	0	0	0	0	0	3	0
Darrell Evans, 1b-5,3b-1	.294	5	17	0	5	0	0	0	4	2	0	0
Kirk Gibson, of	.286	5	21	4	6	1	0	1	4	3	8	3
Johnny Grubb, dh-1	.571	4	7	0	4	0	0	0	0	0	1	0
Mike Heath, c	.286	3	7	1	2	0	0	1	2	0	0	0
Mike Henneman, p	.000	3	0	0	0	0	0	0	0	0	0	0
Willie Hernandez, p	.000	1	0	0	0	0	0	0	0	0	0	0
Larry Herndon, of-2,dh-1	.333	3	9	1	3	1	0	0	2	1	1	0
Eric King, p	.000	2	0	0	0	0	0	0	0	0	0	0
Chet Lemon, of	.278	5	18	4	5	0	0	2	4	1	4	0
Bill Madlock, dh	.000	1	5	0	0	0	0	0	0	0	3	0
Jack Morris, p-1,dh-1	.000	2	1	0	0	0	0	0	0	0	0	0
Jim Morrison, 3b-1,dh-1	.400	2	5	1	2	0	0	0	0	0	1	0
Matt Nokes, c-3,dh-2	.143	5	14	2	2	0	0	1	2	1	4	0
Dan Petry, p	.000	1	0	0	0	0	0	0	0	0	0	0
Jeff Robinson, p	.000	1	0	0	0	0	0	0	0	0	0	0
Pat Sheridan, of-4	.300	5	10	2	3	1	0	1	2	0	2	1
Frank Tanana, p	.000	1	0	0	0	0	0	0	0	0	0	0
Walt Terrell, p	.000	1	0	0	0	0	0	0	0	0	0	0
Mark Thurmond, p	.000	1	0	0	0	0	0	0	0	0	0	0
Alan Trammell, ss	.200	5	20	3	4	1	0	0	2	2	2	0
Lou Whitaker, 2b	.176	5	17	4	3	0	0	1	1	3	1	0
TOTAL	.240		167	23	40	4	0	7	21	18	35	5

PITCHER	W	L	ERA	G	GS	CG	SV	SHO	IP	H	ER	BB	SO
Doyle Alexander	0	2	10.00	2	2	0	0	0	9.0	14	10	1	5
Mike Henneman	1	0	10.80	3	0	0	0	0	5.0	6	6	6	3
Willie Hernandez	0	0	0.00	1	0	0	0	0	0.1	2	0	0	0
Eric King	0	0	1.69	2	0	0	0	0	5.1	3	1	2	4
Jack Morris	0	1	6.75	1	1	1	0	0	8.0	6	6	3	7
Dan Petry	0	0	0.00	1	0	0	0	0	3.1	1	0	0	1
Jeff Robinson	0	0	0.00	1	0	0	0	0	0.1	1	0	0	0
Frank Tanana	0	1	5.06	1	1	0	0	0	5.1	6	3	4	1
Walt Terrell	0	0	9.00	1	1	0	0	0	6.0	7	6	4	4
Mark Thurmond	0	0	0.00	1	0	0	0	0	0.1	0	0	0	0
TOTAL	1	4	6.70	14	5	1	0	0	43.0	46	32	20	25

GAME 1 AT MIN OCT 7

DET	001	001	120	5	10	0
MIN	010	030	04X	8	10	0

Pitchers: ALEXANDER, Henneman (8), Hernandez (8), King (8) vs Viola, REARDON (8)
Home Runs: Heath-DET, Gibson-DET, Gaetti-MIN (2)
Attendance: 53,269

GAME 2 AT MIN OCT 8

DET	020	000	010	3	7	1
MIN	030	210	00X	6	6	0

Pitchers: MORRIS vs BLYLEVEN, Berenguer (8)
Home Runs: Lemon-DET, Whitaker-DET, Hrbek-MIN
Attendance: 55,245

GAME 3 AT DET OCT 10

MIN	000	202	200	6	8	1
DET	005	000	02X	7	7	0

Pitchers: Straker, Schatzeder (3), Berenguer (7), REARDON (8) vs Terrell, HENNEMAN (7)
Home Runs: Gagne-MIN, Brunansky-MIN, Sheridan-DET
Attendance: 49,730

GAME 4 AT DET OCT 11

MIN	001	111	010	5	7	1
DET	100	011	000	3	7	3

Pitchers: VIOLA, Atherton (6), Berenguer (6), Reardon (9) vs TANANA, Petry (6), Thurmond (9)
Home Runs: Puckett-MIN, Gagne-MIN
Attendance: 51,939

GAME 5 AT DET OCT 12

MIN	040	000	113	9	15	1
DET	000	300	011	5	9	1

Pitchers: BLYLEVEN, Schatzeder (7), Berenguer (8), Reardon (8) vs ALEXANDER, King (2), Henneman (7), Robinson (9)
Home Runs: Brunansky-MIN, Nokes-DET, Lemon-DET
Attendance: 47,448

Although the Twins compiled a dismal record on the road during the season (29–52), their play at home (56–25) topped the majors. In postseason play they won all six games played in their Metrodome, including the four that won them the world championship. They overwhelmed St. Louis in the Series opener, the first World Series game ever played indoors. The Cardinals scored first, in the second inning, but Twins ace Frank Viola (with relief from Keith Atherton in the ninth) stopped them after that as his teammates unloaded for seven runs in the fourth inning (capped by Dan Gladden's grand slam) on their way to a 10–1 win. The Cardinals scored four runs in Game 2, but again the Twins enjoyed a big fourth inning—bunching six of their 10 hits together for six runs—and scored two other runs on homers by Gary Gaetti and Tim Laudner.

When the Series moved to St. Louis, the Cardinals grabbed the home advantage to post their three wins. In Game 3, Cardinal pitchers John Tudor and Todd Worrell combined for a five-hitter as the Cards came from behind with a three-run seventh to win, 3–1. The next day St. Louis broke a 1–1 tie with their own fourth-inning explosion, for six runs. The big blow was a three-run homer by utility infielder Tom Lawless—only the second home run of his big league career—as the Cards won, 7–2. After five scoreless innings in Game 5, St. Louis moved out to a 4–0 lead in the sixth and seventh innings. Gaetti's eighth-inning triple put two Minnesota runs across, but the Cards held on for a 4–2 win.

Back in Minneapolis, St. Louis built up a 5–2 lead in Game 6 before the Twins retaliated with four runs in the fifth inning (with Don Baylor's three-run homer providing the tying runs) and four more an inning later on Kent Hrbek's grand slam. A final Twins run in the eighth ended the scoring at 11–5.

The Cardinals scored first in Game 7, with a pair of runs in the second inning, but the Twins edged their way to a tie with single runs in the second and fifth, and an inning later took the lead on three walks and an infield single. As Twins starter Frank Viola held St. Louis scoreless on two hits after the second inning, Minnesota made the score 4–2 with a final run in the eighth, and ace reliever Jeff Reardon retired the Cards in order in the ninth to bring Minnesota its first world championship.

Minnesota Twins (AL) 4;
St. Louis Cardinals (NL), 3

MIN (A)

PLAYER/POS	AVG	G	AB	R	H	2B	3B	HR	RB	BB	SO	SB
Keith Atherton, p	.000	2	0	0	0	0	0	0	0	0	0	0
Don Baylor, dh-3	.385	5	13	3	5	0	0	1	3	1	1	0
Juan Berenguer, p	.000	3	0	0	0	0	0	0	0	0	0	0
Bert Blyleven, p	.000	2	1	0	0	0	0	0	0	0	1	0
Tom Brunansky, of	.200	7	25	5	5	0	0	0	2	4	4	1
Randy Bush, dh-2	.167	4	6	1	1	1	0	0	0	2	1	0
Sal Butera, c	.000	1	0	0	0	0	0	0	0	0	0	0
Mark Davidson, of-1	.000	2	1	0	0	0	0	0	0	0	0	0
George Frazier, p	.000	1	0	0	0	0	0	0	0	0	0	0
Gary Gaetti, 3b	.259	7	27	4	7	2	1	1	4	2	5	2
Greg Gagne, ss	.200	7	30	5	6	1	0	1	3	1	6	0
Dan Gladden, of	.290	7	31	3	9	2	1	1	7	3	4	2
Kent Hrbek, 1b	.208	7	24	4	5	0	0	1	6	5	3	0
Gene Larkin, 1b-1,dh-1	.000	5	3	1	0	0	0	0	0	1	0	0
Tim Laudner, c	.318	7	22	4	7	1	0	1	4	5	4	0
Steve Lombardozzi, 2b	.412	6	17	3	7	1	0	1	4	2	2	0
Al Newman, 2b-3	.200	4	5	0	1	0	0	0	0	1	1	0
Joe Niekro, p	.000	1	0	0	0	0	0	0	0	0	0	0
Kirby Puckett, of	.357	7	28	5	10	1	1	0	3	2	1	1
Jeff Reardon, p	.000	4	0	0	0	0	0	0	0	0	0	0
Dan Schatzeder, p	.000	3	0	0	0	0	0	0	0	0	0	0
Roy Smalley, ph	.500	4	2	0	1	1	0	0	0	2	0	0
Les Straker, p	.000	2	2	0	0	0	0	0	0	0	2	0
Frank Viola, p	.000	3	1	0	0	0	0	0	0	0	1	0
TOTAL	.269		238	38	64	10	3	7	38	29	36	6

PITCHER	W	L	ERA	G	GS	CG	SV	SHO	IP	H	ER	BB	SO
Keith Atherton	0	0	6.75	2	0	0	0	0	1.1	0	1	1	0
Juan Berenguer	0	1	10.38	3	0	0	0	0	4.1	10	5	0	1
Bert Blyleven	1	1	2.77	2	2	0	0	0	13.0	13	4	2	12
George Frazier	0	0	0.00	1	0	0	0	0	2.0	1	0	0	2
Joe Niekro	0	0	0.00	1	0	0	0	0	2.0	1	0	1	1
Jeff Reardon	0	0	0.00	4	0	0	1	0	4.2	5	0	0	3
Dan Schatzeder	1	0	6.23	3	0	0	0	0	4.1	4	3	3	3
Les Straker	0	0	4.00	2	2	0	0	0	9.0	9	4	3	6
Frank Viola	2	1	3.72	3	3	0	0	0	19.1	17	8	3	16
TOTAL	4	3	3.75	21	7	0	1	0	60.0	60	25	13	44

STL (N)

PLAYER/POS	AVG	G	AB	R	H	2B	3B	HR	RB	BB	SO	SB
Vince Coleman, of	.143	7	28	5	4	2	0	0	2	2	10	6
Danny Cox, p	.000	3	2	0	0	0	0	0	0	0	1	0
Ken Dayley, p	.000	4	1	0	0	0	0	0	0	0	1	0
Dan Driessen, 1b	.231	4	13	3	3	2	0	0	1	1	1	0
Curt Ford, of-4	.308	5	13	1	4	0	0	0	2	1	1	0
Bob Forsch, p	.000	3	2	0	0	0	0	0	0	0	0	0
Tommy Herr, 2b	.250	7	28	2	7	0	0	1	1	2	2	0
Rick Horton, p	.000	2	0	0	0	0	0	0	0	0	0	0
Lance Johnson, pr	.000	1	0	0	0	0	0	0	0	0	0	1
Steve Lake, c	.333	3	3	0	1	0	0	0	1	0	0	0
Tom Lawless, 3b	.100	3	10	1	1	0	0	1	3	0	4	0
Jim Lindeman, 1b-6,of-1	.333	6	15	3	5	1	0	0	2	0	3	0
Joe Magrane, p	.000	2	0	0	0	0	0	0	0	0	0	0
Greg Mathews, p	.000	1	0	0	0	0	0	0	0	0	0	0
Willie McGee, of	.370	7	27	2	10	2	0	0	4	0	9	0
John Morris, of	.000	1	2	0	0	0	0	0	0	0	0	0
Jose Oquendo, 3b-4,of-3	.250	7	24	2	6	0	0	0	2	1	4	0
Tom Pagnozzi, dh-1	.250	2	4	0	1	0	0	0	0	0	0	0
Tony Pena, c-6,dh-1	.409	7	22	2	9	1	0	0	4	3	2	1
Terry Pendleton, dh-2	.429	3	7	2	3	0	0	0	1	1	1	2
Ozzie Smith, ss	.214	7	28	3	6	0	0	0	2	2	3	2
John Tudor, p	.000	2	2	0	0	0	0	0	0	0	2	0
Lee Tunnell, p	.000	2	0	0	0	0	0	0	0	0	0	0
Todd Worrell, p	.000	4	0	0	0	0	0	0	0	0	0	0
TOTAL	.259		232	26	60	8	0	2	25	13	44	12

PITCHER	W	L	ERA	G	GS	CG	SV	SHO	IP	H	ER	BB	SO
Danny Cox	1	2	7.71	3	2	0	0	0	11.2	13	10	8	9
Ken Dayley	0	0	1.93	4	0	0	1	0	4.2	1	1	0	3
Bob Forsch	1	0	9.95	3	0	0	0	0	6.1	8	7	3	3
Rick Horton	0	0	6.00	2	0	0	0	0	3.0	5	2	0	1
Joe Magrane	0	1	8.59	2	2	0	0	0	7.1	9	7	5	5
Greg Mathews	0	0	2.45	1	1	0	0	0	3.2	2	1	2	3
John Tudor	1	1	5.73	2	2	0	0	0	11.0	15	7	3	8
Lee Tunnell	0	0	2.08	2	0	0	0	0	4.1	4	1	2	1
Todd Worrell	0	0	1.29	4	0	0	2	0	7.0	6	1	4	3
TOTAL	3	4	5.64	23	7	0	3	0	59.0	64	37	29	36

GAME 1 AT MIN OCT 17

STL	010 000 000	1 5 1
MIN	000 720 10X	10 11 0

Pitchers: MAGRANE, Forsch (4), Horton (7) vs VIOLA, Atherton (9)
Home Runs: Gladden-MIN, Lombardozzi-MIN
Attendance: 55,171

GAME 2 AT MIN OCT 18

STL	000 010 120	4 9 0
MIN	010 601 00X	8 10 0

Pitchers: COX, Tunnell (4), Dayley (7), Worrell (8) vs BLYLEVEN, Berenguer (8), Reardon (9)
Home Runs: Gaetti-MIN, Laudner-MIN
Attendance: 55,257

GAME 3 AT STL OCT 20

MIN	000 001 000	1 5 1
STL	000 000 30X	3 9 1

Pitchers: Straker, BERENGUER (7), Schatzeder (7) vs TUDOR, Worrell (8)
Attendance: 55,347

GAME 4 AT STL OCT 21

MIN	001 010 000	2 7 1
STL	001 600 00X	7 10 1

Pitchers: VIOLA, Schatzeder (4), Niekro (5), Frazier (7) vs Mathews, FORSCH (4), Dayley (7)
Home Runs: Gagne-MIN, Lawless-STL
Attendance: 55,347

GAME 5 AT STL OCT 22

MIN	000 000 020	2 6 1
STL	000 003 10X	4 10 0

Pitchers: BLYLEVEN, Atherton (7), Reardon (7) vs COX, Dayley (8), Worrell (8)
Attendance: 55,347

GAME 6 AT MIN OCT 24

STL	110 210 000	5 11 2
MIN	200 044 01X	11 15 0

Pitchers: TUDOR, Horton (5), Forsch (6), Dayley (6), Tunnell (7) vs Straker, SCHATZEDER (4), Berenguer (6), Reardon (9)
Home Runs: Herr-STL, Baylor-MIN, Hrbek-MIN
Attendance: 55,293

GAME 7 AT MIN OCT 25

STL	020 000 000	2 6 1
MIN	010 011 01X	4 10 0

Pitchers: Magrane, COX (5), Worrell (6) vs VIOLA, Reardon (9)
Attendance: 55,376

The Mets had defeated the Dodgers in 10 of 11 regular season games, but in the NLCS the pitching of Dodger ace Orel Hershiser and rookie Tim Belcher, and the timely hitting of Mike Scioscia and Kirk Gibson, propelled L.A. to the pennant. The Dodgers scored a first-inning run in the opener and carried a 2–0 lead into the ninth. But three Mets runs in the top of the ninth (the final two scoring with two outs on a fly to short center that bounced off the glove of a diving John Shelby) gave New York the victory.

Dodgers pitcher Tim Belcher singled with two away in the second inning of Game 2 to start a four-run rally—the margin of victory in Belcher's 6–3 win. In Game 3 (played in a steady downpour after a rainout the night before), the Mets overcame a 4–3 deficit, rapping four Dodgers pitchers for five runs in the last of the eighth to take the series lead.

Kirk Gibson's 12th-inning solo homer the next night put the Dodgers ahead, 5–4, after Mike Scioscia's ninth-inning home run had pulled them into a tie. In the last of the 12th, Orel Hershiser (who had pitched seven innings to no decision in the previous game) took the mound with two outs and the bases full, and saved the game as center fielder Shelby, on the run, snared Kevin McReynolds' looping fly.

Gibson homered again in Game 5—for three runs that provided the winning margin in a 7–4 Dodgers victory. One game from the pennant, as the series moved back to Los Angeles, the Dodgers for the first time failed to score first and saw the series evened a third time as David Cone held them to five hits and one run while the Mets scored five. But in the finale, the Dodgers unloaded on Ron Darling for six runs in the first two innings and Hershiser blanked the Mets on five hits.

Los Angeles Dodgers (West), 4; New York Mets (East), 3

LA (W)

PLAYER/POS	AVG	G	AB	R	H	2B	3B	HR	RB	BB	SO	SB
Tim Belcher, p	.125	2	8	1	1	0	0	0	0	0	3	0
Mike Davis, ph	.000	4	2	0	0	0	0	0	0	1	0	0
Rick Dempsey, c-3	.400	4	5	1	2	2	0	0	2	1	0	0
Kirk Gibson, of	.154	7	26	2	4	0	0	2	6	3	6	2
Jose Gonzalez, of-4	.000	5	0	2	0	0	0	0	0	0	0	0
Alfredo Griffin, ss	.160	7	25	1	4	1	0	0	3	0	5	0
Jeff Hamilton, 3b	.217	7	23	2	5	0	0	0	1	3	4	0
Mickey Hatcher, 1b-6,of-1	.238	6	21	4	5	2	0	0	3	3	0	0
Danny Heep, ph	.000	3	1	0	0	0	0	0	0	1	1	0
Orel Hershiser, p	.000	4	9	1	0	0	0	0	1	1	2	0
Brian Holton, p	1.000	3	1	1	1	0	0	0	0	0	0	0
Rick Horton, p	.000	4	0	0	0	0	0	0	0	0	0	0
Jay Howell, p	.000	2	0	0	0	0	0	0	0	0	0	0
Tim Leary, p	.000	2	1	0	0	0	0	0	0	0	0	0
Mike Marshall, of	.233	7	30	3	7	1	1	0	5	2	9	0
Jesse Orosco, p	.000	4	0	0	0	0	0	0	0	0	0	0
Alejandro Pena, p	.000	3	0	0	0	0	0	0	0	0	0	0
Steve Sax, 2b	.267	7	30	7	8	0	0	0	3	3	3	5
Mike Scioscia, c	.364	7	22	3	8	1	0	1	2	1	2	0
Mike Sharperson, ss-1,3b-1	.000	2	1	0	0	0	0	0	1	1	0	0
John Shelby, of	.167	7	24	3	4	0	0	0	3	5	12	2
Franklin Stubbs, 1b-3	.250	4	8	0	2	0	0	0	0	0	4	0
John Tudor, p	.000	1	2	0	0	0	0	0	0	0	2	0
Tracy Woodson, 1b	.250	3	4	0	1	0	0	0	0	0	1	0
TOTAL	.214		243	31	52	7	1	3	30	25	54	9

PITCHER	W	L	ERA	G	GS	CG	SV	SHO	IP	H	ER	BB	SO
Tim Belcher	2	0	4.11	2	2	0	0	0	15.1	12	7	4	16
Orel Hershiser	1	0	1.09	4	3	1	1	1	24.2	18	3	7	15
Brian Holton	0	0	2.25	3	0	0	1	0	4.0	2	1	1	2
Rick Horton	0	0	0.00	4	0	0	0	0	4.1	4	0	2	3
Jay Howell	0	1	27.00	2	0	0	0	0	0.2	1	2	2	1
Tim Leary	0	1	6.23	2	1	0	0	0	4.1	8	3	3	3
Jesse Orosco	0	0	7.71	4	0	0	0	0	2.1	4	2	3	0
Alejandro Pena	1	1	4.15	3	0	0	1	0	4.1	4	2	5	1
John Tudor	0	0	7.20	1	1	0	0	0	5.0	8	4	1	1
TOTAL	4	3	3.32	25	7	1	3	1	65.0	58	24	28	42

NY (E)

PLAYER/POS	AVG	G	AB	R	H	2B	3B	HR	RB	BB	SO	SB
Rick Aguilera, p	.000	3	1	0	0	0	0	0	0	0	1	0
Wally Backman, 2b	.273	7	22	2	6	1	0	0	2	2	5	1
Gary Carter, c	.222	7	27	0	6	1	1	0	4	1	3	0
David Cone, p	.000	3	4	0	0	0	0	0	0	0	0	0
Ron Darling, p-2	.000	2	3	0	0	0	0	0	0	0	2	0
Lennie Dykstra, of	.429	7	14	6	6	3	0	1	3	4	0	0
Kevin Elster, ss	.250	5	8	1	2	1	0	0	1	3	0	0
Sid Fernandez, p	.000	1	1	0	0	0	0	0	0	0	0	0
Dwight Gooden, p	.200	3	5	0	1	0	0	0	0	0	2	0
Keith Hernandez, 1b	.269	7	26	2	7	0	0	1	5	6	7	1
Gregg Jefferies, 3b	.333	7	27	2	9	2	0	0	1	4	0	0
Howard Johnson, ss-5,3b-1	.056	6	18	3	1	0	0	0	0	1	6	1
Terry Leach, p	.000	3	0	0	0	0	0	0	0	0	0	0
Dave Magadan, ph	.000	3	0	0	0	0	0	0	0	0	2	0
Lee Mazzilli, ph	.500	3	2	0	1	0	0	0	0	0	0	1
Roger McDowell, p	.000	4	0	0	0	0	0	0	0	0	0	0
Kevin McReynolds, of	.250	7	28	4	7	2	0	0	4	3	5	2
Randy Myers, p	.000	3	0	0	0	0	0	0	0	0	0	0
Mackey Sasser, c-1	.200	4	5	0	1	0	0	0	0	0	1	0
Darryl Strawberry, of	.300	7	30	5	9	2	0	1	6	2	5	0
Tim Teufel, 2b	.000	1	3	0	0	0	0	0	0	0	1	0
Mookie Wilson, of-3	.154	4	13	2	2	0	0	0	1	2	2	0
TOTAL	.242		240	27	58	12	1	5	27	28	42	6

PITCHER	W	L	ERA	G	GS	CG	SV	SHO	IP	H	ER	BB	SO
Rick Aguilera	0	0	1.29	3	0	0	0	0	7.0	3	1	2	4
David Cone	1	1	4.50	3	2	1	0	0	12.0	10	6	5	9
Ron Darling	0	1	7.71	2	2	0	0	0	7.0	11	6	4	7
Sid Fernandez	0	1	13.50	1	1	0	0	0	4.0	7	6	1	5
Dwight Gooden	0	0	2.95	3	2	0	0	0	18.1	10	6	8	20
Terry Leach	0	0	0.00	3	0	0	0	0	5.0	4	0	1	4
Roger McDowell	0	1	4.50	4	0	0	0	0	6.0	6	3	2	5
Randy Myers	2	0	0.00	3	0	0	0	0	4.2	1	0	2	0
TOTAL	3	4	3.94	22	7	1	0	0	64.0	52	28	25	54

GAME 1 AT LA OCT 4

NY	000	000	003	3	8	1
LA	100	000	100	2	4	0

Pitchers: Gooden, MYERS (8) vs Hershiser, HOWELL (9)
Attendance: 55,582

GAME 2 AT LA OCT 5

NY	000	200	001	3	6	0
LA	140	010	00X	6	7	0

Pitchers: CONE, Aguilera (3), Leach (6), McDowell (8) vs BELCHER, Orosco (9), Pena (9)
Home Runs: Hernandez-NY
Attendance: 55,780

GAME 3 AT NY OCT 8

LA	021	000	010	4	7	2
NY	001	002	05X	8	9	2

Pitchers: Hershiser, Howell (8), PENA (8), Orosco (8), Horton (8) vs Darling, McDowell (7), MYERS (8), Cone (9)
Attendance: 44,672

GAME 4 AT NY OCT 9

LA	200	000	002	001	5	7	1
NY	000	301	000	000	4	10	2

Pitchers: Tudor, Holton (6), Horton (7), PENA (9), Hershiser (12) vs Gooden, Myers (9), McDOWELL (11)
Home Runs: Strawberry-NY, McReynolds-NY, Scioscia-LA, Gibson-LA
Attendance: 54,014

GAME 5 AT NY OCT 10

LA	000	330	001	7	12	0
NY	000	030	010	4	9	1

Pitchers: BELCHER, Horton (8), Holton (8) vs FERNANDEZ, Leach (5), Aguilera (6), McDowell (8)
Home Runs: Gibson-LA, Dykstra-NY
Attendance: 52,069

GAME 6 AT LA OCT 11

NY	101	021	000	5	11	0
LA	000	010	000	1	5	2

Pitchers: CONE vs LEARY, Holton (5), Horton (6), Orosco (8)
Home Runs: McReynolds-NY
Attendance: 55,885

GAME 7 AT LA OCT 12

NY	000	000	000	0	5	2
LA	150	000	00X	6	10	0

Pitchers: DARLING, Gooden (2), Leach (5), Aguilera (7) vs HERSHISER
Attendance: 55,693

Jose Canseco's three home runs and Dennis Eckersley's sparkling relief pitching highlighted Oakland's sweep to the pennant. In his six shutout innings, Eckersley gave up just one hit and a pair of walks while fanning five, to record an ALCS record four saves.

Canseco's fourth-inning solo shot off Bruce Hurst put the A's out in front in Game 1. Boston tied it up in the seventh, but two former Boston players—Carney Lansford, who doubled, and Dave Henderson, who singled him home—put Oakland back in front in the eighth, and Eckersley (also an ex-Bostonian) held the Sox through the final two innings.

Oakland's Storm Davis and Boston's Roger Clemens dueled scorelessly through five innings of Game 2. The Sox took advantage of an Oakland error to score twice in the sixth, but four Oakland hits in the seventh (including a two-run homer by Canseco), a balk, and a wild pitch put the A's up, 3–2. Rich Gedman's home run for Boston in the last of the seventh tied the score, but in the ninth Oakland's rookie shortstop Walt Weiss singled home what proved the game winner off Sox ace reliever Lee Smith.

Boston unloaded for five runs in the first two innings of Game 3. But Weiss' double and home runs by Mark McGwire and Carney Lansford in the last of the second brought the A's within one run of a tie, and Ron Hassey's two-run homer an inning later gave the A's a lead that they held to the end. Dave Henderson's two-run blast in the eighth capped Oakland's 10–6 victory.

Canseco's first-inning homer in Game 4 put the A's ahead to stay, as starter Dave Stewart and relievers Rick Honeycutt and Eckersley combined for a four-hit, 4–1 pennant clincher.

Oakland Athletics (West), 4; Boston Red Sox (East), 0

OAK (W)

PLAYER/POS	AVG	G	AB	R	H	2B	3B	HR	RB	BB	SO	SB
Don Baylor, dh	.000	2	6	0	0	0	0	0	1	1	2	0
Greg Cadaret, p	.000	1	0	0	0	0	0	0	0	0	0	0
Jose Canseco, of	.313	4	16	4	5	1	0	3	4	1	2	1
Storm Davis, p	.000	1	0	0	0	0	0	0	0	0	0	0
Dennis Eckersley, p	.000	4	0	0	0	0	0	0	0	0	0	0
Mike Gallego, 2b	.083	4	12	1	1	0	0	0	0	0	3	0
Ron Hassey, c	.500	4	8	2	4	1	0	1	3	1	1	0
Dave Henderson, of	.375	4	16	2	6	1	0	1	4	1	7	0
Rick Honeycutt, p	.000	3	0	0	0	0	0	0	0	0	0	0
Stan Javier, of	.500	2	4	0	2	0	0	0	0	1	1	0
Carney Lansford, 3b	.294	4	17	4	5	1	0	1	2	0	2	0
Mark McGwire, 1b	.333	4	15	4	5	0	0	1	3	1	5	0
Gene Nelson, p	.000	2	0	0	0	0	0	0	0	0	0	0
Dave Parker, dh-2,of-1	.250	3	12	1	3	1	0	0	0	0	4	0
Tony Phillips, of-2,2b-1	.286	2	7	0	2	1	0	0	0	1	3	0
Eric Plunk, p	.000	1	0	0	0	0	0	0	0	0	0	0
Luis Polonia, of-1	.400	3	5	0	2	0	0	0	0	1	2	0
Terry Steinbach, c	.250	2	4	0	1	0	0	0	0	2	0	0
Dave Stewart, p	.000	2	0	0	0	0	0	0	0	0	0	0
Walt Weiss, ss	.333	4	15	2	5	2	0	0	2	0	4	0
Bob Welch, p	.000	1	0	0	0	0	0	0	0	0	0	0
Curt Young, p	.000	1	0	0	0	0	0	0	0	0	0	0
TOTAL	.299		137	20	41	8	0	7	20	10	35	1

PITCHER	W	L	ERA	G	GS	CG	SV	SHO	IP	H	ER	BB	SO
Greg Cadaret	0	0	27.00	1	0	0	0	0	0.1	1	1	0	0
Storm Davis	0	0	0.00	1	1	0	0	0	6.1	2	0	5	4
Dennis Eckersley	0	0	0.00	4	0	0	4	0	6.0	1	0	2	5
Rick Honeycutt	1	0	0.00	3	0	0	0	0	2.0	0	0	2	0
Gene Nelson	2	0	0.00	2	0	0	0	0	4.2	5	0	1	0
Eric Plunk	0	0	0.00	1	0	0	0	0	0.1	0	0	0	0
Dave Stewart	1	0	1.35	2	2	0	0	0	13.1	9	2	6	11
Bob Welch	0	0	27.00	1	1	0	0	0	1.2	6	5	2	0
Curt Young	0	0	0.00	1	0	0	0	0	1.1	2	0	0	2
TOTAL	4	0	2.00	16	4	0	4	0	36.0	26	8	18	23

BOS (E)

PLAYER/POS	AVG	G	AB	R	H	2B	3B	HR	RB	BB	SO	SB
Marty Barrett, 2b	.067	4	15	2	1	0	0	0	0	1	0	0
Todd Benzinger, 1b-3	.091	4	11	0	1	0	0	0	0	1	3	0
Mike Boddicker, p	.000	1	0	0	0	0	0	0	0	0	0	0
Wade Boggs, 3b	.385	4	13	2	5	0	0	0	3	3	4	0
Ellis Burks, of	.235	4	17	2	4	1	0	0	1	0	3	0
Roger Clemens, p	.000	1	0	0	0	0	0	0	0	0	0	0
Dwight Evans, of	.167	4	12	1	2	1	0	0	1	3	5	0
Wes Gardner, p	.000	1	0	0	0	0	0	0	0	0	0	0
Rich Gedman, c	.357	4	14	1	5	0	0	1	1	2	1	0
Mike Greenwell, of	.214	4	14	2	3	1	0	1	3	3	0	0
Bruce Hurst, p	.000	2	0	0	0	0	0	0	0	0	0	0
Spike Owen, dh	.000	1	0	0	0	0	0	0	0	1	0	0
Larry Parrish, 1b-2	.000	4	6	0	0	0	0	0	0	0	2	0
Jody Reed, ss	.273	4	11	0	3	1	0	0	0	2	1	0
Jim Rice, dh	.154	4	13	0	2	0	0	0	1	2	4	0
Ed Romero, pr	.000	1	0	0	0	0	0	0	0	0	0	0
Kevin Romine, pr	.000	2	0	1	0	0	0	0	0	0	0	0
Lee Smith, p	.000	2	0	0	0	0	0	0	0	0	0	0
Mike Smithson, p	.000	1	0	0	0	0	0	0	0	0	0	0
Bob Stanley, p	.000	2	0	0	0	0	0	0	0	0	0	0
TOTAL	.206		126	11	26	4	0	2	10	18	23	0

PITCHER	W	L	ERA	G	GS	CG	SV	SHO	IP	H	ER	BB	SO
Mike Boddicker	0	1	20.25	1	1	0	0	0	2.2	8	6	1	2
Roger Clemens	0	0	3.86	1	1	0	0	0	7.0	6	3	0	8
Wes Gardner	0	0	5.79	1	0	0	0	0	4.2	6	3	2	8
Bruce Hurst	0	2	2.77	2	2	1	0	0	13.0	10	4	5	12
Lee Smith	0	1	8.10	2	0	0	0	0	3.1	6	3	1	4
Mike Smithson	0	0	0.00	1	0	0	0	0	2.1	3	0	0	1
Bob Stanley	0	0	9.00	2	0	0	0	0	1.0	2	1	1	0
TOTAL	0	4	5.29	10	4	1	0	0	34.0	41	20	10	35

GAME 1 AT BOS OCT 5

OAK	000	100	010	2	6	0
BOS	000	000	100	1	6	0

Pitchers: Stewart, HONEYCUTT (7), Eckersley (8) vs HURST
Home Runs: Canseco-OAK
Attendance: 34,104

GAME 2 AT BOS OCT 6

OAK	000	000	301	4	10	1
BOS	000	002	100	3	4	1

Pitchers: Davis, Cadaret (7), NELSON (7), Eckersley (9) vs Clemens, Stanley (8), SMITH (8)
Home Runs: Canseco-OAK, Gedman-BOS
Attendance: 34,605

GAME 3 AT OAK OCT 8

BOS	320	000	100	6	12	0
OAK	042	010	12X	10	15	1

Pitchers: BODDICKER, Gardner (3), Stanley (8) vs Welch, NELSON (2), Young (6), Plunk (7), Honeycutt (7), Eckersley (8)
Home Runs: Greenwell-BOS, McGwire-OAK, Lansford-OAK, Hassey-OAK, Henderson-OAK
Attendance: 49,261

GAME 4 AT OAK OCT 9

BOS	000	001	000	1	4	0
OAK	101	000	02X	4	10	1

Pitchers: HURST, Smithson (5), Smith (7) vs STEWART, Honeycutt (8), Eckersley (9)
Home Runs: Canseco-OAK
Attendance: 49,406

Mickey Hatcher's home run in the first inning of Game 1 set the tone for the Dodgers' surprising triumph over Oakland's mighty A's. Hatcher, who homered only once during the season, initiated the Series scoring with a two-run blast to left center. Half an inning later the A's Jose Canseco—baseball's leading slugger, with 42 homers—erased the Dodger lead with his first career grand slam. But while Hatcher went on to hit safely six more times in the Series—including another home run—Canseco's first hit was also his last, as he went 0-for-19 the rest of the way. The Dodgers scored once in the sixth inning to draw within one run of a tie, but remained behind until the last of the ninth when, with two outs and one on, Kirk Gibson pinch hit for pitcher Alejandro Peña. Gibson, the Dodgers' top source of power during the season, was so hobbled by leg injuries that he had, till that moment, sat out the game in the training room. But with two strikes on him he belted a home run off baseball's premier reliever, Dennis Eckersley, to win the game. It was Gibson's only Series appearance.

Dodgers ace Orel Hershiser blanked the A's on three hits in Game 2 and led the offense with three hits of his own. His single in the third inning began a five-run rally (capped by Mike Marshall's three-run homer), and his fourth-inning double drove in the Dodgers' sixth and final run.

When the Series moved to Oakland, the A's recovered for a dramatic win in Game 3, as Mark McGwire (who had homered 32 times during the season) broke a 1–1 tie with his only Series hit, a solo homer in the last of the ninth. In Game 4, Dodgers reliever Jay Howell, who had yielded the losing home run the day before, got McGwire to pop up with the bases full to end the seventh inning, and blanked the A's the rest of the way to preserve a narrow 4–3 victory.

Hershiser returned to pitch Game 5. He allowed two runs in his four-hitter, but Mickey Hatcher had given the Dodgers the lead with a two-run homer in the first inning, and Mike Davis (who had homered just twice during the season) drove a 3–0 pitch into the stands for two more runs in the fourth. Veteran catcher Rick Dempsey (substituting for injured first-stringer Mike Scioscia) doubled home a fifth Los Angeles run in the sixth, and the Dodgers were on their way to a seventh world title.

Los Angeles Dodgers (NL), 4;
Oakland Athletics (AL), 1

LA (N)

PLAYER/POS	AVG	G	AB	R	H	2B	3B	HR	RB	BB	SO	SB
Dave Anderson, dh	.000	1	1	0	0	0	0	0	0	0	1	0
Tim Belcher, p	.000	2	0	0	0	0	0	0	0	0	0	0
Mike Davis, dh-2,of-1	.143	4	7	3	1	0	0	2	2	4	0	2
Rick Dempsey, c	.200	2	5	0	1	1	0	0	1	1	2	0
Kirk Gibson, ph	1.000	1	1	1	1	0	0	1	2	0	0	0
Jose Gonzalez, of-3	.000	4	2	0	0	0	0	0	0	0	0	0
Alfredo Griffin, ss	.188	5	16	2	3	0	0	0	0	2	4	0
Jeff Hamilton, 3b	.105	5	19	1	2	0	0	0	0	1	4	0
Mickey Hatcher, of	.368	5	19	5	7	1	0	2	5	1	3	0
Danny Heep, of-1,dh-1	.250	3	8	0	2	1	0	0	0	0	2	0
Orel Hershiser, p	1.000	2	3	1	3	2	0	0	1	0	0	0
Brian Holton, p	.000	1	0	0	0	0	0	0	0	0	0	0
Jay Howell, p	.000	2	0	0	0	0	0	0	0	0	0	0
Tim Leary, p	.000	2	0	0	0	0	0	0	0	0	0	0
Mike Marshall, of	.231	5	13	2	3	0	0	1	3	0	5	0
Alejandro Pena, p	.000	2	0	0	0	0	0	0	0	0	0	0
Steve Sax, 2b	.300	5	20	3	6	0	0	0	0	1	1	0
Mike Scioscia, c	.214	4	14	0	3	0	0	0	1	0	2	0
John Shelby, of	.222	5	18	0	4	1	0	0	1	2	7	1
Franklin Stubbs, 1b	.294	5	17	3	5	2	0	0	2	1	3	0
John Tudor, p	.000	1	0	0	0	0	0	0	0	0	0	0
Tracy Woodson, 1b-3	.000	4	4	0	0	0	0	0	0	1	0	0
TOTAL	.246		167	21	41	8	1	6	19	13	36	4

PITCHER	W	L	ERA	G	GS	CG	SV	SHO	IP	H	ER	BB	SO
Tim Belcher	1	0	6.23	2	2	0	0	0	8.2	10	6	6	10
Orel Hershiser	2	0	1.00	2	2	2	0	1	18.0	7	2	6	17
Brian Holton	0	0	0.00	1	0	0	0	0	2.0	0	0	1	0
Jay Howell	0	1	3.38	2	0	0	1	0	2.2	3	1	1	2
Tim Leary	0	0	1.35	2	0	0	0	0	6.2	6	1	2	4
Alejandro Pena	1	0	0.00	2	0	0	0	0	5.0	2	0	1	7
John Tudor	0	0	0.00	1	1	0	0	0	1.1	0	0	0	1
TOTAL	4	1	2.03	12	5	2	1	1	44.1	28	10	17	41

OAK (A)

PLAYER/POS	AVG	G	AB	R	H	2B	3B	HR	RB	BB	SO	SB
Don Baylor, ph	.000	1	1	0	0	0	0	0	0	0	1	0
Todd Burns, p	.000	1	0	0	0	0	0	0	0	0	0	0
Greg Cadaret, p	.000	3	0	0	0	0	0	0	0	0	0	0
Jose Canseco, of	.053	5	19	1	1	0	0	1	5	2	5	1
Storm Davis, p	.000	2	1	0	0	0	0	0	0	0	1	0
Dennis Eckersley, p	.000	2	0	0	0	0	0	0	0	0	0	0
Mike Gallego, 2b	.000	1	0	0	0	0	0	0	0	0	0	0
Ron Hassey, c-4	.250	5	8	0	2	0	0	0	1	3	3	0
Dave Henderson, of	.300	5	20	1	6	2	0	0	1	2	7	0
Rick Honeycutt, p	.000	3	0	0	0	0	0	0	0	0	0	0
Glenn Hubbard, 2b	.250	4	12	2	3	0	0	0	0	1	2	1
Stan Javier, of-2	.500	3	4	0	2	0	0	0	0	2	1	0
Carney Lansford, 3b	.167	5	18	2	3	0	0	0	1	2	2	0
Mark McGwire, 1b	.059	5	17	1	1	0	0	1	1	3	4	0
Gene Nelson, p	.000	3	0	0	0	0	0	0	0	0	0	0
Dave Parker, of-2,dh-2	.200	4	15	0	3	0	0	0	0	2	4	0
Tony Phillips, 2b-1,of-1	.250	2	4	1	1	0	0	0	0	1	2	0
Eric Plunk, p	.000	2	0	0	0	0	0	0	0	0	0	0
Luis Polonia, of-2	.111	3	9	1	1	0	0	0	0	0	2	0
Terry Steinbach, c-2,dh-1	.364	3	11	0	4	1	0	0	0	0	2	0
Dave Stewart, p	.000	2	3	1	0	0	0	0	0	1	3	0
Walt Weiss, ss	.063	5	16	1	1	0	0	0	0	0	2	1
Bob Welch, p	.000	1	0	0	0	0	0	0	0	0	0	0
Curt Young, p	.000	1	0	0	0	0	0	0	0	0	0	0
TOTAL	.177		158	11	28	3	0	2	11	17	41	3

PITCHER	W	L	ERA	G	GS	CG	SV	SHO	IP	H	ER	BB	SO
Todd Burns	0	0	0.00	1	0	0	0	0	0.1	0	0	0	0
Greg Cadaret	0	0	0.00	3	0	0	0	0	2.0	2	0	0	3
Storm Davis	0	2	11.25	2	2	0	0	0	8.0	14	10	1	7
Dennis Eckersley	0	1	10.80	2	0	0	0	0	1.2	2	2	1	2
Rick Honeycutt	1	0	0.00	3	0	0	0	0	3.1	1	0	0	5
Gene Nelson	0	0	1.42	3	0	0	0	0	6.1	4	1	3	3
Eric Plunk	0	0	0.00	2	0	0	0	0	1.2	0	0	0	3
Dave Stewart	0	1	3.14	2	2	0	0	0	14.1	12	5	5	5
Bob Welch	0	0	1.80	1	1	0	0	0	5.0	6	1	3	8
Curt Young	0	0	0.00	1	0	0	0	0	1.0	1	0	0	0
TOTAL	1	4	3.92	20	5	0	0	0	43.2	41	19	13	36

GAME 1 AT LA OCT 15

```
OAK   040 000 000    4 7 0
LA    200 001 002    5 7 0
```
Pitchers: Stewart, ECKERSLEY (9) vs Belcher, Leary (3), Holton (6), PENA (8) Home Runs: Hatcher-LA, Canseco-OAK, Gibson-LA
Attendance: 55,983

GAME 2 AT LA OCT 16

```
OAK   000 000 000    0 3 0
LA    005 100 00X    6 10 1
```
Pitchers: DAVIS, Nelson (4), Young (6), Plunk (7), Honeycutt (8) vs HERSHISER
Home Runs: Marshall-LA
Attendance: 56,051

GAME 3 AT OAK OCT 18

```
LA    000 010 000    1 8 1
OAK   001 000 001    2 5 0
```
Pitchers: Tudor, Leary (2), Pena (6), J.HOWELL (9) vs Welch, Cadaret (6), Nelson (6), HONEYCUTT (8)
Home Runs: McGwire-OAK
Attendance: 49,316

GAME 4 AT OAK OCT 19

```
LA    201 000 100    4 8 1
OAK   100 001 100    3 9 2
```
Pitchers: BELCHER, J.Howell (7) vs STEWART, Cadaret (7), Eckersley (9)
Attendance: 49,317

GAME 5 AT OAK OCT 20

```
LA    200 201 000    5 8 0
OAK   001 000 010    2 4 0
```
Pitchers: HERSHISER vs DAVIS, Cadaret (5), Nelson (5), Honeycutt (8), Plunk (9), Burns (9)
Home Runs: Hatcher-LA, Davis-LA
Attendance: 49,317

From the first inning of Game 1 when they drove in their teams' first runs, first basemen Will Clark of the Giants and Mark Grace of the Cubs dominated the offense, finishing with eight RBIs apiece and NLCS record-shattering batting average of .650 and .647, respectively. Although Grace homered for two Chicago runs in the opener, the game belonged to Clark, whose four hits—two of them home runs, one a grand slam—drove in six of the 11 San Francisco runs.

Grace led the Cubs' retaliation the next day with his second three-hit game, driving in four of Chicago's nine runs with doubles in the first and sixth innings. Kevin Mitchell, Matt Williams, and Robby Thompson—runners-up to Clark for Giants offensive honors in the series—all homered in the losing cause.

Chicago scored first in the next three games but lost them all narrowly. Thompson's two-run homer in the last of the seventh put the Giants ahead for good in Game 3. The next day, Williams's two-run single in the third inning overcame Chicago's lead, and his two-run homer in the fifth broke a 4–4 tie to conclude the scoring.

Cubs starter Mike Bielecki stopped San Francisco on a pair of singles through six innings of Game 5; he carried a 1–0 lead into the seventh, when Clark's triple and Mitchell's sacrifice fly tied the score. An inning later, after Bielecki loaded the bases with three two-out walks, relief ace Mitch Williams was called on to face Clark and got two strikes on him. But after fouling off a slider and fastball, Clark lined a single up the middle for two go-ahead runs. San Francisco closer Steve Bedrosian yielded Chicago a second run in the ninth on a trio of two-out singles, but Ryne Sandberg (until then batting .421 in the series) grounded out, and the Giants owned their first pennant in 27 years.

San Francisco Giants (West), 4; Chicago Cubs (East), 1

SF (W)

PLAYER/POS	AVG	G	AB	R	H	2B	3B	HR	RB	BB	SO	SB
Bill Bathe, ph	.000	2	1	0	0	0	0	0	0	0	1	0
Steve Bedrosian, p	.000	4	0	0	0	0	0	0	0	0	0	0
Jeff Brantley, p	.000	3	0	0	0	0	0	0	0	1	0	0
Brett Butler, of	.211	5	19	6	4	0	0	0	0	3	3	0
Will Clark, 1b	.650	5	20	8	13	3	1	2	8	2	2	0
Kelly Downs, p	.000	2	3	0	0	0	0	0	0	0	1	0
Scott Garrelts, p	.000	2	4	0	0	0	0	0	0	1	1	0
Atlee Hammaker, p	.000	1	0	0	0	0	0	0	0	0	0	0
Terry Kennedy, c	.188	5	16	0	3	1	0	0	0	1	4	0
Mike LaCoss, p	.000	1	1	0	0	0	0	0	0	0	0	0
Craig Lefferts, p	.000	2	0	0	0	0	0	0	0	0	0	0
Greg Litton, 3b	1.000	1	1	0	1	0	0	0	0	0	0	0
Candy Maldonado, of	.000	3	3	1	0	0	0	0	1	2	0	0
Kirt Manwaring, c	.000	3	2	0	0	0	0	0	0	0	0	0
Kevin Mitchell, of	.353	5	17	5	6	0	0	2	7	3	3	0
Donell Nixon, of-2	.000	3	3	0	0	0	0	0	0	0	1	1
Ken Oberkfell, 3b-1	.000	3	4	0	0	0	0	0	0	0	0	0
Rick Reuschel, p	.000	2	2	0	0	0	0	0	0	0	0	0
Ernest Riles, ph	.000	1	1	0	0	0	0	0	0	0	0	0
Don Robinson, p	.000	1	0	0	0	0	0	0	0	0	0	0
Pat Sheridan, of	.154	5	13	1	2	0	1	0	0	0	4	0
Robby Thompson, 2b	.278	5	18	5	5	0	0	2	3	3	2	0
Jose Uribe, ss	.235	5	17	2	4	1	0	0	1	1	5	1
Matt Williams, 3b-5,ss-1	.300	5	20	2	6	1	0	2	9	0	2	0
TOTAL	.267		165	30	44	6	2	8	29	17	29	2

PITCHER	W	L	ERA	G	GS	CG	SV	SHO	IP	H	ER	BB	SO
Steve Bedrosian	0	0	2.70	4	0	0	3	0	3.1	4	1	2	2
Jeff Brantley	0	0	0.00	3	0	0	0	0	5.0	1	0	2	3
Kelly Downs	1	0	3.12	2	0	0	0	0	8.2	8	3	6	6
Scott Garrelts	1	0	5.40	2	2	0	0	0	11.2	16	7	2	8
Atlee Hammaker	0	0	0.00	1	0	0	0	0	1.0	1	0	0	0
Mike LaCoss	0	0	9.00	1	1	0	0	0	3.0	7	3	0	2
Craig Lefferts	0	0	9.00	2	0	0	0	0	1.0	1	1	2	1
Rick Reuschel	1	1	5.19	2	2	0	0	0	8.2	12	5	2	5
Don Robinson	1	0	0.00	1	0	0	0	0	1.2	3	0	0	0
TOTAL	4	1	4.09	18	5	0	3	0	44.0	53	20	16	27

CHI (E)

PLAYER/POS	AVG	G	AB	R	H	2B	3B	HR	RB	BB	SO	SB
Paul Assenmacher, p	.000	2	0	0	0	0	0	0	0	0	0	0
Mike Bielecki, p	.200	2	5	0	1	0	0	0	0	2	2	0
Andre Dawson, of	.105	5	19	0	2	1	0	0	3	2	6	0
Shawon Dunston, ss	.316	5	19	2	6	0	0	0	0	1	1	1
Joe Girardi, c	.100	4	10	1	1	0	0	0	0	1	2	0
Mark Grace, 1b	.647	5	17	3	11	3	1	1	8	4	1	1
Paul Kilgus, p	.000	1	0	0	0	0	0	0	0	0	0	0
Lester Lancaster, p	.000	3	1	0	0	0	0	0	0	0	1	0
Vance Law, 3b-1	.000	2	3	0	0	0	0	0	0	0	3	0
Greg Maddux, p-2	.000	2	3	1	0	0	0	0	0	0	0	0
L. McClendon, c-2,of-1	.667	3	3	0	2	0	0	0	1	0	0	0
Domingo Ramos, ph	.000	1	1	0	0	0	0	0	0	0	0	0
Luis Salazar, 3b	.368	5	19	2	7	0	1	1	2	0	0	0
Ryne Sandberg, 2b	.400	5	20	6	8	3	1	1	4	3	4	0
Scott Sanderson, p	.000	1	0	0	0	0	0	0	0	0	0	0
Dwight Smith, of	.200	4	15	2	3	1	0	0	0	2	2	1
Rick Sutcliffe, p	.500	1	2	0	1	1	0	0	0	0	0	0
Jerome Walton, of	.364	5	22	4	8	0	0	0	0	2	2	0
Mitch Webster, of-2	.333	3	3	0	1	0	0	0	0	0	0	0
Curtis Wilkerson, 3b-1	.500	3	2	1	1	0	0	0	0	0	0	0
Mitch Williams, p	.000	2	0	0	0	0	0	0	0	0	0	0
Steve Wilson, p	.000	2	0	0	0	0	0	0	0	0	0	0
Rick Wrona, c	.000	2	5	0	0	0	0	0	0	0	3	0
Marvell Wynne, of-2	.167	4	6	0	1	0	0	0	0	0	0	0
TOTAL	.303		175	22	53	9	3	3	21	16	27	3

PITCHER	W	L	ERA	G	GS	CG	SV	SHO	IP	H	ER	BB	SO
P. Assenmacher	0	0	13.50	2	0	0	0	0	0.2	3	1	0	0
Mike Bielecki	0	1	3.65	2	2	0	0	0	12.1	7	5	6	11
Paul Kilgus	0	0	0.00	1	0	0	0	0	3.0	4	0	1	1
Lester Lancaster	1	1	6.00	3	0	0	0	0	6.0	6	4	1	3
Greg Maddux	0	1	13.50	2	2	0	0	0	7.1	13	11	4	5
Scott Sanderson	0	0	0.00	1	0	0	0	0	2.0	2	0	0	1
Rick Sutcliffe	0	0	4.50	1	1	0	0	0	6.0	5	3	4	2
Mitch Williams	0	0	0.00	2	0	0	0	0	1.0	1	0	2	2
Steve Wilson	0	1	4.91	2	0	0	0	0	3.2	3	2	1	4
TOTAL	1	4	5.57	16	5	0	0	0	42.0	44	26	17	29

GAME 1 AT CHI OCT 4

SF	301	400	030	11	13	0
CHI	201	000	000	3	10	1

Pitchers: GARRELTS, Brantley (8), Hammaker (9) vs MADDUX, Kilgus (5), Wilson (8)
Home Runs: Grace-CHI, Clark-SF (2), Sandberg-CHI, Mitchell-SF
Attendance: 39,195

GAME 2 AT CHI OCT 5

SF	000	200	021	5	10	0
CHI	600	003	00X	9	11	0

Pitchers: REUSCHEL, Downs (1), Lefferts (6), Brantley (7), Bedrosian (8) vs Bielecki, Assenmacher (5), LANCASTER (6)
Home Runs: Mitchell-SF, Williams-SF, Thompson-SF
Attendance: 39,195

GAME 3 AT SF OCT 7

CHI	200	100	100	4	10	0
SF	300	000	20X	5	8	3

Pitchers: Sutcliffe, Assenmacher (7), LANCASTER (7) vs LaCoss, Brantley (4), ROBINSON (7), Lefferts (8), Bedrosian (9)
Home Runs: Thompson-SF
Attendance: 62,065

GAME 4 AT SF OCT 8

CHI	110	020	000	4	12	1
SF	102	120	00X	6	9	1

Pitchers: Maddux, WILSON (4), Sanderson (6), Williams (8) vs Garrelts, DOWNS (5), Bedrosian (9)
Home Runs: Salazar-CHI, Williams-SF
Attendance: 62,078

GAME 5 AT SF OCT 9

CHI	001	000	001	2	10	1
SF	000	000	12X	3	4	1

Pitchers: BIELECKI, Williams (8), Lancaster (8) vs REUSCHEL, Bedrosian (9)
Attendance: 62,084

The awesome A's produced their share of heroes. Jose Canseco powered a truly heroic home run into the top deck of Toronto's SkyDome in Game 4; Dave Parker, in his seventh postseason series, at last hit his first postseason homer (and later his second); closer Dennis Eckersley added three saves to his four from 1988 to establish a new LCS record; and Carney Lansford was batting .455, with four RBIs, when a hamstring pull in Game 3 ended his series play. But the hero of heroes was leadoff batter Rickey Henderson.

Oakland might have won the opener without Henderson, even though his hard slide into second in the sixth inning broke up a double play and forced a wide throw that gave the A's two runs and their first lead of the game. And the A's might also have won the next day even if Henderson had not rattled Toronto with four stolen bases. The A's suffered their loss in Game 3 despite an early 2–0 lead with Henderson scoring both runs—the first after walking, the second after a double and stolen base.

But in the final two games, Rickey Henderson's contribution made the difference between defeat and victory. A pair of two-run Henderson homers (together with Canseco's memorable blast and later RBI single) gave the A's their 6–5 win in Game 4. And in the first inning of Game 5, Henderson, after walking, stole his eighth base—a postseason series record—before Canseco singled him home with the A's first run. Two innings later Henderson tripled home the second Oakland run. The A's scored twice more in the seventh, but Toronto had narrowed Oakland's lead to one run when Eckersley fanned a final Blue Jay to secure the second straight Oakland pennant. Rickey Henderson was the unanimous choice for series MVP.

Oakland Athletics (West), 4;
Toronto Blue Jays (East), 1

OAK (W)

PLAYER/POS	AVG	G	AB	R	H	2B	3B	HR	RB	BB	SO	SB
Lance Blankenship, 2b	.000	1	0	0	0	0	0	0	0	0	0	0
Jose Canseco, of	.294	5	17	1	5	0	0	1	3	3	7	0
Storm Davis, p	.000	1	0	0	0	0	0	0	0	0	0	0
Dennis Eckersley, p	.000	4	0	0	0	0	0	0	0	0	0	0
Mike Gallego, 2b-2,ss-2	.273	4	11	3	3	1	0	0	1	0	2	0
Ron Hassey, c	.167	2	6	0	1	0	0	0	1	1	2	0
Dave Henderson, of	.263	5	19	4	5	3	0	1	1	2	5	0
Rickey Henderson, of	.400	5	15	8	6	1	1	2	5	7	0	8
Rick Honeycutt, p	.000	3	0	0	0	0	0	0	0	0	0	0
Stan Javier, of	.000	1	2	0	0	0	0	0	0	0	1	0
Carney Lansford, 3b	.455	3	11	2	5	0	0	0	4	2	1	2
Mark McGwire, 1b	.389	5	18	3	7	1	0	1	3	1	4	0
Mike Moore, p	.000	1	0	0	0	0	0	0	0	0	0	0
Gene Nelson, p	.000	1	0	0	0	0	0	0	0	0	0	0
Dave Parker, dh	.188	4	16	2	3	0	0	2	3	0	0	0
Ken Phelps, ph	1.000	1	1	0	1	1	0	0	0	0	0	0
Tony Phillips, 2b-3,3b-3	.167	5	18	1	3	1	0	0	1	2	4	2
Terry Steinbach, c-3,dh-1	.200	4	15	0	3	0	0	0	1	1	5	0
Dave Stewart, p	.000	2	0	0	0	0	0	0	0	0	0	0
Walt Weiss, ss	.111	4	9	2	1	1	0	0	0	1	1	1
Bob Welch, p	.000	1	0	0	0	0	0	0	0	0	0	0
Matt Young, p	.000	1	0	0	0	0	0	0	0	0	0	0
TOTAL	.272		158	26	43	9	1	7	23	20	32	13

PITCHER	W	L	ERA	G	GS	CG	SV	SHO	IP	H	ER	BB	SO
Storm Davis	0	1	7.11	1	1	0	0	0	6.1	5	5	2	3
Dennis Eckersley	0	0	1.59	4	0	0	3	0	5.2	4	1	0	2
Rick Honeycutt	0	0	32.40	3	0	0	0	0	1.2	6	6	5	1
Mike Moore	1	0	0.00	1	1	0	0	0	7.0	3	0	2	3
Gene Nelson	0	0	0.00	1	0	0	0	0	1.1	1	0	0	2
Dave Stewart	2	0	2.81	2	2	0	0	0	16.0	13	5	3	9
Bob Welch	1	0	3.18	1	1	0	0	0	5.2	8	2	1	4
Matt Young	0	0	0.00	1	0	0	0	0	0.1	0	0	2	0
TOTAL	4	1	3.89	14	5	0	3	0	44.0	40	19	15	24

TOR (E)

PLAYER/POS	AVG	G	AB	R	H	2B	3B	HR	RB	BB	SO	SB
Jim Acker, p	.000	5	0	0	0	0	0	0	0	0	0	0
George Bell, dh-3,of-2	.200	5	20	2	4	0	0	1	2	0	3	0
Pat Borders, c	1.000	1	1	0	1	0	0	0	1	0	0	0
John Cerutti, p	.000	2	0	0	0	0	0	0	0	0	0	0
Junior Felix, of	.273	3	11	0	3	1	0	0	3	0	2	0
Tony Fernandez, ss	.350	5	20	6	7	3	0	0	1	1	2	5
Mike Flanagan, p	.000	1	0	0	0	0	0	0	0	0	0	0
Kelly Gruber, 3b	.294	5	17	2	5	1	0	0	1	3	2	1
Tom Henke, p	.000	3	0	0	0	0	0	0	0	0	0	0
Jimmy Key, p	.000	1	0	0	0	0	0	0	0	0	0	0
Manny Lee, 2b	.250	2	8	2	2	0	0	0	0	0	1	0
Nelson Liriano, 2b	.429	3	7	1	3	0	0	0	1	2	0	3
Lee Mazzilli, dh-2	.000	3	8	0	0	0	0	0	0	0	2	0
Fred McGriff, 1b	.143	5	21	3	3	0	0	0	3	0	4	0
Lloyd Moseby, of	.313	5	16	4	5	0	0	1	2	5	2	1
Rance Mulliniks, ph	.000	1	1	0	0	0	0	0	0	0	1	0
Dave Stieb, p	.000	2	0	0	0	0	0	0	0	0	0	0
Todd Stottlemyre, p	.000	1	0	0	0	0	0	0	0	0	0	0
Duane Ward, p	.000	2	0	0	0	0	0	0	0	0	0	0
David Wells, p	.000	1	0	0	0	0	0	0	0	0	0	0
Ernie Whitt, c	.125	5	16	1	2	0	0	1	3	2	3	0
Mookie Wilson, of	.263	5	19	2	5	0	0	0	2	2	2	1
TOTAL	.242		165	21	40	5	0	3	19	15	24	11

PITCHER	W	L	ERA	G	GS	CG	SV	SHO	IP	H	ER	BB	SO
Jim Acker	0	0	1.42	5	0	0	0	0	6.1	4	1	1	4
John Cerutti	0	0	0.00	2	0	0	0	0	2.2	0	0	3	1
Mike Flanagan	0	1	10.38	1	1	0	0	0	4.1	7	5	1	3
Tom Henke	0	0	0.00	3	0	0	0	0	2.2	0	0	0	3
Jimmy Key	1	0	4.50	1	1	0	0	0	6.0	7	3	2	2
Dave Stieb	0	2	6.35	2	2	0	0	0	11.1	12	8	6	10
Todd Stottlemyre	0	1	7.20	1	1	0	0	0	5.0	7	4	2	3
Duane Ward	0	0	7.36	2	0	0	0	0	3.2	6	3	3	5
David Wells	0	0	0.00	1	0	0	0	0	1.0	0	0	2	1
TOTAL	1	4	5.02	18	5	0	0	0	43.0	43	24	20	32

GAME 1 AT OAK OCT 3

```
TOR   020 100 000    3  5  1
OAK   010 013 02X    7 11  0
```
Pitchers: STIEB, Acker (6), Ward (8) vs STEWART, Eckersley (9)
Home Runs: D.Henderson-OAK, Whitt-TOR, McGwire-OAK
Attendance: 49,435

GAME 2 AT OAK OCT 4

```
TOR   001 000 020    3  5  1
OAK   000 203 10X    6  9  1
```
Pitchers: STOTTLEMYRE, Acker (6), Wells (6), Cerutti (8) vs MOORE, Honeycutt (8), Eckersley (8)
Home Runs: Parker-OAK
Attendance: 49,444

GAME 3 AT TOR OCT 6

```
OAK   101 100 000    3  8  1
TOR   000 400 30X    7  8  0
```
Pitchers: DAVIS, Honeycutt (7), Nelson (7), M.Young (8) vs KEY, Acker (7), Henke (9)
Home Runs: Parker-OAK
Attendance: 50,268

GAME 4 AT TOR OCT 7

```
OAK   003 020 100    6 11  1
TOR   000 101 120    5 13  0
```
Pitchers: WELCH, Honeycutt (6), Eckersley (8) vs FLANAGAN, Ward (5), Cerutti (8), Acker (9)
Home Runs: R.Henderson-OAK (2), Canseco-OAK
Attendance: 50,076

GAME 5 AT TOR OCT 8

```
OAK   101 000 200    4  4  0
TOR   000 000 012    3  9  0
```
Pitchers: STEWART, Eckersley (9) vs STIEB, Acker (7), Henke (9)
Home Runs: Moseby-TOR, Bell-TOR
Attendance: 50,024

Not even the devastating earthquake that blindsided baseball's first San Francisco Bay World Series could halt the Oakland juggernaut. The A's scored first in every game and, except for an inning and a half of Game 2 in which the score stood at 1–1, held their lead to the finish.

A's ace Dave Stewart shut out the Giants on five hits in the opener. Three second-inning Oakland runs initiated the Series scoring, and Dave Parker and Walt Weiss expanded Stewart's margin of comfort with solo homers in the third and fourth. In Game 2, doubles by Carney Lansford in the first inning and Parker in the fourth drove home the two runs the A's would need for victory; Terry Steinbach's three-run blast later in the fourth added frosting to Oakland's cake. A's starter Mike Moore yielded a pair of singles and the first Giant run of the Series in the third inning but held the Giants to just two more singles in his seven-plus innings of work. Relievers Rick Honeycutt and Dennis Eckersley hurled perfect ball in the eighth and ninth.

After a day off, the Series shifted 11 miles across the Bay to San Francisco for Game 3. But just as fans were settling into their seats, the earthquake struck, knocking out power to Candlestick Park and (as gradually became known) killing 67 people in scattered pockets of destruction throughout the Bay Area. The fans were sent home, but despite the pleas of a few Eastern reporters that the rest of the Series be cancelled, the overwhelming desire of Bay Area residents prevailed, and Game 3 came off at last, 10 days late. Starter Dave Stewart gave up three runs in seven innings, but by the time he was relieved, his A's had sent nine men across the plate. Four more runs in the eighth completed the Oakland scoring. The Giants put together their first big inning of the Series, scoring four runs in the last of the ninth. Although the Giants' effort fell far short of what was needed, pinch hitter Bill Bathe's home run—the game's seventh, including five by the A's—set a new World Series record.

Oakland's Rickey Henderson led off Game 4 with a home run, and by the time Kevin Mitchell homered in San Francisco's first pair of runs in the sixth inning, the A's had scored eight times. The Giants struggled back, though, scoring four times in the seventh on a walk and a cycle of hits—home run, triple, double, and single—to draw within two runs of a tie. But they came no closer. Oakland scored a ninth run an inning later, and Todd Burns and Dennis Eckersley hurled the Series to its

Oakland Athletics (AL), 4;
San Francisco Giants (NL), 0

OAK (A)

PLAYER/POS	AVG	G	AB	R	H	2B	3B	HR	RB	BB	SO	SB
Lance Blankenship, 2b	.500	1	2	1	1	0	0	0	0	0	0	0
Todd Burns, p	.000	2	0	0	0	0	0	0	0	0	0	0
Jose Canseco, of	.357	4	14	5	5	0	0	1	3	4	3	1
Dennis Eckersley, p	.000	2	0	0	0	0	0	0	0	0	0	0
Mike Gallego, 2b-1,3b-1	.000	2	1	0	0	0	0	0	0	0	0	0
Dave Henderson, of	.308	4	13	6	4	2	0	2	4	4	3	0
Rickey Henderson, of	.474	4	19	4	9	1	2	1	3	2	2	3
Rick Honeycutt, p	.000	3	0	0	0	0	0	0	0	0	0	0
Stan Javier, of	.000	1	0	0	0	0	0	0	0	0	0	0
Carney Lansford, 3b	.438	4	16	5	7	1	0	1	4	3	1	0
Mark McGwire, 1b	.294	4	17	0	5	1	0	0	1	1	3	0
Mike Moore, p	.333	2	3	1	1	1	0	0	2	0	1	0
Gene Nelson, p	.000	2	0	0	0	0	0	0	0	0	0	0
Dave Parker, dh-2	.222	3	9	2	2	1	0	1	2	0	2	0
Ken Phelps, ph	.000	1	1	0	0	0	0	0	0	0	0	0
Tony Phillips, 2b-3,3b-2,of-1	.235	4	17	2	4	1	0	1	3	0	3	0
Terry Steinbach, c	.250	4	16	3	4	0	1	1	7	2	1	0
Dave Stewart, p	.000	2	3	0	0	0	0	0	0	0	1	0
Walt Weiss, ss	.133	4	15	3	2	0	0	1	1	2	2	0
TOTAL	.301		146	32	44	8	3	9	30	18	22	4

PITCHER	W	L	ERA	G	GS	CG	SV	SHO	IP	H	ER	BB	SO
Todd Burns	0	0	0.00	2	0	0	0	0	1.2	1	0	1	0
Dennis Eckersley	0	0	0.00	2	0	0	1	0	1.2	0	0	0	0
Rick Honeycutt	0	0	6.75	3	0	0	0	0	2.2	4	2	0	2
Mike Moore	2	0	2.08	2	2	0	0	0	13.0	9	3	3	10
Gene Nelson	0	0	54.00	2	0	0	0	0	1.0	4	6	2	1
Dave Stewart	2	0	1.69	2	2	1	0	1	16.0	10	3	2	14
TOTAL	4	0	3.50	13	4	1	1	1	36.0	28	14	8	27

SF (N)

PLAYER/POS	AVG	G	AB	R	H	2B	3B	HR	RB	BB	SO	SB
Bill Bathe, ph	.500	2	2	1	1	0	0	1	3	0	0	0
Steve Bedrosian, p	.000	2	0	0	0	0	0	0	0	0	0	0
Jeff Brantley, p	.000	3	0	0	0	0	0	0	0	0	0	0
Brett Butler, of	.286	4	14	1	4	1	0	0	1	2	1	2
Will Clark, 1b	.250	4	16	2	4	1	0	0	0	1	3	0
Kelly Downs, p	.000	3	0	0	0	0	0	0	0	0	1	0
Scott Garrelts, p	.000	2	1	0	0	0	0	0	0	0	1	0
Atlee Hammaker, p	.000	2	0	0	0	0	0	0	0	0	0	0
Terry Kennedy, c	.167	4	12	1	2	0	0	0	2	1	3	0
Mike LaCoss, p	.000	2	1	0	0	0	0	0	0	0	0	0
Craig Lefferts, p	.000	3	0	0	0	0	0	0	0	0	0	0
Greg Litton, 2b-2,3b-1	.500	2	6	1	3	1	0	1	3	0	0	0
Candy Maldonado, of-3	.091	4	11	1	1	0	1	0	0	0	4	0
Kirt Manwaring, c	1.000	1	1	1	1	1	0	0	0	0	0	0
Kevin Mitchell, of	.294	4	17	2	5	0	0	1	2	0	3	0
Donell Nixon, of	.200	2	5	1	1	0	0	0	0	1	1	0
Ken Oberkfell, 3b	.333	4	6	1	2	0	0	0	0	3	0	0
Rick Reuschel, p	.000	1	0	0	0	0	0	0	0	0	0	0
Ernie Riles, dh-2	.000	4	8	0	0	0	0	0	0	0	1	0
Don Robinson, p	.000	1	0	0	0	0	0	0	0	0	0	0
Pat Sheridan, of	.000	1	2	0	0	0	0	0	0	0	0	0
Robby Thompson, 2b	.091	4	11	0	1	0	0	0	0	2	4	0
Jose Uribe, ss	.200	3	5	1	1	0	0	0	0	0	0	0
Matt Williams, ss-4,ss-3	.125	4	16	1	2	0	0	1	1	0	6	0
TOTAL	.209		134	14	28	4	1	4	14	8	27	2

PITCHER	W	L	ERA	G	GS	CG	SV	SHO	IP	H	ER	BB	SO
Steve Bedrosian	0	0	0.00	2	0	0	0	0	2.2	0	0	2	2
Jeff Brantley	0	0	4.15	3	0	0	0	0	4.1	5	2	3	1
Kelly Downs	0	0	7.71	3	0	0	0	0	4.2	3	4	2	4
Scott Garrelts	0	2	9.82	2	2	0	0	0	7.1	13	8	1	8
Atlee Hammaker	0	0	15.43	2	0	0	0	0	2.1	8	4	0	2
Mike LaCoss	0	0	6.23	2	0	0	0	0	4.1	4	3	3	2
Craig Lefferts	0	0	3.38	3	0	0	0	0	2.2	2	1	2	1
Rick Reuschel	0	1	11.25	1	1	0	0	0	4.0	5	5	4	2
Don Robinson	0	1	21.60	1	1	0	0	0	1.2	4	4	1	0
TOTAL	0	4	8.21	19	4	0	0	0	34.0	44	31	18	22

conclusion with two and a third innings of perfect relief.

GAME 1 AT OAK OCT 14

SF	000	000	000	0	5	1
OAK	031	100	00X	5	11	1

Pitchers: GARRELTS, Hammaker (5), Brantley (6), LaCoss (8) vs STEWART
Home Runs: Parker-OAK, Weiss-OAK
Attendance: 49,385

GAME 2 AT OAK OCT 15

SF	001	000	000	1	4	0
OAK	100	400	00X	5	7	0

Pitchers: REUSCHEL, Downs (5), Lefferts (7), Bedrosian (8) vs MOORE, Honeycutt (8), Eckersley (9)
Home Runs: Steinbach-OAK
Attendance: 49,388

GAME 3 AT SF OCT 27

OAK	200	241	040	13	14	0
SF	010	200	004	7	10	3

Pitchers: STEWART, Honeycutt (8), Nelson (9), Burns (9) vs GARRELTS, Downs (4), Brantley (5), Hammaker (8), Lefferts (9)
Home Runs: Williams-SF, D.Henderson-OAK (2), Phillips-OAK, Canseco-OAK, Lansford-OAK, Bathe-SF
Attendance: 62,038

GAME 4 AT SF OCT 28

OAK	130	031	010	9	12	0
SF	000	002	400	6	9	0

Pitchers: MOORE, Nelson (7), Honeycutt (7), Burns (7), Eckersley (9) vs ROBINSON, LaCoss (2), Brantley (6), Downs (6), Lefferts (8), Bedrosian (8)
Home Runs: R.Henderson-OAK, Mitchell-SF, Litton-SF
Attendance: 62,032

Fielding plays and misplays provided some of the most crucial moments of the series. After the Pirates had overcome a three-run deficit to tie the score in Game 1, they won the game when Eric Davis misplayed Andy Van Slyke's fly to left field for a run-scoring double. Cincinnati right fielder Paul O'Neill evened the series in Game 2 by singling home the game's first run in the first inning, then (with the game tied 1–1 in the fifth) doubling in the go-ahead—and final—run on a fly Pirates left fielder Barry Bonds lost in the late afternoon sun. Finally, O'Neill gunned down Pittsburgh's potential tying run at third base when Van Slyke attempted to move up after Bonds's fly-out to right.

Two- and three-run homers by Reds Billy Hatcher and Mariano Duncan gave Cincinnati the series advantage in Game 3, and Chris Sabo's sacrifice fly and two-run blast proved the decisive blows a day later as the Reds pushed their series lead to 3–1. In that game left fielder Eric Davis, backing up Bobby Bonilla's double off the center field wall, prevented what would have become a game-tying run when, with a perfect throw to third, he nailed Bonilla trying for a triple.

The Pirates staved off elimination with a narrow 3–2 win in Game 5, a win preserved by a spectacular bases-loaded game-ending double play. But in Game 6, Pittsburgh's uncertain fielding in the first inning gave the Reds their first and, as it turned out, decisive run. In the ninth inning, with the Reds ahead 2–1, Reds right fielder Glen Braggs snared a deep fly with a leaping catch that prevented at least one, and perhaps two, Pirates runs from scoring. One strikeout later the Reds had snared the National League pennant.

Cincinnati Reds (West), 4; Pittsburgh Pirates (East), 2

CIN (W)

PLAYER/POS	AVG	G	AB	R	H	2B	3B	HR	RB	BB	SO	SB
Billy Bates, pr	.000	2	0	1	0	0	0	0	0	0	0	0
Todd Benzinger, 1b-2	.333	5	9	0	3	0	0	0	0	2	0	0
Glenn Braggs, of	.200	2	5	0	1	0	0	0	0	0	1	0
Tom Browning, p	.000	2	3	0	0	0	0	0	0	0	1	0
Norm Charlton, p	.000	4	0	0	0	0	0	0	0	0	0	0
Eric Davis, of	.174	6	23	2	4	1	0	0	2	1	9	0
Rob Dibble, p	.000	4	2	0	0	0	0	0	0	0	1	0
Mariano Duncan, 2b	.300	6	20	1	6	0	0	1	4	0	8	0
Billy Hatcher, of	.333	4	15	2	5	1	0	1	2	0	2	0
Danny Jackson, p	.000	2	3	0	0	0	0	0	0	0	2	0
Barry Larkin, ss	.261	6	23	5	6	2	0	0	1	3	1	3
Rick Mahler, p	.000	1	0	0	0	0	0	0	0	0	0	0
Hal Morris, 1b-4	.417	5	12	3	5	0	0	0	1	1	0	0
Randy Myers, p	.000	4	0	0	0	0	0	0	0	0	0	0
Ron Oester, 2b-2	.333	4	3	1	1	0	0	0	0	0	1	0
Joe Oliver, c	.143	5	14	1	2	0	0	0	0	0	2	0
Paul O'Neill, of	.471	5	17	1	8	3	0	1	4	1	1	1
Luis Quinones, ph	.500	3	2	1	1	0	0	0	0	2	0	1
Jeff Reed, c	.000	4	7	0	0	0	0	0	0	0	2	0
Jose Rijo, p	.000	2	5	0	0	0	0	0	0	0	1	0
Chris Sabo, 3b	.227	6	22	1	5	0	0	1	3	1	4	0
Scott Scudder, p	.000	1	0	0	0	0	0	0	0	0	0	0
Herm Winningham, of-2	.286	3	7	1	2	1	0	0	1	1	1	1
TOTAL	.255		192	20	49	9	0	4	20	10	37	6

PITCHER	W	L	ERA	G	GS	CG	SV	SHO	IP	H	ER	BB	SO
Tom Browning	1	1	3.27	2	2	0	0	0	11.0	9	4	6	5
Norm Charlton	1	1	1.80	4	0	0	0	0	5.0	4	1	3	3
Rob Dibble	0	0	0.00	4	0	0	1	0	5.0	0	0	1	10
Danny Jackson	1	0	2.38	2	2	0	0	0	11.1	8	3	7	8
Rick Mahler	0	0	0.00	1	0	0	0	0	1.2	2	0	0	0
Randy Myers	0	0	0.00	4	0	0	3	0	5.2	2	0	3	7
Jose Rijo	1	0	4.38	2	2	0	0	0	12.1	10	6	7	15
Scott Scudder	0	0	0.00	1	0	0	0	0	1.0	1	0	0	1
TOTAL	4	2	2.38	20	6	0	4	0	53.0	36	14	27	49

PIT (E)

PLAYER/POS	AVG	G	AB	R	H	2B	3B	HR	RB	BB	SO	SB
Wally Backman, 3b-2	.143	3	7	1	1	1	0	0	0	1	3	1
Stan Belinda, p	.000	3	0	0	0	0	0	0	0	0	0	0
Jay Bell, ss	.250	6	20	3	5	1	0	1	1	4	3	0
Barry Bonds, of	.167	6	18	4	3	0	0	0	1	6	5	2
Bobby Bonilla, of-5,3b-3	.190	6	21	0	4	1	0	0	1	3	1	0
Sid Bream, 1b	.500	4	8	1	4	1	0	1	3	2	3	0
Doug Drabek, p	.167	2	6	0	1	0	0	0	0	0	2	0
Jeff King, 3b-4	.100	5	10	0	1	0	0	0	0	1	5	0
Bill Landrum, p	.000	2	0	0	0	0	0	0	0	0	0	0
Mike LaValliere, c	.000	3	6	1	0	0	0	0	0	3	1	0
Jose Lind, 2b	.238	6	21	1	5	1	1	1	2	1	4	0
Carmelo Martinez, 1b	.250	2	8	0	2	2	0	0	2	0	1	0
Bob Patterson, p	.000	2	0	0	0	0	0	0	0	0	0	0
Ted Power, p	.000	2	1	0	0	0	0	0	0	0	1	0
Gary Redus, 1b-2	.250	5	8	1	2	0	0	0	0	1	3	1
R. J. Reynolds, of-3	.200	6	10	0	2	0	0	0	0	2	2	1
Don Slaught, c	.091	4	11	0	1	1	0	0	1	2	3	0
John Smiley, p	.000	1	0	0	0	0	0	0	0	0	0	0
Zane Smith, p	.000	2	3	0	0	0	0	0	0	0	1	0
Andy Van Slyke, of	.208	6	24	3	5	1	1	0	3	1	7	1
Bob Walk, p	.000	2	4	0	0	0	0	0	0	0	4	0
TOTAL	.194		186	15	36	9	2	3	14	27	49	6

PITCHER	W	L	ERA	G	GS	CG	SV	SHO	IP	H	ER	BB	SO
Stan Belinda	0	0	2.45	3	0	0	0	0	3.2	3	1	0	4
Doug Drabek	1	1	1.65	2	2	1	0	0	16.1	12	3	3	13
Bill Landrum	0	0	0.00	2	0	0	0	0	2.0	0	0	0	1
Bob Patterson	0	0	0.00	2	0	0	1	0	1.0	1	0	2	0
Ted Power	0	0	3.60	2	1	0	1	0	5.0	6	2	2	3
John Smiley	0	0	0.00	1	0	0	0	0	2.0	2	0	0	0
Zane Smith	0	2	6.00	2	1	0	0	0	9.0	14	6	1	8
Bob Walk	1	1	4.85	2	2	0	0	0	13.0	11	7	2	8
TOTAL	2	4	3.29	16	6	1	2	0	52.0	49	19	10	37

GAME 1 AT CIN OCT 4

```
PIT   001 200 100   4 7 1
CIN   300 000 000   3 5 0
```

Pitchers: WALK, Belinda (7), Patterson (9), Power (9) vs Rijo, CHARLTON (6), Dibble (9)
Home Runs: Bream-PIT
Attendance: 55,700

GAME 2 AT CIN OCT 5

```
PIT   000 010 000   1 6 0
CIN   100 010 00X   2 5 0
```

Pitchers: DRABEK vs BROWNING, Dibble (8), Myers (8)
Home Runs: Lind-PIT
Attendance: 54,456

GAME 3 AT PIT OCT 8

```
CIN   020 030 001   6 13 1
PIT   000 200 010   3 8 0
```

Pitchers: JACKSON, Dibble (6), Charlton (8), Myers (9) vs SMITH, Landrum (6), Smiley (7), Belinda (9)
Home Runs: Duncan-CIN, Hatcher-CIN
Attendance: 45,611

GAME 4 AT PIT OCT 9

```
CIN   000 200 201   5 10 1
PIT   100 100 010   3 8 0
```

Pitchers: RIJO, Myers (8), Dibble (9) vs WALK, Power (8)
Home Runs: O'Neill-CIN, Sabo-CIN, Bell-PIT
Attendance: 50,461

GAME 5 AT PIT OCT 10

```
CIN   100 000 010   2 7 0
PIT   200 100 00X   3 6 1
```

Pitchers: BROWNING, Mahler (6), Charlton (7), Scudder (8) vs DRABEK, Patterson (9)
Attendance: 48,221

GAME 6 AT CIN OCT 12

```
PIT   000 010 000   1 1 3
CIN   100 000 10X   2 9 0
```

Pitchers: Power, SMITH (3), Belinda (7), Landrum (8) vs Jackson, CHARLTON (7), Myers (8)
Attendance: 56,079

The ejection of Boston ace Roger Clemens from Game 4 for mouthing off to an umpire provided a moment of raucous counterpoint to the surgical precision with which Oakland dismembered the Red Sox. While the A's pitchers anesthetized Boston's hitters, parceling out just one run per game, their batters sliced up the Sox with singles, steals, and sacrifices.

In the fourth inning of Game 1, Boston's Wade Boggs interrupted a pitchers' duel between Clemens and Oakland's Dave Stewart with the series' only home run. But in the top of the seventh—after a tiring Clemens had been relieved—the A's evened the score with a walk, single, and sacrifice fly, took the lead an inning later with a pair of singles sandwiched around a bunt and stolen base, then buried the Sox with seven runs in the ninth. DH Harold Baines provided Oakland's most productive offense in the second game, singling home the tying run in the fourth inning, driving in the tiebreaker with a groundout in the seventh, and doubling home a third run in the ninth. In Game 3, a double steal by Baines and Jose Canseco set up the A's tying and tiebreaking runs, which scored on a sacrifice fly and a single.

The A's scored first for the only time in the series in Game 4, on a pair of singles and a grounder to short in the second inning. Following the shouting match between the Sox and umpires that erupted when pitcher Clemens was thrown out for disputing a walk, Mike Gallego doubled home two more Oakland runs. A trio of Boston relievers stopped the A's the rest of the way, and a pair of Red Sox hits in the ninth ended Dave Stewart's shutout bid. But Rick Honeycutt came on to preserve Stewart's second win of the series and sew up Oakland's third successive American League championship.

Oakland Athletics (West), 4;
Boston Red Sox (East), 0

OAK (W)

PLAYER/POS	AVG	G	AB	R	H	2B	3B	HR	RB	BB	SO	SB
Harold Baines, dh	.357	4	14	2	5	1	0	0	3	2	1	1
Lance Blankenship, dh	.000	3	0	1	0	0	0	0	0	0	0	1
Jose Canseco, of	.182	4	11	3	2	0	0	0	1	5	5	2
Dennis Eckersley, p	.000	3	0	0	0	0	0	0	0	0	0	0
Mike Gallego, ss-3,2b-2	.400	4	10	1	4	1	0	0	2	1	1	0
Ron Hassey, c-1,dh-1	.333	2	3	0	1	0	0	0	0	2	0	0
Dave Henderson, of	.167	2	6	1	0	0	0	0	1	0	2	1
Rickey Henderson, of	.294	4	17	1	5	0	0	0	3	1	2	2
Rick Honeycutt, p	.000	3	0	0	0	0	0	0	0	0	0	0
Doug Jennings, of	.000	1	1	0	0	0	0	0	0	0	0	0
Carney Lansford, 3b	.438	4	16	2	7	1	0	0	2	0	1	0
Willie McGee, of-2,dh-1	.222	3	9	3	2	1	0	0	0	1	2	2
Mark McGwire, 1b	.154	4	13	2	2	0	0	0	2	3	3	0
Mike Moore, p	.000	1	0	0	0	0	0	0	0	0	0	0
Gene Nelson, p	.000	1	0	0	0	0	0	0	0	0	0	0
Jamie Quirk, ph	1.000	1	1	0	1	0	0	0	0	0	0	0
Willie Randolph, 2b	.375	4	8	1	3	0	0	0	3	1	0	0
Terry Steinbach, c	.455	3	11	2	5	0	0	0	1	1	2	0
Dave Stewart, p	.000	2	0	0	0	0	0	0	0	0	0	0
Walt Weiss, ss	.000	2	7	2	0	0	0	0	0	2	2	0
Bob Welch, p	.000	1	0	0	0	0	0	0	0	0	0	0
TOTAL	.299		127	20	38	4	0	0	18	19	21	9

PITCHER	W	L	ERA	G	GS	CG	SV	SHO	IP	H	ER	BB	SO
Dennis Eckersley	0	0	0.00	3	0	0	2	0	3.1	2	0	0	3
Rick Honeycutt	0	0	0.00	3	0	0	1	0	1.2	0	0	0	0
Mike Moore	1	0	1.50	1	1	0	0	0	6.0	4	1	1	5
Gene Nelson	0	0	0.00	1	0	0	0	0	1.2	3	0	0	0
Dave Stewart	2	0	1.13	2	2	0	0	0	16.0	8	2	4	4
Bob Welch	1	0	1.23	1	1	0	0	0	7.1	6	1	3	4
TOTAL	4	0	1.00	11	4	0	3	0	36.0	23	4	6	16

BOS (E)

PLAYER/POS	AVG	G	AB	R	H	2B	3B	HR	RB	BB	SO	SB
Larry Andersen, p	.000	3	0	0	0	0	0	0	0	0	0	0
Marty Barrett, 2b	.000	3	0	0	0	0	0	0	0	0	0	0
Mike Boddicker, p	.000	1	0	0	0	0	0	0	0	0	0	0
Wade Boggs, 3b	.438	4	16	1	7	1	0	1	1	0	3	0
Tom Bolton, p	.000	2	0	0	0	0	0	0	0	0	0	0
Tom Brunansky, of	.083	4	12	0	1	0	0	0	1	1	3	0
Ellis Burks, of	.267	4	15	1	4	2	0	0	0	1	1	1
Roger Clemens, p	.000	2	0	0	0	0	0	0	0	0	0	0
Dwight Evans, dh	.231	4	13	0	3	1	0	0	0	1	3	0
Jeff Gray, p	.000	2	0	0	0	0	0	0	0	0	0	0
Mike Greenwell, of	.000	4	14	1	0	0	0	0	0	2	2	0
Greg Harris, p	.000	1	0	0	0	0	0	0	0	0	0	0
Danny Heep, ph	.000	2	2	0	0	0	0	0	0	0	0	0
Dana Kiecker, p	.000	1	0	0	0	0	0	0	0	0	0	0
Randy Kutcher, pr	.000	2	0	0	0	0	0	0	0	0	0	0
Dennis Lamp, p	.000	1	0	0	0	0	0	0	0	0	0	0
Mike Marshall, ph	.333	3	3	0	1	0	0	0	0	0	0	0
Rob Murphy, p	.000	1	0	0	0	0	0	0	0	0	0	0
Tony Pena, c	.214	4	14	0	3	0	0	0	0	0	0	0
Carlos Quintana, 1b	.000	4	13	0	0	0	0	0	1	1	0	0
Jeff Reardon, p	.000	1	0	0	0	0	0	0	0	0	0	0
Jody Reed, 2b-4,ss-3	.133	4	15	0	2	0	0	0	1	0	2	0
Luis Rivera, ss	.222	4	9	1	2	1	0	0	0	0	0	0
TOTAL	.183		126	4	23	5	0	1	4	6	16	1

PITCHER	W	L	ERA	G	GS	CG	SV	SHO	IP	H	ER	BB	SO
Larry Andersen	0	1	6.00	3	0	0	0	0	3.0	3	2	3	3
Mike Boddicker	0	1	2.25	1	1	1	0	0	8.0	6	2	3	7
Tom Bolton	0	0	0.00	2	0	0	0	0	3.0	2	0	2	3
Roger Clemens	0	1	3.52	2	2	0	0	0	7.2	7	3	5	4
Jeff Gray	0	0	2.70	2	0	0	0	0	3.1	4	1	1	2
Greg Harris	0	1	27.00	1	0	0	0	0	0.1	3	1	0	0
Dana Kiecker	0	0	1.59	1	1	0	0	0	5.2	6	1	1	2
Dennis Lamp	0	0	108.00	1	0	0	0	0	0.1	2	4	2	0
Rob Murphy	0	0	13.50	1	0	0	0	0	0.2	2	1	1	0
Jeff Reardon	0	0	9.00	1	0	0	0	0	2.0	3	2	1	0
TOTAL	0	4	4.50	15	4	1	0	0	34.0	38	17	19	21

In the most stunning World Series sweep since 1954, Cincinnati's fired-up Reds roasted the team many were proclaiming baseball's newest dynasty. Reds left fielder Eric Davis, playing despite shoulder and knee injuries, provided the A's their first hint of what was to come when—on the first pitch thrown to him in the first inning—he homered over the center field wall for two runs. Billy Hatcher, on base with a walk, scored ahead of Davis, the first of his Series-high six runs. Hatcher would not be retired at the plate until Game 3. For Oakland starter Dave Stewart, the 7–0 loss in Game 1 ended a personal postseason six-game win streak. For the club, the loss ended a streak of 10 postseason wins in a row.

The A's put up their best fight of the Series in Game 2, scoring first, then overcoming a 2–1 deficit in the third inning with three more runs for a 4–2 lead. Cincinnati narrowed the gap with a run in the fourth and tied the score in the eighth when Hatcher tripled—setting a World Series record with his seventh straight hit—and came home on a grounder to short. The A's held on until the 10th inning, when ace reliever Dennis Eckersley gave up three straight hits to lose the game.

Game 3 was another Cincinnati blowout, an 8–3 contest in which all 11 runs were scored in the second and third innings. Chris Sabo led the Reds assault with two home runs, and handled a Series-record 10 chances at third base.

For seven innings of Game 4 the tide of battle seemed to be turning in Oakland's favor. Billy Hatcher —who was batting .750—left the game after a pitch hit his hand in the first inning. Later in the inning Eric Davis tore a kidney diving for a Willie McGee shot that went for a double. McGee went on to score, and Davis departed for the hospital. A renewed Dave Stewart, supported by sharp fielding, seemed capable of sustaining his 1–0 lead to the finish. But in the eighth the Reds, with just one solid hit, eked out the two runs they would need for victory. After loading the bases with a leadoff single, a third-strike bunt that went for a hit, and a sacrifice bunt that Stewart misplayed for an error, the Reds drove home the tying run with a grounder to short and took the lead on a sacrifice fly. Meanwhile Reds starter Jose Rijo held the A's hitless after the first inning, leveling 20 men in order from the second into the ninth, when ace closer Randy Myers relieved him for the final two outs of the sweep.

Cincinnati Reds (NL), 4; Oakland Athletics (AL), 0

CIN (N)

PLAYER/POS	AVG	G	AB	R	H	2B	3B	HR	RB	BB	SO	SB
Jack Armstrong, p	.000	1	0	0	0	0	0	0	0	0	0	0
Billy Bates, ph	1.000	1	1	1	1	0	0	0	0	0	0	0
Todd Benzinger, 1b-3	.182	4	11	1	2	0	0	0	0	0	0	0
Glenn Braggs, of-1	.000	2	4	0	0	0	0	0	0	2	1	0
Tom Browning, p	.000	1	0	0	0	0	0	0	0	0	0	0
Norm Charlton, p	.000	1	0	0	0	0	0	0	0	0	0	0
Eric Davis, of	.286	4	14	3	4	0	0	1	5	0	0	0
Rob Dibble, p	.000	3	0	0	0	0	0	0	0	0	0	0
Mariano Duncan, 2b	.143	4	14	1	2	0	0	0	1	2	2	1
Billy Hatcher, of	.750	4	12	6	9	4	1	0	2	2	0	0
Danny Jackson, p	.000	1	1	0	0	0	0	0	0	0	1	0
Barry Larkin, ss	.353	4	17	3	6	1	1	0	1	2	0	0
Hal Morris, 1b-2,dh-2	.071	4	14	0	1	0	0	0	2	1	1	0
Randy Myers, p	.000	3	0	0	0	0	0	0	0	0	0	0
Ron Oester, ph	1.000	1	1	0	1	0	0	0	0	1	0	0
Joe Oliver, c	.333	4	18	2	6	3	0	0	2	0	1	0
Paul O'Neill, of	.083	4	12	2	1	0	0	0	1	5	2	1
Jose Rijo, p	.333	2	3	0	1	0	0	0	0	0	0	0
Chris Sabo, 3b	.563	4	16	2	9	1	0	2	5	2	2	0
Scott Scudder, p	.000	1	0	0	0	0	0	0	0	0	0	0
Herm Winningham, of-1	.500	2	4	1	2	0	0	0	0	0	0	0
TOTAL	.317		142	22	45	9	2	3	22	15	9	2

PITCHER	W	L	ERA	G	GS	CG	SV	SHO	IP	H	ER	BB	SO
Jack Armstrong	0	0	0.00	1	0	0	0	0	3.0	1	0	0	3
Tom Browning	1	0	4.50	1	1	0	0	0	6.0	6	3	2	2
Norm Charlton	0	0	0.00	1	0	0	0	0	1.0	1	0	0	0
Rob Dibble	1	0	0.00	3	0	0	0	0	4.2	3	0	1	4
Danny Jackson	0	0	10.13	1	1	0	0	0	2.2	6	3	2	0
Randy Myers	0	0	0.00	3	0	0	1	0	3.0	2	0	0	3
Jose Rijo	2	0	0.59	2	2	0	0	0	15.1	9	1	5	14
Scott Scudder	0	0	0.00	1	0	0	0	0	1.1	0	0	2	2
TOTAL	4	0	1.70	13	4	0	1	0	37.0	28	7	12	28

OAK (A)

PLAYER/POS	AVG	G	AB	R	H	2B	3B	HR	RB	BB	SO	SB
Harold Baines, dh-2	.143	3	7	1	1	0	0	0	1	2	1	2	0
Lance Blankenship, ph	.000	1	1	0	0	0	0	0	0	0	1	0
Mike Bordick, ss	.000	3	0	0	0	0	0	0	0	0	0	0
Todd Burns, p	.000	2	0	0	0	0	0	0	0	0	0	0
Jose Canseco, of-3,dh-1	.083	4	12	1	1	0	0	1	2	2	3	0
Dennis Eckersley, p	.000	2	0	0	0	0	0	0	0	0	0	0
Mike Gallego, ss	.091	4	11	0	1	0	0	0	1	1	3	1
Ron Hassey, c-1	.333	3	6	0	2	0	0	0	1	0	0	0
Dave Henderson, of-3	.231	4	13	2	3	1	0	0	0	1	3	0
Rickey Henderson, of	.333	4	15	2	5	2	0	1	1	3	4	3
Rick Honeycutt, p	.000	1	0	0	0	0	0	0	0	0	0	0
Doug Jennings, ph	1.000	1	1	0	1	0	0	0	0	0	0	0
Joe Klink, p	.000	1	0	0	0	0	0	0	0	0	0	0
Carney Lansford, 3b	.267	4	15	0	4	0	0	0	1	1	0	1
Willie McGee, of-3	.200	4	10	1	2	1	0	0	0	0	2	1
Mark McGwire, 1b	.214	4	14	1	3	0	0	0	0	2	4	0
Mike Moore, p	.000	1	0	0	0	0	0	0	0	0	0	0
Gene Nelson, p	.000	2	0	0	0	0	0	0	0	0	0	0
Jamie Quirk, c	.000	1	3	0	0	0	0	0	0	0	2	0
Willie Randolph, 2b	.267	4	15	0	4	0	0	0	0	1	0	1
Scott Sanderson, p	.000	2	0	0	0	0	0	0	0	0	0	0
Terry Steinbach, c	.125	3	8	0	1	0	0	0	0	0	1	0
Dave Stewart, p	.000	2	1	0	0	0	0	0	0	0	1	0
Bob Welch, p	.000	1	3	0	0	0	0	0	0	0	2	0
Curt Young, p	.000	1	0	0	0	0	0	0	0	0	0	0
TOTAL	.207		135	8	28	4	0	3	8	12	28	7

PITCHER	W	L	ERA	G	GS	CG	SV	SHO	IP	H	ER	BB	SO
Todd Burns	0	0	16.20	2	0	0	0	0	1.2	5	3	2	0
Dennis Eckersley	0	1	6.75	2	0	0	0	0	1.1	3	1	0	1
Rick Honeycutt	0	0	0.00	1	0	0	0	0	1.2	2	0	1	0
Joe Klink	0	0	—	1	0	0	0	0	0.0	0	0	1	0
Mike Moore	0	1	6.75	1	1	0	0	0	2.2	8	2	0	1
Gene Nelson	0	0	0.00	2	0	0	0	0	5.0	3	0	2	0
Scott Sanderson	0	0	10.80	2	0	0	0	0	1.2	4	2	1	0
Dave Stewart	0	2	3.46	2	2	1	0	0	13.0	10	5	6	5
Bob Welch	0	0	4.91	1	1	0	0	0	7.1	9	4	2	2
Curt Young	0	0	0.00	1	0	0	0	0	1.0	1	0	0	0
TOTAL	0	4	4.33	15	4	1	0	0	35.1	45	17	15	9

GAME 1 AT CIN OCT 16

OAK	000	000	000	0	9 1
CIN	202	030	00X	7	10 0

Pitchers: STEWART, Burns (5), Nelson (5), Sanderson (7), Eckersley (8) vs RIJO, Dibble (8), Myers (9)
Home Runs: Davis-CIN
Attendance: 55,830

GAME 2 AT CIN OCT 17

OAK	103	000	000	0	4 10 2
CIN	200	100	010	1	5 14 2

Pitchers: Welch, Honeycutt (8), ECKERSLEY (10) vs Jackson, Scudder (3), Armstrong (5), Charlton (8), DIBBLE (9)
Home Runs: Canseco-OAK
Attendance: 55,832

GAME 3 AT OAK OCT 19

CIN	017	000	000	8 14 1
OAK	021	000	000	3 7 1

Pitchers: BROWNING, Dibble (7), Myers (8) vs MOORE, Sanderson (3), Klink (4), Nelson (4), Burns (8), Young (9)
Home Runs: Sabo-CIN (2), Baines-OAK, R.Henderson-OAK
Attendance: 48,269

GAME 4 AT OAK OCT 20

CIN	000	000	020	2 7 1
OAK	100	000	000	1 2 1

Pitchers: RIJO, Myers (9) vs STEWART
Attendance: 48,613

Pitching dominated this back-and-forth series which featured four shutouts, including three 1–0 games. Three times Atlanta hurlers blanked Pittsburgh on the Pirates' home grounds. Andy Van Slyke opened the series scoring with a first-inning home run. Pirates starter Doug Drabek held the Braves scoreless through six innings of the opener, before injuring himself on the basepaths. By the time David Justice homered in the ninth for Atlanta's only score, the Pirates had the game well in hand.

Atlanta evened the series in Game 2 behind the pitching of Steve Avery and Alejandro Pena, and the bat and glove of Mark Lemke. The Braves' second baseman doubled home that game's only run in the sixth inning and prevented a Pittsburgh run from scoring in the eighth with a diving stop of a grounder up the middle. In Atlanta for Game 3, the Braves took the series lead with a 10–3 rout that featured home runs by Ron Gant, Greg Olson, and Sid Bream. (Orlando Merced and Jay Bell homered for Pittsburgh.)

Game 4 was much closer. The Braves took a quick lead with two first-inning runs, but Pittsburgh scored once in the second and tied the game in the fifth on a throwing error. In the top of the 10th, Andy Van Slyke led off with a walk. With two away he stole second, and then scored what proved the winning run on Don Slaught's double. With the series even again, Atlanta lost a run in Game 5 when David Justice was ruled out for missing third base as he dashed home from second. An inning later the Pirates parlayed a walk and a pair of singles into the only run they would need to carry the series advantage back to Pittsburgh.

In Game 6, though, the Braves returned the favor, tying the series once more with a gem of their own. Avery and Pena combined for their second 1–0 victory, while Drabek held the Braves scoreless into the ninth, when Olson doubled home the game's only run.

In the finale, John Smoltz enjoyed a three-run lead when he took the mound in the bottom of the first inning. Rookie first baseman Brian Hunter (who had homered for two of the first-inning runs) doubled in an additional Atlanta run in the fifth. Meanwhile Smoltz stopped the Pirates on six hits to bring the Braves their first pennant since their move to Atlanta in 1966.

Atlanta Braves (West), 4; Pittsburgh Pirates (East), 3

ATL (W)

PLAYER/POS	AVG	G	AB	R	H	2B	3B	HR	RB	BB	SO	SB
Steve Avery, p	.143	2	7	0	1	0	0	0	0	0	4	0
Rafael Belliard, ss	.211	7	19	0	4	0	0	0	1	3	3	0
Jeff Blauser, ss	.000	2	2	0	0	0	0	0	0	0	0	0
Sid Bream, 1b	.300	4	10	1	3	0	0	1	3	0	1	0
Jim Clancy, p	.000	1	0	0	0	0	0	0	0	0	0	0
Ron Gant, of	.259	7	27	4	7	1	0	1	3	2	4	7
Tom Glavine, p	.250	2	4	0	1	0	0	0	0	0	2	0
Tommy Gregg, ph	.250	4	4	0	1	0	0	0	0	0	2	0
Brian Hunter, 1b	.333	5	18	2	6	2	0	1	4	0	2	0
David Justice, of	.200	7	25	4	5	1	0	1	2	3	7	0
Charlie Leibrandt, p	.000	1	1	0	0	0	0	0	0	0	0	0
Mark Lemke, 2b	.200	7	20	1	4	1	0	0	1	4	0	0
Kent Mercker, p	.000	1	0	0	0	0	0	0	0	0	0	0
Keith Mitchell, of	.000	5	4	0	0	0	0	0	0	0	1	0
Greg Olson, c	.333	7	24	3	8	1	0	1	4	4	3	1
Alejandro Pena, p	.000	4	0	0	0	0	0	0	0	0	0	0
Terry Pendleton, 3b	.167	7	30	1	5	1	1	0	1	1	3	0
Lonnie Smith, of	.250	7	24	3	6	3	0	0	4	5	1	0
John Smoltz, p	.200	2	5	0	1	0	0	0	0	1	4	1
Mike Stanton, p	.000	3	0	0	0	0	0	0	0	0	0	0
Jeff Treadway, 2b	.333	1	3	0	1	0	0	0	0	0	0	0
Jerry Willard, ph	.000	2	2	0	0	0	0	0	0	0	1	0
Mark Wohlers, p	.000	3	0	0	0	0	0	0	0	0	0	0
TOTAL	.231		229	19	53	10	1	5	19	22	42	10

PITCHER	W	L	ERA	G	GS	CG	SV	SHO	IP	H	ER	BB	SO
Steve Avery	2	0	0.00	2	2	0	0	0	16.1	9	0	4	17
Jim Clancy	0	0	0.00	1	0	0	0	0	0.1	0	0	0	0
Tom Glavine	0	2	3.21	2	2	0	0	0	14.0	12	5	6	11
Charlie Leibrandt	0	0	1.35	1	1	0	0	0	6.2	8	1	3	6
Kent Mercker	0	1	13.50	1	0	0	0	0	0.2	0	1	2	0
Alejandro Pena	0	0	0.00	4	0	0	3	0	4.1	1	0	0	4
John Smoltz	2	0	1.76	2	2	1	0	1	15.1	14	3	3	15
Mike Stanton	0	0	2.45	3	0	0	0	0	3.2	4	1	3	3
Mark Wohlers	0	0	0.00	3	0	0	0	0	1.2	3	0	1	1
TOTAL	4	3	1.57	19	7	1	3	1	63.0	51	11	22	57

PIT (E)

PLAYER/POS	AVG	G	AB	R	H	2B	3B	HR	RB	BB	SO	SB
Stan Belinda, p	.000	3	0	0	0	0	0	0	0	0	0	0
Jay Bell, ss	.414	7	29	2	12	2	0	1	1	0	10	0
Barry Bonds, of	.148	7	27	1	4	1	0	0	0	2	4	3
Bobby Bonilla, of	.304	7	23	2	7	2	0	0	1	6	2	0
Steve Buechele, 3b	.304	7	23	2	7	2	0	0	4	6	0	
Doug Drabek, p	.200	2	5	0	1	1	0	0	1	0	2	0
Cecil Espy, ph	.000	2	2	0	0	0	0	0	0	0	0	0
Bob Kipper, p	.000	1	0	0	0	0	0	0	0	0	0	0
Bill Landrum, p	.000	1	0	0	0	0	0	0	0	0	0	0
Mike LaValliere, c	.333	3	6	0	2	0	0	0	0	2	0	0
Jose Lind, 2b	.160	7	25	0	4	0	0	0	3	0	6	0
Roger Mason, p	.000	3	1	0	0	0	0	0	0	0	1	0
Lloyd McClendon, 1b-1	.000	3	2	0	0	0	0	0	0	1	0	0
Orlando Merced, 1b-2	.222	3	9	1	2	0	0	1	1	0	1	0
Bob Patterson, p	.000	1	0	0	0	0	0	0	0	0	0	0
Gary Redus, 1b	.158	5	19	1	3	0	0	0	0	1	4	2
Rosario Rodriguez, p	.000	1	0	0	0	0	0	0	0	0	0	0
Don Slaught, c	.235	6	17	0	4	0	0	0	1	1	4	0
John Smiley, p	.000	2	0	0	0	0	0	0	0	0	2	0
Zane Smith, p	.000	2	5	0	0	0	0	0	0	0	4	0
Randy Tomlin, p	.000	1	2	0	0	0	0	0	0	0	2	0
Andy Van Slyke, of	.160	7	25	3	4	2	0	1	2	5	5	1
Gary Varsho, ph	.500	2	2	0	1	0	0	0	0	0	1	0
Bob Walk, p	.000	3	2	0	0	0	0	0	0	0	2	0
Curtis Wilkerson, ph	.000	4	4	0	0	0	0	0	0	0	3	0
TOTAL	.224		228	12	51	10	0	3	11	22	57	6

PITCHER	W	L	ERA	G	GS	CG	SV	SHO	IP	H	ER	BB	SO
Stan Belinda	1	0	0.00	3	0	0	0	0	5.0	0	0	3	4
Doug Drabek	1	1	0.60	2	2	1	0	0	15.0	10	1	5	10
Bob Kipper	0	0	4.50	1	0	0	0	0	2.0	2	1	0	1
Bill Landrum	0	0	9.00	1	0	0	0	0	1.0	2	1	2	2
Roger Mason	0	0	0.00	3	0	0	0	1	4.1	3	0	1	2
Bob Patterson	0	0	0.00	1	0	0	0	0	2.0	1	0	0	3
Rosario Rodriguez	0	0	27.00	1	0	0	0	0	1.0	1	3	2	1
John Smiley	0	2	23.63	2	2	0	0	0	2.2	8	7	1	3
Zane Smith	1	1	0.61	2	2	0	0	0	14.2	15	1	3	10
Randy Tomlin	0	0	3.00	1	0	0	0	0	6.0	6	2	2	1
Bob Walk	0	0	1.93	2	0	0	0	0	9.1	5	2	3	5
TOTAL	3	4	2.57	20	7	1	2	0	63.0	53	18	22	42

GAME 1 AT PIT OCT 9

ATL	000	000	001	1	5	1
PIT	102	001	01X	5	8	1

Pitchers: GLAVINE, Wohlers (7), Stanton (8) vs DRABEK, Walk (7)
Home Runs: Van Slyke-PIT, Justice-ATL
Attendance: 57,347

GAME 2 AT PIT OCT 10

ATL	000	001	000	1	8	0
PIT	000	000	000	0	6	0

Pitchers: AVERY, Pena (9) vs SMITH, Mason (8), Belinda (9)
Attendance: 57,533

GAME 3 AT ATL OCT 12

PIT	100	100	100	3	10	2
ATL	411	000	13X	10	11	0

Pitchers: SMILEY, Landrum (3), Patterson (4), Kipper (6), Rodriguez (8) vs SMOLTZ, Stanton (7), Wohlers (8), Pena (8)
Home Runs: Merced-PIT, Bell-PIT, Gant-ATL, Olson-ATL, Bream-ATL
Attendance: 50,905

GAME 4 AT ATL OCT 13

PIT	010	010	000	1	3	11	1
ATL	200	000	000	0	2	7	1

Pitchers: Tomlin, Walk (7), BELINDA (9) vs Leibrandt, Clancy (7), Stanton (8), MERCKER (10), Wohlers (10)
Attendance: 51,109

GAME 5 AT ATL OCT 14

PIT	000	010	000	1	6	2
ATL	000	000	000	0	9	1

Pitchers: SMITH, Mason (8) vs GLAVINE, Pena (9)
Attendance: 51,109

GAME 6 AT PIT OCT 16

ATL	000	000	001	1	7	0
PIT	000	000	000	0	4	0

Pitchers: AVERY, Pena (9) vs DRABEK
Attendance: 54,508

GAME 7 AT PIT OCT 17

ATL	300	010	000	4	6	1
PIT	000	000	000	0	6	0

Pitchers: SMOLTZ vs SMILEY, Walk (1), Mason (6), Belinda (8)
Home Runs: Hunter-ATL
Attendance: 46,932

Minnesota struggled to achieve a 2–1 advantage in the first three games, then blew the Jays out of the SkyDome in the next two. Game 1 looked as though it would be an easy win for the Twins, who drove out starter Tom Candiotti with five runs on eight hits in the first two and two thirds innings. But Toronto scored once in the fourth and chased Twins starter Jack Morris in the sixth with five straight singles and three more runs. Relievers Carl Willis and Rick Aguilera, though, held Toronto to just one more single to preserve the victory for Minnesota.

The Jays scored three times in Game 2 before Minnesota put its first run across in the last of the third, and scored twice more in the seventh, taking their first—and, as it turned out, only—win behind the strong pitching of rookie Juan Guzman and relievers Tom Henke and Duane Ward. Toronto again scored early in Game 3, with a pair of two-out runs (one of them Joe Carter's homer) in the first inning. Jays starter Jimmy Key held the Twins scoreless until they got to him for a run in the fifth, and another in the sixth which evened the score. Meanwhile a string of Minnesota pitchers stifled the Blue Jays from the second inning on. In the 10th, pinch hitter Mike Pagliarulo won it for the Twins with a home run to right.

For the third game in a row, Toronto scored first, with a run in the second inning of Game 4. But Minnesota's Kirby Puckett homered in the fourth to tie the score, and by the time Toronto scored again two innings later, the Twins had upped its run total to six. Puckett's home run in the first inning of Game 5 gave the Twins the first of two early runs, but the Jays came back with three runs in the third and two more in the fourth to drive out starter Kevin Tapani. They scored no more, however, as three Twins relievers held them to one single in the final five frames. In the sixth inning, Minnesota reawakened to tie the game with a trio of runs, and salted it—and the pennant—away in the eighth: with two out, Puckett doubled home the go-ahead run, and Kent Hrbek singled in two more for insurance.

Minnesota Twins (West), 4;
Toronto Blue Jays (East), 1

MIN (W)

PLAYER/POS	AVG	G	AB	R	H	2B	3B	HR	RB	BB	SO	SB
Rick Aguilera, p	.000	3	0	0	0	0	0	0	0	0	0	0
Steve Bedrosian, p	.000	2	0	0	0	0	0	0	0	0	0	0
Jarvis Brown, dh	.000	1	0	1	0	0	0	0	0	0	0	0
Chili Davis, dh	.294	5	17	3	5	2	0	0	2	5	8	1
Scott Erickson, p	.000	1	0	0	0	0	0	0	0	0	0	0
Greg Gagne, ss	.235	5	17	1	4	0	0	0	1	1	5	0
Dan Gladden, of	.261	5	23	4	6	0	0	0	3	1	3	3
Mark Guthrie, p	.000	2	0	0	0	0	0	0	0	0	0	0
Brian Harper, c	.278	5	18	1	5	2	0	0	1	0	2	0
Kent Hrbek, 1b	.143	5	21	0	3	0	0	0	3	1	3	0
Chuck Knoblauch, 2b	.350	5	20	5	7	2	0	0	3	3	3	2
Gene Larkin, ph	.000	3	3	0	0	0	0	0	0	0	1	0
Scott Leius, 3b	.000	3	4	0	0	0	0	0	0	1	1	0
Shane Mack, of	.333	5	18	4	6	1	1	0	3	2	4	2
Jack Morris, p	.000	2	0	0	0	0	0	0	0	0	0	0
Al Newman, 2b-1,3b-1	.000	2	0	0	0	0	0	0	0	0	0	0
Junior Ortiz, c	.000	3	3	0	0	0	0	0	0	0	0	0
Mike Pagliarulo, 3b	.333	5	15	4	5	1	0	1	3	0	2	0
Kirby Puckett, of	.429	5	21	4	9	1	0	2	6	1	4	0
Paul Sorrento, ph	.000	1	1	0	0	0	0	0	0	0	1	0
Kevin Tapani, p	.000	2	0	0	0	0	0	0	0	0	0	0
David West, p	.000	2	0	0	0	0	0	0	0	0	0	0
Carl Willis, p	.000	3	0	0	0	0	0	0	0	0	0	0
TOTAL	.276		181	27	50	9	1	3	25	15	37	8

PITCHER	W	L	ERA	G	GS	CG	SV	SHO	IP	H	ER	BB	SO
Rick Aguilera	0	0	0.00	3	0	0	3	0	3.1	1	0	0	3
Steve Bedrosian	0	0	0.00	2	0	0	0	0	1.1	3	0	2	2
Scott Erickson	0	0	4.50	1	1	0	0	0	4.0	3	2	5	2
Mark Guthrie	1	0	0.00	2	0	0	0	0	2.2	0	0	0	0
Jack Morris	2	0	4.05	2	2	0	0	0	13.1	17	6	1	7
Kevin Tapani	0	1	7.84	2	2	0	0	0	10.1	16	9	3	9
David West	1	0	0.00	2	0	0	0	0	5.2	1	0	4	4
Carl Willis	0	0	0.00	3	0	0	0	0	5.1	2	0	0	3
TOTAL	4	1	3.33	17	5	0	3	0	46.0	43	17	15	30

TOR (E)

PLAYER/POS	AVG	G	AB	R	H	2B	3B	HR	RB	BB	SO	SB
Jim Acker, p	.000	1	0	0	0	0	0	0	0	0	0	0
Roberto Alomar, 2b	.474	5	19	3	9	0	0	0	4	2	3	2
Pat Borders, c	.263	5	19	0	5	1	0	0	2	0	0	0
Tom Candiotti, p	.000	2	0	0	0	0	0	0	0	0	0	0
Joe Carter, of-3,dh-2	.263	5	19	3	5	2	0	1	4	1	5	0
Rob Ducey, of	.000	1	1	0	0	0	0	0	0	0	0	0
Rene Gonzales, 1b-1,ss-1	.000	2	0	0	0	0	0	0	0	0	0	0
Kelly Gruber, 3b	.286	5	21	1	6	1	0	0	4	0	4	1
Juan Guzman, p	.000	1	0	0	0	0	0	0	0	0	0	0
Tom Henke, p	.000	2	0	0	0	0	0	0	0	0	0	0
Jimmy Key, p	.000	1	0	0	0	0	0	0	0	0	0	0
Manuel Lee, ss	.125	5	16	3	2	0	0	0	0	1	5	0
Rob MacDonald, p	.000	1	0	0	0	0	0	0	0	0	0	0
Candy Maldonado, of	.100	5	20	1	2	1	0	0	1	1	6	0
Rance Mulliniks, dh-3	.125	5	8	1	1	0	0	0	0	3	0	0
John Olerud, 1b	.153	5	19	1	3	0	0	0	3	3	1	0
Todd Stottlemyre, p	.000	1	0	0	0	0	0	0	0	0	0	0
Pat Tabler, dh	.000	2	1	0	0	0	0	0	0	1	0	0
Mike Timlin, p	.000	4	0	0	0	0	0	0	0	0	0	0
Duane Ward, p	.000	2	0	0	0	0	0	0	0	0	0	0
David Wells, p	.000	4	0	0	0	0	0	0	0	0	0	0
Devon White, of	.364	5	22	5	8	1	0	0	0	2	3	3
Mookie Wilson, of-2	.250	3	8	1	2	0	0	0	0	1	3	1
TOTAL	.249		173	19	43	6	0	1	18	15	30	7

PITCHER	W	L	ERA	G	GS	CG	SV	SHO	IP	H	ER	BB	SO
Jim Acker	0	0	0.00	1	0	0	0	0	0.2	1	0	0	1
Tom Candiotti	0	1	8.22	2	2	0	0	0	7.2	17	7	2	5
Juan Guzman	1	0	3.18	1	1	0	0	0	5.2	4	2	4	2
Tom Henke	0	0	0.00	2	0	0	0	0	2.2	2	0	1	5
Jimmy Key	0	0	3.00	1	1	0	0	0	6.0	5	2	1	1
Rob MacDonald	0	0	9.00	1	0	0	0	0	1.0	1	1	1	0
Todd Stottlemyre	0	1	9.82	1	1	0	0	0	3.2	7	4	1	3
Mike Timlin	0	1	3.18	4	0	0	0	0	5.2	5	2	2	5
Duane Ward	0	1	6.23	2	0	0	1	0	4.1	4	3	1	6
David Wells	0	0	2.35	4	0	0	0	0	7.2	6	2	2	9
TOTAL	1	4	4.60	19	5	0	1	0	45.0	50	23	15	37

GAME 1 AT MIN OCT 8

TOR	000 103 000	4	9	3
MIN	221 000 00X	5	11	0

Pitchers: CANDIOTTI, Wells (3), Timlin (6) vs MORRIS, Willis (6), Aguilera (8)
Attendance: 54,766

GAME 2 AT MIN OCT 9

TOR	102 000 200	5	9	0
MIN	001 001 000	2	5	1

Pitchers: GUZMAN, Henke (6), Ward (8) vs TAPANI, Bedrosian (7), Guthrie (7)
Attendance: 54,816

GAME 3 AT TOR OCT 11

MIN	000 011 000 1	3	7	0
TOR	200 000 000 0	2	9	0

Pitchers: Erickson, West (5), Willis (7), GUTHRIE (9), Aguilera (10) vs Key, Wells (7), Henke (8), TIMLIN (10)
Home Runs: Carter-TOR, Pagliarulo-MIN
Attendance: 51,454

GAME 4 AT TOR OCT 12

MIN	000 402 111	9	13	1
TOR	010 001 001	3	11	2

Pitchers: MORRIS, Bedrosian (9) vs STOTTLEMYRE, Wells (4), Acker (6), Timlin (7), MacDonald (9)
Home Runs: Puckett-MIN
Attendance: 51,526

GAME 5 AT TOR OCT 13

MIN	110 003 030	8	14	2
TOR	003 200 000	5	9	1

Pitchers: Tapani, WEST (5), Willis (8), Aguilera (9) vs Candiotti, Timlin (6), WARD (6), Wells (8)
Home Runs: Puckett-MIN
Attendance: 51,425

By any measure, this World Series was one of the great ones. Five of the seven games were decided by a single run, three of them—including Games 6 and 7—in extra innings. The opener in Minnesota gave no indication of the suspense to come, as the Twins opened up a 4–0 lead in the fifth inning en route to a 5–2 win. Game 2 proved more difficult. Chili Davis put the Twins in front with a two-run homer in the first inning, but in the fifth Atlanta tied the score. Braves hurler Tom Glavine lost the game when the Twins' Scott Leius lofted a homer to lead off the eighth.

Minnesota took a quick lead in Game 3, but Atlanta tied the game an inning later, and went ahead on solo homers by David Justice in the fourth inning and Lonnie Smith in the fifth. Home runs by Kirby Puckett and Chili Davis in the fifth and sixth re-tied the score, which remained at 4–4 into the last of the 11th inning, when Justice scored from second on Mark Lemke's two-out single. Lemke's heroics also made the difference in Game 4. Mike Pagliarulo drove in a pair of runs for Minnesota with a single in the second and a home run in the seventh, but Braves Terry Pendleton and Lonnie Smith neutralized the runs with solo homers in the third and seventh. Lemke came to bat in the bottom of the ninth with one out and the score still 2–2. He tripled, and scored in a tight play to even the Series.

In Game 5 the Braves assaulted five Minnesota pitchers for 14 runs and the Series lead, but when play returned to Minnesota for Game 6 the Twins revived with two first-inning runs. In the third inning Puckett prevented two Atlanta runs with a leaping catch above the wall, but in the fifth, Atlanta's Terry Pendleton evened the score with a two-run homer. Later in the inning the Twins regained the lead on Puckett's sacrifice fly. Atlanta knotted the score again in the seventh. In the last of the 11th, Puckett lined the ball over the wall near where he had earlier made his game-saving catch.

No one scored through 9½ innings of Game 7 as Minnesota's Jack Morris dueled John Smoltz, Mike Stanton, and Alejandro Pena. Lonnie Smith singled to lead off the 7th inning and could have come around on Terry Pendleton's double to the wall in left center. But, decoyed by the Twins' middle infielders into thinking there was a play at second, he paused just long enough after passing second to enable him to advance only to third. No one was out, but a grounder to first, an intentional walk to load the bases, and a smart 3-2-3 double play ended the Braves' threat.

Thus the game was still scoreless in the last of the 10th when

Dan Gladden hustled his way into a broken-bat double and moved to third on Chuck Knoblauch's sacrifice bunt. Then, after the bases were loaded intentionally, pinch hitter Gene Larkin lobbed a hit over the head of the drawn-in left fielder. Gladden came home with the title for Minnesota.

Minnesota Twins (AL), 4; Atlanta Braves (NL), 3

MIN (A)

PLAYER/POS	AVG	G	AB	R	H	2B	3B	HR	RB	BB	SO	SB
Rick Aguilera, p	.000	4	1	0	0	0	0	0	0	0	0	0
Steve Bedrosian, p	.000	3	0	0	0	0	0	0	0	0	0	0
Jarvis Brown, of-2,dh-1	.000	3	2	0	0	0	0	0	0	0	0	0
Randy Bush, of-2	.250	3	4	0	1	0	0	0	0	0	1	0
Chili Davis, dh-4,of-1	.222	6	18	4	4	0	0	2	4	2	3	0
Scott Erickson, p	.000	2	1	0	0	0	0	0	0	0	1	0
Greg Gagne, ss	.167	7	24	1	4	1	0	1	3	0	7	0
Dan Gladden, of	.233	7	30	5	7	2	2	0	0	3	4	2
Mark Guthrie, p	.000	4	0	0	0	0	0	0	0	0	0	0
Brian Harper, c	.381	7	21	2	8	2	0	0	1	2	2	0
Kent Hrbek, 1b	.115	7	26	2	3	1	0	1	2	2	6	0
Chuck Knoblauch, 2b	.308	7	26	3	8	1	0	0	2	4	2	4
Gene Larkin, dh-1	.500	4	4	0	2	0	0	0	1	0	0	0
Terry Leach, p	.000	2	0	0	0	0	0	0	0	0	0	0
Scott Leius, 3b	.357	7	14	2	5	0	0	1	2	1	2	0
Shane Mack, of	.130	6	23	0	3	1	0	0	1	0	7	0
Jack Morris, p	.000	3	2	0	0	0	0	0	0	0	1	0
Al Newman, 3b-2,2b-1,ss-1	.500	4	2	0	1	0	1	0	1	0	0	0
Junior Ortiz, c	.200	3	5	0	1	0	0	0	1	0	1	0
Mike Pagliarulo, 3b	.273	6	11	1	3	0	0	1	2	1	2	0
Kirby Puckett, of	.250	7	24	4	6	0	1	2	4	5	7	1
Paul Sorrento, 1b-1	.000	3	2	0	0	0	0	0	0	1	2	0
Kevin Tapani, p	.000	2	1	0	0	0	0	0	0	0	0	0
David West, p	.000	2	0	0	0	0	0	0	0	0	0	0
Carl Willis, p	.000	4	0	0	0	0	0	0	0	0	0	0
TOTAL	.232		241	24	56	8	4	8	24	21	48	7

PITCHER	W	L	ERA	G	GS	CG	SV	SHO	IP	H	ER	BB	SO
Rick Aguilera	1	1	1.80	4	0	0	2	0	5.0	6	1	1	3
Steve Bedrosian	0	0	5.40	3	0	0	0	0	3.1	3	2	0	2
Scott Erickson	0	0	5.06	2	2	0	0	0	10.2	10	6	4	5
Mark Guthrie	0	1	2.25	4	0	0	0	0	4.0	3	1	4	3
Terry Leach	0	0	3.86	2	0	0	0	0	2.1	2	1	0	2
Jack Morris	2	0	1.17	3	3	1	0	1	23.0	18	3	9	15
Kevin Tapani	1	1	4.50	2	2	0	0	0	12.0	13	6	2	7
David West	0	0	∞	2	0	0	0	0	0.0	2	4	4	0
Carl Willis	0	0	5.14	4	0	0	0	0	7.0	6	4	2	2
TOTAL	4	3	3.74	26	7	1	2	1	67.1	63	28	26	39

ATL (N)

PLAYER/POS	AVG	G	AB	R	H	2B	3B	HR	RB	BB	SO	SB
Steve Avery, p	.000	2	3	0	0	0	0	0	0	0	2	0
Rafael Belliard, ss	.375	7	16	0	6	1	0	0	4	1	2	0
Jeff Blauser, ss	.167	5	6	0	1	0	0	0	0	1	1	0
Sid Bream, 1b	.125	7	24	0	3	2	0	0	3	4	4	0
Francisco Cabrera, c-1	.000	3	1	0	0	0	0	0	0	0	0	0
Jim Clancy, p	.000	3	1	0	0	0	0	0	0	0	1	0
Ron Gant, of	.267	7	30	3	8	0	1	0	4	2	3	1
Tom Glavine, p	.000	2	2	0	0	0	0	0	0	0	0	0
Tommy Gregg, ph	.000	4	3	0	0	0	0	0	0	0	0	0
Brian Hunter, 1b-4,of-4	.190	7	21	2	4	1	0	1	3	0	2	0
David Justice, of	.259	7	27	5	7	0	0	2	6	5	5	2
Charlie Leibrandt, p	.000	2	0	0	0	0	0	0	0	0	0	0
Mark Lemke, 2b	.417	7	24	4	10	1	3	0	4	2	4	0
Kent Mercker, p	.000	2	0	0	0	0	0	0	0	0	0	0
Keith Mitchell, of	.000	3	2	0	0	0	0	0	0	0	1	0
Greg Olson, c	.222	7	27	3	6	2	0	0	1	5	4	1
Alejandro Pena, p	.000	3	0	0	0	0	0	0	0	0	0	0
Terry Pendleton, 3b	.367	7	30	6	11	3	0	2	3	3	1	0
Randy St. Claire, p	.000	1	0	0	0	0	0	0	0	0	0	0
Lonnie Smith, dh-4,of-3	.231	7	26	5	6	0	0	3	3	3	4	1
John Smoltz, p	.000	2	2	0	0	0	0	0	0	0	1	0
Mike Stanton, p	.000	5	0	0	0	0	0	0	0	0	0	0
Jeff Treadway, 2b-1	.250	3	4	1	1	1	0	0	0	1	2	0
Jerry Willard, ph	.000	1	1	0	0	0	0	0	1	0	0	0
Mark Wohlers, p	.000	3	0	0	0	0	0	0	0	0	0	0
TOTAL	.253		249	29	63	10	4	8	29	26	39	5

PITCHER	W	L	ERA	G	GS	CG	SV	SHO	IP	H	ER	BB	SO
Steve Avery	0	0	3.46	2	2	0	0	0	13.0	10	5	1	8
Jim Clancy	1	0	4.15	3	0	0	0	0	4.1	3	2	4	2
Tom Glavine	1	1	2.70	2	2	1	0	0	13.1	8	4	7	8
Charlie Leibrandt	0	2	11.25	2	1	0	0	0	4.0	8	5	1	3
Kent Mercker	0	0	0.00	2	0	0	0	0	1.0	0	0	0	1
Alejandro Pena	0	1	3.38	3	0	0	0	0	5.1	6	2	3	7
Randy St. Claire	0	0	9.00	1	0	0	0	0	1.0	1	1	0	0
John Smoltz	0	0	1.26	2	2	0	0	0	14.1	13	2	1	11
Mike Stanton	1	0	0.00	5	0	0	0	0	7.1	5	0	2	7
Mark Wohlers	0	0	0.00	3	0	0	0	0	1.2	2	0	2	1
TOTAL	3	4	2.89	25	7	1	0	0	65.1	56	21	21	48

GAME 1 AT MIN OCT 19

ATL	000 001 010	2	6	1
MIN	001 031 00X	5	9	1

Pitchers: LEIBRANDT, Clancy (5), Wohlers (7), Stanton (8) vs MORRIS, Guthrie (8), Aguilera (8)
Home Runs: Gagne-MIN, Hrbek-MIN
Attendance: 55,108

GAME 2 AT MIN OCT 20

ATL	010 010 000	2	8	1
MIN	200 000 01X	3	4	1

Pitchers: GLAVINE vs TAPANI, Aguilera (9)
Home Runs: Davis-MIN, Leius-MIN
Attendance: 55,145

GAME 3 AT ATL OCT 22

MIN	100 000 120 000	4	10	1
ATL	010 120 000 001	5	8	2

Pitchers: Erickson, West (5), Leach (5), Bedrosian (6), Willis (8), AGUILERA (12) vs Avery, Pena (8), Stanton (10), Wohlers (12), Mercker (12), CLANCY (12)
Home Runs: Justice-ATL, Smith-ATL, Puckett-MIN, Davis-MIN
Attendance: 50,878

GAME 4 AT ATL OCT 23

MIN	010 000 100	2	7	0
ATL	001 000 101	3	8	0

Pitchers: Morris, Willis (7), GUTHRIE (8), Bedrosian (9) vs Smoltz, Wohlers (8), STANTON (8)
Home Runs: Pendleton-ATL, Pagliarulo-MIN, Smith-ATL
Attendance: 50,878

GAME 5 AT ATL OCT 24

MIN	000 003 011	5	7	1
ATL	000 410 63X	14	17	1

Pitchers: TAPANI, Leach (5), West (7), Bedrosian (7), Willis (8) vs GLAVINE, Mercker (6), Clancy (7), St. Claire (9)
Home Runs: Justice-ATL, Smith-ATL, Hunter-ATL
Attendance: 50,878

GAME 6 AT MIN OCT 26

ATL	000 020 100 00	3	9	1
MIN	200 010 000 01	4	9	0

Pitchers: Avery, Stanton (7), Pena (9), LEIBRANDT (11) vs Erickson, Guthrie (7), Willis (7), AGUILERA (10)
Home Runs: Pendleton-ATL, Puckett-MIN
Attendance: 55,155

GAME 7 AT MIN OCT 27

ATL	000 000 000 0	0	7	0
MIN	000 000 000 1	1	10	0

Pitchers: Smoltz, Stanton (8), PENA (9) vs MORRIS
Attendance: 55,118

Atlanta opened the series with a pair of one-sided wins but Pittsburgh pulled out a close victory in Game 3. After a third loss, the Pirates pummelled the Braves for two wins even more lopsided than their losses in the first two games. With the series now even, the stage was set for what turned out to be one of the most dramatic finishes in postseason history.

Jose Lind spoiled John Smoltz's Game 1 shutout with his first home run of the season in the eighth inning. But by then the Braves had scored five times and held victory firmly in hand. Game 2 was even easier. By the time the Pirates came up with four runs in the seventh inning (ending Steve Avery's LCS-record streak of scoreless innings at 22⅓), Atlanta had already compiled two four-run innings of their own (one of them on Ron Gant's grand slam). The Braves added five more runs in the last of the seventh to put the game out of reach.

At home for Game 3, the Pirates pulled themselves together behind the five-hit pitching of rookie knuckleballer Tim Wakefield. Sid Bream's solo homer in the fourth inning gave Atlanta a 1–0 lead, but Don Slaught homered to even the score an inning later and a pair of sixth-inning doubles put the Pirates ahead. Ron Gant's homer for Atlanta in the top of the seventh tied the score again, but a single, double, and sacrifice fly in the bottom of the inning put Pittsburgh on top to stay.

A 6–4 loss in Game 4 brought the Pirates to the brink of elimination, but in Game 5 they counter-attacked, driving out Atlanta starter Steve Avery in the first inning with five hits (four of them doubles) and four runs, on their way to a 7–1 victory. The Pirates unloaded on Atlanta's Tom Glavine for eight runs in the second inning of Game 6 before the first out was recorded, and pushed the assault to a 13–4 conclusion and a tied series.

While the Pirates scored single runs in the first and sixth innings of the final game, Pirates starter Doug Drabek (who had taken losses in Games 1 and 4) held Atlanta scoreless through eight innings. Then, in the last of the ninth, leadoff Brave Terry Pendleton doubled. He moved to third as David Justice reached on a grounder bobbled by the usually sure-handed second baseman Jose Lind. A walk to Sid Bream filled the bases. Stan Belinda replaced Drabek on the mound and retired Ron Gant on a fly to left, but Pendleton scored Atlanta's first run after the catch. Damon Berryhill walked to reload the bases, and pinch hitter Brian Hunter popped out. Had there been no error, the game would have

Atlanta Braves (West), 4;
Pittsburgh Pirates (East), 3

ATL (W)

PLAYER/POS	AVG	G	AB	R	H	2B	3B	HR	RB	BB	SO	SB
Steve Avery, p	.000	3	2	0	0	0	0	0	0	1	0	1	0
R. Belliard, ss-3,2b-1	.000	4	2	1	0	0	0	0	0	0	1	0	0
Damon Berryhill, c	.167	7	24	1	4	1	0	0	1	3	2	0
Jeff Blauser, ss	.208	7	24	3	5	0	1	1	4	3	2	0
Sid Bream, 1b	.273	7	22	5	6	3	0	1	2	3	0	0
Francisco Cabrera, ph	.500	2	2	0	1	0	0	0	2	0	0	0
Ron Gant, of	.182	7	22	5	4	0	0	2	6	4	4	1
Tom Glavine, p	.000	2	2	0	0	0	0	0	0	0	0	0
Brian Hunter, 1b-2	.200	3	5	1	1	0	0	0	0	0	1	0
David Justice, of	.280	7	25	5	7	1	0	2	6	6	2	0
Charlie Leibrandt, p	.000	2	1	0	0	0	0	0	0	0	1	0
Mark Lemke, 2b-7,3b-1	.333	7	21	2	7	1	0	0	2	5	3	0
Javier Lopez, c	.000	1	1	0	0	0	0	0	0	0	0	0
Kent Mercker, p	.000	2	0	0	0	0	0	0	0	0	0	0
Otis Nixon, of	.286	7	28	5	8	2	0	0	2	4	4	3
Terry Pendleton, 3b	.233	7	30	2	7	2	0	0	3	0	2	0
Jeff Reardon, p	.000	3	0	0	0	0	0	0	0	0	0	0
Deion Sanders, of-3	.000	4	5	0	0	0	0	0	0	0	3	0
Lonnie Smith, ph	.333	6	6	1	2	0	1	0	1	0	0	0
Pete Smith, p	.000	2	1	0	0	0	0	0	0	0	0	0
John Smoltz, p	.286	3	7	1	2	0	0	0	1	0	2	1
Mike Stanton, p	1.000	5	1	1	1	1	0	0	1	0	0	0
Jeff Treadway, 2b-1	.667	3	3	1	2	0	0	0	0	0	1	0
Mark Wohlers, p	.000	3	0	0	0	0	0	0	0	0	0	0
TOTAL	.244		234	34	57	11	2	6	32	29	28	5

PITCHER	W	L	ERA	G	GS	CG	SV	SHO	IP	H	ER	BB	SO
Steve Avery	1	1	9.00	3	2	0	0	0	8.0	13	8	2	3
Marvin Freeman	0	0	14.73	3	0	0	0	0	3.2	8	6	2	1
Tom Glavine	0	2	12.27	2	2	0	0	0	7.1	13	10	3	2
Charlie Leibrandt	0	0	1.93	2	0	0	0	0	4.2	4	1	3	3
Kent Mercker	0	0	0.00	2	0	0	0	0	3.0	1	0	1	1
Jeff Reardon	1	0	0.00	3	0	0	1	0	3.0	0	0	2	3
Pete Smith	0	0	2.45	2	0	0	0	0	3.2	2	1	3	3
John Smoltz	2	0	2.66	3	3	0	0	0	20.1	14	6	10	19
Mike Stanton	0	0	0.00	5	0	0	0	0	4.1	2	0	3	5
Mark Wohlers	0	0	0.00	3	0	0	0	0	3.0	2	0	1	2
TOTAL	4	3	4.72	28	7	0	1	0	61.0	59	32	29	42

PIT (E)

PLAYER/POS	AVG	G	AB	R	H	2B	3B	HR	RB	BB	SO	SB
Stan Belinda, p	.000	2	0	0	0	0	0	0	0	0	0	0
Jay Bell, ss	.172	7	29	3	5	2	0	1	4	3	4	0
Barry Bonds, of	.261	7	23	5	6	1	0	1	2	6	4	1
Alex Cole, of	.200	4	10	2	2	0	0	0	1	3	2	0
Danny Cox, p	.000	2	0	0	0	0	0	0	0	0	0	0
Doug Drabek, p	.000	3	6	0	0	0	0	0	0	1	4	0
Cecil Espy, of-2	.667	4	3	0	2	0	0	0	0	1	0	0
Carlos Garcia, 2b	.000	1	1	0	0	0	0	0	0	0	0	0
Danny Jackson, p	.000	1	1	0	0	0	0	0	0	0	0	0
Jeff King, 3b	.241	7	29	4	7	4	0	0	2	0	1	0
Mike LaValliere, c	.200	3	10	1	2	0	0	0	0	3	0	0
Jose Lind, 2b	.222	7	27	5	6	2	1	1	5	1	4	0
Roger Mason, p	.000	2	0	0	0	0	0	0	0	0	0	0
Lloyd McClendon, of	.727	5	11	4	8	2	0	1	4	4	1	0
Orlando Merced, 1b	.100	4	10	0	1	1	0	0	2	2	4	0
Denny Neagle, p	.000	2	0	0	0	0	0	0	0	0	0	0
Bob Patterson, p	.000	2	0	0	0	0	0	0	0	0	0	0
Gary Redus, 1b	.438	5	16	4	7	4	1	0	3	2	3	0
Don Slaught, c	.333	5	12	5	4	1	0	1	5	6	3	0
Randy Tomlin, p	.000	2	0	0	0	0	0	0	0	0	0	0
Andy Van Slyke, of	.276	7	29	1	8	3	1	0	4	1	5	0
Gary Varsho, of-1	.500	2	2	1	1	0	0	0	0	0	0	0
Tim Wakefield, p	.000	2	6	1	0	0	0	0	0	0	1	0
Bob Walk, p	.000	2	5	0	0	0	0	0	0	0	2	0
John Wehner, ph	.000	2	2	0	0	0	0	0	0	0	2	0
TOTAL	.255		231	35	59	20	3	5	32	29	42	1

PITCHER	W	L	ERA	G	GS	CG	SV	SHO	IP	H	ER	BB	SO
Stan Belinda	0	0	0.00	2	0	0	0	0	1.2	2	0	1	2
Danny Cox	0	0	0.00	2	0	0	0	0	1.1	1	0	1	1
Doug Drabek	0	3	3.71	3	3	0	0	0	17.0	18	7	6	10
Danny Jackson	0	1	21.60	1	1	0	0	0	1.2	4	4	2	0
Roger Mason	0	0	0.00	2	0	0	0	0	3.1	0	0	2	1
Denny Neagle	0	0	27.00	2	0	0	0	0	1.2	4	5	3	0
Bob Patterson	0	0	5.40	2	0	0	0	0	1.2	3	1	1	1
Randy Tomlin	0	0	6.75	2	0	0	0	0	2.2	5	2	1	0
Tim Wakefield	2	0	3.00	2	2	2	0	0	18.0	14	6	5	7
Bob Walk	1	0	3.86	2	1	1	0	0	11.2	6	5	7	6
TOTAL	3	4	4.45	20	7	3	0	0	60.2	57	30	29	28

been over, with Pittsburgh waving the pennant. Instead, little-used pinch hitter Francisco Cabrera lined the ball safely to left, scoring Justice and Bream for a repeat pennant in Atlanta.

GAME 1 AT ATL OCT 6

PIT	000	000	010	1	5	1
ATL	010	210	10X	5	8	0

Pitchers: DRABEK, Patterson (5), Neagle (7), Cox (8) vs SMOLTZ, Stanton (9)
Home Runs: Lind-PIT, Blauser-ATL
Attendance: 51,971

GAME 2 AT ATL OCT 7

PIT	000	000	410	5	7	0
ATL	040	040	50X	13	14	0

Pitchers: JACKSON, Mason (2), Walk (3), Tomlin (5), Neagle (7), Patterson (7), Belinda (8) vs AVERY, Freeman (7), Stanton (7), Wohlers (8), Reardon (9)
Home Runs: Gant-ATL
Attendance: 51,975

GAME 3 AT PIT OCT 9

ATL	000	100	100	2	5	0
PIT	000	011	10X	3	8	1

Pitchers: GLAVINE, Stanton (7), Wohlers (8) vs WAKEFIELD
Home Runs: Bream-ATL, Gant-ATL, Slaught-PIT
Attendance: 56,610

GAME 4 AT PIT OCT 10

ATL	020	022	000	6	11	1
PIT	021	000	100	4	6	1

Pitchers: SMOLTZ, Stanton (7), Reardon (9) vs DRABEK, Tomlin (5), Cox (6), Mason (7)
Attendance: 57,164

GAME 5 AT PIT OCT 11

ATL	000	000	010	1	3	0
PIT	401	001	10X	7	13	0

Pitchers: AVERY, Smith (1), Leibrandt (5), Freeman (6), Mercker (8) vs WALK
Attendance: 52,929

GAME 6 AT ATL OCT 13

PIT	080	041	000	13	13	1
ATL	000	100	102	4	9	1

Pitchers: WAKEFIELD vs GLAVINE, Leibrandt (2), Freeman (5), Mercker (7), Wohlers (9)
Home Runs: Bell-PIT, Bonds-PIT, McClendon-PIT, Justice-ATL (2)
Attendance: 51,975

GAME 7 AT ATL OCT 14

PIT	100	001	000	2	7	1
ATL	000	000	003	3	7	0

Pitchers: DRABEK, Belinda (9) vs Smoltz, Stanton (7), Smith (7), Avery (7), REARDON (9)
Attendance: 51,975

Oakland had competed in three ALCS in the previous four years and won them all. Toronto in its first 15 seasons of existence had competed three times in the ALCS and never won. In the first game of the 1992 matchup, the Athletics scored first on Mark McGwire's two-run homer and the next batter, Terry Steinbach, pushed the score to 3–0 with another home run. Toronto's Pat Borders and Dave Winfield retaliated with solo homers in the fifth and sixth innings to narrow the gap, and the Blue Jays tied the score in the eighth when Winfield, who had doubled with two outs, came home on John Olerud's single. But in the top of the ninth, Harold Baines led off with the game's fifth home run to put Oakland back into the lead, and A's reliever Dennis Eckersley preserved it for his 10th ALCS save.

After this encouraging beginning, though, the A's went into a three-game decline. In Game 2, fireballer David Cone held Oakland scoreless through eight innings while the Jays built a 3–0 lead on Kelly Gruber's two-run homer in the fifth inning and a third score two innings later. Oakland finally touched Cone for a run in the ninth, but reliever Tom Henke smothered the threat. The A's recovered from an early deficit in Game 3 to tie the score in the fourth inning, but fell behind on Candy Maldonado's leadoff homer in the sixth and never regained the lead. In Game 4 the A's rocked Toronto starter Jack Morris for five runs in the fifth, and added another in the sixth to take a 6–1 lead. But in the eighth, reliever Eckersley, who came on with one run in and two on, yielded singles on his first two pitches to let in two more runs, and in the ninth gave up a leadoff single and a game-tying home run to Roberto Alomar. Toronto finally took the lead in the eleventh as Derek Bell fouled off several pitches before drawing a walk, took third on Maldonado's single, and scored on Pat Borders' fly to left. Reliever Tom Henke held the lead.

Down three games to one, Oakland came out slugging in Game 5. Ruben Sierra homered for a pair of runs in the first inning and the A's added a third run two innings later. Dave Winfield homered in the Toronto fourth, but the A's took advantage of two Toronto errors to score three more runs an inning later. But they couldn't sustain their comeback. Joe Carter's two-run homer in the first inning of Game 6, and Candy Maldonado's three-run blast two innings later, highlighted a 9–2 Toronto romp that ended the team's string of

Toronto Blue Jays (East), 4
Oakland Athletics (West), 2

TOR (E)

PLAYER/POS	AVG	G	AB	R	H	2B	3B	HR	RB	BB	SO	SB
Roberto Alomar, 2b	.423	6	26	4	11	1	0	2	4	2	1	5
Derek Bell, of	.000	2	0	1	0	0	0	0	0	1	0	0
Pat Borders, c	.318	6	22	3	7	0	0	1	3	1	1	0
Joe Carter, of-6,1b-2	.192	6	26	2	5	0	0	1	3	2	4	2
David Cone, p	.000	2	0	0	0	0	0	0	0	0	0	0
Mark Eichhorn, p	.000	1	0	0	0	0	0	0	0	0	0	0
Alfredo Griffin, ss-1	.000	2	2	0	0	0	0	0	0	0	0	0
Kelly Gruber, 3b	.091	6	22	3	2	1	0	1	2	2	3	0
Juan Guzman, p	.000	2	0	0	0	0	0	0	0	0	0	0
Tom Henke, p	.000	4	0	0	0	0	0	0	0	0	0	0
Jimmy Key, p	.000	1	0	0	0	0	0	0	0	0	0	0
Manuel Lee, ss	.278	6	18	2	5	1	1	0	3	1	2	0
Candy Maldonado, of	.273	6	22	3	6	0	0	2	6	2	4	0
Jack Morris, p	.000	2	0	0	0	0	0	0	0	0	0	0
John Olerud, 1b	.348	6	23	4	8	2	0	1	4	2	5	0
Ed Sprague, ph	.500	2	2	0	1	0	0	0	0	0	1	0
Todd Stottlemyre, p	.000	1	0	0	0	0	0	0	0	0	0	0
Mike Timlin, p	.000	2	0	0	0	0	0	0	0	0	0	0
Duane Ward, p	.000	3	0	0	0	0	0	0	0	0	0	0
Devon White, of	.348	6	23	2	8	2	0	0	2	5	6	0
Dave Winfield, dh	.250	6	24	7	6	1	0	2	3	5	2	0
TOTAL	.281		210	31	59	8	1	10	30	23	29	7

PITCHER	W	L	ERA	G	GS	CG	SV	SHO	IP	H	ER	BB	SO
David Cone	1	1	3.00	2	2	0	0	0	12.0	11	4	5	9
Mark Eichhorn	0	0	0.00	1	0	0	0	0	1.0	0	0	0	0
Juan Guzman	2	0	2.08	2	2	0	0	0	13.0	12	3	5	11
Tom Henke	0	0	0.00	4	0	0	3	0	4.2	3	0	2	2
Jimmy Key	0	0	0.00	1	0	0	0	0	3.0	2	0	2	1
Jack Morris	0	1	6.57	2	2	1	0	0	12.1	11	9	6	6
Todd Stottlemyre	0	0	2.45	1	0	0	0	0	3.2	3	1	0	1
Mike Timlin	0	0	6.75	2	0	0	0	0	1.1	4	1	0	1
Duane Ward	1	0	6.75	3	0	0	0	0	4.0	6	3	1	2
TOTAL	4	2	3.44	18	6	1	3	0	55.0	52	21	24	33

OAK (W)

PLAYER/POS	AVG	G	AB	R	H	2B	3B	HR	RB	BB	SO	SB
Harold Baines, dh	.440	6	25	6	11	2	0	1	4	0	3	0
Lance Blankenship, 2b	.231	5	13	2	3	0	0	0	0	3	4	1
Mike Bordick, ss-4,2b-2	.053	6	19	1	1	0	0	0	0	1	2	1
Jerry Browne, 3b-2,of-1	.400	4	10	3	4	0	0	0	2	2	0	0
Jim Corsi, p	.000	3	0	0	0	0	0	0	0	0	0	0
Ron Darling, p	.000	1	0	0	0	0	0	0	0	0	0	0
Kelly Downs, p	.000	2	0	0	0	0	0	0	0	0	0	0
Dennis Eckersley, p	.000	3	0	0	0	0	0	0	0	0	0	0
Eric Fox, of-1,dh-1	.000	4	1	0	0	0	0	0	0	1	0	2
Rickey Henderson, of	.261	6	23	5	6	0	0	0	1	4	4	2
Rick Honeycutt, p	.000	2	0	0	0	0	0	0	0	0	0	0
Carney Lansford, 3b	.167	5	18	0	3	0	0	0	1	1	1	0
Mark McGwire, 1b	.150	6	20	1	3	0	0	1	3	5	4	0
Mike Moore, p	.000	2	0	0	0	0	0	0	0	0	0	0
Jeff Parrett, p	.000	3	0	0	0	0	0	0	0	0	0	0
Jamie Quirk, ph	.000	1	1	0	0	0	0	0	0	0	0	0
Randy Ready, ph	.000	1	1	0	0	0	0	0	0	0	1	0
Jeff Russell, p	.000	3	0	0	0	0	0	0	0	0	0	0
Ruben Sierra, of	.333	6	24	4	8	2	1	1	7	2	1	1
Terry Steinbach, c	.292	6	24	1	7	0	0	1	5	2	7	0
Dave Stewart, p	.000	2	0	0	0	0	0	0	0	0	0	0
Walt Weiss, ss	.167	3	6	1	1	0	0	0	0	2	1	2
Bob Welch, p	.000	1	0	0	0	0	0	0	0	0	0	0
Willie Wilson, of	.227	6	22	0	5	1	0	0	0	1	5	7
Bobby Witt, p	.000	1	0	0	0	0	0	0	0	0	0	0
TOTAL	.251		207	24	52	5	1	4	23	24	33	16

PITCHER	W	L	ERA	G	GS	CG	SV	SHO	IP	H	ER	BB	SO
Jim Corsi	0	0	0.00	3	0	0	0	0	2.0	2	0	3	0
Ron Darling	0	1	3.00	1	1	0	0	0	6.0	4	2	2	3
Kelly Downs	0	1	3.86	2	0	0	0	0	2.1	3	1	1	0
Dennis Eckersley	0	0	6.00	3	0	0	1	0	3.0	8	2	0	2
Rick Honeycutt	0	0	0.00	2	0	0	0	0	2.0	0	0	0	1
Mike Moore	0	2	7.45	2	2	0	0	0	9.2	11	8	5	7
Jeff Parrett	0	0	11.57	3	0	0	0	0	2.1	6	3	0	1
Jeff Russell	1	0	9.00	3	0	0	0	0	2.0	2	2	4	0
Dave Stewart	1	0	2.70	2	2	1	0	0	16.2	14	5	6	7
Bob Welch	0	0	2.57	1	1	0	0	0	7.0	7	2	1	7
Bobby Witt	0	0	18.00	1	0	0	0	0	1.0	2	2	1	1
TOTAL	2	4	4.50	23	6	1	1	0	54.0	59	27	23	29

failed opportunities and carried the American League pennant to Canada for the first time.

GAME 1 AT TOR OCT 7

OAK 030 000 001	4	6	1
TOR 000 011 010	3	9	0

Pitchers: Stewart, RUSSELL (8), Eckersley (9) vs MORRIS
Home Runs: Baines-OAK, McGwire-OAK, Steinbach-OAK, Winfield-TOR, Borders-TOR
Attendance: 51,039

GAME 2 AT TOR OCT 8

OAK 000 000 001	1	6	0
TOR 000 020 10X	3	4	0

Pitchers: MOORE, Corsi (8), Parrett (8) vs CONE, Henke (9)
Home Runs: Gruber-TOR
Attendance: 51,114

GAME 3 AT OAK OCT 10

TOR 010 110 211	7	9	1
OAK 000 200 210	5	13	3

Pitchers: GUZMAN, Ward (7), Timlin (8), Henke (8) vs DARLING, Downs (7), Corsi (8), Russell (8), Honeycutt (9), Eckersley (9)
Home Runs: Alomar-TOR, Maldonado-TOR
Attendance: 46,911

GAME 4 AT OAK OCT 11

TOR 010 000 032 01	7	17	4
OAK 005 001 000 00	6	12	2

Pitchers: Morris, Stottlemyre (4), Timlin (8), WARD (11) vs Welch, Parrett (8), Eckersley (8), Corsi (9), DOWNS (10)
Home Runs: Alomar-TOR, Olerud-TOR
Attendance: 47,732

GAME 5 AT OAK OCT 12

TOR 000 100 100	2	7	3
OAK 201 030 00X	6	8	0

Pitchers: CONE, Key (5), Eichhorn (8) vs STEWART
Home Runs: Winfield-TOR, Sierra-OAK
Attendance: 44,955

GAME 6 AT TOR OCT 14

OAK 000 001 010	2	7	1
TOR 204 010 02X	9	13	0

Pitchers: MOORE, Parrett (3), Honeycutt (5), Russell (7), Witt (8) vs GUZMAN, Ward (8), Henke (9)
Home Runs: Carter-TOR, Maldonado-TOR
Attendance: 51,335

Atlanta outscored Toronto in the Series, 20 runs to 16, but the Blue Jays eked out four one-run victories to bring Canada its first baseball world championship.

In the fourth inning of Game 1, Atlanta's Tom Glavine gave up a leadoff homer to Joe Carter for the game's first run, but held the Jays to just one single the rest of the way. Meanwhile, Toronto starter Jack Morris shut out the Braves for five innings. But in the top of the sixth he gave up a deciding three-run homer to catcher Damon Berryhill. The next night, though, down 4–5 in the ninth inning, Toronto pinch hitter Derek Bell drew a walk from Braves closer Jeff Reardon, and pinch hitter Ed Sprague lined Reardon's first pitch over the left field wall.

Toronto moved ahead with another close victory in Game 3, the first World Series game ever played outside the United States. Atlanta threatened in the fourth inning when, with two on and none out, David Justice flied deep to center Devon White leaped high to snare it. Baserunner Terry Pendleton was ruled out for passing Deion Sanders on the basepath, and third baseman Kelly Gruber tagged Sanders, who was diving back into second base, to complete what seemed to be a triple play. The umpire didn't see the tag, however, and called Sanders safe. Still, no Braves scored, and Joe Carter homered for the game's first run in the last of the fourth. Atlanta tied the game in the sixth and took the lead in the top of the eighth. Gruber homered to re-tie it in the bottom of the inning, and after the Jays had filled the bases in the last of the ninth, Candy Maldonado tagged Reardon for a hit over the drawn-in outfield to bring home the winning run.

The Jays pushed their Series advantage to 3–1 in Game 4. Catcher Pat Borders opened the Toronto third with a home run, and Gruber scored from second on Devon White's seventh-inning single. The Braves got to Toronto starter Jimmy Key for a run in the eighth, but relievers Duane Ward and Tom Henke shut them out thereafter.

In the fifth game the Blue Jays twice came from one run down to even the score. But in the fifth inning, after the Braves had once again built a one-run lead, Lonnie Smith extended it with a grand slam that sent the Series back to Atlanta.

Toronto scored a run in the first inning of Game 6. Atlanta tied the game in the third, but Candy Maldonado's leadoff homer in the fourth restored the advantage to Toronto. In the bottom of the ninth, the Braves scrabbled back to tie it up again. The score was 2–2 until the top of the 11th, when Toronto's

Dave Winfield delivered two runners with a two-out double into the left field corner. As it turned out, the Jays needed both runs, for Atlanta scored in the bottom of the 11th. But with two out and the potential tying run on third, Otis Nixon, was out at first attempting a bunt, and the Series was over.

Toronto Blue Jays (AL), 4; Atlanta Braves (NL), 2

TOR (A)

PLAYER/POS	AVG	G	AB	R	H	2B	3B	HR	RB	BB	SO	SB
Roberto Alomar, 2b	.208	6	24	3	5	1	0	0	0	3	3	3
Derek Bell, ph	.000	2	1	1	0	0	0	0	0	1	0	0
Pat Borders, c	.450	6	20	2	9	3	0	1	3	2	1	0
Joe Carter, of-4	.273	6	22	2	6	0	0	2	3	3	2	1
David Cone, p	.500	2	4	0	2	0	0	0	1	1	0	0
Mark Eichhorn, p	.000	1	0	0	0	0	0	0	0	0	0	0
Alfredo Griffin, ss	.000	2	0	0	0	0	0	0	0	0	0	0
Kelly Gruber, 3b	.105	6	19	2	2	0	0	1	1	2	5	1
Juan Guzman, p	.000	1	0	0	0	0	0	0	0	0	0	0
Tom Henke, p	.000	3	0	0	0	0	0	0	0	0	0	0
Jimmy Key, p	.000	2	1	0	0	0	0	0	0	0	0	0
Manuel Lee, ss	.105	6	19	1	2	0	0	0	0	1	2	0
Candy Maldonado, of-5	.158	6	19	1	3	0	0	1	2	2	5	0
Jack Morris, p	.000	2	2	0	0	0	0	0	0	0	2	0
John Olerud, 1b	.308	4	13	2	4	0	0	0	0	0	4	0
Ed Sprague, 1b-1	.500	3	2	1	1	0	0	1	2	1	0	0
Todd Stottlemyre, p	.000	4	0	0	0	0	0	0	0	0	0	0
Pat Tabler, ph	.000	2	2	0	0	0	0	0	0	0	0	0
Mike Timlin, p	.000	2	0	0	0	0	0	0	0	0	0	0
Duane Ward, p	.000	4	0	0	0	0	0	0	0	0	0	0
David Wells, p	.000	4	0	0	0	0	0	0	0	0	0	0
Devon White, of	.231	6	26	2	6	1	0	0	2	0	6	1
Dave Winfield, of-3,dh-3	.227	6	22	0	5	1	0	0	3	2	3	0
TOTAL	.230		196	17	45	8	0	6	17	18	33	6

PITCHER	W	L	ERA	G	GS	CG	SV	SHO	IP	H	ER	BB	SO
David Cone	0	0	3.48	2	2	0	0	0	10.1	9	4	8	8
Mark Eichhorn	0	0	0.00	1	0	0	0	0	1.0	0	0	0	1
Juan Guzman	0	0	1.13	1	1	0	0	0	8.0	8	1	1	7
Tom Henke	0	0	2.70	3	0	0	2	0	3.1	2	1	2	1
Jimmy Key	2	0	1.00	2	1	0	0	0	9.0	6	1	0	6
Jack Morris	0	2	8.44	2	2	0	0	0	10.2	13	10	6	12
Todd Stottlemyre	0	0	0.00	4	0	0	0	0	3.2	4	0	0	4
Mike Timlin	0	0	0.00	2	0	0	1	0	1.1	0	0	0	0
Duane Ward	2	0	0.00	4	0	0	0	0	3.1	1	0	1	6
David Wells	0	0	0.00	4	0	0	0	0	4.1	1	0	2	3
TOTAL	4	2	2.78	25	6	0	3	0	55	44	17	20	48

ATL (N)

PLAYER/POS	AVG	G	AB	R	H	2B	3B	HR	RB	BB	SO	SB
Steve Avery, p	.000	2	1	0	0	0	0	0	0	0	1	0
Rafael Belliard, ss-3,2b-1	.000	4	0	0	0	0	0	0	0	0	0	0
Damon Berryhill, c	.091	6	22	1	2	0	0	1	3	1	11	0
Jeff Blauser, ss	.250	6	24	2	6	0	0	0	0	1	9	2
Sid Bream, 1b	.200	5	15	1	3	0	0	0	0	4	0	0
Francisco Cabrera, ph	.000	1	1	0	0	0	0	0	0	0	0	0
Ron Gant, of-3	.125	4	8	2	1	1	0	0	0	1	2	2
Tom Glavine, p	.000	2	2	0	0	0	0	0	0	1	0	0
Brian Hunter, 1b-3	.200	4	5	0	1	0	0	0	2	0	1	0
David Justice, of	.158	6	19	4	3	0	0	1	3	6	5	1
Charlie Leibrandt, p	.000	1	0	0	0	0	0	0	0	0	0	0
Mark Lemke, 2b	.211	6	19	0	4	0	0	0	2	1	3	0
Otis Nixon, of	.296	6	27	3	8	1	0	0	1	1	3	5
Terry Pendleton, 3b	.240	6	25	2	6	2	0	0	2	1	5	0
Jeff Reardon, p	.000	2	0	0	0	0	0	0	0	0	0	0
Deion Sanders, of	.533	4	15	4	8	2	0	0	1	2	1	5
Lonnie Smith, dh-3	.167	5	12	1	2	0	0	1	5	1	4	0
Pete Smith, p	.000	1	1	0	0	0	0	0	0	0	1	0
John Smoltz, p-2	.000	3	3	0	0	0	0	0	0	0	2	0
Mike Stanton, p	.000	4	0	0	0	0	0	0	0	0	0	0
Jeff Treadway, ph	.000	1	1	0	0	0	0	0	0	0	0	0
Mark Wohlers, p	.000	2	0	0	0	0	0	0	0	0	0	0
TOTAL	.220		200	20	44	6	0	3	19	20	48	15

PITCHER	W	L	ERA	G	GS	CG	SV	SHO	IP	H	ER	BB	SO
Steve Avery	0	1	3.75	2	2	0	0	0	12.0	11	5	3	11
Tom Glavine	1	1	1.59	2	2	0	0	0	17.0	10	3	4	8
Charlie Leibrandt	0	1	9.00	1	0	0	0	0	2.0	3	2	0	0
Jeff Reardon	0	1	13.50	2	0	0	0	0	1.1	2	2	1	1
Pete Smith	0	0	0.00	1	0	0	0	0	3.0	3	0	0	0
John Smoltz	1	0	2.70	2	2	0	0	0	13.1	13	4	7	12
Mike Stanton	0	0	0.00	4	0	0	1	0	5.0	3	0	2	1
Mark Wohlers	0	0	0.00	2	0	0	0	0	0.2	0	0	1	0
TOTAL	2	4	2.65	16	6	2	1	0	54.1	45	16	18	33

GAME 1 AT ATL OCT 17

TOR	000	100	000	1	4	0
ATL	000	003	00X	3	4	0

Pitchers: MORRIS, Stottlemyre (7), Wells (8) vs GLAVINE
Home Runs: Carter-TOR, Berryhill-ATL
Attendance: 51,763

GAME 2 AT ATL OCT 18

TOR	000	020	012	5	9	2
ATL	010	120	000	4	5	1

Pitchers: Cone, Wells (5), Stottlemyre (7), WARD (8), Henke (9) vs Smoltz, Stanton (8), REARDON (8)
Home Runs: Sprague-TOR
Attendance: 51,763

GAME 3 AT TOR OCT 20

ATL	000	001	010	2	9	0
TOR	000	100	011	3	6	1

Pitchers: AVERY, Wohlers (9), Stanton (9), Reardon (9) vs Guzman, WARD (9)
Home Runs: Carter-TOR, Gruber-TOR
Attendance: 51,813

GAME 4 AT TOR OCT 21

ATL	000	000	010	1	5	0
TOR	001	000	10X	2	6	0

Pitchers: GLAVINE vs KEY, Ward (8), Henke (9)
Home Runs: Borders-TOR
Attendance: 52,090

GAME 5 AT TOR OCT 22

ATL	100	150	000	7	13	0
TOR	010	100	000	2	6	0

Pitchers: SMOLTZ, Stanton (7) vs MORRIS, Wells (5), Timlin (7), Eichhorn (8), Stottlemyre (9)
Home Runs: Justice-ATL, L.Smith-ATL
Attendance: 52,268

GAME 6 AT ATL OCT 24

TOR	100	100	000	02	4	14	1
ATL	001	000	001	01	3	8	1

Pitchers: Cone, Stottlemyre (7), Wells (7), Ward (8), Henke (9), KEY (10), Timlin (11) vs Avery, P.Smith (5), Stanton (8), Wohlers (9), LEIBRANDT (10)
Home Runs: Maldonado-TOR
Attendance: 51,763

Atlanta outhit the Phillies by 47 percentage points, outscored them by 10 runs, and yielded 1.6 fewer earned runs per game. But the Phillies won the pennant. In the opener, Philadelphia starter Curt Schilling fanned 10 batters—including the first five he faced—and left the game after eight innings with a 3–2 lead. An errant throw by Phillies third baseman Kim Batiste (who had just entered the game to strengthen the defense) set up an unearned tying run in the ninth inning. But in the last of the 10th, after John Kruk had doubled, Batiste redeemed himself with a game-winning hit down the left field line.

While the Philadelphia offense remained steady over the next two games, the Braves erupted for 23 runs. By the time Philadelphia scored its first runs in the fourth inning of Game 2, Atlanta had already sent eight men across the plate. In Game 3 the Phillies scored first, and held a 2–0 lead before the Braves destroyed them with five runs in the sixth inning and four more in the seventh.

Game 4 featured only four fewer hits than Game 3, but 10 fewer runs, as Philadelphia evened the series with its second close win. Phillies starter Danny Jackson yielded nine hits and a pair of walks, but only one second-inning run. In the top of the fourth, Darren Daulton, who had reached on an infield error, took third on Milt Thompson's double and scored on Kevin Stocker's two-out single. Pitcher Jackson then singled home Thompson with what proved the winning run.

In the fifth game, Curt Schilling held Atlanta to four hits through eight innings, and carried a 3–0 lead into the bottom of the ninth. But when a walk and infield error put the first two men on, Mitch Williams relieved Schilling and gave up a trio of singles which tied the game. In the top of the 10th inning, though, Lenny Dykstra's solo homer restored the Phillies' lead, and veteran reliever Larry Andersen blanked the Braves in the bottom of the 10th—striking out the final two batters—to preserve the win.

After their two narrow wins on the road, the Phillies clinched the pennant with relative ease when the series returned to Philadelphia for Game 6. Darren Daulton's two-out double in the third inning put the Phillies up 2–0. Atlanta scored once in the fifth, but Dave Hollins' two-run homer in the last of the fifth increased Philadelphia's lead to three runs, and Mickey Morandini's two-out two-run triple an inning later pushed the score to 6–1. Atlanta's Jeff Blauser brought the score to 6–3 with a home run in the

Philadelphia Phillies (East), 4; Atlanta Braves (West), 2

PHI (E)

PLAYER/POS	AVG	G	AB	R	H	2B	3B	HR	RB	BB	SO	SB
Larry Andersen, p	.000	3	0	0	0	0	0	0	0	0	0	0
Kim Batiste, 3b	1.000	4	1	0	1	0	0	0	1	0	0	0
Wes Chamberlain, of-2	.364	4	11	1	4	3	0	0	1	1	3	0
Darren Daulton, c	.263	6	19	2	5	1	0	1	3	6	3	0
Mariano Duncan, 2b	.267	3	15	3	4	0	2	0	0	0	5	0
Lenny Dykstra, of	.280	6	25	5	7	1	0	2	2	5	8	0
Jim Eisenreich, of-5	.133	6	15	0	2	1	0	0	1	0	2	0
Tommy Greene, p	.000	2	1	0	0	0	0	0	0	1	0	0
Dave Hollins, 3b	.200	6	20	2	4	1	0	2	4	5	4	1
Pete Incaviglia, of	.167	3	12	2	2	0	0	1	1	0	3	0
Danny Jackson, p	.250	1	4	0	1	0	0	0	1	0	3	0
Ricky Jordan, ph	.000	2	1	0	0	0	0	0	0	0	1	0
John Kruk, 1b	.250	6	24	4	6	2	1	1	5	4	5	0
Tony Longmire, ph	.000	1	1	0	0	0	0	0	0	0	1	0
Roger Mason, p	.000	2	0	0	0	0	0	0	0	0	0	0
Mickey Morandini, 2b	.250	4	16	1	4	0	1	0	2	0	3	1
Terry Mulholland, p	.000	1	2	0	0	0	0	0	0	0	1	0
Todd Pratt, c	.000	1	1	0	0	0	0	0	0	0	1	0
Ben Rivera, p	.000	1	0	0	0	0	0	0	0	0	0	0
Curt Schilling, p	.000	2	5	0	0	0	0	0	0	0	2	0
Kevin Stocker, ss	.182	6	22	0	4	1	0	0	1	2	5	0
Bobby Thigpen, p	.000	2	0	0	0	0	0	0	0	0	0	0
Milt Thompson, of-5	.231	6	13	2	3	1	0	0	1	0	2	0
David West, p	.000	3	0	0	0	0	0	0	0	0	0	0
Mitch Williams, p	.000	4	0	0	0	0	0	0	0	0	0	0
TOTAL	.227		207	23	47	11	4	7	22	26	51	2

PITCHER	W	L	ERA	G	GS	CG	SV	SHO	IP	H	ER	BB	SO
Larry Andersen	0	0	15.43	3	0	0	1	0	2.1	4	4	1	3
Tommy Greene	1	1	9.64	2	2	0	0	0	9.1	12	10	7	7
Danny Jackson	1	0	1.17	1	1	0	0	0	7.2	9	1	2	6
Roger Mason	0	0	0.00	2	0	0	0	0	3.0	1	0	0	2
Terry Mulholland	0	1	7.20	1	1	0	0	0	5.0	9	4	1	2
Ben Rivera	0	0	4.50	1	0	0	0	0	2.0	1	1	1	2
Curt Schilling	0	0	1.69	2	2	0	0	0	16.0	11	3	5	19
Bobby Thigpen	0	0	5.40	2	0	0	0	0	1.2	1	1	1	3
David West	0	0	13.50	3	0	0	0	0	2.2	5	4	2	5
Mitch Williams	2	0	1.69	4	0	0	2	0	5.1	6	1	2	5
TOTAL	4	2	4.75	21	6	0	3	0	55.0	59	29	22	54

ATL (W)

PLAYER/POS	AVG	G	AB	R	H	2B	3B	HR	RB	BB	SO	SB
Steve Avery, p	.500	2	4	1	2	1	0	0	0	0	1	0
Rafael Belliard, 2b-1,ss-1	.000	2	1	1	0	0	0	0	0	0	1	0
Damon Berryhill, c	.211	6	19	2	4	0	0	1	3	1	5	0
Jeff Blauser, ss	.280	6	25	5	7	1	0	2	4	4	7	0
Sid Bream, 1b	1.000	1	1	1	1	0	0	0	0	0	0	0
Francisco Cabrera, c-1	.667	3	3	0	2	0	0	0	1	0	1	0
Ron Gant, of	.185	6	27	4	5	3	0	0	3	2	9	0
Tom Glavine, p	.000	1	3	0	0	0	0	0	0	0	0	0
David Justice, of	.143	6	21	2	3	1	0	0	4	3	3	0
Mark Lemke, 2b	.208	6	24	2	5	2	0	0	4	1	6	0
Greg Maddux, p	.250	2	4	1	1	0	0	0	0	0	1	0
Fred McGriff, 1b	.435	6	23	6	10	2	0	1	4	4	7	0
Greg McMichael, p	.000	4	0	0	0	0	0	0	0	0	0	0
Kent Mercker, p	.000	5	0	0	0	0	0	0	0	0	0	0
Otis Nixon, of	.348	6	23	3	8	2	0	0	4	5	6	0
Greg Olson, c	.333	2	3	0	1	1	0	0	0	0	1	0
Bill Pecota, ph	.333	4	3	1	1	0	0	0	0	0	1	0
Terry Pendleton, 3b	.346	6	26	4	9	1	0	1	5	0	2	0
Deion Sanders, of-1	.000	5	3	0	0	0	0	0	0	0	1	0
John Smoltz, p	.000	1	1	0	0	0	0	0	0	1	1	0
Mike Stanton, p	.000	5	0	0	0	0	0	0	0	0	0	0
Tony Tarasco, of	.000	2	1	0	0	0	0	0	0	0	1	0
Mark Wohlers, p	.000	4	0	0	0	0	0	0	0	0	0	0
TOTAL	.274		215	33	59	14	0	5	32	22	54	0

PITCHER	W	L	ERA	G	GS	CG	SV	SHO	IP	H	ER	BB	SO
Steve Avery	0	0	2.77	2	2	0	0	0	13.0	9	4	6	10
Tom Glavine	0	0	2.57	1	1	0	0	0	7.0	6	2	0	5
Greg Maddux	1	1	4.97	2	2	0	0	0	12.2	11	7	7	11
Greg McMichael	0	1	6.75	4	0	0	0	0	4.0	7	3	2	1
Kent Mercker	0	0	1.80	5	0	0	0	0	5.0	3	1	2	4
John Smoltz	0	1	0.00	1	1	0	0	0	6.1	8	0	5	10
Mike Stanton	0	0	0.00	1	0	0	0	0	1.0	1	0	1	0
Mark Wohlers	0	1	3.38	4	0	0	0	0	5.1	2	2	3	10
TOTAL	2	4	3.15	20	6	0	0	0	54.1	47	19	26	51

seventh inning, but Phillies relievers David West and Mitch Williams set the Braves down in order in the final two innings.

GAME 1 AT PHI OCT 6

ATL	001 100 001	0	3	9	0
PHI	100 100 001	1	4	9	1

Pitchers: Avery, Mercker (7), McMICHAEL (9) vs Schilling, WILLIAMS (9)
Home Runs: Incaviglia-PHI
Attendance: 62,012

GAME 2 AT PHI OCT 7

ATL	206 010 041	14	16	0
PHI	000 200 001	3	7	2

Pitchers: MADDUX, Stanton (8), Wohlers (9) vs GREENE, Thigpen (3), Rivera (4), Mason (6), West (8), Andersen (9)
Home Runs: Blauser-ATL, McGriff-ATL, Pendleton-ATL, Berryhill-ATL, Dykstra-PHI, Hollins-PHI
Attendance: 62,436

GAME 3 AT ATL OCT 9

PHI	000 101 011	4	10	1
ATL	000 005 40X	9	12	0

Pitchers: MULHOLLAND, Mason (6), Andersen (7), West (7), Thigpen (8) vs GLAVINE, Mercker (8), McMichael (9)
Home Runs: Kruk-PHI
Attendance: 52,032

GAME 4 AT ATL OCT 10

PHI	000 200 000	2	8	1
ATL	010 000 000	1	10	1

Pitchers: JACKSON, Williams (8) vs SMOLTZ, Mercker (7), Wohlers (8)
Attendance: 52,032

GAME 5 AT ATL OCT 11

PHI	100 100 001	1	4	6	1
ATL	000 000 003	0	3	7	1

Pitchers: Schilling, WILLIAMS (9), Andersen (10) vs Avery, Mercker (8), McMicahel (9), WOHLERS (10)
Home Runs: Dykstra-PHI, Daulton-PHI
Attendance: 52,032

GAME 6 AT PHI OCT 13

ATL	000 010 200	3	5	3
PHI	002 022 00X	6	7	1

Pitchers: MADDUX, Mercker (6), McMichael (7), Wohlers (7) vs GREENE, West (8), Williams (9)
Home Runs: Blauser-ATL, Hollins-PHI
Attendance: 62,502

The visiting team won the first four games of the series, but in Game 5, home team Toronto held off a ninth-inning White Sox rally to take a 3–2 series lead. Then, in Chicago two days later, the Jays put the Sox away.

In Chicago for the series opener, Toronto scored first when Ed Sprague tripled home a pair of runs in the fourth inning. The White Sox bounced ahead with three runs in the last of the fourth, but the Blue Jays regained the lead a half inning later on John Olerud's two-run double, then pulled away to a 17-hit, 7–3 win. Toronto also scored first in Game 2, with an unearned run in the first inning. But in the last of the inning, Dave Stewart walked the bases full, then handed Chicago the tying run with a wild pitch. With two out in the fourth inning, though, back-to-back doubles by Paul Molitor and Tony Fernandez restored the lead to Toronto, and a walk, an infield hit and an error increased the Jays' lead to 3–1. This ended the scoring, although the White Sox loaded the bases in the sixth before Stewart retired the next three batters.

The White Sox leaped to life when the series moved to Toronto for Game 3. After the first two men had been retired in the third inning, Sox batters combined five singles with a pair of walks for a 5–0 lead, which Chicago starter Wilson Alvarez held for a 6–1 complete game victory. Lance Johnson's two-run homer in the second inning of Game 4 put Chicago ahead. The Jays overtook them with three runs an inning later, but in the sixth inning Frank Thomas homered to even the score at 3–3, and after two batters walked, Johnson's two-out triple put the Sox ahead to stay.

The Blue Jays finally broke the visiting team's lock on victory, scoring single runs in each of the first four innings, and another in the seventh, while starter Juan Guzman held Chicago to three hits and a single run in his seven innings. Robin Ventura's two-run homer off Jays' reliever Duane Ward in the Chicago ninth narrowed Toronto's lead to 5–3, but Ward then retired Bo Jackson with his third strikeout.

Errors ended the White Sox season in Game 6. With the score tied 2–2 in the fourth inning, a bobble by Chicago third baseman Robin Ventura put Paul Molitor on base. Molitor subsequently scored the go-ahead run when second baseman Joey Cora threw a ball into the dugout. Devon White homered in the ninth inning to stretch Toronto's lead to 4–2, and an error by Sox reliever Scott Radinsky on what should have been the third out

set the stage for Molitor to triple home a pair of baserunners. Warren Newson's leadoff homer against Toronto reliever Duane Ward in the bottom of the ninth narrowed the score to 6–3, but the White Sox came no closer. The win, starter Dave Stewart's second of the series, was his eighth triumph without a loss in LCS play.

Toronto Blue Jays (East), 4; Chicago White Sox (West), 2

TOR (E)

PLAYER/POS	AVG	G	AB	R	H	2B	3B	HR	RB	BB	SO	SB
Roberto Alomar, 2b	.292	6	24	3	7	1	0	0	4	4	3	4
Pat Borders, c	.250	6	24	1	6	1	0	0	3	0	6	1
Joe Carter, of	.259	6	27	2	7	0	0	0	2	1	5	0
Tony Castillo, p	.000	2	0	0	0	0	0	0	0	0	0	0
Danny Cox, p	.000	2	0	0	0	0	0	0	0	0	0	0
Mark Eichhorn, p	.000	1	0	0	0	0	0	0	0	0	0	0
Tony Fernandez, ss	.318	6	22	1	7	0	0	0	1	2	4	0
Juan Guzman, p	.000	2	0	0	0	0	0	0	0	0	0	0
Rickey Henderson, of	.120	6	25	4	3	2	0	0	4	4	5	2
Pat Hentgen, p	.000	1	0	0	0	0	0	0	0	0	0	0
Al Leiter, p	.000	2	0	0	0	0	0	0	0	0	0	0
Paul Molitor, dh	.391	6	23	7	9	2	1	1	5	3	3	0
John Olerud, 1b	.348	6	23	5	8	1	0	0	4	3	4	0
Ed Sprague, 3b	.286	6	21	0	6	0	1	0	4	2	4	0
Dave Stewart, p	.000	2	0	0	0	0	0	0	0	0	0	0
Todd Stottlemyre, p	.000	1	0	0	0	0	0	0	0	0	0	0
Mike Timlin, p	.000	1	0	0	0	0	0	0	0	0	0	0
Duane Ward, p	.000	4	0	0	0	0	0	0	0	0	0	0
Devon White, of	.444	6	27	3	12	1	1	1	2	1	5	0
TOTAL	.301		216	26	65	8	3	2	24	21	36	7

PITCHER	W	L	ERA	G	GS	CG	SV	SHO	IP	H	ER	BB	SO
Tony Castillo	0	0	0.00	2	0	0	0	0	2.0	0	0	1	1
Danny Cox	0	0	0.00	2	0	0	0	0	5.0	3	0	2	5
Mark Eichhorn	0	0	0.00	1	0	0	0	0	2.0	1	0	1	1
Juan Guzman	2	0	2.08	2	2	0	0	0	13.0	8	3	9	9
Pat Hentgen	0	1	18.00	1	1	0	0	0	3.0	9	6	2	3
Al Leiter	0	0	3.38	2	0	0	0	0	2.2	4	1	2	2
Dave Stewart	2	0	2.03	2	2	0	0	0	13.1	8	3	8	8
Todd Stottlemyre	0	1	7.50	1	1	0	0	0	6.0	6	5	4	4
Mike Timlin	0	0	3.86	1	0	0	0	0	2.1	3	1	0	2
Duane Ward	0	0	5.79	4	0	0	2	0	4.2	4	3	3	8
TOTAL	4	2	3.67	18	6	0	2	0	54.0	46	22	32	43

CHI (W)

PLAYER/POS	AVG	G	AB	R	H	2B	3B	HR	RB	BB	SO	SB
Wilson Alvarez, p	.000	1	0	0	0	0	0	0	0	0	0	0
Tim Belcher, p	.000	1	0	0	0	0	0	0	0	0	0	0
Jason Bere, p	.000	1	0	0	0	0	0	0	0	0	0	0
Ellis Burks, of	.304	6	23	4	7	1	0	1	3	3	5	0
Joey Cora, 2b	.136	6	22	1	3	0	0	0	1	3	6	0
Jose DeLeon, p	.000	2	0	0	0	0	0	0	0	0	0	0
Alex Fernandez, p	.000	2	0	0	0	0	0	0	0	0	0	0
Craig Grebeck, 3b	1.000	1	1	0	1	0	0	0	0	0	0	0
Ozzie Guillen, ss	.273	6	22	4	6	1	0	0	2	0	2	1
Roberto Hernandez, p	.000	4	0	0	0	0	0	0	0	0	0	0
Bo Jackson, dh	.000	3	10	1	0	0	0	0	0	3	6	0
Lance Johnson, of	.217	6	23	2	5	1	1	1	6	2	1	1
Ron Karkovice, c	.000	6	15	0	0	0	0	0	0	1	7	0
Mike LaValliere, c	.333	2	3	0	1	0	0	0	0	1	0	0
Kirk McCaskill, p	.000	3	0	0	0	0	0	0	0	0	0	0
Jack McDowell, p	.000	2	0	0	0	0	0	0	0	0	0	0
Warren Newson, dh-1	.200	2	5	1	1	0	0	1	1	0	1	0
Dan Pasqua, 1b	.000	2	6	1	0	0	0	0	0	1	2	0
Scott Radinsky, p	.000	4	0	0	0	0	0	0	0	0	0	0
Tim Raines, of	.444	6	27	5	12	3	0	0	1	2	2	1
Frank Thomas, 1b-4,dh-2	.353	6	17	2	6	0	0	1	3	10	5	0
Robin Ventura, 3b-6,1b-1	.200	6	20	2	4	0	0	1	5	6	6	0
TOTAL	.237		194	23	46	6	1	5	22	32	43	3

PITCHER	W	L	ERA	G	GS	CG	SV	SHO	IP	H	ER	BB	SO
Wilson Alvarez	1	0	1.00	1	1	1	0	0	9.0	7	1	2	6
Tim Belcher	1	0	2.45	1	0	0	0	0	3.2	3	1	3	1
Jason Bere	0	0	11.57	1	1	0	0	0	2.1	5	3	2	3
Jose DeLeon	0	0	1.03	2	0	0	0	0	4.2	7	1	1	6
Alex Fernandez	0	2	1.80	2	2	0	0	0	15.0	15	3	6	10
Roberto Hernandez	0	0	0.00	4	0	0	1	0	4.0	4	0	0	1
Kirk McCaskill	0	0	0.00	3	0	0	0	0	3.2	3	0	1	3
Jack McDowell	0	2	10.00	2	2	0	0	0	9.0	18	10	5	5
Scott Radinsky	0	0	10.80	4	0	0	0	0	1.2	3	2	1	1
TOTAL	1	4	3.57	20	6	1	1	0	53.0	65	21	21	36

GAME 1 AT CHI OCT 5

```
TOR   000 230 200   7 17 1
CHI   000 300 000   3  6 1
```

Pitchers: GUZMAN, Cox (7), Ward (9) vs McDOWELL, DeLeon (7), Radinsky (8), McCaskill (9)
Home Runs: Molitor-TOR
Attendance: 46,246

GAME 2 AT CHI OCT 6

```
TOR   100 200 000   3 8 0
CHI   100 000 000   1 7 2
```

Pitchers: STEWART, Leiter (7), Ward (9) vs FERNANDEZ, Hernandez (9)
Attendance: 46,101

GAME 3 AT TOR OCT 8

```
CHI   005 100 000   6 12 0
TOR   001 000 000   1  7 1
```

Pitchers: ALVAREZ vs HENTGEN, Cox (4), Eichhorn (7), Castillo (9)
Attendance: 51,783

GAME 4 AT TOR OCT 9

```
CHI   020 003 101   7 11 0
TOR   003 001 000   4  9 0
```

Pitchers: Bere, BELCHER (3), McCaskill (7), Radinsky (8), Hernandez (9) vs STOTTLEMYRE, Leiter (7), Timlin (7)
Home Runs: Thomas-CHI, Johnson-CHI
Attendance: 51,889

GAME 5 AT TOR OCT 10

```
CHI   000 010 002   3  5 1
TOR   111 100 10X   5 14 0
```

Pitchers: McDOWELL, DeLeon (3), Radinsky (7), Hernandez (7) vs GUZMAN, Castillo (8), Ward (9)
Home Runs: Ventura-CHI, Burks-CHI
Attendance: 51,375

GAME 6 AT CHI OCT 12

```
TOR   020 100 003   6 10 0
CHI   002 000 001   3  5 3
```

Pitchers: STEWART, Ward (8) vs FERNANDEZ, McCaskill (8), Radinsky (9), Hernandez (9)
Home Runs: White-TOR, Newson-CHI
Attendance: 45,527

The Phillies and Blue Jays split the first two games, played in Toronto. But the defending champions captured the lead when play moved to Philadelphia for Game 3. In a contest delayed more than an hour by rain, Paul Molitor tripled home two Blue Jay runs before the first out had been recorded, and the Jays pushed on from there to an easy 10–3 win.

By just about any measure except pitching effectiveness, Game 4—played in a steady drizzle that for a time increased to a downpour—was one of the great ones. At 4 hours 14 minutes, it was the longest in World Series history, and its 29 total runs scored established a new record for major league postseason championship play, as did Philadelphia's 14 runs for a losing team. Toronto scored three times after two men had been retired in the top of the first inning, but Philadelphia retaliated immediately with four two-out runs in the bottom of the inning, as Jays' starter Todd Stottlemyre walked four batters, and Milt Thompson tripled. Lenny Dykstra's two-run homer an inning later pushed the Phillies' lead to 6–3, but Toronto scrambled back to regain a 7–6 advantage in the third inning on two walks and four singles. Philadelphia scored a tying run in the fourth inning, then scored five times an inning later with a barrage of hits highlighted by Darren Daulton's two-run homer and Dykstra's second two-run blast of the game. Toronto scored twice in the sixth inning, but single runs in the sixth and seventh restored Philadelphia's five-run lead. Then, in the top of the eighth, the Blue Jays parlayed two walks, two singles and a two-base error (later changed by the official scorer to a double) into a pair of runs and a diamond full of baserunners. Mitch Williams fanned Ed Sprague for the second out of the inning, but Rickey Henderson lined a two-run single to center to bring the Jays within one run of a tie, and Devon White looped a triple to right center for the tying and go-ahead runs. Relievers Mike Timlin and Duane Ward retired the final seven Phillies on five strikeouts and a pair of pop flies.

The Phillies salvaged their final home game, scoring single runs in the first two innings as Curt Schilling shut out the Blue Jays and forced the Series back to Toronto for a sixth game. Paul Molitor's RBI triple gave the Jays a first-inning lead, and his solo homer in the fifth stretched it to 5–1. Lenny Dykstra's three-run shot in the seventh (his fourth home run of the Series) brought Philadelphia to within a run of Toronto and Mariano Duncan scored the tying run

on Dave Hollins' single. Pinch hitter Pete Incaviglia's sacrifice fly gave the Phillies their first lead of the game, 6–5. In the bottom of the ninth, Mitch Williams walked Rickey Henderson and, with one away, gave up a single to Molitor (which raised his Series batting average to .500). Molitor scored the Series-winning run when Joe Carter, the next man up, lined Williams' would-be third strike over the left field fence for an 8–6 victory and Toronto's second straight world championship.

Toronto Blue Jays, 4; Philadelphia Phillies, 2

TOR (A)

PLAYER/POS	AVG	G	AB	R	H	2B	3B	HR	RB	BB	SO	SB
Roberto Alomar, 2b	.480	6	25	5	12	2	1	0	6	2	3	4
Pat Borders, c	.304	6	23	2	7	0	0	0	1	2	1	0
Rob Butler, ph	.500	2	2	1	1	0	0	0	0	0	0	0
Willie Canate, pr	.000	1	0	0	0	0	0	0	0	0	0	0
Joe Carter, of	.280	6	25	6	7	1	0	2	8	0	4	0
Tony Castillo, p	.000	2	1	0	0	0	0	0	0	0	1	0
Danny Cox, p	.000	3	1	0	0	0	0	0	0	0	0	0
Mark Eichhorn, p	.000	1	0	0	0	0	0	0	0	0	0	0
Tony Fernandez, ss	.333	6	21	2	7	1	0	0	9	3	3	0
Alfredo Griffin, 3b-2	.000	3	0	0	0	0	0	0	0	0	0	0
Juan Guzman, p	.000	2	2	0	0	0	0	0	0	0	1	0
Rickey Henderson, of	.227	6	22	6	5	2	0	0	2	5	2	1
Pat Hentgen, p	.000	1	3	0	0	0	0	0	0	0	1	0
Randy Knorr, c	.000	1	0	0	0	0	0	0	0	0	0	0
Al Leiter, p	1.000	3	1	0	1	1	0	0	0	0	0	0
Paul Molitor, dh-3	.500	6	24	10	12	2	2	2	8	3	0	1
John Olerud, 1b	.235	5	17	5	4	1	0	1	2	4	1	0
Ed Sprague, 3b-4,1b-1	.067	5	15	0	1	0	0	0	2	1	6	0
Dave Stewart, p	.000	2	0	0	0	0	0	0	0	0	0	0
Todd Stottlemyre, p	.000	1	0	0	0	0	0	0	0	0	0	0
Mike Timlin, p	.000	2	0	0	0	0	0	0	0	1	0	0
Duane Ward, p	.000	4	0	0	0	0	0	0	0	0	0	0
Devon White, of	.292	6	24	8	7	3	2	1	7	4	7	1
TOTAL	.311		206	45	64	13	5	6	45	25	30	7

PITCHER	W	L	ERA	G	GS	CG	SV	SHO	IP	H	ER	BB	SO
Tony Castillo	1	0	8.10	2	0	0	0	0	3.1	6	3	3	1
Danny Cox	0	0	8.10	3	0	0	0	0	3.1	6	3	5	6
Mark Eichhorn	0	0	0.00	1	0	0	0	0	0.1	1	0	0	0
Juan Guzman	0	1	3.75	2	2	0	0	0	12.0	10	5	8	12
Pat Hentgen	1	0	1.50	1	1	0	0	0	6.0	5	1	3	6
Al Leiter	1	0	7.71	3	0	0	0	0	7.0	12	6	2	5
Dave Stewart	0	1	6.75	2	2	0	0	0	12.0	10	9	8	8
Todd Stottlemyre	0	0	27.00	1	1	0	0	0	2.0	3	6	4	1
Mike Timlin	0	0	0.00	2	0	0	0	0	2.1	2	0	0	4
Duane Ward	1	0	1.93	4	0	0	2	0	4.2	3	1	0	7
TOTAL	4	2	5.77	21	6	0	2	0	53.0	58	34	34	50

PHI (N)

PLAYER/POS	AVG	G	AB	R	H	2B	3B	HR	RB	BB	SO	SB
Larry Andersen, p	.000	4	0	0	0	0	0	0	0	0	0	0
Kim Batiste, 3b	.000	3	0	0	0	0	0	0	0	0	0	0
Wes Chamberlain, ph	.000	2	2	0	0	0	0	0	0	0	1	0
Darren Daulton, c	.217	6	23	4	5	2	0	1	4	4	5	0
Mariano Duncan, 2b-5,dh-1	.345	6	29	5	10	1	0	1	2	1	7	3
Lenny Dykstra, of	.348	6	23	9	8	1	0	4	8	7	4	4
Jim Eisenreich, of	.231	6	26	3	6	0	0	1	7	2	4	0
Tommy Greene, p	1.000	1	1	1	1	0	0	0	0	0	0	0
Dave Hollins, 3b	.261	6	23	5	6	1	0	0	2	6	5	0
Pete Incaviglia, of	.125	4	8	0	1	0	0	0	1	0	4	0
Danny Jackson, p	.000	1	1	0	0	0	0	0	0	0	1	0
Ricky Jordan, dh-2	.200	3	10	0	2	0	0	0	0	0	2	0
John Kruk, 1b	.348	6	23	4	8	1	0	0	4	7	7	0
Roger Mason, p	.000	4	1	0	0	0	0	0	0	0	0	0
Mickey Morandini, 2b-1	.200	3	5	1	1	0	0	0	0	1	2	0
Terry Mulholland, p	.000	2	0	0	0	0	0	0	0	0	0	0
Ben Rivera, p	.000	1	0	0	0	0	0	0	0	0	0	0
Curt Schilling, p	.500	2	2	0	1	0	0	0	0	0	1	0
Kevin Stocker, ss	.211	6	19	1	4	1	0	0	1	5	5	0
Bobby Thigpen, p	.000	2	0	0	0	0	0	0	0	0	0	0
Milt Thompson, of	.313	6	16	3	5	1	1	1	6	1	2	0
David West, p	.000	3	0	0	0	0	0	0	0	0	0	0
Mitch Williams, p	.000	3	0	0	0	0	0	0	0	0	0	0
TOTAL	.274		212	36	58	7	2	7	35	34	50	7

PITCHER	W	L	ERA	G	GS	CG	SV	SHO	IP	H	ER	BB	SO
Larry Andersen	0	0	12.27	4	0	0	0	0	3.2	5	5	3	3
Tommy Greene	0	0	27.00	1	1	0	0	0	2.1	7	7	4	1
Danny Jackson	0	1	7.20	1	1	0	0	0	5.0	6	4	1	1
Roger Mason	0	0	1.17	4	0	0	0	0	7.2	4	1	1	7
Terry Mulholland	1	0	6.75	2	2	0	0	0	10.2	14	8	3	5
Ben Rivera	0	0	27.00	1	0	0	0	0	1.1	4	4	2	3
Curt Schilling	1	1	3.52	2	2	1	0	1	15.1	13	6	5	9
Bobby Thigpen	0	0	0.00	2	0	0	0	0	2.2	1	0	1	0
David West	0	0	27.00	3	0	0	0	0	1.0	5	3	1	1
Mitch Williams	0	2	20.25	3	0	0	1	0	2.2	5	6	4	1
TOTAL	2	4	7.57	23	6	1	1	1	52.1	64	44	25	30

GAME 1 AT TOR OCT 16

PHI	201	010	001	5	11	1
TOR	021	011	30X	8	10	3

Pitchers: SCHILLING, West (7), Andersen (7), Mason (8) vs Guzman, LEITER (6), Ward (8)
Home Runs: White-TOR, Olerud-TOR
Attendance: 52,011

GAME 2 AT TOR OCT 17

PHI	005	000	100	6	12	0
TOR	000	201	010	4	8	0

Pitchers: MULHOLLAND, Mason (6), Williams (7) vs STEWART, Castillo (7), Eichhorn (8), Timlin (8)
Home Runs: Dykstra-PHI, Eisenreich-PHI, Carter-TOR
Attendance: 52,062

GAME 3 AT PHI OCT 19

TOR	301	001	302	10	13	1
PHI	000	010	101	3	9	0

Pitchers: HENTGEN, Cox (7), Ward (9) vs JACKSON, Rivera (6), Thigpen (7), Andersen (9)
Home Runs: Molitor-TOR, Thompson-PHI
Attendance: 62,689

GAME 4 AT PHI OCT 20

TOR	304	002	060	15	18	0
PHI	420	151	100	14	14	0

Pitchers: Stottlemyre, Leiter (3), CASTILLO (5), Timlin (8), Ward (8) vs Greene, Mason (3), West (5), Andersen (7), WILLIAMS (8), Thigpen (9)
Home Runs: Dykstra-PHI (2), Daulton-PHI
Attendance: 62,731

GAME 5 AT PHI OCT 21

TOR	000	000	000	0	5	1
PHI	110	000	00X	2	5	1

Pitchers: GUZMAN, Cox (8) vs SCHILLING
Attendance: 62,706

GAME 6 AT TOR OCT 23

PHI	000	100	500	6	7	0
TOR	300	001	003	8	10	2

Pitchers: Mulholland, Mason (6), West (8), Andersen (8), WILLIAMS (9) vs Stewart, Cox (7), Leiter (7), WARD (9)
Home Runs: Molitor-TOR, Dykstra-PHI, Carter-TOR
Attendance: 52,195

Pitching-rich Atlanta's appearance in the division playoffs surprised few, but the hard-hitting expansion Rockies made history by reaching the postseason in just their third year of existence.

Two individuals shared the spotlight in Game 1: Braves rookie third baseman Chipper Jones and Rockies manager Don Baylor, but for wildly different reasons. Jones collected two homers and made a spectacular stop to rob Andres Galarraga of a double. Baylor was less fortunate. He ran out of hitters in the bottom of the ninth—having to use pitcher Lance Painter as his last batter—after Jones homered with two outs in the top of the inning. Atlanta won, 5-4.

Atlanta trailed, 4-3, going into the top of the ninth in Game 2, but they came thundering back with four runs as Mike Mordecai pinch homered, and Rockies second baseman Eric Young botched a routine ground ball. The Braves triumphed, 7-4, taking a 2-0 lead in the series.

In Game 3 Atlanta came through in the ninth once more on pinch-hitter Luis Polonia's two-strike run-scoring single, and the game went into extra innings. But Colorado bounced back to score twice in the 10th on Dante Bichette's double down the left field line and run-scoring singles by Andres Galarraga and Vinny Castilla (who had homered in the sixth).

Cy Young Award winners battled in Game 4 as Greg Maddux and Bret Saberhagen started, but Saberhagen was ineffective and Atlanta eliminated the Rockies with a 10-4 win. Maddux struck out seven and walked none before leaving for a pinch hitter in the seventh inning. Not helping Saberhagen was a controversial "safe" call on a play in which he attempted to cover first. Fred McGriff followed with the first of his two homers in the contest.

Atlanta Braves (E), 3;
Colorado Rockies (WC), 1

ATL (E)

PLAYER/POS	AVG	G	AB	R	H	2B	3B	HR	RB	BB	SO	SB
Steve Avery, p	.000	1	0	0	0	0	0	0	0	0	0	0
Rafael Belliard, ss	.000	4	5	1	0	0	0	0	0	0	1	0
Jeff Blauser, ss	.000	3	6	0	0	0	0	0	0	1	3	0
Pedro Borbon, p	.000	1	0	0	0	0	0	0	0	0	0	0
Brad Clontz, p	.000	1	0	0	0	0	0	0	0	0	0	0
Mike Devereaux, of-3	.200	4	5	1	1	0	0	0	0	0	0	0
Tom Glavine, p	.333	1	3	0	1	0	0	0	0	0	1	0
Marquis Grissom, of	.524	4	21	5	11	2	0	3	4	0	3	2
Chipper Jones, 3b	.389	4	18	4	7	2	0	2	4	2	2	0
David Justice, of	.231	4	13	2	3	0	0	0	0	5	2	0
Ryan Klesko, of	.467	4	15	5	7	1	0	0	0	1	3	0
Mark Lemke, 2b	.211	4	19	3	4	1	0	0	1	1	3	0
Javy Lopez, c	.444	3	9	0	4	0	0	0	3	0	3	0
Greg Maddux, p	.167	2	6	1	1	0	0	0	0	0	1	0
Fred McGriff, 1b	.333	4	18	4	6	0	0	2	6	2	3	0
Greg McMichael, p	.000	2	0	0	0	0	0	0	0	0	0	0
Kent Mercker, p	.000	1	0	0	0	0	0	0	0	0	0	0
Mike Mordecai, ss-1	.667	2	3	1	2	1	0	0	2	0	0	0
Charlie O'Brien, c	.200	2	5	0	1	0	0	0	0	1	1	0
Alejandro Pena, p	.000	3	0	0	0	0	0	0	0	0	0	0
Luis Polonia, ph	.333	3	3	0	1	0	0	0	2	0	1	1
Dwight Smith, ph	.667	4	3	0	2	1	0	0	1	0	0	0
John Smoltz, p	.000	1	2	0	0	0	0	0	0	0	0	0
Mark Wohlers, p	.000	3	0	0	0	0	0	0	0	0	0	0
TOTAL	.331		154	27	51	8	0	7	24	12	27	3

PITCHER	W	L	ERA	G	GS	CG	SV	SHO	IP	H	ER	BB	SO
Steve Avery	0	0	13.50	1	0	0	0	0	0.2	1	1	0	1
Pedro Borbon	0	0	0.00	1	0	0	0	0	1.0	1	0	0	3
Brad Clontz	0	0	0.00	1	0	0	0	0	1.1	0	0	0	2
Tom Glavine	0	0	2.57	1	1	0	0	0	7.0	5	2	1	3
Greg Maddux	1	0	4.50	2	2	0	0	0	14.0	19	7	2	7
Greg McMichael	0	0	6.75	2	0	0	0	0	1.1	1	1	2	1
Kent Mercker	0	0	0.00	1	0	0	0	0	0.1	0	0	0	0
Alejandro Pena	2	0	0.00	3	0	0	0	0	3.0	3	0	1	2
John Smoltz	0	0	7.94	1	1	0	0	0	5.2	5	5	1	6
Mark Wohlers	0	1	6.75	3	0	0	2	0	2.2	6	2	2	4
TOTAL	3	1	4.38	16	4	0	2	0	37.0	41	18	9	29

COL (W)

PLAYER/POS	AVG	G	AB	R	H	2B	3B	HR	RB	BB	SO	SB
Jason Bates, 2b-1,3b-1	.250	4	4	0	1	0	0	0	0	0	0	0
Dante Bichette, of	.588	4	17	6	10	3	0	1	3	1	3	0
Ellis Burks, of	.333	2	6	1	2	1	0	0	2	0	1	0
Vinny Castilla, 3b	.467	4	15	3	7	1	0	3	6	0	1	0
Andres Galarraga, 1b	.278	4	18	1	5	1	0	0	2	0	6	0
Joe Girardi, c	.125	4	16	0	2	0	0	0	0	0	2	0
Darren Holmes, p	.000	3	0	0	0	0	0	0	0	0	0	0
Trenidad Hubbard, ph	.000	3	2	0	0	0	0	0	0	0	0	0
Mike Kingery, of	.200	4	10	1	2	0	0	0	0	1	0	0
Curt Leskanic, p	.000	3	0	0	0	0	0	0	0	0	0	0
Mike Munoz, p	.000	4	0	0	0	0	0	0	0	0	0	0
J Owens, c	.000	1	1	0	0	0	0	0	0	0	1	0
Lance Painter, p-1	.000	2	2	0	0	0	0	0	0	0	1	0
Steve Reed, p	.000	3	0	0	0	0	0	0	0	0	0	0
Armando Reynoso, p	.000	1	0	0	0	0	0	0	0	0	0	0
Kevin Ritz, p	.000	2	0	0	0	0	0	0	0	0	0	0
Bruce Ruffin, p	.000	4	0	0	0	0	0	0	0	0	0	0
Bret Saberhagen, p	.000	1	1	0	0	0	0	0	0	0	0	0
Bill Swift, p	.000	1	3	0	0	0	0	0	0	0	2	0
Mark Thompson, p	.000	1	0	0	0	0	0	0	0	0	0	0
John Vander Wal, ph	.000	4	4	0	0	0	0	0	0	0	2	0
Larry Walker, of	.214	4	14	3	3	0	0	1	3	3	4	1
Walt Weiss, ss	.167	4	12	1	2	0	0	0	0	3	3	1
Eric Young, 2b	.438	4	16	3	7	1	0	1	2	2	2	1
TOTAL	.287		143	19	41	7	0	6	18	9	29	3

PITCHER	W	L	ERA	G	GS	CG	SV	SHO	IP	H	ER	BB	SO
Darren Holmes	1	0	0.00	3	0	0	0	0	1.2	6	0	0	2
Curt Leskanic	0	1	6.00	3	0	0	0	0	3.0	3	2	0	4
Mike Munoz	0	1	13.50	4	0	0	0	0	1.1	4	2	1	1
Lance Painter	0	0	5.40	1	1	0	0	0	5.0	5	3	2	4
Steve Reed	0	0	0.00	3	0	0	0	0	2.2	2	0	1	3
Armando Reynoso	0	0	0.00	1	0	0	0	0	1.0	2	0	0	0
Kevin Ritz	0	0	7.71	2	1	0	0	0	7.0	12	6	3	5
Bruce Ruffin	0	0	2.70	4	0	0	0	0	3.1	3	1	2	2
Bret Saberhagen	0	1	11.25	1	1	0	0	0	4.0	7	5	1	3
Bill Swift	0	0	6.00	1	1	0	0	0	6.0	7	4	2	3
Mark Thompson	0	0	0.00	1	0	0	1	0	1.0	0	0	0	0
TOTAL	1	3	5.75	24	4	0	1	0	36.0	51	23	12	27

GAME 1 AT COL OCT 3

ATL	001 002 011	5	12	1
COL	000 300 010	4	13	4

Pitchers: Maddux, McMichael (8), PENA (8), Wohlers (9) vs Ritz, Reed (6), Ruffin (7), Munoz (8), Holmes (8), LESKANIC (9)
Home Runs: Grissom-ATL, Jones-ATL (2), Castilla-COL
Attendance: 50,040

GAME 2 AT COL OCT 4

ATL	101 100 004	7	13	1
COL	000 003 010	4	8	2

Pitchers: Glavine, Avery (8), PENA (8), Wohlers (9) vs Painter, Reed (6), Ruffin (7), Leskanic (8), MUNOZ (9), Holmes (9)
Home Runs: Grissom-ATL (2), Walker-COL
Attendance: 50,040

GAME 3 AT ATL OCT 6

COL	102 002 000 2	7	9	0
ATL	000 300 101 0	5	11	0

Pitchers: Swift, Reed (7), Munoz (7), Leskanic (7), Ruffin (8), HOLMES (9), Thompson (10) vs Smoltz, Clontz (6), Borbon (8), McMichael (9), WOHLERS (10), Mercker (10)
Home Runs: Young-COL, Castilla-COL
Attendance: 51,300

GAME 4 AT ATL OCT 7

COL	003 001 000	4	11	1
ATL	004 213 00X	10	15	0

Pitchers: SABERHAGEN, Ritz (5), Munoz (6), Reynoso (7), Ruffin (8) vs MADDUX, Pena (8)
Home Runs: Bichette-COL, Castilla-COL, McGriff-ATL (2)
Attendance: 50,027

Davey Johnson's Cincinnati Reds made short work of Tommy Lasorda's Los Angeles Dodgers in the 1995 NL division series, sweeping them, 3-0, and outscoring them, 22-7.

Game 1 saw the Reds score four times in the first inning as they walloped the Dodgers, 7-2. Los Angeles starter Ramon Martinez was ineffective, being cuffed for 10 hits and two walks in just four and a third innings.

Game 2 was a more even affair until the Los Angeles bullpen went to work. Barry Larkin's eighth-inning single to right broke open a 2-2 tie, and in the top of the ninth the Reds added two insurance runs.

The Reds wrapped up the series by humiliating the Dodgers 10-1 in Game 3. The Dodgers had their chances in the contest, but squandered their opportunities, leaving 11 runners on base. The Reds broke the game open in the sixth as pinch hitter Mark Lewis delivered a grand slam to left-center off Mark Guthrie.

Cincinnati Reds (C), 3; Los Angeles (W), 0

CIN (C)

PLAYER/POS	AVG	G	AB	R	H	2B	3B	HR	RB	BB	SO	SB
Bret Boone, 2b	.300	3	10	4	3	1	0	1	1	1	3	1
Jeff Branson, 3b	.286	3	7	0	2	1	0	0	2	2	0	0
Jeff Brantley, p	.000	3	0	0	0	0	0	0	0	0	0	0
Dave Burba, p	.000	1	0	0	0	0	0	0	0	0	0	0
Mariano Duncan, 2b-1	.667	2	3	1	2	0	0	0	1	0	0	1
Ron Gant, of	.231	3	13	3	3	0	0	1	2	0	3	0
Thomas Howard, of	.100	3	10	0	1	1	0	0	0	0	2	0
Mike Jackson, p	1.000	3	1	0	1	1	0	0	3	0	0	0
Barry Larkin, ss	.385	3	13	2	5	0	0	0	1	1	2	4
Darren Lewis, of	.000	3	3	0	0	0	0	0	0	0	1	0
Mark Lewis, 3b	.500	2	2	2	1	0	0	1	5	1	0	0
Hal Morris, 1b	.500	3	10	5	5	1	0	0	2	3	1	1
Reggie Sanders, of	.154	3	13	3	2	1	0	1	2	1	9	2
Benito Santiago, c	.333	3	9	2	3	0	0	1	3	3	3	0
Pete Schourek, p	.000	1	2	0	0	0	0	0	0	0	1	0
John Smiley, p	.000	1	2	0	0	0	0	0	0	0	1	0
Jerome Walton, of	.000	3	3	0	0	0	0	0	0	1	1	0
David Wells, p	.333	1	3	0	1	0	0	0	0	0	1	0
TOTAL	.279		104	22	29	6	0	5	22	13	28	9

PITCHER	W	L	ERA	G	GS	CG	SV	SHO	IP	H	ER	BB	SO
Jeff Brantley	0	0	6.00	3	0	0	1	0	3.0	5	2	0	2
Dave Burba	1	0	0.00	1	0	0	0	0	1.0	2	0	1	0
Mike Jackson	0	0	0.00	3	0	0	0	0	3.2	4	0	0	1
Pete Schourek	1	0	2.57	1	1	0	0	0	7.0	5	2	3	5
John Smiley	0	0	3.00	1	1	0	0	0	6.0	9	2	0	1
David Wells	1	0	0.00	1	1	0	0	0	6.1	6	0	1	8
TOTAL	3	0	2.00	10	3	0	1	0	27.0	31	6	5	17

LA (W)

PLAYER/POS	AVG	G	AB	R	H	2B	3B	HR	RB	BB	SO	SB
Billy Ashley, ph	.000	1	0	0	0	0	0	0	0	1	0	0
Pedro Astacio, p	.000	3	0	0	0	0	0	0	0	0	0	0
Brett Butler, of	.267	3	15	1	4	0	0	0	1	0	3	0
John Cummings, p	.000	2	0	0	0	0	0	0	0	0	0	0
Delino DeShields, 2b	.250	3	12	1	3	0	0	0	0	1	3	0
Chad Fonville, ss	.500	3	12	1	6	0	0	0	0	0	1	0
Mark Guthrie, p	.000	3	0	0	0	0	0	0	0	0	0	0
Chris Gwynn, ph	.000	1	1	0	0	0	0	0	0	0	1	0
Dave Hansen, ph	.667	3	3	0	2	0	0	0	0	0	0	0
Todd Hollandsworth, of	.000	2	2	0	0	0	0	0	0	0	0	0
Eric Karros, 1b	.500	3	12	3	6	1	0	2	4	1	0	0
Roberto Kelly, of	.364	3	11	0	4	0	0	0	0	1	0	0
Ramon Martinez, p	.000	1	1	0	0	0	0	0	0	0	0	0
Raul Mondesi, of	.222	3	9	0	2	0	0	0	1	0	2	0
Hideo Nomo, p	.000	1	2	0	0	0	0	0	0	0	2	0
Jose Offerman, pr	.000	1	0	0	0	0	0	0	0	0	0	0
Antonio Osuna, p	.000	3	0	0	0	0	0	0	0	0	0	0
Mike Piazza, c	.214	3	14	1	3	1	0	1	1	1	2	0
Kevin Tapani, p	.000	2	0	0	0	0	0	0	0	0	0	0
Ismael Valdes, p	.000	1	3	0	0	0	0	0	0	0	0	0
Tim Wallach, 3b	.083	3	12	0	1	0	0	0	0	1	3	0
Mitch Webster, ph	.000	2	2	0	0	0	0	0	0	0	0	0
TOTAL	.279		111	7	31	2	0	3	7	5	17	0

PITCHER	W	L	ERA	G	GS	CG	SV	SHO	IP	H	ER	BB	SO
Pedro Astacio	0	0	0.00	3	0	0	0	0	3.1	1	0	0	5
John Cummings	0	0	20.25	2	0	0	0	0	1.1	3	3	2	3
Mark Guthrie	0	0	6.75	3	0	0	0	0	1.1	2	1	1	1
Ramon Martinez	0	1	14.54	1	1	0	0	0	4.1	10	7	2	3
Hideo Nomo	0	1	9.00	1	1	0	0	0	5.0	7	5	2	6
Antonio Osuna	0	0	2.70	3	0	0	0	0	3.1	3	1	1	3
Kevin Tapani	0	0	81.00	2	0	0	0	0	0.1	0	3	4	1
Ismael Valdes	0	0	0.00	1	1	0	0	0	7.0	3	0	1	6
TOTAL	0	3	6.92	16	3	0	0	0	26.0	29	20	13	28

GAME 1 AT LA OCT 3

CIN	400 030 000	7	12	0
LA	000 011 000	2	8	0

Pitchers: SCHOUREK, Jackson (8), Brantley (9) vs MARTINEZ, Cummings (5), Astacio (6), Guthrie (8), Osuna (9)
Home Runs: Santiago-CIN, Piazza-LA
Attendance: 44,199

GAME 2 AT LA OCT 4

CIN	000 200 012	5	6	0
LA	100 100 002	4	14	2

Pitchers: Smiley, BURBA (7), Jackson (8), Brantley (9) vs Valdes, OSUNA (8), Tapani (9), Guthrie (9), Astacio (9)
Home Runs: Sanders-CIN, Karros-LA (2)
Attendance: 46,051

GAME 3 AT CIN OCT 6

LA	000 100 000	1	9	1
CIN	002 104 30X	10	11	2

Pitchers: NOMO, Tapani (6), Guthrie (6), Astacio (6), Cummings (7), Osuna (7) vs WELLS, Jackson (7), Brantley (9)
Home Runs: Gant-CIN, Boone-CIN, M.Lewis-CIN
Attendance: 53,276

The Cleveland Indians had enjoyed a 100-44 record in the strike-shortened 1995 season and captured the AL's new Central Division by a record 30 games. Not surprisingly, they were heavily favored against the AL East champion Red Sox. And not surprisingly, the Curse of Rocky Colavito fell in three straight to the Curse of the Bambino—in other words, the Tribe won.

Yet there were moments of high drama in the series. Game 1 was a titanic struggle that had nearly everything: two rain delays (39 minutes at the start and 23 minutes in the eighth), three extra inning homers, and a controversial piece of lumber. The five-hour and one-minute game ended at 2:08 a.m. the next day. But no one in Cleveland was complaining.

Boston jumped off to a 2-0 lead on John Valentin's two-run homer, but Red Sox starter Roger Clemens surrendered three runs in the sixth. Boston's Luis Alicea evened the score up with a leadoff homer in the eighth. In the top of the 11th, Tim Naehring homered to give the Sox the lead, but Albert Belle retaliated in the bottom of the frame with a homer of his own. The next move was Boston's, which contended Belle's bat was corked. AL authorities confiscated it and sawed it in half but found no cork. In the 12th the Indians loaded the bases with one out but did not score. In the 13th former Red Sox catcher Tony Pena ended it all with an improbable homer off a 3-0 pitch from Zane Smith.

Game 2 was a much easier win as veteran Orel Hershiser faced Boston's Erik Hanson. Omar Vizquel doubled in two runs in the fifth. Eddie Murray added a two-run homer off Hanson in the eighth. That was more than Hershiser needed as he struck out seven in seven and a third innings while walking just two and allowing three hits.

Game 3 moved from Jacobs Field to Fenway Park, but the home field proved to be no advantage. Red Sox knuckleballer Tim Wakefield surrendered seven runs in five and a third innings as the Indians, behind Charles Nagy, eliminated Boston with an 8-2 win. Mo Vaughn and Jose Canseco went hitless, running their record to 0-for-27, with nine strikeouts in the series. But Boston's defeat was not the duo's fault entirely. Overall, Sox batters were 2-for-28 with runners in scoring position.

Cleveland Indians (C), 3; Boston Red Sox (E), 0

CLE (C)

PLAYER/POS	AVG	G	AB	R	H	2B	3B	HR	RB	BB	SO	SB
Sandy Alomar, c	.182	3	11	1	2	1	0	0	1	0	1	0
Paul Assenmacher, p	.000	3	0	0	0	0	0	0	0	0	0	0
Carlos Baerga, 2b	.286	3	14	2	4	1	0	0	1	0	1	0
Albert Belle, of	.273	3	11	3	3	1	0	1	3	4	3	0
Alvaro Espinoza, 3b	.000	1	1	0	0	0	0	0	0	0	0	0
Orel Hershiser, p	.000	1	0	0	0	0	0	0	0	0	0	0
Ken Hill, p	.000	1	0	0	0	0	0	0	0	0	0	0
Wayne Kirby, of-2	1.000	3	1	0	1	0	0	0	0	0	0	0
Kenny Lofton, of	.154	3	13	1	2	0	0	0	0	1	3	0
Dennis Martinez, p	.000	1	0	0	0	0	0	0	0	0	0	0
Jose Mesa, p	.000	2	0	0	0	0	0	0	0	0	0	0
Eddie Murray, dh	.385	3	13	3	5	0	1	1	3	2	1	0
Charles Nagy, p	.000	1	0	0	0	0	0	0	0	0	0	0
Tony Pena, c	.500	2	2	1	1	0	0	1	1	0	0	0
Herb Perry, ph	.000	1	1	0	0	0	0	0	0	0	0	0
Eric Plunk, p	.000	1	0	0	0	0	0	0	0	0	0	0
Jim Poole, p	.000	1	0	0	0	0	0	0	0	0	0	0
Manny Ramirez, of	.000	3	12	1	0	0	0	0	0	1	2	0
Paul Sorrento, 1b	.300	3	10	2	3	0	0	0	1	2	3	0
Julian Tavarez, p	.000	3	0	0	0	0	0	0	0	0	0	0
Jim Thome, 3b	.154	3	13	1	2	0	0	1	3	1	6	0
Omar Vizquel, ss	.167	3	12	2	2	1	0	0	4	2	2	1
TOTAL	.219		114	17	25	4	1	4	17	13	22	1

PITCHER	W	L	ERA	G	GS	CG	SV	SHO	IP	H	ER	BB	SO
Paul Assenmacher	0	0	0.00	3	0	0	0	0	1.2	0	0	0	3
Orel Hershiser	1	0	0.00	1	1	0	0	0	7.1	3	0	2	7
Ken Hill	1	0	0.00	1	1	0	0	0	1.1	1	0	0	2
Dennis Martinez	0	0	3.00	1	1	0	0	0	6.0	5	2	0	4
Jose Mesa	0	0	0.00	2	0	0	0	0	2.0	0	0	2	0
Charles Nagy	1	0	1.29	1	1	0	0	0	7.0	4	1	5	6
Eric Plunk	0	0	0.00	1	0	0	0	0	1.1	1	0	1	1
Jim Poole	0	0	5.40	1	0	0	0	0	1.2	2	1	1	2
Julian Tavarez	0	0	6.75	3	0	0	0	0	2.2	5	2	0	3
TOTAL	3	0	1.74	14	3	0	0	0	31.0	21	6	11	26

BOS (E)

PLAYER/POS	AVG	G	AB	R	H	2B	3B	HR	RB	BB	SO	SB
Rick Aguilera, p	.000	1	0	0	0	0	0	0	0	0	0	0
Luis Alicea, 2b	.600	3	10	1	6	1	0	1	1	2	2	1
Stan Belinda, p	.000	1	0	0	0	0	0	0	0	0	0	0
Jose Canseco, dh-2,of-1	.000	3	13	0	0	0	0	0	0	2	2	0
Roger Clemens, p	.000	1	0	0	0	0	0	0	0	0	0	0
Rheal Cormier, p	.000	2	0	0	0	0	0	0	0	0	0	0
Mike Greenwell, of	.200	3	15	0	3	0	0	0	0	0	1	0
Erik Hanson, p	.000	1	0	0	0	0	0	0	0	0	0	0
Bill Haselman, c	.000	1	2	0	0	0	0	0	0	0	0	0
Dwayne Hosey, of	.000	3	12	1	0	0	0	0	0	2	3	1
Joe Hudson, p	.000	1	0	0	0	0	0	0	0	0	0	0
Reggie Jefferson, dh	.250	1	4	1	1	0	0	0	0	0	1	0
Mike Macfarlane, c	.333	3	9	0	3	0	0	0	1	0	3	0
Mike Maddux, p	.000	2	0	0	0	0	0	0	0	0	0	0
Willie McGee, of	.250	2	4	0	1	0	0	0	1	0	2	0
Tim Naehring, 3b	.308	3	13	2	4	0	0	1	1	0	1	0
Zane Smith, p	.000	1	0	0	0	0	0	0	0	0	0	0
Matt Stairs, ph	.000	1	1	0	0	0	0	0	0	0	1	0
Mike Stanton, p	.000	1	0	0	0	0	0	0	0	0	0	0
Lee Tinsley, of	.000	1	5	0	0	0	0	0	0	1	2	0
John Valentin, ss	.250	3	12	1	3	1	0	1	2	3	1	0
Mo Vaughn, 1b	.000	3	14	0	0	0	0	0	0	1	7	0
Tim Wakefield, p	.000	1	0	0	0	0	0	0	0	0	0	0
TOTAL	.184		114	6	21	2	0	3	6	11	26	2

PITCHER	W	L	ERA	G	GS	CG	SV	SHO	IP	H	ER	BB	SO
Rick Aguilera	0	0	13.50	1	0	0	0	0	0.2	3	1	0	1
Stan Belinda	0	0	0.00	1	0	0	0	0	0.1	0	0	0	0
Roger Clemens	0	0	3.86	1	1	0	0	0	7.0	5	3	1	5
Rheal Cormier	0	0	13.50	2	0	0	0	0	0.2	2	1	1	2
Erik Hanson	0	1	4.50	1	1	1	0	0	8.0	4	4	4	5
Joe Hudson	0	0	0.00	1	0	0	0	0	1.0	2	0	1	0
Mike Maddux	0	0	0.00	2	0	0	0	0	3.0	2	0	1	1
Zane Smith	0	1	6.75	1	0	0	0	0	1.1	1	1	0	0
Mike Stanton	0	0	0.00	1	0	0	0	0	2.1	1	0	0	4
Tim Wakefield	0	1	11.81	1	1	0	0	0	5.1	5	7	5	4
TOTAL	0	3	5.16	12	3	1	0	0	29.2	25	17	13	22

GAME 1 AT CLE OCT 3

BOS	002 000 010 010 0	4	11	2
CLE	000 003 000 010 1	5	10	2

Pitchers: Clemens, Cormier (8), Belinda (8), Stanton (8), Aguilera (11), Maddux (11), SMITH (12) vs Martinez, Tavarez (7), Assenmacher (8), Plunk (8), Mesa (10), Poole (11), HILL (12)
Home Runs: Valentin-BOS, Alicea-BOS, Naehring-BOS, Belle-CLE, Pena-CLE
Attendance: 44,218

GAME 2 AT CLE OCT 4

BOS	000 000 000	0	3	1
CLE	000 020 02X	4	4	2

Pitchers: HANSON vs HERSHISER, Tavarez (8), Assenmacher (8), Mesa (9)
Home Runs: Murray-CLE
Attendance: 44,264

GAME 3 AT BOS OCT 6

BOS	000 100 010	2	7	1
CLE	021 005 000	8	11	2

Pitchers: NAGY, Tavarez (8), Assenmacher (9) vs WAKEFIELD, Cormier (6), Maddux (6), Hudson (9)
Home Runs: Thome-CLE
Attendance: 34,211

The hitherto laughable Seattle Mariners shocked the New York Yankees in a gritty, exciting five-game division series that could only be likened to two prize fighters standing toe-to-toe and slugging it out.

Seattle found its rotation askew after being forced into a one-game playoff against California to determine the AL West championship. In Game 1 the Yankees' David Cone started against Seattle's Chris Bosio and triumphed 9-6 despite Ken Griffey, Jr.'s two homers. Ultimately, Griffey would hit five in the series.

The Yankees won Game 2 by breaking up a 5-5 marathon on a two-run Jim Leyritz homer in the bottom of the 15th. In the 12th Griffey had homered to right-center on a 3-1 pitch to give Seattle the lead, but New York evened it in the bottom of the inning on Ruben Sierra's run-scoring double to left.

Seattle's ace, Cy Young Award winner Randy Johnson, finally appeared in Game 3, striking out 10 as Seattle won, 7-6, before a delirious Kingdome crowd. New York jumped off to a 5-0 lead in Game 4, but Seattle battled back to even the series at 2-2. The big blow was Edgar Martinez's grand-slam to center in the Mariners' five-run eighth inning. The game went down to the last out as New York left runners on second and third in the ninth.

After Seattle scored twice in the eighth to deadlock deciding Game 5 at 4-4, Mariners manager Lou Piniella brought in Randy Johnson (who had pitched seven innings just two days before) to shut the door on New York. Not to be outdone, Yankees manager Buck Showalter countered with starter Jack McDowell. Once again, Edgar Martinez (series average of .571) came through in the clutch. hitting a two-run double down the left field line to end the game—and the series.

Seattle Mariners (W), 3;
New York Yankees (WC), 2

SEA (W)

PLAYER/POS	AVG	G	AB	R	H	2B	3B	HR	RBI	BB	SO	SB
Bobby Ayala, p	.000	2	0	0	0	0	0	0	0	0	0	0
Tim Belcher, p	.000	2	0	0	0	0	0	0	0	0	0	0
Andy Benes, p	.000	2	0	0	0	0	0	0	0	0	0	0
Mike Blowers, 3b-5,1b-1	.167	5	18	0	3	0	0	0	1	3	7	0
Chris Bosio, p	.000	2	0	0	0	0	0	0	0	0	0	0
Jay Buhner, of	.458	5	24	2	11	1	0	1	3	2	4	0
Norm Charlton, p	.000	4	0	0	0	0	0	0	0	0	0	0
Vince Coleman, of	.217	5	23	6	5	0	1	1	1	2	4	1
Joey Cora, 2b	.316	5	19	7	6	1	0	1	1	3	0	1
Alex Diaz, of-1	.333	2	3	0	1	0	0	0	0	1	1	0
Felix Fermin, ss-2,2b-1	.000	3	1	0	0	0	0	0	0	0	1	0
Ken Griffey, of	.391	5	23	9	9	0	0	5	7	2	4	1
Randy Johnson, p	.000	2	0	0	0	0	0	0	0	0	0	0
Tino Martinez, 1b	.409	5	22	4	9	1	0	1	5	3	4	0
Edgar Martinez, dh	.571	5	21	6	12	3	0	2	10	6	2	0
Jeff Nelson, p	.000	3	0	0	0	0	0	0	0	0	0	0
Warren Newson, ph	.000	1	1	0	0	0	0	0	0	0	1	0
Bill Risley, p	.000	4	0	0	0	0	0	0	0	0	0	0
Alex Rodriguez, ss	.000	1	1	1	0	0	0	0	0	0	0	0
Luis Sojo, ss	.250	5	20	0	5	0	0	0	0	3	0	0
Doug Strange, 3b	.000	2	4	0	0	0	0	0	0	1	1	0
Bob Wells, p	.000	1	0	0	0	0	0	0	0	0	0	0
Chris Widger, c	.000	2	3	0	0	0	0	0	0	0	3	0
Dan Wilson, c	.118	5	17	0	2	0	0	0	1	2	6	0
TOTAL	.315		200	35	63	6	1	11	33	25	41	3

PITCHER	W	L	ERA	G	GS	CG	SV	SHO	IP	H	ER	BB	SO
Bobby Ayala	0	0	54.00	2	0	0	0	0	0.2	6	4	1	0
Tim Belcher	0	1	6.23	2	0	0	0	0	4.1	4	3	5	0
Andy Benes	0	0	5.40	2	2	0	0	0	11.2	10	7	9	8
Chris Bosio	0	0	10.57	2	2	0	0	0	7.2	10	9	4	2
Norm Charlton	1	0	2.45	4	0	0	1	0	7.1	4	2	3	9
Randy Johnson	2	0	2.70	2	1	0	0	0	10.0	5	3	6	16
Jeff Nelson	0	1	3.18	3	0	0	0	0	5.2	7	2	3	7
Bill Risley	0	0	6.00	4	0	0	1	0	3.0	2	2	0	1
Bob Wells	0	0	9.00	1	0	0	0	0	1.0	2	1	1	0
TOTAL	3	2	5.79	22	5	0	2	0	51.1	50	33	32	43

NY (E)

PLAYER/POS	AVG	G	AB	R	H	2B	3B	HR	RBI	BB	SO	SB
Wade Boggs, 3b	.263	4	19	4	5	2	0	1	3	3	5	0
David Cone, p	.000	2	0	0	0	0	0	0	0	0	0	0
Russ Davis, 3b	.200	2	5	0	1	0	0	0	0	0	2	0
Tony Fernandez, ss	.238	5	21	0	5	2	0	0	0	2	2	0
Sterling Hitchcock, p	.000	2	0	0	0	0	0	0	0	0	0	0
Steve Howe, p	.000	2	0	0	0	0	0	0	0	0	0	0
Dion James, of	.083	4	12	0	1	0	0	0	0	1	1	0
Scott Kamieniecki, p	.000	1	0	0	0	0	0	0	0	0	0	0
Pat Kelly, 2b-4	.000	5	3	3	0	0	0	0	0	1	1	0
Jim Leyritz, c	.143	2	7	1	1	0	0	1	2	1	5	0
Don Mattingly, 1b	.417	5	24	3	10	4	0	1	6	1	5	0
Jack McDowell, p	.000	2	0	0	0	0	0	0	0	0	0	0
Paul O'Neill, of	.333	5	18	5	6	0	0	3	6	5	5	0
Andy Pettitte, p	.000	1	0	0	0	0	0	0	0	0	0	0
Jorge Posada, pr	.000	1	0	1	0	0	0	0	0	0	0	0
Mariano Rivera, p	.000	3	0	0	0	0	0	0	0	0	0	0
Ruben Sierra, dh	.174	5	23	2	4	2	0	0	2	5	7	0
Mike Stanley, c	.313	5	16	2	5	0	0	1	3	2	1	0
Darryl Strawberry, ph	.000	2	2	0	0	0	0	0	0	0	1	0
Randy Velarde, 2b-4, 3b-2,of-2	.176	5	17	3	3	0	0	0	1	6	4	0
John Wetteland, p	.000	3	0	0	0	0	0	0	0	0	0	0
Bob Wickman, p	.000	3	0	0	0	0	0	0	0	0	0	0
Bernie Williams, of	.429	5	21	8	9	2	0	2	5	7	3	1
Gerald Williams, of	.000	5	5	0	0	0	0	0	0	2	1	0
TOTAL	.259		193	33	50	12	0	11	32	32	43	1

PITCHER	W	L	ERA	G	GS	CG	SV	SHO	IP	H	ER	BB	SO
David Cone	1	0	4.60	2	2	0	0	0	15.2	15	8	9	14
Sterling Hitchcock	0	0	5.40	2	0	0	0	0	1.2	2	1	2	1
Steve Howe	0	0	18.00	2	0	0	0	0	1.0	4	2	0	0
Scott Kamieniecki	0	0	7.20	1	1	0	0	0	5.0	9	4	4	4
Jack McDowell	0	2	9.00	2	2	0	0	0	7.0	8	7	4	6
Andy Pettitte	0	0	5.14	1	1	0	0	0	7.0	9	4	3	0
Mariano Rivera	1	0	0.00	3	0	0	0	0	5.1	3	0	1	8
John Wetteland	0	1	14.54	3	0	0	0	0	4.1	8	7	2	5
Bob Wickman	0	0	0.00	3	0	0	0	0	3.0	5	0	0	3
TOTAL	2	3	5.94	19	5	0	0	0	50.0	63	33	25	41

GAME 1 AT NY OCT 3

SEA	000 101 202	6	9	0
NY	002 002 41X	9	13	0

Pitchers: Bosio, NELSON (6), Ayala (7), Risley (7), Wells (8) vs CONE, Wetteland (9)
Home Runs: Griffey-SEA (2), Boggs-NY, Sierra-NY
Attendance: 57,178

GAME 2 AT NY OCT 4

SEA	001 001 200 001 000	5	16	2
NY	000 012 100 001 002	7	11	0

Pitchers: Benes, Risley (6), Charlton (7), Nelson (11), BELCHER (11) vs Pettitte, Wickman (8), Wetteland (9), RIVERA (12)
Home Runs: Coleman-SEA, Griffey-SEA, Sierra-NY, Mattingly-NY, O'Neill-NY, Leyritz-NY
Attendance: 57,126

GAME 3 AT SEA OCT 6

NY	000 100 120	4	6	2
SEA	000 024 10X	7	7	0

Pitchers: McDOWELL, Howe (6), Wickman (6), Hitchcock (7), Rivera (7) vs JOHNSON, Risley (8), Charlton (8)
Home Runs: B.Williams-NY (2), Stanley-NY, T.Martinez-SEA
Attendance: 57,944

GAME 4 AT SEA OCT 7

NY	302 000 012	8	14	1
SEA	004 011 05X	11	16	0

Pitchers: Kamieniecki, Hitchcock (6), Wickman (7), WETTELAND (8), Howe (8) vs Bosio, Nelson (3), Belcher (7), CHARLTON (8), Ayala (9), Risley (9)
Home Runs: O'Neill-NY, E.Martinez-SEA (2), Griffey-SEA, Buhner-SEA
Attendance: 57,180

GAME 5 AT SEA OCT 8

NY	000 202 000 01	5	6	0
SEA	001 100 020 02	6	15	0

Pitchers: Cone, Rivera (8), McDOWELL (9) vs Benes, Charlton (7), JOHNSON (9)
Home Runs: O'Neill-NY, Cora-SEA, Griffey-SEA
Attendance: 57,411

Both the Braves and the Reds had moved through the National League's first-ever division series with ease, with Atlanta knocking off Colorado, 3-1, and Cincinnati sweeping the Dodgers in three games as the Reds made their first postseason appearance since 1990. The Braves, meanwhile, became the first team to play in the NLCS four straight times.

In Game 1 of the NLCS, a scant crowd of only 40,382 Riverfront Stadium patrons saw the Braves edge the Reds, 2-1. Atlanta prevailed despite failing to move a runner past second base until the ninth inning, as the Reds' Pete Schourek held the Braves to four singles through eight. Atlanta broke through in the 11th on Mike Devereaux's pinch-hit single, a feat which helped earn him NLCS MVP honors.

Game 2 was another extra inning affair as Atlanta cracked the game open with four in the 10th to triumph, 6-2. In that inning the Braves loaded the bases, scoring their first run on Mark Portugal's wild pitch. Javier Lopez followed with a three-run homer off the left-field foul screen. Game 3 remained scoreless until the sixth, when catcher Charlie O'Brien homered to left off David Wells, scoring Fred McGriff and Mike Devereaux. Chipper Jones followed with a two-run homer to complete the Braves' scoring.

Game 4 saw a 6-0 Atlanta win, completing the first sweep since 1982. Steve Avery allowed just three singles, two of which failed to make it out of the infield. Mike Devereaux delivered the key blow, a three-run homer to left in the seventh. Atlanta, seeking its first Series win since 1957, would now face Cleveland, making its first Fall Classic appearance since 1954.

Atlanta Braves (E), 4; Cincinnati Reds (C), 0

ATL (E)

PLAYER/POS	AVG	G	AB	R	H	2B	3B	HR	RB	BB	SO	SB
Steve Avery, p	.500	2	2	0	1	0	0	0	0	0	0	0
Rafael Belliard, ss	.273	4	11	1	3	0	0	0	0	0	3	0
Jeff Blauser, ss	.000	1	4	0	0	0	0	0	0	1	2	0
Brad Clontz, p	.000	1	0	0	0	0	0	0	0	0	0	0
Mike Devereaux, of	.308	4	13	2	4	1	0	1	5	1	2	0
Tom Glavine, p	.000	1	1	0	0	0	0	0	0	1	0	0
Marquis Grissom, of	.263	4	19	2	5	0	1	0	0	1	4	0
Chipper Jones, 3b	.438	4	16	3	7	0	0	1	3	3	1	1
David Justice, of	.273	3	11	1	3	0	0	0	1	2	1	0
Ryan Klesko, of-3	.000	4	7	0	0	0	0	0	0	3	4	0
Mark Lemke, 2b	.167	4	18	2	3	0	0	0	1	1	0	0
Javy Lopez, c	.357	3	14	2	5	1	0	1	3	0	1	0
Greg Maddux, p	.000	1	3	0	0	0	0	0	0	0	1	0
Fred McGriff, 1b	.438	4	16	5	7	4	0	0	0	3	0	0
Greg McMichael, p	.000	3	0	0	0	0	0	0	0	0	0	0
Mike Mordecai, ss-1	.000	2	2	0	0	0	0	0	0	0	1	0
Charlie O'Brien, c-1	.400	2	5	1	2	0	0	1	3	0	1	0
Alejandro Pena, p	.000	3	0	0	0	0	0	0	0	0	0	0
Luis Polonia, of-1	.500	3	2	0	1	0	0	0	1	0	0	0
Dwight Smith, ph	.000	2	2	0	0	0	0	0	0	0	0	0
John Smoltz, p	.333	1	3	0	1	0	0	0	0	0	1	1
Mark Wohlers, p	.000	4	0	0	0	0	0	0	0	0	0	0
TOTAL	.282		149	19	42	6	1	4	17	16	22	2

PITCHER	W	L	ERA	G	GS	CG	SV	SHO	IP	H	ER	BB	SO
Steve Avery	1	0	0.00	2	1	0	0	0	6.0	2	0	4	6
Brad Clontz	0	0	0.00	1	0	0	0	0	0.1	1	0	0	0
Tom Glavine	0	0	1.29	1	1	0	0	0	7.0	7	1	2	5
Greg Maddux	1	0	1.13	1	1	0	0	0	8.0	7	1	2	4
Greg McMichael	1	0	0.00	3	0	0	1	0	2.2	0	0	1	2
Alejandro Pena	0	0	0.00	3	0	0	0	0	3.0	2	0	1	4
John Smoltz	0	0	2.57	1	1	0	0	0	7.0	7	2	2	2
Mark Wohlers	1	0	1.80	4	0	0	0	0	5.0	2	1	0	8
TOTAL	4	0	1.15	16	4	0	1	0	39.0	28	5	12	31

CIN (C)

PLAYER/POS	AVG	G	AB	R	H	2B	3B	HR	RB	BB	SO	SB
Eric Anthony, ph	.000	2	1	0	0	0	0	0	0	1	1	0
Bret Boone, 2b	.214	4	14	1	3	0	0	0	0	1	2	0
Jeff Branson, 3b	.111	4	9	2	1	1	0	0	0	0	2	1
Jeff Brantley, p	.000	2	0	0	0	0	0	0	0	0	0	0
Dave Burba, p	.000	2	0	0	0	0	0	0	0	0	0	0
Hector Carrasco, p	.000	1	0	0	0	0	0	0	0	0	0	0
Mariano Duncan, 1b-1	.000	3	3	0	0	0	0	0	0	1	1	0
Ron Gant, of	.188	4	16	1	3	0	0	0	1	0	3	0
Lenny Harris, ph	1.000	3	2	0	2	0	0	0	1	0	0	1
Xavier Hernandez, p	.000	1	0	0	0	0	0	0	0	0	0	0
Thomas Howard, of-3	.250	4	8	0	2	1	0	0	1	2	0	0
Mike Jackson, p	.000	3	0	0	0	0	0	0	0	0	0	0
Barry Larkin, ss	.389	4	18	1	7	2	1	0	0	1	1	1
Darren Lewis, of	.000	2	1	0	0	0	0	0	0	0	0	0
Mark Lewis, 3b	.250	2	4	0	1	0	0	0	0	1	1	0
Hal Morris, 1b	.167	4	12	0	2	1	0	0	1	1	1	1
Mark Portugal, p	.000	1	0	0	0	0	0	0	0	0	0	0
Reggie Sanders, of	.125	4	16	0	2	0	0	0	0	2	10	0
Benito Santiago, c	.231	4	13	0	3	0	0	0	0	2	3	0
Pete Schourek, p	.000	2	2	0	0	0	0	0	0	0	4	0
John Smiley, p	.000	1	1	0	0	0	0	0	0	0	0	0
Eddie Taubensee, c-1	.500	2	2	0	1	0	0	0	0	0	0	0
Jerome Walton, of	.000	2	7	0	0	0	0	0	0	0	2	0
David Wells, p	.500	1	2	0	1	0	0	0	0	0	0	0
TOTAL	.209		134	5	28	5	1	0	4	12	31	4

PITCHER	W	L	ERA	G	GS	CG	SV	SHO	IP	H	ER	BB	SO
Jeff Brantley	0	0	0.00	2	0	0	0	0	2.2	0	0	2	1
Dave Burba	0	0	0.00	2	0	0	0	0	3.2	3	0	4	0
Hector Carrasco	0	0	0.00	1	0	0	0	0	1.1	1	0	0	3
Xavier Hernandez	0	0	27.00	1	0	0	0	0	0.2	3	2	0	0
Mike Jackson	0	1	23.14	3	0	0	0	0	2.1	5	6	4	1
Mark Portugal	0	1	36.00	1	0	0	0	0	1.0	3	4	1	0
Pete Schourek	0	1	1.26	2	2	0	0	0	14.1	14	2	3	13
John Smiley	0	0	3.60	1	1	0	0	0	5.0	5	2	0	1
David Wells	0	1	4.50	1	1	0	0	0	6.0	8	3	2	3
TOTAL	0	4	4.62	14	4	0	0	0	37.0	42	19	16	22

GAME 1 AT CIN OCT 10

ATL	000 000 001 01	2	7	0
CIN	000 100 000 00	1	8	0

Pitchers: Glavine, Pena (8), WOHLERS (9), Clontz (11), Avery (11), McMichael (11) vs Schourek, Brantley (9), JACKSON (11)
Attendance: 40,382

GAME 2 AT CIN OCT 11

ATL	100 100 000 4	6	11	1
CIN	000 020 000 0	2	9	1

Pitchers: Smoltz, Pena (8), McMICHAEL (9), Wohlers (10) vs Smiley, Burba (6), Jackson (8), Brantley (9), PORTUGAL (10)
Home Runs: Lopez-ATL
Attendance: 44,624

GAME 3 AT ATL OCT 13

CIN	000 000 011	2	8	0
ATL	000 003 20X	5	12	1

Pitchers: WELLS, Hernandez (7), Carrasco (7) vs MADDUX, Wohlers (9)
Home Runs: O'Brien-ATL, Jones-ATL
Attendance: 51,424

GAME 4 AT ATL OCT 14

CIN	000 000 000	0	3	1
ATL	001 000 50X	6	12	1

Pitchers: SCHOUREK, Jackson (7), Burba (7) vs AVERY, McMichael (7), Pena (8), Wohlers (9)
Home Runs: Devereaux-ATL
Attendance: 52,067

Cleveland had romped in a three-one sweep of Boston. Seattle had engaged in a thrilling, exhausting five-game series against New York, fraying their pitching—and probably their nerves—in the process.

Most observers expected the Tribe to take Game 1. Seattle's rotation had been decimated in defeating the Yankees, and Mariners manager Lou Piniella had to start rookie Bob Wolcott rather than ace Randy Johnson. Wolcott gave up a game-tying seventh inning homer to Albert Belle, but otherwise Piniella had nothing to complain about. Seattle answered in the bottom of that frame and made the run hold up.

Cleveland stranded 10 runners in Game 2 (making a total of 22 left on in the first two contests) but still triumphed, 5-2. Manny Ramirez came into the game mired in a 1-for-16 postseason slump but went 4-for-4 with solo homers in the sixth and eighth innings.

Randy Johnson finally appeared in the series in Game 3 but wasn't around for a decision. The Mariners jumped off to a 2-0 lead thanks to two Cleveland errors, but at the end of eight the score was tied. In the top of the 11th an intentional walk to Tino Martinez backfired as Jay Buhner followed with a three-run homer.

In Game 4 Cleveland evened the series with a 7-0 triumph against an ineffective Andy Benes, aided by Eddie Murray's two-run first inning homer, Jim Thome's two-run third inning homer, and Omar Vizquel's run-scoring sixth inning double.

In Game 5 Orel Hershiser ran his career postseason record to 7-0 as he struck out eight and walked only two. He needed help, however, leaving the game with a 3-2 lead that Paul Assenmacher and Jose Mesa protected skillfully.

In the final game, the Indians' Dennis Martinez defeated Randy Johnson, 4-0. Through eight innings only one run had scored (an unearned one by Cleveland), but in that inning Mariners hopes unraveled. Johnson surrendered a leadoff double to Tony Pena, then an infield single to Kenny Lofton, who stole second. Next came a wild pitch. Ruben Amaro (running for Pena) scored, but so did Lofton, motoring all the way from second, embarrassing Mariners catcher Dan Wilson. That play sealed the Mariners' doom. Carlos Baerga then homered, and, two innings later, the Indians had their first AL pennant in 41 years.

Cleveland Indians (C), 4;
Seattle Mariners (W), 2

CLE (C)

PLAYER/POS	AVG	G	AB	R	H	2B	3B	HR	RB	BB	SO	SB
Sandy Alomar, c	.267	5	15	0	4	1	1	0	1	1	1	0
Ruben Amaro, dh-1	.000	3	1	1	0	0	0	0	0	0	0	0
Paul Assenmacher, p	.000	3	0	0	0	0	0	0	0	0	0	0
Carlos Baerga, 2b	.400	6	25	3	10	0	0	1	4	2	3	0
Albert Belle, of	.222	5	18	1	4	1	0	1	1	3	5	0
Alan Embree, p	.000	1	0	0	0	0	0	0	0	0	0	0
Alvaro Espinoza, 3b	.125	4	8	1	1	0	0	0	0	0	3	0
Orel Hershiser, p	.000	2	0	0	0	0	0	0	0	0	0	0
Ken Hill, p	.000	1	0	0	0	0	0	0	0	0	0	0
Wayne Kirby, of	.200	5	5	2	1	0	0	0	0	0	0	1
Kenny Lofton, of	.458	6	24	4	11	0	2	0	3	4	6	5
Dennis Martinez, p	.000	2	0	0	0	0	0	0	0	0	0	0
Jose Mesa, p	.000	4	0	0	0	0	0	0	0	0	0	0
Eddie Murray, dh	.250	6	24	2	6	1	0	1	3	2	3	0
Charles Nagy, p	.000	1	0	0	0	0	0	0	0	0	0	0
Chad Ogea, p	.000	1	0	0	0	0	0	0	0	0	0	0
Tony Pena, c	.333	4	6	1	2	1	0	0	0	1	0	0
Herb Perry, 1b	.000	3	8	0	0	0	0	0	0	1	3	0
Eric Plunk, p	.000	3	0	0	0	0	0	0	0	0	0	0
Jim Poole, p	.000	1	0	0	0	0	0	0	0	0	0	0
Manny Ramirez, of	.286	6	21	2	6	0	0	2	2	2	5	0
Paul Sorrento, 1b	.154	4	13	2	2	1	0	0	0	2	3	0
Julian Tavarez, p	.000	4	0	0	0	0	0	0	0	0	0	0
Jim Thome, 3b	.267	5	15	2	4	0	0	2	5	2	3	0
Omar Vizquel, ss	.087	6	23	2	2	1	0	0	2	5	2	3
TOTAL	.257		206	23	53	6	3	7	21	25	37	9

PITCHER	W	L	ERA	G	GS	CG	SV	SHO	IP	H	ER	BB	SO
Paul Assenmacher	0	0	0.00	3	0	0	0	0	1.1	0	0	1	2
Alan Embree	0	0	0.00	1	0	0	0	0	0.1	0	0	0	1
Orel Hershiser	2	0	1.29	2	2	0	0	0	14.0	9	2	3	15
Ken Hill	1	0	0.00	1	1	0	0	0	7.0	5	0	3	6
Dennis Martinez	1	1	2.03	2	2	0	0	0	13.1	10	3	3	7
Jose Mesa	0	0	2.25	4	0	0	1	0	4.0	3	1	1	1
Charles Nagy	0	0	1.13	1	1	0	0	0	8.0	5	1	0	6
Chad Ogea	0	0	0.00	1	0	0	0	0	0.2	1	0	0	2
Eric Plunk	0	0	9.00	3	0	0	0	0	2.0	1	2	3	2
Jim Poole	0	0	0.00	1	0	0	0	0	1.0	0	0	0	2
Julian Tavarez	0	1	2.70	4	0	0	0	0	3.1	3	1	1	2
TOTAL	4	2	1.64	23	6	0	1	0	55.0	37	10	15	46

SEA (W)

PLAYER/POS	AVG	G	AB	R	H	2B	3B	HR	RB	BB	SO	SB
Rich Amaral, ph	.000	2	2	0	0	0	0	0	0	0	1	0
Bobby Ayala, p	.000	2	0	0	0	0	0	0	0	0	0	0
Tim Belcher, p	.000	1	0	0	0	0	0	0	0	0	0	0
Andy Benes, p	.000	1	0	0	0	0	0	0	0	0	0	0
Mike Blowers, 3b	.222	6	18	1	4	0	0	1	2	0	4	0
Chris Bosio, p	.000	1	0	0	0	0	0	0	0	0	0	0
Jay Buhner, of	.304	6	23	5	7	2	0	3	5	2	8	0
Norm Charlton, p	.000	3	0	0	0	0	0	0	0	0	0	0
Vince Coleman, of-5	.100	6	20	0	2	0	0	0	0	2	6	4
Joey Cora, 2b	.174	6	23	3	4	1	0	0	0	1	0	2
Alex Diaz, of-3	.429	4	7	0	3	1	0	0	0	1	1	0
Felix Fermin, 2b-1,ss-1	.000	2	0	0	0	0	0	0	0	0	0	0
Ken Griffey, of	.333	6	21	2	7	2	0	1	2	4	4	2
Randy Johnson, p	.000	2	0	0	0	0	0	0	0	0	0	0
Tino Martinez, 1b	.136	6	22	1	3	0	0	0	0	3	7	0
Edgar Martinez, dh	.087	6	23	0	2	0	0	0	0	2	5	1
Jeff Nelson, p	.000	3	0	0	0	0	0	0	0	0	0	0
Bill Risley, p	.000	3	0	0	0	0	0	0	0	0	0	0
Alex Rodriguez, ph	.000	1	1	0	0	0	0	0	0	0	1	0
Luis Sojo, ss	.250	6	20	0	5	2	0	0	1	0	2	0
Doug Strange, 3b-2	.000	4	4	0	0	0	0	0	0	2	0	0
Bob Wells, p	.000	1	0	0	0	0	0	0	0	0	0	0
Chris Widger, c	.000	3	1	0	0	0	0	0	0	0	1	0
Dan Wilson, c	.000	6	16	0	0	0	0	0	0	0	4	0
Bob Wolcott, p	.000	1	0	0	0	0	0	0	0	0	0	0
TOTAL	.184		201	12	37	8	0	5	10	15	46	9

PITCHER	W	L	ERA	G	GS	CG	SV	SHO	IP	H	ER	BB	SO
Bobby Ayala	0	0	2.45	2	0	0	0	0	3.2	3	1	3	3
Tim Belcher	0	1	6.35	1	1	0	0	0	5.2	9	4	2	1
Andy Benes	0	1	23.14	1	1	0	0	0	2.1	6	6	2	3
Chris Bosio	0	1	3.38	1	1	0	0	0	5.1	7	2	2	3
Norm Charlton	1	0	0.00	3	0	0	1	0	6.0	1	0	1	5
Randy Johnson	0	1	2.35	2	2	0	0	0	15.1	12	4	2	13
Jeff Nelson	0	0	0.00	3	0	0	0	0	3.0	3	0	5	3
Bill Risley	0	0	0.00	3	0	0	0	0	2.2	2	0	1	2
Bob Wells	0	0	3.00	1	0	0	0	0	3.0	2	1	2	2
Bob Wolcott	1	0	2.57	1	1	0	0	0	7.0	8	2	5	2
TOTAL	2	4	3.33	18	6	0	1	0	54.0	53	20	25	37

GAME 1 AT SEA OCT 10

CLE	001 000 100	2	10 1
SEA	020 000 10X	3	7 0

Pitchers: MARTINEZ, Tavarez (7), Assenmacher (8), Plunk (8) vs WOLCOTT, Nelson (8), Charlton (8)
Home Runs: Belle-CLE, Blowers-SEA
Attendance: 57,065

GAME 2 AT SEA OCT 11

CLE	000 022 010	5	12 0
SEA	000 001 001	2	6 1

Pitchers: HERSHISER, Mesa (9) vs BELCHER, Ayala (6), Risley (9)
Home Runs: Ramirez-CLE (2), Griffey-SEA, Buhner-SEA
Attendance: 58,144

GAME 3 AT CLE OCT 13

SEA	011 000 000 03	5	9 1
CLE	000 100 010 00	2	4 2

Pitchers: Johnson, CHARLTON (9) vs Nagy, Mesa (10), Assenmacher (11), Plunk (11)
Home Runs: Buhner-SEA (2)
Attendance: 43,643

GAME 4 AT CLE OCT 14

SEA	000 000 000	0	6 1
CLE	312 001 00X	7	9 0

Pitchers: BENES, Wells (3), Ayala (6), Nelson (7), Risley (8) vs HILL, Poole (8), Ogea (9), Embree (9)
Home Runs: Murray-CLE, Thome-CLE
Attendance: 43,686

GAME 5 AT CLE OCT 15

SEA	001 010 000	2	5 2
CLE	100 002 00X	3	10 4

Pitchers: BOSIO, Nelson (6), Risley (7) vs HERSHISER, Tavarez (7), Assenmacher (7), Plunk (8), Mesa (9)
Home Runs: Thome-CLE
Attendance: 43,607

GAME 6 AT SEA OCT 17

CLE	000 010 030	4	8 0
SEA	000 000 000	0	4 1

Pitchers: MARTINEZ, Tavarez (8), Mesa (9) vs JOHNSON, Charlton (8)
Home Runs: Baerga-CLE
Attendance: 58,489

The Indians and Braves met for a rematch of their tussle in the 1948 World Series, but this time the transplanted Braves went home with the honors. Game 1 quickly established that Atlanta's vaunted pitching staff was no myth. Perennial Cy Young Award winner Greg Maddux used just 95 pitches in shutting down the hard-hitting Indians. Only three runners reached against him, on opposite field singles by Kenny Lofton and Jim Thome, and on an error by Rafael Belliard. Cleveland starter Orel Hershiser tired in the seventh and walked two, leading to the second and third Atlanta runs and his first loss after seven straight postseason victories.

In Game 2 Atlanta took a 2-0 Series lead as catcher Javier Lopez anticipated a Dennis Martinez fastball on the outside part of the plate. He hammered it to straight-away center field for a two-run homer, shattering a 2-2 tie and providing the Braves with all the margin they would need for a 4-3 win.

The Indians bats finally came alive in Game 3. It looked like the Tribe would be facing a 3-0 deficit, as they trailed 6-5 in the bottom of the eighth. But in that inning Kenny Lofton (who reached base six times in the contest) scored the tying run on Sandy Alomar's first hit of the series. In the 11th Murray singled off Alejandro Pena's first pitch to score pinch-runner Alvaro Espinoza with the winning run.

Atlanta's Ryan Klesko and Cleveland's Albert Belle traded solo sixth-inning homers in Game 4 to set up a 1-1 tie going into the top of the seventh. Atlanta then scored three runs on Luis Polonia's run-scoring double and David Justice's two-out, two-run single to center to break the contest open and ultimately give Atlanta a 5-2 win.

The Tribe stayed alive in Game 5 as Jim Thome singled in the go-ahead run in the sixth and provided a crucial insurance run with an eighth inning homer. Ryan Klesko nicked Jose Mesa for a two-run homer in the ninth—the third straight game in which he'd homered—but it wasn't enough.

The keys to Game 6 were two players with something to prove: Tom Glavine, who had survived Atlanta's horrible days in the late 1980s, and David Justice, who was taking heat for comments he had made about Atlanta fans' lack of spirit. Glavine allowed only a sixth inning single to Tony Pena, walked three and struck out eight. Justice brought home the game's only run with a sixth inning homer off reliever Jim Poole. The Braves now had their first world championship since 1957 and had become the first franchise to win the crown in

Atlanta Braves (N,) 4;
Cleveland Indians (A), 2

ATL (N)

PLAYER/POS	AVG	G	AB	R	H	2B	3B	HR	RB	BB	SO	SB
Steve Avery, pn	.000	1	0	0	0	0	0	0	0	0	0	0
Rafael Belliard, ss	.000	6	16	0	0	0	0	0	0	1	4	0
Pedro Borbon, p	.000	1	0	0	0	0	0	0	0	0	0	0
Brad Clontz, p	.000	2	0	0	0	0	0	0	0	0	0	0
Mike Devereaux, of-4,dh-1	.250	5	4	0	1	0	0	0	1	2	1	0
Tom Glavine, p	.000	2	4	0	0	0	0	0	0	1	2	0
Marquis Grissom, of	.360	6	25	3	9	1	0	0	1	1	3	3
Chipper Jones, 3b	.286	6	21	3	6	3	0	0	1	4	3	0
David Justice, of	.250	6	20	3	5	1	0	1	5	5	1	0
Ryan Klesko, of-3,dh-3	.313	6	16	4	5	0	0	3	4	3	4	0
Mark Lemke, 2b	.273	6	22	1	6	0	0	0	0	3	2	0
Javy Lopez, c	.176	6	17	1	3	2	0	1	3	1	1	0
Greg Maddux, p	.000	2	3	0	0	0	0	0	0	0	1	0
Fred McGriff, 1b	.261	6	23	5	6	2	0	2	3	3	7	1
Greg McMichael, p	.000	3	0	0	0	0	0	0	0	0	0	0
Kent Mercker, p	.000	1	0	0	0	0	0	0	0	0	0	0
Mike Mordecai, ss-2, dh-1	.333	3	3	0	1	0	0	0	0	0	1	0
Charlie O'Brien, c	.000	2	3	0	0	0	0	0	0	0	1	0
Alejandro Pena, p	.000	2	0	0	0	0	0	0	0	0	0	0
Luis Polonia, of-4	.286	6	14	3	4	1	0	1	4	1	3	1
Dwight Smith, ph	.500	3	2	0	1	0	0	0	0	0	1	0
John Smoltz, p	.000	1	0	0	0	0	0	0	0	0	0	0
Mark Wohlers, p	.000	4	0	0	0	0	0	0	0	0	0	0
TOTAL	.244		193	23	47	10	0	8	23	25	34	5

PITCHER	W	L	ERA	G	GS	CG	SV	SHO	IP	H	ER	BB	SO
Steve Avery	1	0	1.50	1	1	0	0	0	6.0	3	1	5	3
Pedro Borbon	0	0	0.00	1	0	0	1	0	1.0	0	0	0	2
Brad Clontz	0	0	2.70	2	0	0	0	0	3.1	2	1	0	2
Tom Glavine	2	0	1.29	2	2	0	0	0	14.0	4	2	6	11
Greg Maddux	1	1	2.25	2	2	1	0	0	16.0	9	4	3	8
Greg McMichael	0	0	2.70	3	0	0	0	0	3.1	3	1	2	2
Kent Mercker	0	0	4.50	1	0	0	0	0	2.0	1	1	2	2
Alejandro Pena	0	1	9.00	2	0	0	0	0	1.0	3	1	2	0
John Smoltz	0	0	15.43	1	1	0	0	0	2.1	6	4	2	4
Mark Wohlers	0	0	1.80	4	0	0	2	0	5.0	4	1	3	3
TOTAL	4	2	2.67	19	6	1	3	0	54.0	35	16	25	37

CLE (A)

PLAYER/POS	AVG	G	AB	R	H	2B	3B	HR	RB	BB	SO	SB
Sandy Alomar, c	.200	5	15	0	3	2	0	0	1	0	2	0
Ruben Amaro, of-1	.000	2	2	0	0	0	0	0	0	0	1	0
Paul Assenmacher, p	.000	4	0	0	0	0	0	0	0	0	0	0
Carlos Baerga, 2b	.192	6	26	1	5	2	0	0	4	1	1	0
Albert Belle, of	.235	6	17	4	4	0	0	2	4	7	5	0
Alan Embree, p	.000	4	0	0	0	0	0	0	0	0	0	0
Alvaro Espinoza, 3b-1	.500	2	2	1	1	0	0	0	0	0	0	0
Orel Hershiser, p	.000	2	2	0	0	0	0	0	0	0	0	0
Ken Hill, p	.000	2	3	0	0	0	0	0	0	0	1	0
Wayne Kirby, of-2	.000	3	1	0	0	0	0	0	0	0	1	0
Kenny Lofton, of	.200	6	25	6	5	1	0	0	0	3	1	6
Dennis Martinez, p	.000	2	3	0	0	0	0	0	0	0	1	0
Jose Mesa, p	.000	2	0	0	0	0	0	0	0	0	0	0
Eddie Murray, 1b-3,dh-3	.105	6	19	1	2	0	0	1	3	5	4	0
Charles Nagy, p	.000	1	0	0	0	0	0	0	0	0	0	0
Tony Pena, c	.167	2	6	0	1	0	0	0	0	0	2	0
Herb Perry, 1b	.000	3	5	0	0	0	0	0	0	0	2	0
Jim Poole, p	.000	2	0	0	0	0	0	0	0	0	0	0
Manny Ramirez, of	.222	6	18	2	4	0	0	1	2	4	5	1
Paul Sorrento, 1b-3	.182	6	11	0	2	1	0	0	0	1	4	0
Julian Tavarez, p	.000	5	0	0	0	0	0	0	0	0	0	0
Jim Thome, 3b	.211	6	19	1	4	1	0	1	2	2	5	0
Omar Vizquel, ss	.174	6	23	3	4	0	1	0	1	3	5	1
TOTAL	.179		195	19	35	7	1	5	17	25	37	8

PITCHER	W	L	ERA	G	GS	CG	SV	SHO	IP	H	ER	BB	SO
Paul Assenmacher	0	0	6.75	4	0	0	0	0	1.1	1	1	3	3
Alan Embree	0	0	2.70	4	0	0	0	0	3.1	2	1	2	2
Orel Hershiser	1	1	2.57	2	2	0	0	0	14.0	8	4	4	13
Ken Hill	0	1	4.26	2	1	0	0	0	6.1	7	3	4	1
Dennis Martinez	0	1	3.48	2	2	0	0	0	10.1	12	4	8	5
Jose Mesa	1	0	4.50	2	0	0	1	0	4.0	5	2	1	4
Charles Nagy	0	0	6.43	1	1	0	0	0	7.0	8	5	1	4
Jim Poole	0	1	3.86	2	0	0	0	0	2.1	1	1	0	1
Julian Tavarez	0	0	0.00	5	0	0	0	0	4.1	3	0	2	1
TOTAL	2	4	3.57	24	6	0	1	0	53.0	47	21	25	34

three different cities—Boston, Milwaukee, and Atlanta.

GAME 1 AT ATL OCT 21

CLE	100 000 001	2	2	0
ATL	010 000 20X	3	3	2

Pitchers: HERSHISER, Assenmacher (7), Tavarez (7), Embree (8) vs MADDUX
Home Runs: McGriff-ATL
Attendance: 51,876

GAME 2 AT ATL OCT 22

CLE	020 000 100	3	6	2
ATL	002 002 00X	4	8	2

Pitchers: MARTINEZ, Embree (6), Poole (7), Tavarez (8) vs GLAVINE, McMichael (7), Pena (7), Wohlers (8)
Home Runs: Murray-CLE, Lopez-ATL
Attendance: 51,877

GAME 3 AT CLE OCT 24

ATL	100 001 130 00	6	12	1
CLE	202 000 110 01	7	12	2

Pitchers: Smoltz, Clontz (3), Mercker (5), McMichael (7), Wohlers (8), PENA (11) vs Nagy, Assenmacher (8), Tavarez (8), MESA (9)
Home Runs: McGriff-ATL, Klesko-ATL
Attendance: 43,584

GAME 4 AT CLE OCT 25

ATL	000 001 301	5	11	1
CLE	000 001 001	2	6	0

Pitchers: AVERY, McMichael (7), Wohlers (9), Borbon (9) vs HILL, Assenmacher (7), Tavarez (8), Embree (8)
Home Runs: Belle-CLE, Ramirez-CLE, Klesko-ATL
Attendance: 43,578

GAME 5 AT CLE OCT 26

ATL	000 110 002	4	7	0
CLE	200 002 01X	5	8	1

Pitchers: MADDUX, Clontz (8) vs HERSHISER, Mesa (9)
Home Runs: Belle-CLE, Thome-CLE, Polonia-ATL, Klesko-ATL
Attendance: 43,595

GAME 6 AT ATL OCT 28

CLE	000 000 000	0	1	1
ATL	000 001 00X	1	6	0

Pitchers: Martinez, POOLE (5), Hill (7), Embree (7), Tavarez (8), Assenmacher (8) vs GLAVINE, Wohlers (9)
Home Runs: Justice-ATL
Attendance: 51,875

The Braves became the first National League team to make five consecutive postseason appearances. The Braves struggled in mid-September, but their opponents in the Division Series, the Dodgers, had really stumbled into the postseason. Los Angeles lost its last four regular-season games, but still captured the Wild Card. Dodger Stadium was abuzz when the Division Series began and the two starting pitchers, LA's Ramon Martinez and Atlanta's John Smoltz, were equal to the task. Martinez allowed just one run and three hits through eight innings while Smoltz pitched nine innings with only one run and four hits against him. Smoltz and the Braves caught the break they needed in the 10th when Javier Lopez homered to right-center for a 2-1 lead. Reliever Mark Wohlers made it hold up with two strikeouts in the tenthth inning.

Pitching was the name of the game again the next night. While Greg Maddux's four-year streak of Cy Young Awards would end in 1996, he reminded the country that his trophy collection was well-deserved. Maddux, however, was touched for unearned runs in the first and fourth innings as the Dodgers took a 2-1 lead into the seventh inning despite just three hits. Dodgers starter Ismael Valdes limited the Braves to three hits as well through six innings, including a home run by Ryan Klesko, but that changed in a span of seven pitches in the seventh inning. Fred McGriff hit a line-drive home run to center field to tie the score. After Valdes recorded his fifth strikeout, Jermaine Dye hit the first pitch he saw over the left field wall for a 3-2 lead. Greg McMichael and Mark Wohlers each had a scoreless inning to close out the win.

A club-record crowd greeted the Braves at Fulton County Stadium for Game 3, but the fans fidgeted in their seats when Hideo Nomo struck out the first two Braves he faced. They were soon on their feet, however, when Chipper Jones singled and McGriff doubled him home. Nomo retired the first two batters he faced in the fourth inning, but he was on his way to the showers by the time the third out was recorded. Pitcher Tom Glavine started the rally with a double and Marquis Grissom walked before Mark Lemke doubled home both runners. Chipper Jones followed with a two-run home run to give Atlanta a 5-0 lead. To their credit, the Dodgers nicked Glavine for a run in the seventh inning and McMichael for another in the eighth, but Mike Bielecki and Mark Wohlers allowed nothing

Atlanta Braves (E), 3; Los Angeles Dodgers (WC), 0

ATL (E)

PLAYER/POS	AVG	G	AB	R	H	2B	3B	HR	RB	BB	SO	SB
Rafael Belliard, ss	.000	3	0	0	0	0	0	0	0	0	0	0
Mike Bielecki, p	.000	1	0	0	0	0	0	0	0	0	0	0
Jeff Blauser, ss	.111	3	9	0	1	0	0	0	0	1	3	0
Jermaine Dye, of	.182	3	11	1	2	0	0	1	1	0	6	1
Tom Glavine, p	.500	1	2	1	1	1	0	0	0	0	0	0
Marquis Grissom, of	.083	3	12	2	1	0	0	0	0	1	2	1
Andruw Jones, of	.000	3	0	0	0	0	0	0	0	1	0	0
Chipper Jones, 3b	.222	3	9	2	2	0	0	1	2	3	4	1
Ryan Klesko, of	.125	3	8	1	1	0	0	1	1	3	4	1
Mark Lemke, 2b	.167	3	12	1	2	1	0	0	2	0	1	0
Javy Lopez, c	.286	2	7	1	2	0	0	1	1	1	0	1
Greg Maddux, p	.000	1	2	0	0	0	0	0	0	0	1	0
Fred McGriff, 1b	.333	3	9	1	3	1	0	1	3	2	1	0
Greg McMichael, p	.000	2	0	0	0	0	0	0	0	0	0	0
Terry Pendleton, ph	.000	1	1	0	0	0	0	0	0	0	0	0
Eddie Perez, c	.333	1	3	0	1	0	0	0	0	0	0	0
Luis Polonia, ph	.000	2	2	0	0	0	0	0	0	0	1	0
John Smoltz, p	.000	1	2	0	0	0	0	0	0	0	0	0
Mark Wohlers, p	.000	3	0	0	0	0	0	0	0	0	0	0
TOTAL	.180		89	10	16	3	0	5	10	12	24	5

PITCHER	W	L	ERA	G	GS	CG	SV	SHO	IP	H	ER	BB	SO
Mike Bielecki	0	0	0.00	1	0	0	0	0	0.2	0	0	1	1
Tom Glavine	1	0	1.35	1	1	0	0	0	6.2	5	1	3	7
Greg Maddux	1	0	0.00	1	1	0	0	0	7.0	3	0	0	7
Greg McMichael	0	0	6.75	2	0	0	0	0	1.1	1	1	1	3
John Smoltz	1	0	1.00	1	1	0	0	0	9.0	4	1	2	7
Mark Wohlers	0	0	0.00	3	0	0	3	0	3.1	1	0	0	4
TOTAL	3	0	0.96	9	3	0	3	0	28.0	14	3	7	29

LA (W)

PLAYER/POS	AVG	G	AB	R	H	2B	3B	HR	RB	BB	SO	SB
Billy Ashley, ph	.000	2	2	0	0	0	0	0	0	0	2	0
Pedro Astacio, p	.000	1	0	0	0	0	0	0	0	0	0	0
Tom Candiotti, p	.000	1	0	0	0	0	0	0	0	0	0	0
Juan Castro, 2b	.200	2	5	0	1	1	0	0	1	1	1	0
Dave Clark, ph	.000	2	2	0	0	0	0	0	0	0	2	0
Chad Curtis, of	.000	1	2	0	0	0	0	0	0	1	1	0
Delino DeShields, 2b	.000	2	4	0	0	0	0	0	0	0	1	0
Darren Dreifort, p	.000	1	0	0	0	0	0	0	0	0	0	0
Greg Gagne, ss	.273	3	11	2	3	1	0	0	0	0	5	0
Mark Guthrie, p	.000	1	0	0	0	0	0	0	0	0	0	0
Dave Hansen, ph	.000	2	2	0	0	0	0	0	0	0	0	0
Todd Hollandsworth, of	.333	3	12	1	4	3	0	0	1	0	3	0
Eric Karros, 1b	.000	3	9	0	0	0	0	0	0	2	3	0
Wayne Kirby, of	.125	3	8	1	1	0	0	0	0	2	1	0
Ramon Martinez, p	.000	1	3	0	0	0	0	0	0	0	2	0
Raul Mondesi, of	.182	3	11	0	2	2	0	0	1	0	4	0
Hideo Nomo, p	.000	1	1	0	0	0	0	0	0	0	1	0
Antonio Osuna, p	.000	2	0	0	0	0	0	0	0	0	0	0
Mike Piazza, c	.300	3	10	1	3	0	0	0	2	1	2	0
Scott Radinsky, p	.000	2	0	0	0	0	0	0	0	0	0	0
Ismael Valdes, p	.000	1	2	0	0	0	0	0	0	0	0	0
Tim Wallach, 3b	.000	3	11	0	0	0	0	0	0	0	1	0
Todd Worrell, p	.000	1	0	0	0	0	0	0	0	0	0	0
TOTAL	.147		95	5	14	7	0	0	5	7	29	0

PITCHER	W	L	ERA	G	GS	CG	SV	SHO	IP	H	ER	BB	SO
Pedro Astacio	0	0	0.00	1	0	0	0	0	1.2	0	0	0	1
Tom Candiotti	0	0	0.00	1	0	0	0	0	2.0	0	0	0	1
Darren Dreifort	0	0	0.00	1	0	0	0	0	0.2	0	0	0	0
Mark Guthrie	0	0	0.00	1	0	0	0	0	0.1	0	0	1	1
Ramon Martinez	0	0	1.13	1	1	0	0	0	8.0	3	1	3	6
Hideo Nomo	0	1	12.27	1	1	0	0	0	3.2	5	5	5	3
Antonio Osuna	0	1	4.50	2	0	0	0	0	2.0	3	1	1	4
Scott Radinsky	0	0	0.00	2	0	0	0	0	1.1	0	0	1	2
Ismael Valdes	0	1	4.26	1	1	0	0	0	6.1	5	3	0	5
Todd Worrell	0	0	0.00	1	0	0	0	0	1.0	0	0	1	1
TOTAL	0	3	3.33	12	3	0	0	0	27.0	16	10	12	24

more and the Braves had another opportunity to celebrate.

GAME ONE AT LA OCT 2

ATL	000	100	000	1	2	4	1
LA	000	010	000	0	1	5	0

Pitchers: SMOLTZ, Wohlers (10) vs Martinez, Radinsky (9), OSUNA (9)
Home Runs: Lopez-ATL
Attendance: 47,428

GAME TWO AT LA OCT 3

ATL	010	000	200	3	5	2
LA	100	100	000	2	3	0

Pitchers: MADDUX, McMichael (8), Wohlers (9) vs VALDES, Astacio (7), Worrell (9)
Home Runs: Klesko-ATL, McGriff-ATL, Dye-ATL
Attendance: 51,916

GAME THREE AT ATL OCT 5

LA	000	000	110	2	6	1
ATL	100	400	00X	5	7	0

Pitchers: NOMO, Guthrie (4), Candiotti (5), Radinsky (7), Osuna (8), Dreifort (8) vs GLAVINE, McMichael (7), Bielecki (8), Wohlers (8)
Home Runs: C.Jones-ATL
Attendance: 52,529

St. Louis finished 19 games under .500 in 1995, but with new manager Tony LaRussa and 14 new players, the Cards of 1996 won 88 games and captured the NL Central by six games. San Diego's storybook season ended with a three-game sweep over the Dodgers to claim the NL West title with a 91-71 mark. The Cardinals took control of the Division Series at Busch Stadium when Gary Gaetti hit a three-run home run, his only hit of the series, to give the Cards a first-inning lead against Joey Hamilton. St. Louis made it hold up. Todd Stottlemyre, who entered the game with a postseason ERA of 7.50, allowed only a Rickey Henderson home run in 6⅔ innings. Then LaRussa's veteran bullpen of Rick Honeycutt and Dennis Eckersley, with 40 years of major league experience between them, kept the Padres at bay.

Game 2 was another well-played contest as the two teams matched each other run for run through the first seven and a half innings in front of a record crowd in St. Louis. Willie McGee singled in the first run of the game for the Cards in the third, but Ken Caminiti answered back with a home run to right field to tie the score at 1-1 in the top of the fifth. St. Louis rallied for three runs in the bottom of the frame when Ron Gant hit a bases-clearing double. The Padres scored twice in the sixth when Tony Gwynn singled in one run and a throwing error allowed another run to score. San Diego tied the game in the top of the eighth on a groundout by Steve Finley, but Tom Pagnozzi's line drive in the bottom of the inning ticked off the glove of reliever Trevor Hoffman and brought home the winning run. Eckersley retired the side in order in the ninth to make a winner of Honeycutt.

In San Diego's only other playoff appearance in 1984, the Padres dropped the first two games in Chicago and then won the last three at home for the pennant. The Padres were looking for that magic again as they took a 4-1 lead after four innings against Cardinals starter Donovan Osborne. The Cards rallied to tie matters in the sixth. St. Louis pushed across a run in the seventh after the Padres misplayed a bunt, but Caminiti hit his second home run of the game—and third of the series—to tie the game in the eighth. San Diego had a chance to take the lead later in the inning, but right fielder Brian Jordan made a sensational diving catch to end the threat. With his shoulder still aching from the catch, Jordan crushed a home run to left off Hoffman for a 7-5 lead in the ninth. Eckersley

made the sweep official by earning the save.

St. Louis Cardinals (C), 3;
San Diego Padres (W), 0

STL (C)

PLAYER/POS	AVG	G	AB	R	H	2B	3B	HR	RB	BB	SO	SB
Luis Alicea, 2b	.182	3	11	1	2	2	0	0	0	1	4	0
Andy Benes, p	.500	1	2	1	1	0	0	0	0	0	0	0
Royce Clayton, ss	.333	2	6	1	2	0	0	0	0	3	1	0
Dennis Eckersley, p	.000	3	0	0	0	0	0	0	0	0	0	0
Gary Gaetti, 3b	.091	3	11	1	1	0	0	1	3	0	3	0
Mike Gallego, 2b-1,3b-1	.000	2	1	0	0	0	0	0	0	0	1	0
Ron Gant, of	.400	3	10	3	4	1	0	1	4	2	0	2
Rick Honeycutt, p	.000	3	1	0	0	0	0	0	0	0	1	0
Brian Jordan, of	.333	3	12	4	4	0	0	1	3	1	3	1
Ray Lankford, of	.500	1	2	1	1	0	0	0	0	1	0	0
John Mabry, 1b	.300	3	10	1	3	0	1	0	1	1	1	0
T. J. Mathews, p	.000	1	0	0	0	0	0	0	0	0	0	0
Willie McGee, of	.100	3	10	1	1	0	0	0	1	1	3	0
Miguel Mejia, pr	.000	1	0	0	0	0	0	0	0	0	0	0
Donovan Osborne, p	.000	1	0	0	0	0	0	0	0	0	0	0
Tom Pagnozzi, c	.273	3	11	0	3	0	0	0	2	1	3	0
Mark Petkovsek, p	.000	1	0	0	0	0	0	0	0	0	0	0
Ozzie Smith, ss-1	.333	2	3	1	1	0	0	0	0	2	0	0
Todd Stottlemyre, p	.000	1	2	0	0	0	0	0	0	0	2	0
Mark Sweeney, ph	1.000	1	1	0	1	0	0	0	0	0	0	0
TOTAL	.255		94	15	24	3	1	3	14	13	23	3

PITCHER	W	L	ERA	G	GS	CG	SV	SHO	IP	H	ER	BB	SO
Andy Benes	0	0	5.14	1	1	0	0	0	7.0	6	4	1	9
Dennis Eckersley	0	0	0.00	3	0	0	3	0	3.2	3	0	0	2
Rick Honeycutt	1	0	3.38	3	0	0	0	0	2.2	3	1	1	2
T. J. Mathews	1	0	0.00	1	0	0	0	0	1.0	1	0	0	2
Donovan Osborne	0	0	9.00	1	1	0	0	0	4.0	7	4	0	5
Mark Petkovsek	0	0	0.00	1	0	0	0	0	2.0	0	0	0	1
Todd Stottlemyre	1	0	1.35	1	1	0	0	0	6.2	5	1	2	7
TOTAL	3	0	3.33	11	3	0	3	0	27.0	25	10	4	28

SD (W)

PLAYER/POS	AVG	G	AB	R	H	2B	3B	HR	RB	BB	SO	SB
Andy Ashby, p	.000	1	1	0	0	0	0	0	0	0	1	0
Willie Blair, p.	.000	1	0	0	0	0	0	0	0	0	0	0
Doug Bochtler, p	.000	1	0	0	0	0	0	0	0	0	0	0
Ken Caminiti, 3b	.300	3	10	3	3	0	0	3	3	2	5	0
Archi Cianfrocco, 1b	.333	3	3	1	1	0	0	0	0	0	1	0
Steve Finley, of	.083	3	12	0	1	0	0	0	1	0	4	1
John Flaherty, c	.000	2	4	0	0	0	0	0	0	0	1	0
Chris Gomez, ss	.167	3	12	0	2	0	0	0	1	0	4	0
Tony Gwynn, of	.308	3	13	0	4	1	0	0	1	0	2	1
Chris Gwynn, ph	1.000	2	2	1	2	0	0	0	0	0	0	0
Joey Hamilton, p	.000	1	2	0	0	0	0	0	0	0	2	0
Rickey Henderson, of	.333	3	12	2	4	0	0	1	1	2	3	0
Trevor Hoffman, p	.000	2	0	0	0	0	0	0	0	0	0	0
Brian Johnson, c	.375	2	8	2	3	1	0	0	0	0	1	0
Wally Joyner, 1b	.111	3	9	0	1	0	0	0	0	0	2	0
Scott Livingstone, ph	.500	2	2	1	1	0	0	0	0	0	0	0
Luis Lopez, pr	.000	1	0	0	0	0	0	0	0	0	0	0
Jody Reed, 2b	.273	3	11	0	3	1	0	0	0	2	1	0
Scott Sanders, p	.000	1	1	0	0	0	0	0	0	0	0	0
Fernando Valenzuela, p	.000	1	0	0	0	0	0	0	0	0	1	0
Greg Vaughn, ph	.000	3	3	0	0	0	0	0	0	0	1	0
Dario Veras, p	.000	2	0	0	0	0	0	0	0	0	0	0
Tim Worrell, p	.000	2	0	0	0	0	0	0	0	0	0	0
TOTAL	.238		105	10	25	3	0	4	9	4	28	2

PITCHER	W	L	ERA	G	GS	CG	SV	SHO	IP	H	ER	BB	SO
Andy Ashby	0	0	6.75	1	1	0	0	0	5.1	7	4	1	5
Willie Blair	0	0	0.00	1	0	0	0	0	2.0	1	0	2	3
Doug Bochtler	0	1	27.00	1	0	0	0	0	0.1	0	1	2	0
Joey Hamilton	0	1	4.50	1	1	0	0	0	6.0	5	3	0	6
Trevor Hoffman	0	1	10.80	2	0	0	0	0	1.2	3	2	1	2
Scott Sanders	0	0	8.31	1	1	0	0	0	4.1	3	4	4	4
Fernando Valenzuela	0	0	0.00	1	0	0	0	0	0.2	0	0	2	0
Dario Veras	0	0	0.00	2	0	0	0	0	1.0	1	0	0	1
Tim Worrell	0	0	2.45	2	0	0	0	0	3.2	4	1	1	2
TOTAL	0	3	5.40	12	3	0	0	0	25.0	24	15	13	23

The Rangers jumped out to a lead in all four games of the Division Series, but the difference was Yankees relief pitching—and Bernie Williams. The New York bullpen allowed just one earned run in 19⅔ innings of relief while Texas relievers failed to hold the lead in all three losses. Williams hit three home runs in the series, including two in decisive Game 4. Juan Gonzalez hit five home runs and drove in nine runs for the Rangers, but the Yankees won by corralling the rest of the Texas bats in the series.

John Burkett, a late-season acquisition, quieted the boisterous Yankee Stadium crowd with a complete-game effort in Game 1. Gonzalez and Dean Palmer both homered off David Cone in the fifth inning for a 6-2 Ranger win. Texas jumped out to a 4-1 lead in Game 2 against Andy Pettitte, courtesy of a pair of Gonzalez home runs, but the Rangers' failure to convert two tailor-made double-play grounders in the fourth inning gave the Yankees a key run. The Yankees tied it against the Texas bullpen and the Rangers defense gave New York the game when Palmer threw away Charlie Hayes' bunt in the 12th inning to score Derek Jeter with the winner.

In Game 3 Williams homered to the opposite field in the top of the first inning and then reached over the fence to rob Rusty Greer of a home run in the bottom of the inning. In the first home postseason game in the history of the franchise, Darren Oliver gave the crowd plenty to cheer about as he held the Yankees to four hits through eight innings. Texas scored two runs off Jimmy Key as Gonzalez provided the expected power with a fourth-inning home run and the other run was set up when no one covered second base on a steal. Rangers manager Johnny Oates knew the shaky state of his bullpen, so he let Oliver start the ninth and yanked him only after the first two runners reached base. Mike Henneman allowed a game-tying sacrifice fly and surrendered a single by Mariano Duncan for a 3-2 Yankees lead. John Wetteland retired the side in the ninth to give New York a two games to one lead.

The Rangers jumped out to a 4-0 lead the next afternoon in Game 4. Gonzalez, as usual, added a home run, but timely hits by Mickey Tettleton, Ivan Rodriguez, and Mark McLemore scored three more runs and ended the Yankees' streak of bullpen dominance. New York simply started a new streak. David Weathers pitched three scoreless innings of relief and wound up with the win when Mariano Rivera and Wetteland also pitched scoreless baseball. The Rangers, mean-

New York Yankees (E), 3; Texas Rangers (W), 1

NY (E)

PLAYER/POS	AVG	G	AB	R	H	2B	3B	HR	RB	BB	SO	SB
Brian Boehringer, p	.000	2	0	0	0	0	0	0	0	0	0	0
Wade Boggs, 3b	.083	3	12	0	1	1	0	0	0	0	2	0
David Cone, p	.000	1	0	0	0	0	0	0	0	0	0	0
Mariano Duncan, 2b	.313	4	16	0	5	0	0	0	3	0	4	0
Cecil Fielder, dh	.364	3	11	2	4	0	0	1	4	1	2	0
Andy Fox, dh-1	.000	2	0	0	0	0	0	0	0	0	0	0
Joe Girardi, c	.222	4	9	1	2	0	0	0	0	4	1	0
Charlie Hayes, 3b-2	.200	3	5	0	1	0	0	0	1	0	0	0
Derek Jeter, ss	.412	4	17	2	7	1	0	0	1	0	2	0
Jimmy Key, p	.000	1	0	0	0	0	0	0	0	0	0	0
Jim Leyritz, c-1	.000	2	3	0	0	0	0	0	0	1	0	0
Graeme Lloyd, p	.000	2	0	0	0	0	0	0	0	0	0	0
Tino Martinez, 1b	.267	4	15	3	4	2	0	0	0	0	3	1
Jeff Nelson, p	.000	2	0	0	0	0	0	0	0	0	0	0
Paul O'Neill, of	.133	4	15	0	2	0	0	0	0	0	2	0
Andy Pettitte, p	.000	1	0	0	0	0	0	0	0	0	0	0
Tim Raines, of	.250	4	16	3	4	0	0	0	0	3	1	0
Mariano Rivera, p	.000	2	0	0	0	0	0	0	0	0	0	0
Ruben Rivera, of	.000	2	1	0	0	0	0	0	0	0	1	0
Kenny Rogers, p	.000	2	0	0	0	0	0	0	0	0	0	0
Luis Sojo, 2b	.000	2	0	0	0	0	0	0	0	0	0	0
Darryl Strawberry, dh	.000	2	5	0	0	0	0	0	0	0	2	0
Dave Weathers, p	.000	2	0	0	0	0	0	0	0	0	0	0
John Wetteland, p	.000	3	0	0	0	0	0	0	0	0	0	0
Bernie Williams, of	.467	4	15	5	7	0	0	3	5	2	1	1
TOTAL	.264		140	16	37	4	0	4	15	13	20	1

PITCHER	W	L	ERA	G	GS	CG	SV	SHO	IP	H	ER	BB	SO
Brian Boehringer	1	0	6.75	2	0	0	0	0	1.1	3	1	2	0
David Cone	0	1	9.00	1	1	0	0	0	6.0	8	6	2	8
Jimmy Key	0	0	3.60	1	1	0	0	0	5.0	5	2	1	3
Graeme Lloyd	0	0	0.00	2	0	0	0	0	1.0	1	0	0	0
Jeff Nelson	1	0	0.00	2	0	0	0	0	3.2	1	0	2	5
Andy Pettitte	0	0	5.68	1	1	0	0	0	6.1	4	4	6	3
Mariano Rivera	0	0	0.00	2	0	0	0	0	4.2	0	0	1	1
Kenny Rogers	0	0	9.00	2	1	0	0	0	2.0	5	2	2	1
Dave Weathers	1	0	0.00	2	0	0	0	0	5.0	1	0	0	5
John Wetteland	0	0	0.00	3	0	0	2	0	4.0	2	0	4	4
TOTAL	3	1	3.46	18	4	0	2	0	39.0	31	15	20	30

TEX (W)

PLAYER/POS	AVG	G	AB	R	H	2B	3B	HR	RB	BB	SO	SB
Damon Buford, pr	.000	2	0	0	0	0	0	0	0	0	0	0
John Burkett, p	.000	1	0	0	0	0	0	0	0	0	0	0
Will Clark, 1b	.125	4	16	1	2	0	0	0	0	3	2	0
Dennis Cook, p	.000	2	0	0	0	0	0	0	0	0	0	0
Kevin Elster, ss	.333	4	12	2	4	2	0	0	3	2	1	0
Rene Gonzales, ss	.000	1	0	0	0	0	0	0	0	0	0	0
Juan Gonzalez, of	.438	4	16	5	7	0	0	5	9	3	2	0
Rusty Greer, of	.125	4	16	2	2	0	0	0	0	3	3	0
Darryl Hamilton, of	.158	4	19	0	3	0	0	0	0	3	2	0
Mike Henneman, p	.000	3	0	0	0	0	0	0	0	0	0	0
Ken Hill, p	.000	1	0	0	0	0	0	0	0	0	0	0
Mark McLemore, 2b	.133	4	15	1	2	0	0	0	2	0	4	0
Warren Newson, ph	.000	2	1	0	0	0	0	0	0	1	0	0
Darren Oliver, p	.000	1	0	0	0	0	0	0	0	0	0	0
Dean Palmer, 3b	.211	4	19	3	4	1	0	1	2	0	5	0
Danny Patterson, p	.000	1	0	0	0	0	0	0	0	0	0	0
Roger Pavlik, p	.000	1	0	0	0	0	0	0	0	0	0	0
Ivan Rodriguez, c	.375	4	16	1	6	1	0	0	2	2	3	0
Jeff Russell, p	.000	2	0	0	0	0	0	0	0	0	0	0
Mike Stanton, p	.000	3	0	0	0	0	0	0	0	0	0	0
Mickey Tettleton, dh	.083	4	12	1	1	0	0	0	1	5	7	0
Ed Vosberg, p	.000	1	0	0	0	0	0	0	0	0	0	0
Bobby Witt, p	.000	1	0	0	0	0	0	0	0	0	0	0
TOTAL	.218		142	16	31	4	0	6	16	20	30	1

PITCHER	W	L	ERA	G	GS	CG	SV	SHO	IP	H	ER	BB	SO
John Burkett	1	0	2.00	1	1	1	0	0	9.0	10	2	1	7
Dennis Cook	0	0	0.00	2	0	0	0	0	1.1	0	0	1	0
Mike Henneman	0	0	0.00	3	0	0	0	0	1.0	1	0	1	1
Ken Hill	0	0	4.50	1	1	0	0	0	6.0	5	3	3	1
Darren Oliver	0	1	3.38	1	1	0	0	0	8.0	6	3	2	3
Danny Patterson	0	0	0.00	1	0	0	0	0	0.1	1	0	0	0
Roger Pavlik	0	1	6.75	1	1	0	0	0	2.2	4	2	0	1
Jeff Russell	0	0	3.00	2	0	0	0	0	3.0	3	1	0	1
Mike Stanton	0	1	2.70	3	0	0	0	0	3.1	2	1	3	3
Ed Vosberg	0	0	INF	1	0	0	0	0	0.0	1	0	0	0
Bobby Witt	0	0	8.10	1	1	0	0	0	3.1	4	3	2	3
TOTAL	1	3	3.55	17	4	1	0	0	38.0	37	15	13	20

while, tried eight pitchers and still couldn't stop the Yankees. Cecil Fielder, Duncan, and Jeter each drove in runs in the fourth to cut the lead to 4-3. Switch-hitting Williams led off the fifth with a home run from the left side to tie the game and—after Fielder had given the Yankees the lead in the seventh—Williams clinched it with a homer from the right side in the ninth inning.

GAME ONE AT NY OCT 1

TEX 000 501 000   6 8 0
NY   100 100 000   2 19 0

Pitchers: BURKETT vs CONE, Lloyd (7), Weathers (8)
Home Runs: Gonzalez-TEX, Palmer-TEX
Attendance: 57,205

GAME TWO AT NY OCT 2

TEX 013 000 000 000   4 8 1
NY   010 100 110 001   5 8 0

Pitchers: Hill, Cook (7), Russell (8), STANTON (10), Henneman (12) vs Pettitte, Rivera (7), Wetteland (10), Lloyd (12), Nelson (12), Rogers (12), BOEHRINGER (12)
Home Runs: Gonzalez-TEX (2), Fielder-NY
Attendance: 57,156

GAME THREE AT TEX OCT 4

NY   100 000 002   3 7 1
TEX 000 110 000   2 6 1

Pitchers: Key, NELSON (6), Wetteland (9) vs OLIVER, Henneman (9), Stanton (9)
Home Runs: Williams-NY, Gonzalez-TEX
Attendance: 50,860

GAME FOUR AT TEX OCT 5

NY   000 310 101   6 12 1
TEX 022 000 000   4 9 0

Pitchers: Rogers, Boehringer (3), WEATHERS (4), Rivera (7), Wetteland (9) vs Witt, Patterson (4), Cook (4), PAVLIK (5), Vosberg (7), Russell (7), Stanton (8), Henneman (9)
Home Runs: Williams-NY (2), Gonzalez-TEX
Attendance: 50,066

An ugly spitting incident by Roberto Alomar overshadowed Baltimore's first trip to the postseason since 1983. Alomar spit at umpire John Hirschbeck during the last series of the regular season and that led the umpires to threaten to strike the postseason if Alomar was not suspended immediately. He was not suspended, the umpires (thanks to a court order) did not strike, and the fans both cheered Alomar (in Baltimore) and booed him (in Cleveland). But in the end, Alomar was the hero in the Orioles' unlikely win over the team with the best record in baseball.

Roberto Alomar was not the only player to come through with a big home run. Brady Anderson, the poster boy for "Year of the Home Run" with 50 regular-season clouts, started the series with a home run to lead off Game 1. The Orioles followed suit three more times, including a grand slam by Bobby Bonilla and two home runs by B.J. Surhoff, as the Orioles cruised to a 10-4 win. The Indians battled back from a 4-0 deficit to tie Game 2, but the difference was the way relief pitchers handled bases loaded situations in the eighth inning. In the top of the inning, the Indians had the bases loaded with no one out and the five-six-seven batters due up. Julio Franco hit a long sacrifice fly to tie the game, but reliever Armando Benitez came back to strike out Manny Ramirez and Sandy Alomar Jr. to end the threat. In the bottom of the eighth, the Orioles loaded the bases with none out and Indians reliever Paul Assenmacher got Surhoff to ground back to the mound. Assenmacher got the force out at home, but catcher Sandy Alomar's return throw to first bounced and could not be handled by Jeff Kent as Cal Ripken crossed the plate. The Indians argued that Surhoff ran on the inside route to the base and should have been ruled out automatically. This time, the umpires were on Baltimore's side and the O's went on to win, 7-4, to take a two games to none lead.

Relief pitching was again the difference in Game 3, but it was the Indians, not the Orioles who got the better of it at Jacobs Field. Jesse Orosco walked the bases loaded in the seventh inning and Benitez entered a 4-4 game with the chance to douse another Tribe rally. Albert Belle's grand slam broke the tie and shattered Baltimore's bid for a sweep. Game 4 was an uncharacteristic pitcher's duel. Charles Nagy, who had been hit hard by the O's in the opener, fanned 12 batters in six innings and

four relievers held Baltimore to two runs through eight innings.

Cleveland closer Jose Mesa had a 3-2 lead and a chance to force Game 5, but Roberto Alomar came through with a single to tie the game in the ninth. Mesa faced Alomar again in the 12th and he responded with a 402-foot home run to center for a 4-3 lead. Third baseman Todd Zeile, a converted catcher and a late-season pickup, made a great play on a bunt by Jose Vizcaino to get the first out in the bottom of the 12th and reliever Randy Myers did the rest. The Orioles, who struck out a postseason-record 23 times in the game, still found a way to get the bat on the ball when it counted.

Baltimore Orioles (WC), 3; Cleveland Indians (C), 1

BAL (E)

PLAYER/POS	AVG	G	AB	R	H	2B	3B	HR	RB	BB	SO	SB
Manny Alexander, dh-1	.000	3	0	2	0	0	0	0	0	0	0	0
Roberto Alomar, 2b	.294	4	17	2	5	0	0	1	4	2	3	0
Brady Anderson, of	.294	4	17	3	5	0	0	2	4	2	3	0
Armando Benitez, p	.000	3	0	0	0	0	0	0	0	0	0	0
Bobby Bonilla, of	.200	4	15	4	3	0	0	2	5	4	6	0
Mike Devereaux, of-3	.000	4	1	0	0	0	0	0	0	0	0	0
Scott Erickson, p	.000	1	0	0	0	0	0	0	0	0	0	0
Chris Hoiles, c	.143	4	7	1	1	0	0	0	0	3	3	0
Pete Incaviglia, of	.200	2	5	1	1	0	0	0	0	0	4	0
Terry Mathews, p	.000	3	0	0	0	0	0	0	0	0	0	0
Eddie Murray, dh	.400	4	15	1	6	1	0	0	1	3	4	1
Mike Mussina, p	.000	1	0	0	0	0	0	0	0	0	0	0
Randy Myers, p	.000	3	0	0	0	0	0	0	0	0	0	0
Jesse Orosco, p	.000	4	0	0	0	0	0	0	0	0	0	0
Rafael Palmeiro, 1b	.176	4	17	4	3	1	0	1	2	1	6	0
Mark Parent, c	.200	4	5	0	1	0	0	0	0	0	2	0
Arthur Lee Rhodes, p	.000	2	0	0	0	0	0	0	0	0	0	0
Cal Ripken, ss	.444	4	18	2	8	3	0	0	2	0	3	0
B.J. Surhoff, of-3	.385	4	13	3	5	0	0	3	5	0	1	0
David Wells, p	.000	2	0	0	0	0	0	0	0	0	0	0
Todd Zeile, 3b	.263	4	19	2	5	1	0	0	0	2	5	0
TOTAL	.289		149	25	43	6	0	9	23	17	40	1

PITCHER	W	L	ERA	G	GS	CG	SV	SHO	IP	H	ER	BB	SO
Armando Benitez	2	0	2.25	3	0	0	0	0	4.0	1	1	2	6
Scott Erickson	0	0	4.05	1	1	0	0	0	6.2	6	3	2	6
Terry Mathews	0	0	0.00	3	0	0	0	0	2.2	3	0	1	2
Mike Mussina	0	0	4.50	1	1	0	0	0	6.0	7	3	2	6
Randy Myers	0	0	0.00	3	0	0	2	0	3.0	0	0	0	3
Jesse Orosco	0	1	36.00	4	0	0	0	0	1.0	2	4	3	2
Arthur Lee Rhodes	0	0	9.00	2	0	0	0	0	1.0	1	1	1	1
David Wells	1	0	4.61	2	2	0	0	0	13.2	15	7	4	6
TOTAL	3	1	4.50	19	4	0	2		38.0	35	19	15	32

CLE (C)

PLAYER/POS	AVG	G	AB	R	H	2B	3B	HR	RB	BB	SO	SB
Sandy Alomar, c	.125	4	16	0	2	0	0	0	3	0	2	0
Paul Assenmacher, p	.000	3	0	0	0	0	0	0	0	0	0	0
Albert Belle, of	.200	4	15	2	3	0	0	2	6	3	2	1
Casey Candaele, dh-1	.000	2	0	1	0	0	0	0	0	1	0	0
Alan Embree, p	.000	3	0	0	0	0	0	0	0	0	0	0
Julio Franco, 1b-3,dh-1	.133	4	15	1	2	0	0	0	1	1	6	0
Brian Giles, ph	.000	1	1	0	0	0	0	0	0	0	1	0
Orel Hershiser, p	.000	1	0	0	0	0	0	0	0	0	0	0
Jeff Kent, 3b-2,1b-1, 2b-1	.125	4	8	2	1	1	0	0	0	0	0	0
Kenny Lofton, of	.167	4	18	3	3	0	0	0	1	2	3	5
Jack McDowell, p	.000	1	0	0	0	0	0	0	0	0	0	0
Jose Mesa, p	.000	2	0	0	0	0	0	0	0	0	0	0
Charles Nagy, p	.000	2	0	0	0	0	0	0	0	0	0	0
Chad Ogea, p	.000	1	0	0	0	0	0	0	0	0	0	0
Tony Pena, c	.000	1	0	0	0	0	0	0	0	0	0	0
Eric Plunk, p	.000	3	0	0	0	0	0	0	0	0	0	0
Manny Ramirez, of	.375	4	16	4	6	2	0	2	2	1	4	0
Kevin Seitzer, dh-3,1b-1	.294	4	17	1	5	1	0	0	4	2	4	1
Paul Shuey, p	.000	3	0	0	0	0	0	0	0	0	0	0
Julian Tavarez, p	.000	2	0	0	0	0	0	0	0	0	0	0
Jim Thome, 3b	.300	4	10	1	3	0	0	0	0	1	5	0
Jose Vizcaino, 2b	.333	3	12	1	4	2	0	0	1	1	1	0
Omar Vizquel, ss	.429	4	14	4	6	1	0	0	2	3	4	4
Nigel Wilson, ph	.000	1	1	0	0	0	0	0	0	0	0	0
TOTAL	.245		143	20	35	7	0	4	20	15	32	11

PITCHER	W	L	ERA	G	GS	CG	SV	SHO	IP	H	ER	BB	SO
Paul Assenmacher	1	0	0.00	3	0	0	0	0	1.2	0	0	1	2
Alan Embree	0	0	9.00	3	0	0	0	0	1.0	0	1	0	1
Orel Hershiser	0	0	5.40	1	1	0	0	0	5.0	7	3	3	3
Jack McDowell	0	0	6.35	1	1	0	0	0	5.2	6	4	1	5
Jose Mesa	0	1	3.86	2	0	0	0	0	4.2	8	2	0	7
Charles Nagy	0	1	7.15	2	2	0	0	0	11.1	15	9	5	13
Chad Ogea	0	0	0.00	1	0	0	0	0	0.1	0	0	1	0
Eric Plunk	0	1	6.75	3	0	0	0	0	4.0	1	3	2	6
Paul Shuey	0	0	9.00	3	0	0	0	0	2.0	5	2	2	2
Julian Tavarez	0	0	0.00	2	0	0	0	0	1.1	1	0	2	1
TOTAL	1	3	5.84	21	4	0	0		37.0	43	24	17	40

GAME ONE AT BAL OCT 1

CLE	010 200 100	4	10	0
BAL	112 005 10X	10	10	1

Pitchers: NAGY, Embree (6), Shuey (6), Tavarez (8) vs WELLS, Orosco (7), Mathews (7), Rhodes (8), Myers (9)
Home Runs: Ramirez-CLE, Anderson-BAL, Surhoff-BAL (2), Bonilla-BAL
Attendance: 47,644

GAME TWO AT BAL OCT 2

CLE	000 003 010	4	8	2
BAL	100 030 03X	7	9	0

Pitchers: Hershiser, PLUNK (6), Assenmacher (8), Tavarez (8) vs Erickson, Orosco (7), BENITEZ (8), Myers (9)
Home Runs: Belle-CLE, Anderson-BAL
Attendance: 48,970

GAME THREE AT CLE OCT 4

BAL	010 300 000	4	8	2
CLE	120 100 41X	9	10	0

Pitchers: Mussina, OROSCO (7), Benitez (7), Rhodes (8), Mathews (8) vs McDowell (6), Shuey (7), ASSENMACHER (7), Plunk (8), Mesa (9)
Home Runs: Surhoff-BAL, Ramirez-CLE, Belle-CLE
Attendance: 44,250

GAME FOUR AT CLE OCT 5

BAL	020 000 001 001	4	14	1
CLE	000 210 000 000	3	7	1

Pitchers: Wells, Mathews (8), Orosco (9), BENITEZ (10), Myers (12) vs Nagy, Embree (7), Shuey (7), Assenmacher (7), Plunk (8), MESA (9), Ogea (12)
Home Runs: Palmeiro-BAL, Bonilla-BAL, R.Alomar-BAL
Attendance: 44,280

The Cards and Braves last met in the NLCS in 1982—a 3-0 Cardinals sweep. Fourteen years later, the Cardinals were just as tough, but John Smoltz beat the Cards in the opener in Atlanta, 4-2. In Game 2, St. Louis turned the tables. Four-time Cy Young winner Greg Maddux was touched for three runs in the first three innings, but the Braves rallied to tie the game on a two-run home run by Marquis Grissom and a single by Ryan Klesko. After the Cards took a 4-3 lead in the seventh on a Ray Lankford sacrifice fly, Maddux fanned Ron Gant and intentionally walked Brian Jordan to pitch to Gary Gaetti. Gaetti hit the first pitch for a grand slam and finished the scoring at 8-3.

The Cards kept the pressure on in St. Louis. Gant hit a pair of home runs off Tom Glavine and Cardinals starter Donovan Osborne pitched seven strong innings in Game 3. Dennis Eckersley came on in the ninth to earn his fourth save of the postseason in the 3-2 Cards win. The Braves handed Denny Neagle a 3-0 lead in Game 4 on home runs by Klesko and Mark Lemke plus an RBI single by Jermaine Dye. But the Cards came back. Neagle got the first two outs in the seventh, but John Mabry singled and Tom Pagnozzi walked. Dmitri Young greeted reliever Greg McMichael with triple that plated two runs. Luis Alicea, followed with a walk and the Cards evened the score on an infield hit by Royce Clayton. In the eighth, Jordan lined a 2-1 pitch over the wall for a 4-3 lead.

The series' second part commenced in Game 5—and it was all Atlanta. The Braves had a 5-0 lead after half an inning and that was more than enough for John Smoltz. But they kept on hitting, collecting 22 hits and sending Stottlemyre to the showers in the second. McGriff and Javier Lopez added home runs in the 14-0 rout to send the series back to Atlanta. In Game 6 the only run the Cards got came on a wild pitch by Mark Wohlers in relief of Greg Maddux.

The Cards never even had a chance to do any damage against Glavine in Game 7. Osborne allowed three runs on RBIs by McGriff, Dye, and Andruw Jones, but the crushing blow came off the bat of Glavine. His line drive to left went for a three-run triple and a 6-0 lead. Atlanta added nine more runs, including home runs by MVP Lopez and Andruw Jones, who, at 19, became the youngest player to hit a postseason round-tripper. The Braves also became the first team to come back from a three games to one deficit to win the NLCS. From Game 5 on, the Braves outscored the Cards, 32-1.

Atlanta Braves (E), 4; St. Louis Cardinals (C), 3

ATL (E)

PLAYER/POS	AVG	G	AB	R	H	2B	3B	HR	RB	BB	SO	SB
Steve Avery, p	.000	2	0	0	0	0	0	0	0	0	0	0
Rafael Belliard, ss	.667	4	6	0	4	0	0	0	0	2	0	0
Mike Bielecki, p	.000	3	0	0	0	0	0	0	0	0	0	0
Jeff Blauser, ss	.176	7	17	5	3	0	1	0	2	4	6	0
Brad Clontz, p	.000	1	0	0	0	0	0	0	0	0	0	0
Jermaine Dye, of	.214	7	28	2	6	1	0	0	4	1	7	0
Tom Glavine, p	.167	2	6	0	1	0	1	0	3	0	3	0
Marquis Grissom, of	.286	7	35	7	10	1	0	1	3	0	8	2
Andruw Jones, of	.222	5	9	3	2	0	0	1	3	3	2	0
Chipper Jones, 3b	.440	7	25	6	11	2	0	0	4	4	1	1
Ryan Klesko, of	.250	6	16	1	4	0	0	1	3	2	6	0
Mark Lemke, 2b	.444	7	27	4	12	2	0	1	5	3	2	0
Javy Lopez, c	.542	7	24	8	13	5	0	2	6	3	1	1
Greg Maddux, p	.000	2	4	0	0	0	0	0	0	0	2	0
Fred McGriff, 1b	.250	7	28	6	7	0	1	2	7	3	5	0
Greg McMichael, p	.000	3	0	0	0	0	0	0	0	0	0	0
Mike Mordecai, 2b-2, 3b-1	.250	4	4	1	1	0	0	0	0	0	0	0
Denny Neagle, p	.500	2	2	0	1	0	0	0	0	0	0	0
Terry Pendleton, 3b-2	.000	6	6	0	0	0	0	0	0	1	3	0
Eddie Perez, c	.000	4	1	0	0	0	0	0	0	0	1	0
Luis Polonia, ph	.000	3	3	0	0	0	0	0	0	0	0	0
John Smoltz, p	.286	2	7	1	2	0	0	0	0	0	3	0
Terrell Wade, p	.000	1	0	0	0	0	0	0	0	0	0	0
Mark Wohlers, p	.000	3	1	0	0	0	0	0	0	0	1	0
TOTAL	.309		249	44	77	11	3	8	43	25	51	4

PITCHER	W	L	ERA	G	GS	CG	SV	SHO	IP	H	ER	BB	SO
Steve Avery	0	0	0.00	2	0	0	0	0	2.0	2	0	1	1
Mike Bielecki	0	0	0.00	3	0	0	0	0	3.0	0	0	1	5
Brad Clontz	0	0	0.00	1	0	0	0	0	0.2	0	0	0	0
Tom Glavine	1	1	2.08	2	2	0	0	0	13.0	10	3	0	9
Greg Maddux	1	1	2.51	2	2	0	0	0	14.1	15	4	2	10
Greg McMichael	0	1	9.00	3	0	0	0	0	2.0	4	2	1	3
Denny Neagle	0	0	2.35	2	1	0	0	0	7.2	2	2	3	8
John Smoltz	2	0	1.20	2	2	0	0	0	15.0	12	2	3	12
Terrell Wade	0	0	0.00	1	0	0	0	0	0.1	0	0	0	1
Mark Wohlers	0	0	0.00	3	0	0	2	0	3.0	0	0	0	4
TOTAL	4	3	1.92	21	7	0	2	0	61.0	45	13	11	53

STL (C)

PLAYER/POS	AVG	G	AB	R	H	2B	3B	HR	RB	BB	SO	SB
Luis Alicea, 2b	.000	5	8	0	0	0	0	0	0	2	1	0
Alan Benes, p	.000	2	1	0	0	0	0	0	0	0	1	0
Andy Benes, p	.250	3	4	0	1	1	0	0	0	1	2	0
Royce Clayton, ss	.350	5	20	4	7	0	0	0	1	1	4	1
Dennis Eckersley, p	.000	3	0	0	0	0	0	0	0	0	0	0
Tony Fossas, p	.000	5	0	0	0	0	0	0	0	0	0	0
Gary Gaetti, 3b	.292	7	24	1	7	0	0	1	4	1	5	0
Mike Gallego, 2b-5,3b-2	.143	7	14	1	2	0	0	0	0	1	3	0
Ron Gant, of	.240	7	25	3	6	1	0	2	4	2	6	0
Rick Honeycutt, p	.000	5	0	0	0	0	0	0	0	0	0	0
Danny Jackson, p	.000	1	0	0	0	0	0	0	0	0	0	0
Brian Jordan, of	.240	7	25	3	6	1	1	1	2	1	3	0
Ray Lankford, of-3	.000	5	13	1	0	0	0	0	1	1	4	0
John Mabry, 1b-6,of-2	.261	7	23	1	6	0	0	0	0	0	6	0
T. J. Mathews, p	.000	2	0	0	0	0	0	0	0	0	0	0
Willie McGee, of-5	.333	6	15	0	5	0	0	0	0	0	3	0
Miguel Mejia, of-2	.000	3	1	1	0	0	0	0	0	0	1	0
Donovan Osborne, p	.000	2	3	0	0	0	0	0	0	0	2	0
Tom Pagnozzi, c	.158	7	19	1	3	1	0	0	1	1	4	0
Mark Petkovsek, p	.000	6	0	0	0	0	0	0	0	0	0	0
Danny Sheaffer, c	.000	2	3	0	0	0	0	0	0	0	0	0
Ozzie Smith, ss-2	.000	3	9	0	0	0	0	0	0	0	1	0
Todd Stottlemyre, p	.000	2	0	0	0	0	0	0	0	0	0	0
Mark Sweeney, of-2	.000	5	4	1	0	0	0	0	0	0	2	0
Dmitri Young, 1b-2	.286	4	7	1	2	0	1	0	2	0	1	0
TOTAL	.204		221	18	45	4	2	4	15	11	53	1

PITCHER	W	L	ERA	G	GS	CG	SV	SHO	IP	H	ER	BB	SO
Alan Benes	0	1	2.84	2	1	0	0	0	6.1	3	2	2	5
Andy Benes	0	0	5.28	3	2	0	0	0	15.1	19	9	3	9
Dennis Eckersley	1	0	0.00	3	0	0	1	0	3.1	2	0	0	4
Tony Fossas	0	0	2.08	5	0	0	0	0	4.1	1	1	3	1
Rick Honeycutt	0	0	9.00	5	0	0	0	0	4.0	5	4	3	3
Danny Jackson	0	0	9.00	1	0	0	0	0	3.0	7	3	3	3
T. J. Mathews	0	0	0.00	2	0	0	0	0	0.2	2	0	1	2
Donovan Osborne	1	1	9.39	2	2	0	0	0	7.2	12	8	4	6
Mark Petkovsek	0	1	7.36	6	0	0	0	0	7.1	11	6	3	7
Todd Stottlemyre	1	1	12.38	3	2	0	0	0	8.0	15	11	3	11
TOTAL	3	4	6.60	32	7	0	1	0	60.0	77	44	25	51

The Yankees and the Orioles had gone a combined 28 years without a pennant, but that was going to change in 1996—for one team at least. The Orioles had the early advantage in Game 1 on home runs from Brady Anderson and Rafael Palmeiro, but the Yankees cut the lead to 4-3 after seven. Derek Jeter led off the eighth with a long fly to right that Tony Tarasco seemed to have lined up at the wall, but fate—in the form of a 12-year-old boy—intervened. Yankees fan Jeff Maier reached over the fence and knocked the ball into the stands. Right field umpire Rich Garcia ruled it a home run despite protests from several Orioles, including manager Davey Johnson, who was ejected. (Upon seeing a replay, Garcia admitted he made the wrong call, but AL president Gene Budig denied Baltimore's protest.) The Orioles got out of further trouble in the eighth, but Game 1 was tied at 4-4. With Randy Myers pitching in the bottom of the 11th, Bernie Williams hit a 1-1 pitch deep to left to give the Yanks the improbable win.

Baltimore bounced back in Game 2. Orioles southpaw David Wells spotted the Yanks a pair of first inning runs, but Wells improved to 10-1 at Yankee Stadium. Todd Zeile's two-run home run off David Cone tied the game in the third and Palmeiro's two-run shot off reliever Jeff Nelson gave Baltimore the lead in the seventh. The Orioles added a run in the eighth to go up 5-3, but Benitez retired Cecil Fielder and Tino Martinez with two on in the ninth to even the series at one game apiece.

The teams traveled to Camden Yards for the next three games, but the Yankees, who were 6-0 in Baltimore during the regular season, continued to treat the park like a home away from home. Zeile's two-run home run in the first looked like it might stand up as Mike Mussina was masterful through seven and two thirds innings. He never got that last out, though. The Yanks rallied to tie in the eighth then Martinez followed with a double to left field and Williams stopped at third; when Zeile's fake throw to second trickled away, Williams dashed home with the go-ahead run.

Darryl Strawberry took Game 4 of the ALCS into his own hands. His solo home run in the second gave the Yanks a 3-1 lead and his two-run blast in the eighth capped off New York's 8-4 victory. Mariano Rivera bailed New York out of a bases-loaded, no-out jam in the eighth and Wetteland retired the Orioles in order in the ninth.

Jim Leyritz started the decisive third-inning rally in Game 5 with a home run off Scott Erickson. Jeter

singled and Wade Boggs ended an 0-for-23 playoff skid with an infield hit to set the stage for the rally that put the Birds away for good. Series MVP Bernie Williams sent a tailor-made double-play grounder to Roberto Alomar, but the second baseman let it go through his legs. One out later, Fielder cleared the basepaths with a three-run home run for a 5-0 lead. Strawberry followed with a 446-foot drive to tie the 1993 Blue Jays for the most home runs (10) in an LCS. Andy Pettitte and John Wetteland held off Baltimore to bring the World Series back to Yankee Stadium for the first time since 1981 and send manager Joe Torre to the Fall Classic for the first time after a record 4,272 games as a player and manager.

New York Yankees (E), 4; Baltimore Orioles (WC), 1

NY (E)

PLAYER/POS	AVG	G	AB	R	H	2B	3B	HR	RB	BB	SO	SB
Mike Aldrete, ph	.000	1	0	0	0	0	0	0	0	0	0	0
Wade Boggs, 3b	.133	3	15	1	2	0	0	0	0	1	3	0
David Cone, p	.000	1	0	0	0	0	0	0	0	0	0	0
Mariano Duncan, 2b	.200	4	15	0	3	2	0	0	0	0	3	0
Cecil Fielder, dh	.167	5	18	3	3	0	0	2	8	4	5	0
Andy Fox, dh	.000	2	0	0	0	0	0	0	0	0	0	0
Joe Girardi, c	.250	4	12	1	3	0	1	0	0	1	3	0
Charlie Hayes, 3b-2, dh-1	.143	4	7	0	1	0	0	0	0	2	2	0
Derek Jeter, ss	.417	5	24	5	10	2	0	1	1	0	5	2
Jimmy Key, p	.000	1	0	0	0	0	0	0	0	0	0	0
Jim Leyritz, c-2,of-1	.250	3	8	1	2	0	0	1	2	1	4	0
Graeme Lloyd, p	.000	2	0	0	0	0	0	0	0	0	0	0
Tino Martinez, 1b	.182	5	22	3	4	1	0	0	0	0	2	0
Jeff Nelson, p	.000	2	0	0	0	0	0	0	0	0	0	0
Paul O'Neill, of	.273	4	11	1	3	0	0	1	2	3	2	0
Andy Pettitte, p	.000	2	0	0	0	0	0	0	0	0	0	0
Tim Raines, of	.267	5	15	2	4	1	0	0	0	1	1	0
Mariano Rivera, p	.000	2	0	0	0	0	0	0	0	0	0	0
Kenny Rogers, p	.000	1	0	0	0	0	0	0	0	0	0	0
Luis Sojo, 2b	.200	3	5	0	1	0	0	0	0	0	1	0
Darryl Strawberry, of	.417	4	12	4	5	0	0	3	5	2	2	0
Dave Weathers, p	.000	2	0	0	0	0	0	0	0	0	0	0
John Wetteland, p	.000	4	0	0	0	0	0	0	0	0	0	0
Bernie Williams, of	.474	5	19	6	9	3	0	2	6	5	4	1
TOTAL	.273		183	27	50	9	1	10	24	20	37	3

PITCHER	W	L	ERA	G	GS	CG	SV	SHO	IP	H	ER	BB	SO
David Cone	0	0	3.00	1	1	0	0	0	6.0	5	2	5	5
Jimmy Key	1	0	2.25	1	1	0	0	0	8.0	3	2	1	5
Graeme Lloyd	0	0	0.00	2	0	0	0	0	1.2	0	0	0	1
Jeff Nelson	0	1	11.57	2	0	0	0	0	2.1	5	3	0	2
Andy Pettitte	1	0	3.60	2	2	0	0	0	15.0	10	6	5	7
Mariano Rivera	1	0	0.00	2	0	0	0	0	4.0	6	0	1	5
Kenny Rogers	0	0	12.00	1	1	0	0	0	3.0	5	4	2	3
Dave Weathers	1	0	0.00	2	0	0	0	0	3.0	3	0	0	0
John Wetteland	0	0	4.50	4	0	0	1	0	4.0	2	2	1	5
TOTAL	4	1	3.64	17	5	0	1	0	47.0	39	19	15	33

BAL (E)

PLAYER/POS	AVG	G	AB	R	H	2B	3B	HR	RB	BB	SO	SB
Roberto Alomar, 2b	.217	5	23	2	5	2	0	0	1	0	4	0
Brady Anderson, of	.190	5	21	5	4	1	0	1	1	3	5	0
Armando Benitez, p	.000	3	0	0	0	0	0	0	0	0	0	0
Bobby Bonilla, of	.050	5	20	1	1	0	0	1	2	1	4	0
Rocky Coppinger, p	.000	1	0	0	0	0	0	0	0	0	0	0
Mike Devereaux, of	.000	3	2	0	0	0	0	0	0	0	1	0
Scott Erickson, p	.000	2	0	0	0	0	0	0	0	0	0	0
Chris Hoiles, c	.167	4	12	1	2	0	0	1	2	1	3	0
Pete Incaviglia, dh	.500	1	2	1	1	0	0	0	0	0	0	0
Terry Mathews, p	.000	3	0	0	0	0	0	0	0	0	0	0
Alan Mills, p	.000	3	0	0	0	0	0	0	0	0	0	0
Eddie Murray, dh	.267	5	15	1	4	0	0	1	2	2	2	0
Mike Mussina, p	.000	1	0	0	0	0	0	0	0	0	0	0
Randy Myers, p	.000	3	0	0	0	0	0	0	0	0	0	0
Jesse Orosco, p	.000	4	0	0	0	0	0	0	0	0	0	0
Rafael Palmeiro, 1b	.235	5	17	4	4	0	0	2	4	4	4	0
Mark Parent, c	.167	2	6	0	1	0	0	0	0	0	2	0
Arthur Lee Rhodes, p	.000	3	0	0	0	0	0	0	0	0	0	0
Cal Ripken, ss	.250	5	20	1	5	1	0	0	0	1	4	0
B.J. Surhoff, of	.267	5	15	0	4	0	0	0	2	1	2	0
Tony Tarasco, of	.000	2	1	0	0	0	0	0	0	0	1	0
David Wells, p	.000	1	0	0	0	0	0	0	0	0	0	0
Todd Zeile, 3b	.364	5	22	3	8	0	0	3	5	2	1	0
TOTAL	.222		176	19	39	4	0	9	19	15	33	0

PITCHER	W	L	ERA	G	GS	CG	SV	SHO	IP	H	ER	BB	SO
Armando Benitez	0	0	7.71	3	0	0	1	0	2.1	3	2	3	2
Rocky Coppinger	0	1	8.44	1	1	0	0	0	5.1	6	5	1	3
Scott Erickson	0	1	2.38	2	2	0	0	0	11.1	14	3	4	8
Terry Mathews	0	0	0.00	3	0	0	0	0	2.1	0	0	2	0
Alan Mills	0	0	3.86	3	0	0	0	0	2.1	3	1	1	3
Mike Mussina	0	1	5.87	1	1	0	0	0	7.2	8	5	2	6
Randy Myers	0	1	2.25	3	0	0	0	0	4.0	4	1	3	2
Jesse Orosco	0	0	4.50	4	0	0	0	0	2.0	2	1	1	2
Arthur Lee Rhodes	0	0	0.00	3	0	0	0	0	2.0	2	0	0	2
David Wells	1	0	4.05	1	1	0	0	0	6.2	8	3	3	6
TOTAL	1	4	4.11	24	5	0	1	0	46.0	50	21	20	37

New York looked disoriented in the opener, squandering opportunities early against John Smoltz, but it wasn't long before the Braves took advantage of Andy Pettitte. Andruw Jones, 19, became the youngest player in Series history to hit a homer in the second, and, an inning later, joined Gene Tenace as the second player to homer his first two times up in the Series. It was 9-0 before Wade Boggs broke up the no-hit bid by Smoltz in the fifth. Things didn't get much better for the Yanks the next night. Greg Maddux handcuffed New York on six hits in eight innings as Fred McGriff drove in three runs. The Braves steamrolled New York 16-1 in the first two games, and had outscored their postseason opposition 48-2 over their last five games.

Things changed in Atlanta. David Cone allowed just four hits through six, and RBI singles by Bernie Williams and Darryl Strawberry gave the Yankees a 2-1 lead against Tom Glavine. The Yankees got insurance in the form of a two-run home run by Williams and an RBI single by Luis Sojo in the eighth. The Braves battered Kenny Rogers for five runs in two-plus innings in Game 4 and Andruw Jones doubled off David Weathers for a 6-0 lead in the fifth. Right field umpire Tim Welke got in the way of Jermaine Dye and kept Derek Jeter's foul fly from being caught. Then Jeter singled; two hits, a walk and an error followed to cut Atlanta's lead in half. Closer Mark Wohlers came in to start the eighth and promptly gave up two hits. It looked like the Braves might escape when Mariano Duncan hit a double-play grounder to Rafael Belliard, but the shortstop botched it and only one out was recorded. Jim Leyritz then homered to tie the game. With runners on first and second in the 10th, Braves manager Bobby Cox opted to walk Williams to load the bases for Boggs. Steve Avery walked Boggs, to bring in the go-ahead run. The Yankees scored again and held on for the biggest comeback in the team's World Series history.

Things continued to go the Yankees' way in Game 5. New York's Andy Pettitte won the last game ever played at Fulton County Stadium because one of the game's best outfielders dropped a ball, and two gimpy outfielders made great catches to preserve the 1-0 victory. The only run Smoltz allowed was set up when a flyball bounced off Grissom's glove; Fielder plated the run with a double. Strawberry, playing despite a broken toe, crashed into the wall to take an extra-base hit away in the eighth, and Paul O'Neill, nursing a torn hamstring, reached to his right to snag Luis Polonia's line drive to end the game with the tying run at third.

The Yankees got good news on the only off-day of the Series. Manager Joe Torre's brother Frank, who won a World Series ring with

the 1957 Braves, received a heart transplant after months of waiting for a donor. The good luck continued for Game 6. O'Neill doubled to start the third and Joe Girardi tripled him home; Jeter and Williams followed with RBI singles against Maddux. The Braves got a run when Dye walked in the fourth, but Terry Pendleton grounded into a double play to end the threat. Key pitched into the sixth and Weathers, Lloyd, and Rivera got the Yanks to the ninth. Series MVP John Wetteland allowed a run but gained his fourth save of the Series when Mark Lemke popped up to Hayes in foul ground.

New York Yankees (A), 4; Atlanta Braves (N), 2

NY (A)

PLAYER/POS	AVG	G	AB	R	H	2B	3B	HR	RB	BB	SO	SB
Mike Aldrete, of-1	.000	2	1	0	0	0	0	0	0	0	0	0
Brian Boehringer, p	.000	2	0	0	0	0	0	0	0	0	0	0
Wade Boggs, 3b	.273	4	11	0	3	1	0	0	2	1	0	0
David Cone, p	.000	1	2	0	0	0	0	0	0	0	1	0
Mariano Duncan, 2b	.053	6	19	1	1	0	0	0	0	0	4	1
Cecil Fielder, 1b-3,dh-3	.391	6	23	1	9	2	0	0	2	2	2	0
Andy Fox, 2b-1,3b-1	.000	4	0	1	0	0	0	0	0	0	0	0
Joe Girardi, c	.200	4	10	1	2	0	1	0	1	1	2	0
Charlie Hayes, 3b-4, 1b-1	.188	5	16	2	3	0	0	0	1	1	5	0
Derek Jeter, ss	.250	6	20	5	5	0	0	0	1	4	6	1
Jimmy Key, p	.000	2	0	0	0	0	0	0	0	0	0	0
Jim Leyritz, c-3	.375	4	8	1	3	0	0	1	3	3	2	1
Graeme Lloyd, p	.000	4	1	0	0	0	0	0	0	0	0	0
Tino Martinez, 1b-5	.091	6	11	0	1	0	0	0	0	2	5	0
Jeff Nelson, p	.000	3	0	0	0	0	0	0	0	0	0	0
Paul O'Neill, of-4	.167	5	12	1	2	2	0	0	0	3	2	0
Andy Pettitte, p	.000	2	4	0	0	0	0	0	0	0	1	0
Tim Raines, of	.214	4	14	2	3	0	0	0	2	2	1	0
Mariano Rivera, p	.000	4	1	0	0	0	0	0	0	0	0	0
Kenny Rogers, p	1.000	1	1	0	1	0	0	0	0	0	0	0
Luis Sojo, 2b-3	.600	5	5	0	3	1	0	0	1	0	0	0
Darryl Strawberry, of	.188	5	16	0	3	0	0	0	1	4	6	0
Dave Weathers, p	.000	5	0	0	0	0	0	0	0	0	0	0
John Wetteland, p	.000	5	0	0	0	0	0	0	0	0	0	0
Bernie Williams, of	.167	6	24	3	4	0	0	1	4	3	6	1
TOTAL	.216		199	18	43	6	1	2	16	26	43	4

PITCHER	W	L	ERA	G	GS	CG	SV	SHO	IP	H	ER	BB	SO
Brian Boehringer	0	0	5.40	2	0	0	0	0	5.0	5	3	0	5
David Cone	1	0	1.50	1	1	0	0	0	6.0	4	1	4	3
Jimmy Key	1	1	3.97	2	2	0	0	0	11.1	15	5	5	1
Graeme Lloyd	1	0	0.00	4	0	0	0	0	2.2	0	0	0	4
Jeff Nelson	0	0	0.00	3	0	0	0	0	4.1	1	0	1	5
Andy Pettitte	1	1	5.91	2	2	0	0	0	10.2	11	7	4	5
Mariano Rivera	0	0	1.59	4	0	0	0	0	5.2	4	1	3	4
Kenny Rogers	0	0	22.50	1	1	0	0	0	2.0	5	5	2	0
Dave Weathers	0	0	3.00	5	0	0	0	0	3.0	2	1	3	3
John Wetteland	0	0	2.08	5	0	0	4	0	4.1	4	1	1	6
TOTAL	4	2	3.93	27	6	0	4	0	55.0	51	24	23	36

ATL (N)

PLAYER/POS	AVG	G	AB	R	H	2B	3B	HR	RB	BB	SO	SB
Steve Avery, p	.000	1	0	0	0	0	0	0	0	0	0	0
Rafael Belliard, ss-3	.000	4	0	0	0	0	0	0	0	0	0	0
Mike Bielecki, p	.000	2	1	0	0	0	0	0	0	0	1	0
Jeff Blauser, ss	.167	6	18	2	3	1	0	0	1	1	4	0
Brad Clontz, p	.000	3	0	0	0	0	0	0	0	0	0	0
Jermaine Dye, of	.118	5	17	0	2	0	0	0	1	1	1	0
Tom Glavine, p	.000	1	1	0	0	0	0	0	0	1	1	0
Marquis Grissom, of	.444	6	27	4	12	2	1	0	5	1	2	1
Andruw Jones, of	.400	6	20	4	8	1	0	2	6	3	6	1
Chipper Jones, 3b-6, ss-1	.286	6	21	3	6	3	0	0	3	4	2	1
Ryan Klesko, of-2, 1b-1,dh-1	.100	5	10	2	1	0	0	0	1	2	4	0
Mark Lemke, 2b	.231	6	26	2	6	1	0	0	2	0	3	0
Javy Lopez, c	.190	6	21	3	4	0	0	0	1	3	4	0
Greg Maddux, p	.000	2	0	0	0	0	0	0	0	0	0	0
Fred McGriff, 1b	.300	6	20	4	6	0	0	2	6	5	4	0
Greg McMichael, p	.000	2	0	0	0	0	0	0	0	0	0	0
Mike Mordecai, ph	.000	1	1	0	0	0	0	0	0	0	1	0
Denny Neagle, p	.000	2	1	0	0	0	0	0	0	0	1	0
Terry Pendleton, dh-2,3b-1	.222	4	9	1	2	1	0	0	1	1	1	0
Eddie Perez, c	.000	2	1	0	0	0	0	0	0	0	0	0
Luis Polonia, ph	.000	6	5	0	0	0	0	0	0	1	2	0
John Smoltz, p	.500	2	2	0	1	0	0	0	0	0	0	0
Terrell Wade, p	.000	2	0	0	0	0	0	0	0	0	0	0
Mark Wohlers, p	.000	4	0	0	0	0	0	0	0	0	0	0
TOTAL	.254		201	26	51	9	1	4	26	23	36	3

PITCHER	W	L	ERA	G	GS	CG	SV	SHO	IP	H	ER	BB	SO
Steve Avery	0	1	13.50	1	0	0	0	0	0.2	1	1	3	0
Mike Bielecki	0	0	0.00	2	0	0	0	0	3.0	0	0	3	6
Brad Clontz	0	0	0.00	3	0	0	0	0	1.2	1	0	1	2
Tom Glavine	0	0	1.29	1	1	0	0	0	7.0	4	1	3	8
Greg Maddux	1	1	1.72	2	2	0	0	0	15.2	14	3	1	5
Greg McMichael	0	0	27.00	2	0	0	0	0	1.0	5	3	0	1
Denny Neagle	0	0	3.00	2	1	0	0	0	6.0	5	2	4	3
John Smoltz	1	1	0.64	2	2	0	0	0	14.0	6	1	8	14
Terrell Wade	0	0	0.00	2	0	0	0	0	0.2	0	0	1	0
Mark Wohlers	0	0	6.23	4	0	0	0	0	4.1	7	3	2	4
TOTAL	2	4	2.33	21	6	0	0	0	54.0	43	14	26	43

GAME ONE AT NY OCT 20

ATL	026	013	000	12	13 0
NY	000	010	000	1	4 1

Pitchers: SMOLTZ, McMichael (7), Neagle (8), Wade (9), Clontz (9) vs PETTITTE, Boehringer (3), Weathers (6), Nelson (8), Wetteland (9)
Home Runs: A.Jones-ATL (2), McGriff-ATL
Attendance: 56,365

GAME TWO AT NY OCT 21

ATL	101	011	000	4	10 0
NY	000	000	000	0	7 1

Pitchers: MADDUX, Wohlers (9) vs KEY, Lloyd (7), Nelson (7), Rivera (9)
Attendance: 56,340

GAME THREE AT ATL OCT 22

NY	100	100	030	5	8 1
ATL	000	001	010	2	6 1

Pitchers: CONE, Rivera (7), Lloyd (8), Wetteland (9) vs GLAVINE, McMichael (8), Clontz (8), Bielecki (9)
Home Runs: Williams-NY
Attendance: 51,843

GAME FOUR AT ATL OCT 23

NY	000	003	030 2	8	12 0
ATL	041	010	000 0	6	9 2

Pitchers: Rogers, Boehringer (3), Weathers (5), Nelson (6), Rivera (8), LLOYD (9), Wetteland (10) vs Neagle (6), Wade (6), Bielecki (6), Wohlers (8), AVERY (10), Clontz (10)
Home Runs: Leyritz-NY, McGriff-ATL
Attendance: 51,881

GAME FIVE AT ATL OCT 24

NY	000	100	000	1	4 1
ATL	000	000	000	0	5 1

Pitchers: PETTITTE, Wetteland (9) vs SMOLTZ, Wohlers (9)
Attendance: 51,881

GAME SIX AT NY OCT 26

ATL	000	100	001	2	8 0
NY	003	000	00X	3	8 1

Pitchers: MADDUX, Wohlers (8) vs KEY, Weathers (6), Lloyd (6), Rivera (7), Wetteland (9)
Attendance: 56,375

The Giants went from last place in 1996 to first place in 1997, but Florida got the key hits late in each game to key a sweep of the division series. The Marlins became the first expansion team to win a post-season series, in their fifth year of existence. Kirk Reuter and Kevin Brown each threw seven innings of four-hit ball and each pitcher was nicked for a run in their last inning in Game 1. Bill Mueller homered for the Giants leading off the top of the seventh, and Charles Johnson answered with a home run in the bottom of the inning. In the last of the ninth, the Marlins loaded the bases with one out, but Devon White grounded into a force play at the plate. Reliever Roberto Hernandez fell behind Edgar Renteria and the Marlins shortstop grounded a single to right to win the game.

Game 2 was a battle of the bullpens; starters Shawn Estes and Al Leiter were both out of the game by the fifth inning. Stan Javier had four hits, and Barry Bonds, who had three RBIs in 21 career post-season games, drove home two runs. Bobby Bonilla's three RBIs and Gary Sheffield's home run gave the Marlins a 6-5 lead entering the ninth, but two errors and a broken-bat hit against Robb Nen tied the game. In the bottom of the ninth, Moises Alou singled with two runners on against Hernandez, and center fielder Dante Powell's strong throw hit the pitcher's mound and bounced straight up in the air, allowing Sheffield to score the winning run.

Wilson Alvarez, who came with Hernandez in a late season blockbuster deal with the White Sox, sailed through the first five and two thirds innings of Game 3, but then he filled the bases. Devon White, batting eighth, just missed getting hit by a pitch, then launched a grand slam to left field. Jeff Kent homered twice, the second coming just after Mueller was thrown out trying to steal, but Alex Fernandez, Dennis Cook, and Nen limited San Francisco to just five more hits.

Florida Marlins (E), 3;
San Francisco Giants (W), 0

FLA (E)

PLAYER/POS	AVG	G	AB	R	H	2B	3B	HR	RB	BB	SO	SB
Kurt Abbott, 2b-2	.250	3	8	0	2	0	0	0	0	0	0	0
Moises Alou, of	.214	3	14	1	3	1	0	0	1	0	3	0
Alex Arias, ph	1.000	1	1	1	1	0	0	0	1	0	0	0
Bobby Bonilla, 3b	.333	3	12	1	4	0	0	1	3	2	1	0
Kevin Brown, p	.000	1	2	0	0	0	0	0	0	0	2	0
John Cangelosi, ph	.000	1	1	0	0	0	0	0	0	0	0	0
Jeff Conine, 1b	.364	3	11	3	4	1	0	0	0	1	0	0
Dennis Cook, p	.000	2	0	0	0	0	0	0	0	0	0	0
Craig Counsell, 2b	.400	3	5	0	2	1	0	0	1	1	0	0
Jim Eisenreich, ph	.000	2	3	0	0	0	0	0	0	0	2	0
Alex Fernandez, p	.000	1	2	0	0	0	0	0	0	0	1	0
Livan Hernandez, p	.000	1	1	0	0	0	0	0	0	0	0	0
Charles Johnson, c	.250	3	8	5	2	1	0	1	2	3	2	0
Al Leiter, p	.000	1	1	0	0	0	0	0	0	0	0	0
Robb Nen, p	.000	2	0	0	0	0	0	0	0	0	0	0
Edgar Renteria, ss	.154	3	13	1	2	0	0	0	1	2	4	0
Gary Sheffield, of	.556	3	9	2	5	1	0	1	1	5	0	1
John Wehner, of	.000	1	0	0	0	0	0	0	0	0	0	0
Devon White, of	.182	3	11	1	2	0	0	1	4	2	3	0
TOTAL	.273		99	15	27	5	0	4	14	19	16	1

PITCHER	W	L	ERA	G	GS	CG	SV	SHO	IP	H	ER	BB	SO
Kevin Brown	0	0	1.29	1	1	0	0	0	7.0	4	1	0	5
Dennis Cook	1	0	0.00	2	0	0	0	0	3.0	0	0	1	3
Alex Fernandez	1	0	2.57	1	1	0	0	0	7.0	7	2	0	5
Livan Hernandez	0	0	2.25	1	0	0	0	0	4.0	3	1	0	3
Al Leiter	0	0	9.00	1	1	0	0	0	4.0	7	4	3	3
Robb Nen	1	0	0.00	2	0	0	0	0	2.0	1	0	2	2
TOTAL	3	0	2.67	8	3	0	0	0	27.0	22	8	6	21

SF (W)

PLAYER/POS	AVG	G	AB	R	H	2B	3B	HR	RB	BB	SO	SB
Wilson Alvarez, p	.000	1	2	0	0	0	0	0	0	0	0	0
Rod Beck, p	.000	1	0	0	0	0	0	0	0	0	0	0
Marvin Benard, ph	.000	2	2	0	0	0	0	0	0	0	1	0
Damon Berryhill, ph	.000	1	1	0	0	0	0	0	0	0	0	0
Barry Bonds, of	.250	3	12	0	3	2	0	0	2	0	3	1
Shawn Estes, p	.000	1	1	0	0	0	0	0	0	0	0	0
Darryl Hamilton, of	.000	2	5	1	0	0	0	0	0	0	1	0
Doug Henry, p	.000	1	0	0	0	0	0	0	0	0	0	0
Roberto Hernandez, p	.000	3	0	0	0	0	0	0	0	0	0	0
Glenallen Hill, of-2	.000	3	7	0	0	0	0	0	0	2	2	0
Stan Javier, of	.417	3	12	2	5	1	0	0	1	0	2	1
Brian Johnson, c	.100	3	10	2	1	0	0	1	1	1	4	0
Jeff Kent, 2b-3,1b-1	.300	3	10	2	3	0	0	2	2	2	1	0
Mark Lewis, 2b	.600	1	5	0	3	0	0	0	1	0	0	0
Bill Mueller, 3b	.250	3	12	1	3	0	0	1	1	0	0	0
Dante Powell, of	.000	1	0	0	0	0	0	0	0	0	0	0
Rich Rodriguez, p	.000	2	0	0	0	0	0	0	0	0	0	0
Kirk Reuter, p	.500	1	2	0	1	0	0	0	0	0	0	0
J. T. Snow, 1b	.167	3	6	0	1	0	0	0	0	1	1	0
Julian Tavarez, p	.000	3	0	0	0	0	0	0	0	0	0	0
Jose Vizcaino, ss	.182	3	11	1	2	1	0	0	0	0	5	0
TOTAL	.224		98	9	22	4	0	4	8	6	21	2

PITCHER	W	L	ERA	G	GS	CG	SV	SHO	IP	H	ER	BB	SO
Wilson Alvarez	0	1	6.00	1	1	0	0	0	6.0	6	4	4	4
Rod Beck	0	0	0.00	1	0	0	0	0	1.1	1	0	0	1
Shawn Estes	0	0	15.00	1	1	0	0	0	3.0	5	5	4	3
Doug Henry	0	0	0.00	1	0	0	0	0	2.0	1	0	3	2
Roberto Hernandez	0	1	20.25	3	0	0	0	0	1.1	5	3	3	1
Rich Rodriguez	0	0	0.00	2	0	0	0	0	1.0	1	0	0	0
Kirk Reuter	0	1	1.29	1	1	0	0	0	7.0	4	1	3	5
Julian Tavarez	0	1	4.50	3	0	0	0	0	4.0	4	2	2	0
TOTAL	0	3	5.26	13	3	0	0	0	25.2	27	15	19	16

GAME 1 AT FLA SEPT 30

SF	000 000 100	1	4	0
FLA	000 000 101	2	7	0

Pitchers: Rueter, TAVAREZ (8), Hernandez (9) vs Brown, COOK (8)
Home Runs: Mueller-SF, Johnson-FLA
Attendance: 42,167

GAME 2 AT FLA OCT 1

SF	111 100 101	6	11	0
FLA	201 201 001	7	10	2

Pitchers: Estes, Henry (4), Tavarez (6), Rodriguez (8), HERNANDEZ (9) vs Leiter, Hernandez (5), NEN (9)
Home Runs: Bonilla-FLA, Johnson-SF, Sheffield-FLA
Attendance: 41,283

GAME 3 AT SF OCT 3

FLA	000 004 020	6	10	2
SF	000 101 000	2	7	0

Pitchers: FERNANDEZ, Cook (8), Nen (8) vs ALVAREZ, Tavarez (7), Hernandez (8), Rodriguez (8), Beck (8)
Home Runs: Kent-SF (2), White-FLA
Attendance: 57,188

The Astros had the worst record of any team to reach the postseason while the Braves had the best record in baseball. It was a mismatch on paper, and it played out that way on the field, too. The Braves outscored the Astros, 19-5, and their pitching proved to be so dominant that 20-game winner Denny Neagle didn't even get a start in the series for Atlanta.

The handwriting was on the wall in Game 1 when Darryl Kile pitched a two-hitter and still lost, 2-1. Kile was also Houston's only hitter in the clutch, driving in the team's run. Kenny Lofton doubled to start the game and two fly outs brought him home. Ryan Klesko homered to lead off the second and that was it for the scoring and the hitting for the Braves, but Greg Maddux scattered seven hits for the complete-game victory.

Even in a 13-3 second game, the pitchers again had a lot to say about the outcome—although much of it was with their bats. Tom Glavine's single in the bottom of the third sparked a three-run Braves rally and Mike Hampton's single in the top of the fourth drove in the tying run. In the fifth inning Hampton got the first two outs, but then walked four straight batters. His replacement, Mike Magnante, allowed a two-run single to pinch hitter Greg Colrunn that gave the Braves a 6-3 lead. Glavine's single started a five-run rally in the sixth inning.

Game 3 belonged to John Smoltz, who pitched a three-hitter for his 10th career postseason victory. Shane Reynolds, starting the first postseason game in the Astrodome since 1986, had early chances to pitch out of trouble. He picked off Kenny Lofton in the first inning, then allowed a home run to Chipper Jones. In the second, he had a base open with Smoltz on deck, but he pitched instead to Jeff Blauser, who singled in the second run. Smoltz, meanwhile, struck out 11 Astros and silenced "The Killer B's." For the series, the top of the Astros order—Craig Biggio, Derek Bell, and Jeff Bagwell—batted a combined .054 (2-for-37).

Atlanta Braves (E), 3; Houston Astros (C), 0

ATL (E)

PLAYER/POS	AVG	G	AB	R	H	2B	3B	HR	RB	BB	SO	SB
Danny Bautista, of	.333	3	3	0	1	0	0	0	0	2	0	1	0
Jeff Blauser, ss	.300	3	10	2	3	0	0	1	4	2	2	0
Mike Cather, p	.000	1	1	0	0	0	0	0	0	0	1	0
Greg Colbrunn, ph	1.000	1	1	0	1	0	0	0	2	0	0	0
Tom Glavine, p	.667	1	3	2	2	0	0	0	0	0	0	0
Tony Graffanino, 2b	.000	3	3	0	0	0	0	0	0	0	2	0
Andruw Jones, of	.000	3	5	1	0	0	0	0	1	1	1	0
Chipper Jones, 3b	.500	3	8	3	4	0	0	1	2	3	2	1
Ryan Klesko, of	.250	3	8	2	2	1	0	1	1	0	2	0
Keith Lockhart, 2b	.000	2	6	0	0	0	0	0	0	0	1	0
Kenny Lofton, of	.154	3	13	2	2	1	0	0	1	2	0	0
Javy Lopez, c	.286	2	7	3	2	2	0	0	1	2	1	0
Greg Maddux, p	.000	1	2	0	0	0	0	0	0	0	1	0
Fred McGriff, 1b	.222	3	9	4	2	0	0	0	1	3	2	0
Eddie Perez, c	.000	1	3	0	0	0	0	0	0	0	1	0
John Smoltz, p	.000	1	4	0	0	0	0	0	0	0	1	0
Michael Tucker, of	.167	2	6	0	1	0	0	0	1	0	1	0
Mark Wohlers, p	.000	1	0	0	0	0	0	0	0	0	0	0
TOTAL	.217		92	19	20	4	0	3	15	15	20	1

PITCHER	W	L	ERA	G	GS	CG	SV	SHO	IP	H	ER	BB	SO
Mike Cather	0	0	0.00	1	0	0	0	0	2.0	0	0	1	2
Tom Glavine	1	0	4.50	1	1	0	0	0	6.0	5	3	5	4
Greg Maddux	1	0	1.00	1	1	1	0	0	9.0	7	1	1	6
John Smoltz	1	0	1.00	1	1	1	0	0	9.0	3	1	1	11
Mark Wohlers	0	0	0.00	1	0	0	0	0	1.0	1	0	0	1
TOTAL	3	0	1.67	5	3	2	0	0	27.0	16	5	8	24

HOU (C)

PLAYER/POS	AVG	G	AB	R	H	2B	3B	HR	RB	BB	SO	SB
Bob Abreu, ph	.333	3	3	0	1	0	0	0	0	0	2	1
Brad Ausmus, c	.400	2	5	1	2	1	0	0	2	0	1	0
Jeff Bagwell, 1b	.083	3	12	0	1	0	0	0	0	1	5	0
Derek Bell, of	.000	3	13	0	0	0	0	0	0	0	3	0
Sean Berry, ph	.000	1	1	0	0	0	0	0	0	0	0	0
Craig Biggio, 2b	.083	3	12	0	1	0	0	0	0	1	0	0
Chuck Carr, of	.250	2	4	1	1	0	0	1	1	1	3	0
Raul Eusebio, c	.667	1	3	1	2	0	0	0	0	0	1	1
Ramon Garcia, p	.000	2	0	0	0	0	0	0	0	0	0	0
Luis Gonzalez, of	.333	3	12	0	4	0	0	0	0	0	1	0
Ricky Gutierrez, ss	.125	3	8	0	1	0	0	0	0	2	1	0
Mike Hampton, p	.500	1	2	0	1	0	0	0	1	0	0	0
Richard Hidalgo, of	.000	2	5	1	0	0	0	0	0	1	2	0
Thomas Howard, ph	.000	2	1	0	0	0	0	0	0	1	1	0
Russ Johnson, ph	.000	1	1	0	0	0	0	0	0	0	1	0
Darryl Kile, p	1.000	1	2	0	2	0	0	0	0	0	0	0
Jose Lima, p	.000	1	0	0	0	0	0	0	0	0	0	0
Mike Magnante, p	.000	2	0	0	0	0	0	0	0	0	0	0
Tom Martin, p	.000	2	0	0	0	0	0	0	0	0	0	0
Tony Pena, c	.000	2	0	0	0	0	0	0	0	0	0	0
Shane Reynolds, p	.000	1	1	0	0	0	0	0	0	0	1	0
Bill Spiers, 3b	.000	3	11	1	0	0	0	0	0	1	2	0
Russ Springer, p	.000	2	0	0	0	0	0	0	0	0	0	0
Billy Wagner, p	.000	1	0	0	0	0	0	0	0	0	0	0
TOTAL	.167		96	5	16	1	0	1	5	8	24	2

PITCHER	W	L	ERA	G	GS	CG	SV	SHO	IP	H	ER	BB	SO
Ramon Garcia	0	0	0.00	2	0	0	0	0	1.0	1	0	1	1
Mike Hampton	0	1	11.57	1	1	0	0	0	4.2	2	6	8	2
Darryl Kile	0	1	2.57	1	1	0	0	0	7.0	2	2	2	4
Jose Lima	0	0	0.00	1	0	0	0	0	1.0	0	0	1	1
Mike Magnante	0	0	4.50	2	0	0	0	0	2.0	4	1	0	2
Tom Martin	0	0	0.00	2	0	0	0	0	0.2	1	0	1	0
Shane Reynolds	0	1	3.00	1	1	0	0	0	6.0	5	2	1	5
Russ Springer	0	0	5.40	2	0	0	0	0	1.2	2	1	1	3
Billy Wagner	0	0	18.00	1	0	0	0	0	1.0	3	2	0	2
TOTAL	0	3	5.04	13	3	0	0	0	25.0	20	14	15	20

GAME 1 AT ATL SEPT 30

HOU	000	010	000	1	7	1
ATL	110	000	00X	2	2	0

Pitchers: KILE, Springer (8), Martin (8) vs MADDUX
Home Runs: Klesko-ATL
Attendance: 46,467

GAME 2 AT ATL OCT 1

HOU	000	300	000	3	6	2
ATL	003	035	02X	13	10	1

Pitchers: HAMPTON, Magnante (5), Garcia (6), Lima (7), Wagner (8) vs GLAVINE, Cather (7), Wohlers (9)
Home Runs: Blauser-ATL
Attendance: 49,200

GAME 3 AT HOU OCT 3

ATL	110	000	110	4	8	2
HOU	000	000	100	1	3	1

Pitchers: SMOLTZ vs REYNOLDS, Springer (7), Martin (8), Garcia (8), Magnante (9)
Home Runs: C.Jones-ATL, Carr-FLA
Attendance: 53,688

The predetermined postseason matchup seemed to favor the Wild Card Yankees, who drew the Indians in the Division Series while the AL East champion Orioles got the power-packed Mariners. The Indians had the worst record of any American League postseason club, but Cleveland got off to a 5-0 lead in the first inning of Game 1. Cleveland held a 6-1 lead by the time David Cone was chased from the mound, and Cone's injured shoulder made it his only appearance of the series. But Orel Hershiser, who came into the series with an 8-1 record with a 1.83 ERA in the postseason, didn't last through the fifth inning. In the sixth inning, Tim Raines, Derek Jeter, and Paul O'Neill hit successive home runs—a first in postseason history—to give the Yankees an 8-6 victory.

In Game 2 the Yankees couldn't hold the lead. New York reached 21-year-old rookie Jaret Wright for three runs in the first inning, but a two-out rally off Andy Pettitte in the fourth inning gave the Indians a 5-3 lead. Matt Williams homered in the fifth inning, and a trio of relievers held off a late Yankees comeback. David Wells pitched a five-hitter in Game 3 to win a Division Series game for the third straight year for his third different team. New York chased Cleveland starter Charles Nagy in the fourth inning, and Paul O'Neill greeted Chad Ogea with a grand slam. It was the last run the Indians bullpen would allow.

In Game 4 Orel Hershiser and Dwight Gooden looked a lot like they did when they faced each other in the 1988 playoffs. Hershiser was good for seven innings, but Gooden left with a 2-1 lead in the sixth. The Yankees were four outs from winning the series with their closer Mariano Rivera on the mound when Sandy Alomar hit an opposite-field home run to tie the game. In the ninth inning Omar Vizquel's hard grounder up the middle glanced off reliever Ramiro Mendoza and rolled into left field, allowing Marquis Grissom to score from second with the winning run.

Manny Ramirez stepped to the plate in the third inning of Game 5 batting .111 for the series, but he hit a ground-rule double on a two-strike pitch from Pettitte to score Grissom and Vizquel. The Indians took a 4-0 lead, but the Yankees made it a one-run game in the sixth inning against Wright. Jose Mesa snuffed a Yankees rally in the eighth, and, after a two-out double by O'Neill in the ninth, he retired Bernie Williams on a flyball to left to end the series.

Cleveland Indians (C), 3; New York Yankees (E), 2

CLE (C)

PLAYER/POS	AVG	G	AB	R	H	2B	3B	HR	RB	BB	SO	SB
Sandy Alomar, c	.316	5	19	4	6	1	0	2	5	0	2	0
Paul Assenmacher, p	.000	4	0	0	0	0	0	0	0	0	0	0
Tony Fernandez, 2b	.182	4	11	0	2	1	0	0	4	0	0	0
Brian Giles, of	.143	3	7	0	1	0	0	0	0	0	1	0
Marquis Grissom, of	.235	5	17	3	4	0	1	0	0	1	2	0
Orel Hershiser, p	.000	2	0	0	0	0	0	0	0	0	0	0
Mike Jackson, p	.000	4	0	0	0	0	0	0	0	0	0	0
David Justice, dh	.263	5	19	3	5	2	0	1	2	2	3	0
Jose Mesa, p	.000	2	0	0	0	0	0	0	0	0	0	0
Alvin Morman, p	.000	1	0	0	0	0	0	0	0	0	0	0
Charles Nagy, p	.000	1	0	0	0	0	0	0	0	0	0	0
Chad Ogea, p	.000	1	0	0	0	0	0	0	0	0	0	0
Eric Plunk, p	.000	1	0	0	0	0	0	0	0	0	0	0
Manny Ramirez, of	.143	5	21	2	3	1	0	0	3	0	3	0
Bip Roberts, of-4,2b-2	.316	5	19	1	6	0	0	0	1	2	2	2
Kevin Seitzer, 1b	.000	1	4	0	0	0	0	0	0	0	0	0
Jim Thome, 1b	.200	5	15	3	3	0	0	0	1	0	5	0
Omar Vizquel, ss	.500	5	18	3	9	0	0	0	1	2	1	4
Matt Williams, 3b	.235	5	17	4	4	1	0	1	3	3	3	0
Jaret Wright, p	.000	2	0	0	0	0	0	0	0	0	0	0
TOTAL	.257		167	21	43	6	1	4	20	10	22	6

PITCHER	W	L	ERA	G	GS	CG	SV	SHO	IP	H	ER	BB	SO
Paul Assenmacher	0	0	5.40	4	0	0	0	0	3.1	2	2	2	2
Orel Hershiser	0	0	3.97	2	2	0	0	0	11.1	14	5	2	4
Mike Jackson	1	0	0.00	4	0	0	0	0	4.1	3	0	1	5
Jose Mesa	0	0	2.70	2	0	0	1	0	3.1	5	1	1	2
Alvin Morman	0	0	INF	1	0	0	0	0	0.0	0	0	1	0
Charles Nagy	0	1	9.82	1	1	0	0	0	3.2	2	4	6	1
Chad Ogea	0	0	1.69	1	0	0	0	0	5.1	2	1	0	1
Eric Plunk	0	1	27.00	1	0	0	0	0	1.1	4	4	0	1
Jaret Wright	2	0	3.97	2	2	0	0	0	11.1	11	5	7	10
TOTAL	3	2	4.50	18	5	0	1	0	44.0	43	22	20	26

NY (E)

PLAYER/POS	AVG	G	AB	R	H	2B	3B	HR	RB	BB	SO	SB
Brian Boehringer, p	.000	1	0	0	0	0	0	0	0	0	0	0
Wade Boggs, 3b-2	.429	3	7	1	3	0	0	0	2	0	0	0
David Cone, p	.000	1	0	0	0	0	0	0	0	0	0	0
Chad Curtis, of	.167	4	6	1	1	0	0	0	0	3	1	0
Cecil Fielder, dh	.125	2	8	0	1	0	0	0	1	0	3	0
Andy Fox, 2b	.000	2	0	0	0	0	0	0	0	0	0	0
Joe Girardi, c	.133	5	15	2	2	0	0	0	0	1	3	0
Dwight Gooden, p	.000	1	0	0	0	0	0	0	0	0	0	0
Charlie Hayes, 3b-5,2b-1	.333	5	15	0	5	0	0	0	1	0	2	0
Derek Jeter, ss	.333	5	21	6	7	1	0	2	3	5	5	1
Graeme Lloyd, p	.000	2	0	0	0	0	0	0	0	0	0	0
Tino Martinez, 1b	.222	5	18	1	4	1	0	1	4	2	4	0
Ramiro Mendoza, p	.000	2	0	0	0	0	0	0	0	0	0	0
Jeff Nelson, p	.000	4	0	0	0	0	0	0	0	0	0	0
Paul O'Neill, of	.421	5	19	5	8	2	0	2	7	3	0	0
Andy Pettitte, p	.000	2	0	0	0	0	0	0	0	0	1	0
Jorge Posada, c	.000	2	2	0	0	0	0	0	0	0	1	0
Scott Pose, pr	.000	1	0	0	0	0	0	0	0	0	0	0
Tim Raines, of-3,dh-2	.211	5	19	4	4	0	0	1	3	3	1	2
Mariano Rivera, p	.000	2	0	0	0	0	0	0	0	0	0	0
Rey Sanchez, 2b	.200	5	15	1	3	1	0	0	1	1	2	0
Mike Stanley, dh-1	.750	2	4	1	3	1	0	0	1	0	1	0
Mike Stanton, p	.000	3	0	0	0	0	0	0	0	0	0	0
David Wells, p	.000	1	0	0	0	0	0	0	0	0	0	0
Bernie Williams, of	.118	5	17	3	2	1	0	0	1	4	3	0
TOTAL	.259		166	24	43	7	0	6	23	20	26	3

PITCHER	W	L	ERA	G	GS	CG	SV	SHO	IP	H	ER	BB	SO
Brian Boehringer	0	0	0.00	1	0	0	0	0	1.2	1	0	1	2
David Cone	0	0	16.20	1	1	0	0	0	3.1	7	6	2	2
Dwight Gooden	0	0	1.59	1	1	0	0	0	5.2	5	1	3	5
Graeme Lloyd	0	0	0.00	2	0	0	0	0	1.1	0	0	0	1
Ramiro Mendoza	1	1	2.45	2	0	0	0	0	3.2	3	1	0	2
Jeff Nelson	0	0	0.00	4	0	0	0	0	4.0	4	0	2	6
Andy Pettitte	0	2	8.49	2	2	0	0	0	11.2	15	11	1	5
Mariano Rivera	0	0	4.50	2	0	0	1	0	2.0	2	1	0	1
Mike Stanton	0	0	0.00	3	0	0	0	0	1.0	1	0	1	3
David Wells	1	0	1.00	1	1	1	0	0	9.0	5	1	0	1
TOTAL	2	3	4.36	19	5	1	1	0	43.1	43	21	10	22

GAME 1 AT NY SEPT 30

CLE	500 100 000	6	11	0
NY	010 115 00X	8	11	0

Pitchers: Hershiser, Morman (5), PLUNK (5), Assenmacher (7), Jackson (7) vs Cone, MENDOZA (4), Nelson (7), Rivera (8)
Home Runs: Alomar-BAL, Martinez-NY, Raines-NY, Jeter-NY, O'Neill-NY
Attendance: 57,398

GAME 2 AT NY OCT 2

CLE	000 520 000	7	11	1
NY	300 000 011	5	7	2

Pitchers: WRIGHT, Jackson (7), Assenmacher (7), Mesa (8) vs PETTITTE, Boehringer (6), Lloyd (7), Nelson (9)
Home Runs: Williams-CLE, Jeter-NY
Attendance: 57,360

GAME 3 AT CLE OCT 4

NY	101 400 000	6	4	1
CLE	010 000 000	1	5	1

Pitchers: WELLS vs NAGY, Ogea (4)
Home Runs: O'Neill-NY
Attendance: 45,274

GAME 4 AT CLE OCT 5

NY	200 000 000	2	9	1
CLE	010 000 011	3	9	0

Pitchers: Gooden, Lloyd (6), Nelson (6), Stanton (7), Rivera (9) vs Hershiser, Assenmacher (8), JACKSON (8)
Home Runs: Justice-CLE, Alomar-CLE
Attendance: 45,231

GAME 5 AT CLE OCT 6

NY	000 021 000	3	12	0
CLE	003 100 00X	4	7	2

Pitchers: PETTITTE, Nelson (7), Stanton (8) vs WRIGHT, Jackson (6), Assenmacher (7), Mesa (8)
Attendance: 45,203

The Orioles found an antidote to Randy Johnson, and they used it twice to beat the Mariners. Meanwhile, Mike Mussina found a way to silence Seattle's powerful lineup twice and that was the difference. Orioles manager Davey Johnson raised eyebrows when he rested Roberto Alomar, Rafael Palmeiro, and B.J. Surhoff against southpaw Randy Johnson, but their replacements and the rest of the Baltimore lineup had little trouble in Game 1. Johnson left in the fifth inning trailing 5-1, and the much-maligned Mariners bullpen lived up to its reputation as the Orioles coasted behind Mussina. Jamie Moyer had a 2-1 lead when he was forced to leave Game 2 with an injured left elbow in the fifth inning. Paul Spoljaric relieved and the next batter, Roberto Alomar, doubled off Ken Griffey, Jr.'s glove in center field to give the Orioles a 3-2 lead. Brady Anderson homered and doubled against two more Mariners relievers, and the Orioles left Seattle with their second straight 9-3 laugher.

Roberto Kelly doubled in a run in the first inning, and Griffey singled in a run in the fifth to stake Jeff Fassero to a 2-0 lead in Game 3. Fassero pitched a brilliant three-hitter for eight innings, but manager Lou Piniella brought in Heathcliff Slocumb to close the game when the Mariners took a 4-0 lead into the bottom of the ninth. Jeffrey Hammonds doubled home two runs, but Harold Baines popped out to end the game.

Mussina, who pitched a five-hitter for seven innings in the series opener, allowed just two hits in seven innings in Game 4. The Orioles helped him out by scoring twice in the first inning on a home run by Jeff Reboulet (Alomar's replacement in Davey Johnson's lineup against Randy Johnson) and a run-scoring single by Cal Ripken. Edgar Martinez led off the second inning with a home run, and Seattle followed that with a walk and a single. Mussina did not allow another hit and fanned seven.

Baltimore Orioles (E), 3;
Seattle Mariners (W), 1

BAL (E)

PLAYER/POS	AVG	G	AB	R	H	2B	3B	HR	RB	BB	SO	SB
Roberto Alomar, 2b	.300	4	10	1	3	2	0	0	2	1	1	0
Brady Anderson, of	.353	4	17	3	6	1	0	1	4	1	4	1
Harold Baines, dh-1	.400	2	5	2	2	0	0	1	1	1	0	0
Armando Benitez, p	.000	3	0	0	0	0	0	0	0	0	0	0
Geronimo Berroa, dh-3,of-1	.385	4	13	4	5	1	0	2	2	2	2	0
Mike Bordick, ss	.400	4	10	4	4	1	0	0	4	4	2	0
Eric Davis, of	.222	3	9	0	2	0	0	0	2	0	5	0
Scott Erickson, p	.000	1	0	0	0	0	0	0	0	0	0	0
Jeffrey Hammonds, of	.100	4	10	3	1	1	0	0	2	2	2	1
Chris Hoiles, c	.143	3	7	1	1	0	0	1	1	2	1	0
Jimmy Key, p	.000	1	0	0	0	0	0	0	0	0	0	0
Terry Mathews, p	.000	1	0	0	0	0	0	0	0	0	0	0
Alan Mills, p	.000	1	0	0	0	0	0	0	0	0	0	0
Mike Mussina, p	.000	2	0	0	0	0	0	0	0	0	0	0
Randy Myers, p	.000	2	0	0	0	0	0	0	0	0	0	0
Jesse Orosco, p	.000	2	0	0	0	0	0	0	0	0	0	0
Rafael Palmeiro, 1b	.250	4	12	2	3	2	0	0	0	0	2	0
Jeff Reboulet, 2b	.200	2	5	1	1	0	0	1	1	0	2	0
Arthur Lee Rhodes, p	.000	1	0	0	0	0	0	0	0	0	0	0
Cal Ripken, 3b	.438	4	16	1	7	2	0	0	1	2	2	0
B.J. Surhoff, of	.273	3	11	0	3	1	0	0	2	0	2	0
Jerome Walton, 1b	.000	2	4	0	0	0	0	0	0	0	0	0
Lenny Webster, c	.167	3	6	1	1	0	0	0	1	1	0	0
TOTAL	.289		135	23	39	11	0	6	23	16	27	2

PITCHER	W	L	ERA	G	GS	CG	SV	SHO	IP	H	ER	BB	SO
Armando Benitez	0	0	3.00	3	0	0	0	0	3.0	3	1	2	4
Scott Erickson	1	0	4.05	1	1	0	0	0	6.2	7	3	2	6
Jimmy Key	0	1	3.86	1	1	0	0	0	4.2	8	2	0	4
Terry Mathews	0	0	18.00	1	0	0	0	0	1.0	2	2	0	1
Alan Mills	0	0	0.00	1	0	0	0	0	1.0	1	0	0	1
Mike Mussina	2	0	1.93	2	2	0	0	0	14.0	7	3	3	16
Randy Myers	0	0	0.00	2	0	0	1	0	2.0	0	0	0	5
Jesse Orosco	0	0	0.00	2	0	0	0	0	1.1	1	0	0	1
Arthur Lee Rhodes	0	0	0.00	1	0	0	0	0	2.1	0	0	0	4
TOTAL	3	1	2.75	14	4	0	1	0	36.0	29	11	7	42

SEA (W)

PLAYER/POS	AVG	G	AB	R	H	2B	3B	HR	RB	BB	SO	SB
Rich Amaral, 1b	.500	2	4	2	2	0	0	0	0	0	1	0
Bobby Ayala, p	.000	1	0	0	0	0	0	0	0	0	0	0
Mike Blowers, 3b	.200	3	5	0	1	0	0	0	0	0	3	0
Jay Buhner, of	.231	4	13	2	3	0	0	2	2	3	6	0
Norm Charlton, p	.000	2	0	0	0	0	0	0	0	0	0	0
Joey Cora, 2b	.176	4	17	1	3	0	0	0	0	0	4	0
Rob Ducey, of-1	.500	2	4	0	2	0	0	0	0	1	0	0
Jeff Fassero, p	.000	1	0	0	0	0	0	0	0	0	0	0
Brent Gates, 3b	.000	2	0	0	0	0	0	0	0	0	0	0
Ken Griffey, of	.133	4	15	0	2	0	0	0	2	1	3	2
Randy Johnson, p	.000	2	0	0	0	0	0	0	0	0	0	0
Roberto Kelly, of-3	.308	4	13	1	4	3	0	0	1	0	3	0
Edgar Martinez, dh	.188	4	16	2	3	0	0	2	3	3	3	0
Jamie Moyer, p	.000	1	0	0	0	0	0	0	0	0	0	0
Alex Rodriguez, ss	.313	4	16	1	5	1	0	1	1	0	5	0
Andy Sheets, 3b	.333	2	3	0	1	0	0	0	0	0	2	0
Heathcliff Slocumb, p	.000	2	0	0	0	0	0	0	0	0	0	0
Paul Sorrento, 1b	.300	4	10	2	3	1	0	1	1	2	3	0
Paul Spoljaric, p	.000	2	0	0	0	0	0	0	0	0	0	0
Mike Timlin, p	.000	1	0	0	0	0	0	0	0	0	0	0
Bob Wells, p	.000	1	0	0	0	0	0	0	0	0	0	0
Rick Wilkins, c	.000	1	1	0	0	0	0	0	0	0	1	0
Dan Wilson, c	.000	4	13	0	0	0	0	0	0	0	9	0
TOTAL	.218		133	11	29	5	0	6	11	7	42	2

PITCHER	W	L	ERA	G	GS	CG	SV	SHO	IP	H	ER	BB	SO
Bobby Ayala	0	0	40.50	1	0	0	0	0	1.1	4	6	1	3
Norm Charlton	0	0	0.00	2	0	0	0	0	2.1	2	0	0	1
Jeff Fassero	1	0	1.13	1	1	0	0	0	8.0	3	1	4	3
Randy Johnson	0	2	5.54	2	2	1	0	0	13.0	14	8	6	16
Jamie Moyer	0	1	5.79	1	1	0	0	0	4.2	5	3	1	2
Heathcliff Slocumb	0	0	4.50	2	0	0	0	0	2.0	3	1	1	0
Paul Spoljaric	0	0	0.00	2	0	0	0	0	1.2	4	0	0	1
Mike Timlin	0	0	54.00	1	0	0	0	0	0.2	3	4	1	1
Bob Wells	0	0	0.00	1	0	0	0	0	1.1	1	0	0	1
TOTAL	1	3	5.91	13	4	1	0	0	35.0	39	23	14	28

GAME 1 AT SEA OCT 1

BAL	001 044 000	9 13 0
SEA	000 100 101	3 7 1

Pitchers: MUSSINA, Orosco (8), Benitez (9) vs JOHNSON, Timlin (6), Spoljaric (6), Wells (7), Charlton (8)

Home Runs: Martinez-SEA, Berroa-BAL, Hoiles-BAL, Buhner-SEA, Rodriguez-SEA

Attendance: 59,579

GAME 2 AT SEA OCT 2

BAL	010 020 240	9 14 0
SEA	200 000 100	3 9 0

Pitchers: ERICKSON, Benitez (7), Orosco (8), Myers (9) vs MOYER, Spoljaric (5), Ayala (7), Charlton (8), Slocumb (9)

Home Runs: Baines-BAL, Anderson-BAL

Attendance: 59,309

GAME 3 AT BAL OCT 4

SEA	001 010 002	4 11 0
BAL	000 000 002	2 5 0

Pitchers: FASSERO, Slocumb (9) vs KEY, Mills (5), Rhodes (6), Mathews (9)

Home Runs: Buhner-SEA, Sorrento-SEA

Attendance: 49,137

GAME 4 AT BAL OCT 5

SEA	010 000 000	1 2 0
BAL	200 010 00X	3 7 0

Pitchers: JOHNSON vs MUSSINA, Benitez (8), Myers (9)

Home Runs: Reboulet-BAL, Martinez-SEA, Berroa-BAL

Attendance: 48,766

The Marlins didn't even exist the last time Jim Leyland led a team to the NLCS against the Braves; since then Atlanta had become the first team in history to win six straight division titles (minus the 1994 strike season). Leyland watched as his Pirates lost to the Braves in the bottom of the ninth in Game 7 of the 1992 NLCS in Fulton County Stadium, but now he was with a different team; the Braves had a different stadium (Turner Field), and the results were different, too.

The fifth-year Marlins struck for five unearned runs off Greg Maddux in the opener, and Kevin Brown and three relievers made it hold up. Charles Johnson, who was the first catcher in major league history to go through an entire season without an error, threw a ball into center field on a stolen base attempt by Kenny Lofton in the first inning of Game 2. Keith Lockhart tripled Lofton home and Ryan Klesko hit his second home run in as many nights. Lockhart singled in the third inning and Chipper Jones followed with his second home run in two games. Alex Fernandez left after two and two thirds innings; it was later revealed that he had a torn rotator cuff and would not pitch for a year.

Fernandez's replacement, Livan Hernandez, made his first appearance of the series in relief in Game 3 in Florida and picked up the win. This time poor defense and bad baserunning cost Atlanta. After Chipper Jones got caught in a rundown at second base with the bases loaded in the top of the sixth inning, Andruw Jones misplayed a flyball in right to tie the game. Johnson, who was hitless in 10 career at bats against John Smoltz, doubled in three runs and chased him from the game. Denny Neagle was masterful for the Braves in Game 4, pitching the first complete game in the NLCS since 1992. Series MVP Hernandez followed with an even more remarkable performance with 15 strikeouts, tying an LCS record set the day before by Baltimore's Mike Mussina in Cleveland. Maddux again pitched in bad luck. He allowed just four hits, but Jeff Conine's single in the seventh drove in Bobby Bonilla with the deciding run.

The Braves, who complained about umpire Eric Gregg's liberal strike zone in Game 5, could only complain about their inability to get timely hits in Game 6. The Marlins batted around and scored four runs in the first inning off Tom Glavine, but the Braves cut the lead to 4-3 by the second inning. Brown, whose start was pushed back three days because of a stomach virus, talked Leyland out of removing him after the sixth inning. He remained in the contest despite a two-out Braves rally in the ninth inning that brought the tying run to the plate. Chipper Jones grounded a ball up the middle but Craig Counsell went behind second base and flipped to Edgar Renteria for the force play to give the Marlins the pennant exactly five years after the Braves had rallied in the ninth to take the flag away from Leyland's Pirates.

Florida Marlins (WC), 4; Atlanta Braves (E), 2

FLA (E)

PLAYER/POS	AVG	G	AB	R	H	2B	3B	HR	RB	BB	SO	SB
Kurt Abbott, 2b	.375	2	8	0	3	1	0	0	0	0	2	0
Moises Alou, of-4	.067	5	15	0	1	1	0	0	5	1	3	0
Alex Arias, 3b-2	1.000	3	1	0	1	0	0	0	0	0	0	0
Bobby Bonilla, 3b	.261	6	23	3	6	1	0	0	4	1	6	0
Kevin Brown, p	.000	2	6	0	0	0	0	0	0	0	3	0
John Cangelosi, of-1	.200	3	5	0	1	0	0	0	0	1	0	0
Jeff Conine, 1b	.111	6	18	1	2	0	0	0	1	1	4	0
Dennis Cook, p	.000	2	0	0	0	0	0	0	0	0	0	0
Craig Counsell, 2b-4	.429	5	14	0	6	0	0	0	2	3	3	0
Darren Daulton, 1b-2	.250	3	4	1	1	1	0	0	1	1	2	0
Jim Eisenreich, of	.000	1	3	0	0	0	0	0	0	0	0	0
Alex Fernandez, p	.000	1	1	0	0	0	0	0	0	0	1	0
Felix Heredia, p	.000	2	0	0	0	0	0	0	0	0	0	0
Livan Hernandez, p	.000	2	3	0	0	0	0	0	0	0	1	0
Charles Johnson, c	.118	6	17	1	2	2	0	0	5	3	8	0
Al Leiter, p	.000	2	1	0	0	0	0	0	0	0	1	0
Robb Nen, p	.000	2	0	0	0	0	0	0	0	0	0	0
Jay Powell, p	.000	1	0	0	0	0	0	0	0	0	0	0
Edgar Renteria, ss	.227	6	22	4	5	1	0	0	0	3	6	1
Tony Saunders, p	.000	1	2	0	0	0	0	0	0	0	2	0
Gary Sheffield, of	.235	6	17	6	4	0	0	1	1	7	3	0
Ed Vosberg, p	.000	2	0	0	0	0	0	0	0	0	0	0
Devon White, of	.190	6	21	4	4	1	0	0	1	2	7	1
Greg Zaun, c	.000	1	0	0	0	0	0	0	0	0	0	0
TOTAL	.199		181	20	36	8	0	1	20	23	52	2

PITCHER	W	L	ERA	G	GS	CG	SV	SHO	IP	H	ER	BB	SO
Kevin Brown	2	0	4.20	2	2	1	0	0	15.0	16	7	5	11
Dennis Cook	0	0	0.00	2	0	0	0	0	2.1	0	0	0	2
Alex Fernandez	0	1	16.88	1	1	0	0	0	2.2	6	5	1	3
Felix Heredia	0	0	5.40	2	0	0	0	0	3.1	3	2	2	4
Livan Hernandez	2	0	0.84	2	1	1	0	0	10.2	5	1	2	16
Al Leiter	0	1	4.32	2	1	0	0	0	8.1	13	4	2	6
Robb Nen	0	0	0.00	2	0	0	2	0	2.0	0	0	0	1
Jay Powell	0	0	0.00	1	0	0	0	0	0.2	0	0	0	0
Tony Saunders	0	0	3.38	1	1	0	0	0	5.1	4	2	3	3
Ed Vosberg	0	0	0.00	2	0	0	0	0	2.2	2	0	1	3
TOTAL	4	2	3.57	17	6	2	2	0	53.0	49	21	16	49

ATL (E)

PLAYER/POS	AVG	G	AB	R	H	2B	3B	HR	RB	BB	SO	SB
Danny Bautista, of	.250	2	4	0	1	0	0	0	0	0	0	0
Jeff Blauser, ss	.300	6	20	5	6	0	0	1	1	3	6	0
Mike Cather, p	.000	4	0	0	0	0	0	0	0	0	0	0
Greg Colbrunn, ph	.667	3	3	0	2	0	0	0	0	0	0	0
Alan Embree, p	.000	1	0	0	0	0	0	0	0	0	0	0
Tom Glavine, p	.333	2	3	0	1	0	0	0	0	0	2	0
Tony Graffanino, 2b	.250	3	8	1	2	1	0	0	0	0	3	0
Tommy Gregg, ph	.000	4	4	0	0	0	0	0	0	0	1	0
Andruw Jones, of	.444	5	9	0	4	0	0	0	1	1	1	0
Chipper Jones, 3b	.292	6	24	5	7	1	0	2	4	2	3	0
Ryan Klesko, of	.235	5	17	2	4	0	0	2	4	2	3	0
Kerry Ligtenberg, p	.000	2	0	0	0	0	0	0	0	0	0	0
Keith Lockhart, 2b	.500	5	16	4	8	1	1	0	3	1	1	0
Kenny Lofton, of	.185	6	27	3	5	0	1	0	1	1	7	1
Javy Lopez, c	.059	5	17	0	1	1	0	0	2	1	7	0
Greg Maddux, p	.000	2	3	0	0	0	0	0	0	0	2	0
Fred McGriff, 1b	.333	6	21	0	7	1	0	0	4	2	7	0
Denny Neagle, p	.000	2	3	0	0	0	0	0	0	0	1	0
Eddie Perez, c	.000	2	3	0	0	0	0	0	0	0	0	0
John Smoltz, p	.000	1	2	0	0	0	0	0	0	0	0	0
Michael Tucker, of-4	.100	5	10	1	1	0	0	1	1	3	4	0
Mark Wohlers, p	.000	2	0	0	0	0	0	0	0	0	0	0
TOTAL	.253		194	21	49	5	2	6	21	16	49	1

PITCHER	W	L	ERA	G	GS	CG	SV	SHO	IP	H	ER	BB	SO
Mike Cather	0	0	0.00	4	0	0	0	0	2.2	3	0	0	3
Alan Embree	0	0	0.00	1	0	0	0	0	1.0	0	0	1	1
Tom Glavine	1	1	5.40	2	2	0	0	0	13.1	13	8	11	9
Kerry Ligtenberg	0	0	0.00	2	0	0	0	0	3.0	1	0	4	4
Greg Maddux	0	2	1.38	2	2	0	0	0	13.0	9	2	4	16
Denny Neagle	1	0	0.00	2	1	1	0	0	12.0	5	0	1	9
John Smoltz	0	1	7.50	1	1	0	0	0	6.0	5	5	5	9
Mark Wohlers	0	0	0.00	1	0	0	0	0	1.0	0	0	1	1
TOTAL	2	4	2.60	15	6	1	0	0	52.0	36	15	23	52

GAME 1 AT ATL OCT 7

FLA 302 000 000   5 6 0
ATL 101 001 000   3 5 2

PITCHERS: BROWN, Cook (7), Powell (8), Nen(9) vs MADDUX, Neagle (7)
HOME RUNS: C.Jones-ATL, Klesko-ATL
ATTENDANCE: 49,244

GAME 2 AT ATL OCT 8

FLA 000 000 010   1 3 1
ATL 302 000 20X   7 13 0

PITCHERS: FERNANDEZ, Leiter (3), Heredia (6), Vosberg (8) vs GLAVINE, Cather (8), Wohlers (9)
HOME RUNS: Klesko-ATL, C.Jones-ATL
ATTENDANCE: 48,933

GAME 3 AT FLA OCT 10

ATL 000 101 000   2 6 1
FLA 000 104 00X   5 8 1

PITCHERS: SMOLTZ, Cather (7), Ligtenberg (8) vs Saunders, HERNANDEZ (6), Cook (8), Nen (9)
HOME RUNS: Sheffield-FLA
ATTENDANCE: 53,857

GAME 4 AT FLA OCT 11

ATL 101 020 000   4 11 0
FLA 000 000 000   0 4 0

PITCHERS: NEAGLE vs LEITER, Heredia (7), Vosberg (9)
HOME RUNS: Blauser-ATL
ATTENDANCE: 54,890

GAME 5 AT FLA OCT 12

ATL 010 000 000   1 3 0
FLA 100 000 10X   2 5 0

PITCHERS: MADDUX, Cather (8) vs HERNANDEZ
HOME RUNS: Tucker-ATL
ATTENDANCE: 51,982

GAME 6 AT ATL OCT 14

FLA 400 003 000   7 10 1
ATL 120 000 001   4 11 1

PITCHERS: BROWN vs GLAVINE, Cather (6), Ligtenberg (7), Embree (9)
ATTENDANCE: 50,446

In a series dominated by pitching, Baltimore's starters were brilliant, but it was Cleveland's relief corps that won the day. Brady Anderson, who made a leaping catch at the wall to end the top of the first inning of Game 1, hit Chad Ogea's first pitch for a home run to lead off the bottom of the inning. Scott Erickson tossed a four-hitter for eight innings, and Randy Myers earned the save. The Indians got off to a solid start in Game 2 with a two-run home run by Manny Ramirez, but Cal Ripken matched it with a two-run homer in the second inning. Mike Bordick broke the tie with a two-run single in the sixth inning. Armando Benitez surrendered a three-run home run to ninth-place hitter Marquis Grissom in the eighth inning to even the series.

Game 3 was a bizarre contest played in the twilight of Jacobs Field that haunted batters and fielders alike. Baltimore's Mike Mussina struck out an LCS-record 15 batters, but a run-scoring single by Matt Williams gave Cleveland a 1-0 lead heading into the ninth. With a runner on second and two out, Grissom misplayed a fly ball to allow the tying run to score. The oddest play of the day was the one that finally ended the game in the 12th inning. On a suicide squeeze, Omar Vizquel missed the bunt attempt and catcher Lenny Webster missed the ball. Webster, thinking it was a foul ball, walked after it and ALCS MVP Grissom slid across the plate with the winning run.

A wild pitch resulted in two runs on one play in Game 4, one on a wild pitch by Arthur Rhodes and the second on Webster's throwing error. Rafael Palmiero's single in the top of the ninth tied the game, but Sandy Alomar singled home Ramirez with the winning run in the bottom of the inning. The Orioles kept the series alive with a 4-2 win in Game 5, but the Indians had the tying runs on base left to end the game.

Mussina's performance in Game 6 was actually better than his Game 3 gem, but again the Orioles could not score for him. Charles Nagy was not as sharp for Cleveland, but 14 Baltimore baserunners were stranded. The play of the game was a perfectly-executed rotation play on Roberto Alomar's bunt in the seventh inning with Williams throwing to Vizquel for the out at third. Tony Fernandez, who got the start at second base because his batting practice line drive damaged the thumb of teammate Bip Roberts, homered to right field in the top of the 11th inning. The Indians bullpen earned all four wins in the series.

Cleveland Indians (C), 4;
Baltimore Orioles (E), 2

CLE (C)

PLAYER/POS	AVG	G	AB	R	H	2B	3B	HR	RB	BB	SO	SB
Sandy Alomar, c	.125	6	24	3	3	0	0	1	4	1	3	0
Brian Anderson, p	.000	3	0	0	0	0	0	0	0	0	0	0
Paul Assenmacher, p	.000	5	0	0	0	0	0	0	0	0	0	0
Jeff Branson, dh	.000	1	2	0	0	0	0	0	0	0	2	0
Tony Fernandez, 2b	.357	5	14	1	5	1	0	1	2	1	2	0
Brian Giles, of	.188	6	16	1	3	3	0	0	0	2	6	0
Marquis Grissom, of	.261	6	23	2	6	0	0	1	4	1	9	3
Orel Hershiser, p	.000	1	0	0	0	0	0	0	0	0	0	0
Mike Jackson, p	.000	5	0	0	0	0	0	0	0	0	0	0
Jeff Juden, p	.000	3	0	0	0	0	0	0	0	0	0	0
David Justice, dh	.333	6	21	3	7	1	0	0	0	2	4	0
Jose Mesa, p	.000	4	0	0	0	0	0	0	0	0	0	0
Alvin Morman, p	.000	2	0	0	0	0	0	0	0	0	0	0
Charles Nagy, p	.000	2	0	0	0	0	0	0	0	0	0	0
Chad Ogea, p	.000	2	0	0	0	0	0	0	0	0	0	0
Eric Plunk, p	.000	1	0	0	0	0	0	0	0	0	0	0
Manny Ramirez, of	.286	6	21	3	6	1	0	2	3	5	5	0
Bip Roberts, 2b-4,of-2	.150	5	20	0	3	1	0	0	0	0	8	1
Kevin Seitzer, 1b-3	.000	4	4	0	0	0	0	0	0	1	2	0
Jim Thome, 1b	.071	6	14	3	1	0	0	0	0	5	4	0
Omar Vizquel, ss	.040	6	25	1	1	0	0	0	0	2	10	0
Matt Williams, 3b	.217	6	23	1	5	1	0	0	2	3	7	1
Jaret Wright, p	.000	1	0	0	0	0	0	0	0	0	0	0
TOTAL	.193		207	18	40	8	0	5	15	23	62	5

PITCHER	W	L	ERA	G	GS	CG	SV	SHO	IP	H	ER	BB	SO
Brian Anderson	1	0	1.42	3	0	0	0	0	6.1	1	1	3	7
Paul Assenmacher	1	0	9.00	5	0	0	0	0	2.0	5	2	1	3
Orel Hershiser	0	0	0.00	1	1	0	0	0	7.0	4	0	1	7
Mike Jackson	0	0	0.00	5	0	0	0	0	4.1	1	0	1	7
Jeff Juden	0	0	0.00	3	0	0	0	0	1.0	2	0	2	2
Jose Mesa	1	0	3.38	4	0	0	2	0	5.1	5	2	3	5
Alvin Morman	0	0	0.00	2	0	0	0	0	1.1	0	0	0	1
Charles Nagy	0	0	2.77	2	2	0	0	0	13.0	17	4	5	5
Chad Ogea	0	2	3.21	2	2	0	0	0	14.0	12	5	5	7
Eric Plunk	1	0	0.00	1	0	0	0	0	0.2	1	0	0	0
Jaret Wright	0	0	15.00	1	1	0	0	0	3.0	6	5	2	3
TOTAL	4	2	2.95	29	6	0	2	0	58.0	54	19	23	47

BAL (E)

PLAYER/POS	AVG	G	AB	R	H	2B	3B	HR	RB	BB	SO	SB
Roberto Alomar, 2b	.182	6	22	2	4	0	0	1	2	7	3	0
Brady Anderson, of	.360	6	25	5	9	2	0	2	3	4	4	2
Harold Baines, dh	.353	6	17	1	6	0	0	1	2	2	1	0
Armando Benitez, p	.000	4	0	0	0	0	0	0	0	0	0	0
Geronimo Berroa, of-4,dh-2	.286	6	21	1	6	2	0	0	3	0	3	0
Mike Bordick, ss	.158	6	19	0	3	1	0	0	2	0	6	0
Eric Davis, of-3,dh-3	.154	6	13	1	2	0	0	1	1	1	3	0
Scott Erickson, p	.000	2	0	0	0	0	0	0	0	0	0	0
Jeffrey Hammonds, of-4	.000	5	3	0	0	0	0	0	0	1	2	1
Chris Hoiles, c	.143	4	14	1	2	0	0	0	0	2	5	0
Scott Kamieniecki, p	.000	2	0	0	0	0	0	0	0	0	0	0
Jimmy Key, p	.000	2	0	0	0	0	0	0	0	0	0	0
Alan Mills, p	.000	3	0	0	0	0	0	0	0	0	0	0
Mike Mussina, p	.000	2	0	0	0	0	0	0	0	0	0	0
Randy Myers, p	.000	4	0	0	0	0	0	0	0	0	0	0
Jesse Orosco, p	.000	2	0	0	0	0	0	0	0	0	0	0
Rafael Palmiero, 1b	.280	6	25	3	7	2	0	1	2	0	10	0
Jeff Reboulet, ss	.000	1	2	1	0	0	0	0	0	0	1	0
Arthur Lee Rhodes, p	.000	2	0	0	0	0	0	0	0	0	0	0
Cal Ripken, 3b	.348	6	23	3	8	2	0	1	3	4	6	0
B.J. Surhoff, of-6,1b-1	.200	6	25	1	5	2	0	0	1	2	2	0
Jerome Walton, of	.000	1	0	0	0	0	0	0	0	0	0	0
Lenny Webster, c-3	.222	4	9	0	2	0	0	0	0	0	1	0
TOTAL	.248		218	19	54	11	0	7	19	23	47	3

PITCHER	W	L	ERA	G	GS	CG	SV	SHO	IP	H	ER	BB	SO
Armando Benitez	0	2	12.00	4	0	0	0	0	3.0	3	4	4	6
Scott Erickson	1	0	4.26	2	2	0	0	0	12.2	15	6	1	6
Scott Kamieniecki	1	0	0.00	2	1	0	0	0	8.0	4	0	2	5
Jimmy Key	0	0	2.57	2	1	0	0	0	7.0	5	2	3	7
Alan Mills	0	1	2.70	3	0	0	0	0	3.1	1	1	2	3
Mike Mussina	0	0	0.60	2	2	0	0	0	15.0	4	1	4	25
Randy Myers	0	1	5.06	4	0	0	1	0	5.1	6	3	3	7
Jesse Orosco	0	0	0.00	2	0	0	0	0	1.1	0	0	1	1
Arthur Lee Rhodes	0	0	0.00	2	0	0	0	0	2.1	2	0	3	2
TOTAL	2	4	2.64	23	6	0	1	0	58.0	40	17	23	62

GAME 1 AT BAL OCT 8

CLE	000	000	000	0	4 1
BAL	102	000	00X	3	6 1

Pitchers: OGEA, Anderson (7) vs ERICKSON, Myers (9)
Home Runs: Anderson-BAL, Alomar-BAL
Attendance: 49,029

GAME 2 AT BAL OCT 9

CLE	200	000	030	5	6 3
BAL	020	002	000	4	8 1

Pitchers: Nagy, Morman (6), Juden (6), ASSENMACHER (6), Jackson (8), Mesa (9) vs Key, Kamieneicki (5), BENITEZ (8), Mills (9)
Home Runs: Ramirez-CLE, Ripken-BAL, Grissom-CLE
Attendance: 49,131

GAME 3 AT CLE OCT 11

BAL	000	000	001 000	1	8 1
CLE	000	000	100 001	2	6 0

Pitchers: Mussina, Benitez (8), Orosco (9), Mills (9), Rhodes (10), MYERS (11) vs Hershiser, Assenmacher (8), Jackson (8), Mesa (9), Juden (11), Morman (11), PLUNK (12)
Attendance: 45,047

GAME 4 AT CLE OCT 12

BAL	014	000	101	7	12 2
CLE	020	140	001	8	13 0

Pitchers: Erickson, Rhodes (5), MILLS (7), Orosco (9), Benitez (9) vs Wright, Anderson (4), Juden (7), Assenmacher (7), Jackson (7), MESA (8)
Home Runs: Alomar-CLE, Anderson-BAL, Baines-BAL, Palmiero-BAL, Ramirez-CLE
Attendance: 45,081

GAME 5 AT CLE OCT 13

BAL	002	000	002	4	10 1
CLE	000	000	002	2	8 1

Pitchers: KAMIENIECKI, Key (6), Myers (9) vs OGEA, Assenmacher (9), Jackson (9)
Home Runs: Davis-BAL
Attendance: 45,068

GAME 6 AT BAL OCT 15

CLE	000	000	000	01	1 3 0
BAL	000	000	000	00	0 10 0

Pitchers: Nagy, Assenmacher (8), Jackson (8), ANDERSON (10), Mesa (11) vs Mussina, Myers (9), BENITEZ (11)
Home Runs: Fernandez-CLE
Attendance: 49,075

The Florida Marlins became the first expansion team to win the World Series, after only five seasons of existence. It didn't come without a fight from the Cleveland Indians.

Back-to-back home runs by Moises Alou and Charles Johnson in the fifth inning off Orel Hershiser helped the Marlins to a 7-4 win in Game 1. Florida starter Livan Hernandez didn't make it out of the sixth, but a trio of Marlins relievers finished off the Tribe before the first of four crowds of 67,000-plus in Miami. The home crowd didn't have much to cheer about in Game 2 as Bip Roberts and Sandy Alomar Jr. each drove in two runs and Chad Ogea pitched the Indians to a 6-1 win.

The temperature in Cleveland for Game 3 was 30 degrees lower and the wind blew almost 20 miles per hour harder than in Miami. The biggest change, though, was on the scorebook. The 25 combined runs and 17 walks were just shy of setting World Series marks, but a defensive play by the not-so-slick-fielding Gary Sheffield was as crucial as any hit. The Marlins right fielder, who had five RBIs in the game, leaped to grab Jim Thome's seventh-inning drive at the wall to keep the score tied at 7-7. Cleveland's bullpen and defense collapsed in the ninth, resulting in seven runs. Marlins closer Rob Nen surrendered four runs in the bottom of the ninth, but Florida hung on for the ugly 14-11 win.

The 15-degree wind chill for Game 4 made it the coldest World Series in history, and home runs by Manny Ramirez and Matt Williams made it a long night for the Marlins. Jaret Wright outdistanced Tony Saunders amid snow flurries as the Indians evened the World Series with a 10-3 win. In Game 5 Alou hit his second three-run home run off Orel Hershiser, his third homer of the Series. Hernandez, who would be named Series MVP, pitched into the ninth inning of Florida's 8-7 win. In Game 6 Ogea had two hits, two RBIs, scored a run, and also earned the 4-1 win for the Indians to set the stage for a seventh game.

Starters Al Leiter and Jaret Wright both pitched well, but Game 7 came down to the bullpen. The Indians were within two outs of their first world championship since 1948 when Craig Counsell's sacrifice fly drove in the tying run in the ninth inning off Jose Mesa. Edgar Renteria ended the second-longest seventh game in World Series history with a bases-loaded single over the glove of Indians pitcher Charles Nagy with two outs in the 11th inning. Counsell crossed home plate with the deciding run in Florida's 3-2 win to make the Marlins the first Wild

Florida Marlins (N), 4; Cleveland Indians (A), 3

FLA (N)

PLAYER/POS	AVG	G	AB	R	H	2B	3B	HR	RB	BB	SO	SB
Kurt Abbott, dh-1	.000	3	3	0	0	0	0	0	0	0	1	0
Antonio Alfonseca, p	.000	3	0	0	0	0	0	0	0	0	0	0
Moises Alou, of	.321	7	28	6	9	2	0	3	9	3	6	1
Alex Arias, 3b-1,dh-1	.000	2	1	1	0	0	0	0	0	0	0	0
Bobby Bonilla, 3b	.207	7	29	5	6	1	0	1	3	3	5	0
Kevin Brown, p	.000	2	3	0	0	0	0	0	0	0	1	0
John Cangelosi, ph	.333	3	3	0	1	0	0	0	0	0	2	0
Jeff Conine, 1b	.231	6	13	1	3	0	0	0	2	0	0	0
Dennis Cook, p	.000	3	0	0	0	0	0	0	0	0	0	0
Craig Counsell, 2b	.182	7	22	4	4	1	0	0	2	6	5	1
Darren Daulton, 1b-5,dh-1	.389	7	18	7	7	2	0	1	2	3	0	1
Jim Eisenreich, 1b-2,dh-2	.500	5	8	1	4	0	0	1	3	3	1	0
Cliff Floyd, dh-1	.000	4	2	1	0	0	0	0	0	1	1	0
Felix Heredia, p	.000	4	0	0	0	0	0	0	0	0	0	0
Livan Hernandez, p	.000	2	2	0	0	0	0	0	0	0	0	0
Charles Johnson, c	.357	7	28	4	10	0	0	1	3	1	6	0
Al Leiter, p	.000	2	0	0	0	0	0	0	0	2	0	0
Robb Nen, p	.000	4	0	0	0	0	0	0	0	0	0	0
Jay Powell, p	.000	4	0	0	0	0	0	0	0	0	0	0
Edgar Renteria, ss	.290	7	31	3	9	2	0	0	3	3	5	0
Tony Saunders, p	.000	1	0	0	0	0	0	0	0	0	0	0
Gary Sheffield, of	.292	7	24	4	7	1	0	1	5	8	5	0
Ed Vosberg, p	.000	2	0	0	0	0	0	0	0	0	0	0
Devon White, of	.242	7	33	0	8	3	1	0	2	3	10	1
Greg Zaun, c-1	.000	2	2	0	0	0	0	0	0	0	0	0
TOTAL	.272		250	37	68	12	1	8	34	36	48	4

PITCHER	W	L	ERA	G	GS	CG	SV	SHO	IP	H	ER	BB	SO
Antonio Alfonseca	0	0	0.00	3	0	0	0	0	6.1	6	0	1	5
Kevin Brown	0	2	8.18	2	2	0	0	0	11.0	15	10	5	6
Dennis Cook	1	0	0.00	3	0	0	0	0	3.2	1	0	1	5
Felix Heredia	0	0	0.00	4	0	0	0	0	5.1	2	0	1	5
Livan Hernandez	2	0	5.27	2	2	0	0	0	13.2	15	8	10	7
Al Leiter	0	0	5.06	2	2	0	0	0	10.2	10	6	10	10
Robb Nen	0	0	7.71	4	0	0	2	0	4.2	8	4	2	7
Jay Powell	1	0	7.36	4	0	0	0	0	3.2	5	3	4	2
Tony Saunders	0	1	27.00	1	1	0	0	0	2.0	7	6	3	2
Ed Vosberg	0	0	6.00	2	0	0	0	0	3.0	3	2	3	2
TOTAL	4	3	5.48	27	7	0	2	0	64.0	72	39	40	51

CLE (A)

PLAYER/POS	AVG	G	AB	R	H	2B	3B	HR	RB	BB	SO	SB
Sandy Alomar, c	.367	7	30	5	11	1	0	2	10	2	3	0
Brian Anderson, p	.000	3	0	0	0	0	0	0	0	0	0	0
Paul Assenmacher, p	.000	5	0	0	0	0	0	0	0	0	0	0
Jeff Branson, ph	.000	1	1	0	0	0	0	0	0	0	1	0
Tony Fernandez, 2b	.471	5	17	1	8	1	0	0	4	0	1	0
Brian Giles, of-2	.500	5	4	1	2	1	0	0	2	4	1	0
Marquis Grissom, of	.360	7	25	5	9	1	0	0	2	4	4	0
Orel Hershiser, p	.000	2	2	0	0	0	0	0	0	0	1	0
Mike Jackson, p	.000	4	2	0	0	0	0	0	0	0	1	0
Jeff Juden, p	.000	2	0	0	0	0	0	0	0	0	0	0
David Justice, of-4,dh-3	.185	7	27	4	5	0	0	0	4	6	8	0
Jose Mesa, p	.000	5	0	0	0	0	0	0	0	0	0	0
Alvin Morman, p	.000	2	0	0	0	0	0	0	0	0	0	0
Charles Nagy, p	.000	2	0	0	0	0	0	0	0	0	0	0
Chad Ogea, p	.500	2	4	1	2	1	0	0	2	0	0	0
Eric Plunk, p	.000	3	0	0	0	0	0	0	0	0	0	0
Manny Ramirez, of	.154	7	26	3	4	0	0	2	6	6	5	0
Bip Roberts, 2b-4,of-2	.273	6	22	3	6	4	0	0	4	3	5	0
Kevin Seitzer, 3b	.000	1	1	0	0	0	0	0	0	0	0	0
Jim Thome, 1b	.286	7	28	8	8	0	1	2	4	5	7	0
Omar Vizquel, ss	.233	7	30	5	7	2	0	0	1	3	5	5
Matt Williams, 3b	.385	7	26	8	10	1	0	1	3	7	6	0
Jaret Wright, p	.000	2	2	0	0	0	0	0	0	0	0	0
TOTAL	.291		247	44	72	12	1	7	42	40	51	5

PITCHER	W	L	ERA	G	GS	CG	SV	SHO	IP	H	ER	BB	SO
Brian Anderson	0	0	2.45	3	0	0	1	0	3.2	2	1	0	2
Paul Assenmacher	0	0	0.00	5	0	0	0	0	4.0	5	0	0	6
Orel Hershiser	0	2	11.70	2	2	0	0	0	10.0	15	13	6	5
Mike Jackson	0	0	1.93	4	0	0	0	0	4.2	5	1	3	4
Jeff Juden	0	0	4.50	2	0	0	0	0	2.0	2	1	2	0
Jose Mesa	0	0	5.40	5	0	0	1	0	5.0	10	3	1	5
Alvin Morman	0	0	0.00	2	0	0	0	0	0.1	0	0	2	1
Charles Nagy	0	1	6.43	2	1	0	0	0	7.0	8	5	5	5
Chad Ogea	2	0	1.54	2	2	0	0	0	11.2	11	2	3	5
Eric Plunk	0	1	9.00	3	0	0	0	0	3.0	3	3	4	3
Jaret Wright	1	0	2.92	2	2	0	0	0	12.1	7	4	10	12
TOTAL	3	4	4.66	32	7	0	2	0	63.2	68	33	36	48

Card team to win the World Series. Tony Fernandez drove in both Cleveland runs, but his crucial error prolonged the deciding rally.

GAME 1 AT FLA OCT 18

CLE	100	011	010	4	11 0
FLA	001	420	00X	7	7 1

Pitchers: HERSHISER, Juden (5), Plunk (6), Assenmacher (8) vs HERNANDEZ, Cook (6), Powell (8), Nen (9)
Home Runs: Alou-FLA, Johnson-FLA, Ramirez-CLE, Thome-CLE
Attendance: 67,245

GAME 2 AT FLA OCT 19

CLE	100	032	000	6	14 0
FLA	100	000	000	1	8 0

Pitchers: OGEA, Jackson (7), Mesa (9) vs BROWN, Heredia (7), Alfonseca (8)
Home Runs: Alomar-CLE
Attendance: 67,025

GAME 3 AT CLE OCT 21

FLA	101	102	207	14	16 3
CLE	200	320	004	11	10 3

Pitchers: Leiter (5), COOK (8), Nen (9) vs Nagy, Anderson (7), Jackson (7), Assenmacher (8), PLUBK (8), Morman (9), Mesa (9)
Home Runs: Sheffield-FLA, Daulton-FLA, Thome-CLE, Esienreich-FLA
Attendance: 44,880

GAME 4 AT CLE OCT 22

FLA	000	102	000	3	6 2
CLE	303	001	12X	10	15 0

Pitchers: SAUNDERS, Alfonseca (3), Vosberg (6), Powell (8) vs WRIGHT, Anderson (7)
Home Runs: Ramirez-CLE, Alou-FLA, Williams-CLE
Attendance: 44,877

GAME 5 AT CLE OCT 23

FLA	020	004	011	8	15 2
CLE	013	000	003	7	9 0

Pitchers: HERNANDEZ, Nen (9) vs HERSHISER, Morman (6), Plunk (6), Juden (7), Assenmacher (9), Mesa (9)
Home Runs: Alomar-CLE, Alou-FLA
Attendance: 44,888

GAME 6 AT FLA OCT 25

CLE	020	101	000	4	7 0
FLA	000	010	000	1	8 0

Pitchers: OGEA, Jackson (6), Assenmacher (8), Mesa (9) vs BROWN, Heredia (6), Powell (8), Vosberg (9)
Attendance: 67,498

GAME 7 AT FLA OCT 26

CLE	002	000	000	00	2	6 2
FLA	000	000	101	01	3	8 0

Pitchers: Wright, Assenmacher (7), Jackson (8), Anderson (8), Mesa (9), NAGY (10) vs Leiter, Cook (7), Alfonseca (8), Heredia (9), Nen (9), POWELL (11)
Home Runs: Bonilla-FLA
Attendance: 67,204

The Astros and Padres had both won division titles by comfortable margins, but Houston was given the pre-series edge because they had won more games and held advantages in many offensive and defensive categories. Plus, the Astros had Randy Johnson, the 6-foot-10-inch left-hander obtained from Seattle who went 10-1 with a 1.28 ERA down the stretch. The Astros also had home-field advantage in the Division Series. Yet none of that prepared the Astros for Kevin Brown or Jim Leyritz. Brown struck out 16 and limited Houston to just two hits in eight innings in Game 1; Leyritz, who drove in at least one run in each game of the series, brought in the first run with a sacrifice fly in the sixth inning. Greg Vaughn added a home run off Johnson in the eighth and the Padres held on for the 2-1 win.

The Astros led Game 2 from the first inning as Jeff Bagwell drove in three runs and Derek Bell added a home run to take a 4-2 lead into the top of the ninth. Leyritz, who hit dramatic postseason home runs for the Yankees in 1995 and '96, lofted an opposite-field, two-run home run just inside the right-field foul pole to tie the game. Houston's Ricky Gutierrez stole third base in the bottom of the ninth and then scored when Bill Spiers singled to end the game and tie the series.

With an extra off day on the schedule, Padres manager Bruce Bochy moved Brown up in the rotation to pitch Game 3. Brown lowered his ERA for the series to 0.61 and reliever Dan Miceli came in with the bases loaded in the top of the seventh to strike out Spiers and keep the game tied at 1-1. Leyritz homered off Scott Elarton in the bottom of the seventh as the Padres took a 2-1 lead in the game and the series. The second consecutive crowd of more than 64,000 in San Diego watched Leyritz hit his third home run of the series in Game 4. Padres left-hander Sterling Hitchcock struck out 11 of the 21 batters he faced and earned the win when Sean Berry threw away Ken Caminiti's grounder to bring in the go-ahead run in the sixth. The Padres tacked on four insurance runs in the eighth on a two-run triple by John Vander Wal and a two-run homer by Wally Joyner. Trevor Hoffman, who pitched in all four games, set down the Astros in the ninth inning.

San Diego Padres (W), 3;
Houston Astros (C), 1

SD (W)

PLAYER/POS	AVG	G	AB	R	H	2B	3B	HR	RB	BB	SO	SB
George Arias, ph	.000	1	1	0	0	0	0	0	0	0	1	0
Andy Ashby, p	.000	1	1	0	0	0	0	0	0	0	0	0
Kevin Brown, p	.000	2	3	0	0	0	0	0	0	0	2	0
Ken Caminiti, 3b	.143	4	14	2	2	0	0	0	0	1	3	0
Steve Finley, of	.100	4	10	2	1	1	0	0	1	1	4	0
Chris Gomez, ss	.273	4	11	3	3	0	0	0	0	4	1	0
Tony Gwynn, of	.200	4	15	1	3	2	0	0	2	0	2	0
Joey Hamilton, p	.000	2	0	0	0	0	0	0	0	0	0	0
Carlos Hernandez, c	.417	4	12	0	5	0	0	0	0	0	0	0
Sterling Hitchcock, p	.000	1	2	0	0	0	0	0	0	0	1	0
Trevor Hoffman, p	.000	4	0	0	0	0	0	0	0	0	0	0
Wally Joyner, 1b	.167	4	6	1	1	0	0	1	2	1	2	0
Jim Leyritz, 1b-3,c-1	.400	4	10	3	4	0	0	3	5	2	2	0
Dan Miceli, p	.000	3	0	0	0	0	0	0	0	0	0	0
Greg Myers, c	.000	1	0	0	0	0	0	0	0	0	0	0
Ruben Rivera, of	.000	3	6	0	0	0	0	0	0	0	3	0
Andy Sheets, 2b-1	.000	2	0	0	0	0	0	0	0	0	0	0
Mark Sweeney, ph	.000	2	1	0	0	0	0	0	0	1	0	0
John Vander Wal, ph	.333	3	3	1	1	0	1	0	2	0	1	0
Greg Vaughn, of	.333	4	15	2	5	1	0	1	1	0	4	0
Quilvio Veras, 2b	.133	4	15	1	2	0	0	0	1	6	0
Donne Wall, p	.000	1	0	0	0	0	0	0	0	0	0	0
TOTAL	.216		125	14	27	4	1	5	13	9	32	0

PITCHER	W	L	ERA	G	GS	CG	SV	SHO	IP	H	ER	BB	SO
Andy Ashby	0	0	6.75	1	1	0	0	0	4.0	6	3	1	4
Kevin Brown	1	0	0.61	2	2	0	0	0	14.2	5	1	7	21
Joey Hamilton	0	0	0.00	2	0	0	0	0	3.1	1	0	2	3
Sterling Hitchcock	1	0	1.50	1	1	0	0	0	6.0	3	1	0	11
Trevor Hoffman	0	0	0.00	4	0	0	2	0	3.0	3	0	1	4
Dan Miceli	1	1	2.70	3	0	0	0	0	3.1	2	1	0	4
Donne Wall	0	0	9.00	1	0	0	0	0	1.0	2	1	0	2
TOTAL	3	1	1.78	14	4	0	2	0	35.1	22	7	11	49

HOU (C)

PLAYER/POS	AVG	G	AB	R	H	2B	3B	HR	RB	BB	SO	SB
Moises Alou, of	.188	4	16	0	3	0	0	0	0	0	2	0
Brad Ausmus, c	.222	4	9	0	2	0	0	0	0	0	4	0
Jeff Bagwell, 1b	.143	4	14	0	2	0	0	0	4	1	6	0
Derek Bell, of	.125	4	16	1	2	0	0	1	1	0	4	0
Sean Berry, 3b	.000	1	2	0	0	0	0	0	0	0	1	0
Craig Biggio, 2b	.182	4	11	3	2	1	0	0	1	4	4	0
Dave Clark, ph	.000	2	0	0	0	0	0	0	0	2	0	0
Scott Elarton, p	.000	1	0	0	0	0	0	0	0	0	0	0
Raul Eusebio, c	.333	1	3	0	1	1	0	0	0	0	2	0
Carl Everett, of-3	.154	4	13	1	2	0	0	0	0	4	0	0
Ricky Gutierrez, ss	.300	4	10	1	3	0	0	0	3	7	1
Mike Hampton, p	.000	1	2	0	0	0	0	0	0	2	0
Doug Henry, p	.000	2	0	0	0	0	0	0	0	0	0
Richard Hidalgo, of	.250	4	4	0	1	0	0	0	0	1	0
Pete Incaviglia, ph	.000	1	1	0	0	0	0	0	0	0	0
Randy Johnson, p	.000	2	4	0	0	0	0	0	0	4	0
Trever Miller, p	.000	1	0	0	0	0	0	0	0	0	0
Jay Powell, p	.000	3	0	0	0	0	0	0	0	0	0
Shane Reynolds, p	.000	1	2	0	0	0	0	0	0	1	0
Bill Spiers, 3b	.286	4	14	2	4	3	0	1	1	3	0
Billy Wagner, p	.000	1	0	0	0	0	0	0	0	0	0
TOTAL	.182		121	8	22	5	0	1	7	11	49	1

PITCHER	W	L	ERA	G	GS	CG	SV	SHO	IP	H	ER	BB	SO
Scott Elarton	0	1	4.50	1	0	0	0	0	2.0	1	1	1	3
Mike Hampton	0	0	1.50	1	1	0	0	0	6.0	2	1	1	2
Doug Henry	0	0	5.40	2	0	0	0	0	1.2	2	1	0	1
Randy Johnson	0	2	1.93	2	2	0	0	0	14.0	12	3	2	17
Trever Miller	0	0	INF	1	0	0	0	0	0.0	0	0	1	0
Jay Powell	0	0	11.57	3	0	0	0	0	2.1	2	3	3	3
Shane Reynolds	0	0	2.57	1	1	0	0	0	7.0	4	2	1	5
Billy Wagner	1	0	18.00	1	0	0	0	0	1.0	4	2	0	1
TOTAL	1	3	3.44	12	4	0	0	0	34.0	27	13	9	32

GAME 1 AT HOU SEPT 29

SD	000 001 010	2 9 1
HOU	000 000 001	1 4 0

Pitchers: BROWN, Hoffman (9) vs JOHNSON, Powell (9), Henry (9)
Home Runs: Vaughn-SD
Attendance: 50,080

GAME 2 AT HOU OCT 1

SD	000 002 002	4 8 1
HOU	102 000 011	5 11 1

Pitchers: Ashby, Hamilton (5), Wall (8), MICELI (9), Hoffman (9) vs Reynolds, Powell (8), WAGNER (9)
Home Runs: Leyritz-SD, Bell-HOU
Attendance: 45,550

GAME 3 AT SD OCT 3

HOU	000 000 100	1 4 0
SD	000 001 10X	2 3 0

Pitchers: Hampton, ELARTON (7) vs Brown, MICELI (7), Hoffman (9)
Home Runs: Leyritz-SD
Attendance: 65,235

GAME 4 AT SD OCT 4

HOU	000 100 000	1 3 1
SD	010 001 04X	6 7 1

Pitchers: JOHNSON, Miller (7), Henry (7), Powell (8) vs HITCHCOCK, Hamilton (7), Miceli (9), Hoffman (9)
Home Runs: Leyritz-SD, Joyner-SD
Attendance: 64,898

The Cubs had just completed a remarkable season that included Sammy Sosa's home run chase with Mark McGwire and a three-way wild card race, while the Braves were just getting ready for business as usual in October. Atlanta, making its seventh consecutive trip to the postseason, was coming off a regular season that included a franchise-best 106 wins. By contrast, the Cubs had won 90 games, and they needed a one-game playoff victory over the Giants to secure a postseason berth for the first time in nine years.

The teams started even in Game 1, but the Braves still had great pitching. John Smoltz, who went 17-3 during the season, handcuffed the Cubs on five hits. Atlanta took the lead on Michael Tucker's home run in the second inning following a two-out error. A grand slam by Ryan Klesko in the seventh put the game out of reach.

Chicago's Kevin Tapani, a 19-game winner, outpitched 20-game winner Tom Glavine in Game 2. Tapani had a four-hit shutout through eight innings, and manager Jim Riggleman, hoping to save an exhausted bullpen, let the right-hander pitch the ninth inning with a 1-0 lead. Javier Lopez homered to left with one out to tie the game. Terry Mulholland relieved in the 10th, but he missed the first base bag on a bunt play to put runners on first and second for Chipper Jones. Jones hit a line drive that landed just inside the left field line to bring in the winning run.

Atlanta's Greg Maddux, who won the first of his four Cy Young Awards as a Cub in 1992, had the task of quieting the raucous crowd at Wrigley Field in Game 3. Maddux outdid Cubs phenom Kerry Wood on the mound and on the basepaths. A superb slide enabled Maddux to stretch a double in the third inning, and, after he crossed to third on a groundout, he scored on a passed ball. In the top of the eighth, Gerald Williams singled in Atlanta's second run, and Eddie Perez lifted a grand slam to left off Rod Beck. Maddux was charged with two runs in the eighth, but Kerry Ligtenberg relieved and finished off the Cubs. Atlanta pitching held Chicago to just three extra-base hits and four runs in the series, while Sosa, who clubbed 66 home runs during the season, was one of six Cubs regulars to bat under .200 in Atlanta's sweep.

Atlanta Braves (E), 3;
Chicago Cubs (C), 0

ATL (E)

PLAYER/POS	AVG	G	AB	R	H	2B	3B	HR	RB	BB	SO	SB
Danny Bautista, of	.500	2	2	0	1	1	0	0	0	0	0	0
Greg Colbrunn, ph	.000	2	2	0	0	0	0	0	0	0	0	0
Andres Galarraga, 1b	.250	3	12	1	3	0	0	0	0	1	3	0
Tom Glavine, p	.000	1	1	0	0	0	0	0	0	0	0	0
Tony Graffanino, ph	.000	1	0	0	0	0	0	0	0	0	0	0
Ozzie Guillen, ph	.000	1	0	0	0	0	0	0	0	0	0	0
Andruw Jones, of	.000	3	9	2	0	0	0	0	1	3	2	2
Chipper Jones, 3b	.200	2	10	2	2	0	0	0	1	4	3	0
Ryan Klesko, of	.273	3	11	1	3	0	0	1	4	0	3	0
Kerry Ligtenberg, p	.000	3	0	0	0	0	0	0	0	0	0	0
Keith Lockhart, 2b	.333	3	12	2	4	0	0	0	0	1	0	0
Javy Lopez, c	.286	2	7	1	2	0	0	1	1	1	1	0
Greg Maddux, p	.250	1	4	1	1	1	0	0	0	0	1	0
Eddie Perez, c	.200	1	5	1	1	0	0	1	4	0	2	0
Odaliz Perez, p	.000	1	0	0	0	0	0	0	0	0	0	0
John Rocker, p	.000	2	0	0	0	0	0	0	0	0	0	0
Rudy Seanez, p	.000	1	0	0	0	0	0	0	0	0	0	0
John Smoltz, p	.500	1	2	0	1	0	0	0	0	1	1	0
Michael Tucker, of	.250	3	8	1	2	0	0	1	2	2	0	1
Walt Weiss, ss	.154	3	13	2	2	0	0	0	0	1	3	0
Gerald Williams, of	.500	2	2	1	1	0	0	0	1	0	1	0
TOTAL	.228		101	15	23	2	0	4	14	14	20	3

PITCHER	W	L	ERA	G	GS	CG	SV	SHO	IP	H	ER	BB	SO
Tom Glavine	0	0	1.29	1	1	0	0	0	7.0	3	1	1	8
Kerry Ligtenberg	0	0	0.00	3	0	0	0	0	3.1	1	0	4	3
Greg Maddux	1	0	2.57	1	1	0	0	0	7.0	7	2	0	4
Odaliz Perez	1	0	0.00	1	0	0	0	0	0.2	0	0	0	1
John Rocker	0	0	0.00	2	0	0	0	0	1.1	1	0	0	2
Rudy Seanez	0	0	0.00	1	0	0	0	0	1.0	0	0	0	0
John Smoltz	1	0	1.17	1	1	0	0	0	7.2	5	1	0	6
TOTAL	3	0	1.29	10	3	0	0	0	28.0	17	4	5	24

CHI (C)

PLAYER/POS	AVG	G	AB	R	H	2B	3B	HR	RB	BB	SO	SB
Manny Alexander, ss-1	.000	2	5	0	0	0	0	0	0	0	1	0
Rod Beck, p	.000	1	0	0	0	0	0	0	0	0	0	0
Jeff Blauser, ph	.000	2	2	0	0	0	0	0	0	0	1	0
Brant Brown, ph	.000	1	1	0	0	0	0	0	0	0	0	0
Mark Clark, p	.500	1	2	0	1	0	0	0	0	0	0	0
Gary Gaetti, 3b	.091	3	11	0	1	0	0	0	0	0	4	0
Mark Grace, 1b	.083	3	12	0	1	0	0	0	0	1	2	0
Felix Heredia, p	.000	1	0	0	0	0	0	0	0	0	0	0
Jose Hernandez, ss	.286	2	7	1	2	0	0	0	0	0	2	0
Glenallen Hill, of	.333	1	3	0	1	0	0	0	0	1	2	1
Tyler Houston, c	.167	3	6	1	1	0	0	1	1	0	3	0
Lance Johnson, of	.167	3	12	0	2	0	0	0	0	1	1	0
Matt Karchner, p	.000	1	0	0	0	0	0	0	0	0	0	0
Angel Martinez, c	1.000	1	1	1	1	0	0	0	0	0	0	0
Mickey Morandini, 2b	.222	3	9	1	2	0	0	0	1	2	2	0
Mike Morgan, p	.000	2	0	0	0	0	0	0	0	0	0	0
Terry Mulholland, p	.000	2	0	0	0	0	0	0	0	0	0	0
Henry Rodriguez, of-2	.143	3	7	0	1	1	0	0	0	1	2	0
Scott Servais, c	.667	1	3	0	2	0	0	0	0	0	0	0
Sammy Sosa, of	.182	3	11	0	2	1	0	0	0	1	4	0
Kevin Tapani, p	.000	1	1	0	0	0	0	0	0	0	0	0
Kerry Wood, p	.000	1	1	0	0	0	0	0	0	0	0	0
TOTAL	.181		94	4	17	2	0	1	4	5	24	1

PITCHER	W	L	ERA	G	GS	CG	SV	SHO	IP	H	ER	BB	SO
Rod Beck	0	0	16.20	1	0	0	0	0	1.2	5	3	2	1
Mark Clark	0	1	3.00	1	1	0	0	0	6.0	7	2	1	4
Felix Heredia	0	0	54.00	1	0	0	0	0	0.1	2	2	0	0
Matt Karchner	0	0	13.50	1	0	0	0	0	0.2	1	1	0	1
Mike Morgan	0	0	0.00	2	0	0	0	0	1.1	0	0	0	1
Terry Mulholland	0	1	11.57	2	0	0	0	0	2.1	2	3	2	2
Kevin Tapani	0	0	1.00	1	1	0	0	0	9.0	5	1	3	8
Kerry Wood	0	1	1.80	1	1	0	0	0	5.0	3	1	4	5
TOTAL	0	3	4.44	10	3	0	0	0	26.1	23	13	14	20

GAME 1 AT ATL SEPT 30

CHI	000	000	010	1	5 1
ATL	020	001	40X	7	8 0

Pitchers: CLARK, Heredia (7), Karchner (7), Morgan (8) vs SMOLTZ, Rocker (8), Ligtenberg (9)
Home Runs: Tucker-ATL, Klesko-ATL, Houston-CHI
Attendance: 45,598

GAME 2 AT ATL OCT 1

CHI	000	001	000	0	1 4 1
ATL	000	000	001	1	2 6 0

Pitchers: Tapani, MULHOLLAND (10) vs Glavine, Rocker (8), Seanez (9), Ligtenberg (10), O.PEREZ (10)
Home Runs: Lopez-ATL
Attendance: 51,713

GAME 3 AT CHI OCT 3

ATL	001	000	050	6 9 0
CHI	000	000	020	2 8 2

Pitchers: MADDUX, Ligtenberg (8) vs WOOD, Mulholland (6), Beck (8), Morgan (9)
Home Runs: E.Perez-ATL
Attendance: 39,597

The Boston Red Sox had to go back to Game 5 of the 1986 World Series for the team's last post-season win, but they broke out of their postseason slump in a big way. Their string of 13 straight postseason losses (two World Series games, eight Championship Series games, and three Division Series games) ended quickly against the Indians in the opening game of the 1998 Division Series. Mo Vaughn launched a home run to left field with two men on in the first inning, then homered again with a runner on in the sixth, before he capped the day with a two-run double in the eighth. Nomar Garciaparra added a home run and a sacrifice fly as the two Boston sluggers drove in each run of their team's 11-3 win. For the series, the pair combined for 19 runs batted in, while the rest of the team drove in just one run.

The Red Sox jumped out to a quick 2-0 lead in the first inning of Game 2 as both Cleveland manager Mike Hargrove and starting pitcher Dwight Gooden were ejected after separate arguments with umpire Joe Brinkman. The Indians were a new team after that. They chased Boston starter Tim Wakefield in a five-run second inning, Dave Burba pitched five and a third innings of relief for the win, and Mike Jackson tossed the final two innings to even the series. In the third game the Indians managed just five hits, but four of those were solo home runs as Cleveland held on for a 4-3 win in Boston. The home run that wound up being the most important was Manny Ramirez's second of the game in the top of the ninth. Garciaparra's two-run home run in the bottom of the ninth cut the lead to 4-3, but two groundouts ended the game.

Both the fans and the press alike were critical of Boston manager Jimy Williams for not starting his ace, Pedro Martinez, on three day's rest in Game 4. Martinez, who won Game 1, watched as Pete Schourek pitched five and a third innings and left with a 1-0 lead supplied by Garciaparra's third home run of the series. Boston closer Tom Gordon had not blown a save since April 14, but he surrendered the lead in the eighth inning on a two-run double by left fielder David Justice, who had also thrown out John Valentin at the plate in the sixth inning. Jackson earned his third save in as many games as the Indians defeated the Red Sox in the postseason for the second time in three years.

Cleveland Indians (C), 3;
Boston Red Sox (E), 1

CLE (C)

PLAYER/POS	AVG	G	AB	R	H	2B	3B	HR	RB	BB	SO	SB
Sandy Alomar, c	.231	4	13	2	3	3	0	0	2	1	4	0
Paul Assenmacher, p	.000	3	0	0	0	0	0	0	0	0	0	0
Dave Burba, p	.000	1	0	0	0	0	0	0	0	0	0	0
Bartolo Colon, p	.000	1	0	0	0	0	0	0	0	0	0	0
Joey Cora, 2b	.000	4	10	2	0	0	0	0	0	3	2	0
Travis Fryman, 3b	.154	4	13	1	2	1	0	0	0	3	4	1
Brian Giles, of-2,dh-1	.200	3	10	1	2	1	0	0	0	1	4	0
Dwight Gooden, p	.000	1	0	0	0	0	0	0	0	0	0	0
Mike Jackson, p	.000	3	0	0	0	0	0	0	0	0	0	0
Doug Jones, p	.000	1	0	0	0	0	0	0	0	0	0	0
David Justice, of-2,dh-2	.313	4	16	2	5	4	0	1	6	0	1	0
Kenny Lofton, of	.375	4	16	5	6	1	0	2	4	1	1	2
Charles Nagy, p	.000	1	0	0	0	0	0	0	0	0	0	0
Jim Poole, p	.000	2	0	0	0	0	0	0	0	0	0	0
Manny Ramirez, of	.357	4	14	2	5	2	0	2	3	1	4	0
Steve Reed, p	.000	2	0	0	0	0	0	0	0	0	0	0
Richie Sexson, 1b	.000	3	2	0	0	0	0	0	0	2	1	0
Paul Shuey, p	.000	3	0	0	0	0	0	0	0	0	0	0
Jim Thome, 1b-3,dh-1	.133	4	15	2	2	0	0	2	2	2	5	0
Omar Vizquel, ss	.067	4	15	1	1	0	0	0	0	1	0	0
Enrique Wilson, 2b	.000	1	2	0	0	0	0	0	0	0	0	0
Jaret Wright, p	.000	1	0	0	0	0	0	0	0	0	0	0
TOTAL	.206		126	18	26	12	0	7	17	15	26	3

PITCHER	W	L	ERA	G	GS	CG	SV	SHO	IP	H	ER	BB	SO
Paul Assenmacher	0	0	0.00	3	0	0	0	0	1.0	2	0	0	2
Dave Burba	1	0	5.06	1	0	0	0	0	5.1	4	3	2	4
Bartolo Colon	0	0	1.59	1	1	0	0	0	5.2	5	1	3	3
Dwight Gooden	0	0	54.00	1	1	0	0	0	0.1	1	2	2	1
Mike Jackson	0	0	4.50	3	0	0	3	0	4.0	3	2	1	1
Doug Jones	0	0	6.75	1	0	0	0	0	2.2	3	2	1	1
Charles Nagy	1	0	1.13	1	1	0	0	0	8.0	4	1	0	3
Jim Poole	0	0	0.00	2	0	0	0	0	1.0	1	0	1	2
Steve Reed	1	0	40.50	1	0	0	0	0	0.2	1	3	1	1
Paul Shuey	0	0	0.00	3	0	0	0	0	3.0	3	0	1	4
Jaret Wright	0	1	12.46	1	1	0	0	0	4.1	7	6	2	6
TOTAL	3	1	5.00	19	4	0	3	0	36.0	34	20	14	28

BOS (E)

PLAYER/POS	AVG	G	AB	R	H	2B	3B	HR	RB	BB	SO	SB
Mike Benjamin, 2b-4,1b-1	.091	4	11	1	1	0	0	0	0	1	3	0
Darren Bragg, of	.083	3	12	0	1	0	0	0	0	0	5	0
Damon Buford, of-1,dh-1	.000	3	1	2	0	0	0	0	0	0	0	0
Jim Corsi, p	.000	2	0	0	0	0	0	0	0	0	0	0
Midre Cummings, ph	.000	3	3	0	0	0	0	0	0	0	0	0
Dennis Eckersley, p	.000	1	0	0	0	0	0	0	0	0	0	0
Nomar Garciaparra, ss	.333	4	15	4	5	1	0	3	11	1	0	0
Tom Gordon, p	.000	2	0	0	0	0	0	0	0	0	0	0
Scott Hatteberg, c	.111	3	9	0	1	0	0	0	0	3	1	0
Darren Lewis, of	.357	4	14	4	5	2	0	0	0	1	3	1
Derek Lowe, p	.000	2	0	0	0	0	0	0	0	0	0	0
Pedro Martinez, p	.000	1	0	0	0	0	0	0	0	0	0	0
Trot Nixon, of	.333	2	3	0	1	0	0	0	0	1	0	0
Troy O'Leary, of	.063	4	16	0	1	0	0	0	0	1	4	0
Bret Saberhagen, p	.000	1	0	0	0	0	0	0	0	0	0	0
Donnie Sadler, 2b	.000	3	0	0	0	0	0	0	0	0	0	0
Pete Schourek, p	.000	1	0	0	0	0	0	0	0	0	0	0
Mike Stanley, dh	.267	4	15	1	4	0	0	0	2	5	0	0
Greg Swindell, p	.000	1	0	0	0	0	0	0	0	0	0	0
John Valentin, 3b	.467	4	15	5	7	1	0	0	0	3	1	0
Jason Varitek, c	.250	4	4	0	1	0	0	0	0	1	0	1
Mo Vaughn, 1b	.412	4	17	3	7	2	0	2	7	1	5	0
Tim Wakefield, p	.000	1	0	0	0	0	0	0	0	0	0	0
John Wasdin, p	.000	1	0	0	0	0	0	0	0	0	0	0
TOTAL	.252		135	20	34	6	0	5	19	14	28	1

PITCHER	W	L	ERA	G	GS	CG	SV	SHO	IP	H	ER	BB	SO
Jim Corsi	0	0	0.00	2	0	0	0	0	3.0	1	0	1	2
Dennis Eckersley	0	0	9.00	1	0	0	0	0	1.0	1	1	0	1
Tom Gordon	0	1	9.00	2	0	0	0	0	3.0	4	3	4	1
Derek Lowe	0	0	2.08	2	0	0	0	0	4.1	3	1	1	2
Pedro Martinez	1	0	3.86	1	1	0	0	0	7.0	6	3	0	8
Bret Saberhagen	0	1	3.86	1	1	0	0	0	7.0	4	3	1	7
Pete Schourek	0	0	0.00	1	1	0	0	0	5.1	2	0	4	1
Greg Swindell	0	0	0.00	1	0	0	0	0	1.1	0	0	1	1
Tim Wakefield	0	1	33.75	1	1	0	0	0	1.1	3	5	2	1
John Wasdin	0	0	10.80	1	0	0	0	0	1.2	2	2	1	2
TOTAL	1	3	4.63	13	4	0	0	0	35.0	26	18	15	26

GAME 1 AT CLE SEPT 29

BOS	300 032 030	11	12	0
CLE	000 002 100	3	7	0

Pitchers: MARTINEZ, Corsi (8) vs WRIGHT, Jones (5), Reed (8), Assenmacher (8), Poole (8), Shuey (8), Assenmacher (9)
Home Runs: Vaughn-BOS (2), Garciaparra-BOS, Lofton-CLE, Thome-CLE
Attendance: 45,185

GAME 2 AT CLE SEPT 30

BOS	201 002 000	5	10	0
CLE	151 001 01X	9	9	1

Pitchers: WAKEFIELD, Wasdin (2), Lowe (4), Swindell (6) vs Gooden, BURBA (1), Shuey (6), Assenmacher (8), Jackson (8)
Home Runs: Justice-CLE
Attendance: 45,229

GAME 3 AT BOS OCT 2

CLE	000 011 101	4	5	0
BOS	000 100 002	3	6	0

Pitchers: NAGY, Jackson (9) vs SABERHAGEN, Corsi (8), Eckersley (9)
Home Runs: Thome-CLE, Lofton-CLE, Ramirez-CLE (2), Garciaparra-BOS
Attendance: 33,114

GAME 4 AT BOS OCT 3

CLE	000 000 020	2	5	0
BOS	000 100 000	1	6	0

Pitchers: Colon, Poole (6), REED (7), Shuey (8), Jackson (8) vs Schourek, Lowe (6), GORDON (8)
Home Runs: Garciaparra-BOS
Attendance: 33,537

Despite an AL-record 114 wins by the Yankees, the Rangers actually batted higher than New York during the regular season (.289 to .288). They were second in the league to New York in runs (965 to 940), but pitching stole the show in the Division Series. The Rangers received three good performances from their starters, but Texas scored just one run in three games and batted a meager .141. David Well set the tone in Game 1 with a five-hitter through eight innings. Texas starter Todd Stottlemyre, son of Yankees pitching coach Mel Stottlemyre, nearly matched Wells with six hits in eight innings, but the two runs the Yankees scratched out in the second inning proved to be his downfall. With one out in the second, Jorge Posada walked and Chad Curtis doubled him to third. Scott Brosius singled in one run and then got in a rundown on an attempted steal of second while Curtis crossed the plate.

Shane Spencer, who hit 10 home runs in just 67 at bats in August and September for the Yankees, homered in the second inning off Rick Helling in Game 2. Spencer singled to start the fourth inning and Brosius followed with a home run. Andy Pettitte rose to the occasion—although he allowed the Rangers' lone run of the series—as he permitted just three hits in seven innings.

Not even a violent lightning storm and torrential rain could save the Rangers in Game 3. The Yankees scored four times in the sixth inning on homers by Paul O'Neill and Spencer before the weather forced a 3-hour, 16-minute delay in Texas. The Yankees, already drained from the news that teammate Darryl Strawberry had been diagnosed with colon cancer, showed no signs of fatigue when Game 3 finally resumed. The Rangers managed just three hits off four New York pitchers as the Yankees beat Texas in the Division Series for the second time in three years.

New York Yankees (E), 3; Texas Rangers (W), 0

NY (E)

PLAYER/POS	AVG	G	AB	R	H	2B	3B	HR	RB	BB	SO	SB
Scott Brosius, 3b	.400	3	10	1	4	0	0	1	3	0	3	0
Homer Bush, dh	.000	1	0	0	0	0	0	0	0	0	0	1
David Cone, p	.000	1	0	0	0	0	0	0	0	0	0	0
Chad Curtis, of	.667	3	3	1	2	1	0	0	0	1	1	1
Chili Davis, dh	.167	2	6	0	1	0	0	0	0	0	2	0
Joe Girardi, c	.429	2	7	0	3	0	0	0	0	0	1	0
Derek Jeter, ss	.111	3	9	0	1	0	0	0	0	2	2	0
Chuck Knoblauch, 2b	.091	3	11	0	1	0	0	0	0	0	4	0
Graeme Lloyd, p	.000	1	0	0	0	0	0	0	0	0	0	0
Tino Martinez, 1b	.273	3	11	1	3	2	0	0	0	0	2	0
Jeff Nelson, p	.000	2	0	0	0	0	0	0	0	0	0	0
Paul O'Neill, of	.364	3	11	1	4	2	0	1	1	1	1	0
Andy Pettitte, p	.000	1	0	0	0	0	0	0	0	0	0	0
Jorge Posada, c	.000	1	2	1	0	0	0	0	0	1	2	0
Tim Raines, dh-1	.250	2	4	1	1	0	0	0	0	1	1	0
Mariano Rivera, p	.000	3	0	0	0	0	0	0	0	0	0	0
Shane Spencer, of	.500	2	6	3	3	0	0	2	4	0	1	0
David Wells, p	.000	1	0	0	0	0	0	0	0	0	0	0
Bernie Williams, of	.000	3	11	0	0	0	0	0	0	1	4	0
TOTAL	.253		91	9	23	6	0	4	8	7	24	2

PITCHER	W	L	ERA	G	GS	CG	SV	SHO	IP	H	ER	BB	SO
David Cone	1	0	0.00	1	1	0	0	0	5.2	2	0	1	6
Graeme Lloyd	0	0	0.00	1	0	0	0	0	0.1	0	0	0	0
Jeff Nelson	0	0	0.00	2	0	0	0	0	2.2	2	0	1	2
Andy Pettitte	1	0	1.29	1	1	0	0	0	7.0	3	1	0	8
Mariano Rivera	0	0	0.00	3	0	0	2	0	3.1	1	0	1	2
David Wells	1	0	0.00	1	1	0	0	0	8.0	5	0	1	9
TOTAL	3	0	0.33	9	3	0	2	0	27.0	13	1	4	27

TEX (W)

PLAYER/POS	AVG	G	AB	R	H	2B	3B	HR	RB	BB	SO	SB
Luis Alicea, ph	.000	1	1	0	0	0	0	0	0	0	0	0
Will Clark, 1b	.091	3	11	0	1	0	0	0	0	1	2	0
Royce Clayton, ss	.222	3	9	0	2	0	0	0	0	0	4	0
Tim Crabtree, p	.000	2	0	0	0	0	0	0	0	0	0	0
Juan Gonzalez, of	.083	3	12	1	1	1	0	0	0	0	3	0
Tom Goodwin, of	.250	2	4	0	1	0	0	0	0	0	1	0
Rusty Greer, of	.091	3	11	0	1	0	0	0	0	1	2	0
Rick Helling, p	.000	1	0	0	0	0	0	0	0	0	0	0
Roberto Kelly, of	.143	2	7	0	1	1	0	0	0	0	2	0
Mark McLemore, 2b	.100	3	10	0	1	1	0	0	0	2	3	0
Ivan Rodriguez, c	.100	3	10	0	1	0	0	0	1	0	5	0
Aaron Sele, p	.000	1	0	0	0	0	0	0	0	0	0	0
Mike Simms, dh	.200	2	5	0	1	0	0	0	0	0	2	0
Lee Stevens, dh	.000	1	3	0	0	0	0	0	0	0	1	0
Todd Stottlemyre, p	.000	1	0	0	0	0	0	0	0	0	0	0
John Wetteland, p	.000	1	0	0	0	0	0	0	0	0	0	0
Todd Zeile, 3b	.333	3	9	0	3	0	0	0	0	0	2	0
TOTAL	.141		92	1	13	3	0	0	1	4	27	0

PITCHER	W	L	ERA	G	GS	CG	SV	SHO	IP	H	ER	BB	SO
Tim Crabtree	0	0	0.00	2	0	0	0	0	4.0	1	0	0	2
Rick Helling	0	1	4.50	1	1	0	0	0	6.0	8	3	1	9
Aaron Sele	0	1	6.00	1	1	0	0	0	6.0	8	4	1	4
Todd Stottlemyre	0	1	2.25	1	1	1	0	0	8.0	6	2	4	8
John Wetteland	0	0	0.00	1	0	0	0	0	1.0	0	0	1	1
TOTAL	0	3	3.24	6	3	1	0	0	25.0	23	9	7	24

GAME 1 AT NY   SEPT 29

TEX	000 000 000	0	5	0
NY	020 000 00X	2	6	0

Pitchers: STOTTLEMYRE vs WELLS, Rivera (9)

Attendance: 57,362

GAME 2 AT NY   SEPT 30

TEX	000 010 000	1	5	0
NY	010 200 00X	3	8	0

Pitchers: HELLING, Crabtree (7) vs PETTITTE, Nelson (8), Rivera (8)

Home Runs: Spencer-NY, Brosius-NY

Attendance: 57,360

GAME 3 AT TEX   OCT 2

NY	000 004 000	4	9	1
TEX	000 000 000	0	3	1

Pitchers: CONE, Lloyd (6), Nelson (7), Rivera (9) vs SELE, Crabtree (7), Wetteland (9)

Home Runs: O'Neill-NY, Spencer-NY

Attendance: 49,450

Good pitching and timely hitting sent the Padres to their first World Series in 14 years. The Braves, who were appearing in their seventh consecutive NLCS, missed the World Series after winning 100 games for the third time in five seasons. The first of four errors in the NLCS by normally reliable first baseman Andres Galarraga gave the Padres a 2-1 lead against John Smoltz in the seventh inning of Game 1. But Trevor Hoffman, who had 53 saves during the season, could not hold the lead as Andruw Jones drove in the tying run in the ninth. Ken Caminiti homered in the 10th, and the Padres held on for the 3-2 win. Game 2 was all Kevin Brown. Not only did he pitch a three-hit shutout, he also had two hits and hustled around the bases in the ninth for an important insurance run as the Padres left Atlanta up, two games to none.

The series shifted to the West Coast and the momentum stayed with the Padres. While Sterling Hitchcock labored through five innings, he trailed only 1-0 thanks to John Vander Wal, who started in left field in place of the injured Greg Vaughn. Vander Wal threw out Walt Weiss at the plate to end the third inning. Hitchcock singled to open the bottom of the fifth and he came around to score on Steve Finley's double. Finley then scored on a single by Tony Gwynn. The Braves threatened in the top of the sixth, but Donne Wall came out of the bullpen and struck out pinch-hitters Ryan Klesko and Michael Tucker with three men on—one of three innings in which Atlanta left the bases loaded. The Braves were down, 3-2, in the seventh inning of Game 4 and were looking at the wrong end of a sweep when they finally exploded. Javier Lopez homered off a tiring Joey Hamilton to tie the game, and Galarraga capped the six-run seventh with a grand slam.

The Padres had a 4-2 lead in Game 5 when manager Bruce Bochy brought in his scheduled Game 6 starter, Kevin Brown, to pitch out of a jam in the seventh inning. He retired all three batters that inning, but, in the eighth he surrendered a three-run home run to Michael Tucker, who drove in five runs in the game. Atlanta added two more runs in the inning, which turned out to be crucial when Jim Leyritz hit a two-run homer off Kerry Ligtenberg in the ninth to make it 7-6. Greg Maddux, with four Cy Young Awards but no saves in his 12-year career, got the last three outs. The Braves became the first team in postseason history to force a sixth game after trailing three games to none.

Tom Glavine and Hitchcock were locked in a scoreless pitcher's duel when the Padres bunched six hits for five runs in the sixth inning. The decisive play, however, occurred when left fielder Danny Bautista dropped Hitchcock's sinking line drive allowing two runs to score. Hitchcock, who combined with four relievers for a two-hitter, earned series MVP. The Braves, meanwhile, missed the World Series after winning 100 games for the third time in five seasons.

San Diego Padres (W), 4; Atlanta Braves (E), 2

SD (W)

PLAYER/POS	AVG	G	AB	R	H	2B	3B	HR	RB	BB	SO	SB
Andy Ashby, p	.000	2	4	0	0	0	0	0	0	0	4	0
Brian Boehringer, p	.000	3	0	0	0	0	0	0	0	0	0	0
Kevin Brown, p	.500	2	4	1	2	0	0	0	0	0	1	0
Ken Caminiti, 3b	.273	6	22	3	6	0	0	2	4	5	4	0
Steve Finley, of	.333	6	21	3	7	1	0	0	2	6	2	1
Chris Gomez, ss	.150	6	20	2	3	0	0	0	0	2	5	0
Tony Gwynn, of	.231	6	26	1	6	1	0	0	2	1	2	0
Joey Hamilton, p	.000	2	2	0	0	0	0	0	0	0	1	0
Carlos Hernandez, c	.333	6	18	2	6	2	0	0	0	1	5	0
Sterling Hitchcock, p	.200	2	5	1	1	0	0	0	0	0	0	0
Trevor Hoffman, p	.000	3	0	0	0	0	0	0	0	0	0	0
Wally Joyner, 1b	.313	6	16	3	5	0	0	0	2	4	3	0
Mark Langston, p	.000	3	0	0	0	0	0	0	0	0	0	0
Jim Leyritz, 1b-3,c-2	.167	5	12	1	2	0	0	1	4	0	2	0
Dan Miceli, p	.000	3	0	0	0	0	0	0	0	0	0	0
Greg Myers, ph	1.000	2	1	1	1	0	0	1	2	1	0	0
Randy Myers, p	.000	4	0	0	0	0	0	0	0	0	0	0
Ruben Rivera, of	.231	6	13	1	3	2	0	0	0	0	7	1
Andy Sheets, ss-2	.000	3	3	0	0	0	0	0	0	0	0	0
Mark Sweeney, ph	.000	3	2	1	0	0	0	0	0	1	1	0
John Vander Wal, of-2	.429	3	7	1	3	0	0	1	2	0	2	0
Greg Vaughn, of-2	.250	3	8	1	2	0	0	0	0	1	1	0
Quilvio Veras, 2b	.250	6	24	2	6	1	0	0	2	5	7	0
Donne Wall, p	.000	3	0	0	0	0	0	0	0	0	0	0
TOTAL	.255		208	24	53	7	0	5	20	27	48	2

PITCHER	W	L	ERA	G	GS	CG	SV	SHO	IP	H	ER	BB	SO
Andy Ashby	0	0	2.08	2	2	0	0	0	13.0	14	3	2	5
Brian Boehringer	0	0	0.00	3	0	0	0	0	3.0	3	0	1	1
Kevin Brown	1	1	2.61	2	2	1	0	0	10.1	5	3	4	12
Joey Hamilton	0	1	4.91	2	1	0	0	0	7.1	7	4	3	6
Sterling Hitchcock	2	0	0.90	2	2	0	0	0	10.0	5	1	8	14
Trevor Hoffman	1	0	2.08	3	0	0	1	0	4.1	2	1	2	7
Mark Langston	0	0	0.00	3	0	0	0	0	1.1	1	0	0	1
Dan Miceli	0	0	13.50	3	0	0	0	0	0.2	4	1	0	1
Randy Myers	0	0	13.50	4	0	0	0	0	2.0	3	3	2	3
Donne Wall	0	0	3.00	3	0	0	1	0	3.0	3	1	4	4
TOTAL	4	2	2.78	27	6	1	2	0	55.0	47	17	26	54

ATL (E)

PLAYER/POS	AVG	G	AB	R	H	2B	3B	HR	RB	BB	SO	SB
Danny Bautista, of-4	.000	5	5	0	0	0	0	0	0	0	1	0
Greg Colbrunn, ph	.333	6	6	0	2	0	0	0	0	0	2	0
Andres Galarraga, 1b	.095	6	21	1	2	0	0	1	4	6	6	0
Tom Glavine, p-2	.250	3	4	0	1	0	0	0	0	1	2	0
Tony Graffanino, 2b-3	.333	4	3	2	1	1	0	0	1	2	1	0
Ozzie Guillen, ss-3	.417	4	12	1	5	0	0	0	1	0	1	0
Andruw Jones, of	.273	6	22	3	6	0	0	1	2	1	4	1
Chipper Jones, 3b	.208	6	24	2	5	1	0	0	1	4	5	0
Ryan Klesko, of	.083	5	12	2	1	0	0	0	1	6	3	0
Kerry Ligtenberg, p	.000	4	0	0	0	0	0	0	0	0	0	0
Keith Lockhart, 2b	.235	6	17	2	4	1	1	0	0	0	4	0
Javy Lopez, c	.300	6	20	2	6	0	0	1	1	0	7	0
Greg Maddux, p	.000	2	1	0	0	0	0	0	0	0	0	0
Marty Malloy, 2b-1	.000	4	1	1	0	0	0	0	0	0	0	0
Dennis Martinez, p	.000	4	0	0	0	0	0	0	0	0	0	0
Denny Neagle, p	.000	2	2	0	0	0	0	0	0	0	1	0
Eddie Perez, c	.750	3	4	0	3	0	0	0	0	0	0	0
Odaliz Perez, p	.000	2	0	0	0	0	0	0	0	0	0	0
John Rocker, p	.000	6	0	0	0	0	0	0	0	1	0	0
Rudy Seanez, p	.000	4	0	0	0	0	0	0	0	0	0	0
John Smoltz, p	.200	2	5	0	1	0	0	0	0	0	1	0
Michael Tucker, of-5	.385	6	13	1	5	1	0	1	5	2	5	0
Walt Weiss, ss	.200	4	15	0	3	0	0	0	1	2	5	1
Gerald Williams, of	.154	5	13	0	2	0	0	0	0	1	6	1
TOTAL	.235		200	18	47	4	1	4	17	26	54	3

PITCHER	W	L	ERA	G	GS	CG	SV	SHO	IP	H	ER	BB	SO
Tom Glavine	0	2	2.31	2	2	0	0	0	11.2	13	3	9	8
Kerry Ligtenberg	0	1	7.36	4	0	0	0	0	3.2	3	3	2	5
Greg Maddux	0	1	3.00	2	1	0	0	0	6.0	5	2	3	4
Dennis Martinez	1	0	0.00	4	0	0	0	0	3.1	1	0	0	4
Denny Neagle	0	0	3.52	2	1	0	0	0	7.2	8	3	2	9
Odaliz Perez	0	0	54.00	2	0	0	0	0	0.1	5	2	2	0
John Rocker	1	0	0.00	6	0	0	0	0	4.2	3	0	1	5
Rudy Seanez	0	0	6.00	4	0	0	0	0	3.0	2	2	1	4
John Smoltz	0	0	3.95	2	2	0	0	0	13.2	13	6	6	13
TOTAL	2	4	3.50	28	6	0	0	0	54.0	53	21	27	48

GAME 1 AT ATL OCT 7

SD	000 010 010	1	3	7	0
ATL	001 000 001	0	2	8	3

Pitchers: Ashby, R.Myers (8), Miceli (8), HOFFMAN (8), Wall (10) vs Smoltz, Rocker (8), Martinez (8), LIGTENBERG (9)
Home Runs: A.Jones-ATL, Caminiti-SD
Attendance: 42,117

GAME 2 AT ATL OCT 8

SD	000 001 002	3	11	0
ATL	000 000 000	0	3	1

Pitchers: BROWN vs GLAVINE, Rocker (7), Seanez (8), O.Perez (9), Ligtenberg (9)
Attendance: 43,083

GAME 3 AT SD OCT 10

ATL	001 000 000	1	8	2
SD	000 020 02X	4	7	0

Pitchers: MADDUX, Martinez (6), Rocker (7), Seanez (8) vs HITCHCOCK, Wall (6), Miceli (8), R.Myers (8), Hoffman (8)
Attendance: 62,799

GAME 4 AT SD OCT 11

ATL	000 101 600	8	12	0
SD	002 000 100	3	8	0

Pitchers: Neagle, MARTINEZ (6), Rocker (7), O.Perez (8), Seanez (8), Ligtenberg (9) vs HAMILTON, Myers (7), Miceli (7), Boehringer (8), Langston (9)
Home Runs: Leyritz-SD, Lopez-ATL, Galarraga-ATL
Attendance: 65,042

GAME 5 AT SD OCT 12

ATL	000 101 050	7	14	1
SD	200 002 002	6	10	1

Pitchers: Smoltz, ROCKER (7), Seanez (8), Ligtenberg (9), Maddux (9) vs Ashby, Langston (7), BROWN (7), Wall (8), Boehringer (9), R.Myers (9)
Home Runs: Caminiti-SD, Vander Wal-SD, Tucker-ATL, G.Myers-SD
Attendance: 58,988

GAME 6 AT ATL OCT 14

SD	000 005 000	5	10	0
ATL	000 000 000	0	2	1

Pitchers: HITCHCOCK, Boehringer (6), Langston (7), Hamilton (7), Hoffman (9) vs GLAVINE, Rocker (6), Martinez (6), Neagle (8)
Attendance: 50,988

The Yankees, coming off a three-game sweep of Texas in the Division Series, handled the Indians easily to start the ALCS. New York scored five times in the first inning of Game 1 of the ALCS to knock out Indians starter Jaret Wright, who had been 2-0 against the Yankees in the 1997 Division Series. That was more than enough for David Wells, who pitched into the ninth inning of the 7-2 victory. Pitching and defense kept the Yankees and Indians tied at 1-1 through 11 innings the next afternoon, but it all fell apart for the Yankees in the top of the 12th. After a leadoff single by Jim Thome, Enrique Wilson came in to pinch run. Travis Fryman laid down a bunt that Tino Martinez errantly fired into Fryman's back. Chuck Knoblauch argued that Fryman had been out of the baseline and should be called out, but the Yankees second baseman made his protest while the play was still going on. By the time Knoblauch picked up the ball and threw home, Wilson had scored. The Indians won the argument and the game.

Bartolo Colon allowed just four hits in Game 3 to record the Tribe's first complete postseason game since the opening game of the 1954 World Series. Three home runs in the fifth inning (by Manny Ramirez, Jim Thome, and Mark Whiten) provided the power to give Cleveland a 2-1 series lead. The Yankees came back with a pitching gem of their own in Game 4 as rookie Orlando Hernandez teamed with two relievers to blank the Indians to even the ALCS. David Wells didn't have his best stuff and he wasn't in a good mood, but he still got the big outs when he needed to in Game 5. Angered by comments made by Cleveland fans as he warmed up, Wells shook off a rocky first inning to give the Yankees the lead in the series with a 5-3 win. Chili Davis drove in three runs in support of ALCS MVP Wells.

David Cone and Charles Nagy had both pitched splendidly in Game 2, but the hitters took charge in their rematch in Game 6. The Yankees grabbed a 6-0 lead after three innings as Cleveland played poor defense, and the Yankees took advantage of the wet grass to advance extra bases. The Indians nearly caught up with one swing on a grand slam by Thome, his fourth homer of the series, to make it 6-5 in the fifth inning. Omar Vizquel's wild throw after a record-tying 74 postseason games without an error set up a three-run sixth inning that put the game, and the Yankees' 35th AL pennant, on ice.

New York Yankees (E), 4; Cleveland Indians (C), 2

NY (E)

PLAYER/POS	AVG	G	AB	R	H	2B	3B	HR	RBI	BB	SO	SB
Scott Brosius, 3b	.300	6	20	2	6	1	0	1	6	2	4	0
Homer Bush, dh-1	.000	2	0	1	0	0	0	0	0	0	0	1
David Cone, p	.000	2	0	0	0	0	0	0	0	0	0	0
Chad Curtis, of	.000	2	4	0	0	0	0	0	0	1	2	0
Chili Davis, dh	.286	5	14	2	4	1	0	1	5	2	3	0
Joe Girardi, c	.250	3	8	2	2	0	0	0	0	1	0	0
Orlando Hernandez, p	.000	1	0	0	0	0	0	0	0	0	0	0
Derek Jeter, ss	.200	6	25	3	5	1	1	0	2	2	5	3
Chuck Knoblauch, 2b	.200	6	25	4	5	1	0	0	0	4	2	0
Ricky Ledee, of-2,dh-1	.000	3	5	0	0	0	0	0	0	0	0	0
Graeme Lloyd, p	.000	1	0	0	0	0	0	0	0	0	0	0
Tino Martinez, 1b	.105	6	19	1	2	1	0	0	1	6	8	2
Ramiro Mendoza, p	.000	2	0	0	0	0	0	0	0	0	0	0
Jeff Nelson, p	.000	3	0	0	0	0	0	0	0	0	0	0
Paul O'Neill, of	.280	6	25	6	7	2	0	1	3	3	4	2
Andy Pettitte, p	.000	1	0	0	0	0	0	0	0	0	0	0
Jorge Posada, c	.182	5	11	1	2	0	0	1	2	4	2	0
Tim Raines, dh-2,of-1	.100	3	10	0	1	0	0	0	1	2	5	0
Mariano Rivera, p	.000	4	0	0	0	0	0	0	0	0	0	0
Luis Sojo, 1b	.000	1	0	0	0	0	0	0	0	0	0	0
Shane Spencer, of	.100	3	10	1	1	0	0	0	0	0	1	3
Mike Stanton, p	.000	3	0	0	0	0	0	0	0	0	0	0
David Wells, p	.000	2	0	0	0	0	0	0	0	0	0	0
Bernie Williams, of	.381	6	21	4	8	1	0	0	5	7	4	1
TOTAL	.218		197	27	43	8	1	4	25	35	42	9

PITCHER	W	L	ERA	G	GS	CG	SV	SHO	IP	H	ER	BB	SO
David Cone	1	0	4.15	2	2	0	0	0	13.0	12	6	6	13
Orlando Hernandez	1	0	0.00	1	1	0	0	0	7.0	3	0	2	6
Graeme Lloyd	0	0	0.00	1	0	0	0	0	0.2	1	0	0	0
Ramiro Mendoza	0	0	0.00	2	0	0	0	0	4.1	4	0	0	1
Jeff Nelson	0	1	20.25	3	0	0	0	0	1.1	3	3	1	3
Andy Pettitte	0	1	11.57	1	1	0	0	0	4.2	8	6	3	1
Mariano Rivera	0	0	0.00	4	0	0	1	0	5.2	0	0	1	5
Mike Stanton	0	0	0.00	3	0	0	0	0	3.2	2	0	1	4
David Wells	2	0	2.87	2	2	0	0	0	15.2	12	5	2	18
TOTAL	4	2	3.21	19	6	0	1	0	56.0	45	20	16	51

CLE (C)

PLAYER/POS	AVG	G	AB	R	H	2B	3B	HR	RBI	BB	SO	SB
Sandy Alomar, c	.063	5	16	1	1	0	0	0	0	0	2	0
Paul Assenmacher, p	.000	3	0	0	0	0	0	0	0	0	0	0
Jeff Branson, ph	.000	1	1	0	0	0	0	0	0	0	0	0
Dave Burba, p	.000	3	0	0	0	0	0	0	0	0	0	0
Bartolo Colon, p	.000	1	0	0	0	0	0	0	0	0	0	0
Joey Cora, 2b	.143	2	7	1	1	0	0	0	0	2	1	0
Einar Diaz, c	.000	5	4	0	0	0	0	0	0	0	1	0
Travis Fryman, 3b	.174	6	23	2	4	0	0	0	0	1	5	1
Brian Giles, of-3	.083	4	12	0	1	0	0	0	0	1	3	0
Dwight Gooden, p	.000	1	0	0	0	0	0	0	0	0	0	0
Mike Jackson, p	.000	1	0	0	0	0	0	0	0	0	0	0
David Justice, dh-4,of-1	.158	6	19	2	3	0	0	1	2	3	3	0
Kenny Lofton, of	.185	6	27	2	5	1	0	1	3	1	7	1
Charles Nagy, p	.000	2	0	0	0	0	0	0	0	0	0	0
Chad Ogea, p	.000	2	0	0	0	0	0	0	0	0	0	0
Jim Poole, p	.000	4	0	0	0	0	0	0	0	0	0	0
Manny Ramirez, of	.333	6	21	2	7	1	0	2	4	4	9	0
Steve Reed, p	.000	3	0	0	0	0	0	0	0	0	0	0
Richie Sexson, 1b	.000	3	6	0	0	0	0	0	0	0	3	0
Paul Shuey, p	.000	5	0	0	0	0	0	0	0	0	0	0
Jim Thome, 1b-4,dh-2	.304	6	23	4	7	0	0	4	8	1	8	0
Omar Vizquel, ss	.440	6	25	2	11	0	1	0	1	0	3	4
Mark Whiten, of	.286	2	7	2	2	1	0	1	1	1	1	0
Enrique Wilson, 2b	.214	5	14	3	3	0	0	0	0	1	3	0
Jaret Wright, p	.000	2	0	0	0	0	0	0	0	0	0	0
TOTAL	.220		205	20	45	3	1	9	19	16	51	6

PITCHER	W	L	ERA	G	GS	CG	SV	SHO	IP	H	ER	BB	SO
Paul Assenmacher	0	0	0.00	3	0	0	0	0	2.0	0	0	0	3
Dave Burba	1	0	3.00	3	0	0	0	0	6.0	3	2	5	8
Bartolo Colon	1	0	1.00	1	1	1	0	0	9.0	4	1	4	3
Dwight Gooden	0	1	5.79	1	1	0	0	0	4.2	3	3	3	3
Mike Jackson	0	0	0.00	1	0	0	1	0	1.0	0	0	0	2
Charles Nagy	0	1	3.72	2	2	0	0	0	9.2	13	4	1	6
Chad Ogea	0	1	8.10	2	1	0	0	0	6.2	9	6	5	4
Jim Poole	0	0	0.00	4	0	0	0	0	1.1	0	0	1	2
Steve Reed	0	0	0.00	3	0	0	0	0	1.2	0	0	1	0
Paul Shuey	0	0	0.00	5	0	0	0	0	6.1	4	0	7	7
Jaret Wright	0	1	8.10	2	1	0	0	0	6.2	7	6	8	4
TOTAL	2	4	3.60	27	6	1	1	0	55.0	43	22	35	42

GAME 1 AT NY OCT 6

CLE	000	000	002	2	5 0
NY	500	001	10X	7	11 0

Pitchers: WRIGHT, Ogea (1), Poole (7), Reed (7), Shuey (8) vs WELLS, Nelson (9)
Home Runs: Posada-NY, Ramirez-CLE
Attendance: 57,138

GAME 2 AT NY OCT 7

CLE	000	100	000	003	4 8 1
NY	000	000	100	000	1 7 1

Pitchers: Nagy, Reed (7), Poole (8), Shuey (8), Assenmacher (10), BURBA (11), Jackson (12) vs Cone, Rivera (9), Stanton (11), NELSON (11), Lloyd (12)
Home Runs: Justice-CLE
Attendance: 57,128

GAME 3 AT CLE OCT 9

NY	100	000	000	1	4 0
CLE	020	040	00X	6	12 0

Pitchers: PETTITTE, Mendoza (5), Stanton (7) vs COLON
Home Runs: Thome-CLE (2), Ramirez-CLE, Whiten-CLE
Attendance: 44,904

GAME 4 AT CLE OCT 10

NY	100	200	001	4	4 0
CLE	000	000	000	0	4 3

Pitchers: HERNANDEZ, Stanton (8), Rivera (9) vs GOODEN, Poole (5), Burba (6), Shuey (9)
Home Runs: O'Neill-NY
Attendance: 44,981

GAME 5 AT CLE OCT 11

NY	310	100	000	5	6 0
CLE	200	001	000	3	8 0

Pitchers: WELLS, Nelson (8), Rivera (8) vs OGEA, Wright (2), Reed (8), Assenmacher (8), Shuey (9)
Home Runs: Lofton-CLE, Davis-NY, Thome-CLE
Attendance: 44,966

GAME 6 AT NY OCT 13

CLE	000	050	000	5	8 3
NY	213	003	00X	9	11 1

Pitchers: NAGY, Burba (4), Poole (6), Shuey (6), Assenmacher (8) vs CONE, Mendoza (6), Rivera (9)
Home Runs: Brosius-NY, Thome-CLE
Attendance: 57,142

The World Series opened with the two hottest pitchers of the post-season facing each other, but neither New York's David Wells nor San Diego's Kevin Brown had their best stuff. The Yankees struck for two runs off Brown in the second inning, but three home runs—two by Greg Vaughn and one by Tony Gwynn—staked the Padres to a 5-2 lead. In the seventh Donne Wall relieved Brown with two runners on and Chuck Knoblauch promptly tied the game with a home run. A few batters later Tino Martinez launched a grand slam off Mark Langston to cap New York's seven-run seventh.

The Yankees jumped on the Padres for seven runs in the first three innings of Game 2. Paul O'Neill made a running catch to rob Wally Joyner of a hit with two runners on base in the top of the first, and a walk and a throwing error by San Diego set up New York for three runs in the bottom of the inning. Bernie Williams capped off a three-run second with a home run and Jorge Posada added a two-run shot of his own three innings later.

The Padres returned home and put the first three runs of the game across the plate in the sixth inning against David Cone. Padres pitcher Sterling Hitchcock started the rally with a single, and a throwing error by O'Neill kept it going. Scott Brosius led off the seventh with a home run, and a passed ball and an error made it a 3-2 game. With closer Trevor Hoffman pitching in the eighth with two runners aboard, Brosius hit his second homer in as many innings and the Yankees held on for a 5-4 win.

Andy Pettitte, pitching for the first time in 10 days, combined with Jeff Nelson and Mariano Rivera to blank the Padres on seven hits in Game 4. The Yankees, showing that they could win in a variety of ways, scored once on a groundout in the sixth and added two insurance runs off Brown on Brosius' sixth RBI in four games plus a sacrifice fly by Ricky Ledee. Mark Sweeney ended the game, fittingly, with a grounder to MVP Brosius, and the Yankees had their 24th world championship.

New York Yankees (A), 4;
San Diego Padres (N), 0

NY (A)

PLAYER/POS	AVG	G	AB	R	H	2B	3B	HR	RB	BB	SO	SB
Scott Brosius, 3b	.471	4	17	3	8	0	0	2	6	0	4	0
Homer Bush, dh-1	.000	2	0	0	0	0	0	0	0	0	0	0
David Cone, p	.500	1	2	0	1	0	0	0	0	0	0	0
Chili Davis, dh-2	.286	3	7	3	2	0	0	0	2	3	2	0
Joe Girardi, c	.000	2	6	0	0	0	0	0	0	0	2	0
Orlando Hernandez, p	.000	1	0	0	0	0	0	0	0	0	0	0
Derek Jeter, ss	.353	4	17	4	6	0	0	0	1	3	3	0
Chuck Knoblauch, 2b	.375	4	16	3	6	0	0	1	3	3	2	1
Ricky Ledee, of	.600	4	10	1	6	3	0	0	4	2	1	0
Graeme Lloyd, p	.000	3	0	0	0	0	0	0	0	0	0	0
Tino Martinez, 1b	.385	4	13	4	5	0	0	1	4	4	2	0
Ramiro Mendoza, p	.000	1	1	0	0	0	0	0	0	0	0	0
Jeff Nelson, p	.000	3	0	0	0	0	0	0	0	0	0	0
Paul O'Neill, of	.211	4	19	3	4	1	0	0	0	1	2	0
Andy Pettitte, p	.000	1	2	0	0	0	0	0	0	0	2	0
Jorge Posada, c	.333	3	9	2	3	0	0	1	2	2	2	0
Mariano Rivera, p	.000	3	0	0	0	0	0	0	0	0	0	0
Shane Spencer, of	.333	1	3	1	1	1	0	0	0	0	2	0
Mike Stanton, p	.000	1	0	0	0	0	0	0	0	0	0	0
David Wells, p	.000	1	0	0	0	0	0	0	0	0	0	0
Bernie Williams, of	.063	4	16	2	1	0	0	1	3	2	5	0
TOTAL	.309		139	26	43	5	0	6	25	20	29	1

PITCHER	W	L	ERA	G	GS	CG	SV	SHO	IP	H	ER	BB	SO
David Cone	0	0	3.00	1	1	0	0	0	6.0	2	2	3	4
Orlando Hernandez	1	0	1.29	1	1	0	0	0	7.0	6	1	3	7
Graeme Lloyd	0	0	0.00	1	0	0	0	0	0.1	0	0	0	0
Ramiro Mendoza	1	0	9.00	1	0	0	0	0	1.0	2	1	0	1
Jeff Nelson	0	0	0.00	3	0	0	0	0	2.1	2	0	1	4
Andy Pettitte	1	0	0.00	1	1	0	0	0	7.1	5	0	3	4
Mariano Rivera	0	0	0.00	3	0	0	3	0	4.1	5	0	0	4
Mike Stanton	0	0	27.00	1	0	0	0	0	0.2	3	2	0	1
David Wells	1	0	6.43	1	1	0	0	0	7.0	7	5	2	4
TOTAL	4	0	2.75	13	4	0	3	0	36.0	32	11	12	29

SD (N)

PLAYER/POS	AVG	G	AB	R	H	2B	3B	HR	RB	BB	SO	SB
Andy Ashby, p	.000	1	0	0	0	0	0	0	0	0	0	0
Brian Boehringer, p	.000	2	0	0	0	0	0	0	0	0	0	0
Kevin Brown, p	.500	2	2	0	1	0	0	0	0	0	0	0
Ken Caminiti, 3b	.143	4	14	1	2	1	0	1	2	7	0	0
Steve Finley, of	.083	3	12	0	1	1	0	0	0	1	1	0
Chris Gomez, ss	.364	4	11	2	4	0	1	0	0	1	1	0
Tony Gwynn, of	.500	4	16	2	8	0	0	1	3	1	0	0
Joey Hamilton, p	.000	1	0	0	0	0	0	0	0	0	0	0
Carlos Hernandez, c	.200	4	10	0	2	0	0	0	0	0	3	0
Sterling Hitchcock, p	.500	1	2	1	1	0	0	0	0	0	0	0
Trevor Hoffman, p	.000	1	0	0	0	0	0	0	0	0	0	0
Wally Joyner, 1b	.000	3	8	0	0	0	0	0	0	3	1	0
Mark Langston, p	.000	1	0	0	0	0	0	0	0	0	0	0
Jim Leyritz, 1b-2,c-1,dh-1	.000	4	10	0	0	0	0	0	0	1	4	0
Dan Miceli, p	.000	2	0	0	0	0	0	0	0	0	0	0
Greg Myers, c-1	.000	2	4	0	0	0	0	0	0	0	2	0
Randy Myers, p	.000	3	0	0	0	0	0	0	0	0	0	0
Ruben Rivera, of	.800	3	5	1	4	2	0	0	1	0	0	0
Andy Sheets, ss	.000	2	2	0	0	0	0	0	0	0	1	0
Mark Sweeney, ph	.667	3	3	0	2	0	0	0	1	0	0	0
John Vander Wal, of-1	.400	4	5	0	2	1	0	0	0	0	0	0
Greg Vaughn, of-3,dh-1	.133	4	15	3	2	0	0	2	4	1	2	0
Quilvio Veras, 2b	.200	4	15	3	3	2	0	0	1	3	4	0
Donne Wall, p	.000	2	0	0	0	0	0	0	0	0	0	0
TOTAL	.239		134	13	32	7	1	3	11	12	29	1

PITCHER	W	L	ERA	G	GS	CG	SV	SHO	IP	H	ER	BB	SO
Andy Ashby	0	1	13.50	1	1	0	0	0	2.2	10	4	1	1
Brian Boehringer	0	0	9.00	2	0	0	0	0	2.0	4	2	2	3
Kevin Brown	0	1	4.40	2	2	0	0	0	14.1	14	7	6	13
Joey Hamilton	0	0	0.00	1	0	0	0	0	1.0	0	0	1	1
Sterling Hitchcock	0	0	1.50	1	1	0	0	0	6.0	7	1	1	7
Trevor Hoffman	0	1	9.00	1	0	0	0	0	2.0	2	2	1	0
Mark Langston	0	0	40.50	1	0	0	0	0	0.2	1	3	2	0
Dan Miceli	0	0	0.00	2	0	0	0	0	1.2	2	0	2	1
Randy Myers	0	0	9.00	2	0	0	0	0	1.0	0	1	3	2
Donne Wall	0	1	6.75	2	0	0	0	0	2.2	3	2	3	1
TOTAL	0	4	5.82	16	4	0	0	0	34.0	43	22	20	29

## CHAPTER 13

Black Ball

Jules Tygiel

More than 50 years have passed since what many have called the finest moment in the history of the national pastime—Jackie Robinson's shattering of the color barrier. Robinson's heroic triumph brought to an end six disgraceful decades of Jim Crow baseball. During that era, some of America's greatest ballplayers plied their trade on all-black teams, in Negro Leagues, on the playing fields of Latin America, and along the barnstorming frontier of the cities and towns of the United States, but never within the major and minor league realm of "organized baseball." When slowly and grudgingly given their chance in the years after 1947, blacks conclusively proved their competitive abilities on the diamond, but discrimination persisted as baseball executives continued to deny them the opportunity to display their talents in both managerial and front office positions.

Scattered evidence exists of blacks playing baseball in the antebellum period, but the first recorded black teams surfaced in Northern cities in the aftermath of the Civil War. In October 1867 the Uniques of Brooklyn hosted the Excelsiors of Philadelphia in a contest billed as the "championship of colored clubs." Before a large crowd of black and white spectators, the Excelsiors marched around the field behind a fife and drum corps before defeating the Uniques, 37-24. Two months later, a second Philadelphia squad, the Pythians, dispatched a representative to the inaugural meetings of the National Association of Base Ball Players, the first organized league. The nominating committee unanimously rejected the Pythian's application, barring "any club which may be composed of one or more colored persons." Using the impeccable logic of a racist society, the committee proclaimed, "If colored clubs were admitted there would be in all probability some division of feeling, whereas, by excluding them no injury could result to anyone." The Philadelphia Pythians, however, continued their quest for interracial competition. In 1869 they became the first black team to face an all-white squad, defeating the cross-town City Items, 27-17.

In 1876 athletic entrepreneurs in the nation's metropolitan centers established the National League which quickly came to represent the pinnacle of the sport. The new entity had no written policy regarding blacks, but precluded them nonetheless through a "gentleman's agreement" among the owners. In the smaller cities and towns of America, however, where under-funded teams and fragile minor league coalitions quickly appeared and faded, individual blacks found scattered opportunities to pursue baseball careers. During the next decade, at least two dozen black ballplayers sought to earn a living in this erratic professional baseball world.

Bud Fowler ranked among the best and most persistent of these trailblazers. Born John Jackson in upstate New York in 1858 and raised, ironically, in Cooperstown, Fowler first achieved recognition as a 20-year-old pitcher for a local team in Chelsea, Massachusetts. In April 1878, Fowler defeated the National League's Boston club, which included future Hall of Famers George Wright and Jim O' Rourke, 2-1, in an exhibition game, besting 40-game winner Tommy Bond. Later that season, Fowler hurled three games for the Lynn Live Oaks of the International Association, the nation's first minor league, and another for Worcester in the New England League. For the next six years, he toiled for a variety of independent and semi-professional teams in the United States and Canada. Despite a reputation as "one of the best pitchers on the continent," he failed to catch on with any major or minor league squads. In 1884, now appearing regularly as a second baseman, as well as a pitcher, Fowler joined Stillwater, Minnesota, in the Northwestern League. Over the next seven seasons, Fowler played for 14 teams in nine leagues, seldom batting less than .300 for a season. He led the Western League in triples in 1886. "He is one of the best general players in the country," reported *Sporting Life*, "and if he had a white face he would be playing with the best of them. . . Those who know, say there is no better second baseman in the country."

In 1886, however, a better second baseman did appear in the form of Frank Grant, perhaps the greatest black player of the nineteenth century. The light-skinned Grant, described as a "Spaniard" in the *Buffalo Express*, batted .325 for Meridien in the Eastern League. When that squad folded he joined Buffalo in the prestigious International Association and improved his average to .340, third best in the league.

Although not as talented as Fowler and Grant, bare-hand-catcher Moses Fleetwood Walker achieved the highest level of play of blacks of this era. The son of an Ohio physician, Fleet Walker had studied at Oberlin College, where in 1881 he and his younger brother Welday helped launch a varsity baseball team. For the next two years, the elder Walker played for the University of Michigan and in 1883 he appeared in 60 games for the pennant-winning Toledo squad in the Northwestern League. In 1884, Toledo entered the American Association, the National League's primary rival, and Walker became the first black major leaguer. In an age when many catchers caught barehanded and lacked chest protectors, Walker suffered frequent injuries and played little after a foul tip broke his

rib in mid-July. Nonetheless, he batted .263 and pitcher Tony Mullane later called him "the best catcher I ever worked with." In July, Toledo briefly signed Walker's brother, Welday, who appeared in six games batting .182. The following year, Toledo dropped from the league, ending the Walkers' major league careers.

These early black players found limited acceptance among teammates, fans, and opponents. In Ontario in 1881, Fowler's teammates forced him off the club. Walker found that Mullane and other pitchers preferred not to pitch to him. Although he acknowledged Walker's skills, Mullane confessed, "I disliked a Negro and whenever I had to pitch to him I used anything I wanted without looking at his signals." At Louisville in 1884, insults from Kentucky fans so rattled Walker that he made five errors in a game. In Richmond, after Walker had actually left the team due to injuries, the Toledo manager received a letter from "75 determined men" threatening "to mob Walker" and cause "much bloodshed" if the black catcher appeared. On Aug. 10, 1883, Chicago White Stockings star and manager Cap Anson had threatened to cancel an exhibition game with Toledo if Walker played. The injured catcher had not been slated to start, but Toledo manager Charlie Morton defied Anson and inserted Walker into the lineup. The game proceeded without incident.

A Hopeful Start

In 1887 Walker, Fowler, Grant, Higgins, Stovey, and three other blacks converged on the International League, a newly reorganized circuit in Canada and upstate New York, one notch below the major league level. At the same time, a new six-team entity, the League of Colored Baseball Clubs, won recognition under baseball's National Agreement, a mutual pact to honor player contracts among team owners. Thus, an air of optimism pervaded the start of the season. But 1887 would prove a fateful year for the future of blacks in baseball.

On May 6 the Colored League made its debut in Pittsburgh with "a grand street parade and a brass band concert." Twelve hundred spectators watched the hometown Keystones lose to the Gorhams of New York, 11-8. Within days, however, the new league began to flounder. The Boston franchise disbanded in Louisville on May 8, stranding its players in the Southern city. Three weeks later, league-founder Walter Brown formally announced the demise of the infant circuit.

Meanwhile, in the International League, black players found their numbers growing, but their status increasingly uncertain. Six of the 10 teams fielded blacks, prompting *Sporting Life* to wonder, "How far will this mania for engaging colored players go?" In Newark, fans marveled at the "colored battery" of Fleet Walker, dubbed the "coon catcher" by one Canadian newspaper, and "headstrong" pitcher George Stovey. Stovey, one of the greatest black pitchers of the 19th century, won 35 games, still an International League record. Frank Grant, in his second season as the Buffalo second baseman, led the league in batting average and home runs. Bud Fowler, one of two blacks on the Binghamton squad, compiled a .350 average through early July and stole 23 bases.

These athletes compiled their impressive statistics under the most adverse conditions. "I could not help pitying some of the poor black fellows that played in the International League," reported a white player. "Fowler used to play second base with the lower part of his legs encased in wooden guards. He knew that about every player that came down to second base on a steal had it in for him." Both Fowler and Grant, "would muff balls intentionally, so that [they] would not have to touch runners, fearing that they might injure [them]." In addition, "About half the pitchers try their best to hit these colored players when [they are] at bat." Grant, whose Buffalo teammates had refused to sit with him for a team portrait in 1886, reportedly saved himself from a "drubbing" at their hands in 1887, only by "the effective use of a club." In Toronto, fans chanted, "Kill the Nigger," at Grant, and a local newspaper headline declared, "THE COLORED PLAYERS DISTASTEFUL." In late June, Bud Fowler's Binghamton teammates refused to take the field unless the club removed him from the lineup. Soon after, on July 7, the Binghamton club submitted to the players' demands, releasing Fowler and a black teammate, a pitcher named Renfroe.

The most dramatic confrontations between black and white players occurred on the Syracuse squad, where a clique of refugees from the Southern League exacerbated racial tensions. In spring training, the club included a catcher named Dick Male, who, rumors had it, was a light-skinned black named Richard Johnson. Male charged "that the man calling him a Negro is himself a black liar," but when released after a poor preseason performance, he returned to his old club, Zanesville in the Ohio State League, and resumed his true identity as Richard Johnson. In May, Syracuse signed 19-year-old black pitcher Robert Higgins, angering the Southern clique. Higgins appeared in his first International League game in Toronto on May 25. "THE SYRACUSE PLOTTERS," as a *Sporting News* headline called his teammates, undermined his debut. According to one account, they "seemed to want the Toronto team to knock Higgins out of the box, and time and again they fielded so badly that the home team were enabled to secure many hits after the side had been retired."

"A disgusting exhibition," admonished the *Toronto World*. "They succeeded in running Male out of the club," reported a Newark paper, "and they will do the same with Higgins." One week later, two Syracuse players refused to pose for a team picture with Higgins. When manager "Ice Water" Joe Simmons suspended pitcher Doug Crothers for this incident, Crothers slugged the manager. Higgins miraculously recovered from his early travails and lack of support to post a 20-7 record.

On July 14, as the directors of the International League discussed the racial situation in Buffalo, the Newark Little Giants planned to send Stovey, their ace, to the mound in an exhibition game against the National League Chicago White Stockings. Once again manager Anson refused to field his squad if either Stovey or Walker appeared. Unlike 1883, Anson's will prevailed. On the same day, team owners, stating that "Many of the best players in the league are anxious to leave on account of the colored element," allowed current black players to remain, but voted by a 6-4 margin to reject all future contracts with

blacks. The teams with black players all voted against the measure, but Binghamton, which had just released Fowler and Renfroe, swung the vote in favor of exclusion.

Events in 1887 continued to conspire against black players. On Sept. 11 the St. Louis Browns of the American Association refused to play a scheduled contest against the all-black Cuban Giants. "We are only doing what is right," they proclaimed. In November, the Buffalo and Syracuse teams unsuccessfully attempted to lift the International League ban on blacks. The Ohio State League, which had fielded three black players, also adopted a rule barring additional contracts with blacks, prompting Welday Walker, who had appeared in the league, to protest, "The law is a disgrace to the present age. . . There should be some broader cause—such as lack of ability, behavior and intelligence—for barring a player, rather than his color."

Only a handful of blacks appeared on integrated squads after 1887. Grant and Higgins returned to their original teams in 1888. Walker jumped from Newark to Syracuse. The following year, only Walker remained for one final season, the last black in the International League until 1946. Richard Johnson, the erstwhile Dick Male, reappeared in the Ohio State League in 1888 and in 1889 joined Springfield in the Central Interstate League, where he hit 14 triples, stole 45 bases, and scored 100 runs in 100 games. In 1890, Harrisburg in the Eastern Interstate League fielded two blacks, while Jamestown in the New York Penn League featured another. Bud Fowler and several other black players appeared in the Nebraska State League in 1892. Three years later, Adrian in the Michigan State League signed five blacks, including Fowler and pitcher George Wilson who posted a 29-4 record. Meanwhile Sol White, who later chronicled these events in his 1906 book, *The History of Colored Baseball*, played for Fort Wayne in the Western State League. In 1896, pitcher-outfielder Bert Jones joined Atchison in the Kansas State League where he played for three seasons before being forced out in 1898. Almost 50 years would pass before another black would appear on an interracial club in organized baseball.

All-Black Teams

While integrated teams grew rare, several leagues allowed entry to all-black squads. In 1889 the Middle States League included the New York Gorhams and the Cuban Giants, the most famous black team of the age. The Giants posted a 55-17 record. A year later, the alliance reorganized as the Eastern Interstate League and again included the Cuban Giants. Giants' star George Williams paced the circuit with a .391 batting average, while teammate Arthur Thomas slugged 26 doubles and 10 triples, both league-leading totals. The Eastern Interstate League folded in midseason, and in 1891 the Giants made one final minor league appearance in the Connecticut State League. When this circuit also disbanded, the brief entry of the Cuban Giants in organized baseball came to an end.

In the 1898 season a team calling itself the Acme Colored Giants affiliated with Pennsylvania's Iron and Oil League, but won only eight of 49 games before dropping out, marking an ignoble conclusion to these early experiments in interracial play.

Overall, at least 70 blacks appeared in organized baseball in the late 19th century. About half played for all-black teams, the remainder for integrated clubs. Few lasted more than one season with the same team. By the 1890s, the pattern for black baseball that would prevail for the next half century had emerged. Blacks were relegated to "colored" teams playing most of their games on the barnstorming circuit, outside of any organized league structure. While exhibition contests allowed them to pit their skills against whites, they remained on the outskirts of baseball's mainstream, unheralded and unknown to most Americans.

As early as the 1880s and 1890s several all-black traveling squads had gained national reputations. The Cuban Giants, formed among the waiters of the Argyle Hotel to entertain guests in 1885, set the pattern and provided the recurrent nickname for these teams. Passing as Cubans, so as not to offend their white clientele, the Giants toured the East in a private railroad car playing amateur and professional opponents. In the 1890s, rivals like the Lincoln Giants from Nebraska, the Page Fence Giants from Michigan, and the Cuban X Giants in New York emerged. From the beginning these teams combined entertainment with their baseball to attract crowds. The Page Fence Giants, founded by Bud Fowler in 1895, would ride through the streets on bicycles to attract attention. In 1899, Fowler organized the All-American Black Tourists, who would arrive in full dress suits with opera hats and silk umbrellas. Their showmanship notwithstanding, the black teams of the 1890s included some of the best players in the nation. The Page Fence Giants won 118 of 154 games in 1895, with two of their losses coming against the major league Cincinnati Reds.

During the early years of the 20th century many blacks still harbored hopes of regaining access to organized baseball. Sol White wrote in 1906 that baseball, "should be taken seriously by the colored player. An honest effort of his great ability will open the avenue in the near future wherein he may walk hand-in-hand with the opposite race in the greatest of all American games—baseball." Rube Foster, the outstanding figure in black baseball from 1910 to 1926, stressed excellence because "we have to be ready when the time comes for integration."

But even clandestine efforts to bring in blacks met a harsh fate. In 1901 Baltimore Orioles manager John McGraw attempted to pass second baseman Charlie Grant of the Columbia Giants off as an Indian named Chief Tokohama, until Chicago White Sox president Charles Comiskey exposed the ruse.

In 1911 the Cincinnati Reds raised black hopes by signing two light-skinned Cubans, Armando Marsans and Rafael Almeida, prompting the *New York Age* to speculate, "Now that the first shock is over it would not be surprising to see a Cuban a few shades darker. . .breaking into the professional ranks. . .it would then be easier for colored players who are citizens of this country to get into fast company." But the Reds rushed to certify that Marsans and Almeida were "genuine Caucasians," and while light-skinned Cubans became a fixture in the majors, their darker brethren remained unwelcome. Over the years, tales circulated of United States blacks passing as Indians or Cubans, but no documented cases exist.

Although most blacks lived in the South, during the first two decades of the 20th century, the great black teams and players congregated in the metropolises and industrial cities of the North. Chicago emerged as the primary center of black baseball with teams like the Leland Giants and the Chicago American Giants. In New York, the Lincoln Giants, which boasted pitching stars Smokey Joe Williams and Cannonball Dick Redding, shortstop John Henry Lloyd and catcher Louis Santop, reigned supreme. Other top clubs of the era included the Philadelphia Giants, the Hilldale Club (also of Philadelphia), the Indianapolis ABC's and the Bacharach Giants of Atlantic City. Player contracts were nonexistent or nonbinding and stars jumped frequently from team to team. "Wherever the money was," recalled John Henry Lloyd, "that's where I was."

Fans and writers often compared the great black players of this era to their white counterparts. Lloyd, one of the outstanding shortstops and hitters of that or any era, came to be known as "The Black Wagner," after his white contemporary Honus Wagner, who called it an "honor" and a "privilege" to be compared to the gangling black infielder. A St. Louis sportswriter once said when asked who was the best player in baseball history, "If you mean in organized baseball, the answer would be Babe Ruth; but if you mean in all baseball. . .the answer would have to be a colored man named John Henry Lloyd." Pitcher "Rube" Foster earned his nickname by outpitching future Hall of Famer Rube Waddell, and Cuban Jose Mendez was called "The Black Matty" after Christy Mathewson.

The talents of Foster and Mendez notwithstanding, the greatest black pitcher of the early twentieth century was 6-foot-5-inch "Smokey" Joe Williams. Born in 1886, Williams spent a good part of his career pitching in his native Texas, unheralded until he joined the Leland Giants in 1909 at the age of 24. From 1912 to 1923 he won renown as a strikeout artist for Harlem's Lincoln Giants. Against major league competition Williams won six games, lost four, and tied two, including a three-hit 1-0 victory over the National League champion Philadelphia Phillies in 1915. In 1925, he signed with the Homestead Grays and although approaching his 40th birthday, starred for seven more seasons. A 1952 poll to name the outstanding black pitcher of the half-century, placed Williams in first place, ahead of the legendary Satchel Paige.

Oscar Charleston ranks as the greatest outfielder of the 1910s and 1920s. With tremendous speed and a strong, accurate arm, Charleston was the quintessential centerfielder. During his 15-year career starting in 1915, Charleston hit for both power and average and may have been the most popular player of the 1920s. After he retired he managed the Philadelphia Stars, Brooklyn Brown Dodgers, and other clubs.

Several major stars of this era labored outside the usual channels of black baseball. In 1914, white Kansas City promoter J. L. Wilkinson organized the All-Nations team, which included whites, blacks, Indians, Asians, and Latin Americans. Pitchers John Donaldson, Jose Mendez, and Bill Drake and outfielder Cristobel Torriente played for the All-Nations team, described by one observer as "strong enough to give any major league team a nip-and-tuck battle." A black Army team from the 25th Infantry Unit in Nogales, Arizona, featured pitcher "Bullet" Joe Rogan and shortstop Dobie Moore. In 1920, when Wilkinson formed the famed Kansas City Monarchs, the players from the All-Nations and 25th Infantry teams formed the nucleus of his club. In 1921, the Monarchs challenged the minor league Kansas City Blues to a tournament for the city championship. The Blues won the series five games to three. In 1922, however, the Monarchs won five of six games to claim boasting honors in Kansas City. One week later, they swept a doubleheader from the touring Babe Ruth All-Stars.

Foster the Giant

In the years after 1910, Andrew "Rube" Foster emerged as the dominant figure in black baseball. Like many of his white contemporaries, Foster rose through the ranks of the national pastime from star player to field manager to club owner. Born in Texas in 1879, Foster accepted an invitation to pitch for Chicago's Union Giants in 1902. "If you play the best clubs in the land, white clubs as you say," he told owner Frank Leland, "it will be a case of Greek meeting Greek. I fear nobody." By 1903 he was hurling for the Cuban X Giants against the Philadelphia Giants in a series billed as the "Colored Championship of the World." His four victories in a best of nine series clinched the title.

The following year, he had switched sides and registered two of three wins for the Philadelphia Giants in a similar matchup, striking out 18 batters in one game and tossing a two-hitter in another. In 1907 he rejoined the Leland Giants and, in 1910, pitched for and managed a reconstituted team of that name to a 123-6 record.

As a pitcher, Foster had ranked among the nation's best; as a manager, his skills achieved legendary proportions. A master strategist and motivator, Foster's teams specialized in the bunt, the steal, and the hit-and-run, which came to characterize black baseball. Fans came to watch him sit on the bench giving signs with a wave of his ever-present pipe. He became the friend and confidant of major league managers like John McGraw. Over the years, Foster trained a generation of black managers, like Dave Malarcher, Biz Mackey, and Oscar Charleston in the subtleties of the game.

Foster entered the ownership ranks, uniting with white saloon keeper John Schorling (the son-in-law of White Sox owner Charles Comiskey) to form the Chicago American Giants in 1911. With Schorling's financial backing, Foster's managerial acumen, a regular home field in Chicago, and high salaries, the American Giants attracted the best black players in the nation. Throughout the decade, whether barnstorming or hosting opponents in Chicago, the American Giants came to represent the pinnacle of black baseball.

By World War I Foster dominated black baseball in Chicago and parts of the Midwest. In most other areas, however, white booking agents controlled access to stadiums, and as one newspaperman charged in 1917, "used circus methods to drag a bunch of our best citizens out, only to undergo humiliation . . . while [they sat] back and [grew] rich off a percentage of the proceeds." In the East, Nat Strong, the part owner of the Brooklyn Royal Giants, Philadelphia Giants, Cuban Stars, Cuban Giants, New

York Black Yankees, and the renowned white semi-pro team, the Bushwicks, held a stranglehold on black competition. To break this monopoly and place the game more firmly under black control, Foster created the National Association of Professional Baseball Clubs, better known as the Negro National League, in 1920.

Foster's new organization marked the third attempt of the century to meld black teams into a viable league. In 1906, the International League of Independent Baseball Clubs, which had four black and two white teams, struggled through one season characterized by shifting and collapsing franchises. Four years later, Beauregard Moseley, secretary of Chicago's Leland Giants, attempted to form a National Negro Baseball League, but the association folded before a single game had been played.

The new Negro National League, which included the top teams from Chicago, St. Louis, Detroit, and other Midwestern cities, fared far better. At Foster's insistence, all clubs, with the exception of the Kansas City Monarchs, whom Foster reluctantly accepted, were controlled by blacks. J. L. Wilkinson, who owned the Monarchs, a major drawing card, had won the respect of his fellow owners and soon overcame Foster's reservations. He became the league secretary and Foster's trusted ally. Operating under the able guidance of Foster and Wilkinson, the league flourished during its early years. In 1923, it attracted 400,000 fans and accumulated $200,000 in gate receipts.

The success of the Negro National League inspired competitors. In 1923 booking agent Nat Strong formed an Eastern Colored League, with teams in New York, Brooklyn, Baltimore, New Jersey, and Philadelphia. With four of the six teams owned by whites, and Strong controlling an erratic schedule, the league had somewhat less legitimacy than Foster's circuit. Playing in larger population centers, however, the more affluent Eastern clubs successfully raided some of the top players of the Negro National League before the circuits negotiated an uneasy truce in 1924. Throughout the remainder of the decade, however, acrimony rather than harmony characterized interleague relations. A third association emerged in the South, where the stronger independent teams in major cities formed the Southern Negro League. While this group became a breeding ground for top players, the impoverished nature of its clientele, and the inability of clubs to bolster revenues with games against white squads, rendered them unable to prevent their best players from jumping to the higher-paying Northern teams.

At their best the Negro Leagues of the 1920s were haphazard affairs. Since most clubs continued to rely on barnstorming for their primary livelihood, scheduling proved difficult. Teams played uneven numbers of games and especially in the Eastern circuit skipped official contests for more lucrative nonleague matchups. Several of the stronger independent teams, like the Homestead Grays, remained unaffiliated. Umpires were often incompetent and lacked authority to control conditions. Finally, players frequently jumped from one franchise to another, peddling their services to the highest bidder. In 1926, Foster grew ill, stripping the Negro National League of his vital leadership. Two years later, the Eastern Colored League disbanded and in 1931, less than a year after Foster's death, the Negro National League departed the scene, once again leaving black baseball with no organized structure.

Two Holdovers Take Over

With the collapse of Foster's Negro National League and the onset of the Great Depression, the always-borderline economics of operating a black baseball club grew more precarious. White booking agents, like Philadelphia's Eddie Gottlieb or Abe Saperstein of the Midwest, again reigned supreme. In the early 1930s, only the stronger independent clubs like the Homestead Grays or Kansas City Monarchs, novelty acts like the Cincinnati Clowns, or those teams backed by the "numbers kings" of the black ghettos could survive.

The Kansas City Monarchs emerged as the healthiest holdover from the old Negro National League. In 1929 owner Wilkinson had commissioned an Omaha, Nebraska, company to design a portable lighting system for night games. The equipment, consisting of a 250-horsepower motor and a 100-kilowatt generator, which illuminated lights atop telescoping poles 50 feet above the field, took about two hours to assemble. To pay for the innovation, Wilkinson mortgaged everything he owned and took in Kansas City businessman Tom Baird as a partner. But the gamble paid off. The novelty of night baseball allowed the Monarchs to play two and three games a day and made them the most popular touring club in the nation.

Meanwhile, in Pittsburgh, former basketball star Cumberland Posey, Jr. had forged the Homestead Grays into one of the best teams in America. Posey, the son of one of Pittsburgh's wealthiest black businessmen, had joined the Grays, then a sandlot team, as an outfielder in 1911. By the early 1920s he owned the club and began recruiting top national players to supplement local talent. In 1925 he signed 39-year-old Smokey Joe Williams, and the following year he lured Oscar Charleston, whom many consider the top black player of that era. Over the next several seasons Posey recruited Judy Johnson, Martin Dihigo, and James "Cool Papa" Bell. In 1930 he added a catcher from the Pittsburgh sandlots named Josh Gibson, and in 1934 brought in first baseman Buck Leonard from North Carolina. Unwilling to subject himself to outside control, Posey preferred to remain free from league affiliations. Yet for two decades, the Homestead Grays reigned as one of the strongest teams in black baseball.

In the 1930s Posey faced competition from crosstown rival Gus Greenlee, "Mr. Big" of Pittsburgh's North Side numbers rackets. Greenlee took over the Pittsburgh Crawfords, a local team, in 1930. Greenlee spent $100,000 to build a new stadium, and wooed established ballplayers with lavish salary offers. In 1931 he landed the colorful Satchel Paige, the hottest young pitcher in the land, and the following year raided the Grays, outbidding Posey for the services of Charleston, Johnson, and Gibson. In 1934 Cool Papa Bell jumped the St. Louis Stars and brought his legendary speed to the Crawfords. With five future Hall of Famers, Greenlee had assembled one of the great squads of baseball history.

The emergence of Gus Greenlee marked a new era for black baseball, the reign of the numbers men. In an age of limited opportunities for blacks, many of the most tal-

ented northern black entrepreneurs turned to gambling and other illegal operations for their livelihood. Novelist Richard Wright explained, "They would have been steel tycoons, Wall Street brokers, auto moguls, had they been white." Like the political bosses of 19th century urban America, numbers operators provided an informal assistance network for needy patrons in the impoverished black communities and represented a major source of capital for black businesses. In city after city, the numbers barons, seeking an element of respectability or an outlet to shield gambling profits from the Internal Revenue Service or merely the thrill of sports ownership, came to dominate black baseball. In Harlem second-generation Cuban immigrant Alex Pompez, a powerful figure in the Dutch Schultz mob, ran the Cuban Stars, while Ed "Soldier Boy" Semler controlled the Black Yankees. Abe Manley of the Newark Eagles, Ed Bolden of the Philadelphia Stars, and Tom Wilson of the Baltimore Elite Giants all garnered their fortunes from the numbers game. Even Cum Posey, who had no connection with the rackets, had to bring in Homestead numbers banker Rufus "Sonnyman" Jackson as a partner and financier to stave off Greenlee's challenge.

In 1933 Greenlee unified the franchises owned by the numbers kings into a rejuvenated Negro National League. Under his leadership, writes Donn Rogosin, "The Negro National League meetings were enclaves of the most powerful black gangsters in the nation." This "unholy alliance" sustained black baseball in the Northeast through depression and war. Even the collapse of the Crawfords and demolition of Greenlee Stadium in 1939 failed to weaken the league which survived until the onset of integration. In 1937 a second circuit, the Negro American League was formed in the Midwest and South. Dominated by Wilkinson and the Kansas City Monarchs, the Negro American League relied less on numbers brokers, but more on white ownership for their financing.

The formation of the Negro American League encouraged the rejuvenation of an annual World Series, matching the champions of the two leagues. But the Negro League World Series never achieved the prominence of its white counterpart. The fact that league standings were often determined among teams playing uneven numbers of games diluted the notion of a champion. Furthermore, impoverished urban blacks could not sustain attendance at a prolonged series. As a result, the Negro League World Series always took a back seat to the annual East-West All-Star Game played in Chicago. The East-West Game, originated by Greenlee in 1933, quickly emerged as the centerpiece of black baseball. Fans chose the players in polls conducted by black newspapers. By 1939, leading candidates received as many as 500,000 votes. Large crowds of blacks and whites watched the finest Negro League stars, and the revenues divided among the teams often spelled the difference between profit and loss at the season's end.

By the 1930s and 1940s, black baseball had become an integral part of Northern ghetto life. With hundreds of employees and millions of dollars in revenue, the Negro Leagues, as Donn Rogosin notes, "may rank among the highest achievements of black enterprise during segregation." In addition, baseball provided an economic ripple effect, boosting business in hotels, cafes, restaurants and bars. In Kansas City and other towns, games became social events, as black citizens, recalls manager Buck O'Neil, "wore their finery." The Monarch Booster Club was a leading civic organization and the "Miss Monarch Bathing Beauty" pageant a popular event.

Black baseball also represented a source of pride for the black community. "The Monarchs was Kansas City's team," boasted bartender Jesse Fisher. "They made Kansas City the talk of the town all over the world." In several cities, white politicians routinely appeared at Opening Day games to curry favor with their often neglected black constituents. When Greenlee Field launched its operations in Pittsburgh, the mayor, city council, and county commissioners lined the field boxes. Negro League owners also played a role in the fight against segregation. In Newark, Effa Manley, who ran the Eagles with her husband Abe, served as treasurer of the New Jersey NAACP and belonged to the Citizen's League for Fair Play which fought for black employment opportunities. Manley sponsored a "Stop Lynching" fundraiser at one Eagles home game.

The impact of the Negro Leagues, however, ranged beyond the communities whose names the teams bore. Throughout the age of Jim Crow baseball, even in those years when a substantial league structure existed, official league games accounted for a relatively small part of the black baseball experience. Black teams would typically play over 200 games a year, only a third of which counted in the league standings. The vast majority of contests occurred on the "barnstorming" circuit, pitting black athletes against a broad array of professional and semi-professional competition, white and black, throughout the nation. In the pre-television era, traveling teams brought a higher level of baseball to fans in the towns and cities of America and allowed local talent to test their skills against the professionals. While some all-white teams, like the "House of David" also trod the barnstorming trail, itinerancy was the key to survival for black squads. The capital needed to finance a Negro League team existed primarily in Northern cities, but the overwhelming majority of blacks lived in the South.

"The schedule was a rugged one," recalled Roy Campanella of the Baltimore Elite Giants. "Rarely were we in the same city two days in a row. Mostly we played by day and traveled by night." After the Monarchs introduced night baseball, teams played both day and night appearing in two and sometimes three different ballparks on the same day. Teams traveled in buses—"our home, dressing room, dining room, and hotel"—or sandwiched into touring cars. "We had little time to waste on the road," states Quincy Trouppe, "so it was a rare treat when the cars would stop at times to let us stretch out and exercise for a few minutes." Most major hotels barred black guests, so even when the schedule allowed overnight stays, the athletes found themselves in less than comfortable accommodations. Large cities usually had better black hotels where ballplayers, entertainers, and other members of the black bourgeoisie congregated. On the road, however, Negro Leaguers more frequently were relegated to Jim Crow roadhouses, "continually under attack by bedbugs."

The black baseball experience extended beyond the confines of the United States and into Central America

and the Caribbean. Negro Leaguers appeared regularly in the Cuban, Puerto Rican, Venezuelan, and Dominican winter leagues where they competed against black and white Latin stars and major leaguers as well.

Some blacks, like Willie Wells and Ray Dandridge, jumped permanently to the Mexican League, where several also became successful managers of interracial teams. As Wells explained, "I am not faced by the racial problem. . . I've found freedom and democracy here, something I never found in the United States. . . In Mexico, I am a man."

Reluctant Clowns

In the United States, however, blacks often found themselves in more distasteful roles. To attract crowds throughout the nation and to keep fans interested in the frequently one-sided contests against amateur competition, some black clubs injected elements of clowning and showmanship into their pre-game and competitive performances. As early as the 1880s, comedy had characterized many barnstorming teams. Black baseball, even in its most serious form, tended to be flashier and less formal than white play. Against inferior teams, players often showboated and flaunted their superior skills. Pitcher Satchel Paige would call in his outfielders or guarantee to strike out the first six or nine batters to face him against semi-professional squads. In the late 1930s, Olympic star Jesse Owens traveled with the Monarchs, racing against horses in pre-game exhibitions.

Black teams, like the Tennessee Rats and Zulu Cannibals, thrived on their minstrel show reputations. The most famous of these franchises were the "Ethiopian Clowns." Originating in Miami in the 1930s, the Clowns later operated out of Cincinnati and then Indianapolis. Their antics included a "pepperball and shadowball" performance (later emulated by basketball's Harlem Globetrotters), and mid-game vaudeville routines by comics Spec Bebop, a dwarf, and King Tut. Players like Pepper Bassett, "the Rocking Chair Catcher" and "Goose" Tatum, a talented first baseman and natural comedian, enlivened the festivities. By the 1940s, the Clowns, through the effort of booking agent Syd Pollack, dominated the baseball comedy market. In 1943, their popularity won the Clowns entrance into the Negro Leagues, although other owners demanded they drop the demeaning "Ethiopian" nickname. Although never one of the better black teams, the Clowns greatly bolstered Negro League attendance.

Their popularity notwithstanding, the comedy teams reflected one of the worst elements of black baseball. The Clowns and Zulus perpetuated stereotypes drawn from Stepin Fetchit and Tarzan movies. "Negroes must realize the danger in insisting that ballplayers paint their faces and go through minstrel show revues before each ballgame," protested sportswriter Wendell Smith. Many black players resented the image that all were clowns. "Didn't nobody clown in our league but the Indianapolis Clowns," objected Piper Davis. "We played baseball."

Even without the clowning, black baseball offered a more freewheeling and, in many respects, more exciting brand of baseball than the major leagues. Since the 1920s, when Babe Ruth had revolutionized the game, the majors had pursued power strategies, emphasizing the home run above all else. Although the great sluggers of the Negro Leagues rivaled those in the National and American Leagues, they comprised but one element in the speed-dominated universe of "tricky baseball." Black teams emphasized the bunt, the stolen base, and the hit-and-run. "We played by the 'coonsbury' rules," boasted second baseman Newt Allen. "That's just any way you think you can win, any kind of play you think you could get by on."

In games between white and black all-star teams, this style of play often confounded the major leaguers. Center fielder Cool Papa Bell personified this approach. Bell was so fast, marveled rival third baseman Judy Johnson, "You couldn't play back in your regular position or you'd never throw him out." In one game against a major league All-Star squad, Bell scored from first base on a sacrifice bunt! In center field, his great speed allowed him to lurk in the shallow reaches of the outfield, ranging great distances to make spectacular catches.

Negro League pitching also took on a peculiar caste. "Anything went in the Negro League," reported catcher Roy Campanella, "Spitballs, shineballs, emery balls; pitchers used any and all of them." Since league officials could not afford to replace the balls as frequently as in organized ball, scuffed and nicked baseballs remained in the game, giving pitchers great latitude for creative efforts. "I never knew what the ball would do once it left the pitcher's hand," recalled Campanella.

Since most rosters included only 14 to 18 men, Negro League players demonstrated a wide range of versatility. Each was required to fill in at a variety of positions. Star pitchers often found themselves in the outfield when not on the mound. Some won renown at more than one position. Ted "Double-Duty" Radcliffe often pitched in the first game of a doubleheader and caught in the second. Cuban Martin Dihigo, whom many rank as the greatest player of all time, excelled at every position. In 1938, in the Mexican League he led the league's pitchers with an 18-2 record and the league's hitters with a .387 average.

The manpower shortage offered opportunities for individuals to display their all-around talents, but it also limited the competitiveness of the black teams. While on a given day a Negro League franchise, featuring one of its top pitchers, might defeat a major league squad, most teams lacked the depth to compete on a regular basis. "The big leagues were strong in every position," remarks Radcliffe. "Most of the colored teams had a few stars but they weren't strong in every position."

While black teams may not have matched the top clubs in organized baseball, the individual stars of the 1930s and 1940s clearly ranked among the best of any age. Homestead Gray teammates Josh Gibson and Buck Leonard won renown as the Babe Ruth and Lou Gehrig of the Negro Leagues. The Grays discovered Gibson in 1929 as an 18-year-old catcher on the sandlots of Pittsburgh, where he had already earned a reputation for 500-foot home runs. For 17 years, he launched prodigious blasts off pitchers in the Negro Leagues, on the barnstorming tour, and in Latin America. As talented as any major league star, Gibson died in January 1947, at age 35, just three months before Jackie Robinson joined the Brooklyn Dodgers. Leonard, four years older than Gibson, starred in both the Negro and Mexican Leagues as a sure-handed,

power-hitting first baseman. The Newark Eagles in the early 1940s, boasted the "million dollar infield" of first baseman Mule Suttles, second baseman Dick Seay, shortstop Willie Wells, and third baseman Ray Dandridge. The acrobatic fielding skills of Seay, Wells and Dandridge led Roy Campanella to call this the greatest infield he ever saw.

Paige Stands Alone

Amidst the many talented Negro Leaguers of 1930s and 1940s, however, one long, lean figure came to personify black baseball to blacks and whites alike. Leroy "Satchel" Paige began his prolonged athletic odyssey in his hometown in 1924 as a 17-year-old pitcher with the semi-professional Mobile Tigers. He joined the Chattanooga Black Lookouts of the Negro Southern League in 1926. Two years later the Lookouts sold his contract to the Birmingham Black Barons. By 1930 his explosive fastball, impeccable control, and eccentric mannerisms had made him a legend in the South. In 1932 Gus Greenlee brought Paige to the Pittsburgh Crawfords where the colorful pitcher embellished his reputation by winning 54 games in his first two years. Greenlee also began the practice of hiring out Paige to semi-professional clubs that needed a one-day box office boost.

For seven years Paige feuded with Greenlee, jumping the club when a better offer appeared, being banished "for life," and then returning. In the mid-1930s, in addition to his stints with the Crawfords, Paige won fame by boosting Bismarck, N.D., to the national semi-professional championships, hurling for the Dominican Republic at the behest of dictator Rafael Trujillo, in the Mexican League, and especially on the postseason barnstorming trail pitted against Dizzy Dean's Major League All-Stars. "That skinny old Satchel Paige with those long arms is my idea of the pitcher with the greatest stuff I ever saw," claimed the unusually immodest Dean.

Paige's appeal stemmed as much from his unusual persona as his pitching prowess. A born showman, Paige's lanky, lackadaisical presence evoked popular racial stereotypes of the age. "As undependable as a pair of second-hand suspenders," Paige often arrived late or failed to show. His names for his pitches (the "bee ball" which buzzed and all of a sudden, "be there"; the "jump ball"; and the "trouble ball") and his minstrel show one-liners enhanced the image. But on the mound, Paige invariably rose to the occasion against top competition or challenged inferior opponents by calling in the outfield or promising to strike out the side.

In 1938 a sore arm threatened to curtail Paige's career, but the Kansas City Monarchs, hoping his reputation alone would draw fans, signed him for their traveling second team. On the road, Paige perfected a repertoire of curves and off-speed pitches, including his famous "hesitation" pitch. When his fastball returned in 1939, he became a better pitcher than ever. Promoted to the main Monarch club, Paige pitched the team to four consecutive Negro American League pennants. From 1941-1947, although officially still a Monarch, Paige spent far more time as an independent performer, hired out by Monarchs' owner J. L. Wilkinson to semi-pro and Negro League clubs. "He kept our league going," recalls Othello Renfroe. "Anytime a team got into trouble, it sent for Satchel to pitch." Paige also continued to hurl against major league all-star teams. In the 1940s, the example of Satchel Paige, whose legend had spread into the white community, offered the most compelling argument for the desegregation of the National Pastime.

Paige's exploits against white players revealed a fundamental irony about baseball in the Jim Crow era. While organized baseball rigidly enforced its ban on black players within the major and minor leagues, opportunities abounded for black athletes to prove themselves against white competition along the unpoliced boundaries of the national pastime. During the 1930s, Western promoters sponsored tournaments for the best semi-professional teams in the nation. These squads often featured former and future major leaguers as well as top local talent. In 1934 the *Denver Post* tourney, "the little World Series of the West," invited the Kansas City Monarchs to compete for the $7,500 first prize. The Monarchs fought their way into the finals against the House of David team (also owned by J. L. Wilkinson) only to find themselves confronted on the mound by Paige, rented out to pitch this one game. Paige outdueled Monarchs ace, Chet Brewer, 2-1. Black teams became a fixture in the Post series, emerging victorious for several consecutive years.

In 1935, the National Baseball Congress began an annual tournament in Wichita, Kan. The competition attracted community squads heartily bankrolled by local business leaders. Neil Churchill, an auto dealer from Bismarck, North Dakota, recruited a half-dozen black stars, including Paige and Brewer, to represent the town in the Wichita competition. Bismarck naturally swept the series, and thereafter teams that were either integrated or all black routinely appeared in the National Baseball Congress invitational each year.

In an age in which the major leagues were confined to the East and Midwest, and television had yet to bring baseball into people's homes, postseason tours by big league stars offered yet another opportunity for black players to prove their equality on the diamond. Games pitting blacks against whites were popular features of the barnstorming circuit. Until the late 1920s, when Commissioner Kenesaw Mountain Landis limited postseason play to all-star squads, black teams frequently met and defeated major league clubs in postseason competition. During the next decade, matchups between the Babe Ruth or Dizzy Dean "All-Stars" and black players became frequent. In the autumns of 1934 and 1935, Dean's team traveled the nation accompanied by the "Satchel Paige All-Stars." In one memorable 1934 game, called by baseball executive Bill Veeck, "the greatest pitching battle I have ever seen," Paige bested Dean, 1-0. Surviving records of interracial contests during the 1930s reveal that blacks won two-thirds of the games. "That's when we played the hardest," asserted Judy Johnson, "to let them know, and to let the public know, that we had the same talent they did and probably a little better at times."

The rivalries proved particularly keen on the West Coast where Monarchs co-owner Tom Baird organized the California Winter League, which included black teams, white major and minor league stars, and some of Mexico's top players. In 1940, pitcher Chet Brewer

formed the Kansas City Royals, which each year fielded one of the best clubs on the coast. One year the Royals defeated the Hollywood Stars, who had won the Pacific Coast League championship, six straight times. In 1945, Brewer's team, including Jackie Robinson and Satchel Paige, regularly defeated major league competition.

The most famous of the interracial barnstorming tours occurred in 1946, when Cleveland Indians pitcher Bob Feller organized a major league All-Star Team, rented two Flying Tiger aircraft and hopped the nation accompanied by the Satchel Paige All-Stars. With Feller and Paige each pitching a few innings a day, the tour proved extremely lucrative for promoters and players alike and gave widespread publicity to the skills of the black athletes.

The World War II years marked the heyday of the Negro Leagues. With black and white workers flooding into Northern industrial centers, relatively full employment, and a scarcity of available consumer goods, attendance at all sorts of entertainment events increased dramatically. In 1942, three million fans saw Negro League teams play, while the East-West game in 1943 attracted over 51,000 fans. "Even the white folks was coming out big," recalled Satchel Paige.

Change in the Air

But World War II also generated forces which would challenge the foundations of Jim Crow baseball. In the armed forces, baseball teams like the Black Bluejackets of the Great Lakes Naval Station team posted outstanding records against teams featuring white major leaguers. In 1945, a well-publicized tournament of teams in the European theatre featured top black players like Leon Day, Joe Green, and Willard Brown in the championship round. More significantly, the hypocrisy of blacks fighting for their country but unable to participate in the national pastime grew steadily more apparent. As wartime manpower shortages forced major league teams to rely on a 15-year-old pitcher, over-the-hill veterans, and one-armed Pete Gray, their refusal to sign black players seemed increasingly irrational. "How do you think I felt when I saw a one-armed outfielder?" moaned Chet Brewer. Pitcher Nate Moreland protested, "I can play in Mexico, but I have to fight for America where I can't play." Pickets at Yankee Stadium carried placards asking, "If we are able to stop bullets, why not balls?"

Amidst this heightened awareness, organized baseball repeatedly walked to the precipice of integration, but always failed to take the final leap. In 1942, Moreland and All-American football star Jackie Robinson requested a tryout at a White Sox training camp in Pasadena, California. Robinson, in particular, impressed White Sox manager Jimmy Dykes but nothing came of the event. Brooklyn Dodgers manager Leo Durocher publicly stated his willingness to sign blacks, only to receive a stinging rebuke from Commissioner Landis. Landis again short-circuited integration talk the following year. At the annual baseball meetings, black leaders led by actor Paul Robeson gained the opportunity to address major league owners on the issue, but Landis ruled all further discussion out of order.

In 1943 several minor and major league teams were rumored close to signing black players. In California, where winter league play had demonstrated the potential of black players, several clubs considered integration. The Los Angeles Angels of the Pacific Coast League announced tryouts for three black players, but pressure from other league owners doomed the plan. Oakland owner Vince DeVicenzi ordered manager Johnny Vergez to consider pitcher Chet Brewer, the most popular black player on the West Coast. Vergez refused and the issue died. Two years later, Bakersfield, a Cleveland Indians farm team in the California League, offered Brewer a position as player-coach, but the parent club vetoed the plan.

At the major league level, Washington Senators owner Clark Griffith called sluggers Josh Gibson and Buck Leonard into his office and asked if they would like to play in the major leagues. They answered affirmatively, but never heard from Griffith again. In Pittsburgh, *Daily Worker* sports editor Nat Low pressured Pirates owner William Benswanger to arrange a tryout for catcher Roy Campanella and pitcher Dave Barnhill. At the last minute, Benswanger canceled the audition, citing "unnamed pressures."

For more than two decades, the imperial Landis had reigned over baseball as an implacable foe of integration. While hypocritically denying the existence of any "rule, formal or informal, or any understanding—unwritten, subterranean, or sub-anything—against the signing of Negro players," Landis had stringently policed the color line. His death in 1944 removed a major barrier for integration advocates.

In April 1945, with World War II entering its final months, the integration crusade gained momentum. On April 6, *People's Voice* sportswriter Joe Bostic appeared at the Brooklyn Dodger training camp at Bear Mountain, New York, with two Negro League players, Terris McDuffie and Dave "Showboat" Thomas, and demanded a tryout. Outraged, but outmaneuvered, Dodgers president Branch Rickey allowed the pair to work out with the club.

One week later, a more serious confrontation occurred in Boston. The Red Sox, under public pressure from popular columnist Dave Egan and city councilman Isidore Muchnick, agreed to audition Sam Jethroe, the Negro League's leading hitter in 1944, second baseman Marvin Williams, and Kansas City Monarchs shortstop Jackie Robinson, all top prospects in their mid-20s. The Fenway Park tryout, however, proved little more than a formality and the players never again heard from the Red Sox.

The publicity surrounding these events, however, forced the major leagues to address the issue at its April meetings. At the urging of black sportswriter Sam Lacy, Leslie O'Connor, Landis' interim successor, established a Major League Committee on Baseball Integration in April 1945, to review the problem. In addition, the racial views of the newly appointed commissioner, A. B. "Happy" Chandler, came under close scrutiny. A former governor of the segregated state of Kentucky, Chandler nonetheless offered at least verbal support to the entry of blacks into organized ball. "If a black boy can make it on Okinawa and Guadalcanal, hell, he can make it in baseball," Chandler told black reporter Rick Roberts. Whether Chandler, however, unlike Landis, would reinforce his rhetoric with positive actions remained uncertain.

Rickey Takes the First Step

Unbeknownst to the integration advocates, baseball officials, and local politicians sand-dancing around the race issue, Branch Rickey, the president of the Brooklyn Dodgers, had already set in motion the events which would lead to the historic breakthrough.

Raised in rural Ohio in a strict Methodist family, Rickey, nicknamed by sportwriters "The Deacon" and "The Mahatma," had financed his way through college and law school playing and coaching baseball. His skills as a catcher merited two years in the major leagues. In 1913 he abandoned a fledgling law career to manage the St. Louis Browns, and in 1917 he began a 25-year relationship with the St. Louis Cardinals. Rickey served as the field manager of the Cardinals from 1919 to 1925, after which he became the club's vice-president and business manager. In the 1920s and 1930s, Rickey perfected the farm system, whereby a major league team controlled young, undeveloped players through a chain of minor league franchises. This innovation allowed the Cardinals to compete equally with richer teams in larger cities, generating pennants for the "Gashouse Gang" and allowing the team to profitably sell off surplus talent.

Although Rickey later claimed that his desire to integrate baseball dated from 1904, when an Indiana hotel had denied lodgings to a black player on his college squad, he gave no indication of any interest in the race issue during his years in St. Louis. Perhaps this stemmed from the fact that St. Louis was a Southern city with firmly entrenched segregationist traditions. Throughout Rickey's reign with the Cardinals, blacks sat in Jim Crow sections at Sportsman's Park, a policy which he never openly challenged.

Nonetheless, in 1942, when Rickey left the Cardinals and assumed control of the Brooklyn Dodgers, he informed the Dodger ownership of his intentions to recruit black players in the near future. Rickey never clearly explained the motivations for this dramatic turnaround. At times Rickey cited moral considerations, stating, "I couldn't face my God much longer knowing that His black creatures are held separate and distinct from His white creatures in the game that has given me all I own." On other occasions, he eschewed the role of "crusader," proclaiming, "My selfish objective is to win baseball games. . .The Negroes will make us winners for years to come."

Some observers saw financial reasons behind Rickey's actions, citing the lure of the growing black population in Northern cities and the prospects of increased attendance. Certainly, Brooklyn offered a more congenial atmosphere for integration than St. Louis. In all probability, a combination of these factors—geographic, moral, competitive, and financial—coupled with Rickey's desire for a broader role in history, impelled him to seek black players.

From 1942-1945, Rickey, a conservative, cautious, and conspiratorial man, moved slowly, studying the philosophical and sociological ramifications of integration and taking few people into his confidence. During the spring and summer of 1945, under the guise of creating a new black baseball circuit, the United States League, Rickey's scouts combed the nation and the Caribbean for black players. Rickey sought one player who would spearhead

the breakthrough and several other potential stars who would follow in his wake. By August 1945 scouting reports and Rickey's own investigations pointed to one man as the ideal candidate for the struggle ahead—Kansas City Monarchs shortstop Jackie Robinson.

In Robinson, Rickey had found a rare combination of athletic ability, competitive fire, intelligence, maturity, and poise. Born in Georgia and raised in Pasadena, Ca., Robinson had won fame at UCLA as the nation's greatest all-around athlete, earning All-America honors in football, establishing broad-jump records, and leading his basketball conference in scoring, all in addition to his baseball exploits. In 1942, he enlisted in the army where he attended officer's candidate school and became a lieutenant. Two years later, while stationed in Texas, Robinson's refusal to move to the back of a bus resulted in a court martial and ultimate acquittal. This incident demonstrated his commitment to the cause of equal rights. After his discharge from the army, Robinson joined the Monarchs and earned a starting spot in the 1945 East-West All-Star Game. Robinson's college education, experience in interracial athletics, and army career complemented his playing talents. But his fiery pride and temper seemed a potential obstacle to his success.

On Aug. 28, 1945, Robinson met with Rickey at the latter's Brooklyn offices. Rickey revealed his bold plan to integrate organized baseball and challenged Robinson to accept the primary role. Rickey flamboyantly playacted, assuming the role of racist players, fans and hotel clerks, impressing upon Robinson the need to "turn the other cheek" in the event of racial confrontations. By the end of the session, Robinson had signed a contract to play for the Montreal Royals in the International League, the top farm team in the Brooklyn system. Rickey promised that if Robinson's performance merited it, he would be promoted to the Dodgers.

Rickey intended to announce the Robinson signing along with that of several other black players, but political pressures stemming from the New York City fall elections forced him to abandon his original plans and, on Oct. 23, 1945, to reveal the signing of Robinson alone. The announcement sent shock waves through the baseball establishment and placed Robinson into a spotlight that he would never relinquish. Numerous sports figures, from players to executives to reporters, predicted the ultimate failure of Rickey's "great experiment."

Robinson's first test came at spring training in Florida in 1946. Thrust into the deep South where Jim Crow reigned supreme, Robinson and black pitcher John Wright, whom Rickey had recruited to room with Robinson, were unable to room with their teammates and barred from playing in Jacksonville and other Florida cities. In addition, a shoulder injury hindered Robinson's performance, raising doubts about his abilities.

On April 18, 1946, at Roosevelt Stadium in Jersey City, Robinson became the first black to appear in modern Organized Baseball (excepting Jimmy Claxton, who passed as white in 1916 for the Oakland Oaks of the Pacific Coast League). In the process he staged one of the most remarkable performances under pressure in the history of the game. In Robinson's second at-bat, he hit a three-run home run. He followed this with three singles and two stolen bases, scoring a total of four runs. As the

New York Times reported, "This would have been a big day for any man, but under the circumstances, it was a tremendous feat."

In many respects, 1946 proved a nightmare season for Robinson. Fans jeered him in Baltimore, and opposing players tormented him with insults. Pitchers made him a frequent target of brushback pitches and baserunners attempted to spike and maim him at second base. As the season drew to a close, Robinson hovered on the brink of a nervous breakdown. Through it all, however, Robinson remained a dominant force on the field. His .349 batting average and 113 runs scored led the league and paced the Royals to the International League pennant. His presence inspired new attendance records throughout the circuit. In the Little World Series, which pitted Montreal against the Louisville Colonels of the American Association, Robinson braved the hostility of Kentucky fans and stroked game-winning hits in the final two games to give the Royals the championship.

Rickey's initiative and Robinson's dramatic success failed to inspire other team owners. In August, major league executives debated a controversial report discussing the "race question" which argued that integration would "lessen the value of several major league franchises." No other clubs moved to sign black players. Only four blacks, all in the Brooklyn system, joined Robinson in organized baseball in 1946. At Nashua, N.H., in the New England League, the Dodgers farm club fielded catcher Roy Campanella and pitcher Don Newcombe. The Nashua Dodgers won the league championship largely due to Campanella's hitting and Newcombe's hurling. In the small town of Trois Rivières in Quebec, pitchers John Wright and Roy Partlow, both of whom had appeared briefly with Robinson at Montreal, led a third Dodgers farm team to the Canadian-American League crown. Nonetheless, at the start of the 1947 season, no additional black players appeared on any major or minor league rosters.

The Big Leagues at Last

Although Robinson's performance at Montreal merited promotion to the Dodgers, Robinson remained a Royal when he reported to spring training in 1947. Rickey hoped that the Brooklyn players themselves, when exposed to Robinson's talents, would request his addition to the team. He switched Robinson to first base, a weak spot on the Dodgers, to make his case more compelling. Robinson compiled a .519 batting average against the major leaguers, but several Dodger players, instead of demanding his promotion, rebelled. Led by Fred "Dixie" Walker, a group of mostly Southern Dodgers circulated a petition against Robinson. Rickey moved quickly to short-circuit the dissension, threatening to trade any athletes who opposed Robinson. In addition, the refusal of Pete Reiser, Pee Wee Reese and other Dodgers to support the protestors, effectively squelched the petition drive. Finally, on April 10, just five days before the start of the 1947 season, Rickey officially announced that Robinson would join the Dodgers.

Throughout the early months of the 1947 campaign Robinson stoically endured crises and challenges. The Philadelphia Phillies, led by manager Ben Chapman, unleashed a barrage of verbal abuse against Robinson which horrified Dodgers players and fans. The Benjamin Franklin Hotel in Philadelphia refused lodgings for Robinson and death threats appeared among his voluminous daily mail. In early May, rumors that the St. Louis Cardinals planned to strike rather than compete against Robinson prompted National League President Ford Frick to warn the players, "If you do this you will be suspended from the league."

Opposing pitchers targeted Robinson's body at a record setting pace and an early season 0 for 20 batting drought led many to question his qualifications as a professional baseball player. "But for the fact that he is the first acknowledged Negro in major league history," observed a Cincinnati sportswriter, "he would have been benched a week ago."

Yet, as the season unfolded, Robinson converted doubters and enemies into admirers. By the end of June, a 21-game hitting streak had raised his batting average to .315 and propelled the Dodgers into first place. Robinson's daring baserunning, typical of Negro League play, evoked images of an "Ebony Ty Cobb." In city after city, record crowds flocked to experience Robinson's charismatic dynamism as five teams set new all-time season attendance marks. While periodic controversies erupted over baserunners who used their spikes "to make a pincushion out of Robinson" at first base, Robinson won the acceptance and respect of teammates and opponents alike. In September, as the Dodgers coasted to the pennant, *The Sporting News* named Robinson the major league Rookie of the Year. To cap his triumphant season, Robinson became the first black player to appear in the World Series.

Robinson's success on the field and at the box office stimulated some movement on the part of other clubs to hire black players. In Cleveland, Bill Veeck recruited 23-year-old Larry Doby, who jumped straight from the Negro League Newark Eagles to the Indians in July. Used sparingly, Doby batted a meager .156, casting doubts upon his future. The St. Louis Browns, seeking to boost flagging attendance, signed Willard Brown and Hank Thompson of the Kansas City Monarchs. When the turnstiles failed to respond, the Browns released both Brown and Thompson, although the latter had established himself as a top prospect. In the National League, the Dodgers signed Dan Bankhead to bolster the club's pitching down the stretch. On Aug. 25, Bankhead, the first black pitcher to appear in the major leagues, surrendered eight runs in three innings but also slammed a home run in his initial at bat.

In addition to the five athletes who appeared in the major leagues, a handful of blacks surfaced in the minors. Campanella succeeded Robinson at Montreal, earning accolades as "the best catcher in the business." Newcombe returned to Nashua where he won 19 games. The independent Stamford Bombers of the Colonial League fielded six black players, and two blacks, including future major leaguer Chuck Harmon, played in the Canadian-American League. Veteran Negro League hurler Nate Moreland won 20 games in California's Class C Sunset League. For the most part, however, organized baseball continued to ignore the treasure trove of black talent

submerged in the Negro Leagues. A full year would pass before additional major league teams would add black players to their chains.

In 1948 the integration focus shifted from the Dodgers, where Robinson now reigned at second base, to the Cleveland Indians. In spring training, Larry Doby, who had performed so dismally in 1947, unexpectedly won a starting berth in the Cleveland outfield. After an erratic early season stretch in which Doby alternated errors and strikeouts with tape-measure home runs, he batted .301 and became a key performer for the American League champion Indians. In July, Cleveland owner Bill Veeck added the legendary Satchel Paige to the team. Amidst charges that his signing had been a publicity stunt, the 42-year-old Paige won six out of seven decisions, including back-to-back shutouts, and posted a 2.47 earned run average. Standing-room-only crowds greeted him in Washington, Chicago, Boston, and even in Cleveland's mammoth Municipal Stadium. The Indians, after defeating the Boston Red Sox in a pennant playoff, won the World Series in six games with Doby's .318 average leading the club.

In 1947 the Dodgers had integrated and reached the World Series; in 1948 the Indians had duplicated and surpassed this achievement. Both teams had set all-time attendance records. Remarkably, as the 1948 season drew to a close, no other franchise had followed their lead. In the minor leagues, Roy Campanella became the first black in the American Association, stopping at St. Paul before permanently joining Robinson on the Dodgers. Newcombe and Bankhead each won more than 20 games for Brooklyn affiliates. The Dodgers also added fleet-footed Sam Jethroe to the Montreal roster, where he batted .322. The Indians began to stockpile black talent as well, signing future major leaguers Al Smith, Dave Hoskins, and Orestes "Minnie" Minoso to minor league contracts. Several other blacks, including San Diego catcher John Ritchey, who broke the Pacific Coast League color line, played for independent teams.

In the interregnum between the 1948 and 1949 seasons four more teams—the Giants, Yankees, Braves, and Cubs—signed blacks to play in their farm systems, and 1949 would herald the beginning of widespread integration in the minor leagues. Blacks starred in all three Triple A leagues. In the Pacific Coast League, Luke Easter won acclaim as the "greatest natural hitter . . . since Ted Williams," amassing 25 home runs and 92 runs batted in in just 80 games before succumbing to a knee injury. Oakland's Artie Wilson led the league in hits, stolen bases, and batting average. In the International League, Jethroe scored 151 runs and stole 89 bases while Montreal teammate Dan Bankhead won 20 games for the second straight year. At Jersey City, Monte Irvin batted .373. The outstanding performer in the American Association was Ray Dandridge. Considered by many the greatest third baseman of all time, the acrobatic Dandridge, now in his late 30s, thrilled Minneapolis fans with his spectacular fielding, batting .364 in the process. Former Negro Leaguers turned in equally stellar performances at lower minor league levels as well.

In the major leagues, the spotlight again returned to Jackie Robinson. For three years, Robinson had honored his pledge to Branch Rickey "to turn the other cheek" and avoid confrontations. With his position in the majors firmly established, Robinson announced, "They better be prepared to be rough this year, because I'm going to be rough on them." The more combative Robinson produced his finest year, batting .342 and earning the Most Valuable Player Award. Complemented by teammates Newcombe and Campanella, Robinson led the Dodgers to another pennant.

Slow to Follow

By the end of the 1949 season integration had achieved spectacular success at both the major and minor league level, but most teams moved "with all deliberate speed" in signing black players. The New York Giants joined the interracial ranks in 1949 when they promoted Monte Irvin and Hank Thompson. The following year, the Boston Braves purchased Jethroe from the Dodgers for $100,000 and installed him in the starting lineup. In 1951, the Chicago White Sox acquired Minnie Minoso in a trade with Cleveland, and Bill Veeck, who had acquired the hapless St. Louis Browns, brought back Satchel Paige for another major league stint. Yet, as late as August 1953, out of 16 major league teams only these six fielded black players. Several teams displayed an interest in signing blacks but bypassed established Negro League stars who might have jumped directly to the majors, concentrating instead on younger prospects for the minor leagues. Still others like the Red Sox, Phillies, Cardinals, and Tigers continued to pursue a whites-only policy.

This failure to hire and promote blacks occurred amidst a continuing backdrop of outstanding performances by black players. The first generation of players from the Negro Leagues proved an extraordinary group. Jackie Robinson quickly established himself as one of the dominant stars in the national pastime, compiling a .311 batting average over his 10-year career while thrilling fans with his baserunning and clutch-hitting talents. Sportswriters called him, "the most dangerous man in baseball today." Campanella won accolades as the best catcher in the National League and won the Most Valuable Player Award in 1951, 1953, and 1955. Both Campanella and Robinson later won election to the Baseball Hall of Fame. Pitcher Don Newcombe averaged better than 20 wins a season during his first five full years with the Dodgers. In addition, from 1950 to 1953 Negro League graduates Sam Jethroe, Willie Mays, Joe Black, and Jim Gilliam each won the National League Rookie of the Year Award.

In the American League, where integration proceeded at a slower pace, several players compiled outstanding records. Larry Doby, while never achieving the superstar status many expected, nonetheless became a steady producer, twice leading the league in home runs and five times driving in more than 100 runs. He was elected to the Baseball Hall of Fame in 1998. Doby's Cleveland teammate Luke Easter, who reached the majors in his mid-30s, slugged 86 home runs and drove in 300 runs in his brief three-season career. Satchel Paige, after a two-year stint with the Indians, joined the hapless St. Louis Browns from 1951 to 1953 and became one of the American League's best relief pitchers. On the Chicago White Sox, Minnie Minoso proved himself a consistent .300 hitter.

Despite their relatively small numbers, teams with black players in both major leagues regularly finished high in the standings and only in 1950 did both pennant winners field all-white squads. In addition, the more aggressive stance of National League teams in recruiting black players gave that circuit a clear superiority in World Series and All-Star contests for more than two decades.

By the end of the 1953 season, the benefits of integration had grown apparent to all but the most recalcitrant of major league owners. In September, the Chicago Cubs purchased shortstop Ernie Banks from the Kansas City Monarchs and finally elevated longtime minor league standout Gene Baker. Connie Mack's Philadelphia Athletics ended their Jim Crow era by acquiring pitcher Bob Trice. At the start of the 1954 season, the Washington Senators, St. Louis Cardinals, Pittsburgh Pirates, and Cincinnati Reds all joined the interracial ranks. The sudden integration of six more clubs left only the Yankees, Tigers, Phillies, and Red Sox with all-white personnel. In addition, 1954 marked the debut of young Henry Aaron with the Braves and the return of Willie Mays, who had sparkled for the Giants in 1951, from military service.

The desegregation of organized baseball opened the way not only to blacks in the United States but to those in other parts of the Americas as well. Throughout the 20th century, baseball had imposed a curious double standard on Latin players, accepting those with light complexions but rejecting their darker countrymen. With the color barrier down, major league clubs found a wealth of talent in the Carribbean. Minnie Minoso, the "Cuban Comet" who integrated the Chicago White Sox, became the first of the great Latin stars. Over a 15-year career, Minoso compiled a .298 batting average. In 1954 slick-fielding Puerto Rican Vic Power launched his career with the Athletics. The following year, Roberto Clemente, the greatest of the Latin stars, debuted with the Pittsburgh Pirates. The proud Puerto Rican won four batting championships and amassed 3,000 hits en route to a .317 lifetime batting average. In the late 1950s the San Francisco Giants revealed the previously ignored treasure trove that existed in the Dominican Republic. In 1958 Felipe Alou became the first of three Alou brothers to play for the Giants, and in 1960 the Giants unveiled pitcher Juan Marichal, "the Dominican Dandy," who won 243 games en route to the Hall of Fame.

Among the early Latin players were two sons of stars of the Jim Crow age. Perucho Cepeda, who had won renown as "The Bull" in his native Puerto Rico, had refused to play in the segregated Negro leagues. His son Orlando, dubbed "The Baby Bull," went on to star for the Giants and Cardinals. Luis Tiant, Sr., a standout performer in both Cuba and the Negro Leagues, lived to see Luis, Jr. win over 200 major league games and excel in the 1975 World Series.

Major Changes in Minor Leagues

As the major leagues moved slowly toward complete desegregation, blacks invaded the minor leagues. In the Northern and Western states, these athletes, a combination of youthful prospects and Negro League veterans, were greeted by a storm of insults, beanballs, and discrimination. "I learned more names than I thought we had," states Piper Davis of his treatment by fans in the Pacific Coast League. At least a half-dozen blacks had to be carried off the field on stretchers after being hit by pitches between 1949 and 1951. In city after city, blacks found hotels and restaurants unwilling to serve them.

"At the same time when they signed blacks and Latins," argues John Roseboro about his Dodger employers, "they should have made sure they would be welcome." But neither the Dodgers nor other clubs provided any special assistance for their black farmhands. Despite these conditions, blacks compiled remarkable records in league after league. In the early 1950s, blacks overcame adversity and dominated the lists of batting leaders at the Triple A level and in many of the lower circuits as well.

In 1952, blacks began to appear on minor league clubs in the Jim Crow South. The Dallas Eagles of the Texas League, hoping to boost sagging attendance, signed former Homestead Gray pitcher Dave Hoskins to become the "Jackie Robinson of the Texas League." Hoskins took the Lone Star State by storm, attracting record crowds en route to a 22-10 record. The black pitcher posted a 2.12 earned run average and also finished third in the league in batting with a .328 mark. By 1955 every Texas League club except Shreveport fielded black players.

Hoskins' performance inspired other teams throughout the South to scramble for black players. In 1953 19-year-old Henry Aaron desegregated the South Atlantic League, which included clubs in Florida, Atlanta, and Georgia, while Bill White appeared in the Carolina League. Playing for Jacksonville (a city which seven years earlier had barred Jackie Robinson), Aaron "led the league in everything but hotel accommodations." By 1954 when the United States Supreme Court issued its historic *Brown* v. *Board of Education* decision ordering school desegregation, blacks had appeared in most Southern minor leagues.

The integration of the South, however, did not proceed without incidents. Black players recall these years as "an ordeal" or a "sentence" and described the South as "enemy country" or a "hellhole." In 1953 the Cotton States League barred brothers Jim and Leander Tugerson from competing.

The following year, Nat Peeples broke the color line in the Southern Association, but lasted only two weeks. For the remainder of the decade, the league adhered to a whites-only policy, a strategy which contributed to the collapse of the Southern Association in 1961. As resistance to the civil rights movement mounted in the 1950s, black players found themselves in increasingly hostile territory. Even in the pioneering Texas League, teams visiting Shreveport, Louisiana, in 1956 had to leave their black players at home due to stricter segregation laws.

In the face of these obstacles, young black stars like Aaron, Curt Flood, Frank Robinson, Bill White, and Leon Wagner overcame their frustrations "by taking it out on the ball." "What had started as a chance to test my baseball ability in a professional setting," wrote Curt Flood, "had become an obligation to test myself as a man." Throughout the 1950s, blacks appeared regularly among the league leaders of the Texas, South Atlantic, Carolina, and other circuits, advancing both their own careers and the cause of integration.

As these events unfolded in the South, the major leagues completed their long overdue integration process. The Yankees, after denying charges of racism for almost a decade, finally promoted Elston Howard to the parent club in 1955. Two more years passed before the Phillies integrated, and not until 1958 did a black player don a Tiger uniform. Thus, at the start of the 1959 season, only the Boston Red Sox, who had yet to hire either black scouts or representatives in the Caribbean, retained their Jim Crow heritage. A storm of protest arose when the Red Sox cut black infielder Elijah "Pumpsie" Green just before Opening Day, but on July 21, 1959, 12 years and 107 days after Jackie Robinson's Dodger debut, Green won promotion to the Boston club, completing the cycle of major league integration.

While integration became a reality in organized baseball, the Negro Leagues gradually faded into oblivion. As early as 1947, Negro League attendance, especially in cities close to National League parks, dropped precipitously. "People wanted to go Brooklynites," recalls Monarchs pitcher Hilton Smith. "Even if we were playing here in Kansas City, people wanted to go over to St. Louis to see Jackie." Negro League owners hoped to offset declining attendance by selling players to organized baseball, but major league teams paid what Effa Manley called "bargain basement" prices for all-star talent. In 1948 the Manleys' Newark Eagles and New York Black Yankees disbanded. The Homestead Grays severed all league connections and returned to its roots as a barnstorming unit. Without these teams the Negro National League collapsed. A reorganized 10-team Negro American League, most of whose franchises were located in minor league cities, vowed to go on, but the spread of integration quickly thinned its ranks. By 1951, the league had dwindled to six teams. Two years later, only the Birmingham Black Barons, Memphis Red Sox, Kansas City Monarchs, and Indianapolis Clowns remained.

For several years in the early 1950s, the Negro Leagues remained a breeding ground for young black talent. The New York Giants plucked Willie Mays from the roster of the Birmingham Black Barons, while the Boston Braves discovered Hank Aaron on the Indianapolis Clowns. The Kansas City Monarchs produced more than two dozen major leaguers, including Robinson, Paige, Banks, and Howard. But for most black players, the demise of the Negro Leagues had disastrous effects. "The livelihoods, the careers, the families of 400 Negro ballplayers are in jeopardy," complained Effa Manley in 1948, "because four players were successful in getting into the major leagues." The slow pace of integration left most in a state of limbo set adrift by their former teams, but still unwelcomed in organized baseball. Some players like Buck Leonard and Cool Papa Bell were too old to be considered, while others like Ray Dandridge and Piper Davis found themselves relegated to the minor leagues, where outstanding records failed to win them promotion.

Throughout the 1950s the Negro American League struggled to survive, recruiting teenagers and second-rate talent for the modest four-team loop. In 1963 Kansas City hosted the 30th and last East-West All-Star Game and the following year the famed Monarchs ceased touring the nation. By 1965 the Indianapolis Clowns remained as a last vestige of Jim Crow baseball. Utilizing white as well as black players, the Clowns continued for another decade. "We are all show now," explained their owner. "We clown, clown, clown."

But the legacy of the Negro Leagues remained. Robinson and other early black players introduced new elements of speed and "tricky baseball" into the major leagues, transforming and improving the quality of play. Since 1947 blacks have led the National League in stolen bases in all but two seasons. In the American League, a black or Latin baserunner has topped the league every year since 1951 with only two exceptions. Nor did this injection of speed come at the expense of power. In the 1950s and 1960s, Hank Aaron, Willie Mays, and Frank Robinson reigned as the greatest power hitters in baseball. Thus, by the 1960s, the national pastime more closely resembled the well-balanced offensive structure of the Negro Leagues than the unidimensional power-oriented attack that had typified the all-white majors.

The demise of the Negro Leagues and the decline of segregation in the majors, however, did not end discrimination. Conditions on and off the field, in spring training and in the executive suites, repeatedly reminded the black athletes of their second-class status. In the early 1950s all-white teams taunted their black opponents with racial insults. Blacks like Jackie and Frank Robinson, Minnie Minoso and Luke Easter repeatedly appeared among the league leaders in being hit by pitches. While black superstars like Willie Mays had little difficulty ascending to the major leagues, players of only slightly above average talent found themselves buried for years in the minors. Many observers charged that teams had imposed quotas on the number of blacks they would field at one time.

In cities like St. Louis, Washington, D. C., and, later, Baltimore, black ballplayers could not stay at hotels with their teammates. In 1954 they achieved a breakthrough of sorts when the luxury Chase Hotel in St. Louis informed Jackie Robinson and other Dodger players that they could room there, but had to refrain from using the dining room or swimming pool or loitering in the lobby. Ten years later, the hotel had removed these restrictions, but still relegated black players, according to Hank Aaron, to rooms "looking out over some old building or some green pastures or a blank wall, so nobody can see us through a window."

Blacks faced even greater discrimination each year in spring training in Florida. While all spring training sites now accepted blacks, segregation statutes and local traditions forced them to live in all-black boarding houses far from the luxury air-conditioned hotels which accommodated white players. "The whole set-up is wrong," protested Jackie Robinson. "There is no reason why we shouldn't be able to live with our teammates." When teams traveled from place to place, blacks could not join their fellow players in restaurants. Instead they had to wait on the bus until someone brought their food out to them. Some teams attempted to reduce the problems faced by blacks. Several clubs moved to Arizona, where conditions were only moderately improved. The Dodgers built a special spring training camp at Vero Beach where players could live together. Most organizations, however, did very little to assist their black employees.

By the time that Jackie Robinson retired in 1956, conditions had barely improved. "After 10 years of traveling

in the South," he charged, " I don't think advances have been fast enough. It's my belief that baseball itself hasn't done all it can to remedy the problems faced by . . . players." Over the next decade, a new generation of black players militantly demanded change. Cardinals stars Bill White, Curt Flood, and Bob Gibson protested against conditions in St. Petersburg, while Aaron and other black Braves demanded changes in Bradenton. In many instances, however, significant changes awaited passage of the Civil Rights Act of 1965 barring segregation in public facilities.

The Next Generation

By 1960 Robinson, Campanella, Doby, and the cadre of Negro League veterans who had formed the vanguard of baseball integration had retired. In their wake, a second generation of black players, most of whom had never appeared in the Negro Leagues, made most Americans forget that Jim Crow baseball had ever existed, as they shattered longstanding "unbreakable" records. In 1962 black shortstop Maury Wills stole 104 bases, eclipsing Ty Cobb's 47-year-old stolen base mark. Twelve years later, outfielder Lou Brock stole 118 bases en route to breaking Cobb's career stolen-base record as well.

In 1966 Frank Robinson, who had won the National League Most Valuable Player Award in 1961, became the first player to win that honor in both leagues when he led the Baltimore Orioles to the American League pennant. By the end of his career, Robinson had slugged 586 home runs. Both Ernie Banks and Willie McCovey also amassed more than 500 home runs during this era. On the pitcher's mound, the indomitable Bob Gibson proved himself one of the greatest strikeout pitchers in the game's history. Upon retirement, Gibson had amassed more strikeouts than anyone except Walter Johnson. Brock, Frank Robinson, Banks, McCovey, and Gibson all won election to the Hall of Fame in their first year of eligibility.

The greatness of these players notwithstanding, two other black players, Willie Mays and Hank Aaron, both of whom ironically had begun their careers in the Negro Leagues, reigned as the dominant stars of baseball in the 1950s and 1960s. Originally signed by the Birmingham Black Barons of the Negro American League, Mays had joined the New York Giants in midseason 1951, sparking their triumph in the most famous pennant race in history and winning the Rookie of the Year Award. After two years in the military, he returned in 1954 to bat a league-leading .345 and hit 41 home runs. The following year, he pounded 51 homers. A spectacular center fielder, Mays won widespread acclaim as the greatest all-around player in the history of the game. In 1969 he became only the second player in major league history to hit 600 home runs and took aim at Babe Ruth's legendary lifetime total of 714. Over the next four seasons, the aging Mays added 60 more homers before retiring, still well short of Ruth's record.

Unlike Mays, who had begun his career amidst the glare of the New York media, Hank Aaron had spent his career first in Milwaukee and later in Atlanta, far distant from the center of national publicity. Nonetheless, he steadily compiled record-threatening statistics in almost every offensive category. In 1972, at age 38, he surpassed Mays' home run total and set his sights on Ruth. Entering the 1973 season, he needed just 41 home runs to catch the Babe. Performing under tremendous pressure and fanfare, Aaron stroked 40 homers, leaving him just one shy of the record. He tied Ruth's mark with his first swing of the 1974 season. Three days later, on April 8, 1974, a nationwide television audience watched Aaron stroke home run number 715. Babe Ruth's "unreachable" record thus fell to a man whose career had started with the Indianapolis Clowns of the Negro Leagues. When Aaron retired in 1976, he boasted 755 home runs and held major league records for games played, at-bats, runs batted in and extra-base hits. He also ranked second to Ty Cobb in hits and runs scored.

By the 1970s black players had become an accepted part of the baseball scene and regularly ranked among the most well-known symbols of the sport. Reggie Jackson, Willie Stargell, and Joe Morgan had succeeded Aaron, Mays, and the Robinsons as Hall of Fame caliber superstars. Yet three decades after Jackie Robinson had broken the color barrier, racism and discrimination remained a persistent problem for baseball. Several studies demonstrated that baseball management channeled blacks into positions thought to require less thinking and fewer leadership qualities. In 1968 blacks accounted for more than half of the major league outfielders, but only 20 percent of other position players. Black catchers were rare and fewer than one in 10 pitchers were black. The disparity had grown greater by 1986. American-born blacks comprised 70 percent of all outfield positions but only 7 percent of all pitcher, second basemen, and third basemen positions. There were no American-born black catchers in the major leagues at the start of the 1986 season; the 1990s, however, saw some progress with the appearance of Charles Johnson and Lenny Webster.

While superior black players had open access to the major leagues, those of average or slightly above average skills often found their paths blocked. "The Negro player may have to be better qualified than a white player to win the same position," argued Aaron Rosenblatt in 1967. "The undistinguished Negro player is less likely to play in the major leagues than the equally undistinguished white player." Rosenblatt demonstrated that black major leaguers on the whole batted 20 points higher than whites. As batting averages dropped, so did the proportion of blacks. This trend continued into the 1980s. A 1982 study revealed that 70 percent of all black non-pitchers were everyday starters, indicating a substantial bias against blacks who filled utility or pinch-hitting roles. Statistics compiled in 1986 showed a strikingly similar pattern.

The subtle nature of this on-the-field discrimination obscured it from public controversy. The failure of baseball to provide jobs for blacks in managerial and front office positions, however, became an increasing embarrassment. In the early years of integration, baseball executives bypassed the substantial pool of experienced Negro Leaguers from consideration for managerial and coaching positions. A handful of blacks, including Sam Bankhead, Nate Moreland, Marvin Williams, and Chet Brewer managed independent, predominantly all-black teams in the minor leagues. The first generation of black major lea-

guers fared no better. "We bring dollars into club treasuries when we play," exclaimed Larry Doby, "but when we stop playing, our dollars stop." No major league organization hired a black pilot at any level until 1961 when the Pittsburgh Pirates placed Gene Baker at the helm of their Batavia franchise. By the mid-1960s no blacks had managed in the majors and only two had held full-time major league coaching positions. The first black umpire did not appear in the majors until 1966, when Emmett Ashford appeared in the American League.

In the final years of his life, Jackie Robinson made repeated pleas for baseball to eliminate these lingering vestiges of Jim Crow. "I'd like to live to see a black manager," he stated before a national television audience at the 1972 World Series. Nine days later he died, his dream unfulfilled. In 1975 the Cleveland Indians hired Frank Robinson to be the first black major league manager. This precedent, however, opened few new doors. Robinson lasted two-and-a-half seasons with the Indians, later managed the San Francisco Giants for four years, and the Baltimore Orioles piloted for three-and-a-half seasons before moving to the club's front office. Maury Wills and Larry Doby each had brief half-season stints as managers. After four decades of integration, only these three men had received major league managerial opportunities.

A similar situation existed in major league front offices. Only one black man, Bill Lucas of the Atlanta Braves, had served as a general manager. As late as 1982, a survey of 24 clubs (the Yankees and Red Sox refused to provide information) found that of 913 available white-collar baseball jobs, blacks held just 32 positions. Among 568 full-time major league scouts, only 15 were black. While many teams hired former players as announcers, few employed blacks in these roles. Five years later, conditions had not improved. Of the top 879 administrative positions in baseball only 17 were filled by blacks and 15 by Hispanics. Four teams in California—the Dodgers, Giants, Athletics, and Angels—accounted for almost two-thirds of the minority hiring. Ten out of 14 American League teams, and five of 12 National League franchises had no blacks in management positions.

These shortcomings came to haunt baseball in 1987. Commissioner Peter Ueberroth had dedicated the season to the commemoration of the 40th anniversary of Jackie Robinson's major league debut. As the celebration began, Los Angeles Dodgers general manager Al Campanis, who had played with Robinson at Montreal, appeared on ABC-TV's "Nightline". When asked about the dearth of black managers, Campanis explained that blacks "may not have some of the necessities to be, let's say, a field manager or general manager." Campanis' statement, which surely reflected the thinking of many baseball executives, evoked a storm of protest, and precipitated his resignation. An embarrassed Ueberroth pledged to take action to bring more blacks into leadership positions and hired University of California sociologist Harry Edwards to facilitate the process. Fifty blacks and Latins with past or present connections to baseball created their own Minority Baseball Network to apprise blacks of employment opportunities and to lobby clubs to recruit more minorities for front office jobs.

When the controversy of 1987 had subsided, few franchises had taken significant steps to increase minority hiring. Several clubs added blacks to administrative positions, but none offered field or general manager positions to nonwhite candidates (although Bill White was named National League president). In 1988 Frank Robinson received his third chance to manage in the major leagues, this time with the Baltimore Orioles. At midseason 1989 Cito Gaston assumed the reins of the Toronto Blue Jays. When the squads managed by Robinson and Gaston had their initial confrontation, it marked, after 40 years of integration, the first time that two teams managed by black men had competed in a major league game. Fittingly, on the final weekend of the season, the Orioles and Blue Jays met face-to-face in a series to decide the championship of the American League Eastern Division. The spectacle offered a resounding rebuke to the short-sightedness and discrimination that continue to plague the national pastime.

By the 1993 season baseball seemed to have finally made some real progress in including minorities in its managerial ranks. The season saw five black and Hispanic field managers: Gaston, who after five years at the helm of the Blue Jays ranked as one of the most successful managers in baseball history, winning four divisional championships, two pennants and two world championships; Felipe Alou, who led the Montreal Expos to consecutive second place finishes; Dusty Baker, who became the winningest rookie manager ever, when his San Francisco Giants won 103 games (after winning only 72 games the year before); Don Baylor, who would pilot the expansion Colorado Rockies into the playoffs in only their third year of existence in 1995; and Tony Perez, who started the season as the manager of the Cincinnati Reds.

Progress extended into other areas of hiring as well. In 1994 Leonard Coleman succeeded Bill White as National League vice-president. By 1995, 27 percent of all coaches were black or latino. Minority hiring in the front office expanded to 17 percent in 1992, a level which held steady through 1994. The Houston Astros named Bob Watson their general manager, making him only the second black man to assume these responsibilities. Watson assumed the same position with the New York Yankees in 1996 and under his stewardship the club won the world championship.

These undeniable gains, however, occurred against a backdrop of continuing racial controversy. The proportion of American-born black players in baseball's major leagues dropped from one in four in the late 1960s to only one in six in the late 1980s and 1990s. In minor league and college baseball, important sources of major league talent, the percentage of African-Americans was even lower. Surveys indicated that African-Americans, who had flocked to major league ballparks in the 1950s, now accounted for one out of every 14 fans. Allegations that Cincinnati Reds owner Marge Schott had repeatedly used racial slurs (and that other owners had ignored these offenses) led to her suspension in 1993.

There remained no American minority owners of major league clubs. All 30 chief executive officers are white. When Watson resigned after the 1997 season, there once again were no black general managers. The surge in the hiring of minority managers that had occurred in the early 1990s also seemed to have abated. Few African-American

or Hispanic managers were hired after 1994.

During the early 1990s baseball undertook several initiatives to improve its image among minorities. The major leagues embraced John Young's RBI (Reviving Baseball in the Inner Cities) program, an effort to entice black youth away from other sports and back to the diamond. Attempts were also made to secure health benefits for surviving Negro League players. To achieve greater recognition for players from the Jim Crow era, the Hall of Fame instructed its Veterans Committee to honor one Negro League star a year for five years. As a result, Leon Day, Willie Wells, Bill Foster, and Bullet Joe Rogan were selected to enter the Hall. African-American reporter Wendell Smith was named to the writer's wing of the Hall of Fame. Nonetheless black athletes still remain woefully underrepresented at Cooperstown.

In 1997 baseball celebrated the 50th anniversary of what most consider its "finest moment"—Jackie Robin-son's Brooklyn Dodgers debut—with extraordinary and unprecedented fanfare. Major League Baseball dedicated the season to Robinson's memory. Players wore arm patches honoring his achievements. Acting Commissioner Bud Selig announced that all teams would henceforth retire his number. On April 15 President Bill Clinton appeared between innings of a Los Angeles Dodgers-New York Mets game at Shea Stadium to address the nation about Robinson's legacy.

A year later the National Baseball Hall of Fame added Larry Doby, who broke the American League color line, and Baltimore Afro-American sportswriter Sam Lacy to its list of honorees. At times the commemorations threatened to be overwhelmed by nostalgia and commercialism. However the 1997 festivities reminded the nation once again of its past heritage—both the shameful and the heroic—and its ongoing obligations to seek greater equality in the future.

## CHAPTER 14

The Minor Leagues
Bob Hoie

The International Association, founded in 1877, is frequently described as the first minor league. For two major reasons it shouldn't be so regarded. First, it was barely a league. Structurally it resembled the old National Association—there was virtually no central authority, no limitation on the number or location of member teams, no set schedule, and haphazard umpire selection. The league was so loosely assembled in fact that some member teams competed at the same time for the championships of other organizations like the New England Association and the League Alliance.

Second, the International Association was originally established as a rival to the National League and never officially recognized itself as being subordinate. It was generally acknowledged that several of its teams were as good as or better than some in the National League. Various off-the-field problems, administrative weaknesses, and a lack of solidarity and resolve on the part of the member clubs assured its subordinate status.

A strong case could be made for the 1879 Northwestern League as the first minor league—it had a preset schedule and had no pretensions of rivaling the National League, but the absence of league-appointed umpires led to frequent forfeits due to charges of biased "hometown" umpiring, and the league folded after only two months.

The Eastern Association was founded in 1881, but this was another loose alliance with no set schedule.

The first recognized minor league was another Northwestern League, this one organized on Oct. 27, 1882. At that time they requested of the National League cooperation and reciprocity in protecting player contracts. This was necessary because independent clubs frequently lost their best players during the course of the season to the National League and later to the American Association clubs. In response to this request, the National League, American Association, and Northwestern League signed a "Tripartite Agreement" in March 1883. This agreement bound the clubs to honor the contracts of players on reserve lists, assured mutual recognition of expulsions and suspensions, established territorial rights, and created an arbitration committee to settle disputes. Minimum salaries were established and pegged at a higher level in the National League and American Association than in the Northwestern League or "any other parties to the agreement," thus by implication assigning a "major" and "minor" status to the leagues.

The Interstate Association was established early in 1883 and was quickly accepted as an "alliance" league by the American Association, becoming a junior partner of the Tripartite Agreement. Both the Northwestern and the Interstate opened their seasons on May 1, 1883. Each had a formal league organization, a schedule that was preset before the season opening, and a complement of umpires appointed and paid for by the league. Both leagues recognized and accepted their status as subordinate to the two "majors." In 1884 the Interstate Association reorganized as the Eastern League and became a fourth member of what now became known as the National Agreement.

In October 1885 a new National Agreement was adopted which made the National League and American Association the principal parties and removed from minor league clubs the protection of the reserve clause. Two years later the reserve clause was reinstated for the minors, but the major-minor league distinction had been formalized. Following the collapse of the American Association in 1892, another National Agreement for the first time established minor league classifications and gave major league clubs the right to draft minor league players at fixed prices.

While these events were taking place, organized baseball expanded dramatically, going from two minor leagues in 1883 to 17 by 1888. Baseball was played throughout the country, of course, but organized ball was confined to the northeast quadrant of the United States in 1884; it expanded to the South in 1885, to Colorado and the upper Midwest in 1886, California in 1887, Texas in 1888, and the Pacific Northwest in 1890. So in the year that the American frontier was officially declared closed, organized baseball had extended to all corners of the country.

In 1887 an organization called the Negro Baseball League, fearing player raids by the still moderately integrated minors, sought and received protection under the National Agreement. The league was to play in eight cities that also had major league teams, but it folded in less than two weeks. This was unfortunately characteristic of the era. Many teams and leagues were underfinanced and were ultrasensitive to changes in the national or local economy. In addition, being unable or unwilling to pay the required fees for reserving their players, they lost their better ones at the close of the season—and those teams that even managed to finish the season could usually consider themselves lucky. During the 19th century, more than 40 percent of the leagues that started a season failed to finish it. There was, however, a solid core of support for minor league baseball. Regardless of how many leagues started each season—usually about 15 but often as many as 20—only eight to 10 usually finished; the rest failed. The 1890s were not a period of expansion nor of stability

as throughout the decade nearly half of the leagues that started a season failed to finish it. A depression in 1893 and the Spanish-American War in 1898 were significant factors, but a proliferation of "fly-by-night" operators played a role as well.

At the close of the 1900 season, the still minor American League withdrew from the National Agreement, announcing through that action its intention not to allow its players to be drafted and not to respect the reserve clause or territorial rights any longer.

In September 1901 the National League announced its intention to abrogate the National Agreement, contending that with the American League invading its cities and raiding its players the National League could not be expected to sit back and abide by restrictions which did not hinder its rival. Essentially this meant that the National, like the American, considered the players on minor league rosters "fair game."

In immediate reaction to this, the presidents of seven minor leagues met in Chicago on Sept. 5, 1901, and in an act of self-protection they organized the National Association of Professional Baseball Leagues. On Oct. 25 representatives of nine minor leagues met in New York and adopted a new "National Agreement." This new agreement established league classifications, roster and salary limits, and a draft system; it recognized reserve lists and created a Board of Arbitration which was given the power to suspend players, clubs, or officials for violations of the agreement. By the beginning of the 1902 season, the National Association included 15 member leagues.

The American and National Leagues ratified a peace agreement early in 1903, and in late August the presidents of the two major leagues and the National Association drafted a National Agreement which was initially rejected by the minors. After some concessions were made by the majors, such as a prohibition on "farming," the plan was adopted in September. The agreement formalized relations between the majors and minors and established a National Commission to serve as a Board of Arbitration.

These agreements were necessary because the majors and minors were mutually dependent on each other. The majors needed the minors as a reliable source of talent, while the minors, many of whom relied on player sales to stay in business, needed assurances from the majors that they would recognize their property rights in players.

Despite this mutual dependence there was a basic buyer-seller conflict. The majors wanted to acquire players as cheaply as possible, while the minors wanted to sell them for as much as possible. This same conflict existed within the minors as well, with the highest-classification clubs wanting to buy cheaply from the lower minors and sell at high prices to the majors. Thus the National Agreement, the major-minor agreement, and the National Association itself were uneasy alliances of clubs and leagues with competing and often conflicting objectives. Nearly annual revisions in draft rules and prices and limits on optional player assignments were required to maintain the equilibrium necessary to keep the alliance intact.

The majors favored an unlimited draft—i.e., any player on a minor league roster could be purchased for a fixed rate. As early as 1896, when Minneapolis of the Western League was decimated through what were in effect forced sales, it became clear that some limitations were necessary, so by 1905 only one player could be drafted from a club per year. The draft prices of top-classification minor leaguers went from $750 to $1,000 in 1905 and then to $2,500 in 1911. While these prices were not particularly low for average prospects in that era, they were well below the value of the best prospects in the minors; thus the draft or the threat of it served as an incentive for minor league clubs at all levels to sell their better players to major or higher-classification minor league clubs at competitive market prices. From the players' standpoint, the draft had the positive effect of allowing them eventually to advance to whatever levels their ability would take them. The lower-classification minor league clubs received lower draft prices for their players but seemed relatively satisfied with the system—after all, this was an era when the contracts of Tris Speaker, Rogers Hornsby, and Ty Cobb were sold to major league clubs for $400, $500, and $700, respectively.

On the other hand, many of the higher-classification minor league clubs had never really been satisfied with the draft. As early as 1908, this dissatisfaction nearly caused the two top minor leagues at that time—the American Association and the Eastern League—to go independent. Several of the top minor league clubs drew more fans annually than some major league clubs and represented substantial investments. As a result these owners were understandably not happy with a system that forced the sale of their top players for below-market prices to the majors; in addition to the challenge to club stability and autonomy caused by the draft, the gap between the market value of the top prospects and the draft price widened throughout the 1910s.

Despite the rumblings of discontent, the establishment of the National Association ushered in a period of minor league expansion to a fairly stable core of 30 leagues. While there were still leagues that failed to finish the season, the failure rate was down to 10–15 percent. For some reason, in 1910 the minors reached a level never to be topped until the post–World War II boom era—52 leagues started the season and 44 finished it. For the next five years more leagues folded, but each season generally closed with 40 leagues operating. Then, for reasons that ranged from the automobile, movies, the war in Europe, and the Federal League War, the bottom started to drop out. Forty-three leagues started in the 1914 season, and by the end of the 1918 season only one was operating (10 leagues had started that year—one folded and eight suspended operations due to the war).

After the 1918 season, with most of the lower minors driven out of business, the National Association, for the first time dominated by the higher minors, adopted a resolution demanding that the majors relinquish the right of the draft and end the practice of "farming out" players. When the majors rejected these demands, the National Association withdrew from the National Agreement. Pending a new major agreement, the majors and minors reached general agreement on property rights in players and territorial rights, and the National Commission ruled that the major league draft would be suspended.

In addition the minor leagues would not accept major league players on option, meaning that any players owned or controlled by major league clubs in excess of the active player roster limit would have to be sold or released to

minor league clubs. A. R. Tierney, president of two minor leagues and a leader in the fight to end the draft, said, "This means that the minor leagues will be able to build fences for themselves instead of for the major leagues." He predicted expansion of the minors and higher sale prices for the players. He was correct on both counts. With no players on option, the majors needed to buy more players from the minors, some of whom they had been forced to sell but now had to buy back at higher prices, and without the draft the minor league clubs could virtually name their own price. The minors expanded, as the leagues that had been driven out of business during the war now reentered the fold.

A Minor Resurgence

The reappearance of the low minors again shifted the balance of power within the minors. The higher minors had never been happy with the one-league, one-vote system in the National Association. Club owners were wary of having their investments affected by the vote of what they perceived as little more than "fly-by-night" operators, and on occasion they tried to change the arrangement. But just as the majors needed the minors, so the high minors needed the low minors. Thus the high minors always stopped short of enacting any measures that might drive their underlings out of the National Association.

As noted previously, many of the low minors needed the revenues they received from the draft to survive. Although the minor league draft still existed, it had ceased to be a dependable source of revenue as the combination of numerous prewar minor league failures and returning military veterans yielded more than enough talent to fill the higher minors' rosters. In addition, many of the low-minor clubs did not have the resources to scout for and sign enough players to remain competitive on the field and/or at the box office; thus they were dependent on receiving some players on option.

So while most of the higher minor leagues were prospering as never before under the new independence, by 1920 the low minors were ready to withdraw from the National Association if a new agreement with the majors restoring the draft was not adopted. In addition, some of the higher minor league clubs were upset that the "no-farming" rules were being circumvented by "gentleman's agreements." These agreements enabled the major league clubs to "sell" a player to a minor league club and "buy" him back at the end of the season with little or no money actually changing hands.

On Jan. 10, 1921, a new major-minor league agreement was signed. The new pact restored the major league draft with a top price of $5,000 but as a compromise gave individual minor leagues the right to be exempt from the draft; in addition major league clubs could option up to eight players for no more than two consecutive years, and a tax on player sales was instituted to help reduce the fake player transfers. Quickly the top three minors—the International League, Pacific Coast League, and the American Association—together with the Western and Three-I Leagues declared their exemption from the draft; this in turn prohibited them from drafting from the lower minors.

The prices the majors paid for top minor league players

nearly doubled between 1919 and 1920, but they skyrocketed during the draft-exemption era. In 1921 the Giants paid $75,000 to San Francisco for Jimmy O'Connell; in 1922 the Giants paid $72,000 to Baltimore for Jack Bentley and the White Sox paid $100,000 to San Francisco for Willie Kamm. The majors clearly were not happy with this situation, and in 1922 they offered to raise the draft price to $7,500, but this failed to lure back the draft-exempt leagues. In early 1923 the majors, after considering but eventually rejecting the idea of a maximum purchase price of $25,000 for any minor league player and/or a boycott of draft-exempt leagues, declared that all players sent to the minors either by sale or option would be subject to the draft. The number of players who could be optioned was increased to 15. Western League clubs immediately began accepting players on option under these conditions.

The prices for ballplayers remained high in 1923. Baltimore of the International League was reportedly offered $100,000 by Brooklyn for Joe Boley and sold Max Bishop to the Philadelphia A's for $50,000. Salt Lake sold Paul Strand to the A's for a reported $70,000, Louisville sold Earle Combs to the Yankees for $50,000, Toronto sold Red Wingo to the Tigers for $50,000 and Rochester sold Maurice Archdeacon to the White Sox for $50,000, but these were isolated cases. Baltimore, aided by five years of draft exemption, had built a powerhouse, but many of the higher-classification minor league clubs had not been nearly as successful and found that they needed to receive players on option to fill holes and remain competitive. Therefore at the close of the 1923 season all exempt leagues but the International agreed to the modified draft which exempted only those players who had come up through the minors. In 1924, after Baltimore sold Lefty Grove to the A's for $100,000, the International League also fell into line.

The modified draft did nothing to reduce the prices paid for top minor league stars: Louisville sold Wayland Dean to the Giants for $72,000 in 1924, San Francisco sold Paul Waner and Hal Rhyne to Pittsburgh for $100,000 in 1925, and Baltimore continued selling star players to the majors for big prices—Tommy Thomas to the White Sox in 1925, Joe Boley to the A's in 1926, John Ogden to the Browns and George Earnshaw to the A's in 1927. Also in 1927 Portland (of the PCL) sold Billy Cissel to the White Sox for a package of cash and players worth over $100,000 and Oakland sold Lyn Lary and Jimmy Reese to the Yankees for $100,000. With prices like these, clubs could afford to lose an occasional Lefty O'Doul or Hack Wilson in the modified draft.

The major-minor agreement expired at the end of the 1927 season, with the National Association members deadlocked on the issue of the draft. The majors and minors were also at an impasse, so the modified draft continued and many of the higher minor league clubs continued to prosper, both through player sales and at the gate. The Pacific Coast League's Los Angeles franchise and ballpark were valued at $2 million, but in the lower minors all was not well through the 1920s. Leagues were operating that never should have been admitted to the National Association—for example, the West Arkansas, which operated in 1924, was comprised of six towns within a 750-square-mile area that had a combined popu-

lation of 16,000 and played just a 60-game schedule.

In 1929 the rift between the high and low minors widened as the low minors, rebuffed in their efforts to nullify the modified draft agreement, now attempted to impose their own draft exemption—essentially exempting from the draft any player with fewer than two seasons of organized baseball.

Early in 1931 the majors and minors finally adopted a new National Agreement, including a provision which eliminated the modified draft and granted to major league clubs greater control of talent through revised option and draft rules. The higher minors had originally objected, but the majors told them to accept the universal draft or they would no longer have any relations with them. In other words, major league teams would not sell or option players to or buy players from the American Association, the International League, or the Pacific Coast League. While such threats had been taken relatively lightly by the minors in the early days of the draft-exempt leagues, they were now taken seriously enough that in less than a month the three recalcitrant leagues capitulated to the majors' terms. In exchange for all this and largely to secure the support of the low minors, the majors agreed to sign only collegian amateurs, leaving all high-schoolers and sandlotters to the minors. Of course, by this time farm systems had developed to the point that most major league clubs could still sign noncollegian amateurs through their farm clubs.

Milwaukee had sold Fred Schulte to the Browns for a reported $100,000 in 1928, but this was the end of an era. There would be no more $100,000 minor leaguers; in fact there would be few if any minor leaguers sold for as much as $50,000 again. At the 1928 National Association Convention, president Mike Sexton wondered when the majors would own enough clubs to control the National Association. The farm system, an old idea now in the process of being perfected by Branch Rickey, had clearly begun to alter the way the minors operated, and despite the efforts of some—most notably Judge Landis—the trend couldn't be reversed.

The Great Depression caused a contraction of the minors in the early 1930s, but even though a near-record low of 14 leagues opened the 1933 season, none of them folded. The minors then entered an era of unprecedented growth and stability, reaching 44 leagues in 1940, with only two leagues failing to finish the season between 1933 and 1941. This can be attributed in part to the substantial involvement of the major leagues through outright ownership or regular infusions of money through working agreements, but there were obviously other factors at work. Judge Bramham, on becoming president of the National Association, instituted a number of reforms, many of which were aimed at getting rid of "fly-by-night" or "shoestring" operators. Minor league baseball was better promoted—they had established a public relations department in 1934—and the advent of night baseball was of incalculable value in generating attendance, which reached 20 million in 1940. Interestingly, that year 54 percent of the minor league clubs were not affiliated with any major league clubs compared to just 37 percent that operated independently in 1936.

World War II caused the minors to drop to just 10 leagues in 1944, but in the first postwar year it was up to 43, increasing to an all-time high of 59 in 1949, and during that time no leagues folded. (In 1946 the Mexican National League, set up by organized baseball to compete with the outlaw Mexican League, is listed by the National Association as having folded during the season, but actually it only withdrew from the association and continued to operate independently.)

According to a general consensus, it was the coming of television that caused the minors to begin to disintegrate. Between 1949 and 1963 the number of minor leagues dropped from 59 to 18. Attendance decreased even more sharply, going from 40 million to less than 10 million over the same time period.

By 1963, the minors had become nothing more than a training ground for the majors—90 percent of the clubs were major league affiliates, and most of those that weren't affiliates were in the largely autonomous Mexican League. While television was commonly cited as the cause of the minors' contraction, some contended it was a natural response to overexpansion. Gerry Hirn, in an April 1954 *Baseball Digest* article, contended that while the number of minor leagues had dropped from 59 to 36, that was still too many and the minors would be stronger and more efficient if only 16 to 20 leagues operated. Interestingly, in 1954 three leagues failed to finish the season, the most failures in peacetime since 1932; they remain the last United States–based minor leagues that failed to finish a season (the Inter-American League, which had a team in Miami but was largely based in the Caribbean, failed to finish the 1979 season—the only year it operated).

An Unexpected But Welcome Boom

For reasons that aren't entirely clear, minor league baseball exploded in popularity in the 1980s. Attendance, which had remained stuck at 10–11 million through the 1960s and most of the 1970s, took off in the late 1970s, topping 20 million in 1987 for the first time since 1953. Louisville, which dropped out of organized ball after drawing just 116,000 in 1972, topped a million in 1983. Nashville, which dropped out in 1963 after drawing just 54,000 for the season, drew over half a million in 1980. Buffalo, which drew only 78,000 in 1969 and saw its franchise shifted to Winnipeg the following year, came back to set an all-time minor league attendance record with 1.1 million in 1988. The Louisville franchise, which didn't exist in 1981 (what became the Louisville franchise was at that time in Springfield, Ill., drawing 120,000), sold for more than $4 million in 1987. In 1990 the far less successful Vancouver franchise sold to Japanese interests for $5.5 million. Minor league franchises that could be picked up in the early 1970s by anyone who would pay the outstanding debts were suddenly selling for several million dollars.

The high prices being paid for franchises may have precipitated the major-minor-league crisis of 1990, reminiscent of the battles earlier in the century. The Professional Baseball Agreement that binds the majors and minors was set to expire at the end of 1990. The majors, who under that agreement provided substantial financial support for the minors, proposed a reduction in those

subsidies. The majors believed that the now financially healthy minor league clubs should assume a greater share of operational expenses.

In addition, the majors wanted the Commissioner's office to have greater control over minor league affairs. The minors felt the majors were trying to usurp their autonomy and, to add injury to insult, charge them for the privilege. If there was no agreement, the majors threatened to place their entire farm systems in spring training complexes in Arizona and Florida. Some minor league operators threatened to go independent and even form a third major league.

In the end, however, the majority of minor league clubs capitulated, believing that they could not afford to operate without players supplied by the major league clubs. The majors would still pick up most of the minor league operators' expenses, but the new agreement (a) eliminated the minors' share of big-league TV revenue, (b) required that the minors pay a share of their ticket revenues to the majors, and (c) established minimum standards that must be met by minor league facilities by 1994 (subsequently extended to 1995).

It was generally believed that these changes, by reducing minor league clubs' profits, might stabilize or reduce the value of franchises. However, in 1992 the Las Vegas franchise sold for a record $7 million and some unsuccessful Class A franchises were sold for well over $1 million each. And the fans kept coming—in 1993 minor league attendance topped 30 million for the first time since 1950, and in 1993 Buffalo went over 1 million in attendance for the sixth consecutive year. In 1994 the Bisons just missed a seventh million-fan season due to two rainouts. In 1998 minor league attendance went over the 35 million mark for the first time since 1949 (with 200 fewer clubs).

The positive trend of the past 15 years is not unprecedented, but the minors have been riding a rollercoaster of success and failure over the past century—the Newark franchise which sold for a reported $600,000 during the depths of the Depression didn't even exist 20 years later. Even today the picture is not all positive: between 1987 and 1996 nearly 60 franchises were shifted, usually due to poor attendance. In the past few years these shifts have fueled large attendance increases as teams have moved from "dead" towns to virgin territories with spanking new state-of-the-art facilities.

The supply of new towns with new ballparks seems to be diminishing and the big success stories of the 1980s have seen their attendance decline. In 1998 Buffalo still drew a robust 743,000 to lead the minors for the 11th straight year but that was down 380,000 from 1992; Louisville, once over a million, dropped to about 400,000; and Nashville, which drew 550,000 as recently as 1990, attracted less than half that in 1997. Some clubs still draw less than 1,000 fans per game; and it is generally believed that many clubs still substantially pad their attendance totals. So the current wave of success is somewhat deceptive and history tells us it won't last forever. However, regardless of fluctuations in popularity and economic viability, the minors have been and one can safely assume will continue to be the primary training ground for major league players.

The Players

Great players have passed through the minors, their careers frequently going in opposite directions and occasionally teaming up or crossing in unlikely locations. In 1924 in Easton, Md., Jimmie Foxx broke into organized baseball as a catcher on a team run by player-manager Frank "Home Run" Baker in his last season as an active player. There were many others: Rube Waddell and Red Faber with Minneapolis in 1911, young Waite Hoyt and ancient Jesse Burkett with Hartford in 1916, Dazzy Vance and Roger Bresnahan with Toledo in 1917, Chief Bender and Lefty Grove with Baltimore in 1923, and more recently Enos Slaughter and Billy Williams with Houston in 1960.

Former Negro Leaguers, teamed up together in the years that followed Jackie Robinson's landmark debut in 1947. Ray Dandridge and Willie Mays were teammates at Minneapolis in 1951 where another teammate was a seven-year minor league veteran, Hoyt Wilhelm. Wilhelm, a 28-year-old knuckleballer with a background that included three years in Class D ball and three more in the military service, at that time appeared to be a member of what in that era was a vast army of career minor leaguers, the best of whom held their own with the acknowledged major league greats passing through the minors, but who for a variety of reasons—some good, some not—would themselves spend the bulk of their careers in the minors.

For some of these players who were left behind, the designated hitter rule came 50 years too late, because while they could hit both for average and power, they generally lacked speed or had defensive shortcomings. For others it is less clear what, if any, deficiencies kept them in the minors, but from these groups a few players emerged as true minor league greats whose impact on fans in minor league cities—Buzz Arlett in Oakland, Joe Hauser in Minneapolis, and Bunny Brief in Kansas City, to name a few—was as great as that of more renowned players in major league cities.

The greatest of the minor league players is generally acknowledged to be Buzz Arlett.

Arlett started his career as a right-handed spitball pitcher with the hometown Oakland Oaks in 1918 and went on to win 108 games, twice going over 25 wins in a season. The Detroit Tigers looked at him, but without the spitball, which he wouldn't be able to use in the majors, they did not consider him a prospect. After suffering arm trouble early in 1923, Buzz switched to the outfield. Although he had been nothing more than a fair-hitting pitcher, once Arlett became a regular he annually averaged nearly .360 with 30 homers and 140 RBIs through the rest of the 1920s.

Early in his career as an outfielder a Cardinals scout labeled him "good hit, no field," and it stuck. Finally in 1931 he was purchased by the Phillies. The 32-year-old switch-hitter batted .313 with 18 homers and 73 RBIs in a season when the National League introduced a "dead ball" in reaction to the hitting orgies of 1929–1930. Despite the dead ball, Arlett, now with Baltimore, still hit four home runs in a game twice within a five-week period in 1932. He led the league with 54 homers for the season, but he would never return to the majors. He spent another year with Baltimore, when he again won the home run

title, a little over a month with Birmingham, and nearly three years with Minneapolis, where he had another home run championship. After a few games with Syracuse in 1937, Arlett's remarkable career was over.

In addition to his 108 wins, he hit 432 homers, a minor league record that held up until Hector Espino topped it in 1977. Arlett walked a lot, didn't strike out much, ran pretty well early in his career, had a .341 lifetime batting average—.350 after he became an outfielder—and was the only player to finish in the top five in home runs and slugging percentage in his only season in the majors. In addition, modern statistical analysis, including range factors, suggests he was nowhere near the defensive liability he was portrayed as being. He was big (6 feet 4 inches, 230) and gave the appearance of being lackadaisical, which apparently irritated some of his managers, but the evidence is strong that Arlett, despite nearly two decades spent in the minors, was a major league-caliber player.

Ike Boone was another player whose hitting feats were not limited to the minors. Boone was a college teammate (at the University of Alabama) of Joe Sewell and Riggs Stephenson; his lifetime major league batting average was .319, and in his only two full seasons in the majors—1924-1925 with the Boston Red Sox—he hit .333 and .330. Yet due to alleged defensive deficiencies most of his career was spent in the minors.

In 1929 with the Missions of San Francisco, Boone probably had the finest season any player has had in the minors. On the all-time minor league list of single-season accomplishments, his 553 total bases that year are first, his 323 hits are second, his 195 runs scored are tied for third, and his 218 RBIs are fourth. On the all-time Pacific Coast League list, his .407 average is second, and his 55 home runs are tied for fourth.

Boone's greatness wasn't confined to a single season; in four of his first eight years in the minors he hit over .400 (he was on his way to perhaps his greatest season in 1930, batting .448 with 22 homers and 96 RBIs when he was sold to Brooklyn in late June). His .402 average with San Antonio in 1923 is the highest in 20th-century Texas League history; his .389 with New Orleans in 1921 is the fifth highest in the Southern Association; he also led the International League in batting twice. His .370 lifetime average is the minor league record for players with ten or more seasons. He had an exceptional arm, but limited range in the outfield. Although he hit 77 home runs in a season and a half with the Missions, he was not generally regarded as a power hitter. He was, however, a great pure hitter; in 11 of his 14 seasons in the minors, he hit over .350, and there is no evidence that he couldn't hit major league pitching.

Smead Jolley was an atrocious outfielder. Stories of his defensive lapses are legion, and the statistical evidence suggests those stories are more than isolated anecdotes. Like Boone, Jolley had a powerful arm but no speed; like Arlett, he was big and awkward; and like both, he could hit—majors or minors. In the equivalent of three full major league seasons with the White Sox and Red Sox, he hit .305 and averaged 15 homers and 105 RBIs. He won six minor league batting championships—leading the Pacific Coast League in hitting three times (winning the Triple Crown with San Francisco in 1928) and the International League once. Twice he had over 300 hits in a season, and twice he drove in more than 180 runs. In the 13 minor league seasons in which he played over 100 games, he had this run: .370, .372, .346, .397, .404, .387, .360, .372, .373, .350, .309, .373, .345. Perhaps because he spent nearly six years in the low minors, the first four as a pitcher, and had a somewhat nomadic career (he was with 13 minor league teams), he has not always been ranked in the top echelon of minor league greats, yet he may have been the finest hitter of them all.

Minor league stars generally fit two stereotypes: one-dimensional players who could hit but could do nothing else well enough to stay in the majors—justly or not, Arlett, Boone, and Jolley were consigned to this group. Then there are those who excelled in the minors but couldn't produce in the majors. Perhaps the classic example is Bunny Brief.

Brief, born Antonio Bordetski, may have been the most dominant power hitter in the minor leagues. In major league trials with the Browns, White Sox, and Pirates between 1912 and 1917, he was consistently unimpressive—in a combined 569, he hit .223 with five homers, 59 RBIs, and nearly 100 strikeouts. In the minors, however, it was a different story. Although he hit 40 or more homers only twice and never had more than 42, he had eight league home run championships. Before going up to the majors, he led the Michigan State League twice; later he led the Pacific Coast League once and the American Association five times. He also led the Association in RBIs five times (four in succession), including a league-record 191 in 1921. He had a six-year stretch (1921–1926) with Kansas City and Milwaukee, where he averaged 90 extra-base hits, 151 RBIs, and a .351 average per season. Brief also drew a lot of walks. Early in his career he had excellent speed, and although he played most of his career at first base, he was the best defensive outfielder of the big minor league sluggers, with good range and an excellent arm. Still, for reasons that remain unclear, Brief never played in a major league game after his 25th birthday.

Nick Cullop was another minor league great who never produced in the majors. He, like many of the great minor league sluggers, began his career as a pitcher. In trials with the Yankees, Senators, Indians, Dodgers, and Reds between 1926 and 1931 he totaled 490 at bats, hit 11 homers, drove in 67 runs, hit .249, and struck out 128 times. He was the first farm-system minor league star, playing 1,450 games in the Cardinals chain from 1932 to 1944. In the minors, he hit 420 home runs and drove in 1,857 runs, 10 times exceeding 100 in a season.

Cullop had good speed early in his career and was a good enough outfielder to play center field into the late 1920s, but he slowed up considerably in the 1930s. While it is not clear why Brief never did well in the majors, Cullop struck out a lot even in the minors and didn't walk much—suggesting that he had holes which could be and were pitched to effectively in the majors.

Ox Eckhardt was a great football star at the University of Texas who after graduation signed with both Austin of the Texas Association and the Cleveland Indians. The resulting dispute delayed his real professional debut for three years until he was 26 years old. Ox quickly made up for lost time, hitting .376 with a league leading 27 triples for Wichita and Amarillo in the Western League in 1928.

That fall he played for the New York Giants of the NFL. His baseball contract had been acquired by the Detroit Tigers and although he was on their 40-man roster in 1929, 1930, and 1931 he never got into a game with the big club. In 1929 he was sent to Seattle, where he hit .354 and again led the league in triples. In 1930 he went to Beaumont, where he led the Texas League with a .379 average. In 1931 he was sold to the Missions, for whom he led the PCL with a .369 average. In the spring of 1932 he was with the Boston Braves—he played eight games at the start of the season as a pinch hitter and was then sent back to the Missions, where over the next four seasons he hit .371, .414, .378, and .399, winning the batting title three times. He went to the Dodgers in 1936, lasted 16 games batting just .182, and was sent to Indianapolis, where he hit .353 and .341 over the next two years. He hit .321 with Toledo and Beaumont in 1938, .361 with Memphis in 1939, and after hitting .293 with Dallas in 1940, he retired with a minor league career batting average of .367 and the highest career average in organized baseball—.365. (Ty Cobb's minor league record drops his overall average to .3630; Ike Boone's major league record drops his organized-baseball average to .3629.) Eckhardt has the highest single-season and career batting average in the PCL, and 10 times he hit over .350.

Unlike many of the minor league stars, Eckhardt did not want for opportunities to play in the majors—counting a trial with the Indians in 1925, he had six shots, but they resulted in his playing in just 24 major league games. The reasons for his failure to make it in the majors are not obscure. Despite being an exceptional athlete with good speed early in his career, he was a poor fielder with a weak arm and no power. Although he was 6-1, 190, the left-handed-hitting Eckhardt slapped the ball to left field. Reportedly managers tried to get him to pull the ball—an idea that should certainly have advanced his career in Detroit or Brooklyn—but it only served to foul up his swing, which he would rediscover after being returned to the minors.

A few minor league greats don't fit the stereotypes: Jigger Statz was the opposite of most—his strengths were speed and defense. Joe Hauser appeared to be on his way to a successful career in the majors, but he broke his leg, never regained his past form, and went to the minors, where he became the only player to have two 60-home run seasons. Hector Espino spent virtually his entire career in Mexico, and while major league scouts believed he could hit in the majors, he apparently had no desire to leave his homeland.

Of the great minor league stars, Statz spent the most time in the majors—683 games—and the most time with one club: all of his 18 minor league seasons were with Los Angeles. His 3,473 games in organized baseball were a record until broken by Hank Aaron in 1976.

Statz was a great fielder; virtually all of his contemporaries considered him the best or one of the best they had seen. Playing very shallow, he reminded many of Tris Speaker. The statistics offer strong support for his claim to greatness. In four full seasons in the majors, he led the league in chances-per-game once and was second the other three years. Between 1922 and 1932 in the majors and minors he had a stretch of 10 seasons in which he played in at least 100 games and never finished lower than

second in chances-per-game. He had excellent speed, but during most of his career with the Angels they were a hard-hitting club that did not feature the running game, but that changed in the mid-1930s, and in the three seasons following his 36th birthday he stole 157 bases. His game was not just limited to speed and defense. A classic leadoff man of his era—a good contact hitter, small and fast—he hit .285 in the majors and .315 in the minors, collecting over 2,300 runs, 4,000 hits, 700 doubles, and 500 stolen bases in his organized-baseball career.

On April 7, 1925, the day of Babe Ruth's "big belly-ache," Joe Hauser a 26-year-old first baseman beginning his fourth season with the Athletics, broke his leg in a non-contact play while fielding during a preseason game against the Phillies at Baker Bowl. He had a .304 average for his first three major league seasons and had hit 27 homers with 115 RBIs in 1924. The injury kept him out for the entire 1925 season. In 1926 he tried to come back but hit only .192. After an excellent season with Kansas City, he went back to the majors but didn't do much in stints with the Philadelphia A's and Indians. Back in the minors, however, he was nothing short of remarkable. In 1930 with Baltimore he set a professional record with 63 homers; then he dropped to 31 in 1931 but still led the league. In 1932 he went to Minneapolis, where he led the American Association in homers with 49. In 1933 he broke his own home run record with 69, and he was off to a great start in 1934—33 homers, 88 RBIs in 82 games—when he broke his kneecap, knocking him out for the season. He continued to play until 1942 but never came close to achieving the success he had in the early 1930s.

Hauser did not hit for a high average, and it has been suggested that he took enormous advantage of short right field fences in Baltimore and Minneapolis—no one would argue that point, since 50 of his 69 homers in 1933 came at home. Yet many greats played in Oriole and Nicollet Parks, and none came close to Hauser's two record-breaking seasons, which remain the two highest home run seasons in the high minors.

Hector Espino holds the minor league career home run record with 484, and all but three of those were hit in Mexico. At the end of the 1964 Mexican League season, the 25-year-old first baseman, who had led the league with 46 homers and a .371 batting average, was sold by Monterrey to the St. Louis Cardinals' Jacksonville farm club. He hit .300 with those three home runs in 100 at bats and was invited to spring training by the Cards for 1965, but he never reported and was eventually returned to Monterrey. In the late 1960s the California Angels coveted Espino, who had led the Mexican League in hitting from 1966 to 1968, but they were never able to consummate a deal. Espino was a legend in Mexico, but it has never been clear why he didn't try the majors—he gave conflicting answers. Possibly he enjoyed being a big fish in a small pond—it wasn't the money, since he never made more than $18,000 a year in Mexico. He was notorious for marching to his own drummer, occasionally leaving clubs for a midseason vacation, and perhaps he was unwilling to sacrifice that independence.

Espino could hit for power and average—he led the Mexican League in batting five times and home runs four times—and scouts said he could have done the same in the majors, but like many players he played too long. His

power started a sharp decline after his 33rd birthday, and he was virtually helpless at the plate during his last two or three seasons. Nevertheless he ranks as perhaps the greatest minor league player who never played in the majors.

Great players do not have to be distributed evenly among all positions or across all eras, but the emphasis being on great hitters, the result is a number of outfielder-first baseman-designated hitter types, most of whom played in the high-scoring 1920s and 1930s.

Ray French was perhaps the best middle infielder in the minors. He spent 28 years in the minors, most of it in the Pacific Coast League. He played 2,736 games at shortstop and was a brilliant fielder. In the 14 seasons that he played more than 100 games at short, he led the league in chances-per-game seven times. He was not an outstanding hitter, but his fielding kept him around long enough for him to collect 3,255 hits—seventh on the all-time minor league list.

The two best 19th-century minor leaguers were first baseman Perry Werden and pitcher Willie Mains. Werden had good speed and power. He had several good years in the majors (twice leading the league in triples), won six minor league home run titles, including two seasons when he went over 40, and his .341 lifetime average was exceptionally high for that era.

Mains was the first minor league pitcher to win 300 games, reaching that figure early in 1905. A seven-time 20-game winner, he was also an excellent hitter in an era when pitchers were frequently expected to take a shift in the outfield. Most of his career was in the New York State League, but in an interesting example of the mobility of players even in the game's early years, in 1892–1893 Mains had back-to-back seasons in Portland—although one season was spent in Oregon and the other in Maine.

A highly productive but not great player who deserves mention is Spencer Harris, a little left-handed-hitting outfielder who holds the minor league career records for runs, hits, doubles, total bases, and walks. He reached those levels primarily because he kept playing until he was forty-eight years old. He did lead the American Association in homers in 1928 while at Minneapolis, but he was aided enormously by the friendly right field fence at Nicollet Park. (He averaged 17 homers a year in 10 seasons with Minneapolis but only six per year in his 16 other minor league seasons.) He was never thought of as the top player on his many minor league clubs—just as a good solid player of the type that formed the backbone of the minors for so many years.

The Pitchers

There have been few minor league pitching stars of the magnitude of the great hitters. Perhaps this is because pitching is a one-dimensional skill—no pitchers were kept in the minors because they couldn't hit or field. Many of the outstanding minor league pitchers stayed there because they didn't have great stuff. Bill Thomas, who won 383 games, and Hal Turpin, who won 271 without ever getting shots at the majors, had the same statistical profile—they struck out few, walked even less, and allowed a lot of hits.

Two pitchers that didn't fit that profile, however, were Joe Martina and Dick Barrett. Martina was a power pitcher who spent most of his career with Beaumont and with his hometown New Orleans Pelicans. He held the minor league career strikeout record until ageless George Brunet broke it while toiling in the Mexican League in 1981. Martina was a workhorse, pitching over 250 innings in 13 different seasons while winning 20 games seven times. He got his first and only big league opportunity at age 35 with the world champion Washington Senators in 1924.

"Kewpie" Dick Barrett didn't really find himself until he joined Seattle of the PCL in 1935, 10 years into his professional career. A little left-hander with less than pinpoint control (he holds the minor league record for career bases on balls), he had good stuff and eight 20-win seasons.

Frank Shellenback is most frequently named as the greatest minor league pitcher. The Pacific Coast League career leader in wins with 295, Shellenback won nine games as a 19-year-old rookie spitballer in 1918. After a poor start the following season, he was sent to Minneapolis. In February 1920 the baseball rules committee outlawed the spitball and other trick pitches. Each major league team was allowed to designate two spitball pitchers who would be able to continue using the pitch in the majors. Unfortunately for Shellenback, he was on the Vernon roster by this time and at age 21 would be consigned forever to pitching in the minors if he couldn't get by without the spitball. Throughout much of his career, articles would be written that usually declared that Shellenback would be a major league star if he was eligible to play there. He did have a great six-year stretch with Hollywood (1928–1933) when he went 142–59. He was a very popular player with the Stars as well as Vernon and a fine hitter with good power, but a review of his record suggests he was never as good as everyone thought he was. He led the PCL in wins and won-loss percentage twice each but never led in another category. He had only five 20-win seasons.

Because of the spitball ban, Shellenback was viewed as a tragic figure, but he wasn't alone. Spitballer Paul Wachtel won 203 games in the Texas League after the ban, including five 20-win seasons. Rube Robinson won 148 games in the Southern Association, including two league-leading 26-win seasons. Wheeler Fuller, who never pitched in the majors, won 156 in the Eastern League after the ban.

Perhaps the greatest minor league pitcher was Tony Freitas, a little left-hander who spent all or part of 15 seasons with Sacramento. He had great control, could get the strikeout, and had nine 20-win seasons (plus two 19-win seasons). If he hadn't lost three years to the military, he probably would have won 400 games in the minors. Freitas had an impressive major league debut, going 12–5 in less than a full season with the 1932 Philadelphia A's, but that was the last success he would have in the majors.

Four other pitchers worthy of mention are Sam Gibson, George Boehler, Bill Bailey, and George Brunet.

Gibson was an underappreciated pitcher who spent most of his career in the PCL, including 12 years with San Francisco. He didn't make his organized-baseball debut until he was 23 years old. After two promising seasons with Detroit, he never had much success in the majors, but

he was extremely effective in the minors. He had six 20-win seasons (plus three 19-win seasons) and, pitching in a high-scoring era, he had eight seasons where his ERA was below 3.00.

Boehler was a hard-throwing workhorse who spent most of his career in the Western League. Twice he pitched over 400 innings, six times over 300. Unfortunately he was terribly inconsistent: with Tulsa he sandwiched a 38-win season in 1922 around seasons in which he combined for just 11 victories. He was consistently ineffective in a number of major league trials.

Bailey had seven league-leading strikeout seasons in four different leagues (International, Texas, Southern, Western), but only three 20-win seasons. After a promising September debut with the Browns in 1907, he pitched over 200 games in the majors with five teams spread over 15 years with no success.

Brunet pitched in organized ball for 33 years (1953-1985), and astonishingly he was a regular-rotation pitcher for all but the last year. When he was 48 years old, he had a 1.94 ERA pitching regularly in the Mexican League. He never won more than 17 games in a season, had only two 200-strikeout seasons (they were 21 years apart), but he had a credible major league career and holds the minor league career strikeout record.

The Teams

There have been a number of debates about the greatest minor league teams. The 1937 Newark Bears, the 1934 Los Angeles Angels, the 1920-1925 Ft. Worth Panthers, and the 1919-1925 Baltimore Orioles usually draw the most support. All were dominant teams with good players.

The Bears included Charlie Keller, Joe Gordon, George McQuinn, Atley Donald, and five other players who would go to the majors the following year. They won the International League pennant by 25½ games with a 109–41 record. The Angels included Frank Demaree, Jigger Statz, Gene Lillard, and Fay Thomas, and they compiled an astounding 137–50 record. The Panthers (or Cats) won six straight pennants and five Dixie Series. They were led by the home run hitting of Big Boy Kraft and a fine pitching staff that included spitballer Paul Wachtel and Joe Pate.

It is doubtful that any of the three could have competed successfully in the majors. It is occasionally claimed that the 1937 Newark Bears were the Yankees' B team and could have finished second in the American League, or at least in the first division. But that ignores the talent that was in the majors. The Red Sox finished fifth in 1937 with a club that included Jimmie Foxx, Joe Cronin, Lefty Grove, Pinky Higgins, Doc Cramer, Ben Chapman, Jack Wilson, and Bobo Newsom, all of whom, it is safe to say, would have started for the Bears. The same is true of the Angels, whose pitching staff chose 1934 to have career years, and of the Cats, who played well as a team but had few players that were even considered minor league standouts.

The Orioles were a different story. Thanks to the draft exemption, Jack Dunn was able to assemble a powerhouse comprised of players ready and capable of playing in the majors. The 1922 team was probably the best minor league club ever assembled. It had Jack Bentley, Max Bishop, Fritz Maisel, and Joe Boley in the infield, and Otis Lawry, Merwyn Jacobson, and Jimmy Walsh in the outfield. The catcher was Lena Styles, and the pitchers were Lefty Grove, John Ogden, Tommy Thomas, Rube Parnham, and Harry Frank with Bentley occasionally seeing action on the mound. Grove, Ogden, and Thomas combined for 60 wins and six years later would win a combined 56 games in the majors. Parnham, a free spirit who pitched when he wanted, was around long enough to win 16 (the following year he won 33). Frank won 22, but his career would soon be cut short by illness. Bentley hit .350 and won 13 games; he went to the Giants in 1923 as a pitcher but hit .427. Bishop and Boley, who hit .261 and .343 respectively, went on to become the double-play combo with the 1929-1930 world champion Philadelphia A's. Styles was just twenty-two years old and hit .315, but that was his peak. Maisel (.306), Walsh (.327), Jacobson (.304), and Lawry (.333) had all played briefly and/or ineffectively in the majors but would all go on to have great careers in the International League. A 20-year-old rookie utility player on the team was Dick Porter, who hit .279 and would have seven excellent seasons with the Orioles before going on to have several good years with the Indians.

As good as the Orioles were and as good as some of their players became, it is doubtful that even they could have finished in the first division of the American or National Leagues in 1922. Yet the strongest evidence of the attraction of minor league baseball and the hold it has long held on fans who were exposed to it is that those great Oriole, Bear, and Angel teams are far better known and more fondly remembered than hundreds of more talented second-division and higher major league clubs.

The Farm System

Farm teams are nearly as old as organized baseball. In 1884 the Boston Beaneaters of the National League owned a team called the Boston Reserves in the Massachusetts State Association. The Reserves, also called the Colts, were apparently intended to serve as a source of replacements for disabled members of the major league club. It has also been suggested that the farm team was a device to keep more players under contract and out of the hands of the Union Association that year. Whatever the origins of the idea, during the next decade a number of major league clubs operated such reserve teams, but they usually competed in local semipro leagues rather than in organized baseball and were viewed more as quick sources of replacements rather than as training grounds for players.

With John B. Day's joint ownership of the New York Gothams of the National League and the New York Metropolitans of the American Association as early as 1883 and with the proliferation of interlocking ownerships of major league clubs in the 1890s, it was only natural that some major and minor league clubs would come under joint ownership as well. The first instance of any significance, however, occurred when John T. Brush, owner of Cincinnati in the National League, entered the Indianapo-

lis club in the newly formed Western League in 1894. While this was not the first case of joint major-minor league club ownership, Brush appears to have been the first to grasp the potential of such an arrangement. Indianapolis served as a place to develop talent that was not quite ready for the majors. The team gave Cincinnati an expanded roster as players were frequently shuffled to and from Indianapolis during the season. It also served as a source of profit because Indianapolis drew well at the gate, having become the dominant club in the Western League, with three pennants and two second-place finishes in five seasons (1895–1899). Indianapolis' success was aided in no small part by Brush's practice of drafting players from other Western League clubs and sending them to Indianapolis, thus simultaneously weakening the opposition and strengthening the Hoosiers. Efforts were made by the other Western League club owners to control "farming" or to modify the draft rules to stop Brush, but none were successful.

Perhaps copying Brush's strategy, in 1896 several National League clubs obtained minor league affiliates: Pittsburgh had Toronto, Boston had Wilkes-Barre, and Cleveland had Ft. Wayne. Philadelphia had a Philadelphia farm club in the Pennsylvania State League, and when that league folded, they shifted the junior club to the Atlantic Association. The New York Giants had the first farm "system," with the New York Mets in the Atlantic Association and Syracuse in the Eastern League.

When the National Agreement was adopted in 1903, it banned the "farming out" of players. Yet "farming" as defined in the agreement referred only to those efforts by major league clubs to exceed the limits on players who could be optioned through subterfuge—"fake transfers" such as loans or sell/buy-back arrangements with minor league clubs where title to a player was never surrendered.

The independent minor league operators saw farming as a curse for two reasons. First, it reduced their autonomy and potential revenue by placing more players under major league ownership, thus reducing the majors' need to buy or draft players from the minors. Second, clubs accepting players from the majors, either openly through options or secretly, might gain an unfair competitive advantage on the field. So while in 1905 the New York Giants' request to establish a working agreement with Bridgeport was validated by the National Commission, most of the legislation was focused on restricting farming, normally by limiting the number of players who could be optioned and the number of times each player could be optioned. For example, in 1904 a rule was adopted which required a player sent out on option to stay with the minor league club for the remainder of that season. In 1907 the rule was relaxed so that a major league club could option a player and recall him, but only once in a season. In 1911 a team could have no more than eight players out on option at one time.

Working agreements became quite common during this period. The major league club furnished the minor league club with its surplus players—youngsters in need of more experience or veterans past their prime who could still strengthen a minor league club—and/or cash. In return the major league club could obtain promising players from the minor league club. During this era the formal working agreement between major and minor league clubs was usually of short duration—a year or two at most—suggesting that major league clubs targeted certain minor league clubs that had two or three players they might be interested in and established a working agreement in order to get first claim on those that developed satisfactorily. There were also informal working agreements, generally based on friendships between major and minor league club operators, and it was usually through such arrangements that the "fake transfers" banned by the National Agreement took place. In the early 1900s there was substantial traffic in players between the White Sox and Milwaukee of the American Association and between the Dodgers and Baltimore in the Eastern League. (Brewers manager Joe Cantillon was a long-time friend of Charles Comiskey, and Brooklyn manager Ned Hanlon was also a minority owner of the Orioles.)

The most efficient and only legal method of circumventing the rules relating to major league control of players was through joint ownership of major and minor league clubs. By 1912 Charles W. Somers owned Cleveland and Toledo, and Charles Ebbets owned both Brooklyn and Newark. This enabled the Indians to hold title to 60 players and the Dodgers to 61. In 1913 a National Commission confidential bulletin directed major league clubs to divest their interest in minor league clubs by Jan. 1, 1914, but neither Somers nor Ebbets complied until several years later (in fact, Somers secretly acquired New Orleans in 1913). In 1921 the joint ownership of major and minor league clubs was again permitted, and the New National Agreement, although retaining option limits, dropped the anti-farming provisions that had been in it since 1903.

In 1921 the Cardinals, who had already acquired an interest in Ft. Smith of the Western Association and Houston of the Texas League, acquired a half interest in Syracuse of the International League. This was the beginning of Branch Rickey's farm system, but initially it attracted little attention as it didn't appear to represent anything particularly new. Major league clubs had long been signing young talent directly off the sandlots and developing it in the minors. In 1910, for example, Cleveland signed Roger Peckinpaugh out of the Cleveland City League, gave him a brief trial, and then optioned him to New Haven and Portland in successive seasons before recalling him when he was deemed ready for the majors. This practice had developed to the point that Mike Sexton, president of the National Association, in 1921 spoke out against the fact that the majors and higher minors had preempted the low minors' traditional role of discovering and signing young talent.

As we have seen, major league clubs had occasionally owned minor league clubs, primarily to expand the number of players under their control, but these were always higher-classification clubs, where talent was refined rather than developed. Rickey's approach was original because he was the first to assemble a system of teams at various levels or classifications. This enabled him to sign young talent and, through a hierarchy of minor league clubs, to develop and retain continuous title to a large number of players, his theory being that out of quantity comes quality. It didn't take long for the system to begin producing talent. The Cards, who had never finished higher than third in this century, won the World Series in

1926 with a team that included future Hall of Famers Jim Bottomley and Chick Hafey as well as regulars Taylor Douthit, Tommy Thevenow, Les Bell, Ray Blades, Flint Rhem, and Art Reinhardt plus reserves Watty Holm, Jake Flowers, Spec Toporcher, Ernie Vick, and Bill Hallahan—all of whom were products of a farm system that was less than seven years old. In addition, Billy Southworth was acquired from the Giants for Heinie Mueller, another product of the Cardinals farm system.

During those seven years when the Cardinals were discovering, signing, and developing unprecedented quantities of players at little expense, the other major league clubs were essentially operating as they always had, signing some players out of the amateur ranks, optioning them out for seasoning, and buying top prospects from minor league clubs, even though the new draft rules were driving the prices of such players to unprecedented levels. For example, the Yankees team the Cardinals defeated in the 1926 World Series had just one home-grown player—Lou Gehrig, who was signed out of Columbia University in 1923 and optioned to Hartford until ready. Although this had been an inexpensive acquisition, the Yankees subsequently had purchased, for $50,000 each, Earle Combs from Louisville, Mark Koenig from St. Paul (with whom the Yankees had a working agreement), and Tony Lazzeri from Salt Lake. In 1925, the year the Pirates won the World Series, they acquired Paul Waner and Hal Rhyne from the San Francisco Seals for $100,000 and also signed Joe Cronin off the San Francisco sandlots for little more than train fare to his first assignment—Johnstown, Pa.

But the escalating prices of players and the success of the Cardinals finally encouraged other clubs to begin acquiring minor league clubs. Shortly after the Cardinals acquired the half interest in Syracuse in 1921, William Wrigley, owner of the Cubs, acquired Los Angeles of the Pacific Coast League, but he treated them virtually as separate investments. By 1927, however, major league acquisition of minor league clubs was causing concern in the minors. The first formal notice came late that year, when the American Association adopted a new Constitution which effectively prohibited major league ownership of its clubs (excluding Columbus, which was already owned by Cincinnati). At the National Association meeting in December 1928, Mike Sexton wondered aloud when the majors would own enough clubs to control the National Association. Early in 1929 major league clubs owned or controlled 27 minor league clubs. At that point Commissioner Landis, who until then had been remarkably quiet on the issue of farm systems, opened fire. He began granting free agency to minor leaguers "covered up" by various major league organizations. Later in 1929, Landis denounced the farm system, and announced his intention of destroying it. In response, Sam Breadon, owner of the Cardinals, cited letters from seven minor leagues saying the farm system was beneficial to them. Interestingly, in 1921 Landis had said, "The object of organized baseball is to facilitate the development of skill among ball players." No one could seriously argue that this wasn't the purpose of the farm system, but by 1929 Landis was accusing Rickey and Breadon of "raping the minors," robbing small-town America of its precious heritage of independent minor league baseball.

Landis tried to make good on his threat to destroy the farm system, but since it was not contrary to baseball law, he had to pick at the edges. Landis levied fines against teams having an interest in more than one team in a minor league or by granting free agency to players who were "covered up" through violations of the option rules or "secret agreements." Attracting much attention in Landis' crusade was his granting of free agency to 74 St. Louis farmhands in 1938 and to 91 Detroit minor leaguers in 1940, but these shots were fired after the war was lost.

More important than the fireworks that erupted between Landis and Breadon at the 1929 major league meeting was Yankees owner Jacob Ruppert's declaration at the same meetings that no ballclub could afford the prices being paid for minor league players. Ruppert added that he was "going to be forced into owning minor league clubs, and so is every other major league owner in this room." At the time he spoke, the Yankees had already purchased the Chambersburg club of the Class D Blue Ridge League. In November 1931 Ruppert purchased Newark of the International League for a reported $600,000 and soon thereafter hired Baltimore general manager George Weiss to develop a farm system. Thus the farm system, a concept that had been created largely out of necessity by Branch Rickey because the Cardinals didn't have the financial resources to compete with other clubs for top minor league prospects, had in less than a decade been embraced by the wealthiest club in baseball as being the most efficient method of acquiring talent. There would still be an occasional Joe DiMaggio or Ted Williams, signed by a minor league club and sold to the majors, but the major league club that didn't establish a farm system did so at its own peril. Not coincidentally, the eight teams which were the slowest to get on the bandwagon and had the thinnest farm systems in the 1930s—the Phillies, Athletics, Senators, White Sox, Giants, Cubs, Braves, and Pirates—were, aside from the Browns, the eight least successful teams in the 1940s. (The Browns and Reds established extensive farm systems in the 1930s, and overall they were the two most improved clubs of the 1940s.)

While several clubs caught on to what the Cardinals were doing, none could catch up to the head start by St. Louis. The Depression had created a large pool of young men with few career options, and Rickey signed players by the hundreds at tryout camps. Whereas during the 1920s the Cardinals system had only increased from three clubs to five, by 1936 it had expanded to 28 teams—remarkable considering that there were only 26 minor leagues that year (the Cardinals had two teams each in the Nebraska State, Georgia-Florida, and Arkansas-Missouri Leagues). The Cardinal system finally topped out with 33 clubs in 1937—more than the two next-largest farm systems combined. Rickey's belief that out of quantity comes quality was proven on the field by the 1942 world champion Cardinals. Every player on the active roster, except for second-line pitchers Harry Gumbert and Whitey Moore, was a product of the St. Louis farm system, and Gumbert had been acquired in exchange for Cardinals farm graduate Bill McGee.

In addition, the sale of players developed by the Cardinals kept the coffers full—in 1940–1941 alone, Johnny Mize, Joe Medwick, and Mickey Owen were ex-

changed to other clubs for $240,000 and nine players.

Thus from the perspective of the majors the farm system was a success, and the minors seemed to be flourishing—going from 14 leagues in 1933 to 44 by 1940. Sam Breadon, responding to another barrage of attacks by Landis in the late 1930s, claimed that the farm system had brought stability and strength to the minors, but there were other factors at work—the proliferation of night games, better promotion, and an influx of good young talent resulted in a per-club increase in attendance of 40 percent from 1937 to 1940. During that same period the portion of minor league clubs affiliated with the majors actually dropped from 61 to 46 percent. Rickey's theory that out of quantity comes quality might have had practical merit during a depression, or again immediately following World War II when there was an influx of returning veterans. However, under normal circumstances huge farm systems were not cost-effective. While the minors were still expanding in the late 1930s, the Cardinals began pruning back their farm system of more than 30 teams. A decade later farm systems were contracting—in 1948 there were six farm systems of 20 or more teams; by 1951 there were none. The portion of minor league teams affiliated with major league teams dropped from 62 percent in 1946 to 47 percent in 1951 as major league farm systems collectively dropped from 280 to 175 clubs and outright major league ownership of minor league clubs dropped from 125 to 75.

In 1950 there were 232 minor league teams not affiliated with the majors. This was the highest number of independent teams in organized baseball in nearly 40 years. Nine of the 58 leagues had no teams with major league affiliations, and more than a dozen others had only one or two affiliates. These leagues operated virtually outside the player-development chain, existing much as a semipro team or league does—to provide entertainment and reflect civic pride. Their only source of revenue was through the turnstiles, and just as 40 years earlier automobiles and the movies helped drive out the marginal teams and leagues, now TV did the same. This can be clearly seen as the densely populated Northeast, the first region to be heavily penetrated by television, suffered the first wave of league failures.

Over the next few years, attendance declined sharply, most of the independent clubs folded, and farm systems continued to contract. In 1956 the majors established a "stabilization fund" of $500,000 to aid clubs and leagues in lower classifications, but the free-fall of leagues, clubs, and attendance continued. In 1959 the majors discontinued the stabilization fund and established a fund of $1 million to finance a player-development and promotional program for the minors. In 1962 the majors and minors adopted the Player Development Plan that, by requiring each major league club to have five farm teams, would guarantee the operation of at least 100 minor league teams, which the majors felt was adequate for their player-development purposes. The plan also included the Player Development Contract under the terms of which the parent major league club became responsible for all spring training costs and all or most of the salaries of players, managers, and coaches. After major league expansion in 1969, major league clubs were only required to support four farm clubs each, but their financial support of each was increased. By 1976 there were only 106 minor league teams with major league affiliations, the lowest peacetime total since 1935. American League expansion the following year created the need for additional minor league affiliates, and in subsequent years major league clubs expanded their farm systems—all of them back up to a minimum of five clubs by 1984. With the dramatic increase in minor league attendance and the resulting increase in the value of franchises in the 1980s, a new Professional Baseball Agreement was ratified by the majors and minors in 1990. The new agreement required the minors to assume a greater share of operational expenses but the majors continued to pay the salaries and meal money of all uniformed personnel. And farm systems continued to grow—by 1994 each major league club had at least six farm clubs and the number of minor league teams with major league affiliations was up to 194, the highest total since 1950. With further major league expansion, the number of major league affiliates reached 207 in 1998.

In 1928 Mike Sexton had asked how long it would be before the majors owned enough minor league clubs to control the National Association. Other than during World War II, when the minors were severely constricted, major league clubs never have "owned" more than 28 percent of the minor league clubs. Yet possibly as early as 1934, probably by 1935, and certainly by 1936, the majors through outright ownership, working agreements, or other interlocking devices "controlled" the National Association, and this situation was generally acknowledged throughout baseball by 1938.

Until about 1960 there was still some room in the National Association for independent clubs and career minor league players, but since then the minors have existed almost exclusively to develop talent for the majors. While this has dismayed many minor league fans and traditionalists, it should be remembered that the principal role of the minors within organized baseball has always been to develop talent for the majors, and to receive money in exchange. The farm system, which owed its success in no small part to the greed of some minor league operators, was merely a different device by which talent moved to the majors and money moved to the minors.

Minor Leagues

Year	Leagues Started	Didn't Finish	Year	Leagues Started	Didn't Finish	Year	Leagues Started	Didn't Finish	Year	Leagues Started	Didn't Finish	Year	Leagues Started	Didn't Finish	Year	Leagues Started	Didn't Finish
1883	2		1902	16	2	1921	26	1	1940	44	1	1959	21		1978	18	
1884	7	3	1903	19	3	1922	30	2	1941	41		1960	22		1979	18	
1885	8	3	1904	23	3	1923	31	2	1942	31	5	1961	22		1980	17	
1886	11	3	1905	29	6	1924	29	3	1943	10	1	1962	20		1981	17	
1887	15	6	1906	33	5	1925	25	1	1944	10		1963	18		1982	17	
1888	17	9	1907	34	6	1926	29	4	1945	12		1964	20		1983	17	
1889	15	5	1908	39	8	1927	24		1946	43	1	1965	19		1984	17	
1890	18	9	1909	34	2	1928	30	3	1947	52		1966	19		1985	18	
1891	13	5	1910	52	8	1929	26	3	1948	58		1967	19		1986	17	
1892	14	10	1911	50	7	1930	23	2	1949	59		1968	21		1987	19	
1893	7	4	1912	45	6	1931	19	3	1950	58	1	1969	21		1988	19	
1894	8	2	1913	42	5	1932	19	6	1951	50	1	1970	20		1989	19	
1895	17	9	1914	43	7	1933	14		1952	43		1971	20		1990	19	
1896	15	8	1915	30	7	1934	20	1	1953	38		1972	20		1991	19	
1897	20	8	1916	25	3	1935	21		1954	36	1	1973	18		1992	19	
1898	20	11	1917	21	10	1936	26		1955	33		1974	18	1	1993	19	
1899	14	5	1918	10	9	1937	37		1956	28		1975	18		1994	19	
1900	15	6	1919	15	2	1938	37		1957	28		1976	19		1995	19	
1901	13	2	1920	22	1	1939	41		1958	24		1977	19	1	1996	19	
															1997	21	
															1998	20	

Minor League Clubs/Major League Affiliations

Year	Minor League Clubs	Affiliated with Majors	Owned by Majors	Year	Minor League Clubs	Affiliated with Majors	Owned by Majors	Year	Minor League Clubs	Affiliated with Majors	Owned by Majors
1936	184	115	38	1956	217	150	33	1976	148	106	24
1937	251	154	39	1957	200	153	32	1977	150	113	23
1938	267	163	48	1958	173	157	34	1978	156	118	24
1939	292	149	47	1959	150	132	30	1979	155	119	
1940	310	143	60	1960	152	126	18	1980	155	125	
1941	304	143	61	1961	147	129	21	1981	152	133	
1942	206	116	46	1962	134	121	22	1982	160	136	
1943	66	42	23	1963	130	114	22	1983	162	139	
1944	70	57	21	1964	136	108	19	1984	164	140	
1945	85	68	33	1965	136	110	28	1985	168	140	
1946	316	197	79	1966	138	116	32	1986	164	143	
1947	388	247	103	1967	141	118	36	1987	176	149	
1948	438	280	125	1968	152	119	39	1988	188	168	
1949	448	243	116	1969	155	128	46	1989	197	179	
1950	446	210	99	1970	153	120	39	1990	202	183	
1951	371	172	75	1971	155	127	45	1991	207	184	
1952	324	166	65	1972	148	125	49	1992	212	192	
1953	292	152	50	1973	147	117	38	1993	214	193	
1954	269	156	49	1974	145	113	27	1994	216	195	
1955	243	155	40	1975	137	109	26	1995	216	193	
								1996	218	198	
								1997	237	206	
								1998	242	207	

Major League Farm Systems
1936–1969

	36	37	38	39	40	41	42	43	44	45	46	47	48	49	50	51	52	53	54	55	56	57	58	59	60	61	62	63	64	65	66	67	68	69
Boston, AL	9	10	7	8	6	7	6	3	5	4	12	13	15	11	8	8	6	6	6	6	5	7	6	6	6	6	5	5	5	6	6	6	6	6
Chicago, AL	5	4	10	8	6	5	5	0	0	1	7	12	15	9	8	8	6	6	6	6	6	5	6	6	6	6	5	5	6	6	4	5	5	5
Cleveland, AL	5	7	13	16	8	9	8	3	3	11	18	20	20	16	12	10	8	8	9	9	8	8	7	5	6	5	4	4	4	4	5	5	5	6
Detroit, AL	11	8	12	7	5	11	8	3	2	7	11	16	14	9	8	7	8	10	9	8	10	7	8	8	6	6	5	5	5	5	5	6	6	6
New York, AL	11	15	15	15	14	12	9	5	5	15	22	24	22	15	14	10	11	9	10	11	10	10	8	7	7	7	5	7	7	6	6	6	6	6
Phila.-K.C.-Oakland, AL	5	3	3	3	4	5	3	2	2	4	7	15	10	11	15	9	8	6	7	9	8	8	8	8	6	5	5	6	6	6	6	6	6	5
St. Louis-Baltimore, AL	3	15	16	12	11	11	6	1	3	3	11	15	20	18	13	10	12	10	12	8	9	9	7	6	6	6	7	6	6	6	7	6	6	6
Wash.-Minnesota, AL	1	5	2	8	4	6	3	1	2	2	5	7	12	9	10	6	8	7	8	7	6	8	8	7	6	7	7	6	8	8	8	8	8	8
Milwaukee-Atlanta, NL	4	6	6	6	5	4	4	1	1	2	13	15	15	11	8	8	10	10	12	15	12	14	12	10	9	7	6	5	6	7	5	6	7	4
Brklyn.-Los Angeles, NL	5	14	14	11	18	14	10	4	7	9	21	25	26	26	22	19	17	15	16	14	13	12	12	11	9	7	6	6	6	6	6	6	6	6
Chicago, NL	5	6	5	2	2	9	11	4	6	7	18	23	19	16	15	14	10	9	9	8	10	8	6	6	6	5	5	5	6	6	6	6	6	5
Cincinnati, NL	16	10	10	10	8	8	5	2	1	3	4	8	11	10	7	4	6	9	9	11	11	8	6	6	6	5	5	5	4	5	5	5	5	5
N.Y.-San Francisco, NL	2	11	4	5	6	7	7	3	5	6	16	19	22	19	14	9	10	10	10	12	9	9	8	7	6	6	6	6	6	6	6	6	6	5
Philadelphia, NL	1	2	3	3	8	3	2	1	3	5	9	11	15	14	12	11	11	9	9	8	9	9	7	10	8	7	6	6	7	7	6	6	7	6
Pittsburgh, NL	4	5	7	7	9	8	2	4	4	13	14	19	13	13	11	15	11	10	13	13	10	11	9	7	7	7	7	6	6	6	6	6	6	6
St. Louis, NL	28	33	32	28	29	25	22	6	7	7	18	19	22	20	21	16	15	16	22	18	15	11	14	12	9	8	6	5	5	6	7	7	7	7
L.A.-California, AL																										2	4	6	6	6	5	5	5	5
Washington, AL																										2	4	4	4	4	5	5	5	
Houston, NL																											2	4	5	5	6	6	5	
New York, NL																										3	4	5	4	4	5	6	6	5
Kansas City, AL																																		7
Seattle, AL																																		4
Montreal, NL																																		3
San Diego, NL																																		4

Annual Overall Minor League Pitching Percentage Leader (20 or more decisions)

Year	Player	Team (League)	W–L	Pct.	Overall W–L	Overall Pct.
1900	Willie Mains	Rome (N.Y. St.)	27–5	.844		
1901	Henry Allemang	Little Rock (So. Assn.)	20–4	.833		
1902	Louis Bruce	Toronto (Eastern)	18–2	.900		
1903	Ernest Nichols	Spokane (Pac. Nat.)	20–4	.833		
1904	Ed Craig	Springfield (Mo. Valley)	19–4	.826		
1905	Fred Steele	Oskaloosa (Iowa St.)	18–3	.857		
1906	Frank Dick	Marshalltown (Iowa St.)	18–3	.857		
1907	Harley Young	Wichita (West. Assn.)	29–4	.879		
1908	Harry Gaspar	Waterloo (Cent. Assn.)	32–4	.889		
1909	Ray Fisher	Hartford (Conn.)	24–5	.828		
1910	Cyrus Dahlgren	Superior (Minn.-Wis.)	22–3	.880		
1911	Howard Northrop	Reading (Inter.-St.)	27–4	.871		
1912	Larue Kirby	Traverse City (Mich. St.)	18–3	.857		
1913	Ralph Bell	Winona (Northern)	28–6	.824		
1914	Joe Chabek	Harrisburg (Tri-St.)	28–3	.903		
1915	Booth Hopper	Minneapolis (A.A.)	18–3	.857		
1916	Howard Ehmke	Syracuse (N.Y. St.)	31–7	.816		
1917	John Verbout	Wilkes-Barre (N.Y. St.)	26–7	.788		
1918	John Beckvermit	Binghamton (Int.)	17–4	.810		
1919	C. A. "Chief" Bender	Richmond (Va.)	29–2	.935		
1920	George Carmen	London (Mich.,-Ont.)	26–2	.926		
1921	Earl Keiser	Mitchell (Dakota)	20–2			
		Oakland (PCL)	3–0		23–2	.920
1922	Byrd Hodges	Joplin (West. Assn.)	26–3	.897		
1923	Emil Levsen	Cedar Rapids (Miss. Val.)	19–4	.826		
1924	Carl Dunagan	Dyersburg (Kitty)	19–2	.905		
1925	Lloyd Brown	Ardmore-Western Assn.	17–1	.944*		
1926	Frank Tubbs	Port Huron (Mich.-Ont.)	8–1			
		Port Huron (Mich. St.)	8–0			
		Oklahoma City (Western)	9–2		25–3	.893
1927	Ben Cantwell	Jacksonville (So'east.)	25–5	.833		
1928	Paul Fittery	Carrollton (Ga.-Ala.)	21–2	.913		
1929	Andrew Bednar	McCook (Neb. St.)	21–4	.840		
1930	Jim Cameron	McCook (Neb. St.)	19–2	.905		
1931	Lyle "Bud" Tinning	Minneapolis (A.A.)	1–2			
		Des Moines (West. Assn.)	24–2		25–4	.862
1932	Marvin Duke	Erie (Central)	23–4	.852		
1933	Al Piechota	Davenport (Miss. Val.)	19–4	.826		
1934	Fay Thomas	Los Angeles (PCL)	28–4	.875		
1935	Lloyd Sterling	Winnipeg (Northern)	24–2	.923		
1936	Bill Yocke	Akron (Mid. Atl.)	1–2			
		Norfolk (Piedmont)	18–1		19–3	.864
1937	Joe Kohlman	Salisbury (E. Shore)	25–1	.962		
1938	Paige Dennis	Thomasville (N.C. St.)	28–2	.933		
1939	Charles Wensloff	Joplin (West. Assn.)	26–4	.867		
1940	Arthur Cyrolewski	Johnson City (App.)	20–3	.870		
	J. Merwin (Merv) Henley	La Crosse (Wis. St.)	20–3	.870		
1941	Frank Marino	Macon (Sally)	19–1	.950		
1942	Paul Minner	Elizabethton (App.)	18–2			
		Knoxville (So. Assn.)	1–0		19–2	.905
1943	Irvin Stein	Portsmouth (Piedmont)	24–6	.800		
1944	Pete Naktenis	Hartford (Eastern)	18–3	.857		
1945	Lewis Carpenter	Atlanta (So. Assn.)	22–2	.917		
1946	Bill Kennedy	Rocky Mount (C. Plain)	28–3	.903		
1947	Chris VanCuyk	Cambridge (E. Shore)	25–2	.926		
1948	Albert Tefft	Blackstone (Va.)	20–1	.952		
1949	Lynn Southworth	Thomasville (N.C. St.)	21–1	.955		
1950	Mike Hudak	Big Stone Gap (Mt. St.)	19–2	.905		
1951	Anderson Bush	Hagerstown (Int. St.)	22–3	.880		
1952	Russell Harris	Ozark (Ala.-Fla.)	27–3	.900		
1953	Steve Kraly	Binghamton (Eastern)	19–2	.905		
1954	Don Vaughn	Merryville-Morristown (Mt. St.)	11–1			
		Highpoint-Thomasville (Carolina)	0–0			
		Vidalia (Ga. St.)	9–1		20–2	.909
1955	Jim Grant	Keokuk (I-I-I)	19–3	.864		
1956	Francisco Ramirez	Mexico City Reds (Mex.)	20–3	.870		
1957	Bob Riesner	Alexandria (Evang.)	20–0			
		New Orleans (So. Assn.)	0–2		20–2	.909
1958	Jerry Walker	Knoxville (Sally)	10–4	.818		
	Art Henriksen	St. Petersburg (Fla. St.)	17–3			
		New Orleans (So. Assn.)	0–1		18–4	.818
1959	Les Bass	Boise (Pioneer)	21–3	.875		
1960	Tom Haake	Grand Forks (Northern)	0–1			
		Dubuque (Midwest)	19–3		19–4	.826
1961	David Seeman	Selma (Ala.-Fla.)	17–3			
		Burlington (Carolina)	7–0		24–3	.889
1962	Bob Schmidt	Modesto (Calif.)	0–0			
		Jamestown (NYP)	17–3		17–3	.850
1963	Bob Lee	Batavia (NYP)	20–2			
		Asheville (Sally)	1–1		21–3	.875
1964	Ed Watt	Aberdeen (Northern)	14–1			
		Elmira (Eastern)	3–1		17–2	.895**
1965	Billy MacLeod	Pittsfield (Eastern)	18–0	1.000***		
1966	Bob Snow	Winston-Salem (Carolina)	20–2	.909		
1967	John Parker	Spartanburg (W. Car.)	17–3	.850		
1968	Pablo Montes De Oca	Campeche (Mex. S.E.)	21–4	.840		
1969	Don Eddy	Appleton (Midwest)	18–3	.857		
1970	Jim Flynn	Albuquerque (Texas)	19–4	.826		
1971	Rich Gossage	Appleton (Midwest)	18–2	.900		
1972	Andres Ayon	Saltillo (Mexican)	22–3	.880		
1973	Silvano Quezada	Tampico (Mexican)	22–2	.917		
1974	Bob Knepper	Fresno (Calif.)	20–5	.800		
1975	Jerry Garvin	Reno (Calif.)	17–5	.773		
1976	Enrique Romo	Mexico City Reds (Mexican)	20–4	.833		
1977	Mike Chris	Lakeland (Fla. St.)	18–5	.783		
1978	Tomas Armas	Saltillo (Mexican)	22–4	.846		
1979	Miguel Solis	Saltillo (Mexican)	25–5	.833		
1980	Gene Nelson	Ft. Lauderdale (Fla. St.)	20–3	.870		
1981	Ted Power	Albuquerque (PCL)	18–3	.857		
1982	Mike Warren	Stockton-Modesto (Calif.)	19–4	.826		
1983	Alfonso Pulido	Mexico City Reds (Mexican)	17–3	.850		
1984	Mike Bielecki	Hawaii (PCL)	19–3	.864		
1985	Eleazar Beltran	Tampico (Mexican)	18–3	.857		
1986	George Ferran	Shreveport (Texas)	16–1	.941		
1987	Bob Faron	Springfield (Midwest)	19–2	.905		
1988	Jimmy Rodgers	Myrtle Beach (So. Atl.)	18–4	.818		
1989	Royal Clayton	Albany (Eastern)	16–4	.800		
1989	Mercedes Esquer	Yucatan (Mexican)	16–4	.800		
1989	Walt Trice	Osceola (Fla. St.)	16–4	.800		
1990	Randy Marshall	Fayetteville (So. Atl.)	13–0			
		Lakeland (Fla. St.)	7–2			
1991	Jose Martinez	Columbus (So. Atl.)	20–4	.833		
1992	John Fritz	Quad Cities (Midwest)	20–4	.833		
1993	John Dettmer	Charlotte (Fla. St.)	16–3	.842		
	Ryan Karp	Albany (Eastern)	0–0			
		Prince William (Carolina)	3–2			
		Greensboro (So. Atl.)	13–1	.842	16–3	****
1994	Francisco Montano	Monclova (Mexican)	19–1	.950		
1995	Rich Hunter	Piedmont (Sally)	10–2			
		Clearwater (Fla. St.)	6–0			
		Reading (Eastern)	3–0		19–2	.905
1996	Ted Silva	Charlotte (Fla. St.)	10–2			
		Tulsa (Texas)	7–2		17–4	.810
1997	Travis Smith	El Paso (Texas)	16–3	+.842		
1998	John Sneed	Hagerstown (Sally)	16–2	++.889		
	Narciso Elvira	Monterrey (Mexican)	16–4	.800		

*Adding two losses to Brown's record giving him 20 decisions yields a .850 percent, better than John Schmutte, Johnstown Middle Atlantic, 19–4, .822

**Adding one loss to Watt's record, giving him 20 decisions, yields an .850 percentage, better than Dave Leonhard, Aberdeen (Northern), 16–4 .800

***Adding two losses to MacLeod's record, giving him 20 decisions, yields a .900 percentage, better than Dave Leonhard, Elmira (Eastern), 20–5 .800

****Adding Dettmer's and Karp's records giving them 20 decisions yields an .800 percentage, better than Urbano Lugo, Jalisco (Mexican) 17-5 .773.

‡Adding three losses to Ferran's record, giving him 20 decisions, yields an .800 percentage, better than Kevin Armstrong, Columbia (Sally), 17-5 .773.

+Adding one loss to Smith's record, giving him 20 decisions, yields an .800 percentage, better than Brian Rose, Pawtucket (International) 17-5. .773 and Reid Cornelius combined 17-5 .773 combined with Portland (Eastern) 5-0 and Charlotte (International) 12-5

++Adding two losses to Sneed's record giving him 20 decisions, yields a .800 percentage

Annual Overall Minor League Batting Leader (400 or more at bats)

Year	Player	Team (League)	G	AB	R	H	2B	3B	HR	RBI	SB	AVG.
1900	Kitty Bransfield	Worcester (Eastern)	122	501	115*	186*	30	8	17	—	40	.371*
1901	Frank Huelsman	Shreveport (So. Assn.)	121*	487	98	191*	31	10	9	—	15	.392*
1902	Emil Frisk	Denver (Western)	123	450	89	168	22	22	14*	—	20	.373*
1903	Frank Huelsman	Spokane (Pac. Int.)	98	418	89	160	35	11	6	—	14	.392*
1904	Billy Hamilton	Haverhill (New Eng.)	113	408	113*	168*	32	8	0	—	74*	.412*
1905	Charlie Hemphill	St. Paul (A. A.)	145	560	122	204*	38	12	5	—	40	.364*
1906	Mike Welday	Des Moines (Western)	129	549	93	197	—	—	—	—	31	.359
1907	Ed Householder	Aberdeen (Northwest)	127	499	64	173	30*	19	9	—	19	.347*
1908	Ward Miller	Wausau (Wis.-Ill.)	124	408	91*	156*	—	—	—	—	4	.382*
1909	Harry Welch	Omaha (Western)	151	527	81	196*	41	15	7	—	51	.372*
1910	Dave Callahan	Eau Claire (Minn.-Wis.)	126	460	92*	168*	25	17*	2	—	52	.365*
1911	Frank Huelsman	Great Falls (U.A.)	135	516	117	212	48	15	17*	125*	25	.411*
1912	Charlie Johnson	Trenton (Tri-State)	109	400	86	161	31	5	14	—	22	.403*
1913	Frank Huelsman	Salt Lake City (U.A.)	122	473	123*	200*	36*	20*	22*	126*	16	.423*
1914	Joe Harris	Bay City (So. Michigan)	139	510	135	197*	39	22*	10	—	42	.386*
1915	Big Bill Kay	Binghamton (N.Y. St.)	125	447	98*	169*	22	25*	7	—	35	.378*
1916	Hank Butcher	Denver (Western)	145	541	116	204	31	20*	15	—	32	.377*
1917	Nap Lajoie	Toronto (Int.)	151	581	83	221*	39*	4	5	—	4	.380*
1918	Polly McLarry	Shreveport (Texas)	29	84	12	24	3	1	1	—	6	.286
		Binghamton (Int.)	103	335	51	129	26	7	4	—	15	.385*
											overall	.365
1919	Joe Wilhoit	Seattle (PCL)	17	67	8	11	1	0	0	—	3	.164
		Wichita (Western)	128	526	126*	222*	41	10	7	—	13	.422*
											overall	.393
1920	Merwyn Jacobson	Baltimore (Int.)	154*	581	161*	235*	35	16*	7	—	18	.404*
1921	Jack Lelivelt	Omaha (Western)	166	659	149	274*	70*	9	14	—	24	.416*
1922	Jack Schaefer	London (Mich.-Ont.)	100	407	79	167	27	21	9	—	9	.410*
1923	Moses Solomon	Hutchinson (So'west.)	134	527	143*	222*	40*	15	49*	—	12	.421*
1924	T. P. Osborne	Mt. Pleasant (E. Tex.)	101	396	93	171*	48	3	23	—	46*	.432*1
1925	Paul Waner	San Francisco (PCL)	174	599	167	280	75*	7	11	130	8	.401*
1926	Bill Diester	Salina (So'west.)	106	428	110*	190*	33*	4	27	—	10	.444*
		Tulsa (Western)	11	44	5	15	4	0	0	—	0	.341
											overall	.434
1927	Elton Langford	Des Moines (Western)	149	611	132	250	47	28*	8	—	31	.409*
1928	Danny Boone	High Point (Piedmont)	128	468	123	196*	40	11	38*	131*	11	.419*
1929	Ed Kallina	Midland(W. Tex.)	94	367	126	159	28	7	44*	—	16	.433*
		Sherman (Lone Star)	17	64	22	22	—	—	6	—	1	.344
											overall	.420
1930	Tony Antista	Bisbee (Arizona St.)	109*	444	127*	191*	36	16*	17	100	18	.430*
1931	Babe Phelps	Youngstown (Mid-Atl.)	115	436	71	178	29	9	15	88	9	.408*
1932	George Puccinelli	Rochester (Int.)	133	478	102	187	34	8	28	115	2	.391*
1933	Ox Eckhardt	Mission (PCL)	189*	760	145	315*	56	16	12	143	15	.414*
1934	Frank Demaree	Los Angeles (PCL)	186	702	190*	269*	51*	4	45*	173*	41	.383*
1935	Ox Eckhardt	Mission (PCL)	172	710	149	283*	40	11	2	114	8	.399*
1936	Cal Lahman	Jamestown (Northern)	127	466	154*	182*	30	9	48*	162*	20	.391*
1937	Earl "Red" Martin	Beckley (Mt. St.)	91	360	80	144	39*	14*	8	96*	7	.400*
		Scranton (NYP)	11	41	7	10	1	0	0	4	1	.244
											overall	.384
1938	Murray Franklin	Beckley (Mt. St.)	94	385	91	169	31	13*	26*	110	13	.439*2
1939	Joe Schmidt	Duluth (Northern)	120	440	114*	194*	29	9	31*	133*	17	.441*
1940	Ed Schweda	Lubbock (W. Tex.-N.M.)	114	469	142	198	39	15	11	118	7	.422*
1941	Lew Flick	Elizabethton (App.)	117	502*	127*	210*	37*	13	5	116*	20	.418*
1942	Don Manno	Welch (Mt. St.)	117	457	136*	174*	32	14*	34*	122*	23	.381*
1943	George Kell	Lancaster (Inter-St.)	138	555	120*	220*	33	23*	5	79	14	.396*
1944	Roland Gladu	Hartford (Eastern)	119	417	92	155	28	14	7	102	8	.372
1945	Arden "Cotton" McCaskey	Bristol (App.)	106	437	72	164*	26*	14*	2	96	5	.375*
1946	Walt Forwood	Carbondale (N. Atl.)	111	419	98	170*	43*	9	3	101	22	.406*
1947	Jim Prince	Midland (Longhorn)	108	415	111	178	31	6	34	141	4	.429*
		Lubbock (W. Tex.-N.M.)	12	37	7	10	3	0	1	12	0	.270
											overall	.416
1948	Hershel Martin	Albuquerque (W. Tex.-N.M.)	132	447	133	190	61*	6	18	128	5	.425*
1949	Bob Montag	Pawtucket (New Eng.)	125	454	139*	192*	36	18*	21*	91	43*	.423*
1950	Oscar Sierra	Hornell (Pony)	93	358	99	151	28	2	21	114	12	.422*
		Newport News (Piedmont)	15	45	5	13	1	0	0	5	0	.289
											overall	.407
1951	D. C. "Pud" Miller	Hickory (N.C. St.)	119	426	115	181	32	1	40*	136*	2	.425*
1952	Don Stafford	Salisbury (N.C. St.)	105	392	99	160	31	3	18	90	1	.408*3
1953	Russ Snyder	McAlester (Sooner St.)	138	556	137	240*	32	16	2	84	74*	.432*
1954	Neal Cobb	Crestview (Ala.-Fla.)	115	435	108	188	27	8	5	124	3	.432*
1955	Tom Jordan	Artesia (Longhorn)	136	543	116	221*	69*	2	28	159*	4	.407*
1956	Len Tucker	Pampa (So'west)	140	565	181*	228	40	13	51	181	47*	.404*
1957	Fran Boniar	Reno (Calif.)	110	443	102	193	33	15	11	138*	4	.436*
		Pueblo (Western)	11	37	5	9	1	1	0	7	3	.243
											overall	.421
1958	Neb Wilson	Ft. Walton Beach-Pensacola (Ala.-Fla.)	119	409	102*	162	38*	3	24*	106*	3	.396*
1959	Tom Hamilton	St. Petersburg (Fla. St.)	125	401	109	155	20	3	20*	96	3	.387*
1960	Al Pinkston	Mexico City Reds (Mexican)	138	567	110	225*	41	11	26	144*	4	.397*
1961	Al Pinkston	Veracruz (Mexican)	109	406	79	152	26*	4	13	86	4	.374*
1962	Ramiro Caballero	Guanajuato (Mex. Center)	113	423	123	175*	25	0	59*	170	3	.414*
1963	Vinicio Garcia	Monterrey (Mexican)	122	475	107*	175	36*	5	21	88	3	.368*
1964	Ramiro Caballero	Leon (Mex. Center)	121	460	135*	175	29	1	35*	145*	3	.380*
1965	Alfonso Peciado	Guanajuato (Mex. Center)	130	529	103	224*	48*	14*	11	147	11	.423*
1966	Heriberto Vargas	Veracruz (Mexican)	7	14	0	3	0	0	0	0	0	.214
		Guanajuato (Mex. Center)	127	481	168*	214	33	1	55*	174*	3	.445*
											overall	.438
1967	Hilario Pena	Campeche (Mex. S.E.)	102	404	60	159	61	3	1	49	9	.394*

1968	Jim Hicks	Tulsa (PCL)	117	407	**100***	149	32	7	23	85	14	**.366***
1969	Bernie Carbo	Indianapolis (A.A.)	111	404	83	145	37	2	21	76	7	**.359***
1970	Miguel Suarez	Tampico (Mex. Center)	126	460	105	**181***	**37***	4	14	101	15	**.393***
1971	Téolindo Acosta	Puebla (Mexican)	133	441	75	173	22	11	7	71	17	**.392***
1972	Don Anderson	Jalisco (Mexican)	130	445	76	161	31	2	8	68	0	**.362***
1973	Hector Espino	Tampico (Mexican)	116	422	82	159	20	2	22	**107***	3	**.377***
1974	Téolindo Acosta	Puebla (Mexican)	122	464	**93***	**170***	17	6	2	43	20	**.366***
1975	Gene Richards	Reno (Calif.)	134	**501***	**148***	**191***	29	10	12	58	**85***	**.381***
1976	Pat Putnam	Asheville (W. Car.)	138	538	100	**194***	**33***	3	**24***	**142***	8	**.361***
1977	Rudy Law	Lodi (California)	122	451	124	174	22	5	9	88	37	**.386***
1978	Champ Summers	Indianapolis (A.A.)	132	462	98	**170***	25	5	**34***	**124***	11	.368
1979	Jimmie Collins	Chihuahua (Mexican)	124	470	95	**206***	35	10	6	60	33	**.438***
1980	Jimmie Collins	Chihuahua (Mex. #1)	91	346	62	131	19	13	4	52	19	.379
		Saltillo (Mex. #2)	39	137	25	**52***	8	**3***	2	**31***	5	.380
											overall	.379
1981	Kent Hrbek	Visalia (Calif.)	121	462	119	175	25	5	27	111	12	**.379***
1982	Randy Ready	El Paso (Texas)	132	475	**122***	**178***	33	5	20	99	13	**.375***
1983	Chris Smith	Phoenix (PCL)	123	449	88	170	31	5	21	102	4	379*
1984	Jimmie Collins	Mexico City Reds-Cordoba (Mexican)	109	403	81	166	35	4	6	59	12	**.412***
1985	Oswaldo Olivares	Aguas.-Campeche (Mexican)	110	441	85	**175***	22	**14***	5	49	20	**.397***
1986	Willie Aikens	Puebla (Mexican)	129	445	134	**202***	38	3	46	**154***	0	**.454***
1987	Orlando Sanchez	Puebla (Mexican)	123	439	95	182	34	1	25	115	6	**.415***
1988	Nelson Barrera	Mexico City Reds (Mexican)	129	460	90	171	26	0	31	**124***	7	.372
1989	Willie Aikens	León (Mexican)	128	423	**108***	167	40	1	37	**131***	1	**.395***
1990	Trench Davis	Saltillo (Mexican)	127	498	84	**189***	33	4	5	50	20	.380
1991	Rich Renteria	Jalisco (Mexican)	104	382	90	169	30	6	24	106	17	**.442***
		Indianapolis (A.A.)	20	72	6	17	5	0	1	5	0	.236
								overall				.410
1992	Raul Perez Tovar	Monclova (Mexican)	129	483	83	201	32	5	8	93	14	**.416***
1993	Nelson Simmons	Jalisco (Mexican)	109	369	81	141	27	0	34	95	1	.382
		Palm Springs (California)	20	76	13	25	8	0	5	23	0	.329
1994	Brian Hunter	Tucson (PCL)	128	513	**113***	**191***	28	9	10	51	**49***	**.372***
1995	Adam Riggs	San Bernardino (Calif.)	134	542	**111***	**196***	**39***	5	24	106	31	**.362***
1996	Vladimir Guerrero	West Palm Beach (Fla. St.)	20	80	16	29	8	0	5	18	2	.363
		Harrisburg (Eastern)	118	417	84	150	32	8	19	78	17	**.360***
1997	Mike Kinkade	El Paso (Texas)	125	468	112	180	35	12	12	109	17	**.385***
1998	Miguel Flores	Monterrey (Mexican)	100	399	87	152	32	4	4	67		.380

*Led league in category

[1]If charged with 400 at bats, Osborne's average would be .428, higher than any player with 400 or more at bats.
(George Rhinehardt, Greenville (Sally) G: 120, AB: 495, R: 110*, H: 200*, 2B: 45*, 3B: 18, HR: 8, RBI: 92, SB: 32*, AVG: .404*)

[2]If charged with 400 at bats, Franklin's average would be .423, higher than any player with 400 or more at bats.
(Butch Moran, Rogers (Ark.-Mo.) G: 105, AB: 406, R: 107, H: 159, 2B: 43*, 3B: 12, HR: 22*, RBI: 114, SB: 8, AVG: .392*)

[3]If charged with 400 at bats, Stafford's average would be .400, higher than any player with 400 or more at bats.
(Clint McCord, Clinton (Miss. Ohio Val.) G:119, AB: 482, R: 123, H: 189*, 2B: 40, 3B: 15, HR: 15, RBI: 109, SB: 20, AVG: .392*)

[4]If charged with 400 at bats, Flores average would be .380, higher than any player with 400 or more at bats.
(Ramon Espinosa, Mexico City Reds (Mexican) G:121, AB: 533, R: 114, H: 202, 2B: 31, 3B: 5, HR: 7, RBI: 62, SB: 16, AVG: .379)

Minor League Career Records

Batters	Years	G	AB	R	H	2B	3B	HR	RBI	SB	AVG
Buzz Arlett	1918–37	2392	8001	1610	2726	598	107	432	1786	200	.341
Ike Boone	1920–37	1857	6807	1362	2521	477	128	215	1334	120	.370
Bunny Brief	1910–28	2426	8945	1776	2963	594	152	340	1776	247	.331
Nick Cullop	1920–44	2484	8571	1607	2670	523	147	420	1857	154	.312
Ox Eckhardt	1925–40	1926	7563	1275	2773	455	146	66	1037	140	.367
Hector Espino	1960–84	2500	8605	1597	2898	403	49	484	1678	54	.337
Ray French	1914–41	3279	12178	1769	3255	590	128	46	1029	363	.267
Spencer Harris	1921–48	3258	11377	2287	3617	743	150	258	1769	241	.318
Joe Hauser	1918–42	1854	6426	1430	1923	340	116	399	1353	109	.299
Smead Jolley	1922–41	2232	8300	1459	3043	640	77	336	1593	61	.367
Jigger Statz	1920–42	2790	10657	1996	3356	595	137	66	1044	466	.315
Perry Werden	1884–1908	1540	6234	1214	2125	392	87	171	—	350	.341

Pitchers	Years	G	IP	W	L	H	R	ER	BB	SO	ERA
Bill Bailey	1906–25	581	3730	242	219	3452	1572	612	1565	2375	2.87
Dick Barrett	1925–53	790	4964	325	257	4578	2176	1747	2099	2513	3.34
George Boehler	1911–30	562	3711	248	202	3421	1745	874	1464	2319	3.74
George Brunet	1953–85	669	4041	244	242	3761	1832	1466	1754	3175	3.27
Tony Freitas	1928–53	736	4905	342	238	5090	2073	1694	932	2324	3.11
Sam Gibson	1923–49	661	4469	307	200	4460	1860	1413	1073	2195	3.08
Willie Mains	1887–1906	551	4044	319	181	4441	2459	—	1220	1680	
Joe Martina	1910–31	833	5417	349	277	4950	2307	1355	1868	2770	3.22
Frank Shellenback	1917–38	638	4514	315	192	4922	2110	1775	1021	1742	3.55
Bill Thomas	1926–52	1016	5995	383	347	6721	3098	2211	1230	2204	3.71
Hal Turpin	1927–46	635	4084	271	203	4512	1917	1367	807	1254	3.28

Year	Number of Leagues	Number of Clubs	Regular Season Total Attendance
1947	52	388	37,815,753
1948	58	438	38,415,716
1949	59	448(6)	39,782,717
1950	58(1)	446(14)	32,960,733
1951	50(1)	371(13)	26,135,174
1952	43	324(5)	24,024,373
1953	38	292(4)	21,109,565
1954	36(3)	269(22)	18,674,503
1955	33	243(5)	18,203,889
1956	28	217(5)	16,402,953
1957	28	200(10)	14,875,346
1958	24	173	12,744,883
1959	21	150	11,622,581
1960	22	152	10,660,811
1961	22	147	9,766,505
1962	20	134	9,732,582
1963	18	130	9,749,381
1964	20	136	10,102,310
1965	19	136	10,029,518
1966	19	138	9,826,124
1967	19	141	9,940,660
1968	21	152	9,887,328
1969	21	155	9,993,615
1970	20	153	10,726,470
1971	20	155	11,134,084
1972	19	148	10,986,628
1973	18	147	10,828,828
1974	18	145	10,562,452
1975	18	137	11,021,848
1976	20	148(1)	11,324,947
1977	19	150	13,004,297
1978	18	156	13,012,727
1979	18(1)	155(6)	15,304,724
1980	17	155(14)	12,265,022
1981	17	152	16,178,790
1982	17	160	17,637,244
1983	17	162	18,599,190
1984	17	164	17,580,299
1985	17	168	18,380,000
1986	17	164	18,456,808
1987	18	176	20,215,564
1988	19	188	21,661,873
1989	19	197	23,103,593
1990	19	202	25,244,569
1991	19	207	26,590,096
1992	19	212	27,180,170
1993	19	214	30,022,761
1994	19	216	33,355,199
1995	19	216	33,126,934
1996	19	218	33,289,278
1997	21	236	34,721,716
1998	20	242	35,427,012

( ) Did not finish season

Source: National Association of Professional Baseball Leagues

## CHAPTER 15

Baseball in Japan

Yoichi Nagata and John B. Holway

The long and sometimes rocky baseball romance between the United States and Japan may take a dramatic upturn. For the first time a U.S. team may play a regular-season series in Japan in 2000. And the recent movement of Japanese stars to the U.S. (e.g. Hideo Nomo and Hideki Irabu) shows no signs of slowing.

Closer Kazuhiro Sasaki of the Central League champion Yokohama Bay Stars has a 100-mph fastball and an almost unhittable forkball with a three-foot drop. Sasaki saved a record 45 games in 1998, giving him 210 career saves, with an 0.64 ERA. The Japanese call him "Daimajin," which, loosely translated, means "an awesome god." At 6 feet 4 inches and 210 pounds, he is considered a sure bet for the U.S. majors. However, he won't be eligible until 2000, when he becomes a free agent at age 31.

Outfielder Ichiro Suzuki (who goes by his first name, Ichiro) won his fifth straight Pacific League batting title with a .358 average. Mets manager Bobby Valentine calls him one of the 10 best offensive players in the world. But major league front offices were forced to put thoughts of reeling in Suzuki on hold; the slugger recently signed a contract making him the highest-paid player in Japanese history.

Under a 1998 U.S.-Japan agreement, U.S. teams must bid for the right to negotiate with a Japanese player who has received permission from his team. Masato Yoshii was a nine-year free agent when he signed with the Mets. Nomo's team had carelessly released him over a salary dispute. Irabu made the jump only after an acrimonious controversy in which he sat out for a year.

Japan's number-one college player, pitcher Koji Uehara, had to choose between the United States and the Tokyo Giants. Uehara had attracted a gaggle of big league scouts in 1997 when he stopped Cuba's 151-game international winning streak. With U.S. teams and the wealthy Giants waving big checks, he weighed all offers but eventually chose the Giants. Others will no doubt face similar bidding wars.

A major source for the Japanese draft is the nation's annual high school tournament, in which more than 4,000 schools took part in 1998. So many promising players remained after the Japanese draft that the Red Sox, Mets, and Reds each signed one, while San Francisco and Tampa Bay set up tryout camps for others. In 1998 eight Japanese were playing in U.S. minor leagues.

Will Japan lose its best players to America? Will that eventually spell the end of pro baseball in Japan?

To date players journeying to America have come mainly from the Pacific League, the less prestigious of Japan's two major leagues. Players from the wealthier Central League have not been anxious to make the change.

A Short History

Japanese baseball was born in the 1870s. Professor Horace Wilson is among those credited with being Nippon's Abner Doubleday. By 1908 Japanese teams beat the visiting University of Washington four games out of 10. The Chicago White Sox and New York Giants visited in 1913. The nation's first pro team formed in 1920. Casey Stengel's All-Stars arrived in 1922. Ty Cobb followed in 1928 to teach his batting secrets. Three years later a team featuring Lou Gehrig, Lefty Grove, Al Simmons, Frankie Frisch, and Lefty O'Doul toured Japan.

In 1934 Babe Ruth, Gehrig, Simmons, O'Doul, Jimmie Foxx, Charlie Gehringer, Earl Averill, and Lefty Gomez arrived. They won all their games handily—except one. Eighteen-year-old high schooler Eiji Sawamura whiffed Gehringer, Ruth, Gehrig, and Foxx in succession but lost, 1-0.

Sawamura starred on the Tokyo Giants when Japan's first professional league formed in 1936. Killed in World War II, he was later honored when Japan's equivalent of the Cy Young Award was named after him. The league lasted until the bombing of 1945. After World War II, General Douglas MacArthur encouraged Japan's major leagues to resume.

Lefty O'Doul brought his Pacific Coast League San Francisco Seals to Japan in 1949. Legendary Russian émigré, Vic Starffin, held them to one hit in eight innings before losing, 1-0. In 1951 O'Doul and Joe DiMaggio led a U.S. squad to Tokyo. The Japanese won their first victory over the Americans, beating Bobby Shantz, 3-1. DiMaggio hit his last homer during the tour.

U.S. teams continued the tradition every other year. In the spring of 1953 the Tokyo Giants visited Florida, winning just one of five against big league clubs, beating the New York Giants, 9-7. That fall an All-Star team including Bob Lemon, Robin Roberts, Yogi Berra, Enos Slaughter, Eddie Mathews, Hank Saucr, and Harvey Kuenn lost their first game, 5-4, to the fifth-place Japanese Orions but won their next 11.

That same year the New York Giants also visited Japan, winning 12 and losing one, with one tie. They came from behind to beat Masaichi Kaneda, 5-3. Then a little submarine-baller, Takumi Otomo, defeated knuckleballer Hoyt

Wilhelm, 1-0, on an eighth-inning home run.

By 1956 the champion Dodgers dropped four games in Japan. In 1989, for the first time, Japan came out ahead of the Americans, beating the Dodgers, nine games to eight. The following year they did it again, whipping an All-Star team including Roger Clemens, Barry Bonds, Cecil Fielder, Roberto Alomar, and Dave Stewart, four games to three.

The Tokyo Giants

The Tokyo Giants, who play in the Tokyo Dome, are the Yankees of Japan. Led by Sadaharu Oh and "Golden Boy" Shigeo Nagashima, they have won 29 pennants in the last 49 years. From 1965 through 1973, the heyday of Oh and Nagashima, they won nine straight Japan Series. Only one pro team in any country in any sport, Josh Gibson's 1937-1945 Negro League Homestead Grays, has equaled that mark. Thanks to immense publicity from their parent company, the Yomiuri newspaper and TV empire, the Giants are also by far the nation's favorite team.

Thanks to the Giants, their league, the Central, attracts 31,000 fans per game, far above the rival Pacific League's 22,800. In the southern city of Fukuoka, the Hawks, managed by the immortal Oh, average 34,000 a game in their new retractable Fukuoka Dome.

For 1997 the Central League demanded a 140-game schedule (up from 130 games) to increase profits. The two leagues compromised on 135. In return, the Pacific demanded interleague play to cash in on the Giants' huge drawing power. However, the Central vetoed that idea.

Gaijin (Foreigners)

Foreign players, known in Japan as Gaijin, have starred in Japan for many years. Consequently there is a long list of "U-turn *Gaijin*" such as Cecil Fielder, Kevin Mitchell, Pete Incaviglia, and Joe Pepitone. They are often overpaid, come for a cup of coffee, earn reputations as whining, roughneck brawlers, and then go home, leaving a bad taste behind.

Some who stayed longer and left happy fans included sluggers Randy Bass, Leron Lee, and Greg "Boomer" Wells. Shane Mack, Warren Cromartie, George Altman, Steve Ontiveros, Jim Paciorek, Daryl Spencer, and Julio Franco also left Japan on good terms.

Japan has also imported stars from the Korean and Taiwan pro leagues. In 1996 several Latin players entered Japan by way of Taiwan. The biggest catch was Korean Sun Dong Yol, a five-time Korean strikeout king. His ERA ranged from 1.70 to 0.78 before switching to relief and leading all Korean hurlers in saves. He had a disappointing injury-filled 1996 season in Japan, but in 1998 he was second to Yokohama' Kazuhiro Sasaki for the Central League lead in saves and ERA (1.48).

In 1990 the Hiroshima Carp opened a baseball academy in the Dominican Republic, scouting for low-priced teenage talent to replace often over-priced U.S. ex-big leaguers. Their biggest catch, pitcher Robinson Checo, debuted in 1995 with a fine 15-8 record and a 2.74 ERA. However, injuries plagued Checo in '96, and then he jumped to the Boston Red Sox for 1997.

Under a new rule allowing each team to sign four foreigners (up from three), 61 foreigners played in Japan in 1998, with Mariano Duncan and Julio Franco leading a generally mediocre American contingent.

The Dominican Republic sent 10 players to Japan. A major scandal erupted in 1998 when after Giants pitcher Balvino Galvez, a Dominican, was ejected for arguing balls and strikes, he threw the next one at the umpire's head. Luckily he still lacked control and missed. Suspended and fined $1.7 million, he left the country.

Oh, McGwire, and Sosa

The Japanese leagues played 130 games a year, and Sadaharu Oh still drew more walks than any man in history, including Babe Ruth. As a result, Oh never came to bat as often as 500 times in one season and several times had less than 400 official at bats. His highest home run total was 55 in 472 at bats in 1964. His best pace was 1974, when he hit 49 in only 385 trips. In 1998 Mark McGwire came to bat 509 times and Sammy Sosa 643. If Oh had had as many at bats as Mac, he conceivably could have hit 65 home runs; if he had as many at bats as Sosa, he could have hit 81 homers.

Oh hit 868 home runs in 9,250 times up in his career, compared to Hank Aaron's 755 in 12,364 at bats. Given Aaron's at bats, Oh's lifetime total would have been 1,160.

It's time to consider Oh for a plaque in Cooperstown.

Sachio Kinugasa: Japan's Lou Gehrig

The diminutive Japanese-American Sachio Kinugasa broke Lou Gehrig's consecutive-game record in 1987, setting a new world mark of 2,215. But not until 1996, when Cal Ripken finally caught him, did the world spotlight belatedly shift to the Orioles shortstop.

No one can argue that Kinugasa's mark was set in an inferior league, but a game in Hiroshima is just as hard to play as a game in Baltimore. In fact, since Japanese teams play only 130 games a year, it took Kinugasa five years longer to set his mark than Gehrig and Ripken took. Sachio had to play to the age of 40 to do it, the two Americans were 35.

Which is harder? Both Kinugasa and Ripken laughed and agreed Japanese conditions were tougher. Actually, Kinugasa almost made it 125 additional games. In 1972 he played the first 124 games, then missed one—the last he would miss for 15 years. Of course he wasn't even thinking of a record then. But it he had played that game, he would have finished with 2,340, and it would have taken until 1997 before Ripken caught him.

Ripken and Kinugasa share one thing in common— they both have red, white, and blue American blood coursing through their veins. Kinugasa's father was a black American GI.

Sachio ran up one mark that Cal (or Lou) will never catch—504 home runs. Pretty good for a little guy who stood four inches shorter than Cal and weighed 60 pounds less.

Cal and Sachio met on the field in Hiroshima in 1983, when the Orioles played the Hiroshima Carp. Baltimore hurler Mike Flanagan remembered the game well. "Kinugasa hit a double off me on an outside fastball on a 1-0 count," he said.

Mashi Murakami

Mashi Murakami, a hard-throwing reliever for the San Francisco Giants in 1964-1965, was the first Japanese to play in the U.S. major leagues. In his rookie year, Mashi struck out 15 men in 15 innings and posted a 1.80 ERA. The next year he whiffed 85 men in 74 innings, won four, lost one, and saved eight.

He became the darling of the San Francisco Nissei community and a favorite of teammates, to whom he removed his cap and bowed after every good play.

Murakami came to the States to gain experience in the Giants' farm system; however, when the Giants wanted to keep him, his parent club demanded his return. Unfortunately, back in Japan he never lived up to expectations.

The Olympics

Ever since baseball became an Olympic sport, Japan has been tough on the Americans, often beating some of the nation's top future stars out of gold and silver medals. The record:

	GOLD	SILVER	U.S. PLAYERS
1984	Japan	U.S.	W. Clark, McGwire, Mack, Larkin, Swift, Witt
1988	U.S.	Japan	Abbott, Benes, T.Martinez, Nagy, Ventura
1992	Cuba	Taiwan	Giambi, Tucker
1996	Cuba	Japan	T.Lee, Kotsay

In 1992 Japan won the bronze, the U.S. finished fourth. Taiwan's pitching star, Chien-fu Kuo-Lee, signed with the Tigers in Japan. In 1996 the U.S. thrashed Japan in their first meeting, 15-5, in a game called under the "mercy" rule. The semifinal rematch was to be another easy triumph as the Americans eyed the final round against Cuba for the gold. Instead, Japan shocked America, 11-2. Masanori Sugiura, 28, a veteran of the '92 Games, gave only two runs in six innings, while Japan smashed five homers and KO'd Kris Benson, top pick in the U.S. draft. The loss forced America to settle for bronze.

Japanese stars to watch: power-hitting shortstop Tadahito Iguchi, and pitchers Takeo Kawamura and Hitoshi Ono. Slugging third baseman Kosuke Fukudome, 19, skipped the big leagues to sign with a company team.

U.S.-Japan Series

After many one-sided victories in the first half of the century, the Americans began discovering they had to work harder to beat the bigger and improved Japanese. They still usually win but now have to send their best talent to play seriously. Over the last 12 years, this is how the series has gone:

	U.S.	Japan	U.S. Players
1986	6	1	Ripken, Canseco, Sandberg, Murphy
1988	3	2	Hershiser, Puckett, Larkin, Molitor
1990	3	4	Bonds, Fielder, R. Johnson, Alomar, Dibble, Thigpen
1992	7	1	Clemens, R.Johnson, Griffey Jr., Franco, Dykstra, O. Smith
1992	0	2	Los Angeles: Hershiser, Butler, Piazza, Offerman
1996	4	2	Nomo, Gonzalez, Galarraga, Piazza, Bonds, Sheffield, Franco, Percival
1998	6	2	Sosa, Garciaparra, Ramirez, Delgado, Hoffman
Total	29	14	*(No extra innings. This resulted in two ties in 1988, one in 1990 and two in '96.)*

In 1990 Hideo Nomo defeated Rob Dibble, 2-1, then lost 5-0 on a combined no-hitter by Randy Johnson and Chuck Finley. The 1996 series was another exciting one, played before crowds averaging 45,000. Japanese fans, who could see all of Hideo Nomo's games with the Dodgers on post-midnight TV, knew all the U.S. stars intimately. Nomo pitched for the American stars, but Japan's best *Gaijin*—Troy Neel, Shane Mack, Alonzo Powell, etc.—didn't play. For the first time, the 1998 series was televised on cable back in the States. Sammy Sosa and Ichiro provided the fireworks as the U.S. All-Stars overpowered Japan, six games to two. Sosa batted an even .500 with two home runs; Ichiro hit .364 with six steals in seven attempts. The visitors outslugged the Japanese, outhomering them, nine to one. The teams used the U.S. Rawlings ball, which is slightly larger and heavier than the Japanese equivalent. Sosa, acclaimed MVP both on and off the field, exchanged bats with Ichiro before game one.

The 1998 Season: Bay Stars Win Central

Yokohama won its first pennant in 38 years since the 1960 "Miracle" Whales went from last place in '59 to the pennant and a four-straight Japan Series victory. The '98 champs featured ex-Angel Bobby Rose in the cleanup spot.

Manager Hiroshi Gondo was once a burgeoning star, notching two 30-victory seasons and 800 innings pitched before overwork abruptly ended his career under the old "the future is now" managerial philosophy. In 17 years as a pitching coach, his star pupils included Nomo and Yoshii. This was his first year as a manager, and he carefully protected his pitchers' arms. With a motto of "Don't sweat it," his starters went five or six innings while the offense took a lead, two short-relievers came in, and the virtually unbeatable Sasaki closed it out.

Incidentally, the Bay Stars' victory pumped an estimated $30 million into Yokohama's economy.

Meanwhile, Giants outfielder Hideki "Godzilla" Matsui won his first home run title with 34 after losing by one homer for two years in a row. In '97 he lost to Ta-keshi Yamazaki of Nagoya when the Nagoya pitchers walked Matsui four straight times in the final game.

Lions Repeat in the Pacific

The Seibu Lions emerged on top of a four-way pennant race after the Fighters of the Nippon Ham company blew a nearly 10-game lead after July 23. The Fighters' "Big

Bang Row" featured sluggers Nigel Wilson (formerly of the Marlins, Reds, and Indians) and Jerry Brooks (former Dodger and Marlin). However, their former star, Hiromitsu Ochi-ai, 44, slowed down, and pitching ace Kip Gross (former Dodger and Red and two-time PL leader in victories) hurt his arm in spring training. Young hurlers took up the slack, and the Fighters had a 51-30 record at the All-Star Game. Then suddenly the Big Bangers stopped banging, and the Fighters plummeted to 16-35 after the break.

Three teams playing .500 ball fought to fill the gap— the defending champion Lions, the Buffaloes, the Hawks under Sadaharu Oh, and even the Blue Wave, who came from 15 games under .500.

The Lions, winners of 11 pennants in 13 years, 1982- 1994, had lost star slugger, Kazuhiro Kiyohara, to free agency. Their ace pitcher and 1997 MVP, Fumiya Nishiguchi, got off to a terrible 1-9 start. However, young pitchers came along, and the Lions had the most steals and least errors in the league.

These four teams were all within a game of each other on Sept. 23. But luck helped the Lions, who had 22 games rained out (their domed stadium is scheduled to be completed by 1999). The make-ups were played after the season ended, permitting the Lions to take the pennant.

Ochi-ai Says Sayonara

Hiromitsu Ochi-ai, Japan's greatest player of the 1980s and the game's number one maverick, called it a career after the 1998 season. He left a record of three Triple Crowns, 510 home runs, a .311 lifetime average for 20 seasons, and a reputation as a "bad guy" in a nation that prizes team players, thus never attaining the popularity of the present fan-darling, Ichiro.

Ochi-ai defied the system throughout his career. As a rookie, he fought his manager over his batting stance and got his way. He walked out of the players' union, the only Japanese player to refuse to belong, and in 1987 became the first player to earn $100 million yen ($870,000) a year.

The Pressures of the Game

Shortly after the 1998 season ended, the general manager of the Orix Blue Wave jumped to his death from a high-rise apartment building. Katsutoshi Miwata had been unable to sign the team's number one draft pick, an 18-year-old pitcher named Nagisa Arakaki.

After winning the Japan Series in 1996, the Blue Wave suffered a disappointing 1998 season. Miwata felt pressured to rebuild the team, and the young pitcher was an important part of those plans. The 53-year-old Miwata had been an outstanding high school player himself, and played professionally until 1973.

1998 Japan Series

After the first game was typhooned out, delirious Yokohama fans celebrated their first Japan Series (the 1960 Whales actually played in nearby Kawasaki). The Series

pumped $500 million into the city's economy, and stores responded with super sales, including one sushi shop that offered dinners for a penny a plate.

Game 1, at Yokohama
Baystars 9, Lions 4
Since the Central League does not use the designated hitter, the Lions played without their cleanup hitter, Domingo Martinez (Blue Jays, White Sox, Cards). Meanwhile the Yokohama machine guns KO'd Lions ace Nishiguchi.

Game 2, at Yokohama
Bay Stars 4, Lions 0
Takashi Saito pitched a three-hit shutout, only the ninth in Japan Series history. Saito underwent elbow surgery in 1997 and was pitching middle relief in early '98 when he was promoted to starter and led the Stars to the pennant with 13 wins.

Led by stolen base champ Takuro Ishii (43), the Stars ran wild with six steals against veteran catcher Tsutomu Ito, who was benched for the rest of the Series.

Game 3, at Seibu
Lions 7, BayStars 2
Sinker baller Tetsuya Shiozaki and substitute catcher Satoshi Nakajima shut down the Yokohama hitting and running games, keeping Ishii off base entirely. Meanwhile, Bay Star pitchers gave up a Series-record 11 bases on balls.

Game 4, at Seibu
Lions 4, BayStars 2
Takashi Ishii allowed only three hits, and Nakajima slammed a two-run shot in the second. After Yokohama tied it, Martinez (0-for-9 in the Series so far) blasted a two-run homer in the sixth to win. Like Yokohama's Saito, Ishii had been a reliever and suffered back problems in June but recovered to lead the Lions in their pennant stretch drive.

Game 5, at Seibu
Bay Stars 17, Lions 5
The machine guns rattled out a Series record 20 hits as Saito won his second game.

Game 6, at Yokohama
Bay Stars 2, Lions 1
Nishiguchi, loser of game one, battled a bad cold and high temperature, but ached for revenge. Yokohama sent Takeo Kawamura to oppose him. The Opening Day pitcher back in April, Kawamura won eight games by the All-Star break, but didn't win a game in the second half. Manager Gondo handed him the ball, saying, "We started the season with you, let's finish it with you."

Both pitchers dueled 0-0 for seven and a half innings. In the home eighth, Seibu thought it had turned an inning-ending double play, but umpires ruled both runners safe. Then Bay Stars' captain and top clutch hitter Norihiro "The Bases Loaded Man" Komada doubled two runs home with two outs for a 2-0 lead.

Sasaki, the "awesome" closer, who had no save opportunities in the Series thus far, entered in the ninth. He gave up a leadoff triple good for one run, then slammed the door as Yokohama fans went wild.

Domed Stadiums

Japan will boast five domed stadiums in 1998 as older, smaller parks are torn down. While nostalgic parks boom in the United States, roofs and AstroTurf are Japan's wave of the future. Most domes boast U.S.-sized playing fields, replacing shorter fences in the older parks. (One exception is Seibu Dome, scheduled for completion in 1999, a new dome over an old park.) Fukuoka Dome in southern Japan, which opened in 1997, has a retractable roof that folds up like a giant fan. The first Japanese dome, Tokyo Dome, nicknamed "the Big Egg," has an inflatable roof similar to the Minnesota's Metrodome.

All the domes are centerpieces of huge entertainment-shopping complexes and are located downtown to amortize construction costs. They also host events, such as Michael Jackson concerts, wrestling, and auto shows.

Central League

Team	Stadium	Seats	LF/RF	CF
Tigers	Koshi-en	55,000	317	396
Swallows	Meiji Shrine	49,000	300	396
Giants	Tokyo Dome	45,000	328	400
Dragons	Nagoya Dome	40,500	330	403
Carp	Hiroshima	32,000	302	381
Bay Stars	Yokohama	29,000	310	389

Pacific League

Team	Stadium	Seats	LF/RF	CF
Hawks	Fukuoka Dome	48,000	314	396
Buffaloes	Osaka Dome	48,000	328	403
Fighters	Tokyo Dome	45,000	330	403
Blue Wave	Green Stadium	35,000	327	403
Lions	Seibu Dome	31,000	313	396
Marines	Chiba	30,000	328	403

Although many of these capacities are considered inflated, most teams are drawing very well. Japan's economic downturn dropped 1998 attendance back almost a decade to about the 1990 level:

	Avg Att
1950	4,350
1960	10,300
1970	12,300
1980	20,700
1990	26,300
1992	29,900 (record)
1998	26,700

Only one club, the champion Yokohama Bay Stars, increased attendance. As usual, the Central League drew the bulk of fans, averaging 32,000 per game, compared to 21,000 for the Pacific.

Salaries

Despite the nation's economic problems, the average Japanese player earned about $390,000 in 1998, depending on the yen's fluctuating value. The three highest paid—Yokohama reliever Kazuhiro Sasaki, Giants first baseman Kazuhiro Kiyohara, and Blue Wave outfielder Ichiro draw about $2.1 million each.

The Giants' payroll exceeded that of the National League champion San Diego Padres and several other U.S. teams, one reason why most Giants players are not interested in jumping to the United States. They also get the best endorsement contracts and highest autograph prices—and, after retiring, the best jobs as TV color commentators.

But Japanese baseball on TV has a programming rival from thousands of miles away. All starting games by Nomo, Irabu, and Yoshii are televised live in Japan, usually in the morning hours, Japan time. In 1998 the Mark McGwire-Sammy Sosa home run race was also televised and followed closely by Japanese fans, suggesting that U.S. games may flourish on Japanese TV, even without Japanese players in the lineup.

Whither Japanese Baseball?

To gain parity with the Central, the Pacific League has proposed merging the two leagues so PL fans can see the more popular CL stars. An alternative is interleague play. However, the Central League has rejected both proposals. It is clear though that some reform is required. If Japan should begin losing too many stars to the States, a Japan-Korea-Taiwan League may emerge.

Single Season Leaders

Batting Champions

YEAR	CENTRAL LEAGUE		PACIFIC LEAGUE	
1950	Fumio Fujimura	.362	Hiroshi Oshita	.339
1951	Tetsuharu Kawakami	.377	Hiroshi Oshita	.383
1952	Michio Nishizawa	.353	Shigeya Iijima	.336
1953	Tetsuharu Kawakami	.347	Isami Okamoto	.318
1954	Wally Yonamine	.361	Larry Raines	.337
1955	Tetsuharu Kawakami	.338	Futoshi Nakanishi	.332
1956	Wally Yonamine	.338	Yasumitsu Toyoda	.325
1957	Wally Yonamine	.343	Kazuhiro Yamauchi	.331
1958	Kenjiro Tamiya	.320	Futoshi Nakanishi	.314
1959	Shigeo Nagashima	.334	Kohei Sugiyama	.323
1960	Shigeo Nagashima	.334	Kihachi Enomoto	.344
1961	Shigeo Nagashima	.353	Isao Harimoto	.336
1962	Katsuya Morinaga	.307	Jack Bloomfield	.374
1963	Shigeo Nagashima	.341	Jack Bloomfield	.335
1964	Shinichi Eto	.323	Yoshinori Hirose	.366
1965	Shinichi Eto	.336	Katsuya Nomura	.320
1966	Shigeo Nagashima	.344	Kihachi Enomoto	.351
1967	Toshio Naka	.343	Isao Harimoto	.336
1968	Sadaharu Oh	.326	Isao Harimoto	.336
1969	Sadaharu Oh	.345	Isao Harimoto	.333
			Yozo Nagafuchi	.333
1970	Sadaharu Oh	.325	Isao Harimoto	.383
1971	Shigeo Nagashima	.320	Shinichi Eto	.337
1972	Tsutomu Wakamatsu	.329	Isao Harimoto	.353
1973	Sadaharu Oh	.355	Hideji Kato	.337
1974	Sadaharu Oh	.332	Isao Harimoto	.340
1975	Koji Yamamoto	.319	Jinten Haku	.319
1976	Kenichi Yazawa	.354	Satoru Yoshioka	.309
1977	Tsutomu Wakamatsu	.358	Michiyo Arito	.329
1978	Jitsuo Mizutani	.348	Kyosuke Sasaki	.354
1979	Felix Millan	.346	Hideo Kahto	.364
1980	Kenichi Yazawa	.369	Leron Lee	.358
1981	Taira Fujita	.358	Hiromitsu Ochi-ai	.326
1982	Keiji Nagasaki	.351	Hiromitsu Ochi-ai	.325
1983	Akinobu Mayumi	.353	Hiromitsu Ochi-ai	.332
1984	Toshio Shinoz'ka	.334	Boomer Wells	.355
1985	Randy Bass	.350	Hiromitsu Ochi-ai	.367
1986	Randy Bass	.389*	Hiromitsu Ochi-ai	.360
1987	Toshio Shinozuka	.333	Hiromasa Arai	.366
	Kozo Shoda	.333		
1988	Kozo Shoda	.340	Hideaki Takazawa	.327
1989	Warren Cromartie	.378	Boomer Wells	.322
1990	Jim Paciorek	.326	Norifumi Nishimura	.338
1991	Atsuya Furuta	.339	Mitsuchika Hirai	.314
1992	Jack Howell	.331	Makoto Sasaki	.322
1993	Tom O'Malley	.329	Hatsush'ko Tsuji	.319
1994	Alonzo Powell	.324	Ichiro Suzuki	.385*
1995	Alonzo Powell	.355	Ichiro Suzuki	.342
1996	Alonzo Powell	.340	Ichiro Suzuki	.356
1997	Takanori Suzuki	.335	Ichiro Suzuki	.345
1998	Takanori Suzuki	.337	Ichiro Suzuki	.358

Home Runs

YEAR	CENTRAL LEAGUE		PACIFIC LEAGUE	
1950	Makoto Kozuru	51	Kaoru Betto	43
1951	Noboru Aota	32	Hiroshi Oshi-ta	26
1952	Satoru Sugiyama	27	Yasuhiro Fukami	25
1953	Fumio Fujimura	27	Futoshi Nakanishi	36
1954	Noboru Aota	31	Futoshi Nakanishi	31
1955	Yukihiko Machida	31	Futoshi Nakanishi	35
1956	Noboru Aota	25	Futoshi Nakanishi	29
1957	Takao Sato	22	Katsuya Nomura	30
	Noboru Aota	22		
1958	Shigeo Nagashima	29	Futoshi Nakanishi	23
1959	Takeshi Kuwata	31	Kazuhiro Yamauchi	25
	Toru Mori	31		
1960	Katsumi Fujimoto	22	Kazuhiro Yamauchi	32
1961	Shigeo Nagashima	28	Katsuya Nomura	29
			Masahiro Nakada	29
1962	Sadaharu Oh	38	Katsuya Nomura	44
1963	Sadaharu Oh	40	Katsuya Nomura	52*
1964	Sadaharu Oh	55*	Katsuya Nomura	41
1965	Sadaharu Oh	42	Katsuya Nomura	42
1966	Sadaharu Oh	48	Katsuya Nomura	34
1967	Sadaharu Oh	47	Katsuya Nomura	35
1968	Sadaharu Oh	49	Katsuya Nomura	38
1969	Sadaharu Oh	44	Tokuji Nagaike	41
1970	Sadaharu Oh	47	Katsuo Osugi	44
1971	Sadaharu Oh	39	Katsuo Osugi	41
1972	Sadaharu Oh	48	Tokuji Nagaike	41
1973	Sadaharu Oh	51	Tokuji Nagaike	43
1974	Sadaharu Oh	49	Clarence Jones	38
1975	Koichi Tabuchi	43	Masahiro Doi	34
1976	Sadaharu Oh	49	Clarence Jones	36
1977	Sadaharu Oh	50	Leron Lee	34
1978	Koji Yamamoto	44	Bobby Mitchell	36
1979	Masayuki Kakefu	48	Charlie Manuel	37
1980	Koji Yamamoto	44	Charlie Manuel	48
1981	Koji Yamamoto	43	Hiromitsu Kadota	44
			Tony Solaita	44
1982	Masayuki Kakefu	35	Hiromitsu Ochi-ai	32
	Yasunori Oshima	36		
1984	Masaru Uno	37	Boomer Wells	37
1985	Randy Bass	54	Hiromitsu Ochi-ai	50
1986	Randy Bass	47	Hiromitsu Ochi-ai	52*
1987	Rick Lancellotti	39	Koji Akiyama	43
1988	Carlos Ponce	33	Hiromitsu Kadota	44
1989	Larry Parrish	42	Ralph Bryant	49
1990	Hiromitsu Ochi-ai	34	Orestes Destrade	42
1991	Hiromitsu Ochi-ai	37	Orestes Destrade	39
1992	Jack Howell	38	Orestes Destrade	41
1993	Akira Eto	34	Ralph Bryant	42
1994	Yasuaki Taihoh	38	Ralph Bryant	35
1995	Akira Eto	39	Hiroki Kokubo	28
1996	Takeshi Yamasaki	39	Troy Neel	32
1997	Dwayne Hosey	38	Nigel Wilson	37
1998	Hideki "Godzilla" Matsui	34	Nigel Wilson	33

*League record

(Teams play 135 games. Home runs can be increased by six or seven to equal a 162-game season.)

RBIs

YEAR	CENTRAL LEAGUE		PACIFIC LEAGUE	
1950	Makoto Kozuru	161*	Kaoru Betto	105
1951	Noboru Aota	105	Tokuji Iida	87
1952	Michio Nishizawa	98	Tokuji Iida	86
1953	Fumio Fujimura	98	Futoshi Nakanishi	86
1954	Hiroyuki Watanabe	91	Kazuhiro Yamauchi	97
	Satoru Sugiyama	91		
1955	Tetsuharu Kawakami	79	Kazuhiro Yamauchi	99
1956	Toshio Miyamoto	69	Futoshi Nakanishi	95
1957	Toshio Miyamoto	78	Futoshi Nakanishi	100
1958	Shigeo Nagashima	92	Takao Katsuragi	85
1959	Toru Mori	87	Takao Katsuragi	95
1960	Katsumi Fujimoto	76	Kazuhiro Yamauchi	103
1961	Takeshi Kuwata	94	Kazuhiro Yamauchi	112
1962	Sadaharu Oh	85	Katsuya Nomura	104
1963	Shigeo Nagashima	112	Katsuya Nomura	135
1964	Sadaharu Oh	119	Katsuya Nomura	115
1965	Sadaharu Oh	104	Katsuya Nomura	110
1966	Sadaharu Oh	116	Katsuya Nomura	97
1967	Sadaharu Oh	108	Katsuya Nomura	100
1968	Shigeo Nagashima	125	George Altman	100
1969	Shigeo Nagashima	115	Atsushi Nagaike	101
1970	Shigeo Nagashima	105	Katsuo Osugi	129
1971	Sadaharu Oh	101	Hiromitsu Kadota	120
1972	Sadaharu Oh	120	Katsuo Osugi	101
			Katsuya Nomura	101
1973	Sadaharu Oh	114	Atsushi Nagai-ke	109
1974	Sadaharu Oh	107	Atsushi Nagai-ke	96
1975	Sadaharu Oh	96	Hideji Kahto	97
1976	Sadaharu Oh	123	Hideji Kahto	82
1977	Sadaharu Oh	124	Leron Lee	109
1978	Sadaharu Oh	118	Bobby Marcano	94
1979	Koji Yamamoto	113	Hideji Kahto	104
1980	Koji Yamamoto	112	Charlie Manuel	129
1981	Koji Yamamoto	103	Tony Solaita	108
1982	Masayuki Kakefu	95	Hiromitsu Ochi-ai	99
1983	Tatsunori Hara	103	Jitsuo Mizutani	114
1984	Sachio Kinugasa	102	Boomer Wells	130
1985	Randy Bass	134	Hiromitsu Ochi-ai	146*
1986	Randy Bass	109	Hiromitsu Ochi-ai	116
1987	Carlos Ponce	98	Boomer Wells	119
1988	Carlos Ponce	102	Hiromitsu Kadota	125
1989	Hiromitsu Ochi-ai	116	Boomer Wells	124
1990	Hiromitsu Ochi-ai	102	Kazuhiko Ishimine	106
			Orestes Destrade	106
1991	Katsumi Hirosawa	102	Orestes Destrade	92
			Jim Traber	92
1992	Larry Sheets	100	Boomer Wells	97
1993	Katsumi Hirosawa	94	Ralph Bryant	107
	Bobby Rose	94		
1994	Yasuaki Taihoh	107	Hiro-o Ishii	111
1995	Akira Eto	106	Ichiro Suzuki	80
			Kiyoshi Hatsushiba	80
			Yukio Tanaka	80
1996	Luis Lopez	109	Troy Neel	111
1997	Luis Lopez	112	Hiroki Kokubo	114
1998	Hideki "Godzilla" Matsui	100	Nigel Wilson	124

Pitching Wins

YEAR	CENTRAL LEAGUE		PACIFIC LEAGUE	
1950	Shigeo Mada	39*	Jun Aramaki	26
1951	Shigeo Mada	28	Masaru Eto	24
1952	Takehiko Bessho	33	Masa-aki Noguchi	23
1953	Takumi Otomo	27	Tokuji Kawasaki	24
1954	Shigeru Sugishi-ta	32	Motoji Taku	26
			Fumio Tanaka	26
1955	Ryohei Hasegawa	30	Motoji Taku	24
	Takumi Otomo	30		
1956	Takehiko Bessho	27	Masayoshi Miura	29
1957	Masaichi Kaneda	28	Kazuhisa Inao	35
1958	Masaichi Kaneda	31	Kazuhisa Inao	33
1959	Motoshi Fujita	27	Tadashi Sugiura	38
1960	Ritsuo Horimoto	29	Shoichi Ono	33
1961	Hiroshi Gondo	35	Kazuhisa Inao	42*
1962	Hiroshi Gondo	30	Masahiro Kubo	28
1963	Masaichi Kaneda	30	Kazuhisa Inao	28
1964	Gene Bacque	29	Masa-aki Koyama	30
1965	Minoru Murayama	25	Yukio Ozaki	27
1966	Minoru Murayama	24	Tetsuya Yoneda	25
1967	Kenjiro Ogawa	29	Masaaki Ikenaga	24
1968	Yutaka Enatsu	25	Mutsuo Minagawa	31
1969	Kazumi Takahashi	22	Keishi Suzuki	24
1970	Masaji Hiramatsu	25	Fumio Narita	25
1971	Masaji Hiramatsu	17	Masaaki Kitaru	24
1972	Tsuneo Horiuchi	26	Hisashi Yamada	20
			Tomohiro Kaneda	20
1973	Yutaka Enatsu	24	Fumio Narita	21
1974	Yukitsuru Matsumoto	20	Tomohiro Kaneda	16
	Motoyasu Kaneshige	20		
1975	Yoshiro Sotokoba	20	Osamu Higashio	23
1976	Kojiro Ikegaya	20	Hisashi Yamada	26
1977	Satoshi Takahashi	20	Keishi Suzuki	20
1978	Osamu Nomura	17	Keishi Suzuki	25
1979	Shigeru Kobayashi	22	Hisashi Yamada	21
1980	Suguru Egawa	16	Isamu Kida	22
1981	Suguru Egawa	20	Yutaro Imai	19
			Choji Murata	19
1982	Manabu Kitabeppu	20	Mikio Kudo	20
1983	Kazuhiko Endo	18	Osamu Higashio	18
			Kazuhiro Yamauchi	18
1984	Kazuhiko Endo	17	Yutaro Imai	21
1985	Tatsuo Komatsu	17	Yoshino Sahto	21
1986	Manabu Kitabeppu	18	Hisanobu Watanabe	16
1987	Tatsuo Komatsu	17	Yukihiko Yamaoki	19
1988	Kazuyuki Ono	18	Hisanobu Watanabe	15
	Akimitsu Ito	18	Yukihiro Nishizaki	15
			Hiroaki Matsuura	15
1989	Masaki Saito	20	Hideyuki Awano	19
	Takashi Nishimoto	20		
1990	Masaki Saito	20	Hideo Nomo	18
			Hisanobu Watanabe	18
1991	Shinji Sasaoka	17	Hideo Nomo	17
1992	Masaki Saito	17	Hideo Nomo	18
1993	Shinji Imanaka	17	Hideo Nomo	17
	Masahiro Yamamoto	17	Koji Noda	17
	Hiroki Nomura	17		
1994	Masahiro Yamamoto	19	Hideki Irabu	15
1995	Masaki Saito	18	Kip Gross	16

1996	Masaki Saito	16	Kip Gross	17
	Balvino Galvez	16		
1997	Masahiro Yamamoto	18	Fumiya Nishiguchi	15
1998	Kenjiro Kawasaki	17	Fumiya Nishiguchi	13
			Kazuhiro Ta-keda	13
			Tomihiro Kuroki	13

Note: In the early years, managers overworked their pitchers. The result: astronomical victory totals and early burnout. Now managers adopt a U.S.-style rotation. It is not clear how much the 130-game schedule affects victory totals, since Japanese teams have many rainouts, and the season lasts six months as does the U.S. season.

Earned Run Average

YEAR	CENTRAL LEAGUE		PACIFIC LEAGUE	
1950	Nobuo Oshima	2.03	Jun Aramaki	2.06
1951	Kiyoshi Matsuda	2.01	Susumu Yuki	2.08
1952	Tadashi Kajioka	1.71	Susumu Yuki	1.91
1953	Takumi Otomo	1.85	Tokuji Kawasaki	1.98
1954	Shigeru Sugishita	1.39	Motoji Taku-wa	1.58
1955	Takehiko Bessho	1.33	Takashi Nakagawa	2.08
1956	Shozo Watanabe	1.45	Kazuhisa Inao	1.06*
1957	Masaichi Kaneda	1.63	Kazuhisa Inao	1.37
1958	Masaichi Kaneda	1.30	Kazuhisa Inao	1.42
1959	Minoru Murayama	1.19	Tadashi Sugiura	1.40
1960	Noboru Akiyama	1.75	Shoichi Ono	1.98
1961	Hiroshi Gondo	1.70	Kazuhisa Inao	1.69
1962	Minoru Murayama	1.20	Osamu Kubota	2.21
1963	Minoru Kakimoto	1.70	Masahiro Kubo	2.36
1964	Gene Bacque	1.89	Yujiro Tsumajima	2.15
1965	Masaichi Kaneda	1.84	Kiyohiro Miura	1.57
1966	Tsuneo Horiuchi	1.39	Kazuhisa Inao	1.79
1967	Masatoshi Gondo	1.40	Mitsuhiro Adachi	1.75
1968	Yoshiro Sotokoba	1.94	Mutsuo Minagawa	1.61
1969	Yutaka Enatsu	1.81	Masa-aki Kitaru	1.72
1970	Minoru Murayama	0.98*	Michio Sahto	2.05
1971	Kazuhiro Fujimoto	1.71	Hisashi Yamada	2.37
1972	Takeshi Yasuda	2.08	Toshihiko Sei	2.36
1973	Takeshi Yasuda	2.02	Tetsuya Yoneda	2.47
1974	Shitoshi Sekimoto	2.28	Michio Sahto	1.91
1975	Sohachi Aniya	1.91	Choji Murata	2.20
1976	Takamasa Suzuki	2.98	Choji Murata	1.82
1977	Hisao Niura	2.32	Hisashi Yamada	2.28
1978	Hisao Niura	2.81	Keishi Suzuki	2.02
1979	Masaji Hiramatsu	2.39	Tetsuji Yamaguchi	2.49
1980	Hiromu Matsuoka	2.35	Isamu Kida	2.28
1981	Suguru Egawa	2.29	Noriaki Okabe	2.70
1982	Akio Saito	2.07	Satoshi Takahashi	1.84
1983	Osamu Fukuma	2.62	Osamu Higashio	2.92
1984	Seiji Kobayashi	2.20	Yutaro Imai	2.93
1985	Tatsuo Komatsu	2.65	Kimiyasu Kudo	2.76
1986	Manabu Kitabeppu	2.43	Yoshinori Sato	2.83
1987	Masumi Kuwata	2.17	Kimiyasu Kudo	2.41
1988	Yutaka Ono	1.70	Hirofumi Kono	2.38
1989	Masaki Saito	1.62	Choji Murata	2.50
1990	Masaki Saito	2.17	Hideo Nomo	2.91
1991	Shinji Sasaoka	2.44	Tomio Watanabe	2.35
1992	Koki Morita	2.05	Motoyuki Akahori	1.80
1993	Masahiro Yamamoto	2.05	Kimiyasu Kudo	2.06
1994	Genji Kaku	2.45	Hiroshi Shintani	2.91
1995	Terry Bross	2.33	Hideki Irabu	2.53
1996	Masaki Saito	2.36	Hideki Irabu	2.40
1997	Yutaka Ohno	2.85	Satoru Komiyama	2.49
1998	Shige-kiNoguchi	2.34	Satoru Ka-nemura	2.73

*League record

Most Valuable Players

YEAR	CENTRAL LEAGUE		PACIFIC LEAGUE	
1950	Makoto Kozuru	OF	Kaoru Betto	OF
1951	Tetsuharu Kawakami	1B	Kazuhito Yamamoto	2B
1952	Takehiko Bessho	P	Susumu Yuki	P
1953	Takumi Otomo	P	Isami Okamoto	2B
1954	Shigeru Shugishita	P	Hiroshi Oshita	OF
1955	Tetsuharu Kawakami	1B	Tokuji Iida	OF
1956	Takehiko Bessho	P	Futoshi Nakanishi	3B
1957	Wally Yonamine	OF	Kazuhisa Inao	P
1958	Motoshi Fujita	P	Kazuhisa Inao	P
1959	Motoshi Fujita	P	Tadashi Sugiura	P
1960	Noboru Akiyama	P	Kazuhiro Yamauchi	OF
1961	Shigeo Nagashima	3B	Katsuya Nomura	C
1962	Minoru Murayama	P	Isao Harimoto	OF
1963	Shigeo Nagashima	3B	Katsuya Nomura	C
1964	Sadaharu Oh	1B	Joe Stanka	P
1965	Sadaharu Oh	1B	Katsuya Nomura	C
1966	Shigeo Nagashima	3B	Katsuya Nomura	C
1967	Sadaharu Oh	1B	Mitsuhiro Adachi	P
1968	Shigeo Nagashima	3B	Tetsuya Yoneda	P
1969	Sadaharu Oh	1B	Tokuji Nagaike	OF
1970	Sadaharu Oh	1B	Masa-aki Kitaru	P
1971	Shigeo Nagashima	3B	Tokuji Nagaike	OF
1972	Tsuneo Horiuchi	P	Yutaka Fukumoto	OF
1973	Sadaharu Oh	1B	Katsuya Nomura	C
1974	Sadaharu Oh	1B	Tomohiro Kaneda	P
1975	Koji Yamamoto	OF	Hideji Kahto	1B
1976	Sadaharu Oh	1B	Hisashi Yamada	P
1977	Sadaharu Oh	1B	Hisashi Yamada	P
1978	Tsutomu Wakamatsu	OF	Hisashi Yamada	P
1979	Yutaka Enatsu	P	Charlie Manuel	OF
1980	Koji Yamamoto	OF	Isamu Kida	P
1981	Suguru Egawa	P	Yutaka Enatsu	P
1982	Takayoshi Nakao	C	Hiromitsu Ochi-ai	2B
1983	Tatsunori Hara	3B	Osamu Higashio	P
1984	Sachio Kinugasa	3B	Boomer Wells	1B
1985	Randy Bass	1B	Hiromitsu Ochi-ai	3B
1986	Manabu Kitabeppu	P	Hiromichi Ishige	SS
1987	Kazuhiro Yamakura	C	Osamu Higashio	P
1988	Genji Kaku	P	Hiromitsu Kadota	OF
1989	Warren Cromartie	OF	Ralph Bryant	OF
1990	Masaki Saito	P	Hideo Nomo	P
1991	Shinji Sasaoka	P	Taigen Kaku	P
1992	Jack Howell	3B	Takehiro Ishii	P
1993	Atsuya Furuta	C	Kimiyasu Kudo	P
1994	Masumi Kuwata	P	Ichiro Suzuki	OF
1995	Tom O'Malley	OF	Ichiro Suzuki	OF
1996	Hideki Matsui	OF	Ichiro Suzuki	OF
1997	Atsuya Furuta	C	Fumiya Nishiguchi	P
1998	Kazuhiro Sasaki	P	Kazuo Matsui	SS

Lifetime Leaders

Home Runs

1.	Sadaharu Oh	868
2.	Katsuya Nomura	657
3.	Hiromitsu Kadota	567
4.	Koji Yamamoto	536
5.	Hiromitsu Ochi-ai	510
6.	Isao Harimoto	504
7.	Sachio Kinugasa	504
8.	Katsuo Osugi	486
9.	Koichi Tabuchi	474
10.	Masahiro Doi	465

RBIs

1.	Sadaharu Oh	2170
2.	Katsuya Nomura	1988
3.	Hiromitsu Kadota	1678
4.	Isa-o Harimoto	
5.	Hiromitsu Ochi-ai	1564
6.	Shigeo Nagashima	1522
7.	Katsuo Osugi	1507
8.	Koji Yamamoto	1475
9.	Sachio Kinugasa	1448
10.	Masahiro Doi	1400

Batting Average

1.	Leron Lee	.320
2.	Tsutomu Wakamatsu	.31918
3.	Isao Harimoto	.31915
4.	Boomer Wells	.317
5.	Tetsuharu Kawakami	.313
6.	Wally Yonamine	.31107
7.	Hiromitsu Ochi-ai	.31087
8.	Leon Lee	.308
9.	Futoshi Nakanishi	.307
10.	Shigeo Nagashima	.305

Note: Leron and Leon Lee are brothers.

Hits

1.	Isao Harimoto	3085
2.	Katsuya Nomura	2901
3.	Sadaharu Oh	2786
4.	Hiromitsu Kadota	2566
5.	Sachio Kinugasa	2543
6.	Yutaka Fukumoto	2543
7.	Shigeo Nagashima	2471
8.	Masahiro Doi	2452
9.	Hiromitsu Ochi-ai	2371
10.	Tetsuharu Kawakami	2351

In stolen bases, little Yutaka Fukumoto retired in 1988 with 1,065 stolen bases, the world record until Rickey Henderson broke it. He was caught 299 times for a .781 percent. Fukumoto also hit 208 homers and holds the Japanese record with 43 leadoff round-trippers.

Wins

		W-L	Pct
1.	Masa-ichi Ka-neda	400-298	.573
2.	Tetsuya Yo-neda	350-285	.551
3.	Masa-aki Koyama	320-232	.580
4.	Keishi Suzuki	317-238	.571
5.	Takehiko Bessho	310-178	.635
6.	Victor Starffin	303-176	.633
7.	Hisashi Yamada	284-166	.631
8.	Kazuhisa Ina-o	276-137	.668
9.	Takao Kajimoto	254-255	.499
10.	Osamu Higashio	251-247	.507

Note: Ka-neda pitched most of his career with a last-place team and often won half their games. Ina-o had an amazing record until he ruined his arm from overwork and retired early.

Strikeouts

1.	Masa-ichi Ka-neda	
2.	Tetsyya Yo-neda	3388
3.	Masa-aki Koyama	3159
4.	Keishi Suzuki	3061
5.	Yutaka Enatsu	2987
6.	Takao Kajimoto	2945
7.	Kazahisa Ina-o	2574
8.	Choji Murata	2363
9.	Minoru Murayama	2271
10.	Shoichi Ono	2244

Ka-neda pitched 5,527 innings. He held the world record until broken by Ryan.

ERA (2,000 IP)

1.	Hideo Fujimoto	1.90
2.	Jiro Noguchi	1.96
3.	Kazuhisa Inao	1.98
4.	Bozo Wakabayashi	1.99
5.	Victor Starffin	2.088
6.	Minoru Murayama	2.092
7.	Takehiko Bessho	2.18
8.	Jun Aramaki	2.30
9.	Shigeru Sugishita	2.33
10.	Masa-ichi Ka-neda	2.34

Pennant Winners: Japan Pro-Baseball League

YEAR	TEAM	WON	LOST	PCT.
1936	FALL TOKYO GIANTS	18	9	—
1937	SPRING TOKYO GIANTS	41	13	.759
	FALL OSAKA TIGERS	39	9	.813
1938	SPRING OSAKA TIGERS	29	6	.829
	FALL TOKYO GIANTS	30	9	.769
1940	TOKYO GIANTS	76	28	.731
1941	TOKYO GIANTS	62	22	.738
1942	TOKYO GIANTS	73	27	.730
1943	TOKYO GIANTS	54	27	.667
1944	HANSHIN	27	6	.818
1945	Play Suspended			
1946	KINKI GREATRING	65	38	.631
1947	OSAKA TIGERS	79	37	.681
1948	NANKAI HAWKS	87	49	.640
1949	YOMIURI GIANTS	85	48	.639

Pennant Winners: Central League

YEAR	TEAM	WON	LOST	PCT.
1950	SHOCHIKU ROBINS	98	35	.737
1951	YOMIURI GIANTS	79	29	.731
1952	YOMIURI GIANTS	83	37	.692
1953	YOMIURI GIANTS	87	37	.702
1954	CHUNICHI DRAGONS	86	40	.683
1955	YOMIURI GIANTS	92	37	.713
1956	YOMIURI GIANTS	82	44	.646
1957	YOMIURI GIANTS	74	53	.581
1958	YOMIURI GIANTS	77	52	.596
1959	YOMIURI GIANTS	77	48	.612
1960	TAIYO WHALES	70	56	.554
1961	YOMIURI GIANTS	71	53	.569
1962	HANSHIN TIGERS	75	55	.577
1963	YOMIURI GIANTS	83	55	.601
1964	HANSHIN TIGERS	80	56	.588
1965	YOMIURI GIANTS	91	47	.659
1966	YOMIURI GIANTS	89	41	.685
1967	YOMIURI GIANTS	84	46	.646
1968	YOMIURI GIANTS	77	53	.592
1969	YOMIURI GIANTS	73	51	.589
1970	YOMIURI GIANTS	79	47	.627
1971	YOMIURI GIANTS	70	52	.574
1972	YOMIURI GIANTS	74	52	.587
1973	YOMIURI GIANTS	66	60	.524
1974	CHUNICHI DRAGONS	70	49	.588
1975	HIROSHIMA CARP	72	47	.605
1976	YOMIURI GIANTS	76	45	.628
1977	YOMIURI GIANTS	80	46	.635
1978	YAKULT SWALLOWS	68	46	.596
1979	HIROSHIMA CARP	67	50	.573
1980	HIROSHIMA CARP	73	44	.624
1981	YOMIURI GIANTS	73	48	.603
1982	CHUNICHI DRAGONS	64	47	.577
1983	YOMIURI GIANTS	72	50	.590
1984	HIROSHIMA CARP	75	45	.625
1985	HANSHIN TIGERS	74	49	.602
1986	HIROSHIMA CARP	73	46	.613
1987	YOMIURI GIANTS	76	43	.639
1988	CHUNICHI DRAGONS	79	46	.632
1989	YOMIURI GIANTS	84	44	.656
1990	YOMIURI GIANTS	88	42	.677
1991	HIROSHIMA CARP	74	56	.569
1992	YAKULT SWALLOWS	69	61	.531
1993	YAKULT SWALLOWS	80	50	.615
1994	YOMIURI GIANTS	70	60	.538
1995	YAKULT SWALLOWS	82	48	.631
1996	YOMIURI GIANTS	77	53	.592
1997	YAKULT SWALLOWS	83	52	.615
1998	YOKOHAMA BAY STARS	79	56	.585

Pennant Winners: Pacific League

YEAR	TEAM	WON	LOST	PCT.
1950	MAINICHI ORIONS	81	34	.704
1951	NANKAI HAWKS	72	24	.750
1952	NANKAI HAWKS	76	44	.633
1953	NANKAI HAWKS	71	48	.597
1954	NISHITETSU LIONS	90	47	.657
1955	NANKAI HAWKS	99	41	.707
1956	NISHITETSU LIONS	96	51	.646
1957	NISHITETSU LIONS	83	44	.648
1958	NISHITETSU LIONS	78	47	.619
1959	NANKAI HAWKS	88	42	.677
1960	DAIMAI ORIONS	82	48	.631
1961	NANKAI HAWKS	85	49	.629
1962	TOEI FLYERS	78	52	.600
1963	NISHITETSU LIONS	86	60	.589
1964	NANKAI HAWKS	84	63	.571
1965	NANKAI HAWKS	88	49	.642
1966	NANKAI HAWKS	79	51	.608
1967	HANKYU BRAVES	75	55	.577
1968	HANKYU BRAVES	80	50	.615
1969	HANKYU BRAVES	76	50	.603
1970	LOTTE ORIONS	80	47	.630
1971	HANKYU BRAVES	80	39	.672
1972	HANKYU BRAVES	80	48	.625
1973	1st HALF [*]NANKAI HAWKS	38	26	.594
	2nd HALF HANKYU BRAVES	43	19	.694
1974	1st HALF HANKYU BRAVES	36	23	.610
	2nd HALF [*]LOTTE ORIONS	38	23	.623
1975	1st HALF [*]HANKYU BRAVES	38	25	.603
	2nd HALF KINTETSU BUFFALOES	40	20	.667
1976	1st HALF HANKYU BRAVES	42	21	.667
	2nd HALF HANKYU BRAVES	37	24	.607
1977	1st HALF [*]HANKYU BRAVES	35	25	.583
	2nd HALF LOTTE ORIONS	33	24	.579
1978	1st HALF HANKYU BRAVES	44	20	.688
	2nd HALF HANKYU BRAVES	38	19	.667
1979	1st HALF [*]KINTETSU BUFFALOES	39	19	.672
	2nd HALF HANKYU BRAVES	36	23	.610
1980	1st HALF LOTTE ORIONS	33	25	.569
	2nd HALF [*]KINTETSU BUFFALOES	35	26	.574
1981	1st HALF LOTTE ORIONS	35	26	.574
	2nd HALF [*]NIPPON HAM FIGHTERS	37	23	.617

YEAR	TEAM	WON	LOST	PCT
1982	1st HALF [*]SEIBU LIONS	36	27	.571
	2nd HALF NIPPON HAM FIGHTERS	35	23	.603
1983	SEIBU LIONS	86	40	.683
1984	HANKYU BRAVES	75	45	.625
1985	SEIBU LIONS	79	45	.637
1986	SEIBU LIONS	68	49	.581
1987	SEIBU LIONS	71	45	.612
1988	SEIBU LIONS	73	51	.589
1989	KINTETSU BUFFALOES	71	54	.568
1990	SEIBU LIONS	81	45	.643
1991	SEIBU LIONS	81	43	.653
1992	SEIBU LIONS	80	47	.630
1993	SEIBU LIONS	74	53	.581
1994	SEIBU LIONS	76	52	.594
1995	ORIX BLUE WAVE	82	47	.636
1996	ORIX BLUE WAVE	74	54	.597
1997	SEIBU LIONS	76	56	.576
1998	SEIBU LIONS	70	61	.534

[*]playoff winner

Japan Series

YEAR	TEAM/LEAGUE	WON	TEAM/LEAGUE	WON
1950	MAINICHI ORIONS, PL	4	SHOCHIKU ROBINS, CL	2
1951	YOMIURI GIANTS, CL	4	NANKAI HAWKS, PL	1
1952	YOMIURI GIANTS, CL	4	NANKAI HAWKS, PL	2
1953	YOMIURI GIANTS, CL	4	NANKAI HAWKS, PL	2 1 TIE
1954	CHUNICHI DRAGONS, CL	4	NISHITETSU LIONS, PL	3
1955	YOMIURI GIANTS, CL	4	NANKAI HAWKS, PL	3
1956	NISHITETSU LIONS, PL	4	YOMIURI GIANTS, CL	2
1957	NISHITETSU LIONS, PL	4	YOMIURI GIANTS, CL	0 1 TIE
1958	NISHITETSU LIONS, PL	4	YOMIURI GIANTS, CL	3
1959	NANKAI HAWKS, PL	4	YOMIURI GIANTS, CL	0
1960	TAIYO WHALES, CL	4	DAIMAI ORIONS, PL	0
1961	YOMIURI GIANTS, CL	4	NANKAI HAWKS, PL	2
1962	TOEI FLYERS, PL	4	HANSHIN TIGERS, CL	2 1 TIE
1963	YOMIURI GIANTS, CL	4	NISHITETSU LIONS, PL	3
1964	NANKAI HAWKS, PL	4	HANSHIN TIGERS	3
1965	YOMIURI GIANTS, CL	4	NANKAI HAWKS, PL	1
1966	YOMIURI GIANTS, CL	4	NANKAI HAWKS, PL	2
1967	YOMIURI GIANTS, CL	4	HANKYU BRAVES, PL	2
1968	YOMIURI GIANTS, CL	4	HANKYU BRAVES, PL	2
1969	YOMIURI GIANTS, CL	4	HANKYU BRAVES, PL	2
1970	YOMIURI GIANTS, CL	4	LOTTE ORIONS, PL	1
1971	YOMIURI GIANTS, CL	4	HANKYU BRAVES, PL	1
1972	YOMIURI GIANTS, CL	4	HANKYU BRAVES, PL	1
1973	YOMIURI GIANTS, CL	4	NANKAI HAWKS, PL	1
1974	LOTTE ORIONS, PL	4	CHUNICHI DRAGONS, CL	2
1975	HANKYU BRAVES, PL	4	HIROSHIMA CARP, CL	0 2 TIES
1976	HANKYU BRAVES, PL	4	YOMIURI GIANTS, CL	3
1977	HANKYU BRAVES, PL	4	YOMIURI GIANTS, CL	1
1978	YAKULT SWALLOWS, CL	4	HANKYU BRAVES, PL	3
1979	HIROSHIMA CARP, CL	4	KINTETSU BUFFALOES, PL	3
1980	HIROSHIMA CARP, CL	4	KINTETSU BUFFALOES, PL	3
1981	YOMIURI GIANTS, CL	4	NIPPON HAM FIGHTERS, PL	2
1982	SEIBU LIONS, PL	4	CHUNICHI DRAGONS, CL	2
1983	SEIBU LIONS, PL	4	YOMIURI GIANTS, CL	3
1984	HIROSHIMA CARP, CL	4	HANKYU BRAVES, PL	3
1985	HANSHIN TIGERS, CL	4	SEIBU LIONS, PL	2
1986	SEIBU LIONS, PL	4	HIROSHIMA CARP, CL	3 1 TIE
1987	SEIBU LIONS, PL	4	YOMIURI GIANTS, CL	2
1988	SEIBU LIONS, PL	4	CHUNICHI DRAGONS, CL	1
1989	YOMIURI GIANTS, CL	4	KINTETSU BUFFALOES, PL	3
1990	SEIBU LIONS, PL	4	YOMIURI GIANTS, CL	0
1991	SEIBU LIONS, PL	4	HIROSHIMA CARP, CL	3
1992	SEIBU LIONS, PL	4	YAKULT SWALLOWS, CL	3
1993	YAKULT SWALLOWS, CL	4	SEIBU LIONS, PL	3
1994	YOMIURI GIANTS, CL	4	SEIBU LIONS, PL	2
1995	YAKULT SWALLOWS	4	ORIX BLUE WAVE	1
1996	ORIX BLUE WAVE	4	YOMIURI GIANTS	1
1997	YAKULT SWALLOWS	4	SEIBU LIONS	1
1998	YOKOHAMA BAY STARS	6	SEIBU LIONS	2

Note on pronunciation. Vowels are the same as Spanish: A=ah, I=ee, U=oo, E=ay, O=oh. Y is a consonant or "ee," thus "kyo" and "ryo" are pronounced something like "keeo" and "reeo." U is usually not emphasized. Some combinations change a bit in actual speech. "Shita" comes out "sh'ta," and "hito" and "hiko" sound like "sh'to" and "sh'ko." G is always hard, as in "gh."

## CHAPTER 16

Baseball in the Caribbean

Rob Ruck

Soon after the World Series marks the season's end in the United States, baseball springs back to life in and around the Caribbean. There, to the beat of *salsa* and *merengue* and against a backdrop of palm trees and seasonal labor, some of the best baseball in the world is played each winter. While most of South America follows football and the British West Indies follows cricket, the rest of the Caribbean basin plays baseball—and has for the better part of a century.

Since baseball fever first infected Cuba in the 1870s, the game has infiltrated the sporting psyches of Mexico, Nicaragua, the Dominican Republic, Venezuela, Puerto Rico, Panama, and Colombia. Although tied to major league baseball in four of these countries through a set of winter leagues and as a source of fresh talent, Caribbean baseball is not simply an appendage of the game that is played in the United States. Rather, baseball has acquired an autonomous persona as the peoples of the region have made the game into their own national pastimes.

More than simply recreation or a display of grace and competence, baseball has catalyzed national consciousness and cohesion in the Caribbean basin. A critical part of the fabric of everyday life, the sport has also influenced how these societies have come to define themselves, their relations with each other, and their ties to the United States. "It's more than a game," Dominican winter league general manager Winston Llenas once remarked. "It's our passion. It's almost our way of life."

Pedro Julio Santana stands at his office window in what was once the colonial zone of Santo Domingo. A sportsman at the center of Dominican baseball's evolution earlier this century, he searches for words to describe how the game penetrated his country and the rest of the basin. Glancing below to the hulking walls of the first Catholic cathedral in the western hemisphere, Santana finds his metaphor. "It is much the same as that which happened with Christianity. Jesus could be compared to the North Americans, but the apostles were the ones that spread the faith, and the apostles of baseball were Cubans. Even though the Dominican Republic and Puerto Rico were occupied by the North Americans, the Cubans first brought baseball here, and to Mexico and Venezuela, too."

Caribbean baseball's first epicenter was Cuba, which had fallen into orbit around the United States by the late 19th century. Baseball arrived there last century, brought by sailors, students, and businessmen from the United States as well as by Cubans who had traveled north. The U.S. military occupations that followed the 1898 conflict with Spain stimulated baseball's expansion there and across the basin. By the time the Good Neighbor Policy had supplanted the Big Stick in the 1930s, baseball was entrenched. Moreover, Cuban baseball had become the focal point of an international network that stretched from the Caribbean basin through the Negro Leagues.

What was likely the first ballgame in Cuba with local participation occurred in June 1866, when sailors of a U.S. ship taking on sugar invited Cuban longshoremen to play. *El Club Habana* (Havana) began two years later, crushing a team from Matanzas in the first organized contest of two Cuban teams.

Havana's victory over Matanzas featured two of Cuba's sporting pioneers, Esteban Bellan and Emilio Sabourín. Bellan became the first Latino in U.S. organized baseball, playing three seasons in the National Association (1871–1873). Sabourín, the A. G. Spalding of Cuban baseball, was the motivating force behind the *Liga de Beisbol Profesional Cubana,* whose inaugural tournament was won by Sabourín's reconstituted Havana club in 1878. Sabourín proselytized for his sport as well as for the cause of Cuban independence from Spain until his contribution of baseball revenues to the independence movement incurred the wrath of Spanish officials. They imprisoned Sabourín until his death and banned baseball in parts of their colony.

While initially a game of the more affluent and those with contact with the United States, baseball soon spread to all classes of Cuban society, both urban and rural. U.S. military occupations, support by companies and businessmen, and close ties to political elites would shape its subsequent development, much as these forces would elsewhere in the basin.

The game was organized on three overlapping levels in its early years. The first was an ad hoc player-organized, self-directed network of teams. The second involved clubs sponsored by businessmen, companies, and politicians who sought the promotional advantages of such patronage. The third level was that of professional (sometimes semiprofessional) baseball, which organized championships from 1878 until 1961, with a changing cast of teams and format. In some years, no tournaments were held, while in others both a summer and winter season took place. Havana, Almendares, Santa Clara, Cienfuegos, and Marianao were the league's mainstays.

Until the 1959 Cuban Revolution and the ensuing U.S. blockade, Cuba set the standard for Caribbean baseball. It sent the most players to the major and Negro leagues

while its winter and summer tournaments featured the highest caliber of Latin ball and attracted players from both the States and the basin. Cuban players, radio broadcasts, and emigrants, in turn, became baseball's emissaries to the rest of the region.

In the Dominican Republic, Cubans who had migrated to escape the turmoil of the Ten Years' War (1868–1878) were the first to form teams. Young Dominicans emulated them and joined with compatriots who had studied in the United States to establish a self-organized matrix of teams and tournaments well in place before the U.S. Marines arrived in 1916 for their eight-year occupation. Santo Domingo's *Licey,* the oldest of the six professional Dominican clubs, formed in 1907, while the forerunners of San Pedro de Macoris's *Estrellas Orientales,* Santiago's *Aguilas Cibaeñas,* and Santo Domingo's other club, *Escogido,* took to the field soon afterward.

While Dominicans refer to these early decades as the romantic epoch of baseball, commercial forces were already at work there and across the basin. Teams occasionally recruited players with the lure of financial reward and soon began importing Cubans and Puerto Ricans for championship tournaments. Moreover, local clubs often induced talented players with payment in cash or work. North American oil companies in Venezuela, rum distilleries and tobacco manufacturers in Cuba, and sugar cane companies in Nicaragua, Puerto Rico, Cuba, and the Dominican Republic sponsored or assisted workplace teams for recreation and community entertainment, but with an industrial agenda, too—winning their workers' hearts and minds.

During these "Yankee years," between 1898 and 1933, when the Marines hit the beaches 34 times in 10 different basin countries, they found baseball already implanted in Cuba, Puerto Rico, Nicaragua, Mexico, and the Dominican Republic. They never made it to Venezuela, but would have found baseball there, too, as early as the organization of the Caracas club in 1895. The occupations, though, helped to push the sport along. While Nicaraguans had played on their Atlantic coast since 1888, the nation's longest-running pro team, *Boer,* was founded by the U.S. consul in Managua. In the Dominican Republic, U.S. marines and sailors played ball to bolster morale; they were frequently challenged by Dominican teams, for whom these contests were both a test of sporting abilities and national character. Far more baseball was in evidence by the end of the U.S. stay on the island.

Professional Imports

While Cubans and some other basin natives had broken into baseball in the States during the first half of the century, the center of gravity for Caribbean baseball remained a regional one. A "Have Glove—Will Travel" mentality soon took hold of basin baseball and its ablest practitioners made the rounds of national tournaments. A core of the finest black players from the States—then barred from major league play by the color line, as were most Latinos—joined them in Cuba, the Dominican Republic, Puerto Rico, Venezuela, and Mexico.

Caribbean baseball's apogee was probably reached in the summer of 1937 in the Dominican Republic during a national championship dedicated to the re-election of the then state-of-the-art dictator Rafael Trujillo. Top Dominican players were joined by the best Cuban, Puerto Rican, and Negro league talent that the Dominican peso could buy to form a three-team league. Santiago boasted the services of Martín Dihigo, Luís Tiant Sr., and Horacio Martínez; San Pedro de Macoris countered with Tetelo Vargas, Ramón Bragaña, and Cocaína García, while the eventual victor, *Ciudad Trujillo* (a merger of *Licey* and *Escogido* that represented the city Trujillo had renamed in his own honor) relied on future Hall of Famers Josh Gibson, Cool Papa Bell, and Satchel Paige, as well as Silvío García, Perucho Cepeda, and Sam Bankhead. Baseball on the island was the equal of that played anywhere that summer. These players barnstormed year-round, and many of them later played together as *Santa Clara* in Cuba and as *La Concordia* in Venezuela.

The proprietary interest taken by caudillos such as Trujillo or Nicaragua's Anastasio Somoza ensured baseball of its most-favored sport status and contributed to the growth of strong regional rivalries. Caribbean participation in the *Mundiales,* the world amateur baseball championships that began in 1938, and later the Caribbean Series of pro circuits, which started in 1949, reinforced the game's hegemony.

Latin ball was an opportunity for North American players to supplement their income and hone their skills in encounters that sometimes surpassed the caliber of major league play. However, it was also a threat to organized baseball in the States. Major league teams had played in Cuba before the turn of the century, and afterward Negro league squads as well as individual black and white pros journeyed south. The 1937 raids on the Negro leagues by Dominican teams destroyed the Pittsburgh Crawfords, and other Negro league squads frequently lost their best players and gate attractions to basin teams. From 1939 until the demise of independent black baseball a decade later, Venezuelan and Mexican franchises vied for Negro leaguers during the summer months, enticing Josh Gibson, Ray Dandridge, and other stars to jump their Negro league teams. They offered better pay and a different atmosphere. "Not only do I get more money playing here, but I live like a king," Willie Wells wrote to *Pittsburgh Courier* sportswriter Wendell Smith in 1939 to explain his switch from the Newark Eagles to Vera Cruz. "I am not faced with the racial problem. . . . I've found freedom and democracy here, something I never found in the United States. . . . Here, in Mexico, I am a man."

The major leagues were less vulnerable to such competition, but even they blanched when Mexican liquor mogul Jorge Pasquel sought major leaguers in addition to Negro leaguers to bolster the six-team summer Mexican League in 1946. Railroad workers from the States taught the game to their Mexican colleagues as early as the 1880s and a strong semipro league formed in the 1920s. In Sonora and Mexico City, the game felt the pull of baseball across the northern border, which Mexican and black teams frequently crossed. In the Yucatan, baseball pointed more toward the Caribbean, especially Cuba. Pasquel, pumping new capital into the league, persuaded Mickey Owen, Sal Maglie, and Max Lanier to desert their major league teams, prompting the latter to ban them. Pasquel also pursued Stan Musial, reportedly placing

$50,000 on the bed in his spring training hotel room at a time when the Cardinals' outfielder was making but $13,000 a season. Other basin leagues also lost top players in the Mexican effort to upgrade. Pasquel's challenge, however, was blunted by organized baseball in the States, which tried to limit any competition for its players, and by the Mexican League's own logistical and financial difficulties. The challenge faded after the 1948 season. In the aftermath of the Mexican raids and with integration imminent, major league baseball began to sign accords with professional leagues throughout the basin, formalizing player movement and institutionalizing winter play.

That was especially important, for with the end of the color line in 1947 Latinos soon renewed their assault on major league ball. By the 1970s, the basin would constitute the freshest source of talent in the majors, especially important as the black community turned away from baseball as part of a general shift toward other sports in the United States. But Latin players—black and white—had played pro ball in the United States long before Jackie Robinson's historic debut.

Colombia's Luis Castro broke ground in baseball's modern era, after the creation of the National and American Leagues, but Cubans for the most part led the way. While Castro played only part of the 1902 season, Rafael Almeida and Armando Marsans spearheaded a Cuban invasion in 1911 that left its imprimatur on the game and numbered over 30 players before integration. Another 90 or so Cubans played major league ball after that divide.

The crucial factor controlling the entry of Cubans and other basin players into the major leagues was skin color. Barnstorming their way through black communities from the early century on, Cuban teams had become a mainstay of the Negro leagues that began in 1920. Popular draws, the Cuban Stars and the New York Cubans featured Latinos too dark to pass the color line into the majors. Playing most of their contests on the road, these Caribbean squads injected talent and a tropical allure to the game. Cubans Martín Dihigo, Alejandro Oms, Luís Tiant Sr., Orestes "Minnie" Miñoso, and Silvío García were joined by Dominicans Horacio Martínez and Tetelo Vargas, Puerto Rican Peruchin Cepeda, Panamanian Pat Scantlebury, and sometimes several black North Americans who passed for Cubans, on these pan-Caribbean aggregations. A few Cubans, such as Cristóbal Torriente, a powerful outfielder, and José de la Caridad Méndez, *"El Diamante Negro,"* who took a no-hitter into the ninth inning the first time he faced the barnstorming Cincinnati Reds, became mainstays of other Negro league franchises.

Lighter-skinned Cubans from that predominantly mixed island played on the other side of sport's racial boundary in the States, in the major leagues. Perhaps the greatest pre–Jackie Robinson Cuban major leaguer was Adolfo Luque, a pitcher whose 20 big league seasons were capped by a brilliant 27–8 record in 1923 and a winning relief stint of shutout ball in the seventh game of the 1933 World Series. Following that game, Clark Griffith, whose Washington Senators had lost the Series, decided to back a scouting exhibition to Cuba. He sent Joe Cambria.

"Papa Joe," as many still refer to Cambria, stocked the Senators with Cubans. Among his first signees was Roberto Estalella, from the sugarcane milltown that Hershey Chocolate operated in Cárdenas. The *Cincinnati Enquirer* had greeted the signings of Almeida and Marsans in 1911 with relief, introducing them as "two of the purest bars of Castilian soap to ever wash upon our shores," but the darker-hued Estalella was more controversial. No one challenged this indirect breaching of the color line, although it prompted Red Smith to write his classic column in which he suspected that "there was a Senegambian somewhere in the Cuban batpile where Senatorial lumber was seasoned."

The player regarded in the Caribbean as the best Cuban ever, and arguably the finest ballplayer of all time, never played major league ball. Martín Dihigo displayed his talents in Cuba, the United States, Mexico, Venezuela, and the Dominican Republic, and is enshrined in the Hall of Fame of three of these nations. Dihigo excelled at the plate, on the mound, and as a manager, but integration came too late for him. His bust at Havana's *Estadio Latinoamericano* reads simply, *El Immortal.*

The contradiction that some Cubans played in the majors and others in the Negro leagues was not lost upon blacks in the States or on Latin ballplayers. As early as Almeida's and Marsans' 1911 debut, the black press began to hope that black ballplayers would soon follow them into baseball's most exclusive league. And while Negro leaguers went south to adulation and greater pay, dark-skinned Latinos who came north encountered prejudice based on both skin color and nationality. As major leaguers such as Ty Cobb, Tris Speaker, and Carl Hubbell traveled south to play in winter ball, black North Americans and Latinos found that they could more than hold their own. These symbolic victories were appreciated both in the States and throughout the basin. North American blacks and the peoples of the region shared each other's athletes and appropriated each other's sporting heroes and symbols. If a proving ground was necessary to show that blacks could compete with whites, that the two could coexist on the same squad, or to dispel any other racial shibboleth, Caribbean baseball was just that.

Following integration, the more farsighted owners began scouring the islands for prospects. Soon a fresh wave of Latinos arrived in the majors, including three future Hall of Famers: Venezuela's Luís Aparicio, Puerto Rico's Roberto Clemente, and the Dominican Republic's Juan Marichal. They signaled, moreover, a shift away from Cuba as the primary spawning waters for Caribbean players.

With the 1959 Cuban Revolution and the subsequent deterioration of relations with the United States, Cuba fell out of organized baseball's system. The Havana Sugar Kings, an International League franchise affiliated with the Reds since 1954, were on their way to winning the Little World Series of the AAA minor leagues in 1959, just months after Fidel Castro came to power. The revolutionary government offered to underwrite the Sugar Kings' debts, and Castro sought to keep the franchise there, "even if I have to pitch," but the International League shipped the club to Jersey City during the 1960 season. Baseball in Cuba was cut off completely from baseball in the United States, and the movement of players and equipment halted. Cuba developed its own sporting goods industry and relied on the repatriated Dihigo, a political exile during the 1950s who had given money to

Che Guevara and who now returned to help teach the game. Cuban baseball soon shed its commercial skin and sought instead to advance the social and political aims of the revolution. Cuba has remained *the* powerhouse in world amateur baseball ever since, but the island stopped producing new major leaguers. After the Zoilo Versalles, Tony Oliva, Tony Pérez generations passed out of baseball, the next set of Cubans to reach the majors were those who, while born on the island, had grown up in the United States.

Dominican Dominance

The fulcrum of baseball power, meanwhile, shifted one island to the east, where the Dominican Republic shared Hispaniola with French-speaking, soccer-playing Haiti. After the star-studded 1937 season, pro ball in the Dominican Republic entered a 14-year hiatus. While an occasional tournament celebrated an event such as the nation's centennial, Dominican pros Horacio Martínez and Tetelo Vargas plied their trade in Cuba, Venezuela, or the United States. But several forces revitalized Dominican baseball in the 1940s, and after the reappearance of a professional league in 1951, these dynamics propelled over 100 players to the major leagues.

The first catalyst was the birth of the *Mundial,* an international championship tournament for amateur baseball. After its inauguration in England in 1938, the *Mundial* moved to the Caribbean. Held in the basin throughout the 1940s, with Cuba hosting five consecutive tournaments, the *Mundial* had a decidedly Latin flavor and became the most important sporting competition in which these nations competed on something approximating equal footing, both with each other and with the United States. Basin nations won every championship from 1940 through 1972, with Cuba winning 11 out of 18 times.

National aspirations and international rivalries sometimes were injected into the *Mundial.* An irate Anastasio Somoza fired the Nicaraguan manager and took to the dugout to direct the team himself. Nicaraguan national honor was restored by a victory over Cuba in the final game of the 1972 series, an event still celebrated as one of the Central American nation's greatest sporting exploits. The Dominican victory in 1948, coming just months after virtually the entire national championship team perished in a plane crash by the Río Verde, captivated the Republic and lent impetus to pro ball's rebirth there.

A second factor in Dominican baseball's rejuvenation was the creation of the *Dirección General de Deportes.* Modeled in part after the comparable Cuban agency, this government body organized regional and then national tournaments for amateur baseball (often with semiprofessional overtones) that gave further purpose to local, company, and armed forces support. Many of the Dominicans that entered the majors from the late 1950s on, including Marichal, Manuel Mota, and the three Rojas Alou brothers, played on these squads.

The final catalysts to Dominican ascendancy were bananas and sugarcane, and the concentrations of baseball fervor and expertise that they fostered. While the sugarcane milltowns of the southeast produce the most prospects today, the banana region along the northwest border with Haiti was instrumental in cultivating the first contingent of pros in the late 1950s. There the Grenada Company, a United Fruit Company subsidiary, began two teams for its workers and their sons in the 1940s. The squad won three national championships, and Juan Marichal and Guayubín Olivo passed through its ranks to the majors.

Dominican sugarcane milltowns, like those in Cuba, had long spawned ballclubs. The six-month long *tiempo muerto,* or dead season, when the cane required minimal attention and most workers were unemployed, contributed to an intense sporting environment, first for cricket and ultimately for baseball. In the 1920s and '30s, *Central La Romana's Papagayo* team was an amateur powerhouse, and in the 1940s the milltowns in and around San Pedro de Macoris made their play. There the descendants of cricket-playing migrants from the British West Indies brought to cut cane and work in the mills displayed an aptitude for playing baseball and an approach to organizing the game that made San Pedro baseball's Mecca. Since Rico Carty's breakthrough in the 1960s, San Pedro has contributed about one-third of the Dominicans to play in the big leagues. The town currently sends more of its native sons to the majors on a per-capita basis than any town ever has. There is probably no other place on earth where the game is played as well and as widely.

Since the end of the color line, ballplayers from Cuba, the Dominican Republic, Venezuela, Puerto Rico, Panama, Nicaragua, Mexico, Colombia, and even the Bahamas have played major league ball. Although the Dominican Republic leads this basin contingent, substantial numbers of Puerto Ricans and Venezuelans are present, too. Mexico, despite a population that dwarfs the rest of the region combined and its well-developed pro leagues, sends few players to the majors. Unlike the other basin leagues, Mexican teams retain first rights to sign any native amateur. A major league club, therefore, must buy the contract from a player's Mexican club, usually for more than it costs to sign a prospect elsewhere in the region. This relationship, the summer Mexican league, and perhaps cultural factors, too, persuade native ballplayers to remain in Mexico.

Cuba opted out of this network after its revolution, and Nicaragua, whose 11-year fling with the pro winter leagues ended in 1967, followed suit after its 1979 revolution. Panama and Colombia have also tried winter ball, but financial pressures made play sporadic.

The flow of players continues to run both north and south. Minor and major leaguers from the United States still play in the winter leagues, which presently operate in Venezuela, Puerto Rico, the Dominican Republic, and Mexico. In their heyday during the 1950s and '60s, these winter leagues featured major leaguers like Tommy Lasorda, Whitey Ford, and Willie Stargell. But as major league salaries soared in the 1970s and unfavorable rates of exchanges weakened basin economies, the winter leagues restricted the number of North American imports. Minor leaguers and inexperienced major leaguers have replaced them. For them, these leagues provide the chance to play in the winter months, developing the potential that might allow them to crack a big league roster. They also earn higher pay than they do in the minors,

encounter competition from top Latino players, and are treated as demigods by the impassioned *fanáticos* of the winter game.

The winners of the winter leagues have met in a *Serie del Caribe* since 1949. Between 1949 and 1960, the pennant-winning squads of Cuba, Panama, Puerto Rico, and Venezuela played in early February to determine a champion of the Caribbean. Cuba won over half of these tournaments, but after the revolution, the series was discontinued. When it resumed in 1970, Mexico and the Dominican Republic replaced Cuba and Panama. The current round-robin format sends the teams that win their postseason tournaments to the *Serie del Caribe* along with a number of reinforcements, including North Americans, from their defeated opponents. Willie Mays, Monte Irvin, Camilo Pasqual, Rico Carty, and Vic Pellot Power are among those who have starred in these postseason celebrations.

Winter ball has descended from its zenith of the 1950s and '60s largely due to economic dynamics beyond the control of the Caribbean franchises. Rising player and fuel costs, devalued currencies, and underdevelopment pushed many into deficits, with government subsidies often vital to their continuation. Government support, long a feature of basin baseball, helps to keep current the Dominican saying that there will never be political trouble during the baseball season, only afterward. But by the middle of the 1980s, fewer of the established Latin major leaguers suited up for the October-through-January campaign. The demands of the regular season, the threat of injury, and the relatively inconsequential pay of winter ball suggest that this trend will continue. The pattern, however, has given younger Latin ballplayers the chance to play before knowledgeable fans and against competition that is often at a major league level.

Major Accomplishments

As the century draws to an end, the impact of players from the Caribbean basin on major league ball has never been greater. Major league baseball, meanwhile, currently exerts an unprecedented influence on the region's sporting culture and economy. These twin dynamics reflect how much the sport's center of gravity has shifted northward throughout the Western Hemisphere.

The 1997 major league playoffs, which featured a pan-Caribbean array of talent, concluded with the surprising World Series triumph of a team based in Miami, the city often dubbed Latin America's capital. That postseason showcasing of Latin players reflected a more fundamental shift in the game's demographics. At the start of the 1998 season, Latin players comprised an astonishing 18-19 percent of all major leaguers, twice what it was a decade ago. If Hispanic-Americans are included in their ranks, Latin ballplayers now outnumber African Americans in the majors. Nor are these players simply filling out rosters. Latin ballplayers are at the forefront of the game's efforts to reinvigorate itself after a decade in which baseball has been subject to ridicule more often than enthusiasm. At the 1998 All-Star game, one third of the players were from Latin America, including Pedro Martinez, Juan Gonzalez, Sammy Sosa, Ivan Rodriguez, Alex Rodri-

guez, Andres Galarraga, and Vinnie Castilla.

Major league baseball's demographic transformation is even more advanced at its grassroots where a greater proportion of minor leaguers is from the Caribbean basin, about 36 percent in 1998. Given these numbers, the continuing growth of baseball in the Caribbean, and the relative waning of interest in the game among youth in the United States, the size of the Latin cohort will undoubtedly swell during the foreseeable future. If the trickle of Cuban ballplayers fleeing their island to seek their fortunes in the majors becomes a mass exodus, Latins could soon make up one-third or more of major league rosters.

But if ballplayers from the Caribbean basin are recasting the professional game in the United States and Canada, reciprocal influences have been just as profound in the region. Where once the winter leagues mattered most in their respective societies, now major league baseball has become the focal point of fan interest and player development. Major league ball injects substantially more revenue, employs more people, and captures much more of the fans' attention than the now diminished winter leagues.

Major leaguers from the Dominican Republic, which spearheads the current Latin contingent to the majors, collectively earned about $70 million in 1997, a figure large enough to be included in the country's estimation of its balance of payments. Almost one-tenth of all major leaguers come from this nation of 8 million people. Only California, with over four times the population, sends more of its sons to the majors. On a per capita basis, the Dominican Republic is clearly number one. Several dozen other Dominicans play professionally in Japan, Korea, and Taiwan while over 1,000 labor in the minor leagues, and hundreds more work in non-playing positions for the 30 major league clubs.

Major league baseball penetration, which once took the form of a network of scouts and bird dogs who periodically scoured the region for talent, has acquired a year-round presence, especially in the Dominican Republic and Venezuela. Virtually every major league club maintains a full-time base of operations in these two countries. That presence includes a 32-team Dominican Summer League (DSL) with 35 players on each roster and an eight-team Venezuelan Summer League (VSL) as well as an infrastructure of baseball academies. The DSL and VSL were begun in 1985 and 1997 to circumvent the limit placed on the number of visas granted to major league organizations to bring their foreign-born minor league players to work in the United States. The 30 clubs divide a total of only 865 visas, but those boys signed to contracts who remain outside the United States do not require visas. Most of them, who range in age from 17 to 19, never make it to a minor league camp in the United States before they are released.

The academies, meanwhile, offer major league organizations a network of training camps for their young Latin players. Since Epy Guerrero developed the first, in Villa Mella outside Santo Domingo in the mid-1980s for the Toronto Blue Jays, and the Los Angeles Dodgers built a state-of-the-art facility in 1987 in Las Palmas, D.R., other organizations have followed suit there and in Venezuela.

Caribbean baseball's integration into an industry built around major league ball has reached the point where

agents from the United States are intervening with talented youngsters before they sign their first professional contracts. For decades, major league clubs have been able to sign Latin prospects for signing bonuses of only $3,000 to $5,000. Though often a windfall to the player's family, such a bonus was and remains a pittance compared to those received by youth in the United States, Canada, and Puerto Rico, where players are subject to the annual amateur draft. The disparity in signing bonuses allowed major league clubs to adopt a different strategy in the region, signing far more payers for far less money in anticipation that their investment would pay off if only a few emerged from the pack. But as some Latin players and their families have become more sophisticated about the market, they have retained agents. Such representation often greatly boosts a legitimate prospect's signing bonus, although it can cause a club to lose interest in a marginal player. Major league clubs, now sometimes forced to spend a great deal more to acquire players, are understandably appalled at their loss of leverage over boys vulnerable because of naivete, poverty, and lack of bargaining clout.

Winter league play, meanwhile, has lost some of its luster. As salaries for major league players skyrocketed, from an average of $51,500 in 1976 to $1,300,000 in 1997, the incentive to play winter ball waned. Though the crisis in winter ball has abated somewhat, the caliber of play is not what it once was. Older fans still recall winter baseball's golden ages when it was an important source of income for ballplayers during the off-season and the route that most aspiring North American minor leaguers took to prove they were good enough to play major league ball. Now, young North Americans seeking to break into the majors are more likely to play in the Arizona Fall League than in the Caribbean.

Winter ball, as a result, means less to the people of the region than it once did, while the fate of their countrymen in the majors means more. The national baseball cultures of the Dominican Republic, Mexico, Puerto Rico, Venezuela, Nicaragua, Colombia, and Panama have been overwhelmed by the pull of major league baseball. Even Cuba, which lost its minor league team after the 1959 revolution and subsequently developed its own "amateur" league, one which has dominated international competition ever since, has begun to lose players and the attention of its fanaticos to the major league game. The goal of young boys throughout the region is first and foremost to become a major leaguer in the United States or Canada. What happens there matters more than what takes place in the Caribbean's respective baseball cultures.

While winter ball will not reprise its golden age in the foreseeable future, and other sports, especially basketball, are making inroads, baseball remains *el rey de deportes* (the king of sports) throughout the basin. From the rocky hillsides and arid plains of northern Mexico through the canefields of the islands to the basin's southernmost flank in the Andes, baseball commands a fascination approaching reverence.

Baseball's significance derives from the role that it has played in the coming together of these societies in the twentieth century. Knitting a common cultural fabric, serving as a vent to social and political tensions, and offering a vehicle not only for individual mobility but collective social affirmation, baseball indeed has been more than a game. It has offered the citizens of the basin a chance to enter a ritual kinship embracing all fans and players. And while reflecting the progressive penetration of the United States in the region, baseball has been more than a cultural transmission belt for North American values. Beating each other and excelling in the major leagues and international competitions at a time when the Caribbean basin has encountered difficulties in asserting either its political or economic autonomy have been tremendous sources of pride. And that symbolic recognition has become a catalyst to national cohesion and consciousness for the region in its troubled evolution this century.

First Major Leaguers from Caribbean Basin Countries

Country	Player	Year	Team
Cuba	Esteban Bellan	1871	Troy Haymakers
	Rafael Almeida	1911	Cincinnati Reds
	Armando Marsans	1911	Cincinnati Reds
Colombia	Luis "Jud" Castro	1902	Philadelphia Athletics
Mexico	Baldomero "Mel" Almada	1933	Boston Red Sox
Venezuela	Alejandro Carrasquel	1939	Washington Senators
Puerto Rico	Hiram Bithorn	1942	Chicago Cubs
Panama	Héctor López	1955	Kansas City Athletics
	Humberto Robinson	1955	Milwaukee Braves
Dominican Republic	Osvaldo Virgil	1956	New York Giants
Virgin Islands	Joe Christopher	1959	Pittsburgh Pirates
Nicaragua	Dennis Martínez	1976	Baltimore Orioles
Honduras	Gerald Young	1987	Houston Astros
Curacao	Hensley Meulens	1990	New York Yankees
Belize	Chito Martinez	1991	Baltimore Orioles
Aruba	Gene Kingsale	1996	Baltimore Orioles

Serie del Caribe

Series	Year	Site	Winning Team/Country
I	1949	Cuba	Almendares/Cuba
II	1950	Puerto Rico	Carta Vieja/Panama
III	1951	Venezuela	Santurce/Puerto Rico
IV	1952	Panama	La Habana/Cuba
V	1953	Cuba	Santurce/Puerto Rico
VI	1954	Puerto Rico	Caguas/Puerto Rico
VII	1955	Venezuela	Santurce/Puerto Rico
VIII	1956	Panama	Cienfuegos/Cuba
IX	1957	Cuba	Marianao/Cuba
X	1958	Puerto Rico	Marianao/Cuba
XI	1959	Venezuela	Almendares/Cuba
XII	1960	Panama	Cienfuegos/Cuba
	1961–69	Not Held	
XIII	1970	Venezuela	Magallanes/Venezuela
XIV	1971	Puerto Rico	Licey/Dominican Republic
XV	1972	Dominican Republic	Ponce/Puerto Rico
XVI	1973	Venezuela	Licey/Dominican Republic
XVII	1974	Mexico	Caguas/Puerto Rico
XVIII	1975	Puerto Rico	Bayamón/Puerto Rico
XIX	1976	Dominican Republic	Hermosillo/Mexico
XX	1977	Venezuela	Licey/Dominican Republic
XXI	1978	Mexico	Mayagüez/Puerto Rico
XXII	1979	Puerto Rico	Magallanes/Venezuela
XXIII	1980	Dominican Republic	Licey/Dominican Republic
	1981	Not Held	
XXIV	1982	Mexico	Caracas/Venezuela
XXV	1983	Venezuela	Arecibo/Puerto Rico
XXVI	1984	Puerto Rico	Zulia/Venezuela
XXVII	1985	Mexico	Licey/Dominican Republic
XXVIII	1986	Venezuela	Mexicali/Mexico
XXIX	1987	Mexico	Caguas/Venezuela
XXX	1988	Dominican Republic	Escogido/Dominican Republic
XXXI	1989	Mazatlan	Zulia/Venezuela
XXXII	1990	Miami	Escogido/Dominican Republic
XXXIII	1991	Miami	Licey/Dominican Republic
XXXIV	1992	Mexico	Mayagüez/Puerto Rico
XXXV	1993	Mexico	Mayagüez/Puerto Rico
XXXVI	1994	Mexico	Licey/Dominican Republic
XXXVII	1995	Puerto Rico	San Juan/Puerto Rico
XXXVIII	1996	Dominican Republic	Culiacan/Mexico
XXXIX	1997	Mexico	Aguilas/Dominican Republic
XL	1998	Venezuela	Aguilas/Dominican Republic

Dominican League Statistics

Year	Champion	BA Leader	HR Leader	Most Games Won
1951	Licey	Luis Villodas .346	Pedro Formental 13	Guayuabín Olivo 10
1952	Aguilas	Luis Olmo .344	Alonzo Perry 11	Terry McDuffie 14
1953	Licey	Tetelo Vargas .355	Alonzo Perry 11	Emilio Cueche 13
1954	Estrellas Orientales	Alonzo Perry .326	Bob Thurman 11	Carrao Bracho G. Olivo 8
1955–56	Escogido*	Bob Wilson .333	Willie Kirkland 9	Fred Waters 11
1956–57	Escogido	Osvaldo Virgil .312	Danny Kravitz 4	Pete Burnside 11
1957–58	Escogido	Alonzo Perry .332	Dick Stuart 14	Fred Kipp 11
1958–59	Licey	Felipe Alou .351	Jim McDaniels 12	Bennie Daniels 12
1959–60	Escogido	Felipe Alou .359	Frank Howard 9	Stan Williams 12
1960–61	Escogido	Manuel Mota .344	Manuel Jiménez 13, J.V. Nicolás, Victor Ramirez, Felipe Alou, N. Saviñón Tied with 4	Danilo Riva
1961–62	Incomplete Season			
1962–63	Not Held			
1963–64	Licey	Manuel Mota .379	O. McFarlane 10	G. Olivo, Steve Blass 9
1964–65	Aguilas	Manuel Mota .364	O. McFarlane 8	Dick LeMay 8
1965–66	Season not organized by league			
1966–67	Aguilas	Mateo Alou .363	Winston Llenas, Bob Robertson 10	Dock Ellis 9
1967–68	Estrellas Orientales	Ricardo Carty .350	Bob Robertson 9	Silvano Quezada 11
1968–69	Escogido	Mateo Alou .390	Nate Colbert 8	Jay Ritchie 9
1969–70	Licey	Ralph Garr .387	Winston Llenas, Byron Browne 9	G. Rounsaville 8
1970–71	Licey	Ralph Garr .457	César Cedeño 8	Rollie Fingers 9
1971–72	Aguilas	Ralph Garr .388	Charlie Sands 10	Gene Garber 9
1972–73	Licey	Von Joshua .358	Adrian Garrett 9	Pedro Borbón 9
1973–74	Licey	Dave Parker .345	Ricardo Carty 9	Rick Waits 8
1974–75	Aguilas	Bruce Bochte .352	Rafael Batista, Bobby Darwin 8	James Richards 8
1975–76	Aguilas	Wilbur Howard .341	Wilbur Howard, John Hale, Gary Alexander, Larry Parrish, G. Thomasson, Bill Nahorodny, Andre Thornton Tied with 4	Nino Espinosa, Tom Dettore 8
1976–77	Licey	Mario Guerrero .365	Pedro Guerrero, Ike Hampton 6	Angel Torres 10
1977–78	Aguilas	Omar Moreno .345	Dick Davis 8	Odell Jones, Al Holland, Mickey Mahler 7
1978–79	Aguilas	Ted Cox .319	Bob Beall, Dick Davis 7	Bo McLaughlin, Mike Proly 9
1979–80	Licey	Tony Peña .317	A. De Freitas, Alberto Lois, Leon Durham	Jerry Hannahs 9
1980–81	Escogido	Ken Landreaux .394	Tony Peña 7	Mario Soto, M. Mahler 7
1981–82	Escogido	Pedro Hernandez .408	Dave Hostetler 9	Pasqual Pérez 10
1982–83	Licey	César Geronimo .341	Howard Johnson 8	Pasqual Pérez 9
1983–84	Licey	Miguel Diloné .343	Reggie Whittemore 12	Orel Hershiser, Frank Wills 8
1984–85	Licey	Junior Noboa .327	Ralph Bryant 9	Tom Filer 8
1985–86	Aguilas	Tony Fernández .364	Tony Peña 9	Mickey Mahler 8
1986–87	Aguilas	Stanley Javier .374	Ralph Bryant 13	Gibson Alba, José Nuñez, Eric Plunk Tied with 5
1987–88	Escogido	Stanley Javier .363	Mark Parent 10	José Bautista 8
1988–89	Licey	Julio Peguero .327	Domingo Michel 9	Melido Perez 8–3
1989–90	Escogido	Angel González .403	Denny González 5	Mel Rojas, Jeff Shaw, Kevin Wickander, Darren Holmes Tied with 6
1990–91	Licey	Hensley Meulens .338	Francisco Cabrera 8	Francesco De la Rosa 7
1991–92	Escogido	Luis Mercedes .333	Francisco Cabrera, Sammy Sosa, Geronimo Berroa, Kevin Koslofski, and Julian Yan tied with 4	José Nuñez 6
1992–93	Aguilas	Tom Marsh .318	Domingo Martinez 6	Efrain Valdez, Jose Martinez, Howard Farmer, and Rafael Valdez 5
1993–94	Licey	Alex Arias .371	Henry Rodriguez 6	Apolinar Garcia 6
1994–95	Azucueros	Luis Mercedes .352	Domingo Martinez 11	Hipolito Pichardo, Julian Heredia 6
1995–96	Aguilas	Domingo Cedeno .419	Sherman Obando 7	Ramon Morel 5
1996–97	Aguilas	Wilton Guerrero .340	Domingo Martinez 6	Dan Hubbs 6
1997–98	Aguilas	Julio Franco .436	Jeff Liefer 6	Efrain Valdez 8

* First year held in winter

Cuban League Statistics

Year	Champion	BA Leader	HR Leader	Most Games Won
1878–79	Habana Undefeated			
1879–80	Habana			
1880–81	Not held			
1882	Disputed: Fe and Habana			
1882–83	Habana			
1885	Habana	Pablo Ronquilla .350		
1885–86	Habana Undefeated	Wenceslao Gálvez .345		Adolfo Luján 5–0
1887	Habana	R. Martínez .439		Adolfo Luján 5–0
1888	Fe	Antonio García .448		Francisco Hernández 10–2
1889	Habana	Francisco Salabarria .305		Adolfo Luján 10–3
1889–90	Habana	Antonio García .364		Miguel Prats 11–2
1890–91	Fe	Alfredo Crespo .375		Miguel Prats 9–4
1892	Habana	Antonio García .362		E. Hernández 4–1
1892–93	Matanzas	Antonio García .385		Francisco Hernández 4–1
1893–94	Almendares	Miguel Pratts .394		José Pastoriza 16–7
1894–95	Suspended due to War of Independence	Alfredo Arcaño .430		Enrique García 12–4
1897–98	Not finished			
1898	Habanista	Valentín González .394		José Romero 5–2
1900	San Francisco	Esteban Pratts .333		Luis Padrón 13–4
1901	Habana	Julián Castillo .454		Carlos Royer 12–3
1902	Habana Undefeated	Luis Padrón .463		Carlos Royer 17–0
1903	Habana	Julián Castillo .330		Cándido Fontanals 14–6
1904	Habana	Regino García .397		Carlos Royer 13–3
1905	Almendares	Regino García .305		Angel D'Meza 10–4
1905–6	Fe	Regino García .304		José Muñoz 8–1
1907	Almendares	Regino García .324		George Mack 4–2
1908	Almendares	Emilio Palomino .350		José Méndez 9–0
1908–9	Habana	Julián Castillo .315		José Méndez L. Haggerman 15–6
1910	Almendares	Emilio Palomino .408		José Méndez 7–0
1910–11	Almendares	Preston Hill .365		José Méndez 11–2
1912	Habana	Emilio Palomino .440		José Junco 6–1
1913	Fe	Armando Marsans .400		Red Redding 7–2
1913–14	Almendares	Manuel Villa .351		José Méndez 10–0
1914–15	Habana	Cristóbal Torriente .387		José Acosta 5–1
1915–16	Almendares	Eustaquio Pedrosos .413		José Acosta 8–3
1917	Orientales	Adolfo Luque .355		José Acosta 2–1
1918–19	Habana	Manuel Cueto .344		José Acosta 16–10
1919–20	Almendares	Cristóbal Torriente .360		Emilio Palmero 5–1
1920–21	Habana	Pelayo Chacon .344	Cristóbal Torrionto M. González B. Jiménez M. Guerra Tied with 1	José "Cheo" Hernández 4–1
1921*	Habana	Bienvenido Jiménez .619	Manuel Cueto 1	Julio Leblanc 2–0
1922–23	Marianao	Bernardo Baró .401	Cristóbal Torriente 4	Lucas Boada 10–4
1923–24	Santa Clara	Oliver Marcells .393	Bienvenido Jiménez 4	Bill Holland 10–2
1924–25	Almendares	Manuel Cueto .364	Esteban Mantalvo 5	José Acosta 4–1
1925–26	Almendares	Johnny Wilson .430	J. H. Lloyd Jud Wilson 3	César Alvarez 10–2
1926–27	Habana	Manuel Cueto .404	J. Hernández 4	Juan Olmo 3–0
1927–28	Habana	Johnny Wilson .424	Oscar Charleston 5	Oscar Levis 7–2
1928–29	Habana	Alejandro Oms .432	Cool Papa Bell 5	Adolfo Luque 9–2
1929–30	Cienfuegos	Alejandro Oms .380	Mule Suttles 7	Heliodoro "Yoyo" Díaz 13–3
1930–31*	Not finished	O. Charleston .373	Ernest Smith José Fernández 1	Martín Dihigo 2–0
1931–32	Almendares	Rámon Cueto .400	Alejandro Oms Ismael Morales 3	Juan Eckelson 5–1
1932–33	Tie: Habana Almendares	M. González .432	R. Estalella 3	Jésus Lorenzo 3–0
1933–34	No championship held			
1934–35	Almendares	Lázaro Salazar .407	Eleven tied with 1	Lázaro Salazar 6–1
1935–36	Santa Clara	Martín Dihigo .358	Willie Wells Jacinto Roque 5	Martín Dihigo 11–2
1936–37	Marianao	Harry Williams .349	H. Andrews R. Estalella 5	Raymond Brown 21–4
1937–38	Santa Clara	Sam Bankhead .366	Willie Wells R. Estalella Raymond Brown 4	Raymond Brown 12–5
1938–39	Santa Clara	Tony Castaños .371	Josh Gibson 11	Martín Dihigo 14–2
1939–40	Almendares	Tony Castaños .340	Mule Suttles 4	Rodolfo Fernández 7–4
1940–41	Habana	Lázaro Salazar .316	A. Crespo 3	Gilberto Torres 10–3
1941–42	Almendares	Silvío García .351		Macon Mayor Agapito Mayor 6–2
1942–43	Almendares	A. Crespo .337	Roberto Ortiz Saguita Hernández 2	Cocaina García 10–3
1943–44	Habana	Roberto Ortiz .337	Saguita Hernández 3	Martín Dihigo 8–1
1944–45	Almendares	Claro Duany .340	Claro Duany 3	Oliverio Ortiz 10–4
1945–46	Cienfuegos	L. Davenport .333	Dick Sisler 9	Adrián Zabala 9–3
1946–47	Almendares	Lou Klein .330	Roberto Ortiz 11	Cocaina García 10–3
1947–48	Habana	Harry Kimbro .346	Jesús Chanquilon Díaz 7	C. Marrero 12–2
1948–49	Almendares	A. Crespo .326	Monte Irvin 10	Octavio Rubert 8–1
1949–50	Almendares	P. Formental .336	Roberto Ortiz Don Lenhardt 15	Octavio Rubert 5–1
1950–51	Habana	Silvío García .347	P. Formental, Bert Hass Ed Mierkowitz Charles Grant Tied with 8	Vincente López 17–3
1951–52	Habana	Bert Hass .323	P. Formental James Basso 9	Joe Black 15–6
1952–53	Habana	Edmundo Amorós .373	Louis Klein 16	R. Alexander 10–3
1953–54	Almendares	Rocky Nelson .352	Earl Rapp Rafael Noble 10	Cliff Fanning 13–4
1954–55	Almendares	Angel Scull .370	Rocky Nelson 13	Joe Hatten 13–5
1955–56	Cienfuegos	Forrest Jacobs .321	Ultus Alvarez 10	Pedro Ramos 13–5
1956–57	Marianao	Orestes Miñoso .312	Archie Wilson 11	Camilo Pascual 15–5
1957–58	Marianao	Milton Smith .320	Daniel Morejon Norman Larker B. Robinson Frank Herrera 9	Billy O'Dell 7–2
1958–59	Almendares	Tony Taylor .303	Jim Baxes 9	Orlando Pena 13–5
1959–60	Cienfuegos	Octavio Rojas .322		
1960–61	Cienfuegos			

* Short season

CHAPTER 17

Baseball in Canada

Bruce L. Prentice and Merritt Clifton

Baseball as we know it—with three bases and home, nine players to a side, and three outs to an inning—has been played in Canada at least since 1860, when the existing teams in London, Hamilton, St. Thomas, and Woodstock, Ontario, all accepted the rules of the New York Game popularized by Henry Chadwick. This was the game played on June 19, 1846 between the New York and Knickerbocker clubs on the Elysian Fields of Hoboken, New Jersey.

But a game differing from early baseball mainly in having five bases was played in Beechville, Ontario, as early as June 4, 1838, according to witness Adam Ford, who described it in a letter to *Sporting Life* published on May 5, 1886. The game included at least two "greyheaded men" who "used to play when they were boys."

Thus the Canadian baseball tradition certainly predates Abner Doubleday's apocryphal invention of the game at Cooperstown in 1839, and may go back as far as the U.S. tradition. Indeed, in both nations, ancestors of baseball including cricket and rounders had been played since the early 1700s, and determining exactly where their derivatives ended and baseball began may be impossible.

Before the arrival of the New York Game, the southwestern Ontario teams played the Canadian Game, with five bases and 11 fielders. All batters had to be retired to end an inning. Only after the New York rules were adopted did the game spread to the other provinces. By 1865 baseball had become so popular in Montreal that an ordinance was passed forbidding games in city parks as a menace to other users.

Baseball reached Manitoba no later than 1874, supplanting a local ancestor game called "bat," which had been played around the Red River Settlement as early as the 1840s. A professional three-team Manitoba League failed in 1886, but the game had firmly caught on by 1902, when the Great Northern Railway sponsored a Winnipeg entry in the professional North Dakota League.

Saskatchewan had semiprofessional baseball by 1887, when future provincial premier Walter Scott led a Regina team to two successive regional championships. Amateur baseball emerged in Alberta at about the same time, with games recorded as early as 1886.

By 1903 baseball was even played in the Yukon, where games attracted heavy gambling. Professional baseball debuted the same year in British Columbia, as 20-year-old Hal Chase—"Prince Hal," the slick-fielding first baseman—starred for a Victoria entry in an otherwise Washington-based league.

While major league baseball came late to Canada, Canadian entries in U.S.-based professional leagues won pennants as early as 1877, when the Tecumsehs of London, Ontario, led the International Association. The Tecumsehs reputedly declined a chance to join the two-year-old National League later that year, and disbanded from lack of fan support in early 1878. Ontario acquired another pennant winner in 1887, as Toronto began an only briefly interrupted 80-year run as a mainstay of the International League, which until 1912 was called the Eastern League. Toronto either finished first during the regular season or won four-team playoffs 15 times, with back-to-back winners in 1917-1918, 1956-1957, and 1965-1966.

Montreal's first Eastern League entry folded within weeks in 1890. A second Eastern League entry was more financially successful, beginning a 20-year run in 1897—but after winning the 1898 league championship, the team rarely escaped the second division. Montreal returned to the league in 1928. The franchise struggled, however, until it was acquired in 1935 by gas station magnate Charlie Trudeau, father of future Canadian prime minister Pierre Elliot Trudeau. Trudeau anchored the lineup with French-speaking Del Bissonnette and Quebec native Gus Dugas, who hit .327 with 191 homers in 13 minor league seasons. Under manager Frank Shaughnessy, who became International League president in 1936 and originated the four-club playoff format many experts credit with saving minor league baseball, the Montreal Royals won the 1935 pennant.

Bought by the Brooklyn Dodgers in 1940, the Royals won either pennant or playoffs in 10 of the next 20 years. Led by Quebecois Roland Gladu (12 homers, 105 RBIs, .338 batting average) and pitcher Jean Pierre Roy (25-11), the 1945 club was probably Montreal's favorite, but the 1946 Royals are best remembered: with them, second baseman Jackie Robinson (.349) broke the Organized Baseball color line that had prevailed since 1899, when Bill "Hippo" Galloway was released after playing five games for Woodstock, Ontario.

The color line had already been broken in Quebec by .392-hitting pitcher/outfielder Fred Wilson, who joined Granby of the then-outlaw Provincial League for the 1935 stretch run. The Provincial League had included a Montreal-based all-black entry, the Black Panthers, in 1936 and 1937, despite a September 1936 incident in which the Montreal Royals players, reportedly led by white southerners Harry Smythe and Ben Sankey, refused to play against the Provincial League All-Stars until Black Panther infielder Carl Logan was removed from the lineup. After the Black Panthers failed financially, the Provincial League was all white again in 1940, during a

one-year fling at Organized Baseball, but was reintegrated in 1946 by minor league hockey star Manny McIntyre, who signed with Sherbrooke only days after the Dodgers had signed Robinson and optioned him to Montreal.

The Provincial League was the longest-running of numerous native Canadian circuits, many of which owed ancestry to the work of longtime Canadian Pacific Railway sports representative Joseph Page, who helped set up teams and leagues wherever the trains stopped. A former semipro teammate of Tip O'Neill, Page was involved with O'Neill in assembling Montreal's 1898 International League pennant winner. He later enlisted former major league pitcher Jean Dubuc to help him organize the Eastern Canada League, a.k.a. the Ontario-Quebec-Vermont League, of 1922-1924. This was an ancestor of three leagues of note, each of which sent over 100 players to the majors—the Provincial, which had already come together for single seasons in 1894 and 1900; the Canadian-American League, which could claim descent from the short lived, Ontario-based Canadian League of 1885; and the outlaw Northern League that flourished in New York and Vermont from 1935 to 1952.

Reorganized a fourth time, the Provincial League grew steadily from 1935 to 1940, was interrupted by World War II, resumed play in 1944, collapsed in 1956 after a disastrous six-year return to Organized Baseball, and struggled on as an outlaw circuit in 1958-1971. Stars were plentiful, from Quebec native Sam LaRoque (1900) to Felix Mantilla (1969), but the zenith came in 1948-1949, as the league attracted black greats who were hoping to prove themselves against whites, displaced wartime major leaguers, and the so-called "Mexican League Jumpers," who were barred from Organized Baseball in 1946-1950 after breaking their major league contracts in an ill-fated stand against the reserve clause. At least 25 major leaguers played in the Provincial League during those two years, among them Sal Maglie, Max Lanier, Vic Power, Gladu and Roy, and Negro League stars Dave Pope, Bus Clarkson, and Quincy Trouppe.

The less colorful Can-Am belonged to Organized Baseball from 1936 through 1951. Several of the Ontario teams continued as an outlaw league into the 1960s.

Page also helped promote the Western Canada League, which began play in 1907, continuing with frequent interruptions and occasional name changes into the late 1940s, when Edmonton and Calgary anchored the Big Four League. The Western Canada League's best year was probably 1921, when its stars included Babe Herman and Heinie Manush.

Canadian teams have also been part of the bygone Northern Copper Country League, which later became the Northern League; the Northwestern League and Western International League, which evolved into today's Northwest League; the Pacific Coast League; the American Association; the Eastern League; the New York-Pennsylvania League; and the Pioneer League.

As well as helping return blacks to Organized Baseball, Canada played a part in popularizing baseball in Japan, through the Asahis (Rising Suns), a team of Vancouver teenagers of Japanese descent (Niseis) formed in 1914. In 1921, a dozen years after the first visit by a U.S. collegiate team and years before the first visit by U.S. major leaguers, the Asahis and a touring team from Seattle barnstormed Japan, playing both Japanese clubs and each other. The Asahis remained a power in Vancouver-area amateur baseball and heroes to the substantial British Columbia Nisei population for over 20 years.

Finding Home-Grown Talent

Of the ten Canadian provinces, only Newfoundland hasn't produced a major leaguer. But Canadian major leaguers are still rare—a reflection of short summers and a paucity of places to play since television killed the old town teams and outlaw leagues in the 1950s. As of 1990, only one high school baseball team existed in Quebec; none in several other provinces.

High school baseball programs have flourished, however, in the Metro Toronto area since 1979, when four schools experimented with a short schedule. There are now close to 70 schools playing a spring schedule that culminates in a championship game played at the SkyDome, prior to a regular-season Blue Jays game. The winning team receives the "Blue Jays Cup."

College baseball was started in 1978, when Seneca College (near Toronto) joined the NJCAA, New York-Penn Conference, for five seasons and was the forerunner to the National Baseball Institute (NBI) located in British Columbia. This college program has produced Canadian major leaguers including outfielders Kevin Reimer and Larry Walker, plus pitchers Steve Wilson and Dennis Boucher.

Listed origins, in any event, can be misleading. Seven players from the late 1800s are listed by most record books as having been born in the U.S., but are believed to have altered their birth records for various reasons, including the 1894 Alien Exemption Act, which barred Canadian athletes from U.S. employment. In addition, several players who were born abroad actually grew up in Canada, e.g., Hank Biasatti and Reno Bertoia, natives of Italy but raised in Windsor, Ontario, and Jimmy Archer, born in Ireland, raised in Toronto, and signed into Organized Baseball from an independent team in Manitoba.

Many of the best Canadian players actually grew up in the U.S., among them infielder Pete Ward, son of former Montreal hockey great Jim Ward, who learned baseball in Oregon; pitcher Dick Lines, born in Montreal but raised in Florida; pitcher Kirk McCaskill, born in Kapuskasing, Ontario, who grew up in Burlington, Vermont; and infielder Sherry Robertson, born in Montreal but raised in Washington, D.C. (as the nephew of Senators and Twins club owner Calvin Griffith, who was also born in Montreal but was brought to Washington in 1921 by Senators owner Clark Griffith, who married Calvin's aunt).

Pitcher Sheldon Burnside reversed that pattern. Born in South Bend, Indiana, Burnside grew up in Toronto.

The first Canadian-born major leaguer was first baseman Bill Phillips, who played for Cleveland, Brooklyn, and Kansas City, from 1879 to 1888. Born in St. John, New Brunswick, Phillips actually grew up in Chicago.

Among the 150 to follow Phillips are active players Rob Ducey, Larry Walker, Kevin Reimer, and Matt Stairs, as well as pitchers Steve Wilson, Kirk McCaskill, Dennis Boucher, Mike Gardiner, Vince Horsman, Paul Quantrill, and Rheal Cormier. While the number of play-

ers by position is roughly proportional to the numbers on major league rosters, pitchers have won the most distinction, perhaps because pitching skills can be developed more readily in short amateur seasons. Bob Emslie of Guelph, Ontario, was the first Canadian pitcher of note, and won more games in a big league season than any other Canadian, posting a 32-17 mark for the 1884 Baltimore Orioles. A poor start in 1885 sent him back to the minors, with a career major league record of just 44-44. Emslie returned to the majors, however, as an umpire, serving 35 years before retiring in 1926.

O'Neill, born at either Woodstock or Springfield, Ontario, in 1858, was the best Canadian hitter before Larry Walker, batting .326 in a big-league career that ran from 1883 to 1892. Breaking into the majors with New York as a pitcher, O'Neill soon switched to the outfield. In 1886 he led the then-major league American Association in hits, doubles, triples, homers, runs scored, batting, and slugging. His batting average, at the time, was actually listed as .492, but 50 walks were counted as hits. Subtracting them, he still hit .435. Though O'Neill fell to .335 in 1887, he repeated as batting champion. Walker won his first batting title in 1998, hitting .363 for Colorado. In 1997 Walker also led the National League with 49 home runs and 409 total bases, and fell 10 RBIs short of winning the first Triple Crown in the NL since 1937. Stairs meanwhile emerged as a slugger too, producing 27 home runs and a .298 average in 1997, followed by 26 and .294 in 1998—which, except for Walker's performance, would have been the most productive seasons for a Canadian-born hitter in 50 years.

The best Canadian player of all was probably Ferguson Jenkins, a 6-foot-5-inch right-hander from Chatham, Ontario, who compiled a 284-226 record over 19 seasons from 1965 to 1983. At his peak, Jenkins, the only Canadian-born Hall of Famer won 20 games or more seven times in eight years. Noted for control, Jenkins fanned over three times as many batters as he walked—and led the NL with 273 whiffs in 1969, retiring ninth on the all-time strikeout list. He earned the 1971 NL Cy Young Award by leading the league in wins (24), innings pitched, and, for the third time each, starts and complete games. He also hit six homers that year, one behind the NL record for home runs by a pitcher.

Other Canadian pitchers of note include Russ Ford, John Hiller, Reggie Cleveland, Phil Marchildon, Dick Fowler, Claude Raymond, and Ron Taylor. Ford, whose older brother also made the big leagues briefly, won 26 games for the New York Highlanders in 1910, his first full season. Hiller saved a then-record 38 games in 1973 and won an AL record 17 games in relief the next year, but is best known for his comeback from a 1971 heart attack. Marchildon and Fowler were half of the Athletics' rotation during the 1940s. On Sept. 9, 1945, Fowler became the only Canadian to hurl a no-hitter, beating the Browns 1-0 for his only victory that year after coming back from military service. Marchildon peaked with 19 wins in 1947. Raymond is remembered as the first native Quebecois to play for the Expos. Taylor relieved for two world champions, the 1964 Cardinals and the 1969 Mets, then became team physician for the Toronto Blue Jays.

Other top Canadian hitters were George Selkirk and Jeff Heath. Selkirk, who replaced Babe Ruth in the Yankees' lineup in 1934, hit .290 over nine seasons, topping .300 five times and twice driving in more than 100 runs. He later served for 10 years as general manager of the Washington Senators. Heath, who reputedly never lived up to his potential, averaged .293 over 14 years, beginning in 1936, with 194 homers. His best years were 1938 (21-112-.343) and 1941 (24-123-.340.) In between he led a player revolt against Indians manager Oscar Vitt. In his final full year, Heath hit .319 with 24 homers, pacing the Braves to the 1948 NL pennant, but broke his leg sliding during the last week of the season, missing his only chance at a World Series.

Canadian managers have included Art Irwin, Freddie Lake, Moon Gibson, and Bill Watkins, who led the Detroit Wolverines to the 1887 NL pennant.

Catcher Nig Clarke, from Amhurstburg, Ontario, won a spot in the minor league record books on June 15, 1902, hitting eight homers for Corsicana of the Texas League in a 51-3 rout of Texarkana. Outfielder Jack Graney, of St. Thomas, Ontario, was reputedly the first major leaguer to wear a number, and was also both the first hitter to face Babe Ruth when the latter debuted as a pitcher, and the first ex-player to become a baseball broadcaster. Outfielder Glen Gorbous, of Drumheller, Alberta, made the *Guinness Book of Records* with the longest measured throw on record. Black pitcher Jimmy Claxton, of New Westminster, British Columbia, briefly broke the color line by passing as an alleged Native American with Oakland of the Pacific Coast League in 1916.

Canada Makes the Big Leagues

National League baseball finally came to Canada with the expansion Montreal Expos in 1969. Hoping to get off to a good start, the Expos drafted mainly veterans, including Maury Wills, who became the only player to appear with Montreal in both the majors and the minors. Wills was soon traded for another veteran, Ron Fairly, who had led the University of Alberta into the 1957 College World Series. A preseason swap of sluggers Donn Clendenon and Rusty Staub had to be rearranged when Clendenon quit rather than join the Astros. Clendenon eventually unretired and was swapped to the Mets. The affair was a milestone in the series of events that led to overturning the reserve clause in 1975. Although the Expos won both their first game and their home opener (on a home run by pitcher Dan McGinn), they finished last. No-hitters by Bill Stoneman in 1969 and 1972 were the club high points until 1973. Then, despite a 79-83 record, the Expos were in contention into the final week, paced by Ken Singleton, Ron Hunt, who set an all-time record by getting hit with pitches 50 times, rookie Steve Rogers, and reliever Mike Marshall, who saved 31 games and won 14 in 92 appearances.

Marshall was promptly traded to the Dodgers for Willie Davis, who staged a sit-down strike in center field before moving on. Singleton and pitcher Mike Torrez were sent to the Orioles a year later for former Cy Young Award winner Dave McNally and outfielder Rich Coggins. A thyroid ailment ended Coggins' career at age 25, while McNally played the 1975 season without a contract, then filed one of the two lawsuits that finally broke the reserve

clause (Andy Messersmith of the Dodgers filed the other).

The Expos regrouped under new manager Dick Williams to win a club record 95 games in 1979. The arrival of young stars including Rogers, Andre Dawson, Gary Carter, Larry Parrish, Tim Raines, and Tim Wallach led management to bill the Expos as "The Team of the Eighties." The promise seemed real when the Expos won a playoff against the Phillies for the NL East title during the strike-shortened split season of 1981, and were leading the Dodgers 1-0 in the fifth inning of the final game of the NL Championship Series. But Rick Monday singled and scored the tying run, then won the game 2-1 with a two-out ninth inning homer off Rogers.

Toronto appeared ready to enter the National League in 1976 by purchasing the San Francisco Giants. When that deal fell through at the last minute, the American League admitted the Blue Jays as an expansion team in 1977. The Blue Jays drafted for the future, enduring six years in the cellar before winning 89 games to place fourth in 1983.

Good trades and a strong farm system loaded the lineup with sluggers George Bell, Jesse Barfield, Lloyd Moseby, and Willie Upshaw, plus hard-hitting infielders Tony Fernandez and Damaso Garcia, and produced a perennially strong pitching staff led by Dave Stieb and Jimmy Key. Ernie Whitt, an expansion draft selection, supplied power behind the plate through 1989. Winning 99 games and the AL East title in 1985, the Jays took a 3-1 lead in the Championship Series against Kansas City, but then dropped three games in a row to lose. The Jays disappointed their fans by dropping the ALCS again in 1989 and 1991, and losing the AL East lead in the last week of 1987 and 1990.

Perhaps those disappointments built character in Toronto. Then again, general manager Pat Gillick, nicknamed "Stand Pat" for his previous conservatism, might have turned the team around with the biggest trade of his career, sending first baseman Fred McGriff and shortstop Tony Fernandez to the San Diego Padres for outfielder Joe Carter and second baseman Roberto Alomar. McGriff was the Jays' top slugger, but Carter virtually duplicated his numbers; Fernandez, a former All Star, was the Jays' senior position player, but Alomar hit with more power, stole more bases, and was equally flashy on defense. Two costly free agent additions—Jack Morris, the pitching ace of the 1991 world champion Minnesota Twins, and veteran designated hitter Dave Winfield—completed a $41 million roster, the most expensive in Canadian baseball history. Morris won 21 games; Winfield, at age 41, became the oldest player to knock in 100 runs.

A six-game victory over the Oakland Athletics in the Championship Series set up the first-ever genuinely international World Series, as Toronto met the Atlanta Braves. The Blue Jays split the first two games in Atlanta, took a pair at home, and then appeared to choke again, dropping the last game in Toronto and losing a 2-1 lead in the sixth Series game in the bottom of the ninth. But with the score still tied in the top of the 11th, Winfield doubled home two runs. Reliever Mike Timlin held off one last Atlanta rally to preserve a 4-3 win. For the first time the world of baseball belonged to a team from outside the U.S.—though to be sure, the Blue Jays had no native Canadian players, having unloaded reserve outfielder Rob Ducey midway through the season.

The 1993 team, shaken up by more Gillick moves, nonetheless picked up where the 1992 edition left off, leading the AL East virtually from start to finish as first baseman John Olerud, a .269 lifetime hitter, averaged .400 for more than half the season. Rolling over the Chicago White Sox in the ALCS, the Blue Jays took the World Series for the second consecutive year on Joe Carter's bottom-of-the-ninth home run off Philadelphia's Mitch Williams in the decisive sixth game.

Contrasting Fortunes

While the Blue Jays struggled to turn near-success into glorious triumph, drawing more than 4 million fans a year, the Expos entered the 1990s just struggling. Discouraged by 22 years without a pennant, and by dropping fan support as the advertised "Team of the Eighties" aged and departed, founding owner Charles Bronfman sold the franchise—after a prolonged hunt for takers—to a group headed by club president Claude Brochu.

The 1991 Expos finished dead last, ending the unpromising campaign with a long unscheduled road trip after a 50-ton block of concrete fell from the Olympic Stadium roof. The 15-year-old ballpark was closed for extensive repairs, while Brochu et al. contemplated relocating to either Buffalo or St. Petersburg.

But Felipe Alou, the first former Montreal player to manage the team, turned everything around after taking over in early 1992, leading the Expos to a 70-55 record in the last four months of the season. In 1993 Alou brought Montreal a club record of 97 victories. And 1994 promised to be Montreal's year, as the Expos held a six-game lead over Atlanta, the second-best team in baseball, when the August 12 strike stopped play. For the first time in several years, fans in other cities began to recognize the Expos regulars, notably the outfield of Moises Alou, Marquis Grissom, and Larry Walker, as well as All Star shortstop Wil Cordero and top starter Ken Hill.

Yet Alou couldn't keep the nucleus together. The club's financial fortunes declined in the mid-1990s with the Quebec economy, exacerbating the perennial loss of stars to free agency and trades intended to cut the payroll. Walker, Hill, and top reliever John Wetteland departed after 1994; Grissom and Cordero left, along with newly emergent .318-hitting third baseman Sean Berry, after the depleted Expos slumped to fifth in 1995.

By 1996, Alou's fifth season as manager, only son Moises, catcher Darrin Fletcher, and pitchers Jeff Fassero and Mel Rojas remained from 1992—but astute scouting and player development brought replacements for most of the missing. Obtained from the Red Sox, Rheal Cormier, 7-10, was the first-ever Quebecois native in the Expos' rotation. Rondell White, Grissom's replacement, hit over .290 for the second year in a row. Mark Grudzielanek, taking over shortstop, hit .306, with 99 runs scored, 201 hits, and 34 doubles, all club records for the position. Henry Rodriguez, written off by the Dodgers after repeated failures to hit major league pitching with authority, won the left field job by leading the National League in home runs for the first third of the season. He cooled off down the stretch, failing to homer from August 25 to

September 12, but still ended up with 42 doubles, 103 RBIs, and a team record 36 home runs, including a September 26 grand slam against Philadelphia that momentarily kept the Expos alive in the National League wild card playoff race.

Never seriously challenging the ever-powerful Braves in the National League East, the Expos had held a one-game lead in the wild card race despite losing 11 of 16 games at the end of August, and recovered with six straight wins in early September—but lost ground thereafter as the Dodgers and Padres each surged in competition for the National League West title. The Expos' hopes were killed chiefly by John Smoltz of the Braves, who beat them with his own three-run homer on September 22, and beat them again on September 27, for his 24th and final victory.

There was no encore. Moises Alou departed through free agency, but the loss of his bat hurt less in 1997 than thin pitching, as the Expos fell into the second division and attendance crashed. Then ace Pedro Martinez, the first Expo to win the Cy Young Award, and sluggers Rodriguez, Fletcher, and David Segui all left after the season. Shortstop Grudzielanek was traded to the Dodgers in the middle of a dismal 65-97 1998 campaign, which barely missed being the team's worst. The frustrated Felipe Alou at season's end nearly left the Expos to manage the Dodgers, but was lured back by a $2 million contract, as one of the chief assets of a team up for sale. Almost the only bright lights on the playing field were the emergence of young slugger Vladimir Guerrero, who hit .302 and .324 in his first two campaigns, and the relief work of Ugueth Urbina, whose 1.30 ERA in 1998 was a team record.

Trying to keep the Expos in Montreal, the ownership group ousted Claude Brochu, club president since 1990, and announced a 150-day timetable to find $50 million to $100 million in operating capital plus financing for a new stadium. The Quebec government earlier refused to contribute to a plan to build a $250 million, 35,000-seat stadium. The plan is now to be scaled back.

The Blue Jays meanwhile staggered through the strike-shortened 1994 and 1995 campaigns, shedding stars from the championship seasons including Roberto Alomar and Paul Molitor, and didn't recover in 1996 despite the continuing consistent power of Carter, career highs of 36 homers and 101 RBIs from third baseman Ed Sprague, and a 20-10 season from Cy Young Award winner Pat Hentgen.

When the Jays disappointed again in 1997, despite a 21-7 performance from high-priced free agent Roger Clemens, manager Cito Gaston got the ax, after eight and a half years, and regrouping began under Tim Johnson. The first former Blue Jay player to manage the team. Johnson predictably built around Clemens, 20-6 in 1998, plus emerging power hitters Carlos Delgado and Shawn Green, both products of the Toronto farm system, but the real impetus toward contention came from Tony Fernandez, who fell just short of career highs in all offensive departments in his third stint with Toronto, and Jose Canseco, whose 46 home runs eclipsed the team record. The Jays' 88-74 record was third best in the AL, albeit four victories short of a wild card playoff spot.

Minor Changes

Edmonton, top farm club for the Oakland Athletics, won the 1996 Pacific Coast League championship, a decade after Vancouver became the only previous Canadian team to lead the PCL, and repeated in 1997, but hit hard times in 1998. Owner Peter Pocklington put the club up for sale, forcing Edmonton to forfeit the opportunity to host the 1999 PCL All-Star Game—but the Anaheim Angels insured that baseball would remain in Edmonton by picking up the franchise in place of Vancouver. Vancouver was to remain in the PCL for 1999 as a lame duck, scheduled for relocation to Sacramento, California, in 2000.

Lethbridge, struggling for years as an independent entry in the otherwise affiliated Pioneer League, also achieved a breakthrough championship in 1996, led by .424-hitting Kevin Sweeney, won a second-half championship in 1997, and lost the deciding game of the 1998 championship series to Idaho Falls. Also including a Blue Jays farm team at Medicine Hat, the Pioneer League was in the mid-1990s the only professional league other than the PCL with more than one Canadian representative.

Independent professional baseball enjoyed mid-decade success in prairie provinces, led by Winnipeg. Without a pro team since 1971, the city took instantly to the Goldeyes, of the Northern League, who won the 1994 league championship, and continued to contend through 1998, making the playoffs each year, paced by ex-major leaguers including former Expos Dann Bilardello (1994) and Terry Lee (1995), who missed the Northern League triple crown by just two home runs. Lee repeated as batting champion in 1997.

Thunder Bay, an Ontario entry in the Northern League, was markedly less successful, as was the Prairie League, a 1997 effort to emulate the Northern League. Four of the eight teams were Canadian, including the Regina Cyclones, the Saskatoon Stallions, the Moose Jaw Diamond dogs, and the Western Manitoba Wranglers. Paced by triple crown-winning third baseman Randy Kapano, Regina won the first and only league championship. The Moose Jaw franchise collapsed after the players went on strike in August, due to non-receipt of pay, and the league itself didn't last much longer.

The professional baseball draft, extended to Canadian players in 1991, tapped 164 Canadians through 1997, including shortstop Kevin Nicholson, of Surrey, B.C., who made a promising pro debut after the San Diego Padres tapped him in the 1997 first round. Team Canada, third in 1996 behind the U.S. and Cuba at the Americas' Baseball Challenge tournament in Edmonton, hosted the World Junior Championship in 1997 at Monckton, New Brunswick, picking up a bronze medal. The Baseball Canada senior team, including ex-professionals for the first time (but no former major leaguers), advanced to the 1998 International Baseball Association championships in Italy, but was eliminated in the quarter finals by Team USA.

[Thanks for research help to Eves Raja; Bill Humber; Donald Guay; Dan Zinuik; and the Brome County Historical Society.]

CHAPTER 18

Baseball in Australia

Robert Laidlaw

As early as the 1850s, homesick Americans played baseball on the Australian goldrush fields of Ballarat. But Australia's first recorded game, as reported in *Bells Life,* was a Feb. 28, 1857 three-inning match between Collingwood and Richmond. Though named "baseball," it was nonetheless an obvious hybrid with cricket. Some said a run was recorded for each base secured. Others said that, like cricket, batters continued batting until they were retired. The final score: Collingwood 350, Richmond 230. A one-and-a-half inning game followed that same day, with Richmond winning, 171-141.

American influences increased in the next 20 years (with games played in the late 1870s in Sydney), but in 1879, the St. Kilda Baseball Club became Australia's first club. After five weeks of training, the team played against the visiting "Hicks Original Georgia Minstrels," a travelling American black brass band. The first match, on June 14, 1879, resulted in a St. Kilda victory. A week later a strengthened Minstrels side (team) won, 29-18. After a June 28 match was rained out, the two teams played again on July 19, before a large and enthusiastic audience. Each scored 27 runs. After recent heavy rains, however, good fielding almost impossible.

A week later the Minstels won in seven innings, 27-20, fielding a very strong team, as well as a full brass band, which enlivened proceedings with several selections.

In the 1880s, two expatriate Americans clubs ("Union" and "Sydney") played in Sydney. Baseball was also played in Melbourne on an ad-hoc basis, with American and Australian cricketers being the main participants.

The Spalding Tour 1888-89

Albert Spalding's 1888-89 tour proved to be a turning point in Australian baseball history. Without this event, the game would probably have continued haphazardly until the 1914 New York Giants-Chicago White Sox tour, or even later.

Al Spalding staged an English tour in 1874 with his Boston club. He gained some support, but, as he found in Australia in 1888, the cricket establishment feared he was trying to supplant their established sport.

Two professional baseball sides made the trip: the White Sox and an assortment of professionals known as "All-America." Also along were two entertainment acts. Negro mascot, Clarence Duval, dressed in a red coat with gold lace, with tight white trousers and high leather boots, danced and baton twirled for the crowd's amusement.

Professor Bartholomew, a daredevil balloonist and parachutist, drew big crowds with his death-defying stunts, going high up in the air in his balloon, swinging from a trapeze, and then parachuting to earth.

When the teams arrived in Sydney on Dec. 14, 1888, a flotilla draped in red, white, and blue sailed out to meet them. A large crowd at Woolloomooloo wharf cheered the tourists as they embarked onto four-horse coaches.

The following day All-America won, 5-4. The party then traveled by rail to Melbourne, receiving a typically generous greeting. The teams played two games, with a scratch match between the Melbourne cricketers and the Americans showing how skilled the tourists were. The Americans scored eight runs, while the Australians struggled to hit against Mark Baldwin.

After Christmas, the teams traveled to Adelaide for three matches, and stopped in Ballarat. Good crowds greeted them at each venue, with Professor Bartholomew helping to increase attendance substantially. At Ballarat, however, he landed on a rooftop, injuring his legs and ending his performances in Australia. Crowds averaged about 5,000, with a peak of 11,000.

On New Year's Day 1889, Aborigines gave the visitors a demonstration of boomerang throwing and rope skipping. The teams played their last game on Jan. 5, at the Melbourne Cricket Ground. Chicago defeated a Melbourne side, 12-0, in a three-inning game. The Americans were challenged to break the Australian record for throwing a cricket ball, which stood at 126 yards, 3 inches. (Ned Williamson had thrown a baseball 133 yards, 11 inches.) Several broke the record, with Ed "Cannonball" Crane reaching 128 yards, 10½ inches.

The party left Melbourne on Jan. 7, arriving back in Chicago on April 20. Spalding had been encouraged sufficiently by Melbourne's reactions to announce Australia had the best hope of taking up baseball of all the places they had visited.

Simpson Follows Spalding

Spalding's hand-picked baseball missionary, Harry Simpson, reveled in his task, instructing and organizing teams in Victoria, South Australia, Broken Hill, and Sydney. Soon after Spalding left Australia, Simpson, with the help of some local Americans, including prominent theatre entrepreneur J.C. Williamson, organized some instruction and games in Melbourne. On Jan. 18 1889, a Williamson-managed team known as "Thespians" (and including Harry Musgrove, who was to manage the Aus-

tralian tour of America in 1897), defeated Albert Park, 26-15.

The Victorian Baseball Club, formed Feb. 12, 1889, with Williamson as president and manager, played against the Hicks Sawyer Minstrels, in mid-February. The Minstrels won, 15-13; then Victoria triumphed, 25-13. Several schools were given a public holiday to witness the second game.

With several clubs forming in Melbourne, Simpson turned to South Australia. In early April, South Australians played twice against the Hicks Sawyer Minstrels. The Southerners won the first game, 19-2, and the Minstrels won the second game, 16-12.

Now the South Australians were ready to battle Victoria in the first Intercolonial series, (best of three games), to determine Australia's first champions. On April 20, 1889, in Melbourne, South Australia came from five runs down to score seven ninth-inning runs to win the first contest between the colonies. Victoria rebounded with a 10-run final inning to win by four. South Australia won the deciding contest, 27-18.

Simpson now headed for Broken Hill. The Victorians chose a winter league to cater to Melbourne cricketers taking up the game, while Adelaide opted for a summer competition, as their players tended to be Australian Rules footballers.

A series of matches were played in Broken Hill late December in 1889 between New South Wales (NSW) and South Australia. NSW won the first game, 28-26. The second was again a close victory for NSW, with the score tied at 38-all, until the winning run broke the deadlock in the bottom of the ninth. The final game completed the route, as the New South Welshmen won, 45-26, although the Southerners claimed to be suffering from illness.

Simpson did his job well, and into 1890 and 1891, enthusiasm mounted for Intercolonial baseball. In early April 1890, South Australia defeated the NSW side from Broken Hill in three straight games in Adelaide. In January 1891, Victoria defeated South Australia in three straight in Melbourne.

After South Australia defeated Victoria in a return series in Adelaide three games to none, (two by only one run), talk grew of an Australian tour of America. After helping set up the NSW Baseball League in Sydney in 1891, Simpson died of typhoid just as the first season began. He lies in an unmarked grave, site 2045, at Waverley Cemetery.

Sydney baseball temporarily fell by the wayside. Although Intercolonial matches ended for three years, competitions in Victoria and South Australia continued.

Some hope remained of an Australian side visiting America. In the meantime, Adelaide Oval another Intercolonial series in September 1894, this time between South Australia and Victoria. Victoria won, 11-10.

Another Intercolonial series was played in early February 1897, with an Australian side to be picked to travel to America. In 1896, an Australian cricket side, managed by Harry Musgrove, a former top Melbourne baseballer, had traveled to America after its English engagements.

The Intercolonial series was easily won by Victoria over South Australia in Melbourne. The Victorians dominated the three games, winning by scores of 32-6, 19-6, and 12-3. Eleven of their players made the tour—Alf

Carter, Walter Ingleton, Harry Irwin, Charles Kemp, Frank Laver, Peter McAlister, James McKay, Charles Over, Harry Stuckey, Jack Wallace, and Arthur Wiseman. Only Rue Ewers and Syd Smith came from South Australia.

The 1897 Tour of America

In 1897 Australians made the first tour by an overseas baseball side to the United States. The Aussies wished to show Americans their progress. But financial losses and stranded players caused the expedition to become known as "The Disastrous Tour."

Musgrove traveled to America to arrange details and reported the tour would be ill-advised. But players ignored his warning and left Sydney on March 15. After stops in New Zealand, Samoa, and Honolulu they arrived in San Francisco on April 8.

On Easter Sunday, April 18, Australia played its first game against the Olympics nine, before 5,000 fans. Australians batted and ran the bases well, but were slow in the field and lacked knowledge on the game's finer points.

The press reported "the Australians go into bat as if they are playing cricket, but the cricket idea will have to be abandoned . . . They are all fairly good throwers, and are nimble and quick, but are buttered-fingered and cannot catch a little bit." The Olympics beat the Australians, 20-9.

Over the next month, Australia played another eight games on the West Coast, winning two. Bad grounds, poor crowds, some questionable umpiring, injuries, and generally too much sightseeing and carousing were straining the purse strings. The team wired Spalding in Chicago for advice. Despite warnings of little Eastern interest, the Aussies continued the tour.

After leaving for Chicago by rail on May 17, the Australians took two games in Ogden and one in Denver, then lost two to Omaha University, and one in Council Bluffs.

Players sat in box seats as guests of James Hart (Chicago club president and a strong supporter of the tour), to witness games between Chicago and Baltimore, which featured Joe Quinn, the first Australian to play in the major leagues.

After losing games in Chicago and Pittsburgh, the team reached New York on June 14. After watching Brooklyn defeat Chicago, 13-3, they played those teams' reserves, winning, 11-8, by taking a big early lead. Darkness intervened before the Americans caught up.

On June 21, the Aussies challenged a team of Boston oldtimers. Despite the additional draw of Hinton and his mechanical pitching machine, only about 500 fans attended. Hinton's "cannon" pitched the last two innings against Australia. The machine's complicated starting mechanism put the Australians at a disadvantage, but the game was well safe before its introduction.

Henry Chadwick threw out the first ball and officially scored the contest. Australians took advantage of their superior fitness level to outclass their famous opponents (Al Spalding, for example, hit cleanly but was unable to reach first), and Australia won, 27-13. After the game, George Wright organized a banquet in honor of the Australians.

Over the next two weeks, the Australians played eight more games, winning two and getting throttled in most of the others. The players now had had enough baseball and spent the remainder of their time sightseeing, including a three-day visit to Niagara Falls.

On July 14, the party left for London, arriving a week later. On their voyage, they discovered a deficiency of 110 pounds in their treasury. On reaching England, Musgrove promised fares back to Australia, but failed to do so. After spending a week sightseeing, the tour played a match against the London Consolidated Club at Crystal Palace. Musgrove had organized the game to raise enough capital for the team to return to Australia. Australia won, 21-8, but during the game Musgrove collected gate receipts, then disappeared, leaving players to find their way back to Australia. Some used their savings, some wired home for money, and a couple actually worked their way back as stokers aboard ship. Syd Smith remained in England and married before returning to Australia in 1912.

Back in Australia, baseball in Melbourne slipped badly, with only a couple of clubs remaining until after the turn of the century. In South Australia competitive baseball ceased until the SABL reformed in 1908.

Although the American tour adversely affected baseball in Victoria and South Australia, New South Wales, which was not involved with the tour, actually took steps in 1897 to establish baseball on a permanent basis. Jim Searle, a local cricket personality, had shunned baseball after seeing Spalding's teams in 1888. But obviously he remembered the effect the game had on cricketers, and helped start baseball up in Sydney in 1897.

The Metropolitan Baseball Association formed the following year in NSW. They played an Interstate series against Victoria in 1900, losing the first game, 11-9, and winning the last two, 9-6 and 8-5. The series continued (except 1902) until 1910, when Interstate clashes were extended to include South Australia regularly, and Tasmania briefly.

Baseball grew in leaps and bounds in NSW and Victoria, with multiple grades now formed as player participation expanded at a rate of 50 percent per year. The 1908 tour of the "Great White Fleet" brought baseball to the forefront with the visit of the American Battle Ships.

The American Great White Fleet

In 1905, the crew of the American warship Brooklyn played a 5-5 tie against a Victorian team, but it was its Great White Fleet, which truly impacted Australian baseball.

When the fleet sailed into Sydney in late August 1908, a crowd of 500,000 lined the wharf to greet them. Over the next two weeks, several of the ships' sides played various club and State sides in NSW and Victoria. A combined fleet squadron played a three "test" series against Australia for the J.C. Williamson Trophy.

The fleet won the first test, 16-4, in Sydney on Aug. 24. The second test, again in Sydney, was played two days later, and Australia won an exciting game 8-7 to force a third game.

The deciding "test" match was played on Sept. 4, in Melbourne. More than 2,000 officers and men marched from the Exhibition Gardens to the Melbourne Cricket Ground, with their bands, to watch the big game. Unfortunately the game did not reach expectations, as the Fleet won the trophy with a resounding 17-1 victory. (Two days earlier, at Melbourne's Cricket Ground, sporting teams from Minnesota and Kentucky staged the first gridiron game played on Australian soil. Wet and muddy conditions resulted in a scoreless draw between the two teams from the fleet.)

Baseball grew steadily in Victoria and NSW before the 1908 tour. Although South Australia did not participate in any of the tour matches, competition re-emerged in that State, with four clubs. It helped cement baseball in those three States until 1936 when Queensland and Western Australia kicked off their competitions.

With Victoria and NSW having established regular Interstate contests, 1910 witnessed an impressive expansion. South Australia and Tasmania joined to lend more variety and lay the foundation for a tradition that lasted until the founding of the Australian Baseball League in 1989.

Many schoolboy and youth teams appeared in Australia from 1910-1925. The schoolboy teams were where many of Australia's best baseballers and cricketers honed their skills. A Western Australia youth group, "The Young Australian League," visited Sydney in 1911 and lost to a schoolboy side, 13-2. They were on the way to America, where they would demonstrate Australian football and baseball, among other activities. In Sydney, a split occurred in their competition, as summer baseball emerged and remained for a number of years.

The 1914 American Visit: New York vs. Chicago

On New Year's Day, 1914, two major league teams, the New York Giants and Chicago White Sox, arrived in Brisbane. Only a few players from those clubs actually came, the rest were from other major league teams. The best-known were Buck Weaver, Tris Speaker, Sam Crawford, Germany Schaefer, Fred Merkle, and Jim Thorpe. They brought along umpires Bill Klem and Jack Sheridan, who had officiated the 1913 World Series.

Chicago owner Charles Comiskey and New York manager John McGraw had organized the global tour to foster an international climate for baseball. Before arriving in Australia, the teams had played in Tokyo, Shanghai, and Manila. Their first Australian game was played the day they arrived in Brisbane—where baseball was relatively unknown—on a quick stop before sailing for Sydney. The score was 1-1 until the top of the ninth, when New York's Fred Merkle knocked in Larry Doyle with the winning run.

After arriving in Sydney, the teams played another exciting game. After trailing 4-0, Chicago made it 4-3, and then in the bottom of the ninth, with two on and two out, Buck Weaver hit a ball along the left field line to score two runs and snatch a 5-4 White Sox victory. Earlier in the day, NSW, with a New York battery, lost, 10-0, to Chicago in a five-inning game. That evening, Australian Prime Minister Joseph Cook toasted the Americans, referring to the international value of sport and the good feeling it created between nations.

The tour headed for Melbourne by rail. At an official luncheon before the first game, McGraw toasted "we have enjoyed ourselves every moment since we struck your island," which caused much amusement.

The last game was on Jan. 8, and like all others, was well attended. Chicago ran up a 3-0 lead going into the bottom of the ninth. New York loaded the bases, and Fred Merkle registered a long hit to score three and tie the score. In the 10th, Buck Weaver tried scoring on a squeeze play, but was out at home. In the bottom of the 11th, Wiltse tripled for the Giants with none out and scored on Magee's hit.

1914 Giants-White Sox Tour Results

Brisbane
Jan. 1 - New York 2, Chicago 1.
Sydney
Jan. 3 - Chicago 5, New York 4. Chicago 10, NSW 1.
Jan. 5 - Chicago 10, New York 5. New York 15, NSW 2.
Melbourne
Jan. 7 - New York 12, Chicago 8. New York 18, Victoria 0.
Jan. 8 - New York 4, Chicago 3 (11 innings). Chicago 16, Victoria 3.

The Impact of World War I

After the 1914 tour, World War I set Australian baseball back for years. There had been talk of John McGraw returning in 1916, but that opportunity was lost. Still, some baseball was played in Australia.

In late February 1915, Americans and Australians staged an exhibition, in connection with the police and fire brigade's patriotic carnival at the Sydney agricultural show. No netting protected spectators. A deflected pitch went into the crowd, striking a woman on the head. Ambulance men hurried to the scene, but the woman was not seriously hurt. A few moments later another ball struck a male spectator on the shoulder. Minister for Health Fred Flowers rushed onto the field and shouted "stop this silly game." Play halted at once.

When Americans and Australians fought side-by-side in the war, they played baseball on the battlefields of the Somme in France. The Australian 7th Brigade and the American 137th Regiment and the 63rd Division played five games in May 1918.

From 1918 through 1925, several American and Japanese battleships visited Australia and played some baseball. On the local scene, local leagues again formed in NSW, Victoria, and South Australia, with interstate competition again flourishing. In 1922, an attempt to start baseball in Queensland was made, including three games against NSW. The Queenslanders failed to score in any of the contests, and baseball died out again in that State.

The 1925 American Fleet Visit

The 1908 Great White Fleet had a major impact on both baseball and Australia, and in 1925 American battleships undertook another tour. The fleet arrived in Australia on July 23, 1925. The majority of the 43-vessel fleet docked in Melbourne, while the rest went to Sydney. Besides baseball, many other activities were undertaken, including American football, ice hockey, and basketball. It was said that there were 525 baseballers onboard.

Games were played between the ships' teams, and against some of the local sides, with the highlight being a three "test" series between Australia and a fleet for the Hugh J. Ward Shield. Australia did not lose a game, while the eight games between fleet sides and locals were split.

The first test was played in Melbourne on July 25 against the USS Pennsylvania. Darkness ended the game at 4-4 after nine innings. Ryder from Australia homered in the fifth to the crowd's delight. When he stepped to the plate again, a spectator called out "come on Babe Ruth, another homer," which caused great merriment. Alas, mighty Ryder struck out.

Australia won the second test, 14-6, against the USS Omaha on July 29. They took the final test, too, besting the Richmond Squadron, 13-2. Australian pitcher Ron Sharpe struck out 13, while a batter named Lansdowne had five hits.

The 1928 Stanford and 1929 Multnomah Tour

On July 26, 1928, Stanford University arrived in Sydney with 13 players (including four pitchers) aged between 20 and 24, and manager Harry Wolters, a former major leaguer. Stanford's visit was just part of Australia's biggest baseball carnival. The annual Interstate series between NSW, South Australia and Victoria was played in Sydney starting July 21. Shortly after Stanford left, the Australian University Baseball Championship took place in mid-August.

Stanford lost its first game against Victoria, but then went undefeated, including a three-test series against Australia. Stanford won 13-6 in front of a crowd of 15,000. Stanford also won the second test, 2-1 in 10 innings. On Aug. 18, Stanford won the final test, 7-0.

Almost a year later (Aug. 7, 1929) another American team arrived in Sydney—the Multnomah Athletic Association baseball team, from Portland, Ore. The side stayed a month, remaining undefeated, with a 5-5 tie with "Metropolitan"—a five-inning game played in heavy rain at Newcastle—the only blemish. Again a three-test series was played against Australia.

Multnomah won the first two tests easily, 4-1, on Aug. 17, and, 10-4, on Aug. 24. The third test (Aug. 31) was much more exciting. The score was 4-4 into seventh, but Multnomah pulled away for another 10-4 victory. The Multnomah team was a class side, and easily bettered its opposition in nearly all the games. Obviously, Australians still had a long way to go.

The Claxton Shield

Although Japanese and American ships visited Australia over the next few years, the main focus of Australian baseball was the annual interstate series between NSW, South Australia and Victoria. For many years, South Australia had been the easy-beat of these series. In 1934,

Norm Claxton, a renowned South Australian sportsman, donated a shield in his name to be awarded to the winning State in the newly named "Claxton Shield Series."

Norm Claxton had been a prominent Australian Rules Footballer with North Adelaide, a State cricketer, one of the State's best baseballers, and the winner of the Bay Sheffield sprint in 1900—an annual South Australia professional footrace. He had also been president of the South Australian Baseball League for many years and that organization's patron when he donated his shield.

The first State to win the shield three times in a row would keep it. To Claxton's joy, not only did South Australia come out of the wilderness to win the inaugural first series in 1934, it also won the next two. It was then decided to award the shield annually. Except for the war years, the Claxton Shield was played annually until the Australian Baseball League superseded State competition in 1989-90. There were 50 Claxton Shield competitions, with both Victoria and South Australia winning 15 times.

In 1937 Western Australia joined, and in 1939 Queensland also competed. Western Australia missed the first series in 1946, while Queensland did not return until 1950. In 1981 Northern Territory entered a team for the first time, while in the final Shield series in 1989 the Australian Capital Territory entered a side.

In one of the most exciting days in Australian baseball history, Victoria played a doubleheader of extra-inning games on the last day of the Claxton Shield in 1935. NSW defeated Victoria, 2-1, in 11 innings, and then a 15-inning scoreless draw, between Victoria and South Australia, clinched the shield for the Southerners. South Australia's Ron Sharpe and Victoria's M. Carr pitched shutouts.

In 1962 America's Helms Foundation originated the Ron Sharpe Medal to honor Sharpe, a leading South Australian player. The medal is awarded to the best player in the Claxton Shield.

Claxton Shield Winners

Year	State	Year	State	Year	State	Year	State
1934	SA	1952	WA	1964	SA	1977	WA
1935	SA	1953	NSW	1965	Vic	1978	WA
1936	SA	1954	Vic	1966	SA	1979	WA
1937	NSW	1955	NSW	1967	SA	1980	SA
1938	NSW	1956	Vic	1968	Vic	1981	Vic
1939	NSW	1957	SA	1969	SA	1982	Qld
1946	NSW	1958	Vic	1970	SA	1983	Qld
1947	Vic	1959	SA	1971	SA	1984	Vic
1948	Vic	1960	SA	1972	Vic	1985	WA
1949	Vic	1961	SA	1973	Vic	1986	Vic
1950	NSW	1962	Vic	1974	Vic	1987	Qld
1951	NSW	1963	NSW	1975	WA	1988	Qld
				1976	SA	1989	NSW

South Australia - SA, New South Wales - NSW, Victoria - Vic, Queensland - Qld, Western Australia - WA

Helms Award—The Ron Sharpe Medal

Year	Player - State	Year	Player - State
1962	Anthony Strand, NSW	1976	Alan Albury, Qld
1963	Kevin Cantwell, NSW	1977	Ronald Owon, Vic
1964	Adrian Pearce, SA	1978	Ray Michell, WA
1965	Graeme Deany, Vic	1979	Brian Wonnacott, Vic
1966	Kevin Greatrex, SA	1980	John Galloway, SA
1967	Garry Thompson, SA	1981	John Hodges, Vic
1968	John Swanson, Vic	1982	Geoffrey Martin, Qld
1969	Neil Page, SA	1983	Doug Mateljan, WA
1970	Paul Russell, NSW	1984	Brett Ward, Vic
1971	Ron McIver, Vic	1985	Tony. Stall, WA
1972	Donald Knapp, WA	1986	Lindsay Orford, Vic
1973	David Mundy, SA	1987	Dave Nilsson, Qld
1974	Neil Buszard, Vic	1988	Tony Adamson, WA
1975	Laurence Home, Qld	1989	Richard Vagg, Vic

Expansion into Other States

In 1936 Western Australia and Queensland both started baseball competitions independently of each other. After an MCC cricket tour in 1935, where they played Western Australia in Perth, the home side showed many flaws in their fielding. Burt Kortland, who had played cricket and baseball, (for the 1909 champions, Tottenham Hotspur), in England, helped form the WABL in 1936 to refine the fielding of cricketers in the winter. Baseball had been played in Western Australia in the 1920s, but it had not amounted to anything like a regular competition.

Mack Gilley immigrated from America to Queensland in 1936 and immediately began organizing clubs, leading to the formation of the Queensland Baseball League. Credited with starting 45 baseball teams during and after the war, Gilley also arranged the export of $1.5 million worth of wooden bats to the United States during a time of American wood shortages.

Going into World War II, five major Australian States now played at the highest level. Then as now, these five States formed the main body of Australian baseball. The game was later played in Northern Territory, but except for the 1980s when it played in the Claxton Shield, it has not developed further.

American Influence during World War II

Though sport generally declined through the World War II, baseball had an opportunity to develop because of the presence of many American battleships in Australia. Several games were played between local and American teams, with some American teams even joining local associations and playing for local teams.

On April 25, 1942, a U.S. military team, defeated a NSW side in 12 innings, 3-2, before 5,000 spectators in Sydney. At one point, the American coach, annoyed at an umpire's call, strode out, and with a cloth wiped the umpire's eyes.

Other States, including Western Australia, witnessed several international games. American teams proved too strong for WA, but on July 4, 1942, two American teams ("Fremantle" and "Cottesloe") played a 60-minute 2-2 match at Subiaco Oval, followed by an Australian Football game between two army teams.

After the war, many Americans settled in Australia, influencing the local baseball scene, especially the game's finer points. American sailors still visited Australian shores, playing against locals, with games becoming almost an annual event for several years after the war.

Night Baseball

Night baseball was the single most important initiative popularizing the sport in Australia, starting in South Australia and soon spreading elsewhere despite lighting levels that were often poor.

In South Australia, the 11 district clubs from the winter competition combined to form six clubs to play on Wednesdays at Norwood Oval in the summer. Attendance for these games hovered around 5,000, even reaching a

crowd of 10,000 on one occasion.

Two matches were played each night, with many other novelty games played to attract spectators. There were All-Star games, the "Ladies" against the "Jockeys", "Schoolboys" against "Veterans", and "State Cricketers" against "State Baseballers." Perhaps the biggest draw was the annual State night baseball championship for the Chrysler Cup. In the nine years of this championship, South Australia won every year. The first interstate game played under lights, on Dec. 12, 1952, saw Victoria defeat South Australia 6-5.

NSW had trouble establishing night baseball. A group separate from the State body attempted to start a night league, but the conflicts restricted night baseball's success. Western Australia ran a fairly successful night league until its major competition switched to summer baseball in 1963. Victoria ran its night competition along similar lines to South Australia. After 16 successful night baseball seasons, a switch to summer competition saw club baseball supersede the successful night league in South Australia from the 1968-69 season.

Night baseball changed the face of the sport. Two significant tours in the 1950s, for different reasons, gave Australia further tastes of international baseball. In the 1960s the televising of games also increased the game's popularity.

The 1954 Tokyo Giants Tour

The Tokyo Giants toured Australia in 1954. Though they were a class outfit, memories of the war remained and the team was not well received, with poor attendance at games. There were some misgivings about the tour (the president of the Returned Soldiers League made some unfavorable comments), but the government felt it was time to heal old wounds. Prime Minister Robert Menzies, with his Minister for the Interior, Kent Hughes—a former Japanese P.O.W.—personally welcomed the Giants.

On Nov. 12, 1954 Tokyo demolished Queensland State, 10-1, before only 500 spectators. Three easy victories over Sydney teams followed. Then came their first "test" against Australia on Nov. 17. The score was 8-8 after nine innings. Unfortunately, the Giants scored six in the 11th to win.

On Nov. 19 the Giants won, 27-6, against a local combination. Two days later they defeated Australia, 13-1, before only 700 people—the best crowd so far. With wet weather in Melbourne, and no promise of better crowds, the tour was cancelled, and players caught the first available flight to Manila.

The USA Olympic Tour of Australia—1956

Prior to the 1956 Melbourne Olympics, a side was chosen from the United States Far East Command stationed in Japan for an invitation game. The Americans sent 18 players, all with college experience. They arrived in Sydney on Nov. 22 and played two warm-up games against NSW, winning both by comfortable margins.

A six-inning demonstration baseball game between Australia and the Americans was played at the main

Olympic Stadium on Dec. 1. It has been claimed that a record baseball crowd attended, but in fact the crowd was still filing in as the game finished, and not even a quarter of the 100,000 spectators had come to watch baseball. The U.S. won, 11-5, with pitcher Van Sutton hitting a grand slam in the third. Australia's Norm "Chalkie" White hit a home run in the second.

After the Olympic demonstration, the teams traveled to Adelaide. The U.S. won the first game, 5-4, with only one of the American runs being earned. In game two, the U.S. scored one run in the first inning on a dropped catch, but was shut out the rest of the way, with Aussy Eddie Moule striking out 14, and allowing only three hits and six walks. Norm Tyshing had tripled home the tying run in the second inning. In an exciting finish, he doubled home the winning run in the ninth for the 2-1 win. The last Adelaide test, and the other two Melbourne tests, resulted in easy American victories.

The Americans had lost only one game, but it was the first victory by Australians over an official American team (they had won games against U.S. naval teams in 1908 and 1925, but the 1956 side was officially representing the United States). Americans conducted clinics for local schoolboys, and practiced with the Australian side, gestures that helped develop the game on the continent. Australians were still fairly raw, but Americans felt their natural talent would help them to compete with top-level competition in the near future.

The Change to Summer Baseball

Summer baseball had been tried in various States, but winter generally remained the main season for baseball until the 1960s. In 1963-64 Western Australia became the first State to permanently move to summer competition. South Australia followed in 1968-69, but the Eastern States resisted until a 1973 directive from the Australian Baseball Council proclaimed that summer was Australia's official season.

In New South Wales, Victoria, and, to a lesser extent, South Australia, a core group of players refused to give up winter ball. So even today, winter competitions flourish. Many play in both seasons, while winter competition also allows cricketers to enjoy both sports, since cricket is played in the summer.

Summer baseball's introduction also allowed Australia more international competition, with nations in the Southern Hemisphere playing in the summer, as is generally the case throughout the world.

Australia's International Development

Fuji Steel, a baseball side from the Japanese Industrial Leagues, visited in 1968. This series was the first of many, and with the Australian tour of the Philippines the following year, laid the foundation of Australia's international development. Several Japanese industrial teams played in Australia over the next decade while Australia also competed in the "Baseball Federation of Asia Series." These series prepared Australia for international competition, and in 1978, Australia played in its first

World Baseball Championships.

Australians played in a warm-up series in Holland — the Haarlem Baseball Tournament—before the WBC, which was held in Italy. Australia won only two of its 10 games, finishing ninth in the 11-nation tournament. But the series laid the foundation for an international future.

Another important development was the international exposure of its juniors. A Japanese high school visited in 1975, playing matches against Australia's under-17 teams. In 1976, an Australian squad of under-18 players toured Florida. Australia continued sending junior sides to America, and in 1979, some Australian coaches toured Florida.

Australia competed in the WBC in Japan (1980) and South Korea (1982), but did not compete again until 1994. In the interim they did play in the Intercontinental Cup and the Asian Baseball Series—including hosting one series in 1984-85 in Perth.

The biggest news in Australia's junior international history occurred in 1981, when an Australian under-19 side won the bronze medal at the World Friendship Series, played in Newark, Ohio. After losing the opener to the United States, 10-7, Australia defeated Taiwan, Italy, El Salvador, Guatemala, and finally Venezuela, for the bronze.

With Cuba boycotting the 1988 Seoul Olympics, Australia was included in the baseball competition, a demonstration sport. After winning, 7-6, over Canada, Australia lost, 10-2, to the USA and 2-1 (10 innings) to South Korea. Australia finished fifth in the eight-nation tournament.

In 1989, Australia's AAA (under 19) side won a bronze medal at the World Championships in Canada. Junior "World" bronze medals also went to Australia in 1995. The under-19 team lost the semifinal to the U.S. and then defeated South Korea, 6-5, for the bronze medal in Fenway Park. In 1997 the under-16's defeated Korea for the bronze by a 4-3 score, after losing to Cuba in the semifinal in Taiwan, 11-3.

In 1994, Australia's senior team returned to the World Championships in Nicaragua. After losing its first three games, Australia won three straight, but lost to Cuba in the last qualifying round to finish fifth.

For the first time in 1995, professional players represented their country. In December, 1995, an Aussy team played in a professional tournament—the Asia Pacific Super Baseball Tournament. Major league players Graeme Lloyd, Dave Nilsson, and Craig Shipley donned the green and gold together for the first time (although Lloyd did not pitch because of injury). Australia lost, 6-0, to the Han Wha Eagles, and, 5-0, to the Daiei Hawks.

With the 1996 Olympic baseball tournament a full medal sport, Australia had to play several qualifying rounds. In the Oceania Championships, Australia disposed of New Zealand (14-0 and 25-0), American Samoa (20-0, 17-1, 13-0, and 10-0) and then Guam (17-1, 13-0, and 6-0). In the deciding series, Australia qualified by defeating South Africa (9-0, 7-0, and 7-0).

Although competitive in most matches, Australia won only two of its seven in the Atlanta Olympics. One win was against eventual silver medallist Japan. Even against gold medallist Cuba, Australia was level-begging (tied) with them after five innings, before a rain delay.

The year 1997 will go down in Australian baseball history as a milestone year. The nation won its first senior international medal—the Intercontinental Cup's bronze. The event was held in Barcelona, Spain, and Australia had a fantastic qualifying series, losing only one game. It lost the semifinal to Japan, but defeated America, 7-6, in 10 innings. Australia's Paul Gonzalez led the tournament in batting and won Most Valuable Player honors.

Australia had high hopes in the 1998 World Baseball Championships in Italy, especially after battling Cuba in a 6-5 loss in 10 innings in the final of the Haarlem Baseball Tournament, held just before the WBC. In a sensational start, Australia won its opening five games before losing a 10-inning heartbreaker to Italy, 9-8, in the quarterfinals.

World Baseball Championships

First played in 1938, the championships had been contested every two years since 1978, (Australia's first as a competitor), until it became a full medal sport at the 1992 Olympics. It is now held every four years.

Australian WBC record

Year	Aust Pos.	Venue	Gold Medal
1978	9th	Italy (25th WBC)	Cuba
1980	8th	Japan	Cuba
1982	10th	South Korea	South Korea
1984	did not qualify	Cuba	Cuba
1986	did not qualify	Netherlands	Cuba
1988	did not qualify	Italy	Cuba
1990	did not qualify	Canada	Cuba
1994	12th	Nicaragua	Cuba
1996	7th	Italy	Cuba

The Australian Baseball League

The Australian Baseball League arose out of controversy. Brisbane sports promoter John Brown attempted to run a National League over the summer of 1988-89, to replace the Claxton Shield. Over the previous summer the Shield series had been played in a home-and-away format similar to a national competition, which was the first step towards the ABL.

With some States in conflict with the Australian Baseball Federation, and confusion reigning, Australian baseball became vulnerable. In the end, an old style Claxton Shield series was held in Sydney in the summer of 1988-89, while the ABF sanctioned the ABL to begin during the following summer, with club sides rather than State teams.

On Oct. 27, 1989, the ABL played its first game at Parry Field in Western Australia between the Adelaide Giants and the Perth Heat. Before 4,800 fans, Adelaide's Tim Day collected the first hit and Perth's Heath Gillard hit the league's first homer. Adelaide, aided by Ron Nelson's two two-run homers, were 8-5 winners.

From the beginning, teams were allowed four American imports, and from the second season, each team had affiliated with a major league franchise. Rules have since been modified, with Americans originally being eligible if they had played A-ball, then Double A, and finally open. Today the standard of play is equal to America's Double A leagues.

Initially, the top two finishers played for the championship. Starting in 1992-93, a playoff featuring the top four clubs determined which teams qualified for the championship final. The Melbourne Reds have been the most successful club, winning three championships, two as Waverley. Every long-term club, except Adelaide, has won a title. During the 1997-98 season, an All-Star contest, where the best of the Americans played the best of the Australians, was instituted. This may become an annual event.

The ABL Clubs

ADELAIDE GIANTS: Twice made the playoffs, but bombed out in straight sets both times.

BRISBANE BANDITS: Won a championship in the first season they reached the playoffs in 1993-94.

CANBERRA BUSHRANGERS: Replaced the Monarchs in second ABL season as the Melbourne Bushrangers. After three unsuccessful seasons in Melbourne, were transplanted to Canberra, where they lasted two more seasons, again finishing near the bottom.

GOLD COAST COUGARS: Known as the Brisbane Clippers in the inaugural ABL season. In the second season, they were bought by the Daikio company, becoming the Gold Coast Dolphins, playing at Carrara. After dominating the league in 1990-91, they lost the championship to Perth, but the following season the roles were reversed. In 1992-93 they were still the Gold Coast Dolphins, but without Daikio ownership. In 1992-93 and 1993-94 they operated as the East Coast Cougars, and have since been the Gold Coast Cougars. The Cougars ran second in 1997-98.

HUNTER EAGLES: The new kids on the block, the Eagles play out of Newcastle in New South Wales, but have won only 35 of their 157 games in three seasons for two wooden spoons (last-place finishes). The Eagles will not participate in the 1998-99 season.

MELBOURNE MONARCHS: Lost the inaugural final to the Waverley Reds. After suspension, because of financial problems, the Monarchs returned for 1992-93 with a bang, winning the championship. After four losing seasons, the Monarchs finished minor premiers last season, but dipped out in the playoffs.

MELBOURNE REDS: Originally known as Waverley, the Reds changed to Melbourne in 1995-96, after winning the 1989-90 and 1994-95 championships. As Melbourne it finished second in 1995-96, last in 1996-97, and champion in 1997-98—a real roller coaster ride for supporters.

PERTH HEAT: Has won two championships, but should have won more as it has been the most consistent finals club in ABL history. Has three times lost the championship series—twice when favored. The only club with a winning record each season, the Heat has only missed the playoffs twice.

SYDNEY STORM: Entering the league as the Parramatta Patriots, they just missed out on the playoff game in that first season, but fell down the list in the second year. A name change to the Sydney Blues brought a wooden spoon in the third year. The Blues contended from 1992-93 through 1996-97, reaching the playoffs each season, and winning the big one in 1995-96. For 1997-98, Sydney

changed its name to the Storm.

SYDNEY WAVE: Started as the Sydney Metros in the first season. They won only 10 of 39 games to finish last in 1989-90, and then lost seven of those wins for breaking ABL rules by playing unregistered players. A name change to Sydney Wave for the second season saw a slight improvement, but could not save the Wave from dissolution.

ABL Playoff Results

ABL 1989-90

TEAM	G	W	L	GB	W%
Waverley Reds	40	34	6	-	.850
Melbourne Monarchs	40	24	16	10	.600
Parramatta Patriots	40	22	18	12	.550
Perth Heat	42	23	19	12	.548
Adelaide Giants	38	19	19	14	.500
Brisbane Clippers	37	16	21	16.5	.432
Brisbane Bandits	42	18	24	17	.429
Sydney Metros	39	3	36	30.5	.077

Sydney lost seven wins due to breaking ABL rules, wins awarded to Giants (two), Bandits (two), Clippers, Monarchs and Patriots.
FINAL - Best of five: Waverley 3, Melbourne 1 (3-1, 3-4, 9-3, 3-2).

ABL 1990-91

TEAM	G	W	L	GB	W%
Gold Coast Dolphins	40	31	9	-	.775
Perth Heat	42	28	14	4	.666
Adelaide Giants	42	26	16	6	.619
Waverley Reds	38*	20	18	10	.526
Parramatta Patriots	41	16	25	15.5	.390
Sydney Wave	42	16	26	16	.381
Brisbane Bandits	39	13	26	17.5	.333
Melbourne Bushrangers	38*	11	27	19	.289

* Indicate tied games.
FINAL - Best of five: Perth 3, Gold Coast 2 (6-4, 7-3, 3-4, 2-6, 11-1).

ABL 1991-92

TEAM	G	W	L	GB	W%
Perth Heat	47	36	11	-	.765
Gold Coast Dolphins	47	28	19	8	.595
Waverley Reds	46*	27	19	8.5	.586
Brisbane Bandits	44*	22	22	12.5	.500
Adelaide Giants	44	20	24	14.5	.454
Melbourne Bushrangers	45	18	27	17	.400
Sydney Wave	44	17	27	17.5	.386
Sydney Blues	45	13	32	22	.288

* Indicate tied games.
FINAL - Best of five: Gold Coast 3, Perth 1 (8-1, 17-10, 5-7, 4-3).

ABL 1992-93

TEAM	G	W	L	GB	W%
Perth Heat	48	30	18	-	.625
Melbourne Monarchs	47	28	19	1.5	.597
Sydney Blues	44	25	19	3	.568
Waverley Reds	47*	26	21	3.5	.553
Brisbane Bandits	46	25	21	4	.543
Gold Coast Dolphins	45	19	26	9.5	.422
Adelaide Giants	46*	19	27	10	.413
Melbourne Bushrangers	47	13	34	16.5	.276

Playoffs - Best of three
Melbourne 2, Sydney 1 (6-5, 6-8, 7-3).
Perth 2, Waverley 0 (7-2, 6-3).
FINAL - Best of three: Melbourne 2, Perth 0 (4-2, 1-0).

ABL 1993-94

TEAM	G	W	L	GB	W%
Sydney Blues	54	35	19	-	.648
Perth Heat	56	36	20	-	.643
Brisbane Bandits	55	34	21	1.5	.618
Adelaide Giants	56	30	26	6	.536
Melbourne Monarchs	55*	29	26	6.5	.527
Waverley Reds	53*	22	31	12.5	.415
Canberra Bushrangers	55	17	38	18.5	.309
East Coast Cougars	52	15	37	19	.288

* Indicate tied games.

Playoffs - Best of three
Sydney 2, Adelaide 0 (2-1, 11-8).
Brisbane 2, Perth 1 (7-1, 1-3, 9-6).
FINAL - Best of three: Brisbane 2, Sidney 0 (5-1, 10-9).

ABL 1994-95

TEAM	G	W	L	GB	W%
Waverley Reds	60*	44	14	-	.750
Perth Heat	63	45	18	1.5	.714
East Coast Cougars	61	34	27	11.5	.557
Sydney Blues	61	34	27	11.5	.557
Adelaide Giants	62	32	30	14	.516
Melbourne Monarchs	64*	27	36	19.5	.430
Brisbane Bandits	60	24	36	21	.400
Canberra Bushrangers	61*	19	41	26	.320
Hunter Eagles	64	17	47	30	.266

* Indicate tied games.
Bandits lost two wins due to breaking ABL rules, wins awarded to Bushrangers and Cougars.
Playoffs - Best of three
Waverley 2, Sydney 0 (5-1, 7-4).
Perth 2, East Coast 1 (7-3, 5-6, 17-6).
FINAL - Best of three: Waverley 2, Perth 0 (5-1, 4-2).

ABL 1995-96

TEAM	G	W	L	GB	W%
Brisbane Bandits	45	29	16	-	.644
Sydney Blues	47	28	19	2	.596
Perth Heat	46	26	20	3.5	.565
Melbourne Reds	48	27	21	3.5	.563
Gold Coast Cougars	44	23	21	5.5	.527
Melbourne Monarchs	48	24	24	6.5	.500
Adelaide Giants	46	21	25	8.5	.457
Hunter Eagles	46	7	39	22.5	.152

Monarchs and Bandits lost a win each to Reds and Cougars due to breaking ABL rules.
Playoffs - Best of three
Melbourne 2, Brisbane 0 (10-8, 15-12).
Sydney 2, Perth 1 (5-2, 2-3, 6-5).
FINAL - Best of three: Sydney Blues 2, Melbourne 0 (8-4, 5-2).

ABL 1996-97

TEAM	G	W	L	GB	W%
Perth Heat	60	40	20	-	.666
Adelaide Giants	59	36	23	3.5	.610
Brisbane Bandits	60	33	27	7	.550
Sydney Blues	59	32	27	7.5	.542
Gold Coast Cougars	59	31	28	8.5	.525
Melbourne Monarchs	57	28	29	10.5	.491
Hunter Eagles	58	18	40	21	.310
Melbourne Reds	58	17	41	22	.293

Playoffs - Best of three
Brisbane 2, Adelaide 0 (9-1, 9-6).
Perth 2, Sydney 0 (6-5, 6-4).
FINAL - Best of three: Perth 2, Brisbane 1 (9-1, 4-6, 9-5).

ABL 1997-98

TEAM	G	W	L	GB	W%
Melbourne Monarchs	52	32	20	-	.615
Sydney Storm	54	32	22	1	.592
Melbourne Reds	51	30	21	1.5	.588
Gold Coast Cougars	53	31	22	1.5	.584
Perth Heat	53	30	23	2.5	.566
Adelaide Giants	53	26	27	6.5	.490
Brisbane Bandits	53	20	33	12.5	.377
Hunter Eagles	53	10	43	22.5	.188

Playoffs - Round Robin
Gold Coast 7, Melbourne Monarchs 5
Melbourne Reds 18, Sydney 5
Melbourne Reds 2, Gold Coast 1
Sydney 5, Melbourne Monarchs 1
Gold Coast 8, Sydney Storm 4
Melbourne Monarchs 12, Melbourne Reds 5.
FINAL - Best of three: Melbourne Reds 2, Gold Coast 0 (4-3, 4-0).

Australians and the Major Leagues

Shayne Bennett: Signed by the Red Sox in 1994, Bennett was traded to Montreal in 1996. With the Expos, Bennett made his major league debut in 1997. In the ABL, Ben-nett won the "Reliever of the Year" in 1995-96, and was named to the league's All-Star team. He also shares the league record for striking out five batters in one inning.

Bennett's ABL Pitching Statistics

Year	Team	G	IP	H	R	ER	ERA	W	L	S
1993-94	Adelaide Giants	9	11.1	14	5	5	3.97	2	0	4
1994-95	East Coast Cougars	22	74.1	70	38	30	3.63	3	6	1
1995-96	East Coast Cougars	19	23.1	31	16	15	5.79	1	4	10
1996-97	Adelaide Giants	9	43.2	36	12	10	2.06	7	1	0
Totals		59	152.2	151	71	60	3.54	13	11	15
Playoff Games		G	IP	H	R	ER	ERA	W	L	S
1994-95	East Coast Cougars	2	2.2	2	0	0	0.00	0	0	1
1996-97	Adelaide Giants	1	7	4	4	1	1.29	0	1	0
Totals		3	9.2	6	4	1	0.93	0	1	1

Mark Ettles: Mark had a "cup of coffee" with the Padres in 1993, relieving in 14 games and recording the first major league win by an Australian-born player. In seven seasons for the ABL's Perth Heat, Ettles won 1991-92 ABL "Reliever of the Year" honors and made two All-Star teams. In 1996-97, he won two playoff games as part of the Heat's championship team.

Ettles' ABL Pitching Statistics

Year	Team	G	IP	H	R	ER	ERA	W	L	S
1989-90	Perth Heat	3	14.2	12	7	5	3.07	1	0	0
1991-92	Perth Heat	12	15.2	15	5	4	2.30	1	0	11
1992-93	Perth Heat	10	9	6	3	2	2.00	0	1	4
1993-94	Perth Heat	1	1	0	0	0	0.00	0	0	0
1994-95	Perth Heat	14	78.2	72	41	39	4.46	6	1	0
1995-96	Perth Heat	7	11.2	13	9	8	6.17	2	1	0
1996-97	Perth Heat	19	28.2	24	15	11	3.45	3	3	6
Totals		66	159.1	142	80	69	3.90	13	6	21
Playoff Games		G	IP	H	R	ER	ERA	W	L	S
1992-93	Perth Heat	2	2	0	0	0	0.00	0	0	1
1995-96	Perth Heat	2	2	2	3	0	0.00	0	1	1
1996-97	Perth Heat	2	2.2	1	0	0	0.00	2	0	0
Totals		6	6.2	3	3	0	0.00	2	1	2
Championship Games		G	IP	H	R	ER	ERA	W	L	S
1996/97	Perth Heat	1	2.1	5	3	3	11.59	0	1	0
Totals		1	2.1	5	3	3	11.59	0	1	0

Mark Hutton: Hutton signed with the Yankees on Dec. 15, 1988 as a free agent. The first Australian-born pitcher to start a major league game, he was traded to the Florida Marlins in mid-season 1996. In mid season 1997, Hutton was again traded, this time to Colorado. He was picked up in 1998 by Cincinnati. Hutton has played only one ABL season, but he may return to the league.

Hutton's ABL Pitching Statistics

Year	Team	G	IP	H	R	ER	ERA	W	L	S
1994-95	Adelaide Giants	11	54	58	35	32	5.33	5	2	0
Totals		11	54	58	35	32	5.33	5	2	0

Graeme Lloyd: Lloyd signed with the Toronto organization on Australia Day (Jan. 26) 1988. After a trade to Milwaukee, in 1993 he became the first Australian to pitch in the major leagues and won Brewers "Rookie of the Year" honors.

After a trade to the Yankees, Lloyd pitched four times in the 1996 World Series with one win and a 0.00 ERA. In the ABL, Lloyd captured the championship series MVP in 1991, when he won two games in Perth's three games to two victory. He holds the ABL lifetime record with 13 shutouts.

Lloyd's ABL Pitching Statistics

Year	Team	G	IP	H	R	ER	ERA	W	L	S
1989-90	Melbourne Monarchs	1	0.1	0	0	0	0.00	0	0	1
1990-91	Perth Heat	9	55	43	21	16	2.62	6	1	0
1991-92	Perth Heat	11	60	45	35	18	2.70	6	2	0
1992-93	Perth Heat	10	61	52	17	10	1.48	8	1	0
1993-94	Perth Heat	6	9.2	12	9	5	4.65	0	1	4
1994-95	Perth Heat	10	47.2	33	12	12	2.27	5	2	2
1995-96	Brisbane Bandits	10	16.1	14	6	4	2.20	2	2	3
Totals		57	250	199	100	65	2.34	27	9	10
Playoff Games		G	IP	H	R	ER	ERA	W	L	S
1992-93	Perth Heat	1	8	6	2	2	2.25	1	0	0
1993-94	Perth Heat	1	2	0	0	0	0.00	0	0	1
1994-95	Perth Heat	1	9	8	3	1	1.00	1	0	0
1995-96	Brisbane Bandits	2	3	9	6	5	15.00	0	2	0
Totals		5	22	23	11	8	3.27	2	2	1
Championship Games		G	IP	H	R	ER	ERA	W	L	S
1989-90	Melbourne Monarchs	1	2.2	1	0	0	0.00	1	0	0
1990-91	Perth Heat	2	15	15	4	3	1.80	2	0	0
1991-92	Perth Heat	1	3.1	8	8	8	21.62	0	1	0
1994-95	Perth Heat	1	8	7	5	3	3.38	0	1	0
Totals		5	29	31	17	14	4.34	3	2	0

Dave Nilsson: Nilsson signed with Milwaukee as a non-drafted free agent, on Jan. 28, 1987. In 1991 Nilsson was named on the USA Today All-Prospect Team as a catcher when he hit .416 for El Paso in Double A, the highest average in pro ball. Nilsson made his major league debut on May 18, 1992, against Detroit with a three-run double, and four days later homered at Yankee Stadium. Nilsson was voted Brewers' MVP in 1994. In the ABL Nilsson has played on three championship teams for three clubs, won a batting title and a League MVP, made three All-Star teams, and hit three home runs in one game.

Nilsson's ABL Batting Statistics

Year	Team	G	AB	H	Ave	R	RBI	HR
1989-90	Brisbane Clippers	NA	34	119	33	.277	15	11
1990-91	Gold Coast Dolphins	40	135	54	.400	28	37	12
1991-92	Gold Coast Dolphins	20	62	25	.403	14	13	2
1992-93	Gold Coast Dolphins	10	25	4	.160	2	3	0
1993-94	Brisbane Bandits	NA	48	141	51	.362	36	47
1994-95	Waverley Reds	NA	54	160	62	.388	41	56
1995-96	Melbourne Reds	NA	11	32	8	.250	5	7
1996-97	Brisbane Bandits	NA	16	50	21	.420	15	10
Totals			233	724	356	156	184	48
Playoff Games		G	AB	H	Ave	R	RBI	HR
1993-94	Brisbane Bandits	3	15	5	.333	4	4	1
1994-95	Waverley Reds	2	6	1	.167	1	1	1
1996-97	Brisbane Bandits	2	9	4	.444	2	1	0
Totals		7	30	10	.333	7	6	2
Championship Games		G	AB	H	Ave	R	RBI	HR
1990-91	Gold Coast Dolphins	5	20	10	500	4	3	1
1991-92	Gold Coast Dolphins	4	13	5		3	4	0
1993-94	Brisbane Bandits	2	7	1	143	1	0	0
1994-95	Waverley Reds	2	7	3	429	1	2	0
1996-97	Brisbane Bandits	3	10	2	.200	0	1	0
Totals		16	57	21		9	10	1

Joseph J. Quinn: Born Christmas Day, 1864, in Sydney, Uncle Joe moved to the United States with his parents when he was a teenager. Quinn started his major league career with St Louis of the Union Association in 1884. He played for St. Louis, Boston, Baltimore, Cleveland, and Cincinnati in the National League, and Washington in the American League. He batted .261 with 30 homers and 796 RBIs in 17 seasons. Mainly a second baseman, he, nonetheless played most other positions. Quinn managed St. Louis in 1895 (39 of their 131 games for a 11-28 record), and Cleveland in 1899 (116 of 154 games for a 12-104 record).

Craig Shipley: Shipley, the 20th century's first Australian-born major leaguer, signed with Los Angeles in 1984, making his major league debut in 1986. He has also played for the Mets, Padres, Astros, and Angels but has yet to play in the Australian Baseball League, although his brother Mark is one of the ABL's top fielders.

Where Australia is Heading

The Australian Baseball League's future remains uncertain, with talk of expansion to include some Asian sides, or a complete re-draft of competition at the highest level in Australia. The ABL has had financial trouble, with travel costs eating into most team budgets. Private ownership of the league has been discussed, with offers coming in from an American consortium.

Two forthcoming international competitions are on tap. In November 1999, Sydney hosts the Intercontinental Cup at Homebush Stadium. The Olympic baseball tournament follows in 2000.

Australian women's baseball predates World War II, but lost popularity to softball. Women again are taking up baseball in the 1990s, with many teams forming in the Eastern States, and individuals also playing in men's leagues.

Australia has carefully nurtured its juniors over the past 20 years, allowing top players to progress through junior ranks into the senior Australian side with little hindrance. South Australia's Seaton High School features baseball on its curriculum, while most States offer a baseball scholarship at sports institutes.

Australians are determined to reach the pinnacle of baseball—and have made much progress toward that goal over the decades.

## CHAPTER 19

History of the Korean Baseball Organization

Thomas St. John

In the early 1980s then-president of Korea Chun Du-hwan and his advisors sought to boost Chun's sagging reputation among the citizenry and, more importantly, to distract the Korean people from the political turmoil plaguing the country. To help further their goal, they decided to form a professional baseball league, the Korean Baseball Organization (KBO). In 1982 the KBO began with six teams, each sponsored by a chaebol, or giant business conglomerate. The following 13 teams have comprised the KBO since its inception in 1982:

> Lotte Giants (1982-present)
> Samsung Lions (1982-present)
> Haitai Tigers (1982-present)
> OB Bears (1982-present)
> MBC Dragons (1982-1989), LG Twins
>   (1990-present)
> Binggrae Eagles (1986-1993) Hanhwa Eagles
>   (1994-present)
> Ssangbangwool Raiders (1991-present)
> Sammi Superstars (1982-1995), Chongbo Pintos
>   (1986-1987)
> Taepyungyang Dolphins (1988-1995), Hyundai
>   Unicorns (1996-present).

Operations, Games, Playoffs and Players

The KBO's season consists of 126 games, playoffs, and the Korean Series in late October. The top four teams in the eight-team league compete in postseason competition. The first-place team is guaranteed a spot in the Series. Third- and fourth-place teams play each other in a three-game series and the first team to win two games plays a best-of-five series against the second-place team with the winner going on to the best-of-seven Korean Series.

All players sign one-year contracts and are effectively owned by their teams. They are not free to change teams or accept endorsements (of which the team gets half of the fee) without their team's approval. Holdouts are almost non-existent and most players are forced to accept what the club offers, though the amount is usually in line with what other teams are offering.

Salary ranges are determined by the previous year's performance and are raised and lowered accordingly. All rookies earn 20 million won ($15,000) per season while top players can expect signing bonuses of several hundred million won. The average salary is about 40 million won with the top being Samsung's Yang Jun-hyuk at 140 million won (about $105,000) a season.

Foreign Players

Beginning with the 1998 season, the KBO opened its doors to foreign players. By the end of the 1998 season, a total of 12 foreign players had taken the field. The first 10 were Joe Strong (Hyundai Unicorns), Scott Coolbaugh (Hyundai Unicorns), Mike Anderson (LG Twins), Doug Brady (Lotte Giants), Joel Chimelis (Hanhwa Eagles), Mike Busch, (Hanhwa Eagles), Scott Baker (Samsung Lions), Jose Parra (Samsung Lions), Edgar Cacerras (OB Bears), and Tyrone Woods (OB Bears). Later in the 1998 season, the Haitai Tigers added Sean Hare and LG signed Junior Felix.

Foreign players were met with anticipation, even loathing, before the season ever began. While the foreign player draft was going on in Florida in late 1997, the Korean economy took a downturn and needed bailing out by the International Monetary Fund (IMF). The whole nation began hoarding dollars and shunning everything foreign, including baseball players.

Teams released many older and popular players just to pay for the foreign players' salaries, which averaged about 133 million won ($100,000). Newspapers ran stories about how the imports would pollute Korea's national pastime and wouldn't be worth the money to pay and house them. As the first season with foreign players ended, reviews were mixed. Four of the 12 had excelled, four were mediocre and four made little impact on their teams due to injuries or not having enough playing time.

The Army Factor

Unlike any other country where professional baseball is played, Korea compels all able-bodied men, including baseball players, to serve in the armed services for 26 months. This has hurt the league and will continue to hurt its development until it is stopped. The situation is unlikely to change any time soon, however. Few exceptions have ever been given. Only the biggest names are excused from serving. Sun Dong-yol was given one because the

government, which was still overseeing the day-to-day operations of the KBO, decided Sun was better throwing baseballs than grenades. A few others received government pardons while others were allowed to play part-time.

During the 1995 season Lee Jeong-bum of the Haitai Tigers, just coming off the best season in KBO history, was not allowed to play in road games. He had to report to his unit when the team was on the road but was allowed to play all home contests. Eventually the public complained, arguing that if baseball players are exempt, why not other citizens as well? Authorities rescinded the rule soon thereafter and now all players are required to serve. Still, some players find ways out of their military obligations.

Some players like OB's Shim Jeong-su, who is one of the most physically fit players in the league, had to serve only six months. After extensive tests, it was determined that Shim had chronic sweaty palms and would not be able to hold an M-16 without the weapon flying out of his hands. So he was released early. This handicap, oddly enough, did not affect his grip on a bat. Another exception was granted to Lotte's Ju Hyung-kwang. Rumors claimed he had an irregular disk in his spine and would not be an effective soldier. This revelation seemed strange to many who had watched Ju win 18 games and strike out 221 batters the season before.

Since 1995, however, no players have been exempt from military service. Los Angeles Dodgers pitcher, Chan-ho Park, should also be changing uniforms very soon, as he is soon approaching his 27th birthday, the cut-off line for enlisting. He says he will willingly return home to serve, but the majority of citizens favor his exemption, opening the debate of when—and if—to grant exceptions at all.

The Haitai Dynasty

When speaking of baseball in Korea, the topic of the Haitai Tigers will almost certainly be brought up. In the 16 years of pro baseball in Korea, the Tigers have dominated by winning nine Korean Series titles. Many credit their success to Kim "the Elephant" Ung-young, the team's manager since 1983. Actually, Kim played only a small role in the Tigers' success. The real story lies in the dedication of a few men from the Cholla region (Korea's southwest corner) who put the area on the map.

In the annual high school baseball tournament, teams from Seoul usually dominated, with the odd exception from another city going all the way. The mere notion of a team from the Cholla region winning was absurd—or so it was thought. Early in the 1980s, a worker at KBO named Lee Young-il, originally from the Cholla region, wanted to see his hometown triumph and gain respectability. In the 1960s he had poured much of his family's wealth into Kunsan High School's baseball team and hired the best coach in the country, Choi Kwon-su, to manage it. Both men tirelessly promoted and strengthened the game in the Cholla region and in 1972 the unthinkable happened: they won the National Championship.

Then three years later another high school from Cholla won. From then on, the teams have gained great respectability and have produced the best players in the country. Most of the players from this area (including Kim Song-

han, Sun Dong-yol, Lee Kang-chul, and Lee Jeong-bum) went on to sign with the hometown Tigers, based in the city of Kwangju, and have since become legends.

Korea-Japan Supergame/Golden Series

Every four years, the best of Korea and Japan get together for a series of friendly games. The first time was in 1992 when the Japanese came to Korea. In 1996 the Koreans returned the favor, visiting Japan for six games. The 1996 series ended with each team posting two wins and two ties. The historic series marked the first time Koreans saw their ability inching closer to that of the Japanese. It was also the first matchup between Suzuki Ichiro of the Orix Blue Wave and his cross-country rival Lee Jeong-bum of the Haitai Tigers. The series is scheduled again in Korea in 2000.

November 1997 witnessed the biggest debacle in the history of Korean pro baseball. The mammoth Hyundai Electronics company sponsored the highly touted return of a national hero, Sun Dong-yol from Japan. It was heavily promoted in the newspapers and on television as the first time he had pitched in over two years. In addition to Sun, the best of the Orix Blue Wave (including Ichiro) and Chunichi Dragons accompanied him to play a team of Korean pros. About 1,000 police mobilized to keep the crowds from eclipsing Sun, but the promotions company ignored one very important detail: World Cup frenzy.

With Korea and Japan co-hosting the World Cup in 2002, a preview match between the two soccer rivals was the hottest ticket in town, easily selling out the main stadium's 100,000 seats. The game was scheduled to take place about 2:30 in the afternoon and the baseball game, just 300 meters away, was hosting the Golden Series featuring Sun. Final attendance figures were never made public, but it is estimated that under 2,000 people attended the baseball game. Sun was so visibly angry sitting on the bench, he refused to go in on the first day and only pitched one inning in the second game. A second Golden Series has not been scheduled.

Rising Stars

Samsung Lions first baseman Lee Seung-yup is only 23 and is already showing great promise as the future franchise player for the Lions. In only his second year he hit .329 with 170 hits, 32 home runs, and 114 RBIs in 126 games. In 1998 he put up similar numbers and is beginning to gain fame outside of Korea. No one should expect to see Lee showcasing his talents overseas, however, as the Samsung group who sponsors the team is not suffering financial difficulties and would gain nothing from releasing Lee from his contract.

Also making a run for diamond fame are Haitai closer Im Chang-young and starter Lee Dae-jin, who are expected to have their contracts sold to either a major league team or a Japanese team to raise money for the Haitai Group, which is operating in debt. (They have already sold the contracts of Sun Dong Yol and Lee Jeong-bum for a total of about $5 million per year.)

The KBO—Present and Future

The KBO flourished well into the 1990s, until attendance began sagging. The top factor was Chan-ho Park's debut with the Dodgers in 1994. Park was followed by pitching legend Sun Dong-yol, who left Korea in 1995 to try his luck in Japan. He was soon followed by former teammate Lee Jeong-bum who departed in 1997.

Also adding to KBO woes was the emergence of the Korean Basketball League (KBL) and the phenominal success of female golfer Se-ri Park. Each factor took a piece of the pie that KBO previously had all to itself, and regrettably the KBO has made few efforts to try to regain its lost market share.

STATISTICAL REGISTER

Korean Series

Champions		W–L–T	Win Pct	MVP
1982	OB Bears	56-24-0	.700	Kim You-dong (OF)
1983	Haitai Tigers	55-44-1	.556	Kim Bong-yeon (IF)
1984	Lotte Giants	50-48-2	.510	You Du-yol (OF)
1985	Samsung Lions	77-32-1	.706	(NO KOREAN SERIES)
1986	Haitai Tigers	67-37-4	.644	Kim Jeong-su (P)
1987	Haitai Tigers	55-48-5	.532	Kim Jeong-hwan (OF)
1988	Haitai Tigers	68-38-2	.639	Moon Hee-su (P)
1989	Haitai Tigers	65-51-4	.558	Park Chul-woo (IF)
1990	LG Twins	71-49-0	.592	Kim Young-su (P)
1991	Haitai Tigers	79-42-5	.647	Chang Chae-kun (C)
1992	Lotte Giants	71-55-0	.563	Park Dong-hee (P)
1993	Haitai Tigers	81-42-3	.655	Lee Jeong-bum (IF)
1994	LG Twins	81-45-0	.643	Kim Young-su (P)
1995	OB Bears	74-47-5	.607	Kim Min-ho (IF)
1996	Haitai Tigers	73-51-2	.587	Lee Kang-chul (P)
1997	Haitai Tigers	75-50-1	.599	Lee Jeong-bum (IF)

Season MVP

1982	Park Chul-soon (P)
1983	Lee Man-su (C)
1984	Choi Dong-won (P)
1985	Kim Song-han (IF)
1986	Sun Dong-yol (P)
1987	Kim Hyo-jo (OF)
1988	Kim Song-han (IF)
1989	Sun Dong-yol (P)
1990	Sun Dong-yol (P)
1991	Chang Jong-hoon (IF)
1992	Chang Jong-hoon (IF)
1993	Kim Song-rae (IF)
1994	Lee Jeong-bum (IF)
1995	Kim Sang-ho (IF)
1996	Ku Dae-song (P)
1997	Lee Seung-yup (IF)

Attendance

1982	1.438 million
1983	2.256
1984	1.664
1985	1.688
1986	2.141
1987	2.019
1988	1.932
1989	2.883
1990	3.189
1991	3.825
1992	3.912
1993	4.437
1994	4.194
1995	5.406
1996	4.498
1997	3.902
1998	2.731 (estimate)

SINGLE SEASON LEADERS

Batting

1982	Baek In-chun	.412
1983	Chong Hyo-jo	.369
1984	Lee Man-su	.340
1985	Chong Hyo-jo	.373
1986	Chong Hyo-jo	.329
1987	Chong hyo-jo	.387
1988	Kim Sang-hoon	.354
1989	Ko Won-bu	.327
1990	Han Dae-hwa	.349
1991	Lee Jeong-hoon	.348
1992	Lee Jeong-hoon	.360
1993	Yang Jun-hyuk	.341
1994	Lee Jeong-bum	.396
1995	Kim Kwang-rim	.337
1996	Yang Jun-hyuk	.346
1997	Kim Ki-tae	.344

Base Hits

1982	Baek In-chun	103
1983	Chang Hyo-jo/ Park Jong-hoon	117
1984	Hong Moon Jong	122
1985	Kim Song-han	133
1986	Lee Kwang-eun	124
1987	Lee Jeong-hoon	124
1988	Kim Song-han	131
1989	Lee Kang-don	137
1990	Lee Kang-don	146
1991	Chang Jong-hoon	160
1992	Lee Sun-chul	152
1993	Kim Hyung-suk	147
1994	Lee Jeong-bum	196
1995	Choi Tae-won	147
1996	Yang Jun-hyuk	151
1997	Lee Seung-yup	170

Home Runs

1982	Kim Bong-yeon	22
1983	Lee Man-su	27
1984	Lee Man-su	23
1985	Lee Man-su/ Kim Song-han	22
1986	Kim Bong-yeon	21
1987	Kim Song-rae	22
1988	Kim Song-han	30
1989	Kim Song-han	26
1990	Chang Jong-hoon	28
1991	Chang Jong-hoon	35
1992	Chang Jong-hoon	41
1993	Kim Song-rae	25
1994	Kim Ki-tae	25
1995	Kim Sang-ho	25
1996	Park Jae-hong	30
1997	Lee Seung-yup	32

Runs Batted In		
1982	Kim Song-han	69
1983	Lee Man-su	74
1984	Lee Man-su	80
1985	Lee Man-su	87
1986	Kim Bong-yeon	67
1987	Lee Man-su	76
1988	Kim Song-han	89
1989	You Seung-han	85
1990	Kim Sang-hoon	91
1991	Kim Sang-hoon	114
1992	Kim Sang-hoon	119
1993	Kim Song-rae	91

Runs Batted In (continued)		
1994	Yang Jun-hyuk	87
1995	Kim Sang-ho	101
1996	Park Jae-hong	108
1997	Lee Seung-yup	114

Stolen Bases		
1982	Kim Il-kwon	53
1983	Kim Il-kwon	48
1984	Kim Il-kwon	41
1985	Kim Jae-park	50
1986	Seo Jong-hwan	43

Stolen Bases (continued)		
1987	Lee Hae-jang	54
1988	Lee Sun-chul	58
1989	Kim Il-kwon	62
1990	Kim Il-kwon	48
1991	Lee Sun-chul	56
1992	Lee Sun-chul	44
1993	Chun Jun-ho	75
1994	Lee Jeong-bum	84
1995	Chun Jun-ho	69
1996	Lee Jeong-bum	57
1997	Lee Jeong-bum	64

PITCHING LEADERS

Won-Lost Record		
1982	Park Chul-soon	24-4
1983	Chong Myung-bu	30-16
1984	Choi Dong-won	27-13
1985	Kim Shi-jin	25-5
	Kim Il-young	25-6
1986	Sun Dong-yol	24-6
1987	Kim Shi-jin	23-6
1988	Yoon Hak-kil	18-10
1989	Sun Dong-yol	21-3
1990	Sun Dong-yol	22-6
1991	Sun Dong-yol	19-4
1992	Song-jin-woo	19-8
1993	Jho Gye-hyun	17-6
1994	Gho Gye-hyun	18-5
	Lee Sang-hoon	18-4
1995	Lee Sang-hoon	20-5
1996	Ku Dae-song	18-3
	Ju Hyung-kwang	18-7
1997	Kim Hyun-uk	20-2†

†All relief wins

Earned Run Average		
1982	Park Chul-soon	1.84
1983	Heo Ki-ryung	2.34
1984	Chang Ho-yeon	1.58
1985	Sun Dong-yol	1.70
1986	Sun Dong-yol	0.99
1987	Sun Dong-yol	0.89
1988	Sun Dong-yol	1.21
1989	Sun Dong-yol	1.17
1990	Sun Dong-yol	1.13
1991	Sun Dong-yol	1.17
1992	Yeom Jeong-sup	2.23
1993	Sun Dong-yol	0.78
1994	Chong Min-chul	2.15
1995	Jho Gye-hyun	1.71
1996	Ku Dae-song	1.88
1997	Kim Hyun-uk	1.88

Strikeout Leaders		
1982	No Sang-su	141
1983	Chong Myung-bu	220
1984	Choi Dong-won	223
1985	Kim Shi-jin	201
1986	Sun Dong-yol	214
1987	Choi Dong-won	163
1988	Sun Dong-yol	200
1989	Sun Dong-yol	198
1990	Sun Dong-yol	189
1991	Sun Dong-yol	210
1992	Lee Kang-chul	155
1993	Kim Sang-yup	170
1994	Chong Min-chul	196
1995	Lee Dae-jin	163
1996	Ju Hyung-kwang	221
1997	Chong Min-chul	160

ALL-TIME LEADERS

Hits	
Kim Song-han	1389
Kim Hyung-suk*	1343
Shin Kyung-sik	1282
Lee Man-su	1276
Kim Kwang-rim*	1270
Lee Sun-chul*	1218
Han Dae-hwa	1190
Kim Sang-hoon	1181
Yoon Duk-kyu	1161
Chang Jong-hoon*	1136
*active player	

Home Runs	
Lee Man-su	252
Chang Jong-hoon*	228
Kim Song-han	207
Han Dae-hwa	163
Lee Sun-chul*	143
Kim Ki-tae*	142
Kim Song-rae*	131
Kim Young-chul	131
Kim Sang-ho*	127
Yang Jun-hyuk*	120
*active player	

Runs Batted In	
Lee Man-su	861
Kim Song-han	781
Chang Jong-hoon*	764
Han Dae-hwa	712
Kim Hyung-suk*	656
*active player	

Steals	
Lee Sun-chul*	368
Kim Il-kwon	363
Lee Jeong-bum	310
Kim Jae-park	284
Chun Jun-ho*	266
*active player	

PITCHING LEADERS

Wins	
1. Sun Dong-yol	146
2. Kim Shi-jin	124
3. Lee Kang-chul*	117
4. Yoon Hak-kil	117
5. Chang Ho-yeon	109
*active player	

Losses	
1. Chong Sam-hum	121
2. Chang Ho-yeon	110
3. Yoon Hak-kil	94
4. Choi Chang-ho*	91
5. Kye Hyung-chul	89
*active player	

Saves	
Kim Young-su*	195
Chong Myung-won*	136
Jho Gye-hyun*	133
Sun Dong-yol	132
Kwon Young-ho	100
*active player	

Strikeouts	
Sun Dong-yol	698
Lee Kang-chul*	1294
Choi Dong-won	1019
Choi Chang-ho*	955
Song Jin-woo	953
*active player	

CHAPTER 20

Baseball in Taiwan

Jeffrey Wilson

Baseball in Taiwan was not an American import. Nor did the sport come from mainland China where the first teams were established in 1895. Baseball in Taiwan began as a Japanese sport, a fact deeply influencing the game's development to the current day. The Treaty of Shimonoseki in 1895 ended the Sino-Japanese War and set Taiwan on a radically different course for the next 50 years—both politically and socially. The treaty forced Qing dynasty China to cede the relatively isolated and backward island to Japan, creating a colony Japan ruled until the end of World War II.

Baseball arrived with the new culture of the colonial masters. But the game was not initially spread to the local Taiwanese population. It was first introduced to the island in 1906 in schools for Japanese children who had immigrated to Taiwan. While a few Taiwanese children soon copied their Japanese counterparts with informal games, they were not formally exposed to the game because they were not allowed to enroll in the official school system.

Within a few years, the sport spread among Taiwan's growing Japanese population. In 1910 Japanese postal and army employees established the first two adult teams in the southern city of Tainan. The next year, the colonial government recruited coaches from Japan to tour the island, instructing local Japanese about the game. Over the next four years, the coaches planted the seeds that would eventually make baseball Taiwan's most popular sport. As a result, the Taiwan Baseball Association was established with 15 amateur teams in 1915. Players were primarily Japanese, but a few were Taiwanese.

While baseball remained predominately Japanese during the pre-war period, there were two brief doses of North American influence. In 1921, a touring team of North American professionals played a Japanese team in Taipei before departing on a tour of central and southern Taiwan. In 1934 Babe Ruth and his team of touring major league all-stars played a game in the southern city of Tainan against a company team during their tour across Asia.

Nengkao Team

The true birth of Taiwanese baseball did not occur until 1921. The spark was lit by Lin Chia-hsing, a resident of the east coast city of Hualien who had played on school squad and a Japanese-owned company team. That year, he saw a group of teens from Taiwan's Ami tribe playing baseball with makeshift bats and rocks. Lin brought to-gether 12 of the players to form a team. His motivation was not primarily to train athletes, but to provide a way out of poverty for the youngsters. The Ami are concentrated on the island's east coast and are Taiwan's largest group of indigenous people, related ethnically to Polynesians. Lin, in contrast, was ethnic Chinese, a descent of emigrants from the mainland who had arrived in Taiwan from southwestern China over the past 400 years.

Lin trained the team for one year until November 1923 when all of the members entered a new school with the squad being known at the "Nengkao team." That year, colonial authorities had changed educational laws allowing Taiwanese students to attend middle schools and technical schools. During this period Japan consolidated its rule over Taiwan and began implementing compulsory Japanese education and cultural assimilation.

In July 1925 Nengkoa's local success gained the colonial government's attention, and it sponsored the team on a tour of Japan. The Nengkao team shocked Japan's baseball community by winning their first game, 28-0, in four innings. The team then entered the prestigious Koshien high school tournament (opened to teams from Taiwan in 1923), advancing to the title game which they lost.

Finishing their tour 5-1, the collection of aboriginal teens made a lasting impact. Not only would they set a precedent for the large role aboriginal players would have in the development of Taiwan baseball, they also created a favorable impression in Japan for the abilities of Ami players and made possible their later acceptance in Japanese professional baseball.

The tour's success resulted in four of the players being recruited to attend school in Kyoto, Japan: Luo Tao-hou, his brother Luo Sha-wei, A-hsien, and Chi Sa. Later, the two Luo brothers and A-hsien starred on a college team in Japan. But, having lost its star players, the Nengkao team disbanded after only two years.

Chia-nung

While the Nengkao team showed that aboriginal players had the ability to compete with Japanese players, it took a southern Taiwanese high school to prove that ethnic Chinese could also play the sport successfully. The Chiayi School for Agriculture and Forestry (known by its Chinese abbreviation of "Chia-nung") was an exception among Taiwan schools in the 1920s; more than 70 percent of its students were ethnic Chinese. Overall, 70 percent of students in Taiwan's schools were Japanese.

In 1928 Chia-nung formed a team with a Japanese

coach and the following year became the first team primarily composed of Taiwanese players to participate in the Taiwan qualifying tournament for the annual Koshien high school competition in Osaka. In 1931, Chia-nan won the qualifying tournament—the first predominately Taiwanese team to do so—and advanced to the title game in Japan, which it lost. Chia-nung also represented Taiwan at the Koshien tournament in 1933, 1935, and 1936.

Over the next two decades, Chia-nung produced a generation of Taiwanese players and coaches who would play large roles in the game's development. The integration of Taiwanese players on the Chia-nung team and their success in the Koshien tournament contrasts sharply with the high school baseball experience in Japanese-occupied northeast China. While Japanese schools also sent teams to the tournament during the pre-war period, no ethnic Chinese players ever participated on teams.

Taiwan Professionals in Japan Before 1945

With no professional baseball in Taiwan, the only career option for the island's best players was to play in Japan. Several found success there in the early years of Japanese professional baseball. Luo Tao-hou—a member of the original group of Taiwan aboriginal players spotted playing on a sandlot in 1921—joined another Ami player (Lan Tien-sung) on the original Tokyo Senators in 1936, the Japanese Professional League's first season.

Another Ami member of the Nengkao team also made Japanese professional ranks: Ye Tien-sung joined the Nankai Hawks in 1940, winning the 1944 batting title with a .369 average.

Hsueh Yung-shun, who was originally born in Fujian province, China, was also on a roster in 1936. He played for the Nagoya Golden Whales and he enjoyed a five-year career.

Players from the Chia-nung school also succeeded in Japan. Among these were Ching Pu-chiang, Wu Hsin-heng, and Wu Chang-cheng. In 1937 Ching was a member of the original Hanshin Tigers and won the fall batting title that season. Wu Hsin-heng batted .325 to finish fourth in batting and tied for the lead in steals while with the Yomuiri Giants in 1944. He had an eight-year career in Japan.

Wu Chang-cheng was a legendary figure who went to Japan before the war and stayed to pursue a coaching career. After appearing in the Koshien tournament with Chia-nung in 1936-37, Wu signed with the Yomiuri Giants in 1937. He won batting titles in 1942 and 1943, a time when many of the Japanese stars were in the military. Following the 1943 season, Wu quit the Giants because he refused to tour with the team to Manchuria to support occupation Japanese troops.

In 1944 he joined Hanshin and tied for the stolen base title with another Taiwan player—Wu Hsin-heng. Five days prior to the end of World War II in August 1945 Wu Chang-cheng burned his left foot during an American bombing raid over Osaka, trying to save a child. The next season, he became a pitcher—a position he hadn't played in more than a decade. He threw a no-hitter and finished the a remarkable comeback season with a record of 14-6.

Wu finally retired to coach in 1957. One of his first projects was to help convert another pitcher into a powerful hitter—Sadaharu Oh, the world's all-time home run king. The secret bond between Wu and Oh was that both were ethnic Chinese. Although he was born in Japan, both of Oh's parents were from Mainland China. (Oh first visited Taiwan in 1965 and spent his honeymoon on the island the next year. He threw out the ceremonial first pitch of the Chinese Professional Baseball League in 1990.)

There were also five Japanese who grew up in Taiwan who played professional baseball in Japan. Among them was Hiroshi Oshita, from the southern Taiwan port city of Kaohsiung. He debuted in the November 1945 all-star games permitted by General Douglas MacArthur. Oshita went on to win the home run title with 20 in 1946.

He helped to put professional baseball in Japan back on its feet. Oshita enjoyed a successful 14-year career with 201 home runs.

After the War

Taiwan was transferred from Japan to the Republic of China (ROC) according to the terms of the Cairo Declaration negotiated by the allied forces on Oct. 25, 1945. The repatriation of thousands of Japanese nationals included many of the players as well as most of the coaches from the school and amateur teams. The disruption in commercial relations meant that baseball equipment became scarce, a problem not fully resolved until Taiwan's own economy took off, and the domestic sporting goods industry was born.

Still, baseball survived and continued to develop as the national sport. In 1946 the first annual Taiwan Provincial Games was held with 19 island teams competing in baseball. The next year, the Taiwan Baseball Association was formed.

With Taiwan's reunification as a province of China, Taiwanese baseball took initial steps to become incorporated with the Chinese sporting structure. In August 1947 Shanghai's Fudan University played a series in Taiwan—the first and still only visit by a collegiate mainland team. In November 1947 the visit was reciprocated by a Taiwan company team that played a series in Shanghai. Taiwan also sent a team to participate in China's Seventh National Athletic Games in Shanghai in 1948. Competing against squads representing Shanghai, Guangdong province, and the Air Force, the Taiwan team won the title. A team representing Taiwan would not return to the mainland until 1991 for the 16th Asian Championships.

In 1949 Taiwan's brief four-year reunification with the mainland ended when China's nationalist government retreated to Taiwan following its military defeat by the Chinese communists. A year earlier, six government-owned banks agreed to form teams and hold regular tournaments. This league, which initially played soft baseball, was the backbone for the initial development of adult baseball on Taiwan under ROC control. Other important regular competitors for these early corporate teams were recreational teams of the U.S. military, which maintained a large and visible presence on the island. The contests against the American military became known as "Coca-Cola" games with Taiwanese able to strike out an Ameri-

can batter receiving a bottle of the drink—a treat normally beyond the reach of most Taiwanese in the decade following World War II.

In 1951 Taiwan teams began representing the ROC—rather than the province—when the first national team was formed to play a series in the Philippines. Taiwan was back in Manila in 1954 for the first Asian Championships. The low level of skill on the national team was soon apparent—Taiwan was no-hit by the Philippines in their first game and finished the four-team tournament without a win. They improved at the second Asian Championships the next year when they defeated the Philippines and South Korea to finish second to Japan.

With players drawn from military, corporate, and college teams, Taiwan continued to field competitive national teams in Asian competition. 1972, Taiwan and Japan became the first Asian countries to compete in the World Championships. The invitation to Taiwan was extended based on its victory over Japan (which had professional baseball) at the 1965 Asian Championships and the island's success at the Little League World Series. Taiwan tied for sixth as its first World Championship, including a 1-0 win over arch-rival Japan.

The 1977 Intercontinental Cup in Nicaragua would be the final time Taiwan's national team baseball would compete as the "Republic of China"—the country's official name. In the 1970s, the People's Republic of China had broken from its self-imposed policy of sporting isolation to challenge Taiwan for the sanctioned representative of "China" in international athletic organizations. By 1976 the PRC had forced Taiwan's ouster from the Olympics. The next year, China had replaced Taiwan as a member of the International Baseball Association, forcing Taiwan out of IBA competition. Taiwan won readmittance to the IBA in time to compete for the 1982 World Championships under the same arrangement that also allowed the island to resume Olympic competition—using the name "Chinese Taipei" under the flag of the Chinese Taipei Olympic Committee. (Taiwan teams competing in the Little League World Series have represented the Far East region rather than a particular country, thereby avoiding political controversies.)

Taking advantage of its return to international competition, Taiwan performed impressively over the next decade. At the 1984 World Championships, it defeated Cuba, 7-4, in Havana in the medal round en route to a second-place finish. Taiwan duplicated the feat by a 4-3 score at the tournament two years later in Amsterdam—the last time Cuba lost in the World Championships.

Among other international competition, Taiwan placed third in the baseball demonstration event in Los Angeles at the 1984 Olympics. In 1987 Taiwan took its first title at the Asian Championships and in 1992 Taiwan reached its highest level of international success when it won a silver medal in the 1992 Barcelona Olympics. It was only Taiwan's fourth Olympic medal ever and the only one the country won at the 1992 Games.

The gradual warming of relations with China has also allowed Taiwan to resume hosting sanctioned tournaments. In 1997 it hosted the Asian Championships for the first time since 1969. China sent its national team to participate—the first time a PRC national team in any sport had competed in Taiwan. Following international

rules, the PRC flag flew in the stadium. Moreover, Taiwan fans were discouraged from displaying their own flag.

The growth of professional baseball in Taiwan has robbed the national team of much of its luster, players, and competitiveness. With no clear direction on the future of the team, Taiwan missed the medal round at the 1998 World Championships in Italy for the first time since it began competing in 1972.

To become more competitive with the goal of qualifying for the 2000 Olympics, Taiwan will follow the international trend by including professionals on its national team. The first test of a team composed primarily of professionals came at the December 1998 Asian Games in Bangkok, Thailand.

Youth Baseball

Taiwan's Little League success is legendary. Its 1996 win was not an overnight, isolated phenomena, but rather a continuation of a long baseball tradition in Taiwan, particularly among the island's aboriginal people. The Japanese colonial government started the first youth tournament in 1921 with five Japanese elementary schools in Taipei participating. Tournaments soon spread: to Kaohsiung and Tainan in 1923, and to Taichung in 1925. The 1924 tournament in Tainan was the first to include teams of Taiwanese students. Tournaments for high school students also began during the decade.

A significant step in the emergence of Taiwan's powerhouse youth program was the August 1968 tour of Taiwan by the Japanese 1967 Little League World Championship team. After winning their opening game against a school team from Chiayi, the Japanese were shutout, 7-0, by the legendary Hung Yeh team—composedly solely of Ami students from a remote school in the mountains on Taiwan's east coast. The Japanese team was then beaten by a Taiwan all-star team, 5-1, and fell again to the Hung Yeh team, 5-2. The Japanese salvaged the final game by beating the Chiayi school, 5-3.

Though Hung Yeh's players were older than the Japanese, two victories by a group of extremely poor children who lacked even basic baseball equipment shocked Taiwan's collective conscience. Moreover, it helped erased Taiwan's lingering feelings of inferiority that its former Japanese colonial masters were physically better than they were.

With new confidence, Taiwan quickly entered the international arena. A national youth team tournament was held in February with the Taitung school from Chiayi taking the first championship. A National Youth Baseball Association formed in April 1969, and Taiwan became a member of Little League Baseball International in June. In July, a national all-star team, the Golden Dragons (Chin-lung), won the Far East regional tournament and qualified for Williamsport. But getting there was another matter. U.S. military stationed in Taiwan donated $7,589 in American dollars after deciding that a flight on one of its planes violated regulations.

After winning the title in Williamsport, the Golden Dragons returned home as national heroes to parades and a visit with President Chiang Kai-shek. The victory also started an annual national ritual with the entire island

crowding around television sets in the early morning hours to watch live broadcasts of Little League World Series games from the United States.

While the Golden Dragons were a national all-star team, Taiwan followed newly adopted Little League regulations to select league championship teams to compete internationally. The Chiayi Seven Tigers lost in the first round in 1970, but the Tainan City Giants were back on top the next year with the second Little League World Series title.

In 1972 Taiwan won its first Senior League title. Two years later Taiwan won its first Big League title, giving it a sweep of the three Little League baseball titles that year. Together with its 17 Little League titles, Taiwan has also won 17 Senior League and Big League championships.

Various theories abound to explain Taiwan's success. One is the tradition of baseball that extends back to the Nengkao team of the 1920s, particularly among aboriginals who have dominated the Little League teams. Second, a winning tradition was established, and Taiwan teams were expected to win. There was no other sport with such an emphasis that could attract the players. Coaching was also stressed, with experienced—often paid—coaches training the players in basic skills. Pitchers were developed, and often overworked. Possibly the biggest key was that the teams practiced longer, playing more games with better competition before they entered the international arena. Some of these squads practiced year-round with competitive seasons in the spring and fall.

In the 1970s incentives to become Little League champions were high. At the time Taiwanese were not allowed to travel abroad for sightseeing—being on a national championship team may have been their only chance to see the outside world. Moreover, advancing along the national programs could ensure future economic success. Being on a junior national team could help obtain college admission or lifetime employment with one of the corporate teams.

The pressure to win often had negative side effects. When Taiwan started winning titles in the 1970s, many schools wanted to establish teams but lacked the necessary funding. Local booster clubs formed by parents and other supporters stepped in. These boosters often paid coaches—in violation of international rules—and often paid players substantial sums of money to win games. The later practice has often been cited as the basis of long-term relationships between players and members of Taiwan's underworld, which exploded in the 1997 professional baseball game-fixing scandal. In fact, game-fixing and gambling at the youth level were not unheard of occurrences.

Other problems surfaced. In preparation for the 1969 national tournament, Hung Yeh school officials altered players' identities and changed birthdates. The school principal, manager, and coach were given a year in prison for forgery along with two-year suspended sentences.

While other schools put on notice after the criminal charges, the age of Taiwan's Little League players has often been a contentious issue in Taiwan as well as overseas. With many of players coming from poor, rural areas, verifying their actual ages has often proved difficult. In some cases, players' birth certificates had been legally obtained, but for various reasons parents had not registered the actual date of birth. These difficulties along with the continued pressure to win led many schools to drop baseball programs during the 1980s. The sharp drop prompted the national Ministry of Education to step-in with a three-year program starting in 1987 to purchase equipment and hire coaches at 20 elementary schools.

In 1997 Taiwan decided to withdraw from Little League baseball due to the island's admitted inability to comply with requirements set by Williamsport. With some Taiwan schools having up to 10,000 students, it was impossible at many schools to field the required one team for each 250 students. Not only did many schools lack the necessary fields, many parents would not allow their children to play, preferring them to spend more time in school.

Moreover, schools wanted qualified physical education teachers to coach the teams, rather than the using volunteers as required. The young players demanded experienced coaches, particularly if they had the professional potential—a realistic goal considering the severe local player shortage in the two professional leagues. After the 1997 withdrawal Taiwan's youth teams continued to play a large role in international competition. Island teams won the Pony and Bronco titles divisions and participate in the International Baseball Association tournaments.

But Taiwan may soon return to Little League. The Chinese Taipei Baseball Association tentatively plans to apply for registration in 1999 for the Little League division only, because there is no IBA division for the 11-12 age group. The CTBA plans to submit an initial application for schools in the Taitung area on Taiwan's southeast coast—the island's traditional baseball powerhouse. Officials estimate that only this area could support the required number of teams required by LLBI regulations.

The Adult Stars

Contrary to Western popular belief, Taiwan's young stars don't necessarily disappear after setting the world ablaze. While many are not encouraged to continue to the game in a society which traditionally values academics over athletics, many have become stars on Taiwan's successful national teams. And a good handful have reached their traditional goal—the Japanese professional leagues.

Many who found their way to Japan were Ami, following in the footsteps of the Kaoneng players who had blazed the path in the initial years of the professional game in Japan. Among these were Kuo Yuan-chih, a member of the Taiwan's first Little League World Series championship team. A member of the Chunichi Dragons, Kuo was the 1982 Rookie of the Year and 1988 save champion. He finished his 16-season Japanese career with 106 wins.

The 42-year-old Kuo is still playing. He returned to Taiwan for the 1997 season and led all local players in salary (base of $180,000 in American dollars), and in performance (14-3, 2.50 with the China Trust Whales.)

Following Kuo to Chunichi in 1989 was Chen Yi-hsin, another Ami. Chen returned to Taiwan in 1992 and led the Brother Elephants to three straight Chinese Professional Baseball League titles while earning two MVP awards. In 1997 he moved to the Taiwan Major League and won the

batting title and MVP award with the Chia-nan Luka in the TML's first season.

Other Taiwanese to pitch in Japan were Kuo Tai-yuan (13 seasons with the Seibu Lions), Chuang Sheng-hsiung (Lotte Orions), Li Tsung-yuan (Lotte Orions), and Chen Chieh-cheng (Yakult Swallows). After leading Taiwan to the silver medal at the 1992 Olympics, Kuo-Lee Chien-fu spent six seasons with the Hanshin Tigers being released at the end of the 1998 season.

While Taiwan pitchers have gained the most fame in Japan, a few position players have also headed north. Outfielder Lu Ming-tse became first player in Japanese baseball history to homer in his first at bat when called up to Yomiuri Giants in 1988. The "Asian Cannon" hit 15 homers in his first two months, dispelling notions Taiwanese players could not hit. After four years in Japan, Lu returned to play professionally in Taiwan.

Two other Taiwan position players in Japan were right fielder Kao Ying-chieh and catcher Li Lai-fa, both of whom played with the Nankai Hawks and became Chinese Taipei national team head coaches. As of November 1998, the lone remaining Taiwanese player in Japanese professional baseball is first baseman Chen Ta-feng of the Hanshin Tigers who originally went to Japan for college.

Despite their success in youth baseball, international competition, and in Japan, the question often arises as to why no Taiwanese has made it to the major leagues in the U.S., particularly since Japanese and South Koreans have recently enjoyed major league success in America.

In fact, one player from Taiwan did play for a major league organization. Following his appearance in the 1972 and 1973 World Championships, pitcher Tan Hsin-ming signed with the San Francisco Giants and played at the Class A level in 1974 and 1975. Tan later went on to become the first head coach of the Mercury Tigers in the CPBL.

Other major league teams have tried to sign Taiwan players. Pitcher Kuo Yuan-chih and catcher Kao Ying-chieh were both recruited by the Cincinnati Reds. The Baltimore Orioles tried to sign Kuo Tai-yuan. Slugger "Smiling George" Chao Chih-chiang's offer to play for the Dodgers fell through after a disappointing performance at the 1984 Olympics. Pitcher Kuo-Lee Chien-fu turned down the Blue Jays following the 1992 Olympics, instead playing in Japan for Hanshin.

There are many hurdles for a Taiwan player to clear before making a bid for the big leagues. The largest barrier was the traditional lure of playing in Japan. Many players' parents were themselves educated under the former Japanese colonial system and felt more comfortable sending their sons to Japan rather than to an uncertain future in North America. In addition, players have long lacked the confidence that they could successfully compete with major leaguers. Players also have 18 months of compulsory military service, cutting into their critical years as prospects.

Taiwan's professional leagues have erected additional barriers to retain the island's best talent. The CPBL instituted lifetime contracts and banned free agency. But major league teams must also share part of the blame for failing to sign a Taiwanese player. With the exception of the Dodgers, major league teams have failed to build the scouting networks and long-term presence required to build relations and trust—the type of effort teams have long made in Latin America.

The success of Hideo Nomo and the Japanese and Korean players who followed him to the major leagues has not gone unnoticed in Taiwan. The younger generation of Taiwanese players with easy access to major league games on television and regular play against import players in the Taiwan professional leagues may give them the confidence to sign with a major league team. Moreover, the Taiwan leagues are warming to the idea of local players in the major leagues as avenues to promote the sport locally and to train stars for a future return to Taiwanese professional and national teams.

Pitchers Chen Chih-chen and Liang Ju-hao of the TML took initial steps by playing a month with the Atlanta Braves in the 1998 fall instructional league. Chen, a 19-year-old phenom, illustrates the difficulties faced by Taiwanese prospects. After pitching a shutout in his only professional game, Chen was caught in tug-of-war between the Chinese Taipei Baseball Association and the TML over whether he could play professionally before serving in the military and on the national team. He was forced to sit out the remainder of the 1998 season. Another possible major leaguer is pitcher Hsu Ming-chieh. A former Little League World Series champion, he received offers from Japan and several major league teams before signing with the TML.

The Professional Game

Despite Taiwan's baseball tradition, the professional leagues are only a relatively recent occurrence. Still, several factors coalesced in the late 1980s for the formation of a league. Taiwan's rapid economic development created a large affluent middle class eager for entertainment and companies with sufficient resources to back teams. The national team's recent international success helped convince fans that a professional league would offer quality competition. Moreover, fans demanded to see regular competition, rather than the short amateur seasons, or infrequent international tournaments. They had watched youth and national team players develop and wanted to see them earn a living at home. Finally, South Korea's successful league showed that pro ball could exist in Asia outside Japan.

The Chinese Professional Baseball League debuted in 1990 with four teams: President Lions, Brother Elephants, Weichuan Dragons, and Mercury Tigers. The teams were named after their sponsoring companies and had no home cities. They barnstormed across the island with an initial 90-game regular season lasting from March to October. Reaction to the league was strong, with teams drawing close to 900,000 fans the first year and developing their own fan clubs in each of the initial five cities they played in. Games had the flavor of contests in Japan, with organized cheer groups and constant noise.

The CPBL expanded with teams drawn from the amateur league. The China Times Eagles and Jungo Bears joined for 1993, with the China Trust Whales added in 1997. The Jungo team was sold and renamed the Sinon Bulls in 1996. The next year Sinon started a working agreement with the Los Angeles Dodgers under which

the Dodgers provided import players, coaches, and training assistance. It is the only working agreement between a Taiwan team and a major league organization.

A dispute over cable television rights for the 1997-99 CPBL seasons led to the country's second professional league—the Taiwan Major League. The league debuted with four teams 1997: Taipei Gida, Taichung Agan, Chia-nan Luka, and Kao-ping Fala. All teams are owned by the league and nominally represent Taiwan cities, although they also play "home" games in other locations.

The TML started by raiding the CPBL for some of its biggest local and foreign stars for guaranteed contracts. The TML initially had promised more of an American-style of baseball to distinguish itself from the CPBL with its conservative, Japanese-oriented style. However, both leagues have ended up offering similar styles and levels of play—generally thought to be between Single and Double A. While the TML has signed some top players off the national team, the consensus is that CPBL has the better local players.

Given the bitter enmity between the CPBL and TML, there is no "Taiwan Series" matching league champions. But both leagues have often staged international exhibition series to end their seasons. Both the Los Angles Dodgers and Yomuiri Giants played CPBL teams in 1993. Given the traditionally popularity of Japanese baseball in Taiwan, the Giants outdrew the Dodgers. In the fall of 1998, the Seibu Lions toured Taiwan to play TML teams.

Due to the CPBL's expansion and the formation of the TML, the lack of Taiwanese players has become acute. Compounding the problem is the lack of comprehensive player development. While the number of youth programs has rebounded in recent years, amateur baseball is very thin. Only five colleges currently have competitive programs. Several corporate teams have disbanded in the past decade, leaving only 11 amateur teams to compete in the two annual tournaments. With the issue still undecided whether high school players may sign directly with professional teams, a total of just 16 amateur and college teams must provide talent for 10 pro teams.

To remedy the player shortage, and to add more flair to the game, both leagues use foreign players. While the original justification was to temporarily fill in the gaps with rosters being fully Taiwanese in the future, import players have grown to become a dominant presence in both leagues. For its first season in 1990, the CPBL teams had four imports per team with three on the field at the same time. Active rosters eventually grew to eight with an unlimited number allowed on the teams each year. A record 117 foreigners were used in 1998 by the CPBL on six teams as most squads engaged in rapid player turnover to find winning combinations.

The TML has allowed four imports on the field at a time. With a limit of nine total foreign players, the four teams in the TML used only 37 foreign players on its four teams during the 1998 season. In both leagues, some pitching staffs have essentially become entirely foreign. Imports dominated the 1998 season winning all statistical categories in both leagues for the first time. Leading the way in the CPBL was first-ever Triple Crown winner Jay Kirkpatrick of the Sinon Bulls. The former Los Angeles Dodgers farmhand batted .387-101-31 in his first Taiwan season and won MVP honors. He set league records in

batting average and RBIs, and tied the home run mark. Players generally hail from the United States and the Dominican Republic, while other Latin American countries, Canada, Australia, Japan, and South Korea are also represented. Most players have Triple A experience with some having spent some time in the majors. Among the most successful is Luis Iglesias, the sole remaining import player from the CPBL's first year. He spent seven years with the Mercury Tigers and the past two seasons with the Chia-nan Luka. The all-time Taiwan professional leader in home runs and RBIs, Iglesias also had the highest base salary for foreign players at a reported US$17,000 per month.

While only a handful of foreigners have come from Japan, five of the six CPBL teams have had Japanese head coaches, with one in the TML. In contrast, while the CPBL has never had a North American head coach, the TML has had two. Canadian Bernie Beckman coached Taipei in 1997 with Tim Ireland taking over the reins in 1998. Former major league managers Jim Lefebvre, Kevin Kennedy, and Bill Russell have taken short team coaching assignments in the two leagues.

Gambling

In August 1996 four star players of the Brother Elephants—the most popular CPBL team—were kidnapped for one night by gangsters upset about a recent gambling loss. The incident blew the lid off a long-suspected problem—game fixing and gambling.

A trial the next September resulted in gambling-related convictions of 21 players and one assistant coach. Players supposedly made up to $120,000 in American money to throw individual games. The trial focused on the China Times team. Indicating the widespread involvement, all 18 local players on the previous season's team were indicted and convicted. Among those convicted were some of the league's biggest stars, including a former two-time MVP, a home run champion, a batting champion, and seven members of the national team which won the silver medal at the 1992 Olympics. After playing out the second half of the season with replacement players, China Times suspended operations for the 1998 season. In October 1998 the team officially folded, reducing the CPBL to six teams.

Receiving the stiffest sentence, 30 months and a fine of more than US$250,000, was China Times star reliever Kuo Chien-chen. Ironically, the ex-Yakult Swallow was the former players' association head and on behalf of his membership had promised fans that games would be clean.

The presiding judge estimated that two-thirds of players in the entire league were involved and turned over to prosecutors a list of players he thought were also guilty. Since then, while police have occasionally raided bookie operations, no further player indictments have followed. Rumors and occasional accusations still surface about widespread game-fixing in both leagues, involving both local and foreign players, umpires, coaches, and front office officials.

The scandal has devastated both leagues and the credibility of professional baseball in the country. In the

CPBL, average game attendance fell from a peak of 5,928 in 1993, to 4,548 in 1996, to an official figure of 2,041 in 1997. Moreover, the CPBL's cable broadcaster has repeatedly demanded reductions in its $62 million three-year contract. While initially removed from the scandal, the TML was suspect and managed to draw officially only 3,630 fans per contest its first year. Both leagues and team sponsors are rumored to have suffered huge financial losses.

Despite the scandal, however, the two leagues continue to receive a huge amount of publicity. More than 20 newspapers, including two national sports dailies, provide coverage. Complementing them are several Chinese-language web sites and eight baseball magazines. Four radio stations broadcast games along with live cable telecasts each day of the season in both leagues.

Local governments continue to construct larger, more modern stadiums. The 1998 schedule included games in 11 cities—up from five in 1990. Taiwan's largest stadium—a 25,000-seat facility in Kaohsiung, is scheduled to open in 1999. The start of construction of a multi-purpose domed stadium for downtown Taipei has been repeatedly delayed.

Professional Champions

Chinese Professional Baseball League

1990	Weichuan Dragons
1991	President Lions
1992	Brother Elephants
1993	Brother Elephants
1994	Brother Elephants
1995	President Lions
1996	President Lions
1997	Weichuan Dragons
1998	Weichuan Dragons

Taiwan Major League

1997	Chia-nan Luka
1998	Taipei Gida

## CHAPTER 21

Spring Training

Myles E. Friedman

Like the origins of baseball itself, the beginnings of spring training are veiled behind the mists of myth and legend. Throughout the 1930s and 1940s, baseball writers generally identified Cap Anson as the father of spring training. As evidence, reporters cited his Chicago White Stockings' 1886 trip to Hot Springs, Ark., as the crystallizing moment. Since Anson has been credited (incorrectly) by several writers as the greatest innovator of baseball in the 19th century, it may have been easy to overlook the journey Harry Wright's Philadelphia nine took that same year to Charleston and New Orleans.

In 1951, *The Sporting News* reported that the Boston Beaneaters, "Honest John" Morrill's National League outfit of 1884, should earn credit for a jaunt that year to New Orleans. Lee Allen's 1955 book, *The Hot Stove League,* reached even farther back, to 1870, and unearthed a preseason trip by Jimmy Wood's newly formed Chicago White Stockings. (Wood's men journeyed to New Orleans in an effort to steel themselves for a run at the Cincinnati Red Stockings, undefeated champions in 1869.) "The plan," wrote Allen, "worked so well that Chicago beat the Red Stockings not once, but twice. So in the years that immediately followed, many of the old National Association teams would winter at New Orleans and play games there."

Later, it was asserted that the Red Stockings themselves trained at New Orleans in 1870, though strictly speaking, they were into their season by the time they reached New Orleans, having already trounced the Louisville Eagle nine, 94-7, in Kentucky. Finally, some historians assert that in 1869 and possibly even before that, the New York Mutuals, who had recently come under the control of a new president, William "Boss" Tweed of Tammany Hall, put in a training session at New Orleans.

In fact, before the first major league was organized in 1871, baseball clubs often packed up in February for southern tours, though at the beginning with less emphasis on training and more on barnstorming. The famous Excelsior Base Ball Club of Brooklyn, led by Jim Creighton, made a "grand tour" in 1860, playing games as far south as Baltimore.

During the early years of major league baseball, the 1870s and '80s, it was hard enough to turn a profit without the additional burden of cold and ice. Weather played the largest role in directing itineraries southward, and big league squads leased locales in Charleston, Mobile, Macon, Savannah, Atlanta, Pensacola, and Jacksonville.

The outlays for training were incredibly modest by today's standards. In 1892 Wright's Phillies ran a spring training season from Feb. 28 through March 29. Included were two weeks in Gainesville, Fla., and two weeks of barnstorming on their way back north; gate receipts for the whole exercise totaled nearly $700, leaving the team with a net loss of $469.

In 1888 the Washington Nationals became the first club to train in Florida. It was not until 1914, however, that more than two teams would train in Florida during the same year. The idea of concentrating clubs in close proximity to each other for the purpose of exhibition play came not from the minds of baseball men, but from civic leaders and promoters of the sun belt.

Al Lang, a Pittsburgh businessman who had moved to St. Petersburg and later became its mayor, began wooing major league clubs in 1913. At first, Lang made the mistake of promising Barney Dreyfuss and his Pittsburgh Pirates beautiful scenery and excellent fishing if they were to shift to Florida from their long-time home in Hot Springs. Dreyfuss replied scornfully that he wasn't interested in giving his boys a good time for fishing and sitting; they were at training camp for hard work and the rougher environs of Arkansas were just fine for that.

Lang did entice Branch Rickey's St. Louis Browns to St. Petersburg for the 1914 season. A Browns official had persuaded several of the town's citizens into agreeing to pay all the expenses for the Browns' retinue of 50. Later, when Lang learned of the deal, he and public officials refused to pay any part of the $6,500 bill. The Browns did not return the following spring.

Soon Lang drew the Boston Braves and New York Yankees to St. Petersburg. The Braves' requirement for relocating in 1922 was a new ballpark. Lang accommodated them with Waterfront Park and in 1925 lured the Yankees by extolling St. Petersburg's relatively chaste society—at least in comparison to New Orleans, the Bombers' long-time preseason home. (It didn't hurt Lang's pitch that manager Miller Huggins had recently bought a home in St. Pete.)

There were several semipermanent training sites before the 1920s, but they were the exceptions. The Pirates lasted at Hot Springs from the turn of the century until 1917, and John McGraw established a Giants camp at Marlin, Texas, that lasted 11 seasons. Marlin, the site of purportedly curative mineral baths like those at Hot Springs, was sufficiently remote for McGraw to keep his men in line. However, when spring training was delayed until mid-March in 1919 in the aftermath of World War I, McGraw opted for the convenience of Gainesville, Fla.

The land boom in the Sunshine State in the 1920s was accompanied by a full-scale rush of baseball clubs. The

Athletics, Braves, Browns, Dodgers, Yankees, Senators, Reds, and Phillies all set up long-term residences during the decade and most never left except during World War II, when long-distance travel was curtailed. One club that did leave was the Giants. In 1924 McGraw moved his outfit to Sarasota, but, after losing $100,000 in a land deal, he said goodbye to Florida; the Giants returned only after McGraw surrendered the reins.

Spring training sites were often determined by the personal holdings of owners or managers. The Cubs only became fixtures on Santa Catalina Island, 20 miles off the coast of Los Angeles, after Phil Wrigley, who owned Catalina, bought the Cubs in 1921. When the Tigers moved to Augusta, Ga., in 1922, it was at the behest of their new manager, Ty Cobb, the "Georgia Peach," who was part owner of the ballpark.

Bill Veeck, who bought the Indians in 1946, owned an Arizona ranch; hence the Indians' move to Tucson, where they stayed for 46 years. The Yankees might still be in St. Petersburg but for owner Dan Topping's yacht and his desire to sail from a Fort Lauderdale mooring (though a promise to provide integrated housing in Fort Lauderdale may have been an equally forceful motivation).

The new congregation of clubs in Florida coincided with an unrelated phenomenon that changed spring training forever: Babe Ruth. When Ruth joined New York in 1920, his arrival had two immediate effects: (1) a 19-game barnstorming trip by the Giants and Red Sox—now without Ruth—became one of the worst spring training fiascoes of all time; and (2) Ruth generated tremendous interest for Yankees exhibitions. When the Yankees finally set up shop in St. Petersburg, spring training reached its zenith for ticket sales. In the spring after Ruth's record-setting 1927 season, 270,000 fans paid to see Yankees exhibition games, enabling Jacob Ruppert to clear an amazing profit of $60,000.

Naturally, other clubs wanted a piece of that action. By the mid-1930s only the Pirates, White Sox, Cubs, and Indians regularly trained outside Florida. Several teams split their spring between Florida and sites offshore—Havana, San Juan, Bermuda, and the Dominican Republic; however, each returned to the mainland for games in Florida and a barnstorming jaunt north. Clubs sometimes scheduled more than 40 games before opening the regular season in mid-April.

World War II travel restrictions forced teams to train nearer home—north of the Potomac River and east of St. Louis. Clubs opened camps later and, from 1943 to 1945, lengthy barnstorming ventures were dropped.

After the war, the major leagues' passion for Florida continued, though with a harsh new aspect. In 1946 Branch Rickey brought Jackie Robinson to camp as a member of the Dodgers' Montreal farm club, thus beginning a 20-year campaign to reverse racism. The Dodgers trained at Daytona Beach, a city which, though allowing Robinson to play in games, still enforced segregationist housing, dining, and travel codes. Robinson was barred from games in Sanford, Jacksonville, and Deland and other games were canceled. In 1947 Rickey moved his club to Cuba and Panama and only returned to Florida after making an inspired decision, one that would have an enduring impact on the game.

Rickey wanted to insulate his club from the hateful Jim Crow racial policies that prevailed in Florida and found the answer in a decommissioned naval base at Vero Beach. In 1948 the Dodgers would live, eat, train, and play at the club's new Dodgertown complex. In addition, the camp would encompass Brooklyn's entire minor league system, more than 400 players, giving Rickey the "baseball college" he had long wanted.

Other clubs encountered similar problems as they tried to integrate the game and, by 1953, five of the seven teams with black players on their rosters trained out west. Gradually most Florida communities, fearful of losing their lucrative spring showpiece, accepted the presence of blacks. But towns that played host to an occasional barnstorming game (and as such, were unaffected by the economic imperatives that worked on training camp cities), were slow to change.

In the spring of 1950, with fans eager to see Robinson, the Dodgers drew 232,000 on a tour north from Florida. But incidents of bigotry only worsened. By the late 1950s racism throughout the region helped end the barnstorming circuits that had operated for nearly a century.

Like Florida, California offered great weather for training, and several teams had sampled West Coast training early in the century. Until 1924, however, there was never more than one per year. By 1932 four clubs trained in California (the Cubs, Pirates, Tigers, and Giants) and, for most of the next 20 years, the Orange League would remain four strong.

The directors of the Pacific Coast League ended spring training by major league teams in California by prohibiting games in PCL cities the week before the PCL season opened (about April 1). That meant that big-league teams had nearly three weeks to kill before their seasons opened. The last major league teams ensconced in California, the Orioles and the White Sox, pulled out after the 1953 season.

Arizona had hosted spring training as early as 1929 when the Tigers trained in Phoenix, but 18 years passed before another club trained in Arizona. In 1947 Horace Stoneham of the Giants and Bill Veeck of the Indians agreed to take their teams to Phoenix and Tucson, respectively. Those clubs, which had or would soon have black players on their rosters, may have stayed in Arizona because of eased race relations. Until 1993, when they moved to Winter Haven, Fla., the Indians (along with the Cubs, who arrived in Arizona in 1952) formed the backbone of the Cactus League. By the 1969 expansion, seven teams were training in Arizona.

In 1951 the Giants and the Yankees engineered one of baseball's great trades. Yankees partner Del Webb was a Phoenix resident and was anxious to give his hometown a close look at his championship squad. He prevailed upon Stoneham to switch training sites for one year and, for the last time, the Yankees trained away from Florida. Incidentally, the two met in the World Series that fall.

The next decisive stage in the evolution of spring training was a consequence of baseball's renaissance following the 1975 World Series. After struggling to compete with America's expanding entertainment marketplace in the 1960s and 1970s, baseball surged in popularity. Attendance in the two years following Carlton Fisk's World Series body-English homer jumped 19 percent, more than twice the growth during all the years since 1950. Then

baseball really took off, reaching in 1994 a per-game figure (31,609) nearly twice that of 1975. The change was reflected in attendance at spring training games in Florida and Arizona; games that were once attended by small crowds of scouts and locals were now attracting better than 2.5 million fans per year.

By 1977 renewed devotion to the game was evident throughout the Cactus League (eight teams) and Grapefruit League (18 teams). Games which were once casual diversions became characterized by sold-out signs, scalpers, and ever-rising ticket prices. In 1990, *USA Today* began running box scores of spring games, providing a level of national coverage beyond the imaginings of earlier fans. Clubs began training in "complexes," following the example of Branch Rickey 30 years later.

By the late 1980s most teams played their spring training games in municipal ballparks or were seeking new ones, complete with practice fields for minor league camps and amenities rivaling major league ballparks. Even as the costs of luring a team to town or keeping it there escalated, cities in Arizona and Florida continued to compete for big league tenants. In 1937 the sum of $5,000 in cash was enough to lure Sam Breadon's St. Louis Cardinals to Daytona Beach. In 1994 Peoria, Ariz., invested $32 million into a stadium and compound for the Mariners and Padres.

Following Peoria's lead, other cities have put together packages designed to attract two clubs to one large facility. In 1998 the Chicago White Sox and the expansion Arizona Diamondbacks opened a shared complex in Tucson, while the St. Louis Cardinals and Montreal Expos became partners in a new spring home at Jupiter, Fla. Other recent developments include the arrival of the Walt Disney empire into Florida's baseball fraternity. Though the company is an owner of the Anaheim Angels, in 1997 it teamed with the Atlanta Braves to open a 200-acre multi-sports compound adjacent to Walt Disney World in Osceola County. The Braves' first full season at Disney's Wide World of Sports, 1998, produced consistent sellouts

as fans flocked to the complex's mixture of sports and entertainment.

Meanwhile, the Grapefruit League's newest member, the Tampa Bay Devil Rays, became the first major league team with a permanent training site in its hometown. In 1998, the Devil Rays ended the Cardinals' 51-year tenure in St. Petersburg, moving into Al Lang Field for their debut season.

The expansion of 1998 (and the migration west of the White Sox) put a record 10 clubs in the Cactus League, and left the Grapefruit League with 20.

Perhaps the most unwelcome change to affect spring training came in 1995 when replacement players were on hand for the first six weeks of the training season. Faced with the ongoing strike by the Major League Baseball Players Association, club owners opened training camps with minor league and amateur replacements. Games were held, though drawing little interest from fans, until March 31, just before clubs broke camp to head north, when the strike ended. Regular players were quickly rushed to their training sites for a short training season before the April 26 regular season opener.

Much of spring training remains unchanged. Scribes and savants continue to debate the necessity of the six-week regimen of calisthenics and infield drills. Though today's athletes generally take better care of themselves than their predecessors, some ballplayers still arrive needing a concentrated cycle of weight reduction. And, despite it all, fans still look to the lengthening days of March for the renewal of hope and a new season in which past promises are at last fulfilled.

Spring Training Sites by Team Nickname

Records of spring training prior to 1900 are incomplete and unclear. While some teams went south as early as the 1860s, it is difficult to separate clubs that were barnstorming from clubs that were training.

NATIONAL LEAGUE

Astros

1962-63 Apache Junction, Ariz.
1964-84 Cocoa Beach, Fla.
1985- Kissimmee, Fla.

Braves

1901 Norfolk, Va.
1902-04 Thomasville, Ga.
1905 Charleston, S.C.
1906 Jacksonville, Fla.
1907 Thomasville, Ga.
1908-12 Augusta, Ga.
1913 Athens, Ga.
1914-15 Macon, Ga.
1916-18 Miami, Fla.
1919-20 Columbus, Ga.
1921 Galveston, Tex.
1922-37 St. Petersburg, Fla.
1938-40 Bradenton, Fla.
1941 San Antonio, Tex.
1942 Sanford, Fla.
1943-44 Wallingford, Conn.
1945 Washington, D.C.
1946-47 Fort Lauderdale, Fla.
1948-62 Bradenton, Fla.
1963-97 West Palm Beach, Fla.
1998- Walt Disney World, Fla.

Brewers (Pilots)

1969-72 Tempe, Ariz.
1973-85 Sun City, Ariz.

1986-1997 Chandler, Ariz.
1998- Maryvale, Ariz.

Cardinals

1901-02 St. Louis, Mo.
1903 Dallas, Tex.
1904 Houston, Tex.
1905 Marlin Springs, Tex.
1906-08 Houston, Tex.
1909-10 Little Rock, Ark.
1911 West Baden, Ind.
1912 Jackson, Miss.
1913 Columbus, Ga.
1914 St. Augustine, Fla.
1915-17 Hot Wells, Tex.
1918 San Antonio, Tex.
1919 St. Louis, Mo.
1920 Brownsville, Tex.
1921-22 Orange, Tex.
1923-24 Bradenton, Fla.
1925 Stockton, Cal.
1926 San Antonio, Tex.
1927-29 Avon Park, Fla.
1930-36 Bradenton, Fla.
1937 Daytona Beach, Fla.
1938-42 St. Petersburg, Fla.
1943-45 Cairo, Ill.
1946-97 St. Petersburg, Fla.
1998- Jupiter, Fla.

Cubs

1901-02 Champaign, Ill.
1903-04 Los Angeles, Cal.

1905 Santa Monica, Cal.
1906 Champaign, Ill.
1907 New Orleans, La.
1908 Vicksburg, Miss.
1909-10 Hot Springs, Ark.
1911-12 New Orleans, La.
1913-16 Tampa, Fla.
1917-21 Pasadena, Cal.
1922-42 Catalina Island, Cal.
1943-45 French Lick, Ind.
1946-47 Catalina Island, Cal.
1948-49 Los Angeles, Cal.
1950-51 Catalina Island, Cal.
1952-65 Mesa, Ariz.
1966 Long Beach, Cal.
1967-78 Scottsdale, Ariz.
1979- Mesa, Ariz.

Diamondbacks

1998- Tucson, Ariz.

Dodgers

1901 Charlotte, N.C.
1902-06 Columbia, S.C.
1907-09 Jacksonville, Fla.
1910-12 Hot Springs, Ark.
1913-14 Augusta, Ga.
1915-16 Daytona Beach, Fla.
1917-18 Hot Springs, Ark.
1919-20 Jacksonville, Fla.
1921 New Orleans, La.
1922 Jacksonville, Fla.
1923-32 Clearwater, Fla.

1933 Miami, Fla.
1934-35 Orlando, Fla.
1936-40 Clearwater, Fla.
1941-42 Havana, Cuba
1943-45 Bear Mountain, N.Y.
1946 Daytona Beach, Fla.
1947 Havana, Cuba
1948 Ciudad Trujillo, D.R.
1949- Vero Beach, Fla.

Expos

1969-72 West Palm Beach, Fla.
1973-80 Daytona Beach, Fla.
1981-97 West Palm Beach, Fla.
1998- Jupiter, Fla.

Giants

1901-02 N.Y., N.Y.
1903-05 Savannah, Ga.
1906 Memphis, Tenn.
1907 Los Angeles, Cal.
1908-18 Marlin Springs, Tex.
1919 Gainesville, Fla.
1920-23 San Antonio, Tex.
1924-27 Sarasota, Fla.
1928 Augusta, Ga.
1929-31 San Antonio, Tex.
1932-33 Los Angeles, Cal.
1934-35 Miami Beach, Fla.
1936 Pensacola, Fla.
1937 Havana, Cuba
1938-39 Baton Rouge, La.
1940 Winter Haven, Fla.

1941-42 Miami, Fla.
1943-45 Lakewood, N.J.
1946 Miami, Fla.
1947-50 Phoenix, Ariz.
1951 St. Petersburg, Fla.
1952-83 Phoenix, Ariz.
1984- Scottsdale, Ariz.

Marlins
1993 Cocoa, Fla.
1994- Viera, Fla.

Mets
1962-87 St. Petersburg, Fla.
1988- Port St. Lucie, Fla.

Padres
1969-93 Yuma, Ariz.
1994- Peoria, Ariz.

Phillies
1901 Philadelphia, Pa.
1902 Washington, N.C.
1903 Richmond, Va.
1904 Savannah, Ga.
1905 Augusta, Ga.
1906-08 Savannah, Ga.
1909-10 Southern Pines, N.C.
1911 Birmingham, Al.
1912 Hot Springs, Ark.
1913 Southern Pines, N.C.
1914 Wilmington, N.C.
1915-18 St. Petersburg, Fla.
1919 Charlotte, N.C.
1920 Birmingham, Al.
1921 Gainesville, Fla.
1922-24 Leesburg, Fla.
1925-27 Bradenton, Fla.
1928-37 Winter Haven, Fla.
1938 Biloxi, Miss.
1939 New Braunfels, Tex.
1940-42 Miami Beach, Fla.
1943 Hershey, Pa.
1944-45 Wilmington, Del.
1946 Miami Beach, Fla.
1947- Clearwater, Fla.

Pirates
1901-16 Hot Springs, Ark.
1917 Columbus, Ga.
1918 Jacksonville, Fla.
1919 Birmingham, Al.
1920-23 Hot Springs, Ark.
1924-34 Paso Robles, Cal.
1935 San Bernardino, Cal.
1936 San Antonio, Tex.
1937-42 San Bernardino, Cal.
1943-45 Muncie, Ind.
1946 San Bernardino, Cal.
1947 Miami Beach, Fla.
1948 Hollywood, Cal.
1949-52 San Bernardino, Cal.
1953 Havana, Cuba
1954 Fort Pierce, Fla.
1955-68 Fort Myers, Fla.
1969- Bradenton, Fla.

Reds
1901-02 Cincinnati, Oh.
1903 Augusta, Ga.
1904 Dallas, Tex.
1905 Jacksonville, Fla.
1906 San Antonio, Tex.
1907 Marlin Springs, Tex.
1908 St. Augustine, Tex.
1909 Atlanta, Ga.
1910-11 Hot Springs, Ark.
1912 Columbus, Ga.
1913 Mobile, Al.
1914-15 Alexandria, La.
1916-17 Shreveport, La.
1918 Montgomery, Al.
1919 Waxahachie, Tex.

1920 Miami, Fla.
1921 Cisco, Tex.
1922 Mineral Wells, Tex.
1923-30 Orlando, Fla.
1931-42 Tampa, Fla.
1943-45 Bloomington, Ind.
1946-87 Tampa, Fla.
1988-97 Plant City, Fla.
1998- Sarasota, Fla.

Rockies
1993- Tucson, Ariz.

AMERICAN LEAGUE

Angels
1961-92 Mesa/Palm Springs, Ariz./Cal.
1993- Mesa/Tempe, Ariz.

Athletics
1901 Philadelphia, Pa.
1902 Charlotte, N.C.
1903 Jacksonville, Fla.
1904 Spartanburg, S.C.
1905 Shreveport, La.
1906 Montgomery, Al.
1907 Dallas, Tex.
1908-09 New Orleans, La.
1910 Atlanta, Ga.
1911 Savannah, Ga.
1912-13 San Antonio, Tex.
1914-18 Jacksonville, Fla.
1919 Philadelphia, Pa.
1920-21 Lake Charles, La.
1922 Eagle Pass, Tex.
1923-24 Montgomery, Al.
1925-36 Fort Myers, Fla.
1937 Mexico City, Mex.
1938-39 Lake Charles, La.
1940-42 Anaheim, Cal.
1943 Wilmington, Del.
1944-45 Frederick, Md.
1946-62 West Palm Beach, Fla.
1963-68 Bradenton, Fla.
1969-78 Mesa, Ariz.
1979-83 Scottsdale, Ariz.
1984- Phoenix, Ariz.

Blue Jays
1977- Dunedin, Fla.

Devil Rays
1998- St. Petersburg, Fla.

Indians
1901 Cleveland, Oh.
1902-03 New Orleans, La.
1904 San Antonio, Tex.
1905-06 Atlanta, Ga.
1907-08 Macon, Ga.
1909 Mobile, Al.
1910-11 Alexandria, La.
1912 Mobile, Al.
1913 Pensacola, Fla.
1914 Athens, Ga.
1915 San Antonio, Tex.
1916-20 New Orleans, La.
1921-22 Dallas, Tex.
1923-27 Lakeland, Fla.
1928-39 New Orleans, La.
1940-41 Fort Myers, Fla.
1942 Clearwater, Fla.
1943-45 Lafayette, Ind.
1946 Clearwater, Fla.
1947-92 Tucson, Ariz.
1993- Winter Haven, Fla.

Mariners
1977-92 Tempe, Ariz.
1993- Peoria, Ariz.

Orioles (Browns)
1901 St. Louis, Mo.

1902 French Lick, Ind.
1903 Baton Rouge, La.
1904 Corsicana, Tex.
1905-06 Dallas, Tex.
1907 San Antonio, Tex.
1908 Shreveport, La.
1909-10 Houston, Tex.
1911 Hot Springs, Ark.
1912 Montgomery, Al.
1913 Waco, Tex.
1914 St. Petersburg, Fla.
1915 Houston, Tex.
1916-17 Palestine, Tex.
1918 Shreveport, La.
1919 San Antonio, Tex.
1920 Taylor, Al.
1921 Bogalusa, Al.
1922-24 Mobile, Al.
1925-27 Tarpon Springs, Fla.
1928-36 West Palm Beach, Fla.
1937-41 San Antonio, Tex.
1942 Deland, Fla.
1943-45 Cape Girardeau, Mo.
1946 Anaheim, Cal.
1947 Miami, Fla.
1948 San Bernardino, Cal.
1949-52 Burbank, Cal.
1953 San Bernardino, Cal.
1954 Yuma, Ariz.
1955 Daytona Beach, Fla.
1956-58 Scottsdale, Ariz.
1959-88 Miami, Fla.
1989-90 Miami/Sarasota, Fla.
1991 Sarasota, Fla.
1992-95 St. Petersburg/Sarasota, Fla.
1996- Ft. Lauderdale, Fla.

Rangers (Senators)
1961-86 Pompano Beach, Fla.
1987- Port Charlotte, Fla.

Red Sox
1901 Charlottesville, Va.
1902 Augusta, Ga.
1903-06 Macon, Ga.
1907-08 Little Rock, Ark.
1909-10 Hot Springs, Ark.
1911 Redondo Beach, Cal.
1912-18 Hot Springs, Ark.
1919 Tampa, Fla.
1920-23 Hot Springs, Ark.
1924 San Antonio, Tex.
1925-27 New Orleans, La.
1928-29 Bradenton, Fla.
1930-31 Pensacola, Fla.
1932 Savannah, Ga.
1933-42 Sarasota, Fla.
1943-44 Medford, Mass.
1945 Atlantic City, N.J.
1946-58 Sarasota, Fla.
1959-65 Scottsdale, Ariz.
1966-92 Winter Haven, Fla.
1993- Fort Myers, Fla.

Royals
1969-87 Fort Myers, Fla.
1988- Baseball City, Fla.

Tigers
1901 Detroit, Mich.
1902 Ypsilanti, Mich.
1903-04 Shreveport, La.
1905-07 Augusta, Ga.
1908 Hot Springs, Ark.
1909-10 San Antonio, Tex.
1911-12 Monroe, La.
1913-15 Gulfport, Miss.
1916-18 Waxahachie, Tex.
1919-20 Macon, Ga.
1921 San Antonio, Tex.
1922-26 Augusta, Ga.
1927-28 San Antonio, Tex.

1929 Phoenix, Ariz.
1930 Tampa, Fla.
1931 Sacramento, Cal.
1932 Palo Alto, Cal.
1933 San Antonio, Tex.
1934-42 Lakeland, Fla.
1943-45 Evansville, Ind.
1946- Lakeland, Fla.

Twins (Senators)
1901 Phoebus, Va.
1902-04 Washington, D.C.
1905 Hampton, Va.
1906 Charlottesville, Va.
1907-09 Galveston, Tex.
1910 Norfolk, Va.
1911 Atlanta, Ga.
1912-16 Charlottesville, Va.
1917 Atlanta, Ga.
1918-19 Augusta, Ga.
1920-29 Tampa, Fla.
1930-35 Biloxi, Miss.
1936-42 Orlando, Fla.
1943-45 College Park, Md.
1946-90 Orlando, Fla.
1991- Fort Myers, Fla.

White Sox
1901-02 Excelsior Springs, Mo.
1903 Mobile, Al.
1904 Marlin Springs, Tex.
1905-06 New Orleans, La.
1907 Mexico City, Mex.
1908 Los Angeles, Cal.
1909-10 San Francisco, Cal.
1911 Mineral Wells, Tex.
1912 Waco, Tex.
1913-15 Paso Robles, Cal.
1916-19 Mineral Wells, Tex.
1920 Waco, Tex.
1921 Waxahachie, Tex.
1922-23 Seguin, Tex.
1924 Winter Haven, Fla.
1925-28 Shreveport, La.
1929 Dallas, Tex.
1930-32 San Antonio, Tex.
1933-42 Pasadena, Cal.
1943-44 French Lick, Ind.
1945 Terre Haute, Ind.
1946-50 Pasadena, Cal.
1951 Pasadena/Palm Springs, Cal.
1952 Pasadena/El Centro, Cal.
1953 El Centro, Cal.
1954-59 Tampa, Fla.
1960-97 Sarasota, Fla.
1998- Tucson, Ariz.

Yankees
1901 Baltimore, Md.
1902 Savannah, Ga.
1903-04 Atlanta, Ga.
1905 Montgomery, Al.
1906 Birmingham, Al.
1907-08 Atlanta, Ga.
1909 Macon, Ga.
1910-11 Athens, Ga.
1912 Atlanta, Ga.
1913 Hamilton, Berm.
1914 Houston, Tex.
1915 Savannah, Ga.
1916-18 Macon, Ga.
1919-20 Jacksonville, Fla.
1921 Shreveport, La.
1922-24 New Orleans, La.
1925-42 St. Petersburg, Fla.
1943 Asbury Park, N.J.
1944-45 Atlantic City, N.J.
1946-50 St Petersburg, Fla.
1951 Phoenix, Ariz.
1952-61 St. Petersburg, Fla.
1962- Fort Lauderdale, Fla.
1996- Tampa, Fla.

## CHAPTER 22

Women in Baseball

Debra A. Shattuck

omen have been associated with baseball, either as players or spectators, since the game's dawn in the early 19th century. Even before baseball emerged in its final form, girls and young women sometimes played precursors of the game like One Old Cat, Town Ball, and Stoolball in Colonial America. As time passed, and the boys' amusement became serious business for grown men, baseball's reputation as a masculine domain was established. In 1865, one year before Charles Peverelly observed that baseball "has now become beyond question the leading feature of the outdoor sports of the United States," *Harper's Weekly* proclaimed: "There is no nobler or manlier game than base-ball."

During the latter half of the 19th century, women's presence as spectators at baseball games was tolerated and sometimes encouraged. Eventually promoters of the game hosted regular "Ladies Days" to attract women fans who would bring in added gate receipts and, hopefully, have a calming effect on the sometimes unruly crowds. Many women were content with their role as spectators and moral uplifters, but others yearned for the opportunity to try their hand at the national pastime. Those who lived out their fantasy often had to endure verbal and written derision from observers anxious to preserve the baseball status quo.

For the most part, the negative attitude toward women baseball players continues to this day. Many still share the opinion of an editorialist who noted in The St. Louis *Globe-Democrat* in 1885 that "The female has no place in base ball, except to the degradation of the game." The criticisms notwithstanding, uncounted women have pursued their own field of dreams, contributing their unique chapter to baseball's rich heritage.

Many of the first women baseball players were college students. The secluded atmosphere of all-girl's schools enabled women to play the game without attracting too much attention. Students at Vassar College organized two baseball clubs as early as 1866. In 1879, according to Vassar alumna Sophia Foster Richardson, the Vassar girls organized at least seven baseball clubs. The private grounds of college campuses did not always protect female players from public criticism, however. In a speech to an alumnae association in 1896, Richardson recalled, "The public, so far as it knew of our playing, was shocked, but in our retired grounds, and protected from observation even in these grounds by sheltering trees, we continued to play in spite of a censorious public." Within a few years, however, the "censorious public" and "disapproving mothers" had succeeded in stifling the game at Vassar.

But Vassar was not the only college where women tried their hand at baseball. In a letter to her former classmates at Smith College, Minnie Stephens (class of 1883) reminisced about the baseball clubs they had organized at the school in 1880. Stephens described the enthusiasm of the players and the keen competition at games. She also related how the Victorian-style clothing of the day, generally a hindrance to sporting endeavors, had actually benefited one of the players during a heated contest, "One vicious batter drove a ball directly into the belt line of her opponent, and had it not been for the rigid steel corset clasp worn in those days, she would have been knocked out completely." Like the women at Vassar, baseball players at Smith College faced opposition which eventually forced them to give up the game for a number of years.

Women baseball players were not limited to college campuses. In Springfield, Illinois, three men organized a women's baseball club in 1875. They were confident that the novelty of women playing baseball would attract large crowds and fatten their bankroll. On Sept. 11, 1875, the club's teams, labeled the "Blondes" and "Brunettes," played their first match. Newspapers heralded the event as the "first game of baseball ever played in public for gate money between feminine ball-tossers." The concept evidently caught on, for numerous other male entrepreneurs copied the idea and organized women's baseball teams. One group started the "Young Ladies' Baseball Club" in Philadelphia in 1883. These owners billed their team's games as entertainment spectacles, not serious competition, and they continually stressed the femininity and moral respectability of their players. A newspaper account of one of the club's first games relayed the management's claim that players were "selected with tender solicitude from 200 applicants, variety actresses and ballet girls being positively barred." Furthermore the article noted, "Only three of the lot had ever been on the stage, and they were in the strictly legitimate business."

The Young Ladies Baseball Club played its first game on Aug. 18, 1883, at Pastime Park in Philadelphia. Despite the supposed "200 applicants," only 16 girls were mustered to form the two teams for the contest; two young men rounded out the rosters. The game was played on a regulation-size diamond, but, as one observer wrote, it was too large for the women. "A ball thrown from pitcher to second base almost invariably fell short and was stopped on the roll. The throw from first to third base was an utter impossibility." Five hundred spectators witnessed the club's debut and were caught up in "uncontrollable laughter" much of the time. From a financial standpoint, however, the venture was a success. More than 1,500 fans

turned out for the club's match at the Manhattan Athletic Club on Sept. 23, 1883, where they "laughed themselves hungry and thirsty." Though one observer conceded that "four of the girls had become expert—for girls," it is obvious that "novelty" and not "ability" was the hallmark of women's baseball at the time.

Bloomer Girls

Another novel group of women baseball players was the Bloomer Girls. Actually "Bloomer Girls" was a misnomer, since Bloomer Girls teams were composed of both men and women. Kansas City Bloomer Girls, New York Bloomer Girls, Texas Bloomer Girls, and Boston Bloomer Girls were just a few of the teams traveling from diamond to diamond in the late 19th and early 20th centuries in search of fame and fortune. Despite the number of Bloomer Girl teams, they did not play each other and no formal league was set up. Instead, they journeyed from town to town, challenging men's amateur and semiprofessional teams. The Bloomer Girls teams relied on sideshow style appeal to draw fans and, not surprisingly, the bottom line was money. The manager of the Texas Bloomer Girls wrote to one prospective promoter in 1913, assuring him that the team's seven girls and four boys, "including the one-armed boy who plays center field," would draw enough fans to ensure the backer "three hundred dollars clear money" each week. A few of the male Bloomer Girls players like "Smoky Joe" Wood and Hall of Famer Rogers Hornsby went on to become successful big league ballplayers, but the future was not as bright for the female players who could not aspire to anything higher in the baseball world.

The Bloomer Girls teams were not the only option available to baseball-playing females around the turn of the century. Women's teams and mixed teams competed occasionally in "pickup" games. One such game took place in Kearsarge, New Hampshire, on Aug. 7, 1903. An article in the *Boston Herald* the following day noted, "The teams were made up of young ladies gowned in white and young men decked out in girls' clothes, all New Englanders, guests at the hotel." On Aug. 31, the newspaper announced an upcoming game at Forest Hills between the "Hickey and Clover clubs," each composed of five women and four men. One year later, in Flat Rock, Indiana, a group of women organized two baseball clubs, one consisting only of married players, the other only of single players.

While some women played on all-female or coed teams, others challenged social constraints of the day by playing on otherwise all-male teams. On June 12, 1903, the *Cincinnati Enquirer* printed an article about the efforts of a local woman, Miss M. E. Phelan, to get a job as center fielder with the all-male Flora Baseball Club of Indiana. Phelan wrote to the club's manager informing him, "I have played with a number of lady ball clubs and am considered the equal of the average country player." Whether the Flora club took Phelan up on her offer to play for them for "$60 per month and expenses" is unknown, but only four years later another Ohioan, Alta Weiss, became an overnight female baseball-playing sensation and, as one article put it, "perhaps the only girl in the

United States to obtain [a] college education through skill as a baseball player."

Weiss, a native of Ragersville, Ohio, became a celebrity in the Cleveland area when she made her pitching debut with the all-male, semiprofessional Vermilion Independents on Sept. 2, 1907. More than 1,200 fans attended the game in which Weiss pitched five innings, giving up only four hits and one run. By the time Weiss made her second appearance on Sept. 8, she was already being heralded as the "Girl Wonder" in the press. According to the *Vermilion News,* so many fans wanted to see Weiss play that special trains had to be run to Vermilion from Cleveland and surrounding towns.

Weiss pitched eight games for the Independents during their 1907 season. More than 13,000 fans saw the games, including a season high of 3,182, who witnessed her debut at Cleveland's League Park on Oct. 2, 1907. At least a dozen newspapers covered her exploits. The following year her father bought a half-interest in a men's semiprofessional team which was known thereafter as the Weiss All-Stars. It was based in Cleveland and, with Alta as a drawing card, played for large crowds throughout Ohio and Kentucky.

Though Weiss was far and away the best-known woman baseball player in northern Ohio at this time, she was not the only one. On June 22, 1908, the *Cleveland Press* introduced 14-year-old Carita Masteller to the public. The paper reported that she had been playing baseball for eight or nine years and was as good as Weiss. That same month Weiss pitched against another female pitcher, Irma Gribble. The two dueled again in August. In another unique game, two sisters from Bellevue, Ohio, Irene and Ruth Basford, pitched for opposing men's teams.

Another well-known woman baseball player who played on men's teams was Rhode Islander Elizabeth Murphy. "Lizzie," as she liked to be called, played amateur and semiprofessional baseball from about 1915 to 1935 and was known as the "Queen of Baseball" throughout New England and eastern Canada. After playing for a number of amateur teams in Rhode Island, Murphy signed with the semiprofessional Providence Independents in 1918. A few years later she joined Ed Carr's All-Stars of Boston and earned quite a reputation for her skills as a first baseman.

In 1928, while Murphy was still impressing the fans in New England, 14-year-old Margaret Gisolo helped her Blanford, Indiana, American Legion boys' baseball team win county, district, sectional, and state championships. In seven tournament games she had 9 hits in 21 at-bats. She scored 10 putouts and 28 assists in the field, with no errors charged against her. A protest against her participation filed by opposing teams went all the way to the American Legion's National Americanism Commission, which referred it to the major league baseball commissioner, Judge Kenesaw Mountain Landis. Landis determined that American Legion rules did not specifically ban the participation of women and disallowed the protest.

Landis had to address a similar situation three years later when the "Barnum of Baseball," Chattanooga Lookouts manager Joe Engel, signed 17-year-old Jackie Mitchell to a contract with his Southern Association minor league team, thus making her the first female profes-

sional baseball player. Mitchell had been taught to pitch by major leaguer Dazzy Vance and had once struck out nine men in a row in an amateur game. She became an overnight celebrity on April 2, 1931, when she pitched in an exhibition game against the visiting New York Yankees—and struck out Babe Ruth and Lou Gehrig, back to back. Speculation continues as to whether Ruth and Gehrig were merely putting on a show or really trying to hit Mitchell's pitches. Mitchell contended that it was not a setup and that the only instructions to the Yankee players had been to try not to hit the ball straight through the pitcher's box. A number of Yankees confirmed her story. Unfortunately Mitchell never had a chance to repeat her performance as a professional baseball player. A few days after her debut, Landis informed Engel that he had disallowed Mitchell's contract on the grounds that life in baseball was too strenuous for women. Organized baseball formalized the ban against women signing professional baseball contracts with men's teams on June 21, 1952; the ruling still stands.

A League is Born

The restriction on women playing professional baseball on men's teams did not prevent the formation of a women's professional baseball league, however. In 1943, with wartime manpower shortages threatening major league baseball, Chicago Cubs owner Philip K. Wrigley decided to form a women's professional softball league which would play its games in the major league stadiums while the men were away at war. Within a year of its founding, the league modified its rules and the All-American Girls Baseball League (AAGBL) was born. The AAGBL made its debut in 1943, when four teams—the Rockford [Illinois] Peaches, the South Bend [Indiana] Blue Sox, the Racine [Wisconsin] Belles, and the Kenosha [Wisconsin] Comets—squared off during the League's 108-game schedule. Attendance that year was 176,000 fans, which, according to one contemporary, meant that the league was "drawing a higher percentage of the population [in league cities] than major league baseball ever did in its greatest attendance years." Attendance figures continued to rise year after year, reaching a peak in 1948, when the league's 10 teams drew almost 1,000,000 fans. That same year, AAGBL teams drew more than 100,000 fans for a series of nine games in Puerto Rico.

Unlike women's teams of the past, the AAGBL relied on players' skills, not just their gender, to draw fans to the ballpark. The more than 500 women who played in the AAGBL during its 12-year existence were top-notch athletes. Many were veterans of championship school, community, or industrial softball teams, and a few had even played on boys' or men's baseball teams. In addition, many of the AAGBL managers were experienced professional baseball players—some, like Bill Wambsganss (the only player ever to achieve an unassisted triple play in a World Series), Max Carey, Jimmie Foxx, and Dave Bancroft, were legends.

The AAGBL represented one of the only times in history that women baseball players received widespread moral and financial support. Once World War II ended, however, social pressures for women to leave nontraditional jobs and return to household duties resumed. This fact, coupled with organizational problems and the rise of televised major league games, led to the demise of the AAGBL. Interest in the league all but disappeared until the 1980s, when a group of former players organized a players association and began lobbying to have the league honored in the National Baseball Hall of Fame. The popular media and serious scholars rediscovered the league and hundreds of articles about the AAGBL appeared in newspapers and magazines across the country. In October 1988, the Hall of Fame unveiled a permanent exhibit of AAGBL league memorabilia. In the summer of 1992, the AAGBL was further memorialized when it became the subject of the feature film, *A League of Their Own*.

Despite the newfound popularity of the AAGBL, modern-day women baseball players still face the same obstacles and criticisms endured by nineteenth century players. For the most part, organized teams and leagues remain closed to women. When Commissioner Ford Frick issued his ban against women players in 1952, his purpose was to prevent teams from using women players as publicity stunts. The end result of his edict was that even highly skilled women players (like those on the all-female team that tried, unsuccessfully, to gain admission to the men's Class A Florida State League in 1984) lost an important avenue for upward mobility and legitimacy in baseball. Women who challenge baseball's "men only" reputation rarely escape the experience unscathed. Julie Croteau, who gained notoriety in the late 1980s by playing first base for the St. Mary's (Maryland) College men's baseball team, earned school and conference honors yet still had to endure derisive comments from teammates. She left school in the middle of her junior year disillusioned with a system she believed treated women as inferior to men.

There is some indication, that the 1990s marked the start of a transformation of baseball from a strictly masculine pastime to a truly "national" pastime. Thanks to a series of court battles in the 1970s, generations of young girls have had the opportunity to play baseball on Little League teams. The 1998 season marked the 25th season in which girls have participated in Little League baseball, and it was the first time a girl played in the championship game of the Little League World Series. A growing number of girls and women are finding opportunities to play baseball in both female leagues and in co-educational leagues. Nearly 3 million girls and 300,000 women play amateur baseball, comprising 17.5 percent of baseball participants in the United States. Women's leagues also exist in Australia and Canada.

In 1994, the Colorado Silver Bullets begin their inaugural season as the first, and only, all-female professional baseball team to be officially recognized by the National Association of Professional Baseball Leagues. Their existence was made possible by the sponsorship of the Coors Brewing Company. Competing against men's teams, the team struggled on the field during its first few seasons, but they attracted national attention.

The team improved its record in 1996 to 18-34, with pitcher Pam Davis (7-7) becoming the first Bullets pitcher to avoid a losing record. The team's third season also saw its offense improve dramatically, from a .183 team batting

average in 1995 to .241 in 1996. And after failing to homer in their first two seasons, the Silver Bullets delivered five in 1996.

The Bullets finished with a winning record for the first time in 1997, and their quality of play continued to improve. Three players hit over .300, and the pitching was impressive, led by Lee Anne Ketcham, who was 7-5, with a 3.35 ERA. As the season ended, though, Coors announced that they would not renew their sponsorship. Without a sponsor, the team did not compete in 1998. "Everybody's put a lot of heart into it," founder Bob Hope said. "You've got little girls out there that had a glass ceiling in between them and the opportunity to play the game. The door's been opened, and we want to work hard to make sure it opens even wider." Phil Niekro, a Hall of Fame pitcher and the only manager in Bullets history said, "Women can play baseball. Someday a woman will play in the big leagues and I only hope I'm around to see it. I want to be sitting right there in the first row because I guarantee you that she will be standing in the batter's box and will be remembering the Silver Bullets. This is where we started."

The first steps towards that goal may have been taken in the past few years. Jodi Haller became the second woman to play college baseball, pitching for NAIA St. Vincent's (Pa.) College in 1990. Then in the fall of 1994, Lee Anne Ketcham and Julie Croteau played for the Maui Stingrays in the Hawaiian Winter Baseball League, a developmental winter league for players at about the Class A level. Both were members of the Colorado Silver Bullets.

The most promising advances were made by Ila Borders, who became the first woman to win a college baseball game in 1994. The left handed pitcher posted a 2-4 record with a 2.92 ERA. during her freshman year for Southern California College, finishing her college career with a 4-5 record at Whittier College in 1997. Later that year, Borders became the first women to pitch in a men's professional baseball game as a member of the St. Paul Saints of the independent Northern League. A mid-season trade sent her to the Duluth-Superior Dukes. In 1998, she joined the Dukes' starting rotation and finished with a record of 1-4 in 14 appearances.

Borders and the Silver Bullets not only showed that women can play baseball, they also suggested that women's baseball could be economically viable. Ladies League Baseball debuted as a professional women's league in 1997 with four teams—two in Los Angeles and one each in San Jose and Phoenix. The 30-game season was a success, and the league expanded eastward in 1998. The league changed its name to Ladies League Baseball and added teams in Buffalo and New Jersey. The expanded league intended to play a 56-game schedule starting in July and ending in September. However, low attendance, and escalating costs forced LPB owners to abbreviate the first half, playing only 16 games in the first half and canceling the second half of the regular season. The popularity of the Silver Bullets, and the recent success of two professional women's basketball leagues, suggest that this story is just beginning.

If girls and women continue to enjoy opportunities to play baseball, the sport will undoubtedly lose its masculine reputation. The question is whether or not current opportunities for female players will last. If they don't, today's female baseball players may find themselves sidelined, once again, with "a league of their own," watching rather than directly experiencing the national pastime.

## CHAPTER 23

The Amateur Draft

Allan Simpson

The year was 1964. Baseball was at a crossroads. By buying up the game's best amateur talent, the New York Yankees and some of the game's wealthier clubs were threatening to make a mockery of competitive balance, one of the game's time-honored virtues. The more they spent, the more successful they became.

To keep pace with the Yankees, who had won nine of the last 10 American League pennants and 14 of 16, some of the smaller-market teams were committing financial suicide. The fledgling Los Angeles Angels opened owner Gene Autry's saddlebags that year and paid untested outfielder Rick Reichardt a record $205,000 bonus—at the time, more than the annual salary of most major leaguers.

The more everyone willfully misspent on raw, unproven amateur prospects, the less there was to prop up a sagging player-development system. Once vibrant and self-sustaining with 460 teams in 1949, the minor leagues were rotting at the core. They had decayed 15 years later to a dangerously low 121 clubs, all of which were dependent on major league subsidization for survival.

By overspending on amateur talent and then underspending to develop it, baseball was playing its own version of Catch-22. The game's future well-being was at stake.

Not coincidentally, 1964 was the year baseball's high-ranking officers instituted a much-debated, much-awaited draft of amateur players. It would become effective in 1965 and become the primary means by which amateurs would infiltrate the professional ranks.

The draft's purpose was twofold: to stop the upward spiral of bonuses and to more evenly distribute talent. It was a reactionary measure to the Reichardt signing and the Yankees' decade of dominance. During the next 34 years, some 44,700 players would be selected in baseball's annual draft. No one—at least in 1964 dollars—would again approach the lavish signing bonus Reichardt received until all aspects of cost containment went out the window in the 1990s. And no team in the draft era would ever dominate the game again as the Yankees did. From 1978 to 1987, 10 different teams would win the World Series.

"Since the draft, there have been no particular dynasties," said Roland Hemond, Angels farm director in 1964 and Baltimore's general manager 30 years later. "That's given every indication that the draft has worked, giving more clubs the opportunity to build."

In 1936, the year the National Football League adopted its draft, the Cleveland Indians signed 17-year-old Iowa farmboy Bob Feller to a contract. The price? One dollar.

Players yearned then for the opportunity to play professional baseball, and were happy just for the chance. There was little competition among clubs for a player's services, no matter how talented he was.

By 1942, America's efforts in World War II siphoned off much of the available talent. The supply of players suddenly became limited. Competition drove the Detroit Tigers to sign outfielder Dick Wakefield to an unprecedented bonus of $52,000. Suddenly, the rush was on.

By the end of World War II, baseball had entered a new era, a golden era. Interest in the game fanned like wildfire. Minor league teams sprung up all over and competition for players became fierce. Teams had to offer bonuses to remain in the game. At the 1946 Winter Meetings, baseball made its first effort to curtail escalating bonuses by instituting a bonus rule. An agreement between the two major leagues and the National Association (the governing body for the minor leagues) designated a bonus player as anyone signed to a contract that exceeded a fixed level. Teams were fined if they paid out an amount that exceeded an imposed limit.

For the next two decades, major league officials wrestled with problems stemming from reckless spending and the competition for new recruits. Various solutions were proposed. None worked. Almost all were revised annually or simply thrown out. They tried several variations of the bonus rule, but that rule was legislated out in 1957 mainly because teams were openly cheating and regularly found ways to circumvent it.

"We'd pass a bonus rule and by the time we got out of the room," Detroit general manager Jim Campbell said, "we already figured out how to skin the cat. There was no way to really police it."

It also didn't help that few high-priced bonus babies reached the major leagues. Pittsburgh made 18-year-old left-hander Paul Pettit the game's first $100,000 bonus player in 1950, but it proved a foolhardy investment. The sore-armed Pettit won only one game in the big leagues.

Beginning in 1958, baseball tried a first-year rule that required teams to retain bonus babies on major league rosters in each of their first two full seasons, or expose them to waivers. But that didn't work either. Opponents said it was anti-development, that too many young players were forced to play in the big leagues before they were ready.

In the meantime, bonuses continued to escalate. In 1957 the Milwaukee Braves spent a record $120,000 for power-hitting outfielder Dave Nicholson, then topped that a few months later by handing $125,000 to shortstop Denis Menke.

At the 1959 winter meetings a proposal introducing a draft of amateur talent was made, but it proved to be five years before its time and was defeated.

In 1960 the Chicago Cubs inked pitcher-outfielder Danny Murphy, 17, to a record $130,000 bonus and immediately placed him in the big leagues. A year later, shortstop Bob Bailey was awarded $175,000 by Pittsburgh. At least six teams that year shelled out the largest bonus in club history. The heavy spending of 1961 sent ripples throughout baseball.

"Maybe we have to be saved from ourselves," Braves general manager John McHale said. "I think it's unfortunate that this is the system. A club like ours must be competitive. To achieve this, we must get ballplayers. If you're not prepared to pay, well, you just stand by and watch somebody else sign 'em. No, I don't know how to stop it. We've tried all kinds of ways, including several bonus rules. But nothing has worked. If a draft system similar to that used by football and basketball would hold up under our justice system, maybe that would be the answer.

"Certainly it would be a much healthier situation if the money that's paid for these tremendous bonuses could be channeled back into baseball. But right now it's as simple as this: If you want the kids, you've got to pay. We want 'em."

From 1958 to 1963, an estimated $45 million was spent on bonuses and first-year player salaries. In 1964 bonus payments continued to go through the roof. Led by Reichardt's lavish deal, a record $7 million-plus was paid out that year to amateur players, more than was spent on major league salaries. Teams such as the Yankees and Los Angeles Dodgers were buying up much of the talent in sight, and were prospering.

The timing was right for a systematic change to the conventional means of procuring talent.

By 1964 all the other major team sports in the United States deployed a draft to equally distribute amateur talent. Football introduced the concept in 1936, basketball followed in 1947 and hockey adopted a draft in 1963. But baseball officials were reluctant to follow suit. It was argued that a draft would penalize the industrious teams and be a form of socialism. Others opposed the draft for legal reasons.

Baseball, unlike the other professional sports, had operated under an anti-trust exemption since Supreme Court Justice Oliver Wendell Holmes bestowed favorable treatment for baseball in 1922. There was concern that a draft, which would restrict a player's freedom and bargaining power, would jeopardize baseball's special judicial standing. The game's hierarchy also feared that Congress would take an adverse stance on the premise that a baseball draft would deal primarily with high school players, or minors.

Football had no such concerns. At the time, most football players were of majority age and had options available to them. Players could consider three professional leagues—the National Football League, American Football League, and Canadian Football League—to market their talents. Baseball had no such options.

Opponents of a draft, however, were in the minority. Teams like the Dodgers and Yankees opposed it not on legal principle, but more for selfish reasons.

"There was some concern whether or not governmental interference would happen, whether some of the players and their representatives would challenge it," said Lee MacPhail, Orioles general manager in 1964 and mastermind of the powerful Yankees teams of the 1950s and early '60s. "But some clubs preferred things go on as they were, if they felt they were getting more than their fair share. They didn't want to change that.

"In the 10 years I was farm director of the Yankees (1949-1958), we won nine pennants and won the World Series five years in a row. Kids wanted to sign with the Yankees, the most glamorous team in baseball at the time. If two or three teams were after them, and one was the Yankees, we generally had the inside track."

Baseball adopted its draft at the 1964 winter meetings.

"The free agent draft will help solve our biggest problem: player procurement and development," Cleveland general manager Gabe Paul said. "It'll help equalize our teams. We have to do something to give the weaker teams greater incentive. Football has gone ahead unafraid of legal obstacles and they had more obstacles when they instituted their draft than we do now. They have benefited by our mistakes. It's about time for us to profit by their experience."

The First Draft

Baseball's new free agent draft would function in a manner similar to football and basketball. All eligible talent would be placed in a common pool with every team selecting from it in turn. When a team picked a player, it would gain exclusive rights to negotiate with him. The baseball draft, however, introduced several notable differences.

First, three drafts would be held each year instead of one. A summer meeting would be held around June 1, a winter session around Jan. 15. A third draft, limited to American Legion players not eligible to sign until Sept. 1, would be held in late summer. The Legion phase lasted only one year and the winter session was phased out in 1986.

The new amateur draft, officially known as the Rule IV draft, initially was open to permanent residents of the United States only, with a focus on high school graduates and college players who had attained sophomore standing or age 21. The college rule was amended two years later to include players of junior class standing. By 1990 players from Canada, Puerto Rico and other U.S. territories had become subject to selection. A full international draft remained the subject of debate through 1998.

Whereas a football team retained permanent negotiating rights to a draftee, a baseball clubs' rights terminated 15 days before the next draft session, later amended to one week. If a player didn't sign by the close period, he went back into a special "secondary" pool for the next time he was eligible to be selected. The secondary phase of the draft was eliminated in 1987.

One of the immediate benefits of a free agent draft, most clubs agreed, would be an improved game at the major league level. No longer would clubs be forced to clutter their 25-man rosters with green, untested youngsters. In 1964 major league teams had been forced to

protect 77 first-year players on their winter rosters.

While most of the emphasis in the early years of the draft was on raw high school talent, a gradual transition took place in the mid-1970s. College players became more and more attractive to scouts as college programs around the country took on a new commitment to fielding competitive teams.

In 1977, for the first time, more college players than high school players were selected, a trend that has never reversed itself. By 1981 the swing to college talent was so pronounced that the ratio of players entering the professional ranks from college programs as compared to high schools was nearly 5 to 1.

No matter what the source of talent, the baseball draft remained, at best, an inexact science. The success rate for first-round picks reaching the big leagues—even for a game or two—was no more than two in three, as compared to a near-100 percent success rate for first-round picks in football and basketball.

"Picking high school and college kids is the most unscientific, inexact of all the evaluations of talent," said Syd Thrift, former Pirates and Yankees general manager. "The reason is these kids are the furthest from the major leagues."

Unlike in football and basketball, whose drafts deal with more finished products, the best players drafted in baseball, even the top college players, invariably need to develop and refine their skills for several seasons in the minor leagues. In the draft's first 32 years, only 18 players went directly to the major leagues. Of that total, 14 had to backtrack to the minor leagues for additional seasoning.

"In football and basketball," Baltimore general manager Pat Gillick said, "they're drafting guys after they've spent three or four years in what is the equivalent of our farm system. The caliber of play in college baseball is not equivalent to that of basketball and football. It's not a very exact science. No matter how much testing you do, you never really know how a young guy's going to react to a pro situation until he plays in one."

Even a former No. 1 overall pick acknowledged how hit-and-miss the baseball draft can be. "The draft is, at best, a shot in the dark," said Bill Almon, the top selection in 1974 by the San Diego Padres. "That's the reason they draft so many players."

Boston Red Sox scout Joe Stephenson might have said it best, when describing how inexact and unpredictable the baseball draft can be. "We belong to the 4-H club. You hope you find a prospect. You hope you get him in the draft. You hope you can sign him. And you hope he can play."

To point out what a crapshoot the baseball draft can be, 1979 provided graphic evidence. Seattle took first baseman Al Chambers with the No. 1 overall pick that year, and he enjoyed only a cup of coffee in the big leagues. Minnesota spent its first-round pick on outfielder Kevin Brandt, whose career was such a washout that he played in only 40 minor league games. Meanwhile, the Dodgers quietly claimed pitcher Orel Hershiser in the 17th round and the Yankees plucked first baseman Don Mattingly in the 19th round.

Several other potential Hall of Famers were late-round finds. For example, second baseman Ryne Sandberg went in the 20th round to Philadelphia in 1978. Catcher Mike

Piazza was one of the great finds of all. He was a 62nd-round pick of Los Angeles in 1988, yet went on to become a star with the Dodgers and Mets—and even owned the richest contract in baseball history for a brief period in 1998. Players such as Kevin Mitchell and Bobby Bonilla, who went on to become impact players in the big leagues, weren't drafted at all.

Astute drafting, though, was largely responsible for a series of mini-dynasties of the draft era. Oakland laid the foundation to World Series championship teams from 1972-74 by selecting Rick Monday, Sal Bando, Gene Tenace and Reggie Jackson in 1965-66, the first two drafts. The Dodgers had a contending team for much of the 1970s because of a 1968 draft that produced 15 future big leaguers, including Bill Buckner, Ron Cey, Steve Garvey, and Dave Lopes. The Mets became a force in the mid to late 1980s because of astute drafting in the early '80s: They landed Darryl Strawberry (1980) and Dwight Gooden (1982) with first-round picks.

In the 1987-1990 period the Chicago White Sox chose pitcher Jack McDowell, third baseman Robin Ventura, first baseman Frank Thomas and pitcher Alex Fernandez with consecutive first-round picks, the corresponding first-round picks for the Dodgers were pitchers Dan Opperman, Bill Bene, Kiki Jones, and Ron Walden—none of whom reached the big leagues.

The Atlanta Braves became a World Series regular in the 1990s because of sound drafting. Third baseman Chipper Jones was the first pick in 1990—Atlanta's reward for finishing last in 1989. The nucleus of the team's celebrated pitching staff was acquired through the draft.

Since its inception, the draft largely has achieved its two underlying goals. Payments to untried amateur players have, except in the 1990s, been kept in line, while new meaning has been given to competitive balance.

Rick Monday, the No. 1 selection in the first draft, received a signing bonus from Kansas City of $104,000, little more than half what Reichardt received in his landmark deal of 1964. It wasn't until Detroit signed outfielder Kirk Gibson in 1978 and the Mets signed Strawberry two years later that players began to approach, in real dollars, the bonus Reichardt received. By then, inflation had reduced those figures to a fraction of Reichardt's windfall package. As late as 1987, Seattle paid just $160,000 to sign Ken Griffey Jr., the first overall pick.

It was only in 1988 and 1989—when Baltimore signed No. 1 overall pick Ben McDonald to an $800,000 three-year major league contract that provided for a $350,000 bonus, and Toronto later went to $575,000 for first baseman John Olerud—that players regularly topped the $200,000 barrier. By then, the financial well-being of the game was on such solid footing that spending lavishly on amateurs wasn't as dangerous as it was in 1964 when the draft was implemented.

In the early 1990s, however, the financial infrastructure of baseball took a quantum leap into uncharted waters. Not only were major league players paid annual salaries that often topped $5-6 million, but bonus payments to draft picks also went off the board.

Atlanta refused to select Arlington, Texas, high school pitcher Todd Van Poppel with the first selection in 1990 because of his insistence on attending the University of

Texas. Undeterred, Oakland swooped in and drafted Van Poppel with its first-round pick (14th overall). He was signed to a record $1.2 million, three-year major league contract that provided for a $500,000 bonus.

A year after, the Yankees stunned the baseball world by signing pitcher Brien Taylor to a whopping $1.55 bonus—more than double the previous record. Average bonus payments to first-round picks began to escalate appreciably, rising from $355,000 in 1991, to $482,000 in 1992, to $611,000 in 1993.

In 1994, with a major league players' strike looming, the average first-round bonus reached $796,000 with five players receiving bonuses of $1 million or more. Paul Wilson, that year's No. 1 pick, tied Taylor's record bonus by signing with the Mets for $1.55 million. Within weeks, that record was broken when the Florida Marlins coughed up $1.6 million to entice shortstop Josh Booty away from a promising football career at Louisiana State University. Booty's record bonus held up until 1998, when all hell broke loose.

A Whole New Ballgame

The entire process of signing amateur players went off the chart in January 1996 when the Marlins outbid every major league team for the rights to Cuban defector Livan Hernandez, 20, who was signed to a four-year major league contract that provided a record $2.5 million bonus. Several more Cubans went on to sign lucrative, seven-figure bonuses in the next few months.

The wave of Cuban defectors was fueled by Oakland's signing of right-hander Ariel Prieto in the 1995 draft. Prieto, 29, had escaped Cuba months earlier and made himself eligible for the draft by pitching for a team in the independent Western League. He was selected fifth overall by Oakland and signed to a contact that provided a $1.2 million bonus.

The draft's restrictive nature caused future Cuban defectors to take up residency in a foreign country that had diplomatic relations with the United States but wasn't subject to the draft. As such, Cubans would be free to sign on the open market and, as expected, bonuses to Cubans rose appreciably. Soon, means of circumventing the draft greatly impacted the draft itself and turned the whole player procurement process upside down. No longer would foreign players be the only ones to benefit from a free-market system.

Prior to 1996 major league teams rarely followed draft rules as outlined in the Professional Baseball Agreement, specifically as they pertained to Rule IV (e). That provision required teams to tender formal, uniform contract offers to draft picks within 15 days of their selection.

At the behest of agents, seven players—six first-round picks and a third-rounder—challenged that rule in 1996. Three elected not to follow through with grievance procedures, but four did and were declared free agents by Major League Baseball. Free to offer their services to all 30 major league clubs, the four were wined and dined extensively and in the end signed the four largest bonuses ever awarded amateur prospects—not just draft picks. All four signed with expansion teams that were still a year away from playing their first games.

First baseman Travis Lee, who had been drafted second overall by Minnesota, signed a stunning $10 million package with the expansion Arizona Diamondbacks. Soon thereafter, right-hander John Patterson (fifth, Expos) signed with the Diamondbacks for $6.075 million and left-hander Bobby Seay (12th, White Sox) signed with the expansion Tampa Bay Devil Rays for $3 million. The fourth player, right-hander Matt White (seventh, Giants), completed the once-in-a-lifetime windfall by agreeing to terms with the Tampa Bay Devil Rays for $10.2 million. Major League Baseball was quick to close that loophole in the future.

Meanwhile, Kris Benson became a mere footnote in draft history. Pittsburgh selected the Clemson right-hander with the first overall pick in the 1996 draft and while he signed with the Pirates for a record bonus of $2 million, his figure became almost pocket change compared to some of the deals signed by his fellow members of the Draft Class of '96.

Fearful of more fallout from a system that ran amok in 1996, teams took a cautious, more tempered approach to the selection of talent in 1997. In many cases, players were chosen on the basis of signability, not ability. Several first-round picks reached verbal agreements before the draft, an illegal tactic but a condition of their being selected in that round nonetheless. Others were passed over because their asking price was deemed too steep. Still, the record for players signing with the club that drafted them was broken again.

Florida high school left-hander Rick Ankiel, selected 72nd overall by the Cardinals, cut a deal for $2.5 million—$500,000 more than Benson. All teams passed on Ankiel in the first round because they couldn't get a handle on his bonus demands.

Ankiel's record lasted only until Rice University right-hander Matt Anderson, the No. 1 overall pick by Detroit, agreed on a $2.505 million deal. Anderson sat out the fall semester at Rice in order to keep his options open with the Tigers and finally agreed to his record deal, even as the Detroit largely held its ground. The Tigers, along with other clubs, were in the position of having to defend themselves against paying $10 million bonuses—even as they were spending record amounts.

"Those were special circumstances involving expansion teams," Tigers general manager Randy Smith said. "Two million dollars is a lot of money. We're not interested in signing any of these players for $10 million. If we're going to spend that kind of money, we're going to spend it on a proven major leaguer, not on someone who is unproven."

But agent Scott Boras, who engineered White's windfall bonus and masterminded several other record deals, said the developments of 1996 proved conclusively that a draft system artificially stunts bonuses. "What we've seen happen in the last two years, first internationally and then domestically, has given us a great barometer on the true worth of a select number of quality amateur players," Boras said. "The market has changed. I know from experience that there are many teams willing to pay optimum dollars for a premium talent."

In outfielder J.D. Drew, Boras had a player who was willing to go to the limit to test the legality of the draft system.

Drew was the consensus top player in the 1997 draft and was selected second overall by Philadelphia. Almost from the start, he was adamant that his rights were being stifled under a system that allowed him to negotiate with only one team. He set his price at $10 million before the draft and told every club not to draft him unless it was prepared to pay that amount. The Phillies took him anyway and negotiations went nowhere from the start. Drew eventually signed a contract with St. Paul of the independent Northern League and played the summer there.

"We made it very clear to the Phillies the day before the draft, and even an hour before the draft, and they still picked me," Drew said. "We had things on the table that other teams would offer. And we let the Phillies know that if they weren't willing to match that, then don't draft us."

Relations between Drew and the Phillies deteriorated. The Phillies viewed Benson's bonus as the benchmark, no matter what happened in 1996.

"This kid is not a free agent," Phillies owner Bill Giles said. "There is a number we think is right, and it's more than Benson got. We're willing to go above that, but not a whole lot above."

Philadelphia had until a week before the 1998 draft to strike a deal with Drew or lose his rights altogether. But the two sides never got close. Drew was simply thrown back into the pool, eligible again for selection. Interestingly, the Phillies had first pick and never considered Drew. They went for University of Miami third baseman Pat Burrell while Drew slipped to the fifth pick overall, where he was selected by the Cardinals.

"Obviously, there's a lot of pressure on the Cardinals to handle the Drew situation with due diligence," one scouting director said. "The whole industry will be paying attention."

What the industry saw was the Cardinals quickly agreeing to terms with Drew on a complicated major league contract with a $3 million signing bonus and major league contract money and incentives that could bring the total value to $8.5 million. Drew made all the contract negotiations appear almost anticlimactic after his long-awaited professional debut. He made quick three-week stops in Double A and Triple A before making his major league debut for the Cardinals the night Mark McGwire hit his 62nd home run. In 36 at bats for St. Louis, Drew hit .417 with five home runs and 13 RBIs, one of the best major league debuts in memory.

The chain reaction to the Drew contract started almost immediately, with the most obvious losers being the Phillies. Faced with the possibility of losing their first pick for the second straight year or topping Drew's St. Louis contract, Philadelphia quickly negotiated a five-year major league deal with Burrell that included a $3.15 million bonus and guarantees that brought the total value to $8

million. Thus they ended up paying Burrell, a lesser player by all accounts than Drew, significantly more than they offered Drew less than two months before.

Not only had the amateur free agent bar been raised, it had shot through the roof. There was little joy in baseball at the reality that Burrell had just been guaranteed more money than the defending World Series champion Florida Marlins were spending on their entire 1998 major league roster.

One important factor that the Burrell and Drew contracts introduced into other players' negotiations in 1998 was the major league contract that allowed payments to be spread over several years.

The Chicago Cubs got bogged down in negotiations with outfielder Corey Patterson, the third overall selection, when they refused to offer a such a contract. But they finally got Patterson to agree to terms on a $2.895 million minor league deal. The unique aspect of the contract was that while the payments were spread over five years, they carried a guaranteed interest rate of 6.5 percent on all deferred payments, making the actual cash value of the deal $3.7 million—a record for a minor league contract.

Oakland also held firm and refused to offer left-hander Mark Mulder, the second overall selection, a major league contract. But Mulder managed to get a $2.944 million signing bonus with interest at the rate of 7 percent until the final payment was due in December 1999. That made the total value of his contract $3.2 million.

The upward spiral in 1998 bonuses set the wheels in motion for major league officials to explore measures to curtail bonus payments or implement fundamental changes in the draft.

"It's definitely an issue that needs to be addressed," said Sandy Alderson, MLB's new executive vice president of baseball operations. "There are a number of ways the draft is no longer serving its original purpose. We're not redistributing the talent the way it was intended.

"Bonuses are skyrocketing and the better players are dropping to the richer, more successful clubs. Even major league players are beginning to wonder if the money that is going to amateur players is being distributed the right way."

The unsettling effects of 1996 and other developments of 1997 and 1998 notwithstanding, adoption of the draft in 1964 proved to be a blessing for baseball. It was the root that enabled the game to grow and prosper in the 1970s and 1980s.

"It's been an unqualified success," Lee MacPhail said. "Certainly, it's evened competition. It's given teams that have a difficult time competing for free-agent talent a fair share, or even more than a fair share. Close races in all divisions today goes back to the free-agent draft. If you didn't have it today, it would be a disaster."

Top 10 Draft Picks 1965-1998

Players are listed in the order in which they were drafted. Those who did not reach the major leagues are listed with the highest minor league classification they attained as of October 1998. DNP signifies that the draft pick did not play in Organized Baseball, or has not as of this edition of TOTAL BASEBALL.

Year/ Selection Number	Player	Team	Position — Highest Minor League Reached
1965			
1	Rick Monday	A's	OF
2	Les Rohr	Mets	P
3	Joe Coleman	Senators	P
4	Alex Barrett	Astros	SS - AAA
5	Billy Conigliaro	Red Sox	OF
6	Rick James	Cubs	P
7	Ray Fosse	Indians	C
8	John Wyatt	Dodgers	SS - A
9	Eddie Leon	Twins	SS
10	Doug Dickerson	Pirates	OF - A
1966			
1	Steve Chilcott	Mets	C - AAA
2	Reggie Jackson	A's	OF
3	Wayne Twitchell	Astros	P
4	Ken Brett	Red Sox	P-OF
5	Dean Burk	Cubs	P - AAA
6	Tom Grieve	Senators	OF
7	Leron Lee	Cardinals	OF
8	Jim De Neff	Angels	SS - AAA
9	Mike Biko	Phillies	P - A
10	Jim Lyttle	Yankees	OF
1967			
1	Ron Blomberg	Yankees	1B
2	Terry Hughes	Cubs	SS
3	Mike Garman	Red Sox	P
4	Jon Matlack	Mets	P
5	John Jones	Senators	C - A
6	John Mayberry	Astros	1B
7	Brian Bickerton	A's	P - AAA
8	Wayne Simpson	Reds	P
9	Mike Nunn	Angel	C - AAA
10	Ted Simmons	Cardinals	C
1968			
1	Tim Foli	Mets	SS
2	Pete Broberg	A's	P
3	Marty Cott	Astros	C - AAA
4	Thurman Munson	Yankees	C
5	Bobby Valentine	Dodgers	OF
6	Robert Weaver	Indians	SS - AA
7	Curtis Moore	Braves	OF - AAA
8	Donnie Castle	Senators	P-OF
9	Dick Sharon	Pirates	OF
10	Junior Kennedy	Orioles	SS

1969			
1	Jeff Burroughs	Senators	OF
2	J.R. Richard	Astros	P
3	Ted Nicholson	White Sox	3B - A
4	Randy Sterling	Mets	P
5	Alan Bannister	Angels	SS
6	Mike Anderson	Phillies	1B
7	Paul Ray Powell	Twins	OF
8	Terry McDermott	Dodgers	C
9	Don Stanhouse	A's	SS
10	Bob May	Pirates	P - A
1970			
1	Mike Ivie	Padres	C
2	Steve Dunning	Indians	P
3	Barry Foote	Expos	C
4	Darrell Porter	Brewers	C
5	Mike Martin	Phillies	P - AAA
6	Lee Richard	White Sox	SS
7	Randy Scarbery	Astros	P
8	Rex Goodson	Royals	C - AA
9	Jim Haller	Dodgers	P - AAA
10	Paul Dade	Angels	3B-OF
1971			
1	Danny Goodwin	White Sox	C
2	Jay Franklin	Padres	P
3	Tom Bianco	Brewers	SS
4	Condredge Holloway	Expos	SS - DNP
5	Roy Branch	Royals	P
6	Roy Thomas	Phillies	P
7	Roger Quiroga	Senators	P - A
8	Ed Kurpiel	Cardinals	1B-P - AAA
9	David Sloan	Indians	P - AA
10	Taylor Duncan	Braves	SS
1972			
1	Dave Roberts	Padres	3B
2	Rick Manning	Indians	SS
3	Larry Christenson	Phillies	P
4	Roy Howell	Rangers	3B
5	Bobby Goodman	Expos	C - AAA
6	Danny Thomas	Brewers	1B
7	Larry Payne	Reds	P - AAA
8	Dick Ruthven	Twins	P
9	Steve Englishbey	Astros	OF - AA
10	Dave Chalk	Angels	3B

1973			
1	David Clyde	Rangers	P
2	John Stearns	Phillies	C
3	Robin Yount	Brewers	SS
4	Dave Winfield	Padres	P-OF
5	Glenn Tufts	Indians	1B-P - AA
6	Johnnie LeMaster	Giants	SS
7	Billy Taylor	Angels	OF - A
8	Gary Roenicke	Expos	SS
9	Lew Olsen	Royals	P-AAA
10	Pat Rockett	Braves	SS
1974			
1	Bill Almon	Padres	SS
2	Tommy Boggs	Rangers	P
3	Lonnie Smith	Phillies	OF
4	Tom Brennan	Indians	P
5	Dale Murphy	Braves	C
6	Butch Edge	Brewers	P
7	Scot Thompson	Cubs	OF
8	Larry Monroe	White Sox	P
9	Ron Sorey	Expos	3B - A
10	Mike Miley	Angels	SS
1975			
1	Danny Goodwin	Angels	C
2	Mike Lentz	Padres	P
3	Les Filkins	Tigers	OF - AAA
4	Brian Rosinski	Cubs	OF - AAA
5	Rich O'Keefe	Brewers	OF- AAA
6	Butch Benton	Mets	C
7	Rick Cerone	Indians	C
8	Ted Barnicle	Giants	P - AAA
9	Clint Hurdle	Royals	OF
10	Art Miles	Expos	SS - A
1976			
1	Floyd Bannister	Astros	P
2	Pat Underwood	Tigers	P
3	Ken Smith	Braves	3B
4	Bill Bordley	Brewers	P
5	Bob Owchinko	Padres	P
6	Ken Landreaux	Angels	OF
7	Herm Segelke	Cubs	P
8	Steve Trout	White Sox	P
9	Bob James	Expos	P
10	Jamie Allen	Twins	P
1977			
1	Harold Baines	White Sox	1B-OF
2	Bill Gullickson	Expos	P
3	Paul Molitor	Brewers	SS
4	Tim Cole	Braves	P - AAA
5	Kevin Richards	Tigers	P - AA
6	Terry Kennedy	Cardinals	C
7	Richard Dotson	Angels	P
8	Brian Greer	Padres	OF
9	David Hibner	Rangers	SS - A
10	Craig Landis	Giants	SS - AAA

1978

1	Bob Horner	Braves	3B
2	Lloyd Moseby	Blue Jays	1B
3	Hubie Brooks	Mets	SS
4	Mike Morgan	A's	P
5	Andy Hawkins	Padres	P
6	Tito Nanni	Mariners	OF-1B - AAA
7	Bob Cummings	Giants	C - AA
8	Nick Hernandez	Brewers	C - A
9	Glenn Franklin	Expos	SS - AAA
10	Phil Lansford	Indians	SS - A

1979

1	Al Chambers	Mariners	OF
2	Tim Leary	Mets	P
3	Jay Schroeder	Blue Jays	C - A
4	Brad Komminsk	Braves	OF
5	Juan Bustabad	A's	SS - AAA
6	Andy Van Slyke	Cardinals	OF
7	Jon Bohnet	Indians	P
8	John Mizerock	Astros	C
9	Steve Buechele	White Sox	SS
10	Tim Wallach	Expos	1B

1980

1	Darryl Strawberry	Mets	OF
2	Garry Harris	Blue Jays	SS - AA
3	Ken Dayley	Braves	P
4	Mike King	A's	P - AAA
5	Jeff Pyburn	Padres	OF - AAA
6	Darnell Coles	Mariners	SS
7	Jay Reid	Giants	1B
8	Cecil Espy	White Sox	OF
9	Ross Jones	Dodgers	SS
10	Kelly Gruber	Indians	SS

1981

1	Mike Moore	Mariners	P
2	Joe Carter	Cubs	OF
3	Dick Schofield	Angels	SS
4	Terry Blocker	Mets	OF
5	Matt Williams	Blue Jays	P
6	Kevin McReynolds	Padres	OF
7	Daryl Boston	White Sox	OF
8	Bobby Meacham	Cardinals	SS
9	Ron Darling	Rangers	P
10	Mark Grant	Giants	P

1982

1	Shawon Dunston	Cubs	SS
2	Augie Schmidt	Blue Jays	SS - AAA
3	Jimmy Jones	Padres	P
4	Bryan Oelkers	Twins	P
5	Dwight Gooden	Mets	P
6	Spike Owen	Mariners	SS
7	Sam Khalifa	Pirates	SS
8	Bob Kipper	Angels	P
9	Duane Ward	Braves	P
10	John Morris	Royals	OF

1983

1	Tim Belcher	Twins	P
2	Kurt Stillwell	Reds	SS
3	Jeff Kunkel	Rangers	SS
4	Eddie Williams	Mets	3B
5	Stan Hilton	A's	P - AAA
6	Jackie Davidson	Cubs	P - AAA
7	Darrel Akerfelds	Mariners	P
8	Robbie Wine	Astros	C
9	Matt Stark	Blue Jays	C
10	Ray Hayward	Padres	P

1984

1	Shawn Abner	Mets	OF
2	Billy Swift	Mariners	P
3	Drew Hall	Cubs	P
4	Cory Snyder	Indians	3B
5	Pat Pacillo	Reds	P
6	Erik Pappas	Angels	C
7	Mike Dunne	Cardinals	P
8	Jay Bell	Twins	SS
9	Alan Cockrell	Giants	OF
10	Mark McGwire	A's	1B

1985

1	B.J. Surhoff	Brewers	SS
2	Will Clark	Giants	1B
3	Bobby Witt	Rangers	P
4	Barry Larkin	Reds	SS
5	Kurt Brown	White Sox	C - AA
6	Barry Bonds	Pirates	OF
7	Mike Campbell	Mariners	P
8	Pete Incaviglia	Expos	OF
9	Mike Poehl	Indians	P - AA
10	Chris Gwynn	Dodgers	OF

1986

1	Jeff King	Pirates	3B
2	Greg Swindell	Indians	P
3	Matt Williams	Giants	SS
4	Kevin Brown	Rangers	P
5	Kent Mercker	Braves	P
6	Gary Sheffield	Brewers	SS
7	Brad Brink	Phillies	P
8	Patrick Lennon	Mariners	SS
9	Derrick May	Cubs	OF
10	Derek Parks	Twins	C

1987

1	Ken Griffey, Jr.	Mariners	OF
2	Mark Merchant	Pirates	OF - AAA
3	Willie Banks	Twins	P
4	Mike Harkey	Cubs	P
5	Jack McDowell	White Sox	P
6	Derek Lilliquist	Braves	P
7	Chris Myers	Orioles	P - AA
8	Dan Opperman	Dodgers	P - AAA
9	Kevin Appier	Royals	P
10	Kevin Garner	Padres	P-OF - AAA

1988

1	Andy Benes	Padres	P
2	Mark Lewis	Indians	SS
3	Steve Avery	Braves	P
4	Gregg Olson	Orioles	P
5	Bill Bene	Dodgers	P - AAA
6	Monty Fariss	Rangers	SS
7	Willie Ansley	Astros	OF - AAA
8	Jim Abbott	Angels	P
9	Ty Griffin	Cubs	2B - AA
10	Robin Ventura	White Sox	3B

1989

1	Ben McDonald	Orioles	P
2	Tyler Houston	Braves	C
3	Roger Salkeld	Mariners	P
4	Jeff Jackson	Phillies	OF - AA
5	Donald Harris	Rangers	OF
6	Paul Coleman	Cardinals	OF - AA
7	Frank Thomas	White Sox	1B
8	Earl Cunningham	Cubs	OF - A
9	Kyle Abbott	Angels	P
10	Charles Johnson	Expos	C

1990

1	Chipper Jones	Braves	SS
2	Tony Clark	Tigers	1B
3	Mike Lieberthal	Phillies	C
4	Alex Fernandez	White Sox	P
5	Kurt Miller	Pirates	P
6	Marc Newfield	Mariners	1B-OF
7	Dan Wilson	Reds	C
8	Tim Costo	Indians	SS
9	Ron Walden	Dodgers	P - A
10	Carl Everett	Yankees	OF

1991

1	Brien Taylor	Yankees	P - AA
2	Mike Kelly	Braves	OF
3	David McCarty	Twins	1B
4	Dmitri Young	Cardinals	3B
5	Kenny Henderson	Brewers	P - A
6	John Burke	Astros	P
7	Joe Vitiello	Royals	1B
8	Joey Hamilton	Padres	P
9	Mark Smith	Orioles	OF
10	Tyler Green	Phillies	P

1992

1	Phil Nevin	Astros	3B
2	Paul Shuey	Indians	P
3	B.J. Wallace	Expos	P - AA
4	Jeffrey Hammonds	Orioles	OF
5	Chad Mottola	Reds	OF
6	Derek Jeter	Yankees	SS
7	Calvin Murray	Giants	OF - AAA
8	Pete Janicki	Angels	P - AAA
9	Preston Wilson	Mets	3B
10	Michael Tucker	Royals	SS

1993

1	Alex Rodriguez	Mariners	SS
2	Darren Dreifort	Dodgers	P
3	Brian Anderson	Angels	P
4	Wayne Gomes	Phillies	P
5	Jeff Granger	Royals	P
6	Steve Soderstrom	Giants	P
7	Trot Nixon	Red Sox	OF
8	Kirk Presley	Mets	P - A
9	Matt Brunson	Tigers	SS - A
10	Brooks Kieschnick	Cubs	1B-OF

1994

1	Paul Wilson	Mets	P
2	Ben Grieve	A's	OF
3	Dustin Hermanson	Padres	P
4	Antone Williamson	Brewers	3B
5	Josh Booty	Marlins	SS
6	McKay Christensen	Angels	OF - A
7	Doug Million	Rockies	P - AA
8	Todd Walker	Twins	2B
9	C.J. Nitkowski	Reds	P
10	Jaret Wright	Indians	P

1995

1	Darin Erstad	Angels	OF
2	Ben Davis	Padres	C-AAA
3	Jose Cruz Jr.	Mariners	OF
4	Kerry Wood	Cubs	P
5	Ariel Prieto	Athletics	P
6	Jaime Jones	Marlins	OF-AA
7	Jonathan Johnson	Rangers	P-AAA
8	Todd Helton	Rockies	1B
9	Geoff Jenkins	Brewers	OF
10	Chad Hermansen	Pirates	SS-AAA

1996

1	Kris Benson	Pirates	P-AAA
2	Travis Lee	Twins	1B
3	Braden Looper	Cardinals	P
4	Bill Koch	Blue Jays	P-AA
5	John Patterson	Expos	P-A
6	Seth Greisinger	Tigers	P
7	Matt White	Giants	P-A
8	Chad Green	Brewers	OF-AA
9	Mark Kotsay	Marlins	OF
10	Eric Chavez	Athletics	3B

1997

1	Matt Anderson	Tigers	P
2	J.D. Drew	Phillies	OF
3	Troy Glaus	Angels	3B
4	Jason Grilli	Giants	P-AAA
5	Vernon Wells	Blue Jays	OF-A
6	Geoff Goetz	Mets	P-A
7	Dan Reichert	Royals	P-AAA
8	J.J. Davis	Pirates	OF-A
9	Michael Cuddyer	Twins	SS-A
10	Jon Garland	Cubs	P-A

1998

1	Pat Burrell	Phillies	3B-A
2	Mark Mulder	Athletics	P-DNP
3	Corey Patterson	Cubs	OF-DNP
4	Jeff Austin	Royals	P-DNS
5	J.D. Drew	Cardinals	OF
6	Ryan Mills	Twins	P-A
7	Austin Kearns	Reds	OF-Rookie
8	Felipe Lopez	Blue Jays	SS-A
9	Sean Burroughs	Padres	3B-DNP
10	Carlos Pena	Rangers	1B-A

## CHAPTER 24

Baseball Reporting

Jack Lang

If baseball really was invented by Abner Doubleday at Cooperstown, N.Y., in 1839, we have only the findings of the Mills Commission to support the theory. That commission, formed in 1905, relied heavily on the rambling recollections of an old mining engineer named Abner Graves to reach the conclusion that Doubleday indeed "devised the first scheme for playing baseball." Graves' testimonies were later found to be chock full of inaccuracies.

There can be no dispute, however, as to when the art of writing about baseball began. In the mid-1850s William Trotter Porter gave a decided lift to the game with extensive coverage in his publication *Spirit of the Times.* Until Porter's reports began appearing regularly, baseball in America was ignored in most publications.

John Rickards Betts of Tulane University, in his *American Quarterly* paper "Sporting Journalism in Nineteenth-Century America," credits Porter with being the greatest "antebellum sports editor" in America. On Dec. 10, 1831, he published the first copy of *Spirit of the Times.* It was, for a time, the country's leading sports journal. But while it reported on racing, prize fighting, and even cricket, it did not devote space to baseball until the 1850s.

When he did start reporting on baseball, Porter is credited with having given it the title of "the national game" and also with having printed the first box scores (although this claim is questionable) and "dope" stories. Shortly thereafter, Frank Queen and Harrison Trent founded the *New York Clipper,* which devoted even more space to baseball. One reason was the addition to the staff of Henry Chadwick, who had begun his career as a journalist in 1844 by contributing to the *Long Island Star.* Chadwick, who had played baseball briefly in his youth, was a devotee of the game and wrote of it voluminously.

Alfred H. Spink, in his book *The National Game* published in 1910, credits William Cauldwell, editor of the *New York Mercury,* as being the first man to write about baseball for a daily newspaper. Spink's authority for this assertion is a gentleman named William M. Rankin, one of the nation's leading reporters on sports in the late 1880s. Rankin, who was the official scorer for the Mutual Club, also wrote extensively for such New York papers as the *Times, Tribune, World, Mail,* and *Express.* He was considered one of the game's leading authorities. According to Rankin, Cauldwell was writing about baseball by 1853. But Cauldwell found the work of editing his newspaper and writing about baseball too exhausting, and he soon hired Chadwick to write on baseball for the *Mercury.* It was not long before Henry Chadwick became the leading baseball authority in America.

If weekly and daily publications were slow to catch on to the popularity of baseball, they caught up in the late 1880s. Magazines like *The Police Gazette* and *Sporting Life* devoted considerable space to the game. Soon editors of daily newspapers recognized the interest in baseball. James Gordon Bennett, one of the world's most respected newspapermen, who was editor of the *New York Tribune,* was one of the first to increase coverage of the game.

In time every newspaper in America devoted a full page to sports . . . focusing on baseball. Charles Dana of the *New York Sun* and Joseph Pulitzer of the *New York World* are recognized as pioneers in the creation of entire sports departments. By the 1890s, most newspapers in America had created a sports staff. It was in the final decade of the 19th century that sports writing began to develop as a full-time occupation on the nation's newspapers.

At the time of his death in 1908, Chadwick was clearly established as the nation's leading baseball authority. Chadwick, who even in his youth had been honored with the nickname "Father Chadwick" for his role in the development of baseball, was such a busy writer that the history of his various affiliations is in conflict. He is credited in some publications as having worked for the *Brooklyn Eagle* in 1856 and the *New York Clipper* in 1857. In others, Chadwick is reported to have written for the *Mercury* before any of the others, or for both at the same time.

Whatever his affiliations, Chadwick was the most prolific of the early-day baseball writers, and eventually he abandoned daily reporting of the game to concentrate on weekly roundups and books about the game.

Chadwick originated what is known today as *The Baseball Guide,* published by *The Sporting News.* He wrote and edited the first baseball guide in 1860, the *Beadle's Dime Base Ball Player.* Later he edited the *DeWitt's Guide* from 1869 to 1880 and, finally, *Spalding's Baseball Guide* from 1881 until his death.

Chadwick's involvement in the game was more than just writing of it. He was instrumental in changing several rules, is credited with having perfected the box score, and was most concerned about drinking, gambling, and rowdyism at ballparks. He led campaigns to clean up the game. Baseball officials of the day heeded his advice.

As early as 1868, Chadwick wrote the first hardcover book in America devoted strictly to baseball. Appropriately, it was titled: *The Game of Base Ball.*

Chadwick's writings on the game led to honors that would be unheard of in the modern era. In 1894, the National League elected Henry an honorary member and two years later voted him a lifetime pension of $600 a

year. If a major league today awarded a baseball writer a pension, it would result in an investigation.

Honors continued for Chadwick 30 years after his death. In 1938, one year before the Hall of Fame opened, Chadwick was elected to the Cooperstown shrine as one of the great contributors to the game along with Alexander Cartwright. It was the same year that Grover Cleveland Alexander was elected. Although baseball writers are now honored with the J.G. Taylor Spink Award and scrolls in their honor are mounted in the Hall of Fame Library, Chadwick is the only former baseball writer with a bronze plaque in the main hall, alongside those of Babe Ruth, Ty Cobb, Joe DiMaggio, Cy Young, Mickey Mantle, Ted Williams, Grover Cleveland Alexander, and others.

Another early-day baseball writer who earned great respect from the leaders of the game was Timothy H. Murnane, known as the Silver King. When Murnane died in 1917, he was so highly regarded that the American League paid for and erected a huge marble tombstone over his grave in Old Calvary Cemetery in Roslindale, Mass. The tombstone cites Murnane as a "pioneer of baseball . . . champion of its integrity . . . gifted and fearless writer."

Murnane was a baseball player who turned to writing after his playing days were over. He founded the *Boston Referee* in 1885, and his writings attracted the editors of the *Boston Globe,* who in 1888 hired him as their baseball writer, a job he held until his death. In his 30 years as baseball editor of the *Globe,* he was one of the most influential writers in the country and even found time to serve as president of the New England League for 24 years.

Upon his death, it was learned that Murnane left only a small estate to his widow. Immediately, a benefit all-star game was scheduled between great players of the American League and the Boston Red Sox with all proceeds to go to Murnane's widow.

On Sept. 17, 1917, a crowd of 17,119 Boston fans (a very good-sized turnout at that time) attended the game which included a pregame show featuring Ziegfeld Follies stars Will Rogers and Fanny Brice. The all-star team included such names as Grover Cleveland Alexander, Walter Johnson, Johnny Evers, Wally Schang, Shoeless Joe Jackson, Buck Weaver, Stuffy McInnis, Eddie Collins, Ty Cobb, and Tris Speaker. Heavyweight boxing champion John L. Sullivan coached first base and Babe Ruth pitched the first six innings for Boston.

All appeared without pay. That was evidence of the esteem in which Murnane was held.

'A Novel Style Among Baseball Writers'

Until the creation of full-time sports staffs in the late 1890s, writing about baseball was, in many cities, a hit-and-miss affair. In many areas, the reports of games were turned in by club secretaries or part-time correspondents. It was often less-than-objective reporting.

With the advent of full-time sports reporters and sports editors in the early 1890s, especially in New York, other major cities suddenly followed suit. This resulted in localized styles of writing and language familiar to the areas.

John Rickards Betts describes it in his *American Quarterly* article on 19th-century journalism: "The most important developments in sporting journalism outside New York were taking place on the Chicago newspapers. Charles Seymour of the *Herald,* Finley Peter Dunne of the *News* and a reporter for the *Times* were creators of a novel style among baseball writers, a style based on picturesque jargon, lively humor and grotesque exaggeration."

Hugh Fullerton, who was one of the great turn-of-the-century baseball writers in Chicago, noted that "the style of reporting baseball changed all over the country."

In New York and Boston the style of baseball writing emphasized expert knowledge of the game. In Chicago and other western cities, the style involved more humor and cynicism. Often the final score of the game was secondary. Reporters described games with a great flourish and seemed intent on capturing readers' interest with their individual writing styles. Here is the way one *Chicago Times* writer reported a Chicago Cubs game on Sept. 26, 1888:

"The ninth inning of yesterday's ball game was a marvel of beauty. To describe it one needs a big stretch of canvas, a white-wash brush, a pan of green paint, and an artist's hand. Words are hardly expressive enough . . . Mr. Schoeneck is a large secretion of fat around considerable bone and muscle, and he knocked the ball out of the diamond and puffed down to first base . . . Immediately after which Mr. Buckley bunted the ball and went to first, his fatness moving to second.

"The inning had not been particularly gorgeous up to this moment, but with the hitting of a fly by Mr. Hines it took on a resplendent and glorious aspect, for Mr. Van Altren [Van Haltren] got under the fly, gauged it with his blue eye, and muffed it beautifully. When the ball reached Capt. Anson it had lost much of its virulence and was bounding gently long, smiling the while. But if it had not been for a chunk of lava fresh from the earth it could not have had more fun with Capt. Anson, for it rollicked out of his hands and into them again and all over his person, blithely tapped him in the face, and danced away. Indeed, it was a beautiful error, that one of Anson's—a regular sunset error flushed and radiant with shadings of purple and a mellow border.

"Mr. Van Altren picked it up and looked about irresolutely. He was debating whether he should sacrifice skill to art, and being a young man of no high culture in this respect, he esteemed art as naught, but hurled the ball to the plate to catch Mr. Hines. But art was triumphant for all, for Mr. Van Altren's irresolution had been fatal. The ball came to the plate a second after Mr. Hines crossed safe, and Mr. Raphael, Mr. M. Angelo, and Mr. Turner will have to take a seat near the door."

A reporter describing a game in that manner today would not be assigned to cover the next day's game. But it was in that style that games were recorded around the turn of the century. A baseball writer, covering a game at three o'clock in the afternoon, had until three o'clock in the morning to write his story. This enabled many to write what some journalists later referred to as "fabulous narratives." Writers were bent on influencing the readers with their imaginative use of the language in long, descriptive phrases. Space in newspapers was plentiful, and baseball writers frequently used two and three columns to describe

a single game. It gave writers an opportunity to develop their own style in an effort to capture the imagination of the readers.

Nowhere was this more evident than in Chicago, where such writers as Sy Sanborn, Ring Lardner, Hugh Fullerton, and Charles Dryden were winning over readers with their often humorous accounts of baseball games. Lardner came out of South Bend, Ind., and covered the Chicago Cubs for the *Inter-Ocean,* the *Examiner,* and later the *Tribune.* Eventually he abandoned daily baseball writing and made his mark as an author of short stories, many with a baseball theme. "You Know Me Al" and "Alibi Ike" are two of his baseball classics.

Fullerton was considered the most remarkable forecaster of his day, and his predictions on the outcome of games were sought in every major league city. When he died at age 72 in 1946, he was hailed in his obituaries as "the game's original dopester." But for all the expertise and humor that he brought to his readers, Fullerton is best remembered in journalistic circles as the writer most responsible for exposing the Chicago White Sox for throwing the 1919 World Series.

Prior to the 1919 Series, the fearless forecaster had predicted an easy victory for the Sox against Cincinnati. But early in the Series Fullerton was convinced that the Sox were not giving it their best effort. In his summary of the Series after Chicago lost, Fullerton suggested as much. But he was not about to let go of it there. Fullerton went to New York, where he followed up leads that tied some of the White Sox to gamblers. The *New York Evening World* published a toned-down version of his theory, and Fullerton was criticized by members of his own craft. But his persistence continued until he convinced American League president Ban Johnson to investigate the matter. Using much of the information Fullerton supplied, Johnson brought the investigation to a head late in the 1920 season. The result was a trial in which eight players were found innocent. But the same eight were later banned from organized baseball for life by Judge Kenesaw Mountain Landis, the newly appointed commissioner of baseball. Fullerton's investigative reporting was responsible for the findings of the commissioner.

Fullerton was a baseball purist, and his "Ten Commandments of Sports" were widely published. They read:

1. *Thou shalt not quit.*
2. *Thou shalt not alibi.*
3. *Thou shalt not gloat over winning.*
4. *Thou shalt not sulk over losing.*
5. *Thou shalt not take unfair advantage.*
6. *Thou shalt not ask odds thou art not willing to give.*
7. *Thou shalt always be willing to give the benefit of doubt.*
8. *Thou shalt not underestimate an opponent or overestimate thyself.*
9. *Remember that the game is the thing and he who thinks otherwise is no true sportsman.*
10. *Honor the game thou players; he who plays the game straight and hard wins even when he loses.*

It was common at the turn of the century for baseball writers to begin their stories with a few lines of verse. Grantland Rice, who came out of Nashville, where he had been sports editor of the *Tennessean,* to join the staff of the *Cleveland Plain Dealer,* was perhaps the most widely known writer in this style. His poetic jingles were read throughout the American League and many attempted to copy his style.

Rice did not remain long in Cleveland. He longed for the South and returned there. But then he returned North to New York, where his syndicated column appeared throughout the country. Rice actually was better known for his football writing than he was for his baseball work.

Besides Rice, another leading baseball writer of the early 20th century who frequently began his stories with a few lines of verse was Franklin Pierce Adams, who wrote under the byline of "F.P.A." He wrote what is known as "Baseball's Sad Lexicon" during a New York Giants-Chicago Cubs series in 1908. Quoted to this day, it read in part:

> *Ruthlessly pricking our gonfalon bubble,*
> *Making a Giant hit into a double,*
> *Words that are weighty with nothing but trouble,*
> *Tinker to Evers to Chance.*

That verse, as much as their actual records on the field, is credited with leading to the induction of the Chicago Cubs' infield trio into the Hall of Fame.

Charles Dryden, born in 1857, moved about as much as any baseball writer in the late 1890s and into the 1900s. He covered the California League for the *San Francisco Examiner* and then moved to the *New York American* and on again to Philadelphia with the *North American.* But in 1905 he was offered what was then considered the highest salary paid a baseball writer and moved to the *Chicago Examiner.* The salary was reported to be $100 weekly.

It was in Chicago that Dryden gained fame with his nicknames for the baseball people he wrote about. He called Charles Comiskey, the White Sox owner, "the Old Roman". He termed the light-hitting White Sox the "Hitless Wonders." Chicago Cubs manager Frank Chance was dubbed "the Peerless Leader." It was also Dryden who coined the phrase about the hapless Washington Senators: "Washington . . . first in war, first in peace and last in the American League."

Keeping the Press in the Press Box

Dryden was a charter member of the Baseball Writers Association of America (BBWAA), which was formed officially in 1908. It was an association born of necessity when baseball writing in the early years of the 20th century was attracting some of the nation's outstanding young writers and baseball itself was dominating the sports pages. Only the baseball owners failed to recognize the importance of this feisty band of scribes. They were treated—or mistreated—as a necessary evil.

At the 1908 playoff game between the Chicago Cubs and the New York Giants at New York's Polo Grounds, Hugh Fullerton arrived to find actor Louis Mann in his seat. This was not uncommon. Giants manager John McGraw loved to hobnob with Broadway actors and often told them to sit in the press box. When Fullerton asked Mann to vacate the seat, Mann refused. No Giants official

would order him to move. At first Fullerton attempted to write his story sitting on Mann's lap, but eventually he sat on a box in the aisle next to him and covered the entire game from that seat.

Baseball writers continued to suffer mistreatment during the Chicago Cubs-Detroit Tigers World Series that followed. The writers covering the Series were outraged at the treatment accorded them. In Chicago, out-of-town writers were placed in the back row of the grandstand. In Detroit, the writers were compelled to climb a ladder to the roof of the first base pavilion, where they were forced to write in the rain and snow that hampered the Series. Finally, unwilling to endure these conditions another year, the writers decided to organize. At the request of Jack Ryder of Cincinnati and Henry Edwards of Cleveland, Joseph S. Jackson, sports editor of the *Detroit Free Press,* arranged a meeting room in the Hotel Ponchartrain on the morning of the final game. That was Oct. 14, 1908. Present at that first meeting, the founding fathers of the Baseball Writers Association of America, were: Tim Murnane and Paul Shannon, Boston; Charles Hughes, Hugh Keough, Malcolm McLean, Hugh Fullerton, Bill Phelon, and Sy Sanborn, Chicago; Ed Bang and Henry Edwards, Cleveland; Jack Ryder and Charles Zuber, Cincinnati; J.W. McConaughy and Sid Mercer, New York; William Weart, Philadelphia; George Moreland, Pittsburgh; Joseph Jackson and Joseph Smith, Detroit; James Crusinberry, Hal Lanigan, W.G. Murphy, and J.B. Sheridan, St. Louis; and Ed Grillo, Washington.

Joseph Jackson was appointed temporary chairman and Sy Sanborn, secretary. Tim Murnane was appointed treasurer, and he passed the hat to collect $1 dues from each of the founding fathers.

A more formal meeting was held in New York in December 1908 at the annual winter meetings of the two leagues. Fullerton, Edwards, and Weart, who had been appointed in Detroit to draw up a constitution, listed four items as the main objective of the BBWAA. They were:

1. *To encourage a square deal in baseball.*
2. *To simplify the rules in scoring baseball games and promote uniformity in scoring.*
3. *To secure better facilities for reporting baseball games and better regulation of the scorers' boxes during both championship seasons and World Series at the parks of the American and National League Clubs, hereinafter to be designated the major leagues.*
4. *To bring together into a closer bond of friendship the writers of baseball throughout the United States and Canada.*

The organization was enthusiastically endorsed from the start by both leagues. Promise of full support was received by league presidents, who appointed the local representatives of chapters in each city to serve as custodians of the league press boxes.

Immediately conditions improved throughout baseball. No longer did writers have the problem of outsiders occupying seats in the press box. Interlopers were immediately escorted out by park security men upon orders of the local BBWAA representative. The writers had the backing of the league to police their own work area.

By 1910-11, the baseball writing fraternity was accepting into its ranks some of the bright young writers of that era—men who would go on to greater heights in the field of literature. Covering the Giants in New York that year were men like Grantland Rice, Damon Runyon, Heywood Broun, and Fred Lieb. Rice later became recognized as the dean of America's sportswriters; Runyon became the chronicler of Broadway night life and the characters who inhabited the Great White Way, while Broun went on to the editorial side of newspapers and founded the Newspaper Guild of America. Lieb was a prolific writer who was one of baseball's leading biographers.

Elsewhere in the country, other fine young writers were honing their skills covering baseball. Some of the greats who were regular beat writers in those days were Red Smith, Frank Graham, John Kieran, J. Roy Stockton, Warren Brown, John Carmichael, Shirley Povich, John Drebinger, and Tom Meany.

There was a coterie of writers in that era whose names were synonymous with baseball for the simple reason that they covered baseball from the first day of spring training until the final out of the World Series. A writer assigned to the Tigers or Cardinals or Pirates or any other club stayed with that team the entire season, traveled to the cities in each league, and made every road trip. Writers associated with one club were almost as well known as the players they wrote about.

Baseball coverage did not vary until after World War II. It was standard practice up to then for the writers on morning newspapers to wait until the end of the game and write on who won or lost, and how. The final score might not appear until well down into the story, but the reporter was writing up the details of the game. Writers for afternoon papers also often sat in the press box after the game and wrote their versions, with considerable editorial opinion and second-guessing. Talking to ballplayers after the game was not considered a necessity. Occasionally, but not always, writers did visit the clubhouses after games for some conversation and verification with ballplayers.

The style of writing changed after World War II. The need to know was of primary importance, and reporters for afternoon papers made it a habit to get down to the clubhouse after a game for what was then known as "the second-day angle." The afternoon papers of the next day had to offer the readers something they had not learned in their morning paper.

But starting in 1946 and in the years that followed, a change in the style of covering a baseball game was evident—especially in New York. No longer did the writers on afternoon papers have the ballplayers to themselves after a game. Dick Young was an enterprising young baseball writer for the *New York Daily News,* a morning newspaper. Because of the multiple editions of his newspaper, he had the time to visit the clubhouse and "pick up quotes" or find out why certain plays had occurred.

Young changed the style of baseball reporting with his hustle, and ever since he arrived, the work of the morning newspaper reporter has not been the same. No beat reporter nowadays would dare turn in a story unless it had clubhouse quotes. Editors demand it.

Along with the enterprise of Dick Young came radio and the television age. Fans were now able to listen to and

watch games at home. What they wanted in their papers the next day was inside stuff from the players and managers. For reporters working night games with deadlines approaching, the job of writing baseball was no longer the sinecure it had been in the first four decades of the century.

Picture the baseball writer of the 1930s. All games started around 3 p.m. There was no need for a pregame story, since most newspapers did not go to press until around midnight. A baseball writer in that era was finished working around 6 or 7 p.m. and was free again until game time the next day.

The baseball beat writer's job was always considered the glamour assignment on any sports staff. Baseball writers were envied for what was considered an easy lifestyle: spring training in some warm climate around the middle of February and then a ballgame every afternoon for six months followed by the World Series. From mid-October until mid-February, the baseball writer had a relative vacation, covering only signings, trades, and trivial matters.

Today's baseball writer, what with virtually every game being played at night and early editions at all papers, finds himself working around the clock. The average writer covering baseball today, especially for a morning newspaper, will find himself writing three or four stories in a single day. He also works year-round, covering labor-management issues.

Night games and travel have also made it difficult for the modern-day writer. Before plane travel, all clubs moved from city to city by train, and the writers traveled with them. Trains left around midnight and arrived early the next morning in the team's next city. At least there was a night of rest and time to fraternize with the ballplayers. Today, teams fly out right after a game, and writers find it impossible to catch the team plane. They most often travel alone.

The result is that fewer writers remain on the baseball beat for any length of time. The travel, the long hours, and the night games have made it an arduous task. Before the age of television, it was quite common for a writer to remain on the beat for 20 to 30 years. Today, a writer feels "burned out" after just a few years.

Awards for Today and for All-Time

Despite the changes in baseball writing, the BBWAA retains the prestige it earned shortly after being founded in 1908. Much of this is due to the organization's annual awards and its responsibility for voting on the Hall of Fame.

The major awards the BBWAA votes on each year are the Most Valuable Player, the Cy Young Award, the Rookie of the Year, the Manager of the Year, and the Hall of Fame, since the Cooperstown shrine's creation in 1936. (For a detailed discussion and the annual balloting for these awards, see Bill Deane's essay in this volume.)

Of all the responsibilities of the Baseball Writers Association, none is taken more seriously than voting for the Hall of Fame. The idea for a baseball Hall of Fame was first discussed in 1935 to celebrate the hundredth anniversary of baseball in 1939. The National Baseball Centennial Commission was formed. Ford Frick, then the National League president, was the moving force behind the creation of the Hall of Fame and the decision to name Cooperstown as the site for the museum. That same year, the Baseball Writers Association was asked by the Commission to vote for players to be elected to the Hall of Fame and inducted officially when the Hall opened in 1939.

The BBWAA has been charged with that responsibility ever since. Another group, known as the Veterans Committee, also votes on players, former executives, managers, and umpires.

Baseball, especially in recent years, has been the most written-about sport in America. No longer is it a sport covered solely by the beat writers for newspapers. It is a game that captures the imagination of authors, a fact born out by the Hall of Fame Library. By the middle of 1990, the library contained approximately 25,000 books about baseball.

By the end of 1990 the library was unable to handle the volume of books and magazine and newspaper articles that were being written about the game. Under the directorship of Hall of Fame chairman Edward Stack, an expansion to the library was undertaken. The completely refurbished library opened late in 1993 and included over 30,000 books. In addition, the written words of the game on file at the library include copies of the *New York Clipper* from the 1850s, *Sporting Life,* and *The Sporting News.*

In 1962 the Hall of Fame decided to honor the outstanding writers with an award and a place of honor in the library. The award was named in honor of J. G. Taylor Spink, former publisher of *The Sporting News.* Since 1962, over 40 writers have had their names enshrined in the writers' wing of the Hall, among them Damon Runyon, Ring Lardner, Grantland Rice, and Dick Young.

Leonard Koppett, the 1993 honoree, noted in his Cooperstown acceptance speech: "The daily baseball writer has played an indispensable role in the creation, growth and maintenance of baseball's popularity. Its commercial success, as well as its place in American culture, have been based on daily newspaper accounts, from Henry B. Chadwick down through Red Smith.

"Even today, when radio and television have surpassed newspapers in impact, it is the daily baseball coverage from which all other media get their information about what they decide to emphasize. And even the call-in talk shows, which set so much of the news agenda, exist only because callers form opinions from what they read about that they cannot see."

One major change in baseball writing and reporting in the 1970s was the need for each paper to have a reporter focus on the labor angle in the game. Writers like Murray Chass of the *New York Times* and Jerome Holtzman of the *Chicago Tribune* devoted much of their attention to reporting the struggles between the Players Association and the club owners. Writing about the labor front has become a full-time job and both men, former beat writers, now concentrate almost exclusively on these off-the-field activities.

Another innovation in baseball writing in the 1970s was the advent of the "notes and quotes" columns which began appearing in Sunday newspapers in most major

league cities. These columns began with beat writers picking up notes and gossip during the week and saving them all for a juicy Sunday column of tidbits. They became as popular as the Broadway gossip columns and soon every paper of any size was running a "notes and quotes" feature. Dick Young of the *New York Daily News* was one of the early innovators of this style of reporting with his popular "Clubhouse Confidential." Peter Gammons of the *Boston Globe* soon concentrated on collecting gossip from other writers around the leagues. The *Globe* devotes an entire page to Gammons' writings each Sunday of the year.

Baseball writers who became tired of the daily beat found a way in the 1990s to keep writing baseball. They convinced editors that a "National Baseball Writer" was needed. These writers spend their time writing about baseball events of national interest such as a big series between two contending teams, a player on a hitting streak about to set a record, a pitcher with a scoreless streak going . . . anything that is of national interest aside from the doings of the local club. Today, virtually every major newspaper has a beat writer covering that city's club plus a national baseball writer focusing on the overall baseball scene.

Baseball is a sport that has inspired political columnists like George Will and Pulitzer Prize-winning authors such as James Michener and David Halberstam to publish books about the game. No sport in America is covered more extensively or comprehensively than baseball. It all begins with the game and the beat writers who cover it.

## CHAPTER 25

Fantasy Baseball Games

Don L. Daglow, Jack Kavanagh, and Garth Chouteau

Young baseball fans lie in bed at night and dream of playing baseball in the big leagues. Old boys—that is, grownups—imagine that they may yet manage their hometown teams. Table-top board games, dice baseball, and the computer have allowed us to live out both fantasies by recreating game situations and allowing us to experiment, rewarding us with different results based on the strategic wisdom of our decisions.

Table Baseball—A World Apart

Baseball simulations have been around longer than Organized Baseball. The first professional league, the National Association, was formed in 1871. The first table baseball game had been patented in 1868. In 1994, baseball simulations took the place of the real thing when major league baseball shut down. Rotisserie type leagues—for which team owners drafted and traded major-league players and conducted their season's play based on real-life performances—could not feed off daily boxscores. However, table gamers rolled dice, shuffled cards, flicked spinners or, in the digital simulations, tapped keyboards or clicked mouse buttons.

The undisputed Father of Table Baseball was Francis C. Sebring, whose board game, Parlour Baseball, was described in an 1866 issue of *Frank Leslie's Illustrated Newspaper.* The game was patented in 1868 (patent No. 74154). The diagram shows it was a mechanical game. One player sent a coin plateward by a spring mechanism while another swung a swiveled bat. The coin, when struck, would end up in a slot, designated an out or a hit. This simple approach was continued in dozens of mechanical games, on tabletops and in pinball arcades, which miniaturized the real game.

However, games played with dice, cards, or spinners have dominated the home baseball game area. These approaches provide greater options and more variable outcomes. Thousands of such games were invented. Most probably remained the private passion of a fan who created his own game to play on his own table. Inventing a simulation of baseball is simple. Baseball itself can be viewed as being transferred from a board game to a playing field. The ancient Hindu game of Pachesi (parcheesi) starts the player at home base and returns him there after he has circled the bases. That's what the play action of baseball amounts to.

As in more complicated board games, the trip around the bases can be made more elaborate and difficult, but the goal is the same: to score more times than your opponents. For the first 60-plus years of table baseball, a problem existed. The players in the lineup did not perform the way they did in actual baseball play. Babe Ruth was no more likely to hit a home run than the weakest hitting infielder. Even worse, the good glove work of the infielder was not reflected in the play of the table game. Pitchers had no traits of superiority nor were any of them easier to hit than others. You could write Walter Johnson's name in the lineup but a pitcher with any other name was as likely to strike out batters.

The first breakthrough to real life came when Clifford A. Van Beek of Green Bay, Wis., marketed *National Pastime* in 1931. He had patented his game in 1923 and was issued No. 1,536,639 in 1925. Although it was advertised in the 1931 issues of *Baseball Magazine,* the fledgling game succumbed to the Great Depression and was not seen again until *APBA* was marketed in 1951. The APBA game imitated *National Pastime* and, as its followers grew into cult-like devotees, its inventor, J. Richard Seitz, allowed them to believe he was the one who had mastered a way to imitate the baseball performances of actual players.

Actually, a game with a different approach, *All-Star Baseball,* marketed by CADACO and designed by a real-life baseball player, Ethan Allen, had appeared in 1941. Seitz had contributed a primitive method of ranking pitchers to his upgrading of the *National Pastime* game. Allen, a .300 hitting outfielder in the National League, did not bother (all pitchers might have looked alike to him). At any rate, in *All-Star Baseball,* the spinner was influenced only by the batter's tendencies. Babe Ruth would hit more home runs than the weak-hitting shortstop because the space for home runs was larger on his player disc. Alas, Allen had not built in a way for the glove man to justify his place on the team. Seitz had tackled that with a grading system. Seitz also widened the play variations by borrowing another idea from the past. Although it was not a real life game, like the one that appeared in the early 1930s, purportedly the brainstorm of pitcher Danny MacFayden, it provided different play charts according to the base/out situation.

The *APBA* game was challenged by *Strat-O-Matic,* also using dice and cards, and its own closely guarded method of rating players. Both games found acceptance and survive to the present. Many other games came and went, but a few had enduring value beyond their playability because, unlike *APBA* and *Strat-O-Matic,* they did not conceal their codes. They revealed the process of rating players for batting, for power factors, for defense, and for

pitching effectiveness as well as strikeout and walks. At least one of these is still marketed, *Extra Innings,* by Big League Game Company of Duluth, Minn.

Which game is best? It is whichever game satisfies the particular player. The cost of advertising and, particularly, the requirement of royalty payments to Major League Baseball Properties and the Major League Baseball Players Association for the use of the names of the teams and the players, drove most small competitors from the market. *ABPA* and *Strat-O-Matic* have been able to pass the costs along to their loyal followers.

Electronic Baseball Games: Before It Was a Business

We often hear that before the excesses of Charlie Finley and the beginning of the age of free agency in the mid-1970s, "Baseball was a game, not just a business." The same is true of the computer baseball simulations of that too-soon ancient era. The nostalgia for those simpler times, however, can't disguise the fact that today's baseball simulations just keep getting better and better.

In 1959, George R. Lindsey published an article in the Operations Research Journal titled "Statistical Data Useful for the Operation of a Baseball Team." Laboriously tracking each detail of hundreds of games by traditional paper and pencil methods, Lindsey and his father tested rules from baseball's unwritten "book." Their research demonstrated that, on average, the traditional righty-lefty matchup did indeed benefit the hitter (by some 15 percentage points). They also established that teams made the correct choice when, with the bases loaded in the early innings, they played the infield back for the double play.

It was also in 1959 that the first baseball model was written on a computer. R. E. Trueman built a mathematical analysis of 5,000 games to answer the same key strategic questions posed by the Lindseys. By 1973 the power of computers had grown to the point where R. Allen Freeze of the University of British Columbia ran a 200,000-game simulation to determine the best batting order for a baseball team, which turned out to be the good-hitting leadoff and powerful cleanup hitter order enshrined in baseball tradition. In those years in the early 1970s the computer had helped lay the foundation for the invention of sabermetrics and the work of Dick Cramer, Bill James, Pete Palmer, John Thorn and many others who deserve mention in such a list.

The computer baseball simulations written before 1970 studied the overall averages of baseball, analyzing which strategy produces the best results most often in a given situation. Created on "batch" machines that read computer cards punched with holes to encode their programs and data, they operated without intervention by any user and printed reports of their calculations. Of course, if a programmer made a mistake in a first draft of a baseball program and the outs didn't count properly, a Giants-Dodgers grudge match could run to 500 innings before a frustrated computer operator saw a ream of printed play-by-play spilling from the printer and realized there was a runaway program.

But human intervention was just around the corner.

The invention of economical "time-sharing" machines in the late 1960s meant that multiple users could run small programs from different terminals tied to a central computer. Results could be displayed on the computer screen instead of printed on paper. The program could even pause mid-stream to ask the user for input.

The computer game was born.

The Digital Equipment Corp. (DEC) PDP-10 computer was the time-sharing machine of choice for colleges during this era, and filled a room the size of a large garage. As a result of their dominance in the universities, the PDP-10's were the platform for almost all of the original computer games, and Microsoft founder Bill Gates started his computing career on the machine often referred to simply as the "10."

The first baseball simulation game was created in 1971 on a DEC PDP-10 at the Claremont Colleges Computer Center in Claremont Calif., about two miles from the house where 8-year-old Mark McGwire then lived. Don Daglow, a student at Pomona College in Claremont, had grown up playing board games like *All-Star Baseball* and *Strat-O-Matic.* He recognized that their systems were good but still not highly accurate because they ignored players' pitching and fielding stats, or at best compromised how they modeled them in the simulation. Daglow set out to create a more sophisticated baseball simulation game using the school computer that would factor for the pitcher's abilities and introduce defense into the game as well.

After two months of surreptitious programming (since writing games was supposed to be forbidden on the academic machines), players of Daglow's program could watch the play-by-play account of any game as it was rattled off on a teletype printer like the ones from which Ernie Harwell and Mel Allen used to report the results of road games on the radio. Users could sit at the computer terminal and press different keys to make managerial decisions such as inserting a pinch hitter, walking the batter, or warming up a reliever in the bullpen. It was the first time a human manager could match wits against a computer in a mathematically defined environment.

The first computer baseball game was a student project inspired solely by a love of baseball, and at the time Daglow did not realize that no one else had preceded him. With the game limited to use on a room-sized machine, no one ever dreamed that within just a few short years computer baseball games would become big business.

1978-1983: The First Great Video Game War

In the early and mid-1970s, a series of coin-operated, arcade-style machines entertained people by showing squares and lines on a TV screen, and allowed users to move the lines or squares to play a game. The most famous of these was *Pong,* where two lines controlled by plastic knobs knocked a square "ball" back and forth across the screen. Home versions followed , consoles that plugged into a TV set and allowed consumers to play *Pong* in their living rooms. Atari, the manufacturer of *Pong,* improved on this concept by creating a console that played different games on interchangeable cartridges, and which could display images in a variety of colors. By the

late 1970s the "Atari VCS" was a huge hit in American toy stores, followed by Mattel's Intellivision and Coleco's Colecovision.

Baseball video games of the late 1970s and early 1980s were arcade contests, where the screen showed the outline of a baseball field, and single-color player silhouettes were drawn in at each position. Everything had to be controlled by a human being; the games had no "artificial (computerized) intelligence" to control the opposing players. One user pressed a button to choose a fast or slow pitch, and perhaps another button to select if the pitch would be straigh or if it would curve. The player controlling the batter pressed a button to swing the bat. Once the ball was in the air, a joystick or "control disk" was used by each player to direct the lead runner and the fielder closest to the ball. Though primitive by today's standards, some of these games sold over 2 million copies, big hits by the standards of any entertainment medium.

With the technology evolving rapidly, the "second generation" of baseball video games arrived almost on top of the first. By 1982 these new versions could show the game on TV in a format similar to an actual TV broadcast, from a center field camera, with insets in the corners to show the runner on first dancing off the bag. By today's standards, the graphics were primitive, with two-color "players" whose outlines still were made from visible square blocks.

With this level of realism, it became practical for the first time in video games to spend the extra money to license the names and stats of real major league players, so that a computer figure that represented Dale Murphy or Andre Dawson really would hit more home runs, while Nolan Ryan's fastball would be greased lightning on the screen. In turn, this assignment of an identity to each player enabled other elements of actual baseball to enter the videogame arena. Pitchers would tire, pinch hitters and runners entered the games, and much more real baseball strategy came into users' living rooms.

The first video game to simulate individual player performance and include these simulation features was Mattel's *World Series Baseball,* and it was also the first electronic sports game to use the television-camera-style display format. Unfortunately for fans, at the last minute Mattel decided not to pay the licensing fee for players' names, and th real stars were cut from the product and replaced with fictional names . . . actually the names of the Intellivision game design team. Don Daglow, now serving as director of game design for Mattel Electronics, designed the project, working with programmer Eddie Dombrower, and much of the baseball simulation was based on his original 1971 program.

By 1983 too many games crowded the shelves, and numerous fast-buck publishers went bankrupt. Unable to return games to the defunct manufacturers, toy stores sold them off at bargain prices on huge discount tables. Soon parents and kids balked at paying $35 for one new game when they could buy seven $5 games for the same price. The final blow was the arrival of inexpensive home computers such as the Commodore 64 and Atari 800, which not only played games but could be used for word processing and educational software.

One by one, the major firms folded their video game divisions, laid off their staffs and struggled to save whatever was left of their companies. Atari split into two separate units that were sold to different investors; Mattel Electronics went from 1,800 people to five in 15 months; Coleco ultimately disappeared entirely into bankruptcy. When Mattel's *World Series Baseball* shipped in 1983 this market disaster was operating at full force, and few copies were ever actually sold.

1982-1994: The Home Computer Comes of Age

When the Apple II home computer was first introduced in 1977, it heralded a defining moment. The prior generation of machines (led by the 1975 release of the MITS Altair 8800, by many definitions the first PC) slipped into obscurity, while the next wave—the Tandy TRS-80, Commodore PET and the Atari 800—pushed on to a whole new level of public acceptance that ushered in "the Age of the PC."

The earliest major baseball simulation on home computers was the Apple II game simply called *Computer Baseball,* published by Strategic Simulations Inc. (SSI) in 1981. Although its designers were not familiar with sabermetrics, it was nonetheless a reasonably accurate simulation that pitted great teams from history against each other and allowed the user to manage either or both teams. Harnessing the 48K of memory in the Apple II (versus 4K to 8K for video game cartridges of the time), *Computer Baseball* nevertheless ignored the flashy graphics, displaying an outline of a stadium while describing the action in text. The ball's location was displayed on the stadium diagram, giving some added inspiration to the user's imagination.

By 1982 the Commodore 64 home computer had challenged the Apple II, offering many of the same capabilities in a cheaper plastic case for much less money ($850 for a complete system, vs. about twice that much for a somewhat more powerful contemporary Apple IIe).

Apple soon focused its efforts on the new Macintosh line, and would-be challenges Mattel and Atari were slow to introduce their planned new computers. Commodore had the field almost to itself, and their Commodores sold in the millions. Their commercials warned, "why buy your child a video game when the kid next door is using a Commodore 64 to prepare for the college courses and jobs of the next century?"

Ironically, these less expensive home computers often turned out to be used primarily as game machines, and the computer game business grew into a real industry as Commodore sales boomed. Electronic Arts (EA) Inc., founded in 1982 by Trip Hawkins, pushed lasting play value, simple interfaces, and graphic quality. Video games seemed simplistic by comparison, and began to fade from prominence.

In 1984 the lack of graphics caught up with *Computer Baseball,* as the first version of *Micro League Baseball* arrived to take the baseball simulation crown. The graphics now told the story so well that text narration was omitted, and only the names and stats of the batter and the pitcher were displayed.

Action-only games, which ignored stats and played as arcade style contests, also flourished during the early 1980s on home computers. Scott Orr's Gamestar Inc.

produced *Star League Baseball* as part of its line of sports games, and no other baseball game of that era, including all the simulations, sold as well.

In the mid-1980s Gamestar was sold to Activision, where *Star League Baseball* was allowed to fade from the public eye. Accolade (then led by Activision co-founder Alan Miller) filled the void with the first *Hardball* game, designed by Bob Whitehead. Although Intellivision *World Series Baseball* was the first game to show the pitches from one angle and the fielding action from another, *Hardball* was the first to do so on home computers, and its graphics were larger and its textures more detailed than prior games. Replacing *Star League* as the leading action baseball game, *Hardball* and its sequels were major products for the next decade, outselling any other series of computer baseball games.

In 1985 the time had come when the newest personal computers (then the Amiga and the IBM PC) could support a game that was both an accurate "sabermetrics-based" simulation and a flashy graphic display of baseball. Daglow, now a producer at Electronic Arts, believed that such a game could support sophisticated "artificial intelligence" imitating the strategy of an individual manager. Hall of Famer Earl Weaver, then newly (and temporarily) retired as Orioles manager, was the unanimous choice as the game's standard-bearer, while Eddie Dombrower again signed on to do the programming. Over the next several years EA published versions of *Earl Weaver Baseball* for the Amiga, the PC, and the Macintosh.

Utilizing a split-screen approach that showed a closeup of the batter and pitcher alongside a picture of the field, Weaver Baseball featured many innovations that later became standard on all games. First of all was the feature of Weaver himself. The design team worked closely with the Orioles manager, boiling his "God bless the three run homer" philosophy down into the key factors he used to make managerial decisions. Once the original "electronic Earl Weaver" had been built, its tendencies were compared against those that Weaver himself showed in real games and the model was refined.

Also important was the game's ability to schedule and simulate a complete season of 162 games and keep records of all the simulated stats, although to play such a full 162 games (at half an hour per contest) would take over eighty hours. All prior programs had required the user to plan out a schedule, play the games, keep the stats, and figure out who were the league leaders. *Weaver* automated this process, and for all its relative slowness it was a huge improvement over paper-and-pencil record-keeping. It was also the first game to support trading players from one team to another. *Weaver* earned a Gold Disk (the software equivalent of a Gold Record) and was honored with a place in *Computer Gaming World* magazine's Computer Game Hall of Fame. Today, more than a decade after its release, *Earl Weaver Baseball* and its sequels are still considered by many avid gamers to be the best baseball simulations ever devised.

The introduction of *Earl Weaver Baseball* put pressure on *Hardball* and *Micro League Baseball,* and the late 1980s saw a "battle of the versions" as all three games maneuvered for position. Activision's *Pete Rose Baseball* and Epyx's *Sporting News Baseball,* each of which also combined stats with graphics, also joined the fray briefly.

The venerable board games *Strat-O-Matic Baseball, Pursue the Pennant* and *APBA* all introduced text-only, then text-with-graphics versions of their best-selling products, and by 1990 baseball fans had a broad choice of computer games to simulate the national pastime.

Each company battled to introduce new features for players to stay on top of the market. Accolade's *Hardball II,* designed by Distinctive Software in Canada, added statistical simulation to its game. *Micro League Baseball II* and *III* added more stats to refine its simulation and a feature that allowed users to draft players onto teams, and *Micro League IV* tried adding miniature videos to its display to keep up on the graphics front. *Weaver II* and Activision's *Pete Rose Baseball* experimented with a "multiple camera" TV broadcast style display that showed the action from behind the fielders and allowed users to choose between several different angles for the display.

For years, baseball games that allowed users to control the fielding had suffered from a basic problem: it was hard to catch a fly or popup on the TV screen just by watching the tiny white circle that was the ball and the tiny black circle that was its shadow. Even experienced players often missed routine flies, undermining the enjoyment of many games.

In 1990 Daglow, having founded Stormfront Studios Inc., began working on *Tony LaRussa Baseball.* La Russa played a continuing role, co-designing the game with the programmers and ultimately joining Stormfront's board of directors. Knowing that computers are good at quickly drawing basic geometric shapes, Daglow attacked the flyball problem by placing a shaded circle on the field to show where the ball was going to land. Routine flyballs became routine, and all games now use some form of flyball "fielding target."

In the early 1990s *LaRussa Baseball* replaced *Weaver Baseball* as *Hardball's* chief rival, but neither matched *Hardball's* sales levels despite their innovations. New versions of each game rolled into the marketplace, each with new features to out-simulate and out-dazzle the competition. But the home computer baseball game again had to take a back seat to its living room-based cousin, the video game.

1989-1994: The Second Great Video Game War

Japanese game makers Nintendo and Sega first started showing their new video game consoles at trade shows in the United States in the mid-1980s, and by 1987 Nintendo's "NES" unit in particular was selling very well to its young audience. Some of the first baseball games for Nintendo, designed in Japan by companies such as Jaleco, already included the names of American major leaguers and used batter power ratings, runners' speed, and pitchers' control abilities to influence play. Although rather simple by comparison with the PC simulations, these cartridges accomplished a very important goal: they got the mainstream of video game playing kids interested in the names and stats of real players in the game.

Soon after, the Sega Genesis appeared, a more powerful videogame system than the original Nintendo NES. One of the first Genesis games was Sega's *Tommy*

Lasorda Baseball, which featured a unique "blimp view" after the ball was hit, displaying the action looking straight down on top of the heads of the players. Stores burned by the crash of 1983-84 began to believe that video games were really back, and stocked both Sega and Nintendo cartridges more deeply as their popularity continued to grow.

These early 1990s cartridges were very different from those programmed only a decade before. An early Intellivision video game contained 4,000 characters of computer code and graphics. When *LaRussa Baseball '95* was introduced for the Sega Genesis in 1994, the game shipped on a cartridge that held the equivalent of 2,000,000 characters of information, an increase of 500 times over the size of the earlier game.

That size, of course, made these new video game platforms potential new battlegrounds for the creators of baseball simulations. Some games, like *Cal Ripken Baseball, Ken Griffey Baseball, Nolan Ryan Baseball* and *Roger Clemens Baseball* used famous players and flashy graphics to appeal to the younger audiences who buy video games. Sega's 1992 *Sports Talk Baseball* featured the voice of veteran broadcaster Lon Simmons, and Accolade's *Hardball III* for Sega and PC featured network broadcaster Al Michaels, but the digitized voices used too much precious cartridge space and were dropped from later versions until CD-ROMs replaced cartridges in the mid-1990s.

By 1994 video games were once again the kings of the toy stores, selling millions of baseball games as part of a multi-billion dollar market. Even the video game juggernaut, however, could not withstand the challenge presented by the baseball strike.

1994-Present: The Strike and Baseball's Comeback

The baseball strike of 1994 was to baseball video games what the asteroid impact of 65 million years ago was to carnivores: it swept away many older franchises, damaged others, and when baseball was reborn in the late 1990s it created an open field where new games flourished.

Although baseball licensees in all parts of the market anecdotally reported a 35 percent reduction in their business, the changes in baseball games were even more profound. The popularity of other sports and their electronic counterparts had flourished in baseball's absence, and when it returned its niche was both more shallow and more precarious in the calendar.

Before 1994 baseball games sold year-round, with spikes at the start of the season, World Series time, and during the Christmas season. After the strike baseball games slowly rebounded until they again were strong sellers from March through July. But once August came and the NFL exhibition season began, baseball sales dropped from the best-seller lists like summer annuals in an autumn freeze.

Microleague Baseball, after 10 years of publication, never recovered from the strike. Long-time franchises *La Russa Baseball* and *Hardball* were published by small companies that couldn't match the promotional budgets of their large competitors. Both lost market share and forged partnerships with larger game companies in order to compete.

The publishers of hit baseball games in the late 1990's are usually billion dollar companies with a wide range of products, because only those companies can afford the development budgets and marketing campaigns needed to win out in the marketplace.

EA Sports, whose *Earl Weaver Baseball* had been pushed from the market in the early 90's, took advantage of the post-strike era to reenter the baseball wars with *Triple Play Baseball.* Backed by an expensive TV ad campaign, it took the number one position on the PSX and PC. On the Sony PlayStation it was Sony itself that provided the chief rival, called *MLB.* On the Nintendo 64 Nintendo itself used its publishing might to introduce mega-hit *Ken Griffey Baseball,* while Acclaim provided a rival game in *All Star Baseball.*

The spring of 1998 provided the irrefutable signal that baseball games were back: as Mark McGwire and Sammy Sosa powered home runs out of the park, baseball games occupied positions one through four on the sports game best-seller list for the first time since the early 1990's.

The Waves of New Technology . . . and What We Cannot Simulate

The "arms race" of computer baseball simulations continues to spiral upwards. The room-sized PDP-10 replayed a season at the rate of five seconds per game in 1971; the desk-sized PC of 1998 uses 20 times as many variables for every batter and pitcher, yet still plays each complete game in less than a sixteenth of a second.

Computer baseball simulation designers have begun harnessing this additional power through the latest in 3D graphics technology, the structure upon which almost all modern video games and computer games are based.

The big sky-blue DEC PDP-10s had 32,000 bytes of RAM (memory), shared by more than 30 users at a time, quickly "swapping" one program into the computer's memory for a few tenths of a second before kicking it out and bringing in the next program. It was the technical equivalent of watching a class of 35 students reciting 35 different poems over 35 different telephones, with each poet getting to speak one word at a time before yielding the floor to the next person. The system was slow: to search a list of 200 names for a single player took almost a minute during peak usage times.

By contrast, only 28 years later, today's typical new home computer may have 16,000,000 to 128,000,000 bytes of memory. In one human generation we took what would have filled hundreds of garages and made it small enough to fit on the top of your desk. The search through 200 names now happens so quickly that to the naked eye it appears to be instantaneous. Many games now offer modem play, where users in different cities can play against each other over telephone lines, and Internet-based fantasy games in which subscribers across the country compete in Rotisserie-style have provided yet another electronic outlet for the baseball fan.

But for all our new technology, there are still parts of

baseball that we cannot simulate, and different schools of thought on what "baseball simulations" ought to be. For example, one game designer who was not himself a baseball fan tried to develop a game by listening carefully to the opinions of coworkers who were baseball experts. He concluded that he could create the best baseball simulation ever . . . by making sure all the statistics from the simulated games came out exactly the same as those from real life! If a player had a .280 batting average in real life and his simulated average was below .280, he would get a hit the next time up, guaranteed, whether the pitcher was Roger Clemens or a converted peanut vendor. If a player who hit 30 round-trippers in real life had 30 home runs on Aug. 20 of the simulated season, he could not hit a homer the rest of the season lest he make the game "inaccurate." Fortunately, the publisher's management listened to the customer complaints and the next year the design was altered to allow more viable results.

Ironically, the same interaction by the user that makes baseball games fun to play on the computer can also play havoc with the "accuracy" of the simulation. At the simplest level, the user might change the 1998 Yankees' usual lineup, batting Derek Jeter, Bernie Williams, and Darryl Strawberry 1-2-3 to see if this will work better than Joe Torre's alignment. This is the whole idea of computer games—to allow people to play with the system and see what happens—but after users make such changes they sometimes complain about the resulting inaccuracy of the final standings in the product!

For those games where the user is also given the chance to control the pitching, hitting, and fielding, even greater chaos can break loose. You can pitch fastball after fastball right down the pipe to Willie Mays or Babe Ruth on every at bat, and watch the home run totals mount. Take the starter who pitched eight tough innings last night and force him to start to day's game at noon, then duck as the line drives scream in all directions. These are the moments when simulation takes a back seat to fun, and that fun is part of the charm of what makes people buy the games.

At one National SABR Convention presentation, a researcher had replayed a recent season 10 times on a leading baseball simulation to see how often the real life pennant winners duplicated their feat. The average was about six times out of 10, but one pennant winner only won two of the 10 simulated seasons, while the second place team won five times. Although even the best baseball simulation is not a magical tool to predict the future or precisely duplicate the past, as long-time students of baseball, these results seemed intuitively reasonable to us. Yet several members of the audience politely indicated their skepticism about the scholar's methodology.

The skeptics missed one key point about real baseball in their assumption that the real winners would never sink so low as to win only two of 10 identically-weighted seasons. After a 162-game season, very often the pennant contending teams' results in wins and losses are so close as to be almost identical. The decade from 1970-1979, for example, is an era remembered for many pennant races that were over in July as teams built big leads and ran away from the competition. Nevertheless, in that 10-year span, 22.5 percent of the division races were decided by two games or less, 30 percent of the League Championship Series went for what was then the complete five games, and five out of the 10 World Series, a full 50 percent, went the maximum seven games. The difference between the performance of the champion and that of the second place team in baseball is often perilously thin.

Let's take one of those season races in which the pennant was decided by a margin of two games. What does it take to swing the margin of victory to the other side? On May 11, a first base ump misses a tough call in deep right field in the top of the ninth, ruling that the outfielder trapped a line drive when the TV replay clearly shows he caught it. The runner ends up at second and scores on a sacrifice fly two batters later, winning the game. On July 30 the runner on third tries to go home after a bad throw from short dribbles out of the first baseman's glove and into foul territory. The game started at 5 p.m. to align with the TV schedule, and the shadow from the top of the stadium lies between first and home. When the first baseman pegs his throw to the plate, the changing light and the white shirts of the crowd throw off the catcher, and he drops the ball as the runner slides in safely. Once again the game is lost.

And on that pair of cosmic events the pennant is decided. An ump guesses wrong on a tough, no-win call, and a catcher loses a ball in the crowd. As a result, all the baseball encyclopedias for all time will proclaim the losing team's clear inferiority, because they came in second.

Observers occasionally remark that computer simulations are inherently inaccurate, because if you turn on the computer and play a game at 10 a.m. in the morning you will get a different result than if you turn it on at noon. In our mythical two-game margin above, however, the same thing is true. If the contestants ignore the TV schedule and start at 7:30, the sun has set by the ninth inning and the catcher sees the ball pegged from foul territory to the plate. If the game starts at 1:05, the afternoon breeze that springs up carries that deep flyball in the top of the seventh and makes it a three-run homer. If star shortstop John Smith doesn't have to wake up early that morning for a 12:15 start time, he doesn't have a fight with his wife and slam the front door on his throwing hand, putting him on the DL for the remainder of the season.

Just as the weather service can simulate what thunderstorms and heat waves are likely to do in the next three days, we can simulate what baseball players and teams are likely to do over the course of a season. But human beings and the weather have a lot in common when it comes to unpredictability, and it is these kinds of factors that no computer will ever be able to predict. Will right fielder John Doe's new baby keep him up at night and reduce his performance, or will his sense of satisfaction and happiness at being a new dad raise his average? These are not the studies of statistical experts but of psychologists, and our inscrutable human individuality should keep that part of baseball sacrosanct for the foreseeable future.

## CHAPTER 26

Reel Baseball

Bob Carroll and Rob Edelman

None of the very first movies shown to a paying audience in the United States featured pitchers and catchers, fielders making acrobatic plays and runners barreling into home plate. Some of their titles were "Sea Waves," "Umbrella Dance," "Butterfly Dance," "Kaiser Wilhelm Reviewing His Troops," and "A Boxing Bout." They were among the dozen short films screened on April 23, 1896 as part of a vaudeville program at Koster and Bial's Music Hall in New York City.

But baseball, that all-American of sports, shortly would make its way onto movie screens. The Koster and Bial's program was presented by Thomas Alva Edison, inventor of the phonograph and lightbulb and one of the key figures in the development of early motion picture technology. It was Edison who produced the first official baseball movie: "The Ball Game" (1898), in which an amateur Newark, N.J. nine battles an unnamed rival.

Since then, baseball has found its way into countless celluloid comedies and mysteries, musicals and dramas. It also has come to be a symbol for all that is good about America. "The Best Years of Our Lives" (1946), one of the all-time-great Hollywood films, is the story of three World War II veterans who meet while returning to their Midwestern hometown. Upon their arrival, they drive past their city's ballyard in a taxi, and their conversation briefly turns to the fortunes of the local nine. From hereon in, instead of focusing on fighting enemies on foreign battlefields, they will be concentrating on struggles for pennants. So even before they come to their doorsteps and greet their relatives, they now officially are "home." Over a half-century after the release of "The Best Years of Our Lives" came another instant-classic chronicle of the World War II era: "Saving Private Ryan" (1998). The film's almost mythical hero is Captain John Miller, an average American and all-around decent human being who is fulfilling his patriotic duty and defending his country as a combat soldier. Miller at one point reveals that, before the war, he was a high school teacher from a small town in Pennsylvania. And of course, to further emphasize his all-American roots, he adds that he was his school's baseball coach.

However, the earliest baseball movies with plots were, as most other movies of the period, one or two reels in length. Many were melodramatic, and predated the Black Sox Scandal as their scenarios involved attempts to pay off players to throw games. A typical entry is "His Last Game" (1909), in which gamblers try but fail to bribe a ballplayer. Others were comedies: for example, in 1917 came a series of humorous "Mudville" comedy shorts.

Some even featured the travails of fans. "How the Office Boy Saw the Ball Game" (1906) and "How Jones Saw the Baseball Game" (1907) chart the plight of employees scheming to skip out of work and attend a game. Real-life ballplayers appeared on screen in "Hal Chase's Home Fun" (1911) and "Home Run Baker's Double" (1914), "The Baseball Bug" (1911), featuring Chief Bender, Jack Coombs and Rube Oldring, and "Baseball's Peerless Leader "(1913), with Frank Chance.

The first feature-length baseball movie came in 1915 with "Right Off the Bat." And with it came the first baseball hero-turned-movie actor: Mike Donlin, an outfielder who hit .333 in a 12-year major league career (which ended the year before his screen debut). "Right Off the Bat" is the earliest example of one of the most venerable of all baseball film genres: the biography, in which a real-life ballplayer's on- and off-the-field heroics are chronicled, with liberal doses of fiction interspersed with fact. Donlin plays himself in "Right Off the Bat," and the scenario follows his rise to baseball prominence. Throughout the 1920s and early '30s, until his death in 1933, Donlin played supporting roles in feature films (with baseball and nonbaseball themes). Also appearing as himself in "Right Off the Bat" is John McGraw (who may be seen in another early feature, 1917's "One Touch of Nature," the story of a junior at Yale who becomes the New York Giants' rookie second baseman).

Almost 70 years before being depicted by director Ron Shelton in "Cobb," Tyrus Raymond Cobb starred in a baseball movie: "Somewhere in Georgia" (1916). Like "Right Off the Bat, Somewhere in Georgia" is an attempt to mythicize a baseball hero. Cobb is cast as a bank clerk who ends up playing for the Detroit Tigers as he thwarts some villains and captures the heart of the heroine. Nowhere in evidence is there the smallest hint of Cobb's legendary contentiousness.

And nowhere to be found in "Headin' Home" (1920) is the real personality or history of its star, Babe Ruth. The Bambino plays a character who is meant to be autobiographical: a humble, mother-adoring small town lad who whittles his own bats out of wood. During the silent era, the Babe was to star in one other feature, "Babe Comes Home" (1927), and appear in a cameo in "Speedy" (1928), a Harold Lloyd comedy. His most notable screen role came in the Lou Gehrig biography "The Pride of the Yankees" (1942). However, in "Home Run on the Keys" (1937), a Vitaphone one-reeler, Ruth gets to offer what he may have hoped would be the final word on his controversial "called shot" home run in the 1932 World Series. He explains that, after taking two called strikes, "I stepped

out of the box, and I looked over to the [Chicago Cubs] bench, and then I looked out at center field, and I pointed. I said, 'I'm gonna hit the next pitched ball right past the flagpole.' Well, the good lord and good luck must have been with me because I did exactly what I said I was gonna do. And I'll tell you one thing. That was the best home run I ever hit in my life."

Other baseball features were made during the 20th century's second decade, most conspicuously the comedy "The Pinch Hitter" (1917) and the comedy-drama "The Busher" (1919), the latter easily the most entertaining of the first baseball features. Both starred Charles Ray, then at his peak playing rural clodhoppers who in the course of the story would come to maturity. In "The Busher," Ray is cast as a talented small-town pitcher who is humbled after his ego becomes oversized upon his making the majors. In "The Pinch Hitter," he is a shy farm boy who goes off to college and becomes a baseball hero.

From the time of "Right Off the Bat" and "The Busher" to the present, baseball has been a constant reference point in movies. However, not all of the films related to baseball have come out of Hollywood. In addition to baseball as a theme within a scenario, there have been documentaries on baseball, which spotlight footage of real ballplayers in action or feature interviews and narration in which the individuals and incidents portrayed are placed within a historical context; and baseball instructionals, which are fashioned as teaching tools for those learning to play the game and understand its rules.

Documentaries

The primary footage included in baseball documentaries is of real-life ballplayers swinging bats, running the bases and making catches. Some simply are compilations of filmed events. While their footage is of historical interest today, much of it was shot strictly for profit-making purposes, to be marketed and sold to the public. In 1908 Essanay, a motion picture production and distribution company, commenced filming the World Series. High points of games were edited into one and two-reel films which were shown in movie theaters. The title tells all in "The Giants-White Sox World Tour" (1914), a celluloid record of an around-the-world trip undertaken during the winter of 1913-1914. Later on, countless baseball-related events were filmed and included in newsreels: visual records of the era's news which were produced prior to the popularity of television, and projected in movie theaters.

Today, the best of this early material which survives, along with footage culled from television broadcasts of ballgames, has been recycled into visual histories of the game. For example, in 1979, Major League Baseball (MLB) put together a film with a self explanatory title: "75 Years of World Series Memories." For star-gazers, films and videos of All-Star Games are available from MLB from 1962 on, although another rare-film vendor offers earlier All-Star highlights. MLB also has marketed individual films and videos which highlight each World Series from 1943 to the present. The earliest, featuring the New York Yankees walloping the St. Louis Cardinals in five games, is in black-and-white and runs 30 minutes.

Fifteen years later, when the Yankees edged the Milwaukee Braves in seven games, Major League Baseball began shooting the Series in color. But it wasn't until 1984 that the Series highlights were expanded to a full 60 minutes.

Major league teams produce short films and videos offering pennant race highlights. The purpose of these promos is not so much to relive the previous season as to help sell tickets for the upcoming one. Therefore, the footage is always upbeat. The local heroes exude spirit against overwhelming odds. While they may have finished last for the third season in a row, the mood is consistently cheerful as the near future is certain to be chock-filled with first place finishes and World Series victories. Fortunately for the makers of highlight films, even the most inept team will produce enough stellar plays over its approximately 500 hours of game-time to fill a 30-minute video.

In recent years, compilations of baseball clips have been marketed on video, under such titles as "Baseball's Greatest Moments, The 50 Greatest Home Runs in Baseball History," and "MLB Unbelievable Bloopers and Great Plays." Just about every top star of the modern era as well as a number of earlier luminaries has his own personal-highlight video. In fact, it seems as if, each week, an altogether new baseball video is offered for sale via television commercial.

Some baseball compilations are sublime. One such title is "When It Was a Game" (1991), which along with a sequel, "When It Was a Game II," was produced for HBO. "When It Was a Game" consists of home movies, filmed by players and fans between 1934 and 1957, and includes eye-popping images of the era's top stars. There are glimpses of what baseball looked like after many of its players went off to World War II, and peeks at extinct pre-expansion ballparks. Plus, there are some incredible images of the 1938 World Series, featuring the New York Yankees and Chicago Cubs. This is the earliest known color footage taken of the fall classic. Indeed, each image in "When It Was a Game" is in color, and this is what makes the program extra-special.

Easily the most famous of the baseball documentaries fashioned as a commentary on the game is "Baseball," the much-ballyhooed, 18-hour epic which first aired on PBS in 1994. The film, while generally enjoyable, was not without controversy. Fans of baseball west of New York and Boston complained that "Baseball" was hampered by an Eastern bias. Other fans observed that Burns devoted too much footage to celebrity talking heads and not enough to the living legends and ordinary baseball figures. If one star emerged from "Baseball," it was Buck O'Neil, the octogenarian Negro Leaguer whose warmth and perceptiveness transformed him into a national celebrity.

However, Ken Burns' "Baseball" is not the lone baseball documentary. Hundreds have been made over the decades, too numerous to cite here. A typically illuminating one, featuring conversations with players from the past, is "The Glory of Their Times" (1977), produced for PBS and based on Lawrence Ritter's classic book. In interviewing players from the 1898-1916 era, Ritter initiated the genre of oral baseball history, and many of the men with whom he spoke in the early 1960s still were alive when this film was produced. An equally excellent

film is "The Boys of Summer" (1983), based on the Roger Kahn book, which spotlights Brooklyn Dodger stars of the 1950s.

Instructionals

"Instructional" films employ real ballplayers, coaches and managers to explain to the uninitiated how real ballplayers fire fastballs, belt home runs, or make letter-perfect pegs to nail runners attempting to take extra bases. These films date from the silent era. Technically, "Babe Ruth, How He Makes His Home Runs," a 1920 one-reeler, qualifies as an instructional; the Bambino is shown swinging a bat in practice and in game action. The real point, however, was to give fans unable to get to the Polo Grounds (where the Yankees then played) or any other American League ballpark a chance to see baseball's newest hero "up close and personal." In 1932, the Bambino also appeared in several short films in the "Babe Ruth Baseball Series," which mixed athletic instruction with slim plots.

Lew Fonseca, while serving as manager of the Chicago White Sox between 1932 and 1934, experimented with using film to detect flaws in his players' techniques. (Considering that the Sox never rose above sixth place under his tutelage, he must have shot a lot of film.) Despite such worthy efforts as "Play Ball, Son!," a 1946 three-reeler that showed viewers how to play the game position by position, instructionals were not an important part of baseball films until the advent of home video.

Today, a Little Leaguer can relax in his or her living room and be tutored in batting by Charley Lau (in "The Art of Hitting .300") and Tony Gwynn ("King of Swing"); in baserunning by Maury Wills ("Baserunning Basics"); in fielding by Ozzie Smith ("Let's Play Baseball"); and in pitching by Mel Stottlemyre ("Pitching for Kids"). A young wannabe major leaguer can learn "George Brett's Secrets of Baseball," or be taught by "Do-It-Better Baseball" or "Little League's Official How-to-Play Baseball."

A parent seeking to improve a child's play will find plenty of instructionals, but the key is to select the one that teaches at the appropriate level for the student. Just as a fourth grader would be overwhelmed by a course in calculus, a baseball beginner will not be ready for a video meant to fine-tune the skills of a more advanced player. Similarly, that already-skilled player will quickly become bored with a video dealing only in the basics. Most instructionals list a range of ages for which they are designed, but the buyer should still ask if his or her youngster plays above or below others in that age range.

For example, "Baseball Tips for All Ages," with Mickey Mantle, Whitey Ford, and Phil Rizzuto, is one of many excellent instructionals for beginners. It includes information on proper equipment, warming up, and safety. On the other hand, "Play Ball with Mickey Mantle," featuring Gary Carter and Tom Seaver, is designed for more advanced students. Another important point is that children are most impressed by current players. No matter how much you may worship Al Kaline, your child is more likely to pay attention to Ken Griffey, Jr.

Movie Movies

The term "baseball movies" usually connotes neither documentaries nor instructionals but fictional scenarios with actors playing ballplayers. Some are among the classics of all sports movies: "Bull Durham," say, or "Field of Dreams," or "The Bad News Bears," or "Bang the Drum Slowly." Others make up the dregs of the genre: the original "Babe Ruth Story," starring William Bendix, or the more recent "Ed" and "The Fan," or "The Bad News Bears in Breaking Training" and "The Bad News Bears Go to Japan."

Ballfields and bleachers may be the settings of these and all of the other baseball movies, but most of the time we are supposed to focus on whether the hero will get the girl or foil the villain or be party to some heroic act—like belting a ninth-inning game-winning homer. The focus of the scenario is on characterization and plot, not baseball as a game.

However, there are certain constants in baseball films. Many of the older ones feature renditions of "Take Me Out to the Ball Game" over the opening credits. Many depict heroes who are youthful outsiders. Early on, they are refused spots on the sandlots by older, louder, tougher kids, but eventually prove to be destined for Hall-of-Fame-caliber careers. Some of the more intelligent baseball films—"Bull Durham" is the best of the lot—spotlight aging ballyard warriors and contrast them to talented young turks in desperate need of seasoning.

Ironically, several of the greatest baseball sequences appear in films whose content is otherwise completely unrelated to the sport. One such example is "Woman of the Year" (1942), a comedy about the evolving relationship between Sam Craig (Spencer Tracy), a sportswriter, and Tess Harding (Katharine Hepburn), a newspaper columnist. The film was released just as America had entered World War II and Tess, who admits that she knows nothing of sports, would have baseball prohibited for the duration. Sam vehemently protests that baseball is synonymous with America. The country is at war to protect all things American. So what would be the purpose of banning on the homefront the very thing that brave young soldiers are defending on foreign battlefields? This sequence is a consummate illustration of baseball employed as a metaphor for patriotism and Americanism. Additionally, Sam attempts to explain baseball to Tess during a visit to Yankee Stadium, in a sequence that is genuinely funny—and far more memorable than most found in the more generic baseball comedies.

Baseball-on-screen also may play a key role in defining social values. "On Moonlight Bay" features a revealing view of the role of women in society both in 1951, when the film was released, and 1917, when it is set. Doris Day plays Marjorie Winfield, a tomboyish teen who, at the outset, is garbed in a baseball uniform and plays in a game with a group of neighborhood boys. Marjorie is quite an athlete. She promptly smacks a triple, and then steals home. However, because she is female, and society deems that athletics are undignified for females, Marjorie's obsession with baseball is portrayed as a passing phase of her young life. Upon meeting William Sherman (Gordon MacRae), the man of her dreams—who, of course, first mistakes her for a boy as she still is garbed in her uni-

form—Marjorie immediately forsakes baseball for frilly dresses and femininity.

Trivia buffs can endlessly cite the errors and inconsistencies in baseball films. The relationship between Lou Gehrig and Babe Ruth constantly varies from screen biography to screen biography. In "The Pride of the Yankees," Gehrig's consecutive games-played streak ends when he is taken out of a game, not when he fails to appear in one. One of the more notorious and well-publicized gaffes of recent years occurs in "Field of Dreams" (1989), in which Shoeless Joe Jackson (Ray Liotta) bats right-handed and throws left-handed. Sticklers can cite all the physically awkward actors cast as ballplayers, from over-aged and athletically inept Gary Cooper as Lou Gehrig in "The Pride of the Yankees" to gangly Anthony Perkins as Jimmy Piersall in "Fear Strikes Out" (1957) and narrow-shouldered Robert Young as a fireballing St. Louis Cardinals rookie hurler in "Death on the Diamond" (1934).

But only a confirmed nitpicker would let an occasional lapse ruin an otherwise enjoyable film. Despite its gaffes, "The Pride of the Yankees" remains a warmhearted love story. "Field of Dreams" expertly captures the game's nostalgia. "Fear Strikes Out" is an effective psychological portrait. "Death on the Diamond," however, would be a lightweight, contrived murder mystery even if Dizzy Dean had replaced Young.

Admittedly, the most intrinsically exciting baseball movies just may be those World Series compilation films featuring Carlton Fisk willing his flyball to stay fair in the 1975 Series, or Mookie Wilson's grounder eluding the glove of Bill Buckner in 1986. But no documentary can convey an altogether different type of passion, one that is found in fictional (or fictionalized) stories which deal with individuals and their baseball dreams.

Angels, Rhubarbs, and Whatever Lola Wants

Among the most entertaining of all older baseball films is a trio of 1930s spoofs starring wide-mouthed comic Joe E. Brown. They are "Fireman, Save My Child" (1932), "Elmer the Great" (1933), and "Alibi Ike" (1935), the latter two based on the writings of sportswriter Ring Lardner. Unlike most of his acting peers, Brown was an excellent athlete who truly loved and understood the game of baseball. His is a likable screen presence, and he actually looked like a ballplayer even when winding up to pitch like some lunatic windmill. Buster Keaton is another comic who genuinely enjoyed the game. He incorporated baseball into two of his silent-era comedies, "College" (1927) and "The Cameraman" (1928), and made the sport the focus of a two-reeler, "One Run Elmer" (1935). "The Cameraman" in particular is a special treat as Keaton, playing a wannabe newsreel photographer, performs a lovely pantomime on the field in Yankee Stadium.

Comedy and fantasy are combined in a series of still-entertaining films from the late 1940s and early 1950s. The first is "It Happens Every Spring" (1949), without a doubt the best-ever title for a baseball movie. Ray Milland plays a chemistry professor who concocts a substance which has the peculiar ability to avoid wood. He becomes an unhittable pitcher by rubbing it on baseballs just before tossing them in the direction of hitters. For once, an actor's awkward throwing style works to the movie's advantage; this character is supposed to be neither pitcher nor athlete.

Paul Douglas, a former professional football player and radio sportscaster, nearly steals "It Happens Every Spring" as Milland's catcher. He also is quite funny in the original "Angels in the Outfield" (1951), far superior to the 1994 remake. In the 1951 original, Douglas plays the hard-headed, hard-hearted, hard-cursing manager. The scenario chronicles how his team, the ever-incompetent Pittsburgh Pirates, is helped to a pennant by angels. Another sweetly likable comedy-fantasy is "Rhubarb" (1951), about a cat which inherits the Brooklyn baseball club.

Well down in the second division of the genre is "Roogie's Bump" (1954), in which a mysterious bump on his arm allows a little boy to throw a fearsome fastball and eventually play for the Brooklyn Dodgers. This scenario is reworked far more successfully in "Rookie of the Year" (1993), in which a fractured arm allows another youngster to toss a ball at 100 miles per hour, and hurl for the Chicago Cubs.

While the fantasy element is less apparent in "The Kid from Left Field" (1953), the scenario is structured around a gimmick—a 9-year-old becomes the manager of a major league team—with the result another diverting illustration of Hollywood escapism. The film was innocuously remade in 1979 as a television movie. It also predates the scenario of the decidedly minor league "Little Big League" (1994), in which a 12-year-old inherits the Minnesota Twins and resolves to manage the team. Arguably the funniest of the comedies of this period is "Kill the Umpire" (1950), starring William Bendix—two years past his disastrous turn as Babe Ruth in "The Babe Ruth Story"—as a former ballplayer and maniacal fan who is forced to become the baseball lover's mortal enemy: an umpire.

Comedy unites with song in the baseball musical. The two best-known baseball song-and-dance fests are "Take Me Out to the Ball Game" (1949) and "Damn Yankees" (1958). The first is a lesser but still enjoyable MGM musical featuring Gene Kelly, Frank Sinatra, and Jules Munshin as a singing and dancing turn-of-the-century Tinker-to-Evers-to-Chance-like threesome. The second is the screen version of the long-running Broadway show about a middle-aged Washington Senators fan/New York Yankees hater who sells his soul to the devilish Mr. Applegate (Ray Walston) and is transformed into Joe Hardy (Tab Hunter), the phenom who will lead the lowly Washingtonians to the pennant. Applegate is aided by the ravishing Lola (Gwen Verdon), and the screen "Damn Yankees" remains a charming union of baseball and sex and an effective allegory about childhood fantasies contrasted to life's real priorities.

However, "Take Me Out to the Ball Game" and "Damn Yankees" are not the sole baseball musicals. "They Learned About Women" (1930) predates "Take Me Out to the Ball Game" as a story of ballplayers who tour the vaudeville circuit in the off-season. The stars are the real-life vaudeville team of Gus Van and Joseph T. Schenck, and the film is a harmonious early talkie crammed with

songs and comedy routines.

Several of the more light-hearted baseball films involve children. "The Great American Pastime" (1956) is a by-the-numbers comedy featuring Tom Ewell as a suburban dad who coaches his son's Little League team. Two others are unintentionally hilarious: "The Kid from Cleveland" (1949), in which the previous year's world champions save the title character (Rusty Tamblyn) from juvenile delinquency; and "Safe at Home!" (1962), in which Mickey Mantle and Roger Maris, the previous year's home run sensations, rescue a Little Leaguer who brags that he can get them to attend his league's banquet. While it is fun to see the M-and-M boys (not to mention Whitey Ford and Ralph Houk) on screen, they were no threat to Gregory Peck or Jack Lemmon come Academy Awards night.

Baseball Biopics

The first sound-era baseball biography came in 1942, with the release of "The Pride of the Yankees," starring Gary Cooper as doomed superstar Lou Gehrig. Despite Cooper's athletic ineptitude, he and Teresa Wright (as Eleanor Gehrig) give winning performances in what essentially is more of a love story than a baseball drama. In fact, a made-for-TV retelling of the Gehrig story, "A Love Affair: The Eleanor and Lou Gehrig Story" (1978), featured not a single scene of baseball action. Back in 1938, Gehrig himself had starred in "Rawhide," a B-Western in which the Iron Horse traded his Yankee pin-stripes for chaps and a cowboy hat. In several scenes—most notably when he thwarts a villain by instinctively belting a ball through a window—you know you are watching a poised, skilled athlete rather than an actor impersonating one.

The next baseball biography is probably the worst baseball movie ever made: "The Babe Ruth Story" (1948). Paul Douglas originally was slated for the role, but poor William Bendix ended up being sent up to bat as the Bambino. Bendix was one of Hollywood's finest character actors, as adept at playing comedy (in the aforementioned "Kill the Umpire") and drama (in a series of films starring his friend Alan Ladd). Bendix also was perfectly cast in such war films as "Guadalcanal Diary" (1943), playing the stereotypical GI from Brooklyn whose every other thought is of his beloved "Bums." But the 42-year-old actor looks ridiculous impersonating the Babe, especially as a teenager, and the character as written is so honorable and heroic that it is unplayable. St. Babe absentmindedly misses a game to take an injured puppy to a hospital. He is unjustly chastised by his manager, Miller Huggins. He bashes a long spring training home run, at which point a young invalid, who is supposed to be crippled for life, rises to his feet in awe. The Babe belts his legendary "called" home run in the 1932 World Series because he had vowed to do so for a sick child. He passes on a job as manager of the Yankees' minor league affiliate in Newark solely to prevent the team's present skipper from being fired. Finally, the fatally ill Babe agrees to take an experimental serum because it "might help other people." (Less than a month before his death from cancer in August 1948, the real Bambino appeared at the pre-

miere of "The Babe Ruth Story," but left the theater well before the finale.)

The story of Babe Ruth has been told twice more: in "Babe Ruth" (1991), a made-for-television movie starring Stephen Lang, and "The Babe" (1992), a theatrical feature with John Goodman. The latter differs from "The Babe Ruth Story" in that its subject is depicted far more realistically. For one thing, his first marriage, which is completely ignored in "The Babe Ruth Story," is a major part of "The Babe." The film offers a warts-and-all characterization of its subject, chronicling the incidents in his life, the idiosyncrasies of his character, and his conquests and frustrations.

However, the bulk of baseball biographies was produced during the late 1940s and early 1950s. "The Stratton Story" (1949) stars James Stewart as pitcher Monty Stratton, who lost his leg in a hunting accident but came back to pitch in the Texas League. As in the Gehrig movies the emphasis is on romance, with June Allyson playing Stratton's ever-supportive, girl-next-door wife.

No baseball movie ever had a lead more believable on the diamond than "The Jackie Robinson Story" (1950), simply because Jackie played himself. He was believable in his dramatic scenes, too, helped by Ruby Dee as his wife Rachel. Today, "The Jackie Robinson Story" serves as a compelling and valuable chronicle of its time, as the scenario clearly and soberly depicts the ballplayer's struggles as he becomes the first 20th-century African American to play in the major leagues.

"The Pride of St. Louis" (1952), starring Dan Dailey as Dizzy Dean, and "The Winning Team" (1952), with Ronald Reagan as Grover Cleveland Alexander, feature remarkably similar scenarios. In each, a gifted young hurler emerges from backwoods America to perform Hall of Fame heroics on the ballfield. Once his career has crested, he sinks to a nadir as he pities himself and abuses alcohol, only to find redemption at the finale. While not strictly a biography, "Big Leaguer" (1953) is worth citing as it depicts a real-life former major leaguer: John B. "Hans" Lobert (Edward G. Robinson), who operates a Florida-based tryout camp for New York Giant wannabes.

Joining "The Babe" as the other major 1990s biography is "Cobb" (1994), starring Tommy Lee Jones and directed by Ron Shelton. The scenario focuses not on the Georgia Peach's on-field heroics but on his infamous belligerence and his relationship with sportswriter Al Stump (Robert Wuhl), hired to author the aged ballplayer's highly fictionalized life story. Like "The Pride of the Yankees" and "Fear Strikes Out," the primary emphasis is not on sports, as Cobb acutely examines the cult of celebrity in America.

Meanwhile, "Space Jam" (1996) may not be a biography; rather, it is a seamless blend of live-action and animation that is tailor-made for kids. But it does depict one of the more publicized athletic retirements of the decade: Michael Jordan's quitting the Chicago Bulls to take his shot at a professional baseball career.

From the 1970s to the present, the majority of baseball biographies have been made-for-television movies. "It's Good to Be Alive" (1974), the story of Roy Campanella's struggle after a near-fatal automobile accident left him paralyzed, benefits from a touching performance by Paul Winfield as the former Dodgers catcher. The perceptive,

sobering "One in a Million: The Ron LeFlore Story" (1978) casts LeVar Burton in the title role of the outfielder who went from doing hard time in prison to swiping bases for the Detroit Tigers. "Don't Look Back: The Story of Leroy 'Satchel' Paige" (1981) is an acceptable biography starring Louis Gossett, Jr. "A Winner Never Quits" (1986) is the inspiring story of Pete Gray (Keith Carradine), the one-armed outfielder who played for the St. Louis Browns during World War II. "Joe Torre: Curveballs Along the Way" (1997), produced in the wake of the New York Yankees' 1996 world championship, is the most disappointing of the lot: an unconvincing drama about the Bronx Bombers manager (Paul Sorvino), his team during that storied season, and his relationship with his seriously ill brother Frank (Robert Loggia), a former big leaguer.

The title tells all in "The Court-Martial of Jackie Robinson" (1990), a solid and revealing drama which focuses on Robinson's refusal to move to the rear of an army bus while stationed at Camp Hood in Texas during World War II. "Soul of the Game" (1996) is the generally effective, occasionally poignant story of three Negro Leaguers—Satchel Paige (Delroy Lindo), Josh Gibson (Mykelti Williamson), and Jackie Robinson (Blair Underwood)— in the mid-1940s, as the Brooklyn Dodgers' Branch Rickey was setting his plan in motion to integrate baseball. (The Paige-Gibson relationship was fictionalized in the 1976 movie "The Bingo Long Traveling All-Stars & Motor Kings," with Billy Dee Williams playing the Paige character and James Earl Jones cast in the Gibson role. While entertaining, "Bingo Long" ultimately is a lightweight concoction rather than a realistic depiction of Negro League baseball.)

The final made-for-television biography does not involve a ballplayer. "Aunt Mary" (1979) is the heartfelt account of Mary Dobkin (Jean Stapleton), a dedicated fan and welfare recipient. The scenario charts how she comes to coach a sandlot team in the Baltimore slums during the 1950s.

The Golden Age of Baseball Movies

While the best baseball movies—"Bull Durham" and "Field of Dreams, The Bad News Bears" and "Bang the Drum Slowly"—have been released from the 1970s onward, it is a misnomer to declare that there were no good baseball films from earlier decades. In addition to the films commended above, even such an obscure feature as "The Battling Orioles" (1924), a slapstick in which the rowdy 19th-century Baltimore Orioles have aged into terminally tired stuffed shirts, is not without its moments of genuine mirth. So is "The Heckler" (1940), a two-reeler starring Charley Chase as a boorish fan. ("The Heckler" is a reworking of another comedy short, 1932's "The Loudmouth," and was remade in 1946 as "Mr. Noisy.")

At the same time, quite a few recent baseball movies have been something less than home runs. "The Slugger's Wife" (1985), "Brewster's Millions" (1985), "Stealing Home" (1988), "Trading Hearts" (1988), and "Night Game" (1989) are strictly second division. Despite its popularity, "Major League" (1989), the chronicle of how

a dreadful Cleveland Indians' team outmaneuvers its scheming new owner and becomes a pennant winner, is an insipid, second division comedy. However, it is the equivalent of "Bull Durham" when contrasted to its astonishingly inept sequels, "Major League II" (1994) and "Major League: Back to the Minors" (1998). "Ed" (1996), about a ballplaying chimpanzee, doesn't even make good kitsch; it rivals "The Babe Ruth Story" in the worst-ever department. "The Fan" (1996) is not only a bad movie: in its unashamedly cynical characterizations of a Bobby Bonds-like ballplayer (Wesley Snipes) and the murderous fan (Robert De Niro) who idolizes him, it exudes distaste for ballplayers and fans alike.

A bit up on the quality scale—but not by much—is "BASEketball" (1998), a crude, gross-out comedy which follows a couple of "dudes" (played by Trey Parker and Matt Stone, the creators of TV's "South Park") who concoct a game whose rules are a combination of baseball and basketball. Much of "BASEketball" is purposefully idiotic and, for a film that intends to chide the commercialization of professional sports, there is an awful lot of product placement. However, "BASEketball" does include a few gags that are clever comic exaggerations of the idiosyncrasies of both sports. And it may be linked to the baseball finale in an earlier comedy made by its director, David Zucker: "The Naked Gun: From the Files of Police Squad!" (1988). Both films are buoyed by the presence of Reggie Jackson, Mr. Humility himself, in a key role.

The Golden Age of Baseball Movies dawns with "Bang the Drum Slowly" (1973), based on the Mark Harris novel and easily the best baseball drama made to date. It is the heartrending, supremely humanistic tale of a star pitcher (Michael Moriarty) and his relationship with a none-too-bright lug of a reserve catcher (Robert De Niro) who is terminally ill. "The Bad News Bears" (1976) is a genuinely funny comedy about a beer-guzzling ex-minor leaguer (Walter Matthau, in training for his role almost two decades later as one of the "Grumpy Old Men") who comes to coach a thoroughly inept Little League team—which improves considerably when a girl (Tatum O'Neal) becomes its pitcher. Unfortunately, just about every child-related baseball film to come in the wake of "The Bad News Bears" has been mindlessly (if not insultingly) unfunny. One exception is "Rookie of the Year;" another is "The Sandlot" (1993), a sweet reminiscence about a gang of kids playing sandlot ball in the summer of 1962.

Two films fit into the "divided-camp" category. "The Natural" (1984), adapted from the Bernard Malamud novel, is an attempt at an adult baseball fable which ends up veering markedly from its source material and, to some critics, wallowing in simplicity and sentimentality; others have declared it a mythic poem superior to its literary source. It is the story of Roy Hobbs (Robert Redford), who might have been the greatest slugger ever had he not been shot and nearly killed by a mysterious woman in black. Sixteen years later, he becomes a middle-aged rookie who belts tape-measure dingers with "Wonderboy," his trusty bat. Regardless of how one regarded "The Natural," it was a significant film in that its box-office success spurred production of other movies with baseball themes. "Mr. Baseball" (1992), a comedy about an ex-major leaguer (Tom Selleck) playing in

Japan, offers some insight into Eastern-versus-Western philosophies, and while some are mystified by its brand of humor, others find it hilarious.

Two little-known movies about life in the minor leagues during the 1950s are effective as odes to their era, to baseball, and to the integrity of the game: "Pastime" (1991), with William Russ as an aging pitcher who befriends a young African-American rookie (Glenn Plummer); and "Long Gone" (1987), a made-for-TV feature starring William L. Petersen as a player-manager who refuses to barter his soul in order to appease his avaricious bosses.

One of the more intelligent baseball films of recent years is "Eight Men Out" (1988), John Sayles' chronicle of the Black Sox Scandal. Unlike most baseball movies set in the past, "Eight Men Out" in no way romanticizes its characters. "A League of Their Own" (1992) entertainingly recreates the first year of the All American Girls Professional Baseball League, which featured women players. The league was launched during World War II, and folded in 1954, and the scenario champions a woman's right to determine her own destiny.

"Bull Durham" (1988) arguably is the greatest baseball movie ever. It was made by Ron Shelton, a five-year veteran of minor league ball, and it is an at-once supremely funny and deeply knowing ode to baseball in the sticks. Kevin Costner has never been better as Crash Davis, a career minor leaguer who truly respects the game but languishes in the obscurity of the bushes. Tim Robbins plays Ebby Calvin "Nuke" LaLoosh, a fireballing young hurler with "a million-dollar arm, but a five-cent head." As Crash is assigned to tutor the youngster, "Bull Durham" becomes the prototype of all baseball films which contrast aging ballplayers whose baseball dreams were never quite realized and young hotshots whose natural ability alone will propel them to the majors. Finally, the scenario features the baseball fan to end all baseball fans: Annie Savoy (Susan Sarandon), whose "church of baseball" monologue as the film opens is a classic, poetic delineation of the game's appeal. (A group of prototypical Baby Boomer baseball fans may be found in 1991's "City Slickers," whose best days have been spent in ballparks. And during the Vietnam era, the sole communication with their fathers centered around a shared love of baseball.)

Finally, "Field of Dreams" is the ultimate union of baseball and poetry, with the sport serving as a seed from which springs the wonder of life. "Field of Dreams," based on W.P. Kinsella's novel Shoeless Joe, is the saga of an Iowa farmer named Ray Kinsella (Kevin Costner) who constructs a ballyard in his cornfield after being told by a mysterious voice that, "If you build it, they will come." Soon enough, the spirits of Shoeless Joe Jackson, other Black Soxers, and other baseball legends are frolicking in the infield.

The fantasy sequence in which the farmer comes to play catch with his now-young and rejuvenated father is nothing short of magical. So is the character of Old Doc Graham (Burt Lancaster), who decades earlier, as "Moonlight" Graham, played in a lone game for the New York Giants. (Back in 1905, a real ballplayer by this name did indeed play one game for the Giants.) While his baseball dreams were thwarted, Doc Graham nonetheless lived a happy and productive life as a small-town doctor.

In the 1990s, professional baseball has been mired in a series of controversies that have tested the patience of fans, with the essence of the game tainted by the idiocy of major league owners and the greed of big league players. Cinematically speaking, this is reflected in "Simon Birch" (1998), the story of an undersized 12-year-old boy growing up in a small Maine town in the early 1960s. However, this is no idealized American community, as most of its residents cruelly view Simon as a freak, a monster.

Baseball is one of the boy's few pleasures. He collects baseball cards, which are his "favorite things in the world," and is the Eddie Gaedel of his Pee Wee League team. Yet a baseball comes to play a crucial role in the story—as an instrument of heartbreak and death. The one time his coach orders him to swing away in a game, Simon connects—and the ball he smashes hits and instantaneously kills his best friend's mother, one of the few adults who is sympathetic to his plight.

According to "Simon Birch," a love of baseball no longer is akin to innocence and purity, and the game is no longer detached from the harsh realities of the world. Nonetheless, during these brutally cynical times, a bit of dialogue from "Field of Dreams" has sustained many of us. It is spoken to Ray Kinsella by Terence Mann (James Earl Jones), a reclusive writer who becomes a part of Kinsella's design to "build it":

The one constant through all the years, Ray, has been baseball. Baseball has marked the time. This field, this game, is a part of our past, Ray. It reminds us of all that once was good, and that could be again."

Baseball Filmography

The list below includes feature films which include baseball in a major portion of their scenarios, and selected feature films in which real ballplayers appear as actors (such as Rawhide, *a B-Western starring Lou Gehrig).*

Right Off the Bat (1915) Arrow Film Corp., B&W, 5 reels. Dir.: Hugh Reticker. Cast: Mike Donlin, John J. McGraw, Claire Mersereau.

Casey at the Bat (1916) Fine Arts Film Co., B&W, 5 reels. Dir.: Lloyd Ingraham. Cast: DeWolf Hopper, Kate Toncray.

Somewhere in Georgia (1916) Sunbeam Motion Picture Corp., B&W, 6 reels. Dir.: George Ridgwell. Cast: Ty Cobb, Elsie MacLeod.

The Pinch Hitter (1917) New York Motion Picture Corp., B&W 5 reels. Dir.: Victor L. Schertzinger. Cast: Charles Ray, Sylvia Bremer.

One Touch of Nature (1917) Thomas A. Edison, Inc., B&W, 5 reels. Dir.: Edward H. Griffith. Cast: John Drew Bennett, Viola Cain, John J. McGraw.

The Busher (1919) Thomas H. Ince Corp., B&W, 5 reels. Dir.: Jerome Storm. Cast: Charles Ray, Colleen Moore, John Gilbert.

Headin' Home (1920) Kessel & Baumann Yankee Photo Corp., B&W, 5 reels. Dir.: Lawrence Windom. Cast: Babe Ruth, Ruth Taylor.

As the World Rolls On (1921) Andlauer Productions Elk Photo Plays, B&W, 7 reels. Dir.: W.A. Andlauer. Cast: Jack Johnson, Blanche Thompson.

Trifling with Honor (1923) Universal Pictures, B&W, 8 reels. Dir.: Harry A. Pollard. Cast: Rockliffe Fellowes, Fritzi Ridgeway.

Hit and Run (1924) Universal Pictures, B&W, 6 reels. Dir.: Edward Sedgwick. Cast: Hoot Gibson, Marion Harlan, Cyril Ring, Mike Donlin.

Life's Greatest Game (1924) Emory Johnson Productions, B&W, 8 reels. Dir.: Emory Johnson. Cast: Tom Santschi, Johnnie Walker, Jane Thomas.

The Battling Orioles (1924) Hal E. Roach Studios, B&W, 6 reels. Dir.: Ted Wilde, Fred Guiol. Cast: Glenn Tryon, Blanche Mahaffey.

The Pinch Hitter (1925) Associated Exhibitors, B&W, 7 reels. Dir.: Joseph Henabery. Cast: Glenn Hunter, Constance Bennett.

Play Ball (1925) Pathe Exchange, B&W, 10 chapter serial, 2 reels per chapter. Dir.: Spencer G. Bennet. Cast: Allene Ray, Walter Miller, John McGraw and the New York Giants.

The New Klondike (1926) Famous Players-Lasky Paramount Pictures, B&W, 8 reels. Dir.: Lewis Milestone. Cast: Thomas Meighan, Lila Lee, Paul Kelly.

Out of the West (1926) R-C Pictures, B&W, 5 reels. Dir.: Robert De Lacy. Cast: Tom Tyler, Bernice Welch, Frankie Darrow.

Babe Comes Home (1927) First National Pictures, B&W, 6 reels. Dir.: Ted Wilde. Cast: Babe Ruth, Anna Q. Nilsson, Louise Fazenda.

The Bush Leaguer (1927) Warner Bros., B&W, 7 reels. Dir.: Howard Bretherton. Cast: Monte Blue, Clyde Cook, Leila Hyams, William Demarest.

Casey at the Bat (1927) Famous Players-Lasky Paramount Pictures, B&W, 6 reels. Dir.: Monte Brice. Cast: Wallace Beery, Ford Sterling, ZaSu Pitts, Sterling Holloway.

Catch-as-Catch-Can (1927) Gotham Productions, B&W, 5 reels. Dir.: Charles Hutchinson. Cast: William Fairbanks, Jack Richardson, Rose Blossom.

College (1927) Buster Keaton Productions United Artists, B&W, 6 reels. Dir.: James W. Horne. Cast: Buster Keaton, Anne Cornwall, Flora Bramley, Harold Goodwin, University of Southern California Baseball Team.

Slide, Kelly, Slide (1927) Metro-Goldwyn-Mayer, B&W, 8 reels. Dir.: Edward Sedgwick. Cast: William Haines, Sally O'Neil, Harry Carey, Karl Dane, Junior Coghlan, Warner Richmond, Paul Kelly, Guinn "Big Boy" Williams, Mike Donlin, Bob Meusel, Irish Meusel, Tony Lazzeri.

The Cameraman (1928) Metro-Goldwyn-Mayer, B&W, 8 reels. Dir.: Edward Sedgwick. Cast: Buster Keaton, Marceline Day, Harry Gribbon, Harold Goodwin.

Speedy (1928) Harold Lloyd Corp. Paramount Famous Lasky Corp., B&W, 8 reels. Dir.: Ted Wilde. Cast: Harold Lloyd, Ann Christy, Babe Ruth.

Warming Up (1928) Paramount Famous Lasky Corp., B&W, 8 reels. Dir.: Fred Newmeyer. Cast: Richard Dix, Jean Arthur, Roscoe Karns, Mike Donlin.

Fast Company (1929) Paramount Famous Lasky Corp., B&W, 8 reels. Dir.: A. Edward Sutherland. Cast: Jack Oakie, Evelyn Brent, Skeets Gallagher, Irish Meusel, Arnold "Jigger" Statz.

Hot Curves (1930) Tiffany Productions, B&W, 9 reels. Dir.: Norman Taurog. Cast: Benny Rubin, Rex Lease, Alice Day, Pert Kelton, Mike Donlin.

They Learned About Women (1930) Metro-Goldwyn-Mayer, B&W, 11 reels. Dir.: Jack Conway, Sam Wood. Cast: Joseph T. Schenck, Gus Van, Bessie Love, Mary Doran, Benny Rubin.

Fireman, Save My Child (1932) First National and Vitaphone, B&W, 67 min. Dir.: Lloyd Bacon. Cast: Joe E. Brown, Evalyn Knapp, Lillian Bond, Guy Kibbee.

Elmer the Great (1933) First National and Vitaphone, B&W, 74 min. Dir.: Mervyn LeRoy. Cast: Joe E. Brown, Patricia Ellis, Frank McHugh, Claire Dodd, Preston S. Foster, Sterling Holloway.

Death on the Diamond (1934) Metro-Goldwyn-Mayer, B&W, 69 min. Dir.: Edward Sedgwick. Cast: Robert Young, Madge Evans, Nat Pendleton, Ted Healy, C. Henry Gordon, Paul Kelly, Mickey Rooney.

Alibi Ike (1935) Warner Brothers and Vitaphone, B&W, 73 min. Dir.: Ray Enright. Cast: Joe E. Brown, Olivia de Havilland, Roscoe Karns, William Frawley.

Swell-Head (1935) Columbia Pictures, B&W, 62 min. Dir.: Ben Stoloff. Cast: Wallace Ford, Dickie Moore, Barbara Kent, J. Farrell MacDonald, Mike Donlin.

The Adventures of Frank Merriwell (1936) Universal Pictures, B&W, 12-chapter serial, 2 reels per chapter. Dir.: Cliff Smith. Cast: Don Briggs, Jean Rogers, John King.

Girls Can Play (1937) Columbia Pictures, B&W, 6 reels. Dir.: Lambert Hillyer. Cast: Jacqueline Wells (Julie Bishop), Charles Quigley, Rita Hayworth.

Manhattan Merry-Go-Round (1937) Republic Pictures, B&W, 82 min., D.: Charles F. Reisner. Cast: Phil Regan, Leo Carillo, Ann Dvorak, James Gleason, Joe DiMaggio.

Rawhide (1938) Principal Productions, Inc. 20th Century-Fox, B&W, 60 min. Dir.: Ray Taylor. Cast: Smith Ballew, Lou Gehrig, Evalyn Knapp.

Brother Rat (1938) Warner Bros., B&W, 90 min. Dir.: William Keighley. Cast: Priscilla Lane, Wayne Morris, Johnnie Davis, Jane Bryan, Eddie Albert, Ronald Reagan, Jane Wyman.

Woman of the Year (1942) Metro-Goldwyn-Mayer, B&W, 1112 m., Dir.: George Stevens. Cast: Spencer Tracy, Katharine Hepburn, Fay Bainter, Reginald Owen, Minor Watson, William Bendix.

The Pride of the Yankees (1942) The Samuel Goldwyn Company RKO-Radio, B&W, 128 min. Dir.: Sam Wood. Cast: Gary Cooper, Teresa Wright, Walter Brennan, Dan

Duryea, Babe Ruth, Elsa Jansen, Ludwig Stossel, Bill Dickey, Bob Meusel, Mark Koenig, Bill Stern.

It Happened in Flatbush (1942) 20th Century-Fox, B&W, 80 min. D.: Ray McCarey. Cast: Lloyd Nolan, Carol Landis, Sara Allgood, William Frawley, Robert Armstrong, Jane Darwell.

Ladies' Day (1943) RKO-Radio, B&W, 62 min. Dir.: Leslie Goodwins. Cast: Lupe Velez, Eddie Albert, Patsy Kelly, Max Baer.

Whistling in Brooklyn (1943) Metro-Goldwyn-Mayer, B&W, 87 min. D.: S. Sylvan Simon. Cast: Red Skelton, Ann Rutherford, Jean Rogers, Rags Ragland, Ray Collins, William Frawley, Sam Levene, Leo Durocher and The Brooklyn Dodgers.

The Naughty Nineties (1945) Universal Pictures, B&W, 76 min. Dir.: Jean Yarbrough. Cast: Bud Abbott, Lou Costello, Alan Curtis, Rita Johnson.

Make Mine Music (1946) Walt Disney Productions RKO-Radio, Color, 75 min. "Casey at the Bat" directed by Clyde Geronimi, narrated by Jerry Colonna.

The Babe Ruth Story (1948) Allied Artists, B&W, 106 min. Dir.: Roy Del Ruth. Cast: William Bendix, Claire Trevor, Charles Bickford, Sam Levene, William Frawley, Mark Koenig, Harry Wismer, Mel Allen, H.V. Kaltenborn, Knox Manning.

It Happens Every Spring (1949) 20th Century-Fox, B&W, 87 min. Dir.: Lloyd Bacon. Cast: Ray Milland, Jean Peters, Paul Douglas, Ed Begley, Ted de Corsia, Ray Collins, Jessie Royce Landis, Alan Hale, Jr.

The Kid from Cleveland (1949) Republic Pictures, B&W, 89 min. Dir.: Herbert Kline. Cast: George Brent, Lynn Bari, Rusty Tamblyn, John Berardino, Bill Veeck, The Cleveland Indians.

The Stratton Story (1949) Metro-Goldwyn-Mayer, B&W, 106 min. Dir.: Sam Wood. Cast: James Stewart, June Allyson, Frank Morgan, Agnes Moorehead, Bill Williams, Gene Bearden, Jimmy Dykes, Mervyn "Spec" Shea, Bill Dickey.

Take Me Out to the Ball Game (1949) Metro-Goldwyn-Mayer, Color, 93 min. Dir.: Busby Berkeley. Cast: Gene Kelly, Frank Sinatra, Esther Williams, Jules Munshin, Betty Garrett, Edward Arnold.

The Jackie Robinson Story (1950) Jewell Pictures Corp. Eagle-Lion Films, B&W, 77 min. Dir.: Alfred E. Green. Cast: Jackie Robinson, Ruby Dee, Minor Watson, Louise Beavers, Richard Lane, Kenny Washington.

Kill the Umpire (1950) Columbia Pictures, B&W, 78 min. Dir.: Lloyd Bacon. Cast: William Bendix, Una Merkel, Ray Collins, William Frawley, Gloria Henry, Tom D'Andrea, Alan Hale, Jr.

Angels in the Outfield (1951) Metro-Goldwyn-Mayer, B&W, 99 min. Dir.: Clarence Brown. Cast: Paul Douglas, Janet Leigh, Donna Corcoran, Keenan Wynn, Lewis Stone, Spring Byington, Bruce Bennett, Ellen Corby, Joe DiMaggio, Bing Crosby, Ty Cobb, Harry Ruby.

Rhubarb (1951) Paramount Pictures, B&W, 94 min. Dir.: Arthur Lubin. Cast: Ray Milland, Jan Sterling, Gene Lockhart, William Frawley, Elsie Holmes, Leonard Nimoy.

On Moonlight Bay (1951) Warner Bros., Color, 95 min. Dir.: Roy Del Ruth. Cast: Doris Day, Gordon MacRae, Jack Smith, Leon Ames, Rosemary DeCamp, Mary Wickes, Ellen Corby, Billy Gray.

The Pride of St. Louis (1952) 20th Century-Fox, B&W, 93 min. Dir.: Harmon Jones. Cast: Dan Dailey, Joanne Dru, Richard Hylton, Richard Crenna, Chet Huntley.

The Winning Team (1952) Warner Bros., B&W, 98 min. Dir.: Lewis Seiler. Cast: Doris Day, Ronald Reagan, Frank Lovejoy, Eve Miller, Bob Lemon, Gerry Priddy, Peanuts Lowery, George (Catfish) Metkovich, Irving (Irv) Noren, Hank Sauer, Al Zarilla, Gene Mauch.

Big Leaguer (1953) Metro-Goldwyn-Mayer, B&W, 70 min. Dir.: Robert Aldrich. Cast: Edward G. Robinson, Vera Ellen, Jeff Richards, Richard Jaeckel, William Campbell, Carl Hubbell, Al Campanis, Bob Tricolor, Tony Ravish.

The Kid from Left Field (1953) 20th Century-Fox, B&W, 80 min. Dir.: Harmon Jones. Cast: Dan Dailey, Anne Bancroft, Billy Chapin, Lloyd Bridges, Ray Collins, Richard Egan, Fess Parker, John Berardino, John "Beans" Reardon.

Roogie's Bump (1954) Republic Pictures, B&W, 71 min. Dir.: Harold Young. Cast: Robert Marriot, Ruth Warrick, Olive Blackeney, Robert Simon, Roy Campanella, Billy Loes, Carl Erskine, Russ Meyer.

Three Stripes in the Sun (1955) Columbia Pictures, B&W, 93 min. Dir.: Richard Murphy. Cast: Aldo Ray, Phil Carey, Dick York, Mitsuko Kimura, Chuck Connors.

The Great American Pastime (1956) Metro-Goldwyn-Mayer, B&W, 89 min. Dir.: Herman Hoffman. Cast: Tom Ewell, Anne Francis, Ann Miller, Dean Jones.

I'll Buy You (1956) Shochiku, B&W, 113 min. Dir.: Masaki Kobayashi. Cast: Keiji Sata, Keiko Kishi, Minoru Oki.

Fear Strikes Out (1957) Paramount Pictures, B&W, 100 min. Dir.: Robert Mulligan. Cast: Anthony Perkins, Karl Malden, Norma Moore, Adam Williams, Perry Wilson.

Damn Yankees (1958) Warner Bros., Color, 110 min. Dir.: George Abbott, Stanley Donen. Cast: Tab Hunter, Gwen Verdon, Ray Walston, Russ Brown, Shannon Bolin, Robert Shafer, Rae Allen, Nathaniel Frey, Jimmie Komack, Jean Stapleton, Bob Fosse.

The Geisha Boy (1958) Paramount Pictures, Color, 95 min. Dir.: Frank Tashlin. Cast: Jerry Lewis, Marie McDonald, Sessue Hayakawa, Suzanne Pleshette, The Los Angeles Dodgers.

Safe at Home! (1962) Naud-Hamilburg Productions Columbia Pictures, B&W, 83 min. Dir.: Walter Doniger. Cast: Mickey Mantle, Roger Maris, William Frawley, Patricia Barry, Don Collier, Bryan Russell, Ralph Houk, Whitey Ford.

That Touch of Mink (1962) Granley Company-Arwin Productions-Nob Hill Productions Universal-International, Color, 99 min. Dir.: Delbert Mann. Cast: Cary

Grant, Doris Day, Gig Young, Audrey Meadows, Mickey Mantle, Roger Maris, Yogi Berra, Art Passarella.

The Ceremony (1971) Sozosha-Atg Shibata Org., Color, 122 min., Dir: Nagisa Oshima. Cast: Kenzo Kawarazaki, Atsuko Kaku, Atsuo Nakamura.

One-Legged Ace (1971) Katsu Productions Daiei, Color, 100 min., Dir.: Kazuo Ikehiro.

Bang the Drum Slowly (1973) Paramount Pictures, Color, 97 min. Dir.: John Hancock. Cast: Michael Moriarty, Robert De Niro, Vincent Gardenia, Phil Foster, Ann Wedgeworth, Tom Ligon.

It's Good to Be Alive (1974, made for TV) Metromedia Producers Corporation/ Larry Harman Pictures CBS, Color, 100 min. Dir.: Michael Landon. Cast: Paul Winfield, Louis Gossett Jr., Ruby Dee, Ramon Bieri.

The Bad News Bears (1976) Paramount Pictures, Color, 102 min. Dir.: Michael Ritchie. Cast: Walter Matthau, Tatum O'Neal, Vic Morrow, Joyce Van Patten, Ben Piazza, Jackie Earle Haley.

The Bingo Long Traveling All-Stars & Motor Kings (1976) Motown Production/Pan Arts Enterprises Universal Pictures, Color, 110 minutes. Dir.: John Badham. Cast: Billy Dee Williams, James Earl Jones, Richard Pryor, Stan Shaw, Ted Ross, Leon Wagner, Emmett Ashford.

The Bad News Bears in Breaking Training (1977) Paramount Pictures, Color, 100 min. Dir.: Michael Pressman. Cast: William Devane, Clifton James, Jackie Earle Haley, Jimmy Baio, Bob Watson, Enos Cabell, Roger Metzger, J.R. Richard, Joe Ferguson, Ken Forsch, Cesar Cedeno, Bill Virdon.

Just the Beginning (1977) Yung Bang Films, Color, 105 min. Dir.: Jung In Yup. Cast: Jin Yoo Young, Ha Myoung Jung, Kang Ju Hee.

Murder at the World Series (1977, made for TV) ABC Circle Films ABC, Color, 100 min. Dir.: Andrew V. McLaglen. Cast: Lynda Day George, Murray Hamilton, Karen Valentine, Gerald S. O'Loughlin, Michael Parks, Janet Leigh, Hugh O'Brian.

The Bad News Bears Go to Japan (1978) Paramount Pictures, Color, 91 min. Dir.: John Berry. Cast: Tony Curtis, Jackie Earle Haley, Tomasaburo Wakayama.

A Boy Called Third Base (1978) Gentosha and ATG, Color, 102 min. Dir.: Yoichi Higashi. Cast: Toshiyuki Nagashima, Tsuguaki Yoshida, Aiko Morishita.

Goodbye, Franklin High (1978) Cal-Am Productions, Color, 94 min. Dir.: Mike MacFarland. Cast: Lane Caudell, Julie Adams, William Windom.

Here Come the Tigers (1978) Filmways Pictures American International, Color, 90 min. Dir.: Sean S. Cunningham. Cast: Richard Lincoln, James Zvanut, Samantha Grey.

A Love Affair: The Eleanor and Lou Gehrig Story (1978, made for TV) Charles Fries Productions/Stonehenge Productions ABC, Color, 100 min. Dir.: Fielder Cook. Cast: Blythe Danner, Edward Herrmann, Patricia Neal, Gerald S. O'Laughlin, Ramon Bieri, Jane Wyatt, Georgia Engel, Michael Lerner.

One in a Million: The Ron LeFlore Story (1978, made for TV) Roger Gimbel Productions/EMI Television CBS, Color, 100 min. Dir.: William A. Grahame. Cast: LeVar Burton, Madge Sinclair, Paul Benjamin, James Luisi, Billy Martin, Larry B. Scott, Al Kaline, Norm Cash, Jim Northrup, Bill Freehan.

Aunt Mary (1979, made for TV) Henry Jaffe Enterprises CBS, Color, 100 min. Dir.: Peter Werner. Cast: Jean Stapleton, Martin Balsam, Harold Gould, Dolph Sweet, Ernie Harwell.

The Kid from Left Field (1979, made for TV) Gary Coleman Productions/ Deena Silver Kramer's Movie Company NBC, Color, 100 min. Dir.: Adell Aldrich. Cast: Gary Coleman, Robert Guillaume, Gary Collins, Ed McMahon, Tab Hunter.

The Comeback Kid (1980, made for TV) ABC Circle Films ABC, Color, 100 min. Dir.: Peter Levin. Cast: John Ritter, Susan Dey, Doug McKeon, James Gregory, Patrick Swayze.

Squeeze Play (1980) Troma, Color, 92 minutes. Dir.: Samuel Weil. Cast: Jim Harris, Jenni Hetrick, Rick Gitlin.

Don't Look Back: The Story of Leroy "Satchel" Paige (1981, made for TV) TBA Productions; Satie Productions; Triseme ABC, Color, 100 min. Dir.: Richard A. Colla. Cast: Louis Gossett Jr., Beverly Todd, Cleavon Little, Ernie Barnes, Clifton Davis, John Beradino, Ossie Davis, Satchel Paige, Bubba Phillips.

Chasing Dreams (1982) Nascent Productions Prism Entertainment Corp., Color, 96 min. Dir.: Therese Conte. Cast: David G. Brown, John Fife, Jim Shane, Kevin Costner.

Million Dollar Infield (1982, made for TV) CBS Entertainment CBS, Color, 100 min. Dir.: Hal Cooper. Cast: Bonnie Bedelia, Robert Costanzo, Rob Reiner, Christopher Guest, Bruno Kirby, Mel Allen.

Zapped! (1982) Embassy Pictures, Color, 96 min. Dir.: Robert J. Rosenthal. Cast: Scott Baio, Willie Aames, Heather Thomas.

Blue Skies Again (1983) Lantana Production Warner Bros., Color, 96 min. Dir.: Richard Michaels. Cast: Harry Hamlin, Mimi Rogers, Robyn Barto, Kenneth McMillan, Dana Elcar, Andy Garcia.

Tiger Town (1983, made for TV) Walt Disney Productions The Disney Channel, Color, 76 min. Dir.: Alan Shapiro. Cast: Roy Scheider, Justin Henry, Ron McLarty, Sparky Anderson, Ernie Harwell.

Max Dugan Returns (1983), Twentieth Century-Fox, Color, 98 min. D.: Herbert Ross. Cast: Marsha Mason, Jason Robards, Donald Sutherland, Matthew Broderick, Charlie Lau.

The Natural (1984) Tri-Star-Delphi II Tri-Star Pictures, Color, 134 min. Dir.: Barry Levinson. Cast: Robert Redford, Robert Duvall, Glenn Close, Kim Basinger, Wilford Brimley, Barbara Hershey, Robert Prosky, Richard Farnsworth, Darren McGavin, Joe Don Baker, Michael Madsen, Sibbi Sisti.

A Soldier's Story (1984) Columbia Pictures, Color, 102 min. Dir.: Norman Jewison. Cast: Howard E. Rollins, Jr., Adolph Caesar, Art Evans, David Alan Grier, David Harris, Larry Riley, Denzel Washington.

The Slugger's Wife (1985) Rastar Columbia Pictures, Color, 105 min. Dir.: Hal Ashby. Cast: Michael O'Keefe, Rebecca De Mornay, Martin Ritt, Randy Quaid, Cleavant Derricks, Mark Fidrych, Al Hrabosky, Ted Turner, Pete Van Wieren, Ernie Johnson, Skip Caray, Nick Charles.

Brewster's Millions (1985) Universal Pictures, Color, 97 min., Dir: Walter Hill. Cast: Richard Pryor, John Candy, Lonette McKee, Stephen Collins, Jerry Orbach, Pat Hingle, Tovah Feldshuh, Hume Cronyn, Rick Moranis.

MacArthur's Children (1985) Orion Classics, Color, 115 min., Dir.: Masahiro Shinoda. Cast: Takaya Yamuchi, Yoshiyuki Omuri, Shiori Sakura.

Insignificance (1985) Zenith Productions Island Alive, Color, 105 min. Dir.: Nicolas Roeg. Cast: Gary Busey, Michael Emil, Theresa Russell, Will Sampson, Tony Curtis.

A Winner Never Quits (1986, made for TV) Blatt/Singer Production Columbia Pictures ABC, Color, 100 min. Dir.: Mel Damski. Cast: Keith Carradine, Huckleberry Fox, Mare Winningham, Dennis Weaver, Ed O'Neill, Dana Delaney.

Long Gone (1987, made for TV) Landsburg Company HBO, Color, 110 min. Dir.: Martin Davidson. Cast: William L. Petersen, Virginia Madsen, Dermot Mulroney, Larry Riley.

Amazing Grace and Chuck (1987) Turnstar Production Tri-Star Pictures/Rastar, Color, 115 min., Dir.: Mike Newell. Cast: Gregory Peck, William L. Petersen, Joshua Zuehlke, Alex English, Jamie Lee Curtis.

Bull Durham (1988) Mount Company Orion Pictures, Color, 115 min. Dir.: Ron Shelton. Cast: Kevin Costner, Susan Sarandon, Tim Robbins, Trey Wilson, Robert Wuhl, Max Patkin.

Eight Men Out (1988) Orion Pictures, Color, 115 min. Dir.: John Sayles. Cast: John Cusack, David Strathairn, D.B. Sweeney, Michael Rooker, Charlie Sheen, John Sayles, Studs Terkel, Michael Lerner, Christopher Lloyd.

Stealing Home (1988) Mount Company Warner Bros., Color, 98 min. Dir.: John Sayles. Cast: Mark Harmon, Jodie Foster, Blair Brown, Jonathan Silverman, Harold Ramis.

Naked Gun: From the Files of Police Squad (1988) Paramount Pictures, Color, 85 min. Dir.: David Zucker. Cast: Leslie Nielsen, George Kennedy, Priscilla Presley, Ricardo Montalban, O.J. Simpson, Reggie Jackson, Jay Johnstone, Hank Robinson, Joe West, Curt Gowdy, Jim Palmer, Tim McCarver, Dick Vitale, Mel Allen, Dick Enberg.

Trading Hearts (1988) The Vista Organization Cineworld Enterprises/IVE, Color, 88 min. D.: Neil Leifer. Cast: Raul Julia, Beverly D'Angelo, Jenny Lewis, Frank DeFord, Ed Koch.

Field of Dreams (1989) Gordon Company Production Universal Pictures, Color, 107 min. Dir.: Phil Alden Robinson. Cast: Kevin Costner, Amy Madigan, Gaby Hoffman, James Earl Jones, Ray Liotta, Burt Lancaster, Timothy Busfield.

Major League (1989) Morgan Creek/Mirage Production Paramount Pictures, Color, 106 min. Dir.: David Ward. Cast: Tom Berenger, Charlie Sheen, Corbin Bernsen, Margaret Whitton, Rene Russo, James Gammon, Bob Uecker, Wesley Snipes, Dennis Haysbert, Steve Yeager, Pete Vukovich.

Night Game (1989) Epic Productions Trans World Entertainment, Color, 95 min., D.: Peter Masterson. Cast: Roy Scheider, Karen Young, Richard Bradford.

The Court-Martial of Jackie Robinson (1990, made for TV) Von Zerneck-Sertner Films; Turner Pictures TNT, Color, 100 min. Dir.: Larry Peerce. Cast: Andre Braugher, Ruby Dee, Stan Shaw, Kasi Lemmons, Daniel Stern, Bruce Dern, Paul Dooley.

Taking Care of Business (1990) Silver Screen Productions IV Hollywood Pictures, Color, 107 min. Dir.: Arthur Hiller. Cast: James Belushi, Charles Grodin, Anne De Salvo, Loryn Locklin, Stephen Elliott, Hector Elizondo, Veronica Hamel, Mako, Gates McFadden, Tony Gwynn, Bert Blyleven.

Babe Ruth (1991, made for TV) Lyttle Productions NBC, Color, 100 min. Dir.: Mark Tinker. Cast: Stephen Lang, Bruce Weitz, Donald Moffat, Lisa Zane, Pete Rose, John Anderson.

Pastime (1991) Bullpen Ltd./Open Road Productions Miramax, Color, 95 min. Dir.: Robin B. Armstrong. Cast: William Russ, Glenn Plummer, Noble Willingham, Jeffrey Tambor, Scott Plank, Dierdre O'Connell, Duke Snider, Don Newcombe, Ernie Banks, Bill Mazeroski, Harmon Killebrew, Bob Feller.

Talent for the Game (1991) Paramount Pictures, Color, 91 min. Dir.: Robert M. Young. Cast: Edward James Olmos, Lorraine Bracco, Jeffrey Corbett, Jamey Sheridan, Terry Kinney, Bobby Tolan, Derrel Thomas, Lenny Randle, Todd Cruz, John D'Aquisto, Phil Lombardi, Lee Lacy, Rudy Law, Steve Ontiveros.

City Slickers (1991) Castle Rock Entertainment/Nelson Entertainment/A Face Production Columbia Pictures, Color, 112 min. Dir.: Ron Underwood. Cast: Billy Crystal, Daniel Stern, Bruno Kirby, Patricia Wettig, Helen Slater, Jack Palance, Josh Mostel, David Paymer.

The Babe (1992) Waterhorse/Finnegan-Pinchuk Universal Pictures, Color, 113 min. Dir.: Arthur Hiller. Cast: John Goodman, Kelly McGillis, Trini Alvarado, Bruce Boxleitner, Peter Donat, James Cromwell, J.C. Quinn, Joe Ragno, Richard Tyson.

The Comrades of Summer (1992, made for TV) Grossbart Barnett Productions HBO, Color, 108 min. Dir.: Tommy Lee Wallace. Cast: Joe Mantegna, Natalya Negoda, Mark Rolston, Michael Lerner, Jim Lampley.

A League of Their Own (1992) Parkway Production Columbia Pictures, Color, 124 min. Dir.: Penny Marshall. Cast: Tom Hanks, Geena Davis, Lori Petty, Madonna, Rosie O'Donnell, Megan Cavanagh, David Strathairn, Garry Marshall, Jon Lovitz, Bill Pullman.

Mr. Baseball (1992) Outlaw Production Universal Pictures, Color, 100 min. Dir.: Fred Schepisi. Cast: Tom Selleck, Ken Takakura, Aya Takanashi, Dennis Haysbert, Toshi Shioya, Tim McCarver, Sean McDonough, Greg Goossen, Frank Thomas.

Cooperstown (1993, made for TV) Brandman Productions, Inc./Ambler Television TNT Screenworks, Color, 90 min. Dir.: Charles Haid. Cast: Alan Arkin, Graham Greene, Hope Lange, Josh Charles, Ed Begley Jr., Maria Pitillo, Ann Wedgeworth, Paul Dooley, Charles Haid, Ernie Harwell.

The Sandlot (1993) Island World 20th Century-Fox, Color, 101 min. Dir.: David Mickey Evans. Cast: Tom Guiry, Mike Vitar, Patrick Renna, Chauncy Leopardi, James Earl Jones, Art LaFleur.

Rookie of the Year (1993) 20th Century-Fox, Color, 103 min. Dir.: Daniel Stern. Cast: Thomas Ian Nicholas, Gary Busey, Albert Hall, Amy Morton, John Candy, Eddie Bracken, Daniel Stern, Barry Bonds, Bobby Bonilla, Pedro Guerrero, Tim Stoddard.

The Man from Left Field (1993) Burt Reynolds Productions, Inc. CBS, Color, 100 min. Dir.: Burt Reynolds. Burt Reynolds, Reba McEntire, Derek Baxter, Sean Dunne, Billy Gardner III.

The Scout (1994) Ruddy Morgan 20th Century-Fox, Color, 101 min. Dir.: Michael Ritchie. Cast: Albert Brooks, Brendan Fraser, Dianne Wiest, Lane Smith, Anne Twomey, Michael Rapaport, Ken Brett, Bob Costas, Roy Firestone, Steve Garvey, Keith Hernandez, Tom Kelly, Tim McCarver, Bobby Murcer, Brett Saberhagen, Bob Sheppard, Ozzie Smith, Reggie Smith, George Steinbrenner III.

Angels in the Outfield (1994) Walt Disney Pictures/Caravan Pictures Buena Vista, Color, 102 min. Dir.: William Dear. Cast: Danny Glover, Brenda Fricker, Tony Danza, Christopher Lloyd, Ben Johnson, Jay O. Sanders, Joseph Gordon-Levitt, Dermot Mulroney, Taylor Negron, Tony Longo, Matthew McConaughy, Mitchell Page, Carney Lansford.

Major League II (1994) Morgan Creek Warner Bros., Color, 104 min. Dir.: David S. Ward. Cast: Charlie Sheen, Tom Berenger, Corbin Bernsen, Dennis Haysbert, James Gammon, Bob Uecker, Margaret Whitton, Randy Quaid, Steve Yeager, Kevin Hickey, Jay Leno.

Little Big League (1994) Castle Rock Entertainment Columbia Pictures, Color, 119 min. Dir.: Andrew Scheinman. Cast: Luke Edwards, Timothy Busfield, John Ashton, Ashley Crow, Kevin Dunn, Jason Robards, Jonathan Silverman, Dennis Farina, Leon "Bull" Durham, Kevin Elster, Ken Griffey, Jr., Lou Pinella, Mickey Tettleton, Ivan Rodriguez, Sandy Alomar, Jr., Eric Anthony, Carlos Baerga, Alex Fernandez, Randy Johnson, Wally Joyner, Dave Magadan, Lenny Webster, Paul O'Neill, Rafael Palmeiro, Dean Palmer, Tim Raines, Chris Berman.

Cobb (1994) Regency Enterprises/Alcor Films Warner Bros., Color, 128 min. Dir.: Ron Shelton. Cast: Tommy Lee Jones, Robert Wuhl, Lolita Davidovich, Lou Myers, Tyler Logan Cobb, Roger Clemens, Jay Tibbs, Ernie Harwell.

The Wormkillers' Last Spring (1994) Clear Gate Films, Color, 94 min. Dir.: Tom Dempsey. Cast: Tom Nowicki, Billy Gillespie, Tracy Roberts.

Past the Bleachers (1995) Signboard Hill Prods. Inc. ABC, Color, 100 min. Dir.: Michael Switzer. Cast: Richard Dean Anderson, Barnard Hughes, Glynnis O'Connor, Ken Jenkins, Grayson Fricke, Noah Fleiss.

Ed (1996) Longview Entertainment Universal Pictures, Color, 94 min. Dir.: Bill Couturie. Cast: Matt LeBlanc, Doren Fein, Jayne Brook, Bill Cobbs, Jack Warden, Charlie Schlatter, Mike McGlone, Tommy Lasorda.

Soul of the Game (1996, made for TV) Gary Hoffman Productions HBO, Color, 105 min. Dir.: Kevin Rodney Sullivan. Cast: Delroy Lindo, Mykelti Williamson, Blair Underwood, Edward Herrmann, R. Lee Ermey, Salli Richardson, Gina Ravera, Obba Babatunde.

The Fan (1996) Mandalay Entertainment/Sony Pictures Entertainment Tri-Star, Color, 120 min. Dir.: Tony Scott. Cast: Robert De Niro, Wesley Snipes, Ellen Barkin, John Leguizamo, Benicio Del Toro, Patti D'Arbanville-Quinn, Chris Mulkey, Andrew J. Ferchland, John Kruk.

Space Jam (1996) Courtside Seats Productions/Northern Lights Entertainment Warner Bros., Color, 87 min. Dir: Joe Pytka, Tony Cervone, Bruce W. Smith. Cast: Michael Jordan, Wayne Knight, Theresa Randle, Brandon Hammond, Larry Bird, Charles Barkley, Patrick Ewing, Tyrone Bogues, Larry Johnson, Shawn Bradley, Ahmad Rashad, Del Harris, Vlade Divac, Cedric Ceballos, Jim Rome, Paul Westphal, Danny Ainge.

Prisoner of Zenda, Inc (Double Play) (1996, made for TV) Hallmark Entertainment, Inc., Showtime, Color, 101 min. Dir: Stefan Scaini. Cast: William Shatner, Jonathan Jackson, Jay Brazeau, Richard Lee Jackson, Don S. Davis, Katherine Isobel, John Tench, Jed Rees, Mark Acheson, Howard Dell.

Joe Torre: Curveballs Along the Way (1997, made for TV) British American Entertainment/Norman Twain Productions/Hallmark Entertainment, Inc, Showtime, Color, 95 min. Dir: Sturla Gunnarsson. Cast: Paul Sorvino, Robert Loggia, Barbara Williams, Isaiah Washington, Gailard Sartain, Marilyn Chris, Eugene A. Clark, Kenneth Welsh, Barry Flatman, Dean McDermott.

Major League: Back to the Minors (1998) Morgan Creek Warner Bros., Color, 95 min. Dir: John Warren. Cast: Scott Bacula, Corbin Bernsen, Dennis Haysbert, Takaaki Ishibashi, Jensen Daggett, Eric Bruskotter, Ted McGinley, Bob Uecker, Walt Goggins, Kenneth Johnson.

BASEketball (1998) Universal Pictures, Color, 105 min. Dir: David Zucker. Cast: Trey Parker, Matt Stone, Yasmine Bleeth, Jenny McCarthy, Robert Vaughn, Ernest Borgnine, Dian Bachar, Trevor Einhorn, Bob Costas, Al Michaels, Marc Allen Goodson, Reggie Jackson, Kareem Abdul-Jabbar, Robert Stack, Tim McCarver, Dan Patrick, Kenny Mayne, Pat O'Brien, Jim Lampley.

Simon Birch (1998) Caravan Pictures/Hollywood Pictures Buena Vista, Color, 110 min. Dir: Mark Steven Johnson. Cast: Ian Michael Smith, Joseph Mazzello, Ashley Judd, Oliver Platt, David Strathairn, Dana Ivey, Beatrice Winde, Jan Hooks, Jim Carrey.

## CHAPTER 27

Baseball Collecting

Barry Halper and Bill Madden

The game's first century did not produce many collectors of baseball memorabilia. Oh, sure, there were a few baseball cards as early as the 1860s and extensive sets by the 1880s; even in the game's infancy there was always that legion of autograph-seekers waiting outside the players' gate at any given ballpark. But the cards were seldom saved (as evidenced by the scarcity today of early cards, even those produced in great quantities in the 1950s) and the autographs were a fancy of one's idol-worshiping days. There were no prices attached to such mementos of youthful infatuation, just as there was no business of collecting.

But then, in 1967, a man by the name of Jefferson Burdick published *The American Card Catalog*—a guide listing the origin, description, and estimated value of every card (baseball or otherwise) ever printed. It was a monumental volume, which took years of painstaking research. What his catalog did was to transform the informal and undocumented hobby of baseball card collecting into the more elevated and established rank of stamp and coin collecting. Prices and values, scarcity and condition—these commercial considerations, once they were applied to cards, quickly moved into just about anything associated with baseball: autographs, bats, balls, uniforms, photos, press pins, chinaware, publications, you name it.

Cards

Despite the growing interest in other memorabilia, cards remain at the center of the baseball collecting hobby. The most extensive early card set (it remains one of the largest ever issued, with 520 players in one to 17 variants each) was the Old Judge Cigarette Brand series of 1887 to 1889. Catalogued by Burdick as N172, these insert cards were photographs mounted on board, in the same manner as the cartes de visite that were popular in the 1860s. In terms of interest today, however, the most popular early baseball card set was the 1909-1911 tobacco issue, No. T206 in the Burdick volume. These 523 cards, approximately 2¼ by 1½ inches, were inserted in packages of Sweet Caporal, Piedmont, Sovereign, Cycle, and other cigarette brands of the American Tobacco Company.

Included in the T206 set are two of the most valuable cards in the history of collecting: the Honus Wagner and the Eddie Plank. Both cards are rare for different reasons. According to legend, Wagner, a nonsmoker, became incensed when he discovered that his picture on a card was being used to promote smoking, and he ordered that the card be removed from the T206 set. (Evidently he had a change of heart years later, as he is depicted in the 1948 Leaf Gum card set with chewing tobacco packed in his jaw.) Today, no more than 25 T206 Wagner cards are said to be in existence. The Plank card is equally rare, a result of an accidental fire in 1909 that destroyed the printing plates.

Burdick, acknowledging the scarcity of both cards, listed the Wagner card's value at $50 and the Plank card at $10. The remainder of the T206 cards are listed at 10 cents apiece. Today, the common T206 lists at $100 mint. The Plank lists at about $25,000, while the Wagner card sold for $451,000 at auction in 1991 and again for $640,500 at auction in September 1996.

Allen & Ginters, Turkey Reds and Old Judges

Besides the T206s, the most popular early lithographed tobacco cards then and now are the 1887-88 Allen & Ginters (N28, N29, and N43) and the 1911 T3 Turkey Reds. The Allen & Ginters maintain their value and popularity because of their beauty. They are the same size as the T206s, but the N28 and N29 series are magnificent watercolor paintings of baseball players printed on glossy stock. The N28 is generally considered the first of the tobacco card baseball sets and includes 10 players, among them Hall of Famers Cap Anson, John Clarkson, Charles Comiskey, King Kelly, John Montgomery Ward, and Tim Keefe. The N29, or second series, adds six players, among them Hall of Famer Buck Ewing. The Anson card is the most expensive today, listing at $2,000 mint. Burdick listed the average Allen & Ginter card at 10 cents.

The T3s are classified as cabinet cards because they measure a much larger 5¾ by 8 inches in size and were obtained by sending in coupons found in Turkey Red, Fez, and Old Mill brand cigarettes. They are also beautiful cards, depicting players in full-color portraits. One hundred of the 126 athletes in the Turkey Red set are baseball players, and the cards average $250 for common cards and considerably more for Hall of Famers (Ty Cobb lists at $5,000). In 1967 Burdick listed the price of T3s at $1 apiece. The N172 Old Judge cards were sepia toned, 1½ by 2½ inch blank backed cards issued by the Goodwin Co. of New York from 1887-1890. The set of 565 major and minor league players from that era included all the prominent Hall of Famers, Harry Wright, John Clarkson, Buck Ewing, John Montgomery Ward, King Kelly, Roger Connor, Ed Delahanty et al. The average value of the Old Judge common players is $150 with the Hall of Famers

ranging from $500-$1,200. At a September 1996 auction, however, an assorted cache of 219 Old Judges sold for $40,250.

Gum and Candy Replaces Tobacco

In the 1930s tobacco companies gave way to gum and confectionery companies as the prime dispensers of baseball cards. The most prominent was the Goudey Gum Company, which issued significant sets from 1933 to 1941. These cards, like all the gum/confectionery cards of the 1930 to 1950 era, measured 2½ by 3¼ inches. The most popular of all the Goudey sets is its initial 1933 effort, which was comprised of 240 cards, including one of the rarest of all, No. 106, Napoleon Lajoie. The Lajoie card was inadvertently omitted from the original 1933 Goudey set, and when collectors inquired about the absence of card No. 106, the company offered it as a premium the following year. The few Lajoie cards that exist today contain the 1934 Goudey card design. Burdick listed the common R319 1933 Goudeys at 20 cents apiece and the Lajoie at $1. Today, the common cards list at $50, the numerous Hall of Famers in the set at $150/$250 and above, and the Lajoie at $30,000.

In 1939 Gum Inc. of Boston entered the baseball card field, issuing the first of its three Play Ball sets. The 1939 and 1940 Play Ball sets were sepia-toned cards, while the 1941 set used color. The 72-card 1941 Play Ball set is the most popular of the sets, listing at $10,000 in mint condition. It also features the first color cards of Joe DiMaggio (mint today $2,500) and Ted Williams ($1,750).

World War II prompted a shutdown of the baseball card industry, and it did not resume production until 1948, when the Chicago-based Leaf Company issued its 168-card set of colorized photo cards with gum. The Leaf set, which contains a number of less-distributed cards, lists at $13,000 in mint condition today. The DiMaggio and Babe Ruth cards list at $1,800 and $2,200 respectively, and the Satchel Paige, because it is his rookie card, $2,400.

In 1950 the Bowman Gum Company of Philadelphia replaced Leaf as the premier baseball card manufacturer. Bowman maintained that position until 1952, when the Topps Gum Company of Brooklyn began making inroads into the burgeoning industry. Topps began modestly with two 52-card sets in 1951, as well as a pair of now highly valuable premium sets called Connie Mack and Current All-Stars. The company broke historical ground in 1952 when it issued a 407-card set.

The 1952 Topps remains the Holy Grail of modern-day card sets for collectors, if only because of the difficulty in completing it. Cards numbered 311-407 were issued late in the year by Topps and only in the New York area and Canada. Because of this they are more difficult to find. Burdick listed the 1952 Topps from 1 to 310 at 10 cents apiece and 311 to 407 at 30 cents in 1967.

Making the final series even more valuable is the fact that Topps included many of the game's superstars of that year, including Mickey Mantle, Jackie Robinson, Pee Wee Reese, Eddie Mathews, and Roy Campanella. All of them list today at over $1,000 mint. The Mantle card, No. 311, at $18,000, is considered the jewel of all modern-day cards. The 311 to 407 commons list at $220 apiece.

When Burdick published his *American Card Catalog,* baseball card collecting was limited to just that—collecting. It was not until the mid-1970s when card values began to be known nationwide that baseball card shows and flea markets began to crop up across the country. Prior to then, only a small network of serious baseball card collectors existed: Frank Nagy of Detroit, Buck Barker of St. Louis and myself [Barry Halper] among them. Cards were never sold within this network, although on many occasions the trading would branch into other collections, trading an autograph for a suitable card or cards.

Autographs

For the longest time, baseball autographs were something to be personally treasured but not necessarily valued. No one, for instance, put a value on a Babe Ruth autograph even 20 years after the Babe's death. For one thing, a Ruth autograph was still one of the most common of all Hall of Famer autographs, simply because the Babe signed willingly for everyone he came in contact with. A Lou Gehrig, by contrast, was not nearly as common, although until the advent of the autograph-collecting boom—which occurred at the same time the baseball card boom hit in the mid 1970s—collectors paid little notice.

Today Ruth, because of who he was and what he is to baseball, remains one of the most sought-after and high-priced baseball autographs. Signatures by Joe DiMaggio, Mickey Mantle, and Willie Mays are also much sought after by collectors. But as autograph collectors will testify, it is turn-of-the-century Hall of Famers such as Pud Galvin, Tommy McCarthy, King Kelly, John Clarkson, Roger Connor, Candy Cummings, and Cap Anson whose signatures command the highest prices. These players have been dead for more than 60 years, and their autographs are scarcer than a Ruth, Lou Gehrig, or Ty Cobb.

Perhaps the best way to sum up the modern-day baseball autograph craze is to recall an incident at the New York Yankees' annual Old Timer's Day game in 1980. All the team's living legends, from Joe DiMaggio to Mickey Mantle, Yogi Berra, and Whitey Ford, were on hand for the occasion and were besieged throughout the day for autographs. Reggie Jackson, the Yankees' star right fielder at the time, was expressing dismay at all the autograph seekers around him. "I don't understand all this idolatry," Jackson told the assembled writers. The next day in the *New York Daily News* coverage of the Old Timer's Day festivities was a picture of Reggie Jackson getting an autograph on a baseball from Joe DiMaggio.

World Series Press Pins

Press pins from the World Series, All-Star Game, and Hall of Fame induction ceremonies are the only baseball collectibles separated from the players. The pins have nothing to do with the games, other than their being displayed on the coats of attending sportswriters, and they cannot be autographed. Nevertheless, in conjunction with the baseball collecting boom of the 1970s and 1980s, World Series press pins are now among the most sought-

after and highly valued of memorabilia.

The origin of the baseball press pin dates back to 1911. According to legend, New York Giants manager John McGraw had invited several of his cronies to attend the hotly contested games of September 1908. Because of the scarcity of tickets, McGraw assigned his friends seats in the press box, where they became rowdy, distracting members of the working press. The Baseball Writers Association of America was formed as a result of this unwelcome intrusion into their working domain, and the new union issued press pins in order to establish proper identity for the World Series. No one was permitted into the press boxes without a press pin.

As years went on, press accreditation for the World Series became far more sophisticated, but press pins continued to be a tradition. Each World Series team designed its own pin for the games in its ballpark, and though most sportswriters kept their pins through the years, they didn't view them as valuable memorabilia. It was not until the early 1970s, when collectors began to realize how genuinely scarce old press pins were (due to limited distribution and the fact that so many of them were thrown away through the years), that they became a prized baseball collectible.

The earliest press pins are now valued at upwards of $10,000 apiece. But even the press pins from the 1940s, '50s, and '60s have considerable value. The most valued of all World Series pins is that of the 1956 Brooklyn Dodgers, primarily because it isn't a pin but a tie clasp. The Dodgers chose to break tradition that year and issue tie clasps with a blue Brooklyn cap affixed to them. Probably because the tie clasps were actually worn by the writers long after the Series was over, many of them disappeared. Today the Brooklyn Dodgers 1956 World Series tie clasp has commanded as much as $2,000 in collectors' markets as opposed to the $300 value established for the World Series press pins of the 1956 New York Yankees, who won the Series.

All-Star Game Press Pins

In 1937 baseball extended its press-pin tradition to the All-Star Game, and those pins have also risen greatly in value. No press pins were issued prior to 1937 because the All-Star Game's creator and founder, sportswriter Arch Ward, had envisioned his "gala" as being a one-time event. The prices of All-Star press pins vary greatly, based primarily on the issuing city. One of the rarest All-Star press pins is the 1948 pin issued by the host St. Louis Browns. It is a beautiful pin depicting the white Brownies cap with the brown bill and gold piping. It is dated 1948 and lists for upwards of $3,500.

Hall of Fame Press Pins

The Hall of Fame joined the press-pin field in 1982. Beginning that year, the Hall of Fame issued commemorative press pins listing the names of each year's inductees. Because a limited number of media personnel cover the Hall of Fame ceremonies, the distribution of the pins is believed to be about one-tenth that of the World Series

pins. The Hall of Fame pins have quickly shot past their contemporary World Series and All-Star pins in value. The first Hall of Fame pin in 1982, engraved with the names of inductees Hank Aaron, Happy Chandler, Frank Robinson, and Travis Jackson, was going for more than $650 in the collectors' market.

'Phantom' Pins

In the early years of press pins the Dieges & Clust Company of John Street in New York was the primary manufacturer. In 1946 the Balfour Company of Attleboro, Mass., assumed the contract from Major League Baseball to produce the pins. The company remains the primary producer of pins and rings for the World Series and All-Star Game, although some teams have, in the interest of cost-cutting, sought local companies to produce their pins.

The advent of the playoff system also caused economic problems for contending clubs that were compelled to commission press pins. It had long been the custom of clubs to date the pins for each year's World Series. In many cases, however, the club wouldn't advance to the Series and the press pins produced were rendered unusable for any future Series. These so-called "phantom" pins, such as the 1951 Brooklyn Dodgers (who lost in a playoff to the Giants on Bobby Thomson's historic home run), the 1938 Pittsburgh Pirates (victims of Chicago Cub Gabby Hartnett's "homer in the gloamin' "), or the 1949 Cardinals are harder to come by and as valuable as the "official" Series press pins of those years.

As John Scarpellini, Balfour's longtime representative to baseball recalled, "The elimination of the dating of the pins came about when Dick O'Connell, general manager of the Red Sox, was asked by us about the kind of press pin he wanted designed for the 1975 World Series. Instead of committing himself, O'Connell opened up a closet door in his office and produced what had to be nearly 50,000 press pins. 'Look at these,' he said. 'They're all dated and therefore no good to us. I've got all these pins, which we've paid for, and we can't do anything with them.'

"After that, we came up with the idea of labeling the pins with the phrase 'Our Second World Series' or whatever number that particular World Series was for that particular team. That way, if the club was beaten out in the playoffs, but had already had to produce their pins, they could just put them away in a vault and use them whenever they made it."

Uniforms

In the entire spectrum of baseball collecting no item is more personal than a uniform. Unfortunately, collecting uniforms from modern-day players has become a risky venture because of the increase in counterfeits on the market. Modern-day doubleknits are so easy to manufacture that it is difficult to tell a counterfeit from the authentic article.

The source for legitimate modern-day uniforms is generally the clubhouse man for the major league ballclubs.

This has created a serious problem for Major League Baseball. Officials are aware of how little clubhouse men are paid and how easily they can become prey for dealers in baseball memorabilia.

In some cases the players themselves can be sources for uniforms. Pete Rose, for example, reportedly had a deal with the Cincinnati Reds that he be given 25 or more uniforms during the course of the season to do with as he wished. During the game in which Rose tied Ty Cobb's all-time hits record, he wore a different jersey for each at bat. Presumably, Rose sold each jersey to a different collector.

Similarly, Gaylord Perry, in winning his 300th game for the Seattle Mariners against the New York Yankees, wore two different uniforms. The reason I know that is that Perry had promised his uniform from that game to me. But a couple of days before he pitched, I got a call from the visiting clubhouse man in Baltimore, who was also a dealer in memorabilia. The clubhouse man offered me Perry's Seattle uniform from his 300th-win game. It seems that Gaylord had decided that two uniforms were better than one when it came to maximizing his profit on 300 wins, and he decided to make a change after four innings. I wound up having to make separate deals with both Perry and the clubhouse man from Baltimore in order to have what was surely the uniform in which Perry won his 300th game.

The values of modern-day players' uniforms vary greatly. Naturally, the uniforms players wore performing historic feats such as Rose's 4,192nd hit are of considerably more value than an everyday game-worn uniform. In the uniform-collecting hobby of the 1990s, common players' uniforms were selling in the $400-$600 range, star-quality players' from 1,500 to $1,500, and superstar/Hall of Fame-caliber players' (the Ripkens, Ozzie Smiths) from $3,000 up.

Old-Time Uniforms

Old-time uniforms are a far more challenging hobby, one that has been the most satisfying and exciting aspect of my collecting career. Why? Because I never believed so many of these old uniforms, particularly the ones from the pre-1900 Hall of Fame players, could still exist. And exist in such remarkable condition! Through the years, I have managed to amass approximately 1,000 uniforms, which I have stored on a dry cleaner conveyer belt that is computerized to stop at whichever uniform number I punch in. Included among these are uniforms of every Hall of Famer who played or managed, and even some minor league uniforms of Hall of Fame executives (such as longtime Yankees business manager Ed Barrow) who never wore a major league uniform.

As one might expect, values for the oldest, turn-of-the-century uniforms far exceed those for any of the more recent Hall of Famers of the 1930s to the present day. Uniforms worn by Babe Ruth, Lou Gehrig, and Ty Cobb have been appraised in excess of $100,000. The uniforms of such Hall of Famers as Pud Galvin (Buffalo, 1879), John Clarkson (Saginaw, 1883), King Kelly (New York Giants, 1893), Charles Comiskey (Cincinnati, 1893), Old Hoss Radbourn (Boston, 1886), Roger Connor (New York Giants, 1893), Joe McGinnity (New York Giants, 1904), and Cy Young (Boston, 1903) are worth much more.

The existence of these uniforms only adds to and rounds out the lore and history of the game of baseball. How they were uncovered after all these years—the treasure hunt—is the most fulfilling aspect of collecting baseballiana.

It was during a conversation I once had with Pete Sheehy, the venerable New York Yankees clubhouse man from the days of Ruth in the '20s right up until the Don Mattingly-Dave Winfield Yankees of the '80s, that I got my most valuable tip in regard to uniform collecting. I asked Sheehy: "Pete, where are all the Pete Sheehys of yesterday? The clubhouse men who kept a vigil over all the old uniforms?"

Not surprisingly, in his days as clubhouse man of the Yankees, Sheehy had become friends with the clubhouse men from other clubs and they would correspond frequently. Most of his contemporaries had died when I talked to him about this, but he kept track of many of their relatives.

One person Sheehy put me in contact with was a man from Coxsackie, N.Y., who, Sheehy thought, was in possession of most of the old Yankees uniforms from 1927, the year of Murderers' Row. Sure enough, upon getting in touch with the man, I was able to acquire the 1927 uniforms of Ruth, Gehrig, Earle Combs, Waite Hoyt, Bob Meusel, Mark Koenig, Bob Shawkey, and about a half dozen others. Sheehy also put me in contact with the relatives of the equipment manager at Columbia University during the early '20s when Gehrig played there. It was through that contact that I was able to uncover Gehrig's Columbia uniform and the first uniform he ever wore as a professional, with Hartford. He had played there under the assumed name of Lewis in 1921 to protect his amateur standing at Columbia; that name is sewn into the bottom flap of the shirt.

All the uniforms from that pre-1920s period are identified by the players' names sewn somewhere on them since numbers did not come into existence until 1929. The Yankees that year introduced numbers on the backs of their uniforms in the order in which the players appeared in the batting order.

Another valuable source of old uniforms was Dick Bartell, the pepperpot New York Giants and Detroit Tigers shortstop of the 1930s and '40s. Bartell put me in touch with Ollie O'Mara, an old ballplayer, then in his 80s, who lived in Reno, Nev. O'Mara had had a brief major league career with the Brooklyn Dodgers from 1914 to 1919, a team that was managed by Hall of Famer Wilbert Robinson. Apparently O'Mara had maintained a close friendship with Robinson. That is the only explanation I can offer for the fact that he had in his possession the 1894 Baltimore Orioles uniforms of Robinson, Joe Kelley, Wee Willie Keeler, Dan Brouthers, and Hughie Jennings—Hall of Famers all. O'Mara never did tell me how he got the uniforms or why he had kept them all those years in near-perfect condition. In 1989 he went to his grave with that secret, but baseball historians can be forever grateful that he preserved so much of the game's valuable past.

Bats, Balls, and Books

Until recently vintage bats, balls, gloves, and other gear were a neglected area for collectors. One could find an antique glove or ball in a thrift store or flea market for only a few dollars. Without an autograph or major league player "association," the items were not viewed as desirable. The same could be said of baseball books and photos, although scorecards, guides (Spalding, Reach, Beadle, and so on), yearbooks, and programs-especially World Series programs-did attract collectors before the baseball-card boom in the 1980s.

A handful of early-baseball enthusiasts picked up as many of these antique items as possible, from club constitutions of the amateur era to thick-handled bats with "mushroom" knobs, from gold-painted trophy balls of the 1860s to sepia-toned photographs of unknown teams. This type of memorabilia has increased in value over the years but not as spectacularly as, for example, the cards of the 1950s. Where a 1952 Mickey Mantle card might fetch $25,000, a rare 1868 book by Henry Chadwick might bring only $5,000.

However, as card prices continue to soar, sophisticated collectors and devoted fans who have been made nervous by the explosive speculation of the 1980s are beginning to see relative safety in the pursuit of older collectibles, where the market is driven more by true scarcity than by widespread demand. Prices may go up or down with general economic conditions, but the lure of baseball and its collectibles remains constant.

The History of Major League Baseball Statistics

John Thorn, Pete Palmer, and Joseph M. Wayman

Part Two, the statistical section of *Total Baseball*, presents the record of major league contests played from 1871 through 1998—all 169,565 of them. It details the accomplishments of the game's 2,295 team seasons and 15,000 players so completely and accurately that Major League Baseball has authorized *Total Baseball* to be the official encyclopedia of the game, its authentic historical record.

Total Baseball won critical acclaim and a devoted following not only for its breadth and depth of information but also for its pioneering "sabermetric" stats that offered alternative, unofficial measures of player performance. Yet, for all its innovation, *Total Baseball* has stood squarely in the tradition of baseball record keeping; it is—like each new spring of our national pastime—a link in a long, long chain. As the New York Knickerbockers' game of 150 years ago lives on in the game of today, so is this volume enriched by the labors of statisticians from Henry Chadwick to Ernie Lanigan, from S.C. Thompson and Seymour Siwoff and the Hirdt brothers to David Neft and Bill James.

How we came from the Knickerbockers' primitive accounting of outs and runs to the vast array of statistics available today is an interesting process, in which Major League Baseball's role has been central. Through its evolving scoring rules and procedures, its judicious endorsement of new measures, and its continuing mission to set the record straight, the Commissioner's Office and its official scorers have provided fans with a wealth of statistical data unmatched by any other sport—perhaps any other human activity—on earth.

Here is how we who love baseball came to this fortunate estate, and how we at *Total Baseball* created what is now the official historical record.

The Origins, 1845-1875

Baseball and stats were a tandem from the very Eden of the game. The first box score appeared in the *New York Morning News* on Oct. 22, 1845, less than a month after Alexander Cartwright and his Knickerbocker teammates codified the first set of rules. Why did these early players and scribes measure individual performance rather than simply count the score? In part to imitate the custom of cricket; yet the larger explanation is that the numbers served to legitimize men's concern with a boys' pastime. The pioneers of baseball reporting—William Cauldwell of the *Sunday Mercury*, William Porter of *Spirit of the Times*, an unknown annalist at the *News*, and later Henry Chadwick—may indeed have reflected that if they did not cloak the game in the "importance" of statistics, it might not seem worthwhile for adults to read about, let alone play. Statistics elevated baseball from other boys' field games of the 1840s and '50s to make it somehow systematic and serious, like business; despite baseball's essential simplicity, it was laced with intricate detail that suited it perfectly to quantification.

In the development of baseball statistics, no man is more important than Father Chadwick. Born in England in 1824, he came to these shores at age thirteen steeped in the tradition of cricket. In his teens he played the English game and in his twenties he reported on it for a variety of newspapers, including the *Long Island Star* and the *New York Times*. In the early 1840s, before the Knickerbocker rules eliminated the practice of retiring a base runner by throwing the ball at him rather than to the base, Chadwick occasionally played baseball too, but he was not favorably impressed, having received "some hard hits in the ribs." Not until 1856, by which time he had been a cricket reporter for a decade, were Chadwick's eyes opened to the possibilities in the American game, which had improved dramatically since his youth.

In 1868 he recalled, "On returning from the early close of a cricket match on Fox Hill, I chanced to go through the Elysian Fields during the progress of a contest between the noted Eagle and Gotham clubs. The game was being sharply played on both sides, and I watched it with deeper interest than any previous ball game between clubs that I had seen. It was not long before I was struck with the idea that baseball was just the game for a national sport for Americans . . . as much so as cricket in England. At the time I refer to I had been reporting cricket for years, and, in my method of taking notes of contests, I had a plan peculiarly my own. It was not long, therefore, after I had become interested in baseball, before I began to invent a method of giving detailed reports of leading contests at baseball . . . ."

Thus Chadwick's cricket background was largely the impetus to his method of scoring a baseball game, the format of his early box scores, and the copious if primitive statistics that appeared in his year-end summaries in the

New York Clipper, Beadle's *Dime Base-Ball Player*, and other publications.

Actually, cricket had begun to shape baseball statistics even before Chadwick's conversion. The first box score reported on two categories, outs and runs: outs, or "hands out," counted both unsuccessful times at bat and outs run into on the basepaths; "runs" were runs scored, not those driven in. The reason for not recording hits in the early years, when coverage of baseball matches appeared alongside reports of cricket matches, was that, unlike baseball, cricket had no such category as the successful hit which did not produce a run. To reach "base" in cricket is to run to the opposite wicket, which tallies a run; if you hit the ball and do not score a run, you have been put out.

Cricket box scores were virtual play-by-plays, a fact made possible by the lesser number of possible events. This play-by-play aspect was applied to a baseball box score as early as 1856; interestingly, despite the abundance of detail, hits were not accounted, nor did they appear in Chadwick's own box scores until 1867. The batting champion as declared by Chadwick, whose computations were immediately and universally accepted as "official," was the man with the highest average of runs per game. An inverse though imprecise measure of batting quality was outs per game. After 1863, when a fair ball caught on one bounce was no longer an out, fielding leaders were those with the greatest total of fly catches, assists, and "foul bounds" (fouls caught on one bounce). Pitching effectiveness was based purely on control, with the leader recognized as the one whose delivery offered the most opportunities for outs at first base and led to the fewest passed balls.

In a sense, Chadwick's measuring of baseball as if it were cricket can be viewed as correct: when you strip the game to its basic elements, those that determine victory or defeat, outs and runs are indeed all that count in the end. No individual statistic is meaningful to the team unless it relates directly to the scoring of runs.

Early player stats were of the most primitive kind, the counting kind. They'd tell you how many runs, or outs, or fly catches had occurred—later, how many hits or total bases. Counting is the most basic of all statistical processes; the next step up is averaging, and Chadwick was the first to put this into practice.

As professionalism infiltrated the game, teams began to bid for star-caliber players. Stars were known not by their stats but by their style until 1865, when Chadwick began to record in the *Clipper* a form of batting average taken from the cricket pages—runs per game. Two years later, in his newly founded baseball weekly, *The Ball Players' Chronicle*, he began to record not only average runs and outs per game, but also home runs, total bases, total bases per game—and hits per game. The averages were expressed not with decimal places but in the standard cricket format of the "average and over." Thus a batter with 23 hits in six games would have an average expressed not as 3.83 but as "3–5"—an average of 3 with an overage, or remainder, of 5. Another innovation was to remove from the individual accounting all bases gained through errors. Runs scored by a team, beginning in 1867, were divided between those scored after a man reached base on a clean hit and those arising from a runner's having reached base on an error. This was a clear precur-

sor of the modern earned run average.

By the end of the decade Chadwick was recording total bases and home runs, but he placed little stock in either, as conscious attempts at slugging violated his cricket-bred image of "form." Just as cricket aficionados watch the game for the many opportunities for fine fielding it affords, so was baseball from its inception perceived as a fielders' sport. The original Knickerbocker rules of 1845, in fact, specified that a ball hit out of the field—in fair territory or foul—was a foul ball! "Long hits are showy," Chadwick wrote in the *Clipper* in 1868, "but they do not pay in the long run. Sharp grounders insuring the first-base certain, and sometimes the second-base easily, are worth all the hits made for home-runs which players strive for."

Chadwick prevailed, and the batting average used from that year on is the same as that used today except in its denominator, where at bats replaced games in 1876. Moreover, Chadwick created a measure in the 1860s that divided total bases by games played; change that denominator to at bats and you have today's slugging average—which, incidentally, was not accepted by the National League as an official statistic until 1923 and by the American until 1946.

Chadwick's "total bases average" represent the game's first attempt at a weighted average—an average in which the elements collected together in the numerator or the denominator are recognized numerically as being unequal. In this instance, a single is the unweighted unit, the double is weighted by a factor of two, the triple by three, and the home run by four. Statistically, this is a distinct leap forward from, first, counting, and next, averaging. The weighted average is in fact the cornerstone of today's statistical innovations, or sabermetrics.

The 1870s gave rise to some new batting stats and to the first attempt to quantify thoroughly the other principal facets of the game, pitching and fielding. Although the *Clipper* recorded base hits and total bases as early as 1868, a significant wrinkle was added in 1870 when at bats were listed as well. This was a critical introduction because it permitted the improvement of the batting average, first introduced in its current form by H.A. Dobson of Washington, D.C., in the *Dime Base-Ball Player* of 1872, and first computed "officially"—that is, for the newly created National League—in 1876, the lone year in which bases on balls were figured as outs. Since then the batting average has not changed, except for 1887, when bases on balls were counted as *hits*. In accord with previously created Major League Baseball policy, *Total Baseball* counts a walk as neither an out nor a hit for all years since 1871.

The objections to the batting average are well known, but to date have not disturbed its place as the most popular measure of hitting ability. First of all, the batting average makes no distinction between the single, the double, the triple, and the home run, treating all as the same unit. This objection had been addressed in 1868 by Chadwick's total bases average. Second, the batting average gives no indication of the effect of that base hit—that is, its value to the team. Third, the batting average does not take into account those occasions when first base is reached via a walk, hit batsman, or error. This last point was addressed at a surprisingly early date, too: in 1879 the National

League adopted as an official statistic a forerunner of the on base percentage; it was called "reached first base," which included times reached by error as well as base on balls and base hits. (Being hit by a pitch did not give the batter first base until the ensuing decade.)

The Flowering, 1876-1920

Ever since the Civil War, serial guides like *Beadle* and *DeWitt* and sporting columns like those in the *Clipper* had carried year-end tabulations of batting, fielding, and pitching exploits, varying from year to year with the brainstorms of Chadwick or other demon compilers like New York's M.J. Kelly or Philadelphia's Al Wright. But the year 1876 was special. It was significant not only for the founding of the National League and the official debut of the batting average in its current form, it was also the Centennial of the United States, which was marked by a giant exposition in Philadelphia celebrating the mechanical marvels of the day. American ingenuity reigned, and technology was seen as the new handmaiden of democracy. Baseball, that mirror of American life, reflected the fervor for things scientific with an explosion of statistics far more complex than those seen before, particularly in the previously neglected areas of pitching and fielding. The increasingly minute statistical examination of the game met a responsive audience, one primed to view complexity as a measure of worth.

In 1876 the number of "official" offensive stats tabulated at season's end—i.e., in any of the publications inspired by Chadwick or Albert Spalding—was six: games, at bats, runs, hits, runs per game, and batting average. (And as with all the various guides until 1941, the stats of men who played in fewer than a specified minimum number of games were not noted.) Of these six, only runs and runs per game were common in the 1860s, while that decade's tabulation of total bases vanished. The number of official offensive stats a hundred years later? Twenty. (Today the number is twenty-one, with the addition of on base percentage).

The number of "official" pitching categories in 1876 was eleven, and there were some modernistic surprises, such as earned run average, hits allowed, hits per game, and opponents' batting average. Strikeouts were not recorded, for Chadwick saw them strictly as a sign of poor batting rather than good pitching. (His view had such an impact that pitcher strikeouts were not kept officially until 1889.) The number of official pitching stats today? Twenty-four.

The number of fielding categories in 1876 was six. One hundred years later it was still six (with the exception of the catcher, who gets a seventh: passed balls), dramatizing how the game, which originated as a showcase for fielders, had changed. The fielding stats of 1876 lumped "battery errors" with fielding errors, so that wild pitches and passed balls—in some years, even walks—diminished one's fielding percentage. This practice continued until 1887, but in *Total Baseball* battery errors are not included in fielding stats. Battery-mates' fielding stats were boosted by the awarding of an assist to the pitcher on strikeouts. This practice lasted until 1889, but is not reflected in *Total Baseball*.

The custom in 1876, as it is now, was to combine putouts, assists, and errors to form a "percentage of chances accepted," or what is today known as fielding average or fielding percentage. A "missing link" variant, devised by Al Wright in 1875, was to form averages by dividing the putouts by the number of games to yield a "putout average"; dividing the assists similarly to arrive at an "assist average"; and dividing putouts plus assists by games to get "fielding average." These averages took no account of errors. (Wright's "fielding average" was reborn a century later as Bill James's "range factor.")

The public's appetite for new statistics was not sated by the outburst of 1876. New measures were introduced in dizzying profusion in the remaining years of the century. Some of these did not catch on and were soon dropped for all time, like the meaningless "total bases run," while others fizzled only to reappear with new vigor in the twentieth century. These include (a) the above-mentioned "reached first base," which resurfaced in the early 1950s in an unofficial, improved form called on base percentage and became an official stat more than thirty years later, and (b) an 1860s stat, earned run average, which was periodically revived before dropping from sight in the 1880s, only to return triumphant to the NL in 1912 and the AL in 1913. (In 1913 Ban Johnson not only proclaimed the ERA official but became so enamored with it that he also instructed American League scorers to compile no official won-lost records. This state of affairs lasted for seven years, 1913-1919, but *Total Baseball* does record wins and losses by pitchers in those years, in accordance with the understood scoring practices of the time.)

Another stat that was "sent back to the minors" before its eventual adoption as an official stat in 1920 was the run batted in. Introduced by a Buffalo newspaper in 1879, the stat was picked up the following year by the *Chicago Tribune* and even became an official NL stat for the opening months of 1891. By season's end it had faded as most NL scorers declined to account for it in their summaries. (The American Association, however, recorded it all year long.) Ernie Lanigan picked up the RBI baton with his reports to the *New York Press* from 1907 through 1919, and he did not figure RBI for men who played in fewer than ten games, or club totals for traded players.

For *Total Baseball* we have placed much reliance upon the source material donated by Information Concepts, Inc. (ICI) to the National Baseball Library in Cooperstown following publication of *The Baseball Encyclopedia* which it developed for publication by Macmillan in 1969. David Neft also kindly supplied us with his unpublished RBI data for the previously missing National League seasons of 1880-1885. The John Tattersall collection of nineteenth century game accounts and box scores was valuable for uncovering RBI as well. (For a detailed accounting of the sources employed for this official historical record of Major League Baseball, see the conclusion of the essay.)

Other statistics introduced officially before the turn of the century were stolen bases (though not caught stealing); doubles, triples, and homers; and sacrifice bunts (though an at-bat was charged from 1889 through 1893). Pitcher strikeouts, bases on balls, and the hit-by-pitch also appeared before 1900, but hit-by-pitch stats were not kept

for batters on a systematic basis until 1917 in the NL and 1920 in the AL. Through newspaper research, we have filled in HBP data from 1884 through 1916 in the National League; the Players League of 1890; the American Association of 1882-1891; from 1901 through 1919 in the American League, and the 1914-1915 Federal League.

Hit into double play—including line outs as well as an groundouts—was an erratically recorded stat in the nineteenth century, but separate stats for groundouts into double plays have been kept by the leagues only since 1933 in the NL and 1939 in the AL. Batters' strikeouts were reported unofficially in 1891, but not as a league stat until 1910 in the NL and 1913 in the AL. Innings pitched were not kept until 1908 in the AL and 1903 in the NL. You can see what a patchwork quilt the records of Major League Baseball were in its early years.

Stolen bases were awarded not only for clean steals but also for extra bases taken through daring, from the first year in which totals were kept, 1886, until 1898. Because the figures reported in the guides were grossly inflated (such as Harry Stovey's ostensible 156 steals in 1888), the figures in *Total Baseball* reflect game-by-game research and refiguring. Caught-stealing (CS) figures are available on a very sketchy basis in some of the later years of the century, as some newspapers carried the data in the box scores of hometown games. From 1912 on, Lanigan recorded CS in box scores of the *New York Press*, but the leagues did not keep the figure officially until 1920. The AL has tabulated CS from that year to the present, excepting 1927, which members of the Society for American Baseball Research reconstructed from newspaper box scores. National League caught-stealing data exists for 1920-1925, and for 1951 to the present.

The new century added little in the way of new official statistics—ERA, RBI, and slugging average are better regarded as revivals despite their respective adoption dates of 1912, 1920, and 1923. But back in 1908 there was a classic case of a statistic rushing in to fill a void, as Phillies' manager Billy Murray observed that his outfielder Sherry Magee had the happy facility of providing a long fly ball whenever presented with a situation of a man on third and fewer than two outs. Taking up the cudgels on his player's behalf, Murray protested to the National League office that it was unfair to charge Magee with an unsuccessful time at bat when he was in fact succeeding, doing precisely what the situation demanded. (More recent stats—the save and the short-lived game-winning run batted in, or GWRBI—have followed from this sort of perception that something important was occurring on the field yet had no verifiable reality because it was not being measured.)

A signal event took place in 1912: the publication by *Baseball Magazine* editor John Lawres of *Who's Who in Baseball,* a small book that became the first to provide career statistics and personal facts for a group of players. Although thoroughly inadequate by today's standards— its only tabulations were games, batting average, and fielding average (even for pitchers, who were given no pitching records!)—*Who's Who* was a groundbreaking work. It gave rise to a much-expanded format in 1916 and inspired two other significant encyclopedic works: in 1914, George Moreland's self-published opus called *Balldom* (grandiosely subtitled "The Britannica of Base-

ball,") and Ernest J. Lanigan's *Baseball Cyclopedia*, also sponsored by *Baseball Magazine*, which debuted in 1922 and was updated annually through 1933.

The Golden Age, 1920-1968

There have been other new statistical tabulations in this century, but generally of the counting sort: complete games (NL 1910, AL 1922), games started (AL 1926, NL 1938), games finished (NL 1920, AL 1926). And there were sacrifice bunts allowed (NL 1913, AL 1921), intentional bases on balls (only since 1955), and, in the next period, saves (1969) and game-winning RBI (1980). The only new average since slugging average was adopted in 1923 has been the on base percentage, adopted in 1985.

The ICI group computed saves for prior years. Another such stat that failed to survive, alas, was stolen bases off pitchers, which the American League recorded only in 1920-1924; it has been recorded on an unofficial basis since the 1980s by the Elias Sports Bureau and Baseball Workshop. The only new fielding measure was team double plays, added to the AL list in 1912 and the NL in 1919. Other new and more interesting stats appeared in the 1940s and '50s but have not yet gained the official stamp of approval, such as Ted Oliver's Weighted Rating System, Alfred P. Berry's Average Bases Allowed (opponents' slugging average), and Branch Rickey and Allan Roth's Isolated Power. (See the ensuing essay, "Sabermetrics" for more about these unorthodox measures, some of which have gained wide acceptance and may, like the on base percentage, one day be embraced by Major League Baseball.)

This period of baseball's history may have fielded its most dazzling array of stars, but strategically and statistically it was rather dim. There was some excitement, however, in baseball record keeping. First came *Daguerreotypes*, issued by *The Sporting News* in 1934, featuring the playing records of many retired players both celebrated and obscure; most if not all of these statistical and biographical profiles originally appeared in the pages of TSN. Although its number of statistical categories was fewer than one might have wished, *Daguerreotypes* was very useful and, through its several editions ably edited by Paul MacFarlane, long-lived.

In 1940 came *The Sporting News's Baseball Register*, which supplied full records for active players, managers, coaches, and umpires, plus a grab bag of former stars. Since the expansion of the major leagues from sixteen teams to twenty-eight, the Register has only accommodated contemporary players and managers, but it remains a valuable source.

Then in 1951 came the first true encyclopedia of baseball, the claims of Moreland and Lanigan notwithstanding. Compiled by Hy Turkin and S.C. Thompson, *The Official Encyclopedia of Baseball* was published by the A.S. Barnes Company. Its 620 pages contained a wealth of features such as manager and umpire rosters, historical essays, playing tips, a bibliography, and much more. But the heart of the volume and the key to its subsequent success was a register of nearly nine thousand men who had played one or more games at the major league level from 1871 through 1949 (the 1950 record of players

appearing in ten games or more was tacked on to the end). In this register, Turkin/Thompson also offered birth and death data and what today seems fairly limited statistical information but by previous standards was a veritable cornucopia: year, club, league, position, games, and batting average or won-lost record. A landmark volume that did much to inspire this one, the Barnes encyclopedia endured through ten revised editions, the last being published in 1979, ten years after the initial appearance of Macmillan's *The Baseball Encyclopedia*.

The Barnes encyclopedia went a long way toward making the study of baseball history and records a respectable pursuit, just as a century earlier the statistical accounting of a boys' game had helped to make baseball a sport for grown men. The researchers' ranks expanded to include such men as Bob Davids, who in 1971, aided by other experts like Cliff Kachline, Bill Haber, Ray Nemec, John Pardon, and Joe Simenic, would create SABR, the Society for American Baseball Research (pronounced "saber"). Formerly the lonely pursuit of a handful of "nuts" like S.C. Thompson, baseball research and sabermetrics—a neologism coined in honor of SABR, signifying the statistical analysis of the game's records—would become the pastime of thousands.

An article in *Life* magazine by Branch Rickey on August 2, 1954, gave further impetus to the study of baseball statistics, but not just to set the historical record straight. Indeed, this article may be viewed as the opening shot of the sabermetric assault of the 1980s. In "Goodby to Some Old Baseball Ideas," Rickey, with the aid of some new mathematical tools supplied by Dodger statistician Allan Roth, sought to puncture some long-held conceptions about how the game was divided among its elements (batting, baserunning, pitching, fielding), who was best at playing it, and what caused one team to win and another to lose. This is a pretty fair statement of what sabermetrics is about.

Rickey attacked the batting average and proposed in its place the on base percentage, but the most important thing Rickey did for baseball statistics was to strip the game and its stats to their pre-1876 essentials and start again, this time remembering that individual stats came into being as an attempt to apportion the players' contributions to achieving a team victory.

Rickey and Roth devised a formula to measure a team's efficiency in turning its offensive and defensive statistics into runs, and thus wins. They realized, and had confirmed for them by mathematicians at the Massachusetts Institute of Technology, that just as the team which scores more runs in a game gets the win, so a team which over the course of a season scores more runs than it allows should win more games than it loses—and by an extent correlated to its run differential.

From this startlingly simple (or rather, seemingly simple) observation of 1954 flowed: first, the trailblazing but little noted work of George Lindsey in the 1950s and early 1960s, when he developed a model for run-scoring probability from the twenty-four combinations of outs and bases occupied; the development of "percentage baseball" stats and strategies by Earnshaw Cook in the 1960s; the play-by-play analysis of complete seasons by the Mills brothers, Eldon and Harlan, in 1969-1970; the recording and analysis of situational statistics by the Elias

Sports Bureau for use by Major League Baseball and its clubs; and, over the next two decades, the statistical and historical works of many sabermetricians.

The Computer Age, 1969-

Despite the death of Turkin in 1957 and Thompson ten years later, their encyclopedia remained the dominant book of baseball statistics, although many fans were frustrated with the fragmentary records it presented. As Frank V. Phelps wrote in the 1987 edition of *The National Pastime*, "Gaps and obvious errors in official averages, the lack of many early records, difficulty in securing the records of players who appeared in only a few games, and frustrating discrepancies among existing guides and registers had long since created a desire for an ultimate, complete, correct set of major league records. But it wasn't until the mid-1960s that the development of sophisticated computers which could absorb, retain, order, and output huge amounts of data finally made a project feasible."

Beginning in 1967, a battalion of researchers commanded by David Neft foraged through the official records and newspaper box scores to provide freshly compiled figures for those who had no ERAs, RBI, slugging averages, saves, and all manner of wonderful things. The material which finally appeared in the tome was entered into a data bank, and the book was the first to be typeset entirely by computer, now a common practice. Published in 1969, *The Baseball Encyclopedia* was a milestone in computer technology, but as indispensable as the computer were the old-fashioned scrapbooks and files of Lee Allen and John Tattersall. The result was a mammoth ledger book of the major leagues more thorough than any that had ever appeared before.

The ICI group not only found new data to correct old inaccuracies but also applied new yardsticks to men who had gone to their graves never having heard of an RBI or a save. The ICI research that went into *The Baseball Encyclopedia* of 1969 created new stars, launching several previously underappreciated heroes of old into the Hall of Fame. Sam Thompson, Addie Joss, Roger Connor, Amos Rusie. Their phenomenal level of play was hidden simply because statisticians back then were not recording the particular numbers which would show them off to best advantage. If sabermetrics consists of finding things in the existing data that were not seen before, or in collecting that data which makes possible the application of new statistics to old performances, the first edition of *The Baseball Encyclopedia* was a monument in the course of sabermetrics.

However, its subsequent editions declined from that standard, dropping valuable data, altering figures for star players in a misguided homage to tradition, and making a shambles of individual/team balance in the totals.

The seventh edition was issued in 1988 and, like the five that preceded it, was less accurate than the classic first issue. The eighth edition, published in 1990, corrected many of the errors in the seventh but retained many once-contested errors that historians had long since expunged from the record, while changing other statistics in a manner at variance with Major League Baseball's

standards and with a rationale that remains unclear. For the ninth edition, Major League Baseball distanced itself from the both the product and its database.

Even when *The Baseball Encyclopedia* had been launched back in 1969, the ICI findings raised the hackles of traditionalists, prompting the formation by Major League Baseball of a Special Baseball Records Committee. Its members ruled upon such matters as whether, for the historical record, bases on balls should be counted as hits (as they were in 1887), outs (as they were in 1876), or neither (as has been the practice in all other years); or whether "sudden-death" home runs—thirty-seven game-winning blows with men on base that they identified as having occurred in the bottom half of the ninth or an extra inning—would be credited as homers or, in the practice before 1920, would count for only as many bases as were needed to push across the winning run. In the latter controversy, committee members first decided to count the disputed blows as homers, but then, when complaints arose that Babe Ruth's famous total of 714 would change to 715, they reversed themselves. They also decided that the National Association of 1871-1875 was not a major league, while the Federal League, Union Association, and Players League were; and they ruled on several other issues, all of which were published in the Appendix to *The Baseball Encyclopedia*.

Because earlier editions of *Total Baseball* enjoyed neither the privilege nor the responsibility of official Major League Baseball status, the editors committed themselves to the *process* of history—its research, reporting, and interpretation—rather than to its product. History is not static and unchanging. Our course then as now seemed unassailable: publish the best-documented data and remain humbly amenable to subsequent revision in the light of new evidence. (This is not very different from the placard in the Baseball Hall of Fame, which states that although later studies have called into question the accuracy of information on the plaques, the facts as engraved were believed to be accurate at the time.)

However, it must be acknowledged that we paid little mind to the consequences of our findings and reasoned judgments, such as the stripping of a batting championship from Ty Cobb in 1910 or Bobby Avila in 1954. For the fourth, landmark edition of *Total Baseball*, our challenge was to devise a more historically sensitive framework that would permit us to incorporate the best modern research while continuing to honor the judgments of the past.

Total Baseball abided by the Special Baseball Records Committee's decision on game-ending homers—not to preserve Ruth's total, but because there were many more such homers before 1920 than the thirty-seven the committee identified, and the disputes surrounding some of them are now beyond settling.

Like Turkin/Thompson and all previous record books, and in accordance with the view of most historians, we rejected the committee's position that the National Association was not a major league. We committed fully to the creation of a full statistical record of that trailblazing circuit, and hope one day soon to integrate the NA and NL records of such players as Al Spalding, Cap Anson, George Wright, and all the others who played in the professional league between 1871 and 1875. For now, we

provide NA stats within the Player and Pitcher Registers, but total them separately from those of the NL (or, in a rare case, the American Association, a major league from 1882 through 1891).

We also differed from the committee's ruling on awarding pitchers wins and losses in the years before 1920. Not finding any official scoring rule or practice for that time, its members chose to apply 1950 guidelines to decisions awarded in 1876-1920. This well-intentioned decision produced substantial alterations in the records of such hurlers as Cy Young, Christy Mathewson, Grover Alexander, and others. In the ensuing years, the notable research of Frank Williams (reported in "All the Record Books Are Wrong," *The National Pastime*, 1982) revealed that there was indeed a pattern and a rationale for the way decisions were awarded in those days; the data in *Total Baseball* conforms with his meticulously substantiated findings.

More involved, and perhaps of most direct interest to fans and media, are the subjects of (a) statistical discrepancies between the official record presented in *Total Baseball* and the figures published in other reference works, or memorialized on Hall of Fame plaques, and (b) the implications of corrected data for the awarding of batting championships. We will address those questions, as well as the larger ones of transcription accuracy and ledger balance, in the "Issues and Answers" section of this essay.

Let's resume our chronicle of how Major League Baseball and others have kept the record of the game. Besides the debut of *The Baseball Encyclopedia* (and the Miracle Mets and the centennial of professional baseball), there were two other interesting baseball developments in 1969. The first and less celebrated was a research project launched by Eldon and Harlan Mills that, like the ICI effort, could not have been contemplated without the computer. The Mills brothers tracked the entire major league seasons of 1969 and 1970 on a play-by-play basis. Then they applied to that record the probabilities of winning which derived from each possible outcome of a plate appearance, as determined by a computer simulation incorporating nearly eight thousand possibilities. What, for example, was the visiting team's chance of winning the game before the first pitch was thrown? Fifty percent, if we are pitting two theoretical teams of equal or unknown ability on a neutral site. If the first man fails to get on base, the chances of the visiting team winning are reduced to 49.8 percent; should he hit a double, the visiting team's chance of victory is raised to 55.9 percent, as determined by the simulation. Every possible situation—combining half-inning, score, men on base, and men out—was tested by the simulator to arrive at "Win Points."

The Millses' purpose was to determine the clutch value of, say, hitting a homer with two men on and one man out in the bottom of the ninth, with the team trailing by two runs, the situation Bobby Thomson faced in the climactic National League game of 1951—oddly, the rookie year of the first modern computer. (That home run gained for him 1,472 Win Points; had it come with no one on in the eighth inning of a game in which his team led 4-0, the homer would have been worth only 12 Win Points.) What the Mills brothers were attempting to do was to evaluate not only the *what* of a performance, which traditional

statistics indicate, but the *when*, or clutch factor, which no measure to that time could provide.

This project, detailed in a small book issued in 1970 called *Player Win Averages*, proceeded from the same impulse that led to other measures of clutch performance: the game-winning RBI, introduced as an official Major League Baseball stat in 1980 and scrapped in 1989; the measures of batting performance in late-inning and men-on-base situations first published by Seymour Siwoff, Steve Hirdt, and Peter Hirdt of the Elias Sports Bureau in 1985; and the historically complete indexes of clutch hitting and clutch pitching developed for the first edition of this book.

The other noteworthy baseball event of 1969 was the official adoption by the major leagues of the save, the stat associated with relief pitching, the game's most significant strategic development since the advent of the gopher ball. Now shown in the papers on a daily basis, saves were not officially recorded at all until 1960. It was at the instigation of Jerome Holtzman of the *Chicago Sun-Times*, with the cooperation of *The Sporting News*, that this statistic was finally accepted. (Although Pat McDonough, a founding member of SABR, had developed a similar stat in 1924 which he called "games finished by relief hurlers"; its first appearance in print came in the *New York Telegram* three years later.) The need for the save arose because relievers operated at a disadvantage when it came to picking up wins. The bullpen specialists were a new breed, and as their role increased, the need emerged to identify excellence, as it had long ago for batters, starting pitchers, and fielders.

The save's prime statistical drawback is that there is no negative to counteract the positive, no stat for saves blown (except, all too often, a victory for the "fireman"); unofficial attempts to develop such a stat have accelerated in recent years, and now are part of the formula for the Fireman of the Year award.

August 10, 1971, marked another milestone, the founding in Cooperstown of SABR, the group in whose annual publications most of today's sabermetricians cut their analytical teeth. Its statistical analysis research committee, headed for more than a decade by Pete Palmer, has served as a sounding board for the inventive approaches of such men as Dallas Adams, Dick Cramer, Steve Mann, Craig Wright, Gary Gillette, and Bill James.

Developments of the ensuing decade include the previously mentioned adoption of the game-winning RBI (GWRBI) in 1980; it rewarded the batter who drove in a run to give his club a lead that it never relinquished. This stat was pilloried in the press from its introduction; Major League Baseball finally gave up on it before the 1989 season. In 1985 on base percentage was made official, thirty-one years after its introduction to the general baseball public by Rickey and Roth.

Situational stats, unofficial but widely reported and employed, have been the specialty of the Elias Sports Bureau, the Baseball Workshop, and Stats, Inc.—performance in day games vs. night, grass vs. artificial turf, lefty vs. righty, day game following night, bases-loaded situations, and so on. When the data is drawn from a large enough sample, these stats can be provocative and meaningful; they represent the wave of the future in baseball, and are fast becoming useful analytical tools for review of the past. Elias has recorded situational data systematically since 1975, Baseball Workshop since 1984.

Total Baseball

The next major event in the history of baseball record keeping was *Total Baseball*. Founded upon a unique historical database that Pete Palmer has cultivated for decades—in the tradition of baseball archivists like S.C. Thompson, Bradshaw Swales, Leonard Gettelson, and John Tattersall—*Total Baseball* is the third-generation encyclopedia of the game. Just as the advent of the Macmillan/ICI encyclopedia supplanted Turkin/ Thompson, the standard for two decades, *Total Baseball* has taken advantage of new technology and new research, notably by members of the Society for American Baseball Research, to present data more accurate than ever before, and more of it.

There are, of course, the traditional stats one would expect in a baseball reference work; there are many of the more revealing sabermetric stats (discussed in detail in the essay that follows this); there are stats never published before their appearance in this book. And as you have seen in Part One, there is a recognition that baseball history and knowledge resides not only in its numbers.

Issues and Answers: Sources of Baseball Statistics

There are six major sources for baseball statistical research, and thus for the official statistics that comprise *Total Baseball*. By far the most significant one is the official Major League Baseball records kept by the leagues, published in the baseball guides, and maintained on microfilm at the Baseball Hall of Fame in Cooperstown and in the league offices. These records cover the years since 1903 for the National League and 1905 for the American League. Any source data before these years were lost.

The second major source is the computer printouts prepared by ICI for *The Baseball Encyclopedia* in 1969. These cover the NL for 1891-1902, the AL for 1901-05, the Federal League for 1914-15, plus all the nineteenth-century leagues (1882-91 American Association, 1884 Union Association, and the 1890 Players League). These records, obtained from newspaper box scores, were turned over to the Baseball Hall of Fame and made public by agreement with its resident historian Lee Allen, who permitted ICI to use his voluminous player demographic files.

The third source is John Tattersall's newspaper box-score research for the NL of 1876-90. Since Tattersall had done such careful work, day-by-day computer printouts were never generated for this period. Any day-by-day records created by John have been lost, but what has survived is a batting and fielding summary and a pitching summary for each club each year listing many categories. This collection, now owned by SABR, also includes the home run log, which lists every home run ever hit from 1871 to date, the date, teams, game location, batter, pitcher, inning, men on base, and other notes. This has

been computerized by SABR and is maintained by David Vincent. John Tattersall, Bob McConnell, and Pete Palmer have discovered over a hundred errors in the homer data from the various accepted sources, either ICI research or guide data.

The fourth source for baseball statistics is a box score collection accumulated by Michael Stagno, covering the National Association of 1871-1875, which was also purchased by SABR. Preliminary basic data was calculated by Stagno. Bob Richardson of Boston and Bob Tiemann of St. Louis have accumulated complete totals in all categories from this data with the exception of caught stealing data.

The fifth source is additional work done by the ICI researchers for the 1969 edition, covering data that were not kept officially during the years since 1903 for the NL and 1905 for the AL. Examples of this data are runs batted in before 1920; extra base hits in the AL for 1905 and 1906, double plays by fielders before 1920 NL and 1923 AL; pitching data except wins and losses for the AL for 1905-07, earned runs for pitchers before 1912 NL and 1913 AL; complete games before 1913 NL and 1926 AL; games started before 1926 AL and 1938 NL; and saves before 1969. Any day-by-day records from this source have been lost, but the season totals have survived.

The sixth source is newspaper box score research to pick up additional categories not covered by the first five sources. Examples of this are hit by pitch for batters before 1917 NL and 1920 AL (by Alex Haas, Tattersall, Palmer, and many others), triple plays by fielders before 1928 AL and 1930 NL (mainly by Jim Smith), home runs allowed by pitchers before 1950 AL and 1952 NL (again by Tattersall). Frank Williams carefully researched AL pitching records for 1901-1919, when the league records were particularly sloppy. *Total Baseball* has day-by-day sheets for most of this data, with the rest residing in the Tattersall collection.

Issues and Answers: Discrepancies

The original data for record books and Hall of Fame plaques, before the 1969 ICI research, were mostly obtained from two sources, the Spalding and Reach annual guides and two *Sporting News* publications: the *Baseball Register* (published yearly 1940-date), which often contained records of oldtimers, and *Daguerreotypes* (published every so often from 1951 to date), which had records of all Hall of Famers and many other notable players. This research was done from guides and newspapers by Paul Rickart, Leonard Gettelson, and Paul MacFarlane.

When the 1969 encyclopedia came out, there were many small differences in player stats when compared to the traditional data. However, since any records used to generate guide data in the early years were lost, the new data appeared to be more reliable. In addition, many more categories were given, like extra base hits, runs batted in, pitcher innings, hits and earned runs allowed, and fielder double plays. Also included in the new data were club splits for traded players and information on those who played in fewer than fifteen games.

In addition to the previously mentioned retroactive

scoring decisions of the Special Baseball Records Committee, it ruled to include in the averages many games that were thrown out before, particularly in 1877, 1879, and 1899. Also included were the NL's tie games of five or more innings in 1878 through 1884 (thirty-eight of them) previously uncounted. Before 1912 in the NL pinch hitters and defensive replacements were included in the official game sheets, but the players were not credited with a game played. The committee decided to add these in, too.

Our research has uncovered a great many small errors and a few major ones in the official statistics. This was done by comparing individual totals to team totals, and by rechecking the addition on the player sheets. Most of these errors were in the American League, particularly before 1920, for which the record keeping was very sloppy. The NL has been much better over the years. For example, from 1910 to date, they took the sum of all the batter and fielder stats for each team, compared them to the sum of the team stats, and resolved almost all the differences. The AL did not start doing this until 1973 when the record keeping was first computerized. The NL went to computers in 1981.

For example, up through 1935, most AL clubs are not in agreement in player sums and team figures for at bats and hits. The differences are usually small, less than 10. (We have corrected the larger discrepancies of those years, but the smaller ones are yet to be resolved.) For 1905 to 1920, the team totals are further removed from the sum of the players, so that *The Baseball Encyclopedia* and *Total Baseball* have replaced the team totals with the sum of the players. We corrected all the post-1935 cases of team at-bat and hit totals not agreeing, but have not yet begun work on the previous years.

An interesting quirk in the way records are kept—and another reminder, as if one needed it, that baseball record keeping remains subject to error and controversy—occurred as recently as the strike-shortened season of 1981. The American League rule was to round off the innings pitched at the end of the season, although the weekly reports showed thirds of innings. Baltimore's Sammy Stewart had 29 earned runs in 112⅓ innings, while Oakland's Steve McCatty had 48 in 185⅔ innings. This gave Stewart the ERA title, 2.323 to 2.327. But when the innings were rounded off, McCatty won, 2.32 to 2.33. McCatty got the title, but the next year both leagues decided to count thirds of innings.

Issues and Answers: Hall of Famers

The data reported by the ICI group in the first edition of *The Baseball Encyclopedia* upset many people in baseball, for their numbers were different from those traditionally accepted; in subsequent editions, many of the prominent players' statistics were fudged back to their traditional values. Yet 1969 had hardly been the first time corrections had been made to official data. In 1929 Grover Cleveland Alexander won his 373rd game, breaking Christy Mathewson's National League record, then thought to be 372. He never won another game. A number of years later, Joseph Reichler found a game in which, by the rules of that time, Matty should have gotten the win,

this game taking place on May 21, 1902. The official record was changed and Matty pulled into a tie with Alex. The problem was that no one checked all of Mathewson's other games to see how many times he received a win under the old rules that wouldn't have been credited that way today. When ICI did its original research in 1968, it found Matty had only 367 wins total by today's rules, while Alexander had 374. (Further research, notably by Frank Williams, has restored Alexander and Mathewson to a tie at 373 wins.)

In another celebrated example of record-book flip-flops, when the American League was formed in 1901, Nap Lajoie was credited with a .422 average, with 220 hits in 543 at bats. After a number of years, someone noticed that if you take these at bats and hits, the average comes out only to .405, so his average was changed. (Turkin/Thompson gave Nap a mark of .409 in its first edition.) Later in the 1950s, John Tattersall had his doubts and decided to go through his newspaper collection of box scores. He found 229 hits for Lajoie, not 220—the error had been in the figure for hits, not in the figure for batting average. Thus his average was restored to .422, which happened to be the highest in American League history. Then ICI research in this area came up with a .426 mark (232 for 544, based on newspaper accounts), which was published in the first edition, then trimmed back to .422 in subsequent editions. The .426 figure is the one this book uses, because the day-by-day source data for the American League of 1901 has been lost.

Lajoie seemed to be involved in a number of controversies. ICI research found four more hits for him in 1902, raising his average from .369 to .378. Later editions of *The Baseball Encyclopedia* have changed Lajoie's stats back to the old values; we have not.

In 1910 there was a very close batting race between Cobb and Lajoie. At the end of the season, most people thought Nap had won, based on his getting seven hits in a doubleheader on the final day of the season. There was talk that the opposing Browns had let him get a number of bunts by playing back, so that the hated Cobb would lose. However, the AL office went over their figures and gave Cobb the title, .385 to .384. Nearly eighty years later, Palmer discovered a critical error: a game in which Cobb had two hits in three at bats had been entered twice. This was found because Sam Crawford had 14 games on his official sheet for the homestand yet the Tigers had only played 13. It turned out that Detroit played a doubleheader on September 24, but the second game inadvertently was inserted in the official sheets as being played on September 25. Later, this second game of the 24th, which appeared to have been missing, was put in the scoresheets again. The League Office discovered this mistake soon after its official announcement that Cobb had won the batting title, because the double entry was corrected for all the other Detroit players. However, Ban Johnson had made a big deal out of how carefully his people had checked the figures in order to settle the controversy, so the AL kept quiet about the gaffe, leaving Cobb the winner.

Appeals to Commissioner Kuhn in 1981 to set the matter straight officially were to no avail, because that would not only have changed the outcome of the 1910 batting race, it would also have altered Cobb's lifetime hit total, then being pursued to massive media attention by Pete Rose. Kuhn's statement read, in part, "The passage of seventy years, in our judgment . . . constitutes a certain statute of limitation as to recognizing any changes in the records with confidence of the accuracy of such changes . . . . Since a variety of questions have been raised through the years about the accuracy of the statistics of that period, the only way to make changes with confidence would be for a complete and thorough review of all team and individual statistics. That is not practical." It may not have not been practical, but we have embarked upon such a course, and Major League Baseball has dedicated itself to that ongoing process.

Asked at the time how we would have resolved the dispute over the 1910 batting race, we responded in this way: remove Cobb's two redundant hits and alter his batting average accordingly, effectively dropping it beneath Lajoie's, and correct his lifetime hit total as well; however, retain Cobb's batting championship, for two reasons—one, because Lajoie's flurry of bunt hits were highly suspect, and two, because Cobb was awarded the title *in his day*, and awards should be permanent, not contingent. Furthermore, a reasonable case can be made that Ban Johnson, if he had believed that Lajoie's tainted hits would have been sufficient to produce a batting championship, would have nullified them; after all, he did banish from baseball the Browns' manager who had instructed his rookie third baseman to play exceptionally deep.

It is this singular event in baseball history that supplied a model for how *Total Baseball* and Major League Baseball developed a policy for incorporating new research finds into the historical record without revoking long-held personal championships. Player records may be changed upon the evidence of historical error, but league awards and titles are forever.

Here is what happened in the now celebrated Honus Wagner case in the 1990 edition of *The Baseball Encyclopedia*, over which Major League Baseball and the Macmillan publishing firm became estranged. The Macmillan editor noticed that previous edition figures for Wagner did not agree with the data presented in the first edition in 1969. He assumed that the data had been corrupted over the years, and thus returned the 1897-1900 data to the original figures, costing Wagner 12 hits. However, the editor did not restore the 1901-02 data, which would have resulted in Wagner losing three more hits. The outcome was that Wagner had a total of 3415 hits in the 1969 edition, 3430 in the 1988 edition (the traditional figure) and 3418 in the 1990 edition (also in 1993). One of the problems with the Macmillan newspaper research was that it did not count protested games in the player data. Although the games were thrown out of the standings, the player stats *did* count in the league compilations at the time, which should be the criterion for inclusion. (Protested games were included in the official records through 1909, then omitted 1910-1919, and were made once again part of the official records in 1920. When our review of these protested games prior to 1909 is completed, the individual stats will be added to our figures.)

Wagner was involved in three of these protested games. There were about twenty-five of them altogether in the nineteenth century. However, the newspaper research did

show up additional differences in player stats beyond those from the protested games.

When checking the plaques for the Hall of Fame players, we found about forty players with differences from the *Total Baseball* data. Most were nineteenth century players with small differences due to discrepancies between the old guide figures and the later newspaper research. Some had to do with rule changes from the 1969 Special Baseball Records Committee, such as not counting walks as hits in 1887. For the twentieth century, there were a number of differences due to official errors, mostly in the area of pitcher won-lost marks in the 1901-1919 American League period. There were only a few outright errors on the plaques (see below for Anson, Clarkson, Hamilton, McCarthy, McGinnity, and Nichols). Exact differences can be found by comparing *Daguerreotypes* (which often agrees with the plaques) with *Total Baseball*.

Below is a guide to variances between the plaques and the official record of Major League Baseball embodied in *Total Baseball* (TB).

19th-Century Hall of Famers

Cap Anson   *Plaque, four batting titles;* **TB**, *three*
In 1879, Anson appears to have been the beneficiary of 20 extra hits, either by error or, as is commonly believed, a civic-minded Chicago official scorer. This error was found by John Tattersall in his review of newspaper box scores. In addition he (and we) incorporated the player records of four Chicago tie games, of which Anson played in two. His traditional mark of .407 was really only .317, and is so recorded in this volume; however, although a modern accounting would result in an 1879 batting title for Paul Hines, with .357, we credit the *championship* that year to Anson, as an instance of the official Major League Baseball policy cited above.

The singular season of 1887 presents a different case. Following the long-standing directive of the Special Baseball Records Committee, we do not count walks as hits, the practice which had been the sole basis of Anson's fourth batting championship. The modern computation reveals Sam Thompson to have had the highest batting average, and in this instance we withdraw the fourth batting title from Anson. Note that only for this year, in which walks were aberrationally recorded as hits, and 1876, when they were aberrationally recorded as outs, will we overturn the scoring practice of the time in favor of a modern reinterpretation of who was the batting leader.

Jake Beckley   *Plaque, .309 lifetime, also for fielding at first base, 2368 games, 23696 putouts, 25000 chances;* **TB**, *.308, 2377, 23709, 25024*
These are about as close as you can get when comparing several sources prior to 1900.

Dan Brouthers   *Plaque, .419 average in 1887;* **TB**, *.338*
This average is inflated by the aforementioned scoring practice of 1887; even if we elected to keep that practice in effect, Brouthers' walks would have lifted him to .426.

John Clarkson   *Plaque, 175 losses, 2013 strikeouts, 4514 innings;* **TB**, *178, 1978, 4536*
The major difference in strikeouts occurred in 1886, where the guide had 340 and we counted only 313. We recorded two additional losses in 1894, in accordance with the scoring rules of the day. Reviewing our sources, we counted 27 more innings in 1887. His plaque bore a clear error concerning his wins in 1888. He had 33 and did not lead the league, although the plaque says 49. This was a confusion with the 49 Clarkson did win in 1889, which was also listed.

Roger Connor   *Plaque, hit .300 twelve times;* **TB**, *eleven*
If we counted walks as hits in 1887, we would also have twelve times.

Ed Delahanty   *Plaque, hit. 408 in 1899;* **TB**, *.410*
The correction is a product of newspaper research.

Hugh Duffy   *Plaque, hit .438 in 1894;* **TB**, *.440*
This was the highest average all-time. The 1895 guide has 236 hits while the newspaper count is 237; both had 539 at bats. Since no backup data has survived for the guide, there is no way to determine where the difference might be.

Jim Galvin   *Plaque, 365-311 won-lost;* **TB**, *360-308*
The plaque data includes a 4-2 mark in the 1875 NA, which has been denied major league status by the Special Baseball Records Committee. There are other smaller differences.

Billy Hamilton   *Plaque, 196 runs in 1894, 115 stolen bases and .338 batting average in 1891, 937 stolen bases total, 1893-1895 batting averages of .395,.399 .393, ten times scoring 100 runs;* **TB**, *192 runs in '94, 111 steals and .340 batting average in '91, 912 lifetime steals, 1893-1895 batting averages of .380, .404, .389, eleven times scoring 100 runs*
Whether Hamilton scored 196 runs or 192, he still holds the all-time record. There were small differences in stolen bases in several years. We speculate that when the folks at Cooperstown counted Hamilton's seasons of scoring 100 or more runs, they overlooked his 1889 A.A. accomplishment.

Hughie Jennings   *Plaque, once hit .397;* **TB**, *.401 in 1896*
The guide had 208 hits in 523 at bats, which actually computes to .398, although .397 was shown. The newspaper research showed 209 for 521.

Tim Keefe   *Plaque, 346 wins;* **TB**, *342*
Daguerreotypes currently also has 342.

Joe Kelley   *Plaque, .391 in 1894;* **TB**, *.393*
Newspaper box score research pointed up discrepancies in the figures recorded in the guides.

King Kelly   *Plaque, .394 average in 1887;* **TB**, *.322*
We do not count walks as hits; if we did, Kelly would have a mark of .393.

Tommy McCarthy **Plaque**, *1268 games, 109 stolen bases in 1888, 53 assists in 1893;* **TB**, *1275 games, 93 steals, 28 assists*
Newspaper research found the early stolen base figures to be inflated, especially for the American Association. His 53 assists in 1893 included many at second base and shortstop. However, he did have 44 in the outfield in 1888, fourth best all-time.

Kid Nichols **Plaque**, *360-202 won-lost, 30 wins in 1895;* **TB** *361-208, 26*
Daguerreotypes now has 361-208 as we do, including 26 wins in 1895. Nichols for years had been credited with winning 30 or more games from 1891 through 1897, but it has been conclusively shown that he had only 26 in 1895. The Spalding guide showed games pitched (which was usually interpreted to be decisions) and percentage. They had 44 and .681 which would give a mark of 30-14. The 1942 *Baseball Register* showed him 30-15. ICI's *The Baseball Encyclopedia* had him at 26-16 in 42 complete games and 0-0 in five relief appearances. Ironically, the corrected figures give him 30 wins in 1898, for seven seasons of 30 victories or more—total, but not consecutive.

Amos Rusie **Plaque**, *led in shutouts five times;* **TB**, *4*
Rusie pitched seven innings of a nine-inning shutout on July 5, 1897. Taking this shutout away, in accordance with current scoring rules (there were no official rules for crediting shutouts until 1951), gave him two shutouts instead of three that year.

Sam Thompson **Plaque**, *.336 lifetime, hit .400 twice;* **TB**, *.331, once*
If walks counted as hits, we would have him at .407 in 1887 and .334 lifetime.

John Ward **Plaque**, *158-102 won-lost, 2151 hits;* **TB**, *164-102, 2105*
Walks in 1887 accounted for 29 of the now "missing" hits. An additional 18 came from the 1890 Players League, for which newspaper research offered a lower total than the league figures. Other discrepancies were spread out over several years. We spotted three extra wins in 1879 and again in 1883.

20th-Century Hall of Famers

Luke Appling **Plaque**, *11,569 chances accepted at shortstop;* **TB**, *11,616*
There was an addition error for his putouts in 1940. He had 307, not 257. *Daguerreotypes* had 11,566, not 11,569.

Jack Chesbro **Plaque**, *192-128 won-lost;* **TB**, *198-132*
Daguerreotypes now has 198-128. The 1947 *Baseball Register*—only one year after Jack's election and the creation of his plaque—had 197-127. Still under review are two other games for which it has been argued that Chesbro should have received wins.

Ty Cobb **Plaque**, *4191 hits;* **TB**, *4189*
See above for discussion of the doubly entered 2-for-3 game. But that is not the whole story of how Cobb's lifetime hit total fell by two, nor of how he comes to retain his twelve batting titles. Modern research of the official day-by-day sheets revealed that Cobb had two games in 1906—on April 22 and 23—in which he went 1-for-8 that were not entered on his sheet. Additionally, there was a game on July 12, 1912 (the first game of a doubleheader) in which Cobb had a run which was entered in his hit column. (If this had indeed been a hit, he would have had a 34-game hitting streak. It was really only 23 games.) Finally, under today's rules, Cobb would not have won the batting title in 1914, because he didn't have enough plate appearances (or at bats). However, he did win it under the rules of the day, as he won the 1910 title, and that is what counts.

Eddie Collins **Plaque**, *3313 hits;* **TB**, *3315*
Collins picked up two hits in 1920 in a game for which his stats were switched with those of Buck Weaver.

Stan Coveleski **Plaque**, *214-141 won-lost, 2.88 ERA;* **TB**, *215-142, 2.89 Daguerreotypes* has 215-141. The 1942 *Baseball Register* has 216-142. Our ERA includes 1912, when Stan had a 3.43 era in 21 innings. The beginning of official status for ERA in the AL was 1913.

Sam Crawford **Plaque**, *2505 games, 2964 hits, 312 triples;* **TB**, *2517, 2961, 309*
Crawford's games played vary from the plaque largely because of the practice of not counting pinch-hit appearances as games played. His ICI sheets reveal five additional games in 1900 and seven in 1901. Also, he loses a triple in each of three seasons (1899, 1902, 1904) before the survival of official sheets; newspaper research does not support the Guide figures. And finally, Crawford lost three hits in 1900 through a recount of box score data, and five more in 1901. He gained back three in 1903 and two in 1904.

Red Faber **Plaque**, *253-211 won-lost, 3.13 era;* **TB**, *254-213, 3.*
15 Faber was credited with one win less than he actually recorded in 1916, one of the years in which the American League, at Ban Johnson's behest, posted no official data in this category. For 1915, we add a loss that clearly was overlooked on the official AL sheet, and for 1926 we add another loss that somehow was not posted when the Guide figures were released. The ERA variance is purely mathematical; it had been computed incorrectly.

Elmer Flick **Plaque**, *.378 in 1900;* **TB**, *.367*
The guide had 207 hits in 547 at bats, while the newspaper research showed 200 in 545.

Harry Heilmann **Plaque**, *2146 games;* **TB**, *2148*
Daguerreotypes has 2145 games. Heilmann appeared in 69 games in 1914, not 66. For 1912-14 the official AL averages did not count a game for any player who had all zeros in his entry. These would be pinch-runners or late-inning defensive replacements. There were a total of over 400 such uncounted appearances in this category altogether.

Walter Johnson   *Plaque, 414 wins;* **TB,** *417*
This research was done by Frank Williams and detailed minutely in his previously cited essay in *The National Pastime* of 1982. Walter had a 16-game winning streak in 1912, but one of the games (August 5) was not marked as a win on his sheet. In 1911, wins were incorrectly marked as losses on June 27 and July 9. For the AL before 1920, there were about twenty or thirty errors in awarding wins and losses in the official statistics each year.

Heinie Manush   *Plaque, 2009 games;* **TB,** *2008*
His games were added incorrectly on the 1927 American League official sheet.

Joe McGinnity   *Plaque, won 20 seven times;* **TB,** *eight*
This looks like an error made by the Hall of Fame. He won 20 in 1902 between two leagues, as shown in the 1941 *Baseball Register* (McGinnity was elected in 1946).

Herb Pennock   *Plaque, 161 losses;* **TB,** *162*
Daguerreotypes agrees with 162 losses. The 1941 *Baseball Register* had 161.

Eppa Rixey   *Plaque, 4494 innings;* **TB,** *4494 2/3*
Official stats rounded innings pitched until 1982. *Total Baseball* records thirds of innings pitched in all seasons.

Red Ruffing   *Plaque, led in shutouts 1938 and 1939;* **TB,** *1939 only*
Lefty Gomez had four shutouts in 1938, not three. This included a rain-shortened complete game on July 15. Ruffing had three. Also, the comment on the plaque about making the all-star team in 1937-38-39 applies to the *Sporting News* All-Star team, not the All-Star Game team.

Tris Speaker   *Plaque, .344 lifetime;* **TB,** *.345*
There was an addition error on his official sheet for 1911. He had 500 at bats, not 510.

Pie Traynor   *Plaque, one of few players with 200 hits in a season;* **TB,** *of course, many players have had 200 or more hits in a season*

Zack Wheat   *Plaque, 2318 games for Brooklyn, 2406 total;* **TB,** *2322 for Brooklyn, 2410 total*
There were four unrecorded games in 1911 in which Wheat appeared only as a pinch hitter.

Issues and Answers: League Batting Leaders

Until the fourth edition of *Total Baseball*, Major League Baseball had established no official historical record, despite its product endorsement of several statistical compendiums over the years. As a result, writers, historians, statisticians, and fans were offered a choice amongst differing annual league batting leaders, depending on the major record book favored. Those most favored by recent chroniclers have been *Total Baseball* and *The Baseball Encyclopedia* because they had all player and club records.

There are two recognized record summary tomes which feature leaders in various statistical categories, lifetime or single-season: *The Book of Baseball Records* (Elias Sports Bureau Inc.) and *The Complete Baseball Record Book* (*The Sporting News*). Though both are respected works, and both organizations have had long, and often official, relationships with Organized Baseball, neither record book enjoys official status, and discrepancies exist between the two.

There was *no* official batting championship rule until 1950. *Total Baseball* and *The Baseball Encyclopedia* remedied this oversight by formulating—independently—their own guidelines for the many years of omission, each based on their own concepts of fairness and equality.

In previous editions, *Total Baseball* established the following criteria for batting championships: 1876-1956, qualification by having plate appearances equal to 3.1 per game times the number of scheduled games, thus conforming to the Major League Baseball practice since 1957. The batting championship criteria for *The Baseball Encyclopedia* over the years have been: 1876-1919, games played equal to at least 60 percent of games the team scheduled; 1920-1949, at least 100 games played, based on acceptance of the unofficial but universally assumed rule requiring appearance in at least 100 games; and 1950-present, the various changing official rule definitions.

In a policy shift endorsed by Major League Baseball, *Total Baseball* identifies league batting champions according to the practice of the time, in each league, and each champion will have his seasonal batting average recorded in boldface in his entry in the Player Register. However, as noted above in the discussion of the 1910 AL batting race, in the Annual Record section of this volume, we record the highest batting averages in each league season as correctly calculated, although not necessarily in descending order.

The history of the official batting championship rule is as follows: (1) 1950-1951, 400 official times at bat; (2) 1952-1954, 400 official times at bat or, if less than 400 times at bat and by adding enough imaginary hitless at bats so as to total 400, "he still would have the highest batting average in his league, he shall be the champion batter"; (3) 1955-1956, 400 official times at bat; (4) 1957-1966, 3.1 plate appearances per game times number of scheduled games, equaling 477 in a 154-game schedule and 502 in a 162-game schedule; and it's 502 plate appearances; and (5) 1967-present, 3.1 plate appearances per scheduled game, except that "if there is any player whose average would be the highest if he were charged with the required number of plate appearances or official at bats, then that player shall be awarded the batting championship."

In the strike-shortened season of 1972, a 156-game standard prevailed instead of the 162 scheduled games. In the strike seasons of 1981 and 1994, the rule of 3.1 plate appearances per game was applied to the number of games played by each team, rather than to those scheduled.

The early record tomes, the *Spalding Record Book* and *The Sporting News Record Book*, placed Jake Stenzel (NL) in the lead for 1893 and Nap Lajoie (AL) on top in 1905. Both Stenzel and Lajoie were the leaders during the

life of the Spalding volumes, 1908-1924, and in the *Sporting News* volume from its debut in 1921 until 1929, when Hugh Duffy replaced Stenzel and 1930, when Elmer Flick supplanted Lajoie. The reasoning behind the *Sporting News* switches was that both Stenzel and Lajoie failed to meet the unwritten criterion of a representative number of games—Stenzel had played in only 60 games and Lajoie in 65, not even half of their club's scheduled games. Otherwise the early record books' leaders were those endorsed by the leagues.

The Spalding Record Book in its 1917 edition made two important batting championship changes, both on the basis of mathematical errors which their editors had noted. To that time, Dan Brouthers had been tied with Cupid Childs for the highest batting average in 1892, but had been awarded the title based on his having played in more games, which was the tie-breaking guideline of the day. In 1917, however, Childs went to the front on the basis of extended batting average (calculating to extra decimal places beyond the thousandths that comprise conventional reporting of batting averages).

Next, Lajoie's average of .422 in 1901 was reduced in 1917 because of a *Reach Guide* typo in the hit column to a .405 figure. The Spalding management (the once independent Reach company had long since been acquired by Spalding) should have known that in 1892, the criterion for awarding a batting championship was indeed games played, not extended batting average, and that in 1901 they would have found Lajoie's correct (as then calculated) average in any number of newspapers. Lajoie's .422 average was restored in 1954 in response to John Tattersall's research, but Childs remained, until this writing, ahead of Brouthers in the NL's *Green Book*. (In this fifth edition of *Total Baseball*, Brouthers is credited as the champion because he played in more games, which was the criterion of the time—not because modern research has lowered Childs' batting average from .335 to .317.)

During its formative years, 1876-1919, the National League omitted any mention of batting championship criteria in its published rules. Certainly, this should have been addressed before 1920. Still, batting championships were tacitly acknowledged by the league, with guidelines drawn primarily from the comments of Henry Chadwick.

From 1876 to ca. 1888, the criterion was understood to be the best seasonal performance; as expressed by Chadwick in the *Spalding Guide* of 1887, "an average rating of a player should be on a season's work." Seasonal leadership may be deduced when the league's recognized champion was not listed first in the official averages. His preeminence was based on a representative number of games played over the season in which he excelled, as opposed to the nominal leader's handful of games.

The yardstick between 1889 and 1919 was playing in at least 100 games. In the 1890 *Spalding Guide* Chadwick wrote: "With the object in view of equalizing the averages and placing the names of the batsmen who have played in 100 games or over, are given the front rank, while those who have played in 50 games and over occupy second place, and those in 25 games and over third place, and so on."

The American League rules in its early years, 1901-1919, omitted any batting championship language. In honoring Cobb as its 1914 bat champ, the AL was un-doubtedly proceeding from the guideline of best seasonal performance.

As discussed in the "Sources of Baseball Statistics" section of this essay, *Total Baseball* relies upon newspaper research and other data for the years before 1903 in the NL and 1905 in the AL. For subsequent seasons, the official league day-by-day sheets are available for study. The record summary books issued by Elias and *Sporting News* accept all the batting leaders recognized in the yearly Guides (Spalding, Reach, etc.). These champions are also accepted in today's league publications (AL *Red Book* and NL *Green Book*). Henceforward, *Total Baseball* recognizes the same champions, with the exception of 1892, discussed above, and 1887, when walks were counted as hits.

For students of the game, Joe Wayman documented the variances among the record books and encyclopedias and highlighted particularly those traditional batting champions whom previous editions of *Total Baseball* had toppled from the pinnacle. Even though most of these champions have been rethroned, the following thumbnail account of the debatable batting leaders will serve to explain the seeming anomaly of a batting champion whose average is lower than that of a rival.

OFFICIAL   TB (eds. 1-5)

		G	AB	H	BA		G	AB	H	BA
1878 NL	Dalrymple	60	267	95	.356	Hines	62	257	92	.358
1879 NL	Anson	49	221	90	.407	Hines	85	409	146	.357
1884 NL	O'Rourke	104	448	197	.350	Kelly	108	452	160	.354
1887 NL	Anson	122	532	224	.421	Thompson*	127	545	203	.372
1892 NL	Brouthers	152	588	197	.335	Brouthers	152	588	197	.335
1892 NL	Childs	144	552	185	.335					
1893 NL	Duffy	131	537	203	.378	Hamilton	82	355	135	.380
1902 AL	Delahanty	123	473	178	.376	Lajoie	87	352	133	.378
1910 AL	Cobb	140	509	196	.385	Lajoie	159	591	227	.384
1914 AL	Cobb	97	345	127	.368	Collins	152	526	181	.344
1926 NL	Hargrave	105	326	115	.353	Waner, P.	144	536	180	.336
1932 AL	Alexander	124	392	144	.367	Foxx	154	585	213	.364
1938 AL	Foxx	149	565	197	.349	Foxx	149	565	197	.349
1940 NL	Garms	103	358	127	.355	Hack	149	603	191	.317
1942 NL	Lombardi	105	309	102	.330	Slaughter	152	591	188	.318
1954 AL	Avila	143	555	189	.341	Williams	117	386	133	.345
1981 NL	Madlock	83	279	95	.341	Rose	107	431	140	.325

*Thompson becomes the official batting champion with a .372 average in accordance with the decision of the Special Baseball Records Committee not to count walks as hits. Anson would be a .347 hitter without the benefit of his walks.

1878: Abner Dalrymple captured the NL's batting title. Modern record tomes (*The Baseball Encyclopedia* and *Total Baseball*) list Paul Hines in the top spot. The NL in 1878 did not include tie games in its official averages, while today's record tomes count them. Thus, by counting tie games, Hines emerges with the higher average, but does not take away Dalrymple's championship.

1879: Cap Anson, the day's recognized batting champion, has been challenged by the moderns (*The Baseball Encyclopedia*, *Total Baseball*, *The Sports Encyclopedia: Baseball*, and *The National League Story*, Lee Allen) as to whether his .407 average is legitimate. In fact, the average was disputed as early as the 1880 DeWitt Guide, the averages for which were compiled by William Stevens of the *Boston Herald*, and *Balldom* (1914), compiled by George Moreland. *Total Baseball* keeps the title with Anson in recognition of the league action at the time, but

reports his batting average correctly in the Player Register and in the Annual Record's listing of top batting averages in the 1879 NL.

1884: The official batting champion remains Orator Jim O'Rourke. Newspaper box scores, game accounts, and the results of tie games elevate King Kelly to a higher average. Tie games were not included in the official averages at the time, and how to handle them today remains a matter of controversy. No matter how we treat Kelly's 2-for-4 in his only tie-game appearance (August 11), his average is higher than O'Rourke's.

1887: In only this season, bases on balls counted as hits. One month into the season, the American Association wanted to scrap the absurd rule, but the NL would not consent. *Total Baseball* gives the championship to Sam Thompson. Without his 60 walks registering as hits, Anson batted .347.

1892: Brouthers and Childs were honored as co-champions at .335, as discussed above. Childs had the higher extended average, .3351, against Brouthers' .3350 mark. By the day's reasoning, however, Brouthers is the leader. As Chadwick noted in the *Spalding Guide*, "the lead in all cases of tie scores in base hits belongs by right to the batsman who has played in the greatest number of games, and in this case Brouthers batted in 152 games to Child's 144." Childs's statistics, as compiled by ICI from newspapers, yield a batting average of .317, placing him third.

1893: Billy Hamilton's average was higher than Duffy's, and he would have met modern criteria for plate appearances. The NL, however, honored Duffy because he appeared in at least 100 games, which was expected of the leading players of that day. The title is thus accorded to him.

1902: The ICI sheets gave Lajoie four more hits than the guides had credited him with originally.

1910: Cobb is the champion, for reasons discussed amply above.

1914: Cobb, due to his proven hitting excellence, was awarded the championship because, in all reasoned probability, he would have been the leader over the full season. Consider, also, that the batting championship for the Chalmers car in 1910 for position players was based on 350 at bats. Cobb would have easily captured the hit crown on a mythical 100 game requirement, even though he was three games shy.

1926: Bubbles Hargrave topped three other questionable contenders—those not credited with at least 400 at bats. All qualified for the title, though, based on the period's acceptance of appearance in at least 100 games. In Hargrave's favor was his position—catcher. Over the years, catchers were considered somewhat differently when it came to handing out awards, because of the demands of their position. In fact, in order for a catcher to qualify for the fielding championship at his position, he need only have appeared in at least 77 games. Hargrave caught in 93 games.

1932: Dale Alexander had the games and at bats to satisfy the AL as to his claim. If the 400 at bat rule had been on the books, Alexander no doubt would have been inserted into the lineup until he secured eight additional at bats. If Jimmie Foxx were recognized as champion today, he would have the first of two consecutive Triple Crowns.

1938: Foxx was the AL leader—no ifs, ands, or buts about it. The AL had a rule in 1938 requiring the batting " . . . winner to be at least 400 times at bat." (*Reach Guide*, 1939) Taffy Wright is the trivia-question champion, batting .350 in 100 games.

1940: Debs Garms raised a few eyebrows as a come-from-nowhere champion. If enough imaginary at bats to reach 400 were to be added to Garms' total, his adjusted average would still be one point higher than that of Stan Hack, the runnerup.

1942: Ernie Lombardi was the recognized NL batting king. As a *Sporting News* headline advised, "Ernie's 105 contests suffice to qualify him for a second title." The announcement called attention to the "inquiries" which had been made regarding a Lombardi award since the AL had put in place a 400 at bat requirement. Bill James noted that the NL announced a "meritorious 400 at bat" requirement after the problematic Garms award two years earlier. NL President Frick, however, contended there was no specific bat rule and catchers, because of their demanding position, deserved special consideration. The catcher's fielding championship by this time was based on 100 games, lessening the Frick contention. Frick may have had in mind the prior, 77-game catching requirement for fielding leadership. Thus, Frick's reasoning could have been to create a proportion: 77 games for catchers is to 100 games for position players what 77 percent of 400 at bats (308) for catchers is to 400 at bats for position players.

1954: Ted Williams, the batter with the highest average in the AL, did not meet the official qualifications to claim the title. The 1954 official Rule 10.17 spelled out the champion as one who, with at least 400 at bats, or with fewer than 400 at bats plus enough imaginary ones to equal 400, has the higher average. Under the official rules definition, Bobby Avila is the batting leader. During the closing weeks of the campaign, Williams was aware of the rule but continued to be selective of pitches, rather than swing at those outside the strike zone simply in order to reach the required 400 at bats. Williams' extended average based on adding imaginary at bats to his 386 is a .331 figure.

1981: Bill Madlock is the official batting champion by the rules of the day. Due to the strike-shortened season, the games a team played, rather than the scheduled games, were the basis for individual championships. Pittsburgh, Madlock's club, played 103 games. Thus, 103 × 3.1 = 319 plate appearances to qualify for the batting championship. Madlock topped the required 319 PA's by one, with 279 at bats, 4 sacrifice flies, 34 bases on balls, 3 hit by pitch, and no sacrifice hits or interference calls. *Total Baseball* awarded the title to Pete Rose in editions 1 and 2, based on average games played per team, then corrected the procedure in its third edition.

The records of the four defunct major leagues show only the American Association had batting champions not agreeing with *Total Baseball* champions. This happened twice: in the 1884 AA, the official winner was Dude Esterbrook though his teammate Dave Orr actually batted 50 points higher; and in 1886 AA, the champ was officially Orr though Guy Hecker's recomputed average nips him by a point. (Pete Browning also surpassed Orr and was listed as champion in earlier editions of *Total Base-*

ball, for which a guideline of 3.1 plate appearances per game was employed throughout.)

A Little Help from Our Friends

The computer has made possible the rapid analysis of mountains of raw baseball data. But as invaluable as the computer has been in producing and cross-checking the statistical data for *Total Baseball*, the editors owe more to the people who have contributed their time, their expertise, their love of the game, and their passion for getting things right. These individuals are listed below, or in the Acknowledgements, or in the table at the end of the book that enumerates those readers of the first three editions who helped us improve the accuracy of *Total Baseball* this time around. A collective debt is owed to the Society for American Baseball Research and the National Baseball Library.

The six principal sources of the statistics herein were discussed earlier. Supplemental sources were:

- For work on the Stagno Collection of NA data, 1871-75, SABR's nineteenth-century research committee, headed successively by John Thorn and Mark Rucker, Bob Tiemann, Bob Richardson, and Fred Ivor-Campbell. New for the fifth edition are strikeouts for 1874-75 and incomplete stolen bases and caught stealing for all years, as well as fielding for all years.
- For batters hit by pitch, 1884-1896 AA/NL/PL, 1909-1916 NL, 1909-1919 AL, research from newspapers by Alex Haas, Pete Palmer, John Schwartz, Bob Davids, John Tattersall, Lyle Spatz, Herb Goldman, Keith Carlson, Tom Chase, Ed Luteran, Frank Phelps, and others. (Note: research continues for the 1897-1908 period, but the data is, at this writing, about 95 percent complete.)
- For home runs allowed by pitchers, 1876-1950 AL/NL, the Tattersall Collection, aided by Bob McConnell.
- For runs batted in, 1903-1919 NL, 1905-1919 AL, ICI research.
- For runs batted in, 1880-1885 NL and 1882-87, 1890 AA, David Neft.
- For pitcher saves (except 1901-1919 AL) 1876-1968 NL/AA/UA/PL/AL, ICI research.
- For stolen bases, 1886 NL, Spalding *Baseball Guide*.

- For wins and losses for pitchers, 1876-1900 NL/AA/PL, and for wins, losses, games started, complete games, shutouts, saves, 1901-1919 AL, and complete pitching data, 1892, research from newspapers and official sheets by Frank Williams.
- For shutouts, 1876-1939, Joe Wayman.
- For biographical data, the biographical research committee of SABR, notably Richard Topp, Bill Carle.
- For caught-stealing data, 1914-1916 AL, 1915-1916 NL, Ernie Lanigan, courtesy of Bob Davids.
- For home/away data, 1876-1891 NL/AA/UA/PL, Bob McConnell.
- For game scores, 1876-1884 NL/AA/UA, Bob Tiemann.
- For game scores, 1885-1891 NL/AA/PL, Richard Topp.
- For runs and homers home/away, 1980s NL/AL, Bill Carr.

Missing data includes:

- Hit batters: 1897-1908, scattered data, especially for New York and Cincinnati.
- Caught stealing: 1886-1914, 1916 (players with fewer than 20 steals), 1917-1919, 1926-1950 NL; 1886-1891 AA; 1890 PL; 1901-1913, 1916 (players with fewer than 20 steals), 1917-1919, 1914-15 FL.
- Sacrifice hits: 1927-1930 (fly balls advancing runners to any base counted as sacrifice hits).
- Sacrifice flies: 1908-1930, 1939.
- Runs batted in, 1882-1884 AA; 1884 UA. Partial data is shown for 1884-84. For 1885-87 and 1890, about 10% of the data is estimated.
- Strikeouts for batters: 1882-1888, 1890 AA; 1884 UA; 1897-1909 NL; 1901-1912 AL. (Team batting strikeouts are presented for 1897-1902 NL and 1901-1904 AL.)

Incomplete data for those years up to 1903 NL and 1905 AL are available from the ICI computer printouts at the National Baseball Library. Additional research could turn up more data. If your research or sharp eye should detect errors or gaps in *Total Baseball*, please write us in care of the publisher (or alternatively, simply e-mail us at jthorn@totalsports.net) and we'll be delighted to improve our data and credit your catch in the next edition.

Sabermetrics
Pete Palmer and John Thorn

Sabermetrics may be a new coinage for the statistical analysis of baseball but it is not a new phenomenon. Henry Chadwick, in the antebellum period, was as much a sabermetrician as Allan Roth or Bill James: he saw as clearly as they did that, because the object of the game is to win, runs are the best measure of player performance, just as they are of team performance at the end of a game.

After many decades in which this fundamental truth was lost (amid the general worship of false idols like batting average and pitcher won-lost percentage), today's sabermetricians have come around full circle to the game as it was originally understood. And what's remarkable about this is that in order to return to the primordial simplicity of the 1840s, '50s, and '60s, when runs and outs were all that went into the box score, they have relied upon computer simulations and higher mathematics. In other words, with the new statistics, simplicity emerges from complexity; what baseball statistics have offered for the last hundred years or so has been, despite the appearance of simplicity, in fact extremely complex.

For the veteran fan as well as for Major League Baseball, new ideas, new statistics, and new discoveries that dispute long-held verities (Ty Cobb's hit total, Hoss Radbourn's number of victories in 1884, etc.) may represent a challenge to tradition and thus a threat to the very soul of baseball, its pride in anachronism. Bernard Malamud wrote, "The whole history of baseball has the quality of mythology." The editors of *Total Baseball* relish the game's myths, from Abner Doubleday to the sacrifice bunt, and believe that in setting the record straight or turning conventional wisdom on its head, they are adding to the fan's enjoyment of the rich texture of the game. If you are one of the skeptics—like Earl Weaver, who once said, "There's no such thing as a new statistic"—please permit us to make the case for sabermetrics. (Much of the material in this section is adapted from our 1984 study, *The Hidden Game of Baseball*.)

What's in a Number?

On April 27, 1983, the Montreal Expos came to bat in the bottom of the eighth inning trailing the Houston Astros, 4-2. First up to face pitcher Nolan Ryan was Tim Blackwell, a lifetime .228 hitter who had struck out in his first time at bat. At this routine juncture of this commonplace game, Ryan stared down at Blackwell, but his invisible—yet, for all that, more substantial—opponent was a man who had died the month before Ryan was born, a man about whom Ryan knew nothing, he confessed, except his statistical line. For at this moment of his glorious big-league career, Ryan had accumulated a total of 3,507 strikeouts, only one short of the mark Walter Johnson had set over 21 seasons, from 1907 to 1927. Long thought invulnerable, Johnson's record was in imminent danger of falling, in 1983, not only to Ryan but also to Steve Carlton and Gaylord Perry.

Ryan fanned Blackwell and then froze the next batter, pinch hitter Brad Mills, with a 1-and-2 curveball. The pinnacle was his. Johnson had been baseball's all-time strikeout leader since 1921, when he surpassed Cy Young. Ryan would hold that title for just a few weeks, then would be overtaken by Carlton, only to display an incredible finishing kick and finish at 5,714 in 1994. But at the time that Ryan topped Johnson, baseball savants scurried to assess the meaning of 3,509 for both the deposed King of K and the new.

In the aftermath of Ryan's feat, some writers pointed out that he only needed 16 full seasons, plus fractions of two others, in which to record 3,509 strikeouts while Johnson needed 21, or that Johnson pitched over 2,500 more innings than Ryan. Coming into the 1983 season, Ryan had fanned 9.44 men per nine innings, while Johnson was way down the list at 5.33. And Ryan had allowed fewer hits per nine innings than Johnson, or, for that matter, anyone in the history of the game. So, it would seem 3,509 was not just one batter better than Johnson, but rather was mere confirmation for the masses of a superiority that was clear to the cognoscenti years before.

However, other writers introduced mitigating factors on Johnson's behalf, much as Ruth found supporters as the home run king even after Aaron hit number 715. These champions of the old order cited Johnson's won-lost record of 417-279 and earned run average of 2.17 while scoffing at Ryan's mark, entering 1983, of 205-186 with an ERA of 3.11. This tack led to further argument in print, bringing in the quality of the teams each man pitched for and against, the resiliency of the ball, the attitudes of the batters in each era toward the strikeout, the advent of night ball, integration, expansion, the designated hitter, the overall talent pool, competition from other professional sports . . . and on down into the black hole of subjectivism.

Why were so many things dragged into that discussion? Because the underlying question about 3,509 was: does this total make Ryan better than Johnson, or even a better strikeout pitcher than Johnson? At the least, does it make him a great pitcher? In our drive to identify excellence on the baseball field (or off it), we inevitably look to the

numbers as a means of encapsulating and comprehending experience. This quantifying habit is at the heart of baseball's hidden game, the one played by Ryan and Johnson and Ruth and Aaron—and, thanks to baseball's voluminous records, more than 15,000 other players—in a stadium bounded only by the imagination.

What's in a number? It's the answer to "How Many?" and sometimes a great deal more. In this case, 3,509 men had come to the plate against Ryan and failed to put the ball in play, one more man than Johnson had returned to the dugout, cursing. So what's the big deal? That Ryan was .0002849 faster, scarier, tougher—better—than Johnson? An absolute number like 3,509, or 714 (the home-run record once thought invulnerable, too), or 4,191 (the erroneous hit total of Ty Cobb that Pete Rose finally surpassed) does not resound with meaning unless it is placed into some context that will give it life.

Baseball statistics are not the instruments of vivisection, taking the life out of the game in order to examine it; rather, statistics are themselves the vital part of baseball, the only tangible and imperishable remains of contests played yesterday or a hundred years ago. Baseball may be loved without statistics, but it cannot be understood without them. As the statistics reflect more accurately the reality of what happened on the field, greater understanding leads to a deeper love and appreciation of this great game—which is, essentially, the case for sabermetrics and the reason for *Total Baseball.*

The Linear Weights System

In 1982 Milwaukee's Robin Yount had the year of his life, batting .331 with 29 homers, 114 RBIs and 129 runs scored; he led the American League in hits, doubles, total bases, and slugging percentage, while finishing just one point behind the league leader in batting average. First of the two times in his career, he was voted the Most Valuable Player in the American League, being named first on all but one of the 28 ballots cast by the baseball writers.

Over in the other league, Mike Schmidt of the Phillies was having an off year, batting only .280 with 35 homers and 87 RBIs; the previous year, when he was awarded the MVP, in only 102 games played he had totaled 31 homers and 91 RBIs. He did lead the league once again in 1982 in slugging percentage, and he did win the Gold Glove at third base for the seventh straight year, yet in the MVP balloting none of the ballots listed him higher than fourth; 10 ballots were cast without listing him at all.

For Yount, 1982 was a crowning achievement; for Schmidt, a disappointment: that was the verdict reached by the baseball writers and conventional baseball statistics. Yet in terms of actual performance, as determined by the number of runs contributed, Schmidt's "off year" was scarcely different from Yount's. With the bat, Yount accounted for 59 park-adjusted runs beyond what an average batter might have contributed; Schmidt, 45. Through base stealing, Yount added 2; Schmidt none. With the glove, Yount was four runs below league average at his position, shortstop; Schmidt was 19 above average at third base. Total runs contributed: Yount 57, Schmidt 64. (Because Yount's batting so far exceeded that of other shortstops, while third base provided several heavy hit-

ters, Yount contributed 7.0 extra wins to his Brewers; Schmidt contributed 6.1 to the Phillies.) Both men had outstanding seasons, the best in their respective leagues, and both outstripped the second-best player by about the same margin.

Viewing player (and team) performance through this sort of prism frequently produces such illuminating results. Cecil Fielder had a wonderful year in 1990, with his 51 homers, 132 RBIs, and league-leading figures in slugging average and extra-base hits. But how did he convince any writer voting for MVP that he had a better year than Rickey Henderson? In *Total Baseball,* you could look it up: Fielder contributed 4.2 extra wins to his team (wins that an average player would not), which was the fourth-best figure in the American League that year; Henderson was responsible for a whopping 8.2, not only the top mark in 1990 but also, at the time, the second-best mark in the AL since Mickey Mantle's epic seasons of 1956-1957!

This is the kind of analysis of player performance possible with a variety of sabermetric measures, not just the Linear Weights System. The common ingredient of most of the new, as yet unofficial, statistics is their creators' recognition of the relationship between runs and wins. These newly calculated measures are not official statistics of Major League Baseball, but they are constructed from the raw data of the official record. Some of the new measures may one day be officially embraced, as the on-base percentage became an official stat three decades after its introduction. Because of fan interest, we include them in the Player and Pitcher Registers that follow, alongside the officially tabulated numbers.

Runs and Wins

George Lindsey, in an article in *Operations Research* in 1963, was the first to assign run values to the various offensive events which lead to runs: Runs = (.41)1B + (.82)2B + (1.06)3B + (1.42)HR. He based these values on recorded play-by-play data and basic probability theory. Unlike Earnshaw Cook, who in the following year assigned run values on the basis of the sum of the individual scoring probabilities—that is, the *direct* run potential of the hit or walk plus those of the baserunners set in motion—Lindsey recognized that a substantial part of the run value of any non-out is that it *brings another man to the plate.* This additional batter has a one-in-three chance of reaching base and thus bringing another man to the plate with the same chance, as do the batters to follow. The *indirect* run potential of these batters cannot be ignored.

Steve Mann's Run Productivity Average (RPA) assigned these values based on observation of some 12,000 plate appearances: RPA = (.51)1B + (.82)2B + (1.38)3B + (2.63)HR + (.25)BB + (.15)SB − (.25)CS, all divided by plate appearances, then plus .016. His values were denominated in terms of the number of runs and RBIs each event produced. Bill James, at about the same time, came up with a similar formula, since shunned, with values based on runs plus RBIs *minus home runs.* The drawbacks to the approaches of Mann and James were the drawbacks of the RBI, which gives the entire credit for producing a run to the man who plates it, and of the run

scored, which gives credit only to the man who touches home, no matter how he came to do so. For example, with no outs, a man reaches first on an error; the next batter hits a double, placing runners on second and third; the following batter taps a roller to short and is thrown out at first, with the run scoring from third. The man who produced the out is given the credit for producing a run, while the man who started the sequence by reaching first on an error is likewise credited with a run. The man who hit the double, which is surely the key event in the sequence which produced the run, and the only one reflecting batting skill, receives no credit whatsoever. In this regard, any formula based on "Runs Produced" (whether R + RBI or R + RBI − HR) is philosophically inferior to the formula Lindsey proposed, despite his failure to account for walks, steals, and other events.

The run values in the Linear Weights formula for identifying batters' real contribution are derived from Pete Palmer's 1978 computer simulation of all major-league games played since 1901. All the data available concerning the frequencies of the various events was collected; following a test run, these were tabulated. Unmeasured quantities, such as the probability of a man going from first to third on a single vs. that of his advancing only one base, were assigned values based on play-by-play analysis of over 100 World Series contests. The goal was to get all the measured quantities very nearly equal to the league statistics; then the simulation would provide run values of each event in terms of net runs produced above average. Expressing the values in those terms would give a meaningful base line to individual performances, because if you are told that a player contributed 87 runs you don't know what that signifies unless you know the average level of run contribution in that year: 87 may sound like a lot, but if the norm was 80, then you know the player contributed only seven runs beyond average.

The values obtained from the simulation are remarkably similar from one era to the next, confounding expectations that the home run would prove more valuable today than in the dead-ball era, or that the steal was once a primary offensive weapon. These values are expressed in beyond-average runs.

Run Values of Various Events, by Periods

Event	Period			
	1901–20	1921–40	1941–60	1961–77
Home Run	1.36	1.40	1.42	1.42
Triple	1.02	1.05	1.03	1.00
Double	.82	.83	.80	.77
Single	.46	.50	.47	.45
Walk/HBP	.32	.35	.35	.33
Stolen Base	.20	.22	.19	.19
Caught Stealing	−.33	−.39	−.36	−.32
Out*	−.24	−.30	−.27	−.25

*An out is considered to be a hitless at bat and its value is set so that the sum of all events times their frequency is zero, thus establishing zero as the base line, or norm, for performance.

In the years since this simulation was conducted, statistician Dave Smith ("Maury Wills and the Value of the Stolen Base," *Baseball Research Journal*, 1980) convinced Pete to adjust the values of the stolen base and caught stealing because of their situation-dependent,

elective nature: attempts are apt to occur more frequently in close games, where they would be worth more than if they were distributed randomly the way an event like a single or a home run would be. Pete revised the value for the steal upward to .30 runs, while for the caught stealing it becomes −.60 runs.

Just as these run values change marginally with changing conditions of play, they differ slightly up and down the batting order (a homer is not worth as much to the leadoff hitter as it is to the fifth-place batter; a walk is worth more for the man batting second than for the man batting eighth); however, these differences have been averaged out in the figures above. For evaluating runs contributed by any batter at any time, there is no better method than Batting Runs, the Linear Weights formula derived from the computer simulation which is the basis of the table above.

The Formula

Batting Runs = (.47)1B + (.78)2B + (1.09)3B + (1.40)HR + (.33)(BB + HB) + (.30)SB − (.60)CS − (.25)(AB − H) − .50(OOB).

The events not included in the formula that you might have thought to see are sacrifices, sacrifice hits, grounded into double plays, and reached on error. The last is not known for most years and in the official statistics is indistinguishable from outs on base (OOB).

The sacrifice has essentially canceling values, trading an out for an advanced base which, often as not, leaves the team in a situation with poorer run potential than it had before the sacrifice.

The sacrifice fly has dubious run value because it is entirely dependent upon a situation not under the batter's control: while a single or a walk always has a potential run value, a long fly does not, unless a man happens to be poised at third base (whether it is achieved by accident or design is open to question, as well, but that is beside the point—getting hit by a pitch is not a product of intent, either).

Last, the grounded into double play is to a far greater extent a function of one's place in the batting order than it is of poor speed or failure in the clutch, and thus it does not find a home in a formula applicable to all batters. It is no accident that Henry Aaron, who ran well for most of his long career and wasn't too bad in the clutch, hit into more DP's than anyone else, nor that Roberto Clemente, Al Kaline, and Frank Robinson, who fit the same description, are also among the 10 "worst" in this department. If a .230-hitting American League shortstop doesn't hit into many twin killings, it's not because of adept bat handling or blazing speed but because he bats ninth.

The Linear Weights formula for batters may be long, but it calls for only addition, subtraction, and multiplication and thus is as simple as the slugging average, whose incorrect weights (1, 2, 3, and 4) it revises and expands upon. Each event has a value and a frequency, just as in slugging average, yet—as in no batting statistic you have ever seen—outs are treated as offensive events with a run value of their own (albeit a negative one), a truth so obvious it somehow escaped notice. Just as the run poten-

tial for a team in a given half inning is boosted by a man reaching base, it is diminished by a man being retired; not only has he failed to change the situation on the bases but he has deprived his team of the services of a man further down the order who might have come up in this half inning, either with men on base and/or with scores already in.

What Batting Runs does is to take every offensive event and to treat it in terms of its impact upon the team—an average team, so that a man does not benefit in his individual record for having the good fortune to bat cleanup with the Giants or suffer for batting seventh with the Marlins. The relationship of individual performance to team play is stated poorly or not at all in conventional baseball statistics. In Batting Runs it is crystal clear: the linear progression, the sum of the various offensive events, when weighted by their accurately predicted run values, will total the runs contributed by that batter or that team beyond the league average.

Recognizing that some dedicated readers of *Total Baseball* will wish to keep track of batting performance by computing Batting Runs themselves over the course of a season, and that they may be frustrated by the difficulty of calculating the "At Bats-Hits" factor for the league, which is necessary to determine the negative value of an out, we advise that using a fixed value of -.25 for outs will tend to work quite well if you wish to include pitcher batting performance, and a fixed value of -.27 will serve if you wish to delete it. Actually, any fixed value will suffice in midseason; it's only when all the numbers are in and you care to compare this year's results with last year's (or with those of the 1927 Yankees) that more precision is desirable. At that point the value of the out may be calculated by the ambitious among you, but ideally, the sporting press will provide accurate Batting Runs figures. Who, after all, calculates ERA for himself?

Batting Runs and Production

For those to whom calculation is anathema, or at the least no pleasure, Batting Runs has a "shadow stat" that tracks its accuracy to a remarkable degree and is a breeze to calculate: Production, which consists simply of On-Base Percentage plus Slugging Average. While it is not expressed in runs and thus lacks the philosophical appeal of Batting Runs, the standard deviation of its most complete version is 20.4 runs compared to the 19.8 of Batting Runs. In other words, the correlation between Batting Runs and Production over the course of an average team season is 99.7 percent.

However, as an average or ratio, Production measures the *rate* of batting success (efficiency), while Batting Runs measures the *amount* of success. For example, a batter who goes 2-for-5 with a walk in one game, those 2 hits being doubles, will have an On-Base Percentage of .500 and a Slugging Average of .800; his Production will be 1.30 or, as stated for convenience in *Total Baseball,* 130. Another batter, who in 162 games gets 200 hits and 100 walks in 500 at bats, with 400 total bases, will have an identical OBP, SLG, and PRO. Which player has contributed more to his team? Clearly, longevity, or amount of production, is no less important than rate of production.

To cite a specific instance in which Production and Batting Runs differ, take George Brett's remarkable 1980 season in which he batted .390, had 298 total bases, 75 bases through walks or HBP, and 118 RBIs—all in only 117 games played. In the table of all-time single-season leaders in Production, the Kansas City third baseman ranks 48th when his PRO of 1.124 is normalized to the league average and adjusted for home-park effects. Yet in the table of park adjusted Batting Runs, Brett's season ranks only 96th all-time because he missed 45 games, in which his team derived no benefit from his high rate of performance. (Had Brett played 162 games and continued to perform at the same level, his Batting Runs would have been not 64 but 88.6, the 21st best mark in history.)

Because PRO is not expressed in runs, it is less versatile than Batting Runs. For just as runs are proportional to the events that form them, so are they proportional to wins and losses. This statement, a truism today, was a novelty in 1954 when Rickey and Roth first stated the correlation between run differentials and team standings. But they did not take the next step, to recognize that not only a team's standing but even its won-lost record could be predicted from the run totals.

"The initial published attempt on this subject," Palmer wrote in the 1982 issue of the SABR annual *The National Pastime,* "was Earnshaw Cook's *Percentage Baseball,* in 1964. Examining major-league results from 1950 through 1960 he found winning percentage equal to .484 times runs scored divided by runs allowed. . . . Arnold Soolman, in an unpublished paper which received some media attention, looked at results from 1901 through 1970 and came up with winning percentage equal to .102 times runs scored per game minus .103 times runs allowed per game plus .505. . . . Bill James, in the *Baseball Abstract,* developed winning percentage equal to runs scored raised to the power *x,* divided by the sum of runs scored and runs allowed, each raised to the power *x.* Originally, *x* was equal to two but then better results were obtained when a value of 1.83 was used. . . .

"My work showed that as a rough rule of thumb, each additional 10 runs scored (or 10 less runs allowed) produced one extra win, essentially the same as the Soolman study. However, breaking the teams into groups showed that high-scoring teams needed more runs to produce a win. This runs-per-win factor I determined to be 10 times the square root of the average number of runs scored per inning by both teams. Thus in normal play, when 4.5 runs per game are scored by each club, each team scores .5 runs per inning—totaling one run, the square root of which is one, times 10."

Note that when we refer to the need for approximately ten additional runs scored (or 10 fewer allowed) to provide a team with an additional win, we do not mean that it takes ten runs to win any given game. Obviously, in a specific case, a one-run margin is all that is required; but statistics are designed for the long haul, not the short.

What does this have to do with Batting Runs? Remembering that Batting Runs are expressed not simply in runs but in beyond-average runs, the conversion from a batter's Linear Weights runs to his wins is a snap: simply divide Batting Runs by the number of runs it takes to gain an extra win in a given year. Taking the exploits of Babe Ruth in 1927, we see that through batting alone he con-

tributed 100.7 runs, or 9.56 wins, since in the American League in 1927 it took 10.53 runs to produce an additional win. If every other player on the Yankees had performed at the league average, the New York record should have been 87-67; if each of the seven other batters had performed only half as well as Ruth and had added five extra wins (discounting reserves, pitchers, fielders, and stealers, whom we shall presume for this discussion to have been average), the Yankees would have gained another 35 wins (7 × 5) to finish with a won-lost mark of 122-32.

Stolen Base Runs

The Linear Weights formula for batters contains a factor for base stealers, expressed in runs. How do you judge the effectiveness of a base stealer? Conventional baseball statistics will lead you to the conclusion that whoever has the most steals is the best thief; that is the sole criterion for *The Sporting News* annual "Golden Shoe Award" in each league. How often the man with the most steals may have been thrown out is of no concern.

An article in the 1981 *Baseball Research Journal* by Bob Davids offered something more sophisticated yet utterly simple: a stolen base percentage, which is simply stolen bases divided by attempts. The best stolen base average of all time, insofar as we know and based on a minimum of 30 attempts, is Max Carey's in 1922 when he stole 51 bases in 53 attempts. The most times caught stealing in the course of a season was Ty Cobb's 38 in 1915, until 1982 when Rickey Henderson was nabbed 42 times. But the best method yet devised, and the one that is pleasingly simple, is to apply the Linear Weights method to get Stolen Base Runs. One multiplies the steals by their run value of .30 and the failed attempts by -.60, and adds the two products. The implication for such men as Ty Cobb, Rickey Henderson, and Vince Coleman is clear: it takes a fabulous stealing performance to produce as many as ten extra runs—i.e., one extra win—for the team.

In 1915 Ty Cobb, when he established the modern stolen base record of 96, can be seen to have contributed to his team 28.8 runs, while his 38 foiled larcenies cost 22.8. Thus Cobb, for all his whirling-dervish activity, accounted for only 6 non-par runs—not even a single win. Whoa! You mean that not a single one of Cobb's steals produced a victory? That is not what is being said: the fact is that while the gain from the stolen base is entirely visible—an extra base which may be followed by a hit that would otherwise not have produced a run—the cost of the caught stealing is entirely invisible, or conjectural, except with the aid of statistics. How many big innings did Cobb run his team out of? How many batters reached base in ensuing innings who might, in an earlier inning, have had their contributions count for runs? What Stolen Base Runs indicate are that, on balance, not on a specific-case basis, the stolen base is at best a dubious method of increasing a team's run production.

Now let's take a look at what Henderson did. His record 130 stolen bases in 1982 produced 39 runs for his team. His 42 failed attempts took away 25.2 possible runs. Net effect: approximately 14 runs, or one and a half wins, a performance nearly three times as good as Cobb's. In

1983, stealing 22 fewer bases, he was even better, accounting for 21.0 runs. However, the all-time best stealing record is that of Maury Wills in 1962, when he stole 104 bases and was caught only 13 times. Wills' 104 stolen bases produced 31.2 runs; his 13 failed attempts cost only 7.8. So, his baserunning contribution was 23.4, or a little over two wins.

Fielding Runs

As mentioned earlier, in 1954 when Branch Rickey and Allan Roth came up with their "efficiency formula" for run scoring and run prevention, the defensive half of the equation was divided into five segments, the last of which was fielding, to which they assigned a mathematical value of zero. "There is nothing on earth," Rickey declared, "anyone can do with fielding."

Since then many have tried, with mixed results, to improve upon the mere toting up of raw data—putouts, assists, errors, double plays. In the second edition of *Total Baseball,* we improved upon the Fielding Runs formula by calculating innings played at each position, plate appearances for all players on the team, and then rating each fielder based on his chances per inning. Where previously all outfield positions had been grouped together, we now rate left fielders against left fielders, center fielders against center fielders, and right fielders against right fielders; we also revised thoroughly the formula for catchers, which retains the highest degree of subjectivism because their primary defensive contribution comes not with the glove but through calling the pitches.

More on this complex subject in the Glossary.

Pitching Runs

Determining the run contributions of pitchers is much easier than determining those of fielders or batters, though not quite so simple as that of base stealers. Actual runs allowed are known, as are innings pitched. Let's assume that a pitcher is responsible only for earned runs. Then why, we hear some of you asking, is the ERA not measure enough of his ability? Because it tells only the pitcher's *rate* of efficiency, not his actual benefit to the team. In a league with an ERA of 3.50, a starter who throws 300 innings with an ERA of 2.50 must be worth twice as much to his team as a starter with the same ERA who appears in only 150 innings. Through Pitching Runs, we seek to determine the number of beyond-average runs a pitcher saved—the number he prevented from scoring that an average pitcher would have allowed.

The formula for Earned Run Average is:

$$ERA = (Earned\ Runs \times 9)/Innings\ Pitched$$

The number of average, or par, runs for a pitcher, which is represented by a Pitching Runs figure of zero, is equal to:

$$(League\ ERA \times IP)/9$$

If the league ERA is 4.21 (as the National League's was in 1994) and a pitcher's ERA is also 4.21, he will by definition have held batters in check at the league average

no matter how many innings he pitched. If, however, his ERA was 1.56 and he hurled 202 innings (as Greg Maddux did for the Braves in '94), he will have saved a certain number of runs that an average pitcher might have allowed in his place; to find that number we employ the Pitching Runs formula:

Pitcher's Runs = Innings Pitched × (League ERA/9) − ER

This represents the difference between the number of earned runs allowed at the league average for the innings pitched and the actual earned runs allowed. For the case of Maddux, we get

Runs = 202 × (4.21/9) − 35 = 59.5

Maddux was 59.5 runs better than the average National League pitcher in 1994, and had he been transported to an average NL team—that mythical entity that scores as many runs as it allows while winning 81 and losing 81—he would have made that team's mark 87-75. (Actually, in the strike shortened 112 game season of 1994, an average team would have been 56-56, and the addition of Maddux would have made that team's record 62-50.) An alternative way to calculate pitchers' Linear Weights, useful with oldtimers for whom you may have the ERA but not the number of earned runs allowed, is to use the pitcher's ERA, subtracted from the league's ERA, multiplying by the innings pitched, then dividing by nine. In Maddux's case, this approach would look like:

(4.21 − 1.56) × 202/9 = 59.5

The two parts of performance—efficiency and durability—are incorporated into all Linear Weights measures. If you are performing at a better than average clip, the more regularly you do so, the more your team will benefit and thus the higher your Linear Weights measure. If you are stealing bases nine times out of ten, your team will benefit more from 60 attempts than from 40; if you are batting at an above average clip, it's better to play in 160 games than 110; if you're allowing one earned run per game less than the average pitcher, your LWTS will increase with innings pitched.

Linear Weights in Practice

Having formulas for pitching, fielding, baserunning, and batting, we can assess the run-scoring contribution of every individual who has ever played the game, and thus the number of wins that he has contributed in a given season or over his career. The number of runs required to produce an additional win has varied over the years between nine and 11 runs, with a very few league seasons outside those parameters.

Limited by conventional baseball statistics, one might, in 1990, have uttered something like, "Barry Bonds hit .293 with 33 homers and 114 RBIs—the guy must have been worth 10 extra wins to Pittsburgh all by himself!" Or: "The White Sox are only one pitcher away from winning the division." Or: "The Yankees are only three players away from being a contender." Or, "Letting Darryl Strawberry get away was the worst thing the Mets ever did; they'll be a second-division club for a decade." With Linear Weights, these statements, or rather the concerns they reflect, can be approached with some data and with some degree of objectivity. First: Barry Bonds had a fine year in 1990, but to have contributed 10 wins by himself he would have had to account for nearly 100 Linear Weights runs, a mark that up till then had been attained by only three men in major-league history. In fact, Bonds contributed 6.5 wins in '90, though he did post 9.0 wins in 1992.

As to the White Sox, they finished 94-68 in 1990, while their Linear Weights projected them to finish at 81-81. The Athletics, who won the AL West at 103-59, actually projected to finish 96-66. So, the Sox management might have asked, how to close ground on the Athletics? Could one pitcher—like Bob Welch, for whom they bid in the free-agent bazaar—make the difference? To do so, he would have to contribute about 150 Pitching Runs, a feat no pitcher has ever accomplished. In 1990, pitching for Oakland—and remember, the Linear Weights formula is divorced from considerations of batter support—Welch contributed 20.7 park-adjusted Pitching Runs. So presuming that he pitched as well for the White Sox as he did for the Athletics, or even slightly better, he would not be enough to "win" Chicago the flag on paper; Chicago would need help from other quarters.

Regarding the other statements, you get the picture: sabermetric analyses like the ones above will tend to puncture fantasies.

Park Factor

A central issue for sabermetricians is the network of illusion created by home-park dimensions, atmospheric conditions, and visibility for batters. How many home runs would Matt Williams hit if he played half his games in Fenway Park? Will the Boston Red Sox and Chicago Cubs keep "failing" to put together solid pitching staffs—or has their pitching been adequate all along? Why had the American League leaders in triples so often worn a Royals uniform? One's home park has a powerful effect on a player or pitcher's record, elevating some good players to greatness and denying the spotlight to some outstanding performers.

It should be understood that the average player does better at home regardless of the park—familiarity breeds success. Individuals bat and pitch at a rate 10 percent higher at home, on average. But parks don't create performance; they only affect it. For example, a left-handed hitter at Fenway can do very well indeed, as Wade Boggs did, by learning to take the outside pitch to left field. Likewise, a right-handed batter can make the friendly Green Monster into his nemesis by trying to pull every pitch.

For hard luck in some parks, it is tough to top the record of Mark McGwire, who has had the misfortune to call the Oakland Coliseum home. McGwire's prodigious and plentiful home run total in 1998 made him the single-season record holder, and the Oakland Coliseum's renovation in 1997 have make it a much more friendly hitters park, but it was not always so. Through 1996, his lifetime Production, normalized to league average but not adjusted for park effects, was 28th best on the all time list of those playing in 1,000 games. Had he played his home

games instead in Fenway Park, his PRO would have projected to the eighth best of all time. Had he even played in an average hitters' park—which is what PRO+ measures—his record would show itself to be the twelfth best ever. In 1998 McGwire hit 38 homers at Busch Stadium and 32 on the road.

If we desire to remove the silver spoon or the millstone that a home park can be, and measure individual ability alone, we must create a statistical balancer that diminishes the individual batting marks created in parks like Fenway and augments those created in Oakland. Pete Palmer developed an adjustment that enables us, for the first time, to measure a player's accomplishments apart from the influence of his home park.

Parks differ in so many ways that it may be hard to imagine how their differences can be quantified. The most obvious way in which they differ is in their dimensions, from home plate to the outfield walls, and from the base lines to the stands. The older arenas—Fenway Park, Wrigley Field, Tiger Stadium—tend to favor hitters in both regards, with reachable fences and little room to pursue a foul pop. Yet two parks can have nearly equal dimensions, like Pittsburgh's Three Rivers Stadium and Atlanta's Fulton County Stadium, yet have highly dissimilar impacts upon hitters because of climate (balls travel farther in hot weather), elevation (travel farther as altitude increases), and playing surface (travel faster and truer on artificial turf). Still another factor is how well batters think they see the ball; Shea Stadium is notorious as a cause of complaints.

And perhaps more important than any of the objective park characteristics, suggested Robert Kingsley in a 1980 study of why so many homers were hit at Fulton County Stadium in Atlanta, is the attitude of the players, the way that the park changes their view of how the game must be played in order to win. In their own home park the Astros might peck and scratch for runs, but playing at Fulton County Stadium in Atlanta they put the steal and hit-and-run in mothballs. Conversely, a team which comes into the Astrodome and plays for the big inning will generally get what it deserves—a loss. The successful team is one that can play its game at home—the game for which the team was constructed—yet is flexible enough to adapt when on the road.

Rather than try to assign a numerical value to each of the six or more variables that might go into establishing an estimator of home park impact, we looked to the single measure in which all these variables are reflected—runs. After all, why would we assign one value to dimensions, another to climate, and so on, except to identify their impact on scoring? If a stadium is a "hitters' park," it stands to reason that more runs would be scored there than in a park perceived as neutral, just as a "pitchers' park" could be expected to depress scoring.

The full and lengthy explanation for the computation of the Park Factor is left to the Glossary, where hardy readers might consider taking a peek right now. For most of us, though, it will be enough to understand that the Park Factor consists mainly of the team's home-road ratio of runs allowed, compared to the league's home-road ratio.

Relativity

Sabermetric statistics can be marvelous tools for cross-era comparisons, enabling us to determine if baseball's history is truly a seamless web or if its seams are real enough, but are camouflaged by traditional statistics.

If Batter A presented himself to you for approval with these statistics—.330 batting average, 16 home runs, 107 RBIs—what would your reaction be? You'd like to have him on your team, right? And what to make of Batter B, who presents these numbers—.257 batting average, 14 home runs, 53 RBIs? Not bad for a middle infielder with a good glove, you say, but otherwise undistinguished? In fact, the "impressive" figures of Batter A represent the average performance of a National League outfielder in 1930, while the "blah" figures of Batter B are those of the average American League outfielder of 1968: the former has more than twice the RBIs of the latter, along with a batting average 73 points higher, yet the two performed at identical levels, and an argument could be made that Batter B was superior.

In a similar comparison involving those two years of extremes, Bill Terry led the National League in 1930 with a batting average of .401, a mark surpassed by Ted Williams in 1941 but not equaled since; Carl Yastrzemski led the American League of 1968 with a performance that oldtimers held to be a disgrace, a lowly batting average of .301, the worst ever to win a batting championship. Terry's mark was achieved at a time when most pitchers had only two pitches, a fastball and a curve, and not enough confidence in the latter to throw it when behind in the count at 2-0 or 3-1. The parks were smaller; there was no night ball; the game was segregated racially; and a team played 22 games with each of its seven rivals, none farther west of the Mississippi than St. Louis. Moreover, 1930 was the year in which National League officials, attempting to match the popularity of the slugging American League, juiced the ball to such an extent that the entire league batted .312 (if you remove pitcher batting). In other words, the average nonpitcher in the NL of 1930 batted higher than the AL leader in 1968! When Yaz hit .301, pitchers dominated the game and the average American League nonpitcher hit .238. How to compare Terry and Yaz, who played under such different conditions 38 years apart?

You could view Terry's .401 in relation to his league's BA of .312, concluding that Memphis Bill was a better hitter (by BA alone, which despite its previously cited deficiencies remains the most comfortable stat by which to introduce this technique) by 28.5 percent. You could compare Yaz's .301 to his league's BA of .238 and conclude that he was a better than average hitter by 26.5 percent. A mere 2 percentage points separate the men— had they both played in the National League of 1983, when the league average was .255, the Terry of 1930 might have hit .328, the Yaz of 1968, .323. (A further refinement of this method would be to delete Terry's at bats and hits from his league's, and those of Yastrzemski from his league's, so that the batters are not in effect compared with themselves. This, however, necessitates the use of at bats and hits rather than simply the averages and does not significantly alter the results.)

Why do we need relative measures? Basically, for the

same reason we need statistics altogether, to compare, to interpret, and to comprehend, but in a more reasonable and accurate manner when the disparity of the data sources makes the use of absolute, unadjusted numbers illogical. If the analysis involves data produced under widely varying conditions, such as a sample including performances 20, 50, or a 100 years apart, any comparison will be meaningless without dragging in a series of rather complex historical understandings to modify the analysis—and in a highly subjective, unreliable manner.

Until the 1970s, when David Shoebotham ("Relative Batting Averages," *Baseball Research Journal,* 1976) and Merritt Clifton ("Relative Baseball," *Samisdat,* 1979) introduced the relativist approach, all baseball stats were absolute. And for cross-era comparison, that favorite Hot Stove League activity, absolute stats were absolutely useless, generating plenty of heat and precious little light.

What the theory of relativity, baseball-style, does beautifully is to eliminate the need for bringing historical baggage to statistical analysis. The normalized or relative versions of any statistic—batting average, Production, ERA, slugging average, you name it; even homers or strikeouts, though there are problems with these—will be greater than 1.00 for all above-average performers (1.41, for example, means 41 percent better than average in the given category) while relative statistics less than 1.00 will indicate a below average level of play (0.88 means 12 percent below the norm).

It is as simple as can be. So Early Wynn had a 3.20 ERA in 1950? What does that mean? Well, the league ERA was 4.58, so Wynn did very well indeed. His normalized ERA thus was 143, a mark better than that earned by Tom Seaver in 1968, when he had an absolute ERA a full run lower at 2.20.

We cannot employ a Relative Won-Lost record, for the league average is every year the same: .500. (A logical corollary is that one cannot fruitfully use relative measures of any sort for a single season's analysis, as all like figures will be compared to the same league average. The numbers may be changed into normalized form, but the players' rankings will be unchanged: the top 10 in batting average in 1990, for example, will retain their ranks in Relative Batting Average.)

Relativism in baseball echoes not only Einstein but also Shakespeare, whose words in *Hamlet* might be modified to read "There is nothing either good or bad, but context makes it so." No longer must we accept arbitrary assessments of performance or regard with awe such old-time figures as Hugh Duffy's BA of .440 in 1894 (not the

accomplishment that Rod Carew's .388 was in 1977) or George Sisler's .407 in 1920 (not as good as Roberto Clemente's .357 in 1967). Conversely, a "mediocre" performance of recent years, such as Bobby Murcer's .292 of 1972, for instance, stacks up as the equal of Eddie Collins' .360 in 1923, while Charlie Grimm's seemingly solid .298 in 1929 compares unfavorably to Mike Cubbage's .260 in 1976.

Relativism redefines our understanding not only of particular accomplishments but also of baseball history itself. We see that the men who batted .400 with numbing regularity in the 1890s and 1920s were not supermen (would you swap Wade Boggs for Tuck Turner? Tony Gwynn for Tip O'Neill?) anymore than the sub-2.00 ERA pitchers of the late 1960s were superhuman (Gary Peters, Bob Bolin, Dave McNally, among other). Absolute figures lie. Are hitters today worse because none has hit .400 since 1941? Or are they superior because a Dave Kingman could average nearly 30 homers a year while Cap Anson only averaged four? Are infielders better today because they make fewer errors than their counterparts of 50, 75, or 100 years ago? Do modern outfielders have limp-noodle arms because their assist totals pale before those registered in the early decades of the 1900s? Is baseball improving or declining, and has its rise or fall been steady? One can spit absolute stats on the hot stove all winter long and get no closer to the answer, but with relative statistics, the issues are clarified.

The Future

The most exciting frontier for sabermetrics is in situational stats, the type employed by The Baseball Workshop, The Elias Sports Bureau, and Stats, Inc. As the years go by and their data bases grow, the sampling sizes of the data will enlarge and their figures for day vs. night, left vs. right, and so on, will be statistically meaningful as well as statistically correct. Cross-era comparison remains a subject of intense interest, and the debate over average-player skill rages on. Fielding stats, as discussed, also provide fertile ground for invention.

Fantasy baseball aficionados seem caught up in the competition and dealmaking (as well as player evaluation), but some of the newsletters provide sound analysis and trend-spotting tips. It would not be surprising if Rotisserie-type leagues and digital game designers compete with SABR to furnish the best sabermetricians of the 1990s.

Evolution of Baseball Records

Marty Appel

Throughout baseball history, if a player was a league leader, his record would forever show an asterisk or boldface so we could readily remember the achievement. But, if the player set an *all-time* record that was later broken, his name would pass from the record books forever. Thus Roger Connor, who was baseball's all-time home run champion before Babe Ruth, is a forgotten man as far as statistical compilations go.

The following is a chronology of major batting, baserunning, and pitching records for a career and for a season. It is an attempt to honor those who set the standards of their times. After the player's name appears, we show the total he concluded with—before the mark was broken—followed by the years in which the record belonged to him. Records at the end of the season are the basis for establishing new leaders to avoid the daily leap-frogging that may have occurred in some cases. This does create the possibility of someone holding a record briefly within a season yet not being included here.

Special thanks to Tom Ruane and Pete Palmer for their assistance in compiling this section.

Career Batting and Baserunning

Games Played

Players	Record	Years Held
Jack Manning, Jim O'Rourke		
Harry Schafer, George Wright	70	1876
Jim O'Rourke, George Wright	131	1877
Jim O'Rourke	191	1878
George Wright	275	1879
Jim O'Rourke	619	1880-84
Paul Hines	731	1884-85
John Morrill	1219	1885-89
Paul Hines	1327	1889-90
Cap Anson	2276	1890-1906
Jake Beckley	2386	1906-09
Bill Dahlen	2443	1909-15
Honus Wagner	2792	1915-26
Ty Cobb	3035	1926-74
Hank Aaron	3298	1974-83
Carl Yastrzemski	3308	1983-84
Pete Rose	3562	1984-present

Consecutive Games (incomplete for 19th century)

Players	Record	Years Held
George Pinkney	577	1889-1920
Everett Scott	1307	1920-33
Lou Gehrig	2130	1933-95
Cal Ripken Jr.	2632	1995-98

At Bats

Players	Record	Years Held
George Wright	1280	1876-80

Paul Hines	6047	1880-91
Cap Anson	9101	1891-1906
Jake Beckley	9526	1906-15
Honus Wagner	10430	1915-26
Ty Cobb	11434	1926-74
Hank Aaron	12364	1974-82
Pete Rose	14053	1982-present

Runs

Players	Record	Years Held
Ross Barnes	142	1876-78
Jim O'Rourke	173	1878-79
George Wright	244	1879-80
Jim O'Rourke	965	1880-88
King Kelly	1160	1888-90
Harry Stovey	1492	1890-94
Cap Anson	1719	1894-1905
Jesse Burkett	1720	1905-16
Honus Wagner	1736	1916-23
Ty Cobb	2246	1923-present

Hits

Players	Record	Years Held
Ross Barnes	138	1876-77
Deacon White	207	1877-78
Deacon White, Cal McVey	288	1878-79
Paul Hines	1027	1879-85
Cap Anson	2995	1885-1914
Honus Wagner	3415	1914-23
Ty Cobb	4189	1923-85
Pete Rose	4256	1985-present

Doubles

Players	Record	Years Held
Ross Barnes, Dick Higham, Paul Hines	21	1876-77
George Wright	33	1877-78
Jim O'Rourke	48	1878-79
Tom York	72	1879-80
Paul Hines	213	1880-85
Cap Anson	528	1885-1911
Nap Lajoie	657	1911-25
Tris Speaker	792	1925-present

Triples

Players	Record	Years Held
Ross Barnes	14	1876-77
George Hall	21	1877-78
Tom York	24	1878-79
Charley Jones	31	1879-80
Charley Jones, Jim O'Rourke	34	1880-81
Jim O'Rourke	55	1881-84
Charley Jones	90	1884-87
Roger Connor	233	1887-1905
Jake Beckley	243	1905-13
Sam Crawford	309	1913-present

Home Runs

Players	Record	Years Held
George Hall	5	1876-77
Charley Jones	40	1877-85

638

Harry Stovey	57	1885-87
Dan Brouthers	74	1887-89
Harry Stovey	122	1889-95
Roger Connor	138	1895-1921
Babe Ruth	714	1921-74
Hank Aaron	755	1974-present

RBI

Players	Record	Years Held
Deacon White	190	1876-80
Cap Anson	1879	1880-1927
Ty Cobb	1937	1927-32
Babe Ruth	2213	1932-75
Hank Aaron	2297	1975-present

Strikeouts

Players	Record	Years Held
Johnny Ryan	23	1876-77
Lew Brown	120	1877-80
Will White	127	1880-81
Pud Galvin	418	1881-86
John Morrill	656	1886-95
Tom Brown	708	1895-1926
Babe Ruth	1330	1926-64
Mickey Mantle	1710	1964-78
Willie Stargell	1912	1978-82
Reggie Jackson	2597	1982-present

Walks

Players	Record	Years Held
Ross Barnes	20	1876-77
Jim O'Rourke	40	1877-79
Charley Jones	55	1879-80
Jim O'Rourke	114	1880-83
Tom York	133	1883-84
George Gore	385	1884-88
Ned Williamson	447	1888-89
George Gore	650	1889-92
Roger Connor	1002	1892-99
Billy Hamilton	1187	1899-1923
Eddie Collins	1499	1923-30
Babe Ruth	2056	1930-present

Stolen Bases (kept separately before and after 1898)

Players	Record	Years Held
Harry Stovey	68	1886-87
Arlie Latham	738	1887-97
Billy Hamilton	787	1897-98
Ed Delahanty	58	1898-99
John McGraw	169	1899-1902
Sam Mertes	294	1902-05
Honus Wagner	698	1905-17
Honus Wagner, Ty Cobb	703	1917-18
Ty Cobb	891	1918-77
Lou Brock	938	1977-91
Rickey Henderson	1297	1991-present

Batting Average (3,000 at bat minimum)

Players	Record	Years Held
Jim O'Rourke	.318	1884-85
Cap Anson	.343	1885-87
Dan Brouthers	.347	1887-88
Cap Anson	.344	1888-89
Dan Brouthers	.345	1889-90
Pete Browning	.345	1890-92
Dan Brouthers	.343	1892-95
Billy Hamilton	.351	1895-97
Jesse Burkett	.352	1897-99
Willie Keeler	.364	1899-1905
Nap Lajoie	.350	1905-11
Ty Cobb	.366	1911-present

Slugging Pct. (3,000 at bat minimum)

Players	Record	Years Held
Paul Hines	.434	1884-85

Cap Anson	.471	1885-87
Dan Brouthers	.520	1887-1903
Nap Lajoie	.529	1903-07
Dan Brouthers	.519	1907-16
Joe Jackson	.522	1916-17
Dan Brouthers	.519	1917-22
Rogers Hornsby	.536	1922-23
Babe Ruth	.690	1923-present

At Bats per Home Run (3,000 at bat minimum)

Players	Record	Years Held
Paul Hines	136.58	1884
Abner Dalrymple	84.35	1885
Charley Jones	63.96	1886
Dan Brouthers	46.46	1887
Dan Brouthers	47.86	1888
Dan Brouthers	49.72	1889
Harry Stovey	49.15	1890
Harry Stovey	47.08	1891
Jimmy Ryan	47.52	1892
Mike Tiernan	44.22	1893
Mike Tiernan	46.70	1894
Sam Thompson	47.02	1895
Sam Thompson	46.64	1896
Sam Thompson	46.75	1897
Sam Thompson	46.87	1898-1903
Buck Freeman	43.49	1904
Sam Thompson	46.87	1905
Sam Thompson	47.12	1906-1916
Gavvy Cravath	33.33	1917
Gavvy Cravath	34.83	1918
Gavvy Cravath	33.10	1919
Gavvy Cravath	33.20	1920
Babe Ruth	12.76	1923
Babe Ruth	12.55	1924
Babe Ruth	12.70	1925
Babe Ruth	12.41	1926
Babe Ruth	11.92	1927
Babe Ruth	11.69	1928
Babe Ruth	11.62	1929
Babe Ruth	11.53	1930-1931
Babe Ruth	11.51	1932
Babe Ruth	11.61	1933
Babe Ruth	11.76	1934-1997
Mark McGwire	11.23	1998

Career Pitching Records

Games Pitched

Players	Record	Years Held
Jim Devlin	129	1876-78
Tommy Bond	294	1878-83
Jim McCormick	386	1883-85
Pud Galvin	697	1885-1905
Cy Young	906	1905-68
Hoyt Wilhelm	1070	1968-1998
Dennis Eckersley	1071	1998-present

Wins

Players	Record	Years Held
Al Spalding	47	1876-77
Tommy Bond	180	1877-84
Will White	228	1884-86
Jim McCormick	252	1886-87
Pud Galvin	360	1887-1903
Cy Young	511	1903-present

Losses

Players	Record	Years Held
Jim Devlin	60	1876-79
George Bradley	82	1879-80
Tommy Bond	97	1880-81
Jim McCormick	173	1881-85
Pud Galvin	308	1885-1911
Cy Young	316	1911-present

Innings Pitched

Players	Record	Years Held
Jim Devlin	1181	1876-78
Tommy Bond	2547.2	1878-83
Jim McCormick	3353.2	1883-85
Pud Galvin	5941.1	1885-1906
Cy Young	7354.2	1906-present

Games Started

Players	Record	Years Held
Jim Devlin	129	1876-78
Tommy Bond	288	1878-83
Jim McCormick	379	1883-85
Pud Galvin	682	1885-1907
Cy Young	815	1907-present

Complete Games

Players	Record	Years Held
Jim Devlin	127	1876-78
Tommy Bond	270	1878-83
Will White	306	1883-84
Jim McCormick	392	1884-86
Pud Galvin	639	1886-1907
Cy Young	749	1907-present

Strikeouts

Players	Record	Years Held
Jim Devlin	263	1876-78
Tommy Bond	715	1878-82
Jim McCormick	1704	1882-88
Tim Keefe	2545	1888-1908
Cy Young	2803	1908-21
Walter Johnson	3509	1921-83
Steve Carlton	3709	1983-84
Nolan Ryan	5714	1984-present

Walks

Players	Record	Years Held
Joe Borden	51	1876-77
Jim Devlin	78	1877-78
Terry Larkin	84	1878-79
Will White	171	1879-81
Jim McCormick	565	1881-86
Mickey Welch	1297	1886-93
Tony Mullane	1408	1893-95
Amos Rusie	1704	1895-1952
Bobo Newsom	1732	1952-55
Bob Feller	1764	1955-63
Early Wynn	1775	1963-81
Nolan Ryan	2795	1981-present

Hits Allowed

Players	Record	Years Held
Bobby Mathews	693	1876-77
Jim Devlin	1183	1877-78
Tommy Bond	2610	1878-83
Pud Galvin	6352	1883-1908
Cy Young	7092	1908-present

Home Runs Allowed

Players	Record	Years Held
Bobby Mathews	8	1876-78
Tommy Bond	20	1878-80
Tommy Bond, George Bradley	21	1880-81
Tommy Bond	24	1881-82
George Bradley	28	1882-83
Will White	39	1883-84
Larry Corcoran	66	1884-86
Jim McCormick	84	1886-88
John Clarkson	88	1888-89
Pud Galvin	105	1889-90
John Clarkson	161	1890-1930
Grover Cleveland Alexander	164	1930-36
George Braeholder	173	1936-38
Earl Whitehill	184	1938-39

Red Ruffing	254	1939-56
Murry Dickson	269	1956-57
Robin Roberts	505	1957-present

Shutouts

Players	Record	Years Held
George Bradley	18	1876-78
Tommy Bond	35	1878-84
Pud Galvin	56	1884-1904
Cy Young	76	1904-14
Christy Mathewson	77	1914-18
Christy Mathewson, Walter Johnson	79	1918-19
Walter Johnson	110	1919-present

Saves

Players	Record	Years Held
Jack Manning	6	1876-89
Tony Mullane	15	1889-98
Tony Millane, Kid Nichols	15	1898-99
Kid Nichols	17	1899-1907
Joe McGinnity	24	1907-10
Mordecai Brown	49	1910-26
Firpo Marberry	101	1926-46
Johnny Murphy	107	1946-62
Roy Face	136	1962-64
Hoyt Wilhelm	227	1964-80
Rollie Ringers	341	1980-92
Jeff Reardon	357	1992-93
Lee Smith	478	1993-present

Runs Allowed

Players	Record	Years Held
Bobby Mathews	395	1876-77
Jim Devlin	597	1877-78
Tommy Bond	634	1878-79
Terry Larkin	857	1879-80
Tommy Bond	1155	1880-82
Will White	1173	1882-83
Pud Galvin	3318	1883-present

Earned Runs Allowed

Players	Record	Years Held
Bobby Mathews	164	1876-77
Jim Devlin	248	1877-78
Tommy Bond	605	1878-83
Pud Galvin	1895	1883-1907
Cy Young	2146	1907-present

Earned Run Average (1,500 innings pitched minimum)

Players	Record	Years Held
Tommy Bond	1.97	1879-80
John Ward	1.90	1880-82
Will White	1.95	1882-84
Old Hoss Radbourn	1.95	1884-86
John Ward	2.10	1886-1905
Christy Mathewson	2.08	1905-06
John Ward	2.10	1906-07
Addie Joss	1.89	1907-09
Mordecai Brown	1.63	1909-10
Ed Walsh	1.70	1910-12
Walter Johnson	1.80	1912-22
Ed Walsh	1.82	1922-present

Winning Pct. (1,500 innings pitched minimum)

Players	Record	Years Held
Tommy Bond	.694	1879-80
John Ward	.659	1880-81
Tommy Bond	.641	1881-83
Larry Corcoran	.692	1883-84
Old Hoss Radbourn	.684	1884-86
Larry Corcoran	.670	1886-87
John Clarkson	.701	1887-88
Bob Caruthers	.708	1888-92
Dave Foutz	.690	1892-1911
Ed Ruelbach	.691	1911-12
Dave Foutz	.690	1912-31

Lefty Grove	.693	1931-36
Dave Foutz	.690	1936-39
Lefty Grove	.691	1939-40
Dave Foutz	.690	1940-53
Vic Raschi	.706	1953-54
Dave Foutz	.690	1954-59
Whitey Ford	.696	1959-67
Dave Foutz	.690	1967-83
Ron Guidry	.705	1983-84
Dave Foutz	.690	1984-85
Ron Guidry	.694	1984-86
Dave Foutz	.690	1986-90
Dwight Gooden	.714	1990-92
Dave Foutz	.690	1992-present

Single Season Batting and Baserunning Records

Games

Players	Record	Years Held
Jack Manning, Jim O'Rourke, Harry Schafer, George Wright	70	1876-79
Paul Hines, Mike McGeary, George Wright	85	1879-80
Emil Gross	87	1880-83
Joe Farrell, Sadie Houck, Martin Powell	101	1883-84
Roger Connor, Alex McKinnon	116	1884-86
Bill McClellan, Bill Phillips, George Pinkney	141	1886-88
George Pinkney	143	1888-92
Roger Connor	155	1892-98
George Van Haltren	156	1898-1904
Jimmy Barrett	162	1904-61
Rocky Colavito, Brooks Robinson	163	1961-62
Maury Wills	165	1962-present

At Bats

Players	Record	Years Held
George Wright	335	1876-79
Paul Hines	409	1879-83
Jud Birchall	449	1883-84
Abner Dalrymple	521	1884-86
George Pinkney	597	1886-87
Arlie Latham	627	1887-92
Tom Brown	660	1892-1921
Jack Tobin	671	1921-22
Rabbit Maranville	672	1922-31
Lloyd Waner	681	1931-35
Lloyd Waner, JoJo Moore	681	1935-36
Woody Jensen	696	1936-69
Matty Alou	698	1969-75
Dave Cash	699	1975-80
Willie Wilson	705	1980-present

Hits

Players	Record	Years Held
Ross Barnes	138	1876-79
Paul Hines	146	1879-83
Dan Brouthers	159	1883-84
Fred Dunlap	185	1884-86
Dave Orr	193	1886-87
Tip O'Neill	225	1887-94
Hugh Duffy	237	1894-96
Jesse Burkett	240	1896-1911
Ty Cobb	248	1911-20
George Sisler	257	1920-present

Doubles

Players	Record	Years Held
Ross Barnes, Dick Higham, Paul Hines	21	1876-78
Dick Higham	22	1878-79
Charlie Eden	31	1879-82
King Kelly	37	1882-83
Ned Williamson	49	1883-87
Tip O'Neill	52	1887-99

Ed Delahanty	55	1899-1923
Tris Speaker	59	1923-26
George Burns	64	1926-31
Earl Webb	67	1931-present

Triples

Players	Record	Years Held
Ross Barnes	14	1876-79
Ross Barnes, Buttercup Dickerson	14	1879-80
Ross Barnes, Buttercup Dickerson, Harry Stovey	14	1880-82
Roger Connor	18	1882-84
Harry Stovey	23	1884-86
Dave Orr	31	1886-94
Dave Orr, Heinie Reitz	31	1894-1912
Chief Wilson	36	1912-present

Home Runs

Players	Record	Years Held
George Hall	5	1876-79
Charley Jones	9	1879-83
Harry Stovey	14	1883-84
Ned Williamson	27	1884-1919
Babe Ruth	29	1919-21
Babe Ruth	59	1921-27
Babe Ruth	60	1927-61
Roger Maris	61	1961-98
Mark McGwire	70	1998-present

RBIs

Players	Record	Years Held
Deacon White	60	1876-79
Charley Jones, John O'Rourke	62	1879-80
Cap Anson	74	1880-82
Cap Anson	83	1882-83
Dan Brouthers	97	1883-84
Cap Anson	102	1884-86
Cap Anson	147	1886-87
Sam Thompson	166	1887-1921
Babe Ruth	171	1921-27
Lou Gehrig	175	1927-30
Hack Wilson	190	1930-present

Strikeouts

Players	Record	Years Held
Johnny Ryan	23	1876-77
Lew Brown	33	1877-78
Will White	41	1878-79
Will White, Pud Galvin	41	1879-80
Pud Galvin	57	1880-81
Pud Galvin	70	1881-83
Pud Galvin	79	1883-84
Sam Wise	104	1884-1914
Gus Williams	120	1914-38
Vince DiMaggio	134	1938-56
Jim Lemon	138	1956-61
Jake Wood	141	1961-62
Harmon Killebrew	142	1962-63
Dave Nicholson	175	1963-69
Bobby Bonds	187	1969-70
Bobby Bonds	189	1970-present

Walks

Players	Record	Years Held
Ross Barnes	20	1876-77
Ross Barnes, Jim O'Rourke	20	1877-79
Charley Jones	29	1879-81
John Clapp	35	1881-83
Tom York	37	1883-84
Candy Nelson	74	1884-85
Ned Williamson	75	1885-86
George Gore	102	1886-87
Paul Radford	106	1887-88
Yank Robinson	116	1888-89
Yank Robinson	118	1889-90
Bill Joyce	123	1890-92
Jack Crooks	136	1892-1911

Players	Record	Years Held
Jimmy Sheckard	147	1911-20
Babe Ruth	148	1920-23
Babe Ruth	170	1923-present

Hit by Pitch (since 1909)

Players	Record	Years Held
Dave Altizer, John Titus	16	1909-10
Louis Evans	31	1910-71
Ron Hunt	50	1971-present

Stolen Bases (starts over in 1897)

Players	Record	Years Held
Harry Stovey	68	1886-87
Hugh Nicol	138	1887-98
Ed Delahanty	58	1898-99
Jimmy Sheckard	77	1899-1910
Eddie Collins	81	1910-11
Ty Cobb	83	1911-12
Clyde Milan	88	1912-15
Ty Cobb	96	1915-62
Maury Wills	104	1962-74
Lou Brock	118	1974-82
Rickey Henderson	130	1982-present

Batting Average

Players	Record	Years Held
Ross Barnes	.429	1876-87
Tip O'Neill	.435	1887-94
Hugh Duffy	.440	1894-present

Slugging Percentage

Players	Record	Years Held
Ross Barnes	.590	1876-84
Fred Dunlap	.621	1884-87
Tip O'Neill	.691	1887-94
Hugh Duffy	.694	1894-1921
Babe Ruth	.846	1921-present

On-Base Percentage

Players	Record	Years Held
Ross Barnes	.462	1876-86
King Kelly	.483	1886-87
Tip O'Neill	.490	1887-94
Billy Hamilton	.523	1894-1923
Babe Ruth	.545	1923-present

Batting Streak

Players	Record	Years Held
Sam Thompson	21	1887-93
George Davis	33	1893-94
Billy Hamilton	36	1894
Bill Dahlen	42	1894-97
Willie Keeler	44	1897-1941
Joe DiMaggio	56	1941-present

Single Season Pitching Records
(acknowledging 1893 change in pitching distance)

Games Pitched

Players	Record	Years Held
Jim Devlin	68	1876-79
Will White	76	1879-93
Amos Rusie	56	1893-1908
Ed Walsh	66	1908-43
Ace Adams	70	1943-50
Jim Konstanty	74	1950-64
John Wyatt	81	1964-65
Ted Abernathy	84	1965-68
Wilbur Wood	88	1968-69
Wayne Granger	90	1969-73
Mike Marshall	92	1973-74
Mike Marshall	106	1974-present

Wins

Players	Record	Years Held
Al Spalding	47	1876-83
Old Hoss Radbourn	48	1883-84
Old Hoss Radbourn	59	1884-93
Frank Killen	36	1893-1904
Jack Chesbro	41	1904-present

Losses

Players	Record	Years Held
Jim Devlin	35	1876-79
Jim McCormick	40	1879-80
Will White	42	1880-83
John Coleman	48	1883-93
Duke Esper	28	1893-95
Ted Breitenstein	30	1895-97
Red Donahue	35	1897-present

Innings Pitched

Players	Record	Years Held
Jim Devlin	622	1876-79
Will White	680	1879-93
Amos Rusie	482	1893-present

Games Started

Players	Record	Years Held
Jim Devlin	68	1876-79
Will White	75	1879-93
Amos Rusie	52	1893-present

Complete Games

Players	Record	Years Held
Jim Devlin	66	1876-79
Will White	75	1879-93
Amos Rusie	50	1893-present

Strikeouts

Players	Record	Years Held
Jim Devlin	122	1876-77
Tommy Bond	170	1877-78
Tommy Bond	182	1878-79
Monte Ward	239	1879-80
Larry Corcoran	268	1880-83
Tim Keefe	361	1883-84
Old Hoss Radbourn	441	1884-86
Matt Kilroy	513	1886-93
Amos Rusie	208	1893-98
Cy Seymour	239	1898-1903
Rube Waddell	302	1903-04
Rube Waddell	349	1904-65
Sandy Koufax	382	1965-73
Nolan Ryan	383	1973-present

Walks

Players	Record	Years Held
Joe Borden	51	1876-77
Terry Larkin, Tricky Nichols	53	1877-78
The Only Nolan	56	1878-79
Jim McCormick	74	1879-80
Larry Corcoran	99	1880-82
Jim McCormick	103	1882-83
Frank Mountain	123	1883-84
Mickey Welch	146	1884-86
Toad Ramsey	207	1886-89
Mark Baldwin	274	1889-90
Amos Rusie	289	1890-93
Amos Rusie	218	1893-present

Hits Allowed

Players	Record	Years Held
Bobby Mathews	693	1876-83
John Coleman	772	1883-93
Amos Rusie	451	1893-94
Ted Breitenstein	497	1894-present

Home Runs Allowed

Players	Record	Years Held
Bobby Mathews	8	1876-79
George Bradley	12	1879-82
Jim McCormick	14	1882-83
John Coleman	17	1883-84
Larry Corcoran	35	1884-93
Harry Staley	22	1893-94
Jack Stivetts	27	1894-1930
Ray Kremer	29	1930-34
Phil Collins	30	1934-37
Lon Warneke	32	1937-48
Murry Dickson	39	1948-55
Robin Roberts	41	1955-56
Robin Roberts	46	1956-86
Bert Blyleven	50	1986-present

Shutouts

Players	Record	Years Held
George Bradley	16	1876-93
Amos Rusie	4	1893-96
Cy Young	5	1896-98
Jack Powell	6	1898-1902
Christy Mathewson	8	1902-04
Cy Young	10	1904-08
Ed Walsh	11	1908-10
Jack Coombs	13	1910-16
Grover Cleveland Alexander	16	1916-present

Saves

Players	Record	Years Held
Jack Manning	5	1876-93
Frank Dwyer	2	1893-94
Bill Hawke, Win Mercer	3	1894-95
Tom Parrott	3	1895-98
Kid Nichols	4	1898-1904
Joe McGinnity	5	1904-05
Claude Elliott	6	1905-06
George Ferguson	7	1906-09
Frank Arellanes	8	1909-11
Mordecai Brown	13	1911-24
Firpo Marberry	15	1924-26
Firpo Marberry	22	1926-49
Joe Page	27	1949-61
Luis Arroyo	29	1961-65
Ted Abernathy	31	1965-66
Jack Aker	32	1966-70
Wayne Granger	35	1970-72
Clay Carroll	37	1972-73

John Hiller	38	1973-83
Dan Quisenberry	45	1983-86
Dave Righetti	46	1986-90
Bobby Thigpen	57	1990-present

Runs

Players	Record	Years Held
Bobby Mathews	395	1876-79
Will White	404	1879-83
John Coleman	510	1883-93
Duke Esper	277	1893-94
Ted Breitenstein	321	1894-present

Earned Runs

Players	Record	Years Held
Bobby Mathews	164	1876-81
Lee Richmond	174	1881-83
John Coleman	291	1883-93
Scott Stratton	196	1893-94
Ted Breitenstein	238	1894-present

Earned Run Average

Players	Record	Years Held
George Bradley	1.23	1876-80
Tim Keefe	0.86	1880-93
Ted Breitenstein	3.18	1893-94
Amos Rusie	2.78	1894-95
Al Maul	2.45	1895-96
Billy Rhines	2.45	1896-98
Clark Griffith	1.88	1898-1901
Cy Young	1.62	1901-02
Jack Taylor	1.33	1902-05
Christy Mathewson	1.28	1905-06
Mordecai Brown	1.04	1906-14
Dutch Leonard	1.00	1914-present

Winning Percentage

Players	Record	Years Held
Al Spalding	.797	1876-80
Fred Goldsmith	.875	1880-84
Perry Werden	.923	1884-93
Hank Gastright	.750	1893-94
Jouett Meekin	.786	1894-95
Bill Hoffer	.838	1895-1907
Bill Donovan	.862	1907-12
Joe Wood	.872	1912-31
Lefty Grove	.886	1931-37
Johnny Allen	.938	1937-present

Going, Going, Gone

Gary Gillette

The home run is the most dramatic event in all major team sports. Of course, all game-winning plays are dramatic but, if you separate the actual event from its context in the game, no other scoring play could possibly have the impact that the home run does in Major League Baseball. What makes the long ball unique is the possibility that one swing of the bat can instantly score four runs, because that number is almost as many runs as the average team scores in a game.

The ultimate home run, the grand slam, is an event of volcanic proportions. Admittedly rare (only 120 were hit in 1998, 2.4 percent of all home runs), grand slams still accounted for 2.1 percent of the 23,297 runs scored in 2,432 games in 1998.

Compare this kind of impact with the National Football League, for instance. The past 20 years has seen each team scoring around 20 points, the number of scoring plays (counting touchdowns and extra points as one play) is somewhat less than the number of runs scored in a baseball game. However, even a seven-point touchdown cannot have the impact of a three-run homer, and few football games are won by a solitary score.

In the National Hockey League, the average number of goals scored per game historically is about a third less than in baseball. In 1997-98, teams scored fewer than three goals per game, a third less than in 1981-82. Because there are no three-goal shots, all scoring plays are equal, and none has the impact of a home run with runners on base. Ditto for professional soccer.

In the National Basketball Association, average points per team have ranged from 95 to 110 for the past 20 years. In roundball, scoring plays far outnumber that of any other major team sport, so no single type of play can have that large an impact. While a three-point play followed by a successful free throw constitutes twice as many points as the standard two-point field goal, even four points is a tiny percentage of overall scoring.

The game-winning hit, basket, touchdown, or shot on goal is climactic regardless of the sport, but the impact of the home run stands alone in team sports.

The Great Home Run Race Of 1998

While fans of other sports might argue, the great home run race of 1998 surely proved that the biggest individual record in all major team sports was Roger Maris' 61 home runs in '61. Baseball's position as king of the hill in American sports may have eroded since 1961, but the worldwide media attention devoted to Mark McGwire and Sammy Sosa showed just how important that record remains.

The only persuasive argument that could be made for another record would be for the career home-run record. If and when anyone challenges the legendary Henry Aaron's mark of 755 home runs, the sports world will again see the universal power and appeal of baseball's transcendent event.

Even more important, however, was the magical way in which McGwire and Sosa seized the hearts of baseball fans and non-fans alike, transfixing hundreds of millions both in North America and abroad as they chased the ghosts of Maris and Ruth throughout the long season. Sept. 8, 1998, is a night that will be remembered forever in sports; it was the night that McGwire broke the record by hitting number 62 against the Cubs—with Sosa playing right field and Maris' children sitting in the stands.

The images of Big Mac bearhugging his indefatigable pursuer—lifting the gracious and grinning Sammy Sosa off his feet—then turning to embrace Maris' children will be cherished by millions for the rest of their lives. To say that McGwire and Sosa saved baseball, as many have, is hyperbole, but to say that they reminded everyone of the beauty inherent in the game is an understatement.

There is no denying the greatness of the accomplishments of McGwire and Sosa, nor, for that matter, of those who came before them. But it is important to remember that all of these great seasons happened in the context of the changing nature of the game. Great athletes and their accomplishments can only be fully understood in the context of their times, and the 1920s, the 1960s, and the 1990s are unique in fundamental ways.

As late as 1918 it was still true that a team might hit as few as 10 homers in a season. The 1906-1910 White Sox (a great team unfairly dubbed as "hitless wonders" due to a low batting average despite decent-to-good offense), hit but 26 home runs in that five-year span. Those Pale Hose set a major-league team record in 1908 when they managed but three round-trippers.

These days, of course, power-hitting teams can easily slug 200 or more homers in a season. Seattle set the all-time mark of 264 in 1997. Six of the top 10 team marks in home runs hit during a season are from the past three seasons, while a seventh is from the offensive binge year of 1987.

In professional baseball's early days, in the 19th century, ballparks were often little more than city parks or cow pastures flanked by hastily-built wooden bleachers. With one battered, discolored baseball commonly kept in

play for a whole game, and, with games played in the late afternoon without artificial lighting, the ability of batters to slug a pitch past the outfielders was minimal.

Prior to Babe Ruth shocking the game with his 29 homers in 1919, the record had been held since 1884 by the National League's Ned Williamson, who launched 27 homers for the Chicago White Stockings (now the Cubs). Of course, Ned was helped not a little by the record short dimensions of his wooden ballpark, where the left field foul line was 180 feet in length and left center measured only 280 feet! In 1883 Williamson had led the league with 49 doubles because the park's ground rules specified that fly balls down the line were doubles, but that rule was changed to make them home runs in 1884.

Williamson and tiny, short-lived Lake Front Park (1883-84) may have been extreme examples, but they illustrate the point that high home-run totals in the 1800s tended to be a reflection of variances in ballparks, not the talents of individual players.

During the first two decades of the 20th century, great hitters like Ty Cobb, Honus Wagner, Tris Speaker, and Shoeless Joe Jackson dominated the game—that is to say, as much as any batter could dominate the pitchers and the lifeless, legally defaced baseballs of the so-called Dead Ball Era. Ty Cobb led the AL in slugging fully eight times even though he topped the league in homers but once and broke into double digits in homers only twice.

Wagner's career high in homers was only 10, while Jackson reached 12 homers only in his last season in 1920. These men were all powerful for their time, but they achieved their greatness by slashing line drives into the gaps, compiling impressive slugging numbers via high batting averages and lots of doubles and triples.

The rate of home runs per game in the first two decades of the new century was 10-20 percent of what it has become since then.

And Then Along Came Ruth

Into this pitching-dominated era strode one George Herman Ruth, a powerful, gifted athlete of gigantic impact, soon to be universally known as "the Babe," "the Bambino," or "the Sultan of Swat."

Ruth, a brilliant young southpaw, had won a combined 47 games in 1916 and 1917 and led the AL in ERA in 1916 and complete games in 1918. Nevertheless, he had nearly completed his conversion from pitching to playing the outfield. Ruth's pitching was a key element of the Red Sox world championships in 1916 and 1918, as he won all three of his starts and fashioned a record-low World Series ERA of 0.87. His ERA record lasted into the 1940s; his record for consecutive scoreless innings (29⅔) was broken by Whitey Ford with 33 much later.

Reading the tea leaves is always easier after the fact, of course, but the facts were very clear if only people had looked closely at them in the last years of the Dead Ball Era. All of Ruth's league-leading 11 homers in 1918 (in 95 games) were hit on the road. Fenway Park was a cavernous pitchers' park then, with the deepest part of center field nearly 500 feet away (488). In 1919 only 13 homers were hit in Fenway, but nine of those were launched by Ruth. (Due to World War I, both the 1918 and 1919 seasons were cut short so Boston played only 126 games in '18 and 138 games in '19.)

Ruth would start 15 games as a pitcher in '19, but he would also get 400 at bats for the first time. In those 432 times at bat, he would hit .322, lead the league in runs and runs batted in, plus slug a record 29 home runs. His prodigious talent at power hitting ended his career on the mound as surely as it ended the era of the dominating dead-ball pitcher.

Baseball's history is a vibrant collage composed in equal parts of fascinating fact and wholly fabricated legend. Just as one of the great myths of American history—that Abner Doubleday invented a game in a cow pasture near Cooperstown—was created to disguise the game's origins, another persistent myth has evolved to explain the home run explosion in the 1920s.

The theory of the "lively ball" has survived all attempts to deflate it because it simply and succinctly explains a very complex historical trend. The only problem with the "lively ball" theory is that there isn't a shred of evidence to support it, except for the coincidental "explosion" of home-run hitting in 1920.

Table 1
League-Leading Home Run Totals
By Era*

Era	AL High	AL Low	AL Avg	NL High	NL Low	NL Avg
1901-19	29	7	11	24	6	13
1920-41	60	33	47	56	15	34
1942-45	36	22	29	33	28	30
1946-60	52	32	39	51	23	44
1961-68	61	32	47	52	36	45
1969-98	56	32	43	70	35	43

* excludes strike seasons of 1981 and 1994

What really happened to cause such an earthquake in the National Pastime in 1920? Babe Ruth, arguably the greatest athlete of all time, was sold by the Red Sox to the Yankees, and he stopped pitching and concentrated on hitting. Ruth knew that he could hit home runs and win games by doing so and, while The Babe was the beneficiary of several supportive external factors, there was no intentional or unintentional change in the composition of the baseball. No "rabbit," no "juice"—just the effort of a man who had the Herculean strength of body and will to forever change the way the game was played.

A quick look at the historical record and a few reasonable projections are enlightening. If Ruth had played 142 games in 1918 (when he hit 11 homers in 95 games), he might have hit 16 home runs; (he hit none in Fenway that year). Assuming a neutral home park, he could have hit 25-30 homers—the same number he hit in 1919.

In 1919 Ruth hit 20 homers on the road and nine at home in 130 games. Pro-rate that to 142 games in a neutral home park, and he could easily have hit 40-45 homers, without even allowing for the obvious improvement he could make by giving up pitching every fourth day and specializing in hitting every day.

Thus, Ruth's 54 home runs with the Yankees in 1920 were not at all out of character with his production of the previous two seasons in Boston. Ruth's change of ballpark, focus on hitting, playing every day and swinging for the fences—that's all there was to it. In short, the

baseball version of the "Year of the Rabbit" never really happened.

Many baseball traditionalists didn't take kindly to this new emphasis on brute power, decrying the changes Ruth wrought in their beloved game. In 1920 Ruth dwarfed everyone else, hitting more homers in '20 than all but one team. Other hitters struggled to learn how to hit with over-the-fence power like the Bambino; the runner-up in homers in 1920 (George Sisler) hit but 19, while the NL leader (Cy Williams) hit only 15. These hitters were aided by two other developments: the prohibition against illegal pitches and the effort to keep clean balls in play.

Prior to the 1920 season, the Joint Rules Committee banned use of most foreign substances on the baseball. A few designated veteran spitball pitchers were allowed to continue to use their wet pitch; otherwise, loading up or defacing the ball was outlawed. As a result, the NL used 40 percent more new baseballs that year, and it's easy to understand that clean, white, unmarred balls were far easier for batters to see. Every hitter knows that seeing a pitch quickly and clearly is crucial to hitting it and hitting it hard; no juice is needed.

This already favorable trend for hitters was given an unintended (and unfortunate) boost on Aug. 16, 1920, when star shortstop Ray Chapman of Cleveland had his skull fractured by a Carl Mays pitch that he probably didn't see clearly. When Chapman died the next day, it gave a life-and-death impetus to keeping clean baseballs in play—baseballs that hitters could still see in the fading late afternoon light.

The well-deserved attention and honors Ruth garnered with his power hitting in 1920 snowballed the next year. Ruth broke his own record with 59 homers as the rate of home runs hit per game rose more than 80 percent in the NL from 1920 to 1921. In the AL, the homer rate rose another 30 percent in 1921 after rising more than 40 percent in 1920. Scoring leaped upward as well, and the Grand Old Game would never be the same.

Four Decades Of Power Baseball

The Yankees' homer-fueled rise to prominence in the 1920s gave the club the "Bronx Bombers" nickname—a name and an identity that remains to this day. Ruth's feats, along with those of Lou Gehrig, Joe DiMaggio, Mickey Mantle, Roger Maris, Reggie Jackson, and the rest of the pantheon of pinstriped sluggers, defined the Yankees, now and forever, as power-based. The Bombers have rarely tried a speed-and-defense approach since the days of the Bambino.

Led by the jaw-dropping power of Babe Ruth, the New York Yankees quickly became the most successful club in history. The Yanks made their World Series debut in 1921, losing to their Polo Grounds landlords in both the '21 and '22 Series. The Yankees won their first world championship against those same Giants in 1923, the year that Yankee Stadium, "The House That Ruth Built," opened to accommodate the adoring crowds that Ruth drew. Ruth broke his own record with 60 home runs in 1927, leading what is widely regarded as the best team in baseball history to a World Series sweep.

New York's success pushed other clubs into adopting the power offense. By 1922, two NL clubs (the Cardinals and Phillies) homered more than 100 times, an amazing feat for that time. when Ruth "slumped" to third in the AL in homers in 1922, two other clubs (the Browns and Athletics) outhomered the Yankees, though the Phillies and Athletics played in hitter-friendly parks (Baker Bowl and Shibe Park, respectively).

Ruth's feats may have seemed superhuman but, once the Sultan of Swat showed the way, other players followed his lead in swinging for the fences. Sluggers such as Rogers Hornsby (42 in 1922), Cy Williams (41 in 1923), Ken Williams (39 in 1922), and even Tilly Walker (37 in 1922), compiled big homer totals in the early 1920s—numbers that five years before would have been viewed as wildly improbable. However, the great Ruth generally maintained his home run pace even when other hitters dropped off. In 1926, for example, Babe led the AL with 47 homers though no one else connected for more than 19. A new generation of sluggers, including Lou Gehrig, Chuck Klein, Mel Ott, Hack Wilson, and Jimmie Foxx, inherited Ruth's mantle by the early 1930s. All of those players hit at least 40 homers in a season, with Wilson ripping 56 in 1930 (setting the NL record that stood till 1998) and Foxx powering 58 in 1938.

Aside from a new generation of muscular sluggers, a second factor that made the National Pastime home run-centric for decades was the relatively unchanging list of ballparks from the 1930s through the early 1950s. For a full half-century from 1903 until 1953, no major league changed cities. Adding to this remarkable stability was that, starting in 1909 with Philadelphia's Shibe Park and Pittsburgh's Forbes Field, teams moved quickly into new, modern concrete-and-steel ballparks. Only one park, Cleveland's Lakefront Stadium (later Municipal Stadium and Cleveland Stadium), opened between 1923, when Yankee Stadium debuted, and 1953. Knowing the home run was critical to winning, some clubs (especially the Boston Braves, Boston Red Sox, Pittsburgh Pirates, and Chicago White Sox) attempted to tailor their ballparks to benefit their top power hitters, shortening fences to the hitters' strong fields. These moves, all eventually reversed, took place between 1927 and 1947.

While overall offense (measured in runs per game) fluctuated somewhat, mostly in the NL, in the 1930s, 1940s, and 1950s, the home run was in the game to stay. The older style of "contact hitting" continued to fade, while strikeouts and walks climbed steadily through the 1940s and into the 1950s.

Table 2
Runs Per Game, Home Runs, and Other Selected Offensive Statistics

DECADE	R/G	HR	HR/G	SO/G	BA	OPS	SB/G
1901-1910	3.92	3207	.13	3.60	.252	.636	1.20
1911-1920	3.97	4255	.18	3.59	.258	.665	1.11
1921-1930	4.93	10829	.44	2.84	.287	.752	.56
1931-1940	4.85	13448	.55	3.36	.276	.735	.39
1941-1950	4.32	13460	.54	3.57	.260	.702	.35
1951-1960	4.39	20915	.85	4.53	.258	.721	.31
1961-1970	4.06	27470	.82	5.76	.249	.691	.43
1971-1980	4.15	29201	.73	5.05	.257	.703	.65
1981-1990	4.30	33172	.82	5.45	.258	.714	.77
1991-1998	4.67	32504	.95	6.17	.264	.745	.72

The war-affected seasons of 1942-1946, of course, in-

troduced quite a few temporary anomalies. Home run production dipped during World War II due to a loss of top talent (Nick Etten, for instance, paced the AL with 22 homers in 1944) and inferior-quality baseballs. The "Balata Ball," introduced for a few disastrous games in 1943, resulted in low-scoring games and fan complaints. The other balls used during wartime were not as dead as the balata, but were close.

Two teams from the Big Apple, the Giants and Yankees, were at or near the top of their leagues in home runs for most of the 1930s and 1940s, even when they weren't winning the pennant. This was partially due to sluggers like Lou Gehrig and Mel Ott, but also a result of the fact that the Polo Grounds and Yankee Stadium were oddly-shaped parks that inhibited scoring due to huge power alleys, while being good for home runs because of their short right field foul lines.

Nevertheless, many of the great NL teams of the 1930s-1950s did not rely on the home run to win. In the 1930s, the strong Cubs and the Gashouse Gang Cardinals were not overwhelming home run hitters. The great star-studded Cardinals of the early and late 1940s, featuring such stars as Walker Cooper, Stan Musial, Enos Slaughter, Harry Walker, and Terry Moore, were not big power hitters. Leo Durocher's Dodgers of the era weren't homer-based either, relying instead on multi-skilled players like Pee Wee Reese, Pete Reiser, and Dixie Walker. The Dodgers of the 1950s, however, were power-based, along with the Giants and Yankees. The fact that the New York teams were so powerful in what is often called the "Golden Age of Baseball" has clearly colored the public perception of home runs and their importance.

The infusion of African-American and Latin players in the 1950s, much more quickly in the National League, increased overall power and speed. Willie Mays, the league's top combination of power and speed of the time, slugged 50 homers in 1955 as well as 10 years later. In the early and mid-1950s, the NL's hitters outslugged their AL counterparts by a wide margin; the AL began to narrow the gap in the later years of the decade and, by 1960, the leagues were virtually even in homers per game.

Big changes came in the 1950s as several struggling franchises moved. First, the Boston Braves moved to Milwaukee for the 1953. Next, the St. Louis Browns defected to Baltimore in 1954, and the Philadelphia Athletics headed west to Kansas City in 1955. Milwaukee and Baltimore's new stadia were far more pitcher-friendly than their predecessors, while the new Kansas City park was about the same as Shibe Park. Following the 1957 season, the Dodgers and Giants headed west to Los Angeles and San Francisco. The L.A. Coliseum, with its 251-foot left-field fence, was a good park for run scoring and a pretty good place for right-handed power hitters. Seals Stadium in San Francisco, on the other hand, was a pitcher's park. Both makeshift facilities would be replaced by 1962.

The Decade Of The Pitcher

Two new teams were added to the AL in 1961, and the result was the greatest season ever up to that time for home run hitters. Yankee Stadium, the House that Maris

and Mantle rebuilt, rocked throughout '61 as the M&M boys staged a thrilling, season-long battle to break Ruth's 1927 record.

Roger Maris hit his record-breaking number 61 on the season's last day as he and his mates hit 240 homers, breaking the all-time club record by a wide margin. Nevertheless, scoring increased less than four percent in the AL, and home runs per game were up less than 10 percent—and both were similar to the NL, which didn't expand in 1961.

Conventional wisdom holds that homers went up because of the poor quality of the expansion pitchers faced by the AL's hitters, but the demonstrable truth is that home runs shot up because of the new ballparks added that year. Los Angeles' Wrigley Field, where the Angels played for one season, was a minor-league bandbox that saw 248 homers in 81 games due to the park's 345-foot power alleys. The addition of Minnesota's Metropolitan Stadium was also a boon to hitters.

The following season, the senior league also expanded. While the fallacy of expansion pumping up offense persists to this day, home runs per game actually *decreased* in the NL as offense decreased slightly in both leagues. One very big reason was that the Dodgers (as well as Angels) moved to Dodger Stadium, a terrific pitcher's park. Houston's temporary park was another pitchers' paradise, and the Giants were playing their second season in windy, cold, pitcher-friendly Candlestick Park.

Then, the roof caved in on the batters. Prior to the 1963 season, the MLB Rules Committee expanded the strike zone from the armpits to the tops of the shoulders. High fastballs became literally unhittable, and batting averages plummeted and scoring dropped sharply to levels not seen since the Dead Ball Era. Homers also declined, though they became paradoxically more valuable in a run-scarce environment.

Exaggerating the trend, changes in ballparks were almost all in favor of the pitcher. The Angels shared Chavez Ravine with the Dodgers from 1962 to 1965 before moving into their own big new park in 1966. Houston moved into the Astrodome, an even worse park to hit in than Colt Stadium. St. Louis' new Busch Stadium (opened in 1966) was far less accommodating to hitters than the old one. The New York Mets moved into Shea Stadium, a fine pitcher's park, in 1964. Four years later, the Athletics left Kansas City for the offense-deadening Oakland Coliseum.

The only new ballpark that helped hitters much from 1961 to 1968 was Atlanta-Fulton County Stadium, a place that put some juice back into Henry Aaron's home run totals. Though his greatness as a hitter masked it, Aaron had suffered for years playing in Milwaukee's large County Stadium. In the AL, home runs dipped 30 percent from 1961 to 1968; they dropped almost 50 percent in the NL in the same period. (See Table 2.) In 1965 Tony Conigliaro led the AL with just 32 four-baggers; two years later, Willie McCovey led the NL with just 36. By 1968, an amazing 21 percent of major league games were shutouts.

In '68, the so-called "Year of the Pitcher," hitters crashed in a collective futility not seen in 50 years. Only Carl Yastrzemski (.301) in the AL managed to hit .300, while Denny McLain racked up 31 victories. In the NL

starting pitchers Bob Gibson and Don Drysdale were truly awesome: Gibson posted a 1.12 ERA while "The Big D" set a record with 58 scoreless innings. Everyone knew things were way out of whack, so the strike zone was restored to its pre-1963 configuration after the season as four expansion teams prepared to start play.

The Leagues Divide And Diverge

In the first year of divisional play in 1969, home runs as well as scoring increased dramatically in both leagues. Unfortunately, the expansion to 24 teams and four divisions tends to get the credit and/or blame, while the big changes in the strike zone and the height of the mound (reduced from 15 to 10 inches) are generally, and unfairly, glossed over.

Two of the four expansion clubs (Kansas City and San Diego) played in below-average home run parks, while the other two (Montreal and Seattle) played in former minor league venues that were extremely good home-run parks. At Chicago's Comiskey Park, moving in the outfield fences helped to nearly double the park's homers from 1968. The same thing happened in Cleveland, where the Indians and their opponents combined for 236 homers in 1970 after just 116 the season before.

As the hitters were regaining dominance, six brand new stadia entered the picture in the following four years as the national game underwent a transition from intimate urban ballparks to plastic-turfed superstadia in many cities. These new venues emphasized what was seen as traditional pitching and defense in the then-dominant NL. Concurrently, the AL went for more offense as it retained more of the older, smaller, historic grass parks.

In 1970 the Seattle Pilots moved to Milwaukee, not nearly as good a place to hit. The Cincinatti Reds left old Crosley Field for Riverfront, Pittsburgh ripped down old Forbes Field and moved into Three Rivers, and the Phillies departed venerable Connie Mack Stadium for Veterans Stadium. In 1972 the Senators moved to Arlington Stadium in Texas, which did not alter offense much. The year after that, the Kansas City Royals moved into their brand-new stadium, a better place to score runs but not as good for homerun hitters.

In the early 1970s home runs and offense dipped again, especially in the AL. By 1973 things were bad enough that the American League chose to adopt the designated hitter rule to pump up both scoring and attendance. The revolutionary change had the desired effect, as the AL's scoring and homers leapt dramatically and, after leveling off somewhat, have stayed higher than that of the NL to the present day.

In the midst of these changes came another historic moment. Atlanta's Hank Aaron, who never once slammed 50 homers in a season but who hit 40 or more eight times, tied Ruth by hitting the 714th home run of his career on his first swing of the season on April 4. Then, four days later, another record once thought unbreakable was shattered as Hammerin' Hank clouted number 715 in the fourth inning of the Braves' home opener.

Like Roger Maris 13 years earlier, Aaron was forced to perform under unbelievable public pressure and media scrutiny as he approached the record, but the Braves great also had to triumph over a wave of virulent racism that produced numerous threats on his life.

Hitters Get The Upper Hand

Scoring stabilized from the late 1970s through the mid-1980s at about 4.5 runs per team per game in the AL, with the DH-less NL generally about half a run per team less. Home run rates were also relatively static over that time span. Then, in 1987, in a summer of record hot weather throughout the east and Midwest, all hell broke loose from the pitchers' viewpoint.

"The Year of the Hitter," as 1987 quickly became known, caused the same kind of consternation among fans, the media, and those in the game that "The Year of the Pitcher" caused in 1968. While scoring rose less than 10 percent in both leagues, homers in the AL were clubbed at a pace of one per team per game, highest in AL history and only slightly below the NL record pace of 1955. In the NL, homers jumped almost 20 percent to the highest rate since 1961. Excepting AL homers, even those offensive peaks were below levels seen in the 1950s.

As in 1968 a change in the strike zone definition was seized upon as the means to reverse the trend. Incongruously, the *de jure* (legal) strike zone was actually reduced (from the "batter's armpits" to the "midpoint between the top of the shoulders and the top of the uniform pants") in an attempt to expand the *de facto* (actual) strike zone, which many claimed had umpires calling balls on any pitch above the waist. Even though the pundits said that the besieged men in blue weren't following the new rules, both scoring and homers plummeted in 1988 to the levels of the early 1980s. The return to less extreme summer temperatures probably had as much to do with the drop. Runs and home runs in both leagues remained relatively stable from 1988 through 1992.

Camden Yards: Back To The Future

April 6, 1992, was a banner day in baseball history. On that day, Oriole Park at Camden Yards opened its gates in Baltimore for the first time. Instantly, every other ballpark in baseball became dated, and any multi-purpose stadium was living on borrowed time as a baseball venue.

As the first of what came to be called the "retro ballparks," Camden Yards received universal acclaim. Its old-time feel and old-fashioned attention to detail combined with its modern amenities to thrill fans and players alike. It succeeded beyond anyone's wildest dreams and spawned a legion of imitators in other cities.

One of the essential elements in creating the fan-friendly atmosphere at Camden Yards was keeping the fans close to the field. Not having to worry about configuring the park for football games, the architects placed the seats close to the action. This seemingly innocent detail automatically boosted offense, as the ability of the fielders to catch foul pop-ups was curtailed, resulting in more swings for the hitters. Of course, more swings mean more hits and more runs.

In 1993 the NL finally expanded to 14 teams (16 years after the AL), placing new franchises in Colorado and

Florida. The effect that playing baseball at a mile-high altitude has on the game can be seen in the statistics from Mile High Stadium, the temporary home of the Rockies for their first two seasons, and Coors Field, the Rockies' "retro" ballpark that opened in 1995. As in 1961, pumped-up offensive stats were seen in an expansion year. As in 1961, many blamed expansion for diluting the level of pitching talent, conveniently ignoring that expansion also dilutes the level of hitting talent. As in 1961, the engines fueling the offensive boom were the two new ballparks, both of which were exceedingly generous to hitters. In fact, Denver and Miami had the two best hitters' parks in the NL in both 1993 and 1994. (Note that the calculation for ballpark effect accounts for the performance of the home team, so having a bad pitching staff won't affect the park calculation.)

Playing in a converted football stadium in Denver in 1993 and 1994 boosted runs by about 30 percent over league average—a very large effect, equivalent to the effect of the best hitters' parks (e.g., Wrigley, Fenway) in the most extreme years in their long history. Playing in a more intimate (even though its dimensions are spacious by normal standards) baseball-only park has boosted scoring by 35-60 percent per year, a stupendous offensive inflation never seen since the advent of permanent concrete-and-steel ballparks in the early 20th century. The mile-high effect on home runs isn't quite as dramatic, but it's still huge.

After the big increase in offense and homers in 1993, the '94 season saw another jump. All summer long, fans and the media were abuzz with speculation about whether anyone could scale the imposing heights of Mount Maris. It was certainly not a coincidence that per-game attendance in 1994 was the highest ever seen in baseball, before or since. At the time play was tragically stopped by the players' strike after games of Aug. 11, two players already had hit 40 home runs: Matt Williams of the Giants (43) and Ken Griffey, Jr., of the Mariners (40). The Astros' Jeff Bagwell had connected for 39, Frank Thomas of the White Sox had clubbed 38, Barry Bonds of the Giants was next with 37, and Albert Belle of the Indians had 36. Since all clubs had between 45 and 50 games left to play, several of these sluggers could easily have cleared 50 home runs. Williams was on a pace to hit 61 home runs, equal to Maris in 1961, with Griffey, Bagwell, and Thomas close behind.

Of course, just because someone was on a pace to hit 62 home runs was no guarantee that breaking the record was inevitable. However, any one of these sluggers could have made a run at the record and generated the kind of excitement that the game saw in 1997 and 1998. Ten players still ended up with 30 or more homers, even in the truncated season.

A Confluence of Trends

Boiling down the wide range of factors influencing baseball games is incredibly complex. Multiply that complexity by 162 games and it boggles the mind. If it were simple to analyze baseball, predicting which team would win each season would be a snap. Prognostications in baseball—whether for a season, a series, or an individual

game—are by far the least accurate in all of team sports.

Stripping away all the hype in recent years about the offensive binge, the home run explosion, and the effects of repeated expansions, it's clear that the sky isn't falling in Major League Baseball. In the 1990s overall offense in the NL has been about the same as in the 1950s—and less than that of the 1920s and 1930s. In the AL, offense is at a level not seen since the slugging, swaggering days of the 1920s, but it's not unprecedented.

Homer-wise, the NL saw balls fly out of parks last year at the second-highest rate ever, but the past six years are completely in character with the 1950s. The AL has seen more homers per game than ever before, with 1996 and 1987 leading the way. Many trends, both intended and unintended, have combined to push scoring and homers up since the mid-1980s. The biggest reasons are: 1) the new ballparks; 2) changes in existing ballparks; 3) stronger hitters; and, 4) better bat selection. Putting them all together at the same time has produced the current big-offense climate in Major League Baseball.

Baseball fans crave intimacy, and intimacy helps hitters. The result: new baseball-only ballparks are almost always far better hitting venues than the parks they replace. Putting domes on ballparks in colder climates helps hitters as well. It's virtually impossible to overemphasize how much new ballparks and changes in existing ballparks have helped hitters. In the past two decades, teams have been constantly modifying parks to accommodate fans, and most of those modifications have directly or indirectly helped the hitters. Every time that premium seating is installed behind home plate and between the dugouts, foul pops that used to be caught fall into the stands. Outfield fences have been moved in more often than out, and fence height has been reduced in many parks. Some of the huge new scoreboards erected have helped block winds blowing in at the batter.

Three factors given far more play than they deserve for increased offense are: 1) expansion; 2) the supposed shrinking of the strike zone; and, 3) the use of performance-enhancing drugs or supplements. Evidence of abuse of steroids in baseball is scant at best; brute strength is not a requirement in baseball as it is in football. The effects of baseball players using legal, if controversial, supplements like creatine are completely unknown. It's entirely possible that creatine might make no difference in a ballplayer's performance. (Think of the placebo effect.)

While the strike zone has clearly been compressed at the top, it has also been expanded at the bottom and on the outside. The unhittable sinker or splitter below the knees has replaced the "high, hard one" of bygone days as the pitcher's best pitch. The downward metamorphosis of the strike zone started with the change in umpire's chest protectors, then continued as pitchers were taught to keep the ball down and to view the high fastball just as if it were a hanging breaking ball—a dangerous mistake.

The relentless "keep the ball down" coaching at all levels worked until good right-handed power hitters, who used to feast on high pitches and eschew low pitches, learned to reach down and *lift* any pitch above the knees. Once they developed that skill, their greatly increased arm and upper-body strength, courtesy of rigorous, year-round training, allowed them to hit those pitches with power. Improved strength and conditioning has also al-

lowed smaller players, whose game often depends on their speed or their defense, to hit more home runs. One rarely hears the term "singles hitter" anymore.

That's also why there's been such an increase in opposite-field home runs in recent years: power hitters with incredibly strong arms now stride into pitches on the outside part of the plate and literally muscle them 400 feet to the opposite power alley. When pitchers stopped busting hitters inside with high fastballs, hitters started crowding the plate and began taking advantage of the increased reach it gave them.

There's nothing mysterious about all of this; left-handed batters have been known as low-ball hitters for decades. It just took an adjustment in hitting styles for righty swingers. That takes years of practice, but professionals can and will make that kind of adjustment when their livelihood depends on it—and those hitters that can't change are quickly replaced

Another little-appreciated improvement in hitting has come from lighter bats. Most fans know that 30-34 ounce bats have replaced the 36-40 ounce cudgels wielded by the sluggers of yesteryear. Scientists studying the physics of hitting have found that the tradeoff in distance in hitting a ball with these lighter bats is very small, but lighter bats allow hitters to hit more pitches squarely because they can swing faster and have better bat control. A 425-foot homer is no better than a 410-foot homer, but hitting more pitches harder means more long flyballs—and that means more home runs.

Finally, while expansion has most certainly diluted the pitching, it has also diluted the hitting to a commensurate degree. This means that Roger Clemens and Randy Johnson will be facing more inferior hitters, just the same way

Mark McGwire and Ken Griffey, Jr. face more inferior pitchers. Thus, individual hitting and pitching records both become easier to break every time the league expands, but that doesn't mean overall offense must go up.

The upward trend in home runs has nothing to do with juicing the ball and everything to do with superb professional athletes reacting to changing circumstances. Hockey scoring has plummeted in the 1980s and 1990s, yet is anyone blaming the puck? If hockey scoring rebounds, as it surely will, will rumors spring up about the "lively puck"?

Baseball players, coaches, and managers are paid lots of money to adjust successfully when their opponents are beating them. Scoring has risen and fallen throughout baseball history for many reasons, and home run rates have done the same. Major fluctuations can be due to seasonal variances in the weather, an especially talented crop of young players entering the league, and to the adoption of different playing, pitching, hitting and coaching strategies. Right now, hitters have the upper hand. No doubt about it; power hitters are thriving. The beleaguered pitchers and their coaches haven't yet figured out how to counter the new generation of sluggers. But what's so bad about that? Fans love the long ball: it's no exaggeration to say that Babe Ruth and his majestic home runs saved baseball in the 1920s. Mark McGwire and Sammy Sosa enchanted fans and non-fans alike with their home-run heroics in 1998.

One of the oldest baseball adages is that pitching and defense win games. Without bothering to analyze the validity of that old chestnut, it's plainly obvious that home runs and scoring win the hearts of the fans.

Long live the home run. It's the best thing in sports.

Table 3
Runs, Home Runs, And Other Selected Offensive Statistics By Year

YEAR	R/G	HR	HR/G	SO/G	BA	OPS	SB/G	YEAR	R/G	HR	HR/G	SO/G	BA	OPS	SB/G
1901	4.99	455	.20	3.14	.272	.686	1.28	1931	4.81	1069	.43	3.20	.278	.730	.44
1902	4.43	354	.16	2.98	.267	.665	1.20	1932	4.91	1358	.55	3.19	.276	.737	.40
1903	4.44	335	.15	3.58	.262	.664	1.23	1933	4.48	1067	.44	3.03	.269	.706	.35
1904	3.73	331	.13	3.72	.247	.622	1.11	1934	4.91	1344	.55	3.45	.279	.738	.37
1905	3.90	338	.14	3.87	.248	.630	1.19	1935	4.90	1325	.54	3.26	.279	.738	.36
1906	3.62	263	.11	3.70	.247	.621	1.22	1936	5.19	1364	.55	3.33	.284	.753	.39
1907	3.53	244	.10	3.53	.245	.614	1.13	1937	4.87	1430	.58	3.63	.277	.742	.41
1908	3.39	267	.11	3.66	.239	.602	1.10	1938	4.89	1475	.60	3.41	.274	.739	.37
1909	3.55	259	.10	3.77	.244	.618	1.23	1939	4.82	1445	.59	3.46	.275	.740	.39
1910	3.84	361	.14	3.92	.249	.644	1.31	1940	4.68	1571	.64	3.66	.267	.726	.39
1911	4.51	514	.21	4.00	.266	.693	1.38	1941	4.49	1331	.53	3.55	.262	.709	.35
1912	4.53	442	.18	3.97	.269	.695	1.37	1942	4.08	1071	.44	3.40	.253	.674	.39
1913	4.04	469	.19	3.83	.259	.670	1.32	1943	3.92	905	.37	3.46	.253	.667	.41
1914	3.75	415	.17	3.92	.249	.647	1.23	1944	4.17	1034	.42	3.29	.260	.684	.37
1915	3.79	385	.15	3.85	.248	.645	1.06	1945	4.18	1007	.41	3.27	.260	.684	.40
1916	3.56	383	.15	3.82	.248	.638	1.10	1946	4.01	1215	.49	3.91	.256	.688	.36
1917	3.59	335	.13	3.46	.249	.635	.97	1947	4.36	1565	.63	3.69	.261	.713	.31
1918	3.63	235	.12	2.89	.254	.642	.98	1948	4.58	1555	.63	3.65	.263	.723	.33
1919	3.87	447	.20	3.07	.263	.670	.93	1949	4.61	1704	.69	3.61	.263	.728	.29
1920	4.36	630	.26	2.95	.277	.707	.70	1950	4.85	2073	.84	3.86	.266	.748	.26
1921	4.86	937	.38	2.83	.291	.750	.60	1951	4.55	1863	.75	3.77	.261	.722	.35
1922	4.87	1055	.43	2.80	.289	.750	.59	1952	4.18	1701	.69	4.19	.253	.696	.31
1923	4.82	980	.40	2.84	.284	.738	.64	1953	4.61	2076	.84	4.12	.264	.733	.27
1924	4.76	896	.36	2.69	.286	.741	.61	1954	4.38	1937	.78	4.13	.261	.726	.28
1925	5.13	1169	.48	2.72	.292	.765	.57	1955	4.49	2224	.90	4.39	.259	.729	.28
1926	4.64	863	.35	2.76	.281	.733	.52	1956	4.45	2294	.93	4.64	.258	.731	.29
1927	4.75	922	.37	2.79	.284	.738	.58	1957	4.31	2202	.89	4.84	.258	.718	.31
1928	4.73	1093	.44	2.88	.281	.741	.51	1958	4.28	2240	.91	4.95	.258	.721	.30
1929	5.19	1349	.55	2.86	.289	.770	.54	1959	4.38	2250	.91	5.09	.257	.718	.34
1930	5.55	1565	.63	3.21	.296	.790	.44	1960	4.31	2128	.86	5.18	.255	.714	.37

YEAR	R/G	HR	HR/G	SO/G	BA	OPS	SB/G
1961	4.53	2730	.95	5.23	.258	.730	.37
1962	4.46	3001	.93	5.42	.258	.722	.42
1963	3.95	2704	.84	5.80	.246	.683	.38
1964	4.04	2762	.85	5.91	.250	.692	.36
1965	3.99	2688	.83	5.94	.246	.685	.45
1966	3.99	2743	.85	5.82	.249	.688	.45
1967	3.77	2299	.71	5.99	.242	.666	.42
1968	3.42	1995	.61	5.89	.237	.641	.47
1969	4.07	3119	.80	5.77	.248	.691	.48
1970	4.34	3429	.88	5.75	.254	.713	.49
1971	3.89	2863	.74	5.41	.249	.684	.46
1972	3.69	2534	.68	5.57	.244	.666	.49
1973	4.21	3102	.80	5.24	.257	.706	.52
1974	4.12	2649	.68	5.01	.257	.696	.64
1975	4.21	2698	.70	4.98	.254	.704	.65
1976	3.99	2235	.58	4.83	.255	.684	.79
1977	4.47	3644	.87	5.16	.264	.733	.72
1978	4.10	2956	.70	4.77	.258	.705	.71
1979	4.46	3433	.82	4.77	.265	.730	.71

YEAR	R/G	HR	HR/G	SO/G	BA	OPS	SB/G
1980	4.29	3087	.73	4.80	.265	.717	.78
1981	4.00	1781	.64	4.75	.256	.691	.72
1982	4.30	3379	.80	5.04	.261	.715	.75
1983	4.31	3301	.78	5.15	.261	.717	.79
1984	4.26	3258	.77	5.34	.260	.710	.72
1985	4.33	3602	.86	5.34	.257	.717	.74
1986	4.41	3813	.91	5.87	.258	.723	.79
1987	4.72	4458	1.06	5.96	.263	.749	.85
1988	4.14	3180	.76	5.56	.254	.698	.79
1989	4.13	3083	.73	5.61	.254	.697	.74
1990	4.26	3317	.79	5.67	.258	.713	.78
1991	4.31	3383	.80	5.80	.256	.711	.74
1992	4.12	3038	.72	5.59	.256	.702	.77
1993	4.60	4030	.89	5.80	.265	.738	.72
1994	4.92	3306	1.03	6.18	.270	.766	.71
1995	4.85	4081	1.01	6.30	.267	.758	.73
1996	5.04	4962	1.09	6.46	.270	.770	.71
1997	4.77	4640	1.02	6.61	.267	.759	.73
1998	4.79	5064	1.04	6.56	.266	.758	.68

The Player Register

The Player Register consists of the central batting, baserunning, and fielding statistics of every man who has batted in major league play since 1871, excepting those men who were primarily pitchers. A pitcher's complete batting record, however, is included for those pitchers who also, over the course of their careers, played in 100 or more games at another position—including pinch hitter—or played in more than half of their total major league games at a position other than pitcher, or played more games at a position other than pitcher in at least one year. (Pitcher batting is also expressed in Batting Wins in the Pitcher Batting column of the Pitcher Register.)

The players are listed alphabetically by surname and, when more than one player bears the name, alphabetically by *given* name—not by "use name," by which we mean the name that may have been applied to him during his playing career. This is the standard method of alphabetizing used in other biographical reference works, and in the case of baseball it makes it easier to find a lesser-known player with a common surname like Smith or Johnson. This method also jibes with that employed in the Annual Record where, for example, Charles "Old Hoss" Radbourn is shown not as the puzzling O. Radbourn or H. Radbourn, as some reference books have it, but as C. Radbourn. On the whole, we have been conservative in ascribing nicknames, doing so only when the player was in fact known by that name during his playing days.

Each page of the Player Register is topped at the corner by a finding aid: in capital letters, the surname of, first, the player whose entry heads up the page and, second, the player whose entry concludes it. Another finding aid is the use of boldface numerals to indicate a league-leading total in those categories in which a player is truly attempting to excel (no boldface is given to the "leaders" in batter strikeouts, times caught stealing, at bats, or games played). An additional finding aid is an asterisk alongside the team for which a player appeared in postseason competition. Additional symbols denote All-Star Game selection and/or play; these appear to the right of the team/league column. Condensed type appears occasionally throughout this section; it has no special significance but is designed simply to accommodate unusually wide figures, such as the 4.000 slugging average of a man who, in his only at bat of the year, hit a home run.

The record for each man who played in more than one season is given in a line for each season, plus a career total line. If he played for more than one team in a given year, his totals for each team are stated on separate lines. And if the teams for which he played in his "traded year" are in the same league, then his full record is stated in both separate and combined fashion. (In the odd case of a man playing for three or more clubs in one year, with some of these clubs being in the same league, the combined total line will reflect only his play in that one league.) Also in this edition, we include position data in the "Yr" line for traded players. A man who played in only one year will have no additional career total line, since it would be identical to his seasonal listing.

Batting records for the National Association are included in The Player Register because the editors, like most baseball historians, regard it as a major league, inasmuch as it was the only professional league of its day and supplied the National League of 1876 with most of its players. In this edition of *Total Baseball*, we benefit from the SABR research project referred to in the Introduction to the Annual Record—which to date has produced extra-base hits, corrected averages, walks, and some stolen bases, strikeouts, and other data heretofore unavailable. Unless Major League Baseball reverses the position it adopted in 1969 and restores the NA to offical major league status, we will continue the practice of carrying separate totals lines for the National Association years rather than integrating them into the career marks of those players whose major league tenures began before 1876 and concluded in that year or later.

Gaps remain elsewhere in the official record of baseball and in the ongoing process of sabermetric reconstruction. The reader will note occasional blank elements in biographical lines, or in single-season columns; these are not typographical lapses but signs that the information does not exist or has not yet been found. In the totals lines of many players, an underlined figure indicates that the total reflects partial data, such as caught stealing for a man whose career covers the National League of 1918–1930 (during which this data was available only for 1920–1925), or batter strikeouts for a man whose career spanned both sides of the year 1909.

For a discussion of which data is missing for particular years, see "The History of Major League Baseball Statistics." Here is a quick summation of the missing data:

Hit batters, 1897–1908 NL/AL, 5 percent missing;
Caught stealing, 1886–1914, 1916 for players with fewer than 20 stolen bases, 1917–1919, 1926–1950 NL; 1886–1891 AA; 1890 PL; 1901–1913, 1916 for players with fewer than 20 stolen bases, 1917–1919 AL (1927 data, missing from the first edition, is now 90 percent complete); 1914–1915 FL;
Sacrifice hit, 1908–1930, 1939 (in these years fly balls scoring runners counted as sacrifice hits, and in 1927–1930 fly balls advancing runners to any base

counted as sacrifices);

Sacrifice fly, 1908–1930, 1939 (counted but inseparable from sacrifice hits), 1940–1953 (not counted);

Runs batted in, 1882–1887, 1890 AA; 1884 UA;

Strikeouts for batters, 1882–1884, 1890 AA; 1884 UA; 1897–1909 NL; 1901-1912 AL.

For a key to the team and league abbreviations used in the Player Register, flip to the last page of this volume. For a guide to the other procedures and abbreviations employed in the Player Register, review the comments on the prodigiously extended playing record below.

■ KID DE LEON

Ponce de Leon, Juan "Castilian Kid" (also played in 1874 as Kid Madrid)
b: 3/13/1460, Madrid, Spain   d: 2/25/1963, St. Augustine, Fl.   BR/TR, 5'11", 173 lbs.   Deb: 5/21/1874 FMUCH

YEAR	TM/L	G	AB	R	H	2B	3B	HR	RBI	BB	SO	AVG	OBP	SLG	PRO+	BR/A	SB	CS	SBR	FA	FR	G/POS	TPR
1874	Bos-n	52	277	73	94	7	4	1	14	2	4	.339	.342	.400	111	4	2	0	1	.892	3	*2-52	0.2
1875	Wes-n	2	3	1	1	0	0	0	1	0	0	.333	.333	.333	95	0	0	0	0	.500	0	/S-2	0.0
1883	Bal-a	28	121	12	33	2	1	1		0	8	.273	.318	.331	101	1				.901	0	C-16,O-10/S-2	0.0
1884	Was-U	86	371	75	107	12	5	1			11	.288	.309	.356	127	5	0			.913	0	1-62,O-15/C-8	0.9
	KC-U	1	4	1	0	0	0	0			0	.000	.000	.000	97	0				1.000	0	/1-1	0.0
	Yr	87	375	76	107	12	5	1			11	.287	.308	.355	126	-0	0			.914	0	1-63,O-15/C-8	0.9
1890	Cin-P	1	1	1	1	0	0	1	1	0	0	1.000	1.000	4.000	700	1	0			.000	0	/2-1	0.0
1908	Phi-N	1	0	0	0	0	0	0	0	0		—	—	—		0	0			.000	-1	/R-1	0.0
	Phi-A	9	31	5	9	3	0	0	2	0		.290	.290	.387	113	0	0			.899	-1	/3-8	0.0
1909	Phi-A	148	541	73	165	27	19	4	85	26		.305	.343	.447	146	26	20			.920	-5	*3-141	3.0
1910	Phi-A	146	561	83	159	25	15	2	74	34		.283	.329	.392	123	13	21			.934	3	*3-144	2.4
1911	Phi-A	148	592	96	198	40	4	11	115	50		.334	.379	.505	157	38	38			.912	-8	*3-147	3.3
1912	Phi-A	149	577	116	200	40	21	10	130	50		.347	.404	.541	171	50	40			.930	9	*3-149	5.4
1913	Phi-A	149	564	116	190	34	9	12	117	63	31	.337	.413	.493	171	48	34			.927	7	*3-148	6.1
1914	Phi-A	150	570	84	182	23	10	9	89	53	37	.319	.380	.442	151	33	19	20	-6	.929	8	*3-150	4.1
1915	Nwk-F	2	8	5	4	2	1	1	4	0	2	.500	.500	1.38	304	3	0			.977	1	/3-2	0.1
1916	NY-A	100	360	46	97	23	2	10	52	36	30	.269	.344	.428	130	12	15			.931	3	3-98	2.1
1917	NY-A	146	553	57	156	24	2	6	71	48	27	.282	.345	.365	109	6	18			.940	11	*3-145	2.7
1918	NY-A	126	504	65	154	24	5	6	62	38	13	.306	.357	.409	138	20	8			.943	11	*3-122	3.4
1939	*NY-A☆	141	567	70	166	22	1	10	83	44	18	.293	.346	.388	100	-0	13			.944	-2	*3-140	0.9
1941	*NY-A★	94	330	46	97	16	2	9	71	26	12	.294	.353	.436	98	-2	8	5	-1	.955	13	3-92	1.6
1942	*NY-A†	69	234	30	65	12	3	7	36	15	14	.278	.327	.444	98	-2	1	3	-2	.940	-8	3-67	-0.4
Total	2 n	54	280	74	95	7	4	1	15	2	4	.339	.348	.404	110	4	/2	0	1	.892	3	*2-52/S-2	0.2
Total	17	1694	6489	981	1983	329	100	100	992	502	184	.306	.354	.446	130	246	235	28		.938	41	*3-1409,1-126/CSO2R	45.1

Looking at the biographical line for any player, we see first his use name in full capitals, then his given name and nickname (and any other name he may have used or been born with, such as the matronymic of a Latin American player). His date and place of birth follow "b" and his date and place of death follow "d." Years through 1900 are expressed fully, in four digits, and years after 1900 are expressed in their last two digits.

Then comes the player's manner of batting and throwing, abbreviated for a lefthanded batter who throws right as BL/TR (a switch-hitter would be shown as BB for "bats both" and a switch thrower as TB for "throws both").

Next, and for most players last, is the player's debut date in the major leagues, all of which are reported now.

Some players continue in major league baseball after their playing days are through, as managers, coaches, or even umpires. A player whose biographical line concludes with an M can be located in the Manager Roster; one whose line bears a C will be listed in the Coach Roster; and one with a U occupies a place in the Umpire Roster. (In the last case we have placed a U on the biographical line only for those players who umpired in at least six games in a year, for in the 19th century—and especially in the years of the National Association—literally hundreds of players were pressed into service as umpires for a game or two. It would be misleading to accord such players the same code we give to Bob Emslie or Babe Pinelli.) The select few who have been enshrined in the Baseball Hall of Fame at Cooperstown, N.Y., are noted with an H. They are also listed in the Hall of Fame Roster found toward the end of Bill Deane's "Awards and Honors" essay. Also in *Total Baseball* since the fourth edition is an F on this line to denote family connection—father-son-grandfather or brother.

The explanations for the statistical column heads follow; for more technical information about formulas and calculations, see the Glossary. The vertical rules in the column-header line separate the stats into seven logical groupings: year, team, league; fundamental counting stats for batters; hits and plate appearances broken out into their component counting stats; basic calculated averages; sabermetric figures of more complex calculation; baserunning stats; fielding stats and Total Player Rating.

Absent from the Player Register in recent editions are some statistics present in the original: production as a raw, unadjusted figure (still available by simply adding OBP plus SLG, as well as in the Annual Record and Leaders sections); Park Factor for batters (still available from the Annual Record); Clutch Hitting Index, newly developed for *Total Baseball* but which we have judged to be of lesser interest and value than the more established sabermetric measures (like PRO, however, it is still present in the Annual Record and Leaders sections); and Total Average, a popular stat but one that is mirrored by Runs Created and Batting Runs, both of which are more accurate (TA is present in the Annual Record and Leaders sections). By deleting these statistics from the Register we have improved legibility, particularly by adding to the margin in the gutter of the book, and reduced some redundancy.

New to the fifth edition was additional hit-by-pitch data for batters in the 1897-1908 period, which is reflected in their on base percentages. We have also made an upward adjustment to overall league performance in the Federal League of 1914-15 and the Union Association of 1884 (thus lowering individual ratings), because while both leagues are regarded as major leagues, there can be no doubt that their caliber of play was not equivalent to that in the rival leagues of those years. Suffice it to say here that league at bats were reduced to 80 percent for the UA

and 90 percent for the FL. A full explanation of the adjustment procedure may be found in the Glossary, under "League Performance."

New to the fifth edition are RBIs for the American Association for 1885-87 and 1890 with data for some players in 1882-1884. Also added are RBIs and strikeouts, stolen bases and caught stealing (incomplete) and fielding data for the National Association.

YEAR Year of play (when a space in the column is blank, this indicates that the man has played for two or more clubs in the last year stated in the column; if those clubs were in the same league, then the man will also have a combined total line, beginning with the abbreviation "Yr" placed in the TEAM/L column)

Yr Year's totals for play with two or more clubs in same league (see comments for YEAR)

* Denotes postseason play, World Series or League Championship Series

TM/L Team and League (see comments for YEAR)

★ Named to All-Star Game, played

☆ Named to All-Star Game, did not play

† Named to All-Star Game, replaced because of injury

G Games

AB At bats

R Runs

H Hits (Bases on balls were counted as hits by scorers in 1887, but in *Total Baseball* they are not figured as times at bat, nor as hits.)

2B Doubles

3B Triples

HR Home Runs

RBI Runs Batted In

BB Bases on Balls (Bases on balls were counted as outs by scorers in 1876, but in *Total Baseball* they are not figured as times at bat nor as outs.)

SO Strikeouts

AVG Batting Average (Figured as hits over at bats; mathematically meaningless averages created through a division by zero are rendered as dashes; see Kid De Leon's entry for 1908 with Pit-N. League leaders in this category, as in others in the Player Register, are noted by bold type. However, some boldface leaders in batting average will have lower marks than other batters who are not credited with having won a championship; for a full explanation of the reasoning for this anomaly, see "The History of Major League Baseball Statistics."

OBP On Base Percentage (See comments for AVG)

SLG Slugging Average (See comments for AVG, and

note the use of condensed type to express Kid De Leon's maximum SLG in 1890.)

PRO⁺ Production Plus, or Adjusted Production (On Base Percentage plus Slugging Average, normalized to league average and adjusted for home-park factor.) See comments for /A.

BR/A Batting Runs (Linear Weights measure of runs contributed beyond what a league-average batter or team might have contributed, defined as zero. Occasionally the curious figure of -0 will appear in this column, or in the columns of other Linear Weights measures of batting, baserunning, fielding, and the TPR. This "negative zero" figure signifies a run contribution that falls below the league average, but to so small a degree that it cannot be said to have cost the team a run. The "/A" signifies that the measure has been adjusted for home-park factor and normalized to league average. A mark of 100 is a league-average performance. Pitcher batting is removed from all league batting statistics before normalization, for a variety of reasons expanded upon in the Glossary. Three-year averages are employed for batting park factors. If a team moved or the park changed dramatically, then two-year averages are employed; if the park was used for only one year, then of course only that run-scoring data is used.)

SB Stolen Bases (for 1886 to the present, plus new data for the NA years, 1871-1875.)

CS Caught Stealing (Available 1915, 1916 for players with 20 or more stolen bases, 1920–1925, 1951–date NL; 1914–1915, 1916 for players with 20 or more stolen bases, 1920 to date AL with scattered data still missing from 1927.)

SBA Stolen Base Average (Stolen bases divided by attempts; availability dependent upon CS as shown above.)

SBR Stolen Base Runs (This is a Linear Weights measure of runs contributed *beyond* what a league-average base stealer might have gained, defined as zero and calculated on the basis of a 66.7 percent success rate, which computer simulations have shown to be the break-even point beyond which stolen bases have positive run value to the team; see the general introduction to Part Two and the Glossary. The presence of a figure in the SBR column in the Player Register is dependent upon the availability of CS as shown above. Lifetime Stolen Base Runs are not totaled where data is incomplete, but seasonal SBRs are reflected in the seasonal Total Player Ratings, which in turn are added to form the lifetime Total Player Rating.)

FA Fielding Average, often called Fielding Percentage as well (putouts plus assists divided by putouts plus assists plus errors, here calculated only for the position at which a man played the most games in a season or career.)

FR Fielding Runs (The Linear Weights measure of

runs saved *beyond* what a league-average player at that position might have saved, defined as zero; this stat is calculated to take account of the particular demands of the different positions; see Glossary for formulas, and note new method for the positional adjustment.)

G/POS Positions played (This is a ranking from left to right by frequency of the positions played in the field or at designated hitter. An asterisk to the left of the position indicates, generally, that in a given year the man played about two-thirds of his team's scheduled games at that position; more precisely, it is figured at 20 games in 1871, 30 in 1872, 35 in 1873, 40 in 1874, and 50 in 1875; two-thirds of the scheduled games in 1876-1900, and 100 or more games since. When a slash separates positions, the man played those positions listed to the left of the slash in 10 or more games and the positions to the right of the slash in fewer than 10 games. If there is no slash, he played all positions listed in 10 or more games. For the lifetime line, the asterisk signifies 1,000 games and the slash marks a dividing point of 100 games. A player's POS column will list him as a pinch runner or pinch hitter in only those years in which he appeared at no other position. New to the fourth edition were listings of the number of games played at the individual's two most common positions. New to the fifth edition were games played at the third and fourth positions when space permits. The positions and their abbreviations are)

1: First base	P: Pitcher
2: Second base	D: Designated hitter
S: Shortstop	R: Runner (pinch)
3: Third base	H: Hitter (pinch)
O: Outfield	M: Manager (playing)
C: Catcher	

TPR Total Player Rating (This is the sum of a player's Adjusted Batting Runs, Fielding Runs, and Base Stealing Runs, minus his positional adjustment, all divided by the Runs Per Win factor for that year—generally around 10, historically in the 9–11 range. For more information on the formula and the Runs Per Win concept, see the general introduction to the statistical section and the Glossary. In the lifetime line, the TPR is the sum of the seasonal TPRs. For men who were primarily pitchers but whose extent of play at other positions warrants a listing in the Player Register as well as the Pitcher Register, the TPR may be listed as 0.0; this signifies that their batting records are summed up in the Total Pitcher Index [TPI] column of the Pitcher Register.) Note that the TPR (and the TPI, Total Pitcher Index) from the fourth edition on will differ from those in earlier volumes, for four reasons which are explained in greater detail in the Glossary. (1) A

broader and more sophisticated computation of the positional adjustment to Batting Runs has improved the accuracy and reasonableness of the method, by which the TPR of those who play skill positions like shortstop and second base tend to be boosted and the TPR of the sluggers who customarily play first base and left field are generally diminished. (2) Because games in left, center, and right fields are now available for all outfielders, center fielders no longer need be compared to an average of the regular center fielders and now may be set against all the men who played center, thus tending to elevate their Fielding Runs. (3) Because Hit Batsmen data is now available for the 1903–1908 period, plus considerable data for the years 1897–1902, men like Frank Chance, who was hit over 100 times in his career, increase their Batter Ratings perceptibly. (4) And for players who were both batters and pitchers, the method of allocating Wins between TPR and TPI (Total Pitcher Index) was improved. Previously, if a pitcher pitched in over half his games, all his batting was included with his pitcher rating (TPI); if he pitched in less than half his games, his Batting Wins were thrown over to his batter rating (TPR), with his TPI including only his Pitching Wins and Pitcher Defense. The new method prorates batting proportionally with the number of games pitched. In addition, fielding ratings at nonpitching positions for players who pitched in over half their games, previously omitted, are now part of the Total Baseball Ranking. In any case, the TPR values of batter-pitchers should remain about the same. Thus in 1918, Babe Ruth now has a batter rating of 2.6 Wins and a pitcher rating of 2.9 (total 5.5). In some previous editions his marks used to be 4.1 and 1.0, respectively, or 5.1 overall, with none of his batting counted in with his pitching record even though he pitched 20 of 95 games. The large jump in his pitcher rating is because now his pitcher batting is compared against average batting for pitchers.

Total For players whose careers include play in the National Association as well as other major leagues, two totals are given, as described above and as illustrated in Kid De Leon's record, where the record of his years in the National Association is shown alongside the notation "Total 2 n," where *2* stands for the number of years totaled and *n* stands for National Association. For players whose careers began in 1876 or later, the lifetime record is shown alongside the notation "Total x," where *x* stands for the number of post-1875 years totaled. Note the underlined entries in the record for Kid De Leon, reflecting the partial data for RBIs, batter strikeouts, stolen bases, and times caught stealing.

YEAR	TM/L	G	AB	R	H	2B	3B	HR	RBI	BB	SO	AVG	OBP	SLG	PRO+	BR/A	SB	CS	SBR	FA	FR	G/POS	TPR
■ **HANK AARON**	Aaron, Henry Louis "Hammerin' Hank" b: 2/5/34, Mobile, Ala. BR/TR, 6', 180 lbs. Deb: 4/13/54 FH																						
1954	Mil-N	122	468	58	131	27	6	13	69	28	39	.280	.325	.447	105	1	2	2	-1	.970	-2	*O-116	-0.6
1955	Mil-N★	153	602	105	189	**37**	9	27	106	49	61	.314	.369	.540	144	36	3	1	0	.967	6	*O-126,2-27	3.8
1956	Mil-N★	153	609	106	**200**	**34**	14	26	92	37	54	**.328**	.369	.558	154	**43**	2	4	-2	.962	10	*O-152	4.4
1957	*Mil-N★	151	615	**118**	198	27	6	**44**	**132**	57	58	.322	.379	.600	170	58	1	1	-0	.983	2	*O-150	5.0
1958	*Mil-N★	153	601	109	196	34	4	30	95	59	49	.326	.387	.546	157	47	4	1	1	.984	2	*O-153	4.1
1959	Mil-N★	154	629	116	**223**	46	7	39	123	51	54	**.355**	.406	**.636**	**188**	**75**	8	0	2	.982	-2	*O-152/3-5	**6.6**
1960	Mil-N★	153	590	102	172	20	11	40	**126**	60	63	.292	.359	.566	160	46	16	7	1	.982	9	*O-153/2-2	4.8
1961	Mil-N★	155	603	115	197	**39**	10	34	120	56	64	.327	.386	.594	**165**	**54**	21	9	1	.982	12	*O-154/3-2	**5.6**
1962	Mil-N★	156	592	127	191	28	6	45	128	66	73	.323	.393	.618	171	58	15	7	0	.980	8	*O-153/1-1	5.5
1963	Mil-N★	161	631	**121**	201	29	4	**44**	**130**	78	94	.319	.394	**.586**	**180**	**64**	31	5	**6**	.979	-1	*O-161	6.5
1964	Mil-N★	145	570	103	187	30	2	24	95	62	46	.328	.394	.514	152	40	22	4	4	.983	11	*O-139,2-11	5.1
1965	Mil-N★	150	570	109	181	**40**	1	32	89	60	81	.318	.384	.560	161	45	24	4	5	.987	10	*O-148	5.5
1966	Atl-N★	158	603	117	168	23	1	**44**	**127**	76	96	.279	.360	.539	144	35	21	3	5	.988	9	*O-158/2-2	4.3
1967	Atl-N★	155	600	**113**	184	37	3	**39**	109	63	97	.307	.373	**.573**	169	**52**	17	6	2	.979	12	*O-152/2-1	6.1
1968	Atl-N★	160	606	84	174	33	4	29	86	64	62	.287	.356	.498	154	39	28	5	5	.991	14	*O-151,1-14	**5.5**
1969	*Atl-N★	147	547	100	164	30	3	44	97	87	47	.300	.398	.607	177	56	9	10	-3	.982	6	*O-144/1-4	5.2
1970	Atl-N★	150	516	103	154	26	1	38	118	74	63	.298	.389	.574	146	33	9	0	3	.977	5	*O-125,1-11	3.2
1971	Atl-N★	139	495	95	162	22	3	47	118	71	58	.327	.414	**.669**	**190**	58	1	1	-0	.996	-8	1-71,O-60	4.2
1972	Atl-N★	129	449	75	119	10	0	34	77	92	55	.265	.391	.514	142	27	4	0	1	.987	1	*1-109,O-15	1.9
1973	Atl-N★	120	392	84	118	12	1	40	96	68	51	.301	.406	.643	173	39	1	1	-0	.977	2	*O-105	3.7
1974	Atl-N★	112	340	47	91	16	0	20	69	39	29	.268	.343	.491	126	11	1	0	0	.986	-4	O-89	0.3
1975	Mil-A★	137	465	45	109	16	2	12	60	70	51	.234	.336	.355	95	-2	0	1	-1	1.000	-1	*D-128/O-3	-0.7
1976	Mil-A	85	271	22	62	8	0	10	35	35	38	.229	.317	.369	102	1	0	1	-1	1.000	-0	D-74/O-1	-0.2
Total	23	3298	12364	2174	3771	624	98	755	2297	1402	1383	.305	.377	.555	156	914	240	73	28	.980	101	*O-2760,1-210,D/23	89.8
■ **TOMMIE AARON**	Aaron, Tommie Lee b: 8/5/39, Mobile, Ala. d: 8/16/84, Atlanta, Ga. BR/TR, 6'1", 200 lbs. Deb: 4/10/62 FC																						
1962	Mil-N	141	334	54	77	20	2	8	38	41	58	.231	.315	.374	86	-7	6	0	2	.989	2	*1-110,O-42/2-1,3-1	-0.8
1963	Mil-N	72	135	6	27	6	1	1	15	11	27	.200	.260	.281	57	-8	0	3	-2	1.000	-6	1-45,O-14/2-6,3-1	-1.8
1965	Mil-N	8	16	1	3	0	0	0	1	1	2	.188	.235	.188	21	-2	0	0	0	.961	0	/1-6	-0.2
1968	Atl-N	98	283	21	69	10	3	1	25	21	37	.244	.296	.311	82	-6	3	4	-2	.942	-4	O-62,1-28/3-1	-1.9
1969	*Atl-N	49	60	13	15	2	0	1	5	6	6	.250	.318	.333	82	-1	0	1	-1	1.000	1	1-16/O-8	-0.2
1970	Atl-N	44	63	3	13	2	0	2	7	3	10	.206	.242	.333	50	-5	0	0	0	.955	-2	1-16,O-12	-0.8
1971	Atl-N	25	53	4	12	2	0	0	3	3	5	.226	.268	.264	48	-4	0	0	0	.974	2	1-11/3-7	-0.2
Total	7	437	944	102	216	42	6	13	94	86	145	.229	.293	.327	75	-31	9	8	-2	.990	-7	1-232,O-138/3-10,2	-5.9
■ **JOHN ABADIE**	Abadie, John b: 11/4/1854, Philadelphia, Pa. d: 5/17/05, Pemberton, N.J. BR/TR, 6', 192 lbs. Deb: 6/10/1875																						
1875	Cen-n	11	45	3	10	0	0	0	4	0	3	.222	.222	.222	60	-2	1	0	0	.912	-0	1-11	-0.1
	Atl-n	1	4	1	1	0	0	0	1	0	0	.250	.250	.250	85	-0	0	0	0	.875	-0	/1-1	0.0
	Yr	12	49	4	11	0	0	0	5	0	3	.224	.224	.224	62	-2	1	0	0	.910	-1	1-12	-0.1
■ **ED ABBATICCHIO**	Abbaticchio, Edward James "Batty" b: 4/15/1877, Latrobe, Pa. d: 1/6/57, Ft.Lauderdale, Fla. BR/TR, 5'11", 170 lbs. Deb: 9/4/1897																						
1897	Phi-N	3	10	0	3	0	0	0	0	1		.300	.364	.300	78	-0	0			.875	-2	/2-3	-0.2
1898	Phi-N	25	92	9	21	4	0	0	14	7		.228	.290	.272	64	-4	4			.818	-13	3-20/2-4,O-1	-1.6
1903	Bos-N	136	489	61	111	18	5	1	46	52		.227	.306	.290	73	-16	23			.934	3	*2-116,S-17	-0.7
1904	Bos-N	154	579	76	148	18	10	3	54	40		.256	.309	.337	103	2	24			.915	2	*S-154	0.9
1905	Bos-N	153	610	70	170	25	12	3	41	35		.279	.326	.374	111	7	30			.919	-12	*S-152/O-1	-0.2
1907	Pit-N	147	496	63	130	14	7	2	82	65		.262	.357	.331	114	10	35			.951	-23	*2-147	-1.6
1908	Pit-N	146	500	43	125	16	7	1	61	58		.250	.336	.316	108	7	22			**.969**	-12	*2-144	-0.8
1909	*Pit-N	36	87	13	20	0	0	1	16	19		.230	.368	.264	89	-0	2			.966	2	S-18/2-4,O-1	0.2
1910	Pit-N	3	3	0	0	0	0	0	0	0	0	.000	.000	.000	-95	-1	0			.500	-0	/S-1	-0.1
	Bos-N	52	178	20	44	4	2	0	10	12	16	.247	.295	.292	68	-7	2			.910	-3	S-46/2-1	-0.9
	Yr	55	181	20	44	4	2	0	10	12	16	.243	.290	.287	66	-8	2			.907	-4	S-47/2-1	-1.0
Total	9	855	3044	355	772	99	43	11	324	289	16	.254	.325	.325	98	-4	142			.949	-59	2-419,S-388/3-20,O	-5.0
■ **CHARLIE ABBEY**	Abbey, Charles S. b: 10/14/1866, Falls City, Neb. d: 4/27/26, San Francisco, Cal. BL/TL, 5'8.5", 169 lbs. Deb: 8/16/1893																						
1893	Was-N	31	116	11	30	1	4	0	12	12	6	.259	.333	.336	80	-3	9			.937	3	O-31	-0.2
1894	Was-N	129	523	95	164	26	18	7	101	58	38	.314	.389	.472	110	9	31			.909	14	*O-129	1.0
1895	Was-N	132	511	102	141	14	10	8	84	43	41	.276	.340	.389	89	-9	28			.903	10	*O-132	-0.8
1896	Was-N	79	301	47	79	12	6	1	49	27	20	.262	.331	.352	80	-9	16			.879	-6	O-78/P-1	-1.8
1897	Was-N	80	300	52	78	14	8	3	34	27		.260	.329	.390	90	-5	9			.946	2	O-80	-0.8
Total	5	451	1751	307	492	67	46	19	280	167	105	.281	.351	.404	94	-17	93			.910	21	O-450/P-1	-2.6
■ **FRED ABBOTT**	Abbott, Harry Frederick (b: Harry Frederick Winbigler) b: 10/22/1874, Versailles, Ohio d: 6/11/35, Los Angeles, Cal. BR/TR, 5'10", 180 lbs. Deb: 4/25/03																						
1903	Cle-A	77	255	25	60	11	3	1	25	7		.235	.270	.314	76	-8	8			.958	9	C-71/1-3	0.8
1904	Cle-A	41	130	14	22	4	2	0	12	6		.169	.206	.231	38	-9	2			.953	-3	C-33/1-7	-1.0
1905	Phi-N	42	128	9	25	6	1	0	12	6		.195	.248	.258	53	-8	4			.954	-0	C-34/1-5	-0.5
Total	3	160	513	48	107	21	6	1	49	19		.209	.248	.279	61	-24	14			.956	6	C-138/1-15	-0.7
■ **JEFF ABBOTT**	Abbott, Jeffrey William b: 8/17/72, Atlanta, Ga. BR/TL, 6'2", 190 lbs. Deb: 6/10/97																						
1997	Chi-A	19	38	8	10	1	0	1	2	0	6	.263	.263	.368	65	-2	0	0	0	1.000	-1	O-10/D-3	-0.3
1998	Chi-A	89	244	33	68	14	1	12	41	9	28	.279	.304	.492	105	1	3	3	-1	.971	-13	O-76/D-2	-1.4
Total	2	108	282	41	78	15	1	13	43	9	34	.277	.299	.475	100	-1	3	3	-1	.974	-14	/O-86,D-5	-1.7
■ **KURT ABBOTT**	Abbott, Kurt Thomas b: 6/2/69, Zanesville, Ohio BR/TR, 6', 185 lbs. Deb: 9/8/93																						
1993	Oak-A	20	61	11	15	1	0	3	9	3	20	.246	.281	.410	89	-1	2	0	1	.971	1	O-13/S-6,2-2	0.1
1994	Fla-N	101	345	41	86	17	3	9	33	16	98	.249	.292	.394	75	-13	3	0	1	.966	-8	S-99	-1.2
1995	Fla-N	120	420	60	107	18	7	17	60	36	110	.255	.321	.452	101	-1	4	3	-1	.959	-11	*S-115	-0.2
1996	Fla-N	109	320	37	81	18	7	8	33	22	99	.253	.307	.428	94	-4	3	3	-1	.969	2	S-44,3-33,2-20	0.2
1997	*Fla-N	94	252	35	69	18	2	6	30	14	68	.274	.315	.433	98	-2	3	1	0	.969	-3	2-54,O-10/S-7,3D	-0.1
1998	Oak-A	35	123	17	33	7	1	2	9	10	34	.268	.328	.390	89	-2	2	1	0	.909	-11	S-28/O-5,3-1,D-3	-1.0
	Col-N	42	71	9	18	6	0	3	15	2	19	.254	.284	.465	75	-3	0	0	0	.929	-0	/O-9,2-7,S-7,3-3,D	-0.2
Total	6	521	1592	210	409	85	20	48	189	103	448	.257	.309	.426	91	-26	17	8	0	.959	-30	S-306/2-83,3-41,OD	-2.4
■ **ODY ABBOTT**	Abbott, Ody Cleon b: 9/5/1888, New Eagle, Pa. d: 4/13/33, Washington, D.C. BR/TR, 6'2", 180 lbs. Deb: 9/10/10																						
1910	StL-N	22	70	2	13	2	1	0	6	6	20	.186	.250	.243	46	-5	3			.982	1	O-21	-0.5
■ **DAVE ABERCROMBIE**	Abercrombie, David b: 5/6/1840, Falkirk, Scotland d: 9/2/16, Baltimore, Md. Deb: 10/21/1871																						
1871	Tro-n	1	4	0	0	0	0	0	0	0	0	.000	.000	.000	-99	-1	0	0	0	.667	-0	/S-1	-0.1
■ **CLIFF ABERSON**	Aberson, Clifford Alexander "Kif" b: 8/28/21, Chicago, Ill. d: 6/23/73, Vallejo, Cal. BR/TR, 6', 200 lbs. Deb: 7/18/47																						
1947	Chi-N	47	140	24	39	6	3	4	20	20	32	.279	.369	.450	121	4	0			.920	-1	O-40	0.1
1948	Chi-N	12	32	1	6	1	0	1	6	5	10	.188	.297	.313	68	-1	0			.867	-1	/O-8	-0.3
1949	Chi-N	4	7	0	0	0	0	0	0	0	2	.000	.000	.000	-99	-2	0			1.000	0	/O-1	-0.2
Total	3	63	179	25	45	7	3	5	26	25	44	.251	.343	.408	103	1	0			.913	-2	/O-49	-0.4
■ **SHAWN ABNER**	Abner, Shawn Wesley b: 6/17/66, Hamilton, Ohio BR/TR, 6'1", 190 lbs. Deb: 9/8/87																						
1987	SD-N	16	47	5	13	3	1	2	7	2	8	.277	.306	.511	116	1	1	0	0	.926	1	O-14	0.1
1988	SD-N	37	83	6	15	3	0	2	5	4	19	.181	.227	.289	48	-6	0	1	-1	.982	-4	O-35	-1.2
1989	SD-N	57	102	13	18	4	0	2	14	5	20	.176	.215	.275	39	-8	1	0	0	1.000	-9	O-51	-1.9
1990	SD-N	91	184	17	45	9	0	1	15	9	28	.245	.287	.310	64	-9	2	3	-1	.991	-7	O-62	-1.9

YEAR	TM/L	G	AB	R	H	2B	3B	HR	RBI	BB	SO	AVG	OBP	SLG	PRO+	BR/A	SB	CS	SBR	FA	FR	G/POS	TPR
1991	SD-N	53	115	15	19	4	1	1	5	7	25	.165	.220	.243	29	-11	0	0	0	1.000	1	O-39	-1.1
	Cal-A	41	101	12	23	6	1	2	9	4	18	.228	.257	.366	71	-4	1	2	-1	1.000	-1	O-38/D-3	-0.7
1992	Chi-A	97	208	21	58	10	1	1	16	12	35	.279	.327	.351	91	-2	1	2	-1	1.000	-13	O-94/D-1	-1.8
Total	6	392	840	89	191	39	4	11	71	43	153	.227	.271	.323	65	-40	6	8	-3	.993	-32	O-333/D-4	-8.5

■ CAL ABRAMS Abrams, Calvin Ross b: 3/2/24, Philadelphia, Pa. d: 2/25/97, Ft.Lauderdale, Fla. BL/TL, 6', 185 lbs. Deb: 4/20/49

YEAR	TM/L	G	AB	R	H	2B	3B	HR	RBI	BB	SO	AVG	OBP	SLG	PRO+	BR/A	SB	CS	SBR	FA	FR	G/POS	TPR
1949	Bro-N	8	24	6	2	1	0	0	0	7	6	.083	.290	.125	15	-3	1			.833	-1	/O-7	-0.4
1950	Bro-N	38	44	5	9	1	0	0	4	9	13	.205	.340	.227	51	-3	0			1.000	-3	O-15	-0.6
1951	Bro-N	67	150	27	42	8	0	3	19	36	26	.280	.419	.393	118	6	3	2	-0	.944	-1	O-34	0.3
1952	Bro-N	10	10	1	2	0	0	0	0	2	4	.200	.333	.200	51	-1	0	0	0	.000	-0	/O-1	-0.1
	Cin-N	71	158	23	44	9	2	2	13	19	25	.278	.356	.399	109	2	1	0	0	1.000	-5	O-46	-0.4
	Yr	81	168	24	46	9	2	2	13	21	29	.274	.354	.387	106	2	1	0	0	1.000	-5	O-47	-0.5
1953	Pit-N	119	448	66	128	10	6	15	43	58	70	.286	.368	.435	109	7	4	4	-1	.973	5	*O-112	0.6
1954	Pit-N	17	42	6	6	1	1	0	2	10	9	.143	.308	.214	39	-4	0	0	0	1.000	0	O-13	-0.4
	Bal-A	115	423	67	124	22	7	6	25	72	67	.293	.401	.421	135	23	1	4	-2	.977	4	*O-115	2.0
1955	Bal-A	118	309	56	75	12	3	6	32	89	69	.243	.416	.359	118	14	2	8	-4	.985	-13	O-96/1-4	-0.8
1956	Chi-A	4	3	0	1	0	0	0	0	2	1	.333	.600	.333	150	1	0	0	0	1.000	-0	/O-2	0.0
Total	8	567	1611	257	433	64	19	32	138	304	290	.269	.387	.392	113	42	12	18		.977	-14	O-441/1-4	0.2

■ BOB ABREU Abreu, Bob Kelly b: 3/11/74, Aragua, Venez. BL/TR, 6', 160 lbs. Deb: 9/1/96

YEAR	TM/L	G	AB	R	H	2B	3B	HR	RBI	BB	SO	AVG	OBP	SLG	PRO+	BR/A	SB	CS	SBR	FA	FR	G/POS	TPR
1996	Hou-N	15	22	1	5	1	0	0	1	2	3	.227	.292	.273	54	-1	0	0	0	1.000	-1	/O-7	-0.3
1997	*Hou-N	59	188	22	47	10	2	3	26	21	48	.250	.329	.372	86	-4	7	2	1	.978	-0	O-53	-0.4
1998	Phi-N	151	497	68	155	29	6	17	74	84	133	.312	.411	.497	132	26	19	10	-0	.973	13	*O-146	3.6
Total	3	225	707	91	207	40	8	20	101	107	184	.293	.387	.457	118	21	26	12	1	.975	11	O-206	2.9

■ JOE ABREU Abreu, Joseph Lawrence b: 5/24/13, Oakland, Cal. d: 3/17/93, Hayward, Cal. BR/TR, 5'8", 160 lbs. Deb: 4/23/42

YEAR	TM/L	G	AB	R	H	2B	3B	HR	RBI	BB	SO	AVG	OBP	SLG	PRO+	BR/A	SB	CS	SBR	FA	FR	G/POS	TPR
1942	Cin-N	9	28	4	6	1	0	1	3	4	4	.214	.313	.357	96	-0	0			.941	-1	/3-6,2-2	-0.1

■ BILL ABSTEIN Abstein, William Henry "Big Bill" b: 2/2/1883, St.Louis, Mo. d: 4/8/40, St.Louis, Mo. BR/TR, 6', 185 lbs. Deb: 9/25/06

YEAR	TM/L	G	AB	R	H	2B	3B	HR	RBI	BB	SO	AVG	OBP	SLG	PRO+	BR/A	SB	CS	SBR	FA	FR	G/POS	TPR
1906	Pit-N	8	20	2	4	0	0	0	3	0		.200	.200	.200	24	-2	2			.769	-2	/2-3,O-2	-0.4
1909	*Pit-N	137	512	51	133	20	10	1	70	27		.260	.302	.344	93	-6	16			.982	-5	*1-135	-1.4
1910	StL-A	25	87	1	13	2	0	0	3	2		.149	.169	.172	7	-9	3			.963	2	1-23	-0.9
Total	3	170	619	54	150	22	10	1	76	29		.242	.281	.315	80	-18	21			.979	-5	1-158/2-3,O-2	-2.7

■ MERITO ACOSTA Acosta, Baldomero Pedro (Fernandez) b: 5/19/1896, Bauta, Cuba d: 11/17/63, Miami, Fla. BL/TL, 5'7", 140 lbs. Deb: 6/15/13 F

YEAR	TM/L	G	AB	R	H	2B	3B	HR	RBI	BB	SO	AVG	OBP	SLG	PRO+	BR/A	SB	CS	SBR	FA	FR	G/POS	TPR
1913	Was-A	12	20	3	6	0	1	0	1	4	2	.300	.417	.400	136	1	2			.714	-3	/O-9	-0.2
1914	Was-A	39	74	10	19	2	2	0	4	11	18	.257	.353	.338	104	1	3	4	-2	.857	-2	O-25	-0.4
1915	Was-A	72	163	20	34	4	1	0	18	28	15	.209	.338	.245	73	-4	8	4	0	.963	-4	O-53	-1.1
1916	Was-A	5	8	0	1	0	0	0	0	2	0	.125	.300	.125	28	-1	0			1.000	1	/O-4	0.0
1918	Was-A	3	2	0	0	0	0	0	0	0	1	.000	.000	.000	-99	-0	0			.000	0	H	-0.1
	Phi-A	49	169	23	51	3	3	0	14	18	10	.302	.369	.355	117	4	4			.944	-3	O-45	-0.2
	Yr	52	171	23	51	3	3	0	14	18	11	.298	.365	.351	115	3	4			.944	-3	O-45	-0.3
Total	5	180	436	56	111	9	7	0	37	63	46	.255	.354	.307	97	0	17	8		.933	-11	O-136	-2.0

■ JIMMY ADAIR Adair, James Aubrey "Choppy" b: 1/25/07, Waxahachie, Tex. d: 12/9/82, Dallas, Tex. BR/TR, 5'10.5", 154 lbs. Deb: 8/24/31 C

YEAR	TM/L	G	AB	R	H	2B	3B	HR	RBI	BB	SO	AVG	OBP	SLG	PRO+	BR/A	SB	CS	SBR	FA	FR	G/POS	TPR
1931	Chi-N	18	76	9	21	3	1	0	3	1	8	.276	.286	.342	67	-4	1			.948	-1	S-18	-0.3

■ JERRY ADAIR Adair, Kenneth Jerry b: 12/17/36, Sand Springs, Okla. d: 5/31/87, Tulsa, Okla. BR/TR, 6', 175 lbs. Deb: 9/2/58 C

YEAR	TM/L	G	AB	R	H	2B	3B	HR	RBI	BB	SO	AVG	OBP	SLG	PRO+	BR/A	SB	CS	SBR	FA	FR	G/POS	TPR
1958	Bal-A	11	19	1	2	0	0	0	0	1	7	.105	.150	.105	-30	-3	0	0	0	.967	2	S-10/2-1	-0.1
1959	Bal-A	12	35	3	11	0	1	0	2	1	5	.314	.333	.371	95	-0	0	0	0	.932	-4	2-11/S-1	-0.3
1960	Bal-A	3	5	1	1	0	0	1	1	0	0	.200	.200	.800	159	0	0	0	0	1.000	0	/2-3	0.1
1961	Bal-A	133	386	41	102	21	1	9	37	35	51	.264	.329	.394	95	-3	5	2	0	.987	-1	*2-107,S-27/3-2	0.8
1962	Bal-A	139	538	67	153	29	4	11	48	27	77	.284	.321	.414	103	-0	7	7	-2	.969	-10	*S-113,2-34/3-1	0.1
1963	Bal-A	109	382	34	87	21	3	6	30	9	51	.228	.249	.346	67	-18	3	3	-1	.985	-0	*2-103	-1.0
1964	Bal-A	155	569	56	141	20	3	9	47	28	72	.248	.284	.341	73	-21	3	2	-0	**.994**	9	*2-153	0.0
1965	Bal-A	157	582	51	151	26	3	7	66	35	65	.259	.304	.351	84	-13	6	4	-1	**.986**	12	*2-157	1.4
1966	Bal-A	17	52	3	15	1	0	0	3	4	8	.288	.339	.308	89	-1	0	0	0	.969	-1	2-13	-0.1
	Chi-A	105	370	27	90	18	2	4	36	17	44	.243	.278	.335	81	-10	3	2	-0	.975	-2	S-75,2-50	-0.4
	Yr	122	422	30	105	19	2	4	39	21	52	.249	.286	.332	82	-11	3	2	-0	.975	-3	S-75,2-63	-0.5
1967	Chi-A	28	98	6	20	4	0	0	9	4	17	.204	.243	.245	46	-7	0	1	-1	.985	-0	2-27	-0.6
	*Bos-A	89	316	41	92	13	1	3	26	13	35	.291	.323	.367	96	-2	1	4	-2	.952	-8	3-35,S-30,2-23	-1.0
	Yr	117	414	47	112	17	1	3	35	17	52	.271	.304	.338	85	-8	1	5	-3	.976	-9	2-50,3-35,S-30	-1.6
1968	Bos-A	74	208	18	45	1	0	2	12	9	28	.216	.252	.250	49	-13	0	0	0	.976	-5	S-46,2-12/3-7,1-1	-1.6
1969	KC-A	126	432	29	108	9	1	5	48	20	36	.250	.288	.310	67	-20	1	3	-2	.984	-22	*2-109/S-8,3-1	-3.6
1970	KC-A	7	27	0	4	0	0	0	1	5	3	.148	.281	.148	22	-3	0	1	-1	1.000	2	/2-7	-0.1
Total	13	1165	4019	378	1022	163	19	57	366	208	499	.254	.294	.347	80	-112	29	29	-9	.985	-30	2-810,S-310/3-46,1	-6.4

■ SPARKY ADAMS Adams, Earl John b: 8/26/1894, Zerbe, Pa. d: 2/24/89, Pottsville, Pa. BR/TR, 5'5.5", 151 lbs. Deb: 9/18/22

YEAR	TM/L	G	AB	R	H	2B	3B	HR	RBI	BB	SO	AVG	OBP	SLG	PRO+	BR/A	SB	CS	SBR	FA	FR	G/POS	TPR
1922	Chi-N	11	44	5	11	0	1	0	3	4	3	.250	.313	.295	56	-3	1	2	-1	.914	-4	2-11	-0.7
1923	Chi-N	95	311	40	90	12	0	4	35	26	10	.289	.346	.367	88	-5	20	19	-5	.935	-6	S-79/O-1	-0.9
1924	Chi-N	117	418	66	117	11	5	1	27	40	20	.280	.344	.337	83	-9	15	17	-6	.941	-8	S-88,2-19	-1.3
1925	Chi-N	149	627	95	180	29	8	2	48	44	15	.287	.341	.368	80	-18	26	12	1	**.983**	**28**	*2-144/S-5	1.3
1926	Chi-N	154	624	95	193	35	3	0	39	52	27	.309	.367	.375	99	1	27			.965	17	*2-136,3-19/S-2	2.2
1927	Chi-N	146	647	100	189	17	7	0	49	42	26	.292	.335	.340	81	-17	26			.994	-1	2-60,3-53,S-40	-0.8
1928	Pit-N	135	539	91	149	14	6	0	38	64	18	.276	.357	.325	76	-16	8			.971	-11	*2-107,S-27/O-1	-2.1
1929	Pit-N	74	196	37	51	8	1	0	11	15	5	.260	.316	.311	55	-14	3			.901	-15	S-30,2-20,3-15,/O-2	-2.3
1930	*StL-N	137	570	98	179	36	9	0	55	45	27	.314	.365	.409	84	-14	7			**.966**	-13	*3-104,2-25/S-7	-1.7
1931	*StL-N	143	608	97	178	**46**	5	1	40	42	24	.293	.340	.390	92	-7	16			**.963**	-12	*3-138/S-6	-1.0
1932	StL-N	31	127	22	35	3	1	0	13	14	5	.276	.352	.315	79	-3	0			.931	-4	3-30	-0.5
1933	StL-N	8	30	1	5	1	0	0	0	1	3	.167	.219	.200	19	-3	0			.955	-2	/S-5,3-3	-0.5
	Cin-N	137	538	59	141	21	1	1	22	44	30	.262	.320	.310	82	-12	3			.963	-3	*3-132/S-8	-0.6
	Yr	145	568	60	146	22	1	1	22	45	33	.257	.315	.305	78	-15	3			.959	-5	*3-135,S-13	-1.1
1934	Cin-N	87	278	38	70	16	1	0	14	20	10	.252	.307	.317	69	-12	2			.955	-3	3-38,2-29	-1.1
Total	13	1424	5557	844	1588	249	48	9	394	453	223	.286	.343	.353	82	-131	154	50		.974	-37	2-551,3-532,S/O	-10.0

■ BUSTER ADAMS Adams, Elvin Clark b: 6/24/15, Trinidad, Col. d: 9/1/90, Rancho Mirage, Cal. BR/TR, 6', 180 lbs. Deb: 4/27/39

YEAR	TM/L	G	AB	R	H	2B	3B	HR	RBI	BB	SO	AVG	OBP	SLG	PRO+	BR/A	SB	CS	SBR	FA	FR	G/POS	TPR
1939	StL-N	2	1	1	0	0	0	0	0	0	0	.000	.000	.000	-94	-0	0			.000	0	H	0.0
1943	StL-N	8	11	1	1	1	0	0	1	4	4	.091	.333	.182	48	-1	0			1.000	-1	/O-6	-0.2
	Phi-N	111	418	48	107	14	7	4	38	39	67	.256	.319	.352	98	-2	2			.984	3	*O-107	-0.5
	Yr	119	429	49	108	15	7	4	39	43	71	.252	.320	.347	96	-3	2			.984	2	*O-113	-0.7
1944	Phi-N	151	584	86	165	35	3	17	64	74	74	.283	.370	.440	132	25	2			.979	11	*O-151	2.8
1945	Phi-N	14	56	6	13	3	1	2	8	5	5	.232	.295	.429	103	-0	0			1.000	-1	O-14	-0.2
	StL-N	140	578	98	169	26	0	20	101	57	75	.292	.359	.441	119	14	3			.978	1	*O-140	0.7
	Yr	154	634	104	182	29	1	22	109	62	80	.287	.353	.440	117	14	3			.979	0	*O-154	0.5
1946	StL-N	81	173	21	32	6	0	5	22	29	27	.185	.312	.306	73	-6	3			.990	-9	O-58	-1.8
1947	Phi-N	69	182	21	45	11	1	2	15	26	29	.247	.341	.352	88	-3	2			.954	-4	O-51	-0.9
Total	6	576	2003	282	532	96	12	50	249	234	281	.266	.346	.400	110	27	12			.979	0	O-527	-0.1

■ GEORGE ADAMS Adams, George b: Grafton, Mass. BR/TR, 5'6", 175 lbs. Deb: 6/14/1879

YEAR	TM/L	G	AB	R	H	2B	3B	HR	RBI	BB	SO	AVG	OBP	SLG	PRO+	BR/A	SB	CS	SBR	FA	FR	G/POS	TPR
1879	Syr-N	4	13	0	3	0	0	0	0	1	1	.231	.286	.231	82	-0				1.000	-1	/O-2,1-2	-0.1

YEAR	TM/L	G	AB	R	H	2B	3B	HR	RBI	BB	SO	AVG	OBP	SLG	PRO+	BR/A	SB	CS	SBR	FA	FR	G/POS	TPR
■ GLENN ADAMS	Adams, Glenn Charles b: 10/4/47, Northbridge, Mass. BL/TR, 6', 185 lbs. Deb: 5/4/75																						
1975	SF-N	61	90	10	27	2	1	4	15	11	25	.300	.382	.478	132	4	1	0	0	.941	-3	O-25	0.1
1976	SF-N	69	74	2	18	4	0	0	3	1	12	.243	.253	.297	54	-5	1	0	0	1.000	-2	/O-6	-0.7
1977	Min-A	95	269	32	91	17	0	6	49	18	30	.338	.380	.468	132	12	0	2	-1	.969	-4	D-47,O-44	0.4
1978	Min-A	116	310	27	80	18	1	7	35	17	32	.258	.297	.390	90	-5	0	1	-1	1.000	-1	*D-101/O-5	-1.0
1979	Min-A	119	326	34	98	13	1	8	50	25	27	.301	.356	.420	104	2	2	2	-1	.958	-8	D-55,O-53	-1.0
1980	Min-A	99	262	32	75	11	2	6	38	15	26	.286	.325	.412	94	-3	2	4	-2	.947	-2	D-81,O-12	-0.9
1981	Min-A	72	220	13	46	10	0	2	24	20	26	.209	.275	.282	57	-12	0	1	-1	.000	0	D-62	-1.6
1982	Tor-A	30	66	2	17	4	0	1	11	4	5	.258	.300	.364	74	-2	0	0	0	.000	0	D-27	-0.3
Total	8	661	1617	152	452	79	5	34	225	111	183	.280	.327	.398	96	-9	6	10	-4	.959	-20	D-373,O-145	-5.0
■ DOUG ADAMS	Adams, Harold Douglas b: 1/27/43, Blue River, Wis. BL/TR, 6'3", 185 lbs. Deb: 9/8/69																						
1969	Chi-A	8	14	1	3	0	0	0	1	1	3	.214	.267	.214	34	-1	0	0	0	1.000	-1	/C-4	-0.2
■ HERB ADAMS	Adams, Herbert Loren b: 4/14/28, Hollywood, Cal. BL/TL, 5'9", 160 lbs. Deb: 9/17/48																						
1948	Chi-A	5	11	1	3	1	0	0	0	1	1	.273	.333	.364	88	-0	0	0	0	1.000	2	/O-4	0.1
1949	Chi-A	56	208	26	61	5	3	0	16	9	16	.293	.323	.346	79	-7	1	2	-1	.975	-0	O-48	-1.0
1950	Chi-A	34	118	12	24	2	3	0	2	12	7	.203	.288	.271	45	-10	3	0	1	.978	-1	O-33	-1.1
Total	3	95	337	39	88	8	6	0	18	22	24	.261	.310	.320	67	-17	4	2	0	.978	0	/O-85	-2.0
■ JIM ADAMS	Adams, James J. b: 1868, E.St.Louis, Ill. TR , Deb: 4/21/1890																						
1890	StL-a	1	4	0	1	0	0	0	0	0		.250	.250	.250	42	-0	0			1.000	-1	/C-1	-0.1
■ BERT ADAMS	Adams, John Bertram b: 6/21/1891, Wharton, Tex. d: 6/24/40, Los Angeles, Cal. BB/TR, 6'1", 185 lbs. Deb: 8/30/10																						
1910	Cle-A	5	13	1	3	0	0	0	0	0		.231	.231	.231	44	-1	0			.964	3	/C-5	0.3
1911	Cle-A	2	5	0	1	0	0	0	0	1		.200	.333	.200	50	-0	0			.900	-1	/C-2	-0.1
1912	Cle-A	20	54	5	11	2	1	0	6	4		.204	.259	.278	52	-4	0			.942	2	C-20	0.0
1915	Phi-N	24	27	1	3	0	0	0	2	2	3	.111	.172	.111	-13	-4	0			.974	-4	C-23/1-1	-0.8
1916	Phi-N	11	13	2	3	0	0	0	1	0	3	.231	.231	.231	40	-1	0			.929	1	C-11	0.0
1917	Phi-N	43	107	4	22	4	1	1	7	0	20	.206	.206	.290	49	-7	0			.994	1	C-38/1-1	-0.4
1918	Phi-N	84	227	10	40	4	0	0	12	10	26	.176	.214	.194	23	-21	5			.976	-1	C-76	-1.8
1919	Phi-N	78	232	14	54	7	2	1	17	6	27	.233	.252	.293	59	-12	4			.966	-2	C-73/1-1	-0.9
Total	8	267	678	37	137	17	4	2	45	23	79	.202	.229	.248	42	-48	9			.970	-2	C-248/1-3	-3.7
■ DICK ADAMS	Adams, Richard Leroy b: 4/8/20, Tuolumne, Cal. BR/TL, 6', 185 lbs. Deb: 5/20/47 F																						
1947	Phi-A	37	89	9	18	2	3	2	11	2	18	.202	.220	.360	58	-6	0	0	0	.995	0	1-24/O-3	-0.6
■ RICKY ADAMS	Adams, Ricky Lee b: 1/21/59, Upland, Cal. BR/TR, 6'2", 180 lbs. Deb: 9/15/82																						
1982	Cal-A	8	14	1	2	0	0	0	0	0	2	.143	.200	.143	-4	-2	1	0	0	.947	-1	/S-8	-0.2
1983	Cal-A	58	112	22	28	2	0	2	6	5	12	.250	.300	.321	72	-4	1	1	-0	.960	22	S-38,3-16/2-4	1.9
1985	SF-N	54	121	12	23	3	1	2	10	5	23	.190	.228	.281	44	-9	1	1	-0	.964	3	S-25,3-16/2-6	-0.5
Total	3	120	247	35	53	5	1	4	16	10	37	.215	.260	.291	54	-16	3	2	-0	.961	24	/S-71,3-32,2-10	1.2
■ BOBBY ADAMS	Adams, Robert Henry b: 12/14/21, Tuolumne, Cal. d: 2/13/97, Gig Harbor, Wash. BR/TR, 5'10", 170 lbs. Deb: 4/16/46 FC																						
1946	Cin-N	94	311	35	76	13	3	4	24	18	32	.244	.292	.344	83	-8	16			.967	24	2-74/O-2,3-1	2.2
1947	Cin-N	81	217	39	59	11	2	4	20	25	23	.272	.358	.396	101	1	9			.967	14	2-69	1.8
1948	Cin-N	87	262	33	78	20	3	1	21	25	23	.298	.361	.408	112	4	6			.965	-12	2-64/3-7	-0.4
1949	Cin-N	107	277	32	70	16	2	0	25	26	36	.253	.317	.325	72	-11	4			.984	-9	2-63,3-14	-1.7
1950	Cin-N	115	348	57	98	21	8	3	25	43	29	.282	.361	.414	103	2	7			.981	-9	2-53,3-42	-0.6
1951	Cin-N	125	403	57	107	12	5	5	24	43	40	.266	.338	.357	86	-7	4	10	-5	.956	-10	3-60,2-42/O-1	-2.1
1952	Cin-N	154	637	85	180	25	4	6	48	49	67	.283	.334	.363	93	-6	11	9	-2	.962	9	*3-154	-0.2
1953	Cin-N	150	607	99	167	14	6	8	49	58	67	.275	.338	.357	81	-16	3	2	-0	.951	8	*3-150	-1.1
1954	Cin-N	110	390	69	105	25	6	3	23	55	46	.269	.364	.387	93	-3	2	5	-2	.951	1	3-93/2-2	-0.6
1955	Cin-N	64	150	23	41	11	2	2	20	20	21	.273	.370	.413	102	1	2	0	1	.969	3	3-42/2-5	0.5
	Chi-A	28	21	8	2	0	1	0	3	4	4	.095	.240	.190	16	-3	0	0	0	.933	5	/3-9,2-1	0.3
1956	Bal-A	41	111	19	25	6	1	0	7	25	15	.225	.368	.297	84	-2	1	1	-0	.984	-6	3-24,2-18	-0.6
1957	Chi-N	60	187	21	47	10	2	1	10	17	28	.251	.320	.342	79	-5	0	3	-2	.949	-8	3-47/2-1	-1.4
1958	Chi-N	62	96	14	27	4	4	0	4	6	15	.281	.324	.406	93	-1	2	0	1	.961	-2	1-11/3-9,2-7	-0.2
1959	Chi-N	3	2	0	0	0	0	0	0	0	1	.000	.000	.000	-99	-1	0	0	0	.667	-0	/1-1	-0.1
Total	14	1281	4019	591	1082	188	49	37	303	414	447	.269	.340	.368	90	-54	67	30		.955	10	3-652,2-399/1-12,O	-4.2
■ BOB ADAMS	Adams, Robert Melvin b: 1/6/52, Pittsburgh, Pa. BR/TR, 6'2", 200 lbs. Deb: 7/10/77																						
1977	Det-A	15	24	2	6	1	0	2	2	0	5	.250	.250	.542	103	-0	0	0	0	1.000	-0	/1-2,C-1	0.0
■ MIKE ADAMS	Adams, Robert Michael b: 7/24/48, Cincinnati, Ohio BR/TR, 5'9", 180 lbs. Deb: 9/10/72 F																						
1972	Min-A	3	6	0	2	0	0	0	0	0	1	.333	.333	.333	94	-0	0	0	0	1.000	-0	/O-1	0.0
1973	Min-A	55	66	21	14	2	0	3	6	17	18	.212	.381	.379	110	2	2	1	0	.978	-1	O-24/D-2	0.0
1976	Chi-N	25	29	1	4	2	0	0	2	8	7	.138	.342	.207	54	-1	0	0	0	1.000	-3	/O-4,3-3,2-1	-0.5
1977	Chi-N	2	2	0	0	0	0	0	0	0	1	.000	.000	.000	-90	-1	0	0	0	.000	-1	/O-2	-0.1
1978	Oak-A	15	15	5	3	1	0	0	1	7	2	.200	.455	.267	113	1	0	0	0	1.000	-1	/2-6,3-3,D-3	0.1
Total	5	100	118	27	23	5	0	3	9	32	29	.195	.375	.314	93	1	2	1	0	.980	-5	/O-31,2-7,3-6,D-5	-0.5
■ SPENCER ADAMS	Adams, Spencer Dewey b: 6/21/1898, Layton, Utah d: 11/24/70, Salt Lake City, Ut BL/TR, 5'9", 158 lbs. Deb: 5/8/23																						
1923	Pit-N	25	56	11	14	0	1	0	4	6	6	.250	.323	.286	60	-3	2	1	0	.879	-6	2-11/S-6	-0.8
1925	*Was-A	39	55	11	15	4	1	0	4	5	4	.273	.333	.382	83	-2	1	1	-0	.941	-2	2-15/S-8,3-3	-0.3
1926	*NY-A	28	25	7	3	1	0	0	1	3	7	.120	.214	.160	-1	-4	1	0	0	1.000	4	/2-4,3-1	0.1
1927	StL-A	88	259	32	69	11	3	0	29	24	33	.266	.333	.332	71	-11	1	8	-5	.948	1	2-54,3-28	-1.1
Total	4	180	395	61	101	16	5	0	38	38	50	.256	.324	.322	66	-19	5	10	-5	.944	-3	/2-84,3-32,S-14	-2.1
■ JOE ADCOCK	Adcock, Joseph Wilbur b: 10/30/27, Coushatta, La. BR/TR, 6'4", 220 lbs. Deb: 4/23/50 M																						
1950	Cin-N	102	372	46	109	16	1	8	55	24	24	.293	.336	.406	94	-4	2			.968	6	O-75,1-24	-0.2
1951	Cin-N	113	395	40	96	16	4	10	47	24	29	.243	.288	.380	77	-14	1	2	-1	.983	1	*O-107	-1.8
1952	Cin-N	117	378	43	105	22	4	13	52	23	38	.278	.321	.460	115	6	1	4	-2	.985	4	O-85,1-17	0.4
1953	Mil-N	157	590	71	168	33	6	18	80	42	82	.285	.334	.453	110	6	3	2	-0	.991	-4	*1-157	-0.5
1954	Mil-N	133	500	73	154	27	5	23	87	44	58	.308	.367	.520	137	25	1	4	-2	.995	-11	*1-133	0.5
1955	Mil-N	84	288	40	76	14	0	15	45	31	44	.264	.340	.469	118	7	0	2	-1	.990	-5	1-78	-0.4
1956	Mil-N	137	454	76	132	23	1	38	103	32	86	.291	.339	.597	**154**	31	1	0	0	**.995**	-6	*1-129	1.8
1957	*Mil-N	65	209	31	60	13	2	12	38	20	51	.287	.352	.541	146	13	0	0	0	.996	-3	1-56	0.6
1958	*Mil-N	105	320	40	88	15	1	19	54	21	63	.275	.322	.506	125	9	0	0	0	.989	-1	1-71,O-22	0.3
1959	Mil-N	115	404	53	118	19	2	25	76	32	77	.292	.344	.535	141	21	0	0	0	.998	10	1-89,O-21	2.5
1960	Mil-N★	138	514	55	153	21	4	25	91	46	86	.298	.357	.500	142	28	2	2	-1	**.993**	3	*1-136	1.9
1961	Mil-N	152	562	77	160	20	0	35	108	59	94	.285	.355	.507	133	25	2	1	0	**.993**	-5	*1-148	0.8
1962	Mil-N	121	391	48	97	12	1	29	78	50	91	.248	.335	.506	126	13	2	0	1	**.997**	-4	*1-112	0.3
1963	Cle-A	97	283	28	71	7	1	13	49	30	53	.251	.323	.420	107	3	1	2	-1	.995	-4	1-78	-0.6
1964	LA-A	118	366	39	98	13	0	21	64	48	61	.268	.353	.475	142	20	0	2	-1	.993	-5	*1-105	1.0
1965	Cal-A	122	349	30	84	14	0	14	47	37	74	.241	.315	.401	104	2	2	2	-1	.996	-4	1-97	-0.9
1966	Cal-A	83	231	33	63	10	3	18	48	31	48	.273	.359	.576	168	20	2	2	-1	.997	-0	1-71	1.6
Total	17	1959	6606	823	1832	295	35	336	1122	594	1059	.277	.339	.485	125	210	20	25		.994	-28	*1-1501,O-310	7.3
■ BOB ADDIS	Addis, Robert Gordon b: 11/6/25, Mineral, Ohio BL/TR, 6', 175 lbs. Deb: 9/1/50																						
1950	Bos-N	16	28	7	7	1	0	0	2	3	5	.250	.323	.286	66	-1	1			1.000	-2	/O-7	-0.3
1951	Bos-N	85	199	23	55	7	0	1	24	9	10	.276	.308	.327	76	-7	3	2	-0	.982	-0	O-46	-0.9

YEAR	TM/L	G	AB	R	H	2B	3B	HR	RBI	BB	SO	AVG	OBP	SLG	PRO+	BR/A	SB	CS	SBR	FA	FR	G/POS	TPR
1952	Chi-N	93	292	38	86	13	2	1	20	23	30	.295	.346	.363	96	-1	4	4	-1	.988	-2	O-79	-0.8
1953	Chi-N	10	12	2	2	1	0	0	1	2	0	.167	.286	.250	40	-1	0	0	0	1.000	1	/O-3	0.0
	Pit-N	4	3	0	0	0	0	0	0	0	2	.000	.000	.000	-99	-1	0	0	0	.000	0	H	-0.1
	Yr	14	15	2	2	1	0	0	1	2	2	.133	.235	.200	15	-2	0	0	0	1.000	1	/O-3	-0.1
Total	4	208	534	70	150	22	2	2	47	37	47	.281	.327	.341	84	-12	8	6		.986	-3	O-135	-2.1

■ JIM ADDUCI Adduci, James David b: 8/9/59, Chicago, Ill. BL/TL, 6'5", 200 lbs. Deb: 9/12/83

YEAR	TM/L	G	AB	R	H	2B	3B	HR	RBI	BB	SO	AVG	OBP	SLG	PRO+	BR/A	SB	CS	SBR	FA	FR	G/POS	TPR
1983	StL-N	10	20	0	1	0	0	0	0	1	6	.050	.095	.050	-59	-4	0	0	0	1.000	0	/1-6,O-1	-0.5
1986	Mil-A	3	11	2	1	1	0	0	0	1	2	.091	.167	.182	-5	-2	0	0	0	1.000	0	/1-3	-0.2
1988	Mil-A	44	94	8	25	6	1	1	15	0	15	.266	.266	.383	79	-3	0	1	-1	.969	-4	O-24,D-10/1-3	-0.8
1989	Phi-N	13	19	1	7	1	0	0	0	0	4	.368	.368	.421	125	1	0	0	0	1.000	0	/1-4,O-1	0.1
Total	4	70	144	11	34	8	1	1	15	2	27	.236	.247	.326	58	-8	0	1	-1	.969	-3	/O-26,1-16,D-10	-1.4

■ BOB ADDY Addy, Robert Edward "Magnet" b: 2/1845, Rochester, N.Y. d: 4/9/10, Pocatello, Idaho BL/TL, 5'8", 160 lbs. Deb: 5/6/1871 M

YEAR	TM/L	G	AB	R	H	2B	3B	HR	RBI	BB	SO	AVG	OBP	SLG	PRO+	BR/A	SB	CS	SBR	FA	FR	G/POS	TPR
1871	Rok-n	25	118	30	32	6	0	0	13	4	0	.271	.295	.322	81	-2	8	1	2	.768	1	*2-22/S-3	-0.1
1873	Phi-n	10	51	12	16	1	0	0	10	2	0	.314	.340	.333	97	-0	0	1	-1	.855	-4	2-10	-0.4
	Bos-n	31	152	37	54	5	2	1	36	1	0	.355	.359	.434	124	3	2	3	-1	.750	-2	O-31	0.1
	Yr	41	203	49	70	6	2	1	46	3	0	.345	.354	.409	118	3	2	4	-2	.750	-5	O-31,2-10	-0.3
1874	Har-n	50	213	25	51	9	2	0	22	1	1	.239	.243	.300	70	-8	4	2	0	.846	2	*2-45/3-5,S-1	-0.6
1875	Phi-n	69	310	60	80	8	4	0	43	0	2	.258	.258	.310	93	-3	16	8	0	.761	-0	*O-68/2-2,M	-0.2
1876	Chi-N	32	142	36	40	4	1	0	16	5	0	.282	.306	.324	98	-1				.800	0	O-32	-0.1
1877	Cin-N	57	245	27	68	2	3	0	31	6	5	.278	.295	.310	102	1				.805	5	*O-57/M	0.3
Total	4 n	185	844	164	233	29	8	1	124	8	3	.276	.283	.333	92	-10	30	15	0	.758	-2	/O-99,2-79,3-5,S-4	-1.2
Total	2	89	387	63	108	6	4	0	47	11	5	.279	.299	.315	100	0				.803	5	/O-89	0.2

■ MORRIE ADERHOLT Aderholt, Morris Woodroe b: 9/13/15, Mt.Olive, N.C. d: 3/18/55, Sarasota, Fla. BL/TR, 6'1", 188 lbs. Deb: 9/13/39

YEAR	TM/L	G	AB	R	H	2B	3B	HR	RBI	BB	SO	AVG	OBP	SLG	PRO+	BR/A	SB	CS	SBR	FA	FR	G/POS	TPR
1939	Was-A	7	25	5	5	0	0	0	4	2	6	.200	.259	.320	51	-2	0	1	-1	.872	0	/2-7	-0.2
1940	Was-A	1	2	0	0	0	0	0	0	0	0	.000	.000	.000	-99	-1	0	0	0	1.000	0	/2-1	0.0
1941	Was-A	11	14	3	2	0	0	0	1	1	3	.143	.200	.143	-8	-2	0	0	0	.818	0	/2-2,3-1	-0.2
1944	Bro-N	17	59	9	16	2	3	0	10	4	4	.271	.317	.407	105	0	0			.871	-1	O-13	-0.1
1945	Bro-N	39	60	4	13	1	0	0	6	3	10	.217	.254	.233	36	-5	0			1.000	-2	/O-8	-0.8
	Bos-N	31	102	15	34	4	0	2	11	9	6	.333	.387	.431	127	4	3			.984	0	O-24/2-1	0.3
	Yr	70	162	19	47	5	0	2	17	12	16	.290	.339	.358	94	-1	3			.985	-2	O-32/2-1	-0.5
Total	5	106	262	36	70	7	3	3	32	19	29	.267	.317	.351	85	-6	3	1		.949	-2	/O-45,2-11,3-1	-1.0

■ DICK ADKINS Adkins, Richard Earl b: 3/3/20, Electra, Tex. d: 9/12/55, Electra, Tex. BR/TR, 5'10", 165 lbs. Deb: 9/19/42

YEAR	TM/L	G	AB	R	H	2B	3B	HR	RBI	BB	SO	AVG	OBP	SLG	PRO+	BR/A	SB	CS	SBR	FA	FR	G/POS	TPR
1942	Phi-A	3	7	2	1	0	0	0	0	2	2	.143	.333	.143	37	-0	0	0	0	.875	-1	/S-3	-0.2

■ HENRY ADKINSON Adkinson, Henry Magee b: 9/1/1874, Chicago, Ill. d: 5/1/23, Salt Lake City, Ut. Deb: 9/25/1895

YEAR	TM/L	G	AB	R	H	2B	3B	HR	RBI	BB	SO	AVG	OBP	SLG	PRO+	BR/A	SB	CS	SBR	FA	FR	G/POS	TPR
1895	StL-N	1	5	1	2	0	0	0	0	0	2	.400	.400	.400	108	0	0			.667	-0	/O-1	0.0

■ DAVE ADLESH Adlesh, David George b: 7/15/43, Long Beach, Cal. BR/TR, 6', 187 lbs. Deb: 5/12/63

YEAR	TM/L	G	AB	R	H	2B	3B	HR	RBI	BB	SO	AVG	OBP	SLG	PRO+	BR/A	SB	CS	SBR	FA	FR	G/POS	TPR
1963	Hou-N	6	8	0	0	0	0	0	0	0	4	.000	.000	.000	-99	-2	0	0	0	.889	-2	/C-6	-0.4
1964	Hou-N	3	10	0	2	0	0	0	0	0	5	.200	.200	.200	14	-1	0	0	0	1.000	-1	/C-3	-0.2
1965	Hou-N	15	34	2	5	1	0	0	3	2	12	.147	.216	.176	13	-4	0	0	0	1.000	-1	C-13	-0.5
1966	Hou-N	3	6	0	0	0	0	0	0	0	4	.000	.000	.000	-99	-2	0	0	0	1.000	1	/C-1	-0.1
1967	Hou-N	39	94	4	17	1	0	1	4	11	28	.181	.267	.223	43	-7	0	0	0	.995	-3	C-31	-0.9
1968	Hou-N	40	104	3	19	1	1	0	4	5	27	.183	.227	.212	33	-8	0	0	0	.990	-3	/C-36	-1.0
Total	6	106	256	9	43	3	1	1	11	18	80	.168	.228	.199	26	-24	0	0	0	.992	-8	/C-90	-3.1

■ TROY AFENIR Afenir, Michael Troy b: 9/21/63, Escondido, Cal. BR/TR, 6'4", 185 lbs. Deb: 9/14/87

YEAR	TM/L	G	AB	R	H	2B	3B	HR	RBI	BB	SO	AVG	OBP	SLG	PRO+	BR/A	SB	CS	SBR	FA	FR	G/POS	TPR
1987	Hou-N	10	20	1	6	1	0	0	1	0	12	.300	.300	.350	74	-1	0	0	0	.974	-1	C-10	-0.1
1990	Oak-A	14	14	0	2	0	0	0	2	0	6	.143	.143	.143	-21	-2	0	0	0	1.000	-1	C-12/D-1	-0.3
1991	Oak-A	5	11	0	1	0	0	0	0	0	2	.091	.091	.091	-53	-2	0	0	0	1.000	1	/C-4,D-1	-0.1
1992	Cin-N	16	34	3	6	1	2	0	4	5	12	.176	.282	.324	69	-1	0	0	0	1.000	-3	C-15	-0.4
Total	4	45	79	4	15	2	2	0	7	5	32	.190	.238	.266	40	-7	0	0	0	.992	-4	/C-41,D-2	-0.9

■ BENNY AGBAYANI Agbayani, Benny Peter b: 12/28/71, Honolulu, Hawaii BR/TR, 6', 225 lbs. Deb: 6/17/98

YEAR	TM/L	G	AB	R	H	2B	3B	HR	RBI	BB	SO	AVG	OBP	SLG	PRO+	BR/A	SB	CS	SBR	FA	FR	G/POS	TPR
1998	NY-N	11	15	1	2	0	0	0	0	1	5	.133	.188	.133	-15	-3	0	2	-1	1.000	-2	/O-9	-0.6

■ TOMMIE AGEE Agee, Tommie Lee b: 8/9/42, Magnolia, Ala. BR/TR, 5'11", 195 lbs. Deb: 9/14/62

YEAR	TM/L	G	AB	R	H	2B	3B	HR	RBI	BB	SO	AVG	OBP	SLG	PRO+	BR/A	SB	CS	SBR	FA	FR	G/POS	TPR
1962	Cle-A	5	14	0	3	0	0	0	2	0	4	.214	.214	.214	16	-2	0	0	0	1.000	-0	/O-3	-0.2
1963	Cle-A	13	27	3	4	1	0	1	3	2	9	.148	.207	.296	39	-2	0	0	0	1.000	-1	O-13	-0.4
1964	Cle-A	13	12	0	2	0	0	0	0	0	3	.167	.167	.167	-7	-2	0	0	0	1.000	-4	O-12	-0.6
1965	Chi-A	10	19	2	3	1	0	0	3	2	6	.158	.238	.211	30	-2	0	1	-1	1.000	-2	/O-9	-0.5
1966	Chi-A★	160	629	98	172	27	8	22	86	41	127	.273	.328	.447	129	21	44	18	2	.982	11	*O-159	2.9
1967	Chi-A★	158	529	73	124	26	2	14	52	44	129	.234	.303	.371	102	0	28	10	2	.969	2	*O-152	-0.3
1968	NY-N	132	368	30	80	12	3	5	17	15	103	.217	.256	.307	68	-15	13	8	-1	.978	-10	*O-127	-3.6
1969	*NY-N	149	565	97	153	23	4	26	76	59	137	.271	.343	.464	121	15	12	9	-2	.986	6	*O-146	1.1
1970	NY-N	153	636	107	182	30	7	24	75	55	156	.286	.345	.469	115	12	31	15	0	.967	13	*O-150	1.7
1971	NY-N	113	425	58	121	19	0	14	50	50	84	.285	.363	.428	125	14	28	6	5	.978	5	*O-107	1.9
1972	NY-N	114	422	52	96	23	0	13	47	53	92	.227	.319	.374	99	-0	8	9	-3	.962	6	*O-109	-0.3
1973	Hou-N	83	204	30	48	5	2	8	15	16	55	.235	.294	.397	90	-3	2	5	-2	.983	-4	O-67	-1.3
	StL-N	26	62	8	11	3	1	3	7	5	13	.177	.239	.403	75	-2	1	0	0	.981	1	O-19	-0.2
	Yr	109	266	38	59	8	3	11	22	21	68	.222	.281	.398	87	-6	3	5	-2	.982	-3	O-86	-1.5
Total	12	1129	3912	558	999	170	27	130	433	342	918	.255	.321	.412	108	35	167	81	2	.975	22	*O-1073	0.2

■ HARRY AGGANIS Agganis, Harry "The Golden Greek" b: 4/20/29, Lynn, Mass. d: 6/27/55, Cambridge, Mass. BL/TL, 6'2", 200 lbs. Deb: 4/13/54

YEAR	TM/L	G	AB	R	H	2B	3B	HR	RBI	BB	SO	AVG	OBP	SLG	PRO+	BR/A	SB	CS	SBR	FA	FR	G/POS	TPR
1954	Bos-A	132	434	54	109	13	8	11	57	47	57	.251	.324	.394	86	-9	6	3	0	.990	7	*1-119	-0.8
1955	Bos-A	25	83	11	26	10	1	0	10	10	10	.313	.387	.458	116	2	2	0	1	.987	0	1-20	0.1
Total	2	157	517	65	135	23	9	11	67	57	67	.261	.334	.404	91	-7	8	3	1	.989	7	1-139	-0.7

■ JOE AGLER Agler, Joseph Abram b: 6/12/1887, Coshocton, Ohio d: 4/26/71, Massillon, Ohio BL/TL, 5'11", 165 lbs. Deb: 10/1/12

YEAR	TM/L	G	AB	R	H	2B	3B	HR	RBI	BB	SO	AVG	OBP	SLG	PRO+	BR/A	SB	CS	SBR	FA	FR	G/POS	TPR
1912	Was-A	2	1	0	0	0	0	0	0	0		.000	.000	.000	-99	-0	0			.000	0	/1-1	0.0
1914	Buf-F	135	463	82	126	17	6	0	20	77	78	.272	.376	.335	93	-8	21			.985	5	1-76,O-54	-0.8
1915	Buf-F	25	73	11	13	1	2	0	2	20	14	.178	.355	.247	69	-3	2			.973	-2	O-20/1-1	-0.7
	Bal-F	72	214	28	46	4	2	0	14	34	38	.215	.325	.252	62	-13	15			.981	5	1-58/O-4,2-3	-1.1
	Yr	97	287	39	59	5	4	0	16	54	52	.206	.333	.251	64	-16	17			.981	3	1-59,O-24/2-3	-1.8
Total	3	234	751	121	185	22	10	0	36	131	130	.246	.359	.302	81	-25	38			.983	7	1-136/O-78,2-3	-2.6

■ SAM AGNEW Agnew, Samuel Lester "Slam" b: 4/12/1887, Farmington, Mo. d: 7/19/51, Sonoma, Cal. BR/TR, 5'11", 185 lbs. Deb: 4/10/13

YEAR	TM/L	G	AB	R	H	2B	3B	HR	RBI	BB	SO	AVG	OBP	SLG	PRO+	BR/A	SB	CS	SBR	FA	FR	G/POS	TPR
1913	StL-A	105	307	27	64	9	5	2	24	20	49	.208	.272	.290	66	-14	11			.952	2	*C-103	-0.3
1914	StL-A	115	311	22	66	5	4	0	16	24	63	.212	.279	.254	63	-14	10	8	-2	.961	3	*C-115	-0.5
1915	StL-A	104	295	18	60	4	2	0	19	12	36	.203	.247	.231	45	-21	5	2	0	.934	5	*C-102	-0.8
1916	Bos-A	40	67	4	14	2	1	0	7	6	4	.209	.293	.269	69	-3	0			.952	8	C-38	0.8
1917	Bos-A	85	260	17	54	6	2	0	16	19	30	.208	.267	.246	57	-13	2			.965	-10	C-85	-1.9
1918	*Bos-A	72	199	11	33	8	0	0	6	11	26	.166	.221	.206	29	-17	0			.965	11	C-72	-0.2
1919	Was-A	42	98	6	23	7	0	0	10	10	8	.235	.312	.306	74	-3	1			.974	8	C-36	0.7
Total	7	563	1537	105	314	41	14	2	98	102	216	.204	.265	.253	56	-85	29	10		.955	26	C-551	-2.2

■ LUIS AGUAYO Aguayo, Luis (Muriel) b: 3/13/59, Vega Baja, P.R. BR/TR, 5'9", 185 lbs. Deb: 4/19/80

YEAR	TM/L	G	AB	R	H	2B	3B	HR	RBI	BB	SO	AVG	OBP	SLG	PRO+	BR/A	SB	CS	SBR	FA	FR	G/POS	TPR
1980	Phi-N	20	47	7	13	1	2	1	8	2	3	.277	.306	.447	102	-0	1	1	-0	.962	1	2-14/S-5	0.2

YEAR	TM/L	G	AB	R	H	2B	3B	HR	RBI	BB	SO	AVG	OBP	SLG	PRO+	BR/A	SB	CS	SBR	FA	FR	G/POS	TPR
1981	*Phi-N	45	84	11	18	4	0	1	7	6	15	.214	.283	.298	62	-4	1	0	0	.938	-4	2-21,S-21/3-3	-0.7
1982	Phi-N	50	56	11	15	1	2	3	7	5	7	.268	.339	.518	133	2	1	1	-0	.966	3	2-21,S-15/3-5	0.6
1983	Phi-N	2	4	0	1	0	0	0	0	1	2	.250	.400	.250	85	-0	0	0	0	1.000	-2	/S-2	-0.2
1984	Phi-N	58	72	15	20	4	0	3	11	8	16	.278	.350	.458	123	2	0	0	0	.909	8	3-14,2-12,S-10	1.0
1985	Phi-N	91	165	27	46	7	3	6	21	22	26	.279	.383	.467	133	8	1	0	0	.957	3	S-60,2-17/3-7	1.6
1986	Phi-N	62	133	17	28	6	1	4	13	8	26	.211	.271	.361	70	-6	1	1	-0	.967	-7	2-31,S-20/3-1	-1.1
1987	Phi-N	94	209	25	43	9	1	12	21	15	56	.206	.275	.431	81	-7	0	0	0	.971	-9	S-78/2-6,3-2	-1.1
1988	Phi-N	49	97	9	24	3	0	3	5	13	17	.247	.336	.371	101	0	2	0	1	.967	2	S-27,3-13/2-2	0.5
	NY-A	50	140	12	35	4	0	3	8	7	33	.250	.291	.343	77	-4	0	2	-1	.961	-2	3-33,2-13/S-6	-0.7
1989	Cle-A	47	97	7	17	4	1	1	8	7	19	.175	.245	.268	44	-7	0	0	0	.950	5	3-19,S-15,2-10,/D-2	-0.1
Total	10	568	1104	142	260	43	10	37	109	94	220	.236	.307	.393	91	-16	7	5	-1	.960	-2	S-259,2-147/3-97,D	-0.0

■ CHARLIE AHEARN Ahearn, Charles b: Troy, N.Y. Deb: 6/19/1880

YEAR	TM/L	G	AB	R	H	2B	3B	HR	RBI	BB	SO	AVG	OBP	SLG	PRO+	BR/A	SB	CS	SBR	FA	FR	G/POS	TPR
1880	Tro-N	1	4	1	1	0	0	0	0	0	0	.250	.250	.250	67	-0				.778	-0	/C-1	0.0

■ WILLIE AIKENS Aikens, Willie Mays b: 10/14/54, Seneca, S.C. BL/TR, 6'3", 220 lbs. Deb: 5/17/77

YEAR	TM/L	G	AB	R	H	2B	3B	HR	RBI	BB	SO	AVG	OBP	SLG	PRO+	BR/A	SB	CS	SBR	FA	FR	G/POS	TPR
1977	Cal-A	42	91	5	18	4	0	0	6	10	23	.198	.277	.242	45	-7	1	2	-1	.971	0	1-13,D-13	-0.9
1979	Cal-A	116	379	59	106	18	0	21	81	61	79	.280	.381	.493	138	21	1	3	-2	.996	-2	1-55,D-51	1.3
1980	*KC-A	151	543	70	151	24	0	20	98	64	88	.278	.362	.433	116	13	1	0	0	.990	-9	*1-138,D-13	-0.4
1981	*KC-A	101	349	45	93	16	0	17	53	62	47	.266	.382	.458	142	21	0	0	0	.992	-5	1-99	1.0
1982	KC-A	134	466	50	131	29	1	17	74	45	70	.281	.348	.457	119	12	0	1	-1	.994	-3	*1-128	0.1
1983	KC-A	125	410	49	124	26	1	23	72	45	75	.302	.374	.539	148	26	0	0	0	.989	-5	*1-112/D-6	1.5
1984	Tor-A	93	234	21	48	7	0	11	26	29	56	.205	.298	.376	82	-6	0	0	0	1.000	0	D-81/1-2	-0.8
1985	Tor-A	12	20	2	4	1	0	1	5	3	6	.200	.304	.400	89	-0	0	0	0	.000	0	D-11	-0.1
Total	8	774	2492	301	675	125	2	110	415	319	444	.271	.358	.455	123	80	3	6	-3	.991	-24	1-547,D-175	1.7

■ DANNY AINGE Ainge, Daniel Ray b: 3/17/59, Eugene, Ore. BR/TR, 6'4", 175 lbs. Deb: 5/21/79

YEAR	TM/L	G	AB	R	H	2B	3B	HR	RBI	BB	SO	AVG	OBP	SLG	PRO+	BR/A	SB	CS	SBR	FA	FR	G/POS	TPR
1979	Tor-A	87	308	26	73	7	1	2	19	12	58	.237	.270	.286	50	-22	1	0	0	.977	-4	2-86/D-1	-1.9
1980	Tor-A	38	111	11	27	6	1	0	4	2	29	.243	.263	.315	55	-7	3	0	1	.986	2	O-29/3-3,2-1,D-2	-0.5
1981	Tor-A	86	246	20	46	6	2	0	14	23	41	.187	.259	.228	39	-19	8	5	-1	.949	1	3-77/S-6,O-4,2-2,D	-2.1
Total	3	211	665	57	146	19	4	2	37	37	128	.220	.265	.269	47	-48	12	5	1	.977	-1	/2-89,3-80,O-33,SD	-4.5

■ EDDIE AINSMITH Ainsmith, Edward Wilbur "Dorf" b: 2/4/1892, Cambridge, Mass. d: 9/6/81, Ft.Lauderdale, Fla BR/TR, 5'11", 180 lbs. Deb: 8/9/10

YEAR	TM/L	G	AB	R	H	2B	3B	HR	RBI	BB	SO	AVG	OBP	SLG	PRO+	BR/A	SB	CS	SBR	FA	FR	G/POS	TPR
1910	Was-A	33	104	4	20	1	2	0	9	6		.192	.236	.240	52	-6	0			.963	-4	C-30	-0.8
1911	Was-A	61	149	12	33	2	3	0	14	10		.221	.275	.275	55	-9	5			.952	0	C-47	-0.4
1912	Was-A	61	186	22	42	7	2	0	22	14		.226	.280	.285	61	-10	4			.958	15	C-59	1.1
1913	Was-A	84	229	26	49	4	4	2	20	12	41	.214	.262	.293	61	-12	17			.967	6	C-79/P-1	0.0
1914	Was-A	62	151	11	34	7	0	0	13	9	28	.225	.273	.272	61	-7	8	5	-1	.969	8	C-51	0.4
1915	Was-A	47	120	13	24	4	2	0	6	10	18	.200	.267	.267	59	-6	7	4	-0	.988	6	C-42	0.2
1916	Was-A	51	100	11	17	4	0	0	8	8	14	.170	.231	.210	33	-8	3			.959	13	C-46	0.7
1917	Was-A	125	350	38	67	17	4	0	42	40	48	.191	.280	.263	66	-14	16			.971	15	*C-119	1.1
1918	Was-A	96	292	22	62	10	9	0	20	29	44	.212	.283	.308	80	-8	6			.975	8	C-89	0.8
1919	Det-A	114	364	42	99	17	12	3	32	45	30	.272	.354	.409	117	8	9			.962	-11	*C-106	0.7
1920	Det-A	69	186	19	43	5	3	1	19	14	19	.231	.285	.306	58	-11	4	3	-1	.955	-3	C-61/1-1	-1.1
1921	Det-A	35	98	6	27	5	2	0	12	13	7	.276	.360	.367	87	-2	1	0	0	.947	-4	C-34	-0.3
	StL-N	27	62	5	18	0	1	0	5	3	4	.290	.323	.323	73	-2	0	0	0	.956	1	C-23/1-1	0.0
1922	StL-N	119	379	46	111	14	4	13	59	28	43	.293	.343	.454	109	4	2	3	-1	.963	-2	*C-116	0.6
1923	StL-N	82	263	22	56	11	6	3	34	22	19	.213	.276	.335	62	-15	4	0	1	.980	-8	C-80	-1.8
	Bro-N	2	10	0	2	0	0	0	2	0	0	.200	.200	.200	6	-1	0	1	-1	1.000	1	/C-2	-0.1
	Yr	84	273	22	58	11	6	3	36	22	19	.212	.274	.330	60	-17	4	1	1	.981	-7	C-82	-1.9
1924	NY-N	10	5	0	3	0	0	0	0	0	0	.600	.600	.600	229	1	0	0	0	1.000	-0	/C-9	0.1
Total	15	1078	3048	299	707	108	54	22	317	263	315	.232	.296	.324	76	-100	86	16		.966	41	C-993/1-2,P-1	1.2

■ GEORGE AITON Aiton, George Wilson b: 12/29/1890, Kingman, Kan. d: 8/16/76, Van Nuys, Cal. BB/TR, 5'11.5", 175 lbs. Deb: 6/29/12

YEAR	TM/L	G	AB	R	H	2B	3B	HR	RBI	BB	SO	AVG	OBP	SLG	PRO+	BR/A	SB	CS	SBR	FA	FR	G/POS	TPR
1912	StL-A	10	17	1	4	0	0	0	1	4		.235	.381	.235	80	-0	0			.917	-0	/O-7	-0.1

■ JOHN AKE Ake, John Leckie b: 8/29/1861, Altoona, Pa. d: 5/11/1887, LaCrosse, Wis. BR/TR, 6'1", 180 lbs. Deb: 5/12/1884

YEAR	TM/L	G	AB	R	H	2B	3B	HR	RBI	BB	SO	AVG	OBP	SLG	PRO+	BR/A	SB	CS	SBR	FA	FR	G/POS	TPR
1884	Bal-a	13	52	1	10	0	1	0	2	0		.192	.208	.231	41	-3				.677	-3	/3-9,O-3,S-1	-0.6

■ BILL AKERS Akers, William G. "Bump" b: 12/25/04, Chattanooga, Tenn. d: 4/13/62, Chattanooga, Tenn. BR/TR, 5'11", 178 lbs. Deb: 9/8/29

YEAR	TM/L	G	AB	R	H	2B	3B	HR	RBI	BB	SO	AVG	OBP	SLG	PRO+	BR/A	SB	CS	SBR	FA	FR	G/POS	TPR
1929	Det-A	24	83	15	22	4	1	1	9	10	9	.265	.351	.373	86	-2	2	0	1	.935	-9	S-24	-0.6
1930	Det-A	85	233	36	65	8	5	9	40	36	34	.279	.375	.472	111	4	5	5	-2	.944	9	S-49,3-26	1.6
1931	Det-A	29	66	5	13	2	2	0	3	7	6	.197	.274	.288	46	-5	0	1	-1	.935	-2	S-21/2-2	-0.6
1932	Bos-N	36	93	8	24	3	1	1	17	10	15	.258	.330	.344	85	-2	0			.927	-5	3-20/2-5,S-5	-0.5
Total	4	174	475	64	124	17	9	11	69	63	64	.261	.349	.404	93	-4	7	6		.936	-6	/S-99,3-46,2-7	-0.1

■ GUS ALBERTS Alberts, Augustus Peter b: 1861, Reading, Pa. d: 5/7/12, Idaho Springs, Colo BR/TR, 5'6.5", 180 lbs. Deb: 5/1/1884

YEAR	TM/L	G	AB	R	H	2B	3B	HR	RBI	BB	SO	AVG	OBP	SLG	PRO+	BR/A	SB	CS	SBR	FA	FR	G/POS	TPR
1884	Pit-a	2	5	1	1	0	0	0		0		.200	.200	.200	30	-0				.500	-1	/S-2	-0.2
	Was-U	4	16	4	4	0	0	0		4		.250	.400	.250	105	-0				.870	2	/S-4	0.2
1888	Cle-a	102	364	51	75	10	6	1	48	41		.206	.299	.275	87	-4	26			.862	4	S-53,3-49	0.3
1891	Mil-a	12	41	6	4	0	0	0	2	7	5	.098	.260	.098	2	-6	1			.814	-3	3-12	-0.7
Total	3	120	426	62	84	10	6	1	50	52	5	.197	.298	.256	76	-10	27			.880	2	/3-61,S-59	-0.4

■ BUTCH ALBERTS Alberts, Francis Burt b: 5/4/50, Williamsport, Pa. BR/TR, 6'2", 205 lbs. Deb: 9/7/78

YEAR	TM/L	G	AB	R	H	2B	3B	HR	RBI	BB	SO	AVG	OBP	SLG	PRO+	BR/A	SB	CS	SBR	FA	FR	G/POS	TPR
1978	Tor-A	6	18	1	5	1	0	0	0	0	2	.278	.278	.333	70	-1	0	0	0	.000	0	/D-4	-0.1

■ JACK ALBRIGHT Albright, Harold John b: 6/30/21, St.Petersburg, Fla. d: 7/22/91, San Diego, Cal. BR/TR, 5'9", 175 lbs. Deb: 5/19/47

YEAR	TM/L	G	AB	R	H	2B	3B	HR	RBI	BB	SO	AVG	OBP	SLG	PRO+	BR/A	SB	CS	SBR	FA	FR	G/POS	TPR
1947	Phi-N	41	99	9	23	4	0	2	5	10	11	.232	.303	.333	71	-4	1			.943	3	S-33	0.0

■ LUIS ALCARAZ Alcaraz, Angel Luis (Acosta) b: 6/20/41, Humacao, P.R. BR/TR, 5'9", 165 lbs. Deb: 9/13/67

YEAR	TM/L	G	AB	R	H	2B	3B	HR	RBI	BB	SO	AVG	OBP	SLG	PRO+	BR/A	SB	CS	SBR	FA	FR	G/POS	TPR
1967	LA-N	17	60	1	14	1	0	0	3	1	13	.233	.246	.250	46	-4	1	1	-0	.990	9	2-17	0.5
1968	LA-N	41	106	4	16	1	0	2	5	9	23	.151	.217	.217	33	-9	1	1	-0	.979	3	2-20,3-13/S-1	-0.5
1969	KC-A	22	79	15	20	2	1	1	7	7	9	.253	.314	.342	83	-2	0	0	0	.988	-5	2-19/3-2,S-1	-0.5
1970	KC-A	35	120	10	20	5	1	1	14	4	13	.167	.194	.250	21	-13	0	0	0	.993	-8	2-31	-2.0
Total	4	115	365	30	70	9	2	4	29	21	58	.192	.236	.260	43	-28	2	2	-1	.988	-1	/2-87,3-15,S-2	-2.5

■ SCOTTY ALCOCK Alcock, John Forbes b: 11/29/1885, Wooster, Ohio d: 1/30/73, Wooster, Ohio BR/TR, 5'9.5", 160 lbs. Deb: 4/19/14

YEAR	TM/L	G	AB	R	H	2B	3B	HR	RBI	BB	SO	AVG	OBP	SLG	PRO+	BR/A	SB	CS	SBR	FA	FR	G/POS	TPR
1914	Chi-A	54	156	12	27	4	2	0	7	7	14	.173	.213	.224	32	-13	4	2	0	.905	4	3-48/2-1	-0.9

■ MIKE ALDRETE Aldrete, Michael Peter b: 1/29/61, Carmel, Cal. BL/TL, 5'11", 185 lbs. Deb: 5/28/86

YEAR	TM/L	G	AB	R	H	2B	3B	HR	RBI	BB	SO	AVG	OBP	SLG	PRO+	BR/A	SB	CS	SBR	FA	FR	G/POS	TPR
1986	SF-N	84	216	27	54	18	3	2	25	33	34	.250	.355	.389	110	4	1	3	-2	1.000	3	1-37,O-31	0.2
1987	*SF-N	126	357	50	116	18	2	9	51	43	50	.325	.398	.462	133	18	6	0	2	.986	-2	O-79,1-33	1.4
1988	SF-N	139	389	44	104	15	0	3	50	56	65	.267	.360	.329	103	4	6	5	-1	.982	-7	*O-115,1-10	-0.9
1989	Mon-N	76	136	12	30	8	1	1	12	19	30	.221	.321	.316	81	-3	1	3	-2	.980	-3	O-37,1-10	-0.9
1990	Mon-N	96	161	22	39	7	1	1	18	37	31	.242	.387	.317	100	2	1	2	-1	.982	-4	O-38,1-18	-0.4
1991	SD-N	12	15	2	0	0	0	0	1	3	4	.000	.167	.000	-48	-3	0	1	-1	1.000	0	/O-5	-0.4
	Cle-A	85	183	22	48	6	1	1	19	36	37	.262	.384	.322	97	1	1	2	-1	.994	-3	1-47,O-16/D-7	-0.5
1993	Oak-A	95	255	40	68	13	1	10	33	34	45	.267	.353	.443	120	7	1	1	-0	.995	-3	1-59,O-20/D-6	0.0
1994	Oak-A	76	178	23	43	5	0	4	18	20	35	.242	.318	.337	76	-6	2	0	1	1.000	-8	O-35,1-27/D-1	-1.5
1995	Oak-A	60	125	18	34	8	0	4	21	19	23	.272	.372	.432	115	3	0	0	0	.989	-6	1-35,O-16	-0.5
	Cal-A	18	24	1	6	0	0	0	3	0	8	.250	.250	.250	31	-2	0	0	0	1.000	1	/O-2,1-1,D-2	-0.2
	Yr	78	149	19	40	8	0	4	24	19	31	.268	.355	.403	101	0	0	0	0	.989	-5	1-36,O-18/D-2	-0.7

YEAR	TM/L	G	AB	R	H	2B	3B	HR	RBI	BB	SO	AVG	OBP	SLG	PRO+	BR/A	SB	CS	SBR	FA	FR	G/POS	TPR
1996	Cal-A	31	40	5	6	1	0	3	8	5	4	.150	.244	.400	59	-3	0	0	0	.750	-2	/O-6,1-1,D-6	-0.5
	*NY-A	32	68	11	17	5	0	3	12	9	15	.250	.338	.456	98	-0	0	1	-1	1.000	-4	/O-9,1-8,P-1,D-9	-0.5
	Yr	63	108	16	23	6	0	6	20	14	19	.213	.303	.435	84	-3	0	1	-1	.909	-6	O-15,D-15/1-9,P-1	-1.0
Total	10	930	2147	277	565	104	9	41	271	314	381	.263	.358	.377	104	20	19	18	-5	.983	-36	O-409,1-286/D-31,P	-4.7

■ CHUCK ALENO Aleno, Charles b: 2/19/17, St.Louis, Mo. BR/TR, 6'1.5", 215 lbs. Deb: 5/15/41

YEAR	TM/L	G	AB	R	H	2B	3B	HR	RBI	BB	SO	AVG	OBP	SLG	PRO+	BR/A	SB	CS	SBR	FA	FR	G/POS	TPR
1941	Cin-N	54	169	23	41	7	3	1	18	11	16	.243	.289	.337	76	-6	3			.975	-4	3-40/1-2	-0.9
1942	Cin-N	7	14	1	2	1	0	0	0	3	3	.143	.294	.214	50	-1	0			.727	1	/3-2,2-1	0.1
1943	Cin-N	7	10	0	3	0	0	0	1	2	1	.300	.417	.300	110	0	0			1.000	-1	/O-2	0.0
1944	Cin-N	50	127	10	21	3	0	1	15	15	15	.165	.259	.213	35	-11	0			.952	-4	3-42/1-3,S-3	-1.5
Total	4	118	320	34	67	11	3	2	34	31	35	.209	.281	.281	60	-17	3			.954	-7	/3-84,1-5,S-3,O2	-2.3

■ DALE ALEXANDER Alexander, David Dale "Moose" b: 4/26/03, Greeneville, Tenn. d: 3/2/79, Greeneville, Tenn. BR/TR, 6'3", 210 lbs. Deb: 4/16/29

YEAR	TM/L	G	AB	R	H	2B	3B	HR	RBI	BB	SO	AVG	OBP	SLG	PRO+	BR/A	SB	CS	SBR	FA	FR	G/POS	TPR
1929	Det-A	155	626	110	**215**	43	15	25	137	56	63	.343	.397	.580	148	42	5	9	-4	.988	-4	*1-155	1.7
1930	Det-A	154	602	86	196	33	8	20	135	42	56	.326	.372	.507	118	15	6	5	-1	.985	-7	*1-154	-0.7
1931	Det-A	135	517	75	168	47	3	3	87	64	35	.325	.401	.445	118	15	5	8	-3	.987	-8	*1-126/O-4	-0.8
1932	Det-A	23	16	0	4	0	0	0	4	6	2	.250	.455	.250	84	0	0	0	0	1.000	-0	/1-2	0.0
	Bos-A	101	376	58	140	27	3	8	56	55	19	.372	.454	.524	157	34	4	5	-2	.992	2	*1-101	2.4
	Yr	124	392	58	144	27	3	8	60	61	21	**.367**	.454	.513	152	33	4	5	-2	.992	2	*1-103	2.4
1933	Bos-A	94	313	40	88	14	1	5	40	25	22	.281	.336	.380	90	-5	0	1	-1	.992	3	1-79	-0.9
Total	5	662	2450	369	811	164	30	61	459	248	197	.331	.394	.497	128	102	20	28	-11	.988	-14	1-617/O-4	1.7

■ GARY ALEXANDER Alexander, Gary Wayne b: 3/27/53, Los Angeles, Cal. BR/TR, 6'2", 200 lbs. Deb: 9/12/75

YEAR	TM/L	G	AB	R	H	2B	3B	HR	RBI	BB	SO	AVG	OBP	SLG	PRO+	BR/A	SB	CS	SBR	FA	FR	G/POS	TPR
1975	SF-N	3	3	1	0	0	0	0	0	1	2	.000	.250	.000	-25	-0	0	0	0	1.000	-1	/C-2	-0.1
1976	SF-N	23	73	12	13	1	1	2	7	10	16	.178	.277	.301	62	-4	1	0	0	.964	-4	C-23	-0.7
1977	SF-N	51	119	17	36	4	2	5	20	20	33	.303	.411	.496	143	8	3	1	0	.968	-8	C-33/O-1	0.1
1978	Oak-A	58	174	18	36	6	1	10	22	22	66	.207	.299	.425	107	1	0	3	-2	1.000	0	D-45/O-6,C-1,1-1	-0.2
	Cle-A	90	324	39	76	14	3	17	62	35	100	.235	.311	.454	114	5	0	2	-1	.983	-9	C-66,D-25	-0.5
	Yr	148	498	57	112	20	4	27	84	57	166	.225	.307	.444	112	6	0	5	-3	.983	-9	D-70,C-67/O-6,1-1	-0.7
1979	Cle-A	110	358	54	82	9	2	15	54	46	100	.229	.319	.391	90	-5	4	2	0	.961	-21	C-91,D-13/O-2	-2.3
1980	Cle-A	76	178	22	40	7	1	5	31	17	52	.225	.292	.360	77	-6	0	4	-2	.971	-2	D-40,C-13/O-2	-1.1
1981	Pit-N	21	47	6	10	4	1	1	6	3	12	.213	.260	.404	84	-1	0	0	0	.964	1	/1-9,O-8	-0.1
Total	7	432	1276	169	293	45	11	55	202	154	381	.230	.315	.411	99	-3	8	12	-5	.969	-42	C-229,D-123/O-19,1	-4.9

■ HUGH ALEXANDER Alexander, Hugh b: 7/10/17, Buffalo, Mo. BR/TR, 6', 190 lbs. Deb: 8/15/37

YEAR	TM/L	G	AB	R	H	2B	3B	HR	RBI	BB	SO	AVG	OBP	SLG	PRO+	BR/A	SB	CS	SBR	FA	FR	G/POS	TPR
1937	Cle-A	7	11	0	1	0	0	0	0	0	5	.091	.091	.091	-54	-3	1	0	0	.667	-2	/O-3	-0.4

■ MANNY ALEXANDER Alexander, Manuel De Jesus (b: Manuel De Jesus (Alexander)) b: 3/20/71, San Pedro De Macoris, D.R. BR/TR, 5'10", 165 lbs. Deb: 9/18/92

YEAR	TM/L	G	AB	R	H	2B	3B	HR	RBI	BB	SO	AVG	OBP	SLG	PRO+	BR/A	SB	CS	SBR	FA	FR	G/POS	TPR
1992	Bal-A	4	5	1	1	0	0	0	0	0	3	.200	.200	.200	12	-1	0	0	0	1.000	1	/S-3	0.0
1993	Bal-A	3	0	1	0	0	0	0	0	0	0	—	—	—	—	0	0	0	0	.000	0	/R	0.0
1995	Bal-A	94	242	35	57	9	1	3	23	20	30	.236	.299	.318	60	-14	11	4	1	.971	-4	2-81/S-7,3-2,D-1	-1.3
1996	*Bal-A	54	68	6	7	0	0	0	4	3	27	.103	.141	.103	-37	-14	3	3	-1	.940	7	S-21/2-7,3-7,OPD	-0.7
1997	NY-N	54	149	26	37	9	3	2	15	9	38	.248	.296	.389	80	-5	11	0	3	.979	-1	2-31,S-26/3-1	0.1
	Chi-N	33	99	11	29	3	1	1	7	8	16	.293	.358	.374	90	-1	2	1	0	.942	2	S-28/2-4	0.3
	Yr	87	248	37	66	12	4	3	22	17	54	.266	.321	.383	84	-6	13	1	3	.959	1	S-54,2-35/3-1	0.4
1998	*Chi-N	108	264	34	60	10	1	5	25	18	66	.227	.279	.330	56	-17	4	1	1	.964	-14	S-50,2-27,3-19,/OD	-2.5
Total	6	350	827	114	191	31	6	11	74	58	180	.231	.286	.323	57	-52	31	9	4	.975	-9	2-150,S-135/3ODP	-4.1

■ MATT ALEXANDER Alexander, Matthew b: 1/30/47, Shreveport, La. BB/TR, 5'11", 169 lbs. Deb: 8/23/73

YEAR	TM/L	G	AB	R	H	2B	3B	HR	RBI	BB	SO	AVG	OBP	SLG	PRO+	BR/A	SB	CS	SBR	FA	FR	G/POS	TPR
1973	Chi-N	12	5	4	1	0	0	0	1	1	1	.200	.333	.200	48	-0	2	0	1	1.000	-1	/O-3	-0.1
1974	Chi-N	45	54	15	11	2	1	0	0	12	12	.204	.358	.278	76	-1	8	4	0	.921	-2	3-19/O-4,2-2	-0.3
1975	Oak-A	63	10	16	1	0	0	0	0	1	1	.100	.182	.100	-19	-2	17	10	-1	1.000	-3	D-17,O-11/2-3,3-2	-0.6
1976	Oak-A	61	30	16	1	0	0	0	0	0	5	.033	.033	.033	-84	-7	20	7	2	1.000	-7	O-23,D-19	-1.4
1977	Oak-A	90	42	24	10	1	0	0	2	4	6	.238	.304	.262	57	-2	26	14	-1	1.000	-11	O-31,S-12/2-4,3D	-1.4
1978	Pit-N	7	0	2	0	0	0	0	0	0	0	—	—	—	—	0	4	1	1	.000	0	R	0.0
1979	*Pit-N	44	13	16	7	0	1	0	1	0	0	.538	.538	.692	223	2	13	1	3	1.000	-3	O-11/S-1	0.2
1980	Pit-N	37	3	13	1	1	0	0	0	0	0	.333	.333	.667	170	0	10	3	1	1.000	-1	/O-4,2-1	0.1
1981	Pit-N	15	11	5	4	0	0	0	0	0	1	.364	.364	.364	104	0	3	2	-0	1.000	-1	/O-6	-0.2
Total	9	374	168	111	36	4	2	0	4	18	26	.214	.294	.262	56	-10	103	42	6	1.000	-29	/O-93,D-37,3-22,S2	-3.7

■ WALT ALEXANDER Alexander, Walter Ernest b: 3/5/1891, Atlanta, Ga. d: 12/29/78, Fort Worth, Tex. BR/TR, 5'10.5", 165 lbs. Deb: 6/21/12

YEAR	TM/L	G	AB	R	H	2B	3B	HR	RBI	BB	SO	AVG	OBP	SLG	PRO+	BR/A	SB	CS	SBR	FA	FR	G/POS	TPR
1912	StL-A	37	97	5	17	4	0	0	5	8		.175	.245	.216	34	-8	1			.969	-3	C-37	-0.8
1913	StL-A	43	110	5	15	2	1	0	7	4	36	.136	.174	.173	2	-14	1			.947	4	C-43	-0.8
1915	StL-A	1	1	0	0	0	0	0	0	0	0	.000	.000	.000	-99	-0	0			.000	0	/C-1	0.0
	NY-A	25	68	7	17	4	0	1	5	13	16	.250	.370	.353	117	2	2	1	0	.967	9	C-24	1.3
	Yr	26	69	7	17	4	0	1	5	13	16	.246	.366	.348	114	2	2	1	0	.967	9	C-25	1.3
1916	NY-A	36	78	8	20	6	1	0	3	13	20	.256	.376	.359	118	2	0			.960	2	C-27	0.6
1917	NY-A	20	51	1	7	2	1	0	4	4	11	.137	.200	.216	27	-5	1			.951	0	C-20	-0.4
Total	5	162	405	26	76	18	3	1	24	42	83	.188	.271	.254	56	-23	5	1		.959	11	C-152	-0.1

■ NIN ALEXANDER Alexander, William Henry b: 11/24/1858, Pana, Ill. d: 12/22/33, Pana, Ill. BR/TR, 5'4.5", 163 lbs. Deb: 6/7/1884

YEAR	TM/L	G	AB	R	H	2B	3B	HR	RBI	BB	SO	AVG	OBP	SLG	PRO+	BR/A	SB	CS	SBR	FA	FR	G/POS	TPR
1884	KC-U	19	65	2	9	0	0	0		1		.138	.152	.138	-13	-11				.907	-2	C-17/S-2,O-2	-1.0
	StL-a	1	4	0	0	0	0	0		0		.000	.000	.000	-97	-1				.667	-0	/C-1,O-1	-0.1
Total	1	20	69	2	9	0	0	0		1		.130	.143	.130	-19	-12				.895	-2	/C-18,O-3,S-2	-1.1

■ EDGARDO ALFONZO Alfonzo, Edgardo Antonio b: 8/11/73, Santa Teresa, Venez. BR/TR, 5'11", 185 lbs. Deb: 4/26/95

YEAR	TM/L	G	AB	R	H	2B	3B	HR	RBI	BB	SO	AVG	OBP	SLG	PRO+	BR/A	SB	CS	SBR	FA	FR	G/POS	TPR
1995	NY-N	101	335	26	93	13	5	4	41	12	37	.278	.305	.382	82	-9	1	1	-0	.962	-6	3-58,2-29/S-6	-1.4
1996	NY-N	123	368	36	96	15	2	4	40	25	56	.261	.308	.345	75	-13	2	0	1	.974	-2	2-66,3-36,S-15	-1.0
1997	NY-N	151	518	84	163	27	2	10	72	63	56	.315	.394	.432	121	18	11	6	-0	.967	6	*3-143,S-12/2-3	2.4
1998	NY-N	144	557	94	155	28	2	17	78	65	77	.278	.357	.427	103	3	8	3	1	.976	-8	*3-144/S-1	-0.1
Total	4	519	1778	240	507	83	11	35	231	165	226	.285	.349	.403	99	-2	22	10	1	.969	-10	3-381/2-98,S-34	-0.1

■ LUIS ALICEA Alicea, Luis Rene (De Jesus) b: 7/29/65, Santurce, P.R. BB/TR, 5'9", 177 lbs. Deb: 4/23/88

YEAR	TM/L	G	AB	R	H	2B	3B	HR	RBI	BB	SO	AVG	OBP	SLG	PRO+	BR/A	SB	CS	SBR	FA	FR	G/POS	TPR
1988	StL-N	93	297	20	63	10	4	1	24	25	32	.212	.278	.283	61	-15	1	1	-0	.970	4	2-91	-0.9
1991	StL-N	56	68	5	13	3	0	0	0	8	19	.191	.276	.235	45	-5	0	1	-1	1.000	-1	2-11/3-2,S-1	-0.7
1992	StL-N	85	265	26	65	9	11	2	32	27	40	.245	.324	.385	103	1	2	5	-2	.989	2	2-75/S-4	0.2
1993	StL-N	115	362	50	101	19	3	3	46	47	54	.279	.368	.373	101	2	11	1	3	.978	2	2-96/O-4,3-1	0.9
1994	StL-N	88	205	32	57	12	5	5	29	30	38	.278	.378	.459	119	6	4	5	-2	.986	4	2-53/O-2	1.0
1995	*Bos-A	132	419	64	113	20	3	6	44	63	61	.270	.374	.375	93	-3	13	10	-2	.977	12	*2-132	1.4
1996	*StL-N	129	380	54	98	26	3	5	42	52	78	.258	.355	.382	95	-1	11	3	2	.957	-21	*2-125	-1.4
1997	Ana-A	128	388	59	98	16	7	5	37	69	65	.253	.376	.369	96	0	22	8	2	.978	-3	*2-105,3-12/D-6	0.5
1998	*Tex-A	101	259	51	71	15	3	6	33	37	40	.274	.375	.425	103	2	4	3	-1	.970	4	2-45,3-26,D-17,/O-2	0.6
Total	9	927	2643	361	679	130	39	33	287	358	427	.257	.354	.373	94	-12	68	37	-2	.975	1	2-733/3-41,D-23,OS	1.6

■ ANDY ALLANSON Allanson, Andrew Neal b: 12/22/61, Richmond, Va. BR/TR, 6'5", 225 lbs. Deb: 4/7/86

YEAR	TM/L	G	AB	R	H	2B	3B	HR	RBI	BB	SO	AVG	OBP	SLG	PRO+	BR/A	SB	CS	SBR	FA	FR	G/POS	TPR
1986	Cle-A	101	293	30	66	7	3	1	29	14	36	.225	.263	.280	49	-21	10	1	2	.960	-7	C-99	-2.0
1987	Cle-A	50	154	17	41	6	0	3	16	9	30	.266	.307	.364	76	-5	1	1	-0	.986	-7	C-50	-0.9
1988	Cle-A	133	434	44	114	11	0	5	50	25	63	.263	.307	.323	75	-14	5	9	-4	.986	1	*C-133	-0.8
1989	Cle-A	111	323	30	75	9	1	3	17	23	47	.232	.291	.294	64	-15	4	4	-1	.986	3	*C-111	-0.7
1991	Det-A	60	151	10	35	10	0	1	16	7	31	.232	.266	.318	60	-8	0	1	-1	.979	6	C-56/1-2,D-1	-0.1
1992	Mil-A	9	25	6	8	1	0	0	0	1	2	.320	.346	.360	100	-0	3	1	0	.943	-2	/C-9	-0.1

YEAR	TM/L	G	AB	R	H	2B	3B	HR	RBI	BB	SO	AVG	OBP	SLG	PRO+	BR/A	SB	CS	SBR	FA	FR	G/POS	TPR
1993	SF-N	13	24	3	4	1	0	0	2	1	2	.167	.200	.208	10	-3	0	0	0	1.000	-1	/C-8,1-2	-0.4
1995	Cal-A	35	82	5	14	3	0	3	10	7	12	.171	.244	.317	45	-7	0	1	-1	.994	6	C-35	0.0
Total	8	512	1486	145	357	48	4	16	140	87	223	.240	.286	.310	64	-74	23	18	-4	.980	-1	C-501/1-4,D-1	-5.0
■ **NICK ALLEN**	Allen, Artemus Ward b: 9/14/1888, Norton, Kan. d: 10/16/39, Hines, Ill. BR/TR, 6′, 180 lbs. Deb: 5/1/14																						
1914	Buf-F	32	63	3	15	1	0	0	4	3	12	.238	.273	.254	43	-6	4			.969	2	C-26	-0.3
1915	Buf-F	84	215	14	44	7	1	0	17	18	34	.205	.269	.247	45	-19	4			.956	7	C-80	-0.7
1916	Chi-N	5	16	1	1	0	0	0	1	0	3	.063	.063	.063	-56	-3	0			.958	-1	/C-4	-0.4
1918	Cin-N	37	96	6	25	2	2	0	5	4	7	.260	.297	.323	91	-1	0			.950	8	C-31	0.9
1919	Cin-N	15	25	7	8	0	1	0	5	2	6	.320	.393	.400	142	1	0			.958	3	C-12	0.5
1920	Cin-N	43	85	10	23	3	1	0	4	6	11	.271	.340	.329	94	-0	0	0	0	.961	6	C-36	0.8
Total	6	216	500	41	116	13	5	0	36	33	73	.232	.288	.278	62	-28	8	0		.958	25	C-189	0.8
■ **BERNIE ALLEN**	Allen, Bernard Keith b: 4/16/39, E.Liverpool, O. BL/TR, 6′, 185 lbs. Deb: 4/10/62																						
1962	Min-A	159	573	79	154	27	7	12	64	62	82	.269	.340	.403	96	-3	0	1	-1	.983	-17	*2-158	-0.4
1963	Min-A	139	421	52	101	20	1	9	43	38	52	.240	.304	.356	83	-10	0	0	0	.976	-24	*2-128	-2.5
1964	Min-A	74	243	28	52	8	1	6	20	33	30	.214	.310	.329	78	-7	1	2	-1	.979	-11	2-71	-1.4
1965	Min-A	19	39	2	9	2	0	0	6	6	8	.231	.333	.282	73	-1	0	0	0	1.000	-2	2-10/3-1	-0.2
1966	Min-A	101	319	34	76	18	1	5	30	26	40	.238	.300	.348	80	-8	2	3	-1	.974	-7	2-89/3-2	-1.1
1967	Was-A	87	254	13	49	5	1	3	18	18	43	.193	.246	.256	51	-16	1	2	-1	.990	19	2-75	0.7
1968	Was-A	120	373	31	90	12	4	6	40	28	35	.241	.301	.343	98	-1	2	0	1	**.991**	5	*2-110/3-2	1.1
1969	Was-A	122	365	33	90	17	4	9	45	50	35	.247	.337	.389	108	4	5	4	-1	.974	3	*2-110/3-6	1.5
1970	Was-A	104	261	31	61	7	1	8	29	43	21	.234	.342	.360	99	0	0	2	-1	.969	-0	2-80,3-12	0.4
1971	Was-A	97	229	18	61	11	1	4	22	33	27	.266	.359	.376	115	5	2	1	0	.961	-11	2-41,3-34	-0.4
1972	NY-A	84	220	26	50	9	0	9	21	23	42	.227	.300	.391	108	2	0	1	-1	.940	-0	3-44,2-20	0.1
1973	NY-A	17	57	5	13	3	0	0	4	5	5	.228	.290	.281	64	-3	0	0	0	.985	0	2-13/D-2	-0.2
	Mon-N	16	50	5	9	1	0	2	9	5	4	.180	.255	.320	56	-3	0	0	0	.970	-1	/2-9,3-8	-0.4
Total	12	1139	3404	357	815	140	21	73	351	370	424	.239	.315	.357	91	-41	13	16	-6	.980	-47	2-914,3-109/D-2	-2.8
■ **JACK ALLEN**	Allen, Cyrus Alban b: 10/2/1855, Woodstock, Ill. d: 4/21/15, Girard, Pa. BR/TR, 160 lbs. Deb: 5/1/1879																						
1879	Syr-N	11	48	7	9	2	1	0	3	1	5	.188	.204	.271	62	-2				.655	-6	/3-8,O-3	-0.7
	Cle-N	16	60	7	7	1	1	0	4	1	9	.117	.131	.167	-3	-6				.845	3	3-14/O-2	-0.3
	Yr	27	108	14	16	3	2	0	7	2	14	.148	.164	.213	24	-8				.790	-3	3-22/O-5	-1.0
■ **ETHAN ALLEN**	Allen, Ethan Nathan b: 1/1/04, Cincinnati, Ohio d: 9/15/93, Brookings, Ore. BR/TR, 6′1″, 180 lbs. Deb: 6/21/26																						
1926	Cin-N	18	13	3	4	1	0	0	0	0	3	.308	.308	.385	88	-0	0			1.000	-3	/O-9	-0.3
1927	Cin-N	111	359	54	106	26	4	2	20	14	23	.295	.325	.407	98	-2	12			.988	-2	O-98	-1.0
1928	Cin-N	129	485	55	148	30	7	1	62	27	29	.305	.343	.402	96	-4	6			.981	3	*O-129	-1.0
1929	Cin-N	143	538	69	157	27	11	6	64	20	21	.292	.317	.416	84	-16	21			**.988**	-10	*O-137	-3.2
1930	Cin-N	21	46	10	10	1	0	3	7	5	2	.217	.294	.435	77	-2	1			.969	-2	O-15	-0.4
	NY-N	76	238	48	73	9	2	7	31	12	23	.307	.340	.450	91	-4	5			.985	-4	O-62	-1.1
	Yr	97	284	58	83	10	2	10	38	17	25	.292	.332	.447	89	-6	6			.981	-6	O-77	-1.5
1931	NY-N	94	298	58	98	18	2	5	43	15	15	.329	.363	.453	121	8	6			.975	-7	O-77	-0.3
1932	NY-N	54	103	13	18	6	2	1	7	1	12	.175	.198	.301	33	-10	0			.957	-4	O-24	-1.5
1933	StL-N	91	261	25	63	7	3	0	36	13	22	.241	.280	.291	60	-13	3			.984	8	O-67	-0.9
1934	Phi-N	145	581	87	192	**42**	4	10	85	33	47	.330	.370	.468	108	6	6			.978	9	*O-145	0.8
1935	Phi-N	156	645	90	198	46	1	8	63	43	54	.307	.351	.419	96	-4	5			.980	17	*O-156	0.6
1936	Phi-N	30	125	21	37	3	1	1	9	4	8	.296	.318	.360	75	-5	4			.954	-0	O-30	-0.6
	Chi-N	91	373	47	110	18	6	3	39	13	30	.295	.322	.399	91	-5	12			.980	-2	O-89	-1.1
	Yr	121	498	68	147	21	7	4	48	17	38	.295	.321	.390	87	-10	16			.972	-3	*O-119	-1.7
1937	StL-A	103	320	39	101	18	1	0	31	21	17	.316	.360	.378	86	-7	3	4	-2	.980	-1	O-78	-1.1
1938	StL-A	19	33	4	10	3	1	0	4	2	4	.303	.343	.455	98	-0	0	0	0	1.000	-1	/O-7	-0.2
Total	13	1281	4418	623	1325	255	45	47	501	223	310	.300	.336	.410	92	-58	84	4		.981	-0	*O-1123	-11.3
■ **SLED ALLEN**	Allen, Fletcher Manson b: 8/23/1886, West Plains, Mo. d: 10/16/59, Lubbock, Tex. BR/TR, 6′1″, 180 lbs. Deb: 5/4/10																						
1910	StL-A	14	23	3	3	1	0	0	1	1		.130	.231	.174	29	-2	0			.903	-6	C-12/1-1	-0.8
■ **HANK ALLEN**	Allen, Harold Andrew b: 7/23/40, Wampum, Pa. BR/TR, 6′, 190 lbs. Deb: 9/9/66 F																						
1966	Was-A	9	31	2	12	0	0	1	6	3	6	.387	.441	.484	167	3	0	0	0	.917	0	/O-9	0.2
1967	Was-A	116	292	34	68	8	4	3	17	13	53	.233	.266	.318	75	-10	3	4	-2	.980	-21	O-99	-4.1
1968	Was-A	68	128	16	28	2	2	1	9	7	16	.219	.265	.289	70	-5	0	0	0	.895	-8	O-25,3-16,2-11	-1.5
1969	Was-A	109	271	42	75	9	3	1	17	13	28	.277	.312	.343	88	-5	12	3	2	.933	-17	O-91/3-6,2-3	-2.5
1970	Was-A	22	38	3	8	2	0	0	4	5	9	.211	.302	.263	60	-2	0	0	0	1.000	-3	O-17	-0.6
	Mil-A	28	61	4	14	4	0	0	4	7	5	.230	.309	.295	67	-3	0	1	-1	1.000	-1	O-14/2-5,1-4	-0.5
	Yr	50	99	7	22	6	0	0	8	12	14	.222	.306	.283	65	-5	0	1	-1	1.000	-4	O-31/2-5,1-4	-1.1
1972	Chi-A	9	21	1	3	0	0	0	0	0	2	.143	.143	.143	-15	-3	0	0	0	.905	3	/3-6	0.0
1973	Chi-A	28	39	2	4	2	0	0	0	1	9	.103	.125	.154	-21	-6	0	1	-1	1.000	-0	/3-9,1-8,O-5,C-1,2	-0.8
Total	7	389	881	104	212	27	9	6	57	49	128	.241	.282	.312	74	-31	15	9	-1	.957	-48	O-260/3-37,2-20,1C	-9.8
■ **HEZEKIAH ALLEN**	Allen, Hezekiah "Ki" b: 2/25/1863, Westport, Conn. d: 9/21/16, Saugatuck, Conn. 5′11″, 160 lbs. Deb: 5/16/1884																						
1884	Phi-N	1	3	0	2	0	0	0	0	0	0	.667	.667	.667	337	1				1.000	-1	/C-1	0.0
■ **HAM ALLEN**	Allen, Homer S. b: 8/1854, Hamden, Conn. d: 1/7/1892, Hamden, Conn. Deb: 4/27/1872																						
1872	Man-n	16	66	8	18	1	0	0	7	0	1	.273	.273	.288	77	-1	0	0	0	.750	6	/O-9,S-8	0.3
■ **HORACE ALLEN**	Allen, Horace Tanner "Pug" b: 6/11/1899, DeLand, Fla. d: 7/5/81, Canton, N.C. BL/TR, 6′, 187 lbs. Deb: 6/15/19																						
1919	Bro-N	4	7	0	0	0	0	0	0	0	2	.000	.000	.000	-98	-2	0			1.000	0	/O-2	-0.2
■ **JAMIE ALLEN**	Allen, James Bradley b: 5/29/58, Yakima, Wash. BR/TR, 6′, 205 lbs. Deb: 5/1/83																						
1983	Sea-A	86	273	23	61	10	0	4	21	33	52	.223	.309	.304	67	-12	6	5	-1	.959	-6	3-82/D-2	-2.0
■ **PETE ALLEN**	Allen, Jesse Hall b: 5/1/1868, Columbiana, Ohio d: 4/16/46, Philadelphia, Pa. BR/TR, 5′8.5″, 185 lbs. Deb: 8/4/1893																						
1893	Cle-N	1	4	0	0	0	0	0	0	0	0	.000	.000	.000	-94	-1	0			1.000	-1	/C-1	-0.2
■ **KIM ALLEN**	Allen, Kim Bryant b: 4/5/53, Fontana, Cal. BR/TR, 5′11″, 175 lbs. Deb: 9/2/80																						
1980	Sea-A	23	51	9	12	3	0	0	3	8	3	.235	.350	.294	78	-1	10	3	1	.970	-2	2-15/O-4,S-1	-0.2
1981	Sea-A	19	3	1	0	0	0	0	0	0	2	.000	.000	.000	-96	-1	2	1	0	.000	-1	/2-2,O-2,D-2	-0.2
Total	2	42	54	10	12	3	0	0	3	8	5	.222	.333	.278	69	-2	12	4	1	.970	-4	/2-17,O-6,D-2,S-1	-0.4
■ **MYRON ALLEN**	Allen, Myron Smith "Zeke" b: 3/22/1854, Kingston, N.Y. d: 3/8/24, Kingston, N.Y. BR/TR, 5′8″, 150 lbs. Deb: 7/19/1883																						
1883	NY-N	1	4	0	0	0	0	0	1	0	2	.000	.000	.000	-99	-1				1.000	-0	/P-1	0.0
1886	Bos-N	1	3	0	0	0	0	0	0	0	1	.000	.000	.000	-99	-1	0			1.000	-0	/2-1	-0.1
1887	Cle-a	117	463	66	128	22	10	4	77	36		.276	.335	.393	106	3	26			.894	8	*O-115/3-3,S-2,P-2	0.8
1888	KC-a	37	136	23	29	6	4	0	10	9		.213	.267	.316	81	-3	4			.931	7	O-35/P-2	0.2
Total	4	156	606	89	157	28	14	4	88	45	3	.259	.317	.371	98	-2	30			.903	15	O-150/P-5,3-3,S2	0.9
■ **DICK ALLEN**	Allen, Richard Anthony b: 3/8/42, Wampum, Pa. BR/TR, 5′11″, 190 lbs. Deb: 9/3/63 F																						
1963	Phi-N	10	24	6	7	2	1	0	2	0	5	.292	.292	.458	114	0	0	0	0	.833	-1	/O-7,3-1	-0.1
1964	Phi-N	162	632	**125**	201	38	**13**	29	91	67	138	.318	.383	.557	163	52	3	4	-2	.921	7	*3-162	5.8
1965	Phi-N★	161	619	93	187	31	14	20	85	74	150	.302	.378	.494	146	38	15	2	3	.943	-2	*3-160/S-2	3.7
1966	Phi-N★	141	524	112	166	25	10	40	110	68	136	.317	.398	**.632**	**181**	**57**	10	6	-1	.967	-8	3-91,O-47	4.5
1967	Phi-N★	122	463	89	142	31	10	23	77	75	117	.307	**.404**	.566	**173**	45	20	5	3	.908	-6	*3-121/2-1,S-1	4.4

YEAR	TM/L	G	AB	R	H	2B	3B	HR	RBI	BB	SO	AVG	OBP	SLG	PRO+	BR/A	SB	CS	SBR	FA	FR	G/POS	TPR
1968	Phi-N	152	521	87	137	17	9	33	90	74	161	.263	.356	.520	160	38	7	7	-2	.973	-5	*O-139,3-10	2.7
1969	Phi-N	118	438	79	126	23	3	32	89	64	144	.288	.378	.573	168	38	9	3	1	.985	-9	*1-117	2.1
1970	StL-N★	122	459	88	128	17	5	34	101	71	118	.279	.378	.560	145	28	5	4	-1	.993	-12	1-79,3-38/O-3	0.9
1971	LA-N	155	549	82	162	24	1	23	90	93	113	.295	.398	.468	154	41	8	1	2	.918	-8	3-67,O-60,1-28	3.1
1972	Chi-A★	148	506	90	156	28	5	**37**	**113**	**99**	126	.308	**.422**	**.603**	**199**	**64**	19	8	1	.995	-4	*1-143/3-2	5.4
1973	Chi-A†	72	250	39	79	20	3	16	41	33	51	.316	.398	.612	175	24	7	2	1	.994	0	1-67/2-2,D-1	2.0
1974	Chi-A★	128	462	84	139	23	1	**32**	88	57	89	.301	.379	**.563**	164	37	7	1	2	.986	-11	*1-125/2-1,D-1	2.0
1975	Phi-N	119	416	54	97	21	3	12	62	58	109	.233	.330	.385	94	-3	11	2	2	.982	-1	*1-113	-1.0
1976	*Phi-N	85	298	52	80	16	1	15	49	37	63	.268	.349	.480	130	11	11	4	1	.989	-3	1-85	0.3
1977	Oak-A	54	171	19	41	4	0	5	31	24	36	.240	.337	.351	89	-2	1	3	-2	.984	2	1-50/D-1	-0.5
Total	15	1749	6332	1099	1848	320	79	351	1119	894	1556	.292	.381	.534	156	469	133	52	9	.989	-62	1-807,3-652,O/2DS	35.3

■ **BOB ALLEN** Allen, Robert (b: Alvah Charles Elliott) b: 10/13/1894, Muscoda, Wis. d: 12/18/75, Naperville, Ill. BR/TR, 5′10″, 180 lbs. Deb: 8/20/19

YEAR	TM/L	G	AB	R	H	2B	3B	HR	RBI	BB	SO	AVG	OBP	SLG	PRO+	BR/A	SB	CS	SBR	FA	FR	G/POS	TPR
1919	Phi-A	9	22	3	3	1	0	0	0	3	7	.136	.269	.182	27	-2	0			.889	-2	/O-6	-0.5

■ **BOB ALLEN** Allen, Robert Gilman b: 7/10/1867, Marion, Ohio d: 5/14/43, Little Rock, Ark. BR/TR, 5′11″, 175 lbs. Deb: 4/19/1890 M

YEAR	TM/L	G	AB	R	H	2B	3B	HR	RBI	BB	SO	AVG	OBP	SLG	PRO+	BR/A	SB	CS	SBR	FA	FR	G/POS	TPR
1890	Phi-N	133	456	69	103	15	11	2	57	87	54	.226	.356	.320	95	-0	13			.924	**39**	*S-133/M	4.0
1891	Phi-N	118	438	46	97	7	4	1	51	43	44	.221	.291	.263	60	-22	12			.896	13	*S-118	-0.2
1892	Phi-N	152	563	77	128	20	14	2	64	61	60	.227	.304	.323	90	-7	15			.919	18	*S-152	1.6
1893	Phi-N	124	471	86	126	19	12	8	90	71	40	.268	.369	.410	107	5	8			.919	18	*S-124	2.4
1894	Phi-N	40	149	26	38	10	3	0	19	17	11	.255	.335	.362	70	-7	4			.915	-2	S-40	-0.6
1897	Bos-N	34	119	33	38	5	0	1	24	18		.319	.409	.387	104	1	1			.924	8	S-32/O-1,2-1	0.8
1900	Cin-N	5	15	0	2	1	0	0	1	0		.133	.188	.200	7	-2	0			.864	-0	/S-5,M	-0.2
Total	7	606	2211	337	532	77	44	14	306	297	209	.241	.334	.334	88	-33	53			.915	93	S-604/2-1,O-1	7.8

■ **ROD ALLEN** Allen, Roderick Bernet b: 10/5/59, Los Angeles, Cal. BR/TR, 6′1″, 185 lbs. Deb: 4/7/83

YEAR	TM/L	G	AB	R	H	2B	3B	HR	RBI	BB	SO	AVG	OBP	SLG	PRO+	BR/A	SB	CS	SBR	FA	FR	G/POS	TPR
1983	Sea-A	11	12	1	2	0	0	0	0	0	1	.167	.167	.167	-8	-2	0	0	0	1.000	0	/O-2,D-3	-0.2
1984	Det-A	15	27	6	8	1	0	0	3	2	8	.296	.367	.333	96	-0	1	0	0	1.000	-0	D-11/O-2	0.0
1988	Cle-A	5	11	1	1	1	0	0	0	0	2	.091	.091	.182	-25	-2	0	0	0	.000	0	/D-4	-0.2
Total	3	31	50	8	11	2	0	0	3	2	11	.220	.264	.260	45	-4	1	0	0	1.000	-0	/D-18,O-4	-0.4

■ **RON ALLEN** Allen, Ronald Frederick b: 12/23/43, Wampum, Pa. BB/TR, 6′3″, 205 lbs. Deb: 8/11/72 F

YEAR	TM/L	G	AB	R	H	2B	3B	HR	RBI	BB	SO	AVG	OBP	SLG	PRO+	BR/A	SB	CS	SBR	FA	FR	G/POS	TPR
1972	StL-N	7	11	2	1	0	0	1	1	3	5	.091	.286	.364	84	-0	0	0	0	.968	-0	/1-5	-0.1

■ **GARY ALLENSON** Allenson, Gary Martin b: 2/4/55, Culver City, Cal. BR/TR, 5′11″, 185 lbs. Deb: 4/8/79 C

YEAR	TM/L	G	AB	R	H	2B	3B	HR	RBI	BB	SO	AVG	OBP	SLG	PRO+	BR/A	SB	CS	SBR	FA	FR	G/POS	TPR
1979	Bos-A	108	241	27	49	10	2	3	22	20	42	.203	.267	.299	50	-17	1	1	-0	.980	9	*C-104/3-3	-0.6
1980	Bos-A	36	70	9	25	6	0	0	10	13	11	.357	.458	.443	141	5	2	2	-1	.981	4	C-24/3-5,D-6	0.9
1981	Bos-A	47	139	23	31	8	0	5	25	23	33	.223	.337	.388	102	1	0	0	0	.969	1	C-47	0.3
1982	Bos-A	92	264	25	54	11	0	6	33	38	39	.205	.307	.314	67	-11	0	3	-2	.992	8	C-91	-0.2
1983	Bos-A	84	230	19	53	11	0	3	30	27	43	.230	.317	.317	70	-9	0	1	-1	.984	4	C-84	-0.2
1984	Bos-A	35	83	9	19	2	0	2	8	9	14	.229	.304	.325	71	-3	0	0	0	.987	0	C-35	-0.2
1985	Tor-A	14	34	2	4	1	0	0	3	0	10	.118	.118	.147	-27	-6	0	0	0	1.000	-2	C-14	-0.7
Total	7	416	1061	114	235	49	2	19	131	130	192	.221	.309	.325	71	-41	3	7	-3	.984	25	C-399/3-8,D-6	-0.7

■ **JERMAINE ALLENSWORTH** Allensworth, Jermaine Lamont b: 1/11/72, Anderson, Ind. BR/TR, 6′, 189 lbs. Deb: 7/23/96

YEAR	TM/L	G	AB	R	H	2B	3B	HR	RBI	BB	SO	AVG	OBP	SLG	PRO+	BR/A	SB	CS	SBR	FA	FR	G/POS	TPR
1996	Pit-N	61	229	32	60	9	3	4	31	23	50	.262	.340	.380	87	-4	11	6	-0	.979	4	O-61	-0.2
1997	Pit-N	108	369	55	94	18	2	3	43	44	79	.255	.345	.339	79	-10	14	7	0	.980	-2	*O-104	-1.5
1998	Pit-N	69	233	30	72	13	3	3	24	17	43	.309	.374	.429	106	3	8	4	0	.980	3	O-66	0.5
	KC-A	30	73	15	15	5	0	0	3	9	17	.205	.326	.274	56	-5	7	0	2	.982	-3	O-27	-0.5
	NY-N	34	54	9	11	2	0	2	4	2	16	.204	.246	.352	53	-4	0	2	-1	1.000	-8	O-31	-1.3
Total	3	302	958	141	252	47	8	12	105	95	205	.263	.344	.366	84	-20	40	19	1	.981	-6	O-289	-3.0

■ **GENE ALLEY** Alley, Leonard Eugene b: 7/10/40, Richmond, Va. BR/TR, 6′, 165 lbs. Deb: 9/4/63

YEAR	TM/L	G	AB	R	H	2B	3B	HR	RBI	BB	SO	AVG	OBP	SLG	PRO+	BR/A	SB	CS	SBR	FA	FR	G/POS	TPR
1963	Pit-N	17	51	3	11	1	0	0	0	2	12	.216	.245	.235	39	-4	0	1	-1	.947	1	/3-7,2-4,S-4	-0.3
1964	Pit-N	81	209	30	44	3	1	6	13	21	56	.211	.289	.321	72	-8	0	1	-1	.966	24	S-61/3-3,2-1	2.0
1965	Pit-N	153	500	47	126	21	6	5	47	32	82	.252	.302	.348	82	-12	7	2	1	.968	**30**	*S-110,2-40/3-1	3.0
1966	Pit-N	147	579	88	173	28	10	7	43	27	83	.299	.336	.418	108	6	8	8	-2	.979	13	*S-143	3.1
1967	Pit-N★	152	550	59	158	25	7	6	55	36	70	.287	.339	.391	108	6	10	5	0	.967	8	*S-146	3.0
1968	Pit-N†	133	474	48	116	20	2	4	39	39	78	.245	.309	.321	91	-5	13	5	1	.974	26	*S-109,2-24	3.8
1969	Pit-N	82	285	28	70	3	2	8	32	19	48	.246	.295	.354	83	-7	4	0	1	.977	7	2-53,S-25/3-5	0.8
1970	*Pit-N	121	426	46	104	16	5	8	41	31	70	.244	.300	.362	78	-14	7	3	0	.975	34	*S-108/2-8,3-2	3.2
1971	*Pit-N	114	348	38	79	8	7	6	28	35	43	.227	.298	.342	81	-9	9	2	2	.958	-16	*S-108/3-1	-1.1
1972	*Pit-N	119	347	30	86	12	2	3	36	38	52	.248	.322	.320	85	-6	4	3	-1	.970	-5	*S-114/3-4	0.3
1973	Pit-N	76	158	25	32	3	2	2	8	20	28	.203	.292	.285	62	-8	1	0	0	.981	5	S-49/3-8	0.2
Total	11	1195	3927	442	999	140	44	55	342	300	622	.254	.312	.354	88	-62	63	30	1	.970	125	S-977,2-130/3-31	18.0

■ **GAIR ALLIE** Allie, Gair Roosevelt b: 10/28/31, Statesville, N.C. BR/TR, 6′1″, 190 lbs. Deb: 4/13/54

YEAR	TM/L	G	AB	R	H	2B	3B	HR	RBI	BB	SO	AVG	OBP	SLG	PRO+	BR/A	SB	CS	SBR	FA	FR	G/POS	TPR
1954	Pit-N	121	418	38	83	8	6	3	30	56	84	.199	.296	.268	49	-31	1	1	-0	.952	-16	S-95,3-19	-4.0

■ **BOB ALLIETTA** Alliotta, Robert George b: 5/1/52, New Bedford, Mass. BR/TR, 6′, 190 lbs. Deb: 5/6/75

YEAR	TM/L	G	AB	R	H	2B	3B	HR	RBI	BB	SO	AVG	OBP	SLG	PRO+	BR/A	SB	CS	SBR	FA	FR	G/POS	TPR
1975	Cal-A	21	45	4	8	1	0	1	2	1	6	.178	.196	.267	32	-4	0	0	0	1.000	2	C-21	-0.2

■ **ANDY ALLISON** Allison, Andrew K. b: 1848, New York, N.Y. 5′10″, 150 lbs. Deb: 5/7/1872

YEAR	TM/L	G	AB	R	H	2B	3B	HR	RBI	BB	SO	AVG	OBP	SLG	PRO+	BR/A	SB	CS	SBR	FA	FR	G/POS	TPR
1872	Eck-n	24	93	11	15	3	0	0	9	0	3	.161	.161	.194	10	-8	0	0	0	.913	-2	1-22/O-1,M	-0.6

■ **ART ALLISON** Allison, Arthur Algernon b: 1/29/1849, Philadelphia, Pa. d: 2/25/16, Washington, D.C. 5′8″, 150 lbs. Deb: 5/4/1871 F

YEAR	TM/L	G	AB	R	H	2B	3B	HR	RBI	BB	SO	AVG	OBP	SLG	PRO+	BR/A	SB	CS	SBR	FA	FR	G/POS	TPR
1871	Cle-n	29	137	28	40	4	5	0	19	2	5	.292	.302	.394	104	1	3	1	0	.885	1	*O-29/2-2	0.3
1872	Cle-n	19	87	13	23	4	0	0	8	0	2	.264	.264	.310	81	-2	0	0	0	.804	0	O-19	0.0
1873	Res-n	23	99	12	32	2	0	0	11	0	0	.323	.323	.343	106	1	0	0	0	.848	-1	O-21/1-3,C-1	0.1
1875	Was-n	26	112	18	24	3	1	0	3	1	2	.214	.221	.259	69	-3	6	0	2	.924	-3	1-23/O-3,C-1	-0.4
	Har-n	40	175	26	42	4	1	1	19	0	3	.240	.240	.291	80	-4	1	2	-1	.785	4	O-37/2-2,C-1,1-1	-0.1
	Yr	66	287	44	66	7	2	1	22	1	5	.230	.233	.279	76	-7	7	2	1	.800	1	O-40,1-24/C-2,2-2	-0.5
1876	Lou-N	31	130	9	27	2	1	0	10	2	6	.208	.220	.238	45	-9				.789	6	O-23/1-8	-0.3
Total	4 n	137	610	97	161	17	7	1	60	3	12	.264	.268	.320	88	-6	10	3	1	.833	1	O-109/1-27,2-4,C-3	-0.1

■ **DOUG ALLISON** Allison, Douglas L. b: 7/1845, Philadelphia, Pa. d: 12/19/16, Washington, D.C. BR/TR, 5′10.5″, 160 lbs. Deb: 5/5/1871 F

YEAR	TM/L	G	AB	R	H	2B	3B	HR	RBI	BB	SO	AVG	OBP	SLG	PRO+	BR/A	SB	CS	SBR	FA	FR	G/POS	TPR
1871	Oly-n	27	133	28	44	10	2	2	27	0	2	.331	.331	.481	137	7	1	1	-0	.806	-3	*C-27	0.2
1872	Tro-n	23	115	23	35	4	2	0	20	1	3	.304	.310	.374	108	1	1	1	-0	.897	6	C-22/S-1	0.4
	Eck-n	18	79	18	27	2	1	0	5	1	2	.342	.350	.392	151	6	0	0	0	.837	-8	C-18	-0.2
	Yr	41	194	41	62	6	3	0	25	2	5	.320	.327	.381	124	6	1	1	-0	.874	-2	C-40/S-1	0.2
1873	Res-n	19	83	11	24	5	0	0	8	0	0	.289	.289	.349	96	0	0	0	0	.810	-0	C-18/O-3,M	0.0
	Mut-n	11	48	6	10	0	0	0	3	1	0	.208	.224	.208	30	-4	0	0	0	.868	1	C-11/O-1	-0.2
	Yr	30	131	17	34	5	0	0	11	1	0	.260	.265	.298	71	-4	0	0	0	.837	1	C-29/O-4	-0.2
1874	Mut-n	65	318	68	90	7	5	0	28	6	5	.283	.296	.336	99	-1	1	0	0	.800	-4	*O-47,C-34/2-1	-0.3
1875	Har-n	61	269	38	67	7	0	0	21	6	3	.249	.265	.275	84	-5	2	0	1	**.896**	17	*C-59/1-2,O-2	1.3
1876	Har-N	44	163	19	43	4	0	0	15	3	9	.264	.277	.288	82	-4				**.881**	11	C-40/O-6	0.7
1877	Har-N	29	115	14	17	2	0	0	6	3	7	.148	.169	.165	7	-11				.896	2	C-29	-0.8
1878	Pro-N	19	76	9	22	2	0	0	7	1	8	.289	.299	.316	102	0				.911	-0	C-19/P-1	0.0
1879	Pro-N	1	5	0	0	0	0	0	0	0	1	.000	.000	.000	-99	-1				.833	0	/C-1	-0.1
1883	Bal-a	1	3	2	2	0	0	0		0		.667	.667	.667	321	1				.000	-1	/O-1,C-1	0.0
Total	5 n	224	1045	192	297	35	10	2	112	15	15	.284	.294	.343	101	3	5	2	0	.861	9	C-189/O-53,1-2,2S	1.2
Total	5	94	362	44	84	8	0	0	28	7	25	.232	.247	.254	63	-15				.892	12	/C-90,O-7,P-1	-0.2

YEAR	TM/L	G	AB	R	H	2B	3B	HR	RBI	BB	SO	AVG	OBP	SLG	PRO+	BR/A	SB	CS	SBR	FA	FR	G/POS	TPR
■ **MILO ALLISON** Allison, Milo Henry b: 10/16/1889, Elk Rapids, Mich. d: 6/18/57, Kenosha, Wis. BL/TR, 5'10", 155 lbs. Deb: 9/26/13																							
1913	Chi-N	2	6	1	2	0	0	0	0	0	1	.333	.333	.333	91	-0	1			1.000	0	/O-1	0.0
1914	Chi-N	1	1	0	1	0	0	0	0	0	0	1.000	1.000	1.000	497	0	0			.000	0	H	0.0
1916	Cle-A	14	18	10	5	0	0	0	0	6	1	.278	.458	.278	115	1	0			1.000	-1	/O-5	0.0
1917	Cle-A	32	35	4	5	0	0	0	0	9	7	.143	.318	.143	38	-2	3			1.000	-3	O-11	-0.6
Total	4	49	60	15	13	0	0	0	0	15	9	.217	.373	.217	74	-1	4			1.000	-4	/O-17	-0.6
■ **BILL ALLISON** Allison, William Andrew b: 9/18/1848, Philadelphia, Pa. d: 6/12/23, Deb: 5/21/1872																							
1872	Eck-n	5	19	5	3	0	0	0	1	0	1	.158	.158	.158	-3	-2	0	0	0	.923	-2	/1-2,O-2,2-1	-0.2
■ **BOB ALLISON** Allison, William Robert b: 7/11/34, Raytown, Mo. d: 4/9/95, Rio Verde, Ariz. BR/TR, 6'4", 220 lbs. Deb: 9/16/58																							
1958	Was-A	11	35	1	7	1	0	0	0	2	5	.200	.243	.229	31	-3	0	2	-1	1.000	-0	O-11	-0.5
1959	Was-A☆	150	570	83	149	18	**9**	30	85	60	92	.261	.334	.482	122	15	13	8	-1	.974	-2	*O-149	0.5
1960	Was-A	144	501	79	126	30	3	15	69	92	94	.251	.370	.413	113	11	11	9	-2	.965	9	*O-140/1-4	1.1
1961	Min-A	159	556	83	136	21	3	29	105	103	100	.245	.367	.450	111	10	2	7	-4	.975	7	*O-150,1-18	0.4
1962	Min-A	149	519	102	138	24	8	29	102	84	115	.266	.372	.511	130	22	8	5	-1	.977	7	*O-147	2.1
1963	Min-A★	148	527	**99**	143	25	4	35	91	90	109	.271	.381	.533	**150**	37	6	1	1	.971	11	*O-147	4.2
1964	Min-A★	149	492	90	141	27	4	32	86	92	99	.287	.406	.553	163	44	10	1	2	.986	-4	1-93,O-61	3.8
1965	*Min-A	135	438	71	102	14	5	23	78	73	114	.233	.345	.445	118	11	10	2	2	.972	11	*O-122/1-3	1.9
1966	Min-A	70	168	34	37	6	1	8	19	30	34	.220	.348	.411	110	3	6	0	2	.967	-1	O-56	0.2
1967	Min-A	153	496	73	128	21	6	24	75	74	114	.258	.357	.470	132	20	6	4	-1	.978	-1	*O-145	1.3
1968	Min-A	145	469	63	116	16	8	22	52	52	98	.247	.325	.456	128	15	9	7	-2	.966	-4	*O-117,1-17	0.4
1969	*Min-A	81	189	18	43	8	2	8	27	29	39	.228	.333	.418	107	2	2	4	-2	1.000	-3	O-58/1-3	-0.6
1970	*Min-A	47	72	15	15	5	0	1	7	14	20	.208	.345	.319	83	-1	1	0	0	1.000	-3	O-17/1-7	-0.5
Total	13	1541	5032	811	1281	216	53	256	796	795	1033	.255	.360	.471	126	186	84	50	-5	.975	27	*O-1320,1-145	14.3
■ **BEAU ALLRED** Allred, Dale Le Beau b: 6/4/65, Mesa, Ariz. BL/TL, 6', 190 lbs. Deb: 9/7/89																							
1989	Cle-A	13	24	0	6	3	0	0	1	2	10	.250	.308	.375	90	-0	0	0	0	1.000	1	/O-5,D-2	0.1
1990	Cle-A	4	16	2	3	1	0	1	2	2	3	.188	.278	.438	98	-0	0	0	0	.833	-1	/O-4	-0.1
1991	Cle-A	48	125	17	29	3	0	3	12	25	35	.232	.364	.328	92	-0	2	2	-1	.972	2	O-42/D-1	0.0
Total	3	65	165	19	38	7	0	4	15	29	48	.230	.349	.345	93	-1	2	2	-1	.969	2	/O-51,D-3	0.0
■ **MEL ALMADA** Almada, Baldomero Melo (Quiros) b: 2/7/13, Huatabampo, Mexico d: 8/13/88, Hermosillo, Mexico BL/TL, 6', 170 lbs. Deb: 9/8/33																							
1933	Bos-A	14	44	11	15	0	0	1	3	11	3	.341	.473	.409	137	3	3	1	0	1.000	-0	O-13	0.2
1934	Bos-A	23	90	7	21	2	1	0	10	6	8	.233	.281	.278	42	-8	3	2	-0	.985	4	O-23	-0.5
1935	Bos-A	151	607	85	176	27	9	3	59	55	34	.290	.350	.379	83	-15	20	9	1	.968	-0	*O-149/1-3	-2.0
1936	Bos-A	96	320	40	81	16	4	1	21	24	15	.253	.305	.338	55	-23	2	4	-2	.987	-2	O-81	-2.7
1937	Bos-A	32	110	17	26	6	2	1	9	15	6	.236	.328	.355	69	-5	0	1	-1	.927	-6	O-27/1-4	-1.2
	Was-A	100	433	74	134	21	4	4	33	38	21	.309	.365	.404	98	-1	12	4	1	.964	14	*O-100	1.0
	Yr	132	543	91	160	27	6	5	42	53	27	.295	.357	.394	91	-7	12	5	1	.960	9	*O-127/1-4	-0.2
1938	Was-A	47	197	24	48	7	4	1	15	8	16	.244	.277	.335	56	-14	4	1	1	.968	5	O-47	-0.9
	StL-A	102	436	77	149	22	2	3	37	38	22	.342	.398	.422	106	5	9	5	-0	.966	-1	*O-101	0.1
	Yr	149	633	101	197	29	6	4	52	46	38	.311	.362	.395	92	-8	13	6	0	.967	4	*O-148	-0.8
1939	StL-A	42	134	17	32	2	1	1	7	10	8	.239	.292	.291	48	-10	1	0	0	.987	-3	O-34	-1.3
	Bro-N	39	112	11	24	4	0	0	3	9	17	.214	.273	.250	40	-9	2			.977	2	O-32	-0.9
Total	7	646	2483	363	706	107	27	15	197	214	150	.284	.342	.367	79	-78	56	27		.970	13	O-607/1-7	-8.2
■ **RAFAEL ALMEIDA** Almeida, Rafael D. "Mike" b: 7/30/1887, Havana, Cuba d: 3/19/68, Havana, Cuba BR/TR, 5'9", 164 lbs. Deb: 7/4/11																							
1911	Cin-N	36	96	9	30	5	1	0	15	9	16	.313	.383	.385	120	3	3			.890	-2	3-27/2-1,S-1	0.1
1912	Cin-N	16	59	9	13	4	3	0	10	5	8	.220	.281	.390	85	-2	0			.891	-2	3-15	-0.3
1913	Cin-N	50	130	14	34	4	2	3	21	11	16	.262	.324	.392	104	0	4			.919	4	3-37/O-3,S-2,2-1	0.5
Total	3	102	285	32	77	13	6	3	46	25	40	.270	.335	.389	106	2	7			.904	0	/3-79,O-3,S-3,2-2	0.3
■ **BILL ALMON** Almon, William Francis b: 11/21/52, Providence, R.I. BR/TR, 6'3", 190 lbs. Deb: 9/2/74																							
1974	SD-N	16	38	4	12	1	0	0	3	2	9	.316	.350	.342	98	-0	1	0	0	.915	-2	S-14	0.0
1975	SD-N	6	10	0	4	0	0	0	0	0	1	.400	.400	.400	131	0	0	0	0	1.000	1	/S-2	0.1
1976	SD-N	14	57	6	14	3	0	1	6	2	9	.246	.271	.351	82	-2	3	1	0	.962	1	S-14	0.2
1977	SD-N	155	613	75	160	18	11	2	43	37	114	.261	.303	.336	79	-20	20	9	1	.954	18	*S-155	1.6
1978	SD-N	138	405	39	102	19	2	0	21	33	74	.252	.308	.309	79	-12	17	5	2	.933	0	*3-114,S-15/2-7	-1.1
1979	SD-N	100	198	20	45	3	0	1	8	21	48	.227	.301	.258	57	-11	6	5	-1	.985	16	2-61,S-25/O-1	0.8
1980	Mon-N	18	38	2	10	1	1	0	3	1	5	.263	.282	.342	73	-1	0	0	0	.911	-2	S-12/2-1	-0.3
	NY-N	48	112	13	19	3	2	0	4	8	27	.170	.225	.232	29	-11	2	0	1	.967	9	S-22,2-18/3-9	0.1
	Yr	66	150	15	29	4	3	0	7	9	32	.193	.239	.260	40	-12	2	0	1	.948	6	S-34,2-19/3-9	-0.2
1981	Chi-A	103	349	46	105	10	2	4	41	21	60	.301	.344	.375	109	4	16	6	1	.969	14	*S-103	3.1
1982	Chi-A	111	308	40	79	10	4	4	26	25	49	.256	.314	.354	83	-7	10	8	-2	.949	20	*S-108/D-1	1.9
1983	Oak-A	143	451	45	120	29	1	4	63	26	67	.266	.309	.361	89	-7	26	8	3	.941	-31	S-52,3-40,1O/2D	-3.5
1984	Oak-A	106	211	24	47	11	0	7	16	10	42	.223	.258	.374	78	-7	5	7	-3	1.000	-9	O-48,1-44,D/3CS	-2.2
1985	Pit-N	88	244	33	66	17	0	6	29	22	61	.270	.333	.414	109	3	10	7	-1	.987	-22	S-43,O-32/1-7,3-7	-1.9
1986	Pit-N	102	196	29	43	7	2	7	27	30	38	.219	.323	.383	92	-2	11	4	1	.983	-13	O-54,3-28,S-19,/1-4	-1.5
1987	Pit-N	19	20	5	4	1	0	0	1	1	5	.200	.238	.250	29	-2	0	0	0	.944	1	/S-4,O-2,3-1	-0.1
	NY-N	49	54	8	13	3	0	0	4	8	16	.241	.339	.296	74	-2	1	0	0	.972	-3	S-22,2-10/1-2,O-1	-0.4
	Yr	68	74	13	17	4	0	0	5	9	21	.230	.313	.284	62	-4	1	0	0	.963	-2	S-26,2-10/O-3,13	-0.5
1988	Phi-N	20	26	1	3	2	0	0	1	3	11	.115	.207	.192	15	-3	0	0	0	.944	1	/3-9,S-5,1-1	-0.2
Total	15	1236	3330	390	846	138	25	36	296	250	636	.254	.307	.343	83	-81	128	60	2	.956	-2	S-616,3-212,O2/1DC	-3.4
■ **ROBERTO ALOMAR** Alomar, Roberto (Velazquez) b: 2/5/68, Ponce, P.R. BB/TR, 6', 185 lbs. Deb: 4/22/88 F																							
1988	SD-N	143	545	84	145	24	6	9	41	47	83	.266	.328	.382	105	3	24	6	4	.980	17	*2-143	3.1
1989	SD-N	158	623	82	184	27	1	7	56	53	76	.295	.352	.376	108	7	42	17	2	.967	6	*2-157	2.1
1990	SD-N★	147	586	80	168	27	5	6	60	48	72	.287	.343	.381	98	-1	24	7	3	.976	-2	*2-137/S-5	0.4
1991	*Tor-A★	161	637	88	188	41	11	9	69	57	86	.295	.357	.436	114	12	53	11	**9**	.981	-22	*2-160	0.2
1992	*Tor-A★	152	571	105	177	27	8	8	76	87	52	.310	.406	.427	128	25	49	9	9	.993	-24	*2-150/D-1	1.3
1993	*Tor-A★	153	589	109	192	35	6	17	93	80	67	.326	.411	.492	141	36	55	15	8	.980	-7	*2-150	4.0
1994	Tor-A★	107	392	78	120	25	4	8	38	51	41	.306	.389	.452	115	10	19	8	1	.991	-4	*2-106	1.1
1995	Tor-A★	130	517	71	155	24	7	13	66	47	45	.300	.358	.449	109	7	30	3	7	**.994**	-5	*2-128	1.5
1996	*Bal-A★	153	588	132	193	43	4	22	94	90	65	.328	.418	.527	138	37	17	6	2	.985	13	*2-141,D-10	5.3
1997	*Bal-A★	112	412	64	137	23	2	14	60	40	43	.333	.396	.500	136	22	9	3	1	.988	4	*2-109/D-2	3.1
1998	Bal-A★	147	588	86	166	36	1	14	56	59	70	.282	.350	.418	101	1	18	5	2	.985	14	*2-144/D-3	2.5
Total	11	1563	6048	979	1825	332	55	127	709	659	700	.302	.373	.438	117	158	340	90	48	.983	-11	*2-1525/D-16,S-5	24.6
■ **SANDY ALOMAR** Alomar, Santos Jr. (Velazquez) b: 6/18/66, Salinas, P.R. BR/TR, 6'5", 215 lbs. Deb: 9/30/88 F																							
1988	SD-N	1	1	0	0	0	0	0	0	0	1	.000	.000	.000	-99	-0	0	0	0	.000	0	H	0.0
1989	SD-N	7	19	1	4	1	0	1	6	3	3	.211	.318	.421	110	0	0	0	0	1.000	-0	/C-6	0.0
1990	Cle-A★	132	445	60	129	26	2	9	66	25	46	.290	.331	.418	109	4	4	1	1	.981	-13	*C-129	0.0
1991	Cle-A★	51	184	10	40	9	0	0	7	8	24	.217	.265	.266	47	-13	0	4	-2	.987	2	C-46/D-4	-1.1
1992	Cle-A★	89	299	22	75	16	0	2	26	13	32	.251	.293	.324	74	-11	3	3	-1	.996	-4	C-88/D-1	-1.1
1993	Cle-A	64	215	24	58	7	1	6	32	11	28	.270	.323	.395	92	-3	3	1	0	.984	-12	C-64	-1.0
1994	Cle-A	80	292	44	84	15	1	14	43	25	31	.288	.348	.490	113	5	8	4	0	.996	-1	C-78	0.9
1995	*Cle-A	66	203	32	61	6	0	10	35	7	26	.300	.333	.478	106	1	3	1	0	.995	1	C-61	0.6
1996	*Cle-A★	127	418	53	110	23	0	11	50	19	42	.263	.300	.397	75	-17	1	0	0	.988	2	*C-124/1-1	-0.8
1997	*Cle-A★	125	451	63	146	37	0	21	83	19	48	.324	.355	.545	126	16	0	2	-1	.985	-16	*C-119/D-1	0.6

YEAR	TM/L	G	AB	R	H	2B	3B	HR	RBI	BB	SO	AVG	OBP	SLG	PRO+	BR/A	SB	CS	SBR	FA	FR	G/POS	TPR
1998	*Cle-A★	117	409	45	96	26	2	6	44	18	45	.235	.272	.352	59	-25	0	3	-2	.992	3	*C-111/D-3	-1.6
Total	11	859	2936	354	803	166	6	80	392	148	326	.274	.315	.416	91	-43	22	19	-5	.989	-37	C-826/D-9,1-1	-3.5

■ SANDY ALOMAR

Alomar, Santos Sr. (Conde) b: 10/19/43, Salinas, P.R. BB/TR, 5'9", 155 lbs. Deb: 9/15/64 FC

YEAR	TM/L	G	AB	R	H	2B	3B	HR	RBI	BB	SO	AVG	OBP	SLG	PRO+	BR/A	SB	CS	SBR	FA	FR	G/POS	TPR
1964	Mil-N	19	53	3	13	1	0	0	6	0	11	.245	.245	.264	43	-4	1	0	0	.967	8	S-19	0.6
1965	Mil-N	67	108	16	26	1	1	0	8	4	12	.241	.268	.269	51	-7	12	5	1	.964	14	S-39,2-19	1.0
1966	Atl-N	31	44	4	4	1	0	0	2	1	10	.091	.111	.114	-37	-8	0	0	0	.981	3	2-21/S-5	-0.4
1967	NY-N	15	22	1	0	0	0	0	0	0	6	.000	.000	.000	-99	-6	0	0	0	1.000	2	S-10/3-3,2-2	-0.3
	Chi-A	12	15	4	3	0	0	0	0	2	0	.200	.294	.200	50	-1	2	0	1	.952	2	/S-8,2-2	0.2
1968	Chi-A	133	363	41	92	8	2	0	12	20	42	.253	.294	.287	76	-11	21	8	2	.958	-16	2-99,3-27/S-9,0-1	-2.2
1969	Chi-A	22	58	8	13	2	0	0	4	4	6	.224	.274	.259	47	-4	2	0	1	.980	3	2-22	0.1
	Cal-A	134	559	60	140	10	2	1	30	36	48	.250	.296	.281	65	-26	18	3	4	.969	-10	*2-134	-2.2
	Yr	156	617	68	153	12	2	1	34	40	54	.248	.294	.279	63	-31	20	3	4	.970	-7	*2-156	-2.1
1970	Cal-A★	162	672	82	169	18	2	2	36	49	65	.251	.303	.293	68	-30	35	12	3	.979	9	*2-153,S-10/3-1	-0.3
1971	Cal-A	162	689	77	179	24	3	4	42	41	60	.260	.301	.321	82	-18	39	10	6	.989	21	*2-137,S-28	2.6
1972	Cal-A	155	610	65	146	20	3	1	25	47	55	.239	.294	.287	78	-17	20	12	-1	.977	3	*2-154/S-4	-0.7
1973	Cal-A	136	470	45	112	7	1	0	28	34	44	.238	.290	.257	60	-25	25	10	2	.979	-8	*2-110,S-31	-2.2
1974	Cal-A	46	54	12	12	0	1	0	1	2	8	.222	.250	.259	49	-4	2	0	1	.977	9	S-19,2-15/3-5,OD	0.7
	NY-A	76	279	35	75	8	0	1	27	14	25	.269	.304	.308	78	-8	6	4	-1	.977	-12	2-76	-1.8
	Yr	122	333	47	87	8	1	1	28	16	33	.261	.295	.300	74	-11	8	4	0	.976	-3	2-91,S-19/3-5,OD	-1.1
1975	NY-A	151	489	61	117	18	4	2	39	26	58	.239	.278	.305	66	-23	28	6	5	**.985**	-12	*2-150/S-1	-2.3
1976	*NY-A	67	163	20	39	4	0	1	10	13	12	.239	.295	.282	70	-6	12	7	-1	.970	-5	2-38/S-6,3-3,1-1,O	-1.0
1977	Tex-A	69	83	21	22	3	0	1	11	8	13	.265	.337	.337	84	-2	4	3	-1	.973	13	D-26,2-18/S-6,O13	1.0
1978	Tex-A	24	29	3	6	1	0	0	1	1	7	.207	.233	.241	34	-3	0	0	0	.975	5	/1-9,2-6,3-3,S-2,D	0.3
Total	15	1481	4760	558	1168	126	19	13	282	302	482	.245	.291	.288	68	-201	227	80	20	.977	31	*2-1156,S-197/3D10	-6.9

■ FELIPE ALOU

Alou, Felipe Rojas (b: Felipe Rojas (Alou)) b: 5/12/35, Haina, D.R. BR/TR, 6', 195 lbs. Deb: 6/8/58 FMC

YEAR	TM/L	G	AB	R	H	2B	3B	HR	RBI	BB	SO	AVG	OBP	SLG	PRO+	BR/A	SB	CS	SBR	FA	FR	G/POS	TPR
1958	SF-N	75	182	21	46	9	2	4	16	19	34	.253	.327	.390	91	-2	4	2	0	.985	-3	O-70	-0.8
1959	SF-N	95	247	38	68	13	2	10	33	17	38	.275	.322	.466	109	2	5	3	-0	.974	-6	O-69	-0.7
1960	SF-N	106	322	48	85	17	3	8	44	16	42	.264	.303	.410	99	-2	10	2	2	.958	-4	O-95	-0.8
1961	SF-N	132	415	59	120	19	0	18	52	26	41	.289	.334	.465	113	7	11	4	1	.990	-4	*O-122	-0.2
1962	*SF-N★	154	561	96	177	30	3	25	98	33	66	.316	.359	.513	133	24	10	7	-1	.971	-2	*O-150	1.3
1963	SF-N	157	565	75	159	31	9	20	82	27	87	.281	.321	.474	127	18	11	2	2	.986	0	*O-153	1.3
1964	Mil-N	121	415	60	105	26	3	9	51	30	41	.253	.310	.395	96	-2	5	2	0	.975	-1	O-92,1-18	-0.9
1965	Mil-N	143	555	80	165	29	2	23	78	31	63	.297	.340	.481	128	19	8	4	0	.980	-4	O-91,1-69/3-2,S-1	0.8
1966	Atl-N☆	154	666	**122**	**218**	32	6	31	74	24	51	.327	.362	.533	143	36	5	7	-3	.988	1	1-90,O-79/3-3,S-1	2.7
1967	Atl-N	140	574	76	157	26	3	15	43	32	50	.274	.320	.408	108	5	6	5	-1	.993	-11	1-85,O-56	-1.7
1968	Atl-N★	160	662	72	**210**	37	5	11	57	48	56	.317	.367	.438	140	32	12	11	-3	.980	8	*O-158	3.2
1969	*Atl-N	123	476	54	134	13	1	5	32	23	23	.282	.320	.345	86	-9	4	6	-2	.989	3	*O-116	-1.6
1970	Oak-A	154	575	70	156	25	3	8	55	32	31	.271	.311	.367	89	-10	10	5	0	.977	-3	*O-145/1-1	-2.1
1971	Oak-A	2	8	0	2	1	0	0	0	0	1	.250	.250	.375	77	-0	0	0	0	1.000	1	/O-2	0.0
	NY-A	131	461	52	133	20	6	8	69	32	24	.289	.337	.410	118	9	5	5	-2	.985	-12	O-80,1-42	-1.3
	Yr	133	469	52	135	21	6	8	69	32	25	.288	.336	.409	117	9	5	5	-2	.986	-11	O-82,1-42	-1.3
1972	NY-A	120	324	33	90	18	1	6	37	22	27	.278	.328	.395	118	6	1	0	0	.990	1	1-95,O-15	0.1
1973	NY-A	93	280	25	66	12	0	4	27	9	25	.236	.260	.321	65	-14	0	0	-1	.988	-1	1-67,O-22	-2.1
	Mon-N	19	48	4	10	1	0	1	4	2	4	.208	.240	.292	45	-4	0	1	-1	1.000	1	O-15/1-1	-0.4
1974	Mil-A	3	3	0	0	0	0	0	0	0	2	.000	.000	.000	-99	-1	0	0	0	.000	-1	/O-1	-0.2
Total	17	2082	7339	985	2101	359	49	206	852	423	706	.286	.330	.433	114	114	107	67	-8	.979	-37	*O-1531,1-468/3-5,S	-3.4

■ JESUS ALOU

Alou, Jesus Maria Rojas (b: Jesus Maria Rojas (Alou)) b: 3/24/42, Haina, D.R. BR/TR, 6'2", 195 lbs. Deb: 9/10/63 FC

YEAR	TM/L	G	AB	R	H	2B	3B	HR	RBI	BB	SO	AVG	OBP	SLG	PRO+	BR/A	SB	CS	SBR	FA	FR	G/POS	TPR
1963	SF-N	16	24	3	6	1	0	0	5	0	3	.250	.280	.292	66	-1	0	1	-1	.875	-4	O-12	-0.6
1964	SF-N	115	376	42	103	11	0	3	28	13	35	.274	.305	.327	77	-11	6	6	-2	.973	-1	*O-108	-1.9
1965	SF-N	143	543	76	162	19	4	9	52	13	40	.298	.318	.398	98	-3	8	5	-1	.980	1	*O-136	-0.9
1966	SF-N	110	370	41	96	13	1	1	20	9	22	.259	.281	.308	62	-19	5	5	-2	.967	-5	*O-100	-3.2
1967	SF-N	129	510	55	149	15	4	5	30	14	39	.292	.316	.367	96	-3	1	7	-4	.948	-6	*O-123	-2.1
1968	SF-N	120	419	26	110	15	4	0	39	9	23	.263	.280	.317	79	-11	1	6	-2	.989	0	*O-105	-2.1
1969	Hou-N	115	452	49	112	19	4	5	34	15	30	.248	.278	.341	74	-17	4	6	-2	.928	-0	*O-112	-2.8
1970	Hou-N	117	458	59	140	27	3	1	44	21	15	.306	.338	.384	97	-3	3	2	-0	.962	-7	*O-108	-1.5
1971	Hou-N	122	433	41	121	21	4	2	40	13	17	.279	.307	.360	91	-6	3	7	-3	.983	6	*O-109	-0.9
1972	Hou-N	52	93	8	29	4	1	0	11	7	5	.312	.366	.376	114	2	0	2	-1	.970	-3	O-23	-0.3
1973	Hou-N	28	55	7	13	2	0	1	8	1	6	.236	.276	.327	67	-3	0	0	0	.941	-3	O-14	-0.6
	*Oak-A	36	108	10	33	3	0	1	11	2	6	.306	.318	.361	96	-1	0	0	0	1.000	-0	O-21/D-6	-0.2
1974	*Oak-A	96	220	13	59	8	0	2	15	5	9	.268	.291	.332	84	-5	0	0	0	1.000	-1	D-41,O-25	-0.8
1975	NY-N	62	102	8	27	3	0	0	11	4	5	.265	.299	.294	68	-5	0	1	-1	.963	-1	O-20	-0.7
1978	Hou-N	77	139	7	45	5	1	2	19	6	5	.324	.352	.417	123	4	0	0	0	.976	-2	O-28	0.1
1979	Hou-N	42	43	3	11	4	0	0	10	6	7	.256	.347	.349	96	-0	0	0	0	1.000	-1	/O-6,1-1	-0.1
Total	15	1380	4345	448	1216	170	26	32	377	138	267	.280	.307	.353	87	-83	31	46	-18	.968	-26	*O-1050/D-47,1-1	-18.6

■ MATTY ALOU

Alou, Mateo Rojas (b: Mateo Rojas (Alou)) b: 12/22/38, Haina, D.R. BL/TL, 5'9", 160 lbs. Deb: 9/26/60 F

YEAR	TM/L	G	AB	R	H	2B	3B	HR	RBI	BB	SO	AVG	OBP	SLG	PRO+	BR/A	SB	CS	SBR	FA	FR	G/POS	TPR
1960	SF-N	4	3	1	1	0	0	0	0	0	0	.333	.333	.333	88	-0	0	0	0	1.000	-0	/O-1	0.0
1961	SF-N	81	200	38	62	7	2	6	24	15	18	.310	.358	.455	118	5	3	2	-0	.978	-4	O-58	-0.2
1962	*SF-N	78	195	28	57	8	1	3	14	14	17	.292	.349	.390	100	0	3	1	0	.976	-6	O-57	-0.8
1963	SF-N	63	76	4	11	1	0	0	2	2	13	.145	.177	.158	-3	-10	0	0	-1	.952	-3	O-20	-1.6
1964	SF-N	110	250	28	66	4	2	1	14	11	25	.264	.303	.308	71	-9	5	3	-0	.976	-9	O-80	-2.2
1965	SF-N	117	324	37	75	12	2	2	18	17	28	.231	.274	.299	60	-17	10	2	2	.986	4	*O-103/P-1	-1.6
1966	Pit-N	141	535	86	183	18	9	2	27	24	44	**.342**	.375	.421	121	15	23	15	-2	.972	-1	*O-136	0.6
1967	Pit-N	139	550	87	186	21	7	2	28	24	42	.338	.372	.413	124	17	16	10	-1	.989	-3	*O-134/1-1	0.7
1968	Pit-N★	146	558	59	185	28	4	0	52	27	26	.332	.365	.396	130	20	18	10	-1	.984	-2	*O-144	1.1
1969	Pit-N★	162	698	105	**231**	**41**	6	1	48	42	35	.331	.371	.411	121	19	22	8	2	.977	5	*O-162	1.7
1970	*Pit-N	155	677	97	201	21	8	1	47	30	18	.297	.331	.356	86	-14	19	11	-1	.975	5	*O-153	-1.8
1971	StL-N	149	609	85	192	28	6	7	74	34	27	.315	.355	.415	113	10	19	10	-0	.981	-0	O-94,1-57	-0.1
1972	StL-N	108	404	46	127	17	2	3	31	24	23	.314	.354	.389	112	6	11	4	1	.988	-2	1-66,O-39	-0.2
	*Oak-A	32	121	11	34	5	0	1	16	11	12	.281	.346	.347	112	2	2	1	0	1.000	-2	O-32/1-1	-0.2
1973	NY-A	123	497	59	147	22	1	2	28	30	43	.296	.340	.356	100	-0	5	2	0	.974	-4	O-85,1-40/D-1	-1.1
	StL-N	11	11	1	3	0	0	0	1	1	0	.273	.333	.273	70	-0	0	0	0	1.000	0	/1-1,O-1	0.0
1974	SD-N	48	81	8	16	3	0	0	3	5	6	.198	.244	.235	36	-7	0	0	0	.947	-2	O-13/1-2	-1.0
Total	15	1667	5789	780	1777	236	50	31	427	311	377	.307	.346	.381	105	35	156	80	-1	.979	-23	*O-1312,1-168/D-1,P	-6.7

■ MOISES ALOU

Alou, Moises Rojas (b: Moises Rojas) b: 7/3/66, Atlanta, Ga. BR/TR, 6'3", 190 lbs. Deb: 7/26/90 F

YEAR	TM/L	G	AB	R	H	2B	3B	HR	RBI	BB	SO	AVG	OBP	SLG	PRO+	BR/A	SB	CS	SBR	FA	FR	G/POS	TPR
1990	Pit-N	2	5	0	1	0	0	0	0	0	0	.200	.200	.200	11	-1	0	0	0	1.000	-0	/O-2	-0.1
	Mon-N	14	15	4	3	0	1	0	0	0	3	.200	.200	.333	46	-1	0	0	0	1.000	-0	/O-5	-0.1
	Yr	16	20	4	4	0	1	0	0	0	3	.200	.200	.300	37	-2	0	0	0	1.000	-0	/O-7	-0.2
1992	Mon-N	115	341	53	96	28	2	9	56	25	46	.282	.332	.455	122	9	16	2	4	.978	-3	*O-100	0.8
1993	Mon-N	136	482	70	138	29	6	18	85	38	53	.286	.345	.483	114	9	17	6	2	.985	-1	*O-136	0.7
1994	Mon-N★	107	422	81	143	31	5	22	78	42	63	.339	.401	.592	153	32	7	6	-2	.986	4	*O-106	3.1
1995	Mon-N	93	344	48	94	22	0	14	58	29	56	.273	.346	.459	106	3	4	3	-1	.981	-0	*O-92	-0.1
1996	Mon-N	143	540	87	152	28	2	21	96	49	83	.281	.343	.457	106	4	9	4	0	.989	-1	*O-142	0.0
1997	*Fla-N★	150	538	88	157	29	5	23	115	70	85	.292	.377	.493	131	25	9	5	-0	.988	-9	*O-150	1.3
1998	*Hou-N★	159	584	104	182	34	5	38	124	84	87	.312	.403	.582	155	48	11	3	2	.980	2	*O-154/D-1	4.9
Total	8	919	3271	535	966	201	26	145	612	337	476	.295	.366	.506	128	128	73	29	5	.984	-8	O-887/D-1	10.5

YEAR	TM/L	G	AB	R	H	2B	3B	HR	RBI	BB	SO	AVG	OBP	SLG	PRO+	BR/A	SB	CS	SBR	FA	FR	G/POS	TPR
■ WHITEY ALPERMAN	Alperman, Charles Augustus b: 11/11/1879, Etna, Pa. d: 12/25/42, Pittsburgh, Pa. BR/TR, 5'10", 180 lbs. Deb: 4/13/06																						
1906	Bro-N	128	441	38	111	15	7	3	46	6		.252	.284	.338	102	-2	13			.940	2	*2-103,S-24/3-1	0.2
1907	Bro-N	141	558	44	130	23	**16**	2	39	13		.233	.266	.342	98	-5	5			.953	14	*2-115,3-14,S-12	0.9
1908	Bro-N	70	213	17	42	3	1	1	15	9		.197	.253	.235	58	-10	2			.934	-5	2-42/3-9,O-5,S-2	-1.8
1909	Bro-N	111	420	35	104	19	12	1	41	2		.248	.262	.357	95	-6	7			.931	8	*2-108	0.0
Total	4	450	1632	134	387	60	36	7	141	30		.237	.268	.331	93	-23	27			.941	19	2-368/S-38,3-24,O-5	-0.7
■ TOM ALSTON	Alston, Thomas Edison b: 1/31/26, Greensboro, N.C. d: 12/30/93, Winston-Salem, N.C. BL/TR, 6'5", 210 lbs. Deb: 4/13/54																						
1954	StL-N	66	244	28	60	14	2	4	34	24	41	.246	.319	.369	78	-8	3	5	-2	.989	10	1-65	-0.3
1955	StL-N	13	8	0	1	0	0	0	0	0	0	.125	.125	.125	-33	-2	0	0	0	1.000	0	/1-7	-0.1
1956	StL-N	3	2	0	0	0	0	0	0	0	0	.000	.000	.000	-99	-1	0	0	0	1.000	0	/1-3	0.0
1957	StL-N	9	17	2	5	1	0	0	2	1	5	.294	.333	.353	83	-0	0	0	0	.947	-1	/1-6	-0.2
Total	4	91	271	30	66	15	2	4	36	25	46	.244	.312	.358	74	-10	3	5	-2	.987	9	/1-81	-0.6
■ WALTER ALSTON	Alston, Walter Emmons "Smokey" b: 12/1/11, Venice, Ohio d: 10/1/84, Oxford, Ohio BR/TR, 6'2", 195 lbs. Deb: 9/27/36 MH																						
1936	StL-N	1	1	0	0	0	0	0	0	0	1	.000	.000	.000	-99	-0	0			.500	-0	/1-1	-0.1
■ DELL ALSTON	Alston, Wendell b: 9/22/52, Valhalla, N.Y. BL/TR, 6', 180 lbs. Deb: 5/17/77																						
1977	NY-A	22	40	10	13	4	0	1	4	3	4	.325	.372	.500	137	2	3	3	-1	1.000	0	D-10/O-2	0.1
1978	NY-A	3	3	0	0	0	0	0	0	0	2	.000	.000	.000	-99	-1	0	0	0	.000	0	H	-0.1
	Oak-A	58	173	17	36	2	0	1	10	10	21	.208	.251	.237	40	-14	11	10	-3	.956	-5	O-50/1-9,D-3	-2.5
	Yr	61	176	17	36	2	0	1	10	10	23	.205	.247	.233	38	-15	11	10	-3	.956	-5	O-50/1-9,D-3	-2.6
1979	Cle-A	54	62	10	18	0	2	1	12	10	10	.290	.389	.403	114	2	4	4	-1	.969	-5	O-30/D-7	-0.5
1980	Cle-A	52	54	11	12	1	2	0	9	5	7	.222	.311	.315	72	-2	2	4	-2	.947	-4	O-26/D-6	-0.8
Total	4	189	332	48	79	7	4	3	35	28	44	.238	.301	.310	71	-13	20	21	-7	.957	-14	O-108/D-26,1-9	-3.8
■ JESSE ALTENBURG	Altenburg, Jesse Howard b: 1/2/1893, Ashley, Mich. d: 3/12/73, Lansing, Mich. BL/TR, 5'9", 158 lbs. Deb: 9/19/16																						
1916	Pit-N	8	14	2	6	1	1	0	0	1	1	.429	.467	.643	237	2	0			1.000	-2	/O-8	0.0
1917	Pit-N	11	17	1	3	0	0	0	3	0	4	.176	.176	.176	8	-2	0			1.000	-1	/O-4	-0.3
Total	2	19	31	3	9	1	1	0	3	1	5	.290	.313	.387	112	0	0			1.000	-3	/O-12	-0.3
■ DAVE ALTIZER	Altizer, David Tilden "Filipino" b: 11/6/1876, Pearl, Ill. d: 5/14/64, Pleasant Hill, Ill BL/TR, 5'10.5", 160 lbs. Deb: 5/29/06																						
1906	Was-A	115	433	56	111	9	5	1	27	35		.256	.324	.307	103	2	37			.931	-20	*S-113/O-2	-1.6
1907	Was-A	147	540	60	145	15	5	2	42	34		.269	.319	.326	115	8	38			.923	-2	S-80,1-50,O-17	0.7
1908	Was-A	67	205	19	46	1	1	0	18	13		.224	.274	.239	73	-6	8			.959	-3	2-38,3-16/1-4,S-1	-1.0
	Cle-A	29	89	11	19	1	2	0	5	7		.213	.278	.270	78	-2	7			.952	4	O-24/S-3	0.1
	Yr	96	294	30	65	2	3	0	23	20		.221	.275	.248	75	-8	15			.959	1	2-38,O-24,3-16,1/S	-0.9
1909	Chi-A	116	382	47	89	6	7	1	20	39		.233	.330	.293	101	2	27			.949	8	O-61,1-46	0.8
1910	Cin-N	3	10	3	6	0	0	0	0	3	0	.600	.692	.600	290	3	0			.933	-2	/S-3	0.2
1911	Cin-N	37	75	8	17	4	1	0	4	9	5	.227	.318	.307	78	-2	2			.907	1	S-23/1-1,2-1,O-1	0.0
Total	6	514	1734	204	433	36	21	4	116	140	5	.250	.318	.302	101	6	119			.925	-14	S-223,O-105,1/23	-0.8
■ GEORGE ALTMAN	Altman, George Lee b: 3/20/33, Goldsboro, N.C. BL/TR, 6'4", 200 lbs. Deb: 4/11/59																						
1959	Chi-N	135	420	54	103	14	4	12	47	34	80	.245	.312	.383	85	-9	1	0	0	.990	4	*O-121	-1.1
1960	Chi-N	119	334	50	89	16	4	13	51	32	67	.266	.332	.455	114	6	4	3	-1	.993	-5	O-79,1-21	-0.4
1961	Chi-N★	138	518	77	157	28	**12**	27	96	40	92	.303	.358	.560	137	26	6	2	1	.978	1	*O-130/1-3	1.9
1962	Chi-N★	147	534	74	170	27	5	22	74	62	89	.318	.394	.511	136	28	19	7	2	.972	-0	*O-129,1-16	2.0
1963	StL-N	135	464	62	127	18	7	9	47	47	93	.274	.343	.401	104	3	13	4	2	.979	2	*O-124	0.0
1964	NY-N	124	422	48	97	14	1	9	47	18	70	.230	.263	.332	68	-19	4	2	0	.968	13	*O-109	-1.2
1965	Chi-N	90	196	24	46	7	1	4	23	19	36	.235	.302	.342	79	-5	3	2	-0	.943	-3	O-45/1-2	-1.1
1966	Chi-N	88	185	19	41	6	0	5	17	14	37	.222	.276	.335	68	-8	2	2	-1	.958	-3	O-42/1-4	-1.4
1967	Chi-N	15	18	1	2	2	0	0	1	2	8	.111	.200	.222	20	-2	0	0	0	1.000	-1	/O-4,1-1	-0.4
Total	9	991	3091	409	832	132	34	101	403	268	572	.269	.331	.432	105	19	52	22	2	.977	7	O-783/1-47	-1.7
■ JOE ALTOBELLI	Altobelli, Joseph Salvatore b: 5/26/32, Detroit, Mich. BL/TL, 6', 185 lbs. Deb: 4/14/55 MC																						
1955	Cle-A	42	75	8	15	3	0	2	5	5	14	.200	.259	.320	53	-5	0	1	-1	.992	-1	1-40	-0.8
1957	Cle-A	83	87	9	18	3	2	0	9	5	14	.207	.258	.287	49	-6	3	2	-0	.994	-0	1-56/O-7	-0.8
1961	Min-A	41	95	10	21	2	1	3	14	13	14	.221	.315	.358	75	-3	0	0	0	.951	-2	O-25/1-2	-0.7
Total	3	166	257	27	54	8	3	5	28	23	42	.210	.280	.323	60	-15	3	3	-1	.993	-3	/1-98,O-32	-2.3
■ NICK ALTROCK	Altrock, Nicholas b: 9/15/1876, Cincinnati, Ohio d: 1/20/65, Washington, D.C. BB/TL, 5'10", 197 lbs. Deb: 7/14/1898 C																						
1898	Lou-N	11	29	4	7	0	0	0	2	2		.241	.313	.241	60	-1	1			1.000	2	P-11	0.0
1902	Bos-A	3	8	0	0	0	0	0	0	0		.000	.000	.000	-97	-2	0			.818	1	/P-3	0.0
1903	Bos-A	1	3	0	2	0	0	0	0	1		.667	.750	.667	311	1	0			1.000	1	/P-1	0.0
	Chi-A	13	30	6	9	0	0	0	3	3		.300	.364	.300	105	0	1			.935	3	P-12	0.0
	Yr	14	33	6	11	0	0	0	3	4		.333	.405	.333	128	1	1			.944	4	P-13	0.0
1904	Chi-A	41	111	13	22	1	0	1	8	4		.198	.239	.234	52	-6	0			.969	4	P-38/1-1	0.0
1905	Chi-A	40	112	8	14	1	0	0	5	6		.125	.190	.134	3	-12	0			.988	8	P-38/1-1	0.0
1906	*Chi-A	38	100	4	16	2	0	0	3	8		.160	.222	.180	27	-8	2			.970	4	P-38/1-1	0.0
1907	Chi-A	30	72	7	13	3	0	0	2	3		.181	.234	.222	47	-4	0			.958	5	P-30	0.0
1908	Chi-A	23	49	6	10	2	0	0	3	0		.204	.235	.245	57	-2	1			.967	5	P-23	0.0
1909	Chi-A	1	3	0	0	0	0	0	0	0		.000	.000	.000	-99	-1	0			1.000	0	/P-1	0.0
	Was-A	12	19	2	1	0	0	0	0	1		.053	.143	.053	-40	-3	0			.905	-0	/P-9,O-3	-0.2
	Yr	13	22	2	1	0	0	0	0	1		.045	.125	.045	-48	-4	0			.920	-0	P-10/O-3	-0.2
1912	Was-A	1	1	0	0	0	0	0	0	0		.000	.000	.000	-99	-0	0			.000	-0	/P-1,1-1	0.0
1913	Was-A	4	1	0	0	0	0	0	0	0	0	.000	.000	.000	-98	-0	0			.833	0	/P-4	0.0
1914	Was-A	1	0	0	0	0	0	0	0	0	0	—	—	—	—	0	0			.000	-0	/P-1	0.0
1915	Was-A	1	1	0	0	0	0	0	0	0	0	.000	.000	.000	-98	-0	0			.000	-0	/P-1	0.0
1918	Was-A	5	8	1	1	0	0	1	1	0	0	.125	.125	.500	90	-0	0			.917	0	/P-5,1-1	0.0
1919	Was-A	1	0	0	0	0	0	0	0	0	0	—	—	—	—	0	0			.000	0	/P-1	0.0
1924	Was-A	1	1	1	1	0	1	0	0	0	0	1.000	1.000	3.000	935	1	0	0	0	.667	0	/P-1	0.0
1929	Was-A	1	1	0	1	0	0	0	0	0	0	1.000	1.000	1.000	413	0	0	0	0	.000	-0	/O-1	0.0
1931	Was-A	1	0	0	0	0	0	0	0	1	0	—	1.000	—	182	0	0	1	-1	.000	0	H	0.0
1933	Was-A	1	1	0	0	0	0	0	0	0	0	.000	.000	.000	-99	-0	0	0	0	.000	0	H	0.0
Total	19	230	550	52	97	9	1	2	27	29	0	.176	.232	.207	39	-38	5	1		.964	33	P-218/1-5,O-4	-0.2
■ GEORGE ALUSIK	Alusik, George Joseph b: 2/11/35, Ashley, Pa. BR/TR, 6'3.5", 175 lbs. Deb: 9/11/58																						
1958	Det-A	2	2	0	0	0	0	0	0	0	1	.000	.000	.000	-93	-1	0	0	0	1.000	-0	/O-1	-0.1
1961	Det-A	15	14	0	2	0	0	0	2	1	4	.143	.200	.143	-6	-2	0	0	0	.000	-0	/O-1	-0.3
1962	Det-A	2	2	0	0	0	0	0	0	0	0	.000	.000	.000	-97	-1	0	0	0	.000	0	H	-0.1
	KC-A	90	209	29	57	10	1	11	35	16	29	.273	.327	.488	111	3	1	1	-0	.968	-3	O-50/1-1	-0.3
	Yr	92	211	29	57	10	1	11	35	16	29	.270	.325	.483	109	2	1	1	-0	.968	-3	O-50/1-1	-0.4
1963	KC-A	87	221	28	59	11	0	9	37	26	33	.267	.347	.439	112	4	0	1	-1	1.000	-3	O-63	-0.3
1964	KC-A	102	204	18	49	10	1	3	19	30	36	.240	.343	.343	89	-2	0	0	0	.984	-4	O-44,1-12	-0.9
Total	5	298	652	75	167	31	2	23	93	73	103	.256	.335	.416	101	1	1	2	-1	.985	-10	O-159/1-13	-2.0
■ LUIS ALVARADO	Alvarado, Luis Cesar (Martinez) b: 1/15/49, Lajas, P.R. BR/TR, 5'9", 162 lbs. Deb: 9/13/68																						
1968	Bos-A	11	46	3	6	2	0	0	1	1	11	.130	.167	.174	3	-5	0	0	0	.976	-4	S-11	-0.9
1969	Bos-A	6	5	0	0	0	0	0	0	0	2	.000	.000	.000	-95	-1	0	1	-1	1.000	2	/S-5	0.0
1970	Bos-A	59	183	19	41	11	0	1	10	9	30	.224	.260	.301	51	-12	1	2	-1	.929	5	3-29,S-27	-0.6
1971	Chi-A	99	264	22	57	14	1	0	8	11	34	.216	.247	.277	47	-19	1	2	-1	.959	15	S-71,2-16	0.4

YEAR	TM/L	G	AB	R	H	2B	3B	HR	RBI	BB	SO	AVG	OBP	SLG	PRO+	BR/A	SB	CS	SBR	FA	FR	G/POS	TPR
1972	Chi-A	103	254	30	54	4	1	4	29	13	36	.213	.254	.283	58	-13	2	2	-1	.957	2	S-81,2-16/3-2	-0.3
1973	Chi-A	80	203	21	47	7	2	0	20	4	20	.232	.250	.286	49	-14	6	2	1	.980	5	2-45,S-18,3-10,/D-1	-0.5
1974	Chi-A	8	10	1	1	0	0	0	0	0	1	.100	.100	.100	-41	-2	0	0	0	.667	-1	/S-4,2-1,3-1	-0.3
	StL-N	17	36	3	5	2	0	0	1	2	6	.139	.184	.194	6	-5	0	0	0	.980	-2	S-17	-0.5
	Cle-A	61	114	12	25	2	0	0	12	6	14	.219	.258	.237	44	-8	1	1	-0	.972	11	2-46/S-7,D-3	0.4
1976	StL-N	16	42	5	12	1	0	0	3	3	6	.286	.333	.310	82	-1	0	0	0	.936	-9	2-16	-1.0
1977	NY-N	1	2	0	0	0	0	0	0	0	0	.000	.000	.000	-99	-1	0	0	0	1.000	0	/2-1	0.0
	Det-A	2	1	0	0	0	0	0	0	0	0	.000	.000	.000	-95	-0	0	0	0	.000	0	/3-2	0.0
Total	9	463	1160	116	248	43	4	5	84	49	160	.214	.248	.271	47	-81	11	10	-3	.957	26	S-241,2-141/3-44,D	-3.3

■ **GABE ALVAREZ** Alvarez, Gabriel De Jesus b: 3/6/74, Navojoa, Mexico BR/TR, 6'1", 205 lbs. Deb: 6/22/98

YEAR	TM/L	G	AB	R	H	2B	3B	HR	RBI	BB	SO	AVG	OBP	SLG	PRO+	BR/A	SB	CS	SBR	FA	FR	G/POS	TPR
1998	Det-A	58	199	16	46	11	0	5	29	18	65	.231	.301	.362	71	-9	1	3	-2	.873	-3	3-55/D-2	-1.2

■ **ORLANDO ALVAREZ** Alvarez, Jesus Manuel Orlando (Monge) b: 2/28/52, Rio Grande, P.R. BR/TR, 6', 165 lbs. Deb: 9/1/73

YEAR	TM/L	G	AB	R	H	2B	3B	HR	RBI	BB	SO	AVG	OBP	SLG	PRO+	BR/A	SB	CS	SBR	FA	FR	G/POS	TPR
1973	LA-N	4	4	0	1	1	0	0	0	0	1	.250	.250	.500	108	-0	0	0	0	.000	0	H	0.0
1974	LA-N	2	1	0	0	0	0	0	0	0	0	.000	.000	.000	-99	-0	0	0	0	1.000	-0	/O-1	0.0
1975	LA-N	4	4	0	0	0	0	0	0	0	1	.000	.000	.000	-99	-1	0	0	0	.000	0	H	-0.1
1976	Cal-A	15	42	4	7	1	0	2	8	0	3	.167	.167	.333	47	-3	0	0	0	1.000	-1	O-11/D-2	-0.5
Total	4	25	51	4	8	2	0	2	8	0	5	.157	.157	.314	36	-4	0	0	0	1.000	-2	/O-12,D-2	-0.6

■ **OSSIE ALVAREZ** Alvarez, Oswaldo (Gonzalez) b: 10/19/33, Matanzas, Cuba BR/TR, 5'10", 165 lbs. Deb: 4/19/58

YEAR	TM/L	G	AB	R	H	2B	3B	HR	RBI	BB	SO	AVG	OBP	SLG	PRO+	BR/A	SB	CS	SBR	FA	FR	G/POS	TPR
1958	Was-A	87	196	20	41	3	0	0	5	16	26	.209	.269	.224	38	-16	1	1	-0	.968	12	S-64,2-14/3-3	0.0
1959	Det-A	8	2	0	1	0	0	0	0	0	1	.500	.500	.500	166	0	0	0	0	.000	0	H	0.0
Total	2	95	198	20	42	3	0	0	5	16	27	.212	.271	.227	39	-16	1	1	-0	.968	12	/S-64,2-14,3-3	0.0

■ **ROGELIO ALVAREZ** Alvarez, Rogelio (Hernandez) b: 4/18/38, Pinar Del Rio, Cuba BR/TR, 5'11", 183 lbs. Deb: 9/18/60

YEAR	TM/L	G	AB	R	H	2B	3B	HR	RBI	BB	SO	AVG	OBP	SLG	PRO+	BR/A	SB	CS	SBR	FA	FR	G/POS	TPR
1960	Cin-N	3	9	1	1	0	0	0	0	0	3	.111	.111	.111	-38	-2	0	0	0	1.000	-1	/1-2	-0.3
1962	Cin-N	14	28	1	6	0	0	0	2	1	10	.214	.241	.214	23	-3	0	0	0	.973	-1	1-13	-0.4
Total	2	17	37	2	7	0	0	0	2	1	13	.189	.211	.189	8	-5	0	0	0	.979	-1	/1-15	-0.7

■ **MAX ALVIS** Alvis, Roy Maxwell b: 2/2/38, Jasper, Tex. BR/TR, 5'11", 187 lbs. Deb: 9/11/62

YEAR	TM/L	G	AB	R	H	2B	3B	HR	RBI	BB	SO	AVG	OBP	SLG	PRO+	BR/A	SB	CS	SBR	FA	FR	G/POS	TPR
1962	Cle-A	12	51	1	11	2	0	0	3	2	13	.216	.245	.255	36	-5	3	1	0	.935	-4	3-12	-0.8
1963	Cle-A	158	602	81	165	32	7	22	67	36	109	.274	.326	.460	118	13	9	7	-2	.942	-5	*3-158	0.7
1964	Cle-A	107	381	51	96	14	3	18	53	29	77	.252	.315	.446	110	4	5	5	-2	.955	-7	*3-105	-0.6
1965	Cle-A★	159	604	88	149	24	2	21	61	47	121	.247	.311	.397	99	-2	12	8	-1	.958	-19	*3-156	-2.7
1966	Cle-A	157	596	67	146	22	3	17	55	50	98	.245	.306	.378	95	-4	4	7	-3	.958	-6	*3-157	-1.8
1967	Cle-A★	161	637	66	163	23	4	21	70	38	107	.256	.302	.403	106	3	3	10	-5	.965	-8	*3-161	-1.3
1968	Cle-A	131	452	38	101	17	3	8	37	41	91	.223	.294	.327	89	-6	5	5	-2	.960	-17	*3-128	-2.8
1969	Cle-A	66	191	13	43	6	0	1	15	14	26	.225	.278	.272	53	-12	1	1	-0	.973	-2	3-58/S-1	-1.5
1970	Mil-A	62	115	16	21	2	0	3	12	5	20	.183	.217	.278	35	-10	1	2	-1	.909	2	3-36	-1.0
Total	9	1013	3629	421	895	142	22	111	373	262	662	.247	.304	.390	97	-19	43	46	-15	.956	-64	3-971/S-1	-11.8

■ **BILLY ALVORD** Alvord, William Charles "Uncle Bill" b: 8/1863, St.Louis, Mo. 5'10", 187 lbs. Deb: 4/30/1885

YEAR	TM/L	G	AB	R	H	2B	3B	HR	RBI	BB	SO	AVG	OBP	SLG	PRO+	BR/A	SB	CS	SBR	FA	FR	G/POS	TPR
1885	StL-N	2	5	0	0	0	0	0	0	1	2	.000	.167	.000	-45	-1				.714	-1	/3-2	-0.1
1889	KC-a	50	186	23	43	8	9	0	18	10	35	.231	.270	.371	77	-7	3			.877	5	3-34/S-8,2-8	0.0
1890	Tol-a	116	495	69	135	13	16	2	52	22		.273	.304	.376	97	-5	21			.872	4	*3-116	0.3
1891	Cle-N	13	59	7	17	2	2	1	7	0	7	.288	.300	.441	110	0	0			.814	-2	3-13	-0.1
	Was-a	81	312	28	73	8	3	0	30	11	38	.234	.260	.279	57	-19	3			.862	17	3-81	0.2
1893	Cle-N	3	12	2	2	0	0	0	2	0	1	.167	.167	.167	-11	-2	0			.875	-2	/3-3	-0.3
Total	5	265	1069	129	270	31	30	3	109	44	83	.253	.283	.346	81	-33	27			.865	22	3-249/2-8,S-8	0.0

■ **BRANT ALYEA** Alyea, Garrabrant Ryerson b: 12/8/40, Passaic, N.J. BR/TR, 6'3", 215 lbs. Deb: 9/11/65

YEAR	TM/L	G	AB	R	H	2B	3B	HR	RBI	BB	SO	AVG	OBP	SLG	PRO+	BR/A	SB	CS	SBR	FA	FR	G/POS	TPR
1965	Was-A	8	13	3	3	0	0	2	6	1	4	.231	.286	.692	171	1	0	0	0	1.000	-1	/1-3,O-1	0.0
1968	Was-A	53	150	18	40	11	1	6	23	10	39	.267	.317	.473	141	7	0	0	0	1.000	1	O-39	0.6
1969	Was-A	104	237	29	59	4	0	11	40	34	67	.249	.346	.405	115	5	1	3	-2	.938	-7	O-69/1-3	-0.8
1970	*Min-A	94	258	34	75	12	1	16	61	28	51	.291	.367	.531	143	14	3	3	-1	.980	-5	O-75	0.5
1971	Min-A	79	158	13	28	4	0	2	15	24	38	.177	.290	.241	50	-10	1	1	-0	.962	-6	O-48	-2.0
1972	Oak-A	20	31	3	6	1	0	1	2	3	5	.194	.265	.323	78	-1	0	0	0	1.000	3	/O-8	0.2
	StL-N	13	19	0	3	1	0	0	1	0	6	.158	.158	.211	4	-2	0	0	0	1.000	1	/O-3	-0.2
Total	6	371	866	100	214	33	2	38	148	100	210	.247	.329	.421	113	14	5	7	-3	.972	-15	O-243/1-6	-1.7

■ **JOEY AMALFITANO** Amalfitano, John Joseph b: 1/23/34, San Pedro, Cal. BR/TR, 5'11", 180 lbs. Deb: 5/3/54 MC

YEAR	TM/L	G	AB	R	H	2B	3B	HR	RBI	BB	SO	AVG	OBP	SLG	PRO+	BR/A	SB	CS	SBR	FA	FR	G/POS	TPR
1954	NY-N	9	5	2	0	0	0	0	0	0	4	.000	.000	.000	-99	-1	0	0	0	1.000	2	/3-4,2-1	0.1
1955	NY-N	36	22	8	5	1	1	0	1	2	2	.227	.292	.364	72	-1	0	0	0	.957	10	/S-5,3-2	0.9
1960	SF-N	106	328	47	91	15	3	1	27	26	31	.277	.336	.351	94	-3	2	3	-1	.935	3	3-63,2-33/S-3,O-1	0.1
1961	SF-N	109	384	64	98	11	4	2	23	44	59	.255	.332	.320	77	-12	7	4	-0	.970	-22	2-95/3-6	-2.4
1962	Hou-N	117	380	44	90	12	5	1	27	45	43	.237	.319	.303	73	-14	4	4	-1	.967	2	*2-110/3-5	-0.3
1963	SF-N	54	137	11	24	3	0	1	7	12	18	.175	.247	.219	36	-11	2	6	-3	.980	-3	2-37/3-7	-1.6
1964	Chi-N	100	324	51	78	19	6	4	27	40	42	.241	.333	.373	95	-1	2	7	-4	.964	2	2-86/1-1,S-1	0.4
1965	Chi-N	67	96	13	26	4	0	0	8	12	14	.271	.364	.313	90	-1	2	2	-1	.989	5	2-24/S-4	0.5
1966	Chi-N	41	38	8	6	2	0	0	3	4	10	.158	.238	.211	26	-4	0	0	0	.977	1	2-12/3-3,S-2	-0.2
1967	Chi-N	4	1	0	0	0	0	0	0	0	1	.000	.000	.000	-96	-0	0	0	0	.000	0	H	0.0
Total	10	643	1715	248	418	67	19	9	123	185	224	.244	.322	.321	78	-48	19	26	-10	.970	0	2-398/3-90,S-15,1O	-2.5

■ **RICH AMARAL** Amaral, Richard Louis b: 4/1/62, Visalia, Cal. BR/TR, 6', 175 lbs. Deb: 5/27/91

YEAR	TM/L	G	AB	R	H	2B	3B	HR	RBI	BB	SO	AVG	OBP	SLG	PRO+	BR/A	SB	CS	SBR	FA	FR	G/POS	TPR
1991	Sea-A	14	16	2	1	0	0	0	0	1	5	.063	.167	.063	-34	-3	0	0	0	1.000	4	/2-5,3-2,S-2,1-1,D	0.1
1992	Sea-A	35	100	9	24	3	0	1	7	5	16	.240	.276	.300	61	-5	4	2	0	.955	2	3-17,S-17/O-3,12	-0.3
1993	Sea-A	110	373	53	108	24	1	1	44	33	54	.290	.352	.367	92	-3	19	11	-1	.975	10	2-77,3-19,S-14,/1D	0.8
1994	Sea-A	77	228	37	60	10	2	4	18	24	28	.263	.336	.377	82	-6	5	1	1	.943	-12	2-42,O-16/S-7,1D	-1.4
1995	*Sea-A	90	238	45	67	14	2	2	19	21	33	.282	.342	.382	87	-4	21	2	5	.992	-7	O-73/D-1	-0.8
1996	Sea-A	118	312	69	91	11	3	1	29	47	55	.292	.393	.356	91	-2	25	6	4	1.000	-5	O-91,2-15,1-10,/3D	-0.4
1997	*Sea-A	89	190	34	54	5	0	1	21	10	34	.284	.330	.326	73	-7	12	8	-1	1.000	-9	O-52,1-14,2/3SD	-1.7
1998	Sea-A	73	134	25	37	6	0	1	4	13	24	.276	.345	.343	80	-4	11	1	3	1.000	-9	O-52,2-11/1-7,3D	-1.0
Total	8	606	1591	274	442	73	8	11	142	154	249	.278	.347	.354	84	-34	97	31	11	.995	-27	O-287,2-162/S31D	-4.7

■ **RUBEN AMARO** Amaro, Ruben Jr. b: 2/12/65, Philadelphia, Pa. BB/TR, 5'10", 175 lbs. Deb: 6/8/91 F

YEAR	TM/L	G	AB	R	H	2B	3B	HR	RBI	BB	SO	AVG	OBP	SLG	PRO+	BR/A	SB	CS	SBR	FA	FR	G/POS	TPR
1991	Cal-A	10	23	0	5	1	0	0	2	3	3	.217	.308	.261	59	-1	0	0	0	1.000	-2	/O-5,2-4,D-1	-0.4
1992	Phi-N	126	374	43	82	15	6	7	34	37	54	.219	.305	.348	85	-7	11	5	0	.992	0	*O-113	-1.0
1993	Phi-N	25	48	7	16	2	2	1	6	6	5	.333	.407	.521	149	3	0	0	0	.963	-2	O-16	0.2
1994	Cle-A	26	23	5	5	1	0	2	5	2	3	.217	.280	.522	100	-0	2	1	0	.909	-4	O-12/D-3	-0.4
1995	*Cle-A	28	60	5	12	3	0	1	7	4	6	.200	.273	.300	48	-5	1	3	-2	1.000	-4	O-22/D-3	-1.0
1996	Phi-N	61	117	14	37	10	0	2	15	9	18	.316	.380	.453	117	3	0	0	0	1.000	-4	O-35/1-1	-0.1
1997	Phi-N	117	175	18	41	6	1	2	21	21	24	.234	.323	.314	68	-8	1	1	-0	.987	-12	O-72/1-1	-2.1
1998	Phi-N	92	107	7	20	5	0	1	10	6	15	.187	.230	.262	27	-12	0	0	0	1.000	-10	O-51	-2.2
Total	8	485	927	99	218	43	9	16	100	88	128	.235	.312	.353	79	-26	15	10	-2	.989	-38	O-326/D-7,2-4,1-2	-7.0

■ **RUBEN AMARO** Amaro, Ruben Sr. (Mora) b: 1/6/36, Veracruz, Mexico BR/TR, 5'11", 170 lbs. Deb: 6/29/58 FC

YEAR	TM/L	G	AB	R	H	2B	3B	HR	RBI	BB	SO	AVG	OBP	SLG	PRO+	BR/A	SB	CS	SBR	FA	FR	G/POS	TPR
1958	StL-N	40	76	8	17	2	1	0	0	5	8	.224	.272	.276	44	-6	0	1	-1	.948	3	S-36/2-1	-0.2
1960	Phi-N	92	264	25	61	9	1	0	16	21	32	.231	.293	.273	56	-16	0	1	-1	.965	-8	S-92	-1.9
1961	Phi-N	135	381	34	98	14	9	1	32	53	59	.257	.351	.349	88	-5	1	0	0	.970	14	*S-132/1-3,2-1	1.9
1962	Phi-N	79	226	24	55	10	0	0	19	30	28	.243	.335	.288	71	-8	5	2	0	.968	6	S-78/1-1	0.5
1963	Phi-N	115	217	25	47	9	2	2	19	19	31	.217	.280	.304	69	-9	0	1	-1	.950	2	S-63,3-45/1-5	-0.5

YEAR	TM/L	G	AB	R	H	2B	3B	HR	RBI	BB	SO	AVG	OBP	SLG	PRO+	BR/A	SB	CS	SBR	FA	FR	G/POS	TPR
1964	Phi-N	129	299	31	79	11	0	4	34	16	37	.264	.308	.341	84	-6	1	6	-3	.971	-4	S-79,1-58/2-3,3O	-1.0
1965	Phi-N	118	184	26	39	7	0	0	15	27	22	.212	.316	.250	63	-8	1	1	-0	.990	-3	1-60,S-60/2-6	-0.9
1966	NY-A	14	23	0	5	0	0	0	3	0	2	.217	.217	.217	26	-2	0	0	0	.977	5	S-14	0.4
1967	NY-A	130	417	31	93	12	0	1	17	43	49	.223	.297	.259	68	-16	3	2	-0	.973	9	*S-123/3-3,1-2	0.5
1968	NY-A	47	41	3	5	1	0	0	0	9	6	.122	.280	.146	33	-3	0	0	0	.962	-0	S-23,1-22	-0.3
1969	Cal-A	41	27	4	6	0	0	0	1	4	6	.222	.323	.222	58	-1	0	0	0	1.000	0	1-18/2-9,S-5,3-2	-0.1
Total	11	940	2155	211	505	75	13	8	156	227	280	.234	.310	.292	70	-81	11	14	-5	.967	24	S-705,1-169/32O	-1.6

■ WAYNE AMBLER Ambler, Wayne Harper b: 11/8/15, Abington, Pa. d: 1/3/98, Ponte Vedra Beach, Fla. BR/TR, 5'8.5", 165 lbs. Deb: 6/4/37

YEAR	TM/L	G	AB	R	H	2B	3B	HR	RBI	BB	SO	AVG	OBP	SLG	PRO+	BR/A	SB	CS	SBR	FA	FR	G/POS	TPR
1937	Phi-A	56	162	3	35	5	0	0	11	13	8	.216	.274	.247	33	-17	1	0	0	.955	-4	2-56	-1.6
1938	Phi-A	120	393	42	92	21	2	0	38	48	31	.234	.317	.298	56	-26	2	1	0	.942	-19	*S-116/2-4	-3.3
1939	Phi-A	95	227	15	48	13	0	0	24	22	25	.211	.281	.269	42	-20	1	0	0	.954	-3	S-77,2-19	-1.5
Total	3	271	782	60	175	39	2	0	73	83	64	.224	.298	.279	47	-63	4	1	1	.946	-26	S-193/2-79	-6.4

■ ED AMELUNG Amelung, Edward Allen b: 4/13/59, Fullerton, Cal. BL/TL, 5'11", 180 lbs. Deb: 7/28/84

YEAR	TM/L	G	AB	R	H	2B	3B	HR	RBI	BB	SO	AVG	OBP	SLG	PRO+	BR/A	SB	CS	SBR	FA	FR	G/POS	TPR
1984	LA-N	34	46	7	10	0	0	0	4	2	4	.217	.250	.217	33	-4	3	2	-0	1.000	-3	O-23	-0.8
1986	LA-N	8	11	0	1	0	0	0	0	0	4	.091	.091	.091	-53	-2	0	0	0	1.000	-1	/O-4	-0.3
Total	2	42	57	7	11	0	0	0	4	2	8	.193	.220	.193	17	-6	3	2	-0	1.000	-4	/O-27	-1.1

■ SANDY AMOROS Amoros, Edmundo (Isasi) b: 1/30/30, Havana, Cuba d: 6/27/92, Miami, Fla. BL/TL, 5'7.5", 170 lbs. Deb: 8/22/52

YEAR	TM/L	G	AB	R	H	2B	3B	HR	RBI	BB	SO	AVG	OBP	SLG	PRO+	BR/A	SB	CS	SBR	FA	FR	G/POS	TPR
1952	*Bro-N	20	44	10	11	3	1	0	3	5	14	.250	.327	.364	90	-1	1	0	0	1.000	-3	O-10	-0.4
1954	Bro-N	79	263	44	72	18	6	9	34	31	24	.274	.353	.490	113	5	1	4	-2	.987	5	O-70	0.4
1955	*Bro-N	119	388	59	96	16	7	10	51	55	45	.247	.350	.402	96	-1	10	5	0	.972	-1	*O-109	-0.7
1956	*Bro-N	114	292	53	76	11	8	16	58	59	51	.260	.386	.517	130	13	3	4	-2	.955	-10	O-86	-0.3
1957	Bro-N	106	238	40	66	7	1	7	26	46	42	.277	.401	.403	107	4	3	2	-0	.984	-1	O-66	0.0
1959	LA-N	5	5	1	1	0	0	0	1	0	1	.200	.200	.200	6	-1	0	0	0	.000	0	H	-0.1
1960	LA-N	9	14	1	2	0	0	0	0	3	2	.143	.294	.143	23	-1	0	0	0	1.000	0	/O-3	-0.1
	Det-A	65	67	7	10	0	0	1	7	12	10	.149	.278	.194	29	-6	0	0	0	1.000	-1	O-10	-0.8
Total	7	517	1311	215	334	55	23	43	180	211	189	.255	.363	.430	105	12	18	15	-4	.976	-11	O-354	-2.0

■ ALF ANDERSON Anderson, Alfred Walton b: 1/28/14, Gainesville, Ga. d: 6/23/85, Albany, Ga. BR/TR, 5'11", 165 lbs. Deb: 4/20/41

YEAR	TM/L	G	AB	R	H	2B	3B	HR	RBI	BB	SO	AVG	OBP	SLG	PRO+	BR/A	SB	CS	SBR	FA	FR	G/POS	TPR
1941	Pit-N	70	223	32	48	7	2	1	10	14	30	.215	.265	.278	53	-14	2			.931	-6	S-58	-1.7
1942	Pit-N	54	166	24	45	4	1	0	7	18	19	.271	.342	.307	89	-2	4			.942	-15	S-48	-1.6
1946	Pit-N	2	1	0	0	0	0	0	0	1	0	.000	.500	.000	47	0	0			.000	0	H	0.0
Total	3	126	390	56	93	11	3	1	17	33	49	.238	.300	.290	68	-16	6			.936	-21	S-106	-3.3

■ ANDY ANDERSON Anderson, Andy Holm b: 11/13/22, Bremerton, Wash. d: 7/18/82, Seattle, Wash. BR/TR, 5'11", 172 lbs. Deb: 5/10/48

YEAR	TM/L	G	AB	R	H	2B	3B	HR	RBI	BB	SO	AVG	OBP	SLG	PRO+	BR/A	SB	CS	SBR	FA	FR	G/POS	TPR
1948	StL-A	51	87	13	24	5	1	1	12	8	15	.276	.337	.391	91	-1	0	0	0	.917	-2	2-21,S-10/1-2	-0.2
1949	StL-A	71	136	10	17	3	0	1	5	14	21	.125	.207	.169	-0	-20	0	1	-1	.957	-7	S-44/2-8,3-8	-2.5
Total	2	122	223	23	41	8	1	2	17	22	36	.184	.257	.256	35	-21	0	1	-1	.946	-9	/S-54,2-29,3-8,1-2	-2.7

■ BRADY ANDERSON Anderson, Brady Kevin b: 1/18/64, Silver Spring, Md. BL/TL, 6'1", 185 lbs. Deb: 4/4/88

YEAR	TM/L	G	AB	R	H	2B	3B	HR	RBI	BB	SO	AVG	OBP	SLG	PRO+	BR/A	SB	CS	SBR	FA	FR	G/POS	TPR
1988	Bos-A	41	148	14	34	5	3	0	12	15	35	.230	.317	.304	72	-5	4	2	0	.989	2	O-41	-0.5
	Bal-A	53	177	17	35	8	1	1	9	8	40	.198	.232	.271	42	-14	6	4	-1	.981	5	O-49	-1.1
	Yr	94	325	31	69	13	4	1	21	23	75	.212	.273	.286	57	-19	10	6	-1	.984	7	O-90	-1.6
1989	Bal-A	94	266	44	55	12	2	4	16	43	45	.207	.324	.312	82	-5	16	4	2	.985	-2	O-79/D-8	-0.7
1990	Bal-A	89	234	24	54	5	2	3	24	31	46	.231	.333	.308	83	-4	15	2	3	.987	2	O-63,D-11	0.0
1991	Bal-A	113	256	40	59	12	3	2	27	38	44	.230	.341	.324	89	-3	12	5	1	.981	-15	*O-101/D-2	-1.9
1992	Bal-A★	159	623	100	169	28	10	21	80	98	98	.271	.378	.449	128	25	53	16	6	.980	14	*O-158	4.2
1993	Bal-A	142	560	87	147	36	8	13	66	82	99	.262	.367	.425	108	7	24	12	0	.993	2	*O-140/D-2	0.7
1994	Bal-A	111	453	78	119	25	5	12	48	57	75	.263	.358	.419	95	-3	31	1	9	.996	-0	*O-109	0.2
1995	Bal-A	143	554	108	145	33	10	16	64	87	111	.262	.372	.444	109	9	26	7	4	.989	-16	*O-142	-0.7
1996	*Bal-A★	149	579	117	172	37	5	50	110	76	106	.297	.399	.637	157	50	21	8	2	.992	6	*O-143/D-2	4.8
1997	*Bal-A★	151	590	97	170	39	7	18	73	84	105	.288	.394	.469	128	27	18	12	-2	.989	-2	*O-124,D-25	1.8
1998	Bal-A	133	479	84	113	28	3	18	51	75	78	.236	.357	.420	103	4	21	7	2	.985	-9	*O-130	-0.6
Total	11	1378	4919	810	1272	268	59	158	580	694	882	.259	.363	.433	111	88	247	80	26	.988	-14	*O-1279/D-50	6.2

■ DAVE ANDERSON Anderson, David Carter b: 8/1/60, Louisville, Ky. BR/TR, 6'2", 185 lbs. Deb: 5/8/83

YEAR	TM/L	G	AB	R	H	2B	3B	HR	RBI	BB	SO	AVG	OBP	SLG	PRO+	BR/A	SB	CS	SBR	FA	FR	G/POS	TPR
1983	LA-N	61	115	12	19	4	2	1	2	12	15	.165	.244	.261	40	-9	6	3	0	.969	3	S-53/3-1	-0.3
1984	LA-N	121	374	51	94	16	2	3	34	45	55	.251	.335	.329	88	-5	15	5	2	.965	19	*S-111,3-11	2.6
1985	*LA-N	77	221	24	44	6	0	4	18	35	42	.199	.311	.281	69	-8	5	4	-1	.957	17	3-51,S-25/2-2	1.0
1986	LA-N	92	216	31	53	9	0	1	15	22	39	.245	.315	.301	76	-7	5	1	1	.976	9	3-51,S-34/2-5	0.5
1987	LA-N	108	265	32	62	12	3	1	13	24	43	.234	.300	.313	64	-13	9	5	-0	.977	6	S-65,3-35/2-5	-0.4
1988	*LA-N	116	285	31	71	10	2	2	20	32	45	.249	.327	.319	89	-3	4	2	0	.986	14	S-82,3-12,2-11	1.8
1989	LA-N	87	140	15	32	2	0	1	14	17	26	.229	.312	.264	67	-5	2	0	1	.990	0	S-33,3-18/2-7	-0.3
1990	SF-N	60	100	14	35	5	1	1	6	3	20	.350	.369	.450	129	4	1	2	-1	1.000	-6	S-29,2-13/1-3,3-2	-0.2
1991	SF-N	100	226	24	56	5	2	2	13	12	35	.248	.286	.314	71	-9	2	4	-2	.956	-10	S-63,1-16,3-11,/2-6	-1.9
1992	LA-N	51	84	10	24	4	0	3	8	4	11	.286	.318	.440	115	1	0	4	-2	.974	2	3-26/S-7	0.1
Total	10	873	2026	244	490	73	12	19	143	206	331	.242	.313	.318	79	-56	49	30	-3	.970	54	S-502,3-218/2-49,1	2.9

■ DWAIN ANDERSON Anderson, Dwain Cleaven b: 11/23/47, Oakland, Cal. BR/TR, 5'11", 165 lbs. Deb: 9/3/71

YEAR	TM/L	G	AB	R	H	2B	3B	HR	RBI	BB	SO	AVG	OBP	SLG	PRO+	BR/A	SB	CS	SBR	FA	FR	G/POS	TPR
1971	Oak-A	16	37	3	10	2	1	0	3	5	9	.270	.372	.378	115	1	0	1	-1	.968	-1	S-10/2-5,3-1	0.1
1972	Oak-A	3	7	2	0	0	0	0	0	1	4	.000	.125	.000	-64	-1	0	0	0	1.000	-0	/S-1,3-1	-0.2
	StL-N	57	135	12	36	4	1	1	8	8	23	.267	.313	.333	85	-3	0	1	-1	.952	-3	S-43,3-13/2-1	-0.3
1973	StL-N	18	17	5	2	0	0	0	0	4	4	.118	.286	.118	16	-2	0	0	0	.500	-3	/S-3,O-2	-0.4
	SD-N	53	107	11	13	0	0	0	3	14	29	.121	.223	.121	-2	-15	2	0	1	.932	3	S-39/3-6	-0.8
	Yr	71	124	16	15	0	0	0	3	18	33	.121	.232	.121	1	-16	2	0	1	.919	1	S-42/3-6,O-2	-1.2
1974	Cle-A	2	3	0	1	0	0	0	0	0	1	.333	.333	.333	93	-0	0	0	0	1.000	-1	/2-1	-0.1
Total	4	149	306	33	62	6	2	1	14	32	70	.203	.282	.245	52	-20	2	2	-1	.940	-4	/S-96,3-21,2-7,O-2	-1.7

■ GOAT ANDERSON Anderson, Edward John b: 1/13/1880, Cleveland, Ohio d: 3/15/23, South Bend, Ind. BL/TR, Deb: 4/11/07

YEAR	TM/L	G	AB	R	H	2B	3B	HR	RBI	BB	SO	AVG	OBP	SLG	PRO+	BR/A	SB	CS	SBR	FA	FR	G/POS	TPR
1907	Pit-N	127	413	73	85	3	1	1	12	80		.206	.343	.225	77	-6	27			.953	-1	*O-117/2-5	-1.3

■ FERRELL ANDERSON Anderson, Ferrell Jack "Andy" b: 1/9/18, Maple City, Kan. d: 3/12/78, Joplin, Mo. BR/TR, 6'1", 200 lbs. Deb: 4/16/46

YEAR	TM/L	G	AB	R	H	2B	3B	HR	RBI	BB	SO	AVG	OBP	SLG	PRO+	BR/A	SB	CS	SBR	FA	FR	G/POS	TPR
1946	Bro-N	79	199	19	51	10	0	2	14	18	21	.256	.330	.337	89	-3	1			.964	-2	C-70	-0.2
1953	StL-N	18	35	1	10	2	0	0	1	0	4	.286	.286	.343	63	-2	0	0	0	1.000	-1	C-12	-0.3
Total	2	97	234	20	61	12	0	2	15	18	25	.261	.324	.338	85	-5	1	0		.968	-3	/C-82	-0.5

■ GARRET ANDERSON Anderson, Garret Joseph b: 6/30/72, Los Angeles, Cal. BL/TL, 6'3", 190 lbs. Deb: 7/27/94

YEAR	TM/L	G	AB	R	H	2B	3B	HR	RBI	BB	SO	AVG	OBP	SLG	PRO+	BR/A	SB	CS	SBR	FA	FR	G/POS	TPR
1994	Cal-A	5	13	0	5	0	0	0	1	0	2	.385	.385	.385	98	-0	0	0	0	1.000	0	/O-4	0.0
1995	Cal-A	106	374	50	120	19	1	16	69	19	65	.321	.355	.505	122	11	6	2	1	.978	7	*O-100/D-1	1.5
1996	Cal-A	150	607	79	173	33	2	12	72	27	84	.285	.315	.405	80	-19	7	9	-3	.979	6	*O-146/D-1	-1.8
1997	Ana-A	154	624	76	189	36	3	8	92	30	70	.303	.337	.409	94	-6	10	4	1	.992	13	*O-148/D-4	0.4
1998	Ana-A	156	622	62	183	41	7	15	79	29	80	.294	.327	.455	99	-2	8	3	1	.983	8	*O-155	0.3
Total	5	571	2240	267	670	129	13	51	313	105	301	.299	.332	.437	96	-17	31	18	-2	.983	34	O-553/D-6	0.4

■ GEORGE ANDERSON Anderson, George Jendrus "Andy" (Born George Andrew Jendrus)
b: 9/26/1889, Cleveland, Ohio d: 5/28/62, Cleveland, Ohio BL/TR, 5'8", 160 lbs. Deb: 5/26/14

YEAR	TM/L	G	AB	R	H	2B	3B	HR	RBI	BB	SO	AVG	OBP	SLG	PRO+	BR/A	SB	CS	SBR	FA	FR	G/POS	TPR
1914	Bro-F	98	364	58	115	13	3	3	24	31	50	.316	.376	.393	110	1	16			.946	4	O-92	0.0
1915	Bro-F	136	511	70	135	23	9	2	39	52	54	.264	.342	.356	97	-9	20			.956	-8	*O-134	-2.5
1918	StL-N	35	132	20	39	4	5	0	6	15	7	.295	.380	.402	143	7	0			.956	-1	O-35	0.4
Total	3	269	1007	148	289	40	17	5	69	98	111	.287	.359	.375	108	-1	36			.952	-5	O-261	-2.1

■ SPARKY ANDERSON Anderson, George Lee b: 2/22/34, Bridgewater, S.Dak BR/TR, 5'9", 170 lbs. Deb: 4/10/59 MC

YEAR	TM/L	G	AB	R	H	2B	3B	HR	RBI	BB	SO	AVG	OBP	SLG	PRO+	BR/A	SB	CS	SBR	FA	FR	G/POS	TPR
1959	Phi-N	152	477	42	104	9	3	0	34	42	53	.218	.283	.249	43	-38	6	9	-4	.984	3	*2-152	-2.9

■ HAL ANDERSON Anderson, Harold b: 2/10/04, St.Louis, Mo. d: 5/1/74, St.Louis, Mo. BR/TR, 5'11", 160 lbs. Deb: 4/12/32

YEAR	TM/L	G	AB	R	H	2B	3B	HR	RBI	BB	SO	AVG	OBP	SLG	PRO+	BR/A	SB	CS	SBR	FA	FR	G/POS	TPR
1932	Chi-A	9	32	4	8	0	0	0	2	0	1	.250	.250	.250	32	-3	0	1	-1	1.000	0	/O-9	-0.4

■ HARRY ANDERSON Anderson, Harry Walter b: 9/10/31, North East, Md. d: 6/11/98, Greenville, Del. BL/TR, 6'3", 210 lbs. Deb: 4/18/57

YEAR	TM/L	G	AB	R	H	2B	3B	HR	RBI	BB	SO	AVG	OBP	SLG	PRO+	BR/A	SB	CS	SBR	FA	FR	G/POS	TPR
1957	Phi-N	118	400	53	107	15	4	17	61	36	61	.268	.337	.452	113	7	2	3	-1	.986	4	*O-109	0.4
1958	Phi-N	140	515	80	155	34	6	23	97	59	95	.301	.376	.524	137	27	0	2	-1	.975	-2	O-87,1-49	1.7
1959	Phi-N	142	508	50	122	28	6	14	63	43	95	.240	.306	.402	85	-12	1	1	-0	.980	18	*O-137	0.0
1960	Phi-N	38	93	10	23	2	0	5	12	10	19	.247	.333	.430	107	1	0	0	0	1.000	-1	O-16,1-12	-0.2
	Cin-N	42	66	6	11	3	0	1	9	11	20	.167	.286	.258	49	-4	0	0	0	.990	-1	1-15/O-4	-0.7
	Yr	80	159	16	34	5	0	6	21	21	39	.214	.313	.358	82	-4	0	0	0	.989	-2	1-27,O-20	-0.9
1961	Cin-N	4	4	0	1	0	0	0	0	0	1	.250	.250	.250	33	-0	0	0	0	.000	0	H	0.0
Total	5	484	1586	199	419	82	16	60	242	159	291	.264	.337	.450	109	18	3	6	-3	.982	19	O-353/1-76	1.2

■ JIM ANDERSON Anderson, James Lea b: 2/23/57, Los Angeles, Cal. BR/TR, 6', 170 lbs. Deb: 7/2/78

YEAR	TM/L	G	AB	R	H	2B	3B	HR	RBI	BB	SO	AVG	OBP	SLG	PRO+	BR/A	SB	CS	SBR	FA	FR	G/POS	TPR
1978	Cal-A	48	108	6	21	7	0	0	7	11	16	.194	.269	.259	51	-7	0	0	0	.955	3	S-47/2-1	0.0
1979	*Cal-A	96	234	33	58	13	1	3	23	17	31	.248	.302	.350	78	-7	3	2	-0	.949	-1	S-82,3-10/2-6,C-3	-0.2
1980	Sea-A	116	317	46	72	7	0	8	30	27	39	.227	.294	.325	69	-14	2	4	-2	.958	3	S-65,3-33/2-2,CD	-0.6
1981	Sea-A	70	162	12	33	7	0	2	19	17	29	.204	.283	.284	61	-8	3	5	-2	.947	4	S-68/3-2	-0.1
1983	Tex-A	50	102	8	22	1	1	0	6	5	8	.216	.252	.245	38	-9	1	2	-1	.962	6	S-27,2-17/3-3,OCD	-0.2
1984	Tex-A	39	47	2	5	0	0	0	1	4	7	.106	.176	.106	-19	-8	0	0	0	.989	10	S-31/3-6,2-1	0.4
Total	6	419	970	107	211	35	2	13	86	81	130	.218	.281	.298	60	-52	9	13	-5	.955	24	S-320/3-54,2DCO	-0.7

■ JOHN ANDERSON Anderson, John Joseph "Honest John" b: 12/14/1873, Sarpsborg, Norway d: 7/23/49, Worcester, Mass. BB/TR, 6'2", 180 lbs. Deb: 9/8/1894

YEAR	TM/L	G	AB	R	H	2B	3B	HR	RBI	BB	SO	AVG	OBP	SLG	PRO+	BR/A	SB	CS	SBR	FA	FR	G/POS	TPR
1894	Bro-N	17	63	14	19	1	3	1	19	3	3	.302	.333	.460	97	-1	7			.778	-5	O-16/3-1	-0.5
1895	Bro-N	102	419	76	120	11	14	9	87	12	29	.286	.314	.444	102	-1	24			.882	-6	*O-101	-1.2
1896	Bro-N	108	430	70	135	23	17	1	55	18	23	.314	.344	.453	116	8	37			.942	-3	O-68,1-42	0.0
1897	Bro-N	117	492	93	160	28	12	4	85	17		.325	.357	.455	120	12	29			.936	0	*O-115/1-3	0.3
1898	Bro-N	6	21	1	3	2	0	0	2	1		.143	.217	.238	31	-2	0			1.000	0	/O-5	-0.2
	Was-N	110	430	70	131	28	18	9	71	23		.305	.357	.516	150	24	18			.948	9	O-93,1-17	2.4
	Bro-N	19	69	11	19	3	4	0	8	5		.275	.333	.435	120	1	2			.966	-1	O-17/1-2	0.0
	Yr	135	520	82	153	33	**22**	9	81	29		.294	.348	**.494**	141	24	20			.952	8	*O-115,1-19	2.2
1899	Bro-N	117	439	65	118	18	7	4	92	27		.269	.317	.369	86	-10	25			.933	-4	O-76,1-41	-1.7
1901	Mil-A	138	576	90	190	46	7	8	99	24		.330	.360	.476	137	26	35			**.982**	5	*1-125,O-13	2.6
1902	StL-A	126	524	60	149	29	6	4	85	21		.284	.316	.385	95	-5	15			.985	-9	*1-126/O-3	-1.6
1903	StL-A	138	550	65	156	34	8	2	78	23		.284	.312	.385	111	6	16			.986	4	*1-133/O-7	0.8
1904	NY-A	143	558	62	155	27	12	3	82	23		.278	.313	.385	115	8	20			.956	-0	*O-112,1-33	0.1
1905	NY-A	32	99	12	23	3	1	0	14	8		.232	.296	.283	75	-3	9			.900	-2	O-22/1-3	-0.6
	Was-A	101	400	50	116	21	6	1	38	22		.290	.330	.380	130	12	22			.960	0	O-97/1-4	0.8
	Yr	133	499	62	139	24	7	1	52	30		.279	.323	.361	117	9	31			.949	-2	*O-119/1-7	0.2
1906	Was-A	151	583	62	158	25	4	3	70	19		.271	.296	.343	105	1	**39**			.953	5	*O-151	-0.2
1907	Was-A	87	333	33	96	12	4	0	44	34		.288	.359	.348	136	14	19			.983	-1	1-61,O-26	1.2
1908	Chi-A	123	355	36	93	17	1	0	47	30		.262	.321	.315	109	4	21			.963	-6	O-87/1-9	-0.6
Total	14	1635	6341	870	1841	328	124	49	976	310	55	.290	.329	.404	114	96	338			.939	-13	*O-1009,1-599/3-1	1.6

■ KENT ANDERSON Anderson, Kent McKay b: 8/12/63, Florence, S.C. BR/TR, 6'1", 180 lbs. Deb: 4/15/89 F

YEAR	TM/L	G	AB	R	H	2B	3B	HR	RBI	BB	SO	AVG	OBP	SLG	PRO+	BR/A	SB	CS	SBR	FA	FR	G/POS	TPR
1989	Cal-A	86	223	27	51	6	1	0	17	17	42	.229	.286	.265	57	-12	1	2	-1	.972	14	S-70/2-7,3-5,O-2,D	0.6
1990	Cal-A	49	143	16	44	6	1	1	5	13	19	.308	.369	.385	113	3	0	2	-1	.964	13	S-28,3-16/2-5	1.6
Total	2	135	366	43	95	12	2	1	22	30	61	.260	.319	.311	79	-9	1	4	-2	.969	27	/S-98,3-21,2-12,OD	2.2

■ MARLON ANDERSON Anderson, Marlon Ordell b: 1/6/74, Montgomery, Ala. BL/TR, 5'11", 190 lbs. Deb: 9/8/98

YEAR	TM/L	G	AB	R	H	2B	3B	HR	RBI	BB	SO	AVG	OBP	SLG	PRO+	BR/A	SB	CS	SBR	FA	FR	G/POS	TPR
1998	Phi-N	17	43	4	14	3	0	1	4	1	6	.326	.341	.465	105	0	2	0	1	.978	1	/2-9	0.3

■ MIKE ANDERSON Anderson, Michael Allen b: 6/22/51, Florence, S.C. BR/TR, 6'2", 200 lbs. Deb: 9/2/71 F

YEAR	TM/L	G	AB	R	H	2B	3B	HR	RBI	BB	SO	AVG	OBP	SLG	PRO+	BR/A	SB	CS	SBR	FA	FR	G/POS	TPR
1971	Phi-N	26	89	11	22	5	1	2	5	13	28	.247	.343	.393	108	1	0	0	0	.986	2	O-26	0.2
1972	Phi-N	36	103	8	20	5	1	2	5	19	36	.194	.320	.320	80	-2	1	0	0	.987	4	O-35	0.0
1973	Phi-N	87	193	32	49	9	1	9	28	19	53	.254	.324	.451	110	2	0	3	-2	.981	-6	O-67	-0.8
1974	Phi-N	145	395	35	99	22	2	5	34	37	75	.251	.315	.354	83	-9	2	1	0	.980	4	*O-133/1-1	-1.0
1975	Phi-N	115	247	24	64	10	3	4	28	17	66	.259	.312	.372	86	-5	1	2	-1	.977	-10	*O-105/1-3	-1.9
1976	StL-N	86	199	17	58	8	1	1	12	26	30	.291	.376	.357	108	3	1	1	-0	.982	0	O-58/1-5	0.1
1977	StL-N	94	154	18	34	4	1	4	17	14	31	.221	.286	.338	68	-7	2	3	-1	.980	-10	O-77	-2.0
1978	Bal-A	53	32	2	3	0	1	0	3	3	10	.094	.171	.156	-8	-5	0	0	0	.962	-15	O-47	-2.1
1979	Phi-N	79	78	12	18	4	0	1	2	13	14	.231	.341	.321	79	-2	1	2	-1	.973	-13	O-70/P-1	-1.8
Total	9	721	1490	159	367	67	11	28	134	161	343	.246	.321	.362	88	-24	8	12	-5	.980	-44	O-618/1-9,P-1	-9.3

■ ERNIE ANDRES Andres, Ernest Henry "Junie" b: 1/11/18, Jeffersonville, Ind. BR/TR, 6'1", 200 lbs. Deb: 4/16/46

YEAR	TM/L	G	AB	R	H	2B	3B	HR	RBI	BB	SO	AVG	OBP	SLG	PRO+	BR/A	SB	CS	SBR	FA	FR	G/POS	TPR
1946	Bos-A	15	41	0	4	2	0	0	1	3	5	.098	.159	.146	-14	-6	0	0	0	1.000	1	3-15	-0.5

■ KIM ANDREW Andrew, Kim Darrell b: 11/14/53, Glendale, Cal. BR/TR, 5'10", 160 lbs. Deb: 4/16/75

YEAR	TM/L	G	AB	R	H	2B	3B	HR	RBI	BB	SO	AVG	OBP	SLG	PRO+	BR/A	SB	CS	SBR	FA	FR	G/POS	TPR
1975	Bos-A	2	2	0	1	0	0	0	0	0	0	.500	.500	.500	169	0	0	0	0	1.000	-0	/2-2	0.0

■ SHANE ANDREWS Andrews, Darrell Shane b: 8/28/71, Dallas, Tex. BR/TR, 6'1", 215 lbs. Deb: 4/26/95

YEAR	TM/L	G	AB	R	H	2B	3B	HR	RBI	BB	SO	AVG	OBP	SLG	PRO+	BR/A	SB	CS	SBR	FA	FR	G/POS	TPR
1995	Mon-N	84	220	27	47	10	1	8	31	17	68	.214	.273	.377	67	-11	1	1	-0	.973	2	3-51,1-29	-1.1
1996	Mon-N	127	375	43	85	15	2	19	64	35	119	.227	.296	.429	86	-9	3	1	0	.955	21	*3-123	1.2
1997	Mon-N	18	64	10	13	3	0	4	9	3	20	.203	.239	.438	73	-3	0	0	0	.895	3	3-18	0.0
1998	Mon-N	150	492	48	117	30	1	25	69	58	137	.238	.318	.455	101	-0	1	6	-3	.954	20	*3-147	1.8
Total	4	379	1151	128	262	58	4	56	173	113	344	.228	.298	.431	88	-23	5	8	-3	.953	45	3-339/1-29	1.9

■ FRED ANDREWS Andrews, Fred b: 5/4/52, Lafayette, La. BR/TR, 5'8", 163 lbs. Deb: 9/26/76

YEAR	TM/L	G	AB	R	H	2B	3B	HR	RBI	BB	SO	AVG	OBP	SLG	PRO+	BR/A	SB	CS	SBR	FA	FR	G/POS	TPR
1976	Phi-N	4	6	1	4	0	0	0	0	2	0	.667	.778	.667	304	2	1	1	-0	1.000	-1	/2-4	0.2
1977	Phi-N	12	23	3	4	0	1	0	2	1	5	.174	.208	.261	24	-2	1	0	0	1.000	3	/2-7	0.1
Total	2	16	29	4	8	0	1	0	2	3	5	.276	.364	.345	90	-0	2	1	0	1.000	2	/2-11	0.3

■ ED ANDREWS Andrews, George Edward b: 4/5/1859, Painesville, Ohio d: 8/12/34, W.Palm Beach, Fla. BR/TR, 5'8", 160 lbs. Deb: 5/1/1884 U

YEAR	TM/L	G	AB	R	H	2B	3B	HR	RBI	BB	SO	AVG	OBP	SLG	PRO+	BR/A	SB	CS	SBR	FA	FR	G/POS	TPR
1884	Phi-N	109	420	74	93	21	2	0	23	9	42	.221	.238	.281	66	-16				.891	-22	*2-109	-3.2
1885	Phi-N	103	421	77	112	15	3	0	23	32	25	.266	.318	.316	108	4				.921	-0	*O-99/2-5	0.2
1886	Phi-N	107	437	93	109	15	4	2	28	31	35	.249	.299	.316	86	-7	**56**			.903	4	*O-104/2-3	-0.5
1887	Phi-N	104	464	110	151	19	7	4	67	21	21	.325	.359	.422	110	5	57			.902	-4	*O-99/2-7,1-1	-0.1
1888	Phi-N	124	528	75	126	14	4	3	44	21	41	.239	.272	.297	77	-14	35			.903	-4	*O-124	-2.2
1889	Phi-N	10	39	10	11	1	0	0	7	2	4	.282	.317	.308	69	-2	7			.808	-1	/O-9,2-1	-0.2
	Ind-N	40	173	32	53	11	0	0	22	5	10	.306	.330	.370	94	-2	7			.885	-3	O-40/2-1	-0.5
	Yr	50	212	42	64	12	0	0	29	7	14	.302	.327	.358	89	-4	14			.867	-4	O-49/2-2	-0.7
1890	Bro-P	94	395	84	100	14	2	3	38	40	32	.253	.323	.322	68	-19	21			.912	1	*O-94	-1.7
1891	Cin-a	83	356	47	75	7	4	0	26	33	35	.211	.279	.253	48	-26	22			.961	17	O-83	-1.0
Total	8	774	3233	602	830	117	26	12	278	194	245	.257	.301	.320	82	-76	205			.912	-13	O-652,2-126/1-1	-9.2

■ JIM ANDREWS Andrews, James Pratt b: 6/5/1865, Shelburne Falls, Mass. d: 12/27/07, Chicago, Ill. Deb: 4/19/1890

YEAR	TM/L	G	AB	R	H	2B	3B	HR	RBI	BB	SO	AVG	OBP	SLG	PRO+	BR/A	SB	CS	SBR	FA	FR	G/POS	TPR
1890	Chi-N	53	202	32	38	4	2	3	17	23	41	.188	.278	.272	58	-11	11			.900	1	O-53	-1.1

YEAR	TM/L	G	AB	R	H	2B	3B	HR	RBI	BB	SO	AVG	OBP	SLG	PRO+	BR/A	SB	CS	SBR	FA	FR	G/POS	TPR
■ MIKE ANDREWS	Andrews, Michael Jay b: 7/9/43, Los Angeles, Cal. BR/TR, 6'3", 195 lbs. Deb: 9/18/66 F																						
1966	Bos-A	5	18	1	3	0	0	0	0	0	2	.167	.167	.167	-4	-2	0	0	0	1.000	2	/2-5	0.0
1967	*Bos-A	142	494	79	130	20	0	8	40	62	72	.263	.348	.352	99	1	7	7	-2	.976	-6	*2-139/S-6	0.2
1968	Bos-A	147	536	77	145	22	1	7	45	81	57	.271	.369	.354	113	11	3	8	-4	.976	1	*2-139/S-4,3-1	2.0
1969	Bos-A★	121	464	79	136	26	2	15	59	71	53	.293	.393	.455	129	20	1	1	-0	.972	5	*2-120	3.6
1970	Bos-A	151	589	91	149	28	1	17	65	81	63	.253	.346	.390	96	-2	2	1	0	.973	-30	*2-148	-2.0
1971	Chi-A	109	330	45	93	16	0	12	47	67	36	.282	.405	.439	135	18	3	5	-2	.956	-3	2-76,1-25	1.8
1972	Chi-A	148	505	58	111	18	0	7	50	70	78	.220	.317	.297	82	-9	2	2	-1	.973	-14	*2-145/1-5	-1.9
1973	Chi-A	52	159	10	32	9	0	0	10	23	28	.201	.302	.258	57	-9	0	1	-1	1.000	-3	D-30/1-9,2-6,3-5	-1.4
	*Oak-A	18	21	1	4	1	0	0	0	3	1	.190	.292	.238	53	-1	0	0	0	.944	-1	/2-9,D-2	-0.2
	Yr	70	180	11	36	10	0	0	10	26	29	.200	.301	.256	57	-10	0	1	-1	.974	-4	D-32,2-15/1-9,3-5	-1.6
Total	8	893	3116	441	803	140	4	66	316	458	390	.258	.356	.369	104	26	18	25	-10	.973	-49	2-787/1-39,D-32,S3	2.1
■ ROB ANDREWS	Andrews, Robert Patrick b: 12/11/52, Santa Monica, Cal. BR/TR, 6', 185 lbs. Deb: 4/7/75 F																						
1975	Hou-N	103	277	29	66	5	4	0	19	31	34	.238	.315	.285	73	-10	12	5	1	.982	7	2-94/S-6	0.2
1976	Hou-N	109	410	42	105	8	5	0	23	33	27	.256	.312	.300	81	-11	7	3	0	.977	8	*2-107/S-3	0.5
1977	SF-N	127	436	60	115	11	3	0	25	56	33	.264	.348	.303	76	-12	5	6	-2	.964	-12	*2-115	-1.9
1978	SF-N	79	177	21	39	3	3	1	11	20	18	.220	.299	.288	67	-8	5	1	1	.977	9	2-62/S-1	0.6
1979	SF-N	75	154	22	40	3	0	2	13	8	9	.260	.296	.318	73	-6	4	1	1	.956	4	2-53/3-3	0.1
Total	5	493	1454	174	365	30	15	3	91	148	121	.251	.320	.298	76	-47	33	16	0	.972	15	2-431/S-10,3-3	-0.5
■ STAN ANDREWS	Andrews, Stanley Joseph "Polo" (b: Stanley Joseph Andruskewicz) b: 4/17/17, Lynn, Mass. d: 6/10/95, Bradenton, Fla. BR/TR, 5'11", 178 lbs. Deb: 6/11/39																						
1939	Bos-N	13	26	1	6	0	0	0	1	1	2	.231	.259	.231	35	-2	0			.857	-2	C-10	-0.4
1940	Bos-N	19	33	1	6	0	0	0	2	0	3	.182	.182	.182	1	-4	1			.944	-1	C-14	-0.5
1944	Bro-N	4	8	1	1	0	0	0	1	1	2	.125	.222	.125	-1	-1	0			1.000	-0	/C-4	-0.1
1945	Bro-N	21	49	5	8	0	1	0	2	5	4	.163	.255	.204	29	-5	0			.948	2	C-21	-0.2
	Phi-N	13	33	3	11	2	0	1	6	1	5	.333	.353	.485	135	1	1			.950	-1	C-12	0.1
	Yr	34	82	8	19	2	1	1	8	6	9	.232	.292	.317	70	-3	1			.949	1	C-33	-0.1
Total	4	70	149	11	32	2	1	1	12	8	16	.215	.259	.262	46	-11	2			.938	-1	/C-61	-1.1
■ WALLY ANDREWS	Andrews, William Walter b: 9/18/1859, Philadelphia, Pa. d: 1/20/40, Indianapolis, Ind. BR/TR, 6'3", 170 lbs. Deb: 5/22/1884																						
1884	Lou-a	14	49	10	10	5	1	0	8	4		.204	.264	.347	102	0				.950	-1	/1-9,3-3,O-1,S-1	-0.1
1888	Lou-a	26	93	12	18	6	3	0	6	13		.194	.292	.323	99	0	5			.997	2	1-26	-0.1
Total	2	40	142	22	28	11	4	0	14	17		.197	.283	.331	100	0	5			.985	1	/1-35,3-3,S-1,O-1	-0.2
■ FRED ANDRUS	Andrus, Frederick Hotham b: 8/23/1850, Washington, Mich. d: 11/10/37, Detroit, Mich. BR/TR, 6'2", 185 lbs. Deb: 7/25/1876																						
1876	Chi-N	8	36	6	11	3	0	0	2	0	5	.306	.306	.389	116	0				.714	-3	/O-8	-0.3
1884	Chi-N	1	5	3	1	0	0	0	0	1	0	.200	.333	.200	67	-0				1.000	0	/P-1	0.0
Total	2	9	41	9	12	3	0	0	2	1	5	.293	.310	.366	110	0				.714	-3	/O-8,P-1	-0.3
■ BILL ANDRUS	Andrus, William Morgan "Andy" b: 7/25/07, Beaumont, Tex. d: 3/12/82, Washington, D.C. BR/TR, 6', 185 lbs. Deb: 9/19/31																						
1931	Was-A	3	7	0	0	0	0	0	1	0	1	.000	.000	.000	-99	-2	0	0	0	.750	-0	/3-2	-0.2
1937	Phi-N	3	2	0	0	0	0	0	0	0	2	.000	.000	.000	-93	-1	0			.000	0	/3-1	-0.1
Total	2	6	9	0	0	0	0	0	1	0	3	.000	.000	.000	-98	-3	0	0		.750	-0	/3-3	-0.3
■ WIMAN ANDRUS	Andrus, William Wiman b: 10/14/1858, Orono, Ontario, Can d: 6/17/35, Miles City, Mont. 5'6.5", 155 lbs. Deb: 9/15/1885																						
1885	Pro-N	1	4	0	0	0	0	0	0	0	1	.000	.000	.000	-99	-1				1.000	1	/3-1	0.0
■ TOM ANGLEY	Angley, Thomas Samuel b: 10/2/04, Baltimore, Md. d: 10/26/52, Wichita, Kan. BL/TR, 5'8", 190 lbs. Deb: 4/23/29																						
1929	Chi-N	5	16	1	4	1	0	0	6	2	2	.250	.333	.313	61	-1	0			.968	1	/C-5	0.1
■ PAT ANKENMAN	Ankenman, Frederick Norman b: 12/23/12, Houston, Tex. d: 1/13/89, Houston, Tex. BR/TR, 5'4", 125 lbs. Deb: 4/16/36																						
1936	StL-N	1	3	0	0	0	0	0	0	0	3	.000	.000	.000	-99	-1	0			.600	-1	/S-1	-0.2
1943	Bro-N	1	2	1	1	0	0	0	0	0	0	.500	.500	.500	189	0	0			1.000	1	/S-1	0.1
1944	Bro-N	13	24	1	6	1	0	0	3	0	2	.250	.250	.292	53	-2	0			.971	0	2-11/S-2	-0.1
Total	3	15	29	2	7	1	0	0	3	0	5	.241	.241	.276	46	-2	0			.800	-1	/2-11,S-4	-0.2
■ BILL ANNIS	Annis, William Perley b: 3/8/1857, Stoneham, Mass. d: 6/10/23, Kennebunkport, Me BR, 5'7", 150 lbs. Deb: 5/1/1884																						
1884	Bos-N	27	96	17	17	2	0	0	3	0	8	.177	.177	.198	18	-9				.897	-3	O-27	-1.2
■ CAP ANSON	Anson, Adrian Constantine b: 4/11/1852, Marshalltown, Iowa d: 4/14/22, Chicago, Ill. BR/TR, 6', 227 lbs. Deb: 5/6/1871 MH																						
1871	Rok-n	25	120	29	39	**11**	3	0	16	2	1	.325	.336	.467	134	6	6	2	1	.763	2	*3-20/C-5,2-2,1O	0.4
1872	Ath-n	46	217	60	90	10	7	0	50	16	3	.415	**.455**	.525	200	26	6	6	-2	.752	-10	*3-46	0.8
1873	Ath-n	52	254	53	101	9	2	0	36	5	1	.398	.409	.449	144	12	0	2	-1	.923	-4	*1-36,3-11/C-3,2O	0.5
1874	Ath-n	55	260	51	87	8	3	0	37	4	1	.335	.345	.388	124	5	6	0	2	.936	-6	1-24,3-20/O-8,SC	0.1
1875	Ath-n	69	326	84	106	15	3	0	58	4	2	.325	.333	.390	135	8	11	6	-0	.922	12	1-32,O-25,C-13,/3M	1.7
1876	Chi-N	66	309	63	110	9	7	2	59	12	8	.356	.380	.450	157	16				.849	13	*3-66/C-2	2.6
1877	Chi-N	59	255	52	86	**19**	1	0	32	9	3	.337	.360	.420	129	7				**.883**	8	*3-40,C-31	1.5
1878	Chi-N	60	261	55	89	12	2	0	40	13	1	.341	.372	.402	145	12				.825	-8	*O-48/2-9,3-3,C-3	0.2
1879	Chi-N	51	227	40	72	20	1	0	34	2	2	**.317**	.323	.414	133	7				.975	0	1-51/M	0.5
1880	Chi-N	86	356	54	120	24	1	1	**74**	14	12	.337	.362	.419	154	19				**.978**	0	*1-81/3-9,S-1,2M	1.2
1881	Chi-N	84	343	67	**137**	21	7	1	**82**	26	4	**.399**	**.442**	.510	**189**	**35**				**.975**	7	*1-84/C-2,S-1,M	3.1
1882	Chi-N	82	348	69	126	29	8	1	**83**	20	7	.362	.397	.500	177	29				.949	-1	*1-82/C-1,M	1.7
1883	Chi-N	98	413	70	127	36	5	0	68	18	9	.308	.336	.419	121	9				.964	3	*1-98/P-2,O-1,CM	0.2
1884	Chi-N	112	475	108	159	30	3	21	**102**	29	13	.335	.373	.543	170	35				.956	-0	*1-112/C-3,S-1,PM	2.0
1885	*Chi-N	112	464	100	144	**35**	7	7	**108**	34	13	.310	.357	.461	143	19				.958	-4	*1-112/C-1,M	0.1
1886	*Chi-N	125	504	117	187	35	11	10	**147**	55	19	.371	.433	.544	171	39	29			.963	8	*1-125,C-12,M	3.1
1887	Chi-N	122	472	107	164	33	13	7	102	60	18	**.347**	.422	.517	141	24	27			.973	10	*1-122/C-1,M	1.8
1888	Chi-N	134	515	101	177	20	12	12	**84**	47	24	**.344**	**.400**	.499	173	41	28			**.986**	9	*1-134,M	3.6
1889	Chi-N	134	518	100	161	32	7	7	117	86	19	.311	.414	.440	132	24	27			**.982**	9	*1-134,M	2.1
1890	Chi-N	139	504	95	157	14	5	7	107	**113**	23	.312	**.443**	.401	141	33	29			.978	0	*1-135/C-3,2-2,M	2.3
1891	Chi-N	136	540	81	157	24	8	8	**120**	75	29	.291	.378	.409	129	21	17			.981	8	*1-136/C-2,M	2.0
1892	Chi-N	146	559	62	152	25	9	1	74	67	30	.272	.354	.354	113	10	13			.973	-5	*1-146/M	-0.2
1893	Chi-N	103	398	70	125	24	2	0	91	68	12	.314	.415	.384	115	12	13			.981	-4	*1-101/M	0.4
1894	Chi-N	83	340	82	132	28	4	5	99	40	15	.388	.457	.538	132	18	17			.990	3	1-82/2-1,M	1.6
1895	Chi-N	122	474	87	159	23	6	2	91	55	23	.335	.408	.422	107	6	12			.985	-1	*1-122/M	0.6
1896	Chi-N	108	402	72	133	18	2	2	90	49	10	.331	.407	.400	109	7	24			.983	-1	*1-98,C-10,M	0.7
1897	Chi-N	114	424	67	121	17	3	3	75	60	11	.285	.379	.361	92	-3	11			.975	1	*1-103,C-11,M	-0.1
Total	5 n	247	1177	277	423	53	18	0	197	31	8	.359	.376	.435	146	56	29	16	-1	.765	-6	3-102/1-93,OCS2	3.5
Total	22	2276	9101	1719	2995	528	124	97	1879	952	294	.329	.395	.446	138	418	247			.974	57	*1-2058,3-118/CO2PS	31.0
■ ERIC ANTHONY	Anthony, Eric Todd b: 11/8/67, San Diego, Cal. BL/TL, 6'2", 195 lbs. Deb: 7/29/89																						
1989	Hou-N	25	61	7	11	2	0	4	7	9	16	.180	.286	.410	100	-0	0	0	0	1.000	-1	O-21	-0.1
1990	Hou-N	84	239	26	46	8	0	10	29	29	78	.192	.285	.351	76	-8	5	0	2	.970	-2	O-71	-1.1
1991	Hou-N	39	118	11	18	6	0	1	7	12	41	.153	.231	.229	31	-11	1	0	0	.986	3	O-37	-0.9
1992	Hou-N	137	440	45	105	15	1	19	80	38	98	.239	.301	.407	103	0	5	4	-1	.973	-6	*O-115	-1.0
1993	Hou-N	145	486	70	121	19	4	15	66	49	88	.249	.320	.397	94	-5	3	5	-2	.988	-7	*O-131	-1.7
1994	Sea-A	79	262	31	62	14	1	10	30	23	66	.237	.298	.412	79	-9	6	2	1	.985	-2	O-71/D-4	-1.1
1995	*Cin-N	47	134	19	36	6	0	5	23	13	30	.269	.333	.425	99	-0	2	1	0	1.000	-1	O-24,1-17	-0.3
1996	Cin-N	47	123	22	30	6	0	8	13	22	36	.244	.359	.488	120	4	0	1	-1	.949	-5	O-37	-0.3
	Col-N	32	62	10	15	2	0	4	9	10	20	.242	.347	.468	91	-1	0	1	-1	1.000	-3	O-19	-0.5

YEAR	TM/L	G	AB	R	H	2B	3B	HR	RBI	BB	SO	AVG	OBP	SLG	PRO+	BR/A	SB	CS	SBR	FA	FR	G/POS	TPR
	Yr	79	185	32	45	8	0	12	22	32	56	.243	.355	.481	107	2	0	2	-1	.967	-8	O-56	-0.8
1997	LA-N	47	74	8	18	3	2	2	5	12	18	.243	.349	.419	108	1	2	0	1	.966	-1	O-21	0.1
Total	9	682	1999	249	462	81	8	78	269	217	491	.231	.308	.397	91	-30	24	14	-1	.981	-25	O-547/1-17,D-4	-6.9
■ JOE ANTOLICK	Antolick, Joseph b: 4/11/16, Hokendauqua, Pa. BR/TR, 6', 185 lbs. Deb: 9/20/44																						
1944	Phi-N	4	6	1	2	0	0	0	0	1	0	.333	.429	.333	120	0	0			1.000	1	/C-3	0.1
■ JOHN ANTONELLI	Antonelli, John Lawrence b: 7/15/15, Memphis, Tenn. d: 4/18/90, Memphis, Tenn. BR/TR, 5'10.5", 165 lbs. Deb: 9/16/44																						
1944	StL-N	8	21	0	4	1	0	0	1	0	4	.190	.190	.238	20	-2	0			1.000	1	/1-3,3-3,2-2	-0.1
1945	StL-N	2	3	0	0	0	0	0	0	0	1	.000	.000	.000	-98	-1	0			.667	-0	/3-1	-0.1
	Phi-N	125	504	50	129	27	2	1	28	24	24	.256	.292	.323	73	-19	1			.959	-9	*3-108,2-23/1-1,S-1	-2.5
	Yr	127	507	50	129	27	2	1	28	24	25	.254	.291	.321	72	-20	1			.957	-9	*3-109,2-23/1-1,S-1	-2.6
Total	2	135	528	50	133	28	2	1	29	24	29	.252	.287	.318	70	-22	1			.958	-8	3-112/2-25,1-4,S-1	-2.7
■ BILL ANTONELLO	Antonello, William James b: 5/19/27, Brooklyn, N.Y. d: 3/4/93, Fridley, Minn. BR/TR, 5'11", 185 lbs. Deb: 4/30/53																						
1953	Bro-N	40	43	9	7	1	1	1	4	2	11	.163	.200	.302	28	-5	0	0	0	.964	-6	O-25	-1.0
■ LUIS APARICIO	Aparicio, Luis Ernesto (Montiel) b: 4/29/34, Maracaibo, Venez. BR/TR, 5'9", 160 lbs. Deb: 4/17/56 H																						
1956	Chi-A	152	533	69	142	19	6	3	56	34	63	.266	.312	.341	71	-23	**21**	4	**4**	.954	0	*S-152	-0.6
1957	Chi-A	143	575	82	148	22	6	3	41	52	55	.257	.319	.332	78	-17	**28**	8	4	.972	-13	*S-142	-1.4
1958	Chi-A★	145	557	76	148	20	9	2	40	35	38	.266	.310	.345	82	-14	**29**	6	**5**	.973	9	*S-145	1.3
1959	*Chi-A★	152	612	98	157	18	5	6	51	53	40	.257	.319	.332	80	-16	**56**	13	**9**	**.970**	-4	*S-152	0.2
1960	Chi-A★	153	600	86	166	20	7	2	61	43	39	.277	.326	.343	82	-15	**51**	8	**11**	**.979**	**30**	*S-153	3.8
1961	Chi-A★	156	625	90	170	24	4	6	45	38	33	.272	.315	.352	79	-19	**53**	13	**8**	**.962**	6	*S-156	0.8
1962	Chi-A★	153	581	72	140	23	5	7	40	32	36	.241	.282	.334	65	-29	**31**	12	2	**.973**	10	*S-152	-0.4
1963	Bal-A★	146	601	73	150	18	8	5	45	36	35	.250	.294	.331	78	-18	**40**	6	**8**	**.983**	-5	*S-145	-0.5
1964	Bal-A†	146	578	93	154	20	3	10	37	49	51	.266	.327	.363	92	-6	**57**	17	**7**	**.979**	3	*S-145	1.5
1965	Bal-A	144	564	67	127	20	10	8	40	46	56	.225	.287	.339	76	-18	26	7	4	**.971**	3	*S-141	-0.2
1966	*Bal-A	151	659	97	182	25	8	6	41	33	42	.276	.312	.366	95	-5	25	11	1	**.978**	10	*S-151	2.2
1967	Bal-A	134	546	55	127	22	5	4	31	29	44	.233	.273	.313	73	-19	18	5	2	.957	-20	*S-131	-2.6
1968	Chi-A	155	622	55	164	24	4	4	36	33	43	.264	.303	.334	92	-7	17	11	-2	.977	25	*S-154	3.7
1969	Chi-A	156	599	77	168	24	5	5	51	66	29	.280	.354	.362	96	-2	24	4	5	.976	29	*S-154	5.1
1970	Chi-A★	146	552	86	173	29	3	5	43	53	34	.313	.375	.404	110	9	8	3	1	.976	18	*S-146	4.6
1971	Bos-A★	125	491	56	114	23	0	4	45	35	43	.232	.286	.303	63	-24	6	4	-1	.971	-18	*S-121	-2.9
1972	Bos-A†	110	436	47	112	26	3	3	39	26	28	.257	.302	.351	89	-6	3	3	-1	.968	-17	*S-109	-1.0
1973	Bos-A	132	499	56	135	17	1	0	49	43	33	.271	.328	.309	76	-15	13	1	3	.966	-17	*S-132	-1.2
Total	18	2599	10230	1335	2677	394	92	83	791	736	742	.262	.313	.343	82	-245	506	136	70	.972	51	*S-2581	12.4
■ LUKE APPLING	Appling, Lucius Benjamin b: 4/2/07, High Point, N.C. d: 1/3/91, Cumming, Ga. BR/TR, 5'10", 183 lbs. Deb: 9/10/30 MCH																						
1930	Chi-A	6	26	2	8	2	0	0	2	0	0	.308	.308	.385	77	-1	2	0	1	.879	-1	/S-6	-0.1
1931	Chi-A	96	297	36	69	13	4	1	28	29	27	.232	.303	.313	66	-15	9	2	2	.900	-6	S-76/2-1	-1.1
1932	Chi-A	139	489	66	134	20	10	3	63	40	36	.274	.329	.374	87	-10	9	8	-2	.929	18	S-85,2-30,3-14	1.4
1933	Chi-A	151	612	90	197	36	10	6	85	56	29	.322	.379	.443	122	19	6	11	-5	.939	11	*S-151	3.4
1934	Chi-A	118	452	75	137	28	6	2	61	59	27	.303	.384	.405	100	2	3	1	0	.945	-9	*S-110/2-8	0.0
1935	Chi-A	153	525	94	161	28	6	1	71	122	40	.307	.437	.389	112	17	12	6	0	.958	**21**	*S-153	4.3
1936	Chi-A★	138	526	111	204	31	7	6	128	85	25	**.388**	.474	.508	137	36	10	6	-1	.951	15	*S-137	5.1
1937	Chi-A	154	574	98	182	42	8	4	77	86	28	.317	.407	.439	113	15	18	10	-1	.944	14	*S-154	3.5
1938	Chi-A	81	294	41	89	14	0	0	44	42	17	.303	.392	.350	85	-5	1	3	-2	.953	1	S-78	0.1
1939	Chi-A☆	148	516	82	162	16	6	0	56	105	37	.314	.430	.368	103	9	16	9	-1	.951	-2	*S-148	1.8
1940	Chi-A★	150	566	96	197	27	13	0	79	69	35	.348	.420	.442	122	22	3	5	-2	.953	-2	*S-150	2.9
1941	Chi-A☆	154	592	93	186	26	8	1	57	82	32	.314	.399	.390	111	13	12	8	-1	.948	0	*S-154	2.2
1942	Chi-A	142	543	78	142	26	4	3	53	63	23	.262	.342	.341	94	-3	17	5	2	.948	-7	*S-141	0.1
1943	Chi-A☆	155	585	63	192	33	2	3	80	90	29	**.328**	**.419**	.407	142	35	27	8	3	.957	7	*S-155	6.0
1945	Chi-A	18	57	12	21	2	2	1	10	12	7	.368	.478	.526	197	8	1	0	0	.930	-1	S-17	0.9
1946	Chi-A★	149	582	59	180	27	5	1	55	71	41	.309	.384	.378	118	16	6	4	-1	.951	7	*S-149	3.2
1947	Chi-A★	139	503	67	154	29	0	8	49	64	28	.306	.386	.412	126	19	8	6	-1	.949	-7	*S-129/3-2	1.8
1948	Chi-A	139	497	63	156	16	2	0	47	94	35	.314	.423	.354	112	14	10	4	1	.943	12	3-72,S-64	2.9
1949	Chi-A	142	492	82	148	21	5	5	58	121	24	.301	.439	.394	125	25	7	12	-5	.964	-1	*S-141	2.8
1950	Chi-A	50	128	11	30	3	4	0	13	12	8	.234	.300	.320	61	-8	2	0	1	.967	0	S-20,1-13/2-1	-0.5
Total	20	2422	8856	1319	2749	440	102	45	1116	1302	528	.310	.399	.398	113	207	179	108	-11	.948	73	*S-2218/3-88,2-40,1	40.7
■ ANGEL ARAGON	Aragon, Angel (Valdes) "Pete" b: 8/2/1890, Havana, Cuba d: 1/24/52, New York, N.Y. BR/TR, 5'5", 150 lbs. Deb: 8/20/14 F																						
1914	NY-A	6	7	1	1	0	0	0	0	1	2	.143	.333	.143	44	-0	0			.000	-1	/O-1	-0.1
1916	NY-A	12	24	1	5	0	0	0	3	2	2	.208	.269	.208	43	-2	2			.864	1	/3-8,O-2	0.0
1917	NY-A	14	45	2	3	1	0	0	2	2	2	.067	.106	.089	-40	-8	0			.933	1	/O-6,3-4,S-2	-0.8
Total	3	32	76	4	9	1	0	0	5	5	6	.118	.183	.132	-4	-10	2			.921	2	/3-12,O-9,S-2	-0.9
■ JACK ARAGON	Aragon, Angel Valdes (Reyes) b: 11/20/15, Havana, Cuba d: 4/4/88, Clearwater, Fla. BR/TR, 5'10", 176 lbs. Deb: 8/13/41 F																						
1941	NY-N	1	0	0	0	0	0	0	0	0	0	—	—	—	—	0	0			.000	0	R	0.0
■ MAURICE ARCHDEACON	Archdeacon, Maurice John "Flash" b: 12/14/1897, St.Louis, Mo. d: 9/5/54, St.Louis, Mo. BL/TL, 5'8", 153 lbs. Deb: 9/17/23																						
1923	Chi-A	22	87	23	35	5	1	0	4	6	8	.402	.441	.483	145	6	2	3	-1	.918	-2	O-20	0.1
1924	Chi-A	95	288	59	92	9	3	0	25	40	30	.319	.410	.372	106	5	11	7	-1	.958	-5	O-77	-0.5
1925	Chi-A	10	9	2	1	0	0	0	0	2	1	.111	.273	.111	0	-1	0	0	0	1.000	-0	/O-1	-0.1
Total	3	127	384	84	128	14	4	0	29	48	39	.333	.413	.391	112	9	13	10	-2	.950	-7	/O-98	-0.5
■ JIMMY ARCHER	Archer, James Patrick b: 5/13/1883, Dublin, Ireland d: 3/29/58, Milwaukee, Wis. BR/TR, 5'10", 168 lbs. Deb: 9/6/04																						
1904	Pit-N	7	20	1	3	0	0	0	1	0		.150	.150	.150	-7	-2	0			.919	0	/C-7,O-1	-0.2
1907	*Det-A	18	42	6	5	0	0	0	0	4		.119	.196	.119	1	-5	0			.975	2	C-17/2-1	-0.1
1909	Chi-N	80	261	31	60	9	2	1	30	12		.230	.266	.291	71	-10	5			.960	-4	C-80	-0.7
1910	*Chi-N	98	313	36	81	17	6	2	41	14	49	.259	.293	.371	94	-4	6			.970	3	C-49,1-40	0.4
1911	Chi-N	116	387	41	98	18	5	4	41	18	43	.253	.288	.357	80	-12	5			.977	-1	*C-102,1-10/2-1	-0.3
1912	Chi-N	120	385	35	109	20	2	5	58	22	36	.283	.330	.384	95	-3	7			.966	-5	*C-118	0.3
1913	Chi-N	111	368	38	98	14	7	2	44	19	27	.266	.311	.359	91	-5	4			.969	-3	*C-103/1-8	0.1
1914	Chi-N	79	248	17	64	9	2	0	19	9	9	.258	.284	.310	77	-8	1			.973	5	C-76	0.4
1915	Chi-N	97	309	21	75	11	5	1	27	11	38	.243	.273	.320	79	-9	5	6	-2	.977	-2	C-88/1-4	-0.6
1916	Chi-N	77	205	11	45	6	2	1	30	12	24	.220	.269	.283	63	-9	3			.979	-3	C-61/3-1	-0.9
1917	Chi-N	2	2	0	0	0	0	0	0	0	1	.000	.000	.000	-93	-0	0			.000	0	H	-0.1
1918	Pit-N	24	58	4	9	1	2	0	3	1	6	.155	.197	.241	32	-5	0			.989	5	C-21/1-1	0.1
	Bro-N	9	22	3	6	0	1	0	0	1	5	.273	.304	.364	104	0	0			.968	1	/C-7	0.1
	Cin-N	9	26	2	7	1	0	0	2	1	3	.269	.296	.308	86	-0	0			1.000	1	/C-7,1-1	0.1
	Yr	42	106	9	22	2	3	0	5	3	14	.208	.243	.283	59	-5	0			.987	7	C-35/1-2	0.3
Total	12	847	2646	246	660	106	34	16	296	124	241	.249	.288	.333	80	-73	36	6		.971	-0	C-736/1-64,2-2,3O	-1.4
■ GEORGE ARCHIE	Archie, George Albert b: 4/27/14, Nashville, Tenn. BR/TR, 6', 170 lbs. Deb: 9/14/38																						
1938	Det-A	3	2	1	0	0	0	0	0	0	1	.000	.000	.000	-95	-1	0	0	0	.000	0	H	-0.1
1941	Was-A	105	379	45	102	20	4	3	48	30	42	.269	.324	.367	87	-8	8	4	0	.936	-4	3-73,1-23	-1.2
	StL-A	9	29	3	11	3	0	0	5	7	3	.379	.500	.483	156	3	2	0	1	.975	0	/1-8	0.3
	Yr	114	408	48	113	23	4	3	53	37	45	.277	.339	.375	92	-5	10	4	1	.936	-4	3-73,1-31	-0.9
1946	StL-A	4	11	1	2	1	0	0	0	0	1	.182	.182	.273	25	-1	0	0	0	1.000	2	/1-3	0.1
Total	3	121	421	50	115	24	4	3	53	37	47	.273	.333	.371	90	-7	10	4	1	.988	-2	/3-73,1-34	-0.9

YEAR	TM/L	G	AB	R	H	2B	3B	HR	RBI	BB	SO	AVG	OBP	SLG	PRO+	BR/A	SB	CS	SBR	FA	FR	G/POS	TPR

■ JOSE ARCIA Arcia, Jose Raimundo (Orta) b: 8/22/43, Havana, Cuba BR/TR, 6'3", 170 lbs. Deb: 4/10/68

1968	Chi-N	59	84	15	16	4	1	0	8	3	24	.190	.218	.274	44	-6	0	0	0	1.000	-2	O-17,2-10/S-7,3-1	-0.9
1969	SD-N	120	302	35	65	11	3	0	10	14	47	.215	.255	.272	49	-21	14	7	0	.977	5	2-68,S-37/3-8,O1	-1.0
1970	SD-N	114	229	28	51	9	3	0	17	12	36	.223	.282	.288	55	-15	3	6	-3	.955	10	S-67,2-20/3-9,O-7	-0.1
Total	3	293	615	78	132	24	6	1	35	29	107	.215	.260	.278	51	-41	17	13	-3	.950	13	S-111/2-98,O-28,31	-2.0

■ DAN ARDELL Ardell, Daniel Miers b: 5/27/41, Seattle, Wash. BL/TL, 6'2", 190 lbs. Deb: 9/14/61

| 1961 | LA-A | 7 | 4 | 1 | 1 | 0 | 0 | 0 | 1 | 2 | .250 | .400 | .250 | 70 | -0 | 0 | 0 | 0 | 1.000 | -0 | /1-1 | 0.0 |

■ JOE ARDNER Ardner, Joseph A. "Old Hoss" b: 2/27/1858, Mt.Vernon, Ohio d: 9/15/35, Cleveland, Ohio BR/TR, 160 lbs. Deb: 5/1/1884

1884	Cle-N	26	92	6	16	1	1	0	4	1	24	.174	.183	.207	21	-8				.866	-5	2-25/3-1	-1.1
1890	Cle-N	84	323	28	72	13	1	0	35	17	40	.223	.266	.269	57	-18	9			.920	-6	2-84	-1.7
Total	2	110	415	34	88	14	2	0	39	18	64	.212	.248	.255	50	-26	9			.908	-11	2-109/3-1	-2.8

■ HANK ARFT Arft, Henry Irven "Bow Wow" b: 1/28/22, Manchester, Mo. BL/TL, 5'10.5", 190 lbs. Deb: 7/27/48

1948	StL-A	69	248	25	59	10	3	5	38	45	43	.238	.355	.363	89	-3	1	2	-1	.995	-1	1-69	-0.5
1949	StL-A	6	5	1	1	1	0	0	2	0	1	.200	.200	.400	55	-0	0	0	0	.000	0	H	-0.0
1950	StL-A	98	280	45	75	16	4	1	32	46	48	.268	.375	.364	87	-5	3	2	-0	.995	-5	1-84	-0.5
1951	StL-A	112	345	44	90	16	5	7	42	41	34	.261	.339	.397	96	-2	4	6	-2	.989	8	1-97	-0.1
1952	StL-A	15	28	1	4	3	1	0	4	5	7	.143	.273	.321	63	-1	0	0	0	.985	-0	1-10	-0.2
Total	5	300	906	116	229	46	13	13	118	137	133	.253	.352	.375	90	-12	8	10	-4	.992	8	1-260	-1.3

■ ALEX ARIAS Arias, Alejandro b: 11/20/67, New York, N.Y. BR/TR, 6'3", 185 lbs. Deb: 5/12/92

1992	Chi-N	32	99	14	29	7	1	0	7	11	13	.293	.375	.354	105	1	0	0	0	.967	-4	S-30	-0.1
1993	Fla-N	96	249	27	67	5	1	2	20	27	18	.269	.348	.321	76	-7	1	1	-0	.987	-9	2-30,3-22,S-18	-1.4
1994	Fla-N	59	113	4	27	0	0	0	15	9	19	.239	.301	.283	52	-8	0	1	-1	.985	-5	S-20,3-15	-1.2
1995	Fla-N	94	216	22	58	9	2	3	26	22	20	.269	.342	.370	87	-4	1	0	0	.947	-5	S-36,3-21/2-6	-0.5
1996	Fla-N	100	224	27	62	11	2	3	26	17	28	.277	.336	.384	92	-2	2	0	1	.956	1	3-59,S-20/1-1,2-1	0.0
1997	*Fla-N	74	93	13	23	2	0	1	11	12	12	.247	.352	.301	76	-3	0	1	-1	.971	1	3-37,S-11	-0.2
1998	Phi-N	56	133	17	39	8	1	0	16	13	18	.293	.361	.376	90	-2	2	0	1	.985	-5	S-38/3-5,2-1	-0.2
Total	7	511	1127	124	305	46	5	10	121	111	128	.271	.344	.347	83	-24	6	3	0	.967	-26	S-173,3-159/2-38,1	-3.6

■ GEORGE ARIAS Arias, George Alberto b: 3/12/72, Tucson, Ariz. BR/TR, 5'11", 190 lbs. Deb: 4/2/96

1996	Cal-A	84	252	19	60	8	1	6	28	16	50	.238	.284	.349	59	-16	2	0	1	.960	28	3-83/D-1	1.1
1997	Ana-A	3	6	1	2	0	0	0	1	0	1	.333	.333	.333	75	-0	0	0	0	1.000	1	/3-1,D-1	-0.0
	SD-N	11	22	2	5	1	0	0	2	0	1	.227	.227	.273	33	-2	0	0	0	.941	2	/3-8	-0.1
1998	*SD-N	20	36	4	7	1	0	1	4	3	16	.194	.293	.361	76	-1	0	0	0	.933	3	3-14/1-1	0.2
Total	3	118	316	26	74	10	2	7	35	19	67	.234	.282	.345	59	-20	2	0	1	.957	33	3-106/D-2,1-1	1.2

■ BUZZ ARLETT Arlett, Russell Loris b: 1/3/1899, Elmhurst, Cal. d: 5/16/64, Minneapolis, Minn. BB/TR, 6'2", 210 lbs. Deb: 4/14/31

| 1931 | Phi-N | 121 | 418 | 65 | 131 | 26 | 7 | 18 | 72 | 45 | 39 | .313 | .387 | .538 | 135 | 20 | 3 | | | .955 | 1 | O-94,1-13 | 1.4 |

■ TONY ARMAS Armas, Antonio Rafael (Machado) b: 7/2/53, Anzoategui, Venez. BR/TR, 6'1", 200 lbs. Deb: 9/6/76 F

1976	Pit-N	4	6	0	2	0	0	0	1	0	2	.333	.333	.333	89	-0	0	0	0	1.000	-0	/O-2	0.0
1977	Oak-A	118	363	26	87	8	2	13	53	20	99	.240	.279	.380	79	-12	1	2	-1	.981	9	*O-112/S-1	-0.7
1978	Oak-A	91	239	17	51	6	1	2	13	10	62	.213	.251	.272	50	-16	1	2	-1	.991	3	O-85/D-3	-1.8
1979	Oak-A	80	278	29	69	9	3	11	34	16	67	.248	.292	.421	95	-3	1	0	0	.976	7	O-80	0.1
1980	Oak-A	158	628	87	175	18	8	35	109	29	128	.279	.313	.500	128	19	5	3	-0	.975	18	*O-158	3.1
1981	*Oak-A★	109	440	51	115	24	3	**22**	76	19	115	.261	.295	.480	126	11	5	1	1	.993	12	*O-109	2.1
1982	Oak-A	138	536	58	125	19	2	28	89	33	128	.233	.279	.433	96	-5	2	2	-1	.983	12	*O-135/D-1	0.2
1983	Bos-A	145	574	77	125	23	2	36	107	29	131	.218	.258	.453	85	-14	0	1	-1	.985	7	*O-116,D-27	-1.3
1984	Bos-A☆	157	639	107	171	29	5	**43**	**123**	32	156	.268	.304	.531	120	14	1	3	-2	.974	2	*O-126,D-31	0.9
1985	Bos-A	103	385	50	102	17	5	23	64	18	90	.265	.301	.514	114	5	0	0	0	.983	-7	O-79,D-19	-0.5
1986	*Bos-A	121	425	40	112	21	4	11	58	24	77	.264	.306	.409	92	-5	0	3	-2	.969	-13	*O-117/D-1	-2.4
1987	Cal-A	28	81	8	16	3	1	3	9	1	11	.198	.207	.370	51	-6	1	0	0	1.000	-4	O-27	-1.0
1988	Cal-A	120	368	42	100	20	2	13	49	22	87	.272	.313	.443	112	5	1	3	-2	.986	-9	*O-113/D-5	-0.9
1989	Cal-A	60	202	22	52	7	1	11	30	7	48	.257	.282	.465	109	1	0	0	0	.990	2	O-47/1-2,D-6	0.2
Total	14	1432	5164	614	1302	204	39	251	815	260	1201	.252	.290	.453	103	-7	18	20	-7	.981	38	*O-1306/D-93,1-2,S	-2.0

■ MARCOS ARMAS Armas, Marcos Rafael (Ruiz) b: 8/5/69, Puerto Piritu, Venez. BR/TR, 6'5", 195 lbs. Deb: 5/25/93 F

| 1993 | Oak-A | 15 | 31 | 7 | 6 | 2 | 0 | 1 | 4 | 1 | 12 | .194 | .242 | .355 | 62 | -2 | 1 | 0 | 0 | 1.000 | 1 | 1-12/O-1,D-2 | -0.2 |

■ ED ARMBRISTER Armbrister, Edison Rosanda b: 7/4/48, Nassau, Bahamas BR/TR, 5'11", 160 lbs. Deb: 8/31/73

1973	*Cin-N	18	37	5	8	3	1	1	3	2	8	.216	.256	.432	92	-1	0	0	0	.917	-2	O-14	-0.3
1974	Cin-N	9	7	0	2	0	0	0	0	1	1	.286	.375	.286	88	-0	0	0	0	1.000	-1	/O-4	-0.2
1975	*Cin-N	59	65	9	12	1	0	0	2	5	19	.185	.254	.200	27	-6	3	1	0	.867	-7	O-19	-1.4
1976	*Cin-N	73	78	20	23	3	2	2	7	6	22	.295	.345	.462	124	2	7	3	0	.972	-4	O-32	-0.2
1977	Cin-N	65	78	12	20	4	3	1	5	10	21	.256	.341	.423	102	0	5	6	-2	.903	-3	O-27	-0.5
Total	5	224	265	46	65	11	6	4	19	24	71	.245	.310	.377	88	-5	15	10	-2	.925	-17	/O-96	-2.6

■ CHARLIE ARMBRUSTER Armbruster, Charles A. b: 8/30/1880, Cincinnati, Ohio d: 10/7/64, Grants Pass, Ore. BR/TR, 5'9", 180 lbs. Deb: 7/17/05

1905	Bos-A	35	91	13	18	4	0	0	6	18		.198	.336	.242	83	-1	3			.944	-6	C-35	-0.4
1906	Bos-A	72	201	9	29	6	1	0	6	25		.144	.242	.184	34	-15	2			.955	1	C-66/1-1	-0.8
1907	Bos-A	23	60	2	6	1	0	0	0	8		.100	.206	.117	3	-6	1			.935	2	C-21	-0.3
	Chi-A		3	0	0	0	0	0	0	1		.000	.250	.000	-20	-0	0			1.000	1	/C-1	0.0
	Yr	24	63	2	6	1	0	0	0	9		.095	.208	.111	2	-7	1			.940	3	C-22	-0.3
Total	3	131	355	24	53	11	1	0	12	52		.149	.262	.186	42	-22	6			.949	-2	C-123/1-1	-1.5

■ HARRY ARMBRUSTER Armbruster, Henry "Army" b: 3/20/1882, Cincinnati, Ohio d: 12/10/53, Cincinnati, Ohio BL/TL, 5'10", 190 lbs. Deb: 4/30/06

| 1906 | Phi-A | 91 | 265 | 40 | 63 | 6 | 3 | 2 | 24 | 43 | | .238 | .353 | .306 | 103 | 3 | 13 | | | .971 | 0 | O-74 | 0.0 |

■ GEORGE ARMSTRONG Armstrong, Noble George "Dodo" b: 6/3/24, Orange, N.J. d: 7/24/93, Orange, N.J. BR/TR, 5'10", 190 lbs. Deb: 4/26/46

| 1946 | Phi-A | 8 | 6 | 0 | 1 | 0 | 0 | 0 | 1 | 1 | | .167 | .286 | .333 | 73 | -0 | 0 | 0 | 0 | 1.000 | 1 | /C-4 | 0.0 |

■ BOB ARMSTRONG Armstrong, Robert b: 1850, Baltimore, Md. 6'2", 160 lbs. Deb: 6/26/1871

| 1871 | Kek-n | 12 | 49 | 9 | 11 | 2 | 1 | 0 | 5 | 0 | 1 | .224 | .224 | .306 | 50 | -3 | 0 | 1 | -1 | .816 | 2 | O-12 | -0.1 |

■ HARRY ARNDT Arndt, Harry J. b: 2/12/1879, South Bend, Ind. d: 3/25/21, South Bend, Ind. TR , Deb: 7/2/02

1902	Det-A	10	34	4	5	1	0	0	7	6		.147	.275	.206	34	-3	0			.958	0	O-10/1-1	-0.3
	Bal-A	68	248	41	63	7	4	2	28	35		.254	.355	.339	89	-3	9			.872	1	O-62/2-4,3-2,S-1	-0.6
	Yr	78	282	45	68	7	5	2	35	41		.241	.346	.323	83	-5	9			.885	1	O-72/2-4,3-2,1-1,S	-0.9
1905	StL-N	113	415	40	101	11	6	2	36	24		.243	.290	.313	82	-10	13			.951	-14	2-90/O-9,3-7,S-5	-2.4
1906	StL-N	69	256	30	69	7	2	2	26	19		.270	.320	.391	127	7	5			.965	12	3-65/1-1,O-1	2.2
1907	StL-N	11	32	3	6	1	0	0	2	1		.188	.212	.219	36	-2	0			1.000	0	/1-4,3-3	-0.2
Total	4	271	985	118	244	26	20	6	99	85		.248	.312	.333	91	-11	27			.952	0	/2-94,O-82,3-77,S1	-1.4

■ LARRY ARNDT Arndt, Larry Wayne b: 2/25/63, Fremont, Ohio BR/TR, 6'1", 195 lbs. Deb: 6/6/89

| 1989 | Oak-A | 2 | 6 | 1 | 1 | 0 | 0 | 0 | 0 | 0 | 1 | .167 | .167 | .167 | -6 | -1 | 0 | 0 | 0 | 1.000 | 0 | /1-1,3-1 | -0.1 |

■ CHRIS ARNOLD Arnold, Christopher Paul b: 11/6/47, Long Beach, Cal. BR/TR, 5'10", 160 lbs. Deb: 9/7/71

1971	SF-N	6	13	2	3	0	0	1	3	1	2	.231	.286	.462	110	0	0	0	0	.917	-1	/2-3	-0.1
1972	SF-N	51	84	8	19	2	0	1	8	12	12	.226	.293	.321	74	-3	0	1	-1	.970	3	3-17/2-7,S-4	0.0
1973	SF-N	49	54	7	16	2	0	1	13	8	11	.296	.387	.389	111	1	0	0	0	.944	-5	/C-9,2-1,3-1	-0.4

YEAR	TM/L	G	AB	R	H	2B	3B	HR	RBI	BB	SO	AVG	OBP	SLG	PRO+	BR/A	SB	CS	SBR	FA	FR	G/POS	TPR
1974	SF-N	78	174	22	42	7	3	1	26	15	27	.241	.305	.333	75	-6	1	1	-0	.974	-6	2-31/3-7,S-1	-1.1
1975	SF-N	29	41	4	8	0	0	0	0	4	8	.195	.267	.195	28	-4	0	0	0	.923	1	/2-4,O-4	-0.4
1976	SF-N	60	69	4	15	0	1	0	5	6	16	.217	.280	.246	49	-4	0	0	0	1.000	3	/2-8,3-4,1-1,S-1	-0.1
Total	6	273	435	47	103	12	5	4	51	42	76	.237	.305	.315	72	-16	1	2	-1	.971	-5	/2-54,3-29,C-9,SO1	-2.1
■ BILLY ARNOLD	Arnold, Willis S. b: 3/2/1851, Middletown, Conn. d: 1/17/1899, Albany, N.Y. Deb: 4/26/1872																						
1872	Man-n	2	7	2	1	0	0	0	0	0	0	.143	.143	.143	-13	-1	0	0	0	1.000	-0	/O-2	-0.1
■ MORRIE ARNOVICH	Arnovich, Morris "Snooker" b: 11/16/10, Superior, Wis. d: 7/20/59, Superior, Wis. BR/TR, 5'10", 168 lbs. Deb: 9/14/36																						
1936	Phi-N	13	48	4	15	3	0	1	7	1	3	.313	.353	.438	102	0	0			1.000	2	O-13	0.2
1937	Phi-N	117	410	60	119	27	4	10	60	34	32	.290	.349	.449	107	3	5			.972	7	*O-107	0.6
1938	Phi-N	139	502	47	138	29	0	4	72	42	37	.275	.333	.357	92	-5	2			.983	17	*O-133	0.8
1939	Phi-N☆	134	491	68	159	25	2	5	67	58	28	.324	.397	.413	122	17	7			.983	15	*O-132	2.7
1940	Phi-N	39	141	13	28	2	1	0	12	14	15	.199	.276	.227	42	-11	0			.959	3	O-37	-1.0
	*Cin-N	62	211	17	60	10	2	0	21	13	10	.284	.326	.351	86	-4	1			1.000	2	O-60	-0.5
	Yr	101	352	30	88	12	3	0	33	27	25	.250	.305	.301	68	-15	1			.983	5	O-97	-1.5
1941	NY-N	85	207	25	58	8	3	2	22	23	14	.280	.352	.377	103	1	2			.982	-4	O-61	-0.6
1946	NY-N	1	3	0	0	0	0	0	0	0	0	.000	.000	.000	-99	-1	0			1.000	-0	/O-1	-0.1
Total	7	590	2013	234	577	104	12	22	261	185	139	.287	.350	.383	100	0	17			.981	42	O-544	2.1
■ TUG ARUNDEL	Arundel, John Thomas b: 6/30/1862, Romulus, N.Y. d: 9/5/12, Auburn, N.Y. Deb: 5/23/1882																						
1882	Phi-a	1	5	0	0	0	0	0		0		.000	.000	.000	-90	-1				.800	-0	/C-1	-0.1
1884	Tol-a	15	47	6	4	0	0	0		3		.085	.140	.085	-24	-6				.946	8	C-15	0.3
1887	Ind-N	43	157	13	31	4	0	0	13	8	12	.197	.241	.223	31	-14	8			.865	-5	C-42/O-2,1-1	-1.4
1888	Was-N	17	51	2	10	0	1	0	3	5	10	.196	.268	.235	65	-2	1			.840	-7	C-17	-0.8
Total	4	76	260	21	45	4	1	0	16	16	22	.173	.224	.196	25	-23	9			.882	-4	/C-75,O-2,1-1	-2.0
■ RANDY ASADOOR	Asadoor, Randall Carl b: 10/20/62, Fresno, Cal. BR/TR, 6'1", 185 lbs. Deb: 9/14/86																						
1986	SD-N	15	55	9	20	5	0	0	7	3	13	.364	.397	.455	137	3	1	2	-1	.889	0	3-15/2-2	0.2
■ JIM ASBELL	Asbell, James Marion "Big Train" b: 6/22/14, Dallas, Tex. d: 7/6/67, San Mateo, Cal. BR/TR, 6', 195 lbs. Deb: 5/8/38																						
1938	Chi-N	17	33	6	6	2	0	0	3	3	9	.182	.250	.242	35	-3	0			1.000	-1	O-10	-0.4
■ CASPER ASBJORNSON	Asbjornson, Robert Anthony (Name Changed To Asby) b: 6/19/09, Concord, Mass. d: 1/21/70, Williamsport, Pa. BR/TR, 6'1", 196 lbs. Deb: 9/17/28																						
1928	Bos-A	6	16	0	3	1	0	0	1	1	1	.188	.235	.250	28	-2	0	0	0	.917	-2	/C-6	-0.3
1929	Bos-A	17	29	1	3	0	0	0	0	1	6	.103	.133	.103	-39	-6	0	0	0	.897	-3	C-15	-0.7
1931	Cin-N	45	118	13	36	7	1	0	22	7	23	.305	.349	.381	102	0	0			.981	-0	C-31	0.2
1932	Cin-N	29	58	5	10	2	0	1	4	0	15	.172	.186	.259	19	-7	0			.961	0	C-16	-0.6
Total	4	97	221	19	52	10	1	1	27	9	45	.235	.272	.303	56	-14	0	0		.960	-5	/C-68	-1.4
■ RICHIE ASHBURN	Ashburn, Don Richard "Whitey" b: 3/19/27, Tilden, Neb. d: 9/9/97, New York, N.Y. BL/TR, 5'10", 170 lbs. Deb: 4/20/48 H																						
1948	Phi-N★	117	463	78	154	17	4	2	40	60	22	.333	.410	.400	122	17	**32**			.981	**18**	*O-116	2.8
1949	Phi-N	154	662	84	188	18	11	1	37	58	38	.284	.343	.349	88	-10	9			.980	**25**	*O-154	0.6
1950	*Phi-N	151	594	84	180	25	**14**	2	41	63	32	.303	.372	.402	105	6	14			.988	8	*O-147	0.7
1951	Phi-N★	154	643	92	**221**	31	5	4	63	50	37	.344	.393	.426	122	21	29	6	5	.988	**32**	*O-154	5.2
1952	Phi-N	154	613	93	173	31	6	1	42	75	30	.282	.362	.357	101	3	16	11	-2	.980	15	*O-154	1.1
1953	Phi-N★	156	622	110	**205**	25	9	2	57	61	35	.330	.394	.408	110	12	14	6	1	.990	**26**	*O-156	3.1
1954	Phi-N	153	559	111	175	16	8	1	41	**125**	46	.313	**.442**	.376	116	22	11	8	-2	.984	17	*O-153	3.0
1955	Phi-N	140	533	91	180	32	9	3	42	105	36	**.338**	**.449**	.448	142	39	12	10	-2	.983	11	*O-140	4.0
1956	Phi-N	154	628	94	190	26	8	3	50	79	45	.303	.385	.384	110	12	10	1	2	.983	25	*O-154	3.2
1957	Phi-N	156	626	93	186	26	8	0	33	**94**	44	.297	.392	.364	108	12	13	10	-2	.987	**32**	*O-156	3.3
1958	Phi-N☆	152	615	98	**215**	24	**13**	2	33	**97**	48	**.350**	**.441**	.441	136	38	30	12	2	.984	22	*O-152	5.3
1959	Phi-N	153	564	86	150	16	2	1	20	79	42	.266	.362	.307	79	-13	9	11	-4	.971	5	*O-149	-2.0
1960	Chi-N	151	547	99	159	16	5	0	40	**116**	50	.291	**.416**	.338	110	15	16	4	2	.976	1	*O-146	1.2
1961	Chi-N	109	307	49	79	7	4	0	19	55	27	.257	.375	.306	83	-5	7	6	-2	.978	-7	O-76	-1.8
1962	NY-N★	135	389	60	119	7	3	7	28	81	39	.306	.426	.393	119	15	12	7	-1	.975	-4	O-97/2-2	0.5
Total	15	2189	8365	1322	2574	317	109	29	586	1198	571	.308	.397	.382	111	184	234	92		.983	227	*O-2104/2-2	30.2
■ ALAN ASHBY	Ashby, Alan Dean b: 7/8/51, Long Beach, Cal. BB/TR, 6'2", 190 lbs. Deb: 7/3/73 C																						
1973	Cle-A	11	29	4	5	1	0	1	3	2	11	.172	.226	.310	49	-2	0	0	0	.978	-2	C-11	-0.4
1974	Cle-A	10	7	1	1	0	0	0	0	1	2	.143	.250	.143	15	-1	0	0	0	1.000	0	/C-9	0.0
1975	Cle-A	90	254	32	57	10	1	5	32	30	42	.224	.309	.331	81	-6	3	2	-0	.990	3	C-87/1-2,3-1,D-1	0.0
1976	Cle-A	89	247	26	59	5	1	4	32	27	49	.239	.314	.316	86	-4	0	2	-1	.987	6	C-86/1-2,3-1	0.3
1977	Tor-A	124	396	25	83	16	3	2	29	50	51	.210	.301	.280	59	-22	0	2	-1	.984	-7	*C-124	-2.6
1978	Tor-A	81	264	27	69	15	0	9	29	28	32	.261	.334	.420	109	3	1	1	-0	.986	-7	C-81	-0.3
1979	Hou-N	108	336	25	68	15	2	2	35	26	70	.202	.264	.277	51	-24	0	0	0	.987	-1	*C-105	-2.2
1980	*Hou-N	116	352	30	90	19	2	3	48	35	40	.256	.323	.347	94	-3	0	0	0	.991	2	*C-114	0.3
1981	*Hou-N	83	255	20	69	13	0	4	33	35	33	.271	.359	.369	112	5	0	2	-1	.982	7	C-81	1.4
1982	Hou-N	100	339	40	87	14	2	12	49	27	53	.257	.313	.416	111	3	2	0	1	.977	-5	C-95	0.3
1983	Hou-N	87	275	31	63	18	1	8	34	31	38	.229	.307	.389	98	-2	0	0	0	.974	-13	C-85	-1.1
1984	Hou-N	66	191	16	50	7	0	4	27	20	22	.262	.335	.361	103	1	0	0	0	.986	-3	C-63	0.1
1985	Hou-N	65	189	20	53	8	0	8	25	24	27	.280	.364	.450	130	8	0	0	0	.978	-0	C-60	1.1
1986	*Hou-N	120	315	24	81	15	0	7	38	39	56	.257	.339	.371	98	-0	1	0	0	.985	-4	*C-103	0.2
1987	Hou-N	125	386	53	111	16	0	14	63	50	52	.288	.371	.438	118	10	0	1	-1	**.993**	-4	*C-110	1.4
1988	Hou-N	73	227	19	54	10	0	7	33	29	36	.238	.324	.374	104	1	0	0	0	.991	-10	C-66	-0.4
1989	Hou-N	22	61	4	10	1	1	0	3	7	8	.164	.261	.213	38	-5	0	0	0	1.000	-3	C-19	-0.7
Total	17	1370	4123	397	1010	183	13	90	513	461	622	.245	.323	.361	93	-37	7	10	-4	.986	-41	*C-1299/1-4,3-2,D-1	-2.6
■ TUCKER ASHFORD	Ashford, Thomas Steven b: 12/4/54, Memphis, Tenn. BR/TR, 6'1", 195 lbs. Deb: 9/21/76																						
1976	SD-N	4	5	0	3	1	0	0	0	1	0	.600	.667	.800	343	2	2	0	1	1.000	0	/3-1	0.3
1977	SD-N	81	249	25	54	18	0	3	24	21	35	.217	.280	.325	69	-12	2	3	-1	.937	2	3-74,S-10/2-4	-1.1
1978	SD-N	75	155	11	38	11	0	3	26	14	31	.245	.308	.374	97	-1	1	0	0	.917	-16	3-32,2-18,1-14	-1.8
1980	Tex-A	15	32	2	4	0	0	0	3	3	3	.125	.200	.125	-9	-5	0	0	0	.943	3	3-12/S-2	-0.2
1981	NY-A	3	0	0	0	0	0	0	0	0	0	—	—	—	—	0	0	0	0	.000	0	/2-2	0.0
1983	NY-N	35	56	3	10	0	1	0	2	7	4	.179	.270	.214	36	-5	0	0	0	.957	-1	3-15,2-13/C-1	-0.6
1984	KC-A	9	13	1	2	1	0	0	0	1	2	.154	.214	.231	23	-1	0	0	0	.909	0	/3-9	-0.1
Total	7	222	510	42	111	31	1	6	55	47	75	.218	.285	.318	70	-22	5	3	-0	.936	-12	3-143/2-37,1-14,SC	-3.5
■ BILLY ASHLEY	Ashley, Billy Manual b: 7/11/70, Trenton, Mich. BR/TR, 6'7", 227 lbs. Deb: 9/1/92																						
1992	LA-N	29	95	6	21	5	0	2	6	5	34	.221	.260	.337	69	-4	0	0	0	.857	-3	O-27	-0.8
1993	LA-N	14	37	0	9	0	0	0	0	2	11	.243	.282	.243	45	-3	0	0	0	1.000	0	O-11	-0.3
1994	LA-N	2	6	0	2	1	0	0	0	0	2	.333	.333	.500	121	0	0	0	0	1.000	-0	/O-2	0.0
1995	*LA-N	81	215	17	51	5	0	8	27	25	88	.237	.322	.372	91	-3	0	0	0	.972	-1	O-69	-0.5
1996	*LA-N	71	110	18	22	2	1	9	25	21	44	.200	.333	.482	121	3	0	0	0	.952	-4	O-38	-0.1
1997	LA-N	71	131	12	32	7	0	6	19	8	46	.244	.293	.435	95	-2	0	0	0	.911	-3	O-35	-0.6
1998	Bos-A	13	24	3	7	3	0	3	7	2	11	.292	.346	.792	184	3	0	0	0	.857	-0	/1-2,O-2,D-5	0.2
Total	7	281	618	56	144	23	1	28	84	63	236	.233	.308	.409	95	-6	0	0	0	.941	-11	O-184/D-5,1-2	-2.1
■ TOM ASMUSSEN	Asmussen, Thomas William b: 9/26/1876, Chicago, Ill. d: 8/21/63, Arlington Heights, Ill. TR , Deb: 8/10/07																						
1907	Bos-N	2	5	0	0	0	0	0	0	0		.000	.000	.000	-99	-1	0			1.000	-1	/C-2	-0.3

YEAR	TM/L	G	AB	R	H	2B	3B	HR	RBI	BB	SO	AVG	OBP	SLG	PRO+	BR/A	SB	CS	SBR	FA	FR	G/POS	TPR
■ KEN ASPROMONTE	Aspromonte, Kenneth Joseph b: 9/22/31, Brooklyn, N.Y. BR/TR, 6', 180 lbs. Deb: 9/2/57 FM																						
1957	Bos-A	24	78	9	21	5	0	0	4	17	10	.269	.400	.333	97	1	0	1	-1	.965	-3	2-24	-0.1
1958	Bos-A	6	16	0	2	0	0	0	0	3	1	.125	.263	.125	10	-2	0	0	0	.952	-3	/2-6	-0.5
	Was-A	92	253	15	57	9	1	5	27	25	28	.225	.297	.328	73	-9	1	1	-0	.964	3	2-72,3-11/S-1	-0.2
	Yr	98	269	15	59	9	1	5	27	28	29	.219	.295	.316	69	-11	1	1	-0	.963	-0	2-78,3-11/S-1	-0.7
1959	Was-A	70	225	31	55	12	0	2	14	26	39	.244	.323	.324	79	-6	2	1	0	.960	-10	2-52,S-12/1-1,O-1	-1.1
1960	Was-A	4	3	0	0	0	0	0	0	0	1	.000	.000	.000	-99	-1	0	0	0	.000	0	H	-0.1
	Cle-A	117	459	65	133	20	1	10	48	53	32	.290	.366	.403	111	8	4	1	1	.976	-12	2-80,3-36	0.4
	Yr	121	462	65	133	20	1	10	48	53	33	.288	.364	.400	110	7	4	1	1	.976	-12	2-80,3-36	0.3
1961	LA-A	66	238	29	53	10	0	2	14	33	21	.223	.322	.290	58	-14	0	0	0	.970	18	2-62	1.1
	Cle-A	22	70	5	16	6	1	0	5	6	3	.229	.289	.343	70	-3	0	0	0	.963	-2	2-21	-0.3
	Yr	88	308	34	69	16	1	2	19	39	24	.224	.315	.302	61	-17	0	0	0	.969	17	2-83	0.8
1962	Cle-A	20	28	4	4	2	0	0	1	6	5	.143	.294	.214	41	-2	0	0	0	1.000	-1	/2-6,3-3	-0.3
	Mil-N	34	79	11	23	2	0	0	7	6	5	.291	.349	.316	82	-2	0	1	-1	1.000	-0	2-12/3-6	-0.1
1963	Chi-N	20	34	2	5	3	0	0	4	4	4	.147	.237	.235	35	-3	0	0	0	.951	3	/2-7,1-2	0.1
Total	7	475	1483	171	369	69	3	19	124	179	149	.249	.332	.338	82	-33	7	5	-1	.969	-7	2-342/3-56,S-13,1O	-1.1
■ BOB ASPROMONTE	Aspromonte, Robert Thomas b: 6/19/38, Brooklyn, N.Y. BR/TR, 6'2", 185 lbs. Deb: 9/19/56 F																						
1956	Bro-N	1	1	0	0	0	0	0	0	0	1	.000	.000	.000	-93	-0	0	0	0	.000	0	H	0.0
1960	LA-N	21	55	1	10	1	0	1	6	0	6	.182	.196	.255	21	-6	1	0	0	.933	-2	S-15/3-4	-0.7
1961	LA-N	47	58	7	14	3	0	0	2	4	12	.241	.290	.293	51	-4	0	0	0	.917	0	/3-9,S-4,2-2	-0.3
1962	Hou-N	149	534	59	142	18	4	11	59	46	54	.266	.333	.376	97	-2	4	5	-2	.967	1	*3-142,S-11/2-1	-0.1
1963	Hou-N	136	468	42	100	9	5	8	49	40	57	.214	.277	.306	72	-17	3	1	0	.938	-16	*3-131/1-1	-3.6
1964	Hou-N	157	553	51	155	20	3	12	69	35	54	.280	.332	.392	109	6	6	7	-2	**.973**	-15	*3-155	-1.4
1965	Hou-N	152	578	53	152	15	2	5	52	38	54	.263	.312	.322	85	-12	2	2	-1	.962	0	*3-146/1-6,S-4	-1.7
1966	Hou-N	152	560	55	141	16	3	8	52	35	63	.252	.298	.334	81	-15	0	4	-2	**.962**	-11	*3-149/1-2,S-2	-3.3
1967	Hou-N	137	486	51	143	24	5	6	58	45	44	.294	.356	.401	121	13	2	2	-1	.963	-4	*3-133	0.8
1968	Hou-N	124	409	25	92	9	2	1	46	35	57	.225	.289	.264	68	-15	1	0	0	.973	0	3-75,O-36/1-1,S-1	-1.9
1969	*Atl-N	82	198	16	50	8	1	3	24	13	19	.253	.305	.348	82	-5	0	1	-1	.975	-6	O-24,3-23,S-18,/2-2	-1.3
1970	Atl-N	62	127	5	27	3	0	0	7	13	13	.213	.286	.236	39	-11	0	0	0	.938	-1	3-30/S-4,1-1,O-1	-1.1
1971	NY-N	104	342	21	77	9	1	5	33	29	25	.225	.286	.301	67	-15	0	2	-1	.965	-5	3-97	-2.3
Total	13	1324	4369	386	1103	135	26	60	457	333	459	.252	.310	.336	86	-84	19	24	-9	.960	-57	*3-1094/O-61,S12	-16.9
■ BRIAN ASSELSTINE	Asselstine, Brian Hanly b: 9/23/53, Santa Barbara, Cal BL/TR, 6'1", 175 lbs. Deb: 9/14/76																						
1976	Atl-N	11	33	2	7	0	0	1	1	3	1	2	.212	.235	.303	49	-2	0	0	0	1.000	-1	/O-9	-0.3
1977	Atl-N	83	124	12	26	6	0	4	17	9	10	.210	.263	.355	57	-8	1	0	0	.983	-2	O-35	-1.1
1978	Atl-N	39	103	11	28	3	3	2	13	11	16	.272	.353	.417	103	0	2	1	0	.968	-5	O-35	-0.7
1979	Atl-N	8	10	1	1	0	0	0	0	1	2	.100	.182	.100	-20	-2	0	0	0	1.000	-0	/O-1	-0.2
1980	Atl-N	87	218	18	62	13	1	3	25	11	37	.284	.322	.394	96	-2	1	3	-2	.962	-9	O-61	-1.5
1981	Atl-N	56	86	8	22	5	0	2	10	5	7	.256	.297	.384	90	-1	1	0	0	.958	-1	O-16	-0.3
Total	6	284	574	52	146	27	4	12	68	38	74	.254	.304	.378	83	-14	5	4	-1	.971	-19	O-157	-4.1
■ JOE ASTROTH	Astroth, Joseph Henry b: 9/1/22, East Alton, Ill. BR/TR, 5'9", 187 lbs. Deb: 8/13/45																						
1945	Phi-A	10	17	1	1	0	0	0	1	0	1	.059	.111	.059	-50	-3	0	0	0	.857	0	/C-8	-0.3
1946	Phi-A	4	7	0	1	0	0	0	0	0	2	.143	.143	.143	-20	-1	0	0	0	.889	-0	/C-4	-0.1
1949	Phi-A	55	148	18	36	4	1	0	12	21	13	.243	.337	.284	67	-7	1	0	0	.979	2	C-44	-0.2
1950	Phi-A	39	110	11	36	3	1	1	18	18	3	.327	.422	.400	113	3	0	0	0	.985	-6	C-38	-0.1
1951	Phi-A	64	187	30	46	10	2	2	19	18	13	.246	.312	.353	78	-6	0	1	-1	.992	4	C-57	-0.1
1952	Phi-A	104	337	24	84	7	2	1	36	25	27	.249	.305	.291	62	-17	2	2	-1	.992	-5	*C-102	-1.8
1953	Phi-A	82	260	28	77	15	2	3	24	27	12	.296	.367	.404	104	2	1	0	0	.987	7	C-79	1.2
1954	Phi-A	77	226	22	50	8	1	1	23	21	19	.221	.296	.279	58	-13	0	0	0	.988	-2	C-71	-1.2
1955	KC-A	101	274	29	69	4	1	5	23	47	33	.252	.373	.328	89	-2	2	3	-1	.989	-4	*C-100	-0.4
1956	KC-A	8	13	0	1	0	0	0	0	0	1	.077	.077	.077	-59	-3	0	0	0	1.000	2	/C-8	-0.1
Total	10	544	1579	163	401	51	10	13	156	177	124	.254	.334	.324	77	-47	6	6	-2	.987	-2	C-511	-3.1
■ CHARLIE ATHERTON	Atherton, Charles Morgan Herbert "Prexy" b: 10/19/1873, New Brunswick, N.J d: 12/19/34, Vienna, Austria BR/TR, 5'10", 160 lbs. Deb: 5/30/1899																						
1899	Was-N	65	242	28	60	5	6	0	23	21		.248	.313	.318	74	-9	2			.890	-6	3-63/O-1	-1.3
■ ED ATKINSON	Atkinson, Edward b: 1851, Baltimore, Md. Deb: 10/22/1873																						
1873	Was-n	2	8	2	0	0	0	0	0	0	0	.000	.000	.000	-99	-2	0	0	0	1.000	-0	/O-2	-0.2
■ LEFTY ATKINSON	Atkinson, Hubert Berley b: 6/2/06, Chicago, Ill. d: 2/12/61, Chicago, Ill. BL/TL, 5'6.5", 149 lbs. Deb: 8/5/27																						
1927	Was-A	1	1	1	0	0	0	0	0	0	0	.000	.000	.000	-99	-0	0	0	0	.000	0	H	0.0
■ DICK ATTREAU	Attreau, Richard Gilbert b: 4/8/1897, Chicago, Ill. d: 7/5/64, Chicago, Ill. BL/TL, 6', 160 lbs. Deb: 9/14/26																						
1926	Phi-N	17	61	9	14	1	1	0	5	6	5	.230	.299	.279	53	-4	0			.989	-1	1-17	-0.6
1927	Phi-N	44	83	17	17	1	1	1	11	14	18	.205	.320	.277	60	-4	1			.989	-2	1-26	-0.7
Total	2	61	144	26	31	2	2	1	16	20	23	.215	.311	.278	57	-8	1			.989	-3	/1-43	-1.3
■ TOBY ATWELL	Atwell, Maurice Dailey b: 3/8/24, Leesburg, Va. BL/TR, 5'9.5", 185 lbs. Deb: 4/15/52																						
1952	Chi-N☆	107	362	36	105	16	3	2	31	40	22	.290	.362	.367	102	2	2	1	0	.977	-7	*C-101	0.0
1953	Chi-N	24	74	10	17	2	0	1	8	13	7	.230	.345	.297	68	-3	0	0	0	.940	1	C-24	-0.1
	Pit-N	53	139	11	34	6	0	0	17	20	12	.245	.352	.288	70	-5	0	0	0	.967	-3	C-45	-0.6
	Yr	77	213	21	51	8	0	1	25	33	19	.239	.349	.291	69	-8	0	0	0	.957	-2	C-69	-0.7
1954	Pit-N	96	287	36	83	8	4	3	26	43	21	.289	.387	.376	101	2	2	3	-1	.990	-2	C-88	0.3
1955	Pit-N	71	207	21	44	8	0	1	18	40	16	.213	.343	.266	65	-9	0	1	-1	.992	6	C-67	-0.2
1956	Pit-N	12	18	0	2	0	0	0	3	1	5	.111	.158	.111	-27	-3	0	0	0	1.000	1	/C-9	-0.2
	Mil-N	15	30	2	5	1	0	2	7	4	1	.167	.265	.400	80	-1	0	0	0	1.000	-1	C-10	-0.1
	Yr	27	48	2	7	1	0	2	10	5	6	.146	.226	.292	40	-4	0	0	0	1.000	0	C-19	-0.3
Total	5	378	1117	116	290	41	7	9	110	161	84	.260	.357	.333	86	-17	4	5	-2	.980	-5	C-344	-0.9
■ BILL ATWOOD	Atwood, William Franklin b: 9/25/11, Rome, Ga. d: 9/14/93, Snyder, Tex. BR/TR, 5'11.5", 190 lbs. Deb: 4/15/36																						
1936	Phi-N	71	192	21	58	9	2	2	29	11	15	.302	.346	.401	92	-2	0			.972	-1	C-53	-0.1
1937	Phi-N	87	279	27	68	15	1	2	32	30	27	.244	.317	.326	69	-12	3			.968	-15	C-80	-2.2
1938	Phi-N	102	281	27	55	8	1	3	28	25	26	.196	.261	.263	46	-21	0			.969	0	C-94	-1.6
1939	Phi-N	4	6	0	0	0	0	0	1	2	3	.000	.250	.000	-29	-1	1			1.000	-0	/C-2	-0.1
1940	Phi-N	78	203	7	39	9	0	0	22	25	18	.192	.284	.236	47	-14	0			.989	1	C-69	-0.9
Total	5	342	961	82	220	41	4	7	112	93	89	.229	.299	.302	63	-50	4			.974	-14	C-298	-4.9
■ JAKE ATZ	Atz, John Jacob (b: Jacob Henry Atz) b: 7/1/1879, Washington, D.C. d: 5/22/45, New Orleans, La. BR/TR, 5'9", 150 lbs. Deb: 9/24/02																						
1902	Was-A	3	10	1	1	0	0	0	0	0		.100	.100	.100	-44	-2	0			1.000	0	/2-3	-0.1
1907	Chi-A	4	8	0	1	0	0	0	0	0		.125	.125	.125	-21	-1	0			1.000	1	/3-2,O-1	0.0
1908	Chi-A	83	206	24	40	3	0	0	27	31		.194	.311	.209	71	-5	9			.936	-3	2-46,S-18/3-1	-0.9
1909	Chi-A	119	381	39	90	18	3	0	22	38		.236	.309	.299	96	-1	14			.954	-7	*2-114/O-3,S-1	-1.2
Total	4	209	605	64	132	21	3	0	49	69		.218	.304	.263	83	-9	23			.949	-8	2-163/S-19,O-4,3-3	-2.2
■ HARRY AUBREY	Aubrey, Harry Herbert "Chub" b: 7/5/1880, St.Joseph, Mo. d: 9/18/53, Baltimore, Md. TR, Deb: 4/22/03																						
1903	Bos-N	96	325	26	69	8	2	0	27	18		.212	.264	.249	49	-22	7			.868	-10	S-94/2-1,O-1	-2.7
■ RICH AUDE	Aude, Richard Thomas b: 7/13/71, Van Nuys, Cal. BR/TR, 6'5", 180 lbs. Deb: 9/9/93																						
1993	Pit-N	13	26	1	3	1	0	0	4	1	7	.115	.148	.154	-19	-4	0	0	0	1.000	-1	/1-7,O-1	-0.6

YEAR	TM/L	G	AB	R	H	2B	3B	HR	RBI	BB	SO	AVG	OBP	SLG	PRO+	BR/A	SB	CS	SBR	FA	FR	G/POS	TPR
1995	Pit-N	42	109	10	27	8	0	2	19	6	20	.248	.287	.376	72	-5	1	2	-1	.996	-3	1-32	-1.1
1996	Pit-N	7	16	0	4	0	0	0	1	0	8	.250	.250	.250	32	-2	0	0	0	.969	0	/1-4	-0.2
Total	3	62	151	11	34	9	0	2	24	7	35	.225	.259	.325	52	-11	1	2	-1	.994	-3	/1-43,O-1	-1.9
■ **RICK AUERBACH**	Auerbach, Frederick Steven b: 2/15/50, Woodland Hills, Cal BR/TR, 6', 165 lbs. Deb: 4/13/71																						
1971	Mil-A	79	236	22	48	10	0	1	9	20	40	.203	.271	.258	51	-15	3	2	-0	.963	-10	S-78	-1.7
1972	Mil-A	153	554	50	121	16	3	2	30	43	62	.218	.277	.269	64	-24	24	8	2	.959	-21	*S-153	-2.5
1973	Mil-A	6	10	2	1	1	0	0	0	0	1	.100	.100	.200	-18	-2	0	1	-1	.833	0	/S-2	-0.2
1974	*LA-N	45	73	12	25	0	0	1	4	8	9	.342	.407	.384	127	3	4	2	0	.950	2	S-19,2-16/3-3	0.6
1975	LA-N	85	170	18	38	9	0	0	12	18	22	.224	.298	.276	63	-8	3	2	-0	.960	-17	S-81/2-1,3-1	-2.1
1976	LA-N	36	47	7	6	0	0	0	1	6	6	.128	.226	.128	2	-6	0	1	-1	.943	11	S-12/3-8,2-7	0.6
1977	Cin-N	33	45	5	7	2	0	0	3	4	7	.156	.224	.200	15	-5	0	0	0	.976	6	2-19,S-12	0.2
1978	Cin-N	63	55	17	18	6	0	2	5	7	12	.327	.413	.545	166	5	1	0	0	.971	10	S-26,2-10/3-3	1.7
1979	*Cin-N	62	100	17	21	8	1	1	12	14	19	.210	.307	.340	76	-3	0	1	-1	.933	-1	3-18,S-16/2-3	-0.3
1980	Cin-N	24	33	5	11	1	1	1	4	3	5	.333	.389	.515	150	2	0	3	-2	1.000	-1	/S-3,3-3,2-1	0.0
1981	Sea-A	38	84	12	13	3	0	1	6	4	15	.155	.202	.226	22	-8	1	1	-0	.979	3	S-38	-0.3
Total	11	624	1407	167	309	56	5	9	86	127	198	.220	.287	.286	65	-62	36	21	-2	.960	-16	S-440/2-57,3-36	-4.0
■ **DAVE AUGUSTINE**	Augustine, David Ralph b: 11/28/49, Follansbee, W.Va. BR/TR, 6'2", 174 lbs. Deb: 9/3/73																						
1973	Pit-N	11	7	1	2	1	0	0	0	0	1	.286	.286	.429	98	-0	0	0	0	1.000	-2	/O-9	-0.2
1974	Pit-N	18	22	3	4	0	0	0	0	0	5	.182	.182	.182	2	-3	0	1	-1	1.000	1	O-11	-0.3
Total	2	29	29	4	6	1	0	0	0	0	6	.207	.207	.241	26	-3	0	1	-1	1.000	-2	/O-20	-0.5
■ **LESLIE AULDS**	Aulds, Leycester Doyle "Tex" b: 12/28/20, Farmerville, La. BR/TR, 6'2", 185 lbs. Deb: 5/25/47																						
1947	Bos-A	3	4	0	1	0	0	0	0	0	1	.250	.250	.250	37	-0	0	0	0	1.000	0	/C-3	0.0
■ **DOUG AULT**	Ault, Douglas Reagan b: 3/9/50, Beaumont, Tex. BR/TL, 6'3", 200 lbs. Deb: 9/9/76																						
1976	Tex-A	9	20	0	6	1	0	0	0	1	3	.300	.333	.350	98	-0	0	0	0	1.000	-1	/1-4,D-3	-0.1
1977	Tor-A	129	445	44	109	22	3	11	64	39	68	.245	.311	.382	87	-8	4	4	-1	.987	7	*1-122/D-4	-1.0
1978	Tor-A	54	104	10	25	1	1	3	7	17	14	.240	.352	.356	98	0	0	0	0	.979	-2	1-25/O-7,D-5	-0.3
1980	Tor-A	64	144	12	28	5	1	3	15	14	23	.194	.275	.306	56	-9	0	1	-1	1.000	3	1-32,D-21/O-1	-0.8
Total	4	256	713	66	168	29	5	17	86	71	108	.236	.311	.362	82	-17	4	5	-2	.988	8	1-183/D-33,O-8	-2.2
■ **RICH AURILIA**	Aurilia, Richard Santo b: 9/2/71, Brooklyn, N.Y. BR/TR, 6', 170 lbs. Deb: 9/6/95																						
1995	SF-N	9	19	4	9	3	0	2	4	1	2	.474	.500	.947	280	5	1	0	0	1.000	1	/S-6	0.6
1996	SF-N	105	318	27	76	7	1	3	26	25	52	.239	.297	.296	59	-19	4	1	1	.973	-4	S-93,2-11	-1.4
1997	SF-N	46	102	16	28	8	0	5	19	8	15	.275	.327	.500	115	2	1	1	-0	.979	11	S-36	1.5
1998	SF-N	122	413	54	110	27	2	9	49	31	62	.266	.321	.407	90	-7	3	3	-1	.979	-0	*S-120	0.3
Total	4	282	852	101	223	45	3	19	98	65	131	.262	.316	.388	86	-19	9	5	-0	.977	9	S-255/2-11	1.0
■ **BRAD AUSMUS**	Ausmus, Bradley David b: 4/14/69, New Haven, Conn. BR/TR, 5'11", 195 lbs. Deb: 7/28/93																						
1993	SD-N	49	160	18	41	8	1	5	12	6	28	.256	.283	.412	82	-5	2	0	1	.975	5	C-49	0.4
1994	SD-N	101	327	45	82	12	1	7	24	30	63	.251	.316	.358	77	-11	5	1	1	.991	2	C-99/1-1	-0.2
1995	SD-N	103	328	44	96	16	4	5	34	31	56	.293	.357	.412	106	3	16	5	2	.992	1	*C-100/1-1	1.2
1996	SD-N	50	149	16	27	4	0	1	13	13	27	.181	.261	.228	32	-15	1	4	-2	.982	2	C-46	-1.2
	Det-A	75	226	30	56	12	0	4	22	26	45	.248	.331	.354	73	-9	3	4	-2	.992	1	C-73	-0.5
1997	*Hou-N	130	425	45	113	25	1	4	44	38	78	.266	.330	.358	83	-10	14	6	1	.992	3	*C-129	0.1
1998	*Hou-N	128	412	62	111	10	4	6	45	53	60	.269	.357	.357	88	-6	10	3	1	.992	6	*C-124	1.0
Total	6	636	2027	260	526	87	11	32	194	197	357	.259	.329	.361	82	-52	51	23	2	.990	19	C-620/1-2	0.8
■ **HENRY AUSTIN**	Austin, Henry C. b: 1844, Brooklyn, N.Y. d: 9/3/1895, Amityville, N.Y. Deb: 4/28/1873																						
1873	Res-n	23	101	10	25	3	3	0	11	0	4	.248	.248	.337	78	-2	0	0	0	.722	-0	O-23	-0.1
■ **JIMMY AUSTIN**	Austin, James Philip "Pepper" b: 12/8/1879, Swansea, Wales d: 3/6/65, Laguna Beach, Cal. BB/TR, 5'7.5", 155 lbs. Deb: 4/19/09 MC																						
1909	NY-A	136	437	37	101	11	5	1	39	32		.231	.285	.286	80	-10	30			.928	13	*3-111,S-23/2-1	0.8
1910	NY-A	133	432	46	94	11	4	2	36	47		.218	.305	.275	77	-11	22			.942	4	*3-133	-0.4
1911	StL-A	148	541	84	141	25	11	2	45	69		.261	.351	.359	102	3	26			.931	16	*3-148	2.0
1912	StL-A	149	536	57	135	14	8	2	44	38		.252	.306	.319	82	-13	28			.911	-1	*3-149	-1.4
1913	StL-A	142	489	56	130	18	6	2	42	45	51	.266	.338	.339	101	1	37			**.944**	7	*3-142,M	1.0
1914	StL-A	130	466	55	111	16	4	0	30	40	59	.238	.300	.290	80	-12	20	23	-8	.935	1	*3-127	-1.6
1915	StL-A	141	477	61	127	6	6	1	30	64	60	.266	.355	.310	103	4	18	15	-4	.917	10	*3-141	1.6
1916	StL-A	129	411	55	85	15	6	1	28	74	59	.207	.333	.280	89	-3	19			.939	-7	*3-124	-0.6
1917	StL-A	127	455	61	109	18	8	0	19	50	46	.240	.319	.314	97	-1	13			.947	3	*3-121/S-6	0.4
1918	StL-A	110	367	42	97	14	4	0	20	53	32	.264	.359	.324	109	6	18			.939	-17	S-57,3-48,M	-0.8
1919	StL-A	106	396	54	94	9	9	1	21	42	31	.237	.314	.313	74	-13	8			.939	7	3-98	-0.3
1920	StL-A	83	280	38	76	11	3	1	32	31	15	.271	.352	.343	82	-6	2	4	-2	.943	2	3-75	-0.2
1921	StL-A	27	66	8	18	2	1	0	2	4	7	.273	.324	.333	64	-4	2	1	0	.938	-3	S-14/2-6,3-2	-0.5
1922	StL-A	15	31	6	9	3	1	0	1	3	2	.290	.353	.452	105	0	0	0	0	.957	-3	/3-9,2-2	-0.2
1923	StL-A	1	0	0	0	0	0	0	0	0	0	—	—	—	—	0	0	0	0	.000	0	/M	0.0
1925	StL-A	1	1	0	0	0	0	0	0	0	0	.000	.000	.000	-95	-0	0	0	0	1.000	0	/3-1	0.0
1926	StL-A	1	2	1	1	1	0	0	1	0	0	.500	.500	1.000	272	0	1	0	0	1.000	0	/3-1	0.1
1929	StL-A	1	1	0	0	0	0	0	0	0	1	.000	.000	.000	-96	-0	0	0	0	1.000	1	/3-1	0.0
Total	18	1580	5388	661	1328	174	76	13	390	592	363	.246	.326	.314	90	-60	244	43		.933	32	*3-1431,S-100/2-9	-0.1
■ **CHICK AUTRY**	Autry, Martin Gordon b: 3/5/03, Martindale, Tex. d: 1/26/50, Savannah, Ga. BR/TR, 6', 180 lbs. Deb: 4/20/24																						
1924	NY-A	2	0	1	0	0	0	0	0	0	0	—	1.000	—	172	0	0	0	0	1.000	-0	/C-2	0.0
1926	Cle-A	3	7	1	1	0	0	0	0	1	0	.143	.250	.143	4	-1	0	0	0	1.000	-0	/C-3	-0.1
1927	Cle-A	16	43	5	11	4	1	0	7	0	6	.256	.256	.395	66	-2	0	0	0	.933	2	C-14	0.1
1928	Cle-A	22	60	6	18	6	1	1	9	1	7	.300	.311	.483	105	0	0	0	0	.972	0	C-18	0.2
1929	Chi-A	43	96	7	20	6	0	1	12	1	8	.208	.224	.302	35	-10	0	0	0	.940	-4	C-30	-1.1
1930	Chi-A	34	71	1	18	1	1	0	5	4	8	.254	.293	.296	52	-5	0	0	0	.992	8	C-29	0.4
Total	6	120	277	21	68	17	3	2	33	7	29	.245	.269	.350	59	-18	0	0	0	.965	5	/C-96	-0.5
■ **CHICK AUTRY**	Autry, William Askew b: 1/2/1885, Humboldt, Tenn. d: 1/16/76, Santa Rosa, Cal. BL/TL, 5'11", 168 lbs. Deb: 9/18/07																						
1907	Cin-N	7	25	3	5	0	0	0	0	1		.200	.231	.200	34	-2	0			.929	-1	/O-7	-0.4
1909	Cin-N	9	33	3	6	2	0	0	4	2		.182	.229	.242	46	-2	1			.956	0	/1-9	-0.2
	Bos-N	65	199	16	39	4	0	0	13	21		.196	.279	.216	51	-11	5			.994	5	1-61/O-4	-0.7
	Yr	74	232	19	45	6	0	0	17	23		.194	.272	.220	51	-13	6			.989	5	1-70/O-4	-0.9
Total	2	81	257	22	50	6	0	0	17	24		.195	.269	.218	49	-15	6			.968	4	/1-70,O-11	-1.3
■ **BRUCE AVEN**	Aven, David Bruce b: 3/4/72, Orange, Tex. BR/TR, 5'9", 180 lbs. Deb: 8/27/97																						
1997	Cle-A	13	19	4	4	1	0	0	2	1	5	.211	.250	.263	33	-2	0	1	-1	1.000	-1	O-13	-0.4
■ **EARL AVERILL**	Averill, Earl Douglas b: 9/9/31, Cleveland, Ohio BR/TR, 5'10", 190 lbs. Deb: 4/19/56 F																						
1956	Cle-A	42	93	12	22	6	0	3	14	14	25	.237	.343	.398	93	-1	0	1	-1	.994	3	C-34	0.2
1958	Cle-A	17	55	2	10	1	0	2	7	4	7	.182	.250	.309	54	-4	1	0	0	.863	0	3-17	-0.3
1959	Chi-N	74	186	22	44	10	0	10	34	15	39	.237	.300	.452	98	-1	0	1	-1	.963	3	C-32,3-13/O-5,2-2	0.3
1960	Chi-N	52	102	14	24	4	0	1	13	11	16	.235	.316	.304	71	-4	1	1	-0	.979	-9	C-34/3-1,O-1	-1.2
	Chi-A	10	14	2	3	0	0	0	2	4	2	.214	.389	.214	68	-0	0	0	0	1.000	2	/C-5	0.2
1961	LA-A	115	323	56	86	9	0	21	59	62	70	.266	.388	.489	119	9	1	0	0	.991	-7	C-88/O-9,2-1	0.7
1962	LA-A	92	187	21	41	9	0	4	22	43	47	.219	.368	.332	93	-0	0	0	0	1.000	-4	O-49/C-6	-0.6

YEAR	TM/L	G	AB	R	H	2B	3B	HR	RBI	BB	SO	AVG	OBP	SLG	PRO+	BR/A	SB	CS	SBR	FA	FR	G/POS	TPR
1963	Phi-N	47	71	8	19	2	0	3	8	9	14	.268	.350	.423	123	2	0	0	0	.966	1	C-20/O-8,1-1,3-1	0.3
Total	7	449	1031	137	249	41	0	44	159	162	220	.242	.349	.409	101	1	3	3	-1	.984	-11	C-219/O-72,3-32,21	-0.4

■ EARL AVERILL Averill, Howard Earl "Rock" b: 5/21/02, Snohomish, Wash. d: 8/16/83, Everett, Wash. BL/TR, 5'9.5", 172 lbs. Deb: 4/16/29 FH

YEAR	TM/L	G	AB	R	H	2B	3B	HR	RBI	BB	SO	AVG	OBP	SLG	PRO+	BR/A	SB	CS	SBR	FA	FR	G/POS	TPR
1929	Cle-A	151	597	110	198	43	13	18	96	63	53	.332	.398	.538	134	29	13	13	-4	.966	-4	*O-151	1.1
1930	Cle-A	139	534	102	181	33	8	19	119	56	48	.339	.404	.537	131	25	10	7	-1	.949	2	*O-134	1.5
1931	Cle-A	155	627	140	209	36	10	32	143	68	38	.333	.404	.576	147	41	9	9	-3	.976	0	*O-155	2.5
1932	Cle-A	153	631	116	198	37	14	32	124	75	40	.314	.392	.569	137	33	5	8	-3	.964	2	*O-153	1.9
1933	Cle-A★	151	599	83	180	39	16	11	92	54	29	.301	.363	.474	115	12	3	1	0	.971	2	*O-149	0.6
1934	Cle-A★	154	598	128	187	48	6	31	113	99	44	.313	.414	.569	149	44	5	3	-0	.970	9	*O-154	4.2
1935	Cle-A†	140	563	109	162	34	13	19	79	70	58	.288	.368	.496	119	15	8	4	0	.982	-2	*O-139	0.7
1936	Cle-A★	152	614	136	**232**	39	**15**	28	126	65	35	.378	.438	.627	159	55	3	3	-1	.969	-4	*O-150	3.9
1937	Cle-A★	156	609	121	182	33	11	21	92	88	65	.299	.387	.493	119	18	5	4	-1	.976	-8	*O-156	0.4
1938	Cle-A★	134	482	101	159	27	15	14	93	81	48	.330	.429	.535	143	34	5	2	0	.975	5	*O-131	3.2
1939	Cle-A	24	55	8	15	8	0	1	7	6	12	.273	.344	.473	111	1	0	1	-1	1.000	-2	O-11	-0.3
	Det-A	87	309	58	81	20	6	10	58	43	30	.262	.354	.463	100	-1	4	2	0	.976	-5	O-80	-0.8
	Yr	111	364	66	96	28	6	11	65	49	42	.264	.353	.464	102	0	4	3	-1	.977	-7	O-91	-1.1
1940	*Det-A	64	118	10	33	4	1	2	20	5	14	.280	.309	.381	71	-5	0	0	0	.962	-5	O-22	-1.1
1941	Bos-N	8	17	2	2	0	0	0	2	1	4	.118	.211	.118	-6	-2	0			1.000	1	/O-4	-0.2
Total	13	1668	6353	1224	2019	401	128	238	1164	774	518	.318	.395	.534	132	296	70	57		.970	-8	*O-1589	17.6

■ BOBBY AVILA Avila, Roberto Francisco (Gonzales) b: 4/2/24, Veracruz, Mexico BR/TR, 5'10", 175 lbs. Deb: 4/30/49

YEAR	TM/L	G	AB	R	H	2B	3B	HR	RBI	BB	SO	AVG	OBP	SLG	PRO+	BR/A	SB	CS	SBR	FA	FR	G/POS	TPR
1949	Cle-A	31	14	3	3	0	0	0	3	1	3	.214	.267	.214	29	-1	0	0	0	1.000	4	/2-5	0.2
1950	Cle-A	80	201	39	60	10	2	1	21	29	17	.299	.390	.383	102	1	5	0	2	.983	-5	2-62/S-2	0.0
1951	Cle-A	141	542	76	165	21	3	10	58	60	31	.304	.374	.410	118	14	14	8	-1	.982	-1	*2-136	1.9
1952	Cle-A★	150	597	102	179	26	**11**	7	45	67	36	.300	.371	.415	127	21	12	10	-2	.966	-18	*2-149	0.9
1953	Cle-A	141	559	85	160	22	3	8	55	58	27	.286	.355	.379	101	1	10	8	-2	**.986**	13	*2-140	2.1
1954	*Cle-A★	143	555	112	189	27	2	15	67	59	31	**.341**	.405	.477	139	30	9	7	-2	.976	8	*2-141/S-7	4.7
1955	Cle-A★	141	537	83	146	22	4	13	61	82	47	.272	.370	.400	103	4	1	4	-2	.982	-3	*2-141	1.0
1956	Cle-A	138	513	74	115	14	2	10	54	70	68	.224	.323	.318	68	-23	17	4	3	.977	-10	*2-135	-1.8
1957	Cle-A	129	463	60	124	19	3	5	48	46	47	.268	.335	.354	89	-6	2	4	-2	.983	-15	*2-107,3-16	-1.5
1958	Cle-A	113	375	54	95	21	3	5	30	55	45	.253	.350	.365	100	1	5	7	-3	.986	-21	2-82,3-33	-1.7
1959	Bal-A	20	47	1	8	0	0	0	0	4	5	.170	.235	.170	14	-6	0	0	0	1.000	-4	O-10/2-8,3-1	-1.0
	Bos-A	22	45	7	11	0	0	3	6	6	11	.244	.333	.444	107	0	0	0	0	.975	-2	2-11	-0.1
	Yr	42	92	8	19	0	0	3	6	10	16	.207	.284	.304	61	-5	0	0	0	.967	-6	2-19,O-10/3-1	-1.1
	Mil-N	51	172	29	41	3	2	3	19	24	31	.238	.332	.331	84	-4	3	0	1	.967	-12	2-51	-1.1
Total	11	1300	4620	725	1296	185	35	80	467	561	399	.281	.360	.388	104	34	78	52	-8	.979	-64	*2-1168/3-50,O-10,S	3.6

■ RAMON AVILES Aviles, Ramon Antonio (Miranda) b: 1/22/52, Manati, P.R. BR/TR, 5'9", 155 lbs. Deb: 7/10/77

YEAR	TM/L	G	AB	R	H	2B	3B	HR	RBI	BB	SO	AVG	OBP	SLG	PRO+	BR/A	SB	CS	SBR	FA	FR	G/POS	TPR
1977	Bos-A	1	0	0	0	0	0	0	0	0	0	—	—	—	—	-0	0	0	0	1.000	0	/2-1	0.0
1979	Phi-N	27	61	7	17	2	0	0	12	8	8	.279	.371	.311	86	-1	0	0	0	.977	-7	2-27	-0.7
1980	*Phi-N	51	101	12	28	6	0	2	9	10	9	.277	.342	.396	100	0	0	0	0	.944	-7	S-29,2-15	-0.4
1981	*Phi-N	38	28	2	6	1	0	0	3	3	5	.214	.290	.250	52	-2	0	0	0	1.000	4	2-20,3-13/S-5	0.3
Total	4	117	190	21	51	9	0	2	24	21	22	.268	.344	.347	88	-2	0	0	0	.971	-10	/2-63,S-34,3-13	-0.8

■ BENNY AYALA Ayala, Benigno (Felix) b: 2/7/51, Yauco, P.R. BR/TR, 6'1", 185 lbs. Deb: 8/27/74

YEAR	TM/L	G	AB	R	H	2B	3B	HR	RBI	BB	SO	AVG	OBP	SLG	PRO+	BR/A	SB	CS	SBR	FA	FR	G/POS	TPR
1974	NY-N	23	68	9	16	1	0	2	8	7	17	.235	.316	.338	84	-1	0	0	0	.927	0	O-20	-0.2
1976	NY-N	22	26	2	3	0	0	1	2	2	6	.115	.179	.231	16	-3	0	1	-1	.889	-1	/O-7	-0.5
1977	StL-N	1	3	0	1	0	0	0	0	0	1	.333	.333	.333	81	-0	0	0	0	1.000	2	/O-1	0.2
1979	*Bal-A	42	86	15	22	5	0	6	13	6	9	.256	.304	.523	123	2	0	0	0	.974	-3	O-24,D-10	0.2
1980	Bal-A	76	170	28	45	8	1	10	33	19	21	.265	.339	.500	128	6	0	0	0	1.000	-2	D-41,O-19	0.2
1981	Bal-A	44	86	12	24	2	0	3	13	11	9	.279	.367	.407	123	3	0	1	-1	1.000	0	D-27/O-4	0.2
1982	Bal-A	64	128	17	39	6	0	6	24	5	14	.305	.331	.492	123	3	1	1	-0	.972	-5	O-25,D-17/1-3	-0.3
1983	*Bal-A	47	104	12	23	7	0	4	13	9	18	.221	.283	.404	88	-2	0	0	0	.953	-3	O-24,D-11	-0.6
1984	Bal-A	60	118	9	25	6	0	4	24	8	24	.212	.262	.364	73	-5	1	1	-0	1.000	-4	D-34,O-13	-1.0
1985	Cle-A	46	76	10	19	7	0	2	15	4	17	.250	.287	.421	92	-1	0	0	0	.917	-4	O-20/D-3	-0.5
Total	10	425	865	114	217	42	1	38	145	71	136	.251	.309	.434	104	2	2	4	-2	.958	-19	O-157,D-143/1-3	-2.7

■ DICK AYLWARD Aylward, Richard John "Dandy" b: 6/4/25, Baltimore, Md. d: 6/11/83, Spring Valley, Cal. BR/TR, 6', 190 lbs. Deb: 5/1/53

YEAR	TM/L	G	AB	R	H	2B	3B	HR	RBI	BB	SO	AVG	OBP	SLG	PRO+	BR/A	SB	CS	SBR	FA	FR	G/POS	TPR
1953	Cle-A	4	3	0	0	0	0	0	0	0	1	.000	.000	.000	-99	-1	0	0	0	1.000	-0	/C-4	-0.1

■ JOE AYRAULT Ayrault, Joseph Allen b: 10/8/71, Rochester, Mich. BR/TR, 6'3", 190 lbs. Deb: 9/1/96

YEAR	TM/L	G	AB	R	H	2B	3B	HR	RBI	BB	SO	AVG	OBP	SLG	PRO+	BR/A	SB	CS	SBR	FA	FR	G/POS	TPR
1996	Atl-N	7	5	0	1	0	0	0	0	0	1	.200	.333	.200	43	-0	0	0	0	1.000	0	/C-7	0.0

■ JOE AZCUE Azcue, Jose Joaquin (Lopez) b: 8/18/39, Cienfuegos, Cuba BR/TR, 6', 200 lbs. Deb: 8/3/60

YEAR	TM/L	G	AB	R	H	2B	3B	HR	RBI	BB	SO	AVG	OBP	SLG	PRO+	BR/A	SB	CS	SBR	FA	FR	G/POS	TPR
1960	Cin-N	14	31	1	3	0	0	0	3	2	6	.097	.152	.097	-30	-5	0	1	-1	1.000	5	C-14	0.0
1962	KC-A	72	223	18	51	9	1	2	25	17	27	.229	.292	.305	58	-13	1	1	0	.985	3	C-70	-0.7
1963	KC-A	2	4	0	0	0	0	0	0	0	1	.000	.000	.000	-95	-1	0	0	0	1.000	0	/C-1	-0.1
	Cle-A	94	320	26	91	16	0	14	46	15	46	.284	.316	.466	117	6	1	1	-0	.992	5	C-91	1.4
	Yr	96	324	26	91	16	0	14	46	15	47	.281	.313	.460	114	5	1	1	-0	.992	5	C-92	1.3
1964	Cle-A	83	271	20	74	9	1	4	34	16	38	.273	.318	.358	88	-4	0	2	-1	.993	-0	C-76	-0.2
1965	Cle-A	111	335	16	77	7	0	2	35	27	54	.230	.293	.269	60	-17	2	1	0	.994	-1	*C-108	-1.3
1966	Cle-A	98	302	22	83	10	1	9	37	20	22	.275	.324	.404	108	3	0	2	-1	.989	-8	C-97	-0.1
1967	Cle-A	86	295	33	74	12	5	11	34	22	35	.251	.309	.437	117	5	0	3	-2	**.999**	5	C-86	1.5
1968	Cle-A★	115	357	23	100	10	0	4	42	28	33	.280	.332	.342	106	3	1	1	-0	**.996**	11	C-97	2.2
1969	Cle-A	7	24	1	7	0	0	1	1	4	3	.292	.393	.417	122	1	0	0	0	.980	2	/C-6	0.3
	Bos-A	19	51	7	11	2	0	0	3	4	5	.216	.273	.255	46	-4	0	0	0	.981	3	C-19	0.0
	Cal-A	80	248	15	54	6	0	1	19	27	28	.218	.300	.254	59	-13	0	1	-1	.992	5	C-80	-0.5
	Yr	106	323	23	72	8	0	2	23	35	36	.223	.303	.266	62	-16	0	1	-1	.989	9	*C-105	-0.2
1970	Cal-A	114	351	19	85	13	1	2	25	24	40	.242	.294	.302	67	-16	0	0	0	.991	-5	*C-112	-1.7
1972	Cal-A	3	2	0	0	0	0	0	0	0	1	.000	.000	.000	-99	-1	0	0	0	1.000	1	/C-2	0.0
	Mil-A	11	14	0	2	0	0	0	0	1	5	.143	.200	.143	3	-2	0	0	0	1.000	2	/C-9	0.0
	Yr	14	16	0	2	0	0	0	0	1	6	.125	.176	.125	-10	-2	0	0	0	1.000	2	C-11	0.0
Total	11	909	2828	201	712	94	9	50	304	207	344	.252	.307	.344	85	-58	5	12	-6	.992	26	C-868	0.8

■ OSCAR AZOCAR Azocar, Oscar Gregorio (Azocar) b: 2/21/65, Soro, Venez. BL/TL, 6'1", 170 lbs. Deb: 7/17/90

YEAR	TM/L	G	AB	R	H	2B	3B	HR	RBI	BB	SO	AVG	OBP	SLG	PRO+	BR/A	SB	CS	SBR	FA	FR	G/POS	TPR
1990	NY-A	65	214	18	53	8	0	5	19	2	15	.248	.258	.355	70	-9	7	0	2	.991	0	O-57/D-1	-0.9
1991	SD-N	38	57	5	14	2	0	0	9	1	9	.246	.271	.281	54	-3	2	0	1	.875	-3	O-13/1-1	-0.6
1992	SD-N	99	168	15	32	6	0	0	8	9	12	.190	.232	.226	30	-15	1	0	0	.942	-1	O-37	-1.8
Total	3	202	439	38	99	16	0	5	36	12	36	.226	.249	.296	52	-28	10	0	3	.964	-4	O-107/1-1,D-1	-3.3

■ CHARLIE BABB Babb, Charles Amos b: 2/20/1873, Milwaukie, Ore. d: 3/20/54, Portland, Ore. BB/TR, 5'10", 165 lbs. Deb: 4/17/03

YEAR	TM/L	G	AB	R	H	2B	3B	HR	RBI	BB	SO	AVG	OBP	SLG	PRO+	BR/A	SB	CS	SBR	FA	FR	G/POS	TPR
1903	NY-N	121	424	68	105	15	8	0	46	45		.248	.350	.321	88	-5	22			.912	-2	*S-113/3-8	-0.1
1904	Bro-N	151	521	49	138	18	3	0	53	53		.265	.345	.311	106	6	34			.927	-3	*S-151	0.7
1905	Bro-N	75	235	27	44	8	2	0	17	27		.187	.303	.238	67	-8	10			.923	-2	S-36,1-31/3-5,2-2	-1.1
Total	3	347	1180	144	287	41	13	0	116	125		.243	.339	.300	92	-7	66			.921	-7	S-300/1-31,3-13,2-2	-0.5

■ LOREN BABE Babe, Loren Rolland "Bee Bee" b: 1/11/28, Pisgah, Iowa d: 2/14/84, Omaha, Neb. BL/TR, 5'10", 180 lbs. Deb: 8/19/52 C

YEAR	TM/L	G	AB	R	H	2B	3B	HR	RBI	BB	SO	AVG	OBP	SLG	PRO+	BR/A	SB	CS	SBR	FA	FR	G/POS	TPR
1952	NY-A	12	21	1	2	1	0	0	0	4	4	.095	.240	.143	9	-3	1	0	0	.909	2	/3-9	-0.1
1953	NY-A	5	18	2	6	1	0	2	6	0	2	.333	.333	.722	185	2	0	0	0	.920	3	/3-5	0.5
	Phi-A	103	343	34	77	16	2	0	20	35	20	.224	.300	.283	56	-21	0	1	-1	.950	1	3-93/S-1	-2.2

YEAR	TM/L	G	AB	R	H	2B	3B	HR	RBI	BB	SO	AVG	OBP	SLG	PRO+	BR/A	SB	CS	SBR	FA	FR	G/POS	TPR
	Yr	108	361	36	83	17	2	2	26	35	22	.230	.302	.305	62	-19	0	1	-1	.948	5	3-98/S-1	-1.7
Total	2	120	382	37	85	18	2	2	26	39	26	.223	.298	.296	59	-21	1	1	-0	.946	6	3-107/S-1	-1.8

■ CHARLIE BABINGTON Babington, Charles Percy b: 5/4/1895, Cranston, R.I. d: 3/22/57, Providence, R.I. BR/TR, 6′, 170 lbs. Deb: 7/20/15

YEAR	TM/L	G	AB	R	H	2B	3B	HR	RBI	BB	SO	AVG	OBP	SLG	PRO+	BR/A	SB	CS	SBR	FA	FR	G/POS	TPR
1915	NY-N	28	33	5	8	3	1	0	2	0	4	.242	.265	.394	104	-0	1			.909	-5	O-12/1-1	-0.6

■ SHOOTY BABITT Babitt, Mack Neal b: 3/9/59, Oakland, Cal. BR/TR, 5′8″, 174 lbs. Deb: 4/9/81

YEAR	TM/L	G	AB	R	H	2B	3B	HR	RBI	BB	SO	AVG	OBP	SLG	PRO+	BR/A	SB	CS	SBR	FA	FR	G/POS	TPR
1981	Oak-A	54	156	10	40	1	3	0	14	13	13	.256	.314	.301	82	-4	5	4	-1	.972	-17	2-52	-2.0

■ WALLY BACKMAN Backman, Walter Wayne b: 9/22/59, Hillsboro, Ore. BB/TR, 5′9″, 160 lbs. Deb: 9/2/80

YEAR	TM/L	G	AB	R	H	2B	3B	HR	RBI	BB	SO	AVG	OBP	SLG	PRO+	BR/A	SB	CS	SBR	FA	FR	G/POS	TPR
1980	NY-N	27	93	12	30	1	1	0	9	11	14	.323	.400	.355	115	3	2	3	-1	1.000	-10	2-20/S-8	-0.7
1981	NY-N	26	36	5	10	2	0	0	0	4	7	.278	.350	.333	96	-0	1	0	0	.946	-3	2-11/3-1	-0.3
1982	NY-N	96	261	37	71	13	2	3	22	49	47	.272	.387	.372	114	7	8	7	-2	.964	-13	2-88/3-6,S-1	-0.5
1983	NY-N	26	42	6	7	0	1	0	3	2	8	.167	.205	.214	16	-5	0	0	0	1.000	-2	2-14/3-2	-0.7
1984	NY-N	128	436	68	122	19	2	1	26	56	63	.280	.362	.339	99	2	32	9	4	.981	-12	*2-115/S-8	-0.2
1985	NY-N	145	520	77	142	24	5	1	38	36	72	.273	.321	.344	88	-8	30	12	2	**.989**	-9	*2-140/S-1	-1.2
1986	*NY-N	124	387	67	124	18	2	1	27	36	32	.320	.378	.385	114	8	13	7	-0	.966	-3	*2-113	0.9
1987	NY-N	94	300	43	75	6	1	1	23	25	43	.250	.308	.287	62	-16	11	3	2	.983	-7	2-87	-1.8
1988	*NY-N	99	294	44	89	12	0	0	17	41	49	.303	.390	.344	118	9	9	5	-0	.989	-9	2-92	0.3
1989	Min-A	87	299	33	69	9	2	1	26	32	45	.231	.307	.284	63	-14	1	1	-0	.982	-22	2-84/D-1	-3.5
1990	*Pit-N	104	315	62	92	21	3	2	28	42	53	.292	.377	.397	118	9	6	3	0	.920	-19	3-71,2-15	-1.0
1991	Phi-N	94	185	20	45	12	0	0	15	30	30	.243	.349	.308	87	-2	3	2	-0	.981	-15	2-36,3-20	-1.7
1992	Phi-N	42	48	6	13	1	0	0	6	6	9	.271	.352	.292	84	-1	1	0	0	.968	0	2-10/3-2	0.0
1993	Sea-A	10	29	2	4	0	0	0	0	1	8	.138	.167	.138	-17	-5	0	0	0	.857	-1	/3-9,2-1	-0.5
Total	14	1102	3245	482	893	138	19	10	240	371	480	.275	.350	.339	94	-13	117	52	4	.980	-125	2-826,3-111/S-18,D	-10.9

■ EDDIE BACON Bacon, Edgar Suter b: 4/8/1895, Franklin Co., Ky. d: 10/2/63, Louisville, Ky. Deb: 8/13/17

YEAR	TM/L	G	AB	R	H	2B	3B	HR	RBI	BB	SO	AVG	OBP	SLG	PRO+	BR/A	SB	CS	SBR	FA	FR	G/POS	TPR
1917	Phi-A	4	6	1	3	1	0	0	2	0	0	.500	.500	.667	259	1	0			1.000	1	/P-1	0.0

■ ART BADER Bader, Arthur Herman b: 9/21/1886, St.Louis, Mo. d: 4/5/57, St.Louis, Mo. BR/TR, 5′9″, 160 lbs. Deb: 8/2/04

YEAR	TM/L	G	AB	R	H	2B	3B	HR	RBI	BB	SO	AVG	OBP	SLG	PRO+	BR/A	SB	CS	SBR	FA	FR	G/POS	TPR
1904	StL-A	2	3	0	0	0	0	0	0	1		.000	.250	.000	-19	-0	0			1.000	1	/O-1	0.0

■ RED BADGRO Badgro, Morris Hiram b: 12/1/02, Orillia, Wash. d: 7/13/98, Kent, Wash. BL/TR, 6′, 190 lbs. Deb: 6/20/29

YEAR	TM/L	G	AB	R	H	2B	3B	HR	RBI	BB	SO	AVG	OBP	SLG	PRO+	BR/A	SB	CS	SBR	FA	FR	G/POS	TPR
1929	StL-A	54	148	27	42	12	0	1	18	11	15	.284	.342	.385	84	-4	1	0	0	.983	-4	O-37	-0.9
1930	StL-A	89	234	30	56	18	3	1	27	13	27	.239	.285	.355	59	-15	3	5	-2	.952	0	O-61	-1.9
Total	2	143	382	57	98	30	3	2	45	24	42	.257	.307	.366	69	-19	4	5	-2	.962	-4	/O-98	-2.8

■ CARLOS BAERGA Baerga, Carlos Obed (Ortiz) b: 11/4/68, Santurce, P.R. BB/TR, 5′11″, 200 lbs. Deb: 4/14/90

YEAR	TM/L	G	AB	R	H	2B	3B	HR	RBI	BB	SO	AVG	OBP	SLG	PRO+	BR/A	SB	CS	SBR	FA	FR	G/POS	TPR
1990	Cle-A	108	312	46	81	17	2	7	47	16	57	.260	.304	.394	94	-3	0	2	-1	.944	-9	3-50,S-48/2-8	-1.2
1991	Cle-A	158	593	80	171	28	2	11	69	48	74	.288	.348	.398	105	4	3	2	-0	.944	11	3-89,2-75/S-2	1.7
1992	Cle-A★	161	657	92	205	32	1	20	105	35	76	.312	.359	.455	129	24	10	2	2	.979	8	*2-160/D-1	3.8
1993	Cle-A★	154	624	105	200	28	6	21	114	34	68	.321	.361	.486	126	21	15	4	2	.979	8	*2-150/D-4	3.4
1994	Cle-A	103	442	81	139	32	2	19	80	10	45	.314	.338	.525	118	10	8	2	1	.973	9	*2-102/D-1	2.2
1995	*Cle-A★	135	557	87	175	28	2	15	90	35	31	.314	.358	.452	108	6	11	2	2	.973	12	*2-134/D-1	2.6
1996	Cle-A	100	424	54	113	25	0	10	55	16	25	.267	.304	.396	76	-17	1	1	-0	.971	-3	*2-100	-1.2
	NY-N	26	83	5	16	3	0	2	11	5	2	.193	.256	.301	48	-6	0	0	0	.990	-5	1-16/3-6,2-1	-1.3
1997	NY-N	133	467	53	131	25	1	9	52	20	54	.281	.314	.396	88	-10	2	6	-3	.978	4	*2-131	-0.1
1998	NY-N	147	511	46	136	27	1	7	53	24	55	.266	.307	.364	74	-20	0	1	-1	.986	-10	*2-144	-2.0
Total	9	1225	4670	649	1367	245	17	121	676	243	487	.293	.335	.430	103	9	50	22	2	.976	27	*2-1005,3-145/S1D	7.9

■ JOSE BAEZ Baez, Jose Antonio (b: Jose Antonio Mota (Baez)) b: 12/31/53, San Cristobal, D.R. BR/TR, 5′8″, 160 lbs. Deb: 4/6/77

YEAR	TM/L	G	AB	R	H	2B	3B	HR	RBI	BB	SO	AVG	OBP	SLG	PRO+	BR/A	SB	CS	SBR	FA	FR	G/POS	TPR
1977	Sea-A	91	305	39	79	14	1	1	17	19	20	.259	.305	.321	71	-12	6	1	1	.973	9	2-77/3-1,D-3	0.3
1978	Sea-A	23	50	8	8	0	1	0	2	6	7	.160	.250	.200	28	-5	1	0	0	.978	12	2-14/3-3,D-1	0.9
Total	2	114	355	47	87	14	2	1	19	25	27	.245	.297	.304	65	-17	7	1	2	.974	21	/2-91,D-4,3-4	1.2

■ KEVIN BAEZ Baez, Kevin Richard b: 1/10/67, Brooklyn, N.Y. BR/TR, 6′, 160 lbs. Deb: 9/3/90

YEAR	TM/L	G	AB	R	H	2B	3B	HR	RBI	BB	SO	AVG	OBP	SLG	PRO+	BR/A	SB	CS	SBR	FA	FR	G/POS	TPR
1990	NY-N	5	12	0	2	1	0	0	0	0	0	.167	.167	.250	13	-1	0	0	0	1.000	0	/S-4	-0.1
1992	NY-N	6	13	0	2	0	0	0	0	0	0	.154	.154	.154	-13	-2	0	0	0	.889	1	/S-5	-0.1
1993	NY-N	52	126	10	23	9	0	0	7	13	17	.183	.259	.254	38	-11	0	0	0	.967	-5	S-52	-1.2
Total	3	63	151	10	27	10	0	0	7	13	17	.179	.244	.245	33	-14	0	0	0	.962	-4	/S-61	-1.4

■ JEFF BAGWELL Bagwell, Jeffery Robert b: 5/27/68, Boston, Mass. BR/TR, 6′, 195 lbs. Deb: 4/8/91

YEAR	TM/L	G	AB	R	H	2B	3B	HR	RBI	BB	SO	AVG	OBP	SLG	PRO+	BR/A	SB	CS	SBR	FA	FR	G/POS	TPR
1991	Hou-N	156	554	79	163	26	4	15	82	75	116	.294	.391	.437	141	32	7	4	-0	.991	-1	*1-155	2.1
1992	Hou-N	162	586	87	160	34	6	18	96	84	97	.273	.375	.444	137	31	10	6	-1	.995	7	*1-159	2.7
1993	Hou-N	142	535	76	171	37	4	20	88	62	73	.320	.393	.516	146	35	13	4	2	.993	6	*1-140	3.1
1994	Hou-N★	110	400	**104**	147	32	2	39	**116**	65	65	.368	**.461**	**.750**	**220**	**71**	15	4	2	.991	17	*1-109/O-1	**7.6**
1995	Hou-N	114	448	88	130	29	0	21	87	79	102	.290	.403	.496	145	32	12	5	1	.994	18	*1-114	3.8
1996	Hou-N★	162	568	111	179	**48**	2	31	120	135	114	.315	.454	.570	182	75	21	7	2	.989	8	*1-162	6.6
1997	*Hou-N★	162	566	109	162	40	2	43	135	127	122	.286	.430	.592	171	63	31	10	3	.993	7	*1-159/D-1	5.6
1998	*Hou-N	147	540	124	164	33	1	34	111	109	90	.304	.427	.557	156	49	19	7	2	.995	9	*1-147	4.5
Total	8	1155	4197	778	1276	279	21	221	835	736	779	.304	.416	.538	161	389	128	47	10	.993	70	*1-1145/D-1,O-1	36.0

■ BILL BAGWELL Bagwell, William Mallory "Big Bill" b: 2/24/1896, Choudrant, La. d: 10/5/76, Choudrant, La. BL/TL, 6′1″, 175 lbs. Deb: 4/17/23

YEAR	TM/L	G	AB	R	H	2B	3B	HR	RBI	BB	SO	AVG	OBP	SLG	PRO+	BR/A	SB	CS	SBR	FA	FR	G/POS	TPR
1923	Bos-N	56	93	8	27	4	2	2	10	6	12	.290	.333	.441	107	1	0	0	0	1.000	-3	O-22	-0.3
1925	Phi-A	36	50	4	15	2	1	0	10	2	2	.300	.327	.380	74	-2	0	0	0	.667	-2	/O-4	-0.4
Total	2	92	143	12	42	6	3	2	20	8	14	.294	.331	.420	95	-2	0	0	0	.973	-5	/O-26	-0.7

■ FRANK BAHRET Bahret, Frank F. b: 1858, Poughkeepsie, N.Y. d: 3/30/1888, Poughkeepsie, N.Y. 6′1″, 184 lbs. Deb: 4/17/1884

YEAR	TM/L	G	AB	R	H	2B	3B	HR	RBI	BB	SO	AVG	OBP	SLG	PRO+	BR/A	SB	CS	SBR	FA	FR	G/POS	TPR
1884	Bal-U	2	8	0	0	0	0	0		0		.000	.000	.000	-91	-2				1.000	0	/O-2	-0.2

■ GENE BAILEY Bailey, Arthur Eugene b: 11/25/1893, Pearsall, Tex. d: 11/14/73, Houston, Tex. BR/TR, 5′8″, 160 lbs. Deb: 9/10/17

YEAR	TM/L	G	AB	R	H	2B	3B	HR	RBI	BB	SO	AVG	OBP	SLG	PRO+	BR/A	SB	CS	SBR	FA	FR	G/POS	TPR
1917	Phi-A	5	12	1	1	0	0	0	0	1	1	.083	.154	.083	-28	-2	0			.833	-1	/O-4	-0.4
1919	Bos-N	4	6	0	2	0	0	0	1	0	2	.333	.333	.333	105	0	1			1.000	0	/O-3	0.0
1920	Bos-N	13	24	2	2	0	0	0	0	3	3	.083	.185	.083	-22	-4	0	1	-1	.929	-2	/O-8	-0.8
	Bos-A	46	135	14	31	2	0	0	5	9	15	.230	.283	.244	42	-11	2	7	-4	.986	-4	O-40	-2.1
1923	Bro-N	127	411	71	109	11	7	1	42	43	34	.265	.343	.333	81	-10	9	7	-2	.959	2	*O-100/1-5	-1.5
1924	Bro-N	18	46	7	11	3	0	1	4	7	6	.239	.340	.370	93	-0	1	0	0	1.000	1	O-17	0.0
Total	5	213	634	95	156	16	7	2	52	63	61	.246	.321	.303	69	-27	13	15		.965	-5	O-172/1-5	-4.8

■ FRED BAILEY Bailey, Frederick Middleton "Penny" b: 8/16/1895, Mt.Hope, W.Va. d: 8/16/72, Huntington, W.Va. BL/TL, 5′11″, 150 lbs. Deb: 8/19/16

YEAR	TM/L	G	AB	R	H	2B	3B	HR	RBI	BB	SO	AVG	OBP	SLG	PRO+	BR/A	SB	CS	SBR	FA	FR	G/POS	TPR
1916	Bos-N	6	10	0	1	0	0	0	1	0	3	.100	.100	.100	-40	-2	0			1.000	-0	/O-2	-0.2
1917	Bos-N	50	110	9	21	2	1	1	5	9	25	.191	.270	.255	65	-4	3			.962	-1	O-27	-0.8
1918	Bos-N	4	4	1	1	0	0	0	0	0	1	.250	.250	.250	55	-0	0			.000	0	H	0.0
Total	3	60	124	10	23	2	1	1	6	9	29	.185	.257	.242	57	-6	3			.963	-2	/O-29	-1.0

■ BILL BAILEY Bailey, Harry Lewis b: 11/19/1881, Shawnee, Ohio d: 10/27/67, Seattle, Wash. BL/TR, 5′10.5″, 170 lbs. Deb: 4/21/11

YEAR	TM/L	G	AB	R	H	2B	3B	HR	RBI	BB	SO	AVG	OBP	SLG	PRO+	BR/A	SB	CS	SBR	FA	FR	G/POS	TPR
1911	NY-A	5	9	1	1	0	0	0	0	0		.111	.111	.111	-36	-2	0			.000	0	/O-2,3-1	-0.1

■ MARK BAILEY Bailey, John Mark b: 11/4/61, Springfield, Mo. BB/TR, 6′5″, 195 lbs. Deb: 4/27/84

YEAR	TM/L	G	AB	R	H	2B	3B	HR	RBI	BB	SO	AVG	OBP	SLG	PRO+	BR/A	SB	CS	SBR	FA	FR	G/POS	TPR
1984	Hou-N	108	344	38	73	16	1	9	34	53	71	.212	.321	.343	93	-3	0	1	-1	.983	-2	*C-108	0.0
1985	Hou-N	114	332	47	88	14	0	10	45	67	70	.265	.390	.398	124	14	0	2	-1	.979	-10	*C-110/1-2	0.8
1986	Hou-N	57	153	9	27	5	0	4	15	28	45	.176	.304	.288	66	-7	1	1	-0	.989	2	C-53/1-1	-0.3
1987	Hou-N	35	64	5	13	1	0	0	3	10	21	.203	.311	.219	45	-5	1	0	0	.985	-0	C-27	-0.4

YEAR	TM/L	G	AB	R	H	2B	3B	HR	RBI	BB	SO	AVG	OBP	SLG	PRO+	BR/A	SB	CS	SBR	FA	FR	G/POS	TPR
1988	Hou-N	8	23	1	3	0	0	0	0	5	6	.130	.286	.130	24	-2	0	1	-1	.981	-1	/C-8	-0.3
1990	SF-N	5	7	1	1	0	0	1	3	0	2	.143	.143	.571	90	-0	0	0	0	1.000	-0	/C-1	-0.1
1992	SF-N	13	26	0	4	1	0	0	1	3	7	.154	.241	.192	26	-3	0	0	0	1.000	-1	/C-7	-0.3
Total	7	340	949	101	209	37	1	24	101	166	222	.220	.338	.337	93	-5	2	5	-2	.983	-13	C-314/1-3	-0.6

■ ED BAILEY Bailey, Lonas Edgar b: 4/15/31, Strawberry Plains, Tenn. BL/TR, 6'2", 205 lbs. Deb: 9/26/53 F

YEAR	TM/L	G	AB	R	H	2B	3B	HR	RBI	BB	SO	AVG	OBP	SLG	PRO+	BR/A	SB	CS	SBR	FA	FR	G/POS	TPR
1953	Cin-N	2	8	1	3	1	0	0	1	1	3	.375	.444	.500	145	1	0	0	0	1.000	-1	/C-2	0.0
1954	Cin-N	73	183	21	36	2	3	9	20	35	34	.197	.326	.388	83	-5	1	0	0	.973	-12	C-61	-1.4
1955	Cin-N	21	39	3	8	1	1	1	4	4	10	.205	.326	.359	77	-1	0	0	0	.962	3	C-11	0.2
1956	Cin-N★	118	383	59	115	8	2	28	75	52	50	.300	.388	.551	140	22	2	0	1	.984	4	*C-106	3.1
1957	Cin-N★	122	391	54	102	15	2	20	48	73	69	.261	.380	.463	117	11	5	3	-0	.991	-12	*C-115	0.3
1958	Cin-N	112	360	39	90	23	1	11	59	47	61	.250	.338	.411	92	-4	2	2	-1	.988	-4	C-99	-0.3
1959	Cin-N	121	379	43	100	13	0	12	40	62	53	.264	.370	.393	101	2	2	0	1	.990	2	*C-117	1.1
1960	Cin-N★	133	441	52	115	19	3	13	67	59	70	.261	.351	.406	105	4	1	0	0	.990	-13	*C-129	-0.1
1961	Cin-N	12	43	4	13	4	0	0	2	3	5	.302	.348	.395	95	-0	0	0	0	.967	-4	C-12	-0.4
	SF-N☆	107	340	39	81	9	1	13	51	42	41	.238	.329	.385	92	-4	1	5	-3	.985	-1	*C-103/O-1	-0.2
	Yr	119	383	43	94	13	1	13	53	45	46	.245	.331	.386	93	-4	1	5	-3	.984	-5	*C-115/O-1	-0.6
1962	*SF-N	96	254	32	59	9	1	17	45	42	42	.232	.354	.476	123	8	1	1	-0	.987	-5	C-75	0.6
1963	SF-N★	105	308	41	81	8	0	21	68	50	64	.263	.368	.494	147	19	0	6	-4	.987	-0	C-88	2.0
1964	Mil-N	95	271	30	71	10	1	5	34	34	39	.262	.346	.362	99	1	2	0	1	.982	-10	C-80	-0.5
1965	SF-N	24	28	1	3	0	0	0	3	6	7	.107	.265	.107	9	-3	0	0	0	1.000	3	C-12/1-2	0.0
	Chi-N	66	150	13	38	6	0	5	23	34	28	.253	.391	.393	119	5	0	1	-1	.981	-5	C-54/1-3	0.2
	Yr	90	178	14	41	6	0	5	26	40	35	.230	.372	.348	102	2	0	1	-1	.984	-2	C-66/1-5	0.2
1966	Cal-A	5	3	0	0	0	0	0	0	1	1	.000	.250	.000	-22	-0	0	0	0	.000	0	H	0.0
Total	14	1212	3581	432	915	128	15	155	540	545	577	.256	.358	.429	110	56	17	18	-6	.986	-54	*C-1064/1-5,O-1	4.6

■ BOB BAILEY Bailey, Robert Sherwood b: 10/13/42, Long Beach, Cal. BR/TR, 6', 188 lbs. Deb: 9/14/62

YEAR	TM/L	G	AB	R	H	2B	3B	HR	RBI	BB	SO	AVG	OBP	SLG	PRO+	BR/A	SB	CS	SBR	FA	FR	G/POS	TPR
1962	Pit-N	14	42	6	7	2	1	0	6	6	10	.167	.271	.262	44	-3	1	1	-0	.921	0	3-12	-0.3
1963	Pit-N	154	570	60	130	15	3	12	45	58	98	.228	.305	.328	82	-13	10	9	-2	.933	6	*3-153/S-3	-1.0
1964	Pit-N	143	530	73	149	26	3	11	51	44	78	.281	.337	.404	108	6	10	8	-2	.943	6	*3-105,O-35/S-2	0.8
1965	Pit-N	159	626	87	160	28	3	11	49	70	93	.256	.330	.363	95	-3	10	14	-5	.939	-18	*3-142,O-28	-3.2
1966	Pit-N	126	380	51	106	19	3	13	46	47	65	.279	.361	.447	123	13	5	3	-0	.956	-0	3-96,O-20	1.0
1967	LA-N	116	322	21	73	8	2	4	28	40	50	.227	.314	.301	84	-6	5	5	-2	.941	0	3-65,O-27/1-4,S-1	-1.0
1968	LA-N	105	322	24	73	9	3	8	39	38	69	.227	.310	.348	105	2	1	2	-1	.953	-3	3-90/S-1,O-1	-0.2
1969	Mon-N	111	358	46	95	16	6	9	53	40	76	.265	.341	.419	111	5	3	3	-1	.992	4	1-85,O-12/3-1	0.1
1970	Mon-N	131	352	77	101	19	3	28	84	72	70	.287	.409	.597	166	34	5	3	-0	.953	-13	3-48,O-44,1-18	1.7
1971	Mon-N	157	545	65	137	21	4	14	83	97	105	.251	.364	.382	111	11	13	7	-0	**.960**	-15	*3-120,O-51/1-9	-0.8
1972	Mon-N	143	489	55	114	10	4	16	57	59	112	.233	.317	.368	92	-5	6	7	-2	.938	-8	*3-134/O-5,1-3	-1.7
1973	Mon-N	151	513	77	140	25	4	26	86	88	99	.273	.380	.489	134	25	5	8	-3	.956	-5	*3-146/O-2	1.7
1974	Mon-N	152	507	69	142	20	2	20	73	100	107	.280	.400	.446	129	23	4	7	-3	.974	-16	O-78,3-68	0.0
1975	Mon-N	106	227	23	62	5	0	5	30	46	38	.273	.398	.361	107	4	4	4	-1	.979	-5	O-61/3-3	-0.4
1976	Cin-N	69	124	17	37	6	1	6	23	16	26	.298	.379	.508	146	7	0	0	0	.974	-5	O-31,3-10	0.2
1977	Cin-N	49	79	9	20	2	1	2	11	12	10	.253	.352	.380	94	-0	1	1	-0	.975	-1	1-19/O-3	-0.2
	Bos-A	2	2	0	0	0	0	0	0	0	1	.000	.000	.000	-90	-1	0	0	0	.000	0	H	-0.1
1978	Bos-A	43	94	12	18	3	0	4	9	19	19	.191	.333	.351	84	-2	2	1	0	1.000	0	D-34/3-1,O-1	-0.3
Total	17	1931	6082	772	1564	234	43	189	773	852	1126	.257	.350	.403	111	97	85	83	-24	.946	-71	*3-1194,O-399,1/DS	-3.7

■ BOB BAILOR Bailor, Robert Michael b: 7/10/51, Connellsville, Pa. BR/TR, 5'11", 170 lbs. Deb: 9/6/75 C

YEAR	TM/L	G	AB	R	H	2B	3B	HR	RBI	BB	SO	AVG	OBP	SLG	PRO+	BR/A	SB	CS	SBR	FA	FR	G/POS	TPR
1975	Bal-A	5	7	0	1	0	0	0	0	1	0	.143	.250	.143	14	-1	0	0	0	1.000	2	/S-2,2-1	0.1
1976	Bal-A	9	6	2	2	0	1	0	0	0	0	.333	.333	.667	200	1	0	1	-1	.000	-0	/S-1,D-1	0.0
1977	Tor-A	122	496	62	154	21	5	5	32	17	26	.310	.336	.403	99	-1	15	6	1	.988	1	O-63,S-53/D-7	0.4
1978	Tor-A	154	621	74	164	29	7	1	52	38	21	.264	.312	.338	81	-16	5	6	-2	.964	15	*O-125,3-28/S-4	-0.8
1979	Tor-A	130	414	50	95	11	5	1	38	36	27	.229	.300	.287	59	-23	14	8	-1	.987	1	*O-118/3-9,D-1	-2.7
1980	Tor-A	117	347	44	82	14	2	1	16	36	33	.236	.312	.297	65	-16	12	8	-1	.991	12	O-98,S-12,3/P2D	-0.8
1981	NY-N	51	81	11	23	3	1	0	8	8	11	.284	.356	.346	101	0	2	0	1	.955	-5	S-22,2-13,O-13,/3-1	-0.2
1982	NY-N	110	376	44	104	14	1	0	31	20	17	.277	.317	.319	79	-10	20	3	4	.984	-19	S-60,2-56,3-21,/O-4	-2.1
1983	NY-N	118	340	33	85	8	0	1	30	20	23	.250	.294	.282	61	-18	18	3	4	.969	-6	S-75,2-50,3-11,/O-3	-1.4
1984	LA-N	65	131	11	36	4	0	0	8	8	1	.275	.317	.305	76	-4	3	1	0	.944	10	2-23,3-17,S-16	0.8
1985	*LA-N	74	118	8	29	3	1	0	7	3	5	.246	.270	.288	58	-7	1	0	0	.962	15	3-45,2-16/S-5,O-1	0.9
Total	11	955	2937	339	775	107	23	9	222	187	164	.264	.312	.325	76	-95	90	36	5	.980	26	O-425,S-250,23/DP	-5.8

■ HAROLD BAINES Baines, Harold Douglass b: 3/15/59, Easton, Md. BL/TL, 6'2", 195 lbs. Deb: 4/10/80

YEAR	TM/L	G	AB	R	H	2B	3B	HR	RBI	BB	SO	AVG	OBP	SLG	PRO+	BR/A	SB	CS	SBR	FA	FR	G/POS	TPR
1980	Chi-A	141	491	55	125	23	6	13	49	19	65	.255	.284	.405	87	-11	2	4	-2	.963	-7	*O-137/D-1	-2.4
1981	Chi-A	82	280	42	80	11	7	10	41	12	41	.286	.320	.482	131	10	6	2	1	.985	-0	O-80/D-1	0.8
1982	Chi-A	161	608	89	165	29	8	25	105	49	95	.271	.326	.469	115	11	10	3	1	.980	2	*O-161	1.0
1983	*Chi-A	156	596	76	167	33	2	20	99	49	85	.280	.336	.443	108	6	7	5	-1	.973	0	*O-155	0.1
1984	Chi-A	147	569	72	173	28	10	29	94	54	75	.304	.364	**.541**	141	30	1	2	-1	.981	0	*O-147	2.5
1985	Chi-A★	160	640	86	198	29	3	22	113	42	89	.309	.353	.467	118	15	1	1	-0	.994	7	*O-159/D-1	1.6
1986	Chi-A★	145	570	72	169	29	2	21	88	38	89	.296	.343	.465	114	10	2	1	0	.984	12	*O-141/D-3	1.7
1987	Chi-A★	132	505	59	148	26	4	20	93	46	82	.293	.353	.479	115	11	0	0	0	1.000	-1	*D-117/O-8	0.6
1988	Chi-A	158	599	55	166	39	1	13	81	67	109	.277	.351	.411	113	11	0	0	0	.882	-1	*D-147/O-9	0.6
1989	Chi-A★	96	333	55	107	20	1	13	56	60	52	.321	.426	.505	165	31	0	1	-1	.981	-0	D-70,O-25	2.8
	Tex-A	50	172	18	49	9	0	3	16	13	27	.285	.335	.390	102	0	0	2	-1	.667	-0	D-46/O-1	-0.2
	Yr	146	505	73	156	29	1	16	72	73	79	.309	.397	.465	144	31	0	3	-2	.964	-1	*D-116,O-26	2.6
1990	Tex-A	103	321	41	93	10	1	13	44	47	63	.290	.380	.449	131	14	0	1	-1	.833	0	D-95/O-2	1.1
	*Oak-A	32	94	11	25	5	0	3	21	20	17	.266	.395	.415	132	5	0	2	-1	.000	0	D-30	0.3
	Yr	135	415	52	118	15	1	16	65	67	80	.284	.384	.441	131	19	0	3	-2	.800	0	*D-125/O-2	1.4
1991	Oak-A★	141	488	76	144	25	1	20	90	72	67	.295	.387	.473	145	31	0	1	-1	.923	-2	*D-125,O-12	2.3
1992	*Oak-A	140	478	58	121	18	0	16	76	59	61	.253	.335	.391	109	5	1	3	-2	.964	-5	*D-116,O-23	-0.5
1993	Bal-A	118	416	64	130	22	0	20	78	57	52	.313	.395	.510	136	21	0	0	0	.000	0	*D-116	1.6
1994	Bal-A	94	326	44	96	12	1	16	54	30	49	.294	.356	.485	109	4	0	0	0	.000	0	D-91	-0.1
1995	Bal-A	127	385	60	115	19	1	24	63	70	45	.299	.407	.540	142	25	0	2	-1	.000	0	*D-122	1.5
1996	Chi-A	143	495	80	154	29	0	22	95	73	62	.311	.401	.503	133	26	3	1	0	.000	0	*D-141	1.6
1997	Chi-A	93	318	40	97	18	0	12	52	41	47	.305	.384	.475	128	14	0	1	-1	.000	0	D-86	0.8
	*Bal-A	44	134	15	39	5	0	4	15	14	15	.291	.358	.418	105	1	0	0	0	.000	-0	D-35/O-1	-0.1
	Yr	137	452	55	136	23	0	16	67	55	62	.301	.377	.458	121	15	0	1	-1	.000	-0	*D-121/O-1	0.7
1998	Bal-A	104	293	40	88	17	0	9	57	32	40	.300	.371	.451	115	7	0	0	0	.000	0	D-80	0.2
Total	19	2567	9111	1208	2649	456	48	348	1480	964	1327	.291	.360	.466	122	277	33	32	-9	.978	6	*D-1423,O-1061	17.8

■ AL BAIRD Baird, Albert Wells b: 6/2/1895, Cleburne, Tex. d: 11/27/76, Shreveport, La. BR/TR, 5'9", 160 lbs. Deb: 9/10/17

YEAR	TM/L	G	AB	R	H	2B	3B	HR	RBI	BB	SO	AVG	OBP	SLG	PRO+	BR/A	SB	CS	SBR	FA	FR	G/POS	TPR
1917	NY-N	10	24	1	7	0	0	0	4	2	2	.292	.346	.292	100	0	2			1.000	2	/2-7,S-3	0.2
1919	NY-N	38	83	8	20	1	0	0	5	5	9	.241	.284	.253	63	-4	3			.898	8	2-24/S-9,3-5	0.6
Total	2	48	107	9	27	1	0	0	9	7	11	.252	.298	.262	71	-4	5			.921	10	/2-31,S-12,3-5	0.8

■ DOUG BAIRD Baird, Howard Douglas b: 9/27/1891, St.Charles, Mo. d: 6/13/67, Thomasville, Ga. BR/TR, 5'9.5", 148 lbs. Deb: 4/18/15

YEAR	TM/L	G	AB	R	H	2B	3B	HR	RBI	BB	SO	AVG	OBP	SLG	PRO+	BR/A	SB	CS	SBR	FA	FR	G/POS	TPR
1915	Pit-N	145	512	49	112	26	12	1	53	37	88	.219	.277	.322	82	-12	29	12	2	.939	-1	*3-120,O-20/2-3	-0.8
1916	Pit-N	128	430	41	93	10	7	1	28	24	49	.216	.263	.279	66	-18	20	16	-4	.933	-5	3-80,2-29,O-16	-2.7
1917	Pit-N	43	135	17	35	6	1	0	18	20	19	.259	.355	.319	104	1	8			.935	-4	3-41/2-2	-0.2
	StL-N	104	364	38	92	19	12	0	24	23	52	.253	.301	.371	108	3	18			.941	13	*3-103/O-2	2.0
	Yr	147	499	55	127	25	13	0	42	43	71	.255	.316	.357	107	4	26			.940	9	*3-144/2-2,O-2	1.8
1918	StL-N	82	316	41	78	12	8	2	25	25	42	.247	.304	.354	104	1	25			.967	16	3-81/S-1,O-1	2.0

YEAR	TM/L	G	AB	R	H	2B	3B	HR	RBI	BB	SO	AVG	OBP	SLG	PRO+	BR/A	SB	CS	SBR	FA	FR	G/POS	TPR
1919	Phi-N	66	242	33	61	13	3	2	30	22	28	.252	.317	.355	95	-1	13			.950	11	3-66	1.3
	StL-N	16	33	4	7	0	1	0	4	2	3	.212	.257	.273	63	-2	2			.773	-4	/3-8,2-1,O-1	-0.6
	Bro-N	20	60	6	11	0	1	0	8	1	10	.183	.197	.217	24	-6	3			1.000	1	3-17	-0.4
	Yr	102	335	43	79	13	5	2	42	25	41	.236	.291	.322	81	-8	18			.946	8	3-91/2-1,O-1	0.3
1920	Bro-N	6	6	1	2	0	0	0	1	2	1	.333	.556	.333	154	1	0	0	0	.800	-0	/3-2	0.1
	NY-N	7	8	0	1	0	0	0	0	1	3	.125	.222	.125	1	-1	0	0	0	1.000	2	/3-4	0.1
	Yr	13	14	1	3	0	0	0	1	3	4	.214	.389	.214	76	-0	0	0	0	.929	1	/3-6	0.2
Total	6	617	2106	230	492	86	45	6	191	157	295	.234	.291	.326	88	-33	118	28		.944	28	3-522/O-40,2-35,S-1	0.8

■ **CHARLIE BAKER** Baker, Charles A. b: 1/15/1856, Sterling, Mass. d: 1/15/37, Manchester, N.H. BR/TR, 5′4″, 140 lbs. Deb: 8/1/1884

YEAR	TM/L	G	AB	R	H	2B	3B	HR	RBI	BB	SO	AVG	OBP	SLG	PRO+	BR/A	SB	CS	SBR	FA	FR	G/POS	TPR
1884	CP-U	15	57	5	8	2	0	1		0		.140	.140	.228	10	-8				.722	-1	O-11/S-3,2-1	-0.8

■ **CHUCK BAKER** Baker, Charles Joseph b: 12/6/52, Seattle, Wash. BR/TR, 5′11″, 180 lbs. Deb: 4/7/78

YEAR	TM/L	G	AB	R	H	2B	3B	HR	RBI	BB	SO	AVG	OBP	SLG	PRO+	BR/A	SB	CS	SBR	FA	FR	G/POS	TPR
1978	SD-N	44	58	8	12	1	0	0	3	2	15	.207	.233	.224	31	-5	0	0	0	.952	14	2-24,S-12	1.0
1980	SD-N	9	22	0	3	1	0	0	0	0	4	.136	.136	.182	-13	-3	0	0	0	.963	2	/S-8	-0.1
1981	Min-A	40	66	6	12	0	3	0	6	1	8	.182	.194	.273	31	-6	0	0	0	.969	7	S-31/2-3,3-1,D-1	0.3
Total	3	93	146	14	27	2	3	0	9	3	27	.185	.201	.240	25	-15	0	0	0	.962	22	/S-51,2-27,D-1,3-1	1.2

■ **DAVE BAKER** Baker, David Glenn b: 11/25/57, Lacona, Iowa BL/TR, 6′, 185 lbs. Deb: 9/12/82 F

YEAR	TM/L	G	AB	R	H	2B	3B	HR	RBI	BB	SO	AVG	OBP	SLG	PRO+	BR/A	SB	CS	SBR	FA	FR	G/POS	TPR
1982	Tor-A	9	20	3	5	1	0	0	2	3	3	.250	.400	.300	88	-0	0	0	0	.808	1	/3-8	0.0

■ **DEL BAKER** Baker, Delmer David b: 5/3/1892, Sherwood, Ore. d: 9/11/73, San Antonio, Tex. BR/TR, 5′11.5″, 176 lbs. Deb: 4/16/14 MC

YEAR	TM/L	G	AB	R	H	2B	3B	HR	RBI	BB	SO	AVG	OBP	SLG	PRO+	BR/A	SB	CS	SBR	FA	FR	G/POS	TPR
1914	Det-A	44	70	4	15	2	1	0	1	6	9	.214	.276	.271	63	-3	0	2	-1	.920	-6	C-38	-0.9
1915	Det-A	68	134	16	33	3	3	0	15	15	15	.246	.327	.313	87	-2	3	1	0	.940	-5	C-61	-0.3
1916	Det-A	61	98	7	15	4	0	0	6	11	8	.153	.245	.194	31	-8	2			.975	-2	C-59	-0.9
Total	3	173	302	27	63	9	4	0	22	32	32	.209	.289	.265	63	-13	5	3		.948	-12	C-158	-2.1

■ **DOUG BAKER** Baker, Douglas Lee b: 4/3/61, Fullerton, Cal. BB/TR, 5′9″, 165 lbs. Deb: 7/2/84 F

YEAR	TM/L	G	AB	R	H	2B	3B	HR	RBI	BB	SO	AVG	OBP	SLG	PRO+	BR/A	SB	CS	SBR	FA	FR	G/POS	TPR
1984	*Det-A	43	108	15	20	4	1	0	12	7	22	.185	.241	.241	34	-10	3	0	1	.969	2	S-39/2-5,D-1	-0.4
1985	Det-A	15	27	4	5	1	0	0	1	0	9	.185	.185	.222	11	-3	0	0	0	.960	-3	S-12/2-1	-0.5
1986	Det-A	13	24	1	3	1	0	0	0	2	7	.125	.192	.167	-1	-3	0	0	0	.970	2	S-10/2-2,D-1	-0.1
1987	Det-A	8	1	0	0	0	0	0	0	0	1	.000	.000	.000	-99	-0	0	0	0	1.000	3	/S-6,2-1,3-1	0.2
1988	Min-A	11	7	1	0	0	0	0	0	0	5	.000	.000	.000	-97	-2	0	0	0	1.000	1	/S-9,2-1,3-1	0.0
1989	Min-A	43	78	17	23	5	1	0	9	9	18	.295	.382	.385	109	1	0	0	0	.982	-2	2-25,S-19/D-1	0.1
1990	Min-A	3	1	0	0	0	0	0	0	0	0	.000	.000	.000	-94	-0	0	0	0	1.000	1	/2-3	0.0
Total	7	136	246	38	51	11	2	0	22	18	62	.207	.270	.268	49	-17	3	0	1	.973	5	/S-95,2-38,D-3,3-2	-0.7

■ **GENE BAKER** Baker, Eugene Walter b: 6/15/25, Davenport, Iowa BR/TR, 6′1″, 170 lbs. Deb: 9/20/53 C

YEAR	TM/L	G	AB	R	H	2B	3B	HR	RBI	BB	SO	AVG	OBP	SLG	PRO+	BR/A	SB	CS	SBR	FA	FR	G/POS	TPR
1953	Chi-N	7	22	1	5	1	0	0	0	1	4	.227	.261	.273	39	-2	1	0	0	.917	-3	/2-6	-0.4
1954	Chi-N	135	541	68	149	32	5	13	61	47	55	.275	.336	.425	96	-4	4	5	-2	.967	-3	*2-134	0.0
1955	Chi-N★	154	609	82	163	29	7	11	52	49	57	.268	.324	.392	89	-10	9	7	-2	.967	7	*2-154	0.8
1956	Chi-N	140	546	65	141	23	3	12	57	39	54	.258	.311	.377	85	-12	4	3	-1	.969	17	*2-140	1.7
1957	Chi-N	12	44	4	11	3	1	1	10	6	3	.250	.353	.432	111	1	0	0	0	.867	-4	3-12	-0.3
	Pit-N	111	365	36	97	19	4	2	36	29	29	.266	.322	.356	84	-8	3	2	-0	.955	-4	3-60,S-28,2-13	-0.8
	Yr	123	409	40	108	22	5	3	46	35	32	.264	.325	.364	87	-7	3	2	-0	.942	-7	3-72,S-28,2-13	-1.1
1958	Pit-N	29	56	3	14	2	1	0	7	8	6	.250	.344	.321	80	-1	0	0	0	1.000	-1	3-11/2-3	-0.2
1960	*Pit-N	33	37	5	9	0	0	0	4	2	9	.243	.282	.243	45	-3	0	0	0	1.000	2	/3-7,2-1	-0.1
1961	Pit-N	9	10	1	1	0	0	0	0	3	2	.100	.308	.100	15	-1	0	0	0	1.000	1	/3-3	0.0
Total	8	630	2230	265	590	109	21	39	227	184	219	.265	.323	.385	88	-40	21	17	-4	.968	12	2-451/3-93,S-28	0.7

■ **FLOYD BAKER** Baker, Floyd Wilson b: 10/10/16, Luray, Va. BL/TR, 5′9″, 160 lbs. Deb: 5/4/43 C

YEAR	TM/L	G	AB	R	H	2B	3B	HR	RBI	BB	SO	AVG	OBP	SLG	PRO+	BR/A	SB	CS	SBR	FA	FR	G/POS	TPR
1943	StL-A	22	46	5	8	2	0	0	4	6	4	.174	.269	.217	42	-3	0	1	-1	.961	0	S-10/3-1	-0.3
1944	*StL-A	44	97	10	17	3	0	0	5	11	5	.175	.259	.206	32	-8	2	0	1	.979	-3	2-17,S-16	-1.0
1945	Chi-A	82	208	22	52	8	0	0	19	23	12	.250	.325	.288	81	-5	3	2	-0	.971	2	3-58,2-11	-0.2
1946	Chi-A	9	24	2	6	1	0	0	3	2	3	.250	.308	.292	71	-1	0	0	0	.962	1	/3-6	0.1
1947	Chi-A	105	371	61	98	12	3	0	22	66	28	.264	.375	.313	96	1	9	7	-2	.980	18	*3-101/2-1,S-1	1.9
1948	Chi-A	104	335	47	72	8	3	0	18	73	26	.215	.359	.257	68	-12	4	10	-5	.961	13	3-71,2-18/S-1	-0.4
1949	Chi-A	125	388	38	101	15	4	1	40	84	32	.260	.392	.327	94	1	3	1	0	**.977**	12	*3-122/S-3,2-1	1.1
1950	Chi-A	83	186	26	59	7	0	0	11	32	10	.317	.417	.355	102	3	1	1	-0	.987	3	3-53/2-3,O-2	0.4
1951	Chi-A	82	133	24	35	6	1	0	14	25	12	.263	.380	.323	93	-0	0	1	-1	.924	-1	3-44/2-5,S-3	-0.2
1952	Was-A	79	263	27	69	8	0	0	33	30	17	.262	.342	.293	81	-6	1	0	0	.994	-16	2-68/S-7,3-1	-1.9
1953	Was-A	9	7	0	0	0	0	0	0	1	0	.000	.222	.000	-37	-1	0	0	0	.000	-0	/3-1	-0.2
	Bos-A	81	172	22	47	4	2	0	24	24	10	.273	.365	.320	82	-3	0	2	-1	.963	1	3-37,2-16	-0.4
	Yr	90	179	22	47	4	2	0	24	25	10	.263	.359	.307	78	-5	0	2	-1	.952	0	3-38,2-16	-0.6
1954	Bos-A	21	20	1	4	2	0	0	3	0	1	.200	.200	.300	32	-2	0	0	0	.889	1	/3-7,2-1	-0.1
	Phi-N	23	22	0	5	0	0	0	0	5	4	.227	.370	.227	60	-1	0	0	0	1.000	4	/3-7,2-2	0.3
1955	Phi-N	5	8	0	0	0	0	0	0	0	1	.000	.000	.000	-99	-2	0	0	0	1.000	1	/3-1	-0.1
Total	13	874	2280	285	573	76	13	1	196	382	165	.251	.360	.297	82	-41	23	25	-8	.971	34	3-510,2-143/S-41,O	-1.0

■ **FRANK BAKER** Baker, Frank b: 1/11/44, Bartow, Fla. BL/TR, 5′10″, 180 lbs. Deb: 7/27/69

YEAR	TM/L	G	AB	R	H	2B	3B	HR	RBI	BB	SO	AVG	OBP	SLG	PRO+	BR/A	SB	CS	SBR	FA	FR	G/POS	TPR
1969	Cle-A	52	172	21	44	5	3	3	15	14	34	.256	.316	.372	89	-3	2	1	0	.950	1	O-46	-0.5
1971	Cle-A	73	181	18	38	12	1	1	23	12	34	.210	.263	.304	55	-11	1	3	-2	.985	-6	O-51	-2.3
Total	2	125	353	39	82	17	4	4	38	26	68	.232	.289	.337	71	-14	3	4	-2	.966	-6	/O-97	-2.8

■ **FRANK BAKER** Baker, Frank Watts b: 10/29/46, Meridian, Miss. BL/TR, 6′2″, 178 lbs. Deb: 8/9/70

YEAR	TM/L	G	AB	R	H	2B	3B	HR	RBI	BB	SO	AVG	OBP	SLG	PRO+	BR/A	SB	CS	SBR	FA	FR	G/POS	TPR
1970	NY-A	35	117	6	27	4	1	0	11	14	26	.231	.323	.282	72	-4	1	2	-1	.973	4	S-35	0.3
1971	NY-A	43	79	9	11	2	0	0	2	16	22	.139	.284	.165	32	-7	3	0	1	.949	11	S-38	0.9
1973	*Bal-A	44	63	10	12	1	2	1	11	7	7	.190	.271	.317	66	-3	0	0	0	.964	4	S-32/2-7,1-1,3-1	0.3
1974	*Bal-A	24	29	3	5	1	0	0	0	3	5	.172	.250	.207	34	-2	0	0	0	.842	2	S-17/2-3,3-1	0.0
Total	4	146	288	28	55	8	3	1	24	40	60	.191	.294	.250	56	-16	4	2	0	.953	20	S-122/2-10,3-2,1-1	1.5

■ **GEORGE BAKER** Baker, George F. b: 1859, St.Louis, Mo. Deb: 5/24/1883

YEAR	TM/L	G	AB	R	H	2B	3B	HR	RBI	BB	SO	AVG	OBP	SLG	PRO+	BR/A	SB	CS	SBR	FA	FR	G/POS	TPR
1883	Bal-a	7	22	0	5	0	0	0		0		.227	.227	.227	45	-1				.667	-3	/S-4,C-3,O-1	-0.3
1884	StL-U	80	317	39	52	6	0	0		5		.164	.177	.183	9	-44				**.897**	16	C-68/2-4,O-4,3-3,S	-1.9
1885	StL-N	38	131	5	16	0	0	0	5	9	28	.122	.179	.122	-1	-14				.865	-11	C-32/3-3,O-2,2-1	-2.1
1886	KC-N	1	4	1	1	0	0	0	0	0	1	.250	.250	.250	49	-0	0			.889	-0	/C-1	0.0
Total	4	126	474	45	74	6	0	0	5	14	29	.156	.180	.169	8	-60	0			.887	3	C-104/O-7,3-6,S2	-4.3

■ **HOWARD BAKER** Baker, Howard Francis b: 3/1/1888, Bridgeport, Conn. d: 1/16/64, Bridgeport, Conn. BR/TR, 5′11″, 175 lbs. Deb: 8/11/12

YEAR	TM/L	G	AB	R	H	2B	3B	HR	RBI	BB	SO	AVG	OBP	SLG	PRO+	BR/A	SB	CS	SBR	FA	FR	G/POS	TPR
1912	Cle-A	11	30	1	5	0	0	0	2	5		.167	.286	.167	29	-3	0			.964	-1	3-10	-0.4
1914	Chi-A	15	47	4	13	1	1	0	5	3	8	.277	.320	.340	100	-0	2	1	0	.879	-4	3-15	-0.5
1915	Chi-A	2	2	0	0	0	0	0	0	0	2	.000	.000	.000	-97	-0	0			.000	0	H	-0.1
	NY-N	1	3	0	0	0	0	0	0	0	0	.000	.000	.000	-99	-1	0			1.000	0	/3-1	-0.1
Total	3	29	82	5	18	1	1	0	7	8	10	.220	.289	.256	61	-4	2	1		.922	-6	/3-26	-1.1

■ **JACK BAKER** Baker, Jack Edward b: 5/4/50, Birmingham, Ala. BR/TR, 6′5″, 225 lbs. Deb: 9/11/76

YEAR	TM/L	G	AB	R	H	2B	3B	HR	RBI	BB	SO	AVG	OBP	SLG	PRO+	BR/A	SB	CS	SBR	FA	FR	G/POS	TPR
1976	Bos-A	12	23	1	3	0	0	1	2	1	5	.130	.167	.261	21	-2	0	0	0	.981	-0	/1-8,D-1	-0.3
1977	Bos-A	2	3	0	0	0	0	0	0	0	1	.000	.000	.000	-90	-1	0	0	0	.857	0	/1-1	-0.1
Total	2	14	26	1	3	0	0	1	2	1	6	.115	.148	.231	8	-3	0	0	0	.966	-0	/1-9,D-1	-0.4

■ **JESSE BAKER** Baker, Jesse (b: Michael Myron Silverman) b: 3/4/1895, Cleveland, Ohio d: 7/29/76, W.Los Angeles, Cal. BR/TR, 5′4″, 140 lbs. Deb: 9/14/19

YEAR	TM/L	G	AB	R	H	2B	3B	HR	RBI	BB	SO	AVG	OBP	SLG	PRO+	BR/A	SB	CS	SBR	FA	FR	G/POS	TPR
1919	Was-A	1	0	0	0	0	0	0	1	0	0	—	—	—	—	0	0			1.000	0	/S-1	0.0

YEAR	TM/L	G	AB	R	H	2B	3B	HR	RBI	BB	SO	AVG	OBP	SLG	PRO+	BR/A	SB	CS	SBR	FA	FR	G/POS	TPR
■ **FRANK BAKER**	Baker, John Franklin "Home Run" b: 3/13/1886, Trappe, Md. d: 6/28/63, Trappe, Md. BL/TR, 5'11", 173 lbs. Deb: 9/21/08 H																						
1908	Phi-A	9	31	5	9	3	0	0	2	0		.290	.290	.387	112	0	0			1.000	2	/3-9	0.3
1909	Phi-A	148	541	73	165	27	**19**	4	85	26		.305	.343	.447	146	25	20			.920	-9	*3-146	2.5
1910	*Phi-A	146	561	83	159	25	15	2	74	34		.283	.329	.392	127	15	21			.920	6	*3-146	2.7
1911	*Phi-A	148	592	96	198	42	14	**11**	115	40		.334	.379	.508	149	35	38			**.942**	-1	*3-148	3.6
1912	Phi-A	149	577	116	200	40	21	**10**	**130**	50		.347	.404	.541	176	54	40			.941	10	*3-149	6.3
1913	*Phi-A	149	564	116	190	34	9	**12**	**117**	63	31	.337	.413	.493	169	48	34			.921	8	*3-149	6.1
1914	*Phi-A	150	570	84	182	23	10	**9**	89	53	37	.319	.380	.442	153	35	19	20	-6	.955	10	*3-149	4.7
1916	NY-A	100	360	46	97	23	2	10	52	36	30	.269	.344	.428	129	11	15			.940	2	3-96	1.8
1917	NY-A	146	553	57	156	24	2	6	71	48	27	.282	.345	.365	116	10	18			.949	11	*3-146	2.6
1918	NY-A	126	504	65	154	24	5	6	62	38	13	.306	.357	.409	128	15	8			**.972**	11	*3-126	3.2
1919	NY-A	141	567	70	166	22	1	10	83	44	18	.293	.346	.388	105	3	13			.955	-2	*3-141	0.7
1921	*NY-A	94	330	46	97	16	2	9	71	26	12	.294	.353	.436	98	-2	8	5	-1	.959	-2	3-83	0.2
1922	*NY-A	69	234	30	65	12	3	7	36	15	14	.278	.327	.444	97	-2	1	3	-2	.962	-10	3-60	-0.9
Total	13	1575	5984	887	1838	315	103	96	987	473	182	.307	.363	.442	136	250	235	28		.943	36	*3-1548	33.8
■ **DUSTY BAKER**	Baker, Johnnie B b: 6/15/49, Riverside, Cal. BR/TR, 6'2", 187 lbs. Deb: 9/7/68 MC																						
1968	Atl-N	6	5	0	2	0	0	0	0	0	1	.400	.400	.400	140	0	0	0	0	.000	-1	/O-3	-0.1
1969	Atl-N	3	7	0	0	0	0	0	0	0	3	.000	.000	.000	-99	-2	0	0	0	1.000	-1	/O-3	-0.3
1970	Atl-N	13	24	3	7	0	0	0	4	2	4	.292	.346	.292	69	-1	0	0	0	.800	-2	O-11	-0.3
1971	Atl-N	29	62	2	14	2	0	0	4	1	14	.226	.238	.258	38	-5	0	1	-1	1.000	-2	O-18	-0.9
1972	Atl-N	127	446	62	143	27	2	17	76	45	68	.321	.388	.504	139	23	4	7	-3	.989	2	*O-123	1.7
1973	Atl-N	159	604	101	174	29	4	21	99	67	72	.288	.364	.454	116	14	24	3	5	.983	10	*O-156	2.3
1974	Atl-N	149	574	80	147	35	0	20	69	71	87	.256	.339	.422	107	5	18	7	1	.981	-18	*O-148	-1.9
1975	Atl-N	142	494	63	129	18	2	19	72	67	57	.261	.349	.421	109	6	12	7	-1	.990	7	*O-136	0.7
1976	LA-N	112	384	36	93	13	0	4	39	31	54	.242	.300	.307	74	-13	2	4	-2	.996	-1	*O-106	-2.1
1977	*LA-N	153	533	86	155	26	1	30	86	58	89	.291	.367	.512	134	25	2	6	-3	.987	-4	*O-152	1.2
1978	*LA-N	149	522	62	137	24	1	11	66	47	66	.262	.327	.375	96	-3	12	3	2	.985	5	*O-145	-0.2
1979	LA-N	151	554	86	152	29	1	23	88	56	70	.274	.342	.455	117	12	11	4	1	.990	13	*O-150	2.0
1980	LA-N	153	579	80	170	26	4	29	97	43	66	.294	.346	.503	137	26	12	10	-2	.991	6	*O-151	2.5
1981	*LA-N★	103	400	48	128	17	3	9	49	29	43	.320	.367	.445	134	17	10	7	-1	.990	1	*O-101	1.5
1982	LA-N★	147	570	80	171	19	1	23	88	56	62	.300	.366	.458	132	24	17	10	-1	.975	-7	*O-144	1.3
1983	*LA-N	149	531	71	138	25	1	15	73	72	59	.260	.350	.395	107	6	7	1	2	.981	-1	*O-143	0.2
1984	SF-N	100	243	31	71	7	2	3	32	40	27	.292	.392	.374	120	8	4	1	1	.974	-1	O-62	0.7
1985	Oak-A	111	343	48	92	15	1	14	52	50	47	.268	.361	.440	128	14	2	1	0	.993	-5	1-58,O-35,D-13	0.4
1986	Oak-A	83	242	25	58	8	0	4	19	27	37	.240	.316	.322	80	-6	0	1	-1	1.000	-3	O-55,D-15/1-3	-1.2
Total	19	2039	7117	964	1981	320	23	242	1013	762	926	.278	.351	.432	116	149	137	73	-3	.985	-2	*O-1842/1-61,D-28	7.5
■ **KIRTLEY BAKER**	Baker, Kirtley "Whitey" b: 6/24/1869, Aurora, Ind. d: 4/15/27, Covington, Ky. BR/TR, 5'9", 160 lbs. Deb: 5/7/1890																						
1890	Pit-N	26	68	6	10	0	0	0	0	10	6	.147	.275	.147	27	-6	1			.878	-0	P-25	0.0
1893	Bal-N	19	57	9	17	1	1	0	6	8	6	.298	.385	.351	94	-0	1			.930	5	P-15/O-3	0.2
1894	Bal-N	2	4	0	0	0	0	0	0	0	1	.000	.000	.000	-96	-1	0			1.000	1	/O-1,P-1	0.0
1898	Was-N	6	18	3	5	0	1	0	3	3		.278	.381	.389	121	1	0			1.000	-1	/P-6	0.0
1899	Was-N	12	19	1	3	0	0	0	1	1		.158	.200	.158	-1	-3	0			.862	2	P-11	0.0
Total	5	65	166	19	35	1	2	0	10	22	13	.211	.311	.241	57	-9	2			.895	7	/P-58,O-4	0.2
■ **PHIL BAKER**	Baker, Philip b: 9/19/1856, Philadelphia, Pa. d: 6/4/40, Washington, D.C. BL/TL, 5'8", 152 lbs. Deb: 5/1/1883																						
1883	Bal-a	28	121	22	33	2	1	1		8		.273	.318	.331	106	1				.883	-7	C-19,O-14/S-1	-0.4
1884	Was-U	86	371	75	107	12	5	1		11		.288	.309	.356	104	-9				.955	-10	1-39,O-32,C-27	-1.9
1886	Was-N	81	325	37	72	6	5	1	34	20	32	.222	.267	.280	70	-11	16			.967	-7	1-56,O-21/C-4	-2.3
Total	3	195	817	134	212	20	11	3	34	39	32	.259	.293	.322	91	-19	16			.963	-23	/1-95,O-67,C-50,S-1	-4.6
■ **TRACY BAKER**	Baker, Tracy Lee b: 11/7/1891, Pendleton, Ore. d: 3/14/75, Placerville, Cal. BR/TR, 6'1", 180 lbs. Deb: 6/19/11																						
1911	Bos-A	1	0	0	0	0	0	0	0	0		—	—	—	—	0	0			1.000	-0	/1-1	0.0
■ **BILL BAKER**	Baker, William Presley b: 2/22/11, Paw Creek, N.C. BR/TR, 6', 200 lbs. Deb: 5/4/40 C																						
1940	*Cin-N	27	69	5	15	1	1	0	7	4	8	.217	.260	.261	44	-5	2			1.000	4	C-24	0.0
1941	Cin-N	2	1	0	0	0	0	0	0	1	1	.000	.500	.000	49	0	0			1.000	0	/C-1	0.0
	Pit-N	35	67	5	15	3	0	0	6	11	0	.224	.333	.269	71	-2	0			.967	0	C-33	0.0
	Yr	37	68	5	15	3	0	0	6	12	1	.221	.338	.265	71	-2	0			.967	0	C-34	0.0
1942	Pit-N	18	17	1	2	0	0	0	2	1	0	.118	.167	.118	-16	-2	0			1.000	1	C-11	-0.1
1943	Pit-N	63	172	12	47	6	3	1	26	22	6	.273	.365	.360	106	2	3			.979	0	C-56	0.6
1946	Pit-N	53	113	7	27	4	0	1	8	12	6	.239	.312	.301	72	-4	0			.965	-6	C-41/1-1	-0.9
1948	StL-N	45	119	13	35	10	1	0	15	15	7	.294	.373	.395	102	1	1			.994	-1	C-36	0.2
1949	StL-N	20	30	2	4	1	0	0	4	2	2	.133	.188	.167	-4	-4	0			1.000	-2	C-10	-0.6
Total	7	263	588	45	145	25	5	2	68	68	30	.247	.328	.316	79	-15	6			.983	-3	C-212/1-1	-0.8
■ **PAUL BAKO**	Bako, Gabor Paul b: 6/20/72, Lafayette, La.. BL/TR, 6'2", 205 lbs. Deb: 4/30/98																						
1998	Det-A	96	305	23	83	12	1	3	30	23	82	.272	.323	.348	74	-11	1	1	-0	.989	-7	C-94	-1.2
■ **JOHN BALAZ**	Balaz, John Lawrence b: 11/24/50, Toronto, Ont., Can. BR/TR, 6'3", 180 lbs. Deb: 9/10/74																						
1974	Cal-A	14	42	4	10	0	0	1	5	2	10	.238	.289	.310	76	-1	0	0	0	1.000	-1	O-12	-0.3
1975	Cal-A	45	120	10	29	8	1	1	10	5	25	.242	.272	.350	80	-4	0	0	0	1.000	-0	O-27,D-11	-0.5
Total	2	59	162	14	39	8	1	2	15	7	35	.241	.276	.340	79	-5	0	0	0	1.000	-1	/O-39,D-11	-0.8
■ **STEVE BALBONI**	Balboni, Stephen Charles b: 1/16/57, Brockton, Mass. BR/TR, 6'3", 225 lbs. Deb: 4/22/81																						
1981	NY-A	4	7	2	2	1	1	0	2	1	4	.286	.375	.714	211	1	0	0	0	1.000	0	/1-3,D-1	0.1
1982	NY-A	33	107	8	20	2	1	2	4	6	34	.187	.230	.280	40	-9	0	0	0	.990	-1	1-26/D-5	-1.1
1983	NY-A	32	86	8	20	2	0	5	17	8	23	.233	.298	.430	101	-0	0	0	0	.984	-1	1-23/D-4	-0.2
1984	*KC-A	126	438	58	107	23	2	28	77	45	139	.244	.320	.498	122	11	0	0	0	.987	-5	*1-125/D-1	-0.1
1985	*KC-A	160	600	74	146	28	2	36	88	52	166	.243	.309	.477	111	7	1	1	-0	.993	-8	*1-160	-1.1
1986	KC-A	138	512	54	117	25	1	29	88	43	146	.229	.290	.451	96	-5	0	0	0	.987	-6	*1-137	-2.0
1987	KC-A	121	386	44	80	11	1	24	60	34	97	.207	.275	.427	80	-12	0	0	0	.989	1	1-55,D-52	-1.6
1988	KC-A	21	63	2	9	2	0	2	5	1	20	.143	.156	.270	17	-7	0	0	0	.980	-1	1-13/D-6	-0.9
	Sea-A	97	350	44	88	15	1	21	61	23	67	.251	.299	.480	110	3	0	1	-1	.994	-1	D-56,1-40	-0.4
	Yr	118	413	46	97	17	1	23	66	24	87	.235	.279	.448	96	-4	0	1	-1	.991	-2	D-62,1-53	-1.3
1989	NY-A	110	300	33	71	12	2	17	59	25	67	.237	.302	.460	113	4	0	0	0	.994	-2	D-82,1-20	-0.1
1990	NY-A	116	266	24	51	6	0	17	34	35	91	.192	.293	.406	93	-3	0	0	0	.984	-3	D-72,1-28	-1.0
1993	Tex-A	2	5	0	3	0	0	0	0	0	2	.600	.600	.600	233	1	0	0	0	.000	0	/D-2	0.1
Total	11	960	3120	351	714	127	11	181	495	273	856	.229	.295	.451	100	-9	1	2	-1	.989	-26	1-630,D-281	-8.3
■ **BOBBY BALCENA**	Balcena, Robert Rudolph b: 8/1/25, San Pedro, Cal. d: 1/4/90, San Pedro, Cal. BR/TL, 5'7", 160 lbs. Deb: 9/16/56																						
1956	Cin-N	7	2	2	0	0	0	0	0	0	1	.000	.000	.000	-94	-1	0	0	0	1.000	-1	/O-2	-0.1
■ **LADY BALDWIN**	Baldwin, Charles Busted b: 4/8/1859, Oramel, N.Y. d: 3/7/37, Hastings, Mich. BL/TL, 5'11", 160 lbs. Deb: 9/30/1884																						
1884	Mil-U	7	27	6	6	3	0	0		0		.222	.222	.333	122	-2				.778	0	/O-5,P-2	-0.1
1885	Det-N	31	124	12	30	6	3	0	18	6	22	.242	.277	.339	98	-0				.879	1	P-21,O-12	-0.1
1886	Det-N	57	204	25	41	6	3	0	25	18	44	.201	.266	.260	59	-10	3			.969	3	P-56/O-2	0.0
1887	*Det-N	24	85	15	23	0	1	0	7	10	6	.271	.354	.294	79	-2	4			.926	1	P-24	0.0
1888	Det-N	6	23	5	6	0	0	0	3	3	3	.261	.346	.261	96	0	0			1.000	-0	/P-6,O-1	0.0
1890	Bro-N	2	3	1	0	0	0	0	0	1	1	.000	.250	.000	-25	-0	0			.625	0	/P-2	0.0

YEAR	TM/L	G	AB	R	H	2B	3B	HR	RBI	BB	SO	AVG	OBP	SLG	PRO+	BR/A	SB	CS	SBR	FA	FR	G/POS	TPR
	Buf-P	7	28	4	8	1	0	0	2	2	1	.286	.333	.321	82	-1	0			1.000	-0	/P-7	0.0
Total	6	134	494	68	114	16	7	0	55	40	77	.231	.290	.291	76	-15	7			.934	6	P-118/O-20	-0.2

■ **KID BALDWIN** Baldwin, Clarence Geoghan b: 11/1/1864, Newport, Ky. d: 7/10/1897, Cincinnati, Ohio BR/TR, 5'6", 147 lbs. Deb: 7/27/1884

YEAR	TM/L	G	AB	R	H	2B	3B	HR	RBI	BB	SO	AVG	OBP	SLG	PRO+	BR/A	SB	CS	SBR	FA	FR	G/POS	TPR
1884	KC-U	50	191	19	37	6	3	0		4		.194	.210	.257	47	-18				.885	1	C-44,O-10/2-1,3-1	-1.3
	CP-U	1	1	0	1	0	0	0		0		1.000	1.000	1.000	511	0				1.000	-0	/C-1	0.0
	Yr	51	192	19	38	6	3	0		4		.198	.214	.260	49	-18				.885	0	C-45,O-10/2-1,3-1	-1.3
1885	Cin-a	34	126	9	17	1	0	1	8	3		.135	.155	.167	2	-14				.863	-2	C-25/O-6,2-2,P-2,3	-1.3
1886	Cin-a	87	315	41	72	8	7	3	32	8		.229	.252	.327	78	-9	12			.891	-6	C-71,3-13/O-6	-0.7
1887	Cin-a	96	388	46	98	15	10	1	57	6		.253	.271	.351	71	-17	13			.874	-2	*C-96/O-2	-0.8
1888	Cin-a	67	271	27	59	11	3	1	25	3		.218	.235	.292	65	-12	4			.918	-2	C-65/O-2,1-1	-0.7
1889	Cin-a	60	223	34	55	14	2	1	34	5	32	.247	.273	.341	72	-9	7			.912	2	C-55/O-4,3-1,1-1	-0.2
1890	Cin-N	22	72	5	11	0	0	0	10	3	6	.153	.187	.153	-1	-9	2			.902	3	C-20/O-2	-0.4
	Phi-a	24	90	5	21	1	2	0	12	4		.233	.274	.289	67	-4	2			.887	1	C-19/3-5	-0.1
Total	7	441	1677	186	371	56	27	7	178	36	38	.221	.243	.299	61	-93	40			.893	-6	C-396/O-32,321P	-5.5

■ **FRANK BALDWIN** Baldwin, Frank De Witt b: 12/25/28, High Bridge, N.J. BR/TR, 5'11", 195 lbs. Deb: 4/22/53

YEAR	TM/L	G	AB	R	H	2B	3B	HR	RBI	BB	SO	AVG	OBP	SLG	PRO+	BR/A	SB	CS	SBR	FA	FR	G/POS	TPR
1953	Cin-N	16	20	0	2	0	0	0	0	1	9	.100	.143	.100	-35	-4	0	0	0	1.000	-1	/C-6	-0.5

■ **HENRY BALDWIN** Baldwin, Henry Clay "Ted" b: 6/13/1894, Chadds Ford, Pa. d: 2/24/64, West Chester, Pa. BR/TR, 5'11", 180 lbs. Deb: 5/22/27

YEAR	TM/L	G	AB	R	H	2B	3B	HR	RBI	BB	SO	AVG	OBP	SLG	PRO+	BR/A	SB	CS	SBR	FA	FR	G/POS	TPR
1927	Phi-N	6	16	1	5	0	0	0	1	1	2	.313	.353	.313	78	-0	0			.857	-2	/S-3,3-2	-0.2

■ **JEFF BALDWIN** Baldwin, Jeffrey Allen b: 9/5/65, Milford, Del. BL/TL, 6'1", 180 lbs. Deb: 5/22/90

YEAR	TM/L	G	AB	R	H	2B	3B	HR	RBI	BB	SO	AVG	OBP	SLG	PRO+	BR/A	SB	CS	SBR	FA	FR	G/POS	TPR
1990	Hou-N	7	8	1	0	0	0	0	0	1	2	.000	.111	.000	-69	-2	0	0	0	1.000	-1	/O-3	-0.3

■ **REGGIE BALDWIN** Baldwin, Reginald Conrad b: 8/19/54, River Rouge, Mich. BR/TR, 6'1", 195 lbs. Deb: 5/25/78

YEAR	TM/L	G	AB	R	H	2B	3B	HR	RBI	BB	SO	AVG	OBP	SLG	PRO+	BR/A	SB	CS	SBR	FA	FR	G/POS	TPR
1978	Hou-N	38	67	5	17	5	0	1	11	3	3	.254	.286	.373	89	-1	0	0	0	.955	-1	C-17	-0.2
1979	Hou-N	14	20	0	4	1	0	0	1	0	1	.200	.200	.250	23	-2	0	0	0	1.000	-1	/C-3,1-1	-0.3
Total	2	52	87	5	21	6	0	1	12	3	4	.241	.267	.345	74	-4	0	0	0	.956	-2	/C-20,1-1	-0.5

■ **BILLY BALDWIN** Baldwin, Robert Harvey b: 6/9/51, Tazewell, Va. BL/TL, 6', 175 lbs. Deb: 7/29/75

YEAR	TM/L	G	AB	R	H	2B	3B	HR	RBI	BB	SO	AVG	OBP	SLG	PRO+	BR/A	SB	CS	SBR	FA	FR	G/POS	TPR
1975	Det-A	30	95	8	21	3	0	4	8	5	14	.221	.260	.379	75	-3	2	1	0	.983	2	O-25/D-1	-0.3
1976	NY-N	9	22	4	6	1	1	1	5	1	2	.273	.304	.545	146	1	0	0	0	.929	1	/O-5	0.2
Total	2	39	117	12	27	4	1	5	13	6	16	.231	.268	.410	87	-2	2	1	0	.972	3	/O-30,D-1	-0.1

■ **MIKE BALENTI** Balenti, Michael Richard b: 7/3/1886, Calumet, Okla. d: 8/4/55, Altus, Okla. BR/TR, 5'11", 175 lbs. Deb: 7/19/11

YEAR	TM/L	G	AB	R	H	2B	3B	HR	RBI	BB	SO	AVG	OBP	SLG	PRO+	BR/A	SB	CS	SBR	FA	FR	G/POS	TPR
1911	Cin-N	8	8	2	2	0	0	0	0	0	1	.250	.250	.250	42	-1	3			.857	0	/S-2,O-1	0.0
1913	StL-A	70	211	17	38	2	4	0	11	6	32	.180	.206	.227	28	-20	3			.923	1	S-56/O-8	-1.6
Total	2	78	219	19	40	2	4	0	11	6	33	.183	.208	.228	28	-21	6			.922	1	/S-58,O-9	-1.6

■ **LEE BALES** Bales, Wesley Owen b: 12/4/44, Los Angeles, Cal. BB/TR, 5'10.5", 165 lbs. Deb: 8/7/66

YEAR	TM/L	G	AB	R	H	2B	3B	HR	RBI	BB	SO	AVG	OBP	SLG	PRO+	BR/A	SB	CS	SBR	FA	FR	G/POS	TPR
1966	Atl-N	12	16	4	1	0	0	0	0	0	5	.063	.063	.063	-64	-3	0	0	0	1.000	3	/2-7,3-3	0.0
1967	Hou-N	19	27	4	3	0	0	0	2	8	7	.111	.314	.111	28	-2	1	1	-0	.944	-2	/2-6,S-1	-0.4
Total	2	31	43	8	4	0	0	0	2	8	12	.093	.235	.093	-3	-6	1	1	-0	.978	1	/2-13,3-3,S-1	-0.4

■ **ART BALL** Ball, Arthur Clark b: 4/1876, Kentucky d: 12/26/15, Chicago, Ill. TR , 168 lbs. Deb: 8/1/1894

YEAR	TM/L	G	AB	R	H	2B	3B	HR	RBI	BB	SO	AVG	OBP	SLG	PRO+	BR/A	SB	CS	SBR	FA	FR	G/POS	TPR
1894	StL-N	1	3	0	1	0	0	0	0	0	1	.333	.333	.333	61	-0	0			.667	-1	/2-1	-0.1
1898	Bal-N	32	81	7	15	2	0	0	8	7		.185	.258	.210	34	-7	2			.906	9	3-15,S-14/2-2,O-1	0.2
Total	2	33	84	7	16	2	0	0	8	7	1	.190	.261	.214	35	-7	2			.929	8	/3-15,S-14,2-3,O-1	0.1

■ **NEAL BALL** Ball, Cornelius b: 4/22/1881, Grand Haven, Mich. d: 10/15/57, Bridgeport, Conn. BR/TR, 5'7", 145 lbs. Deb: 9/12/07

YEAR	TM/L	G	AB	R	H	2B	3B	HR	RBI	BB	SO	AVG	OBP	SLG	PRO+	BR/A	SB	CS	SBR	FA	FR	G/POS	TPR
1907	NY-A	15	44	5	9	1	1	0	4	1		.205	.222	.273	53	-2	1			.817	-3	S-11/2-5	-0.6
1908	NY-A	132	446	34	110	16	2	0	38	21		.247	.284	.291	86	-7	32			.898	-6	*S-130/2-1	-1.3
1909	NY-A	8	29	5	6	1	1	0	3	3		.207	.281	.310	86	-0	2			.917	-3	/2-8	-0.5
	Cle-A	96	324	29	83	13	2	1	25	17		.256	.295	.318	90	-4	17			.914	-11	S-95	-1.5
	Yr	104	353	34	89	14	3	1	28	20		.252	.294	.317	90	-5	19			.914	-14	S-95/2-8	-2.0
1910	Cle-A	53	119	13	25	3	1	0	12	9		.210	.266	.252	61	-5	4			.927	-2	S-27/2-6,O-6,3-3	-0.7
1911	Cle-A	116	412	45	122	14	9	3	45	27		.296	.339	.396	104	1	21			.945	6	2-94,3-17/S-1	0.5
1912	Cle-A	40	132	12	30	4	1	0	14	9		.227	.277	.273	55	-8	7			.938	0	2-37	-0.8
	*Bos-A	18	45	10	9	2	0	0	6	3		.200	.250	.244	40	-4	5			.927	-4	2-17	-0.7
	Yr	58	177	22	39	6	1	0	20	12		.220	.270	.266	51	-11	12			.936	-3	2-54	-1.5
1913	Bos-A	23	58	9	10	2	0	0	4	9	13	.172	.294	.207	46	-4	3			.902	-2	2-10/S-7,3-1	-0.5
Total	7	501	1609	162	404	56	17	4	151	99	13	.251	.296	.314	83	-34	92			.902	-25	S-271,2-178/3-21,O	-6.1

■ **JIM BALL** Ball, James Chandler b: 2/22/1884, Harford Co., Md. d: 4/7/63, Glendale, Cal. BR/TR, 5'11", 175 lbs. Deb: 9/21/07

YEAR	TM/L	G	AB	R	H	2B	3B	HR	RBI	BB	SO	AVG	OBP	SLG	PRO+	BR/A	SB	CS	SBR	FA	FR	G/POS	TPR
1907	Bos-N	10	36	3	6	2	0	0	3	2		.167	.211	.222	36	-3	0			.963	-2	C-10	-0.4
1908	Bos-N	6	15	1	1	0	0	0	0	1		.067	.125	.067	-39	-2	0			.917	-1	/C-6	-0.3
Total	2	16	51	4	7	2	0	0	3	3		.137	.185	.176	14	-5	0			.949	-2	/C-16	-0.7

■ **JEFF BALL** Ball, Jeffrey D. b: 4/17/69, Merced, Cal. BR/TR, 5'10", 185 lbs. Deb: 6/10/98

YEAR	TM/L	G	AB	R	H	2B	3B	HR	RBI	BB	SO	AVG	OBP	SLG	PRO+	BR/A	SB	CS	SBR	FA	FR	G/POS	TPR
1998	SF-N	2	4	0	1	0	0	0	0	0	0	.250	.250	.250	32	-0	0	0	0	1.000	-0	/1-1	-0.1

■ **PELHAM BALLENGER** Ballenger, Pelham Ashby b: 2/6/1894, Gilreath Mill, S.C. d: 12/8/48, Greenville County, S.C. BR/TR, 5'11", 160 lbs. Deb: 5/7/28

YEAR	TM/L	G	AB	R	H	2B	3B	HR	RBI	BB	SO	AVG	OBP	SLG	PRO+	BR/A	SB	CS	SBR	FA	FR	G/POS	TPR
1928	Was-A	3	9	0	1	0	0	0	0	0	1	.111	.111	.111	-42	-2	0	0	0	1.000	1	/3-3	0.0

■ **HAL BAMBERGER** Bamberger, Harold Earl "Dutch" b: 10/29/24, Lebanon, Pa. BL/TR, 6', 173 lbs. Deb: 9/15/48

YEAR	TM/L	G	AB	R	H	2B	3B	HR	RBI	BB	SO	AVG	OBP	SLG	PRO+	BR/A	SB	CS	SBR	FA	FR	G/POS	TPR
1948	NY-N	7	12	0	1	0	0	0	0	1	2	.083	.154	.083	-34	-2	0			1.000	-0	/O-3	-0.3

■ **STUD BANCKER** Bancker, John b: Philadelphia, Pa. Deb: 4/21/1875

YEAR	TM/L	G	AB	R	H	2B	3B	HR	RBI	BB	SO	AVG	OBP	SLG	PRO+	BR/A	SB	CS	SBR	FA	FR	G/POS	TPR
1875	NH-n	19	72	3	11	0	0	0	2	0	3	.153	.153	.153	7	-6	1	0	0	.796	-4	C-14/2-4,3-3,S-1,1	-0.9

■ **DAVE BANCROFT** Bancroft, David James "Beauty" b: 4/20/1891, Sioux City, Iowa d: 10/9/72, Superior, Wis. BB/TR, 5'9.5", 160 lbs. Deb: 4/14/15 MCH

YEAR	TM/L	G	AB	R	H	2B	3B	HR	RBI	BB	SO	AVG	OBP	SLG	PRO+	BR/A	SB	CS	SBR	FA	FR	G/POS	TPR
1915	*Phi-N	153	563	85	143	18	2	7	30	77	62	.254	.346	.330	104	5	15	27	-12	.928	5	*S-153	1.1
1916	Phi-N	142	477	53	101	10	0	3	33	74	57	.212	.323	.252	75	-11	15			.933	25	*S-142	2.4
1917	Phi-N	127	478	56	116	22	5	4	43	44	42	.243	.307	.335	93	-4	14			.936	**28**	*S-120/2-3,O-2	3.3
1918	Phi-N	125	499	69	132	19	4	0	26	54	36	.265	.338	.319	94	-2	11			.928	18	*S-125	2.4
1919	Phi-N	92	335	45	91	13	7	0	25	31	30	.272	.333	.352	99	0	8			.951	10	S-88	1.7
1920	Phi-N	42	171	23	51	7	2	0	5	9	12	.298	.337	.363	96	-1	1	7	-4	.981	9	S-42	0.9
	NY-N	108	442	79	132	29	7	0	31	33	32	.299	.349	.396	115	8	7	5	-1	.946	30	*S-108	4.8
	Yr	150	613	102	183	36	9	0	36	42	44	.299	.346	.387	109	7	8	12	-5	**.955**	**39**	*S-150	5.7
1921	*NY-N	153	606	121	193	26	15	6	67	66	23	.318	.389	.441	119	18	17	10	-1	.960	17	*S-153	4.8
1922	*NY-N	156	651	117	209	41	5	4	60	79	27	.321	.397	.418	109	12	16	11	-2	.941	22	*S-156	4.5
1923	*NY-N	107	444	80	135	33	3	1	31	62	23	.304	.391	.399	110	9	8	7	-2	.936	**21**	*S-96,2-11	3.6
1924	Bos-N	79	319	49	89	11	1	2	21	37	24	.279	.356	.339	91	-3	4	4	-1	.961	-5	S-79,M	-0.1
1925	Bos-N	128	479	75	153	29	8	2	49	64	22	.319	.400	.426	122	18	7	4	-0	**.945**	10	*S-125,M	3.8
1926	Bos-N	127	453	70	141	18	6	1	44	64	29	.311	.399	.384	122	17	3			.956	-3	*S-123/3-2,M	2.7
1927	Bos-N	111	375	44	91	13	4	1	31	43	36	.243	.322	.307	75	-13	5			.939	6	*S-104/3-1,M	0.4
1928	Bro-N	149	515	47	127	19	5	0	51	59	20	.247	.326	.303	66	-24	7			.948	4	*S-149	-0.3
1929	Bro-N	104	358	35	99	11	3	1	44	29	11	.277	.331	.332	66	-19	7			.955	-0	*S-102	-0.6
1930	NY-N	10	17	0	1	1	0	0	0	2	1	.059	.158	.118	-33	-4	0			.966	1	/S-8	-0.2
Total	16	1913	7182	1048	2004	320	77	32	591	827	487	.279	.355	.358	98	8	145	75		.944	198	*S-1873/2-14,3-3,O	35.2

YEAR	TM/L	G	AB	R	H	2B	3B	HR	RBI	BB	SO	AVG	OBP	SLG	PRO+	BR/A	SB	CS	SBR	FA	FR	G/POS	TPR
■ **CHRIS BANDO**	Bando, Christopher Michael b: 2/4/56, Cleveland, Ohio BB/TR, 6', 195 lbs. Deb: 8/13/81 FC																						
1981	Cle-A	21	47	3	10	3	0	0	6	2	2	.213	.245	.277	51	-3	0	0	0	.967	-2	C-15/D-2	-0.5
1982	Cle-A	66	184	13	39	6	1	3	16	24	30	.212	.303	.304	68	-8	0	0	0	.990	-6	C-63/3-2	-1.2
1983	Cle-A	48	121	15	31	3	0	4	15	15	19	.256	.338	.380	94	-1	0	1	-1	.995	-2	C-43	-0.2
1984	Cle-A	75	220	38	64	11	0	12	41	33	35	.291	.383	.505	141	13	1	2	-1	.982	-4	C-63/1-1,3-1,D-1	1.1
1985	Cle-A	73	173	11	24	4	1	0	13	22	21	.139	.236	.173	14	-20	0	1	-1	.986	-3	C-67	-2.1
1986	Cle-A	92	254	28	68	9	0	2	26	22	49	.268	.329	.327	81	-6	0	1	-1	.990	-10	C-86	-1.2
1987	Cle-A	89	211	20	46	9	0	5	16	12	28	.218	.260	.332	55	-14	0	0	0	.990	-2	C-86	-1.1
1988	Cle-A	32	72	6	9	1	0	1	8	8	12	.125	.222	.181	14	-8	0	0	0	.979	1	C-32	-0.6
	Det-A	1	0	0	0	0	0	0	0	0	0	—	—	—	—	0	0	0	0	.000	0	/C-1	0.0
	Yr	33	72	6	9	1	0	1	8	8	12	.125	.222	.181	14	-8	0	0	0	.979	1	C-33	-0.6
1989	Oak-A	1	2	0	1	0	0	0	1	0	1	.500	.500	.500	189	0	0	0	0	1.000	1	/C-1	0.1
Total	9	498	1284	134	292	46	2	27	142	138	197	.227	.303	.329	73	-47	1	5	-3	.987	-28	C-457/3-3,D-3,1-1	-5.7
■ **SAL BANDO**	Bando, Salvatore Leonard b: 2/13/44, Cleveland, O. BR/TR, 6', 205 lbs. Deb: 9/3/66 FC																						
1966	KC-A	11	24	1	7	1	1	0	1	1	3	.292	.320	.417	113	0	0	0	0	.933	4	/3-7	0.5
1967	KC-A	47	130	11	25	3	2	0	6	16	24	.192	.295	.246	64	-5	1	0	0	.959	8	3-44	0.3
1968	Oak-A	162	605	67	152	25	5	9	67	51	78	.251	.317	.354	108	5	13	4	2	.964	-12	*3-162/O-1	-0.5
1969	Oak-A★	162	609	106	171	25	3	31	113	111	82	.281	.401	.484	153	47	1	4	-2	.954	-13	*3-162	3.3
1970	Oak-A	155	502	93	132	20	2	20	75	118	88	.263	.409	.430	137	31	6	10	-4	.954	-22	*3-152	0.4
1971	*Oak-A	153	538	75	146	23	1	24	94	86	55	.271	.380	.452	137	28	3	7	-3	.971	-17	*3-153	0.8
1972	*Oak-A★	152	535	64	126	20	3	15	77	78	55	.236	.342	.368	118	13	3	1	0	.960	6	*3-151/2-1	2.0
1973	*Oak-A★	162	592	97	170	**32**	3	29	98	82	84	.287	.378	.498	153	41	4	2	0	.949	-23	*3-159/D-3	1.8
1974	*Oak-A†	146	498	84	121	21	2	22	103	86	79	.243	.360	.426	134	24	2	3	-1	.946	-13	*3-141/D-3	0.8
1975	*Oak-A	160	562	64	129	24	1	15	78	87	80	.230	.338	.356	98	1	7	1	2	.967	-16	*3-160	-1.4
1976	Oak-A	158	550	75	132	18	2	27	84	76	74	.240	.337	.427	128	19	20	6	2	.962	-5	*3-155/S-5,D-2	1.7
1977	Mil-A	159	580	65	145	27	3	17	82	75	89	.250	.339	.395	99	0	4	2	0	.966	-2	*3-135,D-24/2-1,S-1	-0.3
1978	Mil-A	152	540	85	154	20	6	17	78	72	52	.285	.375	.439	128	22	3	2	-0	.968	12	*3-134,D-12/1-5	3.1
1979	Mil-A	130	476	57	117	14	3	9	43	57	42	.246	.330	.345	82	-11	2	0	1	.963	-9	*3-109,D-19/1-4,P2	-2.0
1980	Mil-A	78	254	28	50	12	1	5	31	29	35	.197	.282	.311	64	-13	5	3	-0	.934	-4	3-57,D-15/1-7	-1.9
1981	*Mil-A	32	65	10	13	4	0	2	9	6	3	.200	.268	.354	82	-2	1	1	-0	.967	0	3-15/1-9,D-2	-0.2
Total	16	2019	7060	982	1790	289	38	242	1039	1031	923	.254	.355	.408	120	200	75	46	-5	.959	-104	*3-1896/D-80,1S2PO	8.4
■ **JEFF BANISTER**	Banister, Jeffery Todd b: 1/15/65, Weatherford, Okla. BR/TR, 6'2", 200 lbs. Deb: 7/23/91																						
1991	Pit-N	1	1	0	1	0	0	0	0	0	0	1.000	1.000	1.000	471	0	0	0	0	.000	0	/H	0.0
■ **BRIAN BANKS**	Banks, Brian Glen b: 9/28/70, Mesa, Ariz. BB/TR, 6'3", 200 lbs. Deb: 9/9/96																						
1996	Mil-A	4	7	2	4	2	0	1	2	1	2	.571	.625	1.286	353	3	0	0	0	1.000	-1	/O-3,1-1	0.1
1997	Mil-A	28	68	9	14	1	0	1	8	6	17	.206	.270	.265	40	-6	0	1	-1	.950	-1	O-15/1-5,3-1,D-1	-0.8
1998	Mil-N	24	24	3	7	2	0	1	5	4	7	.292	.393	.500	129	1	0	0	0	1.000	-2	/C-5,1-2,3-1,O-1	-0.1
Total	3	56	99	14	25	5	0	3	15	11	26	.253	.327	.394	86	-2	0	1	-1	.913	-4	/O-19,1-8,C-5,3D	-0.8
■ **ERNIE BANKS**	Banks, Ernest "Mr. Cub" b: 1/31/31, Dallas, Tex. BR/TR, 6'1", 180 lbs. Deb: 9/17/53 CH																						
1953	Chi-N	10	35	3	11	1	1	2	6	4	5	.314	.385	.571	142	2	0	0	0	.981	3	S-10	0.5
1954	Chi-N	154	593	70	163	19	7	19	79	40	50	.275	.328	.427	94	-6	6	10	-4	.959	-1	*S-154	0.1
1955	Chi-N★	154	596	98	176	29	9	44	117	45	72	.295	.347	.596	145	35	9	3	1	**.972**	5	*S-154	5.3
1956	Chi-N☆	139	538	82	160	25	8	28	85	52	62	.297	.359	.530	137	27	6	9	-4	.962	-16	*S-139	2.0
1957	Chi-N★	156	594	113	169	34	6	43	102	70	85	.285	.363	.579	150	40	8	4	0	.975	-17	*S-100,3-58	3.5
1958	Chi-N★	154	617	119	193	23	11	**47**	**129**	52	87	.313	.370	**.614**	157	48	4	4	-1	.960	-2	*S-154	5.7
1959	Chi-N★	155	589	97	179	25	6	45	**143**	64	72	.304	.379	.596	156	46	2	4	-2	**.985**	6	*S-154	6.2
1960	Chi-N★	156	597	94	162	32	7	**41**	117	71	69	.271	.353	.554	145	36	1	3	-2	**.977**	11	*S-156	5.8
1961	Chi-N★	138	511	75	142	22	4	29	80	54	75	.278	.349	.507	122	15	1	2	-1	.965	13	*S-104,O-23/1-7	3.3
1962	Chi-N★	154	610	87	164	20	6	37	104	30	71	.269	.311	.503	110	6	5	1	1	.993	0	*1-149/3-3	-0.3
1963	Chi-N	130	432	41	98	20	1	18	64	39	73	.227	.297	.403	94	-4	0	3	-2	.993	-2	*1-125	-1.4
1964	Chi-N	157	591	67	156	29	6	23	95	36	84	.264	.310	.450	107	4	1	2	-1	.994	11	*1-157	0.8
1965	Chi-N★	163	612	79	162	25	3	28	106	55	64	.265	.331	.453	116	12	3	5	-2	.992	-7	*1-162	-0.7
1966	Chi-N	141	511	52	139	23	7	15	75	29	59	.272	.317	.432	105	3	0	1	-1	.992	2	*1-130/3-8	-0.5
1967	Chi-N★	151	573	68	158	26	4	23	95	27	93	.276	.312	.455	112	7	2	2	-1	.993	1	*1-147	-0.2
1968	Chi-N	150	552	71	136	27	0	32	83	27	67	.246	.288	.469	116	9	2	0	1	.996	-1	*1-147	-0.4
1969	Chi-N★	155	565	60	143	19	2	23	106	42	101	.253	.313	.416	91	-8	0	0	0	**.997**	1	*1-153	-2.1
1970	Chi-N	72	222	25	56	6	2	12	44	20	33	.252	.317	.459	94	-3	0	0	0	.993	-2	1-62	-1.0
1971	Chi-N	39	83	4	16	2	0	3	6	6	14	.193	.247	.325	53	-5	0	0	0	1.000	1	1-20	-0.7
Total	19	2528	9421	1305	2583	407	90	512	1636	763	1236	.274	.333	.500	122	262	50	53	-17	.994	4	*1-1259,*S-1125/30	25.9
■ **GEORGE BANKS**	Banks, George Edward b: 9/24/38, Pacolet Mills, S.C. d: 3/1/85, Spartanburg, S.C. BR/TR, 5'11", 185 lbs. Deb: 4/15/62																						
1962	Min-A	63	103	22	26	0	2	4	15	21	27	.252	.384	.408	109	2	0	0	0	.962	-3	O-17/3-6	-0.1
1963	Min-A	25	71	5	11	4	0	3	8	9	21	.155	.259	.338	65	-3	0	0	0	.910	2	3-21	-0.2
1964	Min-A	1	1	0	0	0	0	0	0	0	1	.000	.000	.000	-99	-0	0	0	0	.000	0	H	0.0
	Cle-A	9	17	6	5	1	0	2	3	6	6	.294	.478	.706	226	3	0	0	0	1.000	-1	/O-3,2-1,3-1	0.3
	Yr	10	18	6	5	1	0	2	3	6	7	.278	.458	.667	210	3	0	0	0	1.000	-1	/O-3,2-1,3-1	0.3
1965	Cle-A	4	5	0	1	1	0	0	0	1	3	.200	.333	.400	107	0	0	1	-1	1.000	0	/3-1	0.0
1966	Cle-A	4	4	0	1	0	0	0	1	0	1	.250	.250	.250	44	-0	0	0	0	.000	0	H	0.0
Total	5	106	201	33	44	6	2	9	27	37	59	.219	.346	.403	102	1	0	1	-1	.919	-1	/3-29,O-20,2-1	0.0
■ **EVERETT BANKSTON**	Bankston, Wilborn Everett b: 5/25/1893, Barnesville, Ga. d: 2/26/70, Griffin, Ga. BL/TR, 5'11", 180 lbs. Deb: 8/15/15																						
1915	Phi-A	11	36	6	5	1	1	1	2	2	5	.139	.205	.306	55	-2	1			.882	-1	/O-8	-0.3
■ **JIM BANNING**	Banning, James M. b: 1866, New York, N.Y. BL/TR, 5'6", 150 lbs. Deb: 9/27/1888																						
1888	Was-N	1	0	0	0	0	0	0	0	0	0	—	—	—	—	0	0			1.000	-0	/C-1	0.0
1889	Was-N	2	1	0	0	0	0	0	0	0	0	.000	.000	.000	-99	-0	0			1.000	1	/C-2	0.1
Total	2	3	1	0	0	0	0	0	0	0	0	.000	.000	.000	-99	-0	0			1.000	1	/C-3	0.1
■ **ALAN BANNISTER**	Bannister, Alan b: 9/3/51, Montebello, Cal. BR/TR, 5'11", 175 lbs. Deb: 7/13/74																						
1974	Phi-N	26	25	4	3	0	0	0	1	3	7	.120	.241	.120	3	-3	0	0	0	1.000	-2	/O-8,S-2	-0.6
1975	Phi-N	24	61	10	16	3	1	0	0	1	9	.262	.274	.344	68	-3	2	2	-1	1.000	1	O-18/2-1,S-1	-0.3
1976	Chi-A	73	145	19	36	6	2	0	8	14	21	.248	.319	.317	86	-2	12	4	1	.988	-2	O-43,S-14/2-4,3D	-0.4
1977	Chi-A	139	560	87	154	20	3	3	57	54	49	.275	.341	.338	86	-10	4	3	-1	.936	-34	*S-133/2-3,O-3	-2.9
1978	Chi-A	49	107	16	24	3	2	0	8	11	12	.224	.303	.290	67	-5	3	3	-1	1.000	-3	D-19,O-15/S-8,2-2	-0.9
1979	Chi-A	136	506	71	144	28	8	2	55	43	40	.285	.344	.383	96	-2	22	6	3	.963	-24	2-65,O-47,3-12,/1D	-2.1
1980	Chi-A	45	130	16	25	6	0	0	9	12	16	.192	.261	.238	38	-11	5	2	0	1.000	-2	O-23,3-17	-1.4
	Cle-A	81	262	41	86	17	4	1	32	28	25	.328	.393	.435	126	10	9	2	2	.968	-17	2-41,O-40/3-3,S-2	-0.4
	Yr	126	392	57	111	23	4	1	41	40	41	.283	.350	.370	97	-1	14	4	2	.981	-19	O-63,2-41,3-20,/S-2	-1.8
1981	Cle-A	68	232	36	61	11	1	1	17	16	19	.263	.310	.332	86	-4	16	2	4	.986	-14	O-35,2-30/1-2,S-1	-1.4
1982	Cle-A	101	348	40	93	16	1	4	41	42	41	.267	.348	.353	94	-2	18	5	2	.991	-11	O-55,2-48/S-2,3D	-1.0
1983	Cle-A	117	377	51	100	25	4	5	45	31	43	.265	.326	.393	93	-4	6	6	-2	.969	-14	O-91,2-27/1-3,D-3	-2.1
1984	Hou-N	9	20	2	4	2	0	0	0	2	2	.200	.273	.300	65	-1	0	0	0	.947	-1	/S-4,O-1	-0.2
	Tex-A	47	112	20	33	2	1	2	9	21	17	.295	.410	.384	118	4	3	0	1	.959	-12	2-25/O-3,1-1,3-1,D	-0.7
1985	Tex-A	57	122	17	32	4	1	1	6	14	17	.262	.338	.336	84	-2	8	2	1	1.000	-2	D-21,O-14,2-10,/31	-0.4
Total	12	972	3007	430	811	143	28	19	288	292	318	.270	.337	.355	90	-35	108	37	10	.983	-138	O-396,2-256,S/D31	-14.8

YEAR	TM/L	G	AB	R	H	2B	3B	HR	RBI	BB	SO	AVG	OBP	SLG	PRO+	BR/A	SB	CS	SBR	FA	FR	G/POS	TPR
■ **JIMMY BANNON** Bannon, James Henry "Foxy Grandpa" b: 5/5/1871, Amesbury, Mass. d: 3/24/48, Glen Rock, N.J. BR/TR, 5'5", 160 lbs. Deb: 6/15/1893 F																							
1893	StL-N	26	107	9	36	3	4	0	15	4	5	.336	.366	.439	113	2	8			.795	-6	O-24/S-2,P-1	-0.4
1894	Bos-N	128	494	130	166	29	10	13	114	62	42	.336	.414	.514	114	9	47			.873	18	*O-128/P-1	1.4
1895	Bos-N	123	489	101	171	35	5	6	74	54	31	.350	.420	.479	122	15	28			.879	10	*O-122/P-1	1.3
1896	Bos-N	89	344	53	87	9	5	0	50	32	23	.253	.318	.308	62	-19	16			.901	-1	O-76/2-6,S-5,3-3	-2.2
Total	4	366	1434	293	460	76	24	19	253	152	101	.321	.390	.447	105	6	99			.877	22	O-350/S-7,2-6,3P	0.1
■ **TOM BANNON** Bannon, Thomas Edward "Ward Six" b: 5/8/1869, Amesbury, Mass. d: 1/26/50, Lynn, Mass. BR/TR, 5'8", 175 lbs. Deb: 5/10/1895 F																							
1895	NY-N	37	159	33	43	6	2	0	8	7	8	.270	.301	.333	65	-9	20			.894	2	O-21,1-16	-0.7
1896	NY-N	2	7	1	1	1	0	0	0	1	1	.143	.250	.286	42	-1	0			.500	-1	/O-2	-0.2
Total	2	39	166	34	44	7	2	0	8	8	9	.265	.299	.331	64	-9	20			.878	1	/O-23,1-16	-0.9
■ **WALTER BARBARE** Barbare, Walter Lawrence "Dinty" b: 8/11/1891, Greenville, S.C. d: 10/28/65, Greenville, S.C. BR/TR, 6', 162 lbs. Deb: 9/17/14																							
1914	Cle-A	15	52	6	16	2	2	0	5	2	5	.308	.345	.423	126	1	1	4	-2	.933	0	3-14/S-1	0.0
1915	Cle-A	77	246	15	47	3	1	0	11	10	27	.191	.235	.211	33	-21	6	5	-1	.960	7	3-68/1-1	-1.3
1916	Cle-A	13	48	3	11	1	0	0	3	4	9	.229	.288	.250	58	-2	0			.977	1	3-12	-0.1
1918	Bos-A	13	29	2	5	3	0	0	2	0	1	.172	.172	.276	36	-2	1			.826	-4	3-11/S-1	-0.7
1919	Pit-N	85	293	34	80	11	5	1	34	18	18	.273	.317	.355	98	-1	11			.961	-7	3-80/2-1	-0.5
1920	Pit-N	57	186	9	51	5	2	0	12	9	11	.274	.308	.323	79	-5	5	3	-0	.923	-5	S-34,2-12/3-5	-0.8
1921	Bos-N	134	550	66	166	22	7	0	49	24	28	.302	.331	.367	89	-9	11	4	1	.957	-17	*S-121/2-8,3-2	-1.3
1922	Bos-N	106	373	38	86	5	4	0	40	21	22	.231	.272	.265	41	-33	2	0	1	.966	2	2-45,3-38,1-14	-2.5
Total	8	500	1777	173	462	52	21	1	156	88	121	.260	.297	.315	71	-72	37	16		.959	-21	3-230,S-157/2-66,1	-7.2
■ **RED BARBARY** Barbary, Donald Odell b: 6/20/20, Simpsonville, S.C BR/TR, 6'2", 195 lbs. Deb: 5/22/43																							
1943	Was-A	1	1	0	0	0	0	0	0	0	0	.000	.000	.000	-99	-0	0	0	0	.000	0	H	0.0
■ **JAP BARBEAU** Barbeau, William Joseph b: 6/10/1882, New York, N.Y. d: 9/10/69, Milwaukee, Wis. BR/TR, 5'5", 140 lbs. Deb: 9/27/05																							
1905	Cle-A	11	37	1	10	1	1	0	2	1		.270	.289	.351	102	-0	1			.905	1	2-11	0.1
1906	Cle-A	42	129	8	25	5	3	0	12	9		.194	.257	.279	69	-5	5			.830	-7	3-32/S-6	-1.2
1909	Pit-N	91	350	60	77	16	3	0	25	37		.220	.302	.283	75	-10	19			.891	-19	3-85	-3.0
	StL-N	48	175	23	44	3	0	0	5	28		.251	.370	.269	105	3	14			.901	-10	3-47	-0.6
	Yr	139	525	83	121	19	3	0	30	65		.230	.326	.278	85	-7	33			.895	-29	*3-132	-3.6
1910	StL-N	7	21	4	4	0	1	0	2	3	3	.190	.292	.286	71	-1	0			.917	2	/3-6,2-1	0.2
Total	4	199	712	96	160	25	8	0	46	78	3	.225	.311	.282	82	-12	39			.884	-33	3-170/2-12,S-6	-4.5
■ **DAVE BARBEE** Barbee, David Monroe b: 5/7/05, Greensboro, N.C. d: 7/1/68, Albemarle, N.C. BR/TR, 5'11.5", 178 lbs. Deb: 7/29/26																							
1926	Phi-A	19	47	7	8	1	1	1	5	2	4	.170	.220	.298	32	-5	0	0	0	1.000	0	O-10	-0.5
1932	Pit-N	97	327	37	84	22	6	5	55	18	38	.257	.300	.407	89	-6	1			.975	4	O-78	-0.7
Total	2	116	374	44	92	23	7	6	60	20	42	.246	.290	.393	82	-11	1	0		.977	4	/O-88	-1.2
■ **CHARLIE BARBER** Barber, Charles D. b: 1854, Philadelphia, Pa. d: 11/23/10, Philadelphia, Pa. BR/TR, Deb: 4/17/1884																							
1884	Cin-U	55	204	38	41	1	4	0	11			.201	.242	.245	44	-20				.837	4	3-55	-1.4
■ **TURNER BARBER** Barber, Tyrus Turner b: 7/9/1893, Lavinia, Tenn. d: 10/20/68, Milan, Tenn. BL/TR, 5'11", 170 lbs. Deb: 8/19/15																							
1915	Was-A	20	53	9	16	1	1	0	6	6	7	.302	.383	.358	120	1	0	3	-2	.952	-2	O-19	-0.3
1916	Was-A	15	33	3	7	0	1	1	5	2	3	.212	.257	.364	87	-1	0			.833	-3	O-10	-0.4
1917	Chi-N	7	28	2	6	1	0	0	2	2	8	.214	.267	.250	54	-1	1			1.000	1	/O-7	-0.1
1918	*Chi-N	55	123	11	29	3	2	0	10	9	16	.236	.293	.293	77	-3	3			.940	-8	O-27/1-4	-1.4
1919	Chi-N	76	230	26	72	9	4	0	21	14	17	.313	.355	.387	122	6	7			.949	-4	O-68	-0.3
1920	Chi-N	94	340	27	90	10	5	0	50	9	26	.265	.290	.324	74	-12	5	6	-2	.988	-7	1-69,O-17/2-2	-2.5
1921	Chi-N	127	452	73	142	14	4	1	54	41	24	.314	.379	.369	99	1	5	9	-4	.970	2	*O-123	-1.0
1922	Chi-N	84	226	35	70	7	4	0	29	30	9	.310	.391	.376	97	0	7	4	-0	.953	-6	O-47,1-16	-0.9
1923	Bro-N	13	46	3	10	2	0	0	8	2	2	.217	.250	.261	36	-4	0	1	-1	1.000	-2	O-12	-0.7
Total	9	491	1531	189	442	47	21	2	185	115	112	.289	.343	.351	93	-12	28	23		.959	-29	O-330/1-89,2-2	-7.6
■ **BRET BARBERIE** Barberie, Bret Edward b: 8/16/67, Long Beach, Cal. BB/TR, 5'11", 180 lbs. Deb: 6/16/91																							
1991	Mon-N	57	136	16	48	12	2	2	18	20	22	.353	.443	.515	171	14	0	0	0	.931	-2	S-19,2-10,3-10,/1-1	1.4
1992	Mon-N	111	285	26	66	11	0	1	24	47	62	.232	.356	.281	83	-4	9	5	-0	.932	5	3-63,2-26/S-1	0.2
1993	Fla-N	99	375	45	104	16	2	5	33	33	58	.277	.347	.371	87	-6	2	4	-2	.982	11	2-97	0.6
1994	Fla-N	107	372	40	112	20	2	5	31	23	65	.301	.356	.406	95	-2	2	0	1	.975	10	*2-106	1.3
1995	Bal-A	90	237	32	57	14	0	2	25	36	50	.241	.355	.325	77	-7	3	3	-1	.977	-4	2-74/3-3,D-5	-0.8
1996	Chi-N	15	29	4	1	0	0	1	2	5	11	.034	.176	.138	-15	-5	0	1	-1	1.000	-3	/2-6,3-2,S-1	-0.8
Total	6	479	1434	163	388	73	6	16	133	164	268	.271	.358	.363	92	-10	16	13	-3	.980	17	2-319/3-78,S-21,D1	1.9
■ **JIM BARBIERI** Barbieri, James Patrick b: 9/15/41, Schenectady, N.Y. BL/TR, 5'7", 155 lbs. Deb: 7/5/66																							
1966	*LA-N	39	82	9	23	5	0	0	3	9	7	.280	.352	.341	102	0	2	0	1	.939	0	O-20	0.1
■ **GEORGE BARCLAY** Barclay, George Oliver "Deerfoot" b: 5/16/1876, Millville, Pa. d: 4/3/09, Philadelphia, Pa. TR , 5'10", 162 lbs. Deb: 4/17/02																							
1902	StL-N	137	543	79	163	14	2	3	53	31		.300	.345	.350	119	12	30			.904	-7	*O-137	-0.5
1903	StL-N	108	419	37	104	10	8	0	42	15		.248	.278	.310	70	-18	12			.901	-8	*O-107	-3.1
1904	StL-N	103	375	41	75	7	4	1	28	12		.200	.237	.248	52	-22	14			.947	-6	*O-103	-3.6
	Bos-N	24	93	5	21	3	1	0	10	2		.226	.258	.280	68	-4	3			.935	-3	O-24	-0.9
	Yr	127	468	46	96	10	5	1	38	14		.205	.241	.254	55	-25	17			.945	-9	*O-127	-4.5
1905	Bos-N	29	108	5	19	1	0	0	7	2		.176	.205	.185	17	-11	2			.854	-5	O-28	-1.8
Total	4	401	1538	167	382	35	15	4	140	62		.248	.286	.298	79	-42	61			.911	-29	O-399	-9.9
■ **JESSE BARFIELD** Barfield, Jesse Lee b: 10/29/59, Joliet, Ill. BR/TR, 6'1", 205 lbs. Deb: 9/3/81																							
1981	Tor-A	25	95	7	22	3	2	2	9	4	19	.232	.270	.368	77	-3	4	3	-1	1.000	5	O-25	0.1
1982	Tor-A	139	394	54	97	13	2	18	58	42	79	.246	.323	.426	95	-3	1	4	-2	.963	-6	*O-137/D-1	-1.4
1983	Tor-A	128	388	58	98	13	3	27	68	22	110	.253	.300	.510	111	4	2	5	-2	.966	4	*O-120/D-5	0.3
1984	Tor-A	110	320	51	91	14	1	14	49	35	81	.284	.359	.466	122	9	8	2	1	.952	6	O-88/D-9	1.4
1985	*Tor-A	155	539	94	156	34	9	27	84	66	143	.289	.371	.536	141	30	22	8	2	.989	22	*O-154	4.8
1986	Tor-A★	158	589	107	170	35	2	**40**	108	69	146	.289	.371	.559	145	36	8	8	-2	.992	21	*O-157	**4.8**
1987	Tor-A	159	590	89	155	25	3	28	84	58	141	.263	.332	.458	104	3	3	5	-2	.992	16	*O-158	1.2
1988	Tor-A	137	468	62	114	21	5	18	56	41	108	.244	.306	.425	102	0	7	3	0	.988	13	*O-136/D-1	0.9
1989	Tor-A	21	80	8	16	4	0	5	11	5	28	.200	.256	.438	94	-1	0	2	-1	.979	3	O-21	0.0
	NY-A	129	441	71	106	19	1	18	56	82	122	.240	.362	.410	119	13	5	3	-0	.972	9	*O-129	1.9
	Yr	150	521	79	122	23	1	23	67	87	150	.234	.347	.415	115	12	5	5	-2	.973	12	*O-150	1.9
1990	NY-A	153	476	69	117	21	2	25	78	82	150	.246	.362	.456	127	18	4	3	-1	.973	9	*O-151	2.3
1991	NY-A	84	284	37	64	12	0	17	48	36	80	.225	.313	.447	107	2	1	0	0	1.000	11	O-81	1.2
1992	NY-A	30	95	8	13	2	0	2	7	9	27	.137	.212	.221	21	-10	1	1	-0	.966	0	O-30	-1.1
Total	12	1428	4759	715	1219	216	30	241	716	551	1234	.256	.338	.466	116	99	66	47	-8	.980	114	*O-1387/D-16	16.4
■ **AL BARKER** Barker, Alfred L b: 1/18/1839, Rockford, Ill. d: 9/15/12, Rockford, Ill. Deb: 6/1/1871																							
1871	Rok-n	1	4	0	1	0	0	0	2	1	0	.250	.400	.250	97	0	0	0	0	1.000	-0	/O-1	0.0
■ **RAY BARKER** Barker, Raymond Herrell "Buddy" b: 3/12/36, Martinsburg, W.Va. BL/TR, 6', 192 lbs. Deb: 9/13/60																							
1960	Bal-A	5	6	0	0	0	0	0	0	0	3	.000	.000	.000	-99	-2	0	0	0	.000	-0	/O-1	-0.2
1965	Cle-A	11	6	0	0	0	0	0	0	2	2	.000	.250	.000	-22	-1	0	0	0	1.000	-0	/1-3	-0.1
	NY-A	98	205	21	52	11	0	7	31	20	46	.254	.329	.410	109	2	1	0	0	.991	6	1-61/3-3	0.7
	Yr	109	211	21	52	11	0	7	31	22	48	.246	.326	.398	105	1	1	0	0	.991	6	1-64/3-3	0.6
1966	NY-A	61	75	11	14	5	0	3	13	4	20	.187	.228	.373	72	-3	0	0	0	.987	5	1-47	0.1

YEAR	TM/L	G	AB	R	H	2B	3B	HR	RBI	BB	SO	AVG	OBP	SLG	PRO+	BR/A	SB	CS	SBR	FA	FR	G/POS	TPR
1967	NY-A	17	26	2	2	0	0	0	0	3	5	.077	.172	.077	-25	-4	0	0	0	.961	1	1-13	-0.4
Total	4	192	318	34	68	16	0	10	44	29	76	.214	.286	.358	84	-7	1	0	0	.987	12	1-124/3-3,O-1	0.1

■ RED BARKLEY
Barkley, John Duncan b: 9/19/13, Childress, Tex. BR/TR, 5'11", 160 lbs. Deb: 9/2/37

YEAR	TM/L	G	AB	R	H	2B	3B	HR	RBI	BB	SO	AVG	OBP	SLG	PRO+	BR/A	SB	CS	SBR	FA	FR	G/POS	TPR
1937	StL-A	31	101	9	27	6	0	0	14	14	17	.267	.357	.327	73	-4	1	0	0	.969	-4	2-31	-0.5
1939	Bos-N	12	11	1	0	0	0	0	0	1	2	.000	.083	.000	-82	-3	0			.842	4	/S-7,3-4	0.1
1943	Bro-N	20	51	6	16	3	0	0	7	4	7	.314	.364	.373	113	1	1			.894	-3	S-18	-0.1
Total	3	63	163	16	43	9	0	0	21	19	26	.264	.341	.319	75	-6	2	0		.882	-3	/2-31,S-25,3-4	-0.5

■ SAM BARKLEY
Barkley, Samuel E b: 5/24/1858, Wheeling, W.Va. d: 4/20/12, Wheeling, W.Va. BR/TR, 5'11.5", 180 lbs. Deb: 5/1/1884 M

YEAR	TM/L	G	AB	R	H	2B	3B	HR	RBI	BB	SO	AVG	OBP	SLG	PRO+	BR/A	SB	CS	SBR	FA	FR	G/POS	TPR
1884	Tol-a	104	435	71	133	**39**	9	1		22		.306	.342	.444	149	22				.930	25	*2-103/C-2	**4.4**
1885	*StL-a	106	418	67	112	18	10	3	53	25		.268	.312	.380	113	5				.921	15	*2-96,1-11	1.9
1886	Pit-a	122	478	77	127	31	8	1	69	58		.266	.345	.370	125	15	22			.936	-4	*2-112/O-8,1-2	1.3
1887	Pit-N	89	340	44	76	10	4	1	35	30	24	.224	.294	.285	66	-15	6			.979	-5	1-53,2-36	-2.0
1888	KC-a	116	482	67	104	21	6	4	51	26		.216	.262	.309	78	-14	15			.938	-7	*2-116/M	-1.6
1889	KC-a	45	176	36	50	6	2	0	23	15	20	.284	.340	.341	89	-3	8			.923	-12	2-41/1-4	-1.1
Total	6	582	2329	362	602	125	39	10	231	176	44	.258	.314	.359	105	10	51			.929	12	2-504/1-70,O-8,C-2	2.9

■ TOM BARLOW
Barlow, Thomas H. Deb: 5/2/1872

YEAR	TM/L	G	AB	R	H	2B	3B	HR	RBI	BB	SO	AVG	OBP	SLG	PRO+	BR/A	SB	CS	SBR	FA	FR	G/POS	TPR
1872	Atl-n	37	171	34	53	1	0	0	10	3	2	.310	.322	.316	83	-7	7	5	-1	.761	-8	*C-36/S-4,3-1	-1.2
1873	Atl-n	55	271	48	74	0	2	1	14	4	0	.273	.284	.299	82	-4	3	3	-1	.762	-15	*C-55/2-1,S-1	-1.4
1874	Har-n	32	155	37	46	5	1	0	12	2	2	.297	.306	.342	102	-0	**17**	4	**3**	.820	9	S-32	0.8
1875	NH-n	1	5	1	1	0	0	0	0	0	0	.200	.200	.200	45	-0	0	0	0	.800	0	/S-1	0.0
	Atl-n	1	4	0	0	0	0	0	0	0	0	.000	.000	.000	-99	-1	0	0	0	.500	-2	/2-1	-0.2
	Yr	2	9	1	1	0	0	0	0	0	0	.111	.111	.111	-26	-1	0	0	0	.800	-1	/S-1,2-1	-0.2
Total	4 n	126	606	120	174	6	3	1	36	9	4	.287	.298	.312	86	-12	27	12	1	.762	-16	/C-91,S-38,2-2,3-1	-2.0

■ BRUCE BARMES
Barmes, Bruce Raymond "Squeaky" b: 10/23/29, Vincennes, Ind. BL/TR, 5'8", 165 lbs. Deb: 9/13/53

YEAR	TM/L	G	AB	R	H	2B	3B	HR	RBI	BB	SO	AVG	OBP	SLG	PRO+	BR/A	SB	CS	SBR	FA	FR	G/POS	TPR
1953	Was-A	5	5	1	1	0	0	0	0	0	0	.200	.200	.200	8	-1	0	0	0	1.000	0	/O-1	-0.1

■ BABE BARNA
Barna, Herbert Paul b: 3/2/15, Clarksburg, W.Va. d: 5/18/72, Charleston, W.Va. BL/TR, 6'2", 210 lbs. Deb: 9/16/37

YEAR	TM/L	G	AB	R	H	2B	3B	HR	RBI	BB	SO	AVG	OBP	SLG	PRO+	BR/A	SB	CS	SBR	FA	FR	G/POS	TPR
1937	Phi-A	14	36	10	14	2	0	2	9	2	6	.389	.421	.611	159	3	1	0	0	.800	-2	/O-9,1-1	0.1
1938	Phi-A	9	30	4	4	0	0	0	2	3	5	.133	.212	.133	-12	-5	0	0	0	.917	-1	/O-7	-0.6
1941	NY-N	10	42	5	9	3	0	1	5	2	6	.214	.250	.357	68	-2	0			1.000	1	O-10	-0.2
1942	NY-N	104	331	39	85	8	7	6	58	38	48	.257	.333	.378	107	3	3			.983	-5	O-89	-0.7
1943	NY-N	40	113	11	23	5	1	1	12	16	9	.204	.302	.292	72	-4	3			.984	-1	O-31	-0.7
	Bos-A	30	112	19	19	4	1	2	10	15	24	.170	.268	.277	58	-6	2	1	0	.940	-4	O-29	-1.3
Total	5	207	664	88	154	22	9	12	96	76	98	.232	.311	.346	88	-11	9	1		.969	-13	O-175/1-1	-3.4

■ RED BARNES
Barnes, Emile b: 12/25/04, Suggsville, Ala. d: 7/3/59, Mobile, Ala. BL/TR, 5'10.5", 158 lbs. Deb: 9/29/27

YEAR	TM/L	G	AB	R	H	2B	3B	HR	RBI	BB	SO	AVG	OBP	SLG	PRO+	BR/A	SB	CS	SBR	FA	FR	G/POS	TPR
1927	Was-A	3	11	5	4	1	0	0	0	1	3	.364	.417	.455	127	0	0	0	0	1.000	0	/O-3	0.0
1928	Was-A	114	417	82	127	22	15	6	51	55	38	.305	.391	.472	127	17	7	3	0	.978	4	*O-104	1.3
1929	Was-A	72	130	16	26	5	2	1	15	13	12	.200	.273	.292	45	-11	1	0	0	.877	-6	O-30	-1.7
1930	Was-A	12	12	1	2	1	0	0	0	0	3	.167	.167	.250	4	-2	0	0	0	.000	0	H	-0.2
	Chi-A	85	266	48	66	12	7	1	31	26	20	.248	.317	.357	73	-11	4	2	0	.939	-0	O-72	-1.4
	Yr	97	278	49	68	13	7	1	31	26	23	.245	.311	.353	70	-13	4	2	0	.939	-0	O-72	-1.6
Total	4	286	836	152	225	41	24	8	97	95	76	.269	.347	.404	95	-6	12	5	1	.953	-2	O-209	-2.0

■ EPPIE BARNES
Barnes, Everett Duane b: 12/1/1900, Ossining, N.Y. d: 11/17/80, Mineola, N.Y. BL/TL, 5'9", 175 lbs. Deb: 9/25/23

YEAR	TM/L	G	AB	R	H	2B	3B	HR	RBI	BB	SO	AVG	OBP	SLG	PRO+	BR/A	SB	CS	SBR	FA	FR	G/POS	TPR
1923	Pit-N	2	2	0	1	0	0	0	0	0	1	.500	.500	.500	161	0	0	0	0	1.000	0	/1-1	0.0
1924	Pit-N	2	5	0	0	0	0	0	0	0	1	.000	.000	.000	-98	-1	0	0	0	1.000	0	/1-1	-0.1
Total	2	4	7	0	1	0	0	0	0	0	2	.143	.143	.143	-23	-1	0	0	0	1.000	1	/1-2	-0.1

■ HONEY BARNES
Barnes, John Francis b: 1/31/1900, Fulton, N.Y. d: 6/18/81, Lockport, N.Y. BL/TR, 5'10", 175 lbs. Deb: 4/20/26

YEAR	TM/L	G	AB	R	H	2B	3B	HR	RBI	BB	SO	AVG	OBP	SLG	PRO+	BR/A	SB	CS	SBR	FA	FR	G/POS	TPR
1926	NY-A	1	0	0	0	0	0	0	0	1	0	—	1.000	—	179	0	0	0	0	.000	0	/C-1	0.0

■ LUTE BARNES
Barnes, Luther Owens b: 4/28/47, Forest City, Iowa BR/TR, 5'10", 160 lbs. Deb: 8/6/72

YEAR	TM/L	G	AB	R	H	2B	3B	HR	RBI	BB	SO	AVG	OBP	SLG	PRO+	BR/A	SB	CS	SBR	FA	FR	G/POS	TPR
1972	NY-N	24	72	5	17	2	2	0	6	6	4	.236	.295	.319	76	-2	0	1	-1	.959	1	2-14/S-6	-0.1
1973	NY-N	3	2	2	1	0	0	0	1	0	1	.500	.500	.500	181	0	0	0	0	.000	0	H	0.0
Total	2	27	74	7	18	2	2	0	7	6	5	.243	.300	.324	79	-2	0	1	-1	.959	1	/2-14,S-6	-0.1

■ ROSS BARNES
Barnes, Roscoe Charles b: 5/8/1850, Mount Morris, N.Y. d: 2/5/15, Chicago, Ill. BR/TR, 5'8.5", 145 lbs. Deb: 5/5/1871 U

YEAR	TM/L	G	AB	R	H	2B	3B	HR	RBI	BB	SO	AVG	OBP	SLG	PRO+	BR/A	SB	CS	SBR	FA	FR	G/POS	TPR
1871	Bos-n	31	157	**66**	63	10	9	0	34	13	1	.401	.447	.580	186	17	11	6	-0	.873	13	2-16,S-15	**1.8**
1872	Bos-n	45	229	81	**99**	**28**	2	1	44	9	4	**.432**	.454	**.585**	**206**	**27**	12	2	**2**	**.901**	25	*2-45	**3.4**
1873	Bos-n	60	322	**125**	**137**	**29**	8	2	62	**18**	2	**.425**	**.456**	**.584**	**191**	**33**	**13**	4	2	.852	20	*2-47,3-13	**3.4**
1874	Bos-n	51	259	72	88	12	4	0	39	8	2	.340	.360	.417	140	10	8	7	-2	**.856**	19	*2-51/O-1	1.9
1875	Bos-n	78	393	**115**	**143**	20	4	1	58	7	3	.364	**.375**	.443	177	28	29	6	**5**	.877	**19**	*2-76/O-3,S-2	**4.2**
1876	Chi-N	66	322	**126**	**138**	**21**	**14**	1	59	**20**	8	**.429**	**.462**	**.590**	**222**	**39**				**.910**	5	*2-66/P-1	**3.7**
1877	Chi-N	22	92	16	25	1	0	0	5	7	4	.272	.323	.283	83	-2				.838	-8	2-22	-0.9
1879	Cin-N	77	323	55	86	9	2	1	30	16	25	.266	.301	.316	109	4				.864	-1	*S-61,2-16	0.7
1881	Bos-N	69	295	42	80	14	1	0	17	16	16	.271	.309	.325	104	2				.854	-0	*S-63/2-7	0.6
Total	5 n	265	1360	459	530	99	27	4	237	55	12	.390	.413	.511	180	115	73	25	7	.871	97	2-235/S-17,3-13,O-4	14.7
Total	4	234	1032	239	329	45	17	2	111	59	53	.319	.356	.401	143	43				.859	-5	S-124,2-111/P-1	4.1

■ SAM BARNES
Barnes, Samuel Thomas b: 12/18/1899, Suggsville, Ala. d: 2/19/81, Montgomery, Ala. BL/TR, 5'8", 150 lbs. Deb: 9/14/21

YEAR	TM/L	G	AB	R	H	2B	3B	HR	RBI	BB	SO	AVG	OBP	SLG	PRO+	BR/A	SB	CS	SBR	FA	FR	G/POS	TPR
1921	Det-A	7	11	2	2	1	0	0	0	2	1	.182	.357	.273	63	-1	0	0	0	.944	2	/2-2	0.1

■ BILL BARNES
Barnes, William H. b: Indianapolis, Ind. Deb: 9/27/1884

YEAR	TM/L	G	AB	R	H	2B	3B	HR	RBI	BB	SO	AVG	OBP	SLG	PRO+	BR/A	SB	CS	SBR	FA	FR	G/POS	TPR
1884	StP-U	8	30	2	6	1	0	0		0		.200	.200	.233	57	-4				.727	-2	/O-8	-0.5

■ SKEETER BARNES
Barnes, William Henry b: 3/3/57, Cincinnati, Ohio BR/TR, 5'10", 180 lbs. Deb: 9/6/83

YEAR	TM/L	G	AB	R	H	2B	3B	HR	RBI	BB	SO	AVG	OBP	SLG	PRO+	BR/A	SB	CS	SBR	FA	FR	G/POS	TPR
1983	Cin-N	15	34	5	7	0	0	1	4	7	3	.206	.372	.294	84	-0	2	2	-1	1.000	-0	/1-7,3-7	-0.2
1984	Cin-N	32	42	5	5	0	0	1	3	4	6	.119	.196	.190	8	-5	0	0	0	1.000	0	3-11/O-3	-0.5
1985	Mon-N	19	26	0	4	1	0	0	0	0	2	.154	.154	.192	-4	-4	0	1	-1	1.000	1	/3-4,O-3,1-1	-0.3
1987	StL-N	4	4	1	1	0	0	1	3	0	0	.250	.250	1.000	208	1	0	0	0	.000	0	/3-1	0.1
1989	Cin-N	5	3	1	0	0	0	0	0	0	0	.000	.000	.000	-97	-1	0	1	-1	.000	0	H	-0.2
1991	Det-A	75	159	28	46	13	2	5	17	9	24	.289	.327	.491	121	4	10	7	-1	1.000	-1	O-33,3-17/1-9,2D	0.1
1992	Det-A	95	165	27	45	8	1	3	25	10	18	.273	.322	.388	97	-1	3	1	0	.919	2	3-39,1-17,O-15,/2D	0.1
1993	Det-A	84	160	24	45	8	1	2	27	11	19	.281	.327	.381	90	-2	5	5	-2	.984	-0	1-27,O-18,3D2/S	-0.5
1994	Det-A	24	21	4	6	0	0	1	4	0	2	.286	.286	.429	81	-1	0	1	-1	1.000	-1	1-15/O-4,D-1	-0.2
Total	9	353	614	95	159	30	4	14	83	41	74	.259	.310	.389	90	-9	20	18	-5	.938	1	/3-92,O-76,1D2S	-1.6

■ ED BARNEY
Barney, Edmund J. b: 1/23/1890, Amery, Wis. d: 10/4/67, Rice Lake, Wis. BL/TR, 5'10.5", 178 lbs. Deb: 7/22/15

YEAR	TM/L	G	AB	R	H	2B	3B	HR	RBI	BB	SO	AVG	OBP	SLG	PRO+	BR/A	SB	CS	SBR	FA	FR	G/POS	TPR
1915	NY-A	11	36	1	7	0	0	0	8	3	6	.194	.256	.194	35	-3	2	1	0	1.000	-0	O-10	-0.4
	Pit-N	32	99	16	27	1	2	0	5	11	12	.273	.363	.323	110	2	7	3	0	.972	2	O-26	0.3
1916	Pit-N	45	137	16	27	4	0	0	9	23	15	.197	.313	.226	66	-4	8			.964	5	O-40	-0.2
Total	2	88	272	33	61	5	2	0	22	37	33	.224	.324	.257	78	-5	17	4		.971	7	/O-76	-0.3

■ CLYDE BARNHART
Barnhart, Clyde Lee "Pooch" b: 12/29/1895, Buck Valley, Pa. d: 1/21/80, Hagerstown, Md. BR/TR, 5'10", 155 lbs. Deb: 9/22/20 F

YEAR	TM/L	G	AB	R	H	2B	3B	HR	RBI	BB	SO	AVG	OBP	SLG	PRO+	BR/A	SB	CS	SBR	FA	FR	G/POS	TPR
1920	Pit-N	12	46	5	15	4	2	0	5	1	2	.326	.340	.500	135	2	1	0	0	.971	0	3-12	0.3
1921	Pit-N	124	449	66	116	15	13	3	62	32	36	.258	.312	.370	78	-15	3	3	-1	.956	-19	*3-118	-2.6
1922	Pit-N	75	209	30	69	7	5	1	38	25	7	.330	.402	.426	112	5	3	2	-0	.918	-12	3-30,O-26	-0.7
1923	Pit-N	114	327	60	106	25	13	9	72	47	21	.324	.409	.563	151	24	5	7	-3	.985	3	O-92	1.8

YEAR	TM/L	G	AB	R	H	2B	3B	HR	RBI	BB	SO	AVG	OBP	SLG	PRO+	BR/A	SB	CS	SBR	FA	FR	G/POS	TPR
1924	Pit-N	102	344	49	95	6	11	3	51	30	17	.276	.338	.384	91	-4	8	4	0	.970	2	O-88	-0.8
1925	*Pit-N	142	539	85	175	32	11	4	114	59	25	.325	.391	.447	106	6	9	5	-0	.962	1	*O-138	-0.2
1926	Pit-N	76	203	26	39	3	0	0	10	23	13	.192	.278	.207	30	-19	1			.991	-4	O-61	-2.7
1927	*Pit-N	108	360	65	115	23	4	3	54	37	19	.319	.384	.431	110	6	2			.978	4	O-94	0.4
1928	Pit-N	61	196	18	58	6	2	4	30	11	9	.296	.333	.408	89	-3	3			.971	-2	O-48/3-1	-0.8
Total	9	814	2673	404	788	121	61	27	436	265	149	.295	.360	.416	100	1	35	21		.973	-27	O-547,3-161	-5.3

■ VIC BARNHART
Barnhart, Victor Dee b: 9/1/22, Hagerstown, Md. BR/TR, 6', 188 lbs. Deb: 10/1/44 F

YEAR	TM/L	G	AB	R	H	2B	3B	HR	RBI	BB	SO	AVG	OBP	SLG	PRO+	BR/A	SB	CS	SBR	FA	FR	G/POS	TPR
1944	Pit-N	1	2	0	1	0	0	0	0	1	1	.500	.667	.500	222	0	0			.889	1	/S-1	0.2
1945	Pit-N	71	201	21	54	7	0	0	19	9	11	.269	.300	.303	65	-9	2			.928	8	S-60/3-4	0.2
1946	Pit-N	2	1	0	0	0	0	0	0	0	0	.000	.000	.000	-98	-0	0			.000	0	H	0.0
Total	3	74	204	21	55	7	0	0	19	10	12	.270	.304	.304	67	-9	2			.927	9	/S-61,3-4	0.4

■ BILLY BARNIE
Barnie, William Harrison "Bald Billy" b: 1/26/1853, New York, N.Y. d: 7/15/1900, Hartford, Conn. TR , 5'7", 157 lbs. Deb: 5/7/1874 MU

YEAR	TM/L	G	AB	R	H	2B	3B	HR	RBI	BB	SO	AVG	OBP	SLG	PRO+	BR/A	SB	CS	SBR	FA	FR	G/POS	TPR
1874	Har-n	45	190	21	35	4	2	0	20	1	13	.184	.188	.226	31	-15	2	2	-1	.733	-6	C-30,O-29/S-1	-1.6
1875	Wes-n	10	36	3	4	1	0	0	2	0	3	.111	.111	.139	-13	-4	0	0	0	.889	1	/O-7,C-3	-0.3
	Mut-n	9	34	1	5	0	0	0	1	1	0	.147	.171	.147	11	-3	0	0	0	.750	-4	/C-6,O-3	-0.6
	Yr	19	70	4	9	1	0	0	3	1	3	.129	.141	.143	-1	-7	0	0	0	.857	-3	O-10/C-9	-0.9
1883	Bal-a	17	55	7	11	0	0	0		2		.200	.228	.200	38	-4				.846	-2	C-13/O-6,S-1,M	-0.4
1886	Bal-a	2	6	0	0	0	0	0	0	1		.000	.143	.000	-55	-1	0			.000	-1	/O-1,C-1	-0.2
Total	2 n	64	260	25	44	5	2	0	23	2	16	.169	.176	.204	23	-22	2	2	-1	.690	-9	/O-39,C-39,S-1	-2.5
Total	2	19	61	7	11	0	0	0	0	3		.180	.219	.180	29	-5	0			.848	-3	/C-14,O-7,S-1	-0.6

■ DICK BARONE
Barone, Richard Anthony b: 10/13/32, San Jose, Cal. BR/TR, 5'9", 165 lbs. Deb: 9/22/60

YEAR	TM/L	G	AB	R	H	2B	3B	HR	RBI	BB	SO	AVG	OBP	SLG	PRO+	BR/A	SB	CS	SBR	FA	FR	G/POS	TPR
1960	Pit-N	3	6	0	0	0	0	0	0	0	1	.000	.000	.000	-99	-2	0	0	0	.875	-0	/S-2	-0.2

■ SCOTTY BARR
Barr, Hyder Edward b: 10/6/1886, Bristol, Tenn. d: 12/2/34, Ft.Worth, Tex. BR/TR, 6', 175 lbs. Deb: 8/22/08

YEAR	TM/L	G	AB	R	H	2B	3B	HR	RBI	BB	SO	AVG	OBP	SLG	PRO+	BR/A	SB	CS	SBR	FA	FR	G/POS	TPR
1908	Phi-A	19	56	4	8	2	0	0	1	3		.143	.200	.179	22	-5	0			.923	-7	2-11/3-4,1-2,O-2	-1.4
1909	Phi-A	22	51	5	4	1	0	0	1	11		.078	.254	.098	12	-5	2			.947	-1	O-15/1-7	-0.7
Total	2	41	107	9	12	3	0	0	2	14		.112	.228	.140	17	-9	2			.947	-8	/O-17,2-11,1-9,3-4	-2.1

■ CUNO BARRAGAN
Barragan, Facundo Anthony b: 6/20/32, Sacramento, Cal. BR/TR, 5'11", 180 lbs. Deb: 9/1/61

YEAR	TM/L	G	AB	R	H	2B	3B	HR	RBI	BB	SO	AVG	OBP	SLG	PRO+	BR/A	SB	CS	SBR	FA	FR	G/POS	TPR
1961	Chi-N	10	28	3	6	0	0	1	2	2	7	.214	.267	.321	54	-2	0	0	0	1.000	-1	C-10	-0.3
1962	Chi-N	58	134	11	27	6	1	0	12	21	28	.201	.310	.261	53	-8	0	2	-1	.971	-7	C-55	-1.5
1963	Chi-N	1	1	0	0	0	0	0	0	0	1	.000	.000	.000	-95	-0	0	0	0	1.000	-0	/C-1	0.0
Total	3	69	163	14	33	6	1	1	14	23	36	.202	.301	.270	53	-11	0	2	-1	.975	-8	/C-66	-1.8

■ GERMAN BARRANCA
Barranca, German (Costales) b: 10/19/56, Veracruz, Mex. BL/TR, 6', 160 lbs. Deb: 9/2/79

YEAR	TM/L	G	AB	R	H	2B	3B	HR	RBI	BB	SO	AVG	OBP	SLG	PRO+	BR/A	SB	CS	SBR	FA	FR	G/POS	TPR
1979	KC-A	5	5	3	3	1	0	0	0	0	0	.600	.600	.800	269	1	3	1	0	1.000	3	/2-1,3-1,D-1	0.4
1980	KC-A	7	0	3	0	0	0	0	0	0	0	—	—	—	—	0	0	0	0	.000	0	/R	0.0
1981	Cin-N	9	6	2	2	0	0	0	1	0	0	.333	.333	.333	88	-0	0	0	0	.000	0	/H	0.0
1982	Cin-N	46	51	11	13	1	3	0	2	2	9	.255	.283	.392	85	-1	2	0	1	.824	-1	/2-6	-0.2
Total	4	67	62	19	18	2	3	0	3	2	9	.290	.313	.419	101	-0	5	1	1	.893	2	/2-7,D-1,3-1	0.2

■ BARRETT
Barrett b: Brooklyn, N.Y. Deb: 9/18/1872

YEAR	TM/L	G	AB	R	H	2B	3B	HR	RBI	BB	SO	AVG	OBP	SLG	PRO+	BR/A	SB	CS	SBR	FA	FR	G/POS	TPR
1872	Atl-n	8	34	7	7	1	0	0	2	0	1	.206	.206	.235	30	-3	1	0	0	.808	-0	/O-8	-0.2

■ JIMMY BARRETT
Barrett, James Erigena b: 3/28/1875, Athol, Mass. d: 10/24/21, Detroit, Mich. BL/TR, 5'9", 170 lbs. Deb: 9/13/1899

YEAR	TM/L	G	AB	R	H	2B	3B	HR	RBI	BB	SO	AVG	OBP	SLG	PRO+	BR/A	SB	CS	SBR	FA	FR	G/POS	TPR
1899	Cin-N	26	92	30	34	2	4	0	10	18		.370	.477	.478	160	9	4			.936	-2	O-26	0.4
1900	Cin-N	137	545	114	172	11	7	5	42	72		.316	.400	.389	121	19	44			.929	4	*O-137	1.2
1901	Det-A	135	542	110	159	16	9	4	65	76		.293	.385	.378	107	8	26			.940	15	*O-135	1.1
1902	Det-A	136	509	93	154	19	6	4	44	74		.303	.397	.387	116	14	24			.961	8	*O-136	1.2
1903	Det-A	136	517	95	163	13	10	2	31	**74**		.315	**.407**	.391	144	32	27			.955	7	*O-136	3.2
1904	Det-A	162	624	83	167	10	5	0	31	**79**		.268	.353	.300	111	12	15			.971	12	*O-162	1.6
1905	Det-A	20	67	2	17	1	0	0	3	6		.254	.324	.269	88	-1	0			1.000	-3	O-18	-0.5
1906	Cin-N	5	12	1	0	0	0	0	0	2		.000	.143	.000	-53	-2	0			1.000	0	/O-4	-0.3
1907	Bos-A	106	390	52	95	11	6	1	28	38		.244	.314	.310	100	1	3			.966	4	O-99	0.1
1908	Bos-A	3	8	0	1	0	0	0	1	1		.125	.222	.125	13	-1	0			1.000	-1	/O-2	-0.2
Total	10	866	3306	580	962	83	47	16	255	440		.291	.379	.359	117	91	143			.954	44	O-855	7.8

■ JOHNNY BARRETT
Barrett, John Joseph "Jack" b: 12/18/15, Lowell, Mass. d: 8/17/74, Seabrook Beach, N.H. BL/TL, 5'10.5", 170 lbs. Deb: 4/14/42

YEAR	TM/L	G	AB	R	H	2B	3B	HR	RBI	BB	SO	AVG	OBP	SLG	PRO+	BR/A	SB	CS	SBR	FA	FR	G/POS	TPR
1942	Pit-N	111	332	56	82	11	6	0	26	48	42	.247	.347	.316	92	-1	10			.973	6	O-94	0.0
1943	Pit-N	130	290	41	67	12	3	1	32	32	23	.231	.316	.303	77	-8	5			.988	-11	O-99	-2.5
1944	Pit-N	149	568	99	153	24	**19**	7	83	86	56	.269	.366	.415	115	13	**28**			.972	-1	*O-147	0.4
1945	Pit-N	142	507	97	130	29	4	15	67	79	68	.256	.357	.418	111	8	25			.976	-2	*O-132	-0.1
1946	Pit-N	32	71	7	12	3	0	0	6	8	11	.169	.253	.211	32	-6	1			.919	-3	O-21	-1.1
	Bos-N	24	43	3	10	3	0	0	6	12	1	.233	.400	.302	100	1	0			.962	-3	O-17	-0.3
	Yr	56	114	10	22	6	0	0	12	20	12	.193	.313	.246	59	-6	1			.937	-6	O-38	-1.4
Total	5	588	1811	303	454	82	32	23	220	265	201	.251	.349	.369	100	5	69			.974	-15	O-510	-3.6

■ MARTY BARRETT
Barrett, Martin F. b: 11/1860, Port Henry, N.Y. d: 1/29/10, Holyoke, Mass. BR/TR, 5'9", 170 lbs. Deb: 6/24/1884

YEAR	TM/L	G	AB	R	H	2B	3B	HR	RBI	BB	SO	AVG	OBP	SLG	PRO+	BR/A	SB	CS	SBR	FA	FR	G/POS	TPR
1884	Bos-N	3	6	0	0	0	0	0	0	0	4	.000	.000	.000	-99	-1				.900	-1	/C-3	-0.2
	Ind-a	5	13	1	1	1	0	0		1		.077	.143	.154	-3	-1				.808	-3	/C-4,O-1	-0.4
Total	1	8	19	1	1	1	0	0	0	1	4	.053	.100	.105	-34	-3				.833	-4	/C-7,O-1	-0.6

■ MARTY BARRETT
Barrett, Martin Glenn b: 6/23/58, Arcadia, Cal. BR/TR, 5'10", 176 lbs. Deb: 9/6/82 F

YEAR	TM/L	G	AB	R	H	2B	3B	HR	RBI	BB	SO	AVG	OBP	SLG	PRO+	BR/A	SB	CS	SBR	FA	FR	G/POS	TPR
1982	Bos-A	8	18	0	1	0	0	0	0	0	1	.056	.056	.056	-66	-4	0	0	0	1.000	5	/2-7	0.1
1983	Bos-A	33	44	7	10	1	1	0	2	3	1	.227	.277	.295	54	-3	0	0	0	.984	4	2-23/D-5	0.2
1984	Bos-A	139	475	56	144	23	3	3	45	42	25	.303	.361	.383	101	2	5	3	-0	**.987**	0	*2-136	0.6
1985	Bos-A	156	534	59	142	26	0	5	56	56	50	.266	.338	.343	84	-11	7	5	-1	.987	15	*2-155	0.8
1986	*Bos-A	158	625	94	179	39	4	4	60	65	31	.286	.355	.381	100	1	15	7	0	.982	-3	*2-158	0.5
1987	Bos-A	137	559	72	164	23	0	3	43	51	38	.293	.354	.351	85	-10	15	2	3	**.988**	**32**	*2-137	3.0
1988	*Bos-A	150	612	83	173	28	1	1	65	40	35	.283	.334	.337	85	-12	7	3	0	.990	2	*2-150	-0.3
1989	Bos-A	86	336	31	86	18	0	1	27	32	12	.256	.324	.318	77	-10	4	1	1	.975	1	2-80/D-4	-0.6
1990	*Bos-A	62	159	15	36	4	0	0	13	15	13	.226	.297	.252	53	-10	4	0	1	.992	9	2-60/3-1,D-1	0.1
1991	SD-N	12	16	1	3	1	0	1	3	0	3	.188	.235	.438	83	-0	0	0	0	1.000	1	/2-2,3-2	0.0
Total	10	941	3378	418	938	163	9	18	314	304	209	.278	.340	.347	86	-57	57	21	5	.986	66	2 908/D-10,3-3	4.4

■ MICHAEL BARRETT
Barrett, Michael P. b: 10/22/76, Atlanta, Ga. BR/TR, 6'3", 185 lbs. Deb: 9/19/98

YEAR	TM/L	G	AB	R	H	2B	3B	HR	RBI	BB	SO	AVG	OBP	SLG	PRO+	BR/A	SB	CS	SBR	FA	FR	G/POS	TPR
1998	Mon-N	8	23	3	7	2	0	1	2	3	6	.304	.407	.522	144	2	0	0	0	.963	-1	/C-3,3-3	0.1

■ BOB BARRETT
Barrett, Robert Schley "Jumbo" b: 1/27/1899, Atlanta, Ga. d: 1/18/82, Atlanta, Ga. BR/TR, 5'11", 175 lbs. Deb: 4/30/23

YEAR	TM/L	G	AB	R	H	2B	3B	HR	RBI	BB	SO	AVG	OBP	SLG	PRO+	BR/A	SB	CS	SBR	FA	FR	G/POS	TPR
1923	Chi-N	3	3	0	1	0	0	0	0	0	0	.333	.333	.333	76	-0	0	0	0	.000	0	H	0.0
1924	Chi-N	54	133	12	32	2	3	5	21	7	29	.241	.279	.414	82	-4	1	0	0	.943	-1	2-25,1-10/3-8	-0.4
1925	Chi-N	14	32	1	10	1	0	0	7	1	4	.313	.333	.344	72	-1	1	2	-1	1.000	-3	/3-6,2-4	-0.5
	Bro-N	1	1	0	0	0	0	0	1	0	0	.000	.000	.000	-99	-0	0	0	0	.000	0	H	0.0
	Yr	15	33	1	10	1	0	0	8	1	4	.303	.324	.333	67	-2	1	2	-1	1.000	-3	/3-6,2-4	-0.5
1927	Bro-N	99	355	29	92	10	2	5	38	14	22	.259	.289	.341	68	-17	1			.920	-8	3-96	-2.0
1929	Bos-A	68	126	15	34	10	0	0	19	10	6	.270	.324	.349	75	-5	3	1	0	.938	6	3-34/1-4,2-2,O-1	0.2
Total	5	239	650	57	169	23	5	10	86	32	61	.260	.296	.357	72	-27	6	3		.924	-6	3-144/2-31,1-14,O-1	-2.7

YEAR	TM/L	G	AB	R	H	2B	3B	HR	RBI	BB	SO	AVG	OBP	SLG	PRO+	BR/A	SB	CS	SBR	FA	FR	G/POS	TPR
■ TOM BARRETT	Barrett, Thomas Loren b: 4/2/60, San Fernando, Cal. BB/TR, 5'9", 157 lbs. Deb: 7/2/88 F																						
1988	Phi-N	36	54	5	11	1	0	0	3	7	8	.204	.306	.222	53	-3	0	0	0	.959	2	2-10	-0.1
1989	Phi-N	14	27	3	6	0	0	0	1	1	7	.222	.250	.222	36	-2	0	0	0	.978	4	/2-9	0.2
1992	Bos-A	4	3	1	0	0	0	0	0	2	0	.000	.400	.000	19	-0	0	0	0	1.000	1	/2-2	0.0
Total	3	54	84	9	17	1	0	0	4	10	15	.202	.295	.214	47	-5	0	0	0	.970	7	/2-21	0.1
■ BILL BARRETT	Barrett, William b: Washington, D.C. Deb: 7/8/1871																						
1871	Kek-n	1	5	1	1	1	0	0	1	0	0	.200	.200	.400	66	-0	0	0	0	1.000	1	/C-1,3-1	0.0
1872	Oly-n	1	4	0	0	0	0	0	0	0	0	.000	.000	.000	-99	-1	0	0	0	.400	-1	/C-1	-0.2
1873	Bal-n	1	4	0	1	0	0	0	0	0	0	.250	.250	.250	49	-0	0	1	-1	.667	-1	/S-1,O-1	-0.1
Total	3 n	3	13	1	2	1	0	0	1	0	0	.154	.154	.231	12	-1	0	1	-1	.769	-1	/C-2,O-1,S-1,3-1	-0.3
■ BILL BARRETT	Barrett, William Joseph "Whispering Bill" b: 5/28/1900, Cambridge, Mass. d: 1/26/51, Cambridge, Mass. BR/TR, 6', 175 lbs. Deb: 5/13/21																						
1921	Phi-A	14	30	3	7	2	1	0	3	0	5	.233	.233	.367	51	-2	0	0	0	.925	2	/S-8,P-4,3-2,1-1	0.1
1923	Chi-A	44	162	17	44	7	2	2	23	9	24	.272	.310	.377	81	-5	12	3	2	.940	0	O-40/3-1	-0.5
1924	Chi-A	119	406	52	110	18	5	2	56	30	38	.271	.326	.355	78	-14	15	10	-2	.904	-15	S-77,O-28/3-8	-2.2
1925	Chi-A	81	245	44	89	23	3	3	40	24	27	.363	.420	.518	145	16	5	6	-2	.943	-7	2-41,O-27/S-4,3-4	0.7
1926	Chi-A	111	368	46	113	31	4	6	61	25	26	.307	.353	.462	115	6	9	7	-2	.969	-6	*O-102/1-2	-0.7
1927	Chi-A	147	556	62	159	35	9	4	83	52	46	.286	.347	.403	96	-4	20	13	-2	.963	7	*O-147	-0.8
1928	Chi-A	76	235	34	65	11	2	3	26	14	30	.277	.320	.379	84	-6	8	3	1	.988	-5	O-37,2-25	-1.1
1929	Chi-A	3	1	0	0	0	0	0	0	2	0	.000	.667	.000	87	0	0	0	0	.000	0	H	0.0
	Bos-A	111	370	57	100	23	4	3	35	51	38	.270	.363	.378	93	-3	11	8	-2	.974	4	*O-109/3-1	-0.7
	Yr	114	371	57	100	23	4	3	35	53	38	.270	.365	.377	94	-2	11	8	-2	.974	4	*O-109/3-1	-0.7
1930	Bos-A	6	18	3	3	1	0	0	1	1	3	.167	.211	.222	10	-2	0	0	0	1.000	-1	/O-5	-0.4
	Was-A	6	4	0	0	0	0	0	0	1	2	.000	.200	.000	-44	-1	0	0	0	1.000	-0	/O-1	-0.1
	Yr	12	22	3	3	1	0	0	1	2	5	.136	.208	.182	-0	-3	0	0	0	1.000	-1	/O-6	-0.5
Total	9	718	2395	318	690	151	30	23	328	209	239	.288	.347	.405	97	-14	80	50	-6	.964	-21	O-496/S-89,23P1	-5.7
■ JOSE BARRIOS	Barrios, Jose Manuel b: 6/26/57, New York, N.Y. BR/TR, 6'4", 195 lbs. Deb: 4/23/82																						
1982	SF-N	10	19	2	3	0	0	0	0	1	4	.158	.200	.158	1	-2	0	0	0	1.000	-1	/1-7	-0.4
■ TONY BARRON	Barron, Anthony Dirk b: 8/17/66, Portland, Ore. BR/TR, 6', 185 lbs. Deb: 6/2/96																						
1996	Mon-N	1	1	0	0	0	0	0	0	0	1	.000	.000	.000	-98	-0	0	0	0	.000	0	/H	0.0
1997	Phi-N	57	189	22	54	12	1	4	24	12	38	.286	.335	.423	97	-1	0	1	-1	.983	6	O-53	0.3
Total	2	58	190	22	54	12	1	4	24	12	39	.284	.333	.421	96	-1	0	1	-1	.983	6	/O-53	0.3
■ RED BARRON	Barron, David Irenus b: 6/21/1900, Clarksville, Ga. d: 10/4/82, Atlanta, Ga. BR/TR, 5'11.5", 185 lbs. Deb: 6/10/29																						
1929	Bos-N	10	21	3	4	1	0	0	1	1	4	.190	.227	.238	16	-3	2			.929	1	/O-6	-0.2
■ FRANK BARROWS	Barrows, Franklin L. b: 10/22/1846, Hudson, Ohio d: 2/6/22, Fitchburg, Mass. Deb: 5/20/1871																						
1871	Bos-n	18	86	13	13	2	1	0	11	0	0	.151	.151	.198	-1	-11	1	0	0	.829	-2	O-17/2-1	-0.8
■ CUKE BARROWS	Barrows, Roland b: 10/20/1883, Gray, Maine d: 2/10/55, Gorham, Maine BL/TR, 5'8", 158 lbs. Deb: 9/18/09																						
1909	Chi-A	5	20	1	3	0	0	0	2	0		.150	.190	.150	8	-2	0			.923	2	/O-5	-0.1
1910	Chi-A	6	20	0	4	0	0	0	1	3		.200	.304	.200	61	-1	0			.875	-1	/O-6	-0.3
1911	Chi-A	13	46	5	9	2	0	0	4	7		.196	.315	.239	57	-2	2			1.000	-2	O-13	-0.5
1912	Chi-A	8	13	0	3	0	0	0	2	2		.231	.333	.231	64	-0	1			1.000	-0	/O-3	-0.1
Total	4	32	99	6	19	2	0	0	9	12		.192	.292	.212	50	-6	3			.950	-2	/O-27	-1.0
■ JEFF BARRY	Barry, Jeffrey Finas b: 9/22/69, Medford, Ore. BB/TR, 6'1", 190 lbs. Deb: 6/9/95																						
1995	NY-N	15	15	2	2	1	0	0	0	1	8	.133	.188	.200	2	-2	0	0	0	1.000	-0	/O-2	-0.2
1998	Col-N	15	34	4	6	1	0	0	2	2	11	.176	.222	.206	10	-5	0	0	0	1.000	-1	O-10	-0.6
Total	2	30	49	6	8	2	0	0	2	3	19	.163	.212	.204	8	-7	0	0	0	1.000	-1	/O-12	-0.8
■ SHAD BARRY	Barry, John C. b: 10/27/1878, Newburgh, N.Y. d: 11/27/36, Los Angeles, Cal. BR/TR, Deb: 5/30/1899																						
1899	Was-N	78	247	31	71	7	5	1	33	12		.287	.328	.368	92	-3	11			.946	-16	O-23,1-22,S-13,3/2	-1.7
1900	Bos-N	81	254	40	66	10	7	1	37	13		.260	.301	.366	74	-10	9			.956	-16	O-24,S-18,2-16,1/3	-2.4
1901	Bos-N	11	40	3	7	2	0	0	6	2		.175	.233	.225	30	-4	1			.926	-0	O-11	-0.5
	Phi-N	67	252	35	62	10	0	1	22	15		.246	.294	.298	70	-10	13			.903	-13	2-35,3-16,O-13,/S-1	-2.1
	Yr	78	292	38	69	12	0	1	28	17		.236	.285	.288	64	-13	14			.903	-13	2-35,O-24,3-16,/S-1	-2.6
1902	Phi-N	138	543	65	156	20	6	3	58	44		.287	.343	.363	118	11	14			.939	-5	*O-137/1-1	-0.3
1903	Phi-N	138	550	75	152	24	5	1	60	30		.276	.321	.344	92	-6	26			.970	-2	*O-107,1-30/3-1	-1.5
1904	Phi-N	35	122	15	25	2	0	0	3	11		.205	.281	.221	58	-6	2			.979	13	O-32/3-1	0.6
	Chi-N	73	263	29	69	7	2	1	26	17		.262	.310	.316	93	-2	12			.917	-1	O-30,1-18,3-16,/S2	-0.5
	Yr	108	385	44	94	9	2	1	29	28		.244	.300	.286	82	-8	14			.955	12	O-62,1-18,3-17,/S2	0.1
1905	Chi-N	27	104	10	22	2	0	0	10	5		.212	.255	.231	43	-7	5			.982	1	1-26	-0.8
	Cin-N	125	494	90	160	11	12	1	56	33		.324	.372	.401	118	9	16			.982	-7	*1-124/O-2	-0.1
	Yr	152	598	100	182	13	12	1	66	38		.304	.352	.371	105	3	21			.982	-7	*1-150/O-2	-0.9
1906	Cin-N	73	279	38	80	10	5	1	33	26		.287	.354	.369	120	7	11			.993	1	1-43,O-30	0.5
	StL-N	62	237	26	59	9	1	0	12	15		.249	.299	.295	89	-3	6			.930	-7	O-35,1-21/3-6	-1.3
	Yr	135	516	64	139	19	6	1	45	41		.269	.329	.335	107	4	17			.922	-6	O-65,1-64/3-6	-0.8
1907	StL-N	81	294	30	73	5	2	0	19	28		.248	.320	.279	91	-2	4			.963	-6	O-81	-1.4
1908	StL-N	74	268	24	61	8	1	0	11	19		.228	.286	.265	80	-6	9			.967	-1	O-69/S-2	-1.1
	NY-N	37	67	5	10	1	1	0	5	9		.149	.260	.194	43	-4	1			.971	-6	O-31	-1.3
	Yr	111	335	29	71	9	2	0	16	28		.212	.281	.251	71	-10	10			.968	-7	*O-100/S-2	-2.4
Total	10	1100	4014	516	1073	128	47	10	391	279		.267	.321	.330	94	-37	140			.955	-65	O-625,1-295/23S	-13.9
■ JACK BARRY	Barry, John Joseph b: 4/26/1887, Meriden, Conn. d: 4/23/61, Shrewsbury, Mass. BR/TR, 5'9", 158 lbs. Deb: 7/13/08 M																						
1908	Phi-A	40	135	13	30	4	3	0	8	10		.222	.291	.296	85	-2	5			.966	-11	2-20,S-14/3-3	-1.5
1909	Phi-A	124	409	56	88	11	2	1	23	44		.215	.307	.259	77	-9	17			.927	-31	*S-124	-4.4
1910	*Phi-A	145	487	64	126	19	5	3	60	52		.259	.336	.337	112	8	14			.916	-22	*S-145	-1.0
1911	*Phi-A	127	442	73	117	18	7	1	63	38		.265	.333	.344	90	-6	30			**.944**	-7	*S-127	-0.4
1912	Phi-A	140	483	75	126	19	9	0	55	47		.261	.335	.337	96	-2	22			.925	-6	*S-139	0.3
1913	*Phi-A	134	455	62	125	20	6	3	85	44	32	.275	.349	.365	111	7	15			.953	-8	*S-134	1.2
1914	*Phi-A	140	467	57	113	12	0	0	42	53	34	.242	.324	.268	81	-9	22	13	-1	.947	5	*S-140	0.6
1915	Phi-A	54	194	16	43	6	2	0	15	15	9	.222	.284	.273	69	-8	6	5	-1	.952	-4	S-54	-1.0
	*Bos-A	78	248	30	65	13	2	0	26	24	11	.262	.342	.331	104	2	0			.962	-4	2-78	-0.2
	Yr	132	442	46	108	19	4	0	41	39	20	.244	.317	.305	89	-6	6	5	-1	.962	-9	2-78,S-54	-1.2
1916	Bos-A	94	330	28	67	6	1	0	20	17	24	.203	.277	.227	52	-19	8			.974	2	2-94	-1.6
1917	Bos-A	116	388	45	83	9	0	2	30	47	27	.214	.305	.253	71	-12	12			**.974**	-11	*2-116,M	-1.9
1919	Bos-A	31	108	13	26	5	1	0	2	5	5	.241	.293	.306	72	-4	2			.922	-7	2-31	-1.0
Total	11	1223	4146	532	1009	142	38	10	429	396	142	.243	.321	.303	88	-54	153	18		.935	-105	S-877,2-339/3-3	-10.9
■ RICH BARRY	Barry, Richard Donovan b: 9/12/40, Berkeley, Cal. BR/TR, 6'4", 205 lbs. Deb: 7/4/69																						
1969	Phi-N	20	32	4	6	1	0	0	0	5	6	.188	.316	.219	54	-2	0	0	0	.938	-0	/O-9	-0.2
■ KIMERA BARTEE	Bartee, Kimera Anotchi b: 7/21/72, Omaha, Neb. BR/TR, 6', 175 lbs. Deb: 4/3/96																						
1996	Det-A	110	217	32	55	6	1	1	14	17	77	.253	.308	.304	56	-14	20	10	0	.991	-5	O-99/D-2	-1.9
1997	Det-A	12	5	4	1	0	0	0	0	2	2	.200	.500	.200	93	0	3	1	0	1.000	-2	/O-6,D-3	-0.1
1998	Det-A	57	98	20	19	5	1	3	15	6	35	.194	.240	.357	52	-7	9	5	-0	.964	-2	O-29,D-10	-1.0
Total	3	179	320	56	75	11	2	4	29	25	114	.234	.292	.319	56	-21	32	16	0	.986	-9	O-134/D-15	-3.0

YEAR	TM/L	G	AB	R	H	2B	3B	HR	RBI	BB	SO	AVG	OBP	SLG	PRO+	BR/A	SB	CS	SBR	FA	FR	G/POS	TPR
■ **DICK BARTELL**	Bartell, Richard William "Rowdy Richard" b: 11/22/07, Chicago, Ill. d: 8/4/95, Alameda, Cal. BR/TR, 5'9", 160 lbs. Deb: 10/2/27 C																						
1927	Pit-N	1	2	0	0	0	0	0	0	2	0	.000	.500	.000	41	0	0			1.000	0	/S-1	0.0
1928	Pit-N	72	233	27	71	8	4	1	36	21	18	.305	.377	.386	96	-1	4			.974	2	2-39,S-27/3-1	0.5
1929	Pit-N	143	610	101	184	40	13	2	57	40	29	.302	.347	.420	87	-13	11			.953	4	S-74,2-70	0.3
1930	Pit-N	129	475	69	152	32	13	4	75	39	34	.320	.378	.467	102	2	8			.941	6	*S-126	1.9
1931	Phi-N	135	554	88	160	43	7	0	34	27	38	.289	.325	.392	85	-12	6			.948	3	*S-133/2-3	0.5
1932	Phi-N	154	614	118	189	48	7	1	53	64	47	.308	.379	.414	101	2	8			.963	10	*S-154	2.5
1933	Phi-N★	152	587	78	159	25	5	1	37	56	46	.271	.340	.336	83	-12	6			.951	9	*S-152	0.8
1934	Phi-N	146	604	102	187	30	4	0	37	64	59	.310	.384	.373	91	-6	13			.954	14	*S-146	1.6
1935	NY-N	137	539	60	141	28	4	14	53	37	52	.262	.316	.406	94	-5	5			.954	10	*S-137	1.2
1936	*NY-N	145	510	71	152	31	3	8	42	40	36	.298	.355	.418	109	6	6			.956	**45**	*S-144	**5.7**
1937	*NY-N★	128	516	91	158	38	2	14	62	40	38	.306	.367	.469	124	17	5			.958	**38**	*S-128	6.1
1938	NY-N	127	481	67	126	26	1	9	49	55	60	.262	.347	.376	98	-0	4			.952	22	*S-127	3.2
1939	Chi-N	105	336	37	80	24	2	3	34	42	25	.238	.335	.348	82	-8	6			.943	-5	*S-101/3-1	-0.4
1940	*Det-A	139	528	76	123	24	3	7	53	76	53	.233	.335	.330	67	-26	12	2	2	.953	12	*S-139	0.0
1941	Det-A	5	12	0	2	1	0	0	1	2	2	.167	.333	.250	51	-1	0	1	-1	.920	1	/S-5	0.0
	NY-N	104	373	44	113	20	0	5	35	52	29	.303	.394	.397	121	12	6			.959	-10	3-84,S-21	0.5
1942	NY-N	90	316	53	77	10	3	5	24	44	34	.244	.351	.342	102	2	4			.965	1	3-52,S-31	0.6
1943	NY-N	99	337	48	91	14	0	5	28	47	27	.270	.371	.356	110	6	5			.980	18	3-54,S-33	2.9
1946	NY-N	5	2	0	0	0	0	0	0	0	0	.000	.000	.000	-99	-1	0			1.000	1	/3-4,2-2	0.0
Total	18	2016	7629	1130	2165	442	71	79	710	748	627	.284	.355	.391	96	-36	109	3		.953	178	*S-1679,3-196,2-114	27.9
■ **TONY BARTIROME**	Bartirome, Anthony Joseph b: 5/9/32, Pittsburgh, Pa. BL/TL, 5'10", 155 lbs. Deb: 4/19/52 C																						
1952	Pit-N	124	355	32	78	10	3	0	16	26	37	.220	.273	.265	48	-25	3	3	-1	.989	2	*1-118	-2.8
■ **BOYD BARTLEY**	Bartley, Boyd Owen b: 2/11/20, Chicago, Ill. BR/TR, 5'8.5", 165 lbs. Deb: 5/30/43																						
1943	Bro-N	9	21	0	1	0	0	0	1	1	3	.048	.091	.048	-59	-4	0			.897	2	/S-9	-0.2
■ **IRV BARTLING**	Bartling, Henry Irving b: 6/27/14, Bay City, Mich. d: 6/12/73, Westland, Mich. BR/TR, 6', 175 lbs. Deb: 9/8/38																						
1938	Phi-A	14	46	5	8	1	1	0	5	3	7	.174	.224	.239	17	-6	0	0	0	.914	-3	S-13/3-1	-0.7
■ **HARRY BARTON**	Barton, Harry Lamb b: 1/20/1875, Chester, Pa. d: 1/25/55, Upland, Pa. BB/TR, 5'6.5", 155 lbs. Deb: 4/15/05																						
1905	Phi-A	29	60	5	10	2	1	0	3	3		.167	.206	.233	39	-4	2			.954	-5	C-13/1-2,3-2,O-1	-1.0
■ **BOB BARTON**	Barton, Robert Wilbur b: 7/30/41, Norwood, O. BR/TR, 6', 175 lbs. Deb: 9/17/65																						
1965	SF-N	4	7	1	4	0	0	0	1	0	0	.571	.571	.571	217	1	0	0	0	1.000	1	/C-2	0.2
1966	SF-N	43	91	1	16	2	1	0	3	5	5	.176	.219	.220	22	-9	0	0	0	.994	7	C-39	-0.1
1967	SF-N	7	19	0	4	0	0	0	1	0	2	.211	.250	.211	34	-2	0	0	0	1.000	1	/C-7	-0.1
1968	SF-N	46	92	4	24	2	0	0	5	7	18	.261	.313	.283	80	-2	0	0	0	.995	12	C-45	1.3
1969	SF-N	49	106	5	18	2	0	0	1	9	19	.170	.241	.189	22	-11	0	0	0	.985	1	C-49	-0.9
1970	SD-N	61	188	15	41	6	0	4	16	15	37	.218	.279	.314	61	-11	1	1	-0	.995	7	C-59	-0.1
1971	SD-N	121	376	23	94	17	2	5	23	35	49	.250	.317	.346	94	-3	0	5	-3	.981	14	*C-119	1.2
1972	SD-N	29	88	1	17	1	0	0	9	2	19	.193	.211	.205	20	-9	2	0	1	.989	1	C-29	-0.7
1973	Cin-N	3	1	0	0	0	0	0	0	1	0	.000	.500	.000	52	0	0	0	0	1.000	1	/C-2	0.1
1974	SD-N	30	81	4	19	1	0	0	7	13	19	.235	.340	.247	69	-3	0	0	0	.981	10	C-29	0.8
Total	10	393	1049	54	237	31	3	9	66	87	168	.226	.288	.287	65	-49	3	6	-3	.987	53	C-380	1.7
■ **VINCE BARTON**	Barton, Vincent David b: 2/1/08, Edmonton, Alberta, Canada d: 9/13/73, Toronto, Ont., Can BL/TR, 6', 180 lbs. Deb: 7/17/31																						
1931	Chi-N	66	239	45	57	10	1	13	50	21	40	.238	.323	.452	104	1	1			.964	-4	O-61	-0.7
1932	Chi-N	36	134	19	30	2	3	3	15	8	22	.224	.273	.351	67	-6	0			1.000	-2	O-34	-1.0
Total	2	102	373	64	87	12	4	16	65	29	62	.233	.306	.416	91	-6	1			.976	-6	/O-95	-1.7
■ **DAVE BARTOSCH**	Bartosch, David Robert b: 3/24/17, St.Louis, Mo. BR/TR, 6'1", 190 lbs. Deb: 4/28/45																						
1945	StL-N	24	47	9	12	1	0	0	1	6	3	.255	.340	.277	71	-2	0			.964	1	O-11	-0.2
■ **MONTY BASGALL**	Basgall, Romanus b: 2/8/22, Pfeifer, Kan. BR/TR, 5'10.5", 175 lbs. Deb: 4/19/48 C																						
1948	Pit-N	38	51	12	11	1	0	2	6	3	5	.216	.259	.353	63	-3	0			1.000	6	2-22	0.3
1949	Pit-N	107	308	25	67	9	1	2	26	31	32	.218	.291	.273	51	-21	1			.972	-7	2-98/3-3	-2.4
1951	Pit-N	55	153	15	32	5	2	0	9	12	14	.209	.271	.268	44	-12	0	0	0	.969	11	2-55	0.1
Total	3	200	512	52	110	15	3	4	41	46	51	.215	.282	.279	50	-36	1	0		.973	9	2-175/3-3	-2.0
■ **AL BASHANG**	Bashang, Albert C. b: 8/22/1888, Cincinnati, Ohio d: 6/23/67, Cincinnati, Ohio BB/TR, 5'8", 150 lbs. Deb: 7/30/12																						
1912	Det-A	6	12	3	1	0	0	0	0	3		.083	.267	.083	2	-1	0			1.000	-1	/O-6	-0.3
1918	Bro-N	2	5	0	1	0	0	0	0	0	0	.200	.200	.200	22	-0	0			1.000	0	/O-1	0.0
Total	2	8	17	3	2	0	0	0	0	3	0	.118	.250	.118	8	-2	0			1.000	-1	/O-7	-0.3
■ **WALT BASHORE**	Bashore, Walter Franklin (b: Walter Franklin Beshore) b: 10/6/09, Harrisburg, Pa. d: 9/26/84, Sebring, Fla. BR/TR, 6', 170 lbs. Deb: 7/14/36																						
1936	Phi-N	10	10	1	2	0	0	0	0	1	3	.200	.273	.200	26	-1	0			1.000	-3	/O-6,3-1	-0.4
■ **EDDIE BASINSKI**	Basinski, Edwin Frank "Bazooka" or "Fiddler" b: 11/4/22, Buffalo, N.Y. BR/TR, 6'1", 172 lbs. Deb: 5/20/44																						
1944	Bro-N	39	105	13	27	4	1	0	9	6	10	.257	.310	.314	77	-3	1			.960	-2	2-37/S-3	-0.3
1945	Bro-N	108	336	30	88	9	4	0	33	11	33	.262	.293	.313	69	-15	0			.926	-10	*S-101/2-6	-1.7
1947	Pit-N	56	161	15	32	6	2	4	17	18	27	.199	.279	.335	61	-9	0			.972	-1	2-56	-0.8
Total	3	203	602	58	147	19	7	4	59	35	70	.244	.292	.319	68	-27	1			.925	-13	S-104/2-99	-2.8
■ **JOHN BASS**	Bass, John E. b: 1850, Baltimore, Md. 5'6", 150 lbs. Deb: 5/4/1871																						
1871	Cle-n	22	89	18	27	1	**10**	3	18	3	4	.303	.326	.640	179	9	0	1	-1	.779	-6	*S-22/C-1	0.1
1872	Atl-n	2	7	0	1	1	0	0	1	0	0	.143	.143	.286	24	-1	0	0	0	.500	-1	/O-2	-0.1
1877	Har-N	1	4	1	1	0	0	0	0	0	0	.250	.250	.250	65	-0				.000	-1	/O-1	-0.1
Total	2 n	24	96	18	28	2	10	3	19	3	4	.292	.313	.615	166	8	0	1	-1	.779	-7	/S-22,O-2,C-1	0.0
■ **KEVIN BASS**	Bass, Kevin Charles b: 5/12/59, Redwood City, Cal. BB/TR, 6', 183 lbs. Deb: 4/9/82																						
1982	Mil-A	18	9	4	0	0	0	0	0	1	1	.000	.100	.000	-74	-2	0	0	0	1.000	-5	O-14/D-2	-0.8
	Hou-N	12	24	2	1	0	0	0	1	0	8	.042	.042	.042	-83	-6	0	0	0	.917	-1	/O-7	-0.8
1983	Hou-N	88	195	25	46	7	3	2	18	6	27	.236	.259	.333	67	-10	2	2	-1	.945	-6	O-52	-1.9
1984	Hou-N	121	331	33	86	17	5	2	29	6	57	.260	.279	.360	84	-9	5	5	-2	.975	-2	O-81	-1.5
1985	Hou-N	150	539	72	145	27	5	16	68	31	63	.269	.316	.427	109	4	19	8	1	**.997**	6	*O-141	0.8
1986	*Hou-N★	157	591	83	184	33	5	20	79	38	72	.311	.359	.486	134	26	22	13	-1	.984	4	*O-155	2.4
1987	Hou-N	157	592	83	168	31	5	19	85	53	77	.284	.347	.449	113	10	21	8	2	.987	10	*O-155	1.6
1988	Hou-N	157	541	57	138	27	2	14	72	42	65	.255	.316	.390	106	3	31	6	6	.979	2	*O-147	0.7
1989	Hou-N	87	313	42	94	19	4	5	44	29	44	.300	.362	.435	131	12	11	4	1	.985	9	O-84	2.1
1990	SF-N	61	214	25	54	9	1	7	32	14	26	.252	.304	.402	96	-2	2	2	-1	.968	-5	O-55	-0.9
1991	SF-N	124	361	43	84	10	4	10	40	36	56	.233	.309	.366	92	-4	7	4	-0	.977	-1	*O-101	-0.8
1992	SF-N	89	265	25	71	11	3	7	30	16	53	.268	.312	.411	109	2	7	7	-2	.983	-5	O-72	-0.7
	NY-N	46	137	15	37	12	2	2	9	7	17	.270	.306	.431	108	1	7	2	1	.987	1	O-39	0.2
	Yr	135	402	40	108	23	5	9	39	23	70	.269	.310	.418	109	3	14	9	-1	.985	-5	*O-111	-0.5
1993	Hou-N	111	229	31	65	18	0	3	37	26	31	.284	.359	.402	107	3	7	1	2	.989	-7	O-64	-0.3
1994	Hou-N	82	203	37	63	15	1	6	35	28	24	.310	.397	.483	135	11	2	3	-1	.977	-4	O-57	0.5
1995	Bal-A	111	295	32	72	12	0	5	32	24	47	.244	.305	.336	66	-15	8	8	-2	.984	-5	O-77,D-19	-2.4
Total	14	1571	4839	609	1308	248	40	118	611	357	668	.270	.325	.411	106	25	151	73	2	.982	-10	*O-1301/D-21	-1.8

■ RANDY BASS
Bass, Randy William b: 3/13/54, Lawton, Okla. BL/TR, 6'1", 210 lbs. Deb: 9/3/77

YEAR	TM/L	G	AB	R	H	2B	3B	HR	RBI	BB	SO	AVG	OBP	SLG	PRO+	BR/A	SB	CS	SBR	FA	FR	G/POS	TPR
1977	Min-A	9	19	0	2	0	0	0	0	0	5	.105	.105	.105	-43	-4	0	0	0	.000	0	/D-6	-0.4
1978	KC-A	2	2	0	0	0	0	0	0	0	0	.000	.000	.000	-97	-1	0	0	0	.000	0	H	-0.1
1979	Mon-N	2	1	0	0	0	0	0	0	0	0	.000	.000	.000	-99	-0	0	0	0	1.000	-0	/1-1	0.0
1980	SD-N	19	49	5	14	0	1	3	8	7	7	.286	.386	.510	157	4	0	0	0	.985	-1	1-15	0.2
1981	SD-N	69	176	13	37	4	1	4	20	20	28	.210	.294	.313	78	-5	0	1	-1	.993	2	1-50	-0.7
1982	SD-N	13	30	1	6	0	0	1	8	2	4	.200	.273	.300	63	-2	0	0	0	1.000	-1	/1-9	-0.3
	Tex-A	16	48	5	10	2	0	1	6	1	7	.208	.240	.313	53	-3	0	0	0	1.000	-0	/1-6,D-7	-0.4
Total	6	130	325	24	69	6	2	9	42	30	51	.212	.287	.326	76	-11	0	1	-1	.993	-0	/1-81,D-13	-1.7

■ DOC BASS
Bass, William Capers (also played one game in 1918 under name of Johnson)
b: 12/4/1899, Macon, Ga. d: 1/12/70, Macon, Ga. BL/TL, 5'10", 165 lbs. Deb: 7/29/18

YEAR	TM/L	G	AB	R	H	2B	3B	HR	RBI	BB	SO	AVG	OBP	SLG	PRO+	BR/A	SB	CS	SBR	FA	FR	G/POS	TPR
1918	Bos-N	2	1	1	1	0	0	0	0	0	0	1.000	1.000	1.000	533	0	1			.000	0	/H	0.1

■ CHARLEY BASSETT
Bassett, Charles Edwin b: 2/9/1863, Central Falls, R.I. d: 5/28/42, Pawtucket, R.I. BR/TR, 5'10", 150 lbs. Deb: 7/22/1884

YEAR	TM/L	G	AB	R	H	2B	3B	HR	RBI	BB	SO	AVG	OBP	SLG	PRO+	BR/A	SB	CS	SBR	FA	FR	G/POS	TPR
1884	Pro-N	27	79	10	11	2	1	0	6	4	15	.139	.181	.190	17	-7				.815	0	3-13/S-7,O-2,2-1	-0.6
1885	Pro-N	82	285	21	41	8	2	0	16	19	60	.144	.197	.186	25	-23				.900	5	2-39,S-23,3-20,/C-1	-1.5
1886	KC-N	90	342	41	89	19	8	2	32	36	43	.260	.331	.380	109	3	6			.886	8	S-82/3-8	1.0
1887	Ind-N	119	452	41	104	14	6	1	47	25	31	.230	.278	.294	61	-23	25			**.931**	16	*2-119	-0.3
1888	Ind-N	128	481	58	116	20	3	2	60	32	41	.241	.297	.308	91	-4	24			.922	-16	*2-128	-1.5
1889	Ind-N	127	477	64	117	12	5	4	68	37	38	.245	.304	.317	72	-19	15			.937	11	*2-127	-0.1
1890	NY-N	100	410	52	98	13	8	0	54	29	25	.239	.300	.310	78	-12	14			**.952**	12	*2-100	0.5
1891	NY-N	130	524	60	136	19	8	4	68	36	29	.260	.312	.349	96	-3	16			**.908**	8	*3-121/2-9	1.0
1892	NY-N	35	130	9	27	2	3	0	16	6	11	.208	.254	.269	59	-7	0			.938	9	2-30/3-5	0.3
	Lou-N	79	313	36	67	5	5	2	35	15	19	.214	.250	.281	66	-14	16			.861	-0	3-73/2-6	-1.1
	Yr	114	443	45	94	7	8	2	51	21	30	.212	.251	.278	64	-20	16			.858	9	3-78,2-36	-0.8
Total	9	917	3493	392	806	114	49	15	402	239	312	.231	.285	.304	76	-109	116			.932	53	2-559,3-240,S/OC	-2.3

■ JOHNNY BASSLER
Bassler, John Landis b: 6/3/1895, Mechanics Grove, Pa. d: 6/29/79, Santa Monica, Cal BL/TR, 5'9", 170 lbs. Deb: 7/11/13 C

YEAR	TM/L	G	AB	R	H	2B	3B	HR	RBI	BB	SO	AVG	OBP	SLG	PRO+	BR/A	SB	CS	SBR	FA	FR	G/POS	TPR
1913	Cle-A	1	2	0	0	0	0	0	0	0	0	.000	.000	.000	-97	-0	0			.500	-1	/C-1	-0.2
1914	Cle-A	43	77	5	14	1	1	0	6	15	8	.182	.323	.221	61	-3	3	2	-0	.946	-1	C-25/3-1,O-1	-0.2
1921	Det-A	119	388	37	119	18	5	0	56	58	16	.307	.401	.379	101	3	2	1	0	.975	2	*C-114	1.1
1922	Det-A	121	372	41	120	14	0	0	41	62	12	.323	.422	.360	109	9	2	1	0	.980	-3	*C-118	1.2
1923	Det-A	135	383	45	114	12	3	0	49	76	13	.298	.414	.345	103	6	2	2	-1	.988	12	*C-128	2.3
1924	Det-A	124	379	43	131	20	3	1	68	62	11	.346	.441	.422	125	18	2	1	0	.979	-4	*C-122	2.1
1925	Det-A	121	344	40	96	19	3	0	52	74	6	.279	.408	.352	96	2	1	1	-0	.983	-8	*C-118	0.0
1926	Det-A	66	174	20	53	8	1	0	22	45	6	.305	.447	.362	111	6	0	0	0	1.000	2	C-63	1.2
1927	Det-A	81	200	19	57	7	0	0	24	45	9	.285	.416	.320	92	0	1	0	0	.974	-2	C-67	0.3
Total	9	811	2319	250	704	99	16	1	318	437	81	.304	.416	.361	104	42	13	8		.980	-1	C-756/O-1,3-1	7.8

■ CHARLIE BASTIAN
Bastian, Charles J. b: 7/4/1860, Philadelphia, Pa. d: 1/18/32, Pennsauken, N.J. BR/TR, 5'6.5", 145 lbs. Deb: 8/18/1884

YEAR	TM/L	G	AB	R	H	2B	3B	HR	RBI	BB	SO	AVG	OBP	SLG	PRO+	BR/A	SB	CS	SBR	FA	FR	G/POS	TPR
1884	Wil-U	17	60	6	12	1	3	2		3		.200	.238	.417	92	-3				.907	10	2-16/P-1,S-1	0.7
	KC-U	11	46	6	9	3	0	1		4		.196	.260	.326	88	-2				.950	-1	2-11	-0.2
	Yr	28	106	12	21	4	3	3		7		.198	.248	.377	90	-5				.923	10	2-27/P-1,S-1	0.5
1885	Phi-N	103	389	63	65	11	5	4	29	35	82	.167	.236	.252	59	-17				.890	6	*S-103	-0.8
1886	Phi-N	105	373	46	81	9	11	2	38	33	73	.217	.281	.316	81	-9	29			**.945**	-5	*2-87,S-10/3-8	-0.9
1887	Phi-N	60	221	33	47	11	1	1	21	19	29	.213	.284	.285	55	-14	11			.921	-13	2-39,S-18/3-4	-2.2
1888	Phi-N	80	275	30	53	4	1	1	17	27	41	.193	.282	.225	60	-12	12			.945	12	2-65,3-14/S-1	0.3
1889	Chi-N	46	155	19	21	0	0	0	10	25	46	.135	.256	.135	10	-18	1			.919	6	S-45/2-1	-0.9
1890	Chi-P	80	283	38	54	10	5	0	29	33	37	.191	.287	.261	45	-23	4			.880	-10	S-64,2-12/3-4	-2.3
1891	Cin-a	1	4	0	0	0	0	0	0	0	0	.000	.000	.000	-92	-1	0			1.000	1	/2-1	0.0
	Phi-N	1	0	0	0	0	0	0	0	0	0	—	—	—	—	0	0			1.000	0	/S-1	0.0
Total	8	504	1806	241	342	49	26	11	144	179	308	.189	.268	.264	57	-97	57			.892	7	S-243,2-232/3-30,P	-6.3

■ EMIL BATCH
Batch, Emil "Heinie" or "Ace" b: 1/21/1880, Brooklyn, N.Y. d: 8/23/26, Brooklyn, N.Y. BR/TR, 5'7", 170 lbs. Deb: 9/13/04

YEAR	TM/L	G	AB	R	H	2B	3B	HR	RBI	BB	SO	AVG	OBP	SLG	PRO+	BR/A	SB	CS	SBR	FA	FR	G/POS	TPR
1904	Bro-N	28	94	9	24	1	2	2	7	1		.255	.271	.372	100	-1	6			.880	-2	3-28	-0.1
1905	Bro-N	145	568	64	143	20	11	5	49	26		.252	.285	.352	96	-5	21			.887	-8	*3-145	-0.9
1906	Bro-N	59	203	23	52	7	6	0	11	15		.256	.311	.350	115	3	3			.964	1	O-50/3-2	0.1
1907	Bro-N	116	388	38	96	10	3	0	31	23		.247	.291	.289	89	-6	7			.937	-3	*O-102/3-2,2-1,S-1	-1.4
Total	4	348	1253	134	315	38	22	7	98	65		.251	.290	.334	98	-9	37			.886	-12	3-177,O-152/S-1,2-1	-2.3

■ JOHN BATEMAN
Bateman, John Alvin b: 7/21/40, Killeen, Tex. d: 12/3/96, Sand Srpings, Tex. BR/TR, 6'3", 220 lbs. Deb: 4/19/63

YEAR	TM/L	G	AB	R	H	2B	3B	HR	RBI	BB	SO	AVG	OBP	SLG	PRO+	BR/A	SB	CS	SBR	FA	FR	G/POS	TPR
1963	Hou-N	128	404	23	85	8	6	10	59	13	103	.210	.251	.334	71	-16	0	0	0	.971	2	*C-115	-1.1
1964	Hou-N	74	221	18	42	8	0	5	19	17	48	.190	.251	.294	56	-13	0	1	-1	.987	6	C-72	-0.5
1965	Hou-N	45	142	15	28	3	1	7	14	12	37	.197	.260	.380	83	-4	0	1	-1	.985	0	C-39	-0.2
1966	Hou-N	131	433	39	121	24	3	17	70	20	74	.279	.319	.467	123	12	0	0	0	.981	1	*C-121	2.1
1967	Hou-N	76	252	16	48	9	0	2	17	17	53	.190	.247	.250	44	-18	0	0	0	.989	1	C-71	-1.4
1968	Hou-N	111	350	28	87	19	0	4	33	23	46	.249	.301	.337	93	-3	1	1	-0	.985	-2	*C-108	0.1
1969	Mon-N	74	235	16	49	4	0	8	19	12	44	.209	.250	.328	60	-13	0	2	-1	.985	-0	C-66	-1.2
1970	Mon-N	139	520	51	123	21	5	15	68	28	75	.237	.277	.383	75	-20	8	4	0	.983	-2	*C-137	-1.5
1971	Mon-N	139	492	34	119	17	3	10	56	19	87	.242	.276	.350	76	-17	1	0	0	.985	-9	*C-137	-2.2
1972	Mon-N	18	29	0	7	1	0	0	3	3	4	.241	.313	.276	67	-1	0	0	0	1.000	-2	/C-7	-0.3
	Phi-N	82	252	10	56	9	0	3	17	8	39	.222	.249	.294	52	-16	0	1	-1	.972	1	C-80	-1.4
	Yr	100	281	10	63	10	0	3	20	11	43	.224	.256	.292	54	-17	0	1	-1	.973	-1	C-87	-1.7
Total	10	1017	3330	250	765	123	18	81	375	172	610	.230	.273	.350	77	-111	10	10	-3	.982	-2	C-953	-7.6

■ CHARLIE BATES
Bates, Charles William b: 9/17/07, Philadelphia, Pa. d: 1/29/80, Topeka, Kan. BR/TR, 5'10", 165 lbs. Deb: 9/22/27

YEAR	TM/L	G	AB	R	H	2B	3B	HR	RBI	BB	SO	AVG	OBP	SLG	PRO+	BR/A	SB	CS	SBR	FA	FR	G/POS	TPR
1927	Phi-A	9	38	5	9	2	2	0	2	3	5	.237	.293	.395	73	-2	3	1	0	.857	-0	/O-9	-0.2

■ DEL BATES
Bates, Delbert Oakley b: 6/12/40, Seattle, Wash. BL/TR, 6'2", 195 lbs. Deb: 5/6/70

YEAR	TM/L	G	AB	R	H	2B	3B	HR	RBI	BB	SO	AVG	OBP	SLG	PRO+	BR/A	SB	CS	SBR	FA	FR	G/POS	TPR
1970	Phi-N	22	60	1	8	2	0	0	1	6	15	.133	.257	.167	16	-7	0	1	-1	.992	-4	C-20	-1.1

■ BUD BATES
Bates, Hubert Edgar b: 3/16/12, Los Angeles, Cal. d: 4/29/87, Long Beach, Cal. BR/TR, 6', 165 lbs. Deb: 9/16/39

YEAR	TM/L	G	AB	R	H	2B	3B	HR	RBI	BB	SO	AVG	OBP	SLG	PRO+	BR/A	SB	CS	SBR	FA	FR	G/POS	TPR
1939	Phi-N	15	58	8	15	2	0	1	2	2	8	.259	.283	.345	70	-3	1			.978	3	O-14	-0.1

■ JASON BATES
Bates, Jason Charles b: 1/5/71, Downey, Cal. BB/TR, 5'11", 170 lbs. Deb: 4/26/95

YEAR	TM/L	G	AB	R	H	2B	3B	HR	RBI	BB	SO	AVG	OBP	SLG	PRO+	BR/A	SB	CS	SBR	FA	FR	G/POS	TPR
1995	*Col-N	116	322	42	86	17	4	8	46	42	70	.267	.355	.419	80	-11	3	6	-3	.991	10	2-82,S-20,3-15	0.1
1996	Col-N	88	160	19	33	8	1	1	9	23	34	.206	.314	.287	48	-13	2	1	0	.978	0	2-37,S-18,3-12	-1.0
1997	Col-N	62	121	17	29	10	0	3	11	15	27	.240	.338	.397	74	-5	0	1	-1	1.000	-5	2-22,S-16/3-6	-0.8
1998	Col-N	53	74	10	14	3	0	0	3	8	21	.189	.268	.230	26	-8	0	0	0	.974	-5	2-17/3-3,S-3	-1.2
Total	4	319	677	88	162	38	5	12	69	88	152	.239	.333	.363	66	-37	5	8	-3	.987	1	2-158/S-57,3-36	-2.9

■ JOHNNY BATES
Bates, John William b: 1/10/1884, Steubenville, Ohio d: 2/10/49, Steubenville, Ohio BL/TL, 5'7", 168 lbs. Deb: 4/12/06

YEAR	TM/L	G	AB	R	H	2B	3B	HR	RBI	BB	SO	AVG	OBP	SLG	PRO+	BR/A	SB	CS	SBR	FA	FR	G/POS	TPR
1906	Bos-N	140	504	52	127	21	5	6	54	36		.252	.315	.349	110	5	9			.958	-10	*O-140	-1.3
1907	Bos-N	126	447	52	116	18	12	2	49	39		.260	.329	.367	118	9	11			.979	-2	*O-120	0.2
1908	Bos-N	127	445	48	115	14	6	1	29	35		.258	.315	.324	106	3	25			.948	-4	*O-117	-0.6
1909	Bos-N	63	236	27	68	15	3	1	23	20		.288	.354	.390	125	7	15			.945	5	O-60	1.0
	Phi-N	77	266	43	78	11	1	1	15	28		.293	.365	.353	122	7	22			.959	-2	O-73	0.3
	Yr	140	502	70	146	26	4	2	38	48		.291	.360	.371	123	14	37			.952	3	*O-133	1.3
1910	Phi-N	135	498	91	152	26	11	3	61	61	49	.305	.385	.420	130	20	31			.954	12	*O-131	2.6
1911	Cin-N	148	518	89	151	24	13	1	61	103	59	.292	.415	.394	131	28	33			.966	5	*O-147	2.5
1912	Cin-N	81	239	45	69	12	7	1	29	47	16	.289	.406	.410	127	11	10			.950	7	O-65	1.4

YEAR	TM/L	G	AB	R	H	2B	3B	HR	RBI	BB	SO	AVG	OBP	SLG	PRO+	BR/A	SB	CS	SBR	FA	FR	G/POS	TPR
1913	Cin-N	131	407	63	113	13	7	6	51	67	30	.278	.387	.388	122	15	21			.946	4	*O-111	1.4
1914	Cin-N	58	155	29	39	7	5	2	15	28	17	.252	.380	.400	128	6	4			.913	-6	O-54	-0.2
	Chi-N	9	8	2	1	0	0	0	1	1	1	.125	.300	.125	28	-1	0			1.000	-0	/O-3	-0.1
	Yr	67	163	31	40	7	5	2	16	29	18	.245	.376	.387	124	6	4			.917	-6	O-57	-0.3
	Bal-F	59	190	24	58	6	3	1	29	38	18	.305	.429	.384	119	5	6			.950	-1	O-59	0.1
Total	9	1154	3913	565	1087	167	73	25	417	503	190	.278	.367	.377	121	114	187			.955	9	*O-1080	7.3

■ RAY BATES
Bates, Raymond b: 2/8/1890, Paterson, N.J. d: 8/15/70, Tucson, Ariz. BR/TR, 6', 165 lbs. Deb: 5/31/13

YEAR	TM/L	G	AB	R	H	2B	3B	HR	RBI	BB	SO	AVG	OBP	SLG	PRO+	BR/A	SB	CS	SBR	FA	FR	G/POS	TPR
1913	Cle-A	27	30	4	5	0	2	0	4	3	9	.167	.265	.300	63	-1	3			.905	-0	3-12/O-2	-0.2
1917	Phi-A	127	485	47	115	20	7	2	66	21	39	.237	.277	.320	83	-12	12			.933	6	*3-124	-0.4
Total	2	154	515	51	120	20	9	2	70	24	48	.233	.277	.318	82	-13	15			.932	6	3-136/O-2	-0.6

■ BILLY BATES
Bates, William Derrick b: 12/7/63, Houston, Tex. BL/TR, 5'7", 155 lbs. Deb: 8/17/89

YEAR	TM/L	G	AB	R	H	2B	3B	HR	RBI	BB	SO	AVG	OBP	SLG	PRO+	BR/A	SB	CS	SBR	FA	FR	G/POS	TPR
1989	Mil-A	7	14	3	3	0	0	0	0	0	1	.214	.214	.214	21	-1	2	0	1	.938	4	/2-7	0.3
1990	Mil-A	14	29	6	3	1	0	0	2	4	7	.103	.212	.138	-0	-4	4	0	1	.962	3	2-14	0.0
	*Cin-N	8	5	2	0	0	0	0	0	0	2	.000	.000	.000	-96	-1	2	1	0	1.000	0	/2-1	-0.1
Total	2	29	48	11	6	1	0	0	2	4	10	.125	.192	.146	-4	-7	8	1	2	.953	7	/2-22	0.2

■ BILL BATHE
Bathe, William David b: 10/14/60, Downey, Cal. BR/TR, 6'2", 200 lbs. Deb: 4/12/86

YEAR	TM/L	G	AB	R	H	2B	3B	HR	RBI	BB	SO	AVG	OBP	SLG	PRO+	BR/A	SB	CS	SBR	FA	FR	G/POS	TPR
1986	Oak-A	39	103	9	19	3	0	5	11	2	20	.184	.208	.359	55	-7	0	0	0	.991	1	C-39	-0.4
1989	*SF-N	30	32	3	9	1	0	0	6	0	7	.281	.281	.313	72	-1	0	0	0	1.000	-1	/C-7	-0.2
1990	SF-N	52	48	3	11	0	1	3	12	7	12	.229	.327	.458	118	1	0	0	0	1.000	-1	/C-8	0.0
Total	3	121	183	15	39	4	1	8	29	9	39	.213	.254	.377	75	-7	0	0	0	.992	-1	/C-54	-0.6

■ TONY BATISTA
Batista, Leocadio Francisco b: 12/9/73, Puerto Plata, D.R. BR/TR, 6', 180 lbs. Deb: 6/3/96

YEAR	TM/L	G	AB	R	H	2B	3B	HR	RBI	BB	SO	AVG	OBP	SLG	PRO+	BR/A	SB	CS	SBR	FA	FR	G/POS	TPR
1996	Oak-A	74	238	38	71	10	2	6	25	19	49	.298	.353	.433	99	-0	7	3	0	.988	10	2-52,3-18/S-4,D-4	1.2
1997	Oak-A	68	188	22	38	10	1	4	18	14	31	.202	.265	.330	55	-13	2	2	-1	.970	11	S-61/3-4,2-1,D-1	0.2
1998	Ari-N	106	293	46	80	16	1	18	41	18	52	.273	.322	.519	113	4	1	1	-0	.994	1	2-41,S-34,3-15	1.0
Total	3	248	719	106	189	36	4	28	84	51	132	.263	.317	.441	93	-9	10	6	-1	.972	23	/S-99,2-94,3-37,D-5	2.4

■ RAFAEL BATISTA
Batista, Rafael (Sanchez) b: 10/20/47, San Pedro De Macoris, D.R. BL/TL, 6'1", 195 lbs. Deb: 6/17/73

YEAR	TM/L	G	AB	R	H	2B	3B	HR	RBI	BB	SO	AVG	OBP	SLG	PRO+	BR/A	SB	CS	SBR	FA	FR	G/POS	TPR
1973	Hou-N	12	15	2	4	0	0	0	2	1	6	.267	.313	.267	62	-1	0	0	0	1.000	-0	/1-8	-0.1
1975	Hou-N	10	10	0	3	1	0	0	0	0	4	.300	.300	.400	100	-0	0	0	0	.000	0	H	0.0
Total	2	22	25	2	7	1	0	0	2	1	10	.280	.308	.320	76	-1	0	0	0	1.000	-0	/1-8	-0.1

■ KEVIN BATISTE
Batiste, Kevin Wade b: 10/21/66, Galveston, Tex. BR/TR, 6'2", 175 lbs. Deb: 6/13/89

YEAR	TM/L	G	AB	R	H	2B	3B	HR	RBI	BB	SO	AVG	OBP	SLG	PRO+	BR/A	SB	CS	SBR	FA	FR	G/POS	TPR
1989	Tor-A	6	8	1	2	0	0	0	0	0	5	.250	.250	.250	42	-1	0	0	0	1.000	-1	/O-5	-0.1

■ KIM BATISTE
Batiste, Kimothy Emil b: 3/15/68, New Orleans, La. BR/TR, 6', 193 lbs. Deb: 9/8/91

YEAR	TM/L	G	AB	R	H	2B	3B	HR	RBI	BB	SO	AVG	OBP	SLG	PRO+	BR/A	SB	CS	SBR	FA	FR	G/POS	TPR
1991	Phi-N	10	27	2	6	0	0	0	1	1	8	.222	.250	.222	34	-2	0	1	-1	.970	1	/S-7	-0.1
1992	Phi-N	44	136	9	28	4	0	1	10	4	18	.206	.229	.257	37	-11	0	0	0	.922	-8	S-41	-1.9
1993	*Phi-N	79	156	14	44	7	1	5	29	3	29	.282	.300	.436	95	-2	0	1	-1	.956	13	3-58,S-24	1.2
1994	Phi-N	64	209	17	49	6	0	1	13	1	32	.234	.242	.278	34	-20	1	1	-0	.919	2	3-42,S-17	-1.7
1996	SF-N	54	130	17	27	6	0	3	11	5	33	.208	.237	.323	48	-10	3	3	-1	.847	-3	3-25/S-7	-1.4
Total	5	251	658	59	154	23	1	10	64	14	120	.234	.252	.318	52	-45	4	6	-2	.908	5	3-125/S-96	-3.9

■ BILL BATSCH
Batsch, William McKinley b: 5/18/1892, Mingo Junction, O. d: 12/31/63, Canton, Ohio BR/TR, 5'10.5", 168 lbs. Deb: 9/9/16

YEAR	TM/L	G	AB	R	H	2B	3B	HR	RBI	BB	SO	AVG	OBP	SLG	PRO+	BR/A	SB	CS	SBR	FA	FR	G/POS	TPR
1916	Pit-N	1	0	0	0	0	0	0	0	1	0	—	1.000	—	218	0	0			.000	0	H	0.0

■ LARRY BATTAM
Battam, Lawrence J. b: 5/1/1878, Brooklyn, N.Y. d: 1/27/38, Brooklyn, N.Y. 5'11", Deb: 9/28/1895

YEAR	TM/L	G	AB	R	H	2B	3B	HR	RBI	BB	SO	AVG	OBP	SLG	PRO+	BR/A	SB	CS	SBR	FA	FR	G/POS	TPR
1895	NY-N	2	4	0	1	0	0	0	0	2	1	.250	.500	.250	99	0	0			.667	-1	/3-2	0.0

■ GEORGE BATTEN
Batten, George Burnett b: 10/7/1891, Haddonfield, N.J. d: 8/4/72, New Port Richey, Fla. BR/TR, 5'11", 165 lbs. Deb: 9/28/12

YEAR	TM/L	G	AB	R	H	2B	3B	HR	RBI	BB	SO	AVG	OBP	SLG	PRO+	BR/A	SB	CS	SBR	FA	FR	G/POS	TPR
1912	NY-A	1	3	0	0	0	0	0	0	0		.000	.000	.000	-94	-1	0			1.000	-1	/2-1	-0.1

■ EARL BATTEY
Battey, Earl Jesse b: 1/5/35, Los Angeles, Cal. BR/TR, 6'1", 205 lbs. Deb: 9/10/55

YEAR	TM/L	G	AB	R	H	2B	3B	HR	RBI	BB	SO	AVG	OBP	SLG	PRO+	BR/A	SB	CS	SBR	FA	FR	G/POS	TPR
1955	Chi-A	5	7	1	2	0	0	0	0	1	1	.286	.444	.286	97	0	0	0	0	1.000	2	/C-5	0.2
1956	Chi-A	4	4	1	1	0	0	0	0	1	1	.250	.400	.250	74	-0	0	0	0	.800	-1	/C-3	-0.1
1957	Chi-A	48	115	12	20	2	3	3	6	11	38	.174	.246	.322	54	-8	0	2	-1	.989	6	C-43	-0.2
1958	Chi-A	68	168	24	38	8	0	8	26	24	34	.226	.330	.417	106	1	1	0	0	.988	2	C-49	0.6
1959	Chi-A	26	64	9	14	1	2	2	7	8	13	.219	.306	.391	91	-1	0	0	0	.990	4	C-20	0.4
1960	Was-A	137	466	49	126	24	2	15	60	48	68	.270	.349	.427	110	6	4	5	-2	.982	5	*C-136	1.8
1961	Min-A	133	460	70	139	24	1	17	55	53	66	.302	.378	.470	118	12	3	3	-1	.993	7	*C-131	2.4
1962	Min-A★	148	522	58	146	20	3	11	57	57	48	.280	.351	.393	96	-2	0	0	0	.991	6	*C-147	1.0
1963	Min-A★	147	508	64	145	17	1	26	84	61	75	.285	.371	.476	133	23	0	0	0	.994	1	*C-146	3.1
1964	Min-A	131	405	33	110	17	1	12	52	51	49	.272	.354	.407	111	7	1	1	-0	.990	-5	*C-125	0.7
1965	*Min-A★	131	394	36	117	22	2	6	60	50	23	.297	.379	.409	119	11	0	0	0	.986	-8	*C-128	1.0
1966	Min-A★	115	364	30	93	12	1	4	34	43	30	.255	.339	.327	87	-5	4	1	1	.995	6	*C-113	0.9
1967	Min-A	48	109	6	18	3	1	0	8	13	24	.165	.254	.211	36	-8	0	0	0	.987	-2	C-41	-1.0
Total	13	1141	3586	393	969	150	17	104	449	421	470	.270	.351	.409	106	37	13	12	-3	.990	23	*C-1087	10.8

■ JOE BATTIN
Battin, Joseph V. b: 11/11/1851, Philadelphia, Pa. d: 12/10/37, Akron, Ohio BR/TR, Deb: 8/11/1871 MU

YEAR	TM/L	G	AB	R	H	2B	3B	HR	RBI	BB	SO	AVG	OBP	SLG	PRO+	BR/A	SB	CS	SBR	FA	FR	G/POS	TPR
1871	Cle-n	1	3	0	0	0	0	0	0	1	0	.000	.250	.000	-21	-0	0	0	0	1.000	-0	/O-1	0.0
1873	Ath-n	1	5	4	3	0	0	0	2	1	0	.600	.667	.600	260	1	0	0	0	.667	0	/O-1	0.1
1874	Ath-n	51	226	40	52	11	1	0	27	1	7	.230	.233	.288	61	-11	3	2	-0	.813	5	*2-41/O-7,S-5	-0.6
1875	StL-n	67	284	31	71	6	3	0	33	0	6	.250	.250	.292	97	0	15	3	3	.861	14	*2-62/3-6,C-2,O-1	1.3
1876	StL-N	64	283	34	85	11	4	0	46	6	6	.300	.315	.367	134	10				**.867**	14	*3-63/2-1	2.2
1877	StL-N	57	226	28	45	3	7	1	22	6	17	.199	.220	.288	62	-9				.823	-3	3-32,2-21/O-5,P-1	-0.9
1882	Pit-a	34	133	13	28	5	1	1		3		.211	.228	.286	76	-3				.876	21	3-34	1.7
1883	Pit-a	98	388	42	83	9	6	1		11		.214	.236	.276	67	-13				**.891**	29	*3-98/P-2,M	1.3
1884	Pit-a	43	158	10	28	1	2	0		3		.177	.198	.209	32	-12				.919	8	3-43,M	-0.3
	CP-U	18	69	8	13	2	0	0		0		.188	.188	.217	23	-8				.908	11	3-18,M	0.2
	Bal-U	17	59	3	6	1	0	0		0		.102	.102	.119	-30	-11				.813	2	3-17	-0.8
	Yr	35	128	11	19	3	0	0		0		.148	.148	.172	-3	-20				.868	13	3-35	-0.6
1890	Syr-a	29	119	15	25	2	1	0	13	8		.210	.260	.244	54	-7	8			.794	-4	3-29	-0.9
Total	4 n	120	518	75	126	17	4	0	62	3	13	.243	.248	.292	80	-10	18	5	2	.842	19	2-103/O-10,3-6,SC	0.8
Total	6	360	1435	153	313	34	21	3	81	37	23	.218	.238	.277	67	-53	8			.870	77	3-334/2-22,O-5,P-3	2.5

■ ALLEN BATTLE
Battle, Allen Zelmo b: 11/29/68, Grantham, N.C. BR/TR, 6', 170 lbs. Deb: 4/26/95

YEAR	TM/L	G	AB	R	H	2B	3B	HR	RBI	BB	SO	AVG	OBP	SLG	PRO+	BR/A	SB	CS	SBR	FA	FR	G/POS	TPR
1995	StL-N	61	118	13	32	5	0	0	2	15	26	.271	.358	.314	79	-3	3	3	-1	.984	-2	O-32	-0.6
1996	Oak-A	47	130	20	25	3	0	1	5	17	26	.192	.295	.238	38	-12	10	2	2	.988	-6	O-47	-1.6
Total	2	108	248	33	57	8	0	1	7	32	52	.230	.325	.274	57	-15	13	5	1	.986	-8	/O-79	-2.2

■ HOWARD BATTLE
Battle, Howard Dion b: 3/25/72, Biloxi, Miss. BR/TR, 6', 210 lbs. Deb: 9/5/95

YEAR	TM/L	G	AB	R	H	2B	3B	HR	RBI	BB	SO	AVG	OBP	SLG	PRO+	BR/A	SB	CS	SBR	FA	FR	G/POS	TPR
1995	Tor-A	9	15	3	3	0	0	0	0	4	8	.200	.368	.200	53	-1	1	0	0	1.000	0	/3-6,D-1	0.0
1996	Phi-N	5	5	0	0	0	0	0	0	0	2	.000	.000	.000	-99	-1	0	0	0	.000	0	/3-1	-0.1
Total	2	14	20	3	3	0	0	0	0	4	10	.150	.292	.150	20	-2	1	0	0	1.000	0	/3-7,D-1	-0.1

■ JIM BATTLE
Battle, James Milton b: 3/26/01, Bailey, Tex. d: 9/30/65, Chico, Cal. BR/TR, 6'1", 170 lbs. Deb: 9/9/27

YEAR	TM/L	G	AB	R	H	2B	3B	HR	RBI	BB	SO	AVG	OBP	SLG	PRO+	BR/A	SB	CS	SBR	FA	FR	G/POS	TPR
1927	Chi-A	6	8	1	3	0	1	0	0	0	1	.375	.375	.625	160	1	0	0	0	1.000	-1	/3-4,S-2	0.0

■ MATT BATTS
Batts, Matthew Daniel b: 10/16/21, San Antonio, Tex. BR/TR, 5'11", 200 lbs. Deb: 9/10/47

YEAR	TM/L	G	AB	R	H	2B	3B	HR	RBI	BB	SO	AVG	OBP	SLG	PRO+	BR/A	SB	CS	SBR	FA	FR	G/POS	TPR
1947	Bos-A	7	16	3	8	1	0	1	5	1	1	.500	.529	.750	236	3	0	0	0	1.000	-1	/C-6	0.2

YEAR	TM/L	G	AB	R	H	2B	3B	HR	RBI	BB	SO	AVG	OBP	SLG	PRO+	BR/A	SB	CS	SBR	FA	FR	G/POS	TPR
1948	Bos-A	46	118	13	37	12	0	1	24	15	9	.314	.391	.441	115	3	0	0	0	.986	-1	C-41	0.4
1949	Bos-A	60	157	23	38	9	1	3	31	25	22	.242	.350	.369	84	-4	1	0	0	.977	2	C-50	0.1
1950	Bos-A	75	238	27	65	15	3	4	34	18	19	.273	.327	.412	80	-8	0	0	0	.994	3	C-73	-0.2
1951	Bos-A	11	29	1	4	1	0	0	2	1	2	.138	.167	.172	-8	-4	0	0	0	.975	-0	C-11	-0.4
	StL-A	79	248	26	75	17	1	5	31	21	21	.302	.357	.440	111	3	2	0	1	.960	-8	C-64	-0.2
	Yr	90	277	27	79	18	1	5	33	22	23	.285	.338	.412	98	-1	2	0	1	.962	-9	C-75	-0.6
1952	Det-A	56	173	11	41	4	1	3	13	14	22	.237	.298	.324	72	-7	1	0	0	.983	3	C-55	-0.1
1953	Det-A	116	374	38	104	24	3	6	43	24	36	.278	.322	.406	97	-3	2	3	-1	.986	-14	*C-103	-1.3
1954	Det-A	12	21	1	6	1	0	0	5	2	4	.286	.348	.333	89	-0	0	0	0	.967	1	/C-8	0.1
	Chi-A	55	158	16	36	7	1	3	19	17	15	.228	.303	.342	74	-6	0	1	-1	.992	7	C-42	0.2
	Yr	67	179	17	42	8	1	3	24	19	19	.235	.308	.341	76	-6	0	1	-1	.989	8	C-50	0.3
1955	Cin-N	26	71	4	18	4	1	0	13	4	11	.254	.293	.338	63	-4	0	0	0	.986	-1	C-21	-0.4
1956	Cin-N	3	2	0	0	0	0	0	0	1	1	.000	.333	.000	0	-0	0	0	0	.000	0	H	0.0
Total	10	546	1605	163	432	95	11	26	220	143	163	.269	.330	.391	89	-27	6	4	-1	.983	-10	C-474	-1.6

■ HANK BAUER

Bauer, Henry Albert b: 7/31/22, E.St.Louis, Ill. BR/TR, 6', 192 lbs. Deb: 9/6/48 MC

YEAR	TM/L	G	AB	R	H	2B	3B	HR	RBI	BB	SO	AVG	OBP	SLG	PRO+	BR/A	SB	CS	SBR	FA	FR	G/POS	TPR
1948	NY-A	19	50	6	9	1	1	1	9	6	13	.180	.268	.300	51	-4	1	0	0	.964	-1	O-14	-0.5
1949	*NY-A	103	301	56	82	6	6	10	45	37	42	.272	.354	.432	107	2	2	2	-1	.977	-9	O-95	-1.1
1950	*NY-A	113	415	72	133	16	2	13	70	35	41	.320	.380	.463	118	11	2	3	-1	.987	-1	*O-110	0.4
1951	*NY-A	118	348	53	103	19	3	10	54	42	39	.296	.373	.454	128	13	5	2	0	.990	-5	*O-107	0.5
1952	*NY-A★	141	553	86	162	31	6	17	74	50	61	.293	.355	.463	134	23	6	7	-2	.984	3	*O-139	1.8
1953	*NY-A★	133	437	77	133	20	6	10	57	59	45	.304	.394	.446	131	20	2	3	-1	.992	0	*O-126	1.5
1954	NY-A★	114	377	73	111	16	5	12	54	40	42	.294	.362	.459	128	14	4	4	-1	.989	-6	*O-108	0.2
1955	*NY-A	139	492	97	137	20	5	20	53	56	65	.278	.362	.461	122	14	8	4	0	.981	4	*O-133/C-1	1.2
1956	*NY-A	147	539	96	130	18	7	26	84	59	72	.241	.318	.445	103	-1	4	2	0	.969	-8	*O-146	-1.6
1957	*NY-A	137	479	70	124	22	**9**	18	65	42	64	.259	.324	.455	112	6	7	2	1	.986	-7	*O-135	-0.8
1958	*NY-A	128	452	62	121	22	6	12	50	32	56	.268	.318	.423	106	2	3	2	-0	.980	-9	*O-123	-1.3
1959	NY-A	114	341	44	81	20	0	9	39	33	54	.238	.309	.375	90	-5	4	2	0	.972	-13	*O-111	-2.3
1960	KC-A	95	255	30	70	15	0	3	31	21	36	.275	.332	.369	89	-4	1	0	0	.978	-6	O-67	-1.3
1961	KC-A	43	106	11	28	3	1	3	18	9	8	.264	.322	.396	89	-2	1	0	0	.958	-7	O-35,M	-1.0
Total	14	1544	5145	833	1424	229	57	164	703	521	638	.277	.347	.439	114	90	50	33	-5	.982	-65	*O-1449/C-1	-4.3

■ JUSTIN BAUGHMAN

Baughman, Justin Reis b: 8/1/74, Mountain View, Cal. BR/TR, 5'11", 175 lbs. Deb: 5/17/98

YEAR	TM/L	G	AB	R	H	2B	3B	HR	RBI	BB	SO	AVG	OBP	SLG	PRO+	BR/A	SB	CS	SBR	FA	FR	G/POS	TPR
1998	Ana-A	63	196	24	50	9	1	1	20	6	36	.255	.281	.327	57	-12	10	4	1	.977	-1	2-59/S-3,D-1	-0.9

■ PADDY BAUMANN

Baumann, Charles John b: 12/20/1885, Indianapolis, Ind. d: 11/20/69, Indianapolis, Ind. BR/TR, 5'9", 160 lbs. Deb: 8/10/11

YEAR	TM/L	G	AB	R	H	2B	3B	HR	RBI	BB	SO	AVG	OBP	SLG	PRO+	BR/A	SB	CS	SBR	FA	FR	G/POS	TPR
1911	Det-A	26	94	8	24	2	4	0	11	6		.255	.307	.362	82	-3	1			.956	6	2-23/O-3	0.2
1912	Det-A	16	42	3	11	1	0	0	7	6		.262	.354	.286	86	-0	4			.786	-2	/3-6,2-5,O-2	-0.2
1913	Det-A	50	191	31	57	7	4	1	22	16	18	.298	.353	.393	120	4	4			.943	-7	2-49	-0.4
1914	Det-A	3	11	1	0	0	0	0	0	2	1	.000	.154	.000	-52	-2	0			1.000	-1	/2-3	-0.4
1915	NY-A	76	219	30	64	13	1	2	28	28	32	.292	.380	.388	130	9	9	10	-3	.978	-2	2-43,3-19/O-1	0.5
1916	NY-A	79	237	35	68	5	3	1	25	19	16	.287	.352	.346	108	2	10			.958	-7	O-28,3-26/2-9	-0.6
1917	NY-A	49	110	10	24	2	1	0	8	4	9	.218	.246	.255	52	-7	2			.941	-12	2-18/O-7,3-1	-2.1
Total	7	299	904	118	248	30	13	4	101	81	76	.274	.340	.350	103	4	30	10		.953	-26	2-150/3-52,O-41	-3.0

■ JIM BAUMER

Baumer, James Sloan b: 1/29/31, Tulsa, Okla. d: 7/8/96, Paoli, Pa. BR/TR, 6'2", 185 lbs. Deb: 9/14/49

YEAR	TM/L	G	AB	R	H	2B	3B	HR	RBI	BB	SO	AVG	OBP	SLG	PRO+	BR/A	SB	CS	SBR	FA	FR	G/POS	TPR
1949	Chi-A	8	10	2	4	1	1	0	2	2	1	.400	.571	.700	243	2	0	0	0	.938	1	/S-7	0.3
1961	Cin-N	10	24	0	3	0	0	0	0	0	9	.125	.125	.125	-33	-4	0	0	0	1.000	-0	/2-9	-0.4
Total	2	18	34	2	7	1	1	0	2	2	10	.206	.289	.294	55	-2	0	0	0	1.000	1	/2-9,S-7	-0.1

■ JOHN BAUMGARTNER

Baumgartner, John Edward b: 5/29/31, Birmingham, Ala. BR/TR, 6'1", 190 lbs. Deb: 4/14/53

YEAR	TM/L	G	AB	R	H	2B	3B	HR	RBI	BB	SO	AVG	OBP	SLG	PRO+	BR/A	SB	CS	SBR	FA	FR	G/POS	TPR
1953	Det-A	7	27	3	5	0	0	0	2	0	5	.185	.185	.185	0	-4	0	0	0	.913	-1	/3-7	-0.5

■ FRANK BAUMHOLTZ

Baumholtz, Frank Conrad b: 10/7/18, Midvale, Ohio d: 12/14/97, Winter Springs, Fla. BL/TL, 5'10.5", 175 lbs. Deb: 4/15/47

YEAR	TM/L	G	AB	R	H	2B	3B	HR	RBI	BB	SO	AVG	OBP	SLG	PRO+	BR/A	SB	CS	SBR	FA	FR	G/POS	TPR
1947	Cin-N	151	643	96	182	32	9	5	45	56	53	.283	.341	.384	93	-7	6			.977	-5	*O-150	-1.9
1948	Cin-N	128	415	57	123	19	5	4	30	27	32	.296	.344	.395	103	1	8			.987	3	*O-110	-0.2
1949	Cin-N	27	81	12	19	5	3	1	8	6	8	.235	.295	.407	86	-2	0			.964	2	O-20	-0.1
	Chi-N	58	164	15	37	4	2	1	15	9	21	.226	.270	.293	52	-11	2			.986	-4	O-43	-1.8
	Yr	85	245	27	56	9	5	2	23	15	29	.229	.279	.331	64	-13	2			.976	-3	O-63	-1.9
1951	Chi-N	146	560	62	159	28	10	2	50	49	36	.284	.346	.380	94	-5	5	4	-1	.975	-7	*O-140	-1.7
1952	Chi-N	103	409	59	133	17	4	4	35	27	27	.325	.371	.416	116	9	5	7	-3	.974	3	*O-101	0.5
1953	Chi-N	133	520	75	159	36	7	3	25	42	36	.306	.359	.419	100	0	3	3	-1	.980	-3	*O-130	-0.8
1954	Chi-N	90	303	38	90	12	6	4	28	20	15	.297	.343	.416	95	-2	1	3	-2	.988	-10	O-71	-1.6
1955	Chi-N	105	280	23	81	12	5	1	27	16	24	.289	.330	.379	88	-5	0	1	-1	.993	2	O-63	-0.6
1956	Phi-N	76	100	13	27	0	0	0	9	6	6	.270	.318	.270	61	-5	0	2	-1	.962	-0	O-15	-0.8
1957	Phi-N	2	2	0	0	0	0	0	0	0	0	.000	.000	.000	-99	-1	0	0	0	.000	0	H	-0.1
Total	10	1019	3477	450	1010	165	51	25	272	258	258	.290	.342	.389	95	-27	30	20		.980	-20	O-843	-9.1

■ DANNY BAUTISTA

Bautista, Daniel (Alcantara) b: 5/24/72, Santo Domingo, D.R. BR/TR, 5'11", 170 lbs. Deb: 9/15/93

YEAR	TM/L	G	AB	R	H	2B	3B	HR	RBI	BB	SO	AVG	OBP	SLG	PRO+	BR/A	SB	CS	SBR	FA	FR	G/POS	TPR
1993	Det-A	17	61	6	19	3	0	1	9	1	10	.311	.323	.410	96	-1	3	1	0	1.000	1	O-16/D-1	0.1
1994	Det-A	31	99	12	23	4	1	4	15	3	18	.232	.255	.414	68	-5	1	2	-1	1.000	-1	O-30/D-1	-0.7
1995	Det-A	89	271	28	55	9	0	7	27	12	68	.203	.237	.314	42	-24	4	1	1	.988	1	O-86/D-1	-2.3
1996	Det-A	25	64	12	16	2	0	2	8	9	15	.250	.342	.375	81	-2	1	2	-1	.974	-2	O-22/D-1	-0.5
	Atl-N	17	20	1	3	0	0	0	1	2	5	.150	.261	.150	11	-3	0	0	0	1.000	-3	O-14	-0.6
1997	*Atl-N	64	103	14	25	3	2	3	9	5	24	.243	.284	.398	75	-4	2	0	1	.984	-8	O-57	-1.2
1998	*Atl-N	82	144	17	36	11	0	3	17	7	21	.250	.285	.389	71	-6	1	0	0	.959	-9	O-58/D-1	-1.6
Total	6	325	762	90	177	32	3	20	86	39	161	.232	.271	.361	62	-44	12	6	0	.986	-23	O-283/D-5	-6.8

■ JIM BAXES

Baxes, Dimitrios Speros b: 7/5/28, San Francisco, Cal d: 11/14/96, Garden Grove, Cal. BR/TR, 6'1", 190 lbs. Deb: 4/11/59 F

YEAR	TM/L	G	AB	R	H	2B	3B	HR	RBI	BB	SO	AVG	OBP	SLG	PRO+	BR/A	SB	CS	SBR	FA	FR	G/POS	TPR
1959	LA-N	11	33	4	10	1	0	2	5	4	7	.303	.395	.515	130	2	1	0	0	.952	7	3-10	0.8
	Cle-A	77	247	35	59	11	0	15	34	21	47	.239	.299	.466	111	2	0	1	-1	.956	-13	2-48,3-22	-0.8
Total	1	88	280	39	69	12	0	17	39	25	54	.246	.310	.471	113	4	1	1	-0	.931	-7	/2-48,3-32	0.0

■ MIKE BAXES

Baxes, Michael b: 12/18/30, San Francisco, Cal BR/TR, 5'10", 175 lbs. Deb: 4/17/56 F

YEAR	TM/L	G	AB	R	H	2B	3B	HR	RBI	BB	SO	AVG	OBP	SLG	PRO+	BR/A	SB	CS	SBR	FA	FR	G/POS	TPR
1956	KC-A	73	106	9	24	3	1	1	5	18	15	.226	.339	.302	70	-4	0	1	-1	.944	4	S-62/2-1	0.2
1958	KC-A	73	231	31	49	10	1	0	8	21	24	.212	.286	.264	52	-15	1	6	-3	.969	-4	2-61/S-4	-1.9
Total	2	146	337	40	73	13	2	1	13	39	39	.217	.303	.276	58	-19	1	7	-4	.946	-0	/S-66,2-62	-1.7

■ MOOSE BAXTER

Baxter, John Morris b: 7/27/1876, Chippewa Falls, Wis. d: 8/7/26, Portland, Ore. BL/TR, 6'2", 200 lbs. Deb: 4/19/07

YEAR	TM/L	G	AB	R	H	2B	3B	HR	RBI	BB	SO	AVG	OBP	SLG	PRO+	BR/A	SB	CS	SBR	FA	FR	G/POS	TPR
1907	StL-N	6	21	1	4	0	0	0	0	0		.190	.190	.190	20	-2	0			.921	-1	/1-6	-0.3

■ HARRY BAY

Bay, Harry Elbert "Deerfoot" b: 1/17/1878, Pontiac, Ill. d: 3/20/52, Peoria, Ill. BL/TL, 5'8", 138 lbs. Deb: 7/23/01

YEAR	TM/L	G	AB	R	H	2B	3B	HR	RBI	BB	SO	AVG	OBP	SLG	PRO+	BR/A	SB	CS	SBR	FA	FR	G/POS	TPR
1901	Cin-N	41	157	25	33	1	2	1	3	13		.210	.275	.261	60	-8	4			.953	-1	O-40	-1.1
1902	Cin-N	6	16	3	6	0	0	0	1	2		.375	.474	.375	148	1	0			.778	0	/O-3	0.1
	Cle-A	108	455	71	132	10	5	0	23	36		.290	.343	.334	92	-4	22			**.973**	4	*O-107	-0.7
1903	Cle-A	140	579	94	169	15	12	1	35	29		.292	.329	.364	110	7	**45**			.950	-3	*O-140	-0.5
1904	Cle-A	132	506	69	122	12	9	3	36	43		.241	.307	.318	99	-0	**38**			**.987**	7	*O-132	0.0
1905	Cle-A	144	552	90	166	18	10	0	22	36		.301	.349	.370	126	16	36			.970	0	*O-144	1.0
1906	Cle-A	68	280	47	77	8	3	0	14	26		.275	.337	.325	109	3	17			.979	-3	O-68	-0.3
1907	Cle-A	34	95	14	17	1	1	0	7	10		.179	.271	.211	53	-5	7			.968	1	O-31	-0.6
1908	Cle-A	2	0	0	0	0	0	0	0	0		—	—	—	—	0	0			.000	0	R	0.0
Total	8	675	2640	413	722	65	42	5	141	195		.273	.328	.336	103	11	169			.968	6	O-665	-2.1

YEAR	TM/L	G	AB	R	H	2B	3B	HR	RBI	BB	SO	AVG	OBP	SLG	PRO+	BR/A	SB	CS	SBR	FA	FR	G/POS	TPR
■ **DICK BAYLESS**	Bayless, Harry Owen b: 9/6/1883, Joplin, Mo. d: 12/16/20, Santa Rita, N.Mex. BL/TR, 5'9", 178 lbs. Deb: 9/9/08																						
1908	Cin-N	19	71	7	16	1	0	1	3	6		.225	.304	.282	90	-1	0			.946	3	O-19	0.1
■ **DON BAYLOR**	Baylor, Don Edward b: 6/28/49, Austin, Tex. BR/TR, 6'1", 195 lbs. Deb: 9/18/70 MC																						
1970	Bal-A	8	17	4	4	0	0	0	4	2	3	.235	.316	.235	54	-1	1	1	-0	1.000	0	/O-6	-0.2
1971	Bal-A	1	2	0	0	0	0	0	1	2	1	.000	.600	.000	83	0	0	0	0	1.000	0	/O-1	0.1
1972	Bal-A	102	320	33	81	13	3	11	38	29	50	.253	.332	.416	118	7	24	2	6	.975	-9	O-84/1-9	0.1
1973	*Bal-A	118	405	64	116	20	4	11	51	35	48	.286	.362	.437	125	14	32	9	4	.981	-1	*O-110/1-6,D-1	1.2
1974	*Bal-A	137	489	66	133	22	1	10	59	43	56	.272	.343	.382	112	8	29	12	2	.978	-17	*O-129/1-8,D-1	-1.4
1975	Bal-A	145	524	79	148	21	6	25	76	53	64	.282	.363	.489	148	32	32	17	-1	.982	-2	*O-135/1-2,D-7	2.4
1976	Oak-A	157	595	85	147	25	1	15	68	58	72	.247	.334	.368	110	8	52	12	8	.981	-9	O-76,1-69,D-23	0.0
1977	Cal-A	154	561	87	141	27	0	25	75	62	76	.251	.339	.433	113	10	26	12	1	.966	-1	O-77,D-61,1-18	0.3
1978	Cal-A	158	591	103	151	26	0	34	99	56	71	.255	.338	.472	131	23	22	9	1	.974	-2	*D-102,O-39,1-17	1.7
1979	*Cal-A★	162	628	**120**	186	33	3	36	**139**	71	51	.296	.377	.530	147	41	22	12	-1	.976	2	O-97,D-65/1-1	3.4
1980	Cal-A	90	340	39	85	12	2	5	51	24	32	.250	.320	.341	83	-7	6	6	-2	.969	3	O-54,D-36	-1.0
1981	Cal-A	103	377	52	90	18	1	17	66	42	51	.239	.326	.427	116	7	3	3	-1	1.000	1	D-97/1-4,O-1	0.4
1982	*Cal-A	157	608	80	160	24	1	24	93	57	69	.263	.333	.424	106	5	10	4	1	.000	0	*D-155	0.0
1983	NY-A	144	534	82	162	33	3	21	85	40	53	.303	.366	.494	139	28	17	7	1	1.000	-0	*D-136/O-5,1-1	2.3
1984	NY-A	134	493	84	129	29	1	27	89	38	68	.262	.343	.489	132	21	1	1	-0	.889	-1	*D-127/O-5	1.6
1985	NY-A	142	477	70	110	24	1	23	91	52	90	.231	.336	.430	111	8	0	4	-2	.000	0	*D-140	0.3
1986	*Bos-A	160	585	93	139	23	1	31	94	62	111	.238	.346	.439	112	10	3	5	-2	.986	-1	*D-143,1-13/O-3	0.4
1987	Bos-A	108	339	64	81	8	0	16	57	40	47	.239	.360	.404	100	1	5	2	0	.000	0	D-97	-0.1
	*Min-A	20	49	3	14	1	0	0	6	5	12	.286	.397	.306	87	-0	0	1	-1	.000	0	D-14	-0.1
	Yr	128	388	67	95	9	0	16	63	45	59	.245	.364	.392	98	1	5	3	-0	.000	0	*D-111	-0.2
1988	*Oak-A	92	264	28	58	7	0	7	34	34	44	.220	.335	.326	89	-3	0	1	-1	.000	0	D-80	-0.5
Total	19	2292	8198	1236	2135	366	28	338	1276	805	1069	.260	.346	.436	119	212	285	120	14	.977	-37	*D-1285,O-822,1-148	10.9
■ **JACK BEACH**	Beach, Stonewall Jackson b: 1862, Alexandria, Va. d: 7/23/1896, Alexandria, Va. Deb: 5/1/1884																						
1884	Was-a	8	31	3	3	2	0	0		0		.097	.097	.161	-20	-4				.667	-1	/O-8	-0.5
■ **JOHNNY BEALL**	Beall, John Woolf b: 3/12/1882, Beltsville, Md. d: 6/14/26, Beltsville, Md. BL/TR, 6', 180 lbs. Deb: 4/17/13																						
1913	Cle-A	6	6	0	1	0	0	0	1	0	2	.167	.167	.167	-2	-1	0			.000	0	H	-0.1
	Chi-A	17	60	10	16	0	1	2	3	0	0	.267	.279	.400	99	-1	1			.953	1	O-17	-0.1
	Yr	23	66	10	17	0	1	2	4	0	2	.258	.269	.379	89	-1	1			.953	1	O-17	-0.2
1915	Cin-N	10	34	3	8	1	0	0	3	5	10	.235	.350	.265	86	-0	0	1	-1	.960	1	O-10	0.0
1916	Cin-N	6	21	3	7	2	0	1	4	3	7	.333	.417	.571	207	3	1			1.000	1	/O-6	0.4
1918	StL-N	19	49	2	11	1	0	0	6	3	6	.224	.269	.245	59	-2	0			1.000	-1	O-18	-0.5
Total	4	58	170	18	43	4	1	3	17	11	25	.253	.306	.341	95	-1	2	1		.972	2	/O-51	-0.3
■ **BOB BEALL**	Beall, Robert Brooks b: 4/24/48, Portland, Ore. BB/TL, 5'11", 180 lbs. Deb: 5/12/75																						
1975	Atl-N	20	31	2	7	2	0	0	1	6	9	.226	.351	.290	77	-1	0	0	0	.984	-0	/1-8	-0.1
1978	Atl-N	108	185	29	45	8	0	1	16	36	27	.243	.369	.303	81	-3	4	5	-2	.987	-1	1-40/O-8	-0.9
1979	Atl-N	17	15	1	2	2	0	0	1	3	4	.133	.278	.267	46	-1	0	0	0	1.000	0	/1-3	-0.1
1980	Pit-N	3	3	0	0	0	0	0	0	0	1	.000	.000	.000	-99	-1	0	0	0	.000	0	/H	-0.1
Total	4	148	234	32	54	12	0	1	18	45	41	.231	.357	.295	76	-6	4	5	-2	.987	-1	/1-51,O-8	-1.2
■ **TOMMY BEALS**	Beals, Thomas L. (a.k.a. W.Thomas In 1871-1873) b: 8/1850, New York d: 10/2/15, San Francisco, Cal. BR, 5'5", 144 lbs. Deb: 7/27/1871																						
1871	Oly-n	10	36	6	7	0	0	0	1	2	0	.194	.237	.194	27	-3	2	0	1	.778	3	/O-8,2-2	0.0
1872	Oly-n	9	36	6	11	1	1	0	5	1	1	.306	.324	.389	125	1	0	0	0	.853	1	/2-5,S-2,O-2	0.1
1873	Was-n	37	169	35	46	9	5	0	24	1	1	.272	.276	.385	97	-0	1	0	0	.871	7	2-26,C-13/O-1	0.4
1874	Bos-n	19	97	20	19	3	4	0	17	0	2	.196	.196	.309	56	-5	0	1	-1	.849	-2	2-12/O-9	0.6
1875	Bos-n	35	155	38	41	2	6	0	16	3	1	.265	.278	.355	114	2	1	0	0	.867	1	O-30/2-8	0.3
1880	Chi-N	13	46	4	7	0	0	0	3	1	6	.152	.170	.152	10	-4				.889	-6	O-10/2-3	-1.0
Total	5 n	110	493	105	124	15	16	0	63	7	5	.252	.262	.347	90	-5	4	1	1	.864	10	/2-53,O-50,C-13,S-2	0.2
■ **CHARLIE BEAMON**	Beamon, Charles Alfonzo Jr. b: 12/4/53, Oakland, Cal. BL/TL, 6'1", 183 lbs. Deb: 9/11/78 F																						
1978	Sea-A	10	11	2	2	0	0	0	0	1	1	.182	.250	.182	23	-1	0	0	0	1.000	1	/1-2,D-6	0.0
1979	Sea-A	27	25	5	5	1	0	0	0	0	5	.200	.200	.240	18	-3	1	0	0	1.000	0	/1-7,O-2,D-5	-0.3
1981	Tor-A	8	15	1	3	1	0	0	0	2	2	.200	.294	.267	59	-1	0	0	0	1.000	-0	/D-4,1-1	-0.1
Total	3	45	51	8	10	2	0	0	0	3	8	.196	.241	.235	32	-5	1	0	0	1.000	1	/D-15,1-10,O-2	-0.4
■ **TREY BEAMON**	Beamon, Clifford b: 2/11/74, Dallas, Tex. BL/TR, 6'3", 195 lbs. Deb: 8/4/96																						
1996	Pit-N	24	51	7	11	2	0	0	6	4	6	.216	.273	.255	39	-4	1	1	-0	.960	-1	O-14	-0.6
1997	SD-N	43	65	5	18	3	0	0	7	2	17	.277	.309	.323	71	-3	1	2	-1	.909	-2	O-20	-0.6
1998	Det-A	28	42	4	11	4	0	0	2	5	13	.262	.340	.357	81	-1	1	0	0	1.000	-0	D-11/O-4	-0.2
Total	3	95	158	16	40	9	0	0	15	11	36	.253	.306	.310	63	-8	3	3	-1	.944	-3	/O-38,D-11	-1.4
■ **JOE BEAN**	Bean, Joseph William b: 3/18/1874, Boston, Mass. d: 2/15/61, Atlanta, Ga. BR/TR, 5'8", 138 lbs. Deb: 4/28/02																						
1902	NY-N	48	176	13	39	2	1	0	5	5		.222	.247	.244	52	-10	9			.889	-9	S-48	-1.7
■ **BILL BEAN**	Bean, William Daro b: 5/11/64, Santa Ana, Cal. BL/TL, 6'1", 185 lbs. Deb: 4/25/87																						
1987	Det-A	26	66	6	17	2	0	0	4	5	11	.258	.310	.288	63	-3	1	1	-0	1.000	0	O-24	-0.4
1988	Det-A	10	11	2	2	0	1	0	0	0	2	.182	.182	.364	51	-1	0	0	0	1.000	-1	/O-4,1-2,D-1	-0.2
1989	Det-A	9	11	0	0	0	0	0	0	2	3	.000	.214	.000	-36	-2	0	0	0	.833	-3	/O-6,1-2	-0.5
	LA-N	51	71	7	14	4	0	0	3	4	10	.197	.250	.254	45	-5	0	2	-1	1.000	-9	O-44	-1.7
1993	SD-N	88	177	19	46	9	0	5	32	6	29	.260	.292	.395	81	-5	2	4	-2	.987	-7	O-54,1-12	-1.6
1994	SD-N	84	135	7	29	5	1	0	14	7	25	.215	.254	.267	37	-13	0	1	-1	1.000	-5	O-39,1-16	-1.9
1995	SD-N	4	7	1	0	0	0	0	0	1	4	.000	.125	.000	-66	-2	0	0	0	.750	-1	/O-4	-0.3
Total	6	272	478	42	108	20	2	5	53	25	84	.226	.270	.308	55	-31	3	8	-4	.988	-25	O-175/1-32,D-1	-6.6
■ **BILLY BEANE**	Beane, William Lamar b: 3/29/62, Orlando, Fla. BR/TR, 6'4", 195 lbs. Deb: 9/13/84																						
1984	NY-N	5	10	0	1	0	0	0	0	0	2	.100	.100	.100	-44	-2	0	1	-1	1.000	-2	/O-5	-0.4
1985	NY-N	8	8	0	2	1	0	0	1	0	3	.250	.250	.375	74	-0	0	0	0	1.000	-1	/O-2	-0.1
1986	Min-A	80	183	20	39	6	0	3	15	11	54	.213	.258	.295	49	-13	2	3	-1	1.000	-5	O-67/D-5	-2.0
1987	Min-A	12	15	1	4	2	0	0	1	0	6	.267	.267	.400	71	-1	0	0	0	1.000	-1	/O-7	-0.2
1988	Det-A	6	6	1	1	0	0	0	1	0	2	.167	.167	.167	-7	-1	0	0	0	1.000	-2	/O-6	-0.3
1989	Oak-A	37	79	8	19	5	0	0	11	0	13	.241	.241	.304	54	-5	3	1	0	1.000	-2	O-25/1-4,C-1,3-1,D	-0.7
Total	6	148	301	30	66	14	0	3	29	11	80	.219	.247	.296	48	-22	5	5	-2	1.000	-11	O-112/D-9,1-4,3C	-3.7
■ **TED BEARD**	Beard, Cramer Theodore b: 1/7/21, Woodsboro, Md. BL/TL, 5'8", 165 lbs. Deb: 9/5/48																						
1948	Pit-N	25	81	15	16	1	3	0	7	12	18	.198	.316	.284	62	-4	5			1.000	2	O-22	-0.4
1949	Pit-N	14	24	1	2	0	0	0	1	2	2	.083	.154	.083	-34	-5	0			.900	-3	O-10	-0.8
1950	Pit-N	61	177	32	41	6	2	4	12	27	45	.232	.333	.356	79	-5	3			.983	2	O-49	-0.5
1951	Pit-N	22	48	7	9	1	0	1	3	6	14	.188	.291	.271	51	-3	0	0	0	1.000	-2	O-15	-0.5
1952	Pit-N	15	44	5	8	2	1	0	3	7	9	.182	.294	.273	57	-2	2	0	1	1.000	0	O-13	-0.2
1957	Chi-A	38	78	15	16	1	0	0	7	18	14	.205	.354	.218	59	-3	3	2	-0	.974	-1	O-28	-0.6
1958	Chi-A	19	22	5	2	0	0	1	2	6	5	.091	.286	.227	44	-2	3	0	1	1.000	-4	O-15	-0.5
Total	7	194	474	80	94	11	6	6	35	78	107	.198	.315	.285	61	-25	16	2		.987	-5	O-152	-3.5
■ **OLLIE BEARD**	Beard, Oliver Perry b: 5/2/1862, Lexington, Ky. d: 5/28/29, Cincinnati, Ohio BR/TR, 5'11", 180 lbs. Deb: 4/17/1889																						
1889	Cin-a	141	558	96	159	13	14	1	77	35	39	.285	.328	.364	94	-6	36			.896	20	*S-141	1.8
1890	Cin-N	122	492	64	132	17	15	3	72	44	13	.268	.331	.382	108	4	30			.897	1	*S-113/3-9	1.0

YEAR	TM/L	G	AB	R	H	2B	3B	HR	RBI	BB	SO	AVG	OBP	SLG	PRO+	BR/A	SB	CS	SBR	FA	FR	G/POS	TPR
1891	Lou-a	68	257	35	62	4	5	0	24	33	9	.241	.330	.296	80	-6	7			.879	7	3-61/S-7	0.3
Total	3	331	1307	195	353	34	34	4	173	112	61	.270	.330	.357	97	-8	73			.896	28	S-261/3-70	3.1

■ LEW BEASLEY Beasley, Lewis Paige b: 8/27/48, Sparta, Va. BL/TR, 5'10", 172 lbs. Deb: 5/21/77

YEAR	TM/L	G	AB	R	H	2B	3B	HR	RBI	BB	SO	AVG	OBP	SLG	PRO+	BR/A	SB	CS	SBR	FA	FR	G/POS	TPR
1977	Tex-A	25	32	5	7	1	0	0	3	2	2	.219	.265	.250	41	-3	1	1	-0	.833	-6	O-18/S-1,D-1	-0.9

■ DAVE BEATLE Beatle, David b: 1861, New York, N.Y. 6'2", 200 lbs. Deb: 6/17/1884

YEAR	TM/L	G	AB	R	H	2B	3B	HR	RBI	BB	SO	AVG	OBP	SLG	PRO+	BR/A	SB	CS	SBR	FA	FR	G/POS	TPR
1884	Det-N	1	3	0	0	0	0	0	0	0	2	.000	.000	.000	-99	-1				.500	-1	/O-1,C-1	-0.1

■ DESMOND BEATTY Beatty, Aloysius Desmond "Desperate" b: 4/7/1893, Baltimore, Md. d: 10/6/69, Norway, Maine BR/TR, 5'8.5", 158 lbs. Deb: 9/28/14

YEAR	TM/L	G	AB	R	H	2B	3B	HR	RBI	BB	SO	AVG	OBP	SLG	PRO+	BR/A	SB	CS	SBR	FA	FR	G/POS	TPR
1914	NY-N	2	3	0	0	0	0	0	1	0	0	.000	.000	.000	-99	-1	0			.400	-1	/S-1,3-1	-0.1

■ JIM BEAUCHAMP Beauchamp, James Edward b: 8/21/39, Vinita, Okla. BR/TR, 6'2", 205 lbs. Deb: 9/22/63 C

YEAR	TM/L	G	AB	R	H	2B	3B	HR	RBI	BB	SO	AVG	OBP	SLG	PRO+	BR/A	SB	CS	SBR	FA	FR	G/POS	TPR
1963	StL-N	4	3	0	0	0	0	0	0	0	2	.000	.000	.000	-91	-1	0	0	0	.000	0	H	-0.1
1964	Hou-N	23	55	6	9	2	0	2	4	5	16	.164	.246	.309	58	-3	0	0	0	.913	-1	O-15/1-2	-0.5
1965	Hou-N	24	53	5	10	1	0	0	4	5	11	.189	.259	.208	36	-4	0	2	-1	1.000	2	/O-9,1-3	-0.5
	Mil-N	4	3	0	0	0	0	0	0	1	1	.000	.250	.000	-23	-0	0	1	-1	1.000	-0	/1-2	-0.1
	Yr	28	56	5	10	1	0	0	4	6	12	.179	.258	.196	32	-5	0	3	-2	1.000	1	/O-9,1-5	-0.6
1967	Atl-N	4	3	0	0	0	0	0	1	0	0	.000	.000	.000	-99	-1	0	0	0	.000	0	H	-0.1
1968	Cin-N	31	57	10	15	2	0	2	14	4	19	.263	.311	.404	107	0	0	0	0	1.000	-0	O-13/1-1	0.0
1969	Cin-N	43	60	8	15	1	0	1	8	5	13	.250	.308	.317	71	-2	0	0	0	1.000	-2	/O-9,1-3	-0.5
1970	Hou-N	31	26	3	5	0	0	1	4	3	7	.192	.276	.308	59	-2	0	1	-1	1.000	-4	O-16	-0.7
	StL-N	44	58	8	15	2	0	1	6	8	11	.259	.348	.345	85	-1	2	0	1	1.000	1	O-10/1-5	-0.1
	Yr	75	84	11	20	2	0	2	10	11	18	.238	.326	.333	78	-3	2	1	0	1.000	-4	O-26/1-5	-0.8
1971	StL-N	77	162	24	38	8	3	2	16	9	26	.235	.279	.358	76	-5	3	1	0	.982	-2	1-44/O-1	-1.1
1972	NY-N	58	120	10	29	1	0	5	19	7	33	.242	.289	.375	90	-2	0	0	0	.979	-3	1-35/O-5	-0.8
1973	*NY-N	50	61	5	17	1	1	0	14	7	11	.279	.353	.328	91	-1	0	0	0	.969	-1	1-11	-0.2
Total	10	393	661	79	153	18	4	14	90	54	150	.231	.292	.334	76	-22	6	5	-1	.980	-11	1-106/O-78	-4.7

■ GINGER BEAUMONT Beaumont, Clarence Howeth b: 7/23/1876, Rochester, Wis. d: 4/10/56, Burlington, Wis. BL/TR, 5'8", 190 lbs. Deb: 4/21/1899

YEAR	TM/L	G	AB	R	H	2B	3B	HR	RBI	BB	SO	AVG	OBP	SLG	PRO+	BR/A	SB	CS	SBR	FA	FR	G/POS	TPR
1899	Pit-N	111	437	90	154	15	8	3	38	41		.352	.416	.444	137	23	31			.924	6	*O-100/1-2	1.9
1900	*Pit-N	138	567	105	158	14	9	5	50	40		.279	.331	.362	90	-8	27			.944	-12	*O-138	-2.8
1901	Pit-N	133	558	120	185	14	5	8	72	44		.332	.382	.418	128	20	36			.943	-5	*O-133	0.5
1902	Pit-N	130	541	100	**193**	21	6	0	67	39		**.357**	.404	.418	148	31	33			.975	0	*O-130	2.3
1903	*Pit-N	141	613	**137**	**209**	30	6	7	68	44		.341	.390	.444	133	25	23			.948	-7	*O-141	0.9
1904	Pit-N	153	615	97	**185**	12	12	3	54	34		.301	.338	.374	117	11	28			.968	-4	*O-153	-0.3
1905	Pit-N	103	384	60	126	12	8	3	40	22		.328	.365	.424	131	14	21			.972	-0	O-97	0.9
1906	Pit-N	80	310	48	82	9	3	2	32	19		.265	.311	.332	96	-2	1			.945	-5	O-78	-1.2
1907	Bos-N	150	580	67	**187**	19	14	4	62	37		.322	.366	.424	148	30	25			.962	5	*O-149	3.2
1908	Bos-N	125	476	66	127	20	6	2	52	42		.267	.328	.347	117	9	13			.965	-1	*O-121	0.4
1909	Bos-N	123	407	35	107	11	4	0	60	35		.263	.321	.310	92	-4	12			.969	1	*O-111	-0.8
1910	*Chi-N	76	172	30	46	5	1	2	22	28	14	.267	.373	.343	110	3	4			.957	-4	O-56	-0.3
Total	12	1463	5660	955	1759	182	82	39	617	425	14	.311	.362	.393	122	151	254			.956	-25	*O-1407/1-2	4.7

■ ED BEAVENS Beavens, Edward P. (a.k.a. Edward P. Bevens) b: 1848, Troy, N.Y. TR , 5'8", 138 lbs. Deb: 5/9/1871

YEAR	TM/L	G	AB	R	H	2B	3B	HR	RBI	BB	SO	AVG	OBP	SLG	PRO+	BR/A	SB	CS	SBR	FA	FR	G/POS	TPR
1871	Tro-n	3	15	7	6	0	0	0	5	0	0	.400	.400	.400	129	1	2	0	1	.818	1	/2-3	0.1
1872	Atl-n	10	43	6	9	2	0	0	2	1	0	.209	.227	.256	41	-4	0	0	0	.683	-5	2-10/S-1,O-1	-0.7
Total	2 n	13	58	13	15	2	0	0	7	1	0	.259	.271	.293	62	-3	2	0	1	.720	-4	/2-13,O-1,S-1	-0.6

■ BUCK BECANNON Becannon, James Melvin b: 8/22/1859, New York, N.Y. d: 11/5/23, New York, N.Y. 5'10", 165 lbs. Deb: 10/15/1884

YEAR	TM/L	G	AB	R	H	2B	3B	HR	RBI	BB	SO	AVG	OBP	SLG	PRO+	BR/A	SB	CS	SBR	FA	FR	G/POS	TPR
1884	*NY-a	1	3	0	0	0	0	0		0		.000	.000	.000	-99	-1				1.000	0	/P-1	0.0
1885	NY-a	10	33	3	10	0	0	0	2	1		.303	.343	.303	114	1				.947	0	P-10	0.0
1887	NY-N	1	5	0	0	0	0	0	0	0	2	.000	.000	.000	-99	-1	0			.667	-0	/3-1	-0.2
Total	3	12	41	3	10	0	0	0	2	1	2	.244	.279	.244	69	-1	0			.952	0	/P-11,3-1	-0.2

■ GEORGE BECHTEL Bechtel, George A. b: 1848, Philadelphia, Pa. 5'11", 165 lbs. Deb: 5/20/1871

YEAR	TM/L	G	AB	R	H	2B	3B	HR	RBI	BB	SO	AVG	OBP	SLG	PRO+	BR/A	SB	CS	SBR	FA	FR	G/POS	TPR
1871	Ath-n	20	94	24	33	9	1	1	21	2	2	.351	.365	.500	147	6	4	0	1	.821	0	O-15/P-3,3-3	0.4
1872	Mut-n	51	248	60	74	11	2	0	41	6	3	.298	.315	.359	114	6	9	1	2	.823	-0	*O-50/1-1	0.7
1873	Phi-n	53	258	53	63	12	1	1	40	9	1	.244	.270	.310	69	-10	2	1	0	.853	8	*O-52/P-3	0.0
1874	Phi-n	32	151	29	42	4	5	1	34	2	1	.278	.288	.391	111	1	0	0	0	.731	-4	O-28/P-6	0.0
1875	Cen-n	14	61	12	17	5	0	0	7	1	1	.279	.290	.361	136	2	0	0	0	.791	-1	P-14	0.0
	Ath-n	35	164	33	46	6	2	0	20	1	3	.280	.285	.341	105	-1	2	0	1	.810	1	O-31/P-4	0.2
	Yr	49	225	45	63	11	2	0	27	2	4	.280	.286	.347	113	2	2	0	1	.810	0	O-31,P-18	0.2
1876	Lou-N	14	55	2	10	1	0	0	2	0	1	.182	.182	.200	23	-5				.882	-2	O-14	-0.6
	NY-N	2	10	2	3	0	0	0	0	0	0	.300	.300	.300	115	0				.429	-1	/O-2	-0.1
	Yr	16	65	4	13	1	0	0	2	0	1	.200	.200	.215	34	-5				.750	-3	O-16	-0.7
Total	5 n	205	976	211	275	47	11	3	163	21	11	.282	.297	.362	104	4	17	2	4	.816	5	O-176/P-30,3-3,1-1	1.3

■ CLYDE BECK Beck, Clyde Eugene "Jersey" b: 1/6/1900, Bassett, Cal. d: 7/15/88, Temple City, Cal. BR/TR, 5'10", 176 lbs. Deb: 5/19/26

YEAR	TM/L	G	AB	R	H	2B	3B	HR	RBI	BB	SO	AVG	OBP	SLG	PRO+	BR/A	SB	CS	SBR	FA	FR	G/POS	TPR
1926	Chi-N	30	81	10	16	0	0	1	4	7	15	.198	.261	.235	34	-7	0			.993	12	2-30	0.5
1927	Chi-N	117	391	44	101	20	5	2	44	43	37	.258	.332	.350	83	-9	0			.969	22	2-99,3-17/S-1	1.7
1928	Chi-N	131	483	72	124	18	4	3	52	58	58	.257	.341	.329	77	-15	3			.958	-1	3-87,S-47/2-1	-0.6
1929	Chi-N	54	190	28	40	7	0	0	9	19	24	.211	.282	.247	32	-20	3			.978	5	3-33,S-14	-1.1
1930	Chi-N	83	244	32	52	7	0	6	34	36	32	.213	.314	.316	53	-19	2			.953	0	S-57,2-24/3-2	-1.1
1931	Cin-N	53	136	17	21	4	2	0	19	21	14	.154	.272	.213	34	-12	1			.960	-2	3-38/S-6	-1.2
Total	6	468	1525	203	354	56	11	12	162	184	180	.232	.317	.307	63	-83	9			.959	36	3-177,2-154,S-125	-1.8

■ ERVE BECK Beck, Ervin Thomas "Dutch" b: 7/19/1878, Toledo, Ohio d: 12/23/16, Toledo, Ohio BR/TR, 5'10", 168 lbs. Deb: 9/19/1899

YEAR	TM/L	G	AB	R	H	2B	3B	HR	RBI	BB	SO	AVG	OBP	SLG	PRO+	BR/A	SB	CS	SBR	FA	FR	G/POS	TPR
1899	Bro-N	8	24	2	4	2	0	0	2	0		.167	.167	.250	13	-3	0			.931	-2	/2-6,S-2	-0.4
1901	Cle-A	135	539	78	156	26	8	6	79	23		.289	.320	.401	103	1	7			.927	-11	*2-132	-0.4
1902	Cin-N	48	187	19	57	10	3	1	20	3		.305	.319	.406	113	2	2			.936	-5	2-32/1-6,O-6	-0.3
	Det-A	41	162	23	48	4	0	2	22	4		.296	.313	.358	84	-4	3			.971	1	1-36/O-5	-0.3
Total	3	232	912	122	265	42	11	9	123	30		.291	.315	.390	99	-4	12			.929	-16	2-170/1-42,O-11,S-2	-1.4

■ FRANK BECK Beck, Frank J. (b: Frank J. Hengstebeck) b: 4/29/1860, Poughkeepsie, N.Y. d: 2/8/41, Detroit, Mich. TR , 5'9", 141 lbs. Deb: 5/2/1884

YEAR	TM/L	G	AB	R	H	2B	3B	HR	RBI	BB	SO	AVG	OBP	SLG	PRO+	BR/A	SB	CS	SBR	FA	FR	G/POS	TPR
1884	Pit-a	3	12	1	4	1	0	0		0		.333	.333	.417	141	0				1.000	0	/P-3	0.0
	Bal-U	5	20	1	2	1	0	0		0		.100	.100	.150	-23	-4				.500	-1	/O-4,P-2	-0.4
Total	1	8	32	2	6	2	0	0		0		.188	.188	.250	33	-3				1.000	-1	/P-5,O-4	-0.4

■ FRED BECK Beck, Frederick Thomas b: 11/17/1886, Havana, Ill. d: 3/12/62, Havana, Ill. BL/TL, 6'1", 180 lbs. Deb: 4/14/09

YEAR	TM/L	G	AB	R	H	2B	3B	HR	RBI	BB	SO	AVG	OBP	SLG	PRO+	BR/A	SB	CS	SBR	FA	FR	G/POS	TPR
1909	Bos-N	96	334	20	66	5	6	2	27	17		.198	.245	.266	56	-18	5			.966	4	O-57,1-33	-1.8
1910	Bos-N	154	571	52	157	32	9	**10**	64	19	55	.275	.307	.415	105	-0	8			.963	2	*O-134,1-19	-0.5
1911	Cin-N	41	87	7	16	1	2	2	20	1	13	.184	.193	.310	41	-7	2			1.000	-2	O-16/1-6	-1.0
	Phi-N	66	210	26	59	8	3	3	25	17	21	.281	.346	.390	105	1	3			.957	-5	O-61	-0.8
	Yr	107	297	33	75	9	5	5	45	18	34	.253	.304	.367	88	-6	5			.966	-7	O-77/1-6	-1.8
1914	Chi-F	157	555	51	155	23	4	11	77	44	66	.279	.341	.395	106	-6	9			.982	-13	*1-157	-2.3
1915	Chi-F	121	373	35	83	9	3	5	38	24	38	.223	.277	.303	67	-24	4			.992	-6	*1-117	-3.6
Total	5	635	2130	191	536	78	27	33	251	122	193	.252	.301	.360	89	-54	31			.984	-20	1-332,O-268	-10.0

■ ZINN BECK Beck, Zinn Bertram b: 9/30/1885, Steubenville, O. d: 3/19/81, W.Palm Beach, Fla. BR/TR, 5'10.5", 160 lbs. Deb: 9/14/13

YEAR	TM/L	G	AB	R	H	2B	3B	HR	RBI	BB	SO	AVG	OBP	SLG	PRO+	BR/A	SB	CS	SBR	FA	FR	G/POS	TPR
1913	StL-N	10	30	4	5	1	0	0	2	4	10	.167	.265	.200	34	-2	1			.833	1	/S-5,3-5	-0.2
1914	StL-N	137	457	42	106	15	11	3	45	28	32	.232	.282	.333	84	-11	14			.935	10	*3-122,S-16	0.5

YEAR	TM/L	G	AB	R	H	2B	3B	HR	RBI	BB	SO	AVG	OBP	SLG	PRO+	BR/A	SB	CS	SBR	FA	FR	G/POS	TPR
1915	StL-N	70	223	21	52	9	4	0	15	12	31	.233	.282	.309	79	-6	3	10	-5	.935	0	3-62/S-4,2-2	-0.9
1916	StL-N	62	184	8	41	7	1	0	10	14	21	.223	.281	.272	71	-6	3			.910	-6	3-52/1-1,2-1	-1.3
1918	NY-A	11	8	0	0	0	0	0	1	0	1	.000	.000	.000	-98	-2	0			1.000	0	/1-5,3-1	-0.2
Total	5	290	902	75	204	32	16	3	73	58	95	.226	.279	.307	76	-27	21	10		.932	5	3-242/S-25,1-6,2-3	-2.1

■ HEINIE BECKENDORF

Beckendorf, Henry Ward b: 6/15/1884, New York, N.Y. d: 9/15/49, Jackson Heights, N.Y. BR/TR, 5'9", 174 lbs. Deb: 4/16/09

YEAR	TM/L	G	AB	R	H	2B	3B	HR	RBI	BB	SO	AVG	OBP	SLG	PRO+	BR/A	SB	CS	SBR	FA	FR	G/POS	TPR
1909	Det-A	15	27	1	7	1	0	0	1	2		.259	.310	.296	88	-0	0			.957	-0	C-15	0.0
1910	Det-A	3	7	0	3	0	0	0	2	1		.429	.500	.429	179	1	0			.909	-1	/C-2	0.0
	Was-A	37	103	8	15	1	0	0	10	5		.146	.207	.155	14	-10	0			.991	0	C-36	-0.7
	Yr	40	110	8	18	1	0	0	12	6		.164	.227	.173	26	-9	0			.988	-0	C-38	-0.7
Total	2	55	137	9	25	2	0	0	13	8		.182	.243	.197	39	-10	0			.983	-1	/C-53	-0.7

■ BEALS BECKER

Becker, David Beals b: 7/5/1886, ElDorado, Kan. d: 8/16/43, Huntington Park, Cal. BL/TL, 5'9", 170 lbs. Deb: 4/19/08

YEAR	TM/L	G	AB	R	H	2B	3B	HR	RBI	BB	SO	AVG	OBP	SLG	PRO+	BR/A	SB	CS	SBR	FA	FR	G/POS	TPR
1908	Pit-N	20	65	4	10	0	1	0	0	2		.154	.191	.185	20	-6	2			1.000	-1	O-17	-0.8
	Bos-N	43	171	13	47	3	1	0	7	7		.275	.303	.304	96	-1	7			.941	-4	O-43	-0.8
	Yr	63	236	17	57	3	2	0	7	9		.242	.272	.271	74	-7	9			.958	-5	O-60	-1.6
1909	Bos-N	152	562	60	138	15	6	6	24	47		.246	.305	.326	91	-7	21			.932	-2	*O-152	-1.6
1910	NY-N	80	126	18	36	2	4	3	24	14	25	.286	.357	.437	131	5	11			.972	-3	O-45/1-1	0.1
1911	*NY-N	88	172	28	45	11	1	1	20	26	22	.262	.359	.355	97	-0	19			.975	-5	O-55	-0.7
1912	*NY-N	125	402	66	106	18	8	6	58	54	35	.264	.354	.393	101	1	30			.958	-1	*O-117	-0.5
1913	Cin-N	30	108	11	32	5	3	0	14	6	12	.296	.333	.398	109	1	0			.971	2	O-28	0.2
	Phi-N	88	306	53	99	19	10	9	44	22	30	.324	.369	.539	151	19	11			.983	-2	O-77/1-1	1.4
	Yr	118	414	64	131	24	13	9	58	28	42	.316	.360	.502	140	20	11			.980	0	*O-105/1-1	1.6
1914	Phi-N	138	514	76	167	25	5	9	66	37	59	.325	.370	.446	133	20	16			.947	9	*O-126	2.4
1915	*Phi-N	112	338	38	83	16	4	11	35	26	48	.246	.301	.414	114	4	12	15	-5	.943	-8	O-98	-1.5
Total	8	876	2764	367	763	114	43	45	292	241	231	.276	.335	.397	112	35	129	15		.955	-13	O-758/1-2	-1.8

■ HEINZ BECKER

Becker, Heinz Reinhard "Dutch" b: 8/26/15, Berlin, Germany d: 11/11/91, Dallas, Tex. BB/TR, 6'2", 200 lbs. Deb: 4/21/43

YEAR	TM/L	G	AB	R	H	2B	3B	HR	RBI	BB	SO	AVG	OBP	SLG	PRO+	BR/A	SB	CS	SBR	FA	FR	G/POS	TPR
1943	Chi-N	24	69	5	10	0	0	0	2	9	6	.145	.244	.145	14	-7	0			.983	1	1-18	-0.8
1945	*Chi-N	67	133	25	38	8	2	2	27	17	16	.286	.375	.421	124	4	0			1.000	-2	1-28	0.1
1946	Chi-N	9	7	0	2	0	0	0	1	1	1	.286	.375	.286	91	-0	0			.000	0	H	0.0
	Cle-A	50	147	15	44	10	1	0	17	23	18	.299	.401	.381	127	6	1	0	0	.995	0	1-44	0.5
1947	Cle-A	2	2	0	0	0	0	0	0	0	1	.000	.000	.000	-99	-1	0	0	0	.000	0	H	-0.1
Total	4	152	358	45	94	18	3	2	47	50	42	.263	.359	.346	102	3	1	0		.994	0	/1-90	-0.3

■ JOE BECKER

Becker, Joseph Edward b: 6/25/08, St.Louis, Mo. d: 1/11/98, Sunset Hills, Mo. BR/TR, 6'1", 180 lbs. Deb: 5/10/36 C

YEAR	TM/L	G	AB	R	H	2B	3B	HR	RBI	BB	SO	AVG	OBP	SLG	PRO+	BR/A	SB	CS	SBR	FA	FR	G/POS	TPR
1936	Cle-A	22	50	5	9	3	1	1	11	5	4	.180	.255	.340	45	-5	0	0	0	.977	-4	C-15	-0.8
1937	Cle-A	18	33	3	11	2	1	0	2	3	4	.333	.405	.455	116	1	0	0	0	.949	-1	C-12	0.1
Total	2	40	83	8	20	5	2	1	13	8	8	.241	.315	.386	73	-4	0	0	0	.964	-5	/C-27	-0.7

■ MARTY BECKER

Becker, Martin Henry b: 12/25/1893, Tiffin, Ohio d: 9/25/57, Cincinnati, Ohio BB/TL, 5'8.5", 155 lbs. Deb: 9/8/15

YEAR	TM/L	G	AB	R	H	2B	3B	HR	RBI	BB	SO	AVG	OBP	SLG	PRO+	BR/A	SB	CS	SBR	FA	FR	G/POS	TPR
1915	NY-N	17	52	5	13	2	0	0	3	2	9	.250	.278	.288	76	-2	3			.917	0	O-16	-0.1

■ RICH BECKER

Becker, Richard Godhard b: 2/1/72, Aurora, Ill. BL/TL, 5'10", 199 lbs. Deb: 9/10/93

YEAR	TM/L	G	AB	R	H	2B	3B	HR	RBI	BB	SO	AVG	OBP	SLG	PRO+	BR/A	SB	CS	SBR	FA	FR	G/POS	TPR
1993	Min-A	3	7	3	2	2	0	0	0	5	4	.286	.583	.571	211	2	1	1	-0	.875	-0	/O-3	0.1
1994	Min-A	28	98	12	26	3	0	1	8	13	25	.265	.351	.327	76	-3	6	1	1	.989	5	O-26/D-1	0.3
1995	Min-A	106	392	45	93	15	1	2	33	34	95	.237	.305	.296	57	-24	8	9	-3	.986	13	*O-105	-1.7
1996	Min-A	148	525	92	153	31	4	12	71	68	118	.291	.375	.434	102	3	19	5	3	.993	**24**	*O-146	2.3
1997	Min-A	132	443	61	117	22	3	10	45	62	130	.264	.356	.395	94	-2	17	5	2	.985	1	*O-128	-0.2
1998	NY-N	49	100	15	19	4	2	3	10	21	42	.190	.331	.360	80	-3	3	1	0	.984	-3	O-41	-0.5
	Bal-A	79	113	22	23	1	0	3	11	22	34	.204	.343	.292	69	-5	2	0	1	.984	-13	O-60/D-1	-1.7
Total	6	545	1678	250	433	78	10	31	178	225	448	.258	.349	.372	85	-32	56	22	4	.987	26	O-509/D-2	-1.4

■ GLENN BECKERT

Beckert, Glenn Alfred b: 10/12/40, Pittsburgh, Pa. BR/TR, 6'1", 190 lbs. Deb: 4/12/65

YEAR	TM/L	G	AB	R	H	2B	3B	HR	RBI	BB	SO	AVG	OBP	SLG	PRO+	BR/A	SB	CS	SBR	FA	FR	G/POS	TPR
1965	Chi-N	154	614	73	147	21	3	3	30	28	52	.239	.276	.298	60	-32	6	8	-3	.973	9	*2-153	-1.3
1966	Chi-N	153	656	73	188	23	7	1	59	26	36	.287	.318	.348	84	-14	10	4	1	.970	-20	*2-152/S-1	-2.4
1967	Chi-N	146	597	91	167	32	3	5	40	30	25	.280	.314	.369	91	-8	10	3	1	.968	4	*2-144	0.8
1968	Chi-N	155	643	**98**	189	28	4	4	37	31	20	.294	.328	.369	102	1	8	4	0	.977	6	*2-155	1.9
1969	Chi-N★	131	543	69	158	22	1	1	37	24	24	.291	.328	.341	78	-16	6	0	2	.965	6	*2-129	0.3
1970	Chi-N★	143	591	99	170	15	6	3	36	32	22	.288	.324	.349	72	-24	4	1	1	.970	10	*2-138/O-1	-0.2
1971	Chi-N★	131	530	80	181	18	5	2	42	24	24	.342	.370	.406	104	3	3	2	-0	.986	-3	*2-129	1.1
1972	Chi-N★	120	474	51	128	22	2	3	43	23	17	.270	.307	.344	76	-15	2	1	0	.976	11	*2-118	0.3
1973	Chi-N	114	372	38	95	13	0	0	29	30	15	.255	.314	.290	64	-17	0	2	-1	.984	-12	2-88	-2.7
1974	SD-N	64	172	11	44	1	0	0	7	11	8	.256	.301	.262	61	-9	0	0	0	.938	-17	2-36/3-1	-2.6
1975	SD-N	9	16	2	6	1	0	0	0	1	0	.375	.412	.438	145	1	0	0	0	1.000	-1	/3-4	0.0
Total	11	1320	5208	685	1473	196	31	22	360	260	243	.283	.319	.345	81	-129	49	25	-0	.973	-7	*2-1242/3-5,O-1,S-1	-4.8

■ JAKE BECKLEY

Beckley, Jacob Peter "Eagle Eye" b: 8/4/1867, Hannibal, Mo. d: 6/25/18, Kansas City, Mo. BL/TL, 5'10", 200 lbs. Deb: 6/20/1888 H

YEAR	TM/L	G	AB	R	H	2B	3B	HR	RBI	BB	SO	AVG	OBP	SLG	PRO+	BR/A	SB	CS	SBR	FA	FR	G/POS	TPR
1888	Pit-N	71	283	35	97	15	3	0	27	7	22	.343	.363	.417	160	18	20			.979	-3	1-71	0.9
1889	Pit-N	123	522	91	157	24	10	9	97	29	29	.301	.345	.437	130	19	11			.982	2	*1-122/O-1	1.1
1890	Pit-P	121	516	109	167	38	**22**	9	120	42	32	.324	.381	.535	156	39	18			.976	-0	*1-121	2.5
1891	Pit-N	133	554	94	162	20	19	4	73	44	46	.292	.353	.419	128	18	13			.982	13	*1-133	2.1
1892	Pit-N	151	614	102	145	21	19	10	96	31	44	.236	.288	.381	102	-2	30			.978	21	*1-151	1.0
1893	Pit-N	131	542	108	164	32	19	5	106	54	26	.303	.386	.459	127	20	15			.986	11	*1-131	2.2
1894	Pit-N	131	533	121	183	36	18	7	120	43	16	.343	.412	.518	124	21	21			.978	5	*1-131	2.0
1895	Pit-N	129	530	104	174	31	19	5	110	24	20	.328	.381	.487	130	22	20			.978	-7	*1-129	1.5
1896	Pit-N	59	217	44	55	7	5	3	32	22	28	.253	.349	.373	94	-1	8			.982	-1	1-56/O-3,2-1	-0.1
	NY-N	46	182	37	55	8	4	6	38	9	7	.302	.352	.489	124	5	11			.982	-1	1-45/O-2	0.4
	Yr	105	399	81	110	15	9	9	70	31	35	.276	.351	.426	108	4	19			.982	-2	*1-101/O-5,2-1	0.3
1897	NY-N	17	68	8	17	2	3	1	11	2		.250	.301	.412	90	-1	2			.973	2	1-17	0.1
	Cin-N	97	365	76	126	17	9	7	76	18		.345	.395	.499	127	12	23			.979	-3	*1-97	0.8
	Yr	114	433	84	143	19	12	8	87	20		.330	.380	.485	121	11	25			.978	-1	*1-114	0.9
1898	Cin-N	118	459	86	135	20	12	4	72	28		.294	.348	.416	111	4	6			.983	-1	*1-118	0.3
1899	Cin-N	134	513	87	171	27	16	3	99	40		.333	.393	.466	133	22	20			.986	5	*1-134	2.5
1900	Cin-N	141	558	98	190	26	10	2	94	40		.341	.389	.434	130	23	23			.980	6	*1-140	2.5
1901	Cin-N	140	580	78	178	36	13	3	79	28		.307	.346	.429	133	22	4			.977	-4	*1-140	1.6
1002	Cin-N	129	531	82	175	23	7	5	69	34		.330	.377	.427	135	20	15			.983	-3	*1-129/P-1	1.5
1903	Cin-N	120	459	85	150	29	10	2	81	42		.327	.384	.447	123	12	23			.976	4	*1-119	1.3
1904	StL-N	142	551	72	179	22	9	1	67	35		.325	.375	.403	147	30	17			.988	-12	*1-142	1.6
1905	StL-N	134	514	48	147	20	10	1	57	30		.286	.333	.370	113	7	12			.982	-8	*1-134	-0.5
1906	StL-N	87	320	29	79	16	6	0	44	13		.247	.283	.334	96	-3	3			.987	-4	1-85	-1.1
1907	StL-N	32	115	6	24	3	0	0	7	1		.209	.222	.235	45	-8	0			.988	-2	1-32	-1.2
Total	20	2386	9526	1600	2930	473	243	87	1575	616	270	.308	.361	.436	126	300	315			.981	19	*1-2377/O-6,P-1,2-1	23.0

■ JULIO BECQUER

Becquer, Julio (Villegas) b: 12/20/31, Havana, Cuba BL/TL, 5'11.5", 178 lbs. Deb: 9/13/55

YEAR	TM/L	G	AB	R	H	2B	3B	HR	RBI	BB	SO	AVG	OBP	SLG	PRO+	BR/A	SB	CS	SBR	FA	FR	G/POS	TPR
1955	Was-A	10	14	1	3	0	0	0	1	0	1	.214	.214	.214	16	-2	0	0	0	1.000	1	/1-2	-0.1
1957	Was-A	105	186	14	42	6	2	2	22	10	29	.226	.269	.312	59	-11	3	3	-1	1.000	-0	1-43	-1.4
1958	Was-A	86	164	10	39	3	0	0	12	8	21	.238	.273	.256	47	-12	1	2	-1	.994	6	1-42/O-1	-1.0
1959	Was-A	108	220	20	59	12	5	1	26	8	17	.268	.297	.382	85	-5	3	2	-0	.990	2	1-53	-0.6
1960	Was-A	110	298	41	75	15	7	4	35	12	35	.252	.283	.389	81	-9	1	3	-2	.989	-3	1-77/P-1	-1.9
1961	LA-A	11	8	0	0	0	0	0	0	1	5	.000	.111	.000	-61	-2	0	0	0	1.000	0	/1-5	-0.2

YEAR	TM/L	G	AB	R	H	2B	3B	HR	RBI	BB	SO	AVG	OBP	SLG	PRO+	BR/A	SB	CS	SBR	FA	FR	G/POS	TPR
	Min-A	57	84	13	20	1	2	5	18	2	12	.238	.256	.476	86	-2	0	1	-1	1.000	-1	1-18/O-5,P-1	-0.4
	Yr	68	92	13	20	1	2	5	18	3	17	.217	.242	.435	72	-4	0	1	-1	1.000	-0	1-23/O-5,P-1	-0.6
1963	Min-A	1	0	1	0	0	0	0	0	0	0	—	—	—	—	0	0	0	0	.000	0	H	0.0
Total	7	488	974	100	238	37	16	12	114	41	120	.244	.277	.352	70	-42	8	11	-4	.993	5	1-240/O-6,P-2	-5.6
■ **HOWIE BEDELL**	Bedell, Howard William b: 9/29/35, Clearfield, Pa. BL/TR, 6′1″, 185 lbs. Deb: 4/10/62 C																						
1962	Mil-N	58	138	15	27	1	2	0	2	11	22	.196	.255	.232	33	-13	1	0	0	.955	-3	O-45	-1.8
1968	Phi-N	9	7	0	1	0	0	0	1	1	0	.143	.250	.143	20	-1	0	0	0	.000	0	H	-0.1
Total	2	67	145	15	28	1	2	0	3	12	22	.193	.255	.228	32	-14	1	0	0	.955	-3	/O-45	-1.9
■ **GENE BEDFORD**	Bedford, William Eugene b: 12/2/1896, Dallas, Tex. d: 10/6/77, San Antonio, Tex. BB/TR, 5′8″, 170 lbs. Deb: 6/25/25																						
1925	Cle-A	2	3	1	0	0	0	0	0	0	1	.000	.000	.000	-99	-1	0	0	0	1.000	-1	/2-2	-0.2
■ **ED BEECHER**	Beecher, Edward "Scrap Iron" b: 5/1876, Indiana Deb: 9/26/1897																						
1897	StL-N	3	12	1	4	0	0	0	1	0		.333	.333	.333	78	-0	1			1.000	-0	/O-3	-0.1
1898	Cle-N	8	25	1	5	2	0	0	0	0		.200	.200	.280	38	-2	0			.846	-2	/O-8	-0.4
Total	2	11	37	2	9	2	0	0	1	0		.243	.243	.297	51	-3	1			.895	-2	/O-11	-0.5
■ **ED BEECHER**	Beecher, Edward Harry b: 7/2/1860, Guilford, Conn. d: 9/12/35, Hartford, Conn. BL/TL, 5′10″, 185 lbs. Deb: 6/28/1887																						
1887	Pit-N	41	169	15	41	8	0	2	22	7	8	.243	.281	.325	72	-6	8			.915	5	O-41	-0.2
1889	Was-N	42	179	20	53	9	0	0	30	5	4	.296	.319	.346	91	-2	3			.861	-1	O-39/1-3	-0.4
1890	Buf-P	126	536	69	159	22	10	3	90	29	23	.297	.341	.392	104	3	14			.810	-5	*O-126/P-1	-0.5
1891	Was-a	58	235	35	57	11	3	2	28	27	9	.243	.333	.340	97	-1	17			.824	3	O-58	0.1
	Phi-a	16	71	9	15	2	4	0	7	3	4	.211	.243	.352	68	-4	7			1.000	-1	O-16	-0.4
	Yr	74	306	44	72	13	7	2	35	30	13	.235	.314	.343	91	-4	24			.845	2	O-74	-0.3
Total	4	283	1190	148	325	52	17	7	177	71	48	.273	.322	.363	94	-10	49			.843	1	O-280/1-3,P-1	-1.4
■ **JODIE BEELER**	Beeler, Joseph Sam b: 11/26/21, Dallas, Tex. BR/TR, 6′, 170 lbs. Deb: 9/21/44																						
1944	Cin-N	3	3	0	0	0	0	0	0	0	2	.000	.000	.000	-99	-1	0			.000	-1	/2-1,3-1	-0.2
■ **GENE BEGLEY**	Begley, Eugene T. b: 6/7/1861, Brooklyn, N.Y. Deb: 9/11/1886																						
1886	NY-N	5	16	1	2	0	0	0	1	1	3	.125	.176	.125	-7	-2	1			.864	-1	/C-3,O-2	-0.2
■ **JIM BEGLEY**	Begley, James Lawrence "Imp" b: 9/19/02, San Francisco, Cal. d: 2/20/57, San Francisco, Cal BR/TR, 5′6″, 145 lbs. Deb: 5/28/24																						
1924	Cin-N	2	5	1	1	0	0	0	0	2	0	.200	.429	.200	75	-0	0	0	0	.933	1	/2-2	0.1
■ **STEVE BEHEL**	Behel, Stephen Arnold Douglas b: 11/6/1860, Earlville, Ill. d: 2/15/45, Los Angeles, Cal. Deb: 9/27/1884																						
1884	Mil-U	9	33	5	8	1	0	0		3		.242	.306	.273	141	-1				1.000	-1	/O-9	-0.1
1886	NY-a	59	224	32	46	5	2	0	17	22		.205	.279	.246	68	-7	16			.858	-4	O-59	-1.1
Total	2	68	257	37	54	6	2	0	17	25		.210	.283	.249	73	-8	16			.865	-5	/O-68	-1.2
■ **OLLIE BEJMA**	Bejma, Alojzy Frank b: 9/12/07, South Bend, Ind. d: 1/3/95, South Bend, Ind. BR/TR, 5′10″, 165 lbs. Deb: 4/24/34																						
1934	StL-A	95	262	39	71	16	3	2	29	40	36	.271	.376	.378	87	-4	3	2	-0	.952	-12	S-32,2-14,3-13,/O-9	-1.3
1935	StL-A	64	198	18	38	8	2	2	26	27	21	.192	.289	.283	46	-16	1	0	0	.952	-4	2-47/S-8,3-2	-1.5
1936	StL-A	67	139	19	36	2	3	2	18	27	21	.259	.380	.360	81	-3	0	0	0	.963	-12	2-32/3-7,S-1	-1.2
1939	Chi-A	90	307	52	77	9	3	8	44	36	27	.251	.331	.378	79	-10	1	3	-2	.981	-14	2-81/S-1,3-1	-2.0
Total	4	316	906	128	222	35	11	14	117	130	105	.245	.343	.354	75	-34	5	5	-2	.967	-42	2-174/S-42,3-23,O-9	-6.0
■ **MARK BELANGER**	Belanger, Mark Henry b: 6/8/44, Pittsfield, Mass. d: 10/6/98, New York, N.Y. BR/TR, 6′1″, 170 lbs. Deb: 8/7/65																						
1965	Bal-A	11	3	1	1	0	0	0	0	0	0	.333	.333	.333	88	-0	0	1	-1	1.000	1	/S-4	0.0
1966	Bal-A	8	19	2	3	1	0	0	0	0	3	.158	.158	.211	5	-2	0	0	0	1.000	4	/S-6	0.2
1967	Bal-A	69	184	19	32	5	0	1	10	12	46	.174	.224	.217	31	-16	6	1	1	.952	7	S-38,2-26/3-2	-0.4
1968	Bal-A	145	472	40	98	13	0	2	21	40	114	.208	.275	.248	59	-22	10	1	2	.969	12	*S-145	0.8
1969	*Bal-A	150	530	76	152	17	4	2	50	53	54	.287	.354	.345	95	-2	14	6	1	.968	-10	*S-148	0.5
1970	*Bal-A	145	459	53	100	6	5	1	36	52	65	.218	.304	.259	56	-26	13	2	3	.970	8	*S-143	-0.1
1971	*Bal-A	150	500	67	133	19	4	0	35	73	48	.266	.367	.320	97	1	10	8	-2	.978	-0	*S-149	2.0
1972	Bal-A	113	285	36	53	9	1	2	16	18	53	.186	.239	.246	43	-20	6	3	0	.975	21	*S-105	1.4
1973	*Bal-A	154	470	60	106	15	1	0	27	49	54	.226	.305	.262	61	-23	13	6	0	.971	3	*S-154	0.0
1974	*Bal-A	155	493	54	111	14	4	5	36	51	69	.225	.300	.300	75	-15	17	7	1	**.984**	9	*S-155	1.6
1975	Bal-A	152	442	44	100	11	1	3	27	36	53	.226	.286	.276	63	-21	16	4	2	.978	**28**	*S-152	2.5
1976	Bal-A★	153	522	66	141	22	2	1	40	51	64	.270	.337	.326	101	1	27	17	-2	.982	16	*S-153	3.6
1977	Bal-A	144	402	39	83	13	4	2	30	43	68	.206	.288	.274	58	-23	15	8	-0	**.985**	21	*S-142	1.1
1978	Bal-A	135	348	39	74	13	0	0	16	40	55	.213	.305	.250	61	-17	6	6	-2	**.985**	**34**	*S-134	3.0
1979	*Bal-A	101	198	28	33	6	2	0	9	29	33	.167	.276	.217	36	-17	5	1	1	.990	3	S-98	-0.6
1980	Bal-A	113	268	37	61	7	3	0	22	12	25	.228	.261	.276	48	-19	6	3	0	.975	-1	*S-109	-1.1
1981	Bal-A	64	139	9	23	3	2	1	10	12	25	.165	.242	.237	39	-11	2	1	0	.973	5	S-63	-0.2
1982	LA-N	54	50	6	12	1	0	0	4	5	10	.240	.309	.260	62	-2	1	0	0	.953	8	S-44/2-1	0.7
Total	18	2016	5784	676	1316	175	33	20	389	576	839	.228	.302	.280	68	-234	167	75	5	.977	167	*S-1942/2-27,3-2	15.0
■ **WAYNE BELARDI**	Belardi, Carroll Wayne b: 9/5/30, St.Helena, Cal. d: 10/21/93, Santa Cruz, Cal. BL/TL, 6′1″, 185 lbs. Deb: 4/18/50																						
1950	Bro-N	10	10	0	0	0	0	0	0	0	4	.000	.000	.000	-98	-3	0			1.000	-0	/1-1	-0.3
1951	Bro-N	3	3	1	1	0	1	0	0	0	2	.333	.333	1.000	240	1	0	0	0	.000	0	H	0.1
1953	*Bro-N	69	163	19	39	3	2	11	34	16	40	.239	.311	.485	101	-0	0	0	0	.984	-0	1-38	-0.2
1954	Bro-N	11	9	0	2	0	0	0	1	2	3	.222	.364	.222	55	-0	0	0	0	.000	0	H	0.0
	Det-A	88	250	27	58	7	1	11	24	33	34	.232	.333	.400	102	0	1	0	0	.988	2	1-79	-0.1
1955	Det-A	3	3	0	0	0	0	0	0	0	1	.000	.000	.000	-99	-1	0	0	0	.000	0	H	-0.1
1956	Det-A	79	154	24	43	3	1	6	15	15	13	.279	.373	.429	111	3	0	0	0	.988	-1	1-31/O-2	0.0
Total	6	263	592	71	143	13	5	28	74	66	97	.242	.332	.422	100	-1	1	0		.987	0	1-149/O-2	-0.6
■ **KEVIN BELCHER**	Belcher, Kevin Donnell b: 8/8/67, Waco, Tex. BR/TR, 6′, 170 lbs. Deb: 9/3/90																						
1990	Tex-A	16	15	4	2	1	0	0	0	2	6	.133	.235	.200	23	-2	0	0	0	1.000	-2	/O-9	-0.3
■ **IRA BELDEN**	Belden, Ira Allison b: 4/16/1874, Cleveland, Ohio d: 7/15/16, Lakewood, Ohio BL/TR, 5′11″, 175 lbs. Deb: 9/17/1897																						
1897	Cle-N	8	30	5	8	0	2	0	4	2		.267	.333	.400	88	-1	0			1.000	2	/O-8	0.0
■ **TIM BELK**	Belk, Timothy William b: 4/6/70, Cincinnati, Ohio BR/TR, 6′3″, 200 lbs. Deb: 6/25/96																						
1996	Cin-N	7	15	2	3	0	0	0	0	1	2	.200	.250	.200	20	-2	0	0	0	1.000	-1	/1-6	-0.3
■ **CHARLIE BELL**	Bell, Charles C. b: 8/12/1868, Cincinnati, Ohio d: 2/7/37, Cincinnati, Ohio TR, Deb: 10/13/1889 F																						
1889	KC-a	2	6	1	1	1	0	0	3	2	2	.167	.375	.333	97	0	0			.000	-0	/O-1,P-1	-0.1
1891	Lou-a	10	28	3	1	0	0	0	0	6	8	.036	.206	.036	-31	-5	0			.783	-2	P-10	0.0
	Cin-a	1	4	1	2	0	0	0	1	0	0	.500	.500	.500	171	0	0			1.000	0	/P-1	0.0
	Yr	11	32	4	3	0	0	0	1	6	8	.094	.237	.094	-5	-4	0			.815	-1	P-11	0.0
Total	2	13	38	5	4	1	0	0	4	8	10	.105	.261	.132	13	-4	0			.844	-1	/P-12,O-1	-0.1
■ **BUDDY BELL**	Bell, David Gus b: 8/27/51, Pittsburgh, Pa. BR/TR, 6′2″, 185 lbs. Deb: 4/15/72 FMC																						
1972	Cle-A	132	466	49	119	21	1	9	36	34	29	.255	.310	.363	96	-2	5	6	-2	.990	7	*O-123/3-6	-0.3
1973	Cle-A★	156	631	86	169	23	7	14	59	49	47	.268	.327	.393	100	-1	7	15	-7	.958	24	*3-154/O-2	1.6
1974	Cle-A	116	423	51	111	15	1	7	46	35	29	.262	.323	.352	95	-3	1	3	-2	.963	4	*3-115/D-1	-0.1
1975	Cle-A	153	553	66	150	20	4	10	59	51	72	.271	.334	.376	100	0	6	5	-1	.950	-3	*3-153	-0.5
1976	Cle-A	159	604	75	170	26	2	7	60	44	49	.281	.332	.366	105	4	3	8	-4	.956	5	*3-158/1-2	0.4
1977	Cle-A	129	479	64	140	23	4	11	64	45	63	.292	.354	.426	115	10	1	8	-5	.960	13	*3-118,O-11	1.6
1978	Cle-A	142	556	71	157	27	8	6	62	39	43	.282	.329	.392	103	2	1	3	-2	.970	28	*3-139/D-1	2.7

YEAR	TM/L	G	AB	R	H	2B	3B	HR	RBI	BB	SO	AVG	OBP	SLG	PRO+	BR/A	SB	CS	SBR	FA	FR	G/POS	TPR
1979	Tex-A	162	670	89	200	42	3	18	101	30	45	.299	.331	.451	110	7	5	4	-1	.969	12	*3-147,S-33	2.0
1980	Tex-A★	129	490	76	161	24	4	17	83	40	39	.329	.379	.498	143	28	3	1	0	**.981**	22	*3-120/S-3	4.7
1981	Tex-A★	97	360	44	106	16	1	10	64	42	30	.294	.373	.428	137	18	3	3	-1	.961	**30**	3-96/S-1	4.6
1982	Tex-A★	148	537	62	159	27	2	13	67	70	50	.296	.379	.426	127	22	5	4	-1	**.976**	**34**	*3-145/S-4	5.1
1983	Tex-A	156	618	75	171	35	3	14	66	50	48	.277	.335	.411	106	5	3	5	-2	.967	16	*3-154	1.6
1984	Tex-A★	148	553	88	174	36	5	11	83	63	54	.315	.388	.458	129	23	2	1	0	.958	21	*3-147	4.1
1985	Tex-A	84	313	33	74	13	3	4	32	33	21	.236	.311	.335	76	-10	3	2	-0	.942	13	3-83	0.2
	Cin-N	67	247	28	54	15	2	6	36	34	27	.219	.313	.368	86	-5	0	1	-1	.946	-9	3-67	-1.6
1986	Cin-N	155	568	89	158	29	3	20	75	73	49	.278	.365	.445	117	14	2	8	-4	.975	1	*3-151/2-1	0.9
1987	Cin-N	143	522	74	148	19	2	17	70	71	39	.284	.370	.425	105	6	4	1	1	**.979**	-17	*3-142	-1.3
1988	Cin-N	21	54	3	10	0	0	0	3	7	3	.185	.279	.185	34	-4	0	0	0	.968	0	3-13/1-2	-0.5
	Hou-N	74	269	24	68	10	1	7	37	19	29	.253	.302	.375	97	-2	1	1	-0	.924	-11	3-66/1-7	-1.6
	Yr	95	323	27	78	10	1	7	40	26	32	.241	.298	.344	86	-6	1	1	-0	.931	-11	3-79/1-9	-2.1
1989	Tex-A	34	82	4	15	4	0	0	3	7	10	.183	.247	.232	35	-7	0	0	0	1.000	1	D-22/3-9,1-1	-0.7
Total	18	2405	8995	1151	2514	425	56	201	1106	836	776	.279	.343	.406	108	105	55	79	-31	.964	191	*3-2183,O-136/SD12	22.9

■ DAVID BELL Bell, David Michael b: 9/14/72, Cincinnati, Ohio BR/TR, 5'10", 170 lbs. Deb: 5/3/95 F

YEAR	TM/L	G	AB	R	H	2B	3B	HR	RBI	BB	SO	AVG	OBP	SLG	PRO+	BR/A	SB	CS	SBR	FA	FR	G/POS	TPR
1995	Cle-A	2	2	0	0	0	0	0	0	0	0	.000	.000	.000	-99	-1	0	0	0	1.000	0	/3-2	0.0
	StL-N	39	144	13	36	7	2	2	19	4	25	.250	.280	.368	69	-7	1	2	-1	.967	-3	2-37/3-3	-0.8
1996	StL-N	62	145	12	31	6	0	1	9	10	22	.214	.269	.276	45	-12	1	1	-0	.953	9	3-45,2-20/S-1	-0.2
1997	StL-N	66	142	9	30	7	2	1	12	10	28	.211	.263	.310	50	-11	1	0	0	.913	3	3-35,2-23,S-13	-0.6
1998	StL-N	4	9	0	2	1	0	0	0	0	3	.222	.222	.333	42	-1	0	0	0	1.000	-1	/3-4,2-1	-0.1
	Cle-A	107	340	37	89	21	2	10	41	22	54	.262	.310	.424	86	-8	0	4	-2	.982	23	*2-101/3-6,1-1,S-1	1.7
	Sea-A	21	80	11	26	8	0	0	8	5	8	.325	.365	.425	105	1	0	0	0	.984	3	2-14/1-5,3-5,O-1	0.4
	Yr	128	420	48	115	29	2	10	49	27	62	.274	.321	.424	89	-7	0	4	-2	.982	**26**	*2-115,3-11/1-6,SO	2.1
Total	4	301	862	82	214	50	6	14	89	51	140	.248	.294	.369	71	-38	3	7	-3	.979	35	2-196,3-100/S1O	0.4

■ GUS BELL Bell, David Russell b: 11/15/28, Louisville, Ky. d: 5/7/95, Montgomery, Ohio BL/TR, 6'2", 196 lbs. Deb: 5/30/50 F

YEAR	TM/L	G	AB	R	H	2B	3B	HR	RBI	BB	SO	AVG	OBP	SLG	PRO+	BR/A	SB	CS	SBR	FA	FR	G/POS	TPR
1950	Pit-N	111	422	62	119	22	11	8	53	28	46	.282	.333	.443	99	-2	4			.977	6	*O-104	0.0
1951	Pit-N	149	600	80	167	27	**12**	16	89	42	41	.278	.330	.443	103	1	1	4	-2	.986	3	*O-145	-0.3
1952	Pit-N	131	468	53	117	21	5	16	59	36	72	.250	.306	.419	97	-4	1	4	-2	.972	-7	*O-123	-1.8
1953	Cin-N★	151	610	102	183	37	5	30	105	48	72	.300	.354	.525	124	20	0	2	-1	.977	14	*O-151	2.5
1954	Cin-N★	153	619	104	185	38	7	17	101	48	58	.299	.353	.465	108	7	5	3	-0	.986	2	*O-153	0.1
1955	Cin-N	154	610	88	188	30	6	27	104	54	57	.308	.364	.510	122	18	4	4	-1	.987	-8	*O-154	0.2
1956	Cin-N★	150	603	82	176	31	4	29	84	50	66	.292	.349	.501	117	14	6	2	1	.986	-7	*O-149	-0.1
1957	Cin-N★	121	510	65	149	20	3	13	61	30	54	.292	.335	.420	95	-4	0	1	-1	.988	0	*O-121	-1.2
1958	Cin-N	112	385	42	97	16	2	10	46	36	40	.252	.318	.382	80	-11	2	3	-1	**.996**	-2	*O-107	-2.0
1959	Cin-N	148	580	59	170	27	2	19	115	29	44	.293	.329	.445	101	-0	2	3	-1	**.996**	7	*O-145	-0.2
1960	Cin-N	143	515	65	135	19	5	12	62	29	40	.262	.303	.388	86	-11	4	3	-1	.988	0	*O-131	-1.8
1961	*Cin-N	103	235	27	60	10	1	3	33	18	21	.255	.308	.345	72	-9	1	1	-0	.991	-6	O-75	-1.9
1962	NY-N	30	101	8	15	2	0	1	6	10	7	.149	.225	.198	14	-12	0	1	-1	.979	4	O-26	-1.1
	Mil-N	79	214	28	61	11	3	5	24	12	17	.285	.323	.435	104	1	0	0	0	.987	-3	O-58	-0.6
	Yr	109	315	36	76	13	3	6	30	22	24	.241	.291	.359	74	-12	0	1	-1	.984	0	O-84	-1.7
1963	Mil-N	3	3	0	1	0	0	0	0	0	0	.333	.333	.333	94	-0	0	0	0	.000	0	H	0.0
1964	Mil-N	3	3	0	0	0	0	0	0	0	1	.000	.000	.000	-99	-1	0	0	0	.000	0	H	-0.1
Total	15	1741	6478	865	1823	311	66	206	942	470	636	.281	.333	.445	102	7	30	31		.985	2	*O-1642	-8.3

■ DEREK BELL Bell, Derek Nathaniel b: 12/11/68, Tampa, Fla. BR/TR, 6'2", 215 lbs. Deb: 6/28/91

YEAR	TM/L	G	AB	R	H	2B	3B	HR	RBI	BB	SO	AVG	OBP	SLG	PRO+	BR/A	SB	CS	SBR	FA	FR	G/POS	TPR
1991	Tor-A	18	28	5	4	0	0	0	1	6	5	.143	.314	.143	30	-2	3	2	-0	.889	-3	O-13	-0.6
1992	*Tor-A	61	161	23	39	6	3	2	15	15	34	.242	.326	.354	86	-3	7	2	1	1.000	-1	O-56/D-1	-0.4
1993	SD-N	150	542	73	142	19	1	21	72	23	122	.262	.307	.417	90	-9	26	5	5	.976	6	*O-125,3-19	0.0
1994	SD-N	108	434	54	135	20	0	14	54	29	88	.311	.356	.454	112	7	24	8	2	.962	-0	*O-108	0.7
1995	Hou-N	112	452	63	151	21	2	8	86	33	71	.334	.389	.442	128	18	27	9	3	.963	1	*O-110	1.9
1996	Hou-N	158	627	84	165	40	3	17	113	40	123	.263	.316	.418	99	-3	29	3	7	.977	9	*O-157	0.9
1997	*Hou-N	129	493	67	136	29	3	15	71	40	94	.276	.345	.438	107	5	15	7	0	.967	-0	*O-125/D-1	0.2
1998	*Hou-N	156	630	111	198	41	2	22	108	51	126	.314	.369	.490	123	21	13	3	2	.973	5	*O-154	2.6
Total	8	892	3367	480	970	176	14	99	520	237	663	.288	.344	.437	108	34	144	39	20	.971	17	O-848/3-19,D-2	5.3

■ FERN BELL Bell, Fernando Jerome Lee (b: Fern Oran Bell) "Danny" b: 1/21/13, Ada, Okla. BR/TR, 6', 180 lbs. Deb: 4/17/39

YEAR	TM/L	G	AB	R	H	2B	3B	HR	RBI	BB	SO	AVG	OBP	SLG	PRO+	BR/A	SB	CS	SBR	FA	FR	G/POS	TPR
1939	Pit-N	83	262	44	75	5	8	2	34	42	18	.286	.385	.389	110	5	2			.975	0	O-67/3-1	0.3
1940	Pit-N	6	3	0	0	0	0	0	1	1	1	.000	.250	.000	-26	-0	0			.000	0	H	-0.1
Total	2	89	265	44	75	5	8	2	35	43	19	.283	.383	.385	109	5	2			.975	0	/O-67,3-1	0.2

■ FRANK BELL Bell, Frank Gustav b: 1863, Cincinnati, Ohio d: 4/14/1891, Cincinnati, Ohio 6', Deb: 7/7/1885 F

YEAR	TM/L	G	AB	R	H	2B	3B	HR	RBI	BB	SO	AVG	OBP	SLG	PRO+	BR/A	SB	CS	SBR	FA	FR	G/POS	TPR
1885	Bro-a	10	29	5	5	0	1	0	2	0		.172	.200	.241	39	-2				.739	-2	/C-5,O-4,3-2	-0.3

■ GEORGE BELL Bell, George Antonio (Mathey) b: 10/21/59, San Pedro De Macoris, D.R. BR/TR, 6'1", 190 lbs. Deb: 4/9/81 F

YEAR	TM/L	G	AB	R	H	2B	3B	HR	RBI	BB	SO	AVG	OBP	SLG	PRO+	BR/A	SB	CS	SBR	FA	FR	G/POS	TPR
1981	Tor-A	60	163	19	38	2	1	5	12	5	27	.233	.256	.350	69	-7	3	2	-0	.969	1	O-44/D-8	-0.8
1983	Tor-A	39	112	5	30	5	4	2	17	4	17	.268	.305	.438	96	-1	1	1	-0	.954	-2	O-34/D-2	-0.4
1984	Tor-A	159	606	85	177	39	4	26	87	24	86	.292	.328	.498	121	15	11	2	2	.971	-1	*O-147/3-3,D-7	1.1
1985	*Tor-A	157	607	87	167	28	6	28	95	43	90	.275	.331	.479	116	12	21	6	3	.968	8	*O-157/3-2	1.7
1986	Tor-A	159	641	101	198	38	6	31	108	41	62	.309	.352	.532	133	27	7	8	-3	.966	7	*O-147,D-11/3-2	2.5
1987	Tor-A★	156	610	111	188	32	4	47	**134**	39	75	.308	.357	.605	146	37	5	1	1	.960	0	*O-148/2-1,3-1,D-7	3.2
1988	Tor-A	156	614	78	165	27	5	24	97	34	66	.269	.308	.446	108	4	4	2	0	.946	-7	*O-149/D-7	-0.8
1989	*Tor-A	153	613	88	182	41	2	18	104	33	60	.297	.337	.458	124	18	4	3	-1	.963	-4	*O-134,D-19	0.9
1990	Tor-A★	142	562	67	149	25	0	21	86	32	80	.265	.308	.422	100	-1	3	2	-0	.979	4	*O-106,D-36	-0.2
1991	Chi-N★	149	558	63	159	27	0	25	86	32	62	.285	.328	.468	116	10	2	6	-3	.962	-5	*O-146	-0.1
1992	Chi-A	155	627	74	160	27	0	25	112	31	97	.255	.297	.418	99	-3	5	2	0	.964	-2	*D-140,O-15	-1.0
1993	Chi-A	102	410	36	89	17	2	13	64	13	49	.217	.248	.363	64	-23	1	1	-0	.000	0	*D-102	-2.7
Total	12	1587	6123	814	1702	308	34	265	1002	331	771	.278	.320	.469	113	88	67	36	-2	.964	-0	*O-1227,D-339/3-8,2	3.4

■ JAY BELL Bell, Jay Stuart b: 12/11/65, Eglin A.F.B., Fla. BR/TR, 6'1", 185 lbs. Deb: 9/29/86

YEAR	TM/L	G	AB	R	H	2B	3B	HR	RBI	BB	SO	AVG	OBP	SLG	PRO+	BR/A	SB	CS	SBR	FA	FR	G/POS	TPR
1986	Cle-A	5	14	3	5	2	0	1	4	2	3	.357	.438	.714	211	2	0	0	0	.778	-0	/2-2,D-2	0.2
1987	Cle-A	38	125	14	27	9	1	2	13	8	31	.216	.269	.352	62	-7	2	0	1	.947	3	S-38	-0.1
1988	Cle-A	73	211	23	46	5	1	2	21	21	53	.218	.292	.280	59	-11	4	2	0	.965	-13	S-72/D-1	-1.9
1989	Pit-N	78	271	33	70	13	3	2	27	19	47	.258	.309	.351	91	-3	5	3	-0	.968	-16	S-78	-1.3
1990	*Pit-N	159	583	93	148	28	7	7	52	65	109	.254	.332	.362	94	-4	10	6	-1	.970	-3	*S-159	0.6
1991	*Pit-N	157	608	96	164	32	8	16	67	52	99	.270	.331	.428	114	10	10	6	-1	.968	8	*S-156	3.0
1992	*Pit-N	159	632	87	167	36	6	9	55	55	103	.264	.327	.383	102	1	7	5	-1	.973	17	*S-159	3.0
1993	Pit-N★	154	604	102	187	32	9	9	51	77	122	.310	.393	.437	122	22	16	10	-1	**.986**	**26**	*S-154	5.7
1994	Pit-N	110	424	68	117	35	4	9	45	49	82	.276	.355	.441	105	3	2	0	1	.973	19	*S-110	3.1
1995	Pit-N	138	530	79	139	28	4	13	55	55	110	.262	.336	.404	92	-6	2	5	-2	.978	7	*S-136/3-3	1.1
1996	Pit-N	151	527	65	132	29	3	13	71	54	108	.250	.326	.391	86	-11	6	4	-1	**.986**	13	*S-151	1.4
1997	KC-A	153	573	89	167	28	3	21	92	71	101	.291	.373	.461	113	12	10	6	-1	.985	2	*S-149/3-4	2.6
1998	Ari-N	155	549	79	138	29	5	20	67	81	129	.251	.355	.432	102	3	3	5	-2	.971	-16	*S-138,2-15	0.0
Total	13	1530	5651	831	1507	306	54	124	620	609	1097	.267	.343	.406	101	11	77	52	-8	.975	48	*S-1500/2-17,3-7,D	17.4

■ RUDY BELL Bell, John (b: Rudolph Fred Baerwald) b: 1/1/1881, Wausau, Wis. d: 7/28/55, Albuquerque, N.Mex. BR/TR, 5'8.5", 158 lbs. Deb: 9/16/07

YEAR	TM/L	G	AB	R	H	2B	3B	HR	RBI	BB	SO	AVG	OBP	SLG	PRO+	BR/A	SB	CS	SBR	FA	FR	G/POS	TPR
1907	NY-A	17	52	4	11	2	1	0	3	3		.212	.268	.288	72	-2	4			.897	-1	O-17	-0.4

YEAR	TM/L	G	AB	R	H	2B	3B	HR	RBI	BB	SO	AVG	OBP	SLG	PRO+	BR/A	SB	CS	SBR	FA	FR	G/POS	TPR
■ JUAN BELL	Bell, Juan (Mathey) b: 3/29/68, San Pedro De Macoris, D.R. BR/TR, 5′11″, 176 lbs. Deb: 9/6/89 F																						
1989	Bal-A	8	4	2	0	0	0	0	0	0	1	.000	.000	.000	-99	-1	1	0	0	1.000	2	/2-2,S-2,D-4	0.1
1990	Bal-A	5	2	1	0	0	0	0	0	0	1	.000	.000	.000	-99	-1	0	0	0	1.000	0	/S-1,D-1	0.0
1991	Bal-A	100	209	26	36	9	2	1	15	8	51	.172	.203	.249	25	-22	0	0	0	.973	-1	2-77,S-15/O-1,D-4	-2.1
1992	Phi-N	46	147	12	30	3	1	1	8	18	29	.204	.295	.259	58	-8	5	0	2	.972	4	S-46	0.1
1993	Phi-N	24	65	5	13	6	1	0	7	5	12	.200	.268	.323	58	-4	0	1	-1	.909	3	S-22	-0.1
	Mil-A	91	286	42	67	6	2	5	29	36	64	.234	.322	.322	75	-10	6	6	-2	.983	2	2-47,S-40/O-3,D-2	-0.5
1994	Mon-N	38	97	12	27	4	0	2	10	15	21	.278	.375	.381	97	0	4	0	1	.991	-2	2-25/3-3,S-1	0.1
1995	Bos-A	17	26	7	4	2	0	1	2	2	10	.154	.214	.346	41	-2	0	0	0	.857	4	/S-6,2-5,3-1	0.2
Total	7	329	836	107	177	30	6	10	71	84	189	.212	.286	.298	60	-47	16	7	1	.981	13	2-156,S-133/D30	-2.2
■ KEVIN BELL	Bell, Kevin Robert b: 7/13/55, Los Angeles, Cal. BR/TR, 6′, 195 lbs. Deb: 6/16/76																						
1976	Chi-A	68	230	24	57	7	6	5	20	18	56	.248	.305	.396	104	0	2	1	0	.970	3	3-67/D-1	0.3
1977	Chi-A	9	28	4	5	1	0	1	6	3	8	.179	.258	.321	57	-2	0	0	0	.909	0	/S-5,3-4,O-1	-0.1
1978	Chi-A	54	68	9	13	0	0	2	5	5	19	.191	.257	.279	50	-5	1	0	0	.946	11	3-52/D-1	0.7
1979	Chi-A	70	200	20	49	8	1	4	22	15	43	.245	.298	.355	75	-7	2	4	-2	.923	12	3-68/S-2	0.3
1980	Chi-A	92	191	16	34	5	2	1	11	29	37	.178	.286	.241	46	-14	0	0	0	.925	7	3-83/S-3,D-3	-0.8
1982	Oak-A	4	9	1	3	1	0	0	0	0	2	.333	.333	.444	117	0	0	0	0	.857	0	/3-3,D-1	0.0
Total	6	297	726	74	161	22	9	13	64	70	165	.222	.292	.331	73	-26	5	5	-2	.940	33	3-277/S-10,D-6,O-1	0.4
■ LES BELL	Bell, Lester Rowland b: 12/14/01, Harrisburg, Pa. d: 12/26/85, Hershey, Pa. BR/TR, 5′11″, 165 lbs. Deb: 9/18/23																						
1923	StL-N	15	51	5	19	2	1	0	9	9	7	.373	.467	.451	146	4	1	0	0	.917	-1	S-15	0.4
1924	StL-N	17	57	5	14	3	2	1	5	3	7	.246	.295	.421	91	-1	0	0	0	.905	-4	S-17	-0.3
1925	StL-N	153	586	80	167	29	9	11	88	43	47	.285	.334	.422	89	-10	4	5	-2	.924	-1	*3-153/S-1	-0.2
1926	*StL-N	155	581	85	189	33	14	17	100	54	62	.325	.383	.518	135	27	9			.950	-22	*3-155	1.5
1927	StL-N	115	390	48	101	26	6	9	65	34	63	.259	.320	.426	95	-4	5			.904	-14	*3-100,S-10	-1.3
1928	Bos-N	153	591	58	164	36	7	10	91	40	45	.277	.323	.413	96	-6	1			.948	5	*3-153	0.8
1929	Bos-N	139	483	58	144	23	5	9	72	50	42	.298	.364	.422	98	-1	4			.953	-20	*3-127/2-1,S-1	-1.5
1930	Chi-N	74	248	35	69	15	4	5	47	24	27	.278	.342	.431	85	-6	1			.948	-0	3-70/1-2	-0.3
1931	Chi-N	75	252	30	71	17	1	4	32	19	22	.282	.332	.405	95	-2	0			.944	4	3-70	0.6
Total	9	896	3239	404	938	184	49	66	509	276	322	.290	.346	.438	102	1	25	5		.939	-53	3-828/S-44,1-2,2-1	-0.3
■ MIKE BELL	Bell, Michael Allen b: 4/22/68, Lewiston, N.Y. BL/TL, 6′1″, 175 lbs. Deb: 5/2/90																						
1990	Atl-N	36	45	8	11	5	1	1	5	2	9	.244	.292	.467	99	-0	0	1	-1	.981	1	1-24	-0.1
1991	Atl-N	17	30	4	4	0	0	1	1	2	7	.133	.188	.233	17	-3	1	0	0	.975	-0	1-14	-0.4
Total	2	53	75	12	15	5	1	2	6	4	16	.200	.250	.373	67	-4	1	1	-0	.979	1	/1-38	-0.5
■ BEAU BELL	Bell, Roy Chester b: 8/20/07, Bellville, Tex. d: 9/14/77, College Station, Tex. BR/TR, 6′2″, 185 lbs. Deb: 4/16/35																						
1935	StL-A	76	220	20	55	8	2	3	17	16	16	.250	.304	.345	65	-12	1	1	-0	.918	-5	O-37,1-15/3-3	-1.9
1936	StL-A	155	616	100	212	40	12	11	123	60	55	.344	.403	.502	119	18	4	1	1	.974	-2	*O-142,1-17	0.8
1937	StL-A☆	156	642	82	**218**	**51**	8	14	117	53	54	.340	.391	.509	124	23	2	2	-1	.984	3	*O-131,1-26/3-2	1.6
1938	StL-A	147	526	91	138	35	3	13	84	71	46	.262	.350	.414	91	-8	1	3	-2	.979	4	*O-132/1-4	-0.9
1939	StL-A	11	32	4	7	1	0	1	5	4	3	.219	.324	.344	69	-1	0	0	0	1.000	-0	/O-9	-0.2
	Det-A	54	134	14	32	4	2	0	24	24	16	.239	.358	.299	65	-7	0	1	-1	1.000	1	O-37	-0.7
	Yr	65	166	18	39	5	2	1	29	28	19	.235	.352	.307	66	-8	0	1	-1	1.000	1	O-46	-0.9
1940	Cle-A	120	444	55	124	22	2	4	58	34	41	.279	.332	.365	83	-11	2	2	-1	.971	-2	O-97,1-14	-1.9
1941	Cle-A	48	104	12	20	4	3	0	9	10	8	.192	.270	.288	50	-8	1	2	-1	1.000	-3	O-14,1-10	-1.3
Total	7	767	2718	378	806	165	32	46	437	272	239	.297	.362	.432	99	-6	11	12	-4	.976	-5	O-599/1-86,3-5	-4.5
■ TERRY BELL	Bell, Terence William b: 10/27/62, Dayton, Ohio BR/TR, 6′, 195 lbs. Deb: 9/3/86																						
1986	KC-A	8	3	0	0	0	0	0	0	2	1	.000	.400	.000	20	-0	0	0	0	1.000	-0	/C-8	0.0
1987	Atl-N	1	1	0	0	0	0	0	0	0	1	.000	.000	.000	-95	-0	0	0	0	.000	0	/H	0.0
Total	2	9	4	0	0	0	0	0	0	2	2	.000	.333	.000	-0	-0	0	0	0	1.000	-0	/C-8	0.0
■ ZEKE BELLA	Bella, John b: 8/23/30, Greenwich, Conn. BR/TL, 5′11″, 185 lbs. Deb: 9/11/57																						
1957	NY-A	5	10	0	1	0	0	0	0	1	2	.100	.182	.100	-21	-2	0	0	0	1.000	1	/O-4	-0.1
1959	KC-A	47	82	10	17	2	1	1	9	9	14	.207	.293	.293	60	-4	0	0	0	1.000	-3	O-25/1-1	-0.9
Total	2	52	92	10	18	2	1	1	9	10	16	.196	.282	.272	52	-6	0	0	0	1.000	-3	/O-29,1-1	-1.0
■ STEVE BELLAN	Bellan, Esteban Enrique b: 1850, Cuba d: 8/8/32, Havana, Cuba 5′6″, 154 lbs. Deb: 5/9/1871																						
1871	Tro-n	29	128	26	32	3	3	0	23	9	2	.250	.299	.320	77	-4	4	4	-1	.713	-2	*3-28/S-1	-0.6
1872	Tro-n	23	114	22	30	4	0	0	16	0	0	.263	.263	.298	71	-4	1	0	0	.673	-6	/S-9,3-8,O-6	-0.7
1873	Mut-n	8	32	4	7	2	0	0	3	2	0	.219	.265	.281	63	-1	0	0	0	.488	-5	/3-7,2-3	-0.5
Total	3 n	60	274	52	69	9	3	0	42	11	2	.252	.281	.307	73	-9	5	4	-1	.671	-14	/3-43,S-10,O-6,2-3	-1.8
■ ALBERT BELLE	Belle, Albert Jojuan "Joey" b: 8/25/66, Shreveport, La. BR/TR, 6′2″, 210 lbs. Deb: 7/15/89																						
1989	Cle-A	62	218	22	49	8	4	7	37	12	55	.225	.272	.394	84	-5	2	2	-1	.979	1	O-44,D-17	-0.7
1990	Cle-A	9	23	1	4	0	0	1	3	1	6	.174	.208	.304	42	-2	0	0	0	.000	-0	/O-1,D-6	-0.2
1991	Cle-A	123	461	60	130	31	2	28	95	25	99	.282	.326	.540	134	19	3	1	0	.952	3	O-89,D-32	1.9
1992	Cle-A	153	585	81	152	23	1	34	112	52	128	.260	.324	.477	124	16	8	2	1	.969	-4	*D-100,O-52	1.0
1993	Cle-A★	159	594	93	172	36	3	38	**129**	76	96	.290	.378	.552	147	39	23	12	-0	.986	19	*O-150/D-9	5.2
1994	Cle-A★	106	412	90	147	35	2	36	101	58	71	.357	.442	.714	191	56	9	6	-1	.973	3	*O-104/D-2	5.0
1995	*Cle-A★	143	546	**121**	173	**52**	1	**50**	**126**	73	80	.317	.403	**.690**	175	59	5	2	0	.981	8	*O-142/D-1	5.8
1996	*Cle-A★	158	602	124	187	38	3	48	**148**	99	87	.311	.414	.623	158	54	11	0	3	.970	7	*O-152/D-6	**5.4**
1997	Chi-A☆	161	634	90	174	45	1	30	116	53	105	.274	.336	.491	117	14	4	4	-1	.972	7	*O-154/D-7	1.5
1998	Chi-A	163	609	113	200	48	2	49	152	81	84	.328	.408	**.655**	**175**	**66**	6	4	-1	.976	7	*O-159/D-4	**6.4**
Total	10	1237	4684	795	1388	316	19	321	1019	530	811	.296	.373	.577	149	315	71	33	2	.974	50	*O-1047,D-184	31.3
■ MARK BELLHORN	Bellhorn, Mark Christian b: 8/23/74, Boston, Mass. BB/TR, 6′1″, 195 lbs. Deb: 6/10/97																						
1997	Oak-A	68	224	33	51	9	1	6	19	32	70	.228	.324	.357	79	-7	7	1	2	.951	6	3-40,2-17/S-1,D-3	0.2
1998	Oak-A	11	12	1	1	1	0	0	1	3	4	.083	.313	.167	31	-1	2	0	1	1.000	1	/3-5,S-2,2-1,D-2	0.0
Total	2	79	236	34	52	10	1	6	20	35	74	.220	.324	.347	76	-8	9	1	2	.955	6	/3-45,2-18,D-5,S-3	0.2
■ RAFAEL BELLIARD	Belliard, Rafael Leonidas (Matias) b: 10/24/61, Pueblo Nuevo, D.R. BR/TR, 5′6″, 150 lbs. Deb: 9/6/82																						
1982	Pit-N	9	2	3	1	0	0	0	0	0	0	.500	.500	.500	175	0	1	0	0	1.000	1	/S-4	0.2
1983	Pit-N	4	1	1	0	0	0	0	0	0	1	.000	.000	.000	-98	-0	0	0	0	1.000	1	/S-3	0.1
1984	Pit-N	20	22	3	5	0	0	0	0	0	1	.227	.227	.227	28	-2	4	1	1	.889	1	S-12/2-1	0.0
1985	Pit-N	17	20	1	4	0	0	0	1	0	5	.200	.200	.200	12	-2	0	0	0	.947	6	S-12	0.4
1986	Pit-N	117	309	33	72	5	2	0	31	26	54	.233	.299	.262	55	-18	12	2	2	.970	13	S-96,2-23	0.5
1987	Pit-N	81	203	26	42	4	3	1	15	20	25	.207	.288	.271	49	-15	5	1	1	.979	6	S-71/2-7	-0.3
1988	Pit-N	122	286	28	61	0	4	0	11	26	47	.213	.288	.241	54	-16	7	1	2	**.977**	-12	*S-117/2-3	-2.0
1989	Pit-N	67	154	10	33	4	0	0	8	8	22	.214	.253	.240	43	-11	5	2	0	.978	7	S-40,2-20/3-6	-0.2
1990	Pit-N	47	54	10	11	3	0	0	6	5	13	.204	.283	.259	52	-3	1	2	-1	1.000	5	2-21,S-10/3-5	0.1
1991	*Atl-N	149	353	36	88	9	2	0	27	22	63	.249	.297	.286	61	-18	3	1	0	.967	26	*S-145	1.7
1992	*Atl-N	144	285	20	60	6	1	0	14	14	43	.211	.255	.239	38	-23	0	1	-1	.969	**27**	*S-139/2-1	1.0
1993	*Atl-N	91	79	6	18	5	0	0	6	4	13	.228	.291	.291	56	-5	0	0	0	1.000	20	S-58,2-24	1.6
1994	Atl-N	46	120	9	29	7	1	0	9	2	29	.242	.266	.317	50	-9	0	2	-1	.984	-5	S-26,2-18	-1.2
1995	*Atl-N	75	180	12	40	2	1	0	7	6	28	.222	.255	.244	32	-18	2	2	-1	.992	13	S-40,2-32	-0.1
1996	*Atl-N	87	142	9	24	7	0	0	3	2	22	.169	.181	.218	4	-19	3	1	0	.983	23	S-63,2-15	0.7
1997	Atl-N	72	71	9	15	3	0	1	3	1	17	.211	.222	.296	34	-7	0	1	-1	.990	13	S-53/2-7	0.7

YEAR	TM/L	G	AB	R	H	2B	3B	HR	RBI	BB	SO	AVG	OBP	SLG	PRO+	BR/A	SB	CS	SBR	FA	FR	G/POS	TPR
1998	Atl-N	7	20	1	5	0	0	0	1	0	1	.250	.250	.250	30	-2	0	0	0	.952	1	/S-7	-0.1
Total	17	1155	2301	217	508	55	14	2	142	136	384	.221	.271	.259	46	-169	43	17	3	.974	146	S-896,2-172/3-11	3.1
■ **RONNIE BELLIARD**	Belliard, Ronald b: 7/4/75, Bronx, N.Y. BR/TR, 5'8", 180 lbs. Deb: 9/12/98																						
1998	Mil-N	8	5	1	1	0	0	0	0	0	0	.200	.200	.200	4	-1	0	0	0	.000	0	/2-1	-0.1
■ **JACK BELLMAN**	Bellman, John Hutchins "Happy Jack" b: 3/4/1864, Taylorsville, Ky. d: 12/8/31, Louisville, Ky. Deb: 4/23/1889																						
1889	StL-a	1	2	1	1	0	0	0	0	1	0	.500	.667	.500	207	0	0			1.000	-0	/C-1	0.0
■ **ROB BELLOIR**	Belloir, Robert Edward b: 7/13/48, Heidelberg, W.Ger. BR/TR, 5'10", 155 lbs. Deb: 8/2/75																						
1975	Atl-N	43	105	11	23	2	1	0	9	7	8	.219	.268	.257	45	-8	0	0	0	.922	-2	S-38/2-1	-0.7
1976	Atl-N	30	60	5	12	2	0	0	4	5	7	.200	.262	.233	39	-5	0	0	0	.929	-1	S-12,3-10/2-5	-0.5
1977	Atl-N	6	1	2	0	0	0	0	0	0	0	.000	.000	.000	-89	-0	0	0	0	1.000	1	/S-3	0.1
1978	Atl-N	2	1	0	1	1	0	0	0	0	0	1.000	1.000	2.000	647	1	0	0	0	1.000	-0	/S-1,3-1	0.1
Total	4	81	167	18	36	5	1	0	13	12	15	.216	.268	.257	45	-12	0	0	0	.924	-3	/S-54,3-11,2-6	-1.0
■ **CARLOS BELTRAN**	Beltran, Carlos Ivan b: 4/24/77, Manati, P.R. BB/TR, 6', 175 lbs. Deb: 9/14/98																						
1998	KC-A	14	58	12	16	5	3	0	7	3	12	.276	.323	.466	97	-0	3	0	1	.978	2	O-14	0.2
■ **ARIAN BELTRE**	Beltre, Arian (Perez) b: 4/7/78, Santo Domingo, D.R. BR/TR, 5'11", 200 lbs. Deb: 6/24/98																						
1998	LA-N	77	195	18	42	9	0	7	22	14	37	.215	.278	.369	71	-9	3	1	0	.925	10	3-74/S-2	0.2
■ **ESTEBAN BELTRE**	Beltre, Esteban (Valera) b: 12/26/67, Ingenio Quisqueya, D.R. BR/TR, 5'10", 172 lbs. Deb: 9/3/91																						
1991	Chi-A	8	6	0	1	0	0	0	0	1	1	.167	.286	.167	29	-1	1	0	0	1.000	-1	/S-8	-0.1
1992	Chi-A	49	110	21	21	2	0	1	10	3	18	.191	.212	.236	26	-11	1	0	0	.924	-1	S-43/D-4	-0.9
1994	Tex-A	48	131	12	37	5	0	0	12	16	25	.282	.361	.321	78	-4	2	5	-2	.961	8	S-41/3-5,2-1	0.5
1995	Tex-A	54	92	7	20	8	0	0	7	4	15	.217	.250	.304	42	-8	0	0	0	.969	3	S-36,2-15/3-1	-0.3
1996	Bos-A	27	62	6	16	2	0	0	6	4	14	.258	.303	.290	50	-5	1	0	0	1.000	-1	3-13/2-8,S-6,D-1	-0.4
Total	5	186	401	46	95	17	0	1	35	28	73	.237	.287	.287	51	-28	5	5	-2	.951	9	S-134/2-24,3-19,D-5	-1.2
■ **HARRY BEMIS**	Bemis, Harry Parker b: 2/1/1874, Farmington, N.H. d: 5/23/47, Cleveland, Ohio BR/TR, 5'7.5", 175 lbs. Deb: 4/23/02																						
1902	Cle-A	93	317	42	99	12	7	1	29	19		.312	.366	.404	118	8	3			.964	6	C-87/O-2,2-1	2.2
1903	Cle-A	92	314	31	82	20	3	1	41	8		.261	.295	.354	96	-2	5			**.988**	-7	C-74,1-10/2-1	-0.2
1904	Cle-A	97	336	35	76	11	6	0	25	8		.226	.259	.295	76	-10	6			.958	-3	C-79,1-13/2-1	-0.4
1905	Cle-A	70	226	27	66	13	3	0	28	13		.292	.344	.376	127	7	3			.972	-6	C-58/2-4,3-2,1-1	0.8
1906	Cle-A	93	297	28	82	13	5	2	30	12		.276	.311	.374	116	4	8			.963	-10	C-81	0.3
1907	Cle-A	65	172	12	43	7	0	0	19	7		.250	.283	.291	82	-4	5			.957	-8	C-51/1-2	-0.8
1908	Cle-A	91	277	23	62	9	1	0	33	7		.224	.253	.264	68	-10	14			.964	-6	C-76/1-2	-1.1
1909	Cle-A	42	123	4	23	2	3	0	13	0		.187	.194	.252	39	-9	2			.971	-0	C-36	-0.7
1910	Cle-A	61	167	12	36	5	1	1	16	5		.216	.238	.275	60	-8	3			.961	-4	C-46	-0.9
Total	9	704	2229	214	569	92	29	5	234	79		.255	.292	.329	92	-24	49			.966	-37	C-588/1-28,2-7,3O	-0.8
■ **MARVIN BENARD**	Benard, Marvin Larry b: 1/20/71, Bluefields, Nic. BL/TL, 5'10", 180 lbs. Deb: 9/5/95																						
1995	SF-N	13	34	5	13	2	0	1	4	1	7	.382	.400	.529	147	2	1	0	0	1.000	1	/O-7	0.3
1996	SF-N	135	488	89	121	17	4	5	27	59	84	.248	.334	.330	79	-14	25	11	1	.984	5	*O-132	-1.1
1997	*SF-N	84	114	13	26	4	0	1	13	13	29	.228	.318	.289	62	-6	3	1	0	.967	-8	O-36/D-1	-1.4
1998	SF-N	121	286	41	92	21	1	3	36	34	39	.322	.398	.434	120	10	11	4	1	.982	-10	O-79/D-2	0.0
Total	4	353	922	148	252	44	5	10	80	107	159	.273	.354	.364	92	-8	40	16	2	.983	-13	O-254/D-3	-2.2
■ **FREDDIE BENAVIDES**	Benavides, Alfredo b: 4/7/66, Laredo, Tex. BR/TR, 6'2", 180 lbs. Deb: 5/14/91																						
1991	Cin-N	24	63	11	18	1	0	0	3	1	15	.286	.308	.302	69	-3	1	0	0	.974	3	S-20/2-3	0.2
1992	Cin-N	74	173	14	40	10	1	1	17	10	34	.231	.277	.318	66	-8	0	1	-1	1.000	4	2-37,S-34/3-1	-0.3
1993	Col-N	74	213	20	61	10	3	3	26	6	27	.286	.306	.404	76	-8	3	2	-0	.937	-3	S-48,2-19/3-5,1-1	-0.7
1994	Mon-N	47	85	8	16	5	1	0	6	3	15	.188	.225	.271	28	-9	0	0	0	.976	-5	2-36/3-5,1-3,S-3	-1.3
Total	4	219	534	53	135	26	5	4	52	20	91	.253	.284	.343	65	-27	4	3	-1	.948	-0	S-105/2-95,3-11,1-4	-2.1
■ **JOHNNY BENCH**	Bench, Johnny Lee b: 12/7/47, Oklahoma City, Okla. BR/TR, 6'1", 208 lbs. Deb: 8/28/67 H																						
1967	Cin-N	26	86	7	14	3	1	1	6	5	19	.163	.209	.256	29	-8	0	1	-1	.995	5	C-26	-0.2
1968	Cin-N★	154	564	67	155	40	2	15	82	31	96	.275	.315	.433	115	9	1	5	-3	.991	7	*C-154	2.6
1969	Cin-N★	148	532	83	156	23	1	26	90	49	86	.293	.357	.487	128	19	6	6	-2	.992	-3	*C-147	2.3
1970	*Cin-N★	158	605	97	177	35	4	**45**	**148**	54	102	.293	.351	.587	146	35	5	2	0	.986	4	*C-139,O-24,1-12,/3	4.5
1971	Cin-N★	149	562	80	134	19	2	27	61	49	83	.238	.300	.423	105	1	2	1	0	.988	-4	*C-141,1-12,O-12,/3	0.3
1972	*Cin-N★	147	538	87	145	22	2	**40**	**125**	100	84	.270	.386	.541	**171**	**51**	6	6	-2	.992	-5	*C-129,O-17/1-7,3-4	5.1
1973	*Cin-N★	152	557	83	141	17	3	25	104	83	83	.253	.350	.429	121	16	4	1	1	.995	-3	*C-134,O-23/1-4,3-1	1.9
1974	Cin-N★	160	621	108	174	38	2	33	**129**	80	90	.280	.365	.507	144	35	5	4	-1	.993	-5	*C-137,3-36/1-5	3.6
1975	*Cin-N★	142	530	83	150	39	1	28	110	65	108	.283	.363	.519	140	27	11	0	3	.989	3	*C-121,O-19/1-9	3.9
1976	*Cin-N★	135	465	62	109	24	1	16	74	81	95	.234	.350	.394	108	7	13	2	3	**.997**	-3	*C-128/O-5,1-1	1.0
1977	Cin-N★	142	494	67	136	34	2	31	109	58	95	.275	.353	.540	133	22	2	4	-2	.987	-13	*C-135/O-8,1-4,3-1	1.1
1978	Cin-N†	120	393	52	102	17	1	23	73	50	83	.260	.345	.483	129	14	4	2	0	.989	-9	*C-107,1-11/O-2	0.8
1979	*Cin-N†	130	464	73	128	19	0	22	80	67	73	.276	.367	.459	123	16	4	2	0	.986	-7	*C-126/1-2	1.4
1980	Cin-N★	114	360	52	90	12	0	24	68	41	64	.250	.330	.483	124	11	4	2	0	.991	-17	*C-105	-0.3
1981	Cin-N	52	178	14	55	8	0	8	25	17	21	.309	.369	.489	139	9	0	2	-1	.983	-2	1-38/C-7	0.4
1982	Cin-N	119	399	44	103	16	0	13	38	37	58	.258	.321	.396	98	-2	1	2	-1	.917	-17	*3-107/1-8,C-1	-2.4
1983	Cin-N★	110	310	32	79	15	2	12	54	24	38	.255	.308	.432	100	-1	0	1	-1	.933	-12	3-42,1-32/C-5,O-1	-1.7
Total	17	2158	7658	1091	2048	381	24	389	1376	891	1278	.267	.345	.476	127	261	68	43	-5	.990	-80	*C-1742,3-195,1O	24.3
■ **ART BENEDICT**	Benedict, Arthur Melville b: 3/31/1862, Cornwall, Ill. d: 1/20/48, Denver, Colo. BR/TR, Deb: 5/14/1883																						
1883	Phi-N	3	15	3	4	1	0	0	4	0	4	.267	.267	.333	89	-0				.571	-5	/2-3	-0.4
■ **BRUCE BENEDICT**	Benedict, Bruce Edwin b: 8/18/55, Birmingham, Ala. BR/TR, 6'1", 190 lbs. Deb: 8/18/78 C																						
1978	Atl-N	22	52	3	13	2	0	0	1	6	6	.250	.328	.288	66	-2	0	0	0	.990	2	C-22	0.0
1979	Atl-N	76	204	14	46	11	0	0	15	33	18	.225	.333	.279	64	-9	1	3	-2	.984	1	C-76	-0.8
1980	Atl-N	120	359	18	91	14	1	2	34	28	36	.253	.309	.315	72	-13	3	3	-1	.988	3	*C-120	-0.7
1981	Atl-N★	90	295	26	78	12	1	5	35	33	21	.264	.344	.363	98	-0	1	1	-0	.986	6	C-90	1.0
1982	*Atl-N	118	386	34	95	11	1	3	44	37	40	.246	.317	.303	71	-14	4	4	-1	**.993**	2	*C-118	-0.9
1983	Atl-N★	134	423	43	126	13	1	2	43	61	24	.298	.388	.348	98	2	1	3	-2	.992	9	*C-134	1.5
1984	Atl-N	95	300	26	67	8	1	4	25	34	25	.223	.304	.297	65	-13	1	2	-1	.991	1	C-95	-1.0
1985	Atl-N	70	208	12	42	6	0	0	20	22	12	.202	.281	.231	42	-16	0	1	-1	.989	-2	C-70	-1.6
1986	Atl-N	64	160	11	36	10	1	0	13	15	10	.225	.299	.300	62	-8	1	0	0	.993	-3	C-57	-0.8
1987	Atl-N	37	95	4	14	1	0	1	5	17	15	.147	.277	.189	25	-10	0	1	-1	.989	4	C-35	-0.5
1988	Atl-N	90	236	11	57	7	0	0	19	19	26	.242	.298	.271	61	-11	0	2	-1	.989	8	C-89	0.0
1989	Atl-N	66	160	12	31	3	0	1	6	23	18	.194	.299	.231	52	-9	0	0	0	.995	16	C-65	1.0
Total	12	982	2878	214	696	98	6	18	260	328	251	.242	.322	.299	71	-104	12	20	-8	.990	47	C-971	-2.8
■ **JOE BENES**	Benes, Joseph Anthony "Bananas" b: 1/8/01, Long Island City, N.Y. d: 3/7/75, Elmhurst, N.Y. BR/TR, 5'8.5", 158 lbs. Deb: 5/9/31																						
1931	StL-N	10	12	1	2	0	0	0	0	2	1	.167	.333	.167	37	-1	0			1.000	1	/S-6,2-2,3-1	0.0
■ **BENNY BENGOUGH**	Bengough, Bernard Oliver b: 7/27/1898, Niagara Falls, N.Y. d: 12/22/68, Philadelphia, Pa. BR/TR, 5'7.5", 168 lbs. Deb: 5/18/23 C																						
1923	NY-A	19	53	1	7	2	0	0	3	4	2	.132	.193	.170	-4	-8	0	0	0	.973	1	C-19	-0.7
1924	NY-A	11	16	4	5	1	1	0	3	2	0	.313	.389	.500	128	1	0	0	0	1.000	3	C-11	0.4
1925	NY-A	95	283	17	73	14	2	0	23	19	9	.258	.305	.322	60	-18	0	2	-1	**.993**	6	C-94	-0.8
1926	NY-A	36	84	9	32	6	0	0	14	7	4	.381	.435	.452	134	4	1	0	0	.973	8	C-35	1.4

YEAR	TM/L	G	AB	R	H	2B	3B	HR	RBI	BB	SO	AVG	OBP	SLG	PRO+	BR/A	SB	CS	SBR	FA	FR	G/POS	TPR
1927	*NY-A	31	85	6	21	3	3	0	10	4	4	.247	.281	.353	66	-5	0	3	-2	.986	12	C-30	0.6
1928	*NY-A	58	161	12	43	3	1	0	9	7	8	.267	.302	.298	60	-9	0	0	0	.992	6	C-58	0.1
1929	NY-A	23	62	5	12	2	1	0	7	0	2	.194	.194	.258	16	-8	0	0	0	.982	-5	C-23	-1.1
1930	NY-A	44	102	10	24	4	2	0	12	3	8	.235	.257	.314	46	-9	1	0	0	.990	9	C-44	0.3
1931	StL-A	40	140	6	35	4	1	0	12	4	4	.250	.271	.293	46	-11	0	3	-2	.986	-1	C-37	-1.1
1932	StL-A	54	139	13	35	7	1	0	15	12	4	.252	.311	.317	60	-8	0	1	-1	.989	6	C-47	0.0
Total	10	411	1125	83	287	46	12	0	108	62	45	.255	.295	.317	59	-70	2	9	-5	.988	45	C-398	-0.9

■ JUAN BENIQUEZ

Beniquez, Juan Jose (Torres) b: 5/13/50, San Sebastian, P.R. BR/TR, 5'11", 165 lbs. Deb: 9/4/71

YEAR	TM/L	G	AB	R	H	2B	3B	HR	RBI	BB	SO	AVG	OBP	SLG	PRO+	BR/A	SB	CS	SBR	FA	FR	G/POS	TPR
1971	Bos-A	16	57	8	17	2	0	0	4	3	4	.298	.333	.333	83	-1	3	1	0	.895	-8	S-15	-0.7
1972	Bos-A	33	99	10	24	4	1	1	8	7	11	.242	.292	.333	81	-2	2	0	1	.900	5	S-27	0.7
1974	Bos-A	106	389	60	104	14	3	5	33	25	61	.267	.313	.357	86	-7	19	11	-1	.978	2	O-97/D-4	-1.1
1975	*Bos-A	78	254	43	74	14	4	2	17	25	26	.291	.359	.402	106	2	7	10	-4	.991	1	O-44,D-20,3-14	-0.3
1976	Tex-A	145	478	49	122	14	4	0	33	39	56	.255	.315	.301	79	-12	17	6	2	.986	20	*O-141/2-1	0.5
1977	Tex-A	123	424	56	114	19	6	10	50	43	43	.269	.338	.413	102	1	26	18	-3	.988	7	*O-123	0.0
1978	Tex-A	127	473	61	123	17	3	11	50	20	59	.260	.294	.378	88	-9	10	12	-4	.972	-0	*O-126	-2.0
1979	NY-A	62	142	19	36	6	1	4	17	9	17	.254	.307	.394	90	-2	3	3	-1	.981	-6	O-60/3-3	-1.0
1980	Sea-A	70	237	26	54	10	0	6	21	17	25	.228	.280	.346	70	-10	2	3	-1	.957	1	O-65/D-1	-1.4
1981	Cal-A	58	166	18	30	5	0	3	13	15	16	.181	.253	.265	49	-11	2	1	0	.959	-7	O-55/D-1	-2.0
1982	*Cal-A	112	196	25	52	11	2	3	24	15	21	.265	.321	.388	93	-2	3	0	1	.983	-27	*O-107	-2.9
1983	Cal-A	92	315	44	96	15	0	3	34	15	29	.305	.344	.381	100	0	4	2	0	.968	-8	O-84/D-6	-1.0
1984	Cal-A	110	354	60	119	17	0	8	39	18	43	.336	.373	.452	128	13	0	3	-2	.971	-12	O-98	-0.3
1985	Cal-A	132	411	54	125	13	5	8	42	34	46	.304	.364	.418	114	9	4	3	-1	1.000	-15	O-71,1-46,D-14,/3S	-1.1
1986	Bal-A	113	343	48	103	15	0	6	36	40	49	.300	.378	.397	113	7	2	3	-1	.963	-6	O-54,3-25,D-16,1-14	-0.3
1987	KC-A	57	174	14	41	7	0	3	26	11	26	.236	.285	.328	60	-10	0	0	0	1.000	-4	O-22,D-15/1-6,3-6	-1.5
	Tor-A	39	81	6	23	5	1	5	21	5	13	.284	.333	.556	127	3	0	0	0	.875	-2	D-15/O-7,1-2	0.0
	Yr	96	255	20	64	12	1	8	47	16	39	.251	.300	.400	82	-7	0	0	0	.976	-6	D-30,O-29/1-8,3-6	-1.5
1988	Tor-A	27	58	9	17	2	0	1	8	8	6	.293	.379	.379	112	1	0	0	0	.000	-0	D-19/O-1	0.0
Total	17	1500	4651	610	1274	190	30	79	476	349	551	.274	.329	.379	95	-29	104	76	-14	.977	-60	*O-1155,D-111/13S2	-14.4

■ YAMIL BENITEZ

Benitez, Yamil Antonio b: 10/5/72, San Juan, P.R. BR/TR, 6'2", 180 lbs. Deb: 9/16/95

YEAR	TM/L	G	AB	R	H	2B	3B	HR	RBI	BB	SO	AVG	OBP	SLG	PRO+	BR/A	SB	CS	SBR	FA	FR	G/POS	TPR
1995	Mon-N	14	39	8	15	2	1	2	7	1	7	.385	.400	.641	163	3	0	2	-1	.950	-2	O-14	0.0
1996	Mon-N	11	12	0	2	0	0	0	2	0	4	.167	.167	.167	-11	-2	0	0	0	.500	-1	/O-4	-0.3
1997	KC-A	53	191	22	51	7	1	8	21	10	49	.267	.307	.440	90	-3	2	2	-1	.965	-1	O-52	-0.5
1998	Ari-N	91	206	17	41	7	1	9	30	14	46	.199	.263	.374	62	-12	2	2	-1	.972	1	O-62/D-2	-1.2
Total	4	169	448	47	109	16	3	19	60	25	106	.243	.291	.420	81	-14	4	6	-2	.963	-2	O-132/D-2	-2.0

■ STAN BENJAMIN

Benjamin, Alfred Stanley b: 5/20/14, Framingham, Mass. BR/TR, 6'2", 194 lbs. Deb: 9/16/39

YEAR	TM/L	G	AB	R	H	2B	3B	HR	RBI	BB	SO	AVG	OBP	SLG	PRO+	BR/A	SB	CS	SBR	FA	FR	G/POS	TPR
1939	Phi-N	12	50	4	7	2	1	0	2	1	6	.140	.157	.220	0	-7	1			.867	-0	/O-7,3-5	-0.8
1940	Phi-N	8	9	1	2	0	0	0	1	1	1	.222	.300	.222	48	-1	0			1.000	1	/O-2	0.0
1941	Phi-N	129	480	47	113	20	7	3	27	20	81	.235	.266	.325	68	-22	17			.980	-4	*O-110/1-8,2-2,3-1	-3.4
1942	Phi-N	78	210	24	47	8	3	2	8	10	27	.224	.262	.319	73	-8	5			.976	-3	O-45,1-15	-1.4
1945	Cle-A	14	21	1	7	2	0	0	3	0	0	.333	.333	.429	126	1	0	1	-1	1.000	2	/O-4	0.1
Total	5	241	770	77	176	32	11	5	41	32	115	.229	.260	.318	66	-37	23	1		.975	-5	O-168/1-23,3-6,2-2	-5.5

■ MIKE BENJAMIN

Benjamin, Michael Paul b: 11/22/65, Euclid, Ohio BR/TR, 6', 169 lbs. Deb: 7/7/89

YEAR	TM/L	G	AB	R	H	2B	3B	HR	RBI	BB	SO	AVG	OBP	SLG	PRO+	BR/A	SB	CS	SBR	FA	FR	G/POS	TPR
1989	SF-N	14	6	6	1	0	0	0	0	0	1	.167	.167	.167	-5	-1	0	0	0	1.000	2	/S-8	0.1
1990	SF-N	22	56	7	12	3	1	2	3	3	10	.214	.254	.411	83	-2	1	0	0	.988	5	S-21	0.5
1991	SF-N	54	106	12	13	3	0	2	8	7	26	.123	.191	.208	13	-13	3	0	1	.984	16	S-51/3-1	0.7
1992	SF-N	40	75	4	13	2	1	1	3	4	15	.173	.215	.267	38	-6	1	0	0	.991	5	S-33/3-2	0.0
1993	SF-N	63	146	22	29	7	0	4	16	9	23	.199	.264	.329	59	-9	0	0	0	.991	20	2-23,S-23,3-16	1.2
1994	SF-N	38	62	9	16	5	1	1	9	5	16	.258	.343	.419	102	0	5	0	2	.968	9	S-18,2-10/3-5	1.1
1995	SF-N	68	186	19	41	6	0	3	12	8	51	.220	.256	.301	48	-14	11	1	3	.964	3	3-43,S-16/2-8	-0.8
1996	Phi-N	35	103	13	23	5	1	4	13	12	21	.223	.316	.408	88	-2	3	1	0	.954	-2	S-31/2-1	-0.1
1997	Bos-A	49	116	12	27	9	1	0	7	4	27	.233	.264	.328	52	-8	2	3	-1	.929	9	3-19,S-16/2-5,1PD	0.1
1998	*Bos-A	124	349	46	95	23	0	4	39	15	73	.272	.314	.372	78	-12	3	0	1	.994	4	2-87,S-20,3-11,1/D	-0.1
Total	10	507	1205	150	270	63	5	21	110	67	263	.224	.276	.337	63	-66	29	5	6	.979	69	S-237,2-134/31DP	2.7

■ IKE BENNERS

Benners, Isaac B. b: 6/7/1856, Philadelphia, Pa. d: 4/18/32, Philadelphia, Pa. BL , 175 lbs. Deb: 5/1/1884

YEAR	TM/L	G	AB	R	H	2B	3B	HR	RBI	BB	SO	AVG	OBP	SLG	PRO+	BR/A	SB	CS	SBR	FA	FR	G/POS	TPR
1884	Bro-a	49	189	25	38	11	5	1		7		.201	.237	.328	82	-4				.815	-5	O-49	-0.9
	Wil-U	6	22	0	1	0	0	0		1		.045	.087	.045	-57	-5				.750	0	/O-6	-0.5
Total	1	55	211	25	39	11	5	1		8		.185	.222	.299	66	-9				.806	-5	/O-55	-1.4

■ CHARLIE BENNETT

Bennett, Charles Wesley b: 11/21/1854, New Castle, Pa. d: 2/24/27, Detroit, Mich. BR/TR, 5'11", 180 lbs. Deb: 5/1/1878

YEAR	TM/L	G	AB	R	H	2B	3B	HR	RBI	BB	SO	AVG	OBP	SLG	PRO+	BR/A	SB	CS	SBR	FA	FR	G/POS	TPR
1878	Mil-N	49	184	16	45	9	0	1	12	10	26	.245	.284	.310	89	-2				.831	-13	C-35,O-20	-1.5
1880	Wor-N	51	193	20	44	9	3	0	18	10	30	.228	.266	.306	86	-3				.913	-0	C-46/O-6	-0.3
1881	Det-N	76	299	44	90	18	7	7	64	18	37	.301	.341	.478	149	16				**.962**	18	*C-70/3-5,O-3	**3.3**
1882	Det-N	84	342	43	103	16	10	5	51	20	33	.301	.340	.450	151	19				.945	7	*C-65,3-11/2-7,S1	2.5
1883	Det-N	92	371	56	113	34	7	5	55	26	59	.305	.350	.474	155	25				**.944**	-3	*C-72,2-15,O-12	2.3
1884	Det-N	90	341	37	90	18	6	3	40	36	40	.264	.334	.378	132	14				.917	-5	*C-80/O-5,S-4,321	1.4
1885	Det-N	91	349	49	94	24	13	5	60	47	37	.269	.356	.456	161	24				.919	-1	C-62,O-19,3-10	2.6
1886	Det-N	72	235	37	57	13	5	4	34	48	29	.243	.371	.391	128	10	4			**.955**	12	C-69/O-4,S-1	2.6
1887	*Det-N	46	160	26	39	6	5	3	20	30	22	.244	.363	.400	108	2	7			.951	2	C-45/O-1,1-1	0.7
1888	Det-N	74	258	32	68	12	4	5	29	31	40	.264	.347	.399	138	12	4			**.966**	7	C-73/1-1	2.5
1889	Bos-N	82	247	42	57	8	2	4	28	21	43	.231	.296	.328	70	-11	7			**.955**	12	C-82	0.6
1890	Bos-N	85	281	59	60	17	2	3	40	72	56	.214	.377	.320	96	1	6			**.959**	10	C-85	1.6
1891	Bos-N	75	256	35	55	9	3	5	39	42	61	.215	.332	.332	84	-6	3			**.960**	14	C-75	1.3
1892	*Bos-N	35	114	19	23	4	0	1	16	27	23	.202	.355	.263	80	-2	6			.948	1	C-35	0.2
1893	Bos-N	60	191	34	40	6	0	4	27	40	36	.209	.352	.304	69	-8	5			.953	-3	C-60	-0.6
Total	15	1062	3821	549	978	203	67	55	533	478	572	.256	.340	.387	118	90	42			.942	57	C-954/O-70,32S1	19.2

■ GARY BENNETT

Bennett, Gary David b: 4/17/72, Waukegan, Ill. BR/TR, 6', 190 lbs. Deb: 9/24/95

YEAR	TM/L	G	AB	R	H	2B	3B	HR	RBI	BB	SO	AVG	OBP	SLG	PRO+	BR/A	SB	CS	SBR	FA	FR	G/POS	TPR
1995	Phi-N	1	1	0	0	0	0	0	0	0	1	.000	.000	.000	-99	-0	0	0	0	.000	0	-0,-0	0.0
1996	Phi-N	6	16	0	4	0	0	0	1	2	6	.250	.333	.250	56	-1	0	0	0	1.000	3	/C-5	0.2
1998	Phi-N	9	31	4	9	0	0	0	3	5	5	.290	.389	.290	79	-1	0	0	0	1.000	-4	/C-9	-0.4
Total	3	16	48	4	13	0	0	0	4	7	12	.271	.364	.271	68	-2	0	0	0	1.000	-2	/C-14	-0.2

■ HERSCHEL BENNETT

Bennett, Herschel Emmett b: 9/21/1896, Elwood, Mo. d: 9/9/64, Springfield, Mo. BL/TR, 5'9.5", 160 lbs. Deb: 4/19/23

YEAR	TM/L	G	AB	R	H	2B	3B	HR	RBI	BB	SO	AVG	OBP	SLG	PRO+	BR/A	SB	CS	SBR	FA	FR	G/POS	TPR
1923	StL-A	5	4	0	0	0	0	0	0	1	1	.000	.200	.000	-42	-1	0	0	0	1.000	-0	/O-1	-0.1
1924	StL-A	41	94	16	31	4	3	1	11	3	6	.330	.364	.468	107	1	1	0	0	.966	-4	O-21	-0.4
1925	StL-A	93	298	46	83	11	6	2	37	18	16	.279	.324	.376	73	-13	4	10	-5	.916	-2	O-73	-2.2
1926	StL-A	80	225	33	60	14	2	1	26	22	21	.267	.337	.360	78	-7	2	1	0	.950	3	O-50	-0.8
1927	StL-A	93	256	40	68	12	2	3	30	14	21	.266	.311	.363	72	-11	6	2	1	.946	1	O-55	-1.2
Total	5	312	877	135	242	41	13	7	104	58	65	.276	.327	.376	77	-31	13	13	-4	.937	-1	O-200	-4.7

■ FRED BENNETT

Bennett, James Fred "Red" b: 3/15/02, Atkins, Ark. d: 5/12/57, Atkins, Ark. BR/TR, 5'9", 185 lbs. Deb: 4/13/28

YEAR	TM/L	G	AB	R	H	2B	3B	HR	RBI	BB	SO	AVG	OBP	SLG	PRO+	BR/A	SB	CS	SBR	FA	FR	G/POS	TPR
1928	StL-A	7	8	0	2	1	0	0	0	0	2	.250	.250	.375	60	-0	0	0	0	1.000	-0	/O-1	-0.1
1931	Pit-N	32	89	6	25	5	0	1	7	7	4	.281	.333	.371	90	-1	0	0		.951	-2	O-21	-0.5
Total	2	39	97	6	27	6	0	1	7	7	6	.278	.327	.371	87	-2	0	0		.953	-2	/O-22	-0.6

■ JOE BENNETT

Bennett, Joseph Rosenblum b: 7/2/1900, New York, N.Y. d: 7/11/87, Morro Bay, Cal. BR/TR, 5'9", 168 lbs. Deb: 7/5/23

YEAR	TM/L	G	AB	R	H	2B	3B	HR	RBI	BB	SO	AVG	OBP	SLG	PRO+	BR/A	SB	CS	SBR	FA	FR	G/POS	TPR
1923	Phi-N	1	0	0	0	0	0	0	0	0	0	—	—	—	—	0	0	0	0	1.000	0	/3-1	0.0

■ PUG BENNETT Bennett, Justin Titus b: 2/20/1874, Ponca, Neb. d: 9/12/35, Kirkland, Wash. BR/TR, 5'11", 165 lbs. Deb: 4/12/06

YEAR	TM/L	G	AB	R	H	2B	3B	HR	RBI	BB	SO	AVG	OBP	SLG	PRO+	BR/A	SB	CS	SBR	FA	FR	G/POS	TPR
1906	StL-N	153	595	66	156	16	7	1	34	56		.262	.334	.318	108	6	20			.948	-7	*2-153	0.0
1907	StL-N	87	324	20	72	8	2	0	21	21		.222	.272	.259	69	-12	7			.939	-16	2-83/3-3	-3.4
Total	2	240	919	86	228	24	9	1	55	77		.248	.312	.297	94	-6	27			.945	-23	2-236/3-3	-3.4

■ VERN BENSON Benson, Vernon Adair b: 9/19/24, Granite Quarry, N.C. BL/TR, 5'11", 180 lbs. Deb: 7/31/43 MC

YEAR	TM/L	G	AB	R	H	2B	3B	HR	RBI	BB	SO	AVG	OBP	SLG	PRO+	BR/A	SB	CS	SBR	FA	FR	G/POS	TPR
1943	Phi-A	2	2	0	0	0	0	0	0	0	0	.000	.000	.000	-99	-0	0	0	0	.000	0	H	-0.1
1946	Phi-A	7	5	1	0	0	0	0	0	1	3	.000	.167	.000	-51	-1	0	0	0	1.000	-0	/O-2	-0.1
1951	StL-N	13	46	8	12	3	1	1	7	6	8	.261	.346	.435	108	1	0	0	0	.950	0	/3-9,O-4	0.1
1952	StL-N	20	47	6	9	2	0	2	5	5	9	.191	.269	.362	73	-2	0	0	0	.889	-1	3-15	-0.3
1953	StL-N	13	4	2	0	0	0	0	0	1	2	.000	.200	.000	-42	-1	0	0	0	.000	0	H	-0.1
Total	5	55	104	17	21	5	1	3	12	13	22	.202	.291	.356	75	-4	0	0	0	.911	-0	/3-24,O-6	-0.5

■ JACK BENTLEY Bentley, John Needles b: 3/8/1895, Sandy Spring, Md. d: 10/24/69, Olney, Md. BL/TL, 5'11.5", 200 lbs. Deb: 9/6/13

YEAR	TM/L	G	AB	R	H	2B	3B	HR	RBI	BB	SO	AVG	OBP	SLG	PRO+	BR/A	SB	CS	SBR	FA	FR	G/POS	TPR
1913	Was-A	3	3	0	0	0	0	0	0	0	0	.000	.000	.000	-98	-1	0			1.000	0	/P-3	0.0
1914	Was-A	30	40	7	11	2	0	0	4	0	5	.275	.275	.325	77	-1	0			.930	-1	P-30	0.0
1915	Was-A	4	2	0	0	0	0	0	0	0	1	.000	.000	.000	-98	-0	0			.750	-0	/P-4	0.0
1916	Was-A	2	0	0	0	0	0	0	0	0	0	—	—	—	—	0	0			1.000	0	/P-2	0.0
1923	*NY-N	52	89	9	38	6	2	1	14	3	4	.427	.446	.573	169	9	0	0	0	.977	-1	P-31	0.0
1924	*NY-N	46	98	12	26	5	1	0	6	3	13	.265	.287	.337	68	-5	0	0	0	.979	-1	P-28	0.0
1925	NY-N	64	99	10	30	5	2	3	18	9	11	.303	.361	.485	119	3	0	0	0	.930	-2	P-28/O-3,1-1	-0.1
1926	Phi-N	75	240	19	62	12	3	2	27	5	4	.258	.273	.358	66	-12	0			.993	-2	1-56/P-7	-1.6
	NY-N	3	4	0	1	0	0	0	0	0	0	.250	.250	.250	35	-0	0			.000	-0	/P-1	0.0
	Yr	78	244	19	63	12	3	2	27	5	4	.258	.273	.357	65	-13	0			.993	-2	1-56/P-8	-1.6
1927	NY-N	8	9	1	2	0	0	1	2	1	1	.222	.300	.556	125	0	0			.750	-0	/P-4,1-2	0.0
Total	9	287	584	58	170	30	8	7	71	21	39	.291	.316	.406	91	-8	0	0		.949	-6	P-138/1-59,O-3	-1.7

■ BUTCH BENTON Benton, Alfred Lee b: 8/24/57, Tampa, Fla. BR/TR, 6'1", 190 lbs. Deb: 9/14/78

YEAR	TM/L	G	AB	R	H	2B	3B	HR	RBI	BB	SO	AVG	OBP	SLG	PRO+	BR/A	SB	CS	SBR	FA	FR	G/POS	TPR
1978	NY-N	4	4	1	2	0	0	0	2	0	0	.500	.600	.500	218	1	0	0	0	1.000	0	/C-1	0.1
1980	NY-N	12	21	0	1	0	0	0	0	2	4	.048	.167	.048	-39	-4	0	0	0	.935	-1	/C-8	-0.5
1982	Chi-N	4	7	0	1	0	0	0	1	0	1	.143	.143	.143	-19	-1	0	0	0	1.000	2	/C-4	0.1
1985	Cle-A	31	67	5	12	4	0	0	7	3	9	.179	.214	.239	24	-7	0	0	0	.957	-3	C-26	-0.9
Total	4	51	99	6	16	4	0	0	10	5	14	.162	.217	.202	16	-11	0	0	0	.959	-2	/C-39	-1.2

■ RABBIT BENTON Benton, Stanley W. "Stan" b: 9/29/01, Cannel City, Ky. d: 6/7/84, Mesquite, Tex. BR/TR, 5'7", 150 lbs. Deb: 9/13/22

YEAR	TM/L	G	AB	R	H	2B	3B	HR	RBI	BB	SO	AVG	OBP	SLG	PRO+	BR/A	SB	CS	SBR	FA	FR	G/POS	TPR
1922	Phi-N	6	19	1	4	1	0	0	3	2	1	.211	.286	.263	39	-2	0	0	0	.889	0	/2-5	-0.1

■ TODD BENZINGER Benzinger, Todd Eric b: 2/11/63, Dayton, Ky. BB/TR, 6'1", 190 lbs. Deb: 6/21/87

YEAR	TM/L	G	AB	R	H	2B	3B	HR	RBI	BB	SO	AVG	OBP	SLG	PRO+	BR/A	SB	CS	SBR	FA	FR	G/POS	TPR
1987	Bos-A	73	223	36	62	11	1	8	43	22	41	.278	.348	.444	105	2	5	4	-1	.987	8	O-61/1-2	0.7
1988	*Bos-A	120	405	47	103	28	1	13	70	22	80	.254	.294	.425	95	-4	2	3	-1	.991	-4	1-85,O-48/D-1	-1.6
1989	Cin-N	161	628	79	154	28	3	17	76	44	120	.245	.297	.381	89	-10	3	7	-3	.995	-13	*1-158	-4.2
1990	*Cin-N	118	376	35	95	14	2	5	46	19	69	.253	.296	.340	71	-15	3	4	-2	.992	-2	1-95,O-10	-2.6
1991	Cin-N	51	123	7	23	3	2	1	11	10	20	.187	.248	.268	43	-9	2	0	1	.986	-1	1-21,O-15	-1.2
	KC-A	78	293	29	86	15	3	2	40	17	46	.294	.339	.386	99	-0	2	6	-3	.996	-5	1-75/D-1	-1.3
1992	LA-N	121	293	24	70	16	2	4	31	15	54	.239	.276	.348	77	-10	2	4	-2	.989	0	O-51,1-42	-1.5
1993	SF-N	86	177	25	51	7	2	6	26	13	35	.288	.337	.452	112	3	0	0	0	1.000	-4	1-40/O-7,3-1	-0.4
1994	SF-N	107	328	32	87	13	2	9	31	17	84	.265	.305	.399	86	-8	2	1	0	.994	-4	1-99	-2.0
1995	SF-N	9	10	2	2	0	0	1	2	2	3	.200	.333	.500	120	0	0	0	0	1.000	-1	/1-5	-0.1
Total	9	924	2856	316	733	135	18	66	376	181	552	.257	.304	.386	88	-51	21	29	-11	.994	-25	1-622,O-192/D-2,3-1	-14.2

■ JOHNNY BERARDINO Berardino, John "Bernie" b: 5/1/17, Los Angeles, Cal. d: 5/19/96, Los Angeles, Cal. BR/TR, 6', 180 lbs. Deb: 4/22/39

YEAR	TM/L	G	AB	R	H	2B	3B	HR	RBI	BB	SO	AVG	OBP	SLG	PRO+	BR/A	SB	CS	SBR	FA	FR	G/POS	TPR
1939	StL-A	126	468	42	120	24	5	5	58	37	36	.256	.314	.361	71	-21	6	2	1	.958	4	*2-114/3-8,S-2	-1.0
1940	StL-A	142	523	71	135	31	4	16	85	32	46	.258	.301	.424	84	-14	6	8	-3	.939	13	*S-112,2-13/3-9	0.6
1941	StL-A	128	469	48	127	30	4	5	89	41	27	.271	.332	.384	86	-10	3	5	-2	.954	-14	*S-123/3-1	-1.6
1942	StL-A	29	74	11	21	6	0	1	10	4	2	.284	.329	.405	104	0	3	1	0	.950	0	/S-6,3-6,1-5,2-4	0.1
1946	StL-A	144	582	70	154	29	5	5	68	34	58	.265	.306	.357	81	-16	2	4	-2	.972	-2	*2-143	-1.0
1947	StL-A	90	306	29	80	22	1	1	20	44	26	.261	.358	.350	95	-1	6	5	-1	.977	-9	2-86	-0.5
1948	Cle-A	66	147	19	28	5	1	2	10	27	16	.190	.328	.279	64	-7	0	1	-1	.988	4	2-20,1-18,S-12,/3-3	-0.3
1949	Cle-A	50	116	11	23	6	1	0	13	14	14	.198	.295	.267	50	-8	0	1	-1	.935	-1	3-25/2-8,S-3	-1.0
1950	Cle-A	4	5	1	2	0	0	0	3	1	0	.400	.500	.400	137	0	0	0	0	1.000	1	/2-1,3-1	0.1
	Pit-N	40	131	12	27	3	1	1	12	19	11	.206	.307	.267	51	-9	0			.964	3	2-36/3-3	-0.5
1951	StL-A	39	119	13	27	7	1	0	13	17	18	.227	.324	.303	68	-5	1	1	-0	.917	-7	3-31/2-2,1-1,O-1	-1.2
1952	Cle-A	35	32	5	3	0	0	0	2	10	8	.094	.310	.094	17	-3	0	1	-1	.960	2	/2-8,S-8,3-4,1-2	-0.2
	Pit-N	19	56	2	8	4	0	0	4	4	6	.143	.200	.214	14	-7	0	0	0	.960	6	2-18	0.1
Total	11	912	3028	334	755	167	23	36	387	284	268	.249	.316	.355	77	-101	27	29		.968	1	2-453,S-266/310	-6.4

■ LOU BERBERET Berberet, Louis Joseph b: 11/20/29, Long Beach, Cal. BL/TR, 5'11", 212 lbs. Deb: 9/17/54

YEAR	TM/L	G	AB	R	H	2B	3B	HR	RBI	BB	SO	AVG	OBP	SLG	PRO+	BR/A	SB	CS	SBR	FA	FR	G/POS	TPR
1954	NY-A	5	5	1	2	0	0	0	3	1	1	.400	.500	.400	154	0	0	0	0	1.000	1	/C-3	0.2
1955	NY-A	2	5	1	2	0	0	0	2	1	0	.400	.500	.400	147	0	0	0	0	1.000	1	/C-1	0.1
1956	Was-A	95	207	25	54	6	3	4	27	46	33	.261	.402	.377	107	4	0	0	0	.997	-1	C-59	0.6
1957	Was-A	99	264	24	69	11	2	7	36	41	38	.261	.365	.398	110	4	0	1	-1	**1.000**	-3	C-77	0.4
1958	Was-A	5	6	0	1	0	0	0	0	4	1	.167	.500	.167	94	0	0	0	0	.917	1	/C-2	0.1
	Bos-A	57	167	11	35	5	3	2	18	31	32	.210	.337	.311	74	-5	0	2	-1	.984	-6	C-49	-0.9
	Yr	62	173	11	36	5	3	2	18	35	33	.208	.344	.306	76	-5	0	2	-1	.981	-5	C-51	-0.8
1959	Det-A	100	338	38	73	8	2	13	44	35	59	.216	.290	.367	75	-12	0	0	0	.989	-11	C-95	-1.8
1960	Det-A	85	232	18	45	4	0	5	23	41	31	.194	.318	.276	60	-12	2	0	1	.993	-0	C-81	-0.7
Total	7	448	1224	118	281	34	10	31	153	200	195	.230	.341	.350	86	-19	2	3	-1	.992	-17	C-367	-2.0

■ JEFF BERBLINGER Berblinger, Jeffrey James b: 11/19/70, Wichita, Kan. BR/TR, 6', 190 lbs. Deb: 9/7/97

YEAR	TM/L	G	AB	R	H	2B	3B	HR	RBI	BB	SO	AVG	OBP	SLG	PRO+	BR/A	SB	CS	SBR	FA	FR	G/POS	TPR
1997	StL-N	7	5	1	0	0	0	0	0	0	1	.000	.000	.000	-99	-1	0	0	0	1.000	2	/2-4	0.0

■ DAVE BERG Berg, David Scott b: 9/3/70, Roseville, Cal. BR/TR, 5'11", 185 lbs. Deb: 4/2/98

YEAR	TM/L	G	AB	R	H	2B	3B	HR	RBI	BB	SO	AVG	OBP	SLG	PRO+	BR/A	SB	CS	SBR	FA	FR	G/POS	TPR
1998	Fla-N	81	182	18	57	11	0	2	21	26	46	.313	.399	.407	115	5	3	0	1	1.000	4	2-27,3-25,S-17	1.3

■ MOE BERG Berg, Morris b: 3/2/02, New York, N.Y. d: 5/29/72, Belleville, N.J. BR/TR, 6'1", 185 lbs. Deb: 6/27/23 C

YEAR	TM/L	G	AB	R	H	2B	3B	HR	RBI	BB	SO	AVG	OBP	SLG	PRO+	BR/A	SB	CS	SBR	FA	FR	G/POS	TPR
1923	Bro-N	49	129	9	24	3	2	0	6	2	5	.186	.198	.240	16	-16	1	0	0	.906	-6	S-47/2-1	-1.8
1926	Chi-A	41	113	4	25	6	0	0	7	6	9	.221	.261	.274	41	-10	0	2	-1	.948	6	S-31/2-2,3-1	-0.3
1927	Chi-A	35	69	4	17	4	0	0	4	4	10	.246	.288	.304	55	-5	0	0	0	.952	-4	2-11,C-10/S-6,3-3	-0.7
1928	Chi-A	76	224	25	55	16	0	0	29	14	25	.246	.302	.317	64	-12	2	1	0	.990	5	C-73	-0.1
1929	Chi-A	107	352	32	101	7	0	0	47	17	16	.287	.323	.307	64	-18	5	1	1	.982	-3	*C-106	-1.0
1930	Chi-A	20	61	4	7	3	0	0	7	1	5	.115	.129	.164	-27	-12	0	0	0	.986	-1	C-20	-1.0
1931	Cle-A	10	13	1	1	1	0	0	0	1	1	.077	.143	.154	-21	-2	0	0	0	.889	0	/C-8	-0.2
1932	Was-A	75	195	16	46	8	1	1	26	8	13	.236	.266	.303	48	-15	1	1	-0	1.000	7	C-75	-0.5
1933	Was-A	40	65	8	12	3	0	2	9	4	5	.185	.232	.323	46	-5	0	0	0	1.000	3	C-35	-0.2
1934	Was-A	33	86	5	21	4	0	0	6	6	4	.244	.301	.291	55	-6	2	0	1	.988	-4	C-31	-0.8
	Cle-A	29	97	4	25	3	1	0	9	1	7	.258	.265	.309	47	-8	0	0	0	.980	5	C-28	-0.1
	Yr	62	183	9	46	7	1	0	15	7	11	.251	.283	.301	51	-13	2	0	1	.983	1	C-59	-0.9
1935	Bos-A	38	98	13	28	5	0	2	12	5	3	.286	.320	.398	79	-3	0	0	0	.991	2	C-37	0.0
1936	Bos-A	39	125	9	30	4	1	0	19	2	6	.240	.264	.288	34	-13	0	0	0	.986	12	C-39	0.0
1937	Bos-A	47	141	13	36	3	1	0	20	5	4	.255	.281	.291	43	-12	0	0	0	.979	3	C-47	-0.7
1938	Bos-A	10	12	0	4	0	0	0	0	0	1	.333	.333	.333	64	-1	0	0	0	1.000	1	/C-7,1-1	0.0

YEAR	TM/L	G	AB	R	H	2B	3B	HR	RBI	BB	SO	AVG	OBP	SLG	PRO+	BR/A	SB	CS	SBR	FA	FR	G/POS	TPR
1939	Bos-A	14	33	3	9	1	0	1	5	2	3	.273	.314	.394	77	-1	0	0	0	.965	4	C-13	0.3
Total	15	663	1813	150	441	71	6	6	206	78	117	.243	.278	.299	49	-140	11	5	0	.986	29	C-529/S-84,2-14,31	-7.1
■ AUGIE BERGAMO	Bergamo, August Samuel b: 2/14/17, Detroit, Mich. d: 8/19/74, Grosse Pointe, Mich. BL/TL, 5'9", 165 lbs. Deb: 4/25/44																						
1944	*StL-N	80	192	35	55	6	3	2	19	35	23	.286	.399	.380	118	6	0			.988	-7	O-50/1-2	-0.4
1945	StL-N	94	304	51	96	17	2	3	44	43	21	.316	.401	.414	124	11	0			.969	-1	O-77/1-2	0.6
Total	2	174	496	86	151	23	5	5	63	78	44	.304	.400	.401	122	17	0			.975	-9	O-127/1-4	0.2
■ MARTY BERGEN	Bergen, Martin b: 10/25/1871, N.Brookfield, Mass d: 1/19/1900, N.Brookfield, Mass TR , 5'10", 170 lbs. Deb: 4/17/1896 F																						
1896	Bos-N	65	245	39	66	6	4	4	37	11	22	.269	.309	.376	75	-10	6			.920	6	C-63/1-1	0.2
1897	*Bos-N	87	327	47	81	11	3	2	45	18		.248	.295	.318	58	-21	5			.963	4	C-85/O-1	-0.6
1898	Bos-N	120	446	62	125	16	5	3	60	13		.280	.302	.359	85	-11	9			.962	2	*C-117/1-2	0.2
1899	Bos-N	72	260	32	67	11	3	1	34	10		.258	.290	.335	65	-14	4			.955	3	C-72	-0.5
Total	4	344	1278	180	339	44	15	10	176	52	22	.265	.299	.347	72	-56	24			.954	15	C-337/1-3,O-1	-0.7
■ BILL BERGEN	Bergen, William Aloysius b: 6/13/1878, N.Brookfield, Mass. d: 12/19/43, Worcester, Mass. BR/TR, 6', 184 lbs. Deb: 5/6/01 F																						
1901	Cin-N	87	308	15	55	6	4	1	17	8		.179	.199	.234	27	-29	2			.970	-4	C-87	-2.4
1902	Cin-N	89	322	19	58	8	3	0	36	14		.180	.214	.224	32	-26	2			.959	17	C-89	0.0
1903	Cin-N	58	207	21	47	4	2	0	19	7		.227	.252	.266	43	-16	2			.980	2	C-58	-0.8
1904	Bro-N	96	329	17	60	4	2	0	12	9		.182	.204	.207	28	-28	3			.959	14	C-93/1-1	-0.4
1905	Bro-N	79	247	12	47	3	2	0	22	7		.190	.213	.219	31	-21	4			.954	12	C-76	-0.3
1906	Bro-N	103	353	9	56	3	3	0	19	7		.159	.175	.184	13	-37	2			.977	6	*C-103	-2.3
1907	Bro-N	51	138	2	22	3	0	0	14	1		.159	.165	.181	9	-15	1			.968	3	C-51	-1.0
1908	Bro-N	99	302	8	53	8	2	0	15	5		.175	.189	.215	30	-24	1			**.989**	16	C-99	0.0
1909	Bro-N	112	346	16	48	1	1	1	15	10		.139	.163	.156	-1	-41	4			.976	22	*C-112	-1.1
1910	Bro-N	89	249	11	40	2	1	0	14	6	39	.161	.180	.177	4	-31	0			.981	18	C-89	-0.5
1911	Bro-N	84	227	8	30	3	1	0	10	14	42	.132	.183	.154	-6	-32	2			**.981**	15	C-84	-1.0
Total	11	947	3028	138	516	45	21	2	193	88	81	.170	.194	.201	20	-301	23			.972	119	C-941/1-1	-9.8
■ CLARENCE BERGER	Berger, Clarence Edward b: 11/1/1894, E.Cleveland, Ohio d: 6/30/59, Washington, D.C. BL/TR, 6', 185 lbs. Deb: 9/23/14																						
1914	Pit-N	6	13	2	1	0	0	0	0	1	4	.077	.143	.077	-36	-2	0			1.000	-2	/O-5	-0.5
■ JOHNNY BERGER	Berger, John Henne b: 8/27/01, Philadelphia, Pa. d: 5/7/79, Lake Charles, La. BR/TR, 5'9", 165 lbs. Deb: 4/20/22																						
1922	Phi-A	2	1	0	1	0	0	0	0	0	0	1.000	1.000	1.000	412	0	1	0	0	1.000	1	/C-2	0.1
1927	Was-A	9	15	1	4	0	0	0	1	2	3	.267	.353	.267	63	-1	0	0	0	.926	0	/C-9	0.0
Total	2	11	16	1	5	0	0	0	1	2	3	.313	.389	.313	85	-0	1	0	0	.935	1	/C-11	0.1
■ TUN BERGER	Berger, John Henry b: 12/6/1867, Pittsburgh, Pa. d: 6/10/07, Pittsburgh, Pa. TR , 204 lbs. Deb: 5/9/1890																						
1890	Pit-N	104	391	64	104	18	4	0	40	35	23	.266	.337	.332	108	5	11			.912	-7	O-41,S-33,C-21,/23	0.1
1891	Pit-N	43	134	15	32	2	1	1	14	12	10	.239	.315	.291	79	-3	4			.920	-13	C-18,2-17/S-6,O-2	-1.2
1892	Was-N	26	97	9	14	2	1	0	3	7	9	.144	.210	.186	20	-9	3			.872	-11	S-18/C-9	-1.8
Total	3	173	622	88	150	22	6	1	57	54	42	.241	.313	.301	87	-8	18			.837	-30	/S-57,C-48,O-43,23	-2.9
■ JOE BERGER	Berger, Joseph August "Fats" b: 12/20/1886, St.Louis, Mo. d: 3/5/56, Rock Island, Ill. BR/TR, 5'10.5", 170 lbs. Deb: 4/11/13																						
1913	Chi-A	79	223	27	48	6	2	2	20	36	28	.215	.330	.287	82	-4	5			.959	3	2-71/S-4,3-1	-0.2
1914	Chi-A	48	148	11	23	3	1	0	3	13	9	.155	.224	.189	25	-14	2	8	-4	.922	-2	S-28,2-12/3-7	-2.0
Total	2	127	371	38	71	9	3	2	23	49	37	.191	.289	.248	60	-18	7	8		.956	1	/2-83,S-32,3-8	-2.2
■ BOZE BERGER	Berger, Louis William b: 5/13/10, Baltimore, Md. d: 11/3/92, Bethesda, Md. BR/TR, 6'2", 180 lbs. Deb: 8/17/32																						
1932	Cle-A	1	1	0	0	0	0	0	0	0	1	.000	.000	.000	-94	-0	0	0	0	1.000	1	/S-1	0.1
1935	Cle-A	124	461	62	119	27	5	5	43	34	97	.258	.310	.371	74	-19	7	5	-1	.964	13	*2-120/S-3,1-2,3-1	0.2
1936	Cle-A	28	52	1	9	2	0	0	3	1	14	.173	.189	.212	-1	-8	0	0	0	.959	4	/1-8,2-8,3-7,S-2	-0.4
1937	Chi-A	52	130	19	31	5	0	5	13	15	24	.238	.322	.392	79	-5	1	1	-0	.931	-1	3-40/2-1,S-1	-0.4
1938	Chi-A	118	470	60	102	15	3	3	36	43	80	.217	.284	.281	41	-43	4	1	1	.946	-10	S-67,2-42/3-9	-4.1
1939	Bos-A	20	30	4	9	2	0	0	2	1	10	.300	.323	.367	73	-1	0	0	0	.947	1	S-10/3-5,2-2	0.0
Total	6	343	1144	146	270	51	8	13	97	94	226	.236	.296	.329	57	-77	12	7	-1	.954	9	2-173/S-84,3-62,1	-4.6
■ WALLY BERGER	Berger, Walter Antone b: 10/10/05, Chicago, Ill. d: 11/30/88, Redondo Beach, Cal BR/TR, 6'2", 198 lbs. Deb: 4/15/30																						
1930	Bos-N	151	555	98	172	27	14	38	119	54	69	.310	.375	.614	139	31	3			.966	4	*O-145	2.2
1931	Bos-N	156	617	94	199	44	8	19	84	55	70	.323	.380	.512	143	36	13			.977	11	*O-156/1-1	3.5
1932	Bos-N	145	602	90	185	34	6	17	73	33	66	.307	.346	.468	121	16	5			**.993**	5	*O-134,1-11	1.2
1933	Bos-N★	137	528	84	165	37	8	27	106	41	77	.313	.365	.566	**177**	49	2			.977	4	*O-136	4.7
1934	Bos-N★	150	615	92	183	35	8	34	121	49	65	.298	.352	.546	148	38	2			.978	1	*O-150	3.1
1935	Bos-N★	150	589	91	174	39	4	**34**	**130**	50	80	.295	.355	.548	151	39	3			.965	9	*O-149	4.0
1936	Bos-N☆	138	534	88	154	23	3	25	91	53	84	.288	.361	.483	134	24	1			.966	7	*O-133	2.5
1937	Bos-N	30	113	14	31	9	1	5	22	11	33	.274	.344	.504	140	6	0			1.000	-2	O-28	0.3
	*NY-N	59	199	40	58	11	2	12	43	18	30	.291	.359	.548	141	11	3			.965	-2	O-52	0.7
	Yr	89	312	54	89	20	3	17	65	29	63	.285	.354	.532	141	16	3			.976	-4	O-80	1.0
1938	NY-N	16	32	5	6	0	0	0	4	2	4	.188	.235	.188	17	-4	0			1.000	1	/O-9	-0.3
	Cin-N	99	407	74	125	23	4	16	56	29	44	.307	.356	.501	137	19	2			.966	-3	O-98	1.3
	Yr	115	439	79	131	23	4	16	60	31	48	.298	.347	.478	128	15	2			.970	-2	*O-107	1.0
1939	*Cin-N	97	329	36	85	15	1	14	44	36	63	.258	.341	.438	107	3	1			.970	-8	O-95	-0.8
1940	Cin-N	2	2	0	0	0	0	0	0	0	1	.000	.000	.000	-99	-1	0			.000	0	H	-0.1
	Phi-N	20	41	3	13	2	0	1	5	4	8	.317	.378	.439	130	2	1			.947	-2	O-11/1-1	-0.1
	Yr	22	43	3	13	2	0	1	5	4	9	.302	.362	.419	119	1	1			.947	-2	O-11/1-1	-0.2
Total	11	1350	5163	809	1550	299	59	242	898	435	694	.300	.359	.522	140	269	36			.974	26	*O-1296/1-13	22.2
■ JOHN BERGH	Bergh, John Baptist b: 10/8/1857, Boston, Mass. d: 4/17/1883, Boston, Mass. Deb: 8/5/1876																						
1876	Phi-N	1	4	0	0	0	0	0	0	0	2	.000	.000	.000	-99	-1				1.000	-0	/O-1,C-1	-0.1
1880	Bos-N	11	40	2	8	3	0	0	0	2	5	.200	.238	.275	76	-1				.844	-3	C-11	-0.4
Total	2	12	44	2	8	3	0	0	0	2	7	.182	.217	.250	59	-2				.841	-4	/C-12,O-1	-0.5
■ MARTY BERGHAMMER	Berghammer, Martin Andrew "Pepper" b: 6/18/1888, Elliott, Pa. d: 12/21/57, Pittsburgh, Pa. BL/TR, 5'9", 172 lbs. Deb: 9/8/11																						
1911	Chi-A	2	5	0	0	0	0	0	0	0		.000	.167	.000	-54	-1	0			1.000	-0	/2-2	-0.1
1913	Cin-N	74	188	25	41	4	1	1	13	10	29	.218	.269	.266	53	-11	16			.909	5	S-54,2-13	-0.3
1914	Cin-N	77	112	15	25	2	0	0	6	10	18	.223	.287	.241	56	-6	4			.906	7	S-33,2-13	0.2
1915	Pit-F	132	469	96	114	10	6	0	33	83	44	.243	.371	.290	88	-10	26			**.943**	-16	*S-132	-1.6
Total	4	285	774	136	180	16	7	1	52	103	91	.233	.335	.275	75	-28	46			.931	-5	S-219/2-28	-1.8
■ AL BERGMAN	Bergman, Alfred Henry "Dutch" b: 9/27/1890, Peru, Ind. d: 6/20/61, Fort Wayne, Ind. BR/TR, 5'7", 155 lbs. Deb: 8/29/16																						
1916	Cle-A	8	14	2	3	0	1	0	0	2	4	.214	.313	.357	95	-0	0			.889	-2	/2-3	-0.2
■ DAVE BERGMAN	Bergman, David Bruce b: 6/6/53, Evanston, Ill. BL/TL, 6'1.5", 185 lbs. Deb: 8/26/75																						
1975	NY-A	7	17	0	0	0	0	0	0	2	4	.000	.105	.000	-69	-4	0	0	0	.917	0	/O-6	-0.4
1977	NY-A	5	4	1	1	0	0	0	1	0	0	.250	.250	.250	37	-0	0	0	0	1.000	-1	/O-3,1-2	-0.1
1978	Hou-N	104	186	15	43	5	1	0	12	39	32	.231	.364	.269	86	-2	2	0	1	.993	-2	1-66,O-29	-0.6
1979	Hou-N	13	15	4	6	0	0	1	2	0	3	.400	.400	.600	179	1	0	0	0	1.000	-0	/1-4	0.1
1980	*Hou-N	90	78	12	20	6	1	0	3	10	10	.256	.341	.359	104	0	1	0	0	.995	2	1-59/O-5	0.2
1981	Hou-N	6	6	1	1	0	0	1	1	0	0	.167	.167	.667	134	0	0	0	0	1.000	0	/1-1	0.1
	SF-N	63	145	16	37	9	0	3	13	19	18	.255	.341	.379	106	1	2	0	1	.992	0	1-33,O-15	0.1
	Yr	69	151	17	38	9	0	4	14	19	18	.252	.335	.391	108	2	2	0	1	.992	1	1-34,O-15	0.2
1982	SF-N	100	121	22	33	3	1	4	14	18	11	.273	.367	.413	118	3	3	0	1	.991	1	1-69/O-6	0.4

YEAR	TM/L	G	AB	R	H	2B	3B	HR	RBI	BB	SO	AVG	OBP	SLG	PRO+	BR/A	SB	CS	SBR	FA	FR	G/POS	TPR
1983	SF-N	90	140	16	40	4	1	6	24	24	21	.286	.394	.457	140	8	2	1	0	.994	2	1-50/O-6	0.9
1984	*Det-A	120	271	42	74	8	5	7	44	33	40	.273	.358	.417	115	6	3	4	-2	.989	8	*1-114/O-2	0.8
1985	Det-A	69	140	8	25	2	0	3	7	14	15	.179	.253	.257	41	-11	0	0	0	.991	1	1-44/O-1,D-5	-1.2
1986	Det-A	65	130	14	30	6	1	1	9	21	16	.231	.338	.315	79	-3	0	0	0	.986	2	1-41/O-2,D-8	-0.3
1987	*Det-A	91	172	25	47	7	3	6	22	30	23	.273	.384	.453	127	7	0	1	-1	.992	-1	1-65/O-7,D-7	0.3
1988	Det-A	116	289	37	85	14	0	5	35	38	34	.294	.376	.394	121	9	0	2	-1	.990	-0	1-64,D-30,O-13	0.3
1989	Det-A	137	385	38	103	13	1	7	37	44	44	.268	.346	.361	102	2	1	3	-2	.993	5	*1-123/O-1,D-7	-0.3
1990	Det-A	100	205	21	57	10	1	2	26	33	17	.278	.378	.366	108	4	3	2	-0	.995	-3	D-51,1-27/O-5	-0.3
1991	Det-A	86	194	23	46	10	1	7	29	35	40	.237	.354	.407	108	3	1	1	-0	.997	-1	1-49,D-13/O-4	-0.1
1992	Det-A	87	181	17	42	3	0	1	10	20	19	.232	.308	.265	62	-9	1	0	0	.986	-2	1-55,D-12/O-1	-1.4
Total	17	1349	2679	312	690	100	16	54	289	380	347	.258	.351	.367	102	17	19	14	-3	.992	10	1-866,D-133,O-106	-1.5

■ FRANK BERKELBACH Berkelbach, Francis P. b: Philadelphia, Pa. 6', 182 lbs. Deb: 7/4/1884

YEAR	TM/L	G	AB	R	H	2B	3B	HR	RBI	BB	SO	AVG	OBP	SLG	PRO+	BR/A	SB	CS	SBR	FA	FR	G/POS	TPR
1884	Cin-a	6	25	3	6	0	1	0	3	0		.240	.296	.320	96	-0				.667	-2	/O-6	-0.2

■ NATE BERKENSTOCK Berkenstock, Nathan b: 1831, Pennsylvania d: 2/23/1900, Philadelphia, Pa. Deb: 10/30/1871

YEAR	TM/L	G	AB	R	H	2B	3B	HR	RBI	BB	SO	AVG	OBP	SLG	PRO+	BR/A	SB	CS	SBR	FA	FR	G/POS	TPR
1871	Ath-n	1	4	0	0	0	0	0	0	0	3	.000	.000	.000	-99	-1	0	0	0	1.000	0	/O-1	0.0

■ BOB BERMAN Berman, Robert Leon b: 1/24/1899, New York, N.Y. d: 8/2/88, Bridgeport, Conn. BR/TR, 5'7.5", 158 lbs. Deb: 6/4/18

YEAR	TM/L	G	AB	R	H	2B	3B	HR	RBI	BB	SO	AVG	OBP	SLG	PRO+	BR/A	SB	CS	SBR	FA	FR	G/POS	TPR
1918	Was-A	2	0	0	0	0	0	0	0	0	0	—	—	—	—	0	0			1.000	0	/C-1	0.0

■ CURT BERNARD Bernard, Curtis Henry b: 2/18/1878, Parkersburg, W.Va. d: 4/10/55, Culver City, Cal. BL/TR, 5'10", 150 lbs. Deb: 9/17/00

YEAR	TM/L	G	AB	R	H	2B	3B	HR	RBI	BB	SO	AVG	OBP	SLG	PRO+	BR/A	SB	CS	SBR	FA	FR	G/POS	TPR
1900	NY-N	20	71	9	18	2	0	0	8	6		.254	.329	.282	73	-2	1			.929	-2	O-19/S-1	-0.6
1901	NY-N	23	76	11	17	0	2	0	6	7		.224	.289	.276	67	-3	2			.800	-1	O-15/2-4,S-2,3-1	-0.5
Total	2	43	147	20	35	2	2	0	14	13		.238	.309	.279	70	-5	3			.857	-3	/O-34,2-4,S-3,3-1	-1.1

■ TONY BERNAZARD Bernazard, Antonio (Garcia) b: 8/24/56, Caguas, P.R. BB/TR, 5'9", 160 lbs. Deb: 7/13/79

YEAR	TM/L	G	AB	R	H	2B	3B	HR	RBI	BB	SO	AVG	OBP	SLG	PRO+	BR/A	SB	CS	SBR	FA	FR	G/POS	TPR
1979	Mon-N	22	40	11	12	2	0	1	8	15	12	.300	.500	.425	156	5	1	2	-1	.982	-1	2-14	0.3
1980	Mon-N	82	183	26	41	7	1	5	18	17	41	.224	.290	.355	79	-5	9	2	2	.976	2	2-39,S-22	0.2
1981	Chi-A	106	384	53	106	14	4	6	34	54	66	.276	.368	.380	118	11	4	4	-1	.987	-1	*2-104/S-1	1.6
1982	Chi-A	137	540	90	138	25	9	11	56	67	88	.256	.340	.396	101	2	11	0	3	.985	25	*2-137	3.7
1983	Chi-A	59	233	30	61	16	2	2	26	17	45	.262	.312	.373	85	-5	2	1	0	.976	-2	2-59	-0.4
	Sea-A	80	300	35	80	18	1	6	30	38	52	.267	.353	.393	101	1	21	8	2	.971	1	2-79	0.7
	Yr	139	533	65	141	34	3	8	56	55	97	.265	.336	.385	94	-4	23	9	2	.973	-1	*2-138	0.3
1984	Cle-A	140	439	44	97	15	4	2	38	43	70	.221	.293	.287	60	-23	20	13	-2	.971	-11	*2-136/D-1	-3.1
1985	Cle-A	153	500	73	137	26	3	11	59	69	72	.274	.363	.404	111	9	17	9	-0	.978	-29	*2-147/S-1	-1.5
1986	Cle-A	146	562	88	169	28	4	17	73	53	77	.301	.367	.456	125	19	17	8	0	.979	1	*2-146	2.6
1987	Cle-A	79	293	39	70	12	1	11	30	25	49	.239	.301	.399	83	-8	7	4	-0	.983	-16	2-78	-1.9
	Oak-A	61	214	34	57	14	1	3	19	30	30	.266	.357	.383	103	2	4	4	-1	.953	-18	2-59/D-3	-1.5
	Yr	140	507	73	127	26	2	14	49	55	79	.250	.325	.393	91	-6	11	8	-2	.971	-34	*2-137/D-3	-3.4
1991	Det-A	6	12	0	2	0	0	0	0	0	4	.167	.167	.167	-7	-2	0	0	0	.900	1	/2-2,D-2	0.0
Total	10	1071	3700	523	970	177	30	75	391	428	606	.262	.341	.387	100	6	113	55	1	.978	-48	2-1000/S-24,D-6	0.7

■ JUAN BERNHARDT Bernhardt, Juan Ramon (Coradin) b: 8/31/53, San Pedro De Macoris, D.R. BR/TR, 5'11", 160 lbs. Deb: 7/10/76

YEAR	TM/L	G	AB	R	H	2B	3B	HR	RBI	BB	SO	AVG	OBP	SLG	PRO+	BR/A	SB	CS	SBR	FA	FR	G/POS	TPR
1976	NY-A	10	21	1	4	1	0	0	1	0	4	.190	.190	.238	25	-2	0	0	0	.800	-1	/O-4,3-1,D-2	-0.3
1977	Sea-A	89	305	32	74	9	2	7	30	5	26	.243	.260	.354	66	-15	2	3	-1	.982	-1	D-54,3-21/1-8	-1.9
1978	Sea-A	54	165	13	38	9	0	2	12	9	10	.230	.274	.321	67	-7	1	1	-0	.989	-0	1-25,3-22/D-2	-1.0
1979	Sea-A	1	1	0	1	0	0	0	0	0	0	1.000	1.000	1.000	434	0	0	0	0	.000	0	/H	0.0
Total	4	154	492	46	117	19	2	9	43	14	40	.238	.263	.339	66	-24	3	4	-2	.965	-2	/D-58,3-44,1-33,O-4	-3.2

■ CARLOS BERNIER Bernier, Carlos (Rodriguez) b: 1/28/27, Juana Diaz, P.R. d: 4/6/89, Juana Diaz, P.R. BR/TR, 5'9", 180 lbs. Deb: 4/22/53

YEAR	TM/L	G	AB	R	H	2B	3B	HR	RBI	BB	SO	AVG	OBP	SLG	PRO+	BR/A	SB	CS	SBR	FA	FR	G/POS	TPR
1953	Pit-N	105	310	48	66	7	8	3	31	51	53	.213	.332	.316	70	-12	15	14	-4	.970	5	O-86	-1.4

■ JOHNNY BERO Bero, John George b: 12/22/22, Gary, W.Va. d: 5/11/85, Gardena, Cal. BL/TR, 6', 170 lbs. Deb: 9/26/48

YEAR	TM/L	G	AB	R	H	2B	3B	HR	RBI	BB	SO	AVG	OBP	SLG	PRO+	BR/A	SB	CS	SBR	FA	FR	G/POS	TPR
1948	Det-A	4	9	2	0	0	0	0	0	1	1	.000	.100	.000	-70	-2	0	0	0	1.000	-1	/2-2	-0.3
1951	StL-A	61	160	24	34	5	0	5	17	26	30	.213	.323	.338	76	-5	1	1	-0	.954	-9	S-55/2-1	-1.1
Total	2	65	169	26	34	5	0	5	17	27	31	.201	.311	.320	69	-7	1	1	-0	1.000	-10	/S-55,2-3	-1.4

■ DALE BERRA Berra, Dale Anthony b: 12/13/56, Ridgewood, N.J. BR/TR, 6', 190 lbs. Deb: 8/22/77 F

YEAR	TM/L	G	AB	R	H	2B	3B	HR	RBI	BB	SO	AVG	OBP	SLG	PRO+	BR/A	SB	CS	SBR	FA	FR	G/POS	TPR
1977	Pit-N	17	40	0	7	1	0	0	3	1	8	.175	.195	.200	6	-5	0	0	0	.973	3	3-14	-0.3
1978	Pit-N	56	135	16	28	2	0	6	14	13	20	.207	.287	.356	75	-5	3	1	0	.908	1	3-55/S-2	-0.4
1979	Pit-N	44	123	11	26	5	0	3	15	11	17	.211	.276	.325	61	-7	0	0	0	.940	1	S-22,3-22	-0.5
1980	Pit-N	93	245	21	54	8	2	6	31	16	52	.220	.271	.343	69	-11	2	0	1	.968	2	3-48,S-45/2-4	-0.5
1981	Pit-N	81	232	21	56	12	0	2	27	17	34	.241	.302	.319	74	-8	11	1	3	.976	2	3-42,S-30,2-18	-0.1
1982	Pit-N	156	529	64	139	25	5	10	61	33	83	.263	.311	.386	91	-7	6	6	-2	.961	-2	*S-153/3-6	0.3
1983	Pit-N	161	537	51	135	25	1	10	52	61	84	.251	.328	.358	88	-8	8	5	-1	.963	16	*S-161	2.3
1984	Pit-N	136	450	31	100	16	0	9	52	34	78	.222	.278	.318	67	-20	1	3	-2	.955	-2	*S-135/3-1	-1.1
1985	NY-A	48	109	8	25	5	1	1	8	7	20	.229	.276	.321	64	-5	1	1	-0	.917	4	3-41/S-6	-0.2
1986	NY-A	42	108	10	25	7	0	2	13	9	14	.231	.297	.352	77	-4	0	0	0	.972	-1	S-19,3-18/D-4	-0.3
1987	Hou-N	19	45	3	8	3	0	0	2	8	12	.178	.302	.244	49	-3	0	0	0	.963	-3	S-18/2-3	-0.5
Total	11	853	2553	236	603	109	9	49	278	210	422	.236	.297	.344	76	-83	32	17	-1	.959	21	S-591,3-247/2-25,D	-1.3

■ YOGI BERRA Berra, Lawrence Peter b: 5/12/25, St.Louis, Mo. BL/TR, 5'8", 194 lbs. Deb: 9/22/46 FMCH

YEAR	TM/L	G	AB	R	H	2B	3B	HR	RBI	BB	SO	AVG	OBP	SLG	PRO+	BR/A	SB	CS	SBR	FA	FR	G/POS	TPR
1946	NY-A	7	22	3	8	1	0	2	4	1	1	.364	.391	.682	193	2	0	0	0	1.000	2	/C-6	0.5
1947	*NY-A	83	293	41	82	15	3	11	54	13	12	.280	.310	.464	115	3	0	1	-1	.972	-6	C-51,O-24	-0.1
1948	NY-A☆	125	469	70	143	24	10	14	98	25	24	.305	.341	.488	120	10	3	3	-1	.979	-9	C-71,O-50	0.2
1949	*NY-A★	116	415	59	115	20	2	20	91	22	25	.277	.323	.480	111	2	2	1	0	.989	11	*C-109	1.9
1950	*NY-A★	151	597	116	192	30	6	28	124	55	12	.322	.383	.533	136	29	4	2	0	.985	1	*C-148	3.4
1951	*NY-A★	141	547	92	161	19	4	27	88	44	20	.294	.350	.492	131	20	5	4	-1	.984	9	*C-141	3.3
1952	*NY-A★	142	534	97	146	17	1	30	98	66	24	.273	.358	.478	139	26	2	3	-1	.992	2	*C-140	3.5
1953	*NY-A★	137	503	80	149	23	5	27	108	50	32	.296	.363	.523	142	27	0	3	-2	.986	3	*C-133	3.4
1954	NY-A★	151	584	88	179	28	6	22	125	56	29	.307	.371	.488	139	29	0	1	-1	.990	-0	*C-149/3-1	3.6
1955	*NY-A★	147	541	84	147	20	3	27	108	60	20	.272	.352	.470	121	14	1	0	0	.984	-0	*C-145	1.9
1956	*NY-A★	140	521	93	155	29	2	30	105	65	29	.298	.381	.534	144	31	3	2	-0	.986	7	*C-135/O-1	4.2
1957	*NY-A★	134	482	74	121	14	2	24	82	57	24	.251	.331	.438	110	6	1	2	-1	.995	16	*C-121/O-6	2.6
1958	*NY-A★	122	433	60	115	17	3	22	90	35	35	.266	.323	.471	120	10	3	0	1	**1.000**	6	C-88,O-21/1-2	2.1
1959	NY-A★	131	472	64	134	25	1	19	69	43	38	.284	.349	.462	125	15	1	2	-1	**.997**	7	*C-116/O-7	2.8
1900	*NY-A★	120	359	46	99	14	1	15	62	38	23	.276	.350	.446	120	10	2	1	0	.989	-10	C-63,O-36	0.2
1961	*NY-A★	119	395	62	107	11	0	22	61	35	28	.271	.333	.466	117	8	2	0	1	.988	3	O-87,C-15	0.7
1962	*NY-A★	86	232	25	52	8	0	10	35	24	18	.224	.302	.388	87	-5	0	1	-1	.990	8	C-31,O-28	0.2
1963	*NY-A	64	147	20	43	6	0	8	28	15	17	.293	.362	.497	139	8	1	0	0	.988	8	C-35	1.8
1965	NY-N	4	9	1	2	0	0	0	0	0	3	.222	.222	.222	27	-1	0	0	0	.941	1	/C-2	0.0
Total	19	2120	7555	1175	2150	321	49	358	1430	704	414	.285	.350	.482	126	245	30	26	-7	.989	57	*C-1699,O-260/1-2,3	36.2

■ DENNIS BERRAN Berran, Dennis Martin b: 10/8/1887, Merrimac, Mass. d: 4/28/43, Boston, Mass. BL/TL, Deb: 8/11/12

YEAR	TM/L	G	AB	R	H	2B	3B	HR	RBI	BB	SO	AVG	OBP	SLG	PRO+	BR/A	SB	CS	SBR	FA	FR	G/POS	TPR
1912	Chi-A	2	4	1	1	0	0	0	0	0		.250	.250	.250	44	-0	0			1.000	-1	/O-2	-0.1

■ RAY BERRES Berres, Raymond Frederick b: 8/31/07, Kenosha, Wis. BR/TR, 5'9", 170 lbs. Deb: 4/24/34 C

YEAR	TM/L	G	AB	R	H	2B	3B	HR	RBI	BB	SO	AVG	OBP	SLG	PRO+	BR/A	SB	CS	SBR	FA	FR	G/POS	TPR
1934	Bro-N	39	79	7	17	4	0	0	3	1	16	.215	.225	.266	32	-8	0			.969	-2	C-37	-0.8
1936	Bro-N	105	267	16	64	10	1	1	13	14	35	.240	.280	.296	55	-17	1			.988	23	*C-105	0.9
1937	Pit-N	2	6	0	1	0	0	0	0	0	0	.167	.167	.167	-9	-1	0			1.000	1	/C-2	0.0
1938	Pit-N	40	100	7	23	2	0	0	6	8	10	.230	.287	.250	48	-7	0			.993	4	C-40	-0.1

YEAR	TM/L	G	AB	R	H	2B	3B	HR	RBI	BB	SO	AVG	OBP	SLG	PRO+	BR/A	SB	CS	SBR	FA	FR	G/POS	TPR
1939	Pit-N	81	231	22	53	6	1	0	16	11	25	.229	.267	.264	44	-18	1			.993	-2	C-80	-1.7
1940	Pit-N	21	32	2	6	0	0	0	2	1	1	.188	.212	.188	11	-4	0			.980	3	C-21	-0.1
	Bos-N	85	229	12	44	4	1	0	14	18	19	.192	.251	.218	32	-21	0			.981	1	C-85	-1.5
	Yr	106	261	14	50	4	1	0	16	19	20	.192	.246	.215	29	-25	0			.981	3	*C-106	-1.6
1941	Bos-N	120	279	21	56	10	0	1	19	17	20	.201	.247	.247	41	-22	2			**.995**	9	*C-120	-0.6
1942	NY-N	12	32	0	6	0	0	0	1	2	3	.188	.235	.188	24	-3	0			.973	-2	C-12	-0.4
1943	NY-N	20	28	1	4	1	0	0	0	1	2	.143	.172	.179	1	-4	0			.981	4	C-17	0.1
1944	NY-N	16	17	4	8	0	0	1	2	1	0	.471	.526	.647	230	3	0			1.000	0	C-12	0.4
1945	NY-N	20	30	4	5	0	0	0	2	2	3	.167	.219	.167	8	-4	0			1.000	1	C-20	-0.2
Total	11	561	1330	96	287	37	3	3	78	76	134	.216	.260	.255	43	-105	4			.989	40	C-551	-4.0

■ GERONIMO BERROA

Berroa, Geronimo Emiliano Letta (b: Geronimo Emiliano Letta (Berroa)) b: 3/18/65, Santo Domingo, D.R. BR/TR, 6', 195 lbs. Deb: 4/5/89

YEAR	TM/L	G	AB	R	H	2B	3B	HR	RBI	BB	SO	AVG	OBP	SLG	PRO+	BR/A	SB	CS	SBR	FA	FR	G/POS	TPR
1989	Atl-N	81	136	7	36	4	0	2	9	7	32	.265	.301	.338	80	-4	0	1	-1	.971	1	O-34	-0.4
1990	Atl-N	7	4	0	0	0	0	0	0	1	1	.000	.200	.000	-38	-1	0	0	0	1.000	-1	/O-3	-0.2
1992	Cin-N	13	15	2	4	1	0	0	0	2	1	.267	.389	.333	103	0	0	1	-1	1.000	0	/O-3	0.0
1993	Fla-N	14	34	3	4	1	0	0	0	2	7	.118	.167	.147	-14	-5	0	0	0	.833	-1	/O-9	-0.7
1994	Oak-A	96	340	55	104	18	2	13	65	41	62	.306	.385	.485	134	18	7	2	1	1.000	1	D-44,O-42/1-9	1.4
1995	Oak-A	141	546	87	152	22	3	22	88	63	98	.278	.354	.451	114	11	7	4	-0	.971	2	D-72,O-71	0.6
1996	Oak-A	153	586	101	170	32	1	36	106	47	122	.290	.347	.532	120	16	0	3	-2	.980	-7	D-91,O-61	0.0
1997	Oak-A	73	261	40	81	12	0	16	42	36	58	.310	.396	.540	144	17	3	2	-0	.986	-3	O-43,D-32	1.0
	*Bal-A	83	300	48	78	13	0	10	48	40	62	.260	.353	.403	100	0	1	2	-1	.959	-2	D-42,O-40	-0.5
	Yr	156	561	88	159	25	0	26	90	76	120	.283	.373	.467	120	18	4	4	-1	.973	-5	O-83,D-74	0.5
1998	Cle-A	20	65	6	13	3	1	0	3	7	17	.200	.278	.277	44	-5	1	0	0	1.000	1	O-14/D-5	-0.5
	Det-A	52	126	17	30	4	1	1	10	17	27	.238	.338	.310	70	-5	0	1	-1	1.000	-1	D-37/O-4	-0.8
	Yr	72	191	23	43	7	2	1	13	24	44	.225	.318	.298	61	-11	1	1	-0	1.000	-0	D-42,O-18	-1.3
Total	9	733	2413	366	672	110	8	100	371	263	487	.278	.353	.455	111	42	19	16	-4	.976	-11	O-324,D-323/1-9	-0.1

■ KEN BERRY

Berry, Allen Kent b: 5/10/41, Kansas City, Mo. BR/TR, 5'11", 180 lbs. Deb: 9/9/62

YEAR	TM/L	G	AB	R	H	2B	3B	HR	RBI	BB	SO	AVG	OBP	SLG	PRO+	BR/A	SB	CS	SBR	FA	FR	G/POS	TPR
1962	Chi-A	3	6	2	2	0	0	0	0	0	0	.333	.333	.333	80	-0	0	0	0	1.000	1	/O-2	0.0
1963	Chi-A	4	5	2	1	0	0	0	0	1	1	.200	.333	.200	55	-0	0	0	0	.857	-0	/O-2,2-1	0.0
1964	Chi-A	12	32	4	12	1	0	1	4	5	3	.375	.459	.500	171	3	0	1	-1	1.000	-3	O-12	0.0
1965	Chi-A	157	472	51	103	17	4	12	42	28	96	.218	.269	.347	79	-15	4	2	0	.980	3	*O-156	-1.9
1966	Chi-A	147	443	50	120	20	2	8	34	28	63	.271	.317	.379	106	2	7	10	-4	.991	-9	*O-141	-1.8
1967	Chi-A★	147	485	49	117	14	4	7	41	46	68	.241	.311	.330	93	-4	9	8	-2	.992	-15	*O-143	-3.1
1968	Chi-A	153	504	49	127	21	2	7	32	25	64	.252	.289	.343	90	-7	6	6	-2	.981	3	*O-151	-1.5
1969	Chi-A	130	297	25	69	12	2	4	18	24	50	.232	.296	.327	71	-12	1	2	-1	**1.000**	-5	*O-120	-2.3
1970	Chi-A	141	463	45	128	12	2	7	50	43	61	.276	.346	.356	90	-5	6	4	-1	.988	6	*O-138	-0.6
1971	Cal-A	111	298	29	66	17	0	3	22	18	33	.221	.273	.309	69	-13	3	2	-0	.988	2	*O-101	-1.6
1972	Cal-A	119	409	41	118	15	3	5	39	35	47	.289	.348	.377	122	11	5	3	-0	**1.000**	14	*O-116	2.2
1973	Cal-A	136	415	48	118	11	2	3	36	26	50	.284	.328	.342	96	-3	1	6	-3	**.997**	3	*O-129	-0.8
1974	Mil-A	98	267	21	64	9	2	1	24	18	26	.240	.295	.300	72	-10	3	1	0	.995	-3	O-82,D-13	-1.7
1975	Cle-A	25	40	6	8	1	0	0	1	1	7	.200	.238	.225	31	-4	0	1	-1	.926	-2	O-18/D-5	-0.7
Total	14	1383	4136	422	1053	150	23	58	343	298	569	.255	.309	.344	90	-56	45	46	-14	.989	-5	*O-1311/D-18,2-1	-13.8

■ CHARLIE BERRY

Berry, Charles Francis b: 10/18/02, Phillipsburg, N.J. d: 9/6/72, Evanston, Ill. BR/TR, 6', 185 lbs. Deb: 6/15/25 FUC

YEAR	TM/L	G	AB	R	H	2B	3B	HR	RBI	BB	SO	AVG	OBP	SLG	PRO+	BR/A	SB	CS	SBR	FA	FR	G/POS	TPR
1925	Phi-A	10	14	1	3	1	0	0	3	0	2	.214	.214	.286	24	-2	0	0	0	.900	-1	/C-4	-0.2
1928	Bos-A	80	177	18	46	7	3	1	19	21	19	.260	.342	.350	84	-4	1	1	-0	.959	-9	C-63	-0.9
1929	Bos-A	77	207	19	50	11	4	1	21	15	29	.242	.302	.348	69	-10	2	4	-2	.983	3	C-72	-0.3
1930	Bos-A	88	256	31	74	9	6	6	35	16	22	.289	.331	.441	98	-2	2	0	1	.988	7	C-85	1.2
1931	Bos-A	111	357	41	101	16	2	6	49	29	38	.283	.337	.389	96	-3	4	0	1	.985	-3	*C-102	0.2
1932	Bos-A	10	32	0	6	3	0	0	6	3	2	.188	.257	.281	40	-3	0	0	0	.944	-1	C-10	-0.3
	Chi-A	72	226	33	69	15	6	4	31	21	23	.305	.364	.478	124	7	3	0	1	.981	-2	C-70	1.0
	Yr	82	258	33	75	18	6	4	37	24	25	.291	.351	.453	114	4	3	0	1	.977	-2	C-80	0.7
1933	Chi-A	86	271	25	69	8	3	2	28	17	16	.255	.301	.328	70	-12	0	0	0	.987	-8	C-83	-1.5
1934	Phi-A	99	269	14	72	10	2	0	34	22	23	.268	.323	.320	69	-12	1	0	0	.987	-0	C-99	-0.8
1935	Phi-A	62	190	14	48	7	3	3	29	10	20	.253	.290	.368	70	-9	0	0	0	.987	-1	C-56	-0.7
1936	Phi-A	13	17	0	1	1	0	0	1	6	2	.059	.304	.118	8	-2	0	0	0	.971	1	C-12	-0.1
1938	Phi-A	1	2	0	0	0	0	0	0	0	0	.000	.000	.000	-99	-1	0	0	0	1.000	0	/C-1	0.0
Total	11	709	2018	196	539	88	29	23	256	160	196	.267	.322	.374	83	-52	13	5	1	.982	-12	C-657	-2.4

■ CHARLIE BERRY

Berry, Charles Joseph b: 9/6/1860, Elizabeth, N.J. d: 1/22/40, Phillipsburg, N.J. BR/TR, 5'11", 175 lbs. Deb: 4/30/1884 F

YEAR	TM/L	G	AB	R	H	2B	3B	HR	RBI	BB	SO	AVG	OBP	SLG	PRO+	BR/A	SB	CS	SBR	FA	FR	G/POS	TPR
1884	Alt-U	7	25	2	6	0	0	0		0		.240	.240	.240	45	-2				.862	-6	/2-7	-0.8
	KC-U	29	118	15	29	6	1	1		1		.246	.252	.339	89	-5				.887	3	2-22/O-8,3-1	-0.2
	CP-U	7	27	4	3	2	0	0		0		.111	.111	.185	-12	-4				.833	1	/2-7	-0.3
	Yr	43	170	21	38	8	1	1		1		.224	.228	.300	64	-13				.871	-3	2-36/O-8,3-1	-1.3

■ CLAUDE BERRY

Berry, Claude Elzy "Admiral" b: 2/14/1880, Losantville, Ind. d: 2/1/74, Richmond, Ind. BR/TR, 5'7", 165 lbs. Deb: 4/22/04

YEAR	TM/L	G	AB	R	H	2B	3B	HR	RBI	BB	SO	AVG	OBP	SLG	PRO+	BR/A	SB	CS	SBR	FA	FR	G/POS	TPR
1904	Chi-A	3	1	1	0	0	0	0	0	1		.000	.500	.000	68	0	0			1.000	1	/C-3	0.1
1906	Phi-A	10	30	2	7	0	0	0	2	2		.233	.281	.233	60	-1	1			.938	6	C-10	0.5
1907	Phi-A	8	19	2	4	2	0	0	1	2		.211	.286	.316	90	-0	0			.944	-2	/C-8	-0.2
1914	Pit-F	124	411	35	98	18	9	2	36	26	50	.238	.284	.341	70	-25	6			.970	1	*C-122	-1.4
1915	Pit-F	100	292	32	56	11	1	1	26	29	42	.192	.269	.247	46	-25	7			.980	-0	C-99	-2.0
Total	5	245	753	72	165	31	10	3	65	60	92	.219	.279	.299	61	-52	14			.971	4	C-242	-3.0

■ NEIL BERRY

Berry, Cornelius John b: 1/11/22, Kalamazoo, Mich. BR/TR, 5'10", 170 lbs. Deb: 4/20/48

YEAR	TM/L	G	AB	R	H	2B	3B	HR	RBI	BB	SO	AVG	OBP	SLG	PRO+	BR/A	SB	CS	SBR	FA	FR	G/POS	TPR
1948	Det-A	87	256	46	68	8	1	0	16	37	23	.266	.358	.305	75	-8	1	3	-2	.930	4	S-41,2-26	-0.2
1949	Det-A	109	329	38	78	9	1	0	18	27	24	.237	.299	.271	51	-23	4	2	0	.970	-0	2-95/S-4	-1.9
1950	Det-A	39	40	9	10	1	0	0	7	6	11	.250	.348	.275	59	-2	0	0	0	.944	2	S-12/2-2,3-1	0.1
1951	Det-A	67	157	17	36	5	2	0	9	10	15	.229	.275	.287	52	-11	4	2	0	.944	8	S-38,2-10/3-7	0.0
1952	Det-A	73	189	22	43	4	3	0	13	22	19	.228	.311	.280	65	-9	1	3	-2	.965	4	S-66/3-2	-0.3
1953	StL-A	57	99	14	28	1	2	0	11	9	10	.283	.343	.333	82	-2	1	2	-1	.825	-1	3-18,2-15/S-6	-0.4
	Chi-A	5	8	1	1	0	0	0	0	1	1	.125	.222	.125	-4	-1	0	0	0	1.000	2	/2-3	0.1
	Yr	62	107	15	29	1	2	0	11	10	11	.271	.333	.318	75	-4	1	2	-1	.825	1	3-18,2-18/S-6	-0.3
1954	Bal-A	5	9	1	1	0	0	0	0	1	2	.111	.200	.111	-14	-1	0	0	0	1.000	0	/S-5	-0.1
Total	7	442	1087	148	265	28	9	0	74	113	105	.244	.317	.286	62	-58	11	12	-4	.949	19	S-172,2-151/3-28	-2.7

■ JOE BERRY

Berry, Joseph Howard Jr. "Nig" b: 12/31/1894, Philadelphia, Pa. d: 4/29/76, Philadelphia, Pa. BB/TR, 5'10.5", 159 lbs. Deb: 7/18/21 F

YEAR	TM/L	G	AB	R	H	2B	3B	HR	RBI	BB	SO	AVG	OBP	SLG	PRO+	BR/A	SB	CS	SBR	FA	FR	G/POS	TPR
1921	NY-N	9	6	0	2	0	1	0	2	1	1	.333	.429	.667	185	1	0	0	0	.875	0	/2-7	0.1
1922	NY-N	6	0	0	0	0	0	0	0	0	0	—	—	—	—	0	0	0	0	.000	0	R	0.0
Total	2	15	6	0	2	0	1	0	2	1	1	.333	.429	.667	185	1	0	0	0	.875	0	/2-7	0.1

■ JOE BERRY

Berry, Joseph Howard Sr. "Hodge" b: 9/10/1872, Wheeling, W.Va. d: 3/13/61, Allenwood, N.J. BB/TR, 5'9", 172 lbs. Deb: 9/4/02 F

YEAR	TM/L	G	AB	R	H	2B	3B	HR	RBI	BB	SO	AVG	OBP	SLG	PRO+	BR/A	SB	CS	SBR	FA	FR	G/POS	TPR
1902	Phi-N	1	4	0	1	0	0	0	1	1		.250	.400	.250	101	0	1			1.000	-1	/C-1	-0.1

■ SEAN BERRY

Berry, Sean Robert b: 3/22/66, Santa Monica, Cal. BR/TR, 5'11", 210 lbs. Deb: 9/17/90

YEAR	TM/L	G	AB	R	H	2B	3B	HR	RBI	BB	SO	AVG	OBP	SLG	PRO+	BR/A	SB	CS	SBR	FA	FR	G/POS	TPR
1990	KC-A	8	23	2	5	1	1	0	4	2	5	.217	.280	.348	76	-1	0	0	0	.944	1	/3-8	0.0
1991	KC-A	31	60	5	8	3	0	0	1	5	23	.133	.212	.183	10	-7	0	0	0	.970	8	3-30	0.1
1992	Mon-N	24	57	5	19	1	0	1	4	1	11	.333	.345	.404	112	1	2	1	0	.879	-3	3-20	-0.2
1993	Mon-N	122	299	50	78	15	2	14	49	41	70	.261	.354	.465	112	5	12	2	2	.936	5	3-96	1.3
1994	Mon-N	103	320	43	89	19	2	11	41	32	50	.278	.349	.453	106	3	14	0	4	.938	-2	*3-100	0.5
1995	Mon-N	103	314	38	100	22	1	14	55	25	53	.318	.372	.529	130	13	3	8	-4	.947	6	3-83/1-3	1.4

YEAR	TM/L	G	AB	R	H	2B	3B	HR	RBI	BB	SO	AVG	OBP	SLG	PRO+	BR/A	SB	CS	SBR	FA	FR	G/POS	TPR
1996	Hou-N	132	431	55	121	38	1	17	95	23	58	.281	.330	.492	123	12	12	6	0	.922	-5	*3-110	0.6
1997	*Hou-N	96	301	37	77	24	1	8	43	25	53	.256	.323	.422	97	-2	1	5	-3	.921	-2	3-85/D-3	-0.6
1998	*Hou-N	102	299	48	94	17	1	13	52	31	50	.314	.392	.508	134	16	3	1	0	.953	3	3-87/D-1	1.9
Total	9	721	2104	283	591	140	9	78	344	185	373	.281	.347	.467	114	39	47	23	0	.936	10	3-619/D-4,1-3	5.0
■ TOM BERRY Berry, Thomas Haney b: 12/31/1842, Chester, Pa. d: 6/6/15, Chester, Pa. 5'6", 140 lbs. Deb: 9/2/1871																							
1871	Ath-n	1	4	0	1	0	0	0	0	0	0	.250	.250	.250	45	-0	0	0	0	.000	-1	/O-1	0.0
■ DAMON BERRYHILL Berryhill, Damon Scott b: 12/3/63, South Laguna, Cal. BB/TR, 6', 205 lbs. Deb: 9/5/87																							
1987	Chi-N	12	28	2	5	1	0	0	1	3	5	.179	.258	.214	26	-3	0	1	-1	.909	-4	C-11	-0.7
1988	Chi-N	95	309	19	80	19	1	7	38	17	56	.259	.298	.395	93	-3	1	0	0	.982	-3	C-90	0.0
1989	Chi-N	91	334	37	86	13	0	5	41	16	54	.257	.295	.341	76	-11	1	0	0	.992	-12	C-89	-1.8
1990	Chi-N	17	53	6	10	4	0	1	9	5	14	.189	.259	.321	54	-3	0	0	0	.978	-3	C-15	-0.5
1991	Chi-N	62	159	13	30	7	0	5	14	11	41	.189	.246	.327	57	-9	1	2	-1	.967	-6	C-48	-1.5
	Atl-N	1	1	0	0	0	0	0	0	0	1	.000	.000	.000	-94	-0	0	0	0	1.000	0	/C-1	0.0
	Yr	63	160	13	30	7	0	5	14	11	42	.188	.244	.325	56	-10	1	2	-1	.967	-6	C-49	-1.5
1992	*Atl-N	101	307	21	70	16	1	10	43	17	67	.228	.271	.384	79	-9	0	2	-1	.998	-8	C-84	-1.5
1993	*Atl-N	115	335	24	82	18	2	8	43	21	64	.245	.293	.382	78	-11	0	0	0	.990	8	*C-105	0.2
1994	Bos-A	82	255	30	67	17	2	6	34	19	59	.263	.314	.416	82	-7	0	1	-1	.995	-1	C-67/D-6	-0.5
1995	Cin-N	34	82	6	15	3	0	2	11	10	19	.183	.272	.293	49	-6	0	0	0	.988	2	C-29/1-1	-0.3
1997	*SF-N	73	167	17	43	8	0	3	23	20	29	.257	.337	.359	84	-4	0	0	0	.990	1	C-51/1-1	0.0
Total	10	683	2030	175	488	106	6	47	257	139	409	.240	.291	.368	77	-67	3	6	-3	.988	-25	C-590/D-6,1-2	-6.6
■ HARRY BERTE Berte, Harry Thomas b: 5/10/1872, Covington, Ky. d: 5/6/52, Los Angeles, Cal. TR , Deb: 9/17/03																							
1903	StL-N	4	15	1	5	0	0	0	1	1		.333	.375	.333	106	0	0			.778	-4	/2-3,S-1	-0.4
■ DICK BERTELL Bertell, Richard George b: 11/21/35, Oak Park, Ill. BR/TR, 6'0.5", 200 lbs. Deb: 9/22/60																							
1960	Chi-N	5	15	0	2	0	0	0	2	3	1	.133	.278	.133	17	-2	0	0	0	1.000	-1	/C-5	-0.3
1961	Chi-N	92	267	20	73	7	1	2	33	15	33	.273	.312	.330	70	-11	0	0	0	.982	4	C-90	-0.4
1962	Chi-N	77	215	19	65	6	2	2	18	13	30	.302	.345	.377	90	-3	0	1	-1	.986	-13	C-76	-1.4
1963	Chi-N	100	322	15	75	7	2	2	14	24	41	.233	.286	.286	62	-15	0	2	-1	.988	16	C-99	0.4
1964	Chi-N	112	353	29	84	11	3	4	35	33	67	.238	.307	.320	74	-12	2	1	0	.981	-5	*C-110	-1.2
1965	Chi-N	34	84	6	18	2	0	0	7	11	10	.214	.305	.238	54	-5	0	0	0	.981	3	C-34	-0.1
	SF-N	22	48	1	9	1	0	0	3	7	5	.188	.291	.208	42	-3	0	0	0	.992	2	C-22	-0.1
	Yr	56	132	7	27	3	0	0	10	18	15	.205	.300	.227	50	-8	0	0	0	.986	5	C-56	-0.2
1967	Chi-N	2	6	1	1	0	1	0	0	0	1	.167	.167	.500	80	-0	0	0	0	1.000	0	/C-2	0.0
Total	7	444	1310	91	327	34	9	10	112	106	188	.250	.307	.312	70	-51	2	4	-2	.985	7	C-438	-3.1
■ HARRY BERTHRONG Berthrong, Henry W. b: 1/1/1844, Mumford, N.Y. d: 4/28/28, Chelsea, Mass. TR , 5'6.5", 140 lbs. Deb: 5/5/1871																							
1871	Oly-n	17	73	17	17	1	1	0	8	4	2	.233	.273	.274	61	-3	3	1	0	.806	-3	O-12/2-5,C-1	-0.4
■ RENO BERTOIA Bertoia, Reno Peter b: 1/8/35, St.Vito Udine, Italy BR/TR, 5'11.5", 185 lbs. Deb: 9/22/53																							
1953	Det-A	1	1	0	0	0	0	0	0	0	1	.000	.000	.000	-99	-0	0	0	0	.500	-0	/2-1	-0.1
1954	Det-A	54	37	13	6	2	0	1	2	5	9	.162	.262	.297	54	-2	1	0	0	.969	17	2-15/3-8,S-3	1.5
1955	Det-A	38	68	13	14	2	1	1	10	5	11	.206	.260	.309	54	-5	0	0	0	.923	7	3-14/2-6,S-5	0.2
1956	Det-A	22	66	7	12	2	0	1	5	6	12	.182	.260	.258	37	-6	0	0	0	.982	10	2-18/3-2	0.5
1957	Det-A	97	295	28	81	16	2	4	28	19	43	.275	.327	.383	91	-4	2	3	-1	.953	-19	3-83/S-7,2-2	-2.3
1958	Det-A	86	240	28	56	6	0	6	27	20	35	.233	.298	.333	68	-10	5	2	0	.950	4	3-68/S-5,O-1	-0.5
1959	Was-A	90	308	33	73	10	0	8	29	29	48	.237	.305	.347	79	-9	2	5	-2	.971	-11	2-71/3-5,S-1	-1.7
1960	Was-A	121	460	44	122	17	7	4	45	26	58	.265	.316	.359	83	-11	3	5	-2	.961	-0	*3-112,2-21	-1.4
1961	Min-A	35	104	17	22	2	0	1	8	20	12	.212	.339	.260	59	-5	0	0	0	.900	-5	3-32	-1.1
	KC-A	39	120	12	29	2	0	0	13	9	15	.242	.295	.258	48	-9	1	0	0	.942	5	3-29/2-6	-0.3
	Det-A	24	46	6	10	1	0	1	4	3	8	.217	.265	.304	50	-3	2	0	1	.931	0	3-13/2-7,S-1	-0.2
	Yr	98	270	35	61	5	0	2	25	32	35	.226	.308	.267	53	-17	3	0	1	.923	-1	3-74,2-13/S-1	-1.6
1962	Det-A	5	0	3	0	0	0	0	0	0	0	—	—	—	—	0	0	0	0	1.000	0	/2-1,S-1,3-1	0.0
Total	10	612	1745	204	425	60	10	27	171	142	252	.244	.306	.336	73	-65	16	15	-4	.949	7	3-367,2-148/S-23,O	-5.4
■ BOB BESCHER Bescher, Robert Henry b: 2/25/1884, London, Ohio d: 11/29/42, London, Ohio BB/TL, 6'1", 200 lbs. Deb: 9/5/08																							
1908	Cin-N	32	114	16	31	5	5	0	17	9		.272	.336	.404	140	5	10			1.000	4	O-32	0.8
1909	Cin-N	124	446	73	107	17	6	1	34	56		.240	.335	.312	102	3	**54**			.953	-0	*O-117	-0.3
1910	Cin-N	150	589	95	147	20	10	4	48	81	75	.250	.344	.338	104	4	**70**			.947	2	*O-150	-0.2
1911	Cin-N	153	599	106	165	32	10	1	45	102	78	.275	.385	.367	115	16	**81**			.954	-8	*O-153	0.0
1912	Cin-N	145	548	**120**	154	29	11	4	38	83	61	.281	.381	.396	116	15	**67**			.963	4	*O-143	1.1
1913	Cin-N	141	511	86	132	22	11	1	37	**94**	68	.258	.377	.350	109	10	38			.968	4	*O-138	0.8
1914	NY-N	135	512	82	138	23	4	6	35	45	48	.270	.336	.365	112	7	36			.960	9	*O-126	1.1
1915	StL-N	130	486	71	128	15	7	4	34	52	53	.263	.342	.348	109	6	27	19	-3	.971	-1	*O-129	-0.6
1916	StL-N	151	561	78	132	24	8	6	43	60	50	.235	.316	.339	102	2	39	12	5	.953	0	*O-151	-0.2
1917	StL-N	42	110	10	17	1	1	1	8	20	13	.155	.290	.209	56	-5	3			.984	-3	O-32	-1.1
1918	Cle-A	25	60	12	20	2	1	0	6	17	5	.333	.487	.400	153	5	3			.969	-0	O-17	0.4
Total	11	1228	4536	749	1171	190	74	28	345	619	451	.258	.353	.351	109	68	428	31		.960	9	*O-1188	1.8
■ BESTICK Bestick b: New York, N.Y. Deb: 6/10/1872																							
1872	Eck-n	4	14	0	4	0	0	0	1	0	0	.286	.286	.286	90	0	0	0	0	.773	-2	/C-4	-0.1
■ JIM BESWICK Beswick, James William b: 2/12/58, Wilkinsburg, Pa. BB/TR, 6'1", 180 lbs. Deb: 8/9/78																							
1978	SD-N	17	20	2	1	0	0	0	0	1	7	.050	.095	.050	-63	-4	0	0	0	1.000	-1	/O-6	-0.6
■ FRANK BETCHER Betcher, Franklin Lyle (b: Franklin Lyle Bettger) b: 2/15/1888, Philadelphia, Pa. d: 11/27/81, Wynnewood, Pa. BB/TR, 5'11", 173 lbs. Deb: 5/21/10																							
1910	StL-N	35	89	7	18	2	0	0	6	7	14	.202	.276	.225	48	-6	1			.928	0	S-12/3-7,2-6,O-2	-0.5
■ BILL BETHEA Bethea, William Lamar "Spot" b: 1/1/42, Houston, Tex. BR/TR, 6', 175 lbs. Deb: 9/13/64																							
1964	Min-A	10	30	4	5	1	0	0	2	4	4	.167	.265	.200	31	-3	0	0	0	1.000	-1	/2-7,S-3	-0.3
■ LARRY BETTENCOURT Bettencourt, Lawrence Joseph b: 9/22/05, Newark, Cal. d: 9/15/78, New Orleans, La. BR/TR, 5'11", 195 lbs. Deb: 6/2/28																							
1928	StL-A	67	159	30	45	9	4	4	24	22	19	.283	.377	.465	117	4	2	1	0	.946	-11	3-41/O-2,C-1	-0.4
1931	StL-A	74	206	27	53	9	2	3	26	31	35	.257	.357	.364	87	-3	4	3	1	.963	-2	O-58	-0.9
1932	StL-A	27	30	4	4	1	0	1	3	7	6	.133	.297	.267	45	-2	1	0	0	1.000	-0	/O-4,3-2	-0.2
Total	3	168	395	61	102	19	6	8	53	60	60	.258	.360	.397	95	-2	7	4	-0	.966	-13	/O-64,3-43,C-1	-1.5
■ BRUNO BETZEL Betzel, Christian Frederick Albert John Henry David b: 12/6/1894, Chattanooga, Ohio d: 2/7/65, W.Hollywood, Fla. BR/TR, 5'9", 158 lbs. Deb: 9/3/14																							
1914	StL-N	7	9	2	0	0	0	0	0	1	1	.000	.100	.000	-70	-2	0			1.000	2	/2-4,3-1	0.0
1915	StL-N	117	367	42	92	12	4	0	27	18	48	.251	.291	.305	80	-9	10	13	-5	.937	5	*3-105/2-3,S-2	-0.5
1916	StL-N	142	510	49	119	15	11	1	37	39	77	.233	.288	.312	85	-10	22	16	-3	.960	28	*2-113,3-33/O-7	2.3
1917	StL-N	106	328	24	71	4	3	1	17	20	47	.216	.266	.256	62	-15	9			.962	12	2-75,O-23/3-4	-0.1
1918	StL-N	76	230	18	51	6	7	0	13	12	16	.222	.260	.309	76	-7	8			.914	-2	3-34,O-21,2-10	-1.0
Total	5	448	1444	135	333	37	25	2	94	90	189	.231	.278	.295	76	-42	49	29		.956	46	2-205,3-177/O-51,S	0.7
■ KURT BEVACQUA Bevacqua, Kurt Anthony b: 1/23/47, Miami Beach, Fla. BR/TR, 6'1", 185 lbs. Deb: 6/22/71																							
1971	Cle-A	55	137	9	28	3	1	3	13	4	28	.204	.227	.307	46	-10	0	0	0	.971	-9	2-36/O-5,3-3,S-2	-1.8
1972	Cle-A	19	35	2	4	0	0	1	1	3	10	.114	.184	.200	14	-4	0	0	0	.900	-1	O-11/3-1	-0.6
1973	KC-A	99	276	39	71	8	3	2	40	25	42	.257	.321	.330	78	-8	2	3	-1	.935	-11	3-40,2-16,D-16,O/1	-2.1

YEAR	TM/L	G	AB	R	H	2B	3B	HR	RBI	BB	SO	AVG	OBP	SLG	PRO+	BR/A	SB	CS	SBR	FA	FR	G/POS	TPR
1974	Pit-N	18	35	1	4	1	0	0	0	2	10	.114	.162	.143	-15	-5	0	0	0	.955	-1	/3-8,O-1	-0.6
	KC-A	39	90	10	19	0	0	0	3	9	20	.211	.290	.211	43	-6	1	1	-0	.987	-4	1-14,3-13/2-7,SD	-1.1
1975	Mil-A	104	258	30	59	14	0	2	24	26	45	.229	.302	.306	72	-9	3	4	-2	.948	1	3-60,2-32/S-5,1D	-0.8
1976	Mil-A	12	7	3	1	0	0	0	0	0	0	.143	.143	.143	-17	-1	0	0	0	1.000	2	/2-2,D-3	0.1
1977	Tex-A	39	96	13	32	7	2	5	28	6	13	.333	.373	.604	159	7	0	1	-1	1.000	-7	O-14,3-11/1-5,2D	0.0
1978	Tex-A	90	248	21	55	12	0	6	30	18	31	.222	.274	.343	72	-10	1	2	-1	.877	-4	3-49,D-16,2-13,/1-1	-1.6
1979	SD-N	114	297	23	75	12	4	1	34	38	25	.253	.337	.330	88	-4	2	5	-2	.954	-5	3-64,2-16/1-8,O-8	-1.2
1980	SD-N	62	71	4	19	6	1	0	12	6	1	.268	.325	.380	102	0	1	1	-0	.929	-3	3-13/O-4,2-2,1-1	-0.4
	Pit-N	22	43	1	7	1	0	0	4	6	7	.163	.280	.186	32	-4	0	0	0	.958	0	/3-9,1-2	-0.4
	Yr	84	114	5	26	7	1	0	16	12	8	.228	.307	.307	75	-4	1	1	-0	.947	-3	3-22/O-4,1-3,2-2	-0.8
1981	Pit-N	29	27	2	7	1	0	1	4	4	6	.259	.355	.407	112	0	0	0	0	.941	1	/2-4,3-2	0.2
1982	SD-N	64	123	15	31	9	0	0	24	17	22	.252	.343	.325	93	-1	2	0	1	.989	-3	1-30/O-3,3-1	-0.4
1983	SD-N	74	156	17	38	7	0	2	24	18	33	.244	.322	.327	83	-3	0	3	-2	.995	-1	1-27,3-12,O-12	-0.8
1984	*SD-N	59	80	7	16	3	0	1	9	14	19	.200	.326	.275	71	-3	0	0	0	1.000	-2	1-20,3-10/O-3	-0.5
1985	SD-N	71	138	17	33	6	0	3	25	25	17	.239	.356	.348	99	1	0	0	0	.946	-2	3-33/1-9,O-1	-0.2
Total	15	970	2117	214	499	90	11	27	275	221	329	.236	.309	.327	78	-59	12	20	-8	.938	-46	3-329,2-133,1/ODS	-12.2

■ **HAL BEVAN** Bevan, Harold Joseph b: 11/15/30, New Orleans, La. d: 10/5/68, New Orleans, La. BR/TR, 6′2″, 198 lbs. Deb: 4/24/52

YEAR	TM/L	G	AB	R	H	2B	3B	HR	RBI	BB	SO	AVG	OBP	SLG	PRO+	BR/A	SB	CS	SBR	FA	FR	G/POS	TPR
1952	Bos-A	1	1	0	0	0	0	0	0	0	0	.000	.000	.000	-93	-0	0	0	0	.000	0	/3-1	0.0
	Phi-A	8	17	1	6	0	0	0	4	0	1	.353	.353	.353	91	-0	2	0	1	1.000	1	/3-6	0.1
	Yr	9	18	1	6	0	0	0	4	0	1	.333	.333	.333	81	-0	2	0	1	1.000	1	/3-7	0.1
1955	KC-A	3	3	0	0	0	0	0	0	0	0	.000	.000	.000	-99	-1	0	0	0	1.000	0	/3-1	-0.1
1961	Cin-N	3	3	1	1	0	0	1	1	0	2	.333	.333	1.333	311	1	0	0	0	.000	0	H	0.1
Total	3	15	24	2	7	0	0	1	5	0	3	.292	.292	.417	89	-0	2	0	1	1.000	1	/3-8	0.1

■ **MONTE BEVILLE** Beville, Henry Monte b: 2/24/1875, Dublin, Ind. d: 1/24/55, Grand Rapids, Mich BL/TR, 5′11″, 180 lbs. Deb: 4/24/03

YEAR	TM/L	G	AB	R	H	2B	3B	HR	RBI	BB	SO	AVG	OBP	SLG	PRO+	BR/A	SB	CS	SBR	FA	FR	G/POS	TPR
1903	NY-A	82	258	23	50	14	1	0	29	16		.194	.252	.256	49	-16	4			.960	-11	C-75/1-3	-2.0
1904	NY-A	9	22	2	6	2	0	0	2	2		.273	.333	.364	115	0	0			.906	-2	/1-4,C-3	-0.1
	Det-A	54	174	14	36	5	1	0	13	8		.207	.250	.247	59	-8	2			.957	-3	C-30,1-24	-1.0
	Yr	63	196	16	42	7	1	0	15	10		.214	.260	.260	66	-8	2			.950	-5	C-33,1-28	-1.1
Total	2	145	454	39	92	21	2	0	44	26		.203	.255	.258	56	-23	6			.957	-16	C-108/1-31	-3.1

■ **BUDDY BIANCALANA** Biancalana, Roland Americo b: 2/2/60, Larkspur, Cal. BB/TR, 5′11″, 160 lbs. Deb: 9/12/82

YEAR	TM/L	G	AB	R	H	2B	3B	HR	RBI	BB	SO	AVG	OBP	SLG	PRO+	BR/A	SB	CS	SBR	FA	FR	G/POS	TPR
1982	KC-A	3	2	0	1	0	1	0	0	1	0	.500	.667	1.500	474	1	0	0	0	1.000	3	/S-3	0.3
1983	KC-A	6	15	2	3	0	0	0	0	0	7	.200	.200	.200	10	-2	1	0	0	.914	4	/S-6	0.3
1984	*KC-A	66	134	18	26	6	1	2	9	6	44	.194	.229	.299	44	-10	1	2	-1	.946	6	S-33,2-29/D-1	-0.2
1985	*KC-A	81	138	21	26	5	1	1	6	17	34	.188	.277	.261	48	-10	1	4	-2	.961	11	S-74/2-4,D-2	0.3
1986	KC-A	100	190	24	46	4	4	2	8	15	50	.242	.298	.337	71	-8	5	1	1	.946	2	S-89,2-12	0.1
1987	KC-A	37	47	4	10	1	0	1	7	1	10	.213	.229	.298	37	-4	0	0	0	.886	4	S-22,2-12/D-1	0.1
	Hou-N	18	24	1	1	0	0	0	0	1	12	.042	.080	.042	-69	-6	0	0	0	.889	-1	S-16/2-3	-0.6
Total	6	311	550	70	113	16	7	6	30	41	157	.205	.261	.293	50	-38	8	7	-2	.945	28	S-243/2-60,D-4	0.3

■ **TOMMY BIANCO** Bianco, Thomas Anthony b: 12/16/52, Rockville Centre, N.Y. BB/TR, 5′11″, 190 lbs. Deb: 5/28/75

YEAR	TM/L	G	AB	R	H	2B	3B	HR	RBI	BB	SO	AVG	OBP	SLG	PRO+	BR/A	SB	CS	SBR	FA	FR	G/POS	TPR
1975	Mil-A	18	34	6	6	1	0	0	0	3	7	.176	.263	.206	34	-3	0	0	0	.941	-1	/3-7,1-5,D-2	-0.4

■ **HANK BIASATTI** Biasatti, Henry Arcado b: 1/14/22, Beano, Italy d: 4/20/96, Dearborn, Mich. BL/TL, 5′11″, 175 lbs. Deb: 4/23/49

YEAR	TM/L	G	AB	R	H	2B	3B	HR	RBI	BB	SO	AVG	OBP	SLG	PRO+	BR/A	SB	CS	SBR	FA	FR	G/POS	TPR
1949	Phi-A	21	24	6	2	2	0	0	2	8	5	.083	.313	.167	30	-2	0	0	0	.979	-1	/1-8	-0.3

■ **DANTE BICHETTE** Bichette, Alphonse Dante b: 11/18/63, W.Palm Beach, Fla. BR/TR, 6′3″, 225 lbs. Deb: 9/5/88

YEAR	TM/L	G	AB	R	H	2B	3B	HR	RBI	BB	SO	AVG	OBP	SLG	PRO+	BR/A	SB	CS	SBR	FA	FR	G/POS	TPR
1988	Cal-A	21	46	1	12	2	0	0	8	0	7	.261	.261	.304	59	-3	0	0	0	.979	-2	O-21	-0.5
1989	Cal-A	48	138	13	29	7	0	3	15	6	24	.210	.243	.326	60	-8	3	0	1	.990	6	O-40/D-1	-0.2
1990	Cal-A	109	349	40	89	15	1	15	53	16	79	.255	.293	.433	103	-0	5	2	0	.965	-4	*O-105	-0.7
1991	Mil-A	134	445	53	106	18	3	15	59	22	107	.238	.276	.393	85	-11	14	8	-1	.976	11	*O-127/3-1	-0.4
1992	Mil-A	112	387	37	111	27	2	5	41	16	74	.287	.320	.406	104	1	18	7	1	.990	-2	*O-101/D-4	-0.1
1993	Col-N	141	538	93	167	43	5	21	89	28	99	.310	.353	.526	113	8	14	8	-1	.973	13	*O-137	1.7
1994	Col-N★	116	484	74	147	33	2	27	95	19	70	.304	.335	.548	107	3	21	8	2	.991	4	*O-116	0.6
1995	*Col-N★	139	579	102	**197**	38	2	**40**	**128**	22	96	.340	.369	**.620**	120	12	13	9	-2	.986	-6	*O-136	0.0
1996	Col-N★	159	633	114	198	39	3	31	141	45	105	.313	.364	.531	107	3	31	12	2	.967	-7	*O-156	-0.6
1997	Col-N	151	561	81	173	31	2	26	118	30	90	.308	.347	.510	98	-4	6	5	-1	.987	-6	*O-139/D-5	-1.4
1998	Col-N★	161	662	97	**219**	48	2	22	122	28	76	.331	.359	.509	102	0	14	4	2	.965	11	*O-156/D-1	1.2
Total	11	1291	4822	705	1448	301	22	205	869	232	827	.300	.337	.499	104	0	139	63	4	.977	17	*O-1234/D-11,3-1	-0.4

■ **OSCAR BIELASKI** Bielaski, Oscar b: 3/21/1847, Washington, D.C. d: 11/8/11, Washington, D.C. BR/TR, 5′10.5″, 170 lbs. Deb: 4/24/1872

YEAR	TM/L	G	AB	R	H	2B	3B	HR	RBI	BB	SO	AVG	OBP	SLG	PRO+	BR/A	SB	CS	SBR	FA	FR	G/POS	TPR
1872	Nat-n	10	46	13	9	0	0	0	3	0	0	.196	.196	.196	18	-5	0	0	0	.737	-1	O-10	-0.4
1873	Was-n	38	173	35	49	3	2	0	23	4	5	.283	.299	.324	88	-2	0	1	-1	.772	4	*O-38	0.2
1874	Bal-n	43	187	24	45	0	0	0	8	2	4	.241	.249	.241	58	-8	3	1	0	.806	6	*O-43/1-1	0.0
1875	Chi-n	51	201	21	48	1	0	0	11	2	5	.239	.246	.244	70	-6	5	5	-2	.748	0	*O-51	-0.6
1876	Chi-N	32	139	24	29	3	0	0	10	2	3	.209	.220	.230	45	-9				.763	-2	O-32	-1.0
Total	4 n	142	607	93	151	4	2	0	45	8	14	.249	.259	.262	67	-21	8	7	-2	.772	10	O-142/1-1	-0.8

■ **LOU BIERBAUER** Bierbauer, Louis W. b: 9/28/1865, Erie, Pa. d: 1/31/26, Erie, Pa. BL/TR, 5′8″, 140 lbs. Deb: 4/17/1886

YEAR	TM/L	G	AB	R	H	2B	3B	HR	RBI	BB	SO	AVG	OBP	SLG	PRO+	BR/A	SB	CS	SBR	FA	FR	G/POS	TPR
1886	Phi-a	137	522	56	118	17	5	2	47	21		.226	.256	.289	70	-19	19			.910	-3	*2-133/C-4,S-2,P-2	-1.4
1887	Phi-a	126	530	74	144	19	7	1	82	13		.272	.289	.340	75	-19	40			.921	-8	*2-126/P-1	-2.0
1888	Phi-a	134	535	83	143	20	9	0	80	25		.267	.301	.338	105	2	34			.916	22	*2-121,3-13/P-1	2.7
1889	Phi-a	130	549	80	167	27	7	7	105	29	30	.304	.344	.417	118	11	17			.941	37	*2-130/C-1	4.5
1890	Bro-P	133	589	128	180	31	11	7	99	40	15	.306	.350	.431	102	-3	16			.931	25	*2-133	2.4
1891	Pit-N	121	500	60	103	13	6	1	47	28	19	.206	.252	.262	51	-32	12			.929	-2	*2-121	-2.5
1892	Pit-N	152	649	81	153	20	9	8	65	25	29	.236	.264	.331	79	-19	11			.950	32	*2-152	1.4
1893	Pit-N	128	528	84	150	19	11	4	94	36	12	.284	.335	.384	93	-7	11			**.959**	16	*2-128	0.9
1894	Pit-N	130	525	86	159	19	13	3	107	26	9	.303	.337	.406	79	-19	19			.938	9	*2-130	-0.3
1895	Pit-N	117	466	53	120	13	11	0	69	19	8	.258	.290	.333	64	-26	18			.946	14	*2-117	-0.5
1896	Pit-N	59	258	33	74	10	6	0	39	5	7	.287	.300	.372	80	-9	7			.966	12	2-59	0.6
1897	StL-N	12	46	1	10	0	0	0	1	0		.217	.217	.217	15	-6	2			.921	-2	2-12	-0.7
1898	StL-N	4	9	0	0	0	0	0	0	1		.000	.100	.000	-69	-2	0			.429	-1	/2-2,S-1,3-1	-0.3
Total	13	1383	5706	819	1521	208	95	33	835	268	129	.267	.301	.354	83	-148	206			.935	150	*2-1364/3-14,CPS	4.8

■ **CHARLIE BIERMAN** Bierman, Charles S. b: 1845, Hoboken, N.J. d: 8/4/1879, Hoboken, N.J. 6′, 180 lbs. Deb: 6/21/1871

YEAR	TM/L	G	AB	R	H	2B	3B	HR	RBI	BB	SO	AVG	OBP	SLG	PRO+	BR/A	SB	CS	SBR	FA	FR	G/POS	TPR
1871	Kek-n	1	2	0	0	0	0	0	0	1	0	.000	.333	.000	6	-0	0	0	0	.818	-0	/1-1	0.0

■ **STEVE BIESER** Bieser, Steven Ray b: 8/4/67, Perryville, Mo. BL/TR, 5′10″, 170 lbs. Deb: 4/1/97

YEAR	TM/L	G	AB	R	H	2B	3B	HR	RBI	BB	SO	AVG	OBP	SLG	PRO+	BR/A	SB	CS	SBR	FA	FR	G/POS	TPR
1997	NY-N	47	69	16	17	3	0	0	4	7	20	.246	.350	.290	72	-2	2	3	-1	1.000	-2	O-21/C-2	-0.5
1998	Pit-N	13	11	2	3	1	0	0	1	2	2	.273	.385	.364	94	-0	0	0	0	.000	-0	/O-1	0.0
Total	2	60	80	18	20	4	0	0	5	9	22	.250	.355	.300	76	-2	2	3	-1	1.000	-2	/O-22,C-2	-0.5

■ **CARSON BIGBEE** Bigbee, Carson Lee "Skeeter" b: 3/31/1895, Waterloo, Ore. d: 10/17/64, Portland, Ore. BL/TR, 5′9″, 157 lbs. Deb: 8/25/16 F

YEAR	TM/L	G	AB	R	H	2B	3B	HR	RBI	BB	SO	AVG	OBP	SLG	PRO+	BR/A	SB	CS	SBR	FA	FR	G/POS	TPR
1916	Pit-N	43	164	17	41	3	6	0	3	7	14	.250	.285	.341	91	-2	8			.946	-5	2-23,O-19/3-1	-0.8
1917	Pit-N	133	469	46	112	11	6	0	21	37	16	.239	.301	.288	79	-11	19			.961	-3	*O-107,2-16/S-2	-2.2
1918	Pit-N	92	310	47	79	11	3	1	19	42	10	.255	.344	.319	99	1	19			.958	0	O-92	-0.4
1919	Pit-N	125	478	61	132	11	4	2	27	37	26	.276	.332	.328	95	-2	31			.971	18	*O-124	0.8
1920	Pit-N	137	550	78	154	19	15	4	32	45	28	.280	.341	.391	106	5	31	15	0	.971	6	*O-133	0.1
1921	Pit-N	147	632	100	204	23	17	3	42	41	19	.323	.364	.427	106	6	21	20	-6	.977	16	*O-146	0.5
1922	Pit-N	150	614	113	215	29	15	5	99	56	13	.350	.405	.471	124	23	24	15	-2	.956	17	*O-150	2.5

YEAR	TM/L	G	AB	R	H	2B	3B	HR	RBI	BB	SO	AVG	OBP	SLG	PRO+	BR/A	SB	CS	SBR	FA	FR	G/POS	TPR
1923	Pit-N	123	499	79	149	18	7	0	54	43	15	.299	.355	.363	88	-8	10	9	-2	.990	10	*O-122	-0.8
1924	Pit-N	89	282	42	74	4	1	0	15	26	12	.262	.331	.284	65	-13	15	7	0	.943	0	O-75	-1.7
1925	*Pit-N	66	126	31	30	7	0	0	8	7	8	.238	.278	.294	43	-11	2	2	-1	.942	-6	O-42	-1.8
1926	Pit-N	42	68	15	15	3	1	2	4	3	0	.221	.264	.382	69	-3	2			.966	-3	O-21	-0.7
Total	11	1147	4192	629	1205	139	75	17	324	344	161	.287	.345	.369	96	-15	182	68		.966	50	*O-1031/2-39,S-2,3	-4.5

■ LYLE BIGBEE

Bigbee, Lyle Randolph "Al" b: 8/22/1893, Sweet Home, Ore. d: 8/5/42, Portland, Ore. BL/TR, 6', 180 lbs. Deb: 4/15/20 F

YEAR	TM/L	G	AB	R	H	2B	3B	HR	RBI	BB	SO	AVG	OBP	SLG	PRO+	BR/A	SB	CS	SBR	FA	FR	G/POS	TPR
1920	Phi-A	38	75	5	14	2	0	1	8	9	12	.187	.282	.253	42	-6	1	0	0	.857	-2	O-13,P-12	-0.7
1921	Pit-N	5	2	0	0	0	0	0	0	0	1	.000	.000	.000	-97	-1	0	0	0	1.000	-0	/P-5	0.0
Total	2	43	77	5	14	2	0	1	8	9	13	.182	.276	.247	39	-7	1	0	0	1.000	-2	/P-17,O-13	-0.7

■ ELLIOT BIGELOW

Bigelow, Elliot Allardice "Babe" or "Gilly"
b: 10/13/1897, Tarpon Springs, Fla. d: 8/10/33, Tampa, Fla. BL/TL, 5'11", 185 lbs. Deb: 4/18/29

YEAR	TM/L	G	AB	R	H	2B	3B	HR	RBI	BB	SO	AVG	OBP	SLG	PRO+	BR/A	SB	CS	SBR	FA	FR	G/POS	TPR
1929	Bos-A	100	211	23	60	16	0	1	26	23	18	.284	.357	.374	91	-2	1	4	-2	.944	-10	O-59	-1.7

■ CRAIG BIGGIO

Biggio, Craig Alan b: 12/14/65, Smithtown, N.Y. BR/TR, 5'11", 180 lbs. Deb: 6/26/88

YEAR	TM/L	G	AB	R	H	2B	3B	HR	RBI	BB	SO	AVG	OBP	SLG	PRO+	BR/A	SB	CS	SBR	FA	FR	G/POS	TPR
1988	Hou-N	50	123	14	26	6	1	3	5	7	29	.211	.254	.350	74	-5	6	1	1	.991	16	C-50	1.6
1989	Hou-N	134	443	64	114	21	2	13	60	49	64	.257	.339	.402	115	9	21	3	5	.990	-6	*C-125/O-5	1.5
1990	Hou-N	150	555	53	153	24	2	4	42	53	79	.276	.342	.348	93	-4	25	11	1	.985	-7	*C-113,O-50	-0.5
1991	Hou-N★	149	546	79	161	23	4	4	46	53	71	.295	.359	.374	113	10	19	6	2	.990	-14	*C-139/2-3,O-2	0.6
1992	Hou-N★	162	613	96	170	32	3	6	39	94	95	.277	.380	.369	118	18	38	15	2	.984	-21	*2-161	0.4
1993	Hou-N	155	610	98	175	41	5	21	64	77	93	.287	.376	.474	130	27	15	17	-6	.982	-2	*2-155	2.4
1994	Hou-N★	114	437	88	139	**44**	5	6	56	62	58	.318	.412	.483	139	28	**39**	4	**9**	**.988**	-5	*2-113	3.6
1995	Hou-N★	141	553	**123**	167	30	2	22	77	80	85	.302	.411	.483	145	39	33	8	5	.986	-4	*2-141	4.8
1996	Hou-N★	162	605	113	174	24	4	15	75	75	72	.288	.390	.415	122	23	25	7	3	.988	-1	*2-162	3.4
1997	*Hou-N★	162	619	**146**	191	37	8	22	81	84	107	.309	.419	.501	145	45	47	10	8	.979	**24**	*2-160/D-1	**8.3**
1998	*Hou-N★	160	646	123	210	**51**	2	20	88	64	113	.325	.405	.503	137	37	50	8	10	.980	-3	*2-159/D-1	5.4
Total	11	1539	5750	997	1680	333	38	136	633	698	866	.292	.382	.434	126	227	318	90	41	.984	-24	*2-1054,C-427/OD	31.5

■ PETE BIGLER

Bigler, Ivan Edward b: 12/13/1892, Bradford, Ohio d: 4/1/75, Coldwater, Mich. BR/TR, 5'9", 150 lbs. Deb: 5/6/17

YEAR	TM/L	G	AB	R	H	2B	3B	HR	RBI	BB	SO	AVG	OBP	SLG	PRO+	BR/A	SB	CS	SBR	FA	FR	G/POS	TPR
1917	StL-A	1	0	0	0	0	0	0	0	0	0	—	—	—	—	0	0			.000	0	/R	0.0

■ GEORGE BIGNELL

Bignell, George William b: 7/18/1858, Taunton, Mass. d: 1/16/25, Providence, R.I. 5'9", 160 lbs. Deb: 9/27/1884

YEAR	TM/L	G	AB	R	H	2B	3B	HR	RBI	BB	SO	AVG	OBP	SLG	PRO+	BR/A	SB	CS	SBR	FA	FR	G/POS	TPR
1884	Mil-U	4	9	4	2	0	0	0		1		.222	.300	.222	112	-0				.951	3	/C-4	0.3

■ LARRY BIITTNER

Biittner, Lawrence David b: 7/27/45, Pocahontas, Ia. BL/TL, 6'2", 205 lbs. Deb: 7/17/70

YEAR	TM/L	G	AB	R	H	2B	3B	HR	RBI	BB	SO	AVG	OBP	SLG	PRO+	BR/A	SB	CS	SBR	FA	FR	G/POS	TPR
1970	Was-A	2	2	0	0	0	0	0	0	0	0	.000	.000	.000	-99	-1	0	0	0	.000	0	H	-0.1
1971	Was-A	66	171	12	44	4	1	0	16	16	20	.257	.324	.292	80	-4	1	0	0	.940	-0	O-41/1-3	-0.7
1972	Tex-A	137	382	34	99	18	1	3	31	29	37	.259	.315	.335	98	-2	1	3	-2	.991	-1	1-65,O-65	-1.2
1973	Tex-A	83	258	19	65	8	2	1	12	20	21	.252	.308	.310	78	-8	1	0	0	.980	1	O-57,1-20/D-3	-1.0
1974	Mon-N	18	26	2	7	1	0	0	3	0	2	.269	.269	.308	58	-1	0	0	0	1.000	1	/O-4	-0.1
1975	Mon-N	121	346	34	109	13	5	3	28	34	33	.315	.376	.408	113	6	2	1	0	.972	0	O-93	0.3
1976	Mon-N	11	32	2	6	1	0	0	1	0	3	.188	.188	.219	14	-4	0	0	0	.947	1	/O-7	-0.3
	Chi-N	78	192	21	47	13	1	0	17	10	6	.245	.286	.323	66	-9	0	2	-1	.985	4	1-33,O-24	-0.9
	Yr	89	224	23	53	14	1	0	18	10	9	.237	.272	.308	59	-12	0	2	-1	.985	5	1-33,O-31	-1.2
1977	Chi-N	138	493	74	147	28	1	12	62	35	36	.298	.346	.432	97	-3	2	1	0	.987	6	1-80,O-52/P-1	-0.3
1978	Chi-N	120	343	32	88	15	1	4	50	23	37	.257	.305	.341	72	-13	0	1	-1	.987	5	1-62,O-29	-1.3
1979	Chi-N	111	272	35	79	13	3	3	50	21	23	.290	.341	.393	91	-3	1	1	-0	.925	-6	O-44,1-32	-1.3
1980	Chi-N	127	273	21	68	12	2	1	34	18	33	.249	.300	.319	68	-12	1	3	-2	.996	1	1-41,O-38	-1.6
1981	Cin-N	42	61	1	13	4	0	0	8	4	4	.213	.262	.279	52	-4	0	0	0	1.000	1	/1-8,O-3	-0.3
1982	Cin-N	97	184	18	57	9	2	2	24	17	16	.310	.374	.413	118	5	1	0	0	.978	-2	O-31,1-15	0.2
1983	Tex-A	66	116	5	32	5	1	0	18	9	16	.276	.328	.336	85	-2	0	0	0	.987	2	1-22/O-2,D-9	-0.1
Total	14	1217	3151	310	861	144	20	29	354	236	287	.273	.326	.359	87	-53	10	12	-4	.970	14	O-490,1-381/D-12,P	-8.7

■ DANN BILARDELLO

Bilardello, Dann James b: 5/26/59, Santa Cruz, Cal. BR/TR, 6', 190 lbs. Deb: 4/11/83

YEAR	TM/L	G	AB	R	H	2B	3B	HR	RBI	BB	SO	AVG	OBP	SLG	PRO+	BR/A	SB	CS	SBR	FA	FR	G/POS	TPR
1983	Cin-N	109	298	27	71	18	0	9	38	15	49	.238	.277	.389	80	-9	2	1	0	.991	-1	*C-105	-0.7
1984	Cin-N	68	182	16	38	7	0	2	10	19	34	.209	.287	.280	57	-10	0	1	-1	.992	1	C-68	-0.7
1985	Cin-N	42	102	6	17	0	0	1	9	4	15	.167	.206	.196	12	-12	0	0	0	.986	8	C-42	-0.2
1986	Mon-N	79	191	12	37	5	0	4	17	14	32	.194	.249	.283	47	-14	1	0	0	.982	2	C-77	-0.9
1989	Pit-N	33	80	11	18	6	0	2	8	2	18	.225	.244	.375	77	-3	1	2	-1	.970	5	C-33	0.3
1990	Pit-N	19	37	1	2	0	0	0	3	4	10	.054	.146	.054	-44	-7	0	0	0	1.000	3	C-19	-0.4
1991	SD-N	15	26	4	7	2	1	0	5	3	4	.269	.345	.423	111	0	0	0	0	1.000	5	C-13	0.6
1992	SD-N	17	33	2	4	1	0	0	1	4	8	.121	.216	.152	6	-4	0	0	0	1.000	5	C-14	0.2
Total	8	382	949	79	194	39	1	18	91	65	170	.204	.258	.305	55	-59	4	4	-1	.988	28	C-371	-1.8

■ STEVE BILKO

Bilko, Stephen Thomas b: 11/13/28, Nanticoke, Pa. d: 3/7/78, Wilkes-Barre, Pa. BR/TR, 6'1", 230 lbs. Deb: 9/22/49

YEAR	TM/L	G	AB	R	H	2B	3B	HR	RBI	BB	SO	AVG	OBP	SLG	PRO+	BR/A	SB	CS	SBR	FA	FR	G/POS	TPR
1949	StL-N	6	17	3	5	2	0	0	2	5	6	.294	.455	.412	128	1	0			1.000	0	/1-5	0.1
1950	StL-N	10	33	1	6	1	0	0	2	4	10	.182	.270	.212	27	-3	0			.989	0	/1-9	-0.3
1951	StL-N	21	72	5	16	4	0	2	12	9	10	.222	.309	.361	79	-2	0	0	0	.984	-0	1-19	-0.3
1952	StL-N	20	72	7	19	6	1	1	6	4	15	.264	.303	.417	97	-1	0	0	0	.995	4	1-20	0.3
1953	StL-N	154	570	72	143	23	3	21	84	70	125	.251	.334	.412	93	-6	0	1	-1	.991	7	*1-154	-0.5
1954	StL-N	8	14	1	2	0	0	0	1	3	1	.143	.294	.143	18	-2	0	0	0	1.000	2	/1-6	0.0
	Chi-N	47	92	11	22	8	1	4	12	11	24	.239	.320	.478	104	0	0	0	0	1.000	6	1-22	0.5
	Yr	55	106	12	24	8	1	4	13	14	25	.226	.317	.434	92	-1	0	0	0	1.000	8	1-28	0.5
1958	Cin-N	31	87	12	23	4	2	4	17	10	20	.264	.340	.494	111	1	0	0	0	.995	-1	1-21	-0.1
	LA-N	47	101	13	21	1	2	7	18	8	37	.208	.266	.465	86	-3	0	0	0	.995	2	1-25	-0.2
	Yr	78	188	25	44	5	4	11	35	18	57	.234	.301	.479	98	-1	0	0	0	.995	0	1-46	-0.3
1960	Det-A	78	222	20	46	11	2	9	25	27	31	.207	.293	.396	82	-6	0	1	-1	.991	0	1-62	-1.1
1961	LA-A	114	294	49	82	16	1	20	59	58	81	.279	.398	.544	134	14	1	1	-0	.989	3	1-86/O-3	1.0
1962	LA-A	64	164	26	47	9	1	8	38	25	35	.287	.387	.500	141	10	1	1	-0	.995	-1	1-50	0.6
Total	10	600	1738	220	432	85	13	76	276	234	395	.249	.339	.444	103	5	2	4		.992	22	1-479/O-3	0.0

■ JOSH BILLINGS

Billings, John Augustus b: 11/30/1892, Grantville, Kan. d: 12/30/81, Santa Monica, Cal. BR/TR, 5'11", 165 lbs. Deb: 9/9/13

YEAR	TM/L	G	AB	R	H	2B	3B	HR	RBI	BB	SO	AVG	OBP	SLG	PRO+	BR/A	SB	CS	SBR	FA	FR	G/POS	TPR
1913	Cle-A	1	3	0	0	0	0	0	0	0	3	.000	.000	.000	-97	-1	0			.857	0	/C-1	0.0
1914	Cle-A	11	8	2	2	1	0	0	0	1	1	.250	.333	.375	109	0	1			.813	2	/C-3	0.3
1915	Cle-A	8	21	2	4	1	0	0	0	0	6	.190	.190	.238	28	-2	1			1.000	-1	/C-7,O-1	-0.3
1916	Cle-A	22	31	2	5	0	0	0	1	2	11	.161	.212	.161	12	-3	0			.981	3	C-12	0.0
1917	Cle-A	66	129	8	23	3	2	0	9	8	21	.178	.243	.233	42	-9	2			.974	2	C-48	-0.4
1918	Cle-A	2	3	0	1	0	0	0	0	0	0	.333	.333	.333	92	-0	0			1.000	-0	/C-1	0.0
1919	StL-A	38	76	9	15	1	1	0	3	1	12	.197	.218	.237	27	-7	0			.982	5	C-26/1-1	-0.1
1920	StL-A	66	155	19	43	5	2	0	11	11	10	.277	.353	.335	81	-4	1	0	0	.967	-5	C-40	-0.6
1921	StL-A	20	46	2	10	0	0	0	4	0	7	.217	.217	.217	11	-6	0	0	0	.982	2	C-12	-0.4
1922	StL-A	5	7	0	3	1	0	0	1	0	0	.429	.429	.571	153	1	0	0	0	1.000	0	/C-3	0.1
1923	StL-A	4	9	0	0	0	0	0	0	0	2	.000	.000	.000	-95	-3	0	0	0	.917	0	/C-4	-0.2
Total	11	243	488	44	106	12	5	0	29	23	73	.217	.268	.262	47	-35	5	0		.970	7	C-157/1-1,O-1	-1.6

■ DICK BILLINGS

Billings, Richard Arlin b: 12/4/42, Detroit, Mich. BR/TR, 6'1", 195 lbs. Deb: 9/11/68

YEAR	TM/L	G	AB	R	H	2B	3B	HR	RBI	BB	SO	AVG	OBP	SLG	PRO+	BR/A	SB	CS	SBR	FA	FR	G/POS	TPR
1968	Was-A	12	33	3	6	1	0	1	3	5	13	.182	.289	.303	82	-1	0	0	0	.929	0	/O-8,3-4	-0.1
1969	Was-A	27	37	3	5	0	0	0	0	6	8	.135	.256	.135	13	-4	0	1	-1	1.000	0	/O-6,3-1	-0.5
1970	Was-A	11	24	3	6	2	0	1	1	2	3	.250	.308	.458	114	0	0	0	0	1.000	-2	/C-8	-0.1
1971	Was-A	116	349	32	86	14	0	6	48	21	54	.246	.299	.338	85	-8	2	5	-2	.992	-3	C-62,O-32/3-2	-1.3
1972	Tex-A	133	469	41	119	15	1	5	58	29	77	.254	.300	.322	89	-7	1	5	-3	.981	-5	C-92,O-41/3-5,1-1	-1.5

YEAR	TM/L	G	AB	R	H	2B	3B	HR	RBI	BB	SO	AVG	OBP	SLG	PRO+	BR/A	SB	CS	SBR	FA	FR	G/POS	TPR
1973	Tex-A	81	280	17	50	11	0	3	32	20	43	.179	.238	.250	39	-23	1	1	-0	.975	-19	C-72/O-4,1-3,D-2	-4.1
1974	Tex-A	16	31	2	7	1	0	0	0	4	6	.226	.314	.258	68	-1	2	0	1	1.000	1	C-13/O-1,D-1	0.1
	StL-N	1	5	0	1	0	0	0	0	0	1	.200	.200	.200	12	-1	0	0	0	1.000	0	/C-1	0.0
1975	StL-N	3	3	0	0	0	0	0	0	0	2	.000	.000	.000	-97	-1	0	0	0	.000	0	H	-0.1
Total	8	400	1231	101	280	44	1	16	142	87	207	.227	.283	.304	73	-45	6	12	-5	.984	-27	C-248/O-92,3-12,1D	-7.6
■ GEORGE BINKS	Binks, George Alvin "Bingo" (b: George Alvin Binkowski) b: 7/11/16, Chicago, Ill. BL/TL, 6', 175 lbs. Deb: 9/23/44																						
1944	Was-A	5	12	0	3	0	0	0	0	0	1	.250	.250	.250	45	-1	0	0	0	1.000	-1	/O-3	-0.2
1945	Was-A	145	550	62	153	32	6	6	81	34	52	.278	.324	.391	117	8	11	7	-1	.977	4	*O-128,1-20	0.4
1946	Was-A	65	134	13	26	3	0	0	12	6	16	.194	.229	.216	26	-13	1	0	0	1.000	-0	O-28	-1.5
1947	Phi-A	104	333	33	86	19	4	2	34	23	36	.258	.308	.357	83	-8	8	2	1	.965	1	O-75,1-13	-1.1
1948	Phi-A	17	41	2	4	1	0	0	2	2	2	.098	.140	.122	-30	-8	1	0	0	1.000	-2	O-14	-1.0
	StL-A	15	23	2	5	0	0	0	1	2	1	.217	.280	.217	32	-2	0	0	0	1.000	-1	/O-5,1-4	-0.4
	Yr	32	64	4	9	1	0	0	3	4	3	.141	.191	.156	-7	-10	1	0	0	1.000	-3	O-19/1-4	-1.4
Total	5	351	1093	112	277	55	10	8	130	67	108	.253	.299	.344	86	-24	21	9	1	.977	1	O-253/1-37	-3.8
■ STEVE BIRAS	Biras, Stephen Alexander b: 2/26/22, E.St.Louis, Ill. d: 4/21/65, St.Louis, Mo. BR/TR, 5'11", 185 lbs. Deb: 9/15/44																						
1944	Cle-A	2	2	0	2	0	0	0	2	0	0	1.000	1.000	1.000	491	1	0	0	0	.667	0	/2-1	0.1
■ JUD BIRCHALL	Birchall, Adoniram Judson b: 1858, Germantown, Pa. d: 12/22/1887, Philadelphia, Pa. Deb: 5/2/1882																						
1882	Phi-a	75	338	65	89	12	1	0	27	8		.263	.280	.305	87	-7				.860	0	*O-74/2-1	-0.6
1883	Phi-a	96	448	95	108	10	1	1	24	20		.241	.274	.275	71	-16				.809	6	*O-96	-1.0
1884	Phi-a	54	221	36	57	2	2	0		4		.258	.287	.285	82	-5				.838	3	O-52/3-2	-0.2
Total	3	225	1007	196	254	24	4	1	51	32		.252	.279	.287	79	-27				.832	9	O-222/3-2,2-1	-1.8
■ FRANK BIRD	Bird, Frank Zepherin "Dodo" b: 3/10/1869, Spencer, Mass. d: 5/20/58, Worcester, Mass. BR/TR, 5'10", 195 lbs. Deb: 4/16/1892																						
1892	StL-N	17	50	9	10	3	1	1	1	6	11	.200	.286	.360	100	-0	2			.920	-4	C-17	-0.3
■ GEORGE BIRD	Bird, George Raymond b: 6/23/1850, Stillman Valley, Ill. d: 11/9/40, Rockford, Ill. BR/TR, 5'9", 150 lbs. Deb: 5/6/1871																						
1871	Rok-n	25	106	19	28	2	5	0	13	3	2	.264	.284	.377	92	-1	1	0	0	.756	-5	*O-25	-0.2
■ DAVE BIRDSALL	Birdsall, David Solomon b: 7/16/1838, New York, N.Y. d: 12/30/1896, Boston, Mass. BR/TR, 5'9", 126 lbs. Deb: 5/5/1871																						
1871	Bos-n	29	152	51	46	3	3	0	24	4	4	.303	.321	.362	93	-2	6	0	2	.769	-1	*O-27/C-7	0.0
1872	Bos-n	16	76	11	16	3	0	0	15	1	0	.211	.221	.250	42	-5	0	2	-1	.838	1	C-12/O-8	-0.4
1873	Bos-n	3	12	4	1	0	0	0	1	0	0	.083	.083	.083	-46	-2	0	0	0	.200	-1	/O-3	-0.3
Total	3 n	48	240	66	63	6	3	0	40	5	4	.262	.278	.313	70	-10	6	2	1	.720	-1	/O-38,C-19	-0.7
■ JOE BIRMINGHAM	Birmingham, Joseph Leo "Dode" b: 8/6/1884, Elmira, N.Y. d: 4/24/46, Tampico, Mexico BR/TR, 5'10", 185 lbs. Deb: 9/12/06 M																						
1906	Cle-A	10	40	5	11	2	1	0	6	1		.275	.293	.375	110	0	2			1.000	1	/O-9,3-1	0.1
1907	Cle-A	137	476	55	112	10	9	1	33	16		.235	.265	.300	79	-12	23			.949	13	*O-133/S-3	-0.5
1908	Cle-A	122	413	32	88	10	1	2	38	19		.213	.253	.257	65	-16	15			.957	6	*O-121/S-1	-1.7
1909	Cle-A	100	343	29	99	10	5	1	38	19		.289	.333	.356	113	5	12			.948	4	O-98	0.6
1910	Cle-A	104	367	41	84	11	2	0	35	23		.229	.284	.270	72	-12	18			.961	14	*O-103/3-1	-0.3
1911	Cle-A	125	447	55	136	18	5	2	51	15		.304	.334	.380	98	-3	16			.973	8	*O-102,3-16	0.0
1912	Cle-A	107	369	49	94	19	3	1	45	26		.255	.311	.331	81	-10	15			.952	5	O-96/1-9,M	-1.0
1913	Cle-A	47	131	16	37	9	1	0	15	8	22	.282	.324	.366	99	-1	7			.974	-3	O-36,M	-0.5
1914	Cle-A	19	47	2	6	0	0	0	4	2	5	.128	.163	.128	-12	-6	0	1	-1	1.000	-2	O-14,M	-1.1
Total	9	771	2633	284	667	89	27	7	265	129	27	.253	.294	.316	84	-55	108	1		.958	46	O-712/3-18,1-9,S-4	-4.4
■ JOHN BISCHOFF	Bischoff, John George "Smiley" b: 10/28/1894, Granite City, Ill. d: 12/28/81, Granite City, Ill. BR/TR, 5'7", 165 lbs. Deb: 4/18/25																						
1925	Chi-A	7	11	1	1	0	0	0	0	1	5	.091	.167	.091	-35	-2	0	0	0	1.000	-0	/C-4	-0.2
	Bos-A	41	133	13	37	9	1	1	16	6	11	.278	.309	.383	75	-6	1	2	-1	.952	-3	C-40	-0.7
	Yr	48	144	14	38	9	1	1	16	7	16	.264	.298	.361	67	-8	1	2	-1	.955	-3	C-44	-0.9
1926	Bos-A	59	127	6	33	11	2	0	19	15	16	.260	.343	.378	91	-2	1	3	-2	.974	-1	C-46	-0.2
Total	2	107	271	20	71	20	3	1	35	22	32	.262	.320	.369	78	-10	2	5	-2	.964	-4	/C-90	-1.1
■ FRANK BISHOP	Bishop, Frank H. b: 9/21/1860, Belvidere, Ill. d: 6/18/29, Chicago, Ill. Deb: 5/27/1884																						
1884	CP-U	4	16	1	3	1	0	0		0		.188	.188	.250	32	-2				.667	-2	/3-3,S-1	-0.3
■ MAX BISHOP	Bishop, Max Frederick "Tilly" or "Camera Eye" b: 9/5/1899, Waynesboro, Pa. d: 2/24/62, Waynesboro, Pa. BL/TR, 5'8.5", 165 lbs. Deb: 4/15/24																						
1924	Phi-A	91	294	52	75	13	2	2	21	54	30	.255	.380	.333	84	-5	4	3	-1	.969	6	2-80	0.1
1925	Phi-A	105	368	66	103	18	4	4	27	87	37	.280	.420	.383	98	3	5	9	-4	.957	5	*2-104	0.5
1926	Phi-A	122	400	77	106	20	2	0	33	116	41	.265	.431	.325	94	4	4	5	-2	**.987**	0	*2-119	0.5
1927	Phi-A	117	372	80	103	15	1	0	22	105	28	.277	.442	.323	95	5	8	6	-1	.967	3	*2-106	1.0
1928	Phi-A	126	472	104	149	27	5	6	50	97	36	.316	.435	.432	125	23	9	9	-3	**.978**	-11	*2-125	1.2
1929	*Phi-A	129	475	102	110	19	6	3	36	**128**	44	.232	.398	.316	83	-6	1	4	-2	.970	-26	*2-129	-2.7
1930	*Phi-A	130	441	117	111	27	6	10	38	128	60	.252	.426	.408	108	11	3	2	-0	.976	-6	*2-127	1.1
1931	*Phi-A	130	497	115	146	30	4	5	37	112	51	.294	.426	.400	111	14	3	1	0	.984	-0	*2-130	2.1
1932	Phi-A	114	409	89	104	24	2	5	37	110	43	.254	.412	.359	98	4	2	2	-1	**.988**	-9	*2-106	0.0
1933	Phi-A	117	391	80	115	27	1	4	42	106	46	.294	.446	.399	124	21	1	5	-3	.975	-13	*2-113	1.1
1934	Bos-A	97	253	65	66	13	1	1	22	82	22	.261	.445	.332	96	4	3	2	-0	.990	0	2-57,1-15	0.5
1935	Bos-A	60	122	19	28	3	1	1	14	28	14	.230	.377	.295	71	-4	0	2	-1	.978	-5	2-34,1-11/S-2	-0.8
Total	12	1338	4494	966	1216	236	35	41	379	1153	452	.271	.423	.366	102	72	43	50	-17	.976	-56	*2-1230/1-26,S-2	4.6
■ MIKE BISHOP	Bishop, Michael David b: 11/5/58, Santa Maria, Cal. BR/TR, 6'2", 188 lbs. Deb: 4/16/83																						
1983	NY-N	3	8	2	1	1	0	0	0	3	4	.125	.364	.250	74	-0	0	0	0	.944	-0	/C-3	0.0
■ RIVINGTON BISLAND	Bisland, Rivington Martin b: 2/17/1890, New York, N.Y. d: 1/11/73, Salzburg, Austria BR/TR, 5'9", 155 lbs. Deb: 9/13/12																						
1912	Pit-N	1	1	0	0	0	0	0	0	0	0	.000	.000	.000	-99	-0	0			.000	0	H	0.0
1913	StL-A	12	44	3	6	0	0	0	3	2	5	.136	.191	.136	-4	-6	0			.963	-5	S-12	-1.1
1914	Cle-A	18	57	9	6	1	0	0	2	6	2	.105	.190	.123	-5	-7	2	5	-2	.962	-0	S-15/3-1	-1.0
Total	3	31	102	12	12	1	0	0	5	8	7	.118	.189	.127	-6	-13	2	5		.962	-5	/S-27,3-1	-2.1
■ DEL BISSONETTE	Bissonette, Delphia Louis b: 9/6/1899, Winthrop, Me. d: 6/9/72, Augusta, Maine BL/TL, 5'11", 180 lbs. Deb: 4/11/28 MC																						
1928	Bro-N	155	587	90	188	30	13	25	106	70	75	.320	.396	.543	145	38	5			.987	-4	*1-155	2.0
1929	Bro-N	116	431	68	121	28	10	12	75	46	58	.281	.351	.476	105	2	2			.987	-9	*1-113	-1.7
1930	Bro-N	146	572	102	192	33	13	16	113	56	66	.336	.396	.523	121	20	4			.987	-9	*1-146	-0.3
1931	Bro-N	152	587	90	170	19	14	12	87	59	53	.290	.354	.431	111	9	4			.990	-7	*1-152	-1.2
1933	Bro-N	35	114	9	28	7	0	1	10	2	17	.246	.259	.333	71	-5	2			.988	0	1-32	-0.8
Total	5	604	2291	359	699	117	50	66	391	233	269	.305	.371	.486	119	64	17			.988	-28	1-598	-2.0
■ RED BITTMAN	Bittman, Henry Peter b: 7/22/1862, Cincinnati, Ohio d: 11/8/29, Cincinnati, Ohio Deb: 10/10/1889																						
1889	KC-a	4	14	2	4	0	0	0	2	1	1	.286	.333	.286	73	-1	1			1.000	1	/2-4	0.1
■ GEORGE BJORKMAN	Bjorkman, George Anton b: 8/26/56, Ontario, Cal. BR/TR, 6'2", 190 lbs. Deb: 7/10/83																						
1983	Hou-N	29	75	8	17	4	0	2	14	16	29	.227	.370	.360	110	2	0	0	0	.993	-3	C-29	0.0
■ JOHN BLACK	Black, John Falcnor "Jack" (b: John Falcnor Haddow) b: 2/23/1890, Covington, Ky. d: 3/20/62, Rutherford, N.J. BR/TR, 6'1", 185 lbs. Deb: 6/20/11																						
1911	StL-A	54	186	13	28	4	0	0	7	10		.151	.202	.172	5	-24	4			.972	0	1-54	-2.4
■ BILL BLACK	Black, John William "Jigger" b: 8/12/1899, Philadelphia, Pa. d: 1/14/68, Philadelphia, Pa. BL/TR, 5'11", 168 lbs. Deb: 5/4/24																						
1924	Chi-A	6	5	0	1	0	0	0	0	0	0	.200	.200	.200	3	-1	0	0	0	.000	0	/2-1	-0.1

YEAR	TM/L	G	AB	R	H	2B	3B	HR	RBI	BB	SO	AVG	OBP	SLG	PRO+	BR/A	SB	CS	SBR	FA	FR	G/POS	TPR
■ BOB BLACK Black, Robert Benjamin b: 12/10/1862, Cincinnati, Ohio d: 3/21/33, Sioux City, Iowa 5'5.5", 155 lbs. Deb: 8/19/1884																							
1884	KC-U	38	146	25	36	14	2	1		10		.247	.295	.390	122	-1				.784	-1	O-19,P-16/2-6,S-1	-0.3
■ ETHAN BLACKABY Blackaby, Ethan Allen b: 7/24/40, Cincinnati, O. BL/TL, 5'11", 190 lbs. Deb: 9/6/62																							
1962	Mil-N	6	13	0	2	1	0	0	0	1	8	.154	.214	.231	20	-1	0	0	0	1.000	-1	/O-3	-0.2
1964	Mil-N	9	12	0	1	0	0	0	1	1	2	.083	.154	.083	-31	-2	0	0	0	.500	-2	/O-5	-0.4
Total	2	15	25	0	3	1	0	0	1	2	10	.120	.185	.160	-4	-4	0	0	0	.800	-2	/O-8	-0.6
■ EARL BLACKBURN Blackburn, Earl Stuart b: 11/1/1892, Leesville, Ohio d: 8/3/66, Mansfield, Ohio BR/TR, 5'11", 180 lbs. Deb: 9/17/12																							
1912	Pit-N	1	0	0	0	0	0	0	0	0	0	—	—	—	—	0	0			1.000	0	/C-1	0.0
	Cin-N	1	0	0	0	0	0	0	0	1	0	—	1.000	—	191	0	0			1.000	0	/C-1	0.1
	Yr	2	0	0	0	0	0	0	0	1	0	—	1.000	—	190	0	0			1.000	0	/C-2	0.1
1913	Cin-N	17	27	1	7	0	0	0	3	2	5	.259	.310	.259	64	-1	2			.848	-1	C-12	-0.2
1915	Bos-N	3	6	0	1	0	0	0	0	2	1	.167	.375	.167	70	-0	0			1.000	-0	C-3	0.0
1916	Bos-N	47	110	12	30	4	4	0	7	9	21	.273	.328	.382	123	3	2			.972	-1	C-44	0.5
1917	Chi-N	2	2	0	0	0	0	0	0	0	0	.000	.000	.000	-93	-0	0			.000	0	H	-0.1
Total	5	71	145	13	38	4	4	0	10	14	27	.262	.327	.345	107	1	4			.954	-2	/C-61	0.3
■ LENA BLACKBURNE Blackburne, Russell Aubrey "Slats" b: 10/23/1886, Clifton Heights, Pa. d: 2/29/68, Riverside, N.J. BR/TR, 5'11", 160 lbs. Deb: 4/14/10 MC																							
1910	Chi-A	75	242	16	42	3	1	0	10	19		.174	.245	.194	39	-16	4			.911	19	S-74	0.6
1912	Chi-A	5	1	0	0	0	0	0	0	1		.000	.500	.000	48	0	1			.800	1	/S-4,3-1	0.1
1914	Chi-A	144	474	52	105	10	5	1	35	66	58	.222	.324	.270	80	-9	25	15	-1	.963	1	*2-143	-1.2
1915	Chi-A	96	283	33	61	5	1	0	25	35	34	.216	.304	.240	61	-13	13	11	-3	.949	-10	3-83/S-9	-2.4
1918	Cin-N	125	435	34	99	8	10	1	45	25	30	.228	.271	.299	75	-14	6			.938	10	*S-125	0.2
1919	Bos-N	31	80	5	21	3	1	0	4	6	7	.262	.322	.325	99	-0	3			.948	3	3-24/1-1,2-1,S-1	0.5
	Phi-N	72	291	32	58	10	5	2	19	10	22	.199	.228	.289	51	-18	2			.933	6	3-72/1-1	-1.0
	Yr	103	371	37	79	13	6	2	23	16	29	.213	.249	.296	61	-18	5			.937	10	3-96/1-2,2-1,S-1	-0.5
1927	Chi-A	1	1	1	1	0	0	0	1	0	0	1.000	1.000	1.000	431	0	0	0	0	.000	0	H	0.0
1929	Chi-A	1	0	0	0	0	0	0	0	0	0	—	—	—	—	0	0	0	0	.000	0	/P-1,M	0.0
Total	8	550	1807	173	387	39	23	4	139	162	151	.214	.284	.268	67	-69	54	26		.927	30	S-213,3-180,2/1P	-3.2
■ GEORGE BLACKERBY Blackerby, George Franklin b: 11/10/03, Luther, Okla. d: 5/30/87, Wichita Falls, Tex. BR/TR, 6'1", 176 lbs. Deb: 8/10/28																							
1928	Chi-A	30	83	8	21	0	0	0	12	4	10	.253	.287	.253	44	-7	2	1	0	.953	-1	O-20	-0.9
■ FRED BLACKWELL Blackwell, Fredrick William "Blacky" b: 9/7/1891, Bowling Green, Ky. d: 12/8/75, Morgantown, Ky. BL/TR, 5'11.5", 160 lbs. Deb: 9/25/17																							
1917	Pit-N	3	10	1	2	0	0	0	2	0	3	.200	.200	.200	22	-1	0			1.000	0	/C-3	-0.1
1918	Pit-N	8	13	1	2	0	0	0	4	3	4	.154	.313	.154	42	-1	0			.926	0	/C-8	0.0
1919	Pit-N	24	65	3	14	3	0	0	4	3	9	.215	.261	.262	55	-3	0			.964	-0	C-22	-0.2
Total	3	35	88	5	18	3	0	0	10	6	16	.205	.263	.239	50	-5	0			.961	0	/C-33	-0.3
■ TIM BLACKWELL Blackwell, Timothy P b: 8/19/52, San Diego, Cal. BB/TR, 5'11", 180 lbs. Deb: 7/3/74																							
1974	Bos-A	44	122	9	30	1	1	0	8	10	21	.246	.308	.270	63	-5	1	1	-0	.971	2	C-44	-0.2
1975	Bos-A	59	132	15	26	3	2	0	6	19	13	.197	.303	.250	53	-8	0	0	0	.984	8	C-57/D-2	0.2
1976	Phi-N	4	8	0	2	0	0	0	1	0	1	.250	.250	.250	41	-1	0	0	0	1.000	1	/C-4	0.0
1977	Phi-N	1	0	1	0	0	0	0	0	0	0	—	—	—	—	0	0	0	0	1.000	0	/C-1	0.0
	Mon-N	16	22	3	2	1	0	0	0	2	7	.091	.167	.136	-18	-4	0	0	0	.925	-1	C-14	-0.4
	Yr	17	22	4	2	1	0	0	0	2	7	.091	.167	.136	-18	-4	0	0	0	.929	-1	C-15	-0.4
1978	Chi-N	49	103	8	23	3	0	0	7	23	17	.223	.370	.252	68	-3	0	0	0	.987	7	C-49	0.5
1979	Chi-N	63	122	8	20	3	1	0	12	32	25	.164	.342	.205	48	-8	0	0	0	.975	1	C-63	-0.5
1980	Chi-N	103	320	24	87	16	4	5	30	41	62	.272	.355	.394	101	1	0	1	-1	.982	17	*C-103	2.2
1981	Chi-N	58	158	21	37	10	2	1	11	23	23	.234	.331	.342	87	-2	2	1	0	.993	2	C-56	0.1
1982	Mon-N	23	42	2	8	2	1	0	3	3	11	.190	.244	.286	47	-3	0	0	0	.985	2	C-18	-0.1
1983	Mon-N	6	15	0	3	1	0	0	2	1	3	.200	.250	.267	43	-1	0	0	0	.935	1	/C-5	-0.1
Total	10	426	1044	91	238	40	11	6	80	154	183	.228	.329	.305	73	-34	3	3	-1	.981	40	C-414/D-2	1.7
■ RAY BLADES Blades, Francis Raymond b: 8/6/1896, Mt.Vernon, Ill. d: 5/18/79, Lincoln, Ill. BR/TR, 5'7.5", 163 lbs. Deb: 8/19/22 MC																							
1922	StL-N	37	130	27	39	2	4	3	21	25	21	.300	.428	.446	132	8	3	3	-1	.931	-1	O-29/S-4,3-1	0.4
1923	StL-N	98	317	48	78	21	5	5	44	37	46	.246	.342	.391	95	-2	4	2	0	.967	6	O-83/3-4	-0.1
1924	StL-N	131	456	86	142	21	13	11	68	35	38	.311	.373	.487	131	19	7	9	-3	.956	-3	*O-109/2-7,3-7	0.7
1925	StL-N	122	462	112	158	37	8	12	57	59	47	.342	.423	.535	140	29	6	8	-3	.979	11	*O-114/3-1	2.7
1926	StL-N	107	416	81	127	17	12	8	43	62	57	.305	.409	.462	129	19	6			.980	4	*O-105	1.6
1927	StL-N	61	180	33	57	8	5	2	29	28	22	.317	.414	.450	127	8	3			.914	-13	O-50	-0.8
1928	*StL-N	51	85	9	20	7	1	1	19	20	26	.235	.393	.376	100	1	0			.972	-2	O-19	-0.2
1930	*StL-N	45	101	26	40	6	2	4	25	21	15	.396	.504	.614	163	12	1			.957	-3	O-32	0.6
1931	*StL-N	35	67	10	19	4	0	1	5	10	7	.284	.392	.388	106	1	1			.871	-4	O-20	-0.4
1932	StL-N	80	201	35	46	10	1	3	29	34	31	.229	.340	.333	80	-5	2			.975	-5	O-62/3-1	-1.3
Total	10	767	2415	467	726	133	51	50	340	331	310	.301	.395	.460	123	90	33	22		.963	-10	O-623/3-14,2-7,S-4	3.2
■ RICK BLADT Bladt, Richard Alan b: 12/9/46, Santa Cruz, Cal. BR/TR, 6'1", 160 lbs. Deb: 6/15/69																							
1969	Chi-N	10	13	1	2	0	0	0	1	0	5	.154	.154	.154	-12	-2	0	0	0	1.000	0	/O-7	-0.2
1975	NY-A	52	117	13	26	3	1	1	11	11	8	.222	.295	.291	67	-5	6	2	1	.973	-2	O-51	-0.8
Total	2	62	130	14	28	3	1	1	12	11	13	.215	.282	.277	58	-7	6	2	1	.976	-2	/O-58	-1.0
■ RAE BLAEMIRE Blaemire, Rae Bertrum b: 2/8/11, Gary, Ind. d: 12/23/75, Champaign, Ill. BR/TR, 6', 178 lbs. Deb: 9/13/41																							
1941	NY-N	2	5	0	2	0	0	0	0	0	0	.400	.400	.400	123	0	0			1.000	-0	/C-2	0.0
■ FOOTSIE BLAIR Blair, Clarence Vick b: 7/13/1900, Enterprise, Okla. d: 7/1/82, Texarkana, Tex. BL/TR, 6'1", 180 lbs. Deb: 4/28/29																							
1929	*Chi-N	26	72	10	23	5	0	1	8	3	4	.319	.347	.431	91	-1	1			.897	1	/3-8,1-7,2-2	0.0
1930	Chi-N	134	578	97	158	24	12	6	59	20	58	.273	.306	.388	66	-33	9			.958	8	*2-115,3-13	-1.6
1931	Chi-N	86	240	31	62	19	4	3	29	14	26	.258	.302	.408	88	-5	1			.956	-6	2-44,1-23/3-1	-0.9
Total	3	246	890	138	243	48	16	10	96	37	88	.273	.308	.397	73	-39	11			.958	4	2-161/1-30,3-22	-2.5
■ BUDDY BLAIR Blair, Louis Nathan b: 9/10/10, Columbia, Miss. d: 6/7/96, Monroe, La. BL/TR, 6', 186 lbs. Deb: 4/14/42																							
1942	Phi-A	137	484	48	135	26	8	5	66	30	30	.279	.325	.397	103	0	1	6	-3	.931	-7	*3-126	-0.8
■ PAUL BLAIR Blair, Paul L D b: 2/1/44, Cushing, Okla. BR/TR, 6', 171 lbs. Deb: 9/9/64																							
1964	Bal-A	8	1	0	0	0	0	0	0	0	1	.000	.000	.000	-99	-0	0	1	-1	1.000	-2	/O-6	-0.3
1965	Bal-A	119	364	49	85	19	2	5	25	32	52	.234	.303	.338	80	-9	8	5	-1	.992	3	*O-116	-1.3
1966	*Bal-A	133	303	35	84	20	2	6	33	15	36	.277	.311	.416	109	2	5	6	-2	.990	-11	*O-127	-1.5
1967	Bal-A	151	552	72	162	27	**12**	11	64	50	68	.293	.357	.446	137	25	8	6	-1	.985	21	*O-146	4.1
1968	Bal-A	141	421	48	89	22	1	7	38	37	60	.211	.278	.318	80	-10	4	2	0	.993	0	*O-132/3-1	-1.8
1969	*Bal-A★	150	625	102	178	32	5	26	76	40	72	.285	.330	.477	122	15	20	6	2	.988	25	*O-150	3.5
1970	*Bal-A	133	480	79	128	24	2	18	65	56	93	.267	.347	.438	114	9	24	11	1	.990	19	*O-128/3-1	2.3
1971	*Bal-A	141	516	75	135	24	8	10	44	32	94	.262	.306	.397	99	-3	14	11	-2	.991	2	*O-138	-1.0
1972	Bal-A	142	477	47	111	20	8	8	49	25	78	.233	.271	.358	84	-11	7	8	-3	.991	9	*O-139	-1.2
1973	*Bal-A★	146	500	73	140	25	3	10	64	43	72	.280	.337	.402	108	5	18	8	1	.990	7	*O-144/D-1	0.7
1974	*Bal-A	151	552	77	144	27	4	17	62	43	59	.261	.317	.417	113	7	27	9	3	.985	7	*O-151	1.2
1975	Bal-A	140	440	51	96	13	4	5	31	25	82	.218	.260	.300	62	-23	17	11	-2	.991	-2	*O-138/1-1,D-1	-3.3
1976	Bal-A	145	375	29	74	16	0	3	16	22	49	.197	.246	.264	52	-23	15	6	1	.979	-8	*O-139/D-1	-3.6
1977	*NY-A	83	164	20	43	4	3	4	25	9	16	.262	.309	.396	91	-2	3	2	-0	.969	-13	O-79/D-1	-1.7
1978	*NY-A	75	125	10	22	5	0	2	13	9	17	.176	.231	.264	40	-10	1	1	-0	.989	-15	O-64/2-5,S-4,3-3	-2.8

YEAR	TM/L	G	AB	R	H	2B	3B	HR	RBI	BB	SO	AVG	OBP	SLG	PRO+	BR/A	SB	CS	SBR	FA	FR	G/POS	TPR
1979	NY-A	2	5	0	1	0	0	0	0	0	1	.200	.200	.200	8	-1	0	0	0	1.000	0	/O-2	0.0
	Cin-N	75	140	7	21	4	1	2	15	11	27	.150	.212	.236	22	-15	0	0	0	.992	-10	O-67	-2.8
1980	NY-A	12	2	2	0	0	0	0	0	0	0	.000	.000	.000	-99	-1	0	0	0	1.000	-4	O-12	-0.5
Total	17	1947	6042	776	1513	282	55	134	620	449	877	.250	.305	.382	96	-45	171	93	-5	.988	29	*O-1878/2-5,3SD1	-10.0
■ WALTER BLAIR	Blair, Walter Allen "Heavy" b: 10/13/1883, Landrus, Pa. d: 8/20/48, Lewisburg, Pa. BR/TR, 6′, 185 lbs. Deb: 9/17/07 M																						
1907	NY-A	7	22	1	4	0	0	0	1	2		.182	.250	.182	35	-2	0			.922	1	/C-7	0.1
1908	NY-A	76	211	9	40	5	1	1	13	11		.190	.237	.237	53	-11	4			.956	-14	C-60/O-9,1-3	-2.3
1909	NY-A	42	110	5	23	2	2	0	11	7		.209	.269	.264	68	-4	2			.964	-8	C-42	-1.0
1910	NY-A	6	22	2	5	0	1	0	2	0		.227	.227	.318	67	-1	0			.970	-2	/C-6	-0.3
1911	NY-A	85	222	18	43	9	2	0	26	16		.194	.257	.252	40	-18	2			.970	4	C-84/1-1	-0.7
1914	Buf-F	128	378	22	92	11	2	0	33	32	64	.243	.304	.283	59	-27	6			.984	5	*C-128	-1.2
1915	Buf-F	98	290	23	65	15	3	2	20	18	32	.224	.274	.317	65	-19	4			**.981**	5	C-97,M	-0.7
Total	7	442	1255	80	272	42	11	3	106	86	96	.217	.272	.275	56	-81	18			.974	-9	C-424/O-9,1-4	-6.1
■ HARRY BLAKE	Blake, Harry Cooper b: 6/16/1874, Portsmouth, Ohio d: 10/14/19, Chicago, Ill. BR/TR, 5′7″, 165 lbs. Deb: 7/7/1894																						
1894	Cle-N	73	296	51	78	15	4	1	51	30	22	.264	.335	.351	63	-19	1			.932	2	O-73	-1.6
1895	*Cle-N	84	315	50	87	10	1	3	45	30	33	.276	.341	.343	72	-14	11			.898	-2	O-83	-1.8
1896	*Cle-N	104	383	66	92	12	5	1	43	46	30	.240	.322	.305	62	-21	10			.944	2	*O-103/S-1	-2.4
1897	Cle-N	32	117	17	30	3	1	1	15	12		.256	.331	.325	70	-5	5			.989	4	O-32	-0.3
1898	Cle-N	136	474	65	116	18	7	0	58	69		.245	.342	.312	89	-5	12			.952	7	*O-136/1-2	-0.7
1899	StL-N	97	292	50	70	9	4	2	41	43		.240	.341	.318	80	-7	16			.979	-2	O-87/2-4,S-1,1-1,C	-1.3
Total	6	526	1877	299	473	67	22	8	253	230	85	.252	.336	.324	73	-71	55			.948	12	O-514/2-4,1-3,SC	-8.1
■ LINC BLAKELY	Blakely, Lincoln Howard b: 2/12/12, Oakland, Cal. d: 9/28/76, Oakland, Cal. BR/TR, 6′, 180 lbs. Deb: 4/29/34																						
1934	Cin-N	34	102	11	23	1	1	0	10	5	14	.225	.269	.255	42	-8	1			.987	3	O-28	-0.6
■ BOB BLAKISTON	Blakiston, Robert J. (b: Robert J. Blackstone) b: 10/2/1855, San Francisco, Cal. d: 12/25/18, San Francisco, Cal 5′8.5″, 180 lbs. Deb: 5/2/1882																						
1882	Phi-a	72	281	40	64	4	1	0	20	9		.228	.252	.249	62	-12				.855	0	O-38,3-34/2-1	-1.1
1883	Phi-a	44	167	26	41	3	3	0	26	9		.246	.284	.299	82	-4				.857	-4	O-37/1-6,3-5	-0.7
1884	Phi-a	32	128	21	33	6	0	0		11		.258	.336	.305	104	1				.902	2	O-28/3-2,1-1,2-1,S	0.2
	Ind-a	6	18	0	4	1	0	0		1		.222	.263	.278	79	-0				.884	-1	/1-5,O-1	-0.1
	Yr	38	146	21	37	7	0	0		12		.253	.327	.301	101	0				.902	1	O-29/1-6,3-2,2-1,S	0.1
Total	3	154	594	87	142	14	4	0	46	30		.239	.280	.276	77	-16				.872	-2	O-104/3-41,1-12,2S	-1.7
■ JOHNNY BLANCHARD	Blanchard, John Edwin b: 2/26/33, Minneapolis, Minn. BL/TR, 6′1″, 198 lbs. Deb: 9/25/55																						
1955	NY-A	1	3	0	0	0	0	0	0	1	0	.000	.250	.000	-29	-1	0	0	0	1.000	0	/C-1	0.0
1959	NY-A	49	59	6	10	1	0	2	4	7	12	.169	.258	.288	51	-4	0	0	0	.963	-2	C-12/O-8,1-1	-0.6
1960	*NY-A	53	99	8	24	3	1	4	14	6	17	.242	.292	.414	94	-1	0	0	0	.988	10	C-28	0.9
1961	*NY-A	93	243	38	74	10	1	21	54	27	28	.305	.383	.613	170	23	1	0	0	.990	-2	C-48,O-15	2.3
1962	*NY-A	93	246	33	57	7	0	13	39	28	32	.232	.313	.419	98	-1	0	0	0	.987	-7	O-47,C-15/1-2	-1.1
1963	*NY-A	76	218	22	49	4	0	16	45	26	30	.225	.307	.463	114	3	0	0	0	.987	-9	O-64	-0.9
1964	*NY-A	77	161	18	41	8	0	7	28	24	24	.255	.351	.435	115	4	1	0	0	.984	-3	C-25,O-14/1-3	0.1
1965	NY-A	12	34	1	5	1	0	1	3	7	3	.147	.293	.265	60	-2	0	0	0	.961	-1	C-12	-0.2
	KC-A	52	120	10	24	2	0	2	11	8	16	.200	.256	.267	49	-8	0	0	0	1.000	-10	O-20,C-14	-2.0
	Yr	64	154	11	29	3	0	3	14	15	19	.188	.265	.266	52	-10	0	0	0	.971	-11	C-26,O-20	-2.2
	Mil-N	10	10	1	1	0	0	1	2	2	1	.100	.250	.400	79	-0	0	0	0	.000	-0	/O-1	-0.1
Total	8	516	1193	137	285	36	2	67	200	136	163	.239	.320	.441	109	13	2	0	1	.987	-25	O-169,C-155/1-6	-1.6
■ DAMASO BLANCO	Blanco, Damaso (Caripe) b: 11/12/41, Curiepe, Venez. BR/TR, 5′10″, 165 lbs. Deb: 5/26/72																						
1972	SF-N	39	20	5	7	1	0	0	2	4	3	.350	.458	.400	144	1	2	1	0	.889	6	3-19/S-8,2-3	0.8
1973	SF-N	28	12	4	0	0	0	0	0	1	2	.000	.077	.000	-74	-3	0	0	0	1.000	2	/3-7,S-5,2-3	-0.1
1974	SF-N	5	1	0	0	0	0	0	0	0	1	.000	.000	.000	-96	-0	1	0	0	.000	0	H	0.0
Total	3	72	33	9	7	1	0	0	2	5	6	.212	.316	.242	58	-2	3	1	0	.929	8	/3-26,S-13,2-6	0.7
■ HENRY BLANCO	Blanco, Henry Ramon b: 8/29/71, Caracas, Venez. BR/TR, 5′11″, 170 lbs. Deb: 7/25/97																						
1997	LA-N	3	5	1	2	0	0	1	1	0	1	.400	.400	1.000	273	1	0	0	0	1.000	-1	/1-1,3-1	0.1
■ OSSIE BLANCO	Blanco, Oswaldo Carlos (Diaz) b: 9/8/45, Caracas, Venez. BR/TR, 6′, 185 lbs. Deb: 5/26/70																						
1970	Chi-A	34	66	4	13	0	0	0	8	3	14	.197	.232	.197	19	-7	0	1	-1	.993	-1	1-22/O-1	-1.0
1974	Cle-A	18	36	1	7	0	0	0	2	7	4	.194	.326	.194	53	-2	0	3	-2	.992	-1	1-16/D-1	-0.6
Total	2	52	102	5	20	0	0	0	10	10	18	.196	.268	.196	31	-9	0	4	-2	.993	-2	/1-38,D-1,O-1	-1.6
■ COONIE BLANK	Blank, Frank Ignatz b: 10/18/1892, St.Louis, Mo. d: 12/8/61, St.Louis, Mo. BR/TR, 5′11″, 165 lbs. Deb: 8/15/09																						
1909	StL-N	1	2	0	0	0	0	0	0	0		.000	.000	.000	-99	-0	0			1.000	-0	/C-1	-0.1
■ CLIFF BLANKENSHIP	Blankenship, Clifford Douglas b: 4/10/1880, Columbus, Ga. d: 4/26/56, Oakland, Cal. BR/TR, 5′10.5″, 165 lbs. Deb: 4/17/05																						
1905	Cin-N	19	56	8	11	1	1	0	7	4		.196	.250	.250	44	-4	1			.960	-2	1-15	-0.7
1907	Was-A	37	102	4	23	2	0	0	6	3		.225	.248	.245	62	-5	3			.991	0	C-22/1-9	-0.3
1909	Was-A	39	60	4	15	1	0	0	9	0		.250	.250	.267	66	-3	2			.907	-9	C-17/O-4	-1.2
Total	3	95	218	16	49	4	1	0	22	7		.225	.249	.252	58	-11	6			.964	-11	/C-39,1-24,O-4	-2.2
■ LANCE BLANKENSHIP	Blankenship, Lance Robert b: 12/6/63, Portland, Ore. BR/TR, 6′, 185 lbs. Deb: 9/4/88																						
1988	Oak-A	10	3	1	0	0	0	0	0	0	1	.000	.000	.000	-99	-1	0	1	-1	1.000	0	/2-4,D-4	-0.1
1989	*Oak-A	58	125	22	29	5	1	1	4	8	31	.232	.278	.312	68	-5	5	1	1	1.000	3	O-25,2-24,D-10	-0.1
1990	*Oak-A	86	136	18	26	3	0	0	10	20	23	.191	.295	.213	46	-9	3	1	0	.947	-2	3-28,O-28,2-20,/1D	-1.1
1991	Oak-A	90	185	33	46	8	0	3	21	23	42	.249	.341	.341	95	-1	12	3	2	.983	8	2-45,O-28,3-14,/D-6	0.9
1992	*Oak-A	123	349	59	84	24	1	3	34	82	57	.241	.394	.341	113	11	21	7	2	.992	-3	2-78,O-51/1-7,D-3	1.1
1993	Oak-A	94	252	43	48	8	1	2	23	67	64	.190	.364	.254	74	-6	13	5	1	.994	4	O-66,2-19/1-6,SD	-0.2
Total	6	461	1050	176	233	48	3	9	92	200	218	.222	.352	.299	86	-11	54	18	5	.987	10	O-198,2-190/3D1S	0.5
■ LARVELL BLANKS	Blanks, Larvell b: 1/28/50, Del Rio, Tex. BR/TR, 5′8″, 167 lbs. Deb: 7/19/72																						
1972	Atl-N	33	85	10	28	5	0	1	7	7	12	.329	.380	.424	117	2	0	0	0	1.000	6	2-18/S-4,3-2	1.0
1973	Atl-N	17	18	1	4	0	0	0	0	1	3	.222	.263	.222	33	-2	0	0	0	.000	-3	/3-3,2-2,S-2	-0.4
1974	Atl-N	3	8	0	2	0	0	0	1	0	0	.250	.250	.250	38	-1	0	0	0	.889	-0	/S-2	-0.1
1975	Atl-N	141	471	49	110	13	3	3	38	38	43	.234	.294	.293	61	-25	4	3	-1	.960	-12	*S-129,2-12	-2.5
1976	Cle-A	104	328	45	92	8	7	5	41	30	31	.280	.341	.393	116	6	1	2	-1	.977	-20	S-56,2-46/3-2,D-3	-0.6
1977	Cle-A	105	322	43	92	10	4	6	38	19	37	.286	.327	.398	100	-1	3	0	1	.960	-25	S-66,3-18,2-12,/D-6	-1.8
1978	Cle-A	70	193	19	49	10	0	2	20	10	16	.254	.291	.337	77	-6	0	0	0	.926	-10	S-43,2-17/3-3,D-1	-1.0
1979	Tex-A	68	120	13	24	5	0	1	15	11	9	.200	.267	.267	45	-9	0	0	0	.972	-10	S-49,2-16/D-1	-1.5
1980	Atl-N	88	221	23	45	6	0	2	12	16	27	.204	.257	.258	43	-17	1	2	-1	.947	7	S-56,3-43/2-1	-0.8
Total	9	629	1766	203	446	57	14	20	172	132	178	.253	.306	.335	78	-51	9	7	-2	.957	-66	S-407,2-124/3-71,D	-7.7
■ DON BLASINGAME	Blasingame, Don Lee b: 3/16/32, Corinth, Miss. BL/TR, 5′10″, 165 lbs. Deb: 9/20/55																						
1955	StL-N	5	16	4	6	1	0	0	0	6	0	.375	.545	.438	165	2	1	1	-0	.955	2	/2-3,S-2	0.4
1956	StL-N	150	587	94	153	22	7	0	27	72	52	.261	.344	.322	81	-14	8	8	-2	.986	22	2-98,S-49/3-2	1.8
1957	StL-N	154	650	108	176	25	7	8	58	71	49	.271	.343	.368	89	-8	21	9	1	.984	26	*2-154	3.1
1958	StL-N★	143	547	71	150	19	10	2	36	57	47	.274	.344	.356	83	-12	20	5	3	.964	-1	*2-137	-0.1
1959	StL-N	150	615	90	178	26	7	1	24	67	42	.289	.361	.359	87	-9	15	15	-5	.979	21	*2-150	1.8
1960	SF-N	136	523	72	123	12	8	2	31	49	53	.235	.303	.300	70	-21	14	2	3	.979	-13	*2-133	-1.9
1961	SF-N	3	1	1	0	0	0	0	0	2	1	.000	.667	.000	100	0	0	0	0	.000	0	H	0.0

YEAR	TM/L	G	AB	R	H	2B	3B	HR	RBI	BB	SO	AVG	OBP	SLG	PRO+	BR/A	SB	CS	SBR	FA	FR	G/POS	TPR
	*Cin-N	123	450	59	100	18	4	1	21	39	38	.222	.287	.287	52	-30	4	3	-1	.972	-19	*2-116	-3.8
	Yr	126	451	60	100	18	4	1	21	41	39	.222	.289	.286	53	-30	4	3	-1	.972	-19	*2-116	-3.8
1962	Cin-N	141	494	77	139	9	7	2	35	63	44	.281	.365	.340	88	-6	4	3	-1	.976	-10	*2-137	-0.2
1963	Cin-N	18	31	4	5	2	0	0	0	7	5	.161	.316	.226	57	-1	0	1	-1	.974	0	2-11/3-2	-0.1
	Was-A	69	254	29	65	10	2	2	12	24	18	.256	.320	.335	84	-5	3	2	-0	.991	1	2-64	0.2
1964	Was-A	143	506	56	135	17	2	1	34	40	44	.267	.321	.314	78	-14	8	5	-1	.977	-30	*2-135	-3.6
1965	Was-A	129	403	47	90	8	8	1	18	35	45	.223	.289	.290	66	-18	5	4	-1	.984	1	*2-110	-1.0
1966	Was-A	68	200	18	43	9	0	1	11	18	21	.215	.280	.275	61	-10	2	1	0	.984	-1	2-58/S-1	-0.8
	KC-A	12	19	1	3	0	0	0	1	2	3	.158	.238	.158	17	-2	0	1	-1	1.000	-1	/2-4	-0.3
	Yr	80	219	19	46	9	0	1	12	20	24	.210	.276	.265	57	-12	2	2	-1	.985	-2	2-62/S-1	-1.1
Total	12	1444	5296	731	1366	178	62	21	308	552	462	.258	.330	.327	78	-149	105	60	-4	.979	-3	*2-1310/S-52,3-4	-4.5

■ **JOHNNY BLATNIK** Blatnik, John Louis b: 3/10/21, Bridgeport, Ohio BR/TR, 6', 195 lbs. Deb: 4/21/48

YEAR	TM/L	G	AB	R	H	2B	3B	HR	RBI	BB	SO	AVG	OBP	SLG	PRO+	BR/A	SB	CS	SBR	FA	FR	G/POS	TPR
1948	Phi-N	121	415	56	108	27	8	6	45	31	77	.260	.315	.407	96	-4	3			.946	-1	*O-105	-1.0
1949	Phi-N	6	8	3	1	0	0	0	0	4	1	.125	.417	.125	53	-0	0			1.000	-0	/O-2	-0.1
1950	Phi-N	4	4	0	1	0	0	0	0	2	3	.250	.500	.250	106	0	0			1.000	-0	/O-1	0.0
	StL-N	7	20	0	3	0	0	0	1	3	2	.150	.261	.150	11	-3	0			.875	-2	/O-7	-0.5
	Yr	11	24	0	4	0	0	0	1	5	5	.167	.310	.167	29	-2	0			.900	-2	/O-8	-0.5
Total	3	138	447	59	113	27	8	6	46	40	83	.253	.317	.389	91	-6	3			.945	-3	O-115	-1.6

■ **BUDDY BLATTNER** Blattner, Robert Garnett b: 2/8/20, St.Louis, Mo. BR/TR, 6'0.5", 180 lbs. Deb: 4/18/42

YEAR	TM/L	G	AB	R	H	2B	3B	HR	RBI	BB	SO	AVG	OBP	SLG	PRO+	BR/A	SB	CS	SBR	FA	FR	G/POS	TPR
1942	StL-N	19	23	3	1	0	0	0	1	3	6	.043	.185	.043	-29	-4	0			.900	-0	S-13/2-3	-0.4
1946	NY-N	126	420	63	107	18	6	11	49	56	52	.255	.351	.405	113	8	12			.976	1	*2-114/1-1	1.7
1947	NY-N	55	153	28	40	9	2	0	13	21	19	.261	.351	.346	85	-3	4			.947	-3	2-34,3-11	-0.4
1948	NY-N	8	20	3	4	1	0	0	0	3	2	.200	.304	.250	51	-1	2			1.000	2	/2-7	0.1
1949	Phi-N	64	97	15	24	6	0	5	21	19	17	.247	.371	.464	126	4	0			.981	-10	2-15,3-12/S-1	-0.6
Total	5	272	713	112	176	34	8	16	84	102	96	.247	.347	.384	102	4	18			.971	-11	2-173/3-23,S-14,1-1	0.4

■ **JEFF BLAUSER** Blauser, Jeffrey Michael b: 11/8/65, Los Gatos, Cal. BR/TR, 6', 170 lbs. Deb: 7/5/87

YEAR	TM/L	G	AB	R	H	2B	3B	HR	RBI	BB	SO	AVG	OBP	SLG	PRO+	BR/A	SB	CS	SBR	FA	FR	G/POS	TPR
1987	Atl-N	51	165	11	40	6	3	2	15	18	34	.242	.328	.352	76	-5	7	3	0	.962	10	S-50	0.9
1988	Atl-N	18	67	7	16	3	1	2	7	2	11	.239	.271	.403	87	-1	0	1	-1	.967	3	/2-9,S-8	0.2
1989	Atl-N	142	456	63	123	24	2	12	46	38	101	.270	.327	.410	107	3	5	2	0	.929	-17	3-78,2-39,S-30,/O-2	-1.0
1990	Atl-N	115	386	46	104	24	3	8	39	35	70	.269	.338	.409	99	-1	3	5	-2	.961	-3	S-93,2-14/3-9,O-1	0.2
1991	*Atl-N	129	352	49	91	14	3	11	54	54	59	.259	.360	.409	109	5	5	6	-2	.948	-36	S-85,2-32,3-18	-2.9
1992	*Atl-N	123	343	61	90	19	3	14	46	46	82	.262	.356	.458	122	10	5	5	-2	.968	-47	*S-106,2-21/3-1	-3.5
1993	*Atl-N★	161	597	110	182	29	2	15	73	85	109	.305	.405	.436	124	24	16	6	1	.970	-23	*S-161	1.5
1994	Atl-N	96	380	56	98	21	4	6	45	38	64	.258	.333	.382	84	-9	1	3	-2	.970	3	S-96	0.1
1995	*Atl-N	115	431	60	91	16	2	12	31	57	107	.211	.320	.341	72	-17	8	5	-1	.970	-1	*S-115	-0.8
1996	*Atl-N	83	265	48	65	14	1	10	35	40	54	.245	.357	.419	98	-0	6	0	2	.926	-22	S-79	-1.2
1997	*Atl-N★	151	519	90	160	31	4	17	70	70	101	.308	.411	.482	131	26	5	1	1	.973	-29	*S-149/D-1	1.1
1998	*Chi-N	119	361	49	79	11	3	4	26	60	93	.219	.343	.299	67	-16	2	2	-1	.965	-22	*S-106	-2.8
Total	12	1303	4322	650	1139	212	31	113	487	543	885	.264	.357	.405	102	21	63	39	-5	.964	-182	*S-1078,2-115,3/OD	-8.2

■ **MARV BLAYLOCK** Blaylock, Marvin Edward b: 9/30/29, Ft.Smith, Ark. d: 10/23/93, Conway, Ark. BL/TL, 6'1.5", 175 lbs. Deb: 9/26/50

YEAR	TM/L	G	AB	R	H	2B	3B	HR	RBI	BB	SO	AVG	OBP	SLG	PRO+	BR/A	SB	CS	SBR	FA	FR	G/POS	TPR
1950	NY-N	1	1	0	0	0	0	0	0	0	0	.000	.000	.000	-99	-0	0			.000	0	H	0.0
1955	Phi-N	113	259	30	54	7	7	3	24	31	43	.208	.296	.324	66	-13	6	1	1	.991	3	1-77/O-6	-1.2
1956	Phi-N	136	460	61	117	14	8	10	50	50	86	.254	.330	.385	93	-4	5	1	1	.992	-5	*1-124/O-1	-1.7
1957	Phi-N	37	26	5	4	0	0	2	4	3	8	.154	.313	.385	89	-0	0	0	0	1.000	0	1-12/O-1	0.0
Total	4	287	746	96	175	21	15	15	78	84	137	.235	.317	.363	83	-18	11	2		.992	-2	1-213/O-8	-2.9

■ **CURT BLEFARY** Blefary, Curtis Le Roy b: 7/5/43, Brooklyn, N.Y. BL/TR, 6'2", 195 lbs. Deb: 4/14/65

YEAR	TM/L	G	AB	R	H	2B	3B	HR	RBI	BB	SO	AVG	OBP	SLG	PRO+	BR/A	SB	CS	SBR	FA	FR	G/POS	TPR
1965	Bal-A	144	462	72	120	23	4	22	70	88	73	.260	.382	.470	138	25	4	2	0	.979	2	*O-136	2.3
1966	*Bal-A	131	419	73	107	14	3	23	64	73	56	.255	.373	.468	142	25	1	4	-2	.976	-3	*O-109,1-20	1.5
1967	Bal-A	155	554	69	134	19	5	22	81	73	94	.242	.339	.413	122	16	4	4	-1	.968	13	*O-103,1-52	2.2
1968	Bal-A	137	451	50	90	8	1	15	39	65	66	.200	.306	.322	90	-4	6	3	0	.962	-9	O-92,C-40,1-12	-1.8
1969	Hou-N	155	542	66	137	26	7	12	67	77	79	.253	.350	.393	110	8	8	7	-2	.987	6	*1-152/O-1	0.0
1970	NY-A	99	269	34	57	6	0	9	37	43	37	.212	.327	.335	87	-4	1	3	-2	.972	-11	O-79/1-6	-2.1
1971	NY-A	21	36	4	7	1	0	1	2	3	5	.194	.256	.306	62	-2	0	0	0	.875	-1	/O-6,1-4	-0.4
	*Oak-A	50	101	15	22	2	0	5	12	15	15	.218	.325	.386	103	0	0	1	-1	.975	-5	C-14,O-14/3-5,2-2	-0.5
	Yr	71	137	19	29	3	0	6	14	18	20	.212	.308	.365	93	-1	0	1	-1	.958	-5	O-20,C-14/3-5,12	-0.9
1972	Oak-A	8	11	1	5	2	0	0	1	0	1	.455	.455	.636	234	2	0	0	0	.000	-0	/1-1,2-1,O-1	0.1
	SD-N	74	102	10	20	3	0	3	9	19	18	.196	.322	.314	88	-1	0	0	0	.982	-8	C-12/1-6,3-3,O-3	-1.0
Total	8	974	2947	394	699	104	20	112	382	456	444	.237	.345	.400	115	65	24	24	-7	.972	-15	O-544,1-253/C32	0.3

■ **IKE BLESSITT** Blessitt, Isaiah b: 9/30/49, Detroit, Mich. BR/TR, 5'11", 185 lbs. Deb: 9/7/72

YEAR	TM/L	G	AB	R	H	2B	3B	HR	RBI	BB	SO	AVG	OBP	SLG	PRO+	BR/A	SB	CS	SBR	FA	FR	G/POS	TPR
1972	Det-A	4	5	0	0	0	0	0	0	0	2	.000	.000	.000	-97	-1	0	0	0	1.000	-0	/O-1	-0.2

■ **NED BLIGH** Bligh, Edwin Forrest b: 6/30/1864, Brooklyn, N.Y. d: 4/18/1892, Brooklyn, N.Y. BR/TR, 5'11", 172 lbs. Deb: 6/26/1886

YEAR	TM/L	G	AB	R	H	2B	3B	HR	RBI	BB	SO	AVG	OBP	SLG	PRO+	BR/A	SB	CS	SBR	FA	FR	G/POS	TPR
1886	Bal-a	3	9	0	0	0	0	0	0	1		.000	.100	.000	-69	-2	0			.833	-2	/C-3	-0.3
1888	Cin-a	3	5	0	0	0	0	0	0	0		.000	.000	.000	-95	-1	0			1.000	-1	/C-2,O-1	-0.2
1889	Col-a	28	93	6	13	1	1	0	5	4	14	.140	.200	.172	7	-11	2			.927	-3	C-28	-1.0
1890	Col-a	8	29	2	6	2	0	0	5	2		.207	.258	.276	62	-1	0			.933	2	/C-8	0.1
	*Lou-a	24	73	9	15	0	0	1	9	9		.205	.293	.247	60	-3	1			.921	-0	C-24	-0.2
	Yr	32	102	11	21	2	0	1	14	11		.206	.283	.255	61	-5	1			.925	1	C-32	-0.1
Total	4	66	209	17	34	3	1	1	19	16	14	.163	.232	.201	28	-19	3			.923	-5	/C-65,O-1	-1.6

■ **ELMER BLISS** Bliss, Elmer Ward b: 3/9/1875, Penfield, Pa. d: 3/18/62, Bradford, Pa. BL/TR, 6', 180 lbs. Deb: 9/28/03

YEAR	TM/L	G	AB	R	H	2B	3B	HR	RBI	BB	SO	AVG	OBP	SLG	PRO+	BR/A	SB	CS	SBR	FA	FR	G/POS	TPR
1903	NY-A	1	3	0	0	0	0	0	0	0		.000	.000	.000	-94	-1	0			.000	-0	/P-1	0.0
1904	NY-A	1	1	0	0	0	0	0	0	0		.000	.000	.000	-96	-0	0			.000	-0	/O-1	-0.1
Total	2	2	4	0	0	0	0	0	0	0		.000	.000	.000	-94	-1	0			—	-1	/O-1,P-1	-0.1

■ **FRANK BLISS** Bliss, Frank Eugene b: 12/10/1852, Chicago, Ill. d: 1/8/29, Nashville, Tenn. Deb: 6/20/1878

YEAR	TM/L	G	AB	R	H	2B	3B	HR	RBI	BB	SO	AVG	OBP	SLG	PRO+	BR/A	SB	CS	SBR	FA	FR	G/POS	TPR
1878	Mil-N	2	8	1	1	0	0	0	0	0	0	.125	.125	.125	-17	-1				1.000	-0	/3-1,C-1	-0.1

■ **JACK BLISS** Bliss, John Joseph Albert b: 1/9/1882, Vancouver, Wash. d: 10/23/68, Temple City, Cal. BR/TR, 5'9", 185 lbs. Deb: 5/10/08

YEAR	TM/L	G	AB	R	H	2B	3B	HR	RBI	BB	SO	AVG	OBP	SLG	PRO+	BR/A	SB	CS	SBR	FA	FR	G/POS	TPR
1908	StL-N	44	136	9	29	4	0	1	5	8		.213	.267	.265	73	-4	3			.992	5	C-43	0.5
1909	StL-N	35	113	12	25	2	1	1	8	12		.221	.307	.283	89	-1	2			.951	1	C-32	0.3
1910	StL-N	16	33	2	2	0	0	0	3	4	8	.061	.162	.061	-36	-6	0			.980	-1	C-13	-0.7
1911	StL-N	97	258	36	59	6	4	1	27	42	25	.229	.341	.295	81	-5	5			.952	-9	C-84/S-1	-0.7
1912	StL-N	49	114	11	28	3	1	0	18	19	14	.246	.372	.289	84	-1	3			.973	-6	C-41	-0.3
Total	5	241	654	70	143	15	6	3	61	85	47	.219	.318	.274	76	-18	13			.966	-10	C-213/S-1	-0.9

■ **BRUNO BLOCK** Block, James John (b: James John Blochowicz) b: 3/13/1885, Wisconsin Rapids, Wis. d: 8/6/37, S.Milwaukee, Wis. BR/TR, 5'9", 185 lbs. Deb: 8/5/07

YEAR	TM/L	G	AB	R	H	2B	3B	HR	RBI	BB	SO	AVG	OBP	SLG	PRO+	BR/A	SB	CS	SBR	FA	FR	G/POS	TPR
1907	Was-A	24	57	3	8	2	1	0	2	2		.140	.169	.211	23	-5	0			.949	-6	C-21	-1.1
1910	Chi-A	55	152	12	32	1	1	0	9	13		.211	.273	.230	60	-7	3			.964	1	C-47	-0.2
1911	Chi-A	39	115	11	35	6	1	1	18	6		.304	.339	.400	109	1	0			.972	-3	C-38	0.2
1912	Chi-A	46	136	8	35	5	6	0	26	7		.257	.294	.382	96	-2	1			.980	2	C-46	0.4
1914	Chi-F	44	105	8	21	4	1	0	14	11	17	.200	.276	.257	49	-9	1			.966	0	C-34	-0.7
Total	5	208	565	42	131	18	10	1	69	39	17	.232	.281	.304	74	-22	5			.969	-5	C-186	-1.4

YEAR	TM/L	G	AB	R	H	2B	3B	HR	RBI	BB	SO	AVG	OBP	SLG	PRO+	BR/A	SB	CS	SBR	FA	FR	G/POS	TPR
■ CY BLOCK	Block, Seymour b: 5/4/19, Brooklyn, N.Y. BR/TR, 6′, 180 lbs. Deb: 9/7/42																						
1942	Chi-N	9	33	6	12	1	1	0	4	3	3	.364	.417	.455	161	3	2			.917	-2	/3-8,2-1	0.0
1945	*Chi-N	2	7	1	1	0	0	0	1	0	0	.143	.143	.143	-21	-1	0			1.000	1	/2-1,3-1	0.0
1946	Chi-N	6	13	2	3	0	0	0	0	4	0	.231	.412	.231	86	0	0			1.000	1	/3-4	0.1
Total	3	17	53	9	16	1	1	0	5	7	3	.302	.383	.358	118	1	2			.947	-0	/3-13,2-2	0.1
■ TERRY BLOCKER	Blocker, Terry Fennell b: 8/18/59, Columbia, S.C. BL/TL, 6′2″, 195 lbs. Deb: 4/11/85																						
1985	NY-N	18	15	1	1	0	0	0	0	1	2	.067	.125	.067	-46	-3	0	0	0	1.000	-1	/O-5	-0.4
1988	Atl-N	66	198	13	42	4	2	2	10	10	20	.212	.250	.283	50	-13	1	1	-0	.994	4	O-61	-1.2
1989	Atl-N	26	31	1	7	1	0	0	1	1	5	.226	.250	.258	44	-2	1	0	0	1.000	-2	/O-8,P-1	-0.4
Total	3	110	244	15	50	5	2	2	11	12	27	.205	.242	.266	44	-18	2	1	0	.994	1	/O-74,P-1	-2.0
■ WES BLOGG	Blogg, Wesley Collins b: 1855, Norfolk, Va. d: 3/10/1897, Baltimore, Md. Deb: 6/20/1883																						
1883	Pit-a	9	34	0	5	0	0	0		0		.147	.147	.147	-5	-4				.881	-1	/C-6,O-3	-0.4
■ RON BLOMBERG	Blomberg, Ronald Mark "Boomer" b: 8/23/48, Atlanta, Ga. BL/TR, 6′1″, 205 lbs. Deb: 9/10/69																						
1969	NY-A	4	6	0	3	0	0	0	0	1	0	.500	.571	.500	210	1	0	0	0	1.000	-0	/O-2	0.1
1971	NY-A	64	199	30	64	6	2	7	31	14	23	.322	.366	.477	146	11	2	4	-2	.970	-5	O-57	0.2
1972	NY-A	107	299	36	80	22	1	14	49	38	26	.268	.356	.488	155	20	0	2	-1	.985	-8	1-95	0.4
1973	NY-A	100	301	45	99	13	1	12	57	34	25	.329	.397	.498	156	22	2	0	1	.980	1	D-55,1-41	1.9
1974	NY-A	90	264	39	82	11	2	10	48	29	33	.311	.383	.481	150	17	2	1	0	1.000	0	D-58,O-19	1.5
1975	NY-A	34	106	18	27	8	2	4	17	13	10	.255	.336	.481	131	4	0	0	0	1.000	0	D-27/O-1	0.3
1976	NY-A	1	2	0	0	0	0	0	0	0	0	.000	.000	.000	-99	-0	0	0	0	.000	0	/D-1	-0.1
1978	Chi-A	61	156	16	36	7	0	5	22	11	17	.231	.281	.372	81	-4	0	0	0	.986	-1	D-36/1-7	-0.7
Total	8	461	1333	184	391	67	8	52	224	140	134	.293	.363	.473	142	70	6	7	-2	.983	-14	D-177,1-143/O-79	3.6
■ JOE BLONG	Blong, Joseph Myles b: 9/17/1853, St.Louis, Mo. d: 9/16/1892, St.Louis, Mo. BR/TR, Deb: 5/4/1875																						
1875	RS-n	16	68	3	10	2	0	0	5	0	7	.147	.147	.176	13	-5	1	0	0	.927	3	P-15/O-4	-0.1
1876	StL-N	62	264	30	62	7	4	0	30	2	9	.235	.241	.292	81	-5				.895	1	*O-62/P-1	-0.4
1877	StL-N	58	218	17	47	8	3	0	13	4	22	.216	.230	.280	63	-9				.835	-3	*O-40,P-25	-0.8
Total	2	120	482	47	109	15	7	0	43	6	31	.226	.236	.286	72	-13				.867	-2	O-102/P-26	-1.2
■ JIMMY BLOODWORTH	Bloodworth, James Henry b: 7/26/17, Tallahassee, Fla. BR/TR, 5′11″, 180 lbs. Deb: 9/14/37																						
1937	Was-A	15	50	3	11	2	1	0	8	5	8	.220	.291	.300	51	-4	0	1	-1	.946	-1	2-14	-0.4
1939	Was-A	83	318	34	92	24	1	4	40	10	26	.289	.313	.409	90	-7	3	1	0	.972	14	2-73/O-5	1.1
1940	Was-A	119	469	47	115	17	8	11	70	16	71	.245	.272	.386	73	-21	3	1	0	.978	13	2-96,1-17/3-6	-0.3
1941	Was-A	142	506	59	124	24	3	7	66	41	58	.245	.303	.346	75	-20	1	1	-0	.971	**35**	*2-132/3-6,S-1	2.3
1942	Det-A	137	533	62	129	23	1	13	57	35	63	.242	.295	.362	78	-17	2	8	-4	.972	10	*2-134/S-2	-0.3
1943	Det-A	129	474	41	114	23	4	6	52	29	59	.241	.289	.344	79	-14	4	7	-3	.972	17	*2-129	0.8
1946	Det-A	76	249	25	61	8	1	5	36	12	26	.245	.285	.345	71	-10	3	3	-1	.974	-1	2-71	-0.7
1947	Pit-N	88	316	27	79	9	0	7	48	16	39	.250	.290	.345	66	-16	1			.979	-14	2-87	-2.4
1949	Cin-N	134	452	40	118	27	1	9	59	27	36	.261	.304	.385	83	-12	1			.981	-3	2-92,1-23/3-8	-1.2
1950	Cin-N	4	14	1	3	1	0	0	1	2	0	.214	.313	.286	58	-1	0			1.000	-3	/2-4	-0.4
	*Phi-N	54	96	6	22	2	0	0	13	6	12	.229	.275	.250	40	-8	0			1.000	-2	2-27/1-7,3-2	-0.9
	Yr	58	110	7	25	3	0	0	14	8	12	.227	.280	.255	42	-9	0			1.000	-5	2-31/1-7,3-2	-1.3
1951	Phi-N	21	42	2	6	0	0	0	1	3	9	.143	.200	.143	-6	-6	1	0	0	1.000	-1	/2-8,1-6	-0.7
Total	11	1002	3519	347	874	160	20	62	451	202	407	.248	.292	.358	74	-136	19	22		.975	64	2-867/1-53,3-22,OS	-3.1
■ BUD BLOOMFIELD	Bloomfield, Clyde Stalcup b: 1/5/36, Oklahoma City, Okla. BR/TR, 5′11.5″, 175 lbs. Deb: 9/25/63																						
1963	StL-N	1	0	0	0	0	0	0	0	0	0	—	—	—	—	0	0	0	0	.000	0	/3-1	0.0
1964	Min-A	7	7	1	1	0	0	0	0	0	0	.143	.143	.143	-20	-1	0	0	0	1.000	1	/2-3,S-2	0.0
Total	2	8	7	1	1	0	0	0	0	0	0	.143	.143	.143	-20	-1	0	0	0	1.000	1	/2-3,S-2,3-1	0.0
■ GREG BLOSSER	Blosser, Gregory Brent b: 6/26/71, Manatee, Fla. BL/TL, 6′3″, 200 lbs. Deb: 9/5/93																						
1993	Bos-A	17	28	1	2	1	0	0	1	2	7	.071	.133	.107	-33	-5	1	0	0	1.000	-1	/O-9,D-1	-0.6
1994	Bos-A	5	11	2	1	0	0	0	1	4	4	.091	.333	.091	16	-1	0	0	0	.727	-0	/O-3,D-1	-0.1
Total	2	22	39	3	3	1	0	0	2	6	11	.077	.200	.103	-16	-7	1	0	0	.870	-1	/O-12,D-2	-0.7
■ JACK BLOTT	Blott, John Leonard b: 8/24/02, Girard, Ohio d: 6/11/64, Ann Arbor, Mich. BR/TR, 6′, 210 lbs. Deb: 7/30/24																						
1924	Cin-N	2	1	0	0	0	0	0	0	0	0	.000	.000	.000	-99	-0	0	0	0	1.000	-0	/C-1	0.0
■ MIKE BLOWERS	Blowers, Michael Roy b: 4/24/65, Wurzburg, W.Germany BR/TR, 6′2″, 210 lbs. Deb: 9/1/89																						
1989	NY-A	13	38	2	10	0	0	0	3	3	13	.263	.317	.263	66	-2	0	0	0	.852	-3	3-13	-0.4
1990	NY-A	48	144	16	27	4	0	5	21	12	50	.188	.255	.319	59	-8	1	0	0	.899	-8	3-45/D-2	-1.6
1991	NY-A	15	35	3	7	0	0	1	1	4	3	.200	.282	.286	57	-2	0	0	0	.870	-3	3-14	-0.5
1992	Sea-A	31	73	7	14	3	0	1	2	6	20	.192	.253	.274	47	-5	0	0	0	.984	6	3-29/1-3	0.0
1993	Sea-A	127	379	55	106	23	3	15	57	44	98	.280	.358	.475	120	10	1	5	-3	.951	12	*3-117/O-2,C-1,1D	2.0
1994	Sea-A	85	270	37	78	13	0	9	49	25	60	.289	.351	.437	100	-0	2	2	-1	.939	10	3-48,1-20/O-9,D-9	0.7
1995	*Sea-A	134	439	59	113	24	1	23	96	53	128	.257	.337	.474	107	4	2	1	0	.947	-13	*3-126/1-7,O-5	-0.9
1996	LA-N	92	317	31	84	19	2	6	38	37	77	.265	.344	.394	102	1	0	0	0	.951	-20	3-90/1-6,S-1	-1.9
1997	*Sea-A	68	150	22	44	5	0	5	20	21	33	.293	.380	.427	111	3	0	0	0	.990	-0	1-49,3-10/O-6,D-1	0.0
1998	Oak-A	129	409	56	97	24	2	11	71	39	116	.237	.305	.386	81	-12	1	0	0	.927	-8	*3-120/1-8,D-2	-1.9
Total	10	742	2254	288	580	115	8	76	358	244	598	.257	.331	.417	97	-11	7	8	-3	.939	-28	3-612/1-94,ODSC	-4.5
■ BERT BLUE	Blue, Bird Wayne b: 12/9/1877, Bettsville, Ohio d: 9/2/29, Detroit, Mich. BR/TR, 6′3″, 200 lbs. Deb: 6/15/08																						
1908	StL-A	11	24	2	9	1	2	0	1	3		.375	.444	.583	232	3	0			.942	1	/C-8	0.5
	Phi-A	6	18	2	3	0	0	0	1	0		.167	.167	.167	8	-2	0			1.000	1	/C-6	0.0
	Yr	17	42	4	12	1	2	0	2	3		.286	.333	.405	136	2	0			.967	2	C-14	0.5
■ LU BLUE	Blue, Luzerne Atwell b: 3/5/1897, Washington, D.C. d: 7/28/58, Alexandria, Va. BB/TL, 5′10″, 165 lbs. Deb: 4/14/21																						
1921	Det-A	153	585	103	180	33	11	5	75	103	47	.308	.416	.427	117	19	13	17	-6	.990	-7	*1-152	0.2
1922	Det-A	145	584	131	175	31	9	6	45	82	48	.300	.392	.414	114	15	8	5	-1	.991	0	*1-144	0.8
1923	Det-A	129	504	100	143	27	7	1	46	96	40	.284	.402	.371	106	10	10	11	-4	.992	5	*1-129	0.3
1924	Det-A	108	395	81	123	26	7	2	53	64	26	.311	.413	.428	119	14	9	4	0	.986	3	*1-108	1.0
1925	Det-A	150	532	91	163	18	9	3	94	83	29	.306	.403	.391	104	7	19	5	3	.988	0	*1-148	0.1
1926	Det-A	128	429	92	123	24	14	1	52	90	18	.287	.413	.415	115	13	13	7	-0	.985	-5	*1-109/O-1	0.1
1927	Det-A	112	365	71	95	17	9	1	42	71	28	.260	.384	.364	94	-1	13	7	-0	.984	-2	*1-104	-0.9
1928	StL-A	154	549	116	154	32	11	14	80	105	43	.281	.400	.455	120	19	12	7	-1	.989	2	*1-154	0.7
1929	StL-A	151	573	111	168	40	10	6	61	126	32	.293	.422	.429	115	19	12	6	0	.994	-3	*1-151	0.1
1930	StL-A	117	425	85	100	27	5	4	42	81	44	.235	.363	.351	79	-12	12	7	-1	.987	0	*1-111	-2.1
1931	Chi-A	155	589	119	179	23	15	1	62	127	60	.304	.430	.399	126	31	13	3	2	.990	-3	*1-155	1.5
1932	Chi-A	112	373	51	93	21	2	0	43	64	21	.249	.364	.316	83	-7	17	6	2	.986	9	*1-105	-0.4
1933	Bro-N	1	1	0	0	0	0	0	0	0	0	.000	.000	.000	-99	-0	0			1.000	-0	/1-1	0.0
Total	13	1615	5904	1151	1696	319	109	44	695	1092	436	.287	.402	.401	109	126	151	85		.989	1	*1-1571/O-1	1.4
■ OSSIE BLUEGE	Bluege, Oswald Louis b: 10/24/1900, Chicago, Ill. d: 10/14/85, Edina, Minn. BR/TR, 5′11″, 162 lbs. Deb: 4/24/22 FMC																						
1922	Was-A	19	61	5	12	1	0	0	2	7	7	.197	.300	.213	37	-5	1	0	0	.925	-3	3-17/S-2	-0.7
1923	Was-A	109	379	48	93	15	7	2	42	48	53	.245	.343	.338	84	-8	5	3	-0	.936	4	*3-106/2-4	0.4
1924	*Was-A	117	402	59	113	15	4	2	49	39	36	.281	.358	.353	86	-7	7	5	-1	.943	-12	*3-102,2-10/S-4	-1.1
1925	*Was-A	145	522	77	150	27	4	4	79	59	56	.287	.362	.377	89	-8	16	15	-4	.953	1	*3-144/S-4	-0.1
1926	Was-A	139	487	69	132	19	8	3	65	70	46	.271	.368	.361	93	-3	12	9	-2	.952	-19	*3-134/S-8	-1.5
1927	Was-A	146	503	71	138	21	10	1	66	57	47	.274	.354	.362	87	-9	15	5	2	.961	15	*3-146	1.4

YEAR	TM/L	G	AB	R	H	2B	3B	HR	RBI	BB	SO	AVG	OBP	SLG	PRO+	BR/A	SB	CS	SBR	FA	FR	G/POS	TPR
1928	Was-A	146	518	78	154	33	7	2	75	46	27	.297	.364	.400	101	1	18	6	2	.960	12	*3-144/2-1	2.2
1929	Was-A	64	220	35	65	6	0	5	31	19	15	.295	.354	.391	91	-3	6	4	-1	.967	2	3-35,2-14,S-10	0.2
1930	Was-A	134	476	64	138	27	7	3	69	51	40	.290	.368	.395	93	-4	15	8	-0	.964	-1	*3-134	0.3
1931	Was-A	152	570	82	155	25	7	8	98	50	39	.272	.336	.382	88	-10	16	10	-1	**.960**	-5	*3-152/S-1	-0.7
1932	Was-A	149	507	64	131	22	4	5	64	83	41	.258	.367	.347	87	-7	9	7	-2	.970	6	*3-149	0.8
1933	*Was-A	140	501	63	131	14	0	6	71	55	34	.261	.338	.325	77	-15	6	7	-2	.965	-8	*3-138	-1.6
1934	Was-A	99	285	39	70	9	2	0	11	23	15	.246	.306	.291	57	-18	2	1	0	.950	8	3-41,S-30/2-5,O-5	-0.6
1935	Was-A★	100	320	44	84	14	3	0	34	37	21	.262	.341	.325	75	-11	2	2	-1	.967	1	S-58,3-25/2-4	-0.6
1936	Was-A	90	319	43	92	12	1	1	55	38	16	.288	.375	.342	83	-7	5	3	-0	.993	0	2-52,S-23,3-15	-0.1
1937	Was-A	42	127	12	36	4	2	1	13	13	9	.283	.355	.370	87	-2	1	1	-0	.952	2	S-28/1-2,3-2	0.1
1938	Was-A	58	184	25	48	12	1	0	21	21	11	.261	.340	.337	75	-7	3	1	0	.990	1	2-38,S-10/1-1,3-1	-0.3
1939	Was-A	18	59	5	9	0	0	0	3	7	2	.153	.242	.153	3	-9	1	0	0	.989	1	1-11/2-2,S-2,3-2	-0.8
Total	18	1867	6440	883	1751	276	67	43	848	723	515	.272	.352	.356	85	-131	140	87	-10	.957	4	*3-1487,S-180,2/10	-2.7

■ OTTO BLUEGE
Bluege, Otto Adam "Squeaky" b: 7/20/09, Chicago, Ill. d: 6/28/77, Chicago, Ill. BR/TR, 5'10", 154 lbs. Deb: 4/12/32 F

YEAR	TM/L	G	AB	R	H	2B	3B	HR	RBI	BB	SO	AVG	OBP	SLG	PRO+	BR/A	SB	CS	SBR	FA	FR	G/POS	TPR
1932	Cin-N	1	0	1	0	0	0	0	0	0	0	—	—	—	—	0	0			.000	0	R	0.0
1933	Cin-N	108	291	17	62	6	2	0	18	26	29	.213	.278	.247	52	-18	0			.937	-9	S-95,2-10/3-1	-2.2
Total	2	109	291	18	62	6	2	0	18	26	29	.213	.278	.247	52	-18	0			.937	-9	/S-95,2-10,3-1	-2.2

■ RED BLUHM
Bluhm, Harvey Fred b: 6/27/1894, Cleveland, Ohio d: 5/7/52, Flint, Mich. BR/TR, 5'11", 165 lbs. Deb: 7/3/18

YEAR	TM/L	G	AB	R	H	2B	3B	HR	RBI	BB	SO	AVG	OBP	SLG	PRO+	BR/A	SB	CS	SBR	FA	FR	G/POS	TPR
1918	Bos-A	1	1	0	0	0	0	0	0	0	0	.000	.000	.000	-99	-0	0			.000	0	H	0.0

■ CHET BOAK
Boak, Chester Robert b: 6/19/35, New Castle, Pa. d: 11/28/83, Emporium, Pa. BR/TR, 6', 180 lbs. Deb: 9/18/60

YEAR	TM/L	G	AB	R	H	2B	3B	HR	RBI	BB	SO	AVG	OBP	SLG	PRO+	BR/A	SB	CS	SBR	FA	FR	G/POS	TPR
1960	KC-A	5	13	1	2	0	0	0	1	0	2	.154	.214	.154	1	-2	0	0	0	.957	1	/2-5	-0.1
1961	Was-A	5	7	0	0	0	0	0	0	1	1	.000	.125	.000	-64	-2	1	0	0	1.000	-1	/2-1	-0.2
Total	2	10	20	1	2	0	0	0	1	1	3	.100	.182	.100	-22	-3	1	0	0	.962	0	/2-6	-0.3

■ FREDERICK BOARDMAN
Boardman, Frederick Deb: 8/29/1874

YEAR	TM/L	G	AB	R	H	2B	3B	HR	RBI	BB	SO	AVG	OBP	SLG	PRO+	BR/A	SB	CS	SBR	FA	FR	G/POS	TPR
1874	Bal-n	1	4	0	1	0	0	0	0	0	0	.250	.250	.250	61	-0	0	0	0	.000	-0	/O-1	0.0

■ RANDY BOBB
Bobb, Mark Randall b: 1/1/48, Los Angeles, Cal. d: 6/13/82, Carnelian Bay, Cal BR/TR, 6'1", 185 lbs. Deb: 8/15/68

YEAR	TM/L	G	AB	R	H	2B	3B	HR	RBI	BB	SO	AVG	OBP	SLG	PRO+	BR/A	SB	CS	SBR	FA	FR	G/POS	TPR
1968	Chi-N	7	8	0	1	0	0	0	0	1	2	.125	.222	.125	6	-1	0	0	0	1.000	0	/C-7	-0.1
1969	Chi-N	3	2	0	0	0	0	0	0	0	1	.000	.000	.000	-89	-0	0	0	0	1.000	1	/C-2	0.0
Total	2	10	10	0	1	0	0	0	0	1	3	.100	.182	.100	-14	-1	0	0	0	1.000	1	/C-9	-0.1

■ JOHN BOCCABELLA
Boccabella, John Dominic b: 6/29/41, San Francisco, Cal BR/TR, 6'1", 200 lbs. Deb: 9/2/63

YEAR	TM/L	G	AB	R	H	2B	3B	HR	RBI	BB	SO	AVG	OBP	SLG	PRO+	BR/A	SB	CS	SBR	FA	FR	G/POS	TPR
1963	Chi-N	24	74	7	14	4	1	1	5	6	21	.189	.250	.311	57	-4	0	1	-1	.996	-1	1-24	-0.7
1964	Chi-N	9	23	4	9	2	1	0	6	0	3	.391	.391	.565	159	2	0	0	0	1.000	-1	/1-5,O-2	0.1
1965	Chi-N	6	12	2	4	0	0	2	4	1	2	.333	.385	.833	227	2	0	0	0	1.000	-0	/1-2,O-1	0.2
1966	Chi-N	75	206	22	47	9	0	6	25	14	39	.228	.277	.359	74	-7	0	1	-1	.981	1	O-33,1-30/C-5	-1.0
1967	Chi-N	25	35	0	6	1	1	0	8	3	7	.171	.256	.257	45	-2	0	0	0	1.000	-1	/O-9,1-3,C-1	-0.4
1968	Chi-N	7	14	0	1	0	0	0	1	2	2	.071	.188	.071	-19	-2	0	0	0	1.000	-1	/C-4,O-1	-0.3
1969	Mon-N	40	86	4	9	2	0	1	6	6	30	.105	.172	.163	-6	-12	1	0	0	1.000	1	C-32	-1.1
1970	Mon-N	61	145	18	39	3	1	5	17	11	24	.269	.321	.407	94	-2	0	1	-1	.993	10	1-33,C-24/3-1	0.6
1971	Mon-N	74	177	15	39	11	0	3	15	14	26	.220	.281	.333	73	-6	0	1	-1	.979	-1	C-37,1-37/3-2	-1.0
1972	Mon-N	83	207	14	47	8	1	1	10	9	29	.227	.263	.290	56	-12	1	2	-1	.983	8	C-73/1-7,3-1	-0.4
1973	Mon-N	118	403	25	94	13	0	7	46	26	57	.233	.281	.318	63	-20	1	1	-0	.980	1	*C-117/1-1	-1.5
1974	SF-N	29	80	6	11	3	0	0	5	4	6	.138	.179	.175	-1	-11	0	0	0	.991	-2	C-26	-1.3
Total	12	551	1462	117	320	56	5	26	148	96	246	.219	.269	.317	62	-76	3	7	-3	.984	14	C-319,1-142/O-46,3	-6.8

■ MILT BOCEK
Bocek, Milton Frank b: 7/16/12, Chicago, Ill. BR/TR, 6'1", 185 lbs. Deb: 9/3/33

YEAR	TM/L	G	AB	R	H	2B	3B	HR	RBI	BB	SO	AVG	OBP	SLG	PRO+	BR/A	SB	CS	SBR	FA	FR	G/POS	TPR
1933	Chi-A	11	22	3	8	1	0	1	3	4	6	.364	.462	.545	173	2	0	0	0	1.000	-2	/O-6	0.0
1934	Chi-A	19	38	3	8	1	0	0	3	5	5	.211	.302	.237	39	-3	0	0	0	1.000	2	O-10	-0.1
Total	2	30	60	6	16	2	0	1	6	9	11	.267	.362	.350	86	-1	0	0	0	1.000	1	/O-16	-0.1

■ BRUCE BOCHTE
Bochte, Bruce Anton b: 11/12/50, Pasadena, Cal. BL/TL, 6'3", 200 lbs. Deb: 7/19/74

YEAR	TM/L	G	AB	R	H	2B	3B	HR	RBI	BB	SO	AVG	OBP	SLG	PRO+	BR/A	SB	CS	SBR	FA	FR	G/POS	TPR
1974	Cal-A	57	196	24	53	4	1	5	26	18	23	.270	.335	.378	111	3	6	3	0	.985	-4	O-39,1-24	-0.4
1975	Cal-A	107	375	41	107	19	3	3	48	45	43	.285	.365	.376	118	10	3	4	-2	.987	-7	*1-105/D-1	-0.5
1976	Cal-A	146	466	53	120	17	1	2	49	64	53	.258	.350	.311	101	3	4	5	-2	.988	-2	O-86,1-59/D-1	-0.9
1977	Cal-A	25	100	12	29	4	0	2	8	7	4	.290	.336	.390	101	0	3	2	-0	1.000	2	O-24/D-1	0.1
	Cle-A	112	392	52	119	19	1	5	43	40	38	.304	.368	.395	112	7	3	2	-0	.966	5	O-76,1-36/D-1	0.7
	Yr	137	492	64	148	23	1	7	51	47	42	.301	.362	.394	110	7	6	4	-1	.974	7	*O-100,1-36/D-2	0.8
1978	Sea-A	140	486	58	128	25	3	11	51	60	47	.263	.346	.395	108	6	3	4	-2	.984	-4	O-91,D-43/1-1	-0.5
1979	Sea-A★	150	554	81	175	38	6	16	100	67	64	.316	.392	.493	134	28	2	2	-1	.991	5	*1-147	2.2
1980	Sea-A	148	520	62	156	34	4	13	78	72	81	.300	.385	.456	128	22	2	3	-1	.996	6	*1-133,D-11	1.8
1981	Sea-A	99	335	39	87	16	0	6	30	47	53	.260	.354	.361	102	2	1	3	-2	.995	-5	1-82,O-14/D-1	-0.9
1982	Sea-A	144	509	58	151	21	0	12	70	67	71	.297	.382	.409	114	12	8	5	-1	.988	-5	O-99,1-34,D-12	0.1
1984	Oak-A	148	469	58	124	23	0	5	52	52	59	.264	.338	.345	96	-2	2	5	-2	.993	-13	*1-144/D-2	-2.6
1985	Oak-A	137	424	48	125	17	1	14	60	49	58	.295	.368	.439	129	17	3	1	0	.990	-9	*1-128	0.2
1986	Oak-A	125	407	57	104	13	1	6	43	65	68	.256	.358	.337	98	1	3	2	-0	.991	2	*1-115/D-1	-0.6
Total	12	1538	5233	643	1478	250	21	100	658	653	662	.282	.363	.396	114	109	43	41	-12	.992	-30	*1-1008,O-429/D-74	-1.3

■ BRUCE BOCHY
Bochy, Bruce Douglas b: 4/16/55, Landes De Bussac, France BR/TR, 6'4", 210 lbs. Deb: 7/19/78 MC

YEAR	TM/L	G	AB	R	H	2B	3B	HR	RBI	BB	SO	AVG	OBP	SLG	PRO+	BR/A	SB	CS	SBR	FA	FR	G/POS	TPR
1978	Hou-N	54	154	8	41	8	0	3	15	11	35	.266	.315	.377	100	-1	0	0	0	.974	3	C-53	0.3
1979	Hou-N	56	129	11	28	4	0	1	6	13	25	.217	.294	.271	59	-7	0	0	0	.970	-1	C-55	-0.7
1980	*Hou-N	22	22	0	4	1	0	0	0	5	7	.182	.357	.227	72	-1	0	0	0	1.000	-2	C-10/1-1	-0.3
1982	NY-N	17	49	4	15	4	0	2	8	4	6	.306	.358	.510	141	3	0	0	0	.961	4	C-16/1-1	0.7
1983	SD-N	23	42	2	9	1	1	0	3	0	9	.214	.214	.286	39	-4	0	0	0	1.000	2	C-11	-0.2
1984	*SD-N	37	92	10	21	5	1	4	15	3	21	.228	.253	.435	90	-2	0	1	-1	.988	5	C-36	0.4
1985	SD-N	48	112	16	30	2	0	6	13	6	30	.268	.305	.446	109	1	0	0	0	.988	1	C-46	0.3
1986	SD-N	63	127	16	32	9	0	8	22	14	23	.252	.326	.512	130	5	1	0	0	.991	3	C-48	1.0
1987	SD-N	38	75	8	12	3	0	2	11	11	21	.160	.267	.280	47	-6	0	1	-1	.962	-4	C-23	-0.9
Total	9	358	802	75	192	37	2	26	93	67	177	.239	.300	.388	92	-12	1	2	-1	.979	9	C-298/1-2	0.6

■ EDDIE BOCKMAN
Bockman, Joseph Edward b: 7/26/20, Santa Ana, Cal. BR/TR, 5'9", 175 lbs. Deb: 9/11/46

YEAR	TM/L	G	AB	R	H	2B	3B	HR	RBI	BB	SO	AVG	OBP	SLG	PRO+	BR/A	SB	CS	SBR	FA	FR	G/POS	TPR
1946	NY-A	4	12	2	1	1	0	0	0	1	4	.083	.154	.167	-10	-2	0	0	0	.933	1	/3-4	0.0
1947	Cle-A	46	66	8	17	2	2	1	14	5	17	.258	.310	.394	97	-1	0	0	0	.946	9	3-12/2-4,S-1,O-1	0.8
1948	Pit-N	70	176	23	42	7	1	4	23	17	35	.239	.309	.358	79	-5	2			.962	8	3-51/2-1	0.2
1949	Pit-N	79	220	21	49	6	1	6	19	23	31	.223	.296	.341	69	-10	3			.959	6	3-68/2-5	-0.5
Total	4	199	474	54	109	16	4	11	56	46	87	.230	.299	.350	74	-18	5	0		.958	24	3-135/2-10,O-1,S-1	0.5

■ PING BODIE
Bodie, Frank Stephan (b: Francesco Stephano Pezzolo)
b: 10/8/1887, San Francisco, Cal. d: 12/17/61, San Francisco, Cal BR/TR, 5'8", 195 lbs. Deb: 4/22/11

YEAR	TM/L	G	AB	R	H	2B	3B	HR	RBI	BB	SO	AVG	OBP	SLG	PRO+	BR/A	SB	CS	SBR	FA	FR	G/POS	TPR
1911	Chi-A	145	551	75	159	27	13	4	97	49		.289	.348	.407	114	9	14			.969	7	*O-128,2-16	0.9
1912	Chi-A	138	472	58	139	24	7	5	72	43		.294	.358	.407	123	13	12			.969	-12	*O-130	-0.6
1913	Chi-A	127	406	39	107	14	8	8	48	35	57	.264	.325	.397	112	4	5			.968	-5	*O-119	-0.6
1914	Chi-A	107	327	21	75	9	5	3	29	21	35	.229	.278	.315	79	-9	12	11	-3	.959	-2	O-95	-2.1
1917	Phi-A	148	557	51	162	28	11	7	74	53	40	.291	.356	.418	138	24	13			.963	5	*O-145/1-1	2.2
1918	NY-A	91	324	36	83	12	6	3	46	27	24	.256	.319	.358	102	-0	6			.971	4	O-90	-0.1
1919	NY-A	134	475	45	132	27	8	6	59	36	46	.278	.334	.406	107	3	15			.959	-8	*O-134	-1.5
1920	NY-A	129	471	63	139	26	12	7	79	40	30	.295	.350	.446	106	3	6	14	-7	.968	-10	*O-129	-2.2

YEAR	TM/L	G	AB	R	H	2B	3B	HR	RBI	BB	SO	AVG	OBP	SLG	PRO+	BR/A	SB	CS	SBR	FA	FR	G/POS	TPR
1921	NY-A	31	87	5	15	2	2	0	12	8	8	.172	.242	.241	23	-10	0	1	-1	.944	-6	O-25	-1.8
Total	9	1050	3670	393	1011	169	72	43	516	312	240	.275	.335	.396	110	36	83	26		.965	-27	O-995/2-16,1-1	-5.8
■ TONY BOECKEL	Boeckel, Norman Doxie b: 8/25/1892, Los Angeles, Cal. d: 2/16/24, Torrey Pines, Cal. BR/TR, 5'10.5", 175 lbs. Deb: 7/23/17																						
1917	Pit-N	64	219	16	58	11	1	0	23	8	31	.265	.297	.324	88	-3	6			.935	-4	3-62	-0.7
1919	Pit-N	45	152	18	38	9	2	0	16	18	20	.250	.333	.336	98	0	11			.930	-8	3-45	-0.7
	Bos-N	95	365	42	91	11	5	1	26	35	13	.249	.317	.315	94	-2	10			.960	-4	3-93	-0.2
	Yr	140	517	60	129	20	7	1	42	53	33	.250	.322	.321	95	-2	21			.951	-12	*3-138	-0.9
1920	Bos-N	153	582	70	156	28	5	3	62	38	50	.268	.314	.349	94	-5	18	15	-4	.936	-7	*3-149/S-3,2-1	-0.8
1921	Bos-N	153	592	93	185	20	13	10	84	52	41	.313	.370	.441	120	17	20	15	-3	.933	-12	*3-153	1.2
1922	Bos-N	119	402	61	116	19	6	6	47	35	32	.289	.349	.410	99	-1	14	8	-1	.952	-11	*3-106	-0.4
1923	Bos-N	148	568	72	169	32	4	7	79	51	31	.298	.357	.405	105	4	11	8	-2	.939	-10	*3-147/S-1	0.6
Total	6	777	2880	372	813	130	36	27	337	237	218	.282	.339	.381	102	10	90	46		.941	-55	3-755/S-4,2-1	-1.0
■ LEN BOEHMER	Boehmer, Leonard Joseph Stephen b: 6/28/41, Flinthill, Mo. BR/TR, 6'1", 192 lbs. Deb: 6/18/67																						
1967	Cin-N	2	3	0	0	0	0	0	0	0	0	.000	.000	.000	-90	-1	0	0	0	1.000	-0	/2-1	-0.1
1969	NY-A	45	108	5	19	4	0	0	7	8	10	.176	.233	.213	26	-11	0	1	-1	.995	1	1-21/3-8,2-1,S-1	-1.2
1971	NY-A	3	5	0	0	0	0	0	0	0	0	.000	.000	.000	-99	-1	0	0	0	1.000	-0	/3-1	-0.2
Total	3	50	116	5	19	4	0	0	7	8	10	.164	.218	.198	18	-13	0	1	-1	.933	1	/1-21,3-9,2-2,S-1	-1.5
■ TIM BOGAR	Bogar, Timothy Paul b: 10/28/66, Indianapolis, Ind. BR/TR, 6'2", 198 lbs. Deb: 4/21/93																						
1993	NY-N	78	205	19	50	13	0	3	25	14	29	.244	.302	.351	75	-7	0	1	-1	.972	15	S-66/3-7,2-6	1.1
1994	NY-N	50	52	5	8	0	0	2	5	4	11	.154	.214	.269	25	-6	1	0	0	.909	8	3-22,1-14/S-7,2O	0.2
1995	NY-N	78	145	17	42	7	0	1	21	9	25	.290	.331	.359	85	-3	1	0	0	.971	1	S-27,3-25,1-10,/2O	-0.1
1996	NY-N	91	89	17	19	4	0	0	6	8	20	.213	.293	.258	49	-6	1	3	-2	1.000	8	1-32,3-25,S-19,/2-8	0.0
1997	Hou-N	97	241	30	60	14	4	4	30	24	42	.249	.325	.390	89	-4	4	1	1	.985	24	S-80,3-14/1-1	2.5
1998	Hou-N	79	156	12	24	4	1	1	8	9	36	.154	.210	.212	10	-21	2	1	0	.989	18	S-55,2-11,3-11,/D-1	0.0
Total	6	473	888	100	203	42	5	11	95	68	163	.229	.291	.324	63	-48	9	6	-1	.982	73	S-254,3-104/12OD	3.7
■ TERRY BOGENER	Bogener, Terry Wayne b: 9/28/55, Hannibal, Mo. BL/TL, 6', 193 lbs. Deb: 6/14/82																						
1982	Tex-A	24	60	6	13	2	1	1	4	4	8	.217	.288	.333	74	-2	2	0	1	1.000	-4	O-16/D-4	-0.5
■ WADE BOGGS	Boggs, Wade Anthony b: 6/15/58, Omaha, Neb. BL/TR, 6'2", 197 lbs. Deb: 4/10/82																						
1982	Bos-A	104	338	51	118	14	1	5	44	35	21	.349	.410	.441	126	13	1	0	0	.994	18	1-49,3-44/O-1,D-3	2.8
1983	Bos-A	153	582	100	210	44	7	5	74	92	36	**.361**	**.449**	.486	147	41	3	3	-1	.947	8	*3-153	4.5
1984	Bos-A	158	625	109	203	31	4	6	55	89	44	.325	.409	.416	123	23	3	2	-0	.959	21	*3-156/D-2	4.2
1985	Bos-A★	161	653	107	**240**	42	3	8	78	96	61	**.368**	**.452**	.478	149	49	2	1	0	.965	8	*3-161	5.3
1986	*Bos-A★	149	580	107	207	47	2	8	71	**105**	44	**.357**	**.455**	.486	156	51	0	4	-2	.953	-1	*3-149	4.3
1987	Bos-A★	147	551	108	200	40	6	24	89	105	48	**.363**	**.467**	.588	**173**	**63**	1	3	-2	.965	3	*3-145/1-1,D-1	**5.8**
1988	*Bos-A★	155	584	**128**	214	**45**	6	5	58	**125**	34	**.366**	**.480**	.490	165	**60**	2	3	-1	.971	-5	*3-151/D-3	5.3
1989	Bos-A★	156	621	**113**	205	**51**	7	3	54	107	51	.330	**.434**	.449	141	39	2	6	-3	.958	-4	*3-152/D-3	3.3
1990	*Bos-A★	155	619	89	187	44	5	6	63	87	68	.302	.389	.418	120	19	0	0	0	.946	-22	*3-152/D-3	-0.2
1991	Bos-A★	144	546	93	181	42	2	8	51	89	32	.332	.425	.460	138	32	1	2	-1	.968	1	*3-140	3.2
1992	Bos-A★	143	514	62	133	22	4	7	50	74	31	.259	.356	.358	94	-2	1	3	-2	.952	-1	*3-117,D-21	-0.5
1993	NY-A★	143	560	83	169	26	1	2	59	74	49	.302	.383	.363	105	7	0	1	-1	**.970**	20	*3-134/D-8	2.6
1994	NY-A★	97	366	61	125	19	1	11	55	61	29	.342	.437	.489	144	27	2	1	0	.962	13	3-93/1-4	3.6
1995	*NY-A★	126	460	76	149	22	4	5	63	74	50	.324	.418	.422	120	17	1	1	-0	**.981**	-6	*3-117/1-9	1.0
1996	*NY-A★	132	501	80	156	29	2	2	41	67	32	.311	.393	.389	99	2	1	2	-1	.974	-6	*3-123/D-4	-0.5
1997	*NY-A	104	353	55	103	23	1	4	28	48	38	.292	.377	.397	103	3	0	1	-1	.978	3	3-76,D-19/P-1	0.4
1998	TB-A	123	435	51	122	23	4	7	52	46	54	.280	.349	.400	90	-6	3	2	-0	.973	-3	3-78,D-33	-1.0
Total	17	2350	8888	1473	2922	564	60	116	985	1374	722	.329	.420	.445	131	439	23	35	-14	.963	47	*3-2141,D-100/1PO	44.1
■ CHARLIE BOHN	Bohn, Charles b: 1857, Cleveland, Ohio d: 8/1/03, Cleveland, Ohio BR/TR, 5'9", 165 lbs. Deb: 6/20/1882																						
1882	Lou-a	4	13	0	2	0	0	0	0			.154	.154	.154	4	-1				.667	1	/O-2,P-2	0.0
■ SAM BOHNE	Bohne, Samuel Arthur (b: Samuel Arthur Cohen) b: 10/22/1896, San Francisco, Cal d: 5/23/77, Palo Alto, Cal. BR/TR, 5'8.5", 175 lbs. Deb: 9/9/16																						
1916	StL-N	14	38	3	9	0	0	0	0	4	6	.237	.310	.237	69	-1	3			.870	-4	S-14	-0.5
1921	Cin-N	153	613	98	175	28	16	3	44	54	38	.285	.347	.398	101	1	26	22	-5	.973	8	*2-102,3-53	1.0
1922	Cin-N	112	383	53	105	14	5	3	51	39	18	.274	.344	.360	83	-9	13	8	-1	.958	11	2-85,S-20	0.5
1923	Cin-N	139	539	77	136	18	10	3	47	48	37	.252	.316	.340	74	-20	16	19	-7	.975	5	2-96,3-35/S-9,1-1	-1.6
1924	Cin-N	100	349	42	89	15	9	4	46	18	24	.255	.293	.384	81	-10	9	6	-1	.941	-9	2-48,S-40,3-12	-1.5
1925	Cin-N	73	214	24	55	9	1	2	24	14	14	.257	.303	.336	65	-12	6	4	-1	.933	-8	S-49,2-10/O-4,13	-1.4
1926	Cin-N	25	54	8	11	0	2	0	5	4	8	.204	.259	.278	46	-4	1			.931	-3	S-20	-0.5
	Bro-N	47	125	4	25	3	2	1	11	12	9	.200	.270	.280	49	-9	1			.965	11	2-31,3-15	0.3
	Yr	72	179	12	36	3	4	1	16	16	17	.201	.267	.279	48	-13	2			.965	8	2-31,S-20,3-15	-0.2
Total	7	663	2315	309	605	87	45	16	228	193	154	.261	.321	.359	81	-64	75	59		.966	11	2-372,S-152,3/O1	-3.7
■ BRUCE BOISCLAIR	Boisclair, Bruce Armand b: 12/9/52, Putnam, Conn. BL/TL, 6'2", 190 lbs. Deb: 9/11/74																						
1974	NY-N	7	12	0	3	1	0	0	1	1	4	.250	.308	.333	81	-0	0	0	0	.923	1	/O-5	0.1
1976	NY-N	110	286	42	82	13	3	2	13	28	55	.287	.350	.374	112	4	9	5	-0	.981	-6	O-87	-0.5
1977	NY-N	127	307	41	90	21	1	4	44	31	57	.293	.360	.407	110	5	6	4	-1	.959	-9	O-91/1-9	-0.8
1978	NY-N	107	214	24	48	7	1	4	15	23	43	.224	.300	.322	77	-7	3	3	-1	.983	-5	O-69/1-1	-1.6
1979	NY-N	59	98	7	18	5	1	0	4	3	24	.184	.216	.255	29	-10	0	2	-1	1.000	-2	O-24/1-1	-1.5
Total	5	410	917	114	241	47	6	10	77	86	183	.263	.327	.360	94	-8	18	14	-3	.975	-21	O-276/1-11	-4.3
■ BOB BOKEN	Boken, Robert Anthony b: 2/23/08, Maryville, Ill. d: 10/6/88, Las Vegas, Nev. BR/TR, 6'2", 165 lbs. Deb: 4/25/33																						
1933	Was-A	55	133	19	37	5	2	3	26	9	16	.278	.324	.414	95	-1	0	0	0	.969	-2	2-31,3-19,S-10	-0.1
1934	Was-A	11	27	5	6	1	1	0	6	3	1	.222	.300	.333	66	-1	2	0	1	.864	1	/3-6,2-1	0.1
	Chi-A	81	297	30	70	9	1	3	40	15	32	.236	.275	.303	47	-24	2	1	0	.929	-10	2-57,S-22	-2.7
	Yr	92	324	35	76	10	2	3	46	18	33	.235	.277	.306	49	-25	4	1	1	.929	-9	2-58,S-22/3-6	-2.6
Total	2	147	457	54	113	15	4	6	72	27	49	.247	.291	.337	62	-26	4	1	1	.941	-11	/2-89,S-32,3-25	-2.7
■ BOLAND	Boland Deb: 9/4/1875																						
1875	Atl-n	1	4	0	0	0	0	0	0	0	0	.000	.000	.000	-99	-1	0	0	0	.750	-0	/3-1	-0.1
■ ED BOLAND	Boland, Edward John b: 4/18/08, Long Island City, N.Y. d: 2/5/93, Clearwater, Fla. BL/TL, 5'10", 165 lbs. Deb: 9/18/34																						
1934	Phi-N	8	30	2	9	1	1	0	5	0	2	.300	.300	.400	76	-1	1			.778	-2	/O-7	-0.3
1935	Phi-N	30	47	5	10	0	0	0	4	4	6	.213	.275	.213	30	-5	1			.833	-3	O-10	-0.7
1944	Was-A	19	59	4	16	4	0	0	14	0	6	.271	.271	.339	77	-2	0	0	0	.889	-1	O-14	-0.4
Total	3	57	136	11	35	5	1	0	23	4	14	.257	.279	.309	59	-8	2	0		.852	-5	/O-31	-1.4
■ CHARLIE BOLD	Bold, Charles Dickens "Dutch" b: 10/27/1894, Karlskrona, Sweden d: 7/29/78, Chelsea, Mass. BR/TR, 6'2", 185 lbs. Deb: 8/24/14																						
1914	StL-A	2	1	0	0	0	0	0	0	0	1	.000	.000	.000	-99	-0	0			.500	-0	/1-1	-0.1
■ CARL BOLES	Boles, Carl Theodore b: 10/31/34, Center Point, Ark. BR/TR, 5'11", 185 lbs. Deb: 8/2/62																						
1962	SF-N	19	24	4	9	0	0	0	1	0	6	.375	.375	.375	104	0	0	0	0	.833	-1	/O-7	-0.2
■ JOE BOLEY	Boley, John Peter (b: John Peter Bolinsky) b: 7/19/1896, Mahanoy City, Pa. d: 12/30/62, Mahanoy City, Pa. BR/TR, 5'11", 170 lbs. Deb: 4/12/27																						
1927	Phi-A	118	370	49	115	18	8	1	52	26	14	.311	.361	.411	95	-3	8	5	-1	.951	-11	*S-114	-0.3
1928	Phi-A	132	425	49	112	20	3	0	49	32	11	.264	.317	.325	67	-20	5	1	1	.949	-17	*S-132	-2.1
1929	*Phi-A	91	303	36	76	17	6	2	47	24	16	.251	.310	.366	71	-14	1	0	0	.963	-10	S-88/3-1	-1.2
1930	*Phi-A	121	420	41	116	22	2	4	55	32	26	.276	.335	.367	74	-16	0	0	0	**.970**	-7	*S-120	-0.9

YEAR	TM/L	G	AB	R	H	2B	3B	HR	RBI	BB	SO	AVG	OBP	SLG	PRO+	BR/A	SB	CS	SBR	FA	FR	G/POS	TPR
1931	*Phi-A	67	224	26	51	9	3	0	20	15	13	.228	.282	.295	49	-17	1	1	-0	.954	-13	S-62/2-1	-2.3
1932	Phi-A	10	34	2	7	2	0	0	4	1	4	.206	.229	.265	26	-4	0	1	-1	.897	-7	S-10	-1.0
	Cle-A	1	4	0	1	0	0	0	0	0	0	.250	.250	.250	28	-0	0	0	0	.000	0	/S-1	0.0
	Yr	11	38	2	8	2	0	0	4	1	4	.211	.231	.263	27	-4	0	1	-1	.897	-7	S-11	-1.0
Total	6	540	1780	203	478	88	22	7	227	130	84	.269	.323	.354	72	-74	15	8	-0	.957	-64	S-527/2-1,3-1	-7.8

■ JIM BOLGER
Bolger, James Cyril "Dutch" b: 2/23/32, Cincinnati, Ohio BR/TR, 6′2″, 180 lbs. Deb: 6/24/50

YEAR	TM/L	G	AB	R	H	2B	3B	HR	RBI	BB	SO	AVG	OBP	SLG	PRO+	BR/A	SB	CS	SBR	FA	FR	G/POS	TPR
1950	Cin-N	2	1	0	0	0	0	0	0	0	0	.000	.000	.000	-99	-0	0			.000	-1	/O-2	-0.1
1951	Cin-N	2	0	1	0	0	0	0	0	0	0	—	—	—		-0	1	0	0	1.000	0	R	0.0
1954	Cin-N	5	3	1	1	0	0	0	0	0	1	.333	.333	.333	72	-0	0	0	0	.000	-1	/O-2	-0.1
1955	Chi-N	64	160	19	33	5	4	0	7	9	17	.206	.257	.287	45	-13	2	2	-1	.955	-3	O-51	-1.8
1957	Chi-N	112	273	28	75	4	1	5	29	10	36	.275	.308	.352	78	-9	0	1	-1	.987	2	O-63/3-3	-1.1
1958	Chi-N	84	120	15	27	4	1	1	11	9	20	.225	.285	.300	56	-8	0	1	-1	.940	-6	O-37	-1.5
1959	Cle-A	8	7	0	0	0	0	0	0	1	1	.000	.125	.000	-65	-2	0	0	0	.000	0	H	-0.2
	Phi-N	35	48	1	4	1	0	0	1	3	8	.083	.137	.104	-34	-9	0	0	0	.938	-1	/O-9	-1.0
Total	7	312	612	65	140	14	6	6	48	32	83	.229	.274	.301	54	-40	3	4		.966	-9	O-164/3-3	-5.8

■ FRANK BOLICK
Bolick, Frank Charles b: 6/28/66, Ashland, Pa. BB/TR, 5′10″, 180 lbs. Deb: 4/5/93

YEAR	TM/L	G	AB	R	H	2B	3B	HR	RBI	BB	SO	AVG	OBP	SLG	PRO+	BR/A	SB	CS	SBR	FA	FR	G/POS	TPR
1993	Mon-N	95	213	25	45	13	0	4	24	23	37	.211	.300	.329	65	-10	1	0	0	.992	3	1-51,3-24	-1.1
1998	Ana-A	21	45	3	7	2	0	1	2	11	8	.156	.321	.267	55	-3	0	0	0	1.000	-0	/3-7,1-1,O-1,D-9	-0.3
Total	2	116	258	28	52	15	0	5	26	34	45	.202	.304	.318	63	-13	1	0	0	.992	2	/1-52,3-31,D-9,O-1	-1.4

■ FRANK BOLLING
Bolling, Frank Elmore b: 11/16/31, Mobile, Ala. BR/TR, 6′1″, 175 lbs. Deb: 4/13/54 F

YEAR	TM/L	G	AB	R	H	2B	3B	HR	RBI	BB	SO	AVG	OBP	SLG	PRO+	BR/A	SB	CS	SBR	FA	FR	G/POS	TPR
1954	Det-A	117	368	46	87	15	2	6	38	36	51	.236	.304	.337	77	-12	3	5	-2	.974	-29	*2-113	-3.8
1956	Det-A	102	366	53	103	21	7	7	45	42	51	.281	.359	.434	108	4	6	2	1	.978	-15	*2-102	-0.2
1957	Det-A	146	576	72	149	27	6	15	40	57	64	.259	.328	.405	96	-3	4	9	-4	.980	-3	*2-146	0.2
1958	Det-A	154	610	91	164	25	4	14	75	54	54	.269	.332	.392	92	-7	6	4	-1	**.985**	8	*2-154	1.2
1959	Det-A	127	459	56	122	18	3	13	55	45	37	.266	.341	.403	98	-1	2	2	-1	.987	-1	*2-126	0.7
1960	Det-A	139	536	64	136	20	4	9	59	40	48	.254	.308	.356	77	-18	7	4	-0	.978	-5	*2-138	-0.9
1961	Mil-N★	148	585	86	153	16	4	15	56	57	62	.262	.330	.379	93	-6	7	3	0	**.988**	1	*2-148	1.1
1962	Mil-N★	122	406	45	110	17	4	9	43	35	45	.271	.335	.399	99	-1	2	2	-1	**.989**	-9	*2-119	0.1
1963	Mil-N	142	542	73	132	18	2	5	43	41	47	.244	.300	.312	77	-15	2	1	0	.981	-5	*2-141	-0.8
1964	Mil-N	120	352	35	70	11	1	5	34	21	44	.199	.248	.278	48	-24	0	1	-1	**.985**	-9	*2-117	-2.7
1965	Mil-N	148	535	55	141	26	3	7	50	24	41	.264	.295	.363	84	-12	0	4	-2	.976	-16	*2-147	-1.9
1966	Atl-N	75	227	16	48	7	0	1	18	10	14	.211	.248	.256	40	-18	1	1	-0	.983	-15	2-67	-3.2
Total	12	1540	5562	692	1415	221	40	106	556	462	558	.254	.315	.366	85	-114	40	38	-11	.982	-98	*2-1518	-10.2

■ JACK BOLLING
Bolling, John Edward b: 2/20/17, Mobile, Ala. d: 4/13/98, Panama City, Fla. BL/TL, 5′11″, 168 lbs. Deb: 6/10/39

YEAR	TM/L	G	AB	R	H	2B	3B	HR	RBI	BB	SO	AVG	OBP	SLG	PRO+	BR/A	SB	CS	SBR	FA	FR	G/POS	TPR
1939	Phi-N	69	211	27	61	11	0	3	13	11	10	.289	.324	.384	92	-3	6			.982	2	1-48	-0.6
1944	Bro-N	56	131	21	46	14	1	1	25	14	4	.351	.418	.496	159	10	0			.991	1	1-27	1.0
Total	2	125	342	48	107	25	1	4	38	25	14	.313	.361	.427	118	8	6			.985	3	/1-75	0.4

■ MILT BOLLING
Bolling, Milton Joseph b: 8/9/30, Mississippi City, Miss. BR/TR, 6′1″, 180 lbs. Deb: 9/10/52 F

YEAR	TM/L	G	AB	R	H	2B	3B	HR	RBI	BB	SO	AVG	OBP	SLG	PRO+	BR/A	SB	CS	SBR	FA	FR	G/POS	TPR
1952	Bos-A	11	36	4	8	1	0	1	3	3	5	.222	.282	.333	66	-2	0	1	-1	.984	6	S-11	0.4
1953	Bos-A	109	323	30	85	12	1	5	28	23	41	.263	.318	.353	77	-11	1	4	-2	.956	5	*S-109	-0.1
1954	Bos-A	113	370	42	92	20	3	6	36	47	55	.249	.340	.368	84	-8	2	4	-2	.946	15	*S-107/3-5	1.5
1955	Bos-A	6	5	0	1	0	0	0	0	0	1	.200	.200	.200	7	-1	0	0	0	.800	0	/S-2	-0.1
1956	Bos-A	45	118	19	25	3	2	3	8	18	20	.212	.321	.347	68	-6	0	1	-1	.947	-8	S-26,3-11/2-1	-1.2
1957	Bos-A	1	1	0	0	0	0	0	0	0	0	.000	.000	.000	-95	-0	0	0	0	.000	0	H	0.0
	Was-A	91	277	29	63	12	1	4	19	18	59	.227	.279	.321	64	-14	2	2	-1	.982	8	2-53,S-37/3-1	-0.1
	Yr	92	278	29	63	12	1	4	19	18	59	.227	.279	.320	64	-14	2	2	-1	.982	8	2-53,S-37/3-1	-0.1
1958	Det-A	24	31	3	6	2	0	0	0	5	7	.194	.306	.258	53	-2	0	0	0	.946	2	S-13/2-1,3-1	0.1
Total	7	400	1161	127	280	50	7	19	94	114	188	.241	.314	.345	74	-43	5	12	-6	.952	28	S-305/2-55,3-18	0.5

■ DON BOLLWEG
Bollweg, Donald Raymond b: 2/12/21, Wheaton, Ill. d: 5/26/96, Wheaton, Ill. BL/TL, 6′1″, 190 lbs. Deb: 9/28/50

YEAR	TM/L	G	AB	R	H	2B	3B	HR	RBI	BB	SO	AVG	OBP	SLG	PRO+	BR/A	SB	CS	SBR	FA	FR	G/POS	TPR
1950	StL-N	4	11	1	2	0	0	0	1	1	1	.182	.250	.182	15	-1	0			1.000	-1	/1-4	-0.2
1951	StL-N	6	9	1	1	1	0	0	2	0	1	.111	.111	.222	-13	-1	0	0	0	.941	-1	/1-2	-0.2
1953	*NY-A	70	155	24	46	6	4	6	24	21	31	.297	.384	.503	143	9	1	0	0	.983	-4	1-43	0.4
1954	Phi-A	103	268	35	60	15	3	5	24	35	33	.224	.320	.358	85	-5	1	0	0	.978	2	1-71	-0.7
1955	KC-A	12	9	1	1	0	0	0	2	3	2	.111	.333	.111	23	-1	0	0	0	1.000	-0	/1-3	-0.1
Total	5	195	452	62	110	22	7	11	53	60	68	.243	.337	.396	100	0	2	0		.980	-3	1-123	-0.8

■ CECIL BOLTON
Bolton, Cecil Glenford "Glenn" b: 2/13/04, Booneville, Miss. d: 8/25/93, Jackson, Miss. BL/TR, 6′4″, 195 lbs. Deb: 9/21/28

YEAR	TM/L	G	AB	R	H	2B	3B	HR	RBI	BB	SO	AVG	OBP	SLG	PRO+	BR/A	SB	CS	SBR	FA	FR	G/POS	TPR
1928	Cle-A	4	13	1	2	0	2	0	0	2	2	.154	.267	.462	87	-0	0	0	0	.955	-1	/1-4	-0.2

■ CLIFF BOLTON
Bolton, William Clifton b: 4/10/07, High Point, N.C. d: 4/21/79, Lexington, N.C. BL/TR, 5′9″, 160 lbs. Deb: 4/20/31

YEAR	TM/L	G	AB	R	H	2B	3B	HR	RBI	BB	SO	AVG	OBP	SLG	PRO+	BR/A	SB	CS	SBR	FA	FR	G/POS	TPR
1931	Was-A	23	43	3	11	1	1	0	6	1	5	.256	.273	.326	56	-3	0	0	0	.947	-6	C-13	-0.7
1933	*Was-A	33	39	4	16	1	1	0	6	6	3	.410	.500	.487	164	4	0	0	0	.889	-2	/C-9,O-1	0.3
1934	Was-A	42	148	12	40	9	1	1	17	11	9	.270	.321	.365	80	-5	2	0	1	.981	-3	C-39	-0.5
1935	Was-A	110	375	47	114	18	11	2	55	58	13	.304	.399	.427	117	11	0	1	-1	.971	-23	*C-106	-0.6
1936	Was-A	86	289	41	84	18	4	2	51	25	12	.291	.349	.401	90	-5	1	2	-1	.979	-3	C-83	-0.4
1937	Det-A	27	57	6	15	2	0	1	7	8	6	.263	.354	.351	76	-2	0	0	0	.982	0	C-13	-0.1
1941	Was-A	14	11	0	0	0	0	0	1	1	2	.000	.083	.000	-80	-3	0	0	0	1.000	0	/C-3	-0.3
Total	7	335	962	113	280	49	18	6	143	110	50	.291	.366	.398	98	-2	3	3	-1	.974	-36	C-266/O-1	-2.3

■ TOMMY BOND
Bond, Thomas Henry b: 4/2/1856, Granard, Ireland d: 1/24/41, Boston, Mass. BR/TR, 5′7.5″, 160 lbs. Deb: 5/5/1874 MU

YEAR	TM/L	G	AB	R	H	2B	3B	HR	RBI	BB	SO	AVG	OBP	SLG	PRO+	BR/A	SB	CS	SBR	FA	FR	G/POS	TPR
1874	Atl-n	55	245	25	54	10	1	0	20	1	5	.220	.224	.269	65	-8	0	0	0	.841	8	*P-55	0.0
1875	Har-n	72	289	32	77	11	3	0	33	0	5	.266	.266	.325	99	-1	5	1	1	.905	8	P-40,O-29/1-4,2-3	0.3
1876	Har-N	45	182	18	50	8	0	0	21	0	4	.275	.275	.319	90	-3				.887	5	P-45	0.0
1877	Bos-N	61	259	32	59	4	3	0	30	1	15	.228	.231	.266	54	-14				.937	3	*P-58/O-3	-0.1
1878	Bos-N	59	236	22	50	4	1	0	23	0	9	.212	.212	.237	44	-15				.941	1	*P-59/O-2	-0.1
1879	Bos-N	65	257	35	62	3	1	0	21	6	8	.241	.259	.261	70	-8				**.957**	5	*P-64/O-5,1-1	-0.2
1880	Bos-N	76	282	27	62	4	1	0	24	8	14	.220	.241	.241	66	-9				.940	13	*P-63,O-26/3-1,1-1	0.0
1881	Bos-N	3	10	0	2	0	0	0	0	0	0	.200	.200	.200	27	-1				1.000	1	/P-3	0.0
1882	Wor-N	8	30	1	4	0	0	0	2	2	3	.133	.188	.133	5	-3				.714	-3	/O-8,P-2,M	-0.5
1884	Bos-U	37	162	21	48	8	0	0		4		.296	.313	.346	101	-4				.863	1	P-23,O 17/3-1	-0.4
	Ind-a	7	23	0	3	1	1	0		0		.130	.130	.261	25	-2				.700	-2	/P-5,O-2	-0.1
Total	2 n	127	534	57	131	21	4	0	53	1	10	.245	.247	.300	84	-9	5	1	1	.867	17	/P-95,O-29,1-4,2-3	0.3
Total	8	361	1441	156	340	32	7	0	121	21	53	.236	.247	.268	66	-59				.927	24	P-322/O-63,3-2,1-2	-1.4

■ WALT BOND
Bond, Walter Franklin b: 10/19/37, Denmark, Tenn. d: 9/14/67, Houston, Tex. BL/TR, 6′7″, 228 lbs. Deb: 4/19/60

YEAR	TM/L	G	AB	R	H	2B	3B	HR	RBI	BB	SO	AVG	OBP	SLG	PRO+	BR/A	SB	CS	SBR	FA	FR	G/POS	TPR
1960	Cle-A	40	131	19	29	2	1	5	18	13	14	.221	.306	.366	84	-3	4	1	1	1.000	2	O-36	-0.2
1961	Cle-A	38	52	7	9	1	1	2	7	6	10	.173	.271	.346	65	-3	1	0	0	1.000	-1	O-12	-0.4
1962	Cle-A	12	50	10	19	3	0	6	17	4	9	.380	.426	.800	228	9	1	0	0	1.000	-0	O-12	0.8
1964	Hou-N	148	543	63	138	16	7	20	85	38	90	.254	.312	.420	110	6	2	2	-1	.989	-8	1-76,O-71	-0.9
1965	Hou-N	117	407	46	107	17	2	7	47	42	51	.263	.339	.366	106	3	2	1	0	.983	-5	1-74,O-38	-0.7
1967	Min-A	10	16	4	5	1	0	1	5	3	1	.313	.421	.563	174	2	0	0	0	.875	0	/O-3	0.2
Total	6	365	1199	149	307	40	11	41	179	106	175	.256	.325	.410	110	14	10	4	1	.974	-11	O-172,1-150	-1.2

■ BARRY BONDS
Bonds, Barry Lamar b: 7/24/64, Riverside, Cal. BL/TL, 6′1″, 190 lbs. Deb: 5/30/86 F

YEAR	TM/L	G	AB	R	H	2B	3B	HR	RBI	BB	SO	AVG	OBP	SLG	PRO+	BR/A	SB	CS	SBR	FA	FR	G/POS	TPR
1986	Pit-N	113	413	72	92	26	3	16	48	65	102	.223	.331	.416	102	2	36	7	7	.983	15	*O-110	2.0
1987	Pit-N	150	551	99	144	34	9	25	59	54	88	.261	.331	.492	114	9	32	10	4	.986	20	*O-145	2.7

YEAR	TM/L	G	AB	R	H	2B	3B	HR	RBI	BB	SO	AVG	OBP	SLG	PRO+	BR/A	SB	CS	SBR	FA	FR	G/POS	TPR
1988	Pit-N	144	538	97	152	30	5	24	58	72	82	.283	.369	.491	147	33	17	11	-2	.980	5	*O-136	3.4
1989	Pit-N	159	580	96	144	34	6	19	58	93	93	.248	.353	.426	126	21	32	10	4	.984	20	*O-156	4.2
1990	*Pit-N★	151	519	104	156	32	3	33	114	93	83	.301	.410	**.565**	**172**	**53**	52	13	8	.983	15	*O-150	**7.2**
1991	*Pit-N	153	510	95	149	28	5	25	116	107	73	.292	**.419**	.514	**163**	**47**	43	13	5	.991	14	*O-150	**6.4**
1992	*Pit-N★	140	473	**109**	147	36	5	34	103	**127**	69	.311	**.461**	**.624**	**207**	**73**	39	8	7	.991	11	*O-139	**9.2**
1993	SF-N★	159	539	129	181	38	4	**46**	**123**	126	79	.336	**.463**	**.677**	**207**	**87**	29	12	2	.984	5	*O-157	**8.8**
1994	SF-N★	112	391	89	122	18	1	37	81	**74**	43	.312	.429	.647	184	50	29	9	3	.986	8	*O-112	5.6
1995	SF-N★	144	506	109	149	30	7	33	104	**120**	83	.294	**.434**	.577	169	**55**	31	10	3	.980	15	*O-143	**6.7**
1996	SF-N★	158	517	122	159	27	3	42	129	**151**	76	.308	.465	.615	189	75	40	7	**8**	.980	10	*O-152	**8.5**
1997	*SF-N★	159	532	123	155	26	5	40	101	**145**	87	.291	.450	.585	172	63	37	8	6	.984	8	*O-159	7.1
1998	SF-N★	156	552	120	167	44	7	37	122	130	92	.303	.442	.609	175	67	28	12	1	.984	9	*O-155	**7.2**
Total	13	1898	6621	1364	1917	403	63	411	1216	1357	1050	.290	.414	.556	164	636	445	130	56	.984	155	*O-1864	79.0

■ BOBBY BONDS

Bonds, Bobby Lee b: 3/15/46, Riverside, Cal. BR/TR, 6'1", 190 lbs. Deb: 6/25/68 FC

YEAR	TM/L	G	AB	R	H	2B	3B	HR	RBI	BB	SO	AVG	OBP	SLG	PRO+	BR/A	SB	CS	SBR	FA	FR	G/POS	TPR
1968	SF-N	81	307	55	78	10	5	9	35	38	84	.254	.338	.407	123	9	16	7	1	.978	-3	O-80	0.3
1969	SF-N	158	622	**120**	161	25	6	32	90	81	187	.259	.353	.473	132	26	45	4	**11**	.978	-0	*O-155	2.9
1970	SF-N	157	663	134	200	36	10	26	78	77	189	.302	.376	.504	135	32	48	10	**8**	.969	7	*O-157	3.8
1971	*SF-N★	155	619	110	178	32	4	33	102	62	137	.288	.357	.512	146	35	26	8	3	**.994**	3	*O-154	3.5
1972	SF-N	153	626	118	162	29	5	26	80	60	137	.259	.329	.446	116	12	44	6	**10**	.978	11	*O-153	2.7
1973	SF-N★	160	643	**131**	182	34	4	39	96	87	148	.283	.372	.530	141	35	43	17	3	.970	9	*O-158	4.1
1974	SF-N	150	567	97	145	22	8	21	71	95	134	.256	.366	.434	118	15	41	11	6	.966	7	*O-148	2.1
1975	NY-A★	145	529	93	143	26	3	32	85	89	137	.270	.378	.512	152	37	30	17	-1	.987	7	*O-129,D-12	3.7
1976	Cal-A	99	378	48	100	10	3	10	54	41	90	.265	.341	.386	120	10	30	15	0	.977	5	O-98/D-1	1.1
1977	Cal-A	158	592	103	156	23	9	37	115	74	141	.264	.347	.520	138	30	41	18	2	.986	5	*O-140,D-18	3.0
1978	Chi-A	26	90	8	25	4	0	2	8	10	10	.278	.350	.389	107	1	6	2	1	.956	1	O-22/D-3	0.1
	Tex-A	130	475	85	126	15	4	29	82	69	110	.265	.361	.497	139	24	37	20	-1	.970	5	*O-111,D-18	2.3
	Yr	156	565	93	151	19	4	31	90	79	120	.267	.359	.480	133	25	43	22	-0	.968	5	*O-133,D-21	2.4
1979	Cle-A	146	538	93	148	24	1	25	85	74	135	.275	.371	.463	123	18	34	23	-4	.979	11	*O-116,D-29	1.9
1980	StL-N	86	231	37	47	5	3	5	24	33	74	.203	.308	.316	72	-8	15	5	2	.967	-5	O-70	-1.5
1981	Chi-N	45	163	26	35	7	1	6	19	24	44	.215	.323	.380	95	-1	5	6	-2	.982	-0	O-45	-0.5
Total	14	1849	7043	1258	1886	302	66	332	1024	914	1757	.268	.356	.471	129	276	461	169	37	.977	61	*O-1736/D-81	29.5

■ GEORGE BONE

Bone, George Drummond b: 8/28/1876, New Haven, Conn. d: 5/26/18, West Haven, Conn. BB/TR, 5'7", 152 lbs. Deb: 9/18/01

YEAR	TM/L	G	AB	R	H	2B	3B	HR	RBI	BB	SO	AVG	OBP	SLG	PRO+	BR/A	SB	CS	SBR	FA	FR	G/POS	TPR
1901	Mil-A	12	43	6	13	2	0	0	6	4		.302	.362	.349	103	0	0			.869	-2	S-12	-0.1

■ NINO BONGIOVANNI

Bongiovanni, Anthony Thomas b: 12/21/11, New Orleans, La. BL/TL, 5'10", 175 lbs. Deb: 4/23/38

YEAR	TM/L	G	AB	R	H	2B	3B	HR	RBI	BB	SO	AVG	OBP	SLG	PRO+	BR/A	SB	CS	SBR	FA	FR	G/POS	TPR
1938	Cin-N	2	7	0	2	1	0	0	0	0	0	.286	.286	.429	97	-0	0			1.000	0	/O-2	0.0
1939	*Cin-N	66	159	17	41	6	0	0	16	9	8	.258	.298	.296	60	-9	0			.989	1	O-39	-0.9
Total	2	68	166	17	43	7	0	0	16	9	8	.259	.297	.301	61	-9	0			.990	1	/O-41	-0.9

■ JUAN BONILLA

Bonilla, Juan Guillermo b: 2/12/55, Santurce, P.R. BR/TR, 5'9", 170 lbs. Deb: 4/9/81

YEAR	TM/L	G	AB	R	H	2B	3B	HR	RBI	BB	SO	AVG	OBP	SLG	PRO+	BR/A	SB	CS	SBR	FA	FR	G/POS	TPR
1981	SD-N	99	369	30	107	13	2	1	25	25	23	.290	.338	.344	101	0	4	9	-4	.976	-11	2-97	-1.0
1982	SD-N	45	182	21	51	6	2	0	8	11	15	.280	.325	.335	90	-3	0	1	-1	.975	-8	2-45	-0.9
1983	SD-N	152	556	55	132	17	4	4	45	50	40	.237	.304	.304	71	-21	3	0	1	.986	-15	*2-149	-3.0
1985	NY-A	8	16	0	2	1	0	0	2	0	3	.125	.125	.188	-16	-3	0	0	0	.955	1	/2-7	-0.1
1986	Bal-A	102	284	33	69	10	1	1	18	25	21	.243	.311	.296	67	-12	0	0	0	.981	-9	2-70,3-33/D-2	-2.0
1987	NY-A	23	55	6	14	3	0	1	3	5	6	.255	.317	.364	81	-2	0	0	0	.965	1	2-22/3-1,D-1	0.0
Total	6	429	1462	145	375	50	9	7	101	116	108	.256	.315	.317	79	-40	7	10	-4	.980	-41	2-390/3-34,D-3	-7.0

■ BOBBY BONILLA

Bonilla, Roberto Martin Antonio b: 2/23/63, Bronx, N.Y. BB/TR, 6'3", 240 lbs. Deb: 4/9/86

YEAR	TM/L	G	AB	R	H	2B	3B	HR	RBI	BB	SO	AVG	OBP	SLG	PRO+	BR/A	SB	CS	SBR	FA	FR	G/POS	TPR
1986	Chi-A	75	234	27	63	10	2	2	26	33	49	.269	.362	.355	93	-1	4	1	1	.989	-1	O-43,1-30	-0.5
	Pit-N	63	192	28	46	6	2	1	17	29	39	.240	.342	.307	79	-5	4	4	-1	.974	-7	O-51/1-4,3-4	-1.6
1987	Pit-N	141	466	58	140	33	3	15	77	39	64	.300	.357	.481	119	12	3	5	-2	.932	-20	3-89,O-46/1-6	-1.2
1988	Pit-N★	159	584	87	160	32	7	24	100	85	82	.274	.370	.476	143	34	3	5	-2	.935	-1	*3-159	3.1
1989	Pit-N★	163	616	96	173	37	10	24	86	76	93	.281	.361	.490	146	36	8	8	-2	.929	6	*3-156/1-8,O-1	4.2
1990	*Pit-N★	160	625	112	175	39	7	32	120	45	103	.280	.329	.518	135	26	4	3	-1	.961	-2	*O-149,3-14/1-3	2.0
1991	*Pit-N★	157	577	102	174	**44**	6	18	100	90	67	.302	.398	.492	151	41	2	4	-2	.989	3	*O-104,3-67/1-4	4.1
1992	NY-N	128	438	62	109	23	0	19	70	66	73	.249	.349	.432	121	13	4	3	-1	.992	7	*O-121/1-6	1.8
1993	NY-N★	139	502	81	133	21	3	34	87	72	96	.265	.352	.522	133	23	3	3	-1	.969	-2	O-85,3-52/1-6	1.8
1994	NY-N	108	403	60	117	24	1	20	67	55	101	.290	.376	.504	128	17	1	3	-2	.942	3	*3-107	1.8
1995	NY-N★	80	317	49	103	25	4	18	53	31	48	.325	.387	.599	160	27	0	3	-2	.882	-8	3-46,O-31,1-10	1.5
	Bal-A	61	237	47	79	12	4	10	46	23	31	.333	.395	.544	139	13	0	2	-1	.971	1	O-39,3-24	1.1
1996	*Bal-A	159	595	107	171	27	5	28	116	75	85	.287	.372	.491	116	15	1	3	-2	.975	-2	*O-108,D-44/1-9,3-4	0.5
1997	*Fla-N	153	562	77	167	39	3	17	96	73	94	.297	.383	.468	127	23	6	6	-2	.938	-17	*3-149/1-2,D-3	0.5
1998	Fla-N	28	97	11	27	5	0	4	15	12	22	.278	.358	.454	113	2	0	1	-1	.922	-5	3-26	-0.3
	LA-N	72	236	28	56	6	1	7	30	29	37	.237	.321	.360	83	-6	1	1	-0	.912	-11	3-59,O-12	-1.6
	Yr	100	333	39	83	11	1	11	45	41	59	.249	.332	.387	92	-4	1	2	-1	.915	-15	3-85,O-12	-1.9
Total	13	1846	6681	1032	1893	383	58	273	1106	833	1084	.283	.365	.481	129	269	44	55	-20	.931	-56	3-956,O-790/1-88,D	17.2

■ LUTHER BONIN

Bonin, Ernest Luther "Bonnie" b: 1/13/1888, Greenhill, Ind. d: 1/3/65, Sycamore, Ohio BL/TR, 5'9.5", 178 lbs. Deb: 4/13/13

YEAR	TM/L	G	AB	R	H	2B	3B	HR	RBI	BB	SO	AVG	OBP	SLG	PRO+	BR/A	SB	CS	SBR	FA	FR	G/POS	TPR
1913	StL-A	1	1	0	0	0	0	0	0	0	0	.000	.000	.000	-99	-0	0			.000	0	H	0.0
1914	Buf-F	20	76	6	14	4	1	0	4	7	11	.184	.253	.263	40	-8	3			.970	1	O-20	-0.9
Total	2	21	77	6	14	4	1	0	4	7	11	.182	.250	.260	38	-8	3			.970	1	/O-20	-0.9

■ BARRY BONNELL

Bonnell, Robert Barry b: 10/27/53, Clermont County, O. BR/TR, 6'3", 200 lbs. Deb: 5/4/77

YEAR	TM/L	G	AB	R	H	2B	3B	HR	RBI	BB	SO	AVG	OBP	SLG	PRO+	BR/A	SB	CS	SBR	FA	FR	G/POS	TPR
1977	Atl-N	100	360	41	108	11	0	1	45	37	32	.300	.368	.339	81	-8	7	5	-1	.989	8	O-75,3-32	-0.4
1978	Atl-N	117	304	36	73	11	3	1	16	20	30	.240	.287	.306	59	-17	12	6	0	.984	-9	*O-105,3-15	-3.1
1979	Atl-N	127	375	47	97	20	3	12	45	26	55	.259	.312	.424	92	-5	8	7	-2	.983	-15	*O-124/3-1	-2.7
1980	Tor-A	130	463	55	124	22	4	13	56	37	59	.268	.325	.417	97	-2	3	4	-2	.973	6	*O-122/D-3	-0.3
1981	Tor-A	66	227	21	50	7	4	4	28	12	25	.220	.262	.339	68	-10	4	3	-1	.975	2	O-66	-1.1
1982	Tor-A	140	437	59	128	26	3	6	49	32	51	.293	.345	.407	97	-2	14	2	3	.979	-18	*O-125/3-9,D-6	-2.0
1983	Tor-A	121	377	49	120	21	3	10	54	33	52	.318	.373	.469	123	12	10	7	-1	.986	-13	*O-117/3-4,D-1	-0.5
1984	Sea-A	110	363	42	96	15	4	8	48	25	51	.264	.315	.394	96	-2	5	2	0	.994	-11	O-94,3-10/1-5,D-8	-1.6
1985	Sea-A	48	111	9	27	8	0	1	10	6	19	.243	.282	.342	70	-5	1	2	-1	.976	-1	O-22/1-5,D-2	-0.7
1986	Sea-A	17	51	4	10	2	0	0	4	1	13	.196	.212	.235	21	-6	0	1	-1	.941	1	/O-9,1-8,D-2	-0.6
Total	10	976	3068	363	833	143	24	56	355	229	387	.272	.325	.389	89	-45	64	39	-4	.982	-51	O-859/3-71,D-22,1	-13.0

■ FRANK BONNER

Bonner, Frank J b: 8/20/1869, Lowell, Mass. d: 12/31/05, Kansas City, Mo. BR/TR, 5'7.5", 169 lbs. Deb: 4/26/1894

YEAR	TM/L	G	AB	R	H	2B	3B	HR	RBI	BB	SO	AVG	OBP	SLG	PRO+	BR/A	SB	CS	SBR	FA	FR	G/POS	TPR
1894	*Bal-N	33	118	27	38	10	2	0	24	17	5	.322	.412	.441	101	0	12			.904	-15	2-27/O-4,3-2,S-1	-1.0
1895	Bal-N	11	42	9	14	1	1	0	7	5	1	.333	.404	.405	106	0	4			.742	-5	3-11	-0.4
	StL-N	15	59	3	8	0	1	1	8	1	8	.136	.164	.220	-1	-9	2			.656	-5	3-10/O-5,C-1	-1.2
	Yr	26	101	12	22	1	2	1	15	6	9	.218	.269	.297	46	-9	6			.698	-10	3-21/O-5,C-1	-1.6
1896	Bro-N	9	34	8	6	2	0	0	5	2	8	.176	.263	.235	34	-3	1			.915	-1	/2-9	-0.3
1899	Was-N	85	347	41	95	20	4	2	44	18		.274	.313	.372	89	-7	6			.940	2	2-85	0.0
1902	Cle-A	34	132	14	37	6	0	0	14	5		.280	.312	.326	80	-4	1			.907	-10	2-34	-1.2
	Phi-A	11	44	2	8	0	0	0	3	0		.182	.200	.182	6	-6	0			.937	-1	2-11	-0.6
	Yr	45	176	16	45	6	0	0	17	5		.256	.284	.290	61	-9	1			.915	-12	2-45	-1.8
1903	Bos-N	48	173	11	38	5	0	1	10	7		.220	.262	.266	53	-11	2			.957	-4	2-24,S-22	-1.2
Total	6	246	949	115	244	44	8	4	115	55	22	.257	.305	.333	73	-38	28			.931	-39	2-190/S-23,3-23,OC	-5.9

YEAR	TM/L	G	AB	R	H	2B	3B	HR	RBI	BB	SO	AVG	OBP	SLG	PRO+	BR/A	SB	CS	SBR	FA	FR	G/POS	TPR
■ **BOBBY BONNER** Bonner, Robert Averill b: 8/12/56, Uvalde, Tex. BR/TR, 6', 185 lbs. Deb: 9/12/80																							
1980	Bal-A	4	4	1	0	0	0	0	1	0	0	.000	.000	.000	-99	-1	0	0	0	.889	1	/S-3	0.0
1981	Bal-A	10	27	6	8	2	0	0	2	1	4	.296	.321	.370	99	-0	1	0	0	.976	1	/S-9	0.2
1982	Bal-A	41	77	8	13	3	1	0	5	3	12	.169	.200	.234	19	-9	0	0	0	.959	-5	S-38/2-3	-1.2
1983	Bal-A	6	0	0	0	0	0	0	0	0	0	—	—	—	—	0	0	0	0	1.000	-0	/2-5,D-1	0.0
Total	4	61	108	15	21	5	1	0	8	4	16	.194	.223	.259	34	-10	1	0	0	.960	-4	/S-50,2-8,D-1	-1.0
■ **ZEKE BONURA** Bonura, Henry John b: 9/20/08, New Orleans, La. d: 3/9/87, New Orleans, La. BR/TR, 6', 210 lbs. Deb: 4/17/34																							
1934	Chi-A	127	510	86	154	35	4	27	110	64	31	.302	.380	.545	132	22	0	2	-1	**.996**	5	*1-127	1.4
1935	Chi-A	138	550	107	162	34	4	21	92	57	28	.295	.364	.485	115	11	4	0	1	.994	2	*1-138	-0.1
1936	Chi-A	148	587	120	194	39	7	12	138	94	29	.330	.426	.482	119	21	4	2	0	**.996**	12	*1-146	1.6
1937	Chi-A	116	447	79	154	41	2	19	100	49	24	.345	.412	.573	146	30	5	1	1	.989	-2	*1-115	1.5
1938	Was-A	137	540	72	156	27	3	22	114	44	29	.289	.346	.472	111	6	2	2	-1	**.993**	3	*1-129	-0.6
1939	NY-N	123	455	75	146	26	6	11	85	46	22	.321	.388	.477	130	20	1			.992	5	*1-122	1.2
1940	Was-A	79	311	41	85	16	3	3	45	40	13	.273	.358	.373	96	-1	2	0	1	.982	-4	1-79	-1.2
	Chi-N	49	182	20	48	14	0	4	20	10	4	.264	.302	.407	96	-2	1			.991	5	1-44	-0.1
Total	7	917	3582	600	1099	232	29	119	704	404	180	.307	.380	.487	121	106	19	7		.992	27	1-900	3.7
■ **EVERETT BOOE** Booe, Everett Little b: 9/28/1891, Mocksville, N.C. d: 5/21/69, Kenedy, Tex. BL/TR, 5'8.5", 165 lbs. Deb: 4/13/13																							
1913	Pit-N	29	80	9	16	0	2	0	2	6	9	.200	.256	.250	47	-6	2			1.000	-1	O-22	-0.8
1914	Ind-F	20	31	5	7	1	0	0	6	7	6	.226	.368	.258	65	-2	4			.778	-2	/O-5,S-3	-0.3
	Buf-F	76	241	29	54	9	2	0	14	21	50	.224	.289	.278	54	-19	8			.959	-4	O-58/S-8,3-2,2-1	-2.6
	Yr	96	272	34	61	10	2	0	20	28	56	.224	.299	.276	55	-21	12			.944	-5	O-63,S-11/3-2,2-1	-2.9
Total	2	125	352	43	77	10	4	0	22	34	65	.219	.289	.270	54	-26	14			.959	-6	/O-85,S-11,3-2,2-1	-3.7
■ **BUDDY BOOKER** Booker, Richard Lee b: 5/28/42, Lynchburg, Va. BL/TR, 5'10", 170 lbs. Deb: 6/4/66																							
1966	Cle-A	18	28	6	6	1	0	2	5	2	6	.214	.267	.464	105	0	0	0	0	.964	-5	C-12	-0.5
1968	Chi-A	5	5	0	0	0	0	0	0	1	2	.000	.167	.000	-46	-1	0	0	0	1.000	-1	/C-3	-0.2
Total	2	23	33	6	6	1	0	2	5	3	8	.182	.250	.394	83	-1	0	0	0	.967	-6	/C-15	-0.7
■ **ROD BOOKER** Booker, Roderick Stewart b: 9/4/58, Los Angeles, Cal. BL/TR, 6', 175 lbs. Deb: 4/29/87																							
1987	StL-N	44	47	9	13	1	1	0	8	7	7	.277	.370	.340	88	-1	2	0	1	.960	3	2-18/3-4,S-1	0.4
1988	StL-N	18	35	6	12	3	0	0	3	4	3	.343	.410	.429	140	2	2	2	-1	.889	-3	3-13/2-1	-0.1
1989	StL-N	10	8	1	2	0	0	0	0	0	1	.250	.250	.250	42	-1	0	0	0	.867	2	/2-5,3-1	0.2
1990	Phi-N	73	131	19	29	5	2	0	10	15	26	.221	.301	.290	64	-6	3	1	0	.976	-6	S-27,2-23,3-10	-1.0
1991	Phi-N	28	53	3	12	1	0	0	7	1	7	.226	.241	.245	37	-4	0	0	0	1.000	-2	S-20/3-3	-0.6
Total	5	173	274	38	68	10	3	0	28	27	44	.248	.316	.307	72	-10	7	3	0	.985	-5	/S-48,2-47,3-31	-1.1
■ **AL BOOL** Bool, Albert J. b: 8/24/1897, Lincoln, Neb. d: 9/27/81, Lincoln, Neb. BR/TR, 5'11", 180 lbs. Deb: 9/29/28																							
1928	Was-A	2	7	0	1	0	0	0	1	0	0	.143	.143	.143	-25	-1	0	0	0	1.000	0	/C-2	-0.1
1930	Pit-N	78	216	30	56	12	4	7	46	25	29	.259	.336	.449	87	-5	0			.967	-1	C-65	0.0
1931	Bos-N	49	85	5	16	1	0	0	6	9	13	.188	.266	.200	28	-8	0			.989	-2	C-37	-0.9
Total	3	129	308	35	73	13	4	7	53	34	42	.237	.313	.373	71	-15	0	0		.973	-2	C-104	-1.0
■ **AARON BOONE** Boone, Aaron John b: 3/9/73, LaMesa, Cal. BR/TR, 6'2", 190 lbs. Deb: 6/20/97 F																							
1997	Cin-N	16	49	5	12	1	0	0	5	2	5	.245	.275	.265	42	-4	1	0	0	.917	-0	3-13/2-1	-0.4
1998	Cin-N	58	181	24	51	13	2	2	28	15	36	.282	.353	.409	95	-1	6	1	1	.950	-1	3-52/2-1,S-1	0.1
Total	2	74	230	29	63	14	2	2	33	17	41	.274	.337	.378	84	-5	7	1	2	.944	-1	/3-65,2-2,S-1	-0.3
■ **BRET BOONE** Boone, Bret Robert b: 4/6/69, ElCajon, Cal. BR/TR, 5'10", 180 lbs. Deb: 8/19/92 F																							
1992	Sea-A	33	129	15	25	4	0	4	15	4	34	.194	.224	.318	50	-9	1	1	-0	.965	-0	2-32/3-6	-0.9
1993	Sea-A	76	271	31	68	12	2	12	38	17	52	.251	.305	.443	97	-2	2	3	-1	.991	-9	2-74/D-1	-1.0
1994	Cin-N	108	381	59	122	25	2	12	68	24	74	.320	.373	.491	124	13	3	4	-2	.974	-17	*2-106/3-2	-0.1
1995	*Cin-N	138	513	63	137	34	2	15	68	41	84	.267	.329	.429	98	-2	5	1	1	**.994**	-16	*2-138	-0.9
1996	Cin-N	142	520	56	121	21	3	12	69	31	100	.233	.280	.354	65	-27	3	2	-0	**.991**	4	*2-141	-1.4
1997	Cin-N	139	443	40	99	25	1	7	46	45	101	.223	.301	.332	65	-23	5	5	-2	**.997**	-3	*2-136	-1.9
1998	Cin-N☆	157	583	76	155	38	1	24	95	48	104	.266	.326	.458	99	-2	6	4	-1	.988	-5	*2-156	0.4
Total	7	793	2840	340	727	159	11	86	399	210	549	.256	.314	.411	88	-52	25	20	-4	.989	-46	2-783/3-8,D-1	-5.8
■ **IKE BOONE** Boone, Isaac Morgan b: 2/17/1897, Samantha, Ala. d: 8/1/58, Northport, Ala. BL/TR, 6', 195 lbs. Deb: 4/22/22 F																							
1922	NY-N	2	2	0	1	0	0	0	0	0	1	.500	.500	.500	157	0	0	0	0	.000	0	H	0.0
1923	Bos-A	5	15	1	4	0	1	0	2	1	0	.267	.313	.400	86	-0	0	1	-1	.929	0	/O-4	-0.1
1924	Bos-A	128	487	72	164	31	4	13	98	54	32	.337	.404	.497	131	22	2	2	-1	.976	-7	*O-124	0.6
1925	Bos-A	133	476	79	157	34	5	9	68	60	19	.330	.406	.479	124	18	1	4	-2	.941	-7	*O-118	0.1
1927	Chi-A	29	53	10	12	4	0	1	11	3	4	.226	.268	.358	63	-3	0	0	0	1.000	-2	O-11	-0.6
1930	Bro-N	40	101	13	30	9	1	3	13	14	8	.297	.383	.495	111	2	0			.960	-2	O-27	-0.1
1931	Bro-N	6	5	0	1	0	0	0	0	1	1	.200	.333	.200	47	-0	0			.000	0	H	0.0
1932	Bro-N	13	21	2	3	1	0	0	2	5	2	.143	.308	.190	38	-2	0			1.000	-1	/O-8	-0.3
Total	8	356	1160	177	372	79	11	26	194	138	67	.321	.394	.475	121	37	3	7		.960	-18	O-292	-0.4
■ **LUTE BOONE** Boone, Lute Joseph "Danny" b: 5/6/1890, Pittsburgh, Pa. d: 7/29/82, Pittsburgh, Pa. BR/TR, 5'9", 160 lbs. Deb: 9/9/13																							
1913	NY-A	6	12	3	4	0	0	0	1	3	1	.333	.467	.333	134	1	0			.857	-1	/S-4	0.0
1914	NY-A	106	370	34	82	8	2	0	21	31	41	.222	.285	.254	63	-17	10	18	-8	.960	23	2-90/3-9,O-1	-0.3
1915	NY-A	130	431	44	88	12	2	5	43	41	53	.204	.285	.276	68	-17	14	17	-6	.965	**21**	*2-115,S-11/3-4	0.0
1916	NY-A	46	124	14	23	4	0	1	8	8	10	.185	.252	.242	47	-8	7			.973	7	3-25,S-12/2-8	0.1
1918	Pit-N	27	91	7	18	3	0	0	3	8	6	.198	.263	.231	49	-5	1			.921	-0	S-26/2-1	-0.5
Total	5	315	1028	102	215	27	4	6	76	91	111	.209	.282	.261	63	-46	32	35		.964	50	2-214/S-53,3-38,O-1	-0.7
■ **RAY BOONE** Boone, Raymond Otis "Ike" b: 7/27/23, San Diego, Cal. BR/TR, 6'1", 188 lbs. Deb: 9/3/48 F																							
1948	*Cle-A	6	5	0	2	1	0	0	1	0	1	.400	.400	.600	168	0	0	0	0	.889	1	/S-4	0.2
1949	Cle-A	86	258	39	65	4	4	4	26	38	17	.252	.352	.345	87	-5	0	2	-1	.947	2	S-76	0.1
1950	Cle-A	109	365	53	110	14	6	7	58	56	27	.301	.397	.430	116	10	4	3	-1	.945	-9	*S-102	0.7
1951	Cle-A	151	544	65	127	14	1	12	51	48	36	.233	.302	.329	75	-21	5	3	-0	.957	-7	*S-151	-1.7
1952	Cle-A	103	316	57	83	8	2	7	45	53	33	.263	.372	.367	113	7	0	1	-1	.941	-10	S-96/3-2,2-1	0.3
1953	Cle-A	34	112	21	27	1	2	4	21	24	21	.241	.375	.393	110	2	1	2	-1	.952	-1	S-31	0.3
	Det-A	101	385	73	120	16	6	22	93	48	47	.312	.395	.556	156	30	2	1	0	.958	1	3-97/S-3	2.8
	Yr	135	497	94	147	17	8	26	114	72	68	.296	.390	.519	146	32	3	3	-1	.958	0	3-97,S-34	3.1
1954	Det-A★	148	543	76	160	19	7	20	85	71	53	.295	.378	.466	133	24	4	2	0	.964	2	*3-148/S-1	2.3
1955	Det-A	135	500	61	142	22	7	20	**116**	50	49	.284	.350	.476	123	14	1	1	-0	.953	-5	*3-126	0.8
1956	Det-A★	131	481	77	148	14	6	25	81	77	46	.308	.406	.518	142	30	0	0	0	.959	-7	*3-130	2.5
1957	Det-A	129	462	48	126	25	3	12	65	57	47	.273	.356	.418	108	6	1	1	-0	.990	-10	*1-117/3-4	-1.2
1958	Det-A	39	114	16	27	4	1	6	20	14	13	.237	.326	.447	103	0	0	2	-1	.988	-1	1-32	-0.4
	Chi-A	77	246	25	60	12	1	7	41	18	33	.244	.298	.386	89	-4	1	1	-0	.986	-2	1-63	-1.1
	Yr	116	360	41	87	16	2	13	61	32	46	.242	.307	.406	93	-4	1	3	-2	.986	-3	1-95	-1.5
1959	Chi-A	9	21	3	5	0	0	1	5	7	5	.238	.429	.381	126	1	1	0	0	.955	0	/1-6	0.1
	KC-A	61	132	19	36	6	0	2	12	27	17	.273	.396	.364	108	3	1	0	0	.983	1	1-38/3-3	0.2
	Yr	70	153	22	41	6	0	3	17	34	22	.268	.401	.366	111	4	2	0	1	.980	1	1-44/3-3	0.3
	Mil-N	13	15	3	3	0	0	1	2	4	2	.200	.368	.400	114	0	0	0	0	1.000	-0	/1-3	0.0
1960	Mil-N	7	12	3	3	1	0	0	4	5	1	.250	.471	.333	135	1	0	0	0	1.000	0	/1-4	0.1
	Bos-A	34	78	6	16	1	0	1	11	11	15	.205	.303	.256	51	-5	0	0	0	.994	-0	1-22	-0.7
Total	13	1373	4589	645	1260	162	46	151	737	608	463	.275	.363	.429	115	95	21	19	-5	.958	-46	3-510,S-464,1/2	5.3

■ BOB BOONE
Boone, Robert Raymond b: 11/19/47, San Diego, Cal. BR/TR, 6'2", 202 lbs. Deb: 9/10/72 FMC

YEAR	TM/L	G	AB	R	H	2B	3B	HR	RBI	BB	SO	AVG	OBP	SLG	PRO+	BR/A	SB	CS	SBR	FA	FR	G/POS	TPR
1972	Phi-N	16	51	4	14	1	0	1	4	5	7	.275	.339	.353	95	-0	1	0	0	.936	-6	C-14	-0.6
1973	Phi-N	145	521	42	136	20	2	10	61	41	36	.261	.315	.365	86	-10	3	4	-2	.990	6	*C-145	0.0
1974	Phi-N	146	488	41	118	24	3	3	52	35	29	.242	.298	.322	70	-20	3	1	0	.976	-7	*C-146	-2.0
1975	Phi-N	97	289	28	71	14	2	2	20	32	14	.246	.323	.329	78	-8	1	3	-2	.990	1	C-92/3-3	-0.6
1976	*Phi-N★	121	361	40	98	18	2	4	54	45	44	.271	.354	.366	101	2	2	5	-2	.993	-9	*C-108/1-4	-0.8
1977	*Phi-N	132	440	55	125	26	4	11	66	42	54	.284	.349	.436	105	3	5	5	-2	.989	3	*C-131/3-2	0.8
1978	*Phi-N★	132	435	48	123	18	4	12	62	46	37	.283	.353	.425	115	9	2	5	-2	**.991**	-9	*C-129/1-3,O-1	0.0
1979	Phi-N★	119	398	38	114	21	3	9	58	49	33	.286	.367	.422	111	7	1	4	-2	.988	-12	*C-117/3-2	-0.3
1980	*Phi-N	141	480	34	110	23	1	9	55	48	41	.229	.301	.338	74	-17	3	4	-2	.979	5	*C-138	-0.9
1981	*Phi-N	76	227	19	48	7	0	4	24	22	16	.211	.281	.295	61	-12	2	2	-1	.985	-2	C-75	-1.3
1982	*Cal-A	143	472	42	121	17	0	7	58	39	34	.256	.313	.337	79	-14	0	2	-1	.989	7	*C-143	-0.2
1983	Cal-A★	142	468	46	120	18	0	9	52	24	42	.256	.293	.353	77	-15	4	3	-1	.980	4	*C-142	-0.5
1984	Cal-A	139	450	33	91	16	1	3	32	25	45	.202	.244	.262	40	-36	3	3	-1	.984	7	*C-137	-2.4
1985	Cal-A	150	460	37	114	17	0	5	55	37	35	.248	.308	.317	72	-17	1	2	-1	.987	5	*C-147	-0.6
1986	*Cal-A	144	442	48	98	12	2	7	49	43	30	.222	.291	.305	63	-22	1	0	0	.988	12	*C-144	-0.1
1987	Cal-A	128	389	42	94	18	0	3	33	35	36	.242	.306	.311	66	-18	0	2	-1	.983	0	*C-127/D-1	-1.1
1988	Cal-A	122	352	38	104	17	0	5	39	29	26	.295	.352	.386	110	5	2	2	-1	.986	-6	*C-121	0.6
1989	KC-A	131	405	33	111	13	2	1	43	49	37	.274	.355	.323	93	-2	3	2	-0	.991	4	*C-129	0.9
1990	KC-A	40	117	11	28	3	0	0	9	17	12	.239	.336	.265	71	-4	1	1	-0	.985	2	C-40	0.0
Total	19	2264	7245	679	1838	303	26	105	826	663	608	.254	.318	.346	82	-170	38	50	-19	.986	6	*C-2225/1-7,3-7,DO	-9.1

■ BOOTH
Booth Deb: 5/1/1875

YEAR	TM/L	G	AB	R	H	2B	3B	HR	RBI	BB	SO	AVG	OBP	SLG	PRO+	BR/A	SB	CS	SBR	FA	FR	G/POS	TPR
1875	NH-n	1	2	0	0	0	0	0	0	0	1	.000	.000	.000	-99	-0	0	0	0	.500	-0	/S-1	-0.1

■ AMOS BOOTH
Booth, Amos Smith "Darling" b: 9/14/1853, Cincinnati, O. d: 7/1/21, Miamisburg, Ohio BR/TR, 5'9", 159 lbs. Deb: 4/25/1876

YEAR	TM/L	G	AB	R	H	2B	3B	HR	RBI	BB	SO	AVG	OBP	SLG	PRO+	BR/A	SB	CS	SBR	FA	FR	G/POS	TPR
1876	Cin-N	63	272	31	71	3	0	0	14	9	11	.261	.285	.272	101	2				.760	-18	3-24,C-24,S-22,/OP	-1.3
1877	Cin-N	44	157	16	27	2	1	0	13	12	10	.172	.231	.197	41	-9				.853	-5	S-13,C-12,P2/3O	-0.9
1880	Cin-N	1	2	0	0	0	0	0	0	0	0	.000	.000	.000	-99	-0				.000	0	/3-1	0.0
1882	Bal-a	1	3	0	0	0	0	0		0		.000	.000	.000	-99	-1				1.000	0	/3-1	-0.1
	Lou-a	1	4	0	0	0	0	0		0		.000	.000	.000	-99	-1				1.000	-1	/2-1	-0.1
	Yr	2	7	0	0	0	0	0		0		.000	.000	.000	-99	-1				1.000	-1	/3-1,2-1	-0.2
Total	4	110	438	47	98	5	1	0	27	21	21	.224	.259	.240	73	-9				.746	-24	/C-36,S-35,3P2O	-2.4

■ EDDIE BOOTH
Booth, Edward H. b: Brooklyn, N.Y. Deb: 4/26/1872

YEAR	TM/L	G	AB	R	H	2B	3B	HR	RBI	BB	SO	AVG	OBP	SLG	PRO+	BR/A	SB	CS	SBR	FA	FR	G/POS	TPR
1872	Man-n	24	117	25	38	4	2	0	12	0	1	.325	.325	.393	127	4	0	0	0	.764	1	2-20/O-4	0.2
	Atl-n	15	62	11	19	4	0	0	8	0	0	.306	.306	.371	92	-2	0	2	-1	.792	1	O-14/2-1	-0.1
	Yr	39	179	36	57	8	2	0	20	0	1	.318	.318	.385	112	2	0	2	-1	.769	2	2-21,O-18	0.1
1873	Res-n	18	72	11	21	3	2	0	4	0	2	.292	.292	.389	109	1	0	0	0	.848	-3	O-17/2-1	-0.1
	Atl-n	16	69	8	14	3	1	0	8	3	0	.203	.236	.275	58	-3	0	1	-1	.788	1	O-16	-0.1
	Yr	34	141	19	35	6	3	0	12	3	2	.248	.264	.333	84	-2	0	1	-1	.818	-2	O-33/2-1	-0.2
1874	Atl-n	44	185	24	47	4	3	1	16	3	3	.254	.266	.324	100	1	0	0	0	.809	-9	*O-44/2-1	-0.6
1875	Mut-n	68	281	33	56	3	4	0	18	0	2	.199	.199	.238	49	-15	4	3	-1	.827	-1	*O-63/2-8	-1.3
1876	NY-N	57	228	17	49	2	1	0	7	2	4	.215	.222	.232	59	-8				.764	-5	*O-53/2-5,P-1	-1.2
Total	4 n	185	786	112	195	21	12	1	66	6	8	.248	.254	.309	82	-13	4	6	-2	.820	-11	O-158/2-31	-2.0

■ JOSH BOOTY
Booty, Joshua Gibson b: 4/29/75, Starkville, Miss. BR/TR, 6'3", 210 lbs. Deb: 9/24/96

YEAR	TM/L	G	AB	R	H	2B	3B	HR	RBI	BB	SO	AVG	OBP	SLG	PRO+	BR/A	SB	CS	SBR	FA	FR	G/POS	TPR
1996	Fla-N	2	2	1	1	0	0	0	0	0	0	.500	.500	.500	170	0	0	0	0	.000	0	/3-1	0.0
1997	Fla-N	4	5	2	3	0	0	0	1	1	1	.600	.667	.600	246	1	0	0	0	.857	1	/3-4	0.2
1998	Fla-N	7	19	0	3	1	0	0	3	3	8	.158	.273	.211	29	-2	0	0	0	.833	-0	/3-7	-0.2
Total	3	13	26	3	7	1	0	0	4	4	9	.269	.367	.308	82	-1	0	0	0	.840	1	/3-12	0.0

■ FRENCHY BORDAGARAY
Bordagaray, Stanley George b: 1/3/10, Coalinga, Cal. BR/TR, 5'7.5", 175 lbs. Deb: 4/17/34

YEAR	TM/L	G	AB	R	H	2B	3B	HR	RBI	BB	SO	AVG	OBP	SLG	PRO+	BR/A	SB	CS	SBR	FA	FR	G/POS	TPR
1934	Chi-A	29	87	12	28	3	1	0	2	3	8	.322	.344	.379	84	-2	1	2	-1	.938	-1	O-17	-0.4
1935	Bro-N	120	422	69	119	19	6	1	39	17	29	.282	.319	.363	85	-9	18			.980	1	*O-105	-1.2
1936	Bro-N	125	372	63	117	21	3	4	31	17	42	.315	.346	.419	104	2	12			.991	0	O-92,2-11/3-6	-0.1
1937	StL-N	96	300	43	88	11	4	1	37	15	25	.293	.331	.367	88	-5	11			.942	-9	3-50,O-28	-1.4
1938	StL-N	81	156	19	44	5	1	0	21	8	9	.282	.325	.327	76	-5	2			.959	0	O-29/3-4	-0.6
1939	*Cin-N	63	122	19	24	5	1	0	12	9	10	.197	.252	.254	36	-11	3			1.000	-6	O-43/2-2	-1.8
1941	*NY-A	36	73	10	19	1	0	0	4	6	8	.260	.325	.274	61	-4	1	0	0	.967	-3	O-19	-0.7
1942	Bro-N	48	58	11	14	2	0	0	5	3	3	.241	.279	.276	62	-3	2			1.000	-4	O-17	-0.7
1943	Bro-N	89	268	47	81	18	2	0	19	30	15	.302	.379	.384	120	8	6			.989	-15	O-53,3-25	-0.9
1944	Bro-N	130	501	85	141	26	4	6	51	36	22	.281	.331	.385	103	1	3			.945	-20	3-98,O-25	-2.0
1945	Bro-N	113	273	32	70	9	6	2	49	29	15	.256	.328	.355	91	-4	7			.886	-11	3-57,O-22	-1.4
Total	11	930	2632	410	745	120	28	14	270	173	186	.283	.331	.366	91	-32	66	2		.982	-66	O-450,3-240/2-13	-11.2

■ PAT BORDERS
Borders, Patrick Lance b: 5/14/63, Columbus, Ohio BR/TR, 6'2", 200 lbs. Deb: 4/6/88

YEAR	TM/L	G	AB	R	H	2B	3B	HR	RBI	BB	SO	AVG	OBP	SLG	PRO+	BR/A	SB	CS	SBR	FA	FR	G/POS	TPR
1988	Tor-A	56	154	15	42	6	3	5	21	3	24	.273	.287	.448	102	-0	0	0	0	.973	2	C-43/2-1,3-1,D-7	0.4
1989	*Tor-A	94	241	22	62	11	1	3	29	11	45	.257	.292	.349	81	-6	2	1	0	.980	0	C-68,D-18	-0.4
1990	Tor-A	125	346	36	99	24	2	15	49	18	57	.286	.321	.497	123	9	0	1	-1	.993	0	*C-115/D-1	1.5
1991	*Tor-A	105	291	22	71	17	0	5	36	11	45	.244	.274	.354	70	-13	0	0	0	.993	13	*C-102	0.5
1992	*Tor-A	138	480	47	116	26	2	13	53	33	75	.242	.293	.385	85	-11	1	1	-0	.991	5	*C-137	0.2
1993	*Tor-A	138	488	38	124	30	0	9	55	20	66	.254	.286	.371	75	-19	2	2	-1	.986	5	*C-138	-0.7
1994	Tor-A	85	295	24	73	13	1	3	26	15	50	.247	.284	.329	57	-19	1	1	-0	.988	7	C-85	-0.6
1995	KC-A	52	143	14	33	8	1	4	13	7	22	.231	.267	.385	66	-8	0	0	0	1.000	-2	C-45/D-3	-0.7
	Hou-N	11	35	1	4	0	0	0	0	2	7	.114	.162	.114	-27	-6	0	0	0	.987	1	C-11	-0.5
1996	StL-N	26	69	3	22	3	0	0	4	1	14	.319	.329	.362	83	-2	0	1	-1	.984	3	C-17/1-1	0.2
	Cal-A	19	57	6	13	3	0	2	8	3	11	.228	.267	.386	62	-3	0	1	-1	.984	4	C-19	0.0
	Chi-A	31	94	6	26	1	0	3	6	5	18	.277	.313	.383	79	-3	0	0	0	.982	-2	C-30/D-1	-0.3
	Yr	50	151	12	39	4	0	5	14	8	29	.258	.296	.384	72	-7	0	1	-1	.983	2	C-49/D-1	-0.3
1997	Cle-A	55	159	17	47	7	1	4	15	9	27	.296	.341	.428	96	-1	0	2	-1	1.000	6	C-53	0.6
1998	Cle-A	54	160	12	38	6	0	0	6	10	40	.237	.291	.275	47	-12	0	2	-1	.974	-1	C-53/3-1	-1.1
Total	11	989	3012	263	770	155	11	66	321	148	501	.256	.293	.380	79	-95	6	12	-5	.988	40	C-916/D-30,3-2,12	-0.9

■ MIKE BORDICK
Bordick, Michael Todd b: 7/21/65, Marquette, Mich. BR/TR, 5'11", 175 lbs. Deb: 4/11/90

YEAR	TM/L	G	AB	R	H	2B	3B	HR	RBI	BB	SO	AVG	OBP	SLG	PRO+	BR/A	SB	CS	SBR	FA	FR	G/POS	TPR
1990	*Oak-A	25	14	0	1	0	0	0	0	1	4	.071	.133	.071	-43	-3	0	0	0	1.000	-0	3-10/S-9,2-7	-0.3
1991	Oak-A	90	235	21	56	5	1	0	21	14	37	.238	.290	.268	59	-13	3	4	-2	.972	-4	S-84/2-5,3-1	-1.2
1992	*Oak-A	154	504	62	151	19	4	3	48	40	59	.300	.362	.371	111	8	12	6	0	.987	8	2-95,S-70	2.3
1993	Oak-A	159	546	60	136	21	2	3	48	60	58	.249	.335	.311	80	-14	10	10	-3	.982	-16	*S-159/2-1	-1.9
1994	Oak-A	114	391	38	99	18	4	2	37	38	44	.253	.324	.335	77	-13	7	2	1	.974	-2	*S-112/2-4	-0.4
1995	Oak-A	126	428	46	113	13	0	8	44	35	48	.264	.327	.350	81	-12	11	3	2	.983	7	*S-126/D-1	0.7
1996	Oak-A	155	525	46	126	18	4	5	54	52	59	.240	.310	.318	60	-31	5	6	-2	.979	12	*S-155	-0.7
1997	*Bal-A	153	509	55	120	19	1	7	46	33	66	.236	.285	.318	59	-31	0	2	-1	.980	-1	*S-153	-1.9
1998	Bal-A	151	465	59	121	29	1	13	51	39	65	.260	.331	.411	93	-5	6	7	-2	.990	21	*S-150	2.4
Total	9	1127	3617	387	923	142	17	41	349	312	440	.255	.322	.338	78	-114	54	40	-8	.980	26	*S-1018,2-112/3D	-1.0

■ GLENN BORGMANN
Borgmann, Glenn Dennis b: 5/25/50, Paterson, N.J. BR/TR, 6'4", 210 lbs. Deb: 7/1/72

YEAR	TM/L	G	AB	R	H	2B	3B	HR	RBI	BB	SO	AVG	OBP	SLG	PRO+	BR/A	SB	CS	SBR	FA	FR	G/POS	TPR
1972	Min-A	56	175	11	41	4	0	3	14	25	25	.234	.330	.309	86	-2	0	0	0	.965	-1	C-56	-0.1
1973	Min-A	12	34	7	9	2	0	0	9	6	10	.265	.375	.324	95	0	0	0	0	1.000	-2	C-12	-0.2
1974	Min-A	128	345	33	87	8	1	3	45	39	44	.252	.330	.307	82	-7	2	1	0	**.997**	-2	*C-128	-0.4
1975	Min-A	125	352	34	73	15	2	2	33	47	59	.207	.304	.278	65	-15	0	1	-1	.989	-2	*C-125	-1.4

YEAR	TM/L	G	AB	R	H	2B	3B	HR	RBI	BB	SO	AVG	OBP	SLG	PRO+	BR/A	SB	CS	SBR	FA	FR	G/POS	TPR
1976	Min-A	24	65	10	16	3	0	1	6	19	7	.246	.417	.338	120	3	1	1	-0	.976	2	C-24	0.5
1977	Min-A	17	43	12	11	1	0	2	7	11	9	.256	.407	.419	128	2	0	0	0	1.000	2	C-17	0.4
1978	Min-A	49	123	16	26	4	1	3	15	18	17	.211	.312	.333	80	-3	0	0	0	.990	5	C-46/D-1	0.3
1979	Min-A	31	70	4	14	3	0	0	8	12	11	.200	.317	.243	52	-4	1	0	0	.993	7	C-31	0.4
1980	Chi-A	32	87	10	19	2	0	2	14	14	9	.218	.327	.310	76	-3	0	0	0	1.000	2	C-32	0.0
Total	9	474	1294	137	296	42	4	16	151	191	191	.229	.329	.304	79	-30	4	3	-1	.989	10	C-471/D-1	-0.5

■ BOB BORKOWSKI Borkowski, Robert Vilarian b: 1/27/26, Dayton, Ohio BR/TR, 6', 182 lbs. Deb: 4/22/50

YEAR	TM/L	G	AB	R	H	2B	3B	HR	RBI	BB	SO	AVG	OBP	SLG	PRO+	BR/A	SB	CS	SBR	FA	FR	G/POS	TPR
1950	Chi-N	85	256	27	70	7	4	4	29	16	30	.273	.319	.379	84	-6	1			.975	1	O-65/1-1	-0.8
1951	Chi-N	58	89	9	14	1	0	0	10	3	16	.157	.185	.169	-4	-13	0	0	0	.933	-4	O-25	-1.8
1952	Cin-N	126	377	42	95	11	4	4	24	26	53	.252	.300	.334	76	-13	1	3	-2	.991	-6	*O-103/1-5	-2.5
1953	Cin-N	94	249	32	67	11	1	7	29	21	41	.269	.328	.406	89	-4	0	1	-1	.982	-7	O-67/1-2	-1.3
1954	Cin-N	73	162	13	43	12	1	1	19	8	18	.265	.304	.370	73	-7	0	2	-1	1.000	0	O-36/1-3	-0.9
1955	Cin-N	25	18	1	3	1	0	0	1	1	2	.167	.211	.222	14	-2	0	0	0	1.000	-4	O-11/1-1	-0.6
	Bro-N	9	19	2	2	0	0	0	0	1	6	.105	.150	.105	-30	-4	0	0	0	1.000	-3	/O-9	-0.6
	Yr	34	37	3	5	1	0	0	1	2	8	.135	.179	.162	-8	-6	0	0	0	1.000	-6	O-20/1-1	-1.2
Total	6	470	1170	126	294	43	10	16	112	76	166	.251	.299	.346	71	-48	2	6		.982	-22	O-316/1-12	-8.5

■ RED BOROM Borom, Edward Jones b: 10/30/16, Spartanburg, S.C. BL/TR, 5'10", 175 lbs. Deb: 4/23/44

YEAR	TM/L	G	AB	R	H	2B	3B	HR	RBI	BB	SO	AVG	OBP	SLG	PRO+	BR/A	SB	CS	SBR	FA	FR	G/POS	TPR
1944	Det-A	7	14	1	1	0	0	0	1	2	2	.071	.188	.071	-23	-2	0	0	0	.950	1	/2-4,S-1	-0.1
1945	*Det-A	55	130	19	35	4	0	0	9	7	8	.269	.307	.300	72	-5	4	2	0	.966	5	2-28/3-4,S-2	0.2
Total	2	62	144	20	36	4	0	0	10	9	10	.250	.294	.278	62	-7	4	2	0	.964	6	/2-32,3-4,S-3	0.1

■ STEVE BOROS Boros, Stephen b: 9/3/36, Flint, Mich. BR/TR, 6', 185 lbs. Deb: 6/19/57 MC

YEAR	TM/L	G	AB	R	H	2B	3B	HR	RBI	BB	SO	AVG	OBP	SLG	PRO+	BR/A	SB	CS	SBR	FA	FR	G/POS	TPR
1957	Det-A	24	41	4	6	1	0	0	2	1	8	.146	.167	.171	-7	-6	0	0	0	.906	3	/3-9,S-5	-0.3
1958	Det-A	6	2	0	0	0	0	0	0	0	0	.000	.000	.000	-93	-1	0	0	0	1.000	0	/2-1	0.0
1961	Det-A	116	396	51	107	18	2	5	62	68	42	.270	.388	.364	99	3	4	2	0	.953	-21	*3-116	-1.7
1962	Det-A	116	356	46	81	14	1	16	47	53	62	.228	.333	.407	95	-3	3	1	0	.931	-15	*3-105/2-6	-1.6
1963	Chi-N	41	90	9	19	5	1	3	7	12	19	.211	.304	.389	93	-1	0	2	-1	.975	-3	1-14,O-11	-0.6
1964	Cin-N	117	370	31	95	12	3	2	31	47	43	.257	.344	.322	86	-5	4	1	1	.961	4	*3-114	-0.3
1965	Cin-N	2	0	0	0	0	0	0	0	0	0	—	—	—	—	0	0	0	0	1.000	0	/3-2	0.0
Total	7	422	1255	141	308	50	7	26	149	181	174	.245	.346	.359	90	-13	11	6	-0	.948	-31	3-346/1-14,O-11,2S	-4.5

■ BABE BORTON Borton, William Baker b: 8/14/1888, Marion, Ill. d: 7/29/54, Berkeley, Cal. BL/TL, 6', 178 lbs. Deb: 9/2/12

YEAR	TM/L	G	AB	R	H	2B	3B	HR	RBI	BB	SO	AVG	OBP	SLG	PRO+	BR/A	SB	CS	SBR	FA	FR	G/POS	TPR
1912	Chi-A	31	105	15	39	3	1	0	17	8		.371	.416	.419	143	6	1			.997	0	1-30	0.6
1913	Chi-A	28	80	9	22	5	0	0	13	23	5	.275	.442	.338	130	5	1			.991	-2	1-26	0.3
	NY-A	33	108	8	14	2	0	0	11	18	19	.130	.260	.148	20	-10	1			.978	4	1-33	-0.7
	Yr	61	188	17	36	7	0	0	24	41	24	.191	.342	.229	68	-5	2			.984	3	1-59	-0.4
1915	StL-F	159	549	**97**	157	20	14	3	83	**92**	64	.286	.395	.390	115	7	17			.993	-10	*1-159	-0.7
1916	StL-A	66	98	10	22	1	2	1	12	19	13	.224	.350	.306	102	1	1			.991	-1	1-22	-0.1
Total	4	317	940	139	254	31	17	4	136	160	101	.270	.381	.352	108	9	21			.991	-8	1-270	-0.6

■ DON BOSCH Bosch, Donald John b: 7/15/42, San Francisco, Cal BB/TR, 5'10", 160 lbs. Deb: 9/19/66

YEAR	TM/L	G	AB	R	H	2B	3B	HR	RBI	BB	SO	AVG	OBP	SLG	PRO+	BR/A	SB	CS	SBR	FA	FR	G/POS	TPR
1966	Pit-N	3	2	0	0	0	0	0	0	0	0	.000	.000	.000	-99	-1	0	0	0	.000	-0	/O-1	-0.1
1967	NY-N	44	93	7	13	0	1	0	2	5	24	.140	.184	.161	-0	-12	3	1	0	1.000	-4	O-39	-1.9
1968	NY-N	50	111	14	19	1	0	3	7	9	33	.171	.233	.261	48	-7	0	2	-1	.974	2	O-33	-0.9
1969	Mon-N	49	112	13	20	5	0	1	4	8	20	.179	.233	.250	35	-10	1	0	0	.964	-3	O-32	-1.4
Total	4	146	318	34	52	6	1	4	13	22	77	.164	.218	.226	28	-29	4	3	-1	.979	-5	O-105	-4.3

■ RICK BOSETTI Bosetti, Richard Alan b: 8/5/53, Redding, Cal. BR/TR, 5'11", 185 lbs. Deb: 9/9/76

YEAR	TM/L	G	AB	R	H	2B	3B	HR	RBI	BB	SO	AVG	OBP	SLG	PRO+	BR/A	SB	CS	SBR	FA	FR	G/POS	TPR
1976	Phi-N	13	18	6	5	1	0	0	0	1	3	.278	.316	.333	82	-0	3	0	1	1.000	-0	/O-6	0.0
1977	StL-N	41	69	12	16	0	0	0	3	6	11	.232	.303	.232	47	-5	4	4	-1	1.000	-4	O-35	-1.1
1978	Tor-A	136	568	61	147	25	5	5	42	30	65	.259	.300	.347	80	-16	6	10	-4	.986	25	*O-135	-0.1
1979	Tor-A	162	619	59	161	35	2	8	65	22	70	.260	.289	.362	73	-24	13	12	-3	.974	17	*O-162	-1.7
1980	Tor-A	53	188	24	40	7	1	4	18	15	29	.213	.278	.324	62	-10	4	6	-2	.985	-1	O-51	-1.6
1981	Tor-A	25	47	5	11	2	0	0	4	2	6	.234	.265	.277	53	-3	0	2	-1	1.000	-2	O-19/D-1	-0.7
	*Oak-A	9	19	4	2	0	0	0	1	3	3	.105	.227	.105	-2	-2	0	0	0	1.000	-0	/O-5,D-2	-0.3
	Yr	34	66	9	13	2	0	0	5	5	9	.197	.254	.227	38	-5	0	2	-1	1.000	-2	O-24/D-3	-1.0
1982	Oak-A	6	15	1	3	0	0	0	0	0	1	.200	.200	.200	11	-2	0	0	0	1.000	1	/O-6	-0.1
Total	7	445	1543	172	385	70	8	17	133	79	188	.250	.290	.338	71	-62	30	34	-11	.982	37	O-419/D-3	-5.6

■ THAD BOSLEY Bosley, Thaddis b: 9/17/56, Oceanside, Cal. BL/TL, 6'3", 175 lbs. Deb: 6/29/77

YEAR	TM/L	G	AB	R	H	2B	3B	HR	RBI	BB	SO	AVG	OBP	SLG	PRO+	BR/A	SB	CS	SBR	FA	FR	G/POS	TPR
1977	Cal-A	58	212	19	63	10	2	0	19	16	32	.297	.349	.363	98	-0	5	4	-1	.963	1	O-55	-0.3
1978	Chi-A	66	219	25	59	5	1	2	13	13	32	.269	.310	.329	79	-6	12	11	-3	.975	0	O-64	-1.2
1979	Chi-A	36	77	13	24	1	1	1	8	9	14	.312	.384	.390	109	1	4	1	1	.967	1	O-28/D-1	0.2
1980	Chi-A	70	147	12	33	2	0	2	14	10	27	.224	.274	.279	52	-10	3	2	-0	.958	-7	O-52	-1.8
1981	*Mil-A	42	105	11	24	2	0	0	3	6	13	.229	.270	.248	53	-6	2	1	0	.966	-6	O-37/D-1	-1.4
1982	Sea-A	22	46	3	8	1	0	0	2	4	8	.174	.240	.196	21	-5	3	1	0	1.000	-5	O-19	-1.1
1983	Chi-N	43	72	12	21	4	1	2	12	10	12	.292	.378	.458	125	3	1	1	-0	1.000	-1	O-20	0.0
1984	*Chi-N	55	98	17	29	2	2	2	14	13	22	.296	.378	.418	113	2	5	1	1	.976	-4	O-33	-0.2
1985	Chi-N	108	180	25	59	6	3	7	27	20	29	.328	.395	.511	137	9	5	1	1	.988	-7	O-55	0.2
1986	Chi-N	87	120	15	33	4	1	1	9	18	24	.275	.370	.350	92	-1	3	0	1	.969	-10	O-41	-1.0
1987	KC-A	80	140	13	39	6	1	1	16	9	26	.279	.322	.357	78	-4	0	0	0	.966	-6	O-28,D-13	-1.1
1988	KC-A	15	21	1	4	0	0	0	2	2	6	.190	.261	.190	28	-2	0	0	0	1.000	-2	/O-6,D-4	-0.4
	Cal-A	35	75	9	21	5	0	0	7	6	12	.280	.333	.347	93	-1	1	1	-0	.965	-1	O-26/D-2	-0.2
	Yr	50	96	10	25	5	0	0	9	8	18	.260	.317	.313	78	-3	1	1	-0	.967	-3	O-32/D-6	-0.6
1989	Tex-A	37	40	5	9	2	0	1	9	3	11	.225	.279	.350	75	-1	2	0	1	1.000	0	/O-8,D-5	-0.1
1990	Tex-A	30	29	3	4	0	0	1	3	4	7	.138	.242	.241	36	-3	1	0	0	1.000	-3	/O-9,D-4	-0.5
Total	14	784	1581	183	430	50	12	20	158	143	275	.272	.333	.357	89	-24	47	24	-0	.972	-48	O-481/D-30	-8.9

■ HARLEY BOSS Boss, Elmer Harley "Lefty" b: 11/19/08, Hodge, La. d: 5/15/64, Nashville, Tenn. BL/TL, 5'11.5", 185 lbs. Deb: 7/19/28

YEAR	TM/L	G	AB	R	H	2B	3B	HR	RBI	BB	SO	AVG	OBP	SLG	PRO+	BR/A	SB	CS	SBR	FA	FR	G/POS	TPR
1928	Was-A	12	12	1	3	0	0	0	2	3	1	.250	.400	.250	75	-0	0	0	0	.970	-1	/1-5	-0.1
1929	Was-A	28	66	9	18	2	1	0	6	2	6	.273	.294	.333	61	-4	0	0	0	.977	0	1-18	-0.5
1930	Was-A	3	3	0	0	0	0	0	0	0	0	.000	.000	.000	-99	-1	0	0	0	1.000	-0	/1-1	-0.1
1933	Cle-A	112	438	54	118	17	7	1	53	25	27	.269	.310	.347	71	-19	2	5	-2	.994	6	*1-110	-2.5
Total	4	155	519	64	139	19	8	1	61	30	34	.268	.309	.341	69	-24	2	5	-2	.992	5	1-134	-3.2

■ HENRY BOSTICK Bostick, Henry Landers (b: Henry Lipschitz) b: 1/12/1895, Boston, Mass. d: 9/16/68, Denver, Colo. BR/TR, Deb: 5/18/15

YEAR	TM/L	G	AB	R	H	2B	3B	HR	RBI	BB	SO	AVG	OBP	SLG	PRO+	BR/A	SB	CS	SBR	FA	FR	G/POS	TPR
1915	Phi-A	2	7	0	0	0	0	0	2	1	1	.000	.125	.000	-65	-1	0			1.000	-1	/3-2	-0.3

■ LYMAN BOSTOCK Bostock, Lyman Wesley b: 11/22/50, Birmingham, Ala. d: 9/23/78, Gary, Ind. BL/TR, 6'1", 180 lbs. Deb: 4/8/75

YEAR	TM/L	G	AB	R	H	2B	3B	HR	RBI	BB	SO	AVG	OBP	SLG	PRO+	BR/A	SB	CS	SBR	FA	FR	G/POS	TPR
1975	Min-A	98	369	52	104	21	5	0	29	28	42	.282	.332	.366	96	-2	2	3	-1	.985	-3	O-92/D-1	-1.0
1976	Min-A	128	474	75	153	21	9	4	60	33	37	.323	.368	.430	131	18	12	6	0	.988	6	*O-124	1.9
1977	Min-A	153	593	104	199	36	12	14	90	51	59	.336	.394	.508	146	38	16	7	1	.989	4	*O-149	3.5
1978	Cal-A	147	568	74	168	24	4	5	71	59	36	.296	.364	.379	113	11	15	12	-3	.989	11	*O-146/D-1	1.3
Total	4	526	2004	305	624	102	30	23	250	171	174	.311	.368	.427	124	64	45	28	-3	.988	18	O-511/D-2	5.7

■ DARYL BOSTON Boston, Daryl Lamont b: 1/4/63, Cincinnati, Ohio BL/TL, 6'3", 203 lbs. Deb: 5/13/84

YEAR	TM/L	G	AB	R	H	2B	3B	HR	RBI	BB	SO	AVG	OBP	SLG	PRO+	BR/A	SB	CS	SBR	FA	FR	G/POS	TPR
1984	Chi-A	35	83	8	14	3	1	0	3	4	20	.169	.207	.229	20	-9	6	0	2	.910	-6	O-34/D-1	-1.4
1985	Chi-A	95	232	20	53	13	1	3	15	14	44	.228	.272	.332	62	-12	8	6	-1	.989	-6	O-93/D-2	-2.1
1986	Chi-A	56	199	29	53	11	3	5	22	21	33	.266	.336	.427	103	1	9	5	-0	.969	5	O-53/D-1	0.3
1987	Chi-A	103	337	51	87	21	2	10	29	25	68	.258	.309	.421	89	-6	12	6	0	.991	-0	O-92/D-5	-0.8

YEAR	TM/L	G	AB	R	H	2B	3B	HR	RBI	BB	SO	AVG	OBP	SLG	PRO+	BR/A	SB	CS	SBR	FA	FR	G/POS	TPR
1988	Chi-A	105	281	37	61	12	2	15	31	21	44	.217	.272	.434	95	-3	9	3	1	.951	-3	O-85/D-5	-0.7
1989	Chi-A	101	218	34	55	3	4	5	23	24	31	.252	.326	.372	99	-0	7	2	1	.971	-7	O-75/D-9	-0.8
1990	Chi-A	5	1	0	0	0	0	0	0	0	0	.000	.000	.000	-99	-0	1	0	0	.000	-0	/O-1,D-3	0.0
	NY-N	115	366	65	100	21	2	12	45	28	50	.273	.328	.440	110	4	18	7	1	.986	-5	*O-109	-0.2
1991	NY-N	137	255	40	70	16	4	4	21	30	42	.275	.351	.416	116	5	15	8	-0	.981	-17	*O-115	-1.4
1992	NY-N	130	289	37	72	14	2	11	35	38	60	.249	.342	.426	118	7	12	6	0	.993	-6	O-95	0.0
1993	Col-N	124	291	46	76	15	1	14	40	26	57	.261	.326	.464	93	-4	1	6	-3	.985	-6	O-79	-1.5
1994	NY-A	52	77	11	14	2	0	4	14	6	20	.182	.250	.364	58	-5	0	1	-1	1.000	-4	O-16/D-9	-0.9
Total	11	1058	2629	378	655	131	22	83	278	237	469	.249	.313	.410	95	-23	98	50	-1	.977	-54	O-847/D-35	-9.5
■ KEN BOSWELL	Boswell, Kenneth George b: 2/23/46, Austin, Tex. BL/TR, 6', 172 lbs. Deb: 9/18/67																						
1967	NY-N	11	40	2	9	3	0	1	4	1	5	.225	.244	.375	76	-1	0	0	0	.971	2	/2-6,3-4	0.1
1968	NY-N	75	284	37	74	7	2	4	11	16	27	.261	.302	.342	93	-3	7	2	1	.965	-1	2-69	0.1
1969	*NY-N	102	362	48	101	14	7	3	32	36	47	.279	.348	.381	102	1	7	3	0	.959	-15	2-96	-0.7
1970	NY-N	105	351	32	89	13	2	5	44	41	32	.254	.335	.345	82	-8	5	4	-1	.996	-15	*2-101	-1.6
1971	NY-N	116	392	46	107	20	1	5	40	36	31	.273	.337	.367	101	1	5	2	0	.973	-29	*2-109	-2.1
1972	NY-N	100	355	35	75	9	1	9	33	32	35	.211	.276	.318	70	-14	2	2	-1	.990	-31	2-94	-4.5
1973	*NY-N	76	110	12	25	2	1	2	14	12	11	.227	.303	.318	74	-4	0	0	0	.973	0	3-17/2-3	-0.4
1974	NY-N	96	222	19	48	6	1	2	15	18	19	.216	.278	.279	57	-13	0	1	-1	1.000	7	2-28,3-20/O-7	-0.6
1975	Hou-N	86	178	16	43	8	2	0	21	30	12	.242	.354	.309	92	-1	0	3	-2	.991	-10	2-31,3-23	-1.2
1976	Hou-N	91	126	12	33	8	1	0	18	8	8	.262	.306	.341	92	-2	1	0	0	.933	-5	3-16/2-3,O-1	-0.7
1977	Hou-N	72	97	7	21	1	1	0	12	10	12	.216	.290	.247	50	-7	0	0	0	1.000	-3	2-26/3-2	-0.9
Total	11	930	2517	266	625	91	19	31	244	240	239	.248	.316	.337	85	-51	27	17	-2	.979	-100	2-566/3-82,O-8	-12.5
■ JOHN BOTTARINI	Bottarini, John Charles b: 9/14/08, Crockett, Cal. d: 10/8/76, Jemez Springs, N.Mex. BR/TR, 6', 190 lbs. Deb: 4/22/37																						
1937	Chi-N	26	40	3	11	3	0	1	7	5	10	.275	.370	.425	111	1	0			1.000	1	C-18/O-1	0.2
■ JIM BOTTOMLEY	Bottomley, James Leroy "Sunny Jim" b: 4/23/1900, Oglesby, Ill. d: 12/11/59, St.Louis, Mo. BL/TL, 6', 180 lbs. Deb: 8/18/22 MCH																						
1922	StL-N	37	151	29	49	8	5	5	35	6	13	.325	.358	.543	136	7	3	1	0	.986	-3	1-34	0.3
1923	StL-N	134	523	79	194	34	14	8	94	45	44	.371	.425	.535	155	42	4	6	-2	.986	-12	*1-130	1.9
1924	StL-N	137	528	87	167	31	12	14	111	35	35	.316	.362	.500	131	21	5	4	-1	.982	-12	*1-133/2-1	0.0
1925	StL-N	153	619	92	**227**	**44**	12	21	128	47	36	.367	.413	.578	147	42	3	4	-2	.987	-4	*1-153	2.6
1926	*StL-N	154	603	98	180	**40**	14	19	**120**	58	52	.299	.364	.506	127	21	4			.989	-15	*1-154	-0.3
1927	StL-N	152	574	95	174	31	15	19	124	74	49	.303	.387	.509	134	28	8			.989	-11	*1-152	0.6
1928	*StL-N	149	576	123	187	42	**20**	**31**	**136**	71	54	.325	.402	.628	163	50	10			.987	-14	*1-148	2.2
1929	StL-N	146	560	108	176	31	12	29	137	70	54	.314	.391	.568	133	28	3			.991	-6	*1-145	0.7
1930	*StL-N	131	487	92	148	33	7	15	97	44	36	.304	.368	.493	102	1	5			.990	-14	*1-124	-2.2
1931	*StL-N	108	382	73	133	34	5	9	75	34	24	.348	.403	.534	144	23	3			.987	-3	1-93	1.1
1932	StL-N	91	311	45	92	16	3	11	48	25	32	.296	.350	.473	115	6	2			.986	-3	1-74	-0.2
1933	Cin-N	145	549	57	137	23	9	13	83	42	28	.250	.311	.395	102	1	3			.991	-9	*1-145	-2.3
1934	Cin-N	142	556	72	158	31	11	11	78	33	40	.284	.324	.439	105	2	1			.989	-4	*1-139	-1.3
1935	Cin-N	107	399	44	103	21	1	1	49	18	24	.258	.294	.323	68	-18	3			.992	-3	1-97	-3.1
1936	StL-A	140	544	72	162	39	11	12	95	44	55	.298	.354	.476	100	-2	0	0	0	.992	-10	*1-140	-2.2
1937	StL-A	65	109	11	26	7	0	1	12	18	15	.239	.346	.330	71	-5	1	0	0	.995	1	1-24,M	-0.5
Total	16	1991	7471	1177	2313	465	151	219	1422	664	591	.310	.369	.500	124	247	58	15		.988	-120	*1-1885/2-1	-2.7
■ ED BOUCHEE	Bouchee, Edward Francis b: 3/7/33, Livingston, Mont. BL/TL, 6'1", 205 lbs. Deb: 9/19/56																						
1956	Phi-N	9	22	0	6	2	0	0	1	5	6	.273	.407	.364	112	1	0	0	0	1.000	-0	/1-6	0.0
1957	Phi-N	154	574	78	168	35	8	17	76	84	91	.293	.396	.470	136	32	1	0	0	.988	4	*1-154	2.7
1958	Phi-N	89	334	55	86	19	5	9	39	51	74	.257	.356	.425	107	4	1	0	0	.993	0	1-89	-0.1
1959	Phi-N	136	499	75	142	29	4	15	74	70	74	.285	.378	.449	117	14	0	4	-2	.986	-0	*1-134	0.2
1960	Phi-N	22	65	1	17	4	0	0	8	9	11	.262	.360	.323	89	-1	0	0	0	.994	1	1-22	-0.1
	Chi-N	98	299	33	71	11	1	5	44	45	51	.237	.341	.331	86	-5	2	0	1	.991	-0	1-80	-1.1
	Yr	120	364	34	88	15	1	5	52	54	62	.242	.344	.330	86	-5	2	0	1	.992	1	*1-102	-1.2
1961	Chi-N	112	319	49	79	12	3	12	38	58	77	.248	.372	.417	108	5	1	4	-2	.983	1	*1-107	-0.4
1962	NY-N	50	87	7	14	2	0	3	10	18	17	.161	.305	.287	59	-5	0	0	0	.976	4	1-19	-0.2
Total	7	670	2199	298	583	114	21	61	290	340	401	.265	.370	.419	112	46	5	8	-3	.988	9	1-611	1.0
■ AL BOUCHER	Boucher, Alexander Francis "Bo" b: 11/13/1881, Franklin, Mass. d: 6/23/74, Torrance, Cal. BR/TR, 5'8.5", 156 lbs. Deb: 4/16/14																						
1914	StL-F	147	516	62	119	26	4	2	49	52	88	.231	.304	.308	64	-34	13			.916	-4	*3-147	-3.4
■ MEDRIC BOUCHER	Boucher, Medric Charles Francis b: 3/12/1886, St.Louis, Mo. d: 3/12/74, Martinez, Cal. BR/TR, 5'10", 165 lbs. Deb: 5/20/14																						
1914	Bal-F	16	16	2	5	1	1	0	2	1	1	.313	.353	.500	127	0	0			.950	0	/C-7,1-1,O-1	0.1
	Pit-F	1	1	0	0	0	0	0	0	0	0	.000	.000	.000	-99	-0	0			.000	0	H	0.0
	Yr	17	17	2	5	1	1	0	2	1	1	.294	.333	.471	114	-0	0			.950	0	/C-7,1-1,O-1	0.1
■ LOU BOUDREAU	Boudreau, Louis b: 7/17/17, Harvey, Ill. BR/TR, 5'11", 185 lbs. Deb: 9/9/38 MH																						
1938	Cle-A	1	1	0	0	0	0	0	0	1	0	.000	.500	.000	36	0	0	0	0	.000	0	/3-1	0.0
1939	Cle-A	53	225	42	58	15	4	0	19	28	24	.258	.340	.360	82	-6	2	1	0	.953	8	S-53	0.6
1940	Cle-A★	155	627	97	185	46	10	9	101	73	39	.295	.370	.443	113	13	6	3	0	**.968**	12	*S-155	3.5
1941	Cle-A★	148	579	95	149	**45**	8	10	56	85	57	.257	.355	.415	108	7	9	4	0	**.966**	13	*S-147	3.1
1942	Cle-A★	147	506	57	143	18	10	2	58	75	39	.283	.379	.370	118	15	7	16	-8	**.965**	-0	*S-146,M	1.6
1943	Cle-A☆	152	539	69	154	32	7	3	67	90	31	.286	.388	.388	135	27	4	7	-3	**.970**	**28**	*S-152/C-1,M	**6.7**
1944	Cle-A☆	150	584	91	191	**45**	5	3	67	73	39	**.327**	.406	.437	146	37	11	3	2	**.978**	26	*S-149/C-1,M	**7.8**
1945	Cle-A†	97	345	50	106	24	1	3	48	35	20	.307	.374	.409	133	14	0	4	-2	.983	1	S-97,M	2.2
1946	Cle-A	140	515	51	151	30	6	6	62	40	14	.293	.345	.410	118	11	6	7	-2	**.970**	16	*S-139,M	3.4
1947	Cle-A★	150	538	79	165	**45**	3	4	67	67	10	.307	.388	.424	129	22	1	0	0	**.982**	17	*S-148,M	4.8
1948	*Cle-A★	152	560	116	199	34	6	18	106	98	9	.355	.453	.534	166	56	3	2	-0	**.975**	9	*S-151/C-1,M	**6.9**
1949	Cle-A	134	475	53	135	20	3	4	60	70	10	.284	.381	.364	100	2	0	1	-1	.982	5	S-88,3-38/1-6,2M	1.1
1950	Cle-A	81	260	23	70	13	2	1	29	31	5	.269	.349	.346	81	-7	1	2	-1	.986	0	S-61/1-8,2-2,3-2,M	-0.3
1951	Bos-A	82	273	37	73	18	1	5	47	30	12	.267	.353	.396	93	-3	1	0	0	.951	-1	S-52,3-15/1-2	0.0
1952	Bos-A	4	2	1	0	0	0	0	2	0	0	.000	.000	.000	-93	-1	0	0	0	1.000	-0	/S-1,3-1,M	-0.1
Total	15	1646	6029	861	1779	385	66	68	789	796	309	.295	.380	.415	121	187	51	50	-15	.973	134	*S-1539/3-57,12C	41.3
■ CHRIS BOURJOS	Bourjos, Christopher b: 10/16/55, Chicago, Ill. BR/TR, 6', 185 lbs. Deb: 8/31/80																						
1980	SF-N	13	22	4	5	1	0	1	2	2	7	.227	.292	.409	96	-0	0	0	0	1.000	-1	/O-6	-0.2
■ RAFAEL BOURNIGAL	Bournigal, Rafael Antonio (Pelletier) b: 5/12/66, Azua, D.R. BR/TR, 5'11", 165 lbs. Deb: 9/1/92																						
1992	LA-N	10	20	1	3	1	0	0	0	1	2	.150	.227	.200	22	-2	0	0	0	.967	2	/S-9	0.1
1993	LA-N	8	18	0	9	1	0	0	3	0	2	.500	.500	.556	193	2	0	0	0	1.000	1	/2-4,S-4	0.3
1994	LA-N	40	116	2	26	3	1	0	11	9	5	.224	.291	.267	50	-8	0	0	0	.981	0	S-40	-0.5
1996	Oak-A	88	252	33	61	14	2	0	18	16	19	.242	.290	.313	54	-18	4	3	-1	.993	4	2-64,S-23	-0.9
1997	Oak-A	79	222	29	62	9	0	1	20	16	19	.279	.339	.333	78	-7	2	1	0	.980	2	S-74/2-7	0.1
1998	Oak-A	85	209	23	47	11	0	1	19	10	11	.225	.267	.292	47	-16	6	1	1	1.000	4	2-48,S-38/D-1	-0.7
Total	6	310	837	88	208	39	3	2	71	52	58	.249	.300	.309	60	-49	12	5	1	.985	13	S-188,2-123/D-1	-1.6
■ PAT BOURQUE	Bourque, Patrick Daniel b: 3/23/47, Worcester, Mass. BL/TL, 6', 210 lbs. Deb: 9/6/71																						
1971	Chi-N	14	37	3	7	0	1	1	3	3	9	.189	.250	.324	54	-2	0	0	0	.957	2	1-11	-0.1
1972	Chi-N	11	27	3	7	1	0	0	5	2	2	.259	.310	.296	66	-1	0	0	0	1.000	1	/1-7	-0.1
1973	Chi-N	57	139	11	29	6	0	7	20	16	21	.209	.299	.403	86	-3	1	1	-0	.986	5	1-38	0.0
	*Oak-A	23	42	8	8	4	1	2	9	15	10	.190	.404	.476	155	4	0	0	0	1.000	-1	D-15/1-5	0.3
1974	Oak-A	73	96	6	22	4	0	1	16	15	20	.229	.333	.302	90	-1	0	2	-1	.988	-1	1-39/D-8	-0.4

YEAR	TM/L	G	AB	R	H	2B	3B	HR	RBI	BB	SO	AVG	OBP	SLG	PRO+	BR/A	SB	CS	SBR	FA	FR	G/POS	TPR
	Min-A	23	64	5	14	2	0	1	8	7	11	.219	.296	.297	69	-2	0	0	0	.987	3	1-21	-0.1
	Yr	96	160	11	36	6	0	2	24	22	31	.225	.319	.300	82	-3	0	2	-1	.988	2	1-60/D-8	-0.5
Total	4	201	405	36	87	17	2	12	61	58	73	.215	.316	.356	87	-6	1	3	-2	.985	11	1-121/D-23	-0.4

■ LARRY BOWA Bowa, Lawrence Robert b: 12/6/45, Sacramento, Cal. BB/TR, 5'10", 155 lbs. Deb: 4/7/70 MC

YEAR	TM/L	G	AB	R	H	2B	3B	HR	RBI	BB	SO	AVG	OBP	SLG	PRO+	BR/A	SB	CS	SBR	FA	FR	G/POS	TPR
1970	Phi-N	145	547	50	137	17	6	0	34	21	48	.250	.278	.303	57	-34	24	13	-1	.979	-21	*S-143/2-1	-3.9
1971	Phi-N	159	650	74	162	18	5	0	25	36	61	.249	.294	.292	66	-28	28	11	2	**.987**	10	*S-157	0.5
1972	Phi-N	152	579	67	145	11	**13**	1	31	32	51	.250	.292	.320	72	-22	17	9	-0	**.987**	5	*S-150	0.4
1973	Phi-N	122	446	42	94	11	3	0	23	24	31	.211	.253	.249	38	-37	10	6	-1	.979	-0	*S-122	-2.3
1974	Phi-N★	162	669	97	184	19	10	1	36	23	52	.275	.300	.338	75	-23	39	11	5	**.984**	-16	*S-162	-1.4
1975	Phi-N★	136	583	79	178	18	9	2	38	24	32	.305	.335	.377	94	-6	24	6	4	.962	-12	*S-135	0.1
1976	*Phi-N★	156	624	71	155	15	9	0	49	32	31	.248	.285	.301	65	-29	30	8	4	.975	-14	*S-156	-2.2
1977	*Phi-N	154	624	93	175	19	3	4	41	32	32	.280	.316	.340	73	-24	32	3	8	.983	1	*S-154	0.3
1978	*Phi-N★	156	654	78	192	31	5	3	43	24	40	.294	.320	.370	91	-9	27	5	5	**.986**	2	*S-156	1.9
1979	Phi-N★	147	539	74	130	17	11	0	31	61	32	.241	.319	.314	71	-20	20	9	1	**.991**	-12	*S-146	-1.6
1980	*Phi-N	147	540	57	144	16	4	2	39	24	28	.267	.302	.322	70	-21	21	6	3	.975	-13	*S-147	-1.6
1981	*Phi-N	103	360	34	102	14	3	0	31	26	17	.283	.332	.339	87	-6	16	7	1	.975	-10	*S-102	-0.5
1982	Chi-N	142	499	50	123	15	7	0	29	39	38	.246	.302	.305	68	-21	8	3	1	.973	-30	*S-140	-3.9
1983	Chi-N	147	499	73	133	20	5	2	43	35	30	.267	.315	.339	77	-15	7	3	0	**.984**	15	*S-145	1.5
1984	*Chi-N	133	391	33	87	14	2	0	17	28	24	.223	.274	.269	49	-26	10	4	1	.974	7	*S-132	-0.8
1985	Chi-N	72	195	13	48	6	4	0	13	11	20	.246	.286	.318	62	-10	5	1	1	.970	12	S-66	0.8
	NY-N	14	19	2	2	1	0	0	2	2	2	.105	.190	.158	-2	-3	0	0	0	.882	1	/S-9,2-4	-0.2
	Yr	86	214	15	50	7	4	0	15	13	22	.234	.278	.304	57	-12	5	1	1	.965	12	S-75/2-4	0.6
Total	16	2247	8418	987	2191	262	99	15	525	474	569	.260	.301	.320	71	-333	318	105	32	.980	-75	*S-2222/2-5	-12.9

■ BENNY BOWCOCK Bowcock, Benjamin James b: 10/28/1879, Fall River, Mass. d: 6/16/61, Taunton, Mass BR/TR, 5'7", 150 lbs. Deb: 9/18/03

YEAR	TM/L	G	AB	R	H	2B	3B	HR	RBI	BB	SO	AVG	OBP	SLG	PRO+	BR/A	SB	CS	SBR	FA	FR	G/POS	TPR
1903	StL-A	14	50	7	16	3	1	1	10	3		.320	.358	.480	154	3	1			.885	-7	2-14	-0.3

■ TIM BOWDEN Bowden, David Timon b: 8/15/1891, McDonough, Ga. d: 10/25/49, Emory, Ga. BL/TR, 5'10", 175 lbs. Deb: 9/17/14

YEAR	TM/L	G	AB	R	H	2B	3B	HR	RBI	BB	SO	AVG	OBP	SLG	PRO+	BR/A	SB	CS	SBR	FA	FR	G/POS	TPR
1914	StL-A	7	9	0	2	0	0	0	0	1	6	.222	.300	.222	60	-0	0			1.000	-1	/O-4	-0.2

■ CHICK BOWEN Bowen, Emmons Joseph b: 7/26/1897, New Haven, Conn. d: 8/9/48, New Haven, Conn. BR/TR, 5'7", 165 lbs. Deb: 9/15/19

YEAR	TM/L	G	AB	R	H	2B	3B	HR	RBI	BB	SO	AVG	OBP	SLG	PRO+	BR/A	SB	CS	SBR	FA	FR	G/POS	TPR
1919	NY-N	3	5	0	1	0	0	0	1	1	2	.200	.333	.200	63	-0	0			1.000	-0	/O-2	-0.1

■ SAM BOWEN Bowen, Samuel Thomas b: 9/18/52, Brunswick, Ga. BR/TR, 5'9", 170 lbs. Deb: 8/25/77

YEAR	TM/L	G	AB	R	H	2B	3B	HR	RBI	BB	SO	AVG	OBP	SLG	PRO+	BR/A	SB	CS	SBR	FA	FR	G/POS	TPR
1977	Bos-A	3	2	0	0	0	0	0	0	0	2	.000	.000	.000	-90	-1	0	0	0	1.000	-1	/O-3	-0.1
1978	Bos-A	6	7	3	1	0	0	1	1	1	2	.143	.250	.571	112	0	0	0	0	1.000	-2	/O-4	-0.2
1980	Bos-A	7	13	0	2	0	0	0	0	2	3	.154	.267	.154	17	-1	1	0	0	1.000	1	/O-6	0.0
Total	3	16	22	3	3	0	0	1	1	3	7	.136	.240	.273	38	-2	1	0	0	1.000	-1	/O-13	-0.3

■ SAM BOWENS Bowens, Samuel Edward b: 3/23/39, Wilmington, N.C. BR/TR, 6'1.5", 195 lbs. Deb: 9/7/63

YEAR	TM/L	G	AB	R	H	2B	3B	HR	RBI	BB	SO	AVG	OBP	SLG	PRO+	BR/A	SB	CS	SBR	FA	FR	G/POS	TPR
1963	Bal-A	15	48	8	16	3	1	1	9	4	5	.333	.385	.500	151	3	1	1	-0	.952	-1	O-13	0.1
1964	Bal-A	139	501	58	132	25	2	22	71	42	99	.263	.325	.453	114	9	4	3	-1	.981	-0	*O-135	0.2
1965	Bal-A	84	203	16	33	4	1	7	20	10	41	.163	.202	.296	39	-17	7	1	2	.982	-2	O-68	-2.1
1966	Bal-A	89	243	26	51	9	1	6	20	17	52	.210	.275	.329	74	-8	9	3	1	.960	-0	O-68	-1.1
1967	Bal-A	62	120	13	22	2	1	5	12	11	43	.183	.258	.342	76	-4	3	4	-2	.977	-2	O-32	-0.9
1968	Was-A	57	115	14	22	4	0	4	7	11	39	.191	.262	.330	81	-3	0	0	0	.957	-1	O-27	-0.6
1969	Was-A	33	57	6	11	1	0	0	4	5	14	.193	.258	.211	34	-5	1	1	-0	.971	-5	O-30	-1.2
Total	7	479	1287	141	287	48	6	45	143	100	293	.223	.284	.375	87	-25	25	13	-0	.974	-12	O-373	-5.6

■ FRANK BOWERMAN Bowerman, Frank Eugene "Mike" b: 12/5/1868, Romeo, Mich. d: 11/30/48, Romeo, Mich. BR/TR, 6'2", 190 lbs. Deb: 8/24/1895 M

YEAR	TM/L	G	AB	R	H	2B	3B	HR	RBI	BB	SO	AVG	OBP	SLG	PRO+	BR/A	SB	CS	SBR	FA	FR	G/POS	TPR
1895	Bal-N	1	1	0	0	0	0	0	0	0	0	.000	.000	.000	-97	-0	0			1.000	0	/C-1	0.0
1896	Bal-N	4	16	0	2	0	0	0	4	1	0	.125	.176	.125	-20	-3	0			.900	0	/C-3,1-1	-0.2
1897	*Bal-N	38	130	16	41	5	0	1	21	1		.315	.331	.377	86	-3	3			.948	3	C-36	0.3
1898	Bal-N	5	16	5	7	1	0	0	1	2		.438	.526	.500	191	2	1			.950	-0	/C-4	0.2
	Pit-N	69	241	17	66	6	3	0	29	7		.274	.297	.324	79	-7	4			.946	5	C-59/1-9	0.3
	Yr	74	257	22	73	7	3	0	30	9		.284	.313	.335	87	-5	5			.946	5	C-63/1-9	0.5
1899	Pit-N	109	424	49	110	16	10	3	53	11		.259	.286	.366	79	-15	10			.948	12	C-79,1-28	0.3
1900	NY-N	80	270	25	65	5	3	1	42	6		.241	.268	.293	57	-16	10			.929	14	C-75/S-2	0.4
1901	NY-N	59	191	20	38	5	3	0	14	7		.199	.235	.257	44	-14	3			.950	13	C-46/2-3,S-3,3-3,1	0.4
1902	NY-N	107	367	38	93	14	6	0	26	13		.253	.279	.324	87	-7	12			.956	2	C-98/1-3	0.5
1903	NY-N	64	210	22	58	6	2	1	31	6		.276	.306	.338	80	-6	5			.977	0	C-55/1-4,O-1	0.0
1904	NY-N	93	289	38	67	11	4	2	27	16		.232	.288	.318	84	-6	7			.977	3	C-79/1-9,2-2,P-1	0.6
1905	NY-N	98	297	37	80	8	1	3	41	12		.269	.322	.333	93	-3	6			.982	-3	C-72,1-17/2-1	0.0
1906	NY-N	103	285	23	65	7	3	1	42	15		.228	.274	.284	72	-10	5			.984	4	C-67,1-20	-0.1
1907	NY-N	96	311	31	81	8	2	0	32	17		.260	.309	.299	88	-4	11			.990	-5	C-62,1-29	-0.5
1908	Bos-N	86	254	16	58	8	1	1	25	13		.228	.274	.280	78	-7	4			.971	-3	C-63,1-11	-0.5
1909	Bos-N	33	99	6	21	2	0	0	4	2		.212	.228	.232	41	-7	0			.928	1	C-27,M	-0.4
Total	15	1045	3401	343	852	102	38	13	392	129	0	.251	.287	.314	77	-105	81			.963	47	C-826,1-132/2S3PO	1.3

■ BRENT BOWERS Bowers, Brent Raymond b: 5/2/71, Bridgeview, Ill. BL/TR, 6'3", 200 lbs. Deb: 8/16/96

YEAR	TM/L	G	AB	R	H	2B	3B	HR	RBI	BB	SO	AVG	OBP	SLG	PRO+	BR/A	SB	CS	SBR	FA	FR	G/POS	TPR
1996	Bal-A	21	39	6	12	2	0	0	3	0	7	.308	.308	.359	68	-2	0	0	0	1.000	-3	O-21	-0.4

■ BILLY BOWERS Bowers, Grover Bill b: 3/25/22, Parkin, Ark. d: 9/17/96, Wayne, Ark. BL/TR, 5'9.5", 176 lbs. Deb: 4/24/49

YEAR	TM/L	G	AB	R	H	2B	3B	HR	RBI	BB	SO	AVG	OBP	SLG	PRO+	BR/A	SB	CS	SBR	FA	FR	G/POS	TPR
1949	Chi-A	26	78	5	15	2	1	0	6	4	5	.192	.232	.244	27	-9	1	1	-0	.980	0	O-20	-1.0

■ STEW BOWERS Bowers, Stewart Cole "Doc" b: 2/26/15, New Freedom, Pa. BB/TR, 6', 170 lbs. Deb: 8/5/35

YEAR	TM/L	G	AB	R	H	2B	3B	HR	RBI	BB	SO	AVG	OBP	SLG	PRO+	BR/A	SB	CS	SBR	FA	FR	G/POS	TPR
1935	Bos-A	11	5	1	1	0	0	0	0	1	2	.200	.333	.200	38	-0	0	0	0	.875	0	P-10	0.0
1936	Bos-A	6	0	1	0	0	0	0	0	0	0	—	—	—	—	0	0	0	0	.000	-0	/P-5	0.0
1937	Bos-A	1	0	1	0	0	0	0	0	0	0	—	—	—	—	0	0	0	0	.000	0	R	0.0
Total	3	18	5	3	1	0	0	0	0	1	2	.200	.333	.200	38	-0	0	0	0	.875	-0	/P-15	0.0

■ FRANK BOWES Bowes, Frank M. b: 1865, Bath, N.Y. d: 1/21/1895, New York, N.Y. TR , 5'9", 160 lbs. Deb: 4/17/1890

YEAR	TM/L	G	AB	R	H	2B	3B	HR	RBI	BB	SO	AVG	OBP	SLG	PRO+	BR/A	SB	CS	SBR	FA	FR	G/POS	TPR
1890	Bro-a	61	232	28	51	5	2	0	24	7		.220	.246	.259	50	-15	11			.813	-9	C-25,O-19,3-13,/1S	-2.0

■ JIM BOWIE Bowie, James R. b: 2/17/65, Tokyo, Japan BL/TL, 6', 205 lbs. Deb: 8/3/94

YEAR	TM/L	G	AB	R	H	2B	3B	HR	RBI	BB	SO	AVG	OBP	SLG	PRO+	BR/A	SB	CS	SBR	FA	FR	G/POS	TPR
1994	Oak-A	6	14	0	3	0	0	0	0	0	2	.214	.214	.214	12	-2	0	0	0	1.000	0	/1-6	-0.2

■ WELDON BOWLIN Bowlin, Lois Weldon "Hoss" b: 12/10/40, Paragould, Ark. BR/TR, 5'9", 155 lbs. Deb: 9/16/67

YEAR	TM/L	G	AB	R	H	2B	3B	HR	RBI	BB	SO	AVG	OBP	SLG	PRO+	BR/A	SB	CS	SBR	FA	FR	G/POS	TPR
1967	KC-A	2	5	0	1	0	0	0	0	0	0	.200	.200	.200	19	-1	0	0	0	1.000	0	/3-2	0.0

■ STEVE BOWLING Bowling, Stephen Shaddon b: 6/26/52, Tulsa, Okla. BR/TR, 6', 185 lbs. Deb: 9/7/76

YEAR	TM/L	G	AB	R	H	2B	3B	HR	RBI	BB	SO	AVG	OBP	SLG	PRO+	BR/A	SB	CS	SBR	FA	FR	G/POS	TPR
1976	Mil-A	14	42	4	7	2	0	0	2	2	5	.167	.205	.214	23	-4	0	0	0	.975	1	O-13/D-1	-0.3
1977	Tor-A	89	194	19	40	8	1	1	13	37	42	.206	.333	.273	67	-8	2	3	-1	.987	-0	O-87	-1.2
Total	2	103	236	23	47	10	1	1	15	39	47	.199	.313	.263	60	-12	2	3	-1	.985	1	O-100/D-1	-1.5

■ ELMER BOWMAN Bowman, Elmari Wilhelm "Big Bow" b: 3/19/1897, Proctor, Vt. d: 12/17/85, Los Angeles, Cal. BR/TR, 6'0.5", 193 lbs. Deb: 8/3/20

YEAR	TM/L	G	AB	R	H	2B	3B	HR	RBI	BB	SO	AVG	OBP	SLG	PRO+	BR/A	SB	CS	SBR	FA	FR	G/POS	TPR
1920	Was-A	2	1	1	0	0	0	0	0	1	0	.000	.500	.000	42	0	0	0	0	.000	0	H	0.0

■ ERNIE BOWMAN Bowman, Ernest Ferrell b: 7/28/35, Johnson City, Tenn. BR/TR, 5'10", 160 lbs. Deb: 4/12/61

YEAR	TM/L	G	AB	R	H	2B	3B	HR	RBI	BB	SO	AVG	OBP	SLG	PRO+	BR/A	SB	CS	SBR	FA	FR	G/POS	TPR
1961	SF-N	38	38	10	8	0	2	0	2	1	8	.211	.231	.316	45	-3	2	0	1	.885	3	2-13,S-12/3-7	0.1
1962	*SF-N	46	42	9	8	1	0	1	4	1	10	.190	.227	.286	37	-4	0	1	-1	1.000	3	2-17,3-11,S-10	-0.1

YEAR	TM/L	G	AB	R	H	2B	3B	HR	RBI	BB	SO	AVG	OBP	SLG	PRO+	BR/A	SB	CS	SBR	FA	FR	G/POS	TPR
1963	SF-N	81	125	10	23	3	0	0	4	0	15	.184	.184	.208	13	-14	1	2	-1	.952	4	S-40,2-26,3-12	-1.0
Total	3	165	205	29	39	4	2	1	10	2	33	.190	.202	.244	24	-21	3	3	-1	.950	9	/S-62,2-56,3-30	-1.0

■ JOE BOWMAN Bowman, Joseph Emil b: 6/17/10, Kansas City, Kan. d: 11/22/90, Kansas City, Mo. BL/TR, 6′2″, 190 lbs. Deb: 4/18/32

YEAR	TM/L	G	AB	R	H	2B	3B	HR	RBI	BB	SO	AVG	OBP	SLG	PRO+	BR/A	SB	CS	SBR	FA	FR	G/POS	TPR
1932	Phi-A	7	1	0	1	0	0	0	0	0	0	1.000	1.000	1.000	405	0	0	0	0	.875	1	/P-7	0.0
1934	NY-N	31	29	4	5	0	1	0	4	2	3	.172	.226	.241	26	-3	0			1.000	-0	P-30	0.0
1935	Phi-N	49	67	6	13	1	1	1	7	4	7	.194	.239	.284	36	-6	1			.947	-1	P-33/O-1	0.0
1936	Phi-N	44	77	9	15	1	0	0	6	6	14	.195	.253	.208	23	-8	0			.886	-2	P-40	0.0
1937	Pit-N	35	47	3	10	1	0	0	4	5	9	.213	.288	.234	43	-4	0			1.000	0	P-30	0.0
1938	Pit-N	18	21	5	7	0	1	0	1	1	3	.333	.364	.429	116	0	0			.909	-1	P-17	0.0
1939	Pit-N	70	96	9	33	8	1	0	18	5	9	.344	.382	.448	124	3	0			**1.000**	0	P-37	0.0
1940	Pit-N	57	90	11	22	5	1	1	14	14	14	.244	.352	.356	96	-0	0			.981	0	P-32	0.0
1941	Pit-N	22	31	4	8	1	0	0	1	1	2	.258	.281	.290	61	-2	0			1.000	-0	P-18	0.0
1944	Bos-A	59	100	7	20	5	2	0	16	5	19	.200	.238	.290	51	-7	1	0	0	.935	-2	P-26	0.0
1945	Bos-A	9	9	0	2	0	0	0	1	1	1	.222	.300	.222	51	-1	0	0	0	1.000	-0	/P-3	0.0
	Cin-N	29	71	4	5	2	1	0	3	2	9	.070	.096	.127	-39	-13	1			.927	-2	P-25	0.0
Total	11	430	639	62	141	24	8	2	75	46	90	.221	.275	.293	55	-39	3	0		.958	-8	P-298/O-1	0.0

■ BOB BOWMAN Bowman, Robert Leroy b: 5/10/31, Laytonville, Cal. BR/TR, 6′1″, 195 lbs. Deb: 4/16/55

YEAR	TM/L	G	AB	R	H	2B	3B	HR	RBI	BB	SO	AVG	OBP	SLG	PRO+	BR/A	SB	CS	SBR	FA	FR	G/POS	TPR
1955	Phi-N	3	3	0	0	0	0	0	0	0	0	.000	.000	.000	-99	-1	0	0	0	1.000	-0	/O-2	-0.1
1956	Phi-N	6	16	2	3	0	1	1	2	0	6	.188	.188	.500	78	-1	0	0	0	.833	-1	/O-5	-0.2
1957	Phi-N	99	237	31	63	8	2	6	23	27	50	.266	.356	.392	104	2	0	0	0	.929	-2	O-81	-0.4
1958	Phi-N	91	184	31	53	11	2	8	24	16	30	.288	.345	.500	122	5	0	1	-1	.988	-6	O-57	-0.3
1959	Phi-N	57	79	7	10	0	0	2	5	5	23	.127	.179	.203	1	-11	0	0	0	1.000	-1	O-20/P-5	-1.2
Total	5	256	519	71	129	19	5	17	54	48	109	.249	.319	.403	93	-5	0	1	-1	.955	-10	O-165/P-5	-2.2

■ BILL BOWMAN Bowman, William George b: 1869, Chicago, Ill. d: 4/6/18, Arlington Heights, Ill. 5′11″, 180 lbs. Deb: 6/18/1891

YEAR	TM/L	G	AB	R	H	2B	3B	HR	RBI	BB	SO	AVG	OBP	SLG	PRO+	BR/A	SB	CS	SBR	FA	FR	G/POS	TPR
1891	Chi-N	15	45	2	4	1	0	0	5	5	9	.089	.196	.111	-10	-6	0			.915	-5	C-15	-0.9

■ RED BOWSER Bowser, James Harvey b: 9/20/1881, Freeport, Pa. d: 5/22/43, Moundsville, W.Va. Deb: 9/13/10

YEAR	TM/L	G	AB	R	H	2B	3B	HR	RBI	BB	SO	AVG	OBP	SLG	PRO+	BR/A	SB	CS	SBR	FA	FR	G/POS	TPR
1910	Chi-A	1	2	0	0	0	0	0	0	0		.000	.000	.000	-99	-0	0			.000	0	/O-1	-0.1

■ FRANK BOYD Boyd, Frank Jay b: 4/2/1868, West Middletown, Pa d: 12/16/37, Oil City, Pa. BR/TR, Deb: 5/18/1893

YEAR	TM/L	G	AB	R	H	2B	3B	HR	RBI	BB	SO	AVG	OBP	SLG	PRO+	BR/A	SB	CS	SBR	FA	FR	G/POS	TPR
1893	Cle-N	2	5	3	1	1	0	0	3	1	0	.200	.333	.400	89	-0	0			1.000	-0	/C-2	0.0

■ JAKE BOYD Boyd, Jacob Henry b: 1/19/1874, Martinsburg, W.Va. d: 8/12/32, Gettysburg, Pa. TL , 160 lbs. Deb: 9/20/1894

YEAR	TM/L	G	AB	R	H	2B	3B	HR	RBI	BB	SO	AVG	OBP	SLG	PRO+	BR/A	SB	CS	SBR	FA	FR	G/POS	TPR
1894	Was-N	6	21	1	3	0	0	0	1	1	4	.143	.182	.143	-22	-4	2			.833	1	/O-3,P-3	-0.2
1895	Was-N	51	157	29	42	5	1	1	16	20	28	.268	.375	.331	84	-3	2			.786	-14	O-21,P-14,2-10,/S3	-1.4
1896	Was-N	4	13	1	1	0	0	0	1	1	1	.077	.200	.077	-25	-2	0			.909	0	/P-4	0.0
Total	3	61	191	31	46	5	1	1	18	22	33	.241	.344	.293	65	-9	4			.794	-12	/O-24,P-21,2-10,S3	-1.6

■ BOB BOYD Boyd, Robert Richard "The Rope" b: 10/1/25, Potts Camp, Miss. BL/TL, 5′10″, 170 lbs. Deb: 9/8/51

YEAR	TM/L	G	AB	R	H	2B	3B	HR	RBI	BB	SO	AVG	OBP	SLG	PRO+	BR/A	SB	CS	SBR	FA	FR	G/POS	TPR
1951	Chi-A	12	18	3	3	0	1	0	4	3	3	.167	.286	.278	54	-1	0	0	0	1.000	-1	/1-6	-0.2
1953	Chi-A	55	165	20	49	6	2	3	23	13	11	.297	.352	.412	103	0	1	4	-2	1.000	-2	1-29,O-16	-0.5
1954	Chi-A	29	56	10	10	3	0	0	5	4	3	.179	.233	.232	27	-6	2	0	1	.955	-1	O-13,1-12	-0.7
1956	Bal-A	70	225	28	70	8	3	2	11	30	14	.311	.395	.400	119	7	0	5	-3	.990	-7	1-60/O-8	-0.7
1957	Bal-A	141	485	73	154	16	8	4	34	55	31	.318	.389	.408	126	18	2	4	-2	.991	-3	*1-132/O-1	0.6
1958	Bal-A	125	401	58	124	21	5	7	36	25	24	.309	.353	.439	123	11	1	1	-0	.994	-2	1-99	0.4
1959	Bal-A	128	415	42	110	20	2	3	41	29	14	.265	.315	.345	83	-10	3	1	0	.985	-9	*1-109	-2.6
1960	Bal-A	71	82	9	26	5	2	0	9	6	5	.317	.364	.427	114	2	0	0	0	1.000	-0	1-17	0.1
1961	KC-A	26	48	7	11	2	0	0	9	1	2	.229	.245	.271	37	-4	0	2	-1	1.000	-1	/1-8	-0.7
	Mil-N	36	41	3	10	0	0	0	3	1	7	.244	.262	.244	38	-4	0	0	0	1.000	1	/1-3	-0.3
Total	9	693	1936	253	567	81	23	19	175	167	114	.293	.351	.388	105	14	9	17	-8	.991	-24	1-475/O-38	-4.6

■ BILL BOYD Boyd, William J. b: 12/22/1852, New York, N.Y. d: 9/30/12, Jamaica, N.Y. Deb: 4/22/1872 MU

YEAR	TM/L	G	AB	R	H	2B	3B	HR	RBI	BB	SO	AVG	OBP	SLG	PRO+	BR/A	SB	CS	SBR	FA	FR	G/POS	TPR
1872	Mut-n	35	165	26	44	6	1	1	32	6	7	.267	.292	.333	98	1	4	2	0	.730	-11	*3-34/O-1	-0.8
1873	Atl-n	50	228	31	63	5	4	1	31	2	2	.276	.283	.346	96	1	1	1	-0	.716	1	*O-43/3-8	0.2
1874	Har-n	26	117	22	41	8	4	0	19	1	2	.350	.356	.487	160	7	1	0	0	.664	-8	3-25/O-1	0.0
1875	Atl-n	36	151	14	44	11	0	1	10	1	0	.291	.296	.384	154	9	0	0	0	.774	-5	2-15,O-12/3-9,1PSM	0.3
Total	4 n	147	661	93	192	30	9	3	92	10	11	.290	.301	.377	120	17	6	3	0	.704	-23	/3-76,O-57,21SP	-0.3

■ CLETE BOYER Boyer, Cletis Leroy b: 2/9/37, Cassville, Mo. BR/TR, 6′, 182 lbs. Deb: 6/5/55 FC

YEAR	TM/L	G	AB	R	H	2B	3B	HR	RBI	BB	SO	AVG	OBP	SLG	PRO+	BR/A	SB	CS	SBR	FA	FR	G/POS	TPR
1955	KC-A	47	79	3	19	1	0	0	6	3	17	.241	.268	.253	40	-7	0	0	0	.963	6	S-12,3-11,2-10	0.0
1956	KC-A	67	129	15	28	3	1	1	4	11	24	.217	.284	.279	49	-10	1	1	-0	.971	18	2-51/3-7	1.0
1957	KC-A	10	0	0	0	0	0	0	0	0	0	—	—	—	—	0	0	0	0	.000	0	/2-1,3-1	0.0
1959	NY-A	47	114	4	20	2	0	0	3	6	23	.175	.217	.193	14	-13	1	0	0	.990	6	S-26,3-16	-0.6
1960	*NY-A	124	393	54	95	20	1	14	46	23	85	.242	.289	.405	90	-7	2	3	-1	.967	28	3-99,S-33	2.0
1961	*NY-A	148	504	61	113	19	5	11	55	63	83	.224	.313	.347	80	-14	1	3	-2	.967	**30**	*3-141,S-12/O-1	1.6
1962	*NY-A	158	566	85	154	24	1	18	68	51	106	.272	.335	.413	104	2	3	2	-0	.964	**36**	*3-157	4.0
1963	*NY-A	152	557	59	140	20	3	12	54	33	91	.251	.296	.363	84	-13	4	2	0	.954	22	*3-141/S-9,2-1	1.1
1964	*NY-A	147	510	43	111	10	5	8	52	36	93	.218	.271	.304	59	-29	6	1	1	.968	19	*3-123,S-21	-0.9
1965	NY-A	148	514	69	129	23	6	18	58	39	79	.251	.306	.424	106	3	4	1	1	.968	**26**	*3-147/S-2	2.7
1966	NY-A	144	500	59	120	22	4	14	57	46	48	.240	.307	.384	101	-0	6	0	2	.966	20	3-85,S-59	2.7
1967	Atl-N	154	572	63	140	18	3	26	96	39	81	.245	.295	.423	105	1	6	3	0	**.970**	5	*3-150/S-6	0.6
1968	Atl-N	71	273	19	62	7	2	4	17	16	32	.227	.275	.311	75	-8	2	0	1	.981	-0	3-69	-0.9
1969	*Atl-N	144	496	57	124	16	1	14	57	55	87	.250	.330	.371	96	-3	3	7	-3	**.965**	3	*3-141	-0.3
1970	Atl-N	134	475	44	117	14	1	16	62	41	71	.246	.308	.381	79	-15	2	5	-2	.954	12	*3-126/S-5	-0.6
1971	Atl-N	30	98	10	24	1	0	6	19	8	11	.245	.302	.439	101	-0	0	0	0	.961	3	3-25/S-1	0.2
Total	16	1725	5780	645	1396	200	33	162	654	470	931	.242	.301	.372	87	-112	41	28	-5	.965	233	*3-1439,S-186/2O	12.6

■ KEN BOYER Boyer, Kenton Lloyd b: 5/20/31, Liberty, Mo. d: 9/7/82, St.Louis, Mo. BR/TR, 6′2″, 200 lbs. Deb: 4/12/55 FMC

YEAR	TM/L	G	AB	R	H	2B	3B	HR	RBI	BB	SO	AVG	OBP	SLG	PRO+	BR/A	SB	CS	SBR	FA	FR	G/POS	TPR
1955	StL-N	147	530	78	140	27	2	18	62	37	67	.264	.313	.425	94	-6	22	17	-4	.952	4	*3-139,S-18	-0.5
1956	StL-N★	150	595	91	182	30	2	26	98	38	65	.306	.349	.494	123	18	8	3	1	.961	9	*3-149	3.0
1957	StL-N	142	544	79	144	18	3	19	62	44	77	.265	.321	.414	94	-5	12	8	-1	**.996**	4	*O-105,3-41	-0.7
1958	StL-N	150	570	101	175	21	9	23	90	49	53	.307	.365	.496	121	16	11	6	-0	.962	23	*3-144/O-6,S-1	4.0
1959	StL-N★	149	563	86	174	18	5	28	94	67	77	.309	.384	.508	127	22	12	6	0	.956	14	*3-143,S-12	3.6
1960	StL-N★	151	552	95	168	26	10	32	97	56	77	.304	.373	.562	139	29	8	7	-2	.959	13	*3-146	4.0
1961	StL-N★	153	589	109	194	26	11	24	95	68	91	.329	.400	.533	132	27	6	3	0	.951	13	*3-153	4.1
1962	StL-N★	160	611	92	178	27	5	24	98	75	104	.291	.370	.470	113	11	12	7	-1	.956	4	*3-160	1.6
1963	StL-N★	159	617	86	176	28	2	24	111	70	90	.285	.360	.454	121	18	1	0	0	.925	-13	*3-159	0.5
1964	*StL-N★	162	628	100	185	30	10	24	**119**	70	85	.295	.367	.489	128	23	3	5	-2	.951	3	*3-162	2.3
1965	StL-N	144	535	71	139	18	2	13	75	57	73	.260	.332	.374	90	-6	2	7	-4	**.968**	-11	*3-143	-2.6
1966	NY-N	136	496	62	132	28	2	14	61	30	64	.266	.308	.415	101	-0	4	3	-1	.951	11	*3-130/1-2	0.7
1967	NY-N	56	166	17	39	7	2	3	13	26	22	.235	.339	.355	100	1	2	1	0	.949	-2	3-44/1-8	-0.3
	Chi-A	57	180	17	47	5	1	4	21	7	25	.261	.289	.367	96	-2	0	2	-1	.957	1	3-33,1-18	-0.3
1968	Chi-A	10	24	0	3	0	0	0	0	1	6	.125	.160	.125	-13	-3	0	0	0	.900	-1	/3-5,1-1	-0.5
	LA-N	83	221	20	60	7	2	6	41	16	34	.271	.324	.403	127	6	2	2	-1	.922	-4	3-34,1-32	0.0
1969	LA-N	25	34	0	7	2	0	0	4	2	7	.206	.250	.265	48	-2	0	0	0	.971	-0	/1-4	-0.3
Total	15	2034	7455	1104	2143	318	68	282	1141	713	1017	.287	.351	.462	115	147	105	77	-15	.952	69	*3-1785,O-111/1S	18.6

■ DOE BOYLAND Boyland, Dorian Scott b: 1/6/55, Chicago, Ill. BL/TL, 6′4″, 200 lbs. Deb: 9/4/78

YEAR	TM/L	G	AB	R	H	2B	3B	HR	RBI	BB	SO	AVG	OBP	SLG	PRO+	BR/A	SB	CS	SBR	FA	FR	G/POS	TPR
1978	Pit-N	6	8	1	2	0	0	0	1	0	1	.250	.250	.250	38	-1	0	0	0	1.000	-0	/1-1	-0.1

YEAR	TM/L	G	AB	R	H	2B	3B	HR	RBI	BB	SO	AVG	OBP	SLG	PRO+	BR/A	SB	CS	SBR	FA	FR	G/POS	TPR
1979	Pit-N	4	3	0	0	0	0	0	0	0	2	.000	.000	.000	-96	-1	0	0	0	.000	0	/H	-0.1
1981	Pit-N	11	8	0	0	0	0	0	0	1	3	.000	.111	.000	-64	-2	0	0	0	.000	0	/H	-0.2
Total	3	21	19	1	2	0	0	0	1	1	6	.105	.150	.105	-26	-3	0	0	0	1.000	-0	/1-1	-0.4

■ EDDIE BOYLE

Boyle, Edward J. b: 5/8/1874, Cincinnati, Ohio d: 2/9/41, Cincinnati, Ohio BR/TR, 6'3", 200 lbs. Deb: 4/17/1896 F

YEAR	TM/L	G	AB	R	H	2B	3B	HR	RBI	BB	SO	AVG	OBP	SLG	PRO+	BR/A	SB	CS	SBR	FA	FR	G/POS	TPR
1896	Lou-N	3	9	0	0	0	0	0	0	2	2	.000	.182	.000	-52	-2	0			.938	1	/C-3	-0.1
	Pit-N	2	5	0	0	0	0	0	0	0	1	.000	.000	.000	-99	-1	0			.833	-0	/C-2	-0.1
	Yr	5	14	0	0	0	0	0	0	2	3	.000	.125	.000	-68	-3	0			.909	0	/C-5	-0.2

■ HENRY BOYLE

Boyle, Henry J. "Handsome Henry" b: 9/20/1860, Philadelphia, Pa. d: 5/25/32, Philadelphia, Pa. TR , Deb: 7/9/1884

YEAR	TM/L	G	AB	R	H	2B	3B	HR	RBI	BB	SO	AVG	OBP	SLG	PRO+	BR/A	SB	CS	SBR	FA	FR	G/POS	TPR
1884	StL-U	65	262	41	68	10	3	4		9		.260	.284	.366	93	-10				.885	5	O-43,P-19/3-4,S21	-0.2
1885	StL-N	72	258	24	52	9	1	1	21	13	38	.202	.240	.256	64	-10				.907	-4	P-42,O-31/2-2	-0.7
1886	StL-N	30	108	8	27	2	2	1	13	5	19	.250	.283	.333	93	-1	0			.852	1	P-25/O-6	0.0
1887	Ind-N	41	141	17	27	9	1	2	13	9	18	.191	.250	.312	57	-8	2			.912	-5	P-38/O-4	-0.2
1888	Ind-N	37	125	13	18	2	0	1	6	6	31	.144	.189	.184	19	-11	1			.933	3	P-37/1-1	0.0
1889	Ind-N	46	155	17	38	10	0	1	17	9	23	.245	.291	.329	72	-6	4			.958	-5	P-46/3-1	0.0
Total	6	291	1049	120	230	42	7	10	70	51	129	.219	.258	.301	69	-47	7			.912	-5	P-207/O-84,3-5,21S	-1.1

■ JIM BOYLE

Boyle, James John b: 1/19/04, Cincinnati, Ohio d: 12/24/58, Cincinnati, Ohio BR/TR, 6', 180 lbs. Deb: 6/20/26 F

YEAR	TM/L	G	AB	R	H	2B	3B	HR	RBI	BB	SO	AVG	OBP	SLG	PRO+	BR/A	SB	CS	SBR	FA	FR	G/POS	TPR
1926	NY-N	1	0	0	0	0	0	0	0	0	0	—	—	—	—	0	0			.000	0	/C-1	0.0

■ JACK BOYLE

Boyle, John Anthony "Honest Jack" b: 3/22/1866, Cincinnati, Ohio d: 1/7/13, Cincinnati, Ohio BR/TR, 6'4", 190 lbs. Deb: 10/8/1886 F

YEAR	TM/L	G	AB	R	H	2B	3B	HR	RBI	BB	SO	AVG	OBP	SLG	PRO+	BR/A	SB	CS	SBR	FA	FR	G/POS	TPR
1886	Cin-a	1	5	0	1	0	0	0	0	0		.200	.200	.200	25	-0	0			.769	-0	/C-1	0.0
1887	*StL-a	88	350	48	66	3	1	2	41	20		.189	.237	.220	25	-37	7			**.897**	-11	C-86/O-2,1-2,3-1	-3.3
1888	*StL-a	71	257	33	62	8	1	1	23	13		.241	.286	.292	77	-8	11			**.932**	14	C-70/O-1	1.1
1889	StL-a	99	347	54	85	11	5	3	42	21	42	.245	.301	.331	71	-16	5			.947	5	C-80,3-12/O-5,12	-0.3
1890	Chi-P	100	369	56	96	9	5	1	49	44	29	.260	.347	.320	76	-13	11			.940	-4	C-50,3-30,S-16,/1O	-0.9
1891	StL-a	123	439	78	123	18	8	5	79	47	36	.280	.365	.392	101	-3	19			.936	-14	C-91,S-26/3-8,O21	-0.7
1892	NY-N	120	436	52	80	8	8	0	32	36	41	.183	.252	.239	49	-27	10			.922	14	C-79,1-40/O-2,S-2	-0.8
1893	Phi-N	116	504	105	144	29	9	4	81	41	30	.286	.351	.403	100	-1	22			.988	6	*1-112/C-6,2-2	0.2
1894	Phi-N	114	495	98	149	21	10	4	88	45	26	.301	.363	.408	88	-10	21			.983	1	*1-114/3-1,2-1	-0.6
1895	Phi-N	133	565	90	143	17	4	0	67	35	23	.253	.302	.297	55	-38	13			.973	-6	*1-133	-3.4
1896	Phi-N	40	145	17	43	4	1	1	28	6	7	.297	.346	.359	87	-3	3			.920	-7	C-28,1-12	-0.5
1897	Phi-N	75	288	37	73	9	1	2	36	19		.253	.306	.313	65	-15	3			.962	-9	C-50,1-24	-1.5
1898	Phi-N	6	22	0	2	0	1	0	3	1		.091	.130	.182	-11	-3	0			.919	-0	/1-4,C-3	-0.3
Total	13	1086	4222	668	1067	137	54	23	569	328	234	.253	.315	.327	72	-174	125			.929	-10	C-544,1-455/3SO2	-11.0

■ JACK BOYLE

Boyle, John Bellew b: 7/9/1889, Morris, Ill. d: 4/3/71, Ft.Lauderdale, Fla. BL/TR, 5'11.5", 165 lbs. Deb: 6/28/12

YEAR	TM/L	G	AB	R	H	2B	3B	HR	RBI	BB	SO	AVG	OBP	SLG	PRO+	BR/A	SB	CS	SBR	FA	FR	G/POS	TPR
1912	Phi-N	15	25	4	7	1	0	0	2	1	5	.280	.308	.320	67	-1	0			.905	5	/3-6,S-2	0.4

■ BUZZ BOYLE

Boyle, Ralph Francis b: 2/9/08, Cincinnati, Ohio d: 11/12/78, Cincinnati, Ohio BL/TL, 5'11.5", 170 lbs. Deb: 9/11/29 F

YEAR	TM/L	G	AB	R	H	2B	3B	HR	RBI	BB	SO	AVG	OBP	SLG	PRO+	BR/A	SB	CS	SBR	FA	FR	G/POS	TPR
1929	Bos-N	17	57	8	15	2	1	1	2	6	11	.263	.333	.386	81	-2	2			1.000	-0	O-17	-0.3
1930	Bos-N	1	1	0	0	0	0	0	0	0	1	.000	.000	.000	-99	-0	0			.000	-1	/O-1	-0.1
1933	Bro-N	93	338	38	101	13	4	0	31	16	24	.299	.331	.361	102	0	7			.975	-6	O-90	-1.1
1934	Bro-N	128	472	88	144	26	10	7	48	51	44	.305	.376	.447	126	18	8			.970	11	*O-121	2.3
1935	Bro-N	127	475	51	129	17	9	4	44	43	45	.272	.332	.371	90	-6	7			.963	3	*O-124	-0.8
Total	5	366	1343	185	389	58	24	12	125	116	125	.290	.347	.395	105	10	24			.970	6	O-353	-0.0

■ GIBBY BRACK

Brack, Gilbert Herman b: 3/29/08, Chicago, Ill. d: 1/20/60, Greenville, Tex. BR/TR, 5'9", 170 lbs. Deb: 4/23/37

YEAR	TM/L	G	AB	R	H	2B	3B	HR	RBI	BB	SO	AVG	OBP	SLG	PRO+	BR/A	SB	CS	SBR	FA	FR	G/POS	TPR
1937	Bro-N	112	372	60	102	27	9	5	38	44	93	.274	.351	.435	111	5	9			.969	1	*O-101	0.3
1938	Bro-N	40	56	10	12	2	1	1	6	4	14	.214	.267	.339	64	-3	1			1.000	2	O-13	-0.1
	Phi-N	72	282	40	81	20	4	4	28	18	30	.287	.332	.429	111	3	2			.964	-2	O-68	-0.1
	Yr	112	338	50	93	22	5	5	34	22	44	.275	.321	.414	102	-0	3			.969	-0	O-81	-0.2
1939	Phi-N	91	270	40	78	21	4	6	41	26	49	.289	.351	.463	121	7	1			.959	-4	O-48,1-19	-0.1
Total	3	315	980	150	273	70	18	16	113	92	186	.279	.341	.436	111	13	13			.967	-4	O-230/1-19	0.0

■ BUDDY BRADFORD

Bradford, Charles William b: 7/25/44, Mobile, Ala. BR/TR, 5'11", 191 lbs. Deb: 9/9/66

YEAR	TM/L	G	AB	R	H	2B	3B	HR	RBI	BB	SO	AVG	OBP	SLG	PRO+	BR/A	SB	CS	SBR	FA	FR	G/POS	TPR
1966	Chi-A	14	28	3	4	0	0	0	0	2	6	.143	.200	.143	0	-4	0	0	0	.833	-3	/O-9	-0.7
1967	Chi-A	24	20	6	2	1	0	0	1	1	7	.100	.143	.150	-14	-3	1	0	0	.900	-4	O-14	-0.8
1968	Chi-A	103	281	32	61	11	0	5	24	23	67	.217	.281	.310	78	-7	8	4	0	.965	-12	O-99	-2.7
1969	Chi-A	93	273	36	70	8	2	11	27	34	75	.256	.347	.421	109	3	5	2	0	.961	-13	O-88	-1.5
1970	Chi-A	32	91	8	17	3	0	2	8	10	30	.187	.267	.286	51	-6	1	2	-1	.979	-4	O-27	-1.3
	Cle-A	75	163	25	32	6	1	7	23	21	43	.196	.292	.374	79	-5	0	1	-1	.984	-4	O-64/3-1	-1.3
	Yr	107	254	33	49	9	1	9	31	31	73	.193	.283	.343	69	-11	1	3	-2	.982	-8	O-91/3-1	-2.6
1971	Cle-A	20	38	4	6	2	1	0	3	6	10	.158	.273	.263	48	-3	0	0	0	.930	-0	O-18	-0.4
	Cin-N	79	100	17	20	3	0	2	12	14	23	.200	.316	.290	74	-3	4	2	0	.986	-13	O-66	-1.9
1972	Chi-A	35	48	13	13	2	0	2	8	4	13	.271	.340	.438	127	2	3	2	-0	1.000	-5	O-28	-0.5
1973	Chi-A	53	168	24	40	3	1	8	15	17	43	.238	.316	.411	100	-0	4	5	-2	.992	4	O-51	0.0
1974	Chi-A	39	96	16	32	2	0	5	10	13	11	.333	.418	.510	162	8	1	2	-1	.980	-3	O-32/D-1	0.3
1975	Chi-A	25	58	8	9	3	1	2	15	8	22	.155	.290	.345	78	-2	3	2	-0	.966	-2	O-18/D-4	-0.4
	StL-N	50	81	12	22	1	0	4	15	12	24	.272	.366	.432	117	2	0	2	-1	.935	-1	O-25	-0.1
1976	Chi-A	55	160	20	35	5	2	4	14	19	37	.219	.309	.350	92	-1	6	0	2	.978	-3	O-48/D-3	-0.5
Total	11	697	1605	224	363	50	8	52	175	184	411	.226	.313	.364	91	-19	36	24	-4	.971	-64	O-587/D-8,3-1	-11.8

■ VIC BRADFORD

Bradford, Henry Victor b: 3/5/15, Brownsville, Tenn. d: 6/10/94, Paris, Ky. BR/TR, 6'2", 190 lbs. Deb: 5/1/43

YEAR	TM/L	G	AB	R	H	2B	3B	HR	RBI	BB	SO	AVG	OBP	SLG	PRO+	BR/A	SB	CS	SBR	FA	FR	G/POS	TPR
1943	NY-N	6	5	1	1	0	0	0	1	1	1	.200	.333	.200	55	-0	0			1.000	0	/O-1	0.0

■ AL BRADLEY

Bradley, Al 5'10", 185 lbs. Deb: 5/21/1884

YEAR	TM/L	G	AB	R	H	2B	3B	HR	RBI	BB	SO	AVG	OBP	SLG	PRO+	BR/A	SB	CS	SBR	FA	FR	G/POS	TPR
1884	Was-U	1	3	0	0	0	0	0		2		.000	.400	.000	32	-0				1.000	0	/O-1	0.0

■ GEORGE BRADLEY

Bradley, George Washington "Grin" b: 7/13/1852, Reading, Pa. d: 10/2/31, Philadelphia, Pa. BR/TR, 5'10.5", 175 lbs. Deb: 5/4/1875

YEAR	TM/L	G	AB	R	H	2B	3B	HR	RBI	BB	SO	AVG	OBP	SLG	PRO+	BR/A	SB	CS	SBR	FA	FR	G/POS	TPR
1875	StL-n	60	254	28	62	7	3	0	24	1	19	.244	.247	.295	96	0	3	3	-1	.896	-2	*P-60/S-2,2-1,O-1	-0.5
1876	StL-N	64	265	29	66	7	6	0	28	3	12	.249	.257	.321	97	-0				.919	1	*P-64	0.0
1877	Chi-N	55	214	31	52	7	3	0	12	6	19	.243	.264	.304	70	-8				**.950**	-2	*P-50,3-16/1-3,O-1	-0.3
1879	Tro-N	63	251	36	62	9	5	0	23	1	20	.247	.250	.323	93	-1				.867	7	P-54/3-5,1-3,O-1,S	0.2
1880	Pro-N	82	309	32	70	7	6	0	23	5	38	.227	.239	.288	80	-6				.858	19	*3-57,P-28/O-7,1-2	1.5
1881	Det-N	1	4	0	0	0	0	0	0	0	0	.000	.000	.000	-96	-1				.667	-1	/S-1	-0.2
	Cle-N	60	241	21	60	10	1	2	18	4	25	.249	.261	.324	88	-3				.865	-9	3-48/P-6,S-6,O-1	-0.9
	Yr	61	245	21	60	10	1	2	18	4	25	.245	.257	.318	84	-4				.865	-10	3-48/S-7,P-6,O-1	-1.1
1882	Cle-N	30	115	16	21	5	0	0	6	4	16	.183	.210	.226	41	-7				.897	3	P-18/O-9,1-6	-0.4
1883	Cle-N	4	16	0	5	0	1	0	1	0	1	.313	.313	.438	126	0				.792	-0	/S-4	0.0
	Phi-a	76	312	47	73	8	5	1	36	8		.234	.253	.301	72	-11				.779	3	3-44,P-26,O-11,/1-2	-0.3
1884	Cin-U	58	226	31	43	4	7	0		7		.190	.215	.270	43	-23				.912	-0	P-41,O-16/S-5,1-2	-0.9
1886	Phi-a	13	48	1	4	0	1	0	1	1		.083	.102	.125	-29	-7	2			.849	1	S-13	-0.5
1888	Bal-a	1	3	0	0	0	0	0	0	0		.000	.000	.000	-99	-1	0			.600	-1	/S-1	-0.1
Total	10	507	2004	244	456	57	35	3	148	39	131	.228	.242	.295	72	-69	2	0		.896	22	P-287,3-170/OS1	-1.9

■ GEORGE BRADLEY

Bradley, George Washington b: 4/1/14, Greenwood, Ark. d: 10/19/82, Lawrenceburg, Tenn BR/TR, 6'1.5", 185 lbs. Deb: 4/28/46

YEAR	TM/L	G	AB	R	H	2B	3B	HR	RBI	BB	SO	AVG	OBP	SLG	PRO+	BR/A	SB	CS	SBR	FA	FR	G/POS	TPR
1946	StL-A	4	12	2	2	1	0	0	3	0	1	.167	.167	.250	15	-1	0	0	0	1.000	-1	/O-3	-0.2

■ HUGH BRADLEY

Bradley, Hugh Frederick "Corns" b: 5/23/1885, Grafton, Mass. d: 1/26/49, Worcester, Mass. BR/TR, 5'10", 175 lbs. Deb: 4/25/10

YEAR	TM/L	G	AB	R	H	2B	3B	HR	RBI	BB	SO	AVG	OBP	SLG	PRO+	BR/A	SB	CS	SBR	FA	FR	G/POS	TPR
1910	Bos-A	32	83	8	14	6	2	0	7	5		.169	.216	.289	57	-5	2			.995	-2	1-21/C-3,O-1	-0.7

YEAR	TM/L	G	AB	R	H	2B	3B	HR	RBI	BB	SO	AVG	OBP	SLG	PRO+	BR/A	SB	CS	SBR	FA	FR	G/POS	TPR
1911	Bos-A	12	41	9	13	2	0	1	4	2		.317	.364	.439	125	1	1			.993	1	1-12	0.2
1912	Bos-A	40	137	16	26	11	1	1	19	15		.190	.275	.307	63	-7	3			.989	0	1-40	-0.8
1914	Pit-F	118	427	41	131	20	6	0	61	27	27	.307	.359	.382	103	-4	7			.990	-0	*1-118	-0.8
1915	Pit-F	26	66	3	18	4	1	0	6	4	5	.273	.314	.364	91	-2	2			.952	-3	O-15	-0.6
	Bro-F	37	126	7	31	3	2	0	18	4	9	.246	.269	.302	61	-9	6			.996	2	1-26/O-7,C-1	-0.8
	New-F	12	33	0	5	0	0	0	2	2	3	.152	.243	.152	13	-4	2			.986	-2	/1-8	-0.7
	Yr	75	225	10	54	7	3	0	26	10	17	.240	.278	.298	63	-15	10			.994	-2	1-34,O-22/C-1	-2.1
Total	5	277	913	84	238	46	12	2	117	59	44	.261	.314	.344	84	-30	23			.991	-3	1-225/O-23,C-4	-4.2

■ JACK BRADLEY
Bradley, John Thomas b: 9/20/1893, Denver, Colo. d: 3/18/69, Tulsa, Okla. BR/TR, 5′11″, 175 lbs. Deb: 6/18/16

YEAR	TM/L	G	AB	R	H	2B	3B	HR	RBI	BB	SO	AVG	OBP	SLG	PRO+	BR/A	SB	CS	SBR	FA	FR	G/POS	TPR
1916	Cle-A	2	3	0	0	0	0	0	0	0	1	.000	.000	.000	-94	-1	0			1.000	-0	/C-1	-0.1

■ MARK BRADLEY
Bradley, Mark Allen b: 12/3/56, Elizabethtown, Ky. BR/TR, 6′1″, 180 lbs. Deb: 9/3/81

YEAR	TM/L	G	AB	R	H	2B	3B	HR	RBI	BB	SO	AVG	OBP	SLG	PRO+	BR/A	SB	CS	SBR	FA	FR	G/POS	TPR
1981	LA-N	9	6	2	1	1	0	0	0	0	1	.167	.167	.333	41	-1	0	0	0	1.000	-1	/O-6	-0.2
1982	LA-N	8	3	1	1	0	0	0	0	0	0	.333	.333	.333	89	-0	0	0	0	1.000	-1	/O-3	-0.1
1983	NY-N	73	104	10	21	4	0	3	5	11	35	.202	.278	.327	68	-5	4	2	0	1.000	-5	O-35	-1.1
Total	3	90	113	13	23	5	0	3	5	11	36	.204	.274	.327	67	-5	4	2	0	1.000	-7	/O-44	-1.4

■ PHIL BRADLEY
Bradley, Philip Poole b: 3/11/59, Bloomington, Ind. BR/TR, 6′, 185 lbs. Deb: 9/2/83

YEAR	TM/L	G	AB	R	H	2B	3B	HR	RBI	BB	SO	AVG	OBP	SLG	PRO+	BR/A	SB	CS	SBR	FA	FR	G/POS	TPR
1983	Sea-A	23	67	8	18	2	0	0	5	8	5	.269	.347	.299	77	-2	3	1	0	.974	-6	O-21/D-1	-0.8
1984	Sea-A	124	322	49	97	12	4	0	24	34	61	.301	.373	.363	106	4	21	8	2	.992	-11	*O-117/D-3	-0.8
1985	Sea-A★	159	641	100	192	33	8	26	88	55	129	.300	.366	.498	133	29	22	9	1	.986	6	*O-159	3.0
1986	Sea-A	143	526	88	163	27	4	12	50	77	134	.310	.406	.445	130	25	21	12	-1	.996	1	*O-140	2.1
1987	Sea-A	158	603	101	179	38	10	14	67	84	119	.297	.390	.463	119	18	40	10	6	.983	1	*O-158	1.9
1988	Phi-N	154	569	77	150	30	5	11	56	54	106	.264	.344	.392	109	7	11	9	-2	.990	9	*O-153	1.0
1989	Bal-A	144	545	83	151	23	10	11	55	70	103	.277	.367	.417	124	19	20	6	2	.990	-2	*O-140/D-2	1.5
1990	Bal-A	72	289	39	78	9	1	4	26	30	35	.270	.353	.349	100	1	10	4	1	.987	2	O-70/D-2	0.2
	Chi-A	45	133	20	30	5	1	0	5	20	26	.226	.344	.278	78	-3	7	3	0	.973	-4	O-38/D-7	-0.8
	Yr	117	422	59	108	14	2	4	31	50	61	.256	.350	.327	93	-2	17	7	1	.982	-2	*O-108/D-9	-0.6
Total	8	1022	3695	565	1058	179	43	78	376	432	718	.286	.371	.421	118	99	155	62	9	.988	-3	O-996/D-15	7.3

■ SCOTT BRADLEY
Bradley, Scott William b: 3/22/60, Glen Ridge, N.J. BL/TR, 5′11″, 185 lbs. Deb: 9/9/84

YEAR	TM/L	G	AB	R	H	2B	3B	HR	RBI	BB	SO	AVG	OBP	SLG	PRO+	BR/A	SB	CS	SBR	FA	FR	G/POS	TPR
1984	NY-A	9	21	3	6	1	0	0	2	1	1	.286	.318	.333	84	-0	0	0	0	1.000	-1	/O-5,C-3	-0.1
1985	NY-A	19	49	4	8	2	1	0	1	1	5	.163	.196	.245	20	-5	0	0	0	.923	-1	/C-3,D-9	-0.6
1986	Chi-A	9	21	3	6	0	0	0	0	1	0	.286	.375	.286	81	-0	0	2	-1	.000	-0	/O-1,D-6	-0.2
	Sea-A	68	199	17	60	8	3	5	28	12	7	.302	.347	.447	113	3	1	0	0	.990	-13	C-59/D-3	-0.6
	Yr	77	220	20	66	8	3	5	28	13	7	.300	.350	.432	110	3	1	2	-1	.990	-14	C-59/D-9,O-1	-0.8
1987	Sea-A	102	342	34	95	15	1	5	43	15	18	.278	.314	.371	77	-11	0	1	-1	.983	-6	C-82/3-8,O-2,D-6	-1.3
1988	Sea-A	103	335	45	86	17	1	4	33	17	16	.257	.297	.349	77	-11	1	1	-0	.991	4	C-85/O-4,3-3,1-2,D	-0.1
1989	Sea-A	103	270	21	74	16	0	3	37	21	23	.274	.329	.367	93	-3	1	1	-0	.993	3	C-70/1-2,O-1,D-6	0.4
1990	Sea-A	101	233	11	52	9	0	1	28	15	20	.223	.270	.275	52	-15	0	1	-1	.995	1	C-63/3-5,1-1,D-6	-1.2
1991	Sea-A	83	172	10	35	7	0	0	11	19	19	.203	.283	.244	47	-12	0	0	0	.993	-5	C-65/3-4,1-1,D-2	-1.4
1992	Sea-A	2	1	0	0	0	0	0	0	1	1	.000	.500	.000	51	0	0	0	0	1.000	1	/C-1	0.1
	Cin-N	5	5	1	2	0	0	0	1	1	0	.400	.500	.400	154	0	0	0	0	1.000	-1	/C-2	0.0
Total	9	604	1648	149	424	75	6	18	184	104	110	.257	.306	.343	76	-54	3	6	-3	.990	-19	C-433/D-42,3-20,O1	-5.0

■ BILL BRADLEY
Bradley, William Joseph b: 2/13/1878, Cleveland, Ohio d: 3/11/54, Cleveland, Ohio BR/TR, 6′, 185 lbs. Deb: 8/26/1899 M

YEAR	TM/L	G	AB	R	H	2B	3B	HR	RBI	BB	SO	AVG	OBP	SLG	PRO+	BR/A	SB	CS	SBR	FA	FR	G/POS	TPR
1899	Chi-N	35	129	26	40	6	1	2	18	12		.310	.378	.419	122	4	4			.884	-3	3-30/S-5	0.1
1900	Chi-N	122	444	63	125	21	8	5	49	27		.282	.330	.399	104	1	14			.882	17	*3-106,1-15	1.7
1901	Cle-A	133	516	95	151	28	13	1	55	26		.293	.336	.403	109	5	15			**.930**	10	*3-133/P-1	1.5
1902	Cle-A	137	550	104	187	39	12	11	77	27		.340	.375	.515	151	35	11			.923	12	*3-137	4.4
1903	Cle-A	136	536	101	168	36	22	6	68	25		.313	.348	.496	154	33	21			.924	12	*3-136	4.7
1904	Cle-A	154	609	94	183	32	8	6	83	26		.300	.334	.409	136	23	23			**.955**	9	*3-154	4.0
1905	Cle-A	146	541	63	145	34	6	0	51	27		.268	.321	.353	112	7	22			**.945**	13	*3-146,M	2.7
1906	Cle-A	82	302	32	83	16	2	2	25	18		.275	.324	.361	116	5	13			.966	4	3-82	1.3
1907	Cle-A	139	498	48	111	20	1	0	34	35		.223	.286	.267	76	-13	20			**.938**	5	*3-139	-0.4
1908	Cle-A	148	548	70	133	24	7	1	46	29		.243	.297	.318	99	-1	18			.939	-31	*3-118,S-30	-3.2
1909	Cle-A	95	334	30	62	6	3	0	22	19		.186	.236	.222	43	-22	8			.957	-11	3-87/1-3,2-3	-3.4
1910	Cle-A	61	214	12	42	3	0	0	12	10		.196	.236	.210	39	-15	6			.956	-1	3-61	-1.6
1914	Bro-F	7	6	1	3	1	0	0	3	0	0	.500	.500	.667	218	1	0			.000	0	HM	0.1
1915	KC-F	66	203	15	38	9	1	0	9	9	18	.187	.225	.241	33	-22	6			.949	-6	3-61	-2.9
Total	14	1461	5430	754	1471	275	84	34	552	290	18	.271	.317	.371	108	41	181			.933	28	*3-1390/S-35,12P	9.0

■ DALLAS BRADSHAW
Bradshaw, Dallas Carl "Windy" b: 11/23/1895, Wolf Creek, Ill. d: 12/11/39, Herrin, Ill. BL/TR, 5′7″, 145 lbs. Deb: 6/5/17

YEAR	TM/L	G	AB	R	H	2B	3B	HR	RBI	BB	SO	AVG	OBP	SLG	PRO+	BR/A	SB	CS	SBR	FA	FR	G/POS	TPR
1917	Phi-A	2	4	0	0	0	0	0	0	0	1	.000	.000	.000	-99	-1	0			1.000	1	/2-1	0.0

■ GEORGE BRADSHAW
Bradshaw, George Thomas b: 9/12/24, Salisbury, N.C. d: 11/4/94, Hendersonville, N.C. BR/TR, 6′2″, 185 lbs. Deb: 8/10/52

YEAR	TM/L	G	AB	R	H	2B	3B	HR	RBI	BB	SO	AVG	OBP	SLG	PRO+	BR/A	SB	CS	SBR	FA	FR	G/POS	TPR
1952	Was-A	10	23	3	5	2	0	0	6	1	2	.217	.280	.304	65	-1	0	0	0	.917	-3	/C-9	-0.4

■ TERRY BRADSHAW
Bradshaw, Terry Leon b: 2/3/69, Franklin, Va. BL/TR, 6′, 180 lbs. Deb: 5/4/95

YEAR	TM/L	G	AB	R	H	2B	3B	HR	RBI	BB	SO	AVG	OBP	SLG	PRO+	BR/A	SB	CS	SBR	FA	FR	G/POS	TPR
1995	StL-N	19	44	6	10	1	1	0	2	2	10	.227	.261	.295	46	-3	1	2	-1	.952	1	O-10	-0.4
1996	StL-N	15	21	4	7	1	0	0	3	3	2	.333	.417	.381	113	1	0	1	-1	1.000	-2	/O-7	-0.2
Total	2	34	65	10	17	2	1	0	5	5	12	.262	.314	.323	69	-3	1	3	-2	.960	-2	/O-17	-0.6

■ BRADY
Brady Deb: 9/25/1875

YEAR	TM/L	G	AB	R	H	2B	3B	HR	RBI	BB	SO	AVG	OBP	SLG	PRO+	BR/A	SB	CS	SBR	FA	FR	G/POS	TPR
1875	Chi-n	1	4	1	1	0	1	0	0	0	0	.250	.250	.750	231	1	0	0	0	.625	1	/O-1	0.1

■ BRIAN BRADY
Brady, Brian Phelan b: 7/11/62, Elmhurst, N.Y. BL/TL, 5′11″, 185 lbs. Deb: 4/16/89

YEAR	TM/L	G	AB	R	H	2B	3B	HR	RBI	BB	SO	AVG	OBP	SLG	PRO+	BR/A	SB	CS	SBR	FA	FR	G/POS	TPR
1989	Cal-A	2	2	0	1	1	0	0	1	0	1	.500	.500	1.000	319	1	0	0	0	.000	-0	/O-1	0.0

■ CLIFF BRADY
Brady, Clifford Francis b: 3/6/1897, St.Louis, Mo. d: 9/25/74, Belleville, Ill. BR/TR, 5′5.5″, 140 lbs. Deb: 8/8/20

YEAR	TM/L	G	AB	R	H	2B	3B	HR	RBI	BB	SO	AVG	OBP	SLG	PRO+	BR/A	SB	CS	SBR	FA	FR	G/POS	TPR
1920	Bos-A	53	180	16	41	5	1	0	12	13	12	.228	.284	.267	48	-13	0	1	-1	.974	17	2-53	0.5

■ BOB BRADY
Brady, Robert Jay b: 11/8/22, Lewistown, Pa. d: 4/22/96, Manchester, Conn. BL/TR, 6′1″, 175 lbs. Deb: 8/24/46

YEAR	TM/L	G	AB	R	H	2B	3B	HR	RBI	BB	SO	AVG	OBP	SLG	PRO+	BR/A	SB	CS	SBR	FA	FR	G/POS	TPR
1946	Bos-N	3	5	0	1	0	0	0	0	1	1	.200	.333	.200	52	-0	0			.857	0	/C-1	0.0
1947	Bos-N	1	1	0	0	0	0	0	0	0	0	.000	.000	.000	-99	-0	0			.000	0	H	0.0
Total	2	4	6	0	1	0	0	0	0	1	1	.167	.286	.167	29	-1	0			.857	0	/C-1	0.0

■ STEVE BRADY
Brady, Stephen A. b: 7/14/1851, Worcester, Mass. d: 11/1/17, Hartford, Conn. 5′9.5″, 165 lbs. Deb: 7/23/1874

YEAR	TM/L	G	AB	R	H	2B	3B	HR	RBI	BB	SO	AVG	OBP	SLG	PRO+	BR/A	SB	CS	SBR	FA	FR	G/POS	TPR
1874	Har-n	27	118	19	37	5	1	0	14	2	10	.314	.325	.373	117	2	1	2	-1	.662	-10	3-16,O-11/S-1	-0.7
1875	Was-n	21	91	7	13	0	0	0	3	0	4	.143	.143	.143	-0	-9	5	0	2	.815	-6	2-18/O-2,C-1,1-1	-1.2
	Har-n	1	4	0	0	0	0	0	0	0	1	.000	.000	.000	-95	-1	0	0	0	1.000	1	/O-1	0.0
	Yr	22	95	7	13	0	0	0	3	0	5	.137	.137	.137	-5	-9	5	0	2	.815	-5	2-18/O-3,C-1,1-1	-1.2
1883	NY-a	97	432	69	117	12	6	0		11		.271	.289	.326	94	-4				.961	3	*1-81,O-16	-0.8
1884	*NY-a	112	485	102	122	11	3	1		21		.252	.283	.293	90	-5				.918	1	*O-110/1-5,2-1	-0.5
1885	NY-a	108	434	60	128	14	5	3	58	25		.295	.342	.371	136	19				.879	-6	*O-105/1-4,2-2,3-1	0.9
1886	NY-a	124	466	56	112	8	5	0	39	35		.240	.298	.279	85	-7	16			.830	-5	*O-123/1-1	-1.3
Total	2 n	49	213	26	50	5	1	0	17	2	15	.235	.242	.268	68	-8	6	2	1	.703	-16	/2-18,3-16,O1CS	-1.9
Total	4	441	1817	287	479	45	19	4	97	92		.264	.302	.316	100	3	16			.875	-6	O-354/1-91,2-3,3-1	-1.7

■ DOUG BRADY
Brady, Stephen Douglas b: 11/23/69, Jacksonville, Ill. BB/TR, 5′11″, 165 lbs. Deb: 9/5/95

YEAR	TM/L	G	AB	R	H	2B	3B	HR	RBI	BB	SO	AVG	OBP	SLG	PRO+	BR/A	SB	CS	SBR	FA	FR	G/POS	TPR
1995	Chi-A	12	21	4	4	1	0	0	3	2	4	.190	.261	.238	32	-2	0	1	-1	1.000	6	/2-6,D-3	0.3

YEAR	TM/L	G	AB	R	H	2B	3B	HR	RBI	BB	SO	AVG	OBP	SLG	PRO+	BR/A	SB	CS	SBR	FA	FR	G/POS	TPR
■ BOBBY BRAGAN	Bragan, Robert Randall "Nig" b: 10/30/17, Birmingham, Ala. BR/TR, 5'10.5", 175 lbs. Deb: 4/16/40 MC																						
1940	Phi-N	132	474	36	105	14	1	7	44	28	34	.222	.265	.300	58	-28	2			.936	1	*S-132/3-2	-1.7
1941	Phi-N	154	557	37	140	19	3	4	69	26	29	.251	.285	.318	72	-22	7			.944	-7	*S-154/2-2,3-1	-1.8
1942	Phi-N	109	335	17	73	12	2	2	15	20	21	.218	.264	.284	63	-16	0			.939	9	S-78,C-22/2-4,3-3	-0.1
1943	Bro-N	74	220	17	58	7	2	2	24	15	16	.264	.311	.341	88	-4	0			.973	4	C-57,3-12	0.5
1944	Bro-N	94	266	26	71	8	4	0	17	13	14	.267	.304	.327	79	-8	2			.954	-0	S-51,C-35/3-6,2-1	-0.3
1947	*Bro-N	25	36	3	7	2	0	0	3	7	3	.194	.326	.250	53	-2	1			1.000	4	C-21	0.2
1948	Bro-N	9	12	0	2	0	0	0	0	1	0	.167	.231	.167	9	-2	0			1.000	-0	/C-5	-0.2
Total	7	597	1900	136	456	62	12	15	172	110	117	.240	.282	.309	69	-82	12			.941	10	S-415,C-140/3-24,2	-3.4
■ DARREN BRAGG	Bragg, Darren William b: 9/7/69, Waterbury, Conn. BL/TR, 5'9", 180 lbs. Deb: 4/12/94																						
1994	Sea-A	8	19	4	3	1	0	0	2	2	5	.158	.238	.211	17	-2	0	0	0	1.000	-1	/O-3,D-3	-0.3
1995	Sea-A	52	145	20	34	5	1	3	12	18	37	.234	.335	.345	77	-5	9	0	3	.989	4	O-47/D-2	0.1
1996	Sea-A	69	195	36	53	12	1	7	25	33	35	.272	.383	.451	110	4	8	5	-1	.992	1	O-63	0.2
	Bos-A	58	222	38	56	14	1	3	22	36	39	.252	.362	.365	83	-5	6	4	-1	.986	-5	O-58	-1.1
	Yr	127	417	74	109	26	2	10	47	69	74	.261	.371	.405	95	-1	14	9	-1	.989	-4	*O-121	-0.9
1997	Bos-A	153	513	65	132	35	2	9	57	61	102	.257	.340	.386	87	-9	10	6	-1	.987	6	*O-150/3-1	-0.7
1998	*Bos-A	129	409	51	114	29	3	8	57	42	99	.279	.354	.423	101	1	5	3	-0	**.996**	-6	*O-124/D-4	-0.7
Total	5	469	1503	214	392	96	8	30	175	192	317	.261	.351	.395	91	-16	38	18	1	.990	-1	O-445/D-9,3-1	-2.5
■ GLENN BRAGGS	Braggs, Glenn Erick b: 10/17/62, San Bernardino, Cal BR/TR, 6'3", 210 lbs. Deb: 7/18/86																						
1986	Mil-A	58	215	19	51	8	2	4	18	11	47	.237	.278	.349	67	-10	1	1	-0	.910	1	O-56/D-2	-1.1
1987	Mil-A	132	505	67	136	28	7	13	77	47	96	.269	.336	.430	98	-1	12	5	1	.972	14	*O-123/D-8	0.9
1988	Mil-A	72	272	30	71	14	0	10	42	14	60	.261	.309	.423	102	0	6	4	-1	.978	4	O-54,D-18	0.1
1989	Mil-A	144	514	77	127	12	3	15	66	42	111	.247	.309	.370	91	-6	17	5	2	.972	-0	*O-132,D-13	-0.8
1990	Mil-A	37	113	17	28	5	0	3	13	12	21	.248	.336	.372	98	-0	5	3	-0	.965	2	O-32/D-2	0.1
	*Cin-N	72	201	22	60	9	1	6	28	26	43	.299	.387	.443	122	7	3	4	-2	.968	6	O-60	1.0
1991	Cin-N	85	250	36	65	10	0	11	39	23	46	.260	.327	.432	108	2	11	3	2	.966	-2	O-74	0.0
1992	Cin-N	92	266	40	63	16	3	8	38	36	48	.237	.332	.410	106	2	3	1	0	.946	-9	O-79	-0.8
Total	7	692	2336	308	601	102	16	70	321	211	472	.257	.325	.405	98	-6	58	26	2	.963	16	O-610/D-43	-0.6
■ DAVE BRAIN	Brain, David Leonard b: 1/24/1879, Hereford, England d: 5/26/59, Los Angeles, Cal. BR/TR, 5'10", 170 lbs. Deb: 4/24/01																						
1901	Chi-A	5	20	2	7	1	0	0	5	1		.350	.381	.400	120	1	0			.909	1	/2-5	0.1
1903	StL-N	119	464	44	107	8	15	1	60	25		.231	.270	.319	70	-20	21			.908	10	S-72,3-46	-0.6
1904	StL-N	127	488	57	130	24	12	7	72	17		.266	.291	.408	120	8	18			.927	3	S-59,3-30,O-19,2/1	1.4
1905	StL-N	44	158	11	36	4	5	1	17	8		.228	.269	.335	82	-4	4			.910	-9	S-29/3-6,O-6	-1.3
	Pit-N	85	307	31	79	17	6	3	46	15		.257	.296	.381	99	-2	8			.923	6	3-78/S-4	0.7
	Yr	129	465	42	115	21	11	4	63	23		.247	.287	.366	93	-6	12			.929	-3	3-84,S-33/O-6	-0.6
1906	Bos-N	139	525	43	131	19	5	5	45	29		.250	.293	.333	98	-3	11			.917	26	*3-139	2.9
1907	Bos-N	133	509	60	142	24	9	**10**	56	29		.279	.324	.420	134	17	10			.916	25	*3-130/O-3	5.0
1908	Cin-N	16	55	4	6	0	0	0	2	8		.109	.222	.109	7	-5	0			.947	-1	O-16	-0.8
	NY-N	11	17	2	3	0	0	0	1	2		.176	.263	.176	39	-1	1			.867	-3	/2-3,O-3,3-2,S-1	-0.4
	Yr	27	72	6	9	0	0	0	2	10		.125	.232	.125	14	-7	1			.947	-3	O-19/2-3,3-2,S-1	-1.2
Total	7	679	2543	254	641	97	52	27	303	134		.252	.292	.363	101	-10	73			.913	58	3-431,S-165/O21	7.0
■ ASA BRAINARD	Brainard, Asa "Count" b: 1841, Albany, N.Y. d: 12/29/1888, Denver, Colo. TR, 5'8.5", 150 lbs. Deb: 5/5/1871																						
1871	Oly-n	30	134	24	30	4	0	0	21	7	2	.224	.262	.254	52	-7	4	0	1	.852	-3	*P-30	0.0
1872	Oly-n	9	43	8	16	3	0	0	6	0	0	.372	.372	.442	157	3	0	0	0	.625	-1	/P-9	0.0
	Man-n	6	25	2	5	0	0	0	0	1	0	.200	.231	.200	36	-2	0	0	0	.682	-3	/2-4,P-2,O-1	-0.3
	Yr	15	68	10	21	3	0	0	6	1	0	.309	.319	.353	112	1	0	0	0	.667	-4	P-11/2-4,O-1	-0.3
1873	Bal-n	16	69	18	18	1	0	0	8	0	2	.261	.261	.275	60	-3	0	0	0	.800	-2	P-14/O-2,2-1	-0.1
1874	Bal-n	47	196	19	47	3	0	0	8	2	3	.240	.247	.255	62	-8	0	3	-2	.820	-7	P-30,2-21/O-2	-0.7
Total	4 n	108	467	71	116	11	0	0	43	10	7	.248	.264	.272	66	-17	4	3	-1	.810	-16	/P-85,2-26,O-5	-1.1
■ FRED BRAINERD	Brainerd, Frederick F. b: 2/17/1892, Champaign, Ill. d: 4/17/59, Galveston, Tex. BR/TR, 6', 176 lbs. Deb: 10/6/14																						
1914	NY-N	2	5	1	1	0	0	0	0	1	1	.200	.333	.200	62	-0	0			.923	1	/2-2	0.1
1915	NY-N	91	249	31	50	7	2	1	21	21	44	.201	.266	.257	62	-11	6	7	-2	.988	7	1-43,3-15/S-9,2O	-0.8
1916	NY-N	2	7	0	0	0	0	0	0	0	0	.000	.000	.000	-99	-2	0			.625	-1	/3-2	-0.3
Total	3	95	261	32	51	7	2	1	21	22	44	.195	.261	.249	58	-13	6	7		.857	7	/1-43,3-17,S-9,2O	-1.0
■ ART BRAMHALL	Bramhall, Arthur Washington b: 2/22/09, Oak Park, Ill. d: 9/4/85, Madison, Wis. BR/TR, 5'11", 170 lbs. Deb: 4/18/35																						
1935	Phi-N	2	1	0	0	0	0	0	0	0	0	.000	.000	.000	-91	-0	0			1.000	1	/S-1,3-1	0.0
■ AL BRANCATO	Brancato, Albert "Bronk" b: 5/29/19, Philadelphia, Pa. BR/TR, 5'9.5", 188 lbs. Deb: 9/7/39																						
1939	Phi-A	21	68	12	14	5	0	1	8	8	4	.206	.299	.324	60	-4	1	0	0	.939	-1	3-20/S-1	-0.5
1940	Phi-A	107	298	42	57	11	2	1	23	28	36	.191	.265	.252	36	-29	3	1	0	.949	0	S-80,3-25	-2.1
1941	Phi-A	144	530	60	124	20	9	2	49	59	49	.234	.311	.317	68	-24	1	5	-3	.915	-19	*S-139/3-7	-3.5
1945	Phi-A	10	34	3	4	1	0	0	0	1	3	.118	.143	.147	-16	-5	0	0	0	.959	1	S-10	-0.6
Total	4	282	930	117	199	37	11	4	80	96	92	.214	.290	.290	54	-62	5	6	-2	.927	-21	S-230/3-52	-6.7
■ RON BRAND	Brand, Ronald George b: 1/13/40, Los Angeles, Cal. BR/TR, 5'8", 170 lbs. Deb: 5/26/63																						
1963	Pit-N	46	66	8	19	2	0	1	7	10	11	.288	.390	.364	118	2	0	0	0	.968	9	C-33/2-2,3-2	1.2
1965	Hou-N	117	391	27	92	6	3	2	37	19	34	.235	.281	.281	63	-19	10	5	0	.988	-7	*C-102/3-6,O-5	-2.3
1966	Hou-N	56	123	12	30	2	0	0	10	9	13	.244	.306	.260	64	-6	0	2	-1	.986	-5	C-25/2-9,O-3,3-1	-1.1
1967	Hou-N	84	215	22	52	8	1	0	18	23	17	.242	.321	.288	78	-5	4	0	1	.998	-3	C-67/2-1,O-1	-0.4
1968	Hou-N	43	81	7	13	2	0	0	4	9	11	.160	.261	.185	36	-6	1	1	-0	1.000	3	C-29/3-1,O-1	-0.2
1969	Mon-N	103	287	19	74	12	0	0	20	30	19	.258	.330	.300	77	-8	2	3	-1	.985	-8	C-84/O-2	-1.3
1970	Mon-N	72	126	10	30	2	3	0	9	9	16	.238	.289	.302	59	-7	2	1	0	.952	-7	S-19,3-12/C-9,O2	-1.3
1971	Mon-N	47	56	3	12	0	0	0	1	3	5	.214	.254	.214	34	-5	1	2	-1	.957	3	S-22/3-4,O-4,C-1,2	-0.1
Total	8	568	1345	108	322	34	7	3	106	112	126	.239	.305	.282	68	-55	20	13	-2	.988	-16	C-350/S-41,3-26,O2	-5.5
■ JACKIE BRANDT	Brandt, John George b: 4/28/34, Omaha, Neb. BR/TR, 5'11", 170 lbs. Deb: 4/21/56																						
1956	StL-N	27	42	9	12	3	0	1	3	4	5	.286	.362	.429	111	1	0	1	-1	1.000	-3	O-26	-0.4
	NY-N	98	351	45	105	16	8	11	47	17	31	.299	.332	.484	116	7	3	4	-2	.989	-6	O-96	-0.5
	Yr	125	393	54	117	19	8	12	50	21	36	.298	.335	.478	116	8	3	5	-2	.990	-9	*O-122	-0.9
1958	SF-N	18	52	7	13	1	0	0	3	6	5	.250	.328	.269	62	-3	1	0	0	1.000	-0	O-14	-0.3
1959	SF-N	137	429	63	116	16	5	12	57	35	69	.270	.325	.415	98	-2	11	4	1	.984	-7	*O-116,3-18/1-3,2-1	-1.3
1960	Bal-A	145	511	73	130	24	6	15	65	47	69	.254	.321	.413	98	-2	5	3	-0	.983	-10	*O-142/3-2,1-1	-2.0
1961	Bal-A★	139	516	93	153	18	5	16	72	62	51	.297	.373	.444	122	16	10	2	2	.974	-16	*O-136/3-1	-0.6
1962	Bal-A	143	505	76	129	29	5	19	75	55	64	.255	.333	.446	115	9	9	3	1	.976	9	*O-138/3-2	1.1
1963	Bal-A	142	451	49	112	15	5	15	61	34	85	.248	.301	.404	99	-2	4	5	-2	.986	-7	*O-134/3-1	-1.8
1964	Bal-A	137	523	66	127	25	1	13	47	45	104	.243	.306	.369	87	-9	1	4	-2	.981	16	*O-134	-0.2
1965	Bal-A	96	243	35	59	17	0	8	24	21	40	.243	.303	.412	99	-1	1	2	-1	.961	-6	O-84	-1.1
1966	Phi-N	82	164	16	41	6	1	1	15	17	36	.250	.320	.317	78	-4	0	2	-1	.988	-12	O-71	-2.1
1967	Phi-N	16	19	1	2	1	0	0	1	0	6	.105	.105	.158	-25	-3	0	0	0	1.000	-1	/O-3	-0.4
	Hou-N	41	89	7	21	4	1	1	15	8	9	.236	.299	.337	85	-2	0	0	0	.991	-2	1-14/O-6,3-1	-0.6
	Yr	57	108	8	23	5	1	1	16	8	15	.213	.267	.306	65	-5	0	0	0	.991	-3	1-14/O-9,3-1	-1.0
Total	11	1221	3895	540	1020	175	37	112	485	351	574	.262	.325	.412	102	5	45	30	-4	.980	-46	*O-1100/3-25,1-18,2	-10.2
■ OTIS BRANNAN	Brannan, Otis Owen b: 3/13/1899, Greenbrier, Ark. d: 6/6/67, Little Rock, Ark. BL/TR, 5'9", 160 lbs. Deb: 4/11/28																						
1928	StL-A	135	483	68	118	18	3	10	66	60	19	.244	.333	.356	79	-15	3	9	-5	.964	-8	*2-135	-2.3

YEAR	TM/L	G	AB	R	H	2B	3B	HR	RBI	BB	SO	AVG	OBP	SLG	PRO+	BR/A	SB	CS	SBR	FA	FR	G/POS	TPR
1929	StL-A	23	51	4	15	1	0	1	8	4	4	.294	.345	.373	82	-1	0	0	0	.975	-1	2-19	-0.2
Total	2	158	534	72	133	19	3	11	74	64	23	.249	.334	.358	79	-16	3	9	-5	.966	-9	2-154	-2.5

■ MIKE BRANNOCK
Brannock, Michael J. b: 1853, Guelph, Ont., Canada 5'8", 162 lbs. Deb: 10/21/1871

YEAR	TM/L	G	AB	R	H	2B	3B	HR	RBI	BB	SO	AVG	OBP	SLG	PRO+	BR/A	SB	CS	SBR	FA	FR	G/POS	TPR
1871	Chi-n	3	14	2	1	0	0	0	0	0	0	.071	.071	.071	-53	-3	0	0	0	.500	-2	/3-3	-0.4
1875	Chi-n	2	9	2	1	0	0	0	0	0	0	.111	.111	.111	-22	-1	2	0	1	.500	-2	/3-2	-0.2
Total	2 n	5	23	4	2	0	0	0	0	0	0	.087	.087	.087	-43	-4	2	0	1	.500	-4	/3-5	-0.6

■ DUD BRANOM
Branom, Edgar Dudley b: 11/30/1897, Sulphur Springs, Tex. d: 2/4/80, Sun City, Ariz. BL/TL, 6'1", 190 lbs. Deb: 4/12/27

YEAR	TM/L	G	AB	R	H	2B	3B	HR	RBI	BB	SO	AVG	OBP	SLG	PRO+	BR/A	SB	CS	SBR	FA	FR	G/POS	TPR
1927	Phi-A	30	94	8	22	1	0	0	13	2	5	.234	.250	.245	27	-10	2	1	0	.973	-0	1-26	-1.1

■ KITTY BRANSFIELD
Bransfield, William Edward b: 1/7/1875, Worcester, Mass. d: 5/1/47, Worcester, Mass. BR/TR, 5'11", 207 lbs. Deb: 8/22/1898 U

YEAR	TM/L	G	AB	R	H	2B	3B	HR	RBI	BB	SO	AVG	OBP	SLG	PRO+	BR/A	SB	CS	SBR	FA	FR	G/POS	TPR
1898	Bos-N	5	9	2	2	0	1	0	1	0		.222	.222	.444	85	-0	0			.889	-1	/C-4,1-1	-0.1
1901	Pit-N	139	566	92	167	26	16	0	91	29		.295	.335	.398	109	5	23			.981	-10	*1-139	-0.7
1902	Pit-N	102	413	49	126	21	8	0	69	17		.305	.336	.395	121	8	23			.984	-6	*1-101	0.1
1903	*Pit-N	127	505	69	134	23	7	2	57	33		.265	.314	.350	87	-10	13			.981	6	*1-127	-0.6
1904	Pit-N	139	520	47	116	17	9	0	60	22		.223	.259	.290	68	-21	11			.981	-3	*1-139	-2.9
1905	Phi-N	151	580	55	150	23	9	3	76	27		.259	.294	.345	93	-7	27			.985	-1	*1-151	-1.3
1906	Phi-N	140	524	47	144	28	5	1	60	16		.275	.300	.353	104	-1	12			.980	-2	*1-139	-0.7
1907	Phi-N	94	348	25	81	15	2	0	38	14		.233	.262	.287	73	-12	8			.978	-3	1-92	-1.9
1908	Phi-N	144	527	53	160	25	7	3	71	23		.304	.335	.395	128	15	30			.986	-1	*1-143	1.3
1909	Phi-N	140	527	47	154	27	6	1	59	18		.292	.319	.372	114	6	17			**.989**	7	*1-138	1.3
1910	Phi-N	123	427	39	102	17	4	3	52	20	34	.239	.275	.319	71	-18	10			.982	-4	*1-110	-2.4
1911	Phi-N	23	43	4	11	1	1	0	3	0	5	.256	.256	.326	61	-2	1			.987	0	/1-8	-0.2
	Chi-N	3	10	0	4	2	0	0	0	2	2	.400	.500	.600	207	2	0			1.000	-0	/1-3	0.1
	Yr	26	53	4	15	3	1	0	3	2	7	.283	.309	.377	91	-1	1			.991	-0	1-11	-0.1
Total	12	1330	4999	529	1351	225	75	13	637	221	41	.270	.304	.353	97	-35	175			.983	-18	*1-1291/C-4	-8.0

■ JEFF BRANSON
Branson, Jeffery Glenn b: 1/26/67, Waynesboro, Miss. BL/TR, 6', 180 lbs. Deb: 4/12/92

YEAR	TM/L	G	AB	R	H	2B	3B	HR	RBI	BB	SO	AVG	OBP	SLG	PRO+	BR/A	SB	CS	SBR	FA	FR	G/POS	TPR
1992	Cin-N	72	115	12	34	7	1	0	15	5	16	.296	.325	.374	95	-1	0	1	-1	.946	2	2-33/3-8,S-1	0.1
1993	Cin-N	125	381	40	92	15	1	3	22	19	73	.241	.278	.310	57	-23	4	1	1	.978	5	S-59,2-45,3-14,/1-1	-1.3
1994	Cin-N	58	109	18	31	4	1	6	16	5	16	.284	.316	.505	110	1	0	0	0	.980	-4	2-19,3-18/S-8,1-2	-0.2
1995	*Cin-N	122	331	43	86	18	2	12	45	44	69	.260	.350	.435	106	3	2	1	0	.971	**22**	3-98,S-32/2-6,1-1	2.6
1996	Cin-N	129	311	34	76	16	4	9	37	31	67	.244	.315	.408	89	-6	2	0	1	.932	2	3-64,S-38,2-31	0.0
1997	Cin-N	65	98	9	15	3	1	1	5	7	23	.153	.210	.235	16	-12	1	0	0	.971	3	3-27,2-14,S-11	-0.8
	*Cle-A	29	72	5	19	4	0	2	7	7	17	.264	.338	.403	89	-1	0	2	-1	.986	4	2-19/3-6,S-2,D-1	0.3
1998	*Cle-A	63	100	6	20	4	1	1	9	3	21	.200	.223	.290	31	-10	0	0	0	.960	-0	2-31,3-20/1-3,S-2	-0.9
Total	7	663	1517	167	373	71	11	34	156	121	302	.246	.303	.374	78	-49	9	5	-0	.957	33	3-255,2-198,S/1D	-0.2

■ MARSHALL BRANT
Brant, Marshall Lee b: 9/17/55, Garberville, Cal. BR/TR, 6'5", 185 lbs. Deb: 10/1/80

YEAR	TM/L	G	AB	R	H	2B	3B	HR	RBI	BB	SO	AVG	OBP	SLG	PRO+	BR/A	SB	CS	SBR	FA	FR	G/POS	TPR
1980	NY-A	3	6	0	0	0	0	0	0	0	3	.000	.000	.000	-99	-2	0	0	0	1.000	0	/1-2,D-1	-0.1
1983	Oak-A	5	14	2	2	0	0	0	2	0	3	.143	.143	.143	-22	-2	0	0	0	.905	-1	/1-3,D-1	-0.4
Total	2	8	20	2	2	0	0	0	2	0	6	.100	.100	.100	-47	-4	0	0	0	.935	-1	/1-5,D-2	-0.5

■ MICKEY BRANTLEY
Brantley, Michael Charles b: 6/17/61, Catskill, N.Y. BR/TR, 5'10", 180 lbs. Deb: 8/9/86

YEAR	TM/L	G	AB	R	H	2B	3B	HR	RBI	BB	SO	AVG	OBP	SLG	PRO+	BR/A	SB	CS	SBR	FA	FR	G/POS	TPR
1986	Sea-A	27	102	12	20	3	2	3	7	10	21	.196	.268	.353	67	-5	1	1	-0	.983	0	O-25	-0.6
1987	Sea-A	92	351	52	106	23	2	14	54	24	44	.302	.347	.499	115	7	13	4	2	.982	-6	O-82/D-8	-0.1
1988	Sea-A	149	577	76	152	25	4	15	56	26	64	.263	.298	.399	89	-10	18	7	1	.982	-5	*O-147/D-2	-1.8
1989	Sea-A	34	108	14	17	5	0	0	8	7	7	.157	.209	.204	16	-12	2	2	-1	1.000	1	O-23/D-7	-1.2
Total	4	302	1138	154	295	56	8	32	125	67	136	.259	.302	.407	89	-20	34	14	2	.984	-9	O-277/D-17	-3.7

■ RUSSELL BRANYAN
Branyan, Russell Oles b: 12/19/75, Warner Robins, Ga. BL/TR, 6'3", 195 lbs. Deb: 9/26/98

YEAR	TM/L	G	AB	R	H	2B	3B	HR	RBI	BB	SO	AVG	OBP	SLG	PRO+	BR/A	SB	CS	SBR	FA	FR	G/POS	TPR
1998	Cle-A	1	4	0	0	0	0	0	0	0	2	.000	.000	.000	-97	-1	0	0	0	1.000	-1	/3-1	-0.2

■ ROY BRASHEAR
Brashear, Roy Parks b: 1/3/1874, Ashtabula, Ohio d: 4/20/51, Los Angeles, Cal. BR/TR, 5'11", 205 lbs. Deb: 4/25/02 F

YEAR	TM/L	G	AB	R	H	2B	3B	HR	RBI	BB	SO	AVG	OBP	SLG	PRO+	BR/A	SB	CS	SBR	FA	FR	G/POS	TPR
1902	StL-N	110	388	36	107	8	2	1	40	32		.276	.333	.314	104	2	9			.980	-9	1-67,2-21,O-16,/S-3	-0.8
1903	Phi-N	20	75	9	17	3	0	0	4	6		.227	.284	.267	59	-4	2			.918	-4	2-18/1-2	-0.7
Total	2	130	463	45	124	11	2	1	44	38		.268	.325	.307	96	-2	11			.978	-13	/1-69,2-39,O-16,S-3	-1.5

■ JOE BRATCHER
Bratcher, Joseph Warlick "Goobers" b: 7/22/1898, Grand Saline, Tex d: 10/13/77, Fort Worth, Tex. BL/TR, 5'8.5", 140 lbs. Deb: 8/26/24

YEAR	TM/L	G	AB	R	H	2B	3B	HR	RBI	BB	SO	AVG	OBP	SLG	PRO+	BR/A	SB	CS	SBR	FA	FR	G/POS	TPR
1924	StL-N	4	1	1	0	0	0	0	0	0	0	.000	.000	.000	-99	-0	0	0	0	.000	-1	/O-1	-0.1

■ FRED BRATSCHI
Bratschi, Frederick Oscar "Fritz" b: 1/16/1892, Alliance, Ohio d: 1/10/62, Massillon, Ohio BR/TR, 5'10", 170 lbs. Deb: 7/24/21

YEAR	TM/L	G	AB	R	H	2B	3B	HR	RBI	BB	SO	AVG	OBP	SLG	PRO+	BR/A	SB	CS	SBR	FA	FR	G/POS	TPR
1921	Chi-A	16	28	0	8	1	0	0	3	0	2	.286	.286	.321	55	-2	0	0	0	1.000	1	/O-5	-0.1
1926	Bos-A	72	167	12	46	10	1	0	19	14	15	.275	.335	.347	81	-5	0	1	-1	.949	-7	O-37	-1.4
1927	Bos-A	1	1	0	0	0	0	0	0	0	0	.000	.000	.000	-99	-0	0	0	0	.000	0	H	0.0
Total	3	89	196	12	54	11	1	0	22	14	17	.276	.327	.342	76	-7	0	1	-1	.956	-6	/O-42	-1.5

■ STEVE BRAUN
Braun, Stephen Russell b: 5/8/48, Trenton, N.J. BL/TR, 5'10", 180 lbs. Deb: 4/6/71 C

YEAR	TM/L	G	AB	R	H	2B	3B	HR	RBI	BB	SO	AVG	OBP	SLG	PRO+	BR/A	SB	CS	SBR	FA	FR	G/POS	TPR
1971	Min-A	128	343	51	87	12	2	5	35	48	50	.254	.354	.344	95	-1	8	3	1	.933	-13	3-73,2-28,S-10,/O-2	-1.1
1972	Min-A	121	402	40	116	21	0	2	50	45	38	.289	.363	.356	109	6	4	5	-2	.970	-12	3-74,2-20,S-11,/O-9	-0.8
1973	Min-A	115	361	46	102	28	5	6	42	74	48	.283	.409	.438	133	19	4	3	-1	.941	-11	*3-102/O-6	0.7
1974	Min-A	129	453	53	127	12	1	8	40	56	51	.280	.362	.364	106	5	4	4	-1	.964	2	*O-108,3-17	0.1
1975	Min-A	136	453	70	137	18	3	11	45	66	55	.302	.392	.428	130	20	0	2	-1	.971	-2	*O-106/1-9,3-2,2D	1.2
1976	Min-A	122	417	73	120	12	3	3	61	67	43	.288	.388	.353	115	11	12	4	1	.971	-3	D-71,O-32,3-16	0.6
1977	Sea-A	139	451	51	106	19	1	5	31	80	59	.235	.353	.315	84	-7	8	3	1	.975	5	*O-100,D-32/3-1	-0.6
1978	Sea-A	32	74	11	17	4	0	3	15	9	5	.230	.313	.405	101	0	1	0	0	1.000	-1	D-14/O-4	-0.1
	*KC-A	64	137	16	36	10	1	0	14	28	16	.263	.388	.350	106	2	3	2	-0	.964	-5	O-33,3-11	-0.5
	Yr	96	211	27	53	14	1	3	29	37	21	.251	.363	.370	105	3	4	2	0	.967	-6	O-37,D-14,3-11	-0.6
1979	KC-A	58	116	15	31	2	0	4	10	22	11	.267	.384	.388	107	2	0	0	0	1.000	1	O-18,D-11/3-2	0.2
1980	KC-A	14	23	0	1	0	0	0	1	2	2	.043	.120	.043	-53	-5	0	0	0	1.000	-2	/O-5,D-1	-0.7
	Tor-A	37	55	4	15	2	0	1	9	8	5	.273	.365	.364	96	-0	0	0	0	1.000	0	D-13/3-1	0.0
	Yr	51	78	4	16	2	0	1	10	10	7	.205	.295	.269	54	-5	0	0	0	1.000	-2	D-14/O-5,3-1	-0.7
1981	StL-N	44	46	9	9	2	1	0	2	15	7	.196	.393	.283	92	0	1	0	0	1.000	-1	O-12/3-1	0.0
1982	*StL-N	58	62	6	17	4	0	0	4	11	10	.274	.384	.339	103	1	0	0	0	1.000	-5	/O-8,3-5	-0.4
1983	StL-N	78	92	8	25	2	1	3	7	21	7	.272	.407	.413	128	4	0	1	-1	1.000	-5	O-22/3-4	-0.2
1984	StL-N	86	98	6	27	3	1	0	16	17	17	.276	.383	.327	104	1	0	0	0	1.000	-5	O-19/3-1	-0.4
1985	*StL-N	64	67	7	16	4	0	1	6	10	9	.239	.346	.343	94	-0	0	0	0	1.000	-2	O-14	-0.2
Total	15	1425	3650	466	989	155	19	52	388	579	433	.271	.373	.367	108	60	45	27	-3	.973	-57	O-498,3-310,D/2S1	-2.2

■ ANGEL BRAVO
Bravo, Angel Alfonso (Urdaneta) b: 8/4/42, Maracaibo, Venez. BL/TL, 5'8", 150 lbs. Deb: 6/6/69

YEAR	TM/L	G	AB	R	H	2B	3B	HR	RBI	BB	SO	AVG	OBP	SLG	PRO+	BR/A	SB	CS	SBR	FA	FR	G/POS	TPR
1969	Chi-A	27	90	10	26	4	2	1	3	3	5	.289	.319	.411	98	-0	2	0	1	.978	-4	O-25	-0.6
1970	*Cin-N	65	65	10	18	1	1	0	3	9	13	.277	.365	.323	86	-1	0	1	-1	.947	-5	O-22	-0.7
1971	Cin-N	5	5	0	1	0	0	0	0	0	1	.200	.200	.200	14	-1	0	0	0	.000	0	H	-0.1
	SD-N	52	58	6	9	2	0	0	6	8	12	.155	.269	.190	34	-5	0	1	-1	.833	-3	/O-9	-0.9
	Yr	57	63	6	10	2	0	0	6	8	13	.159	.264	.190	33	-5	0	1	-1	.833	-3	/O-9	-1.0
Total	3	149	218	26	54	7	3	1	12	20	31	.248	.317	.321	77	-7	2	2	-1	.957	-12	/O-56	-2.3

■ BUSTER BRAY
Bray, Clarence Wilbur b: 4/1/13, Birmingham, Ala. d: 9/4/82, Evansville, Ind. BL/TL, 6', 170 lbs. Deb: 4/18/41

YEAR	TM/L	G	AB	R	H	2B	3B	HR	RBI	BB	SO	AVG	OBP	SLG	PRO+	BR/A	SB	CS	SBR	FA	FR	G/POS	TPR
1941	Bos-N	4	11	2	1	1	0	0	1	1	2	.091	.167	.182	-2	-2	0			1.000	-0	/O-3	-0.2

YEAR	TM/L	G	AB	R	H	2B	3B	HR	RBI	BB	SO	AVG	OBP	SLG	PRO+	BR/A	SB	CS	SBR	FA	FR	G/POS	TPR
■ **FRANK BRAZILL**	Brazill, Frank Leo b: 8/11/1899, Spangler, Pa. d: 11/3/76, Oakland, Cal. BL/TR, 5'11.5", 175 lbs. Deb: 4/13/21																						
1921	Phi-A	66	177	17	48	3	1	0	19	23	21	.271	.361	.299	70	-7	2	4	-2	.984	-1	1-36/3-9	-1.0
1922	Phi-A	6	13	0	1	0	0	0	1	0	1	.077	.077	.077	-58	-3	0	0	0	.750	-2	/3-2	-0.5
Total	2	72	190	17	49	3	1	0	20	23	22	.258	.344	.284	62	-10	2	4	-2	.892	-3	/1-36,3-11	-1.5
■ **SID BREAM**	Bream, Sidney Eugene b: 8/3/60, Carlisle, Pa. BL/TL, 6'4", 220 lbs. Deb: 9/1/83																						
1983	LA-N	15	11	0	2	0	0	0	2	2	2	.182	.308	.182	39	-1	0	0	0	1.000	-0	/1-4	-0.1
1984	LA-N	27	49	2	9	3	0	0	6	6	9	.184	.273	.245	47	-3	1	0	0	1.000	2	1-14	-0.2
1985	LA-N	24	53	4	7	0	0	3	6	7	10	.132	.233	.302	50	-4	0	0	0	.994	2	1-16	-0.3
	Pit-N	26	95	14	27	7	0	3	15	11	14	.284	.358	.453	127	3	0	2	-1	.992	2	1-25	0.2
	Yr	50	148	18	34	7	0	6	21	18	24	.230	.313	.399	100	-0	0	2	-1	.993	4	1-41	-0.1
1986	Pit-N	154	522	73	140	37	5	16	77	60	73	.268	.345	.450	115	10	13	7	-0	.989	23	*1-153/O-2	2.3
1987	Pit-N	149	516	64	142	25	3	13	65	49	69	.275	.338	.411	97	-3	9	8	-2	.988	11	*1-144	-0.4
1988	Pit-N	148	462	50	122	37	0	10	65	47	64	.264	.333	.409	114	8	9	9	-3	.995	21	*1-138	1.7
1989	Pit-N	19	36	3	8	3	0	0	4	12	10	.222	.417	.306	113	2	0	4	-2	.992	-0	1-13	-0.2
1990	*Pit-N	147	389	39	105	23	2	15	67	48	65	.270	.353	.455	125	13	8	4	0	.993	10	*1-142	1.5
1991	*Atl-N	91	265	32	67	12	0	11	45	25	31	.253	.317	.423	100	-0	0	3	-2	.996	-0	1-85	-0.7
1992	*Atl-N	125	372	30	97	25	1	10	61	46	51	.261	.344	.414	107	4	6	0	2	.989	-3	*1-120	-0.5
1993	*Atl-N	117	277	33	72	14	1	9	35	31	43	.260	.334	.415	98	-1	4	2	0	.996	5	1-90	-0.1
1994	Hou-N	46	61	7	21	5	0	0	7	9	9	.344	.429	.426	131	3	0	1	-1	.986	2	1-10	0.4
Total	12	1088	3108	351	819	191	12	90	455	353	450	.264	.340	.420	107	32	50	40	-9	.992	74	1-954/O-2	3.6
■ **JIM BREAZEALE**	Breazeale, James Leo b: 10/3/49, Houston, Tex. BL/TR, 6'2", 210 lbs. Deb: 9/13/69																						
1969	Atl-N	2	1	1	0	0	0	0	0	2	0	.000	.667	.000	101	0	0	0	0	.833	-0	/1-1	0.0
1971	Atl-N	10	21	1	4	0	0	1	3	0	3	.190	.190	.333	43	-2	0	0	0	1.000	-0	/1-4	-0.2
1972	Atl-N	52	85	10	21	2	0	5	17	6	12	.247	.297	.447	100	-0	0	1	-1	1.000	-2	1-16/3-1	-0.4
1978	Chi-A	25	72	8	15	3	0	3	13	8	10	.208	.287	.375	84	-2	0	0	0	.992	-3	1-19/D-4	-0.6
Total	4	89	179	20	40	5	0	9	33	16	25	.223	.287	.402	88	-3	0	1	-1	.993	-5	/1-40,D-4,3-1	-1.2
■ **BRENT BREDE**	Brede, Brent David b: 9/13/71, Belleville, Ill. BL/TL, 6'4", 190 lbs. Deb: 9/8/96																						
1996	Min-A	10	20	2	6	0	1	0	2	1	5	.300	.333	.400	83	-1	0	0	0	1.000	0	/O-7	0.0
1997	Min-A	61	190	25	52	11	1	3	21	21	38	.274	.349	.389	91	-2	7	2	1	.957	-6	O-42,1-15/D-1	-0.9
1998	Ari-N	98	212	23	48	9	3	2	17	24	43	.226	.311	.325	65	-11	1	0	0	.964	-8	O-58,1-12/D-1	-1.9
Total	3	169	422	50	106	20	5	5	40	46	86	.251	.329	.358	78	-13	8	2	1	.964	-14	O-107/1-27,D-2	-2.8
■ **DANNY BREEDEN**	Breeden, Danny Richard b: 6/27/42, Albany, Ga. BR/TR, 5'11.5", 185 lbs. Deb: 7/24/69 F																						
1969	Cin-N	3	8	0	1	0	0	0	1	0	3	.125	.125	.125	-28	-1	0	0	0	.941	0	/C-3	-0.1
1971	Chi-N	25	65	3	10	1	0	0	4	9	18	.154	.267	.169	23	-6	0	0	0	.975	4	C-25	-0.2
Total	2	28	73	3	11	1	0	0	5	9	21	.151	.253	.164	18	-8	0	0	0	.972	5	/C-28	-0.3
■ **HAL BREEDEN**	Breeden, Harold Noel b: 6/28/44, Albany, Ga. BR/TL, 6'2", 200 lbs. Deb: 4/7/71 F																						
1971	Chi-N	23	36	1	5	1	0	1	2	2	7	.139	.184	.250	19	-4	0	0	0	.982	1	/1-8	-0.3
1972	Mon-N	42	87	6	20	2	0	3	10	7	15	.230	.287	.356	80	-2	0	0	0	.994	-1	1-26/O-1	-0.6
1973	Mon-N	105	258	36	71	10	6	15	43	29	45	.275	.353	.535	138	12	0	1	-1	.991	3	1-66	1.1
1974	Mon-N	79	190	14	47	13	0	2	20	24	35	.247	.332	.347	85	-3	0	1	-1	.987	1	1-56	-0.7
1975	Mon-N	24	37	4	5	2	0	0	1	7	5	.135	.273	.189	29	-3	0	0	0	.989	-0	1-12	-0.5
Total	5	273	608	61	148	28	6	21	76	69	107	.243	.323	.413	99	-1	0	2	-1	.990	4	1-168/O-1	-1.0
■ **MARV BREEDING**	Breeding, Marvin Eugene b: 3/8/34, Decatur, Ala. BR/TR, 6', 175 lbs. Deb: 4/19/60																						
1960	Bal-A	152	551	69	147	25	2	3	43	35	80	.267	.314	.336	77	-18	10	4	1	.977	5	*2-152	0.2
1961	Bal-A	90	244	32	51	8	0	1	16	14	33	.209	.252	.254	37	-22	5	2	0	.970	7	2-80	-0.8
1962	Bal-A	95	240	27	59	10	1	2	18	8	41	.246	.273	.321	63	-13	2	2	-1	.977	21	2-73/S-1,3-1	1.3
1963	Was-A	58	197	20	54	7	2	1	14	7	21	.274	.299	.345	80	-5	1	1	-0	.914	-9	3-29,2-22/S-2	-1.3
	LA-N	20	36	6	6	0	0	0	1	2	5	.167	.211	.167	11	-4	1	0	0	.972	-4	2-17/S-1,3-1	-0.8
Total	4	415	1268	154	317	50	5	7	92	66	180	.250	.289	.314	65	-63	19	9	0	.975	20	2-344/3-31,S-4	-1.4
■ **HERB BREMER**	Bremer, Herbert Frederick b: 10/26/13, Chicago, Ill. d: 11/28/79, Columbus, Ga. BR/TR, 6', 195 lbs. Deb: 9/16/37																						
1937	StL-N	11	33	2	7	1	0	0	3	2	4	.212	.257	.242	36	-3	0			.979	-0	C-10	-0.3
1938	StL-N	50	151	14	33	5	1	2	14	9	36	.219	.262	.305	53	-10	1			.977	3	C-50	-0.5
1939	StL-N	9	9	0	1	0	0	0	1	0	2	.111	.111	.111	-38	-2	0			1.000	1	/C-8	-0.1
Total	3	70	193	16	41	6	1	2	18	11	42	.212	.255	.285	45	-15	1			.979	3	/C-68	-0.9
■ **SAM BRENEGAN**	Brenegan, Olaf Selmar b: 9/1/1890, Galesville, Wis. d: 4/20/56, Galesville, Wis. BL/TR, 6'2", 185 lbs. Deb: 4/24/14																						
1914	Pit-N	1	0	0	0	0	0	0	0	0	0	—	—	—	—	0	0			.000	-0	/C-1	0.0
■ **BOB BRENLY**	Brenly, Robert Earl b: 2/25/54, Coshocton, Ohio BR/TR, 6'2", 210 lbs. Deb: 8/14/81 C																						
1981	SF-N	19	45	5	15	2	1	1	4	6	4	.333	.423	.489	161	4	0	1	-1	.964	-4	C-14/3-3,O-1	0.0
1982	SF-N	65	180	26	51	4	1	4	15	18	26	.283	.352	.383	106	2	6	2	1	.961	0	C-61/3-1	0.5
1983	SF-N	104	281	36	63	12	2	7	34	37	48	.224	.319	.356	89	-4	10	7	-1	.983	1	C-90,1-10/O-2	-0.1
1984	SF-N★	145	506	74	147	28	0	20	80	48	52	.291	.355	.464	133	21	6	9	-4	.986	-18	*C-127,1-22/O-3	0.5
1985	SF-N	133	440	41	97	16	1	19	56	57	62	.220	.313	.391	100	-0	1	4	-2	.984	-7	*C-110,3-17,1-10	-0.4
1986	SF-N	149	472	60	116	26	0	16	62	74	97	.246	.352	.403	113	9	10	6	-1	**.995**	-7	*C-101,3-45,1-19	0.6
1987	*SF-N	123	375	55	100	19	1	18	51	47	85	.267	.353	.467	121	11	10	7	-1	.988	9	*C-108/1-6,3-2	2.5
1988	SF-N	73	206	13	39	7	0	5	22	20	40	.189	.268	.296	64	-10	1	2	-1	.984	-4	C-69	-1.1
1989	Tor-A	48	88	9	15	3	1	1	6	10	17	.170	.255	.261	47	-6	1	0	0	.975	2	D-28,C-13/1-5	-0.5
	SF-N	12	22	2	4	2	0	0	3	1	7	.182	.217	.273	40	-2	0	0	0	1.000	0	C-12	-0.1
Total	9	871	2615	321	647	119	7	91	333	318	438	.247	.333	.403	107	25	45	38	-9	.984	-26	C-705/1-72,3-68,DO	1.9
■ **JIM BRENNAN**	Brennan, James Augustus (b: John Gottlieb Dorn) b: 1862, St.Louis, Mo. d: 10/18/04, Philadelphia, Pa. Deb: 4/20/1884																						
1884	StL-U	56	231	38	50	6	1	0	12			.216	.255	.251	52	-20				.891	-2	C-33,O-16/3-7,S-1	-1.8
1885	StL-N	3	10	0	1	0	0	0	1	1	1	.100	.182	.100	-7	-1				.750	-1	/O-2,3-1	-0.2
1888	KC-a	34	118	5	20	2	0	0	6	3		.169	.203	.186	24	-10	3			.884	-3	C-25/O-5,3-5	-1.0
1889	Phi-a	31	113	12	25	4	0	0	15	10	15	.221	.285	.257	55	-6	1			.818	-4	C-13/O-7,2-7,3-4	-0.8
1890	Cle-P	59	233	32	59	3	7	0	26	13	29	.253	.304	.326	74	-9	8			.845	-4	C-42,3-14/O-6	-0.7
Total	5	183	705	87	155	15	8	0	48	39	45	.220	.267	.264	55	-46	12			.869	-15	C-113/O-36,3-31,2S	-4.5
■ **BILL BRENZEL**	Brenzel, William Richard b: 3/3/10, Oakland, Cal. d: 6/12/79, Oakland, Cal. BR/TR, 5'10", 173 lbs. Deb: 4/13/32																						
1932	Pit-N	9	24	0	1	1	0	0	2	0	4	.042	.042	.083	-69	-6	0			1.000	2	/C-9	-0.3
1934	Cle-A	15	51	4	11	3	0	0	3	2	1	.216	.245	.275	33	-5	0	0	0	1.000	3	C-15	-0.2
1935	Cle-A	52	142	12	31	5	1	0	14	6	10	.218	.250	.268	33	-14	2	2	-1	.975	-7	C-51	-1.8
Total	3	76	217	16	43	9	1	0	19	8	15	.198	.227	.249	23	-25	2	2		.985	-2	/C-75	-2.3
■ **ROGER BRESNAHAN**	Bresnahan, Roger Philip "The Duke Of Tralee" b: 6/11/1879, Toledo, Ohio d: 12/4/44, Toledo, Ohio BR/TR, 5'9", 200 lbs. Deb: 8/27/1897 MCH																						
1897	Was-N	6	16	1	6	0	0	0	3	1		.375	.412	.375	109	0	0			1.000	-1	/P-6,O-1	0.0
1900	Chi-N	2	2	0	0	0	0	0	0	0		.000	.000	.000	-99	-1	0			.000	-0	/C-1	-0.1
1901	Bal-A	86	295	40	79	9	9	1	32	23		.268	.323	.369	88	-5	10			.919	-19	C-69/O-8,3-4,P-2,2	-1.6
1902	Bal-A	65	235	30	64	8	6	4	34	21		.272	.337	.409	102	0	12			.880	-7	3-30,C-22,O-15	-0.5
	NY-N	51	178	16	51	9	3	1	22	16		.287	.352	.388	129	6	6			.946	0	O-27,C-16/1-4,S3	0.7
1903	NY-N	113	406	87	142	30	8	4	55	61		.350	.443	.493	160	34	34			.965	0	O-84,1-13,C-11,/3-4	2.8
1904	NY-N	109	402	81	114	22	7	5	33	58		.284	.381	.410	138	20	13			.954	0	O-93,1-10/S-4,23	1.5
1905	*NY-N	104	331	58	100	18	3	0	46	50		.302	.411	.375	132	16	11			.970	-1	C-87/O-8	2.5

YEAR	TM/L	G	AB	R	H	2B	3B	HR	RBI	BB	SO	AVG	OBP	SLG	PRO+	BR/A	SB	CS	SBR	FA	FR	G/POS	TPR
1906	NY-N	124	405	69	114	22	4	0	43	81		.281	**.419**	.356	139	25	25			.974	5	C-82,O-40	3.9
1907	NY-N	110	328	57	83	9	7	4	38	61		.253	.380	.360	128	13	15			.986	-7	C-95/1-6,O-2,3-1	1.7
1908	NY-N	140	449	70	127	25	3	1	54	**83**		.283	.401	.359	136	23	14			.985	-18	*C-139	2.1
1909	StL-N	72	234	27	57	4	1	0	23	46		.244	.370	.269	105	5	11			.960	-6	C-59/2-9,3-1,M	0.3
1910	StL-N	88	234	35	65	15	3	0	27	55	17	.278	.419	.368	135	14	13			.961	-9	C-77/O-2,P-1,M	1.2
1911	StL-N	81	227	22	63	17	8	3	41	45	19	.278	.404	.463	146	15	4			.968	-2	C-77/2-2,M	2.0
1912	StL-N	48	108	8	36	7	2	1	15	14	9	.333	.419	.463	145	7	4			.974	7	C-28,M	1.7
1913	Chi-N	69	162	20	37	5	2	1	21	21	11	.228	.324	.302	79	-4	7			.963	-5	C-58	-0.5
1914	Chi-N	101	248	42	69	10	4	0	24	49	20	.278	.401	.351	125	11	14			.978	-3	C-85,2-14/O-1	1.5
1915	Chi-N	77	221	19	45	8	1	1	19	29	23	.204	.296	.262	70	-7	19	3	**4**	.982	3	C-68,M	0.5
Total	17	1446	4481	682	1252	218	71	26	530	714	99	.279	.386	.377	126	172	212	3		.971	-63	C-974,O-281/312PS	19.7

■ RUBE BRESSLER
Bressler, Raymond Bloom b: 10/23/1894, Coder, Pa. d: 11/7/66, Cincinnati, Ohio BR/TL, 6′, 187 lbs. Deb: 4/24/14

1914	Phi-A	29	51	6	11	1	1	0	4	6	7	.216	.310	.275	79	-1	0			.941	-2	P-29	0.0
1915	Phi-A	33	55	9	8	0	1	1	4	9	13	.145	.277	.236	56	-3	0			.900	0	P-32	0.0
1916	Phi-A	4	5	1	1	0	1	0	1	0	0	.200	.200	.600	147	0	0			1.000	-0	/P-4	0.0
1917	Cin-N	3	5	0	1	0	0	0	0	0	2	.200	.200	.200	24	-0	0			1.000	-0	/P-2	0.0
1918	Cin-N	23	62	10	17	5	0	0	6	5	4	.274	.328	.355	110	1	0			.982	2	P-17/O-3	-0.1
1919	Cin-N	61	165	22	34	3	4	2	17	23	15	.206	.311	.309	89	-2	2			.965	1	O-48,P-13	-0.5
1920	Cin-N	21	30	4	8	1	0	0	3	1	4	.267	.290	.300	71	-1	1	0	0	1.000	-1	P-10/O-3,1-2	-0.2
1921	Cin-N	109	323	41	99	18	6	1	54	39	20	.307	.385	.409	115	8	5	5	-2	.953	-6	O-85/1-6	-0.6
1922	Cin-N	52	53	7	14	0	2	0	8	4	4	.264	.316	.340	70	-2	1	0	0	1.000	-2	/1-3,O-2	-0.4
1923	Cin-N	54	119	25	33	3	1	0	18	20	4	.277	.399	.319	93	0	3	1	0	.983	-3	1-22/O-6	-0.3
1924	Cin-N	115	383	41	133	14	13	4	49	22	20	.347	.389	.483	134	18	9	10	-3	.990	4	1-50,O-49	1.3
1925	Cin-N	97	319	43	111	17	6	4	61	40	16	.348	.424	.476	133	17	9	5	-0	.982	-3	1-52,O-38	0.8
1926	Cin-N	86	297	58	106	15	9	1	51	37	20	.357	.433	.478	149	22	3			.970	-4	O-80/1-4	1.3
1927	Cin-N	124	467	43	136	14	8	3	77	32	22	.291	.338	.375	94	-4	4			.972	7	*O-120	-0.5
1928	Bro-N	145	501	78	148	29	13	4	70	80	33	.295	.398	.429	118	16	2			**.985**	-6	*O-137	0.1
1929	Bro-N	136	456	72	145	22	8	9	77	67	27	.318	.406	.461	117	14	4			.954	3	*O-122	0.8
1930	Bro-N	109	335	53	100	12	8	3	52	51	19	.299	.394	.409	96	-0	4			.995	6	O-90/1-7	0.0
1931	Bro-N	67	153	22	43	4	5	0	26	11	10	.281	.329	.373	89	-2	0			.982	-4	O-35/1-1	-0.9
1932	Phi-N	27	83	9	19	6	1	0	6	2	5	.229	.247	.325	47	-6	0			1.000	3	O-18	-0.4
	StL-N	10	19	0	3	0	0	0	2	0	1	.158	.158	.158	-14	-3	0			1.000	-0	/O-4	-0.3
	Yr	37	102	9	22	6	1	0	8	2	6	.216	.231	.294	37	-9	0			1.000	3	O-22	-0.7
Total	19	1305	3881	544	1170	164	87	32	586	449	246	.301	.378	.413	110	71	47	21		.971	-4	O-840,1-147,P-107	0.1

■ EDDIE BRESSOUD
Bressoud, Edward Francis b: 5/2/32, Los Angeles, Cal. BR/TR, 6′1″, 175 lbs. Deb: 6/14/56

1956	NY-N	49	163	15	37	4	2	0	9	12	20	.227	.284	.276	52	-11	1	0	0	.950	-9	S-48	-1.7
1957	NY-N	49	127	11	34	2	2	5	10	4	19	.268	.301	.433	94	-1	0	1	-1	.940	1	S-33,3-12	0.2
1958	SF-N	66	137	19	36	5	3	0	8	14	22	.263	.331	.343	81	-4	0	1	-1	.966	-2	2-57/3-6,S-4	-0.3
1959	SF-N	104	315	36	79	17	2	9	26	28	55	.251	.312	.403	91	-5	0	0	0	.974	-6	S-92/1-1,2-1,3-1	-0.4
1960	SF-N	116	386	37	87	19	6	9	43	35	72	.225	.293	.376	87	-8	1	2	-1	.960	6	*S-115	0.6
1961	SF-N	59	114	14	24	6	0	3	11	11	23	.211	.280	.342	66	-6	1	1	-0	.964	-9	S-34/3-3,2-1	-1.3
1962	Bos-A	153	599	79	166	40	9	14	68	46	118	.277	.331	.444	103	1	2	3	-1	.965	25	*S-153	3.8
1963	Bos-A	140	497	61	129	23	6	20	60	52	93	.260	.332	.451	113	9	1	1	-0	.962	-9	*S-137	0.9
1964	Bos-A☆	158	566	86	166	41	3	15	55	72	99	.293	.374	.456	123	19	1	1	-0	.972	-14	*S-158	1.7
1965	Bos-A	107	296	29	67	11	1	8	25	29	77	.226	.298	.351	79	-8	0	1	-1	.963	-5	S-86/3-2,O-1	-0.9
1966	NY-N	133	405	48	91	15	5	10	49	47	107	.225	.307	.360	87	-7	2	2	-1	.960	8	S-94,3-32/1-9,2-7	0.7
1967	*StL-N	52	67	8	9	1	1	1	1	9	18	.134	.237	.224	33	-6	0	0	0	.929	-4	S-48/3-1	-0.9
Total	12	1186	3672	443	925	184	40	94	365	359	723	.252	.321	.401	96	-26	9	13	-5	.963	-19	*S-1002/2-66,310	2.4

■ JIM BRETON
Breton, John Frederick b: 7/15/1891, Chicago, Ill. d: 5/30/73, Beloit, Wis. BR/TR, 5′10.5″, 178 lbs. Deb: 8/25/13

1913	Chi-A	12	30	1	5	1	1	0	2	1	5	.167	.194	.267	35	-3	0			.938	3	/S-7,3-3	0.0
1914	Chi-A	81	231	21	49	7	2	0	24	24	42	.212	.292	.260	67	-9	9	6	-1	.910	3	3-79	-0.5
1915	Chi-A	16	36	3	5	1	0	0	1	5	9	.139	.262	.167	27	-3	2	1	0	.882	-2	3-14/2-1,S-1	-0.5
Total	3	109	297	25	59	9	3	0	27	30	56	.199	.279	.249	59	-15	11	7		.906	4	/3-96,S-8,2-1	-1.0

■ GEORGE BRETT
Brett, George Howard b: 5/15/53, Glen Dale, W.Va. BL/TR, 6′, 200 lbs. Deb: 8/2/73 F

1973	KC-A	13	40	2	5	2	0	0	0	0	5	.125	.125	.175	-15	-6	0	0	0	.974	3	3-13	-0.3
1974	KC-A	133	457	49	129	21	5	2	47	21	38	.282	.314	.363	89	-7	8	5	-1	.948	-9	*3-132/S-1	-1.9
1975	KC-A	159	634	84	**195**	35	**13**	11	89	46	49	.308	.356	.456	125	19	13	10	-2	.949	-6	*3-159/S-1	1.1
1976	*KC-A★	159	645	94	**215**	34	**14**	7	67	49	36	**.333**	.381	.462	145	35	21	11	-0	.948	3	*3-157/S-4	4.0
1977	*KC-A★	139	564	105	176	32	13	22	88	55	24	.312	.375	.532	143	33	14	12	-3	.957	17	*3-135/S-1,D-3	4.4
1978	*KC-A★	128	510	79	150	**45**	8	9	62	39	35	.294	.345	.467	123	14	23	7	3	.961	5	*3-128/S-1	2.1
1979	KC-A★	154	645	119	**212**	42	**20**	23	107	51	36	.329	.378	.563	147	40	17	10	-1	.944	13	*3-149/1-8,D-1	4.9
1980	*KC-A†	117	449	87	175	33	9	24	118	58	22	**.390**	**.461**	**.664**	**203**	**64**	15	6	1	.955	4	*3-112/1-1	6.4
1981	*KC-A★	89	347	42	109	27	7	6	43	27	23	.314	.365	.484	144	19	14	6	1	.946	-9	3-88	0.9
1982	KC-A★	144	552	101	166	32	9	21	82	71	51	.301	.381	.505	141	32	6	1	1	.959	-6	*3-134,O-12	2.3
1983	KC-A★	123	464	90	144	38	2	25	93	57	39	.310	.387	**.563**	157	36	0	1	-1	.919	-25	*3-102,1-14,O-13,/D	0.8
1984	*KC-A★	104	377	42	107	21	3	13	69	38	37	.284	.349	.459	121	10	0	2	-1	.949	-4	*3-101	0.4
1985	*KC-A★	155	550	108	184	38	5	30	112	103	49	.335	.442	**.585**	**178**	**63**	9	1	2	.967	12	*3-152/D-1	7.2
1986	KC-A†	124	441	70	128	28	4	16	73	80	45	.290	.404	.481	137	25	1	2	-1	.952	-2	*3-115/S-2,D-7	1.9
1987	KC-A	115	427	71	124	18	2	22	78	72	47	.290	.394	.496	131	21	6	3	0	.993	-5	1-83,D-21,3-11	0.8
1988	KC-A★	157	589	90	180	42	3	24	103	82	51	.306	.393	.509	149	40	14	3	2	.992	-9	*1-124,D-33/S-1	2.2
1989	KC-A	124	457	67	129	26	3	12	80	59	47	.282	.368	.431	125	16	14	4	2	.998	4	*1-104,D-17/O-2	1.3
1990	KC-A	142	544	82	179	**45**	7	14	87	56	63	**.329**	.392	.515	154	39	9	2	2	.993	-1	*1-102,D-32/O-9,3-1	3.0
1991	KC-A	131	505	77	129	40	2	10	61	58	75	.255	.332	.402	102	1	2	0	1	.989	-1	*D-118,1-10	-0.5
1992	KC-A	152	592	55	169	35	5	7	61	35	69	.285	.332	.397	101	-0	8	6	-1	.987	0	*D-132,1-15/3-3	-0.7
1993	KC-A	145	560	69	149	31	3	19	75	39	67	.266	.317	.434	94	-6	7	5	-1	.000	0	*D-140	-1.3
Total	21	2707	10349	1583	3154	665	137	317	1595	1096	908	.305	.373	.487	135	488	201	97	2	.951	-17	*3-1692,D-506,1/OS	39.0

■ TONY BREWER
Brewer, Anthony Bruce b: 11/25/57, Coushatta, La. BR/TR, 5′11″, 190 lbs. Deb: 8/1/84 F

1984	LA-N	24	37	3	4	1	0	1	4	4	9	.108	.195	.216	16	-4	1	0	0	1.000	-2	O-10	-0.6

■ MIKE BREWER
Brewer, Michael Quinn b: 10/24/59, Shreveport, La. BR/TR, 6′5″, 190 lbs. Deb: 6/11/86 F

1986	KC-A	12	18	0	3	1	0	0	0	2	6	.167	.250	.222	29	-2	0	1	-1	1.000	-2	/O-9,D-1	-0.4

■ ROD BREWER
Brewer, Rodney Lee b: 2/24/66, Eustis, Fla. BL/TL, 6′3″, 210 lbs. Deb: 9/5/90

1990	StL-N	14	25	4	6	1	0	0	2	0	4	.240	.240	.280	42	-2	0	0	0	.981	1	/1-9	-0.2
1991	StL-N	19	13	0	1	0	0	0	1	0	5	.077	.077	.077	-56	-3	0	0	0	1.000	-0	1-15/O-3	-0.3
1992	StL-N	29	103	11	31	6	0	0	10	8	12	.301	.357	.359	107	1	0	1	-1	1.000	1	1-27/O-4	-0.1
1993	StL-N	110	147	15	42	8	0	2	20	17	26	.286	.364	.381	102	1	1	0	0	.960	-6	O-33,1-32/P-1	-0.6
Total	4	172	288	30	80	15	0	2	33	25	47	.278	.340	.351	92	-3	1	1	-0	.995	-4	/1-83,O-40,P-1	-1.2

■ CHARLIE BREWSTER
Brewster, Charles Lawrence b: 12/27/16, Marthaville, La. BR/TR, 5′8.5″, 175 lbs. Deb: 5/2/43

1943	Cin-N	7	8	0	1	0	0	0	0	0	1	.125	.125	.125	-28	-1	0			1.000	-0	/2-2	-0.1
	Phi-N	49	159	13	35	2	0	0	12	10	19	.220	.275	.233	49	-10	1			.901	-20	S-46	-3.0
	Yr	56	167	13	36	2	0	0	12	10	20	.216	.268	.228	45	-12	1			.901	-20	S-46/2-2	-3.1
1944	Chi-N	10	44	4	11	2	0	0	2	5	7	.250	.327	.295	76	-1	0			.903	0	S-10	0.0
1946	Cle-A	3	2	0	0	0	0	0	0	1	1	.000	.333	.000	-1	-0	0	0	0	1.000	0	/S-1	0.0
Total	3	69	213	17	47	4	0	0	14	16	28	.221	.281	.239	52	-13	1	0		.902	-20	/S-57,2-2	-3.1

YEAR	TM/L	G	AB	R	H	2B	3B	HR	RBI	BB	SO	AVG	OBP	SLG	PRO+	BR/A	SB	CS	SBR	FA	FR	G/POS	TPR
■ **FRITZ BRICKELL**	Brickell, Fritz Darrell b: 3/19/35, Wichita, Kan. d: 10/15/65, Wichita, Kan. BR/TR, 5'5.5", 157 lbs. Deb: 4/30/58 F																						
1958	NY-A	2	0	0	0	0	0	0	0	0	0	—	—	—	—	0	0	0	0	1.000	0	/2-2	0.0
1959	NY-A	18	39	4	10	1	0	1	4	1	10	.256	.275	.359	75	-1	0	0	0	.925	0	S-15/2-3	0.0
1961	LA-A	21	49	3	6	0	0	0	3	6	9	.122	.218	.122	-6	-7	0	0	0	.901	0	S-17	-0.6
Total	3	41	88	7	16	1	0	1	7	7	19	.182	.242	.227	26	-9	0	0	0	.911	0	/S-32,2-5	-0.6
■ **FRED BRICKELL**	Brickell, George Frederick b: 11/9/06, Saffordville, Kan. d: 4/8/61, Wichita, Kan. BL/TR, 5'7", 160 lbs. Deb: 8/19/26 F																						
1926	Pit-N	24	55	11	19	3	1	0	4	3	6	.345	.400	.436	119	2	0			.920	-0	O-14	0.1
1927	*Pit-N	32	21	6	6	1	0	1	4	1	0	.286	.318	.476	103	-0	0			1.000	-1	/O-3	0.0
1928	Pit-N	81	202	34	65	4	4	3	41	20	18	.322	.383	.426	107	2	5			.958	1	O-50	0.1
1929	Pit-N	60	118	13	37	4	2	0	17	7	12	.314	.352	.381	80	-4	3			1.000	0	O-27	-0.5
1930	Pit-N	68	219	36	65	9	3	1	14	15	20	.297	.342	.379	74	-9	3			.951	-4	O-61	-1.5
	Phi-N	53	240	33	59	12	6	0	17	13	21	.246	.290	.346	49	-20	1			.963	5	O-53	-1.7
	Yr	121	459	69	124	21	9	1	31	28	41	.270	.315	.362	61	-29	4			.958	0	*O-114	-3.2
1931	Phi-N	130	514	77	130	14	5	1	31	42	39	.253	.316	.305	63	-26	5			.978	4	*O-122	-3.1
1932	Phi-N	45	66	9	22	6	1	0	2	4	5	.333	.389	.455	112	1	2			.935	-0	O-12	0.0
1933	Phi-N	8	13	2	4	1	1	0	1	1	0	.308	.357	.538	136	1	0			1.000	1	/O-4	0.1
Total	8	501	1448	221	407	54	23	6	131	106	121	.281	.335	.363	75	-53	19			.967	5	O-346	-6.5
■ **GEORGE BRICKLEY**	Brickley, George Vincent b: 7/19/1894, Everett, Mass. d: 2/23/47, Everett, Mass. BR/TR, 5'9", 180 lbs. Deb: 9/26/13																						
1913	Phi-A	5	12	0	2	0	1	0	0	0	4	.167	.231	.333	66	-1	0			1.000	-1	/O-4	-0.2
■ **JIM BRIDEWESER**	Brideweser, James Ehrenfeld b: 2/13/27, Lancaster, Ohio d: 8/25/89, ElToro, Cal. BR/TR, 6', 165 lbs. Deb: 9/29/51																						
1951	NY-A	2	8	1	3	0	0	0	0	0	1	.375	.375	.375	107	0	0	0	0	.818	0	/S-2	0.0
1952	NY-A	42	38	12	10	0	0	0	2	3	5	.263	.317	.263	67	-2	0	0	0	.935	2	S-22/2-4,3-1	0.1
1953	NY-A	7	3	3	3	0	1	0	3	1	0	1.000	1.000	1.667	631	2	0	0	0	.833	0	/S-3	0.3
1954	Bal-A	73	204	18	54	7	2	0	12	15	27	.265	.318	.319	81	-6	1	1	-0	.944	-12	S-48,2-19	-1.4
1955	Chi-A	34	58	6	12	3	2	0	4	3	7	.207	.246	.328	52	-4	0	0	0	.949	6	S-26/3-3,2-2	0.3
1956	Chi-A	10	11	0	2	1	0	0	1	0	3	.182	.250	.273	37	-1	0	0	0	.938	0	S-10	-0.1
	Det-A	70	156	23	34	4	0	0	10	20	19	.218	.307	.244	47	-12	3	1	0	.987	14	S-32,2-31/3-4	0.6
	Yr	80	167	23	36	5	0	0	11	20	22	.216	.303	.246	46	-13	3	1	0	.979	14	S-42,2-31/3-4	0.5
1957	Bal-A	91	142	16	38	7	1	1	18	21	15	.268	.362	.352	102	1	2	0	1	.943	5	S-74/3-3,2-1	1.1
Total	7	329	620	79	156	22	6	1	50	63	77	.252	.323	.311	75	-21	6	2	1	.946	15	S-217/2-57,3-11	0.9
■ **ROCKY BRIDGES**	Bridges, Everett Lamar b: 8/7/27, Refugio, Tex. BR/TR, 5'8", 175 lbs. Deb: 4/17/51 C																						
1951	Bro-N	63	134	13	34	7	0	1	15	10	10	.254	.306	.328	69	-6	0	0	0	.871	3	3-40,2-10/S-9	-0.2
1952	Bro-N	51	56	9	11	3	0	0	2	7	9	.196	.286	.250	49	-4	0	1	-1	.986	12	2-24,S-13/3-6	0.8
1953	Cin-N	122	432	52	98	13	2	1	21	37	42	.227	.288	.273	47	-33	6	3	0	.976	11	*2-115/S-6,3-3	-1.6
1954	Cin-N	53	52	4	12	1	0	0	2	7	7	.231	.322	.250	50	-4	0	1	-1	1.000	11	S-20,2-19,3-13	0.7
1955	Cin-N	95	168	20	48	4	0	1	18	15	19	.286	.344	.327	75	-6	1	1	-0	.965	7	3-59,S-26/2-9	0.1
1956	Cin-N	71	19	9	4	0	0	0	1	4	3	.211	.348	.211	52	-1	1	2	-1	.966	8	3-51/2-8,S-7,O-1	0.6
1957	Cin-N	5	1	1	0	0	0	0	0	1	1	.000	.500	.000	46	0	0	0	0	1.000	-1	/2-2,S-1,3-1	-0.1
	Was-A	120	391	40	89	17	2	3	47	40	32	.228	.303	.304	67	-17	0	2	-1	.971	**29**	*S-108,2-14/3-1	2.2
1958	Was-A☆	116	377	38	99	14	3	5	28	27	32	.263	.317	.355	86	-7	0	3	-2	.976	3	*S-112/2-3,3-3	0.4
1959	Det-A	116	381	38	102	16	3	3	35	30	35	.268	.323	.349	80	-10	1	2	-1	.952	-6	*S-110/2-5	-0.7
1960	Det-A	10	5	0	1	0	0	0	0	0	0	.200	.200	.200	8	-1	0	0	0	1.000	3	/3-7,S-3	0.2
	Cle-A	10	27	1	9	0	0	0	3	1	2	.333	.357	.333	91	-0	0	0	0	1.000	3	/S-7,3-3	0.3
	Yr	20	32	1	10	0	0	0	3	1	2	.313	.333	.313	76	-1	0	0	0	1.000	6	3-10,S-10	0.5
	StL-N	3	0	0	0	0	0	0	0	0	0	—	—	—	—	0	0	0	0	1.000	1	/2-3	0.1
1961	LA-A	84	229	20	55	5	1	2	15	26	37	.240	.320	.297	59	-13	1	0	0	.988	10	2-58,S-25/3-4	0.4
Total	11	919	2272	245	562	80	11	16	187	205	229	.247	.312	.313	67	-102	10	15	-6	.968	95	S-447,2-270,3/O	3.2
■ **AL BRIDWELL**	Bridwell, Albert Henry b: 1/4/1884, Friendship, Ohio d: 1/23/69, Portsmouth, Ohio BL/TR, 5'9", 170 lbs. Deb: 4/16/05																						
1905	Cin-N	82	254	17	64	3	1	0	17	19		.252	.309	.272	66	-11	8			.944	0	3-43,O-18/2-7,S1	-1.0
1906	Bos-N	120	459	41	104	9	1	0	22	44		.227	.297	.251	73	-14	6			.930	17	*S-119/O-1	0.8
1907	Bos-N	140	509	49	111	8	2	0	26	61		.218	.309	.242	73	-13	17			**.942**	7	*S-140	-0.4
1908	NY-N	147	467	53	133	14	1	0	46	52		.285	.364	.319	113	9	20			.933	11	*S-147	2.6
1909	NY-N	145	476	59	140	11	5	0	55	67		.294	.386	.338	123	16	32			.940	2	*S-145	2.3
1910	NY-N	142	492	74	136	15	7	0	48	73	23	.276	.374	.335	107	7	14			.946	6	*S-141	2.0
1911	NY-N	76	263	28	71	10	1	0	31	33	10	.270	.358	.316	86	-4	8			.917	6	S-76	0.7
	Bos-N	51	182	29	53	5	0	0	10	33	8	.291	.403	.319	95	0	2			.950	-11	S-51	-0.7
	Yr	127	445	57	124	15	1	0	41	66	18	.279	.377	.317	90	-3	10			.929	-5	*S-127	0.0
1912	Bos-N	31	106	6	25	5	1	0	14	5	5	.236	.270	.302	55	-7	2			.936	-6	S-31	-1.0
1913	Chi-N	136	405	35	97	6	6	1	37	74	28	.240	.358	.291	87	-4	12			.948	2	*S-136	1.1
1914	StL-F	117	381	46	90	6	5	1	33	71	18	.236	.359	.286	73	-17	9			.944	-11	*S-103,2-11	-2.1
1915	StL-F	65	175	20	40	3	2	0	9	25	6	.229	.328	.269	65	-10	6			.952	1	2-42,3-15/1-1	-0.8
Total	11	1252	4169	457	1064	95	32	2	348	557	98	.255	.347	.295	89	-45	136			.939	23	*S-1094/2-60,301	3.5
■ **BUNNY BRIEF**	Brief, Anthony Vincent (b: Anthony John Grzeszkowski) b: 7/3/1892, Remus, Mich. d: 2/10/63, Milwaukee, Wis. BR/TR, 6', 185 lbs. Deb: 9/22/12																						
1912	StL-A	15	42	9	13	3	0	0	5	6		.310	.408	.381	131	2	2			.826	-1	/O-9,1-4	0.1
1913	StL-A	85	258	24	56	11	6	1	26	21	46	.217	.284	.318	78	-8	3			.986	-1	1-62/O-8	-1.1
1915	Chi-A	48	154	13	33	6	2	2	17	16	28	.214	.305	.318	84	-3	8	6	-1	.986	-2	1-46	-0.8
1917	Pit-N	36	115	15	25	5	1	2	11	15	21	.217	.318	.330	96	-0	4			.988	2	1-34	0.0
Total	4	184	569	61	127	25	9	5	59	58	95	.223	.306	.325	87	-9	17	6		.987	-2	1-146/O-17	-1.8
■ **CHARLIE BRIGGS**	Briggs, Charles R. b: 1861, Batavia, Ill. 5'7", 170 lbs. Deb: 5/2/1884																						
1884	CP-U	49	182	29	31	8	2	1		11		.170	.218	.253	42	-18				.814	-5	O-37,2-12/S-2	-2.1
■ **DAN BRIGGS**	Briggs, Dan Lee b: 11/18/52, Scotia, Cal. BL/TL, 6', 180 lbs. Deb: 9/10/75																						
1975	Cal-A	13	31	3	7	1	0	1	3	2	6	.226	.273	.355	82	-1	0	2	-1	.953	-1	/1-6,O-5,D-2	-0.4
1976	Cal-A	77	248	19	53	13	2	1	14	13	47	.214	.256	.294	65	-12	0	3	-2	.993	-0	1-44,O-40/D-1	-1.9
1977	Cal-A	59	74	6	12	2	0	1	4	8	14	.162	.244	.230	31	-7	0	0	0	.993	0	1-45,O-13	-0.8
1978	Cle-A	15	49	4	8	0	1	1	1	4	9	.163	.226	.265	38	-4	0	0	0	1.000	2	O-15	-0.3
1979	SD-N	104	227	34	47	4	3	8	30	18	45	.207	.280	.357	77	-8	2	1	0	.986	-1	1-50,O-44	-1.2
1981	Mon-N	9	11	0	1	0	0	0	0	0	3	.091	.091	.091	-48	-2	0	1	-1	1.000	-1	/1-3,O-3	-0.4
1982	Chi-N	48	48	1	6	0	0	0	1	0	9	.125	.143	.125	-24	-8	0	0	0	.875	2	O-10/1-4	-1.0
Total	7	325	688	67	134	20	6	12	53	45	133	.195	.251	.294	56	-42	2	7	-4	.989	-2	1-152,O-130/D-3	-6.0
■ **GRANT BRIGGS**	Briggs, Grant b: 3/16/1865, Pittsburgh, Pa. d: 5/31/28, Pittsburgh, Pa. 5'11", 170 lbs. Deb: 4/17/1890																						
1890	Syr-a	86	316	44	57	6	5	0	21	16		.180	.222	.231	37	-25	7			.928	-4	C-46,O-33/3-5,S-4	-2.3
1891	Lou-a	1	4	0	1	0	0	0	0	0	0	.250	.250	.250	44	-0				1.000	-0	/C-1	0.0
1892	StL-N	22	55	2	4	1	0	0	1	5	16	.073	.164	.091	-24	-8	2			.902	-11	C-15/O-8	-1.8
1895	Lou-N	1	3	0	0	0	0	0	0	0	1	.000	.000	.000	-99	-1	0			1.000	-1	/C-1	-0.2
Total	4	110	378	46	62	7	5	0	22	21	17	.164	.212	.209	27	-35	9			.925	-15	/C-63,O-41,3-5,S-4	-4.3
■ **JOHNNY BRIGGS**	Briggs, John Edward b: 3/10/44, Paterson, N.J. BL/TL, 6'1", 195 lbs. Deb: 4/17/64																						
1964	Phi-N	61	66	16	17	2	0	1	6	9	12	.258	.347	.333	94	-0	1	1	-0	.957	-2	O-19/1-1	-0.3
1965	Phi-N	93	229	47	54	9	4	4	23	42	44	.236	.354	.362	104	3	3	2	-0	.982	-3	O-66	-0.4
1966	Phi-N	81	255	43	72	13	5	10	23	41	55	.282	.382	.490	140	15	3	2	-0	.977	-4	O-69	0.7
1967	Phi-N	106	332	47	77	12	4	9	30	41	72	.232	.316	.373	96	-2	3	5	-2	.979	-2	O-94	-1.1
1968	Phi-N	110	338	36	86	13	1	7	31	58	72	.254	.365	.361	119	10	8	5	-1	.968	-3	O-65,1-36	0.1

YEAR	TM/L	G	AB	R	H	2B	3B	HR	RBI	BB	SO	AVG	OBP	SLG	PRO+	BR/A	SB	CS	SBR	FA	FR	G/POS	TPR
1969	Phi-N	124	361	51	86	20	3	12	46	64	78	.238	.353	.410	116	9	9	6	-1	.971	0	*O-108/1-2	0.2
1970	Phi-N	110	341	43	92	15	7	9	47	39	65	.270	.345	.434	110	5	5	4	-1	.980	6	O-95	0.5
1971	Phi-N	10	22	3	4	1	0	0	3	6	2	.182	.357	.227	69	-1	0	0	0	.846	-1	/O-8	-0.2
	Mil-A	125	375	51	99	11	1	21	59	71	79	.264	.383	.467	141	22	1	2	-1	.958	1	O-65,1-60	1.5
1972	Mil-A	135	418	58	111	14	1	21	65	54	67	.266	.351	.455	141	21	1	2	-1	.980	-2	*O-106,1-28	1.3
1973	Mil-A	142	488	78	120	20	7	18	57	87	83	.246	.362	.426	124	17	15	9	-1	.968	7	*O-137/D-1	1.7
1974	Mil-A	154	554	72	140	30	8	17	73	71	102	.253	.338	.428	120	14	9	7	-2	.973	5	*O-149/D-2	1.2
1975	Mil-A	28	74	12	22	1	0	3	5	20	13	.297	.447	.432	149	6	0	2	-1	.962	2	O-21/D-1	0.6
	Min-A	87	264	44	61	9	2	7	39	60	41	.231	.373	.360	106	5	6	2	1	.983	7	1-49,O-35/D-2	0.8
	Yr	115	338	56	83	10	2	10	44	80	54	.246	.390	.376	116	11	6	4	-1	.983	9	O-56,1-49/D-3	1.4
Total	12	1366	4117	601	1041	170	43	139	507	663	785	.253	.357	.416	121	123	64	49	-10	.973	12	*O-1037,1-176/D-6	6.6

■ **HARRY BRIGHT** Bright, Harry James b: 9/22/29, Kansas City, Mo. BR/TR, 6', 190 lbs. Deb: 8/7/58

YEAR	TM/L	G	AB	R	H	2B	3B	HR	RBI	BB	SO	AVG	OBP	SLG	PRO+	BR/A	SB	CS	SBR	FA	FR	G/POS	TPR
1958	Pit-N	15	24	4	6	1	0	1	3	1	6	.250	.280	.417	84	-1	0	0	0	1.000	0	/3-7	0.0
1959	Pit-N	40	48	4	12	1	0	3	8	5	10	.250	.321	.458	105	0	0	0	0	1.000	-2	/O-4,3-3,2-1	-0.2
1960	Pit-N	4	4	0	0	0	0	0	0	0	2	.000	.000	.000	-99	-1	0	0	0	.000	0	H	-0.1
1961	Was-A	72	183	20	44	6	0	4	21	19	23	.240	.312	.339	75	-7	0	2	-1	.928	7	3-40/C-8,2-1	0.0
1962	Was-A	113	392	55	107	15	4	17	67	26	51	.273	.321	.462	109	3	2	1	0	.989	-1	1-99/C-3,3-1	-0.4
1963	Cin-N	1	1	0	0	0	0	0	0	0	1	.000	.000	.000	-97	-0	0	0	0	1.000	-0	/1-1	0.0
	*NY-A	60	157	15	37	7	0	7	23	13	31	.236	.298	.414	98	-1	0	0	0	.985	-5	1-35,3-12	-0.7
1964	NY-A	4	5	0	1	0	0	0	0	1	1	.200	.333	.200	52	-0	0	0	0	1.000	-0	/1-2	-0.1
1965	Chi-N	27	25	1	7	1	0	0	4	0	8	.280	.280	.320	67	-1	0	0	0	.000	0	H	-0.1
Total	8	336	839	99	214	31	4	32	126	65	133	.255	.311	.416	96	-7	2	3	-1	.988	-1	1-137/3-63,C-11,O2	-1.6

■ **GREG BRILEY** Briley, Gregory "Peewee" b: 5/24/65, Greenville, N.C. BL/TR, 5'8", 165 lbs. Deb: 6/27/88

YEAR	TM/L	G	AB	R	H	2B	3B	HR	RBI	BB	SO	AVG	OBP	SLG	PRO+	BR/A	SB	CS	SBR	FA	FR	G/POS	TPR
1988	Sea-A	13	36	6	9	2	0	1	4	5	6	.250	.341	.389	100	0	0	1	-1	.929	-2	O-11	-0.3
1989	Sea-A	115	394	52	105	22	4	13	52	39	82	.266	.340	.442	115	7	11	5	0	.958	-5	*O-105,2-10/D-2	0.1
1990	Sea-A	125	337	40	83	18	2	5	29	37	48	.246	.323	.356	89	-5	16	4	2	.989	-4	*O-107/D-4	-0.9
1991	Sea-A	139	381	39	99	17	3	2	26	27	51	.260	.309	.336	78	-11	23	11	0	.980	-17	*O-125/2-1,3-1,D-2	-3.0
1992	Sea-A	86	200	18	55	10	0	5	12	4	31	.275	.293	.400	92	-3	9	2	2	.967	-9	O-42,D-12/2-4,3-4	-1.1
1993	Fla-N	120	170	17	33	6	0	3	12	12	42	.194	.251	.282	40	-14	6	2	1	.986	-12	O-67	-2.7
Total	6	598	1518	172	384	75	9	29	135	124	260	.253	.313	.372	88	-26	65	25	4	.975	-48	O-457/D-20,2-15,3-5	-7.9

■ **BILL BRINKER** Brinker, William Hutchinson "Dode" b: 8/30/1883, Warrensburg, Mo. d: 2/5/65, Arcadia, Cal. BB/TR, 6'1", 190 lbs. Deb: 4/24/12

YEAR	TM/L	G	AB	R	H	2B	3B	HR	RBI	BB	SO	AVG	OBP	SLG	PRO+	BR/A	SB	CS	SBR	FA	FR	G/POS	TPR
1912	Phi-N	9	18	1	4	1	0	0	2	2	3	.222	.300	.278	55	-1	0			.778	-1	/3-2,O-2	-0.2

■ **CHUCK BRINKMAN** Brinkman, Charles Ernest b: 9/16/44, Cincinnati, O. BR/TR, 6'1", 185 lbs. Deb: 7/10/69 F

YEAR	TM/L	G	AB	R	H	2B	3B	HR	RBI	BB	SO	AVG	OBP	SLG	PRO+	BR/A	SB	CS	SBR	FA	FR	G/POS	TPR
1969	Chi-A	14	15	2	1	0	0	0	0	1	5	.067	.125	.067	-43	-3	0	0	0	1.000	1	C-14	-0.2
1970	Chi-A	9	20	4	5	1	0	0	0	3	3	.250	.348	.300	77	-1	0	0	0	.974	1	/C-9	0.1
1971	Chi-A	15	20	0	4	0	0	0	1	3	5	.200	.304	.200	44	-1	0	0	0	1.000	2	C-14	0.1
1972	Chi-A	35	52	1	7	0	0	0	0	4	7	.135	.196	.135	-0	-6	0	0	0	.985	7	C-33	0.2
1973	Chi-A	63	139	13	26	6	0	1	10	11	37	.187	.252	.252	41	-11	0	0	0	.987	10	C-63	0.1
1974	Chi-A	8	14	1	2	0	0	0	0	1	3	.143	.200	.143	-0	-2	0	0	0	1.000	-1	/C-8	-0.3
	Pit-N	4	7	1	1	0	0	0	1	0	0	.143	.143	.143	-21	-1	0	0	0	1.000	-0	/C-4	-0.2
Total	6	148	267	22	46	7	0	1	12	23	60	.172	.241	.210	28	-25	0	0	0	.988	20	C-145	-0.2

■ **ED BRINKMAN** Brinkman, Edwin Albert b: 12/8/41, Cincinnati, O. BR/TR, 6', 170 lbs. Deb: 9/6/61 FC

YEAR	TM/L	G	AB	R	H	2B	3B	HR	RBI	BB	SO	AVG	OBP	SLG	PRO+	BR/A	SB	CS	SBR	FA	FR	G/POS	TPR
1961	Was-A	4	11	0	1	0	0	0	0	1	1	.091	.167	.091	-30	-2	0	0	0	.889	0	/3-3	-0.2
1962	Was-A	54	133	8	22	7	1	0	4	11	28	.165	.229	.233	25	-14	1	0	0	.942	2	S-38,3-10	-1.0
1963	Was-A	145	514	44	117	20	3	7	45	31	86	.228	.277	.319	67	-23	5	3	-0	.950	7	*S-143	-0.7
1964	Was-A	132	447	54	100	20	3	8	34	26	99	.224	.273	.336	68	-20	2	2	-1	.969	-3	*S-125	-1.5
1965	Was-A	154	444	35	82	13	2	5	35	38	82	.185	.252	.257	46	-32	1	2	-1	.964	4	*S-150	-2.1
1966	Was-A	158	582	42	133	18	9	7	48	29	105	.229	.265	.326	70	-24	7	9	-3	.965	12	*S-158	-0.1
1967	Was-A	109	320	21	60	9	2	1	18	24	58	.188	.253	.237	47	-21	1	3	-2	**.979**	14	*S-109	0.0
1968	Was-A	77	193	12	36	3	0	0	6	19	31	.187	.259	.202	43	-13	0	0	0	.967	3	S-74/2-2,O-1	-0.5
1969	Was-A	151	576	71	153	18	5	2	43	50	42	.266	.330	.325	88	-9	2	2	-1	.976	15	*S-150	2.3
1970	Was-A	158	625	63	164	17	2	1	40	60	41	.262	.332	.301	79	-16	8	9	-3	.974	31	*S-157	3.2
1971	Det-A	159	527	40	120	18	2	1	37	44	54	.228	.296	.275	60	-27	1	4	-2	.980	12	*S-159	0.3
1972	*Det-A	156	516	42	105	19	1	6	49	38	51	.203	.262	.279	59	-26	0	0	0	**.990**	2	*S-156	-0.2
1973	Det-A★	162	515	55	122	16	4	7	40	34	79	.237	.285	.324	67	-23	0	1	-1	.968	-13	*S-162	-1.7
1974	Det-A	153	502	55	111	15	3	14	54	29	71	.221	.268	.347	73	-19	2	0	1	.972	13	*S-151/3-2	1.5
1975	StL-N	28	75	6	18	4	0	1	6	7	10	.240	.313	.333	77	-2	0	0	0	.948	0	S-24	0.0
	Tex-A	1	2	0	0	0	0	0	0	0	1	.000	.000	.000	-99	-1	0	0	0	1.000	-0	/3-1	-0.1
	NY-A	44	63	2	11	4	1	0	2	3	6	.175	.224	.270	40	-5	0	0	0	.933	-3	S-39/2-3,3-3	-0.6
	Yr	45	65	2	11	4	1	0	2	3	7	.169	.217	.262	35	-6	0	0	0	.933	-3	S-39/3-4,2-3	-0.7
Total	15	1845	6045	550	1355	201	38	60	461	444	845	.224	.282	.300	65	-276	30	35	-12	.970	94	*S-1795/3-19,2-5,O	-1.4

■ **LEON BRINKOPF** Brinkopf, Leon Clarence b: 10/20/26, Cape Girardeau, Mo BR/TR, 5'11.5", 185 lbs. Deb: 4/18/52

YEAR	TM/L	G	AB	R	H	2B	3B	HR	RBI	BB	SO	AVG	OBP	SLG	PRO+	BR/A	SB	CS	SBR	FA	FR	G/POS	TPR
1952	Chi-N	9	22	1	4	0	0	0	2	4	5	.182	.308	.182	38	-2	0	0	0	.955	-2	/S-6	-0.4

■ **FATTY BRIODY** Briody, Charles F. "Alderman" b: 8/13/1858, Lansingburg, N.Y. d: 6/22/03, Chicago, Ill. TR , 5'8.5", 190 lbs. Deb: 6/16/1880

YEAR	TM/L	G	AB	R	H	2B	3B	HR	RBI	BB	SO	AVG	OBP	SLG	PRO+	BR/A	SB	CS	SBR	FA	FR	G/POS	TPR
1880	Tro-N	1	4	0	0	0	0	0	0	0	0	.000	.000	.000	-95	-1				.700	-1	/C-1	-0.2
1882	Cle-N	53	194	30	50	13	0	0	13	9	13	.258	.291	.325	100	0				.902	2	C-53	0.3
1883	Cle-N	40	145	23	34	5	1	0	10	3	13	.234	.250	.283	62	-6				.900	4	C-33/2-4,1-2,3-1	-0.1
1884	Cle-N	43	148	17	25	6	0	1	12	6	19	.169	.201	.230	34	-11				.922	10	C-42/O-1	0.2
	Cin-U	22	89	11	30	2	2	0		1		.337	.344	.404	117	-1				.943	17	C-22	1.5
1885	StL-N	62	215	14	42	9	0	1	17	12	23	.195	.238	.251	62	-8				.893	-9	C-60/O-1,3-1,2-1	-1.2
1886	KC-N	56	215	14	51	10	3	0	29	3	35	.237	.248	.312	65	-10	0			.919	2	C-54/O-2,1-1	-0.2
1887	Det-N	33	128	24	29	6	1	1	26	9	10	.227	.283	.313	63	-7	6			.907	6	C-33	0.2
1888	KC-a	13	48	1	10	1	0	0	8	1		.208	.224	.229	43	-3	0			.896	-4	C-13	-0.5
Total	8	323	1186	134	271	52	7	3	115	44	113	.228	.257	.292	68	-47	6			.910	25	C-311/2-5,O-4,13	0.0

■ **GEORGE BRISTOW** Bristow, George T. b: 5/1870, Paw Paw, Ill. TR , Deb: 4/15/1899

YEAR	TM/L	G	AB	R	H	2B	3B	HR	RBI	BB	SO	AVG	OBP	SLG	PRO+	BR/A	SB	CS	SBR	FA	FR	G/POS	TPR
1899	Cle-N	3	8	0	1	1	0	0	0	0		.125	.222	.250	32	-1	0			1.000	0	/O-3	-0.1

■ **BERNARDO BRITO** Brito, Bernardo b: 12/4/63, San Cristobal, D.R. BR/TR, 6'1", 190 lbs. Deb: 9/15/92

YEAR	TM/L	G	AB	R	H	2B	3B	HR	RBI	BB	SO	AVG	OBP	SLG	PRO+	BR/A	SB	CS	SBR	FA	FR	G/POS	TPR
1992	Min-A	8	14	1	2	1	0	0	2	0	4	.143	.143	.214	-1	-2	0	1	-1	.750	-1	/O-3,D-1	-0.4
1993	Min-A	27	54	8	13	2	0	4	9	1	20	.241	.255	.500	97	-1	0	0	0	1.000	-1	O-10/D-7	-0.2
1995	Min-A	5	5	1	1	0	0	1	1	0	3	.200	.333	.800	183	1	0	0	0	.000	0	/D-3	0.0
Total	3	40	73	10	16	3	0	5	12	1	27	.219	.240	.466	85	-2	0	1	-1	.941	-2	/O-13,D-11	-0.6

■ **JORGE BRITO** Brito, Jorge Manuel (Uceta) b: 6/22/66, Moncion, D.R. BR/TR, 6'1", 190 lbs. Deb: 4/30/95

YEAR	TM/L	G	AB	R	H	2B	3B	HR	RBI	BB	SO	AVG	OBP	SLG	PRO+	BR/A	SB	CS	SBR	FA	FR	G/POS	TPR
1995	Col-N	18	51	5	11	3	0	0	7	2	17	.216	.259	.275	32	-5	1	0	0	.991	5	C-18	0.1
1996	Col-N	8	14	1	1	0	0	0	0	1	8	.071	.235	.071	-12	-2	0	0	0	1.000	4	/C-8	0.2
Total	2	26	65	6	12	3	0	0	7	3	25	.185	.254	.231	23	-8	1	0	0	.994	8	/C-26	0.3

■ **TILSON BRITO** Brito, Tilson Manuel (Jiminez) b: 5/28/72, Santo Domingo, D.R. BR/TR, 6', 175 lbs. Deb: 4/1/96

YEAR	TM/L	G	AB	R	H	2B	3B	HR	RBI	BB	SO	AVG	OBP	SLG	PRO+	BR/A	SB	CS	SBR	FA	FR	G/POS	TPR
1996	Tor-A	26	80	10	19	7	0	1	7	10	18	.237	.344	.363	79	-2	1	1	-0	.956	-1	2-18/S-5,D-2	-0.2
1997	Tor-A	49	126	9	28	3	0	0	8	9	28	.222	.285	.246	40	-11	1	0	0	.989	1	2-25,3-17/S-8	-0.7
	Oak-A	17	46	8	13	2	1	2	6	1	10	.283	.298	.500	105	0	0	0	0	.920	3	3-10/S-6,2-2	0.3
	Yr	66	172	17	41	5	1	2	14	10	38	.238	.288	.314	57	-11	1	0	0	.961	4	2-27,3-27,S-14	-0.4
Total	2	92	252	27	60	12	1	3	21	20	56	.238	.307	.329	64	-13	2	1	0	.974	4	/2-45,3-27,S-19,D-2	-0.6

■ GUS BRITTAIN Brittain, August Schuster b: 11/29/09, Wilmington, N.C. d: 2/16/74, Wilmington, N.C. BR/TR, 5'10", 192 lbs. Deb: 7/22/37

YEAR	TM/L	G	AB	R	H	2B	3B	HR	RBI	BB	SO	AVG	OBP	SLG	PRO+	BR/A	SB	CS	SBR	FA	FR	G/POS	TPR
1937	Cin-N	3	6	0	1	0	0	0	0	0	3	.167	.167	.167	-10	-1	0			1.000	-0	/C-1	-0.1

■ GIL BRITTON Britton, Stephen Gilbert b: 9/21/1891, Parsons, Kan. d: 6/20/83, Parsons, Kan. BR/TR, 5'10", 160 lbs. Deb: 9/20/13

YEAR	TM/L	G	AB	R	H	2B	3B	HR	RBI	BB	SO	AVG	OBP	SLG	PRO+	BR/A	SB	CS	SBR	FA	FR	G/POS	TPR
1913	Pit-N	3	12	0	0	0	0	0	0	0	2	.000	.000	.000	-99	-3	0			.824	-1	/S-3	-0.4

■ GREG BROCK Brock, Gregory Allen b: 6/14/57, McMinnville, Ore. BL/TR, 6'3", 205 lbs. Deb: 9/1/82

YEAR	TM/L	G	AB	R	H	2B	3B	HR	RBI	BB	SO	AVG	OBP	SLG	PRO+	BR/A	SB	CS	SBR	FA	FR	G/POS	TPR
1982	LA-N	18	17	1	2	1	0	0	1	1	5	.118	.167	.176	-4	-2	0	0	0	1.000	-0	/1-3	-0.3
1983	*LA-N	146	455	64	102	14	2	20	66	83	81	.224	.345	.396	105	5	5	1	1	.991	5	*1-140	0.3
1984	LA-N	88	271	33	61	6	0	14	34	39	37	.225	.323	.402	104	1	8	0	2	.995	7	1-83	0.7
1985	*LA-N	129	438	64	110	19	0	21	66	54	72	.251	.333	.438	118	10	4	2	0	.994	2	*1-122	0.4
1986	LA-N	115	325	33	76	13	0	16	52	37	60	.234	.312	.422	108	2	2	5	-2	.996	12	1-99	0.6
1987	Mil-A	141	532	81	159	29	3	13	85	57	63	.299	.373	.438	111	10	5	4	-1	.993	4	*1-141	0.2
1988	Mil-A	115	364	53	77	16	1	6	50	63	48	.212	.333	.310	81	-8	6	2	1	.993	9	*1-114/D-1	-0.7
1989	Mil-A	107	373	40	99	16	0	12	52	43	49	.265	.346	.405	112	6	6	1	1	.995	-5	*1-100/D-7	-0.5
1990	Mil-A	123	367	42	91	23	0	7	50	43	45	.248	.330	.368	96	-2	4	2	0	.995	-4	*1-115	-1.4
1991	Mil-A	31	60	9	17	4	0	1	6	14	9	.283	.419	.400	131	3	1	1	-0	1.000	-1	1-25	0.1
Total	10	1013	3202	420	794	141	6	110	462	434	469	.248	.340	.399	105	25	41	18	2	.994	29	1-942/D-8	-0.6

■ JOHN BROCK Brock, John Roy b: 10/16/1896, Hamilton, Ill. d: 10/27/51, Clayton, Mo. BR/TR, 5'6.5", 165 lbs. Deb: 8/10/17

YEAR	TM/L	G	AB	R	H	2B	3B	HR	RBI	BB	SO	AVG	OBP	SLG	PRO+	BR/A	SB	CS	SBR	FA	FR	G/POS	TPR
1917	StL-N	7	15	4	6	1	0	0	2	0	2	.400	.400	.467	170	1	2			.944	-1	/C-4	0.1
1918	StL-N	27	52	9	11	2	0	0	4	3	10	.212	.255	.250	56	-3	5			.951	-2	C-18/O-1	-0.4
Total	2	34	67	13	17	3	0	0	6	3	12	.254	.286	.299	81	-2	7			.949	-2	/C-22,O-1	-0.3

■ LOU BROCK Brock, Louis Clark b: 6/18/39, ElDorado, Ark. BL/TL, 5'11.5", 170 lbs. Deb: 9/10/61 H

YEAR	TM/L	G	AB	R	H	2B	3B	HR	RBI	BB	SO	AVG	OBP	SLG	PRO+	BR/A	SB	CS	SBR	FA	FR	G/POS	TPR
1961	Chi-N	4	11	1	1	0	0	0	0	1	3	.091	.167	.091	-29	-2	0	0	0	.750	-1	/O-3	-0.3
1962	Chi-N	123	434	73	114	24	7	9	35	35	96	.263	.322	.412	92	-5	16	7	1	.965	2	*O-106	-1.0
1963	Chi-N	148	547	79	141	19	11	9	37	31	122	.258	.302	.382	91	-7	24	12	0	.973	13	*O-140	-0.1
1964	Chi-N	52	215	30	54	9	2	2	14	13	40	.251	.300	.340	77	-7	10	3	1	.959	2	O-52	-0.6
	*StL-N	103	419	81	146	21	9	12	44	27	87	.348	.391	.527	143	23	33	15	1	.949	6	*O-102	2.6
	Yr	155	634	111	200	30	11	14	58	40	127	.315	.360	.464	121	17	43	18	2	.953	8	*O-154	2.0
1965	StL-N	155	631	107	182	35	8	16	69	45	116	.288	.345	.445	110	8	63	27	3	.959	8	*O-153	1.3
1966	StL-N	156	643	94	183	24	12	15	46	31	134	.285	.321	.429	106	4	**74**	18	**11**	.936	3	*O-154	1.2
1967	*StL-N★	159	689	**113**	206	32	12	21	76	24	109	.299	.328	.472	128	22	**52**	18	5	.956	7	*O-157	2.7
1968	*StL-N	159	660	92	184	**46**	**14**	6	51	46	124	.279	.329	.418	125	18	**62**	12	**11**	.952	6	*O-156	3.1
1969	StL-N	157	655	97	195	33	10	12	47	50	115	.298	.349	.434	118	14	**53**	14	8	.949	5	*O-157	1.8
1970	StL-N	155	664	114	202	29	5	13	57	60	99	.304	.363	.422	107	7	51	15	6	.962	3	*O-152	0.8
1971	StL-N★	157	640	**126**	200	37	7	7	61	76	107	.313	.386	.425	125	23	**64**	19	**8**	.951	-1	*O-157	2.3
1972	StL-N☆	153	621	81	193	26	8	3	42	47	93	.311	.360	.393	115	12	**63**	18	8	.952	-4	*O-149	1.1
1973	StL-N	160	650	110	193	29	8	7	63	71	112	.297	.366	.398	112	12	**70**	20	9	.963	1	*O-159	1.5
1974	StL-N★	153	635	105	194	25	7	3	48	61	88	.306	.368	.381	111	10	**118**	33	**16**	.967	2	*O-152	2.2
1975	StL-N★	136	528	78	163	27	6	3	47	38	64	.309	.359	.400	106	5	56	16	7	.966	1	*O-128	0.7
1976	StL-N	133	498	73	150	24	5	4	67	35	75	.301	.348	.394	109	6	56	19	5	.983	0	*O-123	0.7
1977	StL-N	141	489	69	133	22	6	2	46	30	74	.272	.317	.354	81	-13	35	24	-4	.954	-11	*O-130	-3.4
1978	StL-N	92	298	31	66	9	0	0	12	17	29	.221	.263	.252	45	-22	17	5	2	.975	-6	O-79	-3.1
1979	StL-N★	120	405	56	123	15	4	5	38	23	43	.304	.346	.398	101	1	21	12	-1	.958	-3	O-98	-0.8
Total	19	2616	10332	1610	3023	486	141	149	900	761	1730	.293	.344	.410	109	110	938	307	97	.959	32	*O-2507	12.7

■ MATT BRODERICK Broderick, Matthew Thomas b: 12/1/1877, Lattimer, Pa. d: 2/26/40, Freeland, Pa. BR/TR, 5'6.5", 135 lbs. Deb: 5/1/03

YEAR	TM/L	G	AB	R	H	2B	3B	HR	RBI	BB	SO	AVG	OBP	SLG	PRO+	BR/A	SB	CS	SBR	FA	FR	G/POS	TPR
1903	Bro-N	2	2	0	0	0	0	0	0	0		.000	.000	.000	-99	-1	0			1.000	0	/2-1	0.0

■ STEVE BRODIE Brodie, Walter Scott b: 9/11/1868, Warrenton, Va. d: 10/30/35, Baltimore, Md. BL/TR, 5'11", 180 lbs. Deb: 4/21/1890

YEAR	TM/L	G	AB	R	H	2B	3B	HR	RBI	BB	SO	AVG	OBP	SLG	PRO+	BR/A	SB	CS	SBR	FA	FR	G/POS	TPR
1890	Bos-N	132	514	77	152	19	9	0	67	66	20	.296	.387	.368	111	8	29			**.953**	3	*O-132	0.6
1891	Bos-N	133	523	84	136	13	6	2	78	63	39	.260	.351	.319	85	-11	25			.951	10	*O-133	-0.4
1892	StL-N	154	602	85	152	10	9	4	60	52	31	.252	.316	.319	97	-2	28			.943	8	*O-137,2-16/3-2	0.1
1893	StL-N	107	469	71	149	16	8	2	79	33	16	.318	.376	.399	106	4	41			.951	9	*O-107	0.6
	Bal-N	25	97	18	35	7	2	0	19	12	2	.361	.446	.474	142	6	8			.963	-3	O-25	0.2
	Yr	132	566	89	184	23	10	2	98	45	18	.325	.389	.412	112	10	49			.953	6	*O-132	0.8
1894	*Bal-N	129	573	134	210	25	11	3	113	18	8	.366	.399	.464	103	1	42			.950	-6	*O-129	-1.0
1895	*Bal-N	131	528	85	184	27	10	2	134	26	15	.348	.394	.449	114	10	35			.965	5	*O-131	0.4
1896	*Bal-N	132	516	98	153	19	11	2	87	36	17	.297	.363	.388	97	-2	25			.972	11	*O-132	-0.2
1897	Pit-N	100	370	47	108	7	12	2	53	25		.292	.348	.392	99	-1	11			**.983**	-0	*O-100	-0.7
1898	Pit-N	42	156	15	41	5	0	0	21	6		.263	.303	.295	73	-6	3			.958	3	O-42	-0.5
	Bal-N	23	98	12	30	3	2	0	19	5		.306	.346	.378	105	0	3			.923	3	O-23	0.1
	Yr	65	254	27	71	8	2	0	40	11		.280	.320	.327	86	-5	6			.946	6	O-65	-0.4
1899	Bal-N	137	531	82	164	26	1	3	87	31		.309	.373	.379	101	1	19			**.979**	1	*O-137	-0.8
1901	Bal-A	83	306	41	95	6	6	2	41	25		.310	.378	.389	108	4	9			.963	-3	O-83	-0.5
1902	NY-N	109	416	37	117	8	2	3	42	22		.281	.327	.332	104	2	11			.953	7	*O-109	0.1
Total	12	1437	5699	886	1726	191	89	25	900	420	148	.303	.364	.381	102	15	289			.959	48	*O-1420/2-16,3-2	-2.0

■ RICO BROGNA Brogna, Rico Joseph b: 4/18/70, Turners Falls, Mass. BL/TL, 6'2", 200 lbs. Deb: 8/8/92

YEAR	TM/L	G	AB	R	H	2B	3B	HR	RBI	BB	SO	AVG	OBP	SLG	PRO+	BR/A	SB	CS	SBR	FA	FR	G/POS	TPR
1992	Det-A	9	26	3	5	1	0	1	3	3	5	.192	.276	.346	73	-1	0	0	0	.982	1	/1-8,D-2	-0.1
1994	NY-N	39	131	16	46	11	2	7	20	6	29	.351	.380	.626	158	10	1	0	0	.997	2	1-35	0.9
1995	NY-N	134	495	72	143	27	2	22	76	39	111	.289	.343	.485	119	12	0	0	0	**.998**	5	*1-131	0.7
1996	NY-N	55	188	18	48	10	1	7	30	19	50	.255	.324	.431	101	-0	0	0	0	.996	-2	1-52	-0.6
1997	Phi-N	148	543	68	137	36	1	20	81	33	116	.252	.295	.433	88	-12	12	3	2	.994	10	*1-145	-1.4
1998	Phi-N	153	565	77	150	36	3	20	104	49	125	.265	.324	.446	95	-5	7	7	-2	.996	16	*1-151	-0.3
Total	6	538	1948	254	529	121	9	77	314	149	436	.272	.324	.461	104	5	20	10	0	.996	31	1-522/D-2	-0.8

■ JACK BROHAMER Brohamer, John Anthony b: 2/26/50, Maywood, Cal. BL/TR, 5'10", 165 lbs. Deb: 4/18/72

YEAR	TM/L	G	AB	R	H	2B	3B	HR	RBI	BB	SO	AVG	OBP	SLG	PRO+	BR/A	SB	CS	SBR	FA	FR	G/POS	TPR
1972	Cle-A	136	527	49	123	13	2	5	35	27	46	.233	.272	.294	66	-22	3	2	-0	.977	6	*2-132/3-1	-1.1
1973	Cle-A	102	300	29	66	12	1	4	29	32	23	.220	.295	.307	69	-12	0	2	-1	.971	17	2-97	0.8
1974	Cle-A	101	315	33	85	11	1	2	30	26	22	.270	.331	.330	92	-3	2	1	0	.987	-4	2-99	-0.3
1975	Cle-A	69	217	15	53	5	0	6	16	14	14	.244	.290	.350	80	-6	2	2	-1	.976	4	2-66	0.0
1976	Chi-A	119	354	33	89	12	2	7	40	44	28	.251	.339	.356	103	2	1	3	-2	.984	18	*2-117/3-1	2.7
1977	Chi-A	59	152	26	39	10	3	2	20	21	8	.257	.351	.401	105	1	0	0	0	.923	2	3-38,2-18/D-1	0.4
1978	Bos-A	81	244	34	57	14	1	1	25	25	13	.234	.305	.311	67	-11	1	3	-2	.974	-3	3-30,D-25,2-23	-1.6
1979	Bos-A	64	192	25	51	7	1	1	11	15	15	.266	.319	.328	71	-8	0	3	-2	.982	-0	2-36,3-22	-0.8
1980	Bos-A	21	57	5	18	2	0	1	6	4	3	.316	.361	.404	104	0	0	0	0	.900	-1	3-13/2-4,D-3	-0.1
	Cle-A	53	142	13	32	5	1	1	15	14	6	.225	.295	.296	62	-7	0	1	-1	.979	-4	2-47/D-1	-0.9
	Yr	74	199	18	50	7	1	2	21	18	9	.251	.313	.327	74	-7	0	1	-1	.981	-5	2-51,3-13/D-4	-1.0
Total	9	805	2500	262	613	91	12	30	227	222	178	.245	.309	.327	79	-65	9	17	-8	.979	33	2-639,3-105/D-30	-0.9

■ HERMAN BRONKIE Bronkie, Herman Charles "Dutch" b: 3/31/1885, S.Manchester, Conn d: 5/27/68, Somers, Conn. BR/TR, 5'9", 165 lbs. Deb: 9/20/10

YEAR	TM/L	G	AB	R	H	2B	3B	HR	RBI	BB	SO	AVG	OBP	SLG	PRO+	BR/A	SB	CS	SBR	FA	FR	G/POS	TPR
1910	Cle-A	5	9	1	2	0	0	0	0	1		.222	.300	.222	63	-0	1			.625	-1	/3-3,S-1	-0.2
1911	Cle-A	2	6	0	1	0	0	0	0	0		.167	.167	.167	-7	-1	0			1.000	-1	/3-2	-0.2
1912	Cle-A	6	16	1	0	0	0	0	0	1		.000	.059	.000	-80	-4	0			.917	2	/3-6	-0.1
1914	Chi-N	1	1	1	1	1	0	0	1	0	0	1.000	1.000	2.000	786	1	0			.000	-0	/3-1	0.0
1918	StL-N	18	68	7	15	3	0	1	7	2	4	.221	.243	.309	70	-3	0			.984	-1	3-18	-0.4
1919	StL-A	67	196	23	50	6	4	0	14	23	23	.255	.336	.327	84	-4	2			.939	4	3-34,2-16/1-2	0.2

YEAR	TM/L	G	AB	R	H	2B	3B	HR	RBI	BB	SO	AVG	OBP	SLG	PRO+	BR/A	SB	CS	SBR	FA	FR	G/POS	TPR
1922	StL-A	23	64	7	18	4	1	0	2	6	7	.281	.343	.375	84	-1	0	2	-1	.917	-0	3-18	-0.2
Total	7	122	360	40	87	14	5	1	24	33	34	.242	.307	.317	75	-12	3	2		.931	2	/3-82,2-16,1-2,S-1	-0.9
■ TOM BROOKENS		Brookens, Thomas Dale b: 8/10/53, Chambersburg, Pa. BR/TR, 5'10", 170 lbs. Deb: 7/10/79																					
1979	Det-A	60	190	23	50	5	2	4	21	11	40	.263	.310	.374	81	-5	10	3	1	.945	12	3-42,2-19/D-1	0.8
1980	Det-A	151	509	64	140	25	9	10	66	32	71	.275	.319	.418	98	-2	13	11	-3	.931	4	*3-138/2-9,S-1,D-1	-0.3
1981	Det-A	71	239	19	58	10	1	4	25	14	43	.243	.290	.343	79	-7	5	3	-0	.952	-4	3-71	-1.3
1982	Det-A	140	398	40	92	15	3	9	58	27	63	.231	.280	.352	72	-16	5	9	-4	.939	10	*3-113,2-26/S-9,O-1	-1.1
1983	Det-A	138	332	50	71	13	3	6	32	29	46	.214	.281	.325	68	-15	10	4	1	.928	5	*3-103,S-30,2-10,/D	-0.9
1984	*Det-A	113	224	32	55	11	4	5	26	19	33	.246	.307	.397	94	-2	6	6	-2	.969	20	3-68,S-28,2-26,/D-1	1.8
1985	Det-A	156	485	54	115	34	6	7	47	27	78	.237	.277	.375	77	-16	14	5	1	.943	3	*3-151/S-8,2-3,CD	-1.4
1986	Det-A	98	281	42	76	11	2	3	25	20	42	.270	.321	.356	84	-6	11	8	-2	.955	2	3-35,2-31,S-14,D/O	-0.5
1987	*Det-A	143	444	59	107	15	3	13	59	33	63	.241	.296	.376	80	-13	7	4	-0	.954	2	*3-122,S-16,2-11	-1.1
1988	Det-A	136	441	62	107	23	5	5	38	44	74	.243	.316	.351	90	-6	4	4	-1	.952	-3	*3-136/S-3,2-1	-1.1
1989	NY-A	66	168	14	38	6	0	4	14	11	27	.226	.274	.333	71	-7	1	3	-2	.926	-4	3-51/S-7,2-5,O-3,D	-1.2
1990	Cle-A	64	154	18	41	7	2	1	20	14	25	.266	.327	.357	92	-2	0	0	0	.923	4	3-35,2-21/S-3,1D	0.3
Total	12	1336	3865	477	950	175	40	71	431	281	605	.246	.299	.367	83	-97	86	60	-10	.943	49	*3-1065,2-162,S/DO1C	-6.0
■ HARRY BROOKS		Brooks, Harry Frank b: 11/30/1865, Philadelphia, Pa. d: 12/5/45, Philadelphia, Pa. Deb: 7/24/1886																					
1886	NY-a	1	1	0	0	0	0	0	0	0		.000	.000	.000	-99	-0	0			.500	-1	/O-1,P-1	0.0
■ HUBIE BROOKS		Brooks, Hubert b: 9/24/56, Los Angeles, Cal. BR/TR, 6', 200 lbs. Deb: 9/4/80																					
1980	NY-N	24	81	8	25	2	1	1	10	5	9	.309	.364	.395	115	2	1	1	-0	.966	-1	3-23	0.0
1981	NY-N	98	358	34	110	21	2	4	38	23	65	.307	.351	.411	117	7	9	5	-0	.924	-2	3-93/O-3,S-1	0.3
1982	NY-N	126	457	40	114	21	2	2	40	28	76	.249	.300	.317	73	-16	6	3	0	.931	-8	*3-126	-2.9
1983	NY-N	150	586	53	147	18	4	5	58	24	96	.251	.285	.321	68	-26	6	4	-1	.950	3	*3-145/2-7	-2.7
1984	NY-N	153	561	61	159	23	2	16	73	48	79	.283	.342	.417	114	10	6	5	-1	.929	-18	*3-129,S-26	-0.9
1985	Mon-N	156	605	67	163	34	7	13	100	34	79	.269	.314	.413	108	4	6	9	-4	.958	-34	*S-155	-2.0
1986	Mon-N★	80	306	50	104	18	5	14	58	25	60	.340	.393	.569	164	25	4	2	0	.958	-14	S-80	2.0
1987	Mon-N★	112	430	57	113	22	3	14	72	24	72	.263	.303	.426	88	-9	4	3	-1	.953	-26	*S-109	-2.7
1988	Mon-N	151	588	61	164	35	2	20	90	35	108	.279	.321	.447	113	8	7	3	0	.968	-2	*O-149	0.3
1989	Mon-N	148	542	56	145	30	1	14	70	39	108	.268	.321	.404	105	2	6	11	-5	.964	-2	*O-140	-0.8
1990	LA-N	153	568	74	151	28	1	20	91	33	108	.266	.313	.424	104	1	2	5	-2	.964	-3	*O-150	-0.8
1991	NY-N	103	357	48	85	11	1	16	50	44	62	.238	.327	.409	106	3	3	1	0	.972	-1	*O-100	0.0
1992	Cal-A	82	306	28	66	13	0	8	36	12	46	.216	.248	.337	62	-16	3	3	-1	.986	-0	D-70/1-6	-2.1
1993	KC-A	75	168	14	48	12	0	1	24	11	27	.286	.333	.375	85	-4	0	1	-1	.966	-3	O-40/1-3,D-9	-0.8
1994	KC-A	34	61	5	14	2	0	1	14	2	10	.230	.254	.311	43	-5	1	0	0	1.000	-0	D-19/1-4	-0.6
Total	15	1645	5974	656	1608	290	31	149	824	387	1005	.269	.318	.403	100	-13	64	56	-14	.966	-112	O-582,3-516,S/D12	-13.7
■ JERRY BROOKS		Brooks, Jerome Edward b: 3/23/67, Syracuse, N.Y. BR/TR, 6', 195 lbs. Deb: 9/6/93																					
1993	LA-N	9	9	2	2	1	0	1	1	0	2	.222	.222	.667	135	0	0	0	0	.000	-1	/O-2	-0.1
1996	Fla-N	8	5	2	2	0	1	0	3	1	1	.400	.571	.800	266	1	0	0	0	1.000	-1	/O-2,1-1	0.1
Total	2	17	14	4	4	1	1	1	4	1	3	.286	.375	.714	191	2	0	0	0	1.000	-1	/O-4,1-1	0.0
■ MANDY BROOKS		Brooks, Jonathan Joseph (b: Jonathan Joseph Brozek) b: 8/18/1897, Milwaukee, Wis. d: 6/17/62, Kirkwood, Mo. BR/TR, 5'9", 165 lbs. Deb: 5/30/25																					
1925	Chi-N	90	349	55	98	25	7	14	72	19	28	.281	.322	.513	108	2	10	3	1	.977	5	O-89	0.2
1926	Chi-N	26	48	7	9	1	0	1	6	5	5	.188	.278	.271	48	-4	0			1.000	-2	O-18	-0.7
Total	2	116	397	62	107	26	7	15	78	24	33	.270	.316	.484	101	-2	10	3		.979	2	O-107	-0.5
■ BOBBY BROOKS		Brooks, Robert b: 11/1/45, Los Angeles, Cal. d: 10/11/94, Harbor City, Cal. BR/TR, 5'8.5", 165 lbs. Deb: 9/1/69																					
1969	Oak-A	29	79	13	19	5	0	3	10	20	24	.241	.400	.418	135	5	0	2	-1	1.000	0	O-21	0.3
1970	Oak-A	7	18	2	6	1	0	2	5	1	7	.333	.368	.722	201	2	0	1	-1	1.000	-1	/O-5	0.0
1972	Oak-A	15	39	4	7	0	0	0	5	8	8	.179	.319	.179	54	-2	0	1	-1	.930	2	O-11	-0.1
1973	Cal-A	4	7	0	1	0	0	0	0	0	3	.143	.143	.143	-21	-1	0	0	0	.000	-0	/O-1	-0.2
Total	4	55	143	19	33	6	0	5	20	29	42	.231	.364	.378	116	4	0	4	-2	.964	1	/O-38	0.0
■ SCOTT BROSIUS		Brosius, Scott David b: 8/15/66, Hillsboro, Ore. BR/TR, 6'1", 185 lbs. Deb: 8/7/91																					
1991	Oak-A	36	68	9	16	5	0	2	4	3	11	.235	.268	.397	86	-2	3	1	0	1.000	-1	2-18,O-13/3-7,D-1	-0.2
1992	Oak-A	38	87	13	19	2	0	4	13	3	13	.218	.261	.379	82	-3	3	0	1	1.000	-8	O-20,3-12/1-3,SD	-1.1
1993	Oak-A	70	213	26	53	10	1	6	25	14	37	.249	.298	.390	89	-4	6	0	2	.991	-2	O-46,1-11,3-10,/SD	-0.5
1994	Oak-A	96	324	31	77	14	1	14	49	24	57	.238	.294	.417	88	-7	2	6	-3	.946	-4	3-93/O-7,1-1	-1.4
1995	Oak-A	123	389	69	102	19	2	17	46	41	67	.262	.345	.452	111	6	4	2	0	.918	-9	3-60,O-49,1/2SD	-0.5
1996	Oak-A	114	428	73	130	25	0	22	71	59	85	.304	.397	.516	131	21	7	2	1	.969	15	*3-109,1-10/O-4	3.3
1997	Oak-A	129	479	59	97	20	1	11	41	34	102	.203	.261	.317	51	-35	9	4	0	.977	11	*3-107,S-30,O-22	-2.2
1998	*NY-A★	152	530	86	159	34	0	19	98	52	97	.300	.373	.472	120	17	11	8	-2	.948	10	*3-150/1-3,O-1	2.4
Total	8	758	2518	366	653	129	5	95	347	230	469	.259	.330	.428	99	-7	45	23	-0	.957	12	3-548,O-162/1S2D	-0.2
■ SIG BROSKIE		Broskie, Sigmund Theodore "Chops" b: 3/23/11, Iselin, Pa. d: 5/17/75, Canton, Ohio BR/TR, 5'11.5", 200 lbs. Deb: 9/11/40																					
1940	Bos-N	11	22	1	6	1	0	0	4	1	2	.273	.304	.318	76	-1	0			.935	0	C-11	0.0
■ TONY BROTTEM		Brottem, Anton Christian b: 4/30/1892, Halstad, Minn. d: 8/5/29, Chicago, Ill. BR/TR, 6'0.5", 176 lbs. Deb: 4/17/16																					
1916	StL-N	26	33	3	6	1	0	0	4	3	10	.182	.250	.212	43	-2	1			.950	-1	C-15/O-2	-0.3
1918	StL-N	2	4	0	0	0	0	0	0	1	0	.000	.200	.000	-39	-1	0			1.000	1	/1-2	0.0
1921	Was-A	4	7	1	1	0	0	0	0	2	1	.143	.333	.143	26	-1	0	0	0	1.000	1	/C-4	0.1
	Pit-N	30	91	6	22	2	0	0	9	3	11	.242	.266	.264	40	-8	0	1	-1	.983	-2	C-29	-0.9
Total	3	62	135	10	29	3	0	0	13	9	22	.215	.264	.237	38	-11	1	1		.977	-1	/C-48,1-2,O-2	-1.1
■ CAL BROUGHTON		Broughton, Cecil Calvert b: 12/28/1860, Magnolia, Wis. d: 3/15/39, Evansville, Wis. BR/TR, Deb: 5/2/1883																					
1883	Cle-N	4	10	2	2	0	0	0	1	2	2	.200	.333	.200	68	-0				.950	-0	/C-4	0.0
	Bal-a	9	32	1	6	0	0	0		1		.188	.212	.188	29	-2				.825	-2	/C-8,O-1	-0.3
1884	Mil-U	11	39	5	12	5	0	0		0		.308	.308	.436	227	2				.937	-1	/C-7,O-5	0.2
1885	StL-a	4	17	1	1	0	0	0	1	0		.059	.059	.059	-60	-3				.889	-1	/C-4	-0.4
	NY-a	11	41	1	6	1	0	0	1	1		.146	.167	.171	7	-4				.860	-2	C-11	-0.4
	Yr	15	58	2	7	1	0	0	2	1		.121	.136	.138	-14	-7				.867	-3	C-15	-0.8
1888	Det-N	1	4	0	0	0	0	0	0	0	0	.000	.000	.000	-99	-1	0			1.000	1	/C-1	0.0
Total	4	40	143	10	27	6	0	0	3	4	2	.189	.211	.231	44	-8	0			.887	-5	/C-35,O-6	-0.9
■ MARK BROUHARD		Brouhard, Mark Steven b: 5/22/56, Burbank, Cal. BR/TR, 6'1", 210 lbs. Deb: 4/12/80																					
1980	Mil-A	45	125	17	29	6	0	5	16	7	24	.232	.278	.400	86	-3	1	0	0	.964	0	D-21,O-12,1-10	-0.3
1981	Mil-A	60	186	19	51	6	3	2	20	7	41	.274	.308	.371	100	-1	1	1	-0	.990	1	O-51/D-7	-0.1
1982	*Mil-A	40	108	16	29	4	1	4	10	9	17	.269	.336	.435	117	2	0	3	-2	.986	2	O-30/D-7	0.2
1983	Mil-A	56	185	25	51	10	1	7	23	9	39	.276	.316	.454	118	4	0	4	-2	.991	2	O-42,D-11	0.2
1984	Mil-A	66	197	20	47	7	0	6	22	16	36	.239	.302	.365	87	-4	0	3	-2	.983	4	O-52/D-8	-0.3
1985	Mil-A	37	108	11	28	7	2	1	13	5	26	.259	.298	.389	87	-2	0	0	0	.964	-3	O-29/D-1	-0.6
Total	6	304	909	108	235	40	7	25	104	53	183	.259	.307	.400	99	-3	2	11	-6	.983	7	O-216/D-55,1-10	-0.9
■ ART BROUTHERS		Brouthers, Arthur H. b: 11/25/1882, Montgomery, Ala. d: 9/28/59, Charleston, S.C. TR, 6'1", Deb: 4/14/06																					
1906	Phi-A	37	144	18	30	5	1	0	14	5		.208	.240	.257	54	-8	4			.900	-5	3-35/2-1	-1.2
■ DAN BROUTHERS		Brouthers, Dennis Joseph "Big Dan" b: 5/8/1858, Sylvan Lake, N.Y. d: 8/2/32, E.Orange, N.J. BL/TL, 6'2", 207 lbs. Deb: 6/23/1879 H																					
1879	Tro-N	39	168	17	46	12	1	4	17	1	18	.274	.278	.429	138	7				.926	-5	1-37/P-3	0.1

YEAR	TM/L	G	AB	R	H	2B	3B	HR	RBI	BB	SO	AVG	OBP	SLG	PRO+	BR/A	SB	CS	SBR	FA	FR	G/POS	TPR
1880	Tro-N	3	12	0	2	0	0	0	1	1	0	.167	.231	.167	35	-1				.893	-1	/1-3	-0.2
1881	Buf-N	65	270	60	86	18	9	**8**	45	18	22	.319	.361	**.541**	182	25				.797	-5	O-35,1-30	1.5
1882	Buf-N	84	351	71	**129**	23	11	6	63	21	7	**.368**	**.403**	**.547**	**198**	**37**				**.974**	1	*1-84	2.6
1883	Buf-N	98	425	85	**159**	41	**17**	3	**97**	16	17	**.374**	**.397**	**.572**	**186**	**42**				.961	2	*1-97/3-1,P-1	2.9
1884	Buf-N	94	398	82	130	22	15	14	79	33	20	.327	.378	**.563**	**186**	38				.964	0	*1-93/3-1	2.4
1885	Buf-N	98	407	87	146	32	11	7	59	34	10	.359	.408	**.543**	199	43				.975	-2	*1-98	2.7
1886	Det-N	121	489	139	181	**40**	15	**11**	72	66	16	.370	.445	**.581**	**204**	**62**	21			.968	-8	*1-121	3.5
1887	*Det-N	123	500	**153**	169	**36**	20	12	101	71	9	.338	**.426**	.562	**167**	**46**	34			.969	-4	*1-123	2.4
1888	Det-N	129	522	**118**	160	**33**	11	9	66	68	13	.307	.399	.464	174	**47**	34			.971	-2	*1-129	3.2
1889	Bos-N	126	485	105	181	26	9	7	118	66	6	**.373**	.462	.507	161	42	22			.974	1	*1-126	2.9
1890	Bos-P	123	460	117	152	36	9	1	97	99	17	.330	**.466**	.454	137	29	28			.963	2	*1-123	2.0
1891	Bos-a	130	486	117	170	26	19	5	109	87	20	**.350**	**.471**	**.512**	**184**	**59**	31			.978	-7	*1-130	3.8
1892	Bro-N	152	588	121	**197**	30	20	5	**124**	84	30	**.335**	.432	.480	**182**	**62**	31			.982	12	*1-152	**6.1**
1893	Bro-N	77	282	57	95	21	11	2	59	52	10	.337	.450	.511	163	28	9			.986	3	1-77	2.4
1894	*Bal-N	123	525	137	182	39	23	9	128	67	9	.347	.425	.560	130	24	38			.976	-2	*1-123	1.8
1895	Bal-N	5	23	2	6	2	0	0	5	1	1	.261	.292	.348	63	-1	0			1.000	0	/1-5	-0.1
	Lou-N	24	97	13	30	10	1	2	15	11	2	.309	.380	.495	133	5	1			.953	-2	1-24	0.2
	Yr	29	120	15	36	12	1	2	20	12	3	.300	.364	.467	119	3	1			.960	-2	1-29	0.1
1896	Phi-N	57	218	42	75	13	3	1	41	44	11	.344	.462	.445	141	16	7			.983	-3	1-57	1.2
1904	NY-N	2	5	0	0	0	0	0	0	0		.000	.000	.000	-96	-1	0			1.000	-0	/1-1	-0.2
Total	19	1673	6711	1523	2296	460	205	106	1296	840	238	.342	.423	.519	170	609	256			.971	-18	*1-1633/O-35,P-4,3	41.2

■ JOE BROVIA

Brovia, Joseph John "Ox" b: 2/18/22, Davenport, Cal. d: 8/15/94, Santa Cruz, Cal. BL/TR, 6'3", 195 lbs. Deb: 7/3/55

YEAR	TM/L	G	AB	R	H	2B	3B	HR	RBI	BB	SO	AVG	OBP	SLG	PRO+	BR/A	SB	CS	SBR	FA	FR	G/POS	TPR
1955	Cin-N	21	18	0	2	0	0	0	4	1	6	.111	.158	.111	-25	-3	0	0	0	.000	0	H	-0.3

■ FRANK BROWER

Brower, Frank Willard "Turkeyfoot" b: 3/26/1893, Gainesville, Va. d: 11/20/60, Baltimore, Md. BL/TR, 6'2", 180 lbs. Deb: 8/14/20

YEAR	TM/L	G	AB	R	H	2B	3B	HR	RBI	BB	SO	AVG	OBP	SLG	PRO+	BR/A	SB	CS	SBR	FA	FR	G/POS	TPR
1920	Was-A	36	119	21	37	7	2	1	13	9	11	.311	.374	.429	115	3	1	1	-0	.900	-0	O-20/1-9,3-1	0.1
1921	Was-A	83	203	33	53	12	3	1	35	18	7	.261	.330	.365	81	-6	1	1	-0	.917	3	O-46/1-4	-0.6
1922	Was-A	139	471	61	138	20	6	9	71	52	25	.293	.375	.418	112	9	8	6	-1	.978	-4	*O-121/1-7	-0.4
1923	Cle-A	126	397	77	113	25	8	16	66	62	32	.285	.392	.509	136	21	6	5	-1	.988	-3	*1-112/O-4	1.1
1924	Cle-A	66	107	16	30	10	1	3	20	27	9	.280	.434	.477	133	6	1	1	-0	.990	-1	1-26/P-4,O-3	0.3
Total	5	450	1297	206	371	74	20	30	205	168	84	.286	.379	.443	117	33	17	14	-3	.952	-4	O-194,1-158/P-4,3-1	0.5

■ LOUIS BROWER

Brower, Louis Lester b: 7/1/1900, Cincinnati, Ohio d: 3/4/94, Tyler, Tex. BR/TR, 5'10", 155 lbs. Deb: 6/13/31

YEAR	TM/L	G	AB	R	H	2B	3B	HR	RBI	BB	SO	AVG	OBP	SLG	PRO+	BR/A	SB	CS	SBR	FA	FR	G/POS	TPR
1931	Det-A	21	62	3	10	1	0	0	6	8	5	.161	.278	.177	21	-7	1	0	0	.886	-7	S-20/2-2	-1.1

■ BOB BROWER

Brower, Robert Richard b: 1/10/60, Jamaica, N.Y. BR/TR, 5'11", 185 lbs. Deb: 9/3/86

YEAR	TM/L	G	AB	R	H	2B	3B	HR	RBI	BB	SO	AVG	OBP	SLG	PRO+	BR/A	SB	CS	SBR	FA	FR	G/POS	TPR
1986	Tex-A	21	9	3	1	1	0	0	0	0	3	.111	.111	.222	-12	-1	1	2	-1	1.000	-5	O-17/D-1	-0.8
1987	Tex-A	127	303	63	79	10	3	14	46	36	66	.261	.339	.452	107	3	15	9	-1	.964	-13	*O-106/D-7	-1.3
1988	Tex-A	82	201	29	45	7	0	1	11	27	38	.224	.316	.274	65	-9	10	5	0	.972	-7	O-59,D-13	-1.8
1989	NY-A	26	69	9	16	3	0	2	3	6	11	.232	.293	.362	85	-2	3	1	0	.970	2	O-25/D-1	0.1
Total	4	256	582	104	141	21	3	17	60	69	118	.242	.323	.376	89	-9	29	17	-2	.968	-24	O-207/D-22	-3.8

■ BROWN

Brown Deb: 7/29/1874

YEAR	TM/L	G	AB	R	H	2B	3B	HR	RBI	BB	SO	AVG	OBP	SLG	PRO+	BR/A	SB	CS	SBR	FA	FR	G/POS	TPR
1874	Bal-n	2	9	0	0	0	0	0	0	0	0	.000	.000	.000	-99	-2	0	0	0	.727	-1	/S-2	-0.2

■ ADRIAN BROWN

Brown, Adrian Demond b: 2/7/74, McComb, Miss. BB/TR, 6', 175 lbs. Deb: 5/16/97

YEAR	TM/L	G	AB	R	H	2B	3B	HR	RBI	BB	SO	AVG	OBP	SLG	PRO+	BR/A	SB	CS	SBR	FA	FR	G/POS	TPR
1997	Pit-N	48	147	17	28	6	0	1	10	13	18	.190	.274	.252	38	-13	8	4	0	.987	2	O-38	-1.2
1998	Pit-N	41	152	20	43	4	1	0	5	9	18	.283	.323	.322	67	-7	4	0	1	.977	3	O-38	-0.4
Total	2	89	299	37	71	10	1	1	15	22	36	.237	.298	.288	53	-20	12	4	1	.982	4	/O-76	-1.6

■ BRANT BROWN

Brown, Brant Michael b: 6/22/71, Porterville, Cal. BL/TL, 6'3", 220 lbs. Deb: 6/15/96

YEAR	TM/L	G	AB	R	H	2B	3B	HR	RBI	BB	SO	AVG	OBP	SLG	PRO+	BR/A	SB	CS	SBR	FA	FR	G/POS	TPR
1996	Chi-N	29	69	11	21	1	0	5	9	2	17	.304	.333	.536	122	2	3	3	-1	1.000	3	1-18	0.2
1997	Chi-N	46	137	15	32	7	1	5	15	7	28	.234	.286	.409	77	-5	2	1	0	1.000	-0	O-27,1-12	-0.7
1998	Chi-N†	124	347	56	101	17	7	14	48	30	95	.291	.349	.501	114	7	4	5	-2	.963	-11	*O-102/1-7	-0.7
Total	3	199	553	82	154	25	8	24	72	39	140	.278	.332	.483	106	4	9	9	-3	.970	-9	O-129/1-37	-1.2

■ CURTIS BROWN

Brown, Curtis b: 9/14/45, Sacramento, Cal. BR/TR, 5'11", 180 lbs. Deb: 5/27/73 F

YEAR	TM/L	G	AB	R	H	2B	3B	HR	RBI	BB	SO	AVG	OBP	SLG	PRO+	BR/A	SB	CS	SBR	FA	FR	G/POS	TPR
1973	Mon-N	1	4	0	0	0	0	0	0	0	0	.000	.000	.000	-97	-1	0	0	0	1.000	0	/O-1	-0.1

■ DARRELL BROWN

Brown, Darrell Wayne b: 10/29/55, Oklahoma City, Okla BB/TR, 6', 184 lbs. Deb: 4/11/81

YEAR	TM/L	G	AB	R	H	2B	3B	HR	RBI	BB	SO	AVG	OBP	SLG	PRO+	BR/A	SB	CS	SBR	FA	FR	G/POS	TPR
1981	Det-A	16	4	4	1	0	0	0	0	0	1	.250	.250	.250	43	-0	1	0	0	1.000	-2	/O-6,D-4	-0.2
1982	Oak-A	8	18	2	6	0	1	0	3	1	2	.333	.368	.444	128	1	1	0	0	1.000	-1	/O-7,D-1	0.0
1983	Min-A	91	309	40	84	6	2	0	22	10	28	.272	.297	.304	64	-15	3	3	-1	.995	-4	O-81/D-3	-2.2
1984	Min-A	95	260	36	71	9	3	1	19	14	16	.273	.310	.342	77	-8	4	1	1	.993	4	O-55,D-13	-0.5
Total	4	210	591	82	162	15	6	1	44	25	47	.274	.305	.325	71	-23	9	4	0	.994	-3	O-149/D-21	-2.9

■ DELOS BROWN

Brown, Delos Hight b: 10/4/1892, Anna, Ill. d: 12/21/64, Carbondale, Ill. BR/TR, 5'9", 160 lbs. Deb: 6/12/14

YEAR	TM/L	G	AB	R	H	2B	3B	HR	RBI	BB	SO	AVG	OBP	SLG	PRO+	BR/A	SB	CS	SBR	FA	FR	G/POS	TPR
1914	Chi-A	1	1	0	0	0	0	0	0	0	1	.000	.000	.000	-99	-0	0			.000	0	H	0.0

■ DERMAL BROWN

Brown, Dermal Bram b: 3/27/78, Bronx, N.Y. BL/TR, 5'11", 210 lbs. Deb: 9/14/98

YEAR	TM/L	G	AB	R	H	2B	3B	HR	RBI	BB	SO	AVG	OBP	SLG	PRO+	BR/A	SB	CS	SBR	FA	FR	G/POS	TPR
1998	KC-A	5	3	2	0	0	0	0	0	0	1	.000	.000	.000	-96	-1	0	0	0	1.000	-1	/O-2,D-3	-0.1

■ DRUMMOND BROWN

Brown, Drummond Nicol b: 1/31/1885, Los Angeles, Cal. d: 1/27/27, Parkville, Mo. BR/TR, 6', 180 lbs. Deb: 4/25/13

YEAR	TM/L	G	AB	R	H	2B	3B	HR	RBI	BB	SO	AVG	OBP	SLG	PRO+	BR/A	SB	CS	SBR	FA	FR	G/POS	TPR
1913	Bos-N	15	34	3	11	1	0	1	2	2	9	.324	.361	.441	126	1	0			.960	-4	C-12	-0.2
1914	KC-F	31	58	4	11	3	0	0	5	7	6	.190	.277	.241	44	-6	1			.954	5	C-23/1-2	0.1
1915	KC-F	77	227	13	55	10	1	1	26	12	23	.242	.289	.308	71	-13	3			.961	-2	C-65/1-1	-1.1
Total	3	123	319	20	77	14	1	2	33	21	38	.241	.294	.310	72	-17	4			.960	-2	C-100/1-3	-1.2

■ ED BROWN

Brown, Edward P. b: Chicago, Ill. TR , 178 lbs. Deb: 8/19/1882

YEAR	TM/L	G	AB	R	H	2B	3B	HR	RBI	BB	SO	AVG	OBP	SLG	PRO+	BR/A	SB	CS	SBR	FA	FR	G/POS	TPR
1882	StL-a	17	60	4	11	0	0	0		4		.183	.234	.183	41	-4				.808	-2	O-15/2-2,P-1	-0.5
1884	Tol-a	42	153	13	27	3	0	0		2		.176	.187	.196	24	-13				.815	-8	3-40/O-2,C-1,P-1	-1.9
Total	2	59	213	17	38	3	0	0		6		.178	.201	.192	29	-16				.815	-11	/3-40,O-17,P-2,2C	-2.4

■ EDDIE BROWN

Brown, Edward William "Glass Arm Eddie" b: 7/17/1891, Milligan, Neb. d: 9/10/56, Vallejo, Cal. BR/TR, 6'3", 190 lbs. Deb: 9/26/20

YEAR	TM/L	G	AB	R	H	2B	3B	HR	RBI	BB	SO	AVG	OBP	SLG	PRO+	BR/A	SB	CS	SBR	FA	FR	G/POS	TPR
1920	NY-N	3	8	1	1	1	0	0	0	0	3	.125	.125	.250	6	-1	0	0	0	1.000	0	/O-2	-0.1
1921	NY-N	70	128	16	36	6	2	0	12	4	11	.281	.324	.359	80	-4	1	0	0	.956	-3	O-30	-0.8
1924	Bro-N	114	455	56	140	30	4	5	78	26	15	.308	.345	.424	108	5	3	5	-2	.975	2	*O-114	-0.3
1925	Bro-N	153	618	88	189	39	11	5	99	22	18	.306	.332	.429	95	-6	3	4	-2	.972	8	*O-153	-0.9
1926	Bos-N	153	612	71	**201**	31	8	2	84	23	20	.328	.355	.415	117	12	5			.965	8	*O-153	1.0
1927	Bos-N	155	558	64	171	35	6	2	75	28	20	.306	.340	.401	106	3	11			.980	3	*O-150/1-1	-0.4
1928	Bos-N	142	523	45	140	28	2	2	59	24	22	.268	.305	.340	72	-22	6			.960	-4	*O-129/1-1	-3.5
Total	7	790	2902	341	878	170	33	16	407	127	109	.303	.334	.400	99	-14	29	9		.970	13	O-731/1-2	-5.0

■ RANDY BROWN

Brown, Edwin Randolph b: 8/29/44, Leesburg, Fla. BL/TR, 5'7", 170 lbs. Deb: 9/11/69

YEAR	TM/L	G	AB	R	H	2B	3B	HR	RBI	BB	SO	AVG	OBP	SLG	PRO+	BR/A	SB	CS	SBR	FA	FR	G/POS	TPR
1969	Cal-A	13	25	3	4	1	0	0	0	6	1	.160	.323	.200	52	-1	0	0	0	1.000	-1	C-10/O-1	-0.2
1970	Cal-A	5	4	0	0	0	0	0	0	0	0	.000	.000	.000	-99	-1	0	0	0	1.000	-0	/C-5	-0.1
Total	2	18	29	3	4	1	0	0	0	6	1	.138	.286	.172	32	-2	0	0	0	1.000	-1	/C-15,O-1	-0.3

■ EMIL BROWN

Brown, Emil Quincy b: 12/29/74, Chicago, Ill. BR/TR, 6'2", 195 lbs. Deb: 4/3/97

YEAR	TM/L	G	AB	R	H	2B	3B	HR	RBI	BB	SO	AVG	OBP	SLG	PRO+	BR/A	SB	CS	SBR	FA	FR	G/POS	TPR
1997	Pit-N	66	95	16	17	2	1	2	6	10	32	.179	.304	.284	54	-6	5	1	1	.948	-4	O-42	-0.9
1998	Pit-N	13	39	2	10	1	0	0	3	1	11	.256	.293	.282	49	-3	0	0	0	1.000	2	O-10	-0.1
Total	2	79	134	18	27	3	1	2	9	11	43	.201	.301	.284	53	-9	5	1	1	.963	-2	/O-52	-1.0

YEAR	TM/L	G	AB	R	H	2B	3B	HR	RBI	BB	SO	AVG	OBP	SLG	PRO+	BR/A	SB	CS	SBR	FA	FR	G/POS	TPR
■ FRED BROWN	Brown, Fred Herbert b: 4/12/1879, Ossipee, N.H. d: 2/3/55, Somersworth, N.H. BR/TR, 5'10.5", 190 lbs. Deb: 5/4/01																						
1901	Bos-N	7	14	1	2	0	0	0	2	0		.143	.143	.143	-16	-2	0			1.000	0	/O-5	-0.2
1902	Bos-N	2	6	1	2	1	0	0	0	0		.333	.333	.500	155	0	0			1.000	0	/O-2	0.0
Total	2	9	20	2	4	1	0	0	2	0		.200	.200	.250	30	-2	0			1.000	0	/O-7	-0.2
■ IKE BROWN	Brown, Isaac b: 4/13/42, Memphis, Tenn. BR/TR, 6'1", 205 lbs. Deb: 6/17/69																						
1969	Det-A	70	170	24	39	4	3	5	12	26	43	.229	.338	.376	96	-1	2	3	-1	.962	-6	2-45,3-12/O-3,S-1	-0.5
1970	Det-A	56	94	17	27	5	0	4	15	13	26	.287	.380	.468	132	4	0	0	0	.935	-3	2-23/O-4,3-1	0.3
1971	Det-A	59	110	20	28	1	0	8	19	19	25	.255	.364	.482	133	5	0	1	-1	1.000	-1	1-17/O-9,2-8,3-4,S	0.2
1972	*Det-A	51	84	12	21	3	0	2	10	17	23	.250	.376	.357	115	2	1	2	-1	1.000	3	O-22,1-13/2-3,S3	0.3
1973	Det-A	42	76	12	22	2	1	1	9	15	13	.289	.407	.382	115	2	0	1	-1	.983	-2	1-21,O-12/3-2,D-2	-0.2
1974	Det-A	2	2	0	0	0	0	0	0	0	0	.000	.000	.000	-97	-0	0	0	0	1.000	0	/3-2	0.0
Total	6	280	536	85	137	15	4	20	65	90	130	.256	.366	.410	115	13	3	7	-3	.956	-9	/2-79,1-51,O3SD	0.1
■ JIM BROWN	Brown, James Donaldson "Don" or "Moose" b: 3/31/1897, Laurel, Md. BR/TR, 6', 178 lbs. Deb: 9/13/15																						
1915	StL-N	1	2	0	1	0	0	0	0	2	1	.500	.750	.500	281	1	0			1.000	-0	/O-1	0.1
1916	Phi-A	14	42	6	10	2	1	1	5	4	9	.238	.304	.405	119	1	0			.895	-1	O-12	-0.1
Total	2	15	44	6	11	2	1	1	5	6	10	.250	.340	.409	131	2	0			.900	-2	/O-13	0.0
■ JIMMY BROWN	Brown, James Roberson b: 4/25/10, Jamesville, N.C. d: 12/29/77, Bath, N.C. BB/TR, 5'8.5", 165 lbs. Deb: 4/23/37 C																						
1937	StL-N	138	525	86	145	20	9	2	53	27	29	.276	.313	.360	81	-15	10			.964	-14	*2-112,S-25/3-1	-1.9
1938	StL-N	108	382	50	115	12	6	0	38	27	9	.301	.350	.364	91	-4	7			.968	1	2-49,S-30,3-24	0.2
1939	StL-N	147	645	88	192	31	8	3	51	32	18	.298	.335	.384	87	-12	4			.957	-5	*S-104,2-50	-0.5
1940	StL-N	107	454	56	127	17	4	0	30	24	15	.280	.317	.335	76	-15	9			.977	-22	2-48,3-41,S-28	-3.2
1941	StL-N	132	549	81	168	28	9	3	56	45	22	.306	.363	.406	109	7	2			.965	3	*3-123,2-11	1.3
1942	*StL-N★	145	606	75	155	28	4	1	71	52	11	.256	.315	.320	80	-15	4			.970	-12	2-82,3-66,S-12	-2.3
1943	StL-N	34	110	6	20	4	2	0	8	6	1	.182	.224	.255	37	-9	0			.978	2	2-19/3-9,S-6	-0.6
1946	Pit-N	79	241	23	58	6	0	0	12	18	5	.241	.293	.266	58	-13	3			.960	-2	S-30,2-21/3-9	-1.3
Total	8	890	3512	465	980	146	42	9	319	231	110	.279	.326	.352	84	-76	39			.968	-50	2-392,3-273,S-235	-8.3
■ JIM BROWN	Brown, James W. H. b: 12/12/1860, Clinton Co., Pa. d: 4/6/08, Williamsport, Pa. Deb: 4/17/1884																						
1884	Alt-U	21	88	12	22	2	2	1		1		.250	.258	.352	82	-5				.615	-3	O-14,P-11	-0.6
	NY-N	1	3	0	0	0	0	0	0	0	1	.000	.000	.000	-98	-1				.333	-0	/P-1	0.0
	StP-U	6	16	5	5	4	0	0		1		.313	.353	.563	320	3				.706	0	/P-6,1-1,O-1	0.0
1886	Phi-a	1	3	0	0	0	0	0	0	0		.000	.000	.000	-99	-1	0			1.000	-0	/P-1	0.0
Total	2	29	110	17	27	6	2	1	0	2	1	.245	.259	.364	92	-3	0			.741	-4	/P-19,O-15,1-1	-0.6
■ JARVIS BROWN	Brown, Jarvis Ardel b: 3/26/67, Waukegan, Ill. BR/TR, 5'7", 170 lbs. Deb: 7/2/91																						
1991	*Min-A	38	37	10	8	0	0	0	0	2	8	.216	.256	.216	31	-3	7	1	2	.955	-11	O-32/D-4	-1.3
1992	Min-A	35	15	8	1	0	0	0	0	2	4	.067	.222	.067	-15	-2	2	2	-1	.952	-10	O-31/D-2	-1.4
1993	SD-N	47	133	21	31	9	2	0	8	15	26	.233	.338	.331	78	-4	3	3	-1	.982	2	O-43	-0.4
1994	Atl-N	17	15	3	2	1	0	1	1	0	2	.133	.133	.400	31	-2	0	0	0	1.000	-2	/O-9	-0.3
1995	Bal-A	18	27	2	4	1	0	0	1	7	9	.148	.324	.185	36	-2	1	1	-0	1.000	-5	O-17	-0.7
Total	5	155	227	44	46	11	2	1	10	26	49	.203	.304	.282	57	-13	13	7	-0	.978	-26	O-132/D-6	-4.1
■ JAKE BROWN	Brown, Jerald Ray b: 3/22/48, Sumrall, Miss. d: 12/18/81, Houston, Tex. BR/TR, 6'2", 200 lbs. Deb: 5/17/75																						
1975	SF-N	41	43	6	9	3	0	0	4	5	13	.209	.292	.279	57	-2	0	0	0	.857	-3	O-14	-0.6
■ CHRIS BROWN	Brown, John Christopher b: 8/15/61, Jackson, Miss. BR/TR, 6'2", 210 lbs. Deb: 9/3/84																						
1984	SF-N	23	84	6	24	7	0	1	11	9	19	.286	.362	.405	119	2	2	1	0	.900	-2	3-23	0.0
1985	SF-N	131	432	50	117	20	3	16	61	38	78	.271	.345	.442	125	14	2	3	-1	**.971**	5	*3-120	1.7
1986	SF-N★	116	416	57	132	16	3	7	49	33	43	.317	.380	.421	127	16	13	9	-2	.933	-14	*3-111/S-2	-0.2
1987	SF-N	38	132	17	32	6	0	6	17	9	16	.242	.306	.424	95	-1	1	3	-2	.905	-2	3-37/S-1	-0.5
	SD-N	44	155	17	36	3	0	6	23	11	30	.232	.296	.368	77	-5	3	1	0	.942	-4	3-43	-0.9
	Yr	82	287	34	68	9	0	12	40	20	46	.237	.300	.394	86	-7	4	4	-1	.923	-6	3-80/S-1	-1.4
1988	SD-N	80	247	14	58	6	0	2	19	19	49	.235	.297	.283	69	-10	0	0	0	.949	5	3-72	-0.6
1989	Det-A	17	57	3	11	3	0	0	4	1	17	.193	.207	.246	28	-6	0	0	0	.909	-1	3-17	-0.7
Total	6	449	1523	164	410	61	6	38	184	120	252	.269	.335	.392	105	9	21	17	-4	.943	-13	3-423/S-3	-1.2
■ LINDSAY BROWN	Brown, John Lindsay "Red" b: 7/22/11, Mason, Tex. d: 1/1/67, San Antonio, Tex. BR/TR, 5'10", 160 lbs. Deb: 7/13/37																						
1937	Bro-N	48	115	16	31	3	1	0	6	3	17	.270	.288	.313	62	-6	1			.937	6	S-45	0.2
■ JOE BROWN	Brown, Joseph E. b: 4/4/1859, Warren, Pa. d: 6/28/1888, Warren, Pa. 5'10", 162 lbs. Deb: 8/16/1884																						
1884	Chi-N	15	61	6	13	1	0	0	3	0	15	.213	.213	.230	36	-5				.750	-3	/O-9,P-7,1-1,C-1	-0.5
1885	Bal-a	5	19	2	3	0	0	0	0	0		.158	.158	.158	-0	-2				1.000	0	/P-4,2-1	0.0
Total	2	20	80	8	16	1	0	0	3	0	15	.200	.200	.213	28	-7				.895	-3	/P-11,O-9,2-1,C1	-0.5
■ KEVIN BROWN	Brown, Kevin Lee b: 4/21/73, Valparaiso, Ind. BR/TR, 6'2", 200 lbs. Deb: 9/12/96																						
1996	Tex-A	3	4	1	0	0	0	0	1	2	2	.000	.429	.000	20	-0	0	0	0	1.000	1	/C-2,D-1	0.1
1997	Tex-A	4	5	1	2	0	0	1	1	0	0	.400	.400	1.000	237	1	0	0	0	.900	0	/C-4	0.1
1998	Tor-A	52	110	17	29	7	1	2	15	9	31	.264	.331	.400	89	-2	0	0	-0	.993	7	C-52	0.7
Total	3	59	119	19	31	7	1	3	17	11	33	.261	.338	.412	93	-1	0	0	-0	.990	8	/C-58,D-1	0.9
■ LARRY BROWN	Brown, Larry Leslie b: 3/1/40, Shinnston, W.Va. BR/TR, 5'11", 165 lbs. Deb: 7/6/63 F																						
1963	Cle-A	74	247	28	63	6	0	5	18	22	27	.255	.319	.340	85	-5	4	3	-1	.938	-8	S-46,2-27	-0.9
1964	Cle-A	115	335	33	77	12	1	12	40	24	55	.230	.285	.379	84	-8	1	2	-1	.981	11	*2-103/S-4	1.0
1965	Cle-A	124	438	52	111	22	2	8	40	38	62	.253	.316	.368	93	-4	5	7	-3	.977	3	S-95,2-26	0.5
1966	Cle-A	105	340	29	78	12	0	3	17	36	58	.229	.309	.291	73	-11	0	1	-1	.961	-4	S-90,2-10	-0.7
1967	Cle-A	152	485	38	110	16	2	7	37	53	62	.227	.311	.311	84	-9	4	4	-1	.967	1	*S-150	0.6
1968	Cle-A	154	495	43	116	18	3	6	35	43	46	.234	.302	.319	90	-6	1	1	-0	.966	-14	*S-154	-0.6
1969	Cle-A	132	469	48	112	10	2	4	24	44	43	.239	.305	.294	66	-21	5	3	-0	.959	-17	*S-101,3-29/2-5	-2.8
1970	Cle-A	72	155	17	40	5	2	0	15	20	14	.258	.343	.316	79	-4	1	0	0	.950	-2	S-27,3-17,2-16	-0.2
1971	Cle-A	13	50	4	11	1	0	0	5	3	3	.220	.278	.240	44	-4	0	0	0	.980	-6	S-13	-0.9
	Oak-A	70	189	14	37	2	1	1	9	7	19	.196	.228	.233	31	-17	1	2	-1	.959	4	S-31,2-23,3-10	-1.1
	Yr	83	239	18	48	3	1	1	14	10	22	.201	.239	.234	35	-21	1	2	-1	.965	-2	S-44,2-23,3-10	-2.0
1972	Oak-A	47	142	11	26	2	0	0	4	13	8	.183	.252	.197	37	-11	0	0	0	.974	-8	2-46/3-1	-1.9
1973	*Bal-A	17	28	4	7	0	0	1	5	5	4	.250	.364	.357	104	0	0	0	0	.880	-2	3-15/2-1	-0.2
1974	Tex-A	54	76	10	15	2	0	0	5	9	13	.197	.282	.224	48	-5	0	0	0	.931	8	3-47/2-8,S-1	0.3
Total	12	1129	3449	331	803	108	13	47	254	317	414	.233	.301	.313	76	-103	22	23	-7	.964	-34	S-712,2-265,3-119	-6.9
■ LEON BROWN	Brown, Leon b: 11/16/49, Sacramento, Cal. BR/TR, 6', 185 lbs. Deb: 5/19/76 F																						
1976	NY-N	64	70	11	15	3	0	0	2	4	4	.214	.257	.257	49	-5	2	4	-2	1.000	-18	O-43	-2.7
■ LEW BROWN	Brown, Lewis J. "Blower" b: 2/1/1858, Leominster, Mass. d: 1/15/1889, Boston, Mass. BR/TR, 5'10.5", 185 lbs. Deb: 6/17/1876																						
1876	Bos-N	45	195	23	41	6	6	2	21	3	22	.210	.222	.333	82	-4				.856	-2	C-45/O-1	-0.4
1877	Bos-N	58	221	27	56	12	8	1	31	6	33	.253	.273	.394	104	0				.897	15	*C-55/1-4	1.6
1878	Pro-N	58	243	44	74	21	6	1	43	7	37	.305	.324	.453	153	13				.880	3	*C-45,1-15/O-1,P-1	1.5
1879	Pro-N	53	229	23	59	13	4	2	38	4	24	.258	.270	.376	112	3				.847	-4	C-48/O-6	0.0
	Chi-N	6	21	2	6	1	0	0	3	1	4	.286	.318	.333	109	0				.974	0	/1-6	0.0
	Yr	59	250	25	65	14	4	2	41	5	28	.260	.275	.372	112	3				.847	-4	C-48/O-6,1-6	0.0
1881	Det-N	27	108	16	26	3	1	3	14	3	16	.241	.261	.370	93	-1				.959	-1	1-27	-0.4
	Pro-N	18	75	9	18	3	1	0	10	4	13	.240	.278	.307	85	-1				.833	-4	O-13/1-5	-0.5

YEAR	TM/L	G	AB	R	H	2B	3B	HR	RBI	BB	SO	AVG	OBP	SLG	PRO+	BR/A	SB	CS	SBR	FA	FR	G/POS	TPR
	Yr	45	183	25	44	6	2	3	24	7	29	.240	.268	.344	90	-2				.960	-4	1-32,O-13	-0.9
1883	Bos-N	14	54	5	13	4	1	0	9	3	6	.241	.281	.352	89	-1				.943	-2	1-14	-0.3
	Lou-a	14	60	6	11	2	1	0			1	.183	.197	.250	46	-3				.891	-2	1-14/C-1	-0.6
1884	Bos-U	85	325	50	75	18	3	1		13		.231	.260	.314	74	-20				.914	13	C-54,1-33/O-2,P-1	-0.5
Total	7	378	1531	205	379	83	31	10	169	45	155	.248	.269	.362	99	-13				.884	17	C-248,1-118/O-23,P	0.4

■ MARTY BROWN Brown, Marty Leo b: 1/23/63, Lawton, Okla. BR/TR, 6'1", 190 lbs. Deb: 9/4/88

YEAR	TM/L	G	AB	R	H	2B	3B	HR	RBI	BB	SO	AVG	OBP	SLG	PRO+	BR/A	SB	CS	SBR	FA	FR	G/POS	TPR
1988	Cin-N	10	16	0	3	1	0	0	2	1	2	.188	.235	.250	38	-1	0	1	-1	1.000	1	/3-8	-0.1
1989	Cin-N	16	30	2	5	1	0	0	4	4	9	.167	.265	.200	34	-3	0	0	0	.913	2	3-11	-0.1
1990	Bal-A	9	15	1	3	0	0	0	0	1	7	.200	.250	.200	28	-1	0	0	0	1.000	0	/2-3,3-2,D-4	-0.1
Total	3	35	61	3	11	2	0	0	6	6	18	.180	.254	.213	34	-5	0	1	-1	.943	3	/3-21,D-4,2-3	-0.3

■ MIKE BROWN Brown, Michael Charles b: 12/29/59, San Francisco, Cal. BR/TR, 6'2", 195 lbs. Deb: 7/21/83

YEAR	TM/L	G	AB	R	H	2B	3B	HR	RBI	BB	SO	AVG	OBP	SLG	PRO+	BR/A	SB	CS	SBR	FA	FR	G/POS	TPR
1983	Cal-A	31	104	12	24	5	1	3	9	7	20	.231	.279	.385	81	-3	1	0	0	.949	-2	O-31	-0.5
1984	Cal-A	62	148	19	42	8	3	7	22	13	23	.284	.342	.520	136	7	0	2	-1	.968	-6	O-44/D-3	-0.1
1985	Cal-A	60	153	23	41	9	1	4	20	7	21	.268	.304	.418	96	-1	0	1	-1	1.000	-3	O-48/D-7	-0.5
	Pit-N	57	205	29	68	18	2	5	33	22	27	.332	.396	.512	154	15	2	2	-1	.938	-2	O-56	1.0
1986	Pit-N	87	243	18	53	7	0	4	26	27	32	.218	.296	.296	62	-12	2	3	-1	.973	-4	O-71	-2.1
1988	Cal-A	18	50	4	11	2	0	0	3	1	12	.220	.235	.260	40	-4	0	0	0	.946	-1	O-18	-0.5
Total	5	315	903	105	239	49	7	23	113	77	135	.265	.323	.411	102	1	5	8	-3	.964	-17	O-268/D-10	-2.7

■ OLIVER BROWN Brown, Oliver S. b: 1849, Brooklyn, N.Y. d: 9/23/32, Brooklyn, N.Y. Deb: 8/1/1872

YEAR	TM/L	G	AB	R	H	2B	3B	HR	RBI	BB	SO	AVG	OBP	SLG	PRO+	BR/A	SB	CS	SBR	FA	FR	G/POS	TPR
1872	Atl-n	4	15	0	2	0	0	0	0	0	1	.133	.133	.133	-15	-2	0	0	0	.889	0	/O-4	-0.1
1875	Atl-n	3	10	0	0	0	0	0	0	0	0	.000	.000	.000	-99	-2	0	0	0	.833	-1	/1-2,O-2	-0.2
Total	2 n	7	25	0	2	0	0	0	0	0	1	.080	.080	.080	-46	-4	0	0	0	.846	-0	/O-6,1-2	-0.3

■ OLLIE BROWN Brown, Ollie Lee "Downtown" b: 2/11/44, Tuscaloosa, Ala. BR/TR, 6'3", 200 lbs. Deb: 9/10/65 F

YEAR	TM/L	G	AB	R	H	2B	3B	HR	RBI	BB	SO	AVG	OBP	SLG	PRO+	BR/A	SB	CS	SBR	FA	FR	G/POS	TPR
1965	SF-N	6	10	0	2	1	0	0	0	0	2	.200	.200	.300	38	-1	0	0	0	1.000	-1	/O-4	-0.2
1966	SF-N	115	348	32	81	7	1	7	33	33	66	.233	.303	.319	71	-13	2	5	-2	.978	-7	*O-114	-2.9
1967	SF-N	120	412	44	110	12	1	13	53	25	65	.267	.315	.396	104	1	0	2	-1	.985	-6	*O-115	-1.3
1968	SF-N	40	95	7	22	4	0	0	11	3	23	.232	.270	.274	64	-4	1	0	0	1.000	-7	O-35	-1.5
1969	SD-N	151	568	76	150	18	3	20	61	44	97	.264	.320	.412	108	4	10	6	-1	.976	7	*O-148	0.2
1970	SD-N	139	534	79	156	34	1	23	89	34	78	.292	.335	.489	123	14	5	3	-0	.964	7	*O-137	1.3
1971	SD-N	145	484	36	132	16	0	9	55	52	74	.273	.347	.362	108	6	3	3	-1	.982	5	*O-134	0.3
1972	SD-N	23	70	3	12	2	0	0	3	5	9	.171	.227	.200	24	-7	0	0	0	1.000	1	O-17	-0.8
	Oak-A	20	54	5	13	1	0	1	4	6	14	.241	.317	.315	93	-0	1	1	-0	1.000	-2	O-16	-0.4
	Mil-A	66	179	21	50	8	0	3	25	17	24	.279	.345	.374	116	4	0	2	-1	.992	7	O-56/3-1	0.8
	Yr	86	233	26	63	9	0	4	29	23	38	.270	.339	.361	111	3	1	3	-2	.994	5	O-72/3-1	0.4
1973	Mil-A	97	296	28	83	10	1	7	32	33	53	.280	.356	.392	113	6	4	1	1	1.000	-1	D-82/O-4	0.3
1974	Hou-N	27	69	8	15	1	0	3	6	4	15	.217	.260	.362	76	-3	0	0	0	1.000	-1	O-20	-0.4
	Phi-N	43	99	11	24	5	2	4	13	6	20	.242	.286	.455	101	-1	0	1	-1	.921	-5	O-33	-0.8
	Yr	70	168	19	39	6	2	7	19	10	35	.232	.275	.417	91	-3	0	1	-1	.961	-6	O-53	-1.2
1975	Phi-N	84	145	19	44	12	0	6	26	15	29	.303	.369	.510	137	7	1	1	-0	1.000	-14	O-63	-0.9
1976	*Phi-N	92	209	30	53	10	1	5	30	33	33	.254	.355	.383	106	2	2	1	0	.949	-6	O-75	-0.6
1977	*Phi-N	53	70	5	17	3	1	1	13	4	14	.243	.284	.357	68	-3	1	1	-0	1.000	-4	O-21	-0.8
Total	13	1221	3642	404	964	144	11	102	454	314	616	.265	.326	.394	103	11	30	27	-7	.977	-29	O-992/D-82,3-1	-7.7

■ OSCAR BROWN Brown, Oscar Lee b: 2/8/46, Long Beach, Cal. BR/TR, 6', 175 lbs. Deb: 9/3/69 F

YEAR	TM/L	G	AB	R	H	2B	3B	HR	RBI	BB	SO	AVG	OBP	SLG	PRO+	BR/A	SB	CS	SBR	FA	FR	G/POS	TPR
1969	Atl-N	7	4	2	1	0	0	0	0	0	1	.250	.250	.250	40	-0	0	0	0	1.000	-1	/O-3	-0.1
1970	Atl-N	28	47	6	18	2	1	1	7	7	7	.383	.473	.532	159	4	0	2	-1	.960	-5	O-25	-0.2
1971	Atl-N	27	43	4	9	4	0	0	5	3	8	.209	.261	.302	56	-3	0	0	0	1.000	-2	O-15	-0.5
1972	Atl-N	76	164	19	37	5	1	3	16	4	29	.226	.244	.323	55	-10	0	2	-1	.899	-4	O-59	-1.8
1973	Atl-N	22	58	3	12	3	0	0	0	3	10	.207	.246	.259	37	-5	0	0	0	1.000	2	O-13	-0.4
Total	5	160	316	34	77	14	2	4	28	17	55	.244	.284	.339	68	-13	0	4	-2	.939	-10	O-115	-3.0

■ DICK BROWN Brown, Richard Ernest b: 1/17/35, Shinnston, W.Va. d: 4/17/70, Baltimore, Md. BR/TR, 6'3", 190 lbs. Deb: 6/20/57 F

YEAR	TM/L	G	AB	R	H	2B	3B	HR	RBI	BB	SO	AVG	OBP	SLG	PRO+	BR/A	SB	CS	SBR	FA	FR	G/POS	TPR
1957	Cle-A	34	114	10	30	4	0	4	22	4	23	.263	.288	.404	88	-2	1	1	-0	.986	1	C-33	0.0
1958	Cle-A	68	173	20	41	5	0	7	20	14	27	.237	.305	.387	91	-2	1	0	0	.987	6	C-62	0.6
1959	Cle-A	48	141	15	31	7	0	5	16	11	39	.220	.290	.376	85	-3	0	0	0	.996	4	C-48	0.3
1960	Chi-A	16	43	4	7	0	0	3	5	3	11	.163	.217	.372	57	-3	0	0	0	.986	3	C-14	0.1
1961	Det-A	93	308	32	82	12	2	16	45	22	57	.266	.315	.474	105	1	0	2	-1	.990	-1	C-91	0.4
1962	Det-A	134	431	40	104	12	0	12	40	21	66	.241	.280	.353	67	-21	0	1	-1	.994	3	*C-132	-1.4
1963	Bal-A	59	171	13	42	7	0	2	13	15	35	.246	.310	.322	80	-4	1	0	0	.986	6	C-58	0.3
1964	Bal-A	88	230	24	59	6	0	8	32	12	45	.257	.296	.387	89	-4	2	0	1	.988	4	C-84	0.3
1965	Bal-A	96	255	17	59	9	1	5	30	17	53	.231	.282	.333	73	-9	2	2	-1	.983	10	C-92	0.4
Total	9	636	1866	175	455	62	3	62	223	119	356	.244	.293	.380	83	-49	7	6	-2	.989	35	C-614	1.0

■ BOBBY BROWN Brown, Robert William "Doc" b: 10/25/24, Seattle, Wash. BL/TR, 6'1", 180 lbs. Deb: 9/22/46

YEAR	TM/L	G	AB	R	H	2B	3B	HR	RBI	BB	SO	AVG	OBP	SLG	PRO+	BR/A	SB	CS	SBR	FA	FR	G/POS	TPR
1946	NY-A	7	24	1	8	1	0	0	1	4	0	.333	.429	.375	124	1	0	0	0	1.000	-4	/S-5,3-2	-0.2
1947	*NY-A	69	150	21	45	6	1	1	18	21	9	.300	.390	.373	114	4	0	2	-1	.932	-11	3-27,S-11/O-3	-0.9
1948	NY-A	113	363	62	109	19	5	3	48	48	16	.300	.383	.405	111	6	0	1	-1	.946	-18	3-41,S-26,2-17,/O-4	-1.0
1949	*NY-A	104	343	61	97	14	4	6	61	38	18	.283	.359	.399	101	0	4	3	-1	.949	-4	3-86/O-3	-0.6
1950	*NY-A	95	277	33	74	4	2	4	37	39	18	.267	.360	.339	82	-7	3	1	0	.958	-4	3-82	-1.0
1951	*NY-A	103	313	44	84	15	2	6	51	47	18	.268	.369	.387	108	5	1	1	-0	.955	-5	3-90	-0.1
1952	NY-A	29	89	6	22	2	0	1	14	9	6	.247	.323	.303	80	-2	1	1	-0	.894	3	3-24	0.0
1954	NY-A	28	60	5	13	1	0	1	7	8	3	.217	.309	.283	65	-3	0	1	-1	1.000	-0	3-17	-0.4
Total	8	548	1619	233	452	62	14	22	237	214	88	.279	.367	.376	100	4	9	10	-3	.948	-43	3-369/S-42,2-17,O	-4.2

■ BOBBY BROWN Brown, Rogers Lee b: 5/24/54, Norfolk, Va. BB/TR, 6'1", 205 lbs. Deb: 4/5/79

YEAR	TM/L	G	AB	R	H	2B	3B	HR	RBI	BB	SO	AVG	OBP	SLG	PRO+	BR/A	SB	CS	SBR	FA	FR	G/POS	TPR
1979	Tor-A	4	10	1	0	0	0	0	0	2	1	.000	.167	.000	-50	-2	0	0	0	1.000	-0	/O-4	-0.2
	NY-A	30	68	7	17	3	1	0	3	2	17	.250	.271	.324	61	-4	2	1	0	.949	-3	O-27/D-1	-0.8
	Yr	34	78	8	17	3	1	0	3	4	18	.218	.256	.282	46	-6	2	1	0	.955	-3	O-31/D-1	-1.0
1980	*NY-A	137	412	65	107	12	5	14	47	29	82	.260	.308	.415	98	-2	27	8	3	.972	-1	*O-131/D-1	-0.4
1981	*NY-A	31	62	5	14	1	0	0	6	5	15	.226	.284	.242	53	-4	4	2	0	.949	-2	O-29/D-2	-0.6
1982	Sea-A	79	245	29	59	7	1	4	17	17	32	.241	.290	.327	67	-11	28	6	5	.968	3	O-68/D-3	-0.5
1983	SD-N	57	225	40	60	5	3	5	22	23	38	.267	.335	.382	102	0	27	9	3	.963	-1	O-54	0.0
1984	*SD-N	85	171	28	43	7	2	3	29	11	33	.251	.297	.368	86	-4	16	4	2	.971	-2	O-53	-0.5
1985	SD-N	79	84	8	13	3	0	0	6	5	20	.155	.202	.190	11	-10	6	4	-1	1.000	-7	O-28	-1.9
Total	7	502	1277	183	313	38	12	26	130	94	238	.245	.297	.355	80	-36	110	34	13	.968	-13	O-394/D-7	-4.9

■ SAM BROWN Brown, Samuel Wakefield b: 5/21/1878, Webster, Pa. d: 11/8/31, Mount Pleasant, Pa. BR/TR, Deb: 4/21/06

YEAR	TM/L	G	AB	R	H	2B	3B	HR	RBI	BB	SO	AVG	OBP	SLG	PRO+	BR/A	SB	CS	SBR	FA	FR	G/POS	TPR
1906	Bos-N	71	231	12	48	6	1	0	20	13		.208	.262	.242	59	-11	4			.970	-1	C-35,O-13,3-12,/2	-0.9
1907	Bos-N	70	208	17	40	6	0	0	14	12		.192	.250	.221	48	-12	0			.970	7	C-63/1-2	0.0
Total	2	141	439	29	88	12	1	0	34	25		.200	.256	.232	54	-24	4			.970	7	/C-98,O-13,3-12,12	-0.9

■ TOMMY BROWN Brown, Thomas Michael "Buckshot" b: 12/6/27, Brooklyn, N.Y. BR/TR, 6'1", 170 lbs. Deb: 8/3/44

YEAR	TM/L	G	AB	R	H	2B	3B	HR	RBI	BB	SO	AVG	OBP	SLG	PRO+	BR/A	SB	CS	SBR	FA	FR	G/POS	TPR
1944	Bro-N	46	146	17	24	4	0	0	8	8	17	.164	.208	.192	13	-17	0			.925	-9	S-46	-2.4
1945	Bro-N	57	196	13	48	3	4	2	19	6	16	.245	.267	.332	66	-10	3			.918	-4	S-55/O-1	-1.0
1947	Bro-N	15	34	3	8	1	0	0	2	1	6	.235	.257	.265	37	-3	0			1.000	2	/3-6,O-3,S-1	-0.1
1948	Bro-N	54	145	18	35	4	0	2	20	7	17	.241	.281	.310	58	-9	1			.936	-1	3-43/1-1	-1.0
1949	*Bro-N	41	89	14	27	2	0	3	18	6	8	.303	.347	.427	102	0	0			.931	-2	O-27	-0.3
1950	Bro-N	48	86	15	25	2	1	8	20	11	9	.291	.378	.616	153	6	0			.917	0	O-16	0.6

YEAR	TM/L	G	AB	R	H	2B	3B	HR	RBI	BB	SO	AVG	OBP	SLG	PRO+	BR/A	SB	CS	SBR	FA	FR	G/POS	TPR
1951	Bro-N	11	25	2	4	2	0	0	1	2	4	.160	.222	.240	24	-3	0	0	0	.909	0	/O-5	-0.3
	Phi-N	78	196	24	43	2	1	10	32	15	21	.219	.278	.393	80	-6	1	2	-1	.966	-12	O-32,2-14,1-12,/3-1	-2.0
	Yr	89	221	26	47	4	1	10	33	17	25	.213	.272	.376	73	-9	1	2	-1	.957	-11	O-37,2-14,1-12,/3-1	-2.3
1952	Phi-N	18	25	2	4	1	0	1	2	4	3	.160	.276	.320	65	-1	0	0	0	1.000	-1	/1-3,O-3	-0.2
	Chi-N	61	200	24	64	11	0	3	24	12	24	.320	.358	.420	114	3	1	2	-1	.911	-19	S-39,2-10/1-5	-1.4
	Yr	79	225	26	68	12	0	4	26	16	27	.302	.349	.409	109	2	1	2	-1	.911	-20	S-39,2-10/1-8,O-3	-1.6
1953	Chi-N	65	138	19	27	7	1	2	13	13	17	.196	.279	.304	51	-10	1	0	0	.903	-6	S-25/O-6	-1.4
Total	9	494	1280	151	309	39	7	31	159	85	142	.241	.292	.355	74	-48	7	4		.916	-52	S-166/O-93,3-50,21	-9.5

■ TOM BROWN

Brown, Thomas Tarlton b: 9/21/1860, Liverpool, England d: 10/25/27, Washington, D.C. BL/TR, 5'10", 168 lbs. Deb: 7/6/1882 MU

YEAR	TM/L	G	AB	R	H	2B	3B	HR	RBI	BB	SO	AVG	OBP	SLG	PRO+	BR/A	SB	CS	SBR	FA	FR	G/POS	TPR
1882	Bal-a	45	181	30	55	5	2	1	23	6		.304	.326	.370	146	9				.728	-0	O-45/P-2	0.8
1883	Col-a	97	420	69	115	12	7	5	32	20		.274	.307	.371	127	14				.808	-1	*O-96/P-3	1.1
1884	Col-a	107	451	93	123	9	11	5	32	24		.273	.315	.375	135	18				.847	-6	*O-107/P-4	1.0
1885	Pit-a	108	437	81	134	16	12	4	68	34		.307	.366	.426	152	26				.828	-3	*O-108/P-2	1.9
1886	Pit-a	115	460	106	131	11	11	1	51	56		.285	.365	.363	129	17	30			.837	6	*O-115/P-1	1.8
1887	Pit-N	47	192	30	47	3	4	0	6	11	40	.245	.289	.302	69	-8	12			.870	5	O-47	-0.3
	Ind-N	36	140	20	25	3	0	2	9	8	25	.179	.228	.243	32	-13	13			.813	-2	O-36	-1.3
	Yr	83	332	50	72	6	4	2	15	19	65	.217	.263	.277	53	-21	25			.851	3	O-83	-1.6
1888	Bos-N	107	420	62	104	10	7	9	49	30	68	.248	.299	.369	110	4	46			.896	-3	*O-107	-0.1
1889	Bos-N	90	362	93	84	10	5	2	24	59	56	.232	.341	.304	76	-11	63			.901	3	O-90	-0.9
1890	Bos-P	128	543	146	149	23	14	4	61	86	84	.274	.377	.390	98	-2	79			.911	4	*O-128	-0.2
1891	Bos-a	137	589	**177**	**189**	30	**21**	5	72	70	96	.321	.397	.469	150	37	**106**			.878	-10	*O-137	1.9
1892	Lou-N	153	660	105	150	16	8	2	45	47	94	.227	.284	.285	78	-17	78			.919	19	*O-153	-0.5
1893	Lou-N	122	529	104	127	15	7	5	54	56	63	.240	.319	.323	77	-17	**66**			.929	27	*O-122	0.3
1894	Lou-N	129	536	122	136	22	14	9	57	60	73	.254	.332	.397	81	-18	66			.912	3	*O-129	-1.8
1895	StL-N	83	350	72	76	11	4	1	31	48	44	.217	.315	.280	55	-23	34			.950	8	O-83	-1.7
	Was-N	34	134	25	32	8	3	2	16	18	16	.239	.329	.388	86	-3	8			.909	-7	O-34	-1.0
	Yr	117	484	97	108	19	7	3	47	66	60	.223	.319	.310	63	-26	42			.942	2	*O-117	-2.7
1896	Was-N	116	435	87	128	17	6	2	59	58	49	.294	.385	.375	101	3	28			.928	-5	*O-116	-1.0
1897	Was-N	116	469	91	137	17	2	5	45	52		.292	.364	.369	94	-3	25			.928	1	*O-115/M	-0.9
1898	Was-N	16	55	8	9	1	0	0	2	5		.164	.233	.182	19	-6	3			.925	0	O-15/M	-0.6
Total	17	1786	7363	1521	1951	239	138	64	736	748	708	.265	.337	.361	101	8	657			.890	39	*O-1783/P-12	-1.5

■ TOM BROWN

Brown, Thomas William b: 12/12/40, Laureldale, Pa. BB/TL, 6'1", 190 lbs. Deb: 4/8/63

YEAR	TM/L	G	AB	R	H	2B	3B	HR	RBI	BB	SO	AVG	OBP	SLG	PRO+	BR/A	SB	CS	SBR	FA	FR	G/POS	TPR
1963	Was-A	61	116	8	17	4	0	1	4	11	45	.147	.227	.207	23	-12	2	1	0	1.000	-2	O-16,1-14	-1.6

■ WILLARD BROWN

Brown, Willard "Big Bill" or "California"
b: 1866, San Francisco, Cal. d: 12/20/1897, San Francisco, Cal BR/TR, 6'2", 190 lbs. Deb: 5/10/1887

YEAR	TM/L	G	AB	R	H	2B	3B	HR	RBI	BB	SO	AVG	OBP	SLG	PRO+	BR/A	SB	CS	SBR	FA	FR	G/POS	TPR
1887	NY-N	49	170	17	37	3	2	0	25	10	15	.218	.273	.259	51	-11	10			.914	-0	C-46/3-3,O-2	-0.6
1888	*NY-N	20	59	4	16	1	0	0	6	1	8	.271	.283	.288	84	-1	1			.893	3	C-20	0.3
1889	*NY-N	40	139	16	36	10	0	1	29	9	9	.259	.318	.353	87	-3	6			.846	-5	C-37/O-3	-0.5
1890	NY-P	60	230	47	64	8	4	4	43	13	13	.278	.320	.400	84	-7	5			.900	-5	C-34,O-13/1-9,32	-0.8
1891	Phi-N	115	441	62	107	20	4	0	50	34	35	.243	.303	.306	75	-14	7			**.989**	5	*1-97,C-19/O-2	-1.2
1893	Bal-N	7	32	5	4	3	0	0	5	1	3	.125	.152	.219	-2	-5	0			.985	-0	/1-7	-0.5
	Lou-N	111	461	80	140	23	7	1	85	50	32	.304	.373	.390	112	9	9			.989	-2	*1-111/C-1	0.3
	Yr	118	493	85	144	26	7	1	90	51	35	.292	.360	.379	104	3	9			**.988**	-2	*1-118/C-1	-0.2
1894	Lou-N	13	48	5	10	2	0	0	9	5	7	.208	.283	.250	32	-5	1			.977	4	1-13	-0.1
	StL-N	3	9	0	1	0	0	0	0	0	2	.111	.111	.111	-46	-2	0			1.000	0	/1-3	-0.1
	Yr	16	57	5	11	2	0	0	9	5	9	.193	.258	.228	19	-8	1			.982	4	1-16	-0.2
Total	7	418	1589	236	415	70	17	6	252	123	124	.261	.319	.338	82	-40	39			.987	-0	1-240,C-157/O32	-3.2

■ WILLARD BROWN

Brown, Willard Jessie b: 6/26/15, Shreveport, La. d: 8/8/96, Houston, Tex. BR/TR, 5'11.5", 200 lbs. Deb: 7/19/47

YEAR	TM/L	G	AB	R	H	2B	3B	HR	RBI	BB	SO	AVG	OBP	SLG	PRO+	BR/A	SB	CS	SBR	FA	FR	G/POS	TPR
1947	StL-A	21	67	4	12	3	0	1	6	0	7	.179	.179	.269	23	-7	2	2	-1	1.000	0	O-18	-0.9

■ GATES BROWN

Brown, William James b: 5/2/39, Crestline, O. BL/TR, 5'11", 220 lbs. Deb: 6/19/63 C

YEAR	TM/L	G	AB	R	H	2B	3B	HR	RBI	BB	SO	AVG	OBP	SLG	PRO+	BR/A	SB	CS	SBR	FA	FR	G/POS	TPR
1963	Det-A	55	82	16	22	3	1	2	14	8	13	.268	.341	.402	104	1	2	1	0	1.000	4	O-16	0.3
1964	Det-A	123	426	65	116	22	6	15	54	31	53	.272	.328	.458	114	7	11	4	1	.981	8	*O-106	1.1
1965	Det-A	96	227	33	58	14	2	10	43	17	33	.256	.307	.467	115	4	6	0	2	.973	2	O-56	0.6
1966	Det-A	88	169	27	45	5	1	7	27	18	19	.266	.344	.432	119	4	3	0	1	.980	-3	O-43	0.1
1967	Det-A	51	91	17	17	1	1	2	9	13	15	.187	.288	.286	68	-3	0	0	0	1.000	-2	O-20	-0.6
1968	*Det-A	67	92	15	34	7	2	6	15	12	4	.370	.442	.685	231	14	0	0	0	1.000	-1	O-17/1-1	1.4
1969	Det-A	60	93	13	19	1	2	1	6	5	17	.204	.253	.290	49	-6	0	0	0	.906	1	O-14	-0.7
1970	Det-A	81	124	18	28	3	0	3	24	20	14	.226	.338	.323	82	-2	0	0	0	.950	-1	O-26	-0.5
1971	Det-A	82	195	37	66	2	3	11	29	21	17	.338	.408	.549	163	16	4	2	0	.986	-6	O-56	0.9
1972	*Det-A	103	252	33	58	5	0	10	31	26	28	.230	.307	.369	97	-1	3	0	1	.977	2	O-72	-0.1
1973	Det-A	125	377	48	89	11	1	12	50	52	41	.236	.330	.366	90	-5	1	1	-0	1.000	-1	*D-119/O-2	-0.9
1974	Det-A	73	99	7	24	2	0	4	17	10	15	.242	.312	.384	96	-1	0	0	0	.000	0	D-13	-0.1
1975	Det-A	47	35	1	6	2	0	1	3	9	6	.171	.356	.314	87	-0	0	0	0	.000	0	H	-0.1
Total	13	1051	2262	330	582	78	19	84	322	242	275	.257	.333	.420	109	27	30	8	4	.977	3	O-428,D-132/1-1	1.4

■ BILL BROWN

Brown, William Verna "Verna" b: 7/8/1893, Coleman, Tex. d: 5/13/65, Lubbock, Tex. BL/TL, 5'8", 185 lbs. Deb: 8/15/12

YEAR	TM/L	G	AB	R	H	2B	3B	HR	RBI	BB	SO	AVG	OBP	SLG	PRO+	BR/A	SB	CS	SBR	FA	FR	G/POS	TPR
1912	StL-A	9	20	0	4	0	0	0	1	0		.200	.200	.200	15	-2	0			.909	-2	/O-7	-0.4

■ BYRON BROWNE

Browne, Byron Ellis b: 12/27/42, St.Joseph, Mo. BR/TR, 6'2", 200 lbs. Deb: 9/9/65

YEAR	TM/L	G	AB	R	H	2B	3B	HR	RBI	BB	SO	AVG	OBP	SLG	PRO+	BR/A	SB	CS	SBR	FA	FR	G/POS	TPR
1965	Chi-N	4	6	0	0	0	0	0	0	0	2	.000	.000	.000	-98	-2	0	0	0	.667	-1	/O-4	-0.3
1966	Chi-N	120	419	46	102	15	7	16	51	40	143	.243	.317	.427	103	2	3	3	-1	.967	-4	*O-114	-0.9
1967	Chi-N	10	19	3	3	2	0	0	2	4	5	.158	.304	.263	61	-1	1	1	-0	1.000	-1	/O-8	-0.3
1968	Hou-N	10	13	0	3	0	0	0	1	4	6	.231	.412	.231	99	0	0	0	0	1.000	2	/O-2	0.2
1969	StL-N	22	53	9	12	0	1	1	7	11	14	.226	.359	.321	92	-0	0	0	0	1.000	3	O-16	0.2
1970	Phi-N	104	270	29	67	17	2	10	36	33	72	.248	.330	.437	107	2	1	2	-1	.975	-2	O-88	-0.5
1971	Phi-N	58	68	5	14	3	0	3	5	8	23	.206	.289	.382	89	-1	0	0	0	1.000	-8	O-30	-1.1
1972	Phi-N	21	21	2	4	0	0	0	0	1	8	.190	.227	.190	19	-2	0	0	0	1.000	-3	/O-9	-0.6
Total	8	349	869	94	205	37	10	30	102	101	273	.236	.319	.405	98	-2	5	6	-2	.973	-16	O-271	-3.3

■ EARL BROWNE

Browne, Earl James "Snitz" b: 3/5/11, Louisville, Ky. d: 1/12/93, Whittier, Cal. BL/TL, 6', 175 lbs. Deb: 9/12/35

YEAR	TM/L	G	AB	R	H	2B	3B	HR	RBI	BB	SO	AVG	OBP	SLG	PRO+	BR/A	SB	CS	SBR	FA	FR	G/POS	TPR
1935	Pit-N	9	32	6	8	2	0	0	6	2	8	.250	.294	.313	61	-2	0			1.000	0	/1-9	-0.3
1936	Pit-N	8	23	7	7	1	2	0	3	1	4	.304	.333	.522	124	1	0			1.000	0	/O-4,1-1	0.1
1937	Phi-N	105	332	42	97	19	3	6	52	21	41	.292	.342	.422	98	-1	4			.980	1	O-54,1-23	-0.5
1938	Phi-N	21	74	4	19	4	0	0	8	5	11	.257	.304	.311	71	-3	0			.978	-0	1-16/O-2	-0.5
Total	4	143	461	59	131	26	5	6	69	29	64	.284	.332	.401	93	-5	4			.983	1	/O-60,1-49	-1.2

■ GEORGE BROWNE

Browne, George Edward b: 1/12/1876, Richmond, Va. d: 12/9/20, Hyde Park, N.Y. BL/TR, 5'10.5", 160 lbs. Deb: 9/27/01

YEAR	TM/L	G	AB	R	H	2B	3B	HR	RBI	BB	SO	AVG	OBP	SLG	PRO+	BR/A	SB	CS	SBR	FA	FR	G/POS	TPR
1901	Phi-N	8	26	2	5	1	0	0	4	1		.192	.250	.231	39	-2	2			1.000	-1	/O-8	-0.4
1902	Phi-N	70	281	41	73	7	1	0	26	16		.260	.304	.292	84	-5	11			.910	8	O-70	-0.3
	NY-N	53	216	30	69	9	5	0	14	9		.319	.355	.407	136	8	13			.895	0	O-53	0.5
	Yr	123	497	71	142	16	6	0	40	25		.286	.326	.342	106	3	24			.904	7	*O-123	0.2
1903	NY-N	141	591	105	185	20	3	3	45	43		.313	.364	.372	106	4	27			.918	-4	*O-141	-0.8
1904	NY-N	150	596	**99**	169	16	5	4	39	39		.284	.332	.347	105	3	24			.925	-5	*O-149	-1.1
1905	*NY-N	127	536	95	157	16	14	4	43	20		.293	.321	.397	111	5	26			.915	-9	*O-127	-1.0
1906	NY-N	122	477	61	126	10	4	0	38	27		.264	.304	.302	87	-8	32			.934	-5	*O-121	-2.1
1907	NY-N	127	458	54	119	11	10	5	37	31		.260	.308	.360	106	2	15			.941	-9	*O-121	-1.4

YEAR	TM/L	G	AB	R	H	2B	3B	HR	RBI	BB	SO	AVG	OBP	SLG	PRO+	BR/A	SB	CS	SBR	FA	FR	G/POS	TPR
1908	Bos-N	138	536	61	122	10	6	1	34	36		.228	.276	.274	77	-14	17			.950	4	*O-138	-1.9
1909	Chi-N	12	39	7	8	0	1	0	1	5		.205	.295	.256	70	-1	3			.944	-2	O-12	-0.4
	Was-A	103	393	40	107	15	5	1	16	17		.272	.308	.344	111	3	13			.935	-2	*O-101	-0.4
1910	Was-A	7	22	1	4	0	0	0	0	1		.182	.217	.182	26	-2	0			.667	-2	/O-5	-0.4
	Chi-A	30	112	17	27	4	1	0	4	12		.241	.315	.295	95	-0	5			.952	-4	O-29	-0.6
	Yr	37	134	18	31	4	1	0	4	13		.231	.299	.276	84	-2	5			.917	-5	O-34	-1.0
1911	Bro-N	8	12	1	4	0	0	0	2	1	1	.333	.385	.333	106	0	2			1.000	-0	/O-2	0.0
1912	Phi-N	6	5	0	1	0	0	0	0	1	0	.200	.333	.200	45	-0	0			.000	0	H	0.0
Total	12	1102	4300	614	1176	119	55	18	303	259	1	.273	.318	.339	100	-8	190			.927	-32	*O-1077	-10.3

■ JERRY BROWNE

Browne, Jerome Austin b: 2/13/66, Christiansted, V.I. BB/TR, 5'10", 170 lbs. Deb: 9/6/86

YEAR	TM/L	G	AB	R	H	2B	3B	HR	RBI	BB	SO	AVG	OBP	SLG	PRO+	BR/A	SB	CS	SBR	FA	FR	G/POS	TPR
1986	Tex-A	12	24	6	10	2	0	0	3	1	4	.417	.440	.500	151	2	0	2	-1	.923	-1	/2-8	0.0
1987	Tex-A	132	454	63	123	16	6	1	38	61	50	.271	.360	.339	87	-7	27	17	-2	.980	-17	*2-130/D-1	-1.9
1988	Tex-A	73	214	26	49	9	2	1	17	25	32	.229	.310	.304	71	-8	7	5	-1	.958	-25	2-70/D-1	-3.2
1989	Cle-A	153	598	83	179	31	4	5	45	68	64	.299	.372	.390	113	12	14	6	1	.979	-48	*2-151/D-2	-3.1
1990	Cle-A	140	513	92	137	26	5	6	50	72	46	.267	.359	.372	105	6	12	7	-1	.985	-21	*2-139	-1.3
1991	Cle-A	107	290	28	66	5	2	1	29	27	29	.228	.296	.269	57	-16	2	4	-2	.964	-10	2-47,O-17,3-15,/D-7	-2.7
1992	*Oak-A	111	324	43	93	12	2	3	40	40	40	.287	.372	.364	113	7	3	3	-1	.965	-11	3-58,O-43,2-19,/SD	-0.6
1993	Oak-A	76	260	27	65	13	0	2	19	22	17	.250	.309	.323	74	-9	4	0	1	.985	-4	O-56,3-13/2-3,1-2	-1.3
1994	Fla-N	101	329	42	97	17	4	3	30	52	23	.295	.394	.398	104	4	3	0	1	.931	-7	3-62,O-30,2-15	-0.2
1995	Fla-N	77	184	21	47	4	0	1	17	25	20	.255	.348	.293	71	-7	1	1	-0	.959	6	O-29,2-27/3-7	-0.1
Total	10	982	3190	431	866	135	25	23	288	393	325	.271	.354	.351	94	-16	73	45	-5	.977	-138	2-609,O-175,3/D1S	-14.4

■ PIDGE BROWNE

Browne, Prentice Almont b: 3/21/29, Peekskill, N.Y. d: 6/3/97, Houston, Tex. BL/TL, 6'1", 190 lbs. Deb: 4/13/62

YEAR	TM/L	G	AB	R	H	2B	3B	HR	RBI	BB	SO	AVG	OBP	SLG	PRO+	BR/A	SB	CS	SBR	FA	FR	G/POS	TPR
1962	Hou-N	65	100	8	21	4	2	1	10	13	9	.210	.301	.320	72	-4	0	0	0	.983	1	1-26	-0.4

■ PETE BROWNING

Browning, Louis Rogers "The Gladiator" b: 6/17/1861, Louisville, Ky. d: 9/10/05, Louisville, Ky. BR/TR, 6', 180 lbs. Deb: 5/2/1882

YEAR	TM/L	G	AB	R	H	2B	3B	HR	RBI	BB	SO	AVG	OBP	SLG	PRO+	BR/A	SB	CS	SBR	FA	FR	G/POS	TPR
1882	Lou-a	69	288	67	109	17	3	5		26		**.378**	**.430**	**.510**	**229**	**40**				.890	12	2-42,S-18,3-13	**4.7**
1883	Lou-a	84	358	95	121	15	9	4		23		.338	.378	.464	183	34				.861	-8	O-48,S-26,3-10,/21	2.3
1884	Lou-a	103	447	101	150	33	8	4	47	13		.336	.357	.472	176	36				.806	-9	3-52,O-24,1-23,/2P	2.1
1885	Lou-a	112	481	98	**174**	34	10	9	73	25		**.362**	**.393**	.530	190	**47**				.900	5	*O-112	**4.3**
1886	Lou-a	112	467	86	159	29	6	2	68	30		.340	.389	.441	151	25	26			.791	-10	*O-112	1.1
1887	Lou-a	134	547	137	220	35	16	4	118	55		.402	.464	.547	178	58	103			.868	-3	*O-134	4.2
1888	Lou-a	99	383	58	120	22	8	3	72	37		.313	.380	.436	164	28	36			.888	-1	*O-99	2.2
1889	Lou-a	83	324	39	83	19	5	2	32	34	30	.256	.327	.364	98	-1	21			.882	-3	O-83	-0.5
1890	Cle-P	118	493	112	184	**40**	8	5	93	75	36	**.373**	.459	.517	**175**	**57**	35			.893	4	*O-118	**4.5**
1891	Pit-N	50	203	35	59	14	1	4	28	27	31	.291	.377	.429	138	10	4			.904	5	O-50	1.2
	Cin-N	55	216	29	74	10	3	0	33	24	23	.343	.413	.417	141	12	12			.924	-1	O-55	0.8
	Yr	105	419	64	133	24	4	4	61	51	54	.317	.395	.422	139	22	16			.913	5	*O-105	2.0
1892	Lou-N	21	77	10	19	4	0	0	4	12	7	.247	.348	.299	104	1	5			.911	-1	O-21	-0.1
	Cin-N	83	307	47	93	12	5	3	52	40	25	.303	.383	.404	140	16	8			.917	-2	O-82/1-2	0.9
	Yr	104	384	57	112	16	5	3	56	52	32	.292	.376	.383	133	17	13			.916	-3	*O-103/1-2	0.8
1893	Lou-N	57	220	38	78	11	3	1	37	44	15	.355	.466	.445	155	21	8			.881	-3	O-57	1.2
1894	StL-N	2	7	1	1	0	0	0	0	0	0	.143	.143	.143	-31	-1	0			1.000	-1	/O-2	-0.2
	Bro-N	1	2	1	2	0	0	0	2	1	0	1.000	1.000	1.000	413	1	0			1.000	-0	/O-1	0.1
	Yr	3	9	2	3	0	0	0	2	1	0	.333	.400	.333	80	-0	0			1.000	-1	/O-3	-0.1
Total	13	1183	4820	954	1646	295	85	46	659	466	167	.341	.403	.467	164	384	258			.883	-16	O-998/3-75,2S1P	28.8

■ BILL BRUBAKER

Brubaker, Wilbur Lee b: 11/7/10, Cleveland, Ohio d: 4/2/78, Laguna Hills, Cal. BR/TR, 6'2", 185 lbs. Deb: 9/8/32 F

YEAR	TM/L	G	AB	R	H	2B	3B	HR	RBI	BB	SO	AVG	OBP	SLG	PRO+	BR/A	SB	CS	SBR	FA	FR	G/POS	TPR
1932	Pit-N	7	24	3	10	3	0	0	4	3	4	.417	.481	.542	178	3	1			.909	-0	/3-7	0.3
1933	Pit-N	2	2	0	0	0	0	0	0	0	0	.000	.000	.000	-99	-1	0			1.000	0	/3-1	0.0
1934	Pit-N	3	6	0	2	1	0	0	1	1	0	.333	.429	.500	144	0	0			1.000	1	/3-3	0.1
1935	Pit-N	6	11	1	0	0	0	0	0	2	5	.000	.154	.000	-53	-2	0			.889	-0	/3-5	-0.3
1936	Pit-N	145	554	77	160	27	4	6	102	50	96	.289	.352	.384	96	-2	5			.940	-15	*3-145	-1.2
1937	Pit-N	120	413	57	105	20	4	6	48	47	51	.254	.335	.366	90	-5	2			.952	2	*3-115/S-3,1-1	0.0
1938	Pit-N	45	112	18	33	5	0	3	19	9	14	.295	.347	.420	109	1	2			.875	-1	3-18/1-9,S-3,O-1	0.0
1939	Pit-N	100	345	41	80	23	1	7	43	29	51	.232	.297	.365	78	-11	3			.950	10	2-65,3-32/S-1	0.2
1940	Pit-N	38	78	8	15	3	1	0	7	8	16	.192	.267	.256	45	-6	0			.955	6	3-19/S-8,1-4	0.0
1943	Bos-N	13	19	3	8	3	0	0	1	2	2	.421	.476	.579	207	3	0			.778	-1	/3-5,1-3	0.2
Total	10	479	1564	208	413	85	10	22	225	151	239	.264	.333	.373	90	-20	13			.938	2	3-350/2-65,1-17,SO	-0.7

■ LOU BRUCE

Bruce, Louis R. b: 1/16/1877, St.Regis, N.Y. d: 2/9/68, Ilion, N.Y. BL/TR, 5'5", 145 lbs. Deb: 6/22/04

YEAR	TM/L	G	AB	R	H	2B	3B	HR	RBI	BB	SO	AVG	OBP	SLG	PRO+	BR/A	SB	CS	SBR	FA	FR	G/POS	TPR
1904	Phi-A	30	101	9	27	3	0	0	8	5		.267	.302	.297	85	-2	2			.969	-2	O-25/P-2,2-1,3-1	-0.6

■ EARLE BRUCKER

Brucker, Earle Francis Jr. b: 8/29/25, Los Angeles, Cal. BL/TR, 6'2", 210 lbs. Deb: 10/2/48 F

YEAR	TM/L	G	AB	R	H	2B	3B	HR	RBI	BB	SO	AVG	OBP	SLG	PRO+	BR/A	SB	CS	SBR	FA	FR	G/POS	TPR
1948	Phi-A	2	6	0	1	1	0	0	0	1	1	.167	.286	.333	64	-0	0	0	0	1.000	-0	/C-2	-0.1

■ EARLE BRUCKER

Brucker, Earle Francis Sr. b: 5/6/01, Albany, N.Y. d: 5/8/81, San Diego, Cal. BR/TR, 5'11", 175 lbs. Deb: 4/19/37 FMC

YEAR	TM/L	G	AB	R	H	2B	3B	HR	RBI	BB	SO	AVG	OBP	SLG	PRO+	BR/A	SB	CS	SBR	FA	FR	G/POS	TPR
1937	Phi-A	102	317	40	82	16	5	6	37	48	30	.259	.356	.397	91	-4	1	2	-1	.971	-6	C-92	-0.6
1938	Phi-A	53	171	26	64	21	1	3	35	19	16	.374	.437	.561	152	14	1	1	-0	.986	-2	C-44/1-1	1.3
1939	Phi-A	62	172	18	50	15	1	3	31	24	16	.291	.381	.442	112	3	0	1	-1	1.000	-5	C-47	0.0
1940	Phi-A	23	46	3	9	1	1	0	2	6	3	.196	.288	.261	44	-4	0	0	0	.966	2	C-13	-0.1
1943	Phi-A	1	1	0	0	0	0	0	0	0	0	.000	.000	.000	-99	-0	0	0	0	.000	0	H	0.0
Total	5	241	707	87	205	53	8	12	105	97	65	.290	.376	.438	108	9	2	4	-2	.980	-11	C-196/1-1	0.6

■ J. T. BRUETT

Bruett, Joseph Timothy b: 10/8/67, Milwaukee, Wis. BL/TL, 5'11", 175 lbs. Deb: 6/3/92

YEAR	TM/L	G	AB	R	H	2B	3B	HR	RBI	BB	SO	AVG	OBP	SLG	PRO+	BR/A	SB	CS	SBR	FA	FR	G/POS	TPR
1992	Min-A	56	76	7	19	4	0	0	2	6	12	.250	.313	.303	71	-3	6	3	0	.979	-12	O-45/D-3	-1.6
1993	Min-A	17	20	2	5	2	0	0	1	1	4	.250	.318	.350	79	-1	0	0	0	.857	-4	O-13	-0.5
Total	2	73	96	9	24	6	0	0	3	7	16	.250	.314	.313	73	-3	6	3	0	.952	-16	/O-58,D-3	-2.1

■ FRANK BRUGGY

Bruggy, Frank Leo b: 5/4/1891, Elizabeth, N.J. d: 4/5/59, Elizabeth, N.J. BR/TR, 5'11", 195 lbs. Deb: 4/13/21

YEAR	TM/L	G	AB	R	H	2B	3B	HR	RBI	BB	SO	AVG	OBP	SLG	PRO+	BR/A	SB	CS	SBR	FA	FR	G/POS	TPR
1921	Phi-N	96	277	28	86	11	2	5	28	23	37	.310	.370	.419	100	1	6	2	1	.953	-9	C-86/1-2	-0.3
1922	Phi-A	53	111	10	31	7	0	0	9	6	11	.279	.322	.342	71	-5	1	2	-1	.925	-2	C-31	-0.6
1923	Phi-A	54	105	4	22	3	0	1	6	4	9	.210	.245	.267	34	-10	1	1	-0	.950	0	C-34/1-5	-0.9
1924	Phi-A	50	113	9	30	6	0	0	8	8	15	.265	.314	.319	63	-6	4	0	1	.928	-8	C-44	-1.0
1925	Cin-N	6	14	2	3	0	0	0	1	2	0	.214	.313	.214	38	-1	0	0	0	.870	-0	/C-6	-0.1
Total	5	259	620	53	172	27	2	6	52	43	72	.277	.329	.356	76	-22	12	5	1	.941	-18	C-201/1-7	-2.9

■ JACOB BRUMFIELD

Brumfield, Jacob Donnell b: 5/27/65, Bogalusa, La. BR/TR, 6', 185 lbs. Deb: 4/6/92

YEAR	TM/L	G	AB	R	H	2B	3B	HR	RBI	BB	SO	AVG	OBP	SLG	PRO+	BR/A	SB	CS	SBR	FA	FR	G/POS	TPR
1992	Cin-N	24	30	6	4	0	0	0	2	2	4	.133	.212	.133	-0	-4	6	0	2	1.000	-2	O-16	-0.4
1993	Cin-N	103	272	40	73	17	3	6	23	21	47	.268	.323	.419	97	-2	20	8	1	.978	-5	O-96/2-4	-0.7
1994	Cin-N	68	122	36	38	10	2	4	11	15	18	.311	.387	.525	136	7	6	3	0	.987	-3	O-43	0.3
1995	Pit-N	116	402	64	109	23	2	4	26	37	71	.271	.340	.368	85	-8	22	12	-1	.969	7	*O-104	-0.5
1996	Pit-N	29	80	11	20	9	0	2	8	5	17	.250	.294	.438	87	-2	3	1	0	.946	-2	O-22	-0.4
	Tor-A	90	308	52	79	19	2	12	52	24	58	.256	.318	.448	91	-5	12	3	2	.982	-3	O-83/D-5	-0.8
1997	Tor-A	58	174	22	36	5	1	2	20	14	31	.207	.270	.282	44	-14	4	4	-1	1.000	2	O-47/D-4	-1.4
Total	6	488	1388	231	359	83	10	30	142	118	246	.259	.322	.398	87	-28	73	31	3	.978	-8	O-411/D-9,2-4	-3.9

■ MIKE BRUMLEY

Brumley, Anthony Michael b: 4/9/63, Oklahoma City, Okla. BB/TR, 5'10", 165 lbs. Deb: 6/16/87 F

YEAR	TM/L	G	AB	R	H	2B	3B	HR	RBI	BB	SO	AVG	OBP	SLG	PRO+	BR/A	SB	CS	SBR	FA	FR	G/POS	TPR
1987	Chi-N	39	104	8	21	2	2	1	9	10	30	.202	.278	.288	49	-8	7	1	2	.965	4	S-34/2-1	0.0
1989	Det-A	92	212	33	42	5	2	1	11	14	45	.198	.251	.255	44	-16	8	4	0	.980	-8	S-42,2-24,3-11,/OD	-2.1
1990	Sea-A	62	147	19	33	5	4	0	7	10	22	.224	.274	.313	63	-7	2	0	1	.983	-1	S-47/2-6,3-3,O-2,D	-0.5

YEAR	TM/L	G	AB	R	H	2B	3B	HR	RBI	BB	SO	AVG	OBP	SLG	PRO+	BR/A	SB	CS	SBR	FA	FR	G/POS	TPR
1991	Bos-A	63	118	16	25	5	0	0	5	10	22	.212	.273	.254	45	-9	2	0	1	.950	15	S-31,3-17/2-7,OD	0.8
1992	Bos-A	2	1	0	0	0	0	0	0	0	0	.000	.000	.000	-94	-0	0	0	0	.000	0	/H	0.0
1993	Hou-N	8	10	1	3	0	0	0	2	1	3	.300	.364	.300	83	-0	0	1	-1	.000	-1	/3-1,S-1,O-1	-0.2
1994	Oak-A	11	25	0	6	0	0	0	2	1	8	.240	.269	.240	36	-2	0	0	0	.929	-3	/2-4,3-4,O-3,S-1	-0.5
1995	Hou-N	18	18	1	1	0	0	1	2	0	6	.056	.056	.222	-33	-4	1	0	0	1.000	-1	/S-3,O-3,1-1,3-1	-0.4
Total	8	295	635	78	131	17	8	3	38	46	136	.206	.262	.272	47	-46	20	6	2	.972	5	S-159/2-42,3OD1	-2.9

■ MIKE BRUMLEY Brumley, Tony Mike b: 7/10/38, Granite, Okla. BL/TR, 5'10", 195 lbs. Deb: 4/18/64 F

YEAR	TM/L	G	AB	R	H	2B	3B	HR	RBI	BB	SO	AVG	OBP	SLG	PRO+	BR/A	SB	CS	SBR	FA	FR	G/POS	TPR
1964	Was-A	136	426	36	104	19	2	2	35	40	54	.244	.310	.312	74	-14	1	1	-0	.991	-13	*C-132	-2.3
1965	Was-A	79	216	15	45	4	0	3	15	20	33	.208	.282	.269	58	-12	1	1	-0	.990	2	C-66	-0.8
1966	Was-A	9	18	1	2	1	0	0	0	0	2	.111	.111	.167	-22	-3	0	0	0	1.000	-1	/C-7	-0.4
Total	3	224	660	52	151	24	2	5	50	60	89	.229	.296	.294	67	-29	2	2	-1	.991	-12	C-205	-3.5

■ GLENN BRUMMER Brummer, Glenn Edward b: 11/23/54, Olney, Ill. BR/TR, 6', 200 lbs. Deb: 5/25/81

YEAR	TM/L	G	AB	R	H	2B	3B	HR	RBI	BB	SO	AVG	OBP	SLG	PRO+	BR/A	SB	CS	SBR	FA	FR	G/POS	TPR
1981	StL-N	21	30	2	6	1	0	0	2	1	2	.200	.226	.233	30	-3	0	0	0	1.000	2	C-19	-0.1
1982	*StL-N	35	64	4	15	4	0	0	8	0	12	.234	.234	.297	47	-5	2	0	1	.970	3	C-32	0.0
1983	StL-N	45	87	7	24	7	0	0	9	10	11	.276	.351	.356	96	-0	1	3	-2	.978	0	C-41	0.0
1984	StL-N	28	58	3	12	0	0	1	3	3	7	.207	.246	.259	43	-4	0	0	0	.973	4	C-26	0.0
1985	Tex-A	49	108	7	30	4	0	0	5	11	22	.278	.355	.315	84	-2	1	5	-3	.989	-4	C-47/O-1,D-1	-0.7
Total	5	178	347	23	87	16	0	1	27	25	54	.251	.305	.305	70	-14	4	8	-4	.981	5	C-165/D-1,O-1	-0.8

■ TOM BRUNANSKY Brunansky, Thomas Andrew b: 8/20/60, Covina, Cal. BR/TR, 6'4", 211 lbs. Deb: 4/9/81

YEAR	TM/L	G	AB	R	H	2B	3B	HR	RBI	BB	SO	AVG	OBP	SLG	PRO+	BR/A	SB	CS	SBR	FA	FR	G/POS	TPR
1981	Cal-A	11	33	7	5	0	0	3	6	8	10	.152	.317	.424	112	1	1	0	0	.938	3	O-11	0.3
1982	Min-A	127	463	77	126	30	1	20	46	71	101	.272	.378	.471	128	19	1	2	-1	.986	13	*O-127	2.7
1983	Min-A	151	542	70	123	24	5	28	82	61	95	.227	.310	.445	101	-0	2	5	-2	.985	18	*O-146/D-4	1.1
1984	Min-A	155	567	75	144	21	0	32	85	57	94	.254	.322	.460	109	5	4	5	-2	.984	5	*O-153/D-1	0.4
1985	Min-A★	157	567	71	137	28	4	27	90	71	86	.242	.326	.448	103	2	5	3	-0	.984	5	*O-155	0.2
1986	Min-A	157	593	69	152	28	1	23	75	53	98	.256	.318	.423	97	-3	12	4	1	.982	8	*O-152/D-2	0.1
1987	*Min-A	155	532	83	138	22	2	32	85	74	104	.259	.354	.489	116	12	11	11	-3	.990	-2	*O-138,D-17	0.2
1988	Min-A	14	49	5	9	1	0	1	6	7	11	.184	.286	.265	54	-3	1	2	-1	.864	-2	O-13/D-1	-0.7
	StL-N	143	523	69	128	22	4	22	79	79	82	.245	.348	.428	121	15	16	6	1	**.996**	4	*O-143	1.7
1989	StL-N	158	556	67	133	29	3	20	85	59	107	.239	.314	.410	102	1	5	9	-4	.977	4	*O-155/1-1	-0.3
1990	StL-N	19	57	5	9	3	0	1	2	12	10	.158	.314	.263	60	-3	0	0	0	.950	1	O-17	-0.2
	*Bos-A	129	461	61	123	24	5	15	71	54	105	.267	.347	.438	113	8	5	10	-5	.982	10	*O-121/D-7	1.0
1991	Bos-A	142	459	54	105	24	1	16	70	49	72	.229	.307	.390	87	-9	1	2	-1	.989	3	*O-137/D-1	-1.0
1992	Bos-A	138	458	47	122	31	3	15	74	66	96	.266	.359	.445	116	10	2	5	-2	.980	3	O-92,1-28,D-17	0.7
1993	Mil-A	80	224	20	41	7	3	6	29	25	59	.183	.265	.321	58	-14	3	4	-2	.987	1	O-71/D-6	-1.6
1994	Mil-A	16	28	2	6	2	0	0	0	1	9	.214	.241	.286	34	-3	0	0	0	1.000	-3	/O-6,1-2,D-2	-0.5
	Bos-A	48	177	22	42	10	1	10	34	23	48	.237	.325	.475	98	-1	0	2	-1	.989	-3	O-42/1-5,D-3	-0.6
	Yr	64	205	24	48	12	1	10	34	24	57	.234	.314	.449	90	-4	0	2	-1	.989	-5	O-48/1-7,D-5	-1.1
Total	14	1800	6289	804	1543	306	33	271	919	770	1187	.245	.331	.434	105	39	69	70	-21	.984	65	*O-1679/D-61,1-36	3.5

■ ARLO BRUNSBERG Brunsberg, Arlo Adolph b: 8/15/40, Fertile, Minn. BL/TR, 6', 195 lbs. Deb: 9/23/66

YEAR	TM/L	G	AB	R	H	2B	3B	HR	RBI	BB	SO	AVG	OBP	SLG	PRO+	BR/A	SB	CS	SBR	FA	FR	G/POS	TPR
1966	Det-A	2	3	1	1	1	0	0	0	0	0	.333	.500	.667	227	1	0	0	0	1.000	-1	/C-2	0.0

■ BOB BRUSH Brush, Robert b: 3/8/1875, Osage, Iowa d: 4/2/44, San Bernardino, Cal. Deb: 4/20/07

YEAR	TM/L	G	AB	R	H	2B	3B	HR	RBI	BB	SO	AVG	OBP	SLG	PRO+	BR/A	SB	CS	SBR	FA	FR	G/POS	TPR
1907	Bos-N	2	2	0	0	0	0	0	0	0		.000	.000	.000	-99	-0	0			1.000	-0	/1-1	-0.1

■ BILL BRUTON Bruton, William Haron b: 11/9/25, Panola, Ala. d: 12/5/95, Marshallton, Del. BL/TR, 6'0.5", 169 lbs. Deb: 4/13/53

YEAR	TM/L	G	AB	R	H	2B	3B	HR	RBI	BB	SO	AVG	OBP	SLG	PRO+	BR/A	SB	CS	SBR	FA	FR	G/POS	TPR
1953	Mil-N	151	613	82	153	18	14	1	41	44	100	.250	.306	.330	70	-27	**26**	11	1	.979	8	*O-150	-2.3
1954	Mil-N	142	567	89	161	20	7	4	30	40	78	.284	.336	.365	88	-11	**34**	13	2	.981	1	*O-141	-1.3
1955	Mil-N	149	636	106	175	30	12	9	47	43	72	.275	.325	.403	97	-4	**25**	11	1	.968	15	*O-149	0.4
1956	Mil-N	147	525	73	143	23	**15**	8	56	26	63	.272	.308	.419	99	-3	8	6	-1	.969	3	*O-145	-0.9
1957	Mil-N	79	306	41	85	16	9	5	30	19	35	.278	.322	.438	110	3	11	4	1	.981	1	O-79	0.0
1958	*Mil-N	100	325	47	91	11	3	3	28	27	37	.280	.339	.360	93	-4	4	1	1	.977	-7	O-96	-1.4
1959	Mil-N	133	478	72	138	22	6	6	41	35	54	.289	.339	.397	104	1	13	5	1	.991	4	*O-133	0.0
1960	Mil-N	151	629	**112**	180	27	**13**	12	54	41	97	.286	.332	.428	115	10	22	13	-1	.986	4	*O-149	0.5
1961	Det-A	160	596	99	153	15	5	17	63	61	66	.257	.329	.384	87	-11	22	6	3	.988	12	*O-155	-0.5
1962	Det-A	147	561	90	156	27	5	16	74	55	67	.278	.348	.430	104	3	14	7	0	.983	19	*O-145	1.4
1963	Det-A	145	524	84	134	21	8	8	48	59	70	.256	.331	.372	93	-4	14	7	0	.991	10	*O-138	-0.1
1964	Det-A	106	296	42	82	11	5	5	33	32	54	.277	.348	.399	105	3	14	5	1	.987	-1	O-81	0.0
Total	12	1610	6056	937	1651	241	102	94	545	482	793	.273	.329	.393	96	-43	207	89	9	.981	68	*O-1561	-4.2

■ ED BRUYETTE Bruyette, Edward T. b: 8/31/1874, Manawa, Wis. d: 8/5/40, Peshastin, Wash. BL/TR, 5'10", 170 lbs. Deb: 8/6/01

YEAR	TM/L	G	AB	R	H	2B	3B	HR	RBI	BB	SO	AVG	OBP	SLG	PRO+	BR/A	SB	CS	SBR	FA	FR	G/POS	TPR
1901	Mil-A	26	82	7	15	3	0	0	4	12		.183	.295	.220	46	-5	1			.778	-6	O-21/2-3,S-1,3-1	-1.2

■ BILLY BRYAN Bryan, William Ronald b: 12/4/38, Morgan, Ga. BL/TR, 6'4", 200 lbs. Deb: 9/12/61

YEAR	TM/L	G	AB	R	H	2B	3B	HR	RBI	BB	SO	AVG	OBP	SLG	PRO+	BR/A	SB	CS	SBR	FA	FR	G/POS	TPR
1961	KC-A	9	19	2	3	0	0	1	2	2	7	.158	.238	.316	46	-2	0	0	0	1.000	-2	/C-4	-0.3
1962	KC-A	25	74	5	11	2	1	2	7	5	32	.149	.203	.284	28	-8	0	0	0	.976	-3	C-22	-1.0
1963	KC-A	24	65	11	11	1	1	3	7	9	22	.169	.270	.354	69	-3	0	0	0	.981	5	C-24	0.3
1964	KC-A	93	220	19	53	9	2	13	36	16	69	.241	.292	.477	107	1	0	0	0	.991	-9	C-65	-0.6
1965	KC-A	108	325	36	82	11	5	14	51	29	87	.252	.317	.446	116	6	0	0	0	.984	-6	C-95	0.6
1966	KC-A	32	76	0	10	4	0	0	7	6	17	.132	.195	.184	10	-9	0	0	0	.965	-1	C-21/1-3	-1.0
	NY-A	27	69	5	15	2	0	4	5	5	19	.217	.270	.420	99	-0	0	0	0	.988	-0	C-14/1-3	0.0
	Yr	59	145	5	25	6	0	4	12	11	36	.172	.231	.297	52	-9	0	0	0	.975	-2	C-35/1-6	-1.0
1967	NY-A	16	12	1	2	0	0	1	2	5	3	.167	.412	.417	151	1	0	0	0	1.000	1	/C-1	0.2
1968	Was-A	40	108	7	22	3	0	3	8	14	27	.204	.301	.315	90	-1	0	1	-1	.983	-4	C-28	-0.4
Total	8	374	968	86	209	32	9	41	125	91	283	.216	.285	.395	91	-14	0	1	-1	.984	-18	C-274/1-6	-2.2

■ DEREK BRYANT Bryant, Derek Roszell b: 10/9/51, Lexington, Ky. BR/TR, 5'11", 185 lbs. Deb: 4/24/79

YEAR	TM/L	G	AB	R	H	2B	3B	HR	RBI	BB	SO	AVG	OBP	SLG	PRO+	BR/A	SB	CS	SBR	FA	FR	G/POS	TPR
1979	Oak-A	39	106	8	19	2	1	0	13	10	10	.179	.250	.217	29	-11	0	0	0	1.000	-2	O-33/D-2	-1.4

■ DON BRYANT Bryant, Donald Ray b: 7/13/41, Jasper, Fla. BR/TR, 6'5", 200 lbs. Deb: 7/17/66 C

YEAR	TM/L	G	AB	R	H	2B	3B	HR	RBI	BB	SO	AVG	OBP	SLG	PRO+	BR/A	SB	CS	SBR	FA	FR	G/POS	TPR
1966	Chi-N	13	26	2	8	2	0	0	4	1	4	.308	.357	.385	105	0	1	0	0	.978	0	C-10	0.1
1969	Hou-N	31	59	2	11	1	0	1	6	4	13	.186	.250	.254	42	-5	0	0	0	.993	3	C-28	-0.1
1970	Hou-N	15	24	2	5	0	0	0	3	1	8	.208	.240	.208	22	-3	0	0	0	.957	-0	C-13	-0.3
Total	3	59	109	6	24	3	0	1	13	6	25	.220	.274	.275	53	-7	1	0	0	.983	3	/C-51	-0.3

■ GEORGE BRYANT Bryant, George F. b: 2/10/1857, Bridgeport, Conn. d: 6/12/07, Boston, Mass. Deb: 8/6/1885

YEAR	TM/L	G	AB	R	H	2B	3B	HR	RBI	BB	SO	AVG	OBP	SLG	PRO+	BR/A	SB	CS	SBR	FA	FR	G/POS	TPR
1885	Det-N	1	4	0	0	0	0	0	1	0	2	.000	.000	.000	-99	-1				1.000	-1	/2-1	-0.2

■ RALPH BRYANT Bryant, Ralph Wendell b: 5/20/61, Fort Gaines, Ga. BL/TR, 6'2", 200 lbs. Deb: 9/8/85

YEAR	TM/L	G	AB	R	H	2B	3B	HR	RBI	BB	SO	AVG	OBP	SLG	PRO+	BR/A	SB	CS	SBR	FA	FR	G/POS	TPR
1985	LA-N	6	6	0	2	0	0	0	1	0	2	.333	.333	.333	90	-0	0	0	0	.000	-1	/O-3	-0.1
1986	LA-N	27	75	15	19	4	2	6	13	5	25	.253	.309	.600	156	5	0	1	-1	.953	-1	O-26	0.3
1987	LA-N	46	69	7	17	2	1	2	10	10	24	.246	.350	.391	99	0	2	1	0	.917	-3	O-19	-0.4
Total	3	79	150	22	38	6	3	8	24	15	51	.253	.329	.493	125	5	2	2	-1	.940	-5	/O-48	-0.2

■ STEVE BRYE Brye, Stephen Robert b: 2/4/49, Alameda, Cal. BR/TR, 6', 190 lbs. Deb: 9/3/70

YEAR	TM/L	G	AB	R	H	2B	3B	HR	RBI	BB	SO	AVG	OBP	SLG	PRO+	BR/A	SB	CS	SBR	FA	FR	G/POS	TPR
1970	Min-A	9	11	1	2	1	0	0	2	2	4	.182	.308	.273	60	-1	0	0	0	1.000	-2	/O-6	-0.2
1971	Min-A	28	107	10	24	1	0	3	11	7	15	.224	.272	.318	65	-5	3	1	0	.966	1	O-28	-0.6
1972	Min-A	100	253	18	61	9	3	0	12	17	38	.241	.292	.300	73	-8	3	1	0	.994	2	O-93	-1.0
1973	Min-A	92	278	39	73	9	5	6	33	35	43	.263	.345	.396	104	2	3	5	-2	.986	1	O-87/D-1	-0.3

YEAR	TM/L	G	AB	R	H	2B	3B	HR	RBI	BB	SO	AVG	OBP	SLG	PRO+	BR/A	SB	CS	SBR	FA	FR	G/POS	TPR
1974	Min-A	135	488	52	138	32	1	2	41	22	59	.283	.320	.365	94	-4	1	3	-2	**.997**	1	*O-129	-1.1
1975	Min-A	86	246	41	62	13	1	9	34	21	37	.252	.316	.423	106	1	2	1	0	.983	-3	O-72/D-6	-0.4
1976	Min-A	87	258	33	68	11	0	2	23	13	31	.264	.299	.329	82	-6	1	2	-1	.987	-13	O-78/D-3	-2.4
1977	Mil-A	94	241	27	60	14	3	7	28	16	39	.249	.298	.419	93	-3	1	0	0	1.000	-1	O-83/D-6	-0.6
1978	Pit-N	66	115	16	27	7	0	1	9	11	10	.235	.307	.322	73	-4	2	1	0	.983	-6	O-47	-1.2
Total	9	697	1997	237	515	97	13	30	193	144	276	.258	.311	.365	90	-29	16	14	-4	.991	-19	O-623/D-16	-7.8

■ HAL BUBSER
Bubser, Harold Fred b: 9/28/1895, Chicago, Ill. d: 6/22/59, Melrose Park, Ill BR/TR, 5'11", 170 lbs. Deb: 4/15/22

YEAR	TM/L	G	AB	R	H	2B	3B	HR	RBI	BB	SO	AVG	OBP	SLG	PRO+	BR/A	SB	CS	SBR	FA	FR	G/POS	TPR
1922	Chi-A	3	3	0	0	0	0	0	0	0	2	.000	.000	.000	-99	-1	0	0	0	.000	0	H	-0.1

■ JOHNNY BUCHA
Bucha, John George b: 1/22/25, Allentown, Pa. d: 4/28/96, Bethlehem, Pa. BR/TR, 5'11", 190 lbs. Deb: 5/2/48

YEAR	TM/L	G	AB	R	H	2B	3B	HR	RBI	BB	SO	AVG	OBP	SLG	PRO+	BR/A	SB	CS	SBR	FA	FR	G/POS	TPR
1948	StL-N	2	1	0	0	0	0	0	0	1	0	.000	.500	.000	43	0	0			1.000	-0	/C-1	0.0
1950	StL-N	22	36	1	5	1	0	0	1	4	7	.139	.225	.167	5	-5	0			.959	0	C-17	-0.5
1953	Det-A	60	158	17	35	9	0	1	14	20	14	.222	.309	.297	65	-8	1	1	-0	.984	-4	C-56	-1.0
Total	3	84	195	18	40	10	0	1	15	25	21	.205	.295	.272	53	-12	1	1		.980	-4	/C-74	-1.5

■ JERRY BUCHEK
Buchek, Gerald Peter b: 5/9/42, St.Louis, Mo. BR/TR, 5'11", 185 lbs. Deb: 6/30/61

YEAR	TM/L	G	AB	R	H	2B	3B	HR	RBI	BB	SO	AVG	OBP	SLG	PRO+	BR/A	SB	CS	SBR	FA	FR	G/POS	TPR
1961	StL-N	31	90	6	12	2	0	0	9	0	28	.133	.152	.156	-16	-15	0	0	0	.912	-6	S-31	-1.9
1963	StL-N	3	4	0	1	0	0	0	0	0	2	.250	.250	.250	41	-0	0	0	0	1.000	0	/S-1	0.0
1964	*StL-N	35	30	7	6	0	2	0	1	3	11	.200	.273	.333	64	-1	0	0	0	.929	7	S-20/2-9,3-1	0.6
1965	StL-N	55	166	17	41	8	3	3	21	13	46	.247	.302	.386	84	-4	1	0	0	.994	10	2-33,S-18/3-1	1.1
1966	StL-N	100	284	23	67	10	4	4	25	23	71	.236	.293	.342	75	-9	0	5	-3	.974	-13	2-49,S-48/3-4	-2.0
1967	NY-N	124	411	35	97	11	2	14	41	26	101	.236	.285	.375	89	-7	3	5	-2	.977	4	2-95,3-17/S-9	0.1
1968	NY-N	73	192	8	35	4	0	1	11	10	53	.182	.234	.219	36	-15	1	1	-0	.935	-1	3-37,2-12/O-9	-1.8
Total	7	421	1177	96	259	35	11	22	108	75	312	.220	.271	.325	67	-51	5	11	-5	.978	2	2-198,S-127/3-60,O	-3.9

■ JIM BUCHER
Bucher, James Quinter b: 3/11/11, Manassas, Va. BL/TR, 5'11", 170 lbs. Deb: 4/18/34

YEAR	TM/L	G	AB	R	H	2B	3B	HR	RBI	BB	SO	AVG	OBP	SLG	PRO+	BR/A	SB	CS	SBR	FA	FR	G/POS	TPR
1934	Bro-N	47	84	12	19	5	2	0	8	4	7	.226	.261	.333	61	-5	1			.920	-1	2-20/3-6	-0.5
1935	Bro-N	123	473	72	143	22	1	7	58	10	33	.302	.317	.397	93	-6	4			.950	-11	2-41,3-39,O-37	-1.4
1936	Bro-N	110	370	49	93	12	8	2	41	29	27	.251	.306	.343	74	-14	5			.910	-8	3-39,2-32,O-30	-2.0
1937	Bro-N	125	380	44	96	11	2	4	37	20	18	.253	.295	.324	67	-18	5			.951	-14	2-49,3-43/O-6	-2.7
1938	StL-N	17	57	7	13	3	1	0	7	2	2	.228	.254	.316	53	-4	0			.955	-4	2-14/3-1	-0.7
1944	Bos-A	80	277	39	76	9	2	4	31	19	13	.274	.326	.365	98	-1	3	3	-1	.958	-9	3-44,2-21	-1.0
1945	Bos-A	52	151	19	34	4	3	0	11	7	13	.225	.264	.291	60	-8	1	3	-2	.940	-2	3-32/2-2	-1.1
Total	7	554	1792	242	474	66	19	17	193	91	113	.265	.302	.351	78	-55	19	6		.939	-48	3-204,2-179/O-73	-9.4

■ KEVIN BUCKLEY
Buckley, Kevin John b: 1/16/59, Quincy, Mass. BR/TR, 6'1", 200 lbs. Deb: 9/4/84

YEAR	TM/L	G	AB	R	H	2B	3B	HR	RBI	BB	SO	AVG	OBP	SLG	PRO+	BR/A	SB	CS	SBR	FA	FR	G/POS	TPR
1984	Tex-A	5	7	1	2	1	0	0	0	2	4	.286	.444	.429	138	0	0	0	0	.000	0	/D-3	0.0

■ DICK BUCKLEY
Buckley, Richard D. b: 9/21/1858, Troy, N.Y. d: 12/12/29, Pittsburgh, Pa. TR , 5'10", 195 lbs. Deb: 4/20/1888

YEAR	TM/L	G	AB	R	H	2B	3B	HR	RBI	BB	SO	AVG	OBP	SLG	PRO+	BR/A	SB	CS	SBR	FA	FR	G/POS	TPR
1888	Ind-N	71	260	28	71	9	3	5	22	6	24	.273	.289	.388	112	3	4			.898	-21	C-51,3-22/O-1,1-1	-1.3
1889	Ind-N	68	260	35	67	11	0	8	41	15	32	.258	.301	.392	91	-5	5			.877	-21	C-55,3-12/O-1,1-1	-1.8
1890	NY-N	70	266	39	68	11	0	2	26	23	35	.256	.324	.320	88	-4	3			.931	9	C-62/3-8	1.0
1891	NY-N	75	253	23	55	9	1	4	31	11	30	.217	.258	.308	67	-11	3			.958	19	C-74/3-1	1.2
1892	StL-N	121	410	43	93	17	4	5	52	22	34	.227	.275	.324	85	-9	7			.937	-5	*C-119/1-2	-0.5
1893	StL-N	9	23	2	4	1	0	0	1	0	0	.174	.174	.217	4	-3	0			.914	1	/C-9	-0.1
1894	StL-N	29	89	5	16	1	2	1	3	6	3	.180	.240	.270	23	-12	1			.936	2	C-27/1-1	-0.6
	Phi-N	43	160	18	47	7	3	1	26	6	13	.294	.327	.394	75	-7	0			.966	3	C-42/1-1	0.0
	Yr	72	249	23	63	8	5	2	29	12	16	.253	.295	.349	56	-19	1			.954	4	C-69/1-2	-0.6
1895	Phi-N	38	112	20	28	6	1	0	14	9	17	.250	.333	.321	69	-5	2			.919	6	C-38	0.3
Total	8	524	1833	213	449	72	14	26	216	98	188	.245	.291	.342	81	-53	25			.931	-7	C-477/3-43,1-6,O-2	-1.8

■ BILL BUCKNER
Buckner, William Joseph b: 12/14/49, Vallejo, Cal. BL/TL, 6', 185 lbs. Deb: 9/21/69 C

YEAR	TM/L	G	AB	R	H	2B	3B	HR	RBI	BB	SO	AVG	OBP	SLG	PRO+	BR/A	SB	CS	SBR	FA	FR	G/POS	TPR
1969	LA-N	1	1	0	0	0	0	0	0	0	0	.000	.000	.000	-99	-0	0	0	0	.000	0	H	0.0
1970	LA-N	28	68	6	13	3	1	0	4	3	7	.191	.225	.265	32	-7	0	1	-1	1.000	1	O-20/1-1	-0.7
1971	LA-N	108	358	37	99	15	1	5	41	11	18	.277	.307	.366	96	-3	4	1	1	.994	2	O-86,1-11	-0.6
1972	LA-N	105	383	47	122	14	3	5	37	17	13	.319	.349	.410	118	8	10	3	1	.992	-3	O-61,1-35	0.1
1973	LA-N	140	575	68	158	20	0	8	46	17	34	.275	.299	.351	83	-15	12	2	2	.998	-3	1-93,O-48	-2.6
1974	*LA-N	145	580	83	182	30	3	7	58	30	24	.314	.352	.412	118	12	31	13	2	.976	-3	*O-137/1-6	0.4
1975	LA-N	92	288	30	70	11	2	6	31	17	15	.243	.290	.358	82	-8	8	3	1	.986	2	O-72	-0.9
1976	LA-N	154	642	76	193	28	4	7	60	26	26	.301	.329	.389	105	2	28	9	3	.985	7	*O-153/1-1	0.6
1977	Chi-N	122	426	40	121	27	0	11	60	21	23	.284	.319	.425	88	-8	7	5	-1	.990	-0	1-99	-1.5
1978	Chi-N	117	446	47	144	26	1	5	74	18	17	.323	.349	.419	102	0	7	5	-1	.995	8	*1-105	0.1
1979	Chi-N	149	591	72	168	34	7	14	66	30	28	.284	.321	.437	96	-5	9	4	0	.995	18	*1-140	0.5
1980	Chi-N	145	578	69	187	41	3	10	68	30	18	**.324**	.357	.457	117	12	1	2	-1	.993	8	1-94,O-50	1.2
1981	Chi-N★	106	421	45	131	**35**	3	10	75	26	16	.311	.353	.480	129	14	5	2	0	.984	1	*1-105	1.0
1982	Chi-N	161	657	93	201	34	5	15	105	36	26	.306	.347	.441	116	13	15	5	2	.993	16	*1-161	2.2
1983	Chi-N	153	626	79	175	**38**	6	16	66	25	30	.280	.313	.436	101	-2	12	4	1	.992	21	*1-144,O-15	1.2
1984	Chi-N	21	43	3	9	0	0	0	2	1	1	.209	.244	.209	26	-4	0	0	0	1.000	2	/1-7,O-2	-0.3
	Bos-A	114	439	51	122	21	2	11	67	24	38	.278	.323	.410	97	-2	2	2	-1	.986	5	*1-113	-0.6
1985	Bos-A	162	673	89	201	46	3	16	110	30	36	.299	.330	.447	106	4	18	4	3	.992	25	*1-162	2.2
1986	*Bos-A	153	629	73	168	39	2	18	102	40	25	.267	.315	.421	98	-3	6	4	-1	.989	20	*1-138,D-15	0.6
1987	Bos-A	75	286	23	78	6	1	2	42	13	19	.273	.304	.322	65	-14	1	3	-2	.991	3	1-74	-1.7
	Cal-A	57	183	16	56	12	1	3	32	9	7	.306	.339	.432	106	1	1	0	0	1.000	-0	D-39/1-5	0.0
	Yr	132	469	39	134	18	2	5	74	22	26	.286	.318	.365	80	-13	2	3	-1	.992	3	1-79,D-39	-1.7
1988	Cal-A	19	43	1	9	0	0	0	9	4	0	.209	.277	.209	39	-3	2	0	0	1.000	0	D-11/1-1	-0.3
	KC-A	89	242	18	62	14	0	3	34	13	19	.256	.294	.351	79	-7	3	1	0	.994	-0	D-42,1-21	-1.0
	Yr	108	285	19	71	14	0	3	43	17	19	.249	.291	.330	73	-10	5	1	1	.994	0	D-53,1-22	-1.3
1989	KC-A	79	176	7	38	4	1	1	16	6	11	.216	.242	.267	43	-13	1	0	0	.985	-0	1-24,D-19	-1.6
1990	Bos-A	22	43	4	8	0	0	1	3	3	2	.186	.239	.256	37	-4	0	0	0	1.000	-0	1-15	-0.5
Total	22	2517	9397	1077	2715	498	49	174	1208	450	453	.289	.324	.408	99	-31	183	73	11	.992	127	*1-1555,O-644,D-126	-2.2

■ MARK BUDASKA
Budaska, Mark David b: 12/27/52, Sharon, Pa. BB/TL, 6', 180 lbs. Deb: 6/6/78

YEAR	TM/L	G	AB	R	H	2B	3B	HR	RBI	BB	SO	AVG	OBP	SLG	PRO+	BR/A	SB	CS	SBR	FA	FR	G/POS	TPR
1978	Oak-A	4	4	0	1	1	0	0	0	1	2	.250	.400	.500	160	0	0	0	0	.500	-1	/O-2	-0.1
1981	Oak-A	9	32	3	5	1	0	0	2	4	10	.156	.250	.188	29	-3	0	1	-1	.000	0	/D-9	-0.4
Total	2	13	36	3	6	2	0	0	2	5	12	.167	.268	.222	44	-3	0	1	-1	.500	-1	/D-9,O-2	-0.5

■ BUDD
Budd b: Cleveland, Ohio Deb: 9/10/1890

YEAR	TM/L	G	AB	R	H	2B	3B	HR	RBI	BB	SO	AVG	OBP	SLG	PRO+	BR/A	SB	CS	SBR	FA	FR	G/POS	TPR
1890	Cle-P	1	4	0	0	0	0	0	0	0	3	.000	.000	.000	-99	-1	0			1.000	-0	/O-1	-0.1

■ DON BUDDIN
Buddin, Donald Thomas b: 5/5/34, Turbeville, S.C. BR/TR, 5'11", 178 lbs. Deb: 4/17/56

YEAR	TM/L	G	AB	R	H	2B	3B	HR	RBI	BB	SO	AVG	OBP	SLG	PRO+	BR/A	SB	CS	SBR	FA	FR	G/POS	TPR
1956	Bos-A	114	377	49	90	24	0	5	37	65	62	.239	.357	.342	76	-12	2	0	1	.953	14	*S-113	1.1
1958	Bos-A	136	497	74	118	25	2	12	43	82	106	.237	.350	.368	92	-4	0	4	-2	.958	15	*S-136	2.1
1959	Bos-A	151	485	75	117	24	1	10	53	92	99	.241	.368	.357	95	0	6	1	1	.949	-17	*S-150	-0.3
1960	Bos-A	124	428	62	105	21	5	6	36	62	59	.245	.342	.360	87	-7	4	2	0	.951	-5	*S-124	-0.2
1961	Bos-A	115	339	58	89	22	3	6	42	72	45	.263	.395	.398	110	8	2	1	0	.956	-1	*S-109	1.5
1962	Hou-N	40	80	10	13	4	1	2	10	17	17	.162	.316	.313	75	-3	0	0	0	.952	3	S-27/3-9	0.2
	Det-A	31	83	14	19	3	0	0	4	20	16	.229	.385	.265	76	-2	1	0	0	.978	-2	S-19/2-5,3-2	-0.2
Total	6	711	2289	342	551	123	12	41	225	410	404	.241	.360	.359	90	-19	15	8	-0	.954	7	S-678/3-11,2-5	4.2

■ STEVE BUECHELE
Buechele, Steven Bernard b: 9/26/61, Lancaster, Cal. BR/TR, 6'2", 190 lbs. Deb: 7/19/85

YEAR	TM/L	G	AB	R	H	2B	3B	HR	RBI	BB	SO	AVG	OBP	SLG	PRO+	BR/A	SB	CS	SBR	FA	FR	G/POS	TPR
1985	Tex-A	69	219	22	48	6	3	6	21	14	38	.219	.272	.356	70	-10	3	2	-0	.969	6	3-69/2-1	-0.4

YEAR	TM/L	G	AB	R	H	2B	3B	HR	RBI	BB	SO	AVG	OBP	SLG	PRO+	BR/A	SB	CS	SBR	FA	FR	G/POS	TPR
1986	Tex-A	153	461	54	112	19	2	18	54	35	98	.243	.303	.410	90	-7	5	8	-3	.968	19	*3-137,2-33/O-2	0.6
1987	Tex-A	136	363	45	86	20	0	13	50	28	66	.237	.293	.399	81	-11	2	2	-1	.964	3	*3-123,2-18/O-2	-0.9
1988	Tex-A	155	503	68	126	21	4	16	58	65	79	.250	.342	.404	105	4	2	4	-2	.962	8	*3-153/2-2	1.0
1989	Tex-A	155	486	60	114	22	2	16	59	36	107	.235	.294	.387	89	-8	1	3	-2	.969	15	*3-145,2-18/S-1,D-1	0.7
1990	Tex-A	91	251	30	54	10	0	7	30	27	63	.215	.296	.339	77	-8	1	0	0	.966	6	3-88/2-4	-0.1
1991	Tex-A	121	416	58	111	17	2	18	66	39	69	.267	.337	.447	117	9	0	4	-2	**.991**	20	*3-111,2-13/S-4	2.7
	*Pit-N	31	114	16	28	5	1	4	19	10	28	.246	.317	.412	105	1	0	1	-1	.956	3	3-31	0.3
1992	Pit-N	80	285	27	71	14	1	8	43	34	61	.249	.333	.389	105	2	0	2	-1	.957	6	3-80	0.8
	Chi-N	65	239	25	66	9	3	1	21	18	44	.276	.340	.351	94	-2	1	1	-0	.960	-2	3-63/2-2	-0.5
	Yr	145	524	52	137	23	4	9	64	52	105	.261	.336	.372	100	1	1	3	-2	.958	4	*3-143/2-2	0.3
1993	Chi-N	133	460	53	125	27	2	15	65	48	87	.272	.347	.437	110	6	1	1	-0	**.975**	1	*3-129/1-6	0.7
1994	Chi-N	104	339	33	82	11	1	14	52	39	80	.242	.327	.404	91	-5	1	0	0	.974	-10	3-99/1-6,2-1	-1.4
1995	Chi-N	32	106	10	20	2	0	1	9	11	19	.189	.265	.236	34	-10	0	0	0	.942	0	3-32	-1.0
	Tex-A	9	24	0	3	0	0	0	0	4	3	.125	.250	.125	1	-3	0	0	0	1.000	-0	/3-9	-0.3
Total	11	1334	4266	501	1046	183	21	137	547	408	842	.245	.317	.394	94	-41	17	28	-12	.968	75	*3-1269/2-92,1SOD	2.2

■ CHARLIE BUELOW

Buelow, Charles John b: 1/12/1877, Dubuque, Iowa d: 5/4/51, Dubuque, Iowa BR/TR, Deb: 6/1/01

YEAR	TM/L	G	AB	R	H	2B	3B	HR	RBI	BB	SO	AVG	OBP	SLG	PRO+	BR/A	SB	CS	SBR	FA	FR	G/POS	TPR
1901	NY-N	22	72	3	8	4	0	0	4	2		.111	.147	.167	-10	-10	0			.853	3	3-17/2-2	-0.7

■ FRITZ BUELOW

Buelow, Frederick William Alexander b: 2/13/1876, Berlin, Germany d: 12/27/33, Detroit, Mich. BR/TR, 5′10.5″, 170 lbs. Deb: 9/28/1899

YEAR	TM/L	G	AB	R	H	2B	3B	HR	RBI	BB	SO	AVG	OBP	SLG	PRO+	BR/A	SB	CS	SBR	FA	FR	G/POS	TPR
1899	StL-N	7	15	4	7	0	2	0	2	2		.467	.556	.733	247	3	0			1.000	-2	/C-4,O-2	0.1
1900	StL-N	6	17	2	4	0	0	0	3	0		.235	.235	.235	30	-2	0			.864	-1	/C-4,O-1	-0.2
1901	Det-A	70	231	28	52	5	5	2	29	11		.225	.269	.316	59	-13	2			.967	5	C-69	-0.2
1902	Det-A	66	224	23	50	5	2	2	29	9		.223	.256	.290	50	-15	3			.927	0	C-63/1-2	-0.8
1903	Det-A	63	192	24	41	3	6	1	13	6		.214	.249	.307	68	-8	4			.961	1	C-60/1-2	-0.1
1904	Det-A	42	136	6	15	1	1	0	5	8		.110	.160	.132	-7	-16	2			.975	1	C-42	-1.3
	Cle-A	42	119	11	21	4	1	0	5	11		.176	.252	.227	52	-6	2			.979	1	C-42	-0.1
	Yr	84	255	17	36	5	2	0	10	19		.141	.204	.176	21	-22	4			.977	1	C-84	-1.4
1905	Cle-A	75	239	11	41	4	1	1	18	6		.172	.198	.209	29	-19	7			.960	-7	C-60/O-8,1-3,3-2	-2.2
1906	Cle-A	34	86	7	14	2	0	0	7	9		.163	.250	.186	38	-6	0			.938	3	C-33/1-1	-0.1
1907	StL-A	26	75	9	11	1	0	0	1	7		.147	.220	.160	21	-6	0			.983	1	C-25	-0.4
Total	9	431	1334	125	256	25	18	6	112	69		.192	.238	.251	46	-89	20			.960	1	C-402/O-11,1-8,3-2	-5.3

■ ART BUES

Bues, Arthur Frederick b: 3/3/1888, Milwaukee, Wis. d: 11/7/54, Whitefish Bay, Wis. BR/TR, 5′11″, 184 lbs. Deb: 4/17/13

YEAR	TM/L	G	AB	R	H	2B	3B	HR	RBI	BB	SO	AVG	OBP	SLG	PRO+	BR/A	SB	CS	SBR	FA	FR	G/POS	TPR
1913	Bos-N	2	1	0	0	0	0	0	0	0	1	.000	.000	.000	-98	-0	0			.000	0	/2-1,3-1	0.0
1914	Chi-N	14	45	3	10	1	1	0	4	5	6	.222	.300	.289	76	-1	1			.968	-2	3-12	-0.4
Total	2	16	46	3	10	1	1	0	4	5	7	.217	.294	.283	72	-2	1			.968	-2	/3-13,2-1	-0.4

■ CHARLIE BUFFINTON

Buffinton, Charles G. b: 6/14/1861, Fall River, Mass. d: 9/23/07, Fall River, Mass. BR/TR, 6′1″, 180 lbs. Deb: 5/17/1882 M

YEAR	TM/L	G	AB	R	H	2B	3B	HR	RBI	BB	SO	AVG	OBP	SLG	PRO+	BR/A	SB	CS	SBR	FA	FR	G/POS	TPR
1882	Bos-N	15	50	5	13	1	0	0	4	2	3	.260	.288	.280	83	-1				.615	-1	/O-7,P-5,1-4	-0.2
1883	Bos-N	86	341	28	81	8	3	1	26	6	24	.238	.251	.287	62	-16				.756	-7	O-51,P-43/1-2	-1.4
1884	Bos-N	87	352	48	94	18	3	1	39	16	12	.267	.299	.344	102	1				.946	-1	P-67,O-13,1-11	-0.5
1885	Bos-N	82	338	26	81	12	3	1	33	3	26	.240	.246	.302	79	-8				.912	-0	P-51,O-18,1-15	-1.1
1886	Bos-N	44	176	27	51	4	1	1	30	6	12	.290	.313	.341	103	1	3			.968	-6	1-19,P-18/O-9	-0.7
1887	Phi-N	66	269	34	72	12	1	1	46	11	3	.268	.299	.331	71	-11	8			.931	2	P-40,O-22,1-10	-0.9
1888	Phi-N	46	160	14	29	4	1	0	12	7	5	.181	.216	.219	37	-11	1			.939	9	P-46/O-1	0.0
1889	Phi-N	47	154	16	32	2	0	0	21	9	5	.208	.256	.221	31	-15	0			.916	1	P-47/O-1	0.0
1890	Phi-P	42	150	24	41	3	2	1	24	9	3	.273	.319	.340	74	-6	1			.864	0	P-36/O-5,1-3,M	-0.1
1891	Bos-a	58	181	16	34	2	1	1	16	19	15	.188	.269	.227	43	-13	0			.934	3	P-48,O-10/1-4	-0.5
1892	Bal-N	13	43	7	15	1	1	0	4	3	6	.349	.391	.419	141	2	1			.892	2	P-13	0.0
Total	11	586	2214	245	543	67	16	7	255	91	114	.245	.276	.299	72	-78	14			.916	2	P-414,O-137/1-68	-5.4

■ DAMON BUFORD

Buford, Damon Jackson b: 6/12/70, Baltimore, Md. BR/TR, 5′10″, 170 lbs. Deb: 5/4/93 F

YEAR	TM/L	G	AB	R	H	2B	3B	HR	RBI	BB	SO	AVG	OBP	SLG	PRO+	BR/A	SB	CS	SBR	FA	FR	G/POS	TPR
1993	Bal-A	53	79	18	18	5	0	2	9	9	19	.228	.315	.367	79	-2	2	2	-1	.984	-1	O-30,D-17	-0.5
1994	Bal-A	4	2	2	1	0	0	0	0	0	1	.500	.500	.500	151	0	0	0	0	.000	-0	/O-1,D-1	0.0
1995	Bal-A	24	32	6	2	0	0	0	2	6	7	.063	.211	.063	-24	-6	3	1	0	1.000	-2	O-24	-0.8
	NY-N	44	136	24	32	5	0	4	12	19	28	.235	.350	.360	91	-1	7	7	-2	.972	-1	O-39	-0.5
1996	*Tex-A	90	145	30	41	9	0	6	20	15	34	.283	.350	.469	99	-0	8	5	-1	1.000	-15	O-80	-1.5
1997	Tex-A	122	366	49	82	18	0	8	39	30	83	.224	.288	.339	60	-22	18	7	1	.990	5	*O-117/D-3	-1.8
1998	*Bos-A	86	216	37	61	14	4	10	42	22	43	.282	.351	.523	123	7	5	5	-2	1.000	-4	O-67,D-15/2-1,3-1	0.0
Total	6	423	976	166	237	51	4	30	124	101	215	.243	.320	.395	83	-25	43	27	-3	.991	-18	O-358/D-36,3-1,2-1	-5.1

■ DON BUFORD

Buford, Donald Alvin b: 2/2/37, Linden, Tex. BB/TR, 5′8″, 165 lbs. Deb: 9/14/63 FC

YEAR	TM/L	G	AB	R	H	2B	3B	HR	RBI	BB	SO	AVG	OBP	SLG	PRO+	BR/A	SB	CS	SBR	FA	FR	G/POS	TPR
1963	Chi-A	12	42	9	12	1	2	0	5	5	7	.286	.362	.405	116	1	1	0	0	.955	-5	/3-9,2-2	-0.3
1964	Chi-A	135	442	62	116	14	6	4	30	46	62	.262	.339	.348	94	-3	12	7	-1	.968	-16	2-92,3-37	-1.3
1965	Chi-A	155	586	93	166	22	5	10	47	67	76	.283	.361	.389	120	17	17	7	1	.981	3	*2-139,3-41	3.3
1966	Chi-A	163	607	85	148	26	7	8	52	69	71	.244	.324	.349	100	1	51	22	2	.939	1	*3-133,2-37,O-11	0.4
1967	Chi-A	156	535	61	129	10	9	4	32	65	51	.241	.324	.316	93	-3	34	21	-2	.948	4	*3-121,2-51/O-1	0.0
1968	Bal-A	130	426	65	120	13	4	15	46	57	46	.282	.372	.437	144	24	27	12	1	1.000	-6	O-65,2-58/3-2	2.0
1969	*Bal-A	144	554	99	161	31	3	11	64	96	62	.291	.400	.417	128	24	19	18	-5	.983	-4	*O-128,2-10/3-6	0.9
1970	*Bal-A	144	504	99	137	15	2	17	66	109	55	.272	.409	.411	125	23	16	8	0	.987	6	*O-130/2-3,3-3	2.3
1971	*Bal-A★	122	449	**99**	130	19	4	19	54	89	62	.290	.415	.477	153	35	15	7	0	.987	3	*O-115	3.5
1972	Bal-A	125	408	46	84	6	2	5	22	69	83	.206	.326	.267	76	-9	8	3	1	.989	-1	*O-105	-1.6
Total	10	1286	4553	718	1203	157	44	93	418	672	575	.264	.364	.379	115	109	200	105	-3	.988	-15	O-555,2-392,3-352	9.2

■ JAY BUHNER

Buhner, Jay Campbell b: 8/13/64, Louisville, Ky. BR/TR, 6′3″, 205 lbs. Deb: 9/11/87

YEAR	TM/L	G	AB	R	H	2B	3B	HR	RBI	BB	SO	AVG	OBP	SLG	PRO+	BR/A	SB	CS	SBR	FA	FR	G/POS	TPR
1987	NY-A	7	22	0	5	2	0	0	1	1	6	.227	.261	.318	53	-2	0	0	0	1.000	0	/O-7	-0.2
1988	NY-A	25	69	8	13	0	0	3	13	3	25	.188	.253	.319	60	-4	0	0	0	.964	1	O-22	-0.4
	Sea-A	60	192	28	43	13	1	10	25	25	68	.224	.323	.458	111	3	1	1	-0	.993	9	O-59	1.0
	Yr	85	261	36	56	13	1	13	38	28	93	.215	.305	.421	98	-1	1	1	-0	.985	10	O-81	0.6
1989	Sea-A	58	204	27	56	15	1	9	33	19	55	.275	.342	.490	128	7	1	4	-2	.966	1	O-57	0.4
1990	Sea-A	51	163	16	45	12	0	7	33	17	50	.276	.359	.479	131	7	2	2	-1	.966	-4	O-40,D-10	0.1
1991	Sea-A	137	406	64	99	14	4	27	77	53	117	.244	.340	.498	128	15	0	1	-1	.981	6	*O-131	1.7
1992	Sea-A	152	543	69	132	16	3	25	79	71	146	.243	.337	.422	111	8	0	6	-4	.994	11	*O-150	1.2
1993	Sea-A	158	563	91	153	28	3	27	98	100	144	.272	.383	.476	128	24	2	5	-2	.978	-2	*O-148,D-10	1.5
1994	Sea-A	101	358	74	100	23	4	21	68	66	63	.279	.399	.542	137	21	0	1	-1	.990	6	O-96/D-4	2.2
1995	*Sea-A	126	470	86	123	23	0	40	121	60	120	.262	.347	.566	131	19	0	1	-1	.989	-3	*O-120/D-4	1.2
1996	Sea-A★	150	564	107	153	29	0	44	138	84	159	.271	.374	.557	131	26	0	1	-1	.989	-0	*O-142/D-8	2.0
1997	*Sea-A	157	540	104	131	18	2	40	109	119	175	.243	.384	.506	131	27	0	0	0	**.997**	4	*O-154/D-2	2.6
1998	Sea-A	72	244	33	59	7	1	15	45	38	71	.242	.346	.463	108	3	0	0	0	.985	2	O-70/D-1	0.3
Total	12	1254	4338	707	1112	200	19	268	840	656	1199	.256	.360	.497	125	154	6	22	-11	.986	29	*O-1196/D-39	13.6

■ HARRY BUKER

Buker, Henry L. "Happy" b: 1859, Chicago, Ill. d: 8/10/1899, Chicago, Ill. 140 lbs. Deb: 6/11/1884

YEAR	TM/L	G	AB	R	H	2B	3B	HR	RBI	BB	SO	AVG	OBP	SLG	PRO+	BR/A	SB	CS	SBR	FA	FR	G/POS	TPR
1884	Det-N	30	111	5	15	1	0	0	3	4	15	.135	.165	.144	-2	-12				.867	1	S-19,O-11	-1.0

■ GEORGE BULLARD

Bullard, George Donald "Curly" b: 10/24/28, Lynn, Mass. BR/TR, 5′9.5″, 165 lbs. Deb: 9/17/54

YEAR	TM/L	G	AB	R	H	2B	3B	HR	RBI	BB	SO	AVG	OBP	SLG	PRO+	BR/A	SB	CS	SBR	FA	FR	G/POS	TPR
1954	Det-A	4	1	0	0	0	0	0	0	0	0	.000	.000	.000	-99	-0	0	0	0	.800	1	/S-1	0.1

■ SIM BULLAS

Bullas, Simeon Edward b: 4/10/1861, Cleveland, Ohio d: 1/14/08, Cleveland, Ohio 5′7.5″, 150 lbs. Deb: 5/2/1884

YEAR	TM/L	G	AB	R	H	2B	3B	HR	RBI	BB	SO	AVG	OBP	SLG	PRO+	BR/A	SB	CS	SBR	FA	FR	G/POS	TPR
1884	Tol-a	13	45	4	4	0	1	0		1		.089	.109	.133	-21	-6				.909	-6	C-12/O-2	-1.0

YEAR	TM/L	G	AB	R	H	2B	3B	HR	RBI	BB	SO	AVG	OBP	SLG	PRO+	BR/A	SB	CS	SBR	FA	FR	G/POS	TPR
■ **SCOTT BULLETT**	Bullett, Scott Douglas b: 12/25/68, Martinsburg, W.Va. BB/TL, 6'2", 200 lbs. Deb: 9/3/91																						
1991	Pit-N	11	4	2	0	0	0	0	0	0	3	.000	.200	.000	-40	-1	1	1	-0	1.000	-1	/O-3	-0.2
1993	Pit-N	23	55	2	11	0	2	0	4	3	15	.200	.241	.273	37	-5	3	2	-0	1.000	-2	O-19	-0.7
1995	Chi-N	104	150	19	41	5	7	3	22	12	30	.273	.331	.460	108	1	8	3	1	.968	-11	O-64	-1.0
1996	Chi-N	109	165	26	35	5	0	3	16	10	54	.212	.257	.297	44	-13	7	3	0	.986	-8	O-58	-2.1
Total	4	247	374	49	87	10	9	6	42	25	102	.233	.284	.356	68	-18	19	9	0	.983	-22	O-144	-4.0
■ **BUD BULLING**	Bulling, Terry Charles "Terry" b: 12/15/52, Lynwood, Cal. BR/TR, 6'1", 200 lbs. Deb: 7/3/77																						
1977	Min-A	15	32	2	5	1	0	0	5	5	5	.156	.270	.188	28	-3	0	0	0	.952	-0	C-10/D-3	-0.3
1981	Sea-A	62	154	15	38	3	0	2	15	21	20	.247	.341	.305	84	-2	0	0	0	.977	-3	C-62	-0.3
1982	Sea-A	56	154	17	34	7	0	1	8	19	16	.221	.306	.286	62	-8	2	1	0	.991	7	C-56	0.1
1983	Sea-A	5	5	0	0	0	0	0	0	0	0	.000	.000	.000	-96	-1	0	0	0	1.000	1	/C-5	0.0
Total	4	138	345	34	77	11	0	3	28	45	41	.223	.315	.281	66	-14	2	1	0	.983	6	C-133/D-3	-0.5
■ **ERIC BULLOCK**	Bullock, Eric Gerald b: 2/16/60, Los Angeles, Cal. BL/TL, 5'11", 185 lbs. Deb: 8/26/85																						
1985	Hou-N	18	25	3	7	2	0	0	2	1	3	.280	.308	.360	89	-0	0	1	-1	.750	-2	/O-7	-0.3
1986	Hou-N	6	21	0	1	0	0	0	1	0	3	.048	.048	.048	-76	-5	2	0	1	.875	-1	/O-6	-0.6
1988	Min-A	16	17	3	5	0	0	0	3	3	1	.294	.400	.294	95	0	1	0	0	.875	-1	/O-4,D-2	-0.1
1989	Phi-N	6	4	1	0	0	0	0	0	0	2	.000	.000	.000	-99	-1	0	0	0	1.000	-1	/O-3	-0.2
1990	Mon-N	4	2	0	1	0	0	0	0	0	0	.500	.500	.500	183	0	0	0	0	.000	0	/H	0.0
1991	Mon-N	73	72	6	16	4	0	1	6	9	13	.222	.309	.319	78	-2	6	1	1	1.000	-1	/O-9,1-3	-0.2
1992	Mon-N	8	5	0	0	0	0	0	0	0	1	.000	.000	.000	-99	-1	0	0	0	.000	0	/H	-0.2
Total	7	131	146	13	30	6	0	1	12	13	23	.205	.270	.267	52	-9	9	2	2	.892	-5	/O-29,1-3,D-2	-1.6
■ **AL BUMBRY**	Bumbry, Alonza Benjamin (b: Alonza Benjamin Bumbrey) b: 4/21/47, Fredericksburg, Va. BL/TR, 5'8", 175 lbs. Deb: 9/5/72 C																						
1972	Bal-A	9	11	5	4	0	1	0	0	0	0	.364	.364	.545	164	1	1	1	-0	1.000	0	/O-2	0.1
1973	*Bal-A	110	356	73	120	15	**11**	7	34	34	49	.337	.399	.500	153	25	23	10	1	.978	-10	O-86/D-7	1.2
1974	*Bal-A	94	270	35	63	10	3	1	19	21	46	.233	.291	.304	74	-9	12	4	1	.953	-1	O-67/D-7	-1.2
1975	Bal-A	114	349	47	94	19	4	2	32	32	81	.269	.338	.364	105	2	16	3	3	1.000	-2	D-48,O-39/3-1	0.1
1976	Bal-A	133	450	71	113	15	7	9	36	43	76	.251	.318	.376	109	4	42	10	7	.989	-12	*O-116,D-10	-0.6
1977	Bal-A	133	518	74	164	31	3	4	41	45	88	.317	.373	.411	121	16	19	8	1	.991	-10	*O-130	0.1
1978	Bal-A	33	114	21	27	5	2	2	6	17	15	.237	.346	.368	108	2	5	3	-0	.985	-2	O-28	-0.2
1979	*Bal-A	148	569	80	162	29	1	7	49	43	74	.285	.338	.376	96	-3	37	12	4	.982	-3	*O-146	-0.8
1980	Bal-A★	160	645	118	205	29	9	9	53	78	75	.318	.394	.433	128	27	44	11	7	.990	15	*O-160	4.2
1981	Bal-A	101	392	61	107	18	2	1	27	51	51	.273	.360	.337	102	3	22	15	-2	.992	4	*O-100	0.1
1982	Bal-A	150	562	77	147	20	4	5	40	44	77	.262	.315	.338	80	-15	10	5	0	.986	8	*O-147/D-1	-1.1
1983	*Bal-A	124	378	63	104	14	4	3	31	31	33	.275	.330	.357	91	-4	12	5	1	.988	-11	*O-104,D-11	-1.8
1984	Bal-A	119	344	47	93	12	1	3	24	25	35	.270	.320	.337	84	-7	9	5	-0	.988	-6	O-99/D-9	-1.7
1985	SD-N	68	95	6	19	3	0	1	10	7	9	.200	.255	.263	46	-7	2	0	1	.939	-2	O-17	-0.9
Total	14	1496	5053	778	1422	220	52	54	402	471	709	.281	.345	.378	104	33	254	92	21	.986	-31	*O-1241/D-93,3-1	-2.5
■ **JOSH BUNCE**	Bunce, Joshua b: 5/10/1847, Brooklyn, N.Y. d: 4/28/12, Brooklyn, N.Y. Deb: 8/27/1877																						
1877	Har-N	1	4	0	0	0	0	0	0	0	0	.000	.000	.000	-99	-1				1.000	-0	/O-1	-0.1
■ **NELSON BURBRINK**	Burbrink, Nelson Edward b: 12/28/21, Cincinnati, Ohio BR/TR, 5'10", 195 lbs. Deb: 6/5/55																						
1955	StL-N	58	170	11	47	8	1	0	15	14	13	.276	.335	.335	79	-5	1	1	-0	.979	-1	C-55	-0.4
■ **AL BURCH**	Burch, Albert William b: 10/7/1883, Albany, N.Y. d: 10/5/26, Brooklyn, N.Y. BL/TR, 5'8.5", 160 lbs. Deb: 6/19/06																						
1906	StL-N	91	335	40	89	5	1	0	11	37		.266	.339	.287	99	1	15			.934	1	O-91	-0.3
1907	StL-N	48	154	18	35	3	1	0	5	17		.227	.304	.260	79	-3	7			.922	0	O-48	-0.6
	Bro-N	40	120	12	35	2	2	0	12	11		.292	.351	.342	127	4	5			.890	2	O-36/2-1	0.5
	Yr	88	274	30	70	5	3	0	17	28		.255	.325	.296	100	0	12			.908	2	O-84/2-1	-0.1
1908	Bro-N	123	456	45	111	8	4	2	18	33		.243	.294	.292	91	-5	15			.971	13	*O-116	0.3
1909	Bro-N	152	601	80	163	20	6	1	30	51		.271	.329	.329	108	5	38			.955	6	*O-151/1-1	0.5
1910	Bro-N	103	352	41	83	8	3	1	20	22	30	.236	.281	.284	67	-16	13			.957	-1	O-70,1-13	-2.1
1911	Bro-N	54	167	18	38	2	3	0	7	15	22	.228	.291	.275	61	-9	3			.972	2	O-43/2-3	-0.9
Total	6	611	2185	254	554	48	20	4	103	186	52	.254	.312	.299	91	-23	96			.950	22	O-555/1-14,2-4	-2.6
■ **ERNIE BURCH**	Burch, Earnest W. b: 1856, DeKalb Co., Ill. BL , Deb: 8/15/1884																						
1884	Cle-N	32	124	9	26	4	0	0	7	5	24	.210	.240	.242	50	-7				.899	4	O-32	-0.3
1886	Bro-a	113	456	78	119	22	6	2	72	39		.261	.321	.349	109	4	16			.884	-13	*O-113	-1.0
1887	Bro-a	49	188	47	55	4	4	2	26	29		.293	.395	.388	118	6	15			.899	1	O-49	0.4
Total	3	194	768	134	200	30	10	4	105	73	24	.260	.328	.341	102	3	31			.891	-8	O-194	-0.9
■ **BOB BURDA**	Burda, Edward Robert b: 7/16/38, St.Louis, Mo. BL/TL, 5'11", 180 lbs. Deb: 8/25/62																						
1962	StL-N	7	14	0	1	0	0	0	0	3	1	.071	.235	.071	-12	-2	1	0	0	.917	-0	/O-6	-0.2
1965	SF-N	31	27	0	3	0	0	0	5	5	6	.111	.250	.111	6	-3	0	0	0	.969	-1	1-11/O-1	-0.4
1966	SF-N	37	43	3	7	3	0	0	2	2	5	.163	.200	.233	19	-5	0	0	0	1.000	-1	/1-7,O-4	-0.6
1969	SF-N	97	161	20	37	8	0	6	27	21	12	.230	.319	.391	100	-0	0	1	-1	.995	-1	1-45,O-19	-0.4
1970	SF-N	28	23	1	6	0	0	0	3	5	2	.261	.414	.261	86	-0	0	0	0	.933	-1	/1-8,O-1	-0.1
	Mil-A	78	222	19	55	9	0	4	20	16	17	.248	.307	.342	78	-7	1	0	0	.987	-7	O-64/1-7	-1.8
1971	StL-N	65	71	6	21	0	0	1	12	10	11	.296	.390	.338	104	1	0	0	0	1.000	0	1-13/O-1	0.0
1972	Bos-A	45	73	4	12	1	0	2	9	8	11	.164	.247	.260	48	-5	0	0	0	.992	-0	1-15/O-1	-0.7
Total	7	388	634	53	142	21	0	13	78	70	65	.224	.306	.319	74	-21	2	1	0	.992	-11	1-106/O-97	-4.2
■ **JACK BURDOCK**	Burdock, John Joseph "Black Jack" b: 4/1852, Brooklyn, N.Y. d: 11/27/31, Brooklyn, N.Y. BR/TR, 5'9.5", 158 lbs. Deb: 5/2/1872 MU																						
1872	Atl-n	37	174	26	46	3	0	0	15	1	1	.264	.269	.282	59	-12	0	1	-1	.738	-4	*S-36/C-4,2-2	-1.2
1873	Atl-n	55	245	56	62	7	1	2	36	7	4	.253	.274	.314	83	-3	3	1	0	.816	1	*2-55/C-2	-0.5
1874	Mut-n	61	273	45	75	11	4	1	26	1	5	.275	.277	.355	98	-1	4	1	1	**.820**	8	*3-60/O-3	0.6
1875	Har-n	74	350	72	103	12	5	0	35	3	13	.294	.300	.357	121	6	20	11	-1	**.895**	-4	*2-73/3-2,C-1	0.0
1876	Har-N	69	309	66	80	9	1	0	23	13	16	.259	.289	.294	87	-5				.895	1	*2-69/3-1	-0.4
1877	Har-N	58	277	35	72	6	0	0	9	2	16	.260	.265	.282	81	-5				**.903**	7	*2-55/3-3	0.3
1878	Bos-N	60	246	37	64	12	6	0	25	3	17	.260	.269	.358	97	-2				**.918**	**21**	*2-60	2.2
1879	Bos-N	84	359	64	86	10	3	0	36	9	28	.240	.258	.284	77	-9				.911	10	*2-84	0.6
1880	Bos-N	86	356	58	90	17	4	2	35	8	26	.253	.269	.340	108	3				**.923**	12	*2-86	1.9
1881	Bos-N	73	282	36	67	12	4	1	24	7	18	.238	.256	.319	84	-5				.911	-11	*2-72/S-1	-1.2
1882	Bos-N	83	319	36	76	6	7	0	27	9	24	.238	.259	.301	79	-7				**.932**	3	*2-83	-0.2
1883	Bos-N	96	400	80	132	27	8	5	88	14	35	.330	.353	.475	145	20				.921	-1	*2-96/M	1.8
1884	Bos-N	87	361	65	97	14	4	6	49	15	52	.269	.298	.380	112	5				**.922**	1	*2-87/3-1	0.7
1885	Bos-N	45	169	18	24	5	0	0	7	8	18	.142	.181	.172	15	-15				.917	-4	2-45	-1.7
1886	Bos-N	59	221	26	48	6	1	0	25	11	27	.217	.254	.253	57	-11	3			.904	-8	2-59	-1.5
1887	Bos-N	65	237	36	61	6	0	0	29	18	22	.257	.320	.283	69	-9	19			.882	-19	2-65	-2.3
1888	Bos-N	22	79	5	16	0	0	0	4	2	5	.203	.232	.203	39	-5	1			.903	0	2-22	-0.4
	Bro-a	70	246	15	30	1	2	1	8	8		.122	.166	.154	3	-26	9			.904	2	2-70	-2.1
1891	Bro-N	3	12	1	1	0	0	0	1	1	1	.083	.154	.083	-31	-2	0			1.000	-1	/2-3	-0.2
Total	4 n	227	1042	199	286	33	10	3	112	12	23	.274	.283	.334	94	-10	27	14	-0	.858	0	2-130/3-62,S-36,CO	-1.1
Total	14	960	3873	578	944	131	40	15	390	128	305	.244	.270	.310	83	-74	32			.912	13	2-956/3-5,S-1	-2.5
■ **JOE BURG**	Burg, Joseph Peter b: 6/4/1882, Chicago, Ill. d: 4/28/69, Joliet, Ill. BR/TR, 5'10", 150 lbs. Deb: 9/26/10																						
1910	Bos-N	13	46	7	15	0	1	0	10	7	12	.326	.415	.370	124	2	5			.867	3	3-12/S-1	0.5

■ SMOKY BURGESS

Burgess, Forrest Harrill b: 2/6/27, Caroleen, N.C. d: 9/15/91, Asheville, N.C. BL/TR, 5'8", 187 lbs. Deb: 4/19/49

YEAR	TM/L	G	AB	R	H	2B	3B	HR	RBI	BB	SO	AVG	OBP	SLG	PRO+	BR/A	SB	CS	SBR	FA	FR	G/POS	TPR
1949	Chi-N	46	56	4	15	0	0	1	12	4	4	.268	.317	.321	73	-2	0		0	1.000	1	/C-8	-0.1
1951	Chi-N	94	219	21	55	4	2	2	20	21	12	.251	.317	.315	69	-9	2	0	1	.980	-3	C-64	-0.9
1952	Phi-N	110	371	49	110	27	2	6	56	49	21	.296	.380	.429	125	14	3	1	0	.978	-6	*C-104	1.4
1953	Phi-N	102	312	31	91	17	5	4	36	37	17	.292	.370	.417	105	3	3	2	-0	**.993**	-8	C-95	-0.1
1954	Phi-N★	108	345	41	127	27	5	4	46	42	11	.368	.437	.510	146	25	1	5	-3	.975	-8	C-91	1.8
1955	Phi-N	7	21	4	4	2	0	1	1	3	1	.190	.292	.429	90	-0	0	0	0	1.000	1	/C-6	0.0
	Cin-N★	116	421	67	129	15	3	20	77	47	35	.306	.377	.499	123	14	1	1	-0	.986	-9	*C-107	0.8
	Yr	123	442	71	133	17	3	21	78	50	36	.301	.373	.495	122	14	1	1	-0	.987	-9	*C-113	0.8
1956	Cin-N	90	229	28	63	10	0	12	39	26	18	.275	.349	.476	112	4	0	1	-1	1.000	-2	C-55	0.3
1957	Cin-N	90	205	29	58	14	1	14	39	24	16	.283	.358	.566	134	9	0	0	0	.988	-5	C-45	0.6
1958	Cin-N	99	251	28	71	12	1	6	31	22	20	.283	.343	.410	93	-2	0	0	0	.988	4	C-58	0.5
1959	Pit-N★	114	377	41	112	28	5	11	59	31	16	.297	.354	.485	122	11	0	0	0	.984	-17	*C-101	0.0
1960	*Pit-N★	110	337	33	99	15	2	7	39	35	13	.294	.360	.412	110	5	0	1	-1	**.994**	1	C-89	1.1
1961	Pit-N★	100	323	37	98	17	3	12	52	30	16	.303	.366	.486	123	11	1	0	0	**.991**	-14	C-92	0.2
1962	Pit-N	103	360	38	118	19	2	13	61	31	19	.328	.381	.500	134	17	0	1	-1	.988	-11	*C-101	0.9
1963	Pit-N	91	264	20	74	10	1	6	37	24	14	.280	.343	.394	111	4	0	1	-1	.990	-11	C-72	-0.6
1964	Pit-N☆	68	171	9	42	3	1	2	17	13	14	.246	.303	.310	73	-6	2	1	0	.992	-8	C-44	-1.2
	Chi-A	7	5	1	1	0	0	1	1	2	0	.200	.429	.800	239	1	0	0	0	.000	0	H	0.1
1965	Chi-A	80	77	2	22	4	0	2	24	11	7	.286	.375	.416	132	3	0	0	0	1.000	-0	/C-5	0.4
1966	Chi-A	79	67	0	21	5	0	0	15	11	8	.313	.418	.388	143	4	0	0	0	1.000	-0	/C-2	0.5
1967	Chi-A	77	60	2	8	1	0	2	11	14	8	.133	.307	.250	69	-2	0	0	0	.000	0	H	-0.2
Total	18	1691	4471	485	1318	230	33	126	673	477	270	.295	.364	.446	116	104	13	14	10	.988	-96	*C-1139	5.5

■ TOM BURGESS

Burgess, Thomas Roland "Tim" b: 9/1/27, London, Ont., Can. BL/TL, 6', 180 lbs. Deb: 4/17/54 C

YEAR	TM/L	G	AB	R	H	2B	3B	HR	RBI	BB	SO	AVG	OBP	SLG	PRO+	BR/A	SB	CS	SBR	FA	FR	G/POS	TPR
1954	StL-N	17	21	2	1	1	0	0	1	3	9	.048	.167	.095	-29	-4	0	0	0	.750	-1	/O-4	-0.6
1962	LA-A	87	143	17	28	7	1	2	13	36	20	.196	.358	.301	82	-2	2	0	1	.997	-3	1-35/O-2	-0.6
Total	2	104	164	19	29	8	1	2	14	39	29	.177	.335	.274	67	-6	2	0	1	.857	-4	/1-35,O-6	-1.2

■ BILL BURGO

Burgo, William Ross b: 11/5/19, Johnstown, Pa. d: 10/19/88, Morgan City, La. BR/TR, 5'8", 185 lbs. Deb: 9/22/43

YEAR	TM/L	G	AB	R	H	2B	3B	HR	RBI	BB	SO	AVG	OBP	SLG	PRO+	BR/A	SB	CS	SBR	FA	FR	G/POS	TPR
1943	Phi-A	17	70	12	26	4	2	1	9	4	1	.371	.421	.529	178	7	0	2	-1	.979	2	O-17	0.7
1944	Phi-A	27	88	6	21	2	0	1	3	7	3	.239	.316	.295	76	-3	1	3	-2	.955	2	O-22	-0.3
Total	2	44	158	18	47	6	2	2	12	11	4	.297	.362	.399	121	4	1	5	-3	.965	4	/O-39	0.4

■ BILL BURICH

Burich, William Max b: 5/29/18, Calumet, Mich. BR/TR, 6', 180 lbs. Deb: 4/15/42

YEAR	TM/L	G	AB	R	H	2B	3B	HR	RBI	BB	SO	AVG	OBP	SLG	PRO+	BR/A	SB	CS	SBR	FA	FR	G/POS	TPR
1942	Phi-N	25	80	3	23	1	0	0	7	6	13	.287	.337	.300	92	-1	2			.917	-5	S-19/3-3	-0.5
1946	Phi-N	2	1	1	0	0	0	0	0	0	0	.000	.000	.000	-99	-0	0			.000	0	/3-1	0.0
Total	2	27	81	4	23	1	0	0	7	6	13	.284	.333	.296	89	-1	2			1.000	-5	/S-19,3-4	-0.5

■ MACK BURK

Burk, Mack Edwin b: 4/21/35, Nacogdoches, Tex. BR/TR, 6'4", 180 lbs. Deb: 5/25/56

YEAR	TM/L	G	AB	R	H	2B	3B	HR	RBI	BB	SO	AVG	OBP	SLG	PRO+	BR/A	SB	CS	SBR	FA	FR	G/POS	TPR
1956	Phi-N	15	1	3	1	0	0	0	0	0	0	1.000	1.000	1.000	449	0	0	0	0	1.000	0	/C-1	0.1
1958	Phi-N	1	1	0	0	0	0	0	0	0	1	.000	.000	.000	-99	-0	0	0	0	.000	0	H	0.0
Total	2	16	2	3	1	0	0	0	0	0	1	.500	.500	.500	171	0	0	0	0	1.000	0	/C-1	0.1

■ CHRIS BURKAM

Burkam, Chauncey De Pew b: 10/13/1892, Benton Harbor, Mich. d: 5/9/64, Kalamazoo, Mich. BL/TR, 5'11", 175 lbs. Deb: 6/24/15

YEAR	TM/L	G	AB	R	H	2B	3B	HR	RBI	BB	SO	AVG	OBP	SLG	PRO+	BR/A	SB	CS	SBR	FA	FR	G/POS	TPR
1915	StL-A	1	1	0	0	0	0	0	0	0	1	.000	.000	.000	-99	-0	0			.000	0	H	0.0

■ DAN BURKE

Burke, Daniel L. b: 10/25/1868, Abington, Mass. d: 3/20/33, Taunton, Mass. BR/TR, 5'10", 190 lbs. Deb: 4/18/1890

YEAR	TM/L	G	AB	R	H	2B	3B	HR	RBI	BB	SO	AVG	OBP	SLG	PRO+	BR/A	SB	CS	SBR	FA	FR	G/POS	TPR
1890	Roc-a	32	102	14	22	1	0	0	9	17		.216	.333	.225	70	-3	2			.944	-5	O-29/C-4,1-2	-0.7
	Syr-a	9	20	1	0	0	0	0	0	5		.000	.231	.000	-35	-3	0			.900	3	/C-9	0.0
	Yr	41	122	15	22	1	0	0	9	22		.180	.315	.189	53	-6	2			.944	-2	O-29,C-13/1-2	-0.7
1892	Bos-N	1	4	0	0	0	0	0	0	0	2	.000	.000	.000	-92	-1	0			.900	1	/C-1	0.0
Total	2	42	126	15	22	1	0	0	9	22	2	.175	.307	.183	48	-7	2			.892	-2	/O-29,C-14,1-2	-0.7

■ EDDIE BURKE

Burke, Edward D. b: 10/6/1866, Northumberland, Pa. d: 11/26/07, Utica, N.Y. BL/TR, 5'6", 161 lbs. Deb: 4/19/1890

YEAR	TM/L	G	AB	R	H	2B	3B	HR	RBI	BB	SO	AVG	OBP	SLG	PRO+	BR/A	SB	CS	SBR	FA	FR	G/POS	TPR
1890	Phi-N	100	430	85	113	16	11	4	50	49	40	.263	.349	.379	109	5	38			.904	4	*O-96/2-4	0.5
	Pit-N	31	124	17	26	5	2	1	7	14	9	.210	.295	.306	85	-2	6			.911	1	O-31	-0.2
	Yr	131	554	102	139	21	13	5	57	63	49	.251	.337	.363	105	4	44			.906	4	*O-127/2-4	0.3
1891	Mil-a	35	144	31	34	9	0	2	21	12	19	.236	.337	.340	78	-6	7			.918	3	O-35	-0.4
1892	Cin-N	15	41	6	6	1	0	0	4	9	4	.146	.300	.171	44	-2	2			1.000	-3	O-14/3-1	-0.5
	NY-N	89	363	81	94	10	5	6	41	46	37	.259	.350	.364	118	9	42			.857	-3	2-59,O-30	0.5
	Yr	104	404	87	100	11	5	6	45	55	41	.248	.345	.344	110	6	44			.857	-6	2-59,O-44/3-1	0.0
1893	NY-N	135	537	122	150	23	10	9	80	51	32	.279	.369	.410	106	5	54			.912	2	*O-135	0.0
1894	*NY-N	136	566	121	172	23	11	4	77	37	35	.304	.357	.405	84	-15	34			.933	-4	*O-136	-2.2
1895	NY-N	39	167	38	43	6	2	1	12	7	9	.257	.299	.335	65	-9	14			.914	2	O-39	-0.8
	Cin-N	56	228	52	61	8	6	1	25	22	14	.268	.343	.368	80	-7	19			.899	2	O-56	-0.8
	Yr	95	395	90	104	14	8	2	37	29	23	.263	.325	.354	74	-16	33			.905	4	O-95	-1.6
1896	Cin-N	122	521	120	177	24	9	1	52	41	29	.340	.392	.426	108	6	53			.935	3	*O-122	-0.1
1897	Cin-N	95	387	71	103	17	1	1	41	29		.266	.327	.323	67	-19	22			.940	7	*O-95	-1.6
Total	8	853	3508	744	979	142	57	30	410	317	228	.279	.352	.378	93	-37	291			.921	14	O-789/2-63,3-1	-5.6

■ FRANK BURKE

Burke, Frank Aloysius b: 2/16/1880, Carbon Co., Pa. d: 9/17/46, Los Angeles, Cal. TR , Deb: 9/14/06

YEAR	TM/L	G	AB	R	H	2B	3B	HR	RBI	BB	SO	AVG	OBP	SLG	PRO+	BR/A	SB	CS	SBR	FA	FR	G/POS	TPR
1906	NY-N	8	9	2	3	1	1	0	1	1		.333	.400	.667	227	1	1			.667	-2	/O-4	0.0
1907	Bos-N	43	129	6	23	0	1	0	8	11		.178	.243	.194	37	-9	3			.955	-4	O-36	-1.6
Total	2	51	138	8	26	1	2	0	9	12		.188	.253	.225	50	-8	4			.942	-5	/O-40	-1.6

■ GLENN BURKE

Burke, Glenn Lawrence b: 11/16/52, Oakland, Cal. d: 5/30/95, San Leandro, Cal. BR/TR, 6', 195 lbs. Deb: 4/9/76

YEAR	TM/L	G	AB	R	H	2B	3B	HR	RBI	BB	SO	AVG	OBP	SLG	PRO+	BR/A	SB	CS	SBR	FA	FR	G/POS	TPR
1976	LA-N	25	46	9	11	2	0	0	5	3	8	.239	.300	.283	67	-2	3	2	-0	.971	-3	O-20	-0.7
1977	*LA-N	83	169	16	43	8	0	1	13	5	22	.254	.280	.320	61	-9	13	5	1	.971	-15	O-74	-2.6
1978	LA-N	16	19	2	4	0	0	0	2	0	4	.211	.211	.211	18	-2	1	0	0	1.000	-5	O-15	-0.7
	Oak-A	78	200	19	47	6	1	1	14	10	26	.235	.271	.290	61	-11	15	8	-0	.987	-4	O-67/1-1,D-2	-1.8
1979	Oak-A	23	89	4	19	2	1	0	4	4	10	.213	.247	.258	39	-8	3	1	0	1.000	1	O-23	-0.7
Total	4	225	523	50	124	18	2	2	38	22	70	.237	.271	.291	56	-32	35	16	1	.983	-26	O-199/D-2,1-1	-6.5

■ JIMMY BURKE

Burke, James Timothy "Sunset Jimmy" b: 10/12/1874, St.Louis, Mo. d: 3/26/42, St.Louis, Mo. BR/TR, 5'7", 160 lbs. Deb: 10/6/1898 MC

YEAR	TM/L	G	AB	R	H	2B	3B	HR	RBI	BB	SO	AVG	OBP	SLG	PRO+	BR/A	SB	CS	SBR	FA	FR	G/POS	TPR
1898	Cle-N	13	38	1	4	1	0	0	1	2		.105	.150	.132	-19	-6	1			.853	-4	3-13	-1.0
1899	StL-N	2	6	1	2	0	0	0	0	1		.333	.429	.333	108	0	0			.923	1	/2-2	0.1
1901	Mil-A	64	233	24	48	8	0	0	26	17		.206	.266	.240	43	-17	6			.860	-7	3-64	-2.2
	Chi-A	42	148	20	39	5	0	0	21	12		.264	.327	.297	76	-4	11			.867	-2	S-31,3-11	-0.3
	Yr	106	381	44	87	13	0	0	47	29		.228	.290	.262	56	-22	17			.859	-9	3-75,S-31	-2.5
	Pit-N	14	51	4	10	0	0	0	4	4		.196	.268	.196	35	-4	0			.877	3	3-14	-0.1
1902	Pit-N	60	203	24	60	12	2	0	26	17		.296	.359	.374	122	5	9			.895	-5	2-27,O-18/3-9,S-4	0.1
1903	StL-N	115	431	55	123	13	3	0	42	23		.285	.326	.329	90	-6	28			.911	6	3-93,2-15/O-5	0.2
1904	StL-N	118	406	37	92	10	3	0	37	15		.227	.271	.266	69	-15	17			.897	-7	*3-118	-2.0
1905	StL-N	122	431	34	97	9	5	1	30	21		.225	.275	.276	67	-18	15			.924	3	*3-122,M	-1.1
Total	7	550	1947	200	475	58	13	1	187	112		.244	.295	.289	73	-65	87			.899	-12	3-444/2-44,S-35,O	-6.3

■ JOHN BURKE

Burke, John Patrick b: 1/27/1877, Hazleton, Pa. d: 8/4/50, Jersey City, N.J. BR/TR, Deb: 6/27/02

YEAR	TM/L	G	AB	R	H	2B	3B	HR	RBI	BB	SO	AVG	OBP	SLG	PRO+	BR/A	SB	CS	SBR	FA	FR	G/POS	TPR
1902	NY-N	4	13	0	2	0	0	0	0	0		.154	.154	.154	-5	-2	0			1.000	-0	/P-2,O-2	-0.1

■ JOE BURKE

Burke, Joseph A. b: Cincinnati, Ohio 5'7", 160 lbs. Deb: 9/26/1890

YEAR	TM/L	G	AB	R	H	2B	3B	HR	RBI	BB	SO	AVG	OBP	SLG	PRO+	BR/A	SB	CS	SBR	FA	FR	G/POS	TPR
1890	StL-a	2	6	3	4	0	0	0	2	1		.667	.750	.667	278	2	0			.750	-0	/3-2	0.1

YEAR	TM/L	G	AB	R	H	2B	3B	HR	RBI	BB	SO	AVG	OBP	SLG	PRO+	BR/A	SB	CS	SBR	FA	FR	G/POS	TPR
1891	Cin-a	1	4	0	1	0	0	0	1	0	2	.250	.250	.250	40	-0	0			1.000	1	/2-1	0.1
Total	2	3	10	3	5	0	0	0	3	1	2	.500	.583	.500	192	1	0			.750	1	/3-2,2-1	0.2

■ LEO BURKE

Burke, Leo Patrick b: 5/6/34, Hagerstown, Md. BR/TR, 5'10", 190 lbs. Deb: 9/7/58

YEAR	TM/L	G	AB	R	H	2B	3B	HR	RBI	BB	SO	AVG	OBP	SLG	PRO+	BR/A	SB	CS	SBR	FA	FR	G/POS	TPR
1958	Bal-A	7	11	4	5	1	0	1	4	1	2	.455	.500	.818	271	2	0	0	0	1.000	-2	/O-3,3-1	0.1
1959	Bal-A	5	10	0	2	0	0	0	1	0	5	.200	.273	.200	33	-1	0	0	0	1.000	-2	/2-2,3-2	-0.3
1961	LA-A	6	5	0	0	0	0	0	0	0	1	.000	.000	.000	-90	-1	0	0	0	.000	0	H	-0.1
1962	LA-A	19	64	8	17	1	0	4	14	5	11	.266	.329	.469	115	1	0	0	0	.958	-1	O-12/3-4,S-1	0.0
1963	StL-N	30	49	6	10	2	1	1	5	4	12	.204	.264	.347	68	-2	0	0	0	1.000	-2	O-11/3-5	-0.5
	Chi-N	27	49	4	9	0	0	2	7	4	13	.184	.245	.306	55	-3	0	1	-1	.925	3	2-10/1-4	0.0
	Yr	57	98	10	19	2	1	3	12	8	25	.194	.255	.327	61	-5	0	1	-1	1.000	1	O-11,2-10/3-5,1-4	-0.5
1964	Chi-N	59	103	11	27	3	1	1	14	7	31	.262	.315	.340	81	-2	0	0	0	1.000	-2	O-18/2-5,3-4,1-2,C	-0.5
1965	Chi-N	12	10	0	2	0	0	0	0	0	4	.200	.200	.200	13	-1	0	0	0	1.000	-0	/C-2,O-1	-0.1
Total	7	165	301	33	72	7	2	9	45	21	79	.239	.295	.365	81	-7	0	1	-1	.985	-6	/O-45,2-17,31CS	-1.4

■ LES BURKE

Burke, Leslie Kingston "Buck" b: 12/18/02, Lynn, Mass. d: 5/6/75, Danvers, Mass. BL/TR, 5'9", 168 lbs. Deb: 5/2/23

YEAR	TM/L	G	AB	R	H	2B	3B	HR	RBI	BB	SO	AVG	OBP	SLG	PRO+	BR/A	SB	CS	SBR	FA	FR	G/POS	TPR
1923	Det-A	7	10	2	1	0	0	0	2	0	1	.100	.100	.100	-48	-2	0	0	0	.500	-1	/3-2,2-1	-0.3
1924	Det-A	72	241	30	61	10	4	0	17	22	20	.253	.321	.328	69	-11	2	4	-2	.957	-6	2-58/S-6	-1.7
1925	Det-A	77	180	32	52	6	3	0	24	17	8	.289	.357	.356	82	-4	4	1	1	.962	2	2-52	-0.2
1926	Det-A	38	75	9	17	1	0	0	4	7	3	.227	.301	.240	42	-6	1	2	-1	.942	4	2-15/3-7,S-1	-0.2
Total	4	194	506	73	131	17	7	0	47	46	32	.259	.327	.320	67	-24	7	7	-2	.958	-1	2-126/3-9,S-7	-2.4

■ MIKE BURKE

Burke, Michael E. b: Cincinnati, Ohio d: 6/9/1889, Albany, N.Y. BR/TR, 6', 190 lbs. Deb: 5/1/1879

YEAR	TM/L	G	AB	R	H	2B	3B	HR	RBI	BB	SO	AVG	OBP	SLG	PRO+	BR/A	SB	CS	SBR	FA	FR	G/POS	TPR
1879	Cin-N	28	117	13	26	3	0	0	8	2	5	.222	.235	.248	63	-4				.786	-8	S-19/O-5,3-5	-1.0

■ PAT BURKE

Burke, Patrick Edward b: 5/13/01, St.Louis, Mo. d: 7/7/65, St.Louis, Mo. BR/TR, 5'10.5", 170 lbs. Deb: 9/23/24

YEAR	TM/L	G	AB	R	H	2B	3B	HR	RBI	BB	SO	AVG	OBP	SLG	PRO+	BR/A	SB	CS	SBR	FA	FR	G/POS	TPR
1924	StL-A	1	3	0	0	0	0	0	1	0	0	.000	.000	.000	-94	-1	0	0	0	.000	0	/3-1	-0.1

■ JESSE BURKETT

Burkett, Jesse Cail "Crab" b: 12/4/1868, Wheeling, W.Va. d: 5/27/53, Worcester, Mass. BL/TL, 5'8", 155 lbs. Deb: 4/22/1890 CH

YEAR	TM/L	G	AB	R	H	2B	3B	HR	RBI	BB	SO	AVG	OBP	SLG	PRO+	BR/A	SB	CS	SBR	FA	FR	G/POS	TPR
1890	NY-N	101	401	67	124	23	13	4	60	33	52	.309	.366	.461	140	19	14			.824	3	O-90,P-21	1.3
1891	Cle-N	40	167	29	45	7	4	0	13	23	19	.269	.358	.359	105	1	1			.892	-3	O-40	-0.3
1892	*Cle-N	145	608	119	167	15	14	6	66	67	59	.275	.348	.375	114	9	36			.904	3	*O-145	0.5
1893	Cle-N	125	511	145	178	25	15	6	82	98	23	.348	.459	.491	144	35	39			.849	-8	*O-125	1.7
1894	Cle-N	125	523	138	187	27	14	8	94	84	27	.358	.447	.509	125	23	28			.915	-4	*O-125/P-1	0.8
1895	*Cle-N	131	550	153	**225**	22	13	5	83	74	31	**.409**	.486	.524	152	45	41			.884	-3	*O-131	2.5
1896	*Cle-N	133	586	**160**	**240**	27	16	6	72	49	19	**.410**	.461	.541	155	46	34			.926	-2	*O-133	2.7
1897	Cle-N	127	517	129	198	28	7	2	60	76		.383	.468	.476	142	35	28			.949	-2	*O-127	2.0
1898	Cle-N	150	624	114	213	18	9	0	42	69		.341	.415	.399	135	32	19			.938	-8	*O-150	1.2
1899	StL-N	141	558	116	221	21	8	7	71	67		.396	.463	.500	160	48	25			.938	-3	*O-140/2-1	3.1
1900	StL-N	141	559	88	203	11	15	7	68	62		.363	.429	.474	150	40	32			.934	4	*O-141	3.0
1901	StL-N	142	601	**142**	**226**	20	15	10	75	59		**.376**	**.440**	.509	**184**	**66**	27			.923	-1	*O-142	5.2
1902	StL-A	138	553	97	169	29	9	5	52	71		.306	.390	.418	126	22	23			.924	6	*O-137/P-1,S-1,3-1	1.7
1903	StL-A	132	515	73	151	20	7	3	40	52		.293	.361	.377	125	17	17			.941	-4	*O-132	0.5
1904	StL-A	147	575	72	156	15	10	2	27	78		.271	.363	.343	132	24	12			.942	5	*O-147	2.3
1905	Bos-A	148	573	78	147	12	13	4	47	67		.257	.339	.344	115	11	13			.929	-2	*O-148	0.3
Total	16	2066	8421	1720	2850	320	182	75	952	1029	230	.338	.415	.446	140	474	389			.917	-19	*O-2053/P-23,3S2	28.5

■ ELLIS BURKS

Burks, Ellis Rena b: 9/11/64, Vicksburg, Miss. BR/TR, 6'2", 205 lbs. Deb: 4/30/87

YEAR	TM/L	G	AB	R	H	2B	3B	HR	RBI	BB	SO	AVG	OBP	SLG	PRO+	BR/A	SB	CS	SBR	FA	FR	G/POS	TPR
1987	Bos-A	133	558	94	152	30	2	20	59	41	98	.272	.324	.441	98	-3	27	6	5	.988	14	*O-132/D-1	1.1
1988	*Bos-A	144	540	93	159	37	5	18	92	62	89	.294	.370	.481	131	22	25	9	2	.977	12	*O-142/D-2	3.2
1989	Bos-A	97	399	73	121	19	6	12	61	36	52	.303	.368	.471	127	14	21	5	3	.977	7	O-95/D-1	2.2
1990	*Bos-A†	152	588	89	174	33	8	21	89	48	82	.296	.350	.486	126	19	9	11	-4	.994	2	*O-143/D-6	1.3
1991	Bos-A	130	474	56	119	33	3	14	56	39	81	.251	.316	.422	97	-3	6	11	-5	.993	-3	*O-126/D-2	-1.3
1992	Bos-A	66	235	35	60	8	3	8	30	25	48	.255	.330	.417	101	0	5	2	0	.984	-7	O-63/D-1	-0.8
1993	*Chi-A	146	499	75	137	24	4	17	74	60	97	.275	.357	.441	116	11	6	9	-4	.982	0	*O-146	0.5
1994	Col-N	42	149	33	48	8	3	13	24	16	39	.322	.388	.678	147	9	3	1	0	.964	-2	O-39	0.6
1995	*Col-N	103	278	41	74	10	6	14	49	39	72	.266	.361	.496	96	-4	7	3	0	.970	-4	O-80	-1.0
1996	Col-N★	156	613	**142**	211	45	8	40	128	61	114	.344	.409	**.639**	138	30	32	6	6	.983	2	*O-152	3.3
1997	Col-N	119	424	91	123	19	2	32	82	47	75	.290	.365	.571	114	6	7	2	1	.982	-18	*O-112	-1.4
1998	Col-N	100	357	54	102	22	5	16	54	39	80	.286	.359	.510	102	0	3	7	-3	.975	-11	O-98	-1.5
	SF-N	42	147	22	45	6	1	5	22	19	31	.306	.396	.463	127	6	8	1	2	.989	-2	O-41	0.6
	Yr	142	504	76	147	28	6	21	76	58	111	.292	.370	.496	108	6	11	8	-2	.979	-13	*O-139	-0.9
Total	12	1430	5261	898	1525	294	56	230	820	532	958	.290	.359	.498	117	110	159	73	4	.983	-12	*O-1369/D-13	6.8

■ RICK BURLESON

Burleson, Richard Paul "Rooster" b: 4/29/51, Lynwood, Cal. BR/TR, 5'10", 165 lbs. Deb: 5/4/74 C

YEAR	TM/L	G	AB	R	H	2B	3B	HR	RBI	BB	SO	AVG	OBP	SLG	PRO+	BR/A	SB	CS	SBR	FA	FR	G/POS	TPR
1974	Bos-A	114	384	36	109	22	0	4	44	21	34	.284	.324	.372	93	-4	3	3	-1	.957	-5	S-88,2-31/3-2	0.2
1975	*Bos-A	158	580	66	146	25	1	6	62	45	44	.252	.309	.329	74	-20	8	5	-1	.963	-1	*S-158	-0.4
1976	Bos-A	152	540	75	157	27	1	7	42	60	37	.291	.367	.383	107	5	14	9	-1	.957	-7	*S-152	1.7
1977	Bos-A★	154	663	80	194	36	7	3	52	47	69	.293	.341	.382	87	-12	13	12	-3	.970	12	*S-154	1.4
1978	Bos-A†	145	626	75	155	32	5	5	49	40	71	.248	.297	.339	71	-25	8	8	-2	.981	19	*S-144	1.1
1979	Bos-A★	153	627	93	174	32	5	5	60	35	54	.278	.319	.368	80	-18	9	5	-0	**.980**	22	*S-153	2.0
1980	Bos-A	155	644	89	179	29	2	8	51	62	51	.278	.343	.366	90	-8	12	13	-4	.974	26	*S-155	3.1
1981	Cal-A★	109	430	53	126	17	1	5	33	42	38	.293	.360	.372	111	7	4	6	-2	.979	21	*S-109	3.8
1982	Cal-A	11	45	4	7	1	0	0	2	6	3	.156	.255	.178	21	-5	0	0	0	.986	7	S-11	0.4
1983	Cal-A	33	119	22	34	7	0	0	11	12	12	.286	.351	.345	93	-1	0	2	-1	.969	-0	S-31	0.1
1984	Cal-A	7	4	2	0	0	0	0	0	0	2	.000	.000	.000	-99	-1	0	0	0	.000	0	/H	-0.1
1986	*Cal-A	93	271	35	77	14	0	5	29	33	32	.284	.364	.391	107	3	1	3	-2	.984	-7	D-38,S-37/2-6,3-4	-0.3
1987	Bal-A	62	206	26	43	14	1	2	14	17	30	.209	.279	.316	59	-12	0	2	-1	.977	-1	2-55/D-7	-1.2
Total	13	1346	5139	656	1401	256	23	50	449	420	477	.273	.331	.361	87	-89	72	68	-19	.971	86	*S-1192/2-92,D-45,3	11.8

■ HERCULES BURNETT

Burnett, Hercules H. b: 8/13/1865, Louisville, Ky. d: 10/4/36, Louisville, Ky. BR , 177 lbs. Deb: 6/26/1888

YEAR	TM/L	G	AB	R	H	2B	3B	HR	RBI	BB	SO	AVG	OBP	SLG	PRO+	BR/A	SB	CS	SBR	FA	FR	G/POS	TPR
1888	Lou-a	1	4	1	0	0	0	0	0	1		.000	.200	.000	-34	-1	1			.667	-0	/O-1	-0.1
1895	Lou-N	5	17	6	7	0	1	2	3	2	2	.412	.474	.882	261	4	2			.769	-0	/O-4,1-1	0.3
Total	2	6	21	7	7	0	1	2	3	3	2	.333	.417	.714	211	3	3			.750	-1	/O-5,1-1	0.2

■ JOHNNY BURNETT

Burnett, John Henderson b: 11/1/04, Bartow, Fla. d: 8/13/59, Tampa, Fla. BL/TR, 5'11", 175 lbs. Deb: 5/7/27

YEAR	TM/L	G	AB	R	H	2B	3B	HR	RBI	BB	SO	AVG	OBP	SLG	PRO+	BR/A	SB	CS	SBR	FA	FR	G/POS	TPR
1927	Cle-A	17	8	5	0	0	0	0	0	0	3	.000	.000	.000	-99	-2	1	0	0	.833	2	/2-2	0.0
1928	Cle-A	3	10	3	5	0	0	0	1	0	1	.500	.500	.500	162	1	0	0	0	.867	0	/S-2	0.1
1929	Cle-A	19	33	2	5	1	0	0	2	1	2	.152	.200	.182	-1	-5	0	0	0	.923	6	S-10/2-8	0.1
1930	Cle-A	54	170	28	53	13	0	0	20	17	8	.312	.378	.388	91	-2	2	2	-1	.973	-5	3-27,S-19	-0.3
1931	Cle-A	111	427	85	128	25	5	1	52	39	25	.300	.360	.389	92	-5	5	2	0	.938	-15	S-63,2-35,3-21,/O-1	-1.0
1932	Cle-A	129	512	81	152	23	5	4	53	46	27	.297	.359	.385	87	-9	2	5	-2	.946	-22	*S-103,2-26	-2.2
1933	Cle-A	83	261	39	71	11	2	1	29	23	14	.272	.333	.341	76	-9	3	2	-0	.938	-5	S-41,2-17,3-12	-0.9
1934	Cle-A	72	208	28	61	11	2	3	30	18	11	.293	.352	.409	94	-2	1	1	-0	.981	-8	3-42/S-9,2-3,O-2	-0.7
1935	StL-A	70	206	17	46	10	1	0	26	19	16	.223	.289	.282	46	-17	1	0	0	.939	-6	3-31,S-18,2-12	-1.8
Total	9	558	1835	288	521	94	15	9	213	163	107	.284	.345	.366	81	-50	15	12	-3	.935	-53	S-265,3-133,2/O	-6.7

■ JACK BURNETT

Burnett, John P. b: 12/2/1889, Missouri d: 9/8/29, Taft, Cal. Deb: 7/2/07

YEAR	TM/L	G	AB	R	H	2B	3B	HR	RBI	BB	SO	AVG	OBP	SLG	PRO+	BR/A	SB	CS	SBR	FA	FR	G/POS	TPR
1907	StL-N	59	206	18	49	8	4	0	12	15		.238	.296	.316	95	-2	5			.955	-4	O-59	-1.0

■ JEROMY BURNITZ

Burnitz, Jeromy Neal b: 4/15/69, Westminster, Cal. BL/TR, 6', 190 lbs. Deb: 6/21/93

YEAR	TM/L	G	AB	R	H	2B	3B	HR	RBI	BB	SO	AVG	OBP	SLG	PRO+	BR/A	SB	CS	SBR	FA	FR	G/POS	TPR
1993	NY-N	86	263	49	64	10	6	13	38	38	66	.243	.341	.475	117	6	3	6	-3	.977	2	O-79	0.4

YEAR	TM/L	G	AB	R	H	2B	3B	HR	RBI	BB	SO	AVG	OBP	SLG	PRO+	BR/A	SB	CS	SBR	FA	FR	G/POS	TPR
1994	NY-N	45	143	26	34	4	0	3	15	23	45	.238	.347	.329	78	-4	1	1	-0	.970	-5	O-42	-1.0
1995	Cle-A	9	7	4	4	1	0	0	0	0	0	.571	.571	.714	229	1	0	0	0	1.000	-1	/O-6,D-2	0.1
1996	Cle-A	71	128	30	36	10	0	7	26	25	31	.281	.406	.523	133	7	2	1	0	1.000	-4	O-30,D-15	0.2
	Mil-A	23	72	8	17	4	0	2	14	8	16	.236	.329	.375	75	-3	2	0	1	.975	-2	O-22	-0.4
	Yr	94	200	38	53	14	0	9	40	33	47	.265	.380	.470	113	4	4	1	1	.988	-6	O-52,D-15	-0.2
1997	Mil-A	153	494	85	139	37	8	27	85	75	111	.281	.382	.553	139	28	20	13	-2	.975	-4	*O-149	1.8
1998	Mil-N	161	609	92	160	28	1	38	125	70	158	.263	.343	.499	114	11	7	4	-0	.972	7	*O-161	1.6
Total	6	548	1716	294	454	94	15	90	303	239	427	.265	.359	.494	119	48	35	25	-5	.975	-6	O-489/D-17	2.7

■ C.B. BURNS Burns, Charles Birmingham b: 5/15/1879, Bay View, Md. d: 6/6/68, Havre De Grace, Md BR/TR, 6′, 175 lbs. Deb: 8/19/02

YEAR	TM/L	G	AB	R	H	2B	3B	HR	RBI	BB	SO	AVG	OBP	SLG	PRO+	BR/A	SB	CS	SBR	FA	FR	G/POS	TPR
1902	Bal-A	1	1	0	1	0	0	0	0	0		1.000	1.000	1.000	436	0	0			.000	0	H	0.0

■ ED BURNS Burns, Edward James b: 10/31/1888, San Francisco, Cal d: 6/1/42, Monterey, Cal. BR/TR, 5′6″, 165 lbs. Deb: 6/25/12

YEAR	TM/L	G	AB	R	H	2B	3B	HR	RBI	BB	SO	AVG	OBP	SLG	PRO+	BR/A	SB	CS	SBR	FA	FR	G/POS	TPR
1912	StL-N	1	1	0	0	0	0	0	1	0	0	.000	.000	.000	-99	-0	0			.000	0	/C-1	0.0
1913	Phi-N	17	30	3	6	3	0	0	3	6	3	.200	.351	.300	83	-0	2			.980	-4	C-15	-0.4
1914	Phi-N	70	139	8	36	3	4	0	16	20	12	.259	.352	.338	99	0	5			.947	-2	C-55	0.2
1915	*Phi-N	67	174	11	42	5	0	0	16	20	12	.241	.327	.270	81	-3	1			.981	-6	C-62	-0.5
1916	Phi-N	78	219	14	51	8	1	0	14	16	18	.233	.294	.279	74	-6	3			.981	-12	C-75/S-1,O-1	-1.5
1917	Phi-N	20	49	2	10	1	0	0	6	1	5	.204	.220	.224	35	-4	2			.971	-1	C-15	-0.5
1918	Phi-N	68	184	10	38	1	1	0	9	20	9	.207	.288	.223	53	-10	1			.981	-4	C-68	-1.0
Total	7	321	796	48	183	21	6	0	65	83	59	.230	.308	.271	73	-23	14			.974	-29	C-291/O-1,S-1	-3.7

■ GEORGE BURNS Burns, George Henry "Tioga George" b: 1/31/1893, Niles, Ohio d: 1/7/78, Kirkland, Wash. BR/TR, 6′1.5″, 180 lbs. Deb: 4/14/14

YEAR	TM/L	G	AB	R	H	2B	3B	HR	RBI	BB	SO	AVG	OBP	SLG	PRO+	BR/A	SB	CS	SBR	FA	FR	G/POS	TPR
1914	Det-A	137	478	55	139	22	5	5	57	32	56	.291	.351	.389	119	10	23	13	-1	.982	-5	*1-137	0.1
1915	Det-A	105	392	49	99	18	3	5	50	22	51	.253	.301	.352	91	-6	9	3	1	.986	-4	*1-104	-1.3
1916	Det-A	135	479	60	137	22	6	4	73	22	30	.286	.327	.382	109	3	12			.985	-10	*1-124	-1.3
1917	Det-A	119	407	42	92	14	10	1	40	15	33	.226	.264	.317	77	-13	3			.990	-4	*1-104	-2.3
1918	Phi-A	130	505	61	**178**	22	9	6	70	23	25	.352	.390	.467	157	32	8			.983	6	*1-128/O-2	3.6
1919	Phi-A	126	470	63	139	29	9	8	57	19	18	.296	.339	.447	118	9	15			.980	2	1-86,O-34	0.7
1920	Phi-A	22	60	1	14	3	0	1	7	6	7	.233	.313	.333	71	-3	4	0	1	.958	1	O-13	-0.2
	*Cle-A	44	56	7	15	4	1	0	13	4	3	.268	.339	.375	86	-1	1	0	0	.979	1	1-12/O-1	0.0
	Yr	66	116	8	29	7	1	1	20	10	10	.250	.326	.353	78	-4	5	0	2	.958	1	O-14,1-12	-0.2
1921	Cle-A	84	244	52	88	21	4	0	49	13	19	.361	.398	.480	121	7	3	1	0	.990	2	1-73	0.7
1922	Bos-A	147	558	71	171	32	5	12	73	20	28	.306	.341	.446	104	1	8	2	1	.987	-1	*1-140	-0.4
1923	Bos-A	146	551	91	181	47	5	7	82	45	33	.328	.386	.470	124	18	9	7	-2	.990	-1	*1-146	0.8
1924	Cle-A	129	462	64	143	37	5	4	68	29	27	.310	.370	.437	106	3	14	5	1	.987	8	*1-127	0.5
1925	Cle-A	127	488	69	164	41	4	6	79	24	24	.336	.371	.473	112	7	16	11	-2	.989	-1	*1-126	-0.2
1926	Cle-A	151	603	97	**216**	**64**	3	4	114	28	33	.358	.394	.494	129	24	13	7	-0	.988	1	*1-151	1.5
1927	Cle-A	140	549	84	175	51	2	3	78	42	27	.319	.375	.435	109	7	13	11	-3	.990	3	*1-139	-0.2
1928	Cle-A	82	209	29	52	12	1	5	30	17	11	.249	.323	.388	85	-5	2	3	-1	.984	2	1-53	-0.8
	NY-A	4	4	1	2	0	0	0	0	0	1	.500	.500	.500	169	0	0	0	0	1.000	-0	/1-2	0.0
	Yr	86	213	30	54	12	1	5	30	17	12	.254	.326	.390	87	-4	2	3	-1	.985	2	1-55	-0.8
1929	NY-A	9	9	0	0	0	0	0	0	0	4	.000	.000	.000	-99	-3	0	0	0	.000	0	H	-0.3
	*Phi-A	29	49	5	13	5	0	1	11	2	3	.265	.294	.429	81	-2	1	0	0	1.000	-0	1-19	-0.2
	Yr	38	58	5	13	5	0	1	11	2	7	.224	.250	.362	55	-4	1	0	0	1.000	-0	1-19	-0.5
Total	16	1866	6573	901	2018	444	72	72	951	363	433	.307	.354	.429	112	91	154	63		.987	0	*1-1671/O-50	0.7

■ GEORGE BURNS Burns, George Joseph b: 11/24/1889, Utica, N.Y. d: 8/15/66, Gloversville, N.Y. BR/TR, 5′7″, 160 lbs. Deb: 10/3/11 C

YEAR	TM/L	G	AB	R	H	2B	3B	HR	RBI	BB	SO	AVG	OBP	SLG	PRO+	BR/A	SB	CS	SBR	FA	FR	G/POS	TPR
1911	NY-N	6	17	2	1	0	0	0	0	1	0	.059	.111	.059	-50	-3	0			1.000	-2	/O-6	-0.5
1912	NY-N	29	51	11	15	4	0	0	3	8	8	.294	.400	.373	109	1	7			1.000	-4	O-23	-0.4
1913	*NY-N	150	605	81	173	37	4	2	54	58	74	.286	.352	.370	106	5	40			.963	7	*O-150	0.5
1914	NY-N	154	561	**100**	170	35	10	3	60	89	53	.303	.403	.417	149	**38**	**62**			.950	8	*O-154	4.1
1915	NY-N	155	622	83	169	27	14	3	51	56	57	.272	.333	.375	121	15	27	20	-4	.960	-6	*O-155	-0.3
1916	NY-N	155	623	**105**	174	24	8	5	41	63	47	.279	.346	.368	126	19	37	26	-5	.962	3	*O-155	1.1
1917	*NY-N	152	597	**103**	180	25	13	5	45	**75**	55	.302	.380	.412	148	35	40			.974	5	*O-152	3.5
1918	NY-N	119	465	80	135	22	6	4	51	43	37	.290	.354	.389	129	16	40			.965	9	*O-119	2.0
1919	NY-N	139	534	**86**	162	30	9	2	46	**82**	37	.303	**.396**	.404	142	31	**40**			**.990**	1	*O-139	2.5
1920	NY-N	154	631	**115**	181	35	9	6	46	**76**	48	.287	.365	.399	121	19	22	22	-7	.983	1	*O-154	0.2
1921	*NY-N	149	605	111	181	28	9	4	61	**80**	24	.299	.386	.395	107	9	19	20	-6	.972	3	*O-149/3-1	-0.5
1922	Cin-N	156	631	104	180	20	10	1	53	78	38	.285	.366	.353	88	-9	30	23	-5	.976	6	*O-156	-1.8
1923	Cin-N	154	614	99	168	27	13	3	45	**101**	46	.274	.376	.375	101	4	12	14	-5	.960	-1	*O-154	-1.2
1924	Cin-N	93	336	43	86	19	2	2	33	29	21	.256	.315	.342	77	-11	3	6	-3	.963	1	O-90	-1.8
1925	Phi-N	88	349	65	102	29	1	1	22	33	20	.292	.353	.390	82	-9	4	8	-4	.990	0	O-88	-1.7
Total	15	1853	7241	1188	2077	362	108	41	611	872	565	.287	.366	.384	115	161	383	139		.970	32	*O-1844/3-1	5.7

■ JIM BURNS Burns, James M. b: Quincy, Ill. 5′7″, 168 lbs. Deb: 9/25/1888

YEAR	TM/L	G	AB	R	H	2B	3B	HR	RBI	BB	SO	AVG	OBP	SLG	PRO+	BR/A	SB	CS	SBR	FA	FR	G/POS	TPR
1888	KC-a	15	66	13	20	0	0	0	4	1		.303	.343	.303	101	-0	6			.853	2	O-15	0.1
1889	KC-a	134	579	103	176	23	11	5	97	20	68	.304	.335	.408	105	-0	56			.913	-7	*O-134/3-1	-0.9
1891	Was-a	20	82	15	26	6	0	0	10	6	10	.317	.378	.390	125	3	2			.771	-4	O-20/S-1	-0.1
Total	3	169	727	131	222	29	11	5	111	27	78	.305	.341	.396	107	3	64			.897	-9	O-169/S-1,3-1	-0.9

■ JACK BURNS Burns, John Irving "Slug" b: 8/31/07, Cambridge, Mass. d: 4/18/75, Brighton, Mass. BL/TL, 5′10.5″, 175 lbs. Deb: 9/17/30 C

YEAR	TM/L	G	AB	R	H	2B	3B	HR	RBI	BB	SO	AVG	OBP	SLG	PRO+	BR/A	SB	CS	SBR	FA	FR	G/POS	TPR
1930	StL-A	8	30	5	9	3	0	0	2	5	5	.300	.400	.400	100	0	0	0	0	1.000	1	/1-8	0.0
1931	StL-A	144	570	75	148	27	7	4	70	42	58	.260	.312	.353	72	-24	19	12	-2	.993	18	*1-143	-1.9
1932	StL-A	150	617	111	188	33	8	11	70	61	43	.305	.368	.438	102	2	17	11	-2	.992	4	*1-150	-0.7
1933	StL-A	144	556	89	160	43	4	7	71	56	51	.288	.353	.417	97	-3	11	11	-3	.992	3	*1-143	-1.6
1934	StL-A	154	612	86	157	28	8	13	73	62	47	.257	.327	.392	78	-22	9	3	1	.992	-0	*1-154	-3.2
1935	StL-A	143	549	77	157	28	1	5	67	68	49	.286	.366	.368	86	-10	3	2	-0	.992	-8	*1-141	-3.1
1936	StL-A	9	14	2	3	1	0	0	1	3	1	.214	.353	.286	58	-1	0	0	0	1.000	0	/1-2	-0.1
	Det-A	138	558	96	158	36	3	4	63	79	45	.283	.375	.380	87	-10	4	8	-4	.994	1	*1-138	-2.3
	Yr	147	572	98	161	37	3	4	64	82	46	.281	.374	.378	86	-11	4	8	-4	.994	1	*1-140	-2.4
Total	7	890	3506	541	980	199	31	44	417	376	299	.280	.351	.392	87	-67	63	47	-9	.992	19	1-879	-12.9

■ JACK BURNS Burns, John Joseph b: 5/13/1880, Avoca, Pa. d: 6/24/57, Waterford, Conn. BR/TR, 5′10″, 160 lbs. Deb: 9/11/03

YEAR	TM/L	G	AB	R	H	2B	3B	HR	RBI	BB	SO	AVG	OBP	SLG	PRO+	BR/A	SB	CS	SBR	FA	FR	G/POS	TPR
1903	Det-A	11	37	2	10	0	0	0	3	1		.270	.325	.270	82	-1	0			.981	1	2-11	0.0
1904	Det-A	4	16	3	2	0	0	0	1	1		.125	.176	.125	-4	-2	1			.952	-1	/2-4	-0.4
Total	2	15	53	5	12	0	0	0	4	2		.226	.281	.226	57	-3	1			.973	-1	/2-15	-0.4

■ JOE BURNS Burns, Joseph Francis b: 3/26/1889, Ipswich, Mass. d: 7/12/87, Beverly, Mass. BL/TL, 5′11″, 170 lbs. Deb: 6/19/10

YEAR	TM/L	G	AB	R	H	2B	3B	HR	RBI	BB	SO	AVG	OBP	SLG	PRO+	BR/A	SB	CS	SBR	FA	FR	G/POS	TPR
1910	Cin-N	1	1	0	1	0	0	0	0	0	0	1.000	1.000	1.000	506	0	1			.000	0	H	0.1
1913	Det-A	4	13	0	5	0	0	0	1	2	4	.385	.500	.385	162	1	0			1.000	-1	/O-4	0.1
Total	2	5	14	0	6	0	0	0	1	2	4	.429	.529	.429	184	2	1			1.000	-1	/O-4	0.2

■ JOE BURNS Burns, Joseph Francis b: 2/25/1900, Trenton, N.J. d: 1/7/86, Trenton, N.J. BR/TR, 6′, 175 lbs. Deb: 4/18/24

YEAR	TM/L	G	AB	R	H	2B	3B	HR	RBI	BB	SO	AVG	OBP	SLG	PRO+	BR/A	SB	CS	SBR	FA	FR	G/POS	TPR
1924	Chi-A	8	19	1	2	0	0	0	0	0	2	.105	.105	.105	-47	-4	0	0	0	.933	-2	/C-6	-0.6

■ JOE BURNS Burns, Joseph James b: 6/17/16, Bryn Mawr, Pa. d: 6/24/74, Bryn Mawr, Pa. BR/TR, 5′10.5″, 175 lbs. Deb: 4/24/43

YEAR	TM/L	G	AB	R	H	2B	3B	HR	RBI	BB	SO	AVG	OBP	SLG	PRO+	BR/A	SB	CS	SBR	FA	FR	G/POS	TPR
1943	Bos-N	52	135	12	28	3	0	1	5	8	25	.207	.262	.252	49	-9	2			.933	-1	3-34/O-4	-1.0
1944	Phi-A	28	75	5	18	2	0	1	8	4	8	.240	.278	.307	68	-3	0	1	-1	.919	-8	3-17/2-9	-1.2
1945	Phi-A	31	90	7	23	1	1	0	3	4	17	.256	.287	.289	68	-4	0	1	-1	1.000	-4	O-19/3-5,1-1	-1.0
Total	3	111	300	24	69	6	1	2	16	16	50	.230	.274	.277	60	-16	2	2		.920	-12	/3-56,O-23,2-9,1-1	-3.2

YEAR	TM/L	G	AB	R	H	2B	3B	HR	RBI	BB	SO	AVG	OBP	SLG	PRO+	BR/A	SB	CS	SBR	FA	FR	G/POS	TPR
■ PAT BURNS Burns, Patrick Deb: 8/11/1884																							
1884	Bal-a	6	25	3	5	2	1	0		3		.200	.286	.360	105	0				.953	-1	/1-6	-0.1
	Bal-U	1	4	0	2	0	0	0		0		.500	.500	.500	185	0				.917	-0	/1-1	0.0
Total	1	7	29	3	7	2	1	0		3		.241	.313	.379	117	0				.947	-1	/1-7	-0.1
■ DICK BURNS Burns, Richard Simon b: 12/26/1863, Holyoke, Mass. d: 11/16/37, Holyoke, Mass. BL/TL, 5′7″, 140 lbs. Deb: 5/3/1883																							
1883	Det-N	37	140	11	26	7	1	0	5	2	22	.186	.197	.250	36	-10				.758	-6	O-24,P-17	-1.0
1884	Cin-U	79	350	84	107	17	**12**	4		5		.306	.315	.457	122	-2				.827	-3	O-44,P-40/S-2	-0.5
1885	StL-N	14	54	2	12	2	1	0	4	3	8	.222	.263	.296	86	-1				.682	-3	O-14/P-1	-0.5
Total	3	130	544	97	145	26	14	4	9	10	30	.267	.280	.388	98	-13				.785	-12	/O-82,P-58,S-2	-2.0
■ TOM BURNS Burns, Thomas Everett b: 3/30/1857, Honesdale, Pa. d: 3/19/02, Jersey City, N.J. BR/TR, 5′7″, 152 lbs. Deb: 5/1/1880 MU																							
1880	Chi-N	85	333	47	103	17	3	0	43	12	23	.309	.333	.378	133	10				.864	-24	*S-79/3-9,C-2,P-1	-0.9
1881	Chi-N	84	342	41	95	20	3	4	42	14	22	.278	.306	.389	112	4				.870	-5	*S-80/3-3,2-3	0.4
1882	Chi-N	84	355	55	88	23	6	0	48	15	28	.248	.278	.346	95	-3				.911	0	2-43,S-41	0.0
1883	Chi-N	97	405	69	119	37	7	2	67	13	31	.294	.316	.435	118	7				.872	-1	*S-79,2-19/O-1	0.7
1884	Chi-N	83	343	54	84	14	2	7	44	13	50	.245	.272	.359	89	-6				.838	-2	*S-80/3-3	-0.6
1885	*Chi-N	111	445	82	121	23	9	7	71	16	48	.272	.297	.411	112	2				.844	-2	*S-111/2-1	0.2
1886	*Chi-N	112	445	64	123	18	10	3	65	14	40	.276	.298	.382	92	-8	15			.890	13	*3-112	0.7
1887	Chi-N	115	424	57	112	20	10	3	60	34	32	.264	.320	.380	83	-13	32			.872	21	*3-107/O-8	0.9
1888	Chi-N	134	483	60	115	12	6	3	70	26	49	.238	.281	.306	81	-11	34			.905	17	*3-134	0.8
1889	Chi-N	136	525	64	127	27	6	4	66	32	57	.242	.288	.339	71	-23	18			.880	3	*3-136	-1.3
1890	Chi-N	139	538	86	149	17	6	5	86	57	45	.277	.348	.359	102	1	44			.898	2	*3-139	0.7
1891	Chi-N	59	243	36	55	8	1	1	17	21	21	.226	.288	.280	66	-11	18			.892	-2	3-53/S-4,O-2	-0.9
1892	Pit-N	12	39	7	8	0	0	0	4	3	8	.205	.262	.205	41	-3	1			.690	-5	/3-8,O-3,M	-0.7
Total	13	1251	4920	722	1299	236	69	39	683	270	454	.264	.303	.364	95	-52	162			.886	16	3-704,S-474/2OCP	0.0
■ OYSTER BURNS Burns, Thomas P. b: 9/6/1864, Philadelphia, Pa. d: 11/11/28, Brooklyn, N.Y. BR/TR, 5′8″, 183 lbs. Deb: 8/18/1884																							
1884	Wil-U	2	7	0	1	0	1	0		1		.143	.250	.429	99	-0				.778	-0	/S-2	0.0
	Bal-a	35	131	34	39	2	6	6	23	7		.298	.348	.542	179	11				.826	-5	O-24,2-10/P-2,3-1	0.5
1885	Bal-a	78	321	47	74	11	6	5	37	16		.231	.280	.349	99	-0				.908	-0	O-45,P-15,S/321	-0.1
1887	Bal-a	140	551	122	188	33	**19**	9	99	63		.341	.414	.519	169	53	58			.841	-19	*S-98,3-42/P-3,2-1	2.8
1888	Bal-a	79	325	54	97	18	9	4	42	24		.298	.349	.446	158	20	23			.855	-5	O-56,S-23/P-5,32	1.3
	Bro-a	52	204	40	58	9	6	2	25	14		.284	.339	.417	142	9	21			.851	-13	S-36,O-14/2-3	-0.3
	Yr	131	529	94	155	27	15	6	67	38		.293	.345	.435	152	30	44			.847	-18	O-70,S-59/P-5,23	1.0
1889	*Bro-a	131	504	105	153	19	13	5	100	68	26	.304	.391	.423	131	22	32			.920	-8	*O-113,S-19	1.0
1890	*Bro-N	119	472	102	134	22	12	**13**	**128**	51	42	.284	.359	.464	139	21	21			.941	-3	*O-116/3-3	1.3
1891	Bro-N	123	470	75	134	24	13	4	83	53	30	.285	.358	.417	126	15	21			.922	2	*O-113/S-6,3-5	1.2
1892	Bro-N	141	542	88	171	27	18	4	96	65	42	.315	.395	.454	163	42	33			.937	-13	*O-129/3-7,S-5	2.2
1893	Bro-N	109	415	68	112	22	8	7	60	36	16	.270	.334	.412	103	-0	14			.932	-1	*O-108/S-1	-0.5
1894	Bro-N	125	505	106	179	32	14	5	107	44	18	.354	.409	.503	128	23	30			.949	-4	*O-125	0.9
1895	Bro-N	20	76	7	14	0	1	0	7	8	2	.184	.271	.211	27	-8	0			.918	1	O-19	-0.7
	NY-N	33	114	21	35	5	3	1	25	14	6	.307	.388	.430	113	3	10			.870	-5	O-32/1-1	-0.3
	Yr	53	190	28	49	5	4	1	32	22	8	.258	.341	.342	80	-5	10			.893	-3	O-51/1-1	-1.0
Total	11	1187	4637	869	1389	224	129	65	832	464	182	.300	.368	.446	135	210	263			.920	-73	O-894,S-200/3P21	9.3
■ ALEX BURR Burr, Alexander Thomson b: 11/1/1893, Chicago, Ill. d: 10/12/18, Cazaux, France BR/TR, 6′3.5″, 190 lbs. Deb: 4/21/14																							
1914	NY-A	1	0	0	0	0	0	0	0	0	0	—	—	—	—	0	0			.000	-1	/O-1	-0.1
■ BUSTER BURRELL Burrell, Frank Andrew b: 12/22/1866, Weymouth, Mass. d: 5/8/62, Weymouth, Mass. BR/TR, 5′10″, 165 lbs. Deb: 8/1/1891																							
1891	NY-N	15	53	1	5	0	0	0	1	3	12	.094	.158	.094	-27	-8	2			.856	-5	C-15/O-1	-1.2
1895	Bro-N	12	28	7	4	0	0	1	5	4	3	.143	.250	.250	32	-3	0			.838	-2	C-12	-0.3
1896	Bro-N	62	206	19	62	11	3	0	23	15	13	.301	.348	.383	98	-1	1			.928	-9	C-60	-0.3
1897	Bro-N	33	103	15	25	2	0	2	18	10		.243	.310	.320	70	-4	1			.884	-4	C-27/1-4	-0.5
Total	4	122	390	42	96	13	3	3	47	32	28	.246	.305	.318	70	-16	4			.896	-19	C-114/1-4,O-1	-2.3
■ LARRY BURRIGHT Burright, Larry Allen "Possum" b: 7/10/37, Roseville, Ill. BR/TR, 5′11″, 170 lbs. Deb: 4/12/62																							
1962	LA-N	115	249	35	51	6	5	4	30	21	67	.205	.267	.317	60	-15	4	3	-1	.962	14	*2-109/S-1	0.6
1963	NY-N	41	100	9	22	2	1	0	3	8	25	.220	.291	.260	59	-5	1	0	0	.946	12	S-19,2-15/3-1	1.0
1964	NY-N	3	7	0	0	0	0	0	0	0	0	.000	.000	.000	-99	-2	0	0	0	1.000	4	/2-3	0.3
Total	3	159	356	44	73	8	6	4	33	29	92	.205	.269	.295	56	-22	5	3	-0	.964	30	2-127/S-20,3-1	1.9
■ PAUL BURRIS Burris, Paul Robert b: 7/21/23, Hickory, N.C. BR/TR, 6′, 190 lbs. Deb: 10/2/48																							
1948	Bos-N	2	4	0	2	0	0	0	0	0	0	.500	.500	.500	174	0	0			1.000	1	/C-2	0.1
1950	Bos-N	10	23	1	4	1	0	0	3	1	2	.174	.208	.217	13	-3	0			1.000	1	/C-8	-0.1
1952	Bos-N	55	168	14	37	4	0	2	21	7	19	.220	.256	.280	50	-12	0	0	0	1.000	-4	C-50	-1.4
1953	Mil-N	2	1	0	0	0	0	0	0	0	0	.000	.000	.000	-99	-0	0	0	0	1.000	-0	/C-2	0.0
Total	4	69	196	15	43	5	0	2	24	8	21	.219	.254	.276	47	-14	0	0		1.000	-2	/C-62	-1.4
■ HENRY BURROUGHS Burroughs, Henry S. b: 1845, New Jersey d: 3/31/1878, Newark, N.J. 5′8″, 147 lbs. Deb: 5/5/1871																							
1871	Oly-n	12	63	11	15	2	3	1	14	1	1	.238	.250	.413	91	-0	0	0	0	.706	-2	/O-8,3-5,2-1	-0.2
1872	Oly-n	2	7	1	1	0	0	0	0	1	0	.143	.250	.143	25	-1	0	0	0	.625	0	/O-2	0.0
Total	2 n	14	70	12	16	2	3	1	14	2	1	.229	.250	.386	85	-1	0	0	0	.680	-2	/O-10,3-5,2-1	-0.2
■ JEFF BURROUGHS Burroughs, Jeffrey Alan b: 3/7/51, Long Beach, Cal. BR/TR, 6′1″, 200 lbs. Deb: 7/20/70																							
1970	Was-A	6	12	1	2	0	0	0	1	2	5	.167	.286	.167	29	-1	0	0	0	1.000	-0	/O-3	-0.1
1971	Was-A	59	181	20	42	9	0	5	25	22	55	.232	.319	.365	99	-1	1	0	0	.966	-5	O-50	-0.8
1972	Tex-A	22	65	4	12	1	0	1	3	5	22	.185	.243	.246	48	-4	0	2	-1	.935	-1	O-19/1-1	-0.8
1973	Tex-A	151	526	71	147	17	1	30	85	67	88	.279	.362	.487	143	29	0	0	0	.975	13	*O-148/1-3,D-1	3.5
1974	Tex-A★	152	554	84	167	33	2	25	**118**	91	104	.301	.405	.504	164	**48**	2	3	-1	.972	-8	*O-150/1-2,D-1	3.3
1975	Tex-A	152	585	81	132	20	0	29	94	79	155	.226	.319	.409	105	3	4	4	-1	.966	-8	*O-148/D-3	-1.3
1976	Tex-A	158	604	71	143	22	2	18	86	69	93	.237	.317	.369	98	-1	0	0	0	.987	-2	*O-155/D-3	-1.0
1977	Atl-N	154	579	91	157	19	1	41	114	86	126	.271	.365	.520	120	16	4	1	1	.974	-4	*O-154	0.6
1978	Atl-N☆	153	488	72	147	30	6	23	77	**117**	92	.301	**.436**	.529	151	38	1	2	-1	.975	-0	*O-146	3.2
1979	Atl-N	116	397	49	89	14	1	11	47	73	75	.224	.349	.348	84	-7	2	2	-1	.963	-1	*O-110	-1.3
1980	Atl-N	99	278	35	73	14	0	13	51	35	57	.263	.349	.453	118	7	1	1	-0	.977	-4	O-73	0.0
1981	Sea-A	89	319	32	81	13	1	10	41	41	64	.254	.339	.395	107	3	0	1	-1	.985	-9	O-87/D-1	-1.0
1982	Oak-A	113	285	42	79	13	2	16	48	45	61	.277	.376	.505	146	18	1	3	-2	.981	-5	D-48,O-34	0.9
1983	Oak-A	121	401	43	108	15	1	10	56	47	79	.269	.346	.387	108	5	0	2	-1	.000	0	*D-114	-0.1
1984	Oak-A	58	71	5	15	1	0	2	8	18	23	.211	.371	.310	97	1	0	0	0	1.000	-2	D-23/O-4	-0.2
1985	*Tor-A	86	191	19	49	9	3	6	28	34	36	.257	.369	.429	115	5	0	1	-1	.000	0	D-75	0.3
Total	16	1689	5536	720	1443	230	20	240	882	831	1135	.261	.359	.439	120	159	16	22	-8	.974	-36	*O-1281,D-269/1-6	5.2
■ DICK BURRUS Burrus, Maurice Lennon b: 1/29/1898, Hatteras, N.C. d: 2/2/72, Elizabeth City, N.C BL/TL, 5′11″, 175 lbs. Deb: 6/23/19																							
1919	Phi-A	70	194	17	50	3	4	0	8	9	25	.258	.294	.314	70	-8	2			.986	-4	1-38,O-10	-1.5
1920	Phi-A	71	135	11	25	8	0	0	10	5	7	.185	.225	.244	24	-15	0	3	-2	.989	-2	1-31/O-2	-1.9
1925	Bos-N	152	588	82	200	41	4	5	87	51	29	.340	.396	.449	126	24	8	9	-3	**.990**	1	*1-151	1.2
1926	Bos-N	131	486	59	131	21	1	3	61	37	16	.270	.324	.335	85	-11	4			.991	12	*1-128	-0.6
1927	Bos-N	72	220	22	70	8	3	0	32	17	10	.318	.370	.382	110	3	3			.972	1	1-61	0.1
1928	Bos-N	64	137	15	37	6	0	3	13	19	8	.270	.367	.380	101	1	1			.977	-2	1-32	-0.4
Total	6	560	1760	206	513	87	12	11	211	138	95	.291	.347	.373	97	-6	18	12		.986	7	1-441/O-12	-3.1

YEAR	TM/L	G	AB	R	H	2B	3B	HR	RBI	BB	SO	AVG	OBP	SLG	PRO+	BR/A	SB	CS	SBR	FA	FR	G/POS	TPR
■ FRANK BURT	Burt, Frank J. b: Camden, N.J. Deb: 5/2/1882																						
1882	Bal-a	10	36	2	4	2	1	0		1		.111	.135	.222	20	-3				.815	-1	O-10	-0.3
■ ELLIS BURTON	Burton, Ellis Narrington b: 8/12/36, Los Angeles, Cal. BB/TR, 5'11", 165 lbs. Deb: 9/18/58																						
1958	StL-N	8	30	5	7	0	1	2	4	3	8	.233	.324	.500	110	0	0	1	-1	1.000	-0	/O-7	-0.1
1960	StL-N	29	28	5	6	1	0	0	2	4	14	.214	.313	.250	52	-2	0	2	-1	1.000	-7	O-23	-1.1
1963	Cle-A	26	31	6	6	3	0	1	1	4	4	.194	.286	.387	87	-1	0	0	0	1.000	-4	O-16	-0.5
	Chi-N	93	322	45	74	16	1	12	41	36	59	.230	.315	.398	98	-1	6	3	0	.975	-9	O-90	-1.5
1964	Chi-N	42	105	12	20	3	2	2	7	17	22	.190	.303	.314	71	-4	4	0	1	.981	-4	O-29	-0.9
1965	Chi-N	17	40	6	7	1	0	0	4	1	10	.175	.195	.200	11	-5	1	0	0	1.000	-0	O-12	-0.5
Total	5	215	556	79	120	24	4	17	59	65	117	.216	.304	.365	85	-11	11	6	-0	.981	-24	O-177	-4.6
■ JIM BUSBY	Busby, James Franklin b: 1/8/27, Kenedy, Tex. d: 7/8/96, Augusta, Ga. BR/TR, 6'1", 175 lbs. Deb: 4/23/50 C																						
1950	Chi-A	18	48	5	10	0	0	0	4	1	5	.208	.224	.208	12	-6	0	2	-1	.964	-1	O-12	-0.8
1951	Chi-A★	143	477	59	135	15	2	5	68	40	46	.283	.344	.354	91	-6	26	11	1	.982	3	*O-139	-0.6
1952	Chi-A	16	39	5	5	0	0	0	0	2	7	.128	.171	.128	-16	-6	0	2	-1	1.000	-0	O-16	-0.9
	Was-A	129	512	58	125	24	4	2	47	22	48	.244	.281	.318	69	-23	5	6	-2	.993	14	*O-128	-1.8
	Yr	145	551	63	130	24	4	2	47	24	55	.236	.273	.305	62	-29	5	8	-3	.994	13	*O-144	-2.7
1953	Was-A	150	586	68	183	28	7	6	82	38	45	.312	.358	.415	111	8	13	6	0	.988	**19**	*O-150	2.1
1954	Was-A	155	628	83	187	22	7	7	80	43	56	.298	.346	.389	107	4	17	2	**4**	.988	12	*O-155	1.4
1955	Was-A	47	191	23	44	6	2	6	14	13	22	.230	.279	.377	79	-7	5	0	2	.993	2	O-47	-0.5
	Chi-A	99	337	38	82	13	4	1	27	25	37	.243	.296	.315	62	-18	7	3	0	.984	2	O-99	-2.0
	Yr	146	528	61	126	19	6	7	41	38	59	.239	.290	.337	68	-25	12	3	2	.987	5	*O-146	-2.5
1956	Cle-A	135	494	72	116	17	3	12	50	43	47	.235	.301	.354	71	-22	8	3	1	.989	5	*O-133	-2.3
1957	Cle-A	30	74	9	14	2	1	2	4	1	8	.189	.200	.324	41	-6	0	1	-1	.978	-3	O-26	-1.2
	Bal-A	86	288	31	72	10	1	3	19	23	36	.250	.305	.323	77	-10	6	3	0	.984	10	O-85	-0.5
	Yr	116	362	40	86	12	2	5	23	24	44	.238	.285	.323	69	-16	6	4	-1	.983	6	*O-111	-1.7
1958	Bal-A	113	215	32	51	7	2	3	19	24	37	.237	.322	.330	84	-4	6	4	-1	**.995**	-9	*O-103/3-1	-1.7
1959	Bos-A	61	102	16	23	8	0	1	5	5	18	.225	.269	.333	61	-6	0	1	-1	.980	-6	O-34	-1.3
1960	Bos-A	1	0	0	0	0	0	0	0	0	0	—	—	—	—	0	0	0	0	.000	-0	/O-1	0.0
	Bal-A	79	159	25	41	7	1	0	12	20	14	.258	.341	.314	79	-4	2	3	-1	.985	-5	O-71	-1.3
	Yr	80	159	25	41	7	1	0	12	20	14	.258	.341	.314	79	-4	2	3	-1	.985	-6	O-72	-1.3
1961	Bal-A	75	89	15	23	3	1	0	6	8	10	.258	.320	.315	73	-3	2	0	1	.987	-16	O-71	-2.1
1962	Hou-N	15	11	2	2	0	0	0	1	2	3	.182	.308	.182	38	-1	0	1	-1	1.000	-4	O-10/C-1	-0.5
Total	13	1352	4250	541	1113	162	35	48	438	310	439	.262	.316	.350	82	-110	97	48	0	.988	22	*O-1280/C-1,3-1	-14.0
■ PAUL BUSBY	Busby, Paul Miller "Red" b: 8/25/18, Waynesboro, Miss. BL/TR, 6'1", 175 lbs. Deb: 9/14/41																						
1941	Phi-N	10	16	3	5	0	0	0	2	0	1	.313	.313	.313	79	-0	0			1.000	-1	/O-3	-0.1
1943	Phi-N	26	40	13	10	1	0	0	5	2	1	.250	.286	.275	65	-2	2			1.000	0	O-10	-0.2
Total	2	36	56	16	15	1	0	0	7	2	2	.268	.293	.286	69	-2	2			1.000	-1	/O-13	-0.3
■ ED BUSCH	Busch, Edgar John b: 11/16/17, Lebanon, Ill. d: 1/17/87, St.Clair Co., Ill. BR/TR, 5'10", 175 lbs. Deb: 9/30/43																						
1943	Phi-A	4	17	2	5	0	0	0	0	1	2	.294	.368	.294	95	-0	0	1	-1	.941	-3	/S-4	-0.3
1944	Phi-A	140	484	41	131	11	3	0	40	29	17	.271	.313	.306	78	-14	5	3	-0	.940	-30	*S-111,2-27/3-4	-3.6
1945	Phi-A	126	416	37	104	10	3	0	35	32	9	.250	.305	.288	73	-14	2	3	-1	.952	1	*S-116/2-2,3-2,1-1	-0.6
Total	3	270	917	80	240	21	6	0	75	62	28	.262	.311	.298	76	-28	7	7	-2	.946	-32	S-231/2-29,3-6,1-1	-4.5
■ MIKE BUSCH	Busch, Michael Anthony b: 7/7/68, Davenport, Iowa BR/TR, 6'5", 249 lbs. Deb: 8/30/95																						
1995	LA-N	13	17	3	4	0	0	3	6	0	7	.235	.235	.765	165	1	0	0	0	.875	-1	3-10/1-2	0.1
1996	LA-N	38	83	8	18	4	0	4	17	5	33	.217	.261	.410	80	-3	0	0	0	.932	-4	3-23/1-1	-0.7
Total	2	51	100	11	22	4	0	7	23	5	40	.220	.257	.470	94	-2	0	0	0	.923	-4	/3-33,1-3	-0.6
■ HOMER BUSH	Bush, Homer Giles b: 11/12/72, East St.Louis, Ill. BR/TR, 5'11", 180 lbs. Deb: 8/16/97																						
1997	NY-A	10	11	2	4	0	0	0	3	0	0	.364	.364	.364	91	-0	0	0	0	.913	4	/2-8,D-1	0.3
1998	*NY-A	45	71	17	27	3	0	1	5	5	19	.380	.421	.465	133	4	6	3	0	.971	6	2-24,D-12/3-3,S-2	0.9
Total	2	55	82	19	31	3	0	1	8	5	19	.378	.414	.451	128	3	6	3	0	.956	10	/2-32,D-13,3-3,S-2	1.2
■ DONIE BUSH	Bush, Owen Joseph b: 10/8/1887, Indianapolis, Ind. d: 3/28/72, Indianapolis, Ind. BB/TR, 5'6", 140 lbs. Deb: 9/18/08 M																						
1908	Det-A	20	68	13	20	1	1	0	4	7		.294	.360	.338	122	2	2			.938	-4	S-20	-0.2
1909	*Det-A	157	532	114	145	18	2	0	33	**88**		.273	.380	.314	114	13	53			.925	4	*S-157	2.3
1910	Det-A	142	496	90	130	13	4	3	34	**78**		.262	.365	.323	108	7	49			**.940**	9	*S-141/3-1	2.4
1911	Det-A	150	561	126	130	18	5	1	36	**98**		.232	.349	.287	74	-16	40			.925	17	*S-150	1.0
1912	Det-A	144	511	107	118	14	8	2	38	**117**		.231	.377	.301	98	5	35			.929	29	*S-144	4.6
1913	Det-A	153	597	98	150	19	10	1	40	80	32	.251	.344	.322	96	-1	44			.938	2	*S-153	1.6
1914	Det-A	157	596	97	150	18	4	0	32	**112**	54	.252	.373	.295	98	4	35	26	-5	.944	**34**	*S-157	4.9
1915	Det-A	155	561	99	128	12	8	1	44	118	44	.228	.364	.283	89	-2	35	27	-6	.937	9	*S-155	1.4
1916	Det-A	145	550	73	124	5	9	0	34	75	42	.225	.319	.267	74	-16	19			.954	-15	*S-144	-2.6
1917	Det-A	147	581	**112**	163	18	3	0	24	80	40	.281	.370	.322	111	11	34			.932	-18	*S-147	0.0
1918	Det-A	128	500	74	117	10	3	0	22	79	31	.234	.340	.266	86	-5	9			.931	-20	*S-128	-2.2
1919	Det-A	129	509	82	124	11	6	0	26	75	36	.244	.343	.289	80	-11	22			.943	-12	*S-129	-1.5
1920	Det-A	141	506	85	133	18	5	1	33	73	32	.263	.357	.324	83	-9	15	7	0	.938	-17	*S-140	-1.4
1921	Det-A	104	402	72	113	6	5	0	27	45	23	.281	.355	.321	74	-14	8	11	-4	.949	-5	S-81,2-23	-1.4
	Was-A	23	84	15	18	1	0	0	2	12	4	.214	.313	.226	41	-7	2	2	-1	.932	-4	S-21	-1.0
	Yr	127	486	87	131	7	5	0	29	57	27	.270	.347	.305	69	-21	10	13	-5	.946	-10	*S-102,2-23	-2.4
1922	Was-A	41	134	17	32	4	1	0	7	21	7	.239	.342	.284	68	-6	1	1	-0	.957	-2	3-37/2-1	-0.5
1923	Was-A	10	22	6	9	0	0	0	0	0	1	.409	.409	.409	122	1	1	1	-0	.813	-2	/3-5,2-2,M	-0.1
Total	16	1946	7210	1280	1804	186	74	9	436	1158	346	.250	.356	.300	91	-42	404	75		.936	5	*S-1867/3-43,2-26	7.3
■ RANDY BUSH	Bush, Robert Randall b: 10/5/58, Dover, Del. BL/TL, 6'1", 186 lbs. Deb: 5/1/82																						
1982	Min-A	55	119	13	29	6	1	4	13	8	28	.244	.308	.412	93	-1	0	0	0	1.000	-1	D-26/O-6	-0.4
1983	Min-A	124	373	43	93	24	3	11	56	34	51	.249	.324	.418	99	-1	0	1	-1	1.000	1	*D-103/1-3	-0.5
1984	Min-A	113	311	46	69	17	1	11	43	31	60	.222	.301	.389	85	-7	1	2	-1	1.000	-0	D-89/1-2	-1.0
1985	Min-A	97	234	26	56	13	3	10	35	24	30	.239	.323	.449	103	1	3	0	1	.969	-6	O-41,D-28/1-1	-0.6
1986	Min-A	130	357	50	96	19	7	7	45	39	63	.269	.348	.420	105	3	5	3	-0	.977	-7	*O-102/1-3,D-6	-0.7
1987	*Min-A	122	293	46	74	10	2	11	46	43	49	.253	.354	.413	99	0	10	3	1	.982	-8	O-75/1-9,D-9	-0.9
1988	Min-A	136	394	51	103	20	3	14	51	58	49	.261	.369	.434	120	12	8	6	-1	.979	-6	*O-109/1-6,D-7	0.2
1989	Min-A	141	391	60	103	17	4	14	54	48	73	.263	.348	.435	112	6	5	8	-3	.986	-9	*O-109,1-25/D-5	-1.0
1990	Min-A	73	181	17	44	8	0	6	18	21	27	.243	.341	.387	97	-0	0	3	-2	1.000	-2	O-32,D-29/1-6	-0.6
1991	*Min-A	93	165	21	50	10	1	6	23	24	25	.303	.401	.485	137	9	0	2	-1	1.000	-5	O-38,1-12,D-10	0.2
1992	Min-A	100	182	14	39	8	1	2	22	11	37	.214	.267	.302	57	-11	1	1	-0	1.000	-3	O-24,D-24/1-8	-1.6
1993	Min-A	35	45	1	7	2	0	0	3	7	13	.156	.269	.200	28	-4	0	0	0	1.000	-1	/1-4,O-1,D-5	-0.5
Total	12	1219	3045	388	763	154	26	96	409	348	505	.251	.337	.413	101	7	33	29	-8	.983	-48	O-537,D-341/1-79	-7.4
■ DOC BUSHONG	Bushong, Albert John b: 9/15/1856, Philadelphia, Pa. d: 8/19/08, Brooklyn, N.Y. BR/TR, 5'11", 165 lbs. Deb: 7/19/1875																						
1875	Atl-n	1	5	0	3	0	1	0	0	0	0	.600	.600	1.000	511	2	0	0	0	.800	-0	/C-1	0.1
1876	Phi-N	5	21	4	1	0	0	0	1	0	0	.048	.048	.048	-69	-4				.769	-1	/C-5	-0.4
1880	Wor-N	41	146	13	25	3	0	0	19	1	16	.171	.177	.192	23	-12				.918	16	C-40/O-1,3-1	0.5
1881	Wor-N	76	275	35	64	7	4	0	21	21	23	.233	.287	.287	77	-7				.918	11	*C-76	0.6
1882	Wor-N	69	253	20	40	4	1	1	15	5	17	.158	.174	.194	18	-23				.897	-3	*C-69	-2.1
1883	Cle-N	63	215	15	37	5	0	0	9	7	19	.172	.198	.195	21	-20				.909	15	C-63	-0.1
1884	Cle-N	62	203	24	48	6	1	0	10	17	11	.236	.295	.276	78	-5				.886	0	C-62/O-1	0.1

YEAR	TM/L	G	AB	R	H	2B	3B	HR	RBI	BB	SO	AVG	OBP	SLG	PRO+	BR/A	SB	CS	SBR	FA	FR	G/POS	TPR
1885	*StL-a	85	300	42	80	13	5	0	21	11		.267	.297	.343	97	-2				.932	14	*C-85/3-1	1.7
1886	*StL-a	107	386	56	86	8	0	1	31	31		.223	.281	.251	64	-16	12			**.942**	16	*C-106/1-1	1.0
1887	*StL-a	53	201	35	51	4	0	0	26	11		.254	.299	.274	55	-13	14			.927	7	C-52/O-2,3-2	-0.2
1888	Bro-a	69	253	23	53	5	1	0	16	5		.209	.231	.237	50	-14	9			.915	-7	C-69	-1.4
1889	*Bro-a	25	84	15	13	1	0	0	8	9	7	.155	.237	.167	16	-9	2			.894	-1	C-25	-0.7
1890	*Bro-N	16	55	5	13	2	0	0	7	6	4	.236	.311	.273	70	-2	2			.913	-1	C-15/O-2	-0.2
Total	12	671	2392	287	511	58	12	2	184	124	97	.214	.254	.250	55	-127	39	0		.916	66	C-667/O-6,3-4,1-1	-1.2

■ JOE BUSKEY
Buskey, Joseph Henry "Jazzbow" b: 12/18/02, Cumberland, Md. d: 4/11/49, Cumberland, Md. BR/TR, 5'10", 175 lbs. Deb: 4/19/26

YEAR	TM/L	G	AB	R	H	2B	3B	HR	RBI	BB	SO	AVG	OBP	SLG	PRO+	BR/A	SB	CS	SBR	FA	FR	G/POS	TPR
1926	Phi-N	5	8	1	0	0	0	0	0	1	1	.000	.111	.000	-65	-2	0			.810	-0	/S-5	-0.2

■ MIKE BUSKEY
Buskey, Michael Thomas b: 1/13/49, San Francisco, Cal. BR/TR, 5'11", 160 lbs. Deb: 9/2/77

YEAR	TM/L	G	AB	R	H	2B	3B	HR	RBI	BB	SO	AVG	OBP	SLG	PRO+	BR/A	SB	CS	SBR	FA	FR	G/POS	TPR
1977	Phi-N	6	7	1	2	0	1	0	1	0	1	.286	.375	.571	143	0	0	0	0	.882	2	/S-6	0.2

■ RAY BUSSE
Busse, Raymond Edward b: 9/25/48, Daytona Beach, Fla. BR/TR, 6'4", 175 lbs. Deb: 7/24/71

YEAR	TM/L	G	AB	R	H	2B	3B	HR	RBI	BB	SO	AVG	OBP	SLG	PRO+	BR/A	SB	CS	SBR	FA	FR	G/POS	TPR
1971	Hou-N	10	34	2	5	3	0	0	4	2	9	.147	.194	.235	22	-4	0	0	0	.929	-2	/S-5,3-3	-0.6
1973	StL-N	24	70	6	10	4	2	2	5	5	21	.143	.200	.343	48	-5	0	1	-1	.898	-2	S-23	-0.6
	Hou-N	15	17	1	1	0	0	0	0	1	12	.059	.111	.059	-52	-3	0	0	0	1.000	1	/S-5,3-3	-0.2
	Yr	39	87	7	11	4	2	2	5	6	33	.126	.183	.287	28	-9	0	1	-1	.906	-1	S-28/3-3	-0.8
1974	Hou-N	19	34	3	7	1	0	0	0	3	12	.206	.270	.235	44	-3	0	0	0	.864	-0	/3-8	-0.3
Total	3	68	155	12	23	8	2	2	9	11	54	.148	.205	.265	31	-15	0	1	-1	.908	-3	/S-33,3-14	-1.7

■ HANK BUTCHER
Butcher, Henry Joseph b: 7/12/1886, Chicago, Ill. d: 12/28/79, Hazel Crest, Ill. BR/TR, 5'10", 180 lbs. Deb: 7/8/11

YEAR	TM/L	G	AB	R	H	2B	3B	HR	RBI	BB	SO	AVG	OBP	SLG	PRO+	BR/A	SB	CS	SBR	FA	FR	G/POS	TPR
1911	Cle-A	38	133	21	32	7	3	1	11	11		.241	.303	.361	84	-3	9			.984	0	O-34	-0.5
1912	Cle-A	26	82	9	16	4	1	1	10	6		.195	.250	.305	57	-5	1			.920	1	O-21	-0.5
Total	2	64	215	30	48	11	4	2	21	17		.223	.283	.340	74	-8	10			.956	2	/O-55	-1.0

■ SAL BUTERA
Butera, Salvatore Philip b: 9/25/52, Richmond Hill, N.Y BR/TR, 6', 190 lbs. Deb: 4/10/80 C

YEAR	TM/L	G	AB	R	H	2B	3B	HR	RBI	BB	SO	AVG	OBP	SLG	PRO+	BR/A	SB	CS	SBR	FA	FR	G/POS	TPR
1980	Min-A	34	85	4	23	1	0	0	2	3	6	.271	.303	.282	57	-5	0	0	0	.950	-1	C-32/D-2	-0.5
1981	Min-A	62	167	13	40	7	1	0	18	22	14	.240	.328	.293	75	-5	0	0	0	.970	5	C-59/1-1,D-1	0.2
1982	Min-A	54	126	9	32	2	0	0	8	17	12	.254	.347	.270	70	-4	0	0	0	.988	6	C-53	0.3
1983	Det-A	4	5	1	1	0	0	0	0	0	0	.200	.200	.200	11	-1	0	0	0	.929	1	/C-4	0.1
1984	Mon-N	3	3	0	0	0	0	0	0	1	0	.000	.250	.000	26	0	0	0	0	1.000	1	/C-2	0.0
1985	Mon-N	67	120	11	24	1	0	3	12	13	12	.200	.284	.283	63	-6	0	0	0	.984	0	C-66/P-1	-0.4
1986	Cin-N	56	113	14	27	6	1	2	16	21	10	.239	.358	.363	95	-0	0	0	0	.979	1	C-53/P-1	0.3
1987	Cin-N	5	11	1	2	0	0	1	2	1	6	.182	.250	.455	78	-0	0	0	0	.920	1	/C-5	0.1
	*Min-A	51	111	7	19	5	0	1	12	7	16	.171	.220	.243	22	-13	0	0	0	.983	1	C-51	-0.9
1988	Tor-A	23	60	3	14	2	1	1	6	1	9	.233	.246	.350	65	-3	0	0	0	.991	3	C-23	0.1
Total	9	359	801	63	182	24	3	8	76	86	85	.227	.304	.295	65	-37	0	0	0	.978	17	C-348/D-3,P-2,1-1	-0.7

■ ED BUTKA
Butka, Edward Luke "Babe" b: 1/7/16, Canonsburg, Pa. BR/TR, 6'3", 193 lbs. Deb: 9/26/43

YEAR	TM/L	G	AB	R	H	2B	3B	HR	RBI	BB	SO	AVG	OBP	SLG	PRO+	BR/A	SB	CS	SBR	FA	FR	G/POS	TPR
1943	Was-A	3	9	0	3	1	0	0	1	0	3	.333	.333	.444	132	0	0	0	0	1.000	1	/1-3	0.1
1944	Was-A	15	41	1	8	1	0	0	1	2	11	.195	.233	.220	31	-4	0	0	0	.972	0	1-14	-0.5
Total	2	18	50	1	11	2	0	0	2	2	14	.220	.250	.260	48	-3	0	0	0	.977	1	/1-17	-0.4

■ ART BUTLER
Butler, Arthur Edward (b: Arthur Edward Bouthillier)
b: 12/19/1887, Fall River, Mass. d: 10/7/84, Fall River, Mass. BR/TR, 5'9", 160 lbs. Deb: 4/14/11

YEAR	TM/L	G	AB	R	H	2B	3B	HR	RBI	BB	SO	AVG	OBP	SLG	PRO+	BR/A	SB	CS	SBR	FA	FR	G/POS	TPR
1911	Bos-N	27	68	11	12	2	0	0	2	6	6	.176	.263	.206	30	-6	0			.930	-3	3-14/2-4,S-1	-1.0
1912	Pit-N	43	154	19	42	4	2	1	17	15	13	.273	.337	.344	88	-2	2			.960	-22	2-43	-2.6
1913	Pit-N	82	214	40	60	9	3	0	20	32	14	.280	.379	.350	114	5	9			.919	-12	2-28,S-26/3-2,O-2	-0.5
1914	StL-N	86	274	29	55	12	3	1	24	39	23	.201	.311	.277	76	-7	14			.927	-19	S-83/O-1	-2.1
1915	StL-N	130	469	73	119	12	5	1	31	47	34	.254	.323	.307	91	-4	26	14	-1	.916	-34	*S-125/2-2	-3.2
1916	StL-N	86	110	9	23	5	0	0	7	7	12	.209	.256	.255	57	-6	3			.882	-6	O-15/2-8,S-1,3-1	-1.4
Total	6	454	1289	181	311	44	13	3	101	146	102	.241	.323	.303	85	-20	54	14		.919	-96	S-236/2-85,O-18,3	-10.8

■ BRETT BUTLER
Butler, Brett Morgan b: 6/15/57, Los Angeles, Cal. BL/TL, 5'10", 160 lbs. Deb: 8/20/81

YEAR	TM/L	G	AB	R	H	2B	3B	HR	RBI	BB	SO	AVG	OBP	SLG	PRO+	BR/A	SB	CS	SBR	FA	FR	G/POS	TPR
1981	Atl-N	40	126	17	32	2	3	0	4	19	17	.254	.352	.317	89	-1	9	1	2	.987	-2	O-37	-0.2
1982	*Atl-N	89	240	35	52	2	0	0	7	25	35	.217	.291	.225	44	-17	21	8	2	1.000	-10	O-77	-2.9
1983	Atl-N	151	549	84	154	21	**13**	5	37	54	56	.281	.347	.393	98	-1	39	23	-2	.987	6	*O-143	-0.2
1984	Cle-A	159	602	108	162	25	9	3	49	86	62	.269	.364	.355	98	2	52	22	2	.991	15	*O-156	1.4
1985	Cle-A	152	591	106	184	28	14	5	50	63	42	.311	.379	.431	122	19	47	20	2	**.998**	22	*O-150/D-1	3.7
1986	Cle-A	161	587	92	163	17	**14**	4	51	70	65	.278	.359	.375	102	3	32	15	1	.993	9	*O-159	0.7
1987	Cle-A	137	522	91	154	25	8	9	41	91	55	.295	.401	.425	119	18	33	16	0	.990	15	*O-136	2.7
1988	SF-N	157	568	**109**	163	27	9	6	43	97	64	.287	.395	.398	134	29	43	20	1	.988	6	*O-155	3.4
1989	*SF-N	154	594	100	168	22	4	4	36	59	69	.283	.351	.354	105	5	31	16	-0	.986	14	*O-152	1.6
1990	SF-N	160	622	108	**192**	20	9	3	44	90	62	.309	.401	.384	122	23	51	19	4	.986	7	*O-159	3.0
1991	LA-N★	161	615	**112**	182	13	5	2	38	**108**	79	.296	.402	.343	114	18	38	28	-5	**1.000**	12	*O-161	2.1
1992	LA-N	157	553	86	171	14	11	3	39	95	67	.309	.413	.391	131	28	41	21	-0	.995	2	*O-155	2.8
1993	LA-N	156	607	80	181	21	10	1	42	86	69	.298	.390	.371	111	14	39	19	0	**1.000**	3	*O-155	1.3
1994	LA-N	111	417	79	131	13	**9**	8	33	68	52	.314	.413	.446	133	23	27	8	3	.993	5	*O-111	2.7
1995	NY-N	90	367	54	114	13	7	1	25	43	42	.311	.383	.392	108	6	21	7	2	.995	6	O-90	1.1
	*LA-N	39	146	24	40	5	2	0	13	24	9	.274	.376	.336	98	1	11	1	3	.987	-1	O-38	0.1
	Yr	129	513	78	154	18	**9**	1	38	67	51	.300	.381	.376	106	7	32	8	5	.993	4	*O-128	1.2
1996	LA-N	34	131	22	35	1	1	0	8	9	22	.267	.319	.290	67	-6	8	3	1	.987	1	O-34	-0.5
1997	LA-N	105	343	52	97	8	3	0	18	42	40	.283	.363	.324	88	-5	15	10	-2	1.000	0	O-91/D-1	-0.8
Total	17	2213	8180	1359	2375	277	131	54	578	1129	907	.290	.379	.376	110	157	558	257	13	.992	110	*O-2159/D-2	22.0

■ FRANK BUTLER
Butler, Frank Dean "Stuffy" or "Goldbrick" b: 7/18/1860, Savannah, Ga. d: 7/10/45, Jacksonville, Fla BL/TL, Deb: 7/30/1895

YEAR	TM/L	G	AB	R	H	2B	3B	HR	RBI	BB	SO	AVG	OBP	SLG	PRO+	BR/A	SB	CS	SBR	FA	FR	G/POS	TPR
1895	NY-N	5	22	5	6	1	0	0	2	1	1	.273	.304	.318	62	-1	0			1.000	-1	/O-5	-0.2

■ KID BUTLER
Butler, Frank Edward b: 5/1861, Boston, Mass. d: 4/9/21, S.Boston, Mass. 5'6", 140 lbs. Deb: 5/20/1884

YEAR	TM/L	G	AB	R	H	2B	3B	HR	RBI	BB	SO	AVG	OBP	SLG	PRO+	BR/A	SB	CS	SBR	FA	FR	G/POS	TPR
1884	Bos-U	71	255	36	43	15	0	0		12		.169	.206	.227	32	-29				.810	-6	O-53,2-12/S-6,3-2	-3.2

■ JOHN BUTLER
Butler, John Albert (a.k.a. Frederick King In 1901) b: 7/26/1879, Boston, Mass. d: 2/2/50, Boston, Mass. BR/TR, 5'7", 170 lbs. Deb: 9/28/01

YEAR	TM/L	G	AB	R	H	2B	3B	HR	RBI	BB	SO	AVG	OBP	SLG	PRO+	BR/A	SB	CS	SBR	FA	FR	G/POS	TPR
1901	Mil-A	1	3	0	0	0	0	0	0	1		.000	.250	.000	-28	-0	0			1.000	-1	/C-1	-0.1
1904	StL-N	12	37	0	6	1	0	0	1	4		.162	.262	.189	42	-2	0			.968	-2	C-12	-0.4
1906	Bro-N	1	0	0	0	0	0	0	0	0		—	—	—	—	0	0			1.000	0	/C-1	0.0
1907	Bro-N	30	79	6	10	1	0	0	2	9		.127	.216	.139	12	-8	0			.946	-5	C-28/O-1	-1.2
Total	4	44	119	6	16	2	0	0	3	14		.134	.231	.151	21	-11	0			.953	-8	/C-42,O-1	-1.7

■ JOHNNY BUTLER
Butler, John Stephen "Trolley Line" b: 3/20/1893, Fall River, Kan. d: 4/29/67, Seal Beach, Cal. BR/TR, 6', 175 lbs. Deb: 4/18/26 C

YEAR	TM/L	G	AB	R	H	2B	3B	HR	RBI	BB	SO	AVG	OBP	SLG	PRO+	BR/A	SB	CS	SBR	FA	FR	G/POS	TPR
1926	Bro-N	147	501	54	135	27	5	1	68	54	44	.269	.346	.349	89	-6	6			.949	-7	*S-102,3-42/2-8	0.0
1927	Bro-N	149	521	39	124	13	6	2	57	34	33	.238	.292	.298	58	-31	9			.959	-2	S-90,3-60	-2.0
1928	Chi-N	62	174	17	47	7	0	0	16	19	7	.270	.352	.310	75	-5	2			.950	10	3-59/S-2	0.7
1929	StL-N	17	55	5	9	1	1	0	5	4	5	.164	.220	.218	9	-8	0			.964	1	/3-9,S-8	-0.5
Total	4	375	1251	115	315	48	12	3	146	111	89	.252	.320	.317	70	-51	17			.954	2	S-202,3-170/2-8	-1.8

■ RICH BUTLER
Butler, Richard Dwight b: 5/1/73, Toronto, Ont., Canada BL/TR, 6'1", 180 lbs. Deb: 9/6/97 F

YEAR	TM/L	G	AB	R	H	2B	3B	HR	RBI	BB	SO	AVG	OBP	SLG	PRO+	BR/A	SB	CS	SBR	FA	FR	G/POS	TPR
1997	Tor-A	7	14	3	4	1	0	0	2	2	3	.286	.375	.357	92	-0	0	1	-1	1.000	-0	/O-3,D-1	-0.1
1998	TB-A	72	217	25	49	3	3	7	20	15	37	.226	.282	.364	64	-12	4	2	0	1.000	2	O-61	-1.1
Total	2	79	231	28	53	4	3	7	22	17	40	.229	.288	.364	65	-12	4	3	-1	1.000	2	/O-64,D-1	-1.2

YEAR	TM/L	G	AB	R	H	2B	3B	HR	RBI	BB	SO	AVG	OBP	SLG	PRO+	BR/A	SB	CS	SBR	FA	FR	G/POS	TPR

■ DICK BUTLER   Butler, Richard H.   b: Brooklyn, N.Y.   Deb: 6/16/1897

1897	Lou-N	10	38	3	7	0	0	0	2	0		.184	.184	.184	-3	-6	1			.818	-2	C-10	-0.6
1899	Was-N	12	36	4	10	0	1	0	1	2		.278	.316	.333	79	-1	1			.892	-3	C-11	-0.3
Total	2	22	74	7	17	0	1	0	3	2		.230	.250	.257	37	-7	2			.852	-6	/C-21	-0.9

■ ROB BUTLER   Butler, Robert Frank John   b: 4/10/70, E.York, Ont., Can.   BL/TL, 5'11", 185 lbs.   Deb: 6/12/93   F

1993	*Tor-A	17	48	8	13	4	0	0	2	7	12	.271	.375	.354	97	0	2	2	-1	.970	-0	O-16	-0.1
1994	Tor-A	41	74	13	13	0	1	0	5	7	8	.176	.256	.203	20	-9	0	1	-1	.977	-5	O-31/D-1	-1.4
1997	Phi-N	43	89	10	26	9	1	0	13	5	8	.292	.330	.416	94	-1	1	0	0	1.000	-0	O-25	-0.1
Total	3	101	211	31	52	13	2	0	20	19	28	.246	.315	.327	68	-10	3	3	-1	.982	-6	/O-72,D-1	-1.6

■ BILL BUTLER   Butler, William J.   b: 1861, New Orleans, La.   Deb: 6/29/1884

| 1884 | Ind-a | 9 | 31 | 7 | 7 | 3 | 2 | 0 | | 1 | | .226 | .250 | .452 | 128 | 1 | | | | .700 | -2 | /O-9 | -0.1 |

■ KID BUTLER   Butler, Willis Everett   b: 8/9/1887, Franklin, Pa.   d: 2/22/64, Richmond, Cal.   BR/TR, 5'11", 155 lbs.   Deb: 4/30/07

| 1907 | StL-A | 20 | 59 | 4 | 13 | 2 | 0 | 0 | 6 | 2 | | .220 | .246 | .254 | 60 | -3 | 1 | | | .940 | -1 | 2-11/3-5,S-1 | -0.4 |

■ FRANK BUTTERY   Buttery, Frank   b: 5/13/1851, Silvermine, Conn.   d: 12/16/02, Silvermine, Conn.   Deb: 4/26/1872

| 1872 | Man-n | 18 | 93 | 19 | 24 | 0 | 0 | 0 | 8 | 0 | 2 | .258 | .258 | .258 | 63 | -3 | 0 | 0 | 0 | .600 | -2 | /O-8,P-7,3-5 | -0.2 |

■ JOE BUZAS   Buzas, Joseph John   b: 10/2/19, Alpha, N.J.   BR/TR, 6'1", 180 lbs.   Deb: 4/17/45

| 1945 | NY-A | 30 | 65 | 8 | 17 | 2 | 1 | 0 | 6 | 2 | 5 | .262 | .284 | .323 | 73 | -2 | 2 | 0 | 1 | .898 | -3 | S-12 | -0.4 |

■ BURLEY BYERS   Byers, Burley (b: Christopher A. Bayer)   b: 12/19/1875, Louisville, Ky.   d: 5/30/33, Louisville, Ky.   175 lbs.   Deb: 6/17/1899

| 1899 | Lou-N | 1 | 3 | 0 | 0 | 0 | 0 | 0 | | 0 | | .000 | .000 | .000 | -99 | -1 | 0 | | | .600 | -1 | /S-1 | -0.2 |

■ BILL BYERS   Byers, James William   b: 10/3/1877, Bridgeton, Ind.   d: 9/8/48, Baltimore, Md.   BR/TR, 5'7",   Deb: 4/15/04

| 1904 | StL-N | 19 | 60 | 3 | 13 | 0 | 0 | 0 | 4 | 1 | | .217 | .230 | .217 | 40 | -4 | 0 | | | .971 | -1 | C-16/1-1 | -0.4 |

■ RANDY BYERS   Byers, Randell Parker   b: 10/2/64, Bridgeton, N.J.   BL/TR, 6'2", 180 lbs.   Deb: 9/7/87

1987	SD-N	10	16	1	5	1	0	0	1	1	5	.313	.353	.375	96	-0	1	0	0	1.000	0	/O-5	0.0
1988	SD-N	11	10	0	2	1	0	0	0	0	5	.200	.200	.300	42	-1	0	0	0	.000	-1	/O-2	-0.2
Total	2	21	26	1	7	2	0	0	1	1	10	.269	.296	.346	77	-1	1	0	0	1.000	-1	/O-7	-0.2

■ JIM BYRD   Byrd, James Edward   b: 10/3/68, Wewahitchka, Fla.   BR/TR, 6'1", 185 lbs.   Deb: 5/31/93

| 1993 | Bos-A | 2 | 0 | 0 | 0 | 0 | 0 | 0 | — | | | 0 | 0 | 0 | 0 | | .000 | 0 | /R | | | | |

■ SAMMY BYRD   Byrd, Samuel Dewey "Babe Ruth's Legs"   b: 10/15/07, Bremen, Ga.   d: 5/11/81, Mesa, Ariz.   BR/TR, 5'10.5", 175 lbs.   Deb: 5/11/29

1929	NY-A	62	170	32	53	12	6	5	28	28	18	.312	.409	.471	135	10	1	4	-2	.950	-1	O-54	0.4
1930	NY-A	92	218	46	62	12	2	6	31	30	18	.284	.371	.440	110	4	5	1	1	.992	-12	O-85	-1.0
1931	NY-A	115	248	51	67	18	2	3	32	29	26	.270	.349	.395	101	0	5	0	2	.974	-13	O-88	-1.4
1932	*NY-A	105	209	49	62	12	1	8	30	30	20	.297	.385	.478	129	9	1	2	-1	.964	-18	O-91	-1.2
1933	NY-A	85	107	26	30	6	1	2	11	15	12	.280	.369	.411	113	2	0	1	-1	.987	-16	O-71	-1.5
1934	NY-A	106	191	32	47	8	0	3	18	22	12	.246	.318	.335	73	-8	1	2	-1	**.988**	-13	*O-104	-2.3
1935	Cin-N	121	416	51	109	25	4	9	52	37	51	.262	.322	.406	97	-2	4			.970	3	*O-115	-0.4
1936	Cin-N	59	141	17	35	8	0	2	13	11	11	.248	.303	.348	80	-4	0			.989	-1	O-37	-0.6
Total	8	745	1700	304	465	101	16	38	220	198	178	.274	.350	.412	104	11	17	10		.975	-71	O-645	-8.0

■ BOBBY BYRNE   Byrne, Robert Matthew   b: 12/31/1884, St.Louis, Mo.   d: 12/31/64, Wayne, Pa.   BR/TR, 5'7.5", 145 lbs.   Deb: 4/11/07

1907	StL-N	149	559	55	143	11	5	0	29	35		.256	.307	.293	91	-6	21			.920	22	*3-148/S-1	2.3
1908	StL-N	127	439	57	84	7	1	0	14	23		.191	.238	.212	46	-27	16			.925	9	*3-122/S-4	-1.6
1909	StL-N	105	421	61	90	13	6	1	33	46		.214	.302	.280	86	-6	21			.922	17	*3-105	1.6
	*Pit-N	46	168	31	43	6	2	0	7	32		.256	.387	.315	109	4	8			.987	6	3-46	1.2
	Yr	151	589	92	133	19	8	1	40	78		.226	.327	.290	93	-2	29			.939	23	*3-151	2.8
1910	Pit-N	148	602	101	**178**	**43**	12	2	52	66	27	.296	.366	.417	121	15	36			.929	-7	*3-148	1.3
1911	Pit-N	153	598	96	155	24	17	2	52	67	41	.259	.342	.366	94	-5	23			.930	-3	*3-152	-0.6
1912	Pit-N	130	528	99	152	31	11	3	35	54	40	.288	.358	.405	110	7	20			**.948**	-23	*3-130	-1.5
1913	Pit-N	113	448	54	121	22	0	1	47	29	28	.270	.322	.326	89	-7	10			.940	-9	*3-110	-1.5
	Phi-N	19	58	9	13	1	0	1	4	5	3	.224	.308	.293	69	-2	2			.963	3	3-15	0.1
	Yr	132	506	63	134	23	0	2	51	34	31	.265	.320	.322	86	-9	12			.943	-7	*3-125	-1.4
1914	Phi-N	126	467	61	127	12	1	0	26	45	44	.272	.339	.302	85	-7	9			.934	-3	*2-101,3-22	-1.1
1915	*Phi-N	105	387	50	81	6	4	0	21	39	28	.209	.290	.245	62	-16	4	12	-6	**.969**	-7	*3-105	-2.8
1916	Phi-N	48	141	22	33	10	1	0	9	14	7	.234	.308	.319	89	-2	6			.933	3	3-40	0.3
1917	Phi-N	13	14	1	5	0	0	0	1	2		.357	.400	.357	128	0	0			1.000	-1	/3-4	-0.1
	Chi-A	1	1	0	0	0	0	0	0	0		.000	.000	.000	-98	-0	0			1.000	0	/2-1	0.0
Total	11	1283	4831	667	1225	186	60	10	329	456	220	.254	.324	.323	91	-51	176	12		.934	6	*3-1147,2-102/S-5	-2.4

■ JIM BYRNES   Byrnes, James Joseph   b: 1/5/1880, San Francisco, Cal.   d: 7/31/41, San Francisco, Cal   BR/TR, 5'9", 150 lbs.   Deb: 4/19/06

| 1906 | Phi-A | 10 | 23 | 2 | 4 | 0 | 1 | 0 | | 0 | | .174 | .174 | .261 | 34 | -2 | 0 | | | .889 | -0 | /C-9 | -0.1 |

■ MILT BYRNES   Byrnes, Milton John "Skippy"   b: 11/15/16, St.Louis, Mo.   d: 2/1/79, St.Louis, Mo.   BL/TL, 5'10.5", 170 lbs.   Deb: 4/21/43

1943	StL-A	129	429	58	120	28	7	4	50	53	49	.280	.362	.406	122	12	1	4	-2	**.997**	8	*O-114	1.3
1944	*StL-A	128	407	63	120	20	4	4	45	68	50	.295	.396	.394	119	12	1	7	-4	.976	-6	*O-122	-0.3
1945	StL-A	133	442	53	110	29	4	8	59	78	84	.249	.363	.387	112	8	1	3	-2	.988	5	*O-125/1-2	0.6
Total	3	390	1278	174	350	77	15	16	154	199	183	.274	.373	.395	117	33	3	14	-8	.987	8	O-361/1-2	1.6

■ PUTSY CABALLERO   Caballero, Ralph Joseph   b: 11/5/27, New Orleans, La.   BR/TR, 5'11", 175 lbs.   Deb: 9/14/44

1944	Phi-N	4	4	0	0	0	0	0	0	0	1	.000	.000	.000	-99	-1	0			.889	2	/3-2	0.1
1945	Phi-N	9	1	1	0	0	0	0	1	0	0	.000	.000	.000	-99	-0	0			.857	2	/3-5	0.1
1947	Phi-N	2	7	2	1	0	0	0	0	1	0	.143	.250	.143	7	-1	0			1.000	-0	/2-2,3-1	-0.1
1948	Phi-N	113	351	33	86	12	1	0	19	24	18	.245	.293	.285	58	-20	7			.962	6	3-79,2-23	-1.4
1949	Phi-N	29	68	8	19	3	0	0	3	3		.279	.279	.324	63	-4	0			.981	2	2-21/S-1	0.1
1950	*Phi-N	46	24	12	4	0	0	0	2	2	2	.167	.231	.167	7	-3	1			.950	6	/2-5,3-4,S-2	0.3
1951	Phi-N	84	161	15	30	3	2	1	11	12	7	.186	.243	.248	33	-15	1	2	-1	.985	9	2-54/3-3,S-1	-0.5
1952	Phi-N	35	42	10	10	0	0	0	4	0	0	.238	.273	.310	62	-2	1	0	0	.857	2	/S-8,2-7,3-7	0.1
Total	8	322	658	81	150	21	3	1	40	41	34	.228	.273	.274	49	-47	10	2		.968	31	2-112,3-101/S-12	-1.3

■ ENOS CABELL   Cabell, Enos Milton   b: 10/8/49, Fort Riley, Kan.   BR/TR, 6'5", 185 lbs.   Deb: 9/17/72

1972	Bal-A	3	5	0	0	0	0	0	1	0		.000	.000	.000	-97	-1	0	0		1.000	-0	/1-1	-0.2
1973	Bal-A	32	47	12	10	2	0	1	3	3	7	.213	.260	.319	63	-2	1	3	-2	.991	-1	1-23/3-1	-0.6
1974	*Bal-A	80	174	24	42	4	2	3	17	7	20	.241	.271	.339	77	-6	5	3	-0	.995	2	1-28,O-22,3-19,/2D	-0.6
1975	Hou-N	117	348	43	92	17	6	2	43	18	53	.264	.306	.365	92	-5	12	3	2	.973	-0	O-67,1-25,3-22	-0.7
1976	Hou-N	144	586	85	160	13	7	2	43	29	79	.273	.310	.329	89	-10	35	8	6	.958	-9	*3-143/1-3	-1.5
1977	Hou-N	150	625	101	176	36	7	16	68	27	55	.282	.315	.438	109	4	42	22	-1	.948	-6	*3-144/1-8,S-1	-0.4
1978	Hou-N	162	660	92	195	31	8	7	71	20	80	.295	.323	.398	109	4	33	15	4	.958	-16	*3-153,1-14/S-1	-1.4
1979	Hou-N	155	603	60	164	30	5	6	67	21	68	.272	.300	.368	86	-14	37	18	0	.957	-23	*3-132,1-51	-4.2
1980	*Hou-N	152	604	69	167	23	8	2	55	26	84	.276	.307	.351	90	-10	21	13	-2	.927	-20	*3-150/1-1	-3.6
1981	SF-N	96	396	41	101	20	1	2	36	10	47	.255	.275	.326	71	-16	6	7	-2	.987	-1	1-69,3-22	-2.6
1982	Det-A	125	464	45	121	17	3	2	37	15	48	.261	.285	.293	67	-21	15	6	-5	.992	-8	1-83,3-59/O-3	-3.3
1983	Det-A	121	392	62	122	23	5	6	46	16	41	.311	.340	.434	114	7	4	8	-4	.997	7	*1-106/3-4,S-1,D-8	0.7
1984	Hou-N	127	436	52	135	17	2	8	44	21	47	.310	.343	.417	121	10	8	11	-3	.993	-1	*1-112	-0.1
1985	Hou-N	60	143	20	35	8	1	2	14	16	15	.245	.321	.357	92	-2	3	1	0	.994	-1	1-49	-0.5

YEAR	TM/L	G	AB	R	H	2B	3B	HR	RBI	BB	SO	AVG	OBP	SLG	PRO+	BR/A	SB	CS	SBR	FA	FR	G/POS	TPR
	*LA-N	57	192	20	56	11	0	0	22	14	21	.292	.340	.349	96	-1	6	2	1	.920	-2	3-32,1-21/O-4	-0.4
	Yr	117	335	40	91	19	1	2	36	30	36	.272	.332	.352	94	-3	9	3	1	.993	-3	1-70,3-32/O-4	-0.9
1986	LA-N	107	277	27	71	11	0	2	29	14	26	.256	.297	.318	75	-10	10	4	1	.987	0	1-61,O-16/3-7	-1.4
Total	15	1688	5952	753	1647	263	56	60	596	259	691	.277	.309	.370	93	-74	238	124	-3	.944	-77	3-888,1-655,O/DS2	-21.1
■ AL CABRERA Cabrera, Alfredo A. b: 1883, Canary Islands d: Havana, Cuba TR , Deb: 5/16/13																							
1913	StL-N	1	2	0	0	0	0	0	0	0	0	.000	.000	.000	-99	-1	0			.000	0	/S-1	-0.1
■ FRANCISCO CABRERA Cabrera, Francisco (Paulino) b: 10/10/66, Santo Domingo, D.R. BR/TR, 6'4", 193 lbs. Deb: 7/24/89																							
1989	Tor-A	3	12	1	2	1	0	0	0	1	3	.167	.231	.250	36	-1	0	0	0	.000	0	/D-3	-0.1
	Atl-N	4	14	0	3	2	0	0	0	0	3	.214	.214	.357	59	-1	0	0	0	1.000	-1	/1-2,C-1	-0.2
1990	Atl-N	63	137	14	38	5	1	7	25	5	21	.277	.303	.482	106	1	1	0	0	.990	-2	1-48/C-3	-0.3
1991	*Atl-N	44	95	7	23	6	0	4	23	6	20	.242	.287	.432	94	-1	1	1	-0	.987	-3	C-17,1-14	-0.4
1992	*Atl-N	12	10	2	3	0	0	2	3	1	1	.300	.364	.900	233	2	0	0	0	.000	0	/C-1	0.2
1993	*Atl-N	70	83	8	20	3	0	4	11	8	21	.241	.308	.422	92	-1	0	0	0	1.000	2	1-12/C-2	0.0
Total	5	196	351	32	89	17	1	17	62	21	69	.254	.296	.453	99	-2	2	1	0	.989	-3	/1-76,C-24,D-3	-0.8
■ JOLBERT CABRERA Cabrera, Jolbert Alexis b: 12/8/72, Cartagena, Colombia BR/TR, 6', 177 lbs. Deb: 4/12/98																							
1998	Cle-A	1	2	0	0	0	0	0	0	0	1	.000	.000	.000	-97	-1	0	0	0	1.000	1	/S-1	0.0
■ ORLANDO CABRERA Cabrera, Orlando Luis b: 11/2/74, Cartagena, Colombia BR/TR, 5'11", 165 lbs. Deb: 9/3/97																							
1997	Mon-N	16	18	4	4	0	0	0	2	1	3	.222	.263	.222	29	-2	1	2	-1	.875	3	/S-6,2-4	0.1
1998	Mon-N	79	261	44	73	16	5	3	22	18	27	.280	.326	.414	94	-3	6	2	1	.984	-3	S-52,2-28	0.2
Total	2	95	279	48	77	16	5	3	24	19	30	.276	.322	.401	90	-5	7	4	-0	.980	1	/S-58,2-32	0.3
■ CRAIG CACEK Cacek, Craig Thomas b: 9/10/54, Hollywood, Cal. BR/TR, 6'1", 200 lbs. Deb: 6/18/77																							
1977	Hou-N	7	20	0	1	0	0	0	1	1	3	.050	.095	.050	-66	-5	0	0	0	.981	-1	/1-6	-0.6
■ EDGAR CACERES Caceres, Edgar F. b: 6/6/64, Barquisimeto, Venez BB/TR, 6'1", 170 lbs. Deb: 6/8/95																							
1995	KC-A	55	117	13	28	6	2	1	17	8	15	.239	.294	.350	66	-6	2	2	-1	.992	1	2-36/S-8,1-6,3-3,D	-0.4
■ CHARLIE CADY Cady, Charles B. b: 12/1865, Chicago, Ill. d: 6/7/09, Kankakee, Ill. 5'11", 180 lbs. Deb: 9/5/1883																							
1883	Cle-N	3	11	0	0	0	0	0	0	1	5	.000	.083	.000	-73	-2				1.000	-1	/O-2,P-1	-0.2
1884	CP-U	6	20	4	2	1	1	0		1		.100	.143	.250	17	-3				.909	-0	/P-4,O-2	-0.1
	KC-U	2	3	0	0	0	0	0		0		.000	.000	.000	-99	-1				.600	-2	/C-1,2-1	-0.2
	Yr	8	23	4	2	1	1	0		1		.087	.125	.217	2	-4				.909	-2	/P-4,O-2,C-1,2-1	-0.3
Total	2	11	34	4	2	1	1	0	0	2	5	.059	.111	.147	-23	-6				.917	-3	/P-5,O-4,2-1,C-1	-0.5
■ HICK CADY Cady, Forrest Leroy (b: Forrest Leroy Bergland) b: 1/26/1886, Bishop Hill, Ill. d: 3/3/46, Cedar Rapids, Iowa BR/TR, 6'2", 179 lbs. Deb: 4/26/12																							
1912	*Bos-A	47	135	19	35	13	2	0	9	10		.259	.324	.385	98	-1	0			.990	11	C-43/1-4	1.4
1913	Bos-A	40	96	10	24	5	2	0	6	5	14	.250	.294	.344	84	-2	1			.992	8	C-39	0.9
1914	Bos-A	61	159	14	41	6	1	0	8	12	22	.258	.310	.308	86	-3	2	1	0	.971	-3	C-58	-0.1
1915	*Bos-A	78	205	25	57	10	2	0	17	19	25	.278	.342	.346	109	2	0	2	-1	.980	-2	C-77	0.5
1916	*Bos-A	78	162	5	31	6	3	0	13	15	16	.191	.264	.265	59	-8	0			.967	-13	C-63/1-3	-2.0
1917	Bos-A	17	46	4	7	1	1	0	2	1	6	.152	.170	.217	18	-5	0			.959	1	C-14	-0.3
1919	Phi-N	34	98	6	21	6	0	1	19	4	8	.214	.252	.306	63	-5	1			.984	-7	C-29	-1.0
Total	7	355	901	83	216	47	11	1	74	66	91	.240	.297	.320	82	-21	4	3		.979	-4	C-323/1-7	-0.6
■ TOM CAFEGO Cafego, Thomas b: 8/21/11, Whipple, W.Va. d: 10/29/61, Detroit, Mich. BL/TR, 5'10", 160 lbs. Deb: 9/3/37																							
1937	StL-A	4	4	1	0	0	0	0	0	0	1	.000	.000	.000	-99	-1	0	0	0	.500	-1	/O-1	-0.2
■ JOE CAFFIE Caffie, Joseph Clifford "Rabbit" b: 2/14/31, Ramer, Ala. BL/TR, 5'10.5", 180 lbs. Deb: 9/13/56																							
1956	Cle-A	12	38	7	13	0	0	0	1	4	8	.342	.432	.342	104	1	3	2	-0	1.000	1	O-10	0.1
1957	Cle-A	32	89	14	24	2	1	3	10	4	11	.270	.301	.416	95	-1	0	1	-1	.976	-0	O-19	-0.3
Total	2	44	127	21	37	2	1	3	11	8	19	.291	.343	.394	99	-0	3	3	-1	.984	1	/O-29	-0.2
■ BEN CAFFYN Caffyn, Benjamin Thomas b: 2/10/1880, Peoria, Ill. d: 11/22/42, Peoria, Ill. BL/TL, 5'10", 175 lbs. Deb: 8/21/06																							
1906	Cle-A	30	103	16	20	4	0	0	3	12		.194	.291	.233	65	-4	2			.909	-4	O-29	-1.0
■ WAYNE CAGE Cage, Wayne Levell b: 11/23/51, Monroe, La. BL/TL, 6'4", 205 lbs. Deb: 4/22/78																							
1978	Cle-A	36	98	11	24	6	1	4	13	9	28	.245	.308	.449	112	1	1	2	-1	.988	1	D-20,1-11	0.0
1979	Cle-A	29	56	6	13	2	0	1	6	5	16	.232	.295	.321	66	-3	0	2	-1	1.000	1	/1-7,D-9	-0.4
Total	2	65	154	17	37	8	1	5	19	14	44	.240	.304	.403	94	-2	1	4	-2	.992	2	/D-29,1-18	-0.4
■ JOHN CAHILL Cahill, John Patrick Parnell "Patsy" b: 4/30/1865, San Francisco, Cal d: 10/31/01, Pleasanton, Cal. BR/TR, 5'7.5", 168 lbs. Deb: 5/31/1884																							
1884	Col-a	59	210	28	46	3	3	0		6		.219	.248	.262	72	-6				.843	-0	O-56/S-5,P-2	-0.6
1886	StL-N	125	463	43	92	17	6	1	32	9	79	.199	.214	.268	49	-28	16			.866	2	*O-124/P-2,S-1,3-1	-2.7
1887	Ind-N	68	263	22	54	4	3	0	26	9	5	.205	.234	.243	34	-23	34			.826	-6	O-56/3-9,P-6,S-1	-2.4
Total	3	252	936	93	192	24	12	1	58	24	84	.205	.227	.260	49	-57	50			.851	-5	O-236/3-10,P-10,S-7	-5.7
■ TOM CAHILL Cahill, Thomas H. b: 10/1868, Fall River, Mass. d: 12/25/1894, Scranton, Pa. Deb: 4/9/1891																							
1891	Lou-a	120	433	70	111	18	7	3	47	41	51	.256	.329	.351	96	-3	39			.931	-3	C-56,S-49,O-12,/23	0.2
■ BOB CAIN Cain, Robert Max "Sugar" b: 10/16/24, Longford, Kan. d: 4/8/97, Cleveland, Ohio BL/TL, 6', 165 lbs. Deb: 9/18/49																							
1949	Chi-A	6	3	0	0	0	0	0	0	0	1	.000	.000	.000	-99	-1	0	0	0	1.000	-0	/P-6	0.0
1950	Chi-A	35	61	7	12	2	0	0	2	3	15	.197	.234	.230	20	-7	0	0	0	.974	0	P-34	0.0
1951	Chi-A	4	9	1	3	1	0	0	0	0	3	.333	.333	.444	111	0	0	0	0	1.000	-0	/P-4	0.0
	Det-A	35	53	9	13	3	0	0	9	6	9	.245	.322	.302	69	-2	0	0	0	.972	0	P-35	0.0
	Yr	39	62	10	16	4	0	0	9	6	12	.258	.324	.323	75	-2	0	0	0	.975	-0	P-39	0.0
1952	StL-A	35	58	7	8	0	1	0	1	4	14	.138	.194	.172	2	-8	0	0	0	.966	-2	P-29	0.0
1953	StL-A	34	30	3	6	2	0	0	2	1	3	.200	.226	.267	32	-3	0	0	0	1.000	-2	P-32	0.0
1954	Chi-A	1	0	1	0	0	0	0	0	0	0	—	—	—	—	0	0	0	0	.000	0	R	0.0
Total	6	150	214	28	42	8	1	0	14	14	45	.196	.246	.243	31	-21	0	0	0	.975	-4	P-140	0.0
■ MIGUEL CAIRO Cairo, Miguel Jesus b: 5/4/74, Anaco, Venez. BR/TR, 6', 160 lbs. Deb: 4/17/96																							
1996	Tor-A	9	27	5	6	2	0	0	1	2	9	.222	.300	.296	52	-2	0	0	0	1.000	0	/2-9	-0.1
1997	Chi-N	16	29	7	7	1	0	0	1	2	3	.241	.313	.276	54	-2	0	0	0	1.000	1	/2-9,S-2	-0.1
1998	TB-A	150	515	49	138	26	5	5	46	24	44	.268	.308	.367	72	-22	19	8	1	.978	19	*2-148/D-2	0.6
Total	3	175	571	61	151	29	5	5	48	28	56	.264	.308	.359	70	-25	19	8	1	.980	20	2-166/D-2,S-2	0.4
■ GEORGE CAITHAMER Caithamer, George Theodore "Sidee" b: 7/22/10, Chicago, Ill. d: 6/1/54, Chicago, Ill. BR/TR, 5'10", 168 lbs. Deb: 9/17/34																							
1934	Chi-A	5	19	1	6	1	0	0	3	1	5	.316	.350	.368	83	-0	0	0	0	.958	-1	/C-5	-0.1
■ IVAN CALDERON Calderon, Ivan (Perez) b: 3/19/62, Fajardo, P.R. BR/TR, 6'1", 220 lbs. Deb: 8/10/84																							
1984	Sea-A	11	24	2	5	1	0	1	1	2	5	.208	.269	.375	77	-1	1	0	0	1.000	-1	O-11	-0.1
1985	Sea-A	67	210	37	60	16	4	8	28	19	45	.286	.351	.514	132	9	4	2	0	.981	1	O-53/1-2,D-3	0.8
1986	Sea-A	37	131	13	31	5	0	2	13	6	33	.237	.275	.321	61	-7	3	1	0	.937	-1	O-32	-0.9
	Chi-A	13	33	3	10	2	1	0	2	3	6	.303	.361	.424	109	0	0	0	0	.900	-0	/O-5,D-6	0.0
	Yr	50	164	16	41	7	1	2	15	9	39	.250	.293	.341	71	-7	3	1	0	.932	-1	O-37/D-6	-0.9
1987	Chi-A	144	542	93	159	38	2	28	83	60	109	.293	.365	.526	129	22	10	5	0	.984	5	*O-139/D-3	2.2
1988	Chi-A	73	264	40	56	14	0	14	35	34	66	.212	.302	.424	101	-0	4	4	-1	.954	2	O-67/D-3	-0.2
1989	Chi-A	157	622	83	178	34	9	14	87	43	94	.286	.335	.437	119	14	7	1	2	.978	0	*O-103,D-36,1-26	1.0
1990	Chi-A	158	607	85	166	44	2	14	74	51	79	.273	.331	.422	111	8	32	16	0	.975	4	*O-130,D-27/1-2	0.8

YEAR	TM/L	G	AB	R	H	2B	3B	HR	RBI	BB	SO	AVG	OBP	SLG	PRO+	BR/A	SB	CS	SBR	FA	FR	G/POS	TPR
1991	Mon-N★	134	470	69	141	22	3	19	75	53	64	.300	.375	.481	141	26	31	16	-0	.974	5	*O-122/1-4	2.8
1992	Mon-N	48	170	19	45	14	2	3	24	14	22	.265	.324	.424	111	2	1	2	-1	.988	0	O-46	0.1
1993	Bos-A	73	213	25	47	8	2	1	19	21	28	.221	.294	.291	54	-14	4	2	0	1.000	-1	O-47,D-19	-1.6
	Chi-A	9	26	1	3	2	0	0	3	0	5	.115	.115	.192	-19	-4	0	0	0	.000	0	/D-6	-0.5
	Yr	82	239	26	50	10	2	1	22	21	33	.209	.276	.280	47	-18	4	2	0	1.000	-1	O-47,D-25	-2.1
Total	10	924	3312	470	901	200	25	104	444	306	556	.272	.336	.442	113	55	97	49	-0	.976	15	O-755,D-103/1-34	4.4

■ SAM CALDERONE
Calderone, Samuel Francis b: 2/6/26, Beverly, N.J. BR/TR, 5′10.5″, 185 lbs. Deb: 4/19/50

YEAR	TM/L	G	AB	R	H	2B	3B	HR	RBI	BB	SO	AVG	OBP	SLG	PRO+	BR/A	SB	CS	SBR	FA	FR	G/POS	TPR
1950	NY-N	34	67	9	20	1	0	1	12	2	5	.299	.319	.358	77	-2	0			.972	-4	C-33	-0.5
1953	NY-N	35	45	4	10	2	0	0	8	1	4	.222	.239	.267	31	-5	0	0	0	.966	-1	C-31	-0.4
1954	Mil-N	22	29	3	11	2	0	0	5	4	4	.379	.455	.448	146	2	0	0	0	1.000	3	C-16	0.5
Total	3	91	141	16	41	5	0	1	25	7	13	.291	.324	.348	76	-5	0	0		.978	-2	/C-80	-0.4

■ BRUCE CALDWELL
Caldwell, Bruce b: 2/8/06, Ashton, R.I. d: 2/15/59, West Haven, Conn. BR/TR, 6′, 195 lbs. Deb: 6/30/28

YEAR	TM/L	G	AB	R	H	2B	3B	HR	RBI	BB	SO	AVG	OBP	SLG	PRO+	BR/A	SB	CS	SBR	FA	FR	G/POS	TPR
1928	Cle-A	18	27	2	6	1	1	0	3	2	2	.222	.300	.333	66	-1	1	0	0	1.000	-2	O-10/1-1	-0.3
1932	Bro-N	7	11	2	1	0	0	0	2	2	2	.091	.231	.091	-10	-2	0			.875	-1	/1-6	-0.3
Total	2	25	38	4	7	1	1	0	5	4	4	.184	.279	.263	44	-3	1	0		.900	-3	/O-10,1-7	-0.6

■ RAY CALDWELL
Caldwell, Raymond Benjamin "Rube" or "Sum" b: 4/26/1888, Corydon, Pa. d: 8/17/67, Salamanca, N.Y. BL/TR, 6′2″, 190 lbs. Deb: 9/9/10

YEAR	TM/L	G	AB	R	H	2B	3B	HR	RBI	BB	SO	AVG	OBP	SLG	PRO+	BR/A	SB	CS	SBR	FA	FR	G/POS	TPR
1910	NY-A	6	6	0	0	0	0	0	0	0		.000	.000	.000	-95	-1	0			1.000	-0	/P-6	0.0
1911	NY-A	59	147	14	40	4	1	0	17	11		.272	.323	.313	73	-5	5			.953	-2	P-41,O-11	-0.1
1912	NY-A	44	76	18	18	1	2	0	6	5		.237	.284	.303	64	-4	4			.938	1	P-30/O-1	0.0
1913	NY-A	59	97	10	28	3	2	0	11	3	15	.289	.310	.361	96	-1	3			**1.000**	-1	P-27/O-3	-0.1
1914	NY-A	59	113	9	22	4	0	0	10	7	24	.195	.248	.230	44	-8	2	1	0	.967	-4	P-31/1-6	-0.3
1915	NY-A	72	144	27	35	4	1	4	20	9	32	.243	.288	.368	96	-2	4	3	-1	**.988**	-3	P-36	0.0
1916	NY-A	45	93	6	19	2	0	0	4	2	17	.204	.221	.226	34	-8	1			.960	-1	P-21/O-2	0.0
1917	NY-A	63	124	12	32	6	1	2	12	16	16	.258	.343	.371	117	3	2			.973	-3	P-32/O-8	-0.2
1918	NY-A	65	151	14	44	10	0	1	18	13	23	.291	.352	.377	117	3	2			.977	-2	P-24,O-19	0.1
1919	Bos-A	33	48	5	13	1	1	0	4	0	9	.271	.271	.333	73	-2	0			.950	-2	P-18/O-2	-0.1
	Cle-A	6	23	4	8	4	0	0	2	0	4	.348	.348	.522	134	1	0			.900	-1	/P-6	0.0
	Yr	39	71	9	21	5	1	0	6	0	13	.296	.296	.394	97	-1	0			.933	-3	P-24/O-2	-0.1
1920	*Cle-A	41	89	17	19	3	0	0	7	10	13	.213	.300	.247	45	-7	0	2	-1	.917	-3	P-34	0.0
1921	Cle-A	38	53	2	11	4	0	1	3	2	5	.208	.236	.340	45	-5	0	0	0	.930	-0	P-37	0.0
Total	12	590	1164	138	289	46	8	8	114	78	158	.248	.297	.322	78	-36	23	6		.960	-20	P-343/O-46,1-6	-0.7

■ JACK CALHOUN
Calhoun, John Charles "Red" b: 12/14/1879, Pittsburgh, Pa. d: 2/27/47, Cincinnati, Ohio BR/TR, 6′, 185 lbs. Deb: 6/27/02

YEAR	TM/L	G	AB	R	H	2B	3B	HR	RBI	BB	SO	AVG	OBP	SLG	PRO+	BR/A	SB	CS	SBR	FA	FR	G/POS	TPR
1902	StL-N	20	64	3	10	2	1	0	8	8		.156	.260	.219	50	-4	1			.972	-2	3-12/1-5,O-1	-0.6

■ BILL CALHOUN
Calhoun, William Davitte "Mary" b: 6/23/1890, Rockmart, Ga. d: 1/28/55, Sandersville, Ga. BL/TL, 6′, 180 lbs. Deb: 4/24/13

YEAR	TM/L	G	AB	R	H	2B	3B	HR	RBI	BB	SO	AVG	OBP	SLG	PRO+	BR/A	SB	CS	SBR	FA	FR	G/POS	TPR
1913	Bos-N	6	13	0	1	0	0	0	0	0	3	.077	.077	.077	-55	-3	0			.970	-0	/1-3	-0.3

■ MARTY CALLAGHAN
Callaghan, Martin Francis b: 6/9/1900, Norwood, Mass. d: 6/23/75, Norfolk, Mass. BL/TL, 5′10″, 157 lbs. Deb: 4/13/22

YEAR	TM/L	G	AB	R	H	2B	3B	HR	RBI	BB	SO	AVG	OBP	SLG	PRO+	BR/A	SB	CS	SBR	FA	FR	G/POS	TPR
1922	Chi-N	74	175	31	45	7	4	0	20	17	17	.257	.326	.343	71	-7	2	3	-1	.946	-9	O-53	-2.0
1923	Chi-N	61	129	18	29	1	3	0	14	8	18	.225	.275	.279	47	-10	2	5	-2	.969	-4	O-38	-1.7
1928	Cin-N	81	238	29	69	11	4	0	24	27	10	.290	.362	.370	93	-2	5			.980	-4	O-69	-1.0
1930	Cin-N	79	225	28	62	9	2	0	16	19	25	.276	.335	.333	66	-12	1			.986	3	O-54	-1.2
Total	4	295	767	106	205	28	13	0	74	71	70	.267	.332	.338	72	-31	10	8		.973	-14	O-214	-5.9

■ DAVE CALLAHAN
Callahan, David Joseph b: 7/20/1888, Ottawa, Ill. d: 10/28/69, Ottawa, Ill. BL/TR, 5′10″, 165 lbs. Deb: 9/14/10

YEAR	TM/L	G	AB	R	H	2B	3B	HR	RBI	BB	SO	AVG	OBP	SLG	PRO+	BR/A	SB	CS	SBR	FA	FR	G/POS	TPR
1910	Cle-A	13	44	6	8	1	0	0	2	4		.182	.265	.205	47	-3	5			1.000	0	O-12	-0.3
1911	Cle-A	6	16	1	4	0	1	0	0	1		.250	.294	.375	85	-0	0			1.000	0	/O-4	0.0
Total	2	19	60	7	12	1	1	0	2	5		.200	.273	.250	58	-3	5			1.000	1	/O-16	-0.3

■ ED CALLAHAN
Callahan, Edward Joseph b: 12/11/1857, Boston, Mass. d: 2/5/47, New York, N.Y. Deb: 7/19/1884

YEAR	TM/L	G	AB	R	H	2B	3B	HR	RBI	BB	SO	AVG	OBP	SLG	PRO+	BR/A	SB	CS	SBR	FA	FR	G/POS	TPR
1884	StL-U	1	3	0	0	0	0	0		0		.000	.000	.000	-97	-1				1.000	0	/O-1	0.0
	KC-U	3	11	0	4	0	0	0		0		.364	.364	.364	139	0				.800	1	/S-3	0.1
	Bos-U	4	13	2	5	0	0	0		1		.385	.429	.385	151	1				.750	-1	/O-4	0.0
	Yr	8	27	2	9	0	0	0		1		.333	.357	.333	117	-0				.778	0	/O-5,S-3	0.1

■ NIXEY CALLAHAN
Callahan, James Joseph b: 3/18/1874, Fitchburg, Mass. d: 10/4/34, Boston, Mass. BR/TR, 5′10.5″, 180 lbs. Deb: 5/12/1894 M

YEAR	TM/L	G	AB	R	H	2B	3B	HR	RBI	BB	SO	AVG	OBP	SLG	PRO+	BR/A	SB	CS	SBR	FA	FR	G/POS	TPR
1894	Phi-N	9	21	4	5	0	0	0	0	0	7	.238	.238	.238	16	-3	0			.923	1	/P-9	0.0
1897	Chi-N	94	360	60	105	18	6	3	47	10		.292	.320	.400	86	-9	12			.918	5	2-30,P-23,O-21,S/3	-0.3
1898	Chi-N	43	164	27	43	7	5	0	22	4		.262	.280	.366	85	-4	3			.947	-2	P-31/O-9,S-1,2-1,1	-0.4
1899	Chi-N	47	150	21	39	4	3	0	18	8		.260	.306	.327	76	-5	9			.904	3	P-35/O-9,S-2,2-1	-0.3
1900	Chi-N	32	115	16	27	3	2	0	9	6		.235	.273	.296	59	-7	5			.975	6	P-32	0.0
1901	Chi-A	45	118	15	39	7	3	1	19	10		.331	.383	.466	138	6	10			.944	4	P-27/3-6,2-2	0.0
1902	Chi-A	70	218	27	51	7	2	0	13	6		.234	.261	.284	53	-14	4			.941	2	P-35,O-23/S-1	-1.0
1903	Chi-A	118	439	47	128	26	5	2	56	20		.292	.324	.387	118	9	24			.895	-6	*3-102/O-8,P-3,M	0.3
1904	Chi-A	132	482	66	126	23	2	0	54	39		.261	.318	.317	105	4	29			.977	-17	*O-104,2-28,M	-2.0
1905	Chi-A	96	345	50	94	18	6	1	43	29		.272	.336	.368	128	11	26			.956	-8	O-93	-0.1
1911	Chi-A	120	466	64	131	13	5	3	60	15		.281	.306	.350	86	-11	45			.963	-9	*O-114	-2.6
1912	Chi-A	111	408	45	111	9	7	1	52	12		.272	.298	.336	84	-10	19			.939	-16	*O-107,M	-3.1
1913	Chi-A	6	9	0	2	0	0	0	1	0	2	.222	.222	.222	30	-1	0			1.000	-0	/O-1,M	-0.1
Total	13	923	3295	442	901	135	46	11	394	159	9	.273	.311	.352	94	-34	186			.953	-36	O-489,P-195,3/2S1	-9.6

■ JIM CALLAHAN
Callahan, James Timothy "Red" (b: James Timothy Callaghan)
b: 1/12/1879, Allegheny Co., Pa. d: 3/9/68, Carnegie, Pa. BR/TR, 5′9″, 145 lbs. Deb: 5/25/02

YEAR	TM/L	G	AB	R	H	2B	3B	HR	RBI	BB	SO	AVG	OBP	SLG	PRO+	BR/A	SB	CS	SBR	FA	FR	G/POS	TPR
1902	NY-N	1	4	0	0	0	0	0	0	1		.000	.200	.000	-38	-1	0			.000	-0	/O-1	-0.1

■ LEO CALLAHAN
Callahan, Leo David b: 8/9/1890, Jamaica Plain, Mass d: 5/2/82, Erie, Pa. BL/TL, 5′8″, 142 lbs. Deb: 4/9/13

YEAR	TM/L	G	AB	R	H	2B	3B	HR	RBI	BB	SO	AVG	OBP	SLG	PRO+	BR/A	SB	CS	SBR	FA	FR	G/POS	TPR
1913	Bro-N	33	41	6	7	3	1	0	3	4	5	.171	.244	.293	52	-3	0			.857	-2	/O-8	-0.5
1919	Phi-N	81	235	26	54	14	4	1	9	29	19	.230	.317	.336	90	-2	5			.950	1	O-58	-0.6
Total	2	114	276	32	61	17	5	1	12	33	24	.221	.306	.330	84	-5	5			.941	-1	/O-66	-1.1

■ PAT CALLAHAN
Callahan, Patrick Henry b: 10/15/1866, Cleveland, Ohio d: 2/4/40, Louisville, Ky. Deb: 5/1/1884

YEAR	TM/L	G	AB	R	H	2B	3B	HR	RBI	BB	SO	AVG	OBP	SLG	PRO+	BR/A	SB	CS	SBR	FA	FR	G/POS	TPR
1884	Ind-a	61	258	38	67	8	5	2		8		.260	.282	.353	109	2				.812	-7	3-61	-0.4

■ WESLEY CALLAHAN
Callahan, Wesley Leroy b: 7/3/1888, Lyons, Ind. d: 9/13/53, Dayton, Ohio BR/TR, 5′7.5″, 155 lbs. Deb: 9/7/13

YEAR	TM/L	G	AB	R	H	2B	3B	HR	RBI	BB	SO	AVG	OBP	SLG	PRO+	BR/A	SB	CS	SBR	FA	FR	G/POS	TPR
1913	StL-N	7	14	0	4	0	0	0	1	2	2	.286	.375	.286	91	-0	1			.920	1	/S-6	0.1

■ FRANK CALLAWAY
Callaway, Frank Burnett b: 2/26/1898, Knoxville, Tenn. d: 8/21/87, Knoxville, Tenn. BR/TR, 6′, 170 lbs. Deb: 9/17/21

YEAR	TM/L	G	AB	R	H	2B	3B	HR	RBI	BB	SO	AVG	OBP	SLG	PRO+	BR/A	SB	CS	SBR	FA	FR	G/POS	TPR
1921	Phi-A	14	50	7	12	1	1	0	4	2	11	.240	.283	.300	49	-4	1	0	0	.878	-5	S-14	-0.7
1922	Phi-A	29	48	5	13	0	2	0	4	0	13	.271	.271	.354	60	-3	0	0	0	.880	1	2-11/3-5,S-4	-0.1
Total	2	43	98	12	25	1	3	0	8	2	24	.255	.277	.327	54	-7	1	0	0	.889	-4	/S-18,2-11,3-5	-0.8

■ JOHNNY CALLISON
Callison, John Wesley b: 3/12/39, Qualls, Okla. BL/TR, 5′10″, 175 lbs. Deb: 9/9/58

YEAR	TM/L	G	AB	R	H	2B	3B	HR	RBI	BB	SO	AVG	OBP	SLG	PRO+	BR/A	SB	CS	SBR	FA	FR	G/POS	TPR
1958	Chi-A	18	64	10	19	4	2	1	12	6	14	.297	.357	.469	128	2	1	0	0	.976	3	O-18	0.4
1959	Chi-A	49	104	12	18	3	0	3	12	13	20	.173	.271	.288	54	-7	0	1	-1	.983	-3	O-41	-1.2
1960	Phi-N	99	288	36	75	11	5	9	30	45	70	.260	.360	.427	114	7	0	4	-2	.989	1	O-86	0.1
1961	Phi-N	138	455	74	121	20	11	9	47	69	76	.266	.366	.418	109	7	10	4	1	.967	5	*O-124	0.6
1962	Phi-N★	157	603	107	181	26	**10**	23	83	54	96	.300	.363	.491	131	25	10	3	1	.980	23	*O-152	3.9
1963	Phi-N	157	626	96	178	36	11	26	78	50	111	.284	.339	.502	140	31	8	3	1	.994	23	*O-157	4.8
1964	Phi-N★	162	654	101	179	30	10	31	104	36	95	.274	.318	.492	126	20	6	3	0	.988	19	*O-162	3.3

YEAR	TM/L	G	AB	R	H	2B	3B	HR	RBI	BB	SO	AVG	OBP	SLG	PRO+	BR/A	SB	CS	SBR	FA	FR	G/POS	TPR
1965	Phi-N☆	160	619	93	162	25	**16**	32	101	57	117	.262	.330	.509	135	26	6	5	-1	.982	19	*O-159	3.8
1966	Phi-N	155	612	93	169	**40**	7	11	55	56	83	.276	.340	.418	109	8	8	8	-2	.990	6	*O-154	0.4
1967	Phi-N	149	556	62	145	30	5	14	64	55	63	.261	.331	.408	109	7	6	12	-5	.977	9	*O-147	0.3
1968	Phi-N	121	398	46	97	18	4	14	40	42	70	.244	.321	.415	119	9	4	3	-1	**1.000**	2	*O-109	0.6
1969	Phi-N	134	495	66	131	29	5	16	64	49	73	.265	.335	.440	119	11	2	1	0	.990	16	*O-129	2.0
1970	Chi-N	147	477	65	126	23	2	19	68	60	63	.264	.350	.440	98	-2	7	2	1	.973	-0	*O-144	-0.8
1971	Chi-N	103	290	27	61	12	1	8	38	36	55	.210	.302	.341	71	-11	2	1	0	.982	-3	O-89	-1.9
1972	NY-A	92	275	28	71	10	0	9	34	18	34	.258	.304	.393	110	2	3	0	1	.992	-3	O-74	-0.3
1973	NY-A	45	136	10	24	4	0	1	10	4	24	.176	.200	.228	21	-14	1	1	-0	.960	-2	O-32,D-10	-1.9
Total	16	1886	6652	926	1757	321	89	226	840	650	1064	.264	.333	.441	114	121	74	51	-8	.984	113	*O-1777/D-10	14.1

■ **JACK CALVO** Calvo, Jacinto (Gonzalez) (Born Jacinto Del Calvo) b: 6/11/1894, Havana, Cuba d: 6/15/65, Miami, Fla. BL/TL, 5'10", 156 lbs. Deb: 5/9/13

YEAR	TM/L	G	AB	R	H	2B	3B	HR	RBI	BB	SO	AVG	OBP	SLG	PRO+	BR/A	SB	CS	SBR	FA	FR	G/POS	TPR
1913	Was-A	17	33	5	8	0	0	1	2	1	4	.242	.265	.333	73	-1	0			.900	-2	O-13	-0.4
1920	Was-A	17	23	5	1	0	1	0	2	2	2	.043	.120	.130	-35	-5	0	0	0	1.000	-4	O-10	-0.9
Total	2	34	56	10	9	0	1	1	4	3	6	.161	.203	.250	27	-6	0	0		.938	-6	/O-23	-1.3

■ **HANK CAMELLI** Camelli, Henry Richard b: 12/12/14, Gloucester, Mass. d: 7/14/96, Wellesley, Mass. BR/TR, 5'11", 190 lbs. Deb: 10/3/43

YEAR	TM/L	G	AB	R	H	2B	3B	HR	RBI	BB	SO	AVG	OBP	SLG	PRO+	BR/A	SB	CS	SBR	FA	FR	G/POS	TPR
1943	Pit-N	1	3	1	0	0	0	0	0	1	0	.000	.250	.000	-24	-0	0			1.000	0	/C-1	0.0
1944	Pit-N	63	125	14	37	5	1	1	10	18	12	.296	.385	.376	110	2	0			.959	4	C-61	0.8
1945	Pit-N	1	2	0	0	0	0	0	0	1	0	.000	.333	.000	-3	-0	0			1.000	-0	/C-1	0.0
1946	Pit-N	42	96	8	20	2	2	0	5	8	9	.208	.269	.271	52	-6	0			.971	4	C-39	-0.1
1947	Bos-N	52	150	10	29	8	1	1	11	18	18	.193	.280	.280	50	-11	0			.977	6	C-51	-0.2
Total	5	159	376	33	86	15	4	2	26	46	39	.229	.313	.306	70	-15	0			.970	14	C-153	0.5

■ **JACK CAMERON** Cameron, John William "Happy Jack" b: 9/1884, Nova Scotia, Can. d: 8/17/51, Boston, Mass. Deb: 9/13/06

YEAR	TM/L	G	AB	R	H	2B	3B	HR	RBI	BB	SO	AVG	OBP	SLG	PRO+	BR/A	SB	CS	SBR	FA	FR	G/POS	TPR
1906	Bos-N	18	61	3	11	0	0	0	4	2		.180	.206	.180	21	-6	0			.852	-1	O-16/P-2	-0.8

■ **MIKE CAMERON** Cameron, Michael Terrance b: 1/8/73, LaGrange, Ga. BR/TR, 6'1", 170 lbs. Deb: 8/27/95

YEAR	TM/L	G	AB	R	H	2B	3B	HR	RBI	BB	SO	AVG	OBP	SLG	PRO+	BR/A	SB	CS	SBR	FA	FR	G/POS	TPR
1995	Chi-A	28	38	4	7	2	0	1	2	3	15	.184	.244	.316	46	-3	0	0	0	1.000	-4	O-28	-0.7
1996	Chi-A	11	11	1	1	0	0	0	0	1	3	.091	.167	.091	-34	-2	0	1	-1	1.000	-3	/O-8,D-2	-0.6
1997	Chi-A	116	379	63	98	18	3	14	55	55	105	.259	.360	.433	110	6	23	2	6	.985	5	*O-112/D-4	1.4
1998	Chi-A	141	396	53	83	16	5	8	43	37	101	.210	.287	.336	63	-22	27	11	2	.988	-3	*O-138	-2.5
Total	4	296	824	121	189	36	8	23	100	96	224	.229	.318	.376	83	-21	50	14	7	.987	5	O-286/D-6	-2.4

■ **DOLPH CAMILLI** Camilli, Adolph Louis b: 4/23/07, San Francisco, Cal d: 10/21/97, San Mateo, Cal. BL/TL, 5'10", 185 lbs. Deb: 9/9/33 F

YEAR	TM/L	G	AB	R	H	2B	3B	HR	RBI	BB	SO	AVG	OBP	SLG	PRO+	BR/A	SB	CS	SBR	FA	FR	G/POS	TPR
1933	Chi-N	16	58	8	13	2	1	2	7	4	11	.224	.274	.397	90	-1	3			.994	2	1-16	-0.1
1934	Chi-N	32	120	17	33	8	0	4	19	5	25	.275	.315	.442	102	-0	1			.988	2	1-32	-0.1
	Phi-N	102	378	52	100	20	3	12	68	48	69	.265	.350	.429	95	-3	3			.985	-4	*1-102	-1.5
	Yr	134	498	69	133	28	3	16	87	53	94	.267	.342	.432	96	-3	4			.986	-2	*1-134	-1.6
1935	Phi-N	156	602	88	157	23	5	25	83	65	113	.261	.336	.440	97	-4	9			.987	-1	*1-156	-2.2
1936	Phi-N	151	530	106	167	29	13	28	102	116	84	.315	.441	.577	156	45	5			.988	-10	*1-150	2.0
1937	Phi-N	131	475	101	161	23	7	27	80	90	82	.339	**.446**	.587	165	45	6			**.994**	4	*1-131	3.3
1938	Bro-N	146	509	106	128	25	11	24	100	**119**	101	.251	.393	.485	137	29	6			.995	-1	*1-145	1.2
1939	Bro-N★	157	565	105	164	30	12	26	104	**110**	107	.290	.409	.524	144	38	1			.990	10	*1-157	3.0
1940	Bro-N	142	512	92	147	29	13	23	96	89	83	.287	.397	.529	145	32	9			.992	-4	*1-140	1.5
1941	*Bro-N†	149	529	92	151	29	6	**34**	**120**	104	115	.285	.407	.556	162	**45**	3			.989	3	*1-148	3.7
1942	Bro-N	150	524	89	132	23	7	26	109	97	85	.252	.372	.471	144	30	10			.992	-1	*1-150	2.2
1943	Bro-N	95	353	56	87	15	6	6	43	65	48	.246	.365	.374	113	8	2			.992	-1	1-95	0.2
1945	Bos-A	63	198	24	42	5	2	2	19	35	38	.212	.330	.288	78	-4	2	0	1	.991	2	1-54	-0.6
Total	12	1490	5353	936	1482	261	86	239	950	947	961	.277	.388	.492	134	260	60	0		.990	1	*1-1476	12.6

■ **DOUG CAMILLI** Camilli, Douglas Joseph b: 9/22/36, Philadelphia, Pa. BR/TR, 5'11", 195 lbs. Deb: 9/25/60 FC

YEAR	TM/L	G	AB	R	H	2B	3B	HR	RBI	BB	SO	AVG	OBP	SLG	PRO+	BR/A	SB	CS	SBR	FA	FR	G/POS	TPR
1960	LA-N	6	24	4	8	2	0	1	3	1	4	.333	.385	.542	141	1	0	0	0	.980	0	/C-6	0.2
1961	LA-N	13	30	3	4	0	0	3	4	1	9	.133	.161	.433	47	-2	0	0	0	.986	2	C-12	0.0
1962	LA-N	45	88	16	25	5	2	4	22	12	21	.284	.370	.523	145	5	0	0	0	.983	-5	C-39	0.1
1963	LA-N	49	117	9	19	1	1	3	10	11	22	.162	.234	.265	47	-8	0	0	0	.977	8	C-47	0.1
1964	LA-N	50	123	1	22	3	0	0	10	8	19	.179	.229	.203	25	-12	0	0	0	.990	8	C-46	-0.2
1965	Was-A	75	193	13	37	6	1	3	18	16	34	.192	.257	.280	53	-12	0	0	0	.980	1	C-59	-0.9
1966	Was-A	44	107	5	22	4	0	2	8	3	19	.206	.234	.299	53	-7	0	0	0	.990	4	C-39	-0.1
1967	Was-A	30	82	5	15	1	0	2	5	4	16	.183	.221	.268	46	-6	0	0	0	.993	0	C-24	-0.5
1969	Was-A	1	3	0	1	0	0	0	0	0	2	.333	.333	.333	92	-0	0	0	0	1.000	-0	/C-1	0.0
Total	9	313	767	56	153	22	4	18	80	56	146	.199	.257	.309	61	-41	0	0	0	.984	19	C-273	-1.3

■ **LOU CAMILLI** Camilli, Louis Steven b: 9/24/46, ElPaso, Tex. BB/TR, 5'10", 170 lbs. Deb: 8/9/69

YEAR	TM/L	G	AB	R	H	2B	3B	HR	RBI	BB	SO	AVG	OBP	SLG	PRO+	BR/A	SB	CS	SBR	FA	FR	G/POS	TPR
1969	Cle-A	13	14	0	0	0	0	0	0	0	3	.000	.000	.000	-97	-4	0	0	0	1.000	3	3-13	0.0
1970	Cle-A	16	15	0	0	0	0	0	0	2	2	.000	.118	.000	-62	-3	0	0	0	1.000	-1	/S-3,2-2,3-1	-0.4
1971	Cle-A	39	81	5	16	2	0	0	0	8	10	.198	.270	.222	37	-6	0	0	0	.938	1	S-23,2-16	-0.4
1972	Cle-A	39	41	2	6	2	0	0	3	3	8	.146	.205	.195	19	-4	0	0	0	1.000	-2	/S-8,2-2	-0.6
Total	4	107	151	7	22	4	0	0	3	13	23	.146	.213	.172	11	-18	0	0	0	.951	2	/S-34,2-20,3-14	-1.4

■ **KEN CAMINITI** Caminiti, Kenneth Gene b: 4/21/63, Hanford, Cal. BB/TR, 6', 200 lbs. Deb: 7/16/87

YEAR	TM/L	G	AB	R	H	2B	3B	HR	RBI	BB	SO	AVG	OBP	SLG	PRO+	BR/A	SB	CS	SBR	FA	FR	G/POS	TPR
1987	Hou-N	63	203	10	50	7	1	3	23	12	44	.246	.288	.335	67	-10	0	0	0	.949	3	3-61	-0.7
1988	Hou-N	30	83	5	15	2	0	1	7	5	18	.181	.227	.241	36	-7	0	0	0	.948	-0	3-28	-0.8
1989	Hou-N	161	585	71	149	31	3	10	72	51	93	.255	.318	.369	99	-1	4	1	1	.954	13	*3-160	1.4
1990	Hou-N	153	541	52	131	20	2	4	51	48	97	.242	.304	.309	71	-21	9	4	0	.945	-11	*3-149	-3.2
1991	Hou-N	152	574	65	145	30	3	13	80	46	85	.253	.314	.383	101	-1	4	5	-2	.948	8	*3-152	0.6
1992	Hou-N	135	506	68	149	31	2	13	62	44	68	.294	.352	.441	129	18	10	4	1	.966	-9	*3-129	1.0
1993	Hou-N	143	543	75	142	31	0	13	75	49	88	.262	.323	.390	93	-6	8	5	-1	.942	5	*3-143	-0.1
1994	Hou-N★	111	406	63	115	28	2	18	75	43	71	.283	.355	.495	125	14	4	3	-1	**.969**	2	*3-108	1.5
1995	SD-N	143	526	74	159	33	0	26	94	69	94	.302	.384	.513	139	30	12	5	1	.936	10	*3-143	3.9
1996	*SD-N★	146	546	109	178	37	2	40	130	78	99	.326	.414	.621	179	62	11	5	0	.954	12	*3-145	7.1
1997	SD-N★	137	486	92	141	28	0	26	90	80	118	.290	.394	.508	145	33	11	2	2	.941	14	*3-133	4.7
1998	*SD-N	131	452	87	114	29	0	29	82	71	108	.252	.359	.509	134	22	6	2	1	.931	-12	*3-126	1.3
Total	12	1505	5451	771	1488	307	15	196	841	596	983	.273	.347	.443	118	133	79	36	2	.948	35	*3-1477	16.7

■ **HOWIE CAMP** Camp, Howard Lee "Red" b: 7/1/1893, Munford, Ala. d: 5/8/60, Eastaboga, Ala. BL/TR, 5'9", 169 lbs. Deb: 9/19/17

YEAR	TM/L	G	AB	R	H	2B	3B	HR	RBI	BB	SO	AVG	OBP	SLG	PRO+	BR/A	SB	CS	SBR	FA	FR	G/POS	TPR
1917	NY-A	5	21	3	6	1	0	0	0	1	2	.286	.318	.333	98	-0	0			.857	1	/O-5	0.0

■ **LEW CAMP** Camp, Llewellyn Robert b: 2/22/1868, Columbus, Ohio d: 10/1/48, Omaha, Neb. BL/TR, 6', 175 lbs. Deb: 8/26/1892 F

YEAR	TM/L	G	AB	R	H	2B	3B	HR	RBI	BB	SO	AVG	OBP	SLG	PRO+	BR/A	SB	CS	SBR	FA	FR	G/POS	TPR
1892	StL-N	42	145	19	30	3	1	2	13	17	27	.207	.294	.283	79	-3	12			.780	-16	3-39/O-3	-1.7
1893	Chi-N	38	156	37	41	7	7	2	17	19	19	.263	.347	.436	109	1	30			.847	-10	3-16,O-11/2-9,S-3	-0.7
1894	Chi-N	8	33	1	6	2	0	0	1	1	6	.182	.206	.242	7	-5	0			.830	-3	/2-8	-0.6
Total	3	88	334	57	77	12	8	4	31	37	52	.231	.311	.350	85	-7	42			.801	-28	/3-55,2-17,O-14,S-3	-3.0

■ **ROY CAMPANELLA** Campanella, Roy b: 11/19/21, Philadelphia, Pa. d: 6/26/93, Woodland Hills, Cal. BR/TR, 5'8", 200 lbs. Deb: 4/20/48 H

YEAR	TM/L	G	AB	R	H	2B	3B	HR	RBI	BB	SO	AVG	OBP	SLG	PRO+	BR/A	SB	CS	SBR	FA	FR	G/POS	TPR
1948	Bro-N	83	279	32	72	11	3	9	45	36	45	.258	.345	.416	102	1	3			.981	10	C-78	1.6
1949	*Bro-N★	130	436	65	125	22	2	22	82	67	36	.287	.385	.498	130	19	3			.985	5	*C-127	3.0
1950	Bro-N★	126	437	70	123	19	3	31	89	55	51	.281	.364	.551	134	21	1			.985	-4	*C-123	2.1
1951	Bro-N★	143	505	90	164	33	1	33	108	53	51	.325	.393	.590	158	40	1	2	-1	.986	9	*C-140	5.2
1952	*Bro-N★	128	468	73	126	18	1	22	97	57	59	.269	.352	.453	120	13	8	4	0	**.994**	-7	*C-122	1.3
1953	*Bro-N★	144	519	103	162	26	3	41	**142**	67	58	.312	.395	.611	154	40	4	2	0	.989	3	*C-140	4.7
1954	Bro-N★	111	397	43	82	14	3	19	51	42	49	.207	.286	.401	74	-17	1	4	-2	.989	-3	*C-111	-1.6

YEAR	TM/L	G	AB	R	H	2B	3B	HR	RBI	BB	SO	AVG	OBP	SLG	PRO+	BR/A	SB	CS	SBR	FA	FR	G/POS	TPR
1955	*Bro-N†	123	446	81	142	20	1	32	107	56	41	.318	.402	.583	153	34	2	3	-1	.992	1	*C-121	3.8
1956	*Bro-N★	124	388	39	85	6	1	20	73	66	61	.219	.334	.394	88	-6	1	0	0	.985	3	*C-121	0.3
1957	Bro-N	103	330	31	80	9	0	13	62	34	50	.242	.321	.388	81	-9	1	0	0	**.993**	16	*C-100	1.2
Total	10	1215	4205	627	1161	178	18	242	856	533	501	.276	.362	.500	123	136	25	15		.988	33	*C-1183	21.6

■ **BERT CAMPANERIS** Campaneris, Dagoberto (Blanco) "Campy" (b: Dagoberto Campaneria (Blanco))
b: 3/9/42, Pueblo Nuevo, Cuba BR/TR, 5'10", 160 lbs. Deb: 7/23/64

YEAR	TM/L	G	AB	R	H	2B	3B	HR	RBI	BB	SO	AVG	OBP	SLG	PRO+	BR/A	SB	CS	SBR	FA	FR	G/POS	TPR
1964	KC-A	67	269	27	69	14	3	4	22	15	41	.257	.306	.375	86	-5	10	2	2	.981	-6	S-38,O-27/3-6	-0.9
1965	KC-A	144	578	67	156	23	**12**	6	42	41	71	.270	.328	.382	103	2	**51**	19	4	.938	-14	*S-109,O-39/PC123	-0.3
1966	KC-A	142	573	82	153	29	10	5	42	25	72	.267	.303	.379	98	-3	**52**	10	**10**	.971	-17	*S-138	0.3
1967	KC-A	147	601	85	149	29	6	3	32	36	82	.248	.298	.331	89	-9	**55**	16	**7**	.954	-19	*S-145	-0.8
1968	Oak-A★	159	642	87	**177**	25	9	4	38	50	69	.276	.332	.361	116	11	**62**	22	**5**	.956	1	*S-155/O-3	3.8
1969	Oak-A	135	547	71	142	15	2	2	25	30	62	.260	.303	.305	74	-20	62	8	**14**	.967	-5	*S-125	0.2
1970	Oak-A	147	603	97	168	28	4	22	64	36	73	.279	.323	.448	115	9	**42**	10	7	.973	-10	*S-143	2.4
1971	*Oak-A	134	569	80	143	18	4	5	47	29	64	.251	.290	.323	75	-20	34	7	6	.960	-5	*S-133	-0.1
1972	*Oak-A☆	149	625	85	150	25	2	8	32	32	88	.240	.279	.325	84	-15	**52**	14	**7**	.977	7	*S-148	2.3
1973	*Oak-A★	151	601	89	150	17	6	4	46	50	79	.250	.311	.318	82	-14	34	10	4	.969	-7	*S-149	0.2
1974	*Oak-A★	134	527	77	153	18	8	2	41	47	81	.290	.348	.366	113	9	34	15	1	.966	-9	*S-133/D-1	1.9
1975	*Oak-A★	137	509	69	135	15	3	4	46	50	71	.265	.339	.330	92	-4	24	12	0	.962	-31	*S-137	-2.1
1976	Oak-A	149	536	67	137	14	1	1	52	63	80	.256	.337	.291	89	-5	54	12	**9**	.969	-6	*S-149	1.6
1977	Tex-A★	150	552	77	140	19	7	5	46	47	86	.254	.317	.341	78	-16	27	20	-4	.968	18	*S-149	1.4
1978	Tex-A	98	269	30	50	5	3	1	17	20	36	.186	.247	.238	37	-22	22	4	4	.954	4	S-89/D-4	-0.4
1979	Tex-A	8	9	2	1	0	0	0	0	1	3	.111	.200	.111	-14	-1	1	0	0	.962	4	/S-8	0.3
	*Cal-A	85	239	27	56	4	4	0	15	19	32	.234	.296	.285	59	-13	12	4	1	.957	4	S-82/D-1	0.0
	Yr	93	248	29	57	4	4	0	15	20	35	.230	.293	.278	57	-15	13	4	2	.957	7	S-90/D-1	0.3
1980	Cal-A	77	210	32	53	8	1	2	18	14	33	.252	.302	.329	75	-7	10	5	0	.957	-5	S-64/2-1,D-2	-0.6
1981	Cal-A	55	82	11	21	2	1	1	10	5	10	.256	.299	.341	84	-2	5	2	0	.900	-2	3-45/S-3,2-2	-0.4
1983	NY-A	60	143	19	46	5	0	0	11	8	9	.322	.358	.357	101	0	6	7	-2	.964	-3	2-32,3-24	-0.4
Total	19	2328	8684	1181	2249	313	86	79	646	618	1142	.259	.313	.342	89	-127	649	199	75	.964	-102	*S-2097/3-76,O2D1CP	8.4

■ **AL CAMPANIS** Campanis, Alexander Sebastian (b: Alessandro Campani)
b: 11/2/16, Kos, Dodecanese Islands d: 6/21/98, Fullerton, Cal. BB/TR, 6', 185 lbs. Deb: 9/23/43 F

YEAR	TM/L	G	AB	R	H	2B	3B	HR	RBI	BB	SO	AVG	OBP	SLG	PRO+	BR/A	SB	CS	SBR	FA	FR	G/POS	TPR
1943	Bro-N	7	20	3	2	0	0	0	0	4	5	.100	.250	.100	3	-2	0			1.000	4	/2-7	0.2

■ **JIM CAMPANIS** Campanis, James Alexander b: 2/9/44, New York, N.Y. BR/TR, 6', 195 lbs. Deb: 9/20/66 F

YEAR	TM/L	G	AB	R	H	2B	3B	HR	RBI	BB	SO	AVG	OBP	SLG	PRO+	BR/A	SB	CS	SBR	FA	FR	G/POS	TPR
1966	LA-N	1	1	0	0	0	0	0	0	0	0	.000	.000	.000	-99	-0	0	0	0	1.000	0	/C-1	0.0
1967	LA-N	41	62	3	10	1	0	2	0	9	14	.161	.268	.274	60	-3	0	0	0	.990	-0	C-23	-0.3
1968	LA-N	4	11	0	1	0	0	0	0	1	2	.091	.167	.091	-23	-2	0	0	0	.960	1	/C-4	0.0
1969	KC-A	30	83	4	13	5	0	0	5	5	19	.157	.205	.217	18	-9	0	0	0	.982	3	C-26	-0.5
1970	KC-A	31	54	6	7	0	0	2	2	4	14	.130	.203	.241	22	-6	0	0	0	.986	1	C-13/O-1	-0.5
1973	Pit-N	6	6	0	1	0	0	0	0	0	0	.167	.167	.167	-8	-1	0	0	0	.000	0	H	-0.1
Total	6	113	217	13	32	6	0	4	9	19	49	.147	.219	.230	27	-21	0	0	0	.983	5	/C-67,O-1	-1.4

■ **COUNT CAMPAU** Campau, Charles Columbus b: 10/17/1863, Detroit, Mich. d: 4/3/38, New Orleans, La. BL/TR, 5'11", 160 lbs. Deb: 7/7/1888 M

YEAR	TM/L	G	AB	R	H	2B	3B	HR	RBI	BB	SO	AVG	OBP	SLG	PRO+	BR/A	SB	CS	SBR	FA	FR	G/POS	TPR
1888	Det-N	70	251	28	51	5	3	1	18	19	36	.203	.259	.259	66	-9	27			.933	-4	O-70	-1.5
1890	StL-a	75	314	68	101	9	12	**9**	75	26		.322	.374	.513	141	12	36			.934	3	O-74/3-1,1-1,M	1.1
1894	Was-N	2	7	1	1	0	0	0	0	1	4	.143	.250	.143	-3	-1	0			1.000	-0	/O-2	-0.1
Total	3	147	572	97	153	14	15	10	93	46	40	.267	.322	.397	109	1	63			.934	-1	O-146/1-1,3-1	-0.5

■ **VIN CAMPBELL** Campbell, Arthur Vincent b: 1/30/1888, St.Louis, Mo. d: 11/16/69, Towson, Md. BL/TR, 6', 185 lbs. Deb: 6/6/08

YEAR	TM/L	G	AB	R	H	2B	3B	HR	RBI	BB	SO	AVG	OBP	SLG	PRO+	BR/A	SB	CS	SBR	FA	FR	G/POS	TPR
1908	Chi-N	1	1	0	0	0	0	0	0	0		.000	.000	.000	-96	-0	0			.000	0	H	0.0
1910	Pit-N	97	282	42	92	9	5	4	21	26	23	.326	.391	.436	133	12	17			.895	-4	O-74	0.4
1911	Pit-N	42	93	12	29	3	1	0	10	8	7	.312	.366	.366	101	0	6			.923	-3	O-21	-0.3
1912	Bos-N	145	624	102	185	32	9	3	48	32	44	.296	.334	.391	96	-5	19			.938	0	*O-144	-1.2
1914	Ind-F	134	544	92	173	23	11	7	44	37	47	.318	.368	.439	108	-2	26			.925	-5	*O-132	-1.4
1915	New-F	127	525	78	163	18	10	1	44	29	35	.310	.352	.389	115	1	24			.947	-5	*O-126	-1.1
Total	6	546	2069	326	642	85	36	15	167	132	156	.310	.357	.408	109	6	92			.929	-17	O-497	-3.6

■ **BRUCE CAMPBELL** Campbell, Bruce Douglas b: 10/20/09, Chicago, Ill. d: 6/17/95, Ft.Myers Beach, Fla. BL/TR, 6'1", 185 lbs. Deb: 9/12/30

YEAR	TM/L	G	AB	R	H	2B	3B	HR	RBI	BB	SO	AVG	OBP	SLG	PRO+	BR/A	SB	CS	SBR	FA	FR	G/POS	TPR
1930	Chi-A	5	10	4	5	1	0	0	5	1	2	.500	.545	.800	245	2	0	0	0	1.000	-0	/O-4	0.2
1931	Chi-A	4	17	4	7	2	0	2	5	0	4	.412	.444	.882	256	4	0	0	0	.900	-0	/O-4	0.3
1932	Chi-A	7	18	3	4	1	0	0	2	0	2	.222	.222	.278	31	-2	0	1	-1	1.000	-1	/O-4	-0.3
	StL-A	139	593	83	169	35	11	14	85	40	102	.285	.336	.452	97	-5	7	5	-1	.935	6	*O-139	-0.8
	Yr	146	611	86	173	36	11	14	87	40	104	.283	.333	.447	95	-6	7	6	-2	.935	5	*O-143	-1.1
1933	StL-A	148	567	87	157	38	8	16	106	69	77	.277	.357	.457	108	5	10	4	1	.950	-1	*O-144	-0.3
1934	StL-A	138	481	62	134	25	6	9	74	51	64	.279	.350	.412	88	-9	5	4	-1	.935	3	*O-123	-1.1
1935	Cle-A	80	308	56	100	26	3	7	54	31	33	.325	.390	.497	126	11	2	1	0	.992	-5	O-75	0.3
1936	Cle-A	76	172	35	64	15	2	6	30	19	17	.372	.440	.587	150	14	2	1	0	.960	-4	O-47	0.7
1937	Cle-A	134	448	82	135	42	11	4	61	67	49	.301	.392	.471	116	12	4	5	-2	.978	-2	*O-123	0.4
1938	Cle-A	133	511	90	148	27	12	12	72	53	57	.290	.360	.460	106	3	11	7	-1	.967	-0	*O-122	-0.1
1939	Cle-A	130	450	84	129	23	13	8	72	67	48	.287	.383	.449	116	12	7	6	-2	.942	-3	*O-115	0.3
1940	*Det-A	103	297	56	84	15	5	8	44	45	28	.283	.381	.448	104	2	2	7	-4	.959	-2	O-74	-0.7
1941	Det-A	141	512	72	141	28	10	15	93	68	67	.275	.364	.457	105	3	3	3	-1	.976	-8	*O-133	-1.3
1942	Was-A	122	378	41	105	17	5	5	63	37	34	.278	.344	.389	107	3	0	6	-4	.955	-1	O-87	-0.6
Total	13	1360	4762	759	1382	295	87	106	766	548	584	.290	.367	.455	108	55	53	50	-14	.956	-19	O-1194	-3.0

■ **SOUP CAMPBELL** Campbell, Clarence b: 3/7/15, Sparta, Va. BL/TR, 6'1", 188 lbs. Deb: 4/21/40

YEAR	TM/L	G	AB	R	H	2B	3B	HR	RBI	BB	SO	AVG	OBP	SLG	PRO+	BR/A	SB	CS	SBR	FA	FR	G/POS	TPR
1940	Cle-A	35	62	8	14	1	0	0	2	7	12	.226	.304	.242	45	-5	0	0	0	1.000	-2	O-16	-0.7
1941	Cle-A	104	328	36	82	10	4	3	35	31	21	.250	.317	.332	75	-12	1	9	-5	.981	2	O-78	-1.9
Total	2	139	390	44	96	11	4	3	37	38	33	.246	.315	.318	70	-17	1	9	-5	.984	0	/O-94	-2.6

■ **DAVE CAMPBELL** Campbell, David Wilson b: 1/14/42, Manistee, Mich. BR/TR, 6', 185 lbs. Deb: 9/17/67

YEAR	TM/L	G	AB	R	H	2B	3B	HR	RBI	BB	SO	AVG	OBP	SLG	PRO+	BR/A	SB	CS	SBR	FA	FR	G/POS	TPR
1967	Det-A	2	2	0	0	0	0	0	0	0	1	.000	.000	.000	-97	-0	0	0	0	.500	-0	/1-1	-0.1
1968	Det-A	9	8	1	1	0	0	1	2	1	3	.125	.222	.500	111	0	0	0	0	1.000	0	/2-5	0.1
1969	Det-A	32	39	4	4	1	0	0	2	4	15	.103	.205	.128	-5	-5	0	1	-1	.967	-2	1-13/2-5,3-1	-0.8
1970	SD-N	154	581	71	127	28	2	12	40	40	115	.219	.270	.336	64	-32	18	6	2	.974	12	*2-153	-0.6
1971	SD-N	108	365	38	83	14	2	7	29	37	75	.227	.299	.334	85	-8	9	6	-1	.968	-2	2-69,3-40/S-4,1O	-0.6
1972	SD-N	33	100	6	24	5	0	0	3	11	12	.240	.315	.290	79	-3	0	4	-2	.988	4	3-31/2-1	-0.1
1973	SD-N	33	98	2	22	3	0	0	8	7	15	.224	.276	.255	52	-6	1	1	-0	.979	-1	2-27/1-3,3-2	-0.7
	StL-N	13	21	1	0	0	0	0	1	1	6	.000	.045	.000	-87	-5	0	0	0	.933	-3	/2-6	-0.8
	Hou-N	9	15	1	4	2	0	0	2	0	4	.267	.267	.400	83	-0	0	0	0	1.000	2	/3-5,1-2,O-1	0.1
	Yr	55	134	4	26	5	0	0	11	8	25	.194	.239	.231	33	-12	1	1	-0	.975	-2	2-33/3-7,1-5,O-1	-1.4
1974	Hou-N	35	23	4	2	1	0	0	2	1	8	.087	.125	.130	-30	-4	1	0	0	.895	6	/2-9,1-6,3-2,O-1	0.2
Total	8	428	1252	128	267	54	4	20	89	102	254	.213	.274	.311	64	-64	29	18	-2	.971	16	2-275/3-81,1-27,OS	-3.3

■ **JIM CAMPBELL** Campbell, James Robert b: 6/24/37, Palo Alto, Cal. BR/TR, 6', 190 lbs. Deb: 7/17/62

YEAR	TM/L	G	AB	R	H	2B	3B	HR	RBI	BB	SO	AVG	OBP	SLG	PRO+	BR/A	SB	CS	SBR	FA	FR	G/POS	TPR
1962	Hou-N	27	86	6	19	4	0	3	6	6	23	.221	.272	.372	77	-3	0	0	0	.970	6	C-25	0.4
1963	Hou-N	55	158	9	35	3	0	4	19	10	40	.222	.268	.316	72	-6	0	0	0	.979	-2	C-42	-0.7
Total	2	82	244	15	54	7	0	7	25	16	63	.221	.269	.336	74	-9	0	0	0	.975	4	/C-67	-0.3

■ **JIM CAMPBELL** Campbell, James Robert b: 1/10/43, Hartsville, S.C. BL/TR, 6', 205 lbs. Deb: 4/11/70

YEAR	TM/L	G	AB	R	H	2B	3B	HR	RBI	BB	SO	AVG	OBP	SLG	PRO+	BR/A	SB	CS	SBR	FA	FR	G/POS	TPR
1970	StL-N	13	13	0	3	0	0	0	1	0	3	.231	.231	.231	24	-1	0	0	0	.000	0	H	-0.1

YEAR	TM/L	G	AB	R	H	2B	3B	HR	RBI	BB	SO	AVG	OBP	SLG	PRO+	BR/A	SB	CS	SBR	FA	FR	G/POS	TPR

■ JOE CAMPBELL   Campbell, Joseph Earl   b: 3/10/44, Louisville, Ky.   BR/TR, 6'1", 175 lbs.   Deb: 5/3/67

| 1967 | Chi-N | 1 | 3 | 0 | 0 | 0 | 0 | 0 | 0 | 0 | 3 | .000 | .000 | .000 | -96 | -1 | 0 | 0 | 0 | .000 | -0 | /O-1 | -0.1 |

■ HUTCH CAMPBELL   Campbell, Marc Thaddeus   b: 11/29/1884, Punxsutawney, Pa.   d: 2/13/46, New Bethlehem, Pa.   BB/TR, 5'9", 155 lbs.   Deb: 9/30/07

| 1907 | Pit-N | 2 | 4 | 0 | 1 | 0 | 0 | 0 | 1 | 1 | | .250 | .400 | .250 | 102 | 0 | 0 | | | .889 | 0 | /S-2 | 0.0 |

■ MAT CAMPBELL   Campbell, Mathew   b: 8/1/1850, Ireland   d: 1/12/26, Scotch Plains, N.J.   Deb: 4/28/1873   F

| 1873 | Res-n | 21 | 83 | 9 | 12 | 0 | 0 | 0 | 3 | 3 | 6 | .145 | .174 | .145 | -5 | -10 | 1 | 0 | 0 | .927 | -2 | 1-18/S-3,O-1 | -0.8 |

■ PAUL CAMPBELL   Campbell, Paul McLaughlin   b: 9/1/17, Paw Creek, N.C.   BL/TL, 5'10", 185 lbs.   Deb: 4/15/41

1941	Bos-A	1	0	0	0	0	0	0	—	—	0	—	—	—	—	0	0	0	0	.000	0	R	0.0
1942	Bos-A	26	15	4	1	0	0	0	0	1	5	.067	.125	.067	-44	-3	1	0	0	1.000	-2	/O-4	-0.5
1946	*Bos-A	28	26	3	3	1	0	0	0	2	7	.115	.179	.154	-6	-4	0	0	0	1.000	-0	/1-5	-0.2
1948	Det-A	59	83	15	22	1	1	1	11	1	10	.265	.274	.337	60	-5	0	0	0	.969	3	1-27	-0.2
1949	Det-A	87	255	38	71	15	4	3	30	24	32	.278	.343	.404	97	-2	3	3	-1	.988	-3	1-74	-0.6
1950	Det-A	3	1	1	0	0	0	0	0	0	0	.000	.000	.000	-97	-0	0	0	0	.000	0	H	0.0
Total	6	204	380	61	97	17	5	4	41	28	54	.255	.308	.358	76	-14	4	3	-1	.984	-2	1-106/O-4	-1.7

■ RON CAMPBELL   Campbell, Ronald Thomas   b: 4/5/40, Chattanooga, Tenn.   BR/TR, 6'1", 180 lbs.   Deb: 9/1/64

1964	Chi-N	26	92	7	25	6	1	1	10	1	21	.272	.280	.391	83	-2	0	1	-1	.941	14	2-26	1.3
1965	Chi-N	2	0	0	0	0	0	0	0	0	0	.000	.000	.000	-98	-1	0	0	0	.000	0	H	-0.1
1966	Chi-N	24	60	4	13	1	0	0	4	6	5	.217	.288	.233	46	-4	1	1	-0	.980	4	S-11/3-7	0.0
Total	3	52	154	11	38	7	1	1	14	7	26	.247	.280	.325	67	-7	1	2	-1	.941	18	/2-26,S-11,3-7	1.2

■ SAM CAMPBELL   Campbell, Samuel   b: Philadelphia, Pa.   Deb: 10/11/1890

| 1890 | Phi-a | 2 | 5 | 0 | 0 | 0 | 0 | 0 | | | 1 | .000 | .167 | .000 | -52 | -1 | 0 | | | .833 | -2 | /2-2 | -0.3 |

■ GILLY CAMPBELL   Campbell, William Gilthorpe   b: 2/13/08, Kansas City, Kan.   d: 2/21/73, Los Angeles, Cal.   BL/TR, 5'7.5", 182 lbs.   Deb: 4/25/33

1933	Chi-N	46	89	11	25	3	1	1	10	7	4	.281	.347	.371	105	1	0			.949	-2	C-20	0.0
1935	Cin-N	88	218	26	56	7	0	3	30	42	7	.257	.379	.330	95	1	3			.986	-0	C-66/1-5,O-1	0.3
1936	Cin-N	89	235	28	63	13	1	1	40	43	14	.268	.384	.345	104	3	2			.984	6	C-71/1-1	1.2
1937	Cin-N	18	40	3	11	2	0	0	2	5	1	.275	.356	.325	90	-0	0			.967	-1	C-17	0.0
1938	Bro-N	54	126	10	31	5	0	0	11	19	9	.246	.354	.286	76	-3	0			.958	-1	C-44	-0.1
Total	5	295	708	78	186	30	2	5	93	116	35	.263	.371	.332	96	1	5			.975	4	C-218/1-6,O-1	1.4

■ FRANK CAMPOS   Campos, Francisco Jose (Lopez)   b: 5/11/24, Havana, Cuba   BL/TL, 5'11", 180 lbs.   Deb: 9/11/51

1951	Was-A	8	26	4	11	3	1	0	3	0	1	.423	.423	.615	182	3	0	0	0	1.000	-2	/O-7	0.1
1952	Was-A	53	112	9	29	6	1	0	8	1	13	.259	.278	.330	71	-5	0	0	0	.978	-2	O-23	-0.8
1953	Was-A	10	9	0	1	0	0	0	2	1	0	.111	.200	.111	-14	-1	0	0	0	.000	0	H	-0.1
Total	3	71	147	13	41	9	2	0	13	2	14	.279	.298	.367	86	-4	0	0	0	.981	-4	/O-30	-0.8

■ SIL CAMPUSANO   Campusano, Silvestre (Diaz)   b: 12/31/65, Santo Domingo, D.R.   BR/TR, 6', 175 lbs.   Deb: 4/4/88

1988	Tor-A	73	142	14	31	10	2	2	12	9	33	.218	.284	.359	78	-4	0	0	0	.934	-10	O-69/D-2	-1.6
1990	Phi-N	66	85	10	18	1	1	2	9	6	16	.212	.272	.318	62	-5	1	0	0	.976	-13	O-47	-1.9
1991	Phi-N	15	35	2	4	0	0	1	2	1	10	.114	.139	.200	-6	-5	0	0	0	1.000	0	O-15	-0.6
Total	3	154	262	26	53	11	3	5	23	16	59	.202	.261	.324	62	-14	1	0	0	.953	-24	O-131/D-2	-4.1

■ GEORGE CANALE   Canale, George Anthony   b: 8/11/65, Memphis, Tenn.   BL/TR, 6'1", 190 lbs.   Deb: 9/3/89

1989	Mil-A	13	26	5	5	1	0	1	3	2	3	.192	.250	.346	67	-1	0	1	-1	.989	-0	1-11	-0.3
1990	Mil-A	10	13	4	1	0	0	0	2	6	6	.077	.200	.154	0	-1	0	1	-1	1.000	1	/1-6,D-3	-0.2
1991	Mil-A	21	34	6	6	2	0	3	10	8	6	.176	.333	.500	130	1	0	0	0	.983	3	1-19	0.3
Total	3	44	73	15	12	4	0	4	13	12	15	.164	.282	.384	85	-2	0	2	-1	.988	3	/1-36,D-3	-0.2

■ WILLIE CANATE   Canate, Emisael William (Librada)   b: 12/11/71, Maracaibo, Venez.   BR/TR, 6', 170 lbs.   Deb: 4/16/93

| 1993 | *Tor-A | 38 | 47 | 12 | 10 | 0 | 0 | 1 | 3 | 6 | 15 | .213 | .315 | .277 | 60 | -2 | 1 | 1 | -0 | 1.000 | -4 | O-31/D-1 | -0.7 |

■ JIM CANAVAN   Canavan, James Edward   b: 11/26/1866, New Bedford, Mass.   d: 5/27/49, New Bedford, Mass.   BR/TR, 5'8", 160 lbs.   Deb: 4/8/1891

1891	Cin-a	101	426	74	97	13	14	7	66	27	44	.228	.282	.373	80	-16	21			.860	-11	*S-101	-1.8
	Mil-a	35	142	33	38	2	4	3	21	16	10	.268	.342	.401	94	-3	7			.864	-2	2-24,S-11	-0.3
	Yr	136	568	107	135	15	18	10	87	43	54	.238	.297	.380	84	-19	28			.860	-13	*S-112,2-24	-2.1
1892	Chi-N	118	439	48	73	10	11	0	32	48	48	.166	.248	.239	47	-28	33			.923	-2	*2-112/O-4,S-2	-2.7
1893	Cin-N	121	461	65	104	13	7	5	64	51	20	.226	.305	.317	64	-25	31			.931	-1	*O-117/2-5,3-1	-2.6
1894	Cin-N	101	356	77	97	16	9	13	70	62	25	.272	.380	.478	102	-0	13			.904	-2	*O-95/S-3,3-2,2-1	-0.7
1897	Bro-N	63	240	25	52	9	3	2	34	26		.217	.299	.304	63	-13	9			.909	-21	2-63	-2.7
Total	5	539	2064	322	461	63	48	30	287	230	147	.223	.304	.344	74	-86	114			.920	-40	O-216,2-205,S/31	-10.8

■ CASEY CANDAELE   Candaele, Casey Todd   b: 1/12/61, Lompoc, Cal.   BB/TR, 5'9", 165 lbs.   Deb: 6/5/86

1986	Mon-N	30	104	9	24	1	0	6	5	15		.231	.266	.288	53	-7	3	5	-2	.983	-2	2-24/3-4	-1.0
1987	Mon-N	138	449	62	122	23	4	1	23	38	28	.272	.328	.347	78	-14	7	10	-4	.985	-1	2-68,O-67,S-25/1-1	-1.7
1988	Mon-N	36	116	9	20	5	1	0	4	10	11	.172	.238	.233	34	-10	1	0	0	.988	1	2-35	-0.8
	Hou-N	21	31	2	5	0	0	1	1	6	.161	.188	.258	28	-3	0	1	-1	1.000	1	2-10/O-5,3-1	-0.3
	Yr	57	147	11	25	5	1	0	5	11	17	.170	.228	.238	33	-13	1	1	-0	.990	2	2-45/O-5,3-1	-1.1
1990	Hou-N	130	262	30	75	8	6	3	22	31	42	.286	.364	.397	112	5	7	5	-1	1.000	-14	O-58,2-49,S-13,/3-1	-1.0
1991	Hou-N	151	461	44	121	20	7	4	50	40	49	.262	.321	.362	97	-2	9	3	1	.982	5	*2-109,O-26,3-11	0.6
1992	Hou-N	135	320	19	68	12	1	1	18	24	36	.213	.274	.266	56	-19	7	1	2	.968	-5	S-65,3-29,O-21,/2-9	-2.0
1993	Hou-N	75	120	18	29	8	0	1	9	10	14	.240	.298	.331	70	-5	2	3	-1	1.000	-8	2-19,O-17,S-14,/3-4	-1.2
1996	*Cle-A	24	44	8	11	2	0	1	4	1	9	.250	.267	.364	58	-3	0	0	0	1.000	7	2-11/3-3,S-1	0.4
1997	Cle-A	14	26	5	8	1	0	0	4	1	5	.308	.333	.346	75	-1	1	0	0	1.000	5	/2-9,3-1,D-1	0.4
Total	9	754	1934	206	483	86	20	11	139	161	211	.250	.309	.332	78	-58	37	28	-6	.987	-8	2-343,O-194,S/3D1	-6.6

■ JOHN CANGELOSI   Cangelosi, John Anthony   b: 3/10/63, Brooklyn, N.Y.   BB/TL, 5'8", 160 lbs.   Deb: 6/3/85

1985	Chi-A	5	2	2	0	0	0	0	0	1	0	.000	.333	.000	1	-0	0	0	0	1.000	-2	/O-3,D-2	-0.2
1986	Chi-A	137	438	65	103	16	3	2	32	71	61	.235	.351	.299	77	-12	50	17	5	.969	-5	*O-129/D-3	-1.6
1987	Pit-N	104	182	44	50	8	3	4	18	46	33	.275	.424	.418	125	9	21	6	3	.962	-4	O-47	0.7
1988	Pit-N	75	118	18	30	4	1	0	8	17	16	.254	.353	.305	92	-1	9	4	0	.963	-2	O-24/P-1	-0.3
1989	Pit-N	112	160	18	35	4	2	0	9	35	20	.219	.369	.269	88	-0	11	8	-2	.973	-6	O-46	-1.0
1990	Pit-N	58	76	13	15	2	0	0	1	11	12	.197	.307	.224	50	-5	7	2	1	1.000	-6	O-12	-0.5
1992	Tex-A	73	85	12	16	2	0	1	6	18	16	.188	.330	.247	66	-3	6	5	-1	.964	-13	O-65/D-6	-1.9
1994	NY-N	62	111	14	28	4	0	4	19	20	.252	.371	.288	76	-3	5	1	1	1.000	-6	O-50	-0.9
1995	Hou-N	90	201	46	64	5	2	2	18	48	42	.318	.458	.393	137	15	21	5	3	.950	-5	O-59/P-1	1.3
1996	Hou-N	108	262	49	69	11	4	1	16	44	41	.263	.379	.347	101	2	17	9	-0	.975	-4	O-78	-0.3
1997	*Fla-N	103	192	28	47	8	0	1	12	19	33	.245	.322	.302	68	-9	5	1	1	1.000	-6	O-58/P-1	-1.4
1998	Fla-N	104	171	19	43	8	0	1	10	30	22	.251	.366	.316	83	-3	2	3	-1	.969	-6	O-45/D-1	-1.3
Total	12	1031	1998	328	500	72	15	12	134	358	318	.250	.372	.319	90	-9	154	61	10	.972	-59	O-616/D-12,P-3	-7.4

■ JAY CANIZARO   Canizaro, Jason Kyle   b: 7/4/73, Beaumont, Tex.   BR/TR, 5'9", 170 lbs.   Deb: 4/28/96

| 1996 | SF-N | 43 | 120 | 11 | 24 | 4 | 1 | 2 | 8 | 9 | 38 | .200 | .262 | .300 | 50 | -9 | 0 | 2 | -1 | .972 | 0 | 2-35/S-7 | -0.8 |

■ RIP CANNELL   Cannell, Virgin Wirt   b: 1/23/1880, S.Bridgton, Maine   d: 8/26/48, Bridgton, Maine   BL/TL, 5'10.5", 180 lbs.   Deb: 4/14/04

1904	Bos-N	100	346	32	81	5	1	0	18	23		.234	.286	.254	70	-12	10			.897	-11	O-93	-3.0
1905	Bos-N	154	567	52	140	14	4	0	36	51		.247	.311	.286	80	-13	17			.935	-8	*O-154	-3.0
Total	2	254	913	84	221	19	5	0	54	74		.242	.302	.274	75	-25	27			.923	-19	O-247	-6.0

■ CHRIS CANNIZZARO

Cannizzaro, Christopher John b: 5/3/38, Oakland, Cal. BR/TR, 6', 190 lbs. Deb: 4/17/60 C

YEAR	TM/L	G	AB	R	H	2B	3B	HR	RBI	BB	SO	AVG	OBP	SLG	PRO+	BR/A	SB	CS	SBR	FA	FR	G/POS	TPR
1960	StL-N	7	9	0	2	0	0	0	1	1	3	.222	.300	.222	42	-1	0	0	0	1.000	1	/C-6	0.1
1961	StL-N	6	2	0	1	0	0	0	0	0	0	.500	.500	.500	151	0	0	0	0	1.000	1	/C-5	0.1
1962	NY-N	59	133	9	32	2	1	0	9	19	26	.241	.340	.271	65	-6	1	1	-0	.973	2	C-56/O-1	-0.3
1963	NY-N	16	33	4	8	1	0	0	4	1	8	.242	.265	.273	54	-2	0	0	0	1.000	-1	C-15	-0.2
1964	NY-N	60	164	11	51	10	0	0	10	14	28	.311	.369	.372	112	3	0	5	-3	.988	2	C-53	0.4
1965	NY-N	114	251	17	46	8	2	0	7	28	60	.183	.270	.231	44	-18	0	2	-1	.977	12	*C-112	-0.3
1968	Pit-N	25	58	5	14	2	2	1	7	9	13	.241	.343	.397	123	2	0	0	0	.976	-0	C-25	0.3
1969	SD-N☆	134	418	23	92	14	3	4	33	42	81	.220	.291	.297	68	-18	0	1	-1	.988	-14	*C-132	-2.7
1970	SD-N	111	341	27	95	13	3	5	42	48	49	.279	.369	.378	105	4	2	7	-4	.980	-16	*C-110	-1.0
1971	SD-N	21	63	2	12	1	0	1	8	11	10	.190	.320	.254	69	-2	0	0	0	.992	-2	C-19	-0.3
	Chi-N	71	197	18	42	8	1	5	23	28	24	.213	.314	.340	74	-7	0	0	0	.983	-11	C-70	-1.6
	Yr	92	260	20	54	9	1	6	31	39	34	.208	.316	.319	73	-9	0	0	0	.985	-12	C-89	-1.9
1972	LA-N	73	200	14	48	6	0	2	18	31	38	.240	.342	.300	86	-3	0	1	-1	.983	-8	C-72	-0.9
1973	LA-N	17	21	0	4	0	0	0	3	3	3	.190	.292	.190	38	-2	0	0	0	1.000	-0	C-13	-0.2
1974	SD-N	26	60	2	11	1	0	0	4	6	11	.183	.258	.200	31	-6	0	0	0	.979	5	C-26	0.0
Total	13	740	1950	132	458	66	12	18	169	241	354	.235	.321	.309	77	-55	3	17	-9	.983	-28	C-714/O-1	-6.6

■ JOE CANNON

Cannon, Joseph Jerome b: 7/13/53, Camp Lejeune, N.C. BL/TR, 6'3", 193 lbs. Deb: 9/22/77

YEAR	TM/L	G	AB	R	H	2B	3B	HR	RBI	BB	SO	AVG	OBP	SLG	PRO+	BR/A	SB	CS	SBR	FA	FR	G/POS	TPR
1977	Hou-N	9	17	3	2	2	0	0	1	0	5	.118	.118	.235	-9	-3	1	1	-0	1.000	0	/O-3	-0.3
1978	Hou-N	8	18	1	4	0	0	0	1	0	1	.222	.222	.222	26	-2	0	1	-1	.778	-1	/O-5	-0.4
1979	Tor-A	61	142	14	30	1	1	1	5	1	34	.211	.217	.254	26	-15	12	2	2	1.000	-4	O-50	-1.8
1980	Tor-A	70	50	16	4	0	0	0	4	0	14	.080	.098	.080	-48	-10	2	2	-1	.968	-10	O-33/D-1	-2.2
Total	4	148	227	34	40	3	1	1	11	1	54	.176	.183	.211	7	-29	15	6	1	.977	-15	/O-91,D-1	-4.7

■ JOSE CANSECO

Canseco, Jose (Capas) b: 7/2/64, Havana, Cuba BR/TR, 6'4", 240 lbs. Deb: 9/2/85 F

YEAR	TM/L	G	AB	R	H	2B	3B	HR	RBI	BB	SO	AVG	OBP	SLG	PRO+	BR/A	SB	CS	SBR	FA	FR	G/POS	TPR
1985	Oak-A	29	96	16	29	3	0	5	13	4	31	.302	.330	.490	130	3	1	1	-0	.951	-0	O-26	0.2
1986	Oak-A☆	157	600	85	144	29	1	33	117	65	175	.240	.322	.457	118	13	15	7	0	.958	-3	*O-155/D-1	0.5
1987	Oak-A	159	630	81	162	35	3	31	113	50	157	.257	.314	.470	111	8	15	3	3	.975	11	*O-130,D-30	1.5
1988	*Oak-A★	158	610	120	187	34	0	**42**	**124**	78	128	.307	.394	**.569**	**172**	59	40	16	2	.978	8	*O-144,D-13	**6.4**
1989	*Oak-A†	65	227	40	61	9	1	17	57	23	69	.269	.341	.542	151	14	6	3	0	.976	4	O-56/D-5	1.6
1990	*Oak-A★	131	481	83	132	14	2	37	101	72	158	.274	.375	.543	160	38	19	10	-0	.995	5	O-88,D-43	4.0
1991	Oak-A	154	572	115	152	32	1	**44**	122	78	152	.266	.363	.556	159	45	26	6	4	.965	-3	*O-131,D-24	4.2
1992	Oak-A†	97	366	66	90	11	0	22	72	48	104	.246	.338	.456	127	13	5	7	-3	.988	4	O-77,D-20	1.2
	Tex-A	22	73	8	17	4	0	4	15	15	24	.233	.385	.452	139	4	1	0	0	.970	1	O-13/D-8	0.5
	Yr	119	439	74	107	15	0	26	87	63	128	.244	.346	.456	129	17	6	7	-2	.985	5	O-90,D-28	1.7
1993	Tex-A	60	231	30	59	14	1	10	46	16	62	.255	.312	.455	107	1	6	6	-2	.970	1	O-49/P-1	0.0
1994	Tex-A	111	429	88	121	19	2	31	90	69	114	.282	.388	.552	139	25	15	8	-0	.000	0	*D-111	1.8
1995	*Bos-A	102	396	64	121	25	1	24	81	42	93	.306	.382	.556	136	20	4	0	1	1.000	-0	*D-101/O-1	1.4
1996	Bos-A	96	360	68	104	22	1	28	82	63	82	.289	.403	.589	144	25	3	1	0	1.000	-1	D-84,O-11	1.7
1997	Oak-A	108	388	56	91	19	0	23	74	51	122	.235	.328	.461	105	2	8	2	1	.938	-4	D-56,O-44	-0.4
1998	Tor-A	151	583	98	138	26	0	46	107	65	159	.237	.320	.518	113	9	29	17	-2	.960	-4	D-78,O-73	-0.2
Total	14	1600	6042	1018	1608	296	13	397	1214	739	1630	.266	.353	.517	135	280	193	87	6	.972	19	O-998,D-574/P-1	24.4

■ OZZIE CANSECO

Canseco, Osvaldo (Capas) b: 7/2/64, Havana, Cuba BR/TR, 6'2", 220 lbs. Deb: 7/18/90 F

YEAR	TM/L	G	AB	R	H	2B	3B	HR	RBI	BB	SO	AVG	OBP	SLG	PRO+	BR/A	SB	CS	SBR	FA	FR	G/POS	TPR
1990	Oak-A	9	19	1	2	1	0	0	1	1	10	.105	.150	.158	-14	-3	0	0	0	1.000	-0	/O-2,D-4	-0.3
1992	StL-N	9	29	7	8	5	0	0	3	7	4	.276	.417	.448	150	2	0	0	0	.889	-2	/O-8	0.0
1993	StL-N	6	17	0	3	0	0	0	0	1	3	.176	.222	.176	8	-2	0	0	0	.500	-2	/O-5	-0.5
Total	3	24	65	8	13	6	0	0	4	9	17	.200	.297	.292	67	-3	0	0	0	.857	-4	/O-15,D-4	-0.8

■ BART CANTZ

Cantz, Bartholomew L. b: 1/29/1860, Philadelphia, Pa. d: 2/12/43, Philadelphia, Pa. Deb: 7/25/1888

YEAR	TM/L	G	AB	R	H	2B	3B	HR	RBI	BB	SO	AVG	OBP	SLG	PRO+	BR/A	SB	CS	SBR	FA	FR	G/POS	TPR
1888	Bal-a	37	126	7	21	2	1	0	9	2		.167	.180	.198	22	-11	0			.904	-9	C-33/O-4	-1.6
1889	Bal-a	20	69	6	12	2	0	0	8	4	14	.174	.219	.203	20	-7	2			.860	-7	C-18/O-2	-1.1
1890	Phi-a	5	22	1	1	0	0	0	1	0		.045	.045	.045	-75	-5	0			.893	-3	/C-5	-0.6
Total	3	62	217	14	34	4	1	0	18	6	14	.157	.179	.184	11	-23	2			.890	-19	/C-56,O-6	-3.3

■ NICK CAPRA

Capra, Nick Lee b: 3/8/58, Denver, Colo. BR/TR, 5'8", 165 lbs. Deb: 9/6/82

YEAR	TM/L	G	AB	R	H	2B	3B	HR	RBI	BB	SO	AVG	OBP	SLG	PRO+	BR/A	SB	CS	SBR	FA	FR	G/POS	TPR
1982	Tex-A	13	15	2	4	0	0	1	1	3	4	.267	.421	.467	151	1	2	1	0	1.000	1	/O-9	0.2
1983	Tex-A	8	2	2	0	0	0	0	0	0	0	.000	.000	.000	-99	-1	0	0	0	.000	-2	/O-4	-0.2
1985	Tex-A	8	8	1	1	0	0	0	0	0	0	.125	.125	.125	-31	-1	0	0	0	1.000	-1	/O-8	-0.3
1988	KC-A	14	29	3	4	1	0	0	0	2	3	.138	.194	.172	3	-4	1	0	0	1.000	-2	O-11/D-1	-0.6
1991	Tex-A	2	0	1	0	0	0	0	0	1	0	—	1.000	—	205	0	0	0	0	1.000	-0	/O-2	0.0
Total	5	45	54	9	9	1	0	1	1	6	7	.167	.262	.241	41	-4	3	1	0	1.000	-5	/O-34,D-1	-0.9

■ PAT CAPRI

Capri, Patrick Nicholas b: 11/27/18, New York, N.Y. d: 6/14/89, New York, N.Y. BR/TR, 6'0.5", 170 lbs. Deb: 7/16/44

YEAR	TM/L	G	AB	R	H	2B	3B	HR	RBI	BB	SO	AVG	OBP	SLG	PRO+	BR/A	SB	CS	SBR	FA	FR	G/POS	TPR
1944	Bos-N	7	1	1	0	0	0	0	0	0	1	.000	.000	.000	-96	-0	0			1.000	1	/2-1	0.1

■ RALPH CAPRON

Capron, Ralph Earl b: 6/16/1889, Minneapolis, Minn d: 9/19/80, Los Angeles, Cal. BL/TR, 5'11.5", 165 lbs. Deb: 4/25/12

YEAR	TM/L	G	AB	R	H	2B	3B	HR	RBI	BB	SO	AVG	OBP	SLG	PRO+	BR/A	SB	CS	SBR	FA	FR	G/POS	TPR
1912	Pit-N	1	0	0	0	0	0	0	0	0	0	—	—	—	—	0	0			.000	0	R	0.0
1913	Phi-N	2	1	1	0	0	0	0	0	0	0	.000	.000	.000	-96	-0	0			.000	-1	/O-1	-0.1
Total	2	3	1	1	0	0	0	0	0	0	0	.000	.000	.000	-96	-0	0			—	-1	/O-1	-0.1

■ RAMON CARABALLO

Caraballo, Ramon (Sanchez) b: 5/23/69, Rio San Juan, D.R. BB/TR, 5'7", 150 lbs. Deb: 9/9/93

YEAR	TM/L	G	AB	R	H	2B	3B	HR	RBI	BB	SO	AVG	OBP	SLG	PRO+	BR/A	SB	CS	SBR	FA	FR	G/POS	TPR
1993	Atl-N	6	0	0	0	0	0	0	0	0	0	—	—	—	—	0	0	0	0	1.000	2	/2-5	0.2
1995	StL-N	34	99	10	20	4	1	2	3	6	33	.202	.269	.323	55	-7	3	2	-0	.956	-1	2-24	-0.7
Total	2	40	99	10	20	4	1	2	3	6	33	.202	.269	.323	55	-7	3	2	-0	.958	1	/2-29	-0.5

■ JOHN CARBINE

Carbine, John C. b: 10/12/1855, Syracuse, N.Y. d: 9/11/15, Chicago, Ill. 6', 187 lbs. Deb: 5/8/1875

YEAR	TM/L	G	AB	R	H	2B	3B	HR	RBI	BB	SO	AVG	OBP	SLG	PRO+	BR/A	SB	CS	SBR	FA	FR	G/POS	TPR
1875	Wes-n	10	36	0	3	0	0	0	2	0	1	.083	.083	.083	-40	-5	0	0	0	.950	1	1-10	-0.4
1876	Lou-N	7	25	3	4	0	0	0	1	0	0	.160	.160	.160	6	-3				.878	-0	/1-6,O-1	-0.3

■ BERNIE CARBO

Carbo, Bernardo b: 8/5/47, Detroit, Mich. BL/TR, 6', 175 lbs. Deb: 9/2/69

YEAR	TM/L	G	AB	R	H	2B	3B	HR	RBI	BB	SO	AVG	OBP	SLG	PRO+	BR/A	SB	CS	SBR	FA	FR	G/POS	TPR
1969	Cin-N	4	3	0	0	0	0	0	0	0	2	.000	.000	.000	-95	-1	0	0	0	.000	0	H	-0.1
1970	*Cin-N	125	365	54	113	19	3	21	63	94	77	.310	.456	.551	168	40	10	4	1	.979	0	*O-119	3.5
1971	Cin-N	106	310	33	68	20	1	5	20	54	56	.219	.339	.339	94	-1	2	1	0	.982	2	O-90	-0.3
1972	Cin-N	19	21	2	3	0	0	0	0	6	3	.143	.357	.143	50	-1	0	0	0	1.000	0	/O-4	-0.1
	StL-N	99	302	42	78	13	1	7	34	57	56	.258	.385	.377	119	10	0	1	-1	.967	8	O-92/3-1	1.4
	Yr	118	323	44	81	13	1	7	34	63	59	.251	.383	.362	115	9	0	1	-1	.969	8	O-96/3-1	1.3
1973	StL-N	111	308	42	88	18	0	8	40	58	52	.286	.401	.422	128	14	2	0	1	.978	3	O-94	1.4
1974	Bos-A	117	338	40	84	20	0	12	61	58	90	.249	.365	.414	116	8	4	3	-1	.994	-1	O-87,D-15	0.3
1975	*Bos-A	107	319	64	82	21	3	15	50	83	69	.257	.412	.483	140	20	2	4	-2	.976	-1	O-85,D-13	1.4
1976	Bos-A	17	55	5	13	4	0	2	6	8	17	.236	.333	.418	106	0	1	0	0	1.000	-0	D-15/O-1	0.0
	Mil-A	69	183	20	43	7	0	3	15	33	55	.235	.352	.322	100	1	1	2	-1	1.000	4	O-33,D-24	0.2
	Yr	86	238	25	56	11	0	5	21	41	72	.235	.348	.345	102	2	2	2	-1	1.000	3	D-39,O-34	0.2
1977	Bos-A	86	228	36	66	6	1	15	34	47	72	.289	.411	.522	136	12	1	2	-1	.951	2	O-67/D-7	1.1
1978	Bos-A	17	46	7	12	3	0	1	6	8	8	.261	.370	.391	103	0	1	1	-0	1.000	1	/O-9,D-8	0.1
	Cle-A	60	174	21	50	8	0	4	16	20	31	.287	.364	.402	117	4	1	0	0	1.000	-2	D-49/O-4	0.2
	Yr	77	220	28	62	11	0	5	22	28	39	.282	.365	.400	113	5	2	1	0	1.000	-0	D-57,O-13	0.3
1979	StL-N	52	64	6	18	1	0	3	12	10	22	.281	.378	.438	121	2	1	0	0	1.000	-5	O-17	-0.3
1980	StL-N	14	11	0	2	0	0	0	0	1	0	.182	.250	.182	22	-1	0	0	0	.000	0	H	-0.2
	Pit-N	7	6	0	2	0	0	0	1	1	1	.333	.429	.333	114	0	0	0	0	.000	0	/H	0.0

YEAR	TM/L	G	AB	R	H	2B	3B	HR	RBI	BB	SO	AVG	OBP	SLG	PRO+	BR/A	SB	CS	SBR	FA	FR	G/POS	TPR
	Yr	21	17	0	4	0	0	0	1	2	1	.235	.316	.235	55	-1	0	0	0	.000	0	-0,-0	-0.2
Total	12	1010	2733	372	722	140	9	96	358	538	611	.264	.389	.427	125	109	26	18	-3	.978	12	O-702,D-131/3-1	8.6

■ JOSE CARDENAL

Cardenal, Jose Rosario Domec (b: Jose Rosario Domec (Cardenal)) b: 10/7/43, Matanzas, Cuba BR/TR, 5'10", 150 lbs. Deb: 4/14/63 C

YEAR	TM/L	G	AB	R	H	2B	3B	HR	RBI	BB	SO	AVG	OBP	SLG	PRO+	BR/A	SB	CS	SBR	FA	FR	G/POS	TPR
1963	SF-N	9	5	1	1	0	0	0	2	1	1	.200	.333	.200	58	-0	0	1	-1	.000	-1	/O-2	-0.2
1964	SF-N	20	15	3	0	0	0	0	0	2	3	.000	.118	.000	-62	-3	2	0	1	.909	-3	O-16	-0.6
1965	Cal-A	134	512	58	128	23	2	11	57	27	72	.250	.290	.367	87	-10	37	17	1	.964	10	*O-129/3-2,2-1	-0.5
1966	Cal-A	154	561	67	155	15	3	16	48	34	69	.276	.322	.399	109	5	24	11	1	.992	12	*O-146	1.2
1967	Cal-A	108	381	40	90	13	5	6	27	15	63	.236	.269	.344	83	-9	10	5	0	.986	0	*O-101	-1.6
1968	Cle-A	157	583	78	150	21	7	7	44	39	74	.257	.306	.353	101	-0	40	18	1	.974	13	*O-153	0.6
1969	Cle-A	146	557	75	143	26	3	11	45	49	58	.257	.317	.373	89	-8	36	6	7	.982	11	*O-142/3-5	0.2
1970	StL-N	148	552	73	162	32	6	10	74	45	70	.293	.348	.428	104	3	26	9	2	.969	-0	*O-134	-0.2
1971	StL-N	89	301	37	73	12	4	7	48	29	35	.243	.309	.379	90	-4	12	3	2	.969	7	O-83	0.1
	Mil-A	53	198	20	51	10	0	3	32	13	20	.258	.307	.354	88	-4	9	5	-0	.979	7	O-52	0.0
1972	Chi-N	143	533	96	155	24	6	17	70	55	58	.291	.358	.454	117	12	25	14	-1	.971	-9	*O-137	-0.5
1973	Chi-N	145	522	80	158	33	2	11	68	58	62	.303	.378	.437	116	13	19	7	2	.980	-3	*O-142	0.4
1974	Chi-N	143	542	75	159	35	3	13	72	56	67	.293	.361	.441	118	13	23	9	2	.965	8	*O-137	1.7
1975	Chi-N	154	574	85	182	30	2	9	68	77	50	.317	.402	.423	124	21	34	12	3	.976	12	*O-151	3.0
1976	Chi-N	136	521	64	156	25	2	8	47	32	39	.299	.341	.401	101	0	23	14	-2	.981	7	*O-128	0.0
1977	Chi-N	100	226	33	54	12	1	3	18	28	30	.239	.325	.341	71	-9	5	4	-1	.989	-6	O-62/2-1,S-1	-1.9
1978	*Phi-N	87	201	27	50	12	0	4	33	23	16	.249	.326	.368	93	-2	2	3	-1	.990	-9	1-50,O-13	-1.5
1979	Phi-N	29	48	4	10	3	0	0	9	8	8	.208	.321	.271	61	-2	1	0	0	1.000	-3	O-12/1-1	-0.6
	NY-N	11	37	8	11	4	0	2	4	6	3	.297	.409	.568	170	4	1	0	0	1.000	-1	/O-9,1-2	0.2
	Yr	40	85	12	21	7	0	2	13	14	11	.247	.360	.400	106	1	2	0	1	1.000	-4	O-21/1-3	-0.4
1980	NY-N	26	42	4	7	1	0	0	4	6	4	.167	.271	.190	32	-4	0	1	-1	1.000	0	/O-6,1-5	-0.5
	*KC-A	25	53	8	18	2	0	0	5	5	5	.340	.397	.377	112	1	0	0	0	.970	-3	O-23	-0.2
Total	18	2017	6964	936	1913	333	46	138	775	608	807	.275	.335	.395	102	16	329	139	15	.976	48	*O-1778/1-58,32S	-0.9

■ LEO CARDENAS

Cardenas, Leonardo Lazaro (Alfonso) "Chico" b: 12/17/38, Matanzas, Cuba BR/TR, 5'10", 163 lbs. Deb: 7/25/60

YEAR	TM/L	G	AB	R	H	2B	3B	HR	RBI	BB	SO	AVG	OBP	SLG	PRO+	BR/A	SB	CS	SBR	FA	FR	G/POS	TPR
1960	Cin-N	48	142	13	33	2	4	1	12	6	32	.232	.264	.324	59	-8	0	0	0	.958	7	S-47	0.2
1961	*Cin-N	74	198	23	61	18	1	5	24	15	39	.308	.357	.485	119	5	1	0	0	.973	-5	S-63	0.5
1962	Cin-N	153	589	77	173	31	4	10	60	39	99	.294	.343	.411	98	-2	2	5	-2	.972	-7	*S-149	0.3
1963	Cin-N	158	565	42	133	22	4	7	48	23	101	.235	.270	.326	69	-23	3	5	-2	**.972**	-3	*S-157	-1.9
1964	Cin-N★	163	597	61	150	32	2	9	69	41	110	.251	.302	.357	82	-14	4	4	-1	.960	-10	*S-163	-1.5
1965	Cin-N★	156	557	65	160	25	11	11	57	60	100	.287	.358	.431	113	10	1	4	-2	.975	-1	*S-155	1.9
1966	Cin-N★	160	568	59	145	25	4	20	81	45	87	.255	.311	.419	93	-6	9	4	0	**.980**	-15	*S-160	-0.6
1967	Cin-N	108	379	30	97	14	3	2	21	34	77	.256	.320	.325	76	-11	4	5	-2	.971	-10	*S-108	-1.3
1968	Cin-N★	137	452	45	106	13	2	7	41	36	83	.235	.294	.319	79	-11	2	1	0	.955	-23	*S-136	-2.3
1969	*Min-A	160	578	67	162	24	4	10	70	66	96	.280	.358	.388	106	6	5	6	-2	.965	**34**	*S-160	5.6
1970	*Min-A	160	588	67	145	34	4	11	65	42	101	.247	.301	.374	84	-14	2	5	-2	.978	3	*S-160	0.6
1971	Min-A☆	153	554	59	146	25	4	18	75	51	69	.264	.327	.421	107	4	3	3	-1	**.985**	-0	*S-153	2.4
1972	Cal-A	150	551	25	123	11	2	6	42	35	73	.223	.272	.283	69	-22	1	2	-1	.970	3	*S-150	0.2
1973	Cle-A	72	195	9	42	4	0	0	12	13	42	.215	.264	.236	41	-15	1	4	-2	.964	-8	S-67/3-5	-1.9
1974	Tex-A	34	92	5	25	3	0	0	7	2	14	.272	.287	.304	72	-3	1	0	0	1.000	2	3-21,S-10/D-4	-0.1
1975	Tex-A	55	102	15	24	2	0	1	5	14	12	.235	.328	.284	75	-3	0	0	0	.956	11	3-43/S-5,2-3	0.8
Total	16	1941	6707	662	1725	285	49	118	689	522	1135	.257	.313	.367	88	-107	39	48	-17	.971	-22	*S-1843/3-69,D-4,2	2.9

■ ROD CAREW

Carew, Rodney Cline b: 10/1/45, Gatun, C.Z. BL/TR, 6', 182 lbs. Deb: 4/11/67 CH

YEAR	TM/L	G	AB	R	H	2B	3B	HR	RBI	BB	SO	AVG	OBP	SLG	PRO+	BR/A	SB	CS	SBR	FA	FR	G/POS	TPR
1967	Min-A★	137	514	66	150	22	7	8	51	37	91	.292	.342	.409	112	7	5	9	-4	.976	-10	*2-134	0.2
1968	Min-A★	127	461	46	126	27	2	1	42	26	71	.273	.314	.347	95	-3	12	4	1	.968	-14	*2-117/S-4	-1.0
1969	*Min-A★	123	458	79	152	30	4	8	56	37	72	**.332**	.386	.467	135	21	19	8	1	.970	-17	*2-118	1.5
1970	*Min-A†	51	191	27	70	12	3	4	28	11	28	.366	.407	.524	153	13	4	6	-2	.961	-11	2-45/1-1	0.3
1971	Min-A★	147	577	88	177	16	10	2	48	45	81	.307	.358	.380	106	5	6	7	-2	.976	-25	*2-142/3-2	-1.2
1972	Min-A★	142	535	61	170	21	6	0	51	43	60	**.318**	.371	.379	118	13	12	6	0	.978	-0	*2-139	2.3
1973	Min-A★	149	580	98	**203**	30	**11**	6	62	62	55	**.350**	.415	.471	143	35	41	16	3	.984	7	*2-147	**5.3**
1974	Min-A★	153	599	86	**218**	30	5	3	55	74	49	**.364**	**.435**	.446	149	41	38	16	2	.960	9	*2-148	**6.0**
1975	Min-A★	143	535	89	192	24	4	14	80	64	40	**.359**	**.428**	.497	159	43	35	9	5	.973	4	*2-123,1-14/D-2	5.7
1976	Min-A★	156	605	97	200	29	12	9	90	67	52	.331	.398	.463	149	38	49	22	2	.989	-2	*1-152/2-7	2.8
1977	Min-A★	155	616	**128**	**239**	38	**16**	14	100	69	55	**.388**	**.452**	.570	**179**	**69**	23	13	-1	.994	6	*1-151/2-4,D-1	**6.3**
1978	Min-A★	152	564	85	188	26	10	5	70	78	62	**.333**	**.415**	.441	138	32	27	7	4	.989	1	*1-148/2-4,O-1	2.8
1979	*Cal-A†	110	409	78	130	15	3	3	44	73	46	.318	.421	.391	125	19	18	8	1	.988	-7	*1-103/D-6	0.6
1980	Cal-A★	144	540	74	179	34	7	3	59	59	38	.331	.398	.437	132	25	23	15	-2	.994	-4	*1-103,D-32	1.1
1981	Cal-A★	93	364	57	111	17	1	2	21	45	45	.305	.381	.374	118	10	16	9	-1	.995	-1	1-90/D-2	0.4
1982	*Cal-A†	138	523	88	167	25	5	3	44	67	49	.319	.399	.403	121	18	10	17	-7	.992	1	*1-134	0.5
1983	Cal-A★	129	472	66	160	24	2	2	44	57	48	.339	.411	.411	128	21	6	7	-2	.994	-9	1-89,D-24/2-2	0.3
1984	Cal-A★	93	329	42	97	8	1	3	31	40	39	.295	.371	.353	102	3	4	3	-1	.981	-4	1-83/D-1	-0.7
1985	Cal-A	127	443	69	124	17	3	2	39	64	47	.280	.372	.345	99	2	5	5	-2	.994	-8	*1-116	-1.5
Total	19	2469	9315	1424	3053	445	112	92	1015	1018	1028	.328	.395	.429	131	411	353	187	-6	.991	-85	*1-1184,*2-1130/DS3O	31.7

■ ANDY CAREY

Carey, Andrew Arthur (b: Andrew Arthur Hexem) b: 10/18/31, Oakland, Cal. BR/TR, 6'1", 195 lbs. Deb: 5/2/52

YEAR	TM/L	G	AB	R	H	2B	3B	HR	RBI	BB	SO	AVG	OBP	SLG	PRO+	BR/A	SB	CS	SBR	FA	FR	G/POS	TPR
1952	NY-A	16	40	6	6	0	0	0	1	3	10	.150	.209	.150	1	-5	0	0	0	.889	-1	3-14/S-1	-0.7
1953	NY-A	51	81	14	26	5	0	4	8	9	12	.321	.389	.531	152	6	2	1	0	.988	8	3-40/S-2,2-1	1.4
1954	NY-A	122	411	60	124	14	6	8	65	43	38	.302	.377	.423	123	13	5	5	-2	.967	17	*3-120	2.7
1955	*NY-A	135	510	73	131	19	**11**	7	47	44	51	.257	.317	.378	88	-10	3	3	-1	.954	14	*3-135	0.2
1956	*NY-A	132	422	54	100	18	2	7	50	45	53	.237	.313	.339	75	-16	9	6	-1	.947	-3	*3-131	-1.8
1957	*NY-A	85	247	30	63	6	5	6	33	15	42	.255	.311	.393	92	-3	2	2	-1	.977	3	3-81	0.1
1958	*NY-A	102	315	39	90	19	4	12	45	34	43	.286	.366	.486	137	16	1	2	-1	.961	10	3-99	2.6
1959	NY-A	41	101	11	26	1	0	3	9	7	17	.257	.306	.356	84	-2	1	1	-0	.916	2	3-34	-0.1
1960	NY-A	4	3	1	1	0	0	0	1	0	1	.333	.333	.333	86	-0	0	0	0	1.000	-1	/3-2,O-1	-0.1
	KC-A	102	343	30	80	14	4	12	53	26	52	.233	.289	.402	84	-9	0	0	0	.975	-0	3-91	-0.9
	Yr	106	346	31	81	14	4	12	54	26	53	.234	.290	.402	85	-9	0	0	0	.975	-1	3-93/O-1	-1.0
1961	KC-A	39	123	20	30	6	2	3	11	15	23	.244	.336	.398	94	-1	0	0	0	.944	-1	3-39	-0.2
	Chi-A	56	143	21	38	12	3	0	14	11	24	.266	.327	.392	93	-2	0	1	-1	.961	-5	3-54	-0.7
	Yr	95	266	41	68	18	5	3	25	26	47	.256	.331	.395	93	-3	0	1	-1	.953	-6	3-93	-0.9
1962	LA-N	53	111	12	26	5	1	2	13	16	23	.234	.336	.351	90	-1	0	0	0	.932	1	3-42	0.0
Total	11	938	2850	371	741	119	38	64	350	268	389	.260	.329	.396	97	-15	23	21	-6	.958	45	3-882/S-3,O-1,2-1	2.5

■ SCOOPS CAREY

Carey, George C. b: 12/4/1870, Pittsburgh, Pa. d: 12/17/16, E.Liverpool, Ohio BR/TR, 175 lbs. Deb: 4/26/1895

YEAR	TM/L	G	AB	R	H	2B	3B	HR	RBI	BB	SO	AVG	OBP	SLG	PRO+	BR/A	SB	CS	SBR	FA	FR	G/POS	TPR
1895	*Bal-N	123	490	59	128	21	6	1	75	27	32	.261	.305	.335	63	-28	2			**.987**	-6	*1-123/O-1,S-1,3-1	-2.6
1898	Lou-N	8	32	1	6	1	1	0	1	1		.188	.212	.281	42	-3	0			.961	0	/1-8	-0.2
1902	Was-A	120	452	46	142	35	11	0	60	20		.314	.350	.440	117	9	3			**.989**	4	*1-120	1.0
1903	Was-A	48	183	8	37	3	2	0	23	4		.202	.223	.240	38	-14	0			.977	-3	1-47	-1.8
Total	4	299	1157	114	313	60	20	1	159	52	32	.271	.308	.360	80	-35	5			.986	-6	1-298/3-1,S-1,O-1	-3.6

■ MAX CAREY

Carey, Max George "Scoops" (b: Maximilian Carnarius)
b: 1/11/1890, Terre Haute, Ind. d: 5/30/76, Miami, Fla. BB/TR, 5'11.5", 170 lbs. Deb: 10/3/10 MCH

YEAR	TM/L	G	AB	R	H	2B	3B	HR	RBI	BB	SO	AVG	OBP	SLG	PRO+	BR/A	SB	CS	SBR	FA	FR	G/POS	TPR
1910	Pit-N	2	6	2	3	0	1	0	2	2	1	.500	.625	.833	307	2	0			1.000	2	/O-2	0.3
1911	Pit-N	129	427	77	110	15	10	5	43	44	75	.258	.337	.375	95	-3	27			.975	7	*O-122	-0.3
1912	Pit-N	150	587	114	177	23	8	5	66	61	79	.302	.372	.394	111	10	45			.968	9	*O-150	1.0
1913	Pit-N	154	620	**99**	172	23	10	5	49	55	67	.277	.339	.371	107	6	**61**			.961	15	*O-154	1.3
1914	Pit-N	156	593	76	144	25	**17**	1	31	59	56	.243	.313	.347	101	-0	38			.966	11	*O-154	0.3

YEAR	TM/L	G	AB	R	H	2B	3B	HR	RBI	BB	SO	AVG	OBP	SLG	PRO+	BR/A	SB	CS	SBR	FA	FR	G/POS	TPR
1915	Pit-N	140	564	76	143	26	5	3	27	57	58	.254	.326	.333	101	2	**36**	17	1	.982	13	*O-139	0.9
1916	Pit-N	154	599	90	158	23	11	7	42	59	58	.264	.337	.374	117	13	**63**	19	**8**	.983	**30**	*O-154	4.7
1917	Pit-N	155	588	82	174	21	12	1	51	58	38	.296	.369	.378	125	19	**46**			.979	25	*O-153	3.9
1918	Pit-N	126	468	70	128	14	6	3	48	**62**	25	.274	.363	.348	113	10	**58**			.958	19	*O-126	2.3
1919	Pit-N	66	244	41	75	10	2	0	9	25	24	.307	.376	.365	119	7	18			.947	2	O-63	0.4
1920	Pit-N	130	485	74	140	18	4	1	35	59	31	.289	.369	.348	104	5	**52**	10	**10**	.967	1	*O-129	0.6
1921	Pit-N	140	521	85	161	34	4	7	56	70	30	.309	.395	.430	115	14	37	12	4	.957	16	*O-139	2.3
1922	Pit-N	155	629	140	207	28	12	10	70	**80**	26	.329	.408	.459	122	23	**51**	2	**14**	.969	19	*O-155	4.1
1923	Pit-N	153	610	120	188	32	**19**	6	63	73	28	.308	.388	.452	119	18	**51**	8	**11**	.962	20	*O-153	3.6
1924	Pit-N	149	599	113	178	30	9	8	55	58	17	.297	.366	.417	108	7	**49**	13	**7**	.965	9	*O-149	1.3
1925	*Pit-N	133	542	109	186	39	13	5	44	66	19	.343	.418	.491	123	20	**46**	11	**7**	.950	9	*O-130	2.6
1926	Pit-N	86	324	46	72	14	5	0	28	30	14	.222	.288	.296	55	-21	10			.943	4	O-82	-2.2
	Bro-N	27	100	18	26	3	1	0	7	8	5	.260	.315	.310	70	-4	0			.933	-1	O-27	-0.7
	Yr	113	424	64	98	17	6	0	35	38	19	.231	.294	.300	58	-25	10			.941	3	*O-109	-2.9
1927	Bro-N	144	538	70	143	30	10	1	54	64	18	.266	.345	.364	90	-7	32			.970	6	*O-141	-1.0
1928	Bro-N	108	296	41	73	11	0	2	19	47	24	.247	.354	.304	74	-9	18			.986	-12	O-95	-2.7
1929	Bro-N	19	23	2	7	0	0	0	1	3	2	.304	.407	.304	81	-0	0			1.000	-1	/O-4	-0.1
Total	20	2476	9363	1545	2665	419	159	70	800	1040	695	.285	.361	.386	107	109	738	92		.966	198	*O-2421	22.6

■ PAUL CAREY Carey, Paul Stephan b: 1/8/68, Boston, Mass. BL/TR, 6'4", 215 lbs. Deb: 5/25/93

YEAR	TM/L	G	AB	R	H	2B	3B	HR	RBI	BB	SO	AVG	OBP	SLG	PRO+	BR/A	SB	CS	SBR	FA	FR	G/POS	TPR
1993	Bal-A	18	47	1	10	1	0	0	3	5	14	.213	.288	.234	41	-4	0	0	0	.970	-2	/1-9,D-5	-0.6

■ ROGER CAREY Carey, Roger J. Deb: 7/9/1887

YEAR	TM/L	G	AB	R	H	2B	3B	HR	RBI	BB	SO	AVG	OBP	SLG	PRO+	BR/A	SB	CS	SBR	FA	FR	G/POS	TPR
1887	NY-N	1	4	0	0	0	0	0	2	0	1	.000	.000	.000	-99	-1	0			.800	1	/2-1	0.0

■ TOM CAREY Carey, Thomas Francis Aloysius "Scoops" b: 10/11/06, Hoboken, N.J. d: 2/21/70, Rochester, N.Y. BR/TR, 5'8.5", 170 lbs. Deb: 7/19/35 C

YEAR	TM/L	G	AB	R	H	2B	3B	HR	RBI	BB	SO	AVG	OBP	SLG	PRO+	BR/A	SB	CS	SBR	FA	FR	G/POS	TPR
1935	StL-A	76	296	29	86	18	4	0	42	13	11	.291	.320	.378	77	-11	0	2	-1	.961	-1	2-76	-0.6
1936	StL-A	134	488	58	133	27	6	1	57	27	25	.273	.315	.359	64	-28	2	1	0	.967	-1	*2-128/S-1	-1.8
1937	StL-A	130	487	54	134	24	1	1	40	21	26	.275	.306	.335	61	-29	1	2	-1	.983	2	2-87,S-44/3-1	-1.8
1939	Bos-A	54	161	17	39	6	2	0	20	3	9	.242	.265	.304	44	-14	0	0	0	1.000	6	2-35,S-10	-1.6
1940	Bos-A	43	62	4	20	4	0	0	7	2	1	.323	.344	.387	86	-1	0	0	0	.953	5	S-20/2-4,3-4	0.4
1941	Bos-A	25	21	7	4	0	0	0	0	0	0	.190	.190	.190	1	-3	0	0	0	1.000	4	/2-9,S-8,3-1	0.1
1942	Bos-A	1	1	0	1	0	0	0	1	0	0	1.000	1.000	1.000	448	0	0	0	0	1.000	-0	/2-1	0.0
1946	Bos-A	3	5	0	1	0	0	0	0	0	1	.200	.200	.200	11	-1	0	0	0	.900	1	/2-3	0.1
Total	8	466	1521	169	418	79	13	2	167	66	73	.275	.308	.348	63	-87	3	5	-2	.973	17	2-343/S-83,3-6	-4.2

■ TOM CAREY Carey, Thomas John (b: J. J. Norton) b: 1849, Brooklyn, N.Y. d: 2/13/1899, Los Angeles, Cal. BR/TR, 5'8", 145 lbs. Deb: 5/4/1871 M

YEAR	TM/L	G	AB	R	H	2B	3B	HR	RBI	BB	SO	AVG	OBP	SLG	PRO+	BR/A	SB	CS	SBR	FA	FR	G/POS	TPR
1871	Kek-n	19	87	16	20	2	0	0	10	2	1	.230	.247	.253	43	-6	5	0	2	.857	0	2-19	-0.4
1872	Bal-n	42	198	42	57	7	0	2	27	0	2	.288	.288	.354	92	-3	4	1	1	.815	-12	2-29/S-9,3-3,O-3,1	-1.1
1873	Bal-n	56	290	76	97	19	3	1	55	1	2	.334	.337	.431	127	9	1	3	-2	.845	-2	*2-54/3-4,S-3,M	0.1
1874	Mut-n	64	287	56	82	10	3	1	38	2	4	.286	.291	.352	102	-0	3	0	1	.776	-17	*S-51,2-13,M	-1.5
1875	Har-n	86	382	63	101	6	2	0	38	1	3	.264	.266	.291	89	-5	13	3	2	.844	-13	*S-86/2-1	-1.7
1876	Har-N	68	289	51	78	7	0	0	26	3	4	.270	.277	.294	84	-6				.882	-1	*S-68	-0.7
1877	Har-N	60	274	38	70	3	2	1	20	0	9	.255	.255	.292	81	-5				.826	-6	*S-60	-0.9
1878	Pro-N	61	253	33	60	10	3	0	24	0	14	.237	.237	.300	76	-7				.874	1	*S-61	-0.2
1879	Cle-N	80	335	30	80	14	1	0	32	5	20	.239	.250	.287	77	-8				.864	-3	*S-80	-0.6
Total	5 n	267	1244	253	357	44	8	4	168	6	12	.287	.290	.345	98	-6	26	7	4	.814	-44	S-149,2-116/3-7,O1	-4.6
Total	4	269	1151	152	288	34	6	1	102	8	47	.250	.255	.293	79	-26				.862	-9	S-269	-2.4

■ BOBBY CARGO Cargo, Robert J. b: 10/1868, Pittsburgh, Pa. d: 4/27/04, Atlanta, Ga. BR/TR, Deb: 10/6/1892

YEAR	TM/L	G	AB	R	H	2B	3B	HR	RBI	BB	SO	AVG	OBP	SLG	PRO+	BR/A	SB	CS	SBR	FA	FR	G/POS	TPR
1892	Pit-N	2	4	0	1	0	0	0	0	0	0	.250	.250	.250	51	-0	0			.636	1	/S-2	0.0

■ FRED CARISCH Carisch, Frederick Behlmer b: 11/14/1881, Fountain City, Wis. d: 4/19/77, San Gabriel, Cal. BR/TR, 5'10.5", 174 lbs. Deb: 8/31/03 C

YEAR	TM/L	G	AB	R	H	2B	3B	HR	RBI	BB	SO	AVG	OBP	SLG	PRO+	BR/A	SB	CS	SBR	FA	FR	G/POS	TPR
1903	Pit-N	5	18	4	6	4	0	1	5	0		.333	.333	.722	192	2	0			.969	1	/C-4	0.3
1904	Pit-N	37	125	9	31	3	1	0	8	9		.248	.299	.288	79	-3	3			.984	2	C-22,1-14	0.1
1905	Pit-N	32	107	7	22	0	3	0	8	2		.206	.227	.262	44	-8	1			.973	2	C-30	-0.4
1906	Pit-N	4	12	0	1	0	0	0	0	1		.083	.154	.083	-25	-2	1			.909	-0	/C-4	-0.2
1912	Cle-A	24	69	4	19	3	1	0	5	1		.275	.286	.348	78	-2	3			.952	6	C-23	0.6
1913	Cle-A	82	222	11	48	4	2	0	26	21	19	.216	.287	.252	56	-12	6			.971	13	C-79	0.8
1914	Cle-A	40	102	8	22	3	2	0	5	12	18	.216	.298	.284	72	-3	2	2	-1	.962	0	C-38	-0.1
1923	Det-A	2	0	0	0	0	0	0	0	0	0	—	—	—	—	0	0	0	0	1.000	-0	/C-2	0.0
Total	8	226	655	43	149	17	9	1	57	46	37	.227	.280	.285	66	-28	16	2		.968	24	C-202/1-14	1.2

■ FRED CARL Carl, Frederick E. b: 9/8/1858, Baltimore, Md. d: 5/4/19, Washington, D.C. BL/TL, 5'6", 158 lbs. Deb: 7/25/1889

YEAR	TM/L	G	AB	R	H	2B	3B	HR	RBI	BB	SO	AVG	OBP	SLG	PRO+	BR/A	SB	CS	SBR	FA	FR	G/POS	TPR
1889	Lou-a	25	99	13	20	2	2	0	13	16	22	.202	.313	.263	66	-4	0			.735	0	O-18/2-6,3-1	-0.3

■ LEW CARL Carl, Lewis b: Baltimore, Md. Deb: 9/9/1874

YEAR	TM/L	G	AB	R	H	2B	3B	HR	RBI	BB	SO	AVG	OBP	SLG	PRO+	BR/A	SB	CS	SBR	FA	FR	G/POS	TPR
1874	Bal-n	1	3	0	0	0	0	0	0	0	0	.000	.000	.000	-99	-1	0	0	0	.250	-1	/C-1	-0.1

■ JIM CARLETON Carleton, James b: 1849, New York 5'8", 155 lbs. Deb: 5/4/1871

YEAR	TM/L	G	AB	R	H	2B	3B	HR	RBI	BB	SO	AVG	OBP	SLG	PRO+	BR/A	SB	CS	SBR	FA	FR	G/POS	TPR
1871	Cle-n	29	127	31	32	8	1	0	18	8	3	.252	.296	.331	85	-1	2	1	0	.898	-3	*1-29	-0.2
1872	Cle-n	7	38	8	12	1	0	0	4	1	0	.316	.333	.342	114	1	1	0	0	.956	2	/1-7	0.2
Total	2 n	36	165	39	44	9	1	0	22	9	3	.267	.305	.333	91	-1	3	1	0	.908	-1	/1-36	0.0

■ JIM CARLIN Carlin, James Arthur b: 2/23/18, Wylam, Ala. BR/TR, 5'11", 165 lbs. Deb: 7/26/41

YEAR	TM/L	G	AB	R	H	2B	3B	HR	RBI	BB	SO	AVG	OBP	SLG	PRO+	BR/A	SB	CS	SBR	FA	FR	G/POS	TPR
1941	Phi-N	16	21	2	3	1	0	1	2	3	4	.143	.250	.333	66	-1	0			1.000	-5	/O-9,3-2	-0.7

■ WALTER CARLISLE Carlisle, Walter G. "Rosy" b: 7/6/1883, Yorkshire, England d: 5/27/45, Los Angeles, Cal. BB/TR, 5'9", 154 lbs. Deb: 5/8/08

YEAR	TM/L	G	AB	R	H	2B	3B	HR	RBI	BB	SO	AVG	OBP	SLG	PRO+	BR/A	SB	CS	SBR	FA	FR	G/POS	TPR
1908	Bos-A	3	10	0	1	0	0	0	0	1		.100	.182	.100	-8	-1	1			1.000	1	/O-3	-0.1

■ SWEDE CARLSTROM Carlstrom, Albin Oscar b: 10/26/1886, Elizabeth, N.J. d: 4/28/35, Elizabeth, N.J. BR/TR, 6', 167 lbs. Deb: 9/13/11

YEAR	TM/L	G	AB	R	H	2B	3B	HR	RBI	BB	SO	AVG	OBP	SLG	PRO+	BR/A	SB	CS	SBR	FA	FR	G/POS	TPR
1911	Bos-A	2	6	0	1	0	0	0	0	0		.167	.167	.167	-7	-1	0			1.000	0	/S-2	0.0

■ CLEO CARLYLE Carlyle, Hiram Cleo b: 9/7/02, Fairburn, Ga. d: 11/12/67, Los Angeles, Cal. BL/TR, 6', 170 lbs. Deb: 5/16/27 F

YEAR	TM/L	G	AB	R	H	2B	3B	HR	RBI	BB	SO	AVG	OBP	SLG	PRO+	BR/A	SB	CS	SBR	FA	FR	G/POS	TPR
1927	Bos-A	95	278	31	65	12	8	1	28	36	40	.234	.324	.345	75	-10	4	4	-1	.965	-7	O-83	-2.2

■ ROY CARLYLE Carlyle, Roy Edward "Dizzy" b: 12/10/1900, Buford, Ga. d: 11/22/56, Norcross, Ga. BL/TR, 6'2.5", 195 lbs. Deb: 4/16/25 F

YEAR	TM/L	G	AB	R	H	2B	3B	HR	RBI	BB	SO	AVG	OBP	SLG	PRO+	BR/A	SB	CS	SBR	FA	FR	G/POS	TPR
1925	Was-A	1	1	0	0	0	0	0	0	0	1	.000	.000	.000	-99	-0	0	0	0	.000	0	H	0.0
	Bos-A	93	276	36	90	20	3	7	49	16	28	.326	.365	.496	117	6	1	1	-0	.909	-6	O-67	-0.4
	Yr	94	277	36	90	20	3	7	49	16	29	.325	.364	.495	116	5	1	1	-0	.909	-6	O-67	-0.4
1926	Bos-A	45	165	22	47	6	2	2	16	4	18	.285	.310	.382	82	-5	0	0	0	.904	-4	O-38	-1.1
	NY-A	35	52	3	20	5	1	0	11	4	9	.385	.439	.519	151	4	0	0	0	.941	-3	O-15	0.0
	Yr	80	217	25	67	11	3	2	27	8	27	.309	.342	.415	99	-1	0	0	0	.911	-7	O-53	-1.1
Total	2	174	494	61	157	31	6	9	76	24	56	.318	.354	.460	109	4	1	1	-0	.910	-12	O-120	-1.5

■ GEORGE CARMAN Carman, George Wartman b: 3/29/1866, Philadelphia, Pa. d: 6/16/29, Lancaster, Pa. Deb: 9/4/1890

YEAR	TM/L	G	AB	R	H	2B	3B	HR	RBI	BB	SO	AVG	OBP	SLG	PRO+	BR/A	SB	CS	SBR	FA	FR	G/POS	TPR
1890	Phi-a	28	97	9	17	2	0	0	7	8		.175	.245	.196	31	-8	5			.767	-9	S-15,O-10/2-2,3-1	-1.5

■ DUKE CARMEL Carmel, Leon James b: 4/23/37, New York, N.Y. BL/TL, 6'3", 202 lbs. Deb: 9/10/59

YEAR	TM/L	G	AB	R	H	2B	3B	HR	RBI	BB	SO	AVG	OBP	SLG	PRO+	BR/A	SB	CS	SBR	FA	FR	G/POS	TPR
1959	StL-N	10	23	2	3	1	0	0	3	1	6	.130	.167	.174	-9	-4	0	1	-1	1.000	-3	O-10	-0.7
1960	StL-N	4	3	0	0	0	0	0	0	1	1	.000	.250	.000	-23	-0	1	1	-0	1.000	0	/1-2,O-1	-0.1
1963	StL-N	57	44	9	10	1	0	1	2	9	11	.227	.358	.318	88	-0	0	0	0	.974	-7	O-38/1-1	-0.8
	NY-N	47	149	11	35	5	3	3	18	16	37	.235	.309	.369	93	-1	2	2	-1	.980	-1	O-21,1-18	-0.5

YEAR	TM/L	G	AB	R	H	2B	3B	HR	RBI	BB	SO	AVG	OBP	SLG	PRO+	BR/A	SB	CS	SBR	FA	FR	G/POS	TPR
	Yr	104	193	20	45	6	3	4	20	25	48	.233	.321	.358	90	-2	2	2	-1	.977	-7	O-59,1-19	-1.3
1965	NY-A	6	8	0	0	0	0	0	0	0	5	.000	.000	.000	-99	-2	0	0	0	1.000	0	/1-2	-0.2
Total	4	124	227	22	48	7	3	4	23	27	60	.211	.295	.322	73	-8	3	4	-2	.981	-10	/O-70,1-23	-2.3

■ EDDIE CARNETT
Carnett, Edwin Elliott "Lefty" b: 10/21/16, Springfield, Mo. BL/TL, 6', 185 lbs. Deb: 4/19/41

YEAR	TM/L	G	AB	R	H	2B	3B	HR	RBI	BB	SO	AVG	OBP	SLG	PRO+	BR/A	SB	CS	SBR	FA	FR	G/POS	TPR
1941	Bos-N	2	0	0	0	0	0	0	0	0	0	—	—	—	—	0	0			.000	0	/P-2	0.0
1944	Chi-A	126	457	51	126	18	8	1	60	26	35	.276	.322	.357	95	-4	5	2	0	.949	-8	O-88,1-25/P-2	-1.8
1945	Cle-A	30	73	5	16	7	0	0	7	2	9	.219	.250	.315	66	-4	0	1	-1	.971	-0	O-16/P-2	-0.6
Total	3	158	530	56	142	25	8	1	67	28	44	.268	.312	.351	91	-7	5	3		.952	-8	O-104/1-25,P-6	-2.4

■ JOHN CARNEY
Carney, John Joseph "Handsome Jack" b: 11/10/1866, Salem, Mass. d: 10/19/25, Litchfield, N.H. BR/TR, 5'10.5", 175 lbs. Deb: 4/24/1889

YEAR	TM/L	G	AB	R	H	2B	3B	HR	RBI	BB	SO	AVG	OBP	SLG	PRO+	BR/A	SB	CS	SBR	FA	FR	G/POS	TPR
1889	Was-N	69	273	25	63	7	0	1	29	14	14	.231	.271	.267	54	-17	12			.957	-7	1-53,O-16	-2.4
1890	Buf-P	28	107	11	29	3	0	0	13	7	14	.271	.333	.299	76	-3	2			.972	-2	1-24/O-4	-0.5
	Cle-P	25	89	15	31	5	3	0	21	14	5	.348	.442	.472	157	8	6			.857	-3	O-19/1-6	0.3
	Yr	53	196	26	60	8	3	0	34	21	19	.306	.385	.378	113	5	8			.969	-6	1-30,O-23	-0.2
1891	Cin-a	99	367	47	102	10	8	3	43	35	18	.278	.346	.373	97	-4	15			.974	1	1-99	-0.7
	Mil-a	31	110	22	33	5	2	3	23	13	8	.300	.389	.464	120	1	5			.986	4	1-31	0.3
	Yr	130	477	69	135	15	10	6	66	48	26	.283	.356	.394	103	-2	20			.977	5	*1-130	-0.4
Total	3	252	946	120	258	30	13	7	129	83	59	.273	.338	.354	92	-14	40			.971	-8	1-213/O-39	-3.0

■ PAT CARNEY
Carney, Patrick Joseph "Doc" b: 8/7/1876, Holyoke, Mass. d: 1/9/53, Worcester, Mass. BL/TL, 6', 200 lbs. Deb: 9/20/01

YEAR	TM/L	G	AB	R	H	2B	3B	HR	RBI	BB	SO	AVG	OBP	SLG	PRO+	BR/A	SB	CS	SBR	FA	FR	G/POS	TPR
1901	Bos-N	13	55	6	16	2	1	0	6	3		.291	.339	.364	95	-0				.933	-3	O-13	-0.4
1902	Bos-N	137	522	75	141	17	4	2	65	42		.270	.339	.330	105	4	27			.930	-9	*O-137/P-2	-1.4
1903	Bos-N	110	392	37	94	12	4	1	49	28		.240	.297	.298	73	-14	10			.953	-6	O-92,P-10/1-1	-2.3
1904	Bos-N	78	279	24	57	5	2	0	11	12		.204	.240	.237	49	-17	6			.953	-2	O-71/P-4,1-1	-2.4
Total	4	338	1248	142	308	36	11	3	131	85		.247	.304	.300	82	-27	43			.942	-20	O-313/P-16,1-2	-6.5

■ BILL CARNEY
Carney, William John b: 3/25/1874, St.Paul, Minn. d: 7/31/38, Hopkins, Minn. BB/TR, 5'10", Deb: 8/22/04

YEAR	TM/L	G	AB	R	H	2B	3B	HR	RBI	BB	SO	AVG	OBP	SLG	PRO+	BR/A	SB	CS	SBR	FA	FR	G/POS	TPR
1904	Chi-N	2	7	0	0	0	0	0	0	1		.000	.125	.000	-60	-1	0			1.000	0	/O-2	-0.2

■ HICK CARPENTER
Carpenter, Warren William b: 8/16/1855, Grafton, Mass. d: 4/18/37, San Diego, Cal. BR/TL, 5'11", 186 lbs. Deb: 5/1/1879

YEAR	TM/L	G	AB	R	H	2B	3B	HR	RBI	BB	SO	AVG	OBP	SLG	PRO+	BR/A	SB	CS	SBR	FA	FR	G/POS	TPR
1879	Syr-N	65	261	30	53	6	0	0	20	2	15	.203	.209	.226	49	-13				.948	-4	1-34,3-18,O-11,/2-3	-1.7
1880	Cin-N	77	300	32	72	6	4	0	23	2	15	.240	.245	.287	80	-6				.853	-1	*3-67/1-9,S-1	-0.5
1881	Wor-N	83	347	40	75	12	2	2	31	3	19	.216	.223	.280	54	-19				.848	3	*3-83	-1.4
1882	Cin-a	80	351	78	**120**	15	5	1	67	10		.342	.360	.422	154	18				**.835**	-1	*3-80	1.7
1883	Cin-a	95	435	99	130	18	4	3	40	19		.299	.328	.379	120	8				.870	-6	*3-95	0.2
1884	Cin-a	108	474	80	121	16	2	4	60	6		.255	.271	.323	89	-7				.881	-9	*3-108/O-1	-1.4
1885	Cin-a	112	473	89	131	12	8	2	61	9		.277	.295	.349	101	-1				.860	-6	*3-112	-0.5
1886	Cin-a	111	458	67	101	8	5	2	61	18		.221	.262	.273	66	-19	8			.841	-6	*3-111	-2.0
1887	Cin-a	127	498	70	124	12	6	1	50	19		.249	.282	.303	62	-27	44			.846	-13	*3-127	-3.0
1888	Cin-a	136	551	68	147	14	5	3	67	5		.267	.280	.327	89	-9	59			.866	-12	*3-136	-1.7
1889	Cin-a	123	486	67	127	23	6	0	63	18	41	.261	.293	.333	76	-17	47			.835	-25	*3-121/1-2	-3.3
1892	StL-N	1	3	0	1	0	0	0	0	1	1	.333	.500	.333	161	0	0			.714	0	/3-1	0.0
Total	12	1118	4637	720	1202	142	47	18	543	112	91	.259	.281	.322	86	-92	158			.853	-80	*3-1059/1-45,O2S	-13.6

■ CHARLIE CARR
Carr, Charles Carbitt b: 12/27/1876, Coatesville, Pa. d: 11/25/32, Memphis, Tenn. BR/TR, 6'2", 195 lbs. Deb: 9/15/1898

YEAR	TM/L	G	AB	R	H	2B	3B	HR	RBI	BB	SO	AVG	OBP	SLG	PRO+	BR/A	SB	CS	SBR	FA	FR	G/POS	TPR
1898	Was-N	20	73	6	14	2	0	0	4	2		.192	.213	.219	24	-7	2			.950	-2	1-20	-0.9
1901	Phi-A	2	8	0	1	0	0	0	0	0		.125	.125	.125	-29	-1	0			.926	0	/1-2	-0.1
1903	Det-A	135	548	59	154	23	11	2	79	10		.281	.296	.374	103	0	10			.982	12	*1-135	1.1
1904	Det-A	92	360	29	77	13	3	0	40	14		.214	.245	.267	64	-15	6			.983	16	1-92	-0.1
	Cle-A	32	120	9	27	5	1	0	7	4		.225	.250	.283	69	-4	0			.973	-0	1-32	-0.6
	Yr	124	480	38	104	18	4	0	47	18		.217	.246	.271	65	-20	6			.980	16	*1-124	-0.7
1905	Cle-A	89	306	29	72	12	4	1	31	13		.235	.266	.310	82	-7	12			.991	-2	1-87	-1.3
1906	Cin-N	22	94	9	18	2	3	0	10	2		.191	.216	.277	51	-6	0			.983	1	1-22	-0.6
1914	Ind-F	115	441	44	129	11	10	3	69	26	47	.293	.333	.383	86	-15	19			**.991**	1	*1-115	-1.8
Total	7	507	1950	185	492	68	32	6	240	71	47	.252	.280	.329	81	-56	49			.984	26	1-505	-4.3

■ CHUCK CARR
Carr, Charles Lee Glenn b: 8/10/67, San Bernardino, Cal. BB/TR, 5'10", 165 lbs. Deb: 4/28/90

YEAR	TM/L	G	AB	R	H	2B	3B	HR	RBI	BB	SO	AVG	OBP	SLG	PRO+	BR/A	SB	CS	SBR	FA	FR	G/POS	TPR
1990	NY-N	4	2	0	0	0	0	0	0	0	2	.000	.000	.000	-99	-1	1	0	0	.000	-0	/O-1	-0.1
1991	NY-N	12	11	1	2	0	0	0	1	0	2	.182	.182	.182	3	-1	1	0	0	1.000	-2	/O-9	-0.3
1992	StL-N	22	64	8	14	3	0	0	3	9	6	.219	.315	.266	68	-2	10	2	2	1.000	-1	O-19	-0.2
1993	Fla-N	142	551	75	147	19	2	4	41	49	74	.267	.329	.330	73	-20	**58**	22	4	.985	16	*O-139	-0.3
1994	Fla-N	106	433	61	114	19	2	2	30	22	71	.263	.307	.330	64	-22	32	8	5	.980	10	*O-104	-1.0
1995	Fla-N	105	308	54	70	20	0	2	20	46	49	.227	.331	.312	71	-12	25	11	1	.987	5	*O-103	-0.9
1996	Mil-A	27	106	18	29	6	1	1	11	6	21	.274	.313	.377	71	-5	5	4	-1	1.000	5	O-27	-0.1
1997	Mil-A	26	46	3	6	3	0	0	0	2	11	.130	.184	.196	-1	-7	1	0	0	1.000	-5	O-23/D-1	-1.2
	*Hou-N	63	192	34	53	11	2	4	17	15	37	.276	.335	.417	99	-1	11	5	0	.966	-1	O-59	-0.2
Total	8	507	1713	254	435	81	7	13	123	149	273	.254	.318	.332	70	-71	144	52	12	.984	26	O-484/D-1	-4.3

■ LEW CARR
Carr, Lewis Smith b: 8/15/1872, Union Springs, N.Y d: 6/15/54, Moravia, N.Y. BR/TR, 6'2", 200 lbs. Deb: 7/4/01

YEAR	TM/L	G	AB	R	H	2B	3B	HR	RBI	BB	SO	AVG	OBP	SLG	PRO+	BR/A	SB	CS	SBR	FA	FR	G/POS	TPR
1901	Pit-N	9	28	2	7	1	1	0	4	2		.250	.344	.357	100	0	0			.886	-5	/S-9,3-1	-0.4

■ CHICO CARRASQUEL
Carrasquel, Alfonso (Colon) b: 1/23/28, Caracas, Venez. BR/TR, 6', 170 lbs. Deb: 4/18/50

YEAR	TM/L	G	AB	R	H	2B	3B	HR	RBI	BB	SO	AVG	OBP	SLG	PRO+	BR/A	SB	CS	SBR	FA	FR	G/POS	TPR
1950	Chi-A	141	524	72	148	21	5	4	46	66	46	.282	.368	.365	91	-6	0	2	-1	.961	11	*S-141	1.4
1951	Chi-A★	147	538	41	142	22	4	2	58	46	39	.264	.325	.331	79	-16	14	4	2	**.975**	13	*S-147	0.9
1952	Chi-A	100	359	36	89	7	4	1	42	33	27	.248	.315	.298	71	-14	2	2	-1	.964	-16	S-99	-2.4
1953	Chi-A★	149	552	72	154	30	4	2	47	38	47	.279	.330	.359	83	-13	5	3	-0	**.976**	3	*S-149	0.1
1954	Chi-A★	155	620	106	158	28	3	12	62	85	67	.255	.349	.368	93	-4	7	6	-2	**.975**	11	*S-155	1.9
1955	Chi-A★	145	523	83	134	11	2	11	52	61	59	.256	.338	.348	83	-12	1	1	-0	.973	0	*S-144	0.0
1956	Cle-A	141	474	60	115	15	1	7	48	52	61	.243	.325	.323	70	-20	0	4	-2	.967	-25	*S-141/3-1	-3.6
1957	Cle-A	125	392	37	108	14	1	8	57	41	53	.276	.356	.378	102	2	0	2	-1	.960	-5	*S-122	0.7
1958	Cle-A	49	156	14	40	6	0	2	21	14	12	.256	.318	.333	81	-4	0	0	0	.931	-19	S-32,3-14	-2.1
	KC-A	59	160	19	34	5	1	2	13	21	15	.213	.304	.294	64	-8	0	1	-1	.976	-6	3-32,S-22	-1.3
	Yr	108	316	33	74	11	1	4	34	35	27	.234	.311	.313	72	-12	0	1	-1	.947	-25	S-54,3-46	-3.4
1959	Bal-A	114	346	28	77	13	0	4	28	34	41	.223	.294	.295	64	-17	2	3	-1	.970	-14	S-89,2-22/3-2,1-1	-2.4
Total	10	1325	4644	568	1199	172	25	55	474	491	467	.258	.334	.342	82	-111	31	28	-8	.969	-47	*S-1241/3-49,2-22,1	-6.8

■ CAM CARREON
Carreon, Camilo b: 8/6/37, Colton, Cal. d: 9/2/87, Tucson, Ariz. BR/TR, 6', 198 lbs. Deb: 9/27/59 F

YEAR	TM/L	G	AB	R	H	2B	3B	HR	RBI	BB	SO	AVG	OBP	SLG	PRO+	BR/A	SB	CS	SBR	FA	FR	G/POS	TPR
1959	Chi-A	1	1	0	0	0	0	0	0	0	0	.000	.000	.000	-99	-0	0	0	0	1.000	0	/C-1	0.0
1960	Chi-A	8	17	2	4	0	0	0	2	1	3	.235	.278	.235	41	-1	0	0	0	1.000	0	/C-7	-0.1
1961	Chi-A	78	229	32	62	5	1	4	27	21	24	.271	.332	.354	85	-5	0	1	-1	.995	9	C-71	0.7
1962	Chi-A	106	313	31	80	19	1	4	37	33	37	.256	.329	.361	86	-6	1	1	-0	.995	8	C-93	0.5
1963	Chi-A	101	270	28	74	10	1	2	35	23	32	.274	.333	.341	91	-3	1	1	-0	.987	0	C-92	0.0
1964	Chi-A	37	95	12	26	5	0	0	4	7	13	.274	.330	.326	86	-2	0	0	0	.987	-4	C-34	-0.5
1965	Cle-A	19	52	6	12	2	1	1	7	9	6	.231	.344	.365	101	0	1	1	-0	1.000	0	C-19	0.1
1966	Bal-A	4	9	2	2	2	0	0	2	3	2	.222	.417	.444	150	1	0	0	0	1.000	0	/C-3	0.1
Total	8	354	986	113	260	43	4	11	114	97	117	.264	.331	.349	87	-16	3	4	-2	.993	14	C-320	0.8

■ MARK CARREON
Carreon, Mark Steven b: 7/19/63, Chicago, Ill. BR/TL, 6', 195 lbs. Deb: 9/8/87 F

YEAR	TM/L	G	AB	R	H	2B	3B	HR	RBI	BB	SO	AVG	OBP	SLG	PRO+	BR/A	SB	CS	SBR	FA	FR	G/POS	TPR
1987	NY-N	9	12	0	3	0	0	0	1	1	1	.250	.308	.250	53	-1	0	1	-1	.800	-1	/O-5	-0.3
1988	NY-N	7	9	5	5	2	0	1	1	2	1	.556	.636	1.111	413	4	0	0	0	1.000	-1	/O-4	0.3
1989	NY-N	68	133	20	41	6	0	6	16	12	17	.308	.370	.489	151	8	2	3	-1	.983	-3	O-39	0.4

YEAR	TM/L	G	AB	R	H	2B	3B	HR	RBI	BB	SO	AVG	OBP	SLG	PRO+	BR/A	SB	CS	SBR	FA	FR	G/POS	TPR
1990	NY-N	82	188	30	47	12	0	10	26	15	29	.250	.312	.473	113	3	1	0	0	1.000	-8	O-60	-0.7
1991	NY-N	106	254	18	66	6	0	4	21	12	26	.260	.299	.331	77	-8	2	1	0	.971	-12	O-77	-2.2
1992	Det-A	101	336	34	78	11	1	10	41	22	57	.232	.281	.360	78	-11	3	1	0	.979	2	O-83,D-13	-1.1
1993	SF-N	78	150	22	49	9	1	7	33	13	16	.327	.384	.540	149	10	1	0	0	.943	-7	O-41/1-3	0.3
1994	SF-N	51	100	8	27	4	0	3	20	7	20	.270	.330	.400	94	-1	0	0	0	.978	-5	O-33	-0.6
1995	SF-N	117	396	53	119	24	0	17	65	23	37	.301	.345	.490	121	11	0	1	-1	.993	-10	1-81,O-22	-0.8
1996	SF-N	81	292	40	76	22	3	9	51	22	33	.260	.319	.449	104	0	2	3	-1	.986	-6	1-73/O-5	-1.3
	Cle-A	38	142	16	46	12	0	2	14	11	9	.324	.385	.451	111	3	1	1	-0	.994	-2	1-34/O-5,D-2	-0.3
Total	10	738	2012	246	557	108	5	69	289	140	246	.277	.330	.438	108	18	12	11	-3	.974	-53	O-374,1-191/D-15	-6.3

■ BILL CARRIGAN
Carrigan, William Francis "Rough" b: 10/22/1883, Lewiston, Me. d: 7/8/69, Lewiston, Me. BR/TR, 5'9", 175 lbs. Deb: 7/7/06 M

YEAR	TM/L	G	AB	R	H	2B	3B	HR	RBI	BB	SO	AVG	OBP	SLG	PRO+	BR/A	SB	CS	SBR	FA	FR	G/POS	TPR
1906	Bos-A	37	109	5	23	0	0	0	10	5		.211	.252	.211	45	-7	3			.940	-2	C-35	-0.5
1908	Bos-A	57	149	13	35	5	2	0	14	3		.235	.255	.295	77	-4	1			.955	6	C-47/1-3	0.6
1909	Bos-A	94	280	25	83	13	2	1	36	17		.296	.341	.368	121	6	2			.972	1	C-77/1-8	1.6
1910	Bos-A	114	342	36	85	11	1	3	53	23		.249	.307	.313	92	-3	10			.962	-21	*C-110	-1.6
1911	Bos-A	72	232	29	67	6	1	1	30	26		.289	.373	.336	99	1	5			.972	-1	C-62/1-6	0.6
1912	*Bos-A	87	266	34	70	7	1	0	24	38		.263	.359	.297	84	-4	7			**.970**	-12	C-87	-0.7
1913	Bos-A	87	256	17	62	15	5	0	28	27	26	.242	.319	.340	91	-3	6			.979	-8	C-82,M	-0.4
1914	Bos-A	82	178	18	45	5	1	1	22	40	18	.253	.395	.309	112	5	1	2	-1	**.984**	3	C-78,M	1.5
1915	*Bos-A	46	95	10	19	3	0	0	7	16	12	.200	.321	.232	68	-3	0			.975	8	C-44,M	0.8
1916	*Bos-A	33	63	7	17	2	1	0	11	11	3	.270	.378	.333	113	2	2			1.000	6	C-27,M	1.0
Total	10	709	1970	194	506	67	14	6	235	206	59	.257	.334	.314	94	-11	37	2		.971	-18	C-649/1-17	2.9

■ MATIAS CARRILLO
Carrillo, Matias (Garcia) b: 2/24/63, Los Mochis, Mexico BL/TL, 5'11", 190 lbs. Deb: 5/23/91

YEAR	TM/L	G	AB	R	H	2B	3B	HR	RBI	BB	SO	AVG	OBP	SLG	PRO+	BR/A	SB	CS	SBR	FA	FR	G/POS	TPR
1991	Mil-A	3	0	0	0	0	0	0	0	0	0	—	—	—	—	0	0	0	0	.000	-1	/O-3	-0.1
1993	Fla-N	24	55	4	14	6	0	0	3	1	7	.255	.281	.364	67	-3	0	0	0	1.000	-3	O-16	-0.6
1994	Fla-N	80	136	13	34	7	0	0	9	9	31	.250	.297	.301	55	-9	3	3	-1	.982	-7	O-49	-1.8
Total	3	107	191	17	48	13	0	0	12	10	38	.251	.292	.319	58	-11	3	3	-1	.987	-12	/O-68	-2.5

■ DIXIE CARROLL
Carroll, Dorsey Lee b: 5/9/1891, Paducah, Ky. d: 10/13/84, Jacksonville, Fla BL/TR, 5'11", 165 lbs. Deb: 9/12/19

YEAR	TM/L	G	AB	R	H	2B	3B	HR	RBI	BB	SO	AVG	OBP	SLG	PRO+	BR/A	SB	CS	SBR	FA	FR	G/POS	TPR
1919	Bos-N	15	49	10	13	3	1	0	7	7	1	.265	.379	.367	130	2	5			.921	2	O-13	0.3

■ CHICK CARROLL
Carroll, Edward b: 1868, Arkansas d: 7/13/08, Chicago, Ill. Deb: 4/17/1884

YEAR	TM/L	G	AB	R	H	2B	3B	HR	RBI	BB	SO	AVG	OBP	SLG	PRO+	BR/A	SB	CS	SBR	FA	FR	G/POS	TPR
1884	Was-U	4	16	1	4	0	0	0		0		.250	.250	.250	54	-1				.500	-1	/O-4	-0.2

■ FRED CARROLL
Carroll, Frederick Herbert b: 7/2/1864, Sacramento, Cal. d: 11/7/04, San Rafael, Cal. BR/TR, 5'11", 185 lbs. Deb: 5/1/1884

YEAR	TM/L	G	AB	R	H	2B	3B	HR	RBI	BB	SO	AVG	OBP	SLG	PRO+	BR/A	SB	CS	SBR	FA	FR	G/POS	TPR
1884	Col-a	69	252	46	70	13	5	6		13		.278	.326	.440	161	17				.944	16	C-54,O-15	3.3
1885	Pit-a	71	280	45	75	13	8	0	30	7		.268	.298	.371	112	3				.926	4	C-60,O-12	1.1
1886	Pit-a	122	486	92	140	28	11	5	64	52		.288	.362	.422	146	26	20			.921	11	C-70,O-27,1-25,/S-1	3.6
1887	Pit-N	102	421	71	138	24	15	6	54	36	21	.328	.383	.499	152	30	23			.833	-12	O-46,C-40,1-17,/S-1	1.7
1888	Pit-N	97	366	62	91	14	5	2	48	32	31	.249	.326	.331	119	10	18			.897	-11	C-54,O-38/1-5,3-1	0.2
1889	Pit-N	91	318	80	105	21	11	2	51	85	26	.330	**.486**	.484	**190**	**48**	19			.930	-13	C-43,O-41/1-7,3-1	3.2
1890	Pit-P	111	416	95	124	20	7	2	71	75	22	.298	.418	.394	128	23	35			.856	-17	C-56,O-49/1-7	0.7
1891	Pit-N	91	353	55	77	13	4	4	48	48	36	.218	.315	.312	85	-6	22			.915	6	O-91	-0.3
Total	8	754	2892	546	820	146	66	27	366	348	136	.284	.370	.408	137	151	137			.913	-16	C-377,O-319/13S	13.5

■ SCRAPPY CARROLL
Carroll, John E. b: 8/27/1860, Buffalo, N.Y. d: 11/14/42, Buffalo, N.Y. 5'7.5", Deb: 9/27/1884

YEAR	TM/L	G	AB	R	H	2B	3B	HR	RBI	BB	SO	AVG	OBP	SLG	PRO+	BR/A	SB	CS	SBR	FA	FR	G/POS	TPR
1884	StP-U	9	31	3	3	1	0	0		2		.097	.152	.129	-26	-7				.824	3	/O-8,3-2	-0.4
1885	Buf-N	13	40	1	3	0	0	0	1	2	8	.075	.119	.075	-35	-6				.917	1	O-13	-0.5
1887	Cle-a	57	216	30	43	5	1	0	19	15		.199	.264	.231	40	-17	19			.843	-5	O-54/3-3,2-1	-1.9
Total	3	79	287	34	49	6	1	0	20	19	8	.171	.232	.199	26	-30	19			.853	-2	/O-75,3-5,2-1	-2.8

■ PAT CARROLL
Carroll, Patrick b: 3/1853, Philadelphia, Pa. d: 2/14/16, Philadelphia, Pa. Deb: 5/10/1884

YEAR	TM/L	G	AB	R	H	2B	3B	HR	RBI	BB	SO	AVG	OBP	SLG	PRO+	BR/A	SB	CS	SBR	FA	FR	G/POS	TPR
1884	Alt-U	11	49	4	13	1	0	0		1		.265	.280	.286	71	-3				.920	-4	/C-8,O-3	-0.5
	Phi-U	5	19	1	3	1	0	0		0		.158	.158	.211	12	-3				.839	3	/C-5	0.0
	Yr	16	68	5	16	2	0	0		1		.235	.246	.265	56	-6				.877	-1	C-13/O-3	-0.5

■ DOC CARROLL
Carroll, Ralph Arthur "Red" b: 12/28/1891, Worcester, Mass. d: 6/27/83, Worcester, Mass. BR/TR, 6', 170 lbs. Deb: 6/27/16

YEAR	TM/L	G	AB	R	H	2B	3B	HR	RBI	BB	SO	AVG	OBP	SLG	PRO+	BR/A	SB	CS	SBR	FA	FR	G/POS	TPR
1916	Phi-A	10	22	1	2	0	0	0	0	1	8	.091	.167	.091	-24	-3	0			.942	0	C-10	-0.3

■ CLIFF CARROLL
Carroll, Samuel Clifford b: 10/18/1859, Clay Grove, Iowa d: 6/12/23, Portland, Ore. BB/TR, 5'8", 163 lbs. Deb: 8/3/1882

YEAR	TM/L	G	AB	R	H	2B	3B	HR	RBI	BB	SO	AVG	OBP	SLG	PRO+	BR/A	SB	CS	SBR	FA	FR	G/POS	TPR
1882	Pro-N	10	41	4	5	0	0	0	2	0	4	.122	.122	.122	-21	-5				1.000	1	O-10	-0.4
1883	Pro-N	58	238	37	63	12	3	1	20	4	28	.265	.277	.353	87	-4				.902	5	O-58	0.0
1884	*Pro-N	113	452	90	118	16	4	3	54	29	39	.261	.306	.334	103	2				.904	2	*O-113	0.2
1885	Pro-N	104	426	62	99	12	3	1	40	29	29	.232	.281	.282	85	-6				.886	4	*O-104	-0.5
1886	Was-N	111	433	73	99	11	6	2	22	44	26	.229	.300	.296	87	-5	31			.862	-1	*O-111	-0.8
1887	Was-N	103	420	79	104	17	4	4	37	17	30	.248	.291	.336	78	-12	40			.902	1	*O-103	-1.1
1888	Pit-N	5	20	1	0	0	0	0	0	0	8	.000	.000	.000	-99	-5	2			.667	-1	/O-5	-0.6
1890	Chi-N	136	582	134	166	16	6	7	65	53	34	.285	.352	.369	106	4	34			.936	15	*O-136	1.2
1891	Chi-N	130	515	87	132	20	8	7	80	50	42	.256	.340	.367	106	4	31			.915	-5	*O-130	-0.4
1892	StL-N	101	407	82	111	14	8	4	49	47	22	.273	.363	.376	130	16	30			.901	4	*O-101	1.4
1893	Bos-N	120	438	80	98	7	5	2	54	88	28	.224	.360	.276	65	-21	29			.917	2	*O-120	-2.1
Total	11	991	3972	729	995	125	47	31	423	361	290	.251	.320	.329	92	-32	197			.905	25	O-991	-3.1

■ TOM CARROLL
Carroll, Thomas Edward b: 9/17/36, Jamaica, N.Y. BR/TR, 6'3", 186 lbs. Deb: 5/7/55

YEAR	TM/L	G	AB	R	H	2B	3B	HR	RBI	BB	SO	AVG	OBP	SLG	PRO+	BR/A	SB	CS	SBR	FA	FR	G/POS	TPR
1955	*NY-A	14	6	3	2	0	0	0	0	0	2	.333	.333	.333	81	-0	0	0	0	.875	2	/S-4	0.2
1956	NY-A	36	17	11	6	0	0	0	0	1	3	.353	.389	.353	100	0	1	0	0	.857	5	3-11/S-1	0.5
1959	KC-A	14	7	1	1	0	0	0	1	0	1	.143	.143	.143	-21	-1	0	0	0	1.000	4	/S-9,3-3	0.3
Total	3	64	30	15	9	0	0	0	1	1	6	.300	.323	.300	69	-1	1	0	0	.813	11	/3-14,S-14	1.0

■ KID CARSEY
Carsey, Wilfred b: 10/22/1870, New York, N.Y. d: 3/29/60, Miami, Fla. BL/TR, 5'7", 168 lbs. Deb: 4/8/1891

YEAR	TM/L	G	AB	R	H	2B	3B	HR	RBI	BB	SO	AVG	OBP	SLG	PRO+	BR/A	SB	CS	SBR	FA	FR	G/POS	TPR
1891	Was-a	61	187	25	28	5	2	0	15	19	38	.150	.236	.198	25	-18	2			.922	5	P-54/O-7,S-2	-0.2
1892	Phi-N	44	131	8	20	2	1	1	10	9	24	.153	.207	.206	25	-12	1			.888	2	P-43/O-2	-0.1
1893	Phi-N	39	145	12	27	1	1	0	10	5	14	.186	.229	.207	16	-18	2			.925	2	P-39	0.0
1894	Phi-N	35	125	30	34	2	2	0	18	16	11	.272	.359	.320	67	-6	3			.937	2	P-35	0.0
1895	Phi-N	44	141	24	41	2	0	0	20	15	12	.291	.363	.305	73	-5	2			.878	-1	P-44	0.0
1896	Phi-N	27	81	13	18	2	2	0	7	11	12	.222	.315	.296	62	-4	1			.908	1	P-27	0.0
1897	Phi-N	4	13	1	3	0	0	0	1	0		.231	.231	.231	23	-1	0			1.000	-0	/P-4	0.0
	StL-N	13	43	2	13	2	2	0	5	1		.302	.318	.442	101	-0	1			.917	1	P-12	0.0
	Yr	17	56	3	16	2	2	0	6	1		.286	.298	.393	83	-2	1			.930	1	P-16	0.0
1898	StL-N	38	105	8	21	0	1	1	10	10		.200	.270	.248	47	-7	3			.935	-6	P-20,2-10/O-8	-1.0
1899	Cle-N	11	36	5	10	0	0	0	4	3		.278	.333	.278	74	-1	0			.879	3	P-10/S-1	0.1
	Was-N	4	11	1	0	0	0	0	0	0		.000	.000	.000	-99	-3	0			.923	1	/P-4	0.0
	NY-N	5	18	2	6	1	0	0	1	2		.333	.400	.389	121	1	2			.667	-1	/3-3,S-2	0.0
	Yr	20	65	8	16	1	0	0	5	5		.246	.300	.262	57	-4	2			.891	3	P-14/S-3,3-3	0.1
1901	Bro-N	2	2	0	0	0	0	0	0	0		.000	.000	.000	-97	-0	0			1.000	-0	/P-2	0.0
Total	10	327	1038	131	221	17	11	2	101	91	111	.213	.281	.256	47	-76	17			.911	7	P-294/O-17,2-10,S3	-1.2

■ KIT CARSON
Carson, Walter Lloyd b: 11/15/12, Colton, Cal. d: 6/21/83, Long Beach, Cal. BL/TL, 6', 180 lbs. Deb: 7/21/34

YEAR	TM/L	G	AB	R	H	2B	3B	HR	RBI	BB	SO	AVG	OBP	SLG	PRO+	BR/A	SB	CS	SBR	FA	FR	G/POS	TPR
1934	Cle-A	5	18	4	5	2	1	0	1	2	3	.278	.350	.500	115	0	0	0	0	1.000	-1	/O-4	-0.1
1935	Cle-A	16	22	1	5	2	0	0	1	2	6	.227	.292	.318	57	-1	0	1	-1	1.000	-0	/O-4	-0.2
Total	2	21	40	5	10	4	1	0	2	4	9	.250	.318	.400	83	-1	0	1	-1	1.000	-2	/O-8	-0.3

YEAR	TM/L	G	AB	R	H	2B	3B	HR	RBI	BB	SO	AVG	OBP	SLG	PRO+	BR/A	SB	CS	SBR	FA	FR	G/POS	TPR
■ FRANK CARSWELL Carswell, Frank Willis "Tex" or "Wheels" b: 11/6/19, Palestine, Tex. BR/TR, 6', 195 lbs. Deb: 4/17/53																							
1953	Det-A	16	15	2	4	0	0	0	2	3	1	.267	.389	.267	81	-0	0	0	0	1.000	-1	/O-3	-0.1
■ GARY CARTER Carter, Gary Edmund b: 4/8/54, Culver City, Cal. BR/TR, 6'2", 215 lbs. Deb: 9/16/74																							
1974	Mon-N	9	27	5	11	0	1	1	6	1	2	.407	.429	.593	174	2	2	0	1	1.000	-1	/C-6,O-2	0.3
1975	Mon-N★	144	503	58	136	20	1	17	68	72	83	.270	.363	.416	111	8	5	2	0	.974	-16	O-92,C-66/3-1	-0.8
1976	Mon-N	91	311	31	68	8	1	6	38	30	43	.219	.289	.309	67	-13	0	2	-1	.994	3	C-60,O-36	-1.2
1977	Mon-N	154	522	86	148	29	2	31	84	58	103	.284	.361	.525	138	27	5	5	-2	.990	3	*C-146/O-1	3.3
1978	Mon-N	157	533	76	136	27	1	20	72	62	70	.255	.338	.422	113	9	10	6	-1	.989	10	*C-152/1-1	2.3
1979	Mon-N★	141	505	74	143	26	5	22	75	40	62	.283	.342	.485	124	15	3	2	-0	.989	13	*C-138	3.4
1980	Mon-N★	154	549	76	145	25	5	29	101	58	78	.264	.336	.486	127	18	3	2	-0	**.993**	14	*C-149	3.9
1981	*Mon-N★	100	374	48	94	20	2	16	68	35	35	.251	.317	.444	113	5	1	5	-3	.993	2	*C-100/1-1	0.9
1982	Mon-N★	154	557	91	163	32	1	29	97	78	64	.293	.385	.510	146	35	2	5	-2	.991	14	*C-153	5.4
1983	Mon-N★	145	541	63	146	37	3	17	79	51	57	.270	.341	.444	116	11	1	1	-0	**.995**	10	*C-144/1-1	2.8
1984	Mon-N★	159	596	75	175	32	1	27	**106**	64	57	.294	.368	.487	145	34	2	2	-1	.993	-5	*C-143,1-25	3.5
1985	NY-N†	149	555	83	156	17	1	32	100	69	46	.281	.367	.488	141	30	1	1	-0	.992	5	*C-143/1-6,O-1	4.3
1986	*NY-N★	132	490	81	125	14	2	24	105	62	63	.255	.346	.439	118	12	1	0	0	.991	6	*C-122/1-9,O-4,3-1	2.7
1987	NY-N★	139	523	55	123	18	2	20	83	42	73	.235	.293	.392	84	-14	0	0	0	.991	-0	*C-135/1-4,O-1	-0.5
1988	*NY-N★	130	455	39	110	16	2	11	46	34	52	.242	.304	.358	94	-4	0	2	-1	.990	-3	*C-119,1-10/3-1	0.0
1989	NY-N	50	153	14	28	8	0	2	15	12	15	.183	.242	.275	50	-10	0	0	0	.980	-2	C-47/1-1	-1.0
1990	SF-N	92	244	24	62	10	0	9	27	25	31	.254	.326	.406	104	1	1	1	-0	.992	-3	C-80/1-3	0.1
1991	LA-N	101	248	22	61	14	0	6	26	22	26	.246	.325	.375	98	-0	2	2	-1	.988	3	C-68,1-10	0.6
1992	Mon-N	95	285	24	62	18	1	5	29	33	37	.218	.303	.340	83	-6	0	4	-2	.989	1	C-85/1-5	-0.4
Total	19	2296	7971	1025	2092	371	31	324	1225	848	997	.262	.338	.439	116	159	39	42	-14	.991	54	*C-2056,O-137/13	29.6
■ HOWIE CARTER Carter, John Howard b: 10/13/04, New York, N.Y. d: 7/24/91, New York, N.Y. BR/TR, 5'10", 154 lbs. Deb: 6/21/26																							
1926	Cin-N	5	1	0	0	0	0	0	0	0	0	.000	.000	.000	-99	-0	0			1.000	0	/2-3,S-1	0.0
■ JOE CARTER Carter, Joseph Chris b: 3/7/60, Oklahoma City, Okla. BR/TR, 6'3", 215 lbs. Deb: 7/30/83																							
1983	Chi-N	23	51	6	9	1	1	0	1	0	21	.176	.176	.235	13	-6	1	0	0	1.000	-2	O-16	-0.8
1984	Cle-A	66	244	32	67	6	1	13	41	11	48	.275	.309	.467	109	2	2	4	-2	.956	1	O-59/1-7	-0.1
1985	Cle-A	143	489	64	128	27	0	15	59	25	74	.262	.300	.409	93	-6	24	6	4	.983	-1	*O-135,1-11/2-1,3D	-0.8
1986	Cle-A	162	663	108	200	36	9	29	**121**	32	95	.302	.339	.514	130	25	29	7	5	.976	-6	*O-104,1-70	1.5
1987	Cle-A	149	588	83	155	27	2	32	106	27	105	.264	.306	.480	103	1	31	6	6	.983	-8	1-84,O-62/D-5	-0.9
1988	Cle-A	157	621	85	168	36	6	27	98	35	82	.271	.317	.478	116	11	27	5	5	.985	14	*O-156	2.5
1989	Cle-A	162	651	84	158	32	4	35	105	39	112	.243	.294	.465	109	4	13	5	1	.978	-1	*O-146,1-11/D-8	-0.1
1990	SD-N	162	634	79	147	27	1	24	115	48	93	.232	.293	.391	86	-14	22	6	3	.988	9	*O-150,1-14	-0.7
1991	*Tor-A★	162	638	89	174	42	3	33	108	49	112	.273	.334	.503	124	18	20	9	1	.974	3	*O-151,D-11	1.8
1992	*Tor-A★	158	622	97	164	30	7	34	119	36	109	.264	.315	.498	119	13	12	5	1	.971	6	*O-129,D-24/1-4	1.5
1993	*Tor-A★	155	603	92	153	33	5	33	121	47	113	.254	.317	.489	113	8	8	3	1	.974	1	*O-151/D-3	0.6
1994	Tor-A★	111	435	70	118	25	2	27	103	33	64	.271	.326	.524	114	7	11	0	3	.991	0	*O-110/D-1	0.7
1995	Tor-A	139	558	70	141	23	0	25	76	37	87	.253	.303	.428	88	-12	12	1	3	.975	3	*O-128/1-7,D-5	-1.0
1996	Tor-A★	157	625	84	158	35	7	30	107	44	106	.253	.309	.475	95	-8	7	6	-2	.961	-12	*O-115,1-41,D-15	-2.6
1997	Tor-A	157	612	76	143	30	4	21	102	40	105	.234	.288	.399	76	-23	8	2	1	.972	-0	D-65,O-51,1-42	-3.0
1998	Bal-A	85	283	36	70	15	1	11	34	18	48	.247	.297	.424	86	-7	3	1	0	.962	2	O-50,D-32/1-1	-0.7
	SF-N	41	105	15	31	7	0	7	29	6	13	.295	.333	.562	131	4	1	0	0	1.000	-4	O-17,1-16	-0.1
Total	16	2189	8422	1170	2184	432	53	396	1445	527	1387	.259	.310	.464	104	19	231	66	30	.977	3	*O-1730,1-308,D/32	-2.2
■ BLACKIE CARTER Carter, Otis Leonard b: 9/30/02, Langley, S.C. d: 9/10/76, Greenville, S.C. BR/TR, 5'10", 175 lbs. Deb: 10/3/25																							
1925	NY-N	1	4	0	0	0	0	0	0	0	1	.000	.000	.000	-99	-1	0	0	0	1.000	1	/O-1	-0.1
1926	NY-N	5	17	4	4	1	0	1	1	1	0	.235	.278	.471	100	-0	0			.917	0	/O-4	0.0
Total	2	6	21	4	4	1	0	1	1	1	1	.190	.227	.381	61	-1	0	0		.929	1	/O-5	-0.1
■ STEVE CARTER Carter, Steven Jerome b: 12/3/64, Charlottesville, Va. BL/TR, 6'4", 201 lbs. Deb: 4/16/89																							
1989	Pit-N	9	16	2	2	1	0	1	3	2	5	.125	.222	.375	70	-1	0	0	0	1.000	-1	/O-5	-0.2
1990	Pit-N	5	5	0	1	0	0	0	0	0	1	.200	.200	.200	11	-1	0	0	0	1.000	-1	/O-3	-0.2
Total	2	14	21	2	3	1	0	1	3	2	6	.143	.217	.333	56	-1	0	0	0	1.000	-2	/O-8	-0.4
■ ED CARTWRIGHT Cartwright, Edward Charles "Jumbo" b: 10/6/1859, Johnstown, Pa. d: 9/3/33, St.Petersburg, Fla BR/TR, 5'10", 220 lbs. Deb: 7/10/1890																							
1890	StL-a	75	300	70	90	12	4	8	60	29		.300	.367	.447	123	5	26			.976	-1	1-75	0.0
1894	Was-N	132	507	88	149	35	13	12	106	57	43	.294	.374	.485	109	6	31			.973	-2	*1-132	0.4
1895	Was-N	122	472	95	156	34	17	3	90	54	41	.331	.400	.494	131	22	50			.984	14	*1-122	3.1
1896	Was-N	133	499	76	138	15	10	1	62	54	44	.277	.350	.353	85	-10	28			.978	-0	*1-133	-0.7
1897	Was-N	33	124	19	29	4	0	0	15	8		.234	.286	.266	46	-10	9			.963	2	1-33	-0.6
Total	5	495	1902	348	562	100	44	24	333	202	128	.295	.368	.432	106	14	144			.977	13	1-495	2.2
■ RICO CARTY Carty, Ricardo Adolfo Jacobo (b: Ricardo Adolfo Jacobo (Carty)) b: 9/1/39, San Pedro De Macoris, D.R. BR/TR, 6'3", 200 lbs. Deb: 9/15/63																							
1963	Mil-N	2	2	0	0	0	0	0	0	0	2	.000	.000	.000	-99	-1	0	0	0	.000	0	H	-0.1
1964	Mil-N	133	455	72	150	28	4	22	88	43	78	.330	.391	.554	162	37	1	2	-1	.978	1	*O-121	3.3
1965	Mil-N	83	271	37	84	18	1	10	35	17	44	.310	.357	.494	136	12	1	4	-2	.958	1	O-73	0.8
1966	Atl-N	151	521	73	170	25	2	15	76	60	74	.326	.396	.468	137	28	4	6	-2	.971	5	*O-126,C-17/1-2,3-1	2.7
1967	Atl-N	134	444	41	113	16	2	15	64	49	70	.255	.330	.401	110	6	4	3	-1	.959	4	*O-112/1-9	0.3
1969	*Atl-N	104	304	47	104	15	0	16	58	32	28	.342	.405	.549	164	26	0	2	-1	.952	-3	O-79	1.8
1970	Atl-N★	136	478	84	175	23	3	25	101	77	46	**.366**	**.456**	.584	167	48	1	2	-1	.974	3	*O-133	4.2
1972	Atl-N	86	271	31	75	12	2	6	29	44	33	.277	.378	.402	111	5	0	0	0	.979	-1	O-78	0.1
1973	Tex-A	86	306	24	71	12	0	3	33	36	39	.232	.315	.301	77	-9	2	0	1	1.000	-2	O-53,D-31	-1.3
	Chi-N	22	70	4	15	0	0	1	8	6	10	.214	.276	.257	45	-5	0	0	0	.947	-0	O-19	-0.7
	Oak-A	7	8	1	2	1	0	1	1	2	1	.250	.400	.750	230	1	0	0	0	.000	0	/D-2	0.1
1974	Cle-A	33	91	6	33	5	0	1	16	5	9	.363	.396	.451	144	5	0	0	0	.985	-2	D-14/1-8	0.3
1975	Cle-A	118	383	57	118	19	1	18	64	45	31	.308	.384	.504	149	25	2	2	-1	.990	-1	D-72,1-26,O-12	2.0
1976	Cle-A	152	552	67	171	34	0	13	83	67	45	.310	.384	.442	143	31	1	1	-0	1.000	-2	*D-137,1-12/O-1	2.5
1977	Cle-A	127	461	50	129	23	1	15	80	56	51	.280	.358	.432	118	12	1	2	-1	1.000	1	*D-123/1-2	0.8
1978	Tor-A	104	387	51	110	16	0	20	68	36	41	.284	.345	.481	127	13	1	1	-0	.000	0	*D-101	1.0
	Oak-A	41	141	19	39	5	1	11	31	21	16	.277	.370	.560	167	12	0	0	0	.000	0	D-41	1.1
	Yr	145	528	70	149	21	1	31	99	57	57	.282	.352	.502	138	25	1	1	-0	.717	0	*D-142	2.1
1979	Tor-A	132	461	48	118	26	0	12	55	46	45	.256	.325	.390	91	-6	3	1	0	.000	0	*D-129	-1.0
Total	15	1651	5606	712	1677	278	17	204	890	642	663	.299	.372	.464	132	240	21	26	-9	.970	3	O-807,D-650/1C3	17.9
■ MIKE CARUSO Caruso, Michael J. b: 5/27/77, Queens, N.Y. BL/TR, 6'1", 172 lbs. Deb: 3/31/98																							
1998	Chi-A	133	523	81	160	17	6	5	55	14	38	.306	.333	.390	89	-8	22	6	3	.944	-11	*S-131	-0.4
■ BOB CARUTHERS Caruthers, Robert Lee "Parisian Bob" b: 1/5/1864, Memphis, Tenn. d: 8/5/11, Peoria, Ill. BL/TR, 5'7", 138 lbs. Deb: 9/7/1884 MU																							
1884	StL-a	23	82	15	22	2	0	2		4		.268	.302	.366	113	1				.750	-6	O-16,P-13	-0.4
1885	*StL-a	60	222	37	50	10	2	1	12	20		.225	.289	.302	83	-4				.902	-0	P-53/O-7	-0.1
1886	*StL-a	87	317	91	106	21	14	4	61	64		.334	.448	.527	196	37	26			.897	-6	P-44,O-43/2-2	1.1
1887	*StL-a	98	364	102	130	23	11	8	73	66		.357	.463	.547	164	31	49			.903	9	O-54,P-39/1-7	1.5
1888	Bro-a	94	335	58	77	10	5	5	53	45		.230	.328	.334	113	6	23			.899	1	O-51,P-44	0.1
1889	*Bro-a	59	172	45	43	8	3	2	31	44	17	.250	.408	.366	121	7	9			.968	0	P-56/O-3,1-2	-0.1
1890	*Bro-N	71	238	46	63	7	4	1	29	47	18	.265	.397	.340	115	7	13			.860	-4	O-39,P-37	-0.4
1891	Bro-N	56	171	24	48	5	3	2	23	25	13	.281	.372	.380	120	5	4			.940	-3	P-38,O-17/2-1	-0.2
1892	StL-N	143	513	76	142	16	8	3	69	86	29	.277	.386	.357	131	24	24			.892	-11	*O-122,P-16/2-6,1M	0.6

YEAR	TM/L	G	AB	R	H	2B	3B	HR	RBI	BB	SO	AVG	OBP	SLG	PRO+	BR/A	SB	CS	SBR	FA	FR	G/POS	TPR
1893	Chi-N	1	3	0	0	0	0	0	0	0	1	.000	.000	.000	-99	-1	0			1.000	-0	/O-1	-0.1
	Cin-N	13	48	14	14	2	0	1	8	16	1	.292	.477	.396	130	3	4			.857	-1	O-13	0.1
	Yr	14	51	14	14	2	0	1	8	16	2	.275	.456	.373	119	3	4			.862	-1	O-14	0.0
Total	10	705	2465	508	695	104	50	29	359	417	79	.282	.391	.400	135	117	152			.875	-22	O-366,P-340/1-13,2	2.1

■ PAUL CASANOVA

Casanova, Paulino (Ortiz) b: 12/21/41, Colon, Matanzas, Cuba BR/TR, 6′4″, 200 lbs. Deb: 9/18/65

YEAR	TM/L	G	AB	R	H	2B	3B	HR	RBI	BB	SO	AVG	OBP	SLG	PRO+	BR/A	SB	CS	SBR	FA	FR	G/POS	TPR
1965	Was-A	5	13	2	4	1	0	0	1	1	3	.308	.357	.385	112	0	0	0	0	.938	-2	/C-4	-0.2
1966	Was-A	122	429	45	109	16	5	13	44	14	78	.254	.279	.406	95	-4	1	2	-1	.981	-10	*C-119	-0.8
1967	Was-A☆	141	528	47	131	19	1	9	53	17	65	.248	.274	.339	84	-13	1	1	-0	.984	-5	*C-137	-1.1
1968	Was-A	96	322	19	63	6	0	4	25	7	52	.196	.213	.252	42	-23	0	1	-1	.989	-9	C-92	-3.2
1969	Was-A	124	379	26	82	9	2	4	37	18	52	.216	.257	.282	54	-25	0	0	0	.992	-6	*C-122	-2.6
1970	Was-A	104	328	25	75	17	3	6	30	10	47	.229	.254	.354	69	-15	0	0	0	.988	-1	*C-100	-1.2
1971	Was-A	94	311	19	63	9	1	5	26	14	52	.203	.239	.286	51	-21	0	3	-2	.985	-4	C-83	-2.7
1972	Atl-N	49	136	8	28	3	0	2	10	4	28	.206	.229	.272	38	-11	0	1	-1	.975	-6	C-43	-1.8
1973	Atl-N	82	236	18	51	7	0	7	18	11	36	.216	.254	.335	58	-14	0	2	-1	.977	6	C-78	-0.7
1974	Atl-N	42	104	5	21	0	0	0	8	5	17	.202	.239	.202	23	-11	0	0	0	.986	-1	C-33	-1.1
Total	10	859	2786	214	627	87	12	50	252	101	430	.225	.254	.319	64	-137	2	10	-5	.985	-38	C-811	-15.4

■ RAUL CASANOVA

Casanova, Raul b: 8/23/72, Humacao, P.R. BB/TR, 6′, 192 lbs. Deb: 5/24/96

YEAR	TM/L	G	AB	R	H	2B	3B	HR	RBI	BB	SO	AVG	OBP	SLG	PRO+	BR/A	SB	CS	SBR	FA	FR	G/POS	TPR
1996	Det-A	25	85	6	16	1	0	4	9	6	18	.188	.242	.341	45	-7	0	0	0	.978	-4	C-22/D-3	-0.9
1997	Det-A	101	304	27	74	10	1	5	24	26	48	.243	.309	.332	68	-14	1	1	-0	.985	1	C-92/D-1	-0.7
1998	Det-A	16	42	4	6	2	0	1	3	5	10	.143	.250	.262	33	-4	0	0	0	.967	1	C-14	-0.2
Total	3	142	431	37	96	13	1	10	36	37	76	.223	.290	.327	60	-26	1	1	-0	.982	-2	C-128/D-4	-1.8

■ GEORGE CASE

Case, George Washington b: 11/11/15, Trenton, N.J. d: 1/23/89, Trenton, N.J. BR/TR, 6′, 183 lbs. Deb: 9/8/37 C

YEAR	TM/L	G	AB	R	H	2B	3B	HR	RBI	BB	SO	AVG	OBP	SLG	PRO+	BR/A	SB	CS	SBR	FA	FR	G/POS	TPR
1937	Was-A	22	90	14	26	6	2	0	11	3	5	.289	.312	.400	82	-3	2	1	0	.945	-0	O-22	-0.4
1938	Was-A	107	433	69	132	27	3	2	40	39	28	.305	.362	.395	96	-3	11	6	-0	.964	-4	*O-101	-0.9
1939	Was-A☆	128	530	103	160	20	7	2	35	56	36	.302	.369	.377	98	-0	**51**	17	**5**	.955	3	*O-123	0.3
1940	Was-A	154	656	109	192	29	5	5	56	52	39	.293	.349	.375	94	-6	**35**	10	**5**	.970	1	*O-154	-0.8
1941	Was-A	153	649	95	176	32	8	2	53	51	37	.271	.325	.354	84	-16	**33**	9	**5**	.975	15	*O-151	-0.6
1942	Was-A	125	513	101	164	26	2	5	43	44	30	.320	.377	.407	122	15	**44**	6	**10**	.951	-2	*O-120	1.7
1943	Was-A★	141	613	**102**	180	36	5	1	52	41	27	.294	.341	.374	113	8	**61**	14	**10**	.985	1	*O-140	1.3
1944	Was-A†	119	464	63	116	14	2	2	32	49	22	.250	.326	.302	83	-9	49	18	4	.970	6	*O-114	-0.6
1945	Was-A†	123	504	72	148	19	5	1	31	49	27	.294	.360	.357	118	12	30	16	-1	.979	13	*O-123	1.8
1946	Cle-A	118	484	46	109	23	4	1	22	34	38	.225	.280	.295	65	-24	**28**	11	**2**	.983	-4	*O-118	-3.4
1947	Was-A	36	80	11	12	1	0	0	2	8	8	.150	.227	.162	10	-10	5	1	1	.963	0	O-21	-1.0
Total	11	1226	5016	785	1415	233	43	21	377	426	297	.282	.341	.358	95	-36	349	109	39	.970	30	*O-1187	-2.6

■ DENNIS CASEY

Casey, Dennis Patrick b: 3/30/1858, Binghamton, N.Y. d: 1/19/09, Binghamton, N.Y. BL/TR, 5′9″, 164 lbs. Deb: 8/18/1884 F

YEAR	TM/L	G	AB	R	H	2B	3B	HR	RBI	BB	SO	AVG	OBP	SLG	PRO+	BR/A	SB	CS	SBR	FA	FR	G/POS	TPR
1884	Wil-U	2	8	1	2	1	0	0		0		.250	.250	.375	85	-0				1.000	-0	/O-2	0.0
	Bal-a	37	149	20	37	7	4	3		5		.248	.273	.409	115	2				.898	-1	O-37	0.1
1885	Bal-a	63	264	50	76	10	5	3	29	21		.288	.347	.398	137	12				.821	-5	O-63	0.4
Total	2	102	421	71	115	18	9	6	29	26		.273	.320	.401	128	13				.847	-6	O-102	0.5

■ DOC CASEY

Casey, James Patrick b: 3/15/1870, Lawrence, Mass. d: 12/31/36, Detroit, Mich. BB/TR, 5′6″, 157 lbs. Deb: 9/14/1898

YEAR	TM/L	G	AB	R	H	2B	3B	HR	RBI	BB	SO	AVG	OBP	SLG	PRO+	BR/A	SB	CS	SBR	FA	FR	G/POS	TPR
1898	Was-N	28	112	13	31	2	0	0	15	3		.277	.302	.295	71	-4	15			.893	-3	3-22/S-4,C-3	-0.6
1899	Was-N	9	34	3	4	2	0	0	2	2		.118	.167	.176	-6	-5	1			.853	-1	/3-9	-0.5
	Bro-N	134	525	75	141	14	8	1	43	25		.269	.313	.331	75	-19	27			.892	-19	*3-134	-3.3
	Yr	143	559	78	145	16	8	1	45	27		.259	.304	.322	70	-24	28			.889	-20	*3-143	-3.8
1900	Bro-N	1	3	0	1	0	0	0	1	0		.333	.500	.333	125	0	0			1.000	-0	/3-1	0.0
1901	Det-A	128	540	105	153	16	9	2	46	32		.283	.335	.357	88	-9	34			.887	5	*3-127	-0.2
1902	Det-A	132	520	69	142	18	7	3	55	44		.273	.338	.352	90	-7	22			.904	2	*3-132	-0.4
1903	Chi-N	112	435	56	126	8	3	1	40	19		.290	.324	.329	89	-7	11			.915	-19	*3-112	-2.4
1904	Chi-N	136	548	71	147	20	4	1	43	18		.268	.300	.325	93	-6	21			.911	-10	*3-134/C-2	-1.2
1905	Chi-N	144	526	66	122	21	10	1	56	41		.232	.295	.316	79	-14	22			**.949**	-9	*3-142/S-1	-1.9
1906	Bro-N	149	571	71	133	17	8	0	34	52		.233	.306	.291	93	-4	22			.919	-17	*3-149	-1.8
1907	Bro-N	141	527	55	122	19	3	0	19	34		.231	.282	.279	82	-12	16			.955	-6	*3-138	-1.6
Total	10	1114	4341	584	1122	137	52	9	354	270		.258	.310	.320	85	-86	191			.915	-77	*3-1100/C-5,S-5	-13.9

■ JOE CASEY

Casey, Joseph Felix b: 8/15/1887, Boston, Mass. d: 6/2/66, Melrose, Mass. BR/TR, 5′9″, 180 lbs. Deb: 10/1/09

YEAR	TM/L	G	AB	R	H	2B	3B	HR	RBI	BB	SO	AVG	OBP	SLG	PRO+	BR/A	SB	CS	SBR	FA	FR	G/POS	TPR
1909	Det-A	3	5	1	0	0	0	0	0	1		.000	.167	.000	-45	-1	0			1.000	2	/C-3	0.1
1910	Det-A	23	62	3	12	3	0	0	2	2		.194	.231	.242	45	-4	1			.964	5	C-22	0.4
1911	Det-A	15	33	2	5	0	0	0	3	3		.152	.222	.152	5	-4	0			.956	-3	C-12/O-3	-0.6
1918	Was-A	9	17	3	4	0	0	0	2	2	2	.235	.316	.235	68	-1	0			1.000	2	/C-8	0.2
Total	4	50	117	9	21	3	0	0	7	8	2	.179	.238	.205	32	-10	1			.970	6	/C-45,O-3	0.1

■ BOB CASEY

Casey, Orrin Robinson b: 1/26/1859, Adolphustown, Ontario, Canada d: 11/28/36, Syracuse, N.Y. 5′11″, 190 lbs. Deb: 7/17/1882

YEAR	TM/L	G	AB	R	H	2B	3B	HR	RBI	BB	SO	AVG	OBP	SLG	PRO+	BR/A	SB	CS	SBR	FA	FR	G/POS	TPR
1882	Det-N	9	39	5	9	2	1	1	7	0	15	.231	.231	.410	101	-0				.667	-5	/3-8,2-1	-0.4

■ SEAN CASEY

Casey, Sean Thomas b: 7/2/74, Willingboro, N.J. BL/TR, 6′4″, 215 lbs. Deb: 9/12/97

YEAR	TM/L	G	AB	R	H	2B	3B	HR	RBI	BB	SO	AVG	OBP	SLG	PRO+	BR/A	SB	CS	SBR	FA	FR	G/POS	TPR
1997	Cle-A	6	10	1	2	0	0	0	1	1	2	.200	.333	.200	42	-1	0	0	0	1.000	-0	/1-1,D-3	-0.1
1998	Cin-N	96	302	44	82	21	1	7	52	43	45	.272	.368	.417	102	2	1	1	-0	.994	-8	1-86	-1.3
Total	2	102	312	45	84	21	1	7	53	44	47	.269	.367	.410	100	1	1	1	-0	.994	-8	/1-87,D-3	-1.4

■ DAVE CASH

Cash, David b: 6/11/48, Utica, N.Y. BR/TR, 5′11″, 175 lbs. Deb: 9/13/69 C

YEAR	TM/L	G	AB	R	H	2B	3B	HR	RBI	BB	SO	AVG	OBP	SLG	PRO+	BR/A	SB	CS	SBR	FA	FR	G/POS	TPR
1969	Pit-N	18	61	8	17	3	1	0	4	9	9	.279	.371	.361	108	1	2	0	1	.990	5	2-17	0.8
1970	*Pit-N	64	210	30	66	7	6	1	28	17	25	.314	.368	.419	113	4	5	2	0	.974	6	2-55	1.4
1971	*Pit-N	123	478	79	138	17	4	2	34	46	33	.289	.351	.354	101	1	13	5	1	.987	6	*2-105,3-24/S-3	1.7
1972	*Pit-N	99	425	58	120	22	4	3	30	22	31	.282	.318	.374	98	-2	9	9	-3	.992	28	2-97	3.0
1973	Pit-N	116	436	59	118	21	2	2	31	38	36	.271	.329	.342	88	-7	2	5	-2	.979	6	2-92,3-17	0.2
1974	Phi-N★	162	687	89	206	26	11	2	58	46	33	.300	.352	.378	100	0	20	8	1	.977	**29**	*2-162	4.0
1975	Phi-N★	162	699	111	**213**	40	3	4	57	56	34	.305	.360	.388	103	4	13	6	0	.981	9	*2-162	2.3
1976	*Phi-N★	160	666	92	189	14	**12**	1	56	54	13	.284	.339	.345	92	-6	10	12	-4	**.988**	-2	*2-158	-0.2
1977	Mon-N	153	650	91	188	42	7	0	43	52	33	.289	.344	.375	96	-4	21	12	-1	.986	-11	*2-153	-0.5
1978	Mon-N	159	658	66	166	26	3	3	43	37	29	.252	.292	.315	70	-27	12	6	0	**.986**	-30	*2-159	-4.9
1979	Mon-N	76	187	24	60	11	1	2	19	12	12	.321	.362	.422	114	4	7	4	-0	.971	-6	2-47	0.0
1980	SD-N	130	397	25	90	14	2	1	23	35	21	.227	.289	.280	63	-20	6	5	-1	.987	4	*2-123	-1.1
Total	12	1422	5554	732	1571	243	56	21	426	424	309	.283	.336	.358	93	-51	120	74	-8	.984	43	*2-1330/3-41,S-3	6.7

■ NORM CASH

Cash, Norman Dalton b: 11/10/34, Justiceburg, Tex. d: 10/12/86, Beaver Island, Mich. BL/TL, 6′, 190 lbs. Deb: 6/18/58

YEAR	TM/L	G	AB	R	H	2B	3B	HR	RBI	BB	SO	AVG	OBP	SLG	PRO+	BR/A	SB	CS	SBR	FA	FR	G/POS	TPR
1958	Chi-A	13	8	2	2	0	0	0	0	0	1	.250	.250	.250	39	-1	0	0	0	1.000	-1	/O-4	-0.2
1959	*Chi-A	58	104	16	25	0	1	4	16	18	9	.240	.378	.375	109	2	1	1	-0	.984	-1	1-31	-0.1
1960	Det-A	121	353	64	101	16	3	18	63	65	58	.286	.406	.501	140	22	4	2	0	.991	-2	1-99/O-4	1.3
1961	Det-A★	159	535	119	**193**	22	8	41	132	124	85	**.361**	**.488**	.662	198	82	11	5	0	.992	5	*1-157	7.1
1962	Det-A	148	507	94	123	16	2	39	89	104	82	.243	.385	.513	134	27	6	3	0	.992	7	*1-146/O-3	2.4
1963	Det-A	147	493	67	133	19	1	26	79	89	76	.270	.388	.471	135	26	2	3	-1	.994	2	*1-142	2.1
1964	Det-A	144	479	63	123	15	5	23	83	70	66	.257	.355	.453	121	15	2	1	0	**.997**	4	*1-137	1.3
1965	Det-A	142	467	79	124	23	1	30	82	77	62	.266	.374	.512	147	30	6	6	-2	.992	5	*1-139	2.8
1966	Det-A★	160	603	98	168	18	3	32	93	66	91	.279	.354	.478	133	26	2	1	0	.988	4	*1-158	2.0
1967	Det-A	152	488	64	118	16	5	22	72	81	100	.242	.354	.430	127	18	3	2	-0	**.995**	9	*1-146	2.0
1968	*Det-A	127	411	50	108	15	1	25	63	39	70	.263	.331	.487	141	19	1	1	-0	.992	9	*1-117	2.2
1969	Det-A	142	483	81	135	15	4	22	74	63	80	.280	.370	.464	126	17	2	1	0	.994	6	*1-134	1.3

YEAR	TM/L	G	AB	R	H	2B	3B	HR	RBI	BB	SO	AVG	OBP	SLG	PRO+	BR/A	SB	CS	SBR	FA	FR	G/POS	TPR
1970	Det-A	130	370	58	96	18	2	15	53	72	58	.259	.387	.441	127	16	0	1	-1	.989	2	*1-114	0.8
1971	Det-A★	135	452	72	128	10	3	32	91	59	86	.283	.375	.531	148	28	1	0	0	.992	-0	*1-131	1.8
1972	*Det-A★	137	440	51	114	16	0	22	61	50	64	.259	.340	.445	128	15	0	2	-1	.993	-0	*1-134	0.3
1973	Det-A	121	363	51	95	19	0	19	40	47	73	.262	.359	.471	124	11	1	0	0	.991	2	*1-114/D-3	0.6
1974	Det-A	53	149	17	34	3	2	7	12	19	30	.228	.327	.416	109	2	1	1	-0	.985	-1	1-44	-0.2
Total	17	2089	6705	1046	1820	241	41	377	1103	1043	1091	.271	.377	.488	138	355	43	30	-5	.992	50	*1-1943/O-11,D-3	27.5
■ RON CASH	Cash, Ronald Forrest b: 11/20/49, Atlanta, Ga. BR/TR, 6', 180 lbs. Deb: 9/4/73																						
1973	Det-A	14	39	8	16	1	1	0	6	5	5	.410	.477	.487	161	3	0	0	0	.900	-2	/O-7,3-6	0.1
1974	Det-A	20	62	6	14	2	0	0	5	0	11	.226	.226	.258	38	-5	0	1	-1	.979	-1	1-15/3-4	-0.8
Total	2	34	101	14	30	3	1	0	11	5	16	.297	.330	.347	89	-2	0	1	-1	.950	-3	/1-15,3-10,O-7	-0.7
■ ED CASKIN	Caskin, Edward James b: 12/30/1851, Danvers, Mass. d: 10/9/24, Danvers, Mass. BR/TR, 5'9.5", 165 lbs. Deb: 5/1/1879																						
1879	Tro-N	70	304	32	78	13	2	0	21	2	14	.257	.261	.313	95	-1				.902	6	S-42,C-22/2-6	0.8
1880	Tro-N	82	333	36	75	5	4	0	28	7	24	.225	.241	.264	68	-12				.885	7	*S-82/C-2	0.1
1881	Tro-N	63	234	33	53	7	1	0	21	13	29	.226	.267	.265	65	-9				.906	1	*S-63	-0.5
1883	NY-N	95	383	47	91	11	2	1	40	14	25	.238	.264	.285	68	-14				.855	-5	*S-81,2-13/C-1	-1.5
1884	NY-N	100	351	49	81	11	1	1	40	34	55	.231	.299	.276	80	-7				.883	5	*S-96/C-6	-0.1
1885	StL-N	71	262	31	47	3	0	0	12	12	22	.179	.215	.191	34	-18				.884	-4	3-69/C-2,S-1	-1.9
1886	NY-N	1	4	1	2	0	0	0	1	0	1	.500	.500	.500	203	0	0			1.000	-1	/S-1	0.0
Total	7	482	1871	229	427	50	10	2	163	82	170	.228	.261	.269	70	-61	0			.883	9	S-366/3-69,C-33,2	-3.1
■ HARRY CASSADY	Cassady, Harry Delbert (b: Harry Delbert Cassaday) b: 7/20/1880, Bellflower, Ill. d: 4/19/69, Fresno, Cal. BL/TL, 5'8", 145 lbs. Deb: 8/8/04																						
1904	Pit-N	12	44	8	9	0	0	0	3	2		.205	.239	.205	36	-3	2			.867	-1	O-12	-0.5
1905	Was-A	10	30	1	4	0	0	0	1	0		.133	.133	.133	-16	-4	0			1.000	0	/O-9	-0.4
Total	2	22	74	9	13	0	0	0	4	2		.176	.197	.176	17	-7	2			.933	-1	/O-21	-0.9
■ JOHN CASSIDY	Cassidy, John P. b: 1857, Brooklyn, N.Y. d: 7/2/1891, Brooklyn, N.Y. BR/TL, 5'8", 168 lbs. Deb: 4/24/1875																						
1875	Atl-n	41	166	14	29	3	2	1	6	0	4	.175	.175	.235	47	-7	0	0	0	.782	-8	P-30,O-12,1-10,/2-2	-1.0
	NH-n	6	22	3	3	1	0	0	1	0	1	.136	.136	.182	11	-2	0	1	-1	.988	1	/1-6	-0.2
	Yr	47	188	17	32	4	2	1	7	0	5	.170	.170	.229	43	-9	0	1	-1	.782	-8	P-30,1-16,O-12,/2-2	-1.2
1876	Har-N	12	47	6	13	2	0	0	8	1	0	.277	.292	.319	95	-0				1.000	1	/O-8,1-4	0.0
1877	Har-N	60	251	43	95	10	5	0	27	3	3	.378	.386	.458	184	24				.722	-5	*O-58/P-2	1.4
1878	Chi-N	60	256	33	68	7	1	0	29	9	11	.266	.291	.301	89	-4				.810	8	*O-60/C-1	0.2
1879	Tro-N	9	37	4	7	1	0	0	1	2	4	.189	.231	.216	52	-2				.889	-2	/O-8,1-2	-0.4
1880	Tro-N	83	352	40	89	14	8	0	29	12	34	.253	.277	.338	102	0				.880	-2	*O-82/2-1	-0.4
1881	Tro-N	85	370	57	82	13	3	1	11	18	21	.222	.258	.281	66	-15				.872	-9	*O-84/S-1	-2.4
1882	Tro-N	29	121	14	21	3	1	0	9	3	16	.174	.194	.215	32	-9				.778	-9	O-16,3-13	-1.6
1883	Pro-N	89	366	46	87	16	5	0	42	9	38	.238	.256	.309	69	-14				.864	1	*O-88/2-1,1-1	-1.2
1884	Bro-a	106	433	57	109	11	6	2		19		.252	.286	.319	96	-2				.847	-8	*O-101/3-4,S-1	-1.1
1885	Bro-a	54	221	36	47	6	2	1	28	8		.213	.250	.271	64	-9				.852	-7	O-54	-1.6
Total	10	587	2454	336	618	83	31	4	184	84	127	.252	.278	.316	89	-30				.845	-31	O-559/3-17,1S2PC	-7.1
■ JOE CASSIDY	Cassidy, Joseph Phillip b: 2/8/1883, Chester, Pa. d: 3/25/06, Chester, Pa. BR/TR, Deb: 4/18/04																						
1904	Was-A	152	581	63	140	12	**19**	1	33	15		.241	.265	.332	90	-9	17			.937	12	S-99,O-32,3-23	0.6
1905	Was-A	151	576	67	124	16	4	1	43	25		.215	.250	.262	65	-24	23			.934	**34**	*S-151	1.5
Total	2	303	1157	130	264	28	23	2	76	40		.228	.258	.297	78	-32	40			.935	46	S-250/O-32,3-23	2.1
■ PETE CASSIDY	Cassidy, Peter Francis b: 4/8/1873, Wilmington, Del. d: 7/9/29, Wilmington, Del. BR/TR, 5'10", 165 lbs. Deb: 4/18/1896																						
1896	Lou-N	49	184	16	39	1	1	0	12	7	7	.212	.256	.228	29	-19	5			.973	-7	1-38,S-11	-2.2
1899	Bro-N	6	20	2	3	1	0	0	4	1		.150	.261	.200	27	-2	1			1.000	-4	/3-3,S-2	-0.5
	Was-N	46	178	21	56	13	0	3	32	9		.315	.365	.438	121	5	5			.970	-2	1-37/3-6,S-3	0.3
	Yr	52	198	23	59	14	0	3	36	10		.298	.353	.414	111	3	6			.970	-5	1-37/3-9,S-5	-0.2
Total	2	101	382	39	98	15	1	3	48	17	7	.257	.307	.325	72	-16	11			.972	-13	/1-75,S-16,3-9	-2.4
■ JACK CASSINI	Cassini, Jack Dempsey "Gabby" or "Scat" b: 10/26/19, Dearborn, Mich. BR/TR, 5'10", 175 lbs. Deb: 4/19/49																						
1949	Pit-N	8	0	3	0	0	0	0	0	0	0	—	—	—	—	0	0			.000	0	R	0.0
■ PEDRO CASTELLANO	Castellano, Pedro Orlando (Arrieta) b: 3/11/70, Lara, Venez. BR/TR, 6'1", 175 lbs. Deb: 5/30/93																						
1993	Col-N	34	71	12	13	2	0	3	7	8	16	.183	.266	.338	52	-5	1	1	-0	.909	-1	3-13,1-10/S-5,2-4	-0.7
1995	Col-N	4	5	0	0	0	0	0	0	2	3	.000	.286	.000	-13	-1	0	0	0	1.000	-1	/3-3	-0.2
1996	Col-N	13	17	1	2	0	0	0	2	3	6	.118	.286	.118	9	-2	0	0	0	1.000	1	/2-3,3-1,O-1	-0.2
Total	3	51	93	13	15	2	0	3	9	13	25	.161	.271	.280	40	-8	1	1	-0	.917	-2	/3-17,1-10,2-7,SO	-1.1
■ JIM CASTIGLIA	Castiglia, James Vincent b: 9/30/18, Passaic, N.J. BL/TR, 5'11", 200 lbs. Deb: 4/14/42																						
1942	Phi-A	16	18	2	7	0	0	0	2	1	3	.389	.421	.389	129	1	0	0	0	.875	-1	/C-3	0.0
■ PETE CASTIGLIONE	Castiglione, Peter Paul b: 2/13/21, Greenwich, Conn. BR/TR, 5'11", 175 lbs. Deb: 9/10/47																						
1947	Pit-N	13	50	6	14	0	0	0	1	2	5	.280	.308	.280	55	-3	0			.970	1	S-13	-0.1
1948	Pit-N	4	2	0	0	0	0	0	0	0	0	.000	.000	.000	-98	-1	1			1.000	0	/S-1	0.0
1949	Pit-N	118	448	57	120	20	2	6	43	20	43	.268	.299	.362	74	-17	2			.957	-1	3-98,S-17/O-2	-1.9
1950	Pit-N	94	263	29	67	10	3	3	22	23	23	.255	.317	.350	73	-10	1			.970	-17	3-35,S-29/2-9,1-3	-2.6
1951	Pit-N	132	482	62	126	19	4	7	42	34	28	.261	.311	.361	78	-15	2	2	-1	.957	4	3-99,S-28	-1.1
1952	Pit-N	67	214	27	57	9	1	4	18	17	8	.266	.323	.374	90	-3	3	3	-1	.951	6	3-57/1-1,O-1	0.1
1953	Pit-N	45	159	14	33	2	1	4	21	5	14	.208	.236	.308	41	-14	1	1	-0	.978	4	3-43	-1.1
	StL-N	67	52	9	9	2	0	0	3	2	5	.173	.204	.212	9	-7	0	0	0	.967	8	3-51/2-9,S-3	0.1
	Yr	112	211	23	42	4	1	4	24	7	19	.199	.228	.284	33	-21	1	1	-0	.976	12	3-94/2-9,S-3	-1.0
1954	StL-N	5	0	1	0	0	0	0	0	0	0	—	—	—	—	0	0	0	0	1.000	0	/3-5	0.0
Total	8	545	1670	205	426	62	11	24	150	103	126	.255	.300	.349	71	-70	10	6		.960	4	3-388/S-91,2-18,10	-6.6
■ VINNY CASTILLA	Castilla, Vinicio (Soria) b: 7/4/67, Oaxaca, Mexico BR/TR, 6'1", 185 lbs. Deb: 9/1/91																						
1991	Atl-N	12	5	1	1	0	0	0	0	0	2	.200	.200	.200	12	-1	0	0	0	1.000	1	S-12	0.1
1992	Atl-N	9	16	1	4	1	0	0	1	1	4	.250	.333	.313	79	-0	0	0	0	.875	0	/3-4,S-4	0.0
1993	Col-N	105	337	36	86	9	7	9	30	13	45	.255	.287	.404	71	-15	2	5	-2	.975	8	*S-104	-0.2
1994	Col-N	52	130	16	43	11	1	3	18	7	23	.331	.365	.500	105	1	2	1	0	.984	0	S-18,2-14/3-9,1-2	0.2
1995	*Col-N★	139	527	82	163	34	2	32	90	30	87	.309	.351	.564	106	-0	2	8	-4	.958	-7	*3-137/S-5	-1.1
1996	Col-N	160	629	97	191	34	0	40	113	35	88	.304	.345	.548	106	1	7	2	1	.060	28	*3-160	2.8
1997	Col-N	159	612	94	186	25	2	40	113	44	108	.304	.358	.547	108	4	2	4	-2	.954	5	*3-157	0.7
1998	Col-N★	162	645	108	206	28	4	46	144	40	89	.319	.365	.589	119	15	5	9	-4	.970	-2	*3-162/S-1	1.2
Total	8	798	2901	435	880	142	16	170	509	170	446	.303	.347	.539	105	5	20	29	-11	.961	33	3-629,S-144/2-14,1	3.7
■ ALBERTO CASTILLO	Castillo, Alberto Terrero b: 2/10/70, San Juan De La Maguana, D.R. BR/TR, 6', 185 lbs. Deb: 5/28/95																						
1995	NY-N	13	29	2	3	0	0	0	0	3	9	.103	.212	.103	-14	-5	1	0	0	.974	4	C-12	0.0
1996	NY-N	6	11	1	4	0	0	0	0	0	4	.364	.364	.364	97	-0	0	0	0	1.000	1	/C-6	0.1
1997	NY-N	35	59	3	12	1	0	0	7	9	16	.203	.309	.220	43	-5	0	1	-1	.987	6	C-34	0.2
1998	NY-N	38	83	13	17	4	0	2	7	9	17	.205	.290	.325	60	-5	0	2	-1	.990	7	C-35/D-1	0.3
Total	4	92	182	19	36	5	0	2	14	21	46	.198	.288	.258	45	-14	1	3	-2	.987	18	/C-87,D-1	0.6
■ TONY CASTILLO	Castillo, Anthony b: 6/14/57, San Jose, Cal. BR/TR, 6'4", 190 lbs. Deb: 9/22/78																						
1978	SD-N	5	8	0	1	0	0	0	1	0	2	.125	.125	.125	-33	-1	0	0	0	.950	1	/C-5	0.0

YEAR	TM/L	G	AB	R	H	2B	3B	HR	RBI	BB	SO	AVG	OBP	SLG	PRO+	BR/A	SB	CS	SBR	FA	FR	G/POS	TPR
■ **BRAULIO CASTILLO**	Castillo, Braulio Robinson Medrano (b: Braulio Robinson Medrano (Castillo)) b: 5/13/68, Elias Pina, D.R. BR/TR, 6', 160 lbs. Deb: 8/18/91																						
1991	Phi-N	28	52	3	9	3	0	0	2	1	15	.173	.189	.231	18	-6	1	1	-0	.977	-2	O-26	-0.9
1992	Phi-N	28	76	12	15	3	1	2	7	4	15	.197	.237	.342	62	-4	1	0	0	.956	-2	O-24	-0.6
Total	2	56	128	15	24	6	1	2	9	5	30	.188	.218	.297	44	-10	2	1	0	.966	-4	/O-50	-1.5
■ **MANNY CASTILLO**	Castillo, Esteban Manuel Antonio (Cabrera) b: 4/1/57, Santo Domingo, D.R. BB/TR, 5'9", 160 lbs. Deb: 9/1/80																						
1980	KC-A	7	10	1	2	0	0	0	0	0	0	.200	.200	.200	10	-1	0	0	0	1.000	2	/3-3,2-1,D-2	0.0
1982	Sea-A	138	506	49	130	29	1	3	49	22	35	.257	.291	.336	70	-21	2	8	-4	.938	-24	*3-130/2-9	-5.3
1983	Sea-A	91	203	13	42	6	3	0	24	7	20	.207	.237	.266	37	-17	1	1	-0	.971	8	3-55,1-11/2-5,PD	-1.1
Total	3	236	719	63	174	35	4	3	73	29	55	.242	.274	.314	59	-40	3	9	-5	.949	-15	3-188/2-15,1-11,DP	-6.4
■ **JUAN CASTILLO**	Castillo, Juan (Bryas) b: 1/25/62, San Pedro De Macoris, D.R. BB/TR, 5'11", 162 lbs. Deb: 4/12/86																						
1986	Mil-A	26	54	6	9	0	1	0	5	5	12	.167	.250	.204	24	-6	1	1	-0	1.000	5	2-17/S-4,3-2,O-1,D	-0.1
1987	Mil-A	116	321	44	72	11	4	3	28	33	76	.224	.303	.312	62	-17	15	7	0	.973	-6	2-97,S-13/3-7	-1.7
1988	Mil-A	54	90	10	20	0	0	0	2	3	14	.222	.247	.222	32	-8	2	0	1	.932	7	2-18,3-17,S-13,/OD	0.0
1989	Mil-A	3	4	0	0	0	0	0	3	0	2	.000	.000	.000	-99	-1	0	0	0	1.000	1	/2-3	0.0
Total	4	199	469	60	101	11	5	3	38	41	104	.215	.284	.279	51	-32	18	8	1	.972	6	2-135/S-30,3-26,DO	-1.8
■ **LUIS CASTILLO**	Castillo, Luis Antonio (Donato) b: 9/12/75, San Pedro De Macoris, D.R. BB/TR, 5'11", 145 lbs. Deb: 8/8/96																						
1996	Fla-N	41	164	26	43	2	1	1	8	14	46	.262	.320	.305	68	-7	17	4	3	.986	1	2-41	-0.1
1997	Fla-N	75	263	27	63	8	0	0	8	27	53	.240	.310	.270	56	-16	16	10	-1	.971	-7	2-70	-2.0
1998	Fla-N	44	153	21	31	3	2	1	10	22	33	.203	.307	.268	53	-10	3	0	1	.975	-2	2-44	-0.8
Total	3	160	580	74	137	13	3	2	26	63	132	.236	.312	.279	59	-34	36	14	2	.977	-8	2-155	-2.9
■ **MARTY CASTILLO**	Castillo, Martin Horace b: 1/16/57, Long Beach, Cal. BR/TR, 6'1", 190 lbs. Deb: 8/19/81																						
1981	Det-A	6	8	1	1	0	0	0	0	0	2	.125	.125	.125	-27	-1	0	0	0	1.000	2	/3-4,C-1,O-1	0.1
1982	Det-A	1	0	0	0	0	0	0	0	0	0	—	—	—	—	0	0	0	0	1.000	-0	/C-1	0.0
1983	Det-A	67	119	10	23	4	0	2	10	7	22	.193	.238	.277	42	-9	2	0	1	.990	4	3-58,C-10	-0.5
1984	*Det-A	70	141	16	33	5	2	4	17	10	33	.234	.285	.383	83	-3	1	0	0	.970	2	C-36,3-33/D-1	0.0
1985	Det-A	57	84	4	10	2	0	2	5	2	19	.119	.140	.214	-5	-12	0	2	-1	.977	7	C-32,3-25	-0.5
Total	5	201	352	31	67	11	2	8	32	19	76	.190	.232	.301	46	-26	3	2	-0	.978	15	3-120/C-80,D-1,O-1	-0.9
■ **CARMEN CASTILLO**	Castillo, Monte Carmelo b: 6/8/58, San Pedro De Macoris, D.R. BR/TR, 6'1", 190 lbs. Deb: 7/17/82																						
1982	Cle-A	47	120	11	25	4	0	2	11	6	17	.208	.258	.292	51	-8	0	0	0	.978	-3	O-43/D-2	-1.2
1983	Cle-A	23	36	9	10	2	1	1	3	4	6	.278	.366	.472	124	1	1	1	-0	.929	-1	O-19/D-1	0.0
1984	Cle-A	87	211	36	55	9	2	10	36	21	32	.261	.333	.464	116	4	1	3	-2	.933	-6	O-70/D-2	-0.5
1985	Cle-A	67	184	27	45	5	1	11	25	11	40	.245	.298	.462	105	1	3	0	1	.953	-2	O-51/D-9	-0.2
1986	Cle-A	85	205	34	57	9	0	8	32	9	48	.278	.312	.439	103	0	2	1	0	.939	-2	O-37,D-35	-0.3
1987	Cle-A	89	220	27	55	17	0	11	31	16	52	.250	.301	.477	101	-0	1	1	-0	1.000	-1	D-43,O-23	-0.3
1988	Cle-A	66	176	12	48	8	0	4	14	5	31	.273	.297	.386	87	-3	6	2	1	.933	-6	O-45/D-9	-1.0
1989	Min-A	94	218	23	56	13	3	8	33	15	40	.257	.308	.454	105	1	1	2	-1	.976	-3	O-67,D-16	-0.5
1990	Min-A	64	137	11	30	4	0	0	12	3	23	.219	.241	.248	35	-12	0	1	-1	.923	-5	D-35,O-21	-1.9
1991	Min-A	9	12	0	2	0	1	0	0	0	2	.167	.231	.333	52	-1	0	0	0	1.000	-1	/O-4,D-2	-0.2
Total	10	631	1519	190	383	71	8	55	197	90	291	.252	.300	.418	93	-18	15	11	-2	.953	-30	O-380,D-154	-6.1
■ **JOHN CASTINO**	Castino, John Anthony b: 10/23/54, Evanston, Ill. BR/TR, 5'11", 175 lbs. Deb: 4/6/79																						
1979	Min-A	148	393	49	112	13	8	5	52	27	72	.285	.333	.397	92	-5	5	2	0	.963	18	*3-143/S-5	1.3
1980	Min-A	150	546	67	165	17	7	13	64	29	67	.302	.337	.430	101	-0	7	5	-1	.961	**28**	*3-138,S-18	2.6
1981	Min-A	101	381	41	102	13	**9**	6	36	18	52	.268	.303	.396	94	-4	4	5	-2	**.975**	11	3-98/2-4	0.4
1982	Min-A	117	410	48	99	12	6	6	37	36	51	.241	.306	.344	76	-13	2	5	-2	.995	4	2-96,3-21/O-6,D-1	-0.8
1983	Min-A	142	563	83	156	30	4	11	57	62	54	.277	.350	.403	103	3	4	2	0	.990	7	*2-132/3-8,D-1	1.6
1984	Min-A	8	27	5	12	1	0	0	3	5	2	.444	.531	.481	174	3	0	0	0	1.000	-1	/3-8	0.2
Total	6	666	2320	293	646	86	34	41	249	177	298	.278	.331	.398	95	-16	22	19	-5	.967	67	3-416,2-232/SOD	5.3
■ **VINCE CASTINO**	Castino, Vincent Charles b: 10/11/17, Willisville, Ill. d: 3/6/67, Sacramento, Cal. BR/TR, 5'9", 175 lbs. Deb: 6/24/43																						
1943	Chi-A	33	101	14	23	1	0	2	16	12	11	.228	.310	.297	78	-3	0	0	0	.971	-9	C-30	-1.1
1944	Chi-A	29	78	8	18	5	0	0	3	10	13	.231	.326	.295	79	-2	0	1	-1	.990	1	C-26	0.0
1945	Chi-A	26	36	2	8	1	0	0	4	3	7	.222	.282	.250	56	-2	0	0	0	.951	-2	C-25	-0.4
Total	3	88	215	24	49	7	0	2	23	25	31	.228	.311	.288	75	-7	0	1	-1	.976	-11	/C-81	-1.5
■ **DON CASTLE**	Castle, Donald Hardy b: 2/1/50, Kokomo, Ind. BL/TL, 6'1", 205 lbs. Deb: 9/11/73																						
1973	Tex-A	4	13	0	4	1	0	0	2	1	3	.308	.357	.385	114	0	0	0	0	.000	0	/D-3	0.0
■ **JOHN CASTLE**	Castle, John Francis b: 6/1/1883, Honey Brook, Pa. d: 4/13/29, Philadelphia, Pa. 5'10.5", Deb: 4/30/10																						
1910	Phi-N	3	4	1	1	0	0	0	0	0	0	.250	.250	.250	44	-0	1			.000	-1	/O-2	-0.1
■ **FOSTER CASTLEMAN**	Castleman, Foster Ephraim b: 1/1/31, Nashville, Tenn. BR/TR, 6', 175 lbs. Deb: 8/4/54																						
1954	NY-N	13	12	0	3	0	0	0	1	0	3	.250	.308	.250	47	-1	0	0	0	.000	0	/3-2	-0.1
1955	NY-N	15	28	3	6	1	0	2	4	2	4	.214	.267	.464	89	-1	0	0	0	1.000	-3	/2-6,3-1	-0.3
1956	NY-N	124	385	33	87	16	3	14	45	15	50	.226	.259	.392	72	-16	2	1	0	.947	7	*3-107/S-2,2-1	-0.9
1957	NY-N	18	37	7	6	2	0	1	1	2	8	.162	.205	.297	33	-4	0	0	0	.867	-2	/3-7,2-1,S-1	-0.6
1958	Bal-A	98	200	15	34	5	0	3	14	16	34	.170	.242	.240	35	-18	2	0	1	.964	-19	S-91/2-4,3-4,O-1	-3.2
Total	5	268	662	58	136	24	3	20	65	35	99	.205	.252	.341	60	-39	4	1	1	.944	-17	3-121/S-94,2-12,O-1	-5.1
■ **JUAN CASTRO**	Castro, Juan Gabriel b: 6/20/72, Los Mochis, Mex. BR/TR, 5'10", 165 lbs. Deb: 9/2/95																						
1995	LA-N	11	4	0	1	0	0	0	0	1	1	.250	.400	.250	84	-0	0	0	0	1.000	2	/3-7,S-4	0.2
1996	*LA-N	70	132	16	26	5	3	0	5	10	27	.197	.254	.280	44	-11	1	0	0	.982	-4	S-30,3-23/2-9,O-1	-1.2
1997	LA-N	40	75	3	11	3	1	0	4	7	20	.147	.220	.213	15	-10	0	0	0	1.000	3	S-22,2-14/3-3	-0.5
1998	LA-N	89	220	25	43	7	0	2	14	15	37	.195	.247	.255	33	-22	0	0	0	.954	14	S-47,2-38,3-12	-0.3
Total	4	210	431	44	81	15	4	2	23	33	85	.188	.246	.255	34	-43	1	0	0	.972	16	S-103/2-61,3-45,O-1	-1.8
■ **LUIS CASTRO**	Castro, Luis Manuel "Jud" b: 1877, Colombia d: Venezuela BR/TR, 5'7", Deb: 4/23/02																						
1902	Phi-A	42	143	18	35	8	1	1	15	4		.245	.265	.336	63	-8	2			.918	-15	2-36/O-3,S-1	-2.0
■ **FRANK CATALANOTTO**	Catalanotto, Frank John b: 4/27/74, Smithtown, N.Y. BL/TR, 6', 170 lbs. Deb: 9/3/97																						
1997	Det-A	13	26	2	8	2	0	0	3	3	7	.308	.379	.385	101	0	0	0	0	1.000	-1	/2-6,D-3	0.0
1998	Det-A	89	213	23	60	13	2	6	25	12	39	.282	.332	.446	99	-1	3	2	-0	.974	-1	2-31,D-23,1-18,/3-3	-0.3
Total	2	102	239	25	68	15	2	6	28	15	46	.285	.337	.439	99	-0	3	2	-0	.978	-2	/2-37,D-26,1-18,3-3	-0.3
■ **DANNY CATER**	Cater, Danny Anderson b: 2/25/40, Austin, Tex. BR/TR, 5'11.5", 180 lbs. Deb: 4/14/64																						
1964	Phi-N	60	152	13	45	9	1	1	13	7	15	.296	.327	.388	102	0	1	0	0	.981	-1	O-39/1-7,3-1	-0.2
1965	Chi-A	142	514	74	139	18	4	14	55	33	65	.270	.318	.403	110	5	3	3	-1	.978	-9	*O-127,3-11/1-3	-1.2
1966	Chi-A	21	60	3	11	1	1	0	4	0	10	.183	.197	.233	25	-6	3	1	0	.909	-3	O-18	-1.1
	KC-A	116	425	47	124	16	3	7	52	28	37	.292	.337	.393	113	6	1	4	-2	.994	-5	1-53,3-42,O-22	-0.6
	Yr	137	485	50	135	17	4	7	56	28	47	.278	.320	.373	102	1	4	5	-2	.994	-8	1-53,3-42,O-40	-1.7
1967	KC-A	142	529	55	143	17	4	4	46	34	56	.270	.319	.340	98	-2	4	5	-2	.916	-15	3-56,O-55,1-44	-2.6
1968	Oak-A	147	504	53	146	28	3	6	62	35	43	.290	.338	.393	127	15	8	7	-2	**.995**	-4	*1-121,O-20/2-1	0.0
1969	Oak-A	152	584	64	153	24	2	10	76	28	40	.262	.298	.361	87	-12	1	4	-2	.992	6	*1-132,O-20/2-4	-2.0
1970	NY-A	155	582	64	175	26	5	6	76	34	44	.301	.341	.393	108	5	4	2	0	.992	-4	*1-131,3-42/O-7	-1.0
1971	NY-A	121	428	39	118	16	5	4	50	19	25	.276	.310	.364	96	-4	0	3	-2	.995	8	1-78,3-52	-0.4
1972	Bos-A	92	317	32	75	17	1	8	39	15	33	.237	.275	.372	87	-6	0	1	-1	.993	6	1-90	-0.9

YEAR	TM/L	G	AB	R	H	2B	3B	HR	RBI	BB	SO	AVG	OBP	SLG	PRO+	BR/A	SB	CS	SBR	FA	FR	G/POS	TPR
1973	Bos-A	63	195	30	61	12	0	1	24	10	22	.313	.350	.390	102	0	0	0	0	.997	1	1-37,3-21/D-3	-0.1
1974	Bos-A	56	126	14	31	5	0	5	20	10	13	.246	.312	.405	98	-1	1	0	0	1.000	1	1-23,D-14	-0.1
1975	StL-N	22	35	3	8	2	0	0	2	1	3	.229	.250	.286	47	-3	0	0	0	.981	0	1-12	-0.3
Total	12	1289	4451	491	1229	191	29	66	519	254	406	.276	.318	.377	102	-1	26	30	-10	.994	-20	1-731,O-308,3/D2	-10.5

■ ELI CATES

Cates, Eli Eldo b: 1/26/1877, Greens Fork, Ind. d: 5/29/64, Anderson, Ind. BR/TR, 5'9.5", 175 lbs. Deb: 4/20/08

YEAR	TM/L	G	AB	R	H	2B	3B	HR	RBI	BB	SO	AVG	OBP	SLG	PRO+	BR/A	SB	CS	SBR	FA	FR	G/POS	TPR
1908	Was-A	40	59	5	11	1	1	0	3	6		.186	.273	.237	72	-2	0			.907	-0	P-19/2-3	-0.2

■ TED CATHER

Cather, Theodore Physick b: 5/20/1889, Chester, Pa. d: 4/9/45, Elkton, Md. BR/TR, 5'10.5", 178 lbs. Deb: 9/23/12

YEAR	TM/L	G	AB	R	H	2B	3B	HR	RBI	BB	SO	AVG	OBP	SLG	PRO+	BR/A	SB	CS	SBR	FA	FR	G/POS	TPR
1912	StL-N	5	19	4	8	1	1	0	2	0	4	.421	.421	.579	176	2	1			.944	2	/O-5	0.3
1913	StL-N	67	183	16	39	8	4	0	12	9	24	.213	.250	.301	58	-11	7			.915	-7	O-57/P-1,1-1	-2.1
1914	StL-N	39	99	11	27	7	0	0	13	3	15	.273	.294	.343	90	-2	4			.981	0	O-28	-0.3
	*Bos-N	50	145	19	43	11	2	0	27	7	28	.297	.338	.400	120	3	7			.953	-9	O-48	-0.8
	Yr	89	244	30	70	18	2	0	40	10	43	.287	.320	.377	108	1	11			.966	-9	O-76	-1.1
1915	Bos-N	40	102	10	21	3	1	2	18	15	19	.206	.319	.314	96	-0	2	4	-2	.902	-7	O-32	-1.2
Total	4	201	548	60	138	30	8	2	72	34	90	.252	.300	.347	91	-7	21	4		.938	-21	O-170/1-1,P-1	-4.1

■ HOWDY CATON

Caton, James Howard "Buster" b: 7/16/1896, Zanesville, Ohio d: 1/8/48, Zanesville, Ohio BR/TR, 5'6", 165 lbs. Deb: 9/17/17

YEAR	TM/L	G	AB	R	H	2B	3B	HR	RBI	BB	SO	AVG	OBP	SLG	PRO+	BR/A	SB	CS	SBR	FA	FR	G/POS	TPR
1917	Pit-N	14	57	6	12	1	2	0	4	6	7	.211	.286	.298	77	-2	0			.895	-2	S-14	-0.4
1918	Pit-N	80	303	37	71	5	7	0	17	32	16	.234	.312	.297	83	-5	12			.928	-7	S-79	-1.0
1919	Pit-N	39	102	13	18	1	2	0	5	12	10	.176	.263	.225	46	-6	2			.927	-11	S-17,3-14/O-1	-1.8
1920	Pit-N	98	352	29	83	11	5	0	27	33	19	.236	.305	.295	71	-13	4	9	-4	.929	-22	S-96	-3.4
Total	4	231	814	85	184	18	16	0	53	83	52	.226	.301	.287	72	-26	18	9		.926	-43	S-206/3-14,O-1	-6.6

■ TOM CATTERSON

Catterson, Thomas Henry b: 8/25/1884, Warwick, R.I. d: 2/5/20, Portland, Maine BL/TL, 5'10", 170 lbs. Deb: 9/19/08

YEAR	TM/L	G	AB	R	H	2B	3B	HR	RBI	BB	SO	AVG	OBP	SLG	PRO+	BR/A	SB	CS	SBR	FA	FR	G/POS	TPR
1908	Bro-N	19	68	5	13	1	1	1	2	5		.191	.257	.279	74	-2	0			.976	0	O-18	-0.3
1909	Bro-N	9	18	0	4	0	0	0	1	3		.222	.333	.222	75	-0	0			.833	-2	/O-6	-0.3
Total	2	28	86	5	17	1	1	1	3	8		.198	.274	.267	75	-2	0			.957	-2	/O-24	-0.6

■ JAKE CAULFIELD

Caulfield, John Joseph b: 11/23/17, Los Angeles, Cal. d: 12/16/86, San Francisco, Cal BR/TR, 5'11", 170 lbs. Deb: 4/24/46

YEAR	TM/L	G	AB	R	H	2B	3B	HR	RBI	BB	SO	AVG	OBP	SLG	PRO+	BR/A	SB	CS	SBR	FA	FR	G/POS	TPR
1946	Phi-A	44	94	13	26	8	0	0	10	4	11	.277	.306	.362	87	-2	0	0	0	.929	-6	S-31/3-1	-0.7

■ WAYNE CAUSEY

Causey, James Wayne b: 12/26/36, Ruston, La. BL/TR, 5'10.5", 175 lbs. Deb: 6/5/55

YEAR	TM/L	G	AB	R	H	2B	3B	HR	RBI	BB	SO	AVG	OBP	SLG	PRO+	BR/A	SB	CS	SBR	FA	FR	G/POS	TPR
1955	Bal-A	68	175	14	34	2	1	1	9	17	25	.194	.269	.234	39	-15	0	1	-1	.912	-8	3-55/2-7,S-1	-2.4
1956	Bal-A	53	88	7	15	0	1	1	4	8	23	.170	.240	.227	26	-10	0	0	0	.980	2	3-30/2-7	-0.7
1957	Bal-A	14	10	2	2	0	0	0	1	5	2	.200	.500	.200	105	1	0	0	0	.960	3	/2-6,3-5	0.4
1961	KC-A	104	312	37	86	14	1	8	49	37	28	.276	.352	.404	100	0	0	0	0	.955	20	3-88,S-11/2-9	2.2
1962	KC-A	117	305	40	77	14	1	4	38	41	30	.252	.345	.344	82	-7	2	0	1	.953	2	S-51,3-26/2-9	0.1
1963	KC-A	139	554	72	155	32	4	8	44	56	54	.280	.346	.395	101	2	4	2	0	.978	5	*S-135/3-2	1.7
1964	KC-A	157	604	82	170	31	4	8	49	88	65	.281	.379	.386	110	12	0	1	-1	.967	-1	*S-131,2-17/3-9	2.2
1965	KC-A	144	513	48	134	17	8	3	34	61	48	.261	.342	.343	97	-1	1	3	-2	.972	-19	S-62,2-45,3-35	-1.5
1966	KC-A	28	79	1	18	0	0	0	5	7	6	.228	.291	.228	53	-5	1	0	0	.871	-6	3-15,S-10	-1.0
	Chi-A	78	164	23	40	8	2	0	13	24	13	.244	.340	.317	97	-0	2	0	1	.980	-16	2-60/S-1,3-1	-1.3
	Yr	106	243	24	58	8	2	0	18	31	19	.239	.325	.288	83	-5	3	0	1	.980	-21	2-60,3-16,S-11	-2.3
1967	Chi-A	124	292	21	66	10	3	1	28	32	35	.226	.305	.291	80	-7	2	5	-2	.978	-8	2-96/S-2	-1.4
1968	Chi-A	59	100	8	18	2	0	0	7	14	7	.180	.287	.200	49	-6	0	0	0	.971	-13	2-41	-2.0
	Cal-A	4	11	0	0	0	0	0	0	0	1	.000	.000	.000	-99	-3	0	0	0	1.000	1	/2-4	-0.2
	Yr	63	111	8	18	2	0	0	7	14	8	.162	.262	.180	36	-8	0	0	0	.975	-13	2-45	-2.2
	Atl-N	16	37	2	4	0	1	1	4	0	4	.108	.108	.243	3	-4	0	0	0	1.000	-4	/2-6,S-2,3-2	-1.0
Total	11	1105	3244	357	819	130	26	35	285	390	341	.252	.335	.341	89	-42	12	12	-4	.969	-42	S-406,2-307,3-268	-4.9

■ JOHN CAVANAUGH

Cavanaugh, John J. b: 6/5/1900, Scranton, Pa. d: 1/14/61, New Brunswick, N.J BR/TR, 5'9", 158 lbs. Deb: 7/7/19

YEAR	TM/L	G	AB	R	H	2B	3B	HR	RBI	BB	SO	AVG	OBP	SLG	PRO+	BR/A	SB	CS	SBR	FA	FR	G/POS	TPR
1919	Phi-N	1	1	0	0	0	0	0	0	0	1	.000	.000	.000	-93	-0	0			.000	0	/3-1	0.0

■ PHIL CAVARRETTA

Cavarretta, Philip Joseph b: 7/19/16, Chicago, Ill. BL/TL, 5'11.5", 175 lbs. Deb: 9/16/34 MC

YEAR	TM/L	G	AB	R	H	2B	3B	HR	RBI	BB	SO	AVG	OBP	SLG	PRO+	BR/A	SB	CS	SBR	FA	FR	G/POS	TPR
1934	Chi-N	7	21	5	8	0	1	1	6	2	3	.381	.435	.619	182	2	1			1.000	1	/1-5	0.3
1935	*Chi-N	146	589	85	162	28	12	8	82	39	61	.275	.322	.404	93	-6	4			.986	2	*1-145	-2.0
1936	Chi-N	124	458	55	125	18	1	9	56	17	36	.273	.306	.376	81	-13	8			.987	-2	*1-115	-2.6
1937	Chi-N	106	329	43	94	18	7	5	56	32	35	.286	.349	.429	106	2	7			.972	-1	O-55,1-43	-0.5
1938	*Chi-N	92	268	29	64	11	4	1	28	14	27	.239	.287	.321	65	-13	4			.962	-7	O-52,1-28	-2.4
1939	Chi-N	22	55	4	15	3	1	0	0	4	3	.273	.322	.364	82	-1	2			.991	-1	1-13/O-1	-0.4
1940	Chi-N	65	193	34	54	11	4	2	22	31	18	.280	.388	.409	122	7	3			.991	-1	1-52	0.1
1941	Chi-N	107	346	46	99	18	4	6	40	53	28	.286	.384	.413	129	15	2			.992	-8	O-66,1-33	0.1
1942	Chi-N	136	482	59	130	28	4	3	54	71	42	.270	.365	.363	118	13	7			.989	6	O-70,1-61	1.2
1943	Chi-N	143	530	93	154	27	9	8	73	75	42	.291	.382	.421	134	24	3			.987	-11	*1-134/O-7	0.6
1944	Chi-N★	152	614	106	**197**	35	15	5	82	67	42	.321	.390	.451	137	31	4			.992	-7	*1-139,O-13	1.6
1945	*Chi-N†	132	498	94	177	34	10	6	97	81	34	**.355**	**.449**	.500	167	49	5			.993	-1	*1-120,O-11	3.8
1946	Chi-N★	139	510	89	150	28	10	8	78	88	54	.294	.401	.435	140	30	2			.967	1	O-86,1-51	2.4
1947	Chi-N★	127	459	56	144	22	5	2	63	58	35	.314	.391	.397	114	11	2			.977	-0	*O-100,1-24	0.4
1948	Chi-N	111	334	41	93	16	5	3	40	35	29	.278	.349	.383	102	1	4			.998	1	1-41,O-40	-0.1
1949	Chi-N	105	360	46	106	22	4	8	49	45	31	.294	.374	.444	122	12	2			.993	9	1-70,O-25	1.8
1950	Chi-N	82	256	49	70	11	1	10	31	40	31	.273	.376	.441	115	6	1			.986	-1	1-67/O-3	0.4
1951	Chi-N	89	206	24	64	7	1	6	28	27	28	.311	.393	.442	122	7	0	0	0	.994	4	1-53,M	0.8
1952	Chi-N	41	63	7	15	1	1	1	8	9	3	.238	.333	.333	84	-1	0	0	0	.991	1	1-13,M	-0.1
1953	Chi-N	27	21	3	6	3	0	0	3	6	3	.286	.444	.429	126	1	0	0	0	.000	0	HM	0.1
1954	Chi-A	71	158	21	50	6	0	3	24	26	12	.316	.419	.411	124	7	4	0	1	.993	-4	1-44/O-9	0.2
1955	Chi-A	6	4	1	0	0	0	0	0	0	1	.000	.000	.000	-97	-1	0	0	0	1.000	-0	/1-3	-0.1
Total	22	2030	6754	990	1977	347	99	95	920	820	598	.293	.372	.416	118	182	65	0		.990	-21	*1-1254,O-538	5.6

■ IKE CAVENEY

Caveney, James Christopher b: 12/10/1894, San Francisco, Cal d: 7/6/49, San Francisco, Cal BR/TR, 5'9", 168 lbs. Deb: 4/12/22

YEAR	TM/L	G	AB	R	H	2B	3B	HR	RBI	BB	SO	AVG	OBP	SLG	PRO+	BR/A	SB	CS	SBR	FA	FR	G/POS	TPR
1922	Cin-N	118	394	41	94	12	9	3	54	29	33	.239	.301	.338	66	-21	6	6	-2	.934	-6	*S-118	-1.6
1923	Cin-N	138	488	58	135	21	9	4	63	26	41	.277	.315	.381	84	-12	5	4	-1	.942	-0	*S-138	0.0
1924	Cin-N	95	337	36	92	19	1	4	32	14	21	.273	.310	.371	83	-9	2	3	-1	.924	3	S-90/2-5	0.3
1925	Cin-N	115	358	38	89	9	5	2	47	28	31	.249	.303	.318	60	-21	2	0	1	.941	9	*S-111	-0.1
Total	4	466	1577	173	410	61	24	13	196	97	126	.260	.307	.354	74	-63	15	13	-3	.936	6	S-457/2-5	-1.4

■ ANDUJAR CEDENO

Cedeno, Andujar (Donastorg) b: 8/21/69, LaRomana, D.R. BR/TR, 6'1", 168 lbs. Deb: 9/2/90 F

YEAR	TM/L	G	AB	R	H	2B	3B	HR	RBI	BB	SO	AVG	OBP	SLG	PRO+	BR/A	SB	CS	SBR	FA	FR	G/POS	TPR
1990	Hou-N	7	8	0	0	0	0	0	0	0	5	.000	.000	.000	00	-2	0	0	0	.833	-0	/S-3	-0.3
1991	Hou-N	67	251	27	61	13	2	9	36	9	74	.243	.272	.418	97	-3	4	3	-1	.930	-14	S-66	-1.3
1992	Hou-N	71	220	15	38	13	2	2	13	14	71	.173	.232	.277	46	-16	2	0	1	.959	-2	S-70	-1.5
1993	Hou-N	149	505	69	143	24	4	11	56	48	97	.283	.349	.412	107	5	9	7	-2	.955	-25	*S-149/3-1	-1.1
1994	Hou-N	98	342	38	90	26	0	9	49	29	79	.263	.335	.418	100	-1	1	1	-0	.947	1	S-95	0.8
1995	SD-N	120	390	42	82	16	2	6	31	28	92	.210	.272	.308	54	-26	5	3	-0	.965	-7	*S-116/3-1	-2.4
1996	SD-N	49	154	10	36	2	1	3	18	9	32	.234	.280	.318	61	-9	3	2	-0	.946	4	S-47/3-2	-0.2
	Det-A	52	179	19	35	4	2	7	20	4	37	.196	.213	.358	41	-17	2	1	0	.948	-1	S-51/3-1	-1.3
	Hou-N	3	2	1	0	0	0	0	0	2	1	.000	.500	.000	50	0	0	0	0	1.000	3	/S-2,3-1	0.3
Total	7	616	2051	221	485	98	13	47	223	143	488	.236	.293	.366	78	-69	26	17	-2	.952	-43	S-599/3-6	-7.0

■ CESAR CEDENO

Cedeno, Cesar (Encarnacion) b: 2/25/51, Santo Domingo, D.R. BR/TR, 6'2", 195 lbs. Deb: 6/20/70

YEAR	TM/L	G	AB	R	H	2B	3B	HR	RBI	BB	SO	AVG	OBP	SLG	PRO+	BR/A	SB	CS	SBR	FA	FR	G/POS	TPR
1970	Hou-N	90	355	46	110	21	4	7	42	15	57	.310	.341	.451	115	6	17	4	3	.968	3	O-90	0.7
1971	Hou-N	161	611	85	161	**40**	6	10	81	25	102	.264	.296	.398	97	-5	20	9	1	.989	-2	*O-157/1-2	-1.5
1972	Hou-N★	139	559	103	179	**39**	8	22	82	56	62	.320	.387	.537	163	45	55	21	4	.981	11	*O-137	**5.6**

YEAR	TM/L	G	AB	R	H	2B	3B	HR	RBI	BB	SO	AVG	OBP	SLG	PRO+	BR/A	SB	CS	SBR	FA	FR	G/POS	TPR

■ COZY DOLAN　Dolan, Patrick Henry　b: 12/3/1872, Cambridge, Mass.　d: 3/29/07, Louisville, Ky.　BL/TL, 5'10", 160 lbs.　Deb: 4/26/1895

1895	Bos-N	26	83	12	20	4	1	0	7	6	7	.241	.300	.313	54	-6	3			.949	3	P-25/O-1	-0.1
1896	Bos-N	6	14	4	2	0	0	0	0	0	1	.143	.143	.143	-23	-3	0			.765	-0	/P-6	0.0
1900	Chi-N	13	48	5	13	1	0	0	2	2		.271	.300	.292	66	-2	2			.826	-2	O-13	-0.4
1901	Chi-N	43	171	29	45	1	2	0	16	7		.263	.296	.292	74	-6	3			.878	2	O-41	-0.7
	Bro-N	66	253	33	66	11	1	0	29	17		.261	.313	.312	79	-7	7			.967	-2	O-64	-1.3
	Yr	109	424	62	111	12	3	0	45	24		.262	.306	.304	77	-12	10			.931	0	*O-105	-2.0
1902	Bro-N	141	592	72	166	16	7	1	54	33		.280	.324	.336	103	1	24			.936	-9	*O-141	-1.8
1903	Chi-N	27	104	16	27	5	1	0	7	6		.260	.313	.327	96	-0	5			.971	2	1-19/O-4	0.1
	Cin-N	93	385	64	111	20	3	0	58	28		.288	.340	.356	88	-7	11			.937	-7	O-93	-1.9
1904	Cin-N	129	465	88	132	8	10	6	51	39		.284	.342	.383	113	6	19			.939	-4	*O-102,1-24	-0.4
1905	Cin-N	22	77	7	18	2	1	0	4	7		.234	.306	.286	69	-3	2			.965	-1	1-13/O-9	-0.8
	Bos-N	112	433	44	119	11	7	3	48	27		.275	.322	.353	103	1	21			.946	4	*O-111/P-2,1-2	0.0
	Yr	134	510	51	137	13	8	3	52	34		.269	.319	.343	97	-2	23			.931	0	*O-120,1-15/P-2	-0.8
1906	Bos-N	152	549	54	136	20	4	0	39	55		.248	.318	.299	95	-2	17			.928	-2	*O-144/2-7,P-2,1-1	-1.2
Total	9	830	3174	428	855	99	37	10	315	227	8	.269	.322	.333	94	-27	114			.931	-18	O-723/1-59,P-35,2-7	-8.5

■ TOM DOLAN　Dolan, Thomas J.　b: 1/10/1859, New York, N.Y.　d: 1/16/13, St.Louis, Mo.　BR/TR,　Deb: 9/30/1879

1879	Chi-N	1	4	0	0	0	0	0	0	0	2	.000	.000	.000	-94	-1				1.000	1	/C-1	0.0
1882	Buf-N	22	89	12	14	0	1	0	8	2	11	.157	.176	.180	14	-8				.941	-8	C-18/O-4,3-2	-1.5
1883	StL-a	81	295	32	63	9	2	1	18	9		.214	.237	.268	59	-14				.957	13	C-42,O-40/P-1	0.0
1884	StL-a	35	137	19	36	6	2	0		6		.263	.299	.336	103	0				.873	-6	C-34/O-2	-0.3
	StL-U	19	69	9	13	3	0	0		4		.188	.233	.232	40	-7				.897	11	C-14/3-3,O-2	0.4
1885	StL-N	3	9	1	2	0	0	0		2	1	.222	.364	.222	99	0				.810	-1	/C-3	0.0
1886	StL-N	15	44	8	11	3	0	0	1	7	9	.250	.353	.318	113	1	2			.928	6	C-15	0.8
	Bal-a	38	125	13	19	3	2	0	12	8		.152	.203	.208	30	-10	8			.918	-6	C-35/O-3	-1.1
1888	StL-a	11	36	1	7	1	0	0	1	1		.194	.216	.222	37	-3	1			.914	-0	C-11	-0.3
Total	7	225	808	95	165	25	7	1	40	39	23	.204	.242	.256	57	-42	11			.916	8	C-173/O-51,3-5,P-1	-1.9

■ LESTER DOLE　Dole, Lester Carrington　b: 7/8/1855, Meriden, Conn.　d: 12/10/18, Concord, N.H.　5'11",　Deb: 5/27/1875

| 1875 | NH-n | 1 | 4 | 1 | 2 | 0 | 0 | 0 | 0 | 0 | 0 | .500 | .500 | .500 | 285 | 1 | 0 | 0 | 0 | .750 | 0 | /O-1 | 0.1 |

■ FRANK DOLJACK　Doljack, Frank Joseph "Dolie"　b: 10/5/07, Cleveland, Ohio　d: 1/23/48, Cleveland, Ohio　BR/TR, 5'11", 175 lbs.　Deb: 9/4/30

1930	Det-A	20	74	10	19	5	1	3	17	2	11	.257	.286	.473	87	-2	0	1	-1	.930	1	O-20	-0.3
1931	Det-A	63	187	20	52	13	3	4	20	15	17	.278	.335	.444	100	-1	3	2	-0	.925	3	O-54	-0.1
1932	Det-A	8	26	5	10	1	0	1	7	2	2	.385	.429	.538	143	2	1	0	0	1.000	-2	O-6	0.0
1933	Det-A	42	147	18	42	0	0	0	22	14	13	.286	.348	.347	83	-3	2	6	-3	.941	2	O-37	-0.6
1934	*Det-A	56	120	15	28	7	1	1	19	13	15	.233	.313	.333	67	-6	2	1	0	.943	-3	O-30/1-3	-0.9
1943	Cle-A	3	7	0	0	0	0	0	0	1	2	.000	.125	.000	-66	-1	0	0	0	1.000	-1	/O-2	-0.2
Total	6	192	561	68	151	31	7	9	85	47	60	.269	.329	.398	87	-12	8	10	-4	.934	-0	O-149/1-3	-2.1

■ ART DOLL　Doll, Arthur James "Moose"　b: 5/7/13, Chicago, Ill.　d: 4/28/78, Calumet City, Ill.　BR/TR, 6'1", 190 lbs.　Deb: 9/21/35

1935	Bos-N	3	10	0	1	0	0	0	0	0	1	.100	.100	.100	-50	-2	0			.867	0	/C-3	-0.2
1936	Bos-N	1	2	0	0	0	0	0	0	0	0	.000	.000	.000	-99	-1	0			1.000	-0	/P-1	0.0
1938	Bos-N	3	1	0	1	0	0	0	0	0	0	1.000	1.000	1.000	501	1	0			1.000	0	/P-3	0.0
Total	3	7	13	0	2	0	0	0	0	0	3	.154	.154	.154	-18	-2	0			1.000	0	/P-4,C-3	-0.2

■ SHE DONAHUE　Donahue, Charles Michael　b: 6/29/1877, Oswego, N.Y.　d: 8/28/47, New York, N.Y.　BR/TR, 5'9",　Deb: 4/29/04

1904	StL-N	4	15	1	4	0	0	0	2	0		.267	.267	.267	68	-1	3			.846	-3	/2-3,S-1	-0.4
	Phi-N	58	200	21	43	4	0	0	14	3		.215	.227	.235	44	-13	7			.857	-17	S-29,3-24/1-3,2-2	-3.1
	Yr	62	215	22	47	4	0	0	16	3		.219	.229	.237	46	-14	10			.852	-20	S-30,3-24/2-5,1-3	-3.5

■ JIM DONAHUE　Donahue, James Augustus　b: 1/8/1862, Lockport, Ill.　d: 4/19/35, Lockport, Ill.　BR/TR, 6', 175 lbs.　Deb: 4/19/1886

1886	NY-a	49	186	14	37	0	0	0	9	10		.199	.251	.199	44	-11	1			.803	-2	O-32,C-19	-1.1
1887	NY-a	60	220	33	62	4	1	1	29	21		.282	.350	.323	92	-1	6			.890	-8	C-51/O-5,1-4,3-1,2	-0.3
1888	KC-a	88	337	29	79	11	3	1	28	21		.234	.281	.294	79	-9	12			.902	-11	C-67,O-18/3-5,2-1	-1.3
1889	KC-a	67	252	30	59	5	4	0	32	21	20	.234	.293	.286	61	-13	12			.887	-8	C-46,O-14,3-10	-1.5
1891	Col-a	77	280	27	61	4	3	0	35	31	18	.218	.298	.254	62	-13	2			.942	3	C-75/O-1,1-1	-0.3
Total	5	341	1275	133	298	24	11	2	133	104	38	.234	.295	.275	69	-48	33			.911	-25	C-258/O-70,3-16,12	-4.5

■ JIGGS DONAHUE　Donahue, John Augustus　b: 7/13/1879, Springfield, Ohio　d: 7/19/13, Columbus, Ohio　BL/TL, 6'1", 178 lbs.　Deb: 9/10/00　F

1900	Pit-N	3	10	1	2	0	1	0	3	0		.200	.200	.400	63	-1	1			.889	-1	/C-2,O-1	-0.2
1901	Pit-N	2	0	0	0	0	0	0	0	0		—	—	—	—	0	0			.000	-1	/C-1,O-1	-0.1
	Mil-A	37	107	10	34	5	4	0	16	10		.318	.387	.439	135	5	4			.933	-2	C-19,1-13	0.5
1902	StL-A	30	89	11	21	1	1	1	7	12		.236	.327	.303	76	-2	2			.956	-1	C-23/1-5	-0.1
1904	Chi-A	102	367	46	91	9	7	1	48	25		.248	.298	.319	99	-1	18			.979	7	*1-101	0.4
1905	Chi-A	149	533	71	153	22	4	1	76	44		.287	.346	.349	126	16	32			**.988**	8	*1-149	2.1
1906	*Chi-A	154	556	70	143	17	7	1	57	48		.257	.320	.318	103	2	36			**.988**	9	*1-154	0.7
1907	Chi-A	157	609	75	158	16	4	0	68	28		.259	.295	.299	93	-6	27			**.994**	21	*1-157	1.1
1908	Chi-A	93	304	22	62	8	2	0	22	25		.204	.271	.243	69	-10	14			.994	5	1-83	-0.8
1909	Chi-A	2	4	0	0	0	0	0	2	1		.000	.200	.000	-38	-1	0			1.000	-0	/1-2	-0.1
	Was-A	84	283	13	67	12	1	0	28	22		.237	.294	.286	87	-4	9			.984	-4	1-81	-1.0
	Yr	86	287	13	67	12	1	0	30	23		.233	.293	.282	86	-5	9			.984	-4	1-83	-1.1
Total	9	813	2862	319	731	90	31	4	327	215		.255	.311	.313	99	-1	143			.987	40	1-745/C-45,O-2	2.5

■ JOHN DONAHUE　Donahue, John Frederick "Jiggs"　b: 4/19/1894, Roxbury, Mass.　d: 10/3/49, Boston, Mass.　BB/TR, 5'8", 170 lbs.　Deb: 9/25/23

| 1923 | Bos-A | 10 | 36 | 5 | 10 | 4 | 0 | 0 | 1 | 4 | 5 | .278 | .350 | .389 | 94 | -0 | 0 | 1 | -1 | 1.000 | 3 | /O-9 | 0.2 |

■ PAT DONAHUE　Donahue, Patrick William　b: 11/8/1884, Springfield, Ohio　d: 1/31/66, Springfield, Ohio　BR/TR, 6', 175 lbs.　Deb: 5/29/08　F

1908	Bos-A	35	86	8	17	2	0	1	6	9		.198	.289	.256	75	-2	0			.959	0	C-32/1-3	0.1
1909	Bos-A	64	176	14	42	4	1	2	25	17		.239	.309	.340	93	-1	2			.982	-3	C-58	0.1
1910	Bos-A	2	4	0	0	0	0	0	0	0		.000	.000	.000	-98	-1	0			1.000	0	/C-1	-0.1
	Phi-A	14	34	2	5	0	0	0	4	3		.147	.237	.147	21	-3	1			1.000	3	C-13	0.2
	Cle-A	2	6	0	1	0	0	0	0	0		.167	.167	.167	4	-1	0			1.000	-1	/C-2,1-1	-0.1
	Phi-A	1	1	0	0	0	0	0	0	0		.000	.000	.000	-99	-0	0			1.000	-1	/C-1	-0.1
	Yr	19	45	2	6	0	0	0	4	3		.133	.204	.133	6	-5	1			1.000	3	C-17/1-1	0.0
Total	3	118	307	24	65	6	1	3	35	29		.212	.288	.267	75	-8	3			.978	3	C-107/1-4	0.1

■ TIM DONAHUE　Donahue, Timothy Cornelius "Bridget"　b: 6/8/1870, Raynham, Mass.　d: 6/12/02, Taunton, Mass.　BL/TR, 5'11", 180 lbs.　Deb: 7/28/1891

1891	Bos-a	4	7	0	0	0	0	0	0	0	5	.000	.000	.000	-99	-2	0			.833	-1	/C-4	-0.3
1895	Chi-N	63	219	29	59	9	1	2	36	20	25	.269	.339	.347	73	-9	5			.915	-2	C-63	-0.4
1896	Chi-N	57	188	27	41	10	1	0	20	11	15	.218	.276	.282	45	-15	11			.934	5	C-57	-0.3
1897	Chi-N	58	188	28	45	7	3	0	21	9		.239	.281	.309	54	-13	5			.947	7	C-55/S-2,1-1	0.0
1898	Chi-N	122	396	52	87	12	3	0	39	49		.220	.318	.265	68	-15	17			.962	6	*C-122	0.3
1899	Chi-N	92	278	39	69	9	3	0	29	34		.248	.345	.302	80	-6	10			.951	4	C-91/1-1	0.4
1900	Chi-N	67	216	21	51	10	1	0	17	19		.236	.313	.292	70	-8	5			.928	-7	C-66/2-1	-0.9
1902	Was-A	3	8	0	2	0	0	0	1	0		.250	.250	.250	39	-1	0			1.000	0	/C-3	0.0
Total	8	466	1500	196	354	57	12	2	163	142	45	.236	.314	.294	66	-70	54			.943	11	C-461/1-2,S-2,2-1	-1.2

■ JOHN DONALDSON　Donaldson, John David　b: 5/5/43, Charlotte, N.C.　BL/TR, 5'11", 165 lbs.　Deb: 8/26/66

| 1966 | KC-A | 15 | 30 | 4 | 4 | 1 | 0 | 0 | 3 | 4 | | .133 | .212 | .133 | 2 | -4 | 1 | 0 | 0 | 1.000 | -2 | /2-9 | -0.6 |

YEAR	TM/L	G	AB	R	H	2B	3B	HR	RBI	BB	SO	AVG	OBP	SLG	PRO+	BR/A	SB	CS	SBR	FA	FR	G/POS	TPR
1973	Hou-N★	139	525	86	168	35	2	25	70	41	79	.320	.377	.537	151	34	56	15	8	.981	15	*O-136	5.3
1974	Hou-N★	160	610	95	164	29	5	26	102	64	103	.269	.342	.461	129	21	57	17	7	.993	21	*O-157	4.3
1975	Hou-N	131	500	93	144	31	3	13	63	62	52	.288	.374	.440	135	24	50	17	5	.982	4	*O-131	2.8
1976	Hou-N★	150	575	89	171	26	5	18	83	55	51	.297	.360	.454	143	30	58	15	8	.980	10	*O-146	4.4
1977	Hou-N	141	530	92	148	36	8	14	71	47	50	.279	.350	.457	126	18	61	14	10	**.997**	12	*O-137	3.4
1978	Hou-N	50	192	31	54	8	2	7	23	15	24	.281	.333	.453	127	6	23	2	6	.987	8	O-50	1.8
1979	Hou-N	132	470	57	123	27	4	6	54	64	52	.262	.354	.374	105	4	30	13	1	.981	-5	1-91,O-40	-0.7
1980	*Hou-N	137	499	71	154	32	8	10	73	66	72	.309	.390	.465	150	34	48	15	5	.977	8	*O-136	4.3
1981	*Hou-N	82	306	42	83	19	0	5	34	24	31	.271	.326	.382	106	2	12	7	-1	.991	-1	1-46,O-34	-0.4
1982	Cin-N	138	492	52	142	35	1	8	57	41	41	.289	.348	.413	110	6	16	11	-2	.990	4	*O-131/1-1	0.5
1983	Cin-N	98	332	40	77	16	0	9	39	33	53	.232	.307	.361	82	-8	13	9	-2	.993	2	O-73,1-17	-1.2
1984	Cin-N	110	380	59	105	24	2	10	47	25	54	.276	.323	.429	105	2	19	3	4	.980	-2	O-77,1-44	-0.1
1985	Cin-N	83	220	24	53	12	0	3	30	19	35	.241	.310	.336	77	-7	9	5	-0	.990	-1	O-53,1-34	-1.0
	*StL-N	28	76	14	33	4	1	6	19	5	7	.434	.469	.750	238	13	5	1	1	.993	-4	1-23/O-2	1.0
	Yr	111	296	38	86	16	1	9	49	24	42	.291	.350	.443	116	6	14	6	1	.993	-4	1-57,O-55	0.0
1986	LA-N	37	78	5	18	2	1	0	6	7	13	.231	.294	.282	64	-4	1	1	-0	.944	-4	O-31	-0.9
Total	17	2006	7310	1084	2087	436	60	199	976	664	938	.285	.350	.443	124	221	550	179	58	.985	79	*O-1718,1-258	28.3

■ DOMINGO CEDENO

Cedeno, Domingo Antonio (Donastorg) b: 11/4/68, LaRomana, D.R. BB/TR, 6′1″, 170 lbs. Deb: 5/19/93 F

YEAR	TM/L	G	AB	R	H	2B	3B	HR	RBI	BB	SO	AVG	OBP	SLG	PRO+	BR/A	SB	CS	SBR	FA	FR	G/POS	TPR
1993	Tor-A	15	46	5	8	0	0	0	7	1	10	.174	.191	.174	-1	-6	1	0	0	.973	-3	S-10/2-5	-0.8
1994	Tor-A	47	97	14	19	2	3	0	10	10	31	.196	.271	.278	42	-8	1	2	-1	.935	-3	2-28/S-8,3-6,O-1	-1.1
1995	Tor-A	51	161	18	38	6	1	4	14	10	35	.236	.289	.360	68	-8	0	1	-1	.980	4	S-30,2-20/3-1	-0.1
1996	Tor-A	77	282	44	79	10	2	2	17	15	60	.280	.321	.351	70	-13	5	3	-0	.969	-2	2-62/3-6,S-5	-1.0
	Chi-A	12	19	2	3	2	0	0	3	0	4	.158	.158	.263	4	-3	1	0	0	.000	-1	/2-2,S-2,D-1	-0.3
	Yr	89	301	46	82	12	2	2	20	15	64	.272	.311	.346	66	-15	6	3	0	.969	-3	2-64/S-7,3-6,D-1	-1.3
1997	Tex-A	113	365	49	103	19	6	4	36	27	77	.282	.335	.400	86	-7	3	3	-1	.960	-12	2-65,S-43/3-3,D-2	-1.3
1998	Tex-A	61	141	19	37	9	1	2	21	10	32	.262	.311	.383	76	-5	2	1	0	.963	-2	S-35,D-14/2-7	-0.5
Total	6	376	1111	151	287	48	13	12	108	73	249	.258	.308	.357	70	-51	13	10	-2	.964	-19	2-189,S-133/D30	-5.1

■ ROGER CEDENO

Cedeno, Roger Leandro b: 8/16/74, Valencia, Venez. BB/TR, 6′1″, 165 lbs. Deb: 6/20/95

YEAR	TM/L	G	AB	R	H	2B	3B	HR	RBI	BB	SO	AVG	OBP	SLG	PRO+	BR/A	SB	CS	SBR	FA	FR	G/POS	TPR
1995	LA-N	40	42	4	10	2	0	0	3	3	10	.238	.289	.286	57	-3	1	0	0	.977	-5	O-36	-0.8
1996	LA-N	86	211	26	52	11	1	2	18	24	47	.246	.326	.336	82	-6	5	1	1	.983	-5	O-71	-1.0
1997	LA-N	80	194	31	53	10	2	3	17	25	44	.273	.365	.392	106	2	9	1	2	.987	2	O-71	0.5
1998	LA-N	105	240	33	58	11	1	2	17	27	57	.242	.318	.321	72	-10	8	2	1	.978	-11	O-77	-2.0
Total	4	311	687	94	173	34	4	7	55	79	158	.252	.332	.344	84	-16	23	4	5	.983	-19	O-255	-3.3

■ ORLANDO CEPEDA

Cepeda, Orlando Manuel (Penne) "Baby Bull" or "Cha Cha" b: 9/17/37, Ponce, P.R. BR/TR, 6′2″, 210 lbs. Deb: 4/15/58 C

YEAR	TM/L	G	AB	R	H	2B	3B	HR	RBI	BB	SO	AVG	OBP	SLG	PRO+	BR/A	SB	CS	SBR	FA	FR	G/POS	TPR
1958	SF-N	148	603	88	188	**38**	4	25	96	29	84	.312	.346	.512	126	20	15	11	-2	.989	-3	*1-147	0.6
1959	SF-N★	151	605	92	192	35	4	27	105	33	100	.317	.358	.522	134	27	23	9	2	.984	-8	*1-122,O-44/3-4	1.2
1960	SF-N★	151	569	81	169	36	3	24	96	34	91	.297	.345	.497	135	25	15	6	1	.983	0	O-91,1-63	1.7
1961	SF-N★	152	585	105	182	28	4	**46**	**142**	39	91	.311	.363	.609	158	45	12	8	-1	.997	-3	1-81,O-80	3.0
1962	*SF-N★	162	625	105	191	26	1	35	114	37	97	.306	.350	.518	132	26	10	4	1	.991	-8	*1-160/O-2	0.8
1963	SF-N☆	156	579	100	183	33	4	34	97	37	70	.316	.367	.563	166	47	8	3	1	.985	-8	*1-150/O-3	3.4
1964	SF-N★	142	529	75	161	27	2	31	97	43	83	.304	.366	.539	148	33	9	4	0	.986	-4	*1-139/O-1	2.4
1965	SF-N	33	34	1	6	1	0	1	5	3	9	.176	.243	.294	49	-2	0	0	0	1.000	-0	/1-4,O-2	-0.3
1966	SF-N	19	49	5	14	2	0	3	15	4	11	.286	.352	.510	132	2	0	1	-1	.778	-3	/O-8,1-6	-0.2
	StL-N	123	452	65	137	24	0	17	58	34	68	.303	.369	.469	130	19	9	8	-2	.989	-6	*1-120	0.2
	Yr	142	501	70	151	26	0	20	73	38	79	.301	.367	.473	130	21	9	9	-3	.990	-9	*1-126/O-8	0.0
1967	*StL-N★	151	563	91	183	37	0	25	**111**	62	75	.325	.403	.524	166	49	11	2	2	.993	-0	*1-151	4.4
1968	*StL-N	157	600	71	149	26	2	16	73	43	96	.248	.308	.378	107	4	8	6	-1	.988	-5	*1-154	-1.6
1969	*Atl-N	154	573	74	147	28	2	22	88	55	76	.257	.327	.428	109	6	12	5	1	.994	3	*1-153	-0.3
1970	Atl-N	148	567	87	173	33	0	34	111	47	75	.305	.368	.543	133	25	6	5	-1	.992	3	*1-148	1.3
1971	Atl-N	71	250	31	69	10	1	14	44	22	29	.276	.335	.492	124	7	3	6	-3	.992	2	1-63	0.1
1972	Atl-N	28	84	6	25	3	0	4	9	7	17	.298	.352	.476	122	2	0	0	0	1.000	1	1-22	0.1
	Oak-A	3	3	0	0	0	0	0	0	0	0	.000	.000	.000	-99	-1	0	0	0	.000	0	H	-0.1
1973	Bos-A	142	550	51	159	25	0	20	86	50	81	.289	.352	.444	116	11	0	2	-1	.000	0	*D-142	0.6
1974	KC-A	33	107	3	23	5	0	1	18	9	16	.215	.282	.290	61	-5	1	0	0	.000	0	D-26	-0.6
Total	17	2124	7927	1131	2351	417	27	379	1365	588	1169	.297	.353	.499	133	338	142	80	-5	.990	-39	*1-1683,O-231,D/3	16.7

■ ED CERMAK

Cermak, Edward Hugo b: 3/10/1882, Cleveland, Ohio d: 11/22/11, Cleveland, Ohio BR/TR, 5′11″, 170 lbs. Deb: 9/9/01

YEAR	TM/L	G	AB	R	H	2B	3B	HR	RBI	BB	SO	AVG	OBP	SLG	PRO+	BR/A	SB	CS	SBR	FA	FR	G/POS	TPR
1901	Cle-A	1	4	0	0	0	0	0	0	0		.000	.000	.000	-99	-1	0			1.000	1	/O-1	0.0

■ RICK CERONE

Cerone, Richard Aldo b: 5/19/54, Newark, N.J. BR/TR, 5′11″, 192 lbs. Deb: 8/17/75

YEAR	TM/L	G	AB	R	H	2B	3B	HR	RBI	BB	SO	AVG	OBP	SLG	PRO+	BR/A	SB	CS	SBR	FA	FR	G/POS	TPR
1975	Cle-A	7	12	1	3	1	0	0	0	1	0	.250	.308	.333	81	-0	0	0	0	1.000	-1	/C-7	-0.1
1976	Cle-A	7	16	1	2	0	0	0	1	0	2	.125	.125	.125	-27	-3	0	0	0	.963	0	/C-6,D-1	-0.2
1977	Tor-A	31	100	7	20	4	0	1	10	6	12	.200	.245	.270	40	-8	0	0	0	.994	-2	C-31	-0.9
1978	Tor-A	88	282	25	63	8	2	3	20	23	32	.223	.284	.298	63	-14	0	3	-2	.992	-0	C-84/D-2	-1.5
1979	Tor-A	136	469	47	112	27	4	7	61	37	40	.239	.296	.358	75	-17	1	4	-2	.980	-8	*C-136	-2.2
1980	*NY-A	147	519	70	144	30	4	14	85	32	56	.277	.327	.432	108	4	1	3	-2	.990	6	*C-147	1.4
1981	*NY-A	71	234	23	57	13	2	2	21	12	24	.244	.280	.342	80	-7	0	2	-1	.992	-6	C-69	-1.2
1982	NY-A	89	300	29	68	10	0	5	28	19	27	.227	.275	.310	61	-16	0	2	-1	.989	-8	C-89	-2.2
1983	NY-A	80	246	18	54	7	0	2	22	15	29	.220	.267	.272	51	-17	0	0	0	.991	-0	C-78/3-1	-1.4
1984	NY-A	38	120	8	25	3	0	2	13	9	15	.208	.269	.283	55	-7	1	0	0	.996	3	C-38	-0.2
1985	Atl-N	96	282	15	61	9	0	3	25	29	25	.216	.292	.280	57	-16	0	3	-2	.986	-8	C-91	-2.2
1986	Mil-A	68	216	22	56	14	0	4	18	15	28	.259	.310	.380	84	-5	1	1	-0	.991	7	C-68	0.6
1987	NY-A	113	284	28	69	12	1	4	23	30	46	.243	.324	.335	76	-9	0	1	-1	**.998**	4	*C-111/P-2,1-2	0.1
1988	Bos-A	84	264	31	71	13	1	3	27	20	32	.269	.328	.360	89	-4	0	0	0	**1.000**	-5	C-83/D-1	-0.3
1989	Bos-A	102	296	28	72	16	1	4	48	34	40	.243	.325	.345	84	-6	0	0	0	.984	3	C-97/O-1,D-1	0.1
1990	NY-A	49	139	12	42	6	0	2	11	5	13	.302	.326	.388	99	-1	0	0	0	.995	-3	C-35/2-1,D-6	-0.2
1991	NY-N	90	227	18	62	13	0	2	16	30	24	.273	.360	.357	103	2	1	1	-0	.987	-2	C-81	0.4
1992	Mon-N	33	63	10	17	4	0	1	7	3	5	.270	.313	.381	97	-0	1	2	-1	1.000	1	C-28	0.0
Total	18	1329	4069	393	998	190	15	59	436	320	450	.245	.304	.343	78	-123	6	22	-11	.990	-19	*C-1279/D-11,1P2O3	-10.0

■ BOB CERV

Cerv, Robert Henry b: 5/5/26, Weston, Neb. BR/TR, 6′, 202 lbs. Deb: 8/1/51

YEAR	TM/L	G	AB	R	H	2B	3B	HR	RBI	BB	SO	AVG	OBP	SLG	PRO+	BR/A	SB	CS	SBR	FA	FR	G/POS	TPR
1951	NY-A	12	28	4	6	1	0	0	2	4	6	.214	.313	.250	55	-2	0	0	0	.875	-1	/O-9	-0.3
1952	NY-A	36	87	11	21	3	2	1	8	9	22	.241	.313	.356	91	-1	0	1	-1	1.000	-2	O-27	-0.5
1953	NY-A	8	6	0	0	0	0	0	0	1	1	.000	.143	.000	-61	-1	0	0	0	.000	0	H	-0.1
1954	NY-A	56	100	14	26	6	0	5	13	11	17	.260	.333	.470	122	3	0	2	-1	.897	-5	O-24	-0.4
1955	*NY-A	55	85	17	29	4	2	3	22	7	16	.341	.411	.541	157	7	4	0	1	1.000	-4	O-20	0.4
1956	*NY-A	54	115	16	35	5	6	3	25	18	13	.304	.398	.530	148	8	0	1	-1	.984	-4	O-44	0.2
1957	KC-A	124	345	35	94	14	2	11	44	20	57	.272	.314	.420	97	-2	1	1	-0	.964	-7	O-89	-1.5
1958	KC-A★	141	515	93	157	20	7	38	104	50	82	.305	.372	.592	158	39	3	3	-1	.985	20	*O-136	5.1
1959	KC-A	125	463	61	132	22	4	20	87	35	87	.285	.339	.479	120	11	3	2	-0	.980	6	*O-119	1.1
1960	KC-A	23	78	14	20	1	1	6	12	10	17	.256	.341	.526	130	3	0	0	0	.977	3	O-21	0.5
	*NY-A	87	216	32	54	11	1	8	28	30	36	.250	.349	.421	114	4	0	0	0	.982	4	O-51/1-3	0.5
	Yr	110	294	46	74	12	2	14	40	40	53	.252	.347	.449	119	7	0	0	0	.980	6	O-72/1-3	1.0
1961	LA-A	18	57	3	9	3	0	2	6	1	8	.158	.172	.316	25	-6	0	0	0	.944	-2	O-15	-1.0
	NY-A	57	118	17	32	5	1	6	20	12	17	.271	.344	.483	125	4	1	0	0	.983	1	O-30/1-3	0.4
	Yr	75	175	20	41	8	1	8	26	13	25	.234	.291	.429	91	-3	1	0	0	.974	-1	O-45/1-3	-0.6
1962	NY-A	14	17	1	2	1	0	0	0	2	3	.118	.250	.176	18	-2	0	0	0	1.000	-0	/O-3	-0.3

YEAR	TM/L	G	AB	R	H	2B	3B	HR	RBI	BB	SO	AVG	OBP	SLG	PRO+	BR/A	SB	CS	SBR	FA	FR	G/POS	TPR
	Hou-N	19	31	2	7	0	0	2	3	2	10	.226	.273	.419	89	-1	0	0	0	.833	-0	/O-6	-0.1
Total	12	829	2261	320	624	96	26	105	374	212	392	.276	.343	.481	122	63	12	10	-2	.976	8	O-594/1-6	4.0

■ RON CEY
Cey, Ronald Charles b: 2/15/48, Tacoma, Wash. BR/TR, 5'10", 185 lbs. Deb: 9/3/71

YEAR	TM/L	G	AB	R	H	2B	3B	HR	RBI	BB	SO	AVG	OBP	SLG	PRO+	BR/A	SB	CS	SBR	FA	FR	G/POS	TPR
1971	LA-N	2	2	0	0	0	0	0	0	0	2	.000	.000	.000	-99	-1	0	0	0	.000	0	H	-0.1
1972	LA-N	11	37	3	10	1	0	1	3	7	10	.270	.400	.378	125	2	0	0	0	.900	-2	3-11	-0.1
1973	LA-N	152	507	60	124	18	4	15	80	74	77	.245	.343	.385	106	5	1	1	-0	.961	16	*3-146	2.1
1974	*LA-N★	159	577	88	151	20	2	18	97	76	68	.262	.355	.397	115	12	1	1	-0	.959	17	*3-158	2.9
1975	LA-N★	158	566	72	160	29	2	25	101	78	74	.283	.376	.473	141	31	5	2	0	.960	-4	*3-158	2.8
1976	LA-N★	145	502	69	139	18	3	23	80	89	74	.277	.389	.462	144	31	0	4	-2	.965	11	*3-144	4.1
1977	*LA-N★	153	564	77	136	22	3	30	110	93	106	.241	.351	.450	114	11	3	4	-2	.964	17	*3-153	2.5
1978	*LA-N★	159	555	84	150	32	0	23	84	96	96	.270	.384	.452	134	28	2	5	-2	.966	5	*3-158	2.9
1979	LA-N★	150	487	77	137	20	1	28	81	86	85	.281	.391	.499	143	31	3	3	-1	**.977**	-1	*3-150	2.9
1980	LA-N	157	551	81	140	25	0	28	77	69	92	.254	.342	.452	122	16	2	2	-1	.972	7	*3-157	2.1
1981	*LA-N	85	312	42	90	15	2	13	50	40	55	.288	.375	.474	145	18	0	2	-1	.941	7	3-84	2.4
1982	LA-N	150	556	62	141	23	1	24	79	57	99	.254	.327	.428	113	8	3	2	-0	.963	11	*3-149	1.6
1983	Chi-N	159	581	73	160	33	1	24	90	62	85	.275	.350	.460	117	13	0	0	0	.955	-21	*3-157	-1.0
1984	*Chi-N	146	505	71	121	27	0	25	97	61	108	.240	.329	.442	105	3	3	2	-0	**.967**	-20	*3-144	-2.0
1985	Chi-N	145	500	64	116	18	2	22	63	58	106	.232	.317	.408	91	-6	1	1	-0	.943	-7	*3-140	-1.7
1986	Chi-N	97	256	42	70	21	0	13	36	44	66	.273	.386	.508	134	12	0	0	0	.952	-6	3-77	0.5
1987	Oak-A	45	104	12	23	6	0	4	11	22	32	.221	.362	.394	108	2	0	0	0	.982	-1	D-30/1-7,3-3	0.0
Total	17	2073	7162	977	1868	328	21	316	1139	1012	1235	.261	.357	.445	121	216	24	29	-10	.961	30	*3-1989/D-30,1-7	21.9

■ ELIO CHACON
Chacon, Elio (Rodriguez) b: 10/26/36, Caracas, Venez. d: 4/24/92, Caracas, Venez. BR/TR, 5'9", 160 lbs. Deb: 4/20/60

YEAR	TM/L	G	AB	R	H	2B	3B	HR	RBI	BB	SO	AVG	OBP	SLG	PRO+	BR/A	SB	CS	SBR	FA	FR	G/POS	TPR
1960	Cin-N	49	116	14	21	1	0	0	7	14	23	.181	.275	.190	29	-11	7	1	2	.980	5	2-43/O-2	-0.1
1961	*Cin-N	61	132	26	35	4	2	2	5	21	22	.265	.374	.371	97	0	1	4	-2	.989	0	2-42/O-7	0.2
1962	NY-N	118	368	49	87	10	3	2	27	76	64	.236	.369	.296	80	-7	12	7	-1	.961	-3	*S-110/2-2,3-1	-0.1
Total	3	228	616	89	143	15	5	4	39	111	109	.232	.353	.292	74	-18	20	12	-1	.985	3	S-110/2-87,O-9,3-1	0.0

■ CHET CHADBOURNE
Chadbourne, Chester James "Pop" b: 10/28/1884, Parkman, Me. d: 6/21/43, Los Angeles, Cal. BL/TR, 5'9", 170 lbs. Deb: 9/17/06

YEAR	TM/L	G	AB	R	H	2B	3B	HR	RBI	BB	SO	AVG	OBP	SLG	PRO+	BR/A	SB	CS	SBR	FA	FR	G/POS	TPR
1906	Bos-A	11	43	7	13	1	0	0	3	3		.302	.348	.326	111	1	1			.926	3	2-11/S-1	0.4
1907	Bos-A	10	38	0	11	0	0	0	1	7		.289	.400	.289	121	1	1			1.000	-0	O-10	0.1
1914	KC-F	147	581	92	161	22	8	1	37	69	49	.277	.359	.348	97	-10	42			.965	9	*O-146	-0.8
1915	KC-F	152	587	75	133	16	9	1	35	62	29	.227	.307	.290	71	-31	29			**.979**	1	*O-152	-4.2
1918	Bos-N	27	104	9	27	2	1	0	6	5	5	.260	.300	.298	86	-2	5			.925	-3	O-27	-0.7
Total	5	347	1353	183	345	41	18	2	82	146	83	.255	.333	.316	86	-41	78			.969	10	O-335/2-11,S-1	-5.2

■ DAVE CHALK
Chalk, David Lee b: 8/30/50, Del Rio, Tex. BR/TR, 5'10", 175 lbs. Deb: 9/4/73

YEAR	TM/L	G	AB	R	H	2B	3B	HR	RBI	BB	SO	AVG	OBP	SLG	PRO+	BR/A	SB	CS	SBR	FA	FR	G/POS	TPR
1973	Cal-A	24	69	14	16	2	0	0	6	9	13	.232	.329	.261	74	-2	0	0	0	.962	2	S-22	0.2
1974	Cal-A★	133	465	44	117	9	3	5	31	30	57	.252	.307	.316	84	-10	10	10	-3	.938	-2	S-99,3-38	-0.2
1975	Cal-A☆	149	513	59	140	24	2	3	56	66	49	.273	.358	.345	107	7	6	9	-4	.976	6	*3-149	0.9
1976	Cal-A	142	438	39	95	14	1	0	33	49	62	.217	.310	.253	71	-14	0	0	0	.971	5	*S-102,3-49	0.1
1977	Cal-A	149	519	58	144	27	2	3	45	52	69	.277	.349	.355	96	-1	12	8	-1	.948	-3	*3-141/2-7,S-4	-0.6
1978	Cal-A	135	470	42	119	12	0	1	34	38	34	.253	.318	.285	74	-15	5	8	-3	.955	-20	S-97,2-29,3-22,/D-1	-2.6
1979	Tex-A	9	8	0	2	0	0	0	0	0	0	.250	.250	.250	36	-1	0	0	0	1.000	0	/S-3,2-1,D-2	-0.1
	Oak-A	66	212	15	47	6	0	2	13	29	14	.222	.318	.278	66	-9	2	1	0	.988	-18	2-37,S-16,3-16	-2.3
	Yr	75	220	15	49	6	0	2	13	29	14	.223	.316	.277	65	-10	2	1	0	.988	-18	2-38,S-19,3-16,/D-2	-2.4
1980	*KC-A	69	167	19	42	10	1	1	20	18	27	.251	.332	.341	84	-3	1	1	-0	.964	-3	3-33,2-17/S-1,D-6	-0.7
1981	KC-A	27	49	2	11	3	0	0	5	4	2	.224	.283	.286	65	-2	0	1	-1	.955	-2	3-14,2-10/S-1	-0.4
Total	9	903	2910	292	733	107	9	15	243	295	327	.252	.328	.310	85	-52	36	38	-12	.962	-34	3-462,S-345,2/D	-5.7

■ JOE CHAMBERLAIN
Chamberlain, Joseph Jeremiah b: 5/10/10, San Francisco, Cal d: 1/28/83, San Francisco, Cal. BR/TR, 6'1", 175 lbs. Deb: 4/17/34

YEAR	TM/L	G	AB	R	H	2B	3B	HR	RBI	BB	SO	AVG	OBP	SLG	PRO+	BR/A	SB	CS	SBR	FA	FR	G/POS	TPR
1934	Chi-A	43	141	13	34	5	1	2	17	6	38	.241	.272	.333	54	-10	1	1	-0	.896	-6	S-26,3-14/2-1	-1.4

■ WES CHAMBERLAIN
Chamberlain, Wesley Polk b: 4/13/66, Chicago, Ill. BR/TR, 6'2", 210 lbs. Deb: 8/31/90

YEAR	TM/L	G	AB	R	H	2B	3B	HR	RBI	BB	SO	AVG	OBP	SLG	PRO+	BR/A	SB	CS	SBR	FA	FR	G/POS	TPR
1990	Phi-N	18	46	9	13	3	0	2	4	1	9	.283	.298	.478	110	0	4	0	1	.958	-1	O-10	0.1
1991	Phi-N	101	383	51	92	16	3	13	50	31	73	.240	.300	.399	96	-3	9	4	0	.985	5	O-98	0.0
1992	Phi-N	76	275	26	71	18	0	9	41	10	55	.258	.287	.422	99	-2	4	0	1	.971	-1	O-73	-0.3
1993	*Phi-N	96	284	34	80	20	2	12	45	17	51	.282	.325	.493	117	6	2	1	0	.993	5	O-76	0.9
1994	Phi-N	24	69	7	19	5	0	2	6	3	12	.275	.306	.435	88	-1	0	0	0	1.000	1	O-18	-0.1
	Bos-A	51	164	13	42	9	1	4	20	12	38	.256	.307	.396	76	-6	0	2	-1	1.000	4	O-34,D-12	-0.5
1995	Bos-A	19	42	4	5	1	0	1	1	3	11	.119	.178	.214	1	-6	1	0	0	.955	0	O-12/D-5	-0.6
Total	6	385	1263	144	322	72	6	43	167	77	249	.255	.300	.424	95	-13	20	7	2	.984	12	O-321/D-17	-0.5

■ AL CHAMBERS
Chambers, Albert Eugene b: 3/24/61, Harrisburg, Pa. BL/TL, 6'4", 217 lbs. Deb: 7/23/83

YEAR	TM/L	G	AB	R	H	2B	3B	HR	RBI	BB	SO	AVG	OBP	SLG	PRO+	BR/A	SB	CS	SBR	FA	FR	G/POS	TPR
1983	Sea-A	31	67	11	14	3	0	1	7	18	20	.209	.376	.299	85	-1	0	1	-1	1.000	-1	D-22/O-3	-0.3
1984	Sea-A	22	49	4	11	1	0	1	4	3	12	.224	.269	.306	60	-3	2	1	0	.947	-2	O-13/D-1	-0.5
1985	Sea-A	4	4	0	0	0	0	0	0	0	2	.000	.000	.000	-99	-1	0	0	0	.000	0	/H	-0.1
Total	3	57	120	15	25	4	0	2	11	21	34	.208	.326	.292	71	-4	2	2	-1	.955	-3	/D-23,O-16	-0.9

■ CHRIS CHAMBLISS
Chambliss, Carroll Christopher b: 12/26/48, Dayton, O. BL/TR, 6'1", 215 lbs. Deb: 5/28/71 C

YEAR	TM/L	G	AB	R	H	2B	3B	HR	RBI	BB	SO	AVG	OBP	SLG	PRO+	BR/A	SB	CS	SBR	FA	FR	G/POS	TPR
1971	Cle-A	111	415	49	114	20	4	9	48	40	83	.275	.341	.407	102	1	2	0	1	.992	-5	*1-108	-1.4
1972	Cle-A	121	466	51	136	27	2	6	44	26	63	.292	.329	.397	112	6	3	4	-2	.993	-6	*1-119	-1.3
1973	Cle-A	155	572	70	156	30	2	11	53	58	76	.273	.343	.390	104	3	4	8	-4	.991	7	*1-154	-0.6
1974	Cle-A	17	67	8	22	4	0	0	7	5	5	.328	.375	.388	121	2	0	1	-1	.982	-2	1-17	-0.2
	NY-A	110	400	38	97	16	3	6	43	23	43	.243	.284	.343	81	-11	0	0	0	.992	7	*1-106	-1.1
	Yr	127	467	46	119	20	3	6	50	28	48	.255	.297	.349	87	-9	0	1	-1	.990	5	*1-123	-1.3
1975	NY-A	150	562	66	171	38	4	9	72	29	50	.304	.340	.434	119	12	0	1	-1	.991	3	*1-147	0.5
1976	*NY-A★	156	641	79	188	32	6	17	96	27	80	.293	.325	.441	124	16	1	0	0	.994	-2	*1-155/D-1	0.4
1977	*NY-A	157	600	90	172	32	6	17	90	45	73	.287	.338	.445	113	10	4	0	1	.989	-5	*1-157	-0.3
1978	*NY-A	162	625	81	171	26	3	12	90	41	60	.274	.323	.382	100	-1	2	1	0	**.997**	4	*1-155/D-7	-0.6
1979	NY-A	149	554	61	155	27	3	18	63	34	53	.280	.327	.437	106	4	3	2	-0	.995	0	*1-134,D-16	-0.5
1980	Atl-N	158	602	83	170	37	2	18	72	49	73	.282	.340	.440	113	9	7	3	0	.993	-2	*1-158	-0.2
1981	Atl-N	107	404	44	110	25	2	8	51	44	41	.272	.345	.403	109	5	4	1	1	.997	7	*1-107	0.7
1982	*Atl-N	157	534	57	144	25	2	20	86	57	57	.270	.340	.436	111	8	7	3	0	.993	14	*1-151	1.5
1983	Atl-N	131	447	59	125	24	3	20	78	63	68	.280	.369	.481	124	15	2	7	-4	.996	0	*1-126	0.5
1984	Atl-N	135	389	47	100	14	0	9	44	58	54	.257	.355	.362	95	-1	1	2	-1	.993	2	*1-109	-0.7
1985	Atl-N	101	170	16	40	7	0	3	21	18	22	.235	.309	.329	74	-6	0	0	0	.997	2	1-39	-0.6
1986	Atl-N	97	122	13	38	8	0	2	14	15	24	.311	.387	.426	117	3	0	2	-1	.993	-2	1-20	-0.1
1988	NY-A	1	1	0	0	0	0	0	0	0	1	.000	.000	.000	-99	-0	0	0	0	.000	0	/H	0.0
Total	17	2175	7571	912	2109	392	42	185	972	632	926	.279	.336	.415	108	75	40	35	-9	.993	25	*1-1962/D-24	-4.0

■ MIKE CHAMPION
Champion, Robert Michael b: 2/10/55, Montgomery, Ala. BR/TR, 6', 185 lbs. Deb: 9/14/76

YEAR	TM/L	G	AB	R	H	2B	3B	HR	RBI	BB	SO	AVG	OBP	SLG	PRO+	BR/A	SB	CS	SBR	FA	FR	G/POS	TPR
1976	SD-N	11	38	4	9	2	0	1	2	1	3	.237	.256	.368	82	-1	0	0	0	.940	-4	2-11	-0.5
1977	SD-N	150	507	35	116	14	6	1	43	27	85	.229	.271	.286	55	-34	3	3	-1	.974	-26	*2-149	-5.3
1978	SD-N	32	53	3	12	0	2	0	4	5	13	.226	.293	.302	72	-2	0	0	0	.932	2	2-20/3-4	0.1
Total	3	193	598	42	137	16	8	2	49	33	101	.229	.272	.293	58	-37	3	3	-1	.968	-28	2-180/3-4	-5.7

■ FRANK CHANCE
Chance, Frank Leroy "Husk" or "The Peerless Leader"
b: 9/9/1877, Fresno, Cal. d: 9/15/24, Los Angeles, Cal. BR/TR, 6', 190 lbs. Deb: 4/29/1898 MH

YEAR	TM/L	G	AB	R	H	2B	3B	HR	RBI	BB	SO	AVG	OBP	SLG	PRO+	BR/A	SB	CS	SBR	FA	FR	G/POS	TPR
1898	Chi-N	53	147	32	41	4	3	1	14	7		.279	.338	.367	102	0	7			.950	-5	C-33,O-17/1-3	-0.4
1899	Chi-N	64	192	37	55	6	2	1	22	15		.286	.351	.354	96	-1	10			.950	-2	C-57/O-1,1-1	0.2

YEAR	TM/L	G	AB	R	H	2B	3B	HR	RBI	BB	SO	AVG	OBP	SLG	PRO+	BR/A	SB	CS	SBR	FA	FR	G/POS	TPR
1900	Chi-N	56	149	26	44	9	3	0	13	15		.295	.413	.396	129	8	8			.932	-1	C-51/1-1	1.0
1901	Chi-N	69	241	38	67	12	4	0	36	29		.278	.376	.361	119	8	27			.932	-5	O-51,C-13/1-6	0.0
1902	Chi-N	75	240	39	69	9	4	1	31	35		.287	.396	.371	141	14	27			.969	-4	1-38,C-29/O-4	1.2
1903	Chi-N	125	441	83	144	24	10	2	81	78		.327	.439	.440	155	37	**67**			.972	-3	*1-121/C-2	3.0
1904	Chi-N	124	451	89	140	16	10	6	49	36		.310	.382	.430	150	27	42			.990	12	*1-123/C-1	3.7
1905	Chi-N	118	392	92	124	16	12	2	70	78		.316	**.450**	.434	157	34	38			.990	2	*1-115,M	3.3
1906	*Chi-N	136	474	**103**	151	24	10	3	71	70		.319	.419	.430	156	34	**57**			.989	-1	*1-136,M	3.2
1907	*Chi-N	111	382	58	112	19	2	1	49	51		.293	.395	.361	129	15	35			**.992**	7	*1-109,M	2.2
1908	*Chi-N	129	452	65	123	27	4	2	55	37		.272	.338	.363	119	10	27			.989	4	*1-126,M	1.3
1909	Chi-N	93	324	53	88	16	4	0	46	30		.272	.341	.346	110	4	29			.994	-2	1-92,M	0.2
1910	*Chi-N	88	295	54	88	12	8	0	36	37	15	.298	.395	.393	131	13	16			.996	-2	1-87,M	1.2
1911	Chi-N	31	88	23	21	6	3	1	17	25	13	.239	.432	.409	136	6	9			.990	-2	1-29,M	0.4
1912	Chi-N	2	5	2	1	0	0	0	0	3	0	.200	.500	.200	96	0	1			1.000	-0	/1-2,M	0.0
1913	NY-A	12	24	3	5	0	0	0	6	8	1	.208	.406	.208	81	0	1			1.000	1	/1-7,M	0.0
1914	NY-A	1	0	0	0	0	0	0	0	0	0	—	—	—	—	0	0			1.000	-0	/1-1,M	0.0
Total	17	1287	4297	797	1273	200	79	20	596	554	29	.296	.394	.394	135	208	401			.987	-1	1-997,C-186/O-73	20.5

■ BOB CHANCE

Chance, Robert b: 9/10/40, Statesboro, Ga. BL/TR, 6'2", 219 lbs. Deb: 9/4/63

YEAR	TM/L	G	AB	R	H	2B	3B	HR	RBI	BB	SO	AVG	OBP	SLG	PRO+	BR/A	SB	CS	SBR	FA	FR	G/POS	TPR
1963	Cle-A	16	52	5	15	4	0	2	7	1	10	.288	.302	.481	116	1	0	1	-1	.909	-2	O-14	-0.2
1964	Cle-A	120	390	45	109	16	1	14	75	40	101	.279	.351	.433	118	9	3	3	-1	.988	-12	1-81,O-31	-0.9
1965	Was-A	72	199	20	51	9	0	4	14	18	44	.256	.318	.362	94	-2	0	1	-1	.988	-2	1-48/O-3	-0.7
1966	Was-A	37	57	1	10	3	0	1	8	2	23	.175	.203	.281	38	-5	0	0	0	.974	-2	1-13	-0.7
1967	Was-A	27	42	5	9	2	0	3	7	7	13	.214	.340	.476	144	2	0	0	0	1.000	-0	1-10	0.2
1969	Cal-A	5	7	0	1	0	0	0	1	0	4	.143	.143	.143	-21	-1	0	0	0	.909	-0	/1-1	-0.2
Total	6	277	747	76	195	34	1	24	112	68	195	.261	.326	.406	106	5	3	5	-2	.987	-18	1-153/O-48	-2.5

■ DARREL CHANEY

Chaney, Darrel Lee b: 3/9/48, Hammond, Ind. BB/TR, 6'1", 190 lbs. Deb: 4/11/69

YEAR	TM/L	G	AB	R	H	2B	3B	HR	RBI	BB	SO	AVG	OBP	SLG	PRO+	BR/A	SB	CS	SBR	FA	FR	G/POS	TPR
1969	Cin-N	93	209	21	40	5	2	0	15	24	75	.191	.278	.234	43	-16	1	0	0	.947	-12	S-91	-2.2
1970	*Cin-N	57	95	7	22	3	0	1	4	3	26	.232	.263	.295	49	-7	1	1	-0	.941	5	S-30,2-18/3-3	0.0
1971	Cin-N	10	24	2	3	0	0	0	1	1	3	.125	.160	.125	-19	-4	0	1	-1	1.000	-1	/S-7,2-1,3-1	-0.4
1972	*Cin-N	83	196	29	49	7	2	2	19	29	28	.250	.347	.337	101	1	1	3	-2	.963	-7	S-64,2-12,3-10	-0.1
1973	*Cin-N	105	227	27	41	7	1	0	14	26	50	.181	.268	.220	39	-19	4	3	-1	.964	12	S-75,2-14,3-12	0.1
1974	Cin-N	117	135	27	27	6	1	2	16	26	33	.200	.329	.304	79	-3	1	2	-1	.952	17	3-81,2-38,S-12	1.5
1975	*Cin-N	71	160	18	35	6	0	2	26	14	38	.219	.282	.294	59	-9	3	0	1	.961	17	S-34,2-23,3-13	1.2
1976	Atl-N	153	496	42	125	20	8	1	50	54	92	.252	.327	.331	82	-11	5	7	-3	.950	-0	*S-151/2-1,3-1	0.4
1977	Atl-N	74	209	22	42	7	2	3	15	17	44	.201	.261	.297	44	-17	0	0	0	.979	4	S-41,2-24	-0.7
1978	Atl-N	89	245	27	55	9	1	3	20	25	48	.224	.296	.306	62	-12	1	0	0	.976	-6	S-77/3-8,2-1	-1.0
1979	Atl-N	63	117	15	19	5	0	0	10	19	34	.162	.279	.205	32	-11	2	1	0	.945	-3	S-39/2-5,3-4,C-1	-1.1
Total	11	915	2113	237	458	75	17	14	190	238	471	.217	.297	.288	61	-107	19	18	-5	.959	26	S-621,2-137,3/C	-2.3

■ LES CHANNELL

Channell, Lester Clark "Goat" or "Gint" b: 3/3/1886, Crestline, Ohio d: 5/8/54, Denver, Colo. BL/TL, 6', 180 lbs. Deb: 5/11/10

YEAR	TM/L	G	AB	R	H	2B	3B	HR	RBI	BB	SO	AVG	OBP	SLG	PRO+	BR/A	SB	CS	SBR	FA	FR	G/POS	TPR
1910	NY-A	6	19	3	6	0	0	0	3	2		.316	.381	.316	112	0	2			1.000	-1	/O-6	-0.1
1914	NY-A	1	1	0	1	1	0	0	0	0	0	1.000	1.000	2.000	803	1	0			.000	0	H	0.1
Total	2	7	20	3	7	1	0	0	3	2	0	.350	.409	.400	145	1	2			1.000	-1	/O-6	0.0

■ CHARLIE CHANT

Chant, Charles Joseph b: 8/7/51, Bell, Cal. BR/TR, 6', 190 lbs. Deb: 9/12/75

YEAR	TM/L	G	AB	R	H	2B	3B	HR	RBI	BB	SO	AVG	OBP	SLG	PRO+	BR/A	SB	CS	SBR	FA	FR	G/POS	TPR
1975	Oak-A	5	5	1	0	0	0	0	0	0	0	.000	.000	.000	-99	-1	0	0	0	1.000	-2	/O-5,D-1	-0.3
1976	StL-N	15	14	0	2	0	0	0	0	0	4	.143	.143	.143	-19	-2	0	0	0	1.000	-2	O-14	-0.5
Total	2	20	19	1	2	0	0	0	0	0	4	.105	.105	.105	-40	-3	0	0	0	1.000	-4	/O-19,D-1	-0.8

■ ED CHAPLIN

Chaplin, Bert Edgar (b: Bert Edgar Chapman) b: 9/25/1893, Pelzer, S.C. d: 8/15/78, Sanford, Fla. BL/TR, 5'7", 158 lbs. Deb: 9/4/20

YEAR	TM/L	G	AB	R	H	2B	3B	HR	RBI	BB	SO	AVG	OBP	SLG	PRO+	BR/A	SB	CS	SBR	FA	FR	G/POS	TPR
1920	Bos-A	4	5	2	1	1	0	0	1	4	1	.200	.556	.400	163	1	0	0	0	.900	-1	/C-2	0.1
1921	Bos-A	3	2	0	0	0	0	0	0	0	1	.000	.000	.000	-99	-1	0	0	0	1.000	0	/C-1	0.0
1922	Bos-A	28	69	8	13	1	1	0	6	9	9	.188	.282	.232	35	-6	2	1	0	.960	-3	C-21	-0.8
Total	3	35	76	10	14	2	1	0	7	13	11	.184	.303	.237	43	-6	2	1	0	.953	-3	/C-24	-0.7

■ CALVIN CHAPMAN

Chapman, Calvin Louis b: 12/20/10, Courtland, Miss. d: 4/1/83, Batesville, Miss. BL/TR, 5'9", 160 lbs. Deb: 9/10/35

YEAR	TM/L	G	AB	R	H	2B	3B	HR	RBI	BB	SO	AVG	OBP	SLG	PRO+	BR/A	SB	CS	SBR	FA	FR	G/POS	TPR
1935	Cin-N	15	53	6	18	1	0	0	3	4	5	.340	.386	.358	105	1	2			.949	-3	S-12/2-4	-0.1
1936	Cin-N	96	219	35	54	7	3	1	22	16	19	.247	.301	.320	72	-9	5			.961	-14	O-31,2-23/3-1	-2.2
Total	2	111	272	41	72	8	3	1	25	20	24	.265	.317	.327	78	-8	7			.968	-16	/O-31,2-27,S-12,3-1	-2.3

■ GLENN CHAPMAN

Chapman, Glenn Justice "Pete" b: 1/21/06, Cambridge City, Ind. d: 11/5/88, Richmond, Ind. BR/TR, 5'11.5", 170 lbs. Deb: 4/18/34

YEAR	TM/L	G	AB	R	H	2B	3B	HR	RBI	BB	SO	AVG	OBP	SLG	PRO+	BR/A	SB	CS	SBR	FA	FR	G/POS	TPR
1934	Bro-N	67	93	19	26	5	1	1	10	7	19	.280	.330	.387	96	-1	1			1.000	-7	O-40,2-14	-0.8

■ HARRY CHAPMAN

Chapman, Harry E. b: 10/26/1887, Severance, Kan. d: 10/21/18, Nevada, Mo. BR/TR, 5'11", 160 lbs. Deb: 10/6/12

YEAR	TM/L	G	AB	R	H	2B	3B	HR	RBI	BB	SO	AVG	OBP	SLG	PRO+	BR/A	SB	CS	SBR	FA	FR	G/POS	TPR
1912	Chi-N	1	4	1	1	0	1	0	1	0	0	.250	.250	.750	169	0	1			1.000	1	/C-1	0.1
1913	Cin-N	2	2	0	1	0	0	0	0	0	1	.500	.500	.500	187	0	0			.000	0	H	0.0
1914	StL-F	64	181	16	38	2	1	0	14	13	27	.210	.270	.232	36	-19	2			.973	-4	C-51/1-1,2-1,O-1	-1.9
1915	StL-F	62	186	19	37	6	3	1	29	22	24	.199	.284	.280	56	-14	4			.989	8	C-53	-0.2
1916	StL-A	18	31	2	3	0	0	0	0	2	5	.097	.152	.097	-27	-5	0			.981	2	C-14	-0.2
Total	5	147	404	38	80	8	5	1	44	37	57	.198	.269	.250	43	-37	7			.982	7	C-119/O-1,2-1,1-1	-2.2

■ JACK CHAPMAN

Chapman, John Curtis "Death To Flying Things" b: 5/8/1843, Brooklyn, N.Y. d: 6/10/16, Brooklyn, N.Y. TR , 5'11", 170 lbs. Deb: 5/5/1874 M

YEAR	TM/L	G	AB	R	H	2B	3B	HR	RBI	BB	SO	AVG	OBP	SLG	PRO+	BR/A	SB	CS	SBR	FA	FR	G/POS	TPR
1874	Atl-n	53	242	32	64	10	2	0	24	4	11	.264	.276	.322	103	3	2	1	0	.741	2	*O-53/1-1	0.5
1875	StL-n	43	195	28	44	5	3	0	30	1	7	.226	.230	.282	84	-2	4	1	1	.733	-3	O-43/1-1	-0.4
1876	Lou-N	17	67	4	16	1	0	0	5	1	3	.239	.250	.254	58	-4				.750	-4	O-17/3-1,M	-0.7
Total	2 n	96	437	60	108	15	5	0	54	5	18	.247	.256	.304	95	1	6	2	1	.738	-1	/O-96,1-2	0.1

■ JOHN CHAPMAN

Chapman, John Joseph b: 10/15/1899, Centralia, Pa. d: 11/3/53, Philadelphia, Pa. BR/TR, 5'10.5", 175 lbs. Deb: 6/28/24

YEAR	TM/L	G	AB	R	H	2B	3B	HR	RBI	BB	SO	AVG	OBP	SLG	PRO+	BR/A	SB	CS	SBR	FA	FR	G/POS	TPR
1924	Phi-A	19	71	7	20	4	1	0	7	4	8	.282	.329	.366	78	-2	0	0	0	.958	-10	S-19	-1.0

■ KELVIN CHAPMAN

Chapman, Kelvin Keith b: 6/2/56, Willits, Cal. BR/TR, 5'11", 173 lbs. Deb: 4/5/79

YEAR	TM/L	G	AB	R	H	2B	3B	HR	RBI	BB	SO	AVG	OBP	SLG	PRO+	BR/A	SB	CS	SBR	FA	FR	G/POS	TPR
1979	NY-N	35	80	7	12	1	2	0	4	5	15	.150	.200	.213	13	-10	0	0	0	.980	-4	2-22/3-1	-1.3
1984	NY-N	75	197	27	57	13	0	3	23	19	30	.289	.358	.401	115	4	8	7	-2	.979	1	2-57/3-3	0.5
1985	NY-N	62	144	16	25	3	0	0	7	9	15	.174	.232	.194	21	-15	5	4	-1	.970	-6	2-48/3-1	-2.2
Total	3	172	421	50	94	17	2	3	34	33	60	.223	.286	.295	64	-21	13	11	-3	.976	-9	2-127/3-5	-3.0

■ RAY CHAPMAN

Chapman, Raymond Johnson b: 1/15/1891, Beaver Dam, Ky. d: 8/17/20, New York, N.Y. BR/TR, 5'10", 170 lbs. Deb: 8/30/12

YEAR	TM/L	G	AB	R	H	2B	3B	HR	RBI	BB	SO	AVG	OBP	SLG	PRO+	BR/A	SB	CS	SBR	FA	FR	G/POS	TPR
1912	Cle-A	31	109	29	34	6	3	0	19	10		.312	.375	.422	124	3	10			.904	-10	S-31	-0.4
1913	Cle-A	141	508	78	131	19	7	3	39	46	51	.258	.322	.341	91	-6	29			.936	-9	*S-138/O-1	-0.2
1914	Cle-A	106	375	59	103	16	10	2	42	48	48	.275	.358	.387	119	9	24	9	2	.913	-15	S-72,2-33	0.2
1915	Cle-A	154	570	101	154	14	17	3	67	70	82	.270	.353	.370	114	10	36	15	2	.944	9	*S-154	3.4
1916	Cle-A	109	346	50	80	10	5	0	27	50	46	.231	.330	.289	81	-7	21	14	-2	.935	13	S-52,3-36,2-16	0.9
1917	Cle-A	156	563	98	170	28	13	2	36	61	65	.302	.370	.409	128	18	52			.938	**24**	*S-156	5.4
1918	Cle-A	128	446	**84**	119	19	8	1	32	**84**	46	.267	.390	.352	113	10	30			.936	6	*S-128/O-1	2.4
1919	Cle-A	115	433	75	130	23	10	3	53	31	38	.300	.351	.420	109	4	18			.944	-0	*S-115	1.2
1920	Cle-A	111	435	97	132	27	8	3	49	52	38	.303	.380	.423	109	6	13	9	-2	.959	12	*S-111	2.5
Total	9	1051	3785	671	1053	162	81	17	364	452	414	.278	.358	.377	110	48	233	47		.939	30	S-957/2-49,3-36,O-2	15.4

■ SAM CHAPMAN

Chapman, Samuel Blake b: 4/11/16, Tiburon, Cal. BR/TR, 6'1", 190 lbs. Deb: 5/16/38

YEAR	TM/L	G	AB	R	H	2B	3B	HR	RBI	BB	SO	AVG	OBP	SLG	PRO+	BR/A	SB	CS	SBR	FA	FR	G/POS	TPR
1938	Phi-A	114	406	60	105	17	7	17	63	55	94	.259	.353	.461	105	2	3	4	-2	.952	-2	*O-110	-0.4
1939	Phi-A	140	498	74	134	24	6	15	64	51	62	.269	.338	.432	98	-3	11	4	1	.955	4	*O-117,1-19	-0.3

YEAR	TM/L	G	AB	R	H	2B	3B	HR	RBI	BB	SO	AVG	OBP	SLG	PRO+	BR/A	SB	CS	SBR	FA	FR	G/POS	TPR
1940	Phi-A	134	508	88	140	26	3	23	75	46	96	.276	.337	.474	110	6	2	6	-3	.963	4	*O-129	0.0
1941	Phi-A	143	552	97	178	29	9	25	106	47	49	.322	.378	.543	145	33	6	9	-4	.967	14	*O-141	3.4
1945	Phi-A	9	30	3	6	2	0	0	1	2	4	.200	.250	.267	50	-2	0	0	0	1.000	-1	/O-8	-0.4
1946	Phi-A★	146	545	77	142	22	5	20	67	54	66	.261	.327	.429	111	6	1	3	-2	.970	10	*O-145	0.8
1947	Phi-A	149	551	84	139	18	5	14	83	65	70	.252	.331	.379	95	-4	3	4	-2	.987	12	*O-146	-0.2
1948	Phi-A	123	445	58	115	18	6	13	70	55	50	.258	.341	.413	100	-1	6	1	1	.982	7	*O-118	0.1
1949	Phi-A	154	589	89	164	24	4	24	108	80	68	.278	.367	.455	121	16	3	4	-2	.979	11	*O-154	1.7
1950	Phi-A	144	553	93	139	20	6	23	95	68	79	.251	.338	.434	98	-4	3	3	-1	.978	10	*O-140	0.0
1951	Phi-A	18	65	7	11	1	0	0	5	12	12	.169	.299	.185	32	-6	0	0	0	.957	-1	O-17	-0.7
	Cle-A	94	246	24	56	9	1	6	36	27	32	.228	.304	.346	80	-8	3	0	1	.985	-18	O-84/1-1	-2.7
	Yr	112	311	31	67	10	1	6	41	39	44	.215	.303	.312	69	-14	3	0	1	.978	-19	*O-101/1-1	-3.4
Total	11	1368	4988	754	1329	210	52	180	773	562	682	.266	.342	.438	107	34	41	38	-11	.972	53	*O-1309/1-20	1.3

■ BEN CHAPMAN

Chapman, William Benjamin b: 12/25/08, Nashville, Tenn. d: 7/7/93, Hoover, Ala. BR/TR, 6', 190 lbs. Deb: 4/15/30 MC

YEAR	TM/L	G	AB	R	H	2B	3B	HR	RBI	BB	SO	AVG	OBP	SLG	PRO+	BR/A	SB	CS	SBR	FA	FR	G/POS	TPR
1930	NY-A	138	513	74	162	31	10	10	81	43	58	.316	.371	.474	118	13	14	6	1	.912	-6	3-91,2-45	1.4
1931	NY-A	149	600	120	189	28	11	17	122	75	77	.315	.396	.483	138	33	**61**	23	**5**	.963	8	*O-137,2-11	3.5
1932	*NY-A	151	581	101	174	41	15	10	107	71	55	.299	.381	.473	126	23	**38**	18	1	.949	-3	*O-150	1.1
1933	NY-A★	147	565	112	176	36	4	9	98	72	45	.312	.393	.437	127	24	**27**	18	-3	.975	11	*O-147	2.3
1934	NY-A★	149	588	82	181	21	**13**	5	86	67	68	.308	.381	.413	113	12	26	16	-2	.967	8	*O-149	1.1
1935	NY-A★	140	553	118	160	38	8	8	74	61	39	.289	.361	.430	110	8	17	10	-1	.964	17	*O-138	1.7
1936	NY-A	36	139	19	37	14	3	1	21	15	20	.266	.338	.432	92	-2	1	2	-1	.965	2	O-36	-0.2
	Was-A★	97	401	91	133	36	7	4	60	69	18	.332	.431	.486	133	24	19	7	2	.959	4	O-97	2.2
	Yr	133	540	110	170	50	10	5	81	84	38	.315	.408	.472	123	21	20	9	1	.961	7	*O-133	2.0
1937	Was-A	35	130	23	34	7	1	0	12	26	7	.262	.385	.331	86	-2	8	0	2	.957	-1	O-32	-0.2
	Bos-A	113	423	76	130	23	11	7	57	57	35	.307	.391	.463	110	7	27	12	1	.985	9	*O-112/S-1	1.2
	Yr	148	553	99	164	30	12	7	69	83	42	.297	.389	.432	105	6	**35**	12	**3**	.978	7	*O-144/S-1	1.0
1938	Bos-A	127	480	92	163	40	8	6	80	65	33	.340	.418	.494	122	17	13	6	0	.966	6	*O-126/3-1	1.8
1939	Cle-A	149	545	101	158	31	9	6	82	87	30	.290	.390	.413	109	10	18	6	2	.971	-4	*O-146	0.3
1940	Cle-A	143	548	82	157	40	6	4	50	78	45	.286	.377	.403	105	7	13	7	-0	.964	2	*O-140	0.0
1941	Was-A	28	110	9	28	6	0	1	10	10	6	.255	.317	.336	76	-4	2	2	-1	.983	1	O-26	-0.5
	Chi-A	57	190	26	43	9	1	2	19	19	14	.226	.297	.316	63	-10	2	2	-1	.992	1	O-49	-1.3
	Yr	85	300	35	71	15	1	3	29	29	20	.237	.304	.323	68	-14	4	4	-1	.989	2	O-75	-1.8
1944	Bro-N	20	38	11	14	4	0	0	11	5	4	.368	.442	.474	161	3	1			.900	-2	P-11	0.0
1945	Bro-N	13	22	2	3	0	0	0	3	2	1	.136	.208	.136	-3	-3	0			.938	1	P-10	0.0
	Phi-N	24	51	4	16	2	0	0	4	2	1	.314	.340	.353	95	-0	0			.933	-3	O-10/3-4,P-3,M	-0.4
	Yr	37	73	6	19	2	0	0	7	4	2	.260	.299	.288	65	-3	0			.941	-3	P-13,O-10/3-4	-0.4
1946	Phi-N	1	1	1	0	0	0	0	0	0	0	.000	.000	.000	-99	-0	0			.000	0	/P-1,M	0.0
Total	15	1717	6478	1144	1958	407	107	90	977	824	556	.302	.383	.440	115	159	287	135		.967	50	*O-1495/3-96,2PS	14.0

■ FRED CHAPMAN

Chapman, William Fred "Chappie" b: 7/17/16, Liberty, S.C. d: 3/27/97, Kannapolis, S.C. BR/TR, 6'1", 185 lbs. Deb: 9/15/39

YEAR	TM/L	G	AB	R	H	2B	3B	HR	RBI	BB	SO	AVG	OBP	SLG	PRO+	BR/A	SB	CS	SBR	FA	FR	G/POS	TPR
1939	Phi-A	15	49	5	14	1	1	0	1	1	3	.286	.300	.347	66	-3	1	0	0	.899	-4	S-15	-0.4
1940	Phi-A	26	69	6	11	1	0	0	4	6	10	.159	.227	.174	6	-10	1	1	-0	.862	-5	S-25	-1.3
1941	Phi-A	35	69	1	11	1	0	0	4	4	15	.159	.205	.174	1	-10	1	2	-1	.917	-2	S-28/3-2,2-1	-1.1
Total	3	76	187	12	36	3	1	0	9	11	28	.193	.237	.219	20	-22	3	3	-1	.889	-11	/S-68,3-2,2-1	-2.8

■ HARRY CHAPPAS

Chappas, Harry Perry b: 10/26/57, Mt.Rainier, Md. BB/TR, 5'3", 150 lbs. Deb: 9/7/78

YEAR	TM/L	G	AB	R	H	2B	3B	HR	RBI	BB	SO	AVG	OBP	SLG	PRO+	BR/A	SB	CS	SBR	FA	FR	G/POS	TPR
1978	Chi-A	20	75	11	20	1	0	0	6	6	11	.267	.329	.280	72	-3	1	2	-1	1.000	0	S-20	-0.1
1979	Chi-A	26	59	9	17	1	0	1	4	5	5	.288	.354	.356	92	-0	1	1	-0	.929	3	S-23	0.3
1980	Chi-A	26	50	6	8	2	0	0	2	4	10	.160	.236	.200	21	-5	0	2	-1	.981	-1	S-19/2-1,D-2	-0.6
Total	3	72	184	26	45	4	0	1	12	15	26	.245	.312	.283	65	-8	2	5	-2	.967	1	/S-62,D-2,2-1	-0.4

■ LARRY CHAPPELL

Chappell, La Verne Ashford b: 2/19/1890, McClusky, Ill. d: 11/8/18, San Francisco, Cal. BL/TR, 6', 186 lbs. Deb: 7/18/13

YEAR	TM/L	G	AB	R	H	2B	3B	HR	RBI	BB	SO	AVG	OBP	SLG	PRO+	BR/A	SB	CS	SBR	FA	FR	G/POS	TPR
1913	Chi-A	60	208	20	48	8	1	0	15	18	22	.231	.295	.279	69	-8	7			.952	-1	O-59	-1.3
1914	Chi-A	21	39	3	9	0	0	0	1	4	11	.231	.302	.231	61	-2	0			.929	-2	/O-9	-0.4
1915	Chi-A	1	1	0	0	0	0	0	0	0	0	.000	.000	.000	-97	-0	0			.000	0	H	0.0
1916	Cle-A	3	2	0	0	0	0	0	0	1	0	.000	.333	.000	1	-0	1			.000	0	H	0.0
	Bos-N	20	53	4	12	1	1	0	9	2	8	.226	.268	.283	72	-2	1			.957	-2	O-14	-0.5
1917	Bos-N	4	2	0	0	0	0	0	1	0	1	.000	.000	.000	-99	-0	0			.000	-1	/O-1	-0.1
Total	5	109	305	27	69	9	2	0	26	25	42	.226	.289	.269	66	-13	9			.951	-5	/O-83	-2.3

■ JOE CHARBONEAU

Charboneau, Joseph b: 6/17/55, Belvidere, Ill. BR/TR, 6'2", 205 lbs. Deb: 4/11/80

YEAR	TM/L	G	AB	R	H	2B	3B	HR	RBI	BB	SO	AVG	OBP	SLG	PRO+	BR/A	SB	CS	SBR	FA	FR	G/POS	TPR
1980	Cle-A	131	453	76	131	17	2	23	87	49	70	.289	.362	.488	130	18	2	4	-2	.963	1	O-67,D-57	1.3
1981	Cle-A	48	138	14	29	7	1	4	18	7	22	.210	.248	.362	75	-5	1	0	0	.963	-2	O-27,D-14	-0.8
1982	Cle-A	22	56	7	12	2	1	2	9	5	7	.214	.290	.393	86	-1	0	0	0	.955	-3	O-18/D-1	-0.5
Total	3	201	647	97	172	26	4	29	114	61	99	.266	.333	.453	115	12	3	4	-2	.962	-4	O-112/D-72	-0.0

■ ED CHARLES

Charles, Edwin Douglas b: 4/29/33, Daytona Beach, Fla. BR/TR, 5'10", 170 lbs. Deb: 4/11/62

YEAR	TM/L	G	AB	R	H	2B	3B	HR	RBI	BB	SO	AVG	OBP	SLG	PRO+	BR/A	SB	CS	SBR	FA	FR	G/POS	TPR
1962	KC-A	147	535	81	154	24	7	17	74	54	70	.288	.358	.454	111	9	20	4	4	.964	4	*3-140/2-2	1.8
1963	KC-A	158	603	82	161	28	2	15	79	58	79	.267	.336	.395	99	-1	15	8	-0	.949	-8	*3-158	-0.9
1964	KC-A	150	557	69	134	25	2	16	63	64	92	.241	.323	.379	92	-6	12	7	-1	.954	-15	*3-147	-2.4
1965	KC-A	134	480	55	129	19	7	8	56	44	72	.269	.335	.387	106	4	13	4	2	.971	-1	*3-128/2-1,S-1	0.2
1966	KC-A	118	385	52	110	18	8	9	42	30	53	.286	.337	.444	127	12	12	5	1	.963	-6	*3-104/1-1,O-1	0.5
1967	KC-A	19	61	5	15	1	0	0	5	12	13	.246	.378	.262	95	0	1	0	0	.966	-0	3-18	0.1
	NY-N	101	323	32	77	13	2	3	31	24	58	.238	.305	.319	80	-8	4	1	1	.944	9	3-89	0.0
1968	NY-N	117	369	41	102	11	1	15	53	28	57	.276	.331	.434	127	12	5	4	-1	.954	1	*3-106/1-2	1.3
1969	*NY-N	61	169	21	35	8	1	3	18	18	31	.207	.287	.320	68	-7	4	2	0	.946	-0	3-52	-0.8
Total	8	1005	3482	438	917	147	30	86	421	332	525	.263	.332	.397	103	16	86	35	5	.957	-15	3-942/1-3,2-3,OS	-0.2

■ CHAPPY CHARLES

Charles, Raymond (b: Charles Shuh Achenbach)
b: 3/25/1881, Phillipsburg, N.J. d: 8/4/59, Bethlehem, Pa. BR/TR, 5'11", 175 lbs. Deb: 4/15/08

YEAR	TM/L	G	AB	R	H	2B	3B	HR	RBI	BB	SO	AVG	OBP	SLG	PRO+	BR/A	SB	CS	SBR	FA	FR	G/POS	TPR
1908	StL-N	121	454	39	93	14	3	1	17	19		.205	.238	.256	61	-21	15			.921	-12	2-65,S-31,3-23	-3.9
1909	StL-N	99	339	33	80	7	3	0	29	31		.236	.309	.274	87	-5	7			.918	-2	2-71,S-26/3-2	-0.8
	Cin-N	13	43	3	11	2	0	0	5	4		.256	.319	.302	94	-0	2			.932	-3	2-10/S-3	-0.4
	Yr	112	382	36	91	9	3	0	34	35		.238	.310	.277	87	-5	9			.920	-4	2-81,S-29/3-2	-1.2
1910	Cin-N	4	15	1	2	0	1	0	0	0	1	.133	.133	.267	17	-2	0			.818	-2	/S-4	-0.3
Total	3	237	851	76	186	23	7	1	51	54	1	.219	.270	.266	72	-28	24			.920	-18	2-146/S-64,3-25	-5.4

■ MIKE CHARTAK

Chartak, Michael George "Shotgun" b: 4/28/16, Brooklyn, N.Y. d: 7/25/67, Cedar Rapids, Ia. BL/TL, 6'2", 180 lbs. Deb: 9/13/40

YEAR	TM/L	G	AB	R	H	2B	3B	HR	RBI	BB	SO	AVG	OBP	SLG	PRO+	BR/A	SB	CS	SBR	FA	FR	G/POS	TPR
1940	NY-A	11	15	2	2	1	0	0	3	5	5	.133	.350	.200	49	-1	0	0	0	1.000	-1	/O-3	-0.2
1942	NY-A	5	5	0	0	0	0	0	0	0	0	.000	.000	.000	-99	-1	0	0	0	.000	0	H	-0.1
	Was-A	24	92	11	20	4	2	1	8	14	16	.217	.321	.337	86	-2	0	1	-1	.926	-0	O-24	-0.4
	StL-A	73	237	37	59	11	2	9	43	40	27	.249	.362	.426	119	7	3	3	-1	.974	7	O-64	1.0
	Yr	102	334	48	79	15	4	10	51	54	43	.237	.346	.395	107	4	3	4	-2	.962	7	O-88	0.5
1943	StL-A	108	344	38	88	16	2	10	37	39	55	.256	.333	.401	112	5	1	3	-2	.970	-4	O-77,1-18	-0.5
1944	*StL-A	35	72	8	17	2	1	1	7	6	9	.236	.304	.333	77	-2	0	0	0	1.000	-2	1-12/O-7	-0.3
Total	4	256	765	96	186	34	7	21	98	104	112	.243	.337	.388	105	5	4	7	-3	.967	3	O-175/1-30	-0.5

■ HAL CHASE

Chase, Harold Homer "Prince Hal" b: 2/13/1883, Los Gatos, Cal. d: 5/18/47, Colusa, Cal. BR/TL, 6', 175 lbs. Deb: 4/14/05 M

YEAR	TM/L	G	AB	R	H	2B	3B	HR	RBI	BB	SO	AVG	OBP	SLG	PRO+	BR/A	SB	CS	SBR	FA	FR	G/POS	TPR
1905	NY-A	128	465	60	116	16	6	3	49	15		.249	.277	.329	83	-11	22			.976	-9	*1-124/S-2,2-1	-2.7
1906	NY-A	151	597	84	193	23	10	0	76	13		.323	.341	.395	118	10	28			.980	-3	*1-150/2-1	0.3
1907	NY-A	125	498	72	143	23	3	2	68	19		.287	.315	.357	106	1	32			.973	0	*1-121/O-4	-0.2

YEAR	TM/L	G	AB	R	H	2B	3B	HR	RBI	BB	SO	AVG	OBP	SLG	PRO+	BR/A	SB	CS	SBR	FA	FR	G/POS	TPR
1908	NY-A	106	405	50	104	11	3	1	36	15		.257	.285	.306	91	-5	27			.980	-4	1-98/2-3,O-3,3-1,P	-1.2
1909	NY-A	118	474	60	134	17	3	4	63	20		.283	.317	.357	112	5	25			.978	-2	*1-118/S-1	0.2
1910	NY-A	130	524	67	152	20	5	3	73	16		.290	.312	.365	106	1	40			.981	-4	*1-130,M	-0.4
1911	NY-A	133	527	82	166	32	7	3	62	21		.315	.342	.419	105	1	36			.974	-2	*1-124/O-7,2-2,M	-0.2
1912	NY-A	131	522	61	143	21	9	4	58	17		.274	.299	.372	86	-12	33			.979	-2	*1-122/2-7	-1.6
1913	NY-A	39	146	15	31	2	4	0	9	11	13	.212	.268	.281	60	-8	5			.982	-5	1-29/2-5,O-5	-1.4
	Chi-A	102	384	49	110	11	10	2	39	16	41	.286	.320	.383	107	1	9			.976	1	*1-102	0.1
	Yr	141	530	64	141	13	14	2	48	27	54	.266	.305	.355	94	-7	14			.977	-4	*1-131/2-5,O-5	-1.3
1914	Chi-A	58	206	27	55	10	5	0	20	23	19	.267	.343	.364	114	4	9	4	0	.981	2	1-58	0.5
	Buf-F	75	291	43	101	19	9	3	48	6	31	.347	.365	.505	133	7	10			.980	-1	1-73	0.5
1915	Buf-F	145	567	85	165	31	10	**17**	89	20	50	.291	.316	.471	118	1	23			.983	0	*1-143/O-1	-0.3
1916	Cin-N	142	542	66	**184**	29	12	4	82	19	48	**.339**	.363	.459	**155**	**32**	22	11	0	.986	-7	1-98,O-25,2-16	2.3
1917	Cin-N	152	602	71	167	28	15	4	86	15	49	.277	.296	.394	115	7	21			.983	-3	*1-151	-0.1
1918	Cin-N	74	259	30	78	12	6	2	38	13	15	.301	.339	.417	133	9	5			.980	-2	1-67/O-2	0.5
1919	NY-N	110	408	58	116	17	7	5	45	17	40	.284	.318	.397	115	6	16			.984	-1	*1-107	0.1
Total	15	1919	7417	980	2158	322	124	57	941	276	306	.291	.319	.391	110	51	363	15		.980	-42	*1-1815/O-47,2SP3	-3.6

■ BUSTER CHATHAM Chatham, Charles L b: 12/25/01, West, Tex. d: 12/15/75, Waco, Tex. BR/TR, 5'5", 150 lbs. Deb: 6/1/30

YEAR	TM/L	G	AB	R	H	2B	3B	HR	RBI	BB	SO	AVG	OBP	SLG	PRO+	BR/A	SB	CS	SBR	FA	FR	G/POS	TPR
1930	Bos-N	112	404	48	108	20	11	5	56	37	41	.267	.332	.408	80	-13	8			.920	-14	3-92,S-17	-1.8
1931	Bos-N	17	44	4	10	1	0	1	3	6	6	.227	.320	.318	75	-1	0			.762	-6	/S-6,3-6	-0.6
Total	2	129	448	52	118	21	11	6	59	43	47	.263	.331	.400	80	-15	8			.924	-20	/3-98,S-23	-2.4

■ JIM CHATTERTON Chatterton, James M. b: 10/14/1864, Brooklyn, N.Y. d: 12/15/44, Tewksbury, Mass. Deb: 6/7/1884

YEAR	TM/L	G	AB	R	H	2B	3B	HR	RBI	BB	SO	AVG	OBP	SLG	PRO+	BR/A	SB	CS	SBR	FA	FR	G/POS	TPR
1884	KC-U	4	15	4	2	1	0	0		2		.133	.235	.200	38	-2				1.000	0	/O-2,1-2,P-1	-0.1

■ OSSIE CHAVARRIA Chavarria, Osvaldo (Quijano) b: 8/5/40, Colon, Panama BR/TR, 5'11", 155 lbs. Deb: 4/14/66

YEAR	TM/L	G	AB	R	H	2B	3B	HR	RBI	BB	SO	AVG	OBP	SLG	PRO+	BR/A	SB	CS	SBR	FA	FR	G/POS	TPR
1966	KC-A	86	191	26	46	10	0	2	10	18	43	.241	.306	.325	84	-4	3	2	-0	.939	-5	O-26,S-23,2-14,/13	-0.8
1967	KC-A	38	59	2	6	2	0	0	4	7	16	.102	.209	.136	4	-7	1	0	0	1.000	2	2-17/3-7,O-3,S-2	-0.4
Total	2	124	250	28	52	12	0	2	14	25	59	.208	.283	.280	65	-11	4	2	0	.990	-2	/2-31,O-29,S-25,31	-1.2

■ ERIC CHAVEZ Chavez, Eric Cesar b: 12/7/77, Los Angeles, Cal. BL/TR, 6'1", 195 lbs. Deb: 9/8/98

YEAR	TM/L	G	AB	R	H	2B	3B	HR	RBI	BB	SO	AVG	OBP	SLG	PRO+	BR/A	SB	CS	SBR	FA	FR	G/POS	TPR
1998	Oak-A	16	45	6	14	4	1	0	6	3	5	.311	.354	.444	109	1	1	1	-0	1.000	2	3-13	0.2

■ RAUL CHAVEZ Chavez, Raul Alexander b: 3/18/73, Valencia, Venez. BR/TR, 5'11", 175 lbs. Deb: 8/30/96

YEAR	TM/L	G	AB	R	H	2B	3B	HR	RBI	BB	SO	AVG	OBP	SLG	PRO+	BR/A	SB	CS	SBR	FA	FR	G/POS	TPR
1996	Mon-N	4	5	1	1	0	0	0	0	1	1	.200	.333	.200	44	-0	1	0	0	1.000	1	/C-3	0.1
1997	Mon-N	13	26	0	7	0	0	0	2	0	5	.269	.269	.269	42	-2	1	0	0	1.000	2	C-13	0.0
1998	Sea-A	1	1	0	0	0	0	0	0	0	0	.000	.000	.000	-99	-0	0	0	0	1.000	0	/C-1	0.0
Total	3	18	32	1	8	0	0	0	2	1	6	.250	.273	.250	38	-3	2	0	1	1.000	2	/C-17	0.1

■ HARRY CHEEK Cheek, Harry G. b: 1879, Sedalia, Mo. d: 6/25/56, Paramas, N.J. TR , Deb: 5/12/10

YEAR	TM/L	G	AB	R	H	2B	3B	HR	RBI	BB	SO	AVG	OBP	SLG	PRO+	BR/A	SB	CS	SBR	FA	FR	G/POS	TPR
1910	Phi-N	2	4	1	2	1	0	0	0	0	0	.500	.500	.750	255	1	0			1.000	-1	/C-2	0.0

■ PAUL CHERVINKO Chervinko, Paul b: 7/28/10, Trauger, Pa. d: 6/3/76, Danville, Ill. BR/TR, 5'8", 185 lbs. Deb: 5/30/37

YEAR	TM/L	G	AB	R	H	2B	3B	HR	RBI	BB	SO	AVG	OBP	SLG	PRO+	BR/A	SB	CS	SBR	FA	FR	G/POS	TPR
1937	Bro-N	30	48	1	7	0	1	0	2	3	16	.146	.196	.188	5	-6	0			1.000	0	C-26	-0.5
1938	Bro-N	12	27	0	4	0	0	0	3	2	0	.148	.207	.148	-1	-4	0			.974	0	C-12	-0.3
Total	2	42	75	1	11	0	1	0	5	5	16	.147	.200	.173	3	-10	0			.990	1	/C-38	-0.8

■ CUPID CHILDS Childs, Clarence Algernon b: 8/14/1867, Calvert Co., Md. d: 11/8/12, Baltimore, Md. BL/TR, 5'8", 185 lbs. Deb: 4/23/1888

YEAR	TM/L	G	AB	R	H	2B	3B	HR	RBI	BB	SO	AVG	OBP	SLG	PRO+	BR/A	SB	CS	SBR	FA	FR	G/POS	TPR
1888	Phi-N	2	4	0	0	0	0	0	0	0	0	.000	.000	.000	-95	-1	0			.857	0	/2-2	-0.1
1890	Syr-a	126	493	109	170	**33**	14	2	89	72		.345	.434	.481	189	**59**	56			.928	12	*2-125/S-1	**6.7**
1891	Cle-N	141	551	120	155	21	12	2	83	97	32	.281	.395	.374	119	17	39			.910	-12	*2-141	1.0
1892	*Cle-N	145	558	**136**	177	14	11	3	53	117	20	.317	**.443**	.398	149	40	26			.938	-6	*2-145	3.4
1893	Cle-N	124	485	145	158	19	10	3	65	120	12	.326	.463	.425	129	26	23			.926	10	*2-123	3.1
1894	Cle-N	118	479	143	169	21	12	2	52	107	11	.353	.475	.459	122	23	17			.916	-3	*2-118	1.9
1895	*Cle-N	119	462	96	133	15	3	4	90	74	24	.288	.393	.359	90	-5	20			.921	10	*2-119	0.9
1896	*Cle-N	132	498	106	177	24	9	1	106	100	18	.355	.467	.446	134	30	25			.942	**42**	*2-132	6.6
1897	Cle-N	114	444	105	150	15	9	1	61	74		.338	.435	.419	119	15	25			.944	17	*2-114	3.2
1898	Cle-N	110	413	90	119	9	4	1	31	69		.288	.395	.337	112	10	9			.931	9	*2-110	2.4
1899	StL-N	125	464	73	123	11	11	1	48	74		.265	.369	.343	93	-2	11			.934	-12	*2-125	-0.6
1900	Chi-N	137	531	67	128	14	5	0	44	57		.241	.323	.286	71	-19	15			.935	16	*2-137	0.3
1901	Chi-N	63	236	24	61	9	0	0	21	30		.258	.359	.297	95	0	3			.939	9	2-63	1.2
Total	13	1456	5618	1214	1720	205	100	20	743	991	117	.306	.416	.389	119	194	269			.930	92	*2-1454/S-1	30.0

■ PETE CHILDS Childs, Peter Pierre b: 11/15/1871, Philadelphia, Pa. d: 2/15/22, Philadelphia, Pa. TR , Deb: 4/24/01

YEAR	TM/L	G	AB	R	H	2B	3B	HR	RBI	BB	SO	AVG	OBP	SLG	PRO+	BR/A	SB	CS	SBR	FA	FR	G/POS	TPR
1901	StL-N	29	79	12	21	1	0	0	8	14		.266	.389	.278	100	1	0			.907	-7	2-19/O-2,S-1	-0.4
	Chi-N	60	210	23	48	5	1	0	14	26		.229	.319	.262	72	-6	4			.959	13	2-60	0.9
	Yr	89	289	35	69	6	1	0	22	40		.239	.339	.266	80	-5	4			.947	6	2-79/O-2,S-1	0.5
1902	Phi-N	123	403	25	78	5	0	0	25	34		.194	.256	.206	43	-26	6			.945	-9	*2-123	-3.3
Total	2	212	692	60	147	11	1	0	47	74		.212	.292	.231	59	-31	10			.946	-3	2-202/O-2,S-1	-2.8

■ PEARCE CHILES Chiles, Pearce Nuget "What's The Use" b: 5/28/1867, Deepwater, Mo. BR/TR, 5'11", 185 lbs. Deb: 4/18/1899

YEAR	TM/L	G	AB	R	H	2B	3B	HR	RBI	BB	SO	AVG	OBP	SLG	PRO+	BR/A	SB	CS	SBR	FA	FR	G/POS	TPR
1899	Phi-N	97	338	57	108	28	7	2	76	16		.320	.352	.462	127	10	6			.944	-15	O-46,1-25,2-16	-0.6
1900	Phi-N	33	111	13	24	6	2	1	23	6		.216	.256	.333	63	-6	4			.987	-3	1-16,2-12/O-3	-0.8
Total	2	130	449	70	132	34	9	3	99	22		.294	.328	.430	111	4	10			.947	-18	/O-49,1-41,2-28	-1.4

■ RICH CHILES Chiles, Richard Francis b: 11/22/49, Sacramento, Cal. BL/TL, 5'11", 170 lbs. Deb: 4/20/71

YEAR	TM/L	G	AB	R	H	2B	3B	HR	RBI	BB	SO	AVG	OBP	SLG	PRO+	BR/A	SB	CS	SBR	FA	FR	G/POS	TPR
1971	Hou-N	67	119	12	27	5	1	2	15	6	20	.227	.270	.336	73	-5	0	1	-1	1.000	-3	O-27	-1.0
1972	Hou-N	9	11	0	3	1	0	0	2	1	1	.273	.333	.364	100	0	0	0	0	1.000	0	/O-2	0.0
1973	NY-N	8	25	2	3	2	0	0	1	0	2	.120	.120	.200	-13	-4	0	0	0	1.000	2	/O-8	-0.2
1976	Hou-N	5	4	1	2	1	0	0	0	0	0	.500	.500	.750	276	1	0	0	0	1.000	-0	/O-1	0.1
1977	Min-A	108	261	31	69	16	1	3	36	23	17	.264	.329	.368	91	-3	0	1	-1	.946	-2	D-61,O-22	-0.8
1978	Min-A	87	198	22	53	12	0	1	22	20	25	.268	.341	.343	91	-2	1	2	-1	.965	-2	O-61/D-8	-0.7
Total	6	284	618	68	157	37	2	6	76	50	65	.254	.315	.350	85	-13	1	4	-2	.972	-5	O-121/D-69	-2.6

■ DINO CHIOZZA Chiozza, Dino Joseph "Dynamo" b: 6/30/12, Memphis, Tenn. d: 4/23/72, Memphis, Tenn. BL/TR, 6', 170 lbs. Deb: 7/14/35 F

YEAR	TM/L	G	AB	R	H	2B	3B	HR	RBI	BB	SO	AVG	OBP	SLG	PRO+	BR/A	SB	CS	SBR	FA	FR	G/POS	TPR
1935	Phi-N	2	0	1	0	0	0	0	0	0	0	—	—	—	—	0	0			1.000	-0	/S-2	0.0

■ LOU CHIOZZA Chiozza, Louis Peo b: 5/17/10, Tallulah, La. d: 2/28/71, Memphis, Tenn. BL/TR, 6', 172 lbs. Deb: 4/17/34 F

YEAR	TM/L	G	AB	R	H	2B	3B	HR	RBI	BB	SO	AVG	OBP	SLG	PRO+	BR/A	SB	CS	SBR	FA	FR	G/POS	TPR
1934	Phi-N	134	484	66	147	28	5	0	44	34	35	.304	.357	.382	86	-9	9			.938	-24	2-85,3-26,O-17	-2.7
1935	Phi-N	124	472	71	134	26	6	3	47	33	44	.284	.333	.383	84	-11	5			.947	3	*2-120/3-2	0.1
1936	Phi-N	144	572	83	170	32	6	1	48	37	39	.297	.346	.379	87	-11	17			.972	1	O-90,2-33,3-26	-1.1
1937	*NY-N	117	439	49	102	11	2	4	29	20	30	.232	.266	.294	51	-30	6			.939	2	3-93,O-12/2-2	-2.6
1938	NY-N	57	179	15	42	7	2	3	17	12	7	.235	.283	.346	72	-7	5			.944	-8	2-34,O-16/3-1	-1.4
1939	NY-N	40	142	19	38	3	1	3	12	9	10	.268	.311	.366	81	-4	3			.915	-3	3-30/S-8	-0.6
Total	6	616	2288	303	633	107	22	14	197	145	165	.277	.324	.361	78	-72	45			.943	-30	2-274,3-178,O/S	-8.3

■ WALT CHIPPLE Chipple, Walter John (b: Walter John Chlipala) b: 9/26/18, Utica, N.Y. d: 6/8/88, Tonawanda, N.Y. BR/TR, 6'0.5", 168 lbs. Deb: 4/17/45

YEAR	TM/L	G	AB	R	H	2B	3B	HR	RBI	BB	SO	AVG	OBP	SLG	PRO+	BR/A	SB	CS	SBR	FA	FR	G/POS	TPR
1945	Was-A	18	44	4	6	0	0	0	5	5	6	.136	.224	.136	6	-5	0	1	-1	.978	3	O-13	-0.4

■ TOM CHISM Chism, Thomas Raymond b: 5/9/55, Chester, Pa. BL/TL, 6'1", 195 lbs. Deb: 9/13/79

YEAR	TM/L	G	AB	R	H	2B	3B	HR	RBI	BB	SO	AVG	OBP	SLG	PRO+	BR/A	SB	CS	SBR	FA	FR	G/POS	TPR
1979	Bal-A	6	3	0	0	0	0	0	0	0	0	.000	.000	.000	-99	-1	0	0	0	1.000	-0	/1-4	-0.1

YEAR	TM/L	G	AB	R	H	2B	3B	HR	RBI	BB	SO	AVG	OBP	SLG	PRO+	BR/A	SB	CS	SBR	FA	FR	G/POS	TPR

■ HARRY CHITI　Chiti, Harry　b: 11/16/32, Kincaid, Ill.　BR/TR, 6'3", 225 lbs.　Deb: 9/27/50

1950	Chi-N	3	6	0	2	0	0	0	0	0	0	.333	.333	.333	77	-0	0			1.000	-1	/C-1	-0.1
1951	Chi-N	9	31	1	11	2	0	0	5	2	2	.355	.394	.419	117	1	0	0	0	.913	0	/C-8	0.1
1952	Chi-N	32	113	14	31	5	0	5	13	5	8	.274	.305	.451	106	0	0	1	-1	.984	6	C-32	0.7
1955	Chi-N	113	338	24	78	6	1	11	41	25	68	.231	.286	.352	68	-16	0	0	0	.984	1	*C-113	-1.2
1956	Chi-N	72	203	17	43	6	4	4	18	19	35	.212	.283	.340	68	-10	0	0	0	.981	2	C-67	-0.5
1958	KC-A	103	295	32	79	11	3	9	44	18	48	.268	.316	.417	98	-1	3	2	-0	.987	3	C-83	0.6
1959	KC-A	55	162	20	44	11	1	5	25	17	26	.272	.344	.444	113	3	0	1	-1	.988	2	C-47	0.7
1960	KC-A	58	190	16	42	7	0	5	28	17	33	.221	.288	.337	68	-9	1	0		.983	-1	C-52	-0.6
	Det-A	37	104	9	17	0	0	2	5	10	12	.163	.237	.221	24	-11	0	3	-2	.984	1	C-36	-1.0
	Yr	95	294	25	59	7	0	7	33	27	45	.201	.270	.296	52	-20	1	3	-2	.984	1	C-88	-1.6
1961	Det-A	5	12	0	1	0	0	0	0	1	2	.083	.154	.083	-34	-2	0	0	0	1.000	1	/C-5	-0.1
1962	NY-N	15	41	2	8	1	0	0	0	1	8	.195	.233	.220	22	-4	0	0	0	.971	-1	C-14	-0.5
Total	10	502	1495	135	356	49	9	41	179	115	242	.238	.296	.365	77	-50	4	7		.983	13	C-458	-1.9

■ FELIX CHOUINARD　Chouinard, Felix George　b: 10/5/1887, Chicago, Ill.　d: 4/28/55, Hines, Ill.　BR/TR, 5'7", 150 lbs.　Deb: 9/11/10

1910	Chi-A	24	82	6	16	3	2	0	9	8		.195	.275	.280	77	-2	4			.962	4	O-23/2-1	0.1
1911	Chi-A	14	17	3	3	0	0	0	0	0		.176	.176	.176	-2	-2	0			.857	1	/2-4,O-4	-0.1
1914	Pit-F	9	30	2	9	1	0	1	3	0	4	.300	.300	.433	99	-1	1			.917	-0	/2-4,O-3,S-1	-0.1
	Bro-F	32	79	7	20	1	2	0	8	4	13	.253	.289	.316	65	-5	3			.929	-1	O-20	-0.7
	Bal-F	5	9	3	4	0	0	0	1	0	1	.444	.444	.444	138	-0	0			1.000	-0	/O-2	0.0
	Yr	46	118	12	33	2	2	1	12	4	18	.280	.303	.356	79	-5	4			.941	-1	O-25/2-4,S-1	-0.8
1915	Bro-F	4	4	1	2	0	0	0	2	0	0	.500	.500	.500	183	-0	0			1.000	-1	/O-2	0.0
Total	4	88	221	22	54	5	4	1	23	12	18	.244	.286	.317	75	-10	8			.948	4	/O-54,2-9,S-1	-0.8

■ HARRY CHOZEN　Chozen, Harry　b: 9/27/15, Winnebago, Minn.　d: 9/16/94, Houston, Tex.　BR/TR, 5'9.5", 190 lbs.　Deb: 9/21/37

| 1937 | Cin-N | 1 | 4 | 0 | 1 | 0 | 0 | 0 | 0 | 0 | 0 | .250 | .250 | .250 | 38 | -0 | 0 | | | .833 | -0 | /C-1 | -0.1 |

■ NEIL CHRISLEY　Chrisley, Barbra O'Neil　b: 12/16/31, Calhoun Falls, S.C　BR/TR, 6'3", 187 lbs.　Deb: 4/15/57

1957	Was-A	26	51	6	8	2	1	0	3	6	9	.157	.259	.235	36	-4	0	0	0	.810	-1	O-11	-0.6
1958	Was-A	105	233	19	50	7	4	5	26	16	18	.215	.265	.343	67	-11	1	3	-2	.992	1	O-69/3-1	-1.6
1959	Det-A	65	106	7	14	3	0	6	11	12	10	.132	.237	.330	48	-8	0	0	0	1.000	-2	O-21	-1.1
1960	Det-A	96	220	27	56	10	3	5	24	19	26	.255	.317	.395	89	-4	2	0	1	.981	2	O-47/1-2	-0.3
1961	Mil-N	10	9	1	2	0	0	0	0	1	1	.222	.300	.222	44	-1	0	0	0	.000	0	H	-0.1
Total	5	302	619	60	130	22	8	16	64	55	62	.210	.277	.349	69	-28	3	3	-1	.975	-0	O-148/1-2,3-1	-3.7

■ LLOYD CHRISTENBURY　Christenbury, Lloyd Reid "Low"　b: 10/19/1893, Mecklenburg Co., N.C.　d: 12/13/44, Birmingham, Ala.　BL/TR, 5'7", 165 lbs.　Deb: 9/20/19

1919	Bos-N	7	31	5	9	1	0	0	4	2	2	.290	.333	.323	102	-0	0			.941	1	/O-7	0.1
1920	Bos-N	65	106	17	22	2	2	0	14	13	12	.208	.300	.264	66	-4	0	1	-1	.895	-7	O-14/S-7,2-6,3-2	-1.2
1921	Bos-N	62	125	34	44	6	2	3	16	21	7	.352	.449	.504	161	12	3	4	-2	.914	-13	2-32/S-2,3-2	-0.1
1922	Bos-N	71	152	22	38	5	2	1	13	18	11	.250	.337	.329	76	-5	2	4	-2	.946	1	O-32/2-5,3-2	-0.8
Total	4	205	414	78	113	14	6	4	47	54	32	.273	.362	.365	101	3	5	9		.936	-18	/O-53,2-43,S-9,3-6	-2.0

■ BRUCE CHRISTENSEN　Christensen, Bruce Ray　b: 2/22/48, Madison, Wis.　BL/TR, 5'11", 160 lbs.　Deb: 7/17/71

| 1971 | Cal-A | 29 | 63 | 4 | 17 | 1 | 0 | 0 | 3 | 6 | 5 | .270 | .333 | .286 | 83 | -1 | 0 | 1 | -1 | .988 | 2 | S-24 | 0.3 |

■ JOHN CHRISTENSEN　Christensen, John Lawrence　b: 9/5/60, Downey, Cal.　BR/TR, 6'3", 205 lbs.　Deb: 9/13/84

1984	NY-N	5	11	2	3	2	0	0	3	1	2	.273	.333	.455	121	0	0	1	-1	.500	-2	/O-5	-0.2
1985	NY-N	51	113	10	21	4	1	3	13	19	23	.186	.303	.319	76	-3	1	2	-1	.956	-6	O-38	-1.2
1987	Sea-A	53	132	19	32	6	1	2	12	12	28	.242	.306	.348	69	-6	2	0	1	1.000	-3	O-43/D-8	-0.8
1988	Min-A	23	38	5	10	4	0	0	5	3	5	.263	.349	.368	98	-0	0	0	0	1.000	-1	O-17/D-1	-0.3
Total	4	132	294	36	66	16	2	5	33	35	58	.224	.311	.344	77	-9	3	3	-1	.977	-13	O-103/D-9	-2.5

■ CUCKOO CHRISTENSEN　Christensen, Walter Niels "Seacap"　b: 10/24/1899, San Francisco, Cal　d: 12/20/84, Menlo Park, Cal.　BL/TL, 5'6.5", 156 lbs.　Deb: 4/13/26

1926	Cin-N	114	329	41	115	15	7	0	41	40	18	.350	.426	.438	136	19	8			.978	-10	O-93	0.3
1927	Cin-N	57	185	25	47	6	0	0	16	20	16	.254	.330	.286	68	-8	4			.957	-3	O-50	-1.4
Total	2	171	514	66	162	21	7	0	57	60	34	.315	.392	.383	112	11	12			.970	-13	O-143	-1.1

■ RYAN CHRISTENSON　Christenson, Ryan Alan　b: 3/28/74, Redlands, Cal.　BR/TR, 5'11", 175 lbs.　Deb: 4/20/98

| 1998 | Oak-A | 117 | 370 | 56 | 95 | 22 | 6 | 5 | 40 | 36 | 106 | .257 | .324 | .368 | 82 | -10 | 5 | 6 | -2 | .983 | 2 | *O-116 | -1.1 |

■ BOB CHRISTIAN　Christian, Robert Charles　b: 10/17/45, Chicago, Ill.　d: 2/20/74, San Diego, Cal.　BR/TR, 5'10", 180 lbs.　Deb: 9/2/68

1968	Det-A	3	3	0	1	1	0	0	0	0	0	.333	.333	.667	191	0	0	0	0	1.000	-0	/1-1,O-1	0.0
1969	Chi-A	39	129	11	28	4	0	3	16	10	19	.217	.279	.318	63	-6	3	0	1	.958	0	O-38	-0.8
1970	Chi-A	12	15	3	4	0	0	1	3	1	4	.267	.313	.467	108	0	0	0	0	1.000	-1	/O-4	-0.1
Total	3	54	147	14	33	5	0	4	19	11	23	.224	.283	.340	70	-6	3	0	1	.959	-1	/O-43,1-1	-0.9

■ MARK CHRISTMAN　Christman, Marquette Joseph　b: 10/21/13, Maplewood, Mo.　d: 10/9/76, St.Louis, Mo.　BR/TR, 5'11", 180 lbs.　Deb: 4/20/38

1938	Det-A	95	318	35	79	6	4	1	44	27	21	.248	.307	.302	50	-24	5	2	0	.983	9	3-69,S-21	-1.2
1939	Det-A	6	16	0	4	2	0	0	0	0	2	.250	.250	.375	54	-1	0	0	0	.900	1	/3-5	-0.2
	StL-A	79	222	27	48	6	3	0	20	20	10	.216	.281	.270	41	-20	2	1	0	.960	21	S-64/2-1	0.6
	Yr	85	238	27	52	8	3	0	20	20	12	.218	.279	.277	42	-21	2	1	0	.960	20	S-64/3-5,2-1	0.4
1943	StL-A	98	336	31	91	11	5	2	35	19	19	.271	.318	.351	94	-3	0	3	-2	.991	-3	3-37,S-24,1-20,2-14	-0.4
1944	*StL-A	148	547	56	148	25	1	6	83	47	37	.271	.332	.353	90	-7	5	2	0	.972	4	*3-145/1-3	-0.1
1945	StL-A	78	289	32	80	7	4	4	34	19	19	.277	.328	.370	98	-1	1	0	0	.973	-3	3-77	-0.2
1946	StL-A	128	458	40	118	22	2	1	41	22	29	.258	.295	.321	68	-20	0	2	-1	.975	9	3-77,S-47	-0.8
1947	Was-A	110	374	27	83	15	2	1	33	32	16	.222	.287	.281	60	-21	4	4	-1	.978	-10	*S-106/2-1	-2.7
1948	Was-A	120	409	38	106	17	2	1	40	25	19	.259	.303	.318	67	-20	0	3	-2	.969	-32	*S-102/3-9,2-3	-4.8
1949	Was-A	49	112	8	24	2	0	3	18	8	7	.214	.273	.313	56	-8	0	0	0	.967	-4	3-23/1-6,S-4,2-1	-0.5
Total	9	911	3081	294	781	113	23	19	348	219	179	.253	.306	.324	71	-125	17	17	-5	.975	-0	3-442,S-368/1-29,2	-10.3

■ STEVE CHRISTMAS　Christmas, Stephen Randall　b: 12/9/57, Orlando, Fla.　BL/TR, 6', 190 lbs.　Deb: 9/1/83

1983	Cin-N	9	17	0	1	0	0	0	1	1	3	.059	.111	.059	-50	-3	0	0	0	1.000	-0	/C-7	-0.4
1984	Chi-A	12	11	1	4	1	0	1	4	0	2	.364	.364	.727	185	1	0	0	0	1.000	0	/C-1	0.1
1986	Chi-N	3	9	0	1	1	0	0	2	0	1	.111	.111	.222	-10	-1	0	0	0	1.000	-0	/C-1,1-1	-0.2
Total	3	24	37	1	6	2	0	1	7	1	6	.162	.184	.297	30	-4	0	0	0	1.000	-0	/C-9,1-1	-0.5

■ JOE CHRISTOPHER　Christopher, Joseph O'Neal　b: 12/13/35, Frederiksted, V.I.　BR/TR, 5'10", 176 lbs.　Deb: 5/26/59

1959	Pit-N	15	12	6	0	0	0	0	0	1	4	.000	.077	.000	-78	-3	0	0	0	1.000	-3	/O-9	-0.6
1960	*Pit-N	50	56	21	13	2	0	0	3	5	8	.232	.295	.321	68	-2	1	0	0	1.000	-2	O-17	-0.5
1961	Pit-N	76	186	25	49	7	3	0	14	18	24	.263	.328	.333	76	-6	4	4	-1	.978	-2	O-55	-1.1
1962	NY-N	119	271	36	66	10	2	6	32	35	42	.244	.339	.362	87	-4	11	3	2	.972	-9	O-94	-1.6
1963	NY-N	64	149	19	33	5	1	1	8	13	21	.221	.297	.289	68	-6	1	3	-2	.983	-1	O-45	-1.5
1964	NY-N	154	543	78	163	26	8	16	76	48	92	.300	.360	.466	135	25	6	5	-1	.974	1	*O-145	1.8
1965	NY-N	148	437	38	109	18	3	5	40	35	82	.249	.314	.339	87	-7	4	4	-1	.989	-3	*O-112	-1.8
1966	Bos-A	12	13	1	1	0	0	0	0	2	4	.077	.200	.077	-15	-2	0	0	0	1.000	-1	/O-2	-0.3
Total	8	638	1667	224	434	68	17	29	173	157	277	.260	.331	.374	96	-6	29	19	-3	.979	-24	O-479	-5.6

■ LOYD CHRISTOPHER　Christopher, Loyd Eugene　b: 12/31/19, Richmond, Cal.　d: 9/5/91, Richmond, Cal.　BR/TR, 6'2", 190 lbs.　Deb: 4/20/45　F

| 1945 | Bos-A | 8 | 14 | 4 | 4 | 1 | 0 | 0 | 4 | 3 | 2 | .286 | .412 | .286 | 101 | 0 | 0 | 0 | 0 | 1.000 | -1 | /O-3 | -0.1 |

YEAR	TM/L	G	AB	R	H	2B	3B	HR	RBI	BB	SO	AVG	OBP	SLG	PRO+	BR/A	SB	CS	SBR	FA	FR	G/POS	TPR
	Chi-N	1	0	0	0	0	0	0	0	0	0	—	—	—	—	0	0			.000	-0	/O-1	0.0
1947	Chi-A	7	23	1	5	0	1	0	0	2	4	.217	.280	.304	65	-1	0	1	-1	1.000	1	/O-7	-0.1
Total	2	16	37	5	9	0	1	0	4	5	6	.243	.333	.297	80	-1	0	1		1.000	0	/O-11	-0.2
■ **HI CHURCH**	Church, Hiram Lincoln b: 11/23/1863, Central Square, N.Y. d: 2/23/26, Jacksonville, Fla. Deb: 8/23/1890																						
1890	Bro-a	3	9	1	1	0	0	0	0	0		.111	.111	.111	-36	-2	0			1.000	-1	/O-3	-0.3
■ **JOHN CHURRY**	Churry, John b: 11/26/1900, Johnstown, Pa. d: 2/8/70, Zanesville, Ohio BR/TR, 5'9", 172 lbs. Deb: 5/24/24																						
1924	Chi-N	6	7	0	1	1	0	0	0	2	0	.143	.333	.286	67	-0	0	0	0	1.000	0	/C-3	0.0
1925	Chi-N	3	6	1	3	0	0	0	1	0	0	.500	.500	.500	154	0	0	0	0	1.000	-0	/C-3	0.0
1926	Chi-N	2	4	0	0	0	0	0	0	1	2	.000	.200	.000	-42	-1	0			1.000	0	/C-1	-0.1
1927	Chi-N	1	1	0	1	0	0	0	0	0	0	1.000	1.000	1.000	436	0	0			1.000	0	/C-1	0.1
Total	4	12	18	1	5	1	0	0	1	3	2	.278	.381	.333	89	-0	0	0		1.000	0	/C-8	0.0
■ **LARRY CIAFFONE**	Ciaffone, Lawrence Thomas "Symphony Larry" b: 8/17/24, Brooklyn, N.Y. d: 12/14/91, Brooklyn, N.Y. BR/TR, 5'9.5", 185 lbs. Deb: 4/17/51																						
1951	StL-N	5	5	0	0	0	0	0	0	1	2	.000	.167	.000	-51	-1	0	0	0	1.000	-0	/O-1	-0.1
■ **ARCHI CIANFROCCO**	Cianfrocco, Angelo Dominic b: 10/6/66, Rome, N.Y. BR/TR, 6'5", 215 lbs. Deb: 4/8/92																						
1992	Mon-N	86	232	25	56	5	2	6	30	11	66	.241	.279	.358	80	-7	3	0	1	.993	1	1-56,3-19/O-5	-0.8
1993	Mon-N	12	17	3	4	1	0	1	1	0	5	.235	.235	.471	80	-1	0	0	0	1.000	-0	1-11	-0.1
	SD-N	84	279	27	68	10	2	11	47	17	64	.244	.294	.412	85	-7	2	0	1	.932	-5	3-64,1-31	-1.3
	Yr	96	296	30	72	11	2	12	48	17	69	.243	.291	.416	85	-7	2	0	1	.932	-6	3-64,1-42	-1.4
1994	SD-N	59	146	9	32	8	0	4	13	3	39	.219	.255	.356	59	-9	2	0	1	.920	2	3-37,1-16/S-1	-0.7
1995	SD-N	51	118	22	31	7	0	5	31	11	28	.263	.336	.449	109	1	0	2	-1	1.000	-2	1-30,S-15/O-7,23	-0.2
1996	*SD-N	79	192	21	54	13	3	2	32	8	56	.281	.317	.411	96	-2	1	0	0	1.000	-8	1-33,3-11,S/O2C	-1.1
1997	SD-N	89	220	25	54	12	0	4	26	25	80	.245	.331	.355	86	-5	7	1	2	.983	10	1-39,3-38,2-12,/SO	0.6
1998	SD-N	40	72	4	9	3	0	1	5	5	22	.125	.192	.208	4	-11	1	0	0	1.000	1	1-19,3-13/2-3,O-3	-1.0
Total	7	500	1276	136	308	59	7	34	185	80	360	.241	.294	.379	81	-39	16	3	3	.994	-1	1-235,3-185/SO2C	-4.6
■ **DARRYL CIAS**	Cias, Darryl Richard b: 4/23/57, New York, N.Y. BR/TR, 5'11", 190 lbs. Deb: 4/27/83																						
1983	Oak-A	19	18	1	6	1	0	0	1	2	4	.333	.400	.389	126	1	1	0	0	.967	-0	C-19	0.1
■ **JOE CICERO**	Cicero, Joseph Francis "Dode" b: 11/18/10, Atlantic City, N.J d: 3/30/83, Clearwater, Fla. BR/TR, 5'8", 167 lbs. Deb: 9/20/29																						
1929	Bos-A	10	32	6	10	2	2	0	4	0	2	.313	.313	.500	108	0	0	0	0	1.000	-1	/O-7	-0.1
1930	Bos-A	18	30	5	5	1	2	0	4	1	5	.167	.194	.333	32	-3	0	0	0	.000	-2	/O-5,3-2	-0.5
1945	Phi-A	12	19	3	3	0	0	0	0	1	6	.158	.238	.158	16	-2	0	0	0	1.000	-2	/O-7	-0.5
Total	3	40	81	14	18	3	4	0	8	2	13	.222	.250	.358	60	-5	0	0	0	1.000	-4	/O-19,3-2	-1.1
■ **TED CIESLAK**	Cieslak, Thaddeus Walter b: 11/22/16, Milwaukee, Wis. BR/TR, 5'10", 175 lbs. Deb: 4/18/44																						
1944	Phi-N	85	220	18	54	10	0	2	11	21	17	.245	.314	.318	81	-5	1			.877	-15	3-48/O-5	-2.1
■ **AL CIHOCKI**	Cihocki, Albert Joseph b: 5/7/24, Nanticoke, Pa. BR/TR, 5'11", 185 lbs. Deb: 4/17/45																						
1945	Cle-A	92	283	21	60	9	3	0	24	11	48	.212	.241	.265	49	-19	2	1	0	.946	1	S-41,3-29,2-23	-1.5
■ **ED CIHOCKI**	Cihocki, Edward Joseph "Cy" b: 5/9/07, Wilmington, Del. d: 11/9/87, Newark, Del. BR/TR, 5'8", 163 lbs. Deb: 5/29/32																						
1932	Phi-A	1	1	0	0	0	0	0	0	0	0	.000	.000	.000	-97	-0	0	0	0	.000	0	H	0.0
1933	Phi-A	33	97	6	14	2	3	0	9	7	16	.144	.202	.227	13	-12	0	0	0	.904	-2	S-28/2-1,3-1	-1.3
Total	2	34	98	6	14	2	3	0	9	7	16	.143	.200	.224	12	-13	0	0	0	.904	-2	/S-28,3-1,2-1	-1.3
■ **GINO CIMOLI**	Cimoli, Gino Nicholas b: 12/18/29, San Francisco, Cal. BR/TR, 6'2", 200 lbs. Deb: 4/19/56																						
1956	*Bro-N	73	36	3	4	1	0	0	4	1	8	.111	.135	.139	-24	-6	1	0	0	.946	-18	O-62	-2.6
1957	Bro-N★	142	532	88	156	22	5	10	57	39	86	.293	.346	.410	93	-5	3	1	0	.979	-3	*O-138	-1.5
1958	LA-N	109	325	35	80	6	3	9	27	18	49	.246	.292	.366	71	-14	3	3	-1	.974	-8	*O-104	-2.8
1959	StL-N	143	519	61	145	40	7	8	72	37	83	.279	.330	.430	94	-5	7	0	2	.979	5	*O-141	-0.5
1960	*Pit-N	101	307	36	82	14	4	0	28	32	43	.267	.338	.339	85	-5	1	0	0	.964	-7	O-91	-1.7
1961	Pit-N	21	67	4	20	3	1	0	6	2	13	.299	.319	.373	83	-2	0	0	0	.971	-0	O-19	-0.3
	Mil-N	37	117	12	23	5	0	3	4	11	15	.197	.266	.316	57	-8	1	0	0	.985	-3	O-31	-1.2
	Yr	58	184	16	43	8	1	3	10	13	28	.234	.284	.337	67	-9	1	0	0	.980	-3	O-50	-1.5
1962	KC-A	152	550	67	151	20	**15**	10	71	40	89	.275	.326	.420	95	-5	2	1	0	.968	-9	*O-147	-2.2
1963	KC-A	145	529	56	139	19	11	4	48	39	72	.263	.316	.363	85	-10	3	1	0	.985	2	*O-136	-1.6
1964	KC-A	4	9	1	0	0	0	0	0	0	1	.000	.000	.000	-97	-2	0	0	0	1.000	-0	/O-4	-0.3
	Bal-A	38	58	6	8	3	2	0	3	2	13	.138	.167	.259	16	-7	0	0	0	.893	-9	O-35	-1.7
	Yr	42	67	7	8	3	2	0	3	2	14	.119	.145	.224	1	-9	0	0	0	.912	-9	O-39	-2.0
1965	Cal-A	4	5	1	0	0	0	0	1	0	2	.000	.000	.000	-99	-1	0	0	0	1.000	0	/O-1	-0.1
Total	10	969	3054	370	808	133	48	44	321	221	474	.265	.317	.383	84	-70	21	6	3	.974	-50	O-909	-16.5
■ **FRANK CIPRIANI**	Cipriani, Frank Dominick b: 4/14/41, Buffalo, N.Y. BR/TR, 6', 180 lbs. Deb: 9/8/61																						
1961	KC-A	13	36	2	9	0	0	0	2	2	4	.250	.289	.250	45	-3	0	0	0	1.000	-1	O-11	-0.4
■ **JEFF CIRILLO**	Cirillo, Jeffrey Howard b: 9/23/69, Pasadena, Cal. BR/TR, 6'2", 190 lbs. Deb: 5/11/94																						
1994	Mil-A	39	126	17	30	9	0	3	12	11	16	.238	.309	.381	73	-5	0	1	-1	.965	-1	3-37/2-1	-0.6
1995	Mil-A	125	328	57	91	19	4	9	39	47	42	.277	.375	.442	106	3	7	2	1	.938	15	*3-108,2-25/1-3,S-2	1.9
1996	Mil-A	158	566	101	184	46	5	15	83	58	69	.325	.395	.504	120	18	4	9	-4	.950	-11	*3-154/1-2,2-1,D-3	0.3
1997	Mil-A★	154	580	74	167	46	2	10	82	60	74	.288	.369	.426	106	6	4	3	-1	.963	18	*3-150/D-2	2.3
1998	Mil-N	156	604	97	194	31	1	14	68	79	88	.321	.403	.445	119	20	10	4	1	.976	24	*3-149/1-6	4.5
Total	5	632	2204	346	666	151	12	51	284	255	289	.302	.382	.451	111	43	25	19	-4	.960	44	3-598/2-27,1-11,DS	8.4
■ **GEORGE CISAR**	Cisar, George Joseph b: 8/25/12, Chicago, Ill. BR/TR, 6', 175 lbs. Deb: 9/9/37																						
1937	Bro-N	20	29	8	6	0	0	0	4	2	6	.207	.258	.207	27	-3	3			1.000	-3	O-13	-0.6
■ **BILL CISSELL**	Cissell, Chalmer William b: 1/3/04, Perryville, Mo. d: 3/15/49, Chicago, Ill. BR/TR, 5'11", 170 lbs. Deb: 4/11/28																						
1928	Chi-A	125	443	66	115	22	3	1	60	29	41	.260	.307	.330	68	-21	18	6	2	.938	-2	*S-123	-0.6
1929	Chi-A	152	618	83	173	27	12	5	62	28	53	.280	.312	.387	80	-20	25	17	-3	.937	-3	*S-152	-0.7
1930	Chi-A	141	562	82	152	28	9	2	48	28	32	.270	.307	.363	72	-25	16	9	-1	.948	-11	*2-107,3-24,S-10	-2.6
1931	Chi-A	109	409	42	90	13	5	1	46	16	26	.220	.256	.284	44	-34	18	6	2	.944	-10	S-83,2-23/3-1	-3.1
1932	Chi-A	12	43	7	11	1	1	1	5	1	0	.256	.273	.395	76	-2	0	0	0	.928	0	S-12	-0.1
	Cle-A	131	541	78	173	35	6	6	93	28	25	.320	.354	.440	98	-3	18	15	-4	.964	11	*2-129/S-6	1.1
	Yr	143	584	85	184	36	7	7	98	29	25	.315	.349	.437	97	-4	18	15	-4	.964	11	*2-129,S-18	1.0
1933	Cle-A	112	409	53	94	21	3	6	33	31	29	.230	.284	.340	62	-23	6	6	-2	.947	-7	2-62,S-46/3-1	-2.5
1934	Bos-A	102	416	71	111	13	4	4	44	28	23	.267	.315	.346	66	-22	11	4	1	.959	-4	2-96/S-7,3-2	-1.8
1937	Phi-A	34	117	15	31	7	0	1	14	17	10	.265	.358	.350	81	-3	0	0	0	.962	3	2-33	0.2
1938	NY-N	38	149	19	40	6	0	2	18	6	11	.268	.297	.349	76	-5	1			.977	9	2-33/3-6	0.6
Total	9	956	3707	516	990	173	43	29	423	212	250	.267	.308	.360	73	-158	113	63		.958	-14	2-483,S-439/3-34	-9.5
■ **MOOSE CLABAUGH**	Clabaugh, John William b: 11/13/01, Albany, Mo. d: 7/11/84, Tucson, Ariz. BL/TR, 6', 185 lbs. Deb: 8/30/26																						
1926	Bro-N	11	14	2	1	1	0	0	1	0	1	.071	.133	.143	-26	-3	0			.600	-1	/O-2	-0.3
■ **BOBBY CLACK**	Clack, Robert S. "Gentlemanly Bob" (b: Robert S. Clark) b: 6/1850, England d: 10/22/33, Danvers, Mass. BR/TR, 5'9", 153 lbs. Deb: 5/13/1874																						
1874	Atl-n	33	135	22	23	1	0	0	13	4	2	.170	.194	.178	23	-10	0	0	0	.779	-1	O-31/1-2	-0.8
1875	Atl-n	17	59	1	6	0	0	0	1	0	3	.102	.102	.102	-33	-7	0	0	0	.867	3	O-17/1-1	-0.4
1876	Cin-N	32	118	10	19	0	1	0	5	5	12	.161	.195	.178	29	-8				.736	0	O-17/2-8,1-5,3-3,P	-0.7
Total	2 n	50	194	23	29	1	0	0	14	4	5	.149	.167	.155	7	-17	0	0	0	.811	2	/O-48,1-3	-1.2

■ DANNY CLAIRE Claire, David Matthew b: 11/17/1897, Ludington, Mich. d: 1/7/56, Las Vegas, Nev. BR/TR, 5'8", 164 lbs. Deb: 9/17/20

YEAR	TM/L	G	AB	R	H	2B	3B	HR	RBI	BB	SO	AVG	OBP	SLG	PRO+	BR/A	SB	CS	SBR	FA	FR	G/POS	TPR
1920	Det-A	3	7	1	1	0	0	0	0	0	0	.143	.143	.143	-25	-1	0	0	0	.800	-0	/S-3	-0.2

■ AL CLANCY Clancy, Albert Harrison b: 8/14/1888, Santa Fe, N.Mex. d: 10/17/51, Las Cruces, N.Mex. BR/TR, 5'10.5", 175 lbs. Deb: 6/20/11

YEAR	TM/L	G	AB	R	H	2B	3B	HR	RBI	BB	SO	AVG	OBP	SLG	PRO+	BR/A	SB	CS	SBR	FA	FR	G/POS	TPR
1911	StL-A	3	5	0	0	0	0	0	0	0		.000	.167	.000	-54	-1	0			.800	0	/3-2	-0.1

■ BUD CLANCY Clancy, John William b: 9/15/1900, Odell, Ill. d: 9/26/68, Ottumwa, Iowa BL/TL, 6', 170 lbs. Deb: 8/29/24

YEAR	TM/L	G	AB	R	H	2B	3B	HR	RBI	BB	SO	AVG	OBP	SLG	PRO+	BR/A	SB	CS	SBR	FA	FR	G/POS	TPR
1924	Chi-A	13	35	5	9	1	0	0	6	3	2	.257	.316	.286	58	-2	3	2	-0	.947	-2	/1-8	-0.4
1925	Chi-A	4	3	0	0	0	0	0	0	1	0	.000	.250	.000	-34	-1	0	0	0	.000	0	H	-0.1
1926	Chi-A	12	38	3	13	2	2	0	7	1	1	.342	.375	.500	131	2	0	0	0	.991	0	1-10	0.1
1927	Chi-A	130	464	46	139	21	2	3	53	24	24	.300	.337	.373	86	-10	4	3	-1	.991	0	*1-123	-1.8
1928	Chi-A	130	487	64	132	19	11	2	37	42	25	.271	.331	.368	85	-11	6	9	-4	.991	5	*1-128	-2.1
1929	Chi-A	92	290	36	82	14	6	3	45	16	19	.283	.320	.403	86	-7	3	1	0	.991	2	1-74	-1.1
1930	Chi-A	68	234	28	57	8	3	3	27	12	18	.244	.286	.342	61	-14	3	1	0	.995	-3	1-60	-2.2
1932	Bro-N	53	196	14	60	4	2	0	16	6	13	.306	.327	.347	83	-5	0			.996	3	1-53	-0.6
1934	Phi-N	20	49	8	12	0	0	1	7	6	4	.245	.339	.306	65	-2	0			1.000	-1	1-10	-0.4
Total	9	522	1796	204	504	69	26	12	198	111	106	.281	.325	.368	81	-50	19	16		.992	4	1-466	-8.6

■ BILL CLANCY Clancy, William Edward b: 4/12/1879, Redfield, N.Y. d: 2/10/48, Oriskany, N.Y. BR/TR, 6'2", 180 lbs. Deb: 4/14/05

YEAR	TM/L	G	AB	R	H	2B	3B	HR	RBI	BB	SO	AVG	OBP	SLG	PRO+	BR/A	SB	CS	SBR	FA	FR	G/POS	TPR
1905	Pit-N	56	227	23	52	11	3	2	34	4		.229	.246	.330	69	-10	3			.983	-4	1-52/O-4	-1.6

■ UKE CLANTON Clanton, Eucal "Cat" b: 2/19/1898, Powell, Mo. d: 2/24/60, Antlers, Okla. BL/TL, 5'8", 165 lbs. Deb: 9/21/22

YEAR	TM/L	G	AB	R	H	2B	3B	HR	RBI	BB	SO	AVG	OBP	SLG	PRO+	BR/A	SB	CS	SBR	FA	FR	G/POS	TPR
1922	Cle-A	1	1	0	0	0	0	0	0	0	1	.000	.000	.000	-99	-0	0	0	0	.500	-0	/1-1	-0.1

■ AARON CLAPP Clapp, Aaron Bronson b: 7/1856, Ithaca, N.Y. d: 1/13/14, Sayre, Pa. TR, 5'8", 175 lbs. Deb: 5/1/1879 F

YEAR	TM/L	G	AB	R	H	2B	3B	HR	RBI	BB	SO	AVG	OBP	SLG	PRO+	BR/A	SB	CS	SBR	FA	FR	G/POS	TPR
1879	Tro-N	36	146	24	39	9	3	0	18	6	10	.267	.296	.370	126	4				.935	-4	1-25,O-11	0.0

■ JOHN CLAPP Clapp, John Edgar b: 7/17/1851, Ithaca, N.Y. d: 12/18/04, Ithaca, N.Y. BR/TR, 5'7", 194 lbs. Deb: 4/26/1872 FM

YEAR	TM/L	G	AB	R	H	2B	3B	HR	RBI	BB	SO	AVG	OBP	SLG	PRO+	BR/A	SB	CS	SBR	FA	FR	G/POS	TPR
1872	Man-n	19	97	28	28	6	1	1	10	1	0	.289	.296	.402	120	3	2	1	0	.860	-1	C-19/S-2,O-1,M	0.1
1873	Ath-n	45	204	36	62	10	2	1	28	2	2	.304	.311	.387	99	-2	4	5	-2	**.908**	3	*C-43/S-6,2-1,O-1	-0.1
1874	Ath-n	39	165	46	48	7	4	3	19	1	1	.291	.295	.436	121	2	2	0	1	.861	7	C-27,O-15/S-1	0.8
1875	Ath-n	60	292	65	77	8	7	0	39	7	1	.264	.281	.339	103	-1	9	5	-0	.874	18	*C-60	1.6
1876	StL-N	64	298	60	91	4	2	0	29	8	2	.305	.324	.332	125	9				.874	9	*C-61/O-4,2-1	1.7
1877	StL-N	60	255	47	81	6	6	0	34	8	6	.318	.338	.388	135	11				.887	-6	*C-53,O-10/1-1	0.5
1878	Ind-N	63	263	42	80	10	2	0	29	13	8	.304	.337	.357	148	15				.890	-7	*O-44,1-12/C-9,S2M	0.5
1879	Buf-N	70	292	47	77	12	5	1	36	11	11	.264	.290	.349	107	2				.906	-9	*C-63/O-7,M	-0.5
1880	Cin-N	80	323	33	91	16	4	1	20	21	10	.282	.326	.365	135	12				.897	17	*C-73,O-10,M	2.9
1881	Cle-N	68	261	47	66	12	2	0	25	**35**	6	.253	.341	.314	113	6				.890	-5	C-48,O-21,M	0.3
1883	NY-N	20	73	6	13	0	0	0	5	5	4	.178	.231	.178	27	-6				.895	5	C-16/O-5,M	0.0
Total	4 n	163	758	175	215	31	14	5	96	11	4	.284	.294	.381	107	2	17	11	-2	.878	27	C-149/O-17,S-9,2-1	2.4
Total	7	425	1765	282	499	60	21	2	178	101	47	.283	.322	.344	122	48				.892	4	C-323,O-101/1S2	5.4

■ DENNY CLARE Clare, Dennis J. b: 1/1853, Brooklyn, N.Y. d: 11/26/28, Brooklyn, N.Y. Deb: 9/14/1872

YEAR	TM/L	G	AB	R	H	2B	3B	HR	RBI	BB	SO	AVG	OBP	SLG	PRO+	BR/A	SB	CS	SBR	FA	FR	G/POS	TPR
1872	Atl-n	2	7	1	1	0	0	0	0	0	0	.143	.143	.143	-10	-1	0	0	0	.857	-3	/2-2,S-1	-0.3

■ DOUG CLAREY Clarey, Douglas William b: 4/20/54, Los Angeles, Cal. BR/TR, 6', 180 lbs. Deb: 4/20/76

YEAR	TM/L	G	AB	R	H	2B	3B	HR	RBI	BB	SO	AVG	OBP	SLG	PRO+	BR/A	SB	CS	SBR	FA	FR	G/POS	TPR
1976	StL-N	9	4	2	1	0	0	1	2	0	1	.250	.250	1.000	240	1	0	0	0	1.000	0	/2-7	0.1

■ ALLIE CLARK Clark, Alfred Aloysius b: 6/16/23, S.Amboy, N.J. BR/TR, 5'11", 185 lbs. Deb: 8/5/47

YEAR	TM/L	G	AB	R	H	2B	3B	HR	RBI	BB	SO	AVG	OBP	SLG	PRO+	BR/A	SB	CS	SBR	FA	FR	G/POS	TPR
1947	*NY-A	24	67	9	25	5	0	1	14	5	2	.373	.417	.493	154	5	0	0	0	1.000	0	O-16	0.4
1948	*Cle-A	81	271	43	84	5	2	9	38	23	13	.310	.364	.443	117	6	0	2	-1	.982	-6	O-65/3-5,1-1	-0.5
1949	Cle-A	35	74	8	13	4	0	1	9	4	7	.176	.218	.270	29	-8	0	0	0	1.000	-4	O-17/1-1	-1.3
1950	Cle-A	59	163	19	35	6	1	6	21	11	10	.215	.264	.374	64	-10	0	1	-1	.987	-3	O-41	-1.4
1951	Cle-A	3	10	3	3	2	0	1	3	1	2	.300	.364	.800	221	1	0	0	0	1.000	-1	/O-3	0.1
	Phi-A	56	161	20	40	10	1	4	22	15	7	.248	.320	.398	91	-2	2	0	1	.984	-1	O-32,3-10	-0.4
	Yr	59	171	23	43	12	1	5	25	16	9	.251	.323	.421	98	-1	2	0	1	.985	-1	O-35,3-10	-0.3
1952	Phi-A	71	186	23	51	12	0	7	29	10	19	.274	.315	.452	105	0	0	2	-1	.988	-3	O-48/1-2	-0.6
1953	Phi-A	20	74	6	15	4	0	3	13	3	5	.203	.234	.378	61	-5	0	0	0	1.000	-0	O-19	-0.6
	Chi-A	9	15	0	1	0	0	0	0	0	5	.067	.067	.067	-62	-3	0	0	0	1.000	-0	/1-1,O-1	-0.4
	Yr	29	89	6	16	4	0	3	13	3	10	.180	.207	.326	40	-8	0	0	0	1.000	-1	O-20/1-1	-1.0
Total	7	358	1021	131	267	48	4	32	149	72	70	.262	.312	.410	92	-16	2	5	-2	.988	-19	O-242/3-15,1-5	-4.7

■ DAD CLARK Clark, Alfred Robert "Fred" b: 7/16/1873, San Francisco, Cal. d: 7/26/56, Ogden, Utah BL/TL, 5'11", 170 lbs. Deb: 7/3/02

YEAR	TM/L	G	AB	R	H	2B	3B	HR	RBI	BB	SO	AVG	OBP	SLG	PRO+	BR/A	SB	CS	SBR	FA	FR	G/POS	TPR
1902	Chi-N	12	43	1	8	1	0	0	2	4		.186	.255	.209	45	-3	1			.938	-1	1-12	-0.5

■ TONY CLARK Clark, Anthony Christopher b: 6/15/72, Newton, Kan. BB/TR, 6'7", 240 lbs. Deb: 9/3/95

YEAR	TM/L	G	AB	R	H	2B	3B	HR	RBI	BB	SO	AVG	OBP	SLG	PRO+	BR/A	SB	CS	SBR	FA	FR	G/POS	TPR
1995	Det-A	27	101	10	24	5	1	3	11	8	30	.238	.294	.396	78	-4	0	0	0	.985	-1	1-27	-0.6
1996	Det-A	100	376	56	94	14	0	27	72	29	127	.250	.304	.503	99	-3	0	1	-1	.993	-2	1-86,D-12	-1.3
1997	Det-A	159	580	105	160	28	3	32	117	93	144	.276	.379	.500	128	25	1	3	-2	.993	-2	*1-158/D-1	0.5
1998	Det-A	157	602	84	175	37	0	34	103	63	128	.291	.361	.522	125	21	3	3	-1	.991	1	*1-142,D-15	0.6
Total	4	443	1659	255	453	84	4	96	303	193	429	.273	.351	.502	117	40	4	7	-3	.992	-4	1-413/D-28	-0.8

■ EARL CLARK Clark, Bailey Earl b: 11/6/07, Washington, D.C. d: 1/16/38, Washington, D.C. BR/TR, 5'10", 160 lbs. Deb: 8/17/27

YEAR	TM/L	G	AB	R	H	2B	3B	HR	RBI	BB	SO	AVG	OBP	SLG	PRO+	BR/A	SB	CS	SBR	FA	FR	G/POS	TPR
1927	Bos-N	13	44	6	12	1	0	0	3	2	4	.273	.304	.295	66	-2	0			1.000	-1	O-13	-0.3
1928	Bos-N	28	112	18	34	9	1	0	10	4	8	.304	.339	.402	98	-1	0			.987	-1	O-27	-0.3
1929	Bos-N	84	279	43	88	13	3	1	30	12	30	.315	.346	.394	86	-6	6			.978	4	O-74	-0.6
1930	Bos-N	82	233	29	69	11	3	3	28	7	22	.296	.320	.408	77	-9	3			.977	1	O-63	-1.1
1931	Bos-N	16	50	8	11	2	0	0	4	7	4	.220	.316	.260	58	-3	1			.970	1	O-14	-0.3
1932	Bos-N	50	44	11	11	2	0	0	4	2	7	.250	.283	.295	58	-3	1			1.000	-2	O-16	-0.5
1933	Bos-N	7	23	3	8	1	0	0	1	2	1	.348	.400	.391	138	1	0			1.000	-1	/O-6	0.0
1934	StL-A	13	41	4	7	2	0	0	1	1	3	.171	.190	.220	5	-6	0	0	0	1.000	1	/O-9	-0.5
Total	8	293	826	122	240	41	7	4	81	37	79	.291	.324	.372	78	-28	11	0		.981	2	O-222	-3.6

■ DANNY CLARK Clark, Daniel Curran b: 1/18/1894, Meridian, Miss. d: 5/23/37, Meridian, Miss. BL/TR, 5'9", 167 lbs. Deb: 4/12/22

YEAR	TM/L	G	AB	R	H	2B	3B	HR	RBI	BB	SO	AVG	OBP	SLG	PRO+	BR/A	SB	CS	SBR	FA	FR	G/POS	TPR
1922	Det-A	83	185	31	54	11	3	3	26	15	11	.292	.345	.432	105	1	1	0	0	.945	-6	2-38/O-5,3-1	-0.4
1924	Bos-A	104	325	36	90	23	3	2	54	51	19	.277	.378	.385	97	-0	4	7	-3	.943	-6	3-94	-0.2
1927	StL-N	58	72	8	17	2	2	0	13	8	7	.236	.313	.319	67	-3	0			.929	1	/O-9	0.3
Total	3	245	582	75	161	36	8	5	93	74	37	.277	.360	.392	96	-3	5	7		.943	-11	/3-95,2-38,O-14	-0.9

■ DAVE CLARK Clark, David Earl b: 9/3/62, Tupelo, Miss. BL/TR, 6'2", 210 lbs. Deb: 9/3/86

YEAR	TM/L	G	AB	R	H	2B	3B	HR	RBI	BB	SO	AVG	OBP	SLG	PRO+	BR/A	SB	CS	SBR	FA	FR	G/POS	TPR
1986	Cle-A	18	58	10	16	1	0	3	9	7	11	.276	.354	.448	119	2	1	0	0	1.000	1	O-10/D-7	0.2
1987	Cle-A	29	87	11	18	5	0	3	12	2	24	.207	.225	.368	53	-6	1	0	0	1.000	0	O-13,D-12	-0.6
1988	Cle-A	63	156	11	41	4	1	3	18	17	28	.263	.335	.359	92	-1	0	2	-1	.947	-4	D-27,O-23	-0.8
1989	Cle-A	102	253	21	60	12	0	8	29	30	63	.237	.318	.379	94	-2	0	2	-1	.964	-5	D-55,O-21	-1.0
1990	Chi-N	84	171	22	47	4	2	5	20	8	40	.275	.307	.409	89	-3	7	1	2	1.000	-2	O-39	-0.5
1991	KC-A	11	10	1	2	0	0	0	1	1	1	.200	.273	.200	33	-1	0	0	0	.000	-0	/O-1,D-1	-0.1
1992	Pit-N	23	33	3	7	0	0	2	7	6	8	.212	.333	.394	106	0	0	0	0	1.000	-1	/O-8	-0.1
1993	Pit-N	110	277	43	75	11	2	11	46	38	58	.271	.361	.444	114	6	1	0	0	.957	-11	O-91	-0.6
1994	Pit-N	86	223	37	66	11	1	10	46	22	48	.296	.359	.489	117	5	2	2	-1	.974	2	O-57	0.5
1995	Pit-N	77	196	30	55	6	0	4	24	24	38	.281	.362	.372	92	-1	3	3	-1	.961	-3	O-61	-0.7
1996	Pit-N	92	211	28	58	12	2	8	35	31	51	.275	.368	.464	115	5	2	1	0	.988	-4	O-61	0.0
	*LA-N	15	15	0	3	0	0	0	1	3	2	.200	.333	.200	49	-1	0	0	0	.000	-0	/O-1	-0.1

YEAR	TM/L	G	AB	R	H	2B	3B	HR	RBI	BB	SO	AVG	OBP	SLG	PRO+	BR/A	SB	CS	SBR	FA	FR	G/POS	TPR
	Yr	107	226	28	61	12	2	8	36	34	53	.270	.365	.447	112	4	2	1	0	.988	-4	O-62	-0.1
1997	Chi-N	102	143	19	43	8	0	5	32	19	34	.301	.390	.462	119	4	1	0	0	.953	0	O-25/D-4	0.5
1998	*Hou-N	93	131	12	27	7	0	0	4	14	45	.206	.288	.260	45	-11	1	1	-0	.885	-3	O-22/D-4	-1.4
Total	13	905	1964	248	518	81	8	62	284	222	451	.264	.340	.408	98	-4	19	12	-2	.969	-31	O-433,D-110	-4.7

■ GLEN CLARK Clark, Glen Ester b: 3/7/41, Austin, Tex. BB/TR, 6'1", 190 lbs. Deb: 6/3/67

YEAR	TM/L	G	AB	R	H	2B	3B	HR	RBI	BB	SO	AVG	OBP	SLG	PRO+	BR/A	SB	CS	SBR	FA	FR	G/POS	TPR
1967	Atl-N	4	4	0	0	0	0	0	0	0	1	.000	.000	.000	-99	-1	0	0	0	.000	0	H	-0.1

■ PEP CLARK Clark, Harry b: 3/20/1883, Union City, Ohio d: 6/8/65, Milwaukee, Wis. BR/TR, 5'7.5", 175 lbs. Deb: 9/11/03

YEAR	TM/L	G	AB	R	H	2B	3B	HR	RBI	BB	SO	AVG	OBP	SLG	PRO+	BR/A	SB	CS	SBR	FA	FR	G/POS	TPR
1903	Chi-A	15	65	7	20	4	2	0	9	2		.308	.338	.431	135	3	5			.877	-0	3-15	0.2

■ JACK CLARK Clark, Jack Anthony b: 11/10/55, New Brighton, Pa. BR/TR, 6'2", 205 lbs. Deb: 9/12/75

YEAR	TM/L	G	AB	R	H	2B	3B	HR	RBI	BB	SO	AVG	OBP	SLG	PRO+	BR/A	SB	CS	SBR	FA	FR	G/POS	TPR
1975	SF-N	8	17	3	4	0	0	0	2	1	2	.235	.278	.235	42	-1	1	0	0	1.000	-0	/O-3,3-2	-0.2
1976	SF-N	26	102	14	23	6	2	2	10	8	18	.225	.282	.382	85	-2	6	2	1	.987	1	O-26	-0.2
1977	SF-N	136	413	64	104	17	4	13	51	49	73	.252	.334	.407	98	-1	12	4	1	.975	7	*O-114	0.3
1978	SF-N★	156	592	90	181	46	8	25	98	50	72	.306	.363	.537	155	40	15	11	-2	.982	14	*O-152	4.7
1979	SF-N★	143	527	84	144	25	2	26	86	63	95	.273	.352	.476	133	22	11	8	-2	.982	5	*O-140/3-2	2.0
1980	SF-N	127	437	77	124	20	8	22	82	74	52	.284	.390	.517	155	33	2	5	-2	.967	1	*O-120	2.8
1981	SF-N	99	385	60	103	19	2	17	53	45	45	.268	.346	.460	129	14	1	1	-0	.981	12	O-98	2.4
1982	SF-N	157	563	90	154	30	3	27	103	90	91	.274	.375	.481	138	30	6	9	-4	.980	3	*O-155	2.6
1983	SF-N	135	492	82	132	25	0	20	66	74	79	.268	.365	.441	126	18	5	3	-0	.967	14	*O-133/1-2	2.8
1984	SF-N	57	203	33	65	9	1	11	44	43	29	.320	.439	.537	179	23	1	1	-0	.990	1	O-54/1-4	2.2
1985	*StL-N★	126	442	71	124	26	3	22	87	83	88	.281	.397	.502	151	32	1	4	-2	.988	-11	*1-121,O-12	1.3
1986	StL-N	65	232	34	55	12	2	9	23	45	61	.237	.363	.422	117	6	1	1	-0	.995	-7	1-64	-0.5
1987	*StL-N★	131	419	93	120	23	1	35	106	**136**	139	.286	**.461**	**.597**	**174**	52	1	2	-1	.989	-8	*1-126/O-1	3.3
1988	NY-A	150	496	81	120	14	0	27	93	113	141	.242	.385	.433	130	24	3	2	-0	.951	-1	*D-112,O-19,1-10	1.9
1989	SD-N	142	455	76	110	19	1	26	94	**132**	145	.242	.413	.459	149	36	6	2	1	.988	1	*1-131,O-12	2.8
1990	SD-N	115	334	59	89	12	1	25	62	**104**	91	.266	.443	.533	166	36	4	3	-1	.994	-3	*1-110	2.5
1991	Bos-A	140	481	75	120	18	1	28	87	96	133	.249	.378	.466	126	19	0	2	-1	.000	0	*D-135	1.2
1992	Bos-A	81	257	32	54	11	0	5	33	56	87	.210	.356	.311	83	-4	1	1	-0	.992	-1	D-64,1-13	-0.8
Total	18	1994	6847	1118	1826	332	39	340	1180	1262	1441	.267	.383	.476	138	377	77	61	-14	.978	27	*O-1039,1-581,D/3	31.1

■ JIM CLARK Clark, James (b: James Petrosky) b: 9/21/27, Baggaley, Pa. d: 10/24/90, Santa Monica, Cal. BR/TR, 5'9", 150 lbs. Deb: 8/17/48

YEAR	TM/L	G	AB	R	H	2B	3B	HR	RBI	BB	SO	AVG	OBP	SLG	PRO+	BR/A	SB	CS	SBR	FA	FR	G/POS	TPR
1948	Was-A	9	12	1	3	0	0	0	0	0	2	.250	.250	.250	34	-1	0	0	0	1.000	-0	/S-1,3-1	-0.1

■ JIM CLARK Clark, James Edward b: 4/30/47, Kansas City, Kan. BR/TR, 6'1", 190 lbs. Deb: 7/16/71

YEAR	TM/L	G	AB	R	H	2B	3B	HR	RBI	BB	SO	AVG	OBP	SLG	PRO+	BR/A	SB	CS	SBR	FA	FR	G/POS	TPR
1971	Cle-A	13	18	2	3	0	1	0	0	2	7	.167	.250	.278	45	-1	0	0	0	1.000	0	/O-3,1-1	-0.1

■ JIM CLARK Clark, James Francis b: 12/26/1887, Brooklyn, N.Y. d: 3/20/69, Beaumont, Tex. BR/TR, 5'11", 175 lbs. Deb: 9/2/11

YEAR	TM/L	G	AB	R	H	2B	3B	HR	RBI	BB	SO	AVG	OBP	SLG	PRO+	BR/A	SB	CS	SBR	FA	FR	G/POS	TPR
1911	StL-N	14	18	2	3	0	1	0	3	3	4	.167	.286	.278	60	-1	2			1.000	-3	/O-8	-0.4
1912	StL-N	2	1	0	0	0	0	0	0	0	1	.000	.000	.000	-99	-0	0			.000	0	H	0.0
Total	2	16	19	2	3	0	1	0	3	3	5	.158	.273	.263	51	-1	2			1.000	-3	/O-8	-0.4

■ JERALD CLARK Clark, Jerald Dwayne b: 8/10/63, Crockett, Tex. BR/TR, 6'4", 202 lbs. Deb: 9/19/88 F

YEAR	TM/L	G	AB	R	H	2B	3B	HR	RBI	BB	SO	AVG	OBP	SLG	PRO+	BR/A	SB	CS	SBR	FA	FR	G/POS	TPR
1988	SD-N	6	15	0	3	1	0	0	3	0	4	.200	.200	.267	33	-1	0	0	0	1.000	1	/O-4	0.0
1989	SD-N	17	41	5	8	2	0	1	7	3	9	.195	.250	.317	61	-2	0	1	-1	.947	-1	O-14	-0.4
1990	SD-N	53	101	12	27	4	1	5	11	5	24	.267	.302	.475	109	1	0	0	0	1.000	-1	1-15,O-13	-0.1
1991	SD-N	118	369	26	84	16	0	10	47	31	90	.228	.298	.352	80	-10	2	1	0	.994	-3	O-96,1-16	-1.7
1992	SD-N	146	496	45	120	22	6	12	58	22	97	.242	.280	.383	85	-12	3	0	1	.990	12	*O-134,1-11	-0.1
1993	Col-N	140	478	65	135	26	6	13	67	20	60	.282	.325	.444	89	-9	9	6	-1	.966	2	O-96,1-37	-1.3
1995	Min-A	36	109	17	37	8	3	3	15	2	11	.339	.357	.550	132	4	3	0	1	1.000	-2	O-23,1-11/D-3	0.3
Total	7	516	1609	170	414	79	16	44	208	83	295	.257	.302	.408	89	-29	17	8	0	.983	9	O-380/1-90,D-3	-3.3

■ CAP CLARK Clark, John Carrol b: 9/19/06, Snow Camp, N.C. d: 2/16/57, Fayetteville, N.C. BL/TR, 5'11", 180 lbs. Deb: 4/23/38

YEAR	TM/L	G	AB	R	H	2B	3B	HR	RBI	BB	SO	AVG	OBP	SLG	PRO+	BR/A	SB	CS	SBR	FA	FR	G/POS	TPR
1938	Phi-N	52	74	11	19	1	1	0	4	9	10	.257	.337	.297	78	-2	0			.936	-3	C-29	-0.4

■ MEL CLARK Clark, Melvin Earl b: 7/7/26, Letart, W.Va. BR/TR, 6', 180 lbs. Deb: 9/11/51

YEAR	TM/L	G	AB	R	H	2B	3B	HR	RBI	BB	SO	AVG	OBP	SLG	PRO+	BR/A	SB	CS	SBR	FA	FR	G/POS	TPR
1951	Phi-N	10	31	2	10	1	0	1	3	0	3	.323	.323	.452	108	0	0	1	-1	1.000	-1	/O-7	-0.1
1952	Phi-N	47	155	20	52	6	4	1	15	6	13	.335	.364	.445	125	5	2	1	0	1.000	4	O-38/3-1	0.7
1953	Phi-N	60	198	31	59	10	4	0	19	11	17	.298	.338	.389	89	-3	1	0	0	.991	1	O-51	-0.3
1954	Phi-N	83	233	26	56	9	7	1	24	17	21	.240	.292	.352	67	-12	0	1	-1	.961	2	O-63	-1.2
1955	Phi-N	10	32	3	5	3	0	0	1	3	4	.156	.229	.250	27	-3	0	0	0	1.000	3	/O-8	-0.1
1957	Det-A	5	7	0	0	0	0	0	1	0	3	.000	.000	.000	-97	-2	0	0	0	1.000	0	/O-2	-0.2
Total	6	215	656	82	182	29	15	3	63	37	61	.277	.318	.381	85	-15	3	3	-1	.983	10	O-169/3-1	-1.2

■ SPIDER CLARK Clark, Owen F. b: 9/16/1867, Brooklyn, N.Y. d: 2/8/1892, Brooklyn, N.Y. TR , 5'10", 150 lbs. Deb: 5/2/1889

YEAR	TM/L	G	AB	R	H	2B	3B	HR	RBI	BB	SO	AVG	OBP	SLG	PRO+	BR/A	SB	CS	SBR	FA	FR	G/POS	TPR
1889	Was-N	38	145	19	37	7	2	3	22	6	18	.255	.285	.393	94	-2	8			.887	6	C-14,S-13/O-9,32	0.5
1890	Buf-P	69	260	45	69	11	1	2	25	20	16	.265	.325	.338	84	-5	8			.938	-4	O-34,C-14,2/13SP	-0.7
Total	2	107	405	64	106	18	3	5	47	26	34	.262	.311	.358	88	-7	16			.952	2	/O-43,C-28,2S13P	-0.2

■ PHIL CLARK Clark, Phillip Benjamin b: 5/6/68, Crockett, Tex. BR/TR, 6', 200 lbs. Deb: 5/27/92 F

YEAR	TM/L	G	AB	R	H	2B	3B	HR	RBI	BB	SO	AVG	OBP	SLG	PRO+	BR/A	SB	CS	SBR	FA	FR	G/POS	TPR
1992	Det-A	23	54	3	22	4	0	1	5	6	9	.407	.467	.537	179	6	1	0	0	.931	-1	O-13/D-7	0.5
1993	SD-N	102	240	33	75	17	0	9	33	8	31	.313	.348	.496	121	6	2	0	1	.963	7	O-36,1-24,C-11,/3-5	1.2
1994	SD-N	61	149	14	32	6	0	5	20	5	17	.215	.255	.356	59	-10	1	2	-1	.992	-2	1-24,O-17/C-5,3-1	-1.4
1995	SD-N	75	97	12	21	3	0	2	7	8	18	.216	.283	.309	58	-6	0	2	-1	1.000	-8	O-34/1-2	-1.5
1996	Bos-A	3	3	0	0	0	0	0	0	0	1	.000	.000	.000	-98	-1	0	0	0	1.000	0	/1-1,3-1,D-1	-0.1
Total	5	264	543	62	150	30	0	17	65	27	76	.276	.321	.425	97	-4	4	4	-1	.951	-3	O-100/1-51,C-16,D3	-1.3

■ BOBBY CLARK Clark, Robert Cale b: 6/13/55, Sacramento, Cal. BR/TR, 6', 190 lbs. Deb: 8/21/79

YEAR	TM/L	G	AB	R	H	2B	3B	HR	RBI	BB	SO	AVG	OBP	SLG	PRO+	BR/A	SB	CS	SBR	FA	FR	G/POS	TPR
1979	*Cal-A	19	54	8	16	2	2	1	5	5	11	.296	.356	.463	123	2	1	1	-0	.978	2	O-19	0.3
1980	Cal-A	78	261	26	60	10	1	5	23	11	42	.230	.266	.333	65	-13	0	1	-1	.982	8	O-77	-0.9
1981	Cal-A	34	88	12	22	2	1	4	19	7	18	.250	.305	.432	110	1	0	0	0	1.000	0	O-34	0.0
1982	*Cal-A	102	90	11	19	1	0	2	8	0	29	.211	.211	.289	36	-8	1	0	0	1.000	-29	*O-102	-3.8
1983	Cal-A	76	212	17	49	9	1	5	21	9	45	.231	.262	.354	68	-10	0	0	0	1.000	-11	O-72/3-1,D-2	-2.2
1984	Mil-A	58	169	17	44	7	2	2	16	16	35	.260	.328	.361	94	-1	1	5	-3	.981	-10	O-56	-1.6
1985	Mil-A	29	93	6	21	3	0	0	8	7	19	.226	.280	.258	49	-6	1	1	-0	1.000	1	O-27	-0.7
Total	7	396	967	97	231	34	7	19	100	55	199	.239	.282	.347	74	-36	4	8	-4	.990	-39	O-387/D-2,3-1	-8.9

■ BOB CLARK Clark, Robert H. b: 3/18/1863, Covington, Ky. d: 8/21/19, Covington, Ky. BR/TR, 5'10", 175 lbs. Deb: 4/17/1886

YEAR	TM/L	G	AB	R	H	2B	3B	HR	RBI	BB	SO	AVG	OBP	SLG	PRO+	BR/A	SB	CS	SBR	FA	FR	G/POS	TPR
1886	Bro-a	71	269	37	58	8	2	0	26	17		.216	.262	.260	63	-12	14			.864	-13	C-44,O-17,S-12	-1.7
1887	Bro-a	48	177	24	47	3	1	0	18	7		.266	.297	.294	64	-9	15			.871	-1	C-45/O-3	-0.5
1888	Bro-a	45	150	23	36	5	3	1	20	9		.240	.292	.333	100	-0	11			.884	-2	C-36/O-8,1-1	0.1
1889	*Bro-a	53	182	32	50	5	2	0	22	26	7	.275	.368	.324	98	0	18			.870	7	C-53	1.0
1890	*Bro-N	43	151	24	33	3	3	0	15	15	8	.219	.306	.278	70	-5	10			.836	-14	C-42/O-1	-1.4
1891	Cin-N	16	54	2	6	0	0	0	3	6	9	.111	.213	.111	-5	-7	3			.868	-5	C-16	-1.0
1893	Lou-N	12	28	3	3	1	0	0	3	5	5	.107	.242	.143	4	-4	0			.947	-2	C-10/O-1,S-1	-0.4
Total	7	288	1011	145	233	25	11	1	107	85	29	.230	.296	.280	71	-36	71			.867	-30	C-246/O-30,S-13,1-1	-3.9

■ RON CLARK Clark, Ronald Bruce b: 1/14/43, Ft.Worth, Tex. BR/TR, 5'10", 175 lbs. Deb: 9/11/66 C

YEAR	TM/L	G	AB	R	H	2B	3B	HR	RBI	BB	SO	AVG	OBP	SLG	PRO+	BR/A	SB	CS	SBR	FA	FR	G/POS	TPR
1966	Min-A	5	1	1	1	0	0	0	1	0	0	1.000	1.000	1.000	448	0	0	0	0	.000	0	/3-1	0.0
1967	Min-A	20	60	7	10	3	1	2	11	4	9	.167	.219	.350	61	-3	0	0	0	.891	-1	3-16	-0.5
1968	Min-A	104	227	14	42	5	1	1	13	16	44	.185	.245	.229	42	-16	3	2	-0	.932	-8	3-52,S-43,2-10	-2.2

YEAR	TM/L	G	AB	R	H	2B	3B	HR	RBI	BB	SO	AVG	OBP	SLG	PRO+	BR/A	SB	CS	SBR	FA	FR	G/POS	TPR
1969	Min-A	5	8	0	1	0	0	0	0	0	0	.125	.125	.125	-29	-1	0	0	0	1.000	-1	/3-2	-0.2
	Sea-A	57	163	9	32	5	0	0	12	13	29	.196	.260	.227	38	-13	1	0	0	.966	-9	S-38,3-15/2-5,1-1	-1.9
	Yr	62	171	9	33	5	0	0	12	13	29	.193	.254	.222	35	-15	1	0	0	.966	-10	S-38,3-17/2-5,1-1	-2.1
1971	Oak-A	2	1	0	0	0	0	0	0	1	0	.000	.500	.000	53	0	0	0	0	.000	0	H	0.0
1972	Oak-A	14	15	1	4	2	0	0	1	2	4	.267	.353	.400	130	1	0	0	0	1.000	0	2-11/3-3	0.1
	Mil-A	22	54	8	10	1	1	2	5	5	11	.185	.254	.352	81	-1	0	0	0	.963	5	2-11,3-10	0.5
	Yr	36	69	9	14	3	1	2	6	7	15	.203	.276	.362	92	-1	0	0	0	.974	6	2-22,3-13	0.6
1975	Phi-N	1	1	0	0	0	0	0	0	0	1	.000	.000	.000	-96	-0	0	0	0	.000	0	H	0.0
Total	7	230	530	40	100	16	3	5	43	41	98	.189	.251	.258	49	-34	4	2	0	.904	-13	/3-99,S-81,2-37,1-1	-4.2

■ ROY CLARK
Clark, Roy Elliott "Pepper" b: 5/11/1874, New Haven, Conn. d: 11/1/25, Bridgeport, Conn. BL/TR, 5'8", 170 lbs. Deb: 4/19/02

YEAR	TM/L	G	AB	R	H	2B	3B	HR	RBI	BB	SO	AVG	OBP	SLG	PRO+	BR/A	SB	CS	SBR	FA	FR	G/POS	TPR
1902	NY-N	21	76	4	11	1	0	0	3	1		.145	.156	.158	-3	-9	5			.962	-3	O-20	-1.4

■ WILL CLARK
Clark, William Nuschler b: 3/13/64, New Orleans, La. BL/TL, 6'1", 190 lbs. Deb: 4/8/86

YEAR	TM/L	G	AB	R	H	2B	3B	HR	RBI	BB	SO	AVG	OBP	SLG	PRO+	BR/A	SB	CS	SBR	FA	FR	G/POS	TPR
1986	SF-N	111	408	66	117	27	2	11	41	34	76	.287	.346	.444	122	11	4	7	-3	.989	-2	*1-102	0.0
1987	*SF-N	150	529	89	163	29	5	35	91	49	98	.308	.372	.580	155	40	5	17	-9	.991	2	*1-139	2.3
1988	SF-N★	162	575	102	162	31	6	29	**109**	**100**	129	.282	.392	.508	163	**49**	9	1	2	.993	-3	*1-158	3.8
1989	*SF-N★	159	588	**104**	196	38	9	23	111	74	103	.333	.412	.546	177	59	8	3	1	.994	0	*1-158	5.0
1990	SF-N★	154	600	91	177	25	5	19	95	62	97	.295	.364	.448	127	22	8	2	1	.992	1	*1-153	1.2
1991	SF-N★	148	565	84	170	32	7	29	116	51	91	.301	.361	**.536**	154	38	4	2	0	**.997**	3	*1-144	3.3
1992	SF-N★	144	513	69	154	40	1	16	73	73	82	.300	.392	.476	153	37	12	7	-1	.993	-0	*1-141	2.8
1993	SF-N	132	491	82	139	27	2	14	73	63	68	.283	.371	.432	118	14	2	2	-1	.988	-3	*1-129	0.0
1994	Tex-A★	110	389	73	128	24	2	13	80	71	59	.329	.436	.501	141	27	5	1	1	.990	1	*1-107/D-1	1.8
1995	Tex-A	123	454	85	137	27	3	16	92	68	50	.302	.397	.480	124	18	0	1	-1	.994	-0	*1-122/D-1	0.5
1996	*Tex-A	117	436	69	124	25	1	13	72	64	67	.284	.382	.436	101	2	2	1	0	.996	-2	*1-117	-1.0
1997	Tex-A	110	393	56	128	29	1	12	51	49	62	.326	.404	.496	127	16	0	0	0	.996	-1	*1-100/D-7	0.5
1998	*Tex-A	149	554	98	169	41	1	23	102	72	97	.305	.388	.507	125	21	1	0	0	.989	-7	*1-134,D-15	0.0
Total	13	1769	6495	1068	1964	395	45	253	1106	830	1079	.302	.386	.494	138	354	60	44	-8	.992	-10	*1-1704/D-24	20.2

■ WILLIE CLARK
Clark, William Otis "Wee Willie" b: 8/16/1872, Pittsburgh, Pa. d: 11/13/32, Pittsburgh, Pa. BL, Deb: 6/20/1895

YEAR	TM/L	G	AB	R	H	2B	3B	HR	RBI	BB	SO	AVG	OBP	SLG	PRO+	BR/A	SB	CS	SBR	FA	FR	G/POS	TPR
1895	NY-N	23	88	9	23	3	2	0	16	5	6	.261	.301	.341	67	-5	1			.974	1	1-23	-0.3
1896	NY-N	72	247	38	72	12	4	0	33	15	12	.291	.352	.372	94	-2	8			.975	-4	1-65	-0.5
1897	NY-N	116	431	63	122	17	12	1	75	37		.283	.352	.385	97	-2	18			.984	2	*1-107/O-7,3-1	0.1
1898	Pit-N	57	209	29	64	9	7	1	31	22		.306	.378	.431	134	9	0			.984	1	1-57	0.9
1899	Pit-N	80	298	49	85	13	10	0	44	35		.285	.379	.396	113	6	11			.989	1	1-78	0.7
Total	5	348	1273	188	366	54	35	2	199	114	18	.288	.359	.390	104	7	38			.983	0	1-330/O-7,3-1	0.9

■ WIN CLARK
Clark, William Winfield b: 4/11/1875, Circleville, Ohio d: 4/15/59, Los Angeles, Cal. BR/TR, 5'10", 175 lbs. Deb: 7/12/1897

YEAR	TM/L	G	AB	R	H	2B	3B	HR	RBI	BB	SO	AVG	OBP	SLG	PRO+	BR/A	SB	CS	SBR	FA	FR	G/POS	TPR
1897	Lou-N	4	16	2	3	0	0	0	2	1		.188	.235	.188	13	-2	1			.810	-2	/2-3,3-1	-0.3

■ ARTIE CLARKE
Clarke, Arthur Franklin b: 5/6/1865, Providence, R.I. d: 11/14/49, Brookline, Mass. BR/TR, 5'8", 155 lbs. Deb: 4/19/1890

YEAR	TM/L	G	AB	R	H	2B	3B	HR	RBI	BB	SO	AVG	OBP	SLG	PRO+	BR/A	SB	CS	SBR	FA	FR	G/POS	TPR
1890	NY-N	101	395	55	89	12	8	0	49	32	38	.225	.290	.296	71	-15	44			.908	-3	C-36,O-33,3-16,2/S	-1.3
1891	NY-N	48	174	17	33	2	2	0	21	15	16	.190	.254	.224	41	-13	5			.916	-12	C-42/3-5,O-2	-1.9
Total	2	149	569	72	122	14	10	0	70	47	54	.214	.279	.274	62	-28	49			.912	-15	/C-78,O-35,3-21,2S	-3.2

■ FRED CLARKE
Clarke, Fred Clifford "Cap" b: 10/3/1872, Winterset, Iowa d: 8/14/60, Winfield, Kan. BL/TR, 5'10.5", 165 lbs. Deb: 6/30/1894 FMCH

YEAR	TM/L	G	AB	R	H	2B	3B	HR	RBI	BB	SO	AVG	OBP	SLG	PRO+	BR/A	SB	CS	SBR	FA	FR	G/POS	TPR
1894	Lou-N	75	310	54	83	11	7	7	48	25	27	.268	.330	.416	85	-9	25			.885	4	O-75	-0.8
1895	Lou-N	132	550	96	191	21	5	4	82	34	24	.347	.396	.425	119	17	40			.881	11	*O-132	1.4
1896	Lou-N	131	517	96	168	15	18	9	79	43	34	.325	.392	.476	133	25	34			.908	0	*O-131	1.2
1897	Lou-N	128	518	120	202	30	13	6	67	45		.390	.462	.533	**168**	**53**	57			.926	6	*O-127,M	4.2
1898	Lou-N	149	599	116	184	23	12	3	47	48		.307	.373	.401	124	19	40			.940	6	*O-149,M	1.3
1899	Lou-N	149	602	122	206	23	9	5	70	49		.342	.406	.435	131	27	49			.964	1	*O-144/S-3,M	1.5
1900	Pit-N	106	399	84	110	15	12	3	32	51		.276	.368	.396	110	6	21			.944	3	*O-104,M	0.1
1901	Pit-N	129	527	118	171	24	15	6	60	51		.324	.395	.461	143	30	23			.970	2	*O-127/S-1,3-1,M	2.1
1902	Pit-N	113	459	103	145	27	14	2	53	51		.316	.401	.449	156	32	29			.958	-1	*O-113,M	2.5
1903	*Pit-N	104	427	88	150	**32**	15	5	70	41		.351	.414	**.532**	**164**	34	21			.962	-8	*O-101/S-2,M	1.9
1904	Pit-N	72	278	51	85	7	11	0	25	22		.306	.367	.410	136	12	11			.979	0	O-70,M	0.8
1905	Pit-N	141	525	95	157	18	15	2	51	55		.299	.368	.402	126	17	24			.976	4	*O-137,M	1.5
1906	Pit-N	118	417	69	129	14	**13**	1	39	40		.309	.371	.412	138	18	18			.974	6	*O-110,M	2.0
1907	Pit-N	148	501	97	145	18	13	2	59	68		.289	.383	.389	140	25	37			**.987**	6	*O-144,M	2.9
1908	Pit-N	151	551	83	146	18	15	2	53	65		.265	.349	.363	127	18	24			.973	10	*O-151,M	2.5
1909	*Pit-N	152	550	97	158	16	11	3	68	**80**		.287	.384	.373	124	18	31			**.987**	7	*O-152,M	2.1
1910	Pit-N	123	429	57	113	23	9	2	63	53	23	.263	.350	.373	105	2	12			.967	3	*O-118,M	0.0
1911	Pit-N	110	392	73	127	25	13	5	49	53	27	.324	.407	.492	146	24	10			.970	0	*O-101,M	1.9
1913	Pit-N	9	13	0	1	1	0	0	0	0	0	.077	.077	.154	-37	-2	0			1.000	-1	/O-2,M	-0.3
1914	Pit-N	2	2	0	0	0	0	0	0	0	0	.000	.000	.000	-99	-0	0			.000	0	HM	-0.1
1915	Pit-N	1	2	0	1	0	0	0	0	0	0	.500	.500	.500	206	0	0			.000	-1	/O-1,M	0.0
Total	21	2242	8568	1619	2672	361	220	67	1015	874	135	.312	.386	.429	132	366	506			.952	59	*O-2189/S-6,3-1	28.7

■ HARRY CLARKE
Clarke, Harry Corson b: 1861, d: 3/3/23, Long Beach, Cal. Deb: 8/28/1889

YEAR	TM/L	G	AB	R	H	2B	3B	HR	RBI	BB	SO	AVG	OBP	SLG	PRO+	BR/A	SB	CS	SBR	FA	FR	G/POS	TPR
1889	Was-N	1	3	0	0	0	0	0	0	0	1	.000	.000	.000	-99	-1	0			1.000	1	/O-1	0.0

■ HENRY CLARKE
Clarke, Henry Tefft b: 8/28/1875, Bellevue, Neb. d: 3/28/50, Colorado Springs, Colo. BR/TR, Deb: 6/26/1897

YEAR	TM/L	G	AB	R	H	2B	3B	HR	RBI	BB	SO	AVG	OBP	SLG	PRO+	BR/A	SB	CS	SBR	FA	FR	G/POS	TPR
1897	Cle-N	7	25	3	7	0	0	0	3	2		.280	.333	.280	60	-1	0			.714	-1	/P-5,O-2	-0.1
1898	Chi-N	2	4	0	1	0	0	0	0	1		.250	.400	.250	87	0	0			.000	-1	/O-1,P-1	-0.1
Total	2	9	29	3	8	0	0	0	3	3		.276	.344	.276	64	-1	0			.750	-2	/P-6,O-3	-0.2

■ HORACE CLARKE
Clarke, Horace Meredith b: 6/2/40, Frederiksted, St.Croix, V.I. BB/TR, 5'9", 178 lbs. Deb: 5/13/65

YEAR	TM/L	G	AB	R	H	2B	3B	HR	RBI	BB	SO	AVG	OBP	SLG	PRO+	BR/A	SB	CS	SBR	FA	FR	G/POS	TPR
1965	NY-A	51	108	13	28	1	0	1	9	6	6	.259	.298	.296	70	-4	2	1	0	.923	3	3-17/2-7,S-1	-0.2
1966	NY-A	96	312	37	83	10	4	6	28	27	24	.266	.326	.381	107	2	5	3	-0	.970	-19	S-63,2-16/3-4	-1.1
1967	NY-A	143	588	74	160	17	0	3	29	42	64	.272	.321	.316	92	-6	21	4	4	**.990**	15	*2-140	2.5
1968	NY-A	148	579	52	133	6	1	2	26	23	46	.230	.259	.254	58	-30	20	7	2	.984	**30**	*2-139	1.1
1969	NY-A	156	641	82	183	26	7	4	48	53	41	.285	.340	.367	101	1	33	13	2	.982	-4	*2-156	1.2
1970	NY-A	158	686	81	172	24	2	4	46	35	35	.251	.289	.309	68	-31	23	7	3	.979	-7	*2-157	-2.2
1971	NY-A	159	625	76	156	23	7	2	41	64	43	.250	.321	.318	87	-11	17	7	1	.981	-3	*2-156	0.1
1972	NY-A	147	547	65	132	20	2	3	37	56	44	.241	.316	.302	87	-8	18	6	2	.985	6	*2-143	1.0
1973	NY-A	148	590	60	155	21	0	2	35	47	48	.263	.319	.308	80	-15	11	10	-3	.979	8	*2-147	-0.1
1974	NY-A	24	47	3	11	1	0	0	1	4	5	.234	.294	.255	60	-2	1	0	0	1.000	-6	2-20/D-1	-0.7
	SD-N	42	90	5	17	1	0	0	4	8	6	.189	.255	.200	30	-8	0	0	0	.978	-4	2-21	-1.3
Total	10	1272	4813	548	1230	150	23	27	304	365	362	.256	.310	.313	82	-112	151	58	11	.983	19	*2-1102/S-64,3-21,D	0.3

■ NIG CLARKE
Clarke, Jay Justin b: 12/15/1882, Amherstburg, Ont., Canada d: 6/15/49, River Rouge, Mich BL/TR, 5'8", 165 lbs. Deb: 4/26/05

YEAR	TM/L	G	AB	R	H	2B	3B	HR	RBI	BB	SO	AVG	OBP	SLG	PRO+	BR/A	SB	CS	SBR	FA	FR	G/POS	TPR
1905	Cle-A	5	9	2	1	1	0	0	1	1		.111	.200	.222	33	-1	0			1.000	-2	/C-5	-0.2
	Det-A	3	7	1	3	0	0	1	1	0		.429	.500	.857	326	2	0			1.000	1	/C-2	0.3
	Cle-A	37	114	9	23	5	1	0	8	10		.202	.266	.263	67	-4	0			.961	-1	C-37	-0.2
	Yr	45	130	12	27	6	1	1	10	11		.208	.275	.292	79	-3	0			.965	-2	C-44	-0.1
1906	Cle-A	57	179	22	64	12	4	1	21	13		.358	.404	.486	181	16	3			.982	-1	C-54	2.2
1907	Cle-A	120	390	44	105	19	6	3	33	35		.269	.333	.372	123	10	3			.961	-11	*C-115	1.0
1908	Cle-A	97	290	34	70	8	6	1	27	30		.241	.315	.321	106	2	6			.969	-8	C-90	0.3
1909	Cle-A	55	164	15	45	4	2	0	14	9		.274	.316	.323	98	-1	1			.952	-3	C-44	0.1
1910	Cle-A	21	58	4	9	2	0	0	2	8		.155	.258	.190	40	-4	0			.974	3	C-17	0.0
1911	StL-A	82	256	22	55	10	1	0	18	26		.215	.287	.262	56	-15	2			.926	-5	C-73/1-4	-1.3

YEAR	TM/L	G	AB	R	H	2B	3B	HR	RBI	BB	SO	AVG	OBP	SLG	PRO+	BR/A	SB	CS	SBR	FA	FR	G/POS	TPR
1919	Phi-N	26	62	4	15	3	0	0	2	4	5	.242	.299	.290	72	-2	1			.969	0	C-22	0.0
1920	Pit-N	3	7	0	0	0	0	0	0	2	4	.000	.222	.000	-32	-1	0	0	0	1.000	1	/C-3	0.0
Total	9	506	1536	157	390	64	20	6	127	138	9	.254	.318	.333	102	3	16	0		.960	-25	C-462/1-4	2.2

■ JOSH CLARKE
Clarke, Joshua Baldwin "Pepper" b: 3/8/1879, Winfield, Kan. d: 7/2/62, Ventura, Cal. BL/TR, 5'10", 180 lbs. Deb: 6/15/1898 F

YEAR	TM/L	G	AB	R	H	2B	3B	HR	RBI	BB	SO	AVG	OBP	SLG	PRO+	BR/A	SB	CS	SBR	FA	FR	G/POS	TPR
1898	Lou-N	6	18	0	3	0	0	0	0	1		.167	.211	.167	9	-2	0			.917	-1	/O-5	-0.3
1905	StL-N	50	167	31	43	3	2	3	18	27		.257	.361	.353	117	4	8			.942	-8	O-26,2-16/S-4	-0.5
1908	Cle-A	131	492	70	119	8	4	1	21	76		.242	.348	.280	104	6	37			.963	-3	*O-131	-0.2
1909	Cle-A	4	12	1	0	0	0	0	0	2		.000	.143	.000	-52	-2	0			.600	-2	/O-4	-0.4
1911	Bos-N	32	120	16	28	7	3	1	4	29	22	.233	.387	.367	103	1	6			.938	4	O-30	0.3
Total	5	223	809	118	193	18	9	5	43	135	22	.239	.351	.302	102	8	51			.949	-9	O-196/2-16,S-4	-1.1

■ GREY CLARKE
Clarke, Richard Grey "Noisy" b: 9/26/12, Fulton, Ala. d: 11/25/93, Kannapolis, N.C. BR/TR, 5'9", 183 lbs. Deb: 4/19/44

YEAR	TM/L	G	AB	R	H	2B	3B	HR	RBI	BB	SO	AVG	OBP	SLG	PRO+	BR/A	SB	CS	SBR	FA	FR	G/POS	TPR
1944	Chi-A	63	169	14	44	10	1	0	27	22	6	.260	.352	.331	97	0	0	4	-2	.941	1	3-45	-0.1

■ SUMPTER CLARKE
Clarke, Sumpter Mills b: 10/18/1897, Savannah, Ga. d: 3/16/62, Knoxville, Tenn. BR/TR, 5'11", 170 lbs. Deb: 9/27/20 F

YEAR	TM/L	G	AB	R	H	2B	3B	HR	RBI	BB	SO	AVG	OBP	SLG	PRO+	BR/A	SB	CS	SBR	FA	FR	G/POS	TPR
1920	Chi-N	1	3	0	1	0	0	0	0	0	1	.333	.333	.333	90	-0	0	0	0	1.000	-0	/3-1	0.0
1923	Cle-A	1	3	0	0	0	0	0	0	0	0	.000	.000	.000	-99	-1	0	0	0	1.000	-0	/O-1	-0.1
1924	Cle-A	35	104	17	24	6	1	0	11	6	12	.231	.273	.308	49	-8	0	0	0	1.000	-5	O-33	-1.5
Total	3	37	110	17	25	6	1	0	11	6	13	.227	.267	.300	46	-9	0	0	0	1.000	-6	/O-34,3-1	-1.6

■ TOMMY CLARKE
Clarke, Thomas Aloysius b: 5/9/1888, New York, N.Y. d: 8/14/45, Corona, N.Y. BR/TR, 5'11", 175 lbs. Deb: 8/26/09

YEAR	TM/L	G	AB	R	H	2B	3B	HR	RBI	BB	SO	AVG	OBP	SLG	PRO+	BR/A	SB	CS	SBR	FA	FR	G/POS	TPR
1909	Cin-N	18	52	8	13	3	2	0	10	6		.250	.328	.385	122	1	3			.965	5	C-17	0.8
1910	Cin-N	64	151	19	42	6	5	1	20	19	17	.278	.370	.404	131	6	1			.971	-1	C-56	1.0
1911	Cin-N	86	203	20	49	6	7	1	25	25	22	.241	.328	.355	94	-2	4			.970	2	C-81/1-1	0.7
1912	Cin-N	72	146	19	41	7	2	0	22	28	14	.281	.400	.356	111	4	9			.983	5	C-63	1.3
1913	Cin-N	114	330	29	87	11	8	1	38	39	40	.264	.345	.355	100	1	2			.979	-13	*C-100	-0.4
1914	Cin-N	113	313	30	82	13	7	2	25	31	30	.262	.332	.367	105	2	6			.973	-4	*C-106	0.7
1915	Cin-N	96	226	23	65	7	2	0	21	33	22	.288	.381	.336	116	6	7	3	0	.981	-4	C-72	0.8
1916	Cin-N	78	177	10	42	10	1	0	17	24	20	.237	.328	.305	97	0	8			.965	-10	C-51	-0.7
1917	Cin-N	58	110	11	32	3	3	1	13	11	12	.291	.361	.400	139	5	2			.991	-5	C-29	0.2
1918	Chi-N	1	0	0	0	0	0	0	0	0	0	—	—	—	—	0	0			.000	0	/C-1	0.0
Total	10	700	1708	169	453	66	37	6	191	216	177	.265	.351	.358	109	24	42	3		.975	-26	C-576/1-1	4.4

■ BOILERYARD CLARKE
Clarke, William Jones b: 10/18/1868, New York, N.Y. d: 7/29/59, Princeton, N.J. BR/TR, 5'11.5", 170 lbs. Deb: 5/1/1893

YEAR	TM/L	G	AB	R	H	2B	3B	HR	RBI	BB	SO	AVG	OBP	SLG	PRO+	BR/A	SB	CS	SBR	FA	FR	G/POS	TPR
1893	Bal-N	49	183	23	32	1	3	1	24	19	14	.175	.274	.230	34	-18	2			.909	-3	C-38,1-11	-1.4
1894	Bal-N	28	100	18	24	8	0	1	19	16	14	.240	.361	.350	69	-5	2			.903	-3	C-23/1-5	-0.4
1895	*Bal-N	67	241	38	70	15	3	0	35	13	18	.290	.350	.378	85	-6	8			.938	6	C-60/1-6	0.5
1896	Bal-N	80	300	48	89	14	7	2	71	14	12	.297	.345	.410	97	-2	7			.948	-11	C-67,1-14	-0.5
1897	*Bal-N	64	241	32	65	7	1	1	38	9		.270	.320	.320	69	-11	5			.939	-15	C-59/1-4	-1.6
1898	Bal-N	82	285	26	69	5	2	0	27	4		.242	.289	.274	60	-15	2			.962	3	C-70,1-10	-0.4
1899	Bos-N	60	223	25	50	3	2	2	32	10		.224	.270	.283	47	-17	2			.940	-1	C-60	-1.2
1900	Bos-N	81	270	35	85	5	2	1	30	9		.315	.344	.359	84	-7	0			.928	7	C-67/1-8	0.6
1901	Was-A	110	422	58	118	15	5	3	54	23		.280	.335	.360	94	-3	7			.952	-9	*C-107/1-3	-0.1
1902	Was-A	87	291	31	78	15	0	6	40	23		.268	.330	.381	96	-2	1			**.972**	-3	C-87	0.4
1903	Was-A	126	465	35	111	14	6	2	38	15		.239	.273	.308	72	-16	12			.981	-11	1-88,C-37	-2.5
1904	Was-A	85	275	23	58	8	1	0	17	17		.211	.269	.247	65	-10	5			.977	0	C-52,1-29	-0.6
1905	NY-N	31	50	2	9	0	0	1	4	4		.180	.241	.240	42	-4	1			.973	-1	1-15,C-12	-0.4
Total	13	950	3346	394	858	110	32	20	429	176	58	.256	.310	.326	75	-115	54			.947	-39	C-739,1-193	-7.6

■ STU CLARKE
Clarke, William Stuart b: 1/24/06, San Francisco, Cal d: 8/26/85, Hayward, Cal. BR/TR, 5'8.5", 160 lbs. Deb: 7/17/29

YEAR	TM/L	G	AB	R	H	2B	3B	HR	RBI	BB	SO	AVG	OBP	SLG	PRO+	BR/A	SB	CS	SBR	FA	FR	G/POS	TPR
1929	Pit-N	57	178	20	47	5	7	2	21	19	21	.264	.338	.404	81	-5	3			.919	-8	S-41,3-15/2-1	-0.8
1930	Pit-N	4	9	2	4	0	1	0	2	1	0	.444	.500	.667	178	1	0			1.000	-1	/2-2	0.0
Total	2	61	187	22	51	5	8	2	23	20	21	.273	.346	.417	86	-4	3			1.000	-9	/S-41,3-15,2-3	-0.8

■ BUZZ CLARKSON
Clarkson, James Buster b: 3/13/15, Hopkins, S.C. d: 1/18/89, Jeannette, Pa. BR/TR, 5'11", 210 lbs. Deb: 4/30/52

YEAR	TM/L	G	AB	R	H	2B	3B	HR	RBI	BB	SO	AVG	OBP	SLG	PRO+	BR/A	SB	CS	SBR	FA	FR	G/POS	TPR
1952	Bos-N	14	25	3	5	0	0	0	1	3	3	.200	.286	.200	38	-2	0	0	0	.938	-2	/S-6,3-2	-0.4

■ ELLIS CLARY
Clary, Ellis "Cat" b: 9/11/16, Valdosta, Ga. BR/TR, 5'8", 160 lbs. Deb: 6/7/42 C

YEAR	TM/L	G	AB	R	H	2B	3B	HR	RBI	BB	SO	AVG	OBP	SLG	PRO+	BR/A	SB	CS	SBR	FA	FR	G/POS	TPR
1942	Was-A	76	240	34	66	9	0	0	16	45	25	.275	.394	.313	101	3	2	0	1	.969	-17	2-69/3-2	-0.9
1943	Was-A	73	254	36	65	19	1	0	19	44	31	.256	.370	.339	112	6	8	4	0	.945	-8	3-68/S-1	-0.1
	StL-A	23	69	15	19	2	0	0	5	11	6	.275	.375	.304	98	0	1	2	-1	.972	-1	3-14/2-3	-0.1
	Yr	96	323	51	84	21	1	0	24	55	37	.260	.371	.331	109	6	9	6	-1	.949	-9	3-82/2-3,S-1	-0.2
1944	*StL-A	25	49	6	13	1	1	0	4	12	9	.265	.410	.327	106	1	1	0	0	1.000	-1	3-11/2-6	0.0
1945	StL-A	26	38	6	8	1	0	1	2	2	3	.211	.250	.316	61	-2	0	2	-1	.947	3	3-16/2-3	0.0
Total	4	223	650	97	171	32	2	1	46	114	74	.263	.376	.323	103	8	12	8	-1	.953	-25	3-111/2-81,S-1	-1.1

■ DAIN CLAY
Clay, Dain Elmer "Sniffy" or "Ding-A-Ling" b: 7/10/19, Hicksville, Ohio d: 8/28/94, Chula Vista, Cal. BR/TR, 5'10.5", 160 lbs. Deb: 6/12/43

YEAR	TM/L	G	AB	R	H	2B	3B	HR	RBI	BB	SO	AVG	OBP	SLG	PRO+	BR/A	SB	CS	SBR	FA	FR	G/POS	TPR
1943	Cin-N	49	93	19	25	2	4	0	9	8	14	.269	.333	.376	106	1	1			.936	-9	O-33	-1.0
1944	Cin-N	110	356	51	89	15	0	0	17	17	18	.250	.290	.292	67	-16	8			.993	-2	O-98	-2.3
1945	Cin-N	153	656	81	184	29	2	1	50	37	58	.280	.321	.335	84	-15	19			.989	6	*O-152	-1.7
1946	Cin-N	121	435	52	99	17	0	2	22	53	40	.228	.318	.280	73	-14	11			**.988**	7	*O-120	-1.3
Total	4	433	1540	203	397	63	6	3	98	115	130	.258	.314	.312	79	-44	39			.987	3	O-403	-6.3

■ BILL CLAY
Clay, Frederick C. b: 11/23/1874, Baltimore, Md. d: 10/12/17, York, Pa. TR , Deb: 8/8/02

YEAR	TM/L	G	AB	R	H	2B	3B	HR	RBI	BB	SO	AVG	OBP	SLG	PRO+	BR/A	SB	CS	SBR	FA	FR	G/POS	TPR
1902	Phi-N	3	8	1	2	0	0	0	1	0		.250	.250	.250	54	-0	0			.750	-1	/O-3	-0.2

■ ROYCE CLAYTON
Clayton, Royce Spencer b: 1/2/70, Burbank, Cal. BR/TR, 6', 183 lbs. Deb: 9/20/91

YEAR	TM/L	G	AB	R	H	2B	3B	HR	RBI	BB	SO	AVG	OBP	SLG	PRO+	BR/A	SB	CS	SBR	FA	FR	G/POS	TPR
1991	SF-N	9	26	0	3	1	0	0	2	1	6	.115	.148	.154	-15	-4	0	0	0	.880	-6	/S-8	-1.0
1992	SF-N	98	321	31	72	7	4	4	24	26	63	.224	.282	.308	71	-13	8	4	0	.973	-9	S-94/3-1	-1.6
1993	SF-N	153	549	54	155	21	5	6	70	38	91	.282	.334	.372	91	-7	11	10	-3	.963	1	*S-153	0.3
1994	SF-N	108	385	38	91	14	6	3	30	30	74	.236	.297	.327	66	-20	23	3	5	.973	7	*S-108	0.1
1995	SF-N	138	509	56	124	29	3	5	58	38	109	.244	.300	.342	71	-22	24	9	2	.969	4	*S-136	-0.4
1996	*StL-N	129	491	64	136	20	4	6	35	33	89	.277	.324	.371	83	-12	33	15	1	.972	1	*S-113	0.0
1997	StL-N★	154	576	75	153	39	5	9	61	33	109	.266	.309	.398	84	-15	30	10	3	.973	7	*S-153	0.9
1998	StL-N	90	355	59	83	19	1	4	29	40	51	.234	.315	.327	68	-16	19	6	2	.970	0	S-90	-0.5
	*Tex-A	52	186	30	53	12	1	5	24	13	32	.285	.335	.441	95	-1	5	5	-2	.972	-4	S-52	-0.2
Total	8	931	3398	407	870	162	29	42	333	252	624	.256	.311	.358	78	-109	153	62	9	.970	1	S-907/3-1	-2.4

■ CHET CLEMENS
Clemens, Chester Spurgeon b: 5/10/17, San Fernando, Cal. BR/TR, 6', 175 lbs. Deb: 9/13/39

YEAR	TM/L	G	AB	R	H	2B	3B	HR	RBI	BB	SO	AVG	OBP	SLG	PRO+	BR/A	SB	CS	SBR	FA	FR	G/POS	TPR
1939	Bos-N	9	23	2	5	0	0	0	1	1	3	.217	.250	.217	29	-2	1			.867	-1	/O-7	-0.4
1944	Bos-N	19	17	7	3	1	1	0	2	2	2	.176	.263	.353	69	-1	0			1.000	-2	/O-7	-0.3
Total	2	28	40	9	8	1	1	0	3	3	5	.200	.256	.275	46	-3	1			.905	-3	/O-14	-0.7

■ CLEM CLEMENS
Clemens, Clement Lambert "Count" (b: Clement Lambert Ulatowski)
b: 11/21/1886, Chicago, Ill. d: 11/2/67, St.Petersburg, Fla. BR/TR, 5'11", 176 lbs. Deb: 5/15/14

YEAR	TM/L	G	AB	R	H	2B	3B	HR	RBI	BB	SO	AVG	OBP	SLG	PRO+	BR/A	SB	CS	SBR	FA	FR	G/POS	TPR
1914	Chi-F	13	27	4	4	0	0	0	2	3	0	.148	.233	.148	6	-4	0			.950	-1	/C-8	-0.5
1915	Chi-F	11	22	3	3	1	0	0	3	1	0	.136	.174	.182	0	-3	0			1.000	-1	/C-9,2-2	-0.4
1916	Chi-N	10	15	0	0	0	0	0	0	1	6	.000	.063	.000	-72	-3	0			.941	1	/C-9	-0.2
Total	3	34	64	7	7	1	0	0	5	5	6	.109	.174	.125	-15	-10	0			.962	-1	/C-26,2-2	-1.1

■ DOUG CLEMENS
Clemens, Douglas Horace b: 6/9/39, Leesport, Pa. BL/TR, 6', 180 lbs. Deb: 10/2/60

YEAR	TM/L	G	AB	R	H	2B	3B	HR	RBI	BB	SO	AVG	OBP	SLG	PRO+	BR/A	SB	CS	SBR	FA	FR	G/POS	TPR
1960	StL-N	1	0	0	0	0	0	0	0	0	0	—	—	—	—	0	0	0	0	1.000	0	/O-1	0.0

YEAR	TM/L	G	AB	R	H	2B	3B	HR	RBI	BB	SO	AVG	OBP	SLG	PRO+	BR/A	SB	CS	SBR	FA	FR	G/POS	TPR
1961	StL-N	6	12	1	2	1	0	0	0	3	1	.167	.333	.250	53	-1	0	0	0	.667	-1	/O-3	-0.2
1962	StL-N	48	93	12	22	1	1	1	12	17	19	.237	.355	.301	71	-3	0	0	0	.974	-6	O-34	-1.1
1963	StL-N	5	6	1	1	0	0	1	2	1	2	.167	.286	.667	151	0	0	0	0	1.000	0	/O-3	0.1
1964	StL-N	33	78	8	16	4	3	1	9	6	16	.205	.271	.372	73	-3	0	0	0	.970	0	O-22	-0.4
	Chi-N	54	140	23	39	10	2	2	12	18	22	.279	.365	.421	116	3	0	0	0	.923	0	O-40	0.2
	Yr	87	218	31	55	14	5	3	21	24	38	.252	.332	.404	100	0	0	0	0	.937	1	O-62	-0.2
1965	Chi-N	128	340	36	75	11	0	4	26	38	53	.221	.303	.288	66	-15	5	8	-3	.981	-6	*O-105	-2.9
1966	Phi-N	79	121	10	31	1	0	1	15	16	25	.256	.353	.289	81	-2	1	0	0	1.000	-1	O-28/1-1	-0.4
1967	Phi-N	69	73	2	13	5	0	0	4	8	15	.178	.268	.247	48	-5	0	0	0	1.000	-3	O-10	-0.8
1968	Phi-N	29	57	6	12	1	1	2	8	7	13	.211	.297	.368	99	-0	0	0	0	1.000	-1	O-17	-0.2
Total	9	452	920	99	211	34	7	12	88	114	166	.229	.319	.321	78	-25	6	8	-3	.969	-16	O-263/1-1	-5.7

■ BOB CLEMENS
Clemens, Robert Baxter b: 8/9/1886, Odessa, Mo. d: 4/5/64, Marshall, Mo. BR/TR, 5'9", 163 lbs. Deb: 9/17/14

YEAR	TM/L	G	AB	R	H	2B	3B	HR	RBI	BB	SO	AVG	OBP	SLG	PRO+	BR/A	SB	CS	SBR	FA	FR	G/POS	TPR
1914	StL-A	7	13	1	3	0	1	0	3	2	1	.231	.375	.385	134	1	0	2	-1	.750	-1	/O-5	-0.2

■ WALLY CLEMENT
Clement, Wallace Oakes b: 7/21/1881, Auburn, Me. d: 11/1/53, Coral Gables, Fla. BL/TR, 5'11", 175 lbs. Deb: 8/17/08

YEAR	TM/L	G	AB	R	H	2B	3B	HR	RBI	BB	SO	AVG	OBP	SLG	PRO+	BR/A	SB	CS	SBR	FA	FR	G/POS	TPR
1908	Phi-N	16	36	0	8	3	0	0	1	0		.222	.222	.306	66	-2	2			1.000	4	/O-8	0.2
1909	Phi-N	3	3	0	0	0	0	0	0	0		.000	.000	.000	-99	-1	0			.000	0	H	-0.1
	Bro-N	92	340	35	88	8	4	0	17	18		.259	.296	.306	90	-5	11			.965	4	O-88	-0.5
	Yr	95	343	35	88	8	4	0	17	18		.257	.294	.303	88	-6	11			.965	4	O-88	-0.6
Total	2	111	379	35	96	11	4	0	18	18		.253	.287	.303	86	-7	13			.970	7	/O-96	-0.4

■ EDGARD CLEMENTE
Clemente, Edgard Alexis (Velazquez) (a.k.a. Edgard Alexis Velazquez) b: 12/15/75, Santurce, P.R. BR/TR, 5'11", 188 lbs. Deb: 9/10/98

YEAR	TM/L	G	AB	R	H	2B	3B	HR	RBI	BB	SO	AVG	OBP	SLG	PRO+	BR/A	SB	CS	SBR	FA	FR	G/POS	TPR
1998	Col-N	11	17	2	6	0	1	0	2	2	8	.353	.421	.471	110	0	0	0	0	.857	-2	/O-7	-0.2

■ ROBERTO CLEMENTE
Clemente, Roberto (Walker) "Bob" b: 8/18/34, Carolina, P.R. d: 12/31/72, San Juan, P.R. BR/TR, 5'11", 175 lbs. Deb: 4/17/55 H

YEAR	TM/L	G	AB	R	H	2B	3B	HR	RBI	BB	SO	AVG	OBP	SLG	PRO+	BR/A	SB	CS	SBR	FA	FR	G/POS	TPR
1955	Pit-N	124	474	48	121	23	11	5	47	18	60	.255	.285	.382	76	-17	2	5	-2	.978	12	*O-118	-1.4
1956	Pit-N	147	543	66	169	30	7	7	60	13	58	.311	.332	.431	105	3	6	6	-2	.957	2	*O-139/2-2,3-1	-0.4
1957	Pit-N	111	451	42	114	17	7	4	30	23	45	.253	.289	.348	72	-18	0	4	-2	.979	13	*O-109	-1.4
1958	Pit-N	140	519	69	150	24	10	6	50	31	41	.289	.329	.408	96	-4	8	2	1	.982	25	*O-135	1.6
1959	Pit-N	105	432	60	128	17	7	4	50	15	51	.296	.324	.396	91	-6	2	3	-1	.948	9	*O-104	-0.3
1960	*Pit-N★	144	570	89	179	22	6	16	94	39	72	.314	.360	.458	121	16	4	5	-2	.971	3	*O-142	1.1
1961	Pit-N★	146	572	100	201	30	10	23	89	35	59	**.351**	.392	.559	148	38	4	1	1	.969	14	*O-144	4.4
1962	Pit-N★	144	538	95	168	28	9	10	74	35	73	.312	.355	.454	115	11	6	4	-1	.973	13	*O-142	1.5
1963	Pit-N★	152	600	77	192	23	8	17	76	31	64	.320	.357	.470	135	26	12	2	2	.958	-3	*O-151	1.9
1964	Pit-N★	155	622	95	**211**	40	7	12	87	51	87	**.339**	.391	.484	145	37	5	2	0	.968	11	*O-154	4.2
1965	Pit-N★	152	589	91	194	21	14	10	65	43	78	**.329**	.380	.463	136	28	8	0	2	.968	9	*O-145	3.4
1966	Pit-N★	154	638	105	202	31	11	29	119	46	109	.317	.363	.536	146	38	7	5	-1	.965	15	*O-154	4.6
1967	Pit-N★	147	585	103	**209**	26	10	23	110	41	103	**.357**	.402	.554	170	52	9	1	2	.970	9	*O-145	5.8
1968	Pit-N	132	502	74	146	18	12	18	57	51	77	.291	.357	.482	152	31	2	3	-1	.984	12	*O-131	3.9
1969	Pit-N★	138	507	87	175	20	**12**	19	91	56	73	.345	.413	.544	170	47	4	1	1	.980	7	*O-135	4.9
1970	*Pit-N★	108	412	65	145	22	10	14	60	38	66	.352	.409	.556	159	34	3	0	1	.966	7	*O-104	3.5
1971	*Pit-N★	132	522	82	178	29	8	13	86	26	65	.341	.372	.502	146	29	1	2	-1	.993	10	*O-124	3.5
1972	*Pit-N†	102	378	68	118	19	7	10	60	29	49	.312	.361	.479	140	18	0	0	0	1.000	6	O-94	2.1
Total	18	2433	9454	1416	3000	440	166	240	1305	621	1230	.317	.362	.475	130	363	83	46	-3	.973	175	*O-2370/2-2,3-1	42.9

■ ED CLEMENTS
Clements, Edward b: Philadelphia, Pa. Deb: 6/24/1890

YEAR	TM/L	G	AB	R	H	2B	3B	HR	RBI	BB	SO	AVG	OBP	SLG	PRO+	BR/A	SB	CS	SBR	FA	FR	G/POS	TPR
1890	Pit-N	1	1	0	0	0	0	0	0	0	0	.000	.000	.000	-99	-0	0			.400	-0	/S-1	-0.1

■ JACK CLEMENTS
Clements, John J. b: 7/24/1864, Philadelphia, Pa. d: 5/23/41, Norristown, Pa. BL/TL, 5'8.5", 204 lbs. Deb: 4/22/1884 M

YEAR	TM/L	G	AB	R	H	2B	3B	HR	RBI	BB	SO	AVG	OBP	SLG	PRO+	BR/A	SB	CS	SBR	FA	FR	G/POS	TPR
1884	Phi-U	41	177	37	50	13	2	3		9		.282	.317	.429	134	2				.764	1	O-22,C-20/S-1	0.3
	Phi-N	9	30	3	7	0	0	0	0	4	8	.233	.324	.233	82	-0				.827	1	/C-9	0.1
1885	Phi-N	52	188	14	36	11	3	1	14	2	30	.191	.200	.298	61	-8				.891	-8	C-41,O-11	-1.2
1886	Phi-N	54	185	15	38	5	1	0	11	7	34	.205	.234	.243	45	-12	4			.930	12	C-47/O-7	0.4
1887	Phi-N	66	246	48	69	13	7	1	47	9	24	.280	.317	.402	93	-3	7			.940	9	C-59/3-4,S-3	0.9
1888	Phi-N	86	326	26	80	8	4	1	32	10	36	.245	.276	.304	81	-8	3			.927	-1	C-85/O-1	0.0
1889	Phi-N	78	310	51	88	17	1	4	35	29	21	.284	.347	.384	96	-3	3			.916	-7	C-78	-0.2
1890	Phi-N	97	381	64	120	23	8	7	74	45	30	.315	.392	.472	148	22	10			.944	3	C-91/1-5,M	2.9
1891	Phi-N	107	423	58	131	29	4	4	75	43	19	.310	.380	.426	131	16	3			.927	-5	*C-107/1-2	1.9
1892	Phi-N	109	402	50	106	25	6	8	76	43	40	.264	.339	.415	128	13	7			.950	6	*C-109	2.4
1893	Phi-N	94	376	64	107	20	3	17	80	39	29	.285	.360	.489	125	11	3			.942	-12	*C-92/1-1	0.6
1894	Phi-N	45	159	26	55	6	5	3	36	24	7	.346	.455	.503	134	11	6			.946	-2	C-45	1.0
1895	Phi-N	88	322	64	127	27	2	13	75	22	7	.394	.446	.612	170	32	3			.969	-10	*C-88	2.4
1896	Phi-N	57	184	35	66	5	7	5	45	17	14	.359	.427	.543	157	15	2			.966	-4	C-53	1.4
1897	Phi-N	55	185	18	44	4	2	6	36	12		.238	.305	.378	82	-6	3			.962	-2	C-49	-0.2
1898	StL-N	99	335	39	86	19	5	3	41	21		.257	.314	.370	94	-4	1			**.971**	-6	C-86	-0.2
1899	Cle-N	4	12	1	3	0	0	0	0	0		.250	.308	.250	58	-1	0			.938	0	/C-4	0.0
1900	Bos-N	16	42	6	13	1	0	1	10	3		.310	.370	.405	101	-0	0			.948	1	C-10	0.2
Total	17	1157	4283	619	1226	226	60	77	687	339	299	.286	.347	.421	116	78	55			.937	-26	*C-1073/O-41,13S	12.7

■ VERNE CLEMONS
Clemons, Verne James "Stinger" or "Tubby" b: 9/8/1891, Clemons, Iowa d: 5/5/59, Bay Pines, Fla. BR/TR, 5'9.5", 190 lbs. Deb: 4/22/16

YEAR	TM/L	G	AB	R	H	2B	3B	HR	RBI	BB	SO	AVG	OBP	SLG	PRO+	BR/A	SB	CS	SBR	FA	FR	G/POS	TPR
1916	StL-A	4	7	0	1	1	0	0	0	0	1	.143	.143	.286	30	-1	0			.889	0	/C-2	0.0
1919	StL-N	88	239	14	63	13	2	2	22	26	13	.264	.336	.360	116	5	4			.982	2	C-75	1.5
1920	StL-N	112	338	17	95	10	6	1	36	30	12	.281	.340	.355	103	2	1	1	-0	.977	-6	*C-103	0.2
1921	StL-N	117	341	29	109	16	2	2	48	33	17	.320	.380	.396	108	5	0	0	0	.985	-4	*C-107	0.6
1922	StL-N	71	160	9	41	4	0	0	15	18	5	.256	.331	.281	62	-8	1	0	0	.996	3	C-63	-0.3
1923	StL-N	57	130	6	37	9	1	0	13	10	11	.285	.345	.369	90	-2	0	0	0	.981	5	C-41	0.5
1924	StL-N	25	56	3	18	3	0	0	6	2	3	.321	.345	.375	94	-0	0	0	0	.983	-2	C-17	-0.1
Total	7	474	1271	78	364	56	11	5	140	119	62	.286	.348	.360	99	0	6	1		.983	-2	C-408	2.4

■ DONN CLENDENON
Clendenon, Donn Alvin b: 7/15/35, Neosho, Mo. BR/TR, 6'3.5", 210 lbs. Deb: 9/22/61

YEAR	TM/L	G	AB	R	H	2B	3B	HR	RBI	BB	SO	AVG	OBP	SLG	PRO+	BR/A	SB	CS	SBR	FA	FR	G/POS	TPR
1961	Pit-N	9	35	7	11	1	1	0	2	5	10	.314	.400	.400	113	1	0	0	0	1.000	1	/O-8	0.1
1962	Pit-N	80	222	39	67	8	5	7	28	26	58	.302	.378	.477	128	9	16	4	2	.990	-1	1-52,O-19	0.6
1963	Pit-N	154	563	65	155	28	7	15	57	39	136	.275	.328	.430	116	10	22	13	-1	.991	7	*1-151	1.0
1964	Pit-N	133	457	53	129	23	8	12	64	26	96	.282	.324	.446	115	8	12	8	-1	.989	-1	*1-119	0.1
1965	Pit-N	162	612	89	184	32	14	14	96	48	128	.301	.356	.467	129	23	9	9	-3	.984	2	*1-158/3-1	1.5
1966	Pit-N	155	571	80	171	22	10	28	98	52	142	.299	.360	.520	141	31	8	7	-2	.985	-1	*1-152	1.8
1967	Pit-N	131	478	46	119	15	2	13	56	34	107	.249	.300	.370	90	-7	4	4	-1	.988	4	*1-123	-1.2
1968	Pit-N	158	584	63	150	20	6	17	87	47	163	.257	.313	.399	114	9	10	3	1	.990	10	*1-155	0.9
1969	Mon-N	38	129	14	31	6	1	4	14	6	32	.240	.274	.395	85	-3	0	2	-1	.987	4	1-24,O-11	-0.3
	*NY-N	72	202	31	51	5	0	12	37	19	62	.252	.323	.455	113	3	3	2	-0	.984	-4	1-58/O-1	-0.5
	Yr	110	331	45	82	11	1	16	51	25	94	.248	.304	.432	103	-0	3	4	-2	.985	-0	1-82,O-12	-0.8
1970	NY-N	121	396	65	114	18	3	22	97	39	91	.288	.353	.515	129	15	4	1	1	.991	-2	*1-100	0.5
1971	NY-N	88	263	29	65	10	0	11	37	21	78	.247	.305	.411	103	0	1	2	-1	.985	-2	1-72	-0.9
1972	StL-N	61	136	13	26	4	0	4	9	17	37	.191	.281	.309	68	-6	1	2	-1	.986	3	1-36	-0.6
Total	12	1362	4648	594	1273	192	57	159	682	379	1140	.274	.331	.442	117	94	90	57	-7	.988	20	*1-1200/O-39,3-1	3.0

■ ELMER CLEVELAND
Cleveland, Elmer Ellsworth b: 9/15/1862, Washington, D.C. d: 10/8/13, Zimmerman, Pa. BR/TR, Deb: 8/29/1884

YEAR	TM/L	G	AB	R	H	2B	3B	HR	RBI	BB	SO	AVG	OBP	SLG	PRO+	BR/A	SB	CS	SBR	FA	FR	G/POS	TPR
1884	Cin-U	29	115	24	37	9	2	0		4		.322	.345	.435	125	-0				.843	2	3-29	0.2
1888	NY-N	9	34	6	8	0	2	2	5	3	1	.235	.297	.529	161	2	1			.667	-7	/3-9	-0.4
	Pit-N	30	108	10	24	2	1	2	11	5	23	.222	.270	.315	93	-1	3			.831	-9	3-30	-0.9

YEAR	TM/L	G	AB	R	H	2B	3B	HR	RBI	BB	SO	AVG	OBP	SLG	PRO+	BR/A	SB	CS	SBR	FA	FR	G/POS	TPR
	Yr	39	142	16	32	2	3	4	16	8	24	.225	.276	.366	110	2	4			.806	-15	3-39	-1.3
1891	Col-a	12	41	12	7	0	0	0	4	12	9	.171	.370	.171	59	-1	4			.843	3	3-12	0.2
Total	3	80	298	52	76	11	5	4	20	24	33	.255	.317	.366	110	0	8			.830	-10	/3-80	-0.9

■ **STAN CLIBURN** Cliburn, Stanley Gene b: 12/19/56, Jackson, Miss. BR/TR, 6', 195 lbs. Deb: 5/6/80 F

YEAR	TM/L	G	AB	R	H	2B	3B	HR	RBI	BB	SO	AVG	OBP	SLG	PRO+	BR/A	SB	CS	SBR	FA	FR	G/POS	TPR
1980	Cal-A	54	56	7	10	2	0	2	6	3	9	.179	.220	.321	48	-4	0	0	0	.971	5	C-54	0.2

■ **HARLOND CLIFT** Clift, Harlond Benton "Darkie" b: 8/12/12, ElReno, Okla. d: 4/27/92, Yakima, Wash. BR/TR, 5'11", 180 lbs. Deb: 4/17/34

YEAR	TM/L	G	AB	R	H	2B	3B	HR	RBI	BB	SO	AVG	OBP	SLG	PRO+	BR/A	SB	CS	SBR	FA	FR	G/POS	TPR
1934	StL-A	147	572	104	149	30	10	14	56	84	100	.260	.357	.421	92	-7	7	2	1	.929	-16	*3-141	-1.6
1935	StL-A	137	475	101	140	26	4	11	69	83	39	.295	.406	.436	113	11	0	3	-2	.934	-6	*3-127/2-6	0.8
1936	StL-A	152	576	145	174	40	11	20	73	115	68	.302	.424	.514	127	27	12	4	1	.951	3	*3-152	3.2
1937	StL-A☆	155	571	103	175	36	7	29	118	98	80	.306	.413	.546	139	35	8	5	-1	.947	**41**	*3-155	**7.2**
1938	StL-A	149	534	119	155	25	7	34	118	118	67	.290	.423	.554	143	38	10	5	0	**.962**	14	*3-149	4.8
1939	StL-A	151	526	90	142	25	2	15	84	**111**	55	.270	.402	.411	106	9	4	3	-1	.953	12	*3-149	2.0
1940	StL-A	150	523	92	143	29	5	20	87	104	62	.273	.396	.463	119	18	9	8	-2	**.959**	4	*3-147	2.1
1941	StL-A	154	584	108	149	33	9	17	84	113	93	.255	.376	.430	109	9	6	4	-1	.959	1	*3-154	1.3
1942	StL-A	143	541	108	148	39	4	7	55	106	48	.274	.394	.399	122	20	6	4	-1	.941	-1	*3-141/S-1	2.0
1943	StL-A	105	379	43	88	11	3	3	25	54	37	.232	.329	.301	83	-7	5	4	-1	.950	19	*3-104	1.3
	Was-A	8	30	4	9	0	0	0	4	5	3	.300	.417	.300	115	1	0	0	0	.968	-1	/3-8	0.1
	Yr	113	409	47	97	11	3	3	29	59	40	.237	.336	.301	85	-6	5	4	-1	.951	18	*3-112	1.4
1944	Was-A	12	44	4	7	3	0	0	3	3	3	.159	.213	.227	27	-4	0	0	0	.842	-3	3-12	-0.7
1945	Was-A	119	375	49	79	12	0	8	53	76	58	.211	.349	.307	99	3	2	1	0	.934	-4	*3-111	0.2
Total	12	1582	5730	1070	1558	309	62	178	829	1070	713	.272	.390	.441	115	152	69	43	-5	.948	63	*3-1550/2-6,S-1	22.7

■ **FLEA CLIFTON** Clifton, Herman Earl b: 12/12/09, Cincinnati, Ohio d: 12/22/97, Cincinnati, Ohio BR/TR, 5'10", 160 lbs. Deb: 4/29/34

YEAR	TM/L	G	AB	R	H	2B	3B	HR	RBI	BB	SO	AVG	OBP	SLG	PRO+	BR/A	SB	CS	SBR	FA	FR	G/POS	TPR
1934	Det-A	16	16	3	1	0	0	0	1	1	2	.063	.118	.063	-52	-4	0	0	0	1.000	2	/3-4,2-1	-0.2
1935	*Det-A	43	110	15	28	5	0	0	9	5	13	.255	.293	.300	56	-7	2	1	0	.934	-1	3-21/2-5,S-4	-0.7
1936	Det-A	13	26	5	5	1	0	0	1	4	3	.192	.300	.231	33	-3	0	1	-1	.926	-0	/S-6,3-2,2-1	-0.3
1937	Det-A	15	43	4	5	1	0	0	2	7	10	.116	.240	.140	-2	-7	3	0	1	.958	-0	/3-7,S-4,2-3	-0.5
Total	4	87	195	27	39	7	0	0	13	17	28	.200	.268	.236	30	-20	5	2	0	.937	-0	/3-34,S-14,2-10	-1.7

■ **MONK CLINE** Cline, John P. b: 3/3/1858, Louisville, Ky. d: 9/23/16, Louisville, Ky. BL/TL, 5'4", 150 lbs. Deb: 7/4/1882

YEAR	TM/L	G	AB	R	H	2B	3B	HR	RBI	BB	SO	AVG	OBP	SLG	PRO+	BR/A	SB	CS	SBR	FA	FR	G/POS	TPR
1882	Bal-a	44	172	18	38	6	2	0		3		.221	.234	.279	79	-3				.825	6	O-39/S-8,2-2,3-1	0.3
1884	Lou-a	94	396	91	115	16	7	2	39	27		.290	.342	.381	142	19				.875	6	*O-90/S-6	2.1
1885	Lou-a	2	9	0	2	1	0	0	2	0		.222	.222	.333	74	-0				1.000	-1	/O-1,3-1	-0.1
1888	KC-a	73	293	45	69	13	2	0	19	20		.235	.289	.294	82	-7	29			.883	5	O-70/2-3,3-1	-0.3
1891	Lou-a	21	76	13	23	3	1	0	12	19	3	.303	.442	.368	134	5	2			.906	-3	O-21	0.1
Total	5	234	946	167	247	39	12	2	72	69	3	.261	.315	.334	111	14	31			.867	14	O-221/S-14,2-5,3-3	2.1

■ **TY CLINE** Cline, Tyrone Alexander b: 6/15/39, Hampton, S.C. BL/TL, 6'0.5", 170 lbs. Deb: 9/14/60

YEAR	TM/L	G	AB	R	H	2B	3B	HR	RBI	BB	SO	AVG	OBP	SLG	PRO+	BR/A	SB	CS	SBR	FA	FR	G/POS	TPR
1960	Cle-A	7	26	2	8	1	1	0	2	0	4	.308	.308	.423	99	-0	0	0	0	1.000	2	/O-6	0.1
1961	Cle-A	12	43	9	9	2	1	0	1	6	1	.209	.333	.302	73	-1	1	0	0	1.000	-2	O-12	-0.4
1962	Cle-A	118	375	53	93	15	5	2	28	28	50	.248	.309	.331	74	-14	5	4	-1	.992	3	*O-107	-1.8
1963	Mil-N	72	174	17	41	2	1	0	10	10	31	.236	.285	.259	58	-9	2	1	0	.992	-0	O-62	-1.3
1964	Mil-N	101	116	22	35	4	2	1	13	8	22	.302	.362	.397	113	2	0	1	-1	.982	-10	O-54/1-6	-1.0
1965	Mil-N	123	220	27	42	5	3	0	10	16	50	.191	.246	.241	37	-18	2	2	-1	.969	-6	O-86/1-5	-2.9
1966	Chi-N	7	17	3	6	0	0	0	2	0	2	.353	.353	.353	96	-0	1	0	0	1.000	-1	/O-5	-0.1
	Atl-N	42	71	12	18	0	0	0	6	3	11	.254	.303	.254	56	-4	2	1	0	1.000	-5	O-19/1-6	-1.0
	Yr	49	88	15	24	0	0	0	8	3	13	.273	.312	.273	63	-4	3	1	0	1.000	-6	O-24/1-6	-1.1
1967	Atl-N	10	8	0	0	0	0	0	0	0	3	.000	.111	.000	-66	-2	0	0	0	1.000	-0	/O-1	-0.2
	SF-N	64	122	18	33	5	5	0	4	9	13	.270	.326	.393	106	1	2	1	0	1.000	-6	O-37	-0.7
	Yr	74	130	18	33	5	5	0	4	9	16	.254	.312	.369	96	-1	2	1	0	1.000	-6	O-38	-0.9
1968	SF-N	116	291	37	65	6	3	1	28	11	26	.223	.254	.275	59	-15	0	2	-1	.971	-4	O-70,1-24	-2.8
1969	Mon-N	101	209	26	50	5	3	2	12	32	22	.239	.346	.321	87	-2	4	3	-1	.988	-0	O-41,1-17	-0.7
1970	Mon-N	2	2	0	1	0	0	0	0	0	0	.500	.500	.500	169	0	0	0	0	.000	0	H	0.0
	*Cin-N	48	63	13	17	7	1	0	8	12	11	.270	.387	.413	114	2	1	2	-1	.966	-2	O-20/1-2	-0.2
	Yr	50	65	13	18	7	1	0	8	12	11	.277	.390	.415	115	2	1	2	-1	.966	-2	O-20/1-2	-0.2
1971	Cin-N	69	97	12	19	1	0	0	1	18	16	.196	.333	.206	57	-5	2	2	-1	1.000	-5	O-28/1-2	-1.2
Total	12	892	1834	251	437	53	25	6	125	153	262	.238	.304	.304	72	-65	22	19	-5	.986	-38	O-548/1-62	-14.2

■ **GENE CLINES** Clines, Eugene Anthony b: 10/6/46, San Pablo, Cal. BR/TR, 5'9", 170 lbs. Deb: 6/28/70 C

YEAR	TM/L	G	AB	R	H	2B	3B	HR	RBI	BB	SO	AVG	OBP	SLG	PRO+	BR/A	SB	CS	SBR	FA	FR	G/POS	TPR
1970	Pit-N	31	37	4	15	2	0	0	3	2	5	.405	.436	.459	143	2	2	1	0	1.000	-2	/O-7	0.0
1971	*Pit-N	97	273	52	84	12	4	1	24	22	36	.308	.366	.392	115	6	15	6	1	.981	2	O-74	0.6
1972	*Pit-N	107	311	52	104	15	6	0	17	16	47	.334	.371	.421	127	11	12	6	0	.958	-9	O-83	-0.1
1973	Pit-N	110	304	42	80	11	3	1	23	26	36	.263	.327	.329	84	-6	8	7	-2	.968	-2	O-77	-1.3
1974	*Pit-N	107	276	29	62	5	1	0	14	30	40	.225	.310	.250	60	-14	14	2	3	.989	2	O-78	-1.2
1975	NY-N	82	203	25	46	6	3	0	10	11	21	.227	.270	.286	57	-12	4	4	-1	.982	-4	O-60	-2.0
1976	Tex-A	116	446	52	123	12	3	0	38	16	52	.276	.307	.316	81	-11	11	9	-2	.987	3	*O-103,D-10	-1.6
1977	Chi-N	101	239	27	70	12	2	3	41	25	25	.293	.362	.397	93	-2	1	2	-1	.986	-8	O-63	-1.3
1978	Chi-N	109	229	31	59	10	2	0	17	21	28	.258	.323	.319	71	-8	4	3	-1	.978	-7	O-66	-2.0
1979	Chi-N	10	10	0	2	0	0	0	0	0	1	.200	.200	.200	9	-1	0	0	0	.000	0	/H	-0.2
Total	10	870	2328	314	645	85	24	5	187	169	291	.277	.331	.341	88	-36	71	40	-3	.979	-24	O-611/D-10	-9.1

■ **BILLY CLINGMAN** Clingman, William Frederick b: 11/21/1869, Cincinnati, Ohio d: 5/14/58, Cincinnati, Ohio BB/TR, 5'11", 150 lbs. Deb: 9/9/1890

YEAR	TM/L	G	AB	R	H	2B	3B	HR	RBI	BB	SO	AVG	OBP	SLG	PRO+	BR/A	SB	CS	SBR	FA	FR	G/POS	TPR
1890	Cin-N	7	27	2	7	1	0	0	5	1	0	.259	.286	.296	70	-1	0			.892	-1	/S-6,2-1	-0.1
1891	Cin-a	1	5	0	1	1	0	0	0	0	0	.200	.200	.400	65	-0	0			.667	-1	/2-1	-0.1
1895	Pit-N	106	382	69	99	16	4	0	45	41	43	.259	.334	.322	74	-14	19			.887	14	*3-106	0.1
1896	Lou-N	121	423	57	99	10	2	2	37	57	51	.234	.329	.281	64	-20	19			.925	24	*3-121	0.5
1897	Lou-N	113	395	59	90	14	7	2	47	37		.228	.302	.314	65	-20	14			**.947**	**29**	*3-113	1.0
1898	Lou-N	154	538	65	138	12	6	0	50	51		.257	.327	.301	81	-12	15			.914	15	3-79,S-74/O-1,2-1	0.7
1899	Lou-N	109	366	67	96	15	4	2	44	46		.262	.349	.342	90	-4	13			.916	-4	*S-109	0.0
1900	Chi-N	47	159	15	33	6	0	0	11	17		.208	.292	.245	51	-10	6			.872	-12	S-47	-1.7
1901	Was-A	137	480	66	116	10	7	2	55	42		.242	.308	.304	71	-18	10			**.932**	18	*S-137	1.0
1903	Cle-A	21	64	10	18	1	1	0	7	11		.281	.387	.328	118	2	2			.932	-0	2-11/S-7,3-3	0.3
Total	10	816	2839	410	697	86	31	8	301	303	94	.246	.323	.306	74	-97	98			.919	80	3-422,S-380/2-14,O	1.7

■ **JIM CLINTON** Clinton, James Lawrence "Big Jim" b: 8/10/1850, New York, N.Y. d: 9/3/21, Brooklyn, N.Y. BR/TR, 5'8.5", 174 lbs. Deb: 5/18/1872 MU

YEAR	TM/L	G	AB	R	H	2B	3B	HR	RBI	BB	SO	AVG	OBP	SLG	PRO+	BR/A	SB	CS	SBR	FA	FR	G/POS	TPR
1872	Eck-n	25	97	12	25	3	1	0	6	0	2	.258	.258	.309	87	-0	0	1	-1	.792	-6	O-11,3-10/2-3,CS	-0.5
1873	Res-n	9	38	5	9	1	0	0	4	0	0	.237	.237	.263	52	-2	0	0	0	.697	-1	/3-9	-0.2
1874	Atl-n	2	11	3	2	1	0	0	2	0	2	.182	.182	.273	49	-1	0	0	0	.444	-2	/2-1,O-1	-0.2
1875	Atl-n	22	81	3	10	0	0	0	0	0	0	.123	.123	.123	-16	-8	0	0	0	.830	3	P-17/O-7,1-5,2-1	-0.1
1876	Lou-N	16	65	8	22	2	0	0	0	0	0	.338	.338	.369	115	0				.783	1	O-14/1-1,P-1	0.0
1882	Wor-N	26	98	9	16	2	0	0	3	7	13	.163	.219	.184	30	-7				.734	-4	O-26	-1.0
1883	Bal-a	94	399	69	125	16	8	0		27		.313	.357	.393	137	16				.842	5	*O-92/2-2	1.8
1884	Bal-a	104	437	82	118	12	6	4		29		.270	.334	.352	119	10				.807	-1	*O-104/2-1	0.6
1885	Cin-a	105	408	48	97	5	5	0	34	15		.238	.277	.275	73	-12				.877	-0	*O-105	-1.4
1886	Bal-a	23	83	8	15	1	0	0	6	4		.181	.227	.193	33	-6	3			.894	-0	O-23	-0.6
Total	4 n	58	227	23	46	5	1	0	12	0	4	.203	.203	.233	45	-11	0	1	-1	.699	-6	/3-19,O-19,P12SC	-1.0
Total	6	368	1490	224	393	38	19	4	43	82	13	.264	.311	.323	101	-0	3			.838	0	O-364/2-3,P-1,1-1	-0.6

■ LOU CLINTON
Clinton, Luciean Louis b: 10/13/37, Ponca City, Okla. d: 12/6/97, Wichita, Kan. BR/TR, 6′1″, 185 lbs. Deb: 4/22/60

YEAR	TM/L	G	AB	R	H	2B	3B	HR	RBI	BB	SO	AVG	OBP	SLG	PRO+	BR/A	SB	CS	SBR	FA	FR	G/POS	TPR
1960	Bos-A	96	298	37	68	17	5	6	37	20	66	.228	.283	.379	75	-11	4	3	-1	.966	2	O-89	-1.4
1961	Bos-A	17	51	4	13	2	1	0	3	2	10	.255	.283	.333	63	-3	0	0	0	1.000	3	O-13	0.0
1962	Bos-A	114	398	63	117	24	10	18	75	34	79	.294	.351	.540	132	16	2	1	0	.979	1	*O-103	1.2
1963	Bos-A	148	560	71	130	23	7	22	77	49	118	.232	.295	.416	94	-6	0	0	0	.982	11	*O-146	-0.3
1964	Bos-A	37	120	15	31	4	3	3	6	9	33	.258	.310	.417	95	-1	1	0	0	1.000	5	O-35	0.3
	LA-A	91	306	30	76	18	0	9	38	31	40	.248	.320	.395	108	2	3	0	1	.985	3	O-86	0.2
	Yr	128	426	45	107	22	3	12	44	40	73	.251	.317	.401	104	1	4	0	1	.990	7	*O-121	0.5
1965	Cal-A	89	222	29	54	12	3	1	8	23	37	.243	.317	.338	88	-3	2	3	-1	.983	-2	O-73	-0.9
	KC-A	1	1	0	0	0	0	0	0	0	0	.000	.000	.000	-99	-0	0	0	0	.000	-0	/O-1	-0.1
	Cle-A	12	34	2	6	1	0	1	2	3	7	.176	.243	.294	51	-2	0	0	0	.941	-0	/O-9	-0.3
	Yr	102	257	31	60	13	3	2	10	26	44	.233	.306	.331	83	-6	2	3	-1	.977	-2	O-83	-1.3
1966	NY-A	80	159	18	35	10	2	5	21	16	27	.220	.291	.403	101	-0	0	0	0	.976	-6	O-63	-0.9
1967	NY-A	6	4	1	2	1	0	0	2	1	1	.500	.600	.750	308	1	0	0	0	.000	-0	/O-1	0.1
Total	8	691	2153	270	532	112	31	65	269	188	418	.247	.310	.418	99	-7	12	7	-1	.980	15	O-619	-2.1

■ ED CLOUGH
Clough, Edgar George "Big Ed" or "Spec" b: 10/28/06, Wiconisco, Pa. d: 1/30/44, Harrisburg, Pa. BL/TL, 6′, 188 lbs. Deb: 8/28/24

YEAR	TM/L	G	AB	R	H	2B	3B	HR	RBI	BB	SO	AVG	OBP	SLG	PRO+	BR/A	SB	CS	SBR	FA	FR	G/POS	TPR
1924	StL-N	7	14	0	1	0	0	0	1	0	3	.071	.071	.071	-63	-3	0	0	0	1.000	0	/O-6	-0.3
1925	StL-N	3	4	0	1	0	0	0	0	0	0	.250	.250	.250	28	-0	0	0	0	1.000	-0	/P-3	0.0
1926	StL-N	1	1	0	0	0	0	0	0	0	0	.000	.000	.000	-96	-0	0			.000	-0	/P-1	0.0
Total	3	11	19	0	2	0	0	0	1	0	3	.105	.105	.105	-44	-4	0	0		1.000	0	/O-6,P-4	-0.3

■ DANNY CLYBURN
Clyburn, Danny b: 4/6/74, Lancaster, S.C. BR/TR, 6′3″, 220 lbs. Deb: 9/15/97

YEAR	TM/L	G	AB	R	H	2B	3B	HR	RBI	BB	SO	AVG	OBP	SLG	PRO+	BR/A	SB	CS	SBR	FA	FR	G/POS	TPR
1997	Bal-A	2	3	0	0	0	0	0	0	0	2	.000	.000	.000	-99	-1	0	0	0	.000	-0	/O-1	-0.1
1998	Bal-A	11	25	6	7	0	0	1	3	1	10	.280	.308	.400	84	-1	0	0	0	1.000	-2	/O-8,D-1	-0.2
Total	2	13	28	6	7	0	0	1	3	1	12	.250	.276	.357	64	-2	0	0	0	1.000	-2	/O-9,D-1	-0.3

■ OTIS CLYMER
Clymer, Otis Edgar b: 1/27/1876, Pine Grove, Pa. d: 2/27/26, St.Paul, Minn. BB/TR, 5′11″, 180 lbs. Deb: 4/14/05

YEAR	TM/L	G	AB	R	H	2B	3B	HR	RBI	BB	SO	AVG	OBP	SLG	PRO+	BR/A	SB	CS	SBR	FA	FR	G/POS	TPR
1905	Pit-N	96	365	74	108	11	5	0	23	19		.296	.332	.353	102	0	23			.986	-2	O-89/1-1	-0.6
1906	Pit-N	11	45	7	11	0	1	0	1	3		.244	.292	.289	78	-1	1			.900	-1	O-11	-0.3
1907	Pit-N	22	66	8	15	2	0	0	4	5		.227	.311	.258	77	-1	4			.923	-3	O-15/1-1	-0.5
	Was-A	57	206	30	65	5	5	1	16	18		.316	.382	.403	163	15	18			.912	-4	O-51/1-1	1.0
1908	Was-A	110	368	32	93	11	4	1	35	20		.253	.291	.313	105	1	19			.933	-8	O-82,2-13/3-2	-1.2
1909	Was-A	45	138	11	27	5	2	0	6	17		.196	.284	.261	76	-4	7			.922	-4	O-41	-1.1
1913	Chi-N	30	105	16	24	5	1	0	7	14	18	.229	.319	.295	76	-3	9			.933	-2	O-26	-0.6
	Bos-N	14	37	4	12	3	1	0	6	3	3	.324	.375	.459	135	2	2			.880	-2	O-11	-0.1
	Yr	44	142	20	36	8	2	0	13	17	21	.254	.333	.338	91	-1	11			.918	-4	O-37	-0.7
Total	6	385	1330	182	355	42	19	2	98	99	21	.267	.322	.332	106	8	83			.939	-25	O-326/2-13,1-3,3-2	-3.4

■ BILL CLYMER
Clymer, William Johnston "Derby Day Bill" b: 12/18/1873, Philadelphia, Pa. d: 12/26/36, Philadelphia, Pa. Deb: 6/26/1891 C

YEAR	TM/L	G	AB	R	H	2B	3B	HR	RBI	BB	SO	AVG	OBP	SLG	PRO+	BR/A	SB	CS	SBR	FA	FR	G/POS	TPR
1891	Phi-a	3	11	0	0	0	0	0	0	1	2	.000	.154	.000	-54	-2	1			.867	-2	/S-3	-0.3

■ PETE COACHMAN
Coachman, Bobby Dean b: 11/11/61, Cottonwood, Ala. BR/TR, 5′9″, 175 lbs. Deb: 8/18/90

YEAR	TM/L	G	AB	R	H	2B	3B	HR	RBI	BB	SO	AVG	OBP	SLG	PRO+	BR/A	SB	CS	SBR	FA	FR	G/POS	TPR
1990	Cal-A	16	45	3	14	3	0	0	5	1	7	.311	.354	.378	107	0	0	1	-1	.958	1	/3-9,2-2,D-2	0.1

■ GIL COAN
Coan, Gilbert Fitzgerald b: 5/18/22, Monroe, N.C. BL/TR, 6′, 180 lbs. Deb: 4/27/46

YEAR	TM/L	G	AB	R	H	2B	3B	HR	RBI	BB	SO	AVG	OBP	SLG	PRO+	BR/A	SB	CS	SBR	FA	FR	G/POS	TPR
1946	Was-A	59	134	17	28	3	2	3	9	7	37	.209	.269	.328	70	-6	2	2	-1	.969	-2	O-29	-1.0
1947	Was-A	11	42	5	21	3	2	0	3	5	6	.500	.553	.667	245	8	2	1	0	1.000	1	O-11	0.8
1948	Was-A	138	513	56	119	13	9	7	60	41	78	.232	.298	.333	70	-24	23	9	2	.970	12	*O-131	-1.7
1949	Was-A	111	358	36	78	7	8	3	25	29	58	.218	.278	.307	56	-24	9	6	-1	.975	2	O-97	-2.8
1950	Was-A	104	366	58	111	17	4	7	50	28	46	.303	.359	.429	106	2	10	5	0	.970	-3	O-98	-0.4
1951	Was-A	135	538	85	163	25	7	9	62	39	62	.303	.357	.426	113	9	8	5	-1	.965	22	*O-132	2.4
1952	Was-A	107	332	50	68	11	6	5	20	32	35	.205	.277	.319	68	-15	9	4	0	.984	0	O-86	-1.9
1953	Was-A	68	168	28	33	1	4	2	17	22	23	.196	.301	.286	60	-9	7	0	2	1.000	4	O-46	-0.5
1954	Bal-A	94	265	29	74	11	1	2	20	16	17	.279	.323	.351	91	-4	9	4	0	.968	-4	O-67	-1.0
1955	Bal-A	61	130	18	31	7	1	1	11	13	15	.238	.313	.331	79	-4	4	2	0	.983	-4	O-43	-1.0
	Chi-A	17	17	0	3	0	0	0	1	0	5	.176	.176	.176	-5	-2	0	0	0	1.000	-1	/O-3	-0.3
	Yr	78	147	18	34	7	1	1	12	13	20	.231	.298	.313	68	-7	4	2	0	.984	-5	O-46	-1.3
	NY-N	9	13	0	2	0	0	0	0	0	1	.154	.154	.154	-18	-2	0	0	0	1.000	-2	/O-6	-0.5
1956	NY-N	4	1	2	0	0	0	0	0	0	1	.000	.000	.000	-99	-0	0	0	0	.000	0	H	0.0
Total	11	918	2877	384	731	98	44	39	278	232	384	.254	.316	.359	84	-73	83	38	2	.973	24	O-749	-7.9

■ JOE COBB
Cobb, Joseph Stanley (b: Joseph Stanley Serafin) b: 1/24/1895, Hudson, Pa. d: 12/24/47, Allentown, Pa. BR/TR, 5′9″, 170 lbs. Deb: 4/25/18

YEAR	TM/L	G	AB	R	H	2B	3B	HR	RBI	BB	SO	AVG	OBP	SLG	PRO+	BR/A	SB	CS	SBR	FA	FR	G/POS	TPR
1918	Det-A	1	0	0	0	0	0	0	0	1	0	—	1.000	—	210	0	0			.000	0	H	0.0

■ TY COBB
Cobb, Tyrus Raymond "The Georgia Peach" b: 12/18/1886, Narrows, Ga. d: 7/17/61, Atlanta, Ga. BL/TR, 6′1″, 175 lbs. Deb: 8/30/05 MH

YEAR	TM/L	G	AB	R	H	2B	3B	HR	RBI	BB	SO	AVG	OBP	SLG	PRO+	BR/A	SB	CS	SBR	FA	FR	G/POS	TPR
1905	Det-A	41	150	19	36	6	0	1	15	10		.240	.287	.300	86	-3	2			.958	2	O-41	-0.3
1906	Det-A	98	358	45	113	15	5	1	34	19		.316	.355	.394	131	12	23			.961	6	O-96	1.5
1907	*Det-A	150	605	97	**212**	28	14	5	**119**	24		**.350**	.380	**.468**	**164**	**40**	**49**			.961	11	*O-150	5.0
1908	*Det-A	150	581	88	**188**	**36**	**20**	4	**108**	34		**.324**	.367	**.475**	**166**	**40**	39			.944	4	*O-150	4.2
1909	*Det-A	156	573	**116**	**216**	33	10	**9**	**107**	48		**.377**	**.431**	**.517**	**190**	**58**	**76**			.946	3	*O-156	**6.1**
1910	Det-A	140	506	**106**	194	35	13	8	91	64		**.383**	**.456**	**.551**	**202**	60	65			.958	9	*O-137	6.7
1911	Det-A	146	591	**147**	**248**	**47**	**24**	8	**127**	44		**.420**	.467	**.621**	**193**	**71**	**83**			.957	11	*O-146	**7.1**
1912	Det-A	140	553	120	**226**	30	23	7	83	43		**.409**	.456	**.584**	**203**	**72**	61			.940	1	*O-140	6.4
1913	Det-A	122	428	70	167	18	16	4	67	58	31	**.390**	**.467**	.535	**196**	53	51			.947	3	*O-119	5.3
1914	Det-A	98	345	69	127	22	11	2	57	57	22	**.368**	.466	**.513**	188	40	35	17	0	.949	-10	O-96	2.8
1915	Det-A	156	563	**144**	**208**	31	13	3	99	118	43	**.369**	**.486**	.487	**182**	**64**	**96**	38	6	.951	-3	*O-156	**6.2**
1916	Det-A	145	542	**113**	201	31	10	5	68	78	39	.371	.452	.493	177	53	**68**	24	**6**	.953	-2	*O-143/1-1	5.4
1917	Det-A	152	588	107	**225**	**44**	**24**	6	102	61	34	**.383**	**.444**	**.570**	**210**	**75**	**55**			.973	13	*O-152	**8.5**
1918	Det-A	111	421	83	161	19	**14**	3	64	41	21	**.382**	**.440**	.515	**196**	**48**	34			.975	2	O-95,1-13/P-2,23	4.8
1919	Det-A	124	497	92	**191**	36	13	1	70	38	22	**.384**	.429	.515	168	44	28			.973	-2	*O-123	3.5
1920	Det-A	112	428	86	143	28	8	2	63	58	28	.334	.416	.451	133	22	15	10	-2	.966	-7	*O-112	0.5
1921	Det-A	128	507	124	197	37	16	12	101	56	19	.389	.452	.596	167	52	22	15	-2	.970	13	*O-121,M	4.9
1922	Det-A	137	526	99	211	42	16	4	99	55	24	.401	.462	.565	172	57	9	13	-5	.980	4	*O-134,M	4.3
1923	Det-A	145	556	103	189	40	7	6	88	66	14	.340	.413	.469	135	29	9	10	-3	.969	4	*O-141,M	2.0
1924	Det-A	155	625	115	211	38	10	4	78	85	18	.338	.418	.450	126	26	23	14	-2	**.986**	5	*O-155,M	1.8
1925	Det-A	121	415	97	157	31	12	12	102	65	12	.378	.468	.598	**171**	47	13	9	-2	.948	-2	*O-105/P-1,M	3.3
1926	Det-A	79	233	48	79	18	5	4	62	26	2	.339	.408	.511	137	12	9	4	0	.950	-5	O-55,M	0.4
1927	Phi-A	134	490	104	175	32	7	5	93	67	12	.357	.440	.482	131	25	22	16	-3	.969	-5	*O-127	0.9
1928	Phi-A	95	353	54	114	27	4	1	40	34	16	.323	.389	.431	112	7	5	8	-3	.964	-1	O-85	-0.3
Total	24	3035	11434	2246	4189	724	295	117	1937	1249	357	.366	.433	.512	167	1004	892	178		.961	56	*O-2935/1-14,P32	91.0

■ DAVE COBLE
Coble, David Lamar b: 12/24/12, Monroe, N.C. d: 10/15/71, Orlando, Fla. BR/TR, 6′1″, 183 lbs. Deb: 5/1/39

YEAR	TM/L	G	AB	R	H	2B	3B	HR	RBI	BB	SO	AVG	OBP	SLG	PRO+	BR/A	SB	CS	SBR	FA	FR	G/POS	TPR
1939	Phi-N	15	25	2	7	1	0	0	0	0	3	.280	.280	.320	63	-1	0			.938	-1	C-13	-0.2

■ GEORGE COCHRAN
Cochran, George Leslie b: 2/12/1889, Rusk, Tex. d: 5/21/60, Harbor City, Cal. TR, Deb: 7/29/18

YEAR	TM/L	G	AB	R	H	2B	3B	HR	RBI	BB	SO	AVG	OBP	SLG	PRO+	BR/A	SB	CS	SBR	FA	FR	G/POS	TPR
1918	Bos-A	24	60	7	7	0	0	0	3	10	6	.117	.264	.117	15	-6	3			.960	-4	3-22/S-1	-1.0

■ DAVE COCHRANE
Cochrane, David Carter b: 1/31/63, Riverside, Cal. BB/TR, 6′2″, 180 lbs. Deb: 9/2/86

YEAR	TM/L	G	AB	R	H	2B	3B	HR	RBI	BB	SO	AVG	OBP	SLG	PRO+	BR/A	SB	CS	SBR	FA	FR	G/POS	TPR
1986	Chi-A	19	62	4	12	2	0	1	2	5	22	.194	.254	.274	42	-5	0	0	0	.872	-3	3-18/S-1	-0.8
1989	Sea-A	54	102	13	24	4	1	3	7	14	27	.235	.333	.382	98	-0	0	2	-1	.905	-13	S-30/1-9,3-9,2OC	-1.5

YEAR	TM/L	G	AB	R	H	2B	3B	HR	RBI	BB	SO	AVG	OBP	SLG	PRO+	BR/A	SB	CS	SBR	FA	FR	G/POS	TPR
1990	Sea-A	15	20	0	3	0	0	0	0	0	8	.150	.150	.150	-16	-3	0	0	0	1.000	0	/S-5,1-3,3-3,C-1	-0.3
1991	Sea-A	65	178	16	44	13	0	2	22	9	38	.247	.287	.354	76	-6	0	1	-1	.969	-14	O-26,C-19,3-13,/1D	-2.1
1992	Sea-A	65	152	10	38	5	0	2	12	12	34	.250	.309	.322	77	-5	1	0	0	.879	-8	O-25,C-21,3/1SD2	-1.2
Total	5	218	514	43	121	24	1	8	43	40	129	.235	.294	.333	73	-19	1	3	-2	.925	-38	/O-54,3-53,CS12D	-5.9
■ MICKEY COCHRANE	Cochrane, Gordon Stanley b: 4/6/03, Bridgewater, Mass. d: 6/28/62, Lake Forest, Ill. BL/TR, 5'10.5", 180 lbs. Deb: 4/14/25 MCH																						
1925	Phi-A	134	420	69	139	21	5	6	55	44	19	.331	.397	.448	107	5	7	4	-0	.984	-10	*C-133	0.1
1926	Phi-A	120	370	50	101	8	9	8	47	56	15	.273	.369	.408	97	-1	5	2	0	.975	12	*C-115	1.7
1927	Phi-A	126	432	80	146	20	6	12	80	50	7	.338	.409	.495	127	17	9	6	-1	.986	3	*C-123	2.6
1928	Phi-A	131	468	92	137	26	12	10	57	76	25	.293	.395	.464	122	16	7	7	-2	.966	2	*C-130	2.6
1929	*Phi-A	135	514	113	170	37	8	7	95	69	8	.331	.412	.475	123	19	7	6	-2	.983	8	*C-135	3.6
1930	*Phi-A	130	487	110	174	42	5	10	85	55	18	.357	.424	.526	133	25	5	0	2	**.993**	6	*C-130	4.0
1931	*Phi-A	122	459	87	160	31	6	17	89	56	21	.349	.423	.553	146	30	2	3	-1	.986	10	*C-117	4.3
1932	Phi-A	139	518	118	152	35	4	23	112	100	22	.293	.412	.510	132	27	0	1	-1	**.993**	10	*C-137/O-1	4.1
1933	Phi-A	130	429	104	138	30	4	15	60	106	22	.322	**.459**	.515	156	41	8	6	-1	.989	-7	*C-128	3.7
1934	*Det-A★	129	437	74	140	32	1	2	76	78	26	.320	.428	.412	117	16	8	4	0	.988	-4	*C-124,M	1.6
1935	*Det-A☆	115	411	93	131	33	3	5	47	96	15	.319	.452	.450	139	30	5	5	-2	.989	-5	*C-110,M	2.7
1936	Det-A	44	126	24	34	8	0	2	17	46	15	.270	.465	.381	111	5	1	1	-0	.983	-9	C-42,M	-0.1
1937	Det-A	27	98	27	30	10	1	2	12	25	4	.306	.452	.490	134	6	0	1	-1	1.000	-2	C-27,M	0.5
Total	13	1482	5169	1041	1652	333	64	119	832	857	217	.320	.419	.478	127	237	64	46	-8	.985	14	*C-1451/O-1	31.4
■ JIM COCKMAN	Cockman, James b: 4/26/1873, Guelph, Ont., Can. d: 9/28/47, Guelph, Ont., Can. BR/TR, 5'6", 145 lbs. Deb: 9/28/05																						
1905	NY-A	13	38	5	4	0	0	0	2	4		.105	.190	.105	-5	-4	2			.875	-2	3-13	-0.7
■ ALAN COCKRELL	Cockrell, Atlee Alan b: 12/5/62, Kansas City, Kan. BR/TR, 6'2", 210 lbs. Deb: 9/7/96																						
1996	Col-N	9	8	0	2	1	0	0	2	0	4	.250	.250	.375	50	-1	0	0	0	.000	-0	/O-1	-0.1
■ JACK COFFEY	Coffey, John Francis b: 1/28/1887, New York, N.Y. d: 2/14/66, Bronx, N.Y. BR/TR, 5'11", 178 lbs. Deb: 6/23/09																						
1909	Bos-N	73	257	21	48	4	4	0	20	11		.187	.229	.233	41	-18	2			.896	-12	S-73	-3.2
1918	Det-A	22	67	7	14	0	2	0	4	8	6	.209	.303	.269	75	-2	2			.957	0	2-22	-0.1
	Bos-A	15	44	5	7	1	0	1	2	3	2	.159	.213	.250	40	-3	2			.955	2	3-14/2-1	-0.1
	Yr	37	111	12	21	1	2	1	6	11	8	.189	.268	.261	62	-5	4			.959	2	2-23,3-14	-0.2
Total	2	110	368	33	69	5	6	1	26	22	8	.188	.241	.242	48	-23	6			.896	-9	/S-73,2-23,3-14	-3.4
■ FRANK COGGINS	Coggins, Franklin b: 5/22/44, Griffin, Ga. BB/TR, 6'2", 187 lbs. Deb: 9/10/67																						
1967	Was-A	19	75	9	23	3	0	1	8	2	17	.307	.325	.387	114	1	1	0	0	.964	3	2-19	0.6
1968	Was-A	62	171	15	30	6	1	0	7	9	33	.175	.217	.222	34	-14	1	1	-0	.953	4	2-52	-0.9
1972	Chi-N	6	1	1	0	0	0	0	0	1	0	.000	.500	.000	48	0	0	0	0	.000	0	H	0.0
Total	3	87	247	25	53	9	1	1	15	12	50	.215	.251	.271	59	-13	2	1	0	.957	7	/2-71	-0.3
■ RICH COGGINS	Coggins, Richard Allen b: 12/7/50, Indianapolis, Ind. BL/TL, 5'8", 170 lbs. Deb: 8/29/72																						
1972	Bal-A	16	39	5	13	4	0	0	1	1	6	.333	.350	.436	129	1	0	2	-1	1.000	2	O-13	0.2
1973	*Bal-A	110	389	54	124	19	9	7	41	28	24	.319	.365	.468	134	16	17	9	-0	.987	-3	*O-101/D-1	0.9
1974	*Bal-A	113	411	53	100	13	3	4	32	29	31	.243	.301	.319	81	-10	26	6	4	.984	-7	*O-105	-1.9
1975	Mon-N	13	37	1	10	3	1	0	4	1	7	.270	.289	.405	87	-1	0	0	0	1.000	-1	O-10	-0.3
	NY-A	51	107	7	24	1	0	1	6	7	16	.224	.272	.262	52	-7	3	3	-1	.970	-3	O-36/D-9	-1.2
1976	NY-A	7	4	1	1	0	0	0	1	0	1	.250	.250	.250	47	-0	1	0	0	1.000	-0	/O-2	0.0
	Chi-A	32	96	4	15	2	0	0	5	6	15	.156	.206	.177	13	-10	3	1	0	1.000	-4	O-26/D-1	-1.6
	Yr	39	100	5	16	2	0	0	6	6	16	.160	.208	.180	14	-11	4	1	1	1.000	-4	O-28/D-1	-1.6
Total	5	342	1083	125	287	42	13	12	90	72	100	.265	.314	.361	93	-11	50	21	2	.986	-17	O-293/D-11	-3.9
■ ED COGSWELL	Cogswell, Edward b: 2/25/1854, England d: 7/27/1888, Fitchburg, Mass. BR/TR, 5'8", 150 lbs. Deb: 7/11/1879																						
1879	Bos-N	49	236	51	76	8	1	1	18	8	5	.322	.344	.377	135	8				.967	1	1-49	0.7
1880	Tro-N	47	209	41	63	7	3	0	13	11	10	.301	.336	.364	130	6				.961	1	1-47	0.3
1882	Wor-N	13	51	10	7	1	0	0	1	6	6	.137	.228	.157	26	-4				.937	-1	1-13	-0.6
Total	3	109	496	102	146	16	4	1	32	25	21	.294	.328	.349	121	11				.960	1	1-109	0.4
■ ALTA COHEN	Cohen, Alta Albert "Schoolboy" b: 12/25/08, New York, N.Y. BL/TL, 5'10.5", 170 lbs. Deb: 4/15/31																						
1931	Bro-N	1	3	1	2	0	0	0	0	0	0	.667	.667	.667	261	1	0			1.000	1	/O-1	0.2
1932	Bro-N	9	32	1	5	1	0	0	1	3	7	.156	.229	.188	14	-4	0			.850	1	/O-8	-0.4
1933	Phi-N	19	32	6	6	1	0	0	1	6	4	.188	.316	.219	49	-2	0			1.000	-0	/O-7	-0.2
Total	3	29	67	8	13	2	0	0	2	9	11	.194	.289	.224	42	-5	0			.925	2	/O-16	-0.4
■ ANDY COHEN	Cohen, Andrew Howard b: 10/25/04, Baltimore, Md. d: 10/29/88, ElPaso, Tex. BR/TR, 5'8", 155 lbs. Deb: 6/6/26 FMC																						
1926	NY-N	32	35	4	9	0	1	0	8	1	2	.257	.278	.314	60	-2	0			.792	2	2-10,S-10/3-2	0.0
1928	NY-N	129	504	64	138	24	7	9	59	31	17	.274	.318	.403	87	-11	3			.969	3	*2-126/S-3,3-1	-0.4
1929	NY-N	101	347	40	102	12	2	5	47	11	15	.294	.319	.383	73	-15	3			.964	12	2-94/S-1,3-1	0.1
Total	3	262	886	108	249	36	10	14	114	43	34	.281	.317	.392	81	-28	6			.964	16	2-230/S-14,3-4	-0.3
■ JIMMIE COKER	Coker, Jimmie Goodwin b: 3/28/36, Holly Hill, S.C. d: 10/29/91, Throckmorton, Tex. BR/TR, 5'11", 195 lbs. Deb: 9/11/58																						
1958	Phi-N	2	6	0	1	0	0	0	0	0	0	.167	.167	.167	-12	-1	0	0	0	1.000	0	/C-2	-0.1
1960	Phi-N	81	252	18	54	5	3	6	34	23	45	.214	.290	.329	69	-11	0	3	-2	.982	2	C-76	-0.6
1961	Phi-N	11	25	3	10	1	0	1	4	7	4	.400	.531	.560	193	4	1	0	0	.984	0	C-11	0.5
1962	Phi-N	5	3	0	0	0	0	0	1	1	2	.000	.250	.000	-27	-1	0	0	0	.000	0	H	-0.1
1963	SF-N	4	5	0	1	0	0	0	0	1	2	.200	.333	.200	58	-0	0	0	0	1.000	-1	/C-2	-0.1
1964	Cin-N	11	32	3	10	2	0	1	4	3	5	.313	.371	.469	130	1	0	0	0	1.000	2	C-11	0.4
1965	Cin-N	24	61	3	15	2	0	2	9	8	16	.246	.333	.377	93	-0	0	0	0	.993	5	C-19	0.6
1966	Cin-N	50	111	9	28	3	0	4	14	8	5	.252	.303	.387	83	-3	0	1	-1	.979	4	C-39/O-2	0.3
1967	Cin-N	45	97	8	18	2	1	2	4	4	20	.186	.218	.289	39	-8	0	1	-1	.976	-0	C-34	-0.8
Total	9	233	592	44	137	15	4	16	70	55	99	.231	.301	.351	77	-18	1	5	-3	.983	13	C-194/O-2	0.1
■ ROCKY COLAVITO	Colavito, Rocco Domenico b: 8/10/33, New York, N.Y. BR/TR, 6'3", 190 lbs. Deb: 9/10/55 C																						
1955	Cle-A	5	9	3	4	2	0	0	0	0	2	.444	.444	.667	189	1	0	0	0	1.000	2	/O-2	0.3
1956	Cle-A	101	322	55	89	11	4	21	65	49	46	.276	.375	.531	134	15	0	1	-1	.968	-1	O-98	0.9
1957	Cle-A	134	461	66	116	26	0	25	84	71	80	.252	.353	.471	124	15	1	6	-3	.962	12	*O-130	1.7
1958	Cle-A	143	489	80	148	26	3	41	113	84	89	.303	.407	**.620**	183	56	0	2	-1	.981	2	*O-129,1-11/P-1	5.0
1959	Cle-A★	154	588	90	151	24	0	**42**	111	71	86	.257	.339	.512	135	26	3	3	-1	.985	12	*O-154	2.9
1960	Det-A	145	555	67	138	18	1	35	87	53	80	.249	.319	.474	108	4	3	6	-3	.976	7	*O-144	0.1
1961	Det-A★	163	583	129	169	30	2	45	140	113	75	.290	.407	.580	156	48	1	2	-1	.975	10	*O-161	4.7
1962	Det-A★	161	601	90	164	30	2	37	112	96	68	.273	.375	.514	132	27	2	0	1	.992	18	*O-161	3.6
1963	Det-A	160	597	91	162	29	2	22	91	84	78	.271	.362	.437	119	16	0	0	0	.988	7	*O-159	1.6
1964	KC-A★	160	588	89	161	31	2	34	102	83	56	.274	.368	.507	136	30	3	1	0	.973	3	*O-159	2.6
1965	Cle-A★	162	592	92	170	25	2	26	**108**	**93**	63	.287	.387	.468	140	34	1	1	-0	**1.000**	4	*O-162	3.1
1966	Cle-A★	151	533	68	127	13	0	30	72	76	81	.238	.337	.432	119	14	2	1	0	.982	7	*O-146	1.5
1967	Cle-A	63	191	10	46	9	0	5	21	24	31	.241	.329	.366	104	1	2	2	-1	.962	-4	O-50	-0.6
	Chi-A	60	190	20	42	4	1	3	29	25	10	.221	.312	.300	85	-3	1	1	-0	.977	-7	O-58	-1.4
	Yr	123	381	30	88	13	1	8	50	49	41	.231	.320	.333	95	-2	3	3	-1	.970	-11	*O-108	-2.0
1968	LA-N	40	113	8	23	3	0	3	11	15	18	.204	.297	.310	89	-1	0	1	-1	1.000	-1	O-33	-0.6
	NY-A	39	91	13	20	2	2	5	13	14	17	.220	.330	.451	139	4	0	0	0	.933	-4	O-28/P-1	-0.2
Total	14	1841	6503	971	1730	283	21	374	1159	951	880	.266	.362	.489	132	287	19	27	-11	.980	66	*O-1774/1-11,P-2	25.2

YEAR	TM/L	G	AB	R	H	2B	3B	HR	RBI	BB	SO	AVG	OBP	SLG	PRO+	BR/A	SB	CS	SBR	FA	FR	G/POS	TPR
■ **MIKE COLBERN**	Colbern, Michael Malloy b: 4/19/55, Santa Monica, Cal. BR/TR, 6'3", 205 lbs. Deb: 7/18/78																						
1978	Chi-A	48	141	11	38	5	1	2	20	1	36	.270	.285	.362	80	-4	0	1	-1	.969	0	C-47/D-1	-0.4
1979	Chi-A	32	83	5	20	5	1	0	8	4	25	.241	.276	.325	61	-5	0	0	0	.971	3	C-32	-0.1
Total	2	80	224	16	58	10	2	2	28	5	61	.259	.281	.348	73	-9	0	1	-1	.970	3	/C-79,D-1	-0.5
■ **CRAIG COLBERT**	Colbert, Craig Charles b: 2/13/65, Iowa City, Iowa BR/TR, 6', 190 lbs. Deb: 4/6/92																						
1992	SF-N	49	126	10	29	5	2	1	16	9	22	.230	.281	.325	76	-4	1	0	0	.994	-7	C-35/3-9,2-2	-1.0
1993	SF-N	23	37	2	6	2	0	1	5	3	13	.162	.225	.297	40	-3	0	0	0	.982	2	C-10/2-2,3-1	-0.1
Total	2	72	163	12	35	7	2	2	21	12	35	.215	.269	.319	67	-8	1	0	0	.990	-5	/C-45,3-10,2-4	-1.1
■ **NATE COLBERT**	Colbert, Nathan b: 4/9/46, St.Louis, Mo. BR/TR, 6'2", 209 lbs. Deb: 4/14/66																						
1966	Hou-N	19	7	3	0	0	0	0	0	0	4	.000	.000	.000	-99	-2	0	0	0	.000	0	H	-0.2
1968	Hou-N	20	53	5	8	1	0	0	4	1	23	.151	.167	.170	1	-6	1	1	-0	.952	-1	O-11/1-5	-1.0
1969	SD-N	139	483	64	123	20	9	24	66	45	123	.255	.322	.482	128	15	6	4	-1	.990	1	*1-134	0.5
1970	SD-N	156	572	84	148	17	6	38	86	56	150	.259	.329	.509	126	18	3	5	-2	.991	-8	*1-153/3-1	-0.6
1971	SD-N★	156	565	81	149	25	3	27	84	63	119	.264	.342	.462	135	24	5	2	0	.993	1	*1-153	1.1
1972	SD-N★	151	563	87	141	27	2	38	111	70	127	.250	.335	.508	147	32	15	6	1	.996	7	*1-150	2.8
1973	SD-N★	145	529	73	143	25	2	22	80	54	146	.270	.347	.450	130	20	9	8	-2	.992	3	*1-144	0.9
1974	SD-N	119	368	53	76	16	0	14	54	62	108	.207	.323	.364	96	-2	10	2	2	.988	8	1-79,O-48	0.2
1975	Det-A	45	156	16	23	4	2	4	18	17	52	.147	.231	.276	41	-13	0	2	-1	.982	-4	1-44/D-1	-2.1
	Mon-N	38	81	10	14	4	1	4	11	5	31	.173	.230	.395	68	-4	0	0	0	.988	-1	1-22	-0.6
1976	Mon-N	14	40	5	8	2	0	2	6	9	16	.200	.347	.400	107	1	3	1	0	1.000	0	/O-7,1-6	0.1
	Oak-A	2	5	0	0	0	0	0	0	1	3	.000	.167	.000	-50	-1	0	0	0	.000	0	/D-2	-0.1
Total	10	1004	3422	481	833	141	25	173	520	383	902	.243	.324	.451	120	81	52	31	-3	.991	5	1-890/O-66,D-3,3-1	1.0
■ **GREG COLBRUNN**	Colbrunn, Gregory Joseph b: 7/26/69, Fontana, Cal. BR/TR, 6', 200 lbs. Deb: 7/9/92																						
1992	Mon-N	52	168	12	45	8	0	2	18	6	34	.268	.301	.351	85	-4	3	2	-0	.992	-1	1-47	-0.9
1993	Mon-N	70	153	15	39	9	0	4	23	6	33	.255	.287	.392	76	-5	4	2	0	.995	1	1-61	-0.8
1994	Fla-N	47	155	17	47	10	0	6	31	9	27	.303	.349	.484	111	2	1	1	-0	.988	-1	1-41	-0.2
1995	Fla-N	138	528	70	146	22	1	23	89	22	69	.277	.313	.453	99	-3	11	3	2	.996	-1	*1-134	-1.4
1996	Fla-N	141	511	60	146	26	2	16	69	25	76	.286	.336	.438	106	3	4	5	-2	.995	5	*1-134	-0.6
1997	Min-A	70	217	24	61	14	0	5	26	8	38	.281	.310	.415	86	-5	1	2	-1	.988	-1	1-64/D-2	-1.1
	*Atl-N	28	54	3	15	3	0	2	9	2	11	.278	.316	.444	95	-1	0	0	0	.984	0	1-14/D-3	-0.1
1998	Col-N	62	122	12	38	8	2	2	13	8	23	.311	.359	.459	92	-2	3	3	-1	.992	0	1-27/O-5,C-1	-0.4
	*Atl-N	28	44	6	13	3	0	1	10	2	11	.295	.367	.432	104	0	1	0	0	1.000	0	/1-9,O-1,D-3	0.0
	Yr	90	166	18	51	11	2	3	23	10	34	.307	.361	.452	96	-1	4	3	-1	.993	1	1-36/O-6,D-3,C-1	-0.4
Total	7	636	1952	219	550	103	5	61	288	88	322	.282	.323	.433	97	-13	28	18	-2	.993	3	1-531/D-8,O-6,C-1	-5.5
■ **ALEX COLE**	Cole, Alexander b: 8/17/65, Fayetteville, N.C. BL/TL, 6', 170 lbs. Deb: 7/27/90																						
1990	Cle-A	63	227	43	68	5	4	0	13	28	38	.300	.379	.357	107	3	40	9	7	.961	2	O-59/D-1	1.0
1991	Cle-A	122	387	58	114	17	3	0	21	58	47	.295	.388	.354	106	6	27	17	-2	.970	1	*O-107/D-6	0.2
1992	Cle-A	41	97	11	20	1	0	0	5	10	21	.206	.287	.216	44	-7	9	2	2	.971	-4	O-24/D-4	-1.0
	*Pit-N	64	205	33	57	3	7	0	10	18	46	.278	.336	.361	99	-0	7	4	-0	.989	-1	O-53	-0.2
1993	Col-N	126	348	50	89	9	4	0	24	43	58	.256	.341	.305	64	-17	30	13	1	.982	2	O-93	-1.6
1994	Min-A	105	345	68	102	15	5	4	23	44	60	.296	.377	.403	101	2	29	8	4	.969	-0	*O-100/D-1	0.3
1995	Min-A	28	79	10	27	3	2	1	14	8	15	.342	.409	.468	127	3	1	3	-2	.938	-3	O-23/D-2	-0.1
1996	Bos-A	24	72	13	16	5	1	0	7	8	11	.222	.300	.319	56	-5	5	3	-0	.974	-3	O-24	-0.8
Total	7	573	1760	286	493	58	26	5	117	217	296	.280	.361	.351	91	-15	148	59	9	.971	-7	O-483/D-14	-2.2
■ **DICK COLE**	Cole, Richard Roy b: 5/6/26, Long Beach, Cal. BR/TR, 6'2", 175 lbs. Deb: 4/27/51 C																						
1951	StL-N	15	36	4	7	1	0	0	3	6	5	.194	.310	.222	45	-3	0	0	0	.969	5	2-14	0.2
	Pit-N	42	106	9	25	4	0	1	11	15	9	.236	.331	.302	69	-4	0	1	-1	.981	-2	2-34/S-8	-0.5
	Yr	57	142	13	32	5	0	1	14	21	14	.225	.325	.282	63	-7	0	1	-1	.978	2	2-48/S-8	-0.3
1953	Pit-N	97	235	29	64	13	1	0	23	38	26	.272	.374	.336	87	-3	2	2	-1	.965	-3	S-77/2-7,1-1	-0.2
1954	Pit-N	138	486	40	131	22	5	1	40	41	48	.270	.326	.342	75	-17	0	0	0	.949	-11	S-66,3-55,2-17	-2.3
1955	Pit-N	77	239	16	54	8	3	0	21	18	22	.226	.286	.285	53	-16	0	0	0	.935	1	3-33,2-24,S-12	-1.3
1956	Pit-N	72	99	7	21	2	1	0	9	11	9	.212	.291	.253	49	-7	0	0	0	.947	-8	3-18,2-12/S-6	-1.4
1957	Mil-N	15	14	1	1	0	0	0	0	3	5	.071	.235	.071	-13	-2	0	0	0	.952	0	2-10/1-1,3-1	-0.2
Total	6	456	1215	106	303	50	10	2	107	132	124	.249	.324	.312	69	-52	2	3	-1	.961	-19	S-169,2-118,3/1	-5.7
■ **STU COLE**	Cole, Stewart Bryan b: 2/7/66, Charlotte, N.C. BR/TR, 6'1", 175 lbs. Deb: 9/5/91																						
1991	KC-A	9	7	1	1	0	0	0	0	2	2	.143	.333	.143	37	-1	0	0	0	1.000	0	/2-5,S-1,D-2	0.0
■ **WILLIS COLE**	Cole, Willis Russell b: 1/6/1882, Milton Junction, Wis. d: 10/11/65, Madison, Wis. BR/TR, 5'8", 170 lbs. Deb: 8/22/09																						
1909	Chi-A	46	165	17	39	7	3	0	16	16		.236	.308	.315	101	0	3			.889	-3	O-46	-0.6
1910	Chi-A	22	80	6	14	2	1	0	2	4		.175	.224	.225	42	-5	0			.974	1	O-22	-0.7
Total	2	68	245	23	53	9	4	0	18	20		.216	.281	.286	82	-5	3			.912	-3	/O-68	-1.3
■ **CHOO CHOO COLEMAN**	Coleman, Clarence b: 8/25/37, Orlando, Fla. BL/TR, 5'9", 165 lbs. Deb: 4/16/61																						
1961	Phi-N	34	47	3	6	1	0	0	4	2	8	.128	.180	.149	-12	-8	0	0	0	.977	-1	C-14	-0.8
1962	NY-N	55	152	24	38	7	2	6	17	11	24	.250	.305	.441	96	-1	2	4	-2	.995	-9	C-44	-1.0
1963	NY-N	106	247	22	44	0	0	3	9	24	49	.178	.264	.215	39	-19	5	5	-2	.969	3	C-91/O-1	-1.6
1966	NY-N	6	16	2	3	0	0	0	0	0	4	.188	.188	.188	5	-2	0	0	0	.963	0	/C-5	-0.2
Total	4	201	462	51	91	8	2	9	30	37	85	.197	.267	.281	52	-30	7	9	-3	.977	-6	C-154/O-1	-3.6
■ **CURT COLEMAN**	Coleman, Curtis Hancock b: 2/18/1887, Salem, Ore. d: 7/1/80, Newport, Ore. BL/TR, 5'11", 180 lbs. Deb: 4/13/12																						
1912	NY-A	12	37	8	9	4	0	0	4	7		.243	.364	.351	99	0	0			.865	0	3-10	0.0
■ **DAVE COLEMAN**	Coleman, David Lee b: 10/26/50, Dayton, Ohio BR/TR, 6'3", 195 lbs. Deb: 4/13/77																						
1977	Bos-A	11	12	1	0	0	0	0	0	1	3	.000	.077	.000	-69	-3	0	0	0	1.000	-3	/O-9	-0.6
■ **JERRY COLEMAN**	Coleman, Gerald Francis b: 9/14/24, San Jose, Cal. BR/TR, 6', 170 lbs. Deb: 4/20/49 M																						
1949	*NY-A	128	447	54	123	21	5	2	42	63	44	.275	.367	.358	92	-4	8	6	-1	**.981**	1	*2-122/S-4	0.2
1950	*NY-A★	153	522	69	150	19	6	6	69	67	38	.287	.372	.381	96	-2	3	2	-0	.977	-15	*2-152/S-6	-1.1
1951	*NY-A	121	362	48	90	11	2	3	43	31	36	.249	.315	.315	73	-14	6	1	1	.968	3	*2-102,S-18	-0.4
1952	NY-A	11	42	6	17	2	1	0	4	5	4	.405	.468	.500	180	5	0	1	-1	.971	3	2-11	0.7
1953	NY-A	8	10	1	2	0	0	0	0	0	2	.200	.200	.200	9	-1	0	0	0	1.000	2	/2-7,S-1	0.1
1954	NY-A	107	300	39	65	7	1	3	21	26	29	.217	.279	.277	54	-19	3	0	1	.977	**18**	2-79,S-30/3-1	0.5
1955	*NY-A	43	96	12	22	5	0	0	8	11	11	.229	.321	.281	64	-5	0	2	-1	.966	-2	S-29,2-13/3-1	-0.5
1956	*NY-A	80	183	15	47	5	1	0	18	12	33	.257	.306	.295	61	-10	1	2	-1	.979	17	2-41,S-24,3-18	0.9
1957	*NY-A	72	157	23	42	7	2	2	12	20	21	.268	.354	.376	101	1	1	1	-0	.969	5	2-45,3-21/S-4	0.8
Total	9	723	2119	267	558	77	18	16	217	235	218	.263	.341	.339	83	-49	22	15	-2	.976	31	2-572,S-116/3-41	1.2
■ **GORDY COLEMAN**	Coleman, Gordon Calvin b: 7/5/34, Rockville, Md. d: 3/12/94, Cincinnati, Ohio BL/TR, 6'2", 218 lbs. Deb: 9/19/59																						
1959	Cle-A	6	15	5	8	0	1	0	2	1	2	.533	.563	.667	245	3	0	0	0	.955	0	/1-3	0.3
1960	Cin-N	66	251	26	68	10	1	6	32	12	32	.271	.309	.390	89	-4	1	1	-0	.998	7	1-66	-0.3
1961	*Cin-N	150	520	63	149	27	4	26	87	45	67	.287	.346	.504	120	14	1	3	-2	.991	7	*1-150	0.7
1962	Cin-N	136	476	73	132	13	1	28	86	36	68	.277	.332	.485	113	7	2	3	-1	.989	-1	*1-128	-0.4
1963	Cin-N	123	365	38	90	20	2	14	59	29	51	.247	.306	.427	105	2	1	0	0	.987	1	*1-107	-0.1
1964	Cin-N	89	198	18	48	6	2	5	27	13	30	.242	.292	.369	82	-5	2	0	1	.990	4	1-49	-0.3
1965	Cin-N	108	325	39	98	19	0	14	57	24	38	.302	.351	.489	125	10	0	0	0	.991	-1	1-89	0.5
1966	Cin-N	91	227	20	57	7	0	5	37	16	45	.251	.300	.348	73	-8	2	1	0	.986	-1	1-65	-1.3

YEAR	TM/L	G	AB	R	H	2B	3B	HR	RBI	BB	SO	AVG	OBP	SLG	PRO+	BR/A	SB	CS	SBR	FA	FR	G/POS	TPR
1967	Cin-N	4	7	0	0	0	0	0	0	1	0	.000	.125	.000	-55	-1	0	0	0	1.000	0	/1-2	-0.2
Total	9	773	2384	282	650	102	11	98	387	177	333	.273	.326	.448	106	18	9	8	-2	.990	16	1-659	-1.1

■ JOHN COLEMAN
Coleman, John Francis b: 3/6/1863, Saratoga Springs, N.Y d: 5/31/22, Detroit, Mich. BL/TR, 5'9.5", 170 lbs. Deb: 5/1/1883

YEAR	TM/L	G	AB	R	H	2B	3B	HR	RBI	BB	SO	AVG	OBP	SLG	PRO+	BR/A	SB	CS	SBR	FA	FR	G/POS	TPR
1883	Phi-N	90	354	33	83	12	8	0	32	15	39	.234	.266	.314	83	-6				.886	10	P-65,O-31/2-1	0.5
1884	Phi-N	43	171	16	42	7	2	0	22	8	20	.246	.279	.310	89	-2				.844	2	O-27,P-21/1-2	-0.1
	Phi-a	28	107	16	22	2	3	2		5		.206	.241	.336	81	-3				.743	-1	O-24/P-3,1-2	-0.4
1885	Phi-a	96	398	71	119	15	11	3	70	25		.299	.345	.415	131	13				.844	-1	*O-93/P-8	0.8
1886	Phi-a	121	492	67	121	18	16	0	65	33		.246	.296	.348	100	-1	28			.862	2	*O-115/1-6,P-3,2-1	-0.2
	Pit-a	11	43	3	15	2	1	0	9	2		.349	.378	.442	157	3	1			.786	-2	O-11	0.0
	Yr	132	535	70	136	20	17	0	74	35		.254	.302	.355	105	2	29			.858	-1	*O-126/1-6,P-3,2-1	-0.2
1887	Pit-N	115	475	75	139	21	11	2	54	31	40	.293	.337	.396	110	7	25			.899	1	*O-115/1-2	0.4
1888	Pit-N	116	438	49	101	11	4	0	26	29	52	.231	.285	.274	85	-6	15			.928	2	O-91,1-25	-0.9
1889	Phi-a	6	19	1	1	0	0	0	1	1	3	.053	.100	.053	-57	-4	1			.929	0	/P-5,O-1	-0.1
1890	Pit-N	3	11	1	2	0	0	0	0	3	0	.182	.357	.182	66	-0	1			1.000	-1	/O-2,P-2	-0.1
Total	8	629	2508	332	645	88	56	7	279	152	154	.257	.302	.345	100	0	71			.873	11	O-510,P-107/1-37,2	-0.1

■ MICHAEL COLEMAN
Coleman, Michael D. b: 8/16/75, Nashville, Tenn. BR/TR, 5'11", 180 lbs. Deb: 9/1/97

YEAR	TM/L	G	AB	R	H	2B	3B	HR	RBI	BB	SO	AVG	OBP	SLG	PRO+	BR/A	SB	CS	SBR	FA	FR	G/POS	TPR
1997	Bos-A	8	24	2	4	1	0	0	2	0	11	.167	.167	.208	-3	-4	1	0	0	.941	-0	/O-7	-0.4

■ ED COLEMAN
Coleman, Parke Edward b: 12/1/01, Canby, Ore. d: 8/5/64, Oregon City, Ore. BL/TR, 6'2", 200 lbs. Deb: 4/15/32

YEAR	TM/L	G	AB	R	H	2B	3B	HR	RBI	BB	SO	AVG	OBP	SLG	PRO+	BR/A	SB	CS	SBR	FA	FR	G/POS	TPR
1932	Phi-A	26	73	13	25	7	1	1	13	1	6	.342	.351	.507	115	1	1	0	0	1.000	1	O-16	0.1
1933	Phi-A	102	388	48	109	26	3	6	68	19	51	.281	.318	.410	91	-7	0	0	0	.948	-1	O-89	-1.2
1934	Phi-A	101	329	53	92	14	6	14	60	29	34	.280	.342	.486	116	6	0	1	-1	.980	-2	O-86	0.0
1935	Phi-A	10	13	0	1	0	0	0	0	0	3	.077	.077	.077	-61	-3	0	0	0	.000	-0	/O-1	-0.3
	StL-A	108	397	66	114	15	9	17	71	53	41	.287	.373	.499	118	10	0	2	-1	.974	-3	*O-102	0.2
	Yr	118	410	66	115	15	9	17	71	53	44	.280	.364	.485	113	7	0	2	-1	.974	-3	*O-103	-0.1
1936	StL-A	92	137	13	40	5	4	2	34	15	17	.292	.366	.431	93	-2	0	0	0	.939	-3	O-18	-0.4
Total	5	439	1337	193	381	67	23	40	246	117	152	.285	.345	.459	105	6	1	3	-2	.966	-8	O-312	-1.6

■ RAY COLEMAN
Coleman, Raymond Leroy b: 6/4/22, Dunsmuir, Cal. BL/TR, 5'11", 170 lbs. Deb: 4/22/47

YEAR	TM/L	G	AB	R	H	2B	3B	HR	RBI	BB	SO	AVG	OBP	SLG	PRO+	BR/A	SB	CS	SBR	FA	FR	G/POS	TPR
1947	StL-A	110	343	34	89	9	7	2	30	26	32	.259	.314	.344	81	-9	2	5	-2	.984	-2	O-93	-1.9
1948	StL-A	17	29	2	5	0	1	0	2	2	5	.172	.226	.241	24	-3	1	0	0	.889	-1	/O-5	-0.4
	Phi-A	68	210	32	51	6	6	0	21	31	17	.243	.340	.329	78	-6	4	3	-1	.978	2	O-53	-0.8
	Yr	85	239	34	56	6	7	0	23	33	22	.234	.327	.318	72	-10	5	3	-0	.972	1	O-58	-1.2
1950	StL-A	117	384	54	104	25	6	8	55	32	37	.271	.330	.430	90	-8	7	5	-1	.985	3	O-98	-0.9
1951	StL-A	91	341	41	96	16	5	5	55	24	32	.282	.329	.402	94	-4	3	4	-2	.975	1	O-87	-0.7
	Chi-A	51	181	21	50	8	7	3	21	15	14	.276	.332	.448	112	2	2	3	-1	.980	-3	O-51	-0.4
	Yr	142	522	62	146	24	12	8	76	39	46	.280	.330	.418	100	-2	5	7	-3	.977	-2	*O-138	-1.1
1952	Chi-A	85	195	19	42	7	1	2	14	13	17	.215	.264	.292	54	-12	0	0	0	.978	-7	O-73	-2.2
	StL-A	20	46	5	9	3	0	0	1	5	4	.196	.288	.261	52	-3	0	0	0	1.000	-2	O-16	-0.6
	Yr	105	241	24	51	10	1	2	15	18	21	.212	.269	.286	54	-15	0	0	0	.982	-9	O-89	-2.8
Total	5	559	1729	208	446	74	33	20	199	148	158	.258	.318	.374	84	-43	19	20	-6	.980	-9	O-476	-7.9

■ BOB COLEMAN
Coleman, Robert Hunter b: 9/26/1890, Huntingburg, Ind. d: 7/16/59, Boston, Mass. BR/TR, 6'2", 190 lbs. Deb: 6/13/13 MC

YEAR	TM/L	G	AB	R	H	2B	3B	HR	RBI	BB	SO	AVG	OBP	SLG	PRO+	BR/A	SB	CS	SBR	FA	FR	G/POS	TPR
1913	Pit-N	24	50	5	9	2	0	0	9	7	8	.180	.281	.220	46	-3	0			.978	-4	C-24	-0.6
1914	Pit-N	73	150	11	40	4	1	1	14	15	32	.267	.333	.327	101	0	3			.977	2	C-72	0.7
1916	Cle-A	19	28	3	6	2	0	0	4	7	6	.214	.371	.286	92	0	0			.972	-3	C-12	-0.2
Total	3	116	228	19	55	8	1	1	27	29	46	.241	.327	.298	87	-3	3			.976	-5	C-108	-0.1

■ VINCE COLEMAN
Coleman, Vincent Maurice b: 9/22/61, Jacksonville, Fla. BB/TR, 6', 185 lbs. Deb: 4/18/85

YEAR	TM/L	G	AB	R	H	2B	3B	HR	RBI	BB	SO	AVG	OBP	SLG	PRO+	BR/A	SB	CS	SBR	FA	FR	G/POS	TPR
1985	*StL-N	151	636	107	170	20	10	1	40	50	115	.267	.321	.335	84	-13	**110**	25	**18**	.979	9	*O-150	0.9
1986	StL-N	154	600	94	139	13	8	0	29	60	98	.232	.304	.280	63	-30	**107**	14	**24**	.972	9	*O-149	-0.2
1987	*StL-N	151	623	121	180	14	10	3	43	70	126	.289	.364	.358	90	-6	**109**	22	**20**	.970	9	*O-150	1.7
1988	StL-N★	153	616	77	160	20	10	3	38	49	111	.260	.315	.339	87	-10	**81**	27	8	.971	5	*O-150	-0.2
1989	StL-N★	145	563	94	143	21	9	2	28	50	90	.254	.317	.334	84	-11	**65**	10	**14**	.962	-5	*O-142	-0.7
1990	StL-N	124	497	73	145	18	9	6	39	35	88	.292	.341	.400	103	2	**77**	17	**13**	.981	8	*O-120	2.0
1991	NY-N	72	278	45	71	7	5	1	17	39	47	.255	.347	.327	91	-2	37	14	3	.979	0	O-70	-0.1
1992	NY-N	71	229	37	63	11	1	2	21	27	41	.275	.357	.358	104	2	24	9	2	.991	-1	O-61	0.2
1993	NY-N	92	373	64	104	14	8	2	25	21	58	.279	.317	.375	86	-8	38	13	4	.982	0	O-90	-0.6
1994	KC-A	104	438	61	105	14	12	2	33	29	72	.240	.288	.340	59	-27	50	8	10	.962	0	O-99/D-5	-1.8
1995	KC-A	75	293	39	84	13	4	4	20	27	48	.287	.349	.399	93	-3	26	9	2	.975	-3	O-69/D-4	-0.5
	*Sea-A	40	162	27	47	10	2	1	9	10	32	.290	.335	.395	88	-3	16	7	1	.988	4	O-38	0.0
	Yr	115	455	66	131	23	6	5	29	37	80	.288	.344	.398	91	-6	42	16	3	.980	1	*O-107/D-4	-0.5
1996	Cin-N	33	84	10	13	1	1	1	4	9	31	.155	.237	.226	23	-9	12	2	2	.968	0	O-20	-0.7
1997	Det-A	6	14	0	1	0	0	0	0	1	3	.071	.133	.071	-45	-3	0	0	0	1.000	-1	/O-3,D-1	-0.4
Total	13	1371	5406	849	1425	176	89	28	346	477	960	.264	.325	.345	83	-122	752	177	119	.974	34	*O-1311/D-10	-0.4

■ CAD COLES
Coles, Cadwallader b: 1/17/1886, Rock Hill, S.C. d: 6/30/42, Miami, Fla. BL/TR, 6'0.5", 174 lbs. Deb: 4/16/14

YEAR	TM/L	G	AB	R	H	2B	3B	HR	RBI	BB	SO	AVG	OBP	SLG	PRO+	BR/A	SB	CS	SBR	FA	FR	G/POS	TPR
1914	KC-F	78	194	17	49	7	3	1	25	5	30	.253	.271	.335	67	-13	6			.889	-7	O-39/1-3	-2.3

■ CHUCK COLES
Coles, Charles Edward b: 6/27/31, Fredericktown, Pa d: 1/25/96, Myrtle Beach, S.C. BL/TL, 5'9", 180 lbs. Deb: 9/19/58

YEAR	TM/L	G	AB	R	H	2B	3B	HR	RBI	BB	SO	AVG	OBP	SLG	PRO+	BR/A	SB	CS	SBR	FA	FR	G/POS	TPR
1958	Cin-N	5	11	0	2	1	0	0	2	2	6	.182	.308	.273	52	-1	0	0	0	1.000	1	/O-4	0.0

■ DARNELL COLES
Coles, Darnell b: 6/2/62, San Bernardino, Cal BR/TR, 6'1", 185 lbs. Deb: 9/4/83

YEAR	TM/L	G	AB	R	H	2B	3B	HR	RBI	BB	SO	AVG	OBP	SLG	PRO+	BR/A	SB	CS	SBR	FA	FR	G/POS	TPR
1983	Sea-A	27	92	9	26	7	0	1	6	7	12	.283	.333	.391	95	-1	0	3	-2	.941	-3	3-26	-0.6
1984	Sea-A	48	143	15	23	3	1	0	6	17	26	.161	.259	.196	28	-14	2	1	0	.918	-3	3-42/O-3,D-3	-1.8
1985	Sea-A	27	59	8	14	4	0	1	5	9	17	.237	.348	.356	93	-0	0	1	-1	.918	1	S-15/3-7,O-2,D-2	0.1
1986	Det-A	142	521	67	142	30	2	20	86	45	84	.273	.337	.453	113	9	6	2	1	.938	-5	*3-133/S-2,O-2,D-7	0.1
1987	Det-A	53	149	14	27	5	1	4	15	15	23	.181	.265	.309	54	-10	0	1	-1	.847	-5	3-36/1-9,O-8,S-1,D	-1.6
	Pit-N	40	119	20	27	8	0	6	24	19	20	.227	.338	.445	105	1	1	3	-2	1.000	-5	O-26,3-10/1-1	-0.7
1988	Pit-N	68	211	20	49	13	1	5	36	20	41	.232	.308	.374	96	-1	1	1	-0	.990	-3	O-55/1-1,3-1	-0.7
	Sea-A	55	195	32	57	10	1	10	34	17	26	.292	.361	.508	134	9	3	2	-0	.986	-3	O-47/1-1,D-7	0.4
1989	Sea-A	146	535	54	135	21	3	10	59	27	61	.252	.296	.359	81	-14	5	4	-1	.975	7	O-89,3-26,1-18,D-12	-1.1
1990	Sea-A	37	107	9	23	5	1	2	16	4	17	.215	.250	.336	62	-6	0	0	0	.970	1	O-20/3-6,1-4,D-1	-0.5
	Det-A	52	108	13	22	2	0	1	4	12	21	.204	.283	.250	50	-7	0	4	-2	1.000	-1	D-30,O-11/3-8	-1.2
	Yr	89	215	22	45	7	1	3	20	16	38	.209	.267	.293	56	-13	0	4	-2	.977	-0	O-31,D-31,3-14,/1-4	-1.7
1991	SF-N	11	14	1	3	0	0	0	0	0	2	.214	.214	.214	22	-1	0	0	0	.000	-1	/O-3,1-1	-0.3
1992	Cin-N	55	141	16	44	11	2	3	18	3	15	.312	.326	.482	123	4	1	0	0	1.000	1	3-23,1-20/O-5	0.4
1993	Tor-A	64	194	26	49	9	1	4	26	16	29	.253	.322	.371	85	-4	1	1	-0	.957	-9	O-44,3-16/1-1,D-1	-1.4
1994	Tor-A	48	143	15	30	6	1	4	15	10	25	.210	.266	.350	57	-10	0	0	0	.980	-3	O-29,1-10/3-7,D-1	-1.3
1995	StL-N	63	138	13	31	7	0	3	16	16	20	.225	.318	.341	74	-5	0	0	0	.951	-6	3-22,1-18/O-1	-1.2
1997	Col-N	21	22	1	7	1	0	1	2	0	6	.318	.348	.500	97	-0	0	0	0	1.000	-1	/3-3,O-2	-0.1
Total	14	957	2891	333	709	142	14	75	368	237	445	.245	.310	.382	88	-51	20	23	-8	.923	-41	3-366,O-347/1DS	-11.5

■ CHRIS COLETTA
Coletta, Christopher Michael b: 8/2/44, Brooklyn, N.Y. BL/TL, 5'11", 190 lbs. Deb: 8/15/72

YEAR	TM/L	G	AB	R	H	2B	3B	HR	RBI	BB	SO	AVG	OBP	SLG	PRO+	BR/A	SB	CS	SBR	FA	FR	G/POS	TPR
1972	Cal-A	14	30	5	9	1	0	1	7	1	4	.300	.323	.433	131	1	0	0	0	1.000	-2	/O-7	-0.1

■ ED COLGAN
Colgan, William H. b: E.St.Louis, Ill. d: 8/8/1895, Great Falls, Mont. 180 lbs. Deb: 5/3/1884

YEAR	TM/L	G	AB	R	H	2B	3B	HR	RBI	BB	SO	AVG	OBP	SLG	PRO+	BR/A	SB	CS	SBR	FA	FR	G/POS	TPR
1884	Pit-a	48	161	10	25	4	1	0		3		.155	.171	.193	18	-14				.906	2	C-44/O-4	-0.8

YEAR	TM/L	G	AB	R	H	2B	3B	HR	RBI	BB	SO	AVG	OBP	SLG	PRO+	BR/A	SB	CS	SBR	FA	FR	G/POS	TPR
■ LOU COLLIER	Collier, Louis Keith b: 8/21/73, Chicago, Ill. BR/TR, 5'10", 170 lbs. Deb: 6/28/97																						
1997	Pit-N	18	37	3	5	0	0	0	3	1	11	.135	.158	.135	-22	-7	1	0	0	1.000	3	S-18	-0.3
1998	Pit-N	110	334	30	82	13	6	2	34	31	70	.246	.321	.338	70	-14	2	2	-1	.960	-4	*S-107	-0.8
Total	2	128	371	33	87	13	6	2	37	32	81	.235	.306	.318	61	-21	3	2	-0	.964	-1	S-125	-1.1
■ COLLINS	Collins Deb: 9/12/1892																						
1892	StL-N	1	2	0	0	0	0	0	0	0	0	.000	.000	.000	-99	-0	0			1.000	0	/O-1	0.0
■ CHUB COLLINS	Collins, Charles Augustine b: 10/12/1857, Dundas, Ont., Canada d: 5/20/14, Dundas, Ont., Can. BB, 5'11.5", 165 lbs. Deb: 5/1/1884																						
1884	Buf-N	45	169	24	30	6	0	0	20	14	36	.178	.240	.213	42	-11				.914	0	2-42/S-3	-0.9
	Ind-a	38	138	18	31	3	1	0		9		.225	.272	.261	77	-3				.886	-8	2-38	-1.0
1885	Det-N	14	55	8	10	0	2	0	6	0	11	.182	.182	.255	40	-4				.792	-8	S-14	-1.1
Total	2	97	362	50	71	9	3	0	26	23	47	.196	.244	.238	55	-18				.901	-16	/2-80,S-17	-3.0
■ WILSON COLLINS	Collins, Cyril Wilson b: 5/7/1889, Pulaski, Tenn. d: 2/28/41, Knoxville, Tenn. BR/TR, 5'9.5", 165 lbs. Deb: 5/12/13																						
1913	Bos-N	16	3	3	1	0	0	0	0	0	1	.333	.333	.333	89	-0	0			1.000	-4	/O-9	-0.4
1914	Bos-N	27	35	5	9	0	0	0	1	2	8	.257	.297	.257	66	-1	0			.917	-4	O-19	-0.7
Total	2	43	38	8	10	0	0	0	1	2	9	.263	.300	.263	68	-1	0			.926	-8	/O-28	-1.1
■ DAN COLLINS	Collins, Daniel Thomas b: 7/12/1854, St.Louis, Mo. d: 9/21/1883, New Orleans, La. Deb: 6/8/1874																						
1874	Chi-n	3	12	1	1	1	0	0	0	0	2	.083	.083	.167	-22	-2	1	0	0	1.000	0	/P-2,O-2,S-1	-0.1
1876	Lou-N	7	28	3	4	1	0	0	9	0	2	.143	.143	.179	5	-3				.909	1	/O-7	-0.2
■ DAVE COLLINS	Collins, David S b: 10/20/52, Rapid City, S.D. BB/TL, 5'11", 175 lbs. Deb: 6/7/75 C																						
1975	Cal-A	93	319	41	85	13	4	3	29	36	55	.266	.343	.361	106	3	24	10	1	.988	4	O-75,D-12	0.5
1976	Cal-A	99	365	45	96	12	1	4	28	40	55	.263	.336	.334	103	2	32	19	-2	.994	3	O-71,D-22	-0.1
1977	Sea-A	120	402	46	96	9	3	5	28	33	66	.239	.301	.313	69	-17	25	10	2	.985	0	O-73,D-40	-1.9
1978	Cin-N	102	102	13	22	1	0	0	7	15	18	.216	.316	.225	54	-6	7	7	-2	.969	-4	O-24	-1.3
1979	*Cin-N	122	396	59	126	16	4	3	35	27	48	.318	.365	.402	108	5	16	9	-1	.976	-9	O-91,1-10	-0.9
1980	Cin-N	144	551	94	167	20	4	3	35	53	68	.303	.367	.370	106	6	79	21	11	.986	3	*O-141	1.6
1981	Cin-N	95	360	63	98	18	6	3	23	41	41	.272	.356	.381	107	4	26	10	2	.977	1	O-94	0.5
1982	NY-A	111	348	41	88	12	3	3	25	28	49	.253	.318	.330	80	-9	13	8	-1	.992	-5	O-60,1-52/D-1	-1.9
1983	Tor-A	118	402	55	109	12	4	1	34	43	67	.271	.345	.328	81	-9	31	7	5	.989	6	*O-112/1-5,D-1	-0.2
1984	Tor-A	128	441	59	136	24	**15**	2	44	33	41	.308	.369	.444	119	12	60	14	10	.991	1	*O-108/1-6,D-4	1.9
1985	Oak-A	112	379	52	95	16	4	4	29	29	37	.251	.306	.346	84	-9	29	8	4	.978	6	O-91	-0.1
1986	Det-A	124	419	44	113	18	2	1	27	44	49	.270	.342	.329	84	-8	27	12	1	.995	3	O-94,D-24	-0.7
1987	Cin-N	57	85	19	25	5	0	0	5	11	12	.294	.388	.353	94	-0	9	0	3	1.000	-1	O-21	0.1
1988	Cin-N	99	174	12	41	6	2	0	14	11	27	.236	.289	.293	65	-8	7	2	1	.965	-4	O-35/1-3	-1.2
1989	Cin-N	78	106	12	25	4	0	0	7	10	17	.236	.302	.274	63	-5	3	1	0	1.000	2	O-16	-0.3
1990	StL-N	99	58	12	13	1	0	0	3	13	10	.224	.366	.241	70	-2	7	1	2	1.000	-6	1-49,O-12	-0.6
Total	16	1701	4907	667	1335	187	52	32	373	467	660	.272	.340	.351	93	-40	395	139	35	.986	3	*O-1118,1-125,D-104	-4.6
■ EDDIE COLLINS	Collins, Edward Trowbridge Jr. b: 11/23/16, Lansdowne, Pa. BL/TR, 5'10", 175 lbs. Deb: 7/4/39 F																						
1939	Phi-A	32	21	6	5	1	0	0	0	0	3	.238	.238	.286	34	-2	1	0	0	1.000	-0	/O-6,2-1	-0.2
1941	Phi-A	80	219	29	53	6	3	0	12	20	24	.242	.305	.297	61	-12	2	1	0	.968	-0	O-50	-1.5
1942	Phi-A	20	34	6	8	2	0	0	4	4	2	.235	.316	.294	72	-1	1	0	0	.800	-4	/O-9	-0.5
Total	3	132	274	41	66	9	3	0	16	24	29	.241	.302	.296	61	-15	4	1	1	.959	-4	/O-65,2-1	-2.2
■ EDDIE COLLINS	Collins, Edward Trowbridge Sr. "Cocky" (a.k.a. Edward T. Sullivan In 1906) b: 5/2/1887, Millerton, N.Y. d: 3/25/51, Boston, Mass. BL/TR, 5'9", 175 lbs. Deb: 9/17/06 FMCH																						
1906	Phi-A	6	15	2	3	0	0	0	0	0		.200	.200	.200	25	-1	0			.900	-0	/S-3,2-1,3-1	-0.2
1907	Phi-A	14	23	0	8	0	1	0	2	0		.348	.348	.435	146	1	0			.833	1	/S-6	0.2
1908	Phi-A	102	330	39	90	18	7	1	40	16		.273	.312	.379	116	5	8			.944	-12	2-47,S-28,O-10	-0.8
1909	Phi-A	153	571	104	198	30	10	3	56	62		.347	.416	.450	170	47	67			**.967**	8	*2-152/S-1	5.7
1910	*Phi-A	153	581	81	188	16	15	3	81	49		.324	.382	.418	152	34	**81**			**.972**	**34**	*2-153	7.0
1911	*Phi-A	132	493	92	180	22	13	3	73	62		.365	.451	.481	163	45	38			.967	3	*2-132	4.4
1912	Phi-A	153	543	**137**	189	25	11	0	64	101		.348	.450	.435	159	48	63			.955	15	*2-153	5.8
1913	*Phi-A	148	534	**125**	184	23	13	3	73	85	37	.345	.441	.453	165	48	55			.965	16	*2-148	6.4
1914	*Phi-A	152	526	**122**	181	23	14	2	85	97	31	.344	**.452**	.452	**179**	**56**	58	30	-1	**.970**	0	*2-152	5.9
1915	Chi-A	155	521	118	173	22	10	4	77	**119**	27	.332	.460	.436	163	48	46	30	-4	**.974**	13	*2-155	6.1
1916	Chi-A	155	545	87	168	14	17	0	52	86	36	.308	.405	.396	139	29	40	21	-1	**.976**	-6	*2-155	3.0
1917	*Chi-A	156	564	91	163	18	12	0	67	89	16	.289	.389	.363	127	22	53			.969	-26	*2-156	0.5
1918	Chi-A	97	330	51	91	8	2	2	30	73	13	.276	.407	.330	121	13	22			.974	-1	2-96	2.0
1919	*Chi-A	140	518	87	165	19	7	4	80	68	27	.319	.400	.405	126	20	**33**			.974	3	*2-140	3.1
1920	Chi-A	153	602	117	224	38	13	3	76	69	19	.372	.438	.493	146	42	20	8	1	**.976**	10	*2-153	5.6
1921	Chi-A	139	526	79	177	20	10	2	58	66	11	.337	.412	.424	115	15	12	10	-2	**.968**	27	*2-136	4.0
1922	Chi-A	154	598	92	194	20	12	1	69	73	16	.324	.401	.403	110	12	20	12	-1	**.976**	-10	*2-154	0.5
1923	Chi-A	145	505	89	182	22	5	5	67	84	8	.360	.455	.453	141	36	**48**	29	-3	.975	-4	*2-142	2.9
1924	Chi-A	152	556	108	194	27	7	6	86	89	16	.349	.441	.455	136	34	**42**	17	**2**	**.977**	-7	*2-150,M	2.9
1925	Chi-A	118	425	80	147	26	3	3	80	87	8	.346	.461	.442	137	31	19	6	2	.970	-9	*2-116,M	2.4
1926	Chi-A	106	375	66	129	32	4	1	62	62	8	.344	.441	.459	140	25	13	8	-1	.973	-6	*2-101,M	2.0
1927	Phi-A	95	226	50	76	12	1	1	15	56	9	.336	.468	.412	123	12	6	2	1	.965	-7	2-56/S-1	0.6
1928	Phi-A	36	33	3	10	3	0	0	7	4	4	.303	.378	.394	100	0	0	0	0	.000	-2	/2-2,S-1	-0.1
1929	Phi-A	9	7	0	0	0	0	0	0	2	0	.000	.222	.000	-37	-1	0	0	0	.000	0	H	-0.1
1930	Phi-A	3	2	1	1	0	0	0	0	0	0	.500	.500	.500	148	0	0	0	0	.000	0	H	0.0
Total	25	2826	9949	1821	3315	438	187	47	1300	1499	286	.333	.424	.429	142	622	744	173		.970	41	*2-2650/S-40,O-10,3	69.8
■ HUB COLLINS	Collins, Hubert B. b: 4/15/1864, Louisville, Ky. d: 5/21/1892, Brooklyn, N.Y. BR/TR, 5'8", 160 lbs. Deb: 9/4/1886																						
1886	Lou-a	27	101	12	29	3	2	0	10	5		.287	.321	.356	106	0	7			.885	-2	O-24/3-2,S-1,2-1,1	-0.2
1887	Lou-a	130	559	122	162	22	8	1	66	39		.290	.338	.363	94	-6	71			.887	-8	*O-109,2-10/1-8,S3	-1.3
1888	Lou-a	116	485	117	149	26	11	2	50	41		.307	.366	.419	154	30	62			.890	13	O-82,2-19,S-15	3.7
	Bro-a	12	42	16	13	5	1	0	3	9		.310	.442	.476	195	5	9			.897	-3	2-12	0.3
	Yr	128	527	133	162	**31**	12	2	53	50		.307	.373	.423	158	35	71			.890	10	O-82,2-31,S-15	**4.0**
1889	*Bro-a	138	560	139	149	18	3	2	73	80	41	.266	.365	.320	95	-0	65			.929	-2	*2-138	0.4
1890	*Bro-N	129	510	**148**	142	32	7	3	69	85	47	.278	.385	.386	124	18	85			.945	5	*2-129	2.7
1891	Bro-N	107	435	82	120	16	5	3	31	59	63	.276	.365	.356	111	8	32			.910	-22	2-72,O-35	-1.1
1892	Bro-N	21	87	17	26	5	1	0	17	14	13	.299	.396	.379	140	5	4			.925	-2	O-21	0.2
Total	7	680	2779	653	790	127	38	11	319	332	164	.284	.365	.369	115	60	335			.928	-21	2-381,O-271/S13	4.7
■ HUGH COLLINS	Collins, Hugh 150 lbs. Deb: 8/1/1887																						
1887	NY-a	1	4	0	1	0	0	0	0	0		.250	.250	.250	41	-0	0			.250	-1	/C-1	-0.1
■ RIPPER COLLINS	Collins, James Anthony b: 3/30/04, Altoona, Pa. d: 4/15/70, New Haven, Conn. BB/TL, 5'9", 165 lbs. Deb: 4/18/31 C																						
1931	*StL-N	89	279	34	84	20	10	4	59	18	24	.301	.350	.487	118	6	1			.995	5	1-68/O-3	0.5
1932	StL-N	149	549	82	153	28	8	21	91	38	67	.279	.329	.474	110	6	4			.999	-5	1-81,O-60	-0.9
1933	StL-N	132	493	66	153	26	7	10	68	38	49	.310	.363	.452	125	16	7			.994	3	*1-123	0.7
1934	*StL-N	154	600	116	200	40	12	**35**	128	57	50	.333	.393	**.615**	155	45	2			.991	8	*1-154	3.8
1935	StL-N★	150	578	109	181	36	10	23	122	65	45	.313	.385	.529	138	30	0			.987	1	*1-150	1.4
1936	StL-N★	103	277	48	81	15	3	13	48	48	30	.292	.399	.509	143	18	1			.990	-2	1-61/O-9	0.9
1937	Chi-N★	115	456	77	125	16	5	16	71	32	46	.274	.329	.436	102	0	2			.991	1	*1-111	-1.2
1938	*Chi-N	143	490	78	131	22	8	13	61	54	48	.267	.344	.424	107	5	1			**.996**	10	*1-135	-0.1

YEAR	TM/L	G	AB	R	H	2B	3B	HR	RBI	BB	SO	AVG	OBP	SLG	PRO+	BR/A	SB	CS	SBR	FA	FR	G/POS	TPR
1941	Pit-N	49	62	5	13	2	2	0	11	6	14	.210	.279	.306	65	-3	0			.947	-0	1-11/O-3	-0.4
Total	9	1084	3784	615	1121	205	65	135	659	356	373	.296	.360	.492	125	123	18			.992	19	1-894/O-75	4.7
■ JIMMY COLLINS Collins, James Joseph b: 1/16/1870, Buffalo, N.Y. d: 3/6/43, Buffalo, N.Y. BR/TR, 5'9", 178 lbs. Deb: 4/19/1895 MH																							
1895	Bos-N	11	38	10	8	3	0	1	8	4	4	.211	.302	.368	67	-2	0			.714	-2	O-10	-0.4
	Lou-N	96	373	65	104	17	5	6	49	33	16	.279	.352	.399	100	0	12			.926	21	3-77,O-18/2-2,S-1	1.7
	Yr	107	411	75	112	20	5	7	57	37	20	.273	.347	.397	96	-2	12			.926	19	3-77,O-28/2-2,S-1	1.3
1896	Bos-N	84	304	48	90	10	9	1	46	30	12	.296	.374	.398	98	-1	10			.909	20	3-80/S-4	1.7
1897	*Bos-N	134	529	103	183	28	13	6	132	41		.346	.400	.482	125	17	14			.917	21	*3-134	3.5
1898	Bos-N	152	597	107	196	35	5	**15**	111	40		.328	.377	.479	138	26	12			.932	15	*3-152	3.8
1899	Bos-N	151	599	98	166	28	11	5	92	40		.277	.335	.386	89	-12	12			.943	21	*3-151	0.9
1900	Bos-N	142	586	104	178	25	5	6	95	34		.304	.352	.394	94	-7	23			.935	10	*3-141/S-1	0.4
1901	Bos-A	138	564	108	187	42	16	6	94	34		.332	.375	.495	142	30	19			.914	14	*3-138,M	4.0
1902	Bos-A	108	429	71	138	21	10	6	61	24		.322	.360	.459	123	12	18			**.954**	9	*3-107,M	2.0
1903	*Bos-A	130	540	88	160	33	17	5	72	24		.296	.329	.448	125	14	23			**.952**	12	*3-130,M	2.9
1904	Bos-A	156	631	85	171	33	13	3	67	27		.271	.306	.379	110	6	19			.945	7	*3-156,M	1.9
1905	Bos-A	131	508	66	140	26	5	4	65	37		.276	.330	.370	120	11	18			.923	4	*3-131,M	2.2
1906	Bos-A	37	142	17	39	8	4	1	16	4		.275	.295	.408	120	2	1			.911	2	3-32,M	0.6
1907	Bos-A	41	158	13	46	8	0	0	10	10		.291	.333	.342	116	3	4			.874	-8	3-41	-0.4
	Phi-A	99	364	38	99	21	0	0	35	24		.272	.331	.330	108	4	4			.904	-2	3-98	0.5
	Yr	140	522	51	145	29	0	0	45	34		.278	.332	.333	110	6	8			.895	-10	*3-139	0.1
1908	Phi-A	115	433	34	94	14	3	0	30	20		.217	.258	.263	65	-17	5			.928	-7	*3-115	-2.2
Total	14	1725	6795	1055	1999	352	116	65	983	426	32	.294	.343	.409	112	85	194			.929	137	*3-1683/O-28,S-6,2	23.1
■ ZIP COLLINS Collins, John Edgar b: 5/2/1892, Brooklyn, N.Y. d: 12/19/83, Manassas, Va. BL/TL, 5'11", 152 lbs. Deb: 7/31/14																							
1914	Pit-N	49	182	14	44	2	0	0	15	8	10	.242	.277	.253	61	-9	3			.962	1	O-49	-1.2
1915	Pit-N	101	354	51	104	8	5	1	23	24	38	.294	.340	.353	112	5	6	7	-2	.942	5	O-89	0.3
	Bos-N	5	14	3	4	1	1	0	0	2	1	.286	.375	.500	171	1	1			1.000	0	/O-4	0.2
	Yr	106	368	54	108	9	6	1	23	26	39	.293	.342	.359	114	6	7	7	-2	.944	6	O-93	0.5
1916	Bos-N	93	268	39	56	1	6	1	18	18	42	.209	.261	.269	66	-11	4			.947	-6	O-78	-2.4
1917	Bos-N	9	27	3	4	0	1	0	2	0	4	.148	.148	.222	14	-3	0			1.000	1	/O-5	-0.3
1921	Phi-A	24	71	14	20	5	1	0	5	6	5	.282	.354	.380	87	-1	1	2	-1	.915	0	O-20	-0.3
Total	5	281	916	124	232	17	14	2	63	58	100	.253	.301	.309	85	-18	15	9		.946	1	O-245	-3.7
■ SHANO COLLINS Collins, John Francis b: 12/4/1885, Charlestown, Mass. d: 9/10/55, Newton, Mass. BR/TR, 6', 185 lbs. Deb: 4/21/10 FM																							
1910	Chi-A	97	315	29	62	10	8	1	24	25		.197	.258	.289	74	-10	10			.949	4	O-66,1-28	-1.0
1911	Chi-A	106	370	48	97	16	12	4	48	20		.262	.309	.403	101	-2	14			.978	4	1-98/2-3,O-3	0.2
1912	Chi-A	153	579	75	168	34	10	2	81	29		.290	.330	.394	110	5	26			.969	3	*O-105,1-46	0.2
1913	Chi-A	148	535	53	128	26	9	1	47	32	60	.239	.286	.327	80	-15	22			.949	1	*O-147	-2.2
1914	Chi-A	154	598	61	164	34	9	3	65	27	49	.274	.312	.376	108	3	30	24	-5	.970	6	*O-154	-0.5
1915	Chi-A	153	576	73	148	24	17	2	85	28	50	.257	.298	.368	96	-6	38	19	0	.963	2	*O-104,1-47	-1.1
1916	Chi-A	143	527	74	128	28	12	0	42	59	51	.243	.323	.342	98	-1	16			.959	8	*O-137/1-4	-0.1
1917	*Chi-A	82	252	38	59	13	3	1	14	10	27	.234	.269	.321	78	-8	14			.992	-2	O-73	-1.4
1918	Chi-A	103	365	30	100	18	11	1	56	17	19	.274	.310	.392	111	2	7			.973	14	O-93/1-5	1.2
1919	*Chi-A	63	179	21	50	6	3	1	16	7	11	.279	.317	.363	90	-3	3			.957	1	O-46/1-8	-0.5
1920	Chi-A	133	495	70	150	21	10	1	63	23	24	.303	.339	.392	93	-6	12	9	-2	.988	-9	*1-116,O-13	-1.9
1921	Bos-A	141	542	63	155	29	12	4	69	18	38	.286	.314	.406	85	-15	15	8	-0	.966	4	*O-139/1-3	-2.0
1922	Bos-A	135	472	33	128	24	7	1	52	7	30	.271	.289	.358	68	-23	7	9	-3	.951	-7	*O-117/1-1	-4.2
1923	Bos-A	97	342	41	79	10	5	0	18	11	29	.231	.265	.289	46	-28	7	8	-3	.953	-2	O-89	-3.7
1924	Bos-A	89	240	37	70	17	5	0	28	18	17	.292	.349	.404	94	-3	4	6	-2	.957	-10	O-56,1-12	-1.8
1925	Bos-A	2	3	1	1	0	0	0	1	0	0	.333	.333	.333	70	-0	0	0	0	.000	-1	/O-1	-0.1
Total	16	1799	6390	747	1687	310	133	22	709	331	405	.264	.306	.364	90	-109	225	83		.962	16	*O-1343,1-368/2-3	-18.9
■ JOE COLLINS Collins, Joseph Edward (b: Joseph Edward Kollonige) b: 12/3/22, Scranton, Pa. d: 8/30/89, Union, N.J. BL/TL, 6', 185 lbs. Deb: 9/25/48																							
1948	NY-A	5	5	0	1	1	0	0	2	0	1	.200	.200	.400	58	-0	0	0	0	.000	0	H	0.0
1949	NY-A	7	10	2	1	0	0	0	4	6	2	.100	.438	.100	46	-0	0	0	0	.920	-1	/1-5	-0.2
1950	*NY-A	108	205	47	48	8	3	8	28	31	34	.234	.335	.420	95	-2	5	0	2	.987	0	1-99/O-2	-0.2
1951	*NY-A	125	262	52	75	8	5	9	48	34	23	.286	.368	.458	127	10	9	7	-2	.987	4	*1-114,O-15	0.8
1952	*NY-A	122	428	69	120	16	8	18	59	55	47	.280	.364	.481	142	23	4	2	0	.990	-3	*1-119	1.7
1953	*NY-A	127	387	72	104	11	2	17	44	59	36	.269	.365	.439	121	11	2	6	-3	.989	1	*1-113/O-4	0.5
1954	NY-A	130	343	67	93	20	2	12	46	51	37	.271	.365	.446	126	12	2	2	-1	.992	1	*1-117	0.9
1955	*NY-A	105	278	40	65	9	1	13	45	44	32	.234	.343	.414	104	2	0	2	-1	.998	5	1-73,O-27	0.2
1956	*NY-A	100	262	38	59	5	3	7	43	34	33	.225	.316	.347	78	-9	3	1	0	.990	2	O-51,1-43	-1.0
1957	*NY-A	79	149	17	30	1	0	2	10	24	18	.201	.312	.248	56	-8	2	1	0	.987	-3	1-32,O-15	-1.4
Total	10	908	2329	404	596	79	24	86	329	338	263	.256	.351	.421	112	37	27	21	-5	.990	7	1-715,O-114	1.3
■ KEVIN COLLINS Collins, Kevin Michael "Casey" b: 8/4/46, Springfield, Mass. BL/TR, 6'2", 190 lbs. Deb: 9/1/65																							
1965	NY-N	11	23	3	4	1	0	0	0	1	9	.174	.208	.217	21	-2	0	1	-1	1.000	-1	/3-7,S-3	-0.5
1967	NY-N	4	10	1	1	0	0	0	0	0	3	.100	.100	.100	-43	-2	1	0	0	1.000	-0	/2-2	-0.2
1968	NY-N	58	154	12	31	5	2	1	13	7	37	.201	.236	.279	54	-9	0	1	-1	.955	-7	3-40/2-6,S-1	-1.8
1969	NY-N	16	40	1	6	3	0	1	2	3	10	.150	.209	.300	40	-3	0	0	0	.925	3	3-14	-0.1
	Mon-N	52	96	5	23	5	1	2	12	8	16	.240	.298	.375	87	-2	0	0	0	1.000	-7	2-20,3-16	-0.9
	Yr	68	136	6	29	8	1	3	14	11	26	.213	.272	.353	73	-5	0	0	0	.917	-4	3-30,2-20	-1.0
1970	Det-A	25	24	2	5	1	0	1	3	1	10	.208	.240	.375	67	-1	0	0	0	1.000	0	/1-1	-0.1
1971	Det-A	35	41	6	11	2	1	1	4	0	12	.268	.268	.439	94	-1	0	0	0	1.000	1	/3-4,O-2,2-1	0.0
Total	6	201	388	30	81	17	4	6	34	20	97	.209	.248	.320	62	-20	1	2	-1	.944	-11	/3-81,2-29,S-4,01	-3.6
■ ORTH COLLINS Collins, Orth Stein "Buck" b: 4/27/1880, Lafayette, Ind. d: 12/13/49, Ft.Lauderdale, Fla BL/TR, 6', 150 lbs. Deb: 6/1/04																							
1904	NY-A	5	17	3	6	1	1	0	1	1		.353	.389	.529	180	1	0			1.000	2	/O-5	0.4
1909	Was-A	8	7	0	0	0	0	0	0	0		.000	.000	.000	-99	-2	0			1.000	-1	/O-2,P-1	-0.2
Total	2	13	24	3	6	1	1	0	1	1		.250	.280	.375	104	-0	0			1.000	1	/O-7,P-1	0.2
■ RIP COLLINS Collins, Robert Joseph b: 9/18/09, Pittsburgh, Pa. d: 4/19/69, Pittsburgh, Pa. BR/TR, 5'11", 176 lbs. Deb: 4/28/40																							
1940	Chi-N	47	120	11	25	3	0	1	14	14	18	.208	.296	.258	55	-7	4			.951	-3	C-42	-0.7
1944	NY-A	3	3	0	1	0	0	0	0	1	0	.333	.500	.333	136	0	0	0	0	1.000	0	/C-3	0.1
Total	2	50	123	11	26	3	0	1	14	15	18	.211	.302	.260	58	-7	4	0		.953	-2	/C-45	-0.6
■ PAT COLLINS Collins, Tharon Leslie b: 9/13/1896, Sweet Sprgs., Mo. d: 5/20/60, Kansas City, Kan. BR/TR, 5'9", 178 lbs. Deb: 9/5/19																							
1919	StL-A	11	21	2	3	1	0	0	1	4	2	.143	.280	.190	32	-2	0			.929	-1	/C-5	-0.2
1920	StL-A	23	28	5	6	1	0	0	6	3	5	.214	.290	.250	43	-2	0	0	0	1.000	-2	/C-7	-0.4
1921	StL-A	58	111	9	27	3	0	1	10	16	17	.243	.339	.297	60	-6	1	0	0	.961	-1	C-31	-0.5
1922	StL-A	63	127	14	39	6	0	8	23	21	21	.307	.405	.543	140	8	0	1	-1	.980	6	C-28/1-5	1.4
1923	StL-A	85	181	9	32	8	0	3	30	15	45	.177	.240	.271	32	-18	0	0	0	.980	-1	C-47	-1.7
1924	StL-A	32	54	9	17	2	0	1	11	11	14	.315	.431	.407	110	1	0	1	-1	.969	-1	C-20	0.1
1926	*NY-A	102	290	41	83	11	3	7	35	73	57	.286	.433	.417	124	15	3	2	-0	.971	2	*C-100	2.2
1927	*NY-A	92	251	38	69	9	3	7	36	54	24	.275	.407	.418	118	9	0	1	-1	.976	-7	C-89	0.7
1928	*NY-A	70	136	18	30	5	0	6	14	35	16	.221	.380	.390	106	2	0	0	0	.977	-5	C-70	0.2
1929	Bos-N	7	5	1	0	0	0	0	2	3	1	.000	.375	.000	2	-1	0			1.000	1	/C-6	0.1
Total	10	543	1204	146	306	46	6	33	168	235	202	.254	.378	.385	98	5	4	5		.974	-7	C-403/1-5	1.9

YEAR	TM/L	G	AB	R	H	2B	3B	HR	RBI	BB	SO	AVG	OBP	SLG	PRO+	BR/A	SB	CS	SBR	FA	FR	G/POS	TPR
■ **BILL COLLINS**	Collins, William J. b: 1863, Dublin, Ireland d: 6/8/1893, New York, N.Y. BR , Deb: 10/5/1889																						
1889	Phi-a	1	4	0	1	0	0	0	1	1	0	.250	.400	.250	88	0	1			.800	-1	/C-1	0.0
1890	Phi-a	1	1	0	0	0	0	0	0	0		.000	.000	.000	-99	-0	0			.500	-0	/S-1	0.0
1891	Cle-N	2	3	0	0	0	0	0	0	0	0	.000	.000	.000	-96	-1	0			.000	1	/O-1,C-1	0.0
Total	3	4	8	0	1	0	0	0	1	1	0	.125	.222	.125	1	-1	1			.867	0	/C-2,O-1,S-1	0.0
■ **BILL COLLINS**	Collins, William Shirley b: 3/27/1882, Chesterton, Ind. d: 6/26/61, San Bernardino, Cal. BB/TR, 6′, 170 lbs. Deb: 4/14/10																						
1910	Bos-N	151	584	67	141	6	7	3	40	43	48	.241	.308	.291	72	-21	36			**.977**	13	*O-151	-1.7
1911	Bos-N	17	44	8	6	1	1	0	8	1	8	.136	.156	.205	0	-6	4			1.000	0	O-13/3-1	-0.6
	Chi-N	7	3	2	1	1	0	0	0	1	0	.333	.500	.667	225	1	0			1.000	-2	/O-4	-0.1
	Yr	24	47	10	7	2	1	0	8	2	8	.149	.184	.234	16	-6	4			1.000	-2	O-17/3-1	-0.7
1913	Bro-N	32	95	8	18	1	0	0	4	8	11	.189	.267	.200	33	-8	2			.921	-3	O-27	-1.3
1914	Buf-F	21	47	6	7	2	2	0	2	1	8	.149	.167	.277	19	-6	0			.864	-1	O-15	-0.8
Total	4	228	773	91	173	11	10	3	54	54	75	.224	.287	.276	60	-41	42			.966	7	O-210/3-1	-4.5
■ **BILL COLLVER**	Collver, William J. b: 3/21/1867, Clyde, Ohio d: 3/24/1888, Detroit, Mich. Deb: 7/4/1885																						
1885	Bos-N	1	4	0	0	0	0	0	0	0	1	.000	.000	.000	-99	-1				.000	-0	/O-1	-0.1
■ **FRANK COLMAN**	Colman, Frank Lloyd b: 3/2/18, London, Ont., Canada d: 2/19/83, London, Ont., Can. BL/TL, 5′11″, 188 lbs. Deb: 9/12/42																						
1942	Pit-N	10	37	2	5	0	0	1	2	2	2	.135	.179	.216	15	-4	0			1.000	1	/O-8	-0.4
1943	Pit-N	32	59	9	16	2	2	0	4	8	7	.271	.358	.373	108	1	0			1.000	0	O-11	0.0
1944	Pit-N	99	226	30	61	9	5	6	53	25	27	.270	.345	.434	113	4	0			.964	-3	O-53/1-6	-0.2
1945	Pit-N	77	153	18	32	11	1	4	30	9	16	.209	.253	.373	70	-7	0			.993	-1	1-22,O-12	-1.0
1946	Pit-N	26	53	3	9	3	0	1	6	2	7	.170	.214	.283	39	-4	0			1.000	0	/O-8,1-2	-0.5
	NY-A	5	15	2	4	0	0	1	5	1	1	.267	.313	.467	114	0	0	0	0	1.000	-0	/O-5	0.0
1947	NY-A	22	28	2	3	0	0	2	6	2	6	.107	.167	.321	34	-3	0	0	0	1.000	-1	/O-6	-0.4
Total	6	271	571	66	130	25	8	15	106	49	66	.228	.291	.378	85	-14	0	0		.980	-4	O-103/1-30	-2.5
■ **CRIS COLON**	Colon, Cristobal b: 1/3/69, LaGuaira, Venez. BB/TR, 6′2″, 180 lbs. Deb: 9/18/92																						
1992	Tex-A	14	36	5	6	0	0	0	1	1	8	.167	.189	.167	0	-5	0	0	0	.946	3	S-14	-0.1
■ **BOB COLUCCIO**	Coluccio, Robert Pasquali b: 10/2/51, Centralia, Wash. BR/TR, 5′11″, 183 lbs. Deb: 4/15/73																						
1973	Mil-A	124	438	65	98	21	8	15	58	54	92	.224	.313	.411	105	2	13	6	0	.992	10	*O-108,D-11	0.7
1974	Mil-A	138	394	42	88	13	4	6	31	43	61	.223	.305	.322	81	-9	15	9	-1	.989	0	*O-131/D-2	-1.5
1975	Mil-A	22	62	8	12	0	1	1	5	11	11	.194	.324	.274	70	-2	1	4	-2	1.000	1	O-22	-0.5
	Chi-A	61	161	22	33	4	2	4	13	13	34	.205	.269	.329	67	-7	4	0	1	.980	-5	O-59/D-1	-1.4
	Yr	83	223	30	45	4	3	5	18	24	45	.202	.285	.314	68	-9	5	4	-1	.987	-5	O-81/D-1	-1.9
1977	Chi-A	20	37	4	10	0	0	0	7	6	2	.270	.372	.270	79	-1	0	2	-1	1.000	-2	O-19	-0.5
1978	StL-N	5	3	0	0	0	0	0	0	1	2	.000	.250	.000	-25	-0	0	0	0	1.000	-1	/O-2	-0.1
Total	5	370	1095	141	241	38	15	26	114	128	202	.220	.306	.353	87	-18	33	21	-3	.990	2	O-341/D-14	-3.3
■ **EARLE COMBS**	Combs, Earle Bryan "The Kentucky Colonel" b: 5/14/1899, Pebworth, Ky. d: 7/21/76, Richmond, Ky. BL/TR, 6′, 185 lbs. Deb: 4/16/24 CH																						
1924	NY-A	24	35	10	14	5	0	0	2	4	2	.400	.462	.543	159	3	0	1	-1	1.000	-3	O-11	-0.1
1925	NY-A	150	593	117	203	36	13	3	61	65	43	.342	.411	.462	123	22	12	13	-4	.979	4	*O-150	1.1
1926	*NY-A	145	606	113	181	31	12	8	55	47	23	.299	.352	.429	105	2	8	6	-1	.970	1	*O-145	-0.8
1927	*NY-A	152	648	137	**231**	36	**23**	6	64	62	31	.356	.414	.511	143	41	15	6	1	.968	2	*O-152	3.2
1928	*NY-A	149	626	118	194	33	**21**	7	56	77	33	.310	.387	.463	127	25	10	8	-2	.980	8	*O-149	2.0
1929	NY-A	142	586	119	202	33	15	3	65	69	32	.345	.414	.468	135	32	11	7	-1	.966	-4	*O-141	1.7
1930	NY-A	137	532	129	183	30	**22**	7	82	74	26	.344	.424	.523	145	38	16	10	-1	.969	-4	*O-135	2.1
1931	NY-A	138	563	120	179	31	13	5	58	68	34	.318	.394	.446	128	24	11	3	2	.974	-0	*O-129	1.5
1932	*NY-A	144	591	143	190	32	10	9	65	81	16	.321	.405	.455	129	28	3	9	-5	.967	-7	*O-139	0.6
1933	NY-A	122	417	86	125	22	16	5	64	47	19	.300	.372	.465	128	16	6	4	-1	.975	-4	*O-104	0.6
1934	NY-A	63	251	47	80	13	5	2	25	40	9	.319	.412	.434	127	12	3	1	0	.993	-2	O-62	0.7
1935	NY-A	89	298	47	84	7	4	3	35	36	10	.282	.359	.362	92	-3	1	3	-2	.993	-4	O-70	-1.0
Total	12	1455	5746	1186	1866	309	154	58	632	670	278	.325	.397	.462	127	241	96	71	-14	.974	-14	*O-1387	11.6
■ **MERL COMBS**	Combs, Merrill Russell b: 12/11/19, Los Angeles, Cal. d: 7/8/81, Riverside, Cal. BL/TR, 6′, 172 lbs. Deb: 9/12/47 C																						
1947	Bos-A	17	68	8	15	1	0	1	6	9	9	.221	.329	.279	65	-3	0	0	0	1.000	4	3-17	0.1
1949	Bos-A	14	24	5	5	1	0	0	1	9	0	.208	.424	.250	75	-0	0	0	0	.923	-0	/3-9,S-1	-0.1
1950	Bos-A	1	0	0	0	0	0	0	0	1	0	—	1.000	—	158	0	0	0	0	.000	0	H	0.0
	Was-A	37	102	19	25	1	0	0	6	22	16	.245	.379	.255	68	-4	0	0	0	.966	-1	S-30	-0.2
	Yr	38	102	19	25	1	0	0	6	23	16	.245	.384	.255	69	-3	0	0	0	.966	-1	S-30	-0.2
1951	Cle-A	19	28	2	5	2	0	0	2	2	3	.179	.233	.250	32	-3	0	0	0	.960	5	S-16	0.2
1952	Cle-A	52	139	11	23	1	1	1	10	14	15	.165	.242	.209	28	-14	0	1	-1	.972	9	S-49/2-3	-0.3
Total	5	140	361	45	73	6	1	2	25	57	43	.202	.314	.241	52	-23	0	1	-1	.968	17	/S-96,3-26,2-3	-0.3
■ **WAYNE COMER**	Comer, Harry Wayne b: 2/3/44, Shenandoah, Va. BR/TR, 5′10″, 175 lbs. Deb: 9/17/67																						
1967	Det-A	4	3	0	1	0	0	0	0	0	0	.333	.333	.333	95	-0	0	0	0	.000	-0	/O-1	0.0
1968	*Det-A	48	48	8	6	0	1	1	3	2	7	.125	.160	.229	16	-5	0	0	0	1.000	-5	O-27/C-1	-1.2
1969	Sea-A	147	481	88	118	18	1	15	54	82	79	.245	.356	.380	108	7	18	7	1	.980	3	*O-139/C-1,3-1	0.4
1970	Mil-A	13	17	1	1	0	0	0	1	0	3	.059	.059	.059	-67	-4	0	0	0	1.000	-1	/O-5	-0.5
	Was-A	77	129	21	30	4	0	0	8	22	16	.233	.349	.264	75	-3	4	1	1	.960	-10	O-58/3-1	-1.5
	Yr	90	146	22	31	4	0	0	9	22	19	.212	.320	.240	59	-7	4	1	1	.962	-11	O-63/3-1	-2.0
1972	Det-A	27	9	1	1	0	0	0	1	0	1	.111	.111	.111	-33	-1	0	1	-1	1.000	-5	O-17	-0.9
Total	5	316	687	119	157	22	2	16	67	106	106	.229	.333	.336	90	-7	22	9	1	.978	-18	O-247/3-2,C-2	-3.7
■ **CHARLIE COMISKEY**	Comiskey, Charles Albert "Commy" or "The Old Roman" b: 8/15/1859, Chicago, Ill. d: 10/26/31, Eagle River, Wis. BR/TR, 6′, 180 lbs. Deb: 5/2/1882 MH																						
1882	StL-a	78	329	58	80	9	5	1	45	4		.243	.252	.310	85	-6				.967	-1	*1-77/P-2	-1.4
1883	StL-a	96	401	87	118	17	9	2	64	11		.294	.313	.397	120	7				.963	-2	*1-96/O-1,M	-0.4
1884	StL-a	108	460	76	109	17	6	2	84	5		.237	.253	.313	81	-11				.969	2	*1-108/2-1,P-1,M	-1.9
1885	*StL-a	83	340	68	87	15	7	2	44	14		.256	.293	.359	101	-1				.969	1	*1-83,M	-0.9
1886	*StL-a	131	578	95	147	15	9	3	76	10		.254	.267	.327	82	-15	41			.975	4	*1-122/2-9,O-2,M	-2.3
1887	*StL-a	125	538	139	180	22	5	4	103	27		.335	.374	.416	109	2	117			.976	3	*1-116/2-9,O-3,M	-0.5
1888	*StL-a	137	576	102	157	22	5	6	83	12		.273	.292	.359	98	-6	72			.970	-6	*1-133/O-5,2-3,M	-2.3
1889	StL-a	137	587	105	168	28	10	3	102	19	19	.286	.312	.383	86	-17	65			.970	-1	*1-134/O-3,2-3,P,M	-2.3
1890	Chi-P	88	377	53	92	11	3	0	59	14	17	.244	.277	.289	49	-29	34			.965	-2	1-88,M	-2.9
1891	StL-a	141	580	86	152	16	2	3	93	33	25	.262	.310	.312	68	-30	41			.980	3	*1-141/O-2,M	-2.9
1892	Cin-N	141	551	61	125	14	6	3	71	32	16	.227	.274	.290	72	-20	30			.984	1	*1-141,M	-2.4
1893	Cin-N	64	259	38	57	12	1	0	26	11	2	.220	.257	.274	40	-23	9			.979	-6	1-64,M	-2.6
1894	Cin-N	61	220	26	58	8	0	0	33	5	5	.264	.289	.300	41	-22	10			.972	-4	1-60/O-1,M	-2.0
Total	13	1390	5796	994	1530	206	68	29	883	197	84	.264	.293	.338	82	-169	419			.973	-8	*1-1363/2-25,O-17,P	-24.8
■ **JIM COMMAND**	Command, James Dalton "Igor" b: 10/15/28, Grand Rapids, Mich BL/TR, 6′2″, 200 lbs. Deb: 6/20/54																						
1954	Phi-N	9	18	1	4	1	0	1	6	2	4	.222	.300	.444	91	-0	0	0	0	.929	-0	/3-6	-0.1
1955	Phi-N	5	5	0	0	0	0	0	0	0	0	.000	.000	.000	-99	-1	0	0	0	.000	0	H	-0.1
Total	2	14	23	1	4	1	0	1	6	2	4	.174	.240	.348	52	-2	0	0	0	.929	-0	/3-6	-0.2
■ **ADAM COMOROSKY**	Comorosky, Adam Anthony b: 12/9/05, Swoyersville, Pa. d: 3/2/51, Swoyersville, Pa. BR/TR, 5′10″, 167 lbs. Deb: 9/13/26																						
1926	Pit-N	8	15	2	4	1	1	0	0	1	2	.267	.313	.467	102	-0	1			1.000	-1	/O-6	-0.2
1927	Pit-N	18	61	5	14	1	0	0	4	3	1	.230	.266	.246	35	-6	0			.978	2	O-16	-0.5
1928	Pit-N	51	176	22	52	6	3	2	34	15	6	.295	.354	.398	92	-2	1			.968	-1	O-49	-0.5

YEAR	TM/L	G	AB	R	H	2B	3B	HR	RBI	BB	SO	AVG	OBP	SLG	PRO+	BR/A	SB	CS	SBR	FA	FR	G/POS	TPR
1929	Pit-N	127	473	86	152	26	11	6	97	40	22	.321	.377	.461	104	3	19			.963	0	*O-121	-0.5
1930	Pit-N	152	597	112	187	47	**23**	12	119	51	33	.313	.371	.529	114	12	14			.969	1	*O-152	0.2
1931	Pit-N	99	350	37	85	12	1	1	48	34	28	.243	.310	.291	63	-17	11			.978	3	O-90	-2.1
1932	Pit-N	108	370	54	106	18	4	4	46	25	20	.286	.337	.389	96	-2	7			.981	7	O-92	0.0
1933	Pit-N	64	162	18	46	8	1	1	15	4	9	.284	.301	.364	89	-3	2			1.000	-1	O-30	-0.5
1934	Cin-N	127	446	46	115	12	6	0	40	34	23	.258	.315	.312	70	-18	1			.970	1	*O-122	-2.2
1935	Cin-N	59	137	22	34	3	1	2	14	7	14	.248	.290	.328	68	-6	1			.953	-2	O-40	-0.9
Total	10	813	2787	404	795	134	51	28	417	214	158	.285	.339	.400	91	-39	57			.972	9	O-718	-7.2

■ PETE COMPTON
Compton, Anna Sebastian "Bash" b: 9/28/1889, San Marcos, Tex. d: 2/3/78, Kansas City, Mo. BL/TL, 5'11", 170 lbs. Deb: 9/6/11

YEAR	TM/L	G	AB	R	H	2B	3B	HR	RBI	BB	SO	AVG	OBP	SLG	PRO+	BR/A	SB	CS	SBR	FA	FR	G/POS	TPR
1911	StL-A	28	107	9	29	4	0	0	5	8		.271	.322	.308	79	-3	2			.917	1	O-28	-0.3
1912	StL-A	103	268	26	75	6	4	2	30	22		.280	.339	.354	102	1	11			.925	1	O-72	-0.2
1913	StL-A	63	100	14	18	5	2	2	17	13	13	.180	.274	.330	79	-3	2			.862	-4	O-21	-0.9
1915	StL-F	2	8	0	2	0	0	0	3	0	0	.250	.250	.250	39	-1	0			1.000	-1	/O-2	-0.2
	Bos-N	35	116	10	28	7	1	1	12	8	11	.241	.290	.345	96	-1	4	1	1	.971	0	O-31	-0.2
1916	Bos-N	34	98	13	20	2	0	0	8	7	7	.204	.264	.224	53	-5	5			.939	-2	O-30	-1.0
	Pit-N	5	16	1	1	0	0	0	0	2	5	.063	.211	.063	-14	-2	0			.917	0	/O-5	-0.3
	Yr	39	114	14	21	2	0	0	8	9	12	.184	.256	.202	43	-7	5			.936	-2	O-35	-1.3
1918	NY-N	21	60	5	13	0	1	0	5	5	4	.217	.277	.250	62	-3	2			.971	-1	O-19	-0.5
Total	6	291	773	78	186	24	8	5	80	65	40	.241	.303	.312	83	-17	26	1		.933	-6	O-208	-3.6

■ MIKE COMPTON
Compton, Michael Lynn b: 8/15/44, Stamford, Tex. BR/TR, 5'10", 180 lbs. Deb: 4/17/70

YEAR	TM/L	G	AB	R	H	2B	3B	HR	RBI	BB	SO	AVG	OBP	SLG	PRO+	BR/A	SB	CS	SBR	FA	FR	G/POS	TPR
1970	Phi-N	47	110	8	18	0	1	1	7	9	22	.164	.240	.209	22	-12	0	0	0	.986	8	C-40	-0.3

■ CLINT CONATSER
Conatser, Clinton Astor "Connie" b: 7/24/21, Los Angeles, Cal. BR/TR, 5'11", 182 lbs. Deb: 4/21/48

YEAR	TM/L	G	AB	R	H	2B	3B	HR	RBI	BB	SO	AVG	OBP	SLG	PRO+	BR/A	SB	CS	SBR	FA	FR	G/POS	TPR
1948	*Bos-N	90	224	30	62	9	3	3	23	32	27	.277	.370	.384	106	3	0			.974	-9	O-76	-0.9
1949	Bos-N	53	152	10	40	6	0	3	16	14	19	.263	.325	.362	89	-3	0			.951	0	O-44	-0.4
Total	2	143	376	40	102	15	3	6	39	46	46	.271	.352	.375	99	0	0			.965	-8	O-120	-1.3

■ DAVE CONCEPCION
Concepcion, David Ismael (Benitez) b: 6/17/48, Aragua, Venez. BR/TR, 6'1", 180 lbs. Deb: 4/6/70

YEAR	TM/L	G	AB	R	H	2B	3B	HR	RBI	BB	SO	AVG	OBP	SLG	PRO+	BR/A	SB	CS	SBR	FA	FR	G/POS	TPR
1970	*Cin-N	101	265	38	69	6	3	1	19	23	45	.260	.326	.317	73	-10	10	2	2	.945	-8	S-93/2-3	-0.6
1971	Cin-N	130	327	24	67	4	4	1	20	18	51	.205	.246	.251	42	-25	9	3	1	.974	-4	*S-112,2-10/3-7,O-5	-1.7
1972	*Cin-N	119	378	40	79	13	2	2	29	32	65	.209	.274	.270	58	-21	13	6	0	.969	3	*S-114/3-9,2-1	-0.3
1973	Cin-N†	89	328	39	94	18	3	8	46	21	55	.287	.331	.433	116	6	22	5	4	.974	2	S-88/O-2	2.3
1974	Cin-N	160	594	70	167	25	1	14	82	44	79	.281	.337	.397	106	4	41	6	9	.963	9	*S-160/O-1	4.3
1975	*Cin-N★	140	507	62	139	23	1	5	49	39	51	.274	.328	.353	88	-9	33	6	6	.977	8	*S-130/3-6	2.1
1976	*Cin-N★	152	576	74	162	28	7	9	69	49	68	.281	.339	.401	107	5	21	10	0	.968	17	*S-150	4.1
1977	Cin-N★	156	572	59	155	26	3	8	64	46	77	.271	.325	.369	84	-13	29	7	5	**.986**	8	*S-156	1.7
1978	Cin-N★	153	565	75	170	33	4	6	67	51	83	.301	.360	.405	113	10	23	10	1	.969	-5	*S-152	2.7
1979	*Cin-N†	149	590	91	166	25	3	16	84	64	73	.281	.352	.415	108	7	19	7	2	.967	13	*S-148	3.8
1980	Cin-N★	156	622	72	162	31	8	5	77	37	107	.260	.303	.360	84	-14	12	2	2	.978	-13	*S-155/2-1	-0.7
1981	Cin-N★	106	421	57	129	28	0	5	67	37	61	.306	.364	.409	117	10	4	5	-2	.960	4	*S-106	2.4
1982	Cin-N★	147	572	48	164	25	4	5	53	45	61	.287	.339	.371	96	-2	13	6	0	.977	13	*S-145/1-1,3-1	2.5
1983	Cin-N	143	528	54	123	22	0	1	47	56	81	.233	.307	.280	61	-26	14	9	-1	.979	-22	*S-139/3-6,1-1	-3.8
1984	Cin-N	154	531	46	130	26	1	4	58	52	72	.245	.312	.320	75	-17	22	6	3	.978	-35	*S-104,3-54/1-6	-4.3
1985	Cin-N	155	560	59	141	19	2	7	48	50	67	.252	.316	.330	77	-16	16	12	-2	.962	-32	*S-151/3-5	-3.9
1986	Cin-N	90	311	42	81	13	2	3	30	26	43	.260	.318	.344	79	-9	13	2	3	.965	-2	S-60,1-12,2-10,3-10	-0.3
1987	Cin-N	104	279	32	89	15	0	1	33	28	24	.319	.381	.384	99	1	4	3	-1	.992	0	2-59,1-26,3-13,/S-2	0.2
1988	Cin-N	84	197	11	39	9	0	0	8	18	23	.198	.265	.244	45	-14	3	2	-0	.994	1	2-46,1-16,S-13,/3P	-1.3
Total	19	2488	8723	993	2326	389	48	101	950	736	1186	.267	.325	.357	88	-133	321	109	31	.971	-44	*S-2178,2-130,3/1OP	9.2

■ ONIX CONCEPCION
Concepcion, Onix Cardona (Cardona) b: 10/5/57, Dorado, P.R. BR/TR, 5'6", 180 lbs. Deb: 8/30/80

YEAR	TM/L	G	AB	R	H	2B	3B	HR	RBI	BB	SO	AVG	OBP	SLG	PRO+	BR/A	SB	CS	SBR	FA	FR	G/POS	TPR
1980	*KC-A	12	15	1	2	0	0	0	2	0	1	.133	.133	.133	-26	-3	0	0	0	.833	1	/S-6	-0.2
1981	KC-A	2	0	0	0	0	0	0	0	0	0	—	—	—	—	0	0	0	0	.000	0	/S-1	0.0
1982	KC-A	74	205	17	48	9	1	0	15	5	18	.234	.256	.288	49	-14	2	1	0	.948	-2	S-46,2-24/D-1	-1.1
1983	KC-A	80	219	22	53	11	3	0	20	12	12	.242	.284	.320	66	-10	10	3	1	.913	1	3-31,2-28,S-21,/D-1	-0.6
1984	*KC-A	90	287	36	81	9	2	1	23	14	33	.282	.322	.338	82	-7	9	6	-1	.972	3	S-85/2-6,3-1	0.4
1985	*KC-A	131	314	32	64	5	1	2	20	16	29	.204	.256	.245	38	-27	4	4	-1	.959	5	*S-128/2-2	-1.2
1987	Pit-N	1	1	0	1	0	0	0	0	0	0	1.000	1.000	1.000	429	0	0	0	0	.000	0	/H	0.0
Total	7	390	1041	108	249	34	7	3	80	47	93	.239	.279	.294	58	-60	25	14	-1	.960	8	S-287/2-60,3-32,D-2	-2.7

■ RAMON CONDE
Conde, Ramon Luis (Roman) "Wito" b: 12/29/34, Juana Diaz, P.R. BR/TR, 5'8", 172 lbs. Deb: 7/17/62

YEAR	TM/L	G	AB	R	H	2B	3B	HR	RBI	BB	SO	AVG	OBP	SLG	PRO+	BR/A	SB	CS	SBR	FA	FR	G/POS	TPR
1962	Chi-A	14	16	0	0	0	0	0	1	3	3	.000	.158	.000	-54	-4	0	0	0	.889	-1	/3-7	-0.4

■ FRED CONE
Cone, Joseph Frederick b: 5/1848, Rockford, Ill. d: 4/13/09, Chicago, Ill. 5'9.5", 171 lbs. Deb: 5/5/1871

YEAR	TM/L	G	AB	R	H	2B	3B	HR	RBI	BB	SO	AVG	OBP	SLG	PRO+	BR/A	SB	CS	SBR	FA	FR	G/POS	TPR
1871	Bos-n	19	77	17	20	3	1	0	16	8	2	.260	.329	.325	86	-1	12	1	3	.854	-0	O-18	0.1

■ BUNK CONGALTON
Congalton, William Millar b: 1/24/1875, Guelph, Ont., Can. d: 8/16/37, Cleveland, Ohio BL/TL, 5'11", 190 lbs. Deb: 4/18/02

YEAR	TM/L	G	AB	R	H	2B	3B	HR	RBI	BB	SO	AVG	OBP	SLG	PRO+	BR/A	SB	CS	SBR	FA	FR	G/POS	TPR
1902	Chi-N	45	179	14	40	3	0	1	24	7		.223	.253	.257	59	-9	3			.987	0	O-45	-1.3
1905	Cle-A	12	47	4	17	0	0	0	5	2		.362	.388	.362	136	2	3			.923	-1	O-12	0.0
1906	Cle-A	117	419	51	134	13	5	3	50	24		.320	.361	.396	139	18	12			.957	-9	*O-114	0.4
1907	Cle-A	9	22	2	4	0	0	0	2	4		.182	.308	.182	56	-1	0			1.000	0	/O-6	-0.1
	Bos-A	124	496	44	142	11	8	2	47	20		.286	.318	.353	115	7	13			.969	-3	*O-123	-0.1
	Yr	133	518	46	146	11	8	2	49	24		.282	.317	.346	112	6	13			.971	-2	*O-129	-0.2
Total	4	307	1163	115	337	27	13	6	128	57		.290	.326	.351	115	17	31			.967	-13	O-300	-1.1

■ TONY CONIGLIARO
Conigliaro, Anthony Richard b: 1/7/45, Revere, Mass. d: 2/24/90, Salem, Mass. BR/TR, 6'3", 185 lbs. Deb: 4/16/64 F

YEAR	TM/L	G	AB	R	H	2B	3B	HR	RBI	BB	SO	AVG	OBP	SLG	PRO+	BR/A	SB	CS	SBR	FA	FR	G/POS	TPR
1964	Bos-A	111	404	69	117	21	2	24	52	35	78	.290	.354	.530	135	18	2	4	-2	.973	3	*O-106	1.5
1965	Bos-A	138	521	82	140	21	5	**32**	82	51	116	.269	.340	.512	131	20	4	2	0	.976	14	*O-137	2.8
1966	Bos-A	150	558	77	148	26	7	28	93	52	112	.265	.333	.487	120	13	0	2	-1	.973	-0	*O-146	0.6
1967	Bos-A★	95	349	59	100	11	5	20	67	27	58	.287	.346	.519	141	17	4	6	-2	.983	3	O-95	1.4
1969	Bos-A	141	506	57	129	21	3	20	82	48	111	.255	.324	.427	103	1	2	4	-2	.981	-8	*O-137	-1.7
1970	Bos-A	146	560	89	149	20	1	36	116	43	93	.266	.327	.498	116	10	4	2	0	.977	3	*O-146	0.6
1971	Cal-A	74	266	23	59	18	0	4	15	23	52	.222	.286	.335	81	-8	3	3	-1	.994	6	O-72	-0.6
1975	Bos-A	21	57	8	7	1	0	2	9	8	9	.123	.231	.246	32	-5	1	0	0	.000	0	D-15	-0.6
Total	8	876	3221	464	849	139	23	166	516	287	629	.264	.330	.476	118	67	20	23	-8	.979	21	O-839/D-15	4.0

■ BILLY CONIGLIARO
Conigliaro, William Michael b: 8/15/47, Revere, Mass. BR/TR, 6', 190 lbs. Deb: 4/11/69 F

YEAR	TM/L	G	AB	R	H	2B	3B	HR	RBI	BB	SO	AVG	OBP	SLG	PRO+	BR/A	SB	CS	SBR	FA	FR	G/POS	TPR
1969	Bos-A	32	80	14	23	6	2	4	7	9	23	.287	.367	.563	149	5	1	1	-0	.926	-7	O-24	-0.3
1970	Bos-A	114	398	59	108	16	3	18	58	35	73	.271	.341	.462	112	6	3	7	-3	.968	0	*O-108	-0.3
1971	Bos-A	101	351	42	92	26	1	11	33	25	68	.262	.311	.436	102	0	3	2	-0	.983	4	*O-100	-0.1
1972	Mil-A	52	191	22	44	6	2	7	16	8	54	.230	.261	.393	95	-2	1	0	0	.992	6	O-50	0.2
1973	*Oak-A	48	110	5	22	2	2	0	14	9	26	.200	.261	.255	48	-8	1	0	0	1.000	-2	O-40/2-1	-1.1
Total	5	347	1130	142	289	56	10	40	128	86	244	.256	.313	.429	103	1	9	10	-3	.980	2	O-322/2-1	-1.6

■ JEFF CONINE
Conine, Jeffrey Guy b: 6/27/66, Tacoma, Wash. BR/TR, 6'1", 220 lbs. Deb: 9/16/90

YEAR	TM/L	G	AB	R	H	2B	3B	HR	RBI	BB	SO	AVG	OBP	SLG	PRO+	BR/A	SB	CS	SBR	FA	FR	G/POS	TPR
1990	KC-A	9	20	3	5	2	0	0	2	2	5	.250	.318	.350	88	-0	0	0	0	.977	0	/1-9	-0.1
1992	KC-A	28	91	10	23	5	2	0	9	8	23	.253	.313	.352	84	-2	0	0	0	1.000	-2	O-23/1-4	-0.5
1993	Fla-N	162	595	75	174	24	3	12	79	52	135	.292	.354	.403	97	-2	2	2	-1	.992	2	*O-147,1-43	-0.5
1994	Fla-N☆	115	451	60	144	27	6	18	82	40	92	.319	.376	.525	128	18	1	2	-1	.974	5	O-97,1-46	1.7
1995	Fla-N★	133	483	72	146	26	2	25	105	66	94	.302	.387	.520	136	26	2	0	1	.976	6	*O-118,1-14	2.7
1996	Fla-N	157	597	84	175	32	2	26	95	62	121	.293	.363	.484	125	21	1	4	-2	.975	5	*O-128,1-48	1.7

YEAR	TM/L	G	AB	R	H	2B	3B	HR	RBI	BB	SO	AVG	OBP	SLG	PRO+	BR/A	SB	CS	SBR	FA	FR	G/POS	TPR
1997	*Fla-N	151	405	46	98	13	1	17	61	57	89	.242	.338	.405	98	-1	2	0	1	.992	10	*1-145/O-1	-0.2
1998	KC-A	93	309	30	79	26	0	8	43	26	68	.256	.318	.417	85	-7	3	0	1	.993	-5	O-80,1-12/D-3	-1.3
Total	8	848	2951	380	844	155	16	106	476	313	627	.286	.357	.457	112	53	11	8	-2	.983	21	O-594,1-321/D-3	3.5
■ JOCKO CONLAN Conlan, John Bertrand b: 12/6/1899, Chicago, Ill. d: 4/16/89, Scottsdale, Ariz. BL/TL, 5'7.5", 165 lbs. Deb: 7/6/34 UH																							
1934	Chi-A	63	225	35	56	11	3	0	16	19	7	.249	.310	.324	62	-13	2	2	-1	.955	-3	O-54	-1.8
1935	Chi-A	65	140	20	40	7	1	0	15	14	6	.286	.355	.350	81	-4	3	3	-1	.961	-3	O-37	-0.8
Total	2	128	365	55	96	18	4	0	31	33	13	.263	.327	.334	69	-17	5	5	-2	.957	-6	/O-91	-2.6
■ JOCKO CONLON Conlon, Arthur Joseph b: 12/10/1897, Woburn, Mass. d: 8/5/87, Falmouth, Mass. BR/TR, 5'7", 145 lbs. Deb: 4/17/23																							
1923	Bos-N	59	147	23	32	3	0	0	17	11	11	.218	.299	.238	45	-11	0	3	-2	.955	1	2-36/S-6,3-4	-1.0
■ BERT CONN Conn, Albert Thomas b: 9/22/1879, Philadelphia, Pa. d: 11/2/44, Philadelphia, Pa. TR , Deb: 9/16/1898																							
1898	Phi-N	1	3	1	1	0	1	0	1	0		.333	.333	1.000	291	1	0			1.000	-0	/P-1	0.0
1900	Phi-N	6	9	4	3	1	0	0	1	0		.333	.333	.444	115	0	0			.667	-1	/P-4	0.0
1901	Phi-N	5	18	2	4	1	0	0	0	0		.222	.263	.278	56	-1	0			.880	-1	/2-5	-0.2
Total	3	12	30	7	8	2	1	0	2	0		.267	.290	.400	95	-0	0			.714	-2	/2-5,P-5	-0.2
■ FRITZIE CONNALLY Connally, Fritzie Lee b: 5/19/58, Bryan, Tex. BR/TR, 6'3", 210 lbs. Deb: 9/9/83																							
1983	Chi-N	8	10	0	1	0	0	0	0	0	5	.100	.100	.100	-42	-2	0	0	0	1.000	0	/3-3	-0.2
1985	Bal-A	50	112	16	26	4	0	3	15	19	21	.232	.348	.348	94	-0	0	0	0	.976	-3	3-46/1-2,D-1	-0.4
Total	2	58	122	16	27	4	0	3	15	19	26	.221	.331	.328	83	-2	0	0	0	.977	-3	/3-49,1-2,D-1	-0.6
■ BRUCE CONNATSER Connatser, Broadus Milburn b: 9/19/02, Sevierville, Tenn d: 1/27/71, Terre Haute, Ind. BR/TR, 5'11.5", 170 lbs. Deb: 9/15/31																							
1931	Cle-A	12	49	5	14	3	0	0	4	2	3	.286	.327	.347	73	-2	0	0	0	1.000	1	1-12	-0.2
1932	Cle-A	23	60	8	14	3	1	0	4	4	8	.233	.281	.317	51	-4	1	0	0	1.000	0	1-14	-0.4
Total	2	35	109	13	28	6	1	0	8	6	11	.257	.302	.330	61	-6	1	0	0	1.000	2	/1-26	-0.6
■ FRANK CONNAUGHTON Connaughton, Frank Henry b: 1/1/1869, Clinton, Mass. d: 12/1/42, Boston, Mass. BR/TR, 5'9", 165 lbs. Deb: 5/28/1894																							
1894	Bos-N	46	171	42	59	9	2	2	33	16	8	.345	.407	.456	100	-0	3			.892	-3	S-33/C-7,O-4	-0.1
1896	NY-N	88	315	53	82	3	2	2	43	25	7	.260	.319	.302	66	-15	22			.892	3	S-54,O-30	-1.1
1906	Bos-N	12	44	3	9	0	0	0	1	3		.205	.271	.205	50	-2	1			.918	-3	S-11/2-1	-0.5
Total	3	146	530	98	150	12	4	4	77	44	15	.283	.344	.343	78	-18	26			.894	-3	/S-98,O-34,C-7,2-1	-1.7
■ GENE CONNELL Connell, Eugene Joseph b: 5/10/06, Hazleton, Pa. d: 8/31/37, Waverly, N.Y. BR/TR, 6'0.5", 180 lbs. Deb: 7/4/31 F																							
1931	Phi-N	6	12	1	3	0	0	0	0	0	3	.250	.250	.250	32	-1	0			1.000	-1	/C-6	-0.1
■ JOE CONNELL Connell, Joseph Bernard b: 1/16/02, Bethlehem, Pa. d: 9/21/77, Trexlertown, Pa. BL/TL, 5'8", 165 lbs. Deb: 6/15/26 F																							
1926	NY-N	2	1	1	0	0	0	0	0	0	0	.000	.000	.000	-99	-0	0			.000	0	H	0.0
■ PETE CONNELL Connell, Peter J. b: Brooklyn, N.Y. Deb: 9/3/1886																							
1886	NY-a	1	5	0	0	0	0	0	0	0		.000	.000	.000	-99	-1	0			.667	-1	/3-1	-0.2
■ TERRY CONNELL Connell, Terence G. b: 6/17/1855, Philadelphia, Pa. d: 3/25/24, Philadelphia, Pa. Deb: 6/20/1874																							
1874	Chi-n	1	4	0	0	0	0	0	0	0	0	.000	.000	.000	-99	-1	0	0	0	.429	-1	/C-1	-0.1
■ TOM CONNELLY Connelly, Thomas Martin b: 10/20/1897, Chicago, Ill. d: 2/18/41, Hines, Ill. BL/TR, 5'11.5", 165 lbs. Deb: 9/24/20																							
1920	NY-A	1	1	0	0	0	0	0	0	0	0	.000	.000	.000	-97	-0	0	0	0	.000	0	H	0.0
1921	NY-A	4	5	0	1	0	0	0	0	1	0	.200	.333	.200	38	-0	0	0	0	1.000	0	/O-3	-0.1
Total	2	5	6	0	1	0	0	0	0	1	0	.167	.286	.167	18	-1	0	0	0	1.000	0	/O-3	-0.1
■ ED CONNOLLY Connolly, Edward Joseph Sr. b: 7/17/08, Brooklyn, N.Y. d: 11/12/63, Pittsfield, Mass. BR/TR, 5'8.5", 180 lbs. Deb: 9/20/29 F																							
1929	Bos-A	5	8	0	0	0	0	0	0	0	2	.000	.000	.000	-99	-2	0	0	0	.889	-1	/C 5	-0.3
1930	Bos-A	27	48	1	9	2	0	0	7	4	3	.188	.250	.229	23	-6	0	0	0	1.000	-1	C-26	-0.5
1931	Bos-A	42	93	3	7	1	0	0	3	5	18	.075	.131	.086	-44	-20	0	0	0	.981	-1	C-41	-1.8
1932	Bos-A	75	222	9	50	8	4	0	21	20	27	.225	.289	.297	54	-15	0	1	-1	.957	4	C-75	-0.8
Total	4	149	371	13	66	11	4	0	31	29	50	.178	.239	.229	23	-43	0	1	-1	.966	1	C-147	-3.4
■ RED CONNOLLY Connolly, John M. b: 1863, New York, N.Y. d: 3/2/1896, New York, N.Y. Deb: 7/1/1886																							
1886	StL-N	2	7	0	0	0	0	0	0	0	3	.000	.000	.000	-99	-2	0			.000	-1	/O-2	-0.2
■ JOE CONNOLLY Connolly, Joseph Aloysius b: 2/12/1886, N.Smithfield, R.I. d: 9/1/43, N.Smithfield, R.I. BL/TR, 5'7.5", 165 lbs. Deb: 4/10/13																							
1913	Bos-N	126	427	79	120	18	11	5	57	66	47	.281	.379	.410	123	14	18			.954	-8	*O-124	0.1
1914	*Bos-N	120	399	64	122	28	10	9	65	49	36	.306	.393	.494	164	32	12			.974	-5	*O-118	2.2
1915	Bos-N	104	305	48	91	14	8	0	23	39	35	.298	.387	.397	144	18	13	12	-3	.971	-4	O-93	0.7
1916	Bos-N	62	110	11	25	5	2	0	12	14	13	.227	.320	.309	98	0	5			.980	-1	O-31	-0.2
Total	4	412	1241	202	358	65	31	14	157	168	131	.288	.380	.425	139	63	48	12		.967	-17	O-366	2.8
■ JOE CONNOLLY Connolly, Joseph George "Coaster Joe" b: 6/4/1896, San Francisco, Cal d: 3/30/60, San Francisco, Cal BR/TR, 6', 170 lbs. Deb: 10/1/21																							
1921	NY-N	2	4	0	0	0	0	0	0	1	1	.000	.200	.000	-42	-1	0	0	0	1.000	-0	/O-1	-0.1
1922	Cle-A	12	45	6	11	2	1	0	6	5	8	.244	.320	.333	70	-2	1	0	0	.972	2	O-12	-0.1
1923	Cle-A	52	109	25	33	10	1	3	25	13	7	.303	.377	.495	129	4	1	2	-1	.957	-10	O-39	-0.8
1924	Bos-A	14	10	1	1	0	0	0	1	2	2	.100	.250	.100	-8	-2	0	0	0	1.000	-1	/O-3	-0.2
Total	4	80	168	32	45	12	2	3	32	21	18	.268	.349	.417	100	-0	2	2	-1	.966	-9	/O-55	-1.2
■ BUD CONNOLLY Connolly, Mervin Thomas "Mike" b: 5/25/01, San Francisco, Cal d: 6/12/64, Berkeley, Cal. BR/TR, 5'8", 154 lbs. Deb: 5/3/25																							
1925	Bos-A	43	107	12	28	7	1	0	21	23	9	.262	.392	.346	88	-1	0	3	-2	.950	-11	S-34/3-2	-0.9
■ TOM CONNOLLY Connolly, Thomas Francis "Blackie" or "Ham" b: 12/30/1892, Boston, Mass. d: 5/14/66, Boston, Mass. BL/TR, 5'11", 175 lbs. Deb: 5/12/15																							
1915	Was-A	50	141	14	26	3	2	0	7	14	19	.184	.268	.234	49	-9	5	4	-1	.970	-7	3-24,O-19/S-4	-1.7
■ NED CONNOR Connor, Edward b: 1850, New York 5'9", 156 lbs. Deb: 5/18/1871																							
1871	Tro-n	7	33	6	7	0	0	0	2	0	0	.212	.212	.212	22	-3	0	0	0	.878	-0	/1-4,O-3	-0.2
■ JIM CONNOR Connor, James Matthew (b: James Matthew O'Connor) b: 5/11/1863, Port Jervis, N.Y. d: 9/3/50, Providence, R.I. BR/TR, Deb: 7/11/1892																							
1892	Chi-N	9	34	0	2	0	0	0	0	1	7	.059	.111	.059	-48	-6	0			.917	-6	/2-9	-1.1
1897	Chi-N	77	285	40	83	10	5	3	38	24		.291	.355	.393	94	-3	10			.936	22	2-76	2.0
1898	Chi-N	138	505	51	114	9	9	0	67	42		.226	.289	.279	63	-24	11			.946	-3	*2-138	-1.7
1899	Chi-N	69	234	26	48	7	1	0	24	18		.205	.265	.244	41	-19	6			.042	4	2-44,3-25	-1.1
Total	4	293	1058	117	247	26	15	3	129	85	7	.233	.296	.295	64	-52	27			.942	18	2-267/3-25	-1.9
■ JOE CONNOR Connor, Joseph Francis b: 12/8/1874, Waterbury, Conn. d: 11/8/57, Waterbury, Conn. BR/TR, 6'2", 185 lbs. Deb: 9/9/1895 F																							
1895	StL-N	2	7	0	0	0	0	0	1	0	2	.000	.000	.000	-99	-2	0			1.000	1	/3-2	-0.1
1900	Bos-N	7	19	2	4	0	0	0	4	2		.211	.286	.211	34	-2	1			.971	2	/C-7	0.1
1901	Mil-A	38	102	10	28	3	1	1	9	6		.275	.321	.353	91	-1	4			.949	0	C-30/2-1,3-1,O-1	0.1
	Cle-A	37	121	13	17	3	1	0	6	7		.140	.200	.182	7	-15	2			.942	-0	C-32/O-4,S-1	-1.2
	Yr	75	223	23	45	6	2	1	15	13		.202	.255	.260	45	-16	6			.946	-0	C-62/O-5,2-1,3-1,S	-1.1
1905	NY-A	8	22	4	5	1	0	0	2	3		.227	.320	.273	79	-0	0			.978	2	/C-6,1-2	0.2
Total	4	92	271	29	54	7	2	1	22	18	2	.199	.257	.251	43	-21	8			.952	5	/C-75,O-5,3-1,S2	-0.9
■ ROGER CONNOR Connor, Roger b: 7/1/1857, Waterbury, Conn. d: 1/4/31, Waterbury, Conn. BL/TR, 6'3", 220 lbs. Deb: 5/1/1880 FMH																							
1880	Tro-N	83	340	53	113	18	8	3	47	13	21	.332	.357	.459	166	22				.821	-10	*3-83	1.4
1881	Tro-N	85	367	55	107	17	6	2	31	15	20	.292	.319	.387	115	5				.950	2	*1-85	-0.1
1882	Tro-N	81	349	65	115	22	**18**	4	42	13	20	.330	.354	.530	188	34				.951	3	1-43,O-24,3-14	2.9

YEAR	TM/L	G	AB	R	H	2B	3B	HR	RBI	BB	SO	AVG	OBP	SLG	PRO+	BR/A	SB	CS	SBR	FA	FR	G/POS	TPR
1883	NY-N	98	409	80	146	28	15	1	50	25	16	.357	.394	.506	173	36				.958	3	*1-98	2.4
1884	NY-N	116	477	98	151	28	4	4	82	38	32	.317	.367	.417	143	23				.860	3	2-67,O-37,3-12	2.4
1885	NY-N	110	455	102	**169**	23	15	1	65	51	8	**.371**	**.435**	.495	**203**	**53**				.975	3	*1-110	**4.0**
1886	NY-N	118	485	105	172	29	**20**	7	71	41	15	.355	.405	.540	183	48	17			.973	10	*1-118	3.9
1887	NY-N	127	471	113	134	26	22	17	104	75	50	.285	.392	.541	164	43	43			**.993**	5	*1-127	2.9
1888	*NY-N	134	481	98	140	15	17	14	71	**73**	44	.291	.389	.480	**178**	45	27			.982	1	*1-133/2-1	3.3
1889	*NY-N	131	496	117	157	32	17	13	**130**	93	46	.317	.426	**.528**	166	46	21			.977	-8	*1-131/3-1	2.5
1890	NY-P	123	484	133	169	24	15	**14**	103	88	32	.349	.450	**.548**	152	35	22			**.985**	11	*1-123	3.1
1891	NY-N	129	479	112	139	29	13	7	94	83	39	.290	.399	.449	153	35	27			.983	1	*1-129	2.7
1892	Phi-N	155	564	123	166	**37**	11	12	73	116	39	.294	.420	.463	167	51	22			**.985**	-6	*1-155	3.4
1893	NY-N	135	511	111	156	25	8	11	105	91	26	.305	.413	.450	129	23	24			.974	2	*1-135/3-1	1.7
1894	NY-N	22	82	10	24	7	0	1	14	8	0	.293	.356	.415	86	-2	2			.976	2	1-21/O-1	0.0
	StL-N	99	380	83	122	28	25	7	79	51	17	.321	.410	.582	137	21	17			.974	5	*1-99	2.0
	Yr	121	462	93	146	35	25	8	93	59	17	.316	.400	.552	128	19	19			.974	7	*1-120/O-1	2.0
1895	StL-N	103	398	78	131	29	9	8	77	63	10	.329	.423	.508	141	26	9			.986	4	*1-103	2.6
1896	StL-N	126	483	71	137	21	9	11	72	52	14	.284	.356	.433	112	7	10			**.988**	13	*1-126,M	1.8
1897	StL-N	22	83	13	19	3	1	1	12	13		.229	.333	.325	76	-3	3			.984	-0	1-22	-0.2
Total	18	1997	7794	1620	2467	441	233	138	1322	1002	449	.317	.397	.486	154	549	244			.978	42	*1-1758,3-111/20	42.7

■ **JERRY CONNORS** Connors, Jeremiah b: Cleveland, Ohio Deb: 7/11/1892

YEAR	TM/L	G	AB	R	H	2B	3B	HR	RBI	BB	SO	AVG	OBP	SLG	PRO+	BR/A	SB	CS	SBR	FA	FR	G/POS	TPR
1892	Phi-N	1	3	0	0	0	0	0	0	0	1	.000	.000	.000	-99	-1	0			.000	-0	/O-1	-0.1

■ **JOE CONNORS** Connors, Joseph P. b: Paterson, N.J. Deb: 5/3/1884

YEAR	TM/L	G	AB	R	H	2B	3B	HR	RBI	BB	SO	AVG	OBP	SLG	PRO+	BR/A	SB	CS	SBR	FA	FR	G/POS	TPR
1884	Alt-U	3	11	0	1	0	0	0		0		.091	.091	.091	-44	-2				1.000	-0	/P-1,3-1,O-1	-0.2
	KC-U	3	11	2	1	0	0	0		1		.091	.167	.091	-23	-2				1.000	0	/O-2,P-2	0.0
	Yr	6	22	2	2	0	0	0		1		.091	.130	.091	-34	-4				.750	0	/P-3,O-3,3-1	-0.2

■ **CHUCK CONNORS** Connors, Kevin Joseph Aloysius b: 4/10/21, Brooklyn, N.Y. d: 11/10/92, Los Angeles, Cal. BL/TL, 6'5", 190 lbs. Deb: 5/1/49

YEAR	TM/L	G	AB	R	H	2B	3B	HR	RBI	BB	SO	AVG	OBP	SLG	PRO+	BR/A	SB	CS	SBR	FA	FR	G/POS	TPR
1949	Bro-N	1	1	0	0	0	0	0	0	0	0	.000	.000	.000	-96	-0	0			.000	0	H	0.0
1951	Chi-N	66	201	16	48	5	1	2	18	12	25	.239	.282	.303	56	-12	4	0	1	.984	-1	1-57	-1.5
Total	2	67	202	16	48	5	1	2	18	12	25	.238	.280	.302	56	-13	4	0		.984	-1	/1-57	-1.5

■ **MERV CONNORS** Connors, Mervyn James b: 1/23/14, Berkeley, Cal. BR/TR, 6'2", 192 lbs. Deb: 9/4/37

YEAR	TM/L	G	AB	R	H	2B	3B	HR	RBI	BB	SO	AVG	OBP	SLG	PRO+	BR/A	SB	CS	SBR	FA	FR	G/POS	TPR
1937	Chi-A	28	103	12	24	4	1	2	12	14	19	.233	.325	.350	70	-5	2	1	0	.926	-3	3-28	-0.7
1938	Chi-A	24	62	14	22	4	0	6	13	9	17	.355	.437	.710	178	7	0	0	0	.979	0	1-16	0.5
Total	2	52	165	26	46	8	1	8	25	23	36	.279	.367	.485	111	2	2	1	0	.926	-3	/3-28,1-16	-0.2

■ **BEN CONROY** Conroy, Bernard Patrick b: 3/14/1871, Philadelphia, Pa. d: 11/25/37, Philadelphia, Pa. 160 lbs. Deb: 4/21/1890

YEAR	TM/L	G	AB	R	H	2B	3B	HR	RBI	BB	SO	AVG	OBP	SLG	PRO+	BR/A	SB	CS	SBR	FA	FR	G/POS	TPR
1890	Phi-a	117	404	45	69	13	1	0	21	45		.171	.262	.208	40	-30	17			.893	-6	S-74,2-42/O-1	-2.6

■ **WID CONROY** Conroy, William Edward b: 4/5/1877, Camden, N.J. d: 12/6/59, Mt.Holly, N.J. BR/TR, 5'9", 158 lbs. Deb: 4/25/01 C

YEAR	TM/L	G	AB	R	H	2B	3B	HR	RBI	BB	SO	AVG	OBP	SLG	PRO+	BR/A	SB	CS	SBR	FA	FR	G/POS	TPR
1901	Mil-A	131	503	74	129	20	6	5	64	36		.256	.316	.350	89	-7	21			.922	19	*S-118,3-12	1.9
1902	Pit-N	99	365	55	89	10	6	1	47	24		.244	.299	.312	86	-6	10			.925	8	S-95/O-3	0.8
1903	NY-A	126	503	74	137	23	12	1	45	32		.272	.322	.372	101	1	33			.919	3	*3-123/S-4	0.6
1904	NY-A	140	489	58	119	18	12	1	52	43		.243	.314	.335	100	1	30			.944	4	*3-110,S-27/O-3	1.0
1905	NY-A	101	385	55	105	19	11	2	25	32		.273	.329	.395	116	6	25			.928	7	3-48,O-25,S-17,1/2	1.5
1906	NY-A	148	567	67	139	17	10	4	54	47		.245	.303	.332	89	-8	32			.968	-1	O-97,S-49/3-2	-1.4
1907	NY-A	140	530	58	124	12	11	3	51	30		.234	.279	.315	83	-11	41			.955	10	*O-100,S-38	-0.5
1908	NY-A	141	531	44	126	22	3	1	39	14		.237	.258	.296	79	-14	23			.939	13	*3-119,2-12,O-10	0.3
1909	Was-A	139	488	44	119	13	4	1	20	37		.244	.298	.293	91	-5	24			.938	-0	*3-120,2-13/O-5,S-1	-0.2
1910	Was-A	103	351	36	89	11	3	1	27	30		.254	.314	.311	100	0	11			.961	2	3-46,O-46/2-5	0.1
1911	Was-A	106	349	40	81	11	4	2	28	20		.232	.282	.304	64	-17	12			.930	6	3-85,O-15/2-1	-1.1
Total	11	1374	5061	605	1257	176	82	22	452	345		.248	.301	.329	91	-62	262			.934	71	3-665,S-349,O/21	3.0

■ **BILL CONROY** Conroy, William Frederick "Pep" b: 1/9/1899, Chicago, Ill. d: 1/23/70, Chicago, Ill. BR/TR, 5'8.5", 160 lbs. Deb: 4/18/23

YEAR	TM/L	G	AB	R	H	2B	3B	HR	RBI	BB	SO	AVG	OBP	SLG	PRO+	BR/A	SB	CS	SBR	FA	FR	G/POS	TPR
1923	Was-A	18	60	6	8	2	2	0	2	4	9	.133	.188	.233	11	-8	0	0	0	.926	-2	3-10/1-6,O-1	-0.9

■ **BILL CONROY** Conroy, William Gordon b: 2/26/15, Bloomington, Ill. d: 11/13/97, Citrus Heights, Cal. BR/TR, 6', 185 lbs. Deb: 9/21/35

YEAR	TM/L	G	AB	R	H	2B	3B	HR	RBI	BB	SO	AVG	OBP	SLG	PRO+	BR/A	SB	CS	SBR	FA	FR	G/POS	TPR
1935	Phi-A	1	4	0	1	1	0	0	0	1	0	.250	.400	.500	133	0	0	0	0	1.000	1	/C-1	0.1
1936	Phi-A	1	2	0	1	0	0	0	0	0	1	.500	.500	.500	151	0	0	0	0	1.000	-0	/C-1	0.0
1937	Phi-A	26	60	4	12	1	1	0	3	7	9	.200	.284	.250	36	-6	1	0	0	1.000	-1	C-18/1-1	-0.6
1942	Bos-A	83	250	22	50	4	2	4	20	40	47	.200	.315	.280	66	-11	2	0	1	.971	1	C-83	-0.3
1943	Bos-A	39	89	13	16	5	0	1	6	18	19	.180	.336	.270	77	-2	0	0	0	.969	2	C-38	0.2
1944	Bos-A	19	47	6	10	2	0	0	4	11	9	.213	.362	.255	79	-1	0	0	0	.972	-0	C-19	0.0
Total	6	169	452	45	90	13	3	5	33	77	85	.199	.322	.274	66	-19	3	0	1	.974	1	C-160/1-1	-0.6

■ **BILLY CONSOLO** Consolo, William Angelo b: 8/18/34, Cleveland, Ohio BR/TR, 5'11", 180 lbs. Deb: 4/20/53 C

YEAR	TM/L	G	AB	R	H	2B	3B	HR	RBI	BB	SO	AVG	OBP	SLG	PRO+	BR/A	SB	CS	SBR	FA	FR	G/POS	TPR
1953	Bos-A	47	65	9	14	2	1	1	6	2	23	.215	.239	.323	48	-5	1	2	-1	.808	10	3-16,2-11	0.4
1954	Bos-A	91	242	23	55	7	1	1	11	33	69	.227	.325	.277	59	-13	2	1	0	.953	-3	S-50,3-18,2-12	-1.2
1955	Bos-A	8	18	4	4	0	0	0	0	5	4	.222	.391	.222	63	-1	0	0	0	.889	-3	/2-4	-0.3
1956	Bos-A	48	11	13	2	0	0	0	1	3	5	.182	.357	.182	41	-1	0	0	0	.920	8	2-25	0.7
1957	Bos-A	68	196	26	53	6	1	4	19	23	48	.270	.347	.372	91	-2	1	3	-2	.933	12	S-42,2-16/3-2	1.3
1958	Bos-A	46	72	13	9	2	1	0	5	6	14	.125	.192	.181	3	-10	0	0	0	.925	7	2-13,S-11/3-1	-0.1
1959	Bos-A	10	14	3	3	1	0	0	0	2	5	.214	.313	.286	63	-1	0	0	0	.818	-2	/S-2	-0.2
	Was-A	79	202	25	43	5	3	0	10	36	54	.213	.332	.267	67	-8	1	0	0	.952	10	S-75/2-4	0.8
	Yr	89	216	28	46	6	3	0	10	38	59	.213	.331	.269	66	-9	1	0	0	.948	9	S-77/2-4	0.6
1960	Was-A	100	174	23	36	4	2	3	15	25	29	.207	.310	.305	68	-8	1	1	-0	.938	-1	S-82,2-12/3-2	-0.5
1961	Min-A	11	5	1	0	0	0	0	0	0	1	.000	.000	.000	-95	-1	0	0	0	1.000	0	/2-3,S-3,3-1	-0.1
1962	Phi-N	13	5	3	2	0	0	0	0	0	1	.400	.400	.400	119	0	0	0	0	.000	0	/3-1	0.0
	LA-A	28	20	4	2	0	0	0	0	3	11	.100	.217	.100	-12	-3	2	0	1	.917	3	3-20/S-4,2-1	0.0
	KC-A	54	154	11	37	4	2	0	16	23	33	.240	.339	.292	68	-6	1	3	-2	.950	-1	S-48	-0.5
	Yr	82	174	15	39	4	2	0	16	26	44	.224	.325	.270	61	-9	3	3	-1	.944	2	S-52,3-20/2-1	-0.5
Total	10	603	1178	158	260	31	11	9	83	161	297	.221	.316	.289	63	-57	9	10	-3	.945	41	S-317,2-101/3-61	0.3

■ **CHARLIE CONWAY** Conway, Charles Connell b: 4/28/1886, Youngstown, Ohio d: 9/12/68, Youngstown, Ohio BR/TR, Deb: 4/15/11

YEAR	TM/L	G	AB	R	H	2B	3B	HR	RBI	BB	SO	AVG	OBP	SLG	PRO+	BR/A	SB	CS	SBR	FA	FR	G/POS	TPR
1911	Was-A	2	3	0	1	0	1	0	0	0		.333	.333	1.000	272	1	0			.000	-1	/O-2	0.0

■ **JACK CONWAY** Conway, Jack Clements b: 7/30/19, Bryan, Tex. d: 6/11/93, Waco, Tex. BR/TR, 5'11.5", 175 lbs. Deb: 9/9/41

YEAR	TM/L	G	AB	R	H	2B	3B	HR	RBI	BB	SO	AVG	OBP	SLG	PRO+	BR/A	SB	CS	SBR	FA	FR	G/POS	TPR
1941	Cle-A	2	2	0	1	0	0	0	1	0	0	.500	.500	.500	174	0	0	0	0	1.000	1	/S-2	0.1
1946	Cle-A	68	258	24	58	6	2	0	18	20	36	.225	.281	.264	56	-15	2	2	-1	.955	-7	2-50,S-14/3-3	-2.0
1947	Cle-A	34	50	3	9	2	0	0	5	3	8	.180	.226	.220	25	-5	0	0	0	.877	0	S-24/2-5,3-1	-0.5
1948	NY-N	24	49	8	12	2	1	1	3	5	10	.245	.315	.388	89	-1	0			.985	6	2-13/S-6,3-3	0.6
Total	4	128	359	35	80	10	3	1	27	28	54	.223	.279	.276	57	-21	2	2		.962	0	/2-68,S-46,3-7	-1.8

■ **OWEN CONWAY** Conway, Owen Sylvester b: 10/23/1890, New York, N.Y. d: 3/12/42, Philadelphia, Pa. TR , Deb: 6/21/15

YEAR	TM/L	G	AB	R	H	2B	3B	HR	RBI	BB	SO	AVG	OBP	SLG	PRO+	BR/A	SB	CS	SBR	FA	FR	G/POS	TPR
1915	Phi-A	4	15	2	1	0	0	0	0	0	3	.067	.067	.067	-62	-3	0			.750	1	/3-4	-0.2

■ **PETE CONWAY** Conway, Peter J. b: 10/30/1866, Burmont, Pa. d: 1/13/03, Clifton Heights, Pa. BR/TR, 5'10.5", 162 lbs. Deb: 8/10/1885 F

YEAR	TM/L	G	AB	R	H	2B	3B	HR	RBI	BB	SO	AVG	OBP	SLG	PRO+	BR/A	SB	CS	SBR	FA	FR	G/POS	TPR
1885	Buf-N	29	90	7	10	5	0	1	7	5	28	.111	.158	.200	15	-8				.889	-1	P-27/O-2,S-1,1-1	-0.2
1886	KC-N	51	194	22	47	8	2	1	18	5	34	.242	.261	.320	71	-7	3			.857	-1	O-31,P-23	-0.4
	Det-N	12	43	10	8	1	0	2	3	1	8	.186	.205	.349	64	-2	0			.846	-1	P-11/O-1	0.0
	Yr	63	237	32	55	9	2	3	21	6	42	.232	.251	.325	70	-9	3			.826	-1	P-34,O-32	-0.4

YEAR	TM/L	G	AB	R	H	2B	3B	HR	RBI	BB	SO	AVG	OBP	SLG	PRO+	BR/A	SB	CS	SBR	FA	FR	G/POS	TPR
1887	*Det-N	24	95	16	22	5	1	1	7	2	9	.232	.247	.337	59	-6	0			.979	2	P-17/O-8	-0.2
1888	Det-N	45	167	28	46	4	2	3	23	8	25	.275	.320	.377	122	4	1			.938	2	P-45/O-1	0.0
1889	Pit-N	3	10	2	1	0	0	1	2	1	3	.100	.182	.400	67	-1	1			.875	-0	/P-3,O-1	0.0
Total	5	164	599	85	134	23	5	9	60	22	107	.224	.255	.324	74	-20	5			.907	2	P-126/O-44,1-1,S-1	-0.8
■ RIP CONWAY	Conway, Richard Daniel b: 4/18/1896, White Bear Lake, Minn. d: 12/3/71, St.Paul, Minn. BL/TR, 5'6", 160 lbs. Deb: 4/16/18																						
1918	Bos-N	14	24	4	4	0	0	0	2	2	4	.167	.231	.167	23	-2	1			.810	-4	/2-5,3-1	-0.7
■ BILL CONWAY	Conway, William F. b: 11/28/1861, Lowell, Mass. d: 12/28/43, Somerville, Mass. BR/TR, 5'8", 170 lbs. Deb: 7/28/1884 F																						
1884	Phi-N	1	4	0	0	0	0	0	0	0	1	.000	.000	.000	-99	-1				1.000	0	/C-1	-0.1
1886	Bal-a	7	14	4	2	0	0	0	3	7		.143	.429	.143	84	0	0			.925	-3	/C-7	-0.2
Total	2	8	18	4	2	0	0	0	3	7	1	.111	.360	.111	52	-0	0			.936	-3	/C-8	-0.3
■ ED CONWELL	Conwell, Edward James "Irish" b: 1/29/1890, Chicago, Ill. d: 5/1/26, Chicago, Ill. BR/TR, 5'11", 155 lbs. Deb: 9/22/11																						
1911	StL-N	1	1	0	0	0	0	0	0	0	1	.000	.000	.000	-99	-0	0			.000	-0	/3-1	-0.1
■ HERB CONYERS	Conyers, Herbert Leroy b: 1/8/21, Cowgill, Mo. d: 9/16/64, Cleveland, Ohio BL/TR, 6'4", 205 lbs. Deb: 4/18/50																						
1950	Cle-A	7	9	2	3	0	0	1	1	1	2	.333	.400	.667	175	1	1	0	0	1.000	-0	/1-1	0.1
■ DALE COOGAN	Coogan, Dale Roger b: 8/14/30, Los Angeles, Cal. d: 3/8/89, Mission Viejo, Cal. BL/TL, 6'1", 190 lbs. Deb: 4/22/50																						
1950	Pit-N	53	129	19	31	6	1	1	13	17	24	.240	.338	.326	73	-5	0			.980	2	1-32	-0.3
■ DAN COOGAN	Coogan, Daniel George b: 2/16/1875, Philadelphia, Pa. d: 10/28/42, Philadelphia, Pa. 128 lbs. Deb: 4/25/1895																						
1895	Was-N	26	77	9	17	2	1	0	7	13	6	.221	.333	.273	58	-4	1			.746	-11	S-18/C-5,O-2,3-1	-1.2
■ JIM COOK	Cook, James Fitchie b: 11/10/1879, Dundee, Ill. d: 6/17/49, St.Louis, Mo. BR/TR, 5'9", 163 lbs. Deb: 7/2/03																						
1903	Chi-N	8	26	3	4	1	0	0	2	2		.154	.241	.192	25	-3	1			1.000	-2	/O-5,2-2,1-1	-0.4
■ DOC COOK	Cook, Luther Almus b: 6/24/1886, Whitt, Tex. d: 6/30/73, Lawrenceburg, Tenn. BL/TR, 6', 170 lbs. Deb: 8/7/13																						
1913	NY-A	20	72	9	19	2	1	0	1	10	4	.264	.369	.319	101	1	1			.939	1	O-20	0.0
1914	NY-A	132	470	59	133	11	3	1	40	44	60	.283	.356	.326	105	4	26	32	-11	.949	-5	*O-127	-2.0
1915	NY-A	132	476	70	129	16	5	2	33	62	43	.271	.364	.338	111	8	29	18	-2	.959	1	*O-131	0.0
1916	NY-A	4	10	0	1	0	0	0	1	0	2	.100	.100	.100	-39	-2	0			1.000	-1	/O-3	-0.3
Total	4	288	1028	138	282	29	9	3	75	116	109	.274	.359	.329	106	11	56	50		.953	-4	O-281	-2.3
■ PAUL COOK	Cook, Paul b: 5/5/1863, Caledonia, N.Y. d: 5/25/05, Rochester, N.Y. BR/TR, Deb: 9/13/1884																						
1884	Phi-N	3	12	0	1	0	0	0	0	0	2	.083	.083	.083	-50	-2				.818	-2	/C-3	-0.3
1886	Lou-a	66	262	28	54	5	2	0	14	10		.206	.235	.240	46	-17	6			.945	-9	1-43,C-21/O-2	-2.6
1887	Lou-a	61	223	34	55	4	2	0	17	11		.247	.294	.283	60	-12	15			.916	-10	C-55/1-6	-1.4
1888	Lou-a	57	185	20	34	2	0	0	13	5		.184	.222	.195	35	-13	9			.901	-14	C-53/O-4,S-1	-2.1
1889	Lou-a	81	286	34	65	10	1	0	15	15	48	.227	.287	.269	60	-15	11			.925	5	C-74/O-7,S-1,1-1	-0.3
1890	Bro-P	58	218	32	55	3	3	0	31	14	18	.252	.303	.294	56	-14	7			.890	-0	C-36,1-21/O-1	-1.0
1891	Lou-a	45	153	21	35	3	1	0	23	11	17	.229	.285	.261	57	-9	4			.909	-9	C-35,1-10	-1.4
	StL-a	7	25	3	5	0	0	0	1	1	2	.200	.259	.200	28	-3	0			.921	3	/C-7	0.1
	Yr	52	178	24	40	3	1	0	24	12	19	.225	.281	.253	52	-11	4			.912	-6	C-42,1-10	-1.3
Total	7	378	1364	172	304	27	9	0	114	67	87	.223	.270	.256	52	-84	52			.906	-35	C-284/1-81,O-14,S-2	-9.0
■ CLIFF COOK	Cook, Raymond Clifford b: 8/20/36, Dallas, Tex. BR/TR, 6', 188 lbs. Deb: 9/9/59																						
1959	Cin-N	9	21	3	8	2	1	0	5	2	8	.381	.435	.571	161	2	1	0	0	.909	1	/3-9	0.3
1960	Cin-N	54	149	9	31	7	0	3	13	8	51	.208	.248	.315	52	-10	0	0	0	.954	4	3-47/O-4	-0.7
1961	Cin-N	4	5	0	0	0	0	0	0	0	4	.000	.000	.000	-99	-1	0	0	0	1.000	0	/3-1	-0.1
1962	Cin-N	6	5	0	0	0	0	0	0	0	2	.000	.000	.000	-97	-1	0	0	0	1.000	-0	/3-4	-0.2
	NY-N	40	112	12	26	6	1	2	9	4	34	.232	.277	.357	68	-5	1	0	0	.875	-8	3-16,O-10	-1.4
	Yr	46	117	12	26	6	1	2	9	4	36	.222	.266	.342	61	-7	1	0	0	.878	-8	3-20,O-10	-1.6
1963	NY-N	50	106	9	15	2	1	2	8	12	37	.142	.229	.236	34	-9	0	1	-1	1.000	4	O-21/3-9,1-5	-0.7
Total	5	163	398	33	80	17	3	7	35	26	136	.201	.255	.312	54	-25	2	1	0	.937	0	/3-86,O-35,1-5	-2.8
■ DUSTY COOKE	Cooke, Allen Lindsey b: 6/23/07, Swepsonville, N.C d: 11/21/87, Raleigh, N.C. BL/TR, 6'1", 205 lbs. Deb: 4/15/30 MC																						
1930	NY-A	92	216	43	55	12	3	6	29	32	61	.255	.353	.421	100	0	4	6	-2	.978	-6	O-73	-1.1
1931	NY-A	27	39	10	13	1	0	1	6	8	11	.333	.447	.436	141	3	4	1	1	1.000	-1	O-11	0.2
1932	NY-A	3	0	1	0	0	0	0	0	1	0	—	1.000	—	191	0	0	0	0	.000	0	H	0.0
1933	Bos-A	119	454	86	133	35	10	5	54	67	71	.293	.386	.447	121	15	7	5	-1	.956	-18	*O-118	-0.9
1934	Bos-A	74	168	34	41	8	5	1	26	36	25	.244	.377	.369	87	-2	7	2	1	.976	-4	O-44	-0.7
1935	Bos-A	100	294	51	90	18	6	3	34	46	24	.306	.400	.439	109	5	6	8	-3	.972	-6	O-82	-0.6
1936	Bos-A	111	341	58	93	20	3	6	47	72	48	.273	.401	.402	93	-2	4	3	-1	.972	2	O-91	-0.4
1938	Cin-N	82	233	41	64	15	1	2	33	28	36	.275	.355	.373	103	2	0			.963	3	O-51	0.3
Total	8	608	1745	324	489	109	28	24	229	290	276	.280	.384	.416	106	21	32	25		.969	-30	O-470	-3.2
■ FRED COOKE	Cooke, Frederick B. b: Paulding, Ohio Deb: 7/30/1897																						
1897	Cle-N	5	17	2	5	2	0	0	3	3		.294	.400	.412	109	0	0			.857	1	/O-5	0.1
■ BRENT COOKSON	Cookson, Brent Adam b: 9/7/69, Van Nuys, Cal. BR/TR, 5'11", 200 lbs. Deb: 8/12/95																						
1995	KC-A	22	35	2	5	1	0	0	5	2	7	.143	.189	.171	-5	-5	1	0	0	1.000	-2	O-12/D-2	-0.7
■ SCOTT COOLBAUGH	Coolbaugh, Scott Robert b: 6/13/66, Binghamton, N.Y. BR/TR, 5'11", 185 lbs. Deb: 9/2/89																						
1989	Tex-A	25	51	7	14	1	0	2	7	4	12	.275	.327	.412	105	0	0	0	0	.958	5	3-23/D-2	0.5
1990	Tex-A	67	180	21	36	6	0	2	13	15	47	.200	.265	.267	49	-12	1	0	0	.941	7	3-66	-0.5
1991	SD-N	60	180	12	39	8	1	2	15	19	45	.217	.295	.306	67	-8	0	3	-2	.952	4	3-54	-0.6
1994	StL-N	15	21	4	4	0	0	2	6	1	4	.190	.227	.476	79	-1	0	0	0	1.000	0	/1-4,3-4	-0.1
Total	4	167	432	44	93	15	1	8	41	39	108	.215	.283	.310	65	-20	1	3	-2	.949	16	3-147/1-4,D-2	-0.7
■ DUFF COOLEY	Cooley, Duff Gordon "Dick" b: 3/29/1873, Leavenworth, Kan. d: 8/9/37, Dallas, Tex. BL/TR, 5'11", 158 lbs. Deb: 7/27/1893																						
1893	StL-N	29	107	20	37	2	3	0	21	8	9	.346	.391	.421	115	2	8			.947	-9	O-15,C-10/S-5	-0.5
1894	StL-N	54	206	35	61	3	1	1	21	12	16	.296	.335	.335	62	-13	7			.833	-11	O-39,3-13/S-1,1-1	-2.0
1895	StL-N	132	563	106	191	9	20	7	75	36	29	.339	.382	.464	119	15	27			.936	11	*O-124/3-5,S-3,C-1	1.3
1896	StL-N	40	166	29	51	5	3	0	13	7	3	.307	.335	.373	90	-3	12			.959	-1	O-40	-0.6
	Phi-N	64	287	63	88	6	4	2	22	18	16	.307	.348	.376	92	-4	18			.901	-5	O-64	-1.1
	Yr	104	453	92	139	11	7	2	35	25	19	.307	.343	.375	91	-0	30			.923	-5	*O-104	-1.7
1897	Phi-N	133	566	124	186	14	13	4	40	51		.329	.386	.420	116	14	31			.960	7	*O-131/1-2	0.9
1898	Phi-N	149	629	123	196	24	12	4	55	48		.312	.364	.407	126	21	17			.943	4	*O-149	1.2
1899	Phi-N	94	406	75	112	15	8	1	31	29		.276	.330	.360	92	-5	15			.971	-5	1-79,O-14/2-1	-1.0
1900	Pit-N	66	249	30	50	8	1	0	22	14		.201	.243	.241	34	-23	9			.989	-5	1-66	-2.6
1901	Bos-N	63	240	27	62	13	3	0	27	14		.258	.302	.338	78	-7	5			.943	2	O-53,1-10	-0.9
1902	Bos-N	135	548	73	162	26	8	0	58	34		.296	.339	.372	118	11	27			.952	-6	*O-127/1-7	-0.4
1903	Bos-N	138	553	76	160	26	10	1	70	44		.289	.342	.378	109	6	27			.952	-5	*O-126,1-13	-0.7
1904	Bos-N	122	467	41	127	18	7	5	70	24		.272	.312	.373	115	7	14			.976	-7	*O-116/1-6	-0.8
1905	Det-A	97	377	25	93	11	9	1	32	26		.247	.297	.332	99	-1	7			.959	7	O-96	0.2
Total	13	1316	5364	847	1576	180	102	26	557	365	73	.294	.341	.380	104	20	224			.945	-22	*O-1094,1-184/3CS2	-7.0
■ CECIL COOMBS	Coombs, Cecil Lysander b: 3/18/1888, Moweaqua, Ill. d: 11/25/75, Fort Worth, Tex. BR/TR, 5'9", 160 lbs. Deb: 8/7/14																						
1914	Chi-A	7	23	1	4	1	0	0	1	1	7	.174	.208	.217	28	-2	0	1	-1	1.000	1	/O-7	-0.3

YEAR	TM/L	G	AB	R	H	2B	3B	HR	RBI	BB	SO	AVG	OBP	SLG	PRO+	BR/A	SB	CS	SBR	FA	FR	G/POS	TPR
■ JACK COOMBS	Coombs, John Wesley "Colby Jack" b: 11/18/1882, LeGrand, Iowa d: 4/15/57, Palestine, Tex. BB/TR, 6', 185 lbs. Deb: 7/5/06 MC																						
1906	Phi-A	24	67	9	16	2	0	0	3	1		.239	.261	.269	64	-3	2			.967	-0	P-23	0.0
1907	Phi-A	24	48	4	8	0	0	1	4	0		.167	.167	.229	25	-4	1			.979	0	P-23	0.0
1908	Phi-A	78	220	24	56	9	5	1	23	9		.255	.287	.355	101	-1	6			.990	6	O-47,P-26/1-1	0.4
1909	Phi-A	37	83	4	14	4	0	0	10	4		.169	.216	.217	36	-6	1			.973	-0	P-30	0.0
1910	*Phi-A	46	132	20	29	3	0	0	9	7		.220	.270	.242	61	-6	3			**.990**	-5	P-45	0.0
1911	*Phi-A	52	141	31	45	6	1	2	23	8		.319	.356	.418	118	3	5			.913	-3	P-47	0.0
1912	Phi-A	56	110	10	28	2	0	0	13	14		.255	.344	.273	80	-2	1			**1.000**	-1	P-40	0.0
1913	Phi-A	2	3	1	1	1	0	0	0	0	2	.333	.333	.667	195	0	0			.500	-0	/P-2	0.0
1914	Phi-A	5	11	0	3	1	0	0	2	1	1	.273	.333	.364	114	0	0	1	-1	1.000	-1	/P-2,O-2	-0.1
1915	Bro-N	29	75	8	21	1	1	0	5	2	17	.280	.299	.320	86	-1	0	1	-1	.980	-4	P-29	0.0
1916	*Bro-N	27	61	2	11	2	0	0	3	2	10	.180	.206	.213	28	-5	0			**1.000**	-6	P-27	0.0
1917	Bro-N	32	44	4	10	0	1	0	2	4	9	.227	.292	.273	72	-1	1			.971	-3	P-31	0.0
1918	Bro-N	46	113	6	19	3	2	0	3	7	5	.168	.223	.230	38	-8	1			.962	-7	P-27,O-13	-0.8
1920	Det-A	2	2	0	0	0	0	0	0	0	0	.000	.000	.000	-99	-1	0	0	0	1.000	-0	/P-2	0.0
Total	14	460	1110	123	261	34	10	4	100	59	44	.235	.278	.295	74	-35	21	2		.966	-24	P-354/O-62,1-1	-0.5
■ RON COOMER	Coomer, Ronald Bryan b: 11/18/66, Crest Hill, Ill. BR/TR, 5'11", 195 lbs. Deb: 8/1/95																						
1995	Min-A	37	101	15	26	3	1	5	19	9	11	.257	.324	.455	100	-0	0	1	-1	.993	1	1-22,3-13/O-1,D-4	-0.1
1996	Min-A	95	233	34	69	12	1	12	41	17	24	.296	.344	.511	110	3	3	0	1	.993	1	1-57,O-23/3-9,D-3	0.0
1997	Min-A	140	523	63	156	30	2	13	85	22	91	.298	.327	.438	96	-4	4	3	-1	.966	-2	*3-119/1-9,O-7,D-7	-0.6
1998	Min-A	137	529	54	146	22	1	15	72	18	72	.276	.300	.406	81	-16	2	2	-1	.972	-5	3-76,1-54,D-13,/O-3	-2.5
Total	4	409	1386	166	397	67	5	45	217	66	198	.286	.319	.439	93	-17	9	6	-1	.968	-6	3-217,1-142/O-34,D	-3.2
■ WILLIAM COON	Coon, William K. b: 3/21/1855, Pennsylvania d: 8/30/15, Burlington, N.J. Deb: 9/4/1875																						
1875	Ath-n	4	12	1	2	0	0	0	1	0	0	.167	.167	.167	15	-1	1	0	0	.810	-0	/C-4,O-1	-0.1
1876	Phi-N	54	220	30	50	5	1	0	22	2	4	.227	.234	.259	65	-8				.761	-15	O-29,C-18/3-4,2P	-2.0
■ JIMMY COONEY	Cooney, James Edward "Scoops" b: 8/24/1894, Cranston, R.I. d: 8/7/91, Warwick, R.I. BR/TR, 5'11", 160 lbs. Deb: 9/22/17 F																						
1917	Bos-A	11	36	4	8	1	0	0	3	6	2	.222	.333	.250	79	-1	0			1.000	5	2-10/S-1	0.5
1919	NY-N	5	14	3	3	0	0	0	1	0	0	.214	.214	.214	29	-1	0			1.000	-1	/S-4,2-1	-0.2
1924	StL-N	110	383	44	113	20	8	1	57	20	20	.295	.330	.397	96	-3	12	10	-2	.969	1	S-99/3-7,2-1	0.6
1925	StL-N	54	187	27	51	11	2	0	18	4	5	.273	.292	.353	62	-11	1	3	-2	.976	-11	S-37,2-15/O-1	-1.8
1926	Chi-N	141	513	52	129	18	5	1	47	23	10	.251	.288	.312	61	-29	11			**.972**	19	*S-141	0.6
1927	Chi-N	33	132	16	32	2	0	0	6	8	7	.242	.286	.258	46	-10	1			.973	-2	S-33	-0.9
	Phi-N	76	259	33	70	12	1	0	15	13	9	.270	.305	.324	68	-12	4			.980	17	S-74	1.2
	Yr	109	391	49	102	14	1	0	21	21	16	.261	.299	.302	61	-22	5			**.978**	15	*S-107	0.3
1928	Bos-N	18	51	2	7	0	0	0	3	2	5	.137	.170	.137	-20	-9	1			.982	2	S-11/2-4	-0.6
Total	7	448	1575	181	413	64	16	2	150	76	58	.262	.298	.327	67	-75	30	13		.974	30	S-400/2-31,3-7,O-1	-0.6
■ JIMMY COONEY	Cooney, James Joseph b: 7/9/1865, Cranston, R.I. d: 7/1/03, Cranston, R.I. BB/TR, 5'9", 155 lbs. Deb: 4/19/1890 F																						
1890	Chi-N	135	574	114	156	19	10	4	52	73	23	.272	.360	.361	106	5	45			**.936**	1	*S-135/C-1	1.2
1891	Chi-N	118	465	84	114	15	3	0	42	48	17	.245	.318	.290	78	-12	21			**.917**	8	*S-118	0.3
1892	Chi-N	65	238	18	41	1	0	0	20	23	5	.172	.248	.176	29	-20	10			.912	-8	S-65	-2.3
	Was-N	6	25	5	4	0	1	0	4	4	3	.160	.276	.240	58	-1	1			.862	-3	/S-6	-0.4
	Yr	71	263	23	45	1	1	0	24	27	8	.171	.251	.183	31	-21	11			.908	-11	S-71	-2.7
Total	3	324	1302	221	315	35	14	4	118	148	48	.242	.324	.300	82	-29	77			.923	-2	S-324/C-1	-1.2
■ JOHNNY COONEY	Cooney, John Walter b: 3/18/01, Cranston, R.I. d: 7/8/86, Sarasota, Fla. BR/TL, 5'10", 165 lbs. Deb: 4/19/21 FMC																						
1921	Bos-N	8	5	0	1	0	0	0	0	0	1	.200	.200	.200	7	-1	0	0	0	1.000	0	/P-8	0.0
1922	Bos-N	4	8	0	0	0	0	0	0	0	1	.000	.000	.000	-99	-2	0	0	0	1.000	0	/P-4	0.0
1923	Bos-N	42	66	7	25	1	0	0	3	4	2	.379	.414	.394	119	2	0	1	-1	1.000	0	P-23,O-11/1-1	0.2
1924	Bos-N	55	130	10	33	2	1	0	4	9	5	.254	.302	.285	61	-7	0	4	-2	.962	0	P-34,O-16/1-1	-0.4
1925	Bos-N	54	103	17	33	7	0	0	13	3	6	.320	.346	.388	96	-1	1	0	0	.949	0	P-31/1-3,O-1	-0.1
1926	Bos-N	64	126	17	38	3	2	0	18	13	7	.302	.367	.357	105	1	6			.996	5	1-31,P-19/O-1	0.3
1927	Bos-N	10	1	3	0	0	0	0	0	0	0	.000	.000	.000	-99	-0	0			.000	0	H	0.0
1928	Bos-N	33	41	2	7	0	0	0	2	4	3	.171	.244	.171	11	-5	0			1.000	2	P-24/1-3,O-2	-0.2
1929	Bos-N	41	72	10	23	4	1	0	6	3	3	.319	.355	.403	91	-1	1			1.000	2	O-16,P-14	-0.1
1930	Bos-N	4	3	0	0	0	0	0	0	0	0	.000	.000	.000	-99	-1	0			1.000	1	/P-2	0.0
1935	Bro-N	10	29	3	9	0	1	0	1	3	2	.310	.375	.379	106	0	0			1.000	-1	O-10	-0.1
1936	Bro-N	130	507	71	143	17	5	0	30	24	15	.282	.315	.335	74	-18	3			**.994**	8	*O-130	-1.6
1937	Bro-N	120	430	61	126	18	5	0	37	22	10	.293	.327	.358	85	-9	5			.976	6	*O-111/1-2	-0.7
1938	Bos-N	120	432	45	117	25	5	0	17	22	12	.271	.308	.352	90	-8	2			.982	-10	*O-110,1-13	-2.2
1939	Bos-N	118	368	39	101	8	1	2	27	21	8	.274	.317	.318	77	-12	2			.992	-6	*O-116/1-2	-2.2
1940	Bos-N	108	365	40	116	14	3	0	21	25	9	.318	.363	.373	109	5	4			.992	-1	O-99/1-7	-0.1
1941	Bos-N	123	442	52	141	25	2	0	29	27	15	.319	.358	.385	114	8	3			**.996**	4	*O-111/1-4	0.5
1942	Bos-N	74	198	23	41	6	0	0	7	23	5	.207	.290	.237	56	-10	2			.984	-14	O-54,1-23	-3.1
1943	Bro-N	37	34	7	7	0	0	0	2	4	3	.206	.289	.206	44	-2	1			1.000	-0	/1-3,O-2	-0.3
1944	Bro-N	7	4	0	3	0	0	0	1	0	0	.750	.750	.750	329	1	0			1.000	-0	/O-2	0.1
	NY-A	10	8	1	1	0	0	0	1	1	0	.125	.222	.125	1	-1	0	0	0	1.000	-0	/O-2	-0.1
Total	20	1172	3372	408	965	130	26	2	219	208	107	.286	.329	.342	87	-63	30	5		.988	-6	O-794,P-159/1-93	-10.1
■ PHIL COONEY	Cooney, Philip Clarence (b: Philip Clarence Cohen) b: 9/14/1882, New York, N.Y. d: 10/6/57, New York, N.Y. BL/TR, 5'8", 155 lbs. Deb: 9/27/05																						
1905	NY-A	1	3	0	0	0	0	0	0	0		.000	.000	.000	-90	-1	0			1.000	-0	/3-1	-0.1
■ BILL COONEY	Cooney, William A. "Cush" b: 4/7/1883, Boston, Mass. d: 11/6/28, Roxbury, Mass. TR , Deb: 9/22/09																						
1909	Bos-N	5	10	0	3	0	0	0	0	0		.300	.300	.300	82	-0	0			.500	-0	/P-3,2-1,S-1	0.0
1910	Bos-N	8	12	2	3	0	0	0	1	2	0	.250	.357	.250	74	-0	0			.000	-1	/O-2	-0.1
Total	2	13	22	2	6	0	0	0	1	2	0	.273	.333	.273	78	-1	0			.500	-1	/P-3,O-2,S-1,2-1	-0.1
■ CECIL COOPER	Cooper, Cecil Celester b: 12/20/49, Brenham, Tex. BL/TL, 6'2", 190 lbs. Deb: 9/8/71																						
1971	Bos-A	14	42	9	13	4	1	0	3	5	4	.310	.396	.452	130	2	1	0	0	.988	-2	1-11	-0.1
1972	Bos-A	12	17	0	4	1	0	0	2	2	5	.235	.316	.294	78	-0	0	0	0	1.000	-1	/1-3	-0.1
1973	Bos-A	30	101	12	24	2	0	3	11	7	12	.238	.287	.347	73	-4	1	2	-1	.984	-0	1-29	-0.7
1974	Bos-A	121	414	55	114	24	1	8	43	32	74	.275	.329	.396	101	-0	2	5	-2	.983	-1	1-74,D-41	-1.0
1975	*Bos-A	106	305	49	95	17	6	14	44	19	33	.311	.358	.544	140	14	1	4	-2	.995	2	D-54,1-35	1.2
1976	Bos-A	123	451	66	127	22	6	15	78	16	62	.282	.308	.457	109	2	7	1	2	.994	-1	1-66,D-53	-0.3
1977	Mil-A	160	643	86	193	31	7	20	78	28	110	.300	.329	.463	113	10	13	8	-1	.992	5	*1-148,D-10	0.5
1978	Mil-A	107	407	60	127	23	2	13	54	32	72	.312	.362	.474	133	17	3	4	-2	.988	2	1-84,D-19	1.2
1979	Mil-A★	150	590	83	182	**44**	1	24	106	56	77	.308	.368	.508	134	27	15	3	3	.993	-8	*1-135,D-15	1.2
1980	Mil-A★	153	622	96	219	33	4	25	**122**	39	42	.352	.392	.539	157	47	17	6	2	**.997**	4	*1-142,D-11	4.3
1981	*Mil-A	106	416	70	133	**35**	1	12	60	28	30	.320	.367	.495	154	27	5	4	-1	.992	-0	*1-101/D-5	2.1
1982	*Mil-A★	155	654	104	205	38	3	32	121	32	53	.313	.345	.528	145	36	2	3	-1	.997	-1	*1-154/D-1	2.5
1983	Mil-A★	160	661	106	203	37	3	30	**126**	37	63	.307	.345	.508	142	34	2	1	0	.993	-10	*1-158/D-2	1.5
1984	Mil-A	148	603	63	166	28	3	11	67	27	59	.275	.309	.386	95	-6	8	2	1	.991	3	*1-122,D-26	-1.0
1985	Mil-A★	154	631	82	185	39	8	16	99	30	77	.293	.327	.456	112	9	10	3	1	.986	-2	*1-123,D-30	0.0
1986	Mil-A	134	542	46	140	24	1	12	75	41	87	.258	.312	.373	83	-13	1	2	-1	.988	-4	1-90,D-44	-2.6
1987	Mil-A	63	250	25	62	13	0	6	36	17	51	.248	.296	.372	74	-10	1	1	-0	.000	0	D-62	-1.1
Total	17	1896	7349	1012	2192	415	47	241	1125	448	911	.298	.340	.466	121	193	89	49	-3	.992	-13	*1-1475,D-373	7.6

YEAR	TM/L	G	AB	R	H	2B	3B	HR	RBI	BB	SO	AVG	OBP	SLG	PRO+	BR/A	SB	CS	SBR	FA	FR	G/POS	TPR
■ **CLAUDE COOPER**	Cooper, Claude William b: 4/1/1892, Troup, Tex. d: 1/21/74, Plainview, Tex. BL/TL, 5′9″, 158 lbs. Deb: 4/14/13																						
1913	*NY-N	27	30	11	9	4	0	0	4	4	6	.300	.382	.433	132	1	3			.895	-5	O-15	-0.4
1914	Bro-F	113	399	56	96	14	11	2	25	26	60	.241	.294	.346	74	-22	25			.926	-1	*O-101	-2.9
1915	Bro-F	153	527	75	155	26	12	2	63	77	78	.294	.388	.400	123	11	31			.958	18	*O-121,1-32	2.4
1916	Phi-N	56	104	9	20	2	0	0	11	7	15	.192	.250	.212	41	-7	1			.945	-3	O-29/1-1	-1.3
1917	Phi-N	24	29	5	3	1	0	0	1	5	4	.103	.235	.138	15	-3	0			.923	-4	O-12	-0.9
Total	5	373	1089	156	283	47	23	4	104	119	163	.260	.338	.356	95	-19	60			.943	5	O-278/1-33	-3.1
■ **GARY COOPER**	Cooper, Gary Clifton b: 8/13/64, Lynwood, Cal. BR/TR, 6′1″, 200 lbs. Deb: 9/15/91																						
1991	Hou-N	9	16	1	4	1	0	0	2	3	6	.250	.368	.313	99	0	0	0	0	.833	-2	/3-4	-0.2
■ **GARY COOPER**	Cooper, Gary Nathaniel b: 12/22/56, Savannah, Ga. BB/TR, 6′3″, 175 lbs. Deb: 8/25/80																						
1980	Atl-N	21	2	3	0	0	0	0	0	0	1	.000	.000	.000	-97	-1	2	1	0	1.000	-4	O-13	-0.4
■ **PAT COOPER**	Cooper, Orge Patterson b: 11/26/17, Albemarle, N.C. d: 3/15/93, Charlotte, N.C. BR/TR, 6′3″, 180 lbs. Deb: 5/11/46																						
1946	Phi-A	1	0	0	0	0	0	0	0	0	0	—	—	—	—	0	0	0	0	.000	-0	/P-1	0.0
1947	Phi-A	13	16	0	4	2	0	0	3	0	5	.250	.250	.375	71	-1	0	0	0	1.000	-0	/1-1	-0.1
Total	2	14	16	0	4	2	0	0	3	0	5	.250	.250	.375	71	-1	0	0	0	1.000	-0	/1-1,P-1	-0.1
■ **SCOTT COOPER**	Cooper, Scott Kendrick b: 10/13/67, St.Louis, Mo. BL/TR, 6′3″, 205 lbs. Deb: 9/5/90																						
1990	Bos-A	2	1	0	0	0	0	0	0	0	1	.000	.000	.000	-96	-0	0	0	0	.000	0	/H	0.0
1991	Bos-A	14	35	6	16	4	2	0	7	2	2	.457	.486	.686	210	5	0	0	0	.933	2	3-13	0.7
1992	Bos-A	123	337	34	93	21	0	5	33	37	33	.276	.348	.383	98	-1	1	1	-0	.990	8	1-62,3-47/2-1,SD	0.4
1993	Bos-A★	156	526	67	147	29	3	9	63	58	81	.279	.357	.397	96	-2	5	2	0	.937	-17	*3-154/1-2,S-1	-1.8
1994	Bos-A★	104	369	49	104	16	4	13	53	30	65	.282	.338	.453	97	-2	0	3	-2	.944	8	*3-104	0.3
1995	StL-N	118	374	29	86	18	2	3	40	49	85	.230	.324	.313	69	-16	0	3	-2	.945	9	*3-110	-0.8
1997	KC-A	75	159	12	32	6	1	3	15	17	32	.201	.287	.308	54	-11	1	1	-0	1.000	-4	3-39/1-8,D-5	-1.4
Total	7	592	1801	197	478	94	12	33	211	193	299	.265	.340	.386	89	-27	7	10	-4	.948	7	3-467/1-72,D-7,S2	-2.6
■ **WALKER COOPER**	Cooper, William Walker "Walk" b: 1/8/15, Atherton, Mo. d: 4/11/91, Scottsdale, Ariz. BR/TR, 6′3″, 210 lbs. Deb: 9/25/40 FC																						
1940	StL-N	6	19	3	6	1	0	0	2	2	2	.316	.381	.368	102	0	1			1.000	-0	/C-6	0.0
1941	StL-N	68	200	19	49	9	1	1	20	13	14	.245	.291	.315	66	-9	1			.966	4	C-63	0.1
1942	*StL-N★	125	438	58	123	32	7	7	65	29	29	.281	.327	.434	113	5	4			.972	3	*C-115	1.8
1943	*StL-N★	122	449	52	143	30	4	9	81	19	19	.318	.349	.463	128	14	1			.975	-3	*C-112	2.0
1944	*StL-N★	112	397	56	126	25	5	13	72	20	19	.317	.352	.504	136	17	4			.980	4	C-97	2.7
1945	StL-N	4	18	3	7	0	0	0	1	0	1	.389	.389	.389	114	0	0			.966	1	/C-4	0.2
1946	NY-N★	87	280	29	75	10	1	8	46	17	12	.268	.310	.396	99	-2	0			.972	-12	C-73	-1.0
1947	NY-N★	140	515	79	157	24	8	35	122	24	43	.305	.339	.586	141	25	2			.979	-9	*C-132	2.4
1948	NY-N★	91	290	40	77	12	0	16	54	28	29	.266	.332	.472	115	5	1			.979	-13	C-79	-0.2
1949	NY-N	42	147	14	31	4	2	4	21	7	8	.211	.261	.347	62	-8	0			.982	-2	C-40	-0.8
	Cin-N☆	82	307	34	86	9	2	16	62	21	24	.280	.330	.479	113	4	0			.978	-3	C-77	0.6
	Yr	124	454	48	117	13	4	20	83	28	32	.258	.308	.436	97	-4	0			.979	-5	*C-117	-0.2
1950	Cin-N	15	47	3	9	3	0	0	4	0	5	.191	.191	.255	16	-6	0			.972	1	C-13	-0.4
	Bos-N☆	102	337	52	111	19	3	14	60	30	26	.329	.389	.528	148	23	1			.973	-5	C-88	2.1
	Yr	117	384	55	120	22	3	14	64	30	31	.313	.367	.495	132	16	1			.973	-4	*C-101	1.7
1951	Bos-N	109	342	42	107	14	1	18	59	28	18	.313	.367	.518	145	20	1	1	-0	.981	-2	C-90	2.2
1952	Bos-N	102	349	33	82	12	1	10	55	22	32	.235	.282	.361	80	-11	1	0	0	.983	-4	C-89	-1.0
1953	Mil-N	53	137	12	30	6	0	3	16	12	15	.219	.287	.328	64	-8	1	0	0	.983	-5	C-35	-1.0
1954	Pit-N	14	15	0	3	2	0	0	1	2	1	.200	.294	.333	64	-1	0	0	0	1.000	-0	/C-2	-0.1
	Chi-N	57	158	21	49	10	2	7	32	21	23	.310	.398	.532	138	9	0	0	0	.978	-2	C-48	0.9
	Yr	71	173	21	52	12	2	7	33	23	24	.301	.389	.514	132	8	0	0	0	.978	-2	C-50	0.8
1955	Chi-N	54	111	11	31	8	1	7	15	6	19	.279	.322	.559	128	4	0	0	0	.961	-11	C-31	-0.6
1956	StL-N	40	68	5	18	5	1	2	14	3	8	.265	.296	.456	98	-0	0	0	0	.984	-3	C-16	-0.3
1957	StL-N	48	78	7	21	5	1	3	10	5	10	.269	.313	.474	106	0	0	0	0	.957	-2	C-13	-0.1
Total	18	1473	4702	573	1341	240	40	173	812	309	357	.285	.332	.464	116	82	18	1		.977	-63	*C-1223	9.3
■ **ALEX CORA**	Cora, Jose Alexander b: 10/18/75, Caguas, P.R. BL/TR, 6′, 180 lbs. Deb: 6/7/98 F																						
1998	LA-N	29	33	1	4	0	1	0	0	2	8	.121	.194	.182	-2	-5	0	0	0	.956	6	S-21/2-4	0.1
■ **JOEY CORA**	Cora, Jose Manuel (Amaro) b: 5/14/65, Caguas, P.R. BB/TR, 5′8″, 152 lbs. Deb: 4/6/87																						
1987	SD-N	77	241	23	57	7	2	0	13	28	26	.237	.319	.282	63	-12	15	11	-2	.975	-2	2-66/S-6	-1.3
1989	SD-N	12	19	5	6	1	0	0	1	1	0	.316	.350	.368	105	0	1	0	0	.960	2	/S-7,3-2,2-1	0.3
1990	SD-N	51	100	12	27	3	0	0	2	6	9	.270	.311	.300	68	-4	8	3	1	.833	-3	S-21,2-15/C-1	-0.6
1991	Chi-A	100	228	37	55	2	3	0	18	20	21	.241	.316	.276	67	-10	11	6	-0	.970	-9	2-80/S-5,D-2	-1.8
1992	Chi-A	68	122	27	30	7	1	0	9	22	13	.246	.378	.320	99	1	10	3	1	.984	5	2-28,D-18/S-6,3-5	0.7
1993	*Chi-A	153	579	95	155	15	13	2	51	67	63	.268	.353	.349	91	-5	20	8	1	.974	-16	*2-151/3-3	-1.5
1994	Chi-A	90	312	55	86	13	4	2	30	38	32	.276	.358	.362	88	-4	8	4	0	.978	-13	2-84/D-1	-1.3
1995	*Sea-A	120	427	64	127	19	2	3	39	37	31	.297	.362	.372	91	-5	18	7	1	.955	-27	*2-112/S-1,D-1	-2.2
1996	Sea-A	144	530	90	154	37	6	6	45	35	32	.291	.343	.417	91	-8	5	5	-2	.979	-20	*2-140/3-1	-1.9
1997	*Sea-A★	149	574	105	172	40	4	11	54	53	49	.300	.364	.441	110	9	6	7	-2	.973	-17	*2-142	-0.2
1998	Sea-A	131	519	95	147	23	6	6	26	62	50	.283	.364	.385	95	-2	13	5	1	.962	-38	*2-130	-2.9
	*Cle-A	24	83	16	19	4	0	0	6	11	9	.229	.326	.277	57	-5	2	1	0	.986	-12	2-21	-1.5
	Yr	155	602	111	166	27	6	6	32	73	59	.276	.359	.370	90	-7	15	6	1	.965	-49	*2-151	-4.4
Total	11	1119	3734	624	1035	171	41	30	294	380	335	.277	.351	.369	90	-45	117	60	-1	.971	-150	2-970/S-46,D-22,3C	-14.2
■ **GENE CORBETT**	Corbett, Eugene Louis b: 10/25/13, Winona, Minn. BL/TR, 6′1.5″, 190 lbs. Deb: 9/19/36																						
1936	Phi-N	6	21	1	3	0	0	0	2	2	3	.143	.217	.143	-1	-3	0			1.000	-1	/1-6	-0.4
1937	Phi-N	7	12	4	4	2	0	0	1	0	0	.333	.333	.500	114	0	0			.800	-1	/3-3,2-1	-0.1
1938	Phi-N	24	75	7	6	1	0	2	7	6	11	.080	.148	.173	-12	-12	0			.995	-1	1-22	-1.5
Total	3	37	108	12	13	3	0	2	10	8	14	.120	.181	.204	5	-15	0			.996	-2	/1-28,3-3,2-1	-2.0
■ **CLAUDE CORBITT**	Corbitt, Claude Elliott b: 7/21/15, Sunbury, N.C. d: 5/1/78, Cincinnati, Ohio BR/TR, 5′10″, 170 lbs. Deb: 9/23/45																						
1945	Bro-N	2	4	1	2	0	0	0	0	1	0	.500	.600	.500	209	1	0			1.000	0	/3-2	0.1
1946	Cin-N	82	274	25	68	10	1	1	16	23	13	.248	.309	.303	77	-9	3			.947	-13	S-77	-1.9
1948	Cin-N	87	258	24	66	11	0	0	18	14	16	.256	.297	.298	64	-13	4			.973	-8	2-52,3-16,S-11	-1.8
1949	Cin-N	44	94	10	17	1	0	0	3	9	1	.181	.252	191	20	-10	1			.084	-6	S-10,2-17/3-1	-1.5
Total	4	215	630	60	153	22	1	1	37	47	30	.243	.297	.286	63	-31	8			.956	-26	S-106/2-69,3-19	-5.1
■ **ART CORCORAN**	Corcoran, Arthur Andrew "Bunny" b: 11/23/1894, Roxbury, Mass. d: 7/27/58, Chelsea, Mass. TR , Deb: 9/9/15																						
1915	Phi-A	1	4	0	0	0	0	0	0	0	2	.000	.000	.000	-99	-1	0			1.000	-0	/3-1	-0.1
■ **JOHN CORCORAN**	Corcoran, John A. b: 1873, Cincinnati, Ohio d: 11/2/01, Cincinnati, Ohio TL , Deb: 9/17/1895																						
1895	Pit-N	6	20	0	3	0	0	0	1	0	2	.150	.150	.150	-24	-4	0			.895	-1	/S-4,3-2	-0.4
■ **JACK CORCORAN**	Corcoran, John H. b: 1860, Lowell, Mass. Deb: 5/1/1884																						
1884	Bro-a	52	185	17	39	4	3	0		8		.211	.251	.265	68	-6				.873	-9	C-38/O-9,2-4,S-2,P	-1.1
■ **LARRY CORCORAN**	Corcoran, Lawrence J. b: 8/10/1859, Brooklyn, N.Y. d: 10/14/1891, Newark, N.J. BL/TR, 120 lbs. Deb: 5/1/1880 F																						
1880	Chi-N	72	286	41	66	11	1	0	25	10	33	.231	.257	.276	76	-7				.957	3	*P-63/O-8,S-8	-0.3
1881	Chi-N	47	189	25	42	8	0	0	9	5	22	.222	.242	.265	57	-9				.893	-1	P-45/S-2,O-1	0.0
1882	Chi-N	40	169	23	35	10	2	1	24	6	18	.207	.234	.308	69	-6				.919	1	P-39/3-1	0.0
1883	Chi-N	68	263	40	55	12	7	0	25	6	62	.209	.227	.308	57	-14				.906	-3	P-56,O-13/S-3,2-1	-0.6

YEAR	TM/L	G	AB	R	H	2B	3B	HR	RBI	BB	SO	AVG	OBP	SLG	PRO+	BR/A	SB	CS	SBR	FA	FR	G/POS	TPR
1884	Chi-N	64	251	43	61	3	4	1	19	10	33	.243	.272	.299	73	-9				.882	7	P-60/O-4,S-2	-0.1
1885	Chi-N	7	22	6	6	1	0	0	4	6	1	.273	.429	.318	127	1				.905	0	/P-7,S-1	0.0
	NY-N	3	14	3	5	0	0	0	2	0	1	.357	.357	.357	133	0				1.000	1	/P-3	0.0
	Yr	10	36	9	11	1	0	0	6	6	2	.306	.405	.333	129	1				.935	1	P-10/S-1	0.0
1886	NY-N	1	4	0	0	0	0	0	0	0	2	.000	.000	.000	-99	-1	0			.000	-1	/O-1	-0.2
	Was-N	21	81	9	15	2	1	0	3	7	14	.185	.250	.235	51	-4	3			.619	-3	O-11/S-9,P-2	-0.6
	Yr	22	85	9	15	2	1	0	3	7	16	.176	.239	.224	44	-5	3			.591	-3	O-12/S-9,P-2	-0.8
1887	Ind-N	3	10	2	2	0	0	0	0	2	1	.200	.333	.200	53	-1	2			1.000	-0	/O-2,P-2	0.0
Total	8	326	1289	192	287	47	15	2	111	52	187	.223	.253	.287	67	-50	5			.910	3	P-277/O-40,S-25,23	-1.8

■ MICKEY CORCORAN

Corcoran, Michael Joseph b: 8/26/1882, Buffalo, N.Y. d: 12/9/50, Buffalo, N.Y. BR/TR, 5'8", 165 lbs. Deb: 9/15/10

YEAR	TM/L	G	AB	R	H	2B	3B	HR	RBI	BB	SO	AVG	OBP	SLG	PRO+	BR/A	SB	CS	SBR	FA	FR	G/POS	TPR
1910	Cin-N	14	46	3	10	3	0	0	7	5	9	.217	.308	.283	76	-1	0			.911	-1	2-14	-0.2

■ TOMMY CORCORAN

Corcoran, Thomas William "Corky" b: 1/4/1869, New Haven, Conn. d: 6/25/60, Plainfield, Conn. BR/TR, 5'9", 164 lbs. Deb: 4/19/1890 U

YEAR	TM/L	G	AB	R	H	2B	3B	HR	RBI	BB	SO	AVG	OBP	SLG	PRO+	BR/A	SB	CS	SBR	FA	FR	G/POS	TPR
1890	Pit-P	123	503	80	117	14	13	1	61	38	45	.233	.289	.318	68	-24	43			.884	4	*S-123	-1.0
1891	Phi-a	133	511	84	130	11	15	7	71	29	56	.254	.307	.376	93	-8	30			**.911**	12	*S-133	1.0
1892	Bro-N	151	613	77	145	11	6	1	74	34	51	.237	.281	.279	72	-21	39			**.925**	-2	*S-151	-1.5
1893	Bro-N	115	459	61	126	11	10	2	58	27	12	.275	.318	.355	82	-13	14			.907	14	*S-115	0.5
1894	Bro-N	129	576	123	173	21	20	5	92	25	17	.300	.329	.432	89	-13	33			.904	-4	*S-129	-0.8
1895	Bro-N	127	535	81	142	17	10	2	69	23	11	.265	.299	.346	72	-23	17			.924	18	*S-127	0.0
1896	Bro-N	132	532	63	154	15	7	3	73	15	13	.289	.310	.361	81	-16	16			.926	24	*S-132	1.0
1897	Cin-N	109	445	76	128	30	5	3	57	13		.288	.311	.398	81	-15	15			.913	6	S-63,2-47	-0.4
1898	Cin-N	153	619	80	155	28	15	2	87	26		.250	.283	.354	77	-22	19			.932	14	*S-153	-0.1
1899	Cin-N	137	537	91	149	11	8	0	81	28		.277	.316	.328	75	-19	32			.931	4	*S-123,2-14	-0.4
1900	Cin-N	127	523	64	128	21	9	1	54	22		.245	.278	.325	68	-24	27			.921	-5	*S-124/2-5	-1.8
1901	Cin-N	31	115	14	24	3	3	0	15	11		.209	.278	.287	68	-5	6			.919	4	S-30	0.2
1902	Cin-N	138	538	54	136	18	4	0	54	11		.253	.268	.301	69	-21	20			.926	-13	*S-137/2-1	-2.8
1903	Cin-N	115	459	61	113	18	7	2	73	12		.246	.267	.329	63	-25	12			.943	6	*S-115	-1.3
1904	Cin-N	150	578	55	133	17	9	2	74	19		.230	.257	.301	66	-25	19			**.936**	2	*S-150	-2.0
1905	Cin-N	151	605	70	150	21	11	2	85	23		.248	.277	.329	72	-23	28			**.952**	20	*S-151	0.0
1906	Cin-N	117	430	29	89	13	1	1	33	19		.207	.242	.249	51	-25	8			.941	8	*S-117	-1.6
1907	NY-N	62	226	21	60	9	2	0	24	7		.265	.288	.323	88	-4	9			.939	-5	2-62	-1.1
Total	18	2200	8804	1184	2252	289	155	34	1135	382	205	.256	.289	.335	74	-327	387			.924	106	*S-2073,2-129	-12.1

■ TIM CORCORAN

Corcoran, Timothy Michael b: 3/19/53, Glendale, Cal. BL/TL, 5'11", 175 lbs. Deb: 5/18/77

YEAR	TM/L	G	AB	R	H	2B	3B	HR	RBI	BB	SO	AVG	OBP	SLG	PRO+	BR/A	SB	CS	SBR	FA	FR	G/POS	TPR
1977	Det-A	55	103	13	29	3	0	3	15	6	9	.282	.321	.398	90	-2	0	1	-1	1.000	-0	O-18/D-3	-0.3
1978	Det-A	116	324	37	86	13	1	1	27	24	27	.265	.326	.321	80	-8	3	2	-0	.985	-6	*O-109/D-1	-1.9
1979	Det-A	18	22	4	5	1	0	0	6	4	2	.227	.346	.273	67	-1	1	1	-0	1.000	-1	/O-9,1-5,D-2	-0.2
1980	Det-A	84	153	20	44	7	1	3	18	22	10	.288	.381	.405	113	3	0	2	-1	.985	-2	1-48,O-18/D-5	-0.2
1981	Min-A	22	51	4	9	3	0	0	4	6	7	.176	.263	.235	42	-4	0	0	0	1.000	1	1-16/D-3	-0.4
1983	Phi-N	3	0	0	0	0	0	0	0	0	0	—	—	—	—	0	0	0	0	1.000	-0	/1-3	0.0
1984	Phi-N	102	208	30	71	13	1	5	36	37	27	.341	.443	.486	158	18	0	1	-1	.997	-4	1-51,O-17	1.1
1985	Phi-N	103	182	11	39	6	1	0	22	29	20	.214	.322	.258	63	-8	0	0	0	.993	-2	1-59/O-3	-1.3
1986	NY-N	6	7	1	0	0	0	0	0	2	0	.000	.222	.000	-34	-1	0	0	0	1.000	0	/1-1	-0.1
Total	9	509	1050	120	283	46	4	12	128	130	102	.270	.354	.355	96	-2	4	7	-3	.993	-15	1-183,O-174/D-14	-3.3

■ WIL CORDERO

Cordero, Wilfredo (Nieva) b: 10/3/71, Mayaguez, P.R. BR/TR, 6'2", 190 lbs. Deb: 7/24/92

YEAR	TM/L	G	AB	R	H	2B	3B	HR	RBI	BB	SO	AVG	OBP	SLG	PRO+	BR/A	SB	CS	SBR	FA	FR	G/POS	TPR
1992	Mon-N	45	126	17	38	4	1	2	8	9	31	.302	.353	.397	113	2	0	0	0	.949	-6	S-35/2-9	-0.2
1993	Mon-N	138	475	56	118	32	2	10	58	34	60	.248	.308	.387	81	-13	12	3	2	.941	-16	*S-134/3-2	-1.7
1994	Mon-N★	110	415	65	122	30	3	15	63	41	62	.294	.366	.489	119	12	16	3	3	.952	-9	*S-109	1.5
1995	Mon-N	131	514	64	147	35	2	10	49	36	88	.286	.343	.420	97	-2	9	5	-0	.960	-22	*S-105,O-26	-1.6
1996	Bos-A	59	198	29	57	14	0	3	37	11	31	.288	.332	.404	83	-5	2	1	0	.949	3	2-37,D-13/1-1	-0.1
1997	Bos-A	140	570	82	160	26	3	18	72	31	122	.281	.322	.432	93	-7	1	3	-2	.992	0	*O-137/2-1,D-2	-1.1
1998	Chi-A	96	341	58	91	18	2	13	49	22	66	.267	.317	.446	98	-2	2	1	0	.992	1	1-83,O-11	-0.9
Total	7	719	2639	371	733	159	13	71	336	184	460	.278	.332	.429	96	-16	42	16	3	.950	-48	S-383,O-174/12D3	-4.1

■ MARTY CORDOVA

Cordova, Martin Keevin b: 7/10/69, Las Vegas, Nev. BR/TR, 6', 200 lbs. Deb: 4/26/95

YEAR	TM/L	G	AB	R	H	2B	3B	HR	RBI	BB	SO	AVG	OBP	SLG	PRO+	BR/A	SB	CS	SBR	FA	FR	G/POS	TPR
1995	Min-A	137	512	81	142	27	4	24	84	52	111	.277	.355	.486	116	11	20	7	2	.986	19	*O-137	2.6
1996	Min-A	145	569	97	176	46	1	16	111	53	96	.309	.376	.478	112	11	11	5	0	.991	13	*O-145	1.9
1997	Min-A	103	378	44	93	18	4	15	51	30	92	.246	.307	.434	89	-7	5	3	-0	.991	12	*O-101/D-2	0.2
1998	Min-A	119	438	52	111	20	2	10	69	50	103	.253	.337	.377	85	-9	3	6	-3	.978	8	*O-115/D-4	-0.6
Total	4	504	1897	274	522	111	11	65	315	185	402	.275	.348	.448	103	6	39	21	-1	.987	51	O-498/D-6	4.1

■ FRED COREY

Corey, Frederick Harrison b: 1857, S.Kingston, R.I. d: 11/27/12, Providence, R.I. BR/TR, Deb: 5/1/1878

YEAR	TM/L	G	AB	R	H	2B	3B	HR	RBI	BB	SO	AVG	OBP	SLG	PRO+	BR/A	SB	CS	SBR	FA	FR	G/POS	TPR
1878	Pro-N	7	21	3	3	0	0	0	1	0	2	.143	.143	.143	-6	-2				1.000	0	/P-5,2-2,1-1	-0.1
1880	Wor-N	41	138	11	24	8	1	0	6	4	27	.174	.197	.246	45	-8				.759	-11	O-29,P-25/S-3,31	-1.3
1881	Wor-N	51	203	22	45	8	4	0	10	5	10	.222	.240	.300	65	-8				.827	2	O-25,P-23/S-7	-0.2
1882	Wor-N	64	255	33	63	7	12	0	29	5	31	.247	.262	.369	97	-1				.847	-13	S-26,P-21,O-15,/31	-1.2
1883	Phi-a	71	298	45	77	16	2	1	40	12		.258	.287	.336	92	-4				.799	-2	3-34,P-18,O/2SC	-0.6
1884	Phi-a	104	439	64	121	17	16	5		17		.276	.306	.421	127	11				**.887**	13	*3-104	2.2
1885	Phi-a	94	384	61	94	14	8	1	38	17		.245	.282	.331	88	-7				.872	8	*3-92/S-1,P-1	0.2
Total	7	432	1738	239	427	70	43	7	124	60	70	.246	.273	.348	93	-20				.863	-4	3-237/P-93,OS21C	-1.0

■ MARK COREY

Corey, Mark Mundell b: 11/3/55, Tucumcari, N.Mex. BR/TR, 6'2", 200 lbs. Deb: 9/1/79

YEAR	TM/L	G	AB	R	H	2B	3B	HR	RBI	BB	SO	AVG	OBP	SLG	PRO+	BR/A	SB	CS	SBR	FA	FR	G/POS	TPR
1979	Bal-A	13	13	1	2	0	0	0	1	0	4	.154	.154	.154	-17	-2	1	0	0	1.000	-3	O-11/D-1	-0.5
1980	Bal-A	36	36	7	10	2	0	1	2	5	7	.278	.366	.417	115	1	0	1	-1	1.000	-10	O-34	-1.0
1981	Bal-A	10	8	2	0	0	0	0	0	2	2	.000	.200	.000	-38	-1	0	0	0	1.000	-2	/O-9	-0.4
Total	3	59	57	10	12	2	0	1	3	7	13	.211	.297	.298	65	-3	1	1	-0	1.000	-15	/O-54,D-1	-1.9

■ CHUCK CORGAN

Corgan, Charles Howard b: 12/4/02, Wagoner, Okla. d: 6/13/28, Wagoner, Okla. BB/TR, 5'11", 180 lbs. Deb: 9/19/25

YEAR	TM/L	G	AB	R	H	2B	3B	HR	RBI	BB	SO	AVG	OBP	SLG	PRO+	BR/A	SB	CS	SBR	FA	FR	G/POS	TPR
1925	Bro-N	14	47	4	8	1	1	0	0	3	9	.170	.220	.234	16	-6	0	0	0	.908	4	S-14	-0.1
1927	Bro-N	19	57	3	15	1	0	0	1	4	4	.263	.311	.281	59	-3	0			.969	-1	2-13/S-3	-0.3
Total	2	33	104	7	23	2	1	0	1	7	13	.221	.270	.260	40	-9	0	0		.900	3	/S-17,2-13	-0.4

■ ROY CORHAN

Corhan, Roy George "Irish" b: 10/21/1887, Indianapolis, Ind. d: 11/24/58, San Francisco, Cal BR/TR, 5'9.5", 165 lbs. Deb: 4/20/11

YEAR	TM/L	G	AB	R	H	2B	3B	HR	RBI	BB	SO	AVG	OBP	SLG	PRO+	BR/A	SB	CS	SBR	FA	FR	G/POS	TPR
1911	Chi-A	43	131	14	28	6	2	0	8	15		.214	.304	.290	68	-5	2			.924	11	S-43	0.8
1916	StL-N	92	295	30	62	6	3	0	18	20	31	.210	.265	.251	59	-14	15			.917	1	S-84	-0.9
Total	2	135	426	44	90	12	5	0	26	35	31	.211	.277	.263	62	-19	17			.920	12	S-127	-0.1

■ POP CORKHILL

Corkhill, John Stewart b: 4/11/1858, Parkesburg, Pa. d: 4/4/21, Pennsauken, N.J. BL/TR, 5'10", 180 lbs. Deb: 5/1/1883

YEAR	TM/L	G	AB	R	H	2B	3B	HR	RBI	BB	SO	AVG	OBP	SLG	PRO+	BR/A	SB	CS	SBR	FA	FR	G/POS	TPR
1883	Cin-a	88	375	53	81	10	8	2	46	3		.216	.222	.301	63	-16				**.930**	1	*O-85/S-2,2-2,1-2	-1.4
1884	Cin-a	110	452	85	124	13	11	4	70	6		.274	.290	.378	111	4				**.934**	10	*O-92,S-11/1-6,3P	1.0
1885	Cin-a	112	440	64	111	10	8	1	53	7		.252	.275	.318	85	-8				.938	17	*O-110/P-8,1-3	0.5
1886	Cin-a	129	540	81	143	9	7	5	97	23		.265	.302	.335	96	-4	24			.919	-0	*O-112,3-12/1-7,SP	-0.6
1887	Cin-a	128	541	79	168	19	11	5	97	14		.311	.333	.414	105	1	30			**.952**	15	*O-128/P-5	1.1
1888	Cin-a	118	490	68	133	11	9	1	74	15		.271	.299	.337	98	-3	27			.958	7	*O-116/P-2,1-1,2-1	0.0
	Bro-a	19	71	17	27	4	3	1	19	4		.380	.429	.563	217	9	3			.980	2	O-19	0.9
	Yr	137	561	85	160	15	12	2	93	19		.285	.316	.365	113	5	30			.961	8	*O-135/P-2,1-1,2-1	0.9
1889	*Bro-a	138	537	91	134	21	9	8	78	42	24	.250	.308	.367	91	-8	22			**.949**	12	*O-138/S-1,1-1	0.1
1890	Bro-N	51	204	23	46	4	2	1	21	15	11	.225	.279	.279	62	-10	6			.977	4	O-48/1-6	-0.7
1891	Phi-a	83	349	50	73	7	7	0	31	26	15	.209	.268	.269	52	-23	12			.956	7	O-83	-1.7
	Cin-N	1	4	0	0	0	0	0	0	0	1	.000	.000	.000	-99	-1	0			1.000	1	/O-1	0.0

YEAR	TM/L	G	AB	R	H	2B	3B	HR	RBI	BB	SO	AVG	OBP	SLG	PRO+	BR/A	SB	CS	SBR	FA	FR	G/POS	TPR
	Pit-N	41	145	16	33	1	1	3	20	7	10	.228	.268	.310	70	-6	7			.935	2	O-41	-0.5
	Yr	42	149	16	33	1	1	3	20	7	11	.221	.261	.302	65	-7	7			.939	3	O-42	-0.5
1892	Pit-N	68	256	23	47	1	4	0	25	12	19	.184	.229	.219	35	-20	6			.953	7	O-68	-1.5
Total	10	1086	4404	650	1120	110	80	31	631	174	80	.254	.288	.337	87	-86	137			.947	83	*O-1041/1-26,PS32	-2.8

■ PAT CORRALES Corrales, Patrick b: 3/20/41, Los Angeles, Cal. BR/TR, 6', 195 lbs. Deb: 8/2/64 MC

YEAR	TM/L	G	AB	R	H	2B	3B	HR	RBI	BB	SO	AVG	OBP	SLG	PRO+	BR/A	SB	CS	SBR	FA	FR	G/POS	TPR
1964	Phi-N	2	1	1	0	0	0	0	0	1	0	.000	.500	.000	55	0	0	0	0	.000	0	H	0.0
1965	Phi-N	63	174	16	39	8	1	2	15	25	42	.224	.325	.316	83	-3	0	0	0	.982	-3	C-62	-0.4
1966	StL-N	28	72	5	13	2	0	0	3	2	17	.181	.224	.208	21	-8	1	0	0	.975	9	C-27	0.3
1968	Cin-N	20	56	3	15	4	0	0	6	6	16	.268	.349	.339	101	0	0	0	0	.991	0	C-20	0.2
1969	Cin-N	29	72	10	19	5	0	1	5	8	17	.264	.346	.375	97	-0	0	1	-1	.986	3	C-29	0.4
1970	*Cin-N	43	106	9	25	5	1	1	10	8	22	.236	.289	.330	65	-5	0	0	0	.983	4	C-42	0.0
1971	Cin-N	40	94	6	17	2	0	0	6	6	17	.181	.230	.202	24	-9	0	0	0	.980	1	C-39	-0.8
1972	Cin-N	2	1	0	0	0	0	0	0	2	0	.000	.667	.000	110	0	0	0	0	1.000	1	/C-2	0.2
	SD-N	44	119	6	23	0	0	0	6	11	26	.193	.267	.193	35	-10	0	0	0	.993	4	C-43	-0.5
	Yr	46	120	6	23	0	0	0	6	13	26	.192	.276	.192	38	-10	0	0	0	.993	5	C-45	-0.3
1973	SD-N	29	72	7	15	2	1	0	3	6	10	.208	.278	.264	55	-4	0	0	0	.986	-1	C-28	-0.5
Total	9	300	767	63	166	28	3	4	54	75	167	.216	.292	.276	61	-39	1	1	-0	.984	18	C-292	-1.1

■ ROD CORREIA Correia, Ronald Douglas b: 9/13/67, Providence, R.I. BR/TR, 5'11", 180 lbs. Deb: 6/20/93

YEAR	TM/L	G	AB	R	H	2B	3B	HR	RBI	BB	SO	AVG	OBP	SLG	PRO+	BR/A	SB	CS	SBR	FA	FR	G/POS	TPR
1993	Cal-A	64	128	12	34	5	0	0	9	6	20	.266	.319	.305	66	-6	2	4	-2	.981	18	S-40,2-11/3-3,D-6	1.2
1994	Cal-A	6	17	4	4	1	0	0	0	0	0	.235	.316	.294	58	-1	0	0	0	1.000	-2	/2-5,S-1	-0.2
1995	Cal-A	14	21	3	5	1	1	0	3	0	5	.238	.238	.381	58	-1	0	0	0	.850	3	/S-7,2-3,3-2,D-1	0.2
Total	3	84	166	19	43	7	1	0	12	6	25	.259	.309	.313	65	-8	2	4	-2	.968	19	/S-48,2-19,D-7,3-5	1.2

■ VIC CORRELL Correll, Victor Crosby b: 2/5/46, Washington, D.C. BR/TR, 5'10", 185 lbs. Deb: 10/4/72

YEAR	TM/L	G	AB	R	H	2B	3B	HR	RBI	BB	SO	AVG	OBP	SLG	PRO+	BR/A	SB	CS	SBR	FA	FR	G/POS	TPR
1972	Bos-A	1	4	1	2	0	0	0	1	0	1	.500	.500	.500	188	0	0	0	0	1.000	1	/C-1	0.1
1974	Atl-N	73	202	20	48	15	1	4	29	21	38	.238	.322	.381	92	-2	0	0	0	.988	6	C-59	0.6
1975	Atl-N	103	325	37	70	12	1	11	39	42	66	.215	.307	.360	82	-8	0	2	-1	.973	-2	C-97	-0.8
1976	Atl-N	69	200	26	45	6	2	5	16	21	37	.225	.302	.350	80	-5	0	1	-1	.981	3	C-65	-0.1
1977	Atl-N	54	144	16	30	7	0	7	16	22	33	.208	.317	.403	82	-4	2	3	-1	.973	2	C-49	-0.2
1978	Cin-N	52	105	9	25	7	0	1	6	8	17	.238	.292	.333	74	-4	0	2	-1	.980	1	C-52	-0.3
1979	Cin-N	48	133	14	31	12	0	1	15	14	26	.233	.311	.346	78	-4	0	0	0	.992	7	C-47	0.4
1980	Cin-N	10	19	1	8	1	0	0	3	0	2	.421	.421	.474	149	1	0	0	0	.919	-0	C-10	0.1
Total	8	410	1132	124	259	60	4	29	125	128	220	.229	.312	.366	83	-26	2	8	-4	.979	18	C-380	-0.2

■ PHIL CORRIDAN Corridan, Philip Deb: 7/16/1884

YEAR	TM/L	G	AB	R	H	2B	3B	HR	RBI	BB	SO	AVG	OBP	SLG	PRO+	BR/A	SB	CS	SBR	FA	FR	G/POS	TPR
1884	CP-U	2	7	1	1	0	0	0		0		.143	.143	.143	-13	-1				.800	-1	/2-2,O-1	-0.2

■ JOHN CORRIDEN Corriden, John Michael Jr. b: 10/6/18, Logansport, Ind. BB/TR, 5'6", 160 lbs. Deb: 4/20/46 F

YEAR	TM/L	G	AB	R	H	2B	3B	HR	RBI	BB	SO	AVG	OBP	SLG	PRO+	BR/A	SB	CS	SBR	FA	FR	G/POS	TPR
1946	Bro-N	1	0	1	0	0	0	0	0	0	0	—	—	—	—	0	0			.000	0	R	0.0

■ RED CORRIDEN Corriden, John Michael Sr. b: 9/4/1887, Logansport, Ind. d: 9/28/59, Indianapolis, Ind BR/TR, 5'9", 165 lbs. Deb: 9/8/10 FMC

YEAR	TM/L	G	AB	R	H	2B	3B	HR	RBI	BB	SO	AVG	OBP	SLG	PRO+	BR/A	SB	CS	SBR	FA	FR	G/POS	TPR
1910	StL-A	26	84	19	13	3	0	1	4	13		.155	.297	.226	68	-2	5			.902	4	S-14,3-12	0.3
1912	Det-A	38	138	22	28	6	0	0	5	15		.203	.286	.246	54	-8	4			.929	-4	3-25/2-7,S-3	-1.2
1913	Chi-N	46	97	13	17	3	0	2	9	10	14	.175	.252	.268	49	-7	4			.907	-1	S-37/2-2,3-1	-0.6
1914	Chi-N	107	318	42	73	9	5	3	29	35	33	.230	.323	.318	91	-3	13			.894	-33	S-91/3-8,2-3	-3.1
1915	Chi-N	6	3	1	0	0	0	0	0	2	1	.000	.571	.000	79	1	0			.667	-1	/3-1,O-1	0.0
Total	5	223	640	97	131	21	5	6	47	75	48	.205	.304	.281	74	-19	26			.896	-35	S-145/3-47,2-12,O-1	-4.6

■ JESS CORTAZZO Cortazzo, John Francis b: 9/26/04, Wilmerding, Pa. d: 3/4/63, Pittsburgh, Pa. BR/TR, 5'3.5", 142 lbs. Deb: 9/1/23

YEAR	TM/L	G	AB	R	H	2B	3B	HR	RBI	BB	SO	AVG	OBP	SLG	PRO+	BR/A	SB	CS	SBR	FA	FR	G/POS	TPR
1923	Chi-A	1	1	0	0	0	0	0	0	0	0	.000	.000	.000	-99	-0	0	0	0	.000	0	H	0.0

■ JOE COSCARART Coscarart, Joseph Marvin b: 11/18/09, Escondido, Cal. d: 4/5/93, Sequim, Wash. BR/TR, 6', 185 lbs. Deb: 4/26/35 F

YEAR	TM/L	G	AB	R	H	2B	3B	HR	RBI	BB	SO	AVG	OBP	SLG	PRO+	BR/A	SB	CS	SBR	FA	FR	G/POS	TPR
1935	Bos-N	86	284	30	67	11	2	1	29	16	28	.236	.277	.299	59	-17	2			.962	-4	3-41,S-27,2-15	-1.7
1936	Bos-N	104	367	28	90	11	2	2	44	19	37	.245	.292	.302	64	-19	0			.935	2	3-97/S-6,2-1	-1.3
Total	2	190	651	58	157	22	4	3	73	35	65	.241	.285	.301	62	-35	2			.943	-3	3-138/S-33,2-16	-3.0

■ PETE COSCARART Coscarart, Peter Joseph b: 6/16/13, Escondido, Cal. BR/TR, 5'11.5", 175 lbs. Deb: 4/26/38 F

YEAR	TM/L	G	AB	R	H	2B	3B	HR	RBI	BB	SO	AVG	OBP	SLG	PRO+	BR/A	SB	CS	SBR	FA	FR	G/POS	TPR
1938	Bro-N	32	79	10	12	3	0	0	6	9	18	.152	.256	.190	24	-8	0			.955	1	2-27	-0.6
1939	Bro-N	115	419	59	116	22	2	4	43	46	56	.277	.354	.368	91	-4	10			.960	-8	*2-107/3-4,S-2	-0.6
1940	Bro-N★	143	506	55	120	24	4	9	58	53	59	.237	.311	.354	78	-15	5			.958	-32	*2-140	-3.8
1941	*Bro-N	43	62	13	8	1	0	0	5	7	12	.129	.217	.145	3	-8	1			.948	5	2-19/S-1	-0.2
1942	Pit-N	133	487	57	111	12	4	3	29	38	56	.228	.288	.287	67	-20	2			.952	-18	*S-108,2-25	-3.3
1943	Pit-N	133	491	57	119	19	6	0	48	46	48	.242	.307	.305	75	-16	4			.961	-6	2-85,S-47/3-1	-1.4
1944	Pit-N	139	554	89	146	30	4	4	42	41	57	.264	.315	.354	85	-12	10			.967	-7	*2-136/S-4,O-1	-1.2
1945	Pit-N	123	392	59	95	17	2	8	38	55	55	.242	.341	.357	91	-4	2			.978	21	*2-122/S-1	2.4
1946	Pit-N	3	2	0	1	1	0	0	0	0	0	.500	.500	1.000	312	1	0			.000	0	/S-1	0.1
Total	9	864	2992	399	728	129	22	28	269	295	361	.243	.314	.329	78	-87	34			.963	-43	2-661,S-164/3-5,O-1	-8.6

■ RAY COSEY Cosey, Donald Ray b: 2/15/56, San Rafael, Cal. BL/TL, 5'10", 185 lbs. Deb: 4/14/80

YEAR	TM/L	G	AB	R	H	2B	3B	HR	RBI	BB	SO	AVG	OBP	SLG	PRO+	BR/A	SB	CS	SBR	FA	FR	G/POS	TPR
1980	Oak-A	9	9	0	1	0	0	0	0	0	0	.111	.111	.111	-42	-2	0	0	0	.000	0	/H	-0.2

■ DAN COSTELLO Costello, Daniel Francis "Dashing Dan" b: 9/9/1891, Jessup, Pa. d: 3/26/36, Pittsburgh, Pa. BL/TR, 6'0.5", 185 lbs. Deb: 7/2/13

YEAR	TM/L	G	AB	R	H	2B	3B	HR	RBI	BB	SO	AVG	OBP	SLG	PRO+	BR/A	SB	CS	SBR	FA	FR	G/POS	TPR
1913	NY-A	2	2	1	1	0	0	0	0	0	0	.500	.500	.500	192	0	0			.000	0	H	0.0
1914	Pit-N	21	64	7	19	1	0	0	5	8	16	.297	.375	.313	110	1	2			.970	-1	O-20	-0.1
1915	Pit-N	71	125	16	27	4	1	0	11	7	23	.216	.258	.264	59	-6	7	1	2	.893	-5	O-22/1-1	-1.3
1916	Pit-N	60	159	11	38	1	3	0	8	6	23	.239	.267	.283	68	-6	3			.976	-2	O-41	-1.2
Total	4	154	350	35	85	6	4	0	24	21	62	.243	.286	.283	73	-11	12	1		.959	-9	/O-83,1-1	-2.6

■ TIM COSTO Costo, Timothy Roger b: 2/16/69, Melrose Park, Ill. BR/TR, 6'5", 220 lbs. Deb: 9/18/92

YEAR	TM/L	G	AB	R	H	2B	3B	HR	RBI	BB	SO	AVG	OBP	SLG	PRO+	BR/A	SB	CS	SBR	FA	FR	G/POS	TPR
1992	Cin-N	12	36	3	8	2	0	0	2	5	6	.222	.317	.278	68	-1	0	0	0	1.000	0	1-12	-0.2
1993	Cin-N	31	98	13	22	5	0	3	12	4	17	.224	.255	.367	64	-5	0	0	0	.980	0	O-26/1-2,3-2	-0.6
Total	2	43	134	16	30	7	0	3	14	9	23	.224	.273	.343	66	-7	0	0	0	1.000	1	/O-26,1-14,3-2	-0.8

■ HENRY COTE Cote, Henry Joseph b: 2/19/1864, Troy, N.Y. d: 4/28/40, Troy, N.Y. 5'9.5", 165 lbs. Deb: 9/16/1894

YEAR	TM/L	G	AB	R	H	2B	3B	HR	RBI	BB	SO	AVG	OBP	SLG	PRO+	BR/A	SB	CS	SBR	FA	FR	G/POS	TPR
1894	Lou-N	10	31	7	9	2	2	0	3	5	6	.290	.389	.484	117	1	2			.918	5	C-10	0.5
1895	Lou-N	10	33	10	10	0	0	0	5	3	3	.303	.361	.303	77	-1	2			.872	-3	C-10	-0.3
Total	2	20	64	17	19	2	2	0	8	8	9	.297	.375	.391	98	0	4			.900	2	/C-20	0.2

■ PETE COTE Cote, Warren Peter b: 8/30/02, Cambridge, Mass. d: 10/17/87, Middleton, Mass. BR/TR, 5'6", 148 lbs. Deb: 6/18/26

YEAR	TM/L	G	AB	R	H	2B	3B	HR	RBI	BB	SO	AVG	OBP	SLG	PRO+	BR/A	SB	CS	SBR	FA	FR	G/POS	TPR
1926	NY-N	2	1	0	0	0	0	0	0	0	0	.000	.000	.000	-99	-0	0			.000	0	H	0.0

■ ED COTTER Cotter, Edward Christopher b: 7/4/04, Hartford, Conn. d: 6/14/59, Hartford, Conn. BR/TR, 6', 185 lbs. Deb: 6/12/26

YEAR	TM/L	G	AB	R	H	2B	3B	HR	RBI	BB	SO	AVG	OBP	SLG	PRO+	BR/A	SB	CS	SBR	FA	FR	G/POS	TPR
1926	Phi-N	17	26	3	8	0	1	0	1	1	4	.308	.333	.385	88	-0	1			.833	0	/3-8,S-5	0.0

■ HOOKS COTTER Cotter, Harvey Louis b: 5/22/1900, Holden, Mo. d: 8/6/55, Los Angeles, Cal. BL/TL, 5'10", 160 lbs. Deb: 4/15/22

YEAR	TM/L	G	AB	R	H	2B	3B	HR	RBI	BB	SO	AVG	OBP	SLG	PRO+	BR/A	SB	CS	SBR	FA	FR	G/POS	TPR
1922	Chi-N	1	1	0	1	1	0	0	0	0	0	1.000	1.000	2.000	644	1	0	0	0	.000	0	H	0.1
1924	Chi-N	98	310	39	81	16	4	4	33	36	31	.261	.338	.377	91	-4	3	5	-2	.989	4	1-90	-0.7
Total	2	99	311	39	82	17	4	4	33	36	31	.264	.340	.383	92	-3	3	5	-2	.989	4	/1-90	-0.6

■ DICK COTTER Cotter, Richard Raphael b: 10/12/1889, Manchester, N.H. d: 4/4/45, Brooklyn, N.Y. BR/TR, 5'11", 172 lbs. Deb: 8/17/11

YEAR	TM/L	G	AB	R	H	2B	3B	HR	RBI	BB	SO	AVG	OBP	SLG	PRO+	BR/A	SB	CS	SBR	FA	FR	G/POS	TPR
1911	Phi-N	20	46	2	13	0	0	0	5	5	7	.283	.353	.283	78	-1	1			.975	-2	C-17	-0.1

YEAR	TM/L	G	AB	R	H	2B	3B	HR	RBI	BB	SO	AVG	OBP	SLG	PRO+	BR/A	SB	CS	SBR	FA	FR	G/POS	TPR
1912	Chi-N	26	54	6	15	0	2	0	10	6	13	.278	.361	.352	96	-0	1			.954	-3	C-24	-0.2
Total	2	46	100	8	28	0	2	0	15	11	20	.280	.357	.320	87	-1	2			.964	-5	/C-41	-0.3
■ TOM COTTER	Cotter, Thomas B. b: 9/30/1866, Waltham, Mass. d: 11/22/06, Brookline, Mass. BR/TR, 5'10.5", 149 lbs. Deb: 9/3/1891																						
1891	Bos-a	6	12	1	3	0	0	0	4	1	2	.250	.308	.250	61	-1	0			.938	-1	/C-5,O-1	-0.1
■ CHUCK COTTIER	Cottier, Charles Keith b: 1/8/36, Delta, Colo. BR/TR, 5'10.5", 175 lbs. Deb: 4/17/59 MC																						
1959	Mil-N	10	24	1	3	1	0	0	1	3	7	.125	.222	.167	6	-3	0	0	0	.976	1	2-10	-0.2
1960	Mil-N	95	229	29	52	8	0	3	19	14	21	.227	.278	.301	63	-12	1	0	0	.968	17	2-92	1.2
1961	Det-A	10	7	2	2	0	0	0	1	1	0	.286	.375	.286	77	-0	0	0	0	.889	2	/S-8,2-2	0.1
	Was-A	101	337	37	79	14	4	2	34	30	51	.234	.299	.318	66	-16	9	1	2	.982	15	*2-100	1.2
	Yr	111	344	39	81	14	4	2	35	31	52	.235	.301	.317	66	-17	9	1	2	.982	17	*2-102/S-8	1.3
1962	Was-A	136	443	50	107	14	6	6	40	44	57	.242	.313	.341	76	-15	14	8	-1	.981	21	*2-134	1.8
1963	Was-A	113	337	30	69	16	4	5	21	24	63	.205	.258	.320	61	-18	2	1	0	.963	11	2-85,S-24/3-1	0.1
1964	Was-A	73	137	16	23	6	2	3	10	19	33	.168	.269	.307	60	-7	2	0	1	.982	14	2-53/3-3,S-2	1.0
1965	Was-A	7	1	1	0	0	0	0	0	0	0	.000	.000	.000	-99	-0	0	0	0	.000	0	H	0.0
1968	Cal-A	33	67	2	13	4	1	0	1	2	15	.194	.217	.284	53	-4	0	0	0	.963	2	3-27/2-4	-0.3
1969	Cal-A	2	2	0	0	0	0	0	0	0	0	.000	.000	.000	-99	-1	0	0	0	1.000	-0	/2-2	-0.1
Total	9	580	1584	168	348	63	17	19	127	137	248	.220	.284	.317	65	-77	28	10	2	.976	81	2-482/S-34,3-31	4.8
■ HENRY COTTO	Cotto, Henry b: 1/5/61, New York, N.Y. BR/TR, 6'2", 178 lbs. Deb: 4/5/84																						
1984	*Chi-N	105	146	24	40	5	0	0	8	10	23	.274	.325	.308	72	-5	9	3	1	.984	-12	O-88	-1.8
1985	NY-A	34	56	4	17	1	0	1	6	3	12	.304	.339	.375	98	-0	1	1	-0	.977	-7	O-30	-0.8
1986	NY-A	35	80	11	17	3	0	1	6	2	17	.213	.232	.287	41	-7	3	0	1	1.000	-2	O-29/D-1	-0.8
1987	NY-A	68	149	21	35	10	0	5	20	6	35	.235	.269	.403	76	-6	4	2	0	.989	-8	O-57	-1.4
1988	Sea-A	133	386	50	100	18	1	8	33	23	53	.259	.304	.373	85	-8	27	3	6	.992	-5	*O-120/D-2	-1.0
1989	Sea-A	100	295	44	78	11	2	9	33	12	44	.264	.300	.407	94	-3	10	4	1	.988	-7	O-90/D-2	-1.1
1990	Sea-A	127	355	40	92	14	3	4	33	22	52	.259	.310	.349	83	-8	21	3	5	.990	-9	*O-118/D-3	-1.5
1991	Sea-A	66	177	35	54	6	2	6	23	10	27	.305	.349	.463	123	5	16	3	3	.981	-5	O-56/D-6	0.2
1992	Sea-A	108	294	42	76	11	1	5	27	14	49	.259	.294	.354	80	-8	23	2	6	1.000	-10	O-92/D-3	-1.4
1993	Sea-A	54	105	10	20	1	0	2	7	2	22	.190	.213	.257	25	-11	5	4	-1	.983	-3	O-34,D-15	-1.6
	Fla-N	54	135	15	40	7	0	3	14	3	18	.296	.317	.415	89	-2	11	1	3	.977	-4	O-46	-0.4
Total	10	884	2178	296	569	87	9	44	210	107	352	.261	.301	.370	83	-54	130	26	23	.989	-70	O-760/D-32	-11.6
■ DENNIS COUGHLIN	Coughlin, Dennis F. Deb: 4/27/1872																						
1872	Nat-n	8	37	5	12	1	0	0	7	0	0	.324	.324	.351	92	-1	0	0	0	.941	1	/O-5,1-1,2-1,S-1	0.0
■ ED COUGHLIN	Coughlin, Edward E. b: 8/5/1861, Hartford, Conn. d: 12/25/52, Hartford, Conn. Deb: 5/15/1884																						
1884	Buf-N	1	4	0	1	0	0	0	1	0	2	.250	.250	.250	56	-0				.750	0	/O-1,P-1	0.0
■ BILL COUGHLIN	Coughlin, William Paul "Scranton Bill" b: 7/12/1878, Scranton, Pa. d: 5/7/43, Scranton, Pa. BR/TR, 5'9", 140 lbs. Deb: 8/9/1899																						
1899	Was-N	6	24	2	3	0	1	0	3	1		.125	.160	.208	1	-3	1			.818	-1	/3-6	-0.4
1901	Was-A	137	506	75	139	17	13	6	68	25		.275	.317	.395	98	-3	16			.922	0	*3-137	-0.1
1902	Was-A	123	469	84	141	27	4	6	71	26		.301	.348	.414	110	5	29			.926	12	3-66,S-31,2-26	1.9
1903	Was-A	125	473	56	116	18	3	1	31	9		.245	.267	.302	69	-18	30			.952	4	*3-119/S-4,2-2	-1.3
1904	Was-A	65	265	28	73	15	4	0	17	9		.275	.307	.362	113	3	10			.939	2	3-64	0.8
	Det-A	56	206	22	47	6	0	0	17	5		.228	.257	.257	65	-8	1			.929	-3	3-56	-1.1
	Yr	121	471	50	120	21	4	0	34	14		.255	.285	.316	92	-5	11			.935	-1	*3-120	-0.3
1905	Det-A	137	489	48	123	20	6	0	44	34		.252	.309	.317	98	-1	16			.914	-9	*3-136	-0.6
1906	Det-A	147	498	54	117	15	5	2	60	36		.235	.293	.297	83	-10	31			.940	-11	*3-147	-1.7
1907	*Det-A	134	519	80	126	10	2	0	46	35		.243	.301	.270	79	-11	15			.930	-9	*3-133	-1.8
1908	*Det-A	119	405	32	87	5	1	0	23	23		.215	.269	.232	61	-17	10			.941	-16	*3-119	-3.3
Total	9	1049	3854	481	972	133	39	15	380	203		.252	.299	.319	86	-63	159			.931	-32	3-983/S-35,2-28	-7.6
■ MARLAN COUGHTRY	Coughtry, James Marlan b: 9/11/34, Hollywood, Cal. BL/TR, 6'1", 170 lbs. Deb: 9/2/60																						
1960	Bos-A	15	19	3	3	0	0	0	0	5	8	.158	.333	.158	36	-1	0	0	0	.909	1	2-13/3-1	0.0
1962	LA-A	11	22	0	4	0	0	0	2	0	6	.182	.182	.182	-2	-3	0	0	0	.867	3	/3-5,2-2	0.0
	KC-A	6	11	1	2	0	0	0	1	4	3	.182	.400	.182	60	-0	0	0	0	.917	1	/3-3	0.1
	Cle-A	3	2	1	1	0	0	0	1	1	1	.500	.667	.500	226	1	0	0	0	.000	0	H	0.1
	Yr	20	35	2	7	0	0	0	4	5	10	.200	.300	.200	38	-3	0	0	0	.889	4	/3-8,2-2	0.2
Total	2	35	54	5	10	0	0	0	4	10	18	.185	.313	.185	37	-4	0	0	0	.915	6	/2-15,3-9	0.2
■ BOB COULSON	Coulson, Robert Jackson b: 6/17/1887, Courtney, Pa. d: 9/11/53, Washington, Pa. BR/TR, 5'10.5", 175 lbs. Deb: 8/4/08																						
1908	Cin-N	8	18	3	6	1	1	0	1	3		.333	.429	.500	202	2	0			1.000	1	/O-6	0.3
1910	Bro-N	25	89	14	22	3	4	1	13	6	14	.247	.302	.404	109	0	9			.922	0	O-25	0.0
1911	Bro-N	146	521	52	122	23	7	0	50	42	78	.234	.301	.305	73	-19	32			.968	1	*O-145	-2.6
1914	Pit-F	18	64	7	13	1	0	0	3	7	10	.203	.282	.219	38	-6	2			.931	-2	O-18	-1.0
Total	4	197	692	76	163	28	12	1	67	58	102	.236	.303	.315	77	-23	43			.960	0	O-194	-3.3
■ CHIP COULTER	Coulter, Thomas Lee b: 6/5/45, Steubenville, O. BB/TR, 5'10", 172 lbs. Deb: 9/18/69																						
1969	StL-N	6	19	3	6	1	1	0	4	2	6	.316	.381	.474	138	1	0	1	-1	.960	-0	/2-6	0.1
■ CRAIG COUNSELL	Counsell, Craig John b: 8/21/70, South Bend, Ind. BL/TR, 6', 180 lbs. Deb: 9/17/95																						
1995	Col-N	3	1	0	0	0	0	0	0	1	0	.000	.500	.000	36	-0	0	0	0	1.000	0	/S-3	0.0
1997	Col-N	1	0	0	0	0	0	0	0	0	0	—	—	—		0	0	0	0	.000	0	/R	0.0
	*Fla-N	51	164	20	49	9	2	1	16	18	17	.299	.378	.396	108	2	1	1	-0	.989	18	2-51	2.2
	Yr	52	164	20	49	9	2	1	16	18	17	.299	.378	.396	107	2	1	1	-0	.989	18	2-51	2.2
1998	Fla-N	107	335	43	84	19	5	4	40	51	47	.251	.356	.373	94	-2	3	0	1	.991	10	*2-104	1.5
Total	3	162	500	63	133	28	7	5	56	70	64	.266	.364	.380	98	0	4	1	1	.990	28	2-155/S-3	3.7
■ CLINT COURTNEY	Courtney, Clinton Dawson "Scrap Iron" b: 3/16/27, Hall Summit, La. d: 6/16/75, Rochester, N.Y. BL/TR, 5'8", 180 lbs. Deb: 9/29/51 C																						
1951	NY-A	1	2	0	0	0	0	0	0	0	1	.000	.333	.000	-5	-0	0	0	0	.800	0	/C-1	0.0
1952	StL-A	119	413	38	118	24	3	5	50	39	26	.286	.349	.395	104	2	0	2	-1	**.996**	3	*C-113	0.9
1953	StL-A	106	355	28	89	12	2	4	19	25	20	.251	.302	.330	69	-16	0	1	-1	.980	-5	*C-103	-1.7
1954	Bal-A	122	397	25	107	18	3	4	37	30	7	.270	.326	.360	95	-4	2	1	0	.990	-3	*C-111	-0.2
1955	Chi-A	19	37	7	14	3	0	1	10	7	0	.378	.477	.541	168	4	0	0	0	1.000	-1	C-17	0.3
	Was-A	75	238	26	71	8	4	2	30	19	9	.298	.353	.391	105	1	0	0	0	.983	-14	C-67	-1.0
	Yr	94	275	33	85	11	4	3	40	26	9	.309	.371	.411	114	5	0	0	0	.985	-15	C-84	-0.7
1956	Was-A	101	283	31	85	20	3	5	44	20	10	.300	.365	.445	113	5	0	5	-3	.979	-15	C-76	-1.0
1957	Was-A	91	232	23	62	14	1	6	27	16	11	.267	.346	.414	108	3	0	0	0	.994	-1	C-59	0.4
1958	Was-A	134	450	46	113	18	0	8	62	48	23	.251	.335	.344	89	-6	1	5	-3	.991	-3	*C-128	-0.4
1959	Was-A	72	189	19	44	4	1	2	18	20	19	.233	.310	.296	68	-8	0	1	-1	.987	-13	C-53	-1.9
1960	Bal-A	83	154	14	35	3	0	1	12	30	14	.227	.380	.266	79	-2	0	1	-1	.975	4	C-58	0.4
1961	KC-A	1	1	0	0	0	0	0	0	0	0	.000	.000	.000	-98	-0	0	0	0	.000	0	H	0.0
	Bal-A	22	45	3	12	2	0	0	4	10	3	.267	.400	.311	96	0	0	0	0	1.000	1	C-16	0.2
	Yr	23	46	3	12	2	0	0	4	10	3	.261	.393	.304	92	0	0	0	0	1.000	1	C-16	0.2
Total	11	946	2796	260	750	126	17	38	313	264	143	.268	.341	.366	94	-21	3	16	-9	.987	-45	C-802	-4.0
■ ERNIE COURTNEY	Courtney, Edward Ernest b: 1/20/1875, Des Moines, Iowa d: 2/29/20, Buffalo, N.Y. BL/TR, 5'10", Deb: 4/17/02																						
1902	Bos-N	48	165	23	36	3	0	0	17	13		.218	.291	.236	62	-7	3			.974	-1	O-39/S-3	-1.1
	Bal-A	1	4	3	2	0	1	0	1	0		.500	.600	1.000	324	1	0			1.000	0	/3-1	0.1
1903	NY-A	25	79	7	21	3	3	1	8	7		.266	.341	.418	119	2	1			.916	-2	S-19/2-4,1-1	0.1

YEAR	TM/L	G	AB	R	H	2B	3B	HR	RBI	BB	SO	AVG	OBP	SLG	PRO+	BR/A	SB	CS	SBR	FA	FR	G/POS	TPR
	Det-A	23	74	7	17	0	0	0	6	5		.230	.305	.230	64	-3	1			.938	-4	3-13/S-9	-0.7
	Yr	48	153	14	38	3	3	1	14	12		.248	.324	.327	94	-1	2			.921	-6	S-28,3-13/2-4,1-1	-0.6
1905	Phi-N	155	601	77	165	14	7	2	77	47		.275	.334	.331	102	2	17			.923	-17	*3-155	-1.0
1906	Phi-N	116	398	53	94	12	2	0	42	45		.236	.315	.276	84	-6	6			.923	-11	3-96,1-13/O-3,S-1	-1.6
1907	Phi-N	130	440	42	107	17	4	2	43	55		.243	.335	.314	105	4	6			.907	-8	3-75,1-48/O-4,2S	-0.3
1908	Phi-N	60	160	14	29	3	0	0	6	15		.181	.260	.200	46	-9	1			.915	-7	3-22,1-13/2-5,S-2	-1.8
Total	6	558	1921	226	471	52	17	5	200	188		.245	.321	.298	91	-15	35			.920	-49	3-362/1-75,O-46,S2	-6.3
■ **DEE COUSINEAU**	Cousineau, Edward Thomas b: 12/16/1898, Watertown, Mass. d: 7/14/51, Watertown, Mass. BR/TR, 6', 170 lbs. Deb: 10/6/23																						
1923	Bos-N	1	2	1	2	0	0	0	2	0	0	1.000	1.000	1.000	447	1	0	0	0	.000	0	/C-1	0.1
1924	Bos-N	3	2	0	0	0	0	0	0	0	0	.000	.000	.000	-99	-1	0	0	0	.500	-1	/C-3	-0.1
1925	Bos-N	1	0	0	0	0	0	0	0	0	0	—	—	—	—	0	0	0	0	.000	0	/C-1	0.0
Total	3	5	4	1	2	0	0	0	2	0	0	.500	.500	.500	174	0	0	0	0	.500	-1	/C-5	0.0
■ **JACK COVENEY**	Coveney, John Patrick b: 6/10/1880, S.Natick, Mass. d: 3/28/61, Wayland, Mass. BR/TR, 5'9", 175 lbs. Deb: 9/19/03																						
1903	StL-N	4	14	0	2	0	0	0	0	0		.143	.143	.143	-19	-2	0			.923	1	/C-4	-0.1
■ **SAM COVINGTON**	Covington, Clarence Otto b: 12/17/1892, Henryville, Tenn. d: 1/4/63, Denison, Tex. BL/TR, 6'1", 190 lbs. Deb: 8/25/13 F																						
1913	StL-A	20	60	3	9	0	1	0	4	4	6	.150	.203	.183	14	-7	3			.994	3	1-16	-0.4
1917	Bos-N	17	66	8	13	2	0	1	10	5	5	.197	.264	.273	69	-2	1			.994	0	1-17	-0.3
1918	Bos-N	3	3	0	1	0	0	0	0	0	0	.333	.333	.333	108	0	0			.000	0	H	0.0
Total	3	40	129	11	23	2	1	1	14	9	11	.178	.237	.233	43	-9	4			.994	3	/1-33	-0.7
■ **WES COVINGTON**	Covington, John Wesley b: 3/27/32, Laurinburg, N.C. BL/TR, 6'1", 205 lbs. Deb: 4/19/56																						
1956	Mil-N	75	138	17	39	4	0	2	16	16	20	.283	.361	.355	100	0	1	0	0	.979	-3	O-35	-0.4
1957	*Mil-N	96	328	51	93	4	8	21	65	29	44	.284	.345	.537	143	18	4	1	1	.981	0	O-89	1.4
1958	*Mil-N	90	294	43	97	12	1	24	74	20	35	.330	.382	.622	175	30	0	0	0	.953	-4	O-82	2.1
1959	Mil-N	103	373	38	104	17	3	7	45	26	41	.279	.331	.397	101	-0	0	1	-1	.962	-3	O-94	-0.8
1960	Mil-N	95	281	25	70	16	1	10	35	15	37	.249	.290	.420	99	-2	1	2	-1	.964	-5	O-72	-1.1
1961	Mil-N	9	21	3	4	1	0	0	0	2	4	.190	.261	.238	36	-2	0	0	0	1.000	-1	/O-5	-0.4
	Chi-A	22	59	5	17	1	0	4	15	4	5	.288	.333	.508	123	2	0	0	0	.900	-1	O-14	0.0
	KC-A	17	44	3	7	0	0	1	6	4	7	.159	.260	.227	31	-4	0	0	0	1.000	-2	O-12	-0.7
	Yr	39	103	8	24	1	0	5	21	8	12	.233	.301	.388	83	-3	0	0	0	.941	-3	O-26	-0.7
	Phi-N	57	165	23	50	9	0	7	26	15	17	.303	.361	.485	124	5	0	0	0	.950	-5	O-45	-0.2
1962	Phi-N	116	304	36	86	12	1	9	44	19	44	.283	.329	.418	102	0	0	0	0	.944	-7	O-88	-1.1
1963	Phi-N	119	353	46	107	24	1	17	64	26	56	.303	.354	.521	150	22	1	0	0	.937	-8	*O-101	1.1
1964	Phi-N	129	339	37	95	18	0	13	58	38	50	.280	.358	.448	127	13	0	0	0	.972	-9	*O-99	0.0
1965	Phi-N	101	235	27	58	10	1	15	45	26	47	.247	.324	.489	128	8	0	0	0	.968	-2	O-64	0.4
1966	Chi-N	9	11	0	1	0	0	0	0	1	2	.091	.167	.091	-26	-2	0	0	0	1.000	0	/O-1	-0.2
	*LA-N	37	33	1	4	0	1	1	6	6	5	.121	.293	.273	63	-2	0	0	0	1.000	-0	/O-2	-0.2
	Yr	46	44	1	5	0	1	1	6	7	7	.114	.264	.227	41	-3	0	0	0	1.000	-0	/O-3	-0.4
Total	11	1075	2978	355	832	128	17	131	499	247	414	.279	.339	.466	123	86	7	4	-0	.961	-49	O-803	-0.1
■ **BILLY COWAN**	Cowan, Billy Rolland b: 8/28/38, Calhoun City, Miss. BR/TR, 6', 170 lbs. Deb: 9/9/63																						
1963	Chi-N	14	36	1	9	1	1	1	2	0	11	.250	.250	.417	84	-1	0	1	-1	.917	-2	O-10	-0.4
1964	Chi-N	139	497	52	120	16	4	19	50	18	128	.241	.269	.404	83	-12	12	3	2	.968	-3	*O-134	-2.1
1965	NY-N	82	156	16	28	8	2	3	9	4	45	.179	.205	.314	45	-12	3	2	-0	1.000	-8	O-61/2-2,S-1	-2.3
	Mil-N	19	27	4	5	1	0	0	0	0	9	.185	.185	.222	14	-3	0	0	0	1.000	-2	O-10	-0.5
	Yr	101	183	20	33	9	2	3	9	4	54	.180	.202	.301	41	-15	3	2	-0	1.000	-10	O-71/2-2,S-1	-2.8
1967	Phi-N	34	59	11	9	0	0	3	6	4	14	.153	.206	.305	44	-4	1	0	0	1.000	-4	O-20/2-1,3-1	-0.9
1969	NY-A	32	48	5	8	0	0	1	3	3	9	.167	.216	.229	25	-5	0	0	0	1.000	-2	O-14	-0.7
	Cal-A	28	56	10	17	1	0	4	10	3	9	.304	.350	.536	152	3	0	0	0	1.000	-0	O-13/1-6	0.3
	Yr	60	104	15	25	1	0	5	13	6	18	.240	.288	.394	93	-1	0	0	0	1.000	-2	O-27/1-6	-0.4
1970	Cal-A	68	134	20	37	9	1	5	25	11	29	.276	.336	.470	124	4	0	1	-1	.929	-6	O-27,1-14/3-2	-0.5
1971	Cal-A	74	174	12	48	8	0	4	20	7	41	.276	.304	.391	103	-0	1	1	-0	1.000	-2	O-40/1-5	-0.5
1972	Cal-A	3	3	0	0	0	0	0	0	0	2	.000	.000	.000	-99	-1	0	0	0	.000	0	H	-0.1
Total	8	493	1190	131	281	44	8	40	125	50	297	.236	.269	.387	83	-31	17	8	0	.977	-28	O-329/1-25,3-3,2S	-7.7
■ **AL COWENS**	Cowens, Alfred Edward b: 10/25/51, Los Angeles, Cal. BR/TR, 6'2", 200 lbs. Deb: 4/6/74																						
1974	KC-A	110	269	28	65	7	1	1	25	23	38	.242	.304	.286	67	-11	5	0	2	.988	-9	*O-102/3-2,D-4	-2.3
1975	KC-A	120	328	44	91	13	8	4	42	28	36	.277	.342	.402	107	3	12	7	-1	.978	-10	*O-113/D-2	-1.1
1976	*KC-A	152	581	71	154	23	6	3	59	26	50	.265	.300	.341	87	-11	23	16	-3	.986	5	*O-148/D-1	-1.5
1977	*KC-A	162	606	98	189	32	14	23	112	41	64	.312	.363	.525	138	30	16	12	-2	.982	3	*O-159/D-1	2.4
1978	*KC-A	132	485	63	133	24	8	5	63	31	54	.274	.326	.388	97	-2	14	6	1	.990	2	*O-127/3-5,D-2	-0.5
1979	KC-A	136	516	69	152	18	7	9	73	40	44	.295	.349	.409	102	1	10	8	-2	.986	-0	*O-134/D-1	-0.6
1980	Cal-A	34	119	11	27	5	0	1	17	12	21	.227	.303	.294	66	-5	1	2	-1	1.000	1	O-30/D-1	-0.7
	Det-A	108	403	58	113	15	3	5	42	37	40	.280	.342	.370	93	-3	5	6	-2	.986	2	*O-107/D-1	-0.8
	Yr	142	522	69	140	20	3	6	59	49	61	.268	.333	.352	87	-8	6	8	-3	.989	3	*O-137/D-2	-1.5
1981	Det-A	85	253	27	66	11	4	1	18	22	36	.261	.322	.348	90	-3	3	3	-1	.994	-6	O-83	-1.3
1982	Sea-A	146	560	72	151	39	8	20	78	46	81	.270	.326	.475	114	9	11	7	-1	.987	7	*O-145/D-1	1.1
1983	Sea-A	110	356	39	73	19	2	7	35	23	38	.205	.257	.329	58	-21	10	2	2	.985	2	O-70,D-34	-2.1
1984	Sea-A	139	524	60	145	34	2	15	78	27	83	.277	.315	.435	106	3	9	5	-0	.987	-2	*O-130/D-7	-0.4
1985	Sea-A	122	452	59	120	32	5	14	69	30	56	.265	.313	.451	105	2	0	0	0	.967	2	*O-110/D-5	0.0
1986	Sea-A	28	82	5	15	4	0	0	6	3	18	.183	.212	.232	20	-9	1	0	0	.971	-0	O-19/D-1	-0.9
Total	13	1584	5534	704	1494	276	68	108	717	389	659	.270	.322	.403	98	-18	120	74	-8	.985	-5	*O-1477/D-61,3-7	-8.7
■ **DICK COX**	Cox, Elmer Joseph b: 9/30/1897, Pasadena, Cal. d: 6/1/66, Morro Bay, Cal. BR/TR, 5'7.5", 158 lbs. Deb: 4/16/25																						
1925	Bro-N	122	434	68	143	23	10	7	64	37	29	.329	.382	.477	121	14	4	3	-1	.968	-4	*O-111	0.2
1926	Bro-N	124	398	53	118	17	4	1	45	46	20	.296	.375	.367	102	3	6			.964	-8	*O-117	-1.2
Total	2	246	832	121	261	40	14	8	109	83	49	.314	.379	.424	112	17	10	3		.966	-12	O-228	-1.0
■ **FRANK COX**	Cox, Francis Bernard "Runt" b: 8/29/1857, Waltham, Mass. d: 6/24/28, Hartford, Conn. 5'6", Deb: 8/13/1884																						
1884	Det-N	27	102	6	13	3	1	0	4	2	36	.127	.144	.176	0	-11				.812	-4	S-27	-1.3
■ **JIM COX**	Cox, James Charles b: 5/28/50, Bloomington, Ill. BR/TR, 5'11", 175 lbs. Deb: 7/19/73																						
1973	Mon-N	9	15	1	2	1	0	0	0	1	4	.133	.188	.200	7	-2	0	0	0	.950	-1	/2-7	-0.2
1974	Mon-N	77	236	29	52	9	1	2	26	23	36	.220	.292	.292	61	-12	2	3	-1	.968	15	2-72	0.4
1975	Mon-N	11	27	1	7	1	0	1	5	1	2	.259	.286	.407	87	-1	1	0	0	1.000	0	/2-8	0.0
1976	Mon-N	13	29	2	5	0	1	0	2	2	2	.172	.226	.241	31	-3	0	0	0	.958	1	2-11	-0.1
Total	4	110	307	33	66	11	2	3	33	27	44	.215	.281	.293	58	-17	3	3	-1	.969	16	/2-98	0.1
■ **JEFF COX**	Cox, Jeffrey Lindon b: 11/9/55, Los Angeles, Cal. BR/TR, 5'11", 170 lbs. Deb: 7/1/80																						
1980	Oak-A	59	169	20	36	3	0	0	9	14	23	.213	.273	.231	43	-13	8	5	-1	.979	-16	2-58	-2.6
1981	Oak-A	2	0	0	0	0	0	0	0	0	0	—	—	—	—	0	0	0	0	1.000	0	/2-1	0.0
Total	2	61	169	20	36	3	0	0	9	14	23	.213	.273	.231	43	-13	8	5	-1	.979	-16	/2-59	-2.6
■ **LARRY COX**	Cox, Larry Eugene b: 9/11/47, Bluffton, Ohio d: 2/17/90, Bellefontaine, Ohio BR/TR, 5'11", 190 lbs. Deb: 4/18/73 C																						
1973	Phi-N	1	0	0	0	0	0	0	0	0	0	—	—	—	—	0	0	0	0	1.000	-0	/C-1	0.0
1974	Phi-N	30	53	5	9	2	0	0	4	4	9	.170	.241	.208	25	-5	0	0	0	.990	0	C-29	-0.4
1975	Phi-N	11	5	0	1	0	0	0	1	1	0	.200	.333	.200	49	-0	1	0	0	1.000	-0	C-10	0.0
1977	Sea-A	35	93	6	23	6	0	2	6	10	12	.247	.320	.376	90	-1	1	1	-0	.970	-1	C-35	-0.2
1978	Chi-N	59	121	10	34	5	0	2	18	12	16	.281	.346	.372	90	-2	0	0	0	.967	2	C-58	0.1

YEAR	TM/L	G	AB	R	H	2B	3B	HR	RBI	BB	SO	AVG	OBP	SLG	PRO+	BR/A	SB	CS	SBR	FA	FR	G/POS	TPR
1979	Sea-A	100	293	32	63	11	3	4	36	22	39	.215	.270	.314	56	-18	2	1	0	.981	-2	C-99	-1.7
1980	Sea-A	105	243	18	49	6	2	4	20	19	36	.202	.260	.292	50	-17	1	2	-1	**.993**	12	*C-104	-0.3
1981	Tex-A	5	13	0	3	1	0	0	0	0	4	.231	.231	.308	57	-1	0	0	0	1.000	3	/C-5	0.3
1982	Chi-N	2	4	1	0	0	0	0	0	2	1	.000	.333	.000	1	-0	0	0	0	1.000	1	/C-2	0.1
Total	9	348	825	72	182	31	5	12	85	70	117	.221	.282	.314	61	-45	5	4	-1	.983	15	C-343	-2.1
■ **BOBBY COX** Cox, Robert Joseph b: 5/21/41, Tulsa, Okla. BR/TR, 5'11", 180 lbs. Deb: 4/14/68 MC																							
1968	NY-A	135	437	33	100	15	1	7	41	41	85	.229	.302	.316	90	-5	3	2	-0	.957	-5	*3-132	-1.2
1969	NY-A	85	191	17	41	7	1	2	17	34	41	.215	.336	.293	80	-4	0	1	-1	.935	11	3-56/2-6	0.7
Total	2	220	628	50	141	22	2	9	58	75	126	.225	.313	.309	87	-9	3	3	-1	.950	6	3-188/2-6	-0.5
■ **BILLY COX** Cox, William Richard b: 8/29/19, Newport, Pa. d: 3/30/78, Harrisburg, Pa. BR/TR, 5'10", 150 lbs. Deb: 9/20/41																							
1941	Pit-N	10	37	4	10	3	1	0	2	3	2	.270	.325	.405	105	0	1			.943	2	S-10	0.3
1946	Pit-N	121	411	32	119	22	6	2	36	26	15	.290	.333	.387	101	-0	4			.935	-16	*S-114	-1.0
1947	Pit-N	132	529	75	145	30	7	15	54	29	28	.274	.313	.442	96	-5	5			.968	-13	*S-129	-1.1
1948	Bro-N	88	237	36	59	13	2	3	15	38	19	.249	.353	.359	90	-3	3			.958	-4	3-70/S-6,2-1	-0.7
1949	*Bro-N	100	390	48	91	18	2	8	40	30	18	.233	.290	.351	68	-18	5			.964	9	*3-100	-1.1
1950	Bro-N	119	451	62	116	17	2	8	44	35	24	.257	.311	.357	74	-17	6			**.957**	12	*3-107,2-13/S-9	-0.6
1951	Bro-N	142	455	62	127	25	4	9	51	37	30	.279	.336	.411	98	-2	5	5	-2	.967	-8	*3-139/S-1	-1.3
1952	*Bro-N	116	455	56	118	12	3	6	34	25	32	.259	.301	.338	76	-15	10	12	-4	.970	-9	*3-100,S-10/2-9	-3.0
1953	*Bro-N	100	327	44	95	18	1	10	44	37	21	.291	.363	.443	106	3	2	2	-1	.974	-2	3-89/S-6,2-1	-0.1
1954	Bro-N	77	226	26	53	9	2	2	17	21	13	.235	.300	.319	59	-13	0	0	0	.961	2	3-58,2-11/S-8	-1.1
1955	Bal-A	53	194	25	41	7	2	3	14	17	16	.211	.275	.314	63	-11	1	2	-1	.969	-9	3-37,2-18/S-6	-2.1
Total	11	1058	3712	470	974	174	32	66	351	298	218	.262	.318	.380	85	-82	42	21		.965	-36	3-700,S-299/2-53	-11.8
■ **TED COX** Cox, William Ted b: 1/24/55, Oklahoma City, Okla BR/TR, 6'3", 195 lbs. Deb: 9/18/77																							
1977	Bos-A	13	58	11	21	3	1	1	6	3	6	.362	.393	.500	127	2	0	0	0	.000	0	D-13	0.2
1978	Cle-A	82	227	14	53	7	0	1	19	16	30	.233	.287	.278	60	-12	0	1	-1	.980	-5	O-38,3-20,D-12,/1S	-2.0
1979	Cle-A	78	189	17	40	6	0	4	22	14	27	.212	.273	.307	56	-12	3	4	-2	.964	1	3-52,O-16/2-4,D-1	-1.3
1980	Sea-A	83	247	17	60	9	0	2	23	19	25	.243	.297	.304	64	-12	0	0	0	.945	-2	3-80	-1.5
1981	Tor-A	16	50	6	15	4	0	2	9	5	10	.300	.364	.500	138	2	0	1	-1	.897	-4	3-14/1-1,D-1	-0.3
Total	5	272	771	65	189	29	1	10	79	57	98	.245	.300	.324	71	-31	3	6	-3	.947	-10	3-166/O-54,D12S	-4.9
■ **TOOTS COYNE** Coyne, Martin Albert b: 10/20/1894, St.Louis, Mo. d: 9/18/39, St.Louis, Mo. TR , Deb: 9/28/14																							
1914	Phi-A	1	2	0	0	0	0	0	0	0	2	.000	.000	.000	-99	-0	0			1.000	-0	/3-1	-0.1
■ **ESTEL CRABTREE** Crabtree, Estel Crayton "Crabby" b: 8/19/03, Crabtree, Ohio d: 1/4/67, Logan, Ohio BL/TR, 6', 168 lbs. Deb: 4/18/29 C																							
1929	Cin-N	1	1	0	0	0	0	0	0	0	0	.000	.000	.000	-99	-0	0			.000	0	H	0.0
1931	Cin-N	117	443	70	119	12	12	4	37	23	33	.269	.309	.377	89	-8	3			.974	10	*O-101/3-4,1-2	-0.5
1932	Cin-N	108	402	38	110	14	9	2	35	23	26	.274	.316	.368	86	-8	2			.990	9	O-95	-0.5
1933	StL-N	23	34	6	9	3	0	0	3	2	3	.265	.306	.353	83	-1	1			.947	-0	/O-7	-0.1
1941	StL-N	77	167	27	57	6	3	5	28	26	24	.341	.439	.503	154	13	1			1.000	-8	O-50/3-1	0.3
1942	StL-N	10	9	1	3	2	0	0	2	1	3	.333	.400	.556	166	1	0			.000	0	H	0.1
1943	Cin-N	95	254	25	70	12	0	2	26	25	17	.276	.345	.346	101	1	1			.939	-5	O-65	-0.8
1944	Cin-N	58	98	7	28	4	1	0	11	13	3	.286	.369	.347	106	1	0			1.000	-4	O-19/1-2	-0.4
Total	8	489	1408	174	396	53	25	13	142	113	109	.281	.339	.382	100	-2	8			.976	1	O-337/3-5,1-4	-1.9
■ **RICKEY CRADLE** Cradle, Rickey Nelson b: 6/20/73, Norfolk, Va. BR/TR, 6'2", 180 lbs. Deb: 7/1/98																							
1998	Sea-A	5	7	0	1	0	0	0	2	1	5	.143	.250	.143	6	-1	1	0	0	1.000	-1	/O-4	-0.2
■ **HARRY CRAFT** Craft, Harry Francis "Wildfire" b: 4/19/15, Ellisville, Miss. d: 8/3/95, Conroe, Tex. BR/TR, 6'1", 185 lbs. Deb: 9/19/37 MC																							
1937	Cin-N	10	42	7	13	2	1	0	4	1	3	.310	.326	.405	102	-0	0			1.000	0	O-10	0.0
1938	Cin-N	151	612	70	165	28	9	15	83	29	46	.270	.305	.418	100	-3	3			.983	16	*O-151	0.9
1939	*Cin-N	134	502	58	129	20	7	13	67	27	54	.257	.299	.402	86	-11	5			.981	3	*O-134	-1.3
1940	*Cin-N	115	422	47	103	18	5	6	48	17	46	.244	.277	.353	72	-17	2			**.997**	6	*O-109/1-2	-1.7
1941	Cin-N	119	413	48	103	15	2	10	59	33	43	.249	.308	.368	90	-7	4			.983	2	*O-115	-1.2
1942	Cin-N	37	113	7	20	2	1	0	6	3	11	.177	.205	.212	22	-11	0			.987	1	O-33	-1.3
Total	6	566	2104	237	533	85	25	44	267	110	203	.253	.294	.380	85	-49	14			.986	28	O-552/1-2	-4.6
■ **ROD CRAIG** Craig, Rodney Paul b: 1/12/58, Los Angeles, Cal. BB/TR, 6'1", 195 lbs. Deb: 9/11/79																							
1979	Sea-A	16	52	9	20	8	1	0	6	1	5	.385	.396	.577	156	4	1	1	-0	.923	-2	O-15	0.1
1980	Sea-A	70	240	30	57	15	1	3	20	17	35	.237	.293	.346	74	-9	3	6	-3	.987	-2	O-63	-1.6
1982	Cle-A	49	65	7	15	2	0	0	1	4	6	.231	.275	.262	49	-5	3	1	0	.966	-4	O-22/D-4	-0.9
1986	Chi-A	10	10	3	2	0	0	0	0	2	2	.200	.333	.200	48	-1	0	0	0	.000	-1	/O-2	-0.1
Total	4	145	367	49	94	25	2	3	27	24	48	.256	.305	.360	80	-10	7	8	-3	.977	-9	O-102/D-4	-2.5
■ **DOC CRAMER** Cramer, Roger Maxwell "Flit" b: 7/22/05, Beach Haven, N.J. d: 9/9/90, Manahawkin, N.J. BL/TR, 6'2", 185 lbs. Deb: 9/18/29 C																							
1929	Phi-A	2	6	0	0	0	0	0	0	0	2	.000	.000	.000	-97	-2	0	0	0	1.000	1	/O-1	-0.1
1930	Phi-A	30	82	12	19	1	1	0	6	2	8	.232	.250	.268	30	-9	0	0	0	.927	-2	O-21/S-1	-1.1
1931	*Phi-A	65	223	37	58	8	2	2	20	11	15	.260	.301	.341	64	-12	2	1	0	.979	1	O-55	-1.4
1932	Phi-A	92	384	73	129	27	6	3	46	17	27	.336	.367	.461	109	4	3	1	0	.976	8	O-86	0.7
1933	Phi-A	152	661	109	195	27	8	8	75	36	24	.295	.331	.396	91	-10	5	4	-1	.971	5	*O-152	-1.4
1934	Phi-A	153	649	99	202	29	9	6	46	40	35	.311	.353	.411	100	-1	1	5	-3	.985	5	*O-152	-0.4
1935	Phi-A★	149	644	96	214	37	4	3	70	37	34	.332	.373	.416	105	4	6	7	-2	.975	4	*O-149	0.0
1936	Bos-A	154	643	99	188	31	7	0	41	49	20	.292	.347	.362	71	-29	4	6	-2	.975	16	*O-154	-1.9
1937	Bos-A☆	133	560	90	171	22	11	0	51	35	14	.305	.351	.384	82	-15	8	6	-1	.969	6	*O-133	-1.4
1938	Bos-A★	148	658	116	198	36	8	0	71	51	19	.301	.354	.380	80	-20	4	9	-4	.986	9	*O-148/P-1	-1.8
1939	Bos-A★	137	589	110	183	30	6	0	56	36	17	.311	.352	.382	85	-13	3	3	-1	.984	2	*O-135	-1.6
1940	Bos-A☆	150	661	94	**200**	27	12	1	51	36	29	.303	.340	.384	84	-16	3	5	-2	.969	-5	*O-149	-3.0
1941	Was-A	154	660	93	180	25	6	2	66	37	15	.273	.317	.338	77	-23	4	1	1	.984	-7	*O-152	-3.8
1942	Det-A	151	630	71	166	26	4	0	43	43	18	.263	.314	.317	72	-24	4	4	-1	.981	-0	*O-150	-3.4
1943	Det-A	140	606	79	182	18	4	1	43	31	13	.300	.335	.348	93	-6	4	3	-1	.989	1	*O-138	-1.4
1944	Det-A	143	578	69	169	20	9	2	42	37	21	.292	.337	.369	96	-3	6	5	-1	.980	-8	*O-141	-2.1
1945	*Det-A	141	541	62	149	22	8	6	58	36	21	.275	.324	.379	97	-3	2	9	-5	**.991**	-8	*O-140	-2.5
1946	Det-A	68	204	26	60	8	2	1	26	15	8	.294	.342	.368	93	-2	3	0	1	1.000	-6	O-50	-1.0
1947	Det-A	73	157	21	42	2	2	2	30	20	5	.268	.350	.344	91	-2	0	4	-2	.965	-2	O-35	-0.8
1948	Det-A	4	4	1	0	0	0	0	1	3	0	.000	.429	.000	19	-0	0	0	0	1.000	-0	/O-1	0.0
Total	20	2239	9140	1357	2705	396	109	37	842	572	345	.296	.340	.375	87	-180	62	73	-25	.979	19	*O-2142/P-1,S-1	-28.4
■ **DICK CRAMER** Cramer, William B. b: Brooklyn, N.Y. d: 8/12/1885, Camden, N.J. Deb: 5/12/1883																							
1883	NY-N	2	6	0	0	0	0	0	0	1	5	.000	.143	.000	-52	-1				.000	-1	/O-2	-0.2
■ **DEL CRANDALL** Crandall, Delmar Wesley b: 3/5/30, Ontario, Cal. BR/TR, 6'1", 195 lbs. Deb: 6/17/49 MC																							
1949	Bos-N	67	228	21	60	10	1	4	34	9	18	.263	.291	.368	80	-7	2			.982	7	C-63	0.3
1950	Bos-N	79	255	21	56	11	0	4	37	13	24	.220	.257	.310	52	-19	0			.967	3	C-75/1-1	-1.3
1953	Mil-N†	116	382	55	104	13	1	15	51	33	47	.272	.330	.429	102	0	2	1	0	.986	15	*C-108	1.9
1954	Mil-N☆	138	463	60	112	18	2	21	64	40	56	.242	.306	.425	94	-6	0	3	-2	.989	14	*C-136	1.2
1955	Mil-N★	133	440	61	104	15	2	26	62	40	56	.236	.303	.457	103	-0	2	1	0	.985	-2	*C-131	0.3
1956	Mil-N†	112	311	37	74	14	2	16	48	35	30	.238	.317	.450	110	3	1	2	-1	**.996**	3	*C-109	1.0
1957	*Mil-N	118	383	45	97	11	2	15	46	30	38	.253	.309	.410	98	-2	1	2	-1	.987	-8	*C-102/O-9,1-1	-0.8
1958	*Mil-N★	131	427	50	116	23	1	18	63	48	38	.272	.351	.457	122	12	4	1	1	**.990**	6	*C-124	2.6
1959	Mil-N★	150	518	65	133	19	2	21	72	46	48	.257	.321	.423	105	2	5	1	1	**.994**	6	*C-146	1.7

YEAR	TM/L	G	AB	R	H	2B	3B	HR	RBI	BB	SO	AVG	OBP	SLG	PRO+	BR/A	SB	CS	SBR	FA	FR	G/POS	TPR
1960	Mil-N★	142	537	81	158	14	1	19	77	34	36	.294	.341	.430	118	12	4	6	-2	.988	-15	*C-141	0.3
1961	Mil-N	15	30	3	6	3	0	0	1	1	0	.200	.226	.300	40	-3	0	0	0	1.000	-2	/C-5	-0.4
1962	Mil-N★	107	350	35	104	12	3	8	45	27	24	.297	.351	.417	108	4	3	4	-2	**.994**	-4	C-90/1-5	0.2
1963	Mil-N	86	259	18	52	4	0	3	28	18	22	.201	.253	.251	46	-18	1	4	-2	.991	5	C-75/1-7	-1.4
1964	SF-N	69	195	12	45	8	1	3	11	22	21	.231	.309	.328	78	-5	0	3	-2	.993	13	C-65	0.8
1965	Pit-N	60	140	11	30	2	0	2	10	14	10	.214	.290	.271	59	-7	1	0	0	.996	5	C-60	0.0
1966	Cle-A	50	108	10	25	2	0	4	8	14	9	.231	.320	.361	95	-1	0	0	0	.991	15	C-49	1.8
Total	16	1573	5026	585	1276	179	18	179	657	424	477	.254	.315	.404	97	-35	26	28		.989	61	*C-1479/1-14,O-9	8.2

■ DOC CRANDALL

Crandall, James Otis b: 10/8/1887, Wadena, Ind. d: 8/17/51, Bell, Cal. BR/TR, 5'10.5", 180 lbs. Deb: 4/24/08

YEAR	TM/L	G	AB	R	H	2B	3B	HR	RBI	BB	SO	AVG	OBP	SLG	PRO+	BR/A	SB	CS	SBR	FA	FR	G/POS	TPR
1908	NY-N	34	72	8	16	4	0	2	6	4		.222	.273	.361	97	-1	0			.985	-2	P-32/2-1	0.0
1909	NY-N	30	41	4	10	0	1	1	1	1		.244	.262	.366	93	-1	0			.941	2	P-30	0.0
1910	NY-N	45	73	10	25	2	4	1	13	5	7	.342	.385	.521	163	5	0			.984	-2	P-42/S-1	0.0
1911	*NY-N	61	113	12	27	1	4	2	21	8	16	.239	.295	.372	83	-3	2			.958	-0	P-41/S-6,2-3	-0.2
1912	*NY-N	50	80	9	25	6	2	0	19	6	7	.313	.360	.438	114	1	0			.957	0	P-37/2-2,1-1	0.0
1913	*NY-N	31	25	4	7	2	1	0	2	1	5	.280	.308	.440	111	0	0			1.000	1	P-24/2-2	0.0
	StL-N	2	2	0	0	0	0	0	0	0	2	.000	.000	.000	-99	-1	0			.000	0	H	-0.1
	*NY-N	15	22	3	8	2	0	0	2	2	3	.364	.417	.455	148	1	0			1.000	1	P-11	0.0
	Yr	48	49	7	15	4	1	0	4	3	10	.306	.346	.429	120	1	0			1.000	2	P-35/2-2	-0.1
1914	StL-F	118	278	40	86	16	5	2	41	58	32	.309	.429	.424	126	9	3			.926	-18	2-63,P-27/S-1,O-1	-1.1
1915	StL-F	84	141	18	40	2	2	1	19	27	15	.284	.406	.348	107	1	4			.958	1	P-51	0.0
1916	StL-A	16	12	0	1	0	0	0	0	2	4	.083	.214	.083	-11	-2	0			.000	-0	/P-2	0.0
1918	Bos-N	14	28	1	8	0	0	0	2	4	3	.286	.375	.286	107	0	0			1.000	0	/P-5,O-3	0.0
Total	10	500	887	109	253	35	19	9	126	118	94	.285	.372	.398	114	13	9			.962	-18	P-302/2-71,S-8,O1	-1.4

■ ED CRANE

Crane, Edward Nicholas "Cannon-Ball" b: 5/27/1862, Boston, Mass. d: 9/20/1896, Rochester, N.Y. BR/TR, 5'10.5", 204 lbs. Deb: 4/17/1884

YEAR	TM/L	G	AB	R	H	2B	3B	HR	RBI	BB	SO	AVG	OBP	SLG	PRO+	BR/A	SB	CS	SBR	FA	FR	G/POS	TPR
1884	Bos-U	101	428	83	122	23	6	12		14		.285	.308	.451	129	2				.826	-5	O-57,C-42/1-5,P-4	-0.2
1885	Pro-N	1	2	0	0	0	0	0	0	1	1	.000	.333	.000	15	-0				.500	0	/O-1	0.0
	Buf-N	13	51	5	14	0	1	2	9	3	8	.275	.315	.431	135	2				.769	-3	O-13	-0.1
	Yr	14	53	5	14	0	1	2	9	4	9	.264	.316	.415	131	2				.750	-2	O-14	-0.1
1886	Was-N	80	292	20	50	11	3	0	20	13	54	.171	.207	.229	34	-22	8			.866	3	O-68,P-10/C-4	-1.7
1888	*NY-N	12	37	3	6	2	0	1	2	3	11	.162	.225	.297	66	-1	1			.867	1	P-12	0.0
1889	*NY-N	29	103	16	21	1	0	2	11	13	21	.204	.293	.272	58	-6	6			.762	-4	P-29/1-1	0.0
1890	NY-P	43	146	27	46	5	4	0	16	10	26	.315	.363	.404	96	-2	5			.846	-3	P-43	0.0
1891	Cin-a	34	110	13	17	0	0	1	7	8	28	.155	.212	.182	12	-13	4			.822	-2	P-32/O-3	-0.1
	Cin-N	15	46	3	5	0	0	0	2	3	12	.109	.163	.109	-20	-7	3			.906	0	P-15	0.0
1892	NY-N	48	163	20	40	1	1	0	14	11	30	.245	.297	.264	71	-6	2			.821	-1	P-47/O-1	-0.1
1893	NY-N	12	26	8	12	1	0	0	3	7	0	.462	.576	.500	186	4	0			.889	-1	P-10/1-1,O-1	0.0
	Bro-N	3	5	1	2	1	0	0	0	0	0	.400	.400	.600	172	0	0			.500	-1	/P-2,O-1	0.0
	Yr	15	31	9	14	2	0	0	3	7	0	.452	.553	.516	186	5	0			.850	-2	P-12/O-2,1-1	0.0
Total	9	391	1409	199	335	45	15	18	84	86	191	.238	.283	.329	80	-49	29			.842	-15	P-204,O-145/C-46,1	-2.2

■ FRED CRANE

Crane, Frederic William Hotchkiss b: 11/4/1840, Old Saybrook, Conn. d: 4/27/25, Brooklyn, N.Y. Deb: 5/26/1873

YEAR	TM/L	G	AB	R	H	2B	3B	HR	RBI	BB	SO	AVG	OBP	SLG	PRO+	BR/A	SB	CS	SBR	FA	FR	G/POS	TPR
1873	Res-n	1	4	0	1	0	0	0	1	0	0	.250	.250	.250	53	-0	0	0	0	.667	-1	/2-1	-0.1
1875	Atl-n	21	81	7	17	1	0	0	4	0	4	.210	.210	.222	58	-3	0	0	0	.953	1	1-20/S-1,O-1	-0.1
Total	2 n	22	85	7	18	1	0	0	5	0	4	.212	.212	.224	57	-3	0	0	0	.953	1	/1-20,O-1,S-1,2-1	-0.2

■ SAM CRANE

Crane, Samuel Byren "Lucky" or "Red" b: 9/13/1894, Harrisburg, Pa. d: 11/12/55, Philadelphia, Pa. BR/TR, 5'11.5", 154 lbs. Deb: 10/2/14

YEAR	TM/L	G	AB	R	H	2B	3B	HR	RBI	BB	SO	AVG	OBP	SLG	PRO+	BR/A	SB	CS	SBR	FA	FR	G/POS	TPR
1914	Phi-A	2	6	0	0	0	0	0	0	2	3	.000	.250	.000	-25	-1	0			.929	1	/S-2	0.0
1915	Phi-A	8	23	3	2	2	0	0	1	0	4	.087	.087	.174	-23	-4	0			.900	2	/S-6,2-1	-0.1
1916	Phi-A	2	4	1	1	0	0	0	0	2	1	.250	.500	.250	132	0	0			1.000	-0	/S-2	0.0
1917	Was-A	32	95	6	17	2	0	0	4	4	14	.179	.212	.200	26	-9	0			.889	-4	S-32	-1.3
1920	Cin-N	54	144	20	31	4	0	0	9	7	9	.215	.261	.243	46	-10	5	4	-1	.945	-9	S-25,3-10/2-4,O-3	-1.9
1921	Cin-N	73	215	20	50	10	2	0	16	14	14	.233	.292	.298	59	-13	2	5	-2	.953	-17	S-63/3-2,O-1	-2.6
1922	Bro-N	3	8	1	2	1	0	0	0	0	1	.250	.333	.375	83	-0	0	0	0	.875	2	/S-3	0.2
Total	7	174	495	51	103	19	2	0	30	29	46	.208	.262	.255	46	-35	7	9		.931	-25	S-133/3-12,2-5,O-4	-5.7

■ SAM CRANE

Crane, Samuel Newhall b: 1/2/1854, Springfield, Mass. d: 6/26/25, New York, N.Y. BR/TR, Deb: 5/1/1880 M

YEAR	TM/L	G	AB	R	H	2B	3B	HR	RBI	BB	SO	AVG	OBP	SLG	PRO+	BR/A	SB	CS	SBR	FA	FR	G/POS	TPR
1880	Buf-N	10	31	4	4	0	0	0	2	1	8	.129	.156	.129	-2	-3				.866	-2	2-10/O-1,M	-0.5
1883	NY-a	96	349	57	82	8	5	0		13		.235	.262	.287	73	-11	8			.859	-10	*2-96/O-1	-1.7
1884	Cin-U	80	309	56	72	9	3	1		11		.233	.259	.291	62	-24	16			.858	-9	*2-80,M	-2.8
1885	Det-N	68	245	23	47	4	6	1	20	13	45	.192	.233	.269	62	-10				.908	-5	2-68	-1.2
1886	Det-N	47	185	24	26	2	2	1	12	8	34	.141	.176	.189	11	-20	8			.903	1	2-38/S-8,O-4	-1.6
	StL-N	39	116	10	20	3	1	0	7	13	27	.172	.256	.216	48	-7	6			.897	-11	2-39	-1.4
	Yr	86	301	34	46	5	3	1	19	21	61	.153	.208	.199	25	-27	14			.900	-10	2-77/S-8,O-4	-3.0
1887	Was-N	7	30	6	9	1	1	0	1	1	6	.300	.323	.400	105	0	5			.865	-1	/S-7	0.0
1890	NY-N	2	6	0	0	0	0	0	0	0	1	.000	.000	.000	-99	-2	1			.778	-1	/1-1,O-1	-0.2
	Pit-N	22	82	3	16	3	0	0	3	0	5	.195	.205	.232	31	-7	5			.880	3	2-15/S-7,O-1	-0.2
	NY-N	2	6	0	0	0	0	0	0	0	1	.000	.000	.000	-99	-2	0			1.000	1	/2-2	-0.1
	Yr	26	94	3	16	3	0	0	3	0	7	.170	.179	.202	12	-11	6			.883	3	2-17/S-7,O-2,1-1	-0.5
Total	7	373	1359	183	276	30	18	3	45	60	127	.203	.237	.258	53	-85	25			.878	-33	2-348/S-22,O-8,1-1	-9.7

■ GAVVY CRAVATH

Cravath, Clifford Carlton "Cactus" b: 3/23/1881, Escondido, Cal. d: 5/23/63, Laguna Beach, Cal. BR/TR, 5'10.5", 186 lbs. Deb: 4/18/08 MC

YEAR	TM/L	G	AB	R	H	2B	3B	HR	RBI	BB	SO	AVG	OBP	SLG	PRO+	BR/A	SB	CS	SBR	FA	FR	G/POS	TPR
1908	Bos-A	94	277	43	71	10	11	1	34	38		.256	.354	.383	136	12	6			.925	-2	O-77/1-5	0.8
1909	Chi-A	19	50	7	9	0	0	1	8	19		.180	.406	.240	109	2	3			.944	-2	O-18	-0.1
	Was-A	4	6	0	0	0	0	0	1	1		.000	.143	.000	-57	-1	0			1.000	1	/O-1	-0.1
	Yr	23	56	7	9	0	0	1	9	20		.161	.382	.214	93	1	3			.947	-2	O-19	-0.2
1912	Phi-N	130	436	63	124	30	9	11	70	47	77	.284	.358	.470	118	9	15			.966	5	*O-113	0.8
1913	Phi-N	147	525	78	**179**	34	14	**19**	**128**	55	63	.341	.407	**.568**	**169**	**46**	10			.958	-4	*O-141	3.7
1914	Phi-N	149	499	76	149	27	8	**19**	100	83	72	.299	.402	.499	**157**	36	14			.930	3	*O-143	3.5
1915	*Phi-N	150	522	**89**	149	31	7	**24**	**115**	**86**	77	.285	**.393**	**.510**	**170**	**46**	11	9	-2	.946	9	*O-149	**4.9**
1916	Phi-N	137	448	70	127	21	8	11	70	64	89	.283	**.379**	.440	146	26	9			.966	-3	*O-130	1.8
1917	Phi-N	140	503	70	141	29	16	**12**	83	70	57	.280	.369	.473	151	31	6			.946	-3	*O-139	2.2
1918	Phi-N	121	426	43	99	27	5	**8**	54	54	46	.232	.320	.376	105	3	7			.931	-4	*O-118	-0.9
1919	Phi-N	83	214	34	73	18	5	**12**	45	35	21	.341	.438	.640	207	28	8			.914	-5	O-56,M	2.2
1920	Phi-N	46	45	2	13	5	0	1	11	9	12	.289	.407	.467	144	3	0	0	0	.007	-2	/O-5,M	0.1
Total	11	1220	3951	575	1134	232	83	119	719	561	514	.287	.380	.478	149	240	89	9		.944	-6	*O-1090/1-5	18.9

■ BILL CRAVER

Craver, William H. b: 6/1844, Troy, N.Y. d: 6/17/01, Troy, N.Y. BR/TR, 5'9", 160 lbs. Deb: 5/9/1871 M

YEAR	TM/L	G	AB	R	H	2B	3B	HR	RBI	BB	SO	AVG	OBP	SLG	PRO+	BR/A	SB	CS	SBR	FA	FR	G/POS	TPR
1871	Tro-n	27	118	26	38	8	1	0	26	3	0	.322	.339	.407	112	2	6	3	0	.870	7	2-18/S-4,C-3,1OM	0.5
1872	Bal-n	35	179	55	50	3	2	0	23	5	2	.279	.299	.318	86	-4	7	1	2	.873	7	C-27/O-4,2-2,3-2,M	0.3
1873	Bal-n	41	196	45	57	9	2	0	28	2	3	.291	.298	.357	94	-1	2	3	-1	.917	5	C-22,S-15/O-7,1-3	0.1
1874	Phi-n	55	265	68	91	19	11	0	56	4	2	.343	.353	.498	164	17	11	3	2	.807	6	*2-54/C-5,1-1	1.7
1875	Cen-n	14	65	8	18	4	2	0	5	2	4	.277	.299	.400	153	4	1	0	0	.773	4	/S-9,3-4,1-1,M	0.6
	Ath-n	54	260	71	83	11	11	2	40	4	5	.319	.330	.469	157	12	8	4	0	.856	-6	*2-54/C-2,3-1	0.4
	Yr	68	325	79	101	15	**13**	2	45	6	9	.311	.323	.455	156	16	9	4	0	.856	-2	2-54/S-9,3-5,C-2,1	1.0
1876	NY-N	56	246	24	55	4	0	0	22	2	7	.224	.230	.240	65	-8				.814	-21	2-42,C-11/S-6,M	-2.6
1877	Lou-N	57	238	33	63	5	2	0	29	5	11	.265	.280	.303	71	-10				.904	-1	*S-57	-0.8
Total	5 n	226	1083	273	337	54	29	2	178	20	16	.311	.324	.420	129	30	35	14	2	.834	22	2-128/C-59,SO31	3.6
Total	2	113	484	57	118	9	2	0	51	7	18	.244	.255	.271	69	-18				.897	-22	/S-63,2-42,C-11	-3.4

■ PAT CRAWFORD
Crawford, Clifford Rankin b: 1/28/02, Society Hill, S.C. d: 1/25/94, Morehead City, N.C BL/TR, 5'11", 170 lbs. Deb: 4/18/29

YEAR	TM/L	G	AB	R	H	2B	3B	HR	RBI	BB	SO	AVG	OBP	SLG	PRO+	BR/A	SB	CS	SBR	FA	FR	G/POS	TPR
1929	NY-N	65	57	13	17	3	0	3	24	11	5	.298	.412	.509	127	3	1			1.000	-0	/1-7,3-1	0.2
1930	NY-N	25	76	11	21	3	2	3	17	7	2	.276	.345	.487	100	-0	0			.966	-4	2-18/1-1	-0.3
	Cin-N	76	224	24	65	7	1	3	26	23	10	.290	.359	.371	81	-6	2			.969	-8	2-54,1-13	-1.2
	Yr	101	300	35	86	10	3	6	43	30	12	.287	.355	.400	86	-7	2			.968	-12	2-72,1-14	-1.5
1933	StL-N	91	224	24	60	8	2	0	21	14	9	.268	.317	.321	78	-6	1			.986	3	1-29,2-15/3-7	-0.6
1934	*StL-N	61	70	3	19	2	0	0	16	5	3	.271	.320	.300	63	-4	0			.900	2	/3-9,2-4	-0.1
Total	4	318	651	75	182	23	5	9	104	60	29	.280	.344	.372	85	-13	4			.969	-8	/2-91,1-50,3-17	-2.0

■ FORREST CRAWFORD
Crawford, Forrest A. b: 5/10/1881, Rockdale, Tex. d: 3/29/08, Austin, Tex. BL/TR, Deb: 7/30/06

YEAR	TM/L	G	AB	R	H	2B	3B	HR	RBI	BB	SO	AVG	OBP	SLG	PRO+	BR/A	SB	CS	SBR	FA	FR	G/POS	TPR
1906	StL-N	45	145	8	30	3	1	0	11	7		.207	.248	.241	55	-8	1			.927	-10	S-39/3-6	-1.8
1907	StL-N	7	22	0	5	0	0	0	3	2		.227	.292	.227	65	-1	0			.912	-1	/S-7	-0.2
Total	2	52	167	8	35	3	1	0	14	9		.210	.254	.240	56	-9	1			.924	-11	/S-46,3-6	-2.0

■ GEORGE CRAWFORD
Crawford, George Deb: 10/8/1890

YEAR	TM/L	G	AB	R	H	2B	3B	HR	RBI	BB	SO	AVG	OBP	SLG	PRO+	BR/A	SB	CS	SBR	FA	FR	G/POS	TPR
1890	Phi-a	5	17	1	2	0	0	0	3	0		.118	.118	.118	-31	-3	1			1.000	1	/O-4,S-1	-0.2

■ GLENN CRAWFORD
Crawford, Glenn Martin "Shorty" b: 12/2/13, North Branch, Mich. d: 1/2/72, Saginaw, Mich. BL/TR, 5'9", 165 lbs. Deb: 4/22/45

YEAR	TM/L	G	AB	R	H	2B	3B	HR	RBI	BB	SO	AVG	OBP	SLG	PRO+	BR/A	SB	CS	SBR	FA	FR	G/POS	TPR
1945	StL-N	4	3	0	0	0	0	0	0	1	0	.000	.250	.000	-26	-0	0			.000	-1	/O-1	-0.1
	Phi-N	82	302	41	89	13	2	2	24	36	15	.295	.372	.371	110	5	5			.976	-2	O-38,S-34,2-14	0.5
	Yr	86	305	41	89	13	2	2	24	37	15	.292	.370	.367	108	4	5			.976	-2	O-39,S-34,2-14	0.4
1946	Phi-N	1	1	0	0	0	0	0	0	0	0	.000	.000	.000	-99	-0	0			.000	0	H	0.0
Total	2	87	306	41	89	13	2	2	24	37	15	.291	.369	.366	108	4	5			—	-2	/O-39,S-34,2-14	0.4

■ KEN CRAWFORD
Crawford, Kenneth Daniel b: 10/31/1894, South Bend, Ind. d: 11/11/76, Pittsburgh, Pa. BL/TR, 5'9", 145 lbs. Deb: 9/6/15

YEAR	TM/L	G	AB	R	H	2B	3B	HR	RBI	BB	SO	AVG	OBP	SLG	PRO+	BR/A	SB	CS	SBR	FA	FR	G/POS	TPR
1915	Bal-F	23	82	4	20	2	1	0	7	1	18	.244	.253	.293	52	-7	0			.978	-2	1-14/O-4	-1.0

■ JAKE CRAWFORD
Crawford, Rufus b: 3/20/28, Campbell, Mo. BR/TR, 6'1.5", 185 lbs. Deb: 9/7/52

YEAR	TM/L	G	AB	R	H	2B	3B	HR	RBI	BB	SO	AVG	OBP	SLG	PRO+	BR/A	SB	CS	SBR	FA	FR	G/POS	TPR
1952	StL-A	7	11	1	2	1	0	0	0	1	5	.182	.250	.273	44	-1	1	0	0	1.000	-0	/O-3	-0.1

■ SAM CRAWFORD
Crawford, Samuel Earl "Wahoo Sam" b: 4/18/1880, Wahoo, Neb. d: 6/15/68, Hollywood, Cal. BL/TL, 6', 190 lbs. Deb: 9/10/1899 H

YEAR	TM/L	G	AB	R	H	2B	3B	HR	RBI	BB	SO	AVG	OBP	SLG	PRO+	BR/A	SB	CS	SBR	FA	FR	G/POS	TPR
1899	Cin-N	31	127	25	39	3	7	1	20	2		.307	.318	.465	111	1	6			.970	2	O-31	0.1
1900	Cin-N	101	389	68	101	15	15	7	59	28		.260	.314	.429	107	1	14			.948	12	*O-95	0.5
1901	Cin-N	131	515	91	170	20	16	**16**	104	37		.330	.378	.524	172	44	13			.923	3	*O-127	3.6
1902	Cin-N	140	555	92	185	18	**22**	3	78	47		.333	.386	.461	147	29	16			.932	4	*O-140	2.5
1903	Det-A	137	550	88	184	23	**25**	4	89	25		.335	.366	.489	159	37	18			.960	4	*O-137	3.3
1904	Det-A	150	562	49	143	22	16	2	73	44		.254	.309	.361	115	9	20			.973	4	*O-150	0.5
1905	Det-A	154	575	73	171	38	10	6	75	50		.297	.357	.430	148	30	22			**.988**	12	*O-103,1-51	3.9
1906	Det-A	145	563	65	166	25	16	2	72	38		.295	.341	.407	130	18	24			.984	1	*O-116,1-32	1.4
1907	*Det-A	144	582	**102**	188	34	17	4	81	37		.323	.366	.460	157	35	18			.965	9	*O-144/1-2	4.1
1908	*Det-A	152	591	102	184	33	16	**7**	80	37		.311	.355	.457	157	34	15			.970	-8	*O-134,1-17	2.3
1909	*Det-A	156	589	83	185	**35**	14	6	97	47		.314	.366	.452	151	32	30			.965	-7	*O-139,1-18	2.3
1910	Det-A	154	588	83	170	26	**19**	5	**120**	37		.289	.332	.423	128	16	20			.963	-11	*O-153/1-1	-0.2
1911	Det-A	146	574	109	217	36	14	7	115	61		.378	.438	.526	160	46	37			.975	-12	*O-146	2.6
1912	Det-A	149	581	81	189	30	21	4	109	42		.325	.373	.470	145	31	41			.984	-17	*O-149	0.7
1913	Det-A	153	609	78	193	32	**23**	9	83	52	28	.317	.371	.489	154	37	13			.964	-10	*O-140,1-13	2.2
1914	Det-A	157	582	74	183	22	**26**	8	**104**	69	31	.314	.388	.483	157	39	25	16	-2	.977	-8	*O-157	2.4
1915	Det-A	156	612	81	183	31	**19**	4	**112**	66	29	.299	.367	.431	132	22	24	14	-1	.974	-14	*O-156	0.0
1916	Det-A	100	322	41	92	11	13	0	42	37	10	.286	.359	.401	124	9	10			.978	-10	O-79/1-2	-0.6
1917	Det-A	61	104	6	18	4	0	2	12	4	6	.173	.204	.269	44	-7	0			.988	-3	1-15/O-3	-1.2
Total	19	2517	9570	1391	2961	458	309	97	1525	760	104	.309	.362	.452	143	464	366	30		.965	-48	*O-2299,1-151	30.4

■ WILLIE CRAWFORD
Crawford, Willie Murphy b: 9/7/46, Los Angeles, Cal. BL/TL, 6'1", 205 lbs. Deb: 9/16/64

YEAR	TM/L	G	AB	R	H	2B	3B	HR	RBI	BB	SO	AVG	OBP	SLG	PRO+	BR/A	SB	CS	SBR	FA	FR	G/POS	TPR
1964	LA-N	10	16	3	5	1	0	0	0	1	7	.313	.353	.375	113	0	1	1	-0	1.000	0	/O-4	0.0
1965	*LA-N	52	27	10	4	0	0	0	0	2	8	.148	.207	.148	2	-4	2	0	1	1.000	-2	/O-8	-0.5
1966	LA-N	6	0	1	0	0	0	0	0	0	0	—	—	—	—	0	0	0	0	.000	0	R	0.0
1967	LA-N	4	4	0	1	0	0	0	0	1	3	.250	.400	.250	98	0	0	0	0	.000	-1	/O-1	-0.1
1968	LA-N	61	175	25	44	12	1	4	14	20	64	.251	.335	.400	130	6	1	3	-2	.966	3	O-48	0.6
1969	LA-N	129	389	64	96	17	5	11	41	49	85	.247	.331	.401	112	6	4	5	-2	.973	-4	*O-113	-0.6
1970	LA-N	109	299	48	70	8	6	8	40	33	88	.234	.314	.381	89	-5	4	4	-1	.960	-1	O-94	-1.1
1971	LA-N	114	342	64	96	16	6	9	40	28	49	.281	.337	.442	126	11	5	2	0	.981	-7	O-97	0.0
1972	LA-N	96	243	28	61	7	3	8	27	35	55	.251	.350	.403	116	6	4	2	0	.983	-8	O-74	-0.5
1973	LA-N	145	457	75	135	26	2	14	66	78	91	.295	.399	.453	142	28	12	5	1	.978	1	*O-138	2.5
1974	*LA-N	139	468	73	138	23	4	11	61	64	88	.295	.380	.432	132	21	7	8	-3	.966	-7	*O-133	0.6
1975	LA-N	124	373	46	98	15	2	9	46	49	43	.263	.348	.386	108	4	5	5	-2	.990	-5	*O-113	-0.6
1976	StL-N	120	392	49	119	17	5	9	50	37	53	.304	.365	.441	127	14	2	1	0	.982	-1	*O-107	0.9
1977	Hou-N	42	114	14	29	3	0	2	18	16	10	.254	.346	.333	91	-1	0	0	0	.959	-2	O-30	-0.4
	Oak-A	59	136	7	25	7	1	1	16	18	20	.184	.279	.272	52	-9	0	0	0	.978	2	O-22,D-18	-0.8
Total	14	1210	3435	507	921	152	35	86	419	431	664	.268	.351	.408	117	77	47	36	-8	.975	-30	O-982/D-18	-0.0

■ GEORGE CREAMER
Creamer, George W. (b: George W. Triebel) b: 1855, Philadelphia, Pa. d: 6/27/1886, Philadelphia, Pa. BR/TR, 6'2", Deb: 5/1/1878 M

YEAR	TM/L	G	AB	R	H	2B	3B	HR	RBI	BB	SO	AVG	OBP	SLG	PRO+	BR/A	SB	CS	SBR	FA	FR	G/POS	TPR
1878	Mil-N	50	193	30	41	7	3	0	15	5	15	.212	.232	.280	63	-8				.839	-5	2-28,O-17/3-6	-1.1
1879	Syr-N	15	60	3	13	2	0	0	3	1	2	.217	.230	.250	65	-2				.825	-10	2-10/S-3,O-2	-1.0
1880	Wor-N	85	306	40	61	6	3	0	27	4	21	.199	.210	.239	47	-17				.883	-7	*2-85	-1.9
1881	Wor-N	80	309	42	64	9	2	0	25	11	27	.207	.234	.249	49	-18				.904	-9	*2-80	-2.2
1882	Wor-N	81	286	27	65	16	6	1	29	14	24	.227	.263	.336	88	-4				.907	11	*2-81	0.8
1883	Pit-a	91	369	54	94	7	9	0		20		.255	.293	.322	103	2				.897	8	*2-91	1.0
1884	Pit-a	98	339	38	62	8	5	0		16		.183	.224	.236	49	-18				**.937**	16	*2-98,M	0.0
Total	7	500	1862	234	400	55	28	1	99	71	89	.215	.244	.276	67	-65				.901	6	2-473/O-19,3-6,S-3	-4.4

■ BIRDIE CREE
Cree, William Franklin b: 10/23/1882, Khedive, Pa. d: 11/8/42, Sunbury, Pa. BR/TR, 5'6", 150 lbs. Deb: 9/17/08

YEAR	TM/L	G	AB	R	H	2B	3B	HR	RBI	BB	SO	AVG	OBP	SLG	PRO+	BR/A	SB	CS	SBR	FA	FR	G/POS	TPR
1908	NY-A	21	78	5	21	0	2	0	4	7		.269	.345	.321	115	2	1			1.000	1	O-21	0.2
1909	NY-A	104	343	48	90	6	3	2	27	30		.262	.338	.315	105	3	10			.949	-7	O-79/S-6,2-4,3-1	-0.7
1910	NY-A	134	467	58	134	19	16	4	73	40		.287	.353	.422	135	18	28			.955	-12	*O-134	-0.1
1911	NY-A	137	520	90	181	30	22	4	88	56		.348	.415	.513	149	33	48			.964	0	*O-132/S-4,2-2	2.6
1912	NY-A	50	190	25	63	11	6	0	22	20		.332	.409	.453	138	10	12			.948	5	O-50	1.2
1913	NY-A	145	534	51	145	25	6	1	63	50	51	.272	.338	.346	100	0	22			**.988**	-4	*O-144	-1.1
1914	NY-A	77	275	45	85	18	5	0	40	30	24	.309	.389	.411	141	14	4	9	-4	.976	7	O-76	1.5
1915	NY-A	74	196	23	42	8	2	0	15	36	22	.214	.353	.276	88	-1	7	8	-3	.945	-3	O-53	-1.0
Total	8	742	2603	345	761	117	62	11	332	269	97	.292	.368	.398	124	78	132	17		.965	-13	O-689/S-10,2-6,3-1	2.6

■ CONNIE CREEDEN
Creeden, Cornelius Stephen b: 7/21/15, Danvers, Mass. d: 11/30/69, Santa Ana, Cal. BL/TL, 6'1", 200 lbs. Deb: 4/28/43

YEAR	TM/L	G	AB	R	H	2B	3B	HR	RBI	BB	SO	AVG	OBP	SLG	PRO+	BR/A	SB	CS	SBR	FA	FR	G/POS	TPR
1943	Bos-N	5	4	0	1	0	0	0	1	1	0	.250	.400	.250	91	0	0			.000	0	H	0.0

■ PAT CREEDEN
Creeden, Patrick Francis "Whoops" b: 5/23/06, Newburyport, Mass. d: 4/20/92, Brockton, Mass. BL/TR, 5'8", 175 lbs. Deb: 4/14/31

YEAR	TM/L	G	AB	R	H	2B	3B	HR	RBI	BB	SO	AVG	OBP	SLG	PRO+	BR/A	SB	CS	SBR	FA	FR	G/POS	TPR
1931	Bos-A	5	8	0	0	0	0	0	0	1	3	.000	.111	.000	-73	-2	0	0	0	.846	0	/2-2	-0.2

■ MARTY CREEGAN
Creegan, Martin b: San Francisco, Cal. 161 lbs. Deb: 4/17/1884

YEAR	TM/L	G	AB	R	H	2B	3B	HR	RBI	BB	SO	AVG	OBP	SLG	PRO+	BR/A	SB	CS	SBR	FA	FR	G/POS	TPR
1884	Was-U	9	33	4	5	0	0	0		1		.152	.176	.152	0	-5				.667	-1	/O-6,C-3,3-2,1-1	-0.5

■ GUS CREELY
Creely, August L. b: 6/6/1870, Florissant, Mo. d: 4/22/34, St.Louis, Mo. 5'6", 150 lbs. Deb: 10/9/1890

YEAR	TM/L	G	AB	R	H	2B	3B	HR	RBI	BB	SO	AVG	OBP	SLG	PRO+	BR/A	SB	CS	SBR	FA	FR	G/POS	TPR
1890	StL-a	4	15	0	0	0	0	0	0	0		.000	.000	.000	-88	-4	1			.769	-3	/S-4	-0.6

YEAR	TM/L	G	AB	R	H	2B	3B	HR	RBI	BB	SO	AVG	OBP	SLG	PRO+	BR/A	SB	CS	SBR	FA	FR	G/POS	TPR
■ PETE CREGAN Cregan, Peter James "Peekskill Pete" b: 4/13/1875, Kingston, N.Y. d: 5/18/45, New York, N.Y. BR/TR, 5'7.5", 150 lbs. Deb: 9/8/1899																							
1899	NY-N	1	2	0	0	0	0	0	0	0		.000	.000	.000	-99	-1	0			1.000	-0	/O-1	-0.1
1903	Cin-N	6	19	0	2	0	0	0	0	1		.105	.190	.105	-13	-3	0			.769	-1	/O-6	-0.4
Total	2	7	21	0	2	0	0	0	0	1		.095	.174	.095	-21	-3	0			.786	-2	/O-7	-0.5
■ BERNIE CREGER Creger, Bernard Odell b: 3/21/27, Wytheville, Va. BR/TR, 6', 175 lbs. Deb: 4/29/47																							
1947	StL-N	15	16	3	3	1	0	0	0	1	3	.188	.235	.250	28	-2	1			.828	-3	S-13	-0.5
■ CREEPY CRESPI Crespi, Frank Angelo Joseph b: 2/16/18, St.Louis, Mo. d: 3/1/90, Florissant, Mo. BR/TR, 5'8.5", 175 lbs. Deb: 9/14/38																							
1938	StL-N	7	19	2	5	2	0	0	1	2	7	.263	.333	.368	88	-0	0			.813	-2	/S-7	-0.2
1939	StL-N	15	29	3	5	1	0	0	6	3	6	.172	.250	.207	23	-3	0			.962	-0	/2-6,S-4	-0.3
1940	StL-N	3	11	2	3	1	0	0	0	1	2	.273	.333	.364	87	-0	1			1.000	-1	/3-2,S-1	-0.1
1941	StL-N	146	560	85	156	24	2	4	46	57	58	.279	.355	.350	93	-4	3			.962	0	*2-145	0.7
1942	*StL-N	93	292	33	71	4	2	0	35	27	29	.243	.309	.271	65	-12	4			.967	-5	2-83/S-5	-1.3
Total	5	264	911	125	240	32	4	4	88	90	102	.263	.336	.321	82	-20	8			.963	-7	2-234/S-17,3-2	-1.2
■ FELIPE CRESPO Crespo, Felipe Javier (Clausio) b: 3/5/73, Rio Piedras, P.R. BB/TR, 5'11", 195 lbs. Deb: 4/28/96																							
1996	Tor-A	22	49	6	9	4	0	0	4	12	13	.184	.375	.265	66	-2	1	0	0	.982	3	2-10/3-6,1-2	0.2
1997	Tor-A	12	28	3	8	0	1	1	5	2	4	.286	.333	.464	105	0	0	0	0	.933	-1	/3-7,2-1,D-2	-0.1
1998	Tor-A	66	130	11	34	8	1	1	15	15	27	.262	.347	.362	85	-3	4	3	-1	1.000	-7	O-42/2-8,3-2,1-1,D	-1.0
Total	3	100	207	20	51	12	2	2	24	29	44	.246	.353	.353	83	-4	5	3	-0	.952	-5	/O-42,2-19,3-15,D1	-0.9
■ LOU CRIGER Criger, Louis b: 2/3/1872, Elkhart, Ind. d: 5/14/34, Tucson, Ariz. BR/TR, 5'10", 165 lbs. Deb: 9/21/1896																							
1896	Cle-N	2	5	0	0	0	0	0	0	1	0	.000	.167	.000	-51	-1	1			1.000	1	/C-1	0.0
1897	Cle-N	39	138	15	31	4	1	0	22	23		.225	.340	.268	58	-8	5			.937	-1	C-37/1-2	-0.4
1898	Cle-N	84	287	43	80	13	4	1	32	40		.279	.377	.362	113	7	2			.957	15	C-82	2.8
1899	StL-N	77	258	39	66	4	5	2	44	28		.256	.333	.333	81	-6	14			.949	2	C-75	0.1
1900	StL-N	80	288	31	78	8	6	2	38	4		.271	.286	.361	78	-10	5			.953	6	C-75/3-1	0.3
1901	Bos-A	76	268	26	62	6	3	0	24	11		.231	.270	.276	52	-17	7			.967	22	C-68/1-8	1.0
1902	Bos-A	83	266	32	68	16	6	0	28	27		.256	.324	.361	87	-5	7			.965	14	C-80/O-1	1.7
1903	*Bos-A	96	317	41	61	7	10	3	31	26		.192	.256	.306	65	-14	5			.979	23	C-96	2.0
1904	Bos-A	98	299	34	63	10	5	2	34	27		.211	.283	.298	79	-7	1			.981	19	C-95	2.5
1905	Bos-A	109	313	33	62	6	7	1	36	54		.198	.322	.272	88	-2	5			.972	5	*C-109	1.5
1906	Bos-A	7	17	0	3	1	0	0	1	1		.176	.222	.235	43	-1	1			.981	5	/C-6	0.4
1907	Bos-A	75	226	12	41	4	0	0	14	19		.181	.251	.199	44	-14	2			.978	-0	C-75	-0.8
1908	Bos-A	84	237	12	45	4	2	0	25	13		.190	.232	.224	47	-14	1			.980	13	C-84	0.7
1909	StL-A	74	212	15	36	1	1	0	9	25		.170	.261	.184	44	-13	2			.986	8	C-73	0.2
1910	NY-A	27	69	3	13	2	0	0	4	10		.188	.291	.217	56	-3	0			.993	-1	C-27	-0.3
1912	StL-A	1	2	1	0	0	0	0	0	0		.000	.000	.000	-99	-1	0			1.000	1	/C-1	0.0
Total	16	1012	3202	337	709	86	50	11	342	309	0	.221	.295	.290	72	-108	58			.971	130	C-984/1-10,O-1,3-1	11.7
■ DAVE CRIPE Cripe, David Gordon b: 4/7/51, Ramona, Cal. BR/TR, 6', 180 lbs. Deb: 9/10/78																							
1978	KC-A	7	13	1	2	0	0	0	1	0	2	.154	.154	.154	-13	-2	0	0	0	1.000	-2	/3-5	-0.4
■ DAVE CRISCIONE Criscione, David Gerald b: 9/2/51, Dunkirk, N.Y. BR/TR, 5'8", 185 lbs. Deb: 7/17/77																							
1977	Bal-A	7	9	1	3	0	0	1	1	0	1	.333	.333	.667	176	1	0	0	0	1.000	-1	/C-7	0.0
■ TONY CRISCOLA Criscola, Anthony Paul b: 7/9/15, Walla Walla, Wash. BL/TR, 5'11.5", 180 lbs. Deb: 4/15/42																							
1942	StL-A	91	158	17	47	9	2	1	13	8	13	.297	.331	.399	103	0	2	2	-1	.955	-14	O-52	-1.7
1943	StL-A	29	52	4	8	0	0	0	1	8	7	.154	.267	.154	24	-5	0	0	0	.960	-2	O-13	-0.8
1944	Cin-N	64	157	14	36	3	2	0	14	14	12	.229	.297	.274	64	-7	0			.977	2	O-35	-0.8
Total	3	184	367	35	91	12	4	1	28	30	32	.248	.307	.311	75	-12	2	2		.966	-15	O-100	-3.3
■ PAT CRISHAM Crisham, Patrick J. b: 6/4/1877, Amesbury, Mass. d: 6/12/15, Syracuse, N.Y. 6', 168 lbs. Deb: 5/5/1899																							
1899	Bal-N	53	172	23	50	5	3	0	20	4		.291	.311	.355	78	-6	4			.979	-5	1-26,C-22	-0.8
■ JOE CRISP Crisp, Joseph Shelby b: 7/8/1889, Higginsville, Mo. d: 2/5/39, Kansas City, Mo. BR/TR, 6'4", 200 lbs. Deb: 9/2/10																							
1910	StL-A	1	1	0	0	0	0	0	0	0		.000	.000	.000	-99	-0	0			1.000	-0	/C-1	0.0
1911	StL-A	1	1	0	1	0	0	0	0	0		1.000	1.000	1.000	477	0	0			.000	0	/H	0.0
Total	2	2	2	0	1	0	0	0	0	0		.500	.500	.500	206	0	0			1.000	-0	/C-1	0.0
■ DODE CRISS Criss, Dode b: 3/12/1885, Sherman, Miss. d: 9/8/55, Sherman, Miss. BL/TR, 6'2", 200 lbs. Deb: 4/20/08																							
1908	StL-A	64	82	15	28	6	0	0	14	9		.341	.407	.415	166	6	1			.933	-1	O-11/P-9,1-1	0.5
1909	StL-A	35	48	2	14	6	1	0	7	0		.292	.306	.458	152	2	0			1.000	-1	P-11	0.0
1910	StL-A	70	91	11	21	4	2	1	11	11		.231	.320	.352	118	2	2			.983	-1	1-11/P-6	0.1
1911	StL-A	58	83	10	21	3	1	2	15	11		.253	.347	.386	109	1	0			.956	-2	1-14/P-4	-0.1
Total	4	227	304	38	84	19	4	3	47	31		.276	.349	.395	133	11	3			.964	-5	/P-30,1-26,O-11	0.5
■ CHES CRIST Crist, Chester Arthur "Squak" b: 2/10/1882, Cozaddale, Ohio d: 1/7/57, Cincinnati, Ohio BR/TR, 5'11", 165 lbs. Deb: 5/18/06																							
1906	Phi-N	6	11	1	0	0	0	0	0	0		.000	.083	.000	-74	-2	0			.800	-3	/C-6	-0.6
■ HUGHIE CRITZ Critz, Hugh Melville b: 9/17/1900, Starkville, Miss. d: 1/10/80, Greenwood, Miss. BR/TR, 5'8", 147 lbs. Deb: 5/31/24																							
1924	Cin-N	102	413	67	133	15	14	3	35	19	18	.322	.352	.448	115	7	19	11	-1	.956	3	2-96/S-1	1.0
1925	Cin-N	144	541	74	150	14	8	2	51	34	17	.277	.321	.344	72	-23	13	13	-4	.970	22	*2-144	-0.3
1926	Cin-N	155	607	96	164	24	14	3	79	39	25	.270	.316	.371	87	-12	7			**.981**	**24**	*2-155	1.6
1927	Cin-N	113	396	50	110	10	8	4	49	16	18	.278	.306	.374	84	-10	7			.969	-2	*2-113	-0.8
1928	Cin-N	153	641	95	190	21	11	5	52	37	24	.296	.335	.387	90	-11	18			.971	-17	*2-153	-2.3
1929	Cin-N	107	425	55	105	17	9	1	50	27	21	.247	.292	.336	58	-29	9			**.974**	4	*2-106/S-1	-1.9
1930	Cin-N	28	104	15	24	3	2	0	11	6	6	.231	.273	.298	40	-10	1			.987	-3	2-28	-1.1
	NY-N	124	558	93	148	17	11	4	50	24	26	.265	.296	.357	58	-39	7			.972	5	*2-124	-2.4
	Yr	152	662	108	172	20	13	4	61	30	32	.260	.292	.347	55	-49	8			**.974**	2	*2-152	-3.5
1931	NY-N	66	238	33	69	7	2	4	17	8	17	.290	.313	.387	89	-4	4			.984	0	2-54	0.0
1932	NY-N	151	659	90	182	32	7	2	50	34	27	.276	.313	.355	81	-18	3			.974	1	*2-151	-0.9
1933	*NY-N	133	558	68	137	18	5	2	33	23	24	.246	.279	.306	68	-23	4			**.982**	**47**	*2-133	3.2
1934	NY-N	137	571	77	138	17	1	6	40	19	24	.242	.269	.306	55	-37	3			**.978**	**25**	*2-137	-0.3
1935	NY-N	65	219	19	41	0	3	2	14	3	10	.187	.198	.242	18	-25	2			.966	3	2-59	-1.8
Total	12	1478	5930	832	1591	195	95	38	531	289	257	.268	.303	.352	74	-235	97	24		.974	111	*2-1453/S-2	-6.0
■ DAVEY CROCKETT Crockett, Daniel Solomon b: 10/5/1875, Roanoke, Va. d: 2/23/61, Charlottesville, Va. BL/TR, 6'1", 175 lbs. Deb: 7/11/01																							
1901	Det-A	28	102	10	29	2	2	0	14	6		.284	.336	.343	85	-2	1			.968	-0	1-27	-0.3
■ ART CROFT Croft, Arthur F. b: 1/23/1855, St.Louis, Mo. d: 3/16/1884, St.Louis, Mo. Deb: 5/4/1875																							
1875	RS-n	19	75	5	15	3	0	0	2	0	2	.200	.200	.240	58	-3	5	1	1	.800	-4	O-19	-0.5
1877	StL-N	54	220	23	51	5	2	0	27	1	15	.232	.235	.273	63	-9				.971	-3	1-28,O-25/2-1	-1.1
1878	Ind-N	60	222	22	35	6	0	0	16	5	23	.158	.176	.185	22	-18				.963	-1	*1-51/O-9	-2.0
Total	2	114	442	45	86	11	2	0	43	6	38	.195	.205	.229	43	-26				.965	-4	/1-79,O-34,2-1	-3.1
■ HARRY CROFT Croft, Henry T. b: 8/1/1875, Chicago, Ill. d: 12/11/33, Oak Park, Ill. Deb: 5/19/1899																							
1899	Lou-N	2	2	0	0	0	0	0	0	0		.000	.000	.000	-99	-1	0			.000	0	/H	0.0
	Phi-N	2	7	0	1	0	0	0	0	1		.143	.250	.143	9	-1	0			1.000	-1	/2-2	-0.1
	Yr	4	9	0	1	0	0	0	0	1		.111	.200	.111	-14	-1	0			1.000	-1	/2-2	-0.1

YEAR	TM/L	G	AB	R	H	2B	3B	HR	RBI	BB	SO	AVG	OBP	SLG	PRO+	BR/A	SB	CS	SBR	FA	FR	G/POS	TPR
1901	Chi-N	3	12	1	4	0	0	0	4	0		.333	.333	.333	97	-0	0			1.000	2	/O-3	0.2
Total	2	7	21	1	5	0	0	0	4	1		.238	.273	.238	47	-1	0			1.000	2	/O-3,2-2	0.1

■ FRED CROLIUS
Crolius, Fred Joseph b: 12/16/1876, Jersey City, N.J. d: 8/25/60, Ormond Beach, Fla. Deb: 4/19/01

YEAR	TM/L	G	AB	R	H	2B	3B	HR	RBI	BB	SO	AVG	OBP	SLG	PRO+	BR/A	SB	CS	SBR	FA	FR	G/POS	TPR
1901	Bos-N	49	200	22	48	4	1	1	13	9		.240	.306	.285	66	-9	6			.850	-8	O-49	-2.0
1902	Pit-N	9	38	4	10	2	1	0	7	0		.263	.263	.368	91	-1	0			1.000	-1	/O-9	-0.2
Total	2	58	238	26	58	6	2	1	20	9		.244	.300	.298	69	-9	6			.868	-8	/O-58	-2.2

■ WARREN CROMARTIE
Cromartie, Warren Livingston b: 9/29/53, Miami Beach, Fla. BL/TL, 6′, 192 lbs. Deb: 9/6/74

YEAR	TM/L	G	AB	R	H	2B	3B	HR	RBI	BB	SO	AVG	OBP	SLG	PRO+	BR/A	SB	CS	SBR	FA	FR	G/POS	TPR
1974	Mon-N	8	17	2	3	0	0	0	0	3	3	.176	.300	.176	34	-1	1	0	0	1.000	-1	/O-6	-0.2
1976	Mon-N	33	81	8	17	1	0	0	2	1	5	.210	.220	.222	25	-8	1	2	-1	.943	-2	O-20	-1.2
1977	Mon-N	155	620	64	175	41	7	5	50	33	40	.282	.323	.395	94	-6	10	3	1	.976	12	*O-155	0.1
1978	Mon-N	159	607	77	180	32	6	10	56	33	60	.297	.340	.418	112	9	8	8	-2	.978	25	*O-158/1-4	2.5
1979	Mon-N	158	659	84	181	46	5	8	46	38	78	.275	.315	.396	94	-7	8	7	-2	.976	20	*O-158	0.5
1980	Mon-N	162	597	74	172	33	5	14	70	51	64	.288	.346	.430	115	12	8	8	-2	.991	-4	*1-158/O-2	-0.5
1981	*Mon-N	99	358	41	109	19	2	6	42	39	27	.304	.373	.419	123	11	2	3	-1	.992	-1	1-62,O-38	0.5
1982	Mon-N	144	497	59	126	24	3	14	62	69	60	.254	.348	.398	106	5	3	0	1	.979	11	*O-136/1-9	1.4
1983	Mon-N	120	360	37	100	26	2	3	43	43	48	.278	.356	.386	106	4	8	3	1	.973	12	*O-101/1-1	1.5
1991	KC-A	69	131	13	41	7	2	1	20	15	18	.313	.384	.420	122	4	1	3	-2	.996	-4	1-29/O-6,D-1	-0.3
Total	10	1107	3927	459	1104	229	32	61	391	325	403	.281	.339	.402	105	22	50	37	-7	.977	68	O-780,1-263/D-1	4.3

■ TRIPP CROMER
Cromer, Roy Bunyan b: 11/21/67, Lake City, S.C. BR/TR, 6′2″, 165 lbs. Deb: 9/7/93

YEAR	TM/L	G	AB	R	H	2B	3B	HR	RBI	BB	SO	AVG	OBP	SLG	PRO+	BR/A	SB	CS	SBR	FA	FR	G/POS	TPR
1993	StL-N	10	23	1	2	0	0	0	0	1	6	.087	.125	.087	-43	-5	0	0	0	.912	1	/S-9	-0.3
1994	StL-N	2	0	1	0	0	0	0	0	0	0	—	—	—	—	0	0	0	0	.000	-1	/S-2	-0.1
1995	StL-N	105	345	36	78	19	0	5	18	14	66	.226	.264	.325	54	-23	0	0	0	.960	2	S-95,2-11	-1.3
1997	LA-N	28	86	8	25	3	0	4	20	6	16	.291	.337	.465	116	2	0	1	-1	.968	-3	2-17,S-10/3-1	0.0
1998	LA-N	6	6	1	1	0	0	1	1	0	2	.167	.167	.667	110	-0	0	0	0	.000	0	/H	0.0
Total	5	151	460	47	106	22	0	10	39	21	90	.230	.270	.343	61	-26	0	1	-1	.957	-1	S-116/2-28,3-1	-1.7

■ NED CROMPTON
Crompton, Edward b: 2/12/1889, Liverpool, England d: 9/28/50, Aspinwall, Pa. BL/TL, 5′10.5″, 175 lbs. Deb: 9/13/09

YEAR	TM/L	G	AB	R	H	2B	3B	HR	RBI	BB	SO	AVG	OBP	SLG	PRO+	BR/A	SB	CS	SBR	FA	FR	G/POS	TPR
1909	StL-A	17	63	7	10	2	1	0	2	7		.159	.254	.222	54	-3	1			.909	1	O-17	-0.3
1910	Cin-N	1	2	0	0	0	0	0	0	0	2	.000	.000	.000	-99	-1	0			.000	-1	/O-1	-0.1
Total	2	18	65	7	10	2	1	0	2	7	2	.154	.247	.215	49	-4	1			.909	1	/O-18	-0.4

■ HERB CROMPTON
Crompton, Herbert Bryan "Workhorse" b: 11/7/11, Taylor Ridge, Ill. d: 8/5/63, Moline, Ill. BR/TR, 6′, 185 lbs. Deb: 4/26/37

YEAR	TM/L	G	AB	R	H	2B	3B	HR	RBI	BB	SO	AVG	OBP	SLG	PRO+	BR/A	SB	CS	SBR	FA	FR	G/POS	TPR
1937	Was-A	2	3	0	1	0	0	0	0	0	0	.333	.333	.333	72	-0	0	0	0	1.000	0	/C-2	0.0
1945	NY-A	36	99	6	19	3	0	0	12	2	7	.192	.208	.222	24	-10	0	0	0	.984	1	C-33	-0.8
Total	2	38	102	6	20	3	0	0	12	2	7	.196	.212	.225	25	-10	0	0	0	.984	1	/C-35	-0.8

■ CHRIS CRON
Cron, Christopher John b: 3/31/64, Albuquerque, N.Mex. BR/TR, 6′2″, 200 lbs. Deb: 8/15/91

YEAR	TM/L	G	AB	R	H	2B	3B	HR	RBI	BB	SO	AVG	OBP	SLG	PRO+	BR/A	SB	CS	SBR	FA	FR	G/POS	TPR
1991	Cal-A	6	15	0	2	0	0	0	0	2	5	.133	.235	.133	5	-2	0	0	0	1.000	2	/1-5,D-1	-0.1
1992	Chi-A	6	10	0	0	0	0	0	0	0	4	.000	.000	.000	-99	-3	0	0	0	.923	-1	/1-5,O-1	-0.3
Total	2	12	25	0	2	0	0	0	0	2	9	.080	.148	.080	-35	-5	0	0	0	.980	1	/1-10,O-1,D-1	-0.4

■ DAN CRONIN
Cronin, Daniel T. b: 4/1/1857, S.Boston, Mass. d: 11/30/1885, Boston, Mass. 5′8″, 170 lbs. Deb: 7/9/1884

YEAR	TM/L	G	AB	R	H	2B	3B	HR	RBI	BB	SO	AVG	OBP	SLG	PRO+	BR/A	SB	CS	SBR	FA	FR	G/POS	TPR
1884	CP-U	1	4	1	1	0	0	0		0		.250	.250	.250	52	-0				.200	-2	/2-1	-0.2
	StL-U	1	5	0	0	0	0	0		0		.000	.000	.000	-97	-1				.000	-1	/O-1	-0.2
	Yr	2	9	1	1	0	0	0		0		.111	.111	.111	-32	-2				.000	-3	/2-1,O-1	-0.4

■ JIM CRONIN
Cronin, James John b: 8/7/05, Richmond, Cal. d: 6/10/83, Concord, Cal. BB/TR, 5′10.5″, 150 lbs. Deb: 7/4/29

YEAR	TM/L	G	AB	R	H	2B	3B	HR	RBI	BB	SO	AVG	OBP	SLG	PRO+	BR/A	SB	CS	SBR	FA	FR	G/POS	TPR
1929	Phi-A	25	56	7	13	2	1	0	4	5	7	.232	.295	.304	52	-4	0	0	0	.966	5	2-10/S-9,3-4	0.2

■ JOE CRONIN
Cronin, Joseph Edward b: 10/12/06, San Francisco, Cal d: 9/7/84, Osterville, Mass. BR/TR, 5′11.5″, 180 lbs. Deb: 4/29/26 MH

YEAR	TM/L	G	AB	R	H	2B	3B	HR	RBI	BB	SO	AVG	OBP	SLG	PRO+	BR/A	SB	CS	SBR	FA	FR	G/POS	TPR
1926	Pit-N	38	83	9	22	2	2	0	11	6	15	.265	.315	.337	72	-3	0			.977	6	2-27/S-7	0.3
1927	Pit-N	12	22	2	5	1	0	0	3	2	3	.227	.292	.273	48	-2	0			1.000	-4	/2-7,S-4,1-1	-0.5
1928	Was-A	63	227	23	55	10	4	0	25	22	27	.242	.309	.322	66	-11	4	0	1	.953	8	S-63	0.5
1929	Was-A	145	494	72	139	29	8	8	61	85	37	.281	.388	.421	107	8	5	9	-4	.923	6	*S-143/2-1	2.6
1930	Was-A	154	587	127	203	41	9	13	126	72	36	.346	.422	.513	135	33	17	10	-1	.960	26	*S-154	6.7
1931	Was-A	156	611	103	187	44	13	12	126	81	52	.306	.391	.480	127	25	10	9	-2	.950	13	*S-155	4.6
1932	Was-A	143	557	95	177	43	**18**	6	116	66	45	.318	.393	.492	129	25	7	5	-1	**.959**	6	*S-141	3.9
1933	*Was-A★	152	602	89	186	**45**	11	5	118	87	49	.309	.398	.445	124	23	5	4	-1	**.960**	10	*S-152,M	4.0
1934	Was-A★	127	504	68	143	30	9	7	101	53	28	.284	.353	.421	103	1	8	0	2	.951	18	*S-127,M	2.7
1935	Bos-A★	144	556	70	164	37	14	9	95	63	40	.295	.370	.460	106	5	3	3	-1	.949	-13	*S-139/1-2,M	-0.2
1936	Bos-A	81	295	36	83	22	4	2	43	32	21	.281	.354	.403	82	-9	1	3	-2	.930	-2	S-60,3-21,M	-0.7
1937	Bos-A★	148	570	102	175	40	4	18	110	84	73	.307	.402	.486	118	17	5	3	-0	.958	-13	*S-148,M	1.3
1938	Bos-A★	143	530	98	172	**51**	5	17	94	91	60	.325	.428	.536	134	29	7	5	-1	.954	7	*S-142,M	4.2
1939	Bos-A★	143	520	97	160	33	3	19	107	87	48	.308	.407	.492	124	20	6	6	-2	.959	6	*S-142,M	3.4
1940	Bos-A	149	548	104	156	35	6	24	111	83	65	.285	.380	.502	122	17	7	5	-1	.948	2	*S-146/3-2,M	2.9
1941	Bos-A★	143	518	98	161	38	8	16	95	82	55	.311	.406	.508	137	29	1	4	-2	.958	-8	*S-119,3-22/O-1,M	2.7
1942	Bos-A	45	79	7	24	3	0	4	24	15	21	.304	.415	.494	150	6	0	1	-1	.865	-1	3-11/1-5,S-1,M	0.4
1943	Bos-A	59	77	8	24	4	0	5	29	11	4	.312	.398	.558	176	7	0	0	0	.968	0	3-10,M	0.8
1944	Bos-A	76	191	24	46	7	0	5	28	34	19	.241	.358	.356	106	3	1	4	-2	.981	-2	1-49,M	-0.4
1945	Bos-A	3	8	1	3	0	0	0	1	3	2	.375	.545	.375	165	1	0	0	0	1.000	1	/3-3,M	0.2
Total	20	2124	7579	1233	2285	515	118	170	1424	1059	700	.301	.390	.468	119	223	87	71		.951	68	*S-1843/3-69,120	39.4

■ BILL CRONIN
Cronin, William Patrick "Crungy" b: 12/26/02, W.Newton, Mass. d: 10/26/66, Newton, Mass. BR/TR, 5′9″, 167 lbs. Deb: 7/4/28

YEAR	TM/L	G	AB	R	H	2B	3B	HR	RBI	BB	SO	AVG	OBP	SLG	PRO+	BR/A	SB	CS	SBR	FA	FR	G/POS	TPR
1928	Bos-N	3	2	1	0	0	0	0	0	1	0	.000	.333	.000	-6	-0	0			1.000	-0	/C-3	0.0
1929	Bos-N	6	9	0	1	0	0	0	0	0	0	.111	.111	.111	-47	-2	0			1.000	1	/C-6	-0.1
1930	Bos-N	66	178	19	45	9	1	0	17	4	8	.253	.277	.315	44	-16	0			.983	7	C-64	-0.4
1931	Bos-N	51	107	8	22	6	1	0	10	7	5	.206	.267	.280	49	-8	0			.941	1	C-50	-0.5
Total	4	126	296	28	68	15	2	0	27	12	13	.230	.269	.294	43	-26	0			.968	9	C-123	-1.0

■ TOM CROOKE
Crooke, Thomas Aloysius b: 7/26/1884, Washington, D.C. d: 4/5/29, Quantico, Va. BR/TR, 6′, 180 lbs. Deb: 9/29/09

YEAR	TM/L	G	AB	R	H	2B	3B	HR	RBI	BB	SO	AVG	OBP	SLG	PRO+	BR/A	SB	CS	SBR	FA	FR	G/POS	TPR
1909	Was-A	3	7	2	2	1	0	0	2	2		.286	.444	.429	184	1	1			.969	-1	/1-3	0.0
1910	Was-A	8	21	1	4	1	0	0	1	1		.190	.227	.238	48	-1	0			1.000	-0	/1-5	-0.2
Total	2	11	28	3	6	2	0	0	3	3		.214	.290	.286	85	-0	1			.988	-1	/1-8	-0.2

■ JACK CROOKS
Crooks, John Charles b: 11/9/1865, St.Paul, Minn. d: 2/2/18, St.Louis, Mo. BR/TR, 5′10″, 170 lbs. Deb: 9/26/1889 M

YEAR	TM/L	G	AB	R	H	2B	3B	HR	RBI	BB	SO	AVG	OBP	SLG	PRO+	BR/A	SB	CS	SBR	FA	FR	G/POS	TPR
1889	Col-a	12	43	13	14	2	3	0	7	10	4	.326	.463	.512	187	6	10			.987	5	2-12	0.9
1890	Col-a	135	485	86	107	5	4	1	62	96		.221	.357	.254	86	-1	57			.937	-4	*2-134/3-1,O-1	0.3
1891	Col-a	138	519	110	127	19	13	0	46	103	47	.245	.379	.331	110	13	50			**.957**	20	*2-138	3.3
1892	StL-N	128	445	82	95	7	4	7	38	**136**	52	.213	.400	.294	116	20	23			.929	-7	*2-101,3-25/O-2,M	1.5
1893	StL-N	128	448	93	106	10	9	1	48	**121**	37	.237	.408	.306	91	2	31			.908	4	*3-123/S-4,C-1	0.7
1895	Was-N	117	409	80	114	19	8	6	57	68	39	.279	.392	.408	108	7	36			**.956**	12	*2-117	2.1
1896	Was-N	25	84	20	24	3	0	3	20	16	8	.286	.406	.429	120	3	2			.916	-3	2-20/3-4	0.1
	Lou-N	39	122	19	29	5	1	2	15	20	8	.238	.354	.344	88	-2	8			.925	5	2-39	0.5
	Yr	64	206	39	53	8	1	5	35	36	16	.257	.376	.379	101	2	10			.922	2	2-59/3-4	0.6
1898	StL-N	72	225	33	52	4	2	1	20	40		.231	.359	.280	82	-3	3			.959	7	2-66/3-3,S-2,O-1	0.7
Total	8	794	2780	536	668	74	44	21	313	610	195	.240	.385	.321	102	44	220			.946	39	2-627,3-156/S-6,OC	10.1

■ ED CROSBY
Crosby, Edward Carlton b: 5/26/49, Long Beach, Cal. BL/TR, 6′2″, 180 lbs. Deb: 7/12/70

YEAR	TM/L	G	AB	R	H	2B	3B	HR	RBI	BB	SO	AVG	OBP	SLG	PRO+	BR/A	SB	CS	SBR	FA	FR	G/POS	TPR
1970	StL-N	38	95	9	24	4	1	0	6	7	5	.253	.311	.316	67	-4	0	0	0	.954	-1	S-35/3-3,2-2	-0.2

YEAR	TM/L	G	AB	R	H	2B	3B	HR	RBI	BB	SO	AVG	OBP	SLG	PRO+	BR/A	SB	CS	SBR	FA	FR	G/POS	TPR
1972	StL-N	101	276	27	60	9	1	0	19	18	27	.217	.270	.257	51	-18	1	1	-0	.979	-6	S-43,2-38,3-14	-1.9
1973	StL-N	22	39	4	5	2	1	0	1	4	4	.128	.209	.231	22	-4	0	0	0	.938	-3	/S-7,2-5,3-4	-0.7
	*Cin-N	36	51	4	11	1	1	0	5	7	12	.216	.333	.275	74	-2	0	1	-1	.953	5	S-29/2-5	0.5
	Yr	58	90	8	16	3	2	0	6	11	16	.178	.282	.256	52	-6	0	1	-1	.950	2	S-36,2-10/3-4	-0.2
1974	Cle-A	37	86	11	18	3	0	0	6	6	12	.209	.261	.244	46	-6	0	1	-1	.926	-10	3-18,S-13/2-3	-1.6
1975	Cle-A	61	128	12	30	3	0	0	7	13	14	.234	.305	.258	60	-6	0	4	-2	.974	4	S-30,2-19,3-13	-0.2
1976	Cle-A	2	2	0	1	0	0	0	0	0	0	.500	.500	.500	195	0	0	0	0	1.000	1	/3-1,D-1	0.1
Total	6	297	677	67	149	22	4	0	44	55	74	.220	.284	.264	55	-40	1	7	-4	.964	-11	S-157/2-72,3-53,D-1	-4.0

■ FRANKIE CROSETTI Crosetti, Frank Peter Joseph "Crow" b: 10/4/10, San Francisco, Cal. BR/TR, 5'10", 165 lbs. Deb: 4/12/32 C

YEAR	TM/L	G	AB	R	H	2B	3B	HR	RBI	BB	SO	AVG	OBP	SLG	PRO+	BR/A	SB	CS	SBR	FA	FR	G/POS	TPR
1932	*NY-A	116	398	47	96	20	9	5	57	51	51	.241	.335	.374	88	-7	3	2	-0	.937	-5	S-84,3-33/2-1	-0.4
1933	NY-A	136	451	71	114	20	5	9	60	55	40	.253	.337	.379	95	-3	4	1	1	.936	-8	*S-133	-0.2
1934	NY-A	138	554	85	147	22	10	11	67	61	58	.265	.344	.401	98	-3	5	6	-2	.945	-10	*S-119,3-23/2-1	-0.6
1935	NY-A	87	305	49	78	17	6	8	50	41	27	.256	.351	.430	107	3	3	1	0	.963	-7	S-87	0.1
1936	*NY-A★	151	632	137	182	35	7	15	78	90	83	.288	.387	.437	107	8	18	7	1	.948	-8	*S-151	1.0
1937	*NY-A	149	611	127	143	29	5	11	49	86	105	.234	.340	.352	74	-24	13	7	-0	.948	2	*S-147	-1.1
1938	*NY-A	157	631	113	166	35	3	9	55	106	97	.263	.382	.371	90	-7	**27**	12	1	.948	18	*S-157	2.2
1939	*NY-A☆	152	656	109	153	25	5	10	56	65	81	.233	.315	.332	67	-33	11	7	-1	**.968**	8	*S-152	-1.2
1940	NY-A	145	546	84	106	23	4	4	31	72	77	.194	.299	.273	52	-39	14	8	-1	.954	-14	*S-145	-4.0
1941	NY-A	50	148	13	33	2	2	1	22	18	14	.223	.320	.284	62	-8	0	2	-1	.944	10	S-32,3-13	0.3
1942	*NY-A	74	285	50	69	5	5	4	23	31	31	.242	.335	.337	91	-3	1	1	-0	.951	-3	3-62/S-8,2-2	-0.4
1943	*NY-A	95	348	36	81	8	1	2	20	36	47	.233	.317	.279	74	-10	4	4	-1	.946	3	S-90	-0.2
1944	NY-A	55	197	20	47	4	2	5	30	11	21	.239	.299	.355	84	-5	3	0	1	.960	-9	S-55	-0.9
1945	NY-A	130	441	57	105	12	0	4	48	59	65	.238	.341	.293	81	-8	7	1	2	.946	-8	*S-126	-0.5
1946	NY-A	28	59	4	17	3	0	0	3	8	2	.288	.382	.339	101	1	0	3	-2	.940	7	S-24	0.7
1947	NY-A	3	1	0	0	0	0	0	0	0	0	.000	.000	.000	-99	-0	0	0	0	.000	0	/2-1,S-1	0.0
1948	NY-A	17	14	4	4	0	1	0	0	2	0	.286	.375	.429	115	0	0	0	0	1.000	0	/2-6,S-5	0.1
Total	17	1683	6277	1006	1541	260	65	98	649	792	799	.245	.341	.354	84	-137	113	62	-3	.949	-24	*S-1516,3-131/2-11	-5.1

■ AMOS CROSS Cross, Amos C. b: 1861, Czechoslovakia d: 7/16/1888, Cleveland, Ohio Deb: 4/22/1885 F

YEAR	TM/L	G	AB	R	H	2B	3B	HR	RBI	BB	SO	AVG	OBP	SLG	PRO+	BR/A	SB	CS	SBR	FA	FR	G/POS	TPR
1885	Lou-a	35	130	11	37	2	1	0	14	0		.285	.290	.315	91	-2				.936	-1	C-35	0.0
1886	Lou-a	74	283	51	78	14	6	1	42	44		.276	.375	.378	129	10	13			.910	-16	C-51,1-20/S-2,O-1	-0.3
1887	Lou-a	8	28	0	3	0	0	0	0	1		.107	.138	.107	-31	-5	0			.808	-4	/C-5,1-2,O-1	-0.8
Total	3	117	441	62	118	16	7	1	56	45		.268	.338	.342	108	4	13			.916	-22	/C-91,1-22,O-2,S-2	-1.1

■ CLARENCE CROSS Cross, Clarence (b: Clarence Crause) b: 3/4/1856, St.Louis, Mo. d: 6/23/31, Seattle, Wash. Deb: 5/5/1884

YEAR	TM/L	G	AB	R	H	2B	3B	HR	RBI	BB	SO	AVG	OBP	SLG	PRO+	BR/A	SB	CS	SBR	FA	FR	G/POS	TPR
1884	Alt-U	2	7	1	4	1	0	0		2		.571	.667	.714	314	2				.500	-2	/3-2	0.0
	Phi-U	2	9	0	2	0	0	0		0		.222	.222	.222	38	-1				.545	-2	/S-2	-0.2
	KC-U	25	93	13	20	1	0	0		6		.215	.263	.226	57	-8				.836	3	S-24/3-1	-0.4
	Yr	29	109	14	26	2	0	0		8		.239	.291	.257	76	-6				.813	-1	S-26/3-3	-0.6
1887	NY-a	16	55	9	11	2	1	0	5	2		.200	.267	.273	53	-3	0			.833	-3	S-13/3-4	-0.5
Total	2	45	164	23	37	4	1	0	5	10		.226	.282	.262	67	-10	0			.818	-4	/S-39,3-7	-1.1

■ FRANK CROSS Cross, Frank Atwell "Mickey" b: 1/20/1873, Cleveland, Ohio d: 11/2/32, Geauga Lake, Ohio TR, Deb: 5/20/01 F

YEAR	TM/L	G	AB	R	H	2B	3B	HR	RBI	BB	SO	AVG	OBP	SLG	PRO+	BR/A	SB	CS	SBR	FA	FR	G/POS	TPR
1901	Cle-A	1	5	0	3	0	0	0	0	0		.600	.600	.600	243	1	0			.000	-0	/O-1	0.0

■ JEFF CROSS Cross, Joffre James b: 8/28/18, Tulsa, Okla. d: 7/23/97, Huntsville, Tex. BR/TR, 5'11", 160 lbs. Deb: 9/27/42

YEAR	TM/L	G	AB	R	H	2B	3B	HR	RBI	BB	SO	AVG	OBP	SLG	PRO+	BR/A	SB	CS	SBR	FA	FR	G/POS	TPR
1942	StL-N	1	4	0	1	0	0	0	1	0	0	.250	.250	.250	43	-0	0			1.000	-1	/S-1	-0.1
1946	StL-N	49	69	17	15	3	0	0	6	10	8	.217	.316	.261	62	-3	4			.970	6	S-17/2-8,3-1	0.3
1947	StL-N	51	49	4	5	1	0	0	3	10	6	.102	.254	.122	3	-7	0			.947	5	3-15,S-14/2-2	-0.1
1948	StL-N	2	0	0	0	0	0	0	0	0	0	—	—	—	—	0	0			.000	0	R	0.0
	Chi-N	16	20	1	2	0	0	0	0	0	4	.100	.100	.100	-48	-4	0			.786	-4	/S-9,2-1	-0.8
	Yr	18	20	1	2	0	0	0	0	0	4	.100	.100	.100	-47	-4	0			.786	-4	/S-9,2-1	-0.8
Total	4	119	142	22	23	4	0	0	10	20	18	.162	.265	.190	26	-14	4			.932	7	/S-41,3-16,2-11	-0.7

■ LAVE CROSS Cross, Lafayette Napoleon b: 5/12/1866, Milwaukee, Wis. d: 9/6/27, Toledo, Ohio BR/TR, 5'8.5", 155 lbs. Deb: 4/23/1887 FM

YEAR	TM/L	G	AB	R	H	2B	3B	HR	RBI	BB	SO	AVG	OBP	SLG	PRO+	BR/A	SB	CS	SBR	FA	FR	G/POS	TPR
1887	Lou-a	54	203	32	54	8	3	0	26	15		.266	.320	.335	81	-5	15			.916	-3	C-44,O-10	-0.3
1888	Lou-a	47	181	20	41	3	0	0	15	2		.227	.239	.243	56	-9	10			.929	1	C-37,O-12/S-2	-0.5
1889	Phi-a	55	199	22	44	8	2	0	23	14	9	.221	.272	.281	58	-11	11			.934	19	C-55	1.1
1890	Phi-P	63	245	42	73	7	8	3	47	12	6	.298	.331	.429	100	-2	5			.885	2	C-49,O-15	0.3
1891	Phi-a	110	402	66	121	20	14	5	52	38	23	.301	.366	.458	131	14	14			.971	-4	O-43,C-43,3-24,/S2	1.2
1892	Phi-N	140	541	84	149	15	10	4	69	39	16	.275	.328	.362	109	5	18			.921	-2	3-65,C-39,O-25,2/S	0.6
1893	Phi-N	96	415	81	124	17	6	4	78	26	7	.299	.342	.398	96	-4	18			.974	15	C-40,3-30,O-10,S/1	1.3
1894	Phi-N	119	529	123	204	34	9	7	125	29	7	.386	.421	.524	130	25	21			.919	20	*3-100,C-16/S-7,2-1	3.6
1895	Phi-N	125	535	95	145	26	9	2	101	35	8	.271	.319	.364	76	-21	21			**.940**	34	*3-125	1.2
1896	Phi-N	106	406	63	104	23	5	1	73	32	14	.256	.312	.345	74	-16	8			.937	13	3-61,S-37/2-6,OC	0.0
1897	Phi-N	88	344	37	89	17	5	3	51	10		.259	.282	.363	71	-16	10			.912	2	3-47,2-38/O-2,S-1	-0.9
1898	StL-N	151	602	71	191	28	8	3	79	28		.317	.348	.405	113	7	14			**.945**	18	*3-149/S-2	2.5
1899	Cle-N	38	154	15	44	5	0	1	20	8		.286	.325	.338	88	-3	2			.955	4	3-38,M	0.1
	StL-N	103	403	61	122	14	5	4	64	17		.303	.333	.392	96	-4	11			.960	29	*3-103	2.4
	Yr	141	557	76	166	19	5	5	84	25		.298	.330	.377	94	-6	13			**.959**	33	*3-141	2.5
1900	StL-N	16	61	6	18	1	0	0	6	1		.295	.306	.311	71	-2	1			.962	1	3-16	-0.1
	*Bro-N	117	461	73	135	14	6	4	67	25		.293	.332	.375	90	-8	20			.943	3	*3-117	-0.4
	Yr	133	522	79	153	15	6	4	73	26		.293	.329	.368	88	-10	21			**.945**	4	*3-133	-0.5
1901	Phi-A	100	424	82	139	28	12	2	73	19		.328	.358	.465	121	10	23			.919	5	*3-100	1.5
1902	Phi-A	137	559	90	191	39	8	0	108	27		.342	.374	.440	120	14	25			.942	7	*3-137	2.1
1903	Phi-A	137	559	60	163	22	4	2	90	10		.292	.304	.356	93	-6	14			.950	-3	*3-136/1-1	-0.7
1904	Phi-A	155	607	73	176	31	10	1	71	13		.290	.310	.379	112	6	10			.936	-10	*3-155	0.1
1905	*Phi-A	147	587	69	156	29	5	0	77	26		.266	.299	.332	98	-2	8			.928	-9	*3-147	-0.6
1906	Was-A	130	494	55	130	14	6	1	46	28		.263	.303	.322	100	-1	19			**.952**	-3	*3-130	0.0
1907	Was-A	41	161	13	32	8	0	0	10	10		.199	.246	.248	62	-7	3			.978	7	3-41	0.1
Total	21	2275	9072	1333	2645	411	135	47	1371	464	90	.292	.328	.382	99	-34	301			.938	146	*3-1721,C-324,O/S21	14.6

■ MONTE CROSS Cross, Montford Montgomery b: 8/31/1869, Philadelphia, Pa. d: 6/21/34, Philadelphia, Pa. BR/TR, 5'8.5", 148 lbs. Deb: 9/27/1892 U

YEAR	TM/L	G	AB	R	H	2B	3B	HR	RBI	BB	SO	AVG	OBP	SLG	PRO+	BR/A	SB	CS	SBR	FA	FR	G/POS	TPR
1892	Bal-N	15	50	5	8	0	0	0	2	4	10	.160	.222	.160	16	-5	2			.864	-3	S-15	-0.7
1894	Pit-N	13	43	14	19	1	5	2	13	5	4	.442	.520	.837	225	9	6			.924	2	S-13	0.8
1895	Pit-N	108	393	67	101	14	13	3	54	38	38	.257	.327	.382	87	-8	39			.883	-13	*S-107/2-1	-1.3
1896	StL-N	125	427	66	104	10	6	6	52	58	48	.244	.342	.337	83	-9	40			.892	-12	*S-125	-1.4
1897	StL-N	131	462	59	132	17	11	4	55	62		.286	.379	.396	107	6	38			.920	28	*S-131	3.1
1898	Phi-N	149	525	68	135	25	5	1	50	55		.257	.337	.330	95	-2	20			.907	15	*S-149	1.8
1899	Phi-N	154	557	85	143	25	6	3	65	56		.257	.335	.339	88	-8	26			.909	2	*S-154	0.5
1900	Phi-N	131	466	59	94	11	3	3	62	51		.202	.289	.258	52	-30	19			.928	-3	*S-131	-2.0
1901	Phi-N	139	483	49	95	14	1	1	44	52		.197	.281	.236	50	-30	24			.924	-16	*S-139	-3.4
1902	Phi-A	137	497	72	115	22	2	3	59	32		.231	.289	.302	61	-26	17			.927	11	*S-137	-0.7
1903	Phi-A	137	470	44	116	21	2	3	45	49		.247	.326	.319	90	-4	31			.940	8	*S-137/2-1	1.0
1904	Phi-A	153	503	33	95	23	4	1	38	46		.189	.266	.256	62	-20	19			.937	-16	*S-153	-3.6
1905	*Phi-A	79	252	28	67	17	2	0	24	19		.266	.332	.349	114	4	8			.929	-4	S-77/2-2	0.2
1906	Phi-A	134	445	32	89	23	3	1	40	50		.200	.291	.272	74	-12	22			.938	4	*S-134	-0.4
1907	Phi-A	77	248	37	51	9	5	0	18	39		.206	.316	.282	89	-2	17			.954	12	S-74	1.3
Total	15	1682	5821	718	1364	232	68	31	621	616	100	.234	.316	.314	80	-138	328			.920	15	*S-1676/2-4	-4.8

YEAR	TM/L	G	AB	R	H	2B	3B	HR	RBI	BB	SO	AVG	OBP	SLG	PRO+	BR/A	SB	CS	SBR	FA	FR	G/POS	TPR
■ FRANK CROSSIN	Crossin, Frank Patrick b: 6/15/1891, Avondale, Pa. d: 12/6/65, Kingston, Pa. BR/TR, 5'10", 160 lbs. Deb: 9/24/12																						
1912	StL-A	8	22	2	5	0	0	0	2	1		.227	.261	.227	41	-2	1			.920	-5	/C-8	-0.6
1913	StL-A	4	4	1	1	0	0	0	0	1	1	.250	.500	.250	124	0	0			.857	-1	/C-2	0.0
1914	StL-A	43	90	5	11	1	1	0	5	10	10	.122	.225	.156	15	-9	3			.934	-1	C-41	-0.7
Total	3	55	116	8	17	1	1	0	7	12	11	.147	.244	.172	25	-10	4			.930	-6	/C-51	-1.3
■ JOE CROTTY	Crotty, Joseph P. b: 12/24/1860, Cincinnati, O. d: 6/22/26, Minneapolis, Minn BR/TR, Deb: 5/4/1882																						
1882	Lou-a	5	20	1	2	0	0	0		0		.100	.100	.100	-34	-3				.882	-0	/C-5	-0.3
	StL-a	8	28	2	4	1	0	0		3		.143	.226	.179	37	-2				.882	-1	/C-7,O-1	-0.3
	Yr	13	48	3	6	1	0	0		3		.125	.176	.146	10	-4				.882	-2	C-12/O-1	-0.6
1884	Cin-U	21	84	11	22	4	2	1		1		.262	.271	.393	92	-4				.896	-7	C-21	-0.8
1885	Lou-a	39	129	14	20	2	0	0	7	3		.155	.193	.171	15	-12				.931	1	C-38/1-1	-0.7
1886	NY-a	14	47	6	8	0	1	0	2	4		.170	.250	.213	48	-3	3			.933	-3	C-14	-0.3
Total	4	87	308	34	56	7	3	1	9	11		.182	.220	.234	42	-23	3			.915	-10	/C-85,1-1,O-1	-2.4
■ JACK CROUCH	Crouch, Jack Albert "Roxy" b: 10/12/03, Salisbury, N.C. d: 8/25/72, Leesburg, Fla. BR/TR, 5'9", 165 lbs. Deb: 9/18/30																						
1930	StL-A	6	14	1	2	1	0	0	1	1	3	.143	.200	.214	5	-2	0	0	0	1.000	1	/C-5	-0.1
1931	StL-A	8	12	0	0	0	0	0	1	0	4	.000	.000	.000	-97	-3	0	0	0	.895	1	/C-7	-0.3
1933	StL-A	19	30	1	5	0	0	1	5	2	6	.167	.219	.267	26	-3	0	0	0	1.000	-1	/C-9	-0.3
	Cin-N	10	16	5	2	0	0	0	1	0	0	.125	.222	.125	1	-2	1			1.000	2	/C-6	0.0
Total	3	43	72	7	9	1	0	1	8	3	13	.125	.182	.181	-3	-11	1	0		.976	3	/C-27	-0.7
■ FRANK CROUCHER	Croucher, Frank Donald "Dingle" b: 7/23/14, San Antonio, Tex. d: 5/21/80, Houston, Tex. BR/TR, 5'11", 165 lbs. Deb: 4/18/39																						
1939	Det-A	97	324	38	87	15	0	5	40	16	42	.269	.303	.361	64	-18	2	2	-1	.934	-8	S-93/2-3	-1.8
1940	*Det-A	37	57	3	6	0	0	0	2	4	5	.105	.164	.105	-26	-11	0	0	0	.936	-2	S-26/2-7,3-1	-1.1
1941	Det-A	136	489	51	124	21	4	2	39	33	72	.254	.305	.325	61	-28	2	0	1	.935	-3	*S-136	-2.0
1942	Was-A	26	65	2	18	1	1	0	5	3	9	.277	.309	.323	79	-2	0	0	0	.950	5	2-18	0.4
Total	4	296	935	94	235	37	5	7	86	56	128	.251	.296	.324	58	-59	4	2	0	.934	-8	S-255/2-28,3-1	-4.5
■ BUCK CROUSE	Crouse, Clyde Elsworth b: 1/6/1897, Anderson, Ind. d: 10/23/83, Muncie, Ind. BL/TR, 5'8", 158 lbs. Deb: 8/1/23																						
1923	Chi-A	23	70	6	18	2	1	1	7	3	4	.257	.297	.357	73	-3	0	0	0	.955	-2	C-22	-0.4
1924	Chi-A	94	305	30	79	10	1	1	44	23	12	.259	.319	.308	64	-16	3	2	-0	.945	1	C-90	-0.9
1925	Chi-A	54	131	18	46	7	0	2	25	12	4	.351	.410	.450	125	5	1	2	-1	.952	-2	C-48	0.4
1926	Chi-A	49	135	10	32	4	1	0	17	14	7	.237	.309	.281	57	-8	0	0	0	.985	3	C-45	-0.3
1927	Chi-A	85	222	22	53	11	0	0	20	21	10	.239	.307	.288	57	-14	4	1	1	.972	7	C-81	-0.2
1928	Chi-A	78	218	17	55	5	2	2	20	19	14	.252	.315	.321	68	-10	3	4	-2	.959	-1	C-76	-0.7
1929	Chi-A	45	107	11	29	7	0	2	12	5	7	.271	.316	.393	82	-3	2	0	1	.979	6	C-40	0.6
1930	Chi-A	42	118	14	30	8	1	0	15	17	10	.254	.348	.339	78	-4	1	1	-0	.979	7	C-38	0.6
Total	8	470	1306	128	342	54	6	8	160	114	68	.262	.326	.331	72	-53	14	10	-2	.964	18	C-440	-0.9
■ DON CROW	Crow, Donald Le Roy b: 8/18/58, Yakima, Wash. BR/TR, 6'4", 200 lbs. Deb: 7/25/82																						
1982	LA-N	4	4	0	0	0	0	0	0	0	3	.000	.000	.000	-99	-1	0	0	0	1.000	1	/C-4	0.0
■ GEORGE CROWE	Crowe, George Daniel "Big George" b: 3/22/21, Whiteland, Ind. BL/TL, 6'2", 212 lbs. Deb: 4/16/52																						
1952	Bos-N	73	217	25	56	13	1	4	20	18	25	.258	.329	.382	100	-0	0	1	-1	.985	2	1-55	-0.1
1953	Mil-N	47	42	6	12	2	0	2	6	2	7	.286	.333	.476	115	1	0	0	0	1.000	0	/1-9	0.1
1955	Mil-N	104	303	41	85	12	4	15	55	45	44	.281	.375	.495	135	16	1	0	0	.989	2	1-79	1.3
1956	Cin-N	77	144	22	36	2	1	10	23	11	28	.250	.312	.486	104	0	0	0	0	.988	2	1-32	0.1
1957	Cin-N	133	494	71	134	20	1	31	92	32	62	.271	.317	.504	108	4	1	1	-0	.989	-2	*1-120	-0.5
1958	Cin-N☆	111	345	31	95	12	5	7	61	41	51	.275	.352	.400	94	-2	1	0	0	.992	-3	1-93/2-1	-1.0
1959	StL-N	77	103	14	31	6	0	8	29	5	12	.301	.333	.592	132	4	0	0	0	1.000	2	1-14	0.6
1960	StL-N	73	72	5	17	3	0	4	13	5	16	.236	.286	.444	89	-1	0	0	0	1.000	0	/1-5	-0.1
1961	StL-N	7	7	0	1	0	0	0	0	0	1	.143	.143	.143	-22	-1	0	0	0	.000	0	H	-0.1
Total	9	702	1727	215	467	70	12	81	299	159	246	.270	.335	.466	109	20	3	2	-0	.990	4	1-407/2-1	0.3
■ ED CROWLEY	Crowley, Edgar Jewel b: 8/20/06, Watkinsville, Ga. d: 4/14/70, Birmingham, Ala. BR/TR, 6'1", 180 lbs. Deb: 6/21/28																						
1928	Was-A	2	1	0	0	0	0	0	0	0	0	.000	.000	.000	-99	-0	0	0	0	.000	-0	/3-2	-0.1
■ JOHN CROWLEY	Crowley, John A. b: 1/12/1862, Lawrence, Mass. d: 9/23/1896, Lawrence, Mass. 5'10", 164 lbs. Deb: 5/1/1884																						
1884	Phi-N	48	168	26	41	7	3	0	19	15	21	.244	.306	.321	102	1				.832	-23	C-48	-1.6
■ TERRY CROWLEY	Crowley, Terrence Michael b: 2/16/47, Staten Island, N.Y. BL/TL, 6', 180 lbs. Deb: 9/4/69 C																						
1969	Bal-A	7	18	2	6	0	0	0	3	1	4	.333	.368	.333	97	-0	0	0	0	1.000	0	/1-3,O-2	0.0
1970	*Bal-A	83	152	25	39	5	0	5	20	35	26	.257	.396	.388	116	5	2	0	1	.973	-5	O-27,1-23	-0.2
1971	Bal-A	18	23	2	4	0	0	0	1	3	4	.174	.269	.174	28	-2	0	0	0	1.000	-2	/O-6,1-2	-0.5
1972	Bal-A	97	247	30	57	10	0	11	29	32	26	.231	.321	.405	112	4	0	0	0	.990	-7	O-68,1-15	-0.7
1973	*Bal-A	54	131	16	27	4	0	3	15	16	14	.206	.297	.305	71	-5	0	0	0	.867	-1	D-23,O-10/1-7	-0.7
1974	Cin-N	84	125	11	30	12	0	1	20	10	16	.240	.301	.360	86	-3	1	0	0	1.000	-2	O-22/1-7	-0.6
1975	*Cin-N	66	71	8	19	6	0	1	11	7	6	.268	.333	.394	100	-0	0	0	0	1.000	1	/1-4,O-4	0.1
1976	Atl-N	7	6	0	0	0	0	0	1	0	0	.000	.000	.000	-94	-2	0	0	0	.000	0	H	-0.2
	Bal-A	33	61	5	15	1	0	0	5	7	11	.246	.333	.262	81	-1	0	0	0	1.000	1	D-17/1-1	-0.1
1977	Bal-A	18	22	3	8	1	0	1	9	1	3	.364	.391	.545	162	2	0	0	0	1.000	-0	/1-1,D-2	0.2
1978	Bal-A	62	95	9	24	2	0	0	12	8	12	.253	.317	.274	72	-3	0	0	0	1.000	0	D-17/O-2,1-1	-0.4
1979	*Bal-A	61	63	8	20	5	1	1	8	14	13	.317	.449	.476	155	6	0	0	0	1.000	-0	D-15/1-2	0.5
1980	Bal-A	92	233	33	67	8	0	12	50	29	21	.288	.366	.476	130	10	0	0	0	1.000	1	D-65/1-3	0.9
1981	Bal-A	68	134	12	33	6	0	4	25	29	12	.246	.380	.381	120	5	0	0	0	1.000	0	D-42/1-4	0.3
1982	Bal-A	65	93	8	22	2	0	3	17	21	9	.237	.377	.355	103	1	0	0	0	.988	0	D-14,1-10	0.1
1983	Mon-N	50	44	2	8	0	0	0	3	9	4	.182	.333	.182	47	-3	0	0	0	1.000	-1	/1-4	-0.4
Total	15	865	1518	174	379	62	1	42	229	222	181	.250	.348	.375	104	13	3	0	1	.980	-13	D-195,O-141/1-87	-1.7
■ BILL CROWLEY	Crowley, William Michael b: 4/8/1857, Philadelphia, Pa. d: 7/14/1891, Gloucester, N.J. BR/TR, 5'7.5", 159 lbs. Deb: 4/26/1875																						
1875	Phi-n	9	37	4	3	0	0	0	3	1	0	.081	.105	.081	-33	-5	0	0	0	.800	-0	/3-4,O-4,1-1	-0.5
1877	Lou-N	61	238	30	67	9	3	1	23	4	13	.282	.293	.357	88	-6				.849	9	*O-58/S-2,C-2,32	0.1
1879	Buf-N	60	261	41	75	9	5	0	30	6	14	.287	.303	.360	115	4				.809	-1	O-43,C-10/1-7,2-3	0.1
1880	Buf-N	85	354	57	95	16	4	0	20	19	23	.268	.306	.336	115	6				.824	1	*O-74,C-22	0.5
1881	Bos-N	72	279	33	71	12	0	0	31	14	15	.254	.290	.297	89	-3				.880	-1	*O-72	-0.5
1883	Phi-a	23	96	16	24	4	3	0	16	3		.250	.273	.354	93	-1				.810	-2	O-22/1-1	-0.3
	Cle-N	11	41	3	12	5	0	0	5	1	7	.293	.310	.415	119	1				.923	-3	O-11	-0.2
1884	Bos-N	108	407	50	110	14	6	6	61	33	74	.270	.325	.378	121	10				.870	-5	*O-108	0.3
1885	Buf-N	92	344	29	83	14	1	1	36	21	32	.241	.285	.297	85	-6				.874	-5	*O-92	-1.2
Total	7	512	2020	259	537	83	22	8	222	101	178	.266	.301	.341	103	5				.853	-6	O-480/C-34,1-8,2S3	-1.2
■ WALTON CRUISE	Cruise, Walton Edwin b: 5/6/1890, Childersburg, Ala. d: 1/9/75, Sylacauga, Ala. BL/TR, 6', 175 lbs. Deb: 4/14/14																						
1914	StL-N	95	256	20	58	9	3	4	28	25	42	.227	.303	.332	90	-3	3			.976	-3	O-81	-1.0
1916	StL-N	3	3	0	2	0	0	0	0	1	0	.667	.750	.667	339	1	0			1.000	-1	/O-2	0.0
1917	StL-N	153	529	70	156	20	10	5	59	38	73	.295	.343	.399	131	18	16			.965	-14	*O-152	-0.4
1918	StL-N	70	240	34	65	5	4	6	39	30	26	.271	.359	.400	136	11	2			.964	-7	O-65	0.0
1919	StL-N	9	21	0	2	1	0	0	0	1	6	.095	.136	.143	-17	-3	0			.833	-2	/O-5,1-2	-0.6
	Bos-N	73	241	23	52	7	0	1	21	17	29	.216	.267	.257	61	-11	8			.978	-5	O-66	-2.4
	Yr	82	262	23	54	8	0	1	21	18	35	.206	.257	.248	55	-14	8			.971	-7	O-71/1-2	-3.0
1920	Bos-N	91	288	40	80	7	5	1	21	31	26	.278	.352	.347	106	3	5	3	-0	.950	-7	O-82	-1.1

YEAR	TM/L	G	AB	R	H	2B	3B	HR	RBI	BB	SO	AVG	OBP	SLG	PRO+	BR/A	SB	CS	SBR	FA	FR	G/POS	TPR
1921	Bos-N	108	344	47	119	16	7	8	55	48	24	.346	.429	.503	154	29	10	8	-2	.963	-6	*O-102/1-2	1.4
1922	Bos-N	104	352	51	98	15	10	4	46	44	20	.278	.360	.412	103	2	4	4	-1	.948	-0	*O-100/1-2	-0.6
1923	Bos-N	21	38	4	8	2	0	0	0	3	2	.211	.268	.263	42	-3	1	0	0	.952	-0	/O-9	-0.4
1924	Bos-N	9	9	4	4	1	0	1	3	0	2	.444	.444	.889	260	2	0	0	0	.000	0	H	0.2
Total	10	736	2321	293	644	83	39	30	272	238	250	.277	.348	.386	114	44	49	15		.962	-45	O-664/1-6	-4.9
■ **GENE CRUMLING**	Crumling, Eugene Leon b: 4/5/22, Wrightsville, Pa. BR/TR, 6′, 180 lbs. Deb: 9/11/45																						
1945	StL-N	6	12	0	1	0	0	0	1	0	1	.083	.083	.083	-52	-2	0			1.000	2	/C-6	-0.1
■ **BUDDY CRUMP**	Crump, Arthur Elliott b: 11/29/01, Norfolk, Va. d: 9/7/76, Raleigh, N.C. BL/TL, 5′10″, 156 lbs. Deb: 9/28/24																						
1924	NY-N	1	4	0	0	0	0	0	1	0	1	.000	.000	.000	-99	-1	0	0	0	.500	-1	/O-1	-0.2
■ **PRESS CRUTHERS**	Cruthers, Charles Preston b: 9/8/1890, Marshallton, Del. d: 12/27/76, Kenosha, Wis. BR/TR, 5′9″, 152 lbs. Deb: 9/29/13																						
1913	Phi-A	3	12	0	3	1	0	0	0	0	0	.250	.250	.333	72	-1	0			.923	-3	/2-3	-0.4
1914	Phi-A	4	15	1	3	0	1	0	0	0	4	.200	.200	.333	63	-1	0	1	-1	1.000	2	/2-4	0.0
Total	2	7	27	1	6	1	1	0	0	0	4	.222	.222	.333	67	-1	0	1		.973	-1	/2-7	-0.4
■ **TOMMY CRUZ**	Cruz, Cirilo (Dilan) b: 2/15/51, Arroyo, P.R. BL/TL, 5′9″, 165 lbs. Deb: 9/4/73 F																						
1973	StL-N	3	0	1	0	0	0	0	0	0	0	—	—	—	—	0	0	0	0	.000	-0	/O-1	0.0
1977	Chi-A	4	2	1	0	0	0	0	0	0	0	.000	.000	.000	-99	-1	0	0	0	1.000	-1	/O-2	-0.1
Total	2	7	2	2	0	0	0	0	0	0	0	.000	.000	.000	-99	-1	0	0	0	1.000	-1	/O-3	-0.1
■ **DEIVI CRUZ**	Cruz, Deivi (Garcia) b: 11/6/75, Bani, D.R. BR/TR, 5′11″, 160 lbs. Deb: 4/1/97																						
1997	Det-A	147	436	35	105	26	0	2	40	14	55	.241	.264	.314	51	-32	3	6	-3	.979	7	*S-147	-1.4
1998	Det-A	135	454	52	118	22	3	5	45	13	55	.260	.285	.355	65	-24	3	4	-2	.983	20	*S-135	0.5
Total	2	282	890	87	223	48	3	7	85	27	110	.251	.275	.335	58	-56	6	10	-4	.981	27	S-282	-0.9
■ **FAUSTO CRUZ**	Cruz, Fausto (Santiago) b: 5/1/72, Monte Cristi, D.R. BR/TR, 5′10″, 165 lbs. Deb: 4/10/94																						
1994	Oak-A	17	28	2	3	0	0	0	0	4	6	.107	.219	.107	-14	-5	0	0	0	.960	3	S-10/3-4,2-1	-0.1
1995	Oak-A	8	23	0	5	0	0	0	5	3	5	.217	.308	.217	42	-2	1	1	-0	.971	-1	/S-8	-0.2
1996	Det-A	14	38	5	9	2	0	0	0	1	11	.237	.256	.289	38	-4	0	0	0	.906	-0	/2-8,S-4,D-1	-0.3
Total	3	39	89	7	17	2	0	0	5	8	22	.191	.258	.213	24	-10	1	1	-0	.934	2	/S-22,2-9,3-4,D-1	-0.6
■ **HECTOR CRUZ**	Cruz, Hector Louis (Dilan) "Heity" b: 4/2/53, Arroyo, P.R. BR/TR, 5′11″, 170 lbs. Deb: 8/11/73 F																						
1973	StL-N	11	11	1	0	0	0	0	0	1	3	.000	.083	.000	-75	-3	0	0	0	1.000	-1	/O-5	-0.4
1975	StL-N	23	48	7	7	2	2	0	6	2	4	.146	.180	.271	23	-5	0	0	0	.800	-1	3-12/O-6	-0.7
1976	StL-N	151	526	54	120	17	1	13	71	42	119	.228	.288	.338	77	-17	1	0	0	.934	-21	*3-148	-4.2
1977	StL-N	118	339	50	80	19	2	6	42	46	56	.236	.329	.357	85	-6	4	3	-1	.964	-9	*O-106/3-2	-2.0
1978	Chi-N	30	76	8	18	5	0	2	9	3	6	.237	.266	.382	70	-3	0	0	0	1.000	0	O-14/3-7	-0.4
	SF-N	79	197	19	44	8	1	6	24	21	39	.223	.301	.365	89	-3	0	2	-1	.978	-5	O-53,3-14	-1.2
	Yr	109	273	27	62	13	1	8	33	24	45	.227	.292	.370	83	-7	0	2	-1	.983	-5	O-67,3-21	-1.6
1979	SF-N	16	25	2	3	0	0	0	1	3	7	.120	.214	.120	-7	-4	0	0	0	1.000	-2	/O-6,3-2	-0.6
	*Cin-N	74	182	24	44	10	2	4	27	31	39	.242	.352	.385	100	1	0	1	-1	.984	-7	O-69	-1.0
	Yr	90	207	26	47	10	2	4	28	34	46	.227	.336	.353	89	-3	0	1	-1	.985	-9	O-75/3-2	-1.6
1980	Cin-N	52	75	5	16	4	1	1	5	8	16	.213	.289	.333	73	-3	0	0	0	.955	-4	O-29	-0.8
1981	Chi-N	53	109	15	25	5	0	7	15	17	24	.229	.333	.468	120	3	2	2	-1	.925	-6	3-18,O-16	-0.4
1982	Chi-N	17	19	1	4	1	0	0	0	2	4	.211	.286	.263	53	-1	0	0	0	1.000	-2	/O-4	-0.3
Total	9	624	1607	186	361	71	9	39	200	176	317	.225	.303	.353	81	-42	7	8	-3	.975	-57	O-308,3-203	-12.0
■ **HENRY CRUZ**	Cruz, Henry (Acosta) b: 2/27/52, Christiansted, V.I. BL/TL, 6′, 175 lbs. Deb: 4/18/75																						
1975	LA-N	53	94	8	25	3	1	0	5	7	6	.266	.317	.319	80	-3	1	1	-0	.960	-11	O-41	-1.5
1976	LA-N	49	88	8	16	2	1	4	14	9	11	.182	.258	.364	76	-3	0	2	-1	.976	-3	O-23	-0.9
1977	Chi-A	16	21	3	6	0	0	2	5	1	3	.286	.318	.571	137	1	0	0	0	.833	-3	/O-9	-0.2
1978	Chi-A	53	77	13	17	2	1	2	10	8	11	.221	.302	.351	82	-2	0	1	-1	1.000	-5	O-40/D-1	-0.8
Total	4	171	280	32	64	7	3	8	34	25	31	.229	.294	.361	84	-7	1	4	-2	.974	-22	O-113/D-1	-3.4
■ **JACOB CRUZ**	Cruz, Jacob b: 1/28/73, Oxnard, Cal. BL/TL, 6′, 175 lbs. Deb: 7/18/96																						
1996	SF-N	33	77	10	18	3	0	3	10	12	24	.234	.352	.390	99	0	0	1	-1	.977	0	O-23	-0.1
1997	SF-N	16	25	3	4	1	0	0	3	3	4	.160	.250	.200	20	-3	0	0	0	.933	-1	O-11	-0.4
1998	SF-N	3	3	0	0	0	0	0	0	0	2	.000	.000	.000	-99	-1	0	0	0	.000	0	/H	-0.1
	Cle-A	1	1	0	0	0	0	0	0	0	1	.000	.000	.000	-97	-0	0	0	0	.000	0	/H	0.0
Total	3	53	106	13	22	4	0	3	13	15	31	.208	.317	.330	73	-4	0	1	-1	.966	-0	/O-34	-0.6
■ **JOSE CRUZ**	Cruz, Jose (Dilan) b: 8/8/47, Arroyo, P.R. BL/TL, 6′, 175 lbs. Deb: 9/19/70 FC																						
1970	StL-N	6	17	2	6	1	0	0	1	4	0	.353	.500	.412	144	2	0	0	0	1.000	2	/O-4	0.3
1971	StL-N	83	292	46	80	13	2	9	27	49	35	.274	.380	.425	123	10	6	3	0	.975	2	O-83	0.9
1972	StL-N	117	332	33	78	14	4	2	23	36	54	.235	.312	.319	81	-8	9	3	1	.979	4	*O-102	-0.8
1973	StL-N	132	406	51	92	22	5	10	57	51	66	.227	.314	.379	92	-5	10	4	1	.979	0	*O-118	-1.0
1974	StL-N	107	161	24	42	4	3	5	20	20	27	.261	.343	.416	112	3	4	2	0	.975	-6	O-53/1-1	-0.5
1975	Hou-N	120	315	44	81	15	2	9	49	52	44	.257	.364	.403	121	10	6	3	0	.980	4	O-94	1.1
1976	Hou-N	133	439	49	133	21	5	4	61	53	46	.303	.378	.401	133	19	28	11	2	.972	10	*O-125	2.7
1977	Hou-N	157	579	87	173	31	10	17	87	69	67	.299	.373	.475	138	30	44	23	-1	.973	4	*O-155	2.7
1978	Hou-N	153	565	79	178	34	9	10	83	57	57	.315	.378	.460	144	32	37	9	6	.975	3	*O-152/1-2	3.6
1979	Hou-N	157	558	73	161	33	7	9	72	72	66	.289	.370	.421	122	18	36	14	2	.959	9	*O-156	2.3
1980	*Hou-N☆	160	612	79	185	29	7	11	91	60	66	.302	.365	.426	130	24	36	11	4	.969	15	*O-158	3.8
1981	*Hou-N	107	409	53	109	16	5	13	55	35	49	.267	.324	.425	117	7	5	7	-3	.984	9	*O-105	1.1
1982	Hou-N	155	570	62	157	27	2	9	68	60	67	.275	.345	.377	110	8	21	11	-0	.964	14	*O-155	1.8
1983	Hou-N	160	594	85	**189**	28	8	14	92	65	86	.318	.386	.463	143	34	30	16	-1	.979	8	*O-160	3.9
1984	Hou-N	160	600	96	187	28	13	12	95	73	68	.312	.386	.462	148	38	22	8	2	.976	13	*O-160	4.9
1985	Hou-N★	141	544	69	163	34	4	9	79	43	74	.300	.351	.426	120	14	16	5	2	.971	10	*O-137	2.2
1986	*Hou-N	141	479	48	133	22	4	10	72	55	86	.278	.352	.403	111	7	3	4	-2	.984	6	*O-134	0.8
1987	Hou-N	126	365	47	88	17	4	11	38	36	65	.241	.309	.400	90	-6	4	1	1	.984	6	O-97	-0.3
1988	NY-A	38	80	9	16	2	0	1	7	8	8	.200	.273	.262	51	-5	0	1	-1	.889	-2	D-12/O-8	-0.8
Total	19	2353	7917	1036	2251	391	94	165	1077	898	1031	.284	.358	.420	122	232	317	136	14	.974	111	*O-2156/D-12,1-3	28.7
■ **JOSE CRUZ**	Cruz, Jose L. b: 4/19/74, Arroyo, P.R. BB/TR, 6′, 190 lbs. Deb: 5/31/97 F																						
1997	Sea-A	49	183	28	49	12	1	12	34	13	45	.268	.316	.541	119	4	1	0	0	.966	-2	O-49	0.1
	Tor-A	55	212	31	49	7	0	14	34	28	72	.231	.321	.462	101	-0	6	2	1	.981	0	O-55	-0.1
	Yr	104	395	59	98	19	1	26	68	41	117	.248	.319	.499	109	4	7	2	1	.974	-2	*O-104	0.0
1998	Tor-A	105	352	55	89	14	3	11	42	57	99	.253	.357	.403	97	-0	11	4	1	.984	2	*O-105	0.1
Total	2	209	747	114	187	33	4	37	110	98	216	.250	.337	.454	104	4	18	6	2	.980	1	O-209	0.1
■ **JULIO CRUZ**	Cruz, Julio Luis b: 12/2/54, Brooklyn, N.Y. BB/TR, 5′9″, 165 lbs. Deb: 7/4/77																						
1977	Sea-A	60	199	25	51	3	1	1	7	24	29	.256	.336	.296	75	-6	15	6	1	.983	2	2-54/D-1	0.1
1978	Sea-A	147	550	77	129	14	1	1	25	69	66	.235	.321	.269	68	-21	59	10	**12**	**.987**	8	*2-141/S-5,D-1	0.9
1979	Sea-A	107	414	70	112	16	2	1	29	62	61	.271	.366	.326	87	-5	49	9	9	.979	17	*2-107	2.7
1980	Sea-A	119	422	66	88	9	3	2	16	59	49	.209	.307	.258	56	-24	45	7	9	.983	1	*2-115/D-3	-0.7
1981	Sea-A	94	352	57	90	12	3	2	24	39	40	.256	.335	.324	87	-5	43	8	**8**	.982	8	2-92/S-1	1.8
1982	Sea-A	154	549	83	133	22	5	8	49	57	71	.242	.317	.344	79	-15	46	13	6	.987	4	*2-151/S-2,3-1,D-2	0.3
1983	Sea-A	61	181	24	46	10	1	2	12	20	22	.254	.335	.354	86	-3	33	6	6	.984	7	2-60/D-1	1.3
	*Chi-A	99	334	47	84	9	4	1	40	29	44	.251	.315	.311	71	-13	24	6	4	.983	10	2-97	0.5
	Yr	160	515	71	130	19	5	3	52	49	66	.252	.322	.326	76	-16	57	12	10	.983	17	*2-157/D-1	1.8

YEAR	TM/L	G	AB	R	H	2B	3B	HR	RBI	BB	SO	AVG	OBP	SLG	PRO+	BR/A	SB	CS	SBR	FA	FR	G/POS	TPR
1984	Chi-A	143	415	42	92	14	4	5	43	45	58	.222	.298	.311	66	-19	14	6	1	.976	22	*2-141	0.9
1985	Chi-A	91	234	28	46	2	3	0	15	32	40	.197	.299	.231	46	-17	8	5	-1	.982	13	2-87/D-2	-0.2
1986	Chi-A	81	209	38	45	2	0	0	19	42	28	.215	.347	.225	58	-11	7	2	1	.985	2	2-78/D-3	-0.5
Total	10	1156	3859	557	916	113	27	23	279	478	508	.237	.324	.299	71	-138	343	78	56	.983	93	*2-1123/D-13,S-8,3	7.1

■ **IVAN CRUZ** Cruz, Luis Ivan b: 5/3/68, Fajardo, P.R. BL/TL, 6'3", 210 lbs. Deb: 7/18/97

YEAR	TM/L	G	AB	R	H	2B	3B	HR	RBI	BB	SO	AVG	OBP	SLG	PRO+	BR/A	SB	CS	SBR	FA	FR	G/POS	TPR
1997	NY-A	11	20	0	5	1	0	0	3	2	4	.250	.318	.300	63	-1	0	0	0	1.000	-0	/1-3,O-1,D-4	-0.1

■ **TODD CRUZ** Cruz, Todd Ruben b: 11/23/55, Highland Park, Mich BR/TR, 6', 175 lbs. Deb: 9/4/78

YEAR	TM/L	G	AB	R	H	2B	3B	HR	RBI	BB	SO	AVG	OBP	SLG	PRO+	BR/A	SB	CS	SBR	FA	FR	G/POS	TPR
1978	Phi-N	3	4	0	2	0	0	0	2	0	0	.500	.500	.500	178	0	0	1	-1	1.000	2	/S-2	0.1
1979	KC-A	55	118	9	24	7	0	2	15	3	19	.203	.230	.314	44	-9	0	1	-1	.974	4	S-48/3-9	-0.3
1980	Cal-A	18	40	5	11	3	0	1	5	5	8	.275	.356	.425	116	1	0	0	0	.860	-6	S-12/3-4,2-1,O-1	-0.4
	Chi-A	90	293	23	68	11	1	2	18	9	54	.232	.260	.297	52	-19	2	1	0	.956	5	S-90	-0.4
	Yr	108	333	28	79	14	1	3	23	14	62	.237	.272	.312	60	-18	2	1	0	.948	-1	*S-102/3-4,2-1,O-1	-0.8
1982	Sea-A	136	492	44	113	20	2	16	57	12	95	.230	.248	.376	67	-24	2	10	-5	.963	19	*S-136	0.3
1983	Sea-A	65	216	21	41	4	2	7	21	7	56	.190	.222	.324	46	-16	1	3	-2	.964	21	S-63	0.9
	*Bal-A	81	221	16	46	9	1	3	27	15	52	.208	.262	.299	55	-14	3	4	-2	.942	5	3-79/2-2	-1.2
	Yr	146	437	37	87	13	3	10	48	22	108	.199	.242	.311	51	-30	4	7	-3	.942	25	3-79,S-63/2-2	-0.3
1984	Bal-A	96	142	15	31	4	0	3	9	8	33	.218	.265	.310	60	-8	1	4	-2	.955	11	3-89/P-1,D-1	0.1
Total	6	544	1526	133	336	58	6	34	154	59	317	.220	.253	.333	59	-89	9	24	-12	.960	60	S-351,3-181/2DPO	-0.9

■ **MIKE CUBBAGE** Cubbage, Michael Lee b: 7/21/50, Charlottesville, Va. BL/TR, 6', 180 lbs. Deb: 4/7/74 MC

YEAR	TM/L	G	AB	R	H	2B	3B	HR	RBI	BB	SO	AVG	OBP	SLG	PRO+	BR/A	SB	CS	SBR	FA	FR	G/POS	TPR
1974	Tex-A	9	15	0	0	0	0	0	0	0	4	.000	.000	.000	-99	-4	0	0	0	1.000	2	/3-3,2-2	-0.2
1975	Tex-A	58	143	12	32	6	0	4	21	18	14	.224	.311	.350	87	-2	0	0	0	.962	2	2-37/3-3,D-2	0.1
1976	Tex-A	14	32	2	7	0	0	0	0	7	7	.219	.359	.219	70	-1	0	0	0	1.000	-0	/2-5,3-1,D-6	-0.1
	Min-A	104	342	40	89	19	5	3	49	42	37	.260	.346	.371	108	4	1	1	-0	.940	2	3-99/2-2,D-2	0.6
	Yr	118	374	42	96	19	5	3	49	49	44	.257	.347	.358	105	3	1	1	-0	.940	2	*3-100/D-8,2-7	0.5
1977	Min-A	129	417	60	110	16	5	9	55	37	49	.264	.324	.391	95	-3	1	4	-2	.952	9	*3-126/D-1	0.2
1978	Min-A	125	394	40	111	12	7	7	57	40	44	.282	.349	.401	108	5	3	1	0	.971	2	*3-115/2-5	0.5
1979	Min-A	94	243	26	67	10	1	2	23	39	26	.276	.376	.350	94	-1	1	8	-5	.928	-12	3-63,D-21/1-1,2-1	-1.8
1980	Min-A	103	285	29	70	9	0	8	42	23	37	.246	.304	.361	76	-10	0	1	-1	.996	7	1-72,3-32/2-1,D-1	-0.7
1981	NY-N	67	80	9	17	2	2	1	4	9	15	.213	.292	.325	76	-3	0	0	0	.963	1	3-12	-0.2
Total	8	703	1951	218	503	74	20	34	251	215	233	.258	.333	.369	94	-14	6	15	-7	.952	12	3-454/1-73,2-53,D	-1.6

■ **AL CUCCINELLO** Cuccinello, Alfred Edward b: 11/26/14, Long Island City, N.Y. BR/TR, 5'10", 165 lbs. Deb: 5/17/35 F

YEAR	TM/L	G	AB	R	H	2B	3B	HR	RBI	BB	SO	AVG	OBP	SLG	PRO+	BR/A	SB	CS	SBR	FA	FR	G/POS	TPR
1935	NY-N	54	165	27	41	7	1	4	20	1	20	.248	.262	.376	70	-7	0			.951	6	2-48/3-2	0.1

■ **TONY CUCCINELLO** Cuccinello, Anthony Francis "Cooch" or "Chick" b: 11/8/07, Long Island City, N.Y. d: 9/21/95, Tampa, Fla. BR/TR, 5'7", 160 lbs. Deb: 4/15/30 FC

YEAR	TM/L	G	AB	R	H	2B	3B	HR	RBI	BB	SO	AVG	OBP	SLG	PRO+	BR/A	SB	CS	SBR	FA	FR	G/POS	TPR
1930	Cin-N	125	443	64	138	22	5	10	78	47	44	.312	.380	.451	105	4	5			.920	-19	*3-109,2-15/S-4	-0.7
1931	Cin-N	154	575	67	181	39	11	2	93	54	28	.315	.374	.431	123	19	1			.969	5	*2-154	3.3
1932	Bro-N	154	597	76	168	32	6	12	77	46	47	.281	.337	.415	103	2	5			.973	19	*2-154	2.9
1933	Bro-N★	134	485	58	122	31	4	9	65	44	40	.252	.316	.388	105	2	4			.977	-19	*2-120,3-14	-0.9
1934	Bro-N	140	528	59	138	32	2	14	94	49	45	.261	.325	.409	100	-1	0			.974	12	*2-101,3-43	1.8
1935	Bro-N	102	360	49	105	20	3	8	53	40	35	.292	.366	.431	116	9	3			.977	6	2-64,3-36	1.9
1936	Bos-N	150	565	68	174	26	3	7	86	58	49	.308	.374	.402	116	14	1			.971	22	*2-150	4.5
1937	Bos-N	152	575	77	156	36	4	11	80	61	40	.271	.341	.405	112	9	2			.967	-10	*2-151	1.0
1938	Bos-N☆	147	555	62	147	25	2	9	76	52	32	.265	.331	.366	102	0	4			.974	-26	*2-147	-1.7
1939	Bos-N	81	310	42	95	17	1	2	40	26	26	.306	.360	.387	109	4	5			.970	-4	2-80	0.5
1940	Bos-N	34	126	14	34	9	0	0	19	8	9	.270	.319	.341	87	-2	1			.978	1	3-33	0.0
	NY-N	88	307	26	64	9	2	5	36	16	42	.208	.248	.300	50	-21	1			.987	5	2-47,3-37	-1.3
	Yr	122	433	40	98	18	2	5	55	24	51	.226	.269	.312	60	-24	2			.971	6	3-70,2-47	-1.3
1942	Bos-N	40	104	8	21	3	0	1	8	9	11	.202	.265	.260	55	-6	1			.907	-4	3-20,2-14	-1.0
1943	Bos-N	13	19	0	0	0	0	0	2	3	1	.000	.136	.000	-60	-4	0			.929	0	/3-4,2-2,S-1	-0.4
	Chi-A	34	103	5	28	5	0	2	11	13	13	.272	.353	.379	114	2	3	1	0	.965	-2	3-30	0.1
1944	Chi-A	38	130	5	34	3	0	0	17	8	16	.262	.304	.285	70	-5	0	0	0	.959	-2	3-30/2-6	-0.7
1945	Chi-A†	118	402	50	124	25	3	2	49	45	19	.308	.379	.400	130	16	6	2	1	.936	-5	*3-112	1.5
Total	15	1704	6184	730	1729	334	46	94	884	579	497	.280	.343	.394	105	41	42	3		.973	-18	*2-1205,3-468/S-5	10.8

■ **JIM CUDWORTH** Cudworth, James Alaric "Cuddy" b: 8/22/1858, Fairhaven, Mass. d: 12/21/43, Middleboro, Mass. BR/TR, 6', 165 lbs. Deb: 7/27/1884

YEAR	TM/L	G	AB	R	H	2B	3B	HR	RBI	BB	SO	AVG	OBP	SLG	PRO+	BR/A	SB	CS	SBR	FA	FR	G/POS	TPR
1884	KC-U	32	116	7	17	3	1	0		2		.147	.161	.190	7	-17				.963	2	1-19,O-12/P-2	-1.4

■ **MANUEL CUETO** Cueto, Manuel "Potato" b: 2/8/1892, Guanajay, Cuba d: 6/29/42, Regla, Cuba BR/TR, 5'5", 157 lbs. Deb: 6/25/14

YEAR	TM/L	G	AB	R	H	2B	3B	HR	RBI	BB	SO	AVG	OBP	SLG	PRO+	BR/A	SB	CS	SBR	FA	FR	G/POS	TPR
1914	StL-F	19	43	2	4	0	0	0	2	5	0	.093	.188	.093	-21	-8	0			.941	-1	3-10/S-5,2-2	-0.9
1917	Cin-N	56	140	10	28	3	0	1	11	16	17	.200	.287	.243	66	-5	4			.963	-1	O-38/2-6,C-5	-0.9
1918	Cin-N	47	108	14	32	5	1	0	14	19	5	.296	.406	.361	137	6	4			.929	-14	O-19,2-10/S-9,C-6	-0.8
1919	Cin-N	29	88	10	22	2	0	0	4	10	4	.250	.340	.273	88	-1	5			.982	4	O-25/3-1	0.1
Total	4	151	379	36	86	10	1	1	31	50	26	.227	.323	.266	80	-8	13			.964	-13	/O-82,2-18,S-14,C3	-2.5

■ **JOHN CUFF** Cuff, John J. b: 6/1864, Jersey City, N.J. Deb: 9/11/1884

YEAR	TM/L	G	AB	R	H	2B	3B	HR	RBI	BB	SO	AVG	OBP	SLG	PRO+	BR/A	SB	CS	SBR	FA	FR	G/POS	TPR
1884	Bal-U	3	11	1	1	1	0	0		1		.091	.167	.182	5	-2				.920	0	/C-3	-0.1

■ **LEON CULBERSON** Culberson, Delbert Leon "Lee" b: 8/6/19, Halls, Ga. d: 9/17/89, Rome, Ga. BR/TR, 5'11", 180 lbs. Deb: 5/16/43

YEAR	TM/L	G	AB	R	H	2B	3B	HR	RBI	BB	SO	AVG	OBP	SLG	PRO+	BR/A	SB	CS	SBR	FA	FR	G/POS	TPR
1943	Bos-A	81	312	36	85	16	6	3	34	31	35	.272	.338	.391	111	4	14	0	4	.978	6	O-79	1.0
1944	Bos-A	75	282	41	67	11	5	2	21	20	20	.238	.288	.333	78	-9	6	4	-1	.979	-3	O-72	-1.7
1945	Bos-A	97	331	26	91	21	6	6	45	20	37	.275	.316	.429	113	4	4	3	-1	.967	5	O-91	0.3
1946	*Bos-A	59	179	34	56	10	1	3	18	16	19	.313	.369	.430	116	4	3	2	-0	.967	-7	O-49/3-4	-0.5
1947	Bos-A	47	84	10	20	2	1	0	11	12	10	.238	.354	.250	65	-3	1	1	-0	.974	-4	O-25/3-4	-0.9
1948	Was-A	12	29	1	5	0	0	0	2	8	5	.172	.351	.172	43	-2	0	0	0	1.000	-3	O-11	-0.5
Total	6	371	1217	148	324	59	18	14	131	107	126	.266	.327	.379	100	-3	28	10	2	.974	-6	O-327/3-8	-2.3

■ **JOHN CULLEN** Cullen, John J. b: Marysville, Cal. Deb: 8/18/1884

YEAR	TM/L	G	AB	R	H	2B	3B	HR	RBI	BB	SO	AVG	OBP	SLG	PRO+	BR/A	SB	CS	SBR	FA	FR	G/POS	TPR
1884	Wil-U	9	31	2	6	0	0	0		1		.194	.219	.194	25	-4				.750	-1	/O-6,S-3	-0.5

■ **TIM CULLEN** Cullen, Timothy Leo b: 2/16/42, San Francisco, Cal. BR/TR, 6'1", 185 lbs. Deb: 8/8/66

YEAR	TM/L	G	AB	R	H	2B	3B	HR	RBI	BB	SO	AVG	OBP	SLG	PRO+	BR/A	SB	CS	SBR	FA	FR	G/POS	TPR
1966	Was-A	18	34	8	8	1	0	0	0	2	8	.235	.278	.265	57	-2	0	0	0	.889	1	/3-8,2-5	0.0
1967	Was-A	124	402	35	95	7	0	2	31	40	47	.236	.307	.269	74	-12	4	5	-2	.951	15	S-69,2-46,3-15,/O-1	1.1
1968	Chi-A	72	155	16	31	7	0	2	13	15	23	.200	.275	.284	69	-6	0	0	0	.966	6	2-71	0.3
	Was-A	47	114	8	31	4	2	1	16	7	12	.272	.325	.368	113	2	0	0	0	.968	-1	S-33,2-16/3-3	0.4
	Yr	119	269	24	62	11	2	3	29	22	35	.230	.296	.320	87	-4	0	0	0	.965	5	2-87,S-33/3-3	0.7
1969	Was-A	119	249	22	52	7	0	1	15	14	27	.209	.257	.249	44	-19	1	1	-0	.981	12	*2-105/S-9,3-1	-0.1
1970	Was-A	123	262	22	56	10	2	1	18	31	38	.214	.304	.279	65	-12	3	2	-0	**.994**	27	*2-112/S-6	2.1
1971	Was-A	125	403	34	77	13	4	2	26	33	47	.191	.252	.258	47	-29	2	0	1	.997	21	2-78,S-62	0.5
1972	*Oak-A	72	142	10	37	8	1	0	15	5	17	.261	.286	.331	88	-3	0	1	-1	.952	-1	2-65/3-4,S-1	-0.2
Total	7	700	1761	155	387	57	9	9	134	147	219	.220	.283	.278	65	-80	10	9	-2	.979	80	2-498,S-180/3-31,O	4.1

■ **ROY CULLENBINE** Cullenbine, Roy Joseph b: 10/18/13, Nashville, Tenn. d: 5/28/91, Mt.Clemens, Mich. BB/TR, 6'1", 190 lbs. Deb: 4/19/38

YEAR	TM/L	G	AB	R	H	2B	3B	HR	RBI	BB	SO	AVG	OBP	SLG	PRO+	BR/A	SB	CS	SBR	FA	FR	G/POS	TPR
1938	Det-A	25	67	12	19	1	3	0	9	12	9	.284	.392	.388	91	-1	2	0	1	1.000	-0	O-17	-0.1
1939	Det-A	75	179	31	43	9	2	6	23	34	29	.240	.362	.413	91	-2	0	1	-1	.902	-5	O-46/1-2	-0.9
1940	Bro-N	22	61	8	11	1	0	1	9	23	11	.180	.405	.246	78	-0	2			1.000	1	O-19	-0.1
	StL-A	86	257	41	59	11	2	7	31	50	34	.230	.359	.370	87	-4	0	1	-1	.975	-2	O-57/1-6	-1.0
1941	StL-A★	149	501	82	159	29	9	9	98	121	43	.317	.452	.465	138	35	6	4	-1	.964	1	*O-120,1-22	2.5

YEAR	TM/L	G	AB	R	H	2B	3B	HR	RBI	BB	SO	AVG	OBP	SLG	PRO+	BR/A	SB	CS	SBR	FA	FR	G/POS	TPR
1942	StL-A	38	109	15	21	7	1	2	14	30	20	.193	.367	.330	95	0	0	1	-1	.930	1	O-27/1-5	-0.1
	Was-A	64	241	30	69	19	0	2	35	44	18	.286	.396	.390	123	9	1	2	-1	.966	8	O-35,3-28	1.5
	*NY-A	21	77	16	28	7	0	2	17	18	2	.364	.484	.532	190	10	0	1	-1	.980	2	O-19/1-1	1.1
	Yr	123	427	61	118	33	1	6	66	92	40	.276	.405	.400	127	20	1	4	-2	.959	11	O-81,3-28/1-6	2.5
1943	Cle-A	138	488	66	141	24	4	8	56	96	58	.289	.407	.404	146	33	3	4	-2	.981	3	*O-121,1-13	2.9
1944	Cle-A☆	154	571	98	162	34	5	16	80	87	49	.284	.380	.445	141	31	4	4	-1	.967	-2	*O-151	2.1
1945	Cle-A	8	13	3	1	1	0	0	0	11	0	.077	.500	.154	97	1	0	0	0	1.000	-2	/O-4,3-3	-0.1
	*Det-A	146	523	80	145	27	5	18	93	102	36	.277	.398	.451	137	28	2	0	1	.980	13	*O-146	3.5
	Yr	154	536	83	146	28	5	18	93	**113**	36	.272	.402	.444	137	29	2	0	1	.980	11	*O-150/3-3	3.4
1946	Det-A	113	328	63	110	21	0	15	56	88	39	.335	.477	.537	172	37	3	0	1	.965	1	O-81,1-21	3.5
1947	Det-A	142	464	82	104	18	1	24	78	137	51	.224	.401	.422	125	21	3	2	-0	.989	16	*1-138	3.3
Total	10	1181	3879	627	1072	209	32	110	599	853	399	.276	.408	.432	132	199	26	20		.969	34	O-843,1-208/3-31	18.1

■ DICK CULLER

Culler, Richard Broadus b: 1/15/15, High Point, N.C. d: 6/16/64, Chapel Hill, N.C. BR/TR, 5′9.5″, 155 lbs. Deb: 9/19/36

YEAR	TM/L	G	AB	R	H	2B	3B	HR	RBI	BB	SO	AVG	OBP	SLG	PRO+	BR/A	SB	CS	SBR	FA	FR	G/POS	TPR
1936	Phi-A	9	38	3	9	0	0	0	1	1	3	.237	.256	.237	23	-5	0	0	0	.946	-3	/2-7,S-2	-0.7
1943	Chi-A	53	148	9	32	5	1	0	11	16	11	.216	.297	.264	65	-6	4	5	-2	.950	11	3-26,2-19/S-3	0.4
1944	Bos-N	8	28	2	2	0	0	0	0	4	2	.071	.188	.071	-24	-5	0			.904	2	/S-8	-0.2
1945	Bos-N	136	527	87	138	12	1	2	30	50	35	.262	.328	.300	75	-17	7			.954	-8	*S-126/3-6	-1.5
1946	Bos-N	134	482	70	123	15	3	0	33	62	18	.255	.342	.299	82	-9	7			.948	-8	*S-132	-1.1
1947	Bos-N	77	214	20	53	5	1	0	19	19	15	.248	.309	.280	59	-12	1			.967	3	S-77	-0.6
1948	Chi-N	48	89	4	15	2	0	0	5	13	3	.169	.275	.191	29	-9	0			.968	16	S-43/2-2	0.9
1949	NY-N	7	1	0	0	0	0	0	0	1	0	.000	.500	.000	45	0	0			.889	2	/S-7	0.2
Total	8	472	1527	195	372	39	6	2	99	166	87	.244	.320	.281	68	-62	19	5		.954	14	S-398/3-32,2-28	-2.6

■ NICK CULLOP

Cullop, Henry Nicholas "Tomato Face" (b: Heinrich Nicholas Kolop)
b: 10/16/1900, St.Louis, Mo. d: 12/8/78, Westerville, Ohio BR/TR, 6′, 200 lbs. Deb: 4/14/26

YEAR	TM/L	G	AB	R	H	2B	3B	HR	RBI	BB	SO	AVG	OBP	SLG	PRO+	BR/A	SB	CS	SBR	FA	FR	G/POS	TPR
1926	NY-A	2	2	0	1	0	0	0	0	0	1	.500	.500	.500	164	0	0	0	0	.000	0	H	0.0
1927	Was-A	15	23	2	5	2	0	0	1	1	6	.217	.250	.304	44	-2	0	0	0	1.000	-1	/O-5,1-1	-0.3
	Cle-A	32	68	9	16	2	3	1	8	9	19	.235	.333	.397	88	-1	0	4	-2	.982	3	O-20/P-1	-0.2
	Yr	47	91	11	21	4	3	1	9	10	25	.231	.314	.374	78	-3	0	4	-2	.984	2	O-25/1-1,P-1	-0.5
1929	Bro-N	13	41	7	8	2	2	1	5	8	7	.195	.327	.415	84	-1	0			1.000	-1	O-11/1-1	-0.2
1930	Cin-N	7	22	2	4	0	0	1	5	1	9	.182	.217	.318	29	-3	0			1.000	0	/O-5	-0.2
1931	Cin-N	104	334	29	88	23	7	8	48	21	86	.263	.309	.446	107	1	1			.968	0	O-83	-0.4
Total	5	173	490	49	122	29	12	11	67	40	128	.249	.308	.424	96	-6	1	4		.975	2	O-124/1-2,P-1	-1.3

■ WIL CULMER

Culmer, Wilfred Hillard b: 11/11/58, Nassau, Bahamas BR/TR, 6′4″, 210 lbs. Deb: 4/12/83

YEAR	TM/L	G	AB	R	H	2B	3B	HR	RBI	BB	SO	AVG	OBP	SLG	PRO+	BR/A	SB	CS	SBR	FA	FR	G/POS	TPR
1983	Cle-A	7	19	0	2	0	0	0	1	0	4	.105	.105	.105	-40	-4	0	1	-1	1.000	-1	/O-4,D-2	-0.6

■ BENNY CULP

Culp, Benjamin Baldy b: 1/19/14, Philadelphia, Pa. BR/TR, 5′9″, 175 lbs. Deb: 9/17/42 C

YEAR	TM/L	G	AB	R	H	2B	3B	HR	RBI	BB	SO	AVG	OBP	SLG	PRO+	BR/A	SB	CS	SBR	FA	FR	G/POS	TPR
1942	Phi-N	1	0	0	0	0	0	0	0	0	0	—	—	—	—	0	0			.500	-0	/C-1	0.0
1943	Phi-N	10	24	4	5	1	0	0	2	3	3	.208	.296	.250	61	-1	0			.958	-3	C-10	-0.3
1944	Phi-N	4	2	1	0	0	0	0	0	0	0	.000	.000	.000	-99	-1	0			1.000	0	/C-1	0.0
Total	3	15	26	5	5	1	0	0	2	3	3	.192	.276	.231	49	-2	0			.926	-3	/C-12	-0.3

■ JACK CUMMINGS

Cummings, John William b: 4/1/04, Pittsburgh, Pa. d: 10/5/62, W.Mifflin, Pa. BR/TR, 6′, 195 lbs. Deb: 9/11/26

YEAR	TM/L	G	AB	R	H	2B	3B	HR	RBI	BB	SO	AVG	OBP	SLG	PRO+	BR/A	SB	CS	SBR	FA	FR	G/POS	TPR
1926	NY-N	7	16	3	5	3	0	0	4	4	2	.313	.450	.500	157	2	0			.958	0	/C-6	0.2
1927	NY-N	43	80	8	29	6	1	2	14	5	10	.363	.407	.538	151	6	0			.974	-5	C-34	0.2
1928	NY-N	33	27	4	9	2	0	2	9	3	4	.333	.400	.630	165	2	0			.833	0	/C-4	0.2
1929	NY-N	3	3	0	1	0	0	0	0	0	0	.333	.333	.333	66	-0	0			1.000	-0	/C-1	0.0
	Bos-N	3	6	0	1	0	0	0	1	0	2	.167	.167	.167	-18	-1	0			.667	-1	/C-3	-0.2
	Yr	6	9	0	2	0	0	0	1	0	2	.222	.222	.222	11	-1	0			.714	-1	/C-4	-0.2
Total	4	89	132	15	45	11	1	4	28	12	18	.341	.400	.530	145	8	0			.947	-6	/C-48	0.4

■ MIDRE CUMMINGS

Cummings, Midre Almeric b: 10/14/71, St.Croix, V.I. BB/TR, 6′, 196 lbs. Deb: 9/10/93

YEAR	TM/L	G	AB	R	H	2B	3B	HR	RBI	BB	SO	AVG	OBP	SLG	PRO+	BR/A	SB	CS	SBR	FA	FR	G/POS	TPR
1993	Pit-N	13	36	5	4	1	0	0	3	4	9	.111	.200	.139	-7	-5	0	0	0	1.000	-1	O-11	-0.7
1994	Pit-N	24	86	11	21	4	0	1	12	4	18	.244	.286	.326	58	-5	0	0	0	.962	0	O-24	-0.6
1995	Pit-N	59	152	13	37	7	1	2	15	13	30	.243	.303	.342	68	-7	1	0	0	.988	-0	O-41	-0.8
1996	Pit-N	24	85	11	19	3	1	3	7	0	16	.224	.224	.388	56	-6	0	0	0	.980	1	O-21	-0.5
1997	Pit-N	52	106	11	20	6	2	3	8	8	26	.189	.252	.368	59	-7	0	0	0	1.000	-1	O-25	-0.8
	Phi-N	63	208	24	63	16	4	1	23	23	30	.303	.372	.433	110	3	2	3	-1	.991	2	O-54	0.3
	Yr	115	314	35	83	22	6	4	31	31	56	.264	.332	.411	93	-4	2	3	-1	.993	1	O-79	-0.5
1998	*Bos-A	67	120	20	34	8	0	5	15	17	19	.283	.381	.475	121	4	3	3	-1	.941	-4	D-29,O-17	-0.3
Total	6	302	793	95	198	45	8	15	83	69	148	.250	.313	.383	81	-23	6	6	-2	.984	-3	O-193/D-29	-3.4

■ GEORGE CUNNINGHAM

Cunningham, George Harold b: 7/13/1894, Sturgeon Lake, Minn. d: 3/10/72, Chattanooga, Tenn. BR/TR, 5′11″, 185 lbs. Deb: 4/14/16

YEAR	TM/L	G	AB	R	H	2B	3B	HR	RBI	BB	SO	AVG	OBP	SLG	PRO+	BR/A	SB	CS	SBR	FA	FR	G/POS	TPR
1916	Det-A	35	41	7	11	2	2	0	3	8	12	.268	.388	.415	136	2	0			.948	1	P-35	0.0
1917	Det-A	44	34	5	6	0	0	1	3	3	13	.176	.243	.265	55	-2	0			.922	0	P-44	0.0
1918	Det-A	56	112	11	25	4	1	0	2	16	34	.223	.320	.277	84	-2	2			.923	-6	P-27,O-20	-0.8
1919	Det-A	26	23	4	5	0	0	0	5	9	8	.217	.438	.217	89	1	0			.857	0	P-17	0.0
1921	Det-A	1	0	0	0	0	0	0	0	0	0	—	—	—	—	0	0	0	0	1.000	-0	/O-1	0.0
Total	5	162	210	27	47	6	3	1	13	36	67	.224	.337	.295	91	-1	2	0		.923	-4	P-123/O-21	-0.8

■ JOE CUNNINGHAM

Cunningham, Joseph Robert b: 8/27/31, Paterson, N.J. BL/TL, 6′1″, 190 lbs. Deb: 6/30/54 C

YEAR	TM/L	G	AB	R	H	2B	3B	HR	RBI	BB	SO	AVG	OBP	SLG	PRO+	BR/A	SB	CS	SBR	FA	FR	G/POS	TPR
1954	StL-N	85	310	40	88	11	3	11	50	43	40	.284	.375	.445	112	6	1	1	-0	.989	2	1-85	0.3
1956	StL-N	4	3	1	0	0	0	0	0	1	1	.000	.250	.000	-25	-1	0	0	0	1.000	-0	/1-1	-0.1
1957	StL-N	122	261	50	83	15	0	9	52	56	29	.318	.447	.479	146	20	3	3	-1	1.000	-3	1-57,O-46	1.2
1958	StL-N	131	337	61	105	20	3	12	57	82	23	.312	.450	.496	144	26	4	4	-1	.997	-6	1-67,O-66	1.3
1959	StL-N★	144	458	65	158	28	6	7	60	88	47	.345	**.456**	.478	140	31	2	6	-3	.972	-7	*O-121,1-35	1.4
1960	StL-N	139	492	68	138	28	3	6	39	59	59	.280	.364	.386	97	-0	1	7	-4	.950	-7	*O-116,1-15	-1.9
1961	StL-N	113	322	60	92	11	2	7	40	53	32	.286	.404	.398	104	4	1	0	0	.964	-9	O-86,1-10	-1.0
1962	Chi-A	149	526	91	155	32	7	8	70	101	59	.295	.415	.428	128	26	3	3	-1	**.994**	-6	*1-143/O-5	0.9
1963	Chi-A	67	210	32	60	12	1	1	31	33	23	.286	.393	.367	116	6	1	0	0	.989	-7	1-58	-0.3
1964	Chi-A	40	108	13	27	7	0	0	10	14	15	.250	.352	.315	90	-1	0	1	-1	.996	-1	1-33	-0.3
	Was-A	49	126	15	27	4	0	0	7	23	13	.214	.344	.246	68	-4	0	1	-1	.997	-4	1-41	-1.1
	Yr	89	234	28	54	11	0	0	17	37	28	.231	.348	.278	78	-5	0	2	-1	.997	-5	1-74	-1.4
1965	Was-A	95	201	29	46	9	1	3	20	46	27	.229	.375	.328	103	3	0	1	-1	.986	-4	1-59	-0.5
1966	Was-A	3	8	0	1	0	0	0	0	0	1	.125	.125	.125	-28	-1	0	0	0	1.000	1	/1-3	0.0
Total	12	1141	3362	525	980	177	26	64	436	599	369	.291	.406	.417	119	116	16	27	-11	.993	-51	1-607,O-440	-0.1

■ RAY CUNNINGHAM

Cunningham, Raymond Lee b: 1/17/05, Mesquite, Tex. BR/TR, 5′7.5″, 150 lbs. Deb: 9/16/31

YEAR	TM/L	G	AB	R	H	2B	3B	HR	RBI	BB	SO	AVG	OBP	SLG	PRO+	BR/A	SB	CS	SBR	FA	FR	G/POS	TPR
1931	StL-N	3	4	0	0	0	0	0	1	0	0	.000	.000	.000	-96	-1	0			1.000	1	/3-3	0.0
1932	StL-N	11	22	4	4	1	0	0	0	3	4	.182	.280	.227	37	-2	0			1.000	3	/3-8,2-2	0.1
Total	2	14	26	4	4	1	0	0	1	3	4	.154	.241	.192	18	-3	0			1.000	4	/3-11,2-2	0.1

■ BILL CUNNINGHAM

Cunningham, William Aloysius b: 7/30/1895, San Francisco, Cal. d: 9/26/53, Colusa, Cal. BR/TR, 5′8″, 155 lbs. Deb: 7/14/21 C

YEAR	TM/L	G	AB	R	H	2B	3B	HR	RBI	BB	SO	AVG	OBP	SLG	PRO+	BR/A	SB	CS	SBR	FA	FR	G/POS	TPR
1921	NY-N	40	76	10	21	2	1	1	12	3	3	.276	.313	.368	79	-2	0	1	-1	1.000	-4	O-20	-0.8
1922	*NY-N	85	229	37	75	15	2	2	33	7	9	.328	.350	.437	101	-0	4	5	-2	.988	-4	O-71/3-1	-0.9
1923	*NY-N	79	203	22	55	7	1	5	27	10	9	.271	.305	.389	83	-6	5	2	0	.992	-7	O-68/2-4	-1.5
1924	Bos-N	114	437	44	119	15	8	1	40	32	27	.272	.326	.350	85	-9	8	5	-1	.970	6	*O-109	-1.1
Total	4	318	945	113	270	39	12	9	112	52	48	.286	.326	.381	88	-17	17	13	-3	.982	-8	O-268/2-4,3-1	-4.3

YEAR	TM/L	G	AB	R	H	2B	3B	HR	RBI	BB	SO	AVG	OBP	SLG	PRO+	BR/A	SB	CS	SBR	FA	FR	G/POS	TPR
■ BILL CUNNINGHAM Cunningham, William John b: 6/9/1888, Schenectady, N.Y. d: 2/21/46, Schenectady, N.Y. BR/TR, 5'9", 170 lbs. Deb: 9/12/10																							
1910	Was-A	21	74	3	22	5	1	0	14	12		.297	.402	.392	156	5	4			.957	-5	2-21	0.0
1911	Was-A	94	331	34	63	10	5	3	37	19		.190	.239	.278	45	-26	10			.932	-13	2-93	-4.1
1912	Was-A	8	27	5	5	1	0	1	8	3		.185	.267	.333	71	-1	2			.962	-3	/2-7,S-1	-0.4
Total	3	123	432	42	90	16	6	4	59	34		.208	.271	.301	64	-21	16			.938	-21	2-121/S-1	-4.5
■ DOC CURLEY Curley, Walter James b: 3/12/1874, Upton, Mass. d: 9/23/20, Framingham, Mass. BR/TR, Deb: 9/12/1899																							
1899	Chi-N	10	37	7	4	0	1	0	2	3		.108	.233	.162	9	-5	0			.907	-6	2-10	-0.9
■ PETE CURREN Curren, Peter b: Baltimore, Md. 175 lbs. Deb: 9/12/1876																							
1876	Phi-N	3	12	5	4	1	0	0	2	0	0	.333	.333	.417	150	1				.588	-1	/C-2,O-1	0.0
■ PERRY CURRIN Currin, Perry Gilmore b: 9/27/28, Washington, D.C. BL/TR, 6', 175 lbs. Deb: 6/29/47																							
1947	StL-A	3	2	0	0	0	0	0	0	1	0	.000	.333	.000	-3	-0	0	0	0	1.000	1	/S-1	0.1
■ TONY CURRY Curry, George Anthony b: 12/22/38, Nassau, Bahamas BL/TL, 5'11", 185 lbs. Deb: 4/12/60																							
1960	Phi-N	95	245	26	64	14	2	6	34	16	53	.261	.309	.408	94	-2	0	2	-1	.925	-8	O-64	-1.4
1961	Phi-N	15	36	3	7	2	0	0	3	1	8	.194	.216	.250	24	-4	0	0	0	.833	-0	/O-8	-0.5
1966	Cle-A	19	16	4	2	0	0	0	3	3	8	.125	.263	.125	16	-2	0	0	0	.000	0	H	-0.2
Total	3	129	297	33	73	16	2	6	40	20	69	.246	.296	.374	82	-8	0	2	-1	.915	-8	/O-72	-2.1
■ JIM CURRY Curry, James L. b: 3/10/1893, Camden, N.J. d: 8/2/38, Grenloch, N.J. BR/TR, 5'11", 160 lbs. Deb: 10/2/09																							
1909	Phi-A	1	4	1	1	0	0	0	0	0		.250	.250	.250	57	-0	0			1.000	-1	/2-1	-0.1
1911	NY-A	4	11	3	2	0	0	0	0	1		.182	.250	.182	20	-1	0			.773	-1	/2-4	-0.3
1918	Det-A	5	20	1	5	1	0	0	0	0	0	.250	.286	.300	80	-1	0			.952	-3	/2-5	-0.3
Total	3	10	35	5	8	1	0	0	0	1	0	.229	.270	.257	56	-2	0			.867	-5	/2-10	-0.7
■ CHAD CURTIS Curtis, Chad David b: 11/6/68, Marion, Ind. BR/TR, 5'10", 175 lbs. Deb: 4/8/92																							
1992	Cal-A	139	441	59	114	16	2	10	46	51	71	.259	.343	.372	100	1	43	18	2	.978	-3	*O-135/D-1	-0.2
1993	Cal-A	152	583	94	166	25	3	6	59	70	89	.285	.365	.369	95	-2	48	24	0	.980	17	*O-151/2-3	1.1
1994	Cal-A	114	453	67	116	23	4	11	50	37	69	.256	.319	.397	82	-13	25	11	1	.988	15	*O-114	0.0
1995	Det-A	144	586	96	157	29	3	21	67	70	93	.268	.353	.435	104	4	27	15	-1	.992	2	*O-144	0.1
1996	Det-A	104	400	65	105	20	1	10	37	53	73	.262	.350	.393	88	-7	16	10	-1	.965	-7	*O-104	-1.6
	*LA-N	43	104	20	22	5	0	2	9	17	15	.212	.322	.317	75	-4	2	1	0	.985	-3	O-40	-0.7
1997	Cle-A	22	29	8	6	1	0	3	5	7	10	.207	.361	.552	129	1	0	0	0	1.000	-5	O-19	-0.3
	*NY-A	93	320	51	93	21	1	12	50	36	49	.291	.371	.475	120	10	12	6	0	.978	-5	O-92	0.2
	Yr	115	349	59	99	22	1	15	55	43	59	.284	.370	.481	120	11	12	6	0	.980	-10	*O-111	-0.1
1998	*NY-A	151	456	79	111	21	1	10	56	75	80	.243	.359	.360	90	-5	21	5	3	.984	2	*O-148/D-2	-0.2
Total	7	962	3372	539	890	161	15	85	379	416	549	.264	.351	.396	96	-14	194	90	4	.982	13	O-947/2-3,D-3	-1.6
■ ERVIN CURTIS Curtis, Ervin Duane b: 12/27/1861, Coldwater, Mich. d: 2/14/45, N.Adams, Mass. BL/TL, 5'8.5", 157 lbs. Deb: 7/15/1891																							
1891	Cin-N	27	108	11	29	3	3	1	13	9	19	.269	.331	.380	106	1	3			.862	-0	O-27	-0.1
	Was-a	29	103	17	26	3	2	0	12	13	16	.252	.347	.320	96	-0	2			.797	-1	O-29	-0.2
Total	1	56	211	28	55	6	5	1	25	22	35	.261	.339	.351	101	0	5			.829	-2	/O-56	-0.3
■ GENE CURTIS Curtis, Eugene Holmes "Eude" b: 5/5/1883, Bethany, W.Va. d: 1/1/19, Steubenville, Ohio BR/TR, 6'3", 220 lbs. Deb: 9/21/03																							
1903	Pit-N	5	19	2	8	1	0	0	3	1		.421	.450	.474	158	1	0			.833	-0	/O-5	0.1
■ FRED CURTIS Curtis, Frederick Marion b: 10/30/1880, Beaver Lake, Mich. d: 4/5/39, Minneapolis, Minn. BR/TR, 6'1", Deb: 7/24/05																							
1905	NY-A	2	9	0	2	1	0	0	2	1		.222	.300	.333	90	-0	1			1.000	-0	/1-2	0.0
■ HARRY CURTIS Curtis, Harry Albert b: 2/19/1883, Portland, Maine d: 8/1/51, Evanston, Ill. TR , 5'10.5", 170 lbs. Deb: 8/28/07																							
1907	NY-N	6	9	2	2	0	0	0	1	2		.222	.364	.222	81	-0	2			.909	0	/C-6	0.0
■ GUY CURTRIGHT Curtright, Guy Paxton b: 10/18/12, Holliday, Mo. d: 8/23/97, Sun City Center, Fla. BR/TR, 5'11", 200 lbs. Deb: 4/21/43																							
1943	Chi-A	138	488	67	142	20	7	3	48	69	60	.291	.382	.379	123	16	13	12	-3	.972	-2	*O-128	0.5
1944	Chi-A	72	198	22	50	8	2	2	23	23	21	.253	.330	.343	94	-1	4	3	-1	.948	1	O-51	-0.3
1945	Chi-A	98	324	51	91	15	7	4	32	39	29	.281	.358	.407	125	10	3	4	-2	.986	1	O-84	0.6
1946	Chi-A	23	55	7	11	2	0	0	5	11	14	.200	.333	.236	63	-2	0	1	-1	1.000	1	O-15	-0.3
Total	4	331	1065	147	294	45	16	9	108	142	124	.276	.363	.374	115	23	20	20	-6	.973	2	O-278	0.5
■ TONY CUSICK Cusick, Andrew Daniel "Andy" b: 12/1857, Fall River, Mass. d: 8/6/29, Chicago, Ill. BR/TR, 5'9.5", 190 lbs. Deb: 8/21/1884																							
1884	Wil-U	11	34	0	5	0	0	0		1		.147	.171	.147	-3	-5				.871	-0	/C-6,S-3,O-3,2-1,3	-0.4
	Phi-N	9	29	2	4	0	0	0	1	0	3	.138	.138	.138	-14	-4				.930	4	/C-9	0.1
1885	Phi-N	39	141	12	25	1	0	0	5	1	24	.177	.183	.184	19	-12				.808	-3	C-38/O-1	-1.2
1886	Phi-N	29	104	10	23	5	1	0	4	3	14	.221	.243	.288	61	-5	1			.891	-6	C-25/O-3,1-1	-0.7
1887	Phi-N	7	24	3	7	1	0	0	5	3	1	.292	.393	.333	98	0	0			.643	-3	/C-4,1-3,2-1	-0.3
Total	4	95	332	27	64	7	1	0	15	8	42	.193	.214	.220	35	-26	1			.844	-8	/C-82,O-7,1-4,S23	-2.5
■ JACK CUSICK Cusick, John Peter b: 6/12/28, Weehawken, N.J. d: 11/17/89, Edgewood, N.J. BR/TR, 6', 170 lbs. Deb: 4/24/51																							
1951	Chi-N	65	164	16	29	3	2	2	16	17	29	.177	.254	.256	37	-15	2	1	0	.953	-2	S-56	-1.3
1952	Bos-N	49	78	5	13	1	0	0	6	6	9	.167	.226	.179	14	-9	0	1	-1	.969	-2	S-28/3-3	-1.1
Total	2	114	242	21	42	4	2	2	22	23	38	.174	.245	.231	30	-24	2	2	-1	.958	-4	/S-84,3-3	-2.4
■ NED CUTHBERT Cuthbert, Edgar Edward b: 6/20/1845, Philadelphia, Pa. d: 2/6/05, St.Louis, Mo. BR/TR, 5'6", 140 lbs. Deb: 5/20/1871 MU																							
1871	Ath-n	28	150	47	37	7	5	3	30	10	2	.247	.294	.420	103	1	16	2	4	.890	4	*O-27/C-1	0.6
1872	Ath-n	47	260	83	88	10	0	1	47	6	10	.338	.353	.388	127	8	14	4	2	.858	-3	*O-47	0.6
1873	Phi-n	51	278	78	77	5	3	2	33	2	4	.277	.282	.338	80	-8	**13**	2	**3**	.848	-6	*O-51	-0.6
1874	Chi-n	58	295	65	79	6	1	2	24	5	5	.268	.280	.315	90	-3	8	0	2	.806	-0	*O-55/C-4	0.0
1875	StL-n	68	319	68	78	9	2	0	17	3	8	.245	.252	.285	95	-0	18	1	5	.860	-13	*O-67/C-3,2-1	-0.6
1876	StL-N	63	283	46	70	10	1	0	25	7	4	.247	.266	.290	90	-2				.843	-8	*O-63	-1.0
1877	Cin-N	12	56	6	10	5	0	0	2	1	2	.179	.193	.268	49	-3				.830	4	O-12	0.1
1882	StL-a	60	233	28	52	16	5	0		17		.223	.276	.335	101	0				.896	-4	*O-60,M	-0.4
1883	StL-a	21	71	3	12	1	0	0	3	4		.169	.213	.183	27	-6				.794	-1	O-20/1-1	-0.6
1884	Bal-U	44	168	29	34	5	0	0		10		.202	.247	.232	42	-17				.750	-5	O-44	-2.1
Total	5 n	252	1302	341	359	37	11	8	151	26	29	.276	.290	.339	98	-2	69	9	15	.846	-17	O-247/C-8,2-1	0.0
Total	5	200	811	112	178	37	6	0	30	39	6	.219	.255	.280	73	-28				.833	-14	O-199/1-1	-4.0
■ GEORGE CUTSHAW Cutshaw, George William "Clancy" b: 7/27/1887, Wilmington, Ill. d: 8/22/73, San Diego, Cal. BR/TR, 5'9", 160 lbs. Deb: 4/25/12																							
1912	Bro-N	102	357	41	100	14	4	0	28	31	16	.280	.341	.342	91	-4	16			.958	8	2-91/3-5,S-1	0.2
1913	Bro-N	147	592	72	158	23	13	7	80	39	22	.267	.315	.385	97	-4	39			.957	18	*2-147	1.2
1914	Bro-N	153	583	69	150	22	12	2	78	30	32	.257	.297	.346	89	-10	34			.959	28	*2-153	1.8
1915	Bro-N	154	566	68	139	18	9	0	62	34	35	.246	.293	.309	81	-13	28	23	-5	**.971**	17	*2-154	0.0
1916	*Bro-N	154	581	58	151	21	4	2	63	25	32	.260	.292	.320	85	-11	27	20	-4	.958	8	*2-154	-0.2
1917	Bro-N	135	487	42	126	17	7	4	49	21	26	.259	.292	.347	93	-5	22			.963	-9	*2-134	-0.9
1918	Pit-N	126	463	56	132	16	10	5	68	27	18	.285	.326	.395	116	7	25			.964	-3	*2-126	1.4
1919	Pit-N	139	512	49	124	15	8	3	51	30	22	.242	.287	.320	79	-13	36			**.980**	-11	*2-139	-2.0
1920	Pit-N	131	488	56	123	16	8	0	47	23	10	.252	.287	.318	71	-18	17	14	-3	.968	1	*2-129	-1.8
1921	Pit-N	98	350	46	119	18	4	0	53	11	11	.340	.362	.414	102	1	14	5	1	.951	-15	2-84	-1.1
1922	Det-A	132	499	57	133	14	8	2	61	20	13	.267	.300	.339	68	-24	11	5	0	.972	9	*2-132	-1.1
1923	Det-A	45	143	15	32	1	2	0	13	9	5	.224	.279	.259	43	-12	2	1	0	.988	12	2-43/3-2	0.0
Total	12	1516	5621	629	1487	195	89	25	653	300	242	.265	.305	.344	86	-106	271	68		.965	61	*2-1486/3-7,S-1	-2.5

■ **KIKI CUYLER** Cuyler, Hazen Shirley b: 8/30/1898, Harrisville, Mich. d: 2/11/50, Ann Arbor, Mich. BR/TR, 5'10.5", 180 lbs. Deb: 9/29/21 CH

YEAR	TM/L	G	AB	R	H	2B	3B	HR	RBI	BB	SO	AVG	OBP	SLG	PRO+	BR/A	SB	CS	SBR	FA	FR	G/POS	TPR
1921	Pit-N	1	3	0	0	0	0	0	0	0	1	.000	.000	.000	-97	-1	0	0	0	1.000	-0	/O-1	-0.1
1922	Pit-N	1	0	0	0	0	0	0	0	0	0	—	—	—	—	0	0	0	0	.000	0	R	0.0
1923	Pit-N	11	40	4	10	1	1	0	2	5	3	.250	.348	.325	77	-1	2	3	-1	.931	-1	O-11	-0.4
1924	Pit-N	117	466	94	165	27	16	9	85	30	62	.354	.402	.539	147	30	32	11	3	.943	5	*O-114	3.0
1925	*Pit-N	153	617	**144**	220	43	**26**	18	102	58	56	.357	.423	.598	148	44	41	13	5	.967	7	*O-153	4.1
1926	Pit-N	157	614	**113**	197	31	15	8	92	50	66	.321	.380	.459	119	16	**35**			.968	13	*O-157	1.8
1927	Pit-N	85	285	60	88	13	7	3	31	37	36	.309	.394	.435	114	7	20			.980	1	O-73	0.3
1928	Chi-N	133	499	92	142	25	9	17	79	51	61	.285	.359	.473	117	12	**37**			.982	6	*O-127	0.9
1929	*Chi-N	139	509	111	183	29	7	15	102	66	56	.360	.438	.532	139	33	**43**			.974	-0	*O-129	2.2
1930	Chi-N	156	642	155	228	50	17	13	134	72	49	.355	.428	.547	133	36	**37**			.980	12	*O-156	3.2
1931	Chi-N	154	613	110	202	37	12	9	88	72	54	.330	.404	.473	133	30	13			.970	-4	*O-153	1.6
1932	*Chi-N	110	446	58	130	19	9	10	77	29	43	.291	.340	.442	109	5	9			.969	-7	*O-109	-0.8
1933	Chi-N	70	262	37	83	13	3	5	35	21	29	.317	.376	.447	135	12	4			.978	-7	O-69	0.1
1934	Chi-N★	142	559	80	189	**42**	8	6	69	31	62	.338	.377	.474	129	22	15			.971	0	*O-142	1.6
1935	Chi-N	45	157	22	42	5	1	4	18	10	16	.268	.331	.389	92	-2	3			.981	-1	O-42	-0.4
	Cin-N	62	223	36	56	8	3	2	22	27	18	.251	.337	.341	85	-4	5			.985	-3	O-57	-0.8
	Yr	107	380	58	98	13	4	6	40	37	34	.258	.335	.361	88	-6	8			.983	-3	O-99	-1.2
1936	Cin-N	144	567	96	185	29	11	7	74	47	67	.326	.380	.453	132	25	16			.974	-4	*O-140	1.5
1937	Cin-N	117	406	48	110	12	4	0	32	36	50	.271	.333	.320	82	-9	10			.973	-8	*O-106	-2.1
1938	Bro-N	82	253	45	69	10	8	2	23	34	23	.273	.363	.399	107	3	6			.993	0	O-68	0.1
Total	18	1879	7161	1305	2299	394	157	128	1065	676	752	.321	.386	.474	125	258	328	27		.972	12	*O-1807	15.8

■ **MILT CUYLER** Cuyler, Milton b: 10/7/68, Macon, Ga. BB/TR, 5'10", 185 lbs. Deb: 9/6/90

YEAR	TM/L	G	AB	R	H	2B	3B	HR	RBI	BB	SO	AVG	OBP	SLG	PRO+	BR/A	SB	CS	SBR	FA	FR	G/POS	TPR
1990	Det-A	19	51	8	13	3	1	0	8	5	10	.255	.321	.353	88	-1	1	2	-1	.976	0	O-17	-0.2
1991	Det-A	154	475	77	122	15	7	3	33	52	92	.257	.336	.337	86	-8	41	10	6	.986	8	*O-151	0.3
1992	Det-A	89	291	39	70	11	1	3	28	10	62	.241	.275	.316	65	-14	8	5	-1	.983	-0	O-89	-1.7
1993	Det-A	82	249	46	53	11	7	0	19	19	53	.213	.277	.313	59	-15	13	2	3	.968	1	O-80	-1.2
1994	Det-A	48	116	20	28	3	1	1	11	13	21	.241	.323	.310	64	-6	5	3	-0	.975	-9	O-45	-1.5
1995	Det-A	41	88	15	18	1	4	0	5	8	16	.205	.271	.307	50	-7	2	1	0	.929	-4	O-36/D-2	-1.1
1996	Bos-A	50	110	19	22	1	2	2	12	13	19	.200	.302	.300	52	-8	7	3	0	.972	-3	O-45/D-2	-1.0
1998	Tex-A	7	6	3	3	2	0	1	3	1	0	.500	.571	1.333	359	2	0	0	0	1.000	-1	/O-3,D-3	0.2
Total	8	490	1386	227	329	47	23	10	119	121	273	.237	.306	.326	71	-56	77	26	8	.977	-7	O-466/D-7	-6.2

■ **AL CYPERT** Cypert, Alfred Boyd "Cy" b: 8/8/1889, Little Rock, Ark. d: 1/9/73, Washington, D.C. BR/TR, 5'10.5", 150 lbs. Deb: 6/27/14

YEAR	TM/L	G	AB	R	H	2B	3B	HR	RBI	BB	SO	AVG	OBP	SLG	PRO+	BR/A	SB	CS	SBR	FA	FR	G/POS	TPR
1914	Cle-A	1	1	0	0	0	0	0	0	0	1	.000	.000	.000	-96	-0	0			.000	0	/3-1	0.0

■ **PAUL DADE** Dade, Lonnie Paul b: 12/7/51, Seattle, Wash. BR/TR, 6', 195 lbs. Deb: 9/12/75

YEAR	TM/L	G	AB	R	H	2B	3B	HR	RBI	BB	SO	AVG	OBP	SLG	PRO+	BR/A	SB	CS	SBR	FA	FR	G/POS	TPR
1975	Cal-A	11	30	5	6	4	0	0	1	6	7	.200	.333	.333	96	-0	0	0	0	1.000	1	/O-3,3-1,D-7	0.0
1976	Cal-A	13	9	2	1	0	0	0	1	3	3	.111	.333	.111	36	-1	0	0	0	.750	0	/O-4,2-2,3-1,D-1	0.0
1977	Cle-A	134	461	65	134	15	3	3	45	32	58	.291	.339	.356	93	-4	16	8	0	.989	-7	O-99,3-26/2-1,D-7	-1.6
1978	Cle-A	93	307	37	78	12	1	3	20	34	45	.254	.332	.329	88	-4	12	9	-2	.962	2	O-81/D-9	-0.8
1979	Cle-A	44	170	22	48	4	1	3	18	12	22	.282	.330	.371	88	-3	12	6	0	.962	2	O-37/3-2,D-4	-0.3
	SD-N	76	283	38	78	19	2	1	19	14	48	.276	.314	.367	91	-4	13	5	1	.949	6	3-70/O-4	0.1
1980	SD-N	68	53	17	10	0	0	0	3	12	10	.189	.338	.189	54	-3	4	5	-2	.846	1	3-21/O-8,2-1	-0.3
Total	6	439	1313	186	355	54	7	10	107	113	193	.270	.331	.345	89	-19	57	33	-3	.970	4	O-236,3-121/D-28,2	-2.9

■ **ANGELO DAGRES** Dagres, Angelo George "Junior" b: 8/22/34, Newburyport, Mass. BL/TL, 5'11", 175 lbs. Deb: 9/11/55

YEAR	TM/L	G	AB	R	H	2B	3B	HR	RBI	BB	SO	AVG	OBP	SLG	PRO+	BR/A	SB	CS	SBR	FA	FR	G/POS	TPR
1955	Bal-A	8	15	5	4	0	0	0	3	1	2	.267	.313	.267	61	-1	0	0	0	.818	-1	/O-5	-0.2

■ **BILL DAHLEN** Dahlen, William Frederick "Bad Bill" b: 1/5/1870, Nellíston, N.Y. d: 12/5/50, Brooklyn, N.Y. BR/TR, 5'9", 180 lbs. Deb: 4/22/1891 M

YEAR	TM/L	G	AB	R	H	2B	3B	HR	RBI	BB	SO	AVG	OBP	SLG	PRO+	BR/A	SB	CS	SBR	FA	FR	G/POS	TPR
1891	Chi-N	135	549	114	143	18	13	9	76	67	60	.260	.348	.390	115	11	21			.887	9	3-84,O-37,S-15	2.0
1892	Chi-N	143	581	114	169	23	19	5	58	45	56	.291	.347	.422	131	19	60			.909	25	S-72,3-68/O-2,2-1	4.6
1893	Chi-N	116	485	113	146	28	15	5	64	58	30	.301	.381	.452	123	15	31			.892	4	*S-88,O-17,2-10,/3	1.8
1894	Chi-N	121	502	149	179	32	14	15	107	76	33	.357	.444	.566	135	28	42			.898	32	S-66,3-55	**4.8**
1895	Chi-N	129	516	106	131	19	10	7	62	61	51	.254	.344	.370	79	-18	38			.904	36	*S-129/O-1	1.9
1896	Chi-N	125	474	137	167	30	19	9	74	64	36	.352	.438	.553	154	37	51			.915	25	*S-125	5.4
1897	Chi-N	75	276	67	80	18	8	6	40	43		.290	.399	.478	126	11	15			.930	28	S-75	3.4
1898	Chi-N	142	521	96	151	35	8	1	79	58		.290	.385	.393	123	18	27			.921	26	*S-142	**4.6**
1899	Bro-N	121	428	87	121	22	7	4	76	67		.283	.398	.395	115	12	29			.941	17	*S-110,3-11	3.4
1900	*Bro-N	133	483	87	125	16	11	1	69	73		.259	.364	.344	90	-5	31			.938	20	*S-133	2.3
1901	Bro-N	131	511	69	136	17	9	4	82	30		.266	.313	.358	92	-6	23			.929	14	*S-129/2-2	1.8
1902	Bro-N	138	527	67	139	25	8	2	74	43		.264	.329	.353	109	6	20			.916	-6	*S-138	0.8
1903	Bro-N	138	474	71	124	17	9	1	64	82		.262	.373	.342	107	8	34			**.948**	18	*S-138	3.0
1904	NY-N	145	523	70	140	26	2	2	**80**	44		.268	.326	.337	100	0	47			.930	28	*S-145	3.3
1905	*NY-N	148	520	67	126	20	4	7	81	62		.242	.337	.337	99	1	37			.948	20	*S-147/O-1	2.4
1906	NY-N	143	471	63	113	18	3	1	49	76		.240	.357	.297	102	5	16			.938	0	*S-143	1.1
1907	NY-N	143	464	40	96	20	1	0	34	51		.207	.291	.254	69	-16	11			.941	7	*S-143	-0.5
1908	Bos-N	144	524	50	125	23	2	3	48	35		.239	.296	.307	94	-4	10			.952	**38**	*S-144	4.2
1909	Bos-N	69	197	22	46	6	1	2	16	29		.234	.332	.305	93	-1	4			.908	9	S-49/2-6,3-2	1.0
1910	Bro-N	3	2	0	0	0	0	0	0	0	0	.000	.000	.000	-99	-1	0			.000	0	HM	-0.1
1911	Bro-N	1	3	0	0	0	0	0	0	0	3	.000	.000	.000	-99	-1	0			1.000	2	/S-1,M	0.1
Total	21	2443	9031	1589	2457	413	163	84	1233	1064	269	.272	.358	.382	109	121	547			.927	348	*S-2132,3-223/O2	51.3

■ **BABE DAHLGREN** Dahlgren, Ellsworth Tenney b: 6/15/12, San Francisco, Cal. d: 9/4/96, Arcadia, Cal. BR/TR, 6', 190 lbs. Deb: 4/16/35 C

YEAR	TM/L	G	AB	R	H	2B	3B	HR	RBI	BB	SO	AVG	OBP	SLG	PRO+	BR/A	SB	CS	SBR	FA	FR	G/POS	TPR
1935	Bos-A	149	525	77	138	27	7	9	63	56	67	.263	.337	.392	83	-14	6	5	-1	.988	-7	*1-149	-3.7
1936	Bos-A	16	57	6	16	3	1	1	7	7	1	.281	.359	.421	87	-1	2	1	0	.980	-1	1-16	-0.3
1937	NY-A	1	1	0	0	0	0	0	0	0	0	.000	.000	.000	-99	-0	0	0	0	.000	0	H	0.0
1938	NY-A	27	43	8	8	1	0	0	1	1	7	.186	.205	.209	4	-6	0	0	0	.826	-1	/3-8,1-6	-0.7
1939	*NY-A	144	531	71	125	18	6	15	89	57	54	.235	.312	.377	76	-20	2	3	-1	.991	-7	*1-144	-4.1
1940	NY-A	155	568	51	150	24	4	12	73	46	54	.264	.325	.384	86	-12	1	1	-0	.990	-10	*1-155	-3.6
1941	Bos-N	44	166	20	39	8	1	7	30	16	13	.235	.306	.422	108	1	0			.993	2	1-39/3-5	0.1
	Chi-N	99	359	50	101	20	1	16	59	43	39	.281	.360	.476	139	18	2			.991	-8	1-98	0.2
	Yr	143	525	70	140	28	2	23	89	59	52	.267	.343	.459	129	19	2			.992	-6	*1-137/3-5	0.3
1942	Chi-N	17	56	4	12	1	0	0	6	4	2	.214	.267	.232	48	-4	0			.086	1	1-14	-0.4
	StL-A	2	2	0	0	0	0	0	0	0	0	.000	.000	.000	-99	-1	0	0	0	.000	0	H	-0.1
	Bro-N	17	19	2	1	0	0	0	0	4	5	.053	.217	.053	-19	-3	0			1.000	1	1-10	-0.2
1943	Phi-N★	136	508	55	146	19	2	5	56	50	39	.287	.354	.362	111	8	2			.988	-23	1-73,3-35,S-25,/C-1	-1.8
1944	Pit-N	158	599	67	173	28	7	12	101	47	56	.289	.347	.419	110	7	2			.987	8	*1-158	0.7
1945	Pit-N	144	531	57	133	24	8	5	75	51	51	.250	.318	.354	84	-12	1			**.996**	1	*1-144	-2.1
1946	StL-A	28	80	2	14	1	0	0	9	8	13	.175	.250	.188	22	-8	0	1	-1	.981	1	1-24	-0.9
Total	12	1137	4045	470	1056	174	37	82	569	390	401	.261	.329	.383	92	-49	18	11		.990	-44	*1-1030/3-48,S-25,C	-16.9

■ **JOHN DAILEY** Dailey, John G. b: Brooklyn, N.Y. Deb: 7/12/1875

YEAR	TM/L	G	AB	R	H	2B	3B	HR	RBI	BB	SO	AVG	OBP	SLG	PRO+	BR/A	SB	CS	SBR	FA	FR	G/POS	TPR
1875	Was-n	27	110	16	20	5	4	0	13	0	1	.182	.182	.300	67	-3	3	2	-0	.810	-3	S-20/3-5,2-2	-0.7
	Atl-n	2	8	3	1	0	0	0	0	0	1	.125	.125	.125	-15	-1	0	0	0	1.000	-4	/O-2,1-1,S-1	-0.4
	Yr	29	118	19	21	5	4	0	13	0	2	.178	.178	.288	62	-4	3	2	-0	.797	-7	S-21/3-5,2-2,O-2,1	-1.1

■ **VINCE DAILEY** Dailey, Vincent Perry b: 12/25/1864, Osceola, Pa. d: 11/14/19, Hornell, N.Y. 6', 200 lbs. Deb: 4/21/1890

YEAR	TM/L	G	AB	R	H	2B	3B	HR	RBI	BB	SO	AVG	OBP	SLG	PRO+	BR/A	SB	CS	SBR	FA	FR	G/POS	TPR
1890	Cle-N	64	246	41	71	5	7	0	32	33	23	.289	.373	.366	118	6	17			.859	1	O-64/P-2	0.4

YEAR	TM/L	G	AB	R	H	2B	3B	HR	RBI	BB	SO	AVG	OBP	SLG	PRO+	BR/A	SB	CS	SBR	FA	FR	G/POS	TPR
■ CON DAILY	Daily, Cornelius F. b: 9/11/1864, Blackstone, Mass. d: 6/14/28, Brooklyn, N.Y. BL , 6', 192 lbs. Deb: 6/9/1884 F																						
1884	Phi-U	2	8	0	0	0	0	0		0		.000	.000	.000	-99	-2				.857	-1	/C-2	-0.3
1885	Pro-N	60	223	20	58	6	1	0	19	12	20	.260	.298	.296	95	-1				.876	-1	C-48/1-7,O-6	0.2
1886	Bos-N	50	180	25	43	4	2	0	21	19	29	.239	.312	.283	85	-2	2			.911	-11	C-49/O-1	-0.7
1887	Bos-N	36	120	12	19	5	0	0	13	9	8	.158	.229	.200	20	-13	7			.889	-2	C-36	-1.0
1888	Ind-N	57	202	14	44	6	1	0	14	10	28	.218	.255	.257	62	-8	15			.893	-1	C-42/O-5,3-5,1-5,2	-0.6
1889	Ind-N	62	219	35	55	6	2	0	26	28	21	.251	.347	.297	79	-5	14			.887	-12	C-51/O-6,1-6,3-1	-1.1
1890	Bro-P	46	168	20	42	6	3	0	35	15	14	.250	.315	.321	66	-9	6			.879	-7	C-40/1-6,O-1	-1.0
1891	Bro-N	60	206	25	66	10	1	0	30	15	13	.320	.378	.379	121	6	7			.925	-0	C-55/O-3,S-2,1-1	0.9
1892	Bro-N	80	278	38	65	10	1	0	28	38	21	.234	.328	.277	87	-3	18			.943	-2	C-68,O-13	0.0
1893	Bro-N	61	215	33	57	4	2	1	32	20	12	.265	.342	.316	79	-6	13			.935	-1	C-51/O-9	-0.2
1894	Bro-N	67	234	40	60	14	7	0	32	31	22	.256	.351	.376	81	-7	8			.930	-2	C-60/1-7	-0.3
1895	Bro-N	40	142	17	30	3	2	1	11	10	18	.211	.268	.282	46	-12	3			.956	-3	C-39/O-1	-0.9
1896	Chi-N	9	27	1	2	0	0	0	1	1	2	.074	.107	.074	-50	-6	1			.969	-2	/C-9	-0.6
Total	13	630	2222	280	541	74	22	2	262	208	208	.243	.314	.299	76	-68	94			.912	-43	C-550/O-45,13S2	-5.6
■ ED DAILY	Daily, Edward M. b: 9/7/1862, Providence, R.I. d: 10/21/1891, Washington, D.C. BR/TR, 5'10.5", 174 lbs. Deb: 5/4/1885 F																						
1885	Phi-N	50	184	22	38	8	2	1	13	0	25	.207	.207	.288	60	-8				.891	-4	P-50	0.0
1886	Phi-N	79	309	40	70	17	1	4	50	7	34	.227	.244	.327	72	-11	23			.827	5	O-56,P-27	-0.5
1887	Phi-N	26	106	18	30	11	1	1	17	3	9	.283	.303	.434	97	-1	8			.659	-6	O-22/P-6	-0.7
	Was-N	78	311	39	78	6	10	2	36	14	27	.251	.285	.354	81	-8	26			.855	-5	O-77/P-1	-1.3
	Yr	104	417	57	108	17	11	3	53	17	36	.259	.290	.374	85	-9	34			.812	-11	O-99/P-7	-2.0
1888	Was-N	110	453	56	102	8	4	7	39	7	42	.225	.239	.307	77	-12	44			.912	4	*O-100/P-9,1-1	-1.1
1889	Col-a	136	578	105	148	22	8	3	70	38	65	.256	.303	.337	87	-11	60			.854	-3	*O-136/P-2	-1.5
1890	Bro-a	91	394	68	94	15	7	1	39	24		.239	.284	.320	81	-11	49			.892	6	O-64,P-27	-0.5
	NY-N	4	15	1	2	1	0	0	1	0	4	.133	.133	.200	-3	-2	0			.500	0	/O-3,P-2	-0.1
	*Lou-a	23	80	24	20	0	2	0	9	13		.250	.355	.300	95	0	13			.925	1	P-12,O-11	-0.1
1891	Lou-a	22	64	10	16	2	0	0	8	8	6	.250	.344	.281	80	-1	4			.884	0	P-15/O-7	-0.1
	Was-a	21	79	13	18	2	0	0	6	11	10	.228	.322	.253	68	-3	8			.719	-4	O-21	-0.6
	Yr	43	143	23	34	4	0	0	14	19	16	.238	.331	.266	73	-4	12			.750	-3	O-28,P-15	-0.7
Total	7	640	2573	396	616	92	35	19	288	125	222	.239	.276	.325	80	-69	235			.857	-6	O-497,P-151/1-1	-6.5
■ GEORGE DAISEY	Daisey, George K. b: Altoona, Pa. 5'11", 190 lbs. Deb: 5/31/1884																						
1884	Alt-U	1	4	0	0	0	0	0		0		.000	.000	.000	-99	-1				.000	-1	/O-1	-0.2
■ PETE DALENA	Dalena, Peter Martin b: 6/26/60, Fresno, Cal. BL/TR, 5'11", 200 lbs. Deb: 7/7/89																						
1989	Cle-A	5	7	0	1	1	0	0	0	0	3	.143	.143	.286	18	-1	0	0	0	.000	0	/D-1	-0.1
■ MARK DALESANDRO	Dalesandro, Mark Anthony b: 5/14/68, Chicago, Ill. BR/TR, 6', 185 lbs. Deb: 6/6/94																						
1994	Cal-A	19	25	5	5	1	0	1	2	2	4	.200	.259	.360	57	-2	0	0	0	1.000	-3	C-11/3-5,O-2	-0.4
1995	Cal-A	11	10	1	1	1	0	0	0	0	2	.100	.100	.200	-25	-2	0	0	0	1.000	0	/C-8,O-1,D-1	-0.2
1998	Tor-A	32	67	8	20	5	0	2	14	1	6	.299	.309	.463	97	-1	0	0	0	.986	-5	C-18/3-8,1-2,O-1	-0.5
Total	3	62	102	14	26	7	0	3	16	3	12	.255	.276	.412	75	-4	0	0	0	.990	-8	/C-37,3-13,O-4,1D	-1.1
■ JOHN DALEY	Daley, John Francis b: 5/25/1887, Pittsburgh, Pa. d: 8/31/88, Mansfield, Ohio BR/TR, 5'7.5", 155 lbs. Deb: 7/19/12																						
1912	StL-A	18	52	7	9	0	0	1	3	9		.173	.317	.231	60	-2	4			.833	-4	S-17	-0.5
■ JUD DALEY	Daley, Judson Lawrence b: 3/14/1884, S.Coventry, Conn. d: 1/26/67, Gadsden, Ala. BL/TR, 5'8", 172 lbs. Deb: 9/19/11																						
1911	Bro-N	19	65	8	15	2	1	0	7	2	8	.231	.286	.292	65	-3	2			.952	2	O-16	-0.3
1912	Bro-N	61	199	22	51	9	1	1	13	24	17	.256	.342	.327	87	-3	2			.947	2	O-55	-0.4
Total	2	80	264	30	66	11	2	1	20	26	25	.250	.329	.318	82	-6	4			.949	3	/O-71	-0.7
■ PETE DALEY	Daley, Peter Harvey b: 1/14/30, Grass Valley, Cal. BR/TR, 6', 195 lbs. Deb: 5/3/55																						
1955	Bos-A	17	50	4	11	2	1	0	5	3	6	.220	.264	.300	47	-4	0	0	0	1.000	3	C-14	0.0
1956	Bos-A	59	187	22	50	11	3	5	29	18	30	.267	.338	.439	92	-3	1	0	0	.992	-10	C-57	-1.0
1957	Bos-A	78	191	17	43	10	0	3	25	16	31	.225	.288	.325	64	-10	0	0	0	**1.000**	-2	C-77	-1.0
1958	Bos-A	27	56	10	18	2	1	2	8	7	11	.321	.397	.500	136	3	0	0	0	.990	2	C-27	0.6
1959	Bos-A	65	169	9	38	7	0	1	11	13	31	.225	.280	.284	53	-11	1	1	-0	.996	2	C-58	-0.6
1960	KC-A	73	228	19	60	10	2	5	25	16	41	.263	.311	.390	88	-4	0	0	0	.990	-5	C-61/O-1	-0.5
1961	Was-A	72	203	12	39	7	1	2	17	14	37	.192	.244	.266	37	-18	0	1	-1	.988	7	C-72	-1.0
Total	7	391	1084	93	259	49	8	18	120	87	187	.239	.297	.349	71	-47	2	2	-1	.993	-2	C-366/O-1	-3.5
■ TOM DALEY	Daley, Thomas Francis "Pete" b: 11/13/1884, DuBois, Pa. d: 12/2/34, Los Angeles, Cal. BL/TR, 5'5", 168 lbs. Deb: 8/29/08																						
1908	Cin-N	14	46	5	5	0	0	0	1	3		.109	.196	.109	-2	-5	1			1.000	-0	O-13	-0.7
1913	Phi-A	62	141	13	36	2	1	0	11	13	28	.255	.327	.284	81	-3	4			.963	-1	O-39	-0.6
1914	Phi-A	28	86	17	22	1	3	0	7	12	14	.256	.347	.337	110	1	4	7	-3	1.000	2	O-24	-0.1
	NY-A	69	191	36	48	6	4	0	9	38	13	.251	.378	.325	112	5	8	8	-2	.958	6	O-58	0.6
	Yr	97	277	53	70	7	7	0	16	50	27	.253	.369	.329	111	6	12	15	-5	.969	7	O-82	0.5
1915	NY-A	10	8	2	2	0	0	0	1	2	2	.250	.400	.250	95	0	1			1.000	-0	/O-2	0.0
Total	4	183	472	73	113	9	8	0	29	68	57	.239	.341	.292	92	-2	18	15		.970	6	O-136	-0.8
■ DOM DALLESSANDRO	Dallessandro, Nicholas Dominic "Dim Dom" b: 10/3/13, Reading, Pa. d: 4/29/88, Indianapolis, Ind. BL/TL, 5'6", 168 lbs. Deb: 4/24/37																						
1937	Bos-A	68	147	18	34	7	1	0	11	27	16	.231	.351	.293	61	-8	2	1	0	.965	-5	O-35	-1.3
1940	Chi-N	107	287	33	77	19	6	1	36	34	13	.268	.348	.387	104	2	4			.969	-3	O-74	-0.4
1941	Chi-N	140	486	73	132	36	2	6	85	68	37	.272	.362	.391	116	12	3			.987	-2	*O-131	0.2
1942	Chi-N	96	264	30	69	12	4	4	43	36	18	.261	.350	.383	119	7	4			.986	-2	O-66	0.2
1943	Chi-N	87	176	13	39	8	3	1	31	40	14	.222	.369	.318	101	2	1			.967	-4	O-45	-0.4
1944	Chi-N	117	381	53	116	19	4	8	74	61	29	.304	.400	.438	137	21	1			.982	-2	*O-106	1.3
1946	Chi-N	65	89	4	20	2	2	1	9	23	12	.225	.384	.326	104	2	1			.971	-3	O-20	-0.2
1947	Chi-N	66	115	18	33	7	1	1	14	21	11	.287	.397	.391	115	3	0			1.000	-2	O-28	0.0
Total	8	746	1945	242	520	110	23	22	303	310	150	.267	.369	.381	112	40	16	1		.980	-22	O-505	-0.6
■ ABNER DALRYMPLE	Dalrymple, Abner Frank b: 9/9/1857, Warren, Ill. d: 1/25/39, Warren, Ill. BL/TR, 5'10.5", 175 lbs. Deb: 5/1/1878																						
1878	Mil-N	61	271	52	96	10	4	0	15	6	29	**.354**	.368	.421	149	13				.832	7	*O-61	1.5
1879	Chi-N	71	333	47	97	25	1	0	23	4	29	.291	.300	.372	113	4				.728	-13	*O-71	-1.2
1880	Chi-N	86	382	**91**	**126**	25	12	0	36	3	18	.330	.335	.458	157	20				.859	4	*O-86	2.1
1881	Chi-N	82	362	72	117	22	4	1	37	15	22	.323	.350	.414	133	13				.835	-7	*O-82	0.4
1882	Chi-N	84	397	96	117	25	11	1	36	14	18	.295	.319	.421	129	12				.877	0	*O-84	1.0
1883	Chi-N	80	363	78	108	24	4	2	37	11	29	.298	.318	.402	111	3				.826	-1	*O-80	0.2
1884	Chi-N	111	521	111	161	18	9	22	69	14	39	.309	.327	.505	146	23				.882	1	*O-111	2.0
1885	*Chi-N	113	492	109	135	27	12	**11**	61	46	42	.274	.336	.445	133	14				.879	-1	*O-113	1.0
1886	*Chi-N	82	331	62	77	7	12	3	26	33	44	.233	.302	.353	86	-8	16			.952	4	O-82	-0.5
1887	Pit-N	92	358	45	76	18	5	2	31	45	43	.212	.311	.307	77	-9	29			.900	4	*O-92	-0.6
1888	Pit-N	57	227	19	50	9	2	0	14	6	28	.220	.247	.278	72	-7	7			.909	-2	O-57	-1.1
1891	Mil-a	32	135	31	42	7	5	1	22	7	18	.311	.345	.459	108	-1	6			.909	-1	O-32	-0.2
Total	12	951	4172	813	1202	217	81	43	407	204	359	.288	.323	.410	121	77	58			.863	-4	O-951	4.6
■ CLAY DALRYMPLE	Dalrymple, Clayton Errol b: 12/3/36, Chico, Cal. BL/TR, 6', 199 lbs. Deb: 4/24/60																						
1960	Phi-N	82	158	11	43	6	2	4	21	15	21	.272	.347	.411	106	2	0	0	0	.966	-5	C-48	-0.1
1961	Phi-N	129	378	23	83	11	1	5	42	30	30	.220	.284	.294	54	-25	0	2	-1	.978	0	*C-122	-2.0
1962	Phi-N	123	370	40	102	13	3	11	54	70	32	.276	.396	.416	122	15	1	3	-2	.987	-12	*C-119	0.6

YEAR	TM/L	G	AB	R	H	2B	3B	HR	RBI	BB	SO	AVG	OBP	SLG	PRO+	BR/A	SB	CS	SBR	FA	FR	G/POS	TPR
1963	Phi-N	142	452	40	114	15	3	10	40	45	55	.252	.327	.365	100	1	0	2	-1	.981	1	*C-142	0.6
1964	Phi-N	127	382	36	91	16	3	6	46	39	40	.238	.309	.343	84	-8	0	1	-1	.991	3	*C-124	0.0
1965	Phi-N	103	301	14	64	5	5	4	23	34	37	.213	.293	.302	69	-12	0	1	-1	.993	18	*C-102	1.0
1966	Phi-N	114	331	30	81	13	3	4	39	60	57	.245	.365	.338	97	1	0	0	0	.993	-4	*C-110	0.4
1967	Phi-N	101	268	12	46	7	1	3	21	36	49	.172	.272	.239	47	-18	1	2	-1	.994	20	C-97	0.7
1968	Phi-N	85	241	19	50	9	1	3	26	22	57	.207	.277	.290	70	-9	1	2	-1	.990	-3	C-80	-0.9
1969	*Bal-A	37	80	8	19	1	1	3	6	13	8	.237	.344	.387	103	1	0	0	0	1.000	2	C-30	0.3
1970	Bal-A	13	32	4	7	1	0	1	3	7	4	.219	.359	.344	94	-0	0	0	0	1.000	6	C-11	0.6
1971	Bal-A	23	49	6	10	1	0	1	6	16	13	.204	.409	.286	101	1	0	0	0	.971	2	C-18	0.4
Total	12	1079	3042	243	710	98	23	55	327	387	403	.233	.324	.335	85	-51	3	13	-7	.987	27	*C-1003	1.6
■ BILL DALRYMPLE	Dalrymple, William Dunn b: 2/7/1891, Baltimore, Md. d: 7/14/67, San Diego, Cal. TR , Deb: 7/6/15																						
1915	StL-A	3	2	0	0	0	0	0	0	0	0	.000	.000	.000	-99	-0	0			1.000	0	/3-1	0.0
■ JACK DALTON	Dalton, Talbot Percy b: 7/3/1885, Henderson, Tenn. BR/TR, 5'10.5", 187 lbs. Deb: 6/20/10																						
1910	Bro-N	77	273	33	62	9	4	1	21	26	30	.227	.304	.300	79	-7	5			.966	3	O-72	-0.9
1914	Bro-N	128	442	65	141	13	8	1	45	53	39	.319	.396	.391	131	19	19			.965	-3	*O-116	1.1
1915	Buf-F	132	437	68	128	17	3	2	46	50	38	.293	.368	.359	103	-3	28			.966	-5	*O-119	-1.5
1916	Det-A	8	11	1	2	0	0	0	0	0	5	.182	.182	.182	9	-1	0			1.000	-1	/O-4	-0.3
Total	4	345	1163	167	333	39	15	4	112	129	112	.286	.362	.356	107	7	52			.966	-7	O-311	-1.6
■ BERT DALY	Daly, Albert Joseph b: 4/8/1881, Bayonne, N.J. d: 9/3/52, Bayonne, N.J. BR/TR, 5'9", 170 lbs. Deb: 8/7/03																						
1903	Phi-A	10	21	2	4	0	2	0	4	1		.190	.227	.381	76	-1	0			.700	-4	/2-4,3-3,S-1	-0.5
■ SUN DALY	Daly, James J. b: 1/6/1865, Rutland, Vt. d: 4/30/38, Albany, N.Y. Deb: 9/30/1892																						
1892	Bal-N	13	48	5	12	0	2	0	7	1	4	.250	.265	.333	79	-2	0			.923	0	O-13	-0.2
■ JOE DALY	Daly, Joseph John b: 9/21/1868, Conshohocken, Pa. d: 3/21/43, Philadelphia, Pa. TR , 5'8", 157 lbs. Deb: 9/19/1890 F																						
1890	Phi-a	21	75	8	21	4	1	0	7	3		.280	.308	.360	99	-1	1			.900	-6	O-14/C-9	-0.5
1891	Cle-N	1	3	0	0	0	0	0	0	0	2	.000	.000	.000	-96	-1	0			1.000	0	/O-1	-0.1
1892	Bos-N	1	0	0	0	0	0	0	0	0	0	—	—	—	—	0	0			1.000	0	/C-1	0.0
Total	3	23	78	8	21	4	1	0	7	3	2	.269	.296	.346	91	-1	1			.909	-6	/O-15,C-10	-0.6
■ TOM DALY	Daly, Thomas Daniel b: 12/12/1891, St.John, N.B., Can. d: 11/7/46, Medford, Mass. BR/TR, 5'11.5", 171 lbs. Deb: 9/23/13 C																						
1913	Chi-A	1	3	0	0	0	0	0	0	0	0	.000	.000	.000	-99	-1	0			1.000	1	/C-1	0.0
1914	Chi-A	62	133	13	31	2	0	0	8	7	13	.233	.271	.248	57	-7	3	4	-2	.909	-10	O-23/3-5,C-4,1-2	-2.2
1915	Chi-A	29	47	5	9	1	0	0	3	5	9	.191	.269	.213	43	-3	0			.958	-3	C-19/1-1	-0.5
1916	Cle-A	31	73	3	16	1	1	0	8	1	2	.219	.230	.260	45	-5	0			.982	-2	C-25/O-1	-0.6
1918	Chi-N	1	1	0	0	0	0	0	0	0	0	.000	.000	.000	-98	-0	0			.667	-0	/C-1	0.0
1919	Chi-N	25	50	4	11	0	1	0	1	2	5	.220	.250	.260	53	-3	0			.956	-2	C-18	-0.5
1920	Chi-N	44	90	12	28	6	0	0	13	2	6	.311	.333	.378	102	0	1	1	-0	.981	-3	C-29	-0.2
1921	Chi-N	51	143	12	34	7	1	0	22	8	8	.238	.278	.301	53	-10	1	2	-1	.973	4	C-47	-0.4
Total	8	244	540	49	129	17	3	0	55	25	43	.239	.274	.281	59	-29	5	<u>7</u>		.972	-15	C-144/O-24,3-5,1-3	-4.4
■ TOM DALY	Daly, Thomas Peter "Tido" b: 2/7/1866, Philadelphia, Pa. d: 10/29/38, Brooklyn, N.Y. BB/TR, 5'7", 170 lbs. Deb: 4/30/1887 F																						
1887	Chi-N	74	256	45	53	10	4	2	17	22	25	.207	.270	.301	52	-19	29			**.935**	33	C-64/O-8,S-2,2-2,1	1.7
1888	Chi-N	65	219	34	42	2	6	0	29	10	26	.192	.230	.256	51	-12	10			.939	20	C-62/O-4	1.3
1889	Was-N	71	250	39	75	13	5	1	40	38	28	.300	.394	.404	131	12	18			.917	3	C-57/1-8,2-4,O-3,S	1.7
1890	*Bro-N	82	292	55	71	9	4	5	43	32	43	.243	.326	.353	97	-1	20			.953	7	C-69,1-12/O-1	1.0
1891	Bro-N	58	200	29	50	11	5	2	27	21	34	.250	.327	.385	108	2	7			.881	-6	C-26,1-15,S-11,/O-7	-0.2
1892	Bro-N	124	446	76	114	15	6	4	51	64	61	.256	.355	.343	116	11	34			.897	-11	3-57,O-30,C-27,2-10	0.3
1893	Bro-N	126	470	94	136	21	14	8	70	76	65	.289	.388	.445	127	19	32			.915	-18	2-82,3-45	0.3
1894	Bro-N	123	492	135	168	22	10	8	82	77	42	.341	.436	.476	129	27	51			.908	-19	*2-123	1.1
1895	Bro-N	120	455	89	128	17	8	2	68	52	52	.281	.359	.367	95	-2	28			.930	-19	*2-120	-1.1
1896	Bro-N	67	224	43	63	13	6	3	29	33	25	.281	.385	.433	122	8	19			.909	-2	2-66/C-1	0.9
1898	Bro-N	23	73	11	24	3	1	0	11	14		.329	.443	.397	142	5	6			.993	3	2-23	0.9
1899	Bro-N	141	498	95	156	24	9	5	88	69		.313	.409	.428	127	21	43			.929	16	*2-141	4.0
1900	*Bro-N	97	343	72	107	17	3	4	55	46		.312	.403	.414	118	10	27			.921	-8	2-93/1-3,O-2	0.6
1901	Bro-N	133	520	88	164	**38**	10	3	90	42		.315	.371	.444	132	21	31			.944	11	*2-133	3.6
1902	Chi-A	137	489	57	110	22	3	1	54	55		.225	.303	.288	68	-20	19			.957	-15	*2-137	-2.9
1903	Chi-A	43	150	20	31	11	0	0	19	20		.207	.304	.280	80	-3	6			.948	-13	2-43	-1.6
	Cin-N	80	307	42	90	14	9	1	38	16		.293	.332	.407	99	-2	5			.937	-10	2-79	-0.9
Total	16	1564	5684	1024	1582	262	103	49	811	687	<u>401</u>	.278	.361	.387	108	77	385			.931	-28	*2-1056,C-306,3/O1S	10.7
■ BILL DAM	Dam, Elbridge Rust b: 4/4/1885, Cambridge, Mass. d: 6/22/30, Quincy, Mass. Deb: 8/23/09																						
1909	Bos-N	1	2	1	1	1	0	0	0	1		.500	.667	1.000	398	1	0			1.000	-0	/O-1	0.1
■ JACK DAMASKA	Damaska, Jack Lloyd b: 8/21/37, Beaver Falls, Pa. BR/TR, 5'11", 168 lbs. Deb: 7/3/63																						
1963	StL-N	5	5	1	1	0	0	0	1	0	4	.200	.200	.200	14	-1	0	0	0	.000	-0	/2-1,O-1	-0.1
■ JOHNNY DAMON	Damon, Johnny David b: 11/5/73, Fort Riley, Kan. BL/TL, 6', 175 lbs. Deb: 8/12/95																						
1995	KC-A	47	188	32	53	11	5	3	23	12	22	.282	.328	.441	97	-1	7	0	2	.991	-2	O-47	-0.3
1996	KC-A	145	517	61	140	22	5	6	50	31	64	.271	.316	.368	72	-22	25	5	5	.983	2	*O-144/D-1	-1.7
1997	KC-A	146	472	70	130	12	8	8	48	42	70	.275	.338	.386	86	-9	16	10	-1	.988	-3	*O-136/D-5	-1.6
1998	KC-A	161	642	104	178	30	10	18	66	58	84	.277	.341	.439	97	-3	26	12	1	.990	1	*O-158	-0.5
Total	4	499	1819	267	501	75	28	35	187	143	240	.275	.332	.405	87	-36	74	27	6	.987	-2	O-485/D-6	-4.1
■ HARRY DAMRAU	Damrau, Harry Robert (Also Known As Arthur Lee Whitehorn) b: 9/11/1890, Newburgh, N.Y. d: 8/21/57, Staten Island, N.Y BR/TR, 5'10", 178 lbs. Deb: 9/17/15																						
1915	Phi-A	16	56	4	11	1	0	0	3	5	17	.196	.262	.214	44	-4	1	1	-0	.870	-4	3-16	-0.8
■ JAKE DANIEL	Daniel, Handley Jacob b: 4/22/11, Roanoke, Ala. d: 4/23/96, LaGrange, Ga. BL/TL, 5'11", 175 lbs. Deb: 7/24/37																						
1937	Bro-N	12	27	3	5	1	0	0	3	3	4	.185	.267	.222	34	-2	0			1.000	-0	/1-7	-0.3
■ BERT DANIELS	Daniels, Bernard Elmer b: 10/31/1882, Danville, Ill. d: 6/6/58, Cedar Grove, N.J. BR/TR, 5'10", 170 lbs. Deb: 6/25/10																						
1910	NY-A	95	356	68	90	13	8	1	17	41		.253	.356	.343	112	7	41			.957	3	O-85/3-6,1-4	0.6
1911	NY-A	131	462	74	132	16	9	2	31	48		.286	.375	.372	102	2	40			.041	1	*O-120	-0.3
1912	NY-A	135	496	72	136	25	11	2	41	51		.274	.363	.381	106	4	37			.945	5	*O-131	0.3
1913	NY-A	94	320	52	69	13	5	0	22	44	36	.216	.343	.287	85	-4	27			.966	1	O-87	-0.7
1914	Cin-N	71	269	29	59	9	7	0	19	19	40	.219	.276	.305	70	-10	14			.974	0	O-71	-1.5
Total	5	526	1903	295	486	76	40	5	130	203	<u>76</u>	.255	.349	.345	98	-1	159			.953	10	O-494/3-6,1-4	-1.6
■ TONY DANIELS	Daniels, Frederick Clinton b: 12/28/24, Gastonia, N.C. BR/TR, 5'9.5", 185 lbs. Deb: 6/12/45																						
1945	Phi-N	76	230	15	46	3	2	0	10	12	22	.200	.249	.230	35	-20	1			.955	7	2-75/3-1	-0.9
■ JACK DANIELS	Daniels, Harold Jack "Sour Mash Jack" b: 12/21/27, Chester, Pa. BL/TL, 5'10", 165 lbs. Deb: 4/18/52																						
1952	Bos-N	106	219	31	41	5	1	2	14	28	30	.187	.288	.247	51	-14	3	3	-1	.977	-9	O-87	-2.8
■ KAL DANIELS	Daniels, Kalvoski b: 8/20/63, Vienna, Ga. BL/TR, 5'11", 195 lbs. Deb: 4/9/86																						
1986	Cin-N	74	181	34	58	10	4	6	23	22	30	.320	.400	.519	145	11	15	2	3	.967	-0	O-47	1.4
1987	Cin-N	108	368	73	123	24	1	26	64	60	62	.334	.429	.617	166	36	26	8	3	.968	3	O-94	3.8
1988	Cin-N	140	495	95	144	29	1	18	64	87	94	.291	**.400**	.463	141	30	27	6	5	.982	4	*O-137	3.6
1989	Cin-N	44	133	26	29	11	0	2	9	36	28	.218	.392	.346	109	3	6	4	-1	1.000	2	O-38	0.4

YEAR	TM/L	G	AB	R	H	2B	3B	HR	RBI	BB	SO	AVG	OBP	SLG	PRO+	BR/A	SB	CS	SBR	FA	FR	G/POS	TPR
	LA-N	11	38	7	13	2	0	2	8	7	5	.342	.444	.553	187	5	3	0	1	1.000	0	O-11	0.5
	Yr	55	171	33	42	13	0	4	17	43	33	.246	.403	.392	125	8	9	4	0	1.000	2	O-49	0.9
1990	LA-N	130	450	81	133	23	1	27	94	68	104	.296	.392	.531	156	35	4	3	-1	.987	2	*O-127	3.4
1991	LA-N	137	461	54	115	15	1	17	73	63	116	.249	.341	.397	109	6	6	1	1	.979	1	*O-132	0.5
1992	LA-N	35	104	9	24	5	0	2	8	10	30	.231	.304	.337	83	-2	0	0	0	.964	-2	O-21/1-8	-0.6
	Chi-N	48	108	12	27	6	0	4	17	12	24	.250	.331	.417	108	1	0	2	-1	1.000	-2	O-28	-0.2
	Yr	83	212	21	51	11	0	6	25	22	54	.241	.318	.377	95	-1	0	2	-1	.984	-4	O-49/1-8	-0.8
Total	7	727	2338	391	666	125	8	104	360	365	493	.285	.385	.479	137	125	87	26	11	.980	8	O-635/1-8	12.8
■ LAW DANIELS	Daniels, Lawrence Long b: 7/14/1862, Newton, Mass. d: 1/7/29, Waltham, Mass. BR/TR, 5'10", 170 lbs. Deb: 4/25/1887																						
1887	Bal-a	48	165	23	41	5	1	0	32	8		.248	.287	.291	65	-7	7			.845	-8	C-26,O-15/1-4,2S3	-1.1
1888	KC-a	61	218	32	45	2	0	2	28	14		.206	.264	.243	59	-10	20			.855	-2	O-30,C-29/3-2,S-1	-1.0
Total	2	109	383	55	86	7	1	2	60	22		.225	.274	.264	62	-18	27			.859	-10	/C-55,O-45,1-4,3S2	-2.1
■ BUCK DANNER	Danner, Henry Frederick b: 6/8/1891, Dedham, Mass. d: 9/19/49, Dedham, Mass. BR/TR, 5'11", 140 lbs. Deb: 9/17/15																						
1915	Phi-A	3	12	1	3	0	0	0	0	0	1	.250	.250	.250	51	-1	1			.750	-3	/S-3	-0.3
■ HARRY DANNING	Danning, Harry "Harry The Horse" b: 9/6/11, Los Angeles, Cal. BR/TR, 6'1", 190 lbs. Deb: 7/30/33 F																						
1933	NY-N	3	2	0	0	0	0	0	0	1	0	.000	.333	.000	2	-0	0			1.000	0	/C-1	0.0
1934	NY-N	53	97	8	32	7	0	1	7	1	9	.330	.337	.433	107	1	1			.989	-0	C-37	0.1
1935	NY-N	65	152	16	37	11	1	2	20	9	16	.243	.286	.368	76	-6	0			.978	3	C-44	-0.1
1936	*NY-N	32	69	3	11	2	2	0	4	1	5	.159	.183	.246	15	-8	0			.988	2	C-24	-0.6
1937	*NY-N	93	292	30	84	12	4	8	51	18	20	.288	.331	.438	106	2	0			.982	-5	C-86	0.1
1938	NY-N☆	120	448	59	137	26	3	9	60	23	40	.306	.345	.438	113	7	1			.984	-8	*C-114	0.5
1939	NY-N☆	135	520	79	163	28	5	16	74	35	42	.313	.359	.479	122	15	4			.991	7	*C-132	2.9
1940	NY-N★	140	524	65	157	34	4	13	91	35	31	.300	.349	.454	119	12	3			.980	7	*C-131	2.9
1941	NY-N★	130	459	58	112	22	4	7	56	30	25	.244	.292	.355	80	-13	1			.993	7	*C-116/1-1	0.4
1942	NY-N	119	408	45	114	20	3	1	34	34	29	.279	.335	.350	100	-0	3			.979	-5	*C-116	0.5
Total	10	890	2971	363	847	162	26	57	397	187	217	.285	.330	.415	104	9	13			.985	8	C-801/1-1	6.7
■ IKE DANNING	Danning, Ike b: 1/20/05, Los Angeles, Cal. d: 3/30/83, Santa Monica, Cal BR/TR, 5'10", 160 lbs. Deb: 9/21/28 F																						
1928	StL-A	2	6	0	3	0	0	0	1	1	2	.500	.571	.500	178	1	0	0	0	.917	1	/C-2	0.1
■ FATS DANTONIO	Dantonio, John James b: 12/31/18, New Orleans, La. d: 5/28/93, New Orleans, La. BR/TR, 5'8", 165 lbs. Deb: 9/18/44																						
1944	Bro-N	3	7	0	1	0	0	0	0	0	1	.143	.143	.143	-20	-1	0			.846	0	/C-3	-0.1
1945	Bro-N	47	128	12	32	6	1	0	12	11	6	.250	.309	.313	74	-5	3			.929	-5	C-45	-0.8
Total	2	50	135	12	33	6	1	0	12	11	7	.244	.301	.304	69	-6	3			.923	-5	/C-48	-0.9
■ BABE DANZIG	Danzig, Harold P. b: 4/30/1887, Binghamton, N.Y. d: 7/14/31, San Francisco, Cal. BR/TR, 6'2", 205 lbs. Deb: 4/12/09																						
1909	Bos-A	6	13	0	2	0	0	0	0	2		.154	.313	.154	47	-1	0			.960	-1	/1-3	-0.2
■ CLIFF DAPPER	Dapper, Clifford Roland b: 1/2/20, Los Angeles, Cal. BR/TR, 6'2", 190 lbs. Deb: 4/19/42																						
1942	Bro-N	8	17	2	8	1	0	1	9	2	2	.471	.526	.706	255	3	0			1.000	-0	/C-8	0.4
■ CLIFF DARINGER	Daringer, Clifford Clarence "Shanty" b: 4/10/1885, Hayden, Ind. d: 12/26/71, Sacramento, Cal. BL/TR, 5'7.5", 155 lbs. Deb: 4/20/14 F																						
1914	KC-F	64	160	12	42	2	1	0	16	11	7	.262	.322	.287	70	-9	9			.944	6	S-24,3-19,2-14	-0.1
■ ROLLA DARINGER	Daringer, Rolla Harrison b: 11/15/1888, N.Vernon, Ind. d: 5/23/74, Seymour, Ind. BL/TR, 5'10", 155 lbs. Deb: 9/19/14 F																						
1914	StL-N	2	4	1	2	1	0	0	0	1	2	.500	.600	.750	304	1	0			.667	-1	/S-1	0.0
1915	StL-N	10	23	3	2	0	0	0	0	9	5	.087	.344	.087	33	-1	0	1	-1	.947	-3	S-10	-0.5
Total	2	12	27	4	4	1	0	0	0	10	7	.148	.378	.185	72	-0	0	1		.927	-4	/S-11	-0.5
■ ALVIN DARK	Dark, Alvin Ralph "Blackie" b: 1/7/22, Comanche, Okla. BR/TR, 5'11", 185 lbs. Deb: 7/14/46 MC																						
1946	Bos-N	15	13	0	3	3	0	0	1	0	3	.231	.231	.462	93	-0	0			.905	2	S-12/O-1	0.2
1948	*Bos-N	137	543	85	175	39	6	3	48	24	36	.322	.353	.433	114	9	4			.963	-12	*S-133	0.4
1949	Bos-N	130	529	74	146	23	5	3	53	31	43	.276	.317	.355	85	-13	5			.961	-4	*S-125/3-4	-0.7
1950	NY-N	154	587	79	164	36	5	16	67	39	60	.279	.331	.440	100	-1	9			.962	-15	*S-154	-0.4
1951	*NY-N★	156	646	114	196	**41**	7	14	69	42	39	.303	.352	.454	114	11	12	7	-1	.944	1	*S-156	2.3
1952	NY-N☆	151	589	92	177	29	3	14	73	47	39	.301	.357	.431	117	13	6	6	-2	.965	3	*S-150	2.6
1953	NY-N	155	647	126	194	41	6	23	88	28	34	.300	.335	.488	109	7	7	2	1	.967	8	*S-110,2-26,O/3P	2.4
1954	*NY-N★	154	644	98	189	26	6	20	70	27	40	.293	.327	.446	98	-3	5	3	-0	.956	4	*S-154	1.3
1955	NY-N	115	475	77	134	20	3	9	45	22	32	.282	.321	.394	88	-9	2	1	0	.962	-14	*S-115	-1.2
1956	NY-N	48	206	19	52	12	0	2	17	8	13	.252	.284	.340	67	-10	0	0	0	.961	-5	S-48	-1.1
	StL-N	100	413	54	118	14	7	4	37	21	33	.286	.323	.383	89	-7	3	1	0	.959	-2	S-99	0.0
	Yr	148	619	73	170	26	7	6	54	29	46	.275	.310	.368	82	-16	3	1	0	.960	-7	*S-147	-1.1
1957	StL-N	140	583	80	169	25	8	4	64	29	56	.290	.328	.381	88	-10	3	4	-2	.965	6	*S-139/3-1	0.8
1958	StL-N	18	64	7	19	0	0	1	5	2	6	.297	.318	.344	72	-2	0	0	0	.943	-3	/S-8,3-8	-0.5
	Chi-N	114	464	54	137	16	4	3	43	29	23	.295	.343	.366	89	-7	1	1	-0	.949	-3	*3-111	-0.9
	Yr	132	528	61	156	16	4	4	48	31	29	.295	.340	.364	87	-9	1	1	-0	.948	-6	*3-119/S-8	-1.4
1959	Chi-N	136	477	60	126	22	9	6	45	55	50	.264	.344	.386	95	-3	1	1	-0	.948	-2	*3-131/1-4,S-1	-0.5
1960	Phi-N	55	198	29	48	5	1	3	14	19	14	.242	.315	.323	75	-6	1	1	-0	.953	-8	3-53/1-1	-1.5
	Mil-N	50	141	16	42	6	2	1	18	7	13	.298	.336	.390	106	1	0	0	0	.960	-1	O-25,1-10/3-4,2-3	-0.2
	Yr	105	339	45	90	11	3	4	32	26	27	.265	.323	.351	88	-6	1	1	-0	.954	-8	3-57,O-25,1-11,/2-3	-1.7
Total	14	1828	7219	1064	2089	358	72	126	757	430	534	.289	.334	.411	98	-30	59	27		.960	-43	*S-1404,3-320/O21P	3.0
■ DELL DARLING	Darling, Conrad b: 12/21/1861, Erie, Pa. d: 11/20/04, Erie, Pa. BR/TR, 5'8", 170 lbs. Deb: 7/3/1883																						
1883	Buf-N	6	18	1	3	0	0	0	1	2	5	.167	.250	.167	29	-1				.875	-2	/C-6	-0.3
1887	Chi-N	38	141	28	45	7	4	3	20	22	18	.319	.411	.489	132	6	19			.786	2	O-20,C-20	0.8
1888	Chi-N	20	75	12	16	3	1	2	7	3	12	.213	.253	.360	87	-1	0			.932	3	C-20	0.3
1889	Chi-N	36	120	14	23	1	1	0	7	25	22	.192	.331	.217	52	-7	5			.960	4	C-36	0.0
1890	Chi-P	58	221	45	57	12	4	2	39	29	28	.258	.352	.376	91	-3	5			.957	-9	1-29,S-15/C-9,O23	-1.0
1891	StL-a	17	53	9	7	1	3	0	9	10	11	.132	.270	.264	46	-4	0			.894	2	C-17/2-2,S-1	-0.1
Total	6	175	628	109	151	24	13	7	83	91	96	.240	.340	.354	87	-12	29			.923	-1	C-108/1-29,OS23	-0.3
■ JACK DARRAGH	Darragh, James S. b: 7/17/1866, Ebensburg, Pa. d: 8/12/39, Rochester, Pa. Deb: 5/13/1891																						
1891	Lou-a	1	2	0	1	0	0	0	0	0	0	.500	.500	.500	189	0	0			1.000	0	/1-1	0.0
■ BOBBY DARWIN	Darwin, Arthur Bobby Lee b: 2/16/43, Los Angeles, Cal. BR/TR, 6'2", 200 lbs. Deb: 9/30/62																						
1962	LA-A	1	1	0	0	0	0	0	0	0	1	.000	.000	.000	-99	-0	0	0	0	.000	-0	/P-1	0.0
1969	LA-N	6	0	1	0	0	0	0	0	0	0	—	—	—	—	0	0	0	0	.000	-0	/P-3	0.0
1971	LA-N	11	20	2	5	1	0	1	4	2	9	.250	.318	.450	123	0	0	0	0	1.000	0	/O-4	0.0
1972	Min-A	145	513	48	137	20	2	22	80	38	145	.267	.327	.442	122	13	2	3	-1	.980	-1	*O-142	0.5
1973	Min-A	145	560	69	141	20	2	18	90	46	137	.252	.312	.391	93	-6	5	2	0	.980	2	*O-140/D-1	-1.0
1974	Min-A	152	575	67	152	13	7	25	94	37	127	.264	.324	.442	115	10	1	3	-2	.970	-2	*O-142	0.0
1975	Min-A	48	169	26	37	6	0	5	18	18	44	.219	.309	.343	83	-4	2	0	1	.969	-4	O-27,D-19	-0.8
	Mil-A	55	186	19	46	6	2	8	23	11	54	.247	.300	.430	104	0	4	1	1	.978	1	O-43/D-9	0.0
	Yr	103	355	45	83	12	2	13	41	29	98	.234	.304	.389	94	-4	6	1	1	.975	-3	O-70,D-28	-0.8
1976	Mil-A	25	73	6	18	3	1	1	5	6	16	.247	.321	.356	100	0	0	0	0	.977	-1	O-21/D-1	-0.2
	Bos-A	43	106	9	19	5	2	3	13	2	35	.179	.216	.349	57	-6	1	0	0	.964	-2	O-17,D-16	-0.9
	Yr	68	179	15	37	8	3	4	18	8	51	.207	.260	.352	73	-7	1	0	0	.972	-3	O-38,D-17	-1.1
1977	Bos-A	4	9	1	2	1	0	0	1	0	4	.222	.222	.333	44	-1	0	0	0	.500	-0	/O-1,D-2	-0.1

YEAR	TM/L	G	AB	R	H	2B	3B	HR	RBI	BB	SO	AVG	OBP	SLG	PRO+	BR/A	SB	CS	SBR	FA	FR	G/POS	TPR
	Chi-N	11	12	2	2	1	0	0	0	0	5	.167	.167	.250	9	-2	0	0	0	.000	-0	/O-1	-0.2
Total	9	646	2224	250	559	76	16	83	328	160	577	.251	.312	.412	103	4	15	9	-1	.976	-8	O-538/D-48,P-4	-2.7
■ DOUG DASCENZO	Dascenzo, Douglas Craig b: 6/30/64, Cleveland, Ohio BB/TL, 5'8", 160 lbs. Deb: 9/2/88																						
1988	Chi-N	26	75	9	16	3	0	0	4	9	4	.213	.298	.253	57	-4	6	1	1	1.000	2	O-20	-0.1
1989	Chi-N	47	139	20	23	1	0	1	12	13	13	.165	.237	.194	23	-14	6	3	0	1.000	-2	O-45	-1.8
1990	Chi-N	113	241	27	61	9	5	1	26	21	18	.253	.316	.344	76	-8	15	6	1	1.000	-18	*O-107/P-1	-2.7
1991	Chi-N	118	239	40	61	11	0	1	18	24	26	.255	.328	.314	78	-6	14	7	0	.985	-19	O-86/P-3	-2.8
1992	Chi-N	139	376	37	96	13	4	0	20	27	32	.255	.305	.311	73	-13	6	8	-3	.978	-17	*O-122	-3.8
1993	Tex-A	76	146	20	29	5	1	2	10	8	22	.199	.240	.288	43	-12	2	0	1	.990	-12	O-68/D-2	-2.4
1996	SD-N	21	9	3	1	0	0	0	0	1	2	.111	.200	.111	-16	-2	0	1	-1	1.000	-3	O-10	-0.5
Total	7	540	1225	156	287	42	10	5	90	103	117	.234	.295	.297	64	-58	49	26	-1	.990	-69	O-458/P-4,D-2	-14.1
■ WALLY DASHIELL	Dashiell, John Wallace b: 5/9/02, Jewett, Tex. d: 5/20/72, Pensacola, Fla. BR/TR, 5'9.5", 170 lbs. Deb: 4/20/24																						
1924	Chi-A	1	2	0	0	0	0	0	0	0	0	.000	.000	.000	-99	-1	0	0	0	.667	-1	/S-1	-0.1
■ JEFF DATZ	Datz, Jeffrey William b: 11/28/59, Camden, N.J. BR/TR, 6'4", 220 lbs. Deb: 9/5/89																						
1989	Det-A	7	10	0	2	0	0	0	0	1	1	.200	.333	.200	55	-0	0	0	0	1.000	0	/C-6,D-1	0.0
■ BRIAN DAUBACH	Daubach, Brian Michael b: 2/11/72, Belleville, Ill. BL/TR, 6'1", 201 lbs. Deb: 9/10/98																						
1998	Fla-N	10	15	0	3	1	0	0	3	1	5	.200	.294	.267	49	-1	0	0	0	1.000	-0	/1-4	-0.2
■ HARRY DAUBERT	Daubert, Harry "Jake" b: 6/19/1892, Columbus, Ohio d: 1/8/44, Detroit, Mich. BR/TR, 6', 160 lbs. Deb: 9/4/15																						
1915	Pit-N	1	1	0	0	0	0	0	0	0	1	.000	.000	.000	-99	-0	0			.000	0	H	0.0
■ JAKE DAUBERT	Daubert, Jacob Ellsworth b: 4/7/1884, Shamokin, Pa. d: 10/9/24, Cincinnati, Ohio BL/TL, 5'10.5", 160 lbs. Deb: 4/14/10																						
1910	Bro-N	144	552	67	146	15	15	8	50	47	53	.264	.328	.389	112	7	23			.989	-3	*1-144	0.4
1911	Bro-N	149	573	89	176	17	8	5	45	51	56	.307	.366	.391	117	12	32			.989	2	*1-149	1.4
1912	Bro-N	145	559	81	172	19	16	3	66	48	45	.308	.369	.415	119	14	29			**.993**	0	*1-143	1.2
1913	Bro-N	139	508	76	178	17	7	2	52	44	40	**.350**	.405	.423	133	23	25			.991	3	*1-139	2.5
1914	Bro-N	126	474	89	156	17	7	6	45	30	34	**.329**	.375	.432	137	20	25			.993	-6	*1-126	1.2
1915	Bro-N	150	544	62	164	21	8	2	47	57	48	.301	.369	.381	125	17	11	13	-5	.993	9	*1-150	1.9
1916	*Bro-N	127	478	75	151	16	7	3	33	38	39	.316	.371	.397	132	19	21	7	2	**.993**	4	*1-126	2.2
1917	Bro-N	125	468	59	122	4	4	2	30	51	30	.261	.341	.299	94	-1	11			.991	6	*1-125	0.1
1918	Bro-N	108	396	50	122	12	**15**	2	47	27	18	.308	.360	.429	141	18	10			.991	0	*1-105	1.6
1919	*Cin-N	140	537	79	148	10	12	2	44	35	23	.276	.322	.350	105	3	11			.989	-2	*1-140	-0.4
1920	Cin-N	142	553	97	168	28	13	4	48	47	29	.304	.362	.423	127	19	11	13	-5	.990	-9	*1-140	0.2
1921	Cin-N	136	516	69	158	18	12	2	64	24	16	.306	.341	.399	100	-1	12	6	0	.993	2	*1-136	-0.2
1922	Cin-N	156	610	114	205	15	**22**	12	66	56	21	.336	.395	.492	130	27	14	17	-6	**.994**	-0	*1-156	1.3
1923	Cin-N	125	500	63	146	27	10	2	54	40	20	.292	.349	.398	99	-1	11	12	-4	.993	6	*1-121	-0.5
1924	Cin-N	102	405	47	114	14	9	1	31	28	17	.281	.331	.368	88	-7	5	10	-5	.990	7	*1-102	-1.1
Total	15	2014	7673	1117	2326	250	165	56	722	623	489	.303	.360	.401	117	170	251	78		.991	19	*1-2002	11.8
■ RICH DAUER	Dauer, Richard Fremont b: 7/27/52, San Bernardino, Cal. BR/TR, 6', 180 lbs. Deb: 9/11/76 C																						
1976	Bal-A	11	39	0	4	0	0	0	3	1	3	.103	.146	.103	-28	-6	0	0	0	1.000	-3	2-10	-0.9
1977	Bal-A	96	304	38	74	15	1	5	25	20	28	.243	.294	.349	79	-9	1	0	0	.982	6	2-83/3-9,D-2	0.2
1978	Bal-A	133	459	57	121	23	0	6	46	26	22	.264	.303	.353	89	-8	0	4	-2	.998	3	2-87,3-52/D-1	-0.2
1979	*Bal-A	142	479	63	123	20	0	9	61	36	36	.257	.310	.355	82	-13	0	1	-1	.979	-5	*2-103,3-44	-1.2
1980	Bal-A	152	557	71	158	32	0	2	63	46	19	.284	.342	.352	91	-6	3	2	-0	.991	-4	*2-137,3-35	-0.2
1981	Bal-A	96	369	41	97	27	0	4	38	27	18	.263	.318	.369	98	-1	0	0	0	**.989**	-14	2-94/3-4	-1.0
1982	Bal-A	158	558	75	156	24	2	8	57	50	34	.280	.340	.373	96	-2	0	1	-1	.987	-36	*2-123,3-61	-3.5
1983	*Bal-A	140	459	49	108	19	0	5	41	47	29	.235	.309	.309	72	-17	0	1	-1	.988	-29	*2-131,3-17	-4.1
1984	Bal-A	127	397	29	101	26	0	2	24	24	23	.254	.297	.335	76	-13	1	3	-2	.980	-19	*2-123/3-3	-2.9
1985	Bal-A	85	208	25	42	7	0	2	14	20	7	.202	.275	.264	50	-14	0	1	-1	.990	5	2-73,3-17/1-1	-0.8
Total	10	1140	3829	448	984	193	3	43	372	297	219	.257	.313	.343	83	-89	6	13	-6	.987	-96	2-964,3-242/D-3,1-1	-14.6
■ DOC DAUGHERTY	Daugherty, Harold Ray b: 10/12/27, Paris, Pa. BR/TR, 6', 180 lbs. Deb: 4/22/51																						
1951	Det-A	1	1	0	0	0	0	0	0	0	1	.000	.000	.000	-99	-0	0	0	0	.000	0	H	0.0
■ JACK DAUGHERTY	Daugherty, John Michael b: 7/3/60, Hialeah, Fla. BB/TL, 6', 195 lbs. Deb: 9/1/87																						
1987	Mon-N	11	10	1	1	1	0	0	1	0	3	.100	.100	.200	-22	-2	0	0	0	1.000	0	/1-1	-0.2
1989	Tex-A	52	106	15	32	4	2	1	10	11	21	.302	.373	.406	117	3	2	1	0	1.000	1	1-23/O-5,D-8	0.2
1990	Tex-A	125	310	36	93	20	2	6	47	22	49	.300	.350	.435	118	7	0	0	0	.982	-3	O-42,1-30,D-21	0.1
1991	Tex-A	58	144	8	28	3	2	1	11	16	23	.194	.275	.264	51	-10	1	0	0	.981	-4	O-37,1-11/D-1	-1.5
1992	Tex-A	59	127	13	26	9	0	0	9	16	21	.205	.299	.276	64	-6	2	1	0	.939	-4	O-26,D-13/1-8	-1.1
1993	Hou-N	4	3	0	1	0	0	0	0	0	0	.333	.333	.333	82	-0	0	0	0	.000	-0	/1-1,O-1	0.0
	Cin-N	46	59	7	13	2	0	2	9	11	15	.220	.343	.356	87	-1	0	0	0	.917	-4	O-16/1-2	-0.5
	Yr	50	62	7	14	2	0	2	9	11	15	.226	.342	.355	87	-1	0	0	0	.923	-4	O-17/1-3	-0.5
Total	6	355	759	80	194	39	6	10	87	76	132	.256	.327	.362	92	-8	5	2	0	.969	-15	O-127/1-76,D-43	-3.0
■ BOB DAUGHTERS	Daughters, Robert Francis "Red" b: 8/5/14, Cincinnati, Ohio d: 8/22/88, Southbury, Conn. BR/TR, 6'2", 185 lbs. Deb: 4/24/37																						
1937	Bos-A	1	0	1	0	0	0	0	0	0	0	—	—	—	—	0	0	0	0	.000	0	R	0.0
■ DARREN DAULTON	Daulton, Darren Arthur b: 1/3/62, Arkansas City, Kan. BL/TR, 6'2", 190 lbs. Deb: 9/25/83																						
1983	Phi-N	2	3	1	1	0	0	0	0	1	1	.333	.500	.333	137	0	0	0	0	1.000	-0	/C-2	0.0
1985	Phi-N	36	103	14	21	3	1	4	11	16	37	.204	.311	.369	87	-2	3	0	1	.994	0	C-28	0.1
1986	Phi-N	49	138	18	31	4	0	8	21	38	41	.225	.395	.428	123	6	2	3	-1	.985	-4	C-48	0.3
1987	Phi-N	53	129	10	25	6	0	3	13	16	37	.194	.283	.310	55	-8	0	0	0	.991	1	C-40/1-1	-0.5
1988	Phi-N	58	144	13	30	6	0	1	12	17	26	.208	.292	.271	61	-7	2	1	0	.977	-6	C-44/1-1	-1.1
1989	Phi-N	131	368	29	74	12	2	8	44	52	58	.201	.303	.310	76	-11	2	1	0	.984	-11	*C-126	-1.7
1990	Phi-N	143	459	62	123	30	1	12	57	72	72	.268	.370	.416	116	12	7	1	2	.989	-9	*C-139	1.4
1991	Phi-N	89	285	36	56	12	0	12	42	41	66	.196	.302	.365	88	-5	5	0	2	.985	-17	C-88	-1.6
1992	Phi-N★	145	485	80	131	32	5	27	**109**	88	103	.270	.389	.524	157	38	11	2	2	.987	-14	*C-141	3.6
1993	*Phi-N★	147	510	90	131	35	4	24	105	117	111	.257	.397	.482	136	30	5	0	2	.991	-9	*C-146	3.1
1994	Phi-N	69	257	43	77	17	1	15	56	33	43	.300	.381	.549	136	13	4	1	1	.994	7	C-68	2.4
1995	Phi-N★	98	342	44	85	19	3	9	55	55	52	.249	.361	.401	100	1	3	0	1	**.994**	-7	C-95	0.1
1996	Phi-N	5	12	3	2	0	0	0	0	7	5	.167	.500	.167	85	1	0	0	0	1.000	-1	/O-5	0.0
1997	Phi-N	84	269	46	71	13	6	11	42	54	57	.264	.389	.480	126	12	4	0	1	.979	5	O-70/1-3,D-6	1.6
	*Fla-N	52	126	22	33	8	2	3	21	22	17	.262	.376	.429	115	3	2	1	0	.984	-4	1-39/O-3,D-1	-0.4
	Yr	136	395	68	104	21	8	14	63	76	74	.263	.385	.463	123	15	6	1	1	.979	1	O-73,1-42/D-7	1.2
Total	14	1161	3630	511	891	197	25	137	588	629	726	.245	.360	.427	114	83	50	10	9	.989	-68	C-965/O-78,1-44,D-7	7.3
■ YO-YO DAVALILLO	Davalillo, Pompeyo Antonio (Romero) b: 6/30/31, Caracas, Venez. BR/TR, 5'3", 140 lbs. Deb: 8/1/53 F																						
1953	Was-A	19	58	10	17	1	0	0	2	1	7	.293	.305	.310	68	-3	1	0	0	.935	2	S-17	0.0
■ VIC DAVALILLO	Davalillo, Victor Jose (Romero) b: 7/31/36, Cabimas, Venez. BL/TL, 5'7", 155 lbs. Deb: 4/9/63 F																						
1963	Cle-A	90	370	44	108	18	5	7	36	16	41	.292	.323	.424	108	3	3	3	-1	.988	17	O-89	1.5
1964	Cle-A	150	577	64	156	26	2	6	51	34	77	.270	.312	.354	85	-12	21	11	-0	.986	16	*O-143	-0.3
1965	Cle-A★	142	505	67	152	19	1	5	40	35	50	.301	.346	.372	103	2	26	7	4	.988	15	*O-134	1.6
1966	Cle-A	121	344	42	86	6	4	3	19	24	37	.250	.299	.317	77	-10	8	6	-1	.986	0	*O-108	-1.6
1967	Cle-A	139	359	47	103	17	5	2	22	10	30	.287	.308	.379	101	-1	6	7	-2	.986	-8	*O-125	-1.7
1968	Cle-A	51	180	15	43	2	3	2	13	3	19	.239	.255	.317	74	-6	8	6	-1	.967	2	O-49	-0.9

YEAR	TM/L	G	AB	R	H	2B	3B	HR	RBI	BB	SO	AVG	OBP	SLG	PRO+	BR/A	SB	CS	SBR	FA	FR	G/POS	TPR
	Cal-A	93	339	34	101	15	4	1	18	15	34	.298	.328	.375	117	6	17	10	-1	.995	6	O-86	0.7
	Yr	144	519	49	144	17	7	3	31	18	53	.277	.303	.355	102	-1	25	16	-2	.987	8	*O-135	-0.2
1969	Cal-A	33	71	10	11	1	1	0	1	6	5	.155	.231	.197	22	-8	3	0	1	1.000	-2	O-22/1-3	-1.0
	StL-N	63	98	15	26	3	0	2	10	7	8	.265	.314	.357	87	-2	1	1	-0	1.000	-2	O-23/P-2	-0.5
1970	StL-N	111	183	29	57	14	3	1	33	13	19	.311	.357	.437	109	2	4	1	1	.972	-8	O-54	-0.7
1971	*Pit-N	99	295	48	84	14	6	1	33	11	31	.285	.315	.383	97	-2	10	2	2	.983	-2	O-61,1-16	-0.6
1972	*Pit-N	117	368	59	117	19	2	4	28	26	44	.318	.368	.413	124	11	14	1	4	.979	-1	O-97/1-8	1.1
1973	Pit-N	59	83	9	15	1	0	1	3	2	7	.181	.200	.229	19	-9	0	2	-1	.977	-0	1-10,O-10	-1.2
	*Oak-A	38	64	5	12	1	0	0	4	3	4	.188	.224	.203	22	-7	0	0	0	.967	-2	O-19/1-8,D-2	-0.9
1974	Oak-A	17	23	0	4	0	0	0	1	2	2	.174	.240	.174	22	-2	0	0	0	1.000	-2	/O-6,D-4	-0.5
1977	*LA-N	24	48	3	15	2	0	0	4	0	6	.313	.313	.354	79	-1	0	0	0	1.000	-3	O-12	-0.5
1978	*LA-N	75	77	15	24	1	1	1	11	3	7	.312	.338	.390	103	0	2	1	0	1.000	-6	O-25/1-1	-0.7
1979	LA-N	29	27	2	7	1	0	0	2	2	0	.259	.310	.296	67	-1	2	0	1	1.000	-1	/O-3	-0.1
1980	LA-N	7	6	1	1	0	0	0	0	0	1	.167	.167	.167	-7	-1	0	0	0	1.000	-0	/1-1	-0.1
Total	16	1458	4017	509	1122	160	37	36	329	212	422	.279	.317	.364	94	-36	125	58	3	.986	19	*O-1066/1-47,D-6,P	-6.4

■ JERRY DaVANON
DaVanon, Frank Gerald b: 8/21/45, Oceanside, Cal. BR/TR, 5'11", 175 lbs. Deb: 4/11/69

YEAR	TM/L	G	AB	R	H	2B	3B	HR	RBI	BB	SO	AVG	OBP	SLG	PRO+	BR/A	SB	CS	SBR	FA	FR	G/POS	TPR
1969	SD-N	24	59	4	8	1	0	0	3	3	12	.136	.177	.153	-7	-8	0	3	-2	.932	0	2-15/S-7	-0.9
	StL-N	16	40	7	12	3	0	1	7	6	8	.300	.391	.450	135	2	0	0	0	.958	1	S-16	0.4
	Yr	40	99	11	20	4	0	1	10	9	20	.202	.269	.273	53	-6	0	3	-2	.959	1	S-23,2-15	-0.5
1970	StL-N	11	18	2	2	1	0	0	0	2	5	.111	.200	.167	-1	-3	0	0	0	1.000	3	/3-5,2-3	0.0
1971	Bal-A	38	81	14	19	5	0	0	4	12	20	.235	.340	.296	82	-1	0	0	0	.970	-3	2-20,S-11/3-3,1-1	-0.3
1973	Cal-A	41	49	6	12	3	0	0	2	3	9	.245	.288	.306	73	-2	1	2	-1	.927	5	S-14,2-12/3-7	0.4
1974	StL-N	30	40	4	6	1	0	0	4	4	5	.150	.261	.175	24	-4	0	1	-1	.840	-2	S-14/3-8,2-7,O-1	-0.6
1975	Hou-N	32	97	15	27	4	2	1	10	16	7	.278	.386	.392	125	4	2	0	1	.944	2	S-21/2-9,3-3	1.0
1976	Hou-N	61	107	19	31	3	3	1	20	21	12	.290	.411	.402	144	7	0	2	-1	.980	3	2-17,S-17/3-9	1.2
1977	StL-N	9	8	2	0	0	0	0	0	1	2	.000	.111	.000	-68	-2	0	0	0	.923	1	/2-5	0.0
Total	8	262	499	73	117	21	5	3	50	68	80	.234	.332	.315	86	-7	3	8	-4	.936	11	S-100/2-88,3-35,O1	1.2

■ JIM DAVENPORT
Davenport, James Houston b: 8/17/33, Siluria, Ala. BR/TR, 5'11", 175 lbs. Deb: 4/15/58 MC

YEAR	TM/L	G	AB	R	H	2B	3B	HR	RBI	BB	SO	AVG	OBP	SLG	PRO+	BR/A	SB	CS	SBR	FA	FR	G/POS	TPR
1958	SF-N	134	434	70	111	22	3	12	41	33	64	.256	.319	.403	92	-6	1	3	-2	.960	-4	*3-130/S-5	-1.0
1959	SF-N	123	469	65	121	16	3	6	38	28	65	.258	.303	.343	73	-18	0	1	-1	**.978**	-3	*3-121/S-1	-2.2
1960	SF-N	112	363	43	91	15	3	6	38	26	58	.251	.308	.358	87	-7	0	2	-1	**.961**	-1	*3-103/S-7	-0.9
1961	SF-N	137	436	64	121	28	4	12	65	45	65	.278	.348	.443	112	7	4	3	-1	**.965**	8	*3-132	1.6
1962	*SF-N★	144	485	83	144	25	5	14	58	45	76	.297	.359	.456	119	13	2	5	-2	.952	4	*3-141	1.6
1963	SF-N	147	460	40	116	19	3	4	36	32	87	.252	.301	.333	83	-10	5	2	0	.962	1	*3-127,2-22/S-1	-0.8
1964	SF-N	116	297	24	70	10	6	2	26	29	46	.236	.304	.330	77	-9	2	0	1	.979	-3	S-64,3-41,2-30	-0.7
1965	SF-N	106	271	29	68	14	3	4	31	21	47	.251	.307	.369	87	-5	0	0	0	.949	-21	3-39,S-37,2-26	-2.4
1966	SF-N	111	305	42	76	6	2	9	30	22	40	.249	.302	.370	83	-7	1	1	-0	.961	-18	S-58,3-36,2-21,/1-2	-2.2
1967	SF-N	124	295	42	81	10	3	5	30	39	50	.275	.367	.380	116	7	1	4	-2	1.000	1	3-64,S-28,2-12	0.9
1968	SF-N	113	272	27	61	1	1	1	17	26	32	.224	.292	.246	63	-12	0	3	-2	.960	-7	3-82,S-17/2-1	-2.2
1969	SF-N	112	303	20	73	10	1	2	42	29	37	.241	.307	.300	72	-11	0	1	-1	.967	1	*3-104/1-1,S-1,O-1	-1.1
1970	SF-N	22	37	3	9	1	0	0	4	7	6	.243	.364	.270	73	-1	0	0	0	1.000	-3	3-10	-0.4
Total	13	1501	4427	552	1142	177	37	77	456	382	673	.258	.320	.367	90	-58	16	25	-10	.964	-43	*3-1130,S-219,2/1O	-9.8

■ ANDRE DAVID
David, Andre Anter b: 5/18/58, Hollywood, Cal. BL/TL, 6', 170 lbs. Deb: 6/29/84

YEAR	TM/L	G	AB	R	H	2B	3B	HR	RBI	BB	SO	AVG	OBP	SLG	PRO+	BR/A	SB	CS	SBR	FA	FR	G/POS	TPR
1984	Min-A	33	48	5	12	2	0	1	5	7	11	.250	.357	.354	93	-0	0	0	0	1.000	-3	O-14/D-2	-0.4
1986	Min-A	5	5	0	1	0	0	0	0	0	2	.200	.333	.200	48	-0	0	0	0	.000	0	/D-1	0.0
Total	2	38	53	5	13	2	0	1	5	7	13	.245	.355	.340	89	-1	0	0	0	1.000	-3	/O-14,D-3	-0.4

■ CLAUDE DAVIDSON
Davidson, Claude Boucher "Davey" b: 10/13/1896, Boston, Mass. d: 4/18/56, Weymouth, Mass. BL/TR, 5'11", 155 lbs. Deb: 4/25/18

YEAR	TM/L	G	AB	R	H	2B	3B	HR	RBI	BB	SO	AVG	OBP	SLG	PRO+	BR/A	SB	CS	SBR	FA	FR	G/POS	TPR
1918	Phi-A	31	81	4	15	1	0	0	4	5	9	.185	.233	.198	29	-7	0			.943	-7	2-15/O-8,3-1	-1.5
1919	Was-A	2	7	1	3	0	0	0	0	1	1	.429	.500	.429	163	1	0			1.000	-0	/3-2	0.1
Total	2	33	88	5	18	1	0	0	4	6	10	.205	.255	.216	41	-6	0			1.000	-7	/2-15,O-8,3-3	-1.4

■ HOMER DAVIDSON
Davidson, Homer Hurd "Divvy" b: 10/14/1884, Cleveland, Ohio d: 7/26/48, Detroit, Mich. BR/TR, 5'10.5", 155 lbs. Deb: 4/25/08

YEAR	TM/L	G	AB	R	H	2B	3B	HR	RBI	BB	SO	AVG	OBP	SLG	PRO+	BR/A	SB	CS	SBR	FA	FR	G/POS	TPR
1908	Cle-A	9	4	2	0	0	0	0	0	0		.000	.000	.000	-99	-1	1			1.000	2	/C-5,O-1	0.1

■ MARK DAVIDSON
Davidson, John Mark b: 2/15/61, Knoxville, Tenn. BR/TR, 6'2", 190 lbs. Deb: 6/20/86

YEAR	TM/L	G	AB	R	H	2B	3B	HR	RBI	BB	SO	AVG	OBP	SLG	PRO+	BR/A	SB	CS	SBR	FA	FR	G/POS	TPR
1986	Min-A	36	68	5	8	3	0	0	2	6	22	.118	.189	.162	-3	-10	2	3	-1	.980	-4	O-31/D-3	-1.5
1987	*Min-A	102	150	32	40	4	1	1	14	13	26	.267	.325	.327	71	-6	9	2	2	1.000	-14	O-86/D-9	-1.8
1988	Min-A	100	106	22	23	7	0	1	10	10	20	.217	.291	.311	67	-5	3	3	-1	.955	-16	O-91/3-1,D-3	-2.3
1989	Hou-N	33	65	7	13	2	1	1	5	7	14	.200	.278	.308	70	-3	1	0	0	1.000	-3	O-23	-0.6
1990	Hou-N	57	130	12	38	5	1	1	11	10	18	.292	.343	.369	99	-0	0	3	-2	.981	-2	O-51	-0.5
1991	Hou-N	85	142	10	27	6	0	2	15	12	28	.190	.263	.275	54	-9	0	0	0	1.000	-11	O-63	-2.2
Total	6	413	661	88	149	27	3	6	57	58	128	.225	.291	.303	64	-32	15	11	-2	.983	-49	O-345/D-15,3-1	-8.9

■ BILL DAVIDSON
Davidson, William Simpson b: 5/10/1884, Lafayette, Ind. d: 5/23/54, Lincoln, Neb. BR/TR, 5'10", 170 lbs. Deb: 9/29/09

YEAR	TM/L	G	AB	R	H	2B	3B	HR	RBI	BB	SO	AVG	OBP	SLG	PRO+	BR/A	SB	CS	SBR	FA	FR	G/POS	TPR
1909	Chi-N	2	7	2	1	0	0	0	0	1		.143	.250	.143	22	-1	1			1.000	-0	/O-2	-0.1
1910	Bro-N	136	509	48	121	13	7	0	34	24	54	.238	.277	.291	68	-22	27			.961	-7	*O-131	-3.8
1911	Bro-N	87	292	33	68	3	4	1	26	16	21	.233	.275	.281	58	-17	18			.956	-5	O-74	-2.6
Total	3	225	808	83	190	16	11	1	60	41	75	.235	.276	.286	64	-40	46			.959	-12	O-207	-6.5

■ CHICK DAVIES
Davies, Lloyd Garrison b: 3/6/1892, Peabody, Mass. d: 9/5/73, Middletown, Conn. BL/TL, 5'8", 145 lbs. Deb: 7/11/14

YEAR	TM/L	G	AB	R	H	2B	3B	HR	RBI	BB	SO	AVG	OBP	SLG	PRO+	BR/A	SB	CS	SBR	FA	FR	G/POS	TPR
1914	Phi-A	19	46	6	11	3	1	0	5	5	13	.239	.314	.348	103	0	1			.926	0	O-10/P-1	0.0
1915	Phi-A	56	132	13	24	5	3	0	11	14	31	.182	.270	.265	62	-6	2	4	-2	.973	4	O-32/P-4	-0.6
1925	NY-N	4	6	1	0	0	0	0	0	0	1	.000	.000	.000	-99	-2	0	0	0	1.000	0	/P-2,O-1	-0.1
1926	NY-N	38	18	4	4	0	0	0	1	3	5	.222	.333	.222	53	-1	0			.938	1	P-38	0.0
Total	4	117	202	24	39	8	4	0	17	22	50	.193	.279	.272	65	-9	3	4		.938	6	/P-45,O-43	-0.7

■ LEFTY DAVIS
Davis, Alphonzo De Ford b: 2/4/1875, Nashville, Tenn. d: 2/4/19, Collins, N.Y. BL/TL, 5'10", 170 lbs. Deb: 4/18/01

YEAR	TM/L	G	AB	R	H	2B	3B	HR	RBI	BB	SO	AVG	OBP	SLG	PRO+	BR/A	SB	CS	SBR	FA	FR	G/POS	TPR
1901	Bro-N	25	91	11	19	2	0	0	7	10		.209	.287	.231	50	-6	4			.822	-5	O-24/2-1	-1.2
	Pit-N	87	335	87	105	8	11	2	33	56		.313	.415	.421	138	19	22			.975	7	O-86	1.9
	Yr	112	426	98	124	10	11	2	40	66		.291	.389	.380	120	13	26			.942	2	*O-110/2-1	0.7
1902	Pit-N	59	232	52	65	7	3	0	20	35		.280	.377	.336	116	6	19			.945	-2	O-59	0.0
1903	NY-A	104	372	54	88	10	0	0	25	43		.237	.319	.263	72	-11	11			.906	-7	*O-102/S-1	-2.6
1907	Cin-N	73	266	28	61	5	5	1	25	23		.229	.293	.297	82	-6	9			.972	5	O-70	-0.4
Total	4	348	1296	232	338	32	19	3	110	167		.261	.348	.322	98	2	65			.939	-2	O-341/S-1,2-1	-2.3

■ ALVIN DAVIS
Davis, Alvin Glenn b: 9/9/60, Riverside, Cal. BL/TR, 6'1", 195 lbs. Deb: 4/11/84

YEAR	TM/L	G	AB	R	H	2B	3B	HR	RBI	BB	SO	AVG	OBP	SLG	PRO+	BR/A	SB	CS	SBR	FA	FR	G/POS	TPR
1984	Sea-A★	152	567	80	161	34	3	27	116	97	78	.284	.395	.497	147	39	5	4	-1	.992	-4	*1-147/D-7	2.5
1985	Sea-A	155	578	78	166	33	1	18	78	90	71	.287	.385	.441	125	22	1	2	-1	.992	-5	*1-154	0.7
1986	Sea-A	135	479	66	130	18	1	18	72	76	68	.271	.375	.426	116	13	0	3	-2	.986	1	*1-101,D-32	0.4
1987	Sea-A	157	580	86	171	37	2	29	100	72	84	.295	.375	.516	126	22	0	0	0	.994	-7	*1-157	0.3
1988	Sea-A	140	478	67	141	24	1	18	69	95	53	.295	.416	.462	139	29	1	1	-0	.994	-6	*1-115,D-25	1.3
1989	Sea-A	142	498	84	152	30	1	21	95	101	49	.305	.428	.496	155	41	0	1	-1	.992	-3	*1-125,D-14	2.7
1990	Sea-A	140	494	63	140	21	0	17	68	85	68	.283	.393	.429	128	22	0	2	-1	.994	-1	D-87,1-52	1.3
1991	Sea-A	145	462	39	102	15	1	12	69	56	78	.221	.305	.335	77	-14	0	3	-2	1.000	-1	*D-126,1-14	-2.3
1992	Cal-A	40	104	5	26	8	0	0	16	13	9	.250	.333	.327	85	-2	0	0	0	.995	-1	1-22/D-9	-0.4
Total	9	1206	4240	568	1189	220	10	160	683	685	558	.280	.384	.450	127	172	7	16	-8	.992	-26	1-887,D-300	6.5

YEAR	TM/L	G	AB	R	H	2B	3B	HR	RBI	BB	SO	AVG	OBP	SLG	PRO+	BR/A	SB	CS	SBR	FA	FR	G/POS	TPR
■ BILL DAVIS	Davis, Arthur Willard b: 6/6/42, Graceville, Minn. BL/TL, 6'7", 215 lbs. Deb: 9/16/65																						
1965	Cle-A	10	10	0	3	1	0	0	0	0	1	.300	.300	.400	96	-0	0	0	0	.000	0	H	0.0
1966	Cle-A	23	38	2	6	1	0	1	4	6	9	.158	.273	.263	55	-2	0	0	0	.981	0	/1-9	-0.3
1969	SD-N	31	57	1	10	1	0	0	1	8	18	.175	.288	.193	39	-4	0	0	0	.992	-1	1-14	-0.7
Total	3	64	105	3	19	3	0	1	5	14	28	.181	.283	.238	50	-7	0	0	0	.988	-1	/1-23	-1.0
■ BENJAMIN DAVIS	Davis, Benjamin Matthew b: 3/10/77, Chester, Pa. BB/TR, 6'4", 195 lbs. Deb: 9/25/98																						
1998	SD-N	1	1	0	0	0	0	0	0	0	0	.000	.000	.000	-99	-0	0	0	0	1.000	-0	/C-1	0.0
■ BROCK DAVIS	Davis, Bryshear Barnett b: 10/19/43, Oakland, Cal. BL/TL, 5'10", 168 lbs. Deb: 4/9/63																						
1963	Hou-N	34	55	7	11	2	0	1	2	4	10	.200	.254	.291	60	-3	0	0	0	.864	-2	O-14	-0.6
1964	Hou-N	1	3	0	0	0	0	0	0	1	1	.000	.250	.000	-24	-0	0	0	0	1.000	0	/O-1	0.0
1966	Hou-N	10	27	2	4	1	0	0	1	5	4	.148	.281	.185	35	-2	1	0	0	1.000	-0	/O-7	-0.3
1970	Chi-N	6	3	0	0	0	0	0	0	0	1	.000	.000	.000	-89	-1	0	0	0	.000	-0	/O-1	-0.1
1971	Chi-N	106	301	22	77	7	5	0	28	35	34	.256	.337	.312	74	-9	0	6	-4	.982	4	O-93	-1.4
1972	Mil-A	85	154	17	49	2	0	0	12	12	23	.318	.367	.331	111	2	6	4	-1	.970	-5	O-43	-0.5
Total	6	242	543	48	141	12	5	1	43	57	73	.260	.332	.306	79	-13	7	10	-4	.973	-3	O-159	-2.9
■ CHILI DAVIS	Davis, Charles Theodore b: 1/17/60, Kingston, Jamaica BB/TR, 6'3", 210 lbs. Deb: 4/10/81																						
1981	SF-N	8	15	1	2	0	0	0	0	1	2	.133	.188	.133	-8	-2	2	0	1	1.000	-1	/O-6	-0.3
1982	SF-N	154	641	86	167	27	6	19	76	45	115	.261	.311	.410	100	-1	24	13	-1	.972	18	*O-153	1.2
1983	SF-N	137	486	54	113	21	2	11	59	55	108	.233	.311	.352	86	-10	10	12	-4	.976	13	*O-133	-0.5
1984	SF-N★	137	499	87	157	21	6	21	81	42	74	.315	.369	.507	149	31	12	8	-1	.971	8	*O-123	3.4
1985	SF-N	136	481	53	130	25	2	13	56	62	74	.270	.354	.412	119	13	15	7	0	.980	13	*O-126	2.2
1986	SF-N★	153	526	71	146	28	3	13	70	84	96	.278	.378	.416	125	20	16	13	-3	.972	-2	*O-148	1.1
1987	*SF-N	149	500	80	125	22	1	24	76	72	109	.250	.347	.442	113	9	16	9	-1	.975	-13	*O-135	-0.9
1988	Cal-A	158	600	81	161	29	3	21	93	56	118	.268	.331	.432	115	11	9	10	-3	.942	-4	*O-153/D-3	-0.1
1989	Cal-A	154	560	81	152	24	1	22	90	61	109	.271	.343	.436	120	14	3	0	1	.979	-4	*O-147/D-6	0.7
1990	Cal-A	113	412	58	109	17	1	12	58	61	89	.265	.359	.398	114	9	1	2	-1	.965	-3	D-60,O-52	0.3
1991	*Min-A	153	534	84	148	34	1	29	93	95	117	.277	.387	.507	139	30	5	6	-2	1.000	-0	*D-150/O-2	2.1
1992	Min-A	138	444	63	128	27	2	12	66	73	76	.288	.392	.439	128	19	4	5	-2	1.000	-1	*D-125/O-4,1-1	1.2
1993	Cal-A	153	573	74	139	32	0	27	112	71	135	.243	.327	.440	101	-0	4	1	1	.000	-0	*D-150/P-1	-0.6
1994	Cal-A★	108	392	72	122	18	1	26	84	69	84	.311	.416	.561	147	29	3	2	-0	1.000	0	*D-106/O-2	2.1
1995	Cal-A	119	424	81	135	23	0	20	86	89	79	.318	.437	.514	148	34	3	3	-1	.000	0	*D-119	2.3
1996	Cal-A	145	530	73	155	24	0	28	95	86	99	.292	.391	.496	122	19	5	2	0	.000	0	*D-143	1.0
1997	KC-A	140	477	71	133	20	0	30	90	85	96	.279	.389	.509	129	22	6	3	0	.000	0	*D-133	1.3
1998	*NY-A	35	103	11	30	7	0	3	9	14	18	.291	.376	.447	115	3	0	1	-1	.000	0	D-34	0.0
Total	18	2290	8197	1181	2252	399	29	331	1294	1121	1598	.275	.363	.452	121	248	138	97	-17	.971	24	*O-1184,D-1029/P1	16.5
■ DOUG DAVIS	Davis, Douglas Raymond b: 9/24/62, Bloomsburg, Pa. BR/TR, 6', 180 lbs. Deb: 7/8/88																						
1988	Cal-A	6	12	1	0	0	0	0	0	0	3	.000	.077	.000	-79	-3	0	0	0	1.000	-3	/C-3,3-3	-0.6
1992	Tex-A	1	1	0	1	0	0	0	0	0	0	1.000	1.000	1.000	479	0	0	0	0	.000	0	/C-1	0.0
Total	2	7	13	1	1	0	0	0	0	0	3	.077	.143	.077	-38	-2	0	0	0	1.000	-3	/C-4,3-3	-0.6
■ ERIC DAVIS	Davis, Eric Keith b: 5/29/62, Los Angeles, Cal. BR/TR, 6'3", 185 lbs. Deb: 5/19/84																						
1984	Cin-N	57	174	33	39	10	1	10	30	24	48	.224	.322	.466	114	3	10	2	2	.992	1	O-51	0.5
1985	Cin-N	56	122	26	30	3	3	8	18	7	39	.246	.287	.516	114	2	16	3	3	.987	-6	O-47	-0.3
1986	Cin-N	132	415	97	115	15	3	27	71	68	100	.277	.380	.523	140	23	80	11	17	.975	-9	*O-121	2.9
1987	Cin-N★	129	474	120	139	23	4	37	100	84	134	.293	.401	.593	152	36	50	6	11	.990	28	*O-128	**6.9**
1988	Cin-N	135	472	81	129	18	3	26	93	65	124	.273	.365	.489	138	23	35	3	9	.981	-0	*O-130	3.0
1989	Cin-N★	131	462	74	130	14	2	34	101	68	116	.281	.375	.541	154	32	21	7	2	.984	2	*O-125	3.4
1990	*Cin-N	127	453	84	118	26	2	24	86	60	100	.260	.350	.486	122	13	21	3	5	.993	7	*O-122	2.2
1991	Cin-N	89	285	39	67	10	0	11	33	48	92	.235	.355	.386	104	3	14	2	3	.985	6	O-81	1.1
1992	LA-N	76	267	21	61	8	1	5	32	36	71	.228	.327	.322	86	-4	19	1	5	.961	-5	O-74	-0.6
1993	LA-N	108	376	57	88	17	0	14	53	41	88	.234	.311	.391	92	-5	33	5	7	.991	9	*O-103	0.9
	Det-A	23	75	14	19	1	1	6	15	14	18	.253	.371	.533	141	4	2	2	-1	.981	1	O-18/D-5	0.4
1994	Det-A	37	120	19	22	4	0	3	13	18	45	.183	.290	.292	50	-9	5	0	2	.989	-1	O-35	-0.9
1996	Cin-N	129	415	81	119	20	0	26	83	70	121	.287	.397	.523	140	25	23	9	2	.989	2	*O-126/1-1	2.5
1997	*Bal-A	42	158	29	48	11	0	8	25	14	47	.304	.364	.525	132	7	6	0	2	.975	-4	O-30,D-12	0.3
1998	Bal-A	131	452	81	148	29	1	28	89	44	108	.327	.393	.582	152	34	7	6	-2	.992	-5	O-72,D-53	2.2
Total	14	1402	4720	856	1272	209	21	267	842	661	1251	.269	.363	.492	129	188	342	60	67	.985	26	*O-1263/D-70,1-1	24.5
■ GEORGE DAVIS	Davis, George Stacey b: 8/23/1870, Cohoes, N.Y. d: 10/17/40, Philadelphia, Pa. BB/TR, 5'9", 180 lbs. Deb: 4/19/1890 MH																						
1890	Cle-N	136	526	98	139	22	9	6	73	53	34	.264	.336	.375	109	6	22			.946	12	*O-133/2-2,S-1	1.2
1891	Cle-N	136	570	115	165	35	12	3	89	53	29	.289	.354	.409	117	11	42			.931	14	*O-116,3-22/P-3	1.9
1892	*Cle-N	144	597	95	144	27	12	5	82	58	51	.241	.312	.352	97	-4	36			.914	-10	3-79,O-44,S-20,/2-3	-1.1
1893	NY-N	133	549	112	195	22	27	11	119	42	20	.355	.410	.554	155	40	37			.884	0	*3-133/S-1	3.4
1894	*NY-N	122	477	120	168	26	19	8	91	66	10	.352	.435	.537	134	28	40			.908	-1	*3-122	2.0
1895	NY-N	110	430	108	146	36	9	5	101	55	12	.340	.417	.500	139	26	48			.881	15	3-80,1-14,2-10,/OM	3.4
1896	NY-N	124	494	98	158	25	12	5	99	50	24	.320	.387	.449	123	17	48			.917	11	3-74,S-45/O-3,1-3	2.6
1897	NY-N	130	519	112	183	31	10	10	**136**	41		.353	.407	.509	145	33	65			.926	22	*S-129	4.8
1898	NY-N	121	486	80	149	20	5	2	86	32		.307	.351	.381	113	7	26			.933	**35**	*S-121	4.4
1899	NY-N	108	416	68	140	21	5	1	57	37		.337	.393	.418	127	16	34			**.945**	**46**	*S-108	**6.2**
1900	NY-N	114	426	69	136	20	4	3	61	35		.319	.376	.406	121	13	29			**.944**	29	*S-114,M	4.6
1901	NY-N	130	491	69	148	26	7	7	65	40		.301	.356	.426	131	19	27			.939	23	*S-113,3-17,M	4.9
1902	Chi-A	132	485	76	145	27	7	3	93	65		.299	.386	.402	124	19	31			**.951**	-2	*S-129/1-3	2.3
1903	NY-N	4	15	2	4	0	0	0	1	1		.267	.313	.267	63	-1	0			.870	-2	/S-4	-0.2
1904	Chi-A	152	563	75	142	27	15	1	69	43		.252	.311	.359	116	10	32			.937	17	*S-152	3.4
1905	Chi-A	151	550	74	153	29	1	1	55	60		.278	.353	.340	125	18	31			**.948**	17	*S-151	**4.1**
1906	*Chi-A	133	484	63	134	26	6	0	80	41		.277	.338	.355	120	12	27			.946	10	*S-129/2-1	2.8
1907	Chi-A	132	466	59	111	16	2	1	52	47		.238	.313	.288	95	-1	15			.949	8	*S-132	1.1
1908	Chi-A	128	419	41	91	14	1	0	26	41		.217	.298	.255	81	-7	22			.960	4	2-95,S-23/1-4	-0.4
1909	Chi-A	28	68	5	9	1	0	0	2	10		.132	.253	.147	28	-5	4			.986	1	1-17/2-2	-0.5
Total	20	2368	9031	1539	2660	451	163	72	1437	870	180	.295	.361	.404	121	254	616			.940	249	*S-1372,3-527,O2/1P	50.9
■ KIDDO DAVIS	Davis, George Willie b: 2/12/02, Bridgeport, Conn. d: 3/4/83, Bridgeport, Conn. BR/TR, 5'11", 178 lbs. Deb: 6/15/26																						
1926	NY-A	1	0	0	0	0	0	0	0	0	0	—	—	—	—	0	0	0	0	.000	-0	/O-1	0.0
1932	Phi-N	137	576	100	178	39	6	5	57	44	56	.309	.359	.424	98	-2	16			.975	14	*O-133	0.4
1933	*NY-N	126	434	61	112	20	4	7	37	25	30	.258	.298	.371	92	-6	10			.988	-10	*O-120	-2.3
1934	StL-N	16	33	6	10	3	0	1	4	3	1	.303	.361	.485	117	1	1			.960	1	/O-9	0.1
	Phi-N	100	393	50	115	25	5	3	48	27	28	.293	.338	.405	86	-8	1			.991	17	*O-100	0.5
	Yr	116	426	56	125	28	5	4	52	30	29	.293	.340	.411	89	-7	2			.988	18	*O-109	0.6
1935	NY-N	47	91	16	24	7	1	2	6	10	4	.264	.343	.429	108	1	2			.977	-1	O-21	-0.1
1936	*NY-N	47	67	6	16	1	0	0	5	6	5	.239	.301	.254	51	-4	0			1.000	-1	O-22	-0.6
1937	NY-N	56	76	20	20	10	0	0	9	10	7	.263	.356	.395	103	0	1			.932	-10	O-37	-1.0
	Cin-N	40	136	19	35	6	0	1	5	16	6	.257	.340	.324	85	-2	1			.959	2	O-35	-0.2
	Yr	96	212	39	55	16	0	1	14	26	13	.259	.346	.349	90	-2	2			.951	-8	O-72	-1.2
1938	Cin-N	5	18	3	5	1	0	0	0	1	4	.278	.316	.333	81	-0	0			1.000	-1	/O-5	-0.1
Total	8	575	1824	281	515	112	16	19	171	142	141	.282	.336	.393	92	-20	32	0		.980	10	O-483	-3.3

YEAR	TM/L	G	AB	R	H	2B	3B	HR	RBI	BB	SO	AVG	OBP	SLG	PRO+	BR/A	SB	CS	SBR	FA	FR	G/POS	TPR
■ GERRY DAVIS	Davis, Gerald Edward b: 12/25/58, Trenton, N.J. BR/TR, 6', 185 lbs. Deb: 9/20/83																						
1983	SD-N	5	15	3	5	2	0	0	1	3	4	.333	.444	.467	158	1	1	0	0	1.000	1	/O-5	0.2
1985	SD-N	44	58	10	17	3	1	0	2	5	7	.293	.349	.379	105	0	0	0	0	.952	-4	O-23	-0.4
Total	2	49	73	13	22	5	1	0	3	8	11	.301	.370	.397	117	2	1	0	0	.967	-3	/O-28	-0.2
■ GLENN DAVIS	Davis, Glenn Earle b: 3/28/61, Jacksonville, Fla. BR/TR, 6'3", 210 lbs. Deb: 9/2/84																						
1984	Hou-N	18	61	6	13	5	0	2	8	4	12	.213	.262	.393	88	-1	0	0	0	.988	2	1-16	0.0
1985	Hou-N	100	350	51	95	11	0	20	64	27	68	.271	.336	.474	128	12	0	0	0	.985	-2	1-89/O-9	0.4
1986	*Hou-N★	158	574	91	152	32	3	31	101	64	72	.265	.348	.493	133	24	3	1	0	.992	2	*1-156	1.6
1987	Hou-N	151	578	70	145	35	2	27	93	47	84	.251	.313	.458	105	2	4	1	1	.991	3	*1-151	-0.6
1988	Hou-N	152	561	78	152	26	0	30	99	53	77	.271	.346	.478	140	27	4	3	-1	**.996**	0	*1-151	1.5
1989	Hou-N★	158	581	87	156	26	1	34	89	69	123	.269	.353	.492	144	32	4	2	0	.992	3	*1-156	2.4
1990	Hou-N	93	327	44	82	15	4	22	64	46	54	.251	.357	.523	143	19	8	3	1	.995	-3	1-91	1.0
1991	Bal-A	49	176	29	40	9	1	10	28	16	29	.227	.310	.460	115	3	4	0	1	.976	4	1-36,D-12	0.5
1992	Bal-A	106	398	46	110	15	2	13	48	37	65	.276	.341	.422	110	5	1	0	0	1.000	-0	*D-103/1-2	0.1
1993	Bal-A	30	113	8	20	3	0	1	9	7	29	.177	.231	.230	24	-12	0	1	-1	.990	-2	1-22/D-7	-1.6
Total	10	1015	3719	510	965	177	13	190	603	370	613	.259	.335	.467	124	111	28	11	2	.991	6	1-870,D-122/O-9	5.3
■ HARRY DAVIS	Davis, Harry Albert "Stinky" b: 5/7/08, Shreveport, La. d: 3/3/97, Shreveport, La. BL/TL, 5'10.5", 160 lbs. Deb: 4/13/32																						
1932	Det-A	141	590	92	159	32	13	4	74	60	53	.269	.339	.388	84	-14	12	7	-1	.989	-5	*1-141	-2.9
1933	Det-A	66	173	24	37	8	2	0	14	22	8	.214	.303	.283	55	-11	2	3	-1	.978	-5	1-44	-2.0
1937	StL-A	120	450	89	124	25	3	3	35	71	26	.276	.374	.364	86	-7	7	6	-2	.991	-4	*1-112/O-1	-2.4
Total	3	327	1213	205	320	65	18	7	123	153	87	.264	.347	.364	81	-32	21	16	-3	.988	-14	1-297/O-1	-7.3
■ HARRY DAVIS	Davis, Harry H (b: Harry Davis) "Jasper" b: 7/19/1873, Philadelphia, Pa. d: 8/11/47, Philadelphia, Pa. BR/TR, 5'10", 180 lbs. Deb: 9/21/1895 M																						
1895	NY-N	7	24	1	7	0	1	0	6	2	0	.292	.346	.375	88	-0	1			.957	0	/1-7	0.0
1896	NY-N	64	233	43	64	11	10	2	50	31	20	.275	.372	.433	115	5	16			.883	-4	O-40,1-23	-0.1
	Pit-N	44	168	24	32	5	6	0	23	13	21	.190	.257	.292	46	-14	9			.966	0	1-35,O-10/S-1	-1.2
	Yr	108	401	67	96	16	16	2	73	44	41	.239	.325	.374	87	-8	25			.973	-4	1-58,O-50/S-1	-1.3
1897	Pit-N	111	429	70	131	10	**28**	2	63	26		.305	.359	.473	123	13	21			.965	-12	1-64,3-32,O-14,/S-1	0.1
1898	Pit-N	58	222	31	65	9	13	1	24	12		.293	.332	.464	130	7	7			.980	-2	1-53/O-6	0.4
	Lou-N	37	138	18	30	5	2	1	16	7		.217	.255	.304	61	-7	6			.967	0	1-34/2-2,O-1	-0.7
	Was-N	1	3	0	0	0	0	0	0	0		.000	.000	.000	-99	-1	0			.875	-0	/1-1	-0.1
	Yr	96	363	49	95	14	15	2	40	19		.262	.300	.399	102	-1	13			.974	-2	1-88/O-7,2-2	-0.4
1899	Was-N	18	64	3	12	2	3	0	8	8		.188	.288	.313	65	-3	2			.988	-1	1-18	-0.4
1901	Phi-A	117	496	92	152	28	10	8	76	23		.306	.340	.452	113	6	21			.976	8	*1-117	1.2
1902	Phi-A	133	561	89	172	**43**	8	6	92	30		.307	.343	.444	112	7	28			.984	7	*1-128/O-5	1.1
1903	Phi-A	106	420	77	125	28	7	6	55	24		.298	.343	.440	128	13	24			.972	-1	*1-104/O-2	1.1
1904	Phi-A	102	404	54	125	21	11	**10**	62	23		.309	.350	.490	156	24	12			.983	-1	*1-102	2.3
1905	*Phi-A	150	607	**93**	173	**47**	6	**8**	**83**	43		.285	.334	.422	137	23	36			.985	1	*1-150	2.1
1906	Phi-A	145	551	94	161	42	7	**12**	**96**	49		.292	.355	.459	150	30	23			.975	-0	*1-145	2.8
1907	Phi-A	149	582	84	155	**35**	8	**8**	87	42		.266	.318	.395	124	14	20			.977	4	*1-149	1.5
1908	Phi-A	147	513	65	127	23	9	5	62	61		.248	.332	.357	116	10	20			.986	1	*1-147	0.9
1909	Phi-A	149	530	73	142	22	11	4	75	51		.268	.338	.374	122	13	20			.988	-5	*1-149	0.8
1910	*Phi-A	139	492	61	122	19	4	1	41	53		.248	.332	.309	102	3	17			.986	-4	*1-139	-0.2
1911	*Phi-A	57	183	27	36	9	1	1	22	24		.197	.297	.273	60	-9	2			.977	2	1-53	-0.8
1912	Cle-A	2	5	0	0	0	0	0	0	0		.000	.000	.000	-97	-1	0			.941	0	/1-2,M	-0.1
1913	Phi-A	7	17	2	6	2	0	0	4	1	4	.353	.389	.471	155	1	0			1.000	1	/1-6	0.2
1914	Phi-A	5	7	0	3	0	0	0	2	1	0	.429	.556	.429	204	1	0	2	-1	1.000	-0	/1-1	0.0
1915	Phi-A	5	3	0	1	0	0	0	4	0	0	.333	.333	.333	103	-0	0			.000	0	/1-1	0.0
1916	Phi-A	1	0	0	0	0	0	0	0	1	0	—	1.000	—	213	0	0			.000	0	H	0.0
1917	Phi-A	1	1	0	0	0	0	0	0	0	0	.000	.000	.000	-99	-0	0			.000	0	H	0.0
Total	22	1755	6653	1001	1841	361	145	75	951	525	45	.277	.335	.408	119	135	285	2		.980	-7	*1-1628/O-78,32S	10.9
■ TOMMY DAVIS	Davis, Herman Thomas b: 3/21/39, Brooklyn, N.Y. BR/TR, 6'2", 205 lbs. Deb: 9/22/59 C																						
1959	LA-N	1	1	0	0	0	0	0	0	0	1	.000	.000	.000	-93	-0	0	0	0	.000	0	H	0.0
1960	LA-N	110	352	43	97	18	1	11	44	13	35	.276	.305	.426	92	-5	6	2	1	.975	-0	O-87/3-5	-0.9
1961	LA-N	132	460	60	128	13	2	15	58	32	53	.278	.328	.413	87	-9	10	4	1	.973	-12	O-86,3-59	-2.4
1962	LA-N★	163	665	120	**230**	27	9	27	**153**	33	65	**.346**	.379	.535	151	45	18	6	2	.961	1	*O-146,3-39	3.9
1963	*LA-N★	146	556	69	181	19	3	16	88	29	59	**.326**	.363	.457	144	30	15	10	-2	.969	-7	*O-129,3-40	1.6
1964	LA-N	152	592	70	163	20	5	14	86	29	68	.275	.314	.397	106	3	11	8	-2	.982	14	*O-148	0.8
1965	LA-N	17	60	3	15	1	1	0	9	2	4	.250	.274	.300	66	-3	2	1	0	1.000	0	O-16	-0.4
1966	*LA-N	100	313	27	98	11	1	3	27	16	36	.313	.347	.383	111	4	3	3	-1	.972	-2	O-79/3-2	-0.3
1967	NY-N	154	577	72	174	32	0	16	73	31	71	.302	.345	.440	125	17	9	3	1	.975	3	*O-149/1-1	0.9
1968	Chi-A	132	456	30	122	5	3	8	50	16	48	.268	.292	.344	91	-6	4	2	0	.962	-4	*O-116/1-6	-1.9
1969	Sea-A	123	454	52	123	29	1	6	80	30	46	.271	.322	.379	97	-3	19	4	3	.967	-7	*O-112/1-1	-1.3
	Hou-N	24	79	2	19	3	0	1	9	8	9	.241	.318	.316	80	-2	1	1	-0	1.000	0	O-21	-0.4
1970	Hou-N	57	213	24	60	12	2	3	30	7	25	.282	.305	.399	91	-4	8	3	1	.949	-1	O-53	-0.7
	Oak-A	66	200	17	58	9	1	1	27	8	18	.290	.321	.360	91	-3	2	4	-2	.963	-7	O-45/1-8	-1.5
	Chi-N	11	42	4	11	2	0	2	8	1	1	.262	.279	.452	83	-1	0	0	0	.938	-1	O-10	-0.2
1971	*Oak-A	79	219	26	71	8	1	3	42	15	19	.324	.368	.411	123	6	7	1	2	.989	2	1-35,O-16/2-3,3-2	0.7
1972	Chi-N	15	26	3	7	1	0	0	6	2	3	.269	.321	.308	72	-1	0	1	-1	1.000	-0	/1-3,O-2	-0.2
	Bal-A	26	82	9	21	3	0	0	6	6	18	.256	.307	.293	77	-2	2	0	1	1.000	0	O-18/1-3	-0.3
1973	*Bal-A	137	552	53	169	20	3	7	89	30	56	.306	.343	.391	107	5	11	3	2	.971	-0	*D-127/1-4	0.2
1974	*Bal-A	158	626	67	181	20	1	11	84	34	49	.289	.329	.377	106	4	6	2	1	.000	0	*D-155	0.0
1975	Bal-A	116	460	43	130	14	1	6	57	23	52	.283	.317	.357	96	-4	2	0	1	.000	0	*D-111	-0.6
1976	Cal-A	72	219	16	58	5	0	3	26	15	18	.265	.315	.329	95	-2	0	1	-1	1.000	-0	D-54/1-1	-0.4
	KC-A	8	19	1	5	0	0	0	0	1	0	.263	.300	.263	65	-1	0	0	0	.000	0	/D-3	-0.1
	Yr	80	238	17	63	5	0	3	26	16	18	.265	.314	.324	92	-3	0	1	-1	1.000	-0	D-57/1-1	-0.5
Total	18	1999	7223	811	2121	272	35	153	1052	381	754	.294	.332	.405	109	68	136	59	5	.970	-27	*O-1233,D-450,3/12	-3.5
■ IKE DAVIS	Davis, Isaac Marion b: 6/14/1895, Pueblo, Col. d: 4/2/84, Tucson, Ariz. BR/TR, 5'7", 140 lbs. Deb: 4/23/19																						
1919	Was-A	8	14	0	0	0	0	0	0	0	6	.000	.000	.000	-99	-4	0			.857	-2	/S-4	-0.6
1924	Chi-A	10	33	5	8	1	1	0	4	2	5	.242	.286	.333	61	-2	0	0	0	.940	1	S-10	0.0
1925	Chi-A	146	562	105	135	31	9	0	61	71	58	.240	.333	.327	72	-24	19	14	-3	.937	8	*S-144	-0.3
Total	3	164	609	110	143	32	10	0	65	73	69	.235	.324	.320	68	-29	19	14		.936	8	S-158	-0.9
■ IRA DAVIS	Davis, J. Ira "Slats" b: 7/8/1870, Philadelphia, Pa. d: 12/21/42, Brooklyn, N.Y. 162 lbs. Deb: 4/22/1899																						
1899	NY-N	6	17	3	4	1	1	0	2	0		.235	.235	.412	79	-1	1			.750	-0	/S-3,1-2	-0.1
■ JACKE DAVIS	Davis, Jacke Sylvesta b: 3/5/36, Carthage, Tex. BR/TR, 5'11", 160 lbs. Deb: 4/19/62																						
1962	Phi-N	48	75	9	16	0	1	1	6	4	20	.213	.253	.280	44	-6	1	0	0	.926	-6	O-26	-1.2
■ JUMBO DAVIS	Davis, James J. b: 9/5/1861, New York, N.Y. d: 2/14/21, St.Louis, Mo. BL/TR, 5'11", 195 lbs. Deb: 7/27/1884 U																						
1884	KC-U	7	29	3	6	0	0	0		0		.207	.207	.207	30	-3				.633	-2	/3-7	-0.5
1886	Bal-a	60	216	23	42	5	2	1	20	11		.194	.240	.250	55	-11	12			.848	5	3-60	-0.4
1887	Bal-a	130	485	81	150	23	**19**	8	109	28		.309	.353	.485	141	25	49			.826	4	3-87,S-43	2.4
1888	KC-a	121	491	70	131	22	8	3	61	20		.267	.304	.363	106	1	42			.843	30	*3-113/S-8	3.0
1889	KC-a	62	241	40	64	4	3	0	30	17	35	.266	.319	.307	74	-9	25			.803	-0	3-62	-0.6
	StL-a	2	4	1	0	0	0	0	0	1	1	.000	.200	.000	-36	-1	0			1.000	-0	/S-1,O-1	-0.1
	Yr	64	245	41	64	4	3	0	30	18	36	.261	.317	.302	72	-9	25			.803	-1	3-62/S-1,O-1	-0.7

YEAR	TM/L	G	AB	R	H	2B	3B	HR	RBI	BB	SO	AVG	OBP	SLG	PRO+	BR/A	SB	CS	SBR	FA	FR	G/POS	TPR
1890	StL-a	21	71	8	18	3	1	0	13	9		.254	.338	.324	83	-2	5			.731	-1	3-21	-0.2
	Bro-a	38	142	33	43	9	2	2	28	15		.303	.385	.437	147	8	10			.845	-5	3-38	0.4
	Yr	59	213	41	61	12	3	2	41	24		.286	.369	.399	123	6	15			.800	-6	3-59	0.2
1891	Was-a	12	44	7	14	3	2	0	9	7	5	.318	.412	.477	162	4	8			.820	-2	3-12	0.2
Total	7	453	1723	266	468	69	37	14	<u>270</u>	108	<u>41</u>	.272	.322	.379	107	12	151			.824	28	3-400/S-52,O-1	4.2

■ JODY DAVIS　　Davis, Jody Richard　b: 11/12/56, Gainesville, Ga.　BR/TR, 6'3", 210 lbs.　Deb: 4/21/81

YEAR	TM/L	G	AB	R	H	2B	3B	HR	RBI	BB	SO	AVG	OBP	SLG	PRO+	BR/A	SB	CS	SBR	FA	FR	G/POS	TPR
1981	Chi-N	56	180	14	46	5	1	4	21	21	28	.256	.337	.361	94	-1	0	1	-1	.972	-1	C-56	-0.1
1982	Chi-N	130	418	41	109	20	2	12	52	36	92	.261	.321	.404	99	-1	0	1	-1	.984	8	*C-129	1.1
1983	Chi-N	151	510	56	138	31	2	24	84	33	93	.271	.317	.480	113	7	0	2	-1	.984	-14	*C-150	-0.2
1984	*Chi-N★	150	523	55	134	25	2	19	94	47	99	.256	.319	.421	97	-3	5	6	-2	.984	4	*C-146	0.7
1985	Chi-N	142	482	47	112	30	0	17	58	48	83	.232	.302	.400	85	-10	1	0	0	.990	-1	*C-138	-0.4
1986	Chi-N★	148	528	61	132	27	2	21	74	41	110	.250	.304	.428	92	-7	0	1	-1	.992	-4	*C-145/1-1	0.6
1987	Chi-N	125	428	57	106	12	2	19	51	52	91	.248	.332	.418	93	-4	1	2	-1	.989	-3	*C-123	0.1
1988	Chi-N	88	249	16	57	9	0	6	33	29	51	.229	.312	.337	83	-5	0	3	-2	.995	-4	C-74	-0.7
	Atl-N	2	8	2	2	0	0	1	3	0	1	.250	.250	.625	137	0	0	0	0	1.000	1	/C-2	0.1
	Yr	90	257	21	59	9	0	7	36	29	52	.230	.310	.346	84	-5	0	3	-2	.995	-4	C-76	-0.6
1989	Atl-N	78	231	12	39	5	0	4	19	23	61	.169	.247	.242	39	-18	0	0	0	.985	-9	C-72/1-2	-2.6
1990	Atl-N	12	28	0	2	0	0	0	1	3	3	.071	.161	.071	-32	-5	0	0	0	1.000	1	/1-6,C-4	-0.4
Total	10	1082	3585	364	877	164	11	127	490	333	712	.245	.310	.403	91	-48	7	16	-8	.987	-15	*C-1039/1-9	-1.8

■ JOHN DAVIS　　Davis, John Humphrey "Red"　b: 7/15/15, Laurel Run, Pa.　BR/TR, 5'11", 172 lbs.　Deb: 9/9/41

| 1941 | NY-N | 21 | 70 | 8 | 15 | 3 | 0 | 0 | 5 | 8 | 12 | .214 | .295 | .257 | 55 | -4 | 0 | | | .970 | 1 | 3-21 | -0.2 |

■ CRASH DAVIS　　Davis, Lawrence Columbus　b: 7/14/19, Canon, Ga.　BR/TR, 6', 173 lbs.　Deb: 6/15/40

1940	Phi-A	23	67	4	18	1	1	0	9	3	10	.269	.310	.313	63	-4	1	0	0	.963	4	2-19/S-1	0.1
1941	Phi-A	39	105	8	23	3	0	0	8	11	16	.219	.293	.248	45	-8	0	0	0	.952	2	2-20,1-12	-0.5
1942	Phi-A	86	272	31	61	8	1	2	26	21	30	.224	.282	.283	60	-15	1	0	0	.965	-6	2-57,S-26/1-3	-1.6
Total	3	148	444	43	102	12	2	2	43	35	56	.230	.289	.279	57	-26	2	0	1	.961	0	/2-96,S-27,1-15	-2.0

■ MARK DAVIS　　Davis, Mark Anthony　b: 11/25/64, San Diego, Cal.　BR/TR, 6', 180 lbs.　Deb: 7/2/91　F

| 1991 | Cal-A | 3 | 2 | 0 | 0 | 0 | 0 | 0 | 0 | 0 | 0 | .000 | .000 | .000 | -99 | -1 | 0 | 0 | 0 | .500 | -1 | /O-3 | -0.2 |

■ MIKE DAVIS　　Davis, Michael Dwayne　b: 6/11/59, San Diego, Cal.　BL/TL, 6'3", 185 lbs.　Deb: 4/10/80　F

1980	Oak-A	51	95	11	20	2	1	1	8	7	14	.211	.265	.284	54	-6	2	1	0	1.000	1	O-18/1-7,D-6	-0.6
1981	*Oak-A	17	20	0	1	1	0	0	0	2	4	.050	.136	.100	-33	-3	0	0	0	1.000	-0	/O-2,1-1,D-3	-0.4
1982	Oak-A	23	75	12	30	4	0	1	10	2	8	.400	.416	.493	155	5	3	2	-0	.946	-1	O-13/1-7	0.4
1983	Oak-A	128	443	61	122	24	4	8	62	27	74	.275	.324	.402	105	2	32	15	1	.974	9	*O-121/D-3	0.8
1984	Oak-A	134	382	47	88	18	3	9	46	31	66	.230	.290	.364	85	-9	14	9	-1	.961	-4	*O-127/D-4	-1.4
1985	Oak-A	154	547	92	157	34	1	24	82	50	99	.287	.349	.484	135	25	24	10	1	.979	2	*O-151	2.3
1986	Oak-A	142	489	77	131	28	3	19	55	34	91	.268	.317	.454	115	8	27	4	6	.973	2	*O-139	1.1
1987	Oak-A	139	494	69	131	32	1	22	72	42	94	.265	.324	.468	114	8	19	7	2	.942	-7	*O-124,D-14	-0.1
1988	*LA-N	108	281	29	55	11	2	2	17	25	59	.196	.261	.270	55	-17	7	3	0	.961	-9	O-76	-3.0
1989	LA-N	67	173	21	43	7	1	5	19	16	28	.249	.312	.387	101	-0	6	5	-1	.987	-3	O-48	-0.6
Total	10	963	2999	419	778	161	16	91	371	236	537	.259	.316	.415	105	14	134	56	7	.968	-8	O-819/D-30,1-15	-1.5

■ ODIE DAVIS　　Davis, Odie Ernest　b: 8/13/55, San Antonio, Tex.　BR/TR, 6'1", 178 lbs.　Deb: 9/3/80

| 1980 | Tex-A | 17 | 8 | 0 | 1 | 0 | 0 | 0 | 0 | 0 | 2 | .125 | .125 | .125 | -32 | -1 | 0 | 0 | 0 | .880 | 5 | S-13/3-1 | 0.3 |

■ OTIS DAVIS　　Davis, Otis Allen "Scat"　b: 9/24/20, Charleston, Ark.　BL/TL, 6', 160 lbs.　Deb: 4/22/46

| 1946 | Bro-N | 1 | 0 | 1 | 0 | 0 | 0 | 0 | 0 | 0 | 0 | — | — | — | — | — | 0 | 0 | | 1.000 | 0 | R | 0.0 |

■ DICK DAVIS　　Davis, Richard Earl　b: 9/25/53, Long Beach, Cal.　BR/TR, 6'3", 195 lbs.　Deb: 7/12/77

1977	Mil-A	22	51	7	14	2	0	0	6	1	8	.275	.288	.314	64	-3	0	0	0	1.000	-2	O-12/D-6	-0.5
1978	Mil-A	69	218	28	54	10	1	5	26	7	23	.248	.278	.372	81	-6	2	5	-2	1.000	-1	D-34,O-28	-1.2
1979	Mil-A	91	335	51	89	13	1	12	41	16	46	.266	.299	.418	91	-5	3	3	-1	.973	-0	D-53,O-35	-0.9
1980	Mil-A	106	365	50	99	26	2	4	30	11	43	.271	.298	.386	89	-7	5	3	-0	.971	-2	D-63,O-38	-1.3
1981	*Phi-N	45	96	12	32	6	1	2	19	8	13	.333	.390	.479	139	5	1	2	-1	.974	-4	O-32	-0.1
1982	Phi-N	28	68	5	19	3	1	2	7	2	9	.279	.300	.441	103	-0	1	0	0	1.000	0	O-16	0.0
	Tor-A	3	7	0	2	0	0	0	2	0	0	.286	.286	.286	53	-0	0	0	0	1.000	0	/O-1,D-1	-0.1
	Pit-N	39	77	7	14	2	1	2	10	5	9	.182	.232	.312	49	-5	1	0	0	.971	-4	O-28	-0.1
Total	6	403	1217	160	323	62	7	27	141	50	152	.265	.298	.394	89	-22	13	13	-4	.981	-14	O-190,D-157	-5.1

■ BRANDY DAVIS　　Davis, Robert Brandon　b: 9/10/28, Newark, Del.　BR/TR, 6', 170 lbs.　Deb: 4/15/52　C

1952	Pit-N	55	95	14	17	1	1	0	1	11	28	.179	.264	.211	32	-9	9	2	2	.932	-3	O-29	-1.1
1953	Pit-N	12	39	5	8	2	0	0	2	0	3	.205	.205	.256	20	-5	0	2	-1	.955	0	/O-9	-0.6
Total	2	67	134	19	25	3	1	0	3	11	31	.187	.248	.224	29	-13	9	4	0	.938	-3	/O-38	-1.7

■ BOB DAVIS　　Davis, Robert John Eugene　b: 3/1/52, Pryor, Okla.　BR/TR, 6', 180 lbs.　Deb: 4/6/73

1973	SD-N	5	11	1	1	0	0	0	0	0	4	.091	.091	.091	-54	-2	0	0	0	.941	2	/C-5	-0.1
1975	SD-N	43	128	6	30	3	2	0	7	11	31	.234	.310	.289	71	-5	0	0	0	.986	3	C-43	0.0
1976	SD-N	51	83	7	17	0	1	0	5	5	13	.205	.250	.229	40	-7	0	0	0	.965	4	C-47	-0.2
1977	SD-N	48	94	9	17	2	0	1	10	5	24	.181	.238	.234	30	-10	0	1	0	.975	-1	C-46	-1.0
1978	SD-N	19	40	3	8	1	0	0	2	1	9	.200	.220	.225	26	-4	0	1	-1	.960	-2	C-16	-0.7
1979	Tor-A	32	89	6	11	2	0	1	8	6	15	.124	.180	.180	-0	-13	0	0	0	.984	-2	C-32	-1.3
1980	Tor-A	91	218	18	47	11	0	4	19	12	25	.216	.260	.321	56	-14	0	3	-2	.983	-2	C-89	-1.3
1981	Cal-A	1	2	0	0	0	0	0	0	0	0	.000	.000	.000	-99	-1	0	0	0	1.000	-0	/C-1	-0.1
Total	8	290	665	50	131	19	3	7	61	40	118	.197	.250	.262	42	-54	0	1		.978	1	C-279	-4.7

■ RON DAVIS　　Davis, Ronald Everette　b: 10/21/41, Roanoke Rapids, N.C.　d: 9/5/92, Houston, Tex.　BR/TR, 6', 180 lbs.　Deb: 8/1/62

1962	Hou-N	6	14	1	3	0	0	1	1	1	7	.214	.267	.214	33	-1	1	0	0	1.000	-1	/O-5	-0.2
1966	Hou-N	48	194	21	48	10	1	2	19	13	26	.247	.308	.340	86	-4	2	2	-1	.982	6	O-48	-0.1
1967	Hou-N	94	285	31	73	19	1	7	38	17	48	.256	.303	.404	104	0	5	3	-0	.976	-0	O-80	-0.4
1968	Hou-N	52	217	22	46	10	1	1	12	13	48	.212	.269	.281	67	-9	0	4	-2	.971	6	O-52	-0.9
	*StL-N	33	79	11	14	4	2	0	5	5	17	.177	.226	.278	51	-5	1	0	0	.979	0	O-25	-0.6
	Yr	85	296	33	60	14	3	1	17	18	65	.203	.258	.280	63	-14	1	4	-2	.973	6	O-77	-1.5
1969	Pit-N	62	64	10	15	1	1	0	4	7	14	.234	.310	.281	68	3	0	0	0	.933	-13	O-51	-1.8
Total	5	295	853	96	199	44	6	10	79	56	160	.233	.288	.334	82	-21	9	9	-3	.974	-2	O-261	-4.0

■ RUSS DAVIS　　Davis, Russell Stuart　b: 9/13/69, Birmingham, Ala.　BR/TR, 6', 170 lbs.　Deb: 7/6/94

1994	NY-A	4	14	0	2	0	0	0	1	0	4	.143	.143	.143	-27	-3	0	0	0	1.000	0	/3-4	-0.3
1995	*NY-A	40	98	14	27	5	2	2	12	10	26	.276	.349	.429	102	0	0	0	0	.968	3	3-34/1-2,D-4	0.3
1996	Sea-A	51	167	24	39	9	0	5	18	17	50	.234	.312	.377	73	-7	2	0	1	.933	-8	3-51	-1.3
1997	Sea-A	119	420	57	114	29	1	20	63	27	100	.271	.318	.488	108	3	6	2	1	.939	-4	*3-117/D-1	0.7
1998	Sea-A	141	502	68	130	30	1	20	82	34	134	.259	.315	.442	93	-7	4	3	-1	.906	-1	*3-137/O-3	-1.4
Total	5	355	1201	163	312	73	4	47	176	88	314	.260	.315	.445	94	-13	12	5	1	.927	-10	3-343/D-5,O-3,1-2	-1.4

■ STEVE DAVIS　　Davis, Steven Michael　b: 12/30/53, Oakland, Cal.　BR/TR, 6'1", 200 lbs.　Deb: 9/23/79

| 1979 | Chi-N | 3 | 4 | 0 | 0 | 0 | 0 | 0 | 0 | 1 | 0 | .000 | .000 | .000 | -91 | -1 | 0 | 0 | 0 | 1.000 | 1 | /2-2,3-1 | -0.1 |

■ TOD DAVIS　　Davis, Thomas Oscar　b: 7/24/24, Los Angeles, Cal.　d: 12/31/78, W. Covina, Cal.　BR/TR, 6'2", 190 lbs.　Deb: 4/27/49

| 1949 | Phi-A | 31 | 75 | 7 | 20 | 1 | 0 | 1 | 6 | 9 | 16 | .267 | .345 | .333 | 83 | -2 | 0 | 0 | 0 | .912 | -1 | S-14,3-12/2-1 | -0.2 |

YEAR	TM/L	G	AB	R	H	2B	3B	HR	RBI	BB	SO	AVG	OBP	SLG	PRO+	BR/A	SB	CS	SBR	FA	FR	G/POS	TPR
1951	Phi-A	11	15	0	1	0	0	0	0	1	3	.067	.125	.067	-46	-3	0	0	0	1.000	-0	/2-2,3-1	-0.3
Total	2	42	90	7	21	0	1	1	6	10	19	.233	.310	.289	61	-5	0	0	0	.966	-1	/S-14,3-13,2-3	-0.5
■ **TRENCH DAVIS**	Davis, Trench Neal b: 9/12/60, Baltimore, Md. BL/TL, 6'3", 171 lbs. Deb: 6/4/85																						
1985	Pit-N	2	7	1	1	0	0	0	0	0	0	.143	.143	.143	-20	-1	1	0	0	.667	-1	/O-2	-0.2
1986	Pit-N	15	23	2	3	0	0	0	1	0	4	.130	.130	.130	-27	-4	0	0	0	.917	-0	/O-7	-0.5
1987	Atl-N	6	3	0	0	0	0	0	0	0	1	.000	.000	.000	-95	-1	0	0	0	.000	0	/H	-0.1
Total	3	23	33	3	4	0	0	0	1	0	5	.121	.121	.121	-32	-6	1	0	0	.867	-1	/O-9	-0.8
■ **SPUD DAVIS**	Davis, Virgil Lawrence b: 12/20/04, Birmingham, Ala. d: 8/14/84, Birmingham, Ala. BR/TR, 6'1", 197 lbs. Deb: 4/30/28 MC																						
1928	StL-N	2	5	1	1	0	0	0	1	1	0	.200	.333	.200	42	-0	0			.750	-1	/C-2	-0.1
	Phi-N	67	163	16	46	2	0	3	18	15	11	.282	.343	.350	79	-5	0			.980	3	C-49	0.2
	Yr	69	168	17	47	2	0	3	19	16	11	.280	.342	.345	78	-5	0			.971	2	C-51	0.1
1929	Phi-N	98	263	31	90	18	0	7	48	19	17	.342	.391	.490	110	4	1			.961	-12	C-89	-0.1
1930	Phi-N	106	329	41	103	16	1	14	65	17	20	.313	.349	.495	94	-4	1			.986	-2	C-96	0.1
1931	Phi-N	120	393	30	128	32	1	4	51	36	28	.326	.382	.443	112	7	0			.994	1	*C-114	1.6
1932	Phi-N	125	402	44	135	23	5	14	70	40	39	.336	.399	.522	130	17	1			.987	-3	*C-120	2.0
1933	Phi-N	141	495	51	173	28	3	9	65	32	24	.349	.395	.473	130	19	2			.983	-11	*C-132	1.7
1934	*StL-N	107	347	45	104	22	4	9	65	34	27	.300	.366	.464	113	6	0			.988	1	C-94	1.2
1935	StL-N	102	315	28	100	24	2	1	60	33	30	.317	.386	.416	111	6	0			**.992**	-5	C-81/1-5	0.4
1936	StL-N	112	363	24	99	26	2	4	59	35	34	.273	.342	.388	97	-2	0			.985	-13	*C-103/3-2	-1.0
1937	Cin-N	76	209	19	56	10	1	3	33	23	15	.268	.341	.368	97	-1	0			.980	12	C-59	1.4
1938	Cin-N	12	36	3	6	1	0	0	1	5	6	.167	.286	.194	35	-3	0			.962	0	C-11	-0.2
	Phi-N	70	215	11	53	7	0	2	23	14	14	.247	.293	.307	67	-10	1			.980	-12	C-63	-1.9
	Yr	82	251	14	59	8	0	2	24	19	20	.235	.292	.291	62	-13	1			.977	-12	C-74	-2.1
1939	Phi-N	87	202	10	62	8	1	0	23	24	20	.307	.383	.356	103	2	0			**1.000**	-2	C-85	0.3
1940	Pit-N	99	285	23	93	14	1	5	39	35	20	.326	.404	.435	132	14	0			.967	-6	C-87	1.4
1941	Pit-N	57	107	3	27	4	1	0	6	11	11	.252	.322	.308	78	-3	0			1.000	-2	C-49	-0.2
1944	Pit-N	54	93	6	28	7	0	2	14	10	8	.301	.369	.441	122	3	0			.966	-1	C-35	0.3
1945	Pit-N	23	33	2	8	2	0	0	6	2	2	.242	.306	.303	67	-1	0			.968	-0	C-13	-0.1
Total	16	1458	4255	388	1312	244	22	77	647	386	326	.308	.369	.430	108	49	6			.984	-55	*C-1282/1-5,3-2	7.0
■ **BUTCH DAVIS**	Davis, Wallace McArthur b: 6/19/58, Martin Co., N.C. BR/TR, 6', 190 lbs. Deb: 8/23/83																						
1983	KC-A	33	122	13	42	2	6	2	18	4	19	.344	.365	.508	137	6	4	3	-1	.977	2	O-33	0.6
1984	KC-A	41	116	11	17	3	0	2	12	10	19	.147	.214	.224	21	-12	4	3	-1	.959	-1	O-35/D-2	-1.5
1987	Pit-N	7	7	3	1	1	0	0	0	1	3	.143	.250	.286	41	-1	0	0	0	1.000	0	/O-1	0.0
1988	Bal-A	13	25	2	6	1	0	0	0	0	8	.240	.240	.280	46	-2	1	0	0	1.000	-0	O-10/D-1	-0.2
1989	Bal-A	5	6	1	1	1	0	0	0	0	3	.167	.167	.333	39	-1	0	0	0	1.000	-1	/O-3,D-1	-0.1
1991	LA-N	1	1	0	0	0	0	0	0	0	0	.000	.000	.000	-99	-0	0	0	0	.000	0	/H	0.0
1993	Tex-A	62	159	24	39	10	4	3	20	5	28	.245	.273	.415	85	-4	3	1	0	.960	-2	O-44,D-11	-0.6
1994	Tex-A	4	17	2	4	3	0	0	0	0	3	.235	.235	.412	63	-1	1	0	0	1.000	1	/O-4	0.0
Total	8	166	453	56	110	21	10	7	50	20	83	.243	.276	.380	78	-15	13	7	-0	.969	-1	O-130/D-15	-1.8
■ **WILLIE DAVIS**	Davis, William Henry b: 4/15/40, Mineral Springs, Ark. BL/TL, 6'2.5", 181 lbs. Deb: 9/8/60																						
1960	LA-N	22	88	12	28	6	1	2	10	4	12	.318	.348	.477	116	2	3	5	-2	.981	1	O-22	-0.1
1961	LA-N	128	339	56	86	19	6	12	45	27	46	.254	.318	.451	93	-4	12	5	1	.983	-3	*O-114	-1.1
1962	LA-N	157	600	103	171	18	**10**	21	85	42	72	.285	.338	.453	117	13	32	7	5	.963	13	*O-156	2.1
1963	*LA-N	156	515	60	126	19	8	9	60	25	61	.245	.284	.365	92	-8	25	11	1	.978	14	*O-153	0.0
1964	LA-N	157	613	91	180	23	7	12	77	22	59	.294	.319	.413	112	7	42	13	5	.983	25	*O-155	3.1
1965	*LA-N	142	558	52	133	24	3	10	57	14	81	.238	.266	.346	76	-20	25	9	2	.967	9	*O-141	-1.6
1966	*LA-N	153	624	74	177	31	6	11	61	15	68	.284	.305	.405	104	-0	21	10	0	.970	9	*O-152	0.3
1967	LA-N	143	569	65	146	27	9	6	41	29	65	.257	.296	.367	97	-5	20	6	2	.971	3	*O-138	-0.7
1968	LA-N	160	643	86	161	24	10	7	31	31	88	.250	.286	.351	98	-5	36	10	5	.973	5	*O-158	-0.4
1969	LA-N	129	498	66	155	23	8	11	59	33	39	.311	.359	.456	136	22	24	10	1	.979	5	*O-125	2.2
1970	LA-N	146	593	92	181	23	**16**	8	93	29	54	.305	.339	.438	111	7	38	14	3	.992	15	*O-143	1.7
1971	LA-N★	158	641	84	198	33	10	10	74	23	47	.309	.333	.438	124	17	20	8	1	.981	12	*O-157	2.3
1972	LA-N	149	615	81	178	22	7	19	79	27	61	.289	.320	.441	117	11	20	3	4	.987	11	*O-146	2.0
1973	LA-N★	152	599	82	171	29	9	16	77	29	62	.285	.324	.444	116	10	17	5	2	.980	4	*O-146	0.9
1974	Mon-N	153	611	86	180	27	9	12	89	27	69	.295	.328	.427	104	1	25	7	3	.969	6	*O-151	0.4
1975	Tex-A	42	169	16	42	8	2	5	17	4	25	.249	.270	.408	90	-3	13	5	1	.990	-1	O-42	-0.5
	StL-N	98	350	41	102	19	6	6	50	14	27	.291	.326	.431	105	1	10	1	2	.970	2	O-89	0.3
1976	SD-N	141	493	61	132	18	10	5	46	19	34	.268	.298	.375	98	-4	14	2	3	.992	8	*O-128	0.2
1979	*Cal-A	43	56	9	14	2	1	0	2	4	7	.250	.300	.321	70	-2	1	0	0	1.000	-1	/O-7,D-6	-0.1
Total	18	2429	9174	1217	2561	395	138	182	1053	418	977	.279	.314	.412	106	40	398	131	41	.978	137	*O-2323/D-6	10.8
■ **ANDRE DAWSON**	Dawson, Andre Nolan b: 7/10/54, Miami, Fla. BR/TR, 6'3", 195 lbs. Deb: 9/11/76																						
1976	Mon-N	24	85	9	20	4	1	0	7	5	13	.235	.278	.306	63	-4	1	2	-1	.969	2	O-24	-0.4
1977	Mon-N	139	525	64	148	26	9	19	65	34	93	.282	.328	.474	116	9	21	7	2	.989	7	*O-136	1.3
1978	Mon-N	157	609	84	154	24	8	25	72	30	128	.253	.301	.442	106	2	28	11	2	.988	21	*O-153	1.9
1979	Mon-N	155	639	90	176	24	12	25	92	27	115	.275	.311	.468	111	6	35	10	5	.988	6	*O-153	1.0
1980	Mon-N	151	577	96	178	41	7	17	87	44	69	.308	.364	.492	137	27	34	9	5	.986	20	*O-147	4.8
1981	*Mon-N★	103	394	71	119	21	3	24	64	35	50	.302	.369	.553	157	28	26	4	5	.980	18	*O-103	5.0
1982	Mon-N★	148	608	107	183	37	7	23	83	34	96	.301	.346	.498	131	23	39	10	6	.982	21	*O-147	4.7
1983	Mon-N★	159	633	104	**189**	36	10	32	113	38	81	.299	.347	.539	143	33	25	11	1	.980	14	*O-157	4.5
1984	Mon-N	138	533	73	132	23	6	17	86	41	80	.248	.304	.409	103	0	13	5	1	.975	16	*O-134	1.3
1985	Mon-N	139	529	65	135	27	2	23	91	29	92	.255	.299	.444	112	5	13	4	2	.973	-4	*O-131	-0.2
1986	Mon-N	130	496	65	141	32	2	20	78	37	79	.284	.341	.478	125	15	18	12	-2	.986	-0	*O-127	0.9
1987	Chi-N★	153	621	90	178	24	2	**49**	**137**	32	103	.287	.329	.568	127	21	11	3	2	.986	6	*O-152	2.3
1988	Chi-N★	157	591	78	179	31	8	24	79	37	73	.303	.348	.504	136	25	12	4	1	.989	1	*O-147	2.5
1989	*Chi-N★	118	416	62	105	18	6	21	77	35	62	.252	.312	.476	114	6	8	5	-1	.987	5	*O-112	0.8
1990	Chi-N★	147	529	72	164	28	5	27	100	42	65	.310	.363	.535	134	23	16	2	4	.981	-0	*O-139	2.4
1991	Chi-N★	149	563	69	153	21	4	31	104	22	80	.272	.305	.488	114	8	4	5	-2	.988	-1	*O-137	0.1
1992	Chi-N	143	542	60	150	27	2	22	90	30	70	.277	.319	.456	114	8	6	2	1	.992	-1	*O-139	0.5
1993	Bos-A	121	461	44	126	29	1	13	67	17	49	.273	.318	.425	92	-6	2	1	0	1.000	0	D-97,O-20	-1.0
1994	Bos-A	75	292	34	70	18	0	16	48	9	53	.240	.272	.466	82	-9	2	2	-1	.000	0	D-74	-1.3
1995	Fla-N	79	226	30	58	10	3	8	37	9	45	.257	.309	.434	93	-3	0	0	0	.908	-6	O-59	-1.0
1996	Fla-N	42	58	6	16	2	0	2	14	2	13	.276	.311	.414	92	-1	0	0	0	.833	-1	/O-6	-0.2
Total	21	2627	9927	1373	2774	503	98	438	1591	589	1509	.279	.327	.482	119	216	314	109	29	.983	123	*O-2323,D-171	29.9
■ **BOOTS DAY**	Day, Charles Frederick b: 8/31/47, Ilion, N.Y. BL/TL, 5'9", 160 lbs. Deb: 6/15/69																						
1969	StL-N	11	6	1	0	0	0	0	0	1	1	.000	.143	.000	-57	-1	0	0	0	.000	-0	/O-1	-0.2
1970	Chi-N	11	8	2	2	0	0	0	0	0	3	.250	.250	.250	31	-1	0	0	0	.875	-1	/O-7	-0.2
	Mon-N	41	108	14	29	4	0	0	5	6	18	.269	.307	.306	65	-5	3	2	-0	.987	1	O-35	-0.6
	Yr	52	116	16	31	4	0	0	5	6	21	.267	.303	.302	61	-6	3	2	-0	.976	-0	O-42	-0.8
1971	Mon-N	127	371	53	105	10	2	4	33	33	39	.283	.343	.353	97	-1	9	4	0	.982	4	*O-120	-0.2
1972	Mon-N	128	386	32	90	7	4	0	30	29	44	.233	.288	.272	59	-20	3	6	-3	.979	-5	*O-117	-3.5
1973	Mon-N	101	207	36	57	7	0	4	28	21	28	.275	.342	.367	93	-2	0	3	-2	1.000	-9	O-51	-1.5
1974	Mon-N	52	65	8	12	0	0	0	2	5	8	.185	.243	.185	20	-7	0	0	0	1.000	-2	O-16	-1.0
Total	6	471	1151	146	295	28	6	8	98	95	141	.256	.314	.312	75	-37	15	15	-5	.983	-13	O-347	-1.2

■ BRIAN DAYETT
Dayett, Brian Kelly b: 1/22/57, New London, Conn. BR/TR, 5'10", 180 lbs. Deb: 9/11/83

YEAR	TM/L	G	AB	R	H	2B	3B	HR	RBI	BB	SO	AVG	OBP	SLG	PRO+	BR/A	SB	CS	SBR	FA	FR	G/POS	TPR
1983	NY-A	11	29	3	6	0	1	0	5	2	4	.207	.258	.276	49	-2	0	0	0	1.000	1	/O-9	-0.1
1984	NY-A	64	127	14	31	8	0	4	23	9	14	.244	.299	.402	96	-1	0	0	0	.988	-9	O-62/D-1	-1.1
1985	Chi-N	22	26	1	6	0	0	1	4	0	6	.231	.259	.346	61	-1	0	0	0	1.000	-2	O-10	-0.4
1986	Chi-N	24	67	7	18	4	0	4	11	6	10	.269	.329	.507	118	1	0	1	-1	1.000	-4	O-24	-0.3
1987	Chi-N	97	177	20	49	14	1	5	25	20	37	.277	.350	.452	106	2	0	0	0	1.000	-13	O-78	-1.3
Total	5	218	426	45	110	26	2	14	68	37	71	.258	.320	.427	99	-2	0	1	-1	.995	-26	O-183/D-1	-3.2

■ CHARLIE DEAL
Deal, Charles Albert b: 10/30/1891, Wilkinsburg, Pa. d: 9/16/79, Covina, Cal. BR/TR, 6', 160 lbs. Deb: 7/19/12

YEAR	TM/L	G	AB	R	H	2B	3B	HR	RBI	BB	SO	AVG	OBP	SLG	PRO+	BR/A	SB	CS	SBR	FA	FR	G/POS	TPR
1912	Det-A	42	142	13	32	4	2	0	11	9		.225	.272	.282	60	-8	4			.942	10	3-41	0.3
1913	Det-A	16	50	3	11	0	2	0	3	1	7	.220	.235	.300	57	-3	2			.862	2	3-15	-0.1
	Bos-N	10	36	6	11	1	0	0	3	2	1	.306	.359	.333	96	-0	1			.935	-6	2-10	-0.7
1914	*Bos-N	79	257	17	54	13	2	0	23	20	23	.210	.270	.276	63	-12	4			.948	-5	3-74/S-1	-1.6
1915	StL-F	65	223	21	72	12	4	1	27	12	16	.323	.357	.426	114	1	10			.951	5	3-65	0.8
1916	StL-A	23	74	7	10	1	0	0	10	6	8	.135	.200	.149	5	-9	4			.970	-2	3-22/2-1	-1.1
	Chi-N	2	8	2	2	1	0	0	3	0	0	.250	.250	.375	82	-0	0			1.000	2	/3-2	0.2
1917	Chi-N	135	449	46	114	11	3	0	47	19	18	.254	.284	.292	71	-16	10			.957	7	*3-130	-0.8
1918	*Chi-N	119	414	43	99	9	3	2	34	21	13	.239	.279	.290	72	-14	11			.942	-2	*3-118	-1.6
1919	Chi-N	116	405	37	117	23	5	2	52	12	12	.289	.316	.385	110	3	11			**.973**	7	*3-116	1.7
1920	Chi-N	129	450	48	108	10	5	3	39	20	14	.240	.285	.304	68	-19	5	8	-3	**.973**	10	*3-128	-0.7
1921	Chi-N	115	422	52	122	19	8	3	66	13	9	.289	.310	.393	85	-10	3	5	-2	**.973**	14	*3-112	0.9
Total	10	851	2930	295	752	104	34	11	318	135	121	.257	.293	.327	79	-86	65	13		.958	41	3-823/2-11,S-1	-2.7

■ LINDSAY DEAL
Deal, Fred Lindsay b: 9/3/11, Lenoir, N.C. d: 4/18/79, Little Rock, Ark. BL/TR, 6', 175 lbs. Deb: 9/13/39

YEAR	TM/L	G	AB	R	H	2B	3B	HR	RBI	BB	SO	AVG	OBP	SLG	PRO+	BR/A	SB	CS	SBR	FA	FR	G/POS	TPR
1939	Bro-N	4	7	0	0	0	0	0	0	0	2	.000	.000	.000	-97	-2	0			1.000	0	/O-1	-0.2

■ SNAKE DEAL
Deal, John Wesley b: 1/21/1879, Lancaster, Pa. d: 5/9/44, Harrisburg, Pa. BR/TR, 6', 164 lbs. Deb: 7/9/06

YEAR	TM/L	G	AB	R	H	2B	3B	HR	RBI	BB	SO	AVG	OBP	SLG	PRO+	BR/A	SB	CS	SBR	FA	FR	G/POS	TPR
1906	Cin-N	65	231	13	48	4	3	0	21	6		.208	.228	.251	47	-15	15			.985	2	1-65	-1.6

■ PAT DEALY
Dealy, Patrick E. b: Burlington, Vt. d: 12/16/24, Buffalo, N.Y. BR/TR, 5'8", 145 lbs. Deb: 9/30/1884

YEAR	TM/L	G	AB	R	H	2B	3B	HR	RBI	BB	SO	AVG	OBP	SLG	PRO+	BR/A	SB	CS	SBR	FA	FR	G/POS	TPR
1884	StP-U	5	15	2	2	0	0	0		0		.133	.133	.133	-35	-4				.871	3	/C-4,O-1	-0.1
1885	Bos-N	35	130	18	29	4	1	1	9	2	14	.223	.235	.292	72	-4				.903	0	C-29/3-3,O-2,S-2,1	-0.1
1886	Bos-N	15	46	9	15	1	1	0	3	4	4	.326	.380	.391	140	2	5			.929	-2	C-14/O-1	0.2
1887	Was-N	58	212	33	55	8	2	1	18	8	8	.259	.293	.330	77	-7	36			.931	-7	C-28,S-23/O-5,3-5	-0.9
1890	Syr-a	18	66	9	12	1	0	0	4	5		.182	.250	.197	36	-5	4			.900	-6	C-10/3-6,O-2	-0.9
Total	5	131	469	71	113	14	4	2	34	19	26	.241	.275	.301	74	-17	45			.914	-12	/C-85,S-25,3-14,O1	-1.8

■ CHUBBY DEAN
Dean, Alfred Lovill b: 8/24/16, Mt.Airy, N.C. d: 12/21/70, Riverside, Cal. BL/TL, 5'11", 181 lbs. Deb: 4/14/36

YEAR	TM/L	G	AB	R	H	2B	3B	HR	RBI	BB	SO	AVG	OBP	SLG	PRO+	BR/A	SB	CS	SBR	FA	FR	G/POS	TPR
1936	Phi-A	111	342	41	98	21	3	1	48	24	24	.287	.337	.374	77	-13	3	2	-0	.989	-1	1-77	-1.9
1937	Phi-A	104	309	36	81	14	4	2	31	42	10	.262	.350	.353	79	-9	2	1	0	.991	-2	1-78/P-2	-1.9
1938	Phi-A	16	20	3	6	2	0	0	1	1	4	.300	.333	.400	85	-1	0	0	0	1.000	1	/P-6	0.0
1939	Phi-A	80	77	12	27	4	0	0	19	8	4	.351	.412	.403	111	2	0	0	0	.935	1	P-54	0.0
1940	Phi-A	67	90	6	26	2	0	0	6	16	9	.289	.396	.311	88	-1	0	0	0	.976	1	P-30/1-1	0.0
1941	Phi-A	27	37	0	9	2	0	0	9	4	3	.243	.317	.297	65	-2	0	0	0	1.000	0	P-18/1-1	0.0
	Cle-A	17	25	2	4	1	0	0	2	3	2	.160	.250	.200	21	-3	0	0	0	1.000	1	/P-8	0.0
	Yr	44	62	2	13	3	0	0	11	7	5	.210	.290	.258	48	-5	0	0	0	1.000	1	P-26/1-1	0.0
1942	Cle-A	70	101	4	27	1	0	0	7	11	7	.267	.339	.277	79	-2	0	0	0	.939	-3	P-27	0.0
1943	Cle-A	41	46	2	9	0	0	0	5	6	2	.196	.288	.196	45	-3	0	0	0	.929	-1	P-17	0.0
Total	8	533	1047	106	287	47	7	3	128	115	65	.274	.347	.341	79	-32	5	3	-0	.964	-5	P-162,1-157	-3.8

■ TOMMY DEAN
Dean, Tommy Douglas b: 8/30/45, Iuka, Miss. BR/TR, 6', 165 lbs. Deb: 9/17/67

YEAR	TM/L	G	AB	R	H	2B	3B	HR	RBI	BB	SO	AVG	OBP	SLG	PRO+	BR/A	SB	CS	SBR	FA	FR	G/POS	TPR
1967	LA-N	12	28	1	4	1	0	0	2	0	9	.143	.143	.179	-9	-4	0	0	0	.981	6	S-12	0.3
1969	SD-N	101	273	14	48	9	2	2	9	27	54	.176	.252	.245	42	-21	0	3	-2	.978	4	S-97/2-2	-1.1
1970	SD-N	61	158	18	35	5	1	2	13	11	29	.222	.272	.304	56	-10	2	0	1	.974	6	S-55	0.2
1971	SD-N	41	70	2	8	0	0	0	1	4	13	.114	.162	.114	-22	-11	1	0	0	.969	6	S-28,3-11/2-1	-0.3
Total	4	215	529	35	95	15	3	4	25	42	105	.180	.241	.242	36	-47	3	3	-1	.976	23	S-192/3-11,2-3	-0.9

■ HARRY DEANE
Deane, John Henry b: 5/6/1846, Trenton, N.J. d: 5/31/25, Indianapolis, Ind. 5'7", 150 lbs. Deb: 7/20/1871 M

YEAR	TM/L	G	AB	R	H	2B	3B	HR	RBI	BB	SO	AVG	OBP	SLG	PRO+	BR/A	SB	CS	SBR	FA	FR	G/POS	TPR
1871	Kek-n	6	22	3	4	0	1	0	2	2	0	.182	.250	.273	49	-1	0	0	0	1.000	2	/O-6,M	0.0
1874	Bal-n	47	203	29	50	8	1	0	13	4	3	.246	.261	.296	79	-4	2	1	0	.818	-4	*O-46/2-2,S-1	-0.6
Total	2 n	53	225	32	54	8	2	0	15	6	3	.240	.260	.293	75	-6	2	1	0	.850	-3	/O-52,2-2,S-1	-0.6

■ BUDDY DEAR
Dear, Paul Stanford b: 12/1/05, Norfolk, Va. d: 8/29/89, Radford, Va. BR/TR, 5'8", 143 lbs. Deb: 9/9/27

YEAR	TM/L	G	AB	R	H	2B	3B	HR	RBI	BB	SO	AVG	OBP	SLG	PRO+	BR/A	SB	CS	SBR	FA	FR	G/POS	TPR
1927	Was-A	2	1	1	0	0	0	0	0	0	0	.000	.000	.000	-99	-0	0	0	0	.000	0	/2-1	0.0

■ CHARLIE DeARMOND
DeArmond, Charles Hommer "Hummer" b: 2/13/1877, Okeana, Ohio d: 12/17/33, Morning Sun, Ohio BR/TR, 5'10", 165 lbs. Deb: 9/19/03

YEAR	TM/L	G	AB	R	H	2B	3B	HR	RBI	BB	SO	AVG	OBP	SLG	PRO+	BR/A	SB	CS	SBR	FA	FR	G/POS	TPR
1903	Cin-N	11	39	10	11	2	1	0	7	3		.282	.349	.385	98	-0	1			.878	-1	3-11	-0.1

■ JOHN DEASLEY
Deasley, John b: 1/1861, Philadelphia, Pa. d: 12/25/10, Philadelphia, Pa. Deb: 6/17/1884 F

YEAR	TM/L	G	AB	R	H	2B	3B	HR	RBI	BB	SO	AVG	OBP	SLG	PRO+	BR/A	SB	CS	SBR	FA	FR	G/POS	TPR
1884	Was-U	31	134	20	29	1	1	0		3		.216	.234	.239	45	-13				.836	0	S-31	-1.1
	KC-U	13	40	3	7	2	0	0		2		.175	.214	.225	38	-4				.833	-0	S-13	-0.4
	Yr	44	174	23	36	3	1	0		5		.207	.229	.236	44	-17				.835	0	S-44	-1.5

■ PAT DEASLEY
Deasley, Thomas H. b: 11/17/1857, Ireland d: 4/1/43, Philadelphia, Pa. BR/TR, 5'8.5", 154 lbs. Deb: 5/18/1881 F

YEAR	TM/L	G	AB	R	H	2B	3B	HR	RBI	BB	SO	AVG	OBP	SLG	PRO+	BR/A	SB	CS	SBR	FA	FR	G/POS	TPR
1881	Bos-N	43	147	13	35	5	2	0	8	5	10	.238	.263	.299	80	-3				.914	-4	C-28/O-7,S-7,1-2	-0.6
1882	Bos-N	67	264	36	70	8	0	0	29	7	22	.265	.284	.295	86	-4				**.958**	2	*C-56,O-14/S-1	-0.1
1883	StL-a	58	206	27	53	2	1	0	15	6		.257	.278	.277	75	-6				**.930**	8	C-56/O-2	0.5
1884	StL-a	75	254	27	52	5	4	0		7		.205	.235	.256	58	-12				.919	14	*C-75/O-2,1-1	0.7
1885	NY-N	54	207	22	53	5	1	0	24	9	20	.256	.287	.290	88	-3				.935	8	C-54/O-2,S-1	0.9
1886	NY-N	41	143	18	38	6	1	0	17	4	12	.266	.286	.322	84	-3	2			.925	7	C-30,O-15	0.5
1887	NY-N	30	118	12	37	5	0	0	23	9	7	.314	.367	.356	107	2	3			.867	-13	C-24/3-7,S-1	-0.8
1888	Was-N	34	127	6	20	1	0	0	4	2	18	.157	.171	.165	8	-13	2			.922	8	C-31/O-1,S-1,2-1	-0.2
Total	8	402	1466	161	358	37	9	0	120	49	89	.244	.271	.282	75	-42	7			.927	28	C-354/O-43,S312	0.9

■ HANK DeBERRY
DeBerry, John Herman b: 12/29/1894, Savannah, Tenn. d: 9/10/51, Savannah, Tenn. BR/TR, 5'11", 195 lbs. Deb: 9/12/16

YEAR	TM/L	G	AB	R	H	2B	3B	HR	RBI	BB	SO	AVG	OBP	SLG	PRO+	BR/A	SB	CS	SBR	FA	FR	G/POS	TPR
1916	Cle-A	15	33	7	9	4	0	0	4	6	9	.273	.385	.394	126	1	0			1.000	-3	C-14	-0.1
1917	Cle-A	25	33	3	9	2	0	0	1	2	7	.273	.333	.333	96	-0	0			.968	1	/C-9	0.1
1922	Bro-N	85	259	29	78	10	1	3	35	20	9	.301	.354	.382	91	-3	4	1	1	.971	-2	C-81	-0.1
1923	Bro-N	78	235	21	67	11	6	1	48	20	12	.285	.346	.396	98	-1	2	1	0	.971	8	C-60	1.0
1924	Bro-N	77	218	20	53	10	3	3	26	20	21	.243	.307	.358	80	-6	0	1	-1	.993	23	C-63	1.9
1925	Bro-N	67	193	26	50	8	1	2	24	16	8	.259	.322	.342	72	-8	2	2	-1	.981	19	C-55	1.3
1926	Bro-N	48	115	6	33	11	0	0	13	8	5	.287	.333	.383	94	-1	0			.976	8	C-37	0.9
1927	Bro-N	68	201	15	47	3	2	1	21	17	8	.234	.294	.284	55	-13	1			.988	23	C-67	1.5
1928	Bro-N	82	258	19	65	8	2	0	23	18	15	.252	.301	.298	58	-16	3			.977	18	C-80	0.9
1929	Bro-N	68	210	13	55	11	1	1	25	17	15	.262	.317	.338	64	-12	1			.991	6	C-68	0.0
1930	Bro-N	35	95	11	28	3	0	0	14	4	10	.295	.323	.326	58	-6	0			.978	12	C-35	0.7
Total	11	648	1850	170	494	81	16	11	234	148	119	.267	.323	.346	76	-65	13	5		.982	113	C-569	8.1

■ ADAM DEBUS
Debus, Adam Joseph b: 10/7/1892, Chicago, Ill. d: 5/13/77, Chicago, Ill. BR/TR, 5'10.5", 150 lbs. Deb: 7/14/17

YEAR	TM/L	G	AB	R	H	2B	3B	HR	RBI	BB	SO	AVG	OBP	SLG	PRO+	BR/A	SB	CS	SBR	FA	FR	G/POS	TPR
1917	Pit-N	38	131	9	30	5	4	0	7	7	14	.229	.279	.328	83	-3	2			.898	-6	S-21,3-18	-0.9

■ DOUG DeCINCES
DeCinces, Douglas Vernon b: 8/29/50, Burbank, Cal. BR/TR, 6'2", 194 lbs. Deb: 9/9/73

YEAR	TM/L	G	AB	R	H	2B	3B	HR	RBI	BB	SO	AVG	OBP	SLG	PRO+	BR/A	SB	CS	SBR	FA	FR	G/POS	TPR
1973	Bal-A	10	18	2	2	0	0	0	3	1	5	.111	.158	.111	-23	-3	0	0	0	.895	3	/3-8,2-2,S-1	0.0
1974	Bal-A	1	1	0	0	0	0	0	0	1	0	.000	.500	.000	55	0	0	0	0	1.000	0	/3-1	0.0
1975	Bal-A	61	167	20	42	6	3	4	23	13	32	.251	.309	.395	105	0	0	1	-1	.947	3	3-34,S-13,2-11,/1-2	0.4
1976	Bal-A	129	440	36	103	17	2	11	42	29	68	.234	.285	.357	93	-6	8	4	0	.941	-1	*3-109,2-17,1/SD	-0.8
1977	Bal-A	150	522	63	135	28	3	19	69	64	86	.259	.342	.433	117	12	8	8	-2	.958	10	*3-148/1-1,2-1,D-1	1.8
1978	Bal-A	142	511	72	146	37	1	28	80	46	81	.286	.347	.526	152	32	7	7	-2	.975	10	*3-130,2-12	4.0
1979	*Bal-A	120	422	67	97	27	1	16	61	54	68	.230	.322	.412	100	-0	5	3	-0	.964	-3	*3-120	-0.4
1980	Bal-A	145	489	64	122	23	2	16	64	49	83	.249	.322	.403	98	-2	11	6	-0	.960	25	*3-142/1-1	2.0
1981	Bal-A	100	346	49	91	23	2	13	55	41	32	.263	.343	.454	128	12	0	3	-2	.942	-2	*3-100/1-1,O-1	0.7
1982	*Cal-A	153	575	94	173	42	5	30	97	66	80	.301	.374	.548	149	38	7	5	-1	.961	21	*3-153/S-2	5.3
1983	Cal-A★	95	370	49	104	19	3	18	65	32	56	.281	.338	.495	127	13	2	0	1	.955	9	3-84,D-10	2.0
1984	Cal-A	146	547	77	147	23	3	20	82	53	79	.269	.333	.431	111	7	4	1	1	.964	-6	*3-140/D-5	0.0
1985	Cal-A	120	427	50	104	22	1	20	78	47	71	.244	.321	.440	107	3	1	4	-2	.958	-10	*3-111/D-3	-1.0
1986	*Cal-A	140	512	69	131	20	3	26	96	52	74	.256	.327	.459	112	8	2	2	-1	.965	-8	*3-132/S-1,D-3	-0.3
1987	Cal-A	133	453	65	106	23	0	16	63	70	87	.234	.339	.391	96	-2	3	4	-2	.948	-3	*3-128/1-4,S-1,D-1	-0.7
	StL-N	4	9	1	2	2	0	0	1	0	2	.222	.222	.444	70	-0	0	0	0	.833	1	/3-3	0.1
Total	15	1649	5809	778	1505	312	29	237	879	618	904	.259	.333	.445	116	113	58	48	-11	.958	49	*3-1543/2-43,D1SO	13.1

■ HARRY DECKER
Decker, Earle Harry b: 9/3/1854, Lockport, Ill. BR/TR, 5'11", 180 lbs. Deb: 8/23/1884

YEAR	TM/L	G	AB	R	H	2B	3B	HR	RBI	BB	SO	AVG	OBP	SLG	PRO+	BR/A	SB	CS	SBR	FA	FR	G/POS	TPR
1884	Ind-a	4	15	1	4	1	0	0		1		.267	.313	.333	114	0				.870	-3	/C-4	-0.3
	KC-U	23	75	8	10	2	0	0		5		.133	.188	.160	7	-11				.813	2	O-16,C-11	-0.8
1886	Det-N	14	54	2	12	1	0	0	5	2	9	.222	.250	.241	48	-3	0			.871	4	C-14/O-1	0.2
	Was-N	7	23	0	5	1	1	0	2	1	5	.217	.250	.348	85	-0	0			.946	1	/C-4,3-2,S-1	0.1
	Yr	21	77	2	17	2	1	0	7	3	14	.221	.250	.273	59	-4	0			.886	5	C-18/3-2,O-1,S-1	0.3
1889	Phi-N	11	30	4	3	0	0	0	2	2	5	.100	.156	.100	-25	-5	1			.857	-1	/2-7,C-3,O-1	-0.5
1890	Phi-N	5	19	5	7	1	0	0	2	4	1	.368	.478	.421	159	2	4			.938	-1	/1-2,O-2,C-1	0.0
	Pit-N	92	354	52	97	14	3	5	38	26	36	.274	.324	.373	116	6	8			.909	-26	C-70,1-16/O-4,2S	-1.3
	Yr	97	373	57	104	15	3	5	40	30	37	.279	.333	.375	119	8	12			.909	-27	C-71,1-18/O-6,2S	-1.3
Total	4	156	570	72	138	20	4	5	49	41	56	.242	.293	.318	87	-11	13			.903	-25	C-107/O-24,12S3	-2.6

■ FRANK DECKER
Decker, Frank b: 2/26/1856, St.Louis, Mo. d: 2/5/40, St.Louis, Mo. BR/TR, Deb: 6/25/1879

YEAR	TM/L	G	AB	R	H	2B	3B	HR	RBI	BB	SO	AVG	OBP	SLG	PRO+	BR/A	SB	CS	SBR	FA	FR	G/POS	TPR
1879	Syr-N	3	10	0	1	0	0	0	0	0	3	.100	.100	.100	-38	-1				.714	-2	/C-2,O-1,1-1	-0.3
1882	StL-a	2	8	0	2	0	0	0	1	0		.250	.250	.250	66	-0				.813	-0	/2-2	0.0
Total	2	5	18	0	3	0	0	0	1	0	3	.167	.167	.167	12	-2				.813	-2	/2-2,C-2,1-1,O-1	-0.3

■ GEORGE DECKER
Decker, George A "Gentleman George" b: 6/1/1869, York, Pa. d: 6/7/09, Patton, Cal. BL/TL, 6'1", 180 lbs. Deb: 7/11/1892

YEAR	TM/L	G	AB	R	H	2B	3B	HR	RBI	BB	SO	AVG	OBP	SLG	PRO+	BR/A	SB	CS	SBR	FA	FR	G/POS	TPR
1892	Chi-N	78	291	32	66	6	7	1	28	20	49	.227	.277	.306	75	-10	9			.876	-12	O-62,2-16	-2.2
1893	Chi-N	81	328	57	89	9	8	2	48	24	22	.271	.325	.366	85	-8	22			.878	-9	O-33,1-27,2-20,/S-2	-1.6
1894	Chi-N	91	384	74	120	17	6	8	92	24	17	.313	.361	.451	90	-8	23			.974	-8	1-48,O-29/3-7,2S	-1.4
1895	Chi-N	73	297	51	82	9	7	2	41	17	22	.276	.324	.374	75	-13	11			.910	-8	O-57,1-11/3-3,S2	-2.0
1896	Chi-N	107	421	68	118	23	11	5	61	23	14	.280	.318	.423	91	-8	20			.928	-3	O-71,1-36	-1.4
1897	Chi-N	111	428	72	124	12	7	5	63	24		.290	.333	.386	86	-10	11			.925	-3	O-75,1-38/2-1	-1.5
1898	StL-N	76	286	26	74	10	0	1	45	20		.259	.314	.304	76	-9	4			.980	-7	1-75	-1.6
	Lou-N	42	148	27	44	4	3	0	19	9		.297	.342	.365	104	1	9			.993	-1	1-32/O-6	-0.1
	Yr	118	434	53	118	14	3	1	64	29		.272	.323	.325	85	-9	13			**.984**	-9	*1-107/O-6	-1.7
1899	Lou-N	38	135	13	36	8	0	1	18	12		.267	.336	.348	88	-2	3			.968	-3	1-38	-0.4
	Was-N	4	9	0	0	0	0	0	0	0		.000	.000	.000	-99	-2	0			.955	-1	/1-2,O-1	-0.3
	Yr	42	144	13	36	8	0	1	18	12		.250	.316	.326	77	-5	3			.967	-3	1-40/O-1	-0.7
Total	8	701	2727	420	753	98	49	25	415	173	124	.276	.324	.376	84	-70	112			.900	-54	O-334,1-307/23S	-12.5

■ STEVE DECKER
Decker, Steven Michael b: 10/25/65, Rock Island, Ill. BR/TR, 6'3", 205 lbs. Deb: 9/18/90

YEAR	TM/L	G	AB	R	H	2B	3B	HR	RBI	BB	SO	AVG	OBP	SLG	PRO+	BR/A	SB	CS	SBR	FA	FR	G/POS	TPR
1990	SF-N	15	54	5	16	2	0	3	8	1	10	.296	.309	.500	123	1	0	0	0	.989	2	C-15	0.4
1991	SF-N	79	233	11	48	7	1	5	24	16	44	.206	.266	.309	63	-12	0	1	-1	.984	-3	C-78	-1.2
1992	SF-N	15	43	3	7	1	0	0	1	6	7	.163	.280	.186	36	-3	0	0	0	1.000	2	C-15	0.0
1993	Fla-N	8	15	0	0	0	0	0	1	3	3	.000	.167	.000	-48	-3	0	0	0	.968	1	/C-5	-0.2
1995	Fla-N	51	133	12	30	2	1	3	13	19	22	.226	.322	.323	71	-5	1	0	0	.985	6	C-46/1-2	0.3
1996	SF-N	57	122	16	28	1	0	1	12	15	26	.230	.314	.262	56	-7	0	0	0	1.000	2	C-30/1-3,3-2	-0.4
	Col-N	10	25	8	8	2	0	1	8	3	3	.320	.393	.520	112	0	1	0	0	1.000	2	C-10	0.3
	Yr	67	147	24	36	3	0	2	20	18	29	.245	.327	.306	68	-6	1	0	0	1.000	5	C-40/1-3,3-2	-0.1
Total	6	235	625	55	137	15	2	13	67	63	115	.219	.295	.312	66	-30	2	1	0	.989	13	C-199/1-5,3-2	-0.8

■ ARTIE DEDE
Dede, Arthur Richard b: 7/12/1895, Brooklyn, N.Y. d: 9/6/71, Keene, N.H. BR/TR, 5'9", 155 lbs. Deb: 10/4/16

YEAR	TM/L	G	AB	R	H	2B	3B	HR	RBI	BB	SO	AVG	OBP	SLG	PRO+	BR/A	SB	CS	SBR	FA	FR	G/POS	TPR
1916	Bro-N	1	1	0	0	0	0	0	0	0	0	.000	.000	.000	-97	-0	0			1.000	-0	/C-1	-0.1

■ ROD DEDEAUX
Dedeaux, Raoul Martial b: 2/17/15, New Orleans, La. BR/TR, 5'11", 160 lbs. Deb: 9/28/35

YEAR	TM/L	G	AB	R	H	2B	3B	HR	RBI	BB	SO	AVG	OBP	SLG	PRO+	BR/A	SB	CS	SBR	FA	FR	G/POS	TPR
1935	Bro-N	2	4	0	1	0	0	0	1	0	0	.250	.250	.250	36	-0	0			.857	0	/S-2	0.0

■ JIM DEE
Dee, James D. b: Buffalo, N.Y. Deb: 7/30/1884

YEAR	TM/L	G	AB	R	H	2B	3B	HR	RBI	BB	SO	AVG	OBP	SLG	PRO+	BR/A	SB	CS	SBR	FA	FR	G/POS	TPR
1884	Pit-a	12	40	0	5	0	0	0		1		.125	.146	.125	-10	-5				.860	1	S-12	-0.3

■ SHORTY DEE
Dee, Maurice Leo b: 10/4/1889, Halifax, N.S., Can. d: 8/12/71, Jamaica Plain, Mass. BR/TR, 5'6", 155 lbs. Deb: 9/14/15

YEAR	TM/L	G	AB	R	H	2B	3B	HR	RBI	BB	SO	AVG	OBP	SLG	PRO+	BR/A	SB	CS	SBR	FA	FR	G/POS	TPR
1915	StL-A	1	3	1	0	0	0	0	0	1	0	.000	.250	.000	-26	-0	0	1	-1	.500	-1	/S-1	-0.3

■ ROB DEER
Deer, Robert George b: 9/29/60, Orange, Cal. BR/TR, 6'3", 210 lbs. Deb: 9/4/84

YEAR	TM/L	G	AB	R	H	2B	3B	HR	RBI	BB	SO	AVG	OBP	SLG	PRO+	BR/A	SB	CS	SBR	FA	FR	G/POS	TPR
1984	SF-N	13	24	5	4	0	0	3	3	7	10	.167	.375	.542	160	2	1	1	-0	.905	0	/O-9	0.2
1985	SF-N	78	162	22	30	5	1	8	20	23	71	.185	.286	.377	88	-3	0	1	-1	.982	-4	O-37,1-10	-1.0
1986	Mil-A	134	466	75	108	17	3	33	86	72	179	.232	.338	.494	119	12	5	2	0	.974	8	*O-131/1-4	1.5
1987	Mil-A	134	474	71	113	15	2	28	80	86	186	.238	.361	.456	112	9	12	4	1	.974	8	*O-123,1-12/D-4	1.3
1988	Mil-A	135	492	71	124	24	0	23	85	51	153	.252	.331	.441	113	8	9	5	-0	.990	7	*O-133/D-1	1.1
1989	Mil-A	130	466	72	98	18	2	26	65	60	158	.210	.306	.425	105	2	4	8	-4	.972	5	*O-125/D-5	0.0
1990	Mil-A	134	440	57	92	15	1	27	69	64	147	.209	.315	.432	108	4	2	3	-1	.970	9	*O-117,1-21/D-1	0.8
1991	Det-A	134	448	64	80	14	2	25	64	89	175	.179	.315	.386	91	-5	1	3	-2	.978	11	*O-132/D-2	0.2
1992	Det-A	110	393	66	97	20	1	32	64	51	131	.247	.338	.547	143	21	4	2	0	.983	5	*O-106/D-2	2.4
1993	Det-A	90	323	48	70	11	0	14	39	38	120	.217	.305	.381	84	-8	3	2	-0	.975	5	O-86/D-4	-0.5
	Bos-A	38	143	18	28	6	1	7	16	20	49	.196	.303	.399	82	-4	2	0	1	.970	5	O-36/D-2	0.1
	Yr	128	466	66	98	17	1	21	55	58	169	.210	.304	.386	83	-12	5	2	0	.973	9	*O-122/D-6	-0.4
1996	SD-N	25	50	9	9	3	0	4	9	14	30	.180	.359	.480	126	2	0	0	0	1.000	-2	O-18	0.0
Total	11	1155	3881	578	853	148	13	230	600	575	1409	.220	.325	.442	108	40	43	31	-6	.977	56	*O-1053/1-47,D-21	6.1

■ CHARLIE DEES
Dees, Charles Henry b: 6/24/35, Birmingham, Ala. BL/TL, 6'1", 173 lbs. Deb: 5/26/63

YEAR	TM/L	G	AB	R	H	2B	3B	HR	RBI	BB	SO	AVG	OBP	SLG	PRO+	BR/A	SB	CS	SBR	FA	FR	G/POS	TPR
1963	LA-A	60	202	23	62	11	1	3	27	11	31	.307	.367	.416	126	7	3	3	-1	.986	-2	1-56	0.2
1964	LA-A	26	26	3	2	1	0	0	1	1	4	.077	.143	.115	-30	-5	1	2	-1	.981	0	1-12	-0.6
1965	Cal-A	12	32	1	5	0	0	0	1	1	8	.156	.182	.156	-3	-4	1	2	-1	.986	-1	/1-8	-0.7
Total	3	98	260	27	69	12	1	3	29	13	43	.265	.323	.354	95	-2	5	7	-3	.986	-3	/1-76	-1.1

■ TONY DeFATE
DeFate, Clyde Herbert b: 2/22/1895, Kansas City, Mo. d: 9/3/63, New Orleans, La. BR/TR, 5'8.5", 158 lbs. Deb: 4/18/17

YEAR	TM/L	G	AB	R	H	2B	3B	HR	RBI	BB	SO	AVG	OBP	SLG	PRO+	BR/A	SB	CS	SBR	FA	FR	G/POS	TPR
1917	StL-N	14	14	0	2	0	0	0	1	4	5	.143	.333	.143	50	-1	0			1.000	-1	/3-5,2-1	-0.1
	Det-A	3	2	1	0	0	0	0	0	0	1	.000	.000	.000	-99	-0	0			1.000	-0	/2-1	-0.1
Total	1	17	16	1	2	0	0	0	1	4	6	.125	.300	.125	33	-1	0			1.000	-1	/3-5,2-2	-0.2

YEAR	TM/L	G	AB	R	H	2B	3B	HR	RBI	BB	SO	AVG	OBP	SLG	PRO+	BR/A	SB	CS	SBR	FA	FR	G/POS	TPR
■ ARTURO DeFREITAS	DeFreitas, Arturo Marcelino (Simon) b: 4/26/53, San Pedro De Macoris, D.R. BR/TR, 6'2", 195 lbs. Deb: 9/7/78																						
1978	Cin-N	9	19	1	4	1	0	1	2	1	4	.211	.250	.421	84	-1	0	0	0	1.000	0	/1-6	-0.1
1979	Cin-N	23	34	2	7	2	0	0	4	0	16	.206	.206	.265	27	-3	0	0	0	.974	-1	/1-6,O-1	-0.5
Total	2	32	53	3	11	3	0	1	6	1	20	.208	.222	.321	47	-4	0	0	0	.988	-1	/1-12,O-1	-0.6
■ RUBE DeGROFF	DeGroff, Edward Arthur b: 9/2/1879, Hyde Park, N.Y. d: 12/17/55, Poughkeepsie, N.Y. BL , 5'11", Deb: 9/22/05																						
1905	StL-N	15	56	3	14	2	1	0	5	5		.250	.311	.321	91	-1	1			.909	0	O-15	-0.1
1906	StL-N	1	4	1	0	0	0	0	0	0		.000	.000	.000	-99	-1	0			.000	-0	/O-1	-0.2
Total	2	16	60	4	14	2	1	0	5	5		.233	.292	.300	80	-2	1			.909	-0	/O-16	-0.3
■ HERMAN DEHLMAN	Dehlman, Herman J. "Dutch" b: 1852, Brooklyn, N.Y. d: 3/13/1885, Wilkes-Barre, Pa. Deb: 5/2/1872																						
1872	Atl-n	37	165	30	36	3	1	0	14	3	1	.218	.232	.248	41	-14	4	2	0	.928	-1	*1-37	-1.0
1873	Atl-n	54	221	50	52	4	1	0	17	9	7	.235	.265	.262	64	-7	5	0	2	.929	-4	*1-54/S-1	-0.5
1874	Atl-n	53	218	40	49	3	1	0	18	7	5	.225	.249	.248	68	-6	2	0	1	.944	-1	*1-53	-0.5
1875	StL-n	67	254	42	57	12	2	0	14	**11**	21	.224	.257	.287	98	1	23	9	2	**.955**	1	*1-67/O-2	0.3
1876	StL-N	64	245	40	45	6	0	0	9	9	10	.184	.213	.208	43	-13				.958	0	*1-64	-1.3
1877	StL-N	32	119	24	22	4	0	0	11	7	21	.185	.230	.218	44	-7				.931	-3	1-31/O-1	-0.9
Total	4 n	211	858	162	194	22	5	0	63	30	34	.226	.252	.263	68	-26	34	11	4	.941	-5	1-211/O-2,S-1	-1.7
Total	2	96	364	64	67	10	0	0	20	16	31	.184	.218	.212	43	-20				.950	-3	/1-95,O-1	-2.2
■ JIM DEIDEL	Deidel, James Lawrence b: 6/6/49, Denver, Col. BR/TR, 6'2", 195 lbs. Deb: 5/31/74																						
1974	NY-A	2	2	0	0	0	0	0	0	0	0	.000	.000	.000	-99	-1	0	0	0	1.000	1	/C-2	0.1
■ PEP DEININGER	Deininger, Otto Charles b: 10/10/1877, Wasseralfingen, Germany d: 9/25/50, Boston, Mass. BL/TL, 5'8.5", 180 lbs. Deb: 4/26/02																						
1902	Bos-A	2	6	0	2	1	1	0	0	0		.333	.333	.833	210	1	0			1.000	-1	/P-2	0.0
1908	Phi-N	1	0	0	0	0	0	0	0	0		—	—	—	—	0	0			.000	-1	/O-1	-0.1
1909	Phi-N	55	169	22	44	9	0	0	16	11		.260	.309	.314	93	-2	5			.989	-2	O-45/2-1	-0.6
Total	3	58	175	22	46	10	1	0	16	11		.263	.310	.331	97	-1	5			.989	-3	/O-46,P-2,2-1	-0.7
■ PAT DEISEL	Deisel, Edward b: 4/29/1876, Ripley, Ohio d: 4/17/48, Cincinnati, Ohio BR/TR, 5'5 ", 145 lbs. Deb: 8/21/02																						
1902	Bro-N	1	3	0	2	0	0	0	1	1		.667	.800	.667	350	1	0			1.000	0	/C-1	0.1
1903	Cin-N	2	0	0	0	0	0	0	0	1		—	1.000	—	174	0	0			.000	0	/C-1	0.0
Total	2	3	3	0	2	0	0	0	1	2		.667	.833	.667	352	2	0			1.000	0	/C-2	0.1
■ BILL DEITRICK	Deitrick, William Alexander b: 4/20/02, Hanover Co., Va. d: 5/6/46, Bethesda, Md. BR/TR, 5'10", 160 lbs. Deb: 9/19/27																						
1927	Phi-N	5	6	1	1	0	0	0	0	0	0	.167	.167	.167	-10	-1	0			.750	-1	/S-5	-0.2
1928	Phi-N	52	100	13	20	6	0	0	7	17	10	.200	.322	.260	52	-7	1			1.000	-2	O-21/S-8	-0.9
Total	2	57	106	14	21	6	0	0	7	17	10	.198	.315	.255	49	-8	1			.895	-3	/O-21,S-13	-1.1
■ MIKE DEJAN	Dejan, Michael Dan b: 1/13/15, Cleveland, Ohio d: 2/2/53, W.Los Angeles, Cal. BL/TL, 6'1", 185 lbs. Deb: 7/13/40																						
1940	Cin-N	12	16	1	3	0	1	0	2	3	3	.188	.316	.313	73	-1	0			1.000	-0	/O-2	-0.1
■ IVAN DeJESUS	DeJesus, Ivan (Alvarez) b: 1/9/53, Santurce, P.R. BR/TR, 5'11", 175 lbs. Deb: 9/13/74																						
1974	LA-N	3	3	1	1	0	0	0	0	0	2	.333	.333	.333	91	-0	0	0	0	1.000	-1	/S-2	-0.1
1975	LA-N	63	87	10	16	2	1	0	2	11	15	.184	.276	.230	43	-7	1	2	-1	.974	7	S-63	0.3
1976	LA-N	22	41	4	7	2	1	0	2	4	9	.171	.244	.268	46	-3	0	1	-1	.950	5	S-13/3-7	0.3
1977	Chi-N	155	624	91	166	31	7	3	40	56	90	.266	.330	.353	75	-21	24	12	0	.962	**36**	*S-154	3.2
1978	Chi-N	160	619	**104**	172	24	7	3	35	74	78	.278	.357	.354	88	-8	41	12	5	.967	13	*S-160	3.1
1979	Chi-N	160	636	92	180	26	10	5	52	59	82	.283	.346	.379	89	-9	24	20	-5	.959	1	*S-160	0.5
1980	Chi-N	157	618	78	160	26	3	3	33	60	81	.259	.328	.325	77	-17	44	16	4	.969	8	*S-156	1.3
1981	Chi-N	106	403	49	78	8	4	0	13	46	61	.194	.276	.233	44	-29	21	9	1	.959	10	*S-106	-0.8
1982	Phi-N	161	536	53	128	21	5	3	59	54	70	.239	.311	.313	73	-18	14	4	2	.973	-8	*S-154/3-7	-1.0
1983	*Phi-N	158	497	60	126	15	7	4	45	53	77	.254	.325	.336	85	-10	11	4	1	.966	-14	*S-158	-0.8
1984	Phi-N	144	435	40	112	15	3	0	35	43	76	.257	.327	.306	77	-12	12	5	1	.951	-21	*S-141	-2.1
1985	*StL-N	59	72	11	16	5	0	0	7	4	16	.222	.263	.292	55	-4	2	2	-1	1.000	2	3-20,S-13	-0.2
1986	NY-A	7	4	1	0	0	0	0	0	1	1	.000	.200	.000	-40	-1	0	0	0	.900	0	/S-7	-0.1
1987	SF-N	9	10	0	2	0	0	0	1	0	2	.200	.200	.200	7	-1	0	1	-1	.840	2	/S-9	0.1
1988	Det-A	7	17	1	3	0	0	0	0	1	4	.176	.222	.176	14	-2	0	0	0	.893	1	/S-7	-0.1
Total	15	1371	4602	595	1167	175	48	21	324	466	664	.254	.324	.326	76	-142	194	88	5	.963	41	*S-1303/3-34	3.6
■ MARK DeJOHN	DeJohn, Mark Stephen b: 9/18/53, Middletown, Conn. BB/TR, 5'11", 170 lbs. Deb: 4/28/82 C																						
1982	Det-A	24	21	1	4	2	0	0	1	4	4	.190	.320	.286	68	-1	1	0	0	.978	6	S-20/3-4,2-1	0.6
■ BILL DeKONING	DeKoning, William Callahan b: 12/19/18, Brooklyn, N.Y. d: 7/26/79, Palm Harbor, Fla. BR/TR, 5'11", 185 lbs. Deb: 5/27/45																						
1945	NY-N	3	1	0	0	0	0	0	0	0	1	.000	.000	.000	-99	-0	0			1.000	-0	/C-2	0.0
■ ED DELAHANTY	Delahanty, Edward James "Big Ed" b: 10/30/1867, Cleveland, Ohio d: 7/2/03, Niagara Falls, Ont., Canada BR/TR, 6'1", 170 lbs. Deb: 5/22/1888 FH																						
1888	Phi-N	74	290	40	66	12	2	1	31	12	26	.228	.261	.293	73	-9	38			.872	-10	2-56,O-17	-1.7
1889	Phi-N	56	246	37	72	13	3	0	27	14	17	.293	.333	.370	89	-5	19			.956	-13	O-31,2-24/S-1	-1.5
1890	Cle-P	115	517	107	153	26	13	3	64	24	30	.296	.337	.414	109	5	25			.830	-7	S-76,2-20,O-18,/31	0.2
1891	Phi-N	128	543	92	132	19	9	5	86	33	50	.243	.296	.339	83	-14	25			.909	1	*O-99,1-27/2-3	-1.5
1892	Phi-N	123	477	79	146	30	**21**	6	91	31	32	.306	.360	**.495**	158	30	29			.944	10	*O-121/3-4	3.3
1893	Phi-N	132	595	145	219	35	18	**19**	**146**	47	20	.368	.423	**.583**	167	**53**	37			.948	31	*O-117,2-15/1-6	**6.3**
1894	Phi-N	114	489	147	199	39	18	4	131	60	16	.407	.478	.585	159	50	21			.925	17	*O-88,1-12/3-9,S2	4.7
1895	Phi-N	116	480	149	194	**49**	10	11	106	86	31	.404	**.500**	.617	**186**	**66**	46			.944	-0	*O-103/S-9,2-6,3-1	4.7
1896	Phi-N	123	499	131	198	**44**	17	**13**	**126**	62	22	.397	.472	**.631**	**192**	**67**	37			.952	14	*O-99,1-22/2-1	6.0
1897	Phi-N	129	530	109	200	40	15	5	96	60		.377	.444	.538	162	49	26			.970	9	*O-129/1-1	4.0
1898	Phi-N	144	548	115	183	36	9	4	92	77		.334	.426	.454	159	**46**	**58**			.964	6	*O-144	3.7
1899	Phi-N	146	581	135	**238**	**55**	9	9	**137**	55		**.410**	.464	**.582**	**193**	**73**	30			.969	0	*O-143	5.6
1900	Phi-N	131	539	82	174	32	10	2	109	41		.323	.378	.430	124	17	16			.981	-3	*1-130	1.2
1901	Phi-N	139	542	106	192	**38**	16	8	108	65		.354	.427	.528	173	51	29			.949	-4	O-84,1-58	3.8
1902	Was-A	123	473	103	178	**43**	14	10	93	62		**.376**	**.453**	**.590**	**186**	**56**	16			.961	2	*O-111,1-13	4.7
1903	Was-A	42	156	22	52	11	1	1	21	12		.333	.388	.436	144	9	3			.962	2	O-40/1-1	0.8
Total	16	1835	7505	1599	2596	522	185	101	1464	741	244	.346	.411	.505	152	543	455			.951	56	*O-1344,1-271,2/S3	44.3
■ FRANK DELAHANTY	Delahanty, Frank George "Pudgie" b: 1/29/1883, Cleveland, Ohio d: 7/22/66, Cleveland, Ohio BR/TR, 5'9", 160 lbs. Deb: 8/23/05 F																						
1905	NY-A	9	27	0	6	1	0	0	2	1		.222	.250	.259	55	-1	0			.932	-1	/1-5,O-3	-0.3
1906	NY-A	92	307	37	73	11	8	2	41	16		.238	.282	.345	87	-6	11			.954	3	O-86	-0.7
1907	Cle-A	15	52	3	9	0	1	0	4	4		.173	.232	.212	41	-3	2			.917	-0	O-15	-0.5
1908	NY-A	37	125	12	32	1	2	0	10	10		.256	.316	.296	98	-0	9			.957	-1	O-36	-0.3
1914	Buf-F	79	274	29	55	4	7	2	27	23	19	.201	.265	.288	50	-24	21			.976	-6	O-78	-3.5
	Pit-F	41	159	25	38	4	4	1	7	11	11	.239	.297	.333	72	-9	7			.984	-3	O-36/2-4	-1.4
	Yr	120	433	54	93	8	11	3	34	34	30	.215	.277	.305	58	-33	28			.979	-8	*O-114/2-4	-4.9
1915	Pit-F	14	42	3	10	1	0	0	3	1	0	.238	.256	.262	46	-4	0			1.000	1	O-11	-0.4
Total	6	287	986	109	223	22	22	5	94	66	30	.226	.280	.308	70	-47	50			.964	-7	O-265/1-5,2-4	-7.1
■ JIM DELAHANTY	Delahanty, James Christopher b: 6/20/1879, Cleveland, Ohio d: 10/17/53, Cleveland, Ohio BR/TR, 5'10.5", 170 lbs. Deb: 4/19/01 F																						
1901	Chi-N	17	63	4	12	2	0	0	4	3		.190	.239	.222	35	-5	5			.877	-1	3-17/2-1	-0.6
1902	NY-N	7	26	3	6	1	0	0	3	1		.231	.259	.269	64	-1	0			.917	-1	/O-7	-0.2
1904	Bos-N	142	499	56	142	27	8	3	60	27		.285	.333	.389	127	15	16			.888	1	*3-113,2-18/O-9,P-1	1.9
1905	Bos-N	125	461	50	119	11	8	5	55	28		.258	.315	.349	100	-1	12			.962	-7	*O-124/P-1	-1.5
1906	Cin-N	115	379	63	106	21	4	1	39	45		.280	.371	.364	124	12	21			.903	-19	*3-105/S-5,O-2	-0.4

YEAR	TM/L	G	AB	R	H	2B	3B	HR	RBI	BB	SO	AVG	OBP	SLG	PRO+	BR/A	SB	CS	SBR	FA	FR	G/POS	TPR
1907	StL-A	33	95	8	21	3	0	0	6	5		.221	.275	.253	68	-3	6			.889	-1	3-21/O-4,2-2	-0.4
	Was-A	108	404	44	118	18	7	2	54	36		.292	.367	.386	152	24	18			.941	-12	2-68,3-27/O-9,1-4	1.3
	Yr	141	499	52	139	21	7	2	60	41		.279	.350	.361	135	20	24			.942	-13	2-70,3-48,O-13,/1-4	0.9
1908	Was-A	83	287	33	91	11	4	1	30	24		.317	.376	.394	164	20	16			.963	3	2-80	2.5
1909	Was-A	90	302	18	67	13	5	1	21	23		.222	.290	.308	93	-3	4			.956	-3	2-85	-0.8
	*Det-A	46	150	29	38	10	1	0	20	17		.253	.364	.333	115	4	9			.943	-7	2-46	-0.5
	Yr	136	452	47	105	23	6	1	41	40		.232	.316	.316	101	2	13			.951	-10	*2-131	-1.3
1910	Det-A	106	378	67	111	16	2	3	45	43		.294	.379	.370	126	13	15			.940	-15	*2-106	-0.5
1911	Det-A	144	542	83	184	30	14	3	94	56		.339	.411	.463	137	27	15			.978	-10	1-71,2-59,3-13	1.6
1912	Det-A	79	266	34	76	14	1	0	41	42		.286	.397	.346	117	9	9			.930	-5	2-44,O-33	0.1
1914	Bro-F	74	214	28	62	13	5	0	15	25	21	.290	.372	.397	110	0	4			.957	-19	2-55/1-5	-2.0
1915	Bro-F	17	25	0	6	1	0	0	2	3	3	.240	.345	.280	77	-1	1			.857	-1	/2-4	-0.2
Total	13	1186	4091	520	1159	191	59	19	489	378	24	.283	.357	.373	122	110	151			.946	-97	2-568,3-296,O/1SP	0.3

■ **JOE DELAHANTY** Delahanty, Joseph Nicholas b: 10/18/1875, Cleveland, Ohio d: 1/9/36, Cleveland, Ohio BR/TR, 5'9", 168 lbs. Deb: 9/30/07 F

YEAR	TM/L	G	AB	R	H	2B	3B	HR	RBI	BB	SO	AVG	OBP	SLG	PRO+	BR/A	SB	CS	SBR	FA	FR	G/POS	TPR
1907	StL-N	7	22	3	7	0	0	1	2	0		.318	.318	.455	147	1	3			.933	-1	/O-7	0.0
1908	StL-N	140	499	37	127	14	11	1	44	32		.255	.309	.333	110	5	11			.977	-5	*O-138	-0.6
1909	StL-N	123	411	28	88	16	4	2	54	42		.214	.292	.287	85	-7	10			.985	-16	O-63,2-48	-3.0
Total	3	270	932	68	222	30	15	4	100	74		.238	.301	.315	100	-2	24			.978	-21	O-208/2-48	-3.6

■ **TOM DELAHANTY** Delahanty, Thomas James b: 3/9/1872, Cleveland, Ohio d: 1/10/51, Sanford, Fla. BL/TR, 5'8", 175 lbs. Deb: 9/29/1894 F

YEAR	TM/L	G	AB	R	H	2B	3B	HR	RBI	BB	SO	AVG	OBP	SLG	PRO+	BR/A	SB	CS	SBR	FA	FR	G/POS	TPR
1894	Phi-N	1	4	0	1	0	0	0	0	0	1	.250	.250	.250	21	-1	0			.875	0	/2-1	0.0
1896	Cle-N	16	56	11	13	4	0	0	4	8	4	.232	.338	.304	66	-3	4			.823	-1	3-16	-0.3
	Pit-N	1	3	1	1	0	0	0	0	0	0	.333	.333	.333	79	-0	0			.750	-0	/S-1	0.0
	Yr	17	59	12	14	4	0	0	4	8	4	.237	.338	.305	67	-3	4			.823	-2	3-16/S-1	-0.3
1897	Lou-N	1	4	1	1	1	0	0	2	0		.250	.250	.500	99	-0	0			.333	-2	/2-1	-0.2
Total	3	19	67	13	16	5	0	0	6	8	5	.239	.329	.313	66	-3	4			.727	-4	/3-16,2-2,S-1	-0.5

■ **MIKE de la HOZ** de la Hoz, Miguel Angel (Piloto) b: 10/2/38, Havana, Cuba BR/TR, 5'11", 175 lbs. Deb: 7/22/60

YEAR	TM/L	G	AB	R	H	2B	3B	HR	RBI	BB	SO	AVG	OBP	SLG	PRO+	BR/A	SB	CS	SBR	FA	FR	G/POS	TPR
1960	Cle-A	49	160	20	41	6	2	6	23	9	12	.256	.300	.431	98	-1	0	0	0	.950	-15	S-38/3-8	-1.3
1961	Cle-A	61	173	20	45	10	0	3	23	7	10	.260	.297	.370	79	-6	0	0	0	.969	3	2-17,S-17,3-16	0.0
1962	Cle-A	12	12	0	1	0	0	0	0	0	3	.083	.083	.083	-57	-3	0	0	0	1.000	-0	/2-2	-0.3
1963	Cle-A	67	150	15	40	10	0	5	25	9	29	.267	.313	.433	107	1	0	0	0	.962	4	2-34/3-6,S-2,O-2	0.9
1964	Mil-N	78	189	25	55	7	1	4	12	14	22	.291	.346	.402	109	2	1	1	-0	.968	-4	2-25,3-25/S-8	0.0
1965	Mil-N	81	176	15	45	3	2	2	11	8	21	.256	.296	.330	75	-6	0	1	-1	.963	-10	S-41,3-22,2-10,/1-1	-1.6
1966	Atl-N	71	110	11	24	3	0	2	7	5	18	.218	.252	.300	52	-7	0	1	-1	.950	-2	3-30/2-8,S-1	-1.1
1967	Atl-N	74	143	10	29	3	0	3	14	4	14	.203	.224	.287	46	-10	1	0	0	1.000	-4	2-23,3-22/S-1	-1.5
1969	Cin-N	1	1	0	0	0	0	0	0	0	1	.000	.000	.000	-95	-0	0	0	0	.000	0	H	0.0
Total	9	494	1114	116	280	42	5	25	115	56	130	.251	.292	.365	82	-29	2	3	-1	.936	-28	3-129,2-119,S/O1	-4.9

■ **BILL DeLANCEY** DeLancey, William Pinkney b: 11/28/11, Greensboro, N.C. d: 11/28/46, Phoenix, Ariz. BL/TR, 5'11.5", 185 lbs. Deb: 9/11/32

YEAR	TM/L	G	AB	R	H	2B	3B	HR	RBI	BB	SO	AVG	OBP	SLG	PRO+	BR/A	SB	CS	SBR	FA	FR	G/POS	TPR
1932	StL-N	8	26	1	5	0	2	0	2	2	1	.192	.250	.346	57	-2	0			.930	1	/C-8	-0.1
1934	*StL-N	93	253	41	80	18	3	13	40	41	37	.316	.414	.565	150	18	1			.980	5	C-77	2.5
1935	StL-N	103	301	37	84	14	5	6	41	42	34	.279	.369	.419	107	4	0			.971	-2	C-83	0.6
1940	StL-N	15	18	0	4	0	0	0	2	0	2	.222	.222	.222	22	-2	0			.929	1	C-12	0.0
Total	4	219	598	79	173	32	10	19	85	85	74	.289	.380	.472	121	19	1			.972	4	C-180	3.0

■ **BILL DELANEY** Delaney, William L. b: 3/4/1863, Cincinnati, O. d: 3/1/42, Canton, Ohio BR/TR, Deb: 8/21/1890

YEAR	TM/L	G	AB	R	H	2B	3B	HR	RBI	BB	SO	AVG	OBP	SLG	PRO+	BR/A	SB	CS	SBR	FA	FR	G/POS	TPR
1890	Cle-N	36	116	16	22	1	1	1	7	21	19	.190	.314	.241	64	-5	5			.926	-10	2-36	-1.1

■ **JESUS de la ROSA** de la Rosa, Jesus (b: Jesus De Los Santos (De La Rosa)) b: 8/5/53, Santo Domingo, D.R. BR/TR, 6'1", 153 lbs. Deb: 8/2/75

YEAR	TM/L	G	AB	R	H	2B	3B	HR	RBI	BB	SO	AVG	OBP	SLG	PRO+	BR/A	SB	CS	SBR	FA	FR	G/POS	TPR
1975	Hou-N	3	3	1	1	1	0	0	0	0	0	.333	.333	.667	186	0	0	0	0	.000	0	H	0.0

■ **ALEX DELGADO** Delgado, Alexander b: 1/11/71, Palmerejo, Venez. BR/TR, 6', 160 lbs. Deb: 4/4/96

YEAR	TM/L	G	AB	R	H	2B	3B	HR	RBI	BB	SO	AVG	OBP	SLG	PRO+	BR/A	SB	CS	SBR	FA	FR	G/POS	TPR
1996	Bos-A	26	20	5	5	0	0	0	1	3	3	.250	.348	.250	54	-1	0	0	0	.889	-2	C-14/O-6,3-4,1-1,2	-0.3

■ **CARLOS DELGADO** Delgado, Carlos Juan (Hernandez) b: 6/25/72, Mayaguez, P.R. BL/TR, 6'3", 220 lbs. Deb: 10/1/93

YEAR	TM/L	G	AB	R	H	2B	3B	HR	RBI	BB	SO	AVG	OBP	SLG	PRO+	BR/A	SB	CS	SBR	FA	FR	G/POS	TPR
1993	Tor-A	2	1	0	0	0	0	0	0	1	0	.000	.500	.000	47	0	0	0	0	1.000	0	/C-1,D-1	0.0
1994	Tor-A	43	130	17	28	2	0	9	24	25	46	.215	.354	.438	103	1	1	1	-0	.966	-4	O-41/C-1	-0.4
1995	Tor-A	37	91	7	15	3	0	3	11	6	26	.165	.216	.297	32	-9	0	0	0	1.000	1	O-17/1-4,D-7	-0.9
1996	Tor-A	138	488	68	132	28	2	25	92	58	139	.270	.359	.490	112	9	0	0	0	.983	-2	*D-108,1-27	-0.3
1997	Tor-A	153	519	79	136	42	3	30	91	64	133	.262	.352	.528	125	18	0	3	-2	.988	-4	*1-119,D-32	-0.2
1998	Tor-A	142	530	94	155	43	1	38	115	73	139	.292	.389	.592	151	40	3	0	1	.992	-3	*1-141/D-1	2.2
Total	6	515	1759	265	466	118	6	105	333	227	483	.265	.359	.518	123	57	4	4	-1	.990	-13	1-291,D-149/O-58,C	0.4

■ **PUCHY DELGADO** Delgado, Luis Felipe (Robles) b: 2/2/54, Hatillo, P.R. BB/TL, 5'11", 170 lbs. Deb: 9/6/77

YEAR	TM/L	G	AB	R	H	2B	3B	HR	RBI	BB	SO	AVG	OBP	SLG	PRO+	BR/A	SB	CS	SBR	FA	FR	G/POS	TPR
1977	Sea-A	13	22	4	4	0	0	0	2	1	8	.182	.217	.182	10	-3	0	0	0	1.000	-2	O-13	-0.5

■ **WILSON DELGADO** Delgado, Wilson (Duran) b: 7/15/75, San Cristobal, D.R. BB/TR, 5'11", 165 lbs. Deb: 9/24/96

YEAR	TM/L	G	AB	R	H	2B	3B	HR	RBI	BB	SO	AVG	OBP	SLG	PRO+	BR/A	SB	CS	SBR	FA	FR	G/POS	TPR
1996	SF-N	6	22	3	8	0	0	0	2	1	5	.364	.440	.364	120	1	1	0	0	.960	-2	/S-6	0.0
1997	SF-N	8	7	1	1	1	0	0	0	0	2	.143	.143	.286	9	-1	0	0	0	1.000	0	/2-3,S-1	-0.1
1998	SF-N	10	12	1	2	1	0	0	1	1	3	.167	.231	.250	26	-1	0	0	0	1.000	0	/S-6	-0.1
Total	3	24	41	5	11	2	0	0	3	2	10	.268	.333	.317	74	-1	1	0	0	.971	-2	/S-13,2-3	-0.2

■ **BOBBY Del GRECO** Del Greco, Robert George b: 4/7/33, Pittsburgh, Pa. BR/TR, 5'11", 190 lbs. Deb: 4/16/52

YEAR	TM/L	G	AB	R	H	2B	3B	HR	RBI	BB	SO	AVG	OBP	SLG	PRO+	BR/A	SB	CS	SBR	FA	FR	G/POS	TPR
1952	Pit-N	99	341	34	74	14	2	1	20	38	70	.217	.301	.279	60	-18	6	5	-1	.977	6	O-93	-1.8
1956	Pit-N	14	20	4	4	0	0	2	3	3	3	.200	.304	.500	114	0	0	0	0	1.000	-2	/O-7,3-3	-0.2
	StL-N	102	270	29	58	16	2	5	18	32	50	.215	.312	.344	76	-9	1	1	-0	.987	-9	O-99	-2.3
	Yr	116	290	33	62	16	2	7	21	35	53	.214	.311	.355	79	-8	1	1	-0	.987	-10	*O-106/3-3	-2.5
1957	Chi-N	20	40	2	8	2	0	0	3	10	17	.200	.360	.250	69	-1	1	0	0	.967	-2	O-16	-0.3
	NY-A	8	7	3	3	0	0	0	0	2	2	.429	.556	.429	175	1	1	0	0	1.000	-2	/O-6	-0.1
1958	NY-A	12	5	1	1	0	0	0	0	1	1	.200	.333	.200	52	-0	0	1	-1	1.000	-4	O-12	-0.5
1960	Phi-N	100	300	48	71	16	4	10	26	54	64	.237	.355	.417	110	5	1	5	-3	.970	12	O-89	1.0
1961	Phi-N	41	112	14	29	5	0	2	11	12	17	.259	.346	.357	88	-2	0	0	0	1.000	1	O-32/2-1,3-1	-0.2
	KC-A	74	239	34	55	14	1	5	21	30	31	.230	.319	.360	79	-7	1	0	0	.983	5	O-73	-0.5
1962	KC-A	132	338	61	86	21	1	9	38	49	62	.254	.370	.402	103	3	4	1	1	.984	0	*O-124	-0.2
1963	KC-A	121	306	40	65	7	1	8	29	40	52	.212	.313	.320	74	-10	1	2	-1	.981	-6	*O-110/3-2	-2.3
1965	Phi-N	8	4	1	0	0	0	0	0	0	3	.000	.000	.000	-99	-1	0	0	0	.000	-1	/O-4	-0.2
Total	9	731	1982	271	454	95	11	42	169	271	372	.229	.331	.352	84	-38	16	15	-4	.981	-2	O-665/3-6,2-1	-7.6

■ **JUAN DELIS** Delis, Juan Francisco b: 2/27/28, Santiago De Cuba, Cuba BR/TR, 5'11", 170 lbs. Deb: 4/16/55

YEAR	TM/L	G	AB	R	H	2B	3B	HR	RBI	BB	SO	AVG	OBP	SLG	PRO+	BR/A	SB	CS	SBR	FA	FR	G/POS	TPR
1955	Was-A	54	132	12	25	3	1	0	11	3	15	.189	.219	.227	21	-15	1	2	-1	.918	-2	3-24/O-8,2-1	-1.8

■ **EDDIE DELKER** Delker, Edward Alberts b: 4/17/06, Palo Alto, Pa. d: 5/14/97, Pottsville, Pa. BR/TR, 5'10.5", 170 lbs. Deb: 4/28/29

YEAR	TM/L	G	AB	R	H	2B	3B	HR	RBI	BB	SO	AVG	OBP	SLG	PRO+	BR/A	SB	CS	SBR	FA	FR	G/POS	TPR
1929	StL-N	22	40	5	6	0	1	0	3	2	12	.150	.227	.200	7	-6	0			.750	-2	/S-9,2-7,3-3	-0.7
1931	StL-N	1	2	0	1	1	0	0	2	0	0	.500	.500	1.000	283	0	0			1.000	-0	/3-1	0.0
1932	StL-N	20	42	1	5	4	0	0	2	8	7	.119	.260	.214	28	-4	0			1.000	4	2-10/3-5,S-4	0.1
	Phi-N	30	62	7	10	1	1	1	7	6	14	.161	.235	.258	29	-6	0			.925	-2	2-27	-0.7
	Yr	50	104	8	15	5	1	1	9	14	21	.144	.246	.240	29	-11	0			.946	3	2-37/3-5,S-4	-0.6
1933	Phi-N	25	41	6	7	3	1	0	1	0	12	.171	.171	.293	27	-4	0			.968	6	2-17/3-4	0.3
Total	4	98	187	19	29	9	3	1	15	16	45	.155	.229	.251	26	-20	0			.952	6	/2-61,3-13,S-13	-1.0

YEAR	TM/L	G	AB	R	H	2B	3B	HR	RBI	BB	SO	AVG	OBP	SLG	PRO+	BR/A	SB	CS	SBR	FA	FR	G/POS	TPR
■ DAVE DELLUCCI	Dellucci, David Michael b: 10/31/73, Baton Rouge, La. BL/TL, 5'10", 180 lbs. Deb: 6/3/97																						
1997	Bal-A	17	27	3	6	1	0	1	3	4	7	.222	.344	.370	89	-0	0	0	0	1.000	1	/O-9,D-5	0.1
1998	Ari-N	124	416	43	108	19	**12**	5	51	33	103	.260	.319	.399	84	-10	3	5	-2	.987	1	*O-117	-1.2
Total	2	141	443	46	114	20	12	6	54	37	110	.257	.320	.397	85	-10	3	5	-2	.988	2	O-126/D-5	-1.1
■ BERT DELMAS	Delmas, Albert Charles b: 5/20/11, San Francisco, Cal d: 12/4/79, Huntington Beach, Cal. BL/TR, 5'11", 165 lbs. Deb: 9/10/33																						
1933	Bro-N	12	28	4	7	0	0	0	0	1	7	.250	.276	.250	53	-2	0			.912	-3	2-10	-0.5
■ LUIS de los SANTOS	de los Santos, Luis Manuel (Martinez) b: 12/29/66, San Cristobal, D.R. BR/TR, 6'5", 205 lbs. Deb: 9/7/88																						
1988	KC-A	11	22	1	2	1	1	0	1	4	4	.091	.231	.227	29	-2	0	0	0	1.000	-0	/1-5,D-3	-0.3
1989	KC-A	28	87	6	22	3	1	0	6	5	14	.253	.293	.310	71	-3	0	0	0	.986	0	1-27	-0.5
1991	Det-A	16	30	1	5	2	0	0	0	2	4	.167	.219	.233	25	-3	0	0	0	1.000	-0	/O-3,1-2,3-2,D-9	-0.4
Total	3	55	139	8	29	6	2	0	7	11	22	.209	.267	.281	53	-9	0	0	0	.988	-1	/1-34,D-12,O-3,3-2	-1.2
■ GARTON Del SAVIO	Del Savio, Garton Orville b: 11/26/13, New York, N.Y. BR/TR, 5'9.5", 165 lbs. Deb: 4/24/43																						
1943	Phi-N	4	11	0	1	0	0	0	0	1	0	.091	.167	.091	-26	-2	0			.857	0	/S-4	-0.1
■ JIM DELSING	Delsing, James Henry b: 11/13/25, Rudolph, Wis. BL/TR, 5'10", 175 lbs. Deb: 4/21/48																						
1948	Chi-A	20	63	5	12	0	0	0	5	5	12	.190	.261	.190	22	-7	0	0	0	1.000	-1	O-15	-0.9
1949	NY-A	9	20	5	7	1	0	1	3	1	2	.350	.381	.550	145	1	0	0	0	1.000	-2	/O-5	-0.1
1950	NY-A	12	10	2	4	0	0	0	2	2	0	.400	.500	.400	137	1	0	0	0	.000	0	H	0.1
	StL-A	69	209	25	55	5	2	0	15	20	23	.263	.328	.306	61	-12	1	4	-2	.994	2	O-53	-1.4
	Yr	81	219	27	59	5	2	0	17	22	23	.269	.336	.311	65	-11	1	4	-2	.994	2	O-53	-1.3
1951	StL-A	131	449	59	112	20	2	8	45	56	39	.249	.338	.356	85	-9	2	9	-5	.983	9	*O-124	-0.9
1952	StL-A	93	298	34	76	13	6	1	34	25	29	.255	.323	.349	85	-6	3	3	-1	.986	-1	O-85	-1.1
	Det-A	33	113	14	31	2	1	3	15	11	8	.274	.344	.389	103	0	1	0	0	.958	-0	O-32	-0.1
	Yr	126	411	48	107	15	7	4	49	36	37	.260	.329	.360	90	-6	4	3	-1	.979	-1	*O-117	-1.2
1953	Det-A	138	479	77	138	26	6	11	62	66	39	.288	.380	.436	121	15	1	3	-2	.992	-2	*O-133	0.7
1954	Det-A	122	371	39	92	24	2	6	38	49	38	.248	.337	.372	96	-2	4	4	-1	**.996**	-0	*O-108	-0.8
1955	Det-A	114	356	49	85	15	2	10	60	48	40	.239	.331	.376	92	-4	2	0	1	.995	-5	*O-101	-1.3
1956	Det-A	10	12	0	0	0	0	0	0	3	3	.000	.250	.000	-29	-2	0	0	0	1.000	-1	/O-3	-0.3
	Chi-A	55	41	11	5	3	0	0	2	10	13	.122	.294	.195	31	-4	1	0	0	.957	-8	O-29	-1.2
	Yr	65	53	11	5	3	0	0	2	13	16	.094	.284	.151	17	-6	1	0	0	.962	-8	O-32	-1.5
1960	KC-A	16	40	2	10	3	0	0	5	3	5	.250	.302	.325	69	-2	0	0	0	1.000	1	O-10	-0.1
Total	10	822	2461	322	627	112	21	40	286	299	251	.255	.340	.366	91	-31	15	23	-9	.989	-8	O-698	-7.4
■ JOE DeMAESTRI	DeMaestri, Joseph Paul "Oats" b: 12/9/28, San Francisco, Cal. BR/TR, 6', 174 lbs. Deb: 4/19/51																						
1951	Chi-A	56	74	8	15	0	2	1	3	5	11	.203	.253	.297	49	-6	0	4	-2	.959	6	S-27,2-11/3-8	-0.1
1952	StL-A	81	186	13	42	9	1	1	18	8	25	.226	.258	.301	54	-12	0	1	-1	.939	2	S-77/2-1,3-1	-0.7
1953	Phi-A	111	420	53	107	17	3	6	35	24	39	.255	.297	.352	72	-17	0	1	-1	.964	-16	*S-108	-2.7
1954	Phi-A	146	539	49	124	16	3	8	40	20	63	.230	.262	.315	57	-33	1	4	-2	.965	-6	*S-142/2-1,3-1	-3.0
1955	KC-A	123	457	42	114	14	1	6	37	20	47	.249	.285	.324	63	-25	3	5	-2	.964	-12	*S-122	-2.9
1956	KC-A	133	434	41	101	16	1	6	39	25	73	.233	.279	.316	57	-28	3	3	-1	.964	6	*S-132/2-2	-1.3
1957	KC-A☆	135	461	44	113	14	6	9	33	22	82	.245	.282	.360	73	-18	6	1	1	**.980**	-7	*S-134	-1.2
1958	KC-A	139	442	32	97	11	1	6	38	16	84	.219	.248	.290	47	-32	1	0	0	**.980**	11	*S-137	-1.0
1959	KC-A	118	352	31	86	16	5	6	34	28	65	.244	.307	.369	83	-8	1	0	0	.957	5	*S-115	0.6
1960	*NY-A	49	35	8	8	1	0	0	2	0	9	.229	.229	.257	33	-3	0	0	0	.952	7	2-19,S-17	0.4
1961	NY-A	30	41	1	6	0	0	0	2	0	13	.146	.146	.146	-23	-7	0	0	0	.981	7	S-18/2-5,3-4	0.1
Total	11	1121	3441	322	813	114	23	49	281	168	511	.236	.275	.325	62	-190	15	19	-7	.967	4	*S-1029/2-39,3-14	-11.8
■ FRANK DEMAREE	Demaree, Joseph Franklin (b: Joseph Franklin Dimaria) b: 6/10/10, Winters, Cal. d: 8/30/58, Los Angeles, Cal. BR/TR, 5'11.5", 185 lbs. Deb: 7/22/32																						
1932	*Chi-N	23	56	4	14	3	0	0	6	2	7	.250	.288	.304	60	-3	0			1.000	-1	O-17	-0.5
1933	Chi-N	134	515	68	140	24	6	6	51	22	42	.272	.304	.377	94	-5	4			.965	0	*O-133	-1.2
1935	*Chi-N	107	385	60	125	19	4	2	66	26	23	.325	.369	.410	108	5	6			.973	-2	O-98	0.0
1936	Chi-N★	154	605	93	212	34	3	16	96	49	30	.350	.400	.496	137	31	4			.968	-2	*O-154	2.2
1937	Chi-N★	154	615	104	199	36	6	17	115	57	31	.324	.382	.485	129	24	6			.980	2	*O-154	2.0
1938	*Chi-N	129	476	63	130	15	7	8	62	45	34	.273	.341	.384	96	-2	1			.972	-8	*O-125	-1.4
1939	NY-N	150	560	68	170	27	2	11	79	66	40	.304	.381	.418	114	12	2			.986	-1	*O-150	0.6
1940	NY-N	121	460	68	139	18	6	7	61	45	39	.302	.364	.413	113	9	5			.980	-6	*O-119	-0.3
1941	NY-N	16	35	3	6	0	0	0	1	4	1	.171	.256	.171	22	-4	0			1.000	-0	O-10	-0.5
	Bos-N	48	113	20	26	5	2	2	15	12	5	.230	.304	.363	91	-2	2			1.000	-4	O-28	-0.7
	Yr	64	148	23	32	5	2	2	16	16	6	.216	.293	.318	74	-5	2			1.000	-5	O-38	-1.2
1942	Bos-N	64	187	18	42	5	0	3	24	17	10	.225	.289	.299	74	-6	2			1.000	4	O-49	-0.6
1943	*StL-N	39	86	5	25	2	0	0	9	8	4	.291	.351	.314	89	-1	1			1.000	-3	O-23	-0.6
1944	StL-A	16	51	4	13	2	0	0	6	6	3	.255	.333	.294	76	-1	0	0	0	.969	-1	O-16	-0.3
Total	12	1155	4144	578	1241	190	36	72	591	359	269	.299	.357	.415	110	57	33	0		.978	-22	*O-1076	-1.3
■ BILLY DeMARS	DeMars, William Lester "Kid" b: 8/26/25, Brooklyn, N.Y. BR/TR, 5'10", 160 lbs. Deb: 5/18/48 C																						
1948	Phi-A	18	29	3	5	0	0	0	1	5	3	.172	.294	.172	26	-3	0	0	0	.927	4	/S-9,2-1,3-1	0.1
1950	StL-A	61	178	25	44	5	1	0	13	22	13	.247	.330	.287	57	-11	0	1	-1	.933	-7	S-54/3-5	-1.4
1951	StL-A	1	4	1	1	0	0	0	0	1	0	.250	.400	.250	76	-0	0	0	0	1.000	-0	/S-1	0.0
Total	3	80	211	29	50	5	1	0	14	28	16	.237	.326	.270	53	-14	0	1	-1	.933	-4	/S-64,3-6,2-1	-1.3
■ JOHN DeMERIT	DeMerit, John Stephen "Thumper" b: 1/8/36, West Bend, Wis. BR/TR, 6'1.5", 195 lbs. Deb: 6/18/57																						
1957	*Mil-N	33	34	8	5	0	0	0	1	0	8	.147	.147	.147	-22	-6	1	0	0	1.000	-3	O-13	-0.9
1958	Mil-N	3	3	1	2	0	0	0	0	0	0	.667	.667	.667	278	1	0	0	0	1.000	-1	/O-2	0.0
1959	Mil-N	11	5	4	1	0	0	0	0	1	2	.200	.333	.200	51	-0	0	0	0	1.000	-0	/O-4	-0.1
1961	Mil-N	32	74	5	12	3	0	2	5	5	19	.162	.225	.284	36	-7	0	0	0	1.000	0	O-21	-0.8
1962	NY-N	14	16	3	3	0	0	1	1	2	4	.188	.278	.375	72	-1	0	0	0	1.000	-3	/O-9	-0.4
Total	5	93	132	21	23	3	0	3	7	8	33	.174	.227	.265	32	-13	1	0	0	1.000	-6	/O-49	-2.2
■ DON DEMETER	Demeter, Donald Lee b: 6/25/35, Oklahoma City, Okla BR/TR, 6'4", 190 lbs. Deb: 9/18/56																						
1956	Bro-N	3	3	1	1	0	0	1	1	0	1	.333	.333	1.333	297	1	0	0	0	1.000	-0	/O-1	0.0
1958	LA-N	43	106	11	20	2	0	5	8	5	32	.189	.225	.349	48	-8	2	3	-1	1.000	-4	O-39	-1.6
1959	*LA-N	139	371	55	95	11	1	18	70	16	87	.256	.298	.437	86	-8	5	6	-2	.983	6	*O-124	-2.1
1960	LA-N	64	168	23	46	7	1	9	29	8	34	.274	.311	.488	108	1	0	1	-1	.989	-8	O-62	-1.0
1961	LA-N	15	29	3	5	0	0	1	2	3	6	.172	.250	.276	36	-3	0	0	0	.950	-1	O-14	-0.4
	Phi-N	106	382	54	98	18	4	20	68	19	74	.257	.300	.482	105	1	2	1	0	.995	6	O-79,1-22	0.1
	Yr	121	411	57	103	18	4	21	70	22	80	.251	.297	.467	99	-2	2	1	0	.990	5	O-93,1-22	-0.3
1962	Phi-N	153	550	85	169	24	3	29	107	41	93	.307	.366	.520	139	29	2	7	-4	.937	-13	*3-105,O-63/1-1	1.0
1963	Phi-N	154	515	63	133	20	2	22	83	31	93	.258	.308	.433	112	7	1	4	-2	**1.000**	-7	*O-119,3-43,1-26	-0.8
1964	Det-A	134	441	57	113	22	1	22	80	17	85	.256	.292	.460	104	0	4	1	1	1.000	-2	O-88,1-23	-0.6
1965	Det-A	122	389	50	108	16	4	16	58	23	65	.278	.328	.463	121	9	4	2	0	.988	-2	O-82,1-34	0.3
1966	Det-A	32	99	12	21	5	0	5	12	3	19	.212	.235	.414	81	-3	1	0	0	.985	5	O-27/1-4	0.1
	Bos-A	73	226	31	66	13	1	9	29	5	42	.292	.310	.478	111	2	1	0	0	.982	-2	O-57/1-2	-0.1
	Yr	105	325	43	87	18	1	14	41	8	61	.268	.287	.458	102	-0	2	0	1	.984	3	O-84/1-6	0.0
1967	Bos-A	20	43	7	12	5	0	1	4	3	11	.279	.326	.465	122	1	0	0	0	1.000	-1	O-12/3-1	0.0
	Cle-A	51	121	15	25	4	0	5	12	6	16	.207	.256	.364	80	-3	0	0	0	.985	-2	O-35/3-1	-0.7
	Yr	71	164	22	37	9	0	6	16	9	27	.226	.274	.390	92	-2	0	0	0	.988	-3	O-47/3-2	-0.7
Total	11	1109	3443	467	912	147	17	163	563	180	658	.265	.309	.459	108	26	22	25	-8	.990	-37	O-802,3-150,1-112	-5.8

YEAR	TM/L	G	AB	R	H	2B	3B	HR	RBI	BB	SO	AVG	OBP	SLG	PRO+	BR/A	SB	CS	SBR	FA	FR	G/POS	TPR
■ STEVE DEMETER Demeter, Stephen b: 1/27/35, Homer City, Pa. BR/TR, 5'9.5", 185 lbs. Deb: 7/29/59 C																							
1959	Det-A	11	18	1	2	1	0	0	1	0	1	.111	.111	.167	-24	-3	0	0	0	.909	1	/3-4	-0.2
1960	Cle-A	4	5	0	0	0	0	0	0	0	1	.000	.000	.000	-99	-1	0	0	0	1.000	0	/3-3	-0.1
Total	2	15	23	1	2	1	0	0	1	0	2	.087	.087	.130	-40	-4	0	0	0	.933	1	/3-7	-0.3
■ RAY DEMMITT Demmitt, Charles Raymond b: 2/2/1884, Illiopolis, Ill. d: 2/19/56, Glen Ellyn, Ill. BL/TR, 5'8", 170 lbs. Deb: 4/12/09																							
1909	NY-A	123	427	68	105	12	12	4	30	55		.246	.340	.358	120	11	16			.908	5	*O-109	1.3
1910	StL-A	10	23	4	4	1	0	0	2	3		.174	.296	.217	65	-1	0			1.000	1	/O-8	0.0
1914	Det-A	1	0	0	0	0	0	0	0	0	0	—	—	—	0	0	0			.000	0	R	0.0
	Chi-A	146	515	63	133	13	12	2	46	61	48	.258	.344	.342	108	6	12	20	-8	.953	-5	*O-142	-1.6
	Yr	147	515	63	133	13	12	2	46	61	48	.258	.344	.342	108	6	12	20	-8	.953	-5	*O-142	-1.6
1915	Chi-A	9	6	0	0	0	0	0	0	1	2	.000	.143	.000	-55	-1	0			1.000	-1	/O-3	-0.2
1917	StL-A	14	53	6	15	1	2	0	7	0	8	.283	.296	.377	109	0	1			1.000	-3	O-14	-0.4
1918	StL-A	116	405	45	114	23	5	1	61	38	35	.281	.346	.370	120	9	10			.951	7	*O-114	1.1
1919	StL-A	79	202	19	48	11	2	1	19	14	27	.238	.290	.327	71	-8	3			.868	-7	O-49	-2.0
Total	7	498	1631	205	419	61	33	8	165	172	120	.257	.334	.349	108	16	42	20		.934	-3	O-439	-1.8
■ GENE DeMONTREVILLE DeMontreville, Eugene Napoleon b: 3/26/1874, St.Paul, Minn. d: 2/18/35, Memphis, Tenn. BR/TR, 5'8", 165 lbs. Deb: 8/20/1894 F																							
1894	Pit-N	2	8	0	2	0	0	0	0	1	4	.250	.333	.250	43	-1	0			.889	-1	/S-2	-0.1
1895	Was-N	12	46	7	10	1	3	0	9	3	4	.217	.265	.370	63	-3	5			.929	4	S-12	0.1
1896	Was-N	133	533	94	183	24	5	8	77	29	27	.343	.381	.452	119	13	28			.890	16	*S-133	2.8
1897	Was-N	133	566	92	193	27	8	3	93	21		.341	.366	.433	111	7	30			.886	10	*S-99,2-33	1.8
1898	Bal-N	151	567	93	186	19	2	0	86	52		.328	.394	.369	117	14	49			.944	0	*2-123,S-28	2.2
1899	Chi-N	82	310	43	87	6	3	0	40	17		.281	.328	.319	80	-8	26			.902	9	S-82	0.7
	Bal-N	60	240	40	67	13	4	1	36	10		.279	.313	.379	85	-6	21			.961	9	2-60	0.5
	Yr	142	550	83	154	19	7	1	76	27		.280	.322	.345	82	-14	47			.902	18	S-82,2-60	1.2
1900	Bro-N	69	234	34	57	8	1	0	28	10		.244	.283	.286	54	-15	21			.952	0	2-48,S-12/3-7,O1	-1.1
1901	Bos-N	140	577	83	173	14	4	5	72	17		.300	.321	.364	90	-9	25			**.954**	5	*2-120,3-20	0.1
1902	Bos-N	124	481	51	125	16	5	0	53	12		.260	.278	.314	82	-12	23			.940	-17	*2-112,S-10	-2.5
1903	Was-A	12	44	0	12	0	0	0	3	0		.273	.273	.318	75	-1	0			.931	-4	2-11/S-1	-0.6
1904	StL-A	4	9	0	1	0	0	0	0	2		.111	.273	.111	25	-1	0			1.000	-1	/2-3	-0.1
Total	11	922	3615	537	1096	130	35	17	497	174	35	.303	.340	.373	97	-21	228			.948	31	2-510,S-379/31O	3.8
■ LEE DeMONTREVILLE DeMontreville, Leon b: 9/23/1875, Washington Co., Minn. d: 3/22/62, Pelham Manor, N.Y. BR/TR, 5'7", 140 lbs. Deb: 7/10/03 F																							
1903	StL-N	26	70	8	17	3	1	0	7	8		.243	.338	.314	89	-1	3			.901	-3	S-15/2-4,O-1	-0.3
■ RICK DEMPSEY Dempsey, John Rikard b: 9/13/49, Fayetteville, Tenn. BR/TR, 6', 190 lbs. Deb: 9/23/69																							
1969	Min-A	5	6	1	3	1	0	0	0	1	0	.500	.571	.667	240	1	0	0	0	.833	-1	/C-3	0.0
1970	Min-A	5	7	1	0	0	0	0	0	1	1	.000	.125	.000	-62	-2	0	0	0	.923	0	/C-3	-0.2
1971	Min-A	6	13	2	4	1	0	0	0	1	1	.308	.357	.385	107	0	0	0	0	.944	2	/C-6	0.2
1972	Min-A	25	40	0	8	1	0	0	0	6	8	.200	.304	.225	56	-2	0	0	0	.986	-1	C-23	-0.3
1973	NY-A	6	11	0	2	0	0	0	0	1	3	.182	.250	.182	24	-1	0	0	0	.818	-2	/C-5	-0.3
1974	NY-A	43	109	12	26	3	0	2	12	8	7	.239	.291	.321	77	-3	1	0	0	.978	4	C-31/O-2,D-1	0.2
1975	NY-A	71	145	18	38	8	0	1	11	21	15	.262	.355	.338	98	0	0	0	0	.977	3	C-19,D-18/O-8,3-1	0.3
1976	NY-A	21	42	1	5	0	0	0	2	5	4	.119	.213	.119	-1	-5	0	0	0	1.000	2	/C-9,O-4	-0.3
	Bal-A	59	174	11	37	2	0	0	10	13	17	.213	.275	.224	50	-11	1	1	-0	.987	5	C-58/O-3	-0.5
	Yr	80	216	12	42	2	0	0	12	18	21	.194	.263	.204	40	-16	1	1	-0	.988	7	C-67/O-7	-0.8
1977	Bal-A	91	270	27	61	7	4	3	34	34	34	.226	.317	.315	78	-8	2	3	-1	.977	-2	C-91	-0.9
1978	Bal-A	136	441	41	114	25	0	6	32	48	54	.259	.331	.356	99	-0	7	3	0	.985	-5	*C-135	-0.1
1979	*Bal-A	124	368	48	88	23	0	6	41	38	37	.239	.310	.351	81	-10	0	1	-1	.990	19	*C-124	1.2
1980	Bal-A	119	362	51	95	26	3	9	40	36	45	.262	.334	.425	108	4	3	1	0	.987	9	*C-112/O-6,1-2,D-1	1.7
1981	Bal-A	92	251	24	54	10	1	6	15	32	36	.215	.306	.335	85	-5	0	1	-1	**.998**	3	C-90/D-1	0.1
1982	Bal-A	125	344	35	88	15	1	5	36	46	37	.256	.344	.349	91	-3	0	3	-2	.991	0	*C-124/D-1	0.0
1983	*Bal-A	128	347	33	80	16	2	4	32	40	54	.231	.315	.323	78	-10	1	1	-0	**.997**	21	*C-128	1.5
1984	Bal-A	109	330	37	76	11	0	11	34	40	58	.230	.315	.364	89	-5	1	2	-1	.992	-4	*C-108	-0.5
1985	Bal-A	132	362	54	92	19	0	12	52	50	87	.254	.346	.406	108	5	0	1	-1	.987	-11	*C-131	0.0
1986	Bal-A	122	327	42	68	15	1	13	29	45	78	.208	.309	.379	87	-6	1	0	0	.990	5	*C-121	0.6
1987	Cle-A	60	141	16	25	10	0	1	9	23	29	.177	.297	.270	51	-10	0	0	0	.984	1	C-59	-0.5
1988	*LA-N	77	167	25	42	13	0	7	30	25	44	.251	.349	.455	133	7	1	0	0	.989	5	C-74	1.7
1989	LA-N	79	151	16	27	7	0	4	16	30	37	.179	.319	.305	80	-3	1	0	0	.984	3	C-62	0.3
1990	LA-N	62	128	13	25	5	0	2	15	23	29	.195	.318	.281	68	-5	1	0	0	.992	0	C-53	-0.2
1991	Mil-A	61	147	15	34	5	0	4	21	23	20	.231	.335	.347	91	-1	0	2	-1	.993	4	C-56/P-2,1-1	0.4
1992	Bal-A	8	9	2	1	0	0	0	0	2	1	.111	.273	.111	11	-1	0	0	0	1.000	-1	/C-8	-0.2
Total	24	1766	4692	525	1093	223	12	96	471	592	736	.233	.321	.347	88	-72	20	19	-5	.988	59	*C-1633/O-23,D1P3	4.2
■ TOD DENNEHEY Dennehey, Thomas Francis b: 5/12/1899, Philadelphia, Pa. d: 8/8/77, Philadelphia, Pa. BL/TL, 5'10", 180 lbs. Deb: 4/21/23																							
1923	Phi-N	9	24	4	7	2	0	0	2	1	3	.292	.320	.375	74	-1	0	0	0	1.000	-1	/O-9	-0.2
■ OTTO DENNING Denning, Otto George "Dutch" b: 12/28/12, Hays, Kan. d: 5/25/92, Chicago, Ill. BR/TR, 6', 180 lbs. Deb: 4/15/42																							
1942	Cle-A	92	214	15	45	14	0	1	19	18	14	.210	.275	.290	62	-11	0	0	0	**.992**	-2	C-78/O-2	-0.9
1943	Cle-A	37	129	8	31	6	0	0	13	5	1	.240	.269	.287	67	-6	3	1	0	.966	-3	1-34	-1.2
Total	2	129	343	23	76	20	0	1	32	23	15	.222	.272	.289	64	-17	3	1	0	**.99**	-6	/C-78,1-34,O-2	-2.1
■ JERRY DENNY Denny, Jeremiah Dennis (b: Jeremiah Dennis Eldridge) b: 3/16/1859, New York, N.Y. d: 8/16/27, Houston, Tex. BR/TR, 5'11.5", 180 lbs. Deb: 5/2/1881																							
1881	Pro-N	85	320	38	77	16	2	1	24	5	44	.241	.252	.313	78	-8				.840	6	*3-85	-0.1
1882	Pro-N	84	329	54	81	10	9	2	42	4	46	.246	.255	.350	92	-3				.861	13	*3-84	1.0
1883	Pro-N	98	393	73	108	26	8	8	55	9	48	.275	.291	.443	116	6				**.876**	10	*3-98	1.4
1884	*Pro-N	110	439	57	109	22	9	6	59	14	58	.248	.272	.380	105	2				.874	-2	*3-99/1-9,2-3,C-1	-0.1
1885	Pro-N	83	318	40	71	14	4	3	24	12	53	.223	.252	.321	87	-5				.869	-0	*3-83	-0.3
1886	StL-N	119	475	58	122	24	6	9	62	14	68	.257	.278	.389	108	4	16			.895	23	*3-117/S-3	2.6
1887	Ind-N	122	510	86	165	34	12	11	97	13	22	.324	.344	.502	137	23	29			.889	23	*3-116/S-4,O-1,2-1	4.0
1888	Ind-N	126	524	92	137	27	7	12	63	9	79	.261	.277	.408	114	6	32			.894	25	*3-96,S-25/2-5,OP	3.2
1889	Ind-N	133	578	96	163	24	0	18	112	27	63	.282	.314	.417	101	-2	22			**.913**	12	*3-123/2-7,S-5	1.3
1890	NY-N	114	437	50	93	18	7	3	42	28	62	.213	.270	.307	68	-19	11			.889	5	*3-106/S-7,2-1	-0.9
1891	NY-N	4	16	0	4	1	0	0	1	0	3	.250	.250	.313	66	-1	2			.700	-3	/3-4	-0.3
	Cle-N	36	138	17	31	5	0	0	21	12	23	.225	.291	.261	59	-7	3			.884	-3	3-29/O-7	-0.8
	Phi-N	19	73	5	21	1	1	0	11	4	6	.288	.325	.329	88	-1	1			.977	-1	1-12/3-7	-0.2
	Yr	59	227	22	56	7	1	0	33	16	32	.247	.299	.286	69	-9	6			.876	-8	3-40,1-12/O-7	-1.3
1893	Lou-N	44	175	22	43	5	4	1	22	9	15	.246	.283	.337	70	-8	4			.920	1	S-42/3-2	-0.5
1894	Lou-N	60	221	26	61	11	7	0	32	13	12	.276	.325	.389	77	-9	10			.874	3	3-60	-0.5
Total	13	1237	4946	714	1286	238	76	74	667	173	602	.260	.287	.384	98	-23	130			.882	109	*3-1109/S-86,12OPC	9.8
■ DREW DENSON Denson, Andrew b: 11/16/65, Cincinnati, Ohio BB/TR, 6'5", 210 lbs. Deb: 9/13/89																							
1989	Atl-N	12	36	1	9	1	0	0	5	3	9	.250	.308	.278	67	-1	1	0	0	.988	2	1-12	0.0
1993	Chi-A	4	5	0	1	0	0	0	0	0	2	.200	.200	.200	8	-1	0	0	0	.800	-0	/1-3	-0.1
Total	2	16	41	1	10	1	0	0	5	3	11	.244	.295	.268	60	-2	1	0	0	.977	2	/1-15	-0.1
■ BUCKY DENT Dent, Russell Earl (b: Russell Earl O'Dey) b: 11/25/51, Savannah, Ga. BR/TR, 5'11", 181 lbs. Deb: 6/1/73 MC																							
1973	Chi-A	40	117	17	29	2	0	0	10	10	18	.248	.313	.265	62	-6	2	3	-1	.963	5	S-36/2-3,3-1	0.3
1974	Chi-A	154	496	55	136	15	3	5	45	28	48	.274	.317	.347	89	-7	3	4	-2	.972	9	*S-154	2.0

YEAR	TM/L	G	AB	R	H	2B	3B	HR	RBI	BB	SO	AVG	OBP	SLG	PRO+	BR/A	SB	CS	SBR	FA	FR	G/POS	TPR
1975	Chi-A★	157	602	52	159	29	4	3	58	36	48	.264	.306	.341	81	-15	2	4	-2	**.981**	27	*S-157	2.7
1976	Chi-A	158	562	44	138	18	4	2	52	43	45	.246	.301	.302	77	-16	3	5	-2	.976	-6	*S-158	-0.5
1977	*NY-A	158	477	54	118	18	4	8	49	39	28	.247	.306	.352	80	-14	1	1	-0	.974	-11	*S-158	-0.8
1978	*NY-A	123	379	40	92	11	1	5	40	23	24	.243	.290	.317	72	-14	3	1	0	.981	-8	*S-123	-0.7
1979	NY-A	141	431	47	99	14	2	2	32	37	30	.230	.292	.285	58	-25	0	0	0	.977	32	*S-141	2.2
1980	*NY-A★	141	489	57	128	26	2	5	52	48	37	.262	.330	.354	89	-7	0	3	-2	**.982**	13	*S-141	2.1
1981	NY-A★	73	227	20	54	11	0	7	27	19	17	.238	.302	.379	97	-1	0	1	-1	.970	-2	S-73	0.4
1982	NY-A	59	160	11	27	1	1	0	9	8	11	.169	.208	.188	10	-20	0	0	0	.962	17	S-58	0.2
	Tex-A	46	146	16	32	9	0	1	14	13	10	.219	.283	.301	64	-7	0	0	0	.980	-2	S-45	-0.5
	Yr	105	306	27	59	10	1	1	23	21	21	.193	.245	.242	35	-27	0	0	0	.970	15	*S-103	-0.3
1983	Tex-A	131	417	36	99	15	2	2	34	23	31	.237	.279	.297	60	-23	3	7	-3	**.979**	-8	*S-129/D-1	-2.2
1984	KC-A	11	9	2	3	0	0	0	1	1	2	.333	.400	.333	105	0	0	0	0	1.000	-1	/S-9,3-2	0.0
Total	12	1392	4512	451	1114	169	23	40	423	328	349	.247	.300	.321	74	-155	17	29	-12	.976	66	*S-1382/3-3,2-3,D-1	5.2

■ SAM DENTE
Dente, Samuel Joseph "Blackie" b: 4/26/22, Harrison, N.J. BR/TR, 5'11", 175 lbs. Deb: 7/10/47

YEAR	TM/L	G	AB	R	H	2B	3B	HR	RBI	BB	SO	AVG	OBP	SLG	PRO+	BR/A	SB	CS	SBR	FA	FR	G/POS	TPR
1947	Bos-A	46	168	14	39	4	2	0	11	19	15	.232	.310	.280	60	-9	0	1	-1	.939	-3	3-46	-1.3
1948	StL-A	98	267	26	72	11	2	0	22	22	8	.270	.328	.326	72	-11	1	3	-2	.958	-2	S-76/3-6	-1.0
1949	Was-A	153	590	48	161	24	4	1	53	31	24	.273	.309	.332	71	-26	4	4	-1	.957	-9	*S-153	-2.6
1950	Was-A	155	603	56	144	20	5	2	59	39	19	.239	.286	.299	52	-45	1	1	-0	.952	1	*S-128,2-29	-3.1
1951	Was-A	88	273	21	65	8	1	0	29	25	10	.238	.302	.275	58	-16	3	0	1	.962	3	S-65,2-10/3-5	-0.7
1952	Chi-A	62	145	12	32	0	1	0	11	5	8	.221	.257	.234	37	-12	0	0	0	.942	2	S-27,3-18/2-6,O1	-0.9
1953	Chi-A	2	0	0	0	0	0	0	0	0	0	—	—	—	—	0	0	0	0	.000	0	/S-1	0.0
1954	*Cle-A	68	169	18	45	7	1	1	19	14	4	.266	.322	.337	79	-5	0	0	0	.971	-3	S-60/2-7	-0.4
1955	Cle-A	73	105	10	27	4	0	0	10	12	8	.257	.333	.295	68	-4	0	0	0	.976	7	S-53,3-13/2-4	0.5
Total	9	745	2320	205	585	78	16	4	214	167	96	.252	.303	.305	62	-128	9	9	-3	.958	-5	S-563/3-88,2-56,O1	-9.5

■ MIKE DePANGHER
DePangher, Michael Anthony b: 9/11/1858, Marysville, Cal. d: 7/7/15, San Francisco, Cal BL , 5'8", 190 lbs. Deb: 8/8/1884

YEAR	TM/L	G	AB	R	H	2B	3B	HR	RBI	BB	SO	AVG	OBP	SLG	PRO+	BR/A	SB	CS	SBR	FA	FR	G/POS	TPR
1884	Phi-N	4	10	0	2	0	0	0	0	1	3	.200	.273	.200	54	-0				.920	1	/C-4	0.0

■ TONY DePHILLIPS
DePhillips, Anthony Andrew b: 9/20/12, New York, N.Y. d: 5/5/94, Port Jefferson, N.Y. BR/TR, 6'2", 185 lbs. Deb: 4/25/43

YEAR	TM/L	G	AB	R	H	2B	3B	HR	RBI	BB	SO	AVG	OBP	SLG	PRO+	BR/A	SB	CS	SBR	FA	FR	G/POS	TPR
1943	Cin-N	35	20	0	2	1	0	0	2	1	5	.100	.143	.150	-16	-3	0			.981	5	C-35	0.3

■ GENE DERBY
Derby, Eugene A. b: 2/3/1860, Fitchburg, Mass. d: 9/13/17, Waterbury, Conn. 5'7", 160 lbs. Deb: 9/3/1885

YEAR	TM/L	G	AB	R	H	2B	3B	HR	RBI	BB	SO	AVG	OBP	SLG	PRO+	BR/A	SB	CS	SBR	FA	FR	G/POS	TPR
1885	Bal-a	10	31	4	4	0	0	0	2	1		.129	.182	.129	-1	-3				.952	1	/C-9,O-1	-0.2

■ BOB DERNIER
Dernier, Robert Eugene b: 1/5/57, Kansas City, Mo. BR/TR, 6', 165 lbs. Deb: 9/7/80

YEAR	TM/L	G	AB	R	H	2B	3B	HR	RBI	BB	SO	AVG	OBP	SLG	PRO+	BR/A	SB	CS	SBR	FA	FR	G/POS	TPR
1980	Phi-N	10	7	5	4	0	0	0	1	1	0	.571	.625	.571	224	1	3	0	1	1.000	0	/O-3	0.3
1981	Phi-N	10	4	0	3	0	0	0	0	0	0	.750	.750	.750	313	1	2	1	0	1.000	-2	/O-5	-0.1
1982	Phi-N	122	370	56	92	10	2	4	21	36	69	.249	.317	.319	77	-11	42	12	5	.981	-0	*O-119	-0.9
1983	*Phi-N	122	221	41	51	10	0	1	15	18	21	.231	.289	.290	61	-11	35	7	6	.988	-11	*O-107	-1.9
1984	*Chi-N	143	536	94	149	26	5	3	32	63	60	.278	.356	.362	94	-3	45	17	3	.986	5	*O-140	0.1
1985	Chi-N	121	469	63	119	20	3	1	21	40	44	.254	.316	.316	70	-18	31	8	5	.972	9	*O-116	-0.9
1986	Chi-N	108	324	32	73	14	1	4	18	22	41	.225	.275	.312	57	-19	27	2	7	.987	1	*O-105	-1.4
1987	Chi-N	93	199	38	63	4	4	8	21	19	19	.317	.379	.497	125	7	16	7	1	.989	-12	O-71	-0.5
1988	Phi-N	68	166	19	48	3	1	1	10	9	19	.289	.330	.337	90	-2	13	6	0	.980	-4	O-54	-0.8
1989	Phi-N	107	187	26	32	5	0	1	13	14	28	.171	.229	.214	27	-18	4	3	-1	.970	-13	O-74	-3.5
Total	10	904	2483	374	634	92	16	23	152	222	301	.255	.318	.333	77	-73	218	63	28	.982	-26	O-794	-9.6

■ MARK DeROSA
DeRosa, Mark Thomas b: 2/26/75, Passaic, N.J. BR/TR, 6'1", 185 lbs. Deb: 9/2/98

YEAR	TM/L	G	AB	R	H	2B	3B	HR	RBI	BB	SO	AVG	OBP	SLG	PRO+	BR/A	SB	CS	SBR	FA	FR	G/POS	TPR
1998	Atl-N	5	3	2	1	0	0	0	0	0	1	.333	.333	.333	72	-0	0	0	0	1.000	-0	/S-4	0.0

■ CLAUD DERRICK
Derrick, Claud Lester "Deek" b: 6/11/1886, Burton, Ga. d: 7/15/74, Clayton, Ga. BR/TR, 6', 175 lbs. Deb: 9/8/10

YEAR	TM/L	G	AB	R	H	2B	3B	HR	RBI	BB	SO	AVG	OBP	SLG	PRO+	BR/A	SB	CS	SBR	FA	FR	G/POS	TPR
1910	Phi-A	2	1	0	0	0	0	0	0	0		.000	.000	.000	-99	-0	0			.500	-0	/S-1	-0.1
1911	Phi-A	36	100	14	23	1	2	0	5	7		.230	.294	.280	61	-5	7			.960	1	2-21/S-6,1-3,3-2	-0.5
1912	Phi-A	21	58	7	14	0	1	0	7	5		.241	.313	.276	71	-2	1			.884	1	S-18	0.0
1913	NY-A	23	65	7	19	1	0	1	7	5	8	.292	.352	.354	106	1	2			.874	0	S-17/3-4,2-1	0.2
1914	Cin-N	3	6	2	2	1	0	0	1	0	0	.333	.333	.500	142	0	1			.889	0	/S-2	0.1
	Chi-N	28	96	5	21	3	1	0	13	5	13	.219	.257	.271	57	-5	2			.895	3	/S-28	-0.1
	Yr	31	102	7	23	4	1	0	14	5	13	.225	.262	.284	62	-5	3			.894	3	S-30	0.0
Total	5	113	326	35	79	6	4	1	33	22	21	.242	.298	.294	72	-12	13			.892	4	/S-72,2-22,3-6,1-3	-0.4

■ MIKE DERRICK
Derrick, James Michael b: 9/19/43, Columbia, S.C. BL/TR, 6', 190 lbs. Deb: 4/9/70

YEAR	TM/L	G	AB	R	H	2B	3B	HR	RBI	BB	SO	AVG	OBP	SLG	PRO+	BR/A	SB	CS	SBR	FA	FR	G/POS	TPR
1970	Bos-A	24	33	3	7	1	0	0	5	0	11	.212	.212	.242	23	-3	0	1	-1	1.000	0	/O-2,1-1	-0.4

■ RUSS DERRY
Derry, Alva Russell b: 10/7/16, Princeton, Mo. BL/TR, 6'1", 180 lbs. Deb: 7/4/44

YEAR	TM/L	G	AB	R	H	2B	3B	HR	RBI	BB	SO	AVG	OBP	SLG	PRO+	BR/A	SB	CS	SBR	FA	FR	G/POS	TPR
1944	NY-A	38	114	14	29	3	0	4	14	20	19	.254	.366	.386	111	2	1	0	0	.949	-1	O-28	0.0
1945	NY-A	78	253	37	57	6	2	13	45	31	49	.225	.312	.419	107	1	1	0	0	.978	0	O-68	-0.2
1946	Phi-A	69	184	17	38	8	5	0	14	27	54	.207	.311	.304	73	-6	0	0	0	.985	4	O-50	-0.5
1949	StL-N	2	2	0	0	0	0	0	0	0	2	.000	.000	.000	-96	-1	0	0	0	.000	0	H	-0.1
Total	4	187	553	68	124	17	7	17	73	78	124	.224	.322	.373	95	-4	2	0	0	.976	3	O-146	-0.8

■ JOE DeSA
DeSa, Joseph b: 7/27/59, Honolulu, Hawaii d: 12/20/86, San Juan, P.R. BL/TL, 5'11", 170 lbs. Deb: 9/6/80

YEAR	TM/L	G	AB	R	H	2B	3B	HR	RBI	BB	SO	AVG	OBP	SLG	PRO+	BR/A	SB	CS	SBR	FA	FR	G/POS	TPR
1980	StL-N	7	11	0	3	0	0	0	0	0	2	.273	.273	.273	51	-1	0	0	0	1.000	-0	/1-1,O-1	-0.1
1985	Chi-A	28	44	5	8	2	0	2	7	3	6	.182	.234	.364	58	-3	0	0	0	1.000	1	/1-9,O-1,D-4	-0.2
Total	2	35	55	5	11	2	0	2	7	3	8	.200	.241	.345	57	-3	0	0	0	1.000	1	/1-10,D-4,O-2	-0.3

■ GENE DESAUTELS
Desautels, Eugene Abraham "Red" b: 6/13/07, Worcester, Mass. d: 11/5/94, Flint, Mich. BR/TR, 5'11", 170 lbs. Deb: 6/22/30

YEAR	TM/L	G	AB	R	H	2B	3B	HR	RBI	BB	SO	AVG	OBP	SLG	PRO+	BR/A	SB	CS	SBR	FA	FR	G/POS	TPR
1930	Det-A	42	126	13	24	4	2	0	9	7	9	.190	.239	.254	25	-15	2	0	1	.996	9	C-42	-0.2
1931	Det-A	3	11	1	1	0	0	0	1	0	1	.091	.091	.091	-50	-2	0	0	0	1.000	-1	/C-3	-0.3
1932	Det-A	28	72	8	17	2	0	0	2	13	11	.236	.360	.264	62	-4	0	0	0	.984	4	C-24	0.2
1933	Det-A	30	42	5	6	1	0	0	4	4	6	.143	.234	.167	8	-6	0	0	0	.976	2	C-30	-0.2
1937	Bos-A	96	305	33	74	10	3	0	27	36	26	.243	.325	.295	55	-20	1	2	-1	**.993**	4	C-94	-1.2
1938	Bos-A	108	333	47	97	16	2	2	48	57	31	.291	.396	.369	89	-4	1	1	-0	.985	6	*C-108	0.6
1939	Bos-A	76	226	26	55	14	0	0	21	33	13	.243	.340	.305	64	-12	3	1	0	.994	10	C-73	0.2
1940	Bos-A	71	222	19	50	7	1	0	17	32	13	.225	.328	.266	54	-14	0	1	-1	.992	-3	C-70	-1.2
1941	Cle-A	66	189	20	38	5	1	1	17	14	12	.201	.260	.254	38	-17	1	0	0	.997	6	C-66	-0.6
1942	Cle-A	62	162	14	40	5	0	0	9	12	13	.247	.303	.278	68	-7	1	0	0	.975	-8	C-61	-1.1
1943	Cle-A	68	185	14	38	6	0	0	19	11	16	.205	.250	.249	49	-12	2	0	1	.982	2	C-66	-0.7
1945	Cle-A	10	9	1	1	0	0	0	0	1	1	.111	.200	.111	-9	-1	0	0	0	1.000	0	C-10	-0.1
1946	Phi-A	52	130	10	28	3	1	0	13	12	16	.215	.282	.254	51	-8	1	1	-0	.989	2	C-52	-0.5
Total	13	712	2012	211	469	73	11	3	187	232	168	.233	.315	.285	57	-122	12	6	0	.989	31	C-699	-5.1

■ DELINO DeSHIELDS
DeShields, Delino Lamont b: 1/15/69, Seaford, Del. BL/TR, 6'1", 170 lbs. Deb: 4/9/90

YEAR	TM/L	G	AB	R	H	2B	3B	HR	RBI	BB	SO	AVG	OBP	SLG	PRO+	BR/A	SB	CS	SBR	FA	FR	G/POS	TPR
1990	Mon-N	129	499	69	144	28	6	4	45	66	96	.289	.376	.393	116	13	42	22	-1	.981	-8	*2-128	0.7
1991	Mon-N	151	563	83	134	15	4	10	51	95	151	.238	.350	.332	94	-1	56	23	3	.962	-22	*2-148	-1.7
1992	Mon-N	135	530	82	155	19	8	7	56	54	108	.292	.361	.398	116	12	46	15	5	.976	-22	*2-134	-0.3
1993	Mon-N	123	481	75	142	17	7	2	29	72	64	.295	.390	.372	101	4	43	10	7	.983	-1	*2-123	1.4
1994	LA-N	89	320	51	80	11	3	2	33	54	53	.250	.358	.322	85	-6	27	7	4	.986	6	2-88,S-10	0.8
1995	*LA-N	127	425	66	109	18	3	8	37	63	83	.256	.354	.369	100	1	39	14	3	.980	1	*2-113	1.1
1996	*LA-N	154	581	75	130	12	8	5	41	53	124	.224	.290	.298	60	-34	48	11	**8**	.975	-18	*2-154	-3.4
1997	StL-N	150	572	92	169	26	**14**	11	58	55	72	.295	.360	.448	111	9	55	14	8	.972	-9	*2-147	1.7

YEAR	TM/L	G	AB	R	H	2B	3B	HR	RBI	BB	SO	AVG	OBP	SLG	PRO+	BR/A	SB	CS	SBR	FA	FR	G/POS	TPR
1998	StL-N	117	420	74	122	21	8	7	44	56	61	.290	.374	.429	109	7	26	10	2	.983	-21	*2-111/1-1	-0.4
Total	9	1175	4391	667	1185	167	61	56	394	568	812	.270	.356	.374	99	5	382	126	39	.977	-93	*2-1146/S-10,1-1	-0.1
■ **ORESTES DESTRADE** Destrade, Orestes (Cucuas) b: 5/8/62, Santiago De Cuba, Cuba BB/TR, 6'4", 210 lbs. Deb: 9/11/87																							
1987	NY-A	9	19	5	5	0	0	0	1	5	5	.263	.417	.263	87	-0	0	0	0	1.000	-0	/1-3,D-2	0.0
1988	Pit-N	36	47	2	7	1	0	1	3	5	17	.149	.231	.234	34	-4	0	0	0	1.000	-1	/1-8	-0.6
1993	Fla-N	153	569	61	145	20	3	20	87	58	130	.255	.327	.406	90	-8	0	2	-1	.987	-7	*1-152	-2.9
1994	Fla-N	39	130	12	27	4	0	5	15	19	32	.208	.318	.354	73	-5	1	0	0	.983	-3	1-37	-1.1
Total	4	237	765	80	184	25	3	26	106	87	184	.241	.322	.383	84	-17	1	2	-1	.987	-11	1-200/D-2	-4.6
■ **BOB DETHERAGE** Detherage, Robert Wayne b: 9/20/54, Springfield, Mo. BR/TR, 6', 180 lbs. Deb: 4/11/80																							
1980	KC-A	20	26	2	8	2	0	1	7	1	4	.308	.333	.500	124	1	1	1	-0	1.000	-7	O-20	-0.7
■ **GEORGE DeTORE** DeTore, George Francis b: 11/11/06, Utica, N.Y. d: 2/7/91, Utica, N.Y. BR/TR, 5'8", 170 lbs. Deb: 9/14/30 C																							
1930	Cle-A	3	12	0	2	1	0	0	2	0	2	.167	.167	.250	4	-2	0	0	0	.750	-2	/3-3	-0.3
1931	Cle-A	30	56	3	15	6	0	0	7	8	2	.268	.359	.375	88	-1	0	2	-1	.958	4	3-13,S-10/2-3	0.3
Total	2	33	68	3	17	7	0	0	9	8	4	.250	.329	.353	74	-3	0	2	-1	.929	2	/3-16,S-10,2-3	0.0
■ **DUCKY DETWEILER** Detweiler, Robert Sterling b: 2/15/19, Trumbauersville, Pa. BR/TR, 5'11", 178 lbs. Deb: 9/12/42																							
1942	Bos-N	12	44	3	14	2	1	0	5	2	7	.318	.348	.409	123	1	0			.929	-4	3-12	-0.3
1946	Bos-N	1	1	0	0	0	0	0	0	0	0	.000	.000	.000	-99	-0	0			.000	0	H	0.0
Total	2	13	45	3	14	2	1	0	5	2	7	.311	.340	.400	118	1	0			.929	-4	/3-12	-0.3
■ **CESAR DEVAREZ** Devarez, Cesar Salvatore (Santana) b: 9/22/69, San Francisco De Macoris, D.R. BR/TR, 5'10", 175 lbs. Deb: 6/2/95																							
1995	Bal-A	6	4	0	0	0	0	0	0	0	0	.000	.000	.000	-99	-1	0	0	0	1.000	1	/C-6	0.0
1996	Bal-A	10	18	3	2	0	1	0	0	1	3	.111	.158	.222	-5	-3	0	0	0	1.000	1	C-10	-0.2
Total	2	16	22	3	2	0	1	0	0	1	3	.091	.130	.182	-22	-4	0	0	0	1.000	2	/C-16	-0.2
■ **MIKE DEVEREAUX** Devereaux, Michael b: 4/10/63, Casper, Wyo. BR/TR, 6', 195 lbs. Deb: 9/2/87																							
1987	LA-N	19	54	7	12	3	0	0	4	3	10	.222	.263	.278	45	-4	3	1	0	1.000	-2	O-18	-0.6
1988	LA-N	30	43	4	5	1	0	0	2	2	10	.116	.156	.140	-15	-6	0	1	-1	1.000	-5	O-26	-1.4
1989	Bal-A	122	391	55	104	14	3	8	46	36	60	.266	.331	.379	103	1	22	11	0	.983	-4	*O-112/D-5	-0.5
1990	Bal-A	108	367	48	88	18	1	12	49	28	48	.240	.294	.392	93	-5	13	12	-3	.983	6	*O-104/D-3	-0.5
1991	Bal-A	149	608	82	158	27	10	19	59	47	115	.260	.315	.431	109	5	16	9	-1	.993	12	*O-149	1.2
1992	Bal-A	156	653	76	180	29	11	24	107	44	94	.276	.325	.464	116	11	10	8	-2	.989	5	*O-155	1.2
1993	Bal-A	131	527	72	132	31	3	14	75	43	99	.250	.308	.400	85	-12	3	3	-1	.988	2	*O-130	-1.3
1994	Bal-A	85	301	35	61	8	2	9	33	22	72	.203	.259	.332	49	-24	1	2	-1	.995	0	O-84/D-1	-2.5
1995	Chi-A	92	333	48	102	21	1	10	55	25	51	.306	.355	.465	117	7	6	6	-2	.985	3	O-90	0.6
	*Atl-N	29	55	7	14	3	0	1	8	2	11	.255	.281	.364	66	-3	2	0	1	1.000	-2	O-27	-0.4
1996	*Bal-A	127	323	49	74	11	2	8	34	34	53	.229	.306	.350	66	-17	8	2	1	.983	-19	*O-112,D-10	-3.4
1997	Tex-A	29	72	8	15	3	0	0	7	7	10	.208	.278	.250	37	-7	1	0	0	1.000	-6	O-28	-1.2
1998	LA-N	9	13	0	4	1	0	0	1	3	2	.308	.438	.385	125	1	0	1	-1	1.000	1	/O-5	0.1
Total	12	1086	3740	491	949	170	33	105	480	296	635	.254	.311	.401	91	-52	85	56	-8	.988	-8	*O-1040/D-19	-8.7
■ **JIM DEVINE** Devine, Walter James b: 10/5/1858, Brooklyn, N.Y. d: 1/11/05, Syracuse, N.Y. TL , Deb: 5/9/1883																							
1883	Bal-a	2	9	4	2	0	0	0		0		.222	.222	.222	42	-1				.500	-1	/P-2,O-1	0.0
1886	NY-N	1	3	0	0	0	0	0	0	0	1	.000	.000	.000	-99	-1	0			.000	-0	/O-1	-0.1
Total	2	3	12	4	2	0	0	0	0	0	1	.167	.167	.167	6	-1	0			—	-1	/O-2,P-2	-0.1
■ **MICKEY DEVINE** Devine, William Patrick b: 5/9/1892, Albany, N.Y. d: 10/1/37, Albany, N.Y. BR/TR, 5'10", 165 lbs. Deb: 8/2/18																							
1918	Phi-N	4	8	0	1	1	0	0	0	0	1	.125	.125	.250	13	-1	0			.909	0	/C-3	-0.1
1920	Bos-A	8	12	1	2	0	0	0	0	1	2	.167	.231	.167	7	-2	1	0	0	.955	1	/C-5	-0.1
1925	NY-N	21	33	6	9	3	0	0	4	2	3	.273	.314	.364	76	-1	0	0	0	.933	2	C-11/3-1	0.1
Total	3	33	53	7	12	4	0	0	4	3	6	.226	.268	.302	51	-4	1	0		.936	2	/C-19,3-1	0.0
■ **BERNIE DeVIVEIROS** DeViveiros, Bernard John b: 4/19/01, Oakland, Cal. d: 7/5/94, Oakland, Cal. BR/TR, 5'7", 160 lbs. Deb: 9/13/24																							
1924	Chi-A	1	1	0	0	0	0	0	0	0	0	.000	.000	.000	-99	-0	0	0	0	.333	-1	/S-1	-0.1
1927	Det-A	24	22	4	5	1	0	0	2	2	8	.227	.292	.273	46	-2	1	0	0	.913	0	S-14/3-1	-0.1
Total	2	25	23	4	5	1	0	0	2	2	8	.217	.280	.261	40	-2	1	0	0	.846	-1	/S-15,3-1	-0.2
■ **ART DEVLIN** Devlin, Arthur McArthur b: 10/16/1879, Washington, D.C. d: 9/18/48, Jersey City, N.J. BR/TR, 6', 175 lbs. Deb: 4/14/04 C																							
1904	NY-N	130	474	81	133	16	8	1	66	62		.281	.371	.354	119	13	33			.907	7	*3-130	2.5
1905	*NY-N	153	525	74	129	14	7	2	61	66		.246	.344	.310	94	-1	**59**			.932	5	*3-153	1.0
1906	NY-N	148	498	76	149	23	8	2	65	74		.299	.396	.390	142	27	54			.944	**28**	*3-148	6.5
1907	NY-N	143	491	61	136	16	2	1	54	63		.277	.376	.324	116	12	38			.940	0	*3-140/S-3	1.9
1908	NY-N	157	534	59	135	18	4	2	45	62		.253	.346	.313	106	6	19			**.947**	13	*3-157	2.8
1909	NY-N	143	491	61	130	19	8	0	56	65		.265	.362	.336	115	11	26			.934	18	*3-143	3.7
1910	NY-N	147	493	71	128	17	5	2	67	62	32	.260	.353	.327	98	1	28			.933	5	*3-147	1.0
1911	NY-N	95	260	42	71	16	2	0	25	42	19	.273	.386	.350	103	3	9			.944	2	3-79/1-6,2-6,S-6	0.6
1912	Bos-N	124	436	59	126	18	8	0	54	51	37	.289	.367	.367	99	1	11			.992	-1	1-69,S-26,3-26,/O-1	0.1
1913	Bos-N	73	210	19	48	7	5	0	12	29	17	.229	.328	.310	81	-4	8			.973	9	3-69	0.5
Total	10	1313	4412	603	1185	164	57	10	505	576	105	.269	.364	.338	109	68	285			.938	86	*3-1192/1-75,S2O	20.6
■ **JIM DEVLIN** Devlin, James Alexander b: 1849, Philadelphia, Pa. d: 10/10/1883, Philadelphia, Pa. BR/TR, 5'11", 175 lbs. Deb: 4/21/1873																							
1873	Phi-n	23	99	18	24	4	4	0	10	2	4	.242	.257	.364	79	-3	0	0	0	.938	-3	1-12/3-6,S-5,O-1	-0.4
1874	Chi-n	45	203	26	58	5	0	0	26	2	9	.286	.293	.310	93	-2	2	1	0	.930	-3	1-24,O-17/3-5	-0.3
1875	Chi-n	69	318	60	92	17	6	0	40	4	4	.289	.298	.381	133	10	6	1	1	.942	-3	1-42,P-28/O-4	0.5
1876	Lou-N	68	298	38	94	14	1	0	28	1	11	.315	.318	.369	109	-1				.941	2	*P-68/1-1	0.0
1877	Lou-N	61	268	38	72	6	3	1	27	7	27	.269	.287	.325	78	-9				.933	2	*P-61	0.0
Total	3 n	137	620	104	174	26	10	0	76	8	17	.281	.290	.355	110	5	8	2	1	.933	-6	/1-78,P-28,O-22,3S	-0.2
Total	2	129	566	76	166	20	4	1	55	8	38	.293	.303	.348	94	-10				.937	4	P-129/1-1	0.0
■ **JIM DEVLIN** Devlin, James Raymond b: 8/25/22, Plains, Pa. BL/TR, 5'11.5", 165 lbs. Deb: 4/27/44																							
1944	Cle-A	1	1	0	0	0	0	0	0	0	0	.000	.000	.000	-99	-0	0	0	0	1.000	0	/C-1	0.0
■ **REX DeVOGT** DeVogt, Rex Eugene b: 1/4/1888, Clare, Mich. d: 11/9/35, Alma, Mich. BR/TR, 5'9", 170 lbs. Deb: 4/17/13																							
1913	Bos-N	3	6	0	0	0	0	0	0	0	3	.000	.000	.000	-98	-2	0			.941	1	/C-3	0.0
■ **JOSH DEVORE** Devore, Joshua D. b: 11/13/1887, Murray City, Ohio d: 10/6/54, Chillicothe, Ohio BL/TL, 5'6", 160 lbs. Deb: 9/25/08																							
1908	NY-N	5	6	1	1	0	0	0	2	1		.167	.286	.167	43	-0	1			1.000	-1	/O-2	-0.1
1909	NY-N	22	28	6	4	1	0	0	1	2		.143	.250	.179	33	-2	3			.824	-4	O-12	-0.7
1910	NY-N	133	490	92	149	11	10	2	27	46	67	.304	.371	.380	119	12	43			.929	-12	*O-130	-0.6
1911	*NY-N	149	565	96	158	19	10	3	50	81	69	.280	.376	.365	104	6	61			.934	1	*O-149	-0.1
1912	*NY-N	106	327	66	90	14	6	2	37	51	43	.275	.381	.373	104	3	27			.918	-8	O-96	-0.9
1913	NY-N	16	21	4	4	0	1	0	1	3	4	.190	.320	.286	73	-1	6			1.000	-2	/O-8	-0.3
	Cin-N	66	217	30	58	6	4	3	14	12	21	.267	.309	.373	95	-2	17			.920	-3	O-57	-0.8
	Phi-N	23	39	9	11	1	0	0	5	4	7	.282	.364	.308	89	-0	0			.889	-3	O-14	-0.4
	Yr	105	277	43	73	7	5	3	20	19	32	.264	.318	.357	92	-3	23			.919	-9	O-79	-1.5
1914	Phi-N	30	53	5	16	2	0	0	7	4	5	.302	.351	.340	99	-0	0			.947	2	/O-9	0.2
	*Bos-N	51	128	22	29	4	0	1	5	18	14	.227	.327	.281	82	-2	2			.915	-8	O-42	-1.3
	Yr	81	181	27	45	6	0	1	12	22	19	.249	.333	.298	87	-2	2			.923	-6	O-51	-1.1
Total	7	601	1874	331	520	58	31	11	149	222	230	.277	.361	.359	103	13	160			.925	-38	O-519	-5.0

YEAR	TM/L	G	AB	R	H	2B	3B	HR	RBI	BB	SO	AVG	OBP	SLG	PRO+	BR/A	SB	CS	SBR	FA	FR	G/POS	TPR

■ AL DeVORMER   DeVormer, Albert E. b: 8/19/1891, Grand Rapids, Mich d: 8/29/66, Grand Rapids, Mich BR/TR, 6'0.5", 175 lbs. Deb: 8/4/18

1918	Chi-A	8	19	2	5	2	0	0	0	0	4	.263	.263	.368	90	-0	1			1.000	-2	/C-6,O-1	-0.2
1921	*NY-A	22	49	6	17	4	0	0	7	2	4	.347	.373	.429	102	2	0	2	0	1	.950	-1	C-17	0.1
1922	NY-A	24	59	8	12	4	1	0	11	1	6	.203	.217	.305	34	-6	0	0	0		.968	-1	C-17/1-1	-0.6
1923	Bos-A	74	209	20	54	7	3	0	18	6	21	.258	.282	.321	58	-13	3	0	1	.979	0	C-55/1-2	-0.9
1927	NY-N	68	141	14	35	3	1	2	21	11	11	.248	.312	.326	71	-6	1			.953	-4	C-54/1-3	-0.8
Total	5	196	477	50	123	20	5	2	57	20	46	.258	.292	.333	65	-25	7	0		.967	-7	C-149/1-6,O-1	-2.4

■ WALT DeVOY   DeVoy, Walter Joseph b: 3/14/1886, St.Louis, Mo. d: 12/17/53, St.Louis, Mo. BR/TR, 5'11", 165 lbs. Deb: 9/13/09

| 1909 | StL-A | 19 | 69 | 7 | 17 | 3 | 1 | 0 | 8 | 3 | | .246 | .278 | .319 | 95 | -1 | 4 | | | .944 | -2 | O-16/1-3 | -0.3 |

■ JEFF DeWILLIS   DeWillis, Jeffrey Allen b: 4/13/65, Houston, Tex. BR/TR, 6'2", 170 lbs. Deb: 4/19/87

| 1987 | Tor-A | 13 | 25 | 2 | 3 | 1 | 0 | 1 | 2 | 2 | 12 | .120 | .185 | .280 | 21 | -3 | 0 | 0 | 0 | .964 | 2 | C-13 | -0.1 |

■ CHARLIE DEXTER   Dexter, Charles Dana b: 6/15/1876, Evansville, Ind. d: 6/9/34, Cedar Rapids, Iowa BR/TR, 5'7", 155 lbs. Deb: 4/17/1896

1896	Lou-N	107	402	65	112	18	7	3	37	17	34	.279	.318	.381	87	-9	21			.903	-3	C-55,O-47	-0.8
1897	Lou-N	76	257	43	72	12	5	2	46	21		.280	.342	.389	96	-2	12			.907	-5	O-32,C-23,3-14,/S-2	-0.5
1898	Lou-N	112	421	76	132	13	5	1	66	26		.314	.363	.375	114	7	44			.958	-1	O-95/2-8,C-7	0.1
1899	Lou-N	80	295	47	76	7	1	1	33	21		.258	.318	.298	69	-12	21			.942	2	O-71/S-6	-1.3
1900	Chi-N	40	125	7	25	5	0	2	20	1		.200	.213	.288	39	-11	2			.943	8	C-22,O-13/2-1	-0.2
1901	Chi-N	116	460	46	123	9	5	1	66	16		.267	.302	.315	82	-11	22			.982	3	1-54,3-25,O-21,2/C	-0.9
1902	Chi-N	69	266	30	60	12	0	2	26	19		.226	.290	.293	82	-5	13			.853	-13	3-39,1-22,O-10	-2.0
	Bos-N	48	183	33	47	3	0	1	18	16		.257	.323	.290	88	-2	16			.901	-4	S-22,2-19/O-7,3-1	-0.4
	Yr	117	449	63	107	15	0	3	44	35		.238	.303	.292	85	-7	29			.854	-16	3-40,1-22,S-22,2O	-2.4
1903	Bos-N	123	457	82	102	15	1	3	34	61		.223	.323	.280	75	-12	32			.941	-10	*O-106/S-9,C-6	-2.7
Total	8	771	2866	429	749	94	24	16	346	198	34	.261	.318	.328	85	-57	183			.942	-22	O-402,C-116/312S	-8.7

■ ALEX DIAZ   Diaz, Alexis b: 10/5/68, Brooklyn, N.Y. BB/TR, 5'11", 180 lbs. Deb: 7/25/92

1992	Mil-A	22	9	5	1	0	0	0	1	0	0	.111	.111	.111	-38	-2	3	2	-0	1.000	-4	O-11/D-2	-0.7
1993	Mil-A	32	69	9	22	2	0	0	1	0	12	.319	.319	.348	80	-2	5	3	-0	.979	-4	O-28/D-1	-0.6
1994	Mil-A	79	187	17	47	5	7	1	17	10	19	.251	.289	.369	65	-10	5	5	-2	.993	-9	O-73/2-2,D-1	-2.0
1995	*Sea-A	103	270	44	67	14	0	3	27	13	27	.248	.288	.333	60	-16	18	8	1	.987	-7	O-88	-2.3
1996	Sea-A	38	79	11	19	2	0	1	5	2	8	.241	.277	.304	47	-6	6	3	0	.982	-1	O-28/D-1	-0.7
1997	Tex-A	28	90	8	20	4	0	2	12	5	13	.222	.271	.333	54	-6	1	1	-0	.980	1	O-23/1-1,2-1	-0.6
1998	SF-N	34	62	5	8	2	0	0	5	0	15	.129	.129	.161	-26	-11	1	1	-0	1.000	-4	O-21	-1.4
Total	7	336	766	99	184	29	7	7	68	30	94	.240	.273	.324	53	-54	39	23	-2	.988	-26	O-272/D-5,2-3,1-1	-8.3

■ BO DIAZ   Diaz, Baudilio Jose (Seijas) b: 3/23/53, Cua, Venezuela d: 11/23/90, Caracas, Venez. BR/TR, 5'11", 190 lbs. Deb: 9/6/77

1977	Bos-A	2	1	0	0	0	0	0	0	0	1	.000	.000	.000	-90	-0	0	0	0	1.000	1	/C-2	0.0
1978	Cle-A	44	127	12	30	4	0	2	11	4	17	.236	.260	.315	61	-7	0	0	0	.971	-1	C-44	-0.7
1979	Cle-A	15	32	0	5	2	0	0	1	2	6	.156	.206	.219	15	-4	0	0	0	.958	4	C-15	0.0
1980	Cle-A	76	207	15	47	11	2	3	32	7	27	.227	.252	.343	61	-12	1	0	0	.989	3	C-75	-0.6
1981	Cle-A★	63	182	25	57	19	0	7	38	13	23	.313	.362	.533	157	13	2	2	-1	.975	-3	C-51/D-3	1.1
1982	Phi-N	144	525	69	151	29	1	18	85	36	87	.288	.337	.450	116	10	3	6	-3	.989	-9	*C-144	0.4
1983	*Phi-N	136	471	49	111	17	0	15	64	38	57	.236	.295	.367	84	-11	4	-2	.986	14	*C-134	0.7
1984	Phi-N	27	75	5	16	4	0	1	9	5	13	.213	.262	.307	58	-4	0	0	0	.992	-0	C-23	-0.4
1985	Phi-N	26	76	9	16	5	1	2	16	6	7	.211	.268	.382	78	-3	0	0	0	.972	2	C-24	0.1
	Cin-N	51	161	12	42	8	0	3	15	15	18	.261	.328	.366	89	-2	0	0	0	.988	9	C-51	0.9
	Yr	77	237	21	58	13	1	5	31	21	25	.245	.309	.371	86	-5	0	0	0	.983	11	C-75	1.0
1986	Cin-N	134	474	50	129	21	0	10	56	40	52	.272	.329	.380	91	-6	1	1	-0	.984	-6	*C-134	-0.4
1987	Cin-N★	140	496	49	134	28	1	15	82	19	73	.270	.304	.421	86	-11	0	0	0	.992	-6	*C-137	-0.7
1988	Cin-N	92	315	26	69	9	0	10	35	7	41	.219	.238	.343	63	-16	0	2	-0	.990	-3	C-88	-1.5
1989	Cin-N	43	132	6	27	5	0	1	8	6	7	.205	.239	.265	43	-10	0	2	-1	.984	-0	C-43	-1.0
Total	13	993	3274	327	834	162	5	87	452	198	429	.255	.300	.387	86	-63	9	17	-8	.986	3	C-965/D-3	-2.1

■ CARLOS DIAZ   Diaz, Carlos Francisco b: 12/24/64, Elizabeth, N.J. BR/TR, 6'3", 195 lbs. Deb: 5/8/90

| 1990 | Tor-A | 9 | 3 | 1 | 1 | 0 | 0 | 0 | 0 | 0 | 2 | .333 | .333 | .333 | 85 | -0 | 0 | 0 | 0 | 1.000 | 2 | /C-9 | 0.2 |

■ EDDY DIAZ   Diaz, Eddy Javier b: 9/29/71, Barquisimeto, Venez. BR/TR, 5'10", 160 lbs. Deb: 4/17/97

| 1997 | Mil-A | 16 | 50 | 4 | 11 | 2 | 1 | 0 | 7 | 1 | 5 | .220 | .235 | .300 | 38 | -5 | 0 | 0 | 0 | 1.000 | 2 | 2-14/3-1,S-1 | -0.2 |

■ EDGAR DIAZ   Diaz, Edgar (Serrano) b: 2/8/64, Santurce, P.R. BR/TR, 6', 155 lbs. Deb: 9/16/86

1986	Mil-A	5	13	0	3	0	0	0	1	3	.231	.286	.231	41	-1	0	0	0	.875	-1	/S-5	-0.1
1990	Mil-A	86	218	27	59	2	2	0	14	21	32	.271	.338	.298	80	-5	3	2	-0	.950	-1	S-65,2-15/3-7,D-1	-0.1
Total	2	91	231	27	62	2	2	0	14	22	35	.268	.335	.294	78	-6	3	2	-0	.946	-1	/S-70,2-15,3-7,D-1	-0.2

■ EDWIN DIAZ   Diaz, Edwin (Rosario) b: 1/15/75, Bayamon, P.R. BR/TR, 5'11", 172 lbs. Deb: 3/31/98

| 1998 | Ari-N | 3 | 7 | 0 | 0 | 0 | 0 | 0 | 0 | 0 | 2 | .000 | .000 | .000 | -99 | -2 | 0 | 0 | 0 | .938 | 2 | /2-3 | 0.0 |

■ EINAR DIAZ   Diaz, Einar Antonio b: 12/28/72, Chiriqui, Panama BR/TR, 5'10", 165 lbs. Deb: 9/9/96

1996	Cle-A	4	1	0	0	0	0	0	0	0	0	.000	.000	.000	-99	-0	0	0	0	1.000	1	/C-4	0.0
1997	Cle-A	5	7	1	1	1	0	0	1	0	2	.143	.143	.286	8	-1	0	0	0	.955	2	/C-5	0.1
1998	*Cle-A	17	48	8	11	1	0	2	9	3	2	.229	.302	.357	72	-2	0	0	0	.973	3	/C-17	0.1
Total	3	26	56	9	12	2	0	2	10	3	4	.214	.279	.357	62	-3	0	0	0	.971	5	/C-26	0.2

■ MARIO DIAZ   Diaz, Mario Rafael (Torres) b: 1/10/62, Humacao, P.R. BR/TR, 5'10", 160 lbs. Deb: 9/12/87

1987	Sea-A	11	23	4	7	0	0	0	3	0	4	.304	.304	.391	79	-1	0	0	0	.972	4	S-10	0.3
1988	Sea-A	28	72	6	22	5	0	0	9	3	5	.306	.333	.375	94	-1	0	0	0	.985	-4	S-21/2-4,1-1,3-1	-0.1
1989	Sea-A	52	74	9	10	0	0	0	7	7	7	.135	.210	.176	9	-9	0	0	0	.930	-9	S-37,2-14/3-3	-1.7
1990	NY-N	16	22	0	3	1	0	0	1	0	3	.136	.136	.182	-13	-3	0	0	0	.958	2	S-10/2-1	-0.2
1991	Tex-A	96	182	24	48	7	0	1	22	15	18	.264	.320	.319	79	-5	0	1	-1	.962	-2	S-65,2-20/3-8,D-1	-0.5
1992	Tex-A	19	31	2	7	1	0	0	1	1	2	.226	.250	.258	44	-2	0	1	-1	.975	1	S-16/2-3,3-1	-0.1
1993	Tex-A	71	205	24	56	10	1	2	24	8	13	.273	.304	.361	81	-6	0	0	0	.986	-4	S-57,3-12/1-1	-0.6
1994	Fla-N	32	77	10	25	4	2	0	6	1	9	.325	.381	.429	107	1	0	0	0	.964	-3	3-11/2-7,S-7	0.1
1995	Fla-N	49	87	5	20	3	0	1	6	1	12	.230	.239	.299	41	-8	0	0	0	.944	-2	/2-9,S-5,3-3	-0.8
Total	9	374	773	84	198	31	4	5	84	41	70	.256	.295	.326	69	-33	1	2	-1	.972	-15	S-228/2-58,3-39,1D	-3.8

■ MIKE DIAZ   Diaz, Michael Anthony b: 4/15/60, San Francisco, Cal. BR/TR, 6'2", 195 lbs. Deb: 9/15/83

1983	Chi-N	6	7	2	2	1	0	0	1	0	0	.286	.286	.429	91	-0	0	0	0	1.000	-0	/C-3	-0.1
1986	Pit-N	97	209	22	56	9	0	12	36	19	43	.268	.335	.483	120	5	0	1	-0	.966	-5	O-38,1-20/3-5,C-1	-0.3
1987	Pit-N	103	241	28	58	8	2	16	48	31	42	.241	.335	.490	114	4	1	0	0	.960	-6	O-37,1-32/C-8	-0.4
1988	Pit-N	47	74	6	17	3	0	0	5	16	13	.230	.367	.270	87	-0	0	0	0	1.000	-0	O-19/1-6,C-1	-0.4
	Chi-A	40	152	12	36	6	0	3	12	5	30	.237	.266	.336	67	-7	0	1	-1	.987	-2	1-39/D-1	-1.3
Total	4	293	683	70	169	27	2	31	102	71	128	.247	.324	.429	103	2	1	2	-1	.988	-18	/1-97,O-94,C-13,3D	-2.7

■ PAUL DICKEN   Dicken, Paul Franklin b: 10/2/43, DeLand, Fla. BR/TR, 6'5", 195 lbs. Deb: 6/7/64

1964	Cle-A	11	11	0	0	0	0	0	0	0	5	.000	.000	.000	-99	-3	0	0	0	.000	0	H	-0.3
1966	Cle-A	2	2	0	0	0	0	0	0	0	1	.000	.000	.000	-99	-1	0	0	0	.000	0	H	-0.1
Total	2	13	13	0	0	0	0	0	0	0	6	.000	.000	.000	-99	-3	0	0	0		0	-0,-0	-0.4

■ BUTTERCUP DICKERSON   Dickerson, Lewis Pessano b: 10/11/1858, Tyaskin, Md. d: 7/23/20, Baltimore, Md. BL/TR, 5'6", 140 lbs. Deb: 7/15/1878

| 1878 | Cin-N | 29 | 123 | 17 | 38 | 5 | 1 | 0 | 9 | 0 | 7 | .309 | .309 | .366 | 134 | 4 | | | | .877 | -1 | O-29 | 0.1 |

YEAR	TM/L	G	AB	R	H	2B	3B	HR	RBI	BB	SO	AVG	OBP	SLG	PRO+	BR/A	SB	CS	SBR	FA	FR	G/POS	TPR
1879	Cin-N	81	350	73	102	18	**14**	2	57	3	27	.291	.297	.440	147	17				.801	-4	*O-81	0.8
1880	Tro-N	30	119	15	23	2	2	0	10	2	3	.193	.207	.244	49	-6				.903	6	O-30/S-1	-0.1
	Wor-N	31	133	22	39	8	6	0	20	1	2	.293	.299	.444	136	4				.852	-2	O-31	0.1
	Yr	61	252	37	62	10	8	0	30	3	5	.246	.255	.349	96	-2				.883	4	O-61/S-1	0.0
1881	Wor-N	80	367	48	116	18	6	1	31	8	8	.316	.331	.406	123	8				.892	10	*O-80	1.5
1883	Pit-a	85	354	62	88	15	1	0		18		.249	.285	.297	92	-2				.798	0	*O-78/S-8,2-2	-0.2
1884	StL-U	46	211	49	77	15	1	0		8		.365	.388	.445	147	6				.895	5	O-42/3-4	0.9
	Bal-a	13	56	9	12	2	1	0		4		.214	.290	.286	85	-1				.941	-2	O-12/3-1	-0.3
	Lou-a	8	28	6	4	0	2	1		3		.143	.226	.393	103	0				.813	-1	/O-8	0.0
	Yr	21	84	15	16	2	3	1		7		.190	.269	.321	91	-1				.879	-3	O-20/3-1	-0.3
1885	Buf-N	5	21	1	1	1	0	0	0	1	4	.048	.091	.095	-38	-3				1.000	1	/O-5	-0.3
Total	7	408	1762	302	500	84	34	4	127	48	51	.284	.304	.377	118	28				.854	12	O-396/S-9,3-5,2-2	2.5

■ GEORGE DICKEY

Dickey, George Willard "Skeets" b: 7/10/15, Kensett, Ark. d: 6/16/76, DeWitt, Ark. BB/TR, 6′2″, 180 lbs. Deb: 9/21/35 F

YEAR	TM/L	G	AB	R	H	2B	3B	HR	RBI	BB	SO	AVG	OBP	SLG	PRO+	BR/A	SB	CS	SBR	FA	FR	G/POS	TPR
1935	Bos-A	5	11	1	0	0	0	0	1	1	3	.000	.083	.000	-72	-3	0	0	0	1.000	-1	/C-4	-0.4
1936	Bos-A	10	23	0	1	1	0	0	0	2	3	.043	.120	.087	-46	-5	0	0	0	.912	0	C-10	-0.4
1941	Chi-A	32	55	6	11	1	0	2	8	5	7	.200	.267	.327	57	-4	0	0	0	1.000	1	C-17	-0.2
1942	Chi-A	59	116	6	27	3	0	1	17	9	11	.233	.288	.284	63	-6	0	0	0	.918	-4	C-29	-0.8
1946	Chi-A	37	78	8	15	1	0	0	1	12	13	.192	.300	.205	45	-5	0	2	-1	1.000	2	C-30	-0.4
1947	Chi-A	83	211	15	47	6	0	1	27	34	25	.223	.331	.265	69	-8	4	2	0	.985	2	C-80	-0.1
Total	6	226	494	36	101	12	0	4	54	63	62	.204	.294	.253	53	-31	4	4	-1	.974	-0	C-170	-2.3

■ BILL DICKEY

Dickey, William Malcolm b: 6/6/07, Bastrop, La. d: 11/12/93, Little Rock, Ark. BL/TR, 6′1.5″, 185 lbs. Deb: 8/15/28 FMCH

YEAR	TM/L	G	AB	R	H	2B	3B	HR	RBI	BB	SO	AVG	OBP	SLG	PRO+	BR/A	SB	CS	SBR	FA	FR	G/POS	TPR
1928	NY-A	10	15	1	3	1	1	0	2	0	2	.200	.200	.400	56	-1	0	0	0	1.000	-1	/C-6	-0.2
1929	NY-A	130	447	60	145	30	6	10	65	14	16	.324	.346	.485	120	10	4	3	-1	.979	1	*C-127	2.1
1930	NY-A	109	366	55	124	25	7	5	65	21	14	.339	.375	.486	122	11	7	1	2	.977	-12	*C-101	0.9
1931	NY-A	130	477	65	156	17	10	6	78	39	20	.327	.378	.442	122	15	2	1	0	**.996**	4	*C-125	2.5
1932	*NY-A	108	423	66	131	20	4	15	84	34	13	.310	.361	.482	123	13	2	4	-2	.987	-2	*C-108	1.4
1933	NY-A☆	130	478	58	152	24	8	14	97	47	14	.318	.381	.490	138	25	3	4	-2	.993	0	*C-127	2.9
1934	NY-A★	104	395	56	127	24	4	12	72	38	18	.322	.384	.494	134	19	0	3	-2	.986	-2	*C-104	1.9
1935	NY-A	120	448	54	125	26	6	14	81	35	11	.279	.339	.458	111	5	1	1	-0	**.995**	-2	*C-118	0.9
1936	*NY-A★	112	423	99	153	26	8	22	107	46	16	.362	.428	.617	161	39	0	2	-1	.976	0	*C-107	3.8
1937	*NY-A★	140	530	87	176	35	2	29	133	73	22	.332	.417	.570	145	37	3	2	-0	.991	12	*C-137	5.1
1938	*NY-A★	132	454	84	142	27	4	27	115	75	22	.313	.412	.568	144	31	3	0	1	.987	4	*C-126	3.7
1939	*NY-A★	128	480	98	145	23	3	24	105	77	37	.302	.403	.512	135	26	5	0	2	**.989**	8	*C-126	3.9
1940	NY-A★	106	372	45	92	11	1	9	54	48	32	.247	.336	.355	83	-9	0	3	-2	.994	-1	*C-102	-0.3
1941	*NY-A★	109	348	35	99	15	5	7	71	45	17	.284	.371	.417	110	5	2	1	0	**.994**	1	*C-104	1.4
1942	*NY-A†	82	268	28	79	13	1	2	37	26	11	.295	.359	.373	108	3	2	2	-1	.976	3	C-80	1.2
1943	*NY-A☆	85	242	29	85	18	2	4	33	41	12	.351	.445	.492	173	24	2	1	0	.994	-1	C-71	2.9
1946	NY-A★	54	134	10	35	8	0	2	10	19	12	.261	.357	.366	101	1	0	1	-1	.987	10	C-39,M	1.3
Total	17	1789	6300	930	1969	343	72	202	1209	678	289	.313	.382	.486	128	252	36	29	-7	.988	24	*C-1708	35.4

■ JOHNNY DICKSHOT

Dickshot, John Oscar "Ugly" (b: John Oscar Dicksus)
b: 1/24/10, Waukegan, Ill. d: 11/4/97, Waukegan, Ill. BR/TR, 6′, 195 lbs. Deb: 4/16/36

YEAR	TM/L	G	AB	R	H	2B	3B	HR	RBI	BB	SO	AVG	OBP	SLG	PRO+	BR/A	SB	CS	SBR	FA	FR	G/POS	TPR
1936	Pit-N	9	9	2	2	0	0	0	1	1	2	.222	.300	.222	42	-1	0			.000	-1	/O-1	-0.1
1937	Pit-N	82	264	42	67	8	4	3	33	26	36	.254	.323	.348	82	-6	0			.950	-2	O-64	-1.1
1938	Pit-N	29	35	3	8	0	0	0	4	8	5	.229	.372	.229	68	-1	3			1.000	-1	O-10	-0.3
1939	NY-N	10	34	3	8	0	0	0	5	5	3	.235	.333	.235	55	-2	0			1.000	-1	O-10	-0.3
1944	Chi-A	62	162	18	41	8	5	0	15	13	10	.253	.313	.364	94	-2	2	0	1	.974	-3	O-40	-0.6
1945	Chi-A	130	486	74	147	19	10	4	58	48	41	.302	.366	.407	128	17	18	3	**4**	.971	1	*O-124	1.5
Total	6	322	990	142	273	35	19	7	116	101	97	.276	.345	.371	104	5	23	3		.968	-7	O-249	-0.9

■ BOB DIDIER

Didier, Robert Daniel b: 2/16/49, Hattiesburg, Miss. BB/TR, 6′, 190 lbs. Deb: 4/7/69 C

YEAR	TM/L	G	AB	R	H	2B	3B	HR	RBI	BB	SO	AVG	OBP	SLG	PRO+	BR/A	SB	CS	SBR	FA	FR	G/POS	TPR
1969	*Atl-N	114	352	30	90	16	1	0	32	34	39	.256	.321	.307	76	-10	1	3	-2	.994	-2	*C-114	-0.9
1970	Atl-N	57	168	9	25	2	1	0	7	12	11	.149	.210	.173	3	-23	1	0	0	.988	1	C-57	-1.9
1971	Atl-N	51	155	9	34	4	1	0	5	6	17	.219	.248	.258	41	-12	0	0	0	1.000	3	C-50	-0.8
1972	Atl-N	13	40	5	12	2	1	0	5	2	4	.300	.349	.400	103	0	0	0	0	1.000	2	C-11	0.2
1973	Det-A	7	22	3	10	1	0	0	1	3	0	.455	.520	.500	177	2	0	0	0	1.000	2	/C-7	0.5
1974	Bos-A	5	14	0	1	0	0	0	1	2	1	.071	.188	.071	-22	-2	0	0	0	.968	1	/C-5	-0.1
Total	6	247	751	56	172	25	4	0	51	59	72	.229	.287	.273	55	-45	2	3	-1	.994	6	C-244	-3.0

■ ERNIE DIEHL

Diehl, Ernest Guy b: 10/2/1877, Cincinnati, Ohio d: 11/6/58, Miami, Fla. BR/TR, 6′1″, 190 lbs. Deb: 5/31/03

YEAR	TM/L	G	AB	R	H	2B	3B	HR	RBI	BB	SO	AVG	OBP	SLG	PRO+	BR/A	SB	CS	SBR	FA	FR	G/POS	TPR
1903	Pit-N	1	3	0	1	0	0	0	0	0		.333	.333	.333	87	-0	0			.000	-1	/O-1	-0.1
1904	Pit-N	12	37	6	6	0	0	0	4	6		.162	.311	.162	46	-2	3			1.000	1	/O-7,S-4	-0.1
1906	Bos-N	3	11	1	5	0	1	0	0	0		.455	.455	.636	247	2	0			1.000	0	/O-2,S-1	0.2
1909	Bos-N	1	4	1	2	1	0	0	0	0		.500	.500	.750	275	1	0			.800	1	/O-1	0.1
Total	4	17	55	8	14	1	1	0	4	6		.255	.349	.309	101	0	3			.944	2	/O-11,S-5	0.1

■ CHUCK DIERING

Diering, Charles Edward Allen b: 2/5/23, St.Louis, Mo. BR/TR, 5′10″, 165 lbs. Deb: 4/15/47

YEAR	TM/L	G	AB	R	H	2B	3B	HR	RBI	BB	SO	AVG	OBP	SLG	PRO+	BR/A	SB	CS	SBR	FA	FR	G/POS	TPR
1947	StL-N	105	74	22	16	3	1	2	11	19	22	.216	.383	.365	95	0	3			1.000	-22	O-75	-2.3
1948	StL-N	7	7	2	0	0	0	0	0	2	2	.000	.222	.000	-33	-1	1			1.000	-1	/O-5	-0.2
1949	StL-N	131	369	60	97	21	8	3	38	35	49	.263	.328	.388	87	-7	1			.987	-2	*O-124	-1.4
1950	StL-N	89	204	34	51	12	0	3	18	35	38	.250	.360	.353	84	-4	1			.989	-1	O-81	-0.7
1951	StL-N	64	85	9	22	5	1	0	8	6	15	.259	.308	.341	74	-3	0	1	-1	1.000	-8	O-44	-1.3
1952	NY-N	41	23	2	4	1	1	0	2	4	3	.174	.296	.304	66	-1	0	2	-1	1.000	-10	O-36	-1.3
1954	Bal-A	128	418	35	108	14	1	2	29	56	57	.258	.351	.311	89	-5	3	7	-3	.983	13	*O-119	0.0
1955	Bal-A	137	371	38	95	16	2	3	31	57	45	.256	.355	.334	93	-3	5	8	-3	.976	3	*O-107,3-34,S-12	-0.6
1956	Bal-A	50	97	15	18	4	0	1	4	23	19	.186	.342	.258	65	-4	2	5	-2	1.000	-4	O-40/3-2	-1.2
Total	9	752	1648	217	411	76	14	14	141	237	250	.249	.346	.338	86	-27	16	23		.987	-31	O-631/3-36,S-12	-9.0

■ DICK DIETZ

Dietz, Richard Allen b: 9/18/41, Crawfordsville, Ind. BR/TR, 6′1″, 195 lbs. Deb: 6/18/66

YEAR	TM/L	G	AB	R	H	2B	3B	HR	RBI	BB	SO	AVG	OBP	SLG	PRO+	BR/A	SB	CS	SBR	FA	FR	G/POS	TPR
1966	SF-N	13	23	1	1	0	0	0	0	0	9	.043	.083	.043	-62	-5	0	0	0	1.000	-1	/C-6	-0.6
1967	SF-N	56	120	10	27	3	0	4	19	25	44	.225	.363	.350	106	2	0	1	-1	.983	0	C-43	0.4
1968	SF-N	98	301	21	82	14	2	6	38	34	68	.272	.348	.392	122	9	1	1	-0	.976	-8	C-90	0.7
1969	SF-N	79	244	28	56	8	1	11	35	53	53	.230	.373	.406	120	8	0	0	0	.973	-5	C-73	0.7
1970	SF-N★	148	493	82	148	36	2	22	107	109	106	.300	.430	.515	154	42	0	1	-1	.984	-18	*C-139	3.0
1971	*SF-N	142	453	58	114	19	0	19	72	97	86	.252	.388	.419	131	22	1	3	-2	.982	-12	*C-135	1.5
1972	LA-N	27	56	4	9	1	0	1	6	14	11	.161	.329	.232	63	-2	2	0	1	1.000	3	C-22	0.3
1973	Atl-N	83	139	22	41	8	1	3	24	49	25	.295	.479	.432	143	12	0	0	0	.989	1	1-36,C-20	1.1
Total	8	646	1829	226	478	89	6	66	301	381	402	.261	.392	.425	130	88	4	6	-2	.980	-39	C-528/1-36	7.1

■ ROY DIETZEL

Dietzel, Leroy Louis b: 1/9/31, Baltimore, Md. BR/TR, 6′, 190 lbs. Deb: 9/2/54

YEAR	TM/L	G	AB	R	H	2B	3B	HR	RBI	BB	SO	AVG	OBP	SLG	PRO+	BR/A	SB	CS	SBR	FA	FR	G/POS	TPR
1954	Was-A	9	21	1	5	0	0	0	1	5	4	.238	.385	.238	78	-0	0	0	0	.960	-2	/2-7,3-2	-0.2

■ JAY DIFANI

Difani, Clarence Joseph b: 12/21/23, Crystal City, Mo. BR/TR, 6′, 170 lbs. Deb: 4/23/48

YEAR	TM/L	G	AB	R	H	2B	3B	HR	RBI	BB	SO	AVG	OBP	SLG	PRO+	BR/A	SB	CS	SBR	FA	FR	G/POS	TPR
1948	Was-A	2	2	0	0	0	0	0	0	0	2	.000	.000	.000	-99	-1	0	0	0	.000	0	H	-0.1
1949	Was-A	2	1	0	1	1	0	0	0	0	0	1.000	1.000	2.000	699	1	0	0	0	1.000	0	/2-1	0.1
Total	2	4	3	0	1	1	0	0	0	0	2	.333	.333	.667	166	0	0	0	0	1.000	0	/2-1	0.0

■ MIKE DIFELICE

Difelice, Michael William b: 5/28/69, Philadelphia, Pa. BR/TR, 6′2″, 205 lbs. Deb: 9/1/96

YEAR	TM/L	G	AB	R	H	2B	3B	HR	RBI	BB	SO	AVG	OBP	SLG	PRO+	BR/A	SB	CS	SBR	FA	FR	G/POS	TPR
1996	StL-N	4	7	0	2	1	0	0	2	0	1	.286	.286	.429	86	-0	0	0	0	1.000	1	/C-4	0.1
1997	StL-N	93	260	16	62	10	1	4	30	19	61	.238	.298	.331	65	-13	1	1	-0	.991	21	C-91/1-1	1.2

YEAR	TM/L	G	AB	R	H	2B	3B	HR	RBI	BB	SO	AVG	OBP	SLG	PRO+	BR/A	SB	CS	SBR	FA	FR	G/POS	TPR
1998	TB-A	84	248	17	57	12	3	3	23	15	56	.230	.277	.339	56	-16	0	0	0	.993	15	C-84	0.3
Total	3	181	515	33	121	23	4	7	55	34	118	.235	.288	.336	61	-30	1	1	-0	.992	37	C-179/1-1	1.6

■ STEVE DIGNAN Dignan, Stephen E. b: 4/16/1859, Boston, Mass. d: 7/11/1881, Boston, Mass. Deb: 6/1/1880

YEAR	TM/L	G	AB	R	H	2B	3B	HR	RBI	BB	SO	AVG	OBP	SLG	PRO+	BR/A	SB	CS	SBR	FA	FR	G/POS	TPR
1880	Bos-N	8	34	4	11	1	0	0	4	0	3	.324	.324	.353	133	1				.684	0	/O-8	0.1
	Wor-N	3	10	1	3	0	1	0	2	0	1	.300	.300	.500	153	0				.750	-1	/O-3	0.0
	Yr	11	44	5	14	1	1	0	6	0	4	.318	.318	.386	137	2				.696	-1	O-11	0.1

■ DON DILLARD Dillard, David Donald b: 1/8/37, Greenville, S.C. BL/TR, 6'1", 200 lbs. Deb: 4/24/59

YEAR	TM/L	G	AB	R	H	2B	3B	HR	RBI	BB	SO	AVG	OBP	SLG	PRO+	BR/A	SB	CS	SBR	FA	FR	G/POS	TPR
1959	Cle-A	10	10	0	4	0	0	0	1	0	2	.400	.400	.400	125	0	0	0	0	.000	0	H	0.0
1960	Cle-A	6	7	0	1	0	0	0	0	1	3	.143	.250	.143	9	-1	0	0	0	.000	-0	/O-1	-0.1
1961	Cle-A	74	147	27	40	5	0	7	17	15	28	.272	.340	.449	112	2	0	0	0	1.000	-4	O-39	-0.3
1962	Cle-A	95	174	22	40	5	1	5	14	11	25	.230	.276	.356	71	-8	0	1	-1	.965	-10	O-50	-2.1
1963	Mil-N	67	119	9	28	6	4	1	12	5	21	.235	.272	.378	86	-2	0	2	-1	.951	-0	O-30	-0.5
1965	Mil-N	20	19	1	3	0	0	1	3	0	6	.158	.158	.316	30	-2	0	0	0	.000	-0	/O-1	-0.2
Total	6	272	476	59	116	16	5	14	47	32	85	.244	.293	.387	86	-10	0	3	-2	.976	-15	O-121	-3.2

■ PAT DILLARD Dillard, Robert Lee b: 6/12/1873, Chattanooga, Tenn d: 7/22/07, Denver, Colo. BL/TR, 6', 180 lbs. Deb: 4/21/00

YEAR	TM/L	G	AB	R	H	2B	3B	HR	RBI	BB	SO	AVG	OBP	SLG	PRO+	BR/A	SB	CS	SBR	FA	FR	G/POS	TPR
1900	StL-N	57	183	24	42	5	2	0	12	13		.230	.284	.279	56	-11	7			.942	-4	O-26,3-21/S-3	-1.5

■ STEVE DILLARD Dillard, Stephen Bradley b: 2/8/51, Memphis, Tenn. BR/TR, 6'1", 180 lbs. Deb: 9/28/75

YEAR	TM/L	G	AB	R	H	2B	3B	HR	RBI	BB	SO	AVG	OBP	SLG	PRO+	BR/A	SB	CS	SBR	FA	FR	G/POS	TPR
1975	Bos-A	1	5	2	2	0	0	0	0	0	0	.400	.400	.400	117	0	1	0	0	1.000	1	/2-1	0.1
1976	Bos-A	57	167	22	46	14	0	1	15	17	20	.275	.342	.377	99	-0	6	4	-1	.918	-4	3-18,2-17,S-12,/D-7	-0.3
1977	Bos-A	66	141	22	34	7	0	1	13	7	13	.241	.277	.312	54	-9	4	3	-1	.967	8	2-45/S-9,D-6	0.1
1978	Det-A	56	130	21	29	5	2	0	7	6	11	.223	.257	.292	53	-8	1	2	-1	.958	17	2-41/D-4	1.0
1979	Chi-N	89	166	31	47	6	1	5	24	17	24	.283	.353	.422	101	0	1	0	0	.988	9	2-60/3-9	1.3
1980	Chi-N	100	244	31	55	8	1	4	27	20	54	.225	.287	.316	63	-12	2	2	-1	.908	2	3-51,2-38/S-2	-1.0
1981	Chi-N	53	119	18	26	7	1	2	11	8	20	.218	.268	.345	70	-5	0	0	0	.974	3	2-32/3-7,S-2	-0.1
1982	Chi-A	16	41	1	7	3	1	0	5	1	5	.171	.190	.293	30	-4	0	1	-1	.959	3	2-16	-0.1
Total	8	438	1013	148	246	50	6	13	102	76	147	.243	.297	.343	73	-38	15	12	-3	.973	37	2-250/3-85,S-25,D	1.0

■ PICKLES DILLHOEFER Dillhoefer, William Martin b: 10/13/1894, Cleveland, Ohio d: 2/23/22, St.Louis, Mo. BR/TR, 5'7", 154 lbs. Deb: 4/16/17

YEAR	TM/L	G	AB	R	H	2B	3B	HR	RBI	BB	SO	AVG	OBP	SLG	PRO+	BR/A	SB	CS	SBR	FA	FR	G/POS	TPR
1917	Chi-N	42	95	3	12	1	1	0	8	2	9	.126	.144	.158	-7	-12	1			.985	8	C-37	-0.2
1918	Phi-N	8	11	0	1	0	0	0	0	1	1	.091	.167	.091	-19	-2	2			.923	-1	/C-6	-0.2
1919	StL-N	45	108	11	23	3	2	0	12	8	6	.213	.267	.278	68	-4	5			.967	-5	C-39	-0.7
1920	StL-N	76	224	26	59	8	3	0	13	13	7	.263	.304	.326	84	-5	2	1	0	.953	-0	C-74	-0.1
1921	StL-N	76	162	19	39	4	4	0	15	11	7	.241	.289	.315	61	-9	2	1	0	.953	2	C-69	-0.5
Total	5	247	600	59	134	16	10	0	48	35	30	.223	.266	.283	58	-32	12	2		.961	4	C-225	-1.7

■ BOB DILLINGER Dillinger, Robert Bernard "Duke" b: 9/17/18, Glendale, Cal. BR/TR, 5'11.5", 170 lbs. Deb: 4/16/46

YEAR	TM/L	G	AB	R	H	2B	3B	HR	RBI	BB	SO	AVG	OBP	SLG	PRO+	BR/A	SB	CS	SBR	FA	FR	G/POS	TPR
1946	StL-A	83	225	33	63	6	3	0	11	19	30	.280	.341	.333	85	-4	8	1	**2**	.922	-3	3-54/S-1	-0.5
1947	StL-A	137	571	70	168	23	6	3	37	56	38	.294	.361	.371	102	2	**34**	13	**2**	.958	2	*3-137	0.8
1948	StL-A	153	644	110	**207**	34	10	2	44	65	34	.321	.385	.415	110	9	**28**	11	2	.955	-16	*3-153	-0.6
1949	StL-A★	137	544	68	176	22	13	1	51	51	40	.324	.385	.417	108	6	**20**	14	-2	.938	-25	*3-133	-2.4
1950	Phi-A	84	356	55	110	21	9	3	41	31	20	.309	.366	.444	109	4	5	3	-0	.957	-2	3-84	0.0
	Pit-N	58	222	23	64	8	2	1	9	13	22	.288	.328	.356	77	-7	4			.957	2	3-51	-0.6
1951	Pit-N	12	43	3	10	3	0	0	0	1	0	.233	.250	.302	47	-3	2	0	1	.963	-2	3-10	-0.5
	Chi-A	89	299	39	90	6	4	0	20	15	17	.301	.337	.348	87	-6	5	5	-2	.930	-6	3-70	-1.4
Total	6	753	2904	401	888	123	47	10	213	251	201	.306	.363	.391	100	1	106	47		.948	-50	3-692/S-1	-5.2

■ POP DILLON Dillon, Frank Edward b: 10/17/1873, Normal, Ill. d: 9/12/31, Pasadena, Cal. BL/TR, 6'1", 185 lbs. Deb: 9/8/1899

YEAR	TM/L	G	AB	R	H	2B	3B	HR	RBI	BB	SO	AVG	OBP	SLG	PRO+	BR/A	SB	CS	SBR	FA	FR	G/POS	TPR
1899	Pit-N	30	121	21	31	5	0	0	20	5		.256	.286	.298	60	-7	5			.988	1	1-30	-0.5
1900	Pit-N	5	18	3	2	1	0	0	1	0		.111	.111	.167	-24	-3	0			.981	1	/1-5	-0.2
1901	Det-A	74	281	40	81	14	6	1	42	15		.288	.324	.391	94	-3	14			.979	3	1-74	-0.2
1902	Det-A	66	243	21	50	6	3	0	22	16		.206	.255	.255	41	-19	2			.976	5	1-66	-1.5
	Bal-A	2	7	1	2	0	1	0	0	2		.286	.444	.571	173	1	0			.960	0	/1-2	0.1
	Yr	68	250	22	52	6	4	0	22	18		.208	.261	.264	45	-19	2			.975	6	1-68	-1.4
1904	Bro-N	135	511	60	132	18	6	0	31	40		.258	.313	.317	97	-2	13			.982	3	*1-134	-0.1
Total	5	312	1181	146	298	44	16	1	116	78		.252	.299	.319	79	-33	34			.980	14	1-311	-2.4

■ JOHN DILLON Dillon, John Deb: 5/8/1875 F

YEAR	TM/L	G	AB	R	H	2B	3B	HR	RBI	BB	SO	AVG	OBP	SLG	PRO+	BR/A	SB	CS	SBR	FA	FR	G/POS	TPR
1875	RS-n	1	1	0	0	0	0	0	0	0	0	.000	.000	.000	-99	-0	0	0	0	.000	0	/S-1	0.0

■ PACKY DILLON Dillon, Packard Andrew b: St.Louis, Mo. d: 1/8/1890, Guelph, Ont., Canada Deb: 5/4/1875 F

YEAR	TM/L	G	AB	R	H	2B	3B	HR	RBI	BB	SO	AVG	OBP	SLG	PRO+	BR/A	SB	CS	SBR	FA	FR	G/POS	TPR
1875	RS-n	3	13	1	3	1	0	0	1	0	0	.231	.231	.308	94	-0	0	0	0	.923	-2	/C-3	-0.2

■ MIGUEL DILONE Dilone, Miguel Angel (Reyes) b: 11/1/54, Santiago, D.R. BB/TR, 6', 160 lbs. Deb: 9/2/74

YEAR	TM/L	G	AB	R	H	2B	3B	HR	RBI	BB	SO	AVG	OBP	SLG	PRO+	BR/A	SB	CS	SBR	FA	FR	G/POS	TPR
1974	Pit-N	12	2	3	0	0	0	0	0	1	0	.000	.333	.000	-1	-0	2	0	1	1.000	-1	/O-2	0.0
1975	Pit-N	18	6	8	0	0	0	0	0	0	1	.000	.000	.000	-99	-2	2	2	-1	1.000	-0	/O-2	-0.3
1976	Pit-N	16	17	7	4	0	0	0	0	0	0	.235	.235	.235	34	-1	5	1	1	1.000	1	/O-3	0.0
1977	Pit-N	29	44	5	6	0	0	0	0	2	3	.136	.174	.136	-15	-7	12	0	4	1.000	-3	O-17	-0.7
1978	Oak-A	135	258	34	59	8	0	1	14	23	30	.229	.294	.271	63	-12	50	23	1	.985	-7	O-99,D-11/3-3	-2.2
1979	Oak-A	30	91	15	17	1	2	1	6	6	7	.187	.237	.275	40	-8	6	5	-1	.959	-2	O-25	-1.2
	Chi-N	43	36	14	11	0	0	0	1	2	5	.306	.342	.306	71	-1	15	5	2	1.000	-5	O-22	-0.5
1980	Cle-A	132	528	82	180	30	9	0	40	28	45	.341	.376	.432	120	15	61	18	8	.973	-0	*O-118,D-11	1.6
1981	Cle-A	72	269	33	78	5	5	0	19	18	28	.290	.334	.346	98	-1	29	10	3	.971	6	O-56,D-11	0.6
1982	Cle-A	104	379	50	89	12	3	3	25	25	36	.235	.286	.306	63	-19	33	5	7	.964	-3	O-97/D-1	-1.8
1983	Cle-A	32	68	15	13	3	1	0	7	10	5	.191	.295	.265	53	-4	5	1	1	1.000	1	O-19	-0.3
	Chi-A	4	3	1	0	0	0	0	0	0	0	.000	.000	.000	-96	-1	1	0	0	1.000	-1	/O-2,D-2	-0.1
	Yr	36	71	16	13	3	1	0	7	10	5	.183	.284	.254	47	-5	6	1	1	1.000	0	O-21/D-2	-0.4
	Pit-N	7	0	1	0	0	0	0	0	0	0	—	—	—	—	0	2	0	1	.000	0	/R	0.0
1984	Mon-N	88	169	28	47	8	2	1	10	17	18	.278	.348	.367	106	1	27	2	7	.987	1	O-41	0.9
1985	Mon-N	51	84	10	16	0	2	0	6	6	11	.190	.244	.238	38	-7	7	3	0	.974	-2	O-22	-1.0
	SD-N	27	46	8	10	0	1	0	1	4	8	.217	.280	.261	53	-3	10	3	1	.917	-2	O-14	-0.4
	Yr	78	130	18	26	0	3	0	7	10	19	.200	.257	.246	43	-10	17	6	2	.952	-4	O-36	-1.4
Total	12	800	2000	314	530	67	25	6	129	142	197	.265	.316	.333	81	-51	267	78	33	.975	-16	O-539/D-36,3-3	-5.4

■ DOM DiMAGGIO DiMaggio, Dominic Paul "The Little Professor" b: 2/12/17, San Francisco, Cal. BR/TR, 5'9", 168 lbs. Deb: 4/16/40 F

YEAR	TM/L	G	AB	R	H	2B	3B	HR	RBI	BB	SO	AVG	OBP	SLG	PRO+	BR/A	SB	CS	SBR	FA	FR	G/POS	TPR
1940	Bos-A	108	418	81	126	32	6	8	46	41	46	.301	.367	.464	109	6	7	6	-2	.977	10	O-94	0.8
1941	Bos-A★	144	584	117	165	37	6	8	58	90	57	.283	.385	.408	107	8	13	6	0	.964	6	*O-144	0.6
1942	Bos-A☆	151	622	110	178	36	8	14	48	70	52	.286	.364	.437	121	17	16	10	-1	.987	17	*O-151	2.5
1946	*Bos-A★	142	534	85	169	24	7	7	73	66	58	.316	.393	.427	122	17	10	6	-1	.985	7	*O-142	1.8
1947	Bos-A	136	513	75	145	21	5	8	71	74	62	.283	.376	.390	105	5	10	6	-1	.977	19	*O-134	1.7
1948	Bos-A	155	648	127	185	40	4	9	87	101	58	.285	.383	.401	104	5	10	2	2	.981	16	*O-155	1.4
1949	Bos-A★	145	605	126	186	34	5	8	60	96	55	.307	.404	.420	110	11	9	7	-2	.977	14	*O-144	1.6
1950	Bos-A★	141	588	**131**	193	30	**11**	7	70	82	68	.328	.414	.452	111	11	**15**	4	**2**	.983	9	*O-140	1.5
1951	Bos-A★	146	639	**113**	189	34	4	12	72	73	53	.296	.370	.418	103	2	4	7	-3	.973	3	*O-146	-0.4
1952	Bos-A★	128	486	81	143	20	1	6	33	57	61	.294	.371	.377	100	2	6	8	-3	.975	0	*O-123	-0.7
1953	Bos-A	3	3	0	1	0	0	0	0	0	1	.333	.333	.333	76	-0	0	0	0	.000	0	H	0.0
Total	11	1399	5640	1046	1680	308	57	87	618	750	571	.298	.383	.419	109	84	100	62	-7	.978	101	*O-1373	10.8

■ JOE DiMAGGIO
DiMaggio, Joseph Paul "Joltin' Joe" or "The Yankee Clipper" b: 11/25/14, Martinez, Cal. BR/TR, 6'2", 193 lbs. Deb: 5/3/36 FCH

YEAR	TM/L	G	AB	R	H	2B	3B	HR	RBI	BB	SO	AVG	OBP	SLG	PRO+	BR/A	SB	CS	SBR	FA	FR	G/POS	TPR
1936	*NY-A★	138	637	132	206	44	**15**	29	125	24	39	.323	.352	.576	130	23	4	0	1	.978	15	*O-138	3.0
1937	*NY-A★	151	621	**151**	215	35	15	**46**	167	64	37	.346	.412	**.673**	168	60	3	0	1	.962	11	*O-150	6.0
1938	*NY-A★	145	599	129	194	32	13	32	140	59	21	.324	.386	.581	140	33	6	1	1	.963	4	*O-145	3.0
1939	*NY-A★	120	462	108	176	32	6	30	126	52	20	**.381**	.448	.671	**185**	58	3	0	1	.986	8	*O-117	**5.7**
1940	NY-A★	132	508	93	179	28	9	31	133	61	30	**.352**	.425	.626	**176**	**56**	1	2	-1	.978	1	*O-130	**4.5**
1941	*NY-A★	139	541	122	193	43	11	30	**125**	76	13	.357	.440	.643	186	66	4	2	0	.978	10	*O-139	6.4
1942	*NY-A★	154	610	123	186	29	13	21	114	68	36	.305	.376	.498	148	37	4	2	0	.981	2	*O-154	3.1
1946	NY-A☆	132	503	81	146	20	8	25	95	59	24	.290	.367	.511	142	27	1	0	0	.982	4	*O-131	2.5
1947	*NY-A★	141	534	97	168	31	10	20	97	64	32	.315	.391	.522	154	38	3	0	1	**.997**	-13	*O-139	1.8
1948	NY-A★	153	594	110	190	26	11	**39**	**155**	67	30	.320	.396	.598	164	50	1	1	-0	.972	4	*O-152	4.3
1949	*NY-A★	76	272	58	94	14	6	14	67	55	18	.346	.459	.596	178	32	0	1	-1	.985	-1	O-76	2.5
1950	*NY-A★	139	525	114	158	33	10	32	122	80	33	.301	.394	**.585**	152	39	0	0	0	.976	1	*O-137/1-1	3.1
1951	*NY-A☆	116	415	72	109	22	4	12	71	61	36	.263	.365	.422	117	10	0	0	0	.990	4	*O-113	1.0
Total	13	1736	6821	1390	2214	389	131	361	1537	790	369	.325	.398	.579	156	529	30	9	4	.978	51	*O-1721/1-1	46.9

■ VINCE DiMAGGIO
DiMaggio, Vincent Paul b: 9/6/12, Martinez, Cal. d: 10/3/86, N.Hollywood, Cal. BR/TR, 5'11", 183 lbs. Deb: 4/19/37 F

YEAR	TM/L	G	AB	R	H	2B	3B	HR	RBI	BB	SO	AVG	OBP	SLG	PRO+	BR/A	SB	CS	SBR	FA	FR	G/POS	TPR
1937	Bos-N	132	493	56	126	18	4	13	69	39	111	.256	.311	.387	98	-4	8			.982	16	*O-130	0.7
1938	Bos-N	150	540	71	123	28	3	14	61	65	134	.228	.313	.369	96	-4	11			.973	13	*O-149/2-1	0.5
1939	Cin-N	8	14	1	1	1	0	0	2	2	10	.071	.188	.143	-10	-2	0			1.000	-0	/O-7	-0.2
1940	Cin-N	2	4	2	1	0	0	0	0	1	0	.250	.400	.250	82	-0	0			1.000	0	/O-1	0.0
	Pit-N	110	356	59	103	26	0	19	54	37	83	.289	.364	.522	143	20	11			.979	-2	*O-108	1.3
	Yr	112	360	61	104	26	0	19	54	38	83	.289	.365	.519	142	20	11			.979	-2	*O-109	1.3
1941	Pit-N	151	528	73	141	27	5	21	100	68	100	.267	.354	.456	128	19	10			.976	7	*O-151	1.7
1942	Pit-N	143	496	57	118	22	3	15	75	52	87	.238	.311	.385	101	-1	10			.978	**20**	*O-138	1.3
1943	Pit-N★	157	580	64	144	41	2	15	88	70	126	.248	.329	.403	107	5	11			.985	15	*O-156/S-1	1.2
1944	Pit-N★	109	342	41	82	20	4	9	50	33	83	.240	.307	.401	94	-4	6			.984	-6	*O-101/3-1	-1.5
1945	Phi-N	127	452	64	116	25	3	19	84	43	91	.257	.321	.451	117	7	12			.994	10	*O-121	1.1
1946	Phi-N	6	19	1	4	1	0	0	1	0	7	.211	.211	.263	35	-2	0			1.000	-1	/O-6	-0.3
	NY-N	15	25	2	0	0	0	0	0	2	5	.000	.074	.000	-78	-6	0			.967	-1	O-13	-0.8
	Yr	21	44	3	4	1	0	0	1	2	12	.091	.130	.114	-31	-8	0			.975	-2	O-19	-1.1
Total	10	1110	3849	491	959	209	24	125	584	412	837	.249	.324	.413	108	29	79			.981	70	*O-1081/3-1,S-1,2-1	5.0

■ MIKE DIMMEL
Dimmel, Michael Wayne b: 10/16/54, Albert Lea, Minn. BR/TR, 6', 180 lbs. Deb: 9/2/77

YEAR	TM/L	G	AB	R	H	2B	3B	HR	RBI	BB	SO	AVG	OBP	SLG	PRO+	BR/A	SB	CS	SBR	FA	FR	G/POS	TPR
1977	Bal-A	25	5	8	0	0	0	0	0	0	1	.000	.000	.000	-99	-1	1	0	0	1.000	-6	O-23	-0.7
1978	Bal-A	8	0	2	0	0	0	0	0	0	0	—	—	—	—	0	0	1	-1	.667	-3	/O-7	-0.4
1979	StL-N	6	3	1	1	0	0	0	0	0	0	.333	.333	.333	82	-0	0	1	-1	1.000	-2	/O-5	-0.3
Total	3	39	8	11	1	0	0	0	0	0	1	.125	.125	.125	-33	-1	1	2	-1	.952	-11	/O-35	-1.4

■ KERRY DINEEN
Dineen, Kerry Michael b: 7/1/52, Englewood, N.J. BL/TL, 5'11", 165 lbs. Deb: 6/14/75

YEAR	TM/L	G	AB	R	H	2B	3B	HR	RBI	BB	SO	AVG	OBP	SLG	PRO+	BR/A	SB	CS	SBR	FA	FR	G/POS	TPR
1975	NY-A	7	22	3	8	1	0	0	1	2	1	.364	.417	.409	136	1	0	0	0	1.000	0	/O-7	0.1
1976	NY-A	4	7	0	2	0	0	0	1	1	2	.286	.375	.286	96	0	1	1	-0	.900	-0	/O-4	-0.1
1978	Phi-N	5	8	0	2	1	0	0	0	1	0	.250	.333	.375	97	-0	0	0	0	1.000	-0	/O-1	0.0
Total	3	16	37	3	12	2	0	0	2	4	3	.324	.390	.378	120	1	1	1	-0	.967	-0	/O-12	0.0

■ VANCE DINGES
Dinges, Vance George b: 5/29/15, Elizabeth, N.J. d: 10/4/90, Harrisonburg, Va. BL/TL, 6'2", 175 lbs. Deb: 4/17/45

YEAR	TM/L	G	AB	R	H	2B	3B	HR	RBI	BB	SO	AVG	OBP	SLG	PRO+	BR/A	SB	CS	SBR	FA	FR	G/POS	TPR
1945	Phi-N	109	397	46	114	15	4	1	36	35	17	.287	.346	.353	97	-1	5			.986	-1	O-65,1-42	-0.8
1946	Phi-N	50	104	7	32	5	1	1	10	9	12	.308	.363	.404	121	3	2			.985	-0	1-26/O-1	0.1
Total	2	159	501	53	146	20	5	2	46	44	29	.291	.350	.363	102	1	7			.986	-1	/1-68,O-66	-0.7

■ BOB DiPIETRO
DiPietro, Robert Louis Paul b: 9/1/27, San Francisco, Cal BR/TR, 5'11", 185 lbs. Deb: 9/23/51

YEAR	TM/L	G	AB	R	H	2B	3B	HR	RBI	BB	SO	AVG	OBP	SLG	PRO+	BR/A	SB	CS	SBR	FA	FR	G/POS	TPR
1951	Bos-A	4	11	0	1	0	0	0	0	1	1	.091	.167	.091	-26	-2	0	0	0	.833	0	/O-3	-0.2

■ GARY DiSARCINA
DiSarcina, Gary Thomas b: 11/19/67, Malden, Mass. BR/TR, 6'1", 178 lbs. Deb: 9/23/89

YEAR	TM/L	G	AB	R	H	2B	3B	HR	RBI	BB	SO	AVG	OBP	SLG	PRO+	BR/A	SB	CS	SBR	FA	FR	G/POS	TPR
1989	Cal-A	2	0	0	0	0	0	0	0	0	0	—	—	—	—	0	0	0	0	.000	0	/S-1	0.0
1990	Cal-A	18	57	8	8	1	1	0	0	3	10	.140	.183	.193	5	-7	1	0	0	.940	2	S-14/2-3	-0.4
1991	Cal-A	18	57	5	12	2	0	0	3	3	4	.211	.274	.246	45	-4	0	0	0	.915	-1	S-10/2-7,3-2	-0.4
1992	Cal-A	157	518	48	128	19	0	3	42	20	50	.247	.284	.301	64	-25	9	7	-2	.967	12	*S-157	-0.4
1993	Cal-A	126	416	44	99	20	1	3	45	15	38	.238	.275	.313	56	-26	5	7	-3	.975	-13	*S-126	-3.1
1994	Cal-A	112	389	53	101	14	2	3	33	18	28	.260	.296	.329	60	-23	3	7	-3	.983	8	*S-110	-0.8
1995	Cal-A★	99	362	61	111	28	6	5	41	20	25	.307	.346	.459	108	4	7	4	-0	.986	-4	S-98	0.7
1996	Cal-A	150	536	62	137	26	4	5	48	21	36	.256	.286	.347	59	-34	2	1	0	.971	5	*S-150	-1.4
1997	Ana-A	154	549	52	135	28	2	4	47	17	29	.246	.274	.326	56	-36	7	8	-3	.977	-9	*S-153	-3.3
1998	Ana-A	157	551	73	158	39	3	3	56	21	51	.287	.322	.385	82	-15	11	7	-1	.980	-6	*S-157	-0.7
Total	10	993	3435	406	889	177	19	26	315	138	271	.259	.294	.344	67	-167	45	41	-11	.975	-7	S-976/2-10,3-2	-9.8

■ BENNY DISTEFANO
Distefano, Benito James b: 1/23/62, Brooklyn, N.Y. BL/TL, 6'1", 195 lbs. Deb: 5/18/84

YEAR	TM/L	G	AB	R	H	2B	3B	HR	RBI	BB	SO	AVG	OBP	SLG	PRO+	BR/A	SB	CS	SBR	FA	FR	G/POS	TPR
1984	Pit-N	45	78	10	13	1	2	3	9	5	13	.167	.226	.346	59	-5	0	1	-1	.946	1	O-20,1-17	-0.5
1986	Pit-N	31	39	3	7	1	0	1	5	1	5	.179	.200	.282	31	-4	0	0	0	1.000	-1	/O-9,1-1	-0.5
1988	Pit-N	16	29	6	10	3	1	1	6	3	4	.345	.406	.621	194	3	0	0	0	1.000	-0	/1-5,O-2	0.3
1989	Pit-N	96	154	12	38	8	0	2	15	17	30	.247	.333	.338	96	-1	1	0	0	.981	-3	1-48/C-3,O-1	-0.6
1992	Hou-N	52	60	4	14	0	2	0	7	5	14	.233	.303	.300	75	-2	0	0	0	1.000	-0	O-12/1-6	-0.3
Total	5	240	360	35	82	13	5	7	42	31	66	.228	.298	.350	85	-7	1	1	-0	.985	-3	/1-77,O-44,C-3	-1.6

■ DUTCH DISTEL
Distel, George Adam b: 4/15/1896, Madison, Ind. d: 2/12/67, Madison, Ind. BR/TR, 5'9", 165 lbs. Deb: 6/21/18

YEAR	TM/L	G	AB	R	H	2B	3B	HR	RBI	BB	SO	AVG	OBP	SLG	PRO+	BR/A	SB	CS	SBR	FA	FR	G/POS	TPR
1918	StL-N	8	17	3	3	1	1	0	1	2	3	.176	.263	.353	90	-0	0			.900	-2	/2-5,S-2,O-1	-0.2

■ JACK DITTMER
Dittmer, John Douglas b: 1/10/28, Elkader, Iowa BL/TR, 6'1", 175 lbs. Deb: 6/17/52

YEAR	TM/L	G	AB	R	H	2B	3B	HR	RBI	BB	SO	AVG	OBP	SLG	PRO+	BR/A	SB	CS	SBR	FA	FR	G/POS	TPR
1952	Bos-N	93	326	26	63	7	2	7	41	26	26	.193	.255	.291	53	-21	1	0	0	.982	6	2-90	-1.1
1953	Mil-N	138	504	54	134	22	1	9	63	18	35	.266	.293	.367	75	-20	1	0	0	.965	-29	*2-138	-4.0
1954	Mil-N	66	192	22	47	8	0	6	20	19	17	.245	.322	.380	88	-4	0	1	-1	.977	-3	2-55	-0.4
1955	Mil-N	38	72	4	9	1	1	1	4	4	15	.125	.171	.208	0	-11	0	0	0	.977	-2	2-28	-1.1
1956	Mil-N	44	102	8	25	4	0	1	6	8	8	.245	.300	.314	69	-4	0	0	0	.979	3	2-42	0.0
1957	Det-A	16	22	3	5	1	0	0	2	2	1	.227	.292	.273	54	-1	0	0	0	1.000	-1	/3-3,2-1	-0.2
Total	6	395	1218	117	283	43	4	24	136	77	102	.232	.281	.333	66	-61	2	1	0	.974	-26	2-354/3-3	-6.8

■ MOXIE DIVIS
Divis, Edward George b: 1/16/1894, Cleveland, Ohio d: 12/19/55, Lakewood, Ohio Deb: 8/4/16

YEAR	TM/L	G	AB	R	H	2B	3B	HR	RBI	BB	SO	AVG	OBP	SLG	PRO+	BR/A	SB	CS	SBR	FA	FR	G/POS	TPR
1916	Phi-A	3	6	0	1	0	0	0	1	0	2	.167	.167	.167	0	-1	0			1.000	1	/O-1	0.0

■ LEO DIXON
Dixon, Leo Moses b: 9/4/1894, Chicago, Ill. d: 4/11/84, Chicago, Ill. BR/TR, 5'11", 170 lbs. Deb: 4/14/25

YEAR	TM/L	G	AB	R	H	2B	3B	HR	RBI	BB	SO	AVG	OBP	SLG	PRO+	BR/A	SB	CS	SBR	FA	FR	G/POS	TPR
1925	StL-A	76	205	27	46	11	1	1	19	24	42	.224	.318	.302	55	-14	3	2	-0	.981	9	C-75	-0.2
1926	StL-A	33	89	7	17	3	1	0	8	11	14	.191	.294	.247	40	-8	1	4	-2	.977	4	C-33	-0.4
1927	StL-A	36	103	6	20	3	1	0	12	7	6	.194	.245	.243	26	-11	0	1	-1	.937	3	C-35	-0.6
1929	Cin-N	14	30	0	5	2	0	0	2	3	7	.167	.242	.233	19	-4	0			1.000	4	C-14	0.1
Total	4	159	427	40	88	19	3	1	41	45	69	.206	.291	.272	43	-37	4	7		.971	21	C-157	-1.1

■ WALT DOANE
Doane, Walter Rudolph b: 3/12/1887, Bellevue, Idaho d: 10/19/35, W.Brandywine Township, Pa. BL/TR, 6', 165 lbs. Deb: 9/20/09

YEAR	TM/L	G	AB	R	H	2B	3B	HR	RBI	BB	SO	AVG	OBP	SLG	PRO+	BR/A	SB	CS	SBR	FA	FR	G/POS	TPR
1909	Cle-A	4	9	1	1	0	0	0	0	1		.111	.200	.111	-1	-1	0			.778	1	/O-2,P-1	0.0
1910	Cle-A	6	7	0	2	1	0	0	2	1		.286	.375	.429	150	0	0			.750	-1	/P-6	0.0
Total	2	10	16	1	3	1	0	0	2	2		.188	.278	.250	64	-1	0			.800	-0	/P-7,O-2	0.0

YEAR	TM/L	G	AB	R	H	2B	3B	HR	RBI	BB	SO	AVG	OBP	SLG	PRO+	BR/A	SB	CS	SBR	FA	FR	G/POS	TPR
■ **DAN DOBBEK**	Dobbek, Daniel John b: 12/6/34, Ontonagon, Mich. BL/TR, 6′, 195 lbs. Deb: 9/9/59																						
1959	Was-A	16	60	8	15	1	2	1	5	5	13	.250	.308	.383	89	-1	0	0	0	1.000	1	O-16	-0.1
1960	Was-A	110	248	32	54	8	2	10	30	35	41	.218	.317	.387	90	-4	4	3	-1	.973	-8	O-78	-1.5
1961	Min-A	72	125	12	21	3	1	4	14	13	18	.168	.257	.304	47	-10	1	2	-1	.985	-9	O-48	-2.1
Total	3	198	433	52	90	12	5	15	49	53	72	.208	.299	.363	77	-14	5	5	-2	.980	-16	O-142	-3.7
■ **JOHN DOBBS**	Dobbs, John Gordon b: 6/3/1875, Chattanooga, Tenn. d: 9/9/34, Charlotte, N.C. BL/TR, 5′9.5″, 170 lbs. Deb: 4/20/01																						
1901	Cin-N	109	435	71	119	17	4	2	27	36		.274	.338	.345	105	3	19			.948	-7	*O-100/3-8	-1.0
1902	Cin-N	63	256	39	76	7	3	1	16	19		.297	.348	.359	108	2	7			.963	8	O-63	0.6
	Chi-N	59	235	31	71	8	2	0	35	18		.302	.352	.353	121	6	3			.977	1	O-59	0.3
	Yr	122	491	70	147	15	5	1	51	37		.299	.350	.356	114	8	10			.970	8	*O-122	0.9
1903	Chi-N	16	61	8	14	1	1	0	4	7		.230	.329	.279	76	-2	0			1.000	1	O-16	-0.2
	Bro-N	111	414	61	98	15	7	2	59	48		.237	.323	.321	86	-6	23			.966	4	*O-110	-0.9
	Yr	127	475	69	112	16	8	2	63	55		.236	.324	.316	85	-8	23			.970	4	*O-126	-1.1
1904	Bro-N	101	363	36	90	16	2	0	30	28		.248	.304	.303	90	-4	11			.936	0	O-92/2-2,S-2	-1.0
1905	Bro-N	123	460	59	117	21	4	2	36	31		.254	.304	.330	96	-3	15			.938	-6	*O-123	-1.6
Total	5	582	2224	305	585	85	23	7	207	187		.263	.325	.331	98	-4	78			.954	-0	O-563/3-8,S-2,2-2	-3.8
■ **LARRY DOBY**	Doby, Lawrence Eugene b: 12/13/23, Camden, S.C. BL/TR, 6′1″, 182 lbs. Deb: 7/5/47 MCH																						
1947	Cle-A	29	32	3	5	1	0	0	2	1	11	.156	.182	.188	3	-4	0	0	0	1.000	-1	/2-4,1-1,S-1	-0.5
1948	*Cle-A	121	439	83	132	23	9	14	66	54	77	.301	.384	.490	135	21	9	9	-3	.955	3	*O-114	1.5
1949	Cle-A★	147	547	106	153	25	3	24	85	91	90	.280	.389	.468	129	23	10	9	-2	.976	-7	*O-147	0.6
1950	Cle-A★	142	503	110	164	25	5	25	102	98	71	.326	**.442**	.545	**156**	**46**	8	6	-1	.987	-6	*O-140	3.1
1951	Cle-A★	134	447	84	132	27	5	20	69	101	81	.295	.428	.512	**163**	43	4	1	1	.977	-1	*O-132	3.6
1952	Cle-A★	140	519	**104**	143	26	8	**32**	104	90	111	.276	.383	**.541**	**166**	45	5	2	0	.986	11	*O-136	**5.1**
1953	Cle-A★	149	513	92	135	18	5	29	102	96	121	.263	.385	.487	138	29	3	2	-0	.984	-7	*O-146	1.6
1954	*Cle-A★	153	577	94	157	18	4	**32**	**126**	85	94	.272	.368	.484	130	23	3	1	0	.995	6	*O-153	2.4
1955	Cle-A☆	131	491	91	143	17	5	26	75	61	100	.291	.372	.505	129	19	2	0	1	.994	3	*O-129	1.7
1956	Chi-A	140	504	89	135	22	3	24	102	102	105	.268	.395	.466	125	20	0	1	-1	.987	6	*O-137	1.8
1957	Chi-A	119	416	57	120	27	2	14	79	56	79	.288	.376	.464	127	16	2	3	-1	.985	-4	*O-110	0.5
1958	Cle-A	89	247	41	70	10	1	13	45	26	49	.283	.352	.490	132	10	0	2	-1	1.000	1	O-68	0.7
1959	Det-A	18	55	5	12	3	1	0	4	8	9	.218	.317	.309	69	-2	0	0	0	.960	-1	O-16	0.4
	Chi-A	21	58	1	14	1	1	0	9	2	13	.241	.267	.293	54	-4	1	0	0	.955	-1	O-12/1-2	-0.5
	Yr	39	113	6	26	4	2	0	13	10	22	.230	.293	.301	62	-6	1	0	0	.957	-1	O-28/1-2	-0.9
Total	13	1533	5348	960	1515	243	52	253	970	871	1011	.283	.387	.490	137	285	47	36	-8	.983	3	*O-1440/2-4,1-3,S-1	21.2
■ **ONA DODD**	Dodd, Ona Melvin. b: 10/14/1886, Springtown, Tex. d: 12/17/56, Carter, Okla. BR/TR, 5′8″, 150 lbs. Deb: 7/26/12																						
1912	Pit-N	5	9	0	0	0	0	0	1	1	3	.000	.100	.000	-73	-2	0			1.000	0	/3-4,2-1	-0.2
■ **TOM DODD**	Dodd, Thomas Marion b: 8/15/58, Portland, Ore. BR/TR, 6′, 190 lbs. Deb: 7/25/86																						
1986	Bal-A	8	13	1	3	0	0	1	2	2	2	.231	.375	.462	128	1	0	0	0	.000	-0	/3-1,D-6	0.0
■ **JOHN DODGE**	Dodge, John Lewis b: 4/27/1889, Bolivar, Tenn. d: 6/19/16, Mobile, Ala. BR/TR, 5′11.5″, 165 lbs. Deb: 8/29/12																						
1912	Phi-N	30	92	3	11	1	0	0	3	4	11	.120	.156	.130	-20	-15	2			1.000	8	3-23/2-5,S-1	-0.8
1913	Phi-N	3	3	0	1	0	0	0	0	2	0	.333	.600	.333	164	1	0			1.000	-1	/S-3	0.0
	Cin-N	94	323	35	78	8	8	4	45	10	34	.241	.269	.353	77	-11	11			.908	1	3-91	-0.9
	Yr	97	326	35	79	8	8	4	45	12	34	.242	.274	.353	78	-10	11			.908	1	3-91/S-3	-0.9
Total	2	127	418	38	90	9	8	4	48	16	45	.215	.248	.304	55	-26	13			.926	8	3-114/2-5,S-4	-1.7
■ **PAT DODSON**	Dodson, Patrick Neal b: 10/11/59, Santa Monica, Cal. BL/TL, 6′4″, 210 lbs. Deb: 9/5/86																						
1986	Bos-A	9	12	3	5	2	0	1	3	3	3	.417	.533	.833	264	3	0	0	0	1.000	-1	/1-7	0.2
1987	Bos-A	26	42	4	7	3	0	2	6	8	13	.167	.300	.381	77	-1	0	0	0	1.000	-1	1-21/D-1	-0.3
1988	Bos-A	17	45	5	8	3	1	1	1	6	17	.178	.275	.356	72	-2	0	0	0	1.000	2	1-17	-0.1
Total	3	52	99	12	20	8	1	4	10	17	33	.202	.319	.424	97	-0	0	0	0	1.000	0	/1-45,D-1	-0.2
■ **BOBBY DOERR**	Doerr, Robert Pershing b: 4/7/18, Los Angeles, Cal. BR/TR, 5′11″, 175 lbs. Deb: 4/20/37 CH																						
1937	Bos-A	55	147	22	33	5	1	2	14	18	25	.224	.313	.313	56	-10	2	4	-2	.973	4	2-47	-0.5
1938	Bos-A	145	509	70	147	26	7	5	80	59	39	.289	.363	.397	86	-11	5	10	-5	.968	6	*2-145	-0.1
1939	Bos-A	127	525	75	167	28	2	12	73	38	32	.318	.365	.448	103	1	1	10	-6	.976	**27**	*2-126	2.7
1940	Bos-A	151	595	87	173	37	10	22	105	57	53	.291	.353	.497	113	10	10	5	0	.977	18	*2-151	3.6
1941	Bos-A★	132	500	74	141	28	4	16	93	43	43	.282	.339	.450	105	2	1	3	-2	.971	-6	*2-132	0.3
1942	Bos-A☆	144	545	71	158	35	5	15	102	67	55	.290	.369	.455	127	19	4	4	-1	**.975**	11	*2-142	3.8
1943	Bos-A★	155	604	78	163	32	3	16	75	62	59	.270	.339	.412	117	12	8	8	-2	**.990**	15	*2-155	3.5
1944	Bos-A★	125	468	95	152	30	10	15	81	58	31	.325	.399	**.528**	166	39	5	2	0	.976	4	*2-125	5.2
1946	*Bos-A★	151	583	95	158	34	9	18	116	66	67	.271	.346	.453	115	11	5	6	-2	**.986**	**27**	*2-151	4.8
1947	Bos-A★	146	561	79	145	23	10	17	95	59	47	.258	.329	.426	101	-1	3	3	-1	.981	**24**	*2-146	3.3
1948	Bos-A★	140	527	94	150	23	6	27	111	83	49	.285	.386	.505	129	21	3	2	-0	.993	8	*2-138	3.6
1949	Bos-A	139	541	91	167	30	9	18	109	75	33	.309	.393	.497	126	19	2	2	-1	.980	**28**	*2-139	5.0
1950	Bos-A★	149	586	103	172	29	**11**	27	120	67	42	.294	.367	.519	114	9	3	4	-2	**.988**	9	*2-149	2.1
1951	Bos-A★	106	402	60	116	21	2	13	73	57	33	.289	.378	.448	112	7	2	1	0	.981	6	*2-106	1.7
Total	14	1865	7093	1094	2042	381	89	223	1247	809	608	.288	.362	.461	114	127	54	64	-22	.980	181	*2-1852	39.0
■ **JOHN DOHERTY**	Doherty, John Michael b: 8/22/51, Woburn, Mass. BL/TL, 5′11″, 185 lbs. Deb: 6/1/74																						
1974	Cal-A	74	223	20	57	14	1	3	15	8	13	.256	.281	.368	91	-4	2	1	0	.991	-1	1-70/D-2	-0.9
1975	Cal-A	30	94	7	19	3	0	1	12	8	12	.202	.265	.266	54	-6	1	1	-0	.983	-1	1-26/D-1	-0.9
Total	2	104	317	27	76	17	1	4	27	16	25	.240	.276	.338	80	-10	3	2	-0	.989	-2	/1-96,D-3	-1.8
■ **COZY DOLAN**	Dolan, Albert J. (b: James Alberts) b: 12/23/1889, Chicago, Ill. d: 12/10/58, Chicago, Ill. BR/TR, 5′10″, 160 lbs. Deb: 8/15/09 C																						
1909	Cin-N	3	6	2	1	0	0	0	0	2		.167	.375	.167	69	-0	0			.750	-1	/3-3	-0.1
1911	NY-A	19	69	19	21	1	2	0	6	8		.304	.385	.377	106	1	12			.947	-1	3-19	0.0
1912	NY-A	18	60	15	12	1	3	0	11	5		.200	.273	.317	64	-3	5			.768	-5	3-17	-0.8
	Phi-N	11	50	8	14	2	2	0	7	1	10	.280	.294	.400	83	-1	3			.872	-1	3-11	-0.2
1913	Phi-N	55	126	15	33	4	0	0	8	1	21	.262	.273	.294	59	-7	9			.905	-7	O-12,S-10/2-9,31	-1.4
	Pit-N	35	133	22	27	5	2	0	9	15	14	.203	.289	.271	63	-6	14			.937	-1	3-35	-0.8
	Yr	90	259	37	60	9	2	0	17	16	35	.232	.282	.282	61	-13	23			.932	-9	3-39,O-12,S-10,/21	-2.2
1914	StL-N	126	421	76	101	16	3	4	32	55	74	.240	.335	.321	96	-0	42			.955	-8	O-96,3-27	-1.3
1915	StL-N	111	322	53	90	14	9	2	38	34	37	.280	.356	.398	127	11	17	11	-2	.929	-11	O-98	-0.6
1922	NY-N	1	0	0	0	0	0	0	0	0	0	—	—	—	—	0	0	0	0	.000	0	R	0.0
Total	7	379	1187	210	299	43	21	6	111	121	156	.252	.328	.339	95	-6	102	11		.940	-34	O-206,3-116/S21	-5.2
■ **JOE DOLAN**	Dolan, Joseph b: 2/24/1873, Baltimore, Md. d: 3/24/38, Omaha, Neb. TR , 5′10″, 155 lbs. Deb: 8/11/1896																						
1896	Lou-N	44	165	14	35	2	1	3	18	9	12	.212	.253	.291	45	-14	6			.940	10	S-44	-0.2
1897	Lou-N	36	133	10	28	2	2	0	7	8		.211	.271	.256	41	-11	6			.849	-3	S-18,2-18	-1.2
1899	Phi-N	61	222	27	57	6	3	1	30	11		.257	.298	.324	73	-9	3			.915	-11	2-61	-1.5
1900	Phi-N	74	257	39	51	7	3	1	27	16		.198	.259	.261	44	-20	10			.931	3	3-31,2-29,S-12	-1.4
1901	Phi-N	10	37	0	3	0	0	0	2	2		.081	.128	.081	-38	-6	0			.973	-3	2-10	-0.9
	Phi-A	98	338	50	73	21	2	1	38	26		.216	.282	.299	58	-19	3			.881	16	S-61,3-35/2-1,O-1	0.1
Total	5	323	1152	140	247	38	11	6	122	72	12	.214	.270	.282	51	-79	28			.902	11	S-135,2-119/3-66,O	-5.1
■ **BIDDY DOLAN**	Dolan, Leon Mark b: 7/9/1881, Onalaska, Wis. d: 7/15/50, Indianapolis, Ind BR/TR, 6′, Deb: 4/16/14																						
1914	Ind-F	32	103	13	23	4	2	1	15	12	13	.223	.316	.330	69	-6	5			.979	1	1-31	-0.6

YEAR	TM/L	G	AB	R	H	2B	3B	HR	RBI	BB	SO	AVG	OBP	SLG	PRO+	BR/A	SB	CS	SBR	FA	FR	G/POS	TPR
1967	KC-A	105	377	27	104	16	5	0	28	37	39	.276	.344	.345	107	4	6	3	0	.982	-18	*2-101/S-1	-0.8
1968	Oak-A	127	363	37	80	9	2	2	27	45	44	.220	.310	.273	82	-7	5	5	-2	.971	-4	2-98/3-5,S-1	-0.8
1969	Oak-A	12	13	1	1	0	0	0	0	2	4	.077	.200	.077	-21	-2	0	0	0	.857	0	/2-1	-0.2
	Sea-A	95	338	22	79	8	3	1	19	36	36	.234	.307	.284	67	-14	6	1	1	.974	-1	2-90/3-2,S-1	-0.6
	Yr	107	351	23	80	8	3	1	19	38	40	.228	.303	.276	64	-16	6	1	1	.972	-0	2-91/3-2,S-1	-0.8
1970	Oak-A	41	89	4	22	2	1	1	11	9	6	.247	.316	.326	80	-2	1	0	0	.986	-3	2-21/S-6,3-1	-0.3
1974	Oak-A	10	15	1	2	0	0	0	0	0	0	.133	.133	.133	-25	-2	0	0	0	.962	1	/2-7,3-3	-0.2
Total	6	405	1225	96	292	35	11	4	86	132	133	.238	.314	.295	81	-28	19	9	0	.976	-26	2-327/3-11,S-9	-3.5

■ LEN DONDERO
Dondero, Leonard Peter "Mike" b: 9/12/03, Newark, Cal. BR/TR, 5'11", 178 lbs. Deb: 4/21/29

YEAR	TM/L	G	AB	R	H	2B	3B	HR	RBI	BB	SO	AVG	OBP	SLG	PRO+	BR/A	SB	CS	SBR	FA	FR	G/POS	TPR
1929	StL-A	19	31	2	6	0	0	1	8	0	4	.194	.194	.290	22	-4	0	0	0	.857	-3	3-10/2-5	-0.6

■ MIKE DONLIN
Donlin, Michael Joseph "Turkey Mike" b: 5/30/1878, Peoria, Ill. d: 9/24/33, Hollywood, Cal. BL/TL, 5'9", 170 lbs. Deb: 7/19/1899

YEAR	TM/L	G	AB	R	H	2B	3B	HR	RBI	BB	SO	AVG	OBP	SLG	PRO+	BR/A	SB	CS	SBR	FA	FR	G/POS	TPR
1899	StL-N	66	266	49	86	9	6	6	27	17		.323	.366	.470	126	8	20			.873	-7	O-51,1-13/S-3,P-3	-0.4
1900	StL-N	78	276	40	90	8	6	10	48	14		.326	.361	.507	139	13	14			.922	-4	O-47,1-21	0.5
1901	Bal-A	121	476	107	162	23	13	5	67	53		.340	.409	.475	138	25	33			.918	9	O-74,1-47	2.5
1902	Cin-N	34	143	30	41	5	4	0	9	9		.287	.333	.378	109	1	9			.877	-1	O-32/P-1,S-1	-0.2
1903	Cin-N	126	496	110	174	25	18	7	67	56		.351	.420	.516	150	30	26			.900	-2	*O-118/1-7	2.0
1904	Cin-N	60	236	42	84	11	7	1	38	18		.356	.406	.475	158	15	21			.872	-3	O-53/1-6	1.0
	NY-N	42	132	17	37	7	3	2	14	10		.280	.340	.424	130	4	1			.918	-7	O-37	-0.4
	Yr	102	368	59	121	18	10	3	52	28		.329	.382	.457	148	20	22			.886	-9	O-90/1-6	0.6
1905	*NY-N	150	606	**124**	216	31	16	7	80	56		.356	.413	.495	166	49	33			.934	-12	*O-150	3.1
1906	NY-N	37	121	15	38	5	1	1	14	11		.314	.371	.397	136	5	9			.929	-6	O-29/1-1	-0.3
1908	NY-N	155	593	71	198	26	13	6	106	23		.334	.364	.452	153	32	30			.977	0	*O-155	3.0
1911	NY-N	12	12	3	4	0	0	1	1	0	1	.333	.333	.583	150	1	2			1.000	-1	/O-3	-0.1
	Bos-N	56	222	33	70	16	1	2	34	22	17	.315	.377	.423	115	4	7			.912	-3	O-56	-0.2
	Yr	68	234	36	74	16	1	3	35	22	18	.316	.375	.432	117	5	9			.913	-4	O-59	-0.3
1912	Pit-N	77	244	27	77	9	8	2	35	20	16	.316	.370	.443	124	7	8			.982	-2	O-62	0.2
1914	NY-N	35	31	1	5	1	1	1	3	3	5	.161	.235	.355	77	-1	0			.000	0	H	-0.1
Total	12	1049	3854	669	1282	176	97	51	543	312	39	.333	.386	.468	142	193	213			.924	-37	O-867/1-95,P-4,S-4	10.6

■ JIM DONNELLY
Donnelly, James B. b: 7/19/1865, New Haven, Conn. d: 3/5/15, New Haven, Conn. BR/TR, 5'10.5", 155 lbs. Deb: 7/11/1884

YEAR	TM/L	G	AB	R	H	2B	3B	HR	RBI	BB	SO	AVG	OBP	SLG	PRO+	BR/A	SB	CS	SBR	FA	FR	G/POS	TPR
1884	KC-U	6	23	2	3	1	0	0		1		.130	.167	.174	4	-3				.536	-4	/3-5,C-1	-0.6
	Ind-a	40	134	22	34	2	2	0		5		.254	.301	.299	99	0				.850	-5	3-24/S-8,O-6,2-2	-0.4
1885	Det-N	56	211	24	49	4	3	1	22	10	29	.232	.267	.294	81	-4				.850	-3	3-55/1-1	-0.6
1886	KC-N	113	438	51	88	11	3	0	38	36	57	.201	.262	.240	50	-26	16			.845	0	*3-113	-2.2
1887	Was-N	117	425	51	85	9	6	1	46	16	26	.200	.234	.256	38	-35	42			.867	16	*3-115/S-2	-1.4
1888	Was-N	122	428	43	86	9	4	0	23	20	16	.201	.242	.241	57	-20	44			.875	-5	*3-117/S-5	-2.2
1889	Was-N	4	13	3	2	0	0	0	0	2	0	.154	.267	.154	20	-1	1			.667	-2	/3-4	-0.2
1890	StL-a	11	42	11	14	0	0	0	3	8		.333	.451	.333	115	1	5			.795	-3	3-11	-0.1
1891	Col-a	17	54	6	13	0	0	0	9	13	5	.241	.388	.241	85	0	7			.855	3	3-17	0.3
1896	Bal-N	106	396	70	130	14	10	0	71	34	11	.328	.387	.414	110	6	38			.884	-2	*3-106	0.5
1897	Pit-N	44	161	22	31	4	0	0	14	16		.193	.270	.217	31	-16	14			.920	1	3-44	-1.2
	NY-N	23	85	19	16	3	0	0	11	9		.188	.266	.224	31	-8	6			.869	-6	3-23	-1.2
	Yr	67	246	41	47	7	0	0	25	25		.191	.268	.220	31	-24	20			.905	-5	3-67	-2.4
1898	StL-N	1	1	0	1	0	0	0	0	0		1.000	1.000	1.000	463	0	0			.500	0	/3-1	0.0
Total	11	660	2411	324	552	57	28	2	237	170	144	.229	.284	.278	65	-107	173			.862	-8	3-635/S-15,O-6,21C	-9.3

■ JOHN DONNELLY
Donnelly, John b: Elizabeth, N.J. Deb: 4/14/1873 F

YEAR	TM/L	G	AB	R	H	2B	3B	HR	RBI	BB	SO	AVG	OBP	SLG	PRO+	BR/A	SB	CS	SBR	FA	FR	G/POS	TPR
1873	Was-n	30	137	15	35	1	0	0	20	1	0	.255	.261	.263	58	-6	0	0	0	.783	1	S-13,2-12/O-6,3-1	-0.5
1874	Phi-n	6	22	2	5	0	0	0	2	0	0	.227	.227	.227	45	-1	0	0	0	.667	-3	/O-3,S-2,2-1	-0.3
Total	2 n	36	159	17	40	1	0	0	22	1	0	.252	.256	.258	56	-8	0	0	0	.763	-2	/S-15,2-13,O-9,3-1	-0.8

■ PETE DONNELLY
Donnelly, Peter J. b: 10/8/1849, Philadelphia, Pa. d: 10/1/1890, Jersey City, N.J. Deb: 5/13/1871 F

YEAR	TM/L	G	AB	R	H	2B	3B	HR	RBI	BB	SO	AVG	OBP	SLG	PRO+	BR/A	SB	CS	SBR	FA	FR	G/POS	TPR
1871	Kek-n	9	34	7	7	1	1	0	3	1	2	.206	.229	.294	48	-2	0	0	0	.714	-5	/O-9,3-2	-0.5

■ CHRIS DONNELS
Donnels, Chris Barton b: 4/21/66, Los Angeles, Cal. BL/TR, 6', 185 lbs. Deb: 5/7/91

YEAR	TM/L	G	AB	R	H	2B	3B	HR	RBI	BB	SO	AVG	OBP	SLG	PRO+	BR/A	SB	CS	SBR	FA	FR	G/POS	TPR
1991	NY-N	37	89	7	20	2	0	0	5	14	19	.225	.330	.247	65	-4	1	1	-0	1.000	3	1-15,3-11	-0.2
1992	NY-N	45	121	8	21	4	0	0	6	17	25	.174	.275	.207	39	-9	1	0	0	.941	4	3-29,2-12	-0.6
1993	Hou-N	88	179	18	46	14	2	2	24	19	33	.257	.328	.391	95	-1	2	0	1	.898	-0	3-31,1-23/2-1	-0.2
1994	Hou-N	54	86	12	23	5	0	3	5	13	18	.267	.364	.430	112	2	1	0	0	1.000	1	3-14/1-4,2-4	0.2
1995	Hou-N	19	30	4	9	0	0	0	2	3	6	.300	.364	.300	83	-1	0	0	0	.818	-2	/3-9,2-1	-0.2
	Bos-A	40	91	13	23	2	2	2	11	9	18	.253	.320	.385	80	-3	0	0	0	.927	1	3-27/1-8,2-3	-0.2
Total	5	283	596	62	142	27	4	7	53	75	119	.238	.323	.332	79	-16	5	1	1	.929	6	3-121/1-50,2-21	-1.2

■ JOE DONOHUE
Donohue, Joseph F. b: 1869, Syracuse, N.Y. Deb: 8/24/1891

YEAR	TM/L	G	AB	R	H	2B	3B	HR	RBI	BB	SO	AVG	OBP	SLG	PRO+	BR/A	SB	CS	SBR	FA	FR	G/POS	TPR
1891	Phi-N	6	22	2	7	1	0	0	2	1	3	.318	.375	.364	113	0	0			1.000	-0	/O-4,S-2	0.0

■ TOM DONOHUE
Donohue, Thomas James b: 11/15/52, Mineola, N.Y. BR/TR, 6', 185 lbs. Deb: 4/6/79

YEAR	TM/L	G	AB	R	H	2B	3B	HR	RBI	BB	SO	AVG	OBP	SLG	PRO+	BR/A	SB	CS	SBR	FA	FR	G/POS	TPR
1979	Cal-A	38	107	13	24	3	1	3	14	3	29	.224	.259	.355	66	-5	2	0	1	.981	-3	C-38	-0.6
1980	Cal-A	84	218	18	41	4	1	2	14	7	63	.188	.217	.243	26	-22	5	1	1	.986	-10	C-84	-2.9
Total	2	122	325	31	65	7	2	5	28	10	92	.200	.231	.280	40	-28	7	1	2	.985	-12	C-122	-3.5

■ FRED DONOVAN
Donovan, Frederick Maurice b: 7/4/1864, New Hampshire d: 3/7/16, Bloomington, Ill. BR/TR, Deb: 6/23/1895

YEAR	TM/L	G	AB	R	H	2B	3B	HR	RBI	BB	SO	AVG	OBP	SLG	PRO+	BR/A	SB	CS	SBR	FA	FR	G/POS	TPR
1895	Cle-N	3	12	1	1	0	0	0	1	1	2	.083	.154	.083	-36	-2	0			.938	-0	/C-3	-0.2

■ JERRY DONOVAN
Donovan, Jeremiah Francis b: 9/3/1876, Lock Haven, Pa. d: 6/27/38, St.Petersburg, Fla. BR/TR, Deb: 4/12/06 F

YEAR	TM/L	G	AB	R	H	2B	3B	HR	RBI	BB	SO	AVG	OBP	SLG	PRO+	BR/A	SB	CS	SBR	FA	FR	G/POS	TPR
1906	Phi-N	61	166	11	33	4	0	0	15	6		.199	.236	.223	43	-11	2			.955	-4	C-53/S-1,O-1	-1.2

■ MIKE DONOVAN
Donovan, Michael Berchman b: 10/18/1881, Brooklyn, N.Y. d: 2/3/38, New York, N.Y. BR/TR, 5'8", 155 lbs. Deb: 5/29/04

YEAR	TM/L	G	AB	R	H	2B	3B	HR	RBI	BB	SO	AVG	OBP	SLG	PRO+	BR/A	SB	CS	SBR	FA	FR	G/POS	TPR
1904	Cle-A	2	2	0	0	0	0	0	0	0		.000	.000	.000	-99	-0	0			.000	0	/S-1	-0.1
1908	NY-A	5	19	2	5	1	0	0	2	0		.263	.263	.316	87	-0	0			1.000	1	/3-5	0.1
Total	2	7	21	2	5	1	0	0	2	0		.238	.238	.286	69	-1	0			1.000	1	/3-5,S-1	0.0

■ PATSY DONOVAN
Donovan, Patrick Joseph b: 3/16/1865, County Cork, Ireland d: 12/25/53, Lawrence, Mass. BL/TL, 5'11.5", 175 lbs. Deb: 4/19/1890 M

YEAR	TM/L	G	AB	R	H	2B	3B	HR	RBI	BB	SO	AVG	OBP	SLG	PRO+	BR/A	SB	CS	SBR	FA	FR	G/POS	TPR
1890	Bos-N	32	140	17	36	0	0	0	9	8	17	.257	.307	.257	60	-7	10			.891	-5	O-32	-1.2
	*Bro-N	28	105	17	23	5	1	0	8	5	5	.219	.268	.286	61	-5	3			1.000	2	O-28	-0.1
	Yr	60	245	34	59	5	1	0	17	13	22	.241	.290	.269	61	-13	13			.952	-3	O-60	-1.6
1891	Lou-a	105	439	73	141	10	3	2	53	30	18	.321	.375	.371	115	9	27			.912	5	*O-105	0.9
	Was-a	17	70	9	14	1	0	0	3	4	5	.200	.243	.214	33	-6	1			.857	-2	O-17	-0.8
	Yr	122	509	82	155	11	3	2	56	34	23	.305	.358	.350	104	3	28			.907	2	*O-122	0.1
1892	Was-N	40	163	29	39	3	3	0	12	11	13	.239	.295	.294	81	-4	16			.844	1	O-40	-0.4
	Pit-N	90	388	77	114	15	3	2	26	20	16	.294	.333	.363	110	4	40			.872	-3	O-90	-0.3
	Yr	130	551	106	153	18	6	2	38	31	29	.278	.322	.343	102	0	56			.862	-2	*O-130	-0.7
1893	Pit-N	113	499	114	158	5	8	2	56	42	8	.317	.373	.371	100	1	46			.937	-1	*O-112	-0.5
1894	Pit-N	132	576	145	174	21	10	4	76	33	12	.302	.345	.394	79	-21	41			.932	8	*O-132	-1.7
1895	Pit-N	125	519	114	160	17	6	1	58	47	19	.308	.375	.370	98	1	36			.961	-5	*O-125	-1.2
1896	Pit-N	131	573	113	183	20	5	3	59	35	18	.319	.370	.387	104	4	48			.954	7	*O-131	0.0
1897	Pit-N	120	479	82	154	16	7	0	57	25		.322	.360	.384	100	0	34			.949	1	*O-120,M	-0.7
1898	Pit-N	147	610	112	184	16	9	0	37	34		.302	.346	.357	104	2	41			.928	0	*O-147	-0.7
1899	Pit-N	121	531	82	156	11	7	1	55	17		.294	.322	.347	84	-13	26			.941	-12	*O-121,M	-3.1
1900	StL-N	126	503	78	159	11	1	0	61	38		.316	.368	.342	97	-1	**45**			.951	-5	*O-124	-1.3

YEAR	TM/L	G	AB	R	H	2B	3B	HR	RBI	BB	SO	AVG	OBP	SLG	PRO+	BR/A	SB	CS	SBR	FA	FR	G/POS	TPR
1901	StL-N	130	531	92	161	23	5	1	73	27		.303	.344	.371	113	8	28			.979	4	*O-129,M	0.2
1902	StL-N	126	502	70	158	12	4	0	35	28		.315	.363	.355	126	16	34			.959	10	*O-126,M	1.9
1903	StL-N	105	410	63	134	15	3	0	39	25		.327	.370	.378	117	9	25			.952	-1	*O-105,M	0.2
1904	Was-A	125	436	30	100	6	0	0	19	24		.229	.271	.243	64	-17	17			.963	9	*O-122,M	-1.7
1906	Bro-N	7	21	1	5	0	0	0	0	0		.238	.238	.238	53	-1	0			1.000	-1	/O-6,M	-0.2
1907	Bro-N	1	1	0	0	0	0	0	0	0		.000	.000	.000	-99	-0	0			1.000	0	/O-1,M	0.0
Total	17	1821	7496	1318	2253	207	75	16	736	453	131	.301	.347	.355	98	-22	518			.941	13	*O-1813	-11.0
■ **TOM DONOVAN**	Donovan, Thomas Joseph b: 1/1/1873, West Troy, N.Y. d: 3/25/33, Watervliet, N.Y. BR/TR, 6'2", 168 lbs. Deb: 9/10/01 F																						
1901	Cle-A	18	71	9	18	3	1	0	5	0		.254	.254	.324	62	-4	1			.862	-1	O-18/P-1	-0.5
■ **BILL DONOVAN**	Donovan, William Edward "Wild Bill" b: 10/13/1876, Lawrence, Mass. d: 12/9/23, Forsyth, N.Y. BR/TR, 5'11", 190 lbs. Deb: 4/22/1898 MC																						
1898	Was-N	39	103	11	17	2	2	2	8	4		.165	.211	.282	41	-8	2			.933	1	O-20,P-17/S-1,2-1	-0.5
1899	Bro-N	5	13	2	3	1	0	0	0	0		.231	.231	.308	46	-1	0			.857	-0	/P-5	0.0
1900	Bro-N	5	13	0	0	0	0	0	2	0		.000	.000	.000	-94	-3	0			1.000	1	/P-5	0.0
1901	Bro-N	46	135	16	23	3	0	2	13	8		.170	.217	.237	31	-12	1			.927	-1	P-45	0.0
1902	Bro-N	48	161	16	28	3	2	1	16	9		.174	.227	.236	42	-11	7			.948	2	P-35/1-8,O-4,2-1	-0.3
1903	Det-A	40	124	11	30	3	2	0	12	4		.242	.266	.298	71	-4	3			.938	-2	P-35/S-2,2-1,O-1	0.1
1904	Det-A	46	140	12	38	2	1	1	6	3		.271	.287	.321	95	-1	2			.967	-3	P-34/1-8,O-1	-0.4
1905	Det-A	44	130	16	25	4	0	0	5	12		.192	.266	.223	55	-6	8			.933	-0	P-34/O-8,2-2	0.1
1906	Det-A	28	91	5	11	0	1	0	0	1		.121	.130	.143	-14	-12	6			.961	-1	P-25/2-3,O-1	-0.2
1907	*Det-A	37	109	20	29	7	2	0	19	6		.266	.304	.367	110	1	4			.945	-6	P-32	0.0
1908	*Det-A	30	82	5	13	1	0	0	2	10		.159	.250	.171	36	-5	2			.917	-6	P-29	0.0
1909	*Det-A	22	45	6	9	0	0	0	1	2		.200	.250	.200	41	-3	0			.974	-2	P-21	0.0
1910	Det-A	26	69	6	10	1	0	0	2	5		.145	.203	.159	13	-7	0			.955	-6	P-26	0.0
1911	Det-A	24	60	11	12	3	1	1	6	11		.200	.324	.333	79	-2	1			.935	-5	P-20	0.0
1912	Det-A	6	13	3	1	0	0	0	0	1		.077	.143	.077	-38	-2	0			1.000	-2	/P-3,1-2,O-2	-0.3
1915	NY-A	10	12	1	1	0	0	0	0	1	6	.083	.154	.083	-29	-2	0			1.000	-1	/P-9,M	0.0
1916	NY-A	1	0	0	0	0	0	0	0	0	0	—	—	—	—	0	0			.000	-0	/P-1,M	0.0
1918	Det-A	2	2	1	1	0	0	0	1	0	0	.500	.500	.500	210	0	0			1.000	-0	/P-2	0.0
Total	18	459	1302	142	251	30	11	7	93	77	6	.193	.241	.249	49	-80	36			.944	-30	P-378/O-37,1-18,2S	-1.5
■ **RED DOOIN**	Dooin, Charles Sebastian b: 6/12/1879, Cincinnati, Ohio d: 5/14/52, Rochester, N.Y. BR/TR, 5'9.5", 165 lbs. Deb: 4/18/02 M																						
1902	Phi-N	94	333	20	77	7	3	0	35	10		.231	.262	.270	64	-14	8			.950	5	C-84/O-6	-0.1
1903	Phi-N	62	188	18	41	5	1	0	14	8		.218	.254	.255	47	-13	9			.940	-4	C-51/1-1,O-1	-1.2
1904	Phi-N	108	355	41	86	11	4	6	36	8		.242	.261	.346	90	-6	15			.938	7	C-96/1-4,O-3,3-1	1.2
1905	Phi-N	113	380	45	95	13	5	0	36	10		.250	.269	.311	75	-13	12			.965	8	*C-107/3-1	0.6
1906	Phi-N	113	351	25	86	19	1	0	32	13		.245	.274	.305	80	-9	15			.948	-10	*C-107	-1.0
1907	Phi-N	101	313	18	66	8	4	0	14	15		.211	.252	.262	62	-14	10			.959	2	C-94/2-1,O-1	-0.4
1908	Phi-N	133	435	28	108	17	4	0	41	17		.248	.283	.306	85	-8	20			.966	12	*C-132	1.8
1909	Phi-N	141	468	42	105	14	1	2	38	21		.224	.264	.271	66	-20	14			.958	4	*C-140	-0.3
1910	Phi-N	103	331	30	80	13	4	0	30	22	17	.242	.289	.305	71	-13	10			.956	-4	C-91/O-3,M	-0.8
1911	Phi-N	74	247	18	81	15	1	1	16	14	12	.328	.366	.409	115	4	6			.967	5	C-74,M	1.6
1912	Phi-N	69	184	20	43	9	0	0	22	5	12	.234	.262	.283	46	-14	8			.958	0	C-58,M	-0.9
1913	Phi-N	55	129	6	33	4	1	0	13	3	9	.256	.273	.302	62	-7	1			.962	3	C-50,M	-0.1
1914	Phi-N	53	118	10	21	2	0	1	8	4	14	.178	.205	.220	25	-11	4			.967	-0	C-40/O-2,M	-1.0
1915	Cin-N	10	31	2	10	0	0	0	0	2	5	.323	.364	.323	106	0	1			.915	-4	C-10	-0.3
	NY-N	46	124	9	27	2	2	0	9	3	15	.218	.236	.266	55	-7	0	2	-1	.964	1	C-46	-0.5
	Yr	56	155	11	37	2	2	0	9	5	20	.239	.262	.277	66	-7	1	2	-1	.956	-3	C-56	-0.8
1916	NY-N	15	17	1	2	0	0	0	0	0	3	.118	.118	.118	-29	-3	0			.972	0	C-15	-0.2
Total	15	1290	4004	333	961	139	31	10	344	155	87	.240	.272	.298	72	-148	133	2		.957	25	*C-1195/O-16,132	-1.6
■ **MICKEY DOOLAN**	Doolan, Michael Joseph "Doc" (b: Michael Joseph Doolittle) b: 5/7/1880, Ashland, Pa. d: 11/1/51, Orlando, Fla. BR/TR, 5'10.5", 170 lbs. Deb: 4/14/05 C																						
1905	Phi-N	136	492	53	125	27	11	1	48	24		.254	.292	.360	97	-4	17			.935	-9	*S-135	-1.1
1906	Phi-N	154	535	41	123	19	7	1	55	27		.230	.270	.297	77	-16	16			.930	6	*S-154	-0.6
1907	Phi-N	145	509	33	104	19	7	1	47	25		.204	.243	.275	63	-23	18			.929	14	*S-145	-0.6
1908	Phi-N	129	445	29	104	25	4	2	49	17		.234	.267	.321	85	-9	5			.939	0	*S-129	-0.7
1909	Phi-N	147	493	39	108	12	10	1	35	37		.219	.276	.290	75	-15	10			.939	**25**	*S-147	1.3
1910	Phi-N	148	536	58	141	31	6	2	57	35	56	.263	.315	.354	92	-7	16			**.948**	21	*S-148	2.1
1911	Phi-N	146	512	51	122	23	6	1	49	44	65	.238	.301	.313	71	-21	14			.936	20	*S-145	0.9
1912	Phi-N	146	532	47	137	26	6	1	62	34	59	.258	.305	.335	70	-23	6			.950	8	*S-146	-0.2
1913	Phi-N	151	518	32	113	12	6	1	43	29	68	.218	.262	.270	50	-34	17			.941	17	*S-148/2-3	-0.3
1914	Bal-F	145	486	58	119	23	6	1	53	40	47	.245	.311	.323	71	-27	30			**.949**	**29**	*S-145	1.5
1915	Bal-F	119	404	41	75	13	7	2	21	24	39	.186	.238	.267	41	-39	10			.946	32	*S-119	0.3
	Chi-F	24	86	9	23	1	1	0	9	2	7	.267	.292	.302	72	-5	5			.914	1	S-24	-0.2
	Yr	143	490	50	98	14	8	2	30	26	46	.200	.248	.273	46	-44	15			.941	**33**	*S-143	0.1
1916	Chi-N	28	70	4	15	2	1	0	5	8	7	.214	.295	.271	67	-3	0			.918	3	S-24	0.2
	NY-N	18	51	4	12	3	1	1	3	2	4	.235	.264	.392	106	0	1			.975	2	S-16/2-2	0.3
	Yr	46	121	8	27	5	2	1	8	10	11	.223	.282	.322	82	-3	1			.939	4	S-40/2-2	0.5
1918	Bro-N	92	308	14	55	8	2	0	18	22	24	.179	.233	.218	38	-23	8			**.968**	10	2-91	-0.8
Total	13	1728	5977	513	1376	244	81	15	554	370	376	.230	.279	.306	71	-248	173			.940	178	*S-1625/2-96	2.1
■ **HARRY DOOMS**	Dooms, Henry E. "Jack" b: 1/30/1867, St.Louis, Mo. d: 12/14/1899, St.Louis, Mo. Deb: 8/7/1892																						
1892	Lou-N	1	4	0	0	0	0	0	0	1	3	.000	.200	.000	-42	-1	0			.000	-1	/O-1	-0.1
■ **TOM DORAN**	Doran, Thomas J. "Long Tom" b: 12/2/1880, Westchester Co., N.Y. d: 6/22/10, New York, N.Y. BL/TR, 5'11", 152 lbs. Deb: 4/19/04																						
1904	Bos-A	12	32	1	4	0	1	0	0	4		.125	.243	.188	35	-2	1			.898	-5	C-11	-0.7
1905	Bos-A	3	3	0	0	0	0	0	0	0		.000	.000	.000	-99	-1	0			1.000	0	/C-1	0.0
	Det-A	34	94	8	15	3	0	0	4	8		.160	.248	.191	40	-6	2			.963	-5	C-32	-0.9
	Yr	37	97	8	15	3	0	0	4	8		.155	.241	.186	35	-7	2			.964	-5	C-33	-0.9
1906	Bos-A	2	3	1	0	0	0	0	0	0		.000	.000	.000	-99	-1	0			1.000	-0	/C-2	-0.1
Total	3	51	132	10	19	3	1	0	4	12		.144	.236	.182	33	-10	3			.950	-10	/C-46	-1.7
■ **BILL DORAN**	Doran, William Donald b: 5/28/58, Cincinnati, Ohio BB/TR, 5'11", 175 lbs. Deb: 9/6/82																						
1982	Hou-N	26	97	11	27	3	0	0	6	4	11	.278	.307	.309	79	-3	5	0	2	.975	-3	2-26	-0.3
1983	Hou-N	154	535	70	145	12	7	8	39	86	67	.271	.372	.364	112	11	12	12	-4	.979	5	*2-153	2.0
1984	Hou-N	147	548	92	143	18	11	4	41	66	69	.261	.343	.356	104	4	21	12	-1	.986	6	*2-139,S-13	1.5
1985	Hou-N	148	578	84	166	31	6	14	59	71	69	.287	.365	.434	126	21	23	15	-2	.980	7	*2-147	3.2
1986	*Hou-N	145	550	92	152	29	3	6	37	81	57	.276	.371	.373	109	9	42	19	1	.974	-42	*2-144	-2.7
1987	Hou-N	162	625	82	177	23	3	16	79	82	64	.283	.369	.406	109	10	31	11	3	**.992**	-16	*2-162/S-3	0.4
1988	Hou-N	132	480	66	119	18	1	7	53	65	60	.248	.339	.333	97	-0	17	4	3	**.987**	-3	*2-130	0.5
1989	Hou-N	142	507	65	111	25	2	8	58	59	63	.219	.303	.323	82	-12	22	3	5	.980	-27	*2-138	-3.2
1990	Hou-N	109	344	49	99	21	2	6	32	71	53	.288	.410	.413	131	18	18	9	0	.989	-11	2-99	0.9
	Cin-N	17	59	10	22	8	0	1	5	8	5	.373	.448	.559	168	6	5	0	2	.985	1	2-12/3-4	0.9
	Yr	126	403	59	121	29	2	7	37	79	58	.300	.415	.434	137	24	23	9	2	.988	-10	*2-111/3-4	1.8
1991	Cin-N	111	361	51	101	12	2	6	35	46	39	.280	.361	.374	103	3	5	4	-1	.981	-14	2-88/O-6,1-4	-1.1
1992	Cin-N	132	387	48	91	16	2	8	47	64	40	.235	.344	.349	94	-1	7	4	-0	.988	-9	*2-104,1-25	-1.0
1993	Mil-A	28	60	7	13	4	0	0	6	6	3	.217	.288	.283	55	-4	1	0	0	.964	-5	2-17/1-4	-0.9
Total	12	1453	5131	727	1366	220	39	84	497	709	600	.266	.356	.373	107	62	209	93	7	.983	-112	*2-1359/1-33,SO3	0.2

■ BILL DORAN

Doran, William James b: 6/14/1898, San Francisco, Cal. d: 3/9/78, Santa Monica, Cal. BL/TR, 5'11.5", 175 lbs. Deb: 6/23/22

YEAR	TM/L	G	AB	R	H	2B	3B	HR	RBI	BB	SO	AVG	OBP	SLG	PRO+	BR/A	SB	CS	SBR	FA	FR	G/POS	TPR
1922	Cle-A	3	2	0	1	0	0	0	0	1	0	.500	.667	.500	206	0	0	0	0	.000	0	/3-2	0.0

■ JERRY DORGAN

Dorgan, Jeremiah F. b: 1856, Meriden, Conn. d: 6/10/1891, New Haven, Conn. BL/TR, 165 lbs. Deb: 7/8/1880 F

YEAR	TM/L	G	AB	R	H	2B	3B	HR	RBI	BB	SO	AVG	OBP	SLG	PRO+	BR/A	SB	CS	SBR	FA	FR	G/POS	TPR
1880	Wor-N	10	35	2	7	1	0	0	1	0	1	.200	.200	.229	41	-2				.750	-3	/O-9,C-1	-0.5
1882	Phi-a	44	181	25	51	9	1	0	24	4		.282	.297	.343	103	-1				.880	-1	C-25,O-22/3-1	-0.1
1884	Ind-a	34	141	22	42	6	1	0		2		.298	.317	.355	122	3				.793	-2	O-29/C-5	0.1
	Bro-a	4	13	2	4	0	0	0		0		.308	.308	.308	101	-0				.921	2	/C-4	0.2
	Yr	38	154	24	46	6	1	0		2		.299	.316	.351	120	3				.793	-0	O-29/C-9	0.3
1885	Det-N	39	161	23	46	6	2	0	24	8	10	.286	.320	.348	115	3				.857	-3	O-39	-0.2
Total	4	131	531	74	150	22	4	0	49	14	11	.282	.303	.339	107	3				.817	-7	/O-99,C-35,3-1	-0.5

■ MIKE DORGAN

Dorgan, Michael Cornelius b: 10/2/1853, Middletown, Conn. d: 4/26/09, Hartford, Conn. BR/TR, 5'9", 180 lbs. Deb: 5/8/1877 FM

YEAR	TM/L	G	AB	R	H	2B	3B	HR	RBI	BB	SO	AVG	OBP	SLG	PRO+	BR/A	SB	CS	SBR	FA	FR	G/POS	TPR
1877	StL-N	60	266	45	82	9	7	0	23	9	13	.308	.331	.395	135	11				.824	-8	*O-50,C-12/3-2,S2	0.1
1879	Syr-N	59	270	38	72	11	5	1	17	4	13	.267	.277	.356	120	6				.954	-5	1-21,O-16,3/SCP2	0.0
1880	Pro-N	79	321	45	79	10	1	0	31	10	18	.246	.269	.283	90	-3				.858	2	*O-77/3-2,P-1,M	-0.3
1881	Wor-N	51	220	36	61	5	0	0	18	8	4	.277	.303	.300	85	-4				.953	1	1-26,O-23/S-2,M	-0.6
	Det-N	8	34	5	8	1	0	0	5	1	0	.235	.257	.265	62	-1				1.000	-0	/O-5,3-2,1-1	-0.2
	Yr	59	254	41	69	6	0	0	23	9	4	.272	.297	.295	82	-5				.897	0	O-28,1-27/S-2,3-2	-0.8
1883	NY-N	64	261	32	61	11	3	0	27	2	23	.234	.240	.299	63	-11				.847	-5	O-59/C-6,P-1	-1.5
1884	NY-N	83	341	61	94	11	6	1	48	13	27	.276	.302	.352	103	0				.851	1	O-64,P-14/C-6,2-3	0.0
1885	NY-N	89	347	60	113	17	8	0	46	11	24	.326	.346	.421	149	18				.905	-2	*O-88/1-1	1.2
1886	NY-N	118	442	61	129	19	4	2	79	29	37	.292	.335	.367	112	6	9			.888	-8	*O-116/1-3	-0.4
1887	NY-N	71	283	41	73	10	0	0	34	15	20	.258	.302	.293	69	-11	22			.870	-1	O-69/1-2	-1.2
1890	Syr-a	33	139	19	30	8	0	0	18	16		.216	.301	.273	77	-3	8			.900	-2	O-33	-0.6
Total	10	715	2924	443	802	112	34	4	346	118	179	.274	.303	.340	102	8	39			.867	-30	O-600/1-54,CP3S2	-3.5

■ CHARLIE DORMAN

Dorman, Charles William "Slats" b: 4/23/1898, San Francisco, Cal d: 11/15/28, San Francisco, Cal BR/TR, 6'2", 185 lbs. Deb: 5/14/23

YEAR	TM/L	G	AB	R	H	2B	3B	HR	RBI	BB	SO	AVG	OBP	SLG	PRO+	BR/A	SB	CS	SBR	FA	FR	G/POS	TPR
1923	Chi-A	1	2	0	1	0	0	0	0	0	0	.500	.500	.500	166	0	0	0	0	1.000	-0	/C-1	0.0

■ RED DORMAN

Dorman, Dwight Dexter "Curlie" b: 10/3/05, Jacksonville, Ill. d: 12/7/74, Anaheim, Cal. BR/TR, 5'10.5", 180 lbs. Deb: 8/21/28

YEAR	TM/L	G	AB	R	H	2B	3B	HR	RBI	BB	SO	AVG	OBP	SLG	PRO+	BR/A	SB	CS	SBR	FA	FR	G/POS	TPR
1928	Cle-A	25	77	12	28	6	0	0	11	9	6	.364	.430	.442	128	4	1	0	0	.915	-3	O-24	0.0

■ BRIAN DORSETT

Dorsett, Brian Richard b: 4/9/61, Terre Haute, Ind. BR/TR, 6'3", 220 lbs. Deb: 9/8/87

YEAR	TM/L	G	AB	R	H	2B	3B	HR	RBI	BB	SO	AVG	OBP	SLG	PRO+	BR/A	SB	CS	SBR	FA	FR	G/POS	TPR
1987	Cle-A	5	11	2	3	0	0	1	3	0	3	.273	.333	.545	127	0	0	0	0	1.000	-2	/C-4	-0.1
1988	Cal-A	7	11	0	1	0	0	0	2	1	5	.091	.167	.091	-26	-2	0	0	0	1.000	1	/C-7	-0.1
1989	NY-A	8	22	3	8	1	0	0	4	1	3	.364	.391	.409	127	1	0	0	0	1.000	-0	/C-8	0.1
1990	NY-A	14	35	2	5	2	0	0	0	2	4	.143	.189	.200	9	-4	0	0	0	1.000	-1	/C-9,D-5	-0.5
1991	SD-N	11	12	0	1	0	0	0	1	0	3	.083	.083	.083	-51	-2	0	0	0	1.000	0	/1-2	-0.2
1993	Cin-N	25	63	7	16	4	0	2	12	3	14	.254	.288	.413	85	-2	0	0	0	1.000	2	C-18/1-3	0.1
1994	Cin-N	76	216	21	53	8	0	5	26	21	33	.245	.315	.352	74	-8	0	0	0	.991	-1	C-73/1-1	-0.5
1996	Chi-N	17	41	3	5	0	0	1	3	4	8	.122	.200	.195	5	-6	0	0	0	1.000	1	C-15	-0.4
Total	8	163	411	38	92	15	0	9	51	32	73	.224	.283	.326	62	-23	0	0	0	.995	-0	C-134/1-6,D-5	-1.6

■ JERRY DORSEY

Dorsey, Jeremiah b: 1885, Oakland, Cal. BL/TL, 5'11", 175 lbs. Deb: 9/23/11

YEAR	TM/L	G	AB	R	H	2B	3B	HR	RBI	BB	SO	AVG	OBP	SLG	PRO+	BR/A	SB	CS	SBR	FA	FR	G/POS	TPR
1911	Pit-N	2	6	0	0	0	0	0	0	0	1	.000	.000	.000	-96	-2	0			1.000	0	/O-1	-0.1

■ JERRY DORSEY

Dorsey, Michael Jeremiah b: 1854, Canada d: 11/3/38, Auburn, N.Y. Deb: 7/9/1884

YEAR	TM/L	G	AB	R	H	2B	3B	HR	RBI	BB	SO	AVG	OBP	SLG	PRO+	BR/A	SB	CS	SBR	FA	FR	G/POS	TPR
1884	Bal-U	1	3	0	0	0	0	0		0		.000	.000	.000	-91	-1				.000	-0	/O-1,P-1	-0.1

■ HERM DOSCHER

Doscher, John Henry Sr. b: 12/20/1852, New York, N.Y. d: 3/20/34, Buffalo, N.Y. BR/TR, 5'10", 182 lbs. Deb: 9/4/1872 FU

YEAR	TM/L	G	AB	R	H	2B	3B	HR	RBI	BB	SO	AVG	OBP	SLG	PRO+	BR/A	SB	CS	SBR	FA	FR	G/POS	TPR
1872	Atl-n	6	25	4	9	0	0	0	5	0	1	.360	.360	.360	104	-0	0	0	0	.769	1	/O-6	0.0
1873	Atl-n	1	6	1	1	0	0	0	1	0	0	.167	.167	.167	-1	-1	0	0	0	.500	-0	/O-1	-0.1
1875	Was-n	22	81	5	15	4	0	0	5	0	6	.185	.185	.235	46	-4	1	0	0	.752	1	3-22	-0.2
1879	Tro-N	47	191	16	42	8	0	0	18	2	10	.220	.228	.262	65	-7				.806	-4	3-47	-0.9
	Chi-N	3	11	1	2	0	0	0	1	0	3	.182	.182	.182	19	-1				.700	-1	/3-3	-0.2
	Yr	50	202	17	44	8	0	0	19	2	13	.218	.225	.257	62	-8				.800	-5	3-50	-1.1
1881	Cle-N	5	19	2	4	0	0	0	0	0	2	.211	.211	.211	35	-1				.895	-0	/3-5	-0.2
1882	Cle-N	25	104	7	25	2	0	0	10	0	11	.240	.240	.260	62	-4				.857	-2	3-22/O-2,S-1	-0.5
Total	3 n	29	112	10	25	4	0	0	11	0	7	.223	.223	.259	60	-5	1	0	0	.733	1	/3-22,O-7	-0.3
Total	3	80	325	26	73	10	0	0	29	2	26	.225	.229	.255	61	-13				.823	-7	/3-77,O-2,S-1	-1.8

■ DAVID DOSTER

Doster, David Eric b: 10/8/70, Ft.Wayne, Ind. BR/TR, 5'10", 185 lbs. Deb: 6/16/96

YEAR	TM/L	G	AB	R	H	2B	3B	HR	RBI	BB	SO	AVG	OBP	SLG	PRO+	BR/A	SB	CS	SBR	FA	FR	G/POS	TPR
1996	Phi-N	39	105	14	28	8	0	1	8	7	21	.267	.313	.371	79	-3	0	0	0	.973	-1	2-24/3-1	-0.3

■ DUTCH DOTTERER

Dotterer, Henry John b: 11/11/31, Syracuse, N.Y. BR/TR, 6', 209 lbs. Deb: 9/25/57

YEAR	TM/L	G	AB	R	H	2B	3B	HR	RBI	BB	SO	AVG	OBP	SLG	PRO+	BR/A	SB	CS	SBR	FA	FR	G/POS	TPR
1957	Cin-N	4	12	0	1	0	0	0	2	1	2	.083	.154	.083	-32	-2	0	0	0	1.000	-1	/C-4	-0.3
1958	Cin-N	11	28	1	7	1	0	1	2	2	4	.250	.300	.393	77	-1	0	0	0	.981	4	/C-8	0.3
1959	Cin-N	52	161	21	43	7	0	2	17	16	23	.267	.333	.348	79	-4	0	0	0	.992	-0	C-51	-0.2
1960	Cin-N	33	79	4	18	5	0	2	11	13	10	.228	.337	.367	91	-1	0	1	-1	.979	1	C-31	0.1
1961	Was-A	7	19	1	5	2	0	0	1	3	5	.263	.364	.368	98	0	0	0	0	1.000	2	/C-7	0.2
Total	5	107	299	27	74	15	0	5	33	35	44	.247	.326	.348	79	-8	0	1	-1	.988	7	C-101	0.1

■ CHARLIE DOUGHERTY

Dougherty, Charles William b: 2/7/1862, Darlington, Wis. d: 2/18/25, Milwaukee, Wis. Deb: 4/17/1884

YEAR	TM/L	G	AB	R	H	2B	3B	HR	RBI	BB	SO	AVG	OBP	SLG	PRO+	BR/A	SB	CS	SBR	FA	FR	G/POS	TPR
1884	Alt-U	23	85	6	22	5	0	0		2		.259	.276	.318	78	-5				.854	0	2-16/O-8,S-1	-0.4

■ PATSY DOUGHERTY

Dougherty, Patrick Henry b: 10/27/1876, Andover, N.Y. d: 4/30/40, Bolivar, N.Y. BL/TR, 6'2", 190 lbs. Deb: 4/19/02

YEAR	TM/L	G	AB	R	H	2B	3B	HR	RBI	BB	SO	AVG	OBP	SLG	PRO+	BR/A	SB	CS	SBR	FA	FR	G/POS	TPR
1902	Bos-A	108	438	77	150	12	6	0	34	42		.342	.407	.397	120	14	20			.899	-9	*O-102/3-1	-0.2
1903	*Bos-A	139	590	**107**	**195**	19	12	4	59	33		.331	.372	.424	131	22	35			.952	4	*O-139	1.8
1904	Bos-A	49	195	33	53	5	4	0	4	25		.272	.355	.338	113	4	10			.925	0	O-49	0.1
	NY-A	106	452	80	128	13	10	6	22	19		.283	.316	.396	119	9	11			.925	-8	*O-106	-0.7
	Yr	155	647	**113**	181	18	14	6	26	44		.280	.329	.379	117	12	21			.925	-8	*O-155	-0.6
1905	NY-A	116	418	56	110	9	6	3	29	28		.263	.319	.335	96	-2	17			.898	-6	*O-108/3-1	-1.4
1906	NY-A	12	52	3	10	2	0	0	4	0		.192	.192	.231	29	-4	0			1.000	2	O-12	-0.3
	*Chi-A	75	253	30	59	9	4	1	27	19		.233	.295	.312	92	-2	11			.985	-1	O-74	-0.8
	Yr	87	305	33	69	11	4	1	31	19		.226	.278	.298	81	-7	11			.987	1	O-86	-1.1
1907	Chi-A	148	533	69	144	17	2	1	59	36		.270	.322	.315	107	4	33			.946	-7	*O-148	-0.9
1908	Chi-A	138	482	68	134	11	6	0	45	58		.278	.367	.326	128	18	**47**			.947	-15	*O-128	-0.2
1909	Chi-A	139	491	71	140	23	13	1	55	51		.285	.359	.391	143	24	36			.942	-16	*O-138	0.4
1910	Chi-A	127	443	45	110	8	6	1	43	41		.248	.318	.300	98	-1	22			.923	-13	*O-121	-2.2
1911	Chi-A	76	211	39	61	10	9	0	32	26		.289	.380	.422	128	8	19			.933	-6	O-56	0.0
Total	10	1233	4558	678	1294	138	78	17	413	378		.284	.346	.360	117	94	261			.935	-75	*O-1181/3-2	-4.4

■ JOHN DOUGLAS

Douglas, John Franklin b: 9/14/17, Thayer, W.Va. d: 2/11/84, Miami, Fla. BL/TL, 6'2.5", 195 lbs. Deb: 4/21/45

YEAR	TM/L	G	AB	R	H	2B	3B	HR	RBI	BB	SO	AVG	OBP	SLG	PRO+	BR/A	SB	CS	SBR	FA	FR	G/POS	TPR
1945	Bro-N	5	9	0	0	0	0	0	0	2	4	.000	.182	.000	-47	-2	0			.971	-1	/1-4	-0.3

■ ASTYANAX DOUGLASS

Douglass, Astyanax Saunders b: 9/19/1899, Covington, Tex. d: 1/26/75, ElPaso, Tex. BL/TR, 6'1", 190 lbs. Deb: 7/30/21

YEAR	TM/L	G	AB	R	H	2B	3B	HR	RBI	BB	SO	AVG	OBP	SLG	PRO+	BR/A	SB	CS	SBR	FA	FR	G/POS	TPR
1921	Cin-N	4	7	1	1	0	0	0	0	0	1	.143	.143	.143	-25	-1	0	0	0	1.000	0	/C-4	-0.1
1925	Cin-N	7	17	1	3	0	0	0	1	1	3	.176	.222	.176	3	-2	0	0	0	.889	-1	/C-7	-0.3
Total	2	11	24	2	4	0	0	0	1	1	4	.167	.200	.167	-4	-4	0	0	0	.926	-0	/C-11	-0.4

■ KLONDIKE DOUGLASS Douglass, William Bingham b: 5/10/1872, Boston, Pa. d: 12/13/53, Bend, Ore. BL/TR, 6', 200 lbs. Deb: 4/23/1896

YEAR	TM/L	G	AB	R	H	2B	3B	HR	RBI	BB	SO	AVG	OBP	SLG	PRO+	BR/A	SB	CS	SBR	FA	FR	G/POS	TPR
1896	StL-N	81	296	42	78	6	4	1	28	35	15	.264	.351	.321	81	-7	18			.894	-7	O-74/C-6,S-2	-1.6
1897	StL-N	125	516	77	170	15	3	6	50	52		.329	.403	.405	116	14	12			.948	-11	C-61,O-43,1-17,/3S	0.6
1898	Phi-N	146	582	105	150	26	4	2	48	55		.258	.333	.326	93	-4	18			.976	2	*1-146	-0.2
1899	Phi-N	77	275	26	70	6	6	0	27	10		.255	.296	.320	71	-11	7			.970	-5	C-66/3-4,1-4,O-1	-1.0
1900	Phi-N	50	160	23	48	9	4	0	25	13		.300	.360	.406	112	3	7			.934	-3	C-47/3-2	0.3
1901	Phi-N	51	173	14	56	6	1	0	23	11		.324	.371	.370	113	3	10			.979	2	C-41/1-6,O-2	0.8
1902	Phi-N	109	408	37	95	12	3	0	37	23		.233	.274	.277	70	-15	6			.986	-7	1-69,C-29,O-10	-2.2
1903	Phi-N	105	377	43	96	5	4	1	36	28		.255	.308	.297	75	-12	6			.985	-1	1-97	-1.4
1904	Phi-N	3	10	1	3	0	0	0	1	0		.300	.364	.300	109	0	0			.970	-0	/1-3	0.0
Total	9	747	2797	368	766	85	29	10	275	227	15	.274	.337	.336	91	-28	84			.981	-31	1-342,C-250,O/3S	-4.7

■ TAYLOR DOUTHIT Douthit, Taylor Lee b: 4/22/01, Little Rock, Ark. d: 5/28/86, Fremont, Cal. BR/TR, 5'11.5", 175 lbs. Deb: 9/14/23

YEAR	TM/L	G	AB	R	H	2B	3B	HR	RBI	BB	SO	AVG	OBP	SLG	PRO+	BR/A	SB	CS	SBR	FA	FR	G/POS	TPR
1923	StL-N	9	27	3	5	0	2	0	0	0	4	.185	.185	.333	35	-3	1	0	0	1.000	-0	/O-7	-0.3
1924	StL-N	53	173	24	48	13	1	0	13	16	19	.277	.349	.364	93	-1	4	3	-1	.976	2	O-50	-0.3
1925	StL-N	30	73	13	20	3	1	1	8	2	6	.274	.312	.384	75	-3	0	0	0	.981	-1	O-21	-0.4
1926	*StL-N	139	530	96	163	20	4	3	52	55	46	.308	.375	.377	99	1	23			.958	18	*O-138	0.9
1927	StL-N	130	488	81	128	29	6	5	50	52	45	.262	.336	.377	88	-8	6			.964	8	*O-125	-0.8
1928	*StL-N	154	648	111	191	35	3	3	43	84	36	.295	.384	.372	97	0	11			.984	24	*O-154	1.4
1929	StL-N	150	613	128	206	42	7	9	62	79	49	.336	.416	.471	118	20	8			.974	4	*O-150	1.3
1930	*StL-N	154	664	109	201	41	10	7	93	60	38	.303	.364	.426	87	-13	4			.964	8	*O-154	-1.4
1931	StL-N	36	133	21	44	11	2	1	21	11	9	.331	.386	.466	123	4	1			.972	0	O-36	0.2
	Cin-N	95	374	42	98	9	1	0	24	42	24	.262	.340	.291	76	-11	4			.983	5	O-95	-1.3
	Yr	131	507	63	142	20	3	1	45	53	33	.280	.352	.337	89	-6	5			.980	5	*O-131	-1.1
1932	Cin-N	96	333	28	81	12	1	0	25	31	29	.243	.311	.285	64	-16	3			.985	1	O-88	-2.0
1933	Cin-N	1	0	1	0	0	0	0	0	0	0	—	—	—	—	0	0			.000	0	R	0.0
	Chi-N	27	71	8	16	5	0	0	5	11	7	.225	.329	.296	80	-1	2			.930	-0	O-18	-0.3
	Yr	28	71	9	16	5	0	0	5	11	7	.225	.329	.296	80	-1	2			.930	-0	O-18	-0.3
Total	11	1074	4127	665	1201	220	38	29	396	443	312	.291	.364	.384	93	-31	67	3		.972	69	*O-1036	-3.0

■ CLARENCE DOW Dow, Clarence G. b: 10/2/1854, Charlestown, Mass. d: 3/11/1893, West Somerville, Mass. Deb: 9/22/1884

YEAR	TM/L	G	AB	R	H	2B	3B	HR	RBI	BB	SO	AVG	OBP	SLG	PRO+	BR/A	SB	CS	SBR	FA	FR	G/POS	TPR
1884	Bos-U	1	6	1	2	0	0	0		0		.333	.333	.333	104	-0				.333	-1	/O-1	-0.1

■ JOHN DOWD Dowd, John Leo (b: John Leo O'Dowd) b: 1/3/1891, Weymouth, Mass. d: 1/31/81, Ft.Lauderdale, Fla BR/TR, 5'8", 170 lbs. Deb: 7/3/12

YEAR	TM/L	G	AB	R	H	2B	3B	HR	RBI	BB	SO	AVG	OBP	SLG	PRO+	BR/A	SB	CS	SBR	FA	FR	G/POS	TPR
1912	NY-A	10	31	1	6	1	0	0	0	6		.194	.342	.226	60	-1	0			.840	-3	S-10	-0.4

■ SNOOKS DOWD Dowd, Raymond Bernard b: 12/20/1897, Springfield, Mass. d: 4/4/62, Northampton, Mass. BR/TR, 5'8", 163 lbs. Deb: 4/27/19

YEAR	TM/L	G	AB	R	H	2B	3B	HR	RBI	BB	SO	AVG	OBP	SLG	PRO+	BR/A	SB	CS	SBR	FA	FR	G/POS	TPR
1919	Det-A	1	0	0	0	0	0	0	0	0	0	—	—	—	—	0	0			.000	0	R	0.0
	Phi-A	13	18	4	3	0	0	0	6	0	5	.167	.167	.167	-6	-3	2			.800	1	/2-3,S-2,3-1,O-1	-0.2
	Yr	14	18	4	3	0	0	0	6	0	5	.167	.167	.167	-6	-3	2			.800	1	/2-3,S-2,3-1,O-1	-0.2
1926	Bro-N	2	8	0	0	0	0	0	0	0	0	.000	.000	.000	-99	-2	0			1.000	-2	/2-2	-0.5
Total	2	16	26	4	3	0	0	0	6	0	5	.115	.115	.115	-36	-5	2			.875	-1	/2-5,S-2,O-1,3-1	-0.7

■ TOMMY DOWD Dowd, Thomas Jefferson "Buttermilk Tommy" b: 4/20/1869, Holyoke, Mass. d: 7/2/33, Holyoke, Mass. BR/TR, 5'8", 173 lbs. Deb: 4/8/1891 M

YEAR	TM/L	G	AB	R	H	2B	3B	HR	RBI	BB	SO	AVG	OBP	SLG	PRO+	BR/A	SB	CS	SBR	FA	FR	G/POS	TPR
1891	Bos-a	4	11	1	1	0	0	0	0	0	1	.091	.091	.091	-49	-2	0			.000	-2	/O-4	-0.3
	Was-a	112	464	66	120	9	10	1	44	19	44	.259	.291	.328	80	-14	39			.885	-17	*2-107/O-5	-2.3
	Yr	116	475	67	121	9	10	1	44	19	45	.255	.286	.322	77	-16	39			.885	-19	*2-107/O-9	-2.6
1892	Was-N	144	584	94	142	9	10	1	50	34	49	.243	.286	.298	79	-16	49			.891	-33	2-98,O-23,3-18,/S-6	-4.4
1893	StL-N	132	581	114	164	18	7	1	54	49	23	.282	.340	.343	81	-16	59			.944	3	*O-132/2-1	-1.6
1894	StL-N	123	524	92	142	16	8	4	62	54	33	.271	.341	.355	68	-27	31			.930	-7	*O-117/2-7,3-1	-3.3
1895	StL-N	129	505	95	163	19	17	7	74	30	31	.323	.364	.469	116	10	30			.927	-7	*O-115,3-17/2-2	-0.5
1896	StL-N	126	521	93	138	17	11	5	46	42	19	.265	.322	.369	85	-12	40			.920	-13	2-78,O-48,M	-2.1
1897	StL-N	35	145	25	38	9	1	0	9	6		.262	.291	.338	67	-7	11			.915	-7	O-30/2-5,M	-1.4
	Phi-N	91	391	68	114	14	4	0	43	19		.292	.324	.348	79	-12	30			.919	-6	O-73,2-19	-1.9
	Yr	126	536	93	152	23	5	0	52	25		.284	.316	.345	76	-19	41			.918	-13	*O-103,2-24	-3.3
1898	StL-N	139	586	70	143	17	7	0	32	30		.244	.287	.297	66	-27	16			.920	-17	*O-129,2-11	-5.0
1899	Cle-N	147	605	81	168	17	6	2	35	48		.278	.333	.336	90	-8	28			.954	-2	*O-147	-2.0
1901	Bos-A	138	594	104	159	18	7	3	52	38		.268	.315	.337	82	-14	33			.937	1	*O-137/1-2,3-1	-2.1
Total	10	1320	5511	903	1492	163	88	24	501	369	200	.271	.319	.345	82	-146	366			.933	-106	O-960,2-328/3S1	-26.9

■ KEN DOWELL Dowell, Kenneth Allen b: 1/19/61, Sacramento, Cal. BR/TR, 5'9", 160 lbs. Deb: 6/24/87

YEAR	TM/L	G	AB	R	H	2B	3B	HR	RBI	BB	SO	AVG	OBP	SLG	PRO+	BR/A	SB	CS	SBR	FA	FR	G/POS	TPR
1987	Phi-N	15	39	4	5	0	0	0	1	2	5	.128	.171	.128	-19	-7	0	0	0	1.000	0	S-15	-0.5

■ JOE DOWIE Dowie, Joseph E. b: 7/15/1865, New Orleans, La. d: 3/4/17, New Orleans, La. 5'8", 150 lbs. Deb: 7/10/1889

YEAR	TM/L	G	AB	R	H	2B	3B	HR	RBI	BB	SO	AVG	OBP	SLG	PRO+	BR/A	SB	CS	SBR	FA	FR	G/POS	TPR
1889	Bal-a	20	75	12	17	5	0	0	8	2	10	.227	.266	.293	58	-4	5			.947	0	O-20	-0.4

■ RED DOWNEY Downey, Alexander Cummings b: 2/6/1889, Aurora, Ind. d: 7/10/49, Detroit, Mich. BL/TL, 5'11", 174 lbs. Deb: 9/14/09

YEAR	TM/L	G	AB	R	H	2B	3B	HR	RBI	BB	SO	AVG	OBP	SLG	PRO+	BR/A	SB	CS	SBR	FA	FR	G/POS	TPR
1909	Bro-N	19	78	7	20	1	0	0	8	2		.256	.275	.269	71	-3	4			1.000	-1	O-19	-0.6

■ TOM DOWNEY Downey, Thomas Edward b: 1/1/1884, Lewiston, Me. d: 8/3/61, Passaic, N.J. BR/TR, 5'10", 178 lbs. Deb: 5/7/09

YEAR	TM/L	G	AB	R	H	2B	3B	HR	RBI	BB	SO	AVG	OBP	SLG	PRO+	BR/A	SB	CS	SBR	FA	FR	G/POS	TPR
1909	Cin-N	119	416	39	96	9	6	1	32	32		.231	.287	.288	79	-10	16			.909	-6	*S-119/C-1	-1.6
1910	Cin-N	111	378	43	102	9	3	2	32	34	28	.270	.335	.325	97	-1	12			.879	-7	S-68,3-41	-0.5
1911	Cin-N	111	360	50	94	16	7	0	36	44	38	.261	.345	.344	97	-1	10			.906	-12	S-93/2-6,3-5,1-2,O	-0.7
1912	Phi-N	54	171	27	50	6	3	1	23	21	20	.292	.370	.380	99	-0	3			.893	-3	3-46/S-3	-0.2
	Chi-N	13	22	4	4	0	2	0	4	1	5	.182	.217	.364	58	-1	0			.792	1	/S-5,3-3,2-1	0.0
	Yr	67	193	31	54	6	5	1	27	22	25	.280	.353	.378	95	-1	3			.892	-2	3-49/S-8,2-1	-0.2
1914	Buf-F	151	541	69	118	20	3	2	42	40	55	.218	.273	.277	49	-47	35			**.962**	13	*2-129,S-16/3-5	-3.6
1915	Buf-F	92	282	24	56	9	1	1	19	26	26	.199	.269	.248	45	-25	11			.930	2	2-48,3-35/S-2,1-1	-2.3
Total	6	651	2170	256	520	69	25	7	188	198	172	.240	.306	.304	74	-86	87			.901	-12	S-306,2-184,3/1OC	-8.9

■ BRIAN DOWNING Downing, Brian Jay b: 10/9/50, Los Angeles, Cal. BR/TR, 5'10", 194 lbs. Deb: 5/31/73

YEAR	TM/L	G	AB	R	H	2B	3B	HR	RBI	BB	SO	AVG	OBP	SLG	PRO+	BR/A	SB	CS	SBR	FA	FR	G/POS	TPR
1973	Chi-A	34	73	5	13	1	0	2	4	10	17	.178	.277	.274	54	-4	0	0	0	1.000	0	O-13,C-11/3-8,D-1	-0.4
1974	Chi-A	108	293	41	66	12	1	10	39	51	72	.225	.344	.375	104	3	0	1	-1	.994	-7	C-63,O-39/D-9	-0.3
1975	Chi-A	138	420	58	101	12	1	7	41	76	75	.240	.361	.324	93	-1	13	4	2	.990	2	*C-137/D-1	0.9
1976	Chi-A	104	317	38	81	14	0	3	30	40	55	.256	.341	.328	96	-1	7	3	0	.988	-12	C-93,D-11	-1.0
1977	Chi-A	69	169	28	48	4	2	4	25	34	21	.284	.410	.402	123	7	1	2	-1	.983	3	C-61/O-3,D-2	1.0
1978	Cal-A	133	412	42	105	15	0	7	46	52	47	.255	.347	.342	98	0	3	2	-0	.993	-7	*C-128/D-2	-0.3
1979	*Cal-A★	148	509	87	166	27	3	12	75	77	57	.326	.420	.462	142	34	3	3	-1	.985	-21	*C-129,D-18	1.5
1980	Cal-A	30	93	5	27	6	0	2	25	12	12	.290	.371	.419	119	3	0	2	-1	1.000	-4	C-16,D-13	-0.2
1981	Cal-A	93	317	47	79	14	0	9	41	46	35	.249	.351	.379	110	5	1	1	-0	.990	-9	O-56,C-37/D-5	-0.4
1982	*Cal-A	158	623	109	175	37	2	28	84	86	58	.281	.373	.482	132	29	2	1	0	**1.000**	2	*O-158	2.6
1983	Cal-A	113	403	68	99	15	1	19	53	62	59	.246	.353	.429	115	9	1	2	-1	.994	-0	O-84,D-26	0.5
1984	Cal-A	156	539	65	148	28	2	23	91	70	66	.275	.365	.462	128	21	0	4	-2	**1.000**	1	*O-131,D-21	1.6
1985	Cal-A	150	520	80	137	23	1	20	85	78	61	.263	.373	.427	119	16	5	3	-0	.992	2	*O-121,D-25	1.3
1986	*Cal-A	152	513	90	137	27	4	20	95	90	84	.267	.394	.452	131	26	4	4	-1	.989	1	*O-138,D-10	2.1
1987	Cal-A	155	567	110	154	29	3	29	77	**106**	85	.272	.401	.487	139	36	5	5	-2	1.000	-3	*D-118,O-34	2.6
1988	Cal-A	135	484	80	117	18	2	25	64	81	63	.242	.366	.442	129	21	3	4	-2	.000	0	*D-132	1.6
1989	Cal-A	142	544	59	154	25	2	14	59	56	87	.283	.356	.414	118	14	0	2	-1	.000	0	*D-141	0.9
1990	Cal-A	96	330	47	90	18	2	14	51	50	45	.273	.378	.467	138	18	0	0	0	.000	0	D-87	1.5
1991	Tex-A	123	407	76	113	17	2	17	49	58	70	.278	.378	.455	132	19	1	1	-0	.000	0	*D-109	1.4

YEAR	TM/L	G	AB	R	H	2B	3B	HR	RBI	BB	SO	AVG	OBP	SLG	PRO+	BR/A	SB	CS	SBR	FA	FR	G/POS	TPR
1992	Tex-A	107	320	53	89	18	0	10	39	62	58	.278	.408	.428	139	20	1	0	0	.000	0	D-93	1.7
Total	20	2344	7853	1188	2099	360	28	275	1073	1197	1127	.267	.373	.425	122	276	50	44	-11	.995	-51	D-824,O-777,C/3	18.6
■ **RED DOWNS** Downs, Jerome Willis b: 8/22/1883, Neola, Iowa d: 10/19/39, Council Bluffs, Ia BR/TR, 5'11", 155 lbs. Deb: 5/2/07																							
1907	Det-A	105	374	28	82	13	5	1	42	13		.219	.249	.289	69	-14	3			.930	-24	2-80,O-20/S-1,3-1	-4.5
1908	*Det-A	84	289	29	64	10	3	1	35	5		.221	.237	.287	67	-11	2			.925	1	2-82/3-1	-1.3
1912	Bro-N	9	32	2	8	3	0	0	3	1	5	.250	.273	.344	71	-1	3			.881	-1	/2-9	-0.3
	Chi-N	43	95	9	25	4	3	1	14	9	17	.263	.327	.400	99	-0	5			.907	2	2-16/S-9,3-5	0.2
	Yr	52	127	11	33	7	3	1	17	10	22	.260	.314	.386	92	-2	8			.896	0	2-25/S-9,3-5	-0.1
Total	3	241	790	68	179	30	11	3	94	28	22	.227	.256	.304	72	-27	13			.924	-23	2-187/O-20,S-10,3-7	-5.9
■ **TOM DOWSE** Dowse, Thomas Joseph b: 8/12/1866, Ireland d: 12/14/46, Riverside, Cal. BR/TR, 5'11", 175 lbs. Deb: 4/21/1890																							
1890	Cle-N	40	159	20	33	2	1	0	9	12	22	.208	.267	.233	47	-11	3			.870	-3	O-26,1-10/C-3,P-1	-1.3
1891	Col-a	55	201	24	45	7	0	0	22	13	22	.224	.278	.259	57	-11	2			.919	-6	C-51/O-5	-1.2
1892	Lou-N	41	145	10	21	2	0	0	7	2	15	.145	.173	.159	1	-17	1			.918	2	C-29,1-11/O-3,2-1	-1.3
	Cin-N	1	4	0	0	0	0	0	0	0	0	.000	.000	.000	-99	-1	0			1.000	-1	/C-1	-0.2
	Phi-N	16	54	3	10	0	0	0	6	2	4	.185	.228	.185	25	-5	1			.973	-1	C-15	-0.4
	Was-N	7	27	5	7	1	0	0	2	0	3	.259	.259	.296	70	-1	0			.800	0	/O-4,C-3	-0.1
	Yr	65	230	18	38	3	0	0	15	4	22	.165	.193	.178	13	-24	2			.931	1	C-48,1-11/O-7,2-1	-2.0
Total	3	160	590	62	116	12	1	0	46	29	66	.197	.243	.220	38	-46	7			.921	-9	C-102/O-38,1-21,2P	-4.5
■ **BRIAN DOYLE** Doyle, Brian Reed b: 1/26/55, Glasgow, Ky. BL/TR, 5'10", 160 lbs. Deb: 4/30/78 F																							
1978	*NY-A	39	52	6	10	0	0	0	0	0	3	.192	.192	.192	9	-6	0	3	-2	.989	13	2-29/S-7,3-5	0.6
1979	NY-A	20	32	2	4	2	0	0	5	3	1	.125	.200	.188	5	-4	0	0	0	.944	1	2-13/3-6	-0.3
1980	NY-A	34	75	8	13	1	0	1	5	6	7	.173	.235	.227	27	-7	1	1	-0	.953	5	2-20,S-12/3-2	-0.1
1981	Oak-A	17	40	2	5	0	0	0	3	1	2	.125	.146	.125	-22	-6	0	1	-1	1.000	1	2-17	-0.5
Total	4	110	199	18	32	3	0	1	13	10	13	.161	.201	.191	10	-24	1	5	-3	.977	20	/2-79,S-19,3-13	-0.3
■ **CONNY DOYLE** Doyle, Cornelius J. b: 1862, Ireland d: 7/29/21, ElPaso, Tex. 5'10", 185 lbs. Deb: 6/23/1883																							
1883	Phi-N	16	68	3	15	3	2	0	3	0	15	.221	.221	.324	69	-2				.788	-1	O-16	-0.3
1884	Pit-a	15	58	8	17	3	2	0		2		.293	.317	.414	134	2				.818	-1	O-14/S-1	0.0
Total	2	31	126	11	32	6	4	0	3	2	15	.254	.266	.365	100	-0				.800	-3	/O-30,S-1	-0.3
■ **DANNY DOYLE** Doyle, Howard James b: 1/24/17, McLoud, Okla. BB/TR, 6'1", 195 lbs. Deb: 9/14/43																							
1943	Bos-A	13	43	2	9	1	0	0	6	7	9	.209	.320	.233	62	-2	0	1	-1	.964	-2	C-13	-0.4
■ **JIM DOYLE** Doyle, James Francis b: 12/25/1881, Detroit, Mich. d: 2/1/12, Syracuse, N.Y. BR/TR, 5'10", 168 lbs. Deb: 5/4/10																							
1910	Cin-N	7	13	1	2	2	0	0	1	0	2	.154	.154	.308	36	-1	0			.875	-1	/3-3,O-1	-0.3
1911	Chi-N	130	472	69	133	23	12	5	62	40	54	.282	.340	.413	110	5	19			.922	10	*3-127	1.6
Total	2	137	485	70	135	25	12	5	63	40	56	.278	.336	.410	109	4	19			.921	8	3-130/O-1	1.3
■ **JEFF DOYLE** Doyle, Jeffrey Donald b: 10/2/56, Havre, Mont. BB/TR, 5'9", 160 lbs. Deb: 9/13/83																							
1983	StL-N	13	37	4	11	1	2	0	2	1	3	.297	.316	.432	105	0	0	0	0	.966	1	2-12	0.2
■ **JACK DOYLE** Doyle, John Joseph "Dirty Jack" b: 10/25/1869, Killorglin, Ireland d: 12/31/58, Holyoke, Mass. BR/TR, 5'9", 155 lbs. Deb: 8/27/1889 MU																							
1889	Col-a	11	36	6	10	1	1	0	3	6	6	.278	.381	.361	118	1	9			.897	-3	/C-7,O-3,2-2	-0.1
1890	Col-a	77	298	47	80	17	7	2	44	13		.268	.299	.393	111	2	27			.887	-6	C-38,S-25/O-9,23	0.1
1891	Cle-N	69	250	43	69	14	4	0	43	26	44	.276	.351	.364	104	1	24			.897	-3	C-29,O-21,3-20,/S-1	0.1
1892	Cle-N	24	88	17	26	4	1	1	14	6	10	.295	.340	.398	118	2	5			.875	-1	O-12/C-9,1-1,S-1	0.1
	NY-N	90	366	61	109	22	1	5	55	18	30	.298	.336	.404	126	10	42			.864	-18	2-31,C-26,O-17,3/S	-0.5
	Yr	114	454	78	135	26	2	6	69	24	40	.297	.337	.403	124	11	47			.890	-18	C-35,2-31,O3/S1	-0.4
1893	NY-N	82	318	56	102	17	5	1	51	27	12	.321	.383	.415	112	5	40			.919	3	C-48,O-29/S-4,31	0.9
1894	*NY-N	105	422	90	155	30	8	3	100	35	3	.367	.420	.498	121	15	42			.965	-1	*1-99/C-6	1.2
1895	NY-N	82	319	52	100	21	3	1	66	24	12	.313	.365	.408	102	1	35			.968	-2	1-58,2-13/3-6,CM	0.1
1896	*Bal-N	118	487	116	165	29	4	1	101	42	15	.339	.400	.421	115	11	73			.974	-11	*1-118/2-1	0.1
1897	*Bal-N	114	460	91	163	29	4	2	87	29		.354	.394	.448	122	14	62			.979	5	*1-114	1.6
1898	Was-N	43	177	26	54	2	2	2	26	7		.305	.335	.373	103	0	9			.963	-2	1-38/2-5,M	-0.2
	NY-N	82	297	42	84	15	3	1	43	12		.283	.317	.364	98	-2	14			.860	0	O-38,1-24,S-15,/3C	-0.3
	Yr	125	474	68	138	17	5	3	69	19		.291	.324	.367	100	-2	23			.970	-2	1-62,O-38,S/23C	-0.5
1899	NY-N	118	448	55	134	15	7	3	76	33		.299	.353	.384	106	3	35			.976	6	*1-113/C-5	0.9
1900	NY-N	133	505	69	135	24	1	1	66	34		.267	.317	.325	81	-13	34			.971	6	*1-133	-0.6
1901	Chi-N	75	285	21	66	9	2	0	39	7		.232	.263	.277	59	-15	8			.973	7	1-75	-0.9
1902	NY-N	49	186	21	56	13	0	0	18	10		.301	.340	.371	120	4	12			.991	4	1-49	0.7
	Was-A	78	312	52	77	15	2	1	20	29		.247	.311	.317	74	-11	6			.929	-11	2-68/1-7,O-4,C-2	-1.9
1903	Bro-N	139	524	84	164	27	6	0	91	54		.313	.383	.387	123	17	34			.981	2	*1-139	1.6
1904	Bro-N	8	22	2	5	1	0	0	2	6		.227	.414	.273	116	1	1			1.000	1	/1-8	0.2
	Phi-N	66	236	20	52	10	3	1	22	19		.220	.281	.301	83	-5	4			.977	4	1-65/2-1	-0.3
	Yr	74	258	22	57	11	3	1	24	25		.221	.295	.298	86	-4	5			.980	5	1-73/2-1	-0.1
1905	NY-A	1	3	0	0	0	0	0	0	0		.000	.000	.000	-90	-1	0			.833	-1	/1-1	-0.1
Total	17	1564	6039	971	1806	315	64	25	967	437	132	.299	.351	.385	106	41	516			.975	-20	*1-1043,C-176,O2/S3	2.7
■ **JOE DOYLE** Doyle, Joseph K. b: Cincinnati, Ohio Deb: 4/20/1872																							
1872	Nat-n	9	41	6	12	1	0	0	9	0	0	.293	.293	.317	75	-2	0	0	0	.667	-4	/S-8,2-1	-0.5
■ **LARRY DOYLE** Doyle, Lawrence Joseph "Laughing Larry" b: 7/31/1886, Caseyville, Ill. d: 3/1/74, Saranac Lake, N.Y. BL/TR, 5'10", 165 lbs. Deb: 7/22/07																							
1907	NY-N	69	227	16	59	3	0	0	16	20		.260	.320	.273	83	-4	3			.917	-22	2-69	-3.1
1908	NY-N	104	377	65	116	16	9	0	33	22		.308	.354	.398	134	13	17			.935	-10	*2-102	0.3
1909	NY-N	147	570	86	**172**	27	11	6	49	45		.302	.360	.419	140	25	31			.940	-18	*2-144	0.5
1910	NY-N	151	575	97	164	21	14	8	69	71	26	.285	.369	.412	128	20	39			.930	-17	*2-151	0.0
1911	*NY-N	143	526	102	163	25	**25**	13	77	71	39	.310	.397	.527	153	36	38			.944	-24	*2-141	0.8
1912	*NY-N	143	558	98	184	33	8	10	90	56	20	.330	.393	.471	132	24	36			.948	-8	*2-143	1.2
1913	*NY-N	132	482	67	135	25	6	5	73	59	29	.280	.364	.388	114	10	38			.955	-13	*2-130	-0.5
1914	NY-N	145	539	87	140	19	8	5	63	58	25	.260	.343	.353	111	8	17			.959	-19	*2-145	-1.3
1915	NY-N	150	591	86	**189**	**40**	10	4	70	32	28	**.320**	.358	.442	150	32	22	18	-4	.947	-7	*2-147	2.5
1916	NY-N	113	441	55	118	24	10	2	47	27	23	.268	.316	.381	120	9	17			.960	16	*2-113	3.1
	Chi-N	9	38	6	15	5	1	1	7	1	1	.395	.410	.658	203	4	2			.982	5	/2-9	1.0
	Yr	122	479	61	133	29	11	3	54	28	24	.278	.323	.403	127	14	19			.962	20	*2-122	4.1
1917	Chi-N	135	476	48	121	19	5	6	61	48	28	.254	.323	.353	99	-0	5			.952	-2	*2-128	0.4
1918	NY-N	75	257	38	67	7	4	3	36	37	10	.261	.354	.354	118	7	10			.969	-12	2-73	-0.1
1919	NY-N	113	381	61	110	14	10	7	52	31	17	.289	.350	.433	136	16	12			.956	2	*2-100	2.5
1920	NY-N	137	471	48	134	21	2	4	50	47	28	.285	.352	.363	107	5	11	9	-2	.967	-26	*2-133	-2.0
Total	14	1766	6509	960	1887	299	123	74	793	625	274	.290	.357	.408	126	206	298	27		.949	-155	*2-1728	5.3
■ **DENNY DOYLE** Doyle, Robert Dennis b: 1/17/44, Glasgow, Ky. BL/TR, 5'9", 175 lbs. Deb: 4/7/70 F																							
1970	Phi-N	112	413	43	86	10	7	2	16	33	64	.208	.267	.281	48	-31	6	5	-1	.978	-16	*2-103	-4.1
1971	Phi-N	95	342	34	79	12	1	3	24	19	31	.231	.281	.298	64	-16	4	2	0	.967	4	2-91	-0.5
1972	Phi-N	123	442	33	110	14	2	1	26	31	33	.249	.298	.296	68	-18	6	7	-2	.982	-9	*2-119	-2.6
1973	Phi-N	116	370	45	101	9	3	3	26	31	32	.273	.329	.338	83	-8	1	3	-2	.974	9	*2-114	0.6
1974	Cal-A	147	511	47	133	19	2	1	34	25	49	.260	.296	.311	79	-14	6	7	-2	.983	16	*2-146/S-2	0.7
1975	Cal-A	8	15	0	1	0	0	0	0	1	1	.067	.125	.067	-48	-3	0	0	0	.926	2	/2-6,3-1	-0.1
	*Bos-A	89	310	50	96	21	2	4	36	14	11	.310	.342	.429	107	2	5	7	-3	.974	-31	2-84/3-6,S-2	-2.8
	Yr	97	325	50	97	21	2	4	36	15	12	.298	.331	.412	102	-0	5	7	-3	.970	-29	2-90/3-7,S-2	-2.9

YEAR	TM/L	G	AB	R	H	2B	3B	HR	RBI	BB	SO	AVG	OBP	SLG	PRO+	BR/A	SB	CS	SBR	FA	FR	G/POS	TPR
1976	Bos-A	117	432	51	108	15	5	0	26	22	39	.250	.286	.308	66	-19	8	5	-1	.977	-25	*2-112	-4.0
1977	Bos-A	137	455	54	109	13	6	2	49	29	50	.240	.291	.308	57	-27	2	4	-2	.979	-10	*2-137	-3.0
Total	8	944	3290	357	823	113	28	16	237	205	310	.250	.296	.316	70	-135	38	40	-13	.977	-61	2-912/3-7,S-4	-15.8
■ D. J. DOZIER	Dozier, William Henry b: 9/21/65, Norfolk, Va. BR/TR, 6′, 202 lbs. Deb: 5/6/92																						
1992	NY-N	25	47	4	9	2	0	0	2	4	19	.191	.269	.234	44	-3	4	0	1	.971	0	O-17	-0.2
■ DELOS DRAKE	Drake, Delos Daniel b: 12/3/1886, Girard, Ohio d: 10/3/65, Findlay, Ohio BR/TL, 5′11.5″, 170 lbs. Deb: 4/30/11																						
1911	Det-A	95	315	37	88	9	9	1	36	17		.279	.324	.375	90	-5	20			.942	-10	O-83/1-2	-1.9
1914	StL-F	138	514	51	129	18	8	3	42	31	57	.251	.295	.335	68	-31	17			.957	-1	*O-116,1-18	-4.0
1915	StL-F	102	343	32	91	23	4	1	41	23	27	.265	.313	.364	86	-12	6			.974	-5	O-97/1-1	-2.3
Total	3	335	1172	120	308	50	21	5	119	71	84	.263	.308	.354	79	-48	43			.959	-16	O-296/1-21	-8.2
■ LARRY DRAKE	Drake, Larry Francis b: 5/4/21, McKinney, Tex. d: 7/14/85, Houston, Tex. BL/TR, 6′1.5″, 195 lbs. Deb: 7/20/45																						
1945	Phi-A	1	2	0	0	0	0	0	0	0	2	.000	.000	.000	-99	-1	0	0	0	1.000	-0	/O-1	-0.1
1948	Was-A	4	7	0	2	0	0	0	1	1	3	.286	.375	.286	79	-0	0	0	0	1.000	-0	/O-2	-0.1
Total	2	5	9	0	2	0	0	0	1	1	5	.222	.300	.222	44	-1	0	0	0	1.000	-0	/O-3	-0.2
■ LYMAN DRAKE	Drake, Lyman Daniel b: 2/9/1852, Berea, Ohio d: 2/6/32, Muskegon, Mich. 6′, Deb: 6/29/1884																						
1884	Was-a	2	7	0	2	1	0	0	2	0		.286	.286	.429	147	0				.000	-1	/O-2	-0.1
■ SAMMY DRAKE	Drake, Samuel Harrison b: 10/7/34, Little Rock, Ark. BB/TR, 5′11″, 175 lbs. Deb: 4/17/60 F																						
1960	Chi-N	15	15	5	1	0	0	0	0	1	4	.067	.125	.067	-46	-3	0	0	0	1.000	-1	/3-6,2-2	-0.4
1961	Chi-N	13	5	1	0	0	0	0	0	1	1	.000	.167	.000	-50	-1	0	0	0	1.000	-0	/O-1	-0.1
1962	NY-N	25	52	2	10	0	0	0	7	6	12	.192	.276	.192	28	-5	0	0	0	.977	-2	2-10/3-6	-0.6
Total	3	53	72	8	11	0	0	0	7	8	17	.153	.237	.153	8	-9	0	0	0	.978	-3	/2-12,3-12,O-1	-1.1
■ SOLLY DRAKE	Drake, Solomon Louis b: 10/23/30, Little Rock, Ark. BB/TR, 6′, 170 lbs. Deb: 4/17/56 F																						
1956	Chi-N	65	215	29	55	9	1	2	15	23	35	.256	.331	.335	81	-5	9	5	-0	.993	2	O-53	-0.6
1959	LA-N	9	8	2	2	0	0	0	0	1	3	.250	.333	.250	54	-0	1	0	0	.667	-1	/O-4	-0.2
	Phi-N	67	62	10	9	1	0	0	3	8	15	.145	.243	.161	10	-8	5	5	-2	1.000	-10	O-37	-2.0
	Yr	76	70	12	11	1	0	0	3	9	18	.157	.253	.171	15	-8	6	5	-1	.974	-11	O-41	-2.2
Total	2	141	285	41	66	10	1	2	18	32	53	.232	.311	.295	64	-14	15	10	-2	.989	-9	/O-94	-2.8
■ JAKE DRAUBY	Drauby, Jacob C. b: 1865, Harrisburg, Pa. 5′10″, 163 lbs. Deb: 10/3/1892																						
1892	Was-N	10	34	3	7	0	1	0	3	2	12	.206	.250	.265	57	-2	0			.763	-2	3-10	-0.3
■ BILL DREESEN	Dreesen, William Richard b: 7/26/04, New York, N.Y. d: 11/9/71, Mt.Vernon, N.Y. BL/TR, 5′7.5″, 160 lbs. Deb: 5/1/31																						
1931	Bos-N	48	180	38	40	10	4	1	10	23	23	.222	.310	.339	77	-6	1			.910	-8	3-47	-1.1
■ BILL DRESCHER	Drescher, William Clayton "Dutch" b: 5/23/21, Congers, N.Y. d: 5/15/68, Haverstraw, N.Y. BL/TR, 6′2″, 190 lbs. Deb: 4/19/44																						
1944	NY-A	4	7	0	1	0	0	0	0	0	0	.143	.143	.143	-18	-1	0	0	0	.875	0	/C-1	-0.1
1945	NY-A	48	126	10	34	3	1	0	15	8	5	.270	.313	.310	77	-4	0	2	-1	.991	-8	C-33	-1.2
1946	NY-A	5	6	0	2	1	0	0	1	0	0	.333	.333	.500	129	0	0	0	0	1.000	1	/C-3	0.1
Total	3	57	139	10	37	4	1	0	16	8	5	.266	.306	.309	75	-5	0	2	-1	.985	-7	/C-37	-1.2
■ CHUCK DRESSEN	Dressen, Charles Walter b: 9/20/1898, Decatur, Ill. d: 8/10/66, Detroit, Mich. BR/TR, 5′5.5″, 146 lbs. Deb: 4/17/25 MC																						
1925	Cin-N	76	215	35	59	8	2	3	19	12	4	.274	.319	.372	78	-7	5	3	-0	.951	2	3-47/2-5,O-4	-0.3
1926	Cin-N	127	474	76	126	27	11	4	48	49	31	.266	.338	.395	99	-1	0			.966	17	*3-123/S-1,O-1	2.3
1927	Cin-N	144	548	78	160	36	10	2	55	71	32	.292	.376	.405	113	12	7			**.967**	12	*3-142/S-2	3.0
1928	Cin-N	135	498	72	145	26	3	1	59	43	22	.291	.355	.361	89	-7	10			.938	-2	*3-135	-0.2
1929	Cin-N	110	401	49	98	22	3	1	36	41	21	.244	.321	.322	63	-23	8			.932	-20	3-98/2-8	-3.6
1930	Cin-N	33	19	0	4	0	0	0	1	1	3	.211	.250	.211	14	-3	0			1.000	3	3-10/2-3	0.0
1931	Cin-N	5	15	0	1	0	0	0	0	1	1	.067	.125	.067	-50	-3	0			.846	-0	/3-4	-0.3
1933	NY-N	16	45	3	10	4	0	0	3	1	4	.222	.239	.311	57	-3	0			.972	0	3-16	-0.2
Total	8	646	2215	313	603	123	29	11	221	219	118	.272	.343	.369	89	-35	30	3		.953	12	3-575/2-16,O-5,S-3	0.7
■ LEE DRESSEN	Dressen, Lee August b: 7/23/1889, Ellinwood, Kan. d: 6/30/31, Diller, Neb. BL/TL, 6′, 165 lbs. Deb: 4/21/14																						
1914	StL-N	46	103	16	24	2	1	0	7	11	20	.233	.307	.272	73	-3	2			.982	-1	1-38	-0.6
1918	Det-A	31	107	10	19	1	2	0	3	21	10	.178	.323	.224	68	-3	2			.988	-3	1-30	-0.9
Total	2	77	210	26	43	3	3	0	10	32	30	.205	.316	.248	71	-6	4			.985	-5	/1-68	-1.5
■ CAMERON DREW	Drew, Cameron Steward b: 2/12/64, Boston, Mass. BL/TR, 6′5″, 230 lbs. Deb: 9/9/88																						
1988	Hou-N	7	16	1	3	0	1	0	1	0	1	.188	.188	.313	43	-1	0	0	0	1.000	0	/O-5	-0.1
■ DAVE DREW	Drew, David Deb: 5/14/1884																						
1884	Phi-U	2	9	1	4	0	0	0		0		.444	.444	.444	184	1				.000	-0	/P-1,2-1,S-1	0.1
	Was-U	13	53	8	16	1	2	0		1		.302	.315	.396	118	-0				.806	1	/S-8,1-5,O-1	0.0
	Yr	15	62	9	20	1	2	0		1		.323	.333	.403	127	0				.813	1	/S-9,1-5,P-1,2-1,O	0.1
■ J.D. DREW	Drew, David J. b: 11/20/75, Tallahassee, Fla. BL/TR, 6′1″, 190 lbs. Deb: 9/8/98																						
1998	StL-N	14	36	9	15	3	1	5	13	4	10	.417	.475	.972	265	9	0	0	0	1.000	-0	O-11	0.8
■ FRANK DREWS	Drews, Frank John b: 5/25/16, Buffalo, N.Y. d: 4/22/72, Buffalo, N.Y. BR/TR, 5′10″, 175 lbs. Deb: 8/13/44																						
1944	Bos-N	46	141	14	29	9	1	0	10	25	14	.206	.329	.284	71	-5	0			.959	1	2-46	-0.2
1945	Bos-N	49	147	13	30	4	1	0	19	16	18	.204	.282	.245	47	-10	0			.976	5	2-48	-0.3
Total	2	95	288	27	59	13	2	0	29	41	32	.205	.306	.264	59	-15	0			.967	5	/2-94	-0.5
■ DAN DRIESSEN	Driessen, Daniel b: 7/29/51, Hilton Head Island, S.C. BL/TR, 5′11″, 190 lbs. Deb: 6/9/73																						
1973	*Cin-N	102	366	49	110	15	2	4	47	24	37	.301	.347	.385	108	4	8	3	1	.946	-10	3-87,1-35/O-1	-0.7
1974	Cin-N	150	470	63	132	23	6	7	56	48	62	.281	.349	.400	111	6	10	5	0	.915	-21	*3-126,1-47/O-3	-1.7
1975	*Cin-N	88	210	38	59	8	1	7	38	35	30	.281	.389	.429	124	8	10	3	1	.986	-5	1-41,O-29	0.1
1976	*Cin-N	98	219	32	54	11	1	7	44	43	32	.247	.370	.402	116	6	14	1	4	.997	-3	1-40,O-20	0.3
1977	Cin-N	151	536	75	161	31	4	17	91	64	85	.300	.378	.468	123	18	31	13	2	.994	-3	*1-148	0.8
1978	Cin-N	153	524	68	131	23	3	16	70	75	79	.250	.348	.397	108	7	28	9	3	**.996**	3	*1-151	0.4
1979	*Cin-N	150	515	72	129	24	3	18	75	62	77	.250	.334	.414	102	2	11	5	0	.993	-3	*1-143	-1.0
1980	Cin-N	154	524	81	139	36	1	14	74	**93**	68	.265	.382	.418	123	20	19	6	2	.995	-4	*1-151	0.9
1981	Cin-N	82	233	35	55	14	0	7	33	40	31	.236	.353	.386	108	3	2	4	-2	.995	-5	1-74	-0.8
1982	Cin-N	149	516	64	139	25	1	17	57	82	62	.269	.372	.421	119	15	11	6	-0	**.998**	-7	*1-144	0.0
1983	Cin-N	122	386	57	107	17	1	12	57	75	51	.277	.395	.420	121	14	6	4	-1	**.996**	-2	*1-112	0.5
1984	Cin-N	81	218	27	61	13	0	7	28	37	25	.280	.384	.436	124	8	2	1	0	.991	-4	1-70	0.1
	Mon-N	51	169	20	43	11	0	9	32	17	15	.254	.323	.479	128	6	0	1	-1	.995	-2	1-45	0.1
	Yr	132	387	47	104	24	0	16	60	54	40	.269	.358	.455	126	14	2	2	-1	.992	-5	*1-115	0.2
1985	Mon-N	91	312	31	78	18	0	6	25	33	29	.250	.326	.365	99	-1	2	2	-1	.997	3	1-88	-0.4
	SF-N	54	181	22	42	8	0	3	22	17	22	.232	.302	.326	79	-5	0	0	0	.998	-2	1-49	-1.0
	Yr	145	493	53	120	26	0	9	47	50	51	.243	.317	.351	92	-6	2	2	-1	.997	1	*1-137	-1.4
1986	SF-N	15	16	2	3	2	0	0	0	4	4	.188	.350	.313	89	-0	0	0	0	1.000	1	/1-4	0.0
	Hou-N	17	24	5	7	1	0	1	3	5	2	.292	.414	.458	144	2	0	0	0	1.000	-0	1-12	0.1
	Yr	32	40	7	10	3	0	1	3	9	6	.250	.388	.400	122	2	0	0	0	1.000	0	1-16	0.1
1987	*StL-N	24	60	5	14	2	0	1	11	7	8	.233	.313	.317	66	-3	0	0	0	.993	-0	1-21	-0.4
Total	15	1732	5479	746	1464	282	23	153	763	761	719	.267	.359	.411	113	109	154	63	8	.995	-64	*1-1375,3-213/O-53	-2.7

YEAR	TM/L	G	AB	R	H	2B	3B	HR	RBI	BB	SO	AVG	OBP	SLG	PRO+	BR/A	SB	CS	SBR	FA	FR	G/POS	TPR

■ **LEW DRILL**   Drill, Lewis L b: 5/9/1877, Browerville, Minn. d: 7/4/69, St.Paul, Minn. BR/TR, 5'6", 186 lbs. Deb: 4/23/02

1902	Was-A	38	123	21	34	7	2	1	16	16		.276	.369	.390	110	2				.919	-11	C-28/2-4,O-4,3-1	-0.6
	Bal-A	2	8	2	2	0	0	0	0	0		.250	.250	.250	37	-1				1.000	1	/C-1,1-1	0.0
	Was-A	33	98	12	24	3	2	0	13	10		.245	.327	.316	78	-3	5			.926	-4	C-25/O-4,2-1	-0.4
	Yr	73	229	35	60	10	4	1	29	26		.262	.347	.354	94	-1	5			.924	-15	C-54/O-8,2-5,3-1,1	-1.0
1903	Was-A	51	154	11	39	9	3	0	23	15		.253	.331	.351	103	1	4			.966	-4	C-47/1-3	0.2
1904	Was-A	46	142	17	38	7	2	1	11	21		.268	.385	.366	140	8	3			.934	-7	C-29,O-14	0.4
	Det-A	51	160	7	39	6	1	0	13	20		.244	.335	.294	103	1	2			.950	-7	C-49/1-2	0.0
	Yr	97	302	24	77	13	3	1	24	41		.255	.359	.328	121	10	5			.944	-14	C-78,O-14/1-2	0.4
1905	Det-A	72	211	17	55	9	0	0	24	32		.261	.346	.303	112	5	7			.970	-2	C-71	1.1
Total	4	293	896	87	231	41	10	2	100	114		.258	.353	.333	108	14	21			.953	-34	C-250/O-22,1-6,23	0.7

■ **JIM DRISCOLL**   Driscoll, James Bernard b: 5/14/44, Medford, Mass. BL/TR, 5'11", 175 lbs. Deb: 6/17/70

1970	Oak-A	21	52	2	10	0	0	0	2	15		.192	.236	.250	35	-5	0	0	0	.967	-3	/2-7,S-7	-0.6
1972	Tex-A	15	18	0	0	0	0	0	0	3		.000	.100	.000	-72	-4	0	0	0	.900	1	/2-4,3-2	-0.3
Total	2	36	70	2	10	0	0	0	2	4	18	.143	.200	.186	9	-8	0	0	0	.950	-1	/2-11,S-7,3-2	-0.9

■ **DENNY DRISCOLL**   Driscoll, John F. b: 11/19/1855, Lowell, Mass. d: 7/11/1886, Lowell, Mass. BL/TL, 5'10.5", 160 lbs. Deb: 7/1/1880

1880	Buf-N	18	65	1	10	1	0	0	4	1	7	.154	.167	.169	14	-2				.895	-2	O-14/P-6	-0.6
1882	Pit-a	23	80	12	11	2	0	1		3		.138	.169	.200	25	-6				.885	-4	P-23	0.0
1883	Pit-a	41	148	19	27	2	1	0		4		.182	.204	.209	35	-10				.890	4	P-41/O-4,3-1	-0.2
1884	Lou-a	13	48	5	9	1	0	0	1	2		.188	.220	.208	42	-1				.816	-2	P-13/O-2	-0.1
1885	Buf-N	7	19	2	3	0	0	0	0	2	5	.158	.238	.158	29	-1				.719	-5	/2-7	-0.6
Total	5	102	360	39	60	6	1	1	5	12	12	.167	.194	.197	30	-26				.872	-5	/P-83,O-20,2-7,3-1	-1.5

■ **PADDY DRISCOLL**   Driscoll, John Leo b: 1/11/1895, Evanston, Ill. d: 6/28/68, Chicago, Ill. BR/TR, 5'8.5", 155 lbs. Deb: 6/12/17

| 1917 | Chi-N | 13 | 28 | 2 | 3 | 1 | 0 | 0 | 3 | 2 | 6 | .107 | .167 | .143 | -4 | -3 | 2 | | | .882 | 2 | /2-8,3-2,S-1 | -0.1 |

■ **MIKE DRISSEL**   Drissel, Michael F. b: 12/19/1864, St.Louis, Mo. d: 2/26/13, St.Louis, Mo. BR/TR, 5'11", 100 lbs. Deb: 9/5/1885

| 1885 | StL-a | 6 | 20 | 0 | 1 | 0 | 0 | 0 | 0 | 0 | | .050 | .050 | .050 | -65 | -4 | | | | .971 | -0 | /C-6 | -0.3 |

■ **WALT DROPO**   Dropo, Walter "Moose" b: 1/30/23, Moosup, Conn. BR/TR, 6'5", 220 lbs. Deb: 4/19/49

1949	Bos-A	11	41	3	6	2	0	0	1	3	7	.146	.205	.195	6	-6	0	0	0	1.000	-1	1-11	-0.7
1950	Bos-A★	136	559	101	180	28	8	34	**144**	45	75	.322	.378	.583	130	21	0	0	0	.988	-4	*1-134	1.3
1951	Bos-A	99	360	37	86	14	0	11	57	38	52	.239	.312	.369	76	-13	0	0	0	.987	-1	1-93	-1.8
1952	Bos-A	37	132	13	35	7	1	6	27	11	22	.265	.331	.470	112	2	0	0	0	.994	-1	1-35	-0.1
	Det-A	115	459	56	128	17	3	23	70	26	63	.279	.320	.479	120	9	2	2	-1	.989	-1	*1-115	0.3
	Yr	152	591	69	163	24	4	29	97	37	85	.276	.323	.477	118	10	2	2	-1	.990	-2	*1-150	0.2
1953	Det-A	152	606	61	150	30	3	13	96	29	69	.248	.289	.371	78	-21	2	0	1	.990	12	*1-150	-1.5
1954	Det-A	107	320	27	90	14	2	4	44	24	41	.281	.331	.375	95	-3	0	1	-1	.996	-5	1-95	-0.7
1955	Chi-A	141	453	55	127	15	2	19	79	42	71	.280	.344	.448	109	4	0	1	-1	.995	-5	*1-140	-0.9
1956	Chi-A	125	361	42	96	13	1	8	52	37	51	.266	.339	.374	87	-7	1	0	0	**.993**	-3	*1-117	-1.6
1957	Chi-A	93	223	24	57	2	0	13	49	16	40	.256	.305	.439	101	-1	0	1	-1	.987	2	1-69	-0.3
1958	Chi-A	28	52	3	10	1	0	2	8	5	11	.192	.276	.327	67	-2	0	0	0	1.000	1	1-16	-0.3
	Cin-N	63	162	18	47	7	2	7	31	12	31	.290	.343	.488	111	3	0	0	0	1.000	1	1-43	0.1
1959	Cin-N	26	39	4	4	1	0	1	2	4	7	.103	.205	.205	9	-5	0	0	0	1.000	1	1-23	-0.4
	Bal-A	62	151	17	42	9	0	6	21	12	20	.278	.331	.457	117	3	0	0	0	.990	-2	1-54/3-2	-0.1
1960	Bal-A	79	179	16	48	8	0	4	21	20	19	.268	.345	.380	97	-3	0	1	-0	.993	-1	1-67/3-1	-0.6
1961	Bal-A	14	27	1	7	0	0	1	2	4	3	.259	.355	.370	97	-0	0	0	0	1.000	1	1-12	0.0
Total	13	1288	4124	478	1113	168	22	152	704	328	582	.270	.327	.432	100	-17	5	6	-2	.992	-1	*1-1174/3-3	-7.3

■ **KEITH DRUMRIGHT**   Drumright, Keith Alan b: 10/21/54, Springfield, Mo. BL/TR, 5'10", 170 lbs. Deb: 9/1/78

1978	Hou-N	17	55	5	9	0	0	0	2	3	4	.164	.207	.164	5	-7	0	1	-1	.944	-1	2-17	-0.8
1981	*Oak-A	31	86	8	25	1	1	0	11	4	4	.291	.322	.326	91	-1	0	0	0	.989	-5	2-19/D-5	-0.6
Total	2	48	141	13	34	1	1	0	13	7	8	.241	.277	.262	58	-8	0	1	-1	.969	-6	/2-36,D-5	-1.4

■ **JEAN DUBUC**   Dubuc, Jean Joseph Octave Arthur "Chauncey" b: 9/15/1888, St.Johnsbury, Vt. d: 8/28/58, Fort Myers, Fla. BR/TR, 5'10.5", 185 lbs. Deb: 6/25/08 C

1908	Cin-N	15	29	2	4	1	0	0	2	0		.138	.138	.172	-1	-3	0			.943	1	P-15	0.0
1909	Cin-N	19	18	1	3	0	0	0	0	2		.167	.250	.167	30	-1	0			.844	-9	P-19	0.0
1912	Det-A	40	108	16	29	6	2	1	9	3		.269	.295	.389	98	-1	0			.972	4	P-37/O-2	0.0
1913	Det-A	68	135	17	36	5	3	2	11	2	17	.267	.277	.393	97	-2	1			.953	6	P-36/O-3	-0.2
1914	Det-A	71	124	9	28	4	1	1	11	7	11	.226	.273	.331	79	-4	1			.942	3	P-36	0.0
1915	Det-A	60	112	7	23	2	1	0	14	6	15	.205	.258	.241	47	-7	0			.969	1	P-39	0.0
1916	Det-A	52	78	3	20	1	0	0	7	7	12	.256	.318	.308	85	-1	0			.952	4	P-36	0.0
1918	*Bos-A	5	6	0	1	0	0	0	0	1	2	.167	.286	.167	37	-0	0			1.000	-0	/P-2	0.0
1919	NY-N	37	42	2	6	1	1	0	2	0	6	.143	.143	.214	7	-5	0			.964	2	P-36	0.0
Total	9	367	652	57	150	23	10	4	56	30	63	.230	.266	.314	72	-25	2			.952	22	P-256/O-5	-0.2

■ **ROB DUCEY**   Ducey, Robert Thomas b: 5/24/65, Toronto, Ont., Can. BL/TR, 6'2", 180 lbs. Deb: 5/1/87

1987	Tor-A	34	48	12	9	1	0	1	6	8	10	.188	.304	.271	53	-3	2	0	1	1.000	-7	O-28/D-1	-0.9
1988	Tor-A	27	54	15	17	4	1	0	6	5	7	.315	.373	.426	123	2	1	0	0	1.000	-6	O-26/D-1	-0.4
1989	Tor-A	41	76	5	16	4	0	0	7	9	25	.211	.294	.263	59	-4	2	1	0	1.000	-2	O-19	-0.6
1990	Tor-A	19	53	7	16	5	0	0	7	7	15	.302	.393	.396	119	2	1	1	-0	1.000	-0	O-19	0.1
1991	*Tor-A	39	68	8	16	2	1	1	4	6	26	.235	.297	.368	80	-2	2	0	1	.892	-3	O-24/D-2	-0.5
1992	Tor-A	23	21	3	1	1	0	0	0	0	10	.048	.048	.095	-58	-4	0	1	-1	1.000	-3	O-13/D-4	-0.9
	Cal-A	31	59	4	14	3	0	2	5	5	12	.237	.297	.288	68	-3	2	3	-2	.944	-1	O-33/D-5	-0.5
	Yr	54	80	7	15	4	0	2	5	5	22	.188	.235	.237	32	-7	2	4	-2	.957	-4	O-33/D-5	-1.4
1993	Tex-A	27	85	15	24	6	3	2	9	10	17	.282	.358	.494	132	4	3	1	-1	1.000	-2	O-26	0.0
1994	Tex-A	11	29	1	5	1	0	0	2	2	4	.172	.226	.207	13	-4	0	0	0	.882	-2	O-10	-0.5
1997	*Sea-A	76	143	25	41	15	2	5	10	6	31	.287	.315	.524	115	-2	3	3	-1	.986	-14	O-69	-1.2
1998	Sea-A	97	217	30	52	18	2	6	23	23	61	.240	.337	.410	93	-2	4	3	-1	.970	-8	O-83	-1.1
Total	10	425	853	125	211	60	10	14	75	81	215	.247	.320	.390	90	-13	19	15	-3	.975	-47	O-353/D-10	-6.5

■ **JOHN DUDRA**   Dudra, John Joseph b: 5/27/16, Assumption, Ill. d: 10/24/65, Pana, Ill. BR/TR, 5'11.5", 175 lbs. Deb: 9/7/41

| 1941 | Bos-N | 14 | 50 | 3 | 18 | 3 | 1 | 0 | 3 | 3 | 4 | .360 | .429 | .560 | 185 | 3 | 0 | | | .933 | 0 | /2-5,3-5,1-1,S-1 | 0.3 |

■ **PAT DUFF**   Duff, Patrick Henry b: 5/6/1875, Providence, R.I. d: 9/11/25, Providence, R.I. TR Deb: 4/16/06

| 1906 | Was-A | 1 | 1 | 0 | 0 | 0 | 0 | 0 | 0 | 0 | | .000 | .000 | .000 | -99 | -0 | 0 | | | .000 | 0 | H | 0.0 |

■ **CHARLIE DUFFEE**   Duffee, Charles Edward "Home Run" b: 1/27/1866, Mobile, Ala. d: 12/24/1894, Mobile, Ala. BR/TR, Deb: 4/17/1889

1889	StL-a	137	509	93	124	15	11	16	86	60	81	.244	.327	.411	97	-7	21			.936	18	*O-132/3-5,2-2	0.6
1890	StL-a	98	378	60	104	11	7	3	54	37		.275	.344	.365	96	-5	20			.951	10	O-66,3-33/S-1	0.3
1891	Col-a	137	552	86	166	28	4	10	90	42	36	.301	.353	.420	129	8	41			.927	11	*O-128/3-7,S-2	2.2
1892	Was-N	132	492	64	122	12	11	6	51	36	33	.248	.302	.354	101	-1	28			.913	19	*O-125/3-6,1-4	1.2
1893	Cin-N	4	12	3	2	1	0	0	0	5		.167	.412	.250	76	-0	0			.400	-2	/O-4	-0.2
Total	5	508	1943	314	518	67	33	35	281	180	150	.267	.332	.389	106	-5	110			.927	56	O-455/3-51,1-4,S2	4.1

■ **ED DUFFY**   Duffy, Edward Charles b: 1844, Ireland d: 6/21/1889, Brooklyn, N.Y. TR, 5'7.5", 152 lbs. Deb: 5/8/1871

| 1871 | Chi-n | 26 | 121 | 30 | 28 | 5 | 0 | 0 | 15 | 3 | 2 | .231 | .250 | .273 | 45 | -10 | 11 | 4 | 1 | .750 | -3 | *S-26/3-1 | -0.8 |

■ **FRANK DUFFY**   Duffy, Frank Thomas b: 10/14/46, Oakland, Cal. BR/TR, 6'1", 180 lbs. Deb: 9/4/70

| 1970 | Cin-N | 6 | 11 | 1 | 2 | 2 | 0 | 0 | 1 | 2 | 1 | .182 | .250 | .364 | 62 | -1 | 1 | 0 | 0 | 1.000 | 1 | /S-5 | 0.1 |

YEAR	TM/L	G	AB	R	H	2B	3B	HR	RBI	BB	SO	AVG	OBP	SLG	PRO+	BR/A	SB	CS	SBR	FA	FR	G/POS	TPR
1971	Cin-N	13	16	0	3	1	0	0	1	1	2	.188	.235	.250	38	-1	0	0	0	.944	5	S-10	0.4
	*SF-N	21	28	4	5	0	0	0	2	0	10	.179	.179	.179	1	-4	0	0	0	.968	5	/S-6,2-1,3-1	0.2
	Yr	34	44	4	8	1	0	0	3	1	12	.182	.200	.205	15	-5	0	0	0	.955	10	S-16/2-1,3-1	0.6
1972	Cle-A	130	385	23	92	16	4	3	27	31	54	.239	.297	.325	82	-8	6	2	1	.977	3	*S-126	1.2
1973	Cle-A	116	361	34	95	16	4	8	50	25	41	.263	.314	.396	97	-2	6	6	-2	**.986**	12	*S-115	2.3
1974	Cle-A	158	549	62	128	18	0	8	48	30	64	.233	.273	.310	68	-23	7	8	-3	.980	-8	*S-158	-1.5
1975	Cle-A	146	482	44	117	22	2	1	47	27	60	.243	.286	.303	66	-22	10	10	-3	.977	14	*S-145	0.4
1976	Cle-A	133	392	38	83	11	2	2	30	29	50	.212	.270	.265	58	-21	10	0	3	**.983**	11	*S-132	0.7
1977	Cle-A	122	334	30	67	13	2	4	31	21	47	.201	.248	.287	47	-25	8	3	1	.967	3	*S-121	-1.1
1978	Bos-A	64	104	12	27	5	0	0	4	6	11	.260	.306	.308	66	-5	1	1	-0	.960	6	3-22,S-21,2-12,/D-6	0.4
1979	Bos-A	6	3	0	0	0	0	0	0	0	1	.000	.000	.000	-95	-1	0	0	0	1.000	1	/2-3,1-1	0.0
Total	10	915	2665	248	619	104	14	26	240	171	342	.232	.281	.311	69	-112	49	30	-3	.977	53	S-839/3-23,2-16,D1	3.1

■ HUGH DUFFY
Duffy, Hugh b: 11/26/1866, Cranston, R.I. d: 10/19/54, Boston, Mass. BR/TR, 5'7", 168 lbs. Deb: 6/23/1888 MCH

YEAR	TM/L	G	AB	R	H	2B	3B	HR	RBI	BB	SO	AVG	OBP	SLG	PRO+	BR/A	SB	CS	SBR	FA	FR	G/POS	TPR
1888	Chi-N	71	298	60	84	10	4	7	41	9	32	.282	.305	.413	119	5	13			.910	5	O-67/S-3,3-1	0.8
1889	Chi-N	136	584	144	172	21	7	12	89	46	30	.295	.348	.416	108	4	52			.894	-15	*O-126,S-10	-1.3
1890	Chi-P	138	596	**161**	**191**	36	16	7	82	59	20	.320	.384	.470	122	16	78			.917	13	*O-137	2.0
1891	Bos-a	127	536	134	180	20	8	9	**110**	61	29	.336	.408	.453	149	34	85			.917	0	*O-124/3-3,S-1	2.6
1892	*Bos-N	147	612	125	184	28	12	5	81	60	37	.301	.364	.410	123	14	51			.942	-9	*O-146/3-2	-0.1
1893	Bos-N	131	560	147	203	23	7	6	118	50	13	**.363**	.416	.461	123	16	44			.953	-2	*O-131	0.6
1894	Bos-N	125	539	160	**237**	**51**	16	**18**	**145**	66	15	**.440**	**.502**	**.694**	172	61	48			.927	4	*O-124/S-2	4.3
1895	Bos-N	130	531	110	187	30	6	9	100	63	16	.352	.425	.482	124	18	42			.945	6	*O-130	1.1
1896	Bos-N	131	527	97	158	16	8	5	113	52	19	.300	.365	.389	93	-6	39			.957	0	*O-120/2-9,S-2	-1.3
1897	*Bos-N	134	550	130	187	25	10	**11**	129	52		.340	.403	.482	125	18	41			.975	-1	*O-129/2-6,S-2	0.7
1898	Bos-N	152	568	97	169	13	3	8	108	59		.298	.365	.373	106	4	29			.956	2	*O-152/3-1,1-1,C-1	-0.4
1899	Bos-N	147	588	103	164	29	7	5	102	39		.279	.327	.378	85	-15	26			.970	-4	*O-147	-2.7
1900	Bos-N	55	181	27	55	5	4	2	31	16		.304	.360	.409	100	-1	11			.957	-1	O-49/2-1	-0.5
1901	Mil-A	79	285	40	86	15	9	2	45	16		.302	.341	.439	121	7	12			.967	-6	O-77,M	-0.4
1904	Phi-N	18	46	10	13	1	1	0	5	13		.283	.441	.348	150	4	3			.850	-3	O-14,M	0.0
1905	Phi-N	15	40	7	12	2	1	0	3	1		.300	.317	.400	117	1	0			.909	1	/O-8,M	0.1
1906	Phi-N	1	1	0	0	0	0	0	0	0		.000	.000	.000	-99	-0	0			.000	0	HM	0.0
Total	17	1737	7042	1552	2282	325	119	106	1302	662	211	.324	.384	.449	121	181	574			.943	-10	*O-1681/S-20,23C1	5.5

■ JOE DUGAN
Dugan, Joseph Anthony "Jumping Joe" b: 5/12/1897, Mahanoy City, Pa. d: 7/7/82, Norwood, Mass. BR/TR, 5'11", 160 lbs. Deb: 7/5/17

YEAR	TM/L	G	AB	R	H	2B	3B	HR	RBI	BB	SO	AVG	OBP	SLG	PRO+	BR/A	SB	CS	SBR	FA	FR	G/POS	TPR
1917	Phi-A	43	134	9	26	8	0	0	16	3	16	.194	.229	.254	48	-9	0			.917	1	S-39/2-2	-0.7
1918	Phi-A	121	411	26	80	11	3	3	34	16	55	.195	.230	.258	47	-28	4			.930	17	S-86,2-34	-0.6
1919	Phi-A	104	387	25	105	17	2	1	30	11	30	.271	.300	.333	77	-13	9			.929	1	S-98/2-4,3-2	-0.6
1920	Phi-A	123	491	65	158	40	5	3	60	19	51	.322	.351	.442	108	4	5	8	-3	.948	-1	3-60,S-32,2-31	0.6
1921	Phi-A	119	461	54	136	22	6	10	58	28	45	.295	.342	.434	96	-4	5	1	1	.953	-25	*3-119	-1.9
1922	Bos-A	84	341	45	98	22	3	3	38	9	28	.287	.308	.396	83	-10	2	3	-1	.943	-9	3-64,S-21	-1.3
	*NY-A	60	252	44	72	9	1	3	25	13	21	.286	.331	.365	79	-8	1	0	0	.967	-10	3-60	-1.2
	Yr	144	593	89	170	31	4	6	63	22	49	.287	.318	.383	81	-17	3	3	-1	.954	-19	*3-124,S-21	-2.5
1923	*NY-A	146	644	111	182	30	7	7	67	25	41	.283	.311	.384	81	-20	4	2	0	**.974**	-11	*3-146	-1.8
1924	NY-A	148	610	105	184	31	7	3	56	31	33	.302	.341	.390	88	-12	1	2	-1	.962	-15	*3-148/2-2	-1.5
1925	NY-A	102	404	50	118	19	4	0	31	19	20	.292	.330	.359	76	-15	2	4	-2	.970	7	3-96	-0.3
1926	*NY-A	123	434	39	125	19	5	1	64	25	16	.288	.328	.362	81	-13	2	4	-2	.955	-16	*3-122	-2.2
1927	*NY-A	112	387	44	104	24	3	2	43	27	37	.269	.321	.362	79	-12	1	4	-2	.938	-19	*3-111	-2.8
1928	*NY-A	94	312	33	86	15	0	6	34	16	15	.276	.317	.381	85	-7	1	0	0	.952	-18	3-91/2-1	-2.0
1929	Bos-N	60	125	14	38	10	0	0	15	8	8	.304	.346	.384	84	-3	0			.918	-9	3-24/S-5,2-2,O-2	-1.0
1931	Det-A	8	17	1	4	0	0	0	0	0	3	.235	.235	.235	23	-2	0	0	0	.900	-1	/3-5	-0.2
Total	14	1447	5410	665	1516	277	46	42	571	250	419	.280	.317	.372	82	-152	37	28		.957	-107	*3-1048,S-281/2O	-17.5

■ BILL DUGAN
Dugan, William H. b: 1864, New York, N.Y. d: 7/24/21, New York, N.Y. Deb: 8/5/1884 F

YEAR	TM/L	G	AB	R	H	2B	3B	HR	RBI	BB	SO	AVG	OBP	SLG	PRO+	BR/A	SB	CS	SBR	FA	FR	G/POS	TPR
1884	Ric-a	9	28	4	3	1	0	0		0		.107	.138	.143	-8	-3				.889	-3	/C-9	-0.5
	KC-U	3	6	0	0	0	0	0		0		.000	.000	.000	-99	-2				.400	-1	/O-3	-0.3
Total	1	12	34	4	3	1	0	0		0		.088	.114	.118	-26	-5				.889	-4	/C-9,O-3	-0.8

■ GUS DUGAS
Dugas, Augustin Joseph b: 3/24/07, St.Jean De Matha, Que., Canada d: 4/14/97, Colchester, Conn. BL/TL, 5'9", 165 lbs. Deb: 9/17/30

YEAR	TM/L	G	AB	R	H	2B	3B	HR	RBI	BB	SO	AVG	OBP	SLG	PRO+	BR/A	SB	CS	SBR	FA	FR	G/POS	TPR
1930	Pit-N	9	31	8	9	2	0	0	1	7	4	.290	.421	.355	90	-0	0			.864	-1	/O-9	-0.2
1932	Pit-N	55	97	13	23	3	3	3	12	7	11	.237	.288	.423	90	-2	0			.952	-3	O-20	-0.5
1933	Phi-N	37	71	4	12	3	0	0	9	1	9	.169	.181	.211	10	-8	0			.984	-0	1-11/O-1	-1.0
1934	Was-A	24	19	2	1	1	0	0	1	3	3	.053	.182	.105	-25	-4	0	0	0	1.000	-0	/O-2	-0.4
Total	4	125	218	27	45	9	3	3	23	18	27	.206	.267	.317	54	-14	0	0		.926	-4	/O-32,1-11	-2.1

■ DAN DUGDALE
Dugdale, Daniel Edward b: 10/28/1864, Peoria, Ill. d: 3/9/34, Seattle, Wash. 5'8", 180 lbs. Deb: 5/20/1886

YEAR	TM/L	G	AB	R	H	2B	3B	HR	RBI	BB	SO	AVG	OBP	SLG	PRO+	BR/A	SB	CS	SBR	FA	FR	G/POS	TPR
1886	KC-N	12	40	4	7	0	0	0	2	2	13	.175	.214	.175	18	-4	1			.884	-2	/C-7,O-6	-0.5
1894	Was-N	38	134	19	32	4	2	0	16	13	14	.239	.306	.299	48	-11	7			.874	-5	C-33/3-3,O-2	-1.1
Total	2	50	174	23	39	4	2	0	18	15	27	.224	.286	.270	42	-15	8			.877	-7	/C-40,O-8,3-3	-1.6

■ OSCAR DUGEY
Dugey, Oscar Joseph "Jake" b: 10/25/1887, Palestine, Tex. d: 1/1/66, Dallas, Tex. BR/TR, 5'8", 160 lbs. Deb: 9/13/13 C

YEAR	TM/L	G	AB	R	H	2B	3B	HR	RBI	BB	SO	AVG	OBP	SLG	PRO+	BR/A	SB	CS	SBR	FA	FR	G/POS	TPR
1913	Bos-N	5	8	1	2	0	0	0	0	1	1	.250	.333	.250	67	-0	0			.500	-1	/3-2,2-1,S-1	-0.1
1914	Bos-N	58	109	17	21	2	0	1	10	10	15	.193	.267	.239	51	-6	10			.933	-2	O-16,2-16/3-1	-1.0
1915	*Phi-N	42	39	4	6	1	0	0	0	7	5	.154	.283	.179	41	-3	2	1	0	.941	3	2-14	0.0
1916	Phi-N	41	50	9	11	3	0	0	1	9	8	.220	.339	.280	88	-0	3			.967	3	2-12	0.3
1917	Phi-N	44	72	12	14	4	1	0	9	4	9	.194	.237	.278	55	-4	2			.871	0	2-15/O-4	-0.4
1920	Bos-N	5	0	2	0	0	0	0	0	0	0	—	—	—	—	0	0	0	0	.000	0	R	0.0
Total	6	195	278	45	54	10	1	1	20	31	38	.194	.277	.248	58	-14	17	1		.915	3	/2-58,O-20,3-3,S-1	-1.2

■ JIM DUGGAN
Duggan, James Elmer "Mer" b: 6/1/1885, Whiteland, Ind. d: 12/5/51, Indianapolis, Ind. BL/TL, 5'10", 165 lbs. Deb: 6/29/11

YEAR	TM/L	G	AB	R	H	2B	3B	HR	RBI	BB	SO	AVG	OBP	SLG	PRO+	BR/A	SB	CS	SBR	FA	FR	G/POS	TPR
1911	StL-A	1	4	1	0	0	0	0	1	1		.000	.200	.000	-44	-1	0			1.000	0	/1-1	-0.1

■ TOM DUNBAR
Dunbar, Thomas Jerome b: 11/24/59, Graniteville, S.C. BL/TL, 6'2", 192 lbs. Deb: 9/7/83

YEAR	TM/L	G	AB	R	H	2B	3B	HR	RBI	BB	SO	AVG	OBP	SLG	PRO+	BR/A	SB	CS	SBR	FA	FR	G/POS	TPR
1983	Tex-A	12	24	3	6	0	0	0	3	5	7	.250	.379	.250	79	-0	3	1	0	.875	-3	/O-9,D-1	-0.3
1984	Tex-A	34	97	9	25	2	0	2	10	6	16	.258	.301	.340	75	-3	1	0	0	.939	-3	O-20/D-6	-0.6
1985	Tex-A	45	104	7	21	4	0	1	5	12	9	.202	.291	.269	54	-6	0	3	-2	.933	-3	D-18,O-14	-1.2
Total	3	91	225	19	52	6	0	3	18	23	32	.231	.305	.298	66	-10	4	4	-1	.929	-9	/O-43,D-25	-2.1

■ DAVE DUNCAN
Duncan, David Edwin b: 9/26/45, Dallas, Tex. BR/TR, 6'2", 200 lbs. Deb: 5/6/64 C

YEAR	TM/L	G	AB	R	H	2B	3B	HR	RBI	BB	SO	AVG	OBP	SLG	PRO+	BR/A	SB	CS	SBR	FA	FR	G/POS	TPR
1964	KC-A	25	53	2	9	0	1	1	5	2	20	.170	.200	.264	27	-5	0	0	0	.981	3	C-22	-0.1
1967	KC-A	34	101	9	19	4	0	5	11	4	50	.188	.219	.376	75	-4	0	1	-1	.979	-6	C-32	-1.0
1968	Oak-A	82	246	15	47	4	0	7	28	25	68	.191	.268	.293	73	-8	1	2	-1	.987	0	C-79	-0.4
1969	Oak-A	58	127	11	16	3	0	3	22	19	41	.126	.240	.220	31	-12	0	0	0	.982	-12	C-56	-2.3
1970	Oak-A	86	232	21	60	7	0	10	29	22	38	.259	.323	.418	107	1	0	0	0	.978	3	C-73	0.8
1971	*Oak-A☆	103	363	39	92	13	1	15	40	28	77	.253	.309	.419	106	2	1	1	-0	.984	3	*C-102	0.9
1972	*Oak-A	121	403	39	88	13	0	19	59	34	68	.218	.287	.392	106	1	0	2	-1	.993	2	*C-113	0.7
1973	Cle-A	95	344	43	80	11	1	17	43	35	86	.233	.309	.419	101	-0	3	3	-1	.988	-1	C-86/D-9	0.2
1974	Cle-A	136	425	45	85	10	1	16	46	42	91	.200	.275	.341	77	-13	0	4	-2	.976	-8	*C-134/1-3,D-1	-1.9
1975	Bal-A	96	307	30	63	7	0	12	41	16	82	.205	.247	.345	70	-14	0	0	0	.982	-7	C-95	-1.7
1976	Bal-A	93	284	20	58	7	0	4	17	25	56	.204	.271	.271	63	-13	0	0	0	.985	-11	C-93	-2.3
Total	11	929	2885	274	617	79	4	109	341	252	677	.214	.280	.357	85	-65	5	13	-6	.984	-32	C-885/D-10,1-3	-7.1

YEAR	TM/L	G	AB	R	H	2B	3B	HR	RBI	BB	SO	AVG	OBP	SLG	PRO+	BR/A	SB	CS	SBR	FA	FR	G/POS	TPR
■ JIM DUNCAN Duncan, James William b: 7/1/1871, Saltsburg, Pa. d: 10/16/01, Foxburg, Pa. BR/TR, 5'8", 140 lbs. Deb: 7/18/1899																							
1899	Was-N	15	47	5	11	2	0	0	5	4		.234	.294	.277	57	-3	1			.940	-1	C-14	-0.2
	Cle-N	31	105	9	24	2	3	2	9	4		.229	.257	.362	74	-4	0			.971	-4	1-17,C-14	-0.7
	Yr	46	152	14	35	4	3	2	14	8		.230	.269	.336	69	-7	1			.904	-5	C-28,1-17	-0.9
■ PAT DUNCAN Duncan, Louis Baird b: 10/6/1893, Coalton, Ohio d: 7/17/60, Columbus, Ohio BR/TR, 5'9", 170 lbs. Deb: 7/16/15																							
1915	Pit-N	3	5	0	1	0	0	0	0	0	1	.200	.200	.200	22	-0	0			1.000	-0	/O-1	-0.1
1919	*Cin-N	31	90	9	22	3	3	2	17	8	7	.244	.306	.411	118	2	2			.982	-1	O-27	-0.1
1920	Cin-N	154	576	75	170	16	11	2	83	42	42	.295	.350	.372	109	7	18	18	-5	.964	5	*O-154	-0.5
1921	Cin-N	145	532	57	164	27	10	2	60	44	33	.308	.367	.408	110	8	7	18	-9	.971	9	*O-145	-0.3
1922	Cin-N	151	607	94	199	44	12	8	94	40	31	.328	.370	.479	120	16	12	28	-13	.971	4	*O-151	-0.4
1923	Cin-N	147	566	92	185	26	8	7	83	30	27	.327	.363	.438	113	9	15	13	-3	**.993**	-1	*O-146	-0.4
1924	Cin-N	96	319	34	86	21	6	2	37	20	23	.270	.313	.392	89	-6	1	7	-4	.927	-14	O-83	-2.9
Total	7	727	2695	361	827	137	50	23	374	184	164	.307	.355	.420	110	36	55	84		.970	1	O-707	-4.7
■ MARIANO DUNCAN Duncan, Mariano (Nalasco) b: 3/13/63, San Pedro De Macoris, D.R. BR/TR, 6', 185 lbs. Deb: 4/9/85																							
1985	*LA-N	142	562	74	137	24	6	6	39	38	113	.244	.295	.340	79	-16	38	8	7	.954	-8	*S-123,2-19	-0.6
1986	LA-N	109	407	47	93	7	0	8	30	30	78	.229	.285	.305	67	-19	48	13	7	.951	-2	*S-106	-0.4
1987	LA-N	76	261	31	56	8	1	6	18	17	62	.215	.268	.322	57	-17	11	1	3	.930	-1	S-67/2-7,O-2	-0.9
1989	LA-N	49	84	9	21	5	1	0	8	0	15	.250	.267	.333	72	-3	3	3	-1	.943	-0	S-16/2-8,O-7	-0.4
	Cin-N	45	174	23	43	10	1	3	13	8	36	.247	.292	.368	85	-4	6	2	1	.955	-7	S-44/2-5	-0.8
	Yr	94	258	32	64	15	2	3	21	8	51	.248	.284	.357	81	-7	9	5	-0	.952	-8	S-60,2-13/O-7	-1.2
1990	*Cin-N	125	435	67	133	22	**11**	10	55	24	67	.306	.348	.476	119	10	13	7	-0	.973	1	*2-115,S-12/O-1	1.4
1991	Cin-N	100	333	46	86	7	4	12	40	12	57	.258	.290	.411	92	-5	5	4	-1	.974	-6	2-62,S-32/O-7	-0.9
1992	Phi-N	142	574	71	153	40	3	8	50	17	108	.267	.294	.389	92	-8	23	3	5	.976	-23	O-65,2-52,S-42,/3-4	-2.5
1993	*Phi-N	124	496	68	140	26	4	11	73	12	88	.282	.305	.417	92	-7	6	5	-1	.969	-28	2-65,S-59	-3.0
1994	Phi-N★	88	347	49	93	22	1	8	48	17	72	.268	.310	.406	83	-9	10	2	2	.972	-17	2-37,3-28,S-19,/1-6	-2.1
1995	Phi-N	52	196	20	56	12	1	3	23	0	43	.286	.289	.403	80	-6	1	2	-1	.957	5	2-24,S-14,1-12,/3-1	0.0
	*Cin-N	29	69	16	20	2	1	3	13	5	19	.290	.338	.478	113	1	0	1	-1	.963	-3	/2-7,1-6,S-6,O-3	-0.2
	Yr	81	265	36	76	14	2	6	36	5	62	.287	.303	.423	88	-5	1	3	-2	.958	2	2-31,S-20,1-18,/O3	-0.2
1996	*NY-A	109	400	62	136	34	3	8	56	9	77	.340	.356	.500	113	7	4	3	-1	.975	-25	*2-104/3-3,O-3,D-2	-1.1
1997	NY-A	50	172	16	42	8	0	1	13	6	39	.244	.270	.308	51	-12	2	1	0	.976	-8	2-41/O-6,D-2	-1.7
	Tor-A	39	167	20	38	6	0	0	12	6	39	.228	.267	.263	39	-15	4	2	0	.984	1	2-39	-1.1
	Yr	89	339	36	80	14	0	1	25	12	78	.236	.268	.286	45	-27	6	3	0	.980	-7	2-80/O-6,D-2	-2.8
Total	12	1279	4677	619	1247	233	37	87	491	201	913	.267	.302	.388	86	-103	174	57	18	.972	-121	2-585,S-540/O31D	-14.3
■ TAYLOR DUNCAN Duncan, Taylor McDowell b: 5/12/53, Memphis, Tenn. BR/TR, 6', 170 lbs. Deb: 9/15/77																							
1977	StL-N	8	12	2	4	0	0	1	2	2	1	.333	.429	.583	172	1	0	0	0	1.000	-2	/3-5	-0.1
1978	Oak-A	104	319	25	82	15	2	2	37	19	38	.257	.299	.335	82	-8	1	2	-1	.953	-21	3-84,2-11/S-1,D-7	-3.2
Total	2	112	331	27	86	15	2	3	39	21	39	.260	.304	.344	86	-7	1	2	-1	.953	-23	/3-89,2-11,D-7,S-1	-3.3
■ VERN DUNCAN Duncan, Vernon Van Duke b: 1/6/1890, Clayton, N.C. d: 6/1/54, Daytona Beach, Fla BL/TR, 5'9", 155 lbs. Deb: 9/11/13																							
1913	Phi-N	8	12	3	5	1	0	0	1	0	3	.417	.417	.500	155	1	0			1.000	-0	/O-3	0.1
1914	Bal-F	157	557	99	160	20	8	2	53	67	55	.287	.375	.363	98	-7	13			.914	-3	*O-148/3-8,2-1	-1.7
1915	Bal-F	146	531	68	142	18	4	2	43	54	40	.267	.337	.328	85	-17	19			.965	-0	*O-124,3-21/2-1	-2.4
Total	3	311	1100	170	307	39	12	4	97	121	98	.279	.357	.347	93	-23	32			.939	-3	O-275/3-29,2-2	-4.0
■ GUS DUNDON Dundon, Augustus Joseph b: 7/10/1874, Columbus, Ohio d: 9/1/40, Pittsburgh, Pa. BR/TR, 5'10", 165 lbs. Deb: 4/14/04																							
1904	Chi-A	108	373	40	85	9	3	0	36	30		.228	.292	.268	81	-7	19			**.973**	-15	*2-103/3-3,S-2	-2.2
1905	Chi-A	106	364	30	70	7	3	0	22	23		.192	.248	.228	53	-19	14			.983	13	*2-100/S-6	-0.5
1906	Chi-A	33	96	7	13	1	0	0	4	11		.135	.224	.146	17	-9	4			.921	7	2-18,S-14	-0.1
Total	3	247	833	77	168	17	6	0	62	64		.202	.265	.236	61	-35	37			.972	6	2-221/S-22,3-3	-2.8
■ ED DUNDON Dundon, Edward Joseph "Dummy" b: 7/10/1859, Columbus, Ohio d: 8/18/1893, Columbus, Ohio TR, Deb: 6/2/1883																							
1883	Col-a	26	93	8	15	1	0	0		3		.161	.188	.172	18	-8				.804	0	P-20/O-9,2-1	-0.2
1884	Col-a	26	86	6	12	2	2	0		5		.140	.196	.209	35	-6				.966	3	O-16,P-11/1-3	-0.2
Total	2	52	179	14	27	3	2	0		8		.151	.191	.190	26	-14				.866	4	/P-31,O-25,1-3,2-1	-0.4
■ SAM DUNGAN Dungan, Samuel Morrison b: 7/29/1866, Ferndale, Cal. d: 3/16/39, Santa Ana, Cal. BR, 5'11", 180 lbs. Deb: 4/12/1892																							
1892	Chi-N	113	433	46	123	19	7	0	53	35	19	.284	.346	.360	112	6	15			.905	-6	*O-113	-0.5
1893	Chi-N	107	465	86	138	23	7	2	64	29	8	.297	.350	.389	98	-2	11			.920	4	*O-107	-0.3
1894	Chi-N	10	39	5	9	2	0	0	3	7	1	.231	.348	.282	51	-3	1			1.000	0	O-10	-0.3
	Lou-N	8	32	6	11	1	0	0	3	4	1	.344	.417	.375	99	0	2			.941	0	/O-8	0.0
	Yr	18	71	11	20	3	0	0	6	11	2	.282	.378	.324	71	-3	3			.971	1	O-18	-0.3
1900	Chi-N	6	15	1	4	0	0	0	1	1		.267	.313	.267	63	-1	0			.800	-1	/O-3	-0.2
1901	Was-A	138	559	70	179	26	12	1	73	40		.320	.368	.415	118	14	9			.947	-5	*O-104,1-35	0.1
Total	5	382	1543	214	464	71	26	3	197	116	29	.301	.356	.386	107	14	38			.924	-8	O-345/1-35	-1.2
■ LEE DUNHAM Dunham, Leland Huffield b: 6/9/02, Atlanta, Ill. d: 5/11/61, Atlanta, Ill. BL/TL, 5'11", 185 lbs. Deb: 4/17/26																							
1926	Phi-N	5	4	0	1	0	0	0	1	0	1	.250	.250	.250	33	-0	0			1.000	-0	/1-2	0.0
■ FRED DUNLAP Dunlap, Frederick C. "Sure Shot" b: 5/21/1859, Philadelphia, Pa. d: 12/1/02, Philadelphia, Pa. BR/TR, 5'8", 165 lbs. Deb: 5/1/1880 M																							
1880	Cle-N	85	373	61	103	**27**	9	4	30	7	32	.276	.289	.429	143	16				.911	8	*2-85	2.7
1881	Cle-N	80	351	60	114	25	4	3	24	18	24	.325	.358	.444	159	24				.909	6	*2-79/3-1	3.0
1882	Cle-N	84	364	68	102	19	4	0	28	23	26	.280	.323	.354	121	9				.900	18	*2-84,M	2.6
1883	Cle-N	93	396	81	129	34	2	4	37	22	21	.326	.361	.452	147	22				.911	8	*2-93/O-1	2.7
1884	StL-U	101	449	**160**	**185**	39	8	**13**		29		**.412**	**.448**	**.621**	**213**	**49**				**.926**	**31**	*2-100/O-1,P-1,M	**6.9**
1885	StL-N	106	423	70	114	11	5	2	25	41	24	.270	.334	.333	124	13				**.934**	**26**	*2-106,M	4.0
1886	StL-N	71	285	53	76	15	2	3	32	28	30	.267	.332	.365	119	8	7			.931	16	2-71/O-1	2.4
	Det-N	51	196	32	56	8	3	4	37	16	21	.286	.340	.418	126	6	13			.918	3	2-51	1.0
	Yr	122	481	85	132	23	5	7	69	44	51	.274	.335	.387	122	14	20			.926	19	*2-122/O-1	3.4
1887	*Det-N	65	272	60	72	13	10	5	45	25	12	.265	.327	.441	108	2	15			.948	24	2-65/P-1	2.3
1888	Pit-N	82	321	41	84	12	4	1	36	16	30	.262	.303	.333	111	4	24			.940	12	2-82	1.9
1889	Pit-N	121	451	59	106	19	0	2	65	46	33	.235	.309	.290	75	-14	21			**.950**	-6	*2-121,M	-1.2
1890	Pit-N	17	64	9	11	1	1	0	3	7	6	.172	.264	.219	46	-4	2			.874	-3	2-17	-0.5
	NY-P	1	4	1	2	0	0	0	0	0	0	.500	.500	.500	154	0	0			1.000	-1	/2-1	-0.1
1891	Was-a	8	25	4	5	1	1	0	4	5	4	.200	.355	.320	98	0	3			.818	-3	/2-8	-0.3
Total	12	965	3974	759	1159	224	53	41	366	283	263	.292	.340	.406	132	136	85			.924	137	2-963/O-3,P-2,3-1	27.4
■ GRANT DUNLAP Dunlap, Grant Lester "Snap" b: 12/20/23, Stockton, Cal. BR/TR, 6'2", 180 lbs. Deb: 4/21/53																							
1953	StL-N	16	17	2	6	0	1	1	3	0	2	.353	.353	.647	154	1	0	0	0	.000	-0	/O-1	0.1
■ BILL DUNLAP Dunlap, William James b: 5/1/09, Palmer, Mass. d: 11/29/80, Reading, Pa. BR/TR, 5'11", 170 lbs. Deb: 9/2/29																							
1929	Bos-N	10	29	6	12	0	1	1	4	4	4	.414	.485	.586	171	3	0			.889	-1	/O-9	0.1
1930	Bos-N	16	29	3	2	1	0	0	0	0	6	.069	.069	.103	-61	-8	0			1.000	-1	/O-7	-0.8
Total	2	26	58	9	14	1	1	1	4	4	10	.241	.290	.345	57	-4	0			.939	-2	/O-16	-0.7
■ JACK DUNLEAVY Dunleavy, John Francis b: 9/14/1879, Harrison, N.J. d: 4/11/44, S.Norwalk, Conn. TL, 5'6", 167 lbs. Deb: 5/30/03																							
1903	StL-N	61	193	23	48	3	3	0	10	13		.249	.306	.295	74	-6	10			.972	6	O-38,P-14	-0.2
1904	StL-N	51	172	23	40	7	3	1	14	16		.233	.305	.326	99	-0	8			.987	1	O-44/P-7	-0.3
1905	StL-N	119	435	52	105	8	8	1	25	55		.241	.328	.303	91	-3	15			.962	2	*O-118/2-1	-0.7
Total	3	231	800	98	193	18	14	2	49	84		.241	.318	.306	89	-9	33			.969	9	O-200/P-21,2-1	-1.2

YEAR	TM/L	G	AB	R	H	2B	3B	HR	RBI	BB	SO	AVG	OBP	SLG	PRO+	BR/A	SB	CS	SBR	FA	FR	G/POS	TPR
■ **GEORGE DUNLOP**	Dunlop, George Henry b: 7/19/1888, Meriden, Conn. d: 12/12/72, Meriden, Conn. BR/TR, 5'10", 170 lbs. Deb: 9/9/13																						
1913	Cle-A	7	17	3	4	1	0	0	0	0	5	.235	.235	.294	53	-1	0			.923	1	/S-4,3-3	0.0
1914	Cle-A	1	3	0	0	0	0	0	0	1	1	.000	.250	.000	-23	-0	0			1.000	-1	/S-1	-0.2
Total	2	8	20	3	4	1	0	0	0	1	6	.200	.238	.250	42	-1	0			.929	0	/S-5,3-3	-0.2
■ **JACK DUNN**	Dunn, John Joseph b: 10/6/1872, Meadville, Pa. d: 10/22/28, Towson, Md. BR/TR, 5'9", Deb: 5/6/1897																						
1897	Bro-N	36	131	20	29	4	0	0	17	4		.221	.244	.252	33	-13	2			.911	-1	P-25/2-4,O-3,3-3,S	-0.5
1898	Bro-N	51	167	21	41	0	1	0	19	7		.246	.280	.257	54	-10	3			.939	-1	P-41/O-4,S-4,3-2	-0.2
1899	Bro-N	43	122	21	30	2	1	0	16	3		.246	.270	.279	49	-9	3			.963	3	P-41/S-1	0.0
1900	Bro-N	10	26	2	6	0	0	0	1	1		.231	.259	.231	34	-2	0			.960	1	P-10	0.0
	Phi-N	10	33	3	10	1	0	0	5	0		.303	.303	.333	76	-1	1			.920	-1	P-10	0.0
	Yr	20	59	5	16	1	0	0	6	1		.271	.283	.288	56	-4	1			.940	1	P-20	0.0
1901	Phi-N	2	1	1	1	0	0	0	0	1		1.000	1.000	1.000	471	1	0			1.000	-0	/P-2	0.0
	Bal-A	96	362	41	90	9	4	0	36	21		.249	.301	.296	63	-18	10			.872	-7	3-67,S-19/P-9,2O	-2.0
1902	NY-N	100	342	26	72	11	1	0	14	20		.211	.256	.249	56	-18	13			.962	-10	O-43,S-36,3-18,/P2	-2.9
1903	NY-N	78	257	35	62	15	1	0	37	15		.241	.291	.307	68	-11	12			.907	-7	S-27,3-25,2-19,/O-1	-1.5
1904	NY-N	64	181	27	56	12	2	1	19	11		.309	.356	.414	132	6	11			.914	-8	3-28,S-10/2-9,OP	-0.1
Total	8	490	1622	197	397	54	10	1	164	83		.245	.287	.292	66	-75	55			.890	-31	3-143,P-142/SO2	-7.2
■ **JOE DUNN**	Dunn, Joseph Edward b: 3/11/1885, Springfield, Ohio d: 3/19/44, Springfield, Ohio BR/TR, 5'9", 160 lbs. Deb: 9/12/08																						
1908	Bro-N	20	64	3	11	3	0	0	5	0		.172	.172	.219	26	-6	0			.957	7	C-20	0.4
1909	Bro-N	10	25	1	4	1	0	0	2	0		.160	.192	.200	23	-2	0			.952	-2	/C-7	-0.4
Total	2	30	89	4	15	4	0	0	7	0		.169	.178	.213	25	-8	0			.956	6	/C-27	0.0
■ **RON DUNN**	Dunn, Ronald Ray b: 1/24/50, Oklahoma City, Okla BR/TR, 5'11", 180 lbs. Deb: 9/3/74																						
1974	Chi-N	23	68	6	20	7	0	2	15	12	8	.294	.400	.485	141	4	0	0	0	.917	-7	2-21/3-6	-0.2
1975	Chi-N	32	44	2	7	3	0	1	6	6	17	.159	.260	.295	52	-3	0	0	0	.957	-1	3-11/O-2,2-1	-0.4
Total	2	55	112	8	27	10	0	3	21	18	25	.241	.346	.411	106	1	0	0	0	.918	-7	/2-22,3-17,O-2	-0.6
■ **STEVE DUNN**	Dunn, Stephen B. b: 12/21/1858, London, Ont., Can. d: 5/5/33, London, Ont., Can. 5'9.5", 173 lbs. Deb: 9/27/1884																						
1884	StP-U	9	32	2	8	2	0	0		0		.250	.250	.313	128	-2				.972	1	/1-9,3-1	-0.1
■ **STEVE DUNN**	Dunn, Steven Robert b: 4/18/70, Champaign, Ill. BL/TL, 6'4", 225 lbs. Deb: 5/3/94																						
1994	Min-A	14	35	2	8	5	0	0	4	1	12	.229	.250	.371	57	-2	0	0	0	.990	1	1-12	-0.2
1995	Min-A	5	6	0	0	0	0	0	0	1	3	.000	.143	.000	-59	-1	0	0	0	1.000	-0	/1-3	-0.2
Total	2	19	41	2	8	5	0	0	4	2	15	.195	.233	.317	40	-4	0	0	0	.990	1	/1-15	-0.4
■ **TODD DUNN**	Dunn, Todd Kent b: 7/29/70, Tulsa, Okla. BR/TR, 6'5", 220 lbs. Deb: 9/8/96																						
1996	Mil-A	6	10	2	3	1	0	0	1	0	3	.300	.300	.400	72	-0	0	0	0	1.000	-1	/O-6	-0.2
1997	Mil-A	44	118	17	27	5	0	3	9	2	39	.229	.242	.347	51	-9	3	0	1	.909	-4	O-27,D-14	-1.2
Total	2	50	128	19	30	6	0	3	10	2	42	.234	.246	.352	53	-9	3	0	1	.920	-5	/O-33,D-14	-1.4
■ **SHAWON DUNSTON**	Dunston, Shawon Donnell b: 3/21/63, Brooklyn, N.Y. BR/TR, 6'1", 175 lbs. Deb: 4/9/85																						
1985	Chi-N	74	250	40	65	12	4	4	18	19	42	.260	.312	.388	85	-5	11	3	2	.958	13	S-73	1.7
1986	Chi-N	150	581	66	145	37	3	17	68	21	114	.250	.279	.411	82	-16	13	11	-3	.961	20	*S-149	1.6
1987	Chi-N	95	346	40	85	18	3	5	22	10	68	.246	.269	.358	62	-19	12	3	2	.969	5	S-94	-0.5
1988	Chi-N☆	155	575	69	143	23	6	9	56	16	108	.249	.272	.357	76	-19	30	9	4	.973	6	*S-151	0.3
1989	*Chi-N	138	471	52	131	20	6	9	60	30	86	.278	.323	.403	99	-1	19	11	-1	.972	7	*S-138	1.6
1990	Chi-N★	146	545	73	143	22	8	17	66	15	87	.262	.286	.426	87	-12	25	5	5	.970	6	*S-144	1.0
1991	Chi-N	142	492	59	128	22	7	12	50	23	64	.260	.299	.407	92	-6	21	6	3	.968	-6	*S-142	0.1
1992	Chi-N	18	73	8	23	3	1	0	2	3	13	.315	.342	.384	103	0	2	3	-1	.986	-5	S-18	-0.5
1993	Chi-N	7	10	3	4	2	0	0	2	0	1	.400	.400	.600	166	1	0	0	0	1.000	-1	/S-2	0.0
1994	Chi-N	88	331	38	92	19	0	11	35	16	48	.278	.315	.435	94	-4	3	8	-4	.966	-7	S-84	-0.7
1995	Chi-N	127	477	58	141	30	6	14	69	10	75	.296	.318	.472	107	3	10	5	0	.969	-12	*S-125	0.2
1996	SF-N	82	287	27	86	12	2	5	25	13	40	.300	.332	.408	98	-2	8	0	2	.957	-2	S-78	0.5
1997	Chi-N	114	419	57	119	18	4	9	41	8	64	.284	.302	.411	82	-12	29	7	5	.970	-26	*S-108/O-7	-2.4
	Pit-N	18	71	14	28	4	1	5	16	0	11	.394	.394	.690	174	7	3	1	0	.965	-0	S-18	0.8
	Yr	132	490	71	147	22	5	14	57	8	75	.300	.315	.451	96	-5	32	8	5	.969	-26	*S-126/O-7	-1.6
1998	Cle-A	62	156	26	37	11	3	3	12	6	18	.237	.270	.404	70	-7	9	2	2	.978	-1	2-24,S-14,O-12,/D-7	-0.5
	SF-N	36	51	10	9	2	0	3	8	0	10	.176	.222	.392	57	-4	0	2	-1	.938	-5	/S-9,O-6,2-1	-0.9
Total	14	1452	5135	640	1379	255	54	123	550	190	849	.269	.299	.411	88	-96	195	76	13	.967	-8	*S-1347/2-25,O-25,D	2.3
■ **TODD DUNWOODY**	Dunwoody, Todd Franklin b: 4/11/75, Lafayette, Ind. BL/TL, 6'1", 190 lbs. Deb: 5/10/97																						
1997	Fla-N	19	50	7	13	2	2	2	7	7	21	.260	.362	.500	129	2	2	0	1	.929	-1	O-14	0.2
1998	Fla-N	116	434	53	109	27	7	5	28	21	113	.251	.292	.380	76	-17	5	1	1	.989	11	*O-111	-0.5
Total	2	135	484	60	122	29	9	7	35	28	134	.252	.300	.393	81	-15	7	1	2	.984	11	O-125	-0.3
■ **DAN DURAN**	Duran, Daniel James b: 3/16/54, Palo Alto, Cal. BL/TL, 5'11", 190 lbs. Deb: 4/17/81																						
1981	Tex-A	13	16	1	4	0	0	0	0	1	1	.250	.294	.250	61	-1	0	0	0	1.000	-1	/O-7,1-1	-0.2
■ **MIKE DURANT**	Durant, Michael Joseph b: 9/14/69, Columbus, Ohio BR/TR, 6'2", 200 lbs. Deb: 4/3/96																						
1996	Min-A	40	81	15	17	3	0	0	5	10	15	.210	.297	.247	39	-7	3	0	1	.975	9	C-37	0.4
■ **KID DURBIN**	Durbin, Blaine Alphonsus b: 9/10/1886, Lamar, Mo. d: 9/11/43, Kirkwood, Mo. BL/TL, 5'8", 155 lbs. Deb: 4/24/07																						
1907	Chi-N	11	18	2	6	0	0	0	0	1		.333	.368	.333	113	0	0			1.000	0	/P-5,O-5	0.0
1908	Chi-N	14	28	3	7	1	0	0	0	2		.250	.323	.286	91	-0	0			1.000	-3	O-14	-0.4
1909	Cin-N	6	5	1	1	0	0	0	0	1		.200	.333	.200	66	-0	0			.000	0	H	0.0
	Pit-N	1	0	0	0	0	0	0	0	0		—	—	—	—	0	0			.000	0	R	0.0
	Yr	7	5	1	1	0	0	0	0	1		.200	.333	.200	65	-0	0			.000	0	-0,-0	0.0
Total	3	32	51	6	14	1	0	0	0	4		.275	.339	.294	96	-0	0			1.000	-2	/O-19,P-5	-0.4
■ **JOE DURHAM**	Durham, Joseph Vann "Pop" b: 7/31/31, Newport News, Va. BR/TR, 6'1", 186 lbs. Deb: 9/10/54																						
1954	Bal-A	10	40	4	9	0	0	1	3	4	7	.225	.295	.300	68	-2	0	0	0	.917	-1	O-10	-0.3
1957	Bal-A	77	157	19	29	2	0	4	17	16	42	.185	.260	.274	49	-11	1	1	-0	1.000	-11	O-59	-2.7
1959	StL-N	6	5	2	0	0	0	0	0	0	1	.000	.000	.000	-94	-1	0	0	0	1.000	0	/O-1	-0.1
Total	3	93	202	25	38	2	0	5	20	20	50	.188	.261	.272	49	-15	1	1	-0	.979	-12	/O-70	-3.1
■ **LEON DURHAM**	Durham, Leon b: 7/31/57, Cincinnati, Ohio BL/TL, 6'2", 210 lbs. Deb: 5/27/80																						
1980	StL-N	96	303	42	82	15	4	8	42	18	55	.271	.314	.426	101	-0	8	5	-1	.987	7	O-78/1-8	0.3
1981	Chi-N	87	328	42	95	14	6	10	35	27	53	.290	.344	.460	121	8	25	11	1	.970	2	O-83/1-3	0.9
1982	Chi-N☆	148	539	84	168	33	7	22	90	66	77	.312	.389	.521	148	35	28	14	0	.963	-3	*O-143/1-1	2.9
1983	Chi-N★	100	337	58	87	18	8	12	55	66	83	.258	.384	.466	128	15	12	6	0	.966	-7	O-95/1-6	0.5
1984	*Chi-N	137	473	86	132	30	4	23	96	69	86	.279	.372	.505	132	20	16	8	0	.994	6	*1-130	2.0
1985	Chi-N	153	542	58	153	32	2	21	75	64	99	.282	.358	.465	116	11	7	6	-2	.995	3	*1-151	0.3
1986	Chi-N	141	484	66	127	18	7	20	65	67	98	.262	.353	.452	112	8	8	7	-2	.995	-7	*1-141	-1.0
1987	Chi-N	131	439	70	120	22	1	27	63	51	92	.273	.349	.513	120	12	2	2	-1	.990	-9	*1-123	-0.6
1988	Chi-N	24	73	10	16	6	1	3	6	9	20	.219	.305	.452	110	1	0	1	-1	.995	1	1-20	-0.1
	Cin-N	21	51	4	11	3	0	1	2	5	12	.216	.286	.333	74	-2	0	0	0	.993	-1	1-17	-0.4
	Yr	45	124	14	27	9	1	4	8	14	32	.218	.297	.403	95	-1	0	1	-1	.994	-0	1-37	-0.5
1989	StL-N	29	18	2	1	1	0	0	1	2	4	.056	.190	.111	-11	-3	0	1	-1	.961	1	1-18	-0.3
Total	10	1067	3587	522	992	192	40	147	530	444	679	.277	.358	.475	122	105	106	61	-5	.994	-8	1-618,O-399	4.5

YEAR	TM/L	G	AB	R	H	2B	3B	HR	RBI	BB	SO	AVG	OBP	SLG	PRO+	BR/A	SB	CS	SBR	FA	FR	G/POS	TPR
■ RAY DURHAM	Durham, Ray b: 11/30/71, Charlotte, N.C. BB/TR, 5′8″, 170 lbs. Deb: 4/26/95																						
1995	Chi-A	125	471	68	121	27	6	7	51	31	83	.257	.311	.384	83	-12	18	5	2	.973	-29	*2-122/D-1	-3.0
1996	Chi-A	156	557	79	153	33	5	10	65	58	95	.275	.354	.406	96	-3	30	4	7	.984	-21	*2-150/D-3	-0.7
1997	Chi-A	155	634	106	172	27	5	11	53	61	96	.271	.341	.382	92	-7	33	16	0	.974	-31	*2-153/D-1	-2.7
1998	Chi-A★	158	635	126	181	35	8	19	67	73	105	.285	.364	.455	114	14	36	9	5	.976	-6	*2-158	2.1
Total	4	594	2297	379	627	122	24	47	236	223	379	.273	.345	.408	98	-8	117	34	15	.977	-87	2-583/D-5	-4.3
■ BOBBY DURNBAUGH	Durnbaugh, Robert Eugene "Scroggy" b: 1/15/33, Dayton, Ohio BR/TR, 5′8″, 170 lbs. Deb: 9/22/57																						
1957	Cin-N	2	1	0	0	0	0	0	0	0	0	.000	.000	.000	-93	-0	0	0	0	.500	-0	/S-2	0.0
■ GEORGE DURNING	Durning, George Dewey b: 5/9/1898, Philadelphia, Pa. d: 4/18/86, Tampa, Fla. BR/TR, 5′11″, 175 lbs. Deb: 9/12/25																						
1925	Phi-N	5	14	3	5	0	0	0	1	2	1	.357	.438	.357	97	0	0	0	0	1.000	2	/O-4	0.2
■ LEO DUROCHER	Durocher, Leo Ernest "Lippy" b: 7/27/05, W.Springfield, Mass. d: 10/7/91, Palm Springs, Cal. BR/TR, 5′10″, 160 lbs. Deb: 10/2/25 MCH																						
1925	NY-A	2	1	1	0	0	0	0	0	0	0	.000	.000	.000	-99	-0	0	0	0	.000	0	H	0.0
1928	*NY-A	102	296	46	80	8	6	0	31	22	52	.270	.327	.338	77	-10	1	4	-2	.948	12	2-66,S-29	0.5
1929	NY-A	106	341	53	84	4	5	0	32	34	33	.246	.320	.287	62	-19	3	1	0	.958	**26**	S-93,2-12	1.7
1930	Cin-N	119	354	31	86	15	3	3	32	20	45	.243	.287	.328	51	-29	0			.959	10	*S-103,2-13	-0.7
1931	Cin-N	121	361	26	82	11	5	1	29	18	32	.227	.264	.294	53	-25	0			.965	-4	*S-120	-1.9
1932	Cin-N	143	457	43	99	22	5	1	33	36	40	.217	.275	.293	55	-29	3			.960	-14	*S-142	-3.1
1933	Cin-N	16	51	6	11	1	0	1	3	4	5	.216	.273	.294	63	-2	0			.953	6	S-16	0.4
	StL-N	123	395	45	102	18	4	2	41	26	32	.258	.306	.339	80	-10	3			.961	-1	*S-123	-0.3
	Yr	139	446	51	113	19	4	3	44	30	37	.253	.302	.334	78	-13	3			**.960**	5	*S-139	0.1
1934	*StL-N	146	500	62	130	26	5	3	70	33	40	.260	.308	.350	71	-20	2			.957	1	*S-146	-1.1
1935	StL-N	143	513	62	136	23	5	8	78	29	46	.265	.304	.376	79	-16	4			.963	9	*S-142	0.1
1936	StL-N★	136	510	57	146	22	3	1	58	29	47	.286	.327	.347	82	-13	3			**.971**	-11	*S-136	-1.5
1937	StL-N	135	477	46	97	11	3	1	47	38	36	.203	.262	.245	38	-41	6			.959	-11	*S-134	-4.3
1938	Bro-N★	141	479	41	105	18	5	1	56	47	30	.219	.293	.284	58	-27	3			**.966**	-5	*S-141	-2.1
1939	Bro-N	116	390	42	108	21	6	1	34	27	24	.277	.325	.369	83	-9	2			.957	-7	*S-113/3-1,M	-0.7
1940	Bro-N☆	62	160	10	37	9	1	1	14	12	13	.231	.285	.319	62	-8	1			.959	1	S-53/2-4,M	-0.4
1941	Bro-N	18	42	2	12	1	0	0	6	1	3	.286	.302	.310	70	-2	0			.917	-0	S-12/2-1,M	-0.1
1943	Bro-N	6	18	1	4	0	0	0	1	1	2	.222	.263	.222	41	-1	0			1.000	2	/S-6,M	0.1
1945	Bro-N	2	5	1	1	0	0	0	2	0	0	.200	.200	.200	11	-1	0			1.000	1	/2-2,M	0.0
Total	17	1637	5350	575	1320	210	56	24	567	377	480	.247	.299	.320	66	-262	31	5		.961	16	*S-1509/2-98,3-1	-13.4
■ RED DURRETT	Durrett, Elmer Cable b: 2/3/21, Sherman, Tex. d: 1/17/92, Waxahachie, Tex. BL/TL, 5′10″, 170 lbs. Deb: 9/14/44																						
1944	Bro-N	11	32	3	5	1	0	1	1	7	10	.156	.308	.281	68	-1	0			.933	1	/O-9	0.0
1945	Bro-N	8	16	2	2	0	0	0	0	3	3	.125	.263	.125	10	-2	0			1.000	-1	/O-4	-0.3
Total	2	19	48	5	7	1	0	1	1	10	13	.146	.293	.229	48	-3	0			.947	1	/O-13	-0.3
■ CEDRIC DURST	Durst, Cedric Montgomery b: 8/23/1896, Austin, Tex. d: 2/16/71, San Diego, Cal. BL/TL, 5′11″, 160 lbs. Deb: 5/30/22																						
1922	StL-A	15	12	5	4	1	0	0	0	0	1	.333	.333	.417	91	-0	0	0	0	.857	-2	/O-6	-0.2
1923	StL-A	45	85	12	18	2	0	5	11	8	14	.212	.280	.412	76	-4	0	0	0	1.000	-2	O-10/1-8	-0.7
1926	StL-A	80	219	32	52	7	5	3	16	22	19	.237	.310	.356	70	-10	0	5	-3	.980	2	O-57/1-4	-1.5
1927	*NY-A	65	129	18	32	4	3	0	25	6	7	.248	.281	.326	59	-8	0	3	-2	.980	-7	O-36/1-2	-1.8
1928	*NY-A	74	135	18	34	2	1	2	10	7	9	.252	.289	.326	63	-7	1	0	0	.983	-3	O-33/1-3	-1.1
1929	NY-A	92	202	32	52	3	3	4	31	15	25	.257	.309	.361	77	-8	3	2	-0	.987	-0	O-72/1-1	-1.1
1930	NY-A	8	19	0	3	1	0	0	5	0	1	.158	.158	.211	-8	-3	0	0	0	1.000	-0	/O-6	-0.3
	Bos-A	102	302	29	74	19	5	1	24	17	24	.245	.290	.351	64	-17	3	1	0	.968	-2	O-75	-2.2
	Yr	110	321	29	77	20	5	1	29	17	25	.240	.282	.343	60	-20	3	1	0	.970	-2	O-81	-2.5
Total	7	481	1103	146	269	39	17	15	122	75	100	.244	.294	.351	67	-57	7	11	-5	.979	-15	O-295/1-18	-8.9
■ ERV DUSAK	Dusak, Ervin Frank "Four Sack" b: 7/29/20, Chicago, Ill. d: 11/6/94, Glendale Heights, Ill. BR/TR, 6′2″, 185 lbs. Deb: 9/18/41																						
1941	StL-N	6	14	1	2	0	0	0	3	2	6	.143	.250	.143	12	-2	1			1.000	1	/O-4	0.0
1942	StL-N	12	27	4	5	3	0	0	3	3	7	.185	.267	.296	60	-1	0			1.000	0	/O-8,3-1	-0.1
1946	*StL-N	100	275	38	66	9	1	9	42	33	63	.240	.321	.378	94	-2	7			.993	3	O-77,3-11/2-2	-0.2
1947	StL-N	111	328	56	93	7	3	6	28	50	34	.284	.378	.378	97	0	1			.970	1	O-89/3-7	-0.3
1948	StL-N	114	311	60	65	9	2	6	19	49	55	.209	.317	.309	66	-14	3			.992	-5	O-68,2-29/3-9,PS	-2.1
1949	StL-N	1	0	1	0	0	0	0	0	0	0	—	—	—	—	0	0			.000	0	R	0.0
1950	StL-N	23	12	0	1	1	0	0	0	0	3	.083	.083	.167	-34	-2	0			1.000	0	P-14/O-2	-0.1
1951	StL-N	5	2	1	1	0	0	1	1	0	1	.500	.500	2.000	537	1	0	0	0	1.000	0	/P-5	0.0
	Pit-N	21	39	6	12	3	0	1	7	3	11	.308	.357	.462	115	1	0	0	0	1.000	-6	O-12/P-3,2-2,3-2	-0.5
	Yr	26	41	7	13	3	0	2	8	3	12	.317	.364	.537	136	2	0	0	0	1.000	-6	O-12/P-8,2-2,3-2	-0.5
1952	Pit-N	20	27	1	6	0	0	1	3	2	8	.222	.276	.333	66	-1	0	0	0	.818	-2	O-11	-0.3
Total	9	413	1035	168	251	32	6	24	106	142	188	.243	.334	.355	84	-21	12	0		.981	-6	O-271/2-33,3-30,PS	-3.6
■ AL DWIGHT	Dwight, Albert Ward b: 1/4/1856, New York, N.Y. d: 2/20/03, San Francisco, Cal Deb: 6/19/1884																						
1884	KC-U	12	43	8	10	2	0	0		2		.233	.267	.279	75	-3				.953	-1	C-10/O-1,2-1	-0.2
■ JIM DWYER	Dwyer, James Edward "Pig Pen" b: 1/3/50, Evergreen Park, Ill. BL/TL, 5′10″, 175 lbs. Deb: 6/10/73																						
1973	StL-N	28	57	7	11	1	1	0	0	1	5	.193	.207	.246	25	-6	0	0	0	1.000	-2	O-20	-0.9
1974	StL-N	74	86	13	24	1	0	2	11	11	16	.279	.367	.360	105	1	0	0	0	1.000	-3	O-25/1-3	-0.3
1975	StL-N	21	31	4	6	1	0	0	1	4	6	.194	.286	.226	42	-2	0	0	0	1.000	-1	/O-9	-0.3
	Mon-N	60	175	22	50	7	1	3	20	23	30	.286	.369	.389	106	2	4	1	1	.959	1	O-52	0.2
	Yr	81	206	26	56	8	1	3	21	27	36	.272	.356	.364	96	-0	4	1	1	.966	1	O-61	-0.1
1976	Mon-N	50	92	7	17	3	1	0	5	11	10	.185	.272	.239	44	-7	0	0	0	.970	-2	O-19	-1.0
	NY-N	11	13	2	2	0	0	0	0	2	1	.154	.267	.154	23	-1	0	0	0	1.000	-0	/O-2	-0.2
	Yr	61	105	9	19	3	1	0	5	13	11	.181	.271	.229	42	-8	0	0	0	.972	-2	O-21	-1.2
1977	StL-N	13	31	3	7	1	0	0	2	4	5	.226	.351	.258	68	-1	0	0	0	1.000	-2	O-12	-0.4
1978	StL-N	34	65	8	14	3	0	1	4	9	3	.215	.320	.308	77	-2	1	0	0	.952	-4	O-22	-0.7
	SF-N	73	173	22	39	9	2	5	22	28	29	.225	.333	.387	105	1	6	0	2	.987	1	O-36,1-29	0.2
	Yr	107	238	30	53	12	2	6	26	37	32	.223	.330	.366	97	-1	7	0	2	.979	-3	O-58,1-29	-0.5
1979	Bos-A	76	113	19	30	7	0	2	14	17	9	.265	.366	.381	96	-0	3	1	0	.981	-0	1-25,O-19/D-4	-0.1
1980	Bos-A	93	260	41	74	11	1	9	38	28	23	.285	.359	.438	111	4	3	2	-0	.975	-3	O-65,D-12/1-9	-0.1
1981	Bal-A	68	134	16	30	0	1	3	10	20	19	.224	.325	.306	83	-2	0	2	-1	.977	-11	O-59/1-3,D-1	-1.6
1982	Bal-A	71	148	28	45	4	3	6	15	27	24	.304	.411	.493	148	11	2	0	1	.976	-8	O-49/1-1,D-1	0.3
1983	*Bal-A	100	196	37	56	17	1	8	38	31	29	.286	.383	.505	145	13	1	1	-0	.966	-7	O-56,D-10/1-4	0.3
1984	Bal-A	76	161	22	41	9	1	2	21	23	24	.255	.348	.360	98	0	0	2	-1	.966	-4	O-52/D-3	-0.6
1985	Bal-A	101	233	35	58	8	3	7	36	37	31	.249	.354	.399	109	4	0	3	-2	.993	-3	O-78/D-3	-0.3
1986	Bal-A	94	160	18	39	13	1	8	31	23	31	.244	.346	.488	126	6	0	2	-1	1.000	-0	O-24,D-24/1-1	0.3
1987	Bal-A	92	241	54	66	7	1	15	33	37	57	.274	.373	.498	132	11	4	1	1	1.000	-1	D-41,O-30	0.9
1988	Bal-A	35	53	3	12	0	0	0	3	12	11	.226	.369	.226	73	-1	0	0	0	1.000	-0	D-17/O-2	-0.2
	Min-A	20	41	6	12	1	0	2	15	13	8	.293	.473	.463	159	4	0	0	0	.000	0	D-13	0.4
	Yr	55	94	9	24	1	0	2	18	25	19	.255	.417	.330	113	3	0	0	0	1.000	-0	D-30/O-2	0.2
1989	Min-A	88	225	34	71	11	0	3	23	28	23	.316	.391	.404	117	6	2	0	1	.000	-0	D-74/O-1	0.4
	Mon-N	13	10	1	3	1	0	0	2	1	1	.300	.364	.400	116	0	0	0	0	.000	0	H	0.0
1990	Min-A	37	63	7	12	0	0	1	5	12	7	.190	.320	.238	55	-3	0	0	0	1.000	-0	D-23/O-2	-0.5
Total	18	1328	2761	409	719	115	17	77	349	402	402	.260	.357	.398	107	37	26	15	-1	.979	-50	O-634,D-226/1-75	-4.2
■ JOHN DWYER	Dwyer, John E. Deb: 5/16/1882																						
1882	Cle-N	1	3	0	0	0	0	0	1	0	0	.000	.000	.000	-99	-1				.000	-1	/O-1,C-1	-0.2

YEAR	TM/L	G	AB	R	H	2B	3B	HR	RBI	BB	SO	AVG	OBP	SLG	PRO+	BR/A	SB	CS	SBR	FA	FR	G/POS	TPR
■ DOUBLE JOE DWYER	Dwyer, Joseph Michael b: 3/27/03, Orange, N.J. d: 10/21/92, Glen Ridge, N.J. BL/TL, 5'9", 186 lbs. Deb: 4/20/37																						
1937	Cin-N	12	11	2	3	0	0	0	1	1	0	.273	.333	.273	70	-0	0			.000	0	H	0.0
■ JERRY DYBZINSKI	Dybzinski, Jerome Matthew b: 7/7/55, Cleveland, Ohio BR/TR, 6'2", 180 lbs. Deb: 4/11/80																						
1980	Cle-A	114	248	32	57	11	1	1	23	13	35	.230	.274	.294	55	-15	4	1	1	.971	21	S-73,2-29/3-4,D-2	1.3
1981	Cle-A	48	57	10	17	0	0	0	6	5	8	.298	.355	.298	91	-0	7	1	2	.970	8	S-34/2-3,3-3,D-1	1.1
1982	Cle-A	80	212	19	49	6	2	0	22	21	25	.231	.309	.278	63	-10	3	5	-2	.957	17	S-77/3-3	1.1
1983	*Chi-A	127	256	30	59	10	1	1	32	18	29	.230	.286	.289	57	-15	11	4	1	.966	1	*S-118/3-9	-0.5
1984	Chi-A	94	132	17	31	5	1	1	10	13	12	.235	.313	.311	70	-5	7	2	1	.974	18	S-76,3-14/2-1,D-1	1.8
1985	Pit-N	5	4	0	0	0	0	0	0	0	0	.000	.000	.000	-99	-1	0	0	0	.900	1	/S-5	0.0
Total	6	468	909	108	213	32	5	3	93	70	109	.234	.296	.290	61	-47	32	13	2	.966	67	S-383/3-33,2-33,D-4	4.8
■ JIM DYCK	Dyck, James Robert b: 2/3/22, Omaha, Neb. BR/TR, 6'2", 205 lbs. Deb: 9/27/51																						
1951	StL-A	4	15	1	1	0	0	0	0	1	1	.067	.125	.067	-46	-3	0	0	0	1.000	0	/3-4	-0.3
1952	StL-A	122	402	60	108	22	3	15	64	50	68	.269	.354	.450	119	10	0	4	-2	.962	9	3-74,O-48	1.4
1953	StL-A	112	334	38	71	15	1	9	27	38	40	.213	.299	.344	72	-14	3	2	-0	.981	-6	O-55,3-51	-2.3
1954	Cle-A	2	1	0	1	0	0	0	1	1	0	1.000	1.000	1.000	441	1	0	0	0	.000	0	H	0.1
1955	Bal-A	61	197	32	55	13	1	2	22	28	21	.279	.372	.386	112	4	1	0	0	.989	-0	O-45,3-17	0.2
1956	Bal-A	11	23	3	5	2	0	0	0	10	5	.217	.455	.304	112	1	0	0	0	.923	-0	/O-9	0.1
	Cin-N	18	11	5	1	0	0	0	0	3	5	.091	.286	.091	7	-1	0	0	0	1.000	0	/1-1,3-1	-0.1
Total	6	330	983	139	242	52	5	26	114	131	140	.246	.339	.389	98	-2	4	6	-2	.982	3	O-157,3-147/1-1	-0.9
■ JERMAINE DYE	Dye, Jermaine Terrell b: 1/28/74, Oakland, Cal. BR/TR, 6'4", 210 lbs. Deb: 5/17/96																						
1996	*Atl-N	98	292	32	82	16	0	12	37	8	67	.281	.307	.459	93	-4	1	4	-2	.950	-6	O-92	-1.3
1997	KC-A	75	263	26	62	14	0	7	22	17	51	.236	.285	.369	67	-13	2	1	0	.966	6	O-75	-0.8
1998	KC-A	60	214	24	50	5	1	5	23	11	46	.234	.274	.336	55	-14	2	2	-1	.987	9	O-59	-0.7
Total	3	233	769	82	194	35	1	24	82	36	164	.252	.290	.394	74	-31	5	7	-3	.968	9	O-226	-2.8
■ BEN DYER	Dyer, Benjamin Franklin b: 2/13/1893, Chicago, Ill. d: 8/7/59, Kenosha, Wis. BR/TR, 5'11", 170 lbs. Deb: 5/23/14																						
1914	NY-N	7	4	1	1	0	0	0	0	0	1	.250	.250	.250	50	-0	1			1.000	1	/S-6,2-1	0.1
1915	NY-N	7	19	4	4	0	1	0	0	4	3	.211	.375	.316	117	1	0			.889	-0	/3-6,S-1	0.1
1916	Det-A	4	14	4	4	1	0	0	1	1	1	.286	.333	.357	104	0	0			1.000	-2	/S-4	-0.2
1917	Det-A	30	67	6	14	5	0	0	0	2	17	.209	.232	.284	57	-4	3			.846	2	S-14/3-8	-0.1
1918	Det-A	13	18	1	5	0	0	0	2	0	6	.278	.278	.278	71	-1	0			1.000	0	/P-2,1-2,O-2,2-1	-0.1
1919	Det-A	44	85	11	21	4	0	0	15	8	19	.247	.312	.294	72	-3	0			.953	6	3-23,S-11/O-1	0.4
Total	6	105	207	27	49	10	1	0	18	15	47	.237	.291	.295	74	-7	4			.937	7	/3-37,S-36,O-3,1P2	0.2
■ DUFFY DYER	Dyer, Don Robert b: 8/15/45, Dayton, Ohio BR/TR, 6', 195 lbs. Deb: 9/21/68 C																						
1968	NY-N	1	3	0	1	0	0	0	0	1	1	.333	.500	.333	153	0	0	0	0	1.000	0	/C-1	0.1
1969	*NY-N	29	74	5	19	3	1	3	12	4	22	.257	.295	.446	103	-0	0	0	0	.991	-1	C-19	0.0
1970	NY-N	59	148	8	31	1	0	2	12	21	32	.209	.308	.257	53	-9	1	1	-0	.991	2	C-57	-0.6
1971	NY-N	59	169	13	39	7	1	2	18	14	45	.231	.293	.320	75	-6	1	0	0	.992	0	C-53	-0.4
1972	NY-N	94	325	33	75	17	3	8	36	28	71	.231	.302	.375	94	-3	0	1	-1	.993	18	C-91/O-1	1.9
1973	NY-N	70	189	9	35	6	1	1	9	13	40	.185	.245	.243	36	-16	0	1	-1	.994	-1	C-60	-1.7
1974	NY-N	63	142	14	30	1	1	0	10	18	15	.211	.304	.232	53	-8	0	0	0	.982	-4	C-45	-1.2
1975	*Pit-N	48	132	8	30	5	2	3	16	6	22	.227	.266	.364	74	-5	0	0	0	.990	6	C-36	0.2
1976	Pit-N	69	184	12	41	8	0	3	9	29	35	.223	.338	.315	85	-3	0	0	0	.994	7	C-58	0.6
1977	Pit-N	94	270	27	65	11	1	3	19	54	49	.241	.373	.322	86	-3	6	0	2	**.996**	5	C-93	0.6
1978	Pit-N	58	175	7	37	8	1	0	13	18	32	.211	.296	.269	56	-10	2	1	0	.991	6	C-55	-0.3
1979	Mon-N	28	74	4	18	6	0	1	8	9	17	.243	.325	.365	89	-1	0	0	0	.993	7	C-27	0.6
1980	Det-A	48	108	11	20	1	0	4	11	13	34	.185	.273	.306	57	-6	0	0	0	.986	3	C-37,D-10	-0.3
1981	Det-A	2	0	0	0	0	0	0	0	0	0	—	—	—	—	0	0	0	0	.000	0	/C-2	0.0
Total	14	722	1993	151	441	74	11	30	173	228	415	.221	.307	.315	73	-71	10	4	1	.992	46	C-634/D-10,O-1	-0.5
■ EDDIE DYER	Dyer, Edwin Hawley b: 10/11/1900, Morgan City, La. d: 4/20/64, Houston, Tex. BL/TL, 5'11.5", 168 lbs. Deb: 7/8/22 M																						
1922	StL-N	6	3	1	1	1	0	0	0	0	0	.333	.333	.667	159	0	0	0	0	1.000	0	/P-2	0.0
1923	StL-N	35	45	17	12	3	0	2	5	3	5	.267	.313	.467	105	0	1	0	0	1.000	-1	/O-8,P-4	-0.1
1924	StL-N	50	76	8	18	2	3	0	8	3	8	.237	.266	.342	63	-4	1	0	0	.909	1	P-29/O-1	-0.1
1925	StL-N	31	31	4	3	1	0	0	0	3	1	.097	.176	.129	-20	-6	1	1	-0	.917	0	P-27	0.0
1926	StL-N	6	2	1	1	0	0	0	0	0	0	.500	.500	.500	164	0	0			1.000	0	/P-6	0.0
1927	StL-N	1	0	0	0	0	0	0	0	1	0	—	1.000	—	181	0	0			.000	-0	/P-1	0.0
Total	6	129	157	31	35	7	3	2	13	10	14	.223	.269	.344	61	-9	3	1		.921	-0	/P-69,O-9	-0.2
■ JIMMY DYKES	Dykes, James Joseph b: 11/10/1896, Philadelphia, Pa. d: 6/15/76, Philadelphia, Pa. BR/TR, 5'9", 185 lbs. Deb: 5/6/18 MC																						
1918	Phi-A	59	186	13	35	3	3	0	13	19	32	.188	.267	.237	51	-11	3			.940	10	2-56/3-1	0.3
1919	Phi-A	17	49	4	9	1	0	0	1	7	11	.184	.286	.204	38	-4	0			.945	6	2-16	0.3
1920	Phi-A	142	546	81	140	25	4	8	35	55	73	.256	.334	.361	83	-13	6	9	-4	.957	17	*2-108,3-34	0.6
1921	Phi-A	155	613	88	168	32	13	16	77	60	75	.274	.353	.447	102	1	6	5	-1	.954	25	*2-155	2.7
1922	Phi-A	145	501	66	138	23	7	12	68	55	98	.275	.359	.421	100	0	6	2	1	.945	-8	*3-141/2-5	0.4
1923	Phi-A	124	416	50	105	28	1	4	43	35	40	.252	.318	.353	76	-15	6	4	-1	.964	4	*2-102,S-20/3-2	-0.9
1924	Phi-A	110	410	68	128	26	6	3	50	38	60	.312	.372	.427	105	3	1	3	-2	.961	16	2-77,3-27/S-4	1.9
1925	Phi-A	122	465	93	150	32	11	5	55	46	49	.323	.393	.471	111	8	3	2	-0	.944	10	3-64,2-58/S-2	2.1
1926	Phi-A	124	429	54	123	32	5	1	44	49	34	.287	.370	.392	93	-3	6	2	1	.950	**26**	3-82,2-44/S-1	2.8
1927	Phi-A	121	417	61	135	33	6	3	60	44	23	.324	.394	.453	113	8	2	3	-1	.989	-3	1-82,3-25/S-5,O2P	0.0
1928	Phi-A	85	242	39	67	11	0	5	30	27	21	.277	.361	.384	93	-2	2	1	0	.982	-2	2-32,S-22,3-20,/1O	0.0
1929	*Phi-A	119	401	76	131	34	6	13	79	51	25	.327	.412	.539	138	23	8	3	1	.928	-11	S-60,3-48,2-12	2.1
1930	*Phi-A	125	435	69	131	28	4	6	73	74	53	.301	.414	.425	109	9	3	3	-1	.960	-13	*3-123/O-1	0.2
1931	*Phi-A	101	355	48	97	28	2	3	46	49	47	.273	.371	.389	94	-2	1	2	-1	.974	-2	3-87,S-15	0.2
1932	Phi-A	153	558	71	148	29	5	7	90	77	65	.265	.358	.373	87	-10	8	2	1	**.980**	-5	*3-141,S-10/2-1	-0.2
1933	Chi-A★	151	554	49	144	22	6	1	68	69	37	.260	.354	.327	85	-9	3	7	-3	.953	-1	*3-151	-0.4
1934	Chi-A☆	127	456	52	122	17	4	7	82	64	28	.268	.363	.368	86	-8	1	1	-0	.944	-5	3-74,1-27,2-27,M	-1.0
1935	Chi-A	117	403	45	116	24	2	4	61	59	28	.288	.381	.387	97	-0	4	3	-1	.953	-5	3-98,1-16/2-3,M	-0.4
1936	Chi-A	127	435	62	116	16	3	7	60	61	36	.267	.362	.366	77	-15	1	3	-2	.951	-6	*3-125,M	-1.7
1937	Chi-A	30	85	10	26	5	0	1	23	9	7	.306	.372	.400	95	-1	0	0	0	.993	0	1-15,3-11,M	-0.1
1938	Chi-A	26	89	9	27	4	2	2	13	10	8	.303	.374	.461	105	1	0	0	0	.941	1	2-23/S-1,3-1,M	0.3
1939	Chi-A	2	1	0	0	0	0	0	0	0	0	.000	.000	.000	-97	-0	0	0	0	.667	0	/3-2,M	0.0
Total	22	2282	8046	1108	2256	453	90	108	1071	958	850	.280	.365	.399	96	-42	70	55		.952	56	*3-1257,2-722,1S/OP	9.2
■ LENNY DYKSTRA	Dykstra, Leonard Kyle b: 2/10/63, Santa Ana, Cal. BL/TL, 5'10", 167 lbs. Deb: 5/3/85																						
1985	NY-N	83	236	40	60	9	3	1	19	30	24	.254	.341	.331	91	-2	15	2	3	.994	4	O-74	0.3
1986	*NY-N	147	431	77	127	27	7	8	45	58	55	.295	.378	.445	130	18	31	7	5	.990	4	*O-139	2.4
1987	NY-N	132	431	86	123	37	3	10	43	40	67	.285	.352	.455	118	10	27	7	4	.988	1	*O-118	1.1
1988	*NY-N	126	429	57	116	19	3	8	33	30	43	.270	.323	.385	107	3	30	8	4	.996	7	*O-112	1.2
1989	NY-N	56	159	27	43	12	1	3	13	23	15	.270	.370	.415	130	7	13	1	3	.984	2	O-51	1.2
	Phi-N	90	352	39	78	20	3	4	19	37	38	.222	.297	.330	79	-10	17	11	-2	.991	7	O-88	-0.7
	Yr	146	511	66	121	32	4	7	32	60	53	.237	.321	.356	95	-3	30	12	2	.988	9	*O-139	0.5
1990	Phi-N★	149	590	106	**192**	35	3	9	60	89	48	.325	.420	.441	137	35	33	5	7	.987	20	*O-149	5.8
1991	Phi-N	63	246	48	73	13	5	3	12	37	20	.297	.391	.427	131	11	24	4	5	.977	8	O-63	2.3
1992	Phi-N	85	345	53	104	18	0	6	39	40	32	.301	.379	.406	123	11	30	5	6	.989	13	O-85	3.0
1993	*Phi-N	161	637	**143**	**194**	44	6	19	66	**129**	64	.305	.423	.482	144	45	37	12	4	.979	17	*O-160	6.1
1994	Phi-N†	84	315	68	86	26	5	5	24	68	44	.273	.405	.435	116	10	15	4	2	.984	9	O-82	1.9

YEAR	TM/L	G	AB	R	H	2B	3B	HR	RBI	BB	SO	AVG	OBP	SLG	PRO+	BR/A	SB	CS	SBR	FA	FR	G/POS	TPR
1995	Phi-N★	62	254	37	67	15	1	2	18	33	28	.264	.355	.354	87	-4	10	5	0	.987	6	O-61	0.1
1996	Phi-N	40	134	21	35	6	3	3	13	26	25	.261	.389	.418	112	3	3	1	0	1.000	7	O-39	0.9
Total	12	1278	4559	802	1298	281	43	81	404	640	503	.285	.376	.419	120	140	285	72	42	.987	103	*O-1221	25.6

■ JOHN DYLER
Dyler, John F. b: 6/1852, Louisville, Ky. Deb: 7/22/1882 U

YEAR	TM/L	G	AB	R	H	2B	3B	HR	RBI	BB	SO	AVG	OBP	SLG	PRO+	BR/A	SB	CS	SBR	FA	FR	G/POS	TPR
1882	Lou-a	1	4	0	0	0	0	0		0		.000	.000	.000	-99	-1				.000	-0	/O-1	-0.1

■ DON EADDY
Eaddy, Donald Johnson b: 2/16/34, Grand Rapids, Mich BR/TR, 5'11", 165 lbs. Deb: 4/24/59

YEAR	TM/L	G	AB	R	H	2B	3B	HR	RBI	BB	SO	AVG	OBP	SLG	PRO+	BR/A	SB	CS	SBR	FA	FR	G/POS	TPR
1959	Chi-N	15	1	3	0	0	0	0	0	0	1	.000	.000	.000	-99	-0	0	0	0	.500	0	/3-1	0.0

■ TRUCK EAGAN
Eagan, Charles Eugene b: 8/10/1877, San Francisco, Cal d: 3/19/49, San Francisco, Cal BR/TR, 5'11", 190 lbs. Deb: 5/1/01

YEAR	TM/L	G	AB	R	H	2B	3B	HR	RBI	BB	SO	AVG	OBP	SLG	PRO+	BR/A	SB	CS	SBR	FA	FR	G/POS	TPR
1901	Pit-N	4	12	0	1	0	0	0	2	0		.083	.083	.083	-50	-2	1			.923	-1	/S-3	-0.3
	Cle-A	5	18	2	3	0	1	0	2	1		.167	.211	.278	36	-2	0			1.000	0	/2-5,3-1	-0.1
Total	1	9	30	2	4	0	1	0	4	1		.133	.161	.200	2	-4	1			1.000	-1	/2-5,S-3,3-1	-0.4

■ BILL EAGAN
Eagan, William "Bad Bill" b: 6/1/1869, Camden, N.J. d: 2/13/05, Denver, Colo. Deb: 4/8/1891

YEAR	TM/L	G	AB	R	H	2B	3B	HR	RBI	BB	SO	AVG	OBP	SLG	PRO+	BR/A	SB	CS	SBR	FA	FR	G/POS	TPR
1891	StL-a	83	302	49	65	11	4	4	43	44	54	.215	.321	.318	72	-14	21			.929	20	2-83	0.8
1893	Chi-N	6	19	3	5	0	0	0	2	5	5	.263	.417	.263	83	-0	4			.912	0	/2-6	0.0
1898	Pit-N	19	61	14	20	2	3	0	5	8		.328	.453	.459	165	6	1			.914	3	2-17	0.9
Total	3	108	382	66	90	13	7	4	50	57	59	.236	.348	.338	86	-8	26			.925	23	2-106	1.7

■ BILL EAGLE
Eagle, William Lycurgus b: 7/25/1877, Rockville, Md. d: 4/27/51, Churchton, Md. Deb: 8/20/1898

YEAR	TM/L	G	AB	R	H	2B	3B	HR	RBI	BB	SO	AVG	OBP	SLG	PRO+	BR/A	SB	CS	SBR	FA	FR	G/POS	TPR
1898	Was-N	4	13	0	4	1	0	0	2	0		.308	.308	.385	98	-0	0			.750	0	/O-4	0.0

■ CHARLIE EAKLE
Eakle, Charles Emory b: 9/27/1887, Maryland d: 6/15/59, Baltimore, Md. Deb: 8/20/15

YEAR	TM/L	G	AB	R	H	2B	3B	HR	RBI	BB	SO	AVG	OBP	SLG	PRO+	BR/A	SB	CS	SBR	FA	FR	G/POS	TPR
1915	Bal-F	2	7	0	2	1	0	0	0	0	0	.286	.286	.429	97	-0	1			.600	-2	/2-2	-0.3

■ HOWARD EARL
Earl, Howard J. "Slim Jim" b: 2/27/1869, Massachusetts d: 12/22/16, North Bay, N.Y. 6'2", 180 lbs. Deb: 4/19/1890

YEAR	TM/L	G	AB	R	H	2B	3B	HR	RBI	BB	SO	AVG	OBP	SLG	PRO+	BR/A	SB	CS	SBR	FA	FR	G/POS	TPR
1890	Chi-N	92	384	57	95	10	3	7	51	18	47	.247	.285	.344	80	-12	17			.861	-4	O-49,2-39/S-4,1-3	-1.3
1891	Mil-a	31	129	21	32	5	2	1	17	5	13	.248	.281	.341	65	-8	3			.978	-1	O-30/1-2	-0.9
Total	2	123	513	78	127	15	5	8	68	23	60	.248	.284	.343	76	-20	20			.904	-5	/O-79,2-39,1-5,S-4	-2.2

■ SCOTT EARL
Earl, William Scott b: 9/18/60, Seymour, Ind. BR/TR, 5'11", 165 lbs. Deb: 9/10/84

YEAR	TM/L	G	AB	R	H	2B	3B	HR	RBI	BB	SO	AVG	OBP	SLG	PRO+	BR/A	SB	CS	SBR	FA	FR	G/POS	TPR
1984	Det-A	14	35	3	4	0	1	0	1	0	9	.114	.114	.171	-22	-6	1	0	0	.959	1	2-14	-0.4

■ BILLY EARLE
Earle, William Moffat "The Little Globetrotter"
b: 11/10/1867, Philadelphia, Pa. d: 5/30/46, Omaha, Neb. BR/TR, 5'10.5", 170 lbs. Deb: 4/27/1889

YEAR	TM/L	G	AB	R	H	2B	3B	HR	RBI	BB	SO	AVG	OBP	SLG	PRO+	BR/A	SB	CS	SBR	FA	FR	G/POS	TPR
1889	Cin-a	53	169	37	45	4	7	4	31	30	24	.266	.386	.444	132	7	26			.776	-2	O-26,C-23/1-5	0.5
1890	StL-a	22	73	16	17	3	1	0	12	7		.233	.317	.301	72	-3	6			.955	5	C-18/O-3,S-1,3-1,2	0.3
1892	Pit-N	5	13	5	7	2	0	0	3	4	1	.538	.647	.692	304	4	2			.909	-1	/C-5	0.3
1893	Pit-N	27	95	21	24	4	4	2	15	7	6	.253	.304	.442	99	-1	1			.959	1	C-27	0.2
1894	Lou-N	21	65	10	23	1	0	0	7	9	3	.354	.432	.369	102	1	2			.954	3	C-18/1-1,2-1,3-1,O	0.4
	Bro-N	14	50	13	17	6	0	0	6	6	2	.340	.421	.460	121	2	4			.930	-2	C-12/2-1	0.1
	Yr	35	115	23	40	7	0	0	13	15	5	.348	.427	.409	110	3	6			.944	2	C-30/2-2,1-1,3-1,O	0.5
Total	5	142	465	102	133	20	12	6	74	63	36	.286	.378	.419	114	10	41			.929	5	C-103/O-30,1-6,23S	1.8

■ JAKE EARLY
Early, Jacob Willard b: 5/19/15, Kings Mountain, N.C. d: 5/31/85, Melbourne, Fla. BL/TR, 5'11", 168 lbs. Deb: 5/4/39

YEAR	TM/L	G	AB	R	H	2B	3B	HR	RBI	BB	SO	AVG	OBP	SLG	PRO+	BR/A	SB	CS	SBR	FA	FR	G/POS	TPR
1939	Was-A	32	84	8	22	7	2	0	14	5	14	.262	.303	.393	83	-3	0	0	0	.963	-1	C-24	-0.2
1940	Was-A	80	206	26	53	8	4	5	14	23	22	.257	.335	.408	98	-1	0	1	-1	.969	5	C-56	0.7
1941	Was-A	104	355	42	102	20	7	10	54	24	38	.287	.338	.468	117	6	0	1	-1	.965	-11	*C-100	0.3
1942	Was-A	104	353	31	72	14	2	3	46	37	37	.204	.281	.280	59	-19	0	0	0	.981	-2	C-98	-1.5
1943	Was-A★	126	423	37	109	23	3	5	60	53	43	.258	.346	.362	111	6	5	3	-0	.980	-8	*C-122	0.7
1946	Was-A	64	189	13	38	6	0	4	18	23	27	.201	.288	.296	67	-9	0	0	0	.960	2	C-64	-0.3
1947	StL-A	87	214	25	48	9	3	3	19	54	34	.224	.381	.336	98	2	0	1	-1	.989	-3	C-85	0.3
1948	Was-A	97	246	22	54	7	2	1	28	36	33	.220	.322	.276	62	-13	2	1	0	.991	2	C-92	-0.5
1949	Was-A	53	138	12	34	4	0	1	11	26	11	.246	.370	.297	79	-3	0	1	-1	.973	-4	C-53	-0.4
Total	9	747	2208	216	532	98	23	32	264	281	259	.241	.330	.350	89	-33	7	8	-3	.976	-19	C-694	-0.9

■ MIKE EASLER
Easler, Michael Anthony b: 11/29/50, Cleveland, Ohio BL/TR, 6'1", 196 lbs. Deb: 9/5/73 C

YEAR	TM/L	G	AB	R	H	2B	3B	HR	RBI	BB	SO	AVG	OBP	SLG	PRO+	BR/A	SB	CS	SBR	FA	FR	G/POS	TPR
1973	Hou-N	6	7	1	0	0	0	0	0	2	4	.000	.222	.000	-34	-1	0	0	0	.500	-1	/O-2	-0.2
1974	Hou-N	15	15	0	1	0	0	0	0	0	5	.067	.067	.067	-65	-3	0	0	0	.000	0	H	-0.4
1975	Hou-N	5	5	0	0	0	0	0	0	0	1	.000	.000	.000	-99	-1	0	0	0	.000	0	H	-0.2
1976	Cal-A	21	54	6	13	1	1	0	4	2	11	.241	.268	.296	69	-2	1	1	-0	.000	0	D-16	-0.3
1977	Pit-N	10	18	3	8	2	0	1	5	0	1	.444	.444	.722	202	2	0	0	0	1.000	-0	/O-4	0.2
1979	*Pit-N	55	54	8	15	1	1	2	11	8	13	.278	.371	.444	116	1	0	1	-1	.000	-2	/O-4	-0.1
1980	Pit-N	132	393	66	133	27	3	21	74	43	65	.338	.404	.583	170	36	5	9	-4	.986	-8	*O-119	2.1
1981	Pit-N★	95	339	43	97	18	5	7	42	24	45	.286	.333	.431	112	5	4	7	-3	.980	7	O-90	0.6
1982	Pit-N	142	475	52	131	27	2	15	58	40	85	.276	.340	.436	112	7	1	1	-0	.973	1	*O-138	0.4
1983	Pit-N	115	381	44	117	17	2	10	54	22	64	.307	.350	.441	115	7	4	2	0	.965	-3	*O-105	0.1
1984	Bos-A	156	601	87	188	31	5	27	91	58	134	.313	.377	.516	138	31	1	1	-0	.976	2	*D-126,1-29	2.7
1985	Bos-A	155	568	71	149	29	4	16	74	53	129	.262	.329	.412	97	-2	0	1	-1	.914	-2	*D-130,O-20	-0.8
1986	NY-A	146	490	64	148	26	2	14	78	49	87	.302	.365	.449	122	15	3	2	-0	.958	-0	*D-129,O-11	1.2
1987	Phi-N	33	110	7	31	4	0	1	10	6	20	.282	.319	.345	74	-4	0	1	-1	.981	2	O-30	-0.4
	NY-A	65	167	13	47	6	0	4	21	14	32	.281	.341	.389	94	-1	1	0	0	1.000	-1	D-32,O-15	-0.3
Total	14	1151	3677	465	1078	189	25	118	522	321	696	.293	.353	.454	118	88	20	26	-10	.974	-5	O-538,D-433/1-29	4.6

■ DAMION EASLEY
Easley, Jacinto Damion b: 11/11/69, New York, N.Y. BR/TR, 5'11", 185 lbs. Deb: 8/13/92

YEAR	TM/L	G	AB	R	H	2B	3B	HR	RBI	BB	SO	AVG	OBP	SLG	PRO+	BR/A	SB	CS	SBR	FA	FR	G/POS	TPR
1992	Cal-A	47	151	14	39	5	0	1	12	8	26	.258	.309	.311	74	-5	9	5	-0	.970	8	3-45/S-3	0.3
1993	Cal-A	73	230	33	72	13	2	2	22	28	35	.313	.395	.413	114	5	6	6	-2	.978	-11	2-54,3-14/D-1	-0.5
1994	Cal-A	88	316	41	68	16	1	6	30	29	48	.215	.289	.329	58	-20	4	5	-2	.953	-7	3-47,2-40	-2.5
1995	Cal-A	114	357	35	77	14	2	4	35	32	47	.216	.291	.300	55	-24	5	2	0	.981	-8	2-88,S-25	-2.4
1996	Cal-A	28	45	4	7	1	0	2	7	6	12	.156	.255	.311	42	-4	0	0	0	.943	3	S-13/2-9,3-3,O-2,D	0.0
	Det-A	21	67	10	23	1	0	2	10	4	13	.343	.389	.448	111	1	3	1	0	.974	-1	/2-8,S-8,3-2,D-1	0.1
	Yr	49	112	14	30	2	0	4	17	10	25	.268	.333	.393	83	-3	3	1	0	.951	2	S-21,2-17/3-5,DO	0.1
1997	Det-A	151	527	97	139	37	3	22	72	68	102	.264	.365	.471	117	14	28	13	1	.981	-13	*2-137,S-21/D-4	1.0
1998	Det-A★	153	594	84	161	38	2	27	100	39	112	.271	.333	.478	107	5	15	5	2	**.985**	22	*2-140,S-30/D-2	3.5
Total	7	675	2287	318	586	125	10	66	288	214	395	.256	.333	.406	92	-28	70	37	-1	.983	-6	2-476,3-111,S/DO	-0.5

■ CARL EAST
East, Carlton William b: 8/27/1894, Marietta, Ga. d: 1/15/53, Whitesburg, Ga. BL/TR, 6'2", 178 lbs. Deb: 8/24/15

YEAR	TM/L	G	AB	R	H	2B	3B	HR	RBI	BB	SO	AVG	OBP	SLG	PRO+	BR/A	SB	CS	SBR	FA	FR	G/POS	TPR
1915	StL-A	1	1	0	0	0	0	0	0	0	0	.000	.000	.000	-99	-0	0			.000	-0	/P-1	0.0
1924	Was-A	2	6	1	2	1	0	0	2	2	1	.333	.500	.500	163	1	0	0	0	.800	-0	/O-2	0.0
Total	2	3	7	1	2	1	0	0	2	2	1	.286	.444	.429	134	0	0	0		.800	-1	/O-2,P-1	0.0

■ HARRY EAST
East, Henry H. b: 4/1863, St.Louis, Mo. Deb: 6/17/1882

YEAR	TM/L	G	AB	R	H	2B	3B	HR	RBI	BB	SO	AVG	OBP	SLG	PRO+	BR/A	SB	CS	SBR	FA	FR	G/POS	TPR
1882	Bal-a	1	4	0	0	0	0	0		0		.000	.000	.000	-99	-1				.600	-0	/3-1	-0.1

■ LUKE EASTER
Easter, Luscious Luke b: 8/4/15, Jonestown, Miss. d: 3/29/79, Euclid, Ohio BL/TR, 6'4.5", 240 lbs. Deb: 8/11/49 C

YEAR	TM/L	G	AB	R	H	2B	3B	HR	RBI	BB	SO	AVG	OBP	SLG	PRO+	BR/A	SB	CS	SBR	FA	FR	G/POS	TPR
1949	Cle-A	21	45	6	10	3	0	0	2	8	6	.222	.340	.289	68	-2	0	1	-1	1.000	-4	O-12	-0.7
1950	Cle-A	141	540	96	151	20	4	28	107	70	95	.280	.373	.487	123	17	0	3	-2	.991	-3	*1-128,O-13	0.8
1951	Cle-A	128	486	65	131	12	5	27	103	37	71	.270	.333	.481	125	13	0	1	-1	.988	-7	*1-125	0.0
1952	Cle-A	127	437	63	115	10	3	31	97	44	84	.263	.337	.513	144	22	1	1	-0	.983	4	*1-118	2.2
1953	Cle-A	68	211	26	64	9	0	7	31	15	35	.303	.361	.445	120	5	0	2	-1	.981	-2	1-56	0.0

YEAR	TM/L	G	AB	R	H	2B	3B	HR	RBI	BB	SO	AVG	OBP	SLG	PRO+	BR/A	SB	CS	SBR	FA	FR	G/POS	TPR
1954	Cle-A	6	6	0	1	0	0	0	0	0	2	.167	.167	.167	-8	-1	0	0	0	.000	0	H	-0.1
Total	6	491	1725	256	472	54	12	93	340	174	293	.274	.350	.481	126	55	1	8	-5	.986	-12	1-427/O-25	2.2
■ **HENRY EASTERDAY**	Easterday, Henry P. b: 9/16/1864, Philadelphia, Pa. d: 3/30/1895, Philadelphia, Pa. BR/TR, 5'6", 145 lbs. Deb: 6/23/1884																						
1884	Phi-U	28	115	12	28	5	0	0		5		.243	.275	.287	76	-7				.875	6	S-28	0.0
1888	KC-a	115	401	42	76	7	6	3	37	31		.190	.256	.259	61	-18	23			**.888**	26	*S-115	1.0
1889	Col-a	95	324	43	56	5	8	4	34	41	57	.173	.270	.275	58	-17	10			.890	12	S-89/2-5,3-1	0.0
1890	Col-a	58	197	25	31	5	1	1	17	23		.157	.249	.208	37	-15	5			.879	6	S-58	-0.5
	Phi-a	19	68	17	10	1	0	1	3	10		.147	.256	.206	37	-5	4			.860	-2	S-19	-0.5
	Lou-a	7	24	2	2	0	0	0	1	2		.083	.185	.083	-21	-4	1			.886	1	/S-6,3-1	-0.2
	Yr	84	289	44	43	6	1	2	21	35		.149	.245	.197	32	-24	10			.875	5	S-83/3-1	-1.2
Total	4	322	1129	141	203	23	15	9	92	112	57	.180	.259	.251	54	-66	43			.884	50	S-315/2-5,3-2	-0.2
■ **PAUL EASTERLING**	Easterling, Paul b: 9/28/05, Reidsville, Ga. d: 3/15/93, Reidsville, Ga. BR/TR, 5'11", 180 lbs. Deb: 4/11/28																						
1928	Det-A	43	114	17	37	7	1	3	12	8	24	.325	.374	.482	122	3	2	1	0	.921	-2	O-34	-0.1
1930	Det-A	29	79	7	16	6	0	1	14	6	18	.203	.259	.316	44	-7	0	1	-1	1.000	-2	O-25	-1.0
1938	Phi-A	4	7	1	2	0	0	0	0	1	2	.286	.375	.286	70	-0	0	0	0	.750	-0	/O-1	0.0
Total	3	76	200	25	55	13	1	4	26	15	44	.275	.329	.410	88	-4	2	2	-1	.938	-4	/O-60	-1.1
■ **TED EASTERLY**	Easterly, Theodore Harrison b: 4/20/1885, Lincoln, Neb. d: 7/6/51, Clearlake Highlands, Cal. BL/TR, 5'8", 165 lbs. Deb: 4/17/09																						
1909	Cle-A	98	287	32	75	14	10	1	27	13		.261	.293	.390	111	2	8			.965	0	C-76	1.0
1910	Cle-A	110	363	34	111	16	6	0	55	21		.306	.344	.383	126	10	10			.964	-8	C-65,O-32	0.7
1911	Cle-A	99	287	34	93	19	5	1	37	8		.324	.345	.436	116	4	6			.910	-12	O-54,C-22	-0.8
1912	Cle-A	65	186	17	55	4	0	2	21	7		.296	.328	.349	91	-3	3			.958	-4	C-51	-0.2
	Chi-A	30	55	5	20	2	0	0	14	2		.364	.386	.400	129	2	1			.964	-4	C-10/O-1	-0.1
	Yr	95	241	22	75	6	0	2	35	9		.311	.341	.361	100	-1	4			.959	-8	C-61/O-1	-0.3
1913	Chi-A	60	97	3	23	1	0	0	8	4	9	.237	.267	.247	51	-6	2			.976	2	C-19	-0.2
1914	KC-F	134	436	58	146	20	12	1	67	31	25	.335	.384	.443	130	11	10			.969	-18	*C-128	0.4
1915	KC-F	110	309	32	84	12	5	3	32	21	15	.272	.320	.372	99	-6	2			.969	4	C-88	0.5
Total	7	706	2020	215	607	88	38	8	261	107	49	.300	.338	.394	112	14	42			.965	-41	C-459/O-87	1.3
■ **ROY EASTERWOOD**	Easterwood, Roy Charles "Shag" b: 1/12/15, Waxahachie, Tex. d: 8/24/84, Graham, Tex. BR/TR, 6'0.5", 196 lbs. Deb: 4/21/44																						
1944	Chi-N	17	33	1	7	2	0	1	2	1	11	.212	.235	.364	67	-2	0			1.000	-1	C-12	-0.2
■ **JOHN EASTON**	Easton, John David "Goose" b: 3/4/33, Trenton, N.J. BR/TR, 6'2", 185 lbs. Deb: 6/19/55																						
1955	Phi-N	1	0	0	0	0	0	0	0	0	0	—	—	—	—	0	0	0	0	.000	0	R	0.0
1959	Phi-N	3	3	0	0	0	0	0	0	0	3	.000	.000	.000	-98	-1	0	0	0	.000	0	H	-0.1
Total	2	4	3	0	0	0	0	0	0	0	3	.000	.000	.000	-98	-1	0	0	0	.000	0	-0,-0	-0.1
■ **EDDIE EAYRS**	Eayrs, Edwin b: 11/10/1890, Blackstone, Mass. d: 11/30/69, Warwick, R.I. BL/TL, 5'7", 160 lbs. Deb: 6/30/13																						
1913	Pit-N	4	6	0	1	0	0	0	0	0	1	.167	.167	.167	-5	-1	0			.667	-0	/P-2	0.0
1920	Bos-N	87	244	31	80	5	2	1	24	30	18	.328	.410	.377	133	12	4	3	-1	.950	-4	O-63/P-7	0.1
1921	Bos-N	15	15	0	1	0	0	0	1	0	4	.067	.067	.067	-68	-4	0	0	0	.000	-0	/P-2	0.0
	Bro-N	8	6	1	1	0	0	0	1	2	0	.167	.375	.167	47	-0	0	0	0	.000	-1	/O-1	-0.1
	Yr	23	21	1	2	0	0	0	2	2	4	.095	.174	.095	-27	-4	0	0	0	.000	-1	/P-2,O-1	-0.1
Total	3	114	271	32	83	5	2	1	26	32	23	.306	.388	.351	116	7	4	3		.950	-5	/O-64,P-11	0.0
■ **HI EBRIGHT**	Ebright, Hiram C. "Buck" b: 6/12/1859, Lancaster Co., Pa d: 10/24/16, Milwaukee, Wis. BR/TR, Deb: 4/24/1889																						
1889	Was-N	16	59	7	15	2	2	1	6	3	8	.254	.302	.407	103	-0	1			.875	4	/C-9,O-4,S-3	0.4
■ **ANGEL ECHEVARRIA**	Echevarria, Angel Santos b: 5/25/71, Bridgeport, Conn. BR/TR, 6'4", 215 lbs. Deb: 7/15/96																						
1996	Col-N	26	21	2	6	0	0	0	6	2	5	.286	.375	.286	63	-1	0	0	0	1.000	-4	O-11	-0.5
1997	Col-N	15	20	4	5	2	0	0	0	2	5	.250	.318	.350	61	-1	0	0	0	1.000	-1	/O-7	-0.2
1998	Col-N	19	29	7	11	3	0	1	9	2	3	.379	.455	.586	140	2	0	0	0	1.000	-1	/1-4,O-4	0.1
Total	3	60	70	13	22	5	0	1	15	6	13	.314	.392	.429	94	-1	0	0	0	1.000	-6	/O-22,1-4	-0.6
■ **JOHNNY ECHOLS**	Echols, John Gresham b: 1/9/17, Atlanta, Ga. d: 11/13/72, Atlanta, Ga. BR/TR, 5'10.5", 175 lbs. Deb: 5/24/39																						
1939	StL-N	2	0	0	0	0	0	0	0	0	0	—	—	—	—	0	0			.000	0	R	0.0
■ **OX ECKHARDT**	Eckhardt, Oscar George b: 12/23/01, Yorktown, Tex. d: 4/22/51, Yorktown, Tex. BL/TR, 6'1", 185 lbs. Deb: 4/16/32																						
1932	Bos-N	8	8	1	2	0	0	0	1	0	1	.250	.250	.250	36	-1	0			.000	0	H	-0.1
1936	Bro-N	16	44	5	8	1	0	1	6	5	2	.182	.265	.273	45	-3	0			1.000	1	O-10	-0.3
Total	2	24	52	6	10	1	0	1	7	5	3	.192	.263	.269	43	-4	0			1.000	1	/O-10	-0.4
■ **CHARLIE EDEN**	Eden, Charles M. b: 1/18/1855, Lexington, Ky. d: 9/17/20, Cincinnati, Ohio BL/TL, 168 lbs. Deb: 8/17/1877																						
1877	Chi-N	15	55	9	12	0	1	0	5	3	6	.218	.259	.255	56	-3				.679	-2	O-15	-0.5
1879	Cle-N	81	353	40	96	**31**	7	3	34	6	20	.272	.284	.425	131	12				.808	-4	*O-80/1-3,C-1	0.3
1884	Pit-a	32	122	12	33	7	4	1		7		.270	.341	.418	144	6				.759	-4	O-31/P-2	0.1
1885	Pit-a	98	405	57	103	18	6	0	38	17		.254	.298	.328	99	-0				.814	-16	*O-96/P-4,3-2	-1.6
Total	4	226	935	118	244	56	18	4	77	33	26	.261	.296	.372	114	14				.793	-25	O-222/P-6,1-3,3C	-1.7
■ **MIKE EDEN**	Eden, Edward Michael b: 5/22/49, Fort Clayton, Canal Zone BB/TR, 5'10", 170 lbs. Deb: 8/2/76																						
1976	Atl-N	5	8	0	0	0	0	0	1	0	0	.000	.000	.000	-94	-2	0	0	0	1.000	1	/2-2	-0.1
1978	Chi-A	10	17	1	2	0	0	0	0	4	0	.118	.286	.118	17	-2	0	0	0	.905	-0	/S-5,2-4	-0.1
Total	2	15	25	1	2	0	0	0	1	4	0	.080	.207	.080	-16	-4	0	0	0	1.000	0	/2-6,S-5	-0.2
■ **STUMP EDINGTON**	Edington, Jacob Frank b: 7/4/1891, Koleen, Ind. d: 11/11/69, Bastrop, La. BL/TL, 5'8", 170 lbs. Deb: 6/20/12																						
1912	Pit-N	15	53	4	16	0	2	0	12	3	1	.302	.339	.377	97	-0	0			1.000	1	O-14	0.0
■ **DAVE EDLER**	Edler, David Delmar b: 8/5/56, Sioux City, Iowa BR/TR, 6', 185 lbs. Deb: 9/4/80																						
1980	Sea-A	28	89	11	20	1	0	3	9	8	16	.225	.289	.337	70	-4	2	3	-1	.965	4	3-28	-0.2
1981	Sea-A	29	78	7	11	3	0	0	5	11	13	.141	.256	.179	26	-7	3	3	-1	.884	-3	3-26/S-1	-1.2
1982	Sea-A	40	104	14	29	2	2	2	18	11	13	.279	.348	.394	100	0	4	2	0	.922	3	3-31/O-2,D-2	0.2
1983	Sea-A	29	63	2	12	1	1	1	4	5	11	.190	.261	.286	49	-4	3	3	-1	.875	-2	3-13/1-5,O-1,D-6	-0.7
Total	4	126	334	34	72	7	3	6	36	35	53	.216	.294	.308	66	-15	12	11	-3	.922	2	/3-98,D-8,1-5,OS	-1.9
■ **JIM EDMONDS**	Edmonds, James Patrick b: 6/27/70, Fullerton, Cal. BL/TL, 6'1", 190 lbs. Deb: 9/9/93																						
1993	Cal-A	18	61	5	15	4	1	0	4	2	16	.246	.270	.344	62	-3	0	2	-1	.981	5	O-17	0.0
1994	Cal-A	94	289	35	79	13	1	5	37	30	72	.273	.344	.377	85	-6	4	2	0	.981	0	O-77,1-22	-0.9
1995	Cal-A★	141	558	120	162	30	4	33	107	51	130	.290	.355	.536	129	22	1	4	-2	.998	19	*O-139	3.3
1996	Cal-A	114	431	73	131	28	3	27	66	46	101	.304	.376	.571	135	22	4	0	1	.997	8	*O-111/D-1	2.5
1997	Ana-A	133	502	82	146	27	0	26	80	60	80	.291	.371	.500	125	18	5	7	-3	.985	14	*O-115,1-11/D-8	2.5
1998	Ana-A	154	599	115	184	42	1	25	91	57	114	.307	.368	.506	123	20	7	5	-1	.988	11	*O-153	2.5
Total	6	654	2440	430	717	144	10	116	385	246	513	.294	.362	.504	121	72	21	20	-6	.990	57	O-612/1-33,D-9	9.9
■ **BOB EDMONDSON**	Edmondson, Robert E. b: 4/30/1879, Paris, Ky. d: 8/14/31, Lawrence, Kan. BR/TR, 5'11", 185 lbs. Deb: 9/15/06																						
1906	Was-A	3	3	1	1	0	0	0	0	0		.333	.333	.333	114	0	0			1.000	-0	/P-2,O-1	0.0
1908	Was-A	26	80	5	15	4	1	0	2	7		.188	.261	.262	77	-2	0			.878	-2	O-24	-0.6
Total	2	29	83	6	16	4	1	0	2	7		.193	.264	.265	78	-2	0			.878	-2	/O-25,P-2	-0.6
■ **EDDIE EDMONSON**	Edmonson, Earl Edward b: 11/20/1889, Hopewell, Pa. d: 5/10/71, Leesburg, Fla. BL/TR, 6', 175 lbs. Deb: 10/4/13																						
1913	Cle-A	2	5	0	0	0	0	0	0	0	0	.000	.000	.000	-97	-1	0			1.000	-1	/1-1,O-1	-0.2

■ BRUCE EDWARDS
Edwards, Charles Bruce "Bull" b: 7/15/23, Quincy, Ill. d: 4/25/75, Sacramento, Cal. BR/TR, 5'7", 194 lbs. Deb: 6/23/46

YEAR	TM/L	G	AB	R	H	2B	3B	HR	RBI	BB	SO	AVG	OBP	SLG	PRO+	BR/A	SB	CS	SBR	FA	FR	G/POS	TPR
1946	Bro-N	92	292	24	78	13	5	1	25	34	20	.267	.348	.356	99	0	1			.982	6	C-91	1.2
1947	*Bro-N★	130	471	53	139	15	8	9	80	49	55	.295	.364	.418	103	3	2			.983	5	*C-128	1.6
1948	Bro-N	96	286	36	79	17	2	8	54	26	28	.276	.341	.434	105	1	4			.984	-8	C-48,O-21,3-14,/1-1	-0.5
1949	*Bro-N	64	148	24	31	3	0	8	25	25	15	.209	.324	.392	87	-3	0			.990	-3	C-41/O-4,3-1	-0.4
1950	Bro-N	50	142	16	26	4	1	8	16	13	22	.183	.256	.394	67	-8	1			.980	-4	C-38/1-2	-0.9
1951	Bro-N	17	36	6	9	2	0	1	8	1	3	.250	.270	.389	74	-1	0	0	0	1.000	0	/C-9	-0.1
	Chi-N☆	51	141	19	33	9	2	3	17	16	14	.234	.316	.390	87	-3	1	2	-1	.962	-3	C-28/1-9	-0.6
	Yr	68	177	25	42	11	2	4	25	17	17	.237	.308	.390	85	-4	1	2	-1	.971	-3	C-37/1-9	-0.7
1952	Chi-N	50	94	7	23	2	2	1	12	8	12	.245	.304	.340	77	-3	0	0	0	.989	-3	C-22/2-1	-0.5
1954	Chi-N	4	3	1	0	0	0	0	1	2	2	.000	.400	.000	15	-0	0	0	0	.000	0	H	0.0
1955	Was-A	30	57	5	10	2	0	0	3	16	6	.175	.356	.211	58	-3	0	1	-1	.980	7	C-22/3-5	0.4
1956	Cin-N	7	5	0	1	0	0	0	0	0	2	.200	.200	.200	8	-1	0	0	0	.000	-1	/C-2,2-1,3-1	-0.1
Total	10	591	1675	191	429	67	20	39	241	190	179	.256	.335	.390	93	-17	9	3		.982	-3	C-429/O-25,3-21,12	0.1

■ DAVE EDWARDS
Edwards, David Leonard b: 2/24/54, Los Angeles, Cal. BR/TR, 6', 177 lbs. Deb: 9/11/78 F

YEAR	TM/L	G	AB	R	H	2B	3B	HR	RBI	BB	SO	AVG	OBP	SLG	PRO+	BR/A	SB	CS	SBR	FA	FR	G/POS	TPR
1978	Min-A	15	44	7	11	3	0	1	3	7	13	.250	.377	.386	113	1	1	1	-0	.950	1	O-15	0.1
1979	Min-A	96	229	42	57	8	0	8	35	24	45	.249	.323	.389	88	-4	6	3	0	.983	-4	O-86/D-3	-1.0
1980	Min-A	81	200	26	50	9	1	2	20	12	51	.250	.296	.335	68	-9	2	1	0	.932	-6	O-72/D-3	-1.7
1981	SD-N	58	112	13	24	4	1	2	13	11	24	.214	.285	.321	77	-4	3	1	0	.970	-5	O-49	-1.0
1982	SD-N	71	55	7	10	2	0	1	2	1	14	.182	.196	.273	32	-5	0	0	0	.944	-14	O-45/1-1	-2.1
Total	5	321	640	95	152	26	2	14	73	55	147	.237	.302	.350	77	-21	12	6	0	.958	-28	O-267/D-6,1-1	-5.7

■ HANK EDWARDS
Edwards, Henry Albert b: 1/29/19, Elmwood Place, O. d: 6/22/88, Santa Ana, Cal. BL/TL, 6', 190 lbs. Deb: 9/10/41

YEAR	TM/L	G	AB	R	H	2B	3B	HR	RBI	BB	SO	AVG	OBP	SLG	PRO+	BR/A	SB	CS	SBR	FA	FR	G/POS	TPR
1941	Cle-A	16	68	10	15	1	1	1	6	2	4	.221	.243	.309	47	-5	0	0	0	.929	-1	O-16	-0.7
1942	Cle-A	13	48	6	12	2	1	0	7	5	8	.250	.321	.333	89	-1	2	1	0	.968	-1	O-12	-0.3
1943	Cle-A	92	297	38	82	18	6	3	28	30	34	.276	.343	.407	127	9	4	8	-4	.983	-5	O-74	-0.3
1946	Cle-A	124	458	62	138	33	**16**	10	54	43	48	.301	.361	.509	151	28	1	3	-2	.968	1	*O-123	2.3
1947	Cle-A	108	393	54	102	12	3	15	59	31	55	.260	.315	.420	106	1	1	3	-2	.990	-7	*O-100	-1.3
1948	Cle-A	55	160	27	43	9	2	3	18	18	18	.269	.346	.406	102	0	1	1	-0	.987	-3	O-41	-0.5
1949	Cle-A	5	15	3	4	0	0	1	1	1	2	.267	.313	.467	107	-0	0	0	0	1.000	-1	/O-5	-0.1
	Chi-N	58	176	25	51	8	4	7	21	19	22	.290	.359	.500	131	7	0			.988	-4	O-51	0.1
1950	Chi-N	41	110	13	40	11	1	2	21	10	13	.364	.417	.536	150	8	0			.976	-3	O-29	0.4
1951	Bro-N	35	31	1	7	3	0	0	3	4	9	.226	.314	.323	70	-1	0	0	0	.000	0	H	-0.1
	Cin-N	41	127	14	40	9	1	3	20	13	17	.315	.379	.472	126	5	0	2	-1	.985	-3	O-34	-0.1
	Yr	76	158	15	47	12	1	3	23	17	26	.297	.366	.443	115	3	0	2	-1	.985	-3	O-34	-0.2
1952	Cin-N	74	184	24	52	7	6	6	28	19	22	.283	.350	.484	129	7	0	3	-2	.988	-4	O-51	-0.1
	Chi-A	8	18	2	6	0	0	0	1	0	2	.333	.333	.333	85	-0	0	0	0	1.000	0	/O-3	0.0
1953	StL-A	65	106	6	21	3	0	0	9	13	10	.198	.286	.226	39	-9	0	1	-1	1.000	-1	O-21	-1.1
Total	11	735	2191	285	613	116	41	51	276	208	264	.280	.343	.440	119	48	9	22		.981	-31	O-560	-1.8

■ DOC EDWARDS
Edwards, Howard Rodney b: 12/10/36, Red Jacket, W.Va. BR/TR, 6'2", 215 lbs. Deb: 4/21/62 MC

YEAR	TM/L	G	AB	R	H	2B	3B	HR	RBI	BB	SO	AVG	OBP	SLG	PRO+	BR/A	SB	CS	SBR	FA	FR	G/POS	TPR
1962	Cle-A	53	143	13	39	6	0	3	9	9	14	.273	.325	.378	91	-2	0	0	0	.992	9	C-39	0.8
1963	Cle-A	10	31	6	8	2	0	0	0	2	6	.258	.303	.323	76	-1	0	0	0	.988	5	C-10	0.4
	KC-A	71	240	16	60	12	0	6	35	11	23	.250	.289	.375	80	-7	0	1	-1	.987	-5	C-63	-1.1
	Yr	81	271	22	68	14	0	6	35	13	29	.251	.290	.369	79	-8	0	1	-1	.987	-0	C-73	-0.7
1964	KC-A	97	294	25	66	10	0	5	28	13	40	.224	.265	.310	57	-17	0	1	-1	.986	1	C-79/1-7	-1.4
1965	KC-A	6	20	1	3	0	0	0	0	1	2	.150	.190	.150	-2	-3	0	0	0	1.000	-0	/C-6	-0.3
	NY-A	45	100	3	19	3	0	1	9	13	14	.190	.289	.250	55	-6	1	2	-1	.986	2	C-43	-0.3
	Yr	51	120	4	22	3	0	1	9	14	16	.183	.274	.233	46	-8	1	2	-1	.988	2	C-49	-0.6
1970	Phi-N	35	78	5	21	0	0	0	6	4	10	.269	.313	.269	59	-4	0	0	0	.970	6	C-34	0.3
Total	5	317	906	69	216	33	0	15	87	53	109	.238	.287	.325	68	-39	1	4	-2	.986	18	C-274/1-7	-1.6

■ JOHNNY EDWARDS
Edwards, John Alban b: 6/10/38, Columbus, Ohio BL/TR, 6'4", 220 lbs. Deb: 6/27/61

YEAR	TM/L	G	AB	R	H	2B	3B	HR	RBI	BB	SO	AVG	OBP	SLG	PRO+	BR/A	SB	CS	SBR	FA	FR	G/POS	TPR
1961	*Cin-N	52	145	14	27	5	0	2	14	18	28	.186	.280	.262	45	-11	1	0	0	.982	-4	C-52	-1.2
1962	Cin-N	133	452	47	115	28	5	8	50	45	70	.254	.323	.392	88	-8	1	1	-0	.987	12	*C-130	0.9
1963	Cin-N★	148	495	46	128	19	4	11	67	45	93	.259	.325	.380	99	-0	1	5	-3	**.995**	13	*C-148	1.7
1964	Cin-N★	126	423	47	119	23	1	7	55	34	65	.281	.336	.390	100	0	1	2	-1	.992	23	*C-120	2.9
1965	Cin-N☆	114	371	47	99	22	2	17	51	50	45	.267	.355	.474	123	12	0	0	0	.990	5	*C-110	2.3
1966	Cin-N	98	282	24	54	8	0	6	39	31	42	.191	.272	.284	50	-19	1	3	-2	.992	9	C-98	-0.6
1967	Cin-N	80	209	10	43	6	0	2	20	16	28	.206	.262	.263	46	-15	1	4	-2	.990	15	C-73	0.2
1968	*StL-N	85	230	14	55	9	1	3	29	16	20	.239	.291	.326	86	-4	1	1	-0	.992	2	C-54	0.1
1969	Hou-N	151	496	52	115	20	6	6	50	53	69	.232	.309	.333	81	-12	2	1	0	**.994**	5	*C-151	0.1
1970	Hou-N	140	458	46	101	16	4	7	49	51	63	.221	.300	.319	69	-21	1	0	0	**.995**	13	*C-139	-0.1
1971	Hou-N	106	317	18	74	13	4	1	23	26	38	.233	.292	.309	72	-12	1	1	-0	**.995**	8	*C-104	-0.1
1972	Hou-N	108	332	33	89	16	2	5	40	50	39	.268	.366	.373	113	7	2	4	-2	.988	-8	*C-105	0.1
1973	Hou-N	79	250	24	61	10	2	5	27	19	23	.244	.303	.360	83	-6	1	0	0	.989	-1	C-76	-0.4
1974	Hou-N	50	117	8	26	7	1	1	10	11	12	.222	.295	.325	76	-4	1	1	-0	.989	5	C-32	0.2
Total	14	1470	4577	430	1106	202	32	81	524	465	635	.242	.314	.353	85	-92	15	23	-9	.992	97	*C-1392	6.1

■ MARSHALL EDWARDS
Edwards, Marshall Lynn b: 8/27/52, Fort Lewis, Wash. BL/TL, 5'9", 157 lbs. Deb: 4/11/81 F

YEAR	TM/L	G	AB	R	H	2B	3B	HR	RBI	BB	SO	AVG	OBP	SLG	PRO+	BR/A	SB	CS	SBR	FA	FR	G/POS	TPR
1981	*Mil-A	40	58	10	14	1	1	0	4	0	2	.241	.241	.293	56	-3	6	2	1	.979	-9	O-36/D-1	-1.3
1982	*Mil-A	69	178	24	44	4	1	2	14	4	8	.247	.264	.315	62	-10	10	4	1	.984	-2	O-54/D-6	-1.2
1983	Mil-A	51	74	14	22	1	1	0	5	1	9	.297	.307	.338	84	-2	5	5	-2	1.000	-3	O-35/D-4	-0.7
Total	3	160	310	48	80	6	3	2	23	5	19	.258	.270	.316	66	-15	21	11	-0	.987	-13	O-125/D-11	-3.2

■ MIKE EDWARDS
Edwards, Michael Lewis b: 8/27/52, Fort Lewis, Wash. BR/TR, 5'10", 154 lbs. Deb: 9/10/77 F

YEAR	TM/L	G	AB	R	H	2B	3B	HR	RBI	BB	SO	AVG	OBP	SLG	PRO+	BR/A	SB	CS	SBR	FA	FR	G/POS	TPR
1977	Pit-N	7	6	1	0	0	0	0	0	0	3	.000	.143	.000	-56	-1	0	2	-1	1.000	3	/2-4	0.1
1978	Oak-A	142	414	48	113	16	2	1	23	16	32	.273	.303	.329	82	-11	27	21	-5	.964	-28	*2-133/S-9,D-4	-3.5
1979	Oak-A	122	400	35	93	12	2	1	23	15	37	.233	.264	.280	49	-29	10	6	-1	.962	-14	*2-113/S-3,D-2	-3.5
1980	Oak-A	46	59	10	14	0	0	0	3	1	5	.237	.250	.237	37	-5	1	1	-0	.971	4	2-23/O-1,D-5	-0.1
Total	4	317	879	94	220	28	4	2	49	32	77	.250	.281	.298	63	-46	38	30	-7	.964	-34	2-273/S-12,D-11,O-1	-7.0

■ RALPH EDWARDS
Edwards, Ralph Strunk b: 12/14/1882, Brewster, N.Y. d: 1/5/49, White Plains, N.Y. BR/TR, 5'9", 165 lbs. Deb: 9/17/15

YEAR	TM/L	G	AB	R	H	2B	3B	HR	RBI	BB	SO	AVG	OBP	SLG	PRO+	BR/A	SB	CS	SBR	FA	FR	G/POS	TPR
1915	Phi-A	2	5	0	0	0	0	0	0	0	3	.000	.000	.000	-99	-1	0			1.000	-1	/2-1	-0.3

■ ROBERT EENHOORN
Eenhoorn, Robert Franciscus b: 2/9/68, Rotterdam, Holland BR/TR, 6'3", 170 lbs. Deb: 4/27/94

YEAR	TM/L	G	AB	R	H	2B	3B	HR	RBI	BB	SO	AVG	OBP	SLG	PRO+	BR/A	SB	CS	SBR	FA	FR	G/POS	TPR
1994	NY-A	3	4	1	2	1	0	0	0	0	0	.500	.500	.750	225	1	0	0	0	1.000	-1	/S-3	0.0
1995	NY-A	5	14	1	2	1	0	0	2	1	3	.143	.200	.214	8	-2	0	0	0	1.000	-1	/2-3,S-2	-0.3
1996	NY-A	12	14	2	1	0	0	0	2	2	3	.071	.188	.071	-31	-3	0	0	0	1.000	2	2-10/3-2	0.0
	Cal-A	6	15	1	4	0	0	0	0	0	2	.267	.267	.267	35	-1	0	0	0	.875	-1	/S-4,2-2	-0.2
	Yr	18	29	3	5	0	0	0	2	2	5	.172	.226	.172	3	-4	0	0	0	.971	1	2-12/S-4,3-2	-0.2
1997	Ana-A	11	20	2	7	1	0	1	6	0	2	.350	.350	.550	130	1	0	0	0	.833	-2	/3-5,2-3,S-2	-0.1
Total	4	37	67	7	16	3	0	1	10	3	10	.239	.271	.328	53	-5	0	0	0	.963	-3	/2-18,S-11,3-7	-0.6

■ BEN EGAN
Egan, Arthur Augustus b: 11/20/1883, Augusta, N.Y. d: 2/18/68, Sherrill, N.Y. BR/TR, 6', 195 lbs. Deb: 9/29/08 C

YEAR	TM/L	G	AB	R	H	2B	3B	HR	RBI	BB	SO	AVG	OBP	SLG	PRO+	BR/A	SB	CS	SBR	FA	FR	G/POS	TPR
1908	Phi-A	2	6	1	1	1	0	0	0	1		.167	.286	.333	95	-0	0			.933	0	/C-2	0.0
1912	Phi-A	49	138	9	24	3	4	0	13	6		.174	.208	.254	33	-13	3			.958	4	C-46	-0.5
1914	Cle-A	29	88	7	20	2	1	0	11	3	20	.227	.277	.273	63	-4	0	1	-1	.975	4	C-27	0.2
1915	Cle-A	42	120	4	13	3	0	0	6	8	14	.108	.164	.133	-11	-16	0			.970	8	C-40	-0.6
Total	4	122	352	21	58	9	5	0	30	18	34	.165	.212	.219	27	-33	3	1		.966	16	C-115	-0.9

YEAR	TM/L	G	AB	R	H	2B	3B	HR	RBI	BB	SO	AVG	OBP	SLG	PRO+	BR/A	SB	CS	SBR	FA	FR	G/POS	TPR
■ JIM EGAN	Egan, James K. "Troy Terrier" b: 1858, Derby, Conn. d: 9/26/1884, New Haven, Conn. TL , Deb: 5/15/1882																						
1882	Tro-N	30	115	15	23	3	2	0	10	1	21	.200	.207	.261	51	-6				.625	-8	O-18,P-12/C-2	-0.8
■ DICK EGAN	Egan, Richard Joseph b: 6/23/1884, Portland, Ore. d: 7/7/47, Oakland, Cal. BR/TR, 5'11", 162 lbs. Deb: 9/15/08																						
1908	Cin-N	18	68	8	14	3	1	0	5	2		.206	.229	.279	64	-3	7			.891	-3	2-18	-0.7
1909	Cin-N	127	480	59	132	14	3	2	53	37		.275	.329	.329	105	3	39			.950	24	*2-116,S-10	2.7
1910	Cin-N	135	474	70	116	11	5	0	46	53	38	.245	.322	.289	82	-10	41			.961	-11	*2-131/S-3	-2.5
1911	Cin-N	153	558	80	139	11	5	1	56	59	50	.249	.322	.292	75	-18	37			.949	10	*2-152	-1.1
1912	Cin-N	149	507	69	125	14	5	0	52	56	26	.247	.324	.294	72	-19	24			**.973**	3	*2-149	-1.9
1913	Cin-N	60	195	15	55	7	3	0	22	15	13	.282	.333	.349	95	-1	6			.972	-5	2-37,S-17/3-2	-0.5
1914	Bro-N	106	337	30	76	10	3	1	21	22	25	.226	.273	.282	64	-15	8			.914	-9	S-83,3-10/O-3,21	-1.9
1915	Bro-N	3	3	0	0	0	0	0	0	0	0	.000	.000	.000	-98	-1	0			.000	0	H	-0.1
	Bos-N	83	220	20	57	9	1	0	21	28	18	.259	.343	.309	102	2	3	4	-2	.974	-2	O-24,2-22,S-10,/13	-0.2
	Yr	86	223	20	57	9	1	0	21	28	18	.256	.339	.305	100	1	3	4	-2	.974	-2	O-24,2-22,S-10,/13	-0.3
1916	Bos-N	83	238	23	53	8	3	0	16	19	21	.223	.280	.282	76	-7	2			.949	-21	2-59,S-12/3-8	-3.0
Total	9	917	3080	374	767	87	29	4	292	291	191	.249	.315	.300	82	-69	167	4		.956	-14	2-686,S-135/O31	-9.2
■ TOM EGAN	Egan, Thomas Patrick b: 6/9/46, Los Angeles, Cal. BR/TR, 6'4", 218 lbs. Deb: 5/27/65																						
1965	Cal-A	18	38	3	10	0	1	0	1	3	12	.263	.317	.316	82	-1	0	0	0	1.000	-0	C-16	0.0
1966	Cal-A	7	11	0	0	0	0	0	0	1	5	.000	.083	.000	-76	-2	0	0	0	1.000	2	/C-6	-0.1
1967	Cal-A	1	1	0	0	0	0	0	0	0	0	.000	.000	.000	-99	-0	0	0	0	1.000	0	/C-1	0.0
1968	Cal-A	16	43	2	5	1	0	1	4	2	15	.116	.156	.209	10	-5	0	0	0	1.000	2	C-14	-0.3
1969	Cal-A	46	120	7	17	1	0	5	16	17	41	.142	.254	.275	50	-8	0	1	-1	.985	6	C-46	0.0
1970	Cal-A	79	210	14	50	6	0	4	20	14	67	.238	.289	.324	71	-9	0	0	0	.988	-1	C-79	-0.7
1971	Chi-A	85	251	29	60	11	1	10	34	26	94	.239	.320	.410	102	1	1	0	0	.986	3	C-77/1-1	0.7
1972	Chi-A	50	141	8	27	3	0	2	9	4	48	.191	.224	.255	42	-10	0	0	0	.986	3	C-46	-0.6
1974	Cal-A	43	94	4	11	0	0	0	4	8	40	.117	.194	.117	-9	-13	1	0	0	.996	16	C-41	0.4
1975	Cal-A	28	70	7	16	3	1	0	3	5	14	.229	.280	.300	69	-3	0	0	0	.965	4	C-28	0.2
Total	10	373	979	74	196	25	3	22	91	80	336	.200	.267	.299	62	-51	2	1	0	.987	35	C-354/1-1	-0.4
■ ELMER EGGERT	Eggert, Elmer Albert "Mose" b: 1/29/02, Rochester, N.Y. d: 4/9/71, Rochester, N.Y. BR/TR, 5'9", 160 lbs. Deb: 4/27/27																						
1927	Bos-A	5	3	0	0	0	0	0	0	1	1	.000	.250	.000	-31	-1	0	0	0	.000	0	/2-1	-0.1
■ DAVE EGGLER	Eggler, David Daniel b: 4/30/1851, Brooklyn, N.Y. d: 4/5/02, Buffalo, N.Y. BR/TR, 5'9", 165 lbs. Deb: 5/18/1871																						
1871	Mut-n	33	147	37	47	7	3	0	18	4	3	.320	.338	.408	124	6	14	3	2	.910	6	*O-33	1.0
1872	Mut-n	56	290	**94**	98	20	0	0	20	8	9	.338	.356	.407	143	16	**18**	5	**2**	**.922**	15	*O-56	2.5
1873	Mut-n	53	268	82	90	13	4	0	34	5	2	.336	.348	.414	126	9	4	1	1	.862	5	*O-53/3-1	1.1
1874	Phi-n	58	299	70	95	13	8	0	31	5	1	.318	.329	.415	132	9	5	6	-2	**.906**	9	*O-57/2-2	1.3
1875	Ath-n	66	295	66	89	13	7	0	33	1	10	.302	.304	.393	126	5	6	5	-1	**.921**	4	*O-66	0.7
1876	Phi-N	39	174	28	52	4	0	0	19	2	4	.299	.307	.322	111	2				.913	5	O-39	0.6
1877	Chi-N	33	136	20	36	3	0	0	20	1	5	.265	.270	.287	67	-6				.861	3	O-33	-0.4
1879	Buf-N	78	317	41	66	5	7	0	27	11	41	.208	.235	.268	64	-12				.919	-6	*O-78	-2.0
1883	Bal-a	53	202	15	38	2	0	0	7	1		.188	.192	.198	25	-17				.916	1	O-53	-1.5
	Buf-N	38	153	13	38	2	1	0	13	2	29	.248	.258	.275	61	-7				.845	-1	O-38	-0.8
1884	Buf-N	63	241	25	47	3	1	0	20	6	54	.195	.215	.216	35	-18				.887	1	O-63	-1.7
1885	Buf-N	6	24	0	2	0	0	0	0	2	4	.083	.154	.083	-21	-3				.938	1	/O-6	-0.3
Total	5 n	266	1299	349	419	66	22	0	136	23	25	.323	.334	.407	131	45	47	20	2	.905	39	O-265/2-2,3-1	6.6
Total	6	310	1247	142	279	19	9	0	106	25	137	.224	.239	.253	56	-61				.894	3	O-310	-6.1
■ RED EHRET	Ehret, Philip Sydney b: 8/31/1868, Louisville, Ky. d: 7/28/40, Cincinnati, Ohio BR/TR, 6', 175 lbs. Deb: 7/7/1888																						
1888	KC-a	17	63	4	12	4	0	0	4	1		.190	.203	.254	43	-4	1			.750	-4	O-10/P-7,2-1,1-1	-0.7
1889	Lou-a	67	258	27	65	6	6	1	31	4	23	.252	.263	.333	71	-11	4			.891	-1	P-45,O-22/S-1,32	-0.7
1890	*Lou-a	43	146	11	31	2	1	0	10	1		.212	.218	.240	36	-12	1			.859	-3	P-43	0.0
1891	Lou-a	26	91	9	22	2	1	0	9	5	15	.242	.281	.286	63	-5	3			.871	0	P-26	0.0
1892	Pit-N	40	132	12	34	2	0	0	19	7	22	.258	.295	.273	72	-5	1			.855	-4	P-39	0.0
1893	Pit-N	40	136	16	24	3	0	1	17	10	18	.176	.233	.221	21	-16	1			.893	1	P-39	0.0
1894	Pit-N	46	135	6	23	4	1	0	11	8	22	.170	.217	.215	4	-21	0			.859	-1	P-46	0.0
1895	StL-N	37	96	13	21	2	1	1	9	6	12	.219	.265	.292	44	-8	0			.848	0	P-37	0.0
1896	Cin-N	34	102	10	20	2	0	1	20	10	12	.196	.268	.245	33	-10	2			.923	1	P-34/1-1	0.0
1897	Cin-N	34	66	6	13	2	0	0	6	4		.197	.254	.227	26	-7	2			.957	-1	P-34	0.0
1898	Lou-N	13	40	3	9	3	1	0	4	1		.225	.262	.350	76	-1	0			.800	-1	P-12	0.0
Total	11	397	1265	117	274	32	11	4	140	57	124	.217	.252	.269	44	-101	15			.882	-12	P-362/O-32,1-2,23S	-1.4
■ HACK EIBEL	Eibel, Henry Hack b: 12/6/1893, Brooklyn, N.Y. d: 10/16/45, Macon, Ga. BL/TL, 5'11", 220 lbs. Deb: 6/13/12																						
1912	Cle-A	1	3	0	0	0	0	0	0	0		.000	.000	.000	-97	-1	0			.000	-0	/O-1	-0.1
1920	Bos-A	29	43	4	8	2	0	0	6	3	6	.186	.239	.233	26	-5	1	1	-0	.800	-2	/O-5,P-3,1-1	-0.6
Total	2	30	46	4	8	2	0	0	6	3	6	.174	.224	.217	19	-5	1	1		.800	-2	/O-6,P-3,1-1	-0.7
■ IKE EICHRODT	Eichrodt, Frederick George b: 1/6/03, Chicago, Ill. d: 7/14/65, Indianapolis, Ind BR/TR, 5'11.5", 167 lbs. Deb: 9/7/25																						
1925	Cle-A	15	52	4	12	3	1	0	4	2	7	.231	.259	.327	48	-4	0	0	0	.938	-2	O-13	-0.7
1926	Cle-A	37	80	14	25	7	1	0	7	2	11	.313	.329	.425	95	-1	1	0	0	.976	-4	O-27	-0.5
1927	Cle-A	85	267	24	59	19	2	0	25	16	25	.221	.265	.307	48	-21	2	3	-1	.979	1	O-81	-2.5
1931	Chi-A	34	117	9	25	5	1	0	15	1	8	.214	.220	.274	31	-12	0	0	0	1.000	-5	O-32	-1.8
Total	4	171	516	51	121	34	5	0	51	21	51	.234	.264	.320	52	-39	3	3	-1	.979	-9	O-153	-5.5
■ JIM EISENREICH	Eisenreich, James Michael b: 4/18/59, St.Cloud, Minn. BL/TL, 5'11", 195 lbs. Deb: 4/6/82																						
1982	Min-A	34	99	10	30	6	0	2	9	11	13	.303	.378	.424	117	3	0	0	0	.973	-1	O-30	0.1
1983	Min-A	2	7	1	2	1	0	0	0	1	1	.286	.375	.429	116	0	0	0	0	1.000	1	/O-2	0.1
1984	Min-A	12	32	1	7	1	0	0	3	2	4	.219	.265	.250	41	-3	2	0	1	1.000	-1	/O-3,D-6	-0.3
1987	KC-A	44	105	10	25	8	2	4	21	7	13	.238	.286	.467	93	-2	1	1	-0	.000	0	D-26	-0.2
1988	KC-A	82	202	26	44	8	1	1	19	6	31	.218	.240	.282	45	-15	9	3	1	.965	-8	O-64,D-13	-2.4
1989	KC-A	134	475	64	139	33	7	9	59	37	44	.293	.344	.448	122	13	27	8	3	.989	-11	*O-123,D-10	0.2
1990	KC-A	142	496	61	139	29	7	5	51	42	51	.280	.338	.397	106	4	12	14	-5	**.996**	-9	*O-138/D-2	-1.4
1991	KC-A	135	375	47	113	22	3	2	47	20	35	.301	.338	.392	101	0	5	3	-0	.973	-17	*O-105,1-15/D-1	-2.0
1992	KC-A	113	353	31	95	13	3	2	28	24	36	.269	.316	.340	81	-9	11	6	-0	.995	-2	O-88/D-8	-1.3
1993	*Phi-N	153	362	51	115	17	4	7	54	26	36	.318	.365	.445	117	9	5	0	2	.996	-6	*O-137/1-1	0.2
1994	Phi-N	104	290	42	87	15	4	4	43	33	31	.300	.373	.421	104	3	6	2	1	.989	0	O-93	0.1
1995	Phi-N	129	377	46	119	22	2	10	55	38	44	.316	.380	.464	120	11	10	0	3	**1.000**	1	*O-111	1.2
1996	Phi-N	113	338	45	122	24	3	3	41	31	32	.361	.416	.476	133	17	11	1	3	.977	1	O-91	1.8
1997	*Fla-N	120	293	36	82	19	1	2	34	30	28	.280	.349	.372	93	-3	0	0	0	.987	-4	O-55,1-29/D-4	-1.0
1998	Fla-N	30	64	9	16	1	0	1	7	4	14	.250	.294	.313	60	-4	2	0	1	.965	-3	1-10/O-8	-0.7
	LA-N	75	127	12	25	2	2	0	6	12	22	.197	.266	.244	37	-12	4	0	1	.971	-2	O-24/1-9,D-2	-1.3
	Yr	105	191	21	41	3	2	1	13	16	36	.215	.275	.267	45	-16	6	0	2	.977	-4	O-32,1-19/D-2	-2.0
Total	15	1422	3995	492	1160	221	39	52	477	324	435	.290	.345	.404	103	13	105	38	9	.988	-62	*O-1072/D-72,1-64	-6.9
■ ELAND	Eland Deb: 4/14/1873																						
1873	Mar-n	1	3	0	0	0	0	0	0	0	0	.000	.000	.000	-99	-1	0	0	0	.667	-0	/O-1	-0.1
■ KID ELBERFELD	Elberfeld, Norman Arthur "The Tabasco Kid" b: 4/13/1875, Pomeroy, Ohio d: 1/13/44, Chattanooga, Tenn. BR/TR, 5'7", 158 lbs. Deb: 5/30/1898 M																						
1898	Phi-N	14	38	1	9	4	0	0	7	5		.237	.420	.342	124	2	0			.795	-5	3-14	-0.3
1899	Cin-N	41	138	23	36	4	2	0	22	15		.261	.378	.319	90	-1	5			.878	-4	S-24,3-18	-0.3

YEAR	TM/L	G	AB	R	H	2B	3B	HR	RBI	BB	SO	AVG	OBP	SLG	PRO+	BR/A	SB	CS	SBR	FA	FR	G/POS	TPR
1901	Det-A	121	432	76	133	21	11	3	76	57		.308	.397	.428	123	15	23			.907	22	*S-121	4.2
1902	Det-A	130	488	70	127	17	6	1	64	55		.260	.348	.326	86	-7	19			.921	9	*S-130	0.9
1903	Det-A	35	132	29	45	5	3	0	19	11		.341	.412	.424	156	10	6			.932	6	S-34/3-1	1.7
	NY-A	90	349	49	100	18	5	0	45	22		.287	.346	.367	107	4	16			.914	7	S-90	1.5
	Yr	125	481	78	145	23	8	0	64	33		.301	.365	.383	120	13	22			.919	13	*S-124/3-1	3.2
1904	NY-A	122	445	55	117	13	5	2	46	37		.263	.337	.328	106	4	18			.933	15	*S-122	2.6
1905	NY-A	111	390	48	102	18	2	0	53	23		.262	.329	.318	95	-2	18			.908	-5	*S-108	-0.5
1906	NY-A	99	346	59	106	11	5	2	31	30		.306	.378	.384	126	11	19			.925	-4	S-98	1.2
1907	NY-A	120	447	61	121	17	6	0	51	36		.271	.343	.336	108	5	22			.930	8	*S-118	1.7
1908	NY-A	19	56	11	11	3	0	0	5	6		.196	.328	.250	87	-0	1			.916	-3	S-17,M	-0.3
1909	NY-A	106	379	47	90	9	5	0	26	28		.237	.314	.288	89	-4	23			.943	-3	S-61,3-44	-0.4
1910	Was-A	127	455	53	114	9	2	2	42	35		.251	.322	.292	97	-1	19			**.943**	-10	*3-113,2-10/S-3	-0.8
1911	Was-A	127	404	58	110	19	4	0	47	65		.272	.405	.339	110	11	24			.957	10	2-68,3-52	2.0
1914	Bro-N	30	62	7	14	1	0	0	1	2	4	.226	.304	.242	62	-3	0			.901	-4	S-18/2-1	-0.6
Total	14	1292	4561	647	1235	169	56	10	535	427	4	.271	.355	.339	105	44	213			.920	41	S-944,3-242/2-79	12.6

■ GEORGE ELDER Elder, George Rezin b: 3/10/21, Lebanon, Ky. BL/TR, 5'11", 180 lbs. Deb: 7/22/49

YEAR	TM/L	G	AB	R	H	2B	3B	HR	RBI	BB	SO	AVG	OBP	SLG	PRO+	BR/A	SB	CS	SBR	FA	FR	G/POS	TPR
1949	StL-A	41	44	9	11	3	0	0	2	4	11	.250	.313	.318	64	-2	0	0	0	1.000	-1	O-10	-0.4

■ LEE ELIA Elia, Lee Constantine b: 7/16/37, Philadelphia, Pa. BR/TR, 5'11", 175 lbs. Deb: 4/23/66 MC

YEAR	TM/L	G	AB	R	H	2B	3B	HR	RBI	BB	SO	AVG	OBP	SLG	PRO+	BR/A	SB	CS	SBR	FA	FR	G/POS	TPR
1966	Chi-A	80	195	16	40	5	2	3	22	15	39	.205	.269	.297	67	-9	0	1	-1	.954	4	S-75	0.0
1968	Chi-N	15	17	1	3	0	0	0	3	0	6	.176	.222	.176	20	-2	0	0	0	1.000	-1	/S-2,2-1,3-1	-0.3
Total	2	95	212	17	43	5	2	3	25	15	45	.203	.265	.288	63	-10	0	1	-1	.954	3	/S-77,3-1,2-1	-0.3

■ PETE ELKO Elko, Peter "Piccolo Pete" b: 6/17/18, Wilkes-Barre, Pa. d: 9/17/93, Wilkes-Barre, Pa. BR/TR, 5'11", 185 lbs. Deb: 9/17/43

YEAR	TM/L	G	AB	R	H	2B	3B	HR	RBI	BB	SO	AVG	OBP	SLG	PRO+	BR/A	SB	CS	SBR	FA	FR	G/POS	TPR
1943	Chi-N	9	30	1	4	0	0	0	0	4	5	.133	.235	.133	8	-3	0			.852	-2	/3-9	-0.6
1944	Chi-N	7	22	2	5	1	0	0	0	0	0	.227	.227	.273	40	-2	0			1.000	-0	/3-6	-0.2
Total	2	16	52	3	9	1	0	0	0	4	5	.173	.232	.192	22	-5	0			.902	-2	/3-15	-0.8

■ ROY ELLAM Ellam, Roy "Whitey" or "Slippery" b: 2/8/1886, W.Conshohocken, Pa. d: 10/28/48, Conshohocken, Pa. BR/TR, 5'10.5", 203 lbs. Deb: 9/18/09

YEAR	TM/L	G	AB	R	H	2B	3B	HR	RBI	BB	SO	AVG	OBP	SLG	PRO+	BR/A	SB	CS	SBR	FA	FR	G/POS	TPR
1909	Cin-N	10	21	4	4	0	1	1	4	7		.190	.393	.429	156	2	1			.895	-1	/S-9	0.1
1918	Pit-N	26	77	9	10	1	1	0	2	17	17	.130	.302	.169	43	-4	2			.924	-8	S-26	-1.3
Total	2	36	98	13	14	1	2	1	6	24	17	.143	.323	.224	67	-3	3			.917	-10	/S-35	-1.2

■ FRANK ELLERBE Ellerbe, Francis Rogers "Governor" b: 12/25/1895, Marion Co., S.C. d: 7/8/88, Latta, S.C. BR/TR, 5'10.5", 165 lbs. Deb: 8/28/19

YEAR	TM/L	G	AB	R	H	2B	3B	HR	RBI	BB	SO	AVG	OBP	SLG	PRO+	BR/A	SB	CS	SBR	FA	FR	G/POS	TPR
1919	Was-A	28	105	13	29	4	1	0	16	2	15	.276	.290	.333	75	-4	5			.945	-4	S-28	-0.7
1920	Was-A	101	336	38	98	14	2	0	36	19	23	.292	.331	.345	82	-9	5	4	-1	.934	-5	3-75,S-19/O-1	-1.0
1921	Was-A	10	10	1	2	0	1	0	1	0	2	.200	.200	.400	52	-1	0	0	0	.000	0	H	-0.1
	StL-A	105	430	65	124	20	12	2	49	22	42	.288	.327	.405	81	-14	1	6	-3	.953	2	*3-105	-0.7
	Yr	115	440	66	126	20	13	2	50	22	44	.286	.325	.405	81	-14	1	6	-3	.953	2	*3-105	-0.8
1922	StL-A	91	342	42	84	16	3	1	33	25	36	.246	.303	.319	60	-20	1	2	-0	.955	16	3-91	0.2
1923	StL-A	18	49	6	9	0	0	0	1	1	5	.184	.200	.184	1	-7	0	1	-1	.967	-3	3-14	-0.9
1924	StL-A	21	61	7	12	3	0	0	2	2	3	.197	.222	.246	19	-7	0	1	-1	.953	3	3-21	-0.4
	Cle-A	46	120	7	31	1	3	1	14	1	10	.258	.270	.342	56	-8	0	0	0	.975	5	3-39/2-2	-0.1
	Yr	67	181	14	43	4	3	1	16	3	13	.238	.254	.309	44	-16	0	1	-1	.967	8	3-60/2-2	-0.5
Total	6	420	1453	179	389	58	22	4	152	72	136	.268	.306	.346	68	-70	12	13		.952	14	3-345/S-47,2-2,O-1	-3.7

■ JOE ELLICK Ellick, Joseph J. b: 4/3/1854, Cincinnati, Ohio d: 4/21/23, Kansas City, Kan. 5'10", 162 lbs. Deb: 5/13/1875 MU

YEAR	TM/L	G	AB	R	H	2B	3B	HR	RBI	BB	SO	AVG	OBP	SLG	PRO+	BR/A	SB	CS	SBR	FA	FR	G/POS	TPR
1875	RS-n	7	27	1	6	1	0	0	1	0	1	.222	.222	.259	74	-1	1	0	0	.471	-3	/3-5,O-2	-0.3
1878	Mil-N	3	13	2	2	0	0	0	1	0	1	.154	.154	.154	1	-1				.769	-3	/C-2,3-1,P-1	-0.3
1880	Wor-N	5	18	1	1	0	0	0	0	1	2	.056	.105	.056	-40	-3				.882	0	/3-5	-0.2
1884	CP-U	92	394	71	93	11	0	0		16		.236	.266	.264	61	-29				.903	-2	O-57,S-33/2-4,M	-2.9
	KC-U	2	8	0	0	0	0	0		0		.000	.000	.000	-99	-2				.778	-1	/2-1,O-1	-0.3
	Bal-U	7	27	2	4	0	0	0		2		.148	.207	.148	8	-4				.714	-1	/S-6,O-1	-0.4
	Yr	101	429	73	97	11	0	0		18		.226	.257	.252	55	-35				.894	-3	O-59,S-39/2-5	-3.6
Total	3	109	460	76	100	11	0	0	1	19	3	.217	.248	.241	50	-40				.889	-6	/O-59,S-39,3-6,2CP	-4.1

■ LARRY ELLIOT Elliot, Lawrence Lee b: 3/5/38, San Diego, Cal. BL/TL, 6'2", 200 lbs. Deb: 4/19/62

YEAR	TM/L	G	AB	R	H	2B	3B	HR	RBI	BB	SO	AVG	OBP	SLG	PRO+	BR/A	SB	CS	SBR	FA	FR	G/POS	TPR
1962	Pit-N	8	10	2	3	0	0	1	2	0	1	.300	.300	.600	135	0	0	0	0	1.000	-1	/O-3	0.0
1963	Pit-N	4	4	0	0	0	0	0	0	0	3	.000	.000	.000	-99	-1	0	0	0	.000	0	H	-0.1
1964	NY-N	80	224	27	51	8	0	9	22	28	55	.228	.322	.384	100	0	1	2	-1	.985	-2	O-63	-0.5
1966	NY-N	65	199	24	49	14	2	5	32	17	46	.246	.306	.412	100	-0	0	1	-1	.912	0	O-54	-0.3
Total	4	157	437	53	103	22	2	15	56	45	105	.236	.311	.398	99	-1	1	3	-2	.956	-2	O-120	-0.9

■ ALLEN ELLIOTT Elliott, Allen Clifford "Ace" b: 12/25/1897, St.Louis, Mo. d: 5/6/79, St.Louis, Mo. BL/TR, 6', 170 lbs. Deb: 6/14/23

YEAR	TM/L	G	AB	R	H	2B	3B	HR	RBI	BB	SO	AVG	OBP	SLG	PRO+	BR/A	SB	CS	SBR	FA	FR	G/POS	TPR
1923	Chi-N	53	168	21	42	8	2	2	29	2	12	.250	.267	.357	63	-9	3	3	-1	.992	-2	1-52	-1.4
1924	Chi-N	10	14	0	2	0	0	0	0	0	1	.143	.143	.143	-23	-2	0	0	0	1.000	-0	1-10	-0.3
Total	2	63	182	21	44	8	2	2	29	2	13	.242	.258	.341	57	-12	3	3	-1	.992	-2	/1-62	-1.7

■ CARTER ELLIOTT Elliott, Carter Ward b: 11/29/1893, Atchison, Kan. d: 5/21/59, Palm Springs, Cal. BL/TR, 5'11", 165 lbs. Deb: 9/10/21

YEAR	TM/L	G	AB	R	H	2B	3B	HR	RBI	BB	SO	AVG	OBP	SLG	PRO+	BR/A	SB	CS	SBR	FA	FR	G/POS	TPR
1921	Chi-N	12	28	5	7	2	0	0	0	5	3	.250	.364	.321	83	-0	0	0	0	.964	4	S-10	0.4

■ GENE ELLIOTT Elliott, Eugene Birminghouse b: 2/8/1889, Fayette Co., Pa. d: 1/5/76, Huntingdon, Pa. BL/TR, 5'7", 150 lbs. Deb: 4/13/11

YEAR	TM/L	G	AB	R	H	2B	3B	HR	RBI	BB	SO	AVG	OBP	SLG	PRO+	BR/A	SB	CS	SBR	FA	FR	G/POS	TPR
1911	NY-A	5	13	1	1	1	0	0	1	2		.077	.200	.154	-1	-2	0			.000	-1	/O-2,3-1	-0.3

■ ROWDY ELLIOTT Elliott, Harold B. b: 7/8/1890, Kokomo, Ind. d: 2/12/34, San Francisco, Cal. BR/TR, 5'9", 160 lbs. Deb: 9/24/10

YEAR	TM/L	G	AB	R	H	2B	3B	HR	RBI	BB	SO	AVG	OBP	SLG	PRO+	BR/A	SB	CS	SBR	FA	FR	G/POS	TPR
1910	Bos-N	3	2	0	0	0	0	0	0	0	0	.000	.000	.000	-96	-0	0			1.000	-0	/C-1	-0.1
1916	Chi-N	23	55	5	14	3	0	0	3	3	5	.255	.293	.309	77	-2	1			.969	-1	C-18	-0.1
1917	Chi-N	85	223	18	56	8	5	0	28	11	11	.251	.292	.332	84	-4	4			.969	4	C-73	0.5
1918	Chi-N	5	10	0	0	0	0	0	0	2	1	.000	.167	.000	-47	-2	0			.952	0	/C-5	-0.1
1920	Bro-N	41	112	13	27	4	0	1	13	3	6	.241	.267	.304	62	-6	0	0	0	.964	5	C-39	0.1
Total	5	157	402	36	97	15	5	1	44	19	23	.241	.281	.311	73	-14	5	0		.967	7	C-136	0.3

■ HARRY ELLIOTT Elliott, Harry Lewis b: 12/30/23, San Francisco, Cal BR/TR, 5'9", 175 lbs. Deb: 8/1/53

YEAR	TM/L	G	AB	R	H	2B	3B	HR	RBI	BB	SO	AVG	OBP	SLG	PRO+	BR/A	SB	CS	SBR	FA	FR	G/POS	TPR
1953	StL-N	24	59	6	15	6	1	1	6	3	8	.254	.302	.441	91	-1	0	0	0	1.000	1	O-17	-0.1
1955	StL-N	68	117	9	30	4	0	1	12	11	9	.256	.326	.316	71	-5	0	2	-1	.978	-2	O-28	-0.9
Total	2	92	176	15	45	10	1	2	18	14	17	.256	.318	.358	78	-6	0	2	-1	.988	-2	/O-45	-1.0

■ RANDY ELLIOTT Elliott, Randy Lee b: 6/5/51, Oxnard, Cal. BR/TR, 6'2", 190 lbs. Deb: 9/10/72

YEAR	TM/L	G	AB	R	H	2B	3B	HR	RBI	BB	SO	AVG	OBP	SLG	PRO+	BR/A	SB	CS	SBR	FA	FR	G/POS	TPR
1972	SD-N	14	49	5	10	3	1	0	6	2	11	.204	.235	.306	57	-3	0	0	0	1.000	1	O-13	-0.3
1974	SD-N	13	33	5	7	1	0	1	2	7	9	.212	.350	.333	96	0	0	1	-1	1.000	-2	O-11/1-1	-0.4
1977	SF-N	73	167	17	40	5	1	7	26	8	24	.240	.278	.407	82	-5	0	2	-1	.973	1	O-46	-0.7
1980	Oak-A	14	39	4	5	3	0	0	1	1	13	.128	.150	.205	-4	-6	0	0	0	.000	0	D-11	-0.6
Total	4	114	288	31	62	12	2	8	35	18	57	.215	.264	.354	69	-14	0	3	-2	.982	-1	/O-70,D-11,1-1	-2.0

■ BOB ELLIOTT Elliott, Robert Irving "Mr. Team" b: 11/26/16, San Francisco, Cal. d: 5/4/66, San Diego, Cal. BR/TR, 6', 185 lbs. Deb: 9/2/39 MC

YEAR	TM/L	G	AB	R	H	2B	3B	HR	RBI	BB	SO	AVG	OBP	SLG	PRO+	BR/A	SB	CS	SBR	FA	FR	G/POS	TPR
1939	Pit-N	32	129	18	43	10	3	3	19	9	4	.333	.377	.527	143	7	0			.978	3	O-30	0.9
1940	Pit-N	148	551	88	161	34	11	5	64	45	28	.292	.348	.421	112	9	13			.978	2	*O-147	0.3
1941	Pit-N★	141	527	74	144	24	10	3	76	64	52	.273	.353	.374	105	5	6			.970	2	*O-139	-0.2
1942	Pit-N★	143	560	75	166	26	7	9	89	52	35	.296	.358	.416	123	16	2			.927	-2	*3-142/O-1	1.7
1943	Pit-N	156	581	82	183	30	12	7	101	56	24	.315	.376	.444	132	23	4			.949	-8	*3-151/2-2,S-1	1.9
1944	Pit-N★	143	538	85	160	28	16	10	108	75	42	.297	.383	.465	132	24	9			.944	-1	*3-140/S-1	2.5

YEAR	TM/L	G	AB	R	H	2B	3B	HR	RBI	BB	SO	AVG	OBP	SLG	PRO+	BR/A	SB	CS	SBR	FA	FR	G/POS	TPR
1945	Pit-N†	144	541	80	157	36	6	8	108	64	38	.290	.366	.423	115	11	5			.928	8	3-81,O-61	1.8
1946	Pit-N	140	486	50	128	25	3	5	68	64	44	.263	.351	.358	99	1	6			.995	3	O-92,3-43	0.0
1947	Bos-N†	150	555	93	176	35	5	22	113	87	60	.317	.410	.517	148	40	3			**.956**	-2	*3-148	3.7
1948	*Bos-N★	151	540	99	153	24	5	23	100	**131**	57	.283	.423	.474	145	40	6			.945	-10	*3-150	2.8
1949	Bos-N	139	482	77	135	29	5	17	76	90	38	.280	.395	.467	138	28	0			.963	11	*3-130	3.5
1950	Bos-N	142	531	94	162	28	5	24	107	68	67	.305	.386	.512	143	33	2			.952	-17	*3-137	1.3
1951	Bos-N★	136	480	73	137	29	2	15	70	65	56	.285	.371	.448	128	19	2	0	1	.941	-8	*3-127	1.1
1952	NY-N	98	272	33	62	6	2	10	35	36	20	.228	.323	.375	92	-3	1	0	0	.978	-6	O-65,3-13	-1.1
1953	StL-A	48	160	19	40	7	1	5	29	30	18	.250	.368	.400	105	2	0	1	-1	.954	-2	3-45	-0.1
	Chi-A	67	208	24	54	11	1	4	32	31	21	.260	.358	.380	96	-0	1	1	-0	.963	-11	3-58/O-2	-1.3
	Yr	115	368	43	94	18	2	9	61	61	39	.255	.363	.389	100	1	1	2	-1	.959	-12	*3-103/O-2	-1.4
Total	15	1978	7141	1064	2061	382	94	170	1195	967	604	.289	.375	.440	124	252	60	2		.947	-38	*3-1365,O-537/S-2,2	18.8

■ BEN ELLIS
Ellis, Benjamin Franklin b: 7/1870, New York, N.Y. 5'10", 165 lbs. Deb: 7/16/1896

YEAR	TM/L	G	AB	R	H	2B	3B	HR	RBI	BB	SO	AVG	OBP	SLG	PRO+	BR/A	SB	CS	SBR	FA	FR	G/POS	TPR
1896	Phi-N	4	16	0	1	0	0	0	0	3	6	.063	.211	.063	-26	-3	0			.800	-1	/S-2,3-2	-0.3

■ RUBE ELLIS
Ellis, George William b: 11/17/1885, Downey, Cal. d: 3/13/38, Rivera, Cal. BL/TL, 6', 170 lbs. Deb: 4/15/09

YEAR	TM/L	G	AB	R	H	2B	3B	HR	RBI	BB	SO	AVG	OBP	SLG	PRO+	BR/A	SB	CS	SBR	FA	FR	G/POS	TPR
1909	StL-N	149	575	76	154	10	9	3	46	54		.268	.334	.332	114	9	16			.955	13	*O-145	1.8
1910	StL-N	142	550	87	142	18	8	4	54	62	70	.258	.339	.342	102	2	25			.942	0	*O-141	-0.5
1911	StL-N	155	555	69	139	20	11	2	66	66	64	.250	.332	.337	90	-7	9			.938	1	*O-148	-1.5
1912	StL-N	109	305	47	82	18	2	4	33	34	36	.269	.342	.380	100	-0	6			.929	0	O-76	-0.4
Total	4	555	1985	279	517	66	30	13	199	216	170	.260	.336	.344	101	4	56			.943	14	O-510	-0.6

■ JOHN ELLIS
Ellis, John Charles b: 8/21/48, New London, Conn. BR/TR, 6'2.5", 225 lbs. Deb: 5/17/69

YEAR	TM/L	G	AB	R	H	2B	3B	HR	RBI	BB	SO	AVG	OBP	SLG	PRO+	BR/A	SB	CS	SBR	FA	FR	G/POS	TPR
1969	NY-A	22	62	2	18	4	0	1	8	1	11	.290	.313	.403	103	-0	0	2	-1	.978	1	C-15	0.0
1970	NY-A	78	226	24	56	12	1	7	29	18	47	.248	.309	.403	100	-1	0	1	-1	.992	1	1-53/3-5,C-2	-0.5
1971	NY-A	83	238	16	58	12	1	3	34	23	42	.244	.326	.340	95	-2	0	0	0	.990	-3	1-65/C-2	-1.1
1972	NY-A	52	136	13	40	5	1	5	25	8	22	.294	.333	.456	138	6	0	0	0	.965	1	C-25/1-8	0.8
1973	Cle-A	127	437	59	118	12	2	14	68	46	57	.270	.344	.403	108	5	0	0	0	.980	-18	C-72,D-38,1-12	-1.2
1974	Cle-A	128	477	58	136	23	6	10	64	32	53	.285	.331	.421	116	9	1	2	-1	.992	-8	1-69,C-42,D-21	-0.4
1975	Cle-A	92	296	22	68	11	1	7	32	14	33	.230	.269	.345	72	-12	0	1	-1	.976	-8	C-84/1-2,D-3	-1.7
1976	Tex-A	11	31	4	13	2	0	1	8	0	4	.419	.419	.581	187	3	0	0	0	1.000	-1	/C-7,D-3	0.2
1977	Tex-A	49	119	7	28	7	0	4	15	8	26	.235	.283	.395	82	-3	0	0	0	1.000	-2	C-16,D-15/1-8	-0.6
1978	Tex-A	34	94	7	23	4	0	3	17	6	20	.245	.290	.383	88	-2	0	1	-1	.958	-2	C-22/D-7	-0.4
1979	Tex-A	111	316	33	90	12	0	12	61	15	55	.285	.321	.437	103	1	2	2	-1	.978	-3	D-62,1-30/C-7	-0.7
1980	Tex-A	73	182	12	43	9	1	1	23	14	23	.236	.294	.313	69	-8	3	0	1	.992	-2	1-39,D-20/C-3	-1.2
1981	Tex-A	23	58	2	8	3	0	1	7	5	10	.138	.219	.241	34	-5	0	1	-1	.993	-1	1-18/D-1	-0.8
Total	13	883	2672	259	699	116	13	69	391	190	403	.262	.315	.392	99	-10	6	10	-4	.989	-46	1-304,C-297,D/3	-7.6

■ ROB ELLIS
Ellis, Robert Walter b: 7/3/50, Grand Rapids, Mich. BR/TR, 5'11", 180 lbs. Deb: 6/18/71

YEAR	TM/L	G	AB	R	H	2B	3B	HR	RBI	BB	SO	AVG	OBP	SLG	PRO+	BR/A	SB	CS	SBR	FA	FR	G/POS	TPR
1971	Mil-A	36	111	9	22	2	0	0	6	12	24	.198	.282	.216	43	-8	0	2	-1	.923	-7	3-19,O-15	-1.9
1974	Mil-A	22	48	4	14	2	0	0	4	4	11	.292	.346	.333	97	-0	0	0	0	1.000	-1	O-11/3-1,D-9	-0.1
1975	Mil-A	6	7	3	2	0	0	0	0	0	0	.286	.286	.286	62	-0	0	0	0	1.000	-2	/O-5,D-1	-0.2
Total	3	64	166	16	38	4	0	0	10	16	35	.229	.301	.253	59	-8	0	2	-1	.976	-10	/O-31,3-20,D-10	-2.2

■ BABE ELLISON
Ellison, Herbert Spencer "Bert" b: 11/15/1895, Rutland, Ark. d: 8/11/55, San Francisco, Cal BR/TR, 5'11", 170 lbs. Deb: 9/18/16

YEAR	TM/L	G	AB	R	H	2B	3B	HR	RBI	BB	SO	AVG	OBP	SLG	PRO+	BR/A	SB	CS	SBR	FA	FR	G/POS	TPR
1916	Det-A	2	7	0	1	0	0	0	1	0	1	.143	.143	.143	-14	-1	0			1.000	-1	/3-2	-0.3
1917	Det-A	9	29	2	5	1	2	1	4	6	3	.172	.333	.448	139	1	0			.980	-2	/1-9	-0.1
1918	Det-A	7	23	1	6	1	0	0	2	3	1	.261	.346	.304	100	0	1			1.000	-0	/O-4,2-3	0.0
1919	Det-A	56	134	18	29	4	0	0	11	13	24	.216	.291	.246	53	-8	4			.966	-7	2-25,O-10/S-1	-1.5
1920	Det-A	61	155	11	34	7	2	0	21	8	26	.219	.258	.290	46	-12	4	1	1	.997	2	1-38/O-4,3-1	-1.1
Total	5	135	348	32	75	13	4	1	39	30	55	.216	.282	.284	58	-20	9	1		.994	-9	/1-47,2-28,O-18,3S	-3.0

■ VERDO ELMORE
Elmore, Verdo Wilson "Ellie" b: 12/10/1899, Gordo, Ala. d: 8/5/69, Birmingham, Ala. BL/TR, 5'11", 185 lbs. Deb: 9/11/24

YEAR	TM/L	G	AB	R	H	2B	3B	HR	RBI	BB	SO	AVG	OBP	SLG	PRO+	BR/A	SB	CS	SBR	FA	FR	G/POS	TPR
1924	StL-A	7	17	2	3	3	0	0	0	1	3	.176	.222	.353	44	-2	0	0	0	.000	-2	/O-3	-0.3

■ ROY ELSH
Elsh, Eugene Reybold b: 3/1/1892, Penns Grove, N.J. d: 11/12/78, Philadelphia, Pa. BR/TR, 5'9", 165 lbs. Deb: 4/19/23

YEAR	TM/L	G	AB	R	H	2B	3B	HR	RBI	BB	SO	AVG	OBP	SLG	PRO+	BR/A	SB	CS	SBR	FA	FR	G/POS	TPR
1923	Chi-A	81	209	28	52	7	2	0	24	16	23	.249	.305	.301	61	-12	16	8	0	.957	1	O-57	-1.4
1924	Chi-A	60	147	21	45	9	1	0	11	10	14	.306	.350	.381	91	-2	6	1	1	.953	-6	O-38/1-2	-0.8
1925	Chi-A	32	48	6	9	1	0	0	4	5	7	.188	.264	.208	22	-6	2	0	1	.964	-1	O-16/1-3	-0.6
Total	3	173	404	55	106	17	3	0	39	31	44	.262	.317	.319	67	-20	24	9	2	.957	-6	O-111/1-5	-2.8

■ KEVIN ELSTER
Elster, Kevin Daniel b: 8/3/64, San Pedro, Cal. BR/TR, 6'2", 200 lbs. Deb: 9/2/86

YEAR	TM/L	G	AB	R	H	2B	3B	HR	RBI	BB	SO	AVG	OBP	SLG	PRO+	BR/A	SB	CS	SBR	FA	FR	G/POS	TPR
1986	*NY-N	19	30	3	5	1	0	0	0	3	8	.167	.242	.200	24	-3	0	0	0	.962	4	S-19	0.2
1987	NY-N	5	10	1	4	2	0	0	1	0	1	.400	.400	.600	169	1	0	0	0	.909	-0	/S-3	0.1
1988	*NY-N	149	406	41	87	11	1	9	37	35	47	.214	.282	.313	74	-14	2	0	1	.977	5	*S-148	0.2
1989	NY-N	151	458	52	106	25	2	10	55	34	77	.231	.287	.360	88	-8	4	3	-1	.976	7	*S-150	1.0
1990	NY-N	92	314	36	65	20	1	9	45	30	54	.207	.278	.363	75	-11	2	0	1	.960	15	S-92	1.1
1991	NY-N	115	348	33	84	16	2	6	36	40	53	.241	.321	.351	90	-4	2	3	-1	.970	11	*S-107	1.3
1992	NY-N	6	18	0	4	0	0	0	0	0	2	.222	.222	.222	27	-2	0	0	0	1.000	-1	/S-5	-0.2
1994	NY-A	7	20	0	0	0	0	0	0	1	6	.000	.048	.000	-90	-6	0	0	0	1.000	5	/S-7	-0.1
1995	NY-A	10	17	1	2	1	0	0	0	1	5	.118	.167	.176	-11	-3	0	0	0	1.000	1	S-10/2-1	-0.1
	Phi-N	26	53	10	11	4	1	1	9	7	14	.208	.311	.377	80	-2	0	0	0	.982	-0	S-19/1-4,3-2	-0.1
1996	*Tex-A	157	515	79	130	32	2	24	99	52	138	.252	.323	.462	91	-9	4	1	1	.981	4	*S-157	0.8
1997	Pit-N	39	138	14	31	6	2	7	25	21	39	.225	.331	.449	100	-0	0	2	-1	.994	2	S-39	0.4
1998	Tex-A	84	297	33	69	10	1	8	37	33	66	.232	.313	.354	70	-13	0	2	-1	.976	-5	S-84	-1.1
Total	12	860	2624	303	598	128	12	74	344	257	510	.228	.300	.370	81	-75	14	11	-2	.975	47	S-840/1-4,3-2,2-1	3.5

■ BONES ELY
Ely, William Frederick b: 6/7/1863, N.Girard, Pa. d: 1/10/52, Berkeley, Cal. BR/TR, 6'1", 155 lbs. Deb: 6/19/1884

YEAR	TM/L	G	AB	R	H	2B	3B	HR	RBI	BB	SO	AVG	OBP	SLG	PRO+	BR/A	SB	CS	SBR	FA	FR	G/POS	TPR
1884	Buf-N	1	4	0	0	0	0	0	0	0	2	.000	.000	.000	-97	-1				.000	-1	/O-1,P-1	-0.1
1886	Lou-a	10	32	5	5	0	0	0	6	2		.156	.206	.156	13	-3	1			1.000	-0	/P-6,O-5	-0.2
1890	Syr-a	119	496	72	130	16	6	0	64	31		.262	.308	.319	95	-4	44			.915	19	O-78,S-36/1-4,23P	1.3
1891	Bro-N	31	111	9	17	0	1	0	11	7	9	.153	.203	.171	9	-13	4			.870	8	S-28/3-2,2-1	-0.3
1893	StL-N	44	178	25	45	1	6	0	16	17	13	.253	.318	.326	71	-8	2			.905	-3	S-44	-0.7
1894	StL-N	127	510	85	156	20	12	12	89	30	34	.306	.344	.463	93	-9	23			.901	1	*S-126/2-1,P-1	-0.1
1895	StL-N	117	467	68	121	16	2	1	46	19	17	.259	.288	.308	55	-32	28			.925	6	*S-117	-1.7
1896	Pit-N	128	537	85	153	15	9	3	77	33	33	.285	.326	.363	85	-12	18			.918	-2	*S-128	-0.8
1897	Pit-N	133	516	63	146	20	8	2	74	25		.283	.317	.364	83	-14	10			.927	3	*S-133	-0.7
1898	Pit-N	148	519	49	110	14	5	2	44	24		.212	.247	.270	49	-36	6			**.943**	8	*S-148	-2.0
1899	Pit-N	138	522	66	145	18	6	3	72	22		.278	.313	.352	83	-14	8			.928	3	*S-132/2-6	0.0
1900	*Pit-N	130	475	60	116	6	6	0	51	17		.244	.272	.282	53	-31	6			.935	13	*S-130	-0.8
1901	Pit-N	65	240	18	50	6	3	0	28	6		.208	.234	.258	41	-18	5			.916	-8	S-64/3-1	-2.1
	Phi-A	45	171	11	37	6	2	0	16	3		.216	.230	.275	38	-15	6			.913	1	S-45	-0.9
1902	Was-A	105	381	39	100	11	2	1	62	21		.262	.301	.310	69	-16	3			.923	-9	*S-105	-1.8
Total	14	1341	5159	655	1331	149	68	24	656	257	108	.258	.295	.327	70	-225	164			.923	39	*S-1236/O-84,2P31	-10.9

■ CHESTER EMERSON
Emerson, Chester Arthur "Chuck" b: 10/27/1889, Stow, Me. d: 7/2/71, Augusta, Me. BL/TR, 5'8", 165 lbs. Deb: 9/27/11

YEAR	TM/L	G	AB	R	H	2B	3B	HR	RBI	BB	SO	AVG	OBP	SLG	PRO+	BR/A	SB	CS	SBR	FA	FR	G/POS	TPR
1911	Phi-A	7	18	2	4	0	0	0	0	6		.222	.417	.222	82	0	1			1.000	1	/O-7	0.0
1912	Phi-A	1	1	0	0	0	0	0	0	0		.000	.000	.000	-99	-0	0			.000	0	H	0.0
Total	2	8	19	2	4	0	0	0	0	6		.211	.400	.211	74	-0	1			1.000	1	/O-7	0.0

YEAR	TM/L	G	AB	R	H	2B	3B	HR	RBI	BB	SO	AVG	OBP	SLG	PRO+	BR/A	SB	CS	SBR	FA	FR	G/POS	TPR
■ **CAL EMERY** Emery, Calvin Wayne b: 6/28/37, Centre Hall, Pa. BL/TL, 6'2", 205 lbs. Deb: 7/15/63 C																							
1963	Phi-N	16	19	0	3	1	0	0	0	0	2	.158	.158	.211	5	-2	0	0	0	1.000	-0	/1-2	-0.3
■ **SPOKE EMERY** Emery, Herrick Smith b: 12/10/1898, Bay City, Mich. d: 6/2/75, Cape Canaveral, Fla. BR/TR, 5'9", 165 lbs. Deb: 7/18/24																							
1924	Phi-N	5	3	3	2	0	0	0	0	0	0	.667	.667	.667	230	1	0	1	-1	1.000	-0	/O-1	0.0
■ **FRANK EMMER** Emmer, Frank William b: 2/17/1896, Crestline, Ohio d: 10/18/63, Homestead, Fla. BR/TR, 5'8", 150 lbs. Deb: 4/25/16																							
1916	Cin-N	42	89	8	13	3	1	0	2	7	27	.146	.208	.202	27	-8	1			.899	5	S-29/O-2,2-1,3-1	-0.2
1926	Cin-N	80	224	22	44	7	6	0	18	13	30	.196	.244	.281	42	-19	1			.918	-7	S-79	-1.9
Total	2	122	313	30	57	10	7	0	20	20	57	.182	.234	.259	38	-26	2			.913	-3	S-108/O-2,3-1,2-1	-2.1
■ **BOB EMMERICH** Emmerich, Robert George b: 8/1/1897, New York, N.Y. d: 11/22/48, Bridgeport, Conn. BR/TR, 5'3", 155 lbs. Deb: 9/22/23																							
1923	Bos-N	13	24	3	2	0	0	0	0	2	3	.083	.154	.083	-37	-5	1	1	-0	1.000	-1	/O-8	-0.6
■ **ANGELO ENCARNACION** Encarnacion, Angelo Benjamin b: 4/18/73, Santo Domingo, D.R. BR/TR, 5'8", 180 lbs. Deb: 5/2/95																							
1995	Pit-N	58	159	18	36	7	2	2	10	13	28	.226	.285	.333	61	-9	1	1	-0	.979	6	C-55	0.0
1996	Pit-N	7	22	3	7	2	0	0	1	0	5	.318	.318	.409	88	-0	0	0	0	.951	-1	/C-7	-0.1
1997	Ana-A	11	17	2	7	1	0	1	4	0	1	.412	.412	.647	171	2	2	0	1	.940	3	C-11	0.5
Total	3	76	198	23	50	10	2	3	15	13	34	.253	.299	.369	73	-8	3	1	0	.971	9	/C-73	0.4
■ **JUAN ENCARNACION** Encarnacion, Juan De Dios b: 3/8/76, Las Matas De Faran, D.R. BR/TR, 6'2", 160 lbs. Deb: 9/2/97																							
1997	Det-A	11	33	3	7	1	1	1	5	3	12	.212	.316	.394	84	-1	3	1	0	1.000	-1	O-10	-0.1
1998	Det-A	40	164	30	54	9	4	7	21	7	31	.329	.360	.561	134	8	7	4	-0	.985	-4	O-39/D-1	0.3
Total	2	51	197	33	61	10	5	8	26	10	43	.310	.352	.533	126	7	10	5	0	.989	-4	/O-49,D-1	0.2
■ **BILL ENDICOTT** Endicott, William Franklin b: 9/4/18, Acorn, Mo. BL/TL, 5'11.5", 175 lbs. Deb: 4/21/46																							
1946	StL-N	20	20	2	4	3	0	0	3	4	4	.200	.333	.350	90	-0	0			1.000	-0	/O-2	0.0
■ **CLYDE ENGLE** Engle, Arthur Clyde "Hack" b: 3/19/1884, Dayton, Ohio d: 12/26/39, Boston, Mass. BR/TR, 5'10", 190 lbs. Deb: 4/12/09																							
1909	NY-A	135	492	66	137	20	5	3	71	47		.278	.347	.358	122	13	18			.946	14	*O-134	2.4
1910	NY-A	5	13	0	3	0	0	0	0	2		.231	.333	.231	73	-0	1			.857	-0	/O-3	-0.1
	Bos-A	106	363	59	96	18	7	2	38	31		.264	.326	.369	115	5	12			.915	0	3-51,2-27,O-15,/S-7	0.7
	Yr	111	376	59	99	18	7	2	38	33		.263	.326	.364	113	5	13			.915	-0	3-51,2-27,O-18,/S-7	0.6
1911	Bos-A	146	514	58	139	13	3	2	48	51		.270	.343	.319	86	-8	24			.975	-4	1-65,3-51,2-13,O-10	-1.2
1912	*Bos-A	58	171	32	40	5	3	0	18	28		.234	.348	.298	81	-3	12			.977	-8	1-25,2-15,3-11,/SO	-1.2
1913	Bos-A	143	498	75	144	17	12	2	50	53	41	.289	.363	.384	116	10	28			.987	-7	*1-133/O-2	0.1
1914	Bos-A	59	134	14	26	2	0	0	9	14	11	.194	.275	.209	46	-8	4	9	-4	.976	-4	1-29/2-5,3-3,O-1	-2.0
	Buf-F	32	110	12	28	4	1	0	12	11	18	.255	.328	.309	73	-6	5			.889	-7	3-23/O-9	-1.3
1915	Buf-F	141	501	56	131	22	8	3	71	34	43	.261	.312	.355	86	-17	24			.969	-3	*O-100,2-21,3-17,/1	-2.7
1916	Cle-A	11	26	1	4	0	0	0	1	0	6	.154	.154	.154	-7	-3	0			.810	-2	/3-7,1-2,O-1	-0.6
Total	8	836	2822	373	748	101	39	12	318	271	119	.265	.335	.341	97	-19	128	9		.959	-21	O-276,1-255,3/2S	-5.9
■ **CHARLIE ENGLE** Engle, Charlie August "Cholly" b: 8/27/03, New York, N.Y. d: 10/12/83, San Antonio, Tex. BR/TR, 5'8", 145 lbs. Deb: 9/14/25																							
1925	Phi-A	1	0	0	0	0	0	0	0	0	0	—	—	—	—	0	0	0	0	.000	0	/S-1	0.0
1926	Phi-A	19	19	7	2	0	0	0	0	10	6	.105	.433	.105	43	-1	0	0	0	.930	2	S-16	0.2
1930	Pit-N	67	216	34	57	10	1	0	15	22	20	.264	.335	.319	59	-14	1			.975	-1	3-24,S-23,2-10	-0.9
Total	3	87	235	41	59	10	1	0	15	32	26	.251	.346	.302	59	-15	1	0		.937	2	/S-40,3-24,2-10	-0.7
■ **DAVE ENGLE** Engle, Ralph David b: 11/30/56, San Diego, Cal. BR/TR, 6'3", 216 lbs. Deb: 4/14/81 C																							
1981	Min-A	82	248	29	64	14	4	5	32	13	37	.258	.298	.407	95	-2	0	1	-1	.980	-0	O-76/3-1,D-1	-0.6
1982	Min-A	58	186	20	42	7	2	4	16	10	22	.226	.269	.349	67	-9	0	0	0	.985	0	O-34,D-20	-1.0
1983	Min-A	120	374	46	114	22	4	8	43	28	39	.305	.355	.449	115	8	2	1	0	.973	-19	C-73,D-29/O-4	-0.9
1984	Min-A☆	109	391	56	104	20	1	4	38	26	22	.266	.312	.353	80	-11	0	1	-1	.981	-7	C-86,D-22	-1.5
1985	Min-A	70	172	28	44	8	2	7	25	21	28	.256	.337	.448	106	1	2	2	-1	.984	-0	D-38,C-17/O-3	0.0
1986	Det-A	35	86	6	22	7	0	0	4	7	13	.256	.312	.337	77	-3	0	0	0	1.000	-1	1-23/O-4,C-3,D-5	-0.5
1987	Mon-N	59	84	7	19	4	0	1	14	6	11	.226	.278	.310	54	-6	1	0	0	1.000	0	O-11/C-6,1-2,3-1	-0.6
1988	Mon-N	34	37	4	8	3	0	0	1	5	5	.216	.310	.297	72	-1	0	0	0	1.000	-1	/C-9,O-4,3-1	-0.2
1989	Mil-A	27	65	5	14	3	0	2	8	4	13	.215	.261	.354	72	-3	0	0	0	.973	0	1-18/C-3,D-3	-0.4
Total	9	594	1643	201	431	88	13	31	181	120	190	.262	.314	.388	90	-25	5	5	-2	.979	-29	C-197,O-136,D/13	-5.7
■ **CHARLIE ENGLISH** English, Charles Dewie b: 4/8/10, Darlington, S.C. BR/TR, 5'9.5", 160 lbs. Deb: 7/23/32																							
1932	Chi-A	24	63	7	20	3	1	1	8	3	7	.317	.348	.444	111	1	0	0	0	.821	-2	3-13/S-1	-0.1
1933	Chi-A	3	9	2	4	2	0	0	1	1	1	.444	.500	.667	216	2	0	0	0	.923	-1	/2-3	0.1
1936	NY-N	6	1	0	0	0	0	0	0	0	0	.000	.000	.000	-99	-0	0			.000	0	/2-1	0.0
1937	Cin-N	17	63	1	15	3	1	0	4	0	2	.238	.238	.317	52	-4	0			.958	2	3-15/2-2	-0.2
Total	4	50	136	10	39	8	2	1	13	4	10	.287	.307	.397	90	-2	0	0		.897	-2	/3-28,2-6,S-1	-0.2
■ **WOODY ENGLISH** English, Elwood George b: 3/2/07, Fredonia, Ohio d: 9/26/97, Newark, Ohio BR/TR, 5'10", 155 lbs. Deb: 4/26/27																							
1927	Chi-N	87	334	46	97	14	4	1	28	16	26	.290	.325	.365	84	-8	1			.940	7	S-84/3-1	0.7
1928	Chi-N	116	475	68	142	22	4	2	34	30	28	.299	.343	.375	89	-8	4			.946	6	*S-114/3-2	1.1
1929	*Chi-N	144	608	131	168	29	3	1	52	68	50	.276	.352	.339	72	-25	13			.955	15	*S-144	0.8
1930	Chi-N	156	638	152	214	36	17	14	59	100	72	.335	.430	.511	125	30	3			.973	-13	3-83,S-78	2.7
1931	Chi-N	156	634	117	202	38	8	2	53	68	80	.319	.391	.413	114	15	12			.965	1	*S-138,3-18	3.1
1932	*Chi-N	127	522	70	142	23	7	3	47	55	73	.272	.344	.360	90	-6	5			.957	-2	3-93,S-38	0.1
1933	Chi-N★	105	398	54	104	19	2	3	41	53	44	.261	.348	.342	98	1	5			**.973**	-15	*3-103/S-1	-0.8
1934	Chi-N	109	421	65	117	26	5	3	31	48	65	.278	.353	.385	99	1	6			.971	-10	S-56,3-46/2-7	-0.4
1935	Chi-N	34	84	11	17	2	0	2	8	20	4	.202	.368	.298	81	-1	1			.868	-5	3-16,S-12	-0.5
1936	Chi-N	64	182	33	45	9	0	0	20	40	28	.247	.394	.297	86	-1	1			.976	1	S-42,3-17/2-1	0.3
1937	Bro-N	129	378	45	90	16	2	1	42	65	55	.238	.350	.299	77	-10	4			.956	-17	*S-116,2-11	-1.9
1938	Bro-N	34	72	9	18	2	0	0	7	8	11	.250	.333	.278	68	-3	2			.958	1	3-21/2-3,S-3	-0.2
Total	12	1261	4746	801	1356	236	52	32	422	571	536	.286	.366	.378	95	-14	57			.957	-31	S-826,3-400/2-22	5.0
■ **GIL ENGLISH** English, Gilbert Raymond b: 7/2/09, Glenola, N.C. d: 8/31/96, Trinity, N.C. BR/TR, 5'11", 180 lbs. Deb: 9/20/31																							
1931	NY-N	3	8	0	0	0	0	0	0	1	3	.000	.111	.000	-69	-2	0			1.000	-1	/3-3	-0.3
1932	NY-N	59	204	22	46	7	5	2	19	5	20	.225	.244	.338	56	-13	0			.931	4	3-39,S-23	-0.5
1936	Det-A	1	1	0	0	0	0	0	0	0	1	.000	.000	.000	-99	-0	0	0	0	1.000	0	/3-1	0.0
1937	Det-A	18	65	6	17	1	0	1	6	6	4	.262	.333	.323	65	-3	1	1	-0	.962	-8	2-12/3-6	-1.0
	Bos-N	79	269	25	78	5	2	2	37	23	27	.290	.348	.346	98	-1	3			.958	-7	3-71	-0.6
1938	Bos-N	53	165	17	41	6	0	2	21	15	16	.248	.315	.321	84	-4	1			.956	-4	3-43/O-3,2-2,S-2	-0.7
1944	Bro-N	27	79	4	12	3	0	1	7	6	7	.152	.212	.228	24	-8	0			.918	-3	S-13,3-11/2-2	-1.1
Total	6	240	791	74	194	22	7	8	90	56	78	.245	.298	.321	72	-31	5	1		.950	-18	3-174/S-38,2-16,O-3	-4.2
■ **DEL ENNIS** Ennis, Delmer b: 6/8/25, Philadelphia, Pa. d: 2/8/96, Huntingdon Valley, Pa. BR/TR, 6', 195 lbs. Deb: 4/28/46																							
1946	Phi-N★	141	540	70	169	30	6	17	73	39	65	.313	.364	.485	144	28	5			.975	14	*O-138	3.7
1947	Phi-N	139	541	71	149	25	6	12	81	37	51	.275	.325	.410	98	-4	9			.979	9	*O-135	-0.1
1948	Phi-N	152	589	86	171	40	4	30	95	47	58	.290	.345	.525	135	25	2			.957	5	*O-151	2.2
1949	Phi-N	154	610	92	184	39	11	25	110	59	61	.302	.367	.525	140	32	2			.966	6	*O-154	3.0
1950	*Phi-N	153	595	92	185	34	8	31	**126**	56	59	.311	.372	.551	142	34	2			.970	-1	*O-149	2.5
1951	Phi-N★	144	532	76	142	20	5	15	73	68	42	.267	.352	.408	105	5	4	2	0	.969	-1	*O-135	-0.2
1952	Phi-N	151	592	90	171	30	10	20	107	47	65	.289	.341	.475	125	18	6	4	-1	.970	-1	*O-149	1.0
1953	Phi-N	152	578	79	165	22	3	29	125	57	53	.285	.355	.484	117	13	1	3	-2	.980	4	*O-150	0.9
1954	Phi-N	145	556	73	145	23	2	25	119	50	60	.261	.324	.444	98	-3	2	1	0	.957	3	*O-142/1-1	-0.6

YEAR	TM/L	G	AB	R	H	2B	3B	HR	RBI	BB	SO	AVG	OBP	SLG	PRO+	BR/A	SB	CS	SBR	FA	FR	G/POS	TPR
1955	Phi-N★	146	564	82	167	24	7	29	120	46	46	.296	.351	.518	129	22	4	2	0	.987	6	*O-145	2.0
1956	Phi-N	153	630	80	164	23	3	26	95	33	62	.260	.300	.430	95	-6	7	3	0	.962	0	*O-153	-1.5
1957	StL-N	136	490	61	140	24	3	24	105	37	50	.286	.337	.494	117	11	1	3	-2	.943	-15	*O-127	-1.3
1958	StL-N	106	329	22	86	18	1	3	47	15	35	.261	.296	.350	67	-15	0	1	-1	.993	3	O-84	-1.7
1959	Cin-N	5	12	1	4	0	0	0	1	2	2	.333	.429	.333	103	0	0	0	0	1.000	-0	/O-3	0.0
	Chi-A	26	96	10	21	6	0	2	7	4	10	.219	.250	.344	62	-5	0	0	0	.909	-3	O-25	-1.0
Total	14	1903	7254	985	2063	358	69	288	1284	597	719	.284	.341	.472	117	154	45	19		.969	28	*O-1840/1-1	8.9
■ **RUSS ENNIS**	Ennis, Russell Elwood "Hack" b: 3/10/1897, Superior, Wis. d: 1/21/49, Superior, Wis. BR/TR, 5'11.5", 160 lbs. Deb: 9/19/26																						
1926	Was-A	1	0	0	0	0	0	0	0	0	0	—	—	—	—	0	0	0	0	.000	0	/C-1	0.0
■ **GEORGE ENRIGHT**	Enright, George Albert b: 5/9/54, New Britain, Conn. BR/TR, 5'11", 175 lbs. Deb: 8/8/76																						
1976	Chi-A	2	1	0	0	0	0	0	0	0	0	.000	.000	.000	-99	-0	0	0	0	1.000	1	/C-2	0.0
■ **MUTZ ENS**	Ens, Anton b: 11/8/1884, St.Louis, Mo. d: 6/28/50, St.Louis, Mo. BL/TL, 6'1", 180 lbs. Deb: 9/2/12 F																						
1912	Chi-A	3	6	0	0	0	0	0	0	0		.000	.000	.000	-99	-2	0			.857	-1	/1-3	-0.2
■ **JEWEL ENS**	Ens, Jewel Winklemeyer b: 8/24/1889, St.Louis, Mo. d: 1/17/50, Syracuse, N.Y. BR/TR, 5'10.5", 165 lbs. Deb: 4/29/22 FMC																						
1922	Pit-N	47	142	18	42	7	3	0	17	7	9	.296	.338	.387	85	-3	3	0	1	.951	-17	2-29/3-3,1-2,S-1	-1.7
1923	Pit-N	12	29	3	8	1	1	0	5	0	3	.276	.276	.379	70	-1	2	0	1	.975	-0	/1-4,3-3	-0.1
1924	Pit-N	5	10	2	3	0	0	0	0	0	3	.300	.300	.300	60	-1	0	0	0	1.000	-0	/1-5	-0.1
1925	Pit-N	3	5	2	1	0	0	1	2	0	1	.200	.200	.800	133	0	0	0	0	1.000	-0	/1-3	0.0
Total	4	67	186	25	54	8	4	1	24	7	16	.290	.323	.392	83	-5	5	0	2	.990	-17	/2-29,1-14,3-6,S-1	-1.9
■ **CHARLIE ENWRIGHT**	Enwright, Charles Massey b: 10/6/1887, Sacramento, Cal. d: 1/19/17, Sacramento, Cal. BL/TR, 5'10", Deb: 4/19/09																						
1909	StL-N	3	7	1	1	0	0	0	1	2		.143	.333	.143	51	-0	0			.444	-3	/S-2	-0.4
■ **JACK ENZENROTH**	Enzenroth, Clarence Herman b: 11/4/1885, Mineral Point, Wis. d: 2/21/44, Detroit, Mich. BR/TR, 5'7", 160 lbs. Deb: 5/1/14																						
1914	StL-A	3	6	0	1	0	0	0	0	2	3	.167	.444	.167	88	0	0	1	-1	.923	-1	/C-3	-0.2
	KC-F	26	67	7	12	4	1	0	5	5	19	.179	.236	.269	39	-7	0			.965	-2	C-24	-0.8
1915	KC-F	14	19	3	3	0	0	0	3	6	0	.158	.360	.158	50	-1	0			.973	2	/C-8	0.1
Total	2	43	92	10	16	4	1	0	8	13	22	.174	.283	.239	47	-8	0	1		.963	-1	/C-35	-0.9
■ **JIM EPPARD**	Eppard, James Gerhard b: 4/27/60, South Bend, Ind. BL/TL, 6'2", 180 lbs. Deb: 9/8/87																						
1987	Cal-A	8	9	2	3	0	0	0	0	2	0	.333	.455	.333	118	0	0	0	0	1.000	-0	/O-1	0.0
1988	Cal-A	56	113	7	32	3	1	0	14	11	15	.283	.347	.327	92	-1	0	0	0	.971	-0	O-17,D-10/1-6	-0.2
1989	Cal-A	12	12	0	3	0	0	0	2	1	4	.250	.308	.250	60	-1	0	0	0	1.000	-0	/1-4	-0.1
1990	Tor-A	6	5	0	1	0	0	0	0	0	2	.200	.333	.200	52	-0	0	0	0	.000	0	/H	0.0
Total	4	82	139	9	39	3	1	0	16	14	21	.281	.351	.317	90	-1	0	0	0	.972	-1	/O-18,1-10,D-10	-0.3
■ **AUBREY EPPS**	Epps, Aubrey Lee "Yo-Yo" b: 3/3/12, Memphis, Tenn. d: 11/13/84, Ackerman, Miss. BR/TR, 5'10", 170 lbs. Deb: 9/29/35																						
1935	Pit-N	1	4	1	3	0	1	0	3	0	0	.750	.750	1.250	414	2	0			.750	-0	/C-1	0.1
■ **HAL EPPS**	Epps, Harold Franklin b: 3/26/14, Athens, Ga. BL/TL, 6', 175 lbs. Deb: 9/9/38																						
1938	StL-N	17	50	8	15	0	0	1	3	2	4	.300	.327	.360	84	-1	2			.963	-0	O-10	-0.2
1940	StL-N	11	15	6	3	0	0	0	1	0	3	.200	.200	.200	10	-2	0			.800	-1	/O-3	-0.3
1943	StL-A	8	35	2	10	4	0	0	1	3	4	.286	.342	.400	114	1	1	1	-0	1.000	-1	/O-8	-0.1
1944	StL-A	22	62	15	11	1	1	0	3	14	14	.177	.338	.226	59	-3	0	1	-1	.962	1	O-18	-0.3
	Phi-A	67	229	27	60	8	8	0	13	18	18	.262	.316	.367	96	-2	2	1	0	.973	-3	O-60	-0.8
	Yr	89	291	42	71	9	9	0	16	32	32	.244	.321	.337	88	-4	2	2	-1	.970	-2	O-78	-1.1
Total	4	125	391	58	99	13	9	1	21	37	43	.253	.319	.340	86	-7	5	3		.968	-4	/O-99	-1.7
■ **MIKE EPSTEIN**	Epstein, Michael Peter "Superjew" b: 4/4/43, Bronx, N.Y. BL/TL, 6'3.5", 230 lbs. Deb: 9/16/66																						
1966	Bal-A	6	11	1	2	0	1	0	3	1	3	.182	.250	.364	75	-0	0	0	0	1.000	0	/1-4	0.0
1967	Bal-A	9	13	0	2	0	0	0	0	3	5	.154	.313	.154	42	-1	0	0	0	1.000	-0	/1-3	-0.1
	Was-A	96	284	32	65	7	4	9	29	38	74	.229	.332	.377	114	5	1	4	-2	.987	-2	1-80	-0.3
	Yr	105	297	32	67	7	4	9	29	41	79	.226	.331	.367	110	5	1	4	-2	.988	-2	1-83	-0.4
1968	Was-A	123	385	40	90	8	2	13	33	48	91	.234	.339	.366	117	9	1	1	-0	.987	1	*1-110	0.3
1969	Was-A	131	403	73	112	18	1	30	85	85	99	.278	.416	.551	178	45	2	5	-2	.990	-1	*1-118	3.4
1970	Was-A	140	430	55	110	15	3	20	56	73	117	.256	.375	.444	131	20	2	3	-1	.992	-3	*1-122	0.5
1971	Was-A	24	85	6	21	1	1	1	9	12	31	.247	.366	.318	101	1	1	0	0	.992	-1	1-24	-0.2
	*Oak-A	104	329	43	77	13	0	18	51	62	71	.234	.368	.438	130	15	0	3	-2	.995	-2	1-96	0.3
	Yr	128	414	49	98	14	1	19	60	74	102	.237	.368	.413	124	15	1	3	-2	.994	-2	*1-120	0.1
1972	*Oak-A	138	455	63	123	18	2	26	70	68	68	.270	.378	.490	166	38	0	1	-1	.990	-2	*1-137	2.6
1973	Tex-A	27	85	9	16	3	0	1	6	14	19	.188	.324	.259	69	-3	0	0	0	.991	-1	1-25	-0.6
	Cal-A	91	312	30	67	8	2	8	32	34	54	.215	.302	.330	84	-7	0	0	0	.993	-0	1-86	-1.4
	Yr	118	397	39	83	11	2	9	38	48	73	.209	.307	.315	81	-10	0	0	0	.993	-1	*1-111	-2.0
1974	Cal-A	18	62	10	10	2	0	4	6	10	13	.161	.288	.387	98	-0	0	0	0	.993	1	1-18	-0.1
Total	9	907	2854	362	695	93	16	130	380	448	645	.244	.360	.424	130	121	7	17	-8	.991	-10	1-823	4.4
■ **JOE ERAUTT**	Erautt, Joseph Michael "Stubby" b: 9/1/21, Vibank, Sask., Can. d: 10/6/76, Portland, Ore. BR/TR, 5'9", 175 lbs. Deb: 5/9/50 F																						
1950	Chi-A	16	18	0	4	0	0	0	1	1	3	.222	.263	.222	26	-2	0	0	0	1.000	1	/C-5	-0.1
1951	Chi-A	16	25	3	4	1	0	0	0	3	2	.160	.276	.200	31	-2	0	0	0	.977	3	C-12	0.1
Total	2	32	43	3	8	1	0	0	1	4	5	.186	.271	.209	29	-4	0	0	0	.983	4	/C-17	0.0
■ **HANK ERICKSON**	Erickson, Henry Nels "Popeye" b: 11/11/07, Chicago, Ill. d: 12/13/64, Louisville, Ky. BR/TR, 6'1", 185 lbs. Deb: 4/17/35																						
1935	Cin-N	37	88	9	23	3	2	1	4	6	4	.261	.323	.375	90	-1	0			.972	2	C-25	0.2
■ **CAL ERMER**	Ermer, Calvin Coolidge b: 11/10/23, Baltimore, Md. BR/TR, 6'0.5", 175 lbs. Deb: 9/26/47 MC																						
1947	Was-A	1	3	0	0	0	0	0	0	0	0	.000	.000	.000	-99	-1	0	0	0	1.000	1	/2-1	0.0
■ **FRANK ERNAGA**	Ernaga, Frank John b: 8/22/30, Susanville, Cal. BR/TR, 6'1", 195 lbs. Deb: 5/24/57																						
1957	Chi-N	20	35	9	11	3	2	2	7	9	14	.314	.455	.686	204	6	0	0	0	.950	-0	O-10	0.5
1958	Chi-N	9	8	0	1	0	0	0	0	0	2	.125	.125	.125	-34	-2	0	0	0	.000	0	H	-0.2
Total	2	29	43	9	12	3	2	2	7	9	16	.279	.404	.581	163	4	0	0	0	.950	-0	/O-10	0.3
■ **DARIN ERSTAD**	Erstad, Darin Charles b: 6/4/74, Jamestown, N.D. BL/TL, 6'2", 195 lbs. Deb: 6/14/96																						
1996	Cal-A	57	208	34	59	5	1	4	20	17	29	.284	.338	.375	80	-6	3	3	-1	.976	3	O-48	-0.5
1997	Ana-A	139	539	99	161	34	4	16	77	51	86	.299	.364	.466	115	12	23	8	2	.990	-8	*1-126/O-1,D-9	-0.7
1998	Ana-A★	133	537	84	159	39	3	19	82	43	77	.296	.355	.486	115	11	20	6	2	.992	-3	O-72,1-70/D-2	0.2
Total	3	329	1284	217	379	78	8	39	179	111	192	.295	.356	.460	109	16	46	17	4	.992	-8	1-196,O-121/D-11	-1.0
■ **TEX ERWIN**	Erwin, Ross Emil b: 12/22/1885, Forney, Tex. d: 4/5/53, Rochester, N.Y. BL/TR, 6', 185 lbs. Deb: 8/26/07																						
1907	Det-A	4	5	0	1	0	0	0	1	1		.200	.333	.200	68	-0	0			.909	0	/C-4	0.0
1910	Bro-N	81	202	15	38	3	1	1	10	24	12	.188	.278	.228	49	-13	3			.949	-1	C-68	-0.8
1911	Bro-N	91	218	30	59	13	2	7	34	31	23	.271	.367	.445	132	9	5			.971	-5	C-74	1.1
1912	Bro-N	59	133	14	28	3	0	2	14	18	16	.211	.305	.278	62	-7	1			.949	-2	C-41	-0.5
1913	Bro-N	20	31	6	8	1	0	0	3	4	5	.258	.343	.290	80	-1	0			.950	-3	C-13	-0.3
1914	Bro-N	9	11	0	5	0	0	0	1	2	1	.455	.538	.455	192	1	1			1.000	-1	/C-4	0.1
	Cin-N	12	35	5	11	3	0	1	7	2	3	.314	.351	.486	144	2	0			.962	1	C-12	0.3
	Yr	21	46	5	16	3	0	1	8	4	4	.348	.400	.478	157	3	1			.966	-0	C-16	0.4
Total	6	276	635	70	150	23	3	11	70	82	60	.236	.326	.334	90	-8	10			.957	-11	C-216	-0.1

YEAR	TM/L	G	AB	R	H	2B	3B	HR	RBI	BB	SO	AVG	OBP	SLG	PRO+	BR/A	SB	CS	SBR	FA	FR	G/POS	TPR
■ **NICK ESASKY**	Esasky, Nicholas Andrew b: 2/24/60, Hialeah, Fla. BR/TR, 6'3", 205 lbs. Deb: 6/19/83																						
1983	Cin-N	85	302	41	80	10	5	12	46	27	99	.265	.331	.450	111	4	6	2	1	.935	-10	3-84	-0.7
1984	Cin-N	113	322	30	62	10	5	10	45	52	103	.193	.305	.348	79	-9	1	2	-1	.910	-8	3-82,1-25	-2.1
1985	Cin-N	125	413	61	108	21	0	21	66	41	102	.262	.334	.465	115	8	3	4	-2	.946	-6	3-62,O-54,1-12	-0.3
1986	Cin-N	102	330	35	76	17	2	12	41	47	97	.230	.328	.403	96	-2	0	2	-1	.991	-3	1-70,O-42/3-1	-1.1
1987	Cin-N	100	346	48	94	19	2	22	59	29	76	.272	.328	.529	117	7	0	0	0	.994	-11	1-93/3-1,O-1	-1.1
1988	Cin-N	122	391	40	95	17	2	15	62	48	104	.243	.332	.412	108	4	7	2	1	.994	-9	*1-116	-1.4
1989	Bos-A	154	564	79	156	26	5	30	108	66	117	.277	.355	.500	130	22	1	2	-1	.996	4	*1-153/O-1	1.3
1990	Atl-N	9	35	2	6	0	0	0	0	4	14	.171	.256	.171	19	-4	0	0	0	.944	-2	/1-9	-0.6
Total	8	810	2703	336	677	120	21	122	427	314	712	.250	.332	.446	109	31	18	14	-3	.993	-45	1-478,3-230/O-98	-6.0
■ **NINO ESCALERA**	Escalera, Saturnino Cuadrado b: 12/1/29, Santurce, P.R. BL/TR, 5'10", 165 lbs. Deb: 4/17/54																						
1954	Cin-N	73	69	15	11	1	1	0	3	7	11	.159	.237	.203	15	-9	1	0	0	.962	0	O-14/1-8,S-1	-0.8
■ **JIM ESCHEN**	Eschen, James Godrich b: 8/21/1891, Brooklyn, N.Y. d: 9/27/60, Sloatsburg, N.Y. BR/TR, 5'10.5", 160 lbs. Deb: 7/10/15 F																						
1915	Cle-A	15	42	11	10	1	0	0	2	5	9	.238	.319	.262	73	-1	0	1	-1	.968	1	O-10	-0.1
■ **LARRY ESCHEN**	Eschen, Lawrence Edward b: 9/22/20, Suffern, N.Y. BR/TR, 6', 180 lbs. Deb: 6/16/42 F																						
1942	Phi-A	12	11	0	0	0	0	0	0	4	6	.000	.267	.000	-22	-2	0	0	0	.824	-1	/S-7,2-1	-0.3
■ **ANGEL ESCOBAR**	Escobar, Angel Rubenque (Rivas) b: 5/12/65, LaSabana, Venez. BB/TR, 6', 160 lbs. Deb: 5/17/88																						
1988	SF-N	3	3	1	1	0	0	0	0	0	0	.333	.333	.333	96	-0	0	0	0	1.000	0	/S-1,3-1	0.0
■ **JOSE ESCOBAR**	Escobar, Jose Elias (Sanchez) b: 10/30/60, Las Flores, Venez. BR/TR, 5'10", 140 lbs. Deb: 4/13/91																						
1991	Cle-A	10	15	0	3	0	0	0	1	1	4	.200	.250	.200	26	-1	0	0	0	1.000	2	/S-5,2-4,3-1	0.0
■ **JIMMY ESMOND**	Esmond, James Joseph b: 10/8/1889, Albany, N.Y. d: 6/26/48, Troy, N.Y. BR/TR, 5'11", 167 lbs. Deb: 4/20/11																						
1911	Cin-N	73	198	27	54	4	6	1	11	17	30	.273	.330	.369	99	-1	7			.918	1	S-44,3-14/2-2	0.2
1912	Cin-N	82	231	24	45	5	3	1	40	20	31	.195	.259	.255	42	-19	11			.930	-7	S-74	-2.0
1914	Ind-F	151	542	74	160	23	**15**	2	49	40	48	.295	.344	.404	93	-13	25			.919	-7	*S-151	-0.9
1915	New-F	155	569	79	147	20	10	5	62	59	54	.258	.329	.355	98	-11	18			.939	6	*S-155	0.8
Total	4	461	1540	204	406	52	34	9	162	136	163	.264	.324	.359	88	-44	61			.929	-8	S-424/3-14,2-2	-1.9
■ **JUAN ESPINO**	Espino, Juan (Reyes) b: 3/16/56, Bonao, D.R. BR/TR, 6'1", 190 lbs. Deb: 6/25/82																						
1982	NY-A	3	2	0	0	0	0	0	0	0	1	.000	.000	.000	-99	-1	0	0	0	1.000	0	/C-3	0.0
1983	NY-A	10	23	1	6	0	0	1	3	1	5	.261	.292	.391	89	-0	0	0	0	1.000	-0	C-10	0.0
1985	NY-A	9	11	0	4	0	0	0	0	0	0	.364	.364	.364	102	0	0	0	0	1.000	1	/C-9	0.1
1986	NY-A	27	37	1	6	2	0	0	5	2	9	.162	.205	.216	15	-4	0	0	0	.987	3	C-27	-0.1
Total	4	49	73	2	16	2	0	1	8	3	15	.219	.250	.288	48	-5	0	0	0	.993	4	/C-49	0.0
■ **ALVARO ESPINOZA**	Espinoza, Alvaro Alberto b: 2/19/62, Valencia, Venez. BR/TR, 6', 181 lbs. Deb: 9/14/84																						
1984	Min-A	1	0	0	0	0	0	0	0	0	0	—	—	—	—	0	0	0	0	.000	0	/S-1	0.0
1985	Min-A	32	57	5	15	2	0	0	9	1	9	.263	.288	.298	58	-3	0	1	-1	.949	7	S-31	0.4
1986	Min-A	37	42	4	9	1	0	0	1	1	10	.214	.233	.238	28	-4	0	1	-1	.941	6	2-19,S-18	0.2
1988	NY-A	3	3	0	0	0	0	0	0	0	0	.000	.000	.000	-99	-1	0	0	0	1.000	1	/2-2,S-1	0.0
1989	NY-A	146	503	51	142	23	1	0	41	14	60	.282	.303	.332	80	-14	3	3	-1	.970	17	*S-146	1.3
1990	NY-A	150	438	31	98	12	2	2	20	16	54	.224	.259	.274	49	-30	1	2	-1	.977	**21**	*S-150	0.2
1991	NY-A	148	480	51	123	23	2	5	33	16	57	.256	.283	.344	72	-19	4	1	1	.969	20	*S-147/3-2,P-1	1.3
1993	Cle-A	129	263	34	73	15	0	4	27	8	36	.278	.301	.380	82	-7	2	2	-1	.937	1	3-99,S-35/2-2	-0.5
1994	Cle-A	90	231	27	55	13	0	1	19	6	33	.238	.261	.307	46	-19	1	3	-2	.915	24	3-37,S-36,2-20,/1-3	0.7
1995	*Cle-A	66	143	15	36	4	0	2	17	2	16	.252	.267	.322	52	-10	0	2	-1	.966	9	2-22,3-22,S-19,/1D	-0.1
1996	Cle-A	59	112	12	25	4	2	4	11	6	18	.223	.281	.402	70	-6	1	1	-0	.947	4	3-20,1-18,S-16,/2D	-0.2
	NY-N	48	134	19	41	7	2	4	16	4	19	.306	.326	.478	114	2	0	2	-1	.900	-6	3-38/S-7,2-2,1-1	-0.5
1997	Sea-A	33	72	3	13	1	0	0	7	2	12	.181	.213	.194	7	-10	1	1	-0	.965	4	S-17,2-14/3-1	-0.4
Total	12	942	2478	252	630	105	9	22	201	76	324	.254	.281	.331	66	-120	13	19	-8	.971	108	S-624,3-219/21DP	2.4
■ **SAMMY ESPOSITO**	Esposito, Samuel b: 12/15/31, Chicago, Ill. BR/TR, 5'9", 165 lbs. Deb: 9/28/52																						
1952	Chi-A	1	4	0	1	0	0	0	0	0	2	.250	.250	.250	39	-0	0	1	-1	.500	-1	/S-1	-0.3
1955	Chi-A	3	4	3	0	0	0	0	0	1	0	.000	.200	.000	-41	-1	0	0	0	1.000	-1	/3-2	-0.2
1956	Chi-A	81	184	30	42	8	2	3	25	41	19	.228	.374	.342	89	-1	1	2	-1	.962	4	3-61,S-19/2-3	0.2
1957	Chi-A	94	176	26	36	3	0	2	15	38	27	.205	.346	.256	66	-7	5	1	1	.960	16	3-53,S-22/2-4,O-1	1.3
1958	Chi-A	98	81	16	20	3	0	0	3	12	6	.247	.358	.284	81	-2	1	1	-0	.979	11	3-63,S-22/2-2,O-1	1.0
1959	*Chi-A	69	66	12	11	1	0	1	5	11	16	.167	.286	.227	43	-5	0	1	-1	.979	9	3-45,S-14/2-2	0.4
1960	Chi-A	57	77	14	14	5	0	1	11	10	20	.182	.276	.286	53	-5	0	0	0	.929	1	3-37,S-11/2-5	-0.4
1961	Chi-A	63	94	12	16	5	0	1	8	12	21	.170	.264	.255	40	-8	0	0	0	.976	12	3-28,S-20,2-11	0.5
1962	Chi-A	75	81	14	19	1	0	0	4	17	13	.235	.367	.247	69	-3	0	1	-1	.846	3	3-41,S-20/2-7	0.2
1963	Chi-A	1	0	0	0	0	0	0	0	0	0	—	—	—	—	0	0	0	0	.000	0	R	0.0
	KC-A	18	25	3	5	1	0	0	2	3	3	.200	.286	.240	47	-2	0	0	0	1.000	-2	/2-7,S-4,3-3	-0.3
	Yr	19	25	3	5	1	0	0	2	3	3	.200	.286	.240	47	-2	0	0	0	1.000	-2	/2-7,S-4,3-3	-0.3
Total	10	560	792	130	164	27	2	8	73	145	127	.207	.333	.277	66	-33	7	7	-2	.957	51	3-333,S-133/2-41,O	2.4
■ **CECIL ESPY**	Espy, Cecil Edward b: 1/20/63, San Diego, Cal. BB/TR, 6'3", 195 lbs. Deb: 9/2/83																						
1983	LA-N	20	11	4	3	1	0	0	1	1	2	.273	.333	.364	94	-0	0	0	0	1.000	-5	O-15	-0.5
1987	Tex-A	14	8	1	0	0	0	0	0	1	3	.000	.111	.000	-67	-2	2	0	1	1.000	-1	/O-8	-0.2
1988	Tex-A	123	347	46	86	17	6	2	39	20	83	.248	.291	.349	76	-11	33	10	4	.972	-4	O-98,D-12/S-3,C12	-1.4
1989	Tex-A	142	475	65	122	12	7	3	31	38	99	.257	.315	.331	81	-12	45	20	2	.990	-3	*O-133/D-3	-1.7
1990	Tex-A	52	71	10	9	0	0	0	1	10	20	.127	.235	.127	4	-9	11	5	0	1.000	-7	O-39/2-1,D-4	-1.7
1991	*Pit-N	43	82	7	20	4	0	1	11	5	17	.244	.287	.329	74	-3	4	0	1	.966	-3	O-35	-0.6
1992	*Pit-N	112	194	21	50	7	3	1	20	15	40	.258	.311	.340	85	-4	6	3	0	.955	-20	O-82	-2.7
1993	Cin-N	40	60	6	14	2	0	0	5	14	13	.233	.378	.267	76	-1	2	2	-1	.931	-1	O-18	-0.3
Total	8	546	1248	160	304	43	16	7	108	104	277	.244	.303	.321	74	-42	103	40	7	.977	-43	O-428/D-19,S-3,2C1	-9.1
■ **CHUCK ESSEGIAN**	Essegian, Charles Abraham b: 8/9/31, Boston, Mass. BR/TR, 5'11", 202 lbs. Deb: 4/15/58																						
1958	Phi-N	39	114	15	28	5	2	5	16	12	34	.246	.317	.456	103	0	0	0	0	.952	1	O-30	-0.1
1959	StL-N	17	39	2	7	2	1	0	5	1	13	.179	.200	.282	25	-4	0	0	0	1.000	-1	/O-9	-0.6
	*LA-N	24	46	6	14	6	0	1	5	4	11	.304	.360	.500	118	1	0	0	0	1.000	-1	O-10	-0.1
	Yr	41	85	8	21	8	1	1	10	5	24	.247	.289	.400	76	-3	0	0	0	1.000	-2	O-19	0.7
1960	LA-N	52	79	8	17	3	0	3	11	8	24	.215	.287	.367	73	-3	0	0	0	.968	0	O-18	-0.4
1961	Bal-A	1	1	0	0	0	0	0	0	0	0	.000	.000	.000	-99	-0	0	0	0	.000	0	H	0.0
	KC-A	4	6	1	2	1	0	0	1	1	2	.333	.429	.500	145	0	0	0	0	1.000	0	/O-1	0.1
	Cle-A	60	166	25	48	7	1	12	35	10	33	.289	.333	.560	138	8	0	0	0	.968	-2	O-49	0.4
	Yr	65	173	26	50	8	1	12	36	11	35	.289	.335	.555	137	8	0	0	0	.969	-1	O-50	0.5
1962	Cle-A	106	336	59	92	12	0	21	50	42	68	.274	.366	.497	134	16	0	0	0	.994	-4	O-90	0.7
1963	KC-A	101	231	23	52	9	0	5	27	19	48	.225	.287	.329	68	-10	0	0	0	.990	-0	O-53	-1.3
Total	6	404	1018	139	260	45	4	47	150	97	233	.255	.326	.446	106	8	0	0	0	.981	-7	O-260	-1.3
■ **JIM ESSIAN**	Essian, James Sarkis b: 1/2/51, Detroit, Mich. BR/TR, 6'2", 195 lbs. Deb: 9/15/73 M																						
1973	Phi-N	2	3	0	0	0	0	0	0	0	1	.000	.000	.000	-97	-1	0	0	0	.000	0	/C-1	-0.1
1974	Phi-N	17	20	1	2	0	0	0	0	2	1	.100	.182	.100	-19	-3	0	0	0	.976	1	C-15/1-1,3-1	-0.2
1975	Phi-N	2	1	1	1	0	0	0	1	1	0	1.000	1.000	1.000	439	1	0	0	0	1.000	0	/C-2	0.1
1976	Chi-A	78	199	20	49	7	0	0	21	23	28	.246	.327	.281	79	-4	2	1	0	.974	3	C-77/1-2,3-1	0.0
1977	Chi-A	114	322	50	88	18	2	10	44	52	35	.273	.376	.435	120	10	1	4	-2	.986	5	*C-111/3-2	1.6

YEAR	TM/L	G	AB	R	H	2B	3B	HR	RBI	BB	SO	AVG	OBP	SLG	PRO+	BR/A	SB	CS	SBR	FA	FR	G/POS	TPR
1978	Oak-A	126	278	21	62	9	1	3	26	44	22	.223	.329	.295	81	-6	2	1	0	.981	14	*C-119/1-3,2-1,D-1	1.1
1979	Oak-A	98	313	34	76	16	0	8	40	25	29	.243	.303	.371	85	-7	0	1	-1	.981	9	C-70,3-10/1-4,OD	0.4
1980	Oak-A	87	285	19	66	11	0	5	29	30	18	.232	.305	.323	78	-9	1	3	-2	.987	6	C-68,D-11/1-1	-0.3
1981	Chi-A	27	52	6	16	3	0	0	5	4	5	.308	.357	.365	111	1	0	1	-1	.990	5	C-25/3-2	0.6
1982	Sea-A	48	153	14	42	8	0	3	20	11	7	.275	.327	.386	92	-2	2	0	1	.994	6	C-48	0.7
1983	Cle-A	48	93	11	19	4	0	2	11	16	8	.204	.321	.312	72	-3	0	1	-1	.989	3	C-47/3-1	0.1
1984	Oak-A	63	136	17	32	9	0	2	10	23	17	.235	.350	.346	100	1	1	1	-0	.985	11	C-59/3-1,D-1	1.3
Total	12	710	1855	194	453	85	3	33	207	231	171	.244	.330	.347	90	-22	9	13	-5	.984	63	C-642/3-18,D1O2	5.3

■ BOBBY ESTALELLA

Estalella, Robert M b: 8/23/74, Hialeah, Fla. BR/TR, 6'1", 200 lbs. Deb: 9/17/96 F

YEAR	TM/L	G	AB	R	H	2B	3B	HR	RBI	BB	SO	AVG	OBP	SLG	PRO+	BR/A	SB	CS	SBR	FA	FR	G/POS	TPR
1996	Phi-N	7	17	5	6	0	0	2	4	1	6	.353	.389	.706	179	2	1	0	0	1.000	-0	/C-4	0.2
1997	Phi-N	13	29	9	10	1	0	4	9	7	7	.345	.472	.793	224	5	0	0	0	1.000	-4	C-11	0.2
1998	Phi-N	47	165	16	31	6	1	8	20	13	49	.188	.251	.382	60	-10	0	0	0	.988	-6	C-47	-1.3
Total	3	67	211	30	47	7	1	14	33	21	62	.223	.296	.464	92	-3	1	0	0	.990	-11	/C-62	-0.9

■ BOBBY ESTALELLA

Estalella, Roberto (Ventoza) b: 4/25/11, Cardenas, Cuba d: 1/6/91, Hialeah, Fla. BR/TR, 5'8", 180 lbs. Deb: 9/7/35 F

YEAR	TM/L	G	AB	R	H	2B	3B	HR	RBI	BB	SO	AVG	OBP	SLG	PRO+	BR/A	SB	CS	SBR	FA	FR	G/POS	TPR
1935	Was-A	15	51	7	16	2	0	2	10	17	7	.314	.485	.471	153	5	1	0	0	.895	2	3-15	0.8
1936	Was-A	13	9	2	2	0	2	0	0	4	5	.222	.462	.667	186	1	0	0	0	.000	0	H	0.1
1939	Was-A	82	280	51	77	18	6	8	41	40	27	.275	.368	.468	121	8	2	3	-1	.964	-3	O-74	0.2
1941	StL-A	46	83	7	20	6	1	0	14	18	13	.241	.376	.337	87	-1	0	0	0	1.000	-4	O-17	-0.6
1942	Was-A	133	429	68	119	24	5	8	65	85	42	.277	.400	.413	130	21	5	2	0	.941	-14	3-78,O-36	0.7
1943	Phi-A	117	367	43	95	14	4	11	63	52	44	.259	.352	.409	123	11	1	3	-2	.975	-1	O-97	0.3
1944	Phi-A	140	506	54	151	17	9	7	60	59	60	.298	.374	.409	125	17	3	3	-1	.988	-2	*O-128/1-6	0.8
1945	Phi-A	126	451	45	135	25	6	8	52	74	46	.299	.399	.435	142	26	1	6	-3	.988	1	*O-124	1.8
1949	Phi-A	8	20	2	5	0	0	0	3	1	2	.250	.286	.250	44	-2	0	0	0	1.000	0	/O-6	-0.2
Total	9	680	2196	279	620	106	33	44	308	350	246	.282	.383	.421	127	88	13	17	-6	.982	-21	O-482/3-93,1-6	3.9

■ DUDE ESTERBROOK

Esterbrook, Thomas John b: 6/20/1857, Staten Is., N.Y. d: 4/30/01, Middletown, N.Y. BR/TR, 5'11", 167 lbs. Deb: 5/1/1880 M

YEAR	TM/L	G	AB	R	H	2B	3B	HR	RBI	BB	SO	AVG	OBP	SLG	PRO+	BR/A	SB	CS	SBR	FA	FR	G/POS	TPR
1880	Buf-N	64	253	20	61	12	1	0	35	0	15	.241	.241	.296	80	-6				.939	-3	1-47,O-15/2-6,SC	-1.2
1882	Cle-N	45	179	13	44	4	3	0	19	5	12	.246	.266	.302	85	-3				.893	10	O-45/1-1	0.6
1883	NY-a	97	407	55	103	9	7	0		15		.253	.280	.310	86	-7				.871	-4	*3-97	-1.1
1884	*NY-a	112	477	110	150	29	11	1		12		.314	.345	.428	154	28				.886	9	*3-112	3.4
1885	NY-N	88	359	48	92	14	5	2	44	4	28	.256	.264	.340	96	-2				.885	2	*3-84/O-4	0.0
1886	NY-N	123	473	62	125	20	6	3	43	8	43	.264	.277	.351	89	-8	13			**.895**	-3	*3-123	-0.7
1887	NY-a	26	101	11	17	1	0	0	7	6		.168	.222	.178	13	-11	8			.950	-7	/1-9,O-7,S-5,2-5	-1.6
1888	Ind-N	64	246	21	54	8	0	0	17	2	20	.220	.232	.252	53	-13	11			.976	-3	1-61/3-3	-2.2
	Lou-a	23	93	9	21	6	0	0	7	3		.226	.265	.290	80	-2	5			.962	0	1-23	-0.4
1889	Lou-a	11	44	8	14	3	0	0	9	5	2	.318	.400	.386	127	2	6			.931	-1	/1-8,O-2,S-1,M	0.1
1890	NY-N	45	197	29	57	14	1	0	29	10	8	.289	.333	.371	105	1	12			.984	0	1-45	-0.2
1891	Bro-N	3	8	1	3	0	0	0	0	0	1	.375	.444	.375	140	0	0			1.000	-1	/O-2,2-1	0.0
Total	11	701	2837	387	741	120	34	6	210	70	129	.261	.284	.334	94	-22	55			.884	-1	3-419,1-194/O2SC	-3.3

■ FRANK ESTRADA

Estrada, Francisco (Soto) b: 2/12/48, Navojoa, Mexico BR/TR, 5'8", 182 lbs. Deb: 9/14/71

YEAR	TM/L	G	AB	R	H	2B	3B	HR	RBI	BB	SO	AVG	OBP	SLG	PRO+	BR/A	SB	CS	SBR	FA	FR	G/POS	TPR
1971	NY-N	1	2	0	1	0	0	0	0	0	0	.500	.500	.500	187	0	0	0	0	1.000	-1	/C-1	-0.1

■ ANDY ETCHEBARREN

Etchebarren, Andrew Auguste b: 6/20/43, Whittier, Cal. BR/TR, 6'1", 197 lbs. Deb: 9/26/62 C

YEAR	TM/L	G	AB	R	H	2B	3B	HR	RBI	BB	SO	AVG	OBP	SLG	PRO+	BR/A	SB	CS	SBR	FA	FR	G/POS	TPR
1962	Bal-A	2	6	0	2	0	0	0	1	0	2	.333	.333	.333	85	-0	0	0	0	.875	-1	/C-2	-0.1
1965	Bal-A	5	6	1	1	0	0	1	4	0	2	.167	.167	.667	123	0	0	0	0	1.000	3	/C-5	0.3
1966	*Bal-A☆	121	412	49	91	14	6	11	50	38	106	.221	.295	.364	89	-6	0	1	-1	.989	-4	*C-121	-0.3
1967	Bal-A☆	112	330	29	71	13	0	7	35	38	80	.215	.300	.318	83	-6	1	0	0	.989	0	*C-110	0.0
1968	Bal-A	74	189	20	44	11	2	5	20	19	46	.233	.313	.392	112	3	0	0	0	.998	9	C-70	1.7
1969	*Bal-A	73	217	29	54	9	2	3	26	28	42	.249	.353	.350	96	-0	1	2	-1	.990	2	C-72	0.5
1970	*Bal-A	78	230	19	56	10	1	4	28	21	41	.243	.315	.348	82	-6	4	1	1	.984	2	C-76	0.0
1971	*Bal-A	70	222	21	60	8	0	9	29	16	40	.270	.322	.428	112	3	1	4	-2	.986	2	C-70	0.5
1972	Bal-A	71	188	11	38	6	1	2	21	17	43	.202	.279	.277	64	-8	0	2	-1	.992	7	C-70	0.0
1973	*Bal-A	54	152	16	39	9	1	2	23	12	21	.257	.319	.368	94	-1	1	1	-0	.991	2	C-51	0.2
1974	*Bal-A	62	180	13	40	8	0	2	15	6	26	.222	.251	.300	60	-10	1	0	0	.976	6	C-60	-0.1
1975	Bal-A	8	20	0	4	1	0	0	3	0	3	.200	.200	.250	28	-2	0	0	0	1.000	0	/C-7	-0.1
	Cal-A	31	100	10	28	0	1	3	17	14	19	.280	.368	.390	123	3	1	0	0	.981	-4	C-31	0.1
	Yr	39	120	10	32	1	1	3	20	14	22	.267	.343	.367	108	1	1	0	0	.983	-3	C-38	0.0
1976	Cal-A	103	247	15	56	9	1	0	21	24	37	.227	.305	.271	74	-7	0	2	-1	.980	6	*C-102	-0.1
1977	Cal-A	80	114	11	29	2	2	0	14	12	19	.254	.325	.307	77	-3	3	1	0	.987	1	C-80	-0.1
1978	Mil-A	4	5	1	2	1	0	0	2	1	2	.400	.500	.600	207	1	0	0	0	1.000	2	/C-4	0.3
Total	15	948	2618	245	615	101	17	49	309	246	529	.235	.308	.343	88	-41	13	14	-5	.987	32	C-931	2.8

■ BUCK ETCHISON

Etchison, Clarence Hampton b: 1/27/15, Baltimore, Md. d: 1/24/80, E.New Market, Md. BL/TL, 6'1", 190 lbs. Deb: 9/22/43

YEAR	TM/L	G	AB	R	H	2B	3B	HR	RBI	BB	SO	AVG	OBP	SLG	PRO+	BR/A	SB	CS	SBR	FA	FR	G/POS	TPR
1943	Bos-N	10	19	2	6	3	0	0	2	2	2	.316	.381	.474	148	1	0			.956	-1	/1-6	0.0
1944	Bos-N	109	308	30	66	16	0	8	33	33	50	.214	.292	.344	76	-10	1			.993	-1	1-85	-1.6
Total	2	119	327	32	72	19	0	8	35	35	52	.220	.298	.352	79	-9	1			.991	-2	/1-91	-1.6

■ BOBBY ETHERIDGE

Etheridge, Bobby Lamar "Luke" b: 11/25/42, Greenville, Miss. BR/TR, 5'9", 170 lbs. Deb: 7/16/67

YEAR	TM/L	G	AB	R	H	2B	3B	HR	RBI	BB	SO	AVG	OBP	SLG	PRO+	BR/A	SB	CS	SBR	FA	FR	G/POS	TPR
1967	SF-N	40	115	13	26	7	2	1	15	7	12	.226	.299	.348	86	-2	0	0	0	.925	-1	3-37	-0.4
1969	SF-N	56	131	13	34	9	0	1	10	19	26	.260	.358	.351	101	1	0	0	0	.899	-2	3-39/S-1	-0.1
Total	2	96	246	26	60	16	2	2	25	26	38	.244	.331	.350	94	-1	0	0	0	.911	-4	/3-76,S-1	-0.5

■ NICK ETTEN

Etten, Nicholas Raymond Thomas b: 9/19/13, Spring Grove, Ill. d: 10/18/90, Hinsdale, Ill. BL/TL, 6'2", 198 lbs. Deb: 9/8/38

YEAR	TM/L	G	AB	R	H	2B	3B	HR	RBI	BB	SO	AVG	OBP	SLG	PRO+	BR/A	SB	CS	SBR	FA	FR	G/POS	TPR
1938	Phi-A	22	81	6	21	6	2	0	11	9	7	.259	.333	.383	81	-3	1	0	0	.987	-2	1-22	-0.6
1939	Phi-A	43	155	20	39	11	2	3	29	16	11	.252	.322	.406	87	-4	0	0	0	.990	-3	1-41	-1.0
1941	Phi-N	151	540	78	168	27	4	14	79	82	33	.311	.405	.454	147	36	9			.984	-3	*1-150	2.3
1942	Phi-N	139	459	37	121	21	3	8	41	67	26	.264	.357	.375	120	13	3			.985	1	*1-135	0.6
1943	*NY-A	154	583	78	158	35	5	14	107	76	31	.271	.355	.420	126	19	3	7	-3	.989	-11	*1-154	-0.5
1944	NY-A	154	573	88	168	25	4	**22**	91	**97**	29	.293	.399	.466	142	34	4	2	0	.989	4	*1-154	3.0
1945	NY-A†	152	565	77	161	24	4	18	**111**	90	23	.285	.387	.437	133	25	2	3	-1	.989	-9	*1-152	0.5
1946	NY-A	108	323	37	75	14	1	9	49	38	35	.232	.315	.365	88	-5	0	1	-1	.991	-0	1-84	-1.2
1947	Phi-N	14	41	5	10	4	0	1	8	5	4	.244	.326	.415	99	-0	0			.990	1	1-11	0.1
Total	9	937	3320	426	921	167	25	89	526	480	199	.277	.371	.423	125	115	22	13		.988	-22	1-903	3.2

■ FRED EUNICK

Eunick, Fernandas Bowen b: 4/22/1892, Baltimore, Md. d: 12/9/59, Baltimore, Md. BR/TR, 5'6", 148 lbs. Deb: 8/29/17

YEAR	TM/L	G	AB	R	H	2B	3B	HR	RBI	BB	SO	AVG	OBP	SLG	PRO+	BR/A	SB	CS	SBR	FA	FR	G/POS	TPR
1917	Cle-A	1	2	0	0	0	0	0	0	0	0	.000	.000	.000	-93	-0	0			1.000	-0	/3-1	-0.1

■ TONY EUSEBIO

Eusebio, Raul Antonio Bare (b: Raul Antontio Bare (Eusebio)) b: 4/27/67, San Jose De Los Llamos, D.R. BR/TR, 6'2", 180 lbs. Deb: 8/8/91

YEAR	TM/L	G	AB	R	H	2B	3B	HR	RBI	BB	SO	AVG	OBP	SLG	PRO+	BR/A	SB	CS	SBR	FA	FR	G/POS	TPR
1991	Hou-N	10	19	4	2	1	0	0	0	6	8	.105	.320	.158	41	-1	0	0	0	.981	2	/C-9	0.1
1994	Hou-N	55	159	18	47	9	1	5	30	8	33	.296	.329	.459	108	1	0	1	-1	.993	-5	C-52	-0.1
1995	Hou-N	113	368	46	110	21	1	6	58	31	59	.299	.358	.410	110	5	0	2	-1	.993	-13	*C-103	-0.3
1996	Hou-N	58	152	15	41	7	2	1	19	18	20	.270	.347	.362	95	-1	0	1	-1	.996	-9	C-47	-0.8
1997	*Hou-N	60	164	12	45	2	0	1	18	19	27	.274	.364	.305	80	-4	0	1	-1	.987	-2	C-43	-0.3
1998	*Hou-N	66	182	13	46	6	1	1	36	18	31	.253	.323	.313	68	-8	1	0	0	.992	1	C-54	-0.3
Total	6	362	1044	108	291	46	5	14	161	100	178	.279	.346	.373	94	-8	1	5	-3	.992	-25	C-308	-1.7

■ FRANK EUSTACE

Eustace, Frank John b: 11/7/1873, New York, N.Y. d: 10/20/32, Pottsville, Pa. 5'9", 160 lbs. Deb: 4/16/1896

YEAR	TM/L	G	AB	R	H	2B	3B	HR	RBI	BB	SO	AVG	OBP	SLG	PRO+	BR/A	SB	CS	SBR	FA	FR	G/POS	TPR
1896	Lou-N	25	100	18	17	2	2	1	11	6	14	.170	.217	.260	26	-11	4			.841	-5	S-22/2-3	-1.3

YEAR	TM/L	G	AB	R	H	2B	3B	HR	RBI	BB	SO	AVG	OBP	SLG	PRO+	BR/A	SB	CS	SBR	FA	FR	G/POS	TPR
■ EVANS	Evans	Deb: 6/1/1875																					
1875	NH-n	1	4	1	2	0	0	0	1	0	0	.500	.500	.500	285	1	0	0	0	.000	-0	/O-1	0.0

■ AL EVANS Evans, Alfred Hubert b: 9/28/16, Kenly, N.C. d: 4/6/79, Wilson, N.C. BR/TR, 5'11", 190 lbs. Deb: 9/13/39

YEAR	TM/L	G	AB	R	H	2B	3B	HR	RBI	BB	SO	AVG	OBP	SLG	PRO+	BR/A	SB	CS	SBR	FA	FR	G/POS	TPR
1939	Was-A	7	21	2	7	0	0	0	1	5	2	.333	.462	.333	115	1	0	0	0	.964	-1	/C-6	0.1
1940	Was-A	14	25	1	8	2	0	0	7	6	7	.320	.452	.400	131	2	1	0	0	1.000	-1	/C-9	0.2
1941	Was-A	53	159	16	44	8	4	1	19	9	18	.277	.315	.396	91	-3	0	3	-2	.969	2	C-51	0.1
1942	Was-A	74	223	22	51	4	1	0	10	25	36	.229	.309	.256	60	-11	3	0	1	.961	-3	C-67	-0.9
1944	Was-A	14	22	5	2	0	0	0	0	2	6	.091	.167	.091	-27	-4	0	0	0	.933	-1	/C-8	-0.5
1945	Was-A	51	150	19	39	11	2	2	19	17	22	.260	.339	.400	125	4	2	1	0	.973	-6	C-41	0.0
1946	Was-A	88	272	30	69	10	4	2	30	30	28	.254	.332	.342	94	-2	1	2	-1	.966	-12	C-81	-1.1
1947	Was-A	99	319	17	77	8	3	2	23	28	25	.241	.303	.304	71	-13	2	1	0	.989	-2	C-94	-0.9
1948	Was-A	93	228	19	59	6	3	2	28	38	20	.259	.367	.338	91	-2	1	1	-0	.983	-3	C-85	0.0
1949	Was-A	109	321	32	87	12	3	2	42	50	19	.271	.369	.346	92	-3	4	1	1	**.992**	-16	*C-107	-1.1
1950	Was-A	90	289	24	68	8	3	2	30	29	21	.235	.309	.304	61	-18	0	0	0	.987	-13	C-88	-2.6
1951	Bos-A	12	24	1	3	1	0	0	2	4	2	.125	.250	.167	13	-3	0	0	0	1.000	1	C-10	-0.2
Total	12	704	2053	188	514	70	23	13	211	243	206	.250	.332	.326	82	-50	14	9	-1	.979	-56	C-647	-6.9

■ BARRY EVANS Evans, Barry Steven b: 11/30/56, Atlanta, Ga. BR/TR, 6'1", 180 lbs. Deb: 9/4/78

YEAR	TM/L	G	AB	R	H	2B	3B	HR	RBI	BB	SO	AVG	OBP	SLG	PRO+	BR/A	SB	CS	SBR	FA	FR	G/POS	TPR
1978	SD-N	24	90	7	24	1	1	0	4	4	10	.267	.298	.300	73	-3	0	0	0	.947	1	3-24	-0.3
1979	SD-N	56	162	9	35	5	0	1	14	5	16	.216	.240	.265	40	-14	0	2	-1	.952	11	3-53/S-2,2-1	-0.4
1980	SD-N	73	125	11	29	3	2	1	14	17	21	.232	.324	.312	83	-3	1	1	-0	.983	-3	3-43,2-19/S-4,1-1	-0.5
1981	SD-N	54	93	11	30	5	0	0	7	9	9	.323	.382	.376	125	3	2	2	-1	.969	-4	3-24,1-10/2-6,S-2	-0.2
1982	NY-A	17	31	2	8	3	0	0	2	6	6	.258	.395	.355	109	1	0	0	0	1.000	1	/2-8,3-6,S-4	0.2
Total	5	224	501	40	126	17	3	2	41	41	62	.251	.309	.309	77	-16	3	5	-2	.960	7	3-150/2-34,S-12,1	-1.2

■ DARRELL EVANS Evans, Darrell Wayne b: 5/26/47, Pasadena, Cal. BL/TR, 6'2", 205 lbs. Deb: 4/20/69 C

YEAR	TM/L	G	AB	R	H	2B	3B	HR	RBI	BB	SO	AVG	OBP	SLG	PRO+	BR/A	SB	CS	SBR	FA	FR	G/POS	TPR
1969	Atl-N	12	26	3	6	0	0	0	1	1	8	.231	.259	.231	38	-2	0	0	0	.917	-2	/3-6	-0.4
1970	Atl-N	12	44	4	14	1	1	0	9	7	5	.318	.423	.386	112	1	0	0	0	.941	-1	3-12	0.0
1971	Atl-N	89	260	42	63	11	1	12	38	39	54	.242	.343	.431	111	4	2	3	-1	.937	4	3-72/O-3	0.6
1972	Atl-N	125	418	67	106	12	0	19	71	90	58	.254	.391	.419	119	14	4	2	0	.941	9	*3-123	2.3
1973	Atl-N★	161	595	114	167	25	8	41	104	**124**	104	.281	.407	.556	153	45	6	3	0	.953	8	*3-146,1-20	5.2
1974	Atl-N	160	571	99	137	21	3	25	79	**126**	88	.240	.383	.419	119	18	4	2	0	.955	16	*3-160	3.4
1975	Atl-N	156	567	82	138	22	2	22	73	105	106	.243	.364	.406	109	9	12	3	2	.938	23	*3-156/1-3	3.5
1976	Atl-N	44	139	11	24	0	0	1	10	30	33	.173	.320	.194	45	-9	3	0	1	.994	0	1-36/3-7	-1.1
	SF-N	92	257	42	57	9	1	10	36	42	38	.222	.331	.381	99	0	6	1	1	.991	9	1-83/3-5	0.5
	Yr	136	396	53	81	9	1	11	46	72	71	.205	.327	.316	80	-9	9	1	2	.992	9	*1-119,3-12	-0.6
1977	SF-N	144	461	64	117	18	3	17	72	69	50	.254	.355	.416	106	5	9	6	-1	.937	-1	O-81,1-41,3-35	-0.2
1978	SF-N	159	547	82	133	24	2	20	78	105	64	.243	.365	.404	119	17	4	5	-2	.952	10	*3-155	2.4
1979	SF-N	160	562	68	142	23	2	17	70	91	80	.253	.359	.391	112	11	6	7	-2	.943	22	*3-159	3.0
1980	SF-N	154	556	69	147	23	0	20	78	83	65	.264	.362	.414	119	15	17	5	2	.946	17	*3-140,1-14	3.3
1981	SF-N	102	357	51	92	13	4	12	48	54	33	.258	.358	.417	122	11	2	3	-1	.953	7	3-87,1-12	1.5
1982	SF-N	141	465	64	119	20	4	16	61	77	64	.256	.364	.419	119	13	5	4	-1	.933	-2	3-84,1-49,S-13	0.7
1983	SF-N★	142	523	94	145	29	3	30	82	84	81	.277	.379	.516	151	36	6	6	-2	.993	1	*1-113,3-32/S-9	3.0
1984	*Det-A	131	401	60	93	11	1	16	63	77	70	.232	.356	.384	105	5	2	2	-1	.997	2	D-62,1-47,3-19	0.2
1985	Det-A	151	505	81	125	17	0	**40**	94	85	85	.248	.357	.519	137	26	0	4	-2	.984	11	*1-113,D-33/3-7	2.7
1986	Det-A	151	507	78	122	15	0	29	85	91	105	.241	.357	.442	116	13	3	2	-0	.998	11	*1-105,D-42/3-2	1.5
1987	*Det-A	150	499	90	128	20	0	34	99	100	84	.257	.383	.501	138	29	6	5	-1	.997	12	*1-105,D-44/3-7	3.0
1988	Det-A	144	437	48	91	9	0	22	64	84	89	.208	.337	.380	104	4	1	4	-2	.993	5	D-72,1-65	-0.1
1989	Atl-N	107	276	31	57	6	1	11	39	41	46	.207	.309	.355	87	-4	0	1	-1	.985	6	1-50,3-28	-0.3
Total	21	2687	8973	1344	2223	329	36	414	1354	1605	1410	.248	.364	.431	119	263	98	68	-11	.946	165	*3-1442,1-856,D/OS	34.7

■ DWIGHT EVANS Evans, Dwight Michael "Dewey" b: 11/3/51, Santa Monica, Cal. BR/TR, 6'2", 205 lbs. Deb: 9/16/72 C

YEAR	TM/L	G	AB	R	H	2B	3B	HR	RBI	BB	SO	AVG	OBP	SLG	PRO+	BR/A	SB	CS	SBR	FA	FR	G/POS	TPR
1972	Bos-A	18	57	2	15	3	1	1	6	7	13	.263	.344	.404	115	1	0	0	0	1.000	1	O-17	0.2
1973	Bos-A	119	282	46	63	13	1	10	32	40	52	.223	.322	.383	92	-3	5	0	2	.995	-6	*O-113/D-2	-1.1
1974	Bos-A	133	463	60	130	19	8	10	70	38	77	.281	.338	.421	110	5	4	4	-1	.990	11	*O-122/D-7	1.0
1975	*Bos-A	128	412	61	113	24	6	13	56	47	60	.274	.354	.456	118	9	3	4	-2	.987	18	*O-115/D-7	2.2
1976	Bos-A	146	501	61	121	34	5	17	62	57	92	.242	.326	.431	107	3	6	7	-2	**.994**	9	*O-145/D-1	0.5
1977	Bos-A	73	230	39	66	9	2	14	36	28	58	.287	.364	.526	125	7	4	2	0	.992	-2	O-63/D-6	0.3
1978	Bos-A★	147	497	75	123	24	2	24	63	65	119	.247	.337	.449	108	4	8	5	-1	.982	8	*O-142/D-4	0.6
1979	Bos-A	152	489	69	134	24	1	21	58	69	76	.274	.365	.456	114	10	6	9	-4	.988	10	*O-149	1.0
1980	Bos-A	148	463	72	123	37	5	18	60	64	98	.266	.361	.484	123	15	3	1	0	.982	2	*O-144/D-2	1.2
1981	Bos-A★	108	412	84	122	19	4	**22**	71	**85**	85	.296	.418	.522	160	**34**	3	2	-0	.993	14	*O-108	4.5
1982	Bos-A	162	609	122	178	37	7	32	98	112	125	.292	**.403**	.534	146	41	3	2	-0	.973	6	*O-161/D-1	4.2
1983	Bos-A	126	470	74	112	19	4	22	58	70	97	.238	.339	.436	104	3	3	0	1	.987	7	O-99,D-21	0.7
1984	Bos-A	162	630	**121**	186	37	8	32	104	96	115	.295	.392	.532	146	41	3	1	0	.994	2	*O-161/D-1	3.7
1985	Bos-A	159	617	110	162	29	1	29	78	**114**	105	.263	.382	.454	123	22	7	2	1	.990	3	*O-152/D-7	2.0
1986	*Bos-A	152	529	86	137	33	2	26	97	97	117	.259	.380	.476	131	25	3	3	-1	.983	5	*O-149/D-1	2.3
1987	Bos-A★	154	541	109	165	37	2	34	123	**106**	98	.305	.422	.569	155	46	4	6	-2	.982	-7	1-79,O-77/D-4	2.7
1988	*Bos-A	149	559	96	164	31	7	21	111	76	99	.293	.379	.487	135	27	5	1	1	.987	-6	O-85,1-64/D-6	1.4
1989	Bos-A	146	520	82	148	27	3	20	100	99	84	.285	.402	.463	135	27	3	3	-1	.981	2	O-77,D-69	2.5
1990	*Bos-A	123	445	66	111	18	3	13	63	67	73	.249	.353	.391	103	3	3	4	-2	.000	0	*D-122	-0.2
1991	Bal-A	101	270	35	73	9	1	6	38	54	54	.270	.396	.378	120	10	2	3	-1	.984	0	O-67,D-21	0.7
Total	20	2606	8996	1470	2446	483	73	385	1384	1391	1697	.272	.373	.470	126	331	78	59	-12	.987	76	*O-2146,D-282,1-143	30.4

■ JOE EVANS Evans, Joseph Patton "Doc" b: 5/15/1895, Meridian, Miss. d: 8/9/53, Gulfport, Miss. BR/TR, 5'9", 160 lbs. Deb: 7/3/15

YEAR	TM/L	G	AB	R	H	2B	3B	HR	RBI	BB	SO	AVG	OBP	SLG	PRO+	BR/A	SB	CS	SBR	FA	FR	G/POS	TPR
1915	Cle-A	42	109	17	28	4	2	0	11	22	18	.257	.382	.330	111	2	6	1	1	.885	-0	3-30/2-2	0.5
1916	Cle-A	33	82	4	12	1	0	0	1	7	12	.146	.213	.159	11	-9	4			.915	4	3-28	-0.5
1917	Cle-A	132	385	36	73	4	5	2	33	42	44	.190	.271	.242	53	-22	12			.939	3	*3-127	-1.9
1918	Cle-A	79	243	38	64	6	7	1	22	30	29	.263	.344	.358	102	1	7			.932	4	3-74	0.7
1919	Cle-A	21	14	9	1	0	0	0	0	2	1	.071	.188	.071	-24	-2	1			.923	4	/S-6	0.1
1920	*Cle-A	56	172	32	60	9	9	0	23	15	3	.349	.404	.506	136	9	6	2	1	.966	-3	O-43/S-6	0.4
1921	Cle-A	57	153	36	51	11	0	0	21	19	5	.333	.410	.405	107	3	4	1	1	.933	-1	O-47	0.0
1922	Cle-A	75	145	35	39	6	2	0	22	8	4	.269	.307	.338	67	-7	11	2	2	.969	-7	O-49	-1.4
1923	Was-A	106	372	42	98	15	3	0	38	27	18	.263	.313	.320	70	-16	6	4	-1	.982	-4	O-72,3-21/1-5	-2.3
1924	StL-A	77	209	30	53	3	3	0	19	24	12	.254	.330	.297	59	-12	4	4	-1	.969	2	O-49	-1.5
1925	StL-A	55	159	27	50	12	0	0	20	16	6	.314	.377	.390	90	-2	6	2	1	1.000	-1	O-47	-0.5
Total	11	733	2043	306	529	71	31	3	210	212	152	.259	.329	.328	79	-57	67	16		.971	0	O-307,3-280/S12	-6.4

■ STEVE EVANS Evans, Louis Richard b: 2/17/1885, Cleveland, Ohio d: 12/28/43, Cleveland, Ohio BL/TL, 5'10", 175 lbs. Deb: 4/16/08

YEAR	TM/L	G	AB	R	H	2B	3B	HR	RBI	BB	SO	AVG	OBP	SLG	PRO+	BR/A	SB	CS	SBR	FA	FR	G/POS	TPR
1908	NY-N	2	2	0	1	0	0	0	0	0		.500	.500	.500	209	0	0			.000	-1	/O-1	0.0
1909	StL-N	143	498	67	129	17	6	2	56	66		.259	.362	.329	122	16	14			.947	-4	*O-141/1-2	0.7
1910	StL-N	151	506	73	122	21	8	2	73	78	63	.241	.376	.326	109	11	10			.968	-6	*O-141,1-10	-0.2
1911	StL-N	154	547	74	161	24	13	5	71	46	52	.294	.369	.413	122	16	13			.972	-2	*O-150	0.6
1912	StL-N	135	491	59	139	23	9	6	72	36	51	.283	.353	.403	109	6	11			.942	-0	*O-134	-0.1
1913	StL-N	97	245	18	61	15	6	1	31	20	28	.249	.321	.371	99	-1	5			.983	-6	O-74/1-1	-1.0
1914	Bro-F	145	514	93	179	41	**15**	12	96	50	49	.348	.416	**.556**	**165**	**38**	18			.941	-5	*O-112,1-27	2.9
1915	Bro-F	63	216	44	64	14	4	3	30	35	22	.296	.411	.440	140	10	7			.960	-2	O-61/1-7	0.6
	Bal-F	88	340	50	107	20	6	1	37	28	34	.315	.379	.418	120	5	8			.925	-6	O-88/1-4	-0.5

YEAR	TM/L	G	AB	R	H	2B	3B	HR	RBI	BB	SO	AVG	OBP	SLG	PRO+	BR/A	SB	CS	SBR	FA	FR	G/POS	TPR
	Yr	151	556	94	171	**34**	10	4	67	63	56	.308	.392	.426	128	15	15			.940	-8	*O-149/1-5	0.1
Total	8	978	3359	478	963	175	67	32	466	359	299	.287	.374	.407	125	101	86			.955	-31	O-902/1-45	3.0

■ TOM EVANS

Evans, Thomas John b: 7/9/74, Kirkland, Wash. BR/TR, 6'1", 200 lbs. Deb: 9/2/97

YEAR	TM/L	G	AB	R	H	2B	3B	HR	RBI	BB	SO	AVG	OBP	SLG	PRO+	BR/A	SB	CS	SBR	FA	FR	G/POS	TPR
1997	Tor-A	12	38	7	11	2	0	1	2	2	10	.289	.341	.421	97	-0	0	1	-1	.917	1	3-12	0.0
1998	Tor-A	7	10	0	0	0	0	0	0	1	2	.000	.091	.000	-74	-3	0	0	0	.889	-0	/3-7	-0.3
Total	2	19	48	7	11	2	0	1	2	3	12	.229	.288	.333	61	-3	0	1	-1	.911	0	/3-19	-0.3

■ JAKE EVANS

Evans, Uriah L. P. "Bloody Jake" b: 9/1856, Baltimore, Md. d: 1/16/07, Baltimore, Md. TR , 5'8", 154 lbs. Deb: 5/1/1879

YEAR	TM/L	G	AB	R	H	2B	3B	HR	RBI	BB	SO	AVG	OBP	SLG	PRO+	BR/A	SB	CS	SBR	FA	FR	G/POS	TPR
1879	Tro-N	72	280	30	65	9	5	0	17	5	18	.232	.246	.300	84	-4				.884	18	*O-72	0.9
1880	Tro-N	47	180	31	46	8	1	0	22	7	15	.256	.283	.311	96	-1				.906	0	O-47/P-1	-0.2
1881	Tro-N	83	315	35	76	11	5	0	28	14	30	.241	.274	.308	78	-8				.926	14	*O-83	0.4
1882	Wor-N	80	334	33	71	10	4	0	25	7	22	.213	.229	.266	57	-16				.910	20	*O-68,S-11/3-1,2P	0.4
1883	Cle-N	90	332	36	79	13	2	0	31	8	38	.238	.256	.289	66	-13				.902	6	*O-86/S-3,3-3,2P	-0.7
1884	Cle-N	80	313	32	81	18	3	1	38	15	49	.259	.293	.345	97	-2				**.917**	8	*O-76/2-4,S-2	0.4
1885	Bal-a	20	77	18	17	1	1	0	7	7		.221	.318	.260	85	-1				.894	2	O-20	0.1
Total	7	472	1831	215	435	70	21	1	168	63	172	.238	.264	.300	78	-45				.907	67	O-452/S-16,2-6,3P	1.3

■ CARL EVERETT

Everett, Carl Edward b: 6/3/70, Tampa, Fla. BB/TR, 6', 190 lbs. Deb: 7/1/93

YEAR	TM/L	G	AB	R	H	2B	3B	HR	RBI	BB	SO	AVG	OBP	SLG	PRO+	BR/A	SB	CS	SBR	FA	FR	G/POS	TPR
1993	Fla-N	11	19	0	2	0	0	0	0	1	9	.105	.150	.105	-29	-3	1	0	0	.857	-3	/O-8	-0.6
1994	Fla-N	16	51	7	11	1	0	2	6	3	15	.216	.259	.353	56	-3	4	0	1	1.000	-0	O-16	-0.3
1995	NY-N	79	289	48	75	13	1	12	54	39	67	.260	.352	.436	110	4	2	5	-2	.981	5	O-77	0.4
1996	NY-N	101	192	29	46	8	1	1	16	21	53	.240	.327	.307	72	-7	6	0	2	.935	-3	O-55	-0.9
1997	NY-N	142	443	58	110	28	3	14	57	32	102	.248	.309	.420	92	-7	17	9	-0	.971	-9	*O-128	-1.8
1998	*Hou-N	133	467	72	138	34	4	15	76	44	102	.296	.360	.482	118	12	14	12	-3	.987	13	*O-123	2.1
Total	6	482	1461	214	382	84	9	44	209	140	348	.261	.333	.422	99	-4	44	26	-2	.974	2	O-407	-1.1

■ BILL EVERITT

Everitt, William Lee "Wild Bill" b: 12/13/1868, Ft.Wayne, Ind. d: 1/19/38, Denver, Colo. BL/TR, 6'0.5", 185 lbs. Deb: 4/18/1895

YEAR	TM/L	G	AB	R	H	2B	3B	HR	RBI	BB	SO	AVG	OBP	SLG	PRO+	BR/A	SB	CS	SBR	FA	FR	G/POS	TPR
1895	Chi-N	133	550	129	197	16	10	3	88	33	42	.358	.399	.440	109	6	47			.854	-8	*3-130/2-3	0.0
1896	Chi-N	132	575	130	184	16	13	2	46	41	43	.320	.367	.403	99	-2	46			.882	-10	*3-97,O-35	-1.1
1897	Chi-N	92	379	63	119	14	7	5	39	36		.314	.373	.427	107	3	26			.864	-5	3-83/O-8	-0.1
1898	Chi-N	149	596	102	190	15	6	0	69	53		.319	.377	.364	113	11	28			.974	-2	*1-149	0.8
1899	Chi-N	136	536	87	166	17	5	1	74	31		.310	.351	.366	99	-1	30			.971	8	*1-136	0.7
1900	Chi-N	23	91	10	24	4	0	0	17	3		.264	.287	.308	67	-4	2			.979	-1	1-23	-0.5
1901	Was-A	33	115	14	22	3	2	0	8	15		.191	.301	.252	55	-6	7			.967	-4	1-33	-1.0
Total	7	698	2842	535	902	85	43	11	341	212	85	.317	.368	.389	103	7	186			.973	-23	1-341,3-310/O-43,2	-1.2

■ JOHNNY EVERS

Evers, John Joseph "Crab" or "Trojan" b: 7/21/1881, Troy, N.Y. d: 3/28/47, Albany, N.Y. BL/TR, 5'9", 125 lbs. Deb: 9/1/02 FMCH

YEAR	TM/L	G	AB	R	H	2B	3B	HR	RBI	BB	SO	AVG	OBP	SLG	PRO+	BR/A	SB	CS	SBR	FA	FR	G/POS	TPR
1902	Chi-N	26	90	7	20	0	0	0	2	3		.222	.263	.222	51	-5	1			.990	-1	2-18/S-8	-0.5
1903	Chi-N	124	464	70	136	27	7	0	52	19		.293	.325	.381	104	1	25			.937	-14	*2-110,S-11/3-2	-0.9
1904	Chi-N	152	532	49	141	14	7	0	47	28		.265	.307	.318	93	-5	26			.943	31	*2-152	3.2
1905	Chi-N	99	340	44	94	11	2	1	37	27		.276	.333	.329	94	-2	19			.937	3	2-99	0.1
1906	*Chi-N	154	533	65	136	17	6	1	51	36		.255	.305	.315	88	-8	49			.947	6	*2-153/3-1	-0.2
1907	*Chi-N	151	508	66	127	18	4	2	51	38		.250	.309	.313	89	-7	46			.964	**28**	*2-151	2.2
1908	*Chi-N	126	416	83	125	19	6	0	37	66		.300	.402	.375	143	23	36			.960	-0	*2-122/O-1	2.5
1909	Chi-N	127	463	88	122	19	6	1	24	73		.263	.369	.337	116	12	28			.942	3	*2-126	1.3
1910	Chi-N	125	433	87	114	11	7	0	28	108	18	.263	.413	.321	115	16	28			.950	-4	*2-125	1.0
1911	Chi-N	46	155	29	35	4	3	0	7	34	10	.226	.372	.290	86	-1	6			.975	-6	2-33,3-11	-0.8
1912	Chi-N	143	478	73	163	23	11	1	63	74	18	.341	**.431**	.441	139	29	16			.959	6	*2-143	3.1
1913	Chi-N	136	446	81	127	20	5	3	49	50	14	.285	.361	.372	109	7	11			.960	**30**	*2-136,M	3.5
1914	*Bos-N	139	491	81	137	20	3	1	40	87	26	.279	.390	.338	118	16	12			**.976**	5	*2-139	2.0
1915	Bos-N	83	278	38	73	4	1	1	22	50	16	.263	.375	.295	109	6	7	8	-3	.959	-1	2-82	0.3
1916	Bos-N	71	241	33	52	4	1	0	15	40	19	.216	.330	.241	80	-4	5			.951	-18	2-71	-2.2
1917	Bos-N	24	83	5	16	0	0	0	0	13	8	.193	.302	.193	56	-4	1			.950	-7	2-24	-1.1
	Phi-N	56	183	20	41	5	1	1	12	30	13	.224	.333	.279	85	-2	8			.983	-5	2-49/3-7	-0.5
	Yr	80	266	25	57	5	1	1	12	43	21	.214	.324	.252	77	-5	9			.973	-12	2-73/3-7	-1.6
1922	Chi-A	1	3	0	0	0	0	0	1	2	0	.000	.400	.000	12	-0	0	0	0	1.000	-0	/2-1	0.0
1929	Bos-N	1	0	0	0	0	0	0	0	0	0	—	—	—	—	0	0			.000	-1	/2-1	-0.1
Total	18	1784	6137	919	1659	216	70	12	538	778	142	.270	.356	.334	106	71	324	8		.955	54	*2-1735/3-21,S-19,O	12.9

■ JOE EVERS

Evers, Joseph Francis b: 9/10/1891, Troy, N.Y. d: 1/4/49, Albany, N.Y. BR/TR, 5'9", 135 lbs. Deb: 4/24/13 F

YEAR	TM/L	G	AB	R	H	2B	3B	HR	RBI	BB	SO	AVG	OBP	SLG	PRO+	BR/A	SB	CS	SBR	FA	FR	G/POS	TPR
1913	NY-N	1	0	0	0	0	0	0	0	0	0	—	—	—	—	0	0			.000	0	R	0.0

■ TOM EVERS

Evers, Thomas Francis b: 3/31/1852, Troy, N.Y. d: 3/23/25, Washington, D.C. TL, Deb: 5/25/1882

YEAR	TM/L	G	AB	R	H	2B	3B	HR	RBI	BB	SO	AVG	OBP	SLG	PRO+	BR/A	SB	CS	SBR	FA	FR	G/POS	TPR
1882	Bal-a	1	4	0	0	0	0	0		0		.000	.000	.000	-99	-1				.500	-2	/2-1	-0.3
1884	Was-U	109	427	54	99	6	1	0		7		.232	.244	.251	52	-37				.869	11	*2-109	-2.1
Total	2	110	431	54	99	6	1	0		7		.230	.242	.248	51	-38				.866	9	2-110	-2.4

■ HOOT EVERS

Evers, Walter Arthur b: 2/8/21, St.Louis, Mo. d: 1/25/91, Houston, Tex. BR/TR, 6'2", 185 lbs. Deb: 9/16/41 C

YEAR	TM/L	G	AB	R	H	2B	3B	HR	RBI	BB	SO	AVG	OBP	SLG	PRO+	BR/A	SB	CS	SBR	FA	FR	G/POS	TPR
1941	Det-A	1	4	0	0	0	0	0	0	0	2	.000	.000	.000	-91	-1	0	0	0	.000	-0	/O-1	-0.2
1946	Det-A	81	304	42	81	8	4	4	33	34	43	.266	.344	.359	91	-3	7	1	2	.975	0	O-76	-0.5
1947	Det-A	126	460	67	136	24	5	10	67	45	49	.296	.366	.435	119	11	8	7	-2	.978	8	*O-123	1.1
1948	Det-A★	139	538	81	169	33	6	10	103	51	31	.314	.378	.454	117	12	3	4	-2	.973	2	*O-138	0.5
1949	Det-A	132	432	68	131	21	6	7	72	70	38	.303	.403	.428	120	14	6	7	-2	.994	11	*O-123	1.6
1950	Det-A★	143	526	100	170	35	**11**	21	103	71	40	.323	.408	.551	139	30	5	9	-4	**.997**	8	*O-139	2.6
1951	Det-A	116	393	47	88	15	2	11	46	40	47	.224	.297	.356	76	-14	5	3	-0	.976	-4	*O-108	-2.3
1952	Det-A	1	1	0	1	0	0	0	0	0	0	1.000	1.000	1.000	454	0	0	0	0	.000	0	H	0.0
	Bos-A	106	401	53	105	17	4	14	59	29	55	.262	.318	.429	99	-2	5	2	0	.974	-5	*O-105	-1.2
	Yr	107	402	53	106	17	4	14	59	29	55	.264	.320	.430	100	-2	5	2	0	.974	-5	*O-105	-1.2
1953	Bos-A	99	300	39	72	10	1	11	31	23	41	.240	.301	.390	81	-9	2	1	0	.988	-7	O-93	-1.9
1954	Bos-A	6	8	1	0	0	0	0	0	0	2	.000	.000	.000	-90	-2	0	0	0	1.000	-0	/O-1	-0.2
	NY-N	12	11	1	1	0	0	1	3	0	6	.091	.091	.364	12	-2	0	0	0	1.000	-1	/O-4	-0.3
	Det-A	30	60	5	11	4	0	0	5	5	8	.183	.258	.250	40	-5	1	0	0	1.000	-4	O-24	-0.9
1955	Bal-A	60	185	21	44	10	1	6	30	19	28	.238	.309	.400	96	-2	2	1	0	.991	-4	O-55	-0.8
	Cle-A	39	66	10	19	7	1	2	9	3	12	.288	.319	.515	117	1	0	1	-1	1.000	-4	O-25	-0.4
	Yr	99	251	31	63	17	2	8	39	22	40	.251	.311	.430	101	-1	2	2	-1	.993	-8	O-80	-1.2
1956	Cle-A	3	0	1	0	0	0	0	0	1	0	—	1.000	—	180	0	0	0	0	.000	0	H	0.0
	Bal-A	48	112	20	27	3	0	1	4	24	18	.241	.375	.295	85	-1	1	0	0	.985	-3	O-36	-0.5
	Yr	51	112	21	27	3	0	1	4	25	18	.241	.380	.295	86	-1	1	0	0	.985	-3	O-36	-0.5
Total	12	1142	3801	556	1055	187	41	98	565	415	420	.278	.353	.426	106	27	45	36	-8	.983	-4	*O-1051	-3.4

■ GEORGE EWELL

Ewell, George b: Philadelphia, Pa. Deb: 6/26/1871

YEAR	TM/L	G	AB	R	H	2B	3B	HR	RBI	BB	SO	AVG	OBP	SLG	PRO+	BR/A	SB	CS	SBR	FA	FR	G/POS	TPR
1871	Cle-n	1	3	0	0	0	0	0	0	0	0	.000	.000	.000	-99	-1	0	0	0	1.000	-0	/O-1	-0.1

■ JOHN EWING

Ewing, John "Long Jong" b: 6/1/1863, Cincinnati, Ohio d: 4/23/1895, Denver, Colo. TR, Deb: 6/18/1883 F

YEAR	TM/L	G	AB	R	H	2B	3B	HR	RBI	BB	SO	AVG	OBP	SLG	PRO+	BR/A	SB	CS	SBR	FA	FR	G/POS	TPR
1883	StL-a	1	5	0	0	0	0	0		0		.000	.000	.000	-95	-1				.333	-1	/O-1	-0.2
1884	Cin-U	1	4	0	0	0	0	0		0		.000	.000	.000	-93	-1				1.000	-0	/O-1	-0.1
	Was-U	1	5	1	1	0	1	0		0		.200	.200	.600	138	0				.500	0	/O-1	0.0
	Yr	2	9	1	1	0	1	0		0		.111	.111	.333	29	-1				.600	0	/O-2	-0.1
1888	Lou-a	21	79	6	16	1	1	0	5	1		.203	.213	.241	46	-5	7			.907	0	P-21	0.0
1889	Lou-a	41	134	12	23	2	0	0	6	9	30	.172	.234	.187	21	-14	5			.953	2	P-40/1-1	0.0
1890	NY-P	35	114	18	24	2	1	2	17	5	35	.211	.244	.298	41	-11	2			.949	0	P-35	0.0

YEAR	TM/L	G	AB	R	H	2B	3B	HR	RBI	BB	SO	AVG	OBP	SLG	PRO+	BR/A	SB	CS	SBR	FA	FR	G/POS	TPR
1891	NY-N	33	113	10	23	1	0	0	8	3	14	.204	.224	.212	28	-10	4			.917	0	P-33	0.0
Total	6	133	454	47	87	6	3	2	36	18	79	.192	.226	.231	31	-41	18			.935	2	P-129/O-3,1-1	-0.3
■ REUBEN EWING	Ewing, Reuben (b: Reuben Cohen) b: 11/30/1899, Odessa, Russia d: 10/5/70, W.Hartford, Conn. BR/TR, 5'4.5", 150 lbs. Deb: 6/21/21																						
1921	StL-N	3	1	0	0	0	0	0	0	0	1	.000	.000	.000	-99	-0	0	0	0	1.000	0	/S-1	0.0
■ SAM EWING	Ewing, Samuel James b: 4/9/49, Lewisburg, Tenn. BL/TL, 6'3", 200 lbs. Deb: 9/11/73																						
1973	Chi-A	11	20	1	3	1	0	0	2	2	6	.150	.227	.200	20	-2	0	0	0	1.000	1	/1-4	-0.2
1976	Chi-A	19	41	3	9	2	1	0	2	2	8	.220	.256	.317	67	-2	0	0	0	1.000	-0	D-12/1-1	-0.2
1977	Tor-A	97	244	24	70	8	2	4	34	19	42	.287	.338	.385	95	-1	1	1	-0	.957	-5	O-46,D-27/1-2	-0.9
1978	Tor-A	40	56	3	10	0	0	2	9	5	9	.179	.246	.286	48	-4	0	0	0	1.000	-1	/O-3,D-9	-0.5
Total	4	167	361	31	92	11	3	6	47	28	65	.255	.308	.352	81	-9	1	1	-0	.959	-5	/O-49,D-48,1-7	-1.8
■ BUCK EWING	Ewing, William b: 10/17/1859, Hoagland, Ohio d: 10/20/06, Cincinnati, Ohio BR/TR, 5'10", 188 lbs. Deb: 9/9/1880 FMH																						
1880	Tro-N	13	45	1	8	1	0	0	5	1	3	.178	.196	.200	33	-3				.864	-4	C-10/O-4	-0.7
1881	Tro-N	67	272	40	68	14	7	0	25	7	8	.250	.269	.353	89	-4				.915	**25**	C-44,S-22/O-2,3-1	2.2
1882	Tro-N	74	328	67	89	16	11	2	29	10	15	.271	.293	.405	127	10				.887	14	3-44,C-25/2-4,O1P	2.3
1883	NY-N	88	376	90	114	11	13	**10**	41	20	14	.303	.338	.481	147	21				.922	1	C-63,O-14,2-11,/S3	2.3
1884	NY-N	94	382	90	106	15	**20**	3	41	28	22	.277	.327	.445	137	16				.933	4	*C-80,O-12/S-3,3P	2.4
1885	NY-N	81	342	81	104	15	12	6	63	13	17	.304	.330	.471	159	21				.918	9	C-63,O-14/3-8,S1P	3.2
1886	NY-N	73	275	59	85	11	7	4	31	16	17	.309	.347	.444	138	12	18			.921	3	C-50,O-23/1-2	1.7
1887	NY-N	77	318	83	97	17	13	6	44	30	33	.305	.370	.497	146	20	26			.863	-1	3-51,2-19/C-8	1.8
1888	*NY-N	103	415	83	127	18	15	6	58	24	28	.306	.348	.465	159	27	53			.947	5	C-78,3-21/S-4,P-2	3.9
1889	*NY-N	99	407	91	133	23	13	4	87	37	32	.327	.383	.477	139	20	34			.937	16	*C-97/P-3,O-1	3.8
1890	NY-P	83	352	98	119	19	15	8	72	39	12	.338	.406	.545	141	17	36			**.949**	14	C-81/2-1,P-1,M	3.0
1891	NY-N	14	49	8	17	2	1	0	18	5	5	.347	.407	.429	150	3	5			.881	-3	/2-8,C-6	0.1
1892	NY-N	105	393	58	122	10	15	8	76	38	26	.310	.371	.473	158	26	42			.974	8	1-73,C-30/2-2	3.0
1893	Cle-N	116	500	117	172	28	15	6	122	41	18	.344	.394	.496	128	17	47			.927	-1	*O-112/2-5,1-1,C-1	0.9
1894	Cle-N	53	211	32	53	12	4	2	39	24	9	.251	.328	.374	66	-13	18			.912	-2	O-52/2-1	-1.4
1895	Cin-N	105	434	90	138	24	13	5	94	30	22	.318	.363	.468	109	3	34			.976	8	*1-105,M	1.1
1896	Cin-N	69	263	41	73	14	4	1	38	29	13	.278	.349	.373	85	-6	41			.980	4	1-69,M	-0.1
1897	Cin-N	1	1	0	0	0	0	0	0	0		.000	.500	.000	36	0	0			.800	-0	/1-1,M	0.0
Total	18	1315	5363	1129	1625	250	178	71	883	392	294	.303	.351	.456	130	186	354			.931	101	C-636,1-253,O3/2SP	29.5
■ ART EWOLDT	Ewoldt, Arthur Lee "Sheriff" b: 1/8/1894, Paullina, Iowa d: 12/8/77, Des Moines, Iowa BR/TR, 5'10", 165 lbs. Deb: 9/17/19																						
1919	Phi-A	9	32	2	7	1	0	0	2	1	5	.219	.242	.250	38	-3	0			1.000	0	/3-9	-0.2
■ HOMER EZZELL	Ezzell, Homer Estell b: 2/28/1896, Victoria, Tex. d: 8/3/76, San Antonio, Tex. BR/TR, 5'10", 158 lbs. Deb: 4/22/23																						
1923	StL-A	88	279	31	68	6	0	0	14	15	20	.244	.287	.265	44	-23	4	3	-1	.961	8	3-73/2-8	-0.9
1924	Bos-A	90	277	35	75	8	4	0	32	14	21	.271	.311	.329	65	-15	12	5	1	.984	9	3-64,S-21/C-1	0.1
1925	Bos-A	58	186	40	53	6	4	0	15	19	18	.285	.351	.360	81	-5	9	7	-2	.916	-7	3-47/2-9	-1.0
Total	3	236	742	106	196	20	8	0	61	48	59	.264	.312	.313	61	-43	25	15	-1	.957	10	3-184/S-21,2-17,C-1	-1.8
■ JAY FAATZ	Faatz, Jayson S. b: 10/24/1860, Weedsport, N.Y. d: 4/10/23, Syracuse, N.Y. BR/TR, 6'4", Deb: 8/22/1884 M																						
1884	Pit-a	29	112	18	27	2	3	0		1		.241	.274	.313	89	-1				.963	-1	1-29	-0.5
1888	Cle-a	120	470	73	124	10	2	0	51	12		.264	.312	.294	97	-1	64			**.989**	2	*1-120	-0.9
1889	Cle-N	117	442	50	102	12	5	2	38	17	28	.231	.275	.294	60	-24	27			.981	6	*1-117	-2.3
1890	Buf-P	32	111	18	21	0	2	1	16	9	5	.189	.297	.252	52	-7	2			.982	-3	1-32,M	-0.9
Total	4	298	1135	159	274	24	12	3	105	39	33	.241	.293	.292	76	-33	93			.982	4	1-298	-4.6
■ JORGE FABREGAS	Fabregas, Jorge b: 3/13/70, Miami, Fla. BL/TR, 6'3", 205 lbs. Deb: 4/24/94																						
1994	Cal-A	43	127	12	36	3	0	0	16	7	18	.283	.321	.307	62	-7	2	1	0	.987	-2	C-41	-0.6
1995	Cal-A	73	227	24	56	10	0	1	22	17	28	.247	.299	.304	58	-14	0	2	-1	.986	2	C-73	-0.9
1996	Cal-A	90	254	18	73	6	0	2	26	17	27	.287	.332	.335	69	-12	0	1	-1	.989	9	C-89/D-1	0.1
1997	Ana-A	21	38	2	3	1	0	0	3	3	3	.079	.146	.105	-33	-7	0	0	0	.989	2	C-21	-0.5
	Chi-A	100	322	31	90	10	1	7	48	11	43	.280	.305	.382	81	-9	1	1	-0	.988	-5	C-92/1-1	-0.8
	Yr	121	360	33	93	11	1	7	51	14	46	.258	.288	.353	68	-17	1	1	-0	.988	-3	*C-113/1-1	-1.3
1998	Ari-N	50	151	8	30	4	0	1	15	13	26	.199	.267	.245	34	-15	0	0	0	.996	1	C-41	-1.1
	NY-N	20	32	3	6	0	0	1	5	1	6	.188	.212	.281	27	-3	0	0	0	.971	4	C-12	0.1
	Yr	70	183	11	36	4	0	2	20	14	32	.197	.258	.251	33	-18	0	0	0	.991	5	C-53	-1.0
Total	5	397	1151	98	294	34	1	12	135	69	151	.255	.299	.318	60	-67	3	5	-2	.988	11	C-369/1-1,D-1	-3.7
■ BUNNY FABRIQUE	Fabrique, Albert La Verne b: 12/23/1887, Clinton, Mich. d: 1/10/60, Ann Arbor, Mich. BB/TR, 5'8.5", 150 lbs. Deb: 10/4/16																						
1916	Bro-N	2	2	0	0	0	0	0	0	0	1	.000	.000	.000	-97	-0	0			1.000	0	/S-2	0.0
1917	Bro-N	25	88	8	18	3	0	1	3	8	9	.205	.271	.273	65	-4	0			.874	-2	S-21	-0.5
Total	2	27	90	8	18	3	0	1	3	8	10	.200	.265	.267	62	-4	0			.878	-2	/S-23	-0.5
■ LENNY FAEDO	Faedo, Leonardo Lago b: 5/13/60, Tampa, Fla. BR/TR, 6', 170 lbs. Deb: 9/6/80																						
1980	Min-A	5	8	1	2	1	0	0	0	0	0	.250	.250	.375	64	-0	0	0	0	.818	-1	/S-5	-0.1
1981	Min-A	12	41	3	8	0	1	0	6	1	5	.195	.214	.244	30	-4	0	0	0	.971	2	S-12	-0.1
1982	Min-A	90	255	16	62	8	0	3	22	16	22	.243	.290	.310	63	-13	1	0	0	.967	3	S-88/D-1	-0.2
1983	Min-A	51	173	16	48	7	0	1	18	4	19	.277	.294	.335	70	-7	0	0	0	.954	-15	S-51	-1.8
1984	Min-A	16	52	6	13	1	0	1	6	4	3	.250	.304	.327	71	-2	0	0	0	.968	-5	S-15/D-1	-0.6
Total	5	174	529	42	133	17	1	5	52	25	49	.251	.286	.316	64	-26	1	0	0	.961	-16	S-171/D-2	-2.8
■ FRED FAGIN	Fagin, Frederick H. b: Cincinnati, Ohio Deb: 6/25/1895																						
1895	StL-N	1	3	0	1	0	0	0	2	0	0	.333	.333	.333	73	-0	0			.636	0	/C-1	0.0
■ FRANK FAHEY	Fahey, Francis Raymond b: 1/22/1896, Milford, Mass. d: 3/19/54, Boston, Mass. BB/TR, 6'1", 190 lbs. Deb: 4/25/18																						
1918	Phi-A	10	17	2	3	1	0	0	1	0	3	.176	.176	.235	24	-2	0			1.000	-2	/O-5,P-3	-0.4
■ HOWARD FAHEY	Fahey, Howard Simpson "Cap" or "Kid" b: 6/24/1892, Medford, Mass. d: 10/24/71, Clearwater, Fla. BR/TR, 5'7.5", 145 lbs. Deb: 7/23/12																						
1912	Phi-A	5	8	0	0	0	0	0	0	0		.000	.000	.000	-99	-2	0			1.000	-1	/3-2,2-1,S-1	-0.3
■ BILL FAHEY	Fahey, William Roger b: 6/14/50, Detroit, Mich. BL/TR, 6', 200 lbs. Deb: 9/26/71 C																						
1971	Was-A	2	8	0	0	0	0	0	0	0	0	.000	.000	.000	-99	-2	0	0	0	.909	-0	/C-2	-0.3
1972	Tex-A	39	119	8	20	2	0	1	10	12	23	.168	.250	.210	40	-9	4	0	1	.992	11	C-39	0.5
1974	Tex-A	6	16	1	4	0	0	0	0	0	1	.250	.250	.250	45	-1	0	0	0	1.000	-1	/C-6	-0.2
1975	Tex-A	21	37	3	11	1	1	0	3	1	10	.297	.316	.378	96	-0	0	0	0	.983	-1	C-21	-0.1
1976	Tex-A	38	80	12	20	2	0	1	9	11	6	.250	.348	.313	92	-0	1	0	0	.993	2	C-38	0.2
1977	Tex-A	37	68	3	15	4	0	0	5	1	8	.221	.232	.279	38	-6	0	0	0	1.000	-1	C-34	-0.6
1979	SD-N	73	209	14	60	8	1	3	19	21	17	.287	.352	.378	106	2	1	1	-0	.994	-3	C-68	0.1
1980	SD-N	93	241	18	62	4	0	1	22	21	16	.257	.317	.286	74	-8	2	0	1	.977	-4	C-85	-1.0
1981	Det-A	27	67	5	17	2	0	1	9	2	4	.254	.275	.328	71	-3	0	1	-1	.981	3	C-27	0.1
1982	Det-A	28	67	7	10	2	0	0	4	0	5	.149	.149	.179	-10	-10	1	0	0	1.000	5	C-28	-0.4
1983	Det-A	19	22	4	6	1	0	0	2	5	3	.273	.407	.318	106	0	0	0	0	1.000	1	C-18	0.1
Total	11	383	934	75	225	26	2	7	83	74	93	.241	.298	.296	69	-37	9	2	2	.989	11	C-366	-1.6
■ FERRIS FAIN	Fain, Ferris Roy "Burrhead" b: 5/29/21, San Antonio, Tex. BL/TL, 5'11", 186 lbs. Deb: 4/15/47																						
1947	Phi-A	136	461	70	134	28	6	7	71	95	34	.291	.414	.423	130	23	4	5	-2	.985	1	*1-132	1.8
1948	Phi-A	145	520	81	146	27	6	7	88	113	37	.281	.412	.396	115	16	10	5	0	.989	9	*1-145	2.3
1949	Phi-A	150	525	81	138	21	5	3	78	136	51	.263	.415	.339	104	11	8	1	**2**	.984	4	*1-150	1.4

YEAR	TM/L	G	AB	R	H	2B	3B	HR	RBI	BB	SO	AVG	OBP	SLG	PRO+	BR/A	SB	CS	SBR	FA	FR	G/POS	TPR
1950	Phi-A★	151	522	83	147	25	4	10	83	133	26	.282	.430	.402	116	20	8	5	-1	.987	8	*1-151	2.3
1951	Phi-A★	117	425	63	146	30	3	6	57	80	20	**.344**	.451	.471	146	32	0	3	-2	.990	13	*1-108,O-11	3.6
1952	Phi-A☆	145	538	82	176	**43**	3	2	59	105	26	**.327**	**.438**	.429	133	30	3	5	-2	.984	16	*1-144	3.9
1953	Chi-A★	128	446	73	114	18	2	6	52	108	28	.256	.405	.345	101	7	3	2	-0	.989	10	*1-127	1.0
1954	Chi-A†	65	235	30	71	10	1	5	51	40	14	.302	.406	.417	121	9	5	1	1	.987	-4	1-64	0.2
1955	Det-A	58	140	23	37	8	0	2	23	52	12	.264	.464	.364	128	10	2	1	0	.988	0	1-44	0.8
	Cle-A	56	118	9	30	3	0	0	8	42	13	.254	.453	.280	97	3	3	0	1	.992	3	1-51	0.5
	Yr	114	258	32	67	11	0	2	31	94	25	.260	.459	.326	113	13	5	1	1	.990	4	1-95	1.3
Total	9	1151	3930	595	1139	213	30	48	570	904	261	.290	.425	.396	120	160	46	28	-3	.987	59	*1-1116/O-11	17.8

■ GEORGE FAIR

Fair, George T. b: 1/14/1856, Boston, Mass. d: 2/12/39, Roslindale, Mass. 5′7.5″, 140 lbs. Deb: 7/29/1876

YEAR	TM/L	G	AB	R	H	2B	3B	HR	RBI	BB	SO	AVG	OBP	SLG	PRO+	BR/A	SB	CS	SBR	FA	FR	G/POS	TPR
1876	NY-N	1	4	0	0	0	0	0	0	0	0	.000	.000	.000	-99	-1				.750	0	/2-1	-0.1

■ JIM FAIREY

Fairey, James Burke b: 9/22/44, Orangeburg, S.C. BL/TL, 5′10″, 190 lbs. Deb: 4/14/68

YEAR	TM/L	G	AB	R	H	2B	3B	HR	RBI	BB	SO	AVG	OBP	SLG	PRO+	BR/A	SB	CS	SBR	FA	FR	G/POS	TPR
1968	LA-N	99	156	17	31	3	3	1	10	9	32	.199	.242	.276	60	-8	1	1	-0	.944	-8	O-63	-2.1
1969	Mon-N	20	49	6	14	1	0	1	6	1	7	.286	.300	.367	86	-1	0	2	-1	.913	-1	O-13	-0.4
1970	Mon-N	92	211	35	51	9	3	3	25	14	38	.242	.295	.355	74	-8	1	3	-2	.978	-8	O-59	-2.0
1971	Mon-N	92	200	19	49	8	1	1	19	12	23	.245	.288	.310	69	-8	3	3	-1	.968	1	O-58	-1.2
1972	Mon-N	86	141	9	33	7	0	1	15	10	21	.234	.285	.305	66	-6	1	3	-2	.932	-7	O-37	-1.7
1973	LA-N	10	9	0	2	0	0	0	0	1	1	.222	.300	.222	49	-1	0	0	0	.000	0	H	-0.1
Total	6	399	766	86	180	28	7	7	75	47	122	.235	.281	.317	69	-32	6	12	-5	.957	-23	O-230	-7.5

■ RON FAIRLY

Fairly, Ronald Ray b: 7/12/38, Macon, Ga. BL/TL, 5′10″, 181 lbs. Deb: 9/9/58

YEAR	TM/L	G	AB	R	H	2B	3B	HR	RBI	BB	SO	AVG	OBP	SLG	PRO+	BR/A	SB	CS	SBR	FA	FR	G/POS	TPR
1958	LA-N	15	53	6	15	1	0	2	8	6	7	.283	.356	.415	100	0	0	0	0	.971	-1	O-15	-0.2
1959	*LA-N	118	244	27	58	12	1	4	23	31	29	.238	.326	.344	73	-9	0	4	-2	.963	-10	O-88	-2.5
1960	LA-N	14	37	6	4	0	3	1	3	7	12	.108	.250	.351	59	-2	0	0	0	1.000	-1	O-13	-0.4
1961	LA-N	111	245	42	79	15	2	10	48	48	22	.322	.435	.522	140	16	0	0	0	.989	-6	O-71,1-23	0.5
1962	LA-N	147	460	80	128	15	7	14	71	75	59	.278	.383	.433	126	19	1	1	-0	.989	-23	*1-120,O-48	-1.3
1963	*LA-N	152	490	62	133	21	0	12	77	58	69	.271	.350	.388	120	13	5	2	0	**.995**	-11	*1-119,O-45	-0.5
1964	LA-N	150	454	62	116	19	5	10	74	65	59	.256	.351	.385	116	11	4	0	1	.987	-1	*1-141	0.5
1965	*LA-N	158	555	73	152	28	1	9	70	76	72	.274	.364	.377	117	14	2	0	1	.982	-1	*O-148,1-13	0.8
1966	*LA-N	117	351	53	101	20	0	14	61	52	38	.288	.383	.464	146	23	3	2	-0	.974	-15	O-98,1-25	0.3
1967	LA-N	153	486	45	107	19	0	10	55	54	51	.220	.299	.321	85	-10	1	4	-2	.986	-4	O-97,1-68	-2.6
1968	LA-N	141	441	32	103	15	1	4	43	41	61	.234	.305	.299	89	-6	0	2	-1	.989	0	*O-105,1-36	-1.7
1969	LA-N	30	64	3	14	3	2	0	8	9	6	.219	.315	.328	86	-1	0	0	0	.981	-1	1-12,O-10	-0.4
	Mon-N	70	253	35	73	13	4	12	39	28	22	.289	.359	.514	142	13	1	0	0	.991	1	1-52,O-21	1.0
	Yr	100	317	38	87	16	6	12	47	37	28	.274	.350	.476	132	13	1	0	0	.989	-0	1-64,O-31	0.6
1970	Mon-N	119	385	54	111	19	0	15	61	72	64	.288	.406	.455	130	19	10	2	2	.995	5	*1-118/O-4	1.6
1971	Mon-N	146	447	58	115	23	0	13	71	81	65	.257	.377	.396	119	14	1	3	-2	.992	5	*1-135,O-10	0.6
1972	Mon-N	140	446	51	124	15	1	17	68	46	45	.278	.349	.430	118	11	3	4	-2	.985	6	O-70,1-68	0.8
1973	Mon-N★	142	413	70	123	13	1	17	49	86	33	.298	.422	.458	139	26	2	2	-1	.974	-8	*O-121/1-5	1.2
1974	Mon-N	101	282	35	69	9	1	12	43	57	28	.245	.374	.411	113	6	2	1	0	.989	1	1-67,O-20	0.2
1975	StL-N	107	229	32	69	13	2	7	37	45	22	.301	.422	.467	142	15	0	1	-1	.980	-0	1-56,O-20	1.1
1976	StL-N	73	110	13	29	4	0	0	21	23	12	.264	.391	.300	97	1	0	0	0	.995	3	1-27	0.2
	Oak-A	15	46	9	11	1	0	3	10	9	12	.239	.364	.457	145	3	0	0	0	1.000	1	1-15	0.3
1977	Tor-A★	132	458	60	128	24	2	19	64	58	58	.279	.363	.465	122	14	0	4	-2	.986	3	D-58,1-40,O-33	1.0
1978	Cal-A	91	235	23	51	5	0	10	40	25	31	.217	.295	.366	88	-4	0	1	-1	.998	-2	1-78/D-5	-1.1
Total	21	2442	7184	931	1913	307	33	215	1044	1052	877	.266	.363	.408	117	186	35	33	-9	.991	-60	*1-1218,O-1037/D-63	-0.6

■ ANTON FALCH

Falch, Anton C. b: 12/4/1860, Milwaukee, Wis. d: 3/31/36, Wauwatosa, Wis. 6′6″, 220 lbs. Deb: 9/30/1884

YEAR	TM/L	G	AB	R	H	2B	3B	HR	RBI	BB	SO	AVG	OBP	SLG	PRO+	BR/A	SB	CS	SBR	FA	FR	G/POS	TPR
1884	Mil-U	5	18	0	2	0	0	0		0		.111	.111	.111	-60	-5				.600	-1	/O-3,C-2	-0.6

■ BIBB FALK

Falk, Bibb August "Jockey" b: 1/27/1899, Austin, Tex. d: 6/8/89, Austin, Tex. BL/TL, 6′, 175 lbs. Deb: 9/17/20 FMC

YEAR	TM/L	G	AB	R	H	2B	3B	HR	RBI	BB	SO	AVG	OBP	SLG	PRO+	BR/A	SB	CS	SBR	FA	FR	G/POS	TPR
1920	Chi-A	7	17	1	5	1	1	0	2	0	5	.294	.294	.471	100	-0	0	0	0	1.000	-1	/O-4	-0.1
1921	Chi-A	152	585	62	167	31	11	5	82	37	69	.285	.330	.402	87	-13	4	4	-1	.958	-14	*O-149	-3.7
1922	Chi-A	131	483	58	144	27	1	12	79	27	55	.298	.335	.433	99	-2	2	6	-3	.963	-9	*O-129	-2.3
1923	Chi-A	87	274	44	84	18	6	5	38	25	12	.307	.367	.471	121	7	5	5	-2	.951	-7	O-80	-0.6
1924	Chi-A	138	526	77	185	37	8	6	99	47	21	.352	.406	.487	134	26	6	6	-2	.970	10	*O-134	2.3
1925	Chi-A	154	602	80	181	35	9	4	99	51	25	.301	.357	.409	99	-2	4	5	-2	.959	-4	*O-153	-1.7
1926	Chi-A	155	566	86	195	43	4	8	108	66	22	.345	.415	.477	137	32	9	10	-3	**.992**	8	*O-155	2.4
1927	Chi-A	145	535	76	175	35	6	9	83	52	19	.327	.391	.465	125	19	5	7	-3	.978	18	*O-145	2.4
1928	Chi-A	98	286	42	83	18	4	1	37	25	16	.290	.347	.392	95	-2	5	1	1	.972	2	O-78	-0.4
1929	Cle-A	125	426	65	133	30	7	13	93	42	14	.312	.374	.507	120	12	4	4	-1	.943	-4	*O-120	-0.1
1930	Cle-A	82	191	34	62	12	1	4	36	23	8	.325	.397	.461	113	4	2	0	1	.967	1	O-42	0.3
1931	Cle-A	79	161	30	49	13	1	2	28	17	13	.304	.371	.435	105	1	1	1	-0	.949	-3	O-33	-0.4
Total	12	1353	4652	655	1463	300	59	69	784	412	279	.314	.372	.449	113	82	47	49	-15	.967	-4	*O-1222	-1.9

■ CHARLIE FALLON

Fallon, Charles Augustus b: 3/7/1881, New York, N.Y. d: 6/10/60, Kings Park, N.Y. BR/TR, 5′6″, Deb: 6/30/05

YEAR	TM/L	G	AB	R	H	2B	3B	HR	RBI	BB	SO	AVG	OBP	SLG	PRO+	BR/A	SB	CS	SBR	FA	FR	G/POS	TPR
1905	NY-A	1	0	0	0	0	0	0	0	0		—	—	—	—	0	0			.000	0	R	0.0

■ GEORGE FALLON

Fallon, George Decatur "Flash" b: 7/8/14, Jersey City, N.J. d: 10/25/94, Lake Worth, Fla. BR/TR, 5′9″, 155 lbs. Deb: 9/27/37

YEAR	TM/L	G	AB	R	H	2B	3B	HR	RBI	BB	SO	AVG	OBP	SLG	PRO+	BR/A	SB	CS	SBR	FA	FR	G/POS	TPR
1937	Bro-N	4	8	0	2	1	0	0	0	1	0	.250	.333	.375	91	-0	0			.895	1	/2-4	0.1
1943	StL-N	36	78	6	18	1	0	0	5	2	9	.231	.259	.244	44	-6	0			.968	15	2-36	1.1
1944	*StL-N	69	141	16	28	6	0	1	9	16	11	.199	.285	.262	54	-8	1			.973	4	2-38,S-24/3-6	-0.2
1945	StL-N	24	55	4	13	2	1	0	7	6	6	.236	.311	.309	71	-2	1			.948	-2	S-20/2-4	-0.3
Total	4	133	282	26	61	10	1	1	21	25	26	.216	.285	.270	56	-16	2			.966	18	/2-82,S-44,3-6	0.7

■ PETE FALSEY

Falsey, Peter James b: 4/24/1891, New Haven, Conn. d: 5/23/76, Los Angeles, Cal. BL/TL, 5′6.5″, 132 lbs. Deb: 7/16/14

YEAR	TM/L	G	AB	R	H	2B	3B	HR	RBI	BB	SO	AVG	OBP	SLG	PRO+	BR/A	SB	CS	SBR	FA	FR	G/POS	TPR
1914	Pit-N	3	1	0	0	0	0	0	0	0	1	.000	.000	.000	-99	-0	0			.000	0	H	0.0

■ RIKKERT FANEYTE

Faneyte, Rikkert b: 5/31/69, Amsterdam, Holland BR/TR, 6′1″, 170 lbs. Deb: 8/29/93

YEAR	TM/L	G	AB	R	H	2B	3B	HR	RBI	BB	SO	AVG	OBP	SLG	PRO+	BR/A	SB	CS	SBR	FA	FR	G/POS	TPR
1993	SF-N	7	15	2	2	0	0	0	0	2	4	.133	.235	.133	2	-2	0	0	0	1.000	-1	/O-6	-0.3
1994	SF-N	19	26	1	3	3	0	0	4	3	11	.115	.207	.231	15	-3	0	0	0	.900	-1	/O-6	-0.5
1995	SF-N	46	86	7	17	4	1	0	4	11	27	.198	.289	.267	49	-6	1	0	0	.981	-4	O-34	-1.0
1996	Tex-A	8	5	0	1	0	0	0	1	0	0	.200	.200	.200	1	-1	0	0	0	1.000	-1	/O-6,D-2	-0.1
Total	4	80	132	10	23	7	1	0	9	16	42	.174	.264	.242	35	-12	1	0	0	.976	-6	/O-52,D-2	-1.9

■ JIM FANNING

Fanning, William James b: 9/14/27, Chicago, Ill. BR/TR, 5′11″, 180 lbs. Deb: 9/11/54 MC

YEAR	TM/L	G	AB	R	H	2B	3B	HR	RBI	BB	SO	AVG	OBP	SLG	PRO+	BR/A	SB	CS	SBR	FA	FR	G/POS	TPR
1954	Chi-N	11	38	2	7	0	0	0	1	1	7	.184	.205	.184	2	-5	0	0	0	1.000	-1	C-11	-0.6
1955	Chi-N	5	10	0	0	0	0	0	0	1	2	.000	.091	.000	-73	-3	0	0	0	1.000	3	/C-5	0.1
1956	Chi-N	1	4	0	1	0	0	0	0	0	0	.250	.250	.250	36	-0	0	0	0	.800	1	/C-1	0.0
1957	Chi-N	47	89	3	16	2	0	0	4	4	17	.180	.223	.202	16	-11	0	0	0	.981	2	C-35	-0.7
Total	4	64	141	5	24	2	0	0	5	6	26	.170	.209	.184	6	-19	0	0	0	.979	5	/C-52	-1.2

■ CARMEN FANZONE

Fanzone, Carmen Ronald b: 8/30/43, Detroit, Mich. BR/TR, 6′, 200 lbs. Deb: 7/21/70

YEAR	TM/L	G	AB	R	H	2B	3B	HR	RBI	BB	SO	AVG	OBP	SLG	PRO+	BR/A	SB	CS	SBR	FA	FR	G/POS	TPR
1970	Bos-A	10	15	0	3	1	0	0	3	2	2	.200	.333	.267	63	-1	0	0	0	.750	0	/3-5	-0.1
1971	Chi-N	12	43	5	8	2	0	2	5	2	7	.186	.222	.372	57	-3	0	0	0	1.000	0	/O-6,3-3,1-2	-0.3
1972	Chi-N	86	222	26	50	11	0	8	42	35	45	.225	.338	.383	95	-1	2	3	-1	.923	3	3-36,1-21,2-13,/SO	0.0
1973	Chi-N	64	150	22	41	7	0	6	22	20	38	.273	.359	.440	112	3	1	2	-1	.922	-3	3-25,1-24/O-6	-0.3
1974	Chi-N	65	158	13	30	6	0	4	22	15	27	.190	.269	.304	57	-9	0	1	-1	.885	-1	3-35,2-10/1-7,O-1	-1.2
Total	5	237	588	66	132	27	0	20	94	74	119	.224	.317	.372	86	-11	3	6	-3	.896	-1	3-104/1-54,2-23,OS	-1.9

YEAR	TM/L	G	AB	R	H	2B	3B	HR	RBI	BB	SO	AVG	OBP	SLG	PRO+	BR/A	SB	CS	SBR	FA	FR	G/POS	TPR
■ **JUNIOR FELIX**	Felix, Junior Francisco (Sanchez) b: 10/3/67, Laguna Salada, D.R. BB/TR, 5'11", 165 lbs. Deb: 5/3/89																						
1989	*Tor-A	110	415	62	107	14	8	9	46	33	101	.258	.317	.395	101	0	18	12	-2	.966	3	*O-107/D-2	-0.1
1990	Tor-A	127	463	73	122	23	7	15	65	45	99	.263	.331	.441	112	7	13	8	-1	.966	2	*O-125/D-1	0.4
1991	Cal-A	66	230	32	65	10	2	2	26	11	55	.283	.324	.370	91	-3	7	5	-1	.977	-6	O-65	-1.1
1992	Cal-A	139	509	63	125	22	5	9	72	33	128	.246	.294	.361	82	-13	8	8	-2	.983	7	*O-128/D-8	-1.2
1993	Fla-N	57	214	25	51	11	1	7	22	10	50	.238	.276	.397	73	-9	2	1	0	.940	-2	O-52	-1.2
1994	Det-A	86	301	54	92	25	1	13	49	26	76	.306	.376	.525	129	13	1	6	-3	.980	5	O-81/D-2	1.1
Total	6	585	2132	309	562	105	24	55	280	158	509	.264	.320	.413	99	-5	49	40	-9	.972	8	O-558/D-13	-2.1
■ **JACK FELLER**	Feller, Jack Leland b: 12/10/36, Adrian, Mich. BR/TR, 5'10.5", 185 lbs. Deb: 9/13/58																						
1958	Det-A	1	0	0	0	0	0	0	0	0	0	—	—	—	—	0	0	0	0	1.000	-0	/C-1	0.0
■ **HAPPY FELSCH**	Felsch, Oscar Emil b: 8/22/1891, Milwaukee, Wis. d: 8/17/64, Milwaukee, Wis. BR/TR, 5'11", 175 lbs. Deb: 4/14/15																						
1915	Chi-A	121	427	65	106	18	11	3	53	51	59	.248	.334	.363	105	2	16	18	-6	.959	-3	*O-118	-1.4
1916	Chi-A	146	546	73	164	24	12	7	70	31	67	.300	.341	.427	129	16	13			**.981**	7	*O-141	1.7
1917	*Chi-A	152	575	75	177	17	10	6	102	33	52	.308	.352	.403	128	17	26			.985	19	*O-152	3.0
1918	Chi-A	53	206	16	52	2	5	1	20	15	13	.252	.306	.325	90	-3	6			.957	5	O-53	-0.1
1919	*Chi-A	135	502	68	138	34	11	7	86	40	35	.275	.336	.428	113	7	19			.968	21	*O-135	2.1
1920	Chi-A	142	556	88	188	40	15	14	115	37	25	.338	.384	.540	143	31	8	13	-5	.981	18	*O-142	3.2
Total	6	749	2812	385	825	135	64	38	446	207	251	.293	.347	.427	123	70	88	31		.975	67	O-741	8.5
■ **JOHN FELSKE**	Felske, John Frederick b: 5/30/42, Chicago, Ill. BR/TR, 6'3", 195 lbs. Deb: 7/26/68 MC																						
1968	Chi-N	4	2	0	0	0	0	0	0	0	1	.000	.000	.000	-94	-0	0	0	0	.833	1	/C-3	0.0
1972	Mil-A	37	80	6	11	3	0	1	5	8	23	.138	.216	.213	28	-7	0	0	0	.972	-2	C-23/1-8	-1.0
1973	Mil-A	13	22	1	3	0	1	0	4	1	11	.136	.174	.227	12	-3	0	0	0	1.000	0	/C-7,1-6	-0.3
Total	3	54	104	7	14	3	1	1	9	9	35	.135	.204	.212	23	-10	0	0	0	.969	-1	/C-33,1-14	-1.3
■ **FRANK FENNELLY**	Fennelly, Francis John b: 2/18/1860, Fall River, Mass. d: 8/4/20, Fall River, Mass. BR/TR, 5'8", 168 lbs. Deb: 5/1/1884																						
1884	Was-a	62	257	52	75	17	7	2		20		.292	.343	.436	172	21				.863	13	S-60/2-4	3.1
	Cin-a	28	122	42	43	5	8	2		11		.352	.415	.574	209	14				.813	-6	S-28	0.8
	Yr	90	379	94	118	22	15	4		31		.311	.367	.480	186	37				.849	7	S-88/2-4	3.9
1885	Cin-a	112	454	82	124	14	17	10	**89**	38		.273	.333	.445	142	21				.873	-11	*S-112	1.0
1886	Cin-a	132	497	113	124	13	17	6	72	60		.249	.351	.380	125	15	32			.848	14	*S-132	2.6
1887	Cin-a	134	526	133	140	15	16	8	97	82		.266	.369	.401	112	10	74			.855	-9	*S-134	0.2
1888	Cin-a	120	448	64	88	8	7	2	56	63		.196	.297	.259	75	-12	43			.858	17	*S-112/2-4,O-4	0.7
	Phi-a	15	47	13	11	2	2	1	12	9		.234	.357	.426	151	3	5			.912	-1	S-15	0.2
	Yr	135	495	77	99	10	9	3	68	72		.200	.303	.275	82	-9	48			.863	16	*S-127/2-4,O-4	0.9
1889	Phi-a	138	513	70	132	20	5	1	64	65	78	.257	.344	.322	91	-4	15			.872	-20	*S-138	-1.4
1890	Bro-a	45	178	40	44	8	3	2	18	30		.247	.356	.360	115	4	6			.858	0	S-38/3-7	0.6
Total	7	786	3042	609	781	102	82	34	408	378	78	.257	.345	.378	118	72	175			.860	-4	S-769/2-8,3-7,O-4	7.8
■ **BOBBY FENWICK**	Fenwick, Robert Richard b: 12/10/46, Naha, Okinawa BR/TR, 5'9", 165 lbs. Deb: 4/26/72																						
1972	Hou-N	36	50	7	9	3	0	0	4	3	13	.180	.226	.240	33	-4	0	1	-1	.945	3	2-17/S-4,3-2	-0.1
1973	StL-N	5	6	0	1	0	0	0	1	0	2	.167	.167	.167	-7	-1	0	0	0	.750	-1	/2-3	-0.2
Total	2	41	56	7	10	3	0	0	5	3	15	.179	.220	.232	29	-5	0	1	-1	.932	3	/2-20,S-4,3-2	-0.3
■ **JOE FERGUSON**	Ferguson, Joseph Vance b: 9/19/46, San Francisco, Cal. BR/TR, 6'2", 200 lbs. Deb: 9/12/70 C																						
1970	LA-N	5	4	0	1	0	0	0	1	2	2	.250	.500	.250	112	0	0	0	0	1.000	0	/C-3	0.0
1971	LA-N	36	102	13	22	3	0	2	7	12	15	.216	.304	.304	77	-3	1	0	0	.983	-2	C-35	-0.4
1972	LA-N	8	24	2	7	3	0	1	5	2	4	.292	.346	.542	152	2	0	0	0	1.000	2	/C-7,O-2	0.3
1973	LA-N	136	487	84	128	26	0	25	88	87	81	.263	.376	.470	139	27	1	1	-0	**.996**	-0	*C-122,O-20	3.2
1974	*LA-N	111	349	54	88	14	1	16	57	75	73	.252	.384	.436	134	18	2	2	-1	.988	-10	C-82,O-32	1.0
1975	LA-N	66	202	15	42	2	1	5	23	35	47	.208	.328	.302	79	-5	2	1	0	.994	-1	C-35,O-34	-0.6
1976	LA-N	54	185	24	41	7	0	6	18	25	41	.222	.318	.357	93	-2	2	0	1	.966	-1	O-39,C-17	-0.3
	StL-N	71	189	22	38	8	4	4	21	32	40	.201	.320	.349	89	-2	4	2	0	.978	3	C-48,O-14	0.2
	Yr	125	374	46	79	15	4	10	39	57	81	.211	.319	.353	91	-4	6	2	1	.975	2	C-65,O-53	-0.1
1977	Hou-N	132	421	59	108	21	3	16	61	85	79	.257	.381	.435	130	20	6	2	1	.985	-10	*C-122/1-1	1.4
1978	Hou-N	51	150	20	31	5	0	7	22	37	30	.207	.367	.380	118	5	0	0	0	.994	-6	C-51	0.1
	*LA-N	67	198	20	47	11	0	7	28	34	41	.237	.352	.399	110	3	1	2	-1	.984	-10	C-62/O-3	-0.7
	Yr	118	348	40	78	16	0	14	50	71	71	.224	.359	.391	113	8	1	2	-1	.989	-16	*C-113/O-3	-0.6
1979	LA-N	122	363	54	95	14	0	20	69	70	68	.262	.384	.466	133	18	1	0	0	.981	-12	C-67,O-52	0.7
1980	LA-N	77	172	20	41	3	2	9	29	38	46	.238	.376	.436	128	8	2	2	-1	.982	-3	C-66/O-1	0.6
1981	LA-N	17	14	2	2	1	0	0	1	2	5	.143	.250	.214	34	-1	0	0	0	.000	-0	/O-1	-0.2
	Cal-A	12	30	5	7	1	0	1	5	9	8	.233	.410	.367	125	2	0	0	0	.976	0	/C-8,O-4	0.2
1982	Cal-A	36	84	10	19	2	0	3	8	12	19	.226	.323	.357	87	-1	0	0	0	.993	5	C-32/O-2	0.5
1983	Cal-A	12	27	3	2	0	0	0	2	5	8	.074	.219	.074	-15	-4	0	0	0	.968	-2	/C-9,O-3	-0.6
Total	14	1013	3001	407	719	121	11	122	445	562	607	.240	.361	.409	117	84	22	12	-1	.987	-47	C-766,O-207/1-1	5.4
■ **BOB FERGUSON**	Ferguson, Robert Vavasour b: 1/31/1845, Brooklyn, N.Y. d: 5/3/1894, Brooklyn, N.Y. BB/TR, 5'9.5", 149 lbs. Deb: 5/18/1871 MU																						
1871	Mut-n	33	158	30	38	6	1	0	25	3	2	.241	.255	.291	62	-6	4	4	-1	.774	4	*3-20,2-11/C-5,PM	-0.4
1872	Atl-n	37	165	33	46	5	0	0	19	3	0	.279	.292	.309	72	-8	4	2	0	.809	**36**	*3-37/C-1,M	1.8
1873	Atl-n	51	228	36	59	3	5	0	25	4	9	.259	.272	.316	83	-3	1	2	-1	.755	**32**	*3-50/P-4,M	1.8
1874	Atl-n	56	245	34	64	4	0	0	19	2	7	.261	.267	.278	85	-2	5	3	-0	.760	3	*3-55/C-2,P-1,M	0.0
1875	Har-n	85	366	65	88	10	4	0	43	3	5	.240	.247	.290	82	-8	2	1	0	**.827**	8	*3-85/P-1,M	0.0
1876	Har-N	69	310	48	82	8	5	0	32	2	11	.265	.269	.323	89	-5				.826	2	*3-69,M	-0.1
1877	Har-N	58	254	40	65	7	2	0	35	3	10	.256	.265	.299	86	-3				.841	17	*3-56/P-3,M	1.4
1878	Chi-N	61	259	44	91	10	2	0	39	10	12	.351	**.375**	.405	147	12				.881	16	*S-57/2-4,C-1,M	2.8
1879	Tro-N	30	123	18	31	5	2	0	4	4	3	.252	.276	.325	104	1				.808	2	3-24/2-6,M	0.4
1880	Tro-N	82	332	55	87	9	0	0	22	**24**	24	.262	.312	.289	100	0				.904	-3	*2-82,M	0.1
1881	Tro-N	85	339	56	96	13	5	1	35	29	12	.283	.340	.360	114	6				.904	-10	*2-85,M	-0.1
1882	Tro-N	81	319	44	82	15	2	0	32	23	21	.257	.307	.317	106	3				.914	-13	*2-79/S-2,M	-0.7
1883	Phi-N	86	329	39	85	9	2	0	27	18	21	.258	.297	.298	89	-3				.862	-8	*2-86/P-1,M	-0.8
1884	Pit-a	10	41	2	6	0	0	0		0		.146	.146	.146	-4	-5				.714	-3	/O-6,1-3,3-1,M	-0.8
Total	5 n	262	1162	198	295	28	10	0	131	15	23	.254	.263	.295	78	-27	16	12	-2	.787	82	3-247/2-11,C-8,P-7	3.2
Total	9	562	2306	346	625	76	20	1	226	113	114	.271	.305	.323	102	6				.895	0	2-342,3-150/SOP1C	2.2
■ **FELIX FERMIN**	Fermin, Felix Jose (Minaya) b: 10/9/63, Mao Valverde, D.R. BR/TR, 5'11", 170 lbs. Deb: 7/8/87																						
1987	Pit-N	23	68	6	17	0	0	0	4	4	9	.250	.301	.250	48	-5	0	0	0	.980	1	S-23	-0.2
1988	Pit-N	43	87	9	24	0	2	0	2	8	10	.276	.357	.322	98	0	3	1	0	.955	-5	S-43	-0.3
1989	Cle-A	156	484	50	115	9	1	0	21	41	27	.238	.302	.260	59	-25	6	4	-1	.967	18	*S-153/2-2	0.4
1990	Cle-A	148	414	47	106	13	2	1	40	26	22	.256	.300	.304	70	-17	3	3	-1	.975	4	*S-147/2-1	-0.2
1991	Cle-A	129	424	30	111	13	2	0	31	26	27	.262	.309	.302	69	-17	5	4	-1	.980	1	*S-129	-0.7
1992	Cle-A	79	215	27	58	7	2	0	13	18	10	.270	.329	.321	84	-4	0	0	0	.971	-5	S-55,3-17/2-7,1-2	-0.6
1993	Cle-A	140	480	48	126	16	2	2	45	24	14	.262	.303	.317	67	-22	4	5	-2	.960	-29	*S-140	-4.1
1994	Sea-A	101	379	52	120	21	0	1	35	11	22	.317	.343	.380	84	-9	4	4	-1	.974	-6	S-77,2-25	-0.8
1995	*Sea-A	73	200	21	39	6	0	0	15	6	6	.195	.233	.225	20	-24	2	0	1	.971	13	S-46,2-29	-0.5
1996	Chi-N	11	16	4	2	1	0	0	1	2	0	.125	.222	.188	9	-2	0	0	0	.875	-3	/2-6,S-2	-0.4
Total	10	903	2767	294	718	86	11	4	207	166	147	.259	.307	.303	67	-124	27	21	-5	.971	-11	S-815/2-70,3-17,1-2	-7.4
■ **ED FERNANDES**	Fernandes, Edward Paul b: 3/11/18, Oakland, Cal. d: 11/27/68, Hayward, Cal. BB/TR, 5'9", 185 lbs. Deb: 6/9/40																						
1940	Pit-N	28	33	1	4	1	0	0	2	7	6	.121	.275	.152	21	-3	0			.981	0	C-27	-0.2

YEAR	TM/L	G	AB	R	H	2B	3B	HR	RBI	BB	SO	AVG	OBP	SLG	PRO+	BR/A	SB	CS	SBR	FA	FR	G/POS	TPR
1946	Chi-A	14	32	4	8	2	0	0	4	8	7	.250	.400	.313	105	1	0	0	0	.922	-1	C-12	0.0
Total	2	42	65	5	12	3	0	0	6	15	13	.185	.338	.231	61	-3	0	0		.952	-0	/C-39	-0.2

■ FRANK FERNANDEZ

Fernandez, Frank b: 4/16/43, Staten Island, N.Y. BR/TR, 6′1″, 192 lbs. Deb: 9/12/67

YEAR	TM/L	G	AB	R	H	2B	3B	HR	RBI	BB	SO	AVG	OBP	SLG	PRO+	BR/A	SB	CS	SBR	FA	FR	G/POS	TPR
1967	NY-A	9	28	1	6	2	0	1	4	2	7	.214	.290	.393	104	0	1	1	-0	1.000	0	/C-7,O-2	0.0
1968	NY-A	51	135	15	23	6	1	7	30	35	50	.170	.341	.385	124	5	1	0	0	.989	6	C-45/O-4	1.5
1969	NY-A	89	229	34	51	6	1	12	29	65	68	.223	.401	.415	133	13	1	3	-2	.994	-8	C-65,O-14	0.8
1970	Oak-A	94	252	30	54	5	0	15	44	40	76	.214	.327	.413	106	2	1	0	0	.993	-1	C-76/O-1	0.5
1971	Oak-A	2	4	0	0	0	0	0	0	1	2	.000	.200	.000	-40	-1	0	0	0	1.000	2	/C-2	0.1
	Was-A	18	30	0	3	0	0	0	4	4	10	.100	.206	.100	-12	-4	0	0	0	1.000	-1	/O-6,C-1	-0.6
	Oak-A	2	5	1	1	1	0	0	1	0	1	.200	.200	.400	68	-0	0	0	0	1.000	-0	/C-1	-0.1
	Yr	22	39	1	4	1	0	0	5	5	13	.103	.205	.128	-4	-5	0	0	0	1.000	0	/O-6,C-4	-0.6
	Chi-N	17	41	11	7	1	0	4	4	17	15	.171	.414	.488	135	2	0	0	0	.980	0	C-16	0.3
1972	Chi-N	3	3	0	0	0	0	0	0	0	2	.000	.000	.000	-90	-1	0	0	0	1.000	-0	/C-1	-0.1
Total	6	285	727	92	145	21	2	39	116	164	231	.199	.351	.395	114	17	4	4	-1	.992	-2	C-214/O-27	2.4

■ NANNY FERNANDEZ

Fernandez, Froilan b: 10/25/18, Wilmington, Cal. d: 9/19/96, Lomita, Cal. BR/TR, 5′9″, 170 lbs. Deb: 4/14/42

YEAR	TM/L	G	AB	R	H	2B	3B	HR	RBI	BB	SO	AVG	OBP	SLG	PRO+	BR/A	SB	CS	SBR	FA	FR	G/POS	TPR
1942	Bos-N	145	577	63	147	29	3	6	55	38	61	.255	.303	.347	92	-8	15			.914	6	3-98,O-44	-0.3
1946	Bos-N	115	372	37	95	15	2	2	42	30	44	.255	.313	.323	79	-10	1			.940	-2	3-81,S-18,O-14	-1.2
1947	Bos-N	83	209	16	43	4	0	2	21	22	20	.206	.281	.254	44	-17	2			.933	-13	S-62/O-8,3-6	-2.7
1950	Pit-N	65	198	23	51	11	0	6	27	19	17	.258	.326	.404	88	-4	2			.925	-3	3-52	-0.7
Total	4	408	1356	139	336	59	5	16	145	109	142	.248	.306	.334	80	-38	20			.925	-13	3-237/S-80,O-66	-4.9

■ CHICO FERNANDEZ

Fernandez, Humberto (Perez) b: 3/2/32, Havana, Cuba BR/TR, 6′, 170 lbs. Deb: 7/14/56

YEAR	TM/L	G	AB	R	H	2B	3B	HR	RBI	BB	SO	AVG	OBP	SLG	PRO+	BR/A	SB	CS	SBR	FA	FR	G/POS	TPR
1956	Bro-N	34	66	11	15	2	0	1	9	3	10	.227	.261	.303	47	-5	2	3	-1	.978	7	S-25	0.2
1957	Phi-N	149	500	42	131	14	4	5	51	31	64	.262	.306	.336	75	-18	18	5	2	.960	-25	*S-149	-2.7
1958	Phi-N	148	522	38	120	18	5	6	51	37	48	.230	.283	.318	60	-31	12	6	0	.975	-12	*S-148	-3.0
1959	Phi-N	45	123	15	26	5	1	0	3	10	11	.211	.271	.268	43	-10	2	1	0	.958	-3	S-40/2-2	-1.0
1960	Det-A	133	435	44	105	13	3	4	35	39	50	.241	.305	.313	66	-21	13	4	2	.947	-4	*S-130	-1.4
1961	Det-A	133	435	41	108	15	4	3	40	36	45	.248	.306	.322	66	-21	8	5	-1	.958	-8	*S-121/3-8	-1.9
1962	Det-A	141	503	64	125	17	2	20	59	42	69	.249	.306	.410	88	-10	10	3	1	.960	-27	*S-138/3-2,1-1	-2.4
1963	Det-A	15	49	3	7	1	0	0	2	6	11	.143	.236	.163	14	-6	0	1	-1	.947	2	S-14	-0.3
	NY-N	58	145	12	29	6	0	1	9	9	30	.200	.247	.262	46	-10	3	0	1	.944	-16	S-45/3-5,2-3	-2.5
Total	8	856	2778	270	666	91	19	40	259	213	338	.240	.295	.329	67	-130	68	28	4	.960	-86	S-810/3-15,2-5,1-1	-15.0

■ CHICO FERNANDEZ

Fernandez, Lorenzo Marto (Mosquera) b: 4/23/39, Havana, Cuba BR/TR, 5′10″, 160 lbs. Deb: 4/20/68

YEAR	TM/L	G	AB	R	H	2B	3B	HR	RBI	BB	SO	AVG	OBP	SLG	PRO+	BR/A	SB	CS	SBR	FA	FR	G/POS	TPR
1968	Bal-A	24	18	0	2	0	0	0	0	1	2	.111	.158	.111	-17	-3	0	0	0	.923	3	/S-7,2-4	0.0

■ TONY FERNANDEZ

Fernandez, Octavio Antonio (Castro) (b: Octavio Antonio Fernando (Castro))
b: 6/30/62, San Pedro De Macoris, D.R. BB/TR, 6′2″, 175 lbs. Deb: 9/2/83

YEAR	TM/L	G	AB	R	H	2B	3B	HR	RBI	BB	SO	AVG	OBP	SLG	PRO+	BR/A	SB	CS	SBR	FA	FR	G/POS	TPR
1983	Tor-A	15	34	5	9	1	1	0	2	2	2	.265	.324	.353	81	-1	0	1	-1	1.000	-3	S-13/D-1	-0.4
1984	Tor-A	88	233	29	63	5	3	3	19	17	15	.270	.320	.356	84	-5	5	7	-3	.974	3	S-73,3-10/D-1	0.1
1985	*Tor-A	161	564	71	163	31	10	2	51	43	41	.289	.342	.390	97	-2	13	6	0	.962	5	*S-160	1.9
1986	Tor-A★	163	687	91	213	33	9	10	65	27	52	.310	.340	.428	105	4	25	12	0	**.983**	3	*S-163	2.2
1987	Tor-A★	146	578	90	186	29	8	5	67	51	48	.322	.382	.426	112	11	32	12	2	.979	6	*S-146	3.0
1988	Tor-A	154	648	76	186	41	4	5	70	45	65	.287	.337	.386	101	1	15	5	2	.981	10	*S-154	2.5
1989	*Tor-A★	140	573	64	147	25	9	11	64	29	51	.257	.296	.389	93	-7	22	6	3	**.992**	18	*S-140	2.6
1990	Tor-A	161	635	84	175	27	**17**	4	66	71	70	.276	.355	.391	106	7	26	13	0	.989	9	*S-161	2.8
1991	SD-N	145	558	81	152	27	5	4	38	55	74	.272	.338	.360	93	-4	23	9	2	.972	3	*S-145	1.2
1992	SD-N★	155	622	84	171	32	4	4	37	56	62	.275	.339	.359	96	-2	20	20	-6	.983	-17	*S-154	-1.6
1993	NY-N	48	173	20	39	5	2	1	14	25	19	.225	.327	.295	69	-7	6	2	1	.975	7	S-48	0.4
	*Tor-A	94	353	45	108	18	9	4	50	31	26	.306	.362	.442	114	7	15	8	-0	.985	5	S-94	1.8
1994	Cin-N	104	366	50	102	18	6	8	50	44	40	.279	.364	.426	106	4	12	7	-1	.991	2	3-93/S-9,2-5	0.6
1995	*NY-A	108	384	57	94	20	2	5	45	42	40	.245	.326	.346	76	-13	6	6	-2	.976	-13	*S-103/2-4	-1.7
1997	*Cle-A	120	409	55	117	21	1	11	44	22	47	.286	.326	.423	90	-6	6	6	-2	.980	17	*2-109,S-10/D-1	1.4
1998	Tor-A	138	486	71	156	36	2	9	72	45	53	.321	.391	.459	120	16	13	8	-1	.975	-17	2-82,3-54/D-1	0.4
Total	15	1940	7303	973	2081	369	92	86	754	605	705	.285	.344	.396	100	2	239	128	-5	.980	38	*S-1573,2-200,3/D	17.2

■ AL FERRARA

Ferrara, Alfred John "The Bull" b: 12/22/39, Brooklyn, N.Y. BR/TR, 6′1″, 203 lbs. Deb: 7/30/63

YEAR	TM/L	G	AB	R	H	2B	3B	HR	RBI	BB	SO	AVG	OBP	SLG	PRO+	BR/A	SB	CS	SBR	FA	FR	G/POS	TPR
1963	LA-N	21	44	2	7	0	0	1	1	6	9	.159	.275	.227	50	-3	0	0	0	.950	1	O-11	-0.3
1965	LA-N	41	81	5	17	2	1	1	10	9	20	.210	.297	.296	72	-3	0	0	0	.927	-3	O-27	-0.8
1966	*LA-N	63	115	15	31	4	0	5	23	9	35	.270	.339	.435	123	3	0	0	0	.956	-3	O-32	-0.1
1967	LA-N	122	347	41	96	16	1	16	50	33	73	.277	.345	.467	142	17	0	1	-1	.978	-10	O-94	0.3
1968	LA-N	2	7	0	1	0	0	0	0	0	2	.143	.143	.143	-15	-1	0	0	0	.500	-1	/O-2	-0.2
1969	SD-N	138	366	39	95	22	1	14	56	45	69	.260	.352	.440	125	12	0	0	0	.958	-2	O-96	0.5
1970	SD-N	138	372	44	103	15	4	13	51	46	63	.277	.373	.444	123	13	0	0	0	.968	-8	O-96	0.0
1971	SD-N	17	17	0	2	1	0	0	2	5	5	.118	.318	.176	47	-1	0	0	0	1.000	-1	/O-2	-0.2
	Cin-N	32	33	2	6	0	0	1	5	3	10	.182	.270	.273	55	-2	0	0	0	1.000	-1	/O-5	-0.3
	Yr	49	50	2	8	1	0	1	7	8	15	.160	.288	.240	53	-3	0	0	0	1.000	-1	/O-7	-0.5
Total	8	574	1382	148	358	60	7	51	198	156	286	.259	.346	.423	120	36	0	1	-1	.962	-28	O-365	-1.1

■ MIKE FERRARO

Ferraro, Michael Dennis b: 8/18/44, Kingston, N.Y. BR/TR, 5′11″, 175 lbs. Deb: 9/6/66 MC

YEAR	TM/L	G	AB	R	H	2B	3B	HR	RBI	BB	SO	AVG	OBP	SLG	PRO+	BR/A	SB	CS	SBR	FA	FR	G/POS	TPR
1966	NY-A	10	28	4	5	0	0	0	0	3	3	.179	.281	.179	37	-2	0	0	0	.926	1	3-10	-0.1
1968	NY-A	23	87	5	14	0	1	0	1	2	17	.161	.180	.184	11	-9	0	0	0	.975	4	3-22	-0.6
1969	Sea-A	5	4	0	0	0	0	0	0	1	0	.000	.200	.000	-41	-1	0	0	0	.000	0	H	-0.1
1972	Mil-A	124	381	19	97	18	1	2	29	17	41	.255	.286	.323	83	-9	0	5	-3	.950	-16	*3-115/S-1	-3.3
Total	4	162	500	28	116	18	2	2	30	23	61	.232	.267	.288	67	-21	0	5	-3	.953	-10	3-147/S-1	-4.1

■ RICK FERRELL

Ferrell, Richard Benjamin b: 10/12/05, Durham, N.C. d: 7/27/95, Bloomfield Hills, Mich. BR/TR, 5′10″, 160 lbs. Deb: 4/19/29 FCH

YEAR	TM/L	G	AB	R	H	2B	3B	HR	RBI	BB	SO	AVG	OBP	SLG	PRO+	BR/A	SB	CS	SBR	FA	FR	G/POS	TPR
1929	StL-A	64	144	21	33	6	1	0	20	32	10	.229	.373	.285	69	-5	1	2	-1	.962	0	C-45	-0.2
1930	StL-A	101	314	43	84	18	4	1	41	46	10	.268	.363	.360	81	-8	1	4	-2	.983	-9	*C-101	-1.0
1931	StL-A	117	386	47	118	30	4	3	57	56	12	.306	.394	.427	112	8	2	3	-1	.973	4	*C-108	1.7
1932	StL-A	126	438	67	138	30	5	2	65	66	18	.315	.406	.420	108	7	5	5	-2	.986	-2	*C-120	1.1
1933	StL-A	22	72	8	18	2	0	1	5	12	4	.250	.357	.319	76	-2	2	0	1	.991	3	C-21	0.2
	Bos-A★	118	421	50	125	19	4	3	72	58	19	.297	.385	.382	105	5	2	2	-1	.990	5	*C-116	1.6
	Yr	140	493	58	143	21	4	4	77	70	23	.290	.381	.373	100	3	4	2	0	.990	8	*C-137	1.8
1934	Bos-A☆	132	437	50	130	29	4	1	48	66	20	.297	.390	.389	95	-2	0	0	0	**.990**	3	*C-128	0.7
1935	Bos-A☆	133	458	54	138	34	4	3	61	65	15	.301	.388	.413	100	2	5	8	-3	.979	13	*C-131	1.7
1936	Bos-A★	121	410	59	128	27	5	8	55	65	17	.312	.406	.461	108	6	0	1	-1	.987	9	*C-121	1.7
1937	Bos-A	18	65	8	20	2	0	1	4	15	4	.308	.438	.385	105	1	0	0	0	.990	0	C-18	0.2
	Was-A☆	86	279	31	64	6	0	1	32	50	18	.229	.348	.262	59	-16	1	1	-0	.987	-6	C-84	-1.6
	Yr	104	344	39	84	8	0	2	36	65	22	.244	.366	.285	68	-14	1	1	-0	.988	-6	*C-102	-1.4
1938	Was-A☆	135	411	55	120	24	5	1	58	75	17	.292	.401	.382	104	6	1	0	0	.981	-5	*C-131	0.7
1939	Was-A	87	274	32	77	13	1	0	31	41	12	.281	.377	.336	90	-2	1	1	-0	.976	-6	C-83	-0.4
1940	Was-A	103	326	35	89	18	2	0	28	47	15	.273	.365	.340	90	-3	1	1	-0	.980	-6	C-99	-0.2
1941	Was-A	21	66	8	18	5	0	0	13	15	4	.273	.407	.348	107	1	1	0	0	.980	-1	C-21	0.2
	StL-A	100	321	30	81	14	3	2	23	52	22	.252	.357	.333	81	-8	2	1	0	.995	-5	C-98	-0.4
	Yr	121	387	38	99	19	3	2	36	67	26	.256	.366	.336	85	-6	3	1	0	.992	-6	*C-119	-0.2
1942	StL-A	99	273	20	61	6	1	0	26	33	13	.223	.307	.253	57	-15	0	1	-1	.986	9	C-95	0.0
1943	StL-A	74	209	12	50	7	0	0	20	34	14	.239	.348	.273	81	-3	0	0	0	.987	13	C-70	1.4
1944	Was-A☆	99	339	14	94	11	1	0	25	46	13	.277	.364	.316	99	2	2	1	0	.981	3	C-96	1.2

YEAR	TM/L	G	AB	R	H	2B	3B	HR	RBI	BB	SO	AVG	OBP	SLG	PRO+	BR/A	SB	CS	SBR	FA	FR	G/POS	TPR
1945	Was-A†	91	286	33	76	12	1	1	38	43	13	.266	.366	.325	110	5	2	4	-2	.990	-2	C-83	0.6
1947	Was-A	37	99	10	30	11	0	0	12	14	7	.303	.389	.414	127	4	0	0	0	.994	3	C-37	0.9
Total	18	1884	6028	687	1692	324	45	28	734	931	277	.281	.378	.363	95	-17	29	35	-12	.984	20	*C-1806	10.1

■ **WES FERRELL** Ferrell, Wesley Cheek b: 2/2/08, Greensboro, N.C. d: 12/9/76, Sarasota, Fla. BR/TR, 6'2", 195 lbs. Deb: 9/9/27 F

YEAR	TM/L	G	AB	R	H	2B	3B	HR	RBI	BB	SO	AVG	OBP	SLG	PRO+	BR/A	SB	CS	SBR	FA	FR	G/POS	TPR
1927	Cle-A	1	0	0	0	0	0	0	0	0	0	—	—	—	—	0	0	0	0	.000	-0	/P-1	0.0
1928	Cle-A	2	4	0	1	0	1	0	0	0	0	.250	.250	.750	152	0	0	0	0	1.000	0	/P-2	0.0
1929	Cle-A	47	93	12	22	5	3	1	12	6	28	.237	.283	.387	68	-5	1	0	0	.973	3	P-43	0.0
1930	Cle-A	53	118	19	35	8	3	0	14	12	15	.297	.362	.415	93	-1	0	0	0	.967	-3	P-43	0.0
1931	Cle-A	48	116	24	37	6	1	9	30	10	21	.319	.373	.621	149	7	0	0	0	.969	5	P-40	0.0
1932	Cle-A	55	128	14	31	5	2	2	18	6	21	.242	.276	.359	59	-8	0	0	0	.986	1	P-38	0.0
1933	Cle-A☆	61	140	26	38	7	0	7	26	20	22	.271	.363	.471	114	3	0	0	0	**1.000**	2	P-28,O-13	0.1
1934	Bos-A	34	78	12	22	4	0	4	17	7	15	.282	.341	.487	104	0	1	0	0	.969	-2	P-26	0.0
1935	Bos-A	75	150	25	52	5	1	7	32	21	16	.347	.427	.533	138	9	0	0	0	.977	2	P-41	0.0
1936	Bos-A	61	135	20	36	6	1	5	24	14	10	.267	.336	.437	84	-4	0	0	0	.962	-3	P-39	0.0
1937	Bos-A	18	33	7	12	2	0	1	9	7	3	.364	.475	.515	144	3	0	0	0	.964	2	P-12	0.0
	Was-A☆	53	106	7	27	5	0	0	16	9	18	.255	.313	.302	58	-7	0	0	0	.975	-1	P-25	0.0
	Yr	71	139	14	39	7	0	1	25	16	21	.281	.355	.353	81	-4	0	0	0	.971	1	P-37	0.0
1938	Was-A	26	49	6	11	2	0	1	6	15	7	.224	.406	.327	92	0	0	0	0	.976	1	P-23	0.0
	NY-A	5	12	1	2	1	0	0	1	1	4	.167	.231	.250	20	-2	0	0	0	.917	1	/P-5	0.0
	Yr	31	61	7	13	3	0	1	7	16	11	.213	.377	.311	79	-1	0	0	0	.962	2	P-28	0.0
1939	NY-A	3	8	0	1	1	0	0	1	0	2	.125	.125	.250	-6	-1	0	0	0	1.000	0	/P-3	0.0
1940	Bro-N	2	2	0	0	0	0	0	0	0	2	.000	.000	.000	-94	-1	0			1.000	1	/P-1	0.0
1941	Bos-N	4	4	2	2	0	0	1	2	1	1	.500	.600	1.250	430	2	0			1.000	-0	/P-4	0.0
Total	15	548	1176	175	329	57	12	38	208	129	185	.280	.351	.446	99	-5	2	0		.975	7	P-374/O-13	0.1

■ **SERGIO FERRER** Ferrer, Sergio (Marrero) b: 1/29/51, Santurce, P.R. BB/TR, 5'7", 145 lbs. Deb: 4/5/74

YEAR	TM/L	G	AB	R	H	2B	3B	HR	RBI	BB	SO	AVG	OBP	SLG	PRO+	BR/A	SB	CS	SBR	FA	FR	G/POS	TPR
1974	Min-A	24	57	12	16	0	2	0	0	8	6	.281	.379	.351	107	1	3	2	-0	.855	-12	S-20/2-1	-1.0
1975	Min-A	32	81	14	20	3	1	0	2	3	11	.247	.282	.309	66	-4	3	4	-2	.924	-1	S-18,2-10/D-2	-0.5
1978	NY-N	37	33	8	7	0	1	0	1	4	7	.212	.316	.273	68	-1	1	0	0	.971	10	S-29/2-3,3-2	1.0
1979	NY-N	32	7	7	0	0	0	0	0	2	3	.000	.222	.000	-35	-1	0	2	-1	.833	6	3-12/S-5,2-4	0.3
Total	4	125	178	41	43	3	4	0	3	17	27	.242	.318	.303	76	-5	7	8	-3	.922	2	/S-72,2-18,3-14,D-2	-0.2

■ **HOBE FERRIS** Ferris, Albert Sayles b: 12/7/1877, Providence, R.I. d: 3/18/38, Detroit, Mich. BR/TR, 5'8", 162 lbs. Deb: 4/26/01

YEAR	TM/L	G	AB	R	H	2B	3B	HR	RBI	BB	SO	AVG	OBP	SLG	PRO+	BR/A	SB	CS	SBR	FA	FR	G/POS	TPR
1901	Bos-A	138	523	68	131	16	15	2	63	23		.250	.290	.350	78	-17	13			.930	9	*2-138/S-1	-0.2
1902	Bos-A	134	499	57	122	16	14	8	63	21		.244	.276	.381	79	-17	11			.952	**27**	*2-134	1.4
1903	*Bos-A	141	525	69	132	19	7	9	66	25		.251	.287	.366	90	-8	11			.950	15	*2-139/S-2	1.3
1904	Bos-A	156	563	50	120	23	10	3	63	23		.213	.245	.306	70	-20	7			.962	2	*2-156	-1.6
1905	Bos-A	142	523	51	115	24	16	6	59	23		.220	.253	.361	93	-7	11			.960	14	*2-142	0.9
1906	Bos-A	130	495	47	121	25	13	2	44	10		.244	.262	.360	94	-6	8			.960	9	*2-126/3-4	0.4
1907	Bos-A	150	561	41	135	25	2	4	60	10		.241	.254	.314	82	-14	11			.967	13	*2-150	-0.2
1908	StL-A	148	555	54	150	26	7	2	74	14		.270	.291	.353	108	3	6			**.952**	16	*3-148	2.7
1909	StL-A	148	556	36	120	18	5	4	58	12		.216	.232	.288	69	-23	11			.937	7	*3-114,2-34	-1.4
Total	9	1287	4800	473	1146	192	89	40	550	161		.239	.265	.341	84	-108	89			.954	111	*2-1019,3-266/S-3	3.3

■ **WILLY FETZER** Fetzer, William McKinnon b: 6/24/1884, Concord, N.C. d: 5/3/59, Butner, N.C. BL/TR, 5'10.5", 180 lbs. Deb: 9/4/06

YEAR	TM/L	G	AB	R	H	2B	3B	HR	RBI	BB	SO	AVG	OBP	SLG	PRO+	BR/A	SB	CS	SBR	FA	FR	G/POS	TPR
1906	Phi-A	1	1	0	0	0	0	0	0	0		.000	.000	.000	-97	-0	0			.000	0	H	0.0

■ **CHICK FEWSTER** Fewster, Wilson Lloyd b: 11/10/1895, Baltimore, Md. d: 4/16/45, Baltimore, Md. BR/TR, 5'11", 160 lbs. Deb: 9/19/17

YEAR	TM/L	G	AB	R	H	2B	3B	HR	RBI	BB	SO	AVG	OBP	SLG	PRO+	BR/A	SB	CS	SBR	FA	FR	G/POS	TPR
1917	NY-A	11	36	2	8	0	0	0	1	5	5	.222	.317	.222	64	-1	1			.919	2	2-11	0.1
1918	NY-A	5	2	1	1	0	0	0	0	0	0	.500	.500	.500	197	0	0			.000	0	/2-2	0.0
1919	NY-A	81	244	38	69	9	3	1	15	34	36	.283	.386	.357	108	5	8			.946	8	O-41,S-24/2-4,3-2	1.1
1920	NY-A	21	21	8	6	1	0	0	1	7	2	.286	.464	.333	110	1	0	1	-1	.840	0	/S-6,2-3	0.1
1921	*NY-A	66	207	44	58	19	0	1	19	28	43	.280	.382	.386	94	-1	4	4	-1	.974	-3	O-43,2-15	-0.7
1922	NY-A	44	132	20	32	4	1	1	9	16	23	.242	.324	.311	65	-7	2	4	-2	.975	1	O-38/2-2	-0.9
	Bos-A	23	83	8	24	4	1	0	9	6	10	.289	.344	.361	85	-2	8	3	1	.959	4	3-23	0.4
	Yr	67	215	28	56	8	2	1	18	22	33	.260	.332	.330	72	-8	10	7	-1	.975	5	O-38,3-23/2-2	-0.5
1923	Bos-A	90	284	32	67	10	1	0	15	39	35	.236	.334	.278	62	-14	7	14	-6	.938	-10	2-49,S-37/3-3	-2.6
1924	Cle-A	101	322	36	86	12	2	0	36	24	36	.267	.324	.317	65	-17	12	12	-4	.961	-22	2-94/3-5	-4.0
1925	Cle-A	93	294	39	73	16	1	1	38	36	25	.248	.330	.320	65	-15	6	9	-4	.939	-9	2-83,3-10/O-1	-2.5
1926	Bro-N	105	337	53	82	16	3	2	24	45	49	.243	.341	.326	82	-7	9			.953	-15	*2-103	-1.9
1927	Bro-N	4	1	1	0	0	0	0	0	0	0	.000	.000	.000	-99	-0	0			.000	0	H	0.0
Total	11	644	1963	282	506	91	12	6	167	240	264	.258	.346	.326	77	-59	57	47		.945	-43	2-366,O-123/S-67,3	-10.9

■ **NEIL FIALA** Fiala, Neil Stephen b: 8/24/56, St.Louis, Mo. BL/TR, 6'1", 185 lbs. Deb: 9/3/81

YEAR	TM/L	G	AB	R	H	2B	3B	HR	RBI	BB	SO	AVG	OBP	SLG	PRO+	BR/A	SB	CS	SBR	FA	FR	G/POS	TPR
1981	StL-N	3	3	0	0	0	0	0	0	0	1	.000	.000	.000	-97	-1	0	0	0	.000	0	/H	-0.1
	Cin-N	2	2	1	1	0	0	0	1	0	1	.500	.500	.500	181	0	0	0	0	.000	0	/H	0.0
	Yr	5	5	1	1	0	0	0	1	0	2	.200	.200	.200	13	-1	0	0	0	.000	0	-0,-0	-0.1

■ **ROB FICK** Fick, Robert Charles John b: 3/15/74, Torrance, Cal. BL/TR, 6'1", 189 lbs. Deb: 9/19/98

YEAR	TM/L	G	AB	R	H	2B	3B	HR	RBI	BB	SO	AVG	OBP	SLG	PRO+	BR/A	SB	CS	SBR	FA	FR	G/POS	TPR
1998	Det-A	7	22	6	8	1	0	3	7	2	7	.364	.417	.818	209	3	1	0	0	.950	-1	/C-3,1-1,D-2	0.3

■ **JIM FIELD** Field, James C. b: 4/24/1863, Philadelphia, Pa. d: 5/13/53, Atlantic City, N.J 6'1", 170 lbs. Deb: 6/2/1883

YEAR	TM/L	G	AB	R	H	2B	3B	HR	RBI	BB	SO	AVG	OBP	SLG	PRO+	BR/A	SB	CS	SBR	FA	FR	G/POS	TPR
1883	Col-a	76	295	31	75	10	6	1		7		.254	.272	.339	104	2				.938	-7	*1-76	-1.1
1884	Col-a	105	417	74	97	9	7	4		23		.233	.292	.317	107	5				.958	-4	*1-105	-1.0
1885	Pit-a	56	209	28	50	9	1	1	15	13		.239	.306	.306	95	-1				.965	-0	1-56	-0.7
	Bal-a	38	144	16	30	3	2	0	10	13		.208	.278	.257	71	-4				.963	1	1-38	-0.7
	Yr	94	353	44	80	12	3	1	25	26		.227	.295	.286	85	-5				.964	1	1-94	-1.4
1890	Roc-a	52	188	30	38	7	5	4	25	21		.202	.309	.356	104	1	8			.964	-4	1-51/P-2	-0.5
1898	Was-N	5	21	1	2	0	0	0	0	0		.095	.095	.095	-46	-4	1			.979	-0	/1-5	-0.4
Total	5	332	1274	180	292	38	21	10	50	77		.229	.288	.316	96	-1	9			.956	-15	1-331/P-2	-4.4

■ **SAM FIELD** Field, Samuel Jay b: 10/12/1848, Philadelphia, Pa. d: 10/28/04, Sinking Spring, Pa BR/TR, 5'9.5", 182 lbs. Deb: 5/19/1875

YEAR	TM/L	G	AB	R	H	2B	3B	HR	RBI	BB	SO	AVG	OBP	SLG	PRO+	BR/A	SB	CS	SBR	FA	FR	G/POS	TPR
1875	Cen-n	3	11	2	1	0	0	0	0	0	0	.091	.091	.091	-40	-1	0	0	0	.714	-1	/C-2,O-1	-0.2
	Was-n	5	16	0	5	0	0	0	1	0	1	.313	.313	.313	122	0	1	0	0	.731	-2	/C-4,O-1	-0.1
	Yr	8	27	2	6	0	0	0	1	0	1	.222	.222	.222	58	-1	1	0	0	.723	-3	/C-6,O-2	-0.3
1876	Cin-N	4	14	2	0	0	0	0	0	1	3	.000	.067	.000	-89	-3				.667	-3	/C-3,2-2	-0.5

■ **CECIL FIELDER** Fielder, Cecil Grant b: 9/21/63, Los Angeles, Cal. BR/TR, 6'3", 240 lbs. Deb: 7/20/85

YEAR	TM/L	G	AB	R	H	2B	3B	HR	RBI	BB	SO	AVG	OBP	SLG	PRO+	BR/A	SB	CS	SBR	FA	FR	G/POS	TPR
1985	*Tor-A	30	74	6	23	4	0	4	16	6	16	.311	.363	.527	137	4	0	0	0	.979	1	1-25	0.3
1986	Tor-A	34	83	7	13	2	0	4	13	6	27	.157	.222	.325	46	-7	0	0	0	1.000	-1	D-22/1-7,3-2,O-1	-0.8
1987	Tor-A	82	175	30	47	7	1	14	32	20	48	.269	.347	.560	132	8	0	1	-1	1.000	-1	D-55,1-16/3-2	0.4
1988	Tor-A	74	174	24	40	6	1	9	23	14	53	.230	.291	.431	99	-1	0	1	-1	.991	0	D-50,1-17/3-3,2-2	-0.3
1990	Det-A★	159	573	104	159	25	1	**51**	**132**	90	182	.277	.380	**.592**	167	50	0	1	-1	.989	3	*1-143,D-15	4.2
1991	Det-A★	162	624	102	163	25	0	**44**	**133**	78	151	.261	.349	.513	133	27	0	0	0	.993	-3	*1-122,D-42	1.4
1992	Det-A	155	594	80	145	22	0	35	**124**	73	151	.244	.329	.458	118	13	0	0	0	.991	2	*1-114,D-43	0.5
1993	Det-A★	154	573	80	153	23	0	30	117	90	125	.267	.370	.464	124	20	0	1	-1	.991	-2	*1-119,D-36	0.7
1994	Det-A	109	425	67	110	16	2	28	90	50	110	.259	.340	.504	113	7	0	0	0	.993	16	*1-102/D-7	1.3
1995	Det-A	136	494	70	120	18	1	31	82	75	116	.243	.348	.472	112	8	0	1	-1	.993	6	1-77,D-58	0.2
1996	Det-A	107	391	55	97	12	0	26	80	63	91	.248	.357	.478	109	5	2	0	1	.989	4	1-71,D-36	0.0
	*NY-A	53	200	30	52	8	0	13	37	24	48	.260	.345	.495	109	2	0	0	0	1.000	-1	D-43/1-9	-0.2
	Yr	160	591	85	149	20	0	39	117	87	139	.252	.353	.484	109	7	2	0	1	.990	3	1-80,D-79	-0.2

YEAR	TM/L	G	AB	R	H	2B	3B	HR	RBI	BB	SO	AVG	OBP	SLG	PRO+	BR/A	SB	CS	SBR	FA	FR	G/POS	TPR
1997	*NY-A	98	361	40	94	15	0	13	61	51	87	.260	.363	.410	102	2	0	0	0	1.000	0	D-87/1-8	-0.3
1998	Ana-A	103	381	48	92	16	1	17	68	52	98	.241	.337	.423	95	-3	0	1	-1	.997	-2	1-72,D-31	-1.3
	Cle-A	14	35	1	5	1	0	0	0	1	13	.143	.189	.171	-5	-5	0	0	0	.933	0	D-10/1-3	-0.6
	Yr	117	416	49	97	17	1	17	68	53	111	.233	.326	.401	87	-8	0	1	-1	.995	-2	1-75,D-41	-1.9
Total	13	1470	5157	744	1313	200	7	319	1008	693	1316	.255	.348	.482	119	131	2	6	-3	.992	24	1-905,D-535/3-7,2O	5.5
■ **BRUCE FIELDS** Fields, Bruce Alan b: 10/6/60, Cleveland, Ohio BL/TR, 6', 185 lbs. Deb: 9/3/86																							
1986	Det-A	16	43	4	12	1	1	0	6	1	6	.279	.295	.349	75	-2	1	1	-0	.962	-1	O-14/D-1	-0.3
1988	Sea-A	39	67	8	18	5	0	1	5	4	11	.269	.310	.388	90	-1	0	1	-1	1.000	-5	O-23/D-6	-0.7
1989	Sea-A	3	3	2	1	1	0	0	0	0	1	.333	.333	.667	170	0	0	0	0	.000	-0	/O-1	0.0
Total	3	58	113	14	31	7	1	1	11	5	18	.274	.305	.381	86	-2	1	2	-1	.980	-6	/O-38,D-7	-1.0
■ **GEORGE FIELDS** Fields, George W. b: 7/1853, Waterbury, Conn. d: 9/22/33, Waterbury, Conn. Deb: 5/2/1872																							
1872	Man-n	18	87	16	21	3	1	0	9	0	2	.241	.241	.299	69	-3	0	0	0	.563	-13	3-12/O-5,S-1	-1.2
■ **JOCKO FIELDS** Fields, John Joseph b: 10/20/1864, Cork, Ireland d: 10/14/50, Jersey City, N.J. BR/TR, 5'10", 160 lbs. Deb: 5/31/1887																							
1887	Pit-N	43	164	26	44	9	2	0	17	7	13	.268	.306	.348	86	-3	7			.933	1	O-27,C-14/1-3,3P	-0.1
1888	Pit-N	45	169	22	33	7	2	1	15	8	19	.195	.232	.278	67	-6	9			.887	-5	O-29,C-14/3-3	-1.0
1889	Pit-N	75	289	41	90	22	5	2	43	29	30	.311	.376	.443	142	16	7			.860	-6	O-60,C-16	0.9
1890	Pit-P	126	526	101	148	18	20	9	86	57	52	.281	.355	.443	123	16	24			.879	-13	O-80,2-30,C-15,/S-4	0.3
1891	Pit-N	23	75	10	18	3	0	0	5	10	13	.240	.337	.280	82	-1	1			.897	-3	C-15/S-8	-0.2
	Phi-N	8	30	4	7	2	1	0	5	4	2	.233	.324	.367	98	-0	0			.769	-4	/C-8	-0.3
	Yr	31	105	14	25	5	1	0	10	14	15	.238	.333	.305	87	-1	1			.857	-7	C-23/S-8	-0.5
1892	NY-N	21	66	8	18	4	2	0	5	9	10	.273	.368	.394	133	3	2			.917	-1	O-11,C-10	0.2
Total	6	341	1319	212	358	65	32	12	176	124	139	.271	.338	.397	114	25	50			.883	-31	O-207/C-92,2S31P	-0.2
■ **MIKE FIGGA** Figga, Michael Anthony b: 7/31/70, Tampa, Fla. BR/TR, 6', 200 lbs. Deb: 9/16/97																							
1997	NY-A	2	4	0	0	0	0	0	0	0	3	.000	.000	.000	-99	-1	0	0	0	1.000	1	/C-1,D-1	-0.1
1998	NY-A	1	4	1	1	0	0	0	0	0	1	.250	.250	.250	31	-0	0	0	0	1.000	-1	/C-1	-0.1
Total	2	3	8	1	1	0	0	0	0	0	4	.125	.125	.125	-35	-2	0	0	0	1.000	-0	/C-2,D-1	-0.2
■ **BIEN FIGUEROA** Figueroa, Bienvenido b: 2/7/64, Santo Domingo, D.R. BR/TR, 5'10", 170 lbs. Deb: 5/17/92																							
1992	StL-N	12	11	1	2	1	0	0	4	1	2	.182	.250	.273	49	-1	0	0	0	.938	1	/S-9,2-3	0.0
■ **JESUS FIGUEROA** Figueroa, Jesus Maria (Figueroa) b: 2/20/57, Santo Domingo, D.R. BL/TL, 5'10", 160 lbs. Deb: 4/22/80																							
1980	Chi-N	115	198	20	50	5	0	1	11	14	16	.253	.308	.293	64	-9	2	1	0	.979	-4	O-57	-1.5
■ **SAM FILE** File, Lawrence Samuel b: 5/18/22, Chester, Pa. BR/TR, 5'11", 160 lbs. Deb: 9/10/40																							
1940	Phi-N	7	13	0	1	0	0	0	1	0	1	.077	.077	.077	-60	-3	0			.850	1	/S-6,3-1	-0.2
■ **STEVE FILIPOWICZ** Filipowicz, Stephen Charles "Flip" b: 6/28/21, Donora, Pa. d: 2/21/75, Wilkes-Barre, Pa. BR/TR, 5'8", 195 lbs. Deb: 9/3/44																							
1944	NY-N	15	41	10	8	2	1	0	7	3	7	.195	.250	.293	52	-3	0			1.000	-1	O-10/C-1	-0.5
1945	NY-N	35	112	14	23	5	0	2	16	4	13	.205	.239	.304	50	-8	0			.935	-6	O-31	-1.6
1948	Cin-N	7	26	0	9	0	1	0	3	2	1	.346	.393	.423	125	1	0			1.000	-0	/O-7	0.0
Total	3	57	179	24	40	7	2	2	26	9	21	.223	.265	.318	61	-10	0			.961	-8	/O-48,C-1	-2.1
■ **JACK FIMPLE** Fimple, John Joseph b: 2/10/59, Darby, Pa. BR/TR, 6'2", 185 lbs. Deb: 7/30/83																							
1983	*LA-N	54	148	16	37	8	1	2	22	11	39	.250	.302	.358	83	-4	1	0	0	.989	12	C-54	1.1
1984	LA-N	12	26	2	5	1	0	0	3	1	6	.192	.222	.231	28	-3	0	0	0	.983	2	C-12	-0.1
1986	LA-N	13	13	2	1	0	0	0	2	6	6	.077	.368	.077	32	-1	0	0	0	1.000	1	/C-7,1-1,2-1	0.0
1987	Cal-A	13	10	1	2	0	0	0	1	1	2	.200	.273	.200	29	-1	0	0	0	.913	1	C-13	0.0
Total	4	92	197	21	45	9	1	2	28	19	53	.228	.296	.315	70	-8	1	0	0	.986	15	/C-86,2-1,1-1	1.0
■ **JIM FINIGAN** Finigan, James Leroy b: 8/19/28, Quincy, Ill. d: 5/16/81, Quincy, Ill. BR/TR, 5'11", 175 lbs. Deb: 4/25/54																							
1954	Phi-A☆	136	487	57	147	25	6	7	51	64	66	.302	.383	.421	120	14	2	8	-4	.948	2	*3-136	1.0
1955	KC-A★	150	545	72	139	30	7	9	68	61	49	.255	.333	.385	92	-7	1	3	-2	.975	-7	2-90,3-59	-0.9
1956	KC-A	91	250	29	54	7	2	2	21	30	28	.216	.302	.284	55	-16	3	1	0	.969	-1	2-52,3-32	-1.2
1957	Det-A	64	174	20	47	4	2	0	17	23	18	.270	.359	.316	84	-3	1	1	-0	.954	4	3-59/2-3	0.2
1958	SF-N	23	25	3	5	2	0	0	1	3	5	.200	.310	.280	59	-1	0	0	0	.917	-2	/2-8,3-4	-0.3
1959	Bal-A	48	119	14	30	6	0	1	10	9	10	.252	.305	.328	75	-4	1	0	0	.959	0	3-42/2-6,S-2	-0.3
Total	6	512	1600	195	422	74	17	19	168	190	176	.264	.344	.367	92	-17	8	13	-5	.948	-3	3-332,2-159/S-2	-1.5
■ **BOB FINLEY** Finley, Robert Edward b: 11/25/15, Ennis, Tex. d: 1/2/86, W.Covina, Cal. BR/TR, 6'1", 200 lbs. Deb: 7/4/43																							
1943	Phi-N	28	81	9	21	2	0	1	7	4	10	.259	.294	.321	81	-2	0			.962	3	C-24	0.2
1944	Phi-N	94	281	18	70	11	1	1	21	12	25	.249	.292	.306	71	-11	1			.967	-2	C-74	-0.9
Total	2	122	362	27	91	13	1	2	28	16	35	.251	.292	.309	73	-13	1			.966	1	/C-98	-0.7
■ **STEVE FINLEY** Finley, Steven Allen b: 3/12/65, Paducah, Ky. BL/TL, 6'2", 180 lbs. Deb: 4/3/89																							
1989	Bal-A	81	217	35	54	5	2	2	25	15	30	.249	.300	.318	77	-7	17	3	3	.986	-8	O-76/D-3	-1.4
1990	Bal-A	142	464	46	119	16	4	3	37	32	53	.256	.307	.328	80	-12	22	9	1	.977	-1	*O-133/D-2	-1.5
1991	Hou-N	159	596	84	170	28	10	8	54	42	65	.285	.334	.406	114	9	34	18	-1	.985	-6	*O-153	0.0
1992	Hou-N	162	607	84	177	29	13	5	55	58	63	.292	.356	.407	121	17	44	9	8	.993	10	*O-160	3.3
1993	Hou-N	142	545	69	145	15	**13**	8	44	28	65	.266	.306	.385	87	-12	19	6	2	.988	9	*O-140	-0.3
1994	Hou-N	94	373	64	103	16	5	11	33	28	52	.276	.330	.434	102	-0	13	7	-0	.982	5	O-92	0.2
1995	SD-N	139	562	104	167	23	8	10	44	59	62	.297	.367	.420	111	9	36	12	4	.977	5	*O-138	1.3
1996	*SD-N	161	655	126	195	45	9	30	95	56	87	.298	.357	.531	138	34	22	8	2	.982	12	*O-160	4.2
1997	SD-N★	143	560	101	146	26	5	28	92	43	92	.261	.317	.475	112	6	15	3	3	.989	16	*O-140	2.1
1998	*SD-N	159	619	92	154	40	6	14	67	45	103	.249	.303	.401	89	-13	12	3	2	.981	11	*O-157	-0.1
Total	10	1382	5198	805	1430	243	75	119	546	406	672	.275	.331	.419	106	32	234	78	23	.984	53	*O-1349/D-5	7.8
■ **BILL FINLEY** Finley, William James b: 10/4/1863, New York, N.Y. d: 10/6/12, Asbury Park, N.J. 5'3", 170 lbs. Deb: 7/12/1886																							
1886	NY-N	13	44	2	8	0	0	0	5	1	8	.182	.200	.182	17	-4	2			.800	-3	/O-8,C-8	-0.6
■ **NEAL FINN** Finn, Cornelius Francis "Mickey" b: 1/24/04, Brooklyn, N.Y. d: 7/7/33, Allentown, Pa. BR/TR, 5'11", 168 lbs. Deb: 4/21/30																							
1930	Bro-N	87	273	42	76	13	0	3	30	26	18	.278	.350	.359	73	-11	3			.948	-6	2-81	-1.2
1931	Bro-N	118	413	46	113	22	2	0	45	21	42	.274	.314	.337	75	-14	2			.975	0	*2-112	-0.7
1932	Bro-N	65	189	22	45	5	2	0	14	11	15	.238	.284	.286	55	-12	2			.933	4	3-50/2-2,S-1	-0.5
1933	Phi-N	51	169	15	40	4	1	0	13	10	14	.237	.287	.272	54	-10	2			.964	-1	2-51	-0.9
Total	4	321	1044	125	274	44	5	3	102	68	89	.262	.314	.323	67	-48	9			.964	-3	2-246/3-50,S-1	-3.3
■ **HAL FINNEY** Finney, Harold Wilson b: 7/30/05, Lafayette, Ala. d: 12/20/91, Lafayette, Ala. BR/TR, 5'11", 170 lbs. Deb: 6/24/31 F																							
1931	Pit-N	10	26	2	8	1	0	0	2	0	1	.308	.333	.346	84	-1	1			1.000	-0	/C-6	0.0
1932	Pit-N	31	33	14	7	3	0	0	4	3	4	.212	.297	.303	63	-2	0			.971	3	C-11	0.1
1933	Pit-N	56	133	17	31	4	1	1	18	3	19	.233	.250	.301	57	-8	0			.993	-2	C-47	-0.8
1934	Pit-N	5	0	3	0	0	0	0	0	0	0	—	1.000	—	188	0	0			.000	0	/C-1	0.0
1936	Pit-N	21	35	3	0	0	0	0	3	0	8	.000	.000	.000	-98	-10	0			.956	1	C-14	-0.8
Total	5	123	227	39	46	8	1	1	27	6	32	.203	.233	.260	37	-19	1			.983	1	/C-79	-1.5
■ **LOU FINNEY** Finney, Louis Klopsche b: 8/13/10, Buffalo, Ala. d: 4/22/66, Lafayette, Ala. BL/TR, 6', 180 lbs. Deb: 9/12/31 F																							
1931	Phi-A	9	24	7	9	0	1	0	3	6	1	.375	.516	.458	149	2	0	0	0	1.000	1	/O-8	0.3
1933	Phi-A	74	240	26	64	12	2	3	32	13	17	.267	.307	.371	78	-8	1	3	-2	.947	2	O-63	-1.0
1934	Phi-A	92	272	32	76	11	4	1	28	14	17	.279	.315	.360	77	-10	4	3	-1	.943	0	O-54,1-15	-1.3
1935	Phi-A	109	410	45	112	11	6	0	31	18	18	.273	.307	.329	65	-22	7	2	1	.943	-2	O-76,1-18	-2.6

YEAR	TM/L	G	AB	R	H	2B	3B	HR	RBI	BB	SO	AVG	OBP	SLG	PRO+	BR/A	SB	CS	SBR	FA	FR	G/POS	TPR
1936	Phi-A	151	653	100	197	26	10	1	41	47	22	.302	.351	.377	81	-19	7	9	-3	.990	-4	1-78,O-73	-3.3
1937	Phi-A	92	379	53	95	14	9	1	20	20	16	.251	.288	.343	59	-25	2	5	-2	.989	-4	1-50,O-39/2-1	-3.6
1938	Phi-A	122	454	61	125	21	12	10	48	39	25	.275	.333	.441	94	-6	5	8	-3	.990	-3	1-64,O-46	-1.9
1939	Phi-A	9	22	1	3	0	0	0	1	2	0	.136	.208	.136	-10	-4	0	0	0	1.000	0	/O-4	-0.3
	Bos-A	95	249	43	81	18	3	1	46	24	11	.325	.385	.434	105	2	2	5	-2	.986	-6	1-32,O-24	-1.0
	Yr	104	271	44	84	18	3	1	47	26	11	.310	.370	.410	96	-1	2	5	-2	.986	-6	1-32,O-28	-1.3
1940	Bos-A★	130	534	73	171	31	15	5	73	33	13	.320	.360	.463	107	5	5	2	0	.975	2	O-69,1-51	-0.2
1941	Bos-A	127	497	83	143	24	10	4	53	38	17	.288	.340	.400	93	-6	2	5	-2	.945	-3	O-92,1-24	-1.8
1942	Bos-A	113	397	58	113	16	7	3	61	29	11	.285	.335	.383	98	-2	3	3	-1	.976	2	O-95/1-2	-0.6
1944	Bos-A	68	251	37	72	11	2	0	32	23	7	.287	.347	.347	100	0	1	0	0	.987	-5	1-59/O-2	-0.8
1945	Bos-A	2	2	0	0	0	0	0	0	0	1	.000	.000	.000	-98	-0	0	0	0	.000	0	H	-0.1
	StL-A	57	213	24	59	8	4	2	22	21	6	.277	.345	.380	105	1	0	0	0	.986	-2	O-36,1-22/3-1	-0.4
	Yr	59	215	24	59	8	4	2	22	21	7	.274	.342	.377	103	1	0	0	0	.986	-2	O-36,1-22/3-1	-0.5
1946	StL-A	16	30	0	9	0	0	0	3	2	4	.300	.344	.300	77	-1	0	0	0	.938	0	/O-7	-0.1
1947	Phi-N	4	4	0	0	0	0	0	0	0	0	.000	.000	.000	-99	-1	0			.000	0	H	-0.1
Total	15	1270	4631	643	1329	203	85	31	494	329	186	.287	.336	.388	88	-92	39	45		.961	-22	O-688,1-415/3-1,2-1	-18.8

■ MIKE FIORE
Fiore, Michael Gary Joseph b: 10/11/44, Brooklyn, N.Y. BL/TL, 6', 185 lbs. Deb: 9/21/68

YEAR	TM/L	G	AB	R	H	2B	3B	HR	RBI	BB	SO	AVG	OBP	SLG	PRO+	BR/A	SB	CS	SBR	FA	FR	G/POS	TPR
1968	Bal-A	6	17	2	1	0	0	0	0	4	4	.059	.273	.059	5	-2	0	0	0	.943	-0	/1-5,O-1	-0.3
1969	KC-A	107	339	53	93	14	1	12	35	84	63	.274	.421	.428	137	21	4	4	-1	.988	10	1-91,O-13	2.3
1970	KC-A	25	72	6	13	2	0	0	4	13	24	.181	.306	.208	44	-5	1	1	-0	.986	1	1-20	-0.7
	Bos-A	41	50	5	7	0	0	0	4	8	4	.140	.259	.140	12	-6	0	0	0	1.000	0	1-17/O-2	-0.7
	Yr	66	122	11	20	2	0	0	8	21	28	.164	.287	.180	30	-11	1	1	-0	.991	1	1-37/O-2	-1.4
1971	Bos-A	51	62	9	11	2	0	1	6	12	14	.177	.311	.258	58	-3	0	3	-2	1.000	-0	1-12	-0.6
1972	StL-N	17	10	0	1	0	0	0	1	2	3	.100	.250	.100	3	-1	0	0	0	1.000	-1	/1-6,O-1	-0.2
	SD-N	7	6	0	0	0	0	0	0	1	3	.000	.143	.000	-61	-1	0	0	0	.000	0	H	-0.1
	Yr	24	16	0	1	0	0	0	1	3	6	.063	.211	.063	-20	-2	0	0	0	1.000	-1	/1-6,O-1	-0.3
Total	5	254	556	75	126	18	1	13	50	124	115	.227	.370	.333	97	3	5	8	-3	.988	9	1-151/O-17	-0.3

■ DAN FIROVA
Firova, Daniel Michael b: 10/16/56, Refugio, Tex. BR/TR, 6', 185 lbs. Deb: 9/1/81

YEAR	TM/L	G	AB	R	H	2B	3B	HR	RBI	BB	SO	AVG	OBP	SLG	PRO+	BR/A	SB	CS	SBR	FA	FR	G/POS	TPR
1981	Sea-A	13	2	0	0	0	0	0	0	0	1	.000	.000	.000	-96	-0	0	0	0	1.000	1	C-13	0.0
1982	Sea-A	3	5	0	0	0	0	0	0	0	0	.000	.000	.000	-97	-1	0	0	0	.900	-0	/C-3	-0.1
1988	Cle-A	1	0	0	0	0	0	0	0	0	0	—	—	—	—	0	0	0	0	.000	0	/C-1	0.0
Total	3	17	7	0	0	0	0	0	0	0	1	.000	.000	.000	-97	-2	0	0	0	.944	1	/C-17	-0.1

■ WILLIAM FISCHER
Fischer, William Charles b: 3/2/1891, New York, N.Y. d: 9/4/45, Richmond, Va. BL/TR, 6', 174 lbs. Deb: 6/11/13

YEAR	TM/L	G	AB	R	H	2B	3B	HR	RBI	BB	SO	AVG	OBP	SLG	PRO+	BR/A	SB	CS	SBR	FA	FR	G/POS	TPR
1913	Bro-N	62	165	16	44	9	4	1	12	10	5	.267	.313	.388	97	-1	0			.974	-3	C-51	0.0
1914	Bro-N	43	105	12	27	1	2	0	8	8	12	.257	.310	.305	81	-2	1			.958	3	C-30	0.3
1915	Chi-F	105	292	30	96	15	4	4	50	24	19	.329	.384	.449	142	11	5			.972	-6	C-80	1.2
1916	Chi-N	65	179	15	35	9	2	1	14	11	8	.196	.246	.285	57	-9	2			.973	4	C-56	-0.2
	Pit-N	42	113	11	29	7	1	1	6	10	3	.257	.323	.363	109	1	1			.974	5	C-35	1.0
	Yr	107	292	26	64	16	3	2	20	21	11	.219	.276	.315	76	-8	3			.973	8	C-91	0.8
1917	Pit-N	95	245	25	70	9	2	3	25	27	19	.286	.359	.376	121	7	11			.961	-9	C-69/1-2	0.4
Total	5	412	1099	109	301	50	15	10	115	90	66	.274	.332	.374	107	7	20			.969	-8	C-321/1-2	2.7

■ MIKE FISCHLIN
Fischlin, Michael Thomas b: 9/13/55, Sacramento, Cal. BR/TR, 6'1", 165 lbs. Deb: 9/3/77

YEAR	TM/L	G	AB	R	H	2B	3B	HR	RBI	BB	SO	AVG	OBP	SLG	PRO+	BR/A	SB	CS	SBR	FA	FR	G/POS	TPR
1977	Hou-N	13	15	0	3	0	0	0	0	0	2	.200	.200	.200	8	-2	0	0	0	1.000	1	S-12	0.0
1978	Hou-N	44	86	3	10	1	0	0	0	4	9	.116	.165	.128	-19	-14	1	0	0	.928	-4	S-41	-1.6
1980	Hou-N	1	1	0	0	0	0	0	0	0	1	.000	.000	.000	-99	-0	0	0	0	1.000	-0	/S-1	0.0
1981	Cle-A	22	43	3	10	1	0	0	5	3	6	.233	.283	.256	57	-2	3	2	-0	.955	-0	S-19/2-1	-0.2
1982	Cle-A	112	276	34	74	12	1	0	21	34	36	.268	.353	.319	86	-4	9	5	-0	.970	-7	*S-101/3-8,2-6,C-1	-0.3
1983	Cle-A	95	225	31	47	5	2	2	23	26	32	.209	.296	.276	56	-13	9	2	2	.965	21	2-71,S-15/3-4,D-1	1.3
1984	Cle-A	85	133	17	30	4	2	1	14	12	20	.226	.290	.308	64	-6	2	2	-1	.981	18	2-55,3-17,S-15	1.3
1985	Cle-A	73	60	12	12	4	1	0	2	5	7	.200	.262	.300	54	-4	0	1	-1	.990	27	2-31,S-22/1-6,3D	2.3
1986	NY-A	71	102	9	21	2	0	0	3	8	29	.206	.264	.225	35	-9	0	1	-1	.955	7	S-42,2-27	-0.1
1987	Atl-N	1	0	0	0	0	0	0	0	0	0	—	—	—	—	0	0	0	0	.000	0	/R	0.0
Total	10	517	941	109	207	29	6	3	68	92	142	.220	.293	.273	57	-54	24	13	-1	.959	63	S-268,2-191/31DC	2.7

■ SAM FISHBURN
Fishburn, Samuel E. b: 5/15/1893, Haverhill, Mass. d: 4/11/65, Bethlehem, Pa. BR/TR, 5'9", 157 lbs. Deb: 9/30/19

YEAR	TM/L	G	AB	R	H	2B	3B	HR	RBI	BB	SO	AVG	OBP	SLG	PRO+	BR/A	SB	CS	SBR	FA	FR	G/POS	TPR
1919	StL-N	9	6	0	2	1	0	0	2	0	0	.333	.333	.500	158	0	0			1.000	0	/1-1,2-1	0.1

■ JOHN FISHEL
Fishel, John Alan b: 11/8/62, Fullerton, Cal. BR/TR, 5'11", 185 lbs. Deb: 7/14/88

YEAR	TM/L	G	AB	R	H	2B	3B	HR	RBI	BB	SO	AVG	OBP	SLG	PRO+	BR/A	SB	CS	SBR	FA	FR	G/POS	TPR
1988	Hou-N	19	26	1	6	0	0	1	2	3	6	.231	.310	.346	92	-0	0	0	0	1.000	-2	/O-6	-0.3

■ GUS FISHER
Fisher, August Harris b: 10/21/1885, Pottsboro, Tex. d: 4/8/72, Portland, Ore. BL/TR, 5'10", 175 lbs. Deb: 4/18/11

YEAR	TM/L	G	AB	R	H	2B	3B	HR	RBI	BB	SO	AVG	OBP	SLG	PRO+	BR/A	SB	CS	SBR	FA	FR	G/POS	TPR
1911	Cle-A	70	203	20	53	6	3	0	12	7		.261	.302	.320	73	-8	6			.956	8	C-58/1-1	0.5
1912	NY-A	4	10	1	1	0	0	0	0	0		.100	.100	.100	-40	-2	0			1.000	1	/C-4	-0.1
Total	2	74	213	21	54	6	3	0	12	7		.254	.293	.310	68	-10	6			.958	8	/C-62,1-1	0.4

■ CHARLES FISHER
Fisher, Charles Deb: 6/15/1889

YEAR	TM/L	G	AB	R	H	2B	3B	HR	RBI	BB	SO	AVG	OBP	SLG	PRO+	BR/A	SB	CS	SBR	FA	FR	G/POS	TPR
1889	Lou-a	1	2	0	1	0	0	0	0	0	0	.500	.500	.500	189	0	0			.000	-1	/O-1	0.0

■ CHARLES FISHER
Fisher, Charles G. (b: Charles G. Fish) b: 3/10/1852, Boxford, Mass. d: 2/18/17, Eagle, Alaska BL/TR, 5'8", 143 lbs. Deb: 6/7/1884

YEAR	TM/L	G	AB	R	H	2B	3B	HR	RBI	BB	SO	AVG	OBP	SLG	PRO+	BR/A	SB	CS	SBR	FA	FR	G/POS	TPR
1884	KC-U	10	40	3	8	2	0	0		0		.200	.200	.250	41	-4				.711	-0	/3-9,S-1	-0.4
	CP-U	1	3	1	2	0	0	0		1		.667	.750	.667	335	1				.500	-1	/3-1	0.0
	Yr	11	43	4	10	2	0	0		1		.233	.250	.279	68	-3				.702	-1	3-10/S-1	-0.4

■ SHOWBOAT FISHER
Fisher, George Aloys b: 1/16/1899, Wesley, Iowa d: 5/15/94, St.Cloud, Minn. BL/TR, 5'10", 170 lbs. Deb: 4/24/23

YEAR	TM/L	G	AB	R	H	2B	3B	HR	RBI	BB	SO	AVG	OBP	SLG	PRO+	BR/A	SB	CS	SBR	FA	FR	G/POS	TPR
1923	Was-A	13	23	4	6	2	0	0	2	4	3	.261	.370	.348	95	-0	0	0	0	.750	0	/O-5	0.0
1924	Was-A	15	41	7	9	1	0	0	6	6	6	.220	.319	.244	48	-3	2	0	1	.933	-2	O-11	-0.5
1930	*StL-N	92	254	49	95	18	6	8	61	25	21	.374	.432	.587	139	16	4			.962	-3	O-67	0.8
1932	StL-A	18	22	2	4	0	0	0	2	2	5	.182	.250	.182	13	-3	0	0	0	1.000	-1	/O-5	-0.4
Total	4	138	340	62	114	21	6	8	71	37	35	.335	.402	.503	119	10	6	0		.946	-6	/O-88	-0.1

■ GEORGE FISHER
Fisher, George C. b: Wilmington, Del. BL , Deb: 8/9/1884

YEAR	TM/L	G	AB	R	H	2B	3B	HR	RBI	BB	SO	AVG	OBP	SLG	PRO+	BR/A	SB	CS	SBR	FA	FR	G/POS	TPR
1884	Cle-N	6	24	2	3	0	0	0	0	0	3	.125	.125	.125	-20	-3				.897	-3	/2-6,C-1	-0.6
	Wil-U	8	29	0	2	0	0	0		0		.069	.069	.069	-56	-6				.818	-1	/O-6,S-2	-0.7
Total	1	14	53	2	5	0	0	0	0	0	3	.094	.094	.094	-40	-10				.818	-4	/O-6,2-6,S-2,C-1	-1.3

■ HARRY FISHER
Fisher, Harry Devereux b: 1/3/26, Newbury, Ont., Can. d: 9/20/81, Waterloo, Ont., Canada BL/TR, 6', 180 lbs. Deb: 9/16/51

YEAR	TM/L	G	AB	R	H	2B	3B	HR	RBI	BB	SO	AVG	OBP	SLG	PRO+	BR/A	SB	CS	SBR	FA	FR	G/POS	TPR
1951	Pit-N	3	3	0	0	0	0	0	0	0	0	.000	.000	.000	-97	-1	0	0	0	.000	0	H	-0.1
1952	Pit-N	15	15	0	5	1	0	0	1	0	3	.333	.333	.400	100	-0	0	0	0	1.000	-1	/P-8	0.0
Total	2	18	18	0	5	1	0	0	1	0	3	.278	.278	.333	66	-1	0	0	0	1.000	-1	/P-8	-0.1

■ RED FISHER
Fisher, John Gus b: 6/22/1887, Pittsburgh, Pa. d: 1/31/40, Louisville, Ky. BL/TR, Deb: 4/25/10

YEAR	TM/L	G	AB	R	H	2B	3B	HR	RBI	BB	SO	AVG	OBP	SLG	PRO+	BR/A	SB	CS	SBR	FA	FR	G/POS	TPR
1910	StL-A	23	72	5	9	2	1	0	3	8		.125	.222	.181	28	-6	5			.935	-1	O-19	-0.9

■ NEWT FISHER
Fisher, Newton "Ike" b: 6/28/1871, Nashville, Tenn. d: 2/28/47, Norwood Park, Ill. BR/TR, 5'9.5", 171 lbs. Deb: 5/17/1898 F

YEAR	TM/L	G	AB	R	H	2B	3B	HR	RBI	BB	SO	AVG	OBP	SLG	PRO+	BR/A	SB	CS	SBR	FA	FR	G/POS	TPR
1898	Phi-N	9	26	0	3	1	0	0	0	0		.115	.148	.154	-14	-4	1			.844	-1	/C-8,3-1	-0.4

■ BOB FISHER
Fisher, Robert Taylor b: 11/3/1886, Nashville, Tenn. d: 8/4/63, Jacksonville, Fla. BR/TR, 5'9.5", 170 lbs. Deb: 6/3/12 F

YEAR	TM/L	G	AB	R	H	2B	3B	HR	RBI	BB	SO	AVG	OBP	SLG	PRO+	BR/A	SB	CS	SBR	FA	FR	G/POS	TPR
1912	Bro-N	82	257	27	60	10	3	0	26	14	32	.233	.273	.296	58	-16	7			.917	-14	S-74/2-1,3-1	-2.4
1913	Bro-N	132	474	42	124	11	10	4	54	10	43	.262	.278	.352	77	-16	16			.923	-19	*S-131	-2.4

YEAR	TM/L	G	AB	R	H	2B	3B	HR	RBI	BB	SO	AVG	OBP	SLG	PRO+	BR/A	SB	CS	SBR	FA	FR	G/POS	TPR
1914	Chi-N	15	50	5	15	2	2	0	5	3	4	.300	.340	.420	126	1	2			.943	-1	S-15	0.1
1915	Chi-N	147	568	70	163	22	5	5	53	30	51	.287	.326	.370	110	6	9	20	-9	.933	-20	*S-145	-1.4
1916	Cin-N	61	136	9	37	4	3	0	11	8	14	.272	.313	.346	104	0	7			.905	-12	S-29/2-6,O-1	-1.1
1918	StL-N	63	246	36	78	11	3	2	20	15	11	.317	.356	.411	138	10	7			.979	19	2-63	3.5
1919	StL-N	3	11	0	3	1	0	0	1	0	2	.273	.273	.364	96	-0	0			.900	0	/2-3	0.1
Total	7	503	1742	189	480	61	26	11	170	80	157	.276	.309	.359	96	-13	48	20		.925	-48	S-394/2-73,O-1,3-1	-3.6

■ WILBUR FISHER
Fisher, Wilbur McCullough b: 7/18/1894, Green Bottom, W.Va. d: 10/24/60, Welch, W.Va. BL/TR, 6', 174 lbs. Deb: 6/13/16

YEAR	TM/L	G	AB	R	H	2B	3B	HR	RBI	BB	SO	AVG	OBP	SLG	PRO+	BR/A	SB	CS	SBR	FA	FR	G/POS	TPR
1916	Pit-N	1	1	0	0	0	0	0	0	0	0	.000	.000	.000	-99	-0	0			.000	0	H	0.0

■ CHEROKEE FISHER
Fisher, William Charles b: 12/1845, Philadelphia, Pa. d: 9/26/12, New York, N.Y. BR/TR, 5'9", 164 lbs. Deb: 5/6/1871

YEAR	TM/L	G	AB	R	H	2B	3B	HR	RBI	BB	SO	AVG	OBP	SLG	PRO+	BR/A	SB	CS	SBR	FA	FR	G/POS	TPR
1871	Rok-n	25	123	24	28	3	3	1	22	3	1	.228	.246	.325	65	-5	1	2	-1	**.927**	4	*P-24/1-2,2-1	0.0
1872	Bal-n	46	225	39	52	10	3	1	36	2	5	.231	.238	.316	66	-10	0	1	-1	.761	-8	P-19,O-19,3-18	-1.2
1873	Ath-n	51	253	50	66	4	3	1	35	4	5	.261	.272	.312	68	-11	1	2	-1	.743	5	*O-45,P-13/2-3,1-1	-0.2
1874	Har-n	52	241	28	54	7	0	0	31	2	7	.224	.230	.253	52	-13	2	3	-1	.833	-6	P-39,O-12/3-7,S-2	-0.7
1875	Phi-n	41	177	26	41	3	1	0	11	1	6	.232	.236	.260	69	-6	4	3	-1	.896	-5	P-41/O-5	-0.1
1876	Cin-N	35	129	12	32	1	0	0	4	0	8	.248	.248	.256	80	-2				.793	-5	P-28,O-11/S-1,1-1	-0.3
1877	Chi-N	1	4	0	0	0	0	0	0	0	2	.000	.000	.000	-89	-1				.667	-0	/3-1	-0.1
1878	Pro-N	1	3	0	0	0	0	0	0	0	0	.000	.000	.000	-99	-1				1.000	0	/P-1	0.0
Total	5 n	215	1019	167	241	27	10	3	135	12	24	.237	.245	.291	64	-45	8	11	-4	.862	-9	P-136/O-81,321S	-2.2
Total	3	37	136	12	32	1	0	0	4	0	10	.235	.235	.243	68	-4				.803	-5	/P-29,O-11,3-1,1S	-0.4

■ CARLTON FISK
Fisk, Carlton Ernest "Pudge" b: 12/26/47, Bellows Falls, Vt. BR/TR, 6'2", 220 lbs. Deb: 9/18/69

YEAR	TM/L	G	AB	R	H	2B	3B	HR	RBI	BB	SO	AVG	OBP	SLG	PRO+	BR/A	SB	CS	SBR	FA	FR	G/POS	TPR
1969	Bos-A	2	5	0	0	0	0	0	0	0	2	.000	.000	.000	-95	-1	0	0	0	1.000	-1	/C-1	-0.3
1971	Bos-A	14	48	7	15	2	1	2	6	1	10	.313	.327	.521	128	1	0	0	0	.975	-1	C-14	0.1
1972	Bos-A★	131	457	74	134	28	**9**	22	61	52	83	.293	.370	.538	159	33	5	2	0	.984	1	*C-131	4.4
1973	Bos-A★	135	508	65	125	21	0	26	71	37	99	.246	.310	.441	103	0	7	2	1	.983	6	*C-131/D-3	1.3
1974	Bos-A†	52	187	36	56	12	1	11	26	24	23	.299	.385	.551	156	13	5	1	1	.980	2	C-50/D-2	1.9
1975	*Bos-A	79	263	47	87	14	4	10	52	27	32	.331	.397	.529	147	16	4	3	-1	.979	-4	C-71/D-6	1.4
1976	Bos-A★	134	487	76	124	17	5	17	58	56	71	.255	.339	.415	107	4	12	5	1	.984	10	*C-133/D-1	1.9
1977	Bos-A★	152	536	106	169	26	3	26	102	75	85	.315	.408	.521	135	27	7	6	-2	.987	0	*C-151	3.0
1978	Bos-A★	157	571	94	162	39	5	20	88	71	83	.284	.370	.475	123	17	7	2	1	.980	11	*C-154/O-1,D-1	3.4
1979	Bos-A	91	320	49	87	23	2	10	42	10	38	.272	.307	.450	96	-3	3	0	1	.982	-12	D-42,C-39/O-1	-1.3
1980	Bos-A★	131	478	73	138	25	3	18	62	36	62	.289	.355	.467	117	11	11	5	0	.983	-7	*C-115/O-5,1-3,3D	0.8
1981	Chi-A★	96	338	44	89	12	0	7	45	38	37	.263	.358	.361	110	6	3	2	-0	.990	-2	C-92/1-1,3-1,O-1	0.7
1982	Chi-A★	135	476	66	127	17	3	14	65	46	60	.267	.339	.403	103	2	17	2	4	.994	-1	*C-133/1-2	1.0
1983	*Chi-A	138	488	85	141	26	4	26	86	46	88	.289	.357	.518	133	21	9	6	-1	.991	-2	*C-133/D-2	2.4
1984	Chi-A	102	359	54	83	20	1	21	43	26	60	.231	.292	.468	102	-1	6	0	2	.987	-17	C-90/D-5	-1.1
1985	Chi-A★	153	543	85	129	23	1	37	107	52	81	.238	.324	.488	114	9	17	9	-0	.989	-4	*C-130,D-28	1.1
1986	Chi-A	125	457	42	101	11	0	14	63	22	92	.221	.266	.337	61	-25	2	4	-2	.991	2	C-71,O-31/D-22	-2.1
1987	Chi-A	135	454	68	116	22	1	23	71	39	72	.256	.325	.460	103	1	1	4	-2	.990	2	*C-122/1-9,O-2,D-7	0.8
1988	Chi-A	76	253	37	70	8	1	19	50	37	40	.277	.380	.542	155	19	0	0	0	.995	-5	C-74	2.0
1989	Chi-A	103	375	47	110	25	2	13	68	36	60	.293	.360	.475	137	18	1	0	0	**.993**	-15	C-90,D-13	0.8
1990	Chi-A	137	452	65	129	21	0	18	65	61	73	.285	.379	.451	134	22	7	2	1	.994	5	*C-116,D-14	3.5
1991	Chi-A★	134	460	42	111	25	0	18	74	32	86	.241	.301	.413	98	-3	1	2	-1	.993	-2	*C-106,D-13,1-12	-0.1
1992	Chi-A	62	188	12	43	4	1	3	21	23	38	.229	.316	.309	77	-5	3	0	1	.993	-6	C-54/D-2	-0.7
1993	Chi-A	25	53	2	10	0	0	1	4	2	11	.189	.232	.245	29	-5	0	1	-1	1.000	-4	C-25	-0.9
Total	24	2499	8756	1276	2356	421	47	376	1330	849	1386	.269	.343	.457	116	176	128	58	4	.988	-44	*C-2226,D-166/O13	24.0

■ WES FISLER
Fisler, Weston Dickson "Icicle" b: 7/5/1841, Camden, N.J. d: 12/25/22, Philadelphia, Pa. 5'6", 137 lbs. Deb: 5/20/1871

YEAR	TM/L	G	AB	R	H	2B	3B	HR	RBI	BB	SO	AVG	OBP	SLG	PRO+	BR/A	SB	CS	SBR	FA	FR	G/POS	TPR
1871	Ath-n	28	147	43	41	8	2	0	16	3	2	.279	.293	.361	88	-2	6	3	0	**.972**	1	*1-26/2-2	0.0
1872	Ath-n	47	243	49	85	13	3	0	48	4	4	.350	.360	.428	141	11	3	0	1	.889	8	*2-47	1.1
1873	Ath-n	44	218	44	75	11	4	1	42	2	2	.344	.350	.445	125	5	2	1	0	**.855**	3	*2-36,1-10	0.3
1874	Ath-n	37	180	26	59	12	1	0	22	0	1	.328	.328	.406	123	3	2	0	1	.953	4	1-28/2-9,O-1	0.5
1875	Ath-n	58	268	54	74	13	3	0	31	4	4	.276	.287	.347	107	-0	1	4	-2	.958	-0	1-46,O-10/2-5	-0.2
1876	Phi-N	59	278	42	80	15	1	1	30	2	4	.288	.293	.360	117	5				.911	1	O-24,2-21,1-14,/S-1	0.4
Total	5 n	214	1056	216	334	57	13	1	159	13	13	.316	.325	.398	118	17	14	8	-1	.951	15	1-110/2-99,O-11	1.7

■ CHARLIE FITZBERGER
Fitzberger, Charles Casper b: 2/13/04, Baltimore, Md. d: 1/25/65, Baltimore, Md. BL/TL, 6'1.5", 170 lbs. Deb: 9/11/28

YEAR	TM/L	G	AB	R	H	2B	3B	HR	RBI	BB	SO	AVG	OBP	SLG	PRO+	BR/A	SB	CS	SBR	FA	FR	G/POS	TPR
1928	Bos-N	7	7	0	2	0	0	0	0	0	3	.286	.286	.286	52	-0	0			.000	0	H	0.0

■ DENNIS FITZGERALD
Fitzgerald, Dennis S. b: 3/1865, England d: 10/16/36, New Haven, Conn. 5'10", 160 lbs. Deb: 4/17/1890

YEAR	TM/L	G	AB	R	H	2B	3B	HR	RBI	BB	SO	AVG	OBP	SLG	PRO+	BR/A	SB	CS	SBR	FA	FR	G/POS	TPR
1890	Phi-a	2	8	0	2	0	0	0	0	0	0	.250	.250	.250	48	-1	0			.667	-2	/S-2	-0.2

■ ED FITZ GERALD
Fitz Gerald, Edward Raymond b: 5/21/24, Santa Ynez, Cal. BR/TR, 6', 180 lbs. Deb: 4/19/48 C

YEAR	TM/L	G	AB	R	H	2B	3B	HR	RBI	BB	SO	AVG	OBP	SLG	PRO+	BR/A	SB	CS	SBR	FA	FR	G/POS	TPR
1948	Pit-N	102	262	31	70	9	3	1	35	32	37	.267	.349	.336	84	-5	3			.961	-2	C-96	-0.1
1949	Pit-N	75	160	16	42	7	0	2	18	8	27	.262	.302	.344	71	-7	1			.974	-5	C-56	-0.9
1950	Pit-N	6	15	1	1	1	0	0	0	0	3	.067	.067	.133	-47	-3	0			.950	-0	/C-5	-0.3
1951	Pit-N	55	97	8	22	6	0	0	13	7	10	.227	.286	.289	53	-6	1	1	-0	.965	-2	C-38	-0.8
1952	Pit-N	51	73	4	17	1	0	1	7	7	15	.233	.300	.288	62	-4	0	2	-1	1.000	-1	C-18/3-2	-0.6
1953	Pit-N	6	17	2	2	1	0	0	1	0	2	.118	.118	.176	-25	-3	0	0	0	1.000	-1	/C-5	-0.4
	Was-A	88	288	23	72	13	0	3	39	19	34	.250	.299	.326	70	-12	2	1	0	.989	-3	C-85	-1.1
1954	Was-A	115	360	33	104	13	5	4	40	33	22	.289	.352	.386	108	3	0	1	-1	.973	-17	*C-107	-0.9
1955	Was-A	74	236	28	56	3	1	4	19	25	23	.237	.318	.309	73	-9	0	1	-1	.982	-7	C-72	-1.4
1956	Was-A	64	148	15	45	8	0	2	12	20	16	.304	.387	.399	108	2	0	0	0	.974	2	C-50	0.6
1957	Was-A	45	125	14	34	8	0	1	13	10	9	.272	.331	.360	90	-2	2	0	1	.963	-8	C-37	-0.8
1958	Was-A	58	114	7	30	3	0	0	11	8	15	.263	.311	.289	68	-5	0	0	0	.970	-6	C-21/1-5	-1.1
1959	Was-A	19	62	5	12	3	0	0	5	4	8	.194	.242	.242	34	-6	0	0	0	1.000	-1	C-16	-0.6
	Cle-A	49	129	12	35	6	1	1	4	12	14	.271	.343	.357	96	-1	0	0	0	.978	0	C-45	0.2
	Yr	68	191	17	47	9	1	1	9	16	22	.246	.311	.319	76	-6	0	0	0	.984	-0	C-61	-0.4
Total	12	807	2086	199	542	82	10	19	217	185	235	.260	.324	.336	80	-56	9	6		.975	-49	C-651/1-5,3-2	-8.2

■ HOWIE FITZGERALD
Fitzgerald, Howard Chumney "Lefty" b: 5/16/02, Eagle Lake, Tex. d: 2/27/59, Matthews, Tex. BL/TL, 5'11.5", 163 lbs. Deb: 9/17/22

YEAR	TM/L	G	AB	R	H	2B	3B	HR	RBI	BB	SO	AVG	OBP	SLG	PRO+	BR/A	SB	CS	SBR	FA	FR	G/POS	TPR
1922	Chi-N	10	24	3	8	1	0	0	4	3	2	.333	.407	.375	101	0	1	0	0	.818	-2	/O-6	-0.1
1924	Chi-N	7	19	1	3	0	0	0	2	0	0	.158	.158	.158	-15	-3	0	0	0	1.000	-2	/O-5	-0.5
1926	Bos-A	31	97	11	25	2	0	0	8	5	7	.258	.294	.278	51	-7	1	4	-2	.882	-5	O-23	-1.5
Total	3	48	140	15	36	3	0	0	14	8	11	.257	.297	.279	52	-10	2	4	-2	.878	-8	/O-34	-2.1

■ MIKE FITZGERALD
Fitzgerald, Justin Howard b: 6/22/1890, San Mateo, Cal. d: 1/17/45, San Mateo, Cal. BL/TR, 5'8", 160 lbs. Deb: 6/20/11

YEAR	TM/L	G	AB	R	H	2B	3B	HR	RBI	BB	SO	AVG	OBP	SLG	PRO+	BR/A	SB	CS	SBR	FA	FR	G/POS	TPR
1911	NY-A	16	37	6	10	1	0	0	6	4		.270	.341	.297	74	-1	4			1.000	-2	/O-9	-0.3
1918	Phi-N	66	133	21	39	8	0	0	6	13	6	.293	.361	.353	110	2	3			.966	-14	O-59	-1.6
Total	2	82	170	27	49	9	0	0	12	17	6	.288	.356	.341	102	1	7			.971	-15	/O-68	-1.9

■ MATTY FITZGERALD
Fitzgerald, Matthew William b: 8/31/1880, Albany, N.Y. d: 9/22/49, Albany, N.Y. BR/TR, 6', 185 lbs. Deb: 9/15/06

YEAR	TM/L	G	AB	R	H	2B	3B	HR	RBI	BB	SO	AVG	OBP	SLG	PRO+	BR/A	SB	CS	SBR	FA	FR	G/POS	TPR
1906	NY-N	4	6	2	4	0	0	0	2	0		.667	.667	.667	309	1	1			1.000	-1	/C-3	0.1
1907	NY-N	7	15	1	2	1	0	0	1	0		.133	.133	.200	4	-2	0			.952	-1	/C-6	-0.3
Total	2	11	21	3	6	1	0	0	3	0		.286	.286	.333	91	-0	1			.967	-2	/C-9	-0.2

■ MIKE FITZGERALD
Fitzgerald, Michael Patrick b: 3/28/64, Savannah, Ga. BR/TR, 6'1", 196 lbs. Deb: 6/23/88

YEAR	TM/L	G	AB	R	H	2B	3B	HR	RBI	BB	SO	AVG	OBP	SLG	PRO+	BR/A	SB	CS	SBR	FA	FR	G/POS	TPR
1988	StL-N	13	46	4	9	1	0	0	1	0	9	.196	.213	.217	23	-5	0	0	0	.990	-2	1-12	-0.8

YEAR	TM/L	G	AB	R	H	2B	3B	HR	RBI	BB	SO	AVG	OBP	SLG	PRO+	BR/A	SB	CS	SBR	FA	FR	G/POS	TPR

■ MIKE FITZGERALD Fitzgerald, Michael Roy b: 7/13/60, Long Beach, Cal. BR/TR, 5′11″, 190 lbs. Deb: 9/13/83

1983	NY-N	8	20	1	2	0	0	1	2	3	6	.100	.217	.250	29	-2	0	0	0	.957	2	/C-8	0.1
1984	NY-N	112	360	20	87	15	1	2	33	24	71	.242	.291	.306	69	-15	1	0	0	**.995**	8	*C-107	-0.2
1985	Mon-N	108	295	25	61	7	1	5	34	38	55	.207	.301	.288	70	-12	5	3	-0	.987	-6	*C-108	-1.3
1986	Mon-N	73	209	20	59	13	1	6	37	27	34	.282	.367	.440	123	7	3	2	-0	.993	-7	C-71	0.4
1987	Mon-N	107	287	32	69	11	0	3	36	42	54	.240	.339	.310	71	-11	3	4	-2	.981	-1	*C-104/1-1,2-1	-0.7
1988	Mon-N	63	155	17	42	6	1	5	23	19	22	.271	.351	.419	115	3	2	2	-1	.979	4	C-47/O-4	1.0
1989	Mon-N	100	290	33	69	18	2	7	42	35	61	.238	.324	.386	101	0	3	4	-2	.984	-6	C-77/3-8,O-6	-0.3
1990	Mon-N	111	313	36	76	18	1	9	41	60	60	.243	.368	.393	114	8	8	1	2	.990	-4	C-98/O-6	1.2
1991	Mon-N	71	198	17	40	5	2	4	28	22	35	.202	.282	.308	67	-9	4	2	0	.994	2	C-54/1-3,O-3	-0.4
1992	Cal-A	95	189	19	40	2	0	6	17	22	34	.212	.294	.317	71	-7	2	2	-1	.990	-15	C-74,O-11/3-3,12D	-2.0
Total	10	848	2316	220	545	95	9	48	293	292	432	.235	.323	.346	87	-37	31	20	-3	.988	-21	C-748/O-30,312D	-2.2

■ RAY FITZGERALD Fitzgerald, Raymond Francis b: 12/5/04, Chicopee, Mass. d: 9/6/77, Westfield, Mass. BR/TR, 5′9″, 168 lbs. Deb: 4/18/31

1931	Cin-N	1	1	0	0	0	0	0	0	0	0	.000	.000	.000	-99	-0	0			.000	0	H	0.0

■ SHAUN FITZMAURICE Fitzmaurice, Shaun Earle b: 8/25/42, Worcester, Mass. BR/TR, 6′, 180 lbs. Deb: 9/9/66

1966	NY-N	9	13	2	2	0	0	0	0	2	6	.154	.267	.154	21	-1	1	0	0	1.000	1	/O-5	-0.1

■ ED FITZPATRICK Fitzpatrick, Edward Henry b: 12/9/1889, Lewistown, Pa. d: 10/23/65, Bethlehem, Pa. BR/TR, 5′8″, 165 lbs. Deb: 4/17/15

1915	Bos-N	105	303	54	67	19	3	0	24	43	36	.221	.344	.304	101	3	13	8	-1	.967	-5	2-71,O-29	-0.4
1916	Bos-N	83	216	17	46	8	0	1	18	15	26	.213	.280	.264	70	-7	5			.950	-12	2-46,O-28	-2.2
1917	Bos-N	63	178	20	45	8	4	0	17	12	22	.253	.318	.343	109	2	4			.929	-13	2-22,O-19,3-15	-1.2
Total	3	251	697	91	158	35	7	1	59	70	84	.227	.319	.301	94	-3	22	8		.956	-30	2-139/O-76,3-15	-3.8

■ TOM FITZSIMMONS Fitzsimmons, Thomas William b: 4/6/1890, Oakland, Cal. d: 12/20/71, Oakland, Cal. BR/TR, 6′1″, 190 lbs. Deb: 6/12/19

1919	Bro-N	4	4	1	0	0	0	0	0	1	2	.000	.200	.000	-36	-1	0			.500	-1	/3-4	-0.2

■ MAX FLACK Flack, Max John b: 2/5/1890, Belleville, Ill. d: 7/31/75, Belleville, Ill. BL/TL, 5′7″, 148 lbs. Deb: 4/16/14

1914	Chi-F	134	502	66	124	15	3	2	39	51	48	.247	.324	.301	75	-25	37			.973	-1	*O-133	-3.3
1915	Chi-F	141	523	88	164	20	14	3	45	40	21	.314	.365	.423	129	11	37			.969	2	*O-138	0.6
1916	Chi-N	141	465	65	120	14	3	3	20	42	43	.258	.320	.320	87	-7	24	19	-4	**.991**	2	*O-136	-1.8
1917	Chi-N	131	447	65	111	18	7	0	21	51	34	.248	.325	.320	91	-4	17			.947	-3	*O-117	-1.5
1918	*Chi-N	123	478	74	123	17	10	4	41	56	19	.257	.343	.360	111	8	17			.978	3	*O-121	0.4
1919	Chi-N	116	469	71	138	20	4	6	35	34	13	.294	.346	.392	121	12	18			.986	-0	*O-116	0.4
1920	Chi-N	135	520	85	157	30	6	4	49	52	15	.302	.373	.406	121	16	13	19	-8	.967	-5	*O-132	-0.8
1921	Chi-N	133	572	80	172	31	4	6	37	32	15	.301	.342	.400	96	-4	17	11	-2	**.989**	4	*O-130	-1.1
1922	Chi-N	17	54	7	12	1	0	0	6	2	4	.222	.250	.241	27	-6	2	1	0	.933	-2	O-15	-0.9
	StL-N	66	267	46	78	12	1	2	21	31	11	.292	.368	.367	95	-1	3	5	-2	.968	-4	O-66	-1.2
	Yr	83	321	53	90	13	1	2	27	33	15	.280	.349	.346	83	-8	5	6	-2	.961	-6	O-81	-2.1
1923	StL-N	128	505	82	147	16	9	3	28	41	16	.291	.348	.376	93	-5	7	8	-3	.951	-6	*O-121	-2.0
1924	StL-N	67	209	31	55	11	3	2	21	21	5	.263	.330	.373	90	-3	3	5	-2	.971	1	O-52	-0.7
1925	StL-N	79	241	23	60	7	8	0	28	21	9	.249	.309	.344	65	-13	5	3	-0	.991	-2	O-59	-1.8
Total	12	1411	5252	783	1461	212	72	35	391	474	253	.278	.342	.366	99	-21	200	71		.972	-12	*O-1336	-13.7

■ WALLY FLAGER Flager, Walter Leonard b: 11/3/21, Chicago Heights, Ill. d: 12/16/90, Keizer, Ore. BL/TR, 5′11″, 160 lbs. Deb: 4/17/45

1945	Cin-N	21	52	5	11	1	0	0	6	8	5	.212	.317	.231	55	-3	0			.933	-7	S-15	-0.9
	Phi-N	49	168	21	42	4	1	2	15	17	15	.250	.323	.321	82	-4	1			.946	1	S-48/2-1	0.1
	Yr	70	220	26	53	5	1	2	21	25	20	.241	.321	.300	75	-7	1			.943	-6	S-63/2-1	-0.8

■ IRA FLAGSTEAD Flagstead, Ira James "Pete" b: 9/22/1893, Montague, Mich. d: 3/13/40, Olympia, Wash. BR/TR, 5′9″, 165 lbs. Deb: 7/20/17

1917	Det-A	4	4	0	0	0	0	0	0	0	1	.000	.000	.000	-99	-1	0			.000	-1	/O-2	-0.2
1919	Det-A	97	287	43	95	22	3	5	41	35	39	.331	.416	.481	155	22	6			.951	2	O-83	1.9
1920	Det-A	110	311	40	73	13	5	3	35	37	27	.235	.318	.338	76	-11	3	4	-2	.967	7	O-82	-1.2
1921	Det-A	85	259	40	79	16	2	0	31	21	21	.305	.371	.382	93	-2	8	4	0	.903	-5	S-55,O-12/2-8,3-1	-0.3
1922	Det-A	44	91	21	28	5	3	3	8	14	16	.308	.411	.527	148	7	0	1	-1	.967	-2	O-32	0.3
1923	Det-A	1	1	0	0	0	0	0	0	0	0	.000	.000	.000	-99	-0	0	0	0	.000	0	H	0.0
	Bos-A	109	382	55	119	23	4	8	53	37	26	.312	.380	.455	119	10	7	10	-4	.965	19	*O-102/S-1	1.7
	Yr	110	383	55	119	23	4	8	53	37	26	.311	.379	.454	118	10	7	10	-4	.965	19	*O-102/S-1	1.7
1924	Bos-A	149	560	106	172	35	7	5	43	77	41	.307	.401	.421	112	13	10	13	-5	.975	-2	*O-144	-0.3
1925	Bos-A	148	572	84	160	38	2	6	61	63	30	.280	.356	.385	88	-10	5	6	-2	.976	**20**	*O-144	-0.2
1926	Bos-A	98	415	65	124	31	7	3	31	36	22	.299	.363	.429	109	5	4	6	-2	.982	9	O-98	0.4
1927	Bos-A	131	466	63	133	26	8	4	69	57	25	.285	.374	.401	103	4	12	2	2	**.986**	11	*O-129	0.8
1928	Bos-A	140	510	84	148	41	4	1	39	60	23	.290	.366	.392	101	2	12	9	-2	.973	5	*O-135	-0.3
1929	Bos-A	14	36	9	11	2	0	0	3	5	1	.306	.390	.361	97	0	1	3	-2	.955	-3	O-13	-0.5
	Was-A	18	39	5	7	1	0	0	9	4	5	.179	.256	.205	20	-5	1	0	0	.971	3	O-11	-0.2
	Yr	32	75	14	18	3	0	0	12	9	6	.240	.321	.280	57	-5	2	3	-1	.965	0	O-24	-0.7
	Pit-N	26	50	8	14	2	1	0	6	4	2	.280	.333	.360	70	-2	1			1.000	0	/O-9	-0.2
1930	Pit-N	44	156	21	39	7	4	2	21	17	9	.250	.324	.385	70	-8	1			.961	-3	O-40	-1.2
Total	13	1218	4139	644	1202	262	50	40	450	467	288	.290	.370	.407	103	23	71	58		.974	59	*O-1036/S-56,2-8,3	0.5

■ JOHN FLAHERTY Flaherty, John Timothy b: 10/21/67, New York, N.Y. BR/TR, 6′1″, 195 lbs. Deb: 4/12/92

1992	Bos-A	35	66	3	13	2	0	0	2	3	7	.197	.232	.227	27	-6	0	0	0	.982	-3	C-34	-0.9
1993	Bos-A	13	25	3	3	2	0	0	2	2	6	.120	.214	.200	11	-3	0	0	0	1.000	-1	C-13	-0.4
1994	Det-A	34	40	2	6	1	0	0	4	1	11	.150	.171	.175	-11	-7	0	1	-1	1.000	6	C-33/D-1	-0.1
1995	Det-A	112	354	39	86	22	1	11	40	18	47	.243	.285	.404	77	-13	0	0	0	.982	-10	*C-112	-1.5
1996	Det-A	47	152	18	38	12	0	4	23	8	25	.250	.292	.408	75	-6	1	0	0	.981	-13	C-46	-1.5
	*SD-N	72	264	22	80	12	0	9	41	9	36	.303	.331	.451	110	3	2	3	-1	.990	-7	C-72	-0.1
1997	SD-N	129	439	38	120	21	1	9	46	33	62	.273	.324	.387	92	-6	4	4	-1	.987	-17	*C-124	-1.6
1998	TB-A	91	304	21	63	11	0	3	24	22	46	.207	.263	.273	38	-28	0	5	-3	.993	-2	C-91	-2.5
Total	7	533	1644	146	409	83	2	36	182	96	240	.249	.293	.367	73	-67	7	13	-6	.988	-47	C-525/D-1	-8.6

■ MARTIN FLAHERTY Flaherty, Martin J. b: 9/24/1853, Worcester, Mass d: 6/10/20, Providence, R.I. BL/TL, Deb: 8/18/1881

1881	Wor-N	1	2	0	0	0	0	0	0	0	2	.000	.000	.000	-95	-0				.000	-1	/O-1	-0.2

■ PAT FLAHERTY Flaherty, Patrick Henry b: 1/31/1866, St.Louis, Mo. d: 1/28/46, Chicago, Ill. 5′9″, 166 lbs. Deb: 7/11/1894

1894	Lou-N	38	145	15	43	5	3	0	15	9	6	.297	.342	.372	77	-5	2			.855	-5	3-38	-0.8

■ PATSY FLAHERTY Flaherty, Patrick Joseph b: 6/29/1876, Mansfield, Pa. d: 1/23/68, Alexandria, La. BL/TL, 5′8″, 165 lbs. Deb: 9/8/1899

1899	Lou-N	7	24	3	5	1	1	0	6	3		.208	.296	.333	73	-1	0			.692	-1	/P-5,O-2	0.0
1900	Pit-N	4	9	0	1	0	0	0	0	1		.111	.200	.111	-13	-1	0			1.000	1	/P-4	0.0
1903	Chi-A	40	102	7	14	4	0	0	5	5		.137	.178	.176	7	-11	4			.914	3	P-40	0.0
1904	Chi-A	5	12	1	4	1	0	0	0	4		.333	.500	.417	199	2	0			.880	1	/P-5	0.0
	Pit-N	36	104	9	22	3	4	2	19	8		.212	.268	.375	95	-1	0			.965	5	P-29/O-2	0.0
1905	Pit-N	30	76	7	15	4	2	0	4	3		.197	.228	.303	56	-4	0			.894	2	P-27/O-2	-0.1
1907	Bos-N	41	115	9	22	3	2	2	11	2		.191	.212	.304	62	-6	1			.907	3	P-27/O-8	-0.1
1908	Bos-N	32	86	8	12	0	2	0	5	6		.140	.196	.186	22	-8	2			.961	2	P-31	0.0
1910	Phi-N	2	2	0	1	0	0	0	0	0	0	.500	.500	.500	186	0	0			.000	-0	/P-1,O-1	0.0
1911	Bos-N	38	94	9	27	3	2	2	20	8	11	.287	.343	.426	106	0	2			.933	-4	O-19/P-4	-0.4
Total	9	235	624	53	123	19	13	6	70	40	11	.197	.247	.298	63	-30	9			.921	11	P-173/O-34	-0.6

YEAR	TM/L	G	AB	R	H	2B	3B	HR	RBI	BB	SO	AVG	OBP	SLG	PRO+	BR/A	SB	CS	SBR	FA	FR	G/POS	TPR
■ AL FLAIR	Flair, Albert Dell "Broadway" b: 7/24/16, New Orleans, La. d: 7/25/88, New Orleans, La. BL/TL, 6'4", 195 lbs. Deb: 9/6/41																						
1941	Bos-A	10	30	3	6	2	1	0	2	1	1	.200	.226	.333	45	-3	1	1	-0	1.000	-0	/1-8	-0.3
■ CHARLIE FLANAGAN	Flanagan, Charles James b: 12/31/1891, Oakland, Cal. d: 1/8/30, San Francisco, Cal. BR/TR, 6', 175 lbs. Deb: 7/9/13																						
1913	StL-A	4	3	0	0	0	0	0	0	1	0	.000	.250	.000	-26	-0	0			.000	-1	/3-1,O-1	-0.1
■ ED FLANAGAN	Flanagan, Edward J. "Sleepy" b: 9/15/1861, Lowell, Mass. d: 11/10/26, Lowell, Mass. 6'1", 190 lbs. Deb: 4/16/1887																						
1887	Phi-a	19	80	12	20	5	0	1	10	3		.250	.286	.350	77	-3	3			.948	-1	1-19	-0.5
1889	Lou-a	23	88	11	22	7	3	0	8	7	11	.250	.305	.398	101	-0	1			.953	-1	1-23	-0.2
Total	2	42	168	23	42	12	3	1	18	10	11	.250	.296	.375	89	-3	4			.951	-2	/1-42	-0.7
■ STEAMER FLANAGAN	Flanagan, James Paul b: 4/20/1881, Kingston, Pa. d: 4/21/47, Wilkes-Barre, Pa. BL/TL, 6'1", 185 lbs. Deb: 9/25/05																						
1905	Pit-N	7	25	7	7	1	1	0	3	1		.280	.308	.400	108	0	3			1.000	1	/O-5	0.1
■ JOHN FLANNERY	Flannery, John Michael b: 1/25/57, Long Beach, Cal. BR/TR, 6'3", 173 lbs. Deb: 9/2/77																						
1977	Chi-A	7	2	1	0	0	0	0	0	1	1	.000	.333	.000	0	-0	0	0	0	1.000	1	/S-4,3-1,D-1	0.1
■ TIM FLANNERY	Flannery, Timothy Earl b: 9/29/57, Tulsa, Okla. BL/TR, 5'11", 175 lbs. Deb: 9/3/79 C																						
1979	SD-N	22	65	2	10	0	1	0	4	4	5	.154	.225	.185	14	-8	0	0	0	.991	2	2-21	-0.4
1980	SD-N	95	292	15	70	12	0	0	25	18	30	.240	.284	.281	62	-15	2	2	-1	.988	-4	2-53,3-41	-1.9
1981	SD-N	37	67	4	17	4	1	0	6	2	4	.254	.275	.343	80	-2	1	0	0	.967	-1	3-15/2-7	-0.3
1982	SD-N	122	379	40	100	11	7	0	30	30	32	.264	.321	.330	87	-7	1	0	0	.974	-24	*2-104/3-5,S-2	-2.7
1983	SD-N	92	214	24	50	7	3	3	19	20	23	.234	.314	.336	83	-5	2	2	-1	.969	10	3-52,2-21/S-7	0.5
1984	*SD-N	86	128	24	35	3	3	2	10	12	17	.273	.350	.391	108	2	4	1	1	.944	-6	2-22,3-14,S-14	-0.2
1985	SD-N	126	384	50	108	14	3	1	40	58	39	.281	.388	.341	107	7	2	5	-2	.977	-19	*2-121/3-1	-1.1
1986	SD-N	134	368	48	103	11	2	3	28	54	61	.280	.379	.345	103	4	3	6	-3	.993	-7	*2-108,3-23/S-8	-0.2
1987	SD-N	106	276	23	63	5	1	0	20	42	30	.228	.334	.254	61	-14	2	4	-2	.986	3	2-84/3-8,S-2	-0.9
1988	SD-N	79	170	16	45	5	4	0	19	24	32	.265	.369	.341	107	3	3	2	-0	.972	-4	3-51/2-2,S-1	-0.2
1989	SD-N	73	130	9	30	5	0	0	8	13	20	.231	.301	.269	64	-6	2	0	1	.920	2	3-33/2-1	-0.4
Total	11	972	2473	255	631	77	25	9	209	277	293	.255	.338	.317	86	-41	22	22	-7	.982	-47	2-544,3-243/S-34	-7.8
■ ROY FLASKAMPER	Flaskamper, Raymond Harold "Flash" b: 10/31/01, St.Louis, Mo. d: 2/3/78, San Antonio, Tex. BB/TR, 5'7", 140 lbs. Deb: 8/16/27																						
1927	Chi-A	26	95	12	21	5	0	0	6	3	8	.221	.260	.274	40	-9	0	0	0	.962	0	S-25	-0.6
■ FRANK FLEET	Fleet, Frank H. b: 1848, New York, N.Y. d: 6/13/1900, New York, N.Y. Deb: 10/18/1871																						
1871	Mut-n	1	6	1	2	0	0	0	1	0	0	.333	.333	.333	101	0	0	0	0	1.000	1	/P-1	0.0
1872	Eck-n	13	53	10	13	1	0	0	5	0	1	.245	.245	.264	67	-1	1	0	0	.760	3	3-10/2-2,O-2	0.1
1873	Res-n	22	90	11	23	2	0	0	10	1	2	.256	.264	.278	66	-3	0	1	-1	.864	1	/2-9,S-9,P-3,3-2,1	-0.3
1874	Atl-n	22	97	18	22	0	0	0	10	1	1	.227	.235	.227	55	-4	1	0	0	.759	-4	C-13,2-11/O-1	-0.6
1875	StL-n	4	16	1	1	0	0	0	1	0	0	.063	.063	.063	-62	-2	0	0	0	.900	-0	/P-3,3-1,O-1	-0.1
	Atl-n	26	111	13	25	2	0	0	9	1	1	.225	.232	.243	75	-2	0	0	0	.719	-8	C-11,2-10/S-9,P3	-0.9
	Yr	30	127	14	26	2	0	0	10	1	1	.205	.211	.220	57	-4	0	0	0	.719	-8	C-11,2-10/S-9,P3O	-1.0
Total	5 n	88	373	54	86	5	0	0	36	3	5	.231	.237	.244	61	-13	2	1	0	.782	-7	/2-32,C-24,S3PO1	-1.8
■ ANGEL FLEITAS	Fleitas, Angel Felix Husta b: 11/10/14, Los Abreus, Cuba BR/TR, 5'9", 160 lbs. Deb: 7/5/48																						
1948	Was-A	15	13	1	1	0	0	0	1	3	5	.077	.250	.077	-11	-2	0	2	-1	.952	3	/S-7	0.0
■ LES FLEMING	Fleming, Leslie Harvey "Moe" b: 8/7/15, Singleton, Tex. d: 3/5/80, Cleveland, Tex. BL/TL, 5'10", 185 lbs. Deb: 4/22/39																						
1939	Det-A	8	16	0	0	0	0	0	1	0	4	.000	.000	.000	-93	-5	0	0	0	1.000	-0	/O-3	-0.5
1941	Cle-A	2	8	0	2	1	0	0	2	0	0	.250	.250	.375	67	-0	0	0	0	1.000	-0	/1-2	-0.1
1942	Cle-A	156	548	71	160	27	4	14	82	106	57	.292	.412	.432	146	38	6	8	-3	**.993**	-9	*1-156	1.7
1945	Cle-A	42	140	18	46	10	2	3	22	11	5	.329	.382	.493	160	10	0	0	0	.938	-2	O-33/1-5	0.6
1946	Cle-A	99	306	40	85	17	5	8	42	50	42	.278	.383	.444	140	17	1	0	0	.984	3	1-80/O-1	1.6
1947	Cle-A	103	281	39	68	14	2	4	43	53	42	.242	.362	.349	101	2	0	0	0	.989	4	1-77	0.3
1949	Pit-N	24	31	0	8	0	2	0	7	6	2	.258	.395	.387	108	1	0			1.000	-1	/1-5	0.0
Total	7	434	1330	168	369	69	15	29	199	226	152	.277	.386	.417	131	63	7	8		.990	-6	1-325/O-37	3.6
■ TOM FLEMING	Fleming, Thomas Vincent "Sleuth" b: 11/20/1873, Philadelphia, Pa. d: 12/26/57, Boston, Mass. BL/TL, 5'11", 155 lbs. Deb: 9/19/1899																						
1899	NY-N	22	77	9	16	1	1	0	4	1		.208	.218	.247	28	-8	1			.909	-1	O-22	-0.9
1902	Phi-N	5	16	2	6	0	0	0	2	1		.375	.412	.375	143	1	0			1.000	0	/O-5	0.1
1904	Phi-N	3	6	0	0	0	0	0	0	0		.000	.000	.000	-99	-1	0			1.000	0	/O-1	-0.1
Total	3	30	99	11	22	1	1	0	6	2		.222	.238	.253	39	-8	1			.920	-0	/O-28	-0.9
■ ART FLETCHER	Fletcher, Arthur b: 1/5/1885, Collinsville, Ill. d: 2/6/50, Los Angeles, Cal. BR/TR, 5'10.5", 170 lbs. Deb: 4/15/09 MC																						
1909	NY-N	33	98	7	21	0	1	0	6	1		.214	.238	.235	46	-6	0			.893	4	S-22/2-7,3-6	-0.2
1910	NY-N	51	125	12	28	2	1	0	13	4	9	.224	.248	.256	47	-9	9			.895	-5	S-22,2-11,3-11	-1.4
1911	*NY-N	112	326	73	104	17	8	1	37	30	27	.319	.400	.429	128	13	20			.926	4	S-74,3-21,2-13	2.2
1912	*NY-N	129	419	64	118	17	9	1	57	16	29	.282	.330	.372	89	-7	16			.927	16	*S-126/2-2,3-1	1.9
1913	*NY-N	136	538	76	160	20	9	4	71	24	35	.297	.345	.390	109	6	32			.932	-7	*S-136	1.1
1914	NY-N	135	514	62	147	26	8	2	79	22	37	.286	.332	.379	115	8	15			.922	6	*S-135	2.7
1915	NY-N	149	562	59	143	17	7	3	74	6	36	.254	.280	.326	88	-10	12	18	-7	.936	**34**	*S-149	3.0
1916	NY-N	133	500	53	143	23	8	3	66	13	36	.286	.323	.382	122	11	15			.940	20	*S-133	4.3
1917	*NY-N	151	557	70	145	24	5	4	56	23	28	.260	.312	.343	104	2	12			**.956**	27	*S-151	4.1
1918	NY-N	124	468	51	123	20	2	0	47	18	26	.263	.311	.314	93	-4	12			**.959**	**22**	*S-124	2.6
1919	NY-N	127	488	54	135	20	5	3	54	9	28	.277	.300	.357	98	-3	6			.944	24	*S-127	3.2
1920	NY-N	41	171	21	44	7	2	0	24	1	15	.257	.282	.322	74	-6	3	2	-0	.914	-2	S-41	-0.5
	Phi-N	102	379	36	112	25	7	4	38	15	28	.296	.329	.430	112	5	4	6	-2	.958	12	*S-102	2.4
	Yr	143	550	57	156	32	9	4	62	16	43	.284	.315	.396	100	-1	7	8	-3	.945	10	*S-143	1.9
1922	Phi-N	110	396	46	111	20	5	7	53	21	14	.280	.325	.409	80	-13	3	2	-0	.939	7	*S-106	0.4
Total	13	1533	5541	684	1534	238	77	32	675	203	348	.277	.319	.365	100	-14	159	28		.939	162	*S-1448/3-39,2-33	25.8
■ DARRIN FLETCHER	Fletcher, Darrin Glen b: 10/3/66, Elmhurst, Ill. BL/TR, 6'1", 199 lbs. Deb: 9/10/89 F																						
1989	LA-N	5	8	1	4	0	0	1	2	1	0	.500	.556	.875	308	2	0	0	0	1.000	0	/C-5	0.2
1990	LA-N	2	1	0	0	0	0	0	0	0	1	.000	.000	.000	-99	-0	0	0	0	.000	0	/C-1	0.0
	Phi-N	9	22	3	3	1	0	0	1	1	5	.136	.174	.182	-2	-3	0	0	0	1.000	1	/C-6	-0.2
	Yr	11	23	3	3	1	0	0	1	1	6	.130	.167	.174	-6	-3	0	0	0	1.000	1	/C-7	-0.2
1991	Phi-N	46	136	5	31	8	0	1	12	5	15	.228	.255	.309	59	-8	0	1	-1	.992	3	C-45	-0.3
1992	Mon-N	83	222	13	54	10	2	2	26	14	28	.243	.294	.333	78	-7	0	2	-1	.995	-0	C-69	-0.5
1993	Mon-N	133	396	33	101	20	1	9	60	34	40	.255	.323	.379	84	-9	0	0	0	.988	-10	*C-127	-1.3
1994	Mon-N★	94	285	28	74	18	1	10	57	25	23	.260	.326	.435	95	-2	0	0	0	**.996**	-8	C-81	-0.6
1995	Mon-N	110	350	42	100	21	1	11	45	32	23	.286	.352	.446	105	3	0	1	-1	.994	-3	C-98	0.5
1996	Mon-N	127	394	41	105	22	0	12	57	27	42	.266	.323	.414	90	-6	0	0	0	.992	-17	*C-112	-1.6
1997	Mon-N	96	310	39	86	20	1	17	55	17	35	.277	.325	.513	116	6	1	1	-0	.994	-1	C-83	0.9
1998	Tor-A	124	407	37	115	23	0	9	52	25	39	.283	.333	.410	92	-5	0	0	0	.991	6	*C-121/D-1	0.8
Total	10	829	2531	242	673	143	7	72	367	181	251	.266	.323	.413	93	-30	1	5	-3	.993	-29	C-748/D-1	-2.1
■ ELBIE FLETCHER	Fletcher, Elburt Preston b: 3/18/16, Milton, Mass. d: 3/9/94, Milton, Mass. BL/TL, 6', 180 lbs. Deb: 9/16/34																						
1934	Bos-N	8	4	4	2	0	0	0	0	0	2	.500	.500	.500	182	0	1			.875	-0	/1-1	0.0
1935	Bos-N	39	148	12	35	7	1	1	9	7	13	.236	.271	.318	63	-8	1			.997	2	1-39	-1.0
1937	Bos-N	148	539	56	133	22	4	1	38	56	64	.247	.321	.308	79	-16	3			.993	1	*1-148	-3.2
1938	Bos-N	147	529	71	144	24	7	6	48	60	40	.272	.351	.378	112	8	5			.990	10	*1-146	0.3
1939	Bos-N	35	106	14	26	2	0	0	6	19	5	.245	.365	.264	77	-2	1			.986	-5	1-31	-1.1

YEAR	TM/L	G	AB	R	H	2B	3B	HR	RBI	BB	SO	AVG	OBP	SLG	PRO+	BR/A	SB	CS	SBR	FA	FR	G/POS	TPR
	Pit-N	102	370	49	112	23	4	12	71	48	28	.303	.386	.484	134	18	3			.993	-4	*1-101	0.4
	Yr	137	476	63	138	25	4	12	77	67	33	.290	.381	.435	122	16	4			.991	-9	*1-132	-0.7
1940	Pit-N	147	510	94	139	22	7	16	104	**119**	54	.273	**.418**	.437	137	33	5			.993	4	*1-147	2.3
1941	Pit-N	151	521	95	150	29	13	11	74	**118**	54	.288	**.421**	.457	148	39	5			.991	9	*1-151	3.7
1942	Pit-N	145	506	86	146	22	5	7	57	105	60	.289	**.417**	.393	134	28	0			.992	12	*1-144	3.2
1943	Pit-N★	154	544	91	154	24	5	9	70	95	49	.283	.395	.395	124	21	1			**.996**	3	*1-154	1.6
1946	Pit-N	148	532	72	136	25	8	4	66	111	37	.256	.384	.355	108	10	4			.995	1	*1-147	0.3
1947	Pit-N	69	157	22	38	9	1	1	22	29	24	.242	.364	.331	83	-3	2			.986	-0	1-50	-0.4
1949	Bos-N	122	413	57	108	19	3	11	51	84	65	.262	.396	.402	121	16	1			.991	0	*1-121	1.5
Total	12	1415	4879	723	1323	228	58	79	616	851	495	.271	.384	.390	118	145	32			.993	33	*1-1380	7.6

■ GEORGE FLETCHER
Fletcher, George Horace Ellis b: 4/21/1845, Deb: 6/21/1872

YEAR	TM/L	G	AB	R	H	2B	3B	HR	RBI	BB	SO	AVG	OBP	SLG	PRO+	BR/A	SB	CS	SBR	FA	FR	G/POS	TPR
1872	Eck-n	2	8	1	3	0	0	0	0	0	0	.375	.375	.375	155	1	0	0	0	.500	-1	/O-2	0.0

■ FRANK FLETCHER
Fletcher, Oliver Frank b: 3/6/1891, Hildreth, Ill. d: 10/7/74, St.Petersburg, Fla. BR/TR, 5'10", 165 lbs. Deb: 7/14/14

YEAR	TM/L	G	AB	R	H	2B	3B	HR	RBI	BB	SO	AVG	OBP	SLG	PRO+	BR/A	SB	CS	SBR	FA	FR	G/POS	TPR
1914	Phi-N	1	1	0	0	0	0	0	0	0	1	.000	.000	.000	-94	-0	0			.000	0	H	0.0

■ SCOTT FLETCHER
Fletcher, Scott Brian b: 7/30/58, Fort Walton Beach, Fla. BR/TR, 5'11", 173 lbs. Deb: 4/25/81

YEAR	TM/L	G	AB	R	H	2B	3B	HR	RBI	BB	SO	AVG	OBP	SLG	PRO+	BR/A	SB	CS	SBR	FA	FR	G/POS	TPR
1981	Chi-N	19	46	6	10	4	0	0	1	2	4	.217	.250	.304	54	-3	0	0	0	.972	6	2-13/S-4,3-1	0.4
1982	Chi-N	11	24	4	4	0	0	0	1	4	5	.167	.286	.167	29	-2	1	0	0	1.000	-0	S-11	-0.2
1983	*Chi-A	114	262	42	62	16	5	3	31	29	22	.237	.317	.370	85	-5	5	1	1	.965	18	*S-100,2-12/3-7,D-1	2.2
1984	Chi-A	149	456	46	114	13	3	3	35	46	46	.250	.329	.311	75	-14	10	4	1	.973	0	*S-134,2-28/3-3	-0.1
1985	Chi-A	119	301	38	77	8	1	2	31	35	47	.256	.333	.309	74	-10	5	5	-2	.934	-3	3-55,S-44,2-37,/D-2	-1.1
1986	Tex-A	147	530	82	159	34	5	3	50	47	59	.300	.361	.400	104	4	12	11	-3	.973	-6	*S-136,3-12,2-11,/D	0.7
1987	Tex-A	156	588	82	169	28	4	5	63	61	66	.287	.359	.374	95	-3	13	12	-3	.966	5	*S-155	1.2
1988	Tex-A	140	515	59	142	19	4	0	47	62	34	.276	.367	.328	94	-1	8	5	-1	.983	1	*S-139	1.1
1989	Tex-A	83	314	47	75	14	1	0	22	38	41	.239	.325	.290	73	-10	1	0	0	.960	-18	S-81	-2.2
	Chi-A	59	232	30	63	11	1	1	21	26	19	.272	.347	.341	97	-0	1	1	-0	1.000	-3	2-53/S-8,D-1	-0.1
	Yr	142	546	77	138	25	2	1	43	64	60	.253	.334	.311	83	-10	2	1	0	.957	-21	S-89,2-53/D-1	-2.3
1990	Chi-A	151	509	54	123	18	3	4	56	45	63	.242	.307	.312	75	-16	1	3	-2	.988	-6	*2-151	-2.2
1991	Chi-A	90	248	14	51	10	1	1	28	17	26	.206	.265	.266	48	-17	0	2	-1	.992	-6	2-86/3-4	-2.3
1992	Mil-A	123	386	53	106	18	3	3	51	30	33	.275	.338	.360	98	-1	17	10	-1	.992	10	*2-106,S-22/3-1	1.1
1993	Bos-A	121	480	81	137	31	5	5	45	37	35	.285	.343	.402	94	-4	16	3	3	.982	5	*2-116/S-2,3-1,D-1	0.7
1994	Bos-A	63	185	31	42	9	1	3	11	16	14	.227	.296	.335	59	-11	8	1	2	.996	19	2-53/D-4	1.1
1995	Det-A	67	182	19	42	10	1	1	17	19	27	.231	.314	.313	64	-9	1	0	0	1.000	9	2-63/S-3,1-1,D-1	0.3
Total	15	1612	5258	688	1376	243	38	34	510	514	541	.262	.334	.342	84	-104	99	58	-5	.971	30	S-839,2-729/3D1	0.6

■ ELMER FLICK
Flick, Elmer Harrison b: 1/11/1876, Bedford, Ohio d: 1/9/71, Bedford, Ohio BL/TR, 5'9", 168 lbs. Deb: 5/2/1898 H

YEAR	TM/L	G	AB	R	H	2B	3B	HR	RBI	BB	SO	AVG	OBP	SLG	PRO+	BR/A	SB	CS	SBR	FA	FR	G/POS	TPR
1898	Phi-N	134	453	84	137	16	13	8	81	86		.302	.430	.448	158	40	23			.931	7	*O-133	3.5
1899	Phi-N	127	485	98	166	22	11	2	98	42		.342	.407	.445	139	27	31			.931	9	*O-125	2.4
1900	Phi-N	138	545	106	200	32	16	11	**110**	56		.367	.441	.545	173	**55**	35			.914	3	*O-138	4.3
1901	Phi-N	138	540	112	180	32	17	8	88	52		.333	.399	.500	157	39	30			.962	15	*O-138	4.2
1902	Phi-A	11	37	15	11	2	1	0	3	6		.297	.435	.405	128	2	4			.947	-0	O-11	0.1
	Cle-A	110	424	70	126	19	11	2	61	47		.297	.371	.408	121	13	20			.929	-4	*O-110	0.1
	Yr	121	461	85	137	21	12	2	64	53		.297	.377	.408	121	15	24			.930	-4	*O-121	0.2
1903	Cle-A	140	523	81	155	23	16	2	51	51		.296	.368	.413	136	24	24			.955	1	*O-140	1.7
1904	Cle-A	150	579	97	177	31	17	6	56	51		.306	.371	.449	160	40	**38**			.955	10	*O-145/2-6	4.5
1905	Cle-A	132	500	72	154	29	**18**	4	64	53		**.308**	.383	**.462**	**165**	**37**	35			.939	1	*O-131/2-1	3.4
1906	Cle-A	157	624	**98**	194	34	**22**	1	62	54		.311	.372	.441	156	40	**39**			.981	-12	*O-150/2-8	2.3
1907	Cle-A	147	549	80	166	15	**18**	3	58	64		.302	.386	.412	153	35	41			.956	1	*O-147	3.3
1908	Cle-A	9	35	4	8	1	1	0	2	3		.229	.289	.314	96	-0	0			1.000	-0	/O-9	-0.1
1909	Cle-A	66	235	28	60	10	2	0	15	22		.255	.322	.315	97	-0	9			.958	-4	O-61	-0.7
1910	Cle-A	24	68	5	18	2	1	1	7	10		.265	.359	.368	126	2	1			.955	-3	O-18	-0.2
Total	13	1483	5597	950	1752	268	164	48	756	597		.313	.389	.445	149	353	330			.947	23	*O-1456/2-15	28.8

■ LEW FLICK
Flick, Lewis Miller "Noisy" b: 2/18/15, Bristol, Tenn. d: 12/7/90, Weber City, Va. BL/TL, 5'9", 155 lbs. Deb: 9/28/43

YEAR	TM/L	G	AB	R	H	2B	3B	HR	RBI	BB	SO	AVG	OBP	SLG	PRO+	BR/A	SB	CS	SBR	FA	FR	G/POS	TPR
1943	Phi-A	1	5	2	3	0	0	0	0	0	0	.600	.600	.600	253	1	0	0	0	1.000	0	/O-1	0.1
1944	Phi-A	19	35	1	4	0	0	0	2	1	2	.114	.139	.114	-28	-6	1	0	0	1.000	-1	/O-6	-0.7
Total	2	20	40	3	7	0	0	0	2	1	2	.175	.195	.175	6	-5	1	0	0	1.000	-1	/O-7	-0.6

■ DON FLINN
Flinn, Don Raphael b: 11/17/1892, Bluff Dale, Tex. d: 3/9/59, Waco, Tex. BR/TR, 6'1", 185 lbs. Deb: 9/2/17

YEAR	TM/L	G	AB	R	H	2B	3B	HR	RBI	BB	SO	AVG	OBP	SLG	PRO+	BR/A	SB	CS	SBR	FA	FR	G/POS	TPR
1917	Pit-N	14	37	1	11	1	1	0	1	1	6	.297	.316	.378	109	0	1			1.000	0	O-12	0.0

■ SILVER FLINT
Flint, Frank Sylvester b: 8/3/1855, Philadelphia, Pa. d: 1/14/1892, Chicago, Ill. BR/TR, 6', 180 lbs. Deb: 5/4/1875 M

YEAR	TM/L	G	AB	R	H	2B	3B	HR	RBI	BB	SO	AVG	OBP	SLG	PRO+	BR/A	SB	CS	SBR	FA	FR	G/POS	TPR
1875	RS-n	17	61	4	5	0	0	0	1	1	10	.082	.097	.082	-41	-8	2	0	1	.820	-2	C-16/O-2,3-1	-0.7
1878	Ind-N	63	254	23	57	7	0	0	18	2	15	.224	.230	.252	67	-8				.908	-1	*C-59/O-9	-0.8
1879	Chi-N	79	324	46	92	22	6	1	41	6	44	.284	.297	.398	120	6				.915	3	*C-78/O-1,M	1.0
1880	Chi-N	74	284	30	46	10	4	0	17	5	32	.162	.176	.225	33	-20				**.934**	8	*C-67,O-13	-1.0
1881	Chi-N	80	306	46	95	18	0	1	34	6	39	.310	.324	.379	115	4				.938	-8	*C-80/O-8,1-1	-0.1
1882	Chi-N	81	331	48	83	18	8	4	44	2	50	.251	.255	.390	99	-1				.935	-3	*C-81,O-10	-0.1
1883	Chi-N	85	332	57	88	23	4	0	32	3	69	.265	.272	.358	85	-7				.877	-8	*C-83,O-23	-0.9
1884	Chi-N	73	279	35	57	5	2	9	45	7	57	.204	.224	.333	67	-12				.884	-2	C-73	-0.6
1885	*Chi-N	68	249	27	52	8	2	1	17	2	52	.209	.215	.269	49	-15				**.927**	14	C-68/O-1	0.3
1886	*Chi-N	54	173	30	35	6	2	1	13	12	36	.202	.254	.277	54	-11	1			.893	15	C-54/1-3	0.9
1887	Chi-N	49	187	22	50	8	6	3	21	4	28	.267	.283	.422	83	-6	7			.909	3	C-47/1-2	0.1
1888	Chi-N	22	77	6	14	3	0	0	3	1	21	.182	.203	.221	33	-6	1			.926	-2	C-22	-0.6
1889	Chi-N	15	56	6	13	1	0	1	9	3	18	.232	.271	.304	58	-3	1			.903	-1	C-15	-0.3
Total	12	743	2852	376	682	129	34	21	294	53	461	.239	.253	.330	78	-80	10	0		.913	19	C-727/O-65,1-6	-2.1

■ CURT FLOOD
Flood, Curtis Charles b: 1/18/38, Houston, Tex. d: 1/20/97, Los Angeles, Cal. BR/TR, 5'9", 165 lbs. Deb: 9/9/56

YEAR	TM/L	G	AB	R	H	2B	3B	HR	RBI	BB	SO	AVG	OBP	SLG	PRO+	BR/A	SB	CS	SBR	FA	FR	G/POS	TPR
1956	Cin-N	5	1	0	0	0	0	0	0	0	1	.000	.000	.000	-94	-0	0	0	0	.000	0	H	0.0
1957	Cin-N	3	3	2	1	0	0	1	1	0	0	.333	.333	1.333	299	1	0	0	0	.000	-1	/3-2,2-1	0.0
1958	StL-N	121	422	50	110	17	2	10	41	31	56	.261	.317	.382	81	-12	2	12	-7	.978	19	*O-120/3-1	-0.5
1959	StL-N	121	208	24	53	7	3	7	26	16	35	.255	.308	.418	86	-5	2	1	0	.967	-19	*O-106/2-1	-2.7
1960	StL-N	140	396	37	94	20	1	8	38	35	54	.237	.306	.354	73	-14	0	3	-2	**.993**	0	*O-134/3-1	-2.2
1961	StL-N	132	335	53	108	15	5	2	21	35	33	.322	.391	.415	104	3	6	2	1	.984	2	*O-119	0.1
1962	StL-N	151	635	99	188	30	5	12	70	42	57	.296	.349	.416	95	-4	8	6	-1	.990	16	*O-151	0.1
1963	StL-N	158	662	112	200	34	9	5	63	42	57	.302	.346	.403	105	5	17	12	-2	.988	20	*O-158	1.4
1964	*StL-N★	162	679	97	**211**	25	3	5	46	43	53	.311	.356	.378	98	-0	8	11	-4	.988	13	*O-162	0.1
1965	StL-N	156	617	90	191	30	3	11	83	51	50	.310	.368	.421	111	10	9	3	1	.986	11	*O-151	1.6
1966	StL-N★	160	626	64	167	21	5	10	78	26	50	.267	.300	.364	83	-15	14	7	0	**1.000**	10	*O-159	-1.2
1967	*StL-N	134	514	68	172	24	1	5	50	37	46	.335	.382	.414	129	20	2	2	-1	.988	11	*O-126	2.5
1968	*StL-N★	150	618	71	186	17	4	5	60	33	58	.301	.341	.366	114	10	11	6	-0	.983	18	*O-149	2.1
1969	StL-N	153	606	80	173	31	3	4	57	48	57	.285	.345	.366	99	-0	9	7	-2	.989	17	*O-152	0.7
1971	Was-A	13	35	4	7	0	0	0	2	5	2	.200	.300	.200	47	-2	0	1	-1	.941	-2	O-10	-0.6
Total	15	1759	6357	851	1861	271	44	85	636	444	609	.293	.344	.389	99	-4	88	73	-17	.987	114	*O-1697/3-4,2-2	1.4

■ TIM FLOOD
Flood, Timothy A. b: 3/13/1877, Montgomery City, Mo. d: 6/15/29, St.Louis, Mo. BR/TR, 5'9", 160 lbs. Deb: 9/24/1899

YEAR	TM/L	G	AB	R	H	2B	3B	HR	RBI	BB	SO	AVG	OBP	SLG	PRO+	BR/A	SB	CS	SBR	FA	FR	G/POS	TPR
1899	StL-N	10	31	0	9	0	0	0	3	4		.290	.371	.290	81	-1	1			.878	-2	2-10	-0.2
1902	Bro-N	132	476	43	104	11	4	3	51	23		.218	.268	.277	68	-18	8			.942	-16	*2-132/O-1	-3.1

YEAR	TM/L	G	AB	R	H	2B	3B	HR	RBI	BB	SO	AVG	OBP	SLG	PRO+	BR/A	SB	CS	SBR	FA	FR	G/POS	TPR
1903	Bro-N	89	309	27	77	15	2	0	32	15		.249	.291	.311	73	-11	14			.924	-9	2-84/S-2,O-1	-1.6
Total	3	231	816	70	190	26	6	3	86	42		.233	.280	.290	70	-30	23			.933	-26	2-226/S-2,O-2	-4.9
■ **KEVIN FLORA** Flora, Kevin Scot b: 6/10/69, Fontana, Cal. BR/TR, 6', 180 lbs. Deb: 9/27/91																							
1991	Cal-A	3	8	1	1	0	0	0	0	1	5	.125	.222	.125	-1	-1	1	0	0	.846	-2	/2-3	-0.3
1995	Cal-A	2	1	1	0	0	0	0	0	0	1	.000	.000	.000	-99	-0	0	0	0	.000	0	/D-1	0.0
	Phi-N	24	75	12	16	3	0	2	7	4	22	.213	.253	.333	53	-5	1	0	0	1.000	-1	O-20	-0.6
Total	2	29	84	14	17	3	0	2	7	5	28	.202	.247	.310	46	-7	2	0	1	1.000	-2	/O-20,2-3,D-1	-0.9
■ **PAUL FLORENCE** Florence, Paul Robert "Pep" b: 4/22/1900, Chicago, Ill. d: 5/28/86, Gainesville, Fla. BB/TR, 6'1", 185 lbs. Deb: 5/22/26																							
1926	NY-N	76	188	19	43	4	3	2	14	23	12	.229	.322	.314	73	-7	2			.937	-9	C-76	-1.1
■ **GIL FLORES** Flores, Gilberto (Garcia) b: 10/27/52, Ponce, P.R. BR/TR, 6', 185 lbs. Deb: 5/8/77																							
1977	Cal-A	104	342	41	95	19	4	1	26	23	39	.278	.325	.365	92	-4	12	10	-2	.978	-2	O-85/D-8	-1.2
1978	NY-N	11	29	8	8	0	1	0	1	3	5	.276	.344	.345	96	-0	1	0	0	.944	-1	/O-8	-0.1
1979	NY-N	70	93	9	18	1	1	1	10	8	17	.194	.265	.258	45	-7	2	0	1	.976	-7	O-32	-1.5
Total	3	185	464	58	121	20	6	2	37	34	61	.261	.314	.343	82	-11	15	10	-2	.976	-10	O-125/D-8	-2.8
■ **DICKIE FLOWERS** Flowers, Charles Richard b: 1850, Philadelphia, Pa. d: 10/5/1892, Philadelphia, Pa. Deb: 6/3/1871																							
1871	Tro-n	21	105	39	33	5	4	0	18	4	0	.314	.339	.438	120	2	8	2	1	.769	-3	*S-20/P-1,2-1	0.1
1872	Ath-n	3	15	1	4	0	0	0	4	2	2	.267	.353	.267	93	0	0	0	0	.643	-2	/S-3	-0.1
Total	2 n	24	120	40	37	5	4	0	22	6	2	.308	.341	.417	117	2	8	2	1	.757	-5	/S-23,2-1,P-1	0.0
■ **JAKE FLOWERS** Flowers, D'Arcy Raymond b: 3/16/02, Cambridge, Md. d: 12/27/62, Clearwater, Fla. BR/TR, 5'11.5", 170 lbs. Deb: 9/7/23 C																							
1923	StL-N	13	32	0	3	1	0	0	2	2	7	.094	.147	.125	-28	-6	1	2	-1	.971	-1	/S-7,2-2,3-2	-0.7
1926	*StL-N	40	74	13	20	1	0	3	9	5	9	.270	.325	.405	92	-1	1			.984	1	2-11/1-3,S-1	0.0
1927	Bro-N	67	231	26	54	5	5	2	20	21	25	.234	.300	.325	67	-11	3			.944	-8	S-65/2-1	-1.2
1928	Bro-N	103	339	51	93	11	6	2	44	47	30	.274	.366	.360	92	-3	10			.971	-6	2-94/S-6	-0.6
1929	Bro-N	46	130	16	26	6	0	1	16	22	6	.200	.316	.269	47	-10	9			.962	-5	2-39	-1.3
1930	Bro-N	89	253	37	81	18	3	2	50	21	18	.320	.372	.439	96	-1	5			.949	-8	2-65/O-1	-0.5
1931	Bro-N	22	31	3	7	0	0	0	1	7	4	.226	.368	.226	64	-1	1			1.000	1	/2-6,S-1	0.1
	*StL-N	45	137	19	34	11	1	2	19	9	6	.248	.295	.387	79	-4	7			.971	3	S-24,2-21/3-1	0.1
	Yr	67	168	22	41	11	1	2	20	16	10	.244	.310	.357	77	-5	8			.991	4	2-27,S-25/3-1	0.2
1932	StL-N	67	247	35	63	11	1	2	18	31	18	.255	.341	.332	79	-6	7			.980	-0	3-54/S-7,2-2	-0.2
1933	Bro-N	78	210	28	49	11	2	2	22	24	15	.233	.312	.333	88	-3	13			.955	-11	S-36,2-19/3-8,O-1	-1.1
1934	Cin-N	13	9	1	3	0	0	0	0	1	1	.333	.455	.333	117	0	1			.000	0	H	0.0
Total	10	583	1693	229	433	75	18	16	201	190	139	.256	.333	.350	80	-47	58	2		.967	-34	2-260,S-147/310	-5.4
■ **CLIFF FLOYD** Floyd, Cornelius Clifford b: 12/5/72, Chicago, Ill. BL/TL, 6'4", 230 lbs. Deb: 9/18/93																							
1993	Mon-N	10	31	3	7	0	0	1	2	0	9	.226	.226	.323	43	-3	0	0	0	1.000	-0	1-10	-0.4
1994	Mon-N	100	334	43	94	19	4	4	41	24	63	.281	.335	.398	89	-5	10	3	1	.991	-3	1-77,O-26	-1.3
1995	Mon-N	29	69	6	9	1	0	1	8	7	22	.130	.221	.188	9	-9	3	0	1	.987	-1	1-18/O-4	-1.0
1996	Mon-N	117	227	29	55	15	4	6	26	30	52	.242	.344	.423	98	-0	7	1	2	.960	-13	O-85/1-2	-1.3
1997	*Fla-N	61	137	23	32	9	1	6	19	24	33	.234	.356	.445	113	3	6	2	1	.970	0	O-38/1-9	0.3
1998	Fla-N	153	588	85	166	45	3	22	90	47	112	.282	.339	.481	114	11	27	14	-0	.974	6	*O-146/D-3	1.5
Total	6	470	1386	189	363	89	12	40	186	132	291	.262	.332	.430	98	-4	53	20	4	.969	-10	O-299,1-116/D-3	-2.2
■ **BUBBA FLOYD** Floyd, Leslie Roe b: 6/23/17, Dallas, Tex. BR/TR, 5'11", 160 lbs. Deb: 6/16/44																							
1944	Det-A	3	9	1	4	1	0	0	0	1	0	.444	.500	.556	191	1	0	0	0	1.000	-1	/S-3	0.0
■ **BOBBY FLOYD** Floyd, Robert Nathan b: 10/20/43, Hawthorne, Cal. BR/TR, 6', 181 lbs. Deb: 9/18/68																							
1968	Bal-A	5	9	0	1	1	0	0	1	0	3	.111	.111	.222	-1	-1	0	0	0	1.000	2	/S-4	0.1
1969	Bal-A	39	84	7	17	4	0	0	1	6	17	.202	.256	.250	41	-7	0	0	0	.984	11	2-15,S-15/3-9	0.7
1970	Bal-A	3	2	0	0	0	0	0	0	0	2	.000	.000	.000	-99	-1	0	0	0	1.000	-1	/S-2,2-1	-0.1
	KC-A	14	43	5	14	4	0	0	9	4	9	.326	.383	.419	121	1	0	1	-1	.880	1	/S-8,3-6	0.3
	Yr	17	45	5	14	4	0	0	9	4	11	.311	.367	.400	111	1	0	1	-1	.882	1	S-10/3-6,2-1	0.2
1971	KC-A	31	66	8	10	3	0	0	2	7	21	.152	.233	.197	23	-7	0	0	0	.970	5	S-15/2-8,3-1	0.0
1972	KC-A	61	134	9	24	3	0	0	5	5	29	.179	.209	.201	23	-13	1	0	0	.967	-2	3-30,S-29/2-2	-1.4
1973	KC-A	51	78	10	26	3	1	0	8	4	14	.333	.366	.397	107	1	1	1	-0	1.000	9	2-25,S-24	1.1
1974	KC-A	10	9	1	1	0	0	0	0	2	4	.111	.273	.111	13	-1	0	0	0	1.000	2	/2-5,3-2,S-1	0.2
Total	7	214	425	40	93	18	1	0	26	28	99	.219	.267	.266	52	-27	2	2	-1	.940	27	/S-98,2-56,3-48	0.9
■ **JOHN FLUHRER** Fluhrer, John L. (a.k.a. Wm. G. Morris 1 Game In 1915) b: 1/3/1894, Adrian, Mich. d: 7/17/46, Columbus, Ohio BR/TR, 5'9", 165 lbs. Deb: 9/5/15																							
1915	Chi-N	6	6	0	2	0	0	0	0	1	0	.333	.429	.333	132	0	1	0	5	.500	-1	/O-2	0.0
■ **ED FLYNN** Flynn, Edward J. b: 1/25/1864, Chicago, Ill. BL, 5'9", 165 lbs. Deb: 5/5/1887																							
1887	Cle-a	7	27	0	5	1	0	0	4	1		.185	.214	.222	22	-3	3			.786	-0	/3-6,O-1	-0.2
■ **GEORGE FLYNN** Flynn, George A. "Dibby" b: 5/24/1871, Chicago, Ill. d: 12/28/01, Chicago, Ill. Deb: 4/17/1896																							
1896	Chi-N	29	106	15	27	1	2	0	4	11	9	.255	.336	.302	66	-5	12			.878	2	O-29	-0.4
■ **JOCKO FLYNN** Flynn, John A. b: 6/30/1864, Lawrence, Mass. d: 12/30/07, Lawrence, Mass. TR, 5'6.5", 143 lbs. Deb: 5/1/1886																							
1886	Chi-N	57	205	40	41	6	2	4	19	18	45	.200	.265	.307	64	-10	9			.916	-5	P-32,O-28	-1.0
1887	Chi-N	1	0	0	0	0	0	0	0	0	0	—	—	—	—	0	0			.000	-1	/O-1	-0.1
Total	2	58	205	40	41	6	2	4	19	18	45	.200	.265	.307	64	-10	9			.850	-6	/P-32,O-29	-1.1
■ **JOHN FLYNN** Flynn, John Anthony b: 9/7/1883, Providence, R.I. d: 3/23/35, Providence, R.I. BR/TR, 6'0.5", 175 lbs. Deb: 4/22/10																							
1910	Pit-N	96	332	32	91	10	2	6	52	30	47	.274	.336	.370	100	-1	6			.977	-3	1-93	-0.4
1911	Pit-N	33	59	5	12	0	1	0	3	9	8	.203	.309	.237	52	-4	0			1.000	0	1-13/O-1	-0.3
1912	Was-A	20	71	9	12	4	1	0	5	7		.169	.253	.254	45	-5	2			.974	1	1-20	-0.4
Total	3	149	462	46	115	14	4	6	60	46	55	.249	.320	.335	85	-9	8			.978	-1	1-126/O-1	-1.1
■ **JOE FLYNN** Flynn, Joseph b: Philadelphia, Pa. Deb: 4/18/1884																							
1884	Phi-U	52	209	38	52	9	4	4		11		.249	.286	.388	111	-4				.778	-15	O-43,C-10/1-1,S-1	-1.7
	Bos-U	9	31	4	7	2	0	0		2		.226	.273	.290	72	-2				.864	4	/C-7,O-4,1-1	0.2
	Yr	61	240	42	59	11	4	4		13		.246	.285	.375	105	-6				.764	-11	O-47,C-17/1-2,S-1	-1.5
■ **MIKE FLYNN** Flynn, Michael J. b: 3/15/1872, County Kildare, Ireland d: 6/16/41, Los Angeles, Cal. Deb: 8/31/1891																							
1891	Bos-a	1	2	0	0	0	0	0	0	0	1	.000	.000	.000	-99	-1	0			1.000	1	/C-1	0.0
■ **DOUG FLYNN** Flynn, Robert Douglas b: 4/18/51, Lexington, Ky. BR/TR, 5'11", 165 lbs. Deb: 4/9/75																							
1975	Cin-N	89	127	17	34	7	0	1	20	11	13	.268	.326	.346	85	-3	3	0	1	.962	10	3-40,2-30,S-17	1.0
1976	*Cin-N	93	219	20	62	5	2	1	20	10	24	.283	.314	.338	83	-5	2	0	1	.988	-4	2-55,3-23,S-20	-0.4
1977	Cin-N	36	32	0	8	1	1	0	5	0	6	.250	.250	.344	56	-2	0	0	0	1.000	7	3-25/2-9,S-4	0.5
	NY-N	90	282	14	54	6	1	0	14	11	23	.191	.222	.220	20	-32	1	3	-2	.954	-13	S-65,2-29/3-2	-4.0
	Yr	126	314	14	62	7	2	0	19	11	29	.197	.225	.232	24	-34	1	3	-2	.956	-6	S-69,2-38,3-27	-3.5
1978	NY-N	156	532	37	126	12	8	0	36	30	50	.237	.279	.289	61	-28	3	5	-2	.986	2	*2-128,S-60	-1.7
1979	NY-N	157	555	35	135	19	5	4	61	17	46	.243	.266	.317	61	-32	0	3	-2	.983	1	*2-148,S-20	-2.3
1980	NY-N	128	443	46	113	9	8	0	24	22	20	.255	.290	.312	70	-18	2	2	-1	**.991**	3	*2-128/S-3	-0.9
1981	NY-N	105	325	24	72	12	4	1	20	11	19	.222	.247	.292	53	-21	1	2	-1	.987	12	*2-100/S-5	-0.3
1982	Tex-A	88	270	13	57	6	2	0	19	4	14	.211	.223	.248	31	-26	6	2	1	.989	4	2-55,S-35	-1.6
	Mon-N	58	193	13	47	6	2	0	20	4	23	.244	.259	.295	54	-12	0	2	-1	.983	5	2-58	-0.6

YEAR	TM/L	G	AB	R	H	2B	3B	HR	RBI	BB	SO	AVG	OBP	SLG	PRO+	BR/A	SB	CS	SBR	FA	FR	G/POS	TPR
1983	Mon-N	143	452	44	107	18	4	0	26	19	38	.237	.268	.294	56	-27	2	1	0	.986	7	*2-107,S-37	-1.4
1984	Mon-N	124	366	23	89	12	1	0	17	12	41	.243	.267	.281	57	-22	0	0	0	.979	-8	2-88,S-34	-2.6
1985	Mon-N	9	6	0	1	0	0	0	0	0	0	.167	.167	.167	-7	-1	0	0	0	1.000	-1	/2-6,S-1	-0.2
	Det-A	32	51	2	13	2	1	0	2	0	3	.255	.255	.333	60	-3	0	0	0	.984	8	2-20/S-8,3-4	0.6
Total	11	1308	3853	288	918	115	39	7	284	151	320	.238	.267	.294	57	-231	20	20	-6	.986	33	2-961,S-309/3-94	-13.9
■ CLIPPER FLYNN	Flynn, William b: 4/29/1849, Lansingburg, N.Y. d: 11/11/1881, Lansingburg, N.Y. TR , 5'7", 140 lbs. Deb: 5/9/1871																						
1871	Tro-n	29	142	43	48	6	1	0	27	4	2	.338	.356	.394	114	2	3	3	-1	.955	5	1-19/O-8,2-1,3-1	0.5
1872	Oly-n	9	40	4	9	1	0	0	2	0	0	.225	.225	.250	48	-2	0	0	0	.900	-1	/1-9	-0.2
Total	2 n	38	182	47	57	7	1	0	29	4	2	.313	.328	.363	101	0	3	3	-1	.934	4	/1-28,O-8,3-1,2-1	0.3
■ JIM FOGARTY	Fogarty, James G. b: 2/12/1864, San Francisco, Cal d: 5/20/1891, Philadelphia, Pa. BR/TR, 5'10.5", 180 lbs. Deb: 5/1/1884 FM																						
1884	Phi-N	97	378	42	80	12	6	1	37	20	54	.212	.251	.283	71	-12				.915	3	*O-78,3-14/2-4,SP	-0.9
1885	Phi-N	111	427	49	99	13	3	0	39	30	37	.232	.282	.276	83	-7				.941	25	*O-88,2-10/S-8,3-5	1.5
1886	Phi-N	77	280	54	82	13	5	3	47	42	16	.293	.385	.407	140	15	30			.953	-3	O-60,2-13/S-3,3P	0.9
1887	Phi-N	126	495	113	129	26	12	8	50	**82**	44	.261	.376	.410	112	9	102			.920	32	*O-123/S-2,3-2,2P	3.3
1888	Phi-N	121	454	72	107	14	6	1	35	53	66	.236	.325	.300	95	-1	58			.930	14	*O-117/3-5,S-1	1.0
1889	Phi-N	128	499	107	129	15	17	3	54	65	60	.259	.352	.375	95	-5	**99**			**.961**	19	*O-128/P-4	1.0
1890	Phi-P	91	347	71	83	17	6	4	58	59	50	.239	.364	.357	91	-4	36			.963	8	O-91/3-1,M	0.1
Total	7	751	2880	508	709	110	55	20	320	351	327	.246	.335	.343	98	-4	325			.940	98	O-685/3-30,2-28,SP	6.9
■ JOE FOGARTY	Fogarty, Joseph J. b: San Francisco, Cal. Deb: 9/18/1885 F																						
1885	StL-N	2	8	1	1	0	0	0	0	0	1	.125	.125	.125	-20	-1				1.000	-0	/O-2	-0.1
■ LEE FOHL	Fohl, Leo Alexander b: 11/28/1876, Lowell, Ohio d: 10/30/65, Cleveland, Ohio BL/TR, 5'10", 175 lbs. Deb: 8/29/02 MC																						
1902	Pit-N	1	3	0	0	0	0	0	1	0	0	.000	.000	.000	-97	-1	0			.875	0	/C-1	0.0
1903	Cin-N	4	14	3	5	1	1	0	2	0	0	.357	.400	.571	158	1	0			.955	-0	/C-4	0.1
Total	2	5	17	3	5	1	1	0	3	0	0	.294	.333	.471	120	0	0			.933	0	/C-5	0.1
■ HANK FOILES	Foiles, Henry Lee b: 6/10/29, Richmond, Va. BR/TR, 6', 195 lbs. Deb: 4/21/53																						
1953	Cin-N	5	13	1	2	0	0	0	0	1	2	.154	.214	.154	-2	-2	0	0	0	.909	-1	/C-3	-0.2
	Cle-A	7	7	2	1	0	0	0	0	1	1	.143	.250	.143	9	-1	0	0	0	.933	1	/C-7	0.0
1955	Cle-A	62	111	13	29	9	0	1	7	17	18	.261	.359	.369	93	-1	0	0	0	.988	14	C-41	1.4
1956	Cle-A	1	0	0	0	0	0	0	0	0	0	—	—	—	—	0	0	0	0	.000	0	/C-1	0.0
	Pit-N	79	222	24	47	10	2	7	25	17	56	.212	.268	.369	71	-10	0	1	-1	.988	-2	C-73	-1.0
1957	Pit-N★	109	281	32	76	10	4	9	36	37	53	.270	.355	.431	113	6	1	3	-2	.981	-6	*C-109	0.2
1958	Pit-N	104	264	31	54	10	2	8	30	45	53	.205	.323	.348	80	-7	0	1	-1	.990	8	*C-103	0.6
1959	Pit-N	53	80	10	18	3	0	3	4	7	16	.225	.287	.375	75	-3	0	0	0	1.000	9	C-51	0.7
1960	KC-A	6	7	1	4	0	0	0	1	3	2	.571	.700	.571	246	2	0	0	0	.900	-0	/C-2	0.2
	Cle-A	24	68	9	19	1	0	1	6	7	5	.279	.347	.338	89	-1	0	0	0	.982	0	C-22	0.1
	Det-A	26	56	5	14	3	0	0	3	1	8	.250	.263	.304	51	-4	1	0	0	1.000	4	C-22	0.2
	Yr	56	131	15	37	4	0	1	10	11	15	.282	.338	.336	83	-3	1	0	0	.987	5	C-46	0.5
1961	Bal-A	43	124	18	34	6	0	6	19	12	27	.274	.338	.468	117	3	0	2	-1	.995	3	C-38	0.6
1962	Cin-N	43	131	17	36	6	1	7	25	13	39	.275	.340	.496	118	3	0	0	0	.981	1	C-41	0.5
1963	Cin-N	1	3	0	0	0	0	0	0	1	0	.000	.250	.000	-21	-0	1	0	0	1.000	-0	/C-1	0.0
	LA-A	41	84	8	18	1	1	4	10	8	13	.214	.290	.393	95	-1	0	0	0	.974	3	C-30	0.3
1964	LA-A	4	4	0	1	0	0	0	0	0	2	.250	.250	.250	44	-0	0	0	0	.000	0	H	0.0
Total	11	608	1455	171	353	59	10	46	166	170	295	.243	.323	.392	92	-17	3	7	-3	.986	35	C-544	3.6
■ CURRY FOLEY	Foley, Charles Joseph b: 1/14/1856, Milltown, Ireland d: 10/20/1898, Boston, Mass. TL , 5'10", 160 lbs. Deb: 5/13/1879																						
1879	Bos-N	35	146	16	46	3	1	0	17	3	4	.315	.329	.349	121	3				.857	-7	P-21,O-17/1-2	-0.4
1880	Bos-N	80	332	44	97	13	2	2	31	8	14	.292	.309	.361	130	10				.953	-3	P-36,O-35,1-25	0.0
1881	Buf-N	83	375	58	96	20	2	1	25	7	27	.256	.270	.328	88	-5				.795	-4	O-55,1-27,P-10	-1.2
1882	Buf-N	84	341	51	104	16	4	3	49	12	26	.305	.329	.402	131	11				.833	0	*O-84/P-1	1.0
1883	Buf-N	23	111	23	30	5	3	0	6	4	12	.270	.296	.369	98	-0				.885	-2	O-23/P-1	-0.2
Total	5	305	1305	192	373	57	12	6	128	34	83	.286	.304	.362	114	19				.819	-16	O-214/P-69,1-54	-0.8
■ MARV FOLEY	Foley, Marvis Edwin b: 8/29/53, Stanford, Ky. BL/TR, 6', 195 lbs. Deb: 9/11/78 C																						
1978	Chi-A	11	34	3	12	0	0	0	6	4	6	.353	.421	.353	119	1	0	1	-1	.938	-3	C-10	-0.2
1979	Chi-A	34	97	6	24	3	0	2	10	7	5	.247	.298	.340	72	-4	0	0	0	.993	-1	C-33	-0.4
1980	Chi-A	68	137	14	29	5	0	4	15	9	22	.212	.270	.336	65	-7	0	0	0	.991	2	C-64/1-3	-0.3
1982	Chi-A	27	36	1	4	0	0	0	1	6	4	.111	.238	.111	-0	-5	0	0	0	.980	1	C-15/3-2,1-1,D-1	-0.3
1984	Tex-A	63	115	13	25	2	0	6	19	15	24	.217	.313	.391	91	-1	0	0	0	.988	1	C-36/1-1,3-1,D-4	0.1
Total	5	203	419	37	94	10	0	12	51	41	61	.224	.298	.334	73	-16	0	1	-1	.986	0	C-158/D-5,1-5,3-3	-1.1
■ RAY FOLEY	Foley, Raymond Kirwin b: 6/23/06, Naugatuck, Conn. d: 3/22/80, Vero Beach, Fla. BL/TR, 5'11", 173 lbs. Deb: 7/4/28																						
1928	NY-N	2	1	1	0	0	0	0	0	1	1	.000	.500	.000	41	0	0			.000	0	H	0.0
■ TOM FOLEY	Foley, Thomas J. b: 1847, Chicago, Ill. d: 1/4/1896, LaGrange, Ill. 5'9.5", 157 lbs. Deb: 5/8/1871																						
1871	Chi-n	18	84	18	22	3	1	0	13	3	2	.262	.287	.321	67	-5	1	4	-2	.633	-5	O-16/C-4,3-1	-0.7
■ TOM FOLEY	Foley, Thomas Michael b: 9/9/59, Columbus, Ga. BL/TR, 6'1", 180 lbs. Deb: 4/9/83																						
1983	Cin-N	68	98	7	20	4	1	0	9	13	17	.204	.297	.265	55	-6	1	0	0	.983	9	S-37/2-5	0.6
1984	Cin-N	106	277	26	70	8	3	5	27	24	36	.253	.312	.357	84	-6	3	2	-0	.965	1	S-83,2-10/3-1	0.1
1985	Cin-N	43	92	7	18	5	1	0	6	6	16	.196	.245	.272	42	-7	1	0	0	.983	3	2-18,S-15/3-1	-0.3
	Phi-N	46	158	17	42	8	0	3	17	13	18	.266	.322	.373	91	-2	1	3	-2	.981	-5	S-45	-0.4
	Yr	89	250	24	60	13	1	3	23	19	34	.240	.294	.336	73	-9	2	3	-1	.978	-3	S-60,2-18/3-1	-0.7
1986	Phi-N	39	61	8	18	2	1	0	5	10	11	.295	.394	.361	106	1	2	0	1	.975	0	S-24/2-1,3-1	0.3
	Mon-N	64	202	18	52	13	2	1	18	20	26	.257	.324	.356	88	-3	8	3	1	.965	-5	S-29,2-25,3-15	-0.5
	Yr	103	263	26	70	15	3	1	23	30	37	.266	.341	.357	92	-2	10	3	1	.970	-5	S-53,2-26,3-16	-0.2
1987	Mon-N	106	280	35	82	18	3	5	28	11	40	.293	.322	.432	95	-3	6	10	-4	.963	1	S-49,2-39/3-9	-0.1
1988	Mon-N	127	377	33	100	21	3	5	43	30	49	.265	.321	.377	95	-2	2	7	-4	.972	3	2-89,S-32/3-9	0.3
1989	Mon-N	122	375	34	86	19	2	7	39	45	53	.229	.317	.347	88	-5	2	3	-1	.988	20	*2-108,3-16,S-14,/P	1.8
1990	Mon-N	73	164	11	35	2	1	0	12	12	22	.213	.267	.238	42	-13	0	1	-1	.987	3	S-45,2-20/3-7,1-1	-0.9
1991	Mon-N	86	168	12	35	11	1	0	15	14	30	.208	.273	.286	58	-9	2	0	1	.967	-2	S-43,1-31/3-6,2-2	-1.0
1992	Mon-N	72	115	7	20	3	1	0	5	8	21	.174	.234	.217	29	-11	3	0	1	.967	6	S-33,2-13,1-12,/3O	-0.2
1993	Pit-N	86	194	18	49	11	1	3	22	11	26	.253	.293	.366	75	-7	0	0	0	.993	1	2-35,1-12/3-7,S-6	-0.5
1994	Pit-N	59	123	13	29	7	0	3	15	13	18	.236	.309	.366	74	-5	0	0	0	.986	11	2-17,3-14/S-8,1-3	0.7
1995	Mon-N	11	24	2	5	2	0	0	2	2	4	.208	.269	.292	46	-2	1	0	0	1.000	-1	/1-4,2-3	-0.3
Total	13	1108	2708	248	661	134	20	32	263	232	387	.244	.305	.344	78	-80	32	29	-8	.972	45	S-463,2-385/31OP	-0.4
■ WILL FOLEY	Foley, William Brown b: 11/15/1855, Chicago, Ill. d: 11/12/16, Chicago, Ill. BR/TR, 5'9.5", 150 lbs. Deb: 8/23/1875																						
1875	Chi-n	3	12	0	3	1	0	0	1	0	2	.250	.250	.333	100	-0	0	0	0	.813	1	/3-3	0.1
1876	Cin-N	58	221	19	50	3	2	0	9	0	14	.226	.226	.258	71	-6				.804	2	3-46,C-20	-0.2
1877	Cin-N	56	216	23	41	5	1	0	18	4	13	.190	.205	.222	39	-14				.836	6	*3-56	-0.5
1878	Mil-N	56	229	33	62	8	5	0	22	7	14	.271	.292	.349	103	0				.812	-9	*3-53/C-7	-0.6
1879	Cin-N	56	218	22	46	5	1	0	25	2	16	.211	.218	.243	55	-10				.820	3	3-29,O-25/2-3	-0.7
1881	Det-N	5	15	0	2	0	0	0	1	2	3	.133	.235	.133	18	-1				.769	-1	/3-5	-0.3
1884	CP-U	19	71	15	20	1	1	0		5		.282	.329	.324	99	-2				.804	-3	3-19	-0.5
Total	6	250	970	112	221	22	10	0	75	20	60	.228	.243	.271	70	-33				.817	-2	3-208/C-27,O-25,2-3	-2.8

YEAR	TM/L	G	AB	R	H	2B	3B	HR	RBI	BB	SO	AVG	OBP	SLG	PRO+	BR/A	SB	CS	SBR	FA	FR	G/POS	TPR
■ **TIM FOLI**	Foli, Timothy John b: 12/8/50, Culver City, Cal. BR/TR, 6', 179 lbs. Deb: 9/11/70 C																						
1970	NY-N	5	11	0	4	0	0	0	1	0	2	.364	.364	.364	95	-0	0	0	0	1.000	2	/S-2,3-2	0.2
1971	NY-N	97	288	32	65	12	2	0	24	18	50	.226	.274	.281	58	-16	5	0	2	.964	14	2-58,3-36,S-12,/O-1	0.4
1972	Mon-N	149	540	45	130	12	2	2	35	25	43	.241	.282	.281	59	-28	11	7	-1	.966	9	*S-148/2-1	0.1
1973	Mon-N	126	458	37	110	11	0	2	36	28	40	.240	.285	.277	55	-28	6	3	0	.960	8	*S-123/2-2,O-1	-0.3
1974	Mon-N	121	441	41	112	10	3	0	39	28	27	.254	.303	.290	63	-21	8	2	1	.971	19	*S-120/3-1	1.6
1975	Mon-N	152	572	64	136	25	2	1	29	36	49	.238	.285	.294	58	-32	13	3	2	.973	6	*S-151/2-1	-0.9
1976	Mon-N	149	546	41	144	36	1	6	54	16	33	.264	.285	.366	80	-16	6	5	-1	.975	7	*S-146/3-1	0.8
1977	Mon-N	13	57	2	10	5	1	0	3	0	4	.175	.175	.298	25	-6	0	0	0	1.000	1	S-13	-0.4
	SF-N	104	368	30	84	17	3	4	27	11	16	.228	.251	.323	53	-25	2	4	-2	.974	2	*S-102/2-1,3-1,O-1	-1.4
	Yr	117	425	32	94	22	4	4	30	11	20	.221	.241	.320	49	-31	2	4	-2	.977	3	*S-115/2-1,3-1,O-1	-1.8
1978	NY-N	113	413	37	106	21	1	1	27	14	30	.257	.284	.320	71	-17	2	5	-2	.966	-15	*S-112	-2.1
1979	NY-N	3	7	0	0	0	0	0	0	0	0	.000	.000	.000	-99	-2	0	0	0	1.000	1	/S-3	-0.1
	*Pit-N	133	525	70	153	23	1	1	65	28	14	.291	.338	.345	83	-12	6	5	-1	.978	-1	*S-132	0.2
	Yr	136	532	70	153	23	1	1	65	28	14	.288	.334	.340	81	-13	6	5	-1	.978	0	*S-135	0.1
1980	Pit-N	127	495	61	131	22	0	3	38	19	23	.265	.300	.327	74	-17	11	7	-1	**.981**	-0	*S-125	-0.4
1981	Pit-N	86	316	32	78	12	2	0	20	17	10	.247	.287	.297	64	-15	7	7	-2	.965	-9	S-81	-2.0
1982	*Cal-A	150	480	46	121	14	2	3	56	14	22	.252	.276	.308	60	-26	2	4	-2	**.985**	8	*S-139/2-8,3-2	-0.7
1983	Cal-A	88	330	29	83	10	0	2	29	5	18	.252	.265	.300	56	-20	2	3	-1	.975	10	S-74,3-13	-0.4
1984	NY-A	61	163	8	41	11	0	0	16	2	16	.252	.265	.319	63	-8	0	0	0	.950	7	S-28,2-21,3-10,/1-2	0.1
1985	Pit-N	19	37	1	7	0	0	0	2	4	2	.189	.268	.189	30	-3	0	0	0	.980	3	S-13	-0.1
Total	16	1696	6047	576	1515	241	20	25	501	265	399	.251	.286	.309	64	-293	81	55	-9	.973	73	*S-1524/2-92,3O1	-5.2
■ **DEE FONDY**	Fondy, Dee Virgil b: 10/31/24, Slaton, Tex. BL/TL, 6'3", 196 lbs. Deb: 4/17/51																						
1951	Chi-N	49	170	23	46	7	2	3	20	11	20	.271	.319	.388	88	-3	5	6	-2	.976	-3	1-44	-1.0
1952	Chi-N	145	554	69	166	21	9	10	67	28	60	.300	.334	.424	108	4	13	11	-3	.990	2	*1-143	-0.2
1953	Chi-N	150	595	79	184	24	11	18	78	44	106	.309	.358	.477	113	10	10	7	-1	.987	4	*1-149	0.6
1954	Chi-N	141	568	77	162	30	4	9	49	35	84	.285	.328	.400	87	-11	20	5	**3**	.993	7	*1-138	-0.8
1955	Chi-N	150	574	69	152	23	8	17	65	35	87	.265	.309	.422	92	-8	8	9	-3	.991	1	*1-147	-1.9
1956	Chi-N	137	543	52	146	22	9	9	46	20	74	.269	.295	.392	84	-13	9	7	-2	.985	-3	*1-133	-2.8
1957	Chi-N	11	51	3	16	3	1	0	2	0	9	.314	.314	.412	94	-1	1	2	-1	.991	-1	1-11	-0.3
	Pit-N	95	323	42	101	13	2	2	35	25	59	.313	.364	.384	104	2	11	5	0	.982	-3	1-73	-0.5
	Yr	106	374	45	117	16	3	2	37	25	68	.313	.357	.388	103	2	12	7	-1	.983	-4	1-84	-0.8
1958	Cin-N	89	124	23	27	1	1	1	11	5	27	.218	.248	.266	34	-12	7	1	2	.987	-1	1-36,O-22	-1.3
Total	8	967	3502	437	1000	144	47	69	373	203	526	.286	.326	.413	95	-30	84	53	-7	.988	3	1-874/O-22	-8.2
■ **LEW FONSECA**	Fonseca, Lewis Albert b: 1/21/1899, Oakland, Cal. d: 11/26/89, Ely, Iowa BR/TR, 5'10.5", 180 lbs. Deb: 4/13/21 M																						
1921	Cin-N	82	297	38	82	10	3	1	41	8	13	.276	.304	.340	74	-12	2	3	-1	.961	-3	2-50,1-16,O-16	-1.6
1922	Cin-N	81	291	55	105	20	3	4	45	14	18	.361	.390	.491	128	12	7	8	-3	.970	8	2-71	1.8
1923	Cin-N	65	237	33	66	11	4	3	28	9	16	.278	.310	.397	87	-5	4	0	1	.957	8	2-45,1-14	0.4
1924	Cin-N	20	57	5	13	2	1	0	9	4	4	.228	.279	.298	55	-4	1	0	0	1.000	-2	2-10/1-6	-0.6
1925	Phi-N	126	467	78	149	30	5	7	60	21	42	.319	.352	.450	95	-4	6	2	1	.956	-8	2-69,1-55	-1.3
1927	Cle-A	112	428	60	133	20	7	2	40	12	17	.311	.333	.404	90	-8	12	4	1	.973	-6	2-96,1-13	-0.9
1928	Cle-A	75	263	38	86	19	4	3	36	13	17	.327	.361	.464	114	5	4	2	0	1.000	5	1-56,3-15/S-4,2-1	0.5
1929	Cle-A	148	566	97	209	44	15	6	103	50	23	**.369**	.427	.532	140	34	19	11	-1	.995	6	*1-147	2.3
1930	Cle-A	40	129	20	36	9	2	0	17	7	7	.279	.316	.380	73	-6	1	0	0	.980	-1	1-28/3-6	-0.5
1931	Cle-A	26	108	21	40	9	1	1	14	8	7	.370	.419	.500	133	5	3	2	-0	.993	0	1-26	0.3
	Chi-A	121	465	65	139	26	5	2	71	32	22	.299	.348	.389	99	-1	4	4	-1	.974	-17	O-95,2-21/1-2,3-1	-2.2
	Yr	147	573	86	179	35	6	3	85	40	29	.312	.361	.410	106	5	7	6	-2	.974	-16	O-95,1-28,2-21,/3-1	-1.9
1932	Chi-A	18	37	0	5	1	0	0	6	1	7	.135	.158	.162	-18	-7	0	0	0	1.000	1	/O-8,P-1,M	-0.6
1933	Chi-A	23	59	8	12	2	0	2	15	7	6	.203	.288	.339	68	-3	1	0	0	1.000	2	1-12,M	-0.1
Total	12	937	3404	518	1075	203	50	31	485	186	199	.316	.355	.432	103	8	64	36	-2	.994	-3	1-375,2-363,O/3SP	-2.5
■ **CHAD FONVILLE**	Fonville, Chad Everette b: 3/5/71, Jacksonville, N.C. BB/TR, 5'6", 155 lbs. Deb: 4/28/95																						
1995	Mon-N	14	12	2	4	0	0	0	0	0	3	.333	.333	.333	74	-0	0	2	-1	.000	0	/2-2	-0.2
	*LA-N	88	308	41	85	6	1	0	16	23	39	.276	.328	.302	74	-11	20	5	3	.971	-3	S-38,2-36,O-11	-0.6
	Yr	102	320	43	89	6	1	0	16	23	42	.278	.328	.303	73	-12	20	7	2	.971	-3	2-38,S-38,O-11	-0.8
1996	LA-N	103	201	34	41	4	1	0	13	17	31	.204	.266	.234	36	-19	7	2	1	.964	-3	O-35,2-23,S-20,/3-2	-1.9
1997	LA-N	9	14	1	2	0	0	0	1	2	3	.143	.250	.143	7	-2	0	1	-1	.833	-2	/2-3	-0.5
	Chi-A	9	9	1	1	0	0	0	1	1	1	.111	.200	.111	-17	-2	2	0	1	1.000	0	/O-3,2-2,S-2,D-1	-0.1
Total	3	223	544	79	133	10	2	0	31	43	77	.244	.301	.270	57	-34	29	10	3	.966	-8	/2-66,S-60,O-49,3D	-3.3
■ **BARRY FOOTE**	Foote, Barry Clifton b: 2/16/52, Smithfield, N.C. BR/TR, 6'3", 210 lbs. Deb: 9/14/73 C																						
1973	Mon-N	6	6	0	4	0	1	0	1	0	0	.667	.667	1.000	343	2	0	0	0	.000	0	H	0.2
1974	Mon-N	125	420	44	110	23	4	11	60	35	74	.262	.323	.414	100	-1	2	1	0	.984	9	*C-122	1.3
1975	Mon-N	118	387	25	75	16	1	7	30	17	48	.194	.230	.295	43	-31	0	1	-1	.985	11	*C-115	-1.7
1976	Mon-N	105	350	32	82	12	2	7	27	17	32	.234	.272	.340	70	-15	2	1	0	.989	7	C-96/3-2,1-1	-0.5
1977	Mon-N	15	49	4	12	3	1	2	8	4	10	.245	.302	.469	106	0	0	0	0	.988	0	C-13	0.1
	Phi-N	18	32	3	7	1	0	1	3	3	6	.219	.286	.344	65	-2	0	0	0	.980	-1	C-17	-0.2
	Yr	33	81	7	19	4	1	3	11	7	16	.235	.295	.420	88	-2	0	0	0	.985	-0	C-30	-0.1
1978	*Phi-N	39	57	4	9	0	0	1	4	1	11	.158	.172	.211	6	-7	0	0	0	1.000	2	C-31	-0.5
1979	Chi-N	132	429	47	109	26	0	16	56	34	49	.254	.316	.427	92	-6	5	2	0	.979	-3	*C-129	-0.4
1980	Chi-N	63	202	16	48	13	1	6	28	13	18	.238	.284	.401	83	-5	1	1	-0	.992	1	C-55	-0.3
1981	Chi-N	9	22	0	0	0	0	0	1	3	7	.000	.120	.000	-61	-5	0	0	0	1.000	-1	/C-8	-0.6
	*NY-A	40	125	12	26	4	0	6	10	8	21	.208	.256	.384	83	-3	0	0	0	.996	9	C-34/1-1,D-4	0.7
1982	NY-A	17	48	4	7	5	0	0	2	1	11	.146	.163	.250	12	-6	0	0	0	.973	-4	C-17	-0.9
Total	10	687	2127	191	489	103	10	57	230	136	287	.230	.279	.368	75	-78	10	6	-1	.985	31	C-637/D-4,1-2,3-2	-2.8
■ **JIM FORAN**	Foran, James H. b: 1848, New York 5'6.5", 159 lbs. Deb: 5/4/1871																						
1871	Kek-n	19	89	21	31	1	3	1	18	2	1	.348	.363	.461	132	3	1	0	0	.878	1	1-16/O-4	0.3
■ **P.J FORBES**	Forbes, Patrick Joseph b: 9/22/67, Pittsburg, Kan. BR/TR, 5'10", 160 lbs. Deb: 7/21/98																						
1998	Bal-A	9	10	0	1	0	0	0	2	0	0	.100	.100	.100	-49	-2	0	0	0	1.000	1	/2-7,3-1,S-1	-0.1
■ **DAVY FORCE**	Force, David W. "Wee Davy" or "Tom Thumb" b: 7/27/1849, New York, N.Y. d: 6/21/18, Englewood, N.J. BR/TR, 5'4", 130 lbs. Deb: 5/5/1871																						
1871	Oly-n	32	162	45	45	9	4	0	29	4	0	.278	.295	.383	98	0	8	0	2	**.844**	**18**	*S-31/3-1	1.3
1872	Tro-n	25	130	40	53	11	0	0	16	1	0	.408	.412	.492	175	11	2	2	-1	.871	4	3-16/S-9	0.9
	Bal-n	19	95	29	41	2	2	0	13	1	0	.432	.438	.495	178	8	3	0	1	.846	5	3-19	0.9
	Yr	44	225	69	94	13	2	0	29	2	0	.418	.423	.493	176	19	5	2	0	**.857**	8	3-35/S-9	1.8
1873	Bal-n	49	234	77	86	8	1	0	31	9	0	.368	.391	.410	139	12	1	0	0	**.820**	6	3-34,S-17/P-3	1.1
1874	Chi-n	59	294	61	92	9	0	0	26	3	1	.313	.320	.344	112	3	4	0	1	.802	11	*3-42,S-18/P-1	1.1
1875	Ath-n	77	386	78	120	22	5	0	49	7	5	.311	.323	.394	133	9	6	3	0	**.887**	10	*S-77/3-2	1.4
1876	Phi-N	60	284	48	66	6	0	0	17	5	3	.232	.246	.254	67	-9				.898	21	*S-60/3-2	1.0
	NY-N	1	3	0	0	0	0	0	0	0	0	.000	.000	.000	-99	-1				.833	0	/S-1	0.0
	Yr	61	287	48	66	6	0	0	17	5	3	.230	.243	.251	66	-10				.897	21	S-61/3-2	1.0
1877	StL-N	58	225	24	59	5	3	0	22	11	15	.262	.297	.311	97	-0				**.914**	6	*S-50/3-8	0.6
1879	Buf-N	79	316	36	66	5	2	0	8	13	37	.209	.240	.237	57	-14				**.929**	2	*S-78/3-1	-0.8
1880	Buf-N	81	290	22	49	10	0	0	17	10	35	.169	.197	.203	35	-19				.939	31	2-53,S-30	1.6
1881	Buf-N	75	278	21	50	9	1	0	15	11	29	.180	.211	.219	36	-20				.937	24	2-51,S-21/O-3,3-1	0.7
1882	Buf-N	73	278	39	67	10	1	1	28	12	17	.241	.272	.295	81	-6				**.908**	7	*S-61,3-11/2-1	0.4
1883	Buf-N	96	378	40	82	11	3	0	35	12	39	.217	.241	.262	52	-22				.884	-6	*S-78,3-13/2-7	-2.3

YEAR	TM/L	G	AB	R	H	2B	3B	HR	RBI	BB	SO	AVG	OBP	SLG	PRO+	BR/A	SB	CS	SBR	FA	FR	G/POS	TPR
1884	Buf-N	106	403	47	83	13	3	0	36	27	41	.206	.256	.253	59	-19				**.898**	-3	*S-105/2-1	-1.9
1885	Buf-N	71	253	20	57	6	1	0	15	13	19	.225	.263	.257	66	-9				.882	-4	2-42,S-24/3-6	-1.0
1886	Was-N	68	242	26	44	5	1	0	16	17	26	.182	.236	.211	39	-17	9			.909	17	S-56/2-8,3-4	0.1
Total	5 n	261	1301	330	437	61	12	0	164	25	6	.336	.348	.401	132	43	24	5	4	.861	53	S-152,3-114/P-4	6.7
Total	10	768	2950	323	623	80	15	1	209	131	261	.211	.245	.249	58	-136	9			.908	96	S-564,2-163/3-46,O	-1.6

■ CURT FORD

Ford, Curtis Glenn b: 10/11/60, Jackson, Miss. BL/TR, 5'10", 150 lbs. Deb: 6/22/85

YEAR	TM/L	G	AB	R	H	2B	3B	HR	RBI	BB	SO	AVG	OBP	SLG	PRO+	BR/A	SB	CS	SBR	FA	FR	G/POS	TPR
1985	StL-N	11	12	2	6	2	0	0	3	4	1	.500	.625	.667	264	3	1	0	0	.750	-2	/O-4	0.2
1986	StL-N	85	214	30	53	15	2	2	29	23	29	.248	.321	.364	89	-3	13	5	1	.975	1	O-64	-0.3
1987	*StL-N	89	228	32	65	9	5	3	26	14	32	.285	.329	.408	92	-3	11	8	-2	.981	1	O-75	-0.5
1988	StL-N	91	128	11	25	6	0	1	18	8	26	.195	.243	.266	45	-9	6	1	1	.965	-4	O-40/1-7	-1.4
1989	Phi-N	108	142	13	31	5	1	1	13	16	33	.218	.302	.289	70	-5	5	3	-0	1.000	-8	O-52/1-1,2-1	-1.6
1990	Phi-N	22	18	0	2	0	0	0	0	1	5	.111	.158	.111	-25	-3	0	0	0	1.000	-1	/O-3	-0.4
Total	6	406	742	88	182	37	8	7	89	66	126	.245	.309	.345	80	-20	36	17	1	.977	-12	O-238/1-8,2-1	-4.0

■ DAN FORD

Ford, Darnell Glenn b: 5/19/52, Los Angeles, Cal. BR/TR, 6'1", 185 lbs. Deb: 4/12/75

YEAR	TM/L	G	AB	R	H	2B	3B	HR	RBI	BB	SO	AVG	OBP	SLG	PRO+	BR/A	SB	CS	SBR	FA	FR	G/POS	TPR
1975	Min-A	130	440	72	123	21	1	15	59	30	79	.280	.333	.434	114	7	6	7	-2	.988	-9	*O-120/D-3	-0.9
1976	Min-A	145	514	87	137	24	7	20	86	36	118	.267	.327	.457	125	15	17	6	2	.968	-5	*O-139/D-3	0.6
1977	Min-A	144	453	66	121	25	7	11	60	41	79	.267	.341	.426	109	6	6	4	-1	.964	-10	*O-137/D-3	-0.9
1978	Min-A	151	592	78	162	36	10	11	82	48	88	.274	.333	.424	109	7	7	7	-2	.977	-2	*O-149/D-1	-0.4
1979	*Cal-A	142	569	100	165	26	5	21	101	40	86	.290	.340	.464	118	13	8	5	-1	.977	7	*O-141	1.3
1980	Cal-A	65	226	22	63	11	0	7	26	19	45	.279	.340	.420	110	3	0	1	-1	.940	-2	O-45,D-15	-0.2
1981	Cal-A	97	375	53	104	14	1	15	48	23	71	.277	.328	.440	119	8	2	2	-1	.960	-2	O-97	0.2
1982	Bal-A	123	421	46	99	21	3	10	43	23	71	.235	.281	.371	78	-14	5	2	0	.975	4	*O-119/D-1	-1.2
1983	*Bal-A	103	407	63	114	30	4	9	55	29	55	.280	.333	.440	113	6	9	2	2	.987	1	*O-103	0.5
1984	Bal-A	25	91	7	21	4	0	1	5	7	13	.231	.286	.308	66	-4	1	0	0	1.000	2	O-15/D-8	-0.3
1985	Bal-A	28	75	4	14	2	0	1	1	7	17	.187	.256	.253	41	-6	0	1	-1	.000	0	D-28	-0.7
Total	11	1153	4163	598	1123	214	38	121	566	303	722	.270	.326	.427	109	40	61	37	-4	.974	-17	*O-1065/D-62	-2.0

■ ED FORD

Ford, Edward L. b: 1862, Richmond, Va. 5'9.5", 160 lbs. Deb: 10/9/1884

YEAR	TM/L	G	AB	R	H	2B	3B	HR	RBI	BB	SO	AVG	OBP	SLG	PRO+	BR/A	SB	CS	SBR	FA	FR	G/POS	TPR
1884	Ric-a	2	5	0	0	0	0	0		0		.000	.000	.000	-99	-1				.556	1	/S-1,1-1	0.0

■ HOD FORD

Ford, Horace Hills b: 7/23/1897, New Haven, Conn. d: 1/29/77, Winchester, Mass. BR/TR, 5'10", 165 lbs. Deb: 9/8/19

YEAR	TM/L	G	AB	R	H	2B	3B	HR	RBI	BB	SO	AVG	OBP	SLG	PRO+	BR/A	SB	CS	SBR	FA	FR	G/POS	TPR
1919	Bos-N	10	28	4	6	0	1	0	3	2	6	.214	.290	.286	77	-1	0			.946	3	/S-8,3-2	0.3
1920	Bos-N	88	257	16	62	12	5	1	30	18	25	.241	.296	.339	86	-5	3	3	-1	.972	15	2-59,S-18/1-4	1.3
1921	Bos-N	152	555	50	155	29	5	2	61	36	49	.279	.328	.360	87	-11	2	11	-6	**.973**	16	*2-119,S-33	0.5
1922	Bos-N	143	515	58	140	23	9	2	60	30	36	.272	.317	.363	78	-17	2	1	0	.953	-4	*S-115,2-28	-0.8
1923	Bos-N	111	380	27	103	16	7	2	50	31	30	.271	.326	.366	86	-8	1	1	-0	.970	-9	2-95,S-19	-1.4
1924	Phi-N	145	530	58	144	27	5	3	53	27	40	.272	.308	.358	70	-23	1	9	-5	.970	12	*2-145	-1.5
1925	Bro-N	66	216	32	59	11	0	1	15	26	15	.273	.357	.338	81	-5	0	3	-2	.966	-0	S-66	-0.1
1926	Cin-N	57	197	14	55	6	1	0	18	14	12	.279	.336	.320	79	-5	1			.963	5	S-57	0.5
1927	Cin-N	115	409	45	112	16	2	1	46	33	34	.274	.331	.330	80	-11	0			.952	-8	*S-104,2-12	-0.8
1928	Cin-N	149	506	49	122	17	4	0	54	47	31	.241	.308	.291	58	-30	1			**.972**	12	*S-149	-0.1
1929	Cin-N	148	529	68	146	14	6	3	50	41	25	.276	.329	.342	70	-25	8			.953	8	*S-108,2-42	-0.1
1930	Cin-N	132	424	36	98	16	7	1	34	24	28	.231	.272	.309	42	-40	2			.974	2	S-74,2-66	-2.6
1931	Cin-N	84	175	18	40	8	1	0	13	13	13	.229	.286	.286	57	-11	0			.954	1	S-73/2-3,3-1	-0.5
1932	StL-N	1	2	0	0	0	0	0	0	0	0	.000	.000	.000	-97	-1	0			.750	0	/S-1	0.0
	Bos-N	40	95	9	26	5	2	0	6	6	9	.274	.324	.368	89	-1	0			.984	-3	2-20,S-16/3-2	-0.2
	Yr	41	97	9	26	5	2	0	6	6	9	.268	.317	.361	85	-2	0			.984	-3	2-20,S-17/3-2	-0.2
1933	Bos-N	5	15	0	1	0	0	0	1	3	1	.067	.222	.067	-16	-2	0			1.000	5	/S-5	0.3
Total	15	1446	4833	484	1269	200	55	16	494	351	354	.263	.316	.337	72	-198	21	28		.960	54	S-846,2-589/3-5,1-4	-5.2

■ TED FORD

Ford, Theodore Henry b: 2/7/47, Vineland, N.J. BR/TR, 5'10", 180 lbs. Deb: 4/7/70

YEAR	TM/L	G	AB	R	H	2B	3B	HR	RBI	BB	SO	AVG	OBP	SLG	PRO+	BR/A	SB	CS	SBR	FA	FR	G/POS	TPR
1970	Cle-A	26	46	5	8	1	0	1	1	3	13	.174	.224	.261	32	-4	0	0	0	1.000	1	O-12	-0.4
1971	Cle-A	74	196	15	38	6	0	2	14	9	34	.194	.229	.255	34	-17	2	2	-1	1.000	-1	O-55	-2.2
1972	Tex-A	129	429	43	101	19	1	14	50	37	80	.235	.301	.382	107	2	4	3	-1	.977	9	*O-119	0.6
1973	Cle-A	11	40	3	9	0	1	0	3	2	7	.225	.262	.275	50	-3	1	0	0	1.000	-4	O-10	-0.7
Total	4	240	711	66	156	26	2	17	68	51	134	.219	.275	.333	76	-22	7	5	-1	.985	6	O-196	-2.7

■ BROOK FORDYCE

Fordyce, Brook Alexander b: 5/7/70, New London, Conn. BR/TR, 6'1", 185 lbs. Deb: 4/26/95

YEAR	TM/L	G	AB	R	H	2B	3B	HR	RBI	BB	SO	AVG	OBP	SLG	PRO+	BR/A	SB	CS	SBR	FA	FR	G/POS	TPR
1995	NY-N	4	2	1	1	1	0	0	0	1	0	.500	.667	1.000	343	1	0	0	0	.000	0	-0,-0	0.1
1996	Cin-N	4	7	0	2	1	0	0	1	3	1	.286	.500	.429	147	1	0	0	0	1.000	-0	/C-4	0.1
1997	Cin-N	47	96	7	20	5	0	1	8	8	15	.208	.269	.292	46	-8	2	0	1	.983	1	C-30/D-1	-0.4
1998	Cin-N	57	146	8	37	9	0	3	14	11	28	.253	.306	.377	75	-6	0	1	-1	.978	6	C-54	0.2
Total	4	112	251	16	60	16	0	4	23	23	44	.239	.303	.351	69	-12	2	1	0	.980	7	/C-88,D-1	0.0

■ FRANK FOREMAN

Foreman, Francis Isaiah "Monkey" b: 5/1/1863, Baltimore, Md. d: 11/19/57, Baltimore, Md. BL/TL, 6', 160 lbs. Deb: 5/15/1884 F

YEAR	TM/L	G	AB	R	H	2B	3B	HR	RBI	BB	SO	AVG	OBP	SLG	PRO+	BR/A	SB	CS	SBR	FA	FR	G/POS	TPR
1884	CP-U	3	11	0	1	0	0	0		0		.091	.091	.091	-45	-2				.857	-1	/P-3,O-2	-0.1
	KC-U	1	3	0	0	0	0	0		0		.000	.000	.000	-99	-1				.900	1	/P-1	0.0
	Yr	4	14	0	1	0	0	0		0		.071	.071	.071	-59	-3				.882	0	/P-4,O-2	-0.1
1885	Bal-a	3	14	4	4	0	1	0	2	0		.286	.286	.429	125	0				.800	-1	/P-3,O-1	0.0
1889	Bal-a	54	181	18	26	2	1	1	11	12	35	.144	.201	.182	9	-22	7			.853	-3	P-51/O-3	-0.1
1890	Cin-N	25	75	13	10	1	3	1	7	10	13	.133	.253	.267	52	-5	0			.867	-3	P-25/O-1	0.0
1891	Cin-N	1	4	0	1	1	0	0	0	0	0	.250	.250	.500	116	0	0			.000	-0	/O-1	0.0
	Was-a	50	153	26	34	4	5	4	19	23	35	.222	.339	.392	114	3	6			.952	-1	P-43/O-8	0.0
1892	Was-N	11	28	5	13	2	2	1	3	3	3	.464	.516	.786	301	7	0			.632	-1	P-11	0.0
	Bal-N	7	23	2	4	1	1	0	1	3	3	.174	.269	.304	71	-1	1			.750	-0	/O-5,P-4	-0.1
	Yr	18	51	7	17	3	3	1	4	6	6	.333	.404	.569	195	6	1			.731	-1	P-15/O-5	-0.1
1893	NY-N	2	3	0	0	0	0	0	0	0	0	.000	.000	.000	-99	-1	0			1.000	-0	/P-2	0.0
1895	Cin-N	32	94	14	29	7	0	2	11	4	14	.309	.350	.447	100	-0	1			.882	-3	P-32	0.0
1896	Cin-N	27	74	9	18	2	0	0	8	4	6	.243	.282	.270	43	-6	2			.912	-1	P-27	0.0
1901	Bos-A	1	4	0	0	0	0	0	0	0		.000	.000	.000	-99	-1	0			1.000	-0	/P-1	0.0
	Bal-A	24	80	12	26	2	2	0	10	3		.325	.349	.400	103	0	1			.887	-3	P-24	0.0
	Yr	25	84	12	26	2	2	0	10	3		.310	.333	.381	94	-1	1			.891	-3	P-25	0.0
1902	Bal-A	2	7	1	3	1	0	0	1	0		.429	.429	.571	168	1	0			.818	1	/P-2	0.0
Total	11	243	754	104	169	23	15	9	73	62	109	.224	.291	.330	74	-29	18			.881	-16	P-229/O-21	-0.3

■ TOM FORSTER

Forster, Thomas W. b: 5/1/1859, New York, N.Y. d: 7/17/46, New York, N.Y. BR , 5'9", 153 lbs. Deb: 8/4/1882

YEAR	TM/L	G	AB	R	H	2B	3B	HR	RBI	BB	SO	AVG	OBP	SLG	PRO+	BR/A	SB	CS	SBR	FA	FR	G/POS	TPR
1882	Det-N	21	76	5	7	0	0	0	2	5	12	.092	.148	.092	-21	-10				.830	-7	2-21	-1.5
1884	Pit-a	35	126	10	28	5	0	0		7		.222	.263	.262	71	-4				.897	6	S-28/3-6,2-1	0.2
1885	NY-a	57	213	28	47	7	2	0	18	17		.221	.281	.272	82	-3				.903	-12	2-52/O-5	-1.2
1886	NY-a	67	251	33	49	3	2	1	20	20		.195	.263	.235	59	-11	9			.891	-7	2-62/O-4,S-1	-1.4
Total	4	180	666	76	131	15	4	1	40	49	12	.197	.256	.236	59	-28	9			.885	-19	2-136/S-29,O-9,3-6	-3.9

■ ED FORSYTHE

Forsythe, Edward James b: 4/30/1887, Kingston, N.Y. d: 6/22/56, Hoboken, N.J. BR/TR, 5'10", 155 lbs. Deb: 10/2/15

YEAR	TM/L	G	AB	R	H	2B	3B	HR	RBI	BB	SO	AVG	OBP	SLG	PRO+	BR/A	SB	CS	SBR	FA	FR	G/POS	TPR
1915	Bal-F	1	3	0	0	0	0	0	0	1	0	.000	.250	.000	-26	-1	0			.667	-0	/3-1	-0.1

■ GEORGE FOSS

Foss, George Dueward "Deeby" b: 6/13/1897, Register, Ga. d: 11/10/69, Brandon, Fla. BR/TR, 5'10.5", 170 lbs. Deb: 4/16/21

YEAR	TM/L	G	AB	R	H	2B	3B	HR	RBI	BB	SO	AVG	OBP	SLG	PRO+	BR/A	SB	CS	SBR	FA	FR	G/POS	TPR
1921	Was-A	4	7	0	0	0	0	0	0	0	1	.000	.000	.000	-99	-2	0	0	0	.750	0	/3-1	-0.2

■ RAY FOSSE

Fosse, Raymond Earl b: 4/4/47, Marion, Ill. BR/TR, 6'2", 215 lbs. Deb: 9/8/67

YEAR	TM/L	G	AB	R	H	2B	3B	HR	RBI	BB	SO	AVG	OBP	SLG	PRO+	BR/A	SB	CS	SBR	FA	FR	G/POS	TPR
1967	Cle-A	7	16	0	1	0	0	0	0	0	5	.063	.063	.063	-62	-3	0	0	0	1.000	5	/C-7	0.2

YEAR	TM/L	G	AB	R	H	2B	3B	HR	RBI	BB	SO	AVG	OBP	SLG	PRO+	BR/A	SB	CS	SBR	FA	FR	G/POS	TPR
1968	Cle-A	1	0	0	0	0	0	0	0	0	0	—	—	—	—	0	0	0	0	1.000	-0	/C-1	0.0
1969	Cle-A	37	116	11	20	3	0	2	9	8	29	.172	.232	.250	34	-10	1	0	0	.977	3	C-37	-0.5
1970	Cle-A★	120	450	62	138	17	1	18	61	39	55	.307	.363	.469	122	13	1	5	-3	.989	6	*C-120	2.3
1971	Cle-A†	133	486	53	134	21	1	12	62	36	62	.276	.331	.397	97	-2	4	1	1	.988	-3	*C-126/1-4	-0.1
1972	Cle-A	134	457	42	110	20	1	10	41	45	46	.241	.313	.354	95	-3	5	1	1	.985	6	*C-124/1-3	1.0
1973	*Oak-A	143	492	37	126	23	2	7	52	25	62	.256	.293	.354	86	-11	2	2	-1	.987	2	*C-141/D-2	-0.3
1974	*Oak-A	69	204	20	40	8	3	4	23	11	31	.196	.244	.324	66	-10	1	1	-0	.973	-1	C-68/D-1	-0.9
1975	*Oak-A	82	136	14	19	3	2	0	12	8	19	.140	.193	.191	9	-16	0	1	-1	.981	6	C-82/1-1,2-1	-1.0
1976	Cle-A	90	276	26	83	9	1	2	30	20	20	.301	.348	.362	109	3	1	2	-1	.987	1	C-85/1-3,D-1	0.6
1977	Cle-A	78	238	25	63	7	1	6	27	7	26	.265	.294	.378	84	-6	0	5	-3	.983	9	C-77/1-1,D-1	0.2
	Sea-A	11	34	3	12	3	0	0	5	2	2	.353	.389	.441	127	1	0	1	-1	.968	-3	/C-8,D-2	-0.2
	Yr	89	272	28	75	10	1	6	32	9	28	.276	.306	.386	90	-4	0	6	-4	.982	5	C-85/D-3,1-1	0.0
1979	Mil-A	19	52	6	12	3	1	0	2	2	6	.231	.286	.327	65	-3	0	0	0	1.000	-1	C-13/1-1,D-5	-0.3
Total	12	924	2957	299	758	117	13	61	324	203	363	.256	.308	.367	90	-46	15	19	-7	.985	28	C-889/1-13,D-12,2-1	1.0

■ POP FOSTER

Foster, Clarence Francis b: 4/8/1878, New Haven, Conn. d: 4/16/44, Princeton, N.J. BR/TR, 5'8.5", Deb: 9/13/1898

YEAR	TM/L	G	AB	R	H	2B	3B	HR	RBI	BB	SO	AVG	OBP	SLG	PRO+	BR/A	SB	CS	SBR	FA	FR	G/POS	TPR
1898	NY-N	32	112	10	30	6	1	0	9	0		.268	.268	.339	76	-4	0			.967	-5	O-21,3-10/S-2	-1.0
1899	NY-N	84	301	48	89	9	7	3	57	20		.296	.348	.402	109	3	7			.949	-10	O-84/S-1,3-1	-1.2
1900	NY-N	31	84	19	22	3	1	0	11	11		.262	.347	.321	89	-1	0			1.000	-3	O-12/S-7,2-5	-0.3
1901	Was-A	103	392	65	109	16	9	6	54	41		.278	.352	.411	113	7	10			.925	-1	*O-102/S-2	-0.1
	Chi-A	12	35	4	10	2	2	1	6	4		.286	.359	.543	152	2	0			.909	-1	/O-9	0.0
	Yr	115	427	69	119	18	11	7	60	45		.279	.353	.422	116	9	10			.924	-2	*O-111/S-2	-0.1
Total	4	262	924	146	260	36	20	10	137	76		.281	.341	.396	107	8	17			.938	-19	O-228/S-12,3-11,2-5	-2.6

■ EDDIE FOSTER

Foster, Edward Cunningham "Kid" b: 2/13/1887, Chicago, Ill. d: 1/15/37, Washington, D.C. BR/TR, 5'6.5", 145 lbs. Deb: 4/14/10

YEAR	TM/L	G	AB	R	H	2B	3B	HR	RBI	BB	SO	AVG	OBP	SLG	PRO+	BR/A	SB	CS	SBR	FA	FR	G/POS	TPR
1910	NY-A	30	83	5	11	2	0	0	1	8		.133	.217	.157	16	-8	2			.909	-2	S-22	-1.1
1912	Was-A	154	618	98	176	34	9	2	70	53		.285	.345	.379	106	4	27			.920	12	*3-154	1.7
1913	Was-A	106	409	56	101	11	5	1	41	36	31	.247	.309	.306	78	-11	22			.901	4	*3-105	-0.6
1914	Was-A	157	616	82	174	16	10	2	50	60	47	.282	.348	.351	106	5	31	18	-2	.929	-18	*3-157	-1.0
1915	Was-A	154	618	75	170	25	10	0	52	48	30	.275	.329	.348	101	-1	20	6	2	.919	-5	3-79,2-75	0.0
1916	Was-A	158	606	75	153	18	9	1	44	68	26	.252	.332	.317	96	-2	23	16	-3	.929	-16	3-84,2-72	-1.7
1917	Was-A	143	554	66	130	16	8	0	43	46	23	.235	.293	.292	80	-14	11			.935	-6	3-86,2-57	-1.7
1918	Was-A	129	519	70	147	13	3	0	29	41	20	.283	.339	.320	101	0	12			.936	2	*3-127/2-2	0.6
1919	Was-A	120	478	57	126	12	5	0	26	33	21	.264	.314	.310	76	-15	20			.946	7	*3-115	-0.3
1920	Bos-A	117	386	48	100	17	6	0	41	42	17	.259	.336	.334	82	-10	10	4	1	.957	15	3-88,2-21	1.0
1921	Bos-A	120	412	51	117	18	6	0	35	57	15	.284	.371	.357	89	-5	13	7	-0	.943	-14	3-94,2-22	-1.2
1922	Bos-A	48	109	11	23	3	0	0	3	9	10	.211	.277	.239	36	-10	1	1	-0	.886	-11	3-28/S-3	-1.9
	StL-A	37	144	29	44	4	0	0	12	20	8	.306	.394	.333	88	-1	3	1	0	.916	-2	3-37	0.0
	Yr	85	253	40	67	7	0	0	15	29	18	.265	.345	.292	67	-11	4	2	0	.905	-12	3-65/S-3	-1.9
1923	StL-A	27	100	9	18	2	0	0	4	7	7	.180	.241	.200	16	-12	0	0	0	.961	-8	2-20/3-7	-1.9
Total	13	1500	5652	732	1490	191	71	6	451	528	255	.264	.329	.326	89	-81	195	53		.930	-41	*3-1161,2-269/S-25	-8.1

■ ELMER FOSTER

Foster, Elmer Ellsworth b: 8/15/1861, Minneapolis, Minn. d: 7/22/46, Deephaven, Minn. BR/TL, 5'10", 178 lbs. Deb: 6/18/1884

YEAR	TM/L	G	AB	R	H	2B	3B	HR	RBI	BB	SO	AVG	OBP	SLG	PRO+	BR/A	SB	CS	SBR	FA	FR	G/POS	TPR
1884	Phi-a	4	11	4	2	0	0	0		3		.182	.357	.182	76	-0				.885	-2	/C-4,O-1	-0.2
	Phi-U	1	3	0	1	0	1	0		0		.333	.333	1.000	313	1				.625	-1	/C-1	0.0
1886	NY-a	35	125	16	23	0	1	0	7	7		.184	.239	.200	40	-8	3			.853	-0	2-21,O-14	-0.7
1888	NY-N	37	136	15	20	3	2	0	10	9	20	.147	.216	.199	33	-10	13			.852	-2	O-37/3-1	-1.3
1889	NY-N	2	4	2	0	0	0	0	0	3	1	.000	.429	.000	25	-0	2			1.000	-0	/O-2	0.0
1890	Chi-N	27	105	20	26	4	2	5	23	9	21	.248	.325	.467	125	2	18			.986	2	O-27	0.3
1891	Chi-N	4	16	3	3	0	0	1	1	1	2	.188	.235	.375	77	-1	1			.875	-0	/O-4	-0.1
Total	6	110	400	60	75	7	6	6	41	32	44	.188	.261	.280	67	-16	37			.883	-4	/O-85,2-21,C-5,3-1	-2.0

■ GEORGE FOSTER

Foster, George Arthur b: 12/1/48, Tuscaloosa, Ala. BR/TR, 6'1", 185 lbs. Deb: 9/10/69

YEAR	TM/L	G	AB	R	H	2B	3B	HR	RBI	BB	SO	AVG	OBP	SLG	PRO+	BR/A	SB	CS	SBR	FA	FR	G/POS	TPR
1969	SF-N	9	5	1	2	0	0	0	1	0	1	.400	.400	.400	127	0	0	0	0	1.000	-3	/O-8	-0.3
1970	SF-N	9	19	2	6	1	1	1	4	2	5	.316	.381	.632	168	2	0	0	0	1.000	-0	/O-7	0.1
1971	SF-N	36	105	11	28	5	0	3	8	6	27	.267	.306	.400	100	-0	0	1	-1	.980	-2	O-30	-0.4
	Cin-N	104	368	39	86	18	4	10	50	23	93	.234	.291	.386	92	-5	7	6	-2	.986	11	*O-102	-0.1
	Yr	140	473	50	114	23	4	13	58	29	120	.241	.295	.389	94	-5	7	7	-2	.985	9	*O-132	-0.5
1972	*Cin-N	59	145	15	29	4	1	2	12	5	44	.200	.232	.283	48	-10	2	1	0	.973	-5	O-47	-1.8
1973	Cin-N	17	39	6	11	3	0	4	9	4	7	.282	.349	.667	185	4	0	1	-1	1.000	-3	O-13	0.0
1974	Cin-N	106	276	31	73	18	0	7	41	30	52	.264	.345	.406	111	4	3	2	-0	.989	-16	O-98	-1.6
1975	*Cin-N	134	463	71	139	24	4	23	78	40	73	.300	.360	.518	139	22	2	1	0	.990	5	*O-125/1-1	2.3
1976	*Cin-N★	144	562	86	172	21	9	29	**121**	52	89	.306	.369	.530	149	34	17	3	3	**.994**	-2	*O-142/1-1	3.1
1977	Cin-N★	158	615	**124**	197	31	2	**52**	**149**	61	107	.320	.386	**.631**	165	**54**	6	4	-1	.992	16	*O-158	6.1
1978	Cin-N★	158	604	97	170	26	7	**40**	**120**	70	138	.281	.363	.546	151	39	4	4	-1	.971	7	*O-157	4.0
1979	*Cin-N★	121	440	68	133	18	3	30	98	59	105	.302	.388	.561	155	33	0	2	-1	.982	4	*O-116	3.1
1980	Cin-N	144	528	79	144	21	5	25	93	75	99	.273	.364	.473	132	23	1	0	0	.997	10	*O-141	2.9
1981	Cin-N★	108	414	64	122	23	2	22	90	51	75	.295	.376	.519	150	26	4	0	1	.991	8	*O-108	3.4
1982	NY-N	151	550	64	136	23	2	13	70	50	123	.247	.312	.367	90	-8	1	1	-0	.974	12	*O-138	0.0
1983	NY-N	157	601	74	145	19	2	28	90	38	111	.241	.291	.419	95	-6	1	1	-0	.988	10	*O-153	-0.1
1984	NY-N	146	553	67	149	22	1	24	86	30	122	.269	.314	.443	112	7	2	2	-1	.976	11	*O-141	1.3
1985	NY-N	129	452	57	119	24	1	21	77	46	87	.263	.334	.460	123	13	0	1	-1	.976	1	*O-123	0.9
1986	NY-N	72	233	28	53	6	1	13	38	21	53	.227	.291	.429	99	-1	1	1	-0	.962	-0	O-62	-0.4
	Chi-A	15	51	2	11	0	2	1	4	3	8	.216	.259	.353	63	-3	0	0	0	1.000	1	O-11/D-3	-0.2
Total	18	1977	7023	986	1925	307	47	348	1239	666	1419	.274	.341	.480	127	227	51	31	-3	.984	65	*O-1880/D-3,1-2	22.3

■ LEO FOSTER

Foster, Leonard Norris b: 2/2/51, Covington, Ky. BR/TR, 5'11", 165 lbs. Deb: 7/9/71

YEAR	TM/L	G	AB	R	H	2B	3B	HR	RBI	BB	SO	AVG	OBP	SLG	PRO+	BR/A	SB	CS	SBR	FA	FR	G/POS	TPR
1971	Atl-N	9	10	1	0	0	0	0	0	0	1	.000	.000	.000	-94	-2	0	0	0	.900	2	/S-3	-0.1
1973	Atl-N	3	6	1	1	1	0	0	0	0	2	.167	.167	.333	33	-1	0	0	0	1.000	-0	/S-1	-0.1
1974	Atl-N	72	112	16	22	2	0	1	5	9	22	.196	.256	.241	38	-9	1	2	-1	.977	-1	S-43,2-10/3-3,O-1	-0.8
1976	NY-N	24	59	11	12	2	0	1	15	8	5	.203	.299	.288	71	-2	3	0	1	.920	1	/3-9,S-7,2-3	0.0
1977	NY-N	36	75	6	17	3	0	0	6	5	14	.227	.284	.267	51	-5	3	1	0	.968	-4	2-20/S-8,3-2	-0.8
Total	5	144	262	35	52	8	0	2	26	22	44	.198	.263	.252	44	-20	7	3	0	.964	-3	/S-62,2-33,3-14,O-1	-1.8

■ REDDY FOSTER

Foster, Oscar E. b: 8/1864, Richmond, Va. d: 12/19/08, Richmond, Va. Deb: 6/3/1896

YEAR	TM/L	G	AB	R	H	2B	3B	HR	RBI	BB	SO	AVG	OBP	SLG	PRO+	BR/A	SB	CS	SBR	FA	FR	G/POS	TPR
1896	NY-N	1	1	0	0	0	0	0	0	0	0	.000	.000	.000	-99	-0	0			.000	0	H	0.0

■ ROY FOSTER

Foster, Roy b: 7/29/45, Bixby, Okla. BR/TR, 6', 185 lbs. Deb: 4/7/70

YEAR	TM/L	G	AB	R	H	2B	3B	HR	RBI	BB	SO	AVG	OBP	SLG	PRO+	BR/A	SB	CS	SBR	FA	FR	G/POS	TPR
1970	Cle-A	139	477	66	128	26	0	23	60	54	75	.268	.357	.468	120	13	3	3	-1	.965	-3	*O-131	0.2
1971	Cle-A	125	396	51	97	21	1	18	45	35	48	.245	.316	.439	103	0	6	1	1	.968	-1	*O-107	-0.5
1972	Cle-A	73	143	19	32	4	0	4	13	21	23	.224	.331	.336	96	-0	0	2	-1	.966	-6	O-45	-1.1
Total	3	337	1016	136	257	51	1	45	118	110	146	.253	.338	.438	110	13	9	6	-1	.967	-11	O-283	-1.4

■ BOB FOTHERGILL

Fothergill, Robert Roy "Fats" b: 8/16/1897, Massillon, Ohio d: 3/20/38, Detroit, Mich. BR/TR, 5'10.5", 230 lbs. Deb: 4/18/22

YEAR	TM/L	G	AB	R	H	2B	3B	HR	RBI	BB	SO	AVG	OBP	SLG	PRO+	BR/A	SB	CS	SBR	FA	FR	G/POS	TPR
1922	Det-A	42	152	20	49	12	4	0	29	8	9	.322	.356	.454	113	2	1	5	-3	.945	-7	O-38	-0.9
1923	Det-A	101	241	34	76	18	2	1	49	12	19	.315	.358	.419	106	2	5	4	-1	.977	-8	O-68	-1.1
1924	Det-A	54	166	28	50	8	3	0	15	5	13	.301	.326	.386	84	-4	2	3	-1	.968	-4	O-45	-1.1
1925	Det-A	71	204	38	72	14	0	2	28	6	3	.353	.377	.451	111	3	3	2	-0	.977	-2	O-59	-0.2
1926	Det-A	110	387	63	142	31	7	3	73	33	23	.367	.421	.506	139	22	4	12	-6	.961	-1	*O-103	0.8
1927	Det-A	143	527	93	189	38	9	9	114	47	31	.359	.413	.516	138	29	9	15	-6	.961	-6	*O-137	0.8
1928	Det-A	111	347	49	110	28	10	3	63	24	19	.317	.366	.481	119	9	8	3	1	.959	-3	O-90	0.0

YEAR	TM/L	G	AB	R	H	2B	3B	HR	RBI	BB	SO	AVG	OBP	SLG	PRO+	BR/A	SB	CS	SBR	FA	FR	G/POS	TPR
1929	Det-A	115	277	42	98	24	9	6	62	11	11	.354	.378	.570	140	15	3	1	0	.967	-4	O-59	0.8
1930	Det-A	55	143	14	37	9	3	2	14	6	10	.259	.289	.406	72	-7	1	1	-0	.947	-5	O-38	-1.3
	Chi-A	52	135	10	40	9	0	0	24	4	8	.296	.326	.363	77	-5	0	0	0	.879	-3	O-31	-0.9
	Yr	107	278	24	77	18	3	2	38	10	18	.277	.307	.385	75	-11	1	1	-0	.913	-8	O-69	-2.2
1931	Chi-A	108	312	25	88	9	4	3	56	17	17	.282	.323	.365	86	-7	2	2	-1	.972	1	O-74	-1.1
1932	Chi-A	116	346	36	102	24	1	7	50	27	10	.295	.348	.431	107	3	4	4	-1	.952	-11	O-86	-1.4
1933	Bos-A	28	32	1	11	1	0	0	5	2	4	.344	.382	.375	102	0	0	0	0	1.000	-1	/O-4	-0.1
Total	12	1106	3269	453	1064	225	52	36	582	202	177	.325	.368	.459	115	62	42	52	-19	.961	-53	O-832	-5.7

■ JACK FOURNIER

Fournier, John Frank b: 9/28/1889, AuSable, Mich. d: 9/5/73, Tacoma, Wash. BL/TR, 6′, 195 lbs. Deb: 4/13/12

YEAR	TM/L	G	AB	R	H	2B	3B	HR	RBI	BB	SO	AVG	OBP	SLG	PRO+	BR/A	SB	CS	SBR	FA	FR	G/POS	TPR
1912	Chi-A	35	73	6	14	5	2	0	2	4		.192	.262	.315	67	-3	1			.988	3	1-17	-0.1
1913	Chi-A	68	172	20	40	8	5	1	23	21	23	.233	.323	.355	99	-0	9			.990	4	1-29,O-23	0.3
1914	Chi-A	109	379	44	118	14	9	6	44	31	44	.311	.368	.443	146	20	10	13	-5	.978	5	1-97/O-6	1.8
1915	Chi-A	126	422	86	136	20	18	5	77	64	37	.322	.429	**.491**	170	38	21	16	-3	.986	3	1-65,O-57	3.5
1916	Chi-A	105	313	36	75	13	9	3	44	36	40	.240	.328	.367	108	3	19			.976	-3	1-85/O-1	-0.4
1917	Chi-A	1	1	0	0	0	0	0	0	0	1	.000	.000	.000	-98	-0	0			.000	0	H	0.0
1918	NY-A	27	100	9	35	6	1	0	12	7	7	.350	.393	.430	145	5	7			.976	-2	1-27	0.2
1920	StL-N	141	530	77	162	33	14	3	61	42	42	.306	.370	.438	136	25	26	20	-4	.983	1	*1-138	2.0
1921	StL-N	149	574	103	197	27	9	16	86	56	48	.343	.409	.505	144	37	20	22	-7	.987	-4	*1-149	2.1
1922	StL-N	128	404	64	119	23	9	10	61	40	21	.295	.368	.470	120	12	6	8	-3	.982	2	*1-109/P-1	0.6
1923	Bro-N	133	515	91	181	30	13	22	102	43	28	.351	.411	.588	165	47	11	4	1	.985	4	*1-133	**4.3**
1924	Bro-N	154	563	93	188	25	4	**27**	116	83	46	.334	.428	.536	162	52	7	5	-1	.985	7	*1-153	4.7
1925	Bro-N	145	545	99	191	21	16	22	130	**86**	39	.350	.446	.569	162	54	4	6	-2	.989	3	*1-145	4.2
1926	Bro-N	87	243	39	69	9	2	11	48	30	16	.284	.365	.473	126	9	0			.986	-2	1-64	0.3
1927	Bos-N	122	374	55	106	18	2	10	53	44	16	.283	.368	.422	121	11	4			.989	0	*1-102	0.4
Total	15	1530	5208	822	1631	252	113	136	859	587	408	.313	.392	.483	143	308	145	94		.984	20	*1-1313/O-87,P-1	23.9

■ BILL FOUSER

Fouser, William C. b: 10/1855, Philadelphia, Pa. d: 3/1/19, Philadelphia, Pa. Deb: 4/22/1876

YEAR	TM/L	G	AB	R	H	2B	3B	HR	RBI	BB	SO	AVG	OBP	SLG	PRO+	BR/A	SB	CS	SBR	FA	FR	G/POS	TPR
1876	Phi-N	21	89	11	12	0	1	0	2	0	0	.135	.135	.157	-3	-9				.827	3	2-14/O-7,1-1	-0.5

■ DAVE FOUTZ

Foutz, David Luther "Scissors" b: 9/7/1856, Carroll Co., Md. d: 3/5/1897, Waverly, Md. BR/TR, 6′2″, 161 lbs. Deb: 7/29/1884 FM

YEAR	TM/L	G	AB	R	H	2B	3B	HR	RBI	BB	SO	AVG	OBP	SLG	PRO+	BR/A	SB	CS	SBR	FA	FR	G/POS	TPR
1884	StL-a	33	119	17	27	4	0	0		8		.227	.276	.261	73	-3				.940	-3	P-25,O-14	-0.5
1885	*StL-a	65	238	42	59	6	4	0	34	11		.248	.281	.307	82	-5				.899	6	P-47,1-15/O-4	-0.4
1886	*StL-a	102	414	66	116	18	9	3	59	9		.280	.297	.389	109	1	17			.949	4	P-59,O-34,1-11	0.0
1887	*StL-a	102	423	79	151	26	13	4	108	23		.357	.393	.508	136	16	22			.899	-4	O-50,P-40,1-15	0.3
1888	Bro-a	140	563	91	156	20	13	3	99	28		.277	.314	.375	121	11	35			.895	3	O-78,1-42,P-23	0.3
1889	*Bro-a	138	553	118	152	19	8	6	113	64	23	.275	.353	.371	106	5	43			.979	-3	*1-134,P-12	-0.7
1890	*Bro-N	129	509	106	154	25	13	5	98	52	25	.303	.368	.432	133	20	42			.978	-1	*1-113,O-13/P-5	1.1
1891	Bro-N	130	521	87	134	26	8	2	73	40	25	.257	.313	.349	93	-6	48			.976	-3	*1-124/P-6,S-1	-1.3
1892	Bro-N	61	220	33	41	5	3	1	26	14	14	.186	.235	.250	48	-14	19			.850	-2	O-29,P-27/1-6	-1.3
1893	Bro-N	130	557	91	137	20	10	7	67	32	34	.246	.287	.355	74	-24	39			.913	-6	O-77,1-54/P-6,M	-2.9
1894	Bro-N	72	293	40	90	12	9	0	51	14	13	.307	.341	.410	86	-7	14			.976	-3	1-72/P-1,M	-0.7
1895	Bro-N	31	115	14	34	4	1	0	21	4	2	.296	.319	.348	78	-4	1			.879	-5	O-20/1-8,M	-0.8
1896	Bro-N	2	8	0	2	1	0	0	0	1	0	.250	.333	.375	92	-0	0			1.000	0	/O-1,1-1,M	0.0
Total	13	1135	4533	784	1253	186	91	31	749	300	136	.276	.323	.378	102	-10	280			.977	-14	1-595,O-320,P/S	-6.9

■ FRANK FOUTZ

Foutz, Frank Hayes b: 4/8/1877, Baltimore, Md. d: 12/25/61, Lima, Ohio BR/TR, 5′11″, 165 lbs. Deb: 4/26/01 F

YEAR	TM/L	G	AB	R	H	2B	3B	HR	RBI	BB	SO	AVG	OBP	SLG	PRO+	BR/A	SB	CS	SBR	FA	FR	G/POS	TPR
1901	Bal-A	20	72	13	17	4	1	2	14	8		.236	.321	.403	96	-1	0			.959	-0	1-20	-0.1

■ BOOB FOWLER

Fowler, Joseph Chester "Gink" b: 11/11/1900, Waco, Tex. d: 10/8/88, Dallas, Tex. BL/TR, 5′11.5″, 180 lbs. Deb: 5/6/23

YEAR	TM/L	G	AB	R	H	2B	3B	HR	RBI	BB	SO	AVG	OBP	SLG	PRO+	BR/A	SB	CS	SBR	FA	FR	G/POS	TPR
1923	Cin-N	11	33	9	11	0	1	1	6	1	3	.333	.353	.485	121	1	1	0	0	.847	-1	S-10	0.1
1924	Cin-N	59	129	20	43	6	1	0	9	5	15	.333	.358	.395	103	1	2	2	-1	.936	-7	S-32/2-4,3-2	-0.4
1925	Cin-N	6	5	0	2	1	0	0	2	0	1	.400	.400	.600	155	0	0	0	0	.000	0	H	0.0
1926	Bos-A	2	8	1	1	0	0	0	1	0	0	.125	.125	.125	-36	-2	0	0	0	.800	0	/3-2	-0.1
Total	4	78	175	30	57	7	2	1	18	6	19	.326	.348	.406	102	0	3	2	-0	.910	-7	/S-42,3-4,2-4	-0.4

■ ANDY FOX

Fox, Andrew Junipero b: 1/12/71, Sacramento, Cal. BL/TR, 6′4″, 205 lbs. Deb: 4/7/96

YEAR	TM/L	G	AB	R	H	2B	3B	HR	RBI	BB	SO	AVG	OBP	SLG	PRO+	BR/A	SB	CS	SBR	FA	FR	G/POS	TPR
1996	*NY-A	113	189	26	37	4	0	3	13	20	28	.196	.276	.265	38	-18	11	3	2	.958	13	2-72,3-31/S-9,OD	-0.1
1997	*NY-A	22	31	13	7	1	0	0	1	7	9	.226	.368	.258	68	-1	2	1	0	1.000	8	3-11/2-5,S-2,O-2,D	0.6
1998	Ari-N	139	502	67	139	21	6	9	44	43	97	.277	.355	.396	94	-3	14	7	0	.982	-25	2-60,O-48,3-26,1-12	-2.5
Total	3	274	722	106	183	26	6	12	58	70	134	.253	.335	.356	78	-22	27	11	2	.972	-4	2-137/3-68,O1SD	-2.0

■ CHARLIE FOX

Fox, Charles Francis "Irish" b: 10/7/21, New York, N.Y. BR/TR, 5′11″, 180 lbs. Deb: 9/24/42 MC

YEAR	TM/L	G	AB	R	H	2B	3B	HR	RBI	BB	SO	AVG	OBP	SLG	PRO+	BR/A	SB	CS	SBR	FA	FR	G/POS	TPR
1942	NY-N	3	7	1	3	0	0	0	1	1	2	.429	.500	.429	172	1	0			1.000	-1	/C-3	0.0

■ ERIC FOX

Fox, Eric Hollis b: 8/15/63, Lemoore, Cal. BB/TL, 5′10″, 180 lbs. Deb: 7/7/92

YEAR	TM/L	G	AB	R	H	2B	3B	HR	RBI	BB	SO	AVG	OBP	SLG	PRO+	BR/A	SB	CS	SBR	FA	FR	G/POS	TPR
1992	*Oak-A	51	143	24	34	5	2	3	13	13	29	.238	.301	.364	90	-2	3	4	-2	.990	-5	O-43/D-4	-1.0
1993	Oak-A	29	56	5	8	1	0	1	5	2	7	.143	.172	.214	3	-8	0	2	-1	1.000	-3	O-26/D-2	-1.2
1994	Oak-A	26	44	7	9	2	0	1	1	3	8	.205	.255	.318	51	-3	2	0	1	1.000	-4	O-24	-0.7
1995	Tex-A	10	15	2	0	0	0	0	0	3	4	.000	.167	.000	-51	-3	0	0	0	1.000	-1	/O-8,D-1	-0.4
Total	4	116	258	38	51	8	2	5	19	21	48	.198	.258	.302	55	-17	5	6	-2	.995	-13	O-101/D-7	-3.3

■ PETE FOX

Fox, Ervin b: 3/8/09, Evansville, Ind. d: 7/5/66, Detroit, Mich. BR/TR, 5′11″, 165 lbs. Deb: 4/12/33

YEAR	TM/L	G	AB	R	H	2B	3B	HR	RBI	BB	SO	AVG	OBP	SLG	PRO+	BR/A	SB	CS	SBR	FA	FR	G/POS	TPR
1933	Det-A	128	535	82	154	26	13	7	57	23	38	.288	.320	.424	94	-7	9	6	-1	.978	1	*O-124	-1.3
1934	*Det-A	128	516	101	147	31	2	2	45	49	53	.285	.351	.364	85	-11	25	10	2	.974	8	*O-121	-0.6
1935	*Det-A	131	517	116	166	38	8	15	73	45	52	.321	.382	.513	134	24	14	4	2	.988	-0	*O-125	2.0
1936	Det-A	73	220	46	67	12	1	4	26	34	23	.305	.405	.423	104	3	1	3	-2	.968	0	O-55	-0.1
1937	Det-A	148	628	116	208	39	8	12	82	41	43	.331	.372	.476	110	8	12	8	-1	.976	-3	*O-143	-0.1
1938	Det-A	155	634	91	186	35	10	7	96	31	39	.293	.328	.413	80	-21	16	7	1	**.994**	-2	*O-155	-2.5
1939	Det-A	141	519	69	153	24	6	7	66	35	41	.295	.342	.405	84	-13	23	12	-0	.970	9	*O-126	-0.9
1940	*Det-A	93	350	49	101	17	4	5	48	21	30	.289	.329	.403	81	-10	7	7	-2	.967	0	O-85	-1.6
1941	Bos-A	73	268	38	81	12	7	0	31	21	32	.302	.357	.399	98	-1	9	2	2	.977	-1	O-62	-0.4
1942	Bos-A	77	256	42	67	15	5	3	42	20	28	.262	.323	.395	98	-1	8	7	-2	.966	-9	O-71	-1.6
1943	Bos-A	127	489	54	141	24	4	2	44	34	40	.288	.337	.366	104	2	22	8	2	.961	-3	*O-125	-0.6
1944	Bos-A☆	121	496	70	156	37	6	1	64	27	34	.315	.354	.419	122	13	10	5	0	.987	-1	*O-119	0.5
1945	Bos-A	66	208	21	51	4	1	0	20	11	18	.245	.296	.274	64	-9	2	2	-1	.989	-6	O-57	-2.1
Total	13	1461	5636	895	1678	314	75	65	694	392	471	.298	.347	.415	98	-25	158	81	-1	.977	-7	*O-1368	-9.3

■ PADDY FOX

Fox, George B. b: 12/1/1868, Pottstown, Pa. d: 5/8/14, Philadelphia, Pa. Deb: 7/13/1891

YEAR	TM/L	G	AB	R	H	2B	3B	HR	RBI	BB	SO	AVG	OBP	SLG	PRO+	BR/A	SB	CS	SBR	FA	FR	G/POS	TPR
1891	Lou-a	6	19	1	2	0	1	0	2	2	3	.105	.261	.211	36	-2	0			.929	-2	/3-6	-0.3
1899	Pit-N	13	41	4	10	0	1	1	3	3		.244	.311	.366	86	-1	2			.971	2	/1-9,C-3	0.1
Total	2	19	60	5	12	0	2	1	5	5	3	.200	.294	.317	70	-2	2			.971	-1	/1-9,3-6,C-3	-0.2

■ NELLIE FOX

Fox, Jacob Nelson b: 12/25/27, St.Thomas, Pa. d: 12/1/75, Baltimore, Md. BL/TR, 5′9″, 150 lbs. Deb: 6/8/47 CH

YEAR	TM/L	G	AB	R	H	2B	3B	HR	RBI	BB	SO	AVG	OBP	SLG	PRO+	BR/A	SB	CS	SBR	FA	FR	G/POS	TPR
1947	Phi-A	7	3	2	0	0	0	0	0	1	0	.000	.250	.000	-26	-0	0	0	0	1.000	0	/2-1	0.0
1948	Phi-A	3	13	0	2	0	0	0	0	1	0	.154	.214	.154	-1	-2	1	0	0	.950	-2	/2-3	-0.3
1949	Phi-A	88	247	42	63	6	2	0	21	32	9	.255	.354	.296	75	-8	2	2	-1	.982	-1	2-77	-0.6
1950	Chi-A	130	457	45	113	12	7	0	30	35	17	.247	.304	.304	58	-30	4	3	-1	.974	-0	*2-121	-2.4
1951	Chi-A★	147	604	93	189	32	12	4	55	43	11	.313	.372	.425	118	15	9	12	-5	.981	-3	*2-147	1.4
1952	Chi-A☆	152	648	76	**192**	25	10	0	39	34	14	.296	.334	.366	94	-6	5	5	-2	**.985**	8	*2-151	0.8
1953	Chi-A★	154	624	92	178	31	8	3	72	49	18	.285	.344	.375	91	-7	4	5	-2	.983	3	*2-154	0.3
1954	Chi-A★	155	631	111	**201**	24	8	2	47	51	12	.319	.374	.391	106	6	16	9	-1	**.989**	-6	*2-155	1.1

YEAR	TM/L	G	AB	R	H	2B	3B	HR	RBI	BB	SO	AVG	OBP	SLG	PRO+	BR/A	SB	CS	SBR	FA	FR	G/POS	TPR
1955	Chi-A★	154	636	100	198	28	7	6	59	38	15	.311	.366	.406	104	4	7	9	-3	.974	**27**	*2-154	3.9
1956	Chi-A★	154	649	109	192	20	10	4	52	44	14	.296	.350	.376	90	-9	8	4	0	**.986**	3	*2-154	0.7
1957	Chi-A★	155	619	110	**196**	27	8	6	61	75	13	.317	.404	.415	124	24	5	6	-2	.986	21	*2-155	5.6
1958	Chi-A★	155	623	82	**187**	21	6	0	49	47	11	.300	.360	.353	99	1	5	6	-2	.985	2	*2-155	1.2
1959	*Chi-A★	156	624	84	191	34	6	2	70	71	13	.306	.383	.389	114	15	5	6	-2	**.988**	-3	*2-156	2.2
1960	Chi-A★	150	605	85	175	24	**10**	2	59	50	13	.289	.353	.372	97	-1	2	4	-2	.985	12	*2-149	2.4
1961	Chi-A★	159	606	67	152	11	5	2	51	59	12	.251	.326	.295	69	-25	2	3	-1	.982	-6	*2-159	-1.5
1962	Chi-A	157	621	79	166	27	7	2	54	38	12	.267	.317	.343	78	-19	1	2	-1	**.990**	1	*2-154	-0.3
1963	Chi-A★	137	539	54	140	19	0	2	42	24	17	.260	.300	.306	72	-20	0	2	-1	**.988**	-8	*2-134	-1.8
1964	Hou-N	133	442	45	117	12	6	0	28	27	13	.265	.322	.319	86	-8	0	2	-1	.977	-6	*2-115	-0.6
1965	Hou-N	21	41	3	11	2	0	0	1	0	2	.268	.286	.317	75	-1	0	0	0	1.000	-0	/3-6,1-2,2-1	-0.2
Total	19	2367	9232	1279	2663	355	112	35	790	719	216	.288	.349	.363	94	-73	76	80	-25	.984	42	*2-2295/3-6,1-2	11.9

■ JACK FOX
Fox, John Paul b: 5/21/1885, Reading, Pa. d: 6/28/63, Reading, Pa. BR/TR, 5'10", 185 lbs. Deb: 6/2/08

YEAR	TM/L	G	AB	R	H	2B	3B	HR	RBI	BB	SO	AVG	OBP	SLG	PRO+	BR/A	SB	CS	SBR	FA	FR	G/POS	TPR
1908	Phi-A	9	30	2	6	0	0	0	0	0		.200	.200	.200	28	-2	2			.923	-1	/O-8	-0.4

■ BILL FOX
Fox, William Henry b: 1/15/1872, Sturbridge, Mass. d: 5/7/46, Minneapolis, Minn. BB/TR, 5'10", 160 lbs. Deb: 8/20/1897

YEAR	TM/L	G	AB	R	H	2B	3B	HR	RBI	BB	SO	AVG	OBP	SLG	PRO+	BR/A	SB	CS	SBR	FA	FR	G/POS	TPR
1897	Was-N	4	14	4	4	0	0	0	0	1		.286	.333	.286	64	-1	0			.700	0	/S-2,2-2	0.0
1901	Cin-N	43	159	9	28	2	1	0	7	4		.176	.201	.201	18	-17	9			.948	5	2-43	-0.9
Total	2	47	173	13	32	2	1	0	7	5		.185	.212	.208	22	-17	9			.944	6	/2-45,S-2	-0.9

■ JIMMIE FOXX
Foxx, James Emory "Beast" or "Double X" b: 10/22/07, Sudlersville, Md. d: 7/21/67, Miami, Fla. BR/TR, 6', 195 lbs. Deb: 5/1/25 CH

YEAR	TM/L	G	AB	R	H	2B	3B	HR	RBI	BB	SO	AVG	OBP	SLG	PRO+	BR/A	SB	CS	SBR	FA	FR	G/POS	TPR
1925	Phi-A	10	9	2	6	1	0	0	0	0	1	.667	.667	.778	249	2	0	0	0	.000	0	/C-1	0.2
1926	Phi-A	26	32	8	10	2	1	0	5	1	6	.313	.333	.438	94	-0	1	0	0	1.000	2	C-12/O-3	0.2
1927	Phi-A	61	130	23	42	6	5	3	20	14	11	.323	.393	.515	127	5	2	1	0	.975	-2	1-32/C-5	0.1
1928	Phi-A	118	400	85	131	29	10	13	79	60	43	.327	.416	.548	147	28	3	8	-4	.940	-2	3-60,1-30,C-19	2.4
1929	*Phi-A	149	517	123	183	23	9	33	118	103	70	.354	**.463**	.625	171	58	9	7	-2	.995	-4	*1-142/3-8	3.6
1930	*Phi-A	153	562	127	188	33	13	37	156	93	66	.335	.429	.637	159	51	7	7	-2	.990	-2	*1-153	2.8
1931	*Phi-A	139	515	93	150	32	10	30	120	73	84	.291	.380	.567	138	26	4	3	-1	.993	-3	*1-112,3-26/O-1	1.3
1932	Phi-A	154	585	**151**	213	33	9	**58**	**169**	116	96	.364	.469	**.749**	203	**90**	3	7	-3	**.994**	-5	*1-141,3-13	**6.5**
1933	Phi-A☆	149	573	125	204	37	9	**48**	**163**	96	93	**.356**	.449	**.703**	**199**	**81**	2	2	-1	.990	6	*1-149/S-1	**6.7**
1934	Phi-A★	150	539	120	180	28	6	44	130	**111**	75	.334	.449	.653	188	72	11	2	2	.993	4	*1-140/3-9	6.1
1935	Phi-A★	147	535	118	185	33	7	**36**	115	114	99	.346	.461	**.636**	**182**	68	6	4	-1	**.997**	6	*1-121,C-26/3-2	**5.7**
1936	Bos-A★	155	585	130	198	32	8	41	143	105	119	.338	.440	.631	153	48	13	4	2	.991	-1	*1-139,O-16/3-1	3.1
1937	Bos-A★	150	569	111	162	24	6	36	127	99	96	.285	.392	.538	127	23	10	8	-2	**.994**	10	*1-150/C-1	1.3
1938	Bos-A★	149	565	139	197	33	9	50	**175**	**119**	76	**.349**	**.462**	**.704**	**180**	**70**	5	4	-1	.987	6	*1-149	**5.2**
1939	Bos-A☆	124	467	130	168	31	10	**35**	105	89	72	.360	**.464**	**.694**	185	**61**	4	3	-1	.992	7	*1-123/P-1	4.9
1940	Bos-A★	144	515	106	153	30	4	36	119	101	87	.297	.412	.581	148	38	4	7	-3	.990	-2	1-95,C-42/3-1	2.6
1941	Bos-A★	135	487	87	146	27	8	19	105	93	103	.300	.412	.505	138	29	2	5	-2	.992	7	*1-124/3-5,O-1	2.3
1942	Bos-A	30	100	18	27	4	0	5	14	18	15	.270	.392	.460	134	5	0	0	0	.996	6	1-27	1.0
	Chi-N	70	205	25	42	8	0	3	19	22	55	.205	.282	.288	69	-8	1			.983	-4	1-52/C-1	-1.6
1944	Chi-N	15	20	0	1	1	0	0	2	2	5	.050	.136	.100	-33	-4	0			1.000	2	/3-2,C-1	-0.2
1945	Phi-N	89	224	30	60	11	1	7	38	23	39	.268	.336	.420	112	3	0			.988	-3	1-40,3-14/P-9	-0.2
Total	20	2317	8134	1751	2646	458	125	534	1922	1452	1311	.325	.428	.609	161	746	87	72		.992	30	*1-1919,3-141,C/OPS	54.0

■ JOE FOY
Foy, Joseph Anthony b: 2/21/43, New York, N.Y. d: 10/12/89, Bronx, N.Y. BR/TR, 6', 215 lbs. Deb: 4/13/66

YEAR	TM/L	G	AB	R	H	2B	3B	HR	RBI	BB	SO	AVG	OBP	SLG	PRO+	BR/A	SB	CS	SBR	FA	FR	G/POS	TPR
1966	Bos-A	151	554	97	145	23	8	15	63	91	80	.262	.368	.413	112	11	2	5	-2	.953	-1	*3-139,S-13	0.7
1967	*Bos-A	130	446	70	112	22	4	16	49	46	87	.251	.325	.426	111	6	8	6	-1	.921	-10	*3-118/O-1	-0.7
1968	Bos-A	150	515	65	116	18	2	10	60	84	91	.225	.338	.326	96	0	26	8	3	.935	2	*3-147/O-3	0.6
1969	KC-A	145	519	72	136	19	2	11	71	74	75	.262	.360	.370	104	5	37	15	2	.964	-9	*3-113,1-16,O/S2	-0.3
1970	NY-N	99	322	39	76	12	0	6	37	68	58	.236	.376	.329	90	-1	22	13	-1	.937	-1	3-97	-0.4
1971	Was-A	41	128	12	30	8	0	0	11	27	14	.234	.368	.297	96	1	4	1	1	.960	4	3-37/2-3,S-1	0.5
Total	6	716	2484	355	615	102	16	58	291	390	405	.248	.354	.372	103	21	99	48	1	.943	-14	3-651/O-20,S-19,12	0.4

■ JULIO FRANCO
Franco, Julio Cesar (b: Julio Cesar Robles (Franco)) b: 8/23/58, Hato Mayor, D.R. BR/TR, 6', 165 lbs. Deb: 4/23/82

YEAR	TM/L	G	AB	R	H	2B	3B	HR	RBI	BB	SO	AVG	OBP	SLG	PRO+	BR/A	SB	CS	SBR	FA	FR	G/POS	TPR
1982	Phi-N	16	29	3	8	1	0	0	3	2	4	.276	.323	.310	76	-1	0	2	-1	1.000	-0	S-11/3-2	-0.2
1983	Cle-A	149	560	68	153	24	8	8	80	27	50	.273	.309	.387	87	-11	32	12	2	.961	-7	*S-149	-0.1
1984	Cle-A	160	658	82	188	22	5	3	79	43	68	.286	.335	.348	88	-10	19	10	-0	.955	-1	*S-159/D-1	0.5
1985	Cle-A	160	636	97	183	33	4	6	90	54	74	.288	.347	.381	100	1	13	9	-2	.949	-22	*S-151/2-8,D-1	-0.7
1986	Cle-A	149	599	80	183	30	5	10	74	32	66	.306	.341	.422	108	6	10	7	-1	.971	-5	*S-134,2-13/D-3	1.2
1987	Cle-A	128	495	86	158	24	3	8	52	57	56	.319	.393	.428	117	14	32	9	4	.963	-24	*S-111/2-9,D-8	0.4
1988	Cle-A	152	613	88	186	23	6	10	54	56	72	.303	.364	.409	113	11	25	11	1	.982	-10	*2-151/D-1	0.9
1989	Tex-A★	150	548	80	173	31	5	13	92	66	69	.316	.390	.462	137	28	21	3	5	.980	-6	*2-140,D-10	3.1
1990	Tex-A★	157	582	96	172	27	1	11	69	82	83	.296	.384	.402	120	18	31	10	3	.975	-2	*2-152/D-3	2.3
1991	Tex-A☆	146	589	108	201	27	3	15	78	65	78	**.341**	.409	.474	146	38	36	9	5	.979	-31	*2-146	1.6
1992	Tex-A	35	107	19	25	7	0	2	8	15	17	.234	.328	.355	95	-1	1	1	-0	.906	-6	D-15/2-9,O-4	-0.7
1993	Tex-A	144	532	85	154	31	3	14	84	62	95	.289	.365	.438	119	15	9	3	1	.000	0	*D-140	1.0
1994	Chi-A	112	433	72	138	19	2	20	98	62	75	.319	.410	.510	138	26	8	1	2	.969	-1	D-99,1-14	1.9
1996	*Cle-A	112	432	72	139	20	1	14	76	61	82	.322	.409	.470	122	17	8	8	-2	.990	4	1-97,D-13	0.7
1997	Cle-A	78	289	46	82	13	1	3	25	38	75	.284	.367	.367	89	-3	8	5	-1	.983	3	D-42,2-35/1-1	-0.1
	Mil-A	42	141	22	34	3	0	4	19	31	41	.241	.382	.348	91	-1	7	1	2	.992	1	D-28,1-13	-0.1
	Yr	120	430	68	116	16	1	7	44	69	116	.270	.372	.360	90	-4	15	6	1	.983	4	D-70,2-35,1-14	-0.2
Total	15	1890	7243	1104	2177	335	47	141	981	753	1005	.301	.369	.418	113	149	260	101	17	.960	-107	S-715,2-663,D1/O3	11.7

■ MATT FRANCO
Franco, Matthew Neil b: 8/19/69, Santa Monica, Cal. BL/TR, 6'2", 200 lbs. Deb: 9/6/95

YEAR	TM/L	G	AB	R	H	2B	3B	HR	RBI	BB	SO	AVG	OBP	SLG	PRO+	BR/A	SB	CS	SBR	FA	FR	G/POS	TPR
1995	Chi-N	16	17	3	5	1	0	0	1	0	4	.294	.294	.353	71	-1	0	0	0	1.000	-1	/2-3,1-1,3-1	-0.2
1996	NY-N	14	31	3	6	1	0	1	2	1	5	.194	.242	.323	50	-2	0	0	0	.824	-1	/3-8,1-2	-0.4
1997	NY-N	112	163	21	45	5	0	5	21	13	23	.276	.330	.399	93	-2	1	0	0	.937	2	3-39,1-13/O-1,D-1	0.0
1998	NY-N	103	161	20	44	7	2	1	13	23	26	.273	.368	.360	91	-1	0	1	-1	1.000	-2	3-13,O-13,1-11,/D-2	-0.4
Total	4	245	372	47	100	14	2	7	37	37	58	.269	.338	.374	88	-6	1	1	-0	.932	-2	/3-61,1-27,O-14,D2	-1.0

■ TITO FRANCONA
Francona, John Patsy b: 11/4/33, Aliquippa, Pa. BL/TL, 5'11", 190 lbs. Deb: 4/17/56 F

YEAR	TM/L	G	AB	R	H	2B	3B	HR	RBI	BB	SO	AVG	OBP	SLG	PRO+	BR/A	SB	CS	SBR	FA	FR	G/POS	TPR
1956	Bal-A	139	445	62	115	16	4	9	57	51	60	.258	.336	.373	94	-5	11	5	0	.977	-8	*O-122,1-21	-1.8
1957	Bal-A	97	279	35	65	8	3	7	38	29	48	.233	.312	.358	88	-5	7	3	0	.992	-10	O-73/1-4	-1.9
1958	Chi-A	41	128	10	33	3	2	1	10	14	24	.258	.331	.336	86	-2	2	3	-1	1.000	-4	O-35	-0.9
	Det-A	45	69	11	17	5	0	0	10	15	16	.246	.381	.319	88	-0	0	0	0	1.000	-3	O-18/1-1	-0.5
	Yr	86	197	21	50	8	2	1	20	29	40	.254	.350	.330	86	-3	2	3	-1	1.000	-7	O-53/1-1	-1.4
1959	Cle-A	122	399	68	145	17	2	20	79	35	42	.363	.419	.566	174	**40**	2	0	1	.972	-4	O-64,1-35	3.1
1960	Cle-A	147	544	84	159	**36**	2	17	79	67	67	.292	.375	.460	128	22	4	1	1	.989	5	*O-138,1-13	2.0
1961	Cle-A☆	155	592	87	178	30	8	16	85	56	52	.301	.365	.459	122	18	2	1	0	.987	4	*O-138,1-14	1.3
1962	Cle-A	158	621	82	169	28	5	14	70	47	74	.272	.330	.401	99	-2	3	2	-0	.986	2	*1-158	-1.1
1963	Cle-A	142	500	57	114	29	0	10	41	47	77	.228	.297	.346	80	-13	9	1	2	.986	-2	*O-122,1-11	-2.2
1964	Cle-A	111	270	35	67	13	2	8	24	44	46	.248	.362	.400	113	6	1	3	-2	.985	-12	O-69,1-17	-1.2
1965	StL-N	81	174	15	45	6	2	5	19	17	30	.259	.325	.402	95	-1	0	0	0	.972	-9	O-34,1-13	-1.3
1966	StL-N	83	156	14	33	4	1	4	17	7	27	.212	.250	.327	59	-9	0	0	0	.987	1	1-30/O-9	-1.0
1967	Phi-N	27	73	7	15	1	0	0	3	7	10	.205	.275	.219	43	-5	0	1	-1	1.000	1	1-24/O-1	-0.6
	Atl-N	82	254	28	63	5	1	6	25	20	34	.248	.305	.346	87	-4	1	0	0	.991	-1	1-56/O-6	-0.9
	Yr	109	327	35	78	6	1	6	28	27	44	.239	.299	.318	77	-10	1	1	-0	.993	1	1-80/O-7	-1.5
1968	Atl-N	122	346	32	99	13	1	2	47	51	45	.286	.378	.347	118	10	3	0	1	.978	-8	O-65,1-33	-0.3
1969	Atl-N	51	88	5	26	1	0	2	22	13	10	.295	.386	.375	114	2	0	1	-1	.957	-0	O-15/1-7	0.0
	Oak-A	32	85	12	29	6	1	3	20	12	11	.341	.423	.541	175	9	0	0	0	.988	-2	1-19/O-1	0.5

YEAR	TM/L	G	AB	R	H	2B	3B	HR	RBI	BB	SO	AVG	OBP	SLG	PRO+	BR/A	SB	CS	SBR	FA	FR	G/POS	TPR
1970	Oak-A	32	33	2	8	0	0	1	6	6	6	.242	.375	.333	100	0	0	0	0	1.000	1	/1-6,O-1	0.1
	Mil-A	52	65	4	15	3	0	0	4	6	15	.231	.296	.277	58	-4	1	0	0	1.000	1	1-13	-0.3
	Yr	84	98	6	23	3	0	1	10	12	21	.235	.324	.296	73	-3	1	0	0	1.000	2	1-19/O-1	-0.2
Total	15	1719	5121	650	1395	224	34	125	656	544	694	.272	.346	.403	108	56	46	21	1	.984	-49	O-911,1-475	-7.0
■ TERRY FRANCONA	Francona, Terry Jon b: 4/22/59, Aberdeen, S.D. BL/TL, 6'1", 190 lbs. Deb: 8/19/81 FMC																						
1981	*Mon-N	34	95	11	26	0	1	1	8	5	6	.274	.317	.326	82	-2	1	0	0	1.000	1	O-26/1-1	-0.2
1982	Mon-N	46	131	14	42	3	0	0	9	8	11	.321	.360	.344	96	-0	2	3	-1	.936	-6	O-33,1-16	-0.9
1983	Mon-N	120	230	21	59	11	1	3	22	6	20	.257	.275	.352	73	-9	0	2	-1	.978	-2	O-51,1-47	-1.5
1984	Mon-N	58	214	18	74	19	2	1	18	5	12	.346	.364	.467	138	10	0	0	0	.994	6	1-50/O-6	1.3
1985	Mon-N	107	281	19	75	15	1	2	31	12	12	.267	.299	.349	86	-6	5	5	-2	.988	2	1-57,O-28/3-1	-0.9
1986	Chi-N	86	124	13	31	3	0	2	8	6	8	.250	.290	.323	64	-6	0	1	-1	1.000	-7	O-30,1-23	-1.6
1987	Cin-N	102	207	16	47	5	0	3	12	10	12	.227	.266	.295	46	-16	2	0	1	.995	3	1-57/O-8	-1.6
1988	Cle-A	62	212	24	66	8	0	1	12	5	18	.311	.327	.363	91	-3	0	0	0	.977	0	D-38/1-5,O-5	-0.4
1989	Mil-A	90	233	26	54	10	1	3	23	8	20	.232	.257	.322	63	-12	2	1	0	.989	-2	1-46,D-23,O-16,/P-1	-1.8
1990	Mil-A	3	4	1	0	0	0	0	0	0	0	.000	.000	.000	-99	-1	0	0	0	1.000	-0	/1-2,D-1	-0.1
Total	10	708	1731	163	474	74	6	16	143	65	119	.274	.302	.351	81	-46	12	12	-4	.992	-4	1-304,O-203/DP3	-7.7
■ CHARLIE FRANK	Frank, Charles b: 5/30/1870, Mobile, Ala. d: 5/24/22, Memphis, Tenn. 5'10", 170 lbs. Deb: 8/18/1893																						
1893	StL-N	40	164	29	55	6	3	1	17	18	8	.335	.408	.427	122	5	8			.930	3	O-40	0.5
1894	StL-N	80	319	52	89	12	7	4	42	44	13	.279	.372	.398	86	-7	14			.869	-2	O-77/1-3,P-2	-1.1
Total	2	120	483	81	144	18	10	5	59	62	21	.298	.384	.408	97	-2	22			.889	1	O-117/1-3,P-2	-0.6
■ FRED FRANK	Frank, Frederick b: 3/11/1874, Louisa, Ky. d: 3/27/50, Ashland, Ky. Deb: 9/27/1898																						
1898	Cle-N	17	53	3	11	1	1	0	3	4		.208	.276	.264	56	-3	1			.915	3	O-17	-0.1
■ MIKE FRANK	Frank, Stephen Michael b: 1/14/74, Pomona, Cal. BL/TL, 6'2", 185 lbs. Deb: 6/19/98																						
1998	Cin-N	28	89	14	20	6	0	0	7	7	12	.225	.281	.292	48	-7	0	0	0	1.000	1	O-28	-0.6
■ FRANKLIN	Franklin Deb: 9/27/1884																						
1884	Was-U	1	3	0	0	0	0	0		0		.000	.000	.000	-99	-1				1.000	0	/O-1	-0.1
■ MICAH FRANKLIN	Franklin, Micah Ishanti b: 4/25/72, San Francisco, Cal. BB/TR, 6', 205 lbs. Deb: 5/13/97																						
1997	StL-N	17	34	6	11	0	0	2	2	3	10	.324	.378	.500	129	1	0	0	0	1.000	-2	O-13	-0.1
■ MOE FRANKLIN	Franklin, Murray Asher b: 4/1/14, Chicago, Ill. d: 3/16/78, Harbor City, Cal. BR/TR, 6', 175 lbs. Deb: 8/12/41																						
1941	Det-A	13	10	1	3	1	0	0	0	2	2	.300	.417	.400	106	0	0	0	0	.750	-1	/S-4,3-1	-0.1
1942	Det-A	48	154	24	40	7	0	2	16	7	5	.260	.301	.344	75	-5	0	0	0	.967	-6	S-32/2-7	-0.9
Total	2	61	164	25	43	8	0	2	16	9	7	.262	.309	.348	77	-5	0	0	0	.961	-7	/S-36,2-7,3-1	-1.0
■ HERMAN FRANKS	Franks, Herman Louis b: 1/4/14, Price, Utah BL/TR, 5'10.5", 187 lbs. Deb: 4/27/39 MC																						
1939	StL-N	17	17	1	1	0	0	0	3	3	3	.059	.200	.059	-26	-3	0			.973	3	C-13	0.0
1940	Bro-N	65	131	11	24	4	0	1	14	20	6	.183	.296	.237	46	-9	2			.990	9	C-43	0.2
1941	*Bro-N	57	139	10	28	7	0	1	11	14	13	.201	.275	.273	52	-9	0			.986	2	C-54/O-1	-0.3
1947	Phi-A	8	15	2	3	0	1	0	1	4	4	.200	.368	.333	94	0	0	0	0	1.000	-1	/C-4	-0.1
1948	Phi-A	40	98	10	22	7	1	1	14	16	11	.224	.345	.347	84	-2	0	0	0	.977	3	C-27	0.2
1949	NY-N	1	3	1	2	0	0	0	0	0	0	.667	.667	.667	259	1	0			1.000	0	/C-1	0.1
Total	6	188	403	35	80	18	2	3	43	57	37	.199	.302	.275	57	-22	2	0		.985	16	C-142/O-1	0.1
■ LOU FRAZIER	Frazier, Arthur Louis b: 1/26/65, St.Louis, Mo. BB/TR, 6'2", 175 lbs. Deb: 4/8/93																						
1993	Mon-N	112	189	27	54	7	1	1	16	16	24	.286	.341	.349	82	-4	17	2	4	.986	-8	O-60/1-8,2-1	-0.9
1994	Mon-N	76	140	25	38	3	1	0	14	18	23	.271	.358	.307	75	-4	20	4	4	1.000	-2	O-36/2-6,1-1	-0.3
1995	Mon-N	35	63	6	12	2	0	0	3	8	12	.190	.301	.222	39	-5	4	0	1	.973	-3	O-25/2-1	-0.8
	Tex-A	49	99	19	21	2	0	0	8	7	20	.212	.278	.232	34	-10	9	1	2	.973	-6	O-47/D-2	-1.3
1996	Tex-A	30	50	5	13	2	1	0	5	8	10	.260	.373	.340	78	-1	4	2	0	.971	1	O-15,D-13/2-1	-0.1
1998	Chi-A	7	7	0	0	0	0	0	0	2	6	.000	.222	.000	-36	-1	4	0	1	1.000	-1	/O-3	-0.1
Total	5	309	548	82	138	16	3	1	46	59	95	.252	.331	.297	65	-26	58	9	12	.982	-17	O-186/D-15,2-9,1-9	-3.5
■ JOE FRAZIER	Frazier, Joseph Filmore b: 10/6/22, Liberty, N.C. BL/TR, 6', 180 lbs. Deb: 8/31/47 M																						
1947	Cle-A	9	14	1	1	1	0	0	0	1	1	.071	.133	.143	-24	-2	0	0	0	.857	-1	/O-5	-0.4
1954	StL-N	81	88	8	26	5	2	3	18	13	17	.295	.392	.500	129	4	0	0	0	.938	-1	O-11/1-1	0.3
1955	StL-N	58	70	12	14	1	0	4	9	6	12	.200	.273	.386	72	-3	0	0	0	1.000	-3	O-14	-0.6
1956	StL-N	14	19	1	4	2	0	1	4	3	3	.211	.318	.474	109	0	0	1	-1	.800	-1	/O-3	-0.1
	Cin-N	10	17	2	4	0	0	1	2	1	7	.235	.278	.412	77	-1	0	0	0	.000	-2	/O-4	-0.2
	Yr	24	36	3	8	2	0	2	6	4	10	.222	.300	.444	94	-0	0	1	-1	.800	-2	/O-7	-0.3
	Bal-A	45	74	7	19	6	0	1	12	11	6	.257	.360	.378	103	0	0	0	0	1.000	-0	O-19	0.0
Total	4	217	282	31	68	15	2	10	45	35	46	.241	.331	.415	97	-1	0	1	-1	.961	-7	/O-56,1-1	-1.0
■ JOHNNY FREDERICK	Frederick, John Henry b: 1/26/02, Denver, Colo. d: 6/18/77, Tigard, Ore. BL/TL, 5'11", 165 lbs. Deb: 4/18/29																						
1929	Bro-N	148	628	127	206	**52**	6	24	75	39	34	.328	.372	.545	126	23	6			.975	8	*O-143	1.9
1930	Bro-N	142	616	120	206	44	11	17	76	46	34	.334	.383	.524	118	17	1			.990	12	*O-142	1.7
1931	Bro-N	146	611	81	165	34	8	17	71	31	46	.270	.312	.435	99	-3	2			.965	2	*O-145	-1.0
1932	Bro-N	118	384	54	115	28	2	16	56	25	35	.299	.349	.508	130	15	1			.976	-3	O-88	0.6
1933	Bro-N	147	556	65	171	22	7	7	64	36	14	.308	.355	.410	123	16	9			.971	-7	*O-138	0.3
1934	Bro-N	104	307	51	91	20	1	4	35	33	13	.296	.370	.407	114	7	4			.957	-3	O-77/1-1	0.1
Total	6	805	3102	498	954	200	35	85	377	210	176	.308	.357	.477	118	75	23			.974	9	O-733/1-1	3.6
■ ED FREED	Freed, Edwin Charles b: 8/22/19, Centre Valley, Pa. BR/TR, 5'6", 165 lbs. Deb: 9/11/42																						
1942	Phi-N	13	33	3	10	3	1	0	1	4	3	.303	.378	.455	151	2	1			1.000	-1	O-11	0.0
■ ROGER FREED	Freed, Roger Vernon b: 6/2/46, Los Angeles, Cal. d: 1/9/96, Chino, Cal. BR/TR, 6', 190 lbs. Deb: 9/18/70																						
1970	Bal-A	4	13	0	2	0	0	0	1	3	4	.154	.313	.154	32	-1	0	0	0	1.000	0	/1-3,O-1	-0.1
1971	Phi-N	118	348	23	77	12	1	6	37	44	86	.221	.314	.313	78	-9	0	3	-2	.989	-5	*O-106/C-1	-2.2
1972	Phi-N	73	129	10	29	4	0	6	18	23	39	.225	.346	.395	108	2	0	1	-1	.971	-2	O-46	-0.2
1974	Cin-N	6	6	1	2	0	0	1	3	1	1	.333	.429	.833	251	1	0	0	0	1.000	-0	/1-1	0.1
1976	Mon-N	8	15	0	3	1	0	0	1	0	3	.200	.200	.267	30	-1	0	0	0	1.000	-0	/1-3,O-1	-0.2
1977	StL-N	49	83	10	33	2	1	5	21	11	9	.398	.468	.627	194	11	0	0	0	1.000	-2	1-18/O-6	0.8
1978	StL-N	52	92	3	22	6	0	2	20	8	17	.239	.300	.370	87	-2	1	0	0	.992	-1	1-15/O-6	-0.4
1979	StL-N	34	31	2	8	2	0	2	8	5	7	.258	.361	.516	135	1	0	0	0	.889	0	/1-1	0.2
Total	8	344	717	49	176	27	2	22	109	95	166	.245	.337	.381	101	2	1	4	-2	.982	-10	O-166/1-41,C-1	-2.0
■ BILL FREEHAN	Freehan, William Ashley b: 11/29/41, Detroit, Mich. BR/TR, 6'2", 205 lbs. Deb: 9/26/61																						
1961	Det-A	4	10	1	4	0	0	0	4	1	0	.400	.455	.400	127	0	0	0	0	1.000	1	/C-3	0.2
1963	Det-A	100	300	37	73	12	2	9	36	39	56	.243	.334	.387	98	-0	2	0	1	.995	-1	C-73,1-19	0.2
1964	Det-A☆	144	520	69	156	14	8	18	80	36	68	.300	.355	.462	123	16	5	1	1	.993	-2	*C-141/1-1	2.2
1965	Det-A★	130	431	45	101	15	0	10	43	39	63	.234	.308	.339	83	-9	4	2	0	.996	-1	*C-129	-0.4
1966	Det-A★	136	492	47	115	22	0	12	46	40	72	.234	.295	.352	83	-11	5	2	0	**.996**	1	*C-132/1-5	-0.2
1967	Det-A★	155	517	66	146	23	1	20	74	73	71	.282	.392	.447	143	31	1	2	-1	.992	-9	*C-147,1-11	3.2
1968	*Det-A★	155	540	73	142	24	2	25	84	65	64	.263	.367	.454	143	30	0	1	-1	.994	6	*C-138,1-21/O-1	4.8
1969	Det-A★	143	489	61	128	16	3	16	49	53	55	.262	.344	.405	104	3	1	2	-1	.992	4	*C-120,1-20	1.2
1970	Det-A★	117	395	44	95	17	3	16	52	52	48	.241	.335	.420	106	3	0	3	-2	**.997**	-16	*C-114	-0.8
1971	Det-A★	148	516	57	143	26	4	21	71	54	48	.277	.356	.465	126	17	2	7	-4	.996	-12	*C-144/O-1	0.8

YEAR	TM/L	G	AB	R	H	2B	3B	HR	RBI	BB	SO	AVG	OBP	SLG	PRO+	BR/A	SB	CS	SBR	FA	FR	G/POS	TPR
1972	*Det-A★	111	374	51	98	18	2	10	56	48	51	.262	.355	.401	121	11	0	1	-1	.989	0	*C-105/1-1	1.6
1973	Det-A☆	110	380	33	89	10	1	6	29	40	30	.234	.325	.313	75	-11	0	0	0	**.995**	9	C-98/1-7,D-3	0.1
1974	Det-A	130	445	58	132	17	5	18	60	42	44	.297	.364	.479	136	20	2	0	1	.994	-8	1-65,C-63/D-1	1.1
1975	Det-A☆	120	427	42	105	17	3	14	47	32	56	.246	.308	.398	94	-4	2	0	1	.991	-8	*C-113/1-5	-0.7
1976	Det-A	71	237	22	64	10	1	5	27	12	27	.270	.308	.384	98	-1	0	0	0	.983	-2	C-61/1-2,D-3	-0.1
Total	15	1774	6073	706	1591	241	35	200	758	626	753	.262	.342	.412	111	94	24	21	-5	.993	-38	*C-1581,1-157/D-7,O	13.2
■ JERRY FREEMAN	Freeman, Frank Ellsworth "Buck" b: 12/26/1879, Placerville, Cal. d: 9/30/52, Los Angeles, Cal. BL/TR, 6'2", 220 lbs. Deb: 4/14/08																						
1908	Was-A	154	531	45	134	15	5	1	45	36		.252	.304	.305	107	3	6			.975	-13	*1-154	-1.4
1909	Was-A	19	48	2	8	0	1	0	3	4		.167	.245	.208	46	-3	3			.956	-2	1-14/O-1	-0.5
Total	2	173	579	47	142	15	6	1	48	40		.245	.299	.297	101	0	9			.974	-15	1-168/O-1	-1.9
■ JOHN FREEMAN	Freeman, John Edward b: 1/24/01, Boston, Mass. d: 4/14/58, Washington, D.C. BR/TR, 5'8", 160 lbs. Deb: 6/17/27																						
1927	Bos-A	4	2	0	0	0	0	0	0	0	0	.000	.000	.000	-99	-1	0	0	0	.000	-2	/O-3	-0.2
■ BUCK FREEMAN	Freeman, John Frank b: 10/30/1871, Catasauqua, Pa. d: 6/25/49, Wilkes-Barre, Pa. BL/TL, 5'9", 169 lbs. Deb: 6/27/1891																						
1891	Was-a	5	18	1	4	1	0	0	1	2	2	.222	.300	.278	69	-1	0			.769	-0	/P-5	0.0
1898	Was-N	29	107	19	39	2	3	3	21	7		.364	.424	.523	171	10	2			.978	1	O-29	0.8
1899	Was-N	155	588	107	187	19	25	**25**	122	23		.318	.362	.563	154	38	21			.944	-12	*O-155/P-2	1.3
1900	Bos-N	117	418	58	126	19	13	6	65	25		.301	.355	.452	109	2	10			.950	-11	O-91,1-19	-1.4
1901	Bos-A	129	490	88	166	23	15	12	114	44		.339	.400	.520	157	37	17			.974	-5	*1-128/2-1,O-1	2.7
1902	Bos-A	138	564	75	174	38	19	11	**121**	32		.309	.352	.502	131	21	17			.944	-1	*O-138	1.1
1903	*Bos-A	141	567	74	163	39	20	**13**	**104**	30		.287	.328	.496	137	23	5			.933	-6	*O-141	0.9
1904	Bos-A	157	597	64	167	20	**19**	7	84	32		.280	.329	.412	126	17	7			.954	-6	*O-157	0.2
1905	Bos-A	130	455	59	109	20	8	3	49	46		.240	.316	.338	106	4	8			.973	-14	1-66,O-57/3-2	-1.6
1906	Bos-A	121	392	42	98	18	9	1	30	28		.250	.302	.349	104	1	5			.989	1	O-65,1-43/3-4	-0.2
1907	Bos-A	4	12	1	2	0	0	1	2	3		.167	.333	.417	140	1	0			1.000	0	/O-3	0.1
Total	11	1126	4208	588	1235	199	131	82	713	272	2	.293	.346	.462	131	152	92			.950	-53	O-837,1-256/P-7,32	3.9
■ LA VEL FREEMAN	Freeman, La Vel Maurice b: 2/18/63, Oakland, Cal. BL/TL, 5'9", 170 lbs. Deb: 4/7/89																						
1989	Mil-A	2	3	1	0	0	0	0	0	0	2	.000	.000	.000	-99	-1	0	0	0	.000	0	/D-2	-0.1
■ GENE FREESE	Freese, Eugene Lewis "Augie" b: 1/8/34, Wheeling, W.Va. BR/TR, 5'11", 175 lbs. Deb: 4/13/55 F																						
1955	Pit-N	134	455	69	115	21	8	14	44	34	57	.253	.310	.426	94	-5	5	1	1	.943	-2	3-65,2-57	-0.2
1956	Pit-N	65	207	17	43	9	0	3	14	16	45	.208	.274	.295	54	-13	2	1	0	.963	-7	3-47,2-26	-1.9
1957	Pit-N	114	346	44	98	18	2	6	31	17	42	.283	.321	.399	95	-3	9	4	0	.924	-3	3-74,2-10,O-10	-0.4
1958	Pit-N	17	18	1	3	0	0	1	2	1	2	.167	.211	.333	42	-2	0	0	0	.800	1	/3-1	-0.1
	StL-N	62	191	28	49	11	1	6	16	10	32	.257	.294	.419	83	-5	1	1	-0	.924	-25	S-28,2-14/3-3	-2.7
	Yr	79	209	29	52	11	1	7	18	11	34	.249	.286	.411	80	-7	1	1	-0	.924	-24	S-28,2-14/3-4	-2.8
1959	Phi-N	132	400	60	107	14	5	23	70	43	61	.268	.346	.500	120	11	8	4	0	.916	-24	*3-109/2-6	-1.2
1960	Chi-A	127	455	60	124	32	6	17	79	29	65	.273	.318	.481	114	7	10	6	-1	.946	0	*3-122	0.5
1961	*Cin-N	152	575	78	159	27	2	26	87	27	78	.277	.309	.466	101	-1	8	2	1	.950	-17	*3-151/2-1	-1.6
1962	Cin-N	18	42	2	6	1	0	0	1	6	8	.143	.250	.167	14	-5	0	0	0	1.000	-2	3-10	-0.7
1963	Cin-N	66	217	20	53	9	1	6	26	17	42	.244	.305	.378	93	-2	4	2	0	.930	-6	3-62/O-1	-0.9
1964	Pit-N	99	289	33	65	13	2	9	40	19	45	.225	.273	.377	81	-8	1	2	-1	.920	-6	3-72	-1.6
1965	Pit-N	43	80	6	21	4	0	0	8	6	18	.262	.330	.313	82	-2	0	2	-1	.951	-1	3-19	-0.4
	Chi-A	17	32	2	9	0	1	1	4	5	9	.281	.378	.438	140	2	0	0	0	.824	-3	/3-8	-0.1
1966	Chi-A	48	106	8	22	2	0	3	10	8	20	.208	.270	.311	71	-4	2	1	0	.894	3	3-34	-0.2
	Hou-N	21	33	1	3	0	0	0	0	5	11	.091	.211	.091	-13	-5	1	0	0	.800	-0	/3-4,2-3,O-1	-0.5
Total	12	1115	3446	429	877	161	28	115	432	243	535	.254	.307	.418	94	-37	51	26	-0	.934	-90	3-781,2-117/S-28,O	-12.0
■ GEORGE FREESE	Freese, George Walter "Bud" b: 9/12/26, Wheeling, W.Va. BR/TR, 6', 190 lbs. Deb: 4/29/53 FC																						
1953	Det-A	1	1	0	0	0	0	0	0	0	0	.000	.000	.000	-99	-0	0	0	0	.000	0	H	0.0
1955	Pit-N	51	179	17	46	8	2	3	22	17	18	.257	.328	.374	87	-3	1	1	-0	.936	-8	3-50	-1.2
1961	Chi-N	9	7	0	2	0	0	0	1	1	4	.286	.375	.286	78	-0	0	0	0	.000	0	H	0.0
Total	3	61	187	17	48	8	2	3	23	18	22	.257	.329	.369	86	-4	1	1	-0	.936	-8	/3-50	-1.2
■ JIM FREGOSI	Fregosi, James Louis b: 4/4/42, San Francisco, Cal. BR/TR, 6'1", 190 lbs. Deb: 9/14/61 M																						
1961	LA-A	11	27	7	6	0	0	0	3	1	4	.222	.250	.222	25	-3	0	0	0	.944	-0	S-11	-0.2
1962	LA-A	58	175	15	51	3	4	3	23	18	27	.291	.358	.406	108	2	2	1	0	.943	4	S-52	1.1
1963	LA-A	154	592	83	170	29	12	9	50	36	104	.287	.328	.422	115	10	2	2	-1	.964	2	*S-151	2.3
1964	LA-A★	147	505	86	140	22	9	18	72	72	87	.277	.372	.463	145	31	8	3	1	.966	1	*S-137	4.4
1965	Cal-A	161	602	66	167	19	7	15	64	54	107	.277	.341	.407	114	11	13	5	1	.968	6	*S-160	3.0
1966	Cal-A★	162	611	78	154	32	7	13	67	67	89	.252	.328	.391	109	7	17	8	0	.959	15	*S-162/1-1	3.9
1967	Cal-A★	151	590	75	171	23	6	9	56	49	77	.290	.349	.395	124	17	9	6	-1	.965	-7	*S-151	2.6
1968	Cal-A★	159	614	77	150	21	**13**	9	49	60	101	.244	.317	.365	110	7	9	4	0	.962	-14	*S-159	1.1
1969	Cal-A★	161	580	78	151	22	6	12	47	93	86	.260	.364	.381	114	13	9	2	2	.972	-16	*S-160	1.7
1970	Cal-A★	158	601	95	167	33	5	22	82	69	92	.278	.355	.459	127	22	0	2	-1	.973	4	*S-150/1-6	4.2
1971	Cal-A	107	347	31	81	15	1	5	33	39	61	.233	.320	.326	90	-5	2	1	0	.938	-10	S-74,1-18/O-7	-0.7
1972	NY-N	101	340	31	79	15	4	5	32	38	71	.232	.311	.344	88	-5	0	1	-1	.935	-7	3-85/S-6,1-3	-1.4
1973	NY-N	45	124	7	29	4	1	0	11	20	25	.234	.340	.282	75	-3	1	2	-1	.906	-6	S-17,3-17/1-3,O-1	-0.9
	Tex-A	45	157	25	42	6	2	6	16	12	31	.268	.324	.446	120	3	0	1	-1	.937	-9	3-34,1-10/S-6	-0.7
1974	Tex-A	78	230	31	60	5	0	12	34	22	41	.261	.325	.439	121	6	0	1	-1	1.000	-1	1-47,3-32	0.1
1975	Tex-A	77	191	25	50	5	0	7	33	20	39	.262	.335	.398	107	2	0	1	-1	.985	2	1-54,D-13/3-4	0.1
1976	Tex-A	58	133	17	31	7	0	2	12	23	33	.233	.346	.331	97	0	2	0	1	.995	-0	1-26,D-18/3-5	-0.1
1977	Tex-A	13	28	4	7	1	0	1	5	3	4	.250	.323	.393	93	-0	0	0	0	1.000	1	/1-5,D-3	0.0
	Pit-N	36	56	10	16	1	1	3	16	13	10	.286	.420	.500	142	4	2	0	1	.981	-1	1-15/3-1	0.3
1978	Pit-N	20	20	3	4	1	0	0	1	6	8	.200	.385	.250	77	-0	0	0	0	.667	-1	/3-5,1-2,2-1	-0.2
Total	18	1902	6523	844	1726	264	78	151	706	715	1097	.265	.340	.398	114	118	76	40	-1	.963	-40	*S-1396,1-190,3/DO2	20.6
■ VERN FREIBURGER	Freiburger, Vern Donald b: 12/19/23, Detroit, Mich. d: 2/27/90, Palm Springs, Cal. BR/TL, 6'1", 170 lbs. Deb: 9/6/41																						
1941	Cle-A	2	8	0	1	0	0	0	1	0	2	.125	.125	.125	-35	-2	0	0	0	.947	1	/1-2	-0.1
■ HOWARD FREIGAU	Freigau, Howard Earl "Ty" b: 8/1/02, Dayton, Ohio d: 7/18/32, Chattanooga, Tenn BR/TR, 5'10.5", 160 lbs. Deb: 9/13/22																						
1922	StL-N	3	1	0	0	0	0	0	0	0	0	.000	.000	.000	-99	-0	0	0	0	1.000	1	/S-2,3-1	0.1
1923	StL-N	113	358	30	94	18	1	1	35	25	36	.263	.314	.327	71	-15	5	4	-1	.929	2	S-87,2-16/1-9,30	-0.6
1924	StL-N	98	376	35	101	17	6	2	39	19	24	.269	.306	.362	80	-11	10	3	1	.958	3	3-98/S-2	0.0
1925	StL-N	9	26	2	4	0	0	0	0	2	1	.154	.214	.154	-4	-4	0	0	0	.936	3	/S-7,2-1	0.0
	Chi-N	117	476	77	146	22	10	8	71	30	31	.307	.349	.445	100	-1	10	6	-1	.913	-5	3-96,S-17/1-7	0.2
	Yr	126	502	79	150	22	10	8	71	32	32	.299	.342	.430	94	-5	10	6	-1	.913	-1	3-96,S-24/1-7,2-1	0.2
1926	Chi-N	140	508	51	137	27	7	3	51	43	42	.270	.327	.368	86	-10	6			**.966**	-3	*3-135/S-2,O-1	-0.4
1927	Chi-N	30	86	12	20	5	0	0	10	9	10	.233	.313	.291	62	-4	0			.883	1	3-30	-0.3
1928	Bro-N	17	34	6	7	2	0	0	3	1	3	.206	.229	.265	29	-4	0			.810	-4	3-10/S-1	-0.7
	Bos-N	52	109	11	28	8	1	1	17	9	14	.257	.319	.376	86	-3	1			.938	-10	S-14,2-11	-1.0
	Yr	69	143	17	35	10	1	1	20	10	17	.245	.299	.350	72	-6	1			.938	-13	S-15,2-11,3-10	-1.7
Total	7	579	1974	224	537	99	25	15	226	138	161	.272	.322	.370	82	-52	32	13		.940	-11	3-371,S-132/210	-2.7
■ CHARLIE FRENCH	French, Charles Calvin b: 10/12/1883, Indianapolis, Ind. d: 3/30/62, Indianapolis, Ind. BL/TR, 5'6", 140 lbs. Deb: 5/23/09																						
1909	Bos-A	51	167	15	42	3	1	0	13	15		.251	.324	.281	90	-1	8			.921	-8	2-28,S-23	-1.1
1910	Bos-A	9	40	4	8	1	0	0	3	1		.200	.220	.225	38	-3	0			.889	1	/2-8	-0.3
	Chi-A	45	170	17	28	1	1	0	4	10		.165	.224	.182	29	-14	5			.930	-14	2-28,O-16	-3.4

YEAR	TM/L	G	AB	R	H	2B	3B	HR	RBI	BB	SO	AVG	OBP	SLG	PRO+	BR/A	SB	CS	SBR	FA	FR	G/POS	TPR
	Yr	54	210	21	36	2	1	0	7	11		.171	.223	.190	31	-17	5			.919	-14	2-36,O-16	-3.7
Total	2	105	377	36	78	5	2	0	20	26		.207	.269	.231	58	-18	13			.920	-22	/2-64,S-23,O-16	-4.8
■ PAT FRENCH	French, Frank Alexander b: 9/22/1893, Dover, N.H. d: 7/13/69, Bath, Maine BR/TR, 6′1″, 180 lbs. Deb: 7/2/17																						
1917	Phi-A	3	2	0	0	0	0	0	0	0	0	.000	.000	.000	-99	-0	0			1.000	-0	/O-1	-0.1
■ RAY FRENCH	French, Raymond Edward b: 1/9/1895, Alameda, Cal. d: 4/3/78, Alameda, Cal. BR/TR, 5′9.5″, 158 lbs. Deb: 9/17/20																						
1920	NY-A	2	2	2	0	0	0	0	1	0	1	.000	.000	.000	-97	-1	0	0	0	.500	-0	/S-1	-0.1
1923	Bro-N	43	73	14	16	2	1	0	7	4	7	.219	.269	.274	45	-6	0	0	0	.874	4	S-30	0.0
1924	Chi-A	37	112	13	20	4	0	0	11	10	13	.179	.246	.214	20	-14	3	1	0	.927	-3	S-28/2-3	-1.2
Total	3	82	187	29	36	6	1	0	19	14	21	.193	.252	.235	28	-20	3	1	0	.897	2	/S-59,2-3	-1.3
■ JIM FRENCH	French, Richard James b: 8/13/41, Warren, Ohio BL/TR, 5′7″, 182 lbs. Deb: 9/12/65																						
1965	Was-A	13	37	4	11	0	0	1	7	9	5	.297	.435	.378	135	2	1	0	0	.974	-0	C-13	0.3
1966	Was-A	10	24	0	5	1	0	0	3	4	5	.208	.321	.250	67	-1	0	1	-1	.979	-1	C-10	-0.2
1967	Was-A	6	16	0	1	0	0	0	1	3	4	.063	.211	.063	-16	-2	0	0	0	.968	-1	/C-6	-0.3
1968	Was-A	59	165	9	32	5	0	1	10	19	19	.194	.281	.242	62	-7	1	2	-1	.984	2	C-53	-0.3
1969	Was-A	63	158	14	29	6	3	2	13	41	15	.184	.352	.297	88	-1	1	0	0	.989	9	C-63	1.2
1970	Was-A	69	166	20	35	3	1	1	13	38	23	.211	.358	.259	76	-4	0	1	-1	.973	-6	C-62/O-1	-0.8
1971	Was-A	14	41	6	6	2	0	0	4	7	7	.146	.271	.195	36	-3	0	2	-1	.985	-1	C-14	-0.5
Total	7	234	607	53	119	17	4	5	51	121	78	.196	.331	.262	74	-16	3	6	-3	.982	2	C-221/O-1	-0.6
■ WALTER FRENCH	French, Walter Edward "Piggy" or "Fitz" b: 7/12/1899, Moorestown, N.J. d: 5/13/84, Mountain Home, Ark BL/TR, 5′7.5″, 155 lbs. Deb: 9/15/23																						
1923	Phi-A	16	39	7	9	3	0	0	2	5	7	.231	.318	.308	64	-2	0	1	-1	1.000	-1	O-10	-0.4
1925	Phi-A	67	100	20	37	9	0	0	14	1	9	.370	.376	.460	104	0	1	1	-0	.971	0	O-19	-0.1
1926	Phi-A	112	397	51	121	18	7	1	36	18	24	.305	.340	.393	86	-9	2	3	-1	.971	3	O-99	-1.4
1927	Phi-A	109	326	48	99	10	5	0	41	16	14	.304	.338	.365	78	-11	9	1	2	.956	0	O-94	-1.3
1928	Phi-A	48	74	9	19	4	0	0	7	2	5	.257	.286	.311	55	-5	1	1	-0	1.000	-1	O-19	-0.7
1929	*Phi-A	45	45	7	12	1	0	1	9	2	3	.267	.298	.356	65	-2	0	0	0	1.000	-3	O-10	-0.5
Total	6	397	981	142	297	45	12	2	109	44	62	.303	.336	.379	81	-29	13	7	-0	.968	-2	O-251	-4.4
■ BILL FRENCH	French, William b: Baltimore, Md. Deb: 4/14/1873																						
1873	Mar-n	5	18	3	4	0	0	0	1	0	0	.222	.222	.222	42	-1	0	0	0	.905	-0	/1-2,O-2,P-1,3-1	0.0
■ LONNY FREY	Frey, Linus Reinhard "Junior" b: 8/23/10, St.Louis, Mo. BL/TR, 5′10″, 160 lbs. Deb: 8/29/33																						
1933	Bro-N	34	135	25	43	5	3	0	12	13	13	.319	.378	.400	128	5	4			.896	-14	S-34	-0.7
1934	Bro-N	125	490	77	139	24	5	8	57	52	54	.284	.358	.402	109	7	11			.945	13	*S-109,3-13	2.6
1935	Bro-N	131	515	88	135	35	11	11	77	66	68	.262	.352	.437	113	10	6			.937	-4	*S-127/2-4	1.3
1936	Bro-N	148	524	63	146	29	4	4	60	71	56	.279	.369	.372	99	2	7			.918	-32	*S-117,2-30/O-1	-2.1
1937	Chi-N	78	198	33	55	9	3	1	22	33	15	.278	.381	.369	100	1	6			.938	-19	S-30,2-13/3-9,O-5	-1.4
1938	Cin-N	124	501	76	133	26	6	4	36	49	50	.265	.331	.365	94	-4	4			.964	-8	*2-121/S-3	-0.4
1939	*Cin-N★	125	484	95	141	27	9	11	55	72	46	.291	.387	.452	124	18	5			.976	15	*2-124	**4.0**
1940	*Cin-N	150	563	102	150	23	6	8	54	80	48	.266	.361	.371	101	3	**22**			.977	18	*2-150	3.1
1941	Cin-N★	146	543	78	138	29	5	6	59	72	37	.254	.345	.359	98	-0	16			**.970**	-2	*2-145	0.8
1942	Cin-N	141	523	66	139	23	6	2	39	87	38	.266	.373	.344	111	11	9			.977	5	*2-140	2.6
1943	Cin-N★	144	586	78	154	20	8	2	43	76	56	.263	.347	.334	99	1	7			**.985**	12	*2-144	2.2
1946	Cin-N	111	333	46	82	10	3	3	24	63	31	.246	.368	.321	100	3	5			.963	-3	2-65,O-28	0.3
1947	Chi-N	24	43	4	9	0	0	0	3	4	6	.209	.277	.209	32	-4	0			1.000	-2	/2-9	-0.6
	*NY-A	24	28	10	5	2	0	0	2	10	1	.179	.410	.250	87	0	3	0	1	.923	3	/2-8	0.5
1948	NY-A	1	0	1	0	0	0	0	0	0	0	—	—	—	—	0	0	0	0	.000	0	R	0.0
	NY-N	29	51	6	13	1	0	1	6	4	6	.255	.309	.333	73	-2	0			.920	-2	2-13	-0.3
Total	14	1535	5517	848	1482	263	69	61	549	752	525	.269	.359	.374	104	50	105	0		.973	-18	2-966,S-420/O-34,3	11.9
■ HANLEY FRIAS	Frias, Hanley (Acevedo) b: 12/5/73, Villa Altagracia, D.R. BB/TR, 6′, 160 lbs. Deb: 6/21/97																						
1997	Tex-A	14	26	4	5	1	0	0	1	1	4	.192	.222	.231	18	-3	0	0	0	1.000	-4	S-12/2-1	-0.6
1998	Ari-N	15	23	4	3	0	1	1	2	0	5	.130	.130	.348	18	-3	0	0	0	1.000	2	/2-3,3-2,S-2	-0.1
Total	2	29	49	8	8	1	1	1	3	1	9	.163	.180	.286	18	-6	0	0	0	1.000	-2	/S-14,2-4,3-2	-0.7
■ PEPE FRIAS	Frias, Jesus Maria (Andujar) b: 7/14/48, San Pedro De Macoris, D.R. BR/TR, 5′10″, 159 lbs. Deb: 4/6/73																						
1973	Mon-N	100	225	19	52	10	1	0	22	10	24	.231	.267	.284	51	-15	1	3	-2	.950	17	S-46,2-44/3-6,O-1	0.6
1974	Mon-N	75	112	12	24	4	1	0	7	7	10	.214	.261	.268	45	-8	1	0	0	.962	17	S-30,3-27,2-15,/O-3	1.1
1975	Mon-N	51	64	4	8	2	0	0	4	3	13	.125	.164	.156	-10	-10	0	1	-1	.938	14	S-29,3-11/2-7	0.5
1976	Mon-N	76	113	7	28	5	0	0	8	4	14	.248	.274	.292	58	-6	1	1	-0	.957	14	2-35,S-35/3-4,O-1	1.1
1977	Mon-N	53	70	10	18	1	0	0	5	0	10	.257	.257	.271	43	-6	1	0	0	.978	8	2-16,S-14/3-1	0.3
1978	Mon-N	73	15	5	4	2	1	0	5	0	3	.267	.267	.533	120	0	0	0	0	1.000	13	2-61/S-3	1.4
1979	Atl-N	140	475	41	123	18	4	1	44	20	36	.259	.292	.320	62	-25	3	2	-0	.954	0	*S-137	-1.0
1980	Tex-A	116	227	27	55	5	1	0	10	4	23	.242	.259	.273	47	-16	5	1	1	.947	-16	*S-106/3-7,2-2	-2.4
	LA-N	14	9	1	2	1	0	0	0	0	0	.222	.222	.333	54	-1	0	0	0	.933	2	S-11	0.2
1981	LA-N	25	36	6	9	1	0	0	3	1	3	.250	.289	.278	64	-2	0	0	0	.906	-5	S-15/2-6,3-1	-0.6
Total	9	723	1346	132	323	49	8	1	108	49	136	.240	.269	.290	52	-88	12	8	-1	.951	63	S-426,2-186/3-57,O	1.2
■ BERNIE FRIBERG	Friberg, Bernard Albert (b: Gustaf Bernhard Friberg) b: 8/18/1899, Manchester, N.H. d: 12/8/58, Lynn, Mass. BR/TR, 5′11″, 178 lbs. Deb: 8/20/19																						
1919	Chi-N	8	20	0	4	1	0	0	1	0	2	.200	.200	.250	35	-2	0			1.000	-1	/O-7	-0.3
1920	Chi-N	50	114	11	24	5	1	0	7	6	20	.211	.250	.272	49	-8	2	2	-1	.963	1	2-24,O-24	-0.8
1922	Chi-N	97	296	51	92	8	2	0	23	37	37	.311	.391	.351	91	-2	8	10	-4	.972	-2	O-74/1-6,3-5,2-3	-1.2
1923	Chi-N	146	547	91	174	27	11	12	88	45	49	.318	.372	.473	122	16	13	19	-8	.955	7	*3-146	2.8
1924	Chi-N	142	495	67	138	19	3	5	82	66	53	.279	.369	.360	95	-1	19	27	-11	.954	4	*3-142	0.3
1925	Chi-N	44	152	12	39	5	3	1	16	14	22	.257	.327	.349	72	-6	0	1	-1	.889	-5	3-26,O-12/1-6,S-2	-1.1
	Phi-N	91	304	41	82	12	1	5	22	39	35	.270	.353	.365	77	-10	1	1	-0	.965	4	2-77,3-14/P-1,C-1	-0.4
	Yr	135	456	53	121	17	4	6	38	53	57	.265	.344	.360	75	-16	1	2	-1	.965	-2	2-77,3-40,O/1SPC	-1.5
1926	Phi-N	144	478	38	128	21	3	1	51	57	77	.268	.346	.331	79	-13	2			.976	22	*2-144	1.3
1927	Phi-N	111	335	31	78	8	2	1	28	41	49	.233	.322	.278	61	-17	3			.959	25	*3-103/2-5	1.3
1928	Phi-N	52	94	11	19	3	0	1	7	12	16	.202	.292	.266	45	-7	0			.908	1	S-31/3-5,2-3,O-3,1	-0.4
1929	Phi-N	128	455	74	137	21	10	7	55	49	54	.301	.370	.437	93	-5	1			.923	-26	S-73,O-40/2-8,1-2	-2.2
1930	Phi-N	105	331	62	113	21	1	4	42	47	35	.341	.425	.447	104	4	1			.953	-4	2-44,O-35,S-12,/3-8	0.1
1931	Phi-N	103	353	33	92	19	5	1	26	33	25	.261	.324	.351	75	-12	1			.955	6	2-64,3-25/1-5,S-3	-0.1
1932	Phi-N	61	154	17	37	8	2	0	14	19	23	.240	.324	.318	66	-7	0			.957	-1	2-56	-0.6
1933	Bos-A	17	41	5	13	3	0	0	9	6	1	.317	.404	.390	112	1	0	0	0	.950	1	/2-6,3-5,S-2	0.3
Total	14	1299	4169	544	1170	181	44	38	471	471	498	.281	.356	.373	87	-69	51	60		.953	32	3-479,2-434,OS/1CP	-1.0
■ JIM FRIDLEY	Fridley, James Riley "Big Jim" b: 9/6/24, Philippi, W.Va. BR/TR, 6′2″, 205 lbs. Deb: 4/15/52																						
1952	Cle-A	62	175	23	44	2	0	4	16	14	40	.251	.311	.331	84	-4	3	3	-1	.978	-5	O-54	-1.3
1954	Bal-A	85	240	25	59	8	5	4	36	21	41	.246	.312	.371	93	-3	0	1	-1	.985	-1	O-67	-0.8
1958	Cin-N	5	9	2	2	2	0	0	1	0	2	.222	.222	.444	67	-0	0	0	0	1.000	-1	/O-2	-0.1
Total	3	152	424	50	105	12	5	8	53	35	83	.248	.310	.356	89	-8	3	4	-2	.982	-7	O-123	-2.2
■ PAT FRIEL	Friel, Patrick Henry b: 6/11/1860, Lewisburg, W.Va. d: 1/15/24, Providence, R.I. BB , 5′11″, 170 lbs. Deb: 7/13/1890 F																						
1890	Syr-a	62	261	51	65	8	2	3	21	17		.249	.302	.330	96	-2	34			.913	-6	O-62	-0.9
1891	Phi-a	2	8	2	2	1	0	0	0	0	0	.250	.250	.375	76	-0	0			1.000	-1	/O-2	-0.1
Total	2	64	269	53	67	9	2	3	21	17	0	.249	.301	.331	96	-2	34			.914	-7	/O-64	-1.0

YEAR	TM/L	G	AB	R	H	2B	3B	HR	RBI	BB	SO	AVG	OBP	SLG	PRO+	BR/A	SB	CS	SBR	FA	FR	G/POS	TPR
■ BILL FRIEL Friel, William Edward b: 4/1/1876, Renovo, Pa. d: 12/24/59, St.Louis, Mo. BL/TR, 5′10″, 165 lbs. Deb: 5/3/01 FUC																							
1901	Mil-A	106	376	51	100	13	7	4	35	23		.266	.310	.370	92	-4	15			.866	-9	3-61,O-29/2-9,S-6	-1.2
1902	StL-A	80	267	26	64	9	2	2	20	14		.240	.283	.311	65	-13	4			.921	-14	O-33,2-25,1/3SPC	-2.5
1903	StL-A	97	351	46	80	11	8	0	25	23		.228	.279	.305	77	-10	4			.915	-11	2-63,3-24/O-9	-1.9
Total	3	283	994	123	244	33	17	6	80	60		.245	.292	.331	80	-27	23			.924	-33	/2-97,3-93,O1SCP	-5.6
■ FRANK FRIEND Friend, Frank B. (b: Frederick Freund) b: 7/5/1875, Jeffersonville, Ind. d: 11/5/33, Jeffersonville, Ind. TR , 5′10″, 180 lbs. Deb: 8/2/1896																							
1896	Lou-N	2	5	1	1	0	0	0	0	1	1	.200	.333	.200	44	-0	0			1.000	-0	/C-2	0.0
■ OWEN FRIEND Friend, Owen Lacey "Red" b: 3/21/27, Granite City, Ill. BR/TR, 6′1″, 180 lbs. Deb: 10/2/49 C																							
1949	StL-A	2	8	1	3	0	0	0	1	0	0	.375	.375	.375	95	-0	0	0	0	1.000	1	/2-2	0.1
1950	StL-A	119	372	48	88	15	2	8	50	40	68	.237	.312	.352	67	-19	2	1	0	.961	10	2-93,3-24/S-3	-0.5
1953	Det-A	31	96	10	17	4	0	3	10	6	9	.177	.233	.313	47	-8	0	1	-1	.947	4	2-26	-0.3
	Cle-A	34	68	7	16	2	0	2	13	5	16	.235	.288	.353	74	-3	0	0	0	1.000	6	2-19/S-8,3-1	0.4
	Yr	65	164	17	33	6	0	5	23	11	25	.201	.256	.329	58	-10	0	1	-1	.964	10	2-45/S-8,3-1	0.1
1955	Bos-A	14	42	3	11	3	0	0	2	4	11	.262	.326	.333	71	-2	0	0	0	.951	2	S-14/2-1	0.1
	Chi-N	6	10	0	1	0	0	0	0	0	3	.100	.100	.100	-47	-2	0	0	0	1.000	-1	/3-2,S-1	-0.3
1956	Chi-N	2	2	0	0	0	0	0	0	0	2	.000	.000	.000	-99	-1	0	0	0	.000	0	H	-0.1
Total	5	208	598	69	136	24	2	13	76	55	109	.227	.295	.339	63	-34	2	2	-1	.963	23	2-141/3-27,S-26	-0.6
■ BUCK FRIERSON Frierson, Robert Lawrence b: 7/29/17, Chicota, Tex. d: 6/26/96, Paris, Tex. BR/TR, 6′3″, 195 lbs. Deb: 9/9/41																							
1941	Cle-A	5	11	2	3	1	0	0	2	1	1	.273	.333	.364	89	-0	0	0	0	1.000	-1	/O-3	-0.1
■ PETE FRIES Fries, Peter Martin b: 10/30/1857, Scranton, Pa. d: 7/30/37, Chicago, Ill. BL/TL, 5′8″, 160 lbs. Deb: 8/10/1883																							
1883	Col-a	3	10	1	3	1	0	0		1		.300	.364	.400	158	1				.857	0	/P-3	0.0
1884	Ind-a	1	3	0	1	1	0	0		1		.333	.500	.667	285	1				.333	0	/O-1	0.1
Total	2	4	13	1	4	2	0	0		2		.308	.400	.462	190	1				.857	0	/P-3,O-1	0.1
■ FRED FRINK Frink, Frederick Ferdinand b: 8/25/11, Macon, Ga. d: 5/19/95, Miami Springs, Fla. BR/TR, 6′1″, 180 lbs. Deb: 7/1/34																							
1934	Phi-N	2	0	0	0	0	0	0	0	0	0	—	—	—	—	0	0			.000	-1	/O-1	-0.1
■ CHARLIE FRISBEE Frisbee, Charles Augustus "Bunt" b: 2/2/1874, Dows, Iowa d: 11/7/54, Alden, Iowa BB/TR, 5′9″, 175 lbs. Deb: 6/22/1899																							
1899	Bos-N	42	152	22	50	4	2	0	20	9		.329	.374	.382	98	-1	10			.875	-2	O-40	-0.5
1900	NY-N	4	13	2	2	1	0	0	3	2		.154	.267	.231	40	-1	0			.400	-2	/O-4	-0.3
Total	2	46	165	24	52	5	2	0	23	11		.315	.365	.370	94	-2	10			.849	-4	/O-44	-0.8
■ FRANKIE FRISCH Frisch, Frank Francis "The Fordham Flash" b: 9/9/1898, Bronx, N.Y. d: 3/12/73, Wilmington, Del. BB/TR, 5′11″, 165 lbs. Deb: 6/14/19 MCH																							
1919	NY-N	54	190	21	43	3	2	2	24	4	14	.226	.242	.295	62	-9	15			.972	4	2-29,3-20/S-1	-0.4
1920	NY-N	110	440	57	123	10	10	4	77	20	18	.280	.311	.375	97	-3	34	11	4	.967	9	*3-109/S-2	1.6
1921	*NY-N	153	618	121	211	31	17	8	100	42	28	.341	.384	.485	128	25	**49**	13	**7**	.936	4	3-93,2-61	4.3
1922	*NY-N	132	514	101	168	16	13	5	51	47	13	.327	.387	.438	111	9	31	17	-1	.975	13	2-85,3-53/S-1	2.5
1923	*NY-N	151	641	116	**223**	32	10	12	111	46	12	.348	.395	.485	133	30	29	12	2	**.973**	-8	*2-135,3-17	2.6
1924	*NY-N	145	603	**121**	198	33	15	7	69	56	24	.328	.387	.468	132	27	22	9	1	.972	25	*2-143,S-10/3-2	5.4
1925	NY-N	120	502	89	166	26	6	11	48	32	14	.331	.374	.472	119	14	21	12	-1	.931	3	3-46,2-42,S-39	2.3
1926	NY-N	135	545	75	171	29	4	5	44	33	16	.314	.353	.409	106	4	23			.975	11	*2-127/3-7	1.9
1927	StL-N	153	617	112	208	31	11	10	78	43	10	.337	.387	.472	125	21	**48**			**.979**	**49**	*2-153/S-1	**7.3**
1928	*StL-N	141	547	107	164	29	9	10	86	64	17	.300	.374	.441	110	9	29			**.976**	3	*2-139	1.5
1929	StL-N	138	527	93	176	40	12	5	74	53	12	.334	.397	.484	116	14	24			.970	-4	*2-121,3-13/S-1	1.4
1930	*StL-N	133	540	121	187	46	9	10	114	55	16	.346	.407	.520	118	16	15			.969	**28**	*2-123,3-10	4.4
1931	*StL-N	131	518	96	161	24	4	4	82	45	13	.311	.368	.396	101	2	**28**			.974	16	*2-129	2.6
1932	StL-N	115	486	59	142	26	2	3	60	25	13	.292	.327	.372	85	-10	18			.971	16	2-75,3-37/S-4	1.3
1933	StL-N★	147	585	74	177	32	6	4	66	48	16	.303	.358	.398	110	8	18			.982	-3	*2-132,S-15,M	1.5
1934	*StL-N★	140	550	74	168	30	6	3	75	45	10	.305	.359	.398	96	-2	11			.977	5	*2-115,3-25,M	1.0
1935	StL-N☆	103	354	52	104	16	2	1	55	33	16	.294	.356	.359	89	-5	2			.982	-7	2-88/3-5,M	-0.5
1936	StL-N	93	303	40	83	10	0	1	26	36	10	.274	.353	.317	82	-6	2			.965	-13	2-60,3-22/S-1,M	-1.4
1937	StL-N	17	32	3	7	2	0	0	4	1	0	.219	.242	.281	41	-3	0			1.000	-1	/2-5,M	-0.3
Total	19	2311	9112	1532	2880	466	138	105	1244	728	272	.316	.369	.432	110	142	419	74		.974	149	*2-1762,3-459/S-75	39.0
■ EMIL FRISK Frisk, John Emil b: 10/15/1874, Kalkaska, Mich. d: 1/27/22, Seattle, Wash. BL/TR, 6′1″, 190 lbs. Deb: 9/2/1899																							
1899	Cin-N	9	25	5	7	1	0	0	2	2		.280	.357	.320	85	-0	0			.950	-0	/P-9	0.0
1901	Det-A	20	48	10	15	3	0	1	7	3		.313	.365	.438	117	1	0			.851	2	P-11/O-2	0.0
1905	StL-A	124	429	58	112	11	6	3	36	42		.261	.342	.336	122	12	7			.923	-7	*O-115	0.0
1907	StL-A	5	4	0	1	0	0	0	0	1		.250	.400	.250	108	0	0			.000	0	H	0.0
Total	4	158	506	73	135	15	6	4	45	48		.267	.346	.344	119	13	7			.918	-5	O-117/P-20	0.0
■ HARRY FRITZ Fritz, Harry Koch "Dutchman" b: 9/30/1890, Philadelphia, Pa. d: 11/4/74, Columbus, Ohio BR/TR, 5′8″, 170 lbs. Deb: 9/29/13																							
1913	Phi-A	5	13	1	0	0	0	0	0	2	4	.000	.188	.000	-45	-2	0			.846	-1	/3-5	-0.4
1914	Chi-F	65	174	16	37	5	1	0	13	18	18	.213	.297	.253	54	-14	2			.912	-9	3-46/S-9,2-1	-2.2
1915	Chi-F	79	236	27	59	8	4	3	26	13	27	.250	.298	.356	89	-8	4			.964	-8	3-70/2-6,S-1	-1.5
Total	3	149	423	44	96	13	5	3	39	33	49	.227	.294	.303	70	-25	6			.941	-18	3-121/S-10,2-7	-4.1
■ LARRY FRITZ Fritz, Lawrence Joseph b: 2/14/49, E.Chicago, Ind. BL/TL, 6′2″, 225 lbs. Deb: 5/30/75																							
1975	Phi-N	1	1	0	0	0	0	0	0	0	0	.000	.000	.000	-96	-0	0	0	0	.000	0	H	0.0
■ DOUG FROBEL Frobel, Douglas Steven b: 6/6/59, Ottawa, Ont., Can. BL/TR, 6′4″, 196 lbs. Deb: 9/5/82																							
1982	Pit-N	16	34	5	7	2	0	2	3	1	11	.206	.229	.441	81	-1	1	1	-0	1.000	-1	O-12	-0.3
1983	Pit-N	32	60	10	17	4	1	3	11	4	17	.283	.328	.533	132	2	1	1	-0	.964	-4	O-24	-0.2
1984	Pit-N	126	276	33	56	9	3	12	28	24	84	.203	.272	.388	83	-7	7	5	-1	.956	1	*O-112	-1.0
1985	Pit-N	53	109	14	22	5	0	0	7	19	24	.202	.320	.248	62	-5	4	3	-1	.941	-3	O-36	-1.0
	Mon-N	12	23	3	3	1	0	1	4	2	6	.130	.200	.304	42	-2	0	0	0	.923	-0	/O-6	-0.3
	Yr	65	132	17	25	6	0	1	11	21	30	.189	.301	.258	59	-7	4	3	-1	.938	-3	O-42	-1.3
1987	Cle-A	29	40	5	4	0	0	2	5	5	13	.100	.200	.250	18	-5	0	0	0	1.000	-3	O-12/D-5	-0.8
Total	5	268	542	70	109	21	4	20	58	55	155	.201	.277	.365	78	-18	13	10	-2	.957	-10	O-202/D-5	-3.6
■ BEN FROELICH Froelich, William Palmer b: 11/12/1887, Pittsburgh, Pa. d: 9/1/16, Pittsburgh, Pa. BR/TR, Deb: 7/2/09																							
1909	Phi-N	1	1	0	0	0	0	0	0	0	0	.000	.000	.000	-99	-0	0			.000	0	/C-1	0.0
■ JERRY FRY Fry, Jerry Ray b: 2/29/56, Salinas, Cal. BR/TR, 6′, 185 lbs. Deb: 9/4/78																							
1978	Mon-N	4	9	0	0	0	0	0	0	1	5	.000	.100	.000	-71	-2	0	0	0	1.000	1	/C-4	-0.1
■ JEFF FRYE Frye, Jeffrey Dustin b: 8/31/66, Oakland, Cal. BR/TR, 5′9″, 165 lbs. Deb: 7/9/92																							
1992	Tex-A	67	199	24	51	9	1	1	12	16	27	.256	.321	.327	85	-4	1	3	-2	.978	8	2-67	0.4
1994	Tex-A	57	205	37	67	20	3	0	18	29	23	.327	.413	.454	124	8	6	1	1	.983	-16	2-54/3-1,D-1	-0.4
1995	Tex-A	90	313	38	87	15	2	4	29	24	45	.278	.339	.377	84	-7	3	3	-1	.975	3	2-83	0.0
1996	Bos-A	105	419	74	120	27	2	4	41	54	57	.286	.374	.389	92	-4	18	4	3	.983	14	*2-100/O-5,S-3,D-1	1.8
1997	Bos-A	127	404	56	126	36	2	3	51	27	44	.312	.358	.433	103	2	19	8	1	.991	8	2-80,3-18,OD/S1	1.4
Total	5	446	1540	229	451	107	10	12	151	150	196	.293	.362	.399	97	-4	47	19	3	.982	16	2-384/3-19,ODS1	3.2
■ TRAVIS FRYMAN Fryman, David Travis b: 3/25/69, Lexington, Ky. BR/TR, 6′1″, 194 lbs. Deb: 7/7/90																							
1990	Det-A	66	232	32	69	11	1	9	27	17	51	.297	.348	.470	126	7	3	3	-1	.915	5	3-48,S-17/D-1	1.3
1991	Det-A	149	557	65	144	36	3	21	91	40	149	.259	.312	.447	106	2	12	5	1	.946	-9	3-85,S-71	-0.1
1992	Det-A★	161	659	87	175	31	4	20	96	45	144	.266	.318	.416	104	1	8	4	0	.970	-4	*S-137,3-26	0.7

YEAR	TM/L	G	AB	R	H	2B	3B	HR	RBI	BB	SO	AVG	OBP	SLG	PRO+	BR/A	SB	CS	SBR	FA	FR	G/POS	TPR
1993	Det-A★	151	607	98	182	37	5	22	97	77	128	.300	.382	.486	133	28	9	4	0	.953	-5	S-81,3-69/D-1	2.9
1994	Det-A★	114	464	66	122	34	5	18	85	45	128	.263	.335	.474	105	2	2	2	-1	.955	-5	*3-114	-0.3
1995	Det-A	144	567	79	156	21	5	15	81	63	100	.275	.351	.409	97	-2	4	2	0	.969	**27**	*3-144	2.3
1996	Det-A★	157	616	90	165	32	3	22	100	57	118	.268	.334	.437	93	-8	4	3	-1	**.979**	17	*3-128,S-29	1.0
1997	Det-A	154	595	90	163	27	3	22	102	46	113	.274	.331	.440	100	-1	16	3	3	**.978**	9	*3-153	1.1
1998	*Cle-A	146	557	74	160	33	2	28	96	44	125	.287	.343	.504	113	9	10	8	-2	.963	-8	*3-144/S-3,D-2	0.0
Total	9	1242	4854	681	1336	262	31	177	775	434	1056	.275	.339	.451	107	41	68	34	0	.965	26	3-911,S-338/D-4	8.9

■ MIKE FUENTES
Fuentes, Michael Jay b: 7/11/58, Miami, Fla. BR/TR, 6'3", 190 lbs. Deb: 9/2/83

YEAR	TM/L	G	AB	R	H	2B	3B	HR	RBI	BB	SO	AVG	OBP	SLG	PRO+	BR/A	SB	CS	SBR	FA	FR	G/POS	TPR
1983	Mon-N	6	4	1	1	0	0	0	0	0	2	.250	.250	.250	39	-0	0	0	0	.000	0	/H	-0.1
1984	Mon-N	3	4	0	1	0	0	0	0	1	2	.250	.400	.250	90	0	0	0	0	1.000	0	/O-1	0.0
Total	2	9	8	1	2	0	0	0	0	1	4	.250	.333	.250	67	-0	0	0	0	1.000	0	/O-1	-0.1

■ TITO FUENTES
Fuentes, Rigoberto (Peat) b: 1/4/44, Havana, Cuba BB/TR, 5'11", 175 lbs. Deb: 8/18/65

YEAR	TM/L	G	AB	R	H	2B	3B	HR	RBI	BB	SO	AVG	OBP	SLG	PRO+	BR/A	SB	CS	SBR	FA	FR	G/POS	TPR
1965	SF-N	26	72	12	15	1	0	0	1	5	14	.208	.269	.222	39	-6	0	1	-1	.919	-7	S-18/2-7,3-1	-1.3
1966	SF-N	133	541	63	141	21	3	9	40	9	57	.261	.277	.360	73	-20	6	3	0	.957	-14	S-76,2-60	-2.3
1967	SF-N	133	344	27	72	12	1	5	29	27	61	.209	.267	.294	61	-17	4	3	-1	.980	25	*2-130/S-5	1.4
1969	SF-N	67	183	28	54	4	3	1	14	15	25	.295	.352	.366	103	1	2	4	-2	.925	-6	3-36,S-30	-0.5
1970	SF-N	123	435	49	116	13	7	2	32	36	52	.267	.327	.343	81	-12	4	5	-2	.966	-2	2-78,S-36,3-24	-0.7
1971	*SF-N	152	630	63	172	28	6	4	52	18	46	.273	.300	.356	86	-13	12	2	2	.973	1	*2-152	0.3
1972	SF-N	152	572	64	151	33	6	7	53	39	56	.264	.314	.379	95	-5	16	5	2	.964	-21	*2-152	-1.6
1973	SF-N	160	656	78	182	25	5	6	63	45	62	.277	.331	.358	87	-11	12	6	0	**.993**	-5	*2-160/3-1	-0.7
1974	SF-N	108	390	33	97	15	2	0	22	22	32	.249	.294	.297	63	-19	7	3	0	.979	-4	*2-103	-1.9
1975	SD-N	146	565	57	158	21	3	4	43	25	51	.280	.314	.349	89	-10	8	8	-2	.970	4	*2-142	-0.1
1976	SD-N	135	520	48	137	18	0	2	36	18	38	.263	.289	.310	76	-18	5	3	-0	.971	2	*2-127	-0.9
1977	Det-A	151	615	83	190	19	10	5	51	38	61	.309	.351	.397	98	-1	4	4	-1	.970	3	*2-151/D-1	1.1
1978	Oak-A	13	43	5	6	1	0	0	2	1	6	.140	.159	.163	-10	-6	0	0	0	.944	-12	2-13	-1.9
Total	13	1499	5566	610	1491	211	46	45	438	298	561	.268	.309	.347	82	-137	80	47	-4	.974	-37	*2-1275,S-165/3D	-9.1

■ OLLIE FUHRMAN
Fuhrman, Alfred George b: 7/20/1896, Jordan, Minn. d: 1/11/69, Peoria, Ill. BB/TR, 5'11", 185 lbs. Deb: 4/13/22

YEAR	TM/L	G	AB	R	H	2B	3B	HR	RBI	BB	SO	AVG	OBP	SLG	PRO+	BR/A	SB	CS	SBR	FA	FR	G/POS	TPR
1922	Phi-A	6	6	1	2	1	0	0	0	0	0	.333	.333	.500	112	0	0	0	0	1.000	0	/C-4	0.0

■ DOT FULGHUM
Fulghum, James Lavoisier b: 7/4/1900, Valdosta, Ga. d: 11/11/67, Miami, Fla. BR/TR, 5'8.5", 165 lbs. Deb: 9/15/21

YEAR	TM/L	G	AB	R	H	2B	3B	HR	RBI	BB	SO	AVG	OBP	SLG	PRO+	BR/A	SB	CS	SBR	FA	FR	G/POS	TPR
1921	Phi-A	2	2	0	0	0	0	0	0	1	1	.000	.333	.000	-9	-0	0	0	0	.000	0	/S-1	0.0

■ NIG FULLER
Fuller, Charles F. b: 3/30/1879, Toledo, Ohio d: 11/12/47, Toledo, Ohio BR/TR, 5'11", 165 lbs. Deb: 7/1/02

YEAR	TM/L	G	AB	R	H	2B	3B	HR	RBI	BB	SO	AVG	OBP	SLG	PRO+	BR/A	SB	CS	SBR	FA	FR	G/POS	TPR
1902	Bro-N	3	9	0	0	0	0	0	1	0		.000	.000	.000	-99	-2	0			1.000	-1	/C-3	-0.3

■ FRANK FULLER
Fuller, Frank Edward "Rabbit" b: 1/1/1893, Detroit, Mich. d: 10/29/65, Warren, Mich. BB/TR, 5'7", 150 lbs. Deb: 4/14/15

YEAR	TM/L	G	AB	R	H	2B	3B	HR	RBI	BB	SO	AVG	OBP	SLG	PRO+	BR/A	SB	CS	SBR	FA	FR	G/POS	TPR
1915	Det-A	14	32	6	5	0	0	0	2	9	7	.156	.341	.156	47	-2	2	3	-1	.962	-6	/2-9,S-1	-0.9
1916	Det-A	20	10	2	1	0	0	0	1	1	4	.100	.182	.100	-15	-1	3			.846	3	/2-8,S-1	0.1
1923	Bos-A	6	21	3	5	0	0	0	0	1	1	.238	.273	.238	35	-2	1	1	-0	.952	2	/2-6	0.0
Total	3	40	63	11	11	0	0	0	3	11	12	.175	.297	.175	35	-5	6	4		.938	-1	/2-23,S-2	-0.8

■ HARRY FULLER
Fuller, Henry W. b: 12/5/1862, Cincinnati, Ohio d: 12/12/1895, Cincinnati, Ohio Deb: 4/8/1891 F

YEAR	TM/L	G	AB	R	H	2B	3B	HR	RBI	BB	SO	AVG	OBP	SLG	PRO+	BR/A	SB	CS	SBR	FA	FR	G/POS	TPR
1891	StL-a	1	2	0	0	0	0	0	0	0	1	.000	.000	.000	-87	-0	0			.000	-1	/3-1	-0.1

■ JIM FULLER
Fuller, James Hardy b: 11/28/50, Bethesda, Md. BR/TR, 6'3", 215 lbs. Deb: 9/10/73

YEAR	TM/L	G	AB	R	H	2B	3B	HR	RBI	BB	SO	AVG	OBP	SLG	PRO+	BR/A	SB	CS	SBR	FA	FR	G/POS	TPR
1973	Bal-A	9	26	2	3	0	0	2	4	1	17	.115	.148	.346	36	-2	0	0	0	1.000	1	/O-5,1-2,D-1	-0.1
1974	Bal-A	64	189	17	42	11	0	7	28	8	68	.222	.265	.392	90	-4	1	0	0	.960	-2	O-59/1-4,D-2	-0.8
1977	Hou-N	34	100	5	16	6	0	2	9	10	45	.160	.243	.280	44	-8	0	1	-1	.983	5	O-27/1-1	-0.5
Total	3	107	315	24	61	17	0	11	41	19	130	.194	.249	.352	70	-14	1	1	-0	.969	4	/O-91,1-7,D-3	-1.4

■ JOHN FULLER
Fuller, John Edward b: 1/29/50, Lynwood, Cal. BL/TL, 6'2", 180 lbs. Deb: 5/9/74

YEAR	TM/L	G	AB	R	H	2B	3B	HR	RBI	BB	SO	AVG	OBP	SLG	PRO+	BR/A	SB	CS	SBR	FA	FR	G/POS	TPR
1974	Atl-N	3	3	1	1	0	0	0	0	0	0	.333	.333	.333	83	-0	0	0	0	1.000	-0	/O-1	0.0

■ VERN FULLER
Fuller, Vernon Gordon b: 3/1/44, Menomonie, Wis. BR/TR, 6'1", 170 lbs. Deb: 9/5/64

YEAR	TM/L	G	AB	R	H	2B	3B	HR	RBI	BB	SO	AVG	OBP	SLG	PRO+	BR/A	SB	CS	SBR	FA	FR	G/POS	TPR
1964	Cle-A	2	1	0	0	0	0	0	0	0	0	.000	.000	.000	-99	-0	0	0	0	.000	0	H	0.0
1966	Cle-A	16	47	7	11	2	1	2	2	7	6	.234	.357	.447	129	2	0	0	0	1.000	-4	2-16	-0.1
1967	Cle-A	73	206	18	46	10	0	7	21	19	55	.223	.301	.374	98	-1	2	3	-1	.986	0	2-64/S-2	0.2
1968	Cle-A	97	244	14	59	8	2	0	18	24	49	.242	.320	.291	87	-3	2	2	-1	.988	-12	2-73,3-23/S-4	-1.4
1969	Cle-A	108	254	25	60	11	1	4	22	20	53	.236	.297	.335	74	-9	2	1	0	.978	9	*2-102/3-7	0.6
1970	Cle-A	29	33	3	6	2	0	1	2	3	9	.182	.250	.333	57	-2	0	0	0	.919	3	2-16/3-4,1-1	0.1
Total	6	325	785	67	182	33	4	14	65	73	172	.232	.307	.338	87	-13	6	6	-2	.982	-4	2-271/3-34,S-6,1-1	-0.6

■ SHORTY FULLER
Fuller, William Benjamin b: 10/10/1867, Cincinnati, Ohio d: 4/11/04, Cincinnati, Ohio BR/TR, 5'6", 157 lbs. Deb: 7/19/1888 F

YEAR	TM/L	G	AB	R	H	2B	3B	HR	RBI	BB	SO	AVG	OBP	SLG	PRO+	BR/A	SB	CS	SBR	FA	FR	G/POS	TPR
1888	Was-N	49	170	11	31	5	2	0	12	10	14	.182	.232	.235	52	-9	6			.845	-6	S-47/2-2	-1.3
1889	StL-a	140	517	91	117	18	6	0	51	52	56	.226	.303	.284	60	-31	38			**.913**	0	*S-140	-1.9
1890	StL-a	130	526	118	146	9	9	1	40	73		.278	.377	.335	96	-4	60			.870	-1	*S-130	0.3
1891	StL-a	137	586	107	127	15	7	2	63	67	28	.217	.301	.276	57	-38	42			.856	-10	*S-103,2-39	-3.5
1892	NY-N	141	508	74	115	11	4	1	48	52	24	.226	.298	.270	73	-16	37			.888	1	*S-141	-0.8
1893	NY-N	130	474	78	112	14	8	0	51	60	21	.236	.325	.300	66	-23	26			.911	11	*S-130	-0.5
1894	*NY-N	93	368	81	104	14	4	2	46	52	16	.283	.374	.359	78	-12	32			.884	-4	*S-89/O-2,3-2,2-1	-0.9
1895	NY-N	126	458	82	103	11	3	0	32	64	34	.225	.323	.262	53	-30	15			.913	34	*S-126	0.8
1896	NY-N	18	72	10	12	0	0	0	7	14	5	.167	.310	.167	28	-7	4			.874	1	S-18	-0.5
Total	9	964	3679	652	867	97	43	6	350	444	198	.236	.323	.290	67	-168	260			.891	26	S-924/2-42,3-2,O-2	-8.3

■ CHICK FULLIS
Fullis, Charles Philip b: 2/27/04, Girardville, Pa. d: 3/28/46, Ashland, Pa. BR/TR, 5'9", 170 lbs. Deb: 4/13/28

YEAR	TM/L	G	AB	R	H	2B	3B	HR	RBI	BB	SO	AVG	OBP	SLG	PRO+	BR/A	SB	CS	SBR	FA	FR	G/POS	TPR
1928	NY-N	11	1	5	0	0	0	0	0	1	1	.000	.500	.000	41	0	0			.000	0	H	0.0
1929	NY-N	86	274	67	79	11	1	7	29	30	26	.288	.365	.412	92	-3	7			.962	-12	O-78	-1.8
1930	NY-N	13	6	2	0	0	0	0	0	0	1	.000	.000	.000	-99	-2	1			.000	-1	/O-2	-0.3
1931	NY-N	89	302	61	99	15	2	3	28	23	13	.328	.383	.421	119	8	13			.988	-4	O-68/2-9	0.1
1932	NY-N	96	235	35	70	14	3	1	21	11	12	.298	.332	.396	97	-1	1			.990	-8	O-55/2-1	-1.2
1933	Phi-N	151	647	91	200	31	6	1	45	36	34	.309	.350	.380	96	-3	18			.977	8	*O-151/3-1	-0.3
1934	Phi-N	28	102	8	23	6	0	0	12	10	4	.225	.301	.284	51	-7	2			.956	-4	O-27	-1.2
	*StL-N	69	199	21	52	9	1	0	26	14	11	.261	.310	.317	64	-10	4			.969	-3	O-56	-1.4
	Yr	97	301	29	75	15	1	0	38	24	15	.249	.307	.306	59	-17	6			.966	-6	O-83	-2.6
1936	StL-N	47	89	15	25	6	1	0	6	7	11	.281	.333	.371	90	-1	0			1.000	-1	O-26	-0.3
Total	8	590	1855	305	548	92	14	12	167	132	113	.295	.347	.380	92	-19	46			.977	-23	O-463/2-10,3-1	-6.4

■ BRAD FULLMER
Fullmer, Bradley Ryan b: 1/17/75, Chatsworth, Cal. BL/TR, 6'1", 185 lbs. Deb: 9/2/97

YEAR	TM/L	G	AB	R	H	2B	3B	HR	RBI	BB	SO	AVG	OBP	SLG	PRO+	BR/A	SB	CS	SBR	FA	FR	G/POS	TPR
1997	Mon-N	19	40	4	12	2	0	3	8	2	7	.300	.349	.575	137	2	0	0	0	.982	-0	/1-8,O-2	0.1
1998	Mon-N	140	505	58	138	44	2	13	73	39	70	.273	.328	.446	102	0	6	6	-2	.985	-7	*1-137	-1.9
Total	2	159	545	62	150	46	2	16	81	41	77	.275	.329	.455	105	2	6	6	-2	.985	-7	1-145/O-2	-1.8

■ CHICK FULMER
Fulmer, Charles John b: 2/12/1851, Philadelphia, Pa. d: 2/15/40, Philadelphia, Pa. BR/TR, 6', 158 lbs. Deb: 8/23/1871 FU

YEAR	TM/L	G	AB	R	H	2B	3B	HR	RBI	BB	SO	AVG	OBP	SLG	PRO+	BR/A	SB	CS	SBR	FA	FR	G/POS	TPR
1871	Rok-n	16	63	11	17	1	3	0	3	5	1	.270	.324	.381	106	1	0	0	0	.770	2	S-16/1-1	0.2
1872	Mut-n	36	166	28	51	1	1	1	14	2	3	.307	.315	.343	109	3	1	1	-0	.752	-1	3-22,S-14	0.0
1873	Phi-n	49	236	42	66	11	3	1	38	2	3	.280	.286	.364	88	-4	3	1	0	.801	19	*S-49/P-2,C-1,1-1	0.9
1874	Phi-n	57	258	49	72	3	2	0	37	2	5	.279	.285	.306	86	-4	0	2	-1	.793	8	S-32,3-25	0.1
1875	Phi-n	69	295	50	65	6	1	0	24	0	6	.220	.220	.247	60	-12	10	4	1	.835	-1	*S-53,3-17	-1.3
1876	Lou-N	66	267	28	73	9	5	1	29	1	10	.273	.276	.356	93	-5				.861	-3	*S-66	-0.8

YEAR	TM/L	G	AB	R	H	2B	3B	HR	RBI	BB	SO	AVG	OBP	SLG	PRO+	BR/A	SB	CS	SBR	FA	FR	G/POS	TPR
1879	Buf-N	76	306	30	82	11	5	0	28	5	34	.268	.280	.337	100	-0				.905	17	*2-76	2.0
1880	Buf-N	11	44	3	7	0	0	0	1	2	4	.159	.196	.159	21	-3				.882	-2	2-11	-0.5
1882	Cin-a	79	324	54	91	13	4	0	27	10		.281	.302	.346	112	3				**.897**	-13	*S-79	-0.6
1883	Cin-a	92	362	52	92	13	5	5	52	12		.254	.278	.359	98	-2				.863	-2	*S-92	-0.1
1884	Cin-a	31	114	13	20	2	1	0	8	1		.175	.183	.211	27	-9				.786	-10	S-29/O-2,3-1	-1.8
	StL-a	1	5	0	0	0	0	0		0		.000	.000	.000	-97	-1				.778	-1	/2-1	-0.2
	Yr	32	119	13	20	2	1	0	8	1		.168	.175	.202	22	-10				.786	-11	S-29/O-2,3-1,2-1	-2.0
Total	5 n	227	1018	180	271	22	10	2	116	11	18	.266	.274	.313	85	-17	14	8	-1	.807	26	S-164/3-64,P-2,1C	-0.1
Total	6	356	1422	180	365	48	20	6	145	31	48	.257	.273	.331	92	-18				.867	-13	S-266/2-88,O-2,3-1	-2.0

■ CHRIS FULMER Fulmer, Christopher b: 7/4/1858, Tamaqua, Pa. d: 11/9/31, Tamaqua, Pa. BR/TR, 5′8″, 165 lbs. Deb: 8/4/1884

YEAR	TM/L	G	AB	R	H	2B	3B	HR	RBI	BB	SO	AVG	OBP	SLG	PRO+	BR/A	SB	CS	SBR	FA	FR	G/POS	TPR
1884	Was-U	48	181	39	50	9	0	0		11		.276	.318	.326	99	-5				.937	0	C-34,O-16/1-5	-0.2
1886	Bal-a	80	270	54	66	9	3	1	30	48		.244	.363	.311	115	8	29			.949	-4	C-68,O-12/P-1	0.9
1887	Bal-a	56	201	52	54	11	4	0	32	36		.269	.382	.363	115	6	35			.913	-11	C-48/O-8	0.0
1888	Bal-a	52	166	20	31	5	1	0	10	21		.187	.286	.229	67	-5	10			.903	-16	C-45/O-7	-1.6
1889	Bal-a	16	58	11	15	3	1	0	13	6	12	.259	.338	.345	93	-1	2			.938	-5	O-14/C-2	-0.5
Total	5	252	876	176	216	37	9	1	85	122	12	.247	.343	.313	102	3	76			.929	-36	C-197/O-57,1-5,P-1	-1.4

■ WASHINGTON FULMER Fulmer, Washington Fayette b: 6/15/1840, Philadelphia, Pa. d: 12/8/07, Philadelphia, Pa. Deb: 7/19/1875 F

YEAR	TM/L	G	AB	R	H	2B	3B	HR	RBI	BB	SO	AVG	OBP	SLG	PRO+	BR/A	SB	CS	SBR	FA	FR	G/POS	TPR
1875	Atl-n	1	4	1	2	0	0	0	1	0	0	.500	.500	.500	285	1	0	0	0	.750	0	/O-1	0.1

■ DAVE FULTZ Fultz, David Lewis b: 5/29/1875, Staunton, Va. d: 10/29/59, DeLand, Fla. BR/TR, 5′11″, 170 lbs. Deb: 7/1/1898

YEAR	TM/L	G	AB	R	H	2B	3B	HR	RBI	BB	SO	AVG	OBP	SLG	PRO+	BR/A	SB	CS	SBR	FA	FR	G/POS	TPR
1898	Phi-N	19	55	7	10	2	2	0	5	6		.182	.262	.291	61	-3	1			.871	-2	O-14/2-3,S-1	-0.5
1899	Phi-N	2	5	0	2	0	0	0	0	0		.400	.400	.400	124	0	1			.750	-1	/2-1,S-1	0.0
	Bal-N	57	210	31	62	3	2	0	18	13		.295	.342	.329	80	-6	17			.940	-7	O-31,3-20/2-2,1-1	-1.3
	Yr	59	215	31	64	3	2	0	18	13		.298	.343	.330	81	-6	18			.940	-7	O-31,3-20/2-3,S1	-1.3
1901	Phi-A	132	561	95	164	17	9	0	52	32		.292	.334	.355	87	-10	36			.935	-6	*O-106,2-18/S-9	-2.1
1902	Phi-A	129	506	**109**	153	20	5	1	49	62		.302	.381	.368	104	5	44			.961	-2	*O-114,2-16	-0.5
1903	NY-A	79	295	39	66	12	1	0	25	25		.224	.295	.271	67	-11	29			.933	-2	O-77/3-2	-1.9
1904	NY-A	97	339	39	93	17	4	2	32	24		.274	.324	.366	113	5	17			.976	3	O-90	0.3
1905	NY-A	129	422	49	98	13	3	0	42	39		.232	.308	.277	77	-10	44			.966	-6	*O-122	-2.4
Total	7	644	2393	369	648	84	26	3	223	201		.271	.332	.331	89	-31	189			.952	-22	O-554/2-40,3-22,S1	-8.4

■ MARK FUNDERBURK Funderburk, Mark Clifford b: 5/16/57, Charlotte, N.C. BR/TR, 6′4″, 226 lbs. Deb: 9/4/81

YEAR	TM/L	G	AB	R	H	2B	3B	HR	RBI	BB	SO	AVG	OBP	SLG	PRO+	BR/A	SB	CS	SBR	FA	FR	G/POS	TPR
1981	Min-A	8	15	2	3	1	0	0	2	2	1	.200	.294	.267	59	-1	0	0	0	1.000	-1	/O-6,D-1	-0.2
1985	Min-A	23	70	7	22	7	1	2	13	5	12	.314	.360	.529	132	3	0	1	-1	1.000	-1	D-15/O-5,1-1	0.1
Total	2	31	85	9	25	8	1	2	15	7	13	.294	.348	.482	120	2	0	1	-1	1.000	-2	/D-16,O-11,1-1	-0.1

■ LIZ FUNK Funk, Elias Calvin b: 10/28/04, LaCygne, Kan. d: 1/16/68, Norman, Okla. BL/TL, 5′8.5″, 160 lbs. Deb: 4/26/29

YEAR	TM/L	G	AB	R	H	2B	3B	HR	RBI	BB	SO	AVG	OBP	SLG	PRO+	BR/A	SB	CS	SBR	FA	FR	G/POS	TPR
1929	NY-A	1	0	0	0	0	0	0	0	0	0	—	—	—	—	0	0	0	0	.000	0	R	0.0
1930	Det-A	140	527	74	145	26	11	4	65	29	39	.275	.319	.389	77	-19	12	6	0	.965	8	*O-129	-1.9
1932	Chi-A	122	440	59	114	21	5	2	40	43	19	.259	.325	.343	78	-14	17	15	-4	.979	7	*O-120	-1.7
1933	Chi-A	10	9	1	2	0	0	0	0	1	0	.222	.300	.222	42	-1	0	0	0	.000	-1	/O-2	-0.2
Total	4	273	976	134	261	47	16	6	105	73	58	.267	.322	.367	77	-34	29	21	-4	.972	14	O-251	-3.8

■ CARL FURILLO Furillo, Carl Anthony "Skoonj" or "The Reading Rifle"
b: 3/8/22, Stony Creek Mills, Pa. d: 1/21/89, Stony Creek Mills, Pa. BR/TR, 6′, 190 lbs. Deb: 4/16/46

YEAR	TM/L	G	AB	R	H	2B	3B	HR	RBI	BB	SO	AVG	OBP	SLG	PRO+	BR/A	SB	CS	SBR	FA	FR	G/POS	TPR
1946	Bro-N	117	335	29	95	18	6	3	35	31	20	.284	.346	.400	110	4	6			.984	9	*O-112	0.9
1947	*Bro-N	124	437	61	129	24	7	8	88	34	24	.295	.347	.437	103	1	7			.977	2	*O-121	-0.2
1948	Bro-N	108	364	55	108	20	4	4	44	43	32	.297	.374	.407	108	5	6			.983	9	*O-104	0.8
1949	*Bro-N	142	549	95	177	27	10	18	106	37	29	.322	.368	.506	127	19	4			.965	5	*O-142	1.7
1950	Bro-N	153	620	99	189	30	6	18	106	41	40	.305	.353	.460	110	8	8			.971	3	*O-153	0.4
1951	Bro-N	158	667	93	197	32	4	16	91	43	33	.295	.344	.427	104	3	8	7	-2	.986	16	*O-157	1.2
1952	*Bro-N☆	134	425	52	105	18	1	8	59	31	33	.247	.304	.351	80	-12	1	4	-2	.988	-1	*O-131	-2.0
1953	*Bro-N☆	132	479	82	165	38	6	21	92	34	32	**.344**	.393	.580	146	31	1	1	-0	.988	4	*O-131	2.9
1954	Bro-N	150	547	56	161	23	1	19	96	49	35	.294	.358	.444	104	3	2	4	-2	.972	4	*O-149	0.0
1955	*Bro-N	140	523	83	164	24	3	26	95	43	43	.314	.373	.520	130	22	4	5	-2	.981	-3	*O-140	1.1
1956	*Bro-N	149	523	66	151	30	0	21	83	57	41	.289	.360	.467	111	9	1	1	-0	.984	-9	*O-146	-0.9
1957	Bro-N	119	395	61	121	17	4	12	66	29	33	.306	.361	.461	108	5	0	2	-1	.988	-5	*O-107	-0.8
1958	LA-N	122	411	54	119	19	3	18	83	35	28	.290	.348	.482	113	7	0	2	-1	.975	-8	*O-119	-0.8
1959	*LA-N	50	93	8	27	4	0	0	13	7	11	.290	.340	.333	75	-3	0	0	0	.920	-5	O-25	-0.9
1960	LA-N	8	10	1	2	0	1	0	1	0	2	.200	.200	.400	56	-1	0	0	0	1.000	-0	/O-2	-0.1
Total	15	1806	6378	895	1910	324	56	192	1058	514	436	.299	.356	.458	112	102	48	26		.979	22	*O-1739	3.3

■ EDDIE FUSSELBACK Fusselback, Edward L. b: 7/17/1856, Philadelphia, Pa. d: 4/14/26, Philadelphia, Pa. 5′6″, 156 lbs. Deb: 5/3/1882

YEAR	TM/L	G	AB	R	H	2B	3B	HR	RBI	BB	SO	AVG	OBP	SLG	PRO+	BR/A	SB	CS	SBR	FA	FR	G/POS	TPR
1882	StL-a	35	136	13	31	2	0	0		5		.228	.255	.243	66	-5				.853	2	C-19,O-15/P-4	-0.1
1884	Bal-U	68	303	60	86	16	3	1		3		.284	.291	.366	89	-14				.912	19	C-54/3-6,S-5,O-4	0.9
1885	Phi-a	5	19	2	6	1	0	0	2	0		.316	.316	.368	109	0				.911	1	/C-5	0.1
1888	Lou-a	1	4	0	1	0	0	0	1	0		.250	.250	.250	62	-0	0			1.000	0	/O-1	0.0
Total	4	109	462	75	124	19	3	1	3	8		.268	.281	.329	84	-19	0			.901	22	/C-78,O-20,3-6,SP	0.9

■ LES FUSSELMAN Fusselman, Lester Leroy b: 3/7/21, Pryor, Okla. d: 5/21/70, Cleveland, Ohio BR/TR, 6′1″, 195 lbs. Deb: 4/16/52

YEAR	TM/L	G	AB	R	H	2B	3B	HR	RBI	BB	SO	AVG	OBP	SLG	PRO+	BR/A	SB	CS	SBR	FA	FR	G/POS	TPR
1952	StL-N	32	63	5	10	3	0	1	3	0	9	.159	.159	.254	13	-8	0	0	0	.991	3	C-32	-0.4
1953	StL-N	11	8	1	2	1	0	0	0	0	0	.250	.250	.375	60	-0	0	0	0	1.000	2	C-11	0.1
Total	2	43	71	6	12	4	0	1	3	0	9	.169	.169	.268	18	-8	0	0	0	.992	5	/C-43	-0.3

■ GABE GABLER Gabler, William Louis b: 8/4/30, St.Louis, Mo. BL/TR, 6′1″, 190 lbs. Deb: 9/16/58

YEAR	TM/L	G	AB	R	H	2B	3B	HR	RBI	BB	SO	AVG	OBP	SLG	PRO+	BR/A	SB	CS	SBR	FA	FR	G/POS	TPR
1958	Chi-N	3	3	0	0	0	0	0	0	0	3	.000	.000	.000	-99	-1	0	0	0	.000	0	H	-0.1

■ LEN GABRIELSON Gabrielson, Leonard Gary b: 2/14/40, Oakland, Cal. BL/TR, 6′4″, 210 lbs. Deb: 9/9/60 F

YEAR	TM/L	G	AB	R	H	2B	3B	HR	RBI	BB	SO	AVG	OBP	SLG	PRO+	BR/A	SB	CS	SBR	FA	FR	G/POS	TPR
1960	Mil-N	4	3	1	0	0	0	0	0	1	0	.000	.250	.000	-27	-1	0	0	0	.000	-0	/O-1	-0.1
1963	Mil-N	46	120	14	26	5	0	3	15	8	23	.217	.266	.333	72	-4	1	1	-0	1.000	-3	O-22,1-16/3-3	-1.0
1964	Mil-N	24	38	0	7	2	0	0	1	1	8	.184	.205	.237	24	-4	1	0	0	1.000	-1	1-12/O-2	-0.5
	Chi-N	89	272	22	67	11	2	5	23	19	37	.246	.298	.357	80	-7	9	4	0	.984	-1	O-68/1-8	-1.2
	Yr	113	310	22	74	13	2	5	24	20	45	.239	.287	.342	74	-11	10	4	1	.984	-2	O-70,1-20	-1.7
1965	Chi-N	28	48	4	12	0	0	3	5	7	16	.250	.345	.438	116	1	0	2	-1	1.000	-3	O-14/1-1	-0.4
	SF-N	88	269	36	81	6	5	4	26	26	48	.301	.367	.405	114	6	4	0	1	.975	1	O-77/1-5	0.4
	Yr	116	317	40	93	6	5	7	31	33	64	.293	.364	.410	114	7	4	2	0	.977	-2	O-91/1-6	0.0
1966	SF-N	94	240	27	52	7	0	4	16	21	51	.217	.280	.296	58	-13	0	1	-1	.948	-9	O-67/1-6	-2.8
1967	Cal-A	11	12	2	1	0	0	0	2	2	4	.083	.214	.083	-9	-2	0	0	0	.000	-0	/O-1	-0.2
	LA-N	90	238	20	62	10	3	7	29	15	41	.261	.307	.416	114	3	3	1	0	.980	-4	O-68	-0.3
1968	LA-N	108	304	38	82	16	1	10	35	32	47	.270	.339	.428	140	14	1	1	-0	.976	-3	O-86	0.7
1969	LA-N	83	178	13	48	5	1	1	18	12	25	.270	.316	.326	86	-4	1	2	-1	.981	-7	O-47/1-2	-1.4
1970	LA-N	43	42	1	8	2	0	0	6	1	15	.190	.209	.238	20	-5	0	0	0	1.000	-0	/O-2,1-1	-0.5
Total	9	708	1764	178	446	64	12	37	176	145	315	.253	.311	.366	94	-15	20	12	-1	.977	-31	O-455/1-51,3-3	-7.3

■ LEN GABRIELSON Gabrielson, Leonard Hilbourne b: 9/8/15, Oakland, Cal. BL/TL, 6′3″, 210 lbs. Deb: 4/21/39 F

YEAR	TM/L	G	AB	R	H	2B	3B	HR	RBI	BB	SO	AVG	OBP	SLG	PRO+	BR/A	SB	CS	SBR	FA	FR	G/POS	TPR
1939	Phi-N	5	18	3	4	0	0	0	1	2	3	.222	.300	.222	43	-1	0			.977	2	/1-5	0.0

■ EDDIE GAEDEL Gaedel, Edward Carl (b: Edward Carl Gaedele) b: 6/8/25, Chicago, Ill. d: 6/18/61, Chicago, Ill. BR/TL, 3′7″, 65 lbs. Deb: 8/19/51

YEAR	TM/L	G	AB	R	H	2B	3B	HR	RBI	BB	SO	AVG	OBP	SLG	PRO+	BR/A	SB	CS	SBR	FA	FR	G/POS	TPR
1951	StL-A	1	0	0	0	0	0	0	0	1	0	—	1.000	—	182	0	0	0	0	.000	0	H	0.0

YEAR	TM/L	G	AB	R	H	2B	3B	HR	RBI	BB	SO	AVG	OBP	SLG	PRO+	BR/A	SB	CS	SBR	FA	FR	G/POS	TPR
■ GARY GAETTI	Gaetti, Gary Joseph b: 8/19/58, Centralia, Ill. BR/TR, 6′, 200 lbs. Deb: 9/20/81																						
1981	Min-A	9	26	4	5	0	0	2	3	0	6	.192	.192	.423	68	-1	0	0	0	1.000	1	/3-8,D-1	0.0
1982	Min-A	145	508	59	117	25	4	25	84	37	107	.230	.286	.443	94	-6	0	4	-2	.963	-3	*3-142/S-2,D-1	-1.5
1983	Min-A	157	584	81	143	30	3	21	78	54	121	.245	.313	.414	95	-5	7	1	2	.967	13	*3-154/S-3,D-1	0.7
1984	Min-A	162	588	55	154	29	4	5	65	44	81	.262	.318	.350	81	-15	11	5	0	.960	15	*3-154/O-8,S-2	-0.1
1985	Min-A	160	560	71	138	31	0	20	63	37	89	.246	.301	.409	87	-11	13	5	1	.962	17	*3-156/O-4,1-1,D-1	0.4
1986	Min-A	157	596	91	171	34	1	34	108	52	108	.287	.350	.518	129	23	14	15	-5	.956	19	*3-156/S-2,2-1,O-1	3.3
1987	*Min-A	154	584	95	150	36	2	31	109	37	92	.257	.304	.485	101	-1	10	7	-1	.973	-4	*3-150/D-2	-0.8
1988	Min-A★	133	468	66	141	29	2	28	88	36	85	.301	.358	.551	146	27	7	4	-0	.977	-6	*3-115/S-2,D-5	2.1
1989	Min-A★	130	498	63	125	11	4	19	75	25	87	.251	.291	.404	88	-10	6	2	1	.973	11	*3-125/1-2,D-3	0.3
1990	Min-A	154	577	61	132	27	5	16	85	36	101	.229	.278	.376	76	-20	6	1	1	.959	14	*3-151/1-2,S-2	-0.4
1991	Cal-A	152	586	58	144	22	1	18	66	33	104	.246	.295	.379	85	-13	5	5	-2	.965	**25**	*3-152	1.1
1992	Cal-A	130	456	41	103	13	2	12	48	21	79	.226	.269	.342	70	-19	3	1	0	.927	13	3-67,1-44,D-17	-1.0
1993	Cal-A	20	50	3	9	2	0	0	4	5	12	.180	.255	.220	28	-5	1	0	0	.857	2	/3-7,1-6,D-5	-0.3
	KC-A	82	281	37	72	18	1	14	46	16	75	.256	.315	.477	103	0	0	3	-2	.974	5	3-72,1-18/D-1	0.3
	Yr	102	331	40	81	20	1	14	50	21	87	.245	.306	.438	92	-5	1	3	-2	.970	7	3-79,1-24/D-6	0.0
1994	KC-A	90	327	53	94	15	3	12	57	19	63	.287	.330	.462	97	-2	0	2	-1	**.982**	3	3-85/1-9	-0.1
1995	KC-A	137	514	76	134	27	0	35	96	47	91	.261	.332	.518	115	9	3	3	-1	.954	-5	*3-123,1-11/D-6	0.2
1996	*StL-N	141	522	71	143	27	4	23	80	35	97	.274	.329	.473	110	6	2	2	-1	.970	-16	*3-133,1-14	-1.3
1997	StL-N	148	502	63	126	24	1	17	69	36	88	.251	.309	.404	86	-12	7	3	0	**.978**	4	*3-132,1-20/P-1	-0.7
1998	StL-N	91	306	39	81	23	1	11	43	31	39	.265	.342	.454	105	2	1	1	-0	.985	-4	3-83/1-3,P-1,2-1,O	-0.1
	*Chi-N	37	128	21	41	11	0	8	27	12	23	.320	.400	.594	149	9	0	0	0	.979	-0	3-36	0.9
	Yr	128	434	60	122	34	1	19	70	43	62	.281	.359	.495	119	12	1	1	-0	**.983**	-5	*3-119/1-3,P-1,2O	0.8
Total	18	2389	8661	1108	2223	434	38	351	1294	613	1548	.257	.313	.437	98	-43	96	64	-10	.965	102	*3-2201,1-130/DOSP2	3.0
■ FABIAN GAFFKE	Gaffke, Fabian Sebastian b: 8/5/13, Milwaukee, Wis. d: 2/8/92, Milwaukee, Wis. BR/TR, 5′10″, 185 lbs. Deb: 9/9/36																						
1936	Bos-A	15	55	5	7	2	0	1	3	4	5	.127	.200	.218	3	-9	0	0	0	1.000	-1	O-15	-1.0
1937	Bos-A	54	184	32	53	10	4	6	34	15	25	.288	.342	.484	102	-0	1	2	-1	.965	-4	O-50	-0.7
1938	Bos-A	15	10	2	1	0	0	0	1	3	2	.100	.308	.100	6	-1	0	0	0	.000	-1	/O-2,C-1	-0.2
1939	Bos-A	1	1	0	0	0	0	0	1	0	0	.000	.000	.000	-96	-0	0	0	0	.000	0	H	0.0
1941	Cle-A	4	4	0	1	0	0	0	0	2	2	.250	.500	.250	109	0	0	0	0	1.000	-1	/O-2	0.0
1942	Cle-A	40	67	4	11	2	0	0	3	6	13	.164	.243	.194	25	-7	1	0	0	1.000	-2	O-16	-0.9
Total	6	129	321	43	73	14	4	7	42	30	47	.227	.297	.361	67	-17	2	2	-1	.979	-9	/O-85,C-1	-2.8
■ PHIL GAGLIANO	Gagliano, Philip Joseph b: 12/27/41, Memphis, Tenn. BR/TR, 6′1″, 185 lbs. Deb: 4/16/63 F																						
1963	StL-N	10	5	1	2	0	0	0	1	1	1	.400	.500	.400	149	0	0	0	0	1.000	2	/2-3,3-1	0.2
1964	StL-N	40	58	5	15	4	0	1	9	3	10	.259	.295	.379	81	-1	0	1	-1	.918	1	2-12/O-2,1-1,3-1	0.0
1965	StL-N	122	363	46	87	14	2	8	53	40	45	.240	.317	.355	81	-9	2	1	0	.960	-12	2-57,O-25,3-19	-1.8
1966	StL-N	90	213	23	54	8	2	2	15	24	29	.254	.332	.338	86	-3	2	1	0	.982	-4	3-41/1-8,O-5,2-1	-0.9
1967	*StL-N	73	217	20	48	7	0	2	21	19	26	.221	.287	.281	64	-10	0	0	0	.972	-13	2-27,3-25/1-4,S-2	-2.4
1968	*StL-N	53	105	13	24	4	2	0	13	7	12	.229	.283	.305	77	-3	0	0	0	.982	-3	2-17,3-10/O-5	-0.6
1969	StL-N	62	128	7	29	2	0	1	10	14	12	.227	.303	.266	60	-6	0	0	0	.989	-2	2-20/1-9,3-9,O-2	-0.8
1970	StL-N	18	32	0	6	0	0	0	2	1	3	.188	.212	.188	8	-4	0	1	-1	1.000	-1	/3-6,1-3,2-2	-0.6
	Chi-N	26	40	5	6	0	0	0	5	5	5	.150	.244	.150	7	-5	0	0	0	1.000	1	2-16/1-1,3-1	-0.4
	Yr	44	72	5	12	0	0	0	7	6	8	.167	.231	.167	8	-9	0	1	-1	.980	-0	2-18/3-7,1-4	-1.0
1971	Bos-A	47	68	11	22	5	0	0	13	11	5	.324	.418	.397	123	3	0	0	0	1.000	-5	O-11/2-7,3-4	-0.2
1972	Bos-A	52	82	9	21	4	1	0	10	10	13	.256	.337	.329	94	-0	1	0	0	.962	2	O-12/3-5,2-4,1-2	0.2
1973	*Cin-N	63	69	8	20	2	0	0	7	13	16	.290	.402	.319	108	2	0	0	0	.824	-1	/3-7,2-4,1-1,O-1	0.0
1974	Cin-N	46	31	2	2	0	0	0	0	15	7	.065	.370	.065	27	-2	0	0	0	1.000	0	/2-2,1-1,3-1	-0.2
Total	12	702	1411	150	336	50	7	14	159	163	184	.238	.319	.313	77	-40	5	4	-1	.969	-34	2-172,3-130/O1S	-7.5
■ RALPH GAGLIANO	Gagliano, Ralph Michael b: 10/8/46, Memphis, Tenn. BL/TR, 5′11″, 170 lbs. Deb: 9/21/65 F																						
1965	Cle-A	1	0	0	0	0	0	0	0	0	0	—	—	—	—	0	0	0	0	.000	0	R	0.0
■ GREG GAGNE	Gagne, Gregory Carpenter b: 11/12/61, Fall River, Mass. BR/TR, 5′11″, 172 lbs. Deb: 6/5/83																						
1983	Min-A	10	27	2	3	1	0	0	3	0	6	.111	.111	.148	-28	-5	0	0	0	.923	-5	S-10	-1.0
1984	Min-A	2	1	0	0	0	0	0	0	0	0	.000	.000	.000	-96	-0	0	0	0	.000	0	/H	0.0
1985	Min-A	114	293	37	66	15	3	2	23	20	57	.225	.282	.317	60	-16	10	4	1	.968	4	*S-106/D-5	-0.3
1986	Min-A	156	472	63	118	22	6	12	54	30	108	.250	.303	.398	87	-9	12	10	-2	.959	-16	*S-155/2-4	-1.3
1987	*Min-A	137	437	68	116	28	7	10	40	25	84	.265	.311	.430	91	-7	6	6	-2	.970	17	*S-136/O-4,2-1,D-1	1.8
1988	Min-A	149	461	70	109	20	6	14	48	27	110	.236	.289	.397	87	-9	15	7	0	.970	-15	*S-146/O-2,2-1,3-1	-1.3
1989	Min-A	149	460	69	125	29	7	9	48	17	80	.272	.301	.424	96	-4	11	4	1	.971	-4	*S-146/O-1	0.3
1990	Min-A	138	388	38	91	22	3	7	38	24	76	.235	.281	.361	73	-15	8	8	-2	.976	2	*S-135/O-1,D-2	-0.6
1991	*Min-A	139	408	52	108	23	3	8	42	26	72	.265	.314	.395	90	-6	11	9	-2	.984	4	*S-137/D-1	0.5
1992	Min-A	146	439	53	108	23	0	7	39	19	83	.246	.280	.346	72	-17	6	7	-2	.973	21	*S-141	1.1
1993	KC-A	159	540	66	151	32	3	10	57	33	93	.280	.321	.406	89	-10	10	12	-4	**.986**	5	*S-159	0.4
1994	KC-A	107	375	39	97	23	3	7	51	27	79	.259	.315	.392	78	-13	10	17	-7	.977	8	*S-106	-0.3
1995	KC-A	120	430	58	110	25	4	6	49	38	60	.256	.319	.374	79	-14	3	5	-2	.969	7	*S-118/D-2	0.1
1996	*LA-N	128	428	48	109	13	2	10	55	50	93	.255	.335	.364	92	-5	4	2	0	.966	13	*S-127	1.8
1997	LA-N	144	514	49	129	20	3	9	57	31	120	.251	.299	.354	76	-20	2	5	-2	.971	-28	*S-143	-3.7
Total	15	1798	5673	712	1440	296	50	111	604	367	1121	.254	.304	.382	82	-149	108	96	-25	.972	13	*S-1765/D-11,O23	-2.5
■ ED GAGNIER	Gagnier, Edward James b: 4/16/1883, Paris, France d: 9/13/46, Detroit, Mich. BR/TR, 5′9″, 170 lbs. Deb: 4/14/14																						
1914	Bro-F	94	337	22	63	12	2	0	25	13	24	.187	.219	.234	24	-42	8			.933	-1	S-88/3-6	-3.7
1915	Bro-F	20	50	8	13	1	0	0	4	10	5	.260	.393	.280	92	-1	2			.930	2	S-13/2-6	0.3
	Buf-F	1	2	0	0	0	0	0	0	0	0	.000	.000	.000	-98	-1	0			.800	-0	/2-1	-0.1
	Yr	21	52	8	13	1	0	0	4	10	5	.250	.381	.269	85	-1	2			.930	2	S-13/2-7	0.2
Total	2	115	389	30	76	13	2	0	29	23	29	.195	.244	.239	33	-43	10			.933	2	S-101/2-7,3-6	-3.5
■ CHICK GAGNON	Gagnon, Harold Dennis b: 9/27/1897, Millbury, Mass. d: 4/30/70, Wilmington, Del. BR/TR, 5′7.5″, 158 lbs. Deb: 6/27/22																						
1922	Det-A	10	4	2	1	0	0	0	0	0	2	.250	.250	.250	32	-0	0	0	0	.000	-1	/S-1,3-1	-0.1
1924	Was-A	4	5	1	1	0	0	0	1	0	0	.200	.200	.200	3	-1	0	0	0	1.000	1	/S-2	0.0
Total	2	14	9	3	2	0	0	0	1	0	2	.222	.222	.222	16	-1	0	0	0	1.000	0	/S-3,3-1	-0.1
■ DEL GAINER	Gainer, Dellos Clinton "Sheriff" b: 11/10/1886, Montrose, W.Va. d: 1/29/47, Elkins, W.Va. BR/TR, 6′, 180 lbs. Deb: 10/2/09																						
1909	Det-A	2	5	0	1	0	0	0	0	0		.200	.200	.200	25	-0	0			.929	-0	/1-2	-0.1
1911	Det-A	70	248	32	75	11	4	2	25	20		.302	.366	.403	109	3	10			.975	-4	1-69	-0.1
1912	Det-A	52	179	28	43	5	6	0	20	18		.240	.320	.335	90	-2	14			.986	-3	1-50/O-1	-0.6
1913	Det-A	105	363	47	97	16	8	2	25	30	45	.267	.333	.372	108	3	10			.988	-5	*1-103	-0.3
1914	Det-A	1	0	0	0	0	0	0	0	0	0	—	—	—	—	0	0			1.000	-0	/1-1	0.0
	Bos-A	38	84	11	20	9	2	2	13	8	14	.238	.312	.464	133	3	2	2	-1	.981	-3	1-18,2-11/O-1	-0.1
	Yr	39	84	11	20	9	2	2	13	8	14	.238	.312	.464	133	3	2	2	-1	.982	-3	1-19,2-11/O-1	-0.1
1915	*Bos-A	82	200	30	59	5	8	1	29	21	31	.295	.371	.415	139	9	7	2	1	.988	0	1-56/O-6	1.0
1916	*Bos-A	56	142	14	36	6	0	3	18	10	24	.254	.303	.359	98	-1	5			.997	1	1-48/2-2	-0.1
1917	Bos-A	52	172	28	53	10	2	2	19	15	21	.308	.374	.424	145	9	1			.989	-1	1-50	0.7
1919	Bos-A	47	118	9	28	6	2	0	13	13	15	.237	.318	.322	85	-2	5			.978	-3	1-21,O-18	-0.7
1922	StL-N	43	97	19	26	7	4	2	23	14	6	.268	.360	.485	122	3	0	2	-1	.979	-1	1-26,O-10	-0.1
Total	10	548	1608	218	438	75	36	14	185	149	156	.272	.342	.390	113	24	54	6		.985	-19	1-444/O-36,2-13	-0.4
■ JAY GAINER	Gainer, Johnathan Keith b: 10/8/66, Panama City, Fla. BL/TL, 6′, 190 lbs. Deb: 5/14/93																						
1993	Col-N	23	41	4	7	0	0	3	6	4	12	.171	.244	.390	57	-3	1	1	-0	.982	-1	/1-7	-0.5

■ JOE GAINES Gaines, Arnesta Joe b: 11/22/36, Bryan, Tex. BR/TR, 6'1", 190 lbs. Deb: 6/29/60

YEAR	TM/L	G	AB	R	H	2B	3B	HR	RBI	BB	SO	AVG	OBP	SLG	PRO+	BR/A	SB	CS	SBR	FA	FR	G/POS	TPR
1960	Cin-N	11	15	2	3	0	0	0	1	0	1	.200	.200	.200	10	-2	0	0	0	1.000	-1	/O-3	-0.3
1961	Cin-N	5	3	2	0	0	0	0	0	2	1	.000	.400	.000	18	-0	0	0	0	.500	-1	/O-3	-0.2
1962	Cin-N	64	52	12	12	3	0	1	7	8	16	.231	.333	.346	80	-1	0	0	0	1.000	-3	O-13	-0.4
1963	Bal-A	66	126	24	36	4	1	6	20	20	39	.286	.384	.476	145	8	2	1	0	.945	-6	O-39	0.1
1964	Bal-A	16	26	2	4	0	0	1	2	3	7	.154	.241	.269	42	-2	0	0	0	.846	0	/O-5	-0.2
	Hou-N	89	307	37	78	9	7	7	34	27	69	.254	.318	.397	106	2	8	2	1	.957	-2	O-81	-0.3
1965	Hou-N	100	229	21	52	8	1	6	31	18	59	.227	.292	.349	86	-5	4	1	1	.913	-8	O-65	-1.5
1966	Hou-N	11	13	4	1	1	0	0	0	3	5	.077	.250	.154	17	-1	0	0	0	.500	-1	/O-3	-0.3
Total	7	362	771	104	186	25	9	21	95	81	197	.241	.317	.379	99	-2	14	4	2	.934	-21	O-212	-3.1

■ TY GAINEY Gainey, Telmanch b: 12/25/60, Cheraw, S.C. BL/TR, 6'1", 190 lbs. Deb: 4/24/85

YEAR	TM/L	G	AB	R	H	2B	3B	HR	RBI	BB	SO	AVG	OBP	SLG	PRO+	BR/A	SB	CS	SBR	FA	FR	G/POS	TPR
1985	Hou-N	13	37	5	6	0	0	0	0	2	9	.162	.244	.162	16	-4	0	0	0	.913	-0	/O-9	-0.5
1986	Hou-N	26	50	6	15	3	1	1	6	6	19	.300	.375	.460	133	2	3	1	0	1.000	-3	O-19	-0.1
1987	Hou-N	18	24	1	3	0	0	0	1	2	9	.125	.192	.125	-14	-4	1	0	0	1.000	-0	/O-6	-0.4
Total	3	57	111	12	24	3	1	1	7	10	37	.216	.293	.288	62	-6	4	1	1	.968	-3	/O-34	-1.0

■ AUGIE GALAN Galan, August John b: 5/25/12, Berkeley, Cal. d: 12/28/93, Fairfield, Cal. BB/TR, 6', 175 lbs. Deb: 4/29/34 C

YEAR	TM/L	G	AB	R	H	2B	3B	HR	RBI	BB	SO	AVG	OBP	SLG	PRO+	BR/A	SB	CS	SBR	FA	FR	G/POS	TPR
1934	Chi-N	66	192	31	50	6	2	5	22	16	15	.260	.317	.391	90	-3	4			.961	-9	2-43/3-3,S-1	-0.9
1935	*Chi-N	154	646	**133**	203	41	11	12	79	87	53	.314	.399	.467	131	31	**22**			.978	7	*O-154	3.1
1936	Chi-N★	145	575	74	152	26	4	8	81	67	50	.264	.344	.365	89	-8	16			.987	5	*O-145	-0.8
1937	Chi-N	147	611	104	154	24	10	18	78	79	48	.252	.339	.412	99	-1	**23**			.980	13	*O-140/2-8,S-2	0.7
1938	*Chi-N	110	395	52	113	16	9	6	69	49	17	.286	.368	.418	112	8	8			.987	2	*O-103	0.7
1939	Chi-N	148	549	104	167	36	8	6	71	75	26	.304	.392	.432	119	17	8			.970	-2	*O-145	0.9
1940	Chi-N	68	209	33	48	14	2	3	22	37	23	.230	.346	.359	96	-0	9			.984	0	O-54/2-2	-0.3
1941	Chi-N	65	120	18	25	3	0	1	13	22	10	.208	.331	.258	70	-4	0			.959	-5	O-31	-1.1
	*Bro-N	17	27	3	7	3	0	0	4	3	1	.259	.333	.370	94	-0	0			1.000	-0	/O-6	-0.1
	Yr	82	147	21	32	6	0	1	17	25	11	.218	.331	.279	74	-4	0			.967	-5	O-37	-1.2
1942	Bro-N	69	209	24	55	16	0	0	22	24	12	.263	.339	.340	97	-0	2			.990	-5	O-55/1-4,2-3	-0.8
1943	Bro-N★	139	495	83	142	26	3	9	67	**103**	39	.287	.412	.406	136	28	6			.981	16	*O-124,1-13	3.9
1944	Bro-N★	151	547	96	174	43	9	12	93	**101**	23	.318	.426	.495	162	49	4			.988	-2	*O-147/2-2	4.0
1945	Bro-N	152	576	114	177	36	7	9	92	114	27	.307	.423	.441	142	38	13			.988	-8	1-66,O-49,3-40	2.3
1946	Bro-N	99	274	53	85	22	5	3	38	68	21	.310	.451	.460	157	25	8			.935	-10	O-60,3-19,1-12	1.3
1947	Cin-N	124	392	60	123	18	2	6	61	94	19	.314	**.449**	.416	132	24	0			.988	-4	*O-118	1.4
1948	Cin-N	54	77	18	22	3	2	2	16	26	4	.286	.471	.455	157	8	0			.967	-2	O-18	0.5
1949	NY-N	22	17	0	1	1	0	0	2	5	3	.059	.273	.118	8	-2	0			1.000	-1	/1-3,O-1	-0.3
	Phi-A	12	26	4	8	2	0	0	0	9	2	.308	.486	.385	136	2	0	0	0	1.000	-1	/O-9	0.1
Total	16	1742	5937	1004	1706	336	74	100	830	979	393	.287	.390	.419	122	212	123	0		.981	-4	*O-1359/1-98,32S	14.6

■ ANDRES GALARRAGA Galarraga, Andres Jose (b: Andres Jose Padovani (Galarraga)) b: 6/18/61, Caracas, Venez. BR/TR, 6'3", 235 lbs. Deb: 8/23/85

YEAR	TM/L	G	AB	R	H	2B	3B	HR	RBI	BB	SO	AVG	OBP	SLG	PRO+	BR/A	SB	CS	SBR	FA	FR	G/POS	TPR
1985	Mon-N	24	75	9	14	1	0	2	4	3	18	.187	.228	.280	44	-6	1	2	-1	.995	4	1-23	-0.5
1986	Mon-N	105	321	39	87	13	0	10	42	30	79	.271	.339	.405	105	2	6	5	-1	.995	-8	*1-102	-1.4
1987	Mon-N	147	551	72	168	40	3	13	90	41	127	.305	.364	.459	113	10	7	10	-4	.993	0	*1-146	-0.4
1988	Mon-N★	157	609	99	**184**	**42**	8	29	92	39	153	.302	.354	.540	147	34	13	4	2	.991	-4	*1-156	2.0
1989	Mon-N	152	572	76	147	30	1	23	85	48	158	.257	.329	.434	115	10	12	5	1	.992	-2	*1-147	-0.4
1990	Mon-N	155	579	65	148	29	0	20	87	40	169	.256	.308	.409	99	-2	10	1	2	.993	-5	*1-154	-1.7
1991	Mon-N	107	375	34	82	13	2	9	33	23	86	.219	.268	.336	70	-16	5	6	-2	.991	2	*1-105	-2.4
1992	StL-N	95	325	38	79	14	2	10	39	11	69	.243	.285	.391	92	-5	5	4	-1	.991	-1	1-90	-1.3
1993	Col-N★	120	470	71	174	35	4	22	98	24	73	**.370**	.408	.602	143	27	2	4	-2	.990	7	*1-119	2.2
1994	Col-N	103	417	77	133	21	0	31	85	19	93	.319	.360	.592	123	12	8	3	1	.992	-5	*1-103	-0.2
1995	*Col-N	143	554	89	155	29	3	31	106	32	146	.280	.334	.511	92	-11	12	2	2	.991	6	*1-142	-1.6
1996	Col-N	159	626	119	190	39	3	**47**	**150**	40	157	.304	.362	.601	120	13	18	8	1	.992	-2	*1-159/3-1	-0.4
1997	Col-N★	154	600	120	191	31	3	41	**140**	54	141	.318	.390	.585	123	17	15	8	-0	.991	-2	*1-154	0.0
1998	*Atl-N★	153	555	103	169	27	1	44	121	63	146	.305	.400	.595	150	42	7	6	-2	.992	-8	*1-149/D-2	1.9
Total	14	1774	6629	1011	1921	364	30	332	1172	467	1615	.290	.349	.504	117	128	121	68	-5	.992	-18	*1-1749/D-2,3-1	-4.2

■ MILT GALATZER Galatzer, Milton b: 5/4/07, Chicago, Ill. d: 1/29/76, San Francisco, Cal BL/TL, 5'10", 168 lbs. Deb: 6/25/33

YEAR	TM/L	G	AB	R	H	2B	3B	HR	RBI	BB	SO	AVG	OBP	SLG	PRO+	BR/A	SB	CS	SBR	FA	FR	G/POS	TPR
1933	Cle-A	57	160	19	38	2	1	1	17	23	21	.237	.333	.281	61	-8	2	3	-1	.975	-0	O-40/1-5	-1.2
1934	Cle-A	49	196	29	53	10	2	0	15	21	8	.270	.344	.342	76	-7	3	2	-0	.980	3	O-49	-0.6
1935	Cle-A	93	259	45	78	9	3	0	19	35	8	.301	.389	.359	93	-1	4	5	-2	.934	-8	O-81	-1.3
1936	Cle-A	49	97	12	23	4	1	0	6	13	8	.237	.333	.299	57	-6	1	2	-1	.964	-8	O-42/P-1,1-1	-1.4
1939	Cin-N	3	5	0	0	0	0	0	0	0	1	.000	.000	.000	-99	-1	0			1.000	-0	/1-2	-0.2
Total	5	251	717	105	192	25	7	1	57	92	46	.268	.354	.326	75	-24	10	12		.959	-14	O-212/1-8,P-1	-4.7

■ AL GALLAGHER Gallagher, Alan Mitchell Edward George Patrick Henry b: 10/19/45, San Francisco, Cal. BR/TR, 6', 180 lbs. Deb: 4/7/70

YEAR	TM/L	G	AB	R	H	2B	3B	HR	RBI	BB	SO	AVG	OBP	SLG	PRO+	BR/A	SB	CS	SBR	FA	FR	G/POS	TPR
1970	SF-N	109	282	31	75	15	2	4	28	30	37	.266	.337	.376	92	-3	2	1	0	.971	1	3-91	-0.3
1971	*SF-N	136	429	47	119	18	5	5	57	40	57	.277	.342	.378	105	3	2	1	0	.951	-16	*3-128	-1.5
1972	SF-N	82	233	19	52	3	1	2	18	33	39	.223	.322	.270	69	-8	2	1	0	.974	-4	3-69	-1.4
1973	SF-N	5	9	1	2	0	0	0	1	0	0	.222	.300	.222	45	-1	0	0	0	.833	-1	/3-5	-0.2
	Cal-A	110	311	16	85	6	1	0	26	35	31	.273	.349	.299	91	-3	1	3	-2	.961	4	3-98/2-1,S-1	0.0
Total	4	442	1264	114	333	42	9	11	130	138	164	.263	.338	.337	91	-12	7	6	-2	.961	-15	3-391/S-1,2-1	-3.4

■ SHORTY GALLAGHER Gallagher, Charles William b: 4/30/1872, Detroit, Mich. d: 6/23/24, Detroit, Mich. Deb: 8/13/01

YEAR	TM/L	G	AB	R	H	2B	3B	HR	RBI	BB	SO	AVG	OBP	SLG	PRO+	BR/A	SB	CS	SBR	FA	FR	G/POS	TPR
1901	Cle-A	2	4	0	0	0	0	0	0	0		.000	.000	.000	-99	-1	0			.667	-1	/O-2	-0.2

■ DAVE GALLAGHER Gallagher, David Thomas b: 9/20/60, Trenton, N.J. BR/TR, 6', 184 lbs. Deb: 4/12/87

YEAR	TM/L	G	AB	R	H	2B	3B	HR	RBI	BB	SO	AVG	OBP	SLG	PRO+	BR/A	SB	CS	SBR	FA	FR	G/POS	TPR
1987	Cle-A	15	36	2	4	1	1	0	1	2	5	.111	.158	.194	-7	-6	2	0	1	.972	1	O-14	-0.4
1988	Chi-A	101	347	59	105	15	3	5	31	29	40	.303	.356	.406	113	6	5	4	-1	1.000	-1	O-95/D-2	0.1
1989	Chi-A	161	601	74	160	22	2	1	46	46	79	.266	.320	.314	82	-14	5	6	-2	.993	1	*O-160/D-1	-2.0
1990	Chi-A	45	75	5	21	3	1	0	5	3	9	.280	.316	.347	87	-1	0	1	-1	.981	-6	O-37/D-4	-0.9
	Bal-A	23	51	7	11	1	0	0	2	4	3	.216	.273	.235	45	-4	1	1	-0	.980	2	O-20/D-2	-0.2
	Yr	68	126	12	32	4	1	0	7	7	12	.254	.299	.302	70	-5	1	2	-1	.980	-4	O-57/D-6	-1.1
1991	Cal-A	90	270	32	79	17	0	1	30	24	43	.293	.355	.367	100	1	2	4	-2	1.000	1	O-87/D-2	-0.2
1992	NY-N	98	175	20	42	11	1	1	21	19	16	.240	.318	.331	85	-3	4	5	-2	.982	-8	O-76	-1.5
1993	NY-N	99	201	34	55	12	2	6	28	20	18	.274	.339	.443	109	2	1	1	-0	1.000	-7	O-72/1-9	-0.6
1994	Atl-N	89	152	27	34	5	0	2	14	22	17	.224	.326	.296	62	-8	0	2	-1	.989	-9	O-77/1-1	-1.9
1995	Phi-N	62	157	12	50	12	0	1	12	16	20	.318	.382	.414	109	2	0	0	0	1.000	-4	O-55	-0.3
	Cal-A	11	16	1	3	1	0	0	0	2	1	.188	.278	.250	39	-1	0	0	0	1.000	0	/O-6,D-1	-0.1
Total	9	794	2081	273	564	100	10	17	190	187	251	.271	.333	.353	90	-25	20	24	-8	.993	-30	O-699/D-12,1-10	-8.0

■ JIM GALLAGHER Gallagher, James E. b: Findlay, Ohio d: 3/29/1894, Scranton, Pa. Deb: 9/4/1886

YEAR	TM/L	G	AB	R	H	2B	3B	HR	RBI	BB	SO	AVG	OBP	SLG	PRO+	BR/A	SB	CS	SBR	FA	FR	G/POS	TPR
1886	Was-N	1	5	1	1	0	0	0	0	0	2	.200	.200	.200	23	-0	0			.875	1	/S-1	0.0

■ JOHN GALLAGHER Gallagher, John Carroll b: 2/18/1892, Pittsburgh, Pa. d: 3/30/52, Norfolk, Va. BR/TR, 5'10.5", 156 lbs. Deb: 8/20/15

YEAR	TM/L	G	AB	R	H	2B	3B	HR	RBI	BB	SO	AVG	OBP	SLG	PRO+	BR/A	SB	CS	SBR	FA	FR	G/POS	TPR
1915	Bal-F	40	126	11	25	4	0	0	4	5	22	.198	.229	.230	28	-14	1			.945	-2	2-37/S-5,3-1	-1.7

■ JACKIE GALLAGHER Gallagher, John Laurence b: 1/28/02, Providence, R.I. d: 9/10/84, Gladwyne, Pa. BL/TR, 5'10", 175 lbs. Deb: 8/24/23

YEAR	TM/L	G	AB	R	H	2B	3B	HR	RBI	BB	SO	AVG	OBP	SLG	PRO+	BR/A	SB	CS	SBR	FA	FR	G/POS	TPR
1923	Cle-A	1	1	0	1	0	0	0	0	0	0	1.000	1.000	1.000	428	0	0	0	0	.000	-1	/O-1	0.0

■ JOE GALLAGHER Gallagher, Joseph Emmett "Muscles" b: 3/7/14, Buffalo, N.Y. d: 2/25/98, Houston, Tex. BR/TR, 6'2", 210 lbs. Deb: 4/20/39

YEAR	TM/L	G	AB	R	H	2B	3B	HR	RBI	BB	SO	AVG	OBP	SLG	PRO+	BR/A	SB	CS	SBR	FA	FR	G/POS	TPR
1939	NY-A	14	41	8	10	0	1	2	9	3	8	.244	.311	.439	91	-1	1	0	0	1.000	-1	O-12	-0.2

YEAR	TM/L	G	AB	R	H	2B	3B	HR	RBI	BB	SO	AVG	OBP	SLG	PRO+	BR/A	SB	CS	SBR	FA	FR	G/POS	TPR
	StL-A	71	266	41	75	17	2	9	40	17	42	.282	.327	.462	98	-2	0	1	-1	.944	2	O-67	-0.3
	Yr	85	307	49	85	17	3	11	49	20	50	.277	.325	.459	97	-3	1	1	-0	.950	1	O-79	-0.5
1940	StL-A	23	70	14	19	3	1	2	8	4	12	.271	.311	.429	88	-2	2	0	1	.966	-1	O-15	-0.3
	Bro-N	57	110	10	29	6	1	3	16	2	14	.264	.283	.418	86	-3	1			.941	-2	O-20	-0.6
Total	2	165	487	73	133	26	5	16	73	26	76	.273	.314	.446	93	-7	4	1		.950	-3	O-114	-1.4
■ GIL GALLAGHER	Gallagher, Lawrence Kirby b: 9/5/1896, Washington, D.C. d: 1/6/57, Washington, D.C. BB/TR, 5′8″, 155 lbs. Deb: 9/13/22																						
1922	Bos-N	7	22	1	1	1	0	0	2	1	7	.045	.087	.091	-57	-5	0	0	0	.893	-2	/S-6	-0.6
■ BOB GALLAGHER	Gallagher, Robert Collins b: 7/7/48, Newton, Mass. BL/TL, 6′3″, 185 lbs. Deb: 5/17/72 F																						
1972	Bos-A	7	5	0	0	0	0	0	0	0	3	.000	.000	.000	-95	-1	0	0	0	.000	0	H	-0.1
1973	Hou-N	71	148	16	39	3	1	2	10	3	27	.264	.278	.338	70	-6	0	1	-1	1.000	-2	O-42/1-1	-1.1
1974	Hou-N	102	87	13	15	2	0	0	3	12	23	.172	.280	.195	36	-7	1	0	0	.978	-21	O-62/1-4	-3.0
1975	NY-N	33	15	5	2	1	0	0	0	1	3	.133	.188	.200	8	-2	0	0	0	.900	-5	O-16	-0.7
Total	4	213	255	34	56	6	1	2	13	16	56	.220	.268	.275	52	-17	1	1	-0	.985	-27	O-120/1-5	-4.9
■ WILLIAM GALLAGHER	Gallagher, William Howard b: 2/4/1874, Boston, Mass. d: 3/11/50, Worcester, Mass. Deb: 8/19/1896																						
1896	Phi-N	14	49	9	15	2	0	0	6	10	0	.306	.433	.347	108	1	0			.894	-4	S-14	-0.2
■ BILL GALLAGHER	Gallagher, William John b: Philadelphia, Pa. TL , Deb: 5/2/1883																						
1883	Bal-a	16	61	9	10	3	1	0		3		.164	.203	.246	43	-4				.824	-2	/O-9,P-7,S-4	-0.3
	Phi-N	2	8	1	0	0	0	0	0	0	4	.000	.000	.000	-99	-2				1.000	-0	/O-2	-0.2
1884	Phi-U	3	11	1	1	0	0	0		0		.091	.091	.091	-48	-2				.800	0	/P-3	0.0
Total	2	21	80	11	11	3	1	0	0	3	4	.138	.169	.200	16	-8				.850	-2	/O-11,P-10,S-4	-0.5
■ STAN GALLE	Galle, Stanley Joseph (b: Stanley Joseph Galazewski) b: 2/7/19, Milwaukee, Wis. BR/TR, 5′7″, 165 lbs. Deb: 4/14/42																						
1942	Was-A	13	18	3	2	0	0	0	1	1	0	.111	.158	.111	-24	-3	0	0	0	.857	-1	/3-3	-0.4
■ MIKE GALLEGO	Gallego, Michael Anthony b: 10/31/60, Whittier, Cal. BR/TR, 5′8″, 160 lbs. Deb: 4/11/85																						
1985	Oak-A	76	77	13	16	5	1	1	9	12	14	.208	.322	.338	87	-1	1	1	-0	.991	12	2-42,S-21,3-12	1.2
1986	Oak-A	20	37	2	10	2	0	0	4	1	6	.270	.289	.324	72	-1	0	2	-1	.986	9	2-19/3-2,S-1	0.6
1987	Oak-A	72	124	18	31	6	0	2	14	12	21	.250	.321	.347	83	-3	0	1	-1	.968	17	2-31,3-24,S-17	1.4
1988	*Oak-A	129	277	38	58	8	0	2	20	34	53	.209	.298	.260	60	-14	2	3	-1	.993	4	2-83,S-42,3-16	-0.8
1989	*Oak-A	133	357	45	90	14	2	3	30	35	43	.252	.329	.328	89	-4	7	5	-1	.967	18	S-94,2-41/3-3,D-1	2.0
1990	*Oak-A	140	389	36	80	13	2	3	34	35	50	.206	.278	.272	57	-22	5	5	-2	.990	14	2-83,S-38,3-27,/OD	-0.6
1991	Oak-A	159	482	67	119	15	4	12	49	67	84	.247	.345	.369	103	4	6	9	-4	.989	-16	*2-135,S-55	-1.1
1992	NY-A	53	173	24	44	7	1	3	14	20	22	.254	.345	.358	98	0	0	1	-1	.990	1	2-40,S-14	0.3
1993	NY-A	119	403	63	114	20	1	10	54	50	65	.283	.368	.412	113	8	3	2	-0	.976	17	S-55,2-52,3-27,/D-1	2.9
1994	NY-A	89	306	39	73	17	1	6	41	38	46	.239	.330	.359	81	-8	0	1	-1	.970	20	S-72,2-26	1.6
1995	Oak-A	43	120	11	28	0	0	0	8	9	24	.233	.292	.233	41	-10	0	1	-1	.960	0	2-18,S-14,3-12	-0.8
1996	*StL-N	51	143	12	30	2	0	0	4	12	31	.210	.276	.224	34	-13	0	0	0	.985	7	2-43/3-7,S-1	-0.4
1997	StL-N	27	43	6	7	2	0	0	1	1	6	.163	.182	.209	2	-6	0	0	0	.962	5	2-11,S-10/3-7	-0.1
Total	13	1111	2931	374	700	111	12	42	282	326	465	.239	.322	.328	81	-72	24	31	-11	.986	107	2-624,S-434,3/DO	6.2
■ JIM GALLIGAN	Galligan, James M. b: 1862, Easton, Pa. d: 7/17/01, New York, N.Y. 5′10″, 160 lbs. Deb: 9/2/1889																						
1889	Lou-a	31	120	6	20	0	2	0	7	6	17	.167	.213	.200	18	-13	1			.915	2	O-31	-1.0
■ CHICK GALLOWAY	Galloway, Clarence Edward b: 8/4/1896, Clinton, S.C. d: 11/7/69, Clinton, S.C. BR/TR, 5′8″, 160 lbs. Deb: 9/9/19																						
1919	Phi-A	17	63	2	9	0	0	0	4	1	8	.143	.156	.143	-16	-10	0			.969	1	S-17	-0.8
1920	Phi-A	98	298	28	60	9	3	0	18	22	22	.201	.259	.252	35	-28	2	2	-1	.928	4	S-84/2-4,3-3	-1.7
1921	Phi-A	131	465	42	123	28	5	3	47	29	43	.265	.310	.366	72	-21	12	7	-1	.922	-22	*S-110,3-20/2-1	-3.1
1922	Phi-A	155	571	83	185	26	9	6	69	39	39	.324	.368	.433	105	4	10	19	-8	.952	1	*S-155	1.3
1923	Phi-A	134	504	64	140	18	9	2	62	37	30	.278	.327	.361	80	-15	12	10	-2	.944	2	*S-134	-0.3
1924	Phi-A	129	464	41	128	16	4	2	48	23	23	.276	.311	.341	67	-23	11	12	-4	.952	2	*S-129	-1.0
1925	Phi-A	149	481	52	116	11	4	3	71	59	28	.241	.324	.299	55	-32	16	9	-1	.954	-3	*S-148	-1.9
1926	Phi-A	133	408	37	98	13	6	0	49	31	20	.240	.295	.301	53	-28	8	7	-2	.935	-13	*S-133	-3.0
1927	Phi-A	77	181	25	48	10	4	0	22	18	9	.265	.332	.365	76	-6	1	3	-2	.946	5	S-61/3-7	0.2
1928	Det-A	53	148	17	39	5	2	1	17	15	3	.264	.331	.345	77	-5	7	2	1	.914	-4	S-22,3-21/1-1,0-1	-0.4
Total	10	1076	3583	391	946	136	46	17	407	274	225	.264	.317	.342	69	-165	79	71		.943	-28	S-993/3-51,2-5,01	-10.7
■ JIM GALLOWAY	Galloway, James Cato "Bad News" b: 9/16/1887, Iredell, Tex. d: 5/3/50, Fort Worth, Tex. BB/TR, 6′3″, 187 lbs. Deb: 8/24/12																						
1912	StL-N	21	54	4	10	2	0	0	4	5	8	.185	.254	.222	32	-5	2			.971	1	2-16/S-1	-0.4
■ JIM GALVIN	Galvin, James Joseph b: 8/11/07, Somerville, Mass. d: 9/30/69, Marietta, Ga. BR/TR, 5′11.5″, 180 lbs. Deb: 9/27/30																						
1930	Bos-A	2	2	0	0	0	0	0	0	0	0	.000	.000	.000	-99	-1	0	0	0	.000	0	H	-0.1
■ JOHN GALVIN	Galvin, John S. b: Brooklyn, N.Y. d: 4/20/04, Brooklyn, N.Y. Deb: 5/7/1872																						
1872	Atl-n	1	4	0	0	0	0	0	0	0	0	.000	.000	.000	-85	-1	0	0	0	.200	-2	/2-1	-0.2
■ JOHN GAMBLE	Gamble, John Robert b: 2/10/48, Reno, Nev. BR/TR, 5′10″, 165 lbs. Deb: 9/7/72																						
1972	Det-A	6	3	0	0	0	0	0	0	0	0	.000	.000	.000	-97	-1	0	0	0	1.000	1	/S-1	0.1
1973	Det-A	7	0	1	0	0	0	0	0	0	0	—	—	—	—	0	0	0	0	.000	0	R	0.0
Total	2	13	3	1	0	0	0	0	0	0	0	.000	.000	.000	-97	-1	0	0	0	1.000	1	/S-1	0.1
■ LEE GAMBLE	Gamble, Lee Jesse b: 6/28/10, Renovo, Pa. d: 10/5/94, Punxsutawney, Pa. BL/TR, 6′1″, 170 lbs. Deb: 9/15/35																						
1935	Cin-N	2	4	2	2	1	0	0	2	1	0	.500	.600	.750	269	1	1			1.000	-0	/O-2	0.1
1938	Cin-N	53	75	13	24	3	1	0	5	0	6	.320	.320	.387	96	-1	0			1.000	-0	/O-9	-0.1
1939	*Cin-N	72	221	24	59	7	2	0	14	9	14	.267	.296	.317	64	-11	5			.989	-3	O-56	-1.6
1940	Cin-N	38	42	12	6	1	0	0	0	0	1	.143	.143	.167	-15	-6	0			1.000	0	O-10	-0.7
Total	4	165	342	51	91	12	3	0	21	10	21	.266	.287	.319	64	-17	6			.993	-4	/O-77	-2.3
■ OSCAR GAMBLE	Gamble, Oscar Charles b: 12/20/49, Ramer, Ala. BL/TR, 5′11″, 165 lbs. Deb: 8/27/69																						
1969	Chi-N	24	71	6	16	1	1	1	5	10	12	.225	.321	.310	69	-3	0	2	-1	.913	-2	O-24	-0.8
1970	Phi-N	88	275	31	72	12	4	1	19	27	37	.262	.330	.345	84	-6	5	4	-1	.956	1	O-74	-1.0
1971	Phi-N	92	280	24	62	11	1	6	23	21	35	.221	.278	.332	72	-11	5	2	0	.970	-4	O-80	-1.9
1972	Phi-N	74	135	17	32	5	2	1	13	19	16	.237	.335	.326	86	-2	0	1	-1	1.000	-1	O-35/1-1	-0.5
1973	Cle-A	113	390	56	104	11	3	20	44	34	37	.267	.330	.464	120	9	3	4	-2	.971	-1	D-70,O-37	0.3
1974	Cle-A	135	454	74	132	16	4	19	59	48	51	.291	.365	.469	140	23	5	6	-2	1.000	-1	*D-115,O-13	1.7
1975	Cle-A	121	348	60	91	16	3	15	45	53	39	.261	.362	.454	130	14	11	5	0	.987	1	O-82,D-29	1.2
1976	*NY-A	110	340	43	79	13	1	17	57	38	38	.232	.317	.426	117	7	5	3	-0	.981	-0	*O-104/D-1	0.3
1977	Chi-A	137	408	75	121	22	2	31	83	54	54	.297	.387	.588	162	35	1	2	-1	.987	-5	D-79,O-49	2.4
1978	SD-N	126	375	46	103	15	3	7	47	51	45	.275	.370	.387	121	12	1	2	-1	.979	-0	*O-107	0.7
1979	Tex-A	64	161	27	54	6	0	8	32	37	15	.335	.462	.522	167	17	2	1	0	1.000	1	D-37,O-21	1.6
	NY-A	36	113	21	44	4	1	11	32	13	13	.389	.452	.735	219	19	0	0	0	.943	0	O-27/D-6	1.7
	Yr	100	274	48	98	10	1	19	64	50	28	.358	.458	.609	188	36	2	1	0	.969	2	O-48,D-43	3.3
1980	*NY-A	78	194	40	54	10	2	14	50	28	21	.278	.381	.567	159	16	2	0	1	1.000	-6	O-49,D-20	0.8
1981	*NY-A	80	189	24	45	8	0	10	27	35	23	.238	.360	.439	131	8	0	2	-1	1.000	-2	O-43,D-33	0.3
1982	NY-A	108	316	49	86	21	2	18	57	58	47	.272	.392	.522	151	23	6	3	0	1.000	5	D-74,O-29	2.4
1983	NY-A	74	180	26	47	10	2	7	26	25	23	.261	.361	.456	128	7	0	0	0	.942	-0	O-32,D-21	0.5
1984	NY-A	54	125	17	23	2	0	10	27	25	18	.184	.320	.440	112	2	1	0	0	1.000	-1	D-28,O-12	0.1
1985	Chi-A	70	148	20	30	5	0	4	20	34	22	.203	.355	.318	83	-2	0	0	0	.000	0	D-48	-0.3
Total	17	1584	4502	656	1195	188	31	200	666	610	546	.265	.358	.454	127	168	47	37	-8	.977	-15	O-818,D-561/1-1	9.5

YEAR	TM/L	G	AB	R	H	2B	3B	HR	RBI	BB	SO	AVG	OBP	SLG	PRO+	BR/A	SB	CS	SBR	FA	FR	G/POS	TPR
■ DAFF GAMMONS	Gammons, John Ashley b: 3/17/1876, New Bedford, Mass. d: 9/24/63, E.Greenwich, R.I. BR/TR, 5'11", 170 lbs. Deb: 4/23/01																						
1901	Bos-N	28	93	10	18	0	1	0	10	3		.194	.242	.215	30	-8	5			.880	-3	O-23/2-2,3-1	-1.2
■ CHICK GANDIL	Gandil, Arnold b: 1/19/1887, St.Paul, Minn. d: 12/13/70, Calistoga, Cal. BR/TR, 6'1.5", 190 lbs. Deb: 4/14/10																						
1910	Chi-A	77	275	21	53	7	3	2	21	24		.193	.267	.262	69	-10	12			.989	7	1-74/O-2	-0.4
1912	Was-A	117	443	59	135	20	15	2	81	27		.305	.350	.431	122	11	21			**.990**	3	*1-117	1.1
1913	Was-A	148	550	61	175	25	8	1	72	36	33	.318	.363	.398	120	13	22			.990	8	*1-145	2.1
1914	Was-A	145	526	48	136	24	10	3	75	44	44	.259	.324	.359	101	-0	30	19	-2	.991	24	*1-145	1.9
1915	Was-A	136	485	53	141	20	15	2	64	29	33	.291	.340	.406	121	10	20	13	-2	.986	-1	*1-134	0.4
1916	Cle-A	146	533	51	138	26	9	0	72	36	48	.259	.312	.341	91	-7	13			**.995**	8	*1-145	-0.5
1917	*Chi-A	149	553	53	151	9	7	0	57	30	36	.273	.316	.315	91	-7	16			**.995**	-6	*1-149	-2.0
1918	Chi-A	114	439	49	119	18	4	0	55	27	19	.271	.319	.330	95	-4	9			.992	-3	*1-114	-1.2
1919	*Chi-A	115	441	54	128	24	7	1	60	20	20	.290	.325	.383	98	-2	10			**.997**	-4	*1-115	-1.1
Total	9	1147	4245	449	1176	173	78	11	557	273	233	.277	.327	.362	103	3	153	32		.992	36	*1-1138/O-2	0.3
■ BOB GANDY	Gandy, Robert Brinkley "String" b: 8/25/1893, Jacksonville, Fla. d: 6/19/45, Jacksonville, Fla BL/TR, 6'3", 180 lbs. Deb: 10/5/16																						
1916	Phi-N	1	2	0	0	0	0	0	0	0	1	.000	.000	.000	-97	-0	0			1.000	0	/O-1	0.0
■ BOB GANLEY	Ganley, Robert Stephen b: 4/23/1875, Lowell, Mass. d: 10/9/45, Lowell, Mass. BL/TL, 5'7", 156 lbs. Deb: 9/1/05																						
1905	Pit-N	32	127	12	40	1	2	0	7	8		.315	.356	.354	109	1	3			1.000	-2	O-32	-0.3
1906	Pit-N	137	511	63	132	7	6	0	31	41		.258	.316	.295	87	-8	19			.965	-2	*O-134	-1.8
1907	Was-A	154	605	73	167	10	5	1	35	54		.276	.337	.314	117	13	40			.940	9	*O-154	1.7
1908	Was-A	150	549	61	131	19	9	1	36	45		.239	.299	.311	107	4	30			.964	4	*O-150	0.2
1909	Was-A	19	63	5	16	3	0	0	5	1		.254	.266	.302	83	-2	4			1.000	-3	O-17	-0.6
	Phi-A	80	274	32	54	4	2	0	9	28		.197	.272	.226	56	-13	16			.980	8	O-77	-1.0
	Yr	99	337	37	70	7	2	0	14	29		.208	.270	.240	61	-15	20			.982	4	O-94	-1.6
Total	5	572	2129	246	540	44	24	2	123	177		.254	.313	.300	97	-4	112			.962	13	O-564	-1.8
■ BILL GANNON	Gannon, William G. b: 1876, New Haven, Conn. d: 4/26/27, Fort Worth, Tex. 5'9", 170 lbs. Deb: 9/9/01																						
1901	Chi-N	15	61	2	9	0	0	0	0	1		.148	.161	.148	-11	-8	5			1.000	-1	O-15	-1.1
■ RON GANT	Gant, Ronald Edwin b: 3/2/65, Victoria, Tex. BR/TR, 6', 192 lbs. Deb: 9/6/87																						
1987	Atl-N	21	83	9	22	4	0	2	9	1	11	.265	.274	.386	69	-4	4	2	0	.972	-0	2-20	-0.3
1988	Atl-N	146	563	85	146	28	8	19	60	46	118	.259	.319	.439	110	6	19	10	-0	.963	-1	*2-122,3-22	1.0
1989	Atl-N	75	260	26	46	8	3	9	25	20	63	.177	.238	.335	61	-14	9	6	-1	.887	3	3-53,O-14	-1.3
1990	Atl-N	152	575	107	174	34	3	32	84	50	86	.303	.359	.539	136	26	33	16	0	.978	7	*O-146	3.0
1991	*Atl-N	154	561	101	141	35	3	32	105	71	104	.251	.341	.496	125	18	34	15	1	.983	8	*O-148	2.4
1992	*Atl-N★	153	544	74	141	22	6	17	80	45	101	.259	.324	.415	102	1	32	10	4	.986	-4	*O-147	-0.2
1993	*Atl-N	157	606	113	166	27	4	36	117	67	117	.274	.348	.510	125	20	26	9	2	.962	-3	*O-155	1.6
1995	*Cin-N★	119	410	79	113	19	4	29	88	74	108	.276	.390	.554	146	28	23	8	2	.985	4	*O-117	3.0
1996	*StL-N	122	419	74	103	14	2	30	82	73	98	.246	.362	.504	126	16	13	4	2	.978	6	*O-116	2.1
1997	StL-N	139	502	68	115	21	4	17	62	58	162	.229	.310	.388	82	-14	14	6	1	.977	7	*O-128/D-1	-0.9
1998	StL-N	121	383	60	92	17	1	26	67	51	92	.240	.333	.493	112	6	8	0	2	.971	-2	*O-104	0.6
Total	11	1359	4906	796	1259	229	38	249	779	556	1060	.257	.336	.471	114	89	215	86	13	.978	24	*O-1075,2-142/3D	11.0
■ JOE GANTENBEIN	Gantenbein, Joseph Steven "Sep" b: 8/25/16, San Francisco, Cal d: 8/2/93, Novato, Cal. BL/TR, 5'9", 168 lbs. Deb: 4/20/39																						
1939	Phi-A	111	348	47	101	14	4	4	36	32	22	.290	.353	.388	91	-4	1	5	-3	.948	-34	2-76,3-14/S-5	-3.4
1940	Phi-A	75	197	21	47	6	2	4	23	11	21	.239	.282	.350	64	-11	1	0	0	.930	-8	3-45/1-6,S-3,O-1	-1.7
Total	2	186	545	68	148	20	6	8	59	43	43	.272	.328	.374	82	-15	2	5	-2	.934	-42	/2-76,3-59,S-8,1O	-5.1
■ JIM GANTNER	Gantner, James Elmer b: 1/5/53, Fond Du Lac, Wis. BL/TR, 6', 180 lbs. Deb: 9/3/76 C																						
1976	Mil-A	26	69	6	17	1	0	0	7	6	11	.246	.316	.261	71	-2	1	0	0	.982	-3	3-24/D-2	-0.6
1977	Mil-A	14	47	4	14	1	0	1	2	2	5	.298	.327	.383	93	-1	2	1	0	.902	1	3-14	0.1
1978	Mil-A	43	97	14	21	1	0	1	8	5	10	.216	.269	.258	49	-7	2	0	1	.980	5	2-21,3-15/1-1,S-1	0.0
1979	Mil-A	70	208	29	59	10	3	2	22	16	17	.284	.341	.389	96	-1	3	5	-2	.952	4	3-42,2-22/S-3,P-1	0.2
1980	Mil-A	132	415	47	117	21	3	4	40	30	29	.282	.332	.376	97	-2	11	10	-3	.938	-1	3-69,2-66/S-1	-0.2
1981	*Mil-A	107	352	35	94	14	1	2	33	29	29	.267	.328	.330	95	-2	3	6	-3	.984	16	*2-107	1.8
1982	*Mil-A	132	447	48	132	17	2	4	43	26	36	.295	.337	.369	100	-0	6	3	0	.982	9	*2-131	1.5
1983	Mil-A	161	603	85	170	23	8	11	74	38	46	.282	.331	.401	109	6	5	6	-2	.984	10	*2-158	2.1
1984	Mil-A	153	613	61	173	27	1	3	56	30	51	.282	.319	.344	87	-11	6	5	-1	.985	10	*2-153	0.3
1985	Mil-A	143	523	63	133	15	4	5	44	33	42	.254	.302	.327	73	-19	11	8	-2	.988	1	*2-124,3-24/S-1	-1.5
1986	Mil-A	139	497	58	136	25	1	7	38	26	50	.274	.318	.370	84	-11	13	7	-0	.985	-12	*2-135/3-3,S-1,D-1	-1.8
1987	Mil-A	81	265	37	72	14	0	4	30	19	22	.272	.332	.370	84	-6	6	2	1	.984	5	2-57,3-38/D-1	0.2
1988	Mil-A	155	539	67	149	28	2	0	47	34	50	.276	.323	.336	84	-11	20	8	1	.986	-8	*2-154/3-1	-1.2
1989	Mil-A	116	409	51	112	18	3	0	34	21	33	.274	.325	.333	86	-7	20	6	2	.987	9	*2-114/D-2	0.8
1990	Mil-A	88	323	36	85	8	5	0	25	29	19	.263	.328	.319	82	-7	18	3	4	.982	-7	2-80/3-9	-0.9
1991	Mil-A	140	526	63	149	27	4	2	47	27	34	.283	.322	.361	91	-7	4	6	-2	.976	4	3-90,2-59	-0.4
1992	Mil-A	101	256	22	63	12	1	1	18	12	17	.246	.280	.313	67	-12	6	2	1	.994	7	2-68,3-31/1-2,D-2	-0.3
Total	17	1801	6189	726	1696	262	38	47	568	383	501	.274	.322	.351	88	-100	137	78	-6	.985	50	*2-1449,3-360/DS1P	0.1
■ CHARLIE GANZEL	Ganzel, Charles William b: 6/18/1862, Waterford, Wis. d: 4/7/14, Quincy, Mass. BR/TR, 6', 161 lbs. Deb: 9/27/1884 F																						
1884	StP-U	7	23	2	5	0	0	0		0		.217	.217	.217	59	-3				.956	-2	/C-6,O-1	-0.4
1885	Phi-N	34	125	15	21	3	1	0	6	4	13	.168	.194	.208	31	-9				.888	0	C-33/O-1	-0.6
1886	Phi-N	1	3	0	0	0	0	0	0	0	1	.000	.000	.000	-99	-1	0			.600	-1	/C-1	-0.1
	Det-N	57	213	28	58	7	2	1	31	7	22	.272	.295	.338	90	-3	5			.911	3	C-45/O-7,1-5	0.4
	Yr	58	216	28	58	7	2	1	31	7	23	.269	.291	.333	87	-4	5			.903	3	C-46/O-7,1-5	0.3
1887	*Det-N	57	227	40	59	6	5	0	20	8	2	.260	.288	.330	69	-10	3			.913	9	C-51/O-4,1-2,3-1	0.3
1888	Det-N	95	386	45	96	13	5	1	46	14	15	.249	.277	.316	89	-5	12			.900	-1	2-49,C-28/3-9,OS1	-0.1
1889	Bos-N	73	275	30	73	3	5	1	43	15	11	.265	.308	.324	72	-11	13			.927	5	C-39,O-26/1-7,S3	-0.3
1890	Bos-N	38	163	21	44	7	3	0	24	5	6	.270	.300	.350	83	-5	1			.958	3	C-22,O-15/S-3,2-1	0.1
1891	Bos-N	70	263	33	68	18	5	1	29	12	13	.259	.304	.376	87	-6	7			.956	4	C-59,O-13	0.2
1892	*Bos-N	54	198	25	53	9	3	0	25	18	12	.268	.332	.343	96	-2	7			.933	-6	C-51/O-2,1-1	-0.4
1893	Bos-N	73	281	50	75	10	2	1	48	22	9	.267	.325	.327	68	-14	6			.952	-2	C-40,O-23,1-10	-1.1
1894	Bos-N	70	266	51	74	7	6	3	56	19	6	.278	.326	.383	65	-17	1			.897	-5	C-59/1-7,O-3,S-2,2	-1.3
1895	Bos-N	80	277	38	73	2	5	1	52	24	6	.264	.325	.318	61	-17	1			.962	19	C-76/S-2,1-2	0.7
1896	Bos-N	47	179	28	47	2	0	1	18	9	5	.263	.305	.291	54	-12	2			.989	6	C-41/1-3,S-2	-0.2
1897	Bos-N	30	105	15	28	4	3	0	14	4		.267	.300	.362	70	-5	2			.942	2	C-27/1-2	0.0
Total	14	786	2984	421	774	91	45	10	412	161	121	.259	.301	.330	73	-120	60			.934	35	C-578,O-100/21S3	-2.8
■ BABE GANZEL	Ganzel, Foster Pirie b: 5/22/01, Malden, Mass. d: 2/6/78, Jacksonville, Fla. BR/TR, 5'10.5", 172 lbs. Deb: 9/19/27 F																						
1927	Was-A	13	48	7	21	4	2	1	13	7	3	.438	.509	.667	206	8	0	0	0	.944	0	O-13	0.7
1928	Was-A	10	26	2	2	1	0	0	4	1	4	.077	.111	.115	-41	-5	0	0	0	1.000	-1	/O-7	-0.7
Total	2	23	74	9	23	5	2	1	17	8	7	.311	.378	.473	122	2	0	0	0	.957	-1	/O-20	0.0
■ JOHN GANZEL	Ganzel, John Henry b: 4/7/1874, Kalamazoo, Mich. d: 1/14/59, Orlando, Fla. BR/TR, 6'0.5", 195 lbs. Deb: 4/21/1898 FM																						
1898	Pit-N	15	45	5	6	0	0	0	2	4		.133	.220	.133	2	-6	0			.963	-1	1-12	-0.7
1900	Chi-N	78	284	29	78	14	4	4	32	10		.275	.316	.394	99	-2	5			.980	-4	1-78	-0.5
1901	NY-N	138	526	42	113	13	3	2	66	20		.215	.256	.262	52	-32	6			**.986**	2	*1-138	-3.2
1903	NY-A	129	476	62	132	25	7	3	71	30		.277	.336	.378	107	4	9			**.988**	7	*1-129	0.9
1904	NY-A	130	465	50	121	16	10	6	48	24		.260	.309	.376	111	5	13			.988	-2	*1-118/2-9,S-1	0.1
1907	Cin-N	145	531	61	135	20	**16**	2	64	29		.254	.297	.363	102	-1	9			.990	1	*1-143	-0.5

YEAR	TM/L	G	AB	R	H	2B	3B	HR	RBI	BB	SO	AVG	OBP	SLG	PRO+	BR/A	SB	CS	SBR	FA	FR	G/POS	TPR
1908	Cin-N	112	388	32	97	16	10	1	53	19		.250	.289	.351	107	1	6			**.990**	-2	*1-108,M	-0.3
Total	7	747	2715	281	682	104	50	18	336	136		.251	.298	.346	93	-29	48			.987	0	1-726/2-9,S-1	-4.2

■ JOE GARAGIOLA
Garagiola, Joseph Henry b: 2/12/26, St.Louis, Mo. BL/TR, 6', 190 lbs. Deb: 5/26/46

YEAR	TM/L	G	AB	R	H	2B	3B	HR	RBI	BB	SO	AVG	OBP	SLG	PRO+	BR/A	SB	CS	SBR	FA	FR	G/POS	TPR
1946	*StL-N	74	211	21	50	4	1	3	22	23	25	.237	.312	.308	73	-7	0			.990	-5	C-70	-0.9
1947	StL-N	77	183	20	47	10	2	5	25	40	14	.257	.398	.415	111	4	0			.987	1	C-74	0.9
1948	StL-N	24	56	9	6	1	0	2	7	12	9	.107	.275	.232	36	-5	0			.990	2	C-23	-0.2
1949	StL-N	81	241	25	63	14	0	3	26	31	19	.261	.348	.357	85	-4	0			.984	7	C-80	0.7
1950	StL-N	34	88	8	28	6	1	2	20	10	7	.318	.388	.477	120	3	0			1.000	-3	C-30	0.1
1951	StL-N	27	72	9	14	3	2	2	9	9	7	.194	.284	.375	75	-3	0	0	0	1.000	-3	C-23	-0.4
	Pit-N	72	212	24	54	8	2	9	35	32	20	.255	.358	.439	110	3	4	1	1	.986	-9	C-61	-0.2
	Yr	99	284	33	68	11	4	11	44	41	27	.239	.339	.423	101	1	4	1	1	**.989**	-11	C-84	-0.6
1952	Pit-N	118	344	35	94	15	4	8	54	50	24	.273	.369	.410	113	7	0	1	-1	.978	-3	*C-105	0.9
1953	Pit-N	27	73	9	17	5	0	2	14	10	11	.233	.341	.384	89	-1	1	0	0	.989	-4	C-22	-0.3
	Chi-N	74	228	21	62	9	4	1	21	21	23	.272	.336	.360	80	-6	0	0	0	.988	0	C-68	-0.3
	Yr	101	301	30	79	14	4	3	35	31	34	.262	.337	.365	82	-7	1	0	0	.988	-4	C-90	-0.6
1954	Chi-N	63	153	16	43	5	0	5	21	28	12	.281	.405	.412	112	4	0	0	0	.982	-8	C-55	-0.1
	NY-N	5	11	1	3	2	0	0	1	1	2	.273	.333	.455	102	0	0	0	0	1.000	0	/C-3	0.0
	Yr	68	164	17	46	7	0	5	22	29	14	.280	.401	.415	112	4	0	0	0	.983	-8	C-58	-0.1
Total	9	676	1872	198	481	82	16	42	255	267	173	.257	.355	.385	96	-5	5	2		.986	-23	C-614	0.2

■ MIKE GARBARK
Garbark, Nathaniel Michael (b: Nathaniel Michael Garbach)
b: 2/3/16, Houston, Tex. d: 8/31/94, Charlotte, N.C. BR/TR, 6', 200 lbs. Deb: 4/18/44 F

YEAR	TM/L	G	AB	R	H	2B	3B	HR	RBI	BB	SO	AVG	OBP	SLG	PRO+	BR/A	SB	CS	SBR	FA	FR	G/POS	TPR
1944	NY-A	89	299	23	78	9	4	1	33	25	27	.261	.320	.328	82	-7	0	1	-1	.988	8	C-85	0.6
1945	NY-A	60	176	23	38	5	3	1	26	23	12	.216	.310	.295	73	-6	0	1	-1	.972	4	C-59	0.1
Total	2	149	475	46	116	14	7	2	59	48	39	.244	.316	.316	79	-12	0	2	-1	.982	12	C-144	0.7

■ BOB GARBARK
Garbark, Robert Michael (b: Robert Michael Garbach) b: 11/13/09, Houston, Tex. d: 8/15/90, Meadville, Pa. BR/TR, 5'11", 178 lbs. Deb: 9/3/34 F

YEAR	TM/L	G	AB	R	H	2B	3B	HR	RBI	BB	SO	AVG	OBP	SLG	PRO+	BR/A	SB	CS	SBR	FA	FR	G/POS	TPR
1934	Cle-A	5	11	1	0	0	0	0	0	1	3	.000	.083	.000	-76	-3	0	0	0	1.000	-2	/C-5	-0.4
1935	Cle-A	6	18	4	6	1	0	0	4	5	1	.333	.478	.389	124	1	0	0	0	1.000	2	/C-6	0.3
1937	Chi-N	1	1	0	0	0	0	0	0	0	0	.000	.000	.000	-96	-0	0			.000	0	H	0.0
1938	Chi-N	23	54	2	14	0	0	0	5	1	0	.259	.273	.259	46	-4	0			1.000	1	C-20/1-1	-0.2
1939	Chi-N	24	21	1	3	0	0	0	0	0	3	.143	.143	.143	-23	-4	0			1.000	1	C-21	-0.3
1944	Phi-A	18	23	2	6	2	0	0	2	1	0	.261	.292	.348	83	-1	0	0	0	1.000	-0	C-15	-0.1
1945	Bos-A	68	199	21	52	6	0	0	17	18	10	.261	.329	.291	79	-5	0	1	-1	.993	-3	C-67	-0.5
Total	7	145	327	31	81	9	0	0	28	26	17	.248	.307	.275	64	-15	0	1		.996	-2	C-134/1-1	-1.2

■ BARBARO GARBEY
Garbey, Barbaro (Garbey) b: 12/4/56, Santiago De Cuba, Cuba BR/TR, 5'10", 170 lbs. Deb: 4/3/84

YEAR	TM/L	G	AB	R	H	2B	3B	HR	RBI	BB	SO	AVG	OBP	SLG	PRO+	BR/A	SB	CS	SBR	FA	FR	G/POS	TPR
1984	*Det-A	110	327	45	94	17	1	5	52	17	35	.287	.327	.391	98	-1	6	7	-2	.989	-5	1-65,3-20,D-17,O/2	-1.3
1985	Det-A	86	237	27	61	9	1	6	29	15	37	.257	.310	.380	88	-4	3	2	-0	.991	-2	1-37,O-24,D-21,/3-1	-0.9
1988	Tex-A	30	62	4	12	2	0	0	5	4	11	.194	.242	.226	31	-6	0	0	0	.900	-0	/O-8,1-7,3-3,D-7	-0.6
Total	3	226	626	76	167	28	2	11	86	36	83	.267	.312	.371	88	-11	9	9	-3	.990	-8	1-109/D-45,O-42,32	-2.8

■ ALEX GARBOWSKI
Garbowski, Alexander b: 6/25/25, Yonkers, N.Y BR/TR, 6'1", 185 lbs. Deb: 4/16/52

YEAR	TM/L	G	AB	R	H	2B	3B	HR	RBI	BB	SO	AVG	OBP	SLG	PRO+	BR/A	SB	CS	SBR	FA	FR	G/POS	TPR
1952	Det-A	2	0	0	0	0	0	0	0	0	0	—	—	—	—	0	0	0	0	.000	0	R	0.0

■ KIKO GARCIA
Garcia, Alfonso Rafael b: 10/14/53, Martinez, Cal. BR/TR, 5'11", 180 lbs. Deb: 9/11/76

YEAR	TM/L	G	AB	R	H	2B	3B	HR	RBI	BB	SO	AVG	OBP	SLG	PRO+	BR/A	SB	CS	SBR	FA	FR	G/POS	TPR
1976	Bal-A	11	32	2	7	1	1	1	4	0	4	.219	.219	.406	86	-1	2	1	0	1.000	1	S-11	0.1
1977	Bal-A	65	131	20	29	6	0	2	10	6	31	.221	.255	.313	58	-8	2	3	-1	.966	20	S-61/2-2	1.5
1978	Bal-A	79	186	17	49	6	4	0	13	7	43	.263	.290	.339	81	-5	7	1	2	.945	4	S-74/2-3	0.7
1979	*Bal-A	126	417	54	103	15	9	5	24	32	87	.247	.304	.362	82	-11	11	9	-2	.955	-18	*S-113,2-25/3-2,O-2	-1.9
1980	Bal-A	111	311	27	62	8	0	1	27	24	57	.199	.257	.235	36	-27	8	4	0	.974	2	S-96,2-27/O-1	-1.6
1981	*Hou-N	48	136	9	37	6	1	0	15	10	16	.272	.327	.331	91	-2	2	2	-1	.950	3	S-28,3-13/2-9	0.4
1982	Hou-N	34	76	5	16	5	0	1	5	3	15	.211	.241	.316	59	-5	1	0	0	.946	5	S-21/3-2,2-1	0.2
1983	Phi-N	84	118	22	34	7	1	2	9	9	20	.288	.344	.415	111	2	1	2	-1	.970	19	2-52,S-22,3-10	2.2
1984	Phi-N	57	60	6	14	2	0	0	5	4	11	.233	.281	.267	54	-4	0	0	0	.965	5	S-30,3-23/2-1	0.2
1985	Phi-N	4	3	0	0	0	0	0	0	0	1	.000	.000	.000	-97	-1	0	0	0	1.000	-1	/S-3,3-1	-0.2
Total	10	619	1470	162	351	56	16	12	112	95	285	.239	.287	.323	70	-61	34	22	-3	.961	39	S-459,2-120/3-51,O	1.6

■ CARLOS GARCIA
Garcia, Carlos Jesus (Guerrero) b: 10/15/67, Tachira, Venez. BR/TR, 6'1", 185 lbs. Deb: 9/20/90

YEAR	TM/L	G	AB	R	H	2B	3B	HR	RBI	BB	SO	AVG	OBP	SLG	PRO+	BR/A	SB	CS	SBR	FA	FR	G/POS	TPR
1990	Pit-N	4	4	1	2	0	0	0	0	0	2	.500	.500	.500	183	0	0	0	0	1.000	1	/S-3	0.1
1991	Pit-N	12	24	2	6	0	2	0	1	1	8	.250	.280	.417	95	-0	0	0	0	.947	2	/S-9,3-2,2-1	0.2
1992	*Pit-N	22	39	4	8	1	0	0	4	0	9	.205	.205	.231	23	-4	0	0	0	.977	2	2-14/S-8	-0.1
1993	Pit-N	141	546	77	147	25	5	12	47	31	67	.269	.319	.399	91	-8	18	11	-1	.983	-26	*2-140/S-3	-3.1
1994	Pit-N★	98	412	49	114	15	2	6	28	16	67	.277	.310	.367	75	-15	18	9	0	.978	8	2-98	-0.3
1995	Pit-N	104	367	41	108	24	2	6	50	25	55	.294	.343	.420	98	-1	8	4	0	.982	14	2-92,S-15	1.9
1996	Pit-N	101	390	66	111	18	4	6	44	23	58	.285	.331	.397	89	-6	16	6	1	.985	3	2-77,S-19,3-14	0.4
1997	Tor-A	103	350	29	77	18	2	3	23	15	60	.220	.256	.309	46	-28	11	3	2	.981	-7	2-96/S-5,3-4	-2.6
1998	Ana-A	19	35	4	5	1	0	0	0	3	11	.143	.231	.171	7	-5	2	0	1	.978	6	2-11/S-5,D-3	0.2
Total	9	604	2167	273	578	102	17	33	197	114	337	.267	.310	.375	79	-67	73	33	2	.982	4	2-529/S-67,3-20,D-3	-3.3

■ DAMASO GARCIA
Garcia, Damaso Domingo (Sanchez) b: 2/7/55, Moca, D.R. BR/TR, 6', 170 lbs. Deb: 6/24/78

YEAR	TM/L	G	AB	R	H	2B	3B	HR	RBI	BB	SO	AVG	OBP	SLG	PRO+	BR/A	SB	CS	SBR	FA	FR	G/POS	TPR
1978	NY-A	18	41	5	8	0	0	0	1	2	6	.195	.233	.195	22	-4	1	0	0	.959	2	2-16/S-3	-0.2
1979	NY-A	11	38	3	10	1	0	0	4	0	2	.263	.263	.289	50	-3	2	0	1	.902	-6	S-10/3-1	-0.6
1980	Tor-A	140	543	50	151	30	7	4	46	12	55	.278	.297	.381	81	-15	13	13	-4	.980	16	*2-138/D-1	0.5
1981	Tor-A	64	250	24	63	8	1	1	13	9	32	.252	.278	.304	64	-12	13	3	2	.972	-15	2-62/D-1	-2.2
1982	Tor-A	147	597	89	185	32	3	5	42	21	44	.310	.339	.399	93	-6	54	20	4	.980	10	*2-141/D-4	1.6
1983	Tor-A	131	525	84	161	23	6	3	38	24	34	.307	.339	.390	94	-4	31	17	-1	.981	-16	*2-130	-1.5
1984	Tor-A★	152	633	79	180	32	5	5	46	16	46	.284	.312	.374	86	-13	46	12	7	.980	-14	*2-149/D-1	-1.5
1985	*Tor-A★	146	600	70	169	25	4	8	65	15	41	.282	.304	.377	83	-15	28	15	-1	.981	-34	*2-143	-4.5
1986	Tor-A	122	424	57	119	22	0	6	46	13	32	.281	.308	.375	83	-10	9	6	-1	.985	-7	*2-106,D-11/1-1	-1.4
1988	Atl-N	21	60	3	7	1	0	1	4	3	10	.117	.159	.183	-2	-8	1	0	0	.984	-4	2-13	-1.2
1989	Mon-N	80	203	26	55	9	1	3	18	15	20	.271	.321	.369	96	-1	5	4	-1	.972	6	2-62/3-1	0.6
Total	11	1032	3914	490	1108	183	27	36	323	130	322	.283	.311	.371	84	-91	203	90	7	.980	-62	2-960/D-18,S-13,31	-10.4

■ DANNY GARCIA
Garcia, Daniel Raphael b: 4/29/54, Brooklyn, N.Y. BL/TL, 6'1", 182 lbs. Deb: 4/26/81

YEAR	TM/L	G	AB	R	H	2B	3B	HR	RBI	BB	SO	AVG	OBP	SLG	PRO+	BR/A	SB	CS	SBR	FA	FR	G/POS	TPR
1981	KC-A	12	14	4	2	0	0	0	0	0	2	.143	.143	.143	-18	-2	0	0	0	1.000	-2	/O-6,1-2	-0.4

■ FREDDY GARCIA
Garcia, Freddy Adrian (Felix) b: 8/1/72, LaRomana, D.R. BR/TR, 6'2", 190 lbs. Deb: 5/3/95

YEAR	TM/L	G	AB	R	H	2B	3B	HR	RBI	BB	SO	AVG	OBP	SLG	PRO+	BR/A	SB	CS	SBR	FA	FR	G/POS	TPR
1995	Pit-N	42	57	5	8	1	1	0	1	8	17	.140	.246	.193	17	-7	0	1	-1	1.000	2	O-10/3-8	-0.6
1997	Pit-N	20	40	4	6	1	0	3	5	2	17	.150	.190	.400	49	-3	0	0	0	.842	-2	3-10/1-2	-0.5
1998	Pit-N	56	172	27	44	11	1	9	26	18	45	.256	.333	.488	108	2	0	2	-1	.949	5	3-47/1-4	0.6
Total	3	118	269	36	58	13	2	12	32	28	79	.216	.294	.413	80	-8	0	3	-2	.938	5	/3-65,O-10,1-6	-0.5

■ GUILLERMO GARCIA
Garcia, Guillermo Antonio (Morel) b: 4/4/72, Santiago, D.R. BR/TR, 6'3", 215 lbs. Deb: 7/19/98

YEAR	TM/L	G	AB	R	H	2B	3B	HR	RBI	BB	SO	AVG	OBP	SLG	PRO+	BR/A	SB	CS	SBR	FA	FR	G/POS	TPR
1998	Cin-N	12	36	3	7	2	0	2	4	2	13	.194	.237	.417	64	-2	0	0	0	.988	3	C-11	0.2

■ KARIM GARCIA
Garcia, Gustavo Karim b: 10/29/75, Ciudad Obregon, Mexico BL/TL, 6', 200 lbs. Deb: 9/2/95

YEAR	TM/L	G	AB	R	H	2B	3B	HR	RBI	BB	SO	AVG	OBP	SLG	PRO+	BR/A	SB	CS	SBR	FA	FR	G/POS	TPR
1995	LA-N	13	20	1	4	0	0	0	0	0	4	.200	.200	.200	6	-3	0	0	0	1.000	1	/O-5	-0.2
1996	LA-N	1	1	0	0	0	0	0	0	0	1	.000	.000	.000	-99	-0	0	0	0	.000	0	/H	0.0
1997	LA-N	15	39	5	5	0	0	1	8	6	14	.128	.244	.205	21	-5	0	0	0	1.000	-2	O-12	-0.7

YEAR	TM/L	G	AB	R	H	2B	3B	HR	RBI	BB	SO	AVG	OBP	SLG	PRO+	BR/A	SB	CS	SBR	FA	FR	G/POS	TPR
1998	Ari-N	113	333	39	74	10	8	9	43	18	78	.222	.262	.381	64	-19	5	4	-1	.975	0	*O-103	-2.0
Total	4	142	393	45	83	10	8	10	51	24	97	.211	.257	.354	57	-26	5	4	-1	.977	-1	O-120	-2.9
■ **LEO GARCIA**	Garcia, Leonardo Antonio (Peralta) b: 11/6/62, Santiago, D.R. BL/TL, 5′8″, 160 lbs. Deb: 4/6/87																						
1987	Cin-N	31	30	8	6	0	0	1	2	4	8	.200	.294	.300	55	-2	3	1	0	1.000	-2	O-14	-0.4
1988	Cin-N	23	28	2	4	1	0	0	0	4	5	.143	.250	.179	24	-3	0	1	-1	1.000	-1	/O-9	-0.5
Total	2	54	58	10	10	1	0	1	2	8	13	.172	.273	.241	41	-5	3	2	-0	1.000	-4	/O-23	-0.9
■ **PEDRO GARCIA**	Garcia, Pedro Modesto (Delfi) b: 4/17/50, Guayama, P.R. BR/TR, 5′10″, 175 lbs. Deb: 4/6/73																						
1973	Mil-A	160	580	67	142	**32**	5	15	54	40	119	.245	.299	.395	96	-5	11	10	-3	.970	-12	*2-160	-1.0
1974	Mil-A	141	452	46	90	15	4	12	54	26	67	.199	.251	.330	66	-21	8	5	-1	.970	-11	*2-140	-2.7
1975	Mil-A	98	302	40	68	15	2	6	38	18	59	.225	.273	.348	74	-11	12	6	0	.985	19	2-94/D-1	1.3
1976	Mil-A	41	106	12	23	7	1	1	9	4	23	.217	.259	.330	73	-4	2	2	-1	.971	-3	2-39	-0.6
	Det-A	77	227	21	45	10	2	3	20	9	40	.198	.242	.300	56	-13	2	3	-1	.958	-0	2-77	-1.1
	Yr	118	333	33	68	17	3	4	29	13	63	.204	.247	.309	61	-17	4	5	-2	.962	-3	*2-116	-1.7
1977	Tor-A	41	130	10	27	10	1	0	9	5	21	.208	.254	.300	50	-9	0	0	0	.971	-2	2-34/D-4	-0.9
Total	5	558	1797	196	395	89	15	37	184	102	329	.220	.270	.348	75	-63	35	26	-5	.971	-8	2-544/D-5	-5.0
■ **CHICO GARCIA**	Garcia, Vinicio Uzcanga b: 12/24/24, Veracruz, Mexico BR/TR, 5′8″, 170 lbs. Deb: 4/24/54																						
1954	Bal-A	39	62	6	7	0	2	0	5	8	3	.113	.214	.177	9	-8	0	0	0	.962	8	2-24	0.0
■ **NOMAR GARCIAPARRA**	Garciaparra, Anthony Nomar b: 7/23/73, Whittier, Cal. BR/TR, 6′, 165 lbs. Deb: 8/31/96																						
1996	Bos-A	24	87	11	21	2	3	4	16	4	14	.241	.275	.471	82	-3	5	0	2	.988	-5	S-22/2-1,D-1	-0.4
1997	Bos-A★	153	684	122	**209**	44	**11**	30	98	35	92	.306	.345	.534	122	20	22	9	1	.971	-0	*S-153	3.3
1998	*Bos-A	143	604	111	195	37	8	35	122	33	62	.323	.366	.584	142	35	12	6	0	.962	-17	*S-143	2.8
Total	3	320	1375	244	425	83	22	69	236	72	168	.309	.350	.552	128	52	39	15	3	.968	-22	S-318/D-1,2-1	5.7
■ **AL GARDELLA**	Gardella, Alfred Stephan b: 1/11/18, New York, N.Y. BL/TL, 5′10″, 172 lbs. Deb: 5/17/45 F																						
1945	NY-N	16	26	2	2	0	0	0	1	4	3	.077	.226	.077	-14	-4	0			.961	-1	/1-9,O-1	-0.6
■ **DANNY GARDELLA**	Gardella, Daniel Lewis b: 2/26/20, New York, N.Y. BL/TL, 5′7.5″, 160 lbs. Deb: 5/14/44 F																						
1944	NY-N	47	112	20	28	2	2	6	14	11	13	.250	.323	.464	120	2	0			.912	2	O-25	0.3
1945	NY-N	121	430	54	117	10	1	18	71	46	55	.272	.349	.426	113	7	2			.954	-2	O-94,1-15	-0.1
1950	StL-N	1	1	0	0	0	0	0	0	0	0	.000	.000	.000	-95	-0	0			.000	0	H	0.0
Total	3	169	543	74	145	12	3	24	85	57	68	.267	.343	.433	114	9	2			.943	-0	O-119/1-15	0.2
■ **RON GARDENHIRE**	Gardenhire, Ronald Clyde b: 10/24/57, Butzbach, W.Germany BR/TR, 6′, 175 lbs. Deb: 9/1/81 C																						
1981	NY-N	27	48	2	13	1	0	0	3	5	9	.271	.340	.292	82	-1	2	2	-1	.969	4	S-18/2-6,3-1	0.4
1982	NY-N	141	384	29	92	17	1	3	33	23	55	.240	.283	.313	67	-17	5	6	-2	.956	15	*S-135/2-1,3-1	0.7
1983	NY-N	17	32	1	2	0	0	0	1	1	4	.063	.091	.063	-57	-7	0	0	0	1.000	0	S-15	-0.6
1984	NY-N	74	207	20	51	7	1	1	10	9	43	.246	.278	.304	64	-10	6	1	1	.947	-4	S-49,2-18/3-7	-0.9
1985	NY-N	26	39	5	7	2	1	0	2	8	11	.179	.319	.282	71	-1	0	0	0	.911	-1	S-13/2-5,3-2	-0.1
Total	5	285	710	57	165	27	3	4	49	46	122	.232	.279	.296	62	-36	13	9	-2	.955	15	S-230/2-30,3-11	-0.5
■ **ALEX GARDNER**	Gardner, Alexander b: 4/28/1861, Toronto, Ont., Can. d: 6/18/26, Danvers, Mass. Deb: 5/10/1884																						
1884	Was-a	1	3	0	0	0	0	0		0		.000	.000	.000	-99	-1				.600	-1	/C-1	-0.1
■ **ART GARDNER**	Gardner, Arthur Junior b: 9/21/52, Madden, Miss. BL/TL, 5′11″, 175 lbs. Deb: 9/2/75																						
1975	Hou-N	13	31	3	6	0	0	0	2	1	8	.194	.242	.194	24	-3	1	0	0	1.000	-1	/O-8	-0.4
1977	Hou-N	66	65	7	10	0	0	0	3	3	15	.154	.203	.154	-3	-10	0	0	0	1.000	-4	O-26	-1.4
1978	SF-N	7	3	2	0	0	0	0	0	0	2	.000	.000	.000	-99	-1	0	1	-1	.000	0	H	-0.2
Total	3	86	99	12	16	0	0	0	5	4	25	.162	.210	.162	2	-14	1	1	-0	1.000	-4	/O-34	-2.0
■ **EARLE GARDNER**	Gardner, Earle McClurkin b: 1/24/1884, Sparta, Ill. d: 3/2/43, Sparta, Ill. BR/TR, 5′11″, 160 lbs. Deb: 9/18/08																						
1908	NY-A	20	75	7	16	2	0	0	4	1		.213	.234	.240	53	-4	0			.947	4	2-20	0.0
1909	NY-A	22	85	12	28	4	0	0	15	3		.329	.352	.376	129	3	4			.945	-8	2-22	-0.6
1910	NY-A	86	271	36	66	4	2	1	24	21		.244	.303	.284	79	-6	9			.936	6	2-70	-0.2
1911	NY-A	102	357	36	94	13	2	0	39	20		.263	.312	.311	69	-15	14			.959	-3	*2-101	-2.0
1912	NY-A	43	160	14	45	3	1	0	26	5		.281	.303	.313	72	-6	11			.922	-4	2-43	-1.1
Total	5	273	948	105	249	26	5	1	108	50		.263	.305	.304	76	-29	38			.944	-5	2-256	-3.9
■ **GID GARDNER**	Gardner, Frank Washington b: 6/9/1859, Attleboro, Mass. d: 8/1/14, Cambridge, Mass. 165 lbs. Deb: 8/23/1879																						
1879	Tro-N	2	6	1	1	0	0	0	0	0	0	.167	.167	.167	11	-1				.429	-1	/P-2	0.0
1880	Cle-N	10	32	0	6	1	1	0	4	2	4	.188	.235	.281	76	-1				.850	-1	/P-9,O-1	0.0
1883	Bal-a	42	161	28	44	10	3	1		18		.273	.346	.391	133	6				.837	-1	O-35/2-4,3-3,P-2	0.5
1884	Bal-a	41	173	32	37	6	8	2		14		.214	.280	.376	108	1				.860	4	O-40/1-2	0.4
	CP-U	38	149	22	38	10	2	0		10		.255	.302	.349	97	-5				.872	-1	O-29/3-8,P-1,2-1	-0.6
	Bal-U	1	4	0	1	0	0	0		0		.250	.250	.250	47	-0				.714	-0	/S-1	0.0
	Yr	39	153	22	39	10	2	0		10		.255	.301	.346	96	-5				.872	-1	O-29/3-8,P-1,2-1,S	-0.6
1885	Bal-a	44	170	22	37	5	4	0	17	12		.218	.269	.294	79	-4				.891	3	2-39/O-5,1-1,P-1	0.1
1887	Ind-N	18	63	8	11	1	0	1	8	12	11	.175	.307	.238	55	-3	7			1.000	-3	O-11/2-7	-0.6
1888	Was-N	1	3	0	1	0	0	0	0	1	1	.333	.500	.333	180	0	0			.750	0	/S-1	0.1
	Phi-N	1	3	0	2	0	0	0	1	0	0	.667	.667	.667	310	1	0			1.000	-1	/2-1	0.0
	Was-N	1	1	0	0	0	0	0	0	0	0	.000	.000	.000	-99	-0	0			1.000	-0	/2-1	-0.1
	Yr	3	7	0	3	0	0	0	1	1	1	.429	.500	.429	202	1	0			1.000	-1	/2-2,S-1	0.0
Total	7	199	765	113	178	33	18	4	30	69	16	.233	.298	.339	99	-5	7			.855	0	O-121/2-53,P31S	-0.2
■ **JEFF GARDNER**	Gardner, Jeffrey Scott b: 2/4/64, Newport Beach, Cal. BL/TR, 5′11″, 165 lbs. Deb: 9/10/91																						
1991	NY-N	13	37	3	6	0	0	0	1	4	6	.162	.244	.162	17	-4	0	0	0	.818	-2	/S-8,2-3	-0.6
1992	SD-N	15	19	0	2	0	0	0	0	1	8	.105	.150	.105	-26	-3	0	0	0	1.000	4	2-11	0.1
1993	SD-N	140	404	53	106	21	7	1	24	45	69	.262	.338	.356	85	-8	2	6	-3	.983	-8	*2-133/3-1,S-1	-1.6
1994	Mon-N	18	32	4	7	0	1	0	1	3	5	.219	.286	.281	48	-2	0	0	0	.714	-5	/3-9,2-4	-0.8
Total	4	186	492	60	121	21	8	1	26	53	88	.246	.321	.327	73	-18	2	6	-3	.984	-11	2-151/3-10,S-9	-2.9
■ **RAY GARDNER**	Gardner, Raymond Vincent b: 10/25/01, Frederick, Md. d: 5/3/68, Frederick, Md. BR/TR, 5′8″, 145 lbs. Deb: 4/16/29																						
1929	Cle-A	82	256	28	67	3	2	1	24	29	16	.262	.337	.301	63	-13	10	13	-5	.952	8	S-82	-0.1
1930	Cle-A	33	13	7	1	0	0	0	1	0	0	.077	.077	.077	-59	-3	0	1	-1	.861	8	S-22/2-5,3-1	0.4
Total	2	115	269	35	68	3	2	1	25	29	16	.253	.326	.290	57	-16	10	14	-5	.945	16	S-104/2-5,3-1	0.3
■ **BILLY GARDNER**	Gardner, William Frederick "Shotgun" b: 7/19/27, Waterford, Conn. BR/TR, 6′, 180 lbs. Deb: 4/22/54 MC																						
1954	NY-N	62	108	10	23	5	0	1	7	6	19	.213	.261	.287	42	-9	0	1	-1	.987	10	3-30,2-13/S-5	0.0
1955	NY-N	59	187	26	38	10	1	3	17	13	19	.203	.262	.316	52	-13	0	0	0	.940	0	S-38,3-10/2-4	-1.0
1956	Bal-A	144	515	53	119	16	2	11	50	29	53	.231	.281	.334	67	-27	5	5	-2	.974	-12	*2-132,S-25/3-6	-2.9
1957	Bal-A	154	644	79	169	**36**	3	6	55	53	67	.262	.326	.356	92	-8	10	7	-1	**.987**	6	*2-148/S-9	0.9
1958	Bal-A	151	560	32	126	28	2	3	33	34	53	.225	.273	.298	60	-31	2	3	-1	.985	-22	*2-151,S-13	-4.6
1959	Bal-A	140	401	34	87	13	2	6	27	38	61	.217	.286	.304	64	-20	2	1	0	.976	**31**	*2-139/S-1,3-1	2.0
1960	Was-A	145	592	71	152	26	5	9	56	43	76	.257	.314	.363	83	-14	0	4	-2	.973	-2	*2-145,S-13	-0.5
1961	Min-A	45	154	13	36	9	0	1	11	10	14	.234	.280	.312	55	-10	0	0	0	.973	-4	2-41/3-2	-1.0
	*NY-A	41	99	11	21	5	0	1	2	6	18	.212	.278	.293	56	-6	0	0	0	.952	3	3-33/2-6	-0.3
	Yr	86	253	24	57	14	0	2	13	16	32	.225	.279	.304	56	-16	0	0	0	.975	-1	2-47,3-35	-1.3
1962	NY-A	4	1	1	0	0	0	0	0	0	1	.000	.000	.000	-99	-0	0	0	0	1.000	1	/2-1,3-1	0.0
	Bos-A	53	199	22	54	9	2	0	12	10	39	.271	.310	.337	72	-8	0	1	-1	.963	-8	2-38/3-7,S-4	-1.2

YEAR	TM/L	G	AB	R	H	2B	3B	HR	RBI	BB	SO	AVG	OBP	SLG	PRO+	BR/A	SB	CS	SBR	FA	FR	G/POS	TPR
	Yr	57	200	23	54	9	2	0	12	10	40	.270	.308	.335	71	-8	0	1	-1	.963	-7	2-39/3-8,S-4	-1.2
1963	Bos-A	36	84	4	16	2	1	0	1	4	19	.190	.236	.238	32	-8	0	0	0	.989	7	2-21/3-2	0.1
Total	10	1034	3544	356	841	159	18	41	271	246	439	.237	.293	.327	70	-155	19	22	-8	.978	8	2-839,S-108/3-92	-8.5
■ **LARRY GARDNER**	Gardner, William Lawrence b: 5/13/1886, Enosburg Falls, Vt d: 3/11/76, St.George, Vt. BL/TR, 5'8", 165 lbs. Deb: 6/25/08																						
1908	Bos-A	3	10	0	3	1	0	0	1	0		.300	.300	.400	124	0	0			.571	-2	/3-3	-0.2
1909	Bos-A	19	37	7	11	1	2	0	5	4		.297	.381	.432	153	2	1			.800	-4	/3-8,S-5	-0.1
1910	Bos-A	113	413	55	117	12	10	2	36	41		.283	.354	.375	125	12	8			.944	-9	*2-113	0.1
1911	Bos-A	138	492	80	140	17	8	4	44	64		.285	.373	.376	110	8	27			.962	24	3-72,2-62	3.1
1912	*Bos-A	143	517	88	163	24	18	3	86	56		.315	.383	.449	131	20	25			.930	-1	*3-143	2.0
1913	Bos-A	131	473	64	133	17	10	0	63	47	34	.281	.347	.359	104	3	18			.943	-16	*3-130	-1.2
1914	Bos-A	155	553	50	143	23	19	3	68	35	39	.259	.303	.385	107	1	16	23	-9	.942	0	*3-153	-0.3
1915	*Bos-A	127	430	51	111	14	6	1	55	39	24	.258	.327	.326	98	-1	11	12	-4	.933	-7	*3-127	-0.7
1916	*Bos-A	148	493	47	152	19	7	2	62	48	27	.308	.372	.387	128	17	12			.953	-14	*3-147	0.8
1917	Bos-A	146	501	53	133	23	7	1	61	54	37	.265	.341	.345	110	7	16			.937	-7	*3-146	0.3
1918	Phi-A	127	463	50	132	22	6	1	52	43	22	.285	.346	.365	113	7	9			.964	10	*3-127	2.2
1919	Cle-A	139	524	67	157	29	7	2	79	39	29	.300	.352	.393	103	1	7			.946	-6	*3-139	0.1
1920	*Cle-A	154	597	72	185	31	11	3	118	53	25	.310	.367	.414	103	3	3	20	-11	**.976**	-2	*3-154	-0.2
1921	Cle-A	153	586	101	187	32	14	3	120	65	16	.319	.391	.437	109	9	3	3	-1	.950	-1	*3-152	1.7
1922	Cle-A	137	470	74	134	31	3	2	68	49	21	.285	.355	.377	90	-6	9	8	-2	.951	-5	*3-128	-0.4
1923	Cle-A	52	79	4	20	5	1	0	12	12	7	.253	.352	.342	83	-2	0	1	-1	.962	3	3-19	0.1
1924	Cle-A	38	50	3	10	0	0	0	4	5	1	.200	.273	.200	23	-6	0	1	-1	.875	-4	/3-8,2-6	-0.9
Total	17	1923	6688	866	1931	301	129	27	934	654	282	.289	.355	.384	109	75	165	68		.948	-39	*3-1656,2-181/S-5	6.4
■ **ART GARIBALDI**	Garibaldi, Arthur Edward b: 8/20/07, San Francisco, Cal d: 10/19/67, Sacramento, Cal. BR/TR, 5'8", 165 lbs. Deb: 6/20/36																						
1936	StL-N	71	232	30	64	12	0	1	20	16	30	.276	.323	.341	79	-7	3			.925	-5	3-46,2-24	-0.9
■ **DEBS GARMS**	Garms, Debs C. "Tex" b: 6/26/08, Bangs, Tex. d: 12/16/84, Glen Rose, Tex. BL/TR, 5'8.5", 165 lbs. Deb: 8/10/32																						
1932	StL-A	34	134	20	38	7	1	1	8	17	7	.284	.364	.373	86	-2	4	3	-1	.953	-1	O-33	-0.5
1933	StL-A	78	189	35	60	10	2	4	24	30	21	.317	.416	.455	123	7	2	5	-2	.960	-2	O-47	0.0
1934	StL-A	91	232	25	68	14	4	0	31	27	19	.293	.372	.388	89	-4	0	0	0	.942	-3	O-56	-0.8
1935	StL-A	10	15	1	4	0	0	0	0	2	2	.267	.353	.267	59	-1	0	0	0	.800	-0	/O-2	-0.1
1937	Bos-N	125	478	60	124	15	8	2	37	37	33	.259	.317	.337	85	-11	2			.977	-8	O-81,3-36	-2.0
1938	Bos-N	117	428	62	135	19	1	0	47	34	22	.315	.371	.364	114	9	4			.985	-7	O-63,3-54/2-1	0.1
1939	Bos-N	132	513	68	153	24	9	2	37	39	20	.298	.350	.392	107	4	2			.964	-4	O-96,3-37	-0.3
1940	Pit-N	103	358	76	127	23	7	5	57	23	6	**.355**	.395	.500	147	22	3			.964	-1	3-64,O-19	2.2
1941	Pit-N	83	220	25	58	9	3	3	42	22	12	.264	.331	.373	98	-1	0			.911	-10	3-29,O-24	-1.2
1943	*StL-N	90	249	26	64	10	2	0	22	13	8	.257	.299	.313	74	-9	1			.980	-5	O-47,3-23/S-1	-1.7
1944	*StL-N	73	149	17	30	3	0	0	5	13	8	.201	.265	.221	37	-12	0			1.000	-8	O-23,3-21	-2.2
1945	StL-N	74	146	23	49	7	2	0	18	31	3	.336	.452	.411	137	9	0			.956	-10	3-32,O-10	0.0
Total	12	1010	3111	438	910	141	39	17	328	288	161	.293	.355	.379	103	13	18	8		.966	-58	O-501,3-296/S-1,2-1	-6.5
■ **PHIL GARNER**	Garner, Philip Mason b: 4/30/49, Jefferson City, Tenn. BR/TR, 5'10", 177 lbs. Deb: 9/10/73 MC																						
1973	Oak-A	9	5	0	0	0	0	0	0	0	3	.000	.000	.000	-99	-1	0	0	0	1.000	1	/3-9	-0.1
1974	Oak-A	30	28	4	5	1	0	0	1	1	5	.179	.207	.214	23	-3	1	1	-0	.955	4	3-19/S-8,2-3,D-2	0.1
1975	*Oak-A	160	488	46	120	21	5	6	54	30	65	.246	.296	.346	83	-12	4	6	-2	.968	-16	*2-160/S-1	-2.2
1976	Oak-A★	159	555	54	145	29	12	8	74	36	71	.261	.309	.400	111	5	35	13	3	.975	-14	*2-159	0.5
1977	Pit-N	153	585	99	152	35	10	17	77	55	65	.260	.326	.441	101	-0	32	9	4	.971	1	*3-107,2-50,S-12	0.7
1978	Pit-N	154	528	66	138	25	9	10	66	66	71	.261	.349	.400	104	4	27	14	-0	.976	10	2-81,3-81/S-4	1.9
1979	*Pit-N	150	549	76	161	32	8	11	59	55	74	.293	.361	.441	112	10	17	8	0	.981	6	2-83,3-78,S-14	2.2
1980	Pit-N★	151	548	62	142	27	6	5	58	46	53	.259	.319	.358	87	-9	32	7	5	.976	16	*2-151/S-1	2.3
1981	Pit-N★	56	181	22	46	6	2	1	20	21	21	.254	.332	.326	84	-3	4	6	-2	.968	-6	2-50	-1.0
	*Hou-N	31	113	13	27	3	1	0	6	15	11	.239	.328	.283	79	-3	6	2	1	.982	0	2-31	0.0
	Yr	87	294	35	73	9	3	1	26	36	32	.248	.330	.310	82	-6	10	8	-2	.973	-6	2-81	-1.0
1982	Hou-N	155	588	65	161	33	8	13	83	40	92	.274	.323	.423	116	10	24	13	-1	.980	1	*2-136,3-18	1.8
1983	Hou-N	154	567	76	135	24	2	14	79	63	84	.238	.320	.362	94	-5	18	12	-2	.945	4	*3-154	-0.5
1984	Hou-N	128	374	60	104	17	6	4	45	43	63	.278	.359	.388	118	10	3	2	-0	.979	23	3-82,2-35	3.3
1985	Hou-N	135	463	65	124	23	10	6	51	34	72	.268	.321	.400	103	1	4	4	-1	.932	-9	*3-123,2-15	-1.1
1986	*Hou-N	107	313	43	83	14	3	9	41	30	45	.265	.331	.415	108	3	12	6	0	.896	1	3-84/2-7	0.2
1987	Hou-N	43	112	15	25	5	0	3	15	8	20	.223	.275	.348	66	-6	1	0	0	.976	2	3-36/2-2	-0.4
	LA-N	70	126	14	24	4	0	2	8	20	24	.190	.301	.270	54	-8	5	1	1	.923	6	3-46,2-12/S-2	-0.1
	Yr	113	238	29	49	9	0	5	23	28	44	.206	.289	.307	60	-14	6	1	1	.947	8	3-82,2-14/S-2	-0.5
1988	SF-N	15	13	0	2	0	0	0	1	1	3	.154	.214	.154	8	-2	0	1	-1	.000	0	/3-2	-0.2
Total	16	1860	6136	780	1594	299	82	109	738	564	842	.260	.326	.389	100	-10	225	105	4	.974	30	2-975,3-839/S-42,D	7.4
■ **RALPH GARR**	Garr, Ralph Allen "Road Runner" b: 12/12/45, Monroe, La. BL/TR, 5'11", 197 lbs. Deb: 9/3/68																						
1968	Atl-N	11	7	3	2	0	0	0	0	1	0	.286	.375	.286	100	0	1	0	0	.000	0	H	0.0
1969	Atl-N	22	27	6	6	1	0	0	2	2	4	.222	.276	.259	50	-2	1	1	-0	.857	-1	/O-7	-0.4
1970	Atl-N	37	96	18	27	3	0	0	8	5	12	.281	.317	.313	65	-5	5	2	0	1.000	0	O-21	-0.5
1971	Atl-N	154	639	101	219	24	6	9	44	30	68	.343	.374	.441	122	18	30	14	1	.968	16	*O-153	2.9
1972	Atl-N	134	554	87	180	22	0	12	53	25	41	.325	.361	.430	113	9	25	9	2	.962	-4	*O-131	0.1
1973	Atl-N	148	668	94	200	32	6	11	55	22	64	.299	.324	.415	96	-5	35	11	4	.968	1	*O-148	-0.7
1974	Atl-N★	143	606	87	**214**	24	**17**	11	54	28	52	**.353**	.384	.503	141	30	26	16	-2	.967	-19	*O-139	0.4
1975	Atl-N	151	625	74	174	26	**11**	6	31	44	50	.278	.329	.384	94	-6	14	9	-1	.966	6	*O-148	-0.7
1976	Chi-A	136	527	63	158	22	6	4	36	17	41	.300	.324	.387	107	3	14	5	1	.978	-6	*O-125/D-6	-0.8
1977	Chi-A	134	543	78	163	29	7	10	54	27	44	.300	.333	.435	108	5	12	7	-1	.987	3	*O-126/D-2	0.1
1978	Chi-A	118	443	67	122	18	9	3	29	24	41	.275	.314	.377	93	-5	7	5	-1	.959	1	*O-109/D-9	-1.0
1979	Chi-A	102	307	34	86	10	2	9	39	17	19	.280	.320	.414	96	-2	2	4	-2	.951	-8	O-67,D-17	-1.4
	Cal-A	6	24	0	3	0	0	0	0	0	3	.125	.125	.125	-33	-4	0	0	0	.000	0	/D-6	-0.5
	Yr	108	331	34	89	10	2	9	39	17	22	.269	.307	.393	87	-7	2	4	-2	.951	-8	O-67,D-23	-1.9
1980	Cal-A	21	42	5	8	1	0	0	3	4	6	.190	.261	.214	33	-4	0	0	0	.750	-0	/O-2,D-8	-0.4
Total	13	1317	5108	717	1562	212	64	75	408	246	445	.306	.340	.416	106	33	172	83	2	.968	-11	*O-1176/D-48	-2.9
■ **ADRIAN GARRETT**	Garrett, Henry Adrian "Pat" b: 1/3/43, Brooksville, Fla. BL/TR, 6'3", 185 lbs. Deb: 4/13/66 FC																						
1966	Atl-N	4	3	0	0	0	0	0	0	0	2	.000	.000	.000	-99	-1	0	0	0	.000	-0	/O-1	-0.1
1970	Chi-N	3	3	0	0	0	0	0	0	0	3	.000	.000	.000	-89	-1	0	0	0	.000	0	H	-0.1
1971	Oak-A	14	21	1	3	0	0	1	2	5	7	.143	.308	.286	70	-1	0	0	0	1.000	-0	/O-5	-0.1
1972	Oak-A	14	11	0	0	0	0	0	0	1	4	.000	.083	.000	-78	-2	0	0	0	1.000	-1	/O-2	-0.3
1973	Chi-N	36	54	7	12	0	0	3	8	4	18	.222	.276	.389	77	-2	1	0	0	1.000	-1	/O-7,C-6	-0.3
1974	Chi-N	10	8	0	0	0	0	0	0	1	1	.000	.111	.000	-64	-2	0	0	0	1.000	0	/C-3,1-1,O-1	-0.1
1975	Chi-N	16	21	1	2	0	0	1	6	1	8	.095	.136	.238	2	-3	0	0	0	1.000	1	/1-4	-0.2
	Cal-A	37	107	17	28	5	0	6	18	14	28	.262	.347	.477	141	5	3	0	1	1.000	-0	D-23,1-10/O-2,C-1	0.5
1976	Cal-A	29	48	4	6	3	0	0	3	5	16	.125	.208	.188	17	-5	0	0	0	.974	-4	C-15/1-1,D-4	-0.9
Total	8	163	276	30	51	8	0	11	37	31	87	.185	.267	.333	71	-11	4	0	1	.959	-5	/D-27,C-25,O-18,1	-1.6
■ **WAYNE GARRETT**	Garrett, Ronald Wayne b: 12/3/47, Brooksville, Fla. BL/TR, 5'11", 183 lbs. Deb: 4/12/69 F																						
1969	*NY-N	124	400	38	87	11	3	1	39	40	75	.218	.293	.268	57	-22	4	2	0	.951	-13	3-72,2-47/S-9	-3.4
1970	NY-N	114	366	74	93	17	4	12	45	81	60	.254	.392	.421	118	12	5	1	1	.944	-19	3-70,2-45/S-1	-0.3
1971	NY-N	56	202	20	43	2	0	1	11	28	31	.213	.312	.238	58	-10	1	3	-2	.967	-4	3-53/2-9	-1.7
1972	NY-N	111	298	41	69	13	3	2	29	70	58	.232	.378	.315	101	4	3	2	-0	.960	2	3-82,2-22	0.7
1973	*NY-N	140	504	76	129	20	3	16	58	72	74	.256	.350	.403	110	8	6	5	-1	.942	11	*3-130/S-9,2-6	1.9

YEAR	TM/L	G	AB	R	H	2B	3B	HR	RBI	BB	SO	AVG	OBP	SLG	PRO+	BR/A	SB	CS	SBR	FA	FR	G/POS	TPR
1974	NY-N	151	522	55	117	14	3	13	53	89	96	.224	.339	.337	91	-4	4	6	-2	.955	14	*3-144/S-9	0.7
1975	NY-N	107	274	49	73	8	3	6	34	50	45	.266	.382	.383	118	8	3	2	-0	.966	11	3-94/S-3,2-1	1.9
1976	NY-N	80	251	36	56	8	1	4	26	52	26	.223	.359	.311	97	1	7	5	-1	.948	3	3-64,2-10/S-1	0.4
	Mon-N	59	177	15	43	4	1	2	11	30	20	.243	.353	.311	86	-2	2	2	-1	.982	1	2-54/3-2	0.2
	Yr	139	428	51	99	12	2	6	37	82	46	.231	.356	.311	92	-1	9	7	-2	.949	4	3-66,2-64/S-1	0.6
1977	Mon-N	68	159	17	43	6	1	2	22	30	18	.270	.389	.358	105	3	2	2	-1	1.000	2	3-49/2-1	0.4
1978	Mon-N	49	69	6	12	0	0	1	2	8	10	.174	.260	.217	35	-6	0	0	0	.969	1	3-13	-0.6
	StL-N	33	63	11	21	4	0	1	10	11	16	.333	.432	.444	148	5	1	0	0	.927	-2	3-19	0.3
	Yr	82	132	17	33	4	0	2	12	19	26	.250	.344	.326	89	-1	1	0	0	.945	-2	3-32	-0.3
Total	10	1092	3285	438	786	107	22	61	340	561	529	.239	.352	.341	95	-4	38	30	-7	.956	7	3-792,2-195/S-32	0.5

■ **GIL GARRIDO** Garrido, Gil Gonzalo b: 6/26/41, Panama City, Pan. BR/TR, 5'8", 160 lbs. Deb: 4/24/64

YEAR	TM/L	G	AB	R	H	2B	3B	HR	RBI	BB	SO	AVG	OBP	SLG	PRO+	BR/A	SB	CS	SBR	FA	FR	G/POS	TPR
1964	SF-N	14	25	1	2	0	0	0	1	2	7	.080	.148	.080	-33	-4	1	0	0	.969	-1	S-14	-0.5
1968	Atl-N	18	53	5	11	0	0	0	2	2	2	.208	.236	.208	34	-4	0	0	0	.987	3	S-17	0.1
1969	*Atl-N	82	227	18	50	5	1	0	10	16	11	.220	.272	.251	47	-16	0	0	0	.973	-11	S-81	-2.1
1970	Atl-N	101	367	38	97	5	4	1	19	15	16	.264	.293	.308	58	-22	0	2	-1	.975	-1	S-80,2-26	-1.3
1971	Atl-N	79	125	8	27	3	0	0	12	15	12	.216	.300	.240	51	-8	0	1	-1	.961	4	S-32,3-28,2-18	0.0
1972	Atl-N	40	75	11	20	1	0	0	7	11	6	.267	.368	.280	79	-1	1	1	-0	.989	1	2-21,S-10/3-3	0.0
Total	6	334	872	81	207	14	5	1	51	61	54	.237	.288	.268	53	-55	2	4	-2	.974	-4	S-234/2-65,3-31	-3.8

■ **CECIL GARRIOTT** Garriott, Virgil Cecil b: 8/15/16, Harristown, Ill. d: 2/20/90, Lake Elsinore, Cal BL/TR, 5'8", 165 lbs. Deb: 9/4/46

YEAR	TM/L	G	AB	R	H	2B	3B	HR	RBI	BB	SO	AVG	OBP	SLG	PRO+	BR/A	SB	CS	SBR	FA	FR	G/POS	TPR
1946	Chi-N	6	5	1	0	0	0	0	0	0	2	.000	.167	.000	-52	-1	0			.000	0	H	-0.1

■ **FORD GARRISON** Garrison, Robert Ford "Rocky" or "Snapper" b: 8/29/15, Greenville, S.C. BR/TR, 5'10.5", 180 lbs. Deb: 4/22/43 C

YEAR	TM/L	G	AB	R	H	2B	3B	HR	RBI	BB	SO	AVG	OBP	SLG	PRO+	BR/A	SB	CS	SBR	FA	FR	G/POS	TPR
1943	Bos-A	36	129	13	36	5	1	1	11	5	14	.279	.306	.357	92	-2	0	1	-1	.988	-0	O-32	-0.5
1944	Bos-A	13	49	5	12	3	0	0	2	6	4	.245	.327	.306	82	-1	0	0	0	.969	1	O-12	-0.1
	Phi-A	121	449	58	121	13	2	4	37	22	40	.269	.307	.334	84	-10	10	4	1	.987	6	*O-119	-1.0
	Yr	134	498	63	133	16	2	4	39	28	44	.267	.309	.331	84	-11	10	4	1	.985	7	*O-131	-1.1
1945	Phi-A	6	23	3	7	1	0	1	6	4	3	.304	.407	.478	157	2	1	0	0	1.000	1	/O-5	0.2
1946	Phi-A	9	37	1	4	0	0	0	0	0	6	.108	.108	.108	-40	-7	0	0	0	1.000	-2	/O-8	-1.0
Total	4	185	687	80	180	22	3	6	56	37	67	.262	.302	.329	81	-18	11	5	0	.986	5	O-176	-2.4

■ **WEBSTER GARRISON** Garrison, Webster Leotis b: 8/24/65, Marrero, La. BR/TR, 5'11", 170 lbs. Deb: 8/2/96

YEAR	TM/L	G	AB	R	H	2B	3B	HR	RBI	BB	SO	AVG	OBP	SLG	PRO+	BR/A	SB	CS	SBR	FA	FR	G/POS	TPR
1996	Oak-A	5	9	0	0	0	0	0	0	1	0	.000	.100	.000	-73	-2	0	0	0	.875	-1	/2-3,1-1	-0.3

■ **HANK GARRITY** Garrity, Francis Joseph b: 2/4/08, Boston, Mass. d: 9/1/62, Boston, Mass. BR/TR, 6'1", 185 lbs. Deb: 7/26/31

YEAR	TM/L	G	AB	R	H	2B	3B	HR	RBI	BB	SO	AVG	OBP	SLG	PRO+	BR/A	SB	CS	SBR	FA	FR	G/POS	TPR
1931	Chi-A	8	14	0	3	1	0	0	2	1	2	.214	.267	.286	48	-1	0	0	0	.941	0	/C-7	-0.1

■ **STEVE GARVEY** Garvey, Steven Patrick b: 12/22/48, Tampa, Fla. BR/TR, 5'10", 192 lbs. Deb: 9/1/69

YEAR	TM/L	G	AB	R	H	2B	3B	HR	RBI	BB	SO	AVG	OBP	SLG	PRO+	BR/A	SB	CS	SBR	FA	FR	G/POS	TPR
1969	LA-N	3	3	0	1	0	0	0	0	0	1	.333	.333	.333	94	-0	0	0	0	.000	0	H	0.0
1970	LA-N	34	93	8	25	5	0	1	6	6	17	.269	.313	.355	82	-3	1	1	-0	.943	6	3-27/2-1	0.3
1971	LA-N	81	225	27	51	12	1	7	26	21	33	.227	.293	.382	95	-2	1	2	-1	.939	19	3-79	1.6
1972	LA-N	96	294	36	79	14	2	9	30	19	36	.269	.315	.422	110	3	4	2	0	.902	13	3-85/1-3	1.6
1973	LA-N	114	349	37	106	17	3	8	50	11	42	.304	.331	.438	116	6	0	2	-1	.993	-8	1-76,O-10	-1.0
1974	*LA-N★	156	642	95	200	32	3	21	111	31	66	.312	.346	.469	132	23	5	4	-1	.995	-13	*1-156	-0.2
1975	LA-N★	160	659	85	210	38	6	18	95	33	66	.319	.354	.476	135	27	11	2	2	**.995**	-10	*1-160	0.9
1976	LA-N★	162	631	85	200	37	4	13	80	50	69	.317	.368	.450	134	27	19	8	1	**.998**	-16	*1-162	0.1
1977	*LA-N★	162	646	91	192	25	3	33	115	38	90	.297	.337	.498	121	17	9	6	-1	**.995**	-16	*1-160	-1.0
1978	*LA-N★	162	639	89	**202**	36	9	21	113	40	70	.316	.357	.499	138	29	10	5	0	.994	-9	*1-161	1.1
1979	LA-N★	162	648	92	204	32	1	28	110	37	59	.315	.354	.497	131	25	3	6	-3	.995	-2	*1-162	1.2
1980	LA-N★	163	658	78	**200**	27	1	26	106	36	67	.304	.343	.467	126	21	6	11	-5	.996	3	*1-162	1.0
1981	*LA-N★	110	431	63	122	23	1	10	64	25	49	.283	.324	.411	111	5	3	5	-2	**.999**	-6	*1-110	-1.1
1982	LA-N	162	625	66	176	35	1	16	86	20	86	.282	.305	.418	103	-0	5	3	-0	.995	1	*1-158	-0.8
1983	SD-N	100	388	76	114	22	0	14	59	29	39	.294	.348	.459	126	12	4	1	1	.994	-11	*1-100	-0.4
1984	*SD-N★	161	617	72	175	27	2	8	86	24	64	.284	.312	.373	92	-8	1	2	-1	**1.000**	-4	*1-159	-2.4
1985	SD-N★	162	654	80	184	34	6	17	81	35	67	.281	.321	.430	110	6	0	0	0	.997	-8	*1-162	-1.3
1986	SD-N	155	557	58	142	22	0	21	81	23	72	.255	.286	.408	91	-9	1	2	-1	.994	-18	*1-148	-4.0
1987	SD-N	27	76	5	16	2	0	1	9	1	10	.211	.231	.276	35	-7	0	0	0	1.000	0	1-20	-0.8
Total	19	2332	8835	1143	2599	440	43	272	1308	479	1003	.294	.333	.446	117	171	83	62	-12	.996	-78	*1-2059,3-191/O2	-5.2

■ **ROD GASPAR** Gaspar, Rodney Earl b: 4/3/46, Long Beach, Cal. BB/TR, 5'11", 165 lbs. Deb: 4/8/69

YEAR	TM/L	G	AB	R	H	2B	3B	HR	RBI	BB	SO	AVG	OBP	SLG	PRO+	BR/A	SB	CS	SBR	FA	FR	G/POS	TPR
1969	*NY-N	118	215	26	49	6	1	1	14	25	19	.228	.314	.279	66	-9	7	3	0	.983	-7	O-91	-2.0
1970	NY-N	11	14	4	0	0	0	0	0	1	4	.000	.067	.000	-80	-4	1	0	0	1.000	-1	/O-8	-0.4
1971	SD-N	16	17	1	2	0	0	0	2	3	3	.118	.250	.118	8	-2	0	1	-1	1.000	0	/O-2	-0.3
1974	SD-N	33	14	4	3	0	0	0	1	4	3	.214	.389	.214	75	-0	0	0	0	1.000	-2	/O-8,1-2	-0.3
Total	4	178	260	35	54	6	1	1	17	33	29	.208	.302	.250	55	-15	8	4	0	.986	-10	O-109/1-2	-3.0

■ **TOM GASTALL** Gastall, Thomas Everett b: 6/13/32, Fall River, Mass. d: 9/20/56, Riviera Beach, Md. BR/TR, 6'2", 187 lbs. Deb: 6/21/55

YEAR	TM/L	G	AB	R	H	2B	3B	HR	RBI	BB	SO	AVG	OBP	SLG	PRO+	BR/A	SB	CS	SBR	FA	FR	G/POS	TPR
1955	Bal-A	20	27	4	4	1	0	0	0	3	5	.148	.233	.185	15	-3	0	0	0	.967	-1	C-15	-0.4
1956	Bal-A	32	56	3	11	2	0	0	4	3	8	.196	.250	.232	30	-6	0	0	0	1.000	1	C-20	-0.4
Total	2	52	83	7	15	3	0	0	4	6	13	.181	.244	.217	25	-9	0	0	0	.990	0	/C-35	-0.8

■ **ED GASTFIELD** Gastfield, Edward b: 8/1/1865, Chicago, Ill. d: 12/1/1899, Chicago, Ill. BR , 5'9.5", 155 lbs. Deb: 8/13/1884

YEAR	TM/L	G	AB	R	H	2B	3B	HR	RBI	BB	SO	AVG	OBP	SLG	PRO+	BR/A	SB	CS	SBR	FA	FR	G/POS	TPR
1884	Det-N	23	82	6	6	1	0	0	2	2	34	.073	.095	.085	-45	-13				.827	9	C-19/O-2,1-2	-0.3
1885	Det-N	1	3	0	0	0	0	0	0	0	2	.000	.000	.000	-99	-1				.714	-0	/C-1	-0.1
	Chi-N	1	3	0	0	0	0	0	0	0	1	.000	.000	.000	-88	-1				1.000	1	/C-1	0.1
	Yr	2	6	0	0	0	0	0	0	0	3	.000	.000	.000	-93	-1				.889	1	/C-2	0.0
Total	2	25	88	6	6	1	0	0	2	2	37	.068	.089	.080	-49	-14				.832	10	/C-21,1-2,O-2	-0.3

■ **ALEX GASTON** Gaston, Alexander Nathaniel b: 3/12/1893, New York, N.Y. d: 2/8/79, Santa Monica, Cal. BR/TR, 5'9", 170 lbs. Deb: 9/26/20 F

YEAR	TM/L	G	AB	R	H	2B	3B	HR	RBI	BB	SO	AVG	OBP	SLG	PRO+	BR/A	SB	CS	SBR	FA	FR	G/POS	TPR
1920	NY-N	4	10	2	1	0	0	0	1	1	2	.100	.182	.100	-18	-1	0	0	0	.917	-1	/C-3	-0.3
1921	NY-N	20	22	1	5	1	0	1	3	1	9	.227	.261	.364	63	-1	0	0	0	.950	-0	C-11	-0.1
1922	NY-N	16	26	1	5	0	0	0	1	0	3	.192	.192	.192	-1	-4	1	0	0	1.000	0	C-13	-0.3
1923	NY-N	22	39	3	8	2	0	1	5	0	6	.205	.225	.333	46	-3	0	0	0	.957	-0	C-21	-0.3
1926	Bos-A	98	301	37	67	5	3	0	21	21	28	.223	.282	.259	43	-25	3	0	1	.981	-10	C-98	-2.8
1929	Bos-A	55	116	14	26	5	2	2	9	6	8	.224	.262	.353	58	-8	1	0	0	.986	-1	C-49	-0.5
Total	6	215	514	58	112	13	6	3	40	29	56	.218	.266	.284	45	-43	5	0	2	.979	-13	C-195	-4.3

■ **CITO GASTON** Gaston, Clarence Edwin b: 3/17/44, San Antonio, Tex. BR/TR, 6'4", 210 lbs. Deb: 9/14/67 MC

YEAR	TM/L	G	AB	R	H	2B	3B	HR	RBI	BB	SO	AVG	OBP	SLG	PRO+	BR/A	SB	CS	SBR	FA	FR	G/POS	TPR
1967	Atl-N	9	25	1	3	0	1	0	1	0	5	.120	.120	.200	-10	-4	1	0	0	.800	-1	/O-7	-0.5
1969	SD-N	129	391	20	90	11	7	2	28	24	117	.230	.276	.309	67	-18	4	4	-1	.959	6	*O-113	-2.1
1970	SD-N★	146	584	92	186	26	9	29	93	41	142	.318	.365	.543	146	34	4	1	1	.975	4	*O-142	3.1
1971	SD-N	141	518	57	118	13	9	17	61	24	121	.228	.265	.386	88	-11	1	0	0	.972	-0	*O-133	-1.9
1972	SD-N	111	379	30	102	14	0	7	44	22	76	.269	.313	.361	98	-2	0	2	-1	.977	1	O-94	-0.8
1973	SD-N	133	476	51	119	18	4	16	57	20	88	.250	.282	.405	96	-6	0	0	0	.947	2	*O-119	-1.0
1974	SD-N	106	267	19	57	11	0	6	33	16	51	.213	.261	.322	65	-14	0	0	0	.992	3	O-63	-1.4
1975	Atl-N	64	141	17	34	4	0	6	15	17	33	.241	.323	.397	95	-1	1	0	0	.974	-1	O-35/1-1	-0.3
1976	Atl-N	69	134	15	39	4	0	4	25	13	21	.291	.354	.410	109	2	1	0	0	.977	-2	O-28/1-2	-0.1
1977	Atl-N	56	85	6	23	4	0	3	21	5	19	.271	.311	.424	85	-2	1	0	0	1.000	-0	/O-9,1-5	-0.2
1978	Atl-N	60	118	5	27	1	0	1	9	3	20	.229	.248	.263	38	-10	0	0	0	.957	-4	O-29/1-4	-1.5
	Pit-N	2	2	1	1	0	0	0	0	0	0	.500	.500	.500	172	0	0	0	0	.000	-0	/O-1	0.0

YEAR	TM/L	G	AB	R	H	2B	3B	HR	RBI	BB	SO	AVG	OBP	SLG	PRO+	BR/A	SB	CS	SBR	FA	FR	G/POS	TPR
	Yr	62	120	6	28	1	0	1	9	3	20	.233	.252	.267	41	-9	0	0	0	.957	-4	O-30/1-4	-1.5
Total	11	1026	3120	314	799	106	30	91	387	185	693	.256	.300	.397	95	-32	13	7	-0	.970	6	O-773/1-12	-6.7
■ **BRENT GATES**	Gates, Brent Robert b: 3/14/70, Grand Rapids, Mich. BB/TR, 6′1″, 180 lbs. Deb: 5/5/93																						
1993	Oak-A	139	535	64	155	29	2	7	69	56	75	.290	.361	.391	109	7	7	3	0	.981	-3	*2-139	0.9
1994	Oak-A	64	233	29	66	11	1	2	24	21	32	.283	.345	.365	91	-3	3	0	1	.974	-17	2-63/1-1	-1.5
1995	Oak-A	136	524	60	133	24	4	5	56	46	84	.254	.314	.344	75	-19	3	3	-1	.982	11	*2-132/1-1,D-3	-0.1
1996	Oak-A	64	247	26	65	19	2	2	30	18	35	.263	.318	.381	77	-9	1	1	-0	.973	-2	2-63	-0.7
1997	*Sea-A	65	151	18	36	8	0	3	20	14	21	.238	.303	.351	71	-7	0	0	0	.934	-2	3-32,2-21/S-5,1OD	-0.8
1998	Min-A	107	333	31	83	15	0	3	42	36	46	.249	.326	.321	69	-14	3	3	-1	.961	-8	3-77,2-21/1-1,SD	-2.1
Total	6	575	2023	228	538	106	9	22	241	191	293	.266	.332	.360	84	-45	17	10	-1	.979	-20	2-439,3-109/SD1O	-4.3
■ **JOE GATES**	Gates, Joseph Daniel b: 10/3/54, Gary, Ind. BL/TR, 5′7″, 175 lbs. Deb: 9/12/78																						
1978	Chi-A	8	24	6	6	0	0	0	1	4	6	.250	.379	.250	80	-0	1	0	0	.972	-2	/2-8	-0.2
1979	Chi-A	16	16	5	1	0	1	0	1	2	3	.063	.167	.188	-5	-2	1	1	-0	.966	5	/2-8,3-1,D-1	0.2
Total	2	24	40	11	7	0	1	0	2	6	9	.175	.298	.225	46	-3	2	1	0	.969	3	/2-16,D-1,3-1	0.0
■ **MIKE GATES**	Gates, Michael Grant b: 9/20/56, Culver City, Cal. BL/TR, 6′, 165 lbs. Deb: 5/6/81																						
1981	Mon-N	1	2	1	1	0	1	0	1	0	1	.500	.500	1.500	445	1	0	0	0	1.000	-0	/2-1	0.0
1982	Mon-N	36	121	16	28	2	3	0	8	9	19	.231	.285	.298	62	-6	0	0	0	1.000	-9	2-36	-1.5
Total	2	37	123	17	29	2	4	0	9	9	20	.236	.288	.317	68	-5	0	0	0	1.000	-10	/2-37	-1.5
■ **FRANK GATINS**	Gatins, Frank Anthony b: 3/6/1871, Johnstown, Pa. d: 11/8/11, Johnstown, Pa. Deb: 9/21/1898																						
1898	Was-N	17	58	6	13	2	0	0	5	3		.224	.274	.259	53	-4	2			.790	-8	S-17	-1.0
1901	Bro-N	50	197	21	45	7	2	1	21	5		.228	.255	.299	59	-11	6			.919	-9	3-46/S-5	-1.9
Total	2	67	255	27	58	9	2	1	26	8		.227	.259	.290	58	-14	8			.841	-17	/3-46,S-22	-2.9
■ **JIM GAUDET**	Gaudet, James Jennings b: 6/3/55, New Orleans, La. BR/TR, 6′, 185 lbs. Deb: 9/10/78																						
1978	KC-A	3	8	0	0	0	0	0	0	0	3	.000	.000	.000	-97	-2	0	0	0	.938	1	/C-3	-0.1
1979	KC-A	3	6	0	1	0	0	0	0	0	0	.167	.167	.167	-10	-1	0	0	0	1.000	1	/C-3	0.0
Total	2	6	14	0	1	0	0	0	0	0	3	.071	.071	.071	-59	-3	0	0	0	.966	2	/C-6	-0.1
■ **MIKE GAULE**	Gaule, Michael John b: 8/4/1869, Baltimore, Md. d: 1/24/18, Baltimore, Md. BL/TL, 6′2″, Deb: 6/15/1889																						
1889	Lou-a	1	2	0	0	0	0	0	0	0	1	.000	.000	.000	-99	-1	0			.000	-1	/O-1	-0.1
■ **DOC GAUTREAU**	Gautreau, Walter Paul "Punk" b: 7/26/01, Cambridge, Mass. d: 8/23/70, Salt Lake City, Ut BR/TR, 5′4″, 129 lbs. Deb: 6/22/25																						
1925	Phi-A	4	7	0	0	0	0	0	0	0	3	.000	.000	.000	-94	-2	0	0	0	.933	1	/2-4	-0.1
	Bos-N	68	279	45	73	13	3	0	23	35	13	.262	.346	.330	81	-7	11	7	-1	.976	-4	2-68	-1.0
1926	Bos-N	79	266	36	71	9	4	0	8	35	24	.267	.356	.331	94	-1	17			.942	-20	2-74	-1.9
1927	Bos-N	87	236	38	58	12	2	0	20	25	20	.246	.321	.314	76	-8	11			.965	-2	2-57	-0.8
1928	Bos-N	23	18	3	5	0	1	0	1	4	3	.278	.409	.389	116	1	1			.750	-1	/2-4,S-1	0.0
Total	4	261	806	122	207	34	10	0	52	99	63	.257	.341	.324	83	-18	40	7		.960	-25	2-207/S-1	-3.8
■ **SID GAUTREAUX**	Gautreaux, Sidney Allen "Pudge" b: 5/4/12, Schriever, La. d: 4/19/80, Morgan City, La. BB/TR, 5′8″, 190 lbs. Deb: 4/15/36																						
1936	Bro-N	75	71	8	19	3	0	0	16	9	7	.268	.358	.310	80	-2	0			.963	-1	C-15	-0.2
1937	Bro-N	11	10	0	1	1	0	0	2	1	1	.100	.182	.200	4	-1	0			.000	0	H	-0.1
Total	2	86	81	8	20	4	0	0	18	10	8	.247	.337	.296	71	-3	0			.963	-1	/C-15	-0.3
■ **GAVERN**	Gavern Deb: 6/15/1874																						
1874	Atl-n	1	4	1	0	0	0	0	0	0	0	.000	.000	.000	-99	-1	0	0	0	.750	2	/2-1	0.0
■ **MIKE GAZELLA**	Gazella, Michael b: 10/13/1896, Olyphant, Pa. d: 9/11/78, Odessa, Tex. BR/TR, 5′7.5″, 165 lbs. Deb: 7/2/23																						
1923	NY-A	8	13	2	1	0	0	0	1	2	3	.077	.200	.077	-25	-2	0	0	0	1.000	-1	/S-4,2-2,3-2	-0.3
1926	*NY-A	66	168	21	39	6	0	0	20	25	24	.232	.335	.268	60	-9	2	2	-1	.913	-4	3-45,S-11	-1.0
1927	NY-A	54	115	17	32	8	4	0	9	23	16	.278	.403	.417	117	4	4	1	1	.961	-6	3-44/S-6	0.0
1928	NY-A	32	56	11	13	0	0	0	2	6	7	.232	.317	.232	48	-4	2	1	0	.969	-1	3-16/2-4,S-3	-0.4
Total	4	160	352	51	85	14	4	0	32	56	50	.241	.350	.304	73	-12	8	4	0	.940	-12	3-107/S-24,2-6	-1.7
■ **DALE GEAR**	Gear, Dale Dudley b: 2/2/1872, Lone Elm, Kan. d: 9/23/51, Topeka, Kan. BR/TR, 5′11″, 165 lbs. Deb: 8/15/1896																						
1896	Cle-N	4	15	5	6	1	1	0	3	1	1	.400	.438	.600	163	1	0			.857	-1	/P-3,1-1	0.0
1897	Cle-N	7	24	3	4	1	0	0	2	3		.167	.286	.208	30	-2	2			.750	0	/O-6	-0.2
1901	Was-A	58	199	17	47	9	2	0	20	4		.236	.251	.302	54	-13	2			.944	1	O-35,P-24	-1.0
Total	3	69	238	25	57	11	3	0	25	8	1	.239	.267	.311	59	-14	4			.900	0	/O-41,P-27,1-1	-1.2
■ **GARY GEARHART**	Gearhart, Lloyd William b: 8/10/23, New Lebanon, Ohio BR/TL, 5′11″, 180 lbs. Deb: 4/18/47																						
1947	NY-N	73	179	26	44	9	0	6	17	17	30	.246	.315	.397	87	-4	1			.961	-1	O-44	-0.7
■ **HUCK GEARY**	Geary, Eugene Francis Joseph b: 1/22/17, Buffalo, N.Y. d: 1/27/81, Cuba, N.Y. BL/TR, 5′10.5″, 170 lbs. Deb: 7/17/42																						
1942	Pit-N	9	22	3	5	0	0	0	2	2	3	.227	.292	.227	52	-1	0			.939	0	/S-8	-0.1
1943	Pit-N	46	166	17	25	4	0	1	13	18	6	.151	.234	.193	23	-16	3			.956	-6	S-46	-2.1
Total	2	55	188	20	30	4	0	1	15	20	9	.160	.240	.197	26	-17	3			.954	-6	/S-54	-2.2
■ **ELMER GEDEON**	Gedeon, Elmer John b: 4/15/17, Cleveland, Ohio d: 4/20/44, St.Pol, France BR/TR, 6′4″, 196 lbs. Deb: 9/18/39																						
1939	Was-A	5	15	1	3	0	0	0	1	2	5	.200	.294	.200	31	-2	0	0	0	1.000	1	/O-5	-0.1
■ **JOE GEDEON**	Gedeon, Elmer Joseph b: 12/5/1893, Sacramento, Cal. d: 5/19/41, San Francisco, Cal BR/TR, 6′, 167 lbs. Deb: 5/13/13																						
1913	Was-A	29	71	3	13	1	3	0	6	1	6	.183	.205	.282	41	-6	3			.929	2	O-15/3-7,2-2,S-2,P	-0.4
1914	Was-A	4	2	0	0	0	0	0	1	0	1	.000	.333	.000	1	-0	0			.667	-1	/O-4	-0.1
1916	NY-A	122	435	50	92	14	4	0	27	40	61	.211	.282	.262	62	-20	14			.955	-10	*2-122	-2.9
1917	NY-A	33	117	15	28	7	0	0	8	7	13	.239	.288	.299	78	-3	4			.983	4	2-31	0.2
1918	StL-A	123	441	39	94	14	3	1	41	27	29	.213	.271	.265	64	-20	7			**.977**	16	*2-123	0.4
1919	StL-A	120	437	57	111	13	4	0	27	50	35	.254	.340	.302	79	-11	4			**.975**	-3	*2-118	-0.8
1920	StL-A	153	606	95	177	33	6	0	61	55	36	.292	.355	.366	89	-9	1	3	-2	.964	-26	*2-153	-3.1
Total	7	584	2109	259	515	82	20	1	171	180	181	.244	.311	.303	75	-69	33	3		.969	-18	2-549/O-19,3-7,SP	-6.7
■ **RICH GEDMAN**	Gedman, Richard Leo b: 9/26/59, Worcester, Mass. BL/TR, 6′, 215 lbs. Deb: 9/7/80																						
1980	Bos-A	9	24	2	5	0	0	0	1	0	5	.208	.208	.208	14	-3	0	0	0	.867	-0	/C-2,D-4	-0.3
1981	Bos-A	62	205	22	59	15	0	5	26	9	31	.288	.321	.434	109	2	0	0	0	.990	-2	C-59	0.2
1982	Bos-A	92	289	30	72	17	2	4	26	10	37	.249	.279	.363	71	-12	0	1	-1	.977	-7	C-86	-1.7
1983	Bos-A	81	204	21	60	16	1	2	18	15	37	.294	.345	.412	100	0	0	1	-1	.980	-3	C-68	0.0
1984	Bos-A	133	449	54	121	26	4	24	72	29	72	.269	.315	.506	118	9	0	0	0	.977	-8	*C-125	0.7
1985	Bos-A★	144	498	66	147	30	5	18	80	50	79	.295	.363	.484	124	17	2	0	1	.983	4	*C-139	2.7
1986	*Bos-A★	135	462	49	119	29	0	16	65	37	61	.258	.318	.424	100	-1	1	0	0	.994	10	*C-134	1.8
1987	Bos-A	52	151	11	31	8	0	1	13	10	24	.205	.255	.278	40	-13	0	0	0	.976	-4	C-51	-1.3
1988	*Bos-A	95	299	33	69	14	0	9	39	18	49	.231	.281	.368	77	-10	0	0	0	.992	2	C-93/D-1	-0.1
1989	Bos-A	93	260	24	55	9	0	4	16	23	47	.212	.276	.292	57	-15	0	1	-1	.981	-0	C-91	-1.2
1990	Bos-A	10	15	3	3	0	0	0	0	5	6	.200	.429	.200	78	0	0	0	0	.970	0	/C-9	0.1
	Hou-N	40	104	4	21	7	0	1	10	15	24	.202	.303	.298	68	-4	0	0	0	1.000	6	C-39	0.4
1991	StL-N	46	94	7	10	1	0	3	8	4	15	.106	.143	.213	-1	-13	0	1	-1	.976	10	C-43	-0.2
1992	StL-N	41	105	5	23	4	0	1	8	11	22	.219	.293	.286	67	-5	0	0	0	.988	11	C-40	0.8
Total	13	1033	3159	331	795	176	12	88	382	236	509	.252	.307	.399	90	-48	3	4	-2	.984	20	C-979/D-5	1.9

■ COUNT GEDNEY Gedney, Alfred W. b: 5/10/1849, Brooklyn, N.Y. d: 3/26/22, Hackensack, N.J. 5'9", 140 lbs. Deb: 4/27/1872

YEAR	TM/L	G	AB	R	H	2B	3B	HR	RBI	BB	SO	AVG	OBP	SLG	PRO+	BR/A	SB	CS	SBR	FA	FR	G/POS	TPR
1872	Tro-n	9	47	14	20	3	0	3	18	0	0	.426	.426	.681	232	7	1	0	0	.933	-1	/O-9	0.4
	Eck-n	18	71	4	13	1	0	0	7	0	1	.183	.183	.197	20	-6	2	1	0	.911	1	O-18	-0.2
	Yr	27	118	18	33	4	0	3	25	0	1	.280	.280	.390	115	3	3	1	0	.915	0	O-27	0.2
1873	Mut-n	53	224	41	60	5	5	1	25	7	5	.268	.290	.348	89	-3	1	0	0	.867	15	*O-53	1.0
1874	Ath-n	54	222	49	61	4	1	1	34	7	11	.275	.297	.315	89	-4	2	2	-1	.822	-2	*O-51/1-4	-0.4
1875	Mut-n	68	267	30	55	12	2	0	17	0	8	.206	.206	.266	60	-11	2	3	-1	.843	12	*O-67/P-2	0.0
Total	4 n	202	831	138	209	25	8	5	101	14	25	.252	.264	.319	83	-17	8	6	-1	.853	25	O-198/1-4,P-2	0.8

■ BILLY GEER Geer, William Henry Harrison (b: George Harrison Geer) b: 8/13/1849, Syracuse, N.Y. TR, 5'8", 160 lbs. Deb: 10/15/1874

YEAR	TM/L	G	AB	R	H	2B	3B	HR	RBI	BB	SO	AVG	OBP	SLG	PRO+	BR/A	SB	CS	SBR	FA	FR	G/POS	TPR
1874	Mut-n	2	8	0	2	0	0	0	1	0	0	.250	.250	.250	59	-0	0	0	0	.889	2	/O-2	0.1
1875	NH-n	37	164	20	40	4	1	0	9	1	4	.244	.248	.280	96	0	2	2	-1	.765	3	O-17,2-13/S-6,13	0.2
1878	Cin-N	61	237	31	52	13	2	0	20	10	18	.219	.251	.291	86	-3				.867	-4	*S-60/2-2	-0.4
1880	Wor-N	2	6	0	0	0	0	0	0	0	0	.000	.000	.000	-92	-1				1.000	-1	/O-1,S-1	-0.2
1884	Phi-U	9	36	7	9	2	1	0		4		.250	.325	.361	116	-0				.772	1	/S-9	0.1
	Bro-a	107	391	68	82	15	7	0		38		.210	.281	.284	84	-6				.870	17	*S-107/P-2,2-2	1.1
1885	Lou-a	14	51	2	6	2	0	0	3	2		.118	.167	.157	3	-6				.872	2	S-14	-0.3
Total	2 n	39	172	20	42	4	1	0	10	1	4	.244	.249	.279	93	-0	2	2	-1	.791	5	/O-19,2-13,S-6,31	0.3
Total	4	193	721	108	149	32	10	0	23	54	18	.207	.264	.279	79	-15				.864	15	S-191/2-4,P-2,O-1	0.3

■ LOU GEHRIG Gehrig, Henry Louis "The Iron Horse" b: 6/19/03, New York, N.Y. d: 6/2/41, Riverdale, N.Y. BL/TL, 6', 200 lbs. Deb: 6/15/23 H

YEAR	TM/L	G	AB	R	H	2B	3B	HR	RBI	BB	SO	AVG	OBP	SLG	PRO+	BR/A	SB	CS	SBR	FA	FR	G/POS	TPR
1923	NY-A	13	26	6	11	4	1	1	9	2	5	.423	.464	.769	217	4	0	0	0	.933	-1	/1-9	0.3
1924	NY-A	10	12	2	6	1	0	0	5	1	3	.500	.538	.583	190	2	0	0	0	1.000	-0	/1-2,O-1	0.1
1925	NY-A	126	437	73	129	23	10	20	68	46	49	.295	.365	.531	127	15	6	3	0	.989	-9	*1-114/O-6	-0.1
1926	*NY-A	155	572	135	179	47	**20**	16	112	105	73	.313	.420	.549	154	46	6	5	-1	.991	-8	*1-155	2.6
1927	*NY-A	155	584	149	218	**52**	18	47	**175**	109	84	.373	.474	.765	224	**107**	10	8	-2	.992	-6	*1-155	8.1
1928	*NY-A	154	562	139	210	**47**	13	27	**142**	95	69	.374	**.467**	.648	197	81	4	11	-5	.989	-8	*1-154	5.1
1929	NY-A	154	553	127	166	32	10	35	126	122	68	.300	.431	.584	170	61	4	4	-1	.994	-5	*1-154	3.7
1930	NY-A	154	581	143	220	42	17	41	**174**	101	63	.379	.473	.721	207	97	12	14	-5	.989	1	*1-153/O-1	6.9
1931	NY-A	155	619	**163**	**211**	31	15	**46**	**184**	117	56	.341	.446	.662	199	90	17	12	-2	.991	-10	*1-154/O-1	5.8
1932	*NY-A	156	596	138	208	42	9	34	151	108	38	.349	.451	.621	184	77	4	11	-5	.987	-6	*1-156	4.9
1933	NY-A★	152	593	**138**	198	41	12	32	139	92	42	.334	.424	.605	181	68	9	13	-5	.993	-3	*1-152	4.3
1934	NY-A★	154	579	128	210	40	6	**49**	**165**	109	31	**.363**	**.465**	**.706**	**213**	**98**	9	5	-0	.994	1	*1-153/S-1	**7.8**
1935	NY-A★	149	535	**125**	176	26	10	30	119	**132**	38	.329	**.466**	.583	180	**70**	8	7	-2	.990	0	*1-149	4.8
1936	*NY-A★	155	579	**167**	205	37	7	**49**	152	**130**	46	.354	**.478**	**.696**	**193**	**89**	3	4	-2	.994	1	*1-155	**6.4**
1937	*NY-A★	157	569	138	200	37	9	37	159	**127**	49	.351	**.473**	.643	**177**	**72**	4	3	-1	.989	-6	*1-157	4.3
1938	*NY-A★	157	576	115	170	32	6	29	114	107	75	.295	.410	.523	133	30	6	1	1	.991	-1	*1-157	1.2
1939	NY-A†	8	28	2	4	0	0	0	1	5	1	.143	.273	.143	9	-4	0	0	0	.971	-1	/1-8	-0.5
Total	17	2164	8001	1888	2721	534	163	493	1995	1508	790	.340	.447	.632	182	1005	102	101	-30	.991	-60	*1-2137/O-9,S-1	65.7

■ CHARLIE GEHRINGER Gehringer, Charles Leonard "The Mechanical Man" b: 5/11/03, Fowlerville, Mich. d: 1/21/93, Bloomfield Hills, Mich. BL/TR, 5'11", 180 lbs. Deb: 9/22/24 CH

YEAR	TM/L	G	AB	R	H	2B	3B	HR	RBI	BB	SO	AVG	OBP	SLG	PRO+	BR/A	SB	CS	SBR	FA	FR	G/POS	TPR
1924	Det-A	5	13	2	6	0	0	0	1	0	2	.462	.462	.462	141	1	1	1	-0	.967	4	/2-5	0.4
1925	Det-A	8	18	3	3	0	0	0	0	2	0	.167	.250	.167	7	-3	0	1	-1	1.000	4	/2-6	0.0
1926	Det-A	123	459	62	127	19	17	1	48	30	42	.277	.322	.399	86	-11	9	7	-2	.973	-10	*2-112/3-6	-1.8
1927	Det-A	133	508	110	161	29	11	4	61	52	31	.317	.383	.441	112	9	17	8	0	.965	**20**	*2-121	3.1
1928	Det-A	154	603	108	193	29	16	6	74	69	22	.320	.395	.451	120	19	15	9	-1	.962	2	*2-154	2.3
1929	Det-A	155	634	**131**	**215**	**45**	**19**	13	106	64	19	.339	.405	.532	139	36	**27**	9	**3**	**.975**	3	*2-154	3.9
1930	Det-A	154	610	144	201	47	15	16	98	69	17	.330	.404	.534	133	31	19	15	-3	**.979**	2	*2-154	3.4
1931	Det-A	101	383	67	119	24	5	4	53	29	15	.311	.359	.431	103	1	13	4	2	.979	-1	2-78/1-9	0.6
1932	Det-A	152	618	112	184	44	11	19	107	68	34	.298	.370	.497	118	15	9	8	-2	.967	-1	*2-152	1.8
1933	Det-A★	155	628	103	204	42	6	12	105	68	27	.325	.393	.468	125	23	5	4	-1	.981	7	*2-155	3.6
1934	*Det-A★	154	601	**134**	**214**	50	7	11	127	99	25	.356	.450	.517	149	47	11	8	-2	.981	7	*2-154	5.7
1935	*Det-A★	150	610	123	201	32	8	19	108	79	16	.330	.409	.502	139	36	11	4	1	**.985**	3	*2-149	4.7
1936	Det-A★	154	641	144	227	**60**	12	15	116	83	13	.354	.431	.555	141	43	4	1	1	**.974**	16	*2-154	6.1
1937	Det-A★	144	564	133	209	40	1	14	96	90	25	**.371**	.458	.520	143	41	11	4	1	**.986**	6	*2-142	5.2
1938	Det-A★	152	568	133	174	32	5	20	107	113	21	.306	.425	.486	121	21	14	1	**4**	.976	-1	*2-152	3.0
1939	Det-A	118	406	86	132	29	6	16	86	68	16	.325	.423	.544	135	22	4	3	-1	**.977**	1	*2-107	2.6
1940	*Det-A	139	515	108	161	33	3	10	81	101	17	.313	.428	.447	116	16	10	0	3	.972	-20	*2-138	0.8
1941	Det-A	127	436	65	96	19	4	3	46	95	26	.220	.363	.303	71	-16	1	2	-1	**.982**	-3	*2-116	-1.1
1942	Det-A	45	45	6	12	0	0	1	7	7	4	.267	.365	.333	90	-0	0	0	0	1.000	1	/2-3	0.1
Total	19	2323	8860	1774	2839	574	146	184	1427	1186	372	.320	.404	.480	123	332	181	89	1	.976	33	*2-2206/1-9,3-6	44.4

■ PHIL GEIER Geier, Philip Louis "Little Phil" b: 11/3/1875, Washington, D.C. d: 9/25/67, Spokane, Wash. BL/TR, 5'7", 145 lbs. Deb: 8/17/1896

YEAR	TM/L	G	AB	R	H	2B	3B	HR	RBI	BB	SO	AVG	OBP	SLG	PRO+	BR/A	SB	CS	SBR	FA	FR	G/POS	TPR
1896	Phi-N	17	56	12	13	0	1	0	6	6	7	.232	.317	.268	56	-3	3			.813	-2	O-12/2-3,C-2	-0.5
1897	Phi-N	92	316	51	88	6	2	1	35	56		.278	.392	.320	91	-0	19			.932	-7	O-45,2-37/S-6,3-2	-0.7
1900	Cin-N	30	113	18	29	1	4	0	10	7		.257	.306	.336	79	-3	3			.941	1	O-27/3-2	-0.4
1901	Phi-A	50	211	42	49	5	2	0	23	24		.232	.314	.275	61	-11	7			.934	-5	O-50/S-2,3-1	-1.7
	Mil-A	11	39	4	7	1	1	0	1	5		.179	.273	.256	50	-3	4			1.000	-1	/O-8,3-3	-0.4
	Yr	61	250	46	56	6	3	0	24	29		.224	.307	.272	60	-13	11			.941	-6	O-58/3-4,S-2	-2.1
1904	Bos-N	149	580	70	141	17	2	1	27	56		.243	.314	.284	88	-6	18			.933	-3	*O-137/3-7,2-5,S-1	-1.8
Total	5	349	1315	197	327	30	12	2	102	154	7	.249	.332	.294	81	-27	54			.932	-16	O-279/2-45,3-15,SC	-5.5

■ GARY GEIGER Geiger, Gary Merle b: 4/4/37, Sand Ridge, Ill. d: 4/24/96, Murphysboro, Ill. BL/TR, 6', 168 lbs. Deb: 4/15/58

YEAR	TM/L	G	AB	R	H	2B	3B	HR	RBI	BB	SO	AVG	OBP	SLG	PRO+	BR/A	SB	CS	SBR	FA	FR	G/POS	TPR
1958	Cle-A	91	195	28	45	3	1	1	6	27	43	.231	.333	.272	70	-7	2	2	-1	.986	4	O-53/3-2,P-1	-0.6
1959	Bos-A	120	335	45	82	10	4	11	48	21	55	.245	.289	.397	83	-9	9	3	1	.989	-10	O-95	-2.3
1960	Bos-A	77	245	32	74	13	3	9	33	23	38	.302	.369	.490	126	9	2	2	-1	1.000	4	O-66	0.9
1961	Bos-A	140	499	82	116	21	6	18	64	87	91	.232	.351	.407	99	1	16	4	2	.988	10	*O-137	0.5
1962	Bos-A	131	466	67	116	18	4	16	54	67	66	.249	.346	.408	99	-0	18	11	-1	.987	8	*O-129	-0.1
1963	Bos-A	121	399	67	105	13	5	16	44	36	63	.263	.329	.441	110	5	9	4	0	.984	14	O-95/1-6	1.4
1964	Bos-A	5	13	3	5	0	1	0	1	2	2	.385	.467	.538	170	1	0	0	0	1.000	-1	/O-4	0.1
1965	Bos-A	24	45	5	9	3	0	1	2	13	10	.200	.379	.333	98	0	3	0	1	.970	0	O-16	0.1
1966	Atl-N	78	126	23	33	5	3	4	10	21	29	.262	.372	.444	124	5	0	1	-1	.982	-9	O-49	-0.6
1967	Atl-N	69	117	17	19	1	1	1	5	20	35	.162	.285	.214	45	-8	1	1	-0	.980	-6	O-38	-1.6
1969	Hou-N	93	125	19	28	4	1	0	16	24	34	.224	.353	.272	79	-2	2	1	0	.968	-7	O-65	-1.2
1970	Hou-N	5	4	0	1	0	0	0	0	0	0	.250	.250	.250	36	-0	0	0	0	1.000	-1	/O-2	-0.1
Total	12	954	2569	388	633	91	29	77	283	341	466	.246	.339	.394	98	-6	62	29	1	.986	8	O-749/1-6,3-2,P-1	-3.5

■ BILL GEIS Geis, William J. (b: William J. Geiss) b: 7/15/1858, Chicago, Ill. d: 9/18/24, Chicago, Ill. 5'10", 164 lbs. Deb: 5/1/1884 F

YEAR	TM/L	G	AB	R	H	2B	3B	HR	RBI	BB	SO	AVG	OBP	SLG	PRO+	BR/A	SB	CS	SBR	FA	FR	G/POS	TPR
1884	Det-N	75	283	22	50	11	4	2	16	6	60	.177	.194	.265	46	-17				.862	-7	2-73/O-1,1-1,P-1	-2.0

■ EMIL GEISS Geiss, Emil August b: 3/20/1867, Chicago, Ill. d: 10/4/11, Chicago, Ill. BR/TR, 5'11", 170 lbs. Deb: 5/18/1887 F

YEAR	TM/L	G	AB	R	H	2B	3B	HR	RBI	BB	SO	AVG	OBP	SLG	PRO+	BR/A	SB	CS	SBR	FA	FR	G/POS	TPR
1887	Chi-N	3	12	0	1	0	0	0	0	0	7	.083	.083	.083	-47	-2	0			.571	-1	/2-1,1-1,P-1	-0.3

■ CHARLIE GELBERT Gelbert, Charles Magnus b: 1/26/06, Scranton, Pa. d: 1/13/67, Easton, Pa. BR/TR, 5'11", 170 lbs. Deb: 4/16/29

YEAR	TM/L	G	AB	R	H	2B	3B	HR	RBI	BB	SO	AVG	OBP	SLG	PRO+	BR/A	SB	CS	SBR	FA	FR	G/POS	TPR
1929	StL-N	146	512	60	134	29	8	3	65	51	46	.262	.329	.367	71	-23	8			.948	7	*S-146	0.1
1930	*StL-N	139	513	92	156	39	11	3	72	43	41	.304	.360	.441	89	-9	6			.947	9	*S-139	1.3
1931	*StL-N	131	447	61	129	29	5	1	62	54	31	.289	.365	.383	97	-0	7			.959	13	*S-130	2.5
1932	StL-N	122	455	60	122	28	9	1	45	39	30	.268	.330	.376	87	-8	8			.945	0	*S-122	0.3
1935	StL-N	62	168	24	49	7	2	2	21	17	18	.292	.357	.393	97	-0	0			.978	5	3-37,S-21/2-3	0.6
1936	StL-N	93	280	33	64	15	2	3	27	25	26	.229	.292	.329	67	-13	2			.965	8	3-60,S-28/2-8	-0.2

YEAR	TM/L	G	AB	R	H	2B	3B	HR	RBI	BB	SO	AVG	OBP	SLG	PRO+	BR/A	SB	CS	SBR	FA	FR	G/POS	TPR
1937	Cin-N	43	114	12	22	4	0	1	13	15	12	.193	.287	.254	51	-8	1			.968	-2	S-37/2-9,3-1	-0.7
	Det-A	20	47	4	4	2	0	0	1	4	11	.085	.157	.128	-27	-9	0	0	0	.934	-0	S-16	-0.8
1939	Was-A	68	188	36	48	7	5	3	29	30	11	.255	.361	.394	100	0	2	0	1	.970	-4	S-28,3-20/2-1	0.0
1940	Was-A	22	54	7	20	7	1	0	7	4	3	.370	.424	.537	157	5	0	0	0	.920	-5	S-12/P-2,2-1	0.0
	Bos-A	30	91	9	18	2	0	0	8	8	16	.198	.263	.220	25	-10	0	0	0	.926	5	3-29/S-1	-0.5
	Yr	52	145	16	38	9	1	0	15	12	19	.262	.323	.338	72	-6	0	0	0	.926	-1	3-29,S-13/P-2,2-1	-0.5
Total	9	876	2869	398	766	169	43	17	350	290	245	.267	.336	.374	82	-76	34	0		.951	35	S-680,3-147/2-22,P	2.6

■ FRANK GENINS Genins, C. Frank "Frenchy" b: 11/2/1866, St.Louis, Mo. d: 9/30/22, St.Louis, Mo. TR , Deb: 7/5/1892

YEAR	TM/L	G	AB	R	H	2B	3B	HR	RBI	BB	SO	AVG	OBP	SLG	PRO+	BR/A	SB	CS	SBR	FA	FR	G/POS	TPR
1892	Cin-N	35	110	12	20	4	0	0	7	12	12	.182	.262	.218	46	-7	7			.901	4	S-17,O-14/3-4	-0.2
	StL-N	15	51	5	10	1	0	0	4	1	11	.196	.212	.216	31	-4	3			.821	-8	S-14/O-1	-1.1
	Yr	50	161	17	30	5	0	0	11	13	23	.186	.247	.217	42	-11	10			.868	-3	S-31,O-15/3-4	-1.3
1895	Pit-N	73	252	43	63	8	0	2	24	22	14	.250	.315	.306	64	-13	19			.931	-8	O-29,3-16,2-16,/S1	-1.8
1901	Cle-A	26	101	15	23	5	0	0	9	8		.228	.284	.277	58	-6	3			.940	1	O-26	-0.6
Total	3	149	514	75	116	18	0	2	44	43	37	.226	.288	.272	56	-30	32			.934	-10	/O-70,S-39,3-20,21	-3.7

■ GEORGE GENOVESE Genovese, George Michael b: 2/22/22, Staten Island, N.Y BL/TR, 5′6.5″, 160 lbs. Deb: 4/29/50

YEAR	TM/L	G	AB	R	H	2B	3B	HR	RBI	BB	SO	AVG	OBP	SLG	PRO+	BR/A	SB	CS	SBR	FA	FR	G/POS	TPR
1950	Was-A	3	1	1	0	0	0	0	0	1	0	.000	.500	.000	39	0	0	0	0	.000	0	H	0.0

■ JIM GENTILE Gentile, James Edward "Diamond Jim" b: 6/3/34, San Francisco, Cal. BL/TL, 6′4″, 215 lbs. Deb: 9/10/57

YEAR	TM/L	G	AB	R	H	2B	3B	HR	RBI	BB	SO	AVG	OBP	SLG	PRO+	BR/A	SB	CS	SBR	FA	FR	G/POS	TPR
1957	Bro-N	4	6	1	1	0	0	1	1	1	1	.167	.286	.667	133	0	0	0	0	1.000	-0	/1-2	0.0
1958	LA-N	12	30	0	4	1	0	0	4	4	6	.133	.235	.167	9	-4	0	0	0	.981	-1	/1-8	-0.6
1960	Bal-A★	138	384	67	112	17	0	21	98	68	72	.292	.407	.500	146	27	0	0	0	.993	-6	*1-124	1.2
1961	Bal-A★	148	486	96	147	25	2	46	141	96	106	.302	.428	.646	189	64	1	1	-0	.989	2	*1-144	5.3
1962	Bal-A★	152	545	80	137	21	1	33	87	77	100	.251	.351	.475	128	21	1	0	0	.988	6	*1-150	1.7
1963	Bal-A	145	496	65	123	16	1	24	72	76	101	.248	.355	.429	123	17	1	0	0	**.995**	7	*1-143	1.9
1964	KC-A	136	439	71	110	10	0	28	71	84	122	.251	.376	.465	128	19	0	0	0	.988	-0	*1-128	1.4
1965	KC-A	38	118	14	29	5	0	10	22	9	26	.246	.305	.542	138	5	0	0	0	.981	-1	1-35	0.2
	Hou-N	81	227	22	55	11	1	7	31	34	72	.242	.353	.392	118	6	0	0	0	.993	2	1-68	0.5
1966	Hou-N	49	144	16	35	6	1	7	18	21	39	.243	.355	.444	129	6	0	0	0	.989	2	1-43	0.6
	Cle-A	33	47	2	6	1	0	2	4	5	18	.128	.212	.277	39	-4	0	0	0	.944	-0	/1-9	-0.5
Total	9	936	2922	434	759	113	6	179	549	475	663	.260	.372	.486	137	157	3	1	0	.990	10	1-854	11.7

■ SAM GENTILE Gentile, Samuel Christopher b: 10/12/16, Charlestown, Mass. d: 5/4/98, Everett, Mass. BL/TR, 5′11″, 180 lbs. Deb: 4/24/43

YEAR	TM/L	G	AB	R	H	2B	3B	HR	RBI	BB	SO	AVG	OBP	SLG	PRO+	BR/A	SB	CS	SBR	FA	FR	G/POS	TPR
1943	Bos-N	8	4	1	1	1	0	0	0	1	0	.250	.400	.500	162	0	0			.000	0	H	0.0

■ HARVEY GENTRY Gentry, Harvey William b: 5/27/26, Winston-Salem, N.C BL/TR, 6′, 170 lbs. Deb: 4/14/54 F

YEAR	TM/L	G	AB	R	H	2B	3B	HR	RBI	BB	SO	AVG	OBP	SLG	PRO+	BR/A	SB	CS	SBR	FA	FR	G/POS	TPR
1954	NY-N	5	4	0	1	0	0	0	1	1	0	.250	.400	.250	73	-0	0	0	0	.000	0	H	0.0

■ ALEX GEORGE George, Alex Thomas M. b: 9/27/38, Kansas City, Mo. BL/TR, 5′11.5″, 170 lbs. Deb: 9/16/55

YEAR	TM/L	G	AB	R	H	2B	3B	HR	RBI	BB	SO	AVG	OBP	SLG	PRO+	BR/A	SB	CS	SBR	FA	FR	G/POS	TPR
1955	KC-A	5	10	0	1	0	0	0	0	1	7	.100	.182	.100	-22	-2	0	0	0	.917	-1	/S-5	-0.3

■ GREEK GEORGE George, Charles Peter b: 12/25/12, Waycross, Ga. BR/TR, 6′2″, 200 lbs. Deb: 6/30/35

YEAR	TM/L	G	AB	R	H	2B	3B	HR	RBI	BB	SO	AVG	OBP	SLG	PRO+	BR/A	SB	CS	SBR	FA	FR	G/POS	TPR
1935	Cle-A	2	0	0	0	0	0	0	0	0	0	—	—	—	—	0	0	0	0	1.000	0	/C-1	0.0
1936	Cle-A	23	77	3	15	3	0	0	5	9	16	.195	.279	.234	28	-9	0	0	0	.994	16	C-22	0.7
1938	Bro-N	7	20	0	4	0	1	0	2	0	4	.200	.200	.300	35	-2	0			1.000	2	/C-7	0.0
1941	Chi-N	35	64	4	10	2	0	0	6	2	10	.156	.182	.188	4	-8	0			.973	2	C-18	-0.5
1945	Phi-A	51	138	8	24	4	1	0	11	17	29	.174	.265	.217	41	-10	0	0	0	.972	-6	C-46	-1.5
Total	5	118	299	15	53	9	2	0	24	28	59	.177	.248	.221	29	-29	0	0		.983	14	/C-94	-1.3

■ BILL GEORGE George, William M. b: 1/27/1865, Bellaire, Ohio d: 8/23/16, Wheeling, W.Va. BR/TL, 5′8″, 165 lbs. Deb: 5/11/1887

YEAR	TM/L	G	AB	R	H	2B	3B	HR	RBI	BB	SO	AVG	OBP	SLG	PRO+	BR/A	SB	CS	SBR	FA	FR	G/POS	TPR
1887	NY-N	13	53	6	9	0	0	0	5	1	6	.170	.185	.170	-1	-7	2			.854	1	P-13/O-1	0.0
1888	*NY-N	9	39	7	9	1	0	1	6	0	2	.231	.231	.333	79	-1	1			1.000	-1	/O-6,P-4	-0.2
1889	NY-N	3	15	1	4	0	0	0	0	0	3	.267	.267	.267	49	-1	1			.875	-0	/O-3	-0.1
	Col-a	5	17	1	4	0	0	0	3	1	1	.235	.278	.235	49	-1	1			.667	-1	/O-4,P-2	-0.2
Total	3	30	124	15	26	1	0	1	14	2	12	.210	.222	.242	36	-10	5			.860	-1	/P-19,O-14	-0.5

■ BEN GERAGHTY Geraghty, Benjamin Raymond b: 7/19/12, Jersey City, N.J. d: 6/18/63, Jacksonville, Fla BR/TR, 5′11″, 175 lbs. Deb: 4/17/36

YEAR	TM/L	G	AB	R	H	2B	3B	HR	RBI	BB	SO	AVG	OBP	SLG	PRO+	BR/A	SB	CS	SBR	FA	FR	G/POS	TPR
1936	Bro-N	51	129	11	25	4	0	0	9	8	16	.194	.241	.225	26	-13	4			.922	-7	S-31/2-9,3-5	-1.8
1943	Bos-N	8	1	2	0	0	0	0	0	0	0	.000	.000	.000	-99	-0	0			1.000	1	/2-1,S-1,3-1	0.1
1944	Bos-N	11	16	3	4	0	0	0	0	1	2	.250	.294	.250	52	-1	0			1.000	0	/2-4,3-3	-0.1
Total	3	70	146	16	29	4	0	0	9	9	18	.199	.245	.226	28	-15	4			.922	-6	/S-32,2-14,3-9	-1.8

■ CRAIG GERBER Gerber, Craig Stuart b: 1/8/59, Chicago, Ill. BL/TR, 6′, 175 lbs. Deb: 4/11/85

YEAR	TM/L	G	AB	R	H	2B	3B	HR	RBI	BB	SO	AVG	OBP	SLG	PRO+	BR/A	SB	CS	SBR	FA	FR	G/POS	TPR
1985	Cal-A	65	91	8	24	1	2	0	6	2	3	.264	.280	.319	64	-5	0	3	-2	.970	19	S-53/3-9,2-1,D-1	1.4

■ WALLY GERBER Gerber, Walter "Spooks" b: 8/18/1891, Columbus, Ohio d: 6/19/51, Columbus, Ohio BR/TR, 5′10″, 152 lbs. Deb: 9/23/14

YEAR	TM/L	G	AB	R	H	2B	3B	HR	RBI	BB	SO	AVG	OBP	SLG	PRO+	BR/A	SB	CS	SBR	FA	FR	G/POS	TPR
1914	Pit-N	17	54	5	13	1	1	0	5	2	8	.241	.281	.296	75	-2	0			.921	1	S-17	0.0
1915	Pit-N	56	144	8	28	2	0	0	7	9	16	.194	.252	.208	40	-10	6	1	1	.930	2	3-23,S-21/2-2	-0.5
1917	StL-A	14	39	2	12	1	1	0	2	3	2	.308	.357	.385	131	1	1			.939	-2	S-12/2-2	0.0
1918	StL-A	56	171	10	41	4	0	0	10	19	11	.240	.316	.263	77	-4	2			.922	-9	S-56	-1.2
1919	StL-A	140	462	43	105	14	6	1	37	49	36	.227	.308	.290	67	-20	1			.940	-8	*S-140	-2.1
1920	StL-A	154	584	70	163	26	2	2	60	58	32	.279	.346	.341	80	-16	4	13	-7	.939	7	*S-154	-0.2
1921	StL-A	114	436	55	121	12	9	2	48	34	19	.278	.337	.360	73	-18	4	7	-3	.943	-3	*S-113	-1.2
1922	StL-A	153	604	81	161	22	8	1	51	52	34	.267	.326	.334	70	-26	6	4	-1	.944	0	*S-153	-1.1
1923	StL-A	154	605	85	170	26	3	1	62	54	50	.281	.342	.339	75	-21	4	6	-2	.950	6	*S-154	-0.2
1924	StL-A	148	496	61	135	20	4	0	55	43	34	.272	.341	.329	69	-22	4	5	-2	.946	-7	*S-147	-1.4
1925	StL-A	72	246	29	67	13	1	0	19	26	15	.272	.344	.333	69	-11	1	2	-1	.949	5	S-71	0.0
1926	StL-A	131	411	37	111	8	0	0	42	40	29	.270	.339	.290	62	-21	0	2	-1	.944	3	*S-129	-0.6
1927	StL-A	142	438	44	98	13	9	0	45	35	25	.224	.284	.295	49	-34	3	6	-3	.946	9	*S-141/3-1	-1.3
1928	StL-A	6	18	1	5	1	0	0	0	1	3	.278	.316	.333	69	-1	0	0	0	.783	-2	/S-6	-0.2
	Bos-A	104	300	21	64	6	1	0	28	32	31	.213	.289	.240	41	-25	6	1	1	.955	34	*S-103	1.9
	Yr	110	318	22	69	7	1	0	28	33	34	.217	.291	.245	43	-26	6	1	1	.948	**32**	*S-109	1.7
1929	Bos-A	61	91	6	15	3	1	0	5	8	12	.165	.232	.220	17	-11	1	0	0	.937	14	S-30,2-22	0.5
Total	15	1522	5099	558	1309	172	46	7	476	465	357	.257	.323	.313	67	-241	43	47		.943	52	*S-1447/2-26,3-24	-7.6

■ BOB GEREN Geren, Robert Peter b: 9/22/61, San Diego, Cal. BR/TR, 6′3″, 221 lbs. Deb: 5/17/88

YEAR	TM/L	G	AB	R	H	2B	3B	HR	RBI	BB	SO	AVG	OBP	SLG	PRO+	BR/A	SB	CS	SBR	FA	FR	G/POS	TPR
1988	NY-A	10	10	0	1	0	0	0	0	2	3	.100	.250	.100	2	-1	0	0	0	1.000	1	C-10	0.0
1989	NY-A	65	205	26	59	5	1	9	27	12	44	.288	.330	.454	120	5	0	0	0	.991	0	C-60/D-2	0.9
1990	NY-A	110	277	21	59	7	0	8	31	13	73	.213	.261	.325	63	-14	0	0	0	.993	12	*C-107/D-1	0.3
1991	NY-A	64	128	7	28	3	0	2	12	9	31	.219	.270	.289	55	-8	0	1	-1	.989	9	C-63	0.2
1993	SD-N	58	145	8	31	6	0	3	6	13	28	.214	.278	.317	58	-9	0	0	0	.993	4	C-49/1-1,3-1	-0.2
Total	5	307	765	62	178	21	1	22	76	49	179	.233	.284	.349	74	-28	0	1	-1	.992	26	C-289/D-3,3-1,1-1	1.2

■ JOE GERHARDT Gerhardt, John Joseph "Move Up Joe" b: 2/14/1855, Washington, D.C. d: 3/11/22, Middletown, N.Y. BR/TR, 6′, 160 lbs. Deb: 9/1/1873 M

YEAR	TM/L	G	AB	R	H	2B	3B	HR	RBI	BB	SO	AVG	OBP	SLG	PRO+	BR/A	SB	CS	SBR	FA	FR	G/POS	TPR
1873	Was-n	13	56	6	12	3	0	0	7	0	5	.214	.214	.268	44	-4	0	0	0	.700	-5	S-13	-0.7
1874	Bal-n	14	61	10	19	0	1	0	6	0	0	.311	.311	.344	111	1	0	0	0	.750	3	S-14	0.3
1875	Mut-n	58	252	29	54	7	3	0	20	0	2	.214	.214	.266	62	-10	0	5	-3	.753	-1	3-47,2-13/S-1,O-1	-1.2
1876	Lou-N	65	292	33	76	10	3	2	18	3	5	.260	.268	.336	85	-8				.944	5	*1-54/2-5,S-3,O3	-0.3
1877	Lou-N	59	250	41	76	6	5	1	35	5	8	.304	.318	.380	101	-2				.888	**20**	*2-57/O-1,S-1,1-1	1.7
1878	Cin-N	60	259	46	77	7	2	0	28	7	14	.297	.316	.340	127	8				.906	5	*2-60	1.6
1879	Cin-N	79	313	22	62	12	3	1	39	3	19	.198	.206	.265	57	-14				.908	7	2-55,3-16/1-8,S-1	-0.3

YEAR	TM/L	G	AB	R	H	2B	3B	HR	RBI	BB	SO	AVG	OBP	SLG	PRO+	BR/A	SB	CS	SBR	FA	FR	G/POS	TPR
1881	Det-N	80	297	35	72	13	6	0	36	7	31	.242	.260	.327	80	-7				.908	8	*2-79/3-1	0.3
1883	Lou-a	78	319	56	84	11	9	0		14		.263	.294	.354	116	7				.906	20	*2-78,M	2.4
1884	Lou-a	106	404	39	89	7	8	0	40	13		.220	.254	.277	76	-10				.920	27	*2-106	1.8
1885	NY-N	112	399	43	62	12	2	0	33	24	47	.155	.203	.195	30	-30				.911	11	*2-112	-1.4
1886	NY-N	123	426	44	81	11	7	0	40	22	63	.190	.230	.249	45	-28	8			.924	14	*2-123	-0.8
1887	NY-N	1	4	0	0	0	0	0	0	0	0	.000	.000	.000	-99	-1	0			1.000	0	/3-1	-0.1
	NY-a	85	307	40	68	13	2	0	27	24		.221	.280	.277	58	-17	15			.896	15	2-84/3-1	0.0
1890	Bro-a	99	369	34	75	10	4	2	40	30		.203	.270	.268	61	-18	9			.938	37	*2-99	2.1
	StL-a	37	125	15	32	0	0	1	11	9		.256	.321	.280	68	-6	5			.955	5	2-20,3-17,M	0.1
	Yr	136	494	49	107	10	4	3	51	39		.217	.283	.271	63	-24	14			**.940**	**42**	*2-119,3-17	2.2
1891	Lou-a	2	6	0	0	0	0	0	0	1	0	.000	.143	.000	-59	-1	0			.833	-0	/2-2	-0.1
Total	3 n	85	369	45	85	10	4	0	33	0	7	.230	.230	.279	67	-13	0	5	-3	.732	-2	/3-47,S-28,2-13,O-1	-1.6
Total	12	986	3770	448	854	112	51	7	347	162	187	.227	.261	.289	72	-127	37			.913	173	2-880/1-63,3-38,SO	7.0

■ KEN GERHART

Gerhart, Harold Kenneth b: 5/19/61, Charleston, S.C. BR/TR, 6′, 190 lbs. Deb: 9/14/86

YEAR	TM/L	G	AB	R	H	2B	3B	HR	RBI	BB	SO	AVG	OBP	SLG	PRO+	BR/A	SB	CS	SBR	FA	FR	G/POS	TPR
1986	Bal-A	20	69	4	16	2	0	1	7	4	18	.232	.274	.304	58	-4	0	1	-1	.971	-3	O-20	-0.8
1987	Bal-A	92	284	41	69	10	2	14	34	17	53	.243	.288	.440	92	-4	9	2	2	.973	-6	O-91	-1.1
1988	Bal-A	103	262	27	51	10	1	9	23	21	57	.195	.260	.344	69	-11	7	3	0	.975	-8	O-93/D-3	-2.1
Total	3	215	615	72	136	22	3	24	64	42	128	.221	.274	.384	79	-20	16	6	1	.974	-16	O-204/D-3	-4.0

■ GEORGE GERKEN

Gerken, George Herbert "Pickles" b: 7/28/03, Chicago, Ill. d: 10/23/77, Arcadia, Cal. BR/TR, 5′11.5″, 175 lbs. Deb: 4/19/27

YEAR	TM/L	G	AB	R	H	2B	3B	HR	RBI	BB	SO	AVG	OBP	SLG	PRO+	BR/A	SB	CS	SBR	FA	FR	G/POS	TPR
1927	Cle-A	6	14	1	3	0	0	0	2	1	3	.214	.267	.214	26	-2	0	0	0	.917	0	/O-5	-0.2
1928	Cle-A	38	115	16	26	7	2	0	9	12	22	.226	.305	.322	64	-6	3	3	-1	.940	-1	O-34	-1.0
Total	2	44	129	17	29	7	2	0	11	13	25	.225	.301	.310	60	-8	3	3	-1	.937	-1	/O-39	-1.2

■ JOHNNY GERLACH

Gerlach, John Glenn b: 5/11/17, Shullsburg, Wis. BR/TR, 5′9″, 165 lbs. Deb: 9/3/38

YEAR	TM/L	G	AB	R	H	2B	3B	HR	RBI	BB	SO	AVG	OBP	SLG	PRO+	BR/A	SB	CS	SBR	FA	FR	G/POS	TPR
1938	Chi-A	9	25	2	7	0	0	0	1	4	2	.280	.379	.280	66	-1	0	0	0	.949	1	/S-8	0.0
1939	Chi-A	3	2	0	2	0	0	0	0	0	0	1.000	1.000	1.000	402	1	0	0	0	1.000	0	/3-1	0.1
Total	2	12	27	2	9	0	0	0	1	4	2	.333	.419	.333	89	-0	0	0	0	.949	1	/S-8,3-1	0.1

■ DICK GERNERT

Gernert, Richard Edward b: 9/28/28, Reading, Pa. BR/TR, 6′3″, 210 lbs. Deb: 4/16/52 C

YEAR	TM/L	G	AB	R	H	2B	3B	HR	RBI	BB	SO	AVG	OBP	SLG	PRO+	BR/A	SB	CS	SBR	FA	FR	G/POS	TPR
1952	Bos-A	102	367	58	89	20	2	19	67	35	83	.243	.317	.463	107	2	4	1	1	.987	-1	1-99	-0.3
1953	Bos-A	139	494	73	125	15	1	21	71	88	82	.253	.371	.415	106	6	0	7	-4	.986	-3	*1-136	-0.6
1954	Bos-A	14	23	2	6	2	0	0	1	6	4	.261	.414	.348	99	0	0	0	0	1.000	-1	/1-6	-0.1
1955	Bos-A	7	20	6	4	2	0	0	1	1	5	.200	.238	.300	40	-2	0	0	0	.974	-0	/1-5	-0.2
1956	Bos-A	106	306	53	89	11	0	16	68	56	57	.291	.404	.484	119	9	1	0	0	.985	1	O-50,1-37	0.5
1957	Bos-A	99	316	45	75	13	3	14	58	39	62	.237	.327	.430	99	-1	1	1	-0	.989	-2	1-71,O-16	-0.8
1958	Bos-A	122	431	59	102	19	1	20	69	59	78	.237	.331	.425	100	-0	2	0	1	.991	8	*1-114	0.1
1959	Bos-A	117	298	41	78	14	1	11	42	52	49	.262	.371	.426	113	6	1	2	-1	.995	3	1-75,O-25	0.4
1960	Chi-N	52	96	8	24	3	0	0	11	10	19	.250	.321	.281	67	-4	1	0	0	.987	3	1-18/O-5	-0.2
	Det-A	21	50	6	15	4	0	1	5	4	5	.300	.352	.440	110	1	0	0	0	1.000	-2	1-13/O-6	-0.2
1961	Det-A	6	5	1	1	0	0	1	1	1	2	.200	.333	.800	187	1	0	0	0	.000	0	H	0.1
	*Cin-N	40	63	4	19	1	0	0	7	7	9	.302	.371	.317	84	-1	0	0	0	.993	3	1-21	0.1
1962	Hou-N	10	24	1	5	0	0	0	1	5	7	.208	.345	.208	57	-1	0	0	0	1.000	-1	/1-9	-0.2
Total	11	835	2493	357	632	104	8	103	402	363	462	.254	.352	.426	104	15	10	11	-4	.990	9	1-604,O-102	-1.4

■ CESAR GERONIMO

Geronimo, Cesar Francisco (Zorrilla) b: 3/11/48, ElSeibo, D.R. BL/TL, 6′2″, 170 lbs. Deb: 4/16/69

YEAR	TM/L	G	AB	R	H	2B	3B	HR	RBI	BB	SO	AVG	OBP	SLG	PRO+	BR/A	SB	CS	SBR	FA	FR	G/POS	TPR
1969	Hou-N	28	8	8	2	1	0	0	0	0	3	.250	.250	.375	74	-0	0	0	0	1.000	-3	/O-9	-0.3
1970	Hou-N	47	37	5	9	0	0	0	2	2	5	.243	.300	.243	49	-3	0	0	0	.920	-6	O-26	-0.9
1971	Hou-N	94	82	13	18	2	2	1	6	5	31	.220	.264	.329	69	-4	2	2	-1	.977	-16	O-64	-2.2
1972	*Cin-N	120	255	32	70	9	7	4	29	24	64	.275	.344	.412	121	7	2	7	-4	.982	-10	*O-106	-1.1
1973	*Cin-N	139	324	35	68	14	3	4	33	23	74	.210	.269	.309	63	-17	5	5	-2	.992	-6	*O-130	-3.0
1974	Cin-N	150	474	73	133	17	8	7	54	46	96	.281	.347	.395	109	5	9	5	-0	.987	12	*O-145	1.1
1975	*Cin-N	148	501	69	129	25	5	6	53	48	97	.257	.327	.363	90	-7	13	5	1	.993	14	*O-148	0.2
1976	*Cin-N	149	486	59	149	24	11	2	49	56	95	.307	.385	.414	124	17	22	5	4	.985	4	*O-146	2.0
1977	Cin-N	149	492	54	131	22	4	10	52	35	89	.266	.321	.388	88	-9	10	4	1	.992	12	*O-147	-0.1
1978	Cin-N	122	296	28	67	15	1	5	27	43	67	.226	.330	.334	86	-5	8	3	1	.981	0	*O-115	-0.8
1979	*Cin-N	123	356	38	85	17	4	4	38	37	56	.239	.314	.343	79	-10	1	1	-0	.993	7	*O-118	-0.8
1980	Cin-N	103	145	16	37	5	0	2	9	14	24	.255	.321	.331	82	-3	2	1	0	1.000	-18	O-86	-2.5
1981	*KC-A	59	118	14	29	0	2	2	13	11	16	.246	.310	.331	85	-2	6	1	1	.980	-6	O-57	-0.9
1982	KC-A	53	119	14	32	6	3	4	23	8	16	.269	.315	.471	112	2	2	0	1	1.000	-2	O-44/D-1	0.0
1983	KC-A	38	87	2	18	4	0	0	4	2	13	.207	.242	.253	36	-8	0	1	-1	.986	-2	O-35	-1.1
Total	15	1522	3780	460	977	161	50	51	392	354	746	.258	.327	.368	93	-37	82	40	1	.988	-20	*O-1376/D-1	-10.4

■ LOU GERTENRICH

Gertenrich, Louis Wilhelm b: 5/4/1875, Chicago, Ill. d: 10/23/33, Chicago, Ill. BR/TR, 5′8″, 175 lbs. Deb: 9/15/01

YEAR	TM/L	G	AB	R	H	2B	3B	HR	RBI	BB	SO	AVG	OBP	SLG	PRO+	BR/A	SB	CS	SBR	FA	FR	G/POS	TPR
1901	Mil-A	2	3	1	1	0	0	0	0	0		.333	.333	.333	90	-0	0			.000	-0	/O-1	0.0
1903	Pit-N	1	3	0	0	0	0	0	0	0		.000	.000	.000	-97	-1	0			1.000	0	/O-1	-0.1
Total	2	3	6	1	1	0	0	0	0	0		.167	.167	.167	-6	-1	0			1.000	-0	/O-2	-0.1

■ DOC GESSLER

Gessler, Harry Homer "Brownie" b: 12/23/1880, Greensburg, Pa. d: 12/25/24, Pittsburgh, Pa. BL/TR, 5′10″, 180 lbs. Deb: 4/23/03 M

YEAR	TM/L	G	AB	R	H	2B	3B	HR	RBI	BB	SO	AVG	OBP	SLG	PRO+	BR/A	SB	CS	SBR	FA	FR	G/POS	TPR
1903	Det-A	29	105	9	25	5	4	0	12	3		.238	.273	.362	92	-1	1			.974	-2	O-28	-0.5
	Bro-N	49	154	20	38	8	3	0	18	17		.247	.366	.338	104	2	9			.984	-3	O-43	-0.3
1904	Bro-N	104	341	41	99	18	4	2	28	30		.290	.355	.384	131	13	13			.920	2	O-88/1-1,2-1	1.0
1905	Bro-N	126	431	44	125	17	4	3	46	38		.290	.366	.369	129	17	26			.973	2	*1-107,O-12	1.5
1906	Bro-N	9	33	3	8	1	2	0	4	3		.242	.324	.394	134	1	3			.946	1	/1-9	0.2
	*Chi-N	34	83	8	21	3	0	0	10	12		.253	.354	.289	95	0	4			1.000	-1	O-21/1-1	-0.2
	Yr	43	116	11	29	4	2	0	14	15		.250	.346	.319	104	1	7			1.000	-1	O-21,1-10	0.0
1908	Bos-A	128	435	55	134	13	14	3	63	51		.308	**.394**	.423	161	31	19			.950	-7	*O-126	2.1
1909	Bos-A	111	396	57	115	24	1	0	46	31		.290	.354	.356	122	10	16			.933	-1	*O-109	0.6
	Was-A	17	54	10	13	2	1	0	8	12		.241	.406	.315	134	3	4			1.000	-1	O-16/1-1	0.2
	Yr	128	450	67	128	26	2	0	54	43		.284	.361	.351	123	13	20			.940	-2	*O-125/1-1	0.8
1910	Was-A	145	487	58	126	17	12	2	50	62		.259	.361	.355	130	20	18			.953	-3	*O-144	1.1
1911	Was-A	128	450	65	127	19	5	4	78	74		.282	.406	.373	120	17	29			.943	-10	*O-126/1-1	0.1
Total	8	880	2969	370	831	127	50	14	363	333		.280	.370	.370	128	113	142			.945	-23	O-713,1-120/2-1	5.8

■ CHARLIE GETTIG

Gettig, Charles Henry b: 12/1870, Baltimore, Md. d: 4/11/35, Baltimore, Md. BR , 5′10″, 172 lbs. Deb: 8/5/1896

YEAR	TM/L	G	AB	R	H	2B	3B	HR	RBI	BB	SO	AVG	OBP	SLG	PRO+	BR/A	SB	CS	SBR	FA	FR	G/POS	TPR
1896	NY-N	6	9	3	3	1	0	0	0	0	0	.333	.333	.444	107	0	0			1.000	0	/P-4	0.0
1897	NY-N	22	75	8	15	6	0	0	12	6		.200	.277	.280	49	-6	3			.556	-8	/3-7,2-6,O-3,S-3,P	-1.2
1898	NY-N	64	196	30	49	6	2	0	26	15		.250	.310	.301	78	-6	5			.833	-10	O-21,P-17,2/S31C	-1.4
1899	NY-N	34	97	7	24	3	0	0	9	7		.247	.305	.278	63	-5	4			.833	-4	P-18/3-8,2-3,1-3,O	-0.5
Total	4	126	377	48	91	16	2	0	47	28	0	.241	.302	.294	68	-16	12			.879	-22	/P-42,O-25,23S1C	-3.1

■ TOM GETTINGER

Gettinger, Lewis Thomas Leyton (b: Lewis Thomas Leyton Gittinger)
b: 12/11/1868, Frederick, Md. d: 7/26/43, Pensacola, Fla. BL/TL, 5′10″, 180 lbs. Deb: 9/21/1889

YEAR	TM/L	G	AB	R	H	2B	3B	HR	RBI	BB	SO	AVG	OBP	SLG	PRO+	BR/A	SB	CS	SBR	FA	FR	G/POS	TPR
1889	StL-a	4	16	2	7	0	0	1	2	2	1	.438	.500	.625	194	2	0			.750	-1	/O-4	0.0
1890	StL-a	58	227	31	54	7	5	3	30	20		.238	.302	.352	81	-8	8			.886	-6	O-58	-1.4
1895	Lou-N	63	260	28	70	11	5	2	32	8	15	.269	.296	.373	77	-10	6			.910	-3	O-63/P-2	-1.5
Total	3	125	503	61	131	18	10	6	64	30	16	.260	.306	.372	82	-16	14			.897	-10	O-125/P-2	-2.9

■ JAKE GETTMAN

Gettman, Jacob John b: 10/25/1876, Frank, Russia d: 10/4/56, Denver, Colo. BB/TL, 5′11″, 185 lbs. Deb: 8/20/1897

YEAR	TM/L	G	AB	R	H	2B	3B	HR	RBI	BB	SO	AVG	OBP	SLG	PRO+	BR/A	SB	CS	SBR	FA	FR	G/POS	TPR
1897	Was-N	36	143	28	45	7	3	3	29	7		.315	.359	.469	118	3	8			.981	-3	O-36	-0.2
1898	Was-N	142	567	75	157	16	5	5	47	29		.277	.319	.349	92	-7	32			.926	2	*O-139/1-3	-1.5

YEAR	TM/L	G	AB	R	H	2B	3B	HR	RBI	BB	SO	AVG	OBP	SLG	PRO+	BR/A	SB	CS	SBR	FA	FR	G/POS	TPR
1899	Was-N	19	62	5	13	1	0	0	2	4		.210	.258	.226	33	-6	4			1.000	-1	O-16/1-2	-0.8
Total	3	197	772	108	215	24	8	8	78	40		.278	.322	.361	92	-10	44			.941	-2	O-191/1-5	-2.5
■ **GUS GETZ**	Getz, Gustave "Gee-Gee" b: 8/3/1889, Pittsburgh, Pa. d: 5/28/69, Red Bank, N.J. BR/TR, 5'11", 165 lbs. Deb: 8/15/09																						
1909	Bos-N	40	148	6	33	2	0	0	9	1		.223	.228	.236	42	-10	2			.934	0	3-36/2-2,S-2	-1.0
1910	Bos-N	54	144	14	28	0	1	0	7	6	10	.194	.232	.208	27	-13	2			.915	3	3-22,2-13/O-8,S-4	-1.1
1914	Bro-N	55	210	13	52	8	1	0	20	2	15	.248	.255	.295	62	-10	9			.949	12	3-55	0.4
1915	Bro-N	130	477	39	123	10	5	2	46	8	14	.258	.275	.312	76	-15	19	15	-3	.951	8	*3-128/S-2	-0.6
1916	*Bro-N	40	96	9	21	1	2	0	8	0	5	.219	.219	.271	49	-6	9			.913	-3	3-20/S-7,1-3	-0.9
1917	Cin-N	7	14	2	4	0	0	0	3	3	0	.286	.412	.286	121	1	0			.875	-3	/2-4,3-3	-0.2
1918	Cle-A	6	15	2	2	1	0	0	0	4	1	.133	.350	.200	60	-0	0			.941	-0	/3-5	-0.1
	Pit-N	7	10	0	2	0	0	0	0	0	1	.200	.200	.200	21	-1	0			.875	1	/3-2	0.0
Total	7	339	1114	85	265	22	9	2	93	24	46	.238	.257	.279	60	-56	41	15		.942	18	3-271/2-19,S-15,O1	-3.5
■ **CHAPPIE GEYGAN**	Geygan, James Edward b: 6/3/03, Ironton, Ohio d: 3/15/66, Columbus, Ohio BR/TR, 5'11", 170 lbs. Deb: 7/16/24																						
1924	Bos-A	33	82	7	21	5	2	0	4	4	16	.256	.307	.366	73	-4	0	2	-1	.952	4	S-32	0.2
1925	Bos-A	3	11	0	2	0	0	0	0	0	2	.182	.182	.182	-8	-2	0	0	0	.813	-1	/S-3	-0.3
1926	Bos-A	4	10	0	3	0	0	0	0	1	1	.300	.364	.300	77	-0	0	0	0	.800	-1	/3-3	-0.1
Total	3	40	103	7	26	5	2	0	4	5	19	.252	.300	.340	65	-6	0	2	-1	.938	2	/S-35,3-3	-0.2
■ **PATSY GHARRITY**	Gharrity, Edward Patrick b: 3/13/1892, Parnell, Iowa d: 10/10/66, Beloit, Wis. BR/TR, 5'10", 170 lbs. Deb: 5/16/16 C																						
1916	Was-A	39	92	8	21	5	1	0	9	8	18	.228	.297	.304	81	-2	2			1.000	-3	C-16,1-16	-0.5
1917	Was-A	76	176	15	50	5	0	0	18	14	18	.284	.337	.313	99	-0	7			.980	1	1-46/C-5,O-1	-0.1
1918	Was-A	4	4	0	1	1	0	0	2	0	1	.250	.250	.500	129	0	0			.000	0	H	0.0
1919	Was-A	111	347	35	94	19	4	2	43	25	39	.271	.325	.366	95	-3	4			.969	-5	C-60,O-33/1-7	-0.5
1920	Was-A	131	428	51	105	18	3	3	44	37	52	.245	.307	.322	69	-20	6	5	-1	.965	-3	*C-121/1-7,O-1	-1.5
1921	Was-A	121	387	62	120	19	8	7	55	45	44	.310	.386	.455	120	12	4	3	-1	.977	-0	*C-115	1.6
1922	Was-A	96	273	40	70	16	6	5	45	36	30	.256	.351	.414	104	1	3	3	-1	.981	3	C-87	0.7
1923	Was-A	93	251	26	52	9	4	3	33	22	27	.207	.276	.311	57	-17	6	2	1	.986	1	C-35,1-33	-1.5
1929	Was-A	3	2	0	0	0	0	0	0	1	2	.000	.333	.000	-7	-0	0	0	0	.000	0	H	0.0
1930	Was-A	2	1	0	0	0	0	0	0	0	0	.000	.000	.000	-99	-0	0	0	0	1.000	-0	/1-1	0.0
Total	10	676	1961	237	513	92	26	20	249	188	231	.262	.331	.366	90	-29	32	13		.974	-7	C-439,1-110/O-35	-1.8
■ **JASON GIAMBI**	Giambi, Jason Gilbert b: 1/8/71, W.Covina, Cal. BL/TR, 6'2", 200 lbs. Deb: 5/8/95 F																						
1995	Oak-A	54	176	27	45	7	0	6	25	28	31	.256	.367	.398	105	2	2	1	0	.960	-3	3-30,1-26/D-2	-0.2
1996	Oak-A	140	536	84	156	40	1	20	79	51	95	.291	.358	.481	112	9	0	1	-1	.993	2	1-45,O-45,3-39,D-12	0.4
1997	Oak-A	142	519	66	152	41	2	20	81	55	89	.293	.367	.495	124	18	0	1	-1	.982	-2	O-68,1-51,D-25	0.7
1998	Oak-A	153	562	92	166	28	0	27	110	81	102	.295	.389	.489	130	27	2	2	-1	.990	-11	*1-146/D-7	0.1
Total	4	489	1793	269	519	116	3	73	295	215	317	.289	.371	.480	121	56	4	5	-2	.990	-14	1-268,O-113/3-69,D	1.0
■ **JEREMY GIAMBI**	Giambi, Jeremy Dean b: 9/30/74, San Jose, Cal. BL/TL, 6', 185 lbs. Deb: 9/1/98 F																						
1998	KC-A	18	58	6	13	4	0	2	8	11	9	.224	.348	.397	89	-1	0	1	-1	1.000	0	/O-9,D-7	-0.1
■ **RAY GIANNELLI**	Giannelli, Raymond John b: 2/5/66, Brooklyn, N.Y. BL/TR, 6', 195 lbs. Deb: 5/4/91																						
1991	Tor-A	9	24	2	4	1	0	0	0	5	9	.167	.310	.208	45	-2	1	0	0	.923	-2	/3-9	-0.3
1995	StL-N	9	11	0	1	0	0	0	0	3	4	.091	.286	.091	5	-1	0	0	0	1.000	-1	/1-2,O-2	-0.2
Total	2	18	35	2	5	1	0	0	0	8	13	.143	.302	.171	32	-3	1	0	0	.923	-2	/3-9,O-2,1-2	-0.5
■ **JOE GIANNINI**	Giannini, Joseph Francis b: 9/8/1888, San Francisco, Cal d: 9/26/42, San Francisco, Cal. BL/TR, 5'8", 155 lbs. Deb: 8/7/11																						
1911	Bos-A	1	2	0	1	1	0	0	0	0		.500	.500	1.000	317	1	0			.500	-0	/S-1	0.0
■ **JOHN GIBBONS**	Gibbons, John Michael b: 6/8/62, Great Falls, Mont. BR/TR, 5'11", 187 lbs. Deb: 4/11/84																						
1984	NY-N	10	31	1	2	0	0	0	1	3	11	.065	.171	.065	-32	-5	0	0	0	.983	-1	/C-9	-0.6
1986	NY-N	8	19	4	9	4	0	1	1	3	5	.474	.545	.842	285	5	0	0	0	1.000	1	/C-8	0.6
Total	2	18	50	5	11	4	0	1	2	6	16	.220	.316	.360	90	-1	0	0	0	.990	-0	/C-17	0.0
■ **JAKE GIBBS**	Gibbs, Jerry Dean b: 11/7/38, Grenada, Miss. BL/TR, 6', 185 lbs. Deb: 9/11/62																						
1962	NY-A	2	0	2	0	0	0	0	0	0	0	—	—	—	—	0	0	0	0	.000	0	/3-1	0.0
1963	NY-A	4	8	1	2	0	0	0	0	0	1	.250	.250	.250	41	-1	0	0	0	1.000	-1	/C-1	-0.1
1964	NY-A	3	6	1	1	0	0	0	0	0	2	.167	.167	.167	-7	-1	0	0	0	1.000	0	/C-2	0.0
1965	NY-A	37	68	6	15	1	0	2	7	4	20	.221	.274	.324	70	-3	0	0	0	.991	2	C-21	0.0
1966	NY-A	62	182	19	47	6	0	3	20	19	16	.258	.328	.341	96	-1	5	2	0	.988	4	C-54	0.8
1967	NY-A	116	374	33	87	7	1	4	25	28	57	.233	.293	.289	75	-11	7	6	-2	.975	1	C-99	-0.8
1968	NY-A	124	423	31	90	12	3	3	29	27	68	.213	.270	.277	68	-17	9	8	-2	.991	-4	*C-121	-1.7
1969	NY-A	71	219	18	49	9	2	0	18	23	30	.224	.298	.283	65	-10	3	4	-2	.990	8	C-66	0.0
1970	NY-A	49	153	23	46	9	2	8	26	7	14	.301	.335	.542	146	8	2	0	1	.987	3	C-44	1.4
1971	NY-A	70	206	23	45	9	0	5	21	12	23	.218	.271	.335	76	-8	2	2	-1	.988	-5	C-51	-1.2
Total	10	538	1639	157	382	53	8	25	146	120	231	.233	.291	.321	81	-42	28	22	-5	.986	8	C-459/3-1	-1.6
■ **STEVE GIBRALTER**	Gibralter, Stephan Benson b: 10/9/72, Dallas, Tex. BR/TR, 6', 185 lbs. Deb: 6/1/95																						
1995	Cin-N	4	3	0	1	0	0	0	0	0	0	.333	.333	.333	77	-0	0	0	0	1.000	-1	/O-2	-0.1
1996	Cin-N	2	2	0	0	0	0	0	0	0	2	.000	.000	.000	-99	-1	0	0	0	.000	-1	/O-2	-0.2
Total	2	6	5	0	1	0	0	0	0	0	2	.200	.200	.200	6	-1	0	0	0	.500	-2	/O-4	-0.3
■ **CHARLIE GIBSON**	Gibson, Charles Ellsworth "Gibby" b: 11/17/1879, Sharon, Pa. d: 11/22/54, Sharon, Pa. BR/TR, 6', 160 lbs. Deb: 9/23/05																						
1905	StL-A	1	3	0	0	0	0	0	0	0		.000	.000	.000	-99	-1	0			1.000	-0	/C-1	-0.1
■ **CHARLIE GIBSON**	Gibson, Charles Griffin b: 11/21/1899, LaGrange, Ga. d: 12/18/90, LaGrange, Ga. BR/TR, 5'8", 160 lbs. Deb: 5/30/24																						
1924	Phi-A	12	15	1	2	0	0	0	1	2	0	.133	.235	.133	-3	-2	0	0	0	.870	-0	C-12	-0.2
■ **DERRICK GIBSON**	Gibson, Derrick Lamont b: 2/5/75, Winter Haven, Fla. BR/TR, 6'2", 244 lbs. Deb: 9/8/98																						
1998	Col-N	7	21	4	9	1	0	0	2	1	4	.429	.478	.476	125	1	0	0	0	.929	1	/O-7	0.2
■ **FRANK GIBSON**	Gibson, Frank Gilbert b: 9/27/1890, Omaha, Neb. d: 4/27/61, Austin, Tex. BB/TR, 6'0.5", 172 lbs. Deb: 4/22/13																						
1913	Det-A	23	57	8	8	1	0	0	2	3	9	.140	.197	.158	4	-7	2			.914	-6	C-19/O-2	-1.3
1921	Bos-N	63	125	14	33	5	4	2	13	3	17	.264	.292	.416	90	-2	0	0	0	.979	1	C-41	0.0
1922	Bos-N	66	164	15	49	7	2	3	20	10	27	.299	.339	.421	99	-1	4	1	1	.981	-1	C-29,1-20	-0.1
1923	Bos-N	41	50	13	15	1	0	0	5	7	7	.300	.386	.320	02	0	0	2	-1	.923	-2	C-20	-0.2
1924	Bos-N	90	229	25	71	15	6	1	30	10	23	.310	.342	.441	113	3	1	1	-0	.972	2	C-46,1-10/3-2	0.7
1925	Bos-N	104	316	36	88	23	5	2	50	15	28	.278	.313	.402	89	-7	3	3	-1	.968	-2	C-86/1-2	-0.5
1926	Bos-N	24	47	3	16	4	0	0	7	4	6	.340	.392	.426	132	2	0			1.000	2	C-13	0.4
1927	Bos-N	60	167	7	37	1	2	0	19	3	10	.222	.235	.251	33	-16	2			.965	-3	C-47	-1.7
Total	8	471	1155	121	317	57	19	8	146	55	127	.274	.310	.377	86	-28	12	7		.967	-10	C-301/1-32,3-2,O-2	-2.7
■ **GEORGE GIBSON**	Gibson, George C. "Moon" b: 7/22/1880, London, Ont., Can. d: 1/25/67, London, Ont., Can. BR/TR, 5'11.5", 190 lbs. Deb: 7/2/05 MC																						
1905	Pit-N	46	135	14	24	2	2	2	14	15		.178	.270	.267	59	-7	2			.966	3	C-44	0.0
1906	Pit-N	81	259	8	46	6	1	0	20	16		.178	.225	.208	34	-20	1			.971	-5	C-81	-2.0
1907	Pit-N	113	382	28	84	8	7	3	35	18		.220	.261	.301	75	-12	2			.972	-3	*C-109/1-1	-0.6
1908	Pit-N	143	486	37	111	19	4	2	45	19		.228	.260	.296	78	-14	4			.973	-14	*C-140	-1.7
1909	*Pit-N	150	510	42	135	25	9	2	52	44		.265	.326	.361	104	1	9			**.983**	2	*C-150	1.9
1910	Pit-N	143	482	53	125	22	6	3	44	47	31	.259	.333	.349	93	-4	7			**.984**	3	*C-143	1.3
1911	Pit-N	100	311	32	65	12	2	0	19	29	16	.209	.281	.260	50	-21	3			.979	0	C-98	-1.1
1912	Pit-N	95	300	23	72	14	3	2	35	20	16	.240	.290	.327	69	-13	0			**.990**	-1	C-94	-0.5

YEAR	TM/L	G	AB	R	H	2B	3B	HR	RBI	BB	SO	AVG	OBP	SLG	PRO+	BR/A	SB	CS	SBR	FA	FR	G/POS	TPR
1913	Pit-N	48	118	6	33	4	2	0	12	10	8	.280	.341	.347	101	0	2			.986	-9	C-48	-0.5
1914	Pit-N	102	274	19	78	9	5	0	30	27	27	.285	.359	.354	117	7	4			.974	-9	*C-101	0.6
1915	Pit-N	120	351	28	88	15	6	1	30	31	25	.251	.313	.336	98	-1	5	2	0	.965	8	*C-118	1.8
1916	Pit-N	33	84	4	17	2	2	0	4	3	7	.202	.239	.274	57	-4	0			.989	7	C-29	0.5
1917	NY-N	35	82	1	14	3	0	0	5	7	2	.171	.236	.207	38	-6	1			.986	1	C-35	-0.4
1918	NY-N	4	2	0	1	1	0	0	0	0	0	.500	.500	1.000	360	1	0			1.000	0	/C-4	0.1
Total	14	1213	3776	295	893	142	49	15	345	286	132	.236	.295	.312	81	-94	40	2		.977	-18	*C-1194/1-1	-0.6

■ **RUSS GIBSON** Gibson, John Russell b: 5/6/39, Fall River, Mass. BR/TR, 6'1", 195 lbs. Deb: 4/14/67

YEAR	TM/L	G	AB	R	H	2B	3B	HR	RBI	BB	SO	AVG	OBP	SLG	PRO+	BR/A	SB	CS	SBR	FA	FR	G/POS	TPR
1967	*Bos-A	49	138	8	28	7	0	1	15	12	31	.203	.267	.275	56	-7	0	0	0	1.000	-6	C-48	-1.2
1968	Bos-A	76	231	15	52	11	1	3	20	8	38	.225	.251	.320	68	-9	1	2	-1	.983	1	C-74/1-1	-0.6
1969	Bos-A	85	287	21	72	9	1	3	27	15	25	.251	.290	.321	67	-13	1	1	-0	.979	-6	C-83	-1.6
1970	SF-N	24	69	3	16	6	0	0	6	7	12	.232	.303	.319	67	-3	0	0	0	.971	2	C-23	0.0
1971	SF-N	25	57	2	11	1	1	1	7	2	13	.193	.220	.298	46	-4	0	0	0	.965	0	C-22	-0.4
1972	SF-N	5	12	0	2	0	1	0	3	0	4	.167	.167	.333	38	-1	0	0	0	1.000	-1	/C-5	-0.2
Total	6	264	794	49	181	34	4	8	78	44	123	.228	.269	.311	64	-38	2	3	-1	.983	-10	C-255/1-1	-4.0

■ **KIRK GIBSON** Gibson, Kirk Harold b: 5/28/57, Pontiac, Mich. BL/TL, 6'3", 215 lbs. Deb: 9/8/79

YEAR	TM/L	G	AB	R	H	2B	3B	HR	RBI	BB	SO	AVG	OBP	SLG	PRO+	BR/A	SB	CS	SBR	FA	FR	G/POS	TPR
1979	Det-A	12	38	3	9	3	0	1	4	1	3	.237	.256	.395	70	-2	3	3	-1	1.000	-1	O-10	-0.4
1980	Det-A	51	175	23	46	2	1	9	16	10	45	.263	.306	.440	100	-1	4	7	-3	.992	-2	O-49/D-1	-0.7
1981	Det-A	83	290	41	95	11	3	9	40	18	64	.328	.371	.479	138	14	17	5	2	.973	-4	O-67/D-9	1.0
1982	Det-A	69	266	34	74	16	2	8	35	25	41	.278	.342	.444	113	5	9	7	-2	.994	3	O-64/D-4	0.5
1983	Det-A	128	401	60	91	12	9	15	51	53	96	.227	.323	.414	104	2	14	3	2	.975	-1	D-66,O-54	-0.1
1984	*Det-A	149	531	92	150	23	10	27	91	63	103	.282	.367	.516	142	30	29	9	3	.954	-9	*O-139/D-6	2.0
1985	Det-A	154	581	96	167	37	5	29	97	71	137	.287	.370	.518	141	33	30	4	7	.963	-7	*O-144/D-8	2.7
1986	Det-A	119	441	84	118	11	2	28	86	68	107	.268	.374	.492	134	22	34	6	7	.990	-9	*O-114/D-4	1.6
1987	*Det-A	128	487	95	135	25	3	24	79	71	117	.277	.375	.489	132	24	26	7	4	.974	5	*O-121/D-4	2.7
1988	*LA-N	150	542	106	157	28	1	25	76	73	120	.290	.381	.483	151	37	31	4	7	.964	8	*O-148	5.0
1989	LA-N	71	253	35	54	8	2	9	28	35	55	.213	.314	.368	96	-1	12	3	2	.980	1	O-70	-0.1
1990	LA-N	89	315	59	82	20	0	8	38	39	65	.260	.347	.400	108	4	26	2	7	.995	5	O-81	1.4
1991	KC-A	132	462	81	109	17	6	16	55	69	103	.236	.343	.403	105	4	18	4	3	.976	-2	O-94,D-30	0.2
1992	Pit-N	16	56	6	11	0	0	2	5	3	12	.196	.237	.304	53	-4	3	1	0	1.000	1	O-13	-0.3
1993	Det-A	116	403	62	105	18	6	13	62	44	87	.261	.339	.432	106	3	15	6	1	.987	-1	D-76,O-32	-0.1
1994	Det-A	98	330	71	91	17	2	23	72	42	69	.276	.363	.548	130	14	4	5	-2	.988	-2	D-56,O-38	0.6
1995	Det-A	70	227	37	59	12	2	9	35	33	61	.260	.361	.449	110	4	9	2	2	.000	-0	D-63/O-1	0.1
Total	17	1635	5798	985	1553	260	54	255	870	718	1285	.268	.355	.463	123	188	284	78	38	.976	-17	*O-1239,D-327	16.1

■ **WHITEY GIBSON** Gibson, Leighton P. b: 10/6/1868, Lancaster, Pa. d: 10/11/07, Talmage, Pa. TR , 5'9", 178 lbs. Deb: 5/2/1888

YEAR	TM/L	G	AB	R	H	2B	3B	HR	RBI	BB	SO	AVG	OBP	SLG	PRO+	BR/A	SB	CS	SBR	FA	FR	G/POS	TPR
1888	Phi-a	1	3	0	0	0	0	0	0	0		.000	.000	.000	-99	-1	0			1.000	1	/C-1	0.0

■ **JOE GIEBEL** Giebel, Joseph Henry b: 11/30/1891, Washington, D.C. d: 3/17/81, Silver Spring, Md. BR/TR, 5'10.5", 175 lbs. Deb: 9/30/13

YEAR	TM/L	G	AB	R	H	2B	3B	HR	RBI	BB	SO	AVG	OBP	SLG	PRO+	BR/A	SB	CS	SBR	FA	FR	G/POS	TPR
1913	Phi-A	1	3	0	1	0	0	0	0	0	1	.333	.333	.333	97	-0	0			1.000	-0	/C-1	0.0

■ **NORM GIGON** Gigon, Norman Phillip b: 5/12/38, Teaneck, N.J. BR/TR, 6', 195 lbs. Deb: 4/12/67

YEAR	TM/L	G	AB	R	H	2B	3B	HR	RBI	BB	SO	AVG	OBP	SLG	PRO+	BR/A	SB	CS	SBR	FA	FR	G/POS	TPR
1967	Chi-N	34	70	8	12	3	1	1	6	4	14	.171	.237	.286	47	-5	0	0	0	.982	-3	2-12/O-4,3-1	-0.8

■ **BENJI GIL** Gil, Romar Benjamin (Aguilar) b: 10/6/72, Tijuana, Mex. BR/TR, 6'2", 180 lbs. Deb: 4/5/93

YEAR	TM/L	G	AB	R	H	2B	3B	HR	RBI	BB	SO	AVG	OBP	SLG	PRO+	BR/A	SB	CS	SBR	FA	FR	G/POS	TPR
1993	Tex-A	22	57	3	7	0	0	0	2	5	22	.123	.194	.123	-13	-9	1	2	-1	.954	8	S-22	0.0
1995	Tex-A	130	415	36	91	20	3	9	46	26	147	.219	.267	.347	57	-27	2	4	-2	.974	16	*S-130	-0.1
1996	Tex-A	5	5	0	2	0	0	0	1	1	1	.400	.500	.400	125	0	0	1	-1	.923	1	/S-5	0.0
1997	Tex-A	110	317	35	71	13	2	5	31	17	96	.224	.266	.325	50	-23	1	2	-1	.963	**22**	*S-106/D-4	0.6
Total	4	267	794	74	171	33	5	14	80	49	266	.215	.263	.322	50	-60	4	9	-4	.967	47	S-263/D-4	0.5

■ **GUS GIL** Gil, Tomas Gustavo (Guillen) b: 4/19/39, Caracas, Venez. BR/TR, 5'10", 180 lbs. Deb: 4/11/67

YEAR	TM/L	G	AB	R	H	2B	3B	HR	RBI	BB	SO	AVG	OBP	SLG	PRO+	BR/A	SB	CS	SBR	FA	FR	G/POS	TPR
1967	Cle-A	51	96	11	11	4	0	0	5	9	18	.115	.198	.156	6	-11	0	0	0	1.000	2	2-49/1-1	-0.8
1969	Sea-A	92	221	20	49	7	0	0	17	16	28	.222	.274	.253	49	-15	2	0	1	.942	1	3-38,2-18,S-12	-1.2
1970	Mil-A	64	119	12	22	4	0	1	12	21	12	.185	.307	.244	53	-7	2	0	1	.978	3	2-38,3-14	-0.1
1971	Mil-A	14	32	3	5	1	0	0	3	10	5	.156	.357	.188	59	-1	1	0	0	.977	-0	/2-8,3-6	0.0
Total	4	221	468	46	87	16	0	1	37	56	63	.186	.274	.226	43	-34	5	0	2	.987	7	2-113/3-58,S-12,1-1	-2.1

■ **SHAWN GILBERT** Gilbert, Albert Shawn b: 3/12/65, Camden, N.J. BR/TR, 5'9", 170 lbs. Deb: 6/4/97

YEAR	TM/L	G	AB	R	H	2B	3B	HR	RBI	BB	SO	AVG	OBP	SLG	PRO+	BR/A	SB	CS	SBR	FA	FR	G/POS	TPR
1997	NY-N	29	22	3	3	0	0	1	1	1	8	.136	.174	.273	15	-3	1	0	0	.875	1	/2-8,S-6,3-3,O-1	-0.2
1998	NY-N	3	3	1	0	0	0	0	0	0	1	.000	.000	.000	-99	-1	0	0	0	.000	-0	/3-1	-0.1
	StL-N	4	2	0	1	0	0	0	0	0	1	.500	.500	.500	163	0	1	0	0	1.000	0	/2-2	0.1
	Yr	7	5	1	1	0	0	0	0	0	2	.200	.200	.200	4	-1	1	0	0	1.000	0	/2-2,3-1	0.0
Total	2	36	27	4	4	0	0	1	1	1	10	.148	.179	.259	13	-4	2	0	1	.889	1	/2-10,S-6,3-4,O-1	-0.2

■ **ANDY GILBERT** Gilbert, Andrew b: 7/18/14, Bradenville, Pa. d: 8/29/92, Davis, Cal. BR/TR, 6', 203 lbs. Deb: 9/14/42 C

YEAR	TM/L	G	AB	R	H	2B	3B	HR	RBI	BB	SO	AVG	OBP	SLG	PRO+	BR/A	SB	CS	SBR	FA	FR	G/POS	TPR
1942	Bos-A	6	11	0	1	0	0	0	1	1	3	.091	.167	.091	-26	-2	0	0	0	1.000	-2	/O-5	-0.4
1946	Bos-A	2	1	1	0	0	0	0	0	0	0	.000	.000	.000	-95	-0	0	0	0	1.000	0	/O-1	-0.1
Total	2	8	12	1	1	0	0	0	1	1	3	.083	.154	.083	-31	-2	0	0	0	1.000	-2	/O-6	-0.5

■ **CHARLIE GILBERT** Gilbert, Charles Mader b: 7/8/19, New Orleans, La. d: 8/13/83, New Orleans, La. BL/TL, 5'9", 165 lbs. Deb: 4/16/40 F

YEAR	TM/L	G	AB	R	H	2B	3B	HR	RBI	BB	SO	AVG	OBP	SLG	PRO+	BR/A	SB	CS	SBR	FA	FR	G/POS	TPR
1940	Bro-N	57	142	23	35	9	1	2	8	8	13	.246	.287	.366	74	-5	0			.960	-2	O-43	-0.8
1941	Chi-N	39	86	11	24	2	1	0	12	11	6	.279	.361	.326	98	0	1			1.000	-1	O-22	-0.2
1942	Chi-N	74	179	18	33	6	3	0	7	25	24	.184	.284	.251	60	-9	1			.981	0	O-47	-1.1
1943	Chi-N	8	20	1	3	0	0	0	0	3	3	.150	.261	.150	20	-2	1			1.000	-1	/O-6	-0.3
1946	Chi-N	15	13	2	1	0	0	0	1	1	4	.077	.143	.077	-38	-2	0			1.000	0	/O-2	-0.3
	Phi-N	88	260	34	63	5	2	1	17	25	18	.242	.314	.288	73	-9	3			1.000	6	O-69	-0.6
	Yr	103	273	36	64	5	2	1	18	26	22	.234	.306	.278	68	-11	3			1.000	6	O-71	-0.9
1947	Phi-N	83	152	20	36	5	2	2	10	13	14	.237	.301	.336	72	-6	1			.961	-0	O-37	-0.8
Total	6	364	852	109	195	27	9	5	55	86	82	.229	.302	.299	70	-33	7			.982	3	O-226	-4.1

■ **BUDDY GILBERT** Gilbert, Drew Edward b: 7/26/35, Knoxville, Tenn. BL/TR, 6'3", 195 lbs. Deb: 9/9/59

YEAR	TM/L	G	AB	R	H	2B	3B	HR	RBI	BB	SO	AVG	OBP	SLG	PRO+	BR/A	SB	CS	SBR	FA	FR	G/POS	TPR
1959	Cin-N	7	20	4	3	0	0	2	2	3	4	.150	.261	.450	82	-1	0	0	0	1.000	1	/O-6	0.0

■ **TOOKIE GILBERT** Gilbert, Harold Joseph b: 4/4/29, New Orleans, La. d: 6/23/67, New Orleans, La. BL/TR, 6'2.5", 185 lbs. Deb: 5/5/50 F

YEAR	TM/L	G	AB	R	H	2B	3B	HR	RBI	BB	SO	AVG	OBP	SLG	PRO+	BR/A	SB	CS	SBR	FA	FR	G/POS	TPR
1950	NY-N	113	322	40	71	12	2	4	32	43	36	.220	.314	.307	64	-16	3			.988	1	*1-111	-1.7
1953	NY-N	70	160	12	27	3	0	3	16	22	21	.169	.269	.244	34	-15	1	0	0	.995	1	1-44	-1.5
Total	2	183	482	52	98	15	2	7	48	65	57	.203	.299	.286	54	-32	4	0		.991	2	1-155	-3.2

■ **HARRY GILBERT** Gilbert, Harry H. b: 7/7/1868, Pottstown, Pa. d: 12/23/09, Pottstown, Pa. Deb: 6/23/1890 F

YEAR	TM/L	G	AB	R	H	2B	3B	HR	RBI	BB	SO	AVG	OBP	SLG	PRO+	BR/A	SB	CS	SBR	FA	FR	G/POS	TPR
1890	Pit-N	2	8	1	2	0	0	0	0	0	3	.250	.250	.250	52	-1	0			1.000	-1	/2-2	-0.1

■ **JOHN GILBERT** Gilbert, John G. b: 1/8/1864, Pottstown, Pa. d: 11/12/03, Pottstown, Pa. Deb: 6/23/1890 F

YEAR	TM/L	G	AB	R	H	2B	3B	HR	RBI	BB	SO	AVG	OBP	SLG	PRO+	BR/A	SB	CS	SBR	FA	FR	G/POS	TPR
1890	Pit-N	2	8	0	0	0	0	0	0	0	2	.000	.000	.000	-99	-2	0			1.000	-0	/S-2	-0.2

■ **JACK GILBERT** Gilbert, John Robert "Jackrabbit" b: 9/4/1875, Rhinecliff, N.Y. d: 7/7/41, Albany, N.Y. Deb: 9/11/1898

YEAR	TM/L	G	AB	R	H	2B	3B	HR	RBI	BB	SO	AVG	OBP	SLG	PRO+	BR/A	SB	CS	SBR	FA	FR	G/POS	TPR
1898	Was-N	2	5	0	1	0	0	0	1	1		.200	.429	.200	82	0	1			.500	-0	/O-2	0.0
	NY-N	1	4	0	1	0	0	0	0	0		.250	.250	.250	45	-0	1			.500	-0	/O-1	-0.1
	Yr	3	9	0	2	0	0	0	1	1		.222	.364	.222	70	-0	2			.500	-1	/O-3	-0.1
1904	Pit-N	25	87	13	21	0	0	0	3	12		.241	.353	.241	82	-1	3			.857	-6	O-25	-0.9
Total	2	28	96	13	23	0	0	0	4	13		.240	.354	.240	81	-1	5			.821	-6	/O-28	-1.0

■ LARRY GILBERT Gilbert, Lawrence William b: 12/3/1891, New Orleans, La. d: 2/17/65, New Orleans, La. BL/TL, 5'9", 158 lbs. Deb: 4/14/14 F

YEAR	TM/L	G	AB	R	H	2B	3B	HR	RBI	BB	SO	AVG	OBP	SLG	PRO+	BR/A	SB	CS	SBR	FA	FR	G/POS	TPR
1914	*Bos-N	72	224	32	60	6	1	5	25	26	34	.268	.347	.371	114	4	3			.979	-0	O-60	0.1
1915	Bos-N	45	106	11	16	4	0	0	4	11	13	.151	.231	.189	29	-9	4	1	1	.941	-2	O-27	-1.3
Total	2	117	330	43	76	10	1	5	29	37	47	.230	.310	.312	88	-5	7	1		.969	-3	/O-87	-1.2

■ MARK GILBERT Gilbert, Mark David b: 8/22/56, Atlanta, Ga. BB/TR, 6', 175 lbs. Deb: 7/21/85

YEAR	TM/L	G	AB	R	H	2B	3B	HR	RBI	BB	SO	AVG	OBP	SLG	PRO+	BR/A	SB	CS	SBR	FA	FR	G/POS	TPR
1985	Chi-A	7	22	3	6	1	0	0	3	4	5	.273	.385	.318	92	-0	0	0	0	1.000	-1	/O-7	-0.1

■ PETE GILBERT Gilbert, Peter b: 9/6/1867, Baltic, Conn. d: 1/1/12, Springfield, Mass. TR, 5'8", 180 lbs. Deb: 9/6/1890

YEAR	TM/L	G	AB	R	H	2B	3B	HR	RBI	BB	SO	AVG	OBP	SLG	PRO+	BR/A	SB	CS	SBR	FA	FR	G/POS	TPR
1890	Bal-a	29	100	25	28	2	1	1	18	10		.280	.363	.350	105	1	12			.899	-3	3-29	-0.1
1891	Bal-a	139	513	81	118	15	7	3	72	37	77	.230	.317	.304	77	-16	31			.862	2	*3-139	-0.6
1892	Bal-N	4	15	0	3	0	0	0	0	1	3	.200	.250	.200	35	-1	1			.889	1	/3-4	0.0
1894	Bro-N	6	25	1	2	0	0	0	1	1	3	.080	.148	.080	-47	-6	2			.938	1	/2-3,3-3	-0.4
	Lou-N	28	108	13	33	3	1	1	14	5	4	.306	.353	.380	82	-3	2			.742	-6	3-28	-0.7
	Yr	34	133	14	35	3	1	1	15	6	7	.263	.315	.323	58	-9	4			.766	-4	3-31/2-3	-1.1
Total	4	206	761	120	184	20	9	5	105	54	87	.242	.321	.311	76	-25	48			.851	-4	3-203/2-3	-1.8

■ WALLY GILBERT Gilbert, Walter John b: 12/19/1900, Oscoda, Mich. d: 9/7/58, Duluth, Minn. BR/TR, 6', 180 lbs. Deb: 8/18/28

YEAR	TM/L	G	AB	R	H	2B	3B	HR	RBI	BB	SO	AVG	OBP	SLG	PRO+	BR/A	SB	CS	SBR	FA	FR	G/POS	TPR
1928	Bro-N	39	153	26	31	4	0	0	3	14	8	.203	.274	.229	33	-15	2			.965	-1	3-39	-1.3
1929	Bro-N	143	569	88	173	31	4	3	58	42	29	.304	.359	.388	87	-11	7			.956	7	*3-142	0.2
1930	Bro-N	150	623	92	183	34	5	3	67	47	33	.294	.345	.379	76	-24	7			.944	9	*3-150	-0.6
1931	Bro-N	145	552	60	147	25	6	0	46	39	38	.266	.322	.333	77	-17	3			.948	8	*3-145	0.0
1932	Cin-N	114	420	35	90	18	2	1	40	20	23	.214	.252	.274	43	-34	2			.929	-6	*3-111	-3.3
Total	5	591	2317	301	624	112	17	7	214	162	131	.269	.322	.341	71	-101	21			.947	17	3-587	-5.0

■ BILLY GILBERT Gilbert, William Oliver b: 6/21/1876, Tullytown, Pa. d: 8/8/27, New York, N.Y. BR/TR, 5'4", 153 lbs. Deb: 4/25/01

YEAR	TM/L	G	AB	R	H	2B	3B	HR	RBI	BB	SO	AVG	OBP	SLG	PRO+	BR/A	SB	CS	SBR	FA	FR	G/POS	TPR
1901	Mil-A	127	492	77	133	14	7	0	43	31		.270	.320	.327	84	-10	19			.936	-0	*2-127	-0.4
1902	Bal-A	129	445	74	109	12	3	2	38	45		.245	.327	.299	71	-16	38			.907	-5	*S-129	-1.3
1903	NY-N	128	413	62	104	9	0	1	40	41		.252	.348	.281	77	-10	37			.935	11	*2-128	0.5
1904	NY-N	146	478	57	121	13	3	1	54	46		.253	.340	.299	94	-1	33			.946	8	*2-146	1.1
1905	*NY-N	115	376	45	93	11	3	0	24	41		.247	.331	.293	84	-6	11			.947	25	*2-115	2.1
1906	NY-N	104	307	44	71	6	1	1	27	42		.231	.341	.267	88	-2	22			.940	23	2-98	2.3
1908	StL-N	89	276	12	59	7	0	0	10	20		.214	.274	.239	67	-10	6			.952	6	2-89	-0.5
1909	StL-N	12	29	4	5	0	0	0	1	4		.172	.333	.172	61	-1	1			.922	0	2-12	-0.1
Total	8	850	2816	375	695	72	17	5	237	270		.247	.328	.290	81	-57	167			.942	68	2-715,S-129	3.7

■ ROD GILBREATH Gilbreath, Rodney Joe b: 9/24/52, Laurel, Miss. BR/TR, 6'2", 185 lbs. Deb: 6/17/72

YEAR	TM/L	G	AB	R	H	2B	3B	HR	RBI	BB	SO	AVG	OBP	SLG	PRO+	BR/A	SB	CS	SBR	FA	FR	G/POS	TPR
1972	Atl-N	18	38	2	9	1	0	0	1	2	10	.237	.293	.263	54	-2	1	1	-0	1.000	3	/2-7,3-4	0.0
1973	Atl-N	29	74	10	21	2	1	0	2	6	10	.284	.346	.338	84	-1	2	1	0	.960	-0	3-22	-0.2
1974	Atl-N	3	6	2	2	0	0	0	0	2	0	.333	.500	.333	131	0	0	0	0	1.000	0	/2-2	0.1
1975	Atl-N	90	202	24	49	3	1	2	16	24	26	.243	.326	.297	71	-7	5	5	-2	.980	2	2-52,3-10/S-1	-0.4
1976	Atl-N	116	383	57	96	11	8	1	32	42	36	.251	.331	.329	83	-8	7	7	-2	.975	7	*2-104/3-7,S-1	0.4
1977	Atl-N	128	407	47	99	15	2	8	43	45	79	.243	.322	.349	71	-16	3	9	-5	.978	3	*2-122/3-1	-1.0
1978	Atl-N	116	326	22	80	13	3	3	31	26	51	.245	.301	.331	69	-14	7	6	-2	.968	-3	3-62,2-39	-1.8
Total	7	500	1436	164	356	45	15	14	125	147	212	.248	.322	.329	74	-48	25	29	-10	.978	11	2-326,3-106/S-2	-2.9

■ DON GILE Gile, Donald Loren "Bear" b: 4/19/35, Modesto, Cal. BR/TR, 6'6", 220 lbs. Deb: 9/25/59

YEAR	TM/L	G	AB	R	H	2B	3B	HR	RBI	BB	SO	AVG	OBP	SLG	PRO+	BR/A	SB	CS	SBR	FA	FR	G/POS	TPR
1959	Bos-A	3	10	1	2	1	0	0	1	0	2	.200	.273	.300	55	-1	0	0	0	1.000	-0	/C-3	-0.1
1960	Bos-A	29	51	6	9	1	1	1	4	1	13	.176	.192	.294	29	-5	0	0	0	1.000	-1	C-15,1-11	-0.7
1961	Bos-A	8	18	2	5	0	0	1	1	1	5	.278	.316	.444	98	-0	0	0	0	.958	-1	/1-6,C-1	-0.1
1962	Bos-A	18	41	3	2	0	0	1	3	3	15	.049	.133	.122	-30	-8	0	0	0	.990	-1	1-14	-0.9
Total	4	58	120	12	18	2	1	3	9	5	35	.150	.197	.258	21	-14	0	0	0	.982	-2	/1-31,C-19	-1.8

■ BRIAN GILES Giles, Brian Jeffrey b: 4/27/60, Manhattan, Kan. BR/TR, 6'1", 165 lbs. Deb: 9/12/81

YEAR	TM/L	G	AB	R	H	2B	3B	HR	RBI	BB	SO	AVG	OBP	SLG	PRO+	BR/A	SB	CS	SBR	FA	FR	G/POS	TPR
1981	NY-N	9	7	0	0	0	0	0	0	0	3	.000	.000	.000	-99	-2	0	0	0	1.000	3	/2-2,S-2	0.2
1982	NY-N	45	138	14	29	5	0	3	10	12	29	.210	.273	.312	64	-7	6	1	1	.992	15	2-45/S-2	1.2
1983	NY-N	145	400	39	98	15	0	2	27	36	77	.245	.311	.298	70	-16	17	10	-1	.980	15	*2-140,S-12	0.4
1985	Mil-A	34	58	6	10	1	0	1	1	7	16	.172	.262	.241	39	-5	2	1	0	.963	8	S-20,2-13/D-2	0.4
1986	Chi-A	9	11	0	3	0	0	0	1	0	2	.273	.273	.273	48	-1	0	0	0	1.000	4	/2-7,S-1	0.2
1990	Sea-A	45	95	15	22	6	0	4	11	15	24	.232	.336	.421	109	1	2	1	0	.978	7	S-37/2-2,3-1,D-1	1.1
Total	6	287	709	74	162	27	0	10	50	70	151	.228	.300	.309	70	-29	27	13	0	.985	52	2-209/S-74,D-3,3-1	3.6

■ BRIAN GILES Giles, Brian Stephen b: 1/21/71, ElCajon, Cal. BL/TL, 5'11", 195 lbs. Deb: 9/16/95

YEAR	TM/L	G	AB	R	H	2B	3B	HR	RBI	BB	SO	AVG	OBP	SLG	PRO+	BR/A	SB	CS	SBR	FA	FR	G/POS	TPR
1995	Cle-A	6	9	6	5	0	0	1	3	0	1	.556	.556	.889	265	2	0	0	0	1.000	0	/O-3,D-1	0.2
1996	*Cle-A	51	121	26	43	14	1	5	27	19	13	.355	.443	.612	164	12	3	0	1	1.000	-1	D-21,O-16	0.9
1997	*Cle-A	130	377	62	101	15	3	17	61	63	50	.268	.374	.459	112	8	13	3	2	.972	-7	*O-115/D-9	0.0
1998	*Cle-A	112	350	56	94	19	0	16	66	73	75	.269	.399	.460	119	12	10	5	0	.978	5	*O-101/D-6	1.4
Total	4	299	857	150	243	48	4	39	157	155	139	.284	.396	.485	123	34	26	8	3	.976	-3	O-235/D-37	2.5

■ GEORGE GILHAM Gilham, George Louis b: 9/17/1899, Shamokin, Pa. d: 4/25/37, Lansdowne, Pa. BR/TR, 5'11", 164 lbs. Deb: 9/24/20

YEAR	TM/L	G	AB	R	H	2B	3B	HR	RBI	BB	SO	AVG	OBP	SLG	PRO+	BR/A	SB	CS	SBR	FA	FR	G/POS	TPR
1920	StL-N	1	3	0	0	0	0	0	0	0	1	.000	.000	.000	-99	-1	0	0	0	.750	-1	/C-1	-0.2
1921	StL-N	1	1	0	0	0	0	0	0	0	0	.000	.000	.000	-99	-0	0	0	0	.000	0	H	0.0
Total	2	2	4	0	0	0	0	0	0	0	1	.000	.000	.000	-99	-1	0	0	0	.750	-1	/C-1	-0.2

■ FRANK GILHOOLEY Gilhooley, Frank Patrick "Flash" b: 6/10/1892, Toledo, Ohio d: 7/11/59, Toledo, Ohio BL/TR, 5'8", 155 lbs. Deb: 9/18/11

YEAR	TM/L	G	AB	R	H	2B	3B	HR	RBI	BB	SO	AVG	OBP	SLG	PRO+	BR/A	SB	CS	SBR	FA	FR	G/POS	TPR
1911	StL-N	1	0	0	0	0	0	0	0	0	0	—	—	—	—	0	0			.000	-0	/O-1	0.0
1912	StL-N	13	49	5	11	0	0	0	2	3	8	.224	.269	.224	37	-4	0			1.000	-2	O-11	-0.7
1913	NY-A	24	85	10	29	2	1	0	14	4	9	.341	.378	.388	124	2	6			.977	-1	O-24	0.1
1914	NY-A	1	3	0	2	0	0	0	0	1	0	.667	.750	.667	327	1	0			.000	-0	/O-1	0.1
1915	NY-A	1	4	0	0	0	0	0	0	0	1	.000	.000	.000	-99	-1	0			1.000	-0	/O-1	-0.1
1916	NY-A	58	223	40	62	5	3	1	10	37	17	.278	.383	.341	115	6	16			.971	3	O-57	0.6
1917	NY-A	54	165	14	40	6	1	0	8	30	13	.242	.362	.291	99	1	6			.933	-1	O-46	-0.3
1918	NY-A	112	427	59	118	13	5	1	23	53	24	.276	.358	.337	107	5	7			.961	1	*O-111	-0.1
1919	Bos-A	48	112	14	27	4	0	0	1	12	8	.241	.315	.277	71	-4	2			.922	-5	O-33	-1.2
Total	9	312	1068	142	289	30	10	2	58	140	80	.271	.357	.323	102	6	37			.957	-7	O-285	-1.6

■ BERNARD GILKEY Gilkey, Otis Bernard b: 9/24/66, St.Louis, Mo. BR/TR, 6', 190 lbs. Deb: 9/4/90

YEAR	TM/L	G	AB	R	H	2B	3B	HR	RBI	BB	SO	AVG	OBP	SLG	PRO+	BR/A	SB	CS	SBR	FA	FR	G/POS	TPR
1990	StL-N	18	64	11	19	5	2	1	3	8	5	.297	.375	.484	134	3	6	1	1	.961	3	O-18	0.7
1991	StL-N	81	268	28	58	7	2	5	20	39	33	.216	.318	.313	78	-7	14	8	-1	.994	9	O-74	-0.1
1992	StL-N	131	384	56	116	19	4	7	43	39	52	.302	.368	.427	128	14	18	12	-2	.978	7	*O-111	1.9
1993	StL-N	137	557	99	170	40	5	16	70	56	66	.305	.373	.481	129	23	15	10	-2	.969	3	*O-134/1-3	2.1
1994	StL-N	105	380	52	96	22	1	6	45	39	65	.253	.338	.363	84	-8	15	8	-0	.983	5	*O-102	-0.5
1995	StL-N	121	480	73	143	33	4	17	69	42	70	.298	.361	.490	122	15	12	6	0	.986	10	*O-118	2.0
1996	NY-N	153	571	108	181	44	3	30	117	73	125	.317	.398	.562	157	47	17	9	-0	.982	24	*O-151	6.4
1997	NY-N	145	518	85	129	31	1	18	78	70	111	.249	.345	.417	102	2	7	11	-5	.989	13	*O-136/D-2	0.7
1998	NY-N	82	264	33	60	15	0	4	28	32	66	.227	.320	.330	70	-11	5	1	1	.992	4	O-77	-0.6
	Ari-N	29	101	8	25	0	0	1	5	11	14	.248	.327	.277	59	-6	4	2	0	.981	3	O-27	-0.3
	Yr	111	365	41	85	15	0	5	33	43	80	.233	.322	.315	67	-17	9	3	1	.989	7	*O-104	-0.9
Total	9	1002	3587	553	997	216	22	105	478	409	607	.278	.358	.438	113	71	113	68	-7	.983	81	O-948/1-3,D-2	12.3

■ BOB GILKS Gilks, Robert James b: 7/2/1864, Cincinnati, Ohio d: 8/21/44, Brunswick, Ga. BR/TR, 5'8", 178 lbs. Deb: 8/25/1887

YEAR	TM/L	G	AB	R	H	2B	3B	HR	RBI	BB	SO	AVG	OBP	SLG	PRO+	BR/A	SB	CS	SBR	FA	FR	G/POS	TPR
1887	Cle-a	22	83	12	26	2	0	0	13	3		.313	.352	.337	96	-0	5			.881	2	P-13/1-6,O-3,2-1	0.0

YEAR	TM/L	G	AB	R	H	2B	3B	HR	RBI	BB	SO	AVG	OBP	SLG	PRO+	BR/A	SB	CS	SBR	FA	FR	G/POS	TPR
1888	Cle-a	119	484	59	111	14	4	1	63	7		.229	.245	.281	70	-17	16			.899	-1	O-87,3-28/S-4,P2	-1.8
1889	Cle-N	53	210	17	50	5	2	0	18	7	20	.238	.273	.281	56	-13	6			1.000	0	O-29,S-13,1-10,/2-1	-1.1
1890	Cle-N	130	544	65	116	10	3	0	41	32	38	.213	.265	.243	49	-35	17			.941	1	*O-123/P-4,S-3,2-2	-3.3
1893	Bal-N	15	64	10	17	2	0	0	7	0	3	.266	.277	.297	52	-5	3			.969	3	O-15	-0.2
Total	5	339	1385	163	320	33	9	1	142	49	61	.231	.265	.270	60	-69	47			.937	5	O-257/3-28,PS12	-6.4
■ JIM GILL	Gill, James C. b: 7/1866, d: 4/10/23, Beaver Falls, Pa. Deb: 6/27/1889																						
1889	StL-a	2	8	2	2	1	0	0	1	1	2	.250	.333	.375	90	-0	1			1.000	-0	/O-1,2-1	-0.1
■ JOHNNY GILL	Gill, John Wesley "Patcheye" b: 3/27/05, Nashville, Tenn. d: 12/26/84, Nashville, Tenn. BL/TR, 6'2", 190 lbs. Deb: 8/28/27																						
1927	Cle-A	21	60	8	13	3	0	1	4	7	13	.217	.319	.317	65	-3	1	1	-0	1.000	-2	O-17	-0.6
1928	Cle-A	2	2	0	0	0	0	0	0	0	1	.000	.000	.000	-99	-1	0	0	0	.000	0	H	-0.1
1931	Was-A	8	30	2	8	2	1	0	5	1	6	.267	.313	.400	86	-1	0	1	-1	1.000	3	/O-8	0.1
1934	Was-A	13	53	7	13	3	0	2	7	2	3	.245	.286	.415	82	-2	0	0	0	1.000	-1	O-13	-0.3
1935	Chi-N	3	3	2	1	1	0	0	1	0	1	.333	.333	.667	161	0	0			.000	0	H	0.0
1936	Chi-N	71	174	20	44	8	0	7	28	13	19	.253	.309	.420	92	-2	0			.938	-3	O-41	-0.6
Total	6	118	322	39	79	17	1	10	45	23	43	.245	.306	.398	84	-8	1	2		.968	-2	/O-79	-1.5
■ WARREN GILL	Gill, Warren Darst "Doc" b: 12/21/1878, Ladoga, Ind. d: 11/26/52, Laguna Beach, Cal. BR/TR, 6'1", 175 lbs. Deb: 8/26/08																						
1908	Pit-N	27	76	10	17	0	1	0	14	11		.224	.366	.250	97	1	3			1.000	-3	1-25	-0.2
■ SAM GILLEN	Gillen, Samuel (b: Samuel Gilleland) b: 1/1871, Pittsburgh, Pa. d: 5/13/05, Pittsburgh, Pa. 5'8", Deb: 8/19/1893																						
1893	Pit-N	3	6	0	0	0	0	0	0	0	1	.000	.000	.000	-99	-2	0			.750	-0	/S-3	-0.2
1897	Phi-N	75	270	32	70	10	3	0	27	35		.259	.353	.319	80	-6	2			.896	-29	S-69/3-6	-3.0
Total	2	78	276	32	70	10	3	0	27	35	1	.254	.346	.312	76	-8	2			.892	-30	/S-72,3-6	-3.2
■ TOM GILLEN	Gillen, Thomas J. b: 5/18/1862, Philadelphia, Pa. d: 1/26/1889, Philadelphia, Pa. 5'8", 160 lbs. Deb: 4/18/1884																						
1884	Phi-U	29	116	5	18	2	0	0		1		.155	.162	.172	2	-17				.895	-4	C-27/O-3	-1.7
1886	Det-N	2	10	2	4	0	0	0	4	0	1	.400	.400	.400	140	0	0			.889	-2	/C-2	-0.1
Total	2	31	126	7	22	2	0	0	4	1	1	.175	.181	.190	14	-17	0			.895	-6	/C-29,O-3	-1.8
■ CARDEN GILLENWATER	Gillenwater, Carden Edison b: 5/13/18, Riceville, Tenn. BR/TR, 6'1", 178 lbs. Deb: 9/22/40																						
1940	StL-N	7	25	1	4	1	0	0	5	0	2	.160	.160	.200	-1	-3	0			1.000	-1	/O-7	-0.5
1943	Bro-N	8	17	1	3	0	0	0	2	2	3	.176	.263	.176	28	-2	0			1.000	-0	/O-4	-0.2
1945	Bos-N	144	517	74	149	20	2	7	72	73	70	.288	.379	.375	110	9	13			.979	24	*O-140	2.5
1946	Bos-N	99	224	30	51	10	1	1	14	39	27	.228	.342	.295	81	-4	3			.979	1	O-78	-0.6
1948	Was-A	77	221	23	54	10	4	3	21	39	36	.244	.358	.367	96	-1	4	2	0	.974	-1	O-67	-0.5
Total	5	335	1004	129	261	41	7	11	114	153	138	.260	.359	.348	96	-1	20	2		.979	23	O-296	0.7
■ JIM GILLESPIE	Gillespie, James Wheatfield b: 9/1858, Canada BL/TR, Deb: 10/1/1890																						
1890	Buf-P	1	3	0	0	0	0	0	0	0	2	.000	.000	.000	-99	-1	0			.250	-0	/O-1	-0.1
■ PAUL GILLESPIE	Gillespie, Paul Allen b: 9/18/20, Sugar Valley, Ga. d: 8/11/70, Anniston, Ala. BL/TR, 6'3", 195 lbs. Deb: 9/11/42																						
1942	Chi-N	5	16	3	4	0	0	2	4	1	2	.250	.294	.625	172	1	0			1.000	-1	/C-4	0.0
1944	Chi-N	9	26	2	7	1	0	1	2	3	3	.269	.345	.423	116	1	0			.903	-1	/C-7	0.0
1945	*Chi-N	75	163	12	47	6	0	3	25	18	9	.288	.366	.380	110	3	2			.989	1	C-45/O-1	0.6
Total	3	89	205	17	58	7	0	6	31	22	14	.283	.358	.405	115	4	2			.978	-1	/C-56,O-1	0.6
■ PETE GILLESPIE	Gillespie, Peter Patrick b: 11/30/1851, Carbondale, Pa. d: 5/5/10, Carbondale, Pa. BL/TR, 6'1.5", 178 lbs. Deb: 5/1/1880																						
1880	Tro-N	82	346	50	84	20	5	2	24	17	35	.243	.278	.347	105	1				.905	7	*O-82	0.5
1881	Tro-N	84	348	43	96	14	3	0	41	9	24	.276	.294	.333	92	-4				.933	4	*O-84	-0.1
1882	Tro-N	74	298	46	82	5	4	2	33	9	14	.275	.296	.339	108	3				.827	-6	*O-74	-0.2
1883	NY-N	98	411	64	129	23	12	1	62	9	27	.314	.329	.436	131	15				.897	7	*O-98	1.8
1884	NY-N	101	413	75	109	7	4	2	44	19	35	.264	.296	.315	90	-5				.893	-3	*O-101	-0.9
1885	NY-N	102	420	67	123	17	6	0	52	15	32	.293	.317	.362	121	9				**.942**	-4	*O-102	0.2
1886	NY-N	97	396	65	108	13	8	0	58	16	30	.273	.301	.346	95	-3	17			.901	-10	*O-97	-1.4
1887	NY-N	76	295	40	78	9	3	3	37	12	21	.264	.304	.346	84	-6	37			.946	-2	O-76/3-1	-0.8
Total	8	714	2927	450	809	108	45	10	351	106	218	.276	.303	.354	104	11	54			.903	-8	O-714/3-1	-0.9
■ JIM GILLIAM	Gilliam, James William "Junior" b: 10/17/28, Nashville, Tenn. d: 10/8/78, Inglewood, Cal. BB/TR, 5'10.5", 175 lbs. Deb: 4/14/53 C																						
1953	*Bro-N	151	605	125	168	31	**17**	6	63	100	38	.278	.383	.415	106	8	21	14	-2	.976	3	*2-149	1.7
1954	Bro-N	146	607	107	171	28	8	13	52	76	30	.282	.364	.418	100	1	8	7	-2	.977	-11	*2-143/O-4	-0.3
1955	*Bro-N	147	538	110	134	20	8	7	40	70	37	.249	.342	.355	83	-12	15	15	-5	.968	-9	2-99,O-46	-2.0
1956	*Bro-N☆	153	594	102	178	23	8	6	43	95	39	.300	.400	.396	107	10	21	9	1	.981	18	*2-102,O-56	3.4
1957	Bro-N	149	617	89	154	26	4	2	37	64	31	.250	.324	.314	66	-28	26	10	2	**.986**	3	*2-148/O-2	-1.2
1958	LA-N	147	555	81	145	25	5	2	43	78	22	.261	.352	.335	81	-13	18	11	-1	.987	8	O-75,3-44,2-32	-0.8
1959	*LA-N★	145	553	91	156	18	4	3	34	**96**	25	.282	.388	.345	91	-3	23	10	1	.958	2	*3-132/2-8,O-3	0.0
1960	LA-N	151	557	96	138	20	2	5	40	96	28	.248	.361	.318	82	-10	12	9	-2	.960	9	*3-130,2-30	0.0
1961	LA-N	144	439	74	107	26	3	4	32	79	34	.244	.359	.344	81	-10	8	4	0	.956	2	3-74,2-71,O-11	-0.2
1962	LA-N	160	588	83	159	24	1	4	43	93	35	.270	.372	.335	97	2	17	7	1	.981	-14	*2-113,3-90/O-1	0.0
1963	*LA-N	148	525	77	148	27	4	6	49	60	28	.282	.358	.383	122	15	19	5	3	.985	-8	*2-119,3-55	2.2
1964	LA-N	116	334	44	76	8	3	2	27	42	21	.228	.319	.287	78	-9	4	4	-1	.936	-20	3-86,2-25/O-2	-3.1
1965	*LA-N	111	372	54	104	19	4	4	39	53	31	.280	.375	.384	123	13	9	5	-0	.960	-13	3-80,O-22/2-5	-0.3
1966	*LA-N	88	235	30	51	9	0	1	16	34	17	.217	.316	.268	70	-9	2	1	0	.953	-12	3-70/1-2,2-2	-2.4
Total	14	1956	7119	1163	1889	304	71	65	558	1036	416	.265	.361	.355	92	-45	203	111	-6	.979	-43	*2-1046,3-761,O/1	-3.0
■ BARNEY GILLIGAN	Gilligan, Andrew Bernard b: 1/3/1856, Cambridge, Mass. d: 4/1/34, Lynn, Mass. BR/TR, 5'6.5", 130 lbs. Deb: 9/25/1875																						
1875	Atl-n	2	8	2	2	0	0	0	0	0	0	.250	.250	.250	85	-0	0	0	0	1.000	-1	/C-1,O-1	-0.1
1879	Cle-N	52	205	20	35	6	2	0	11	0	13	.171	.171	.220	28	-15				.870	-0	C-27,O-23/S-2	-1.5
1880	Cle-N	30	99	9	17	4	3	1	13	6	12	.172	.219	.303	77	-2				.969	4	C-23/O-4,S-4	0.3
1881	Pro-N	46	183	19	40	7	2	0	20	9	24	.219	.255	.279	69	-6				.930	-1	C-36,S-10/O-1	-0.5
1882	Pro-N	56	201	32	45	7	6	0	26	4	26	.224	.239	.318	77	-5				.932	10	C-54/S-2	0.6
1883	Pro-N	74	263	34	52	13	3	0	24	26	32	.198	.270	.270	63	-11				.900	10	*C-74	0.3
1884	*Pro-N	82	294	47	72	13	2	1	38	35	41	.245	.325	.313	104	3				.928	17	*C-81/3-1,1-1	2.4
1885	Pro-N	71	252	23	54	7	3	0	12	23	33	.214	.280	.266	80	-5				.872	-3	C-65/S-5,O-1,2-1	-0.2
1886	Was-N	81	273	23	52	9	2	0	17	39	35	.190	.292	.238	66	-9	6			.925	-9	C-71,O-14/S-1,3-1	-0.9
1887	Was-N	28	90	7	18	2	0	1	6	5	18	.200	.242	.256	40	-7	2			.874	-4	C-26/S-3,O-1	-0.7
1888	Det-N	1	5	1	1	0	0	0	0	0	1	.200	.200	.200	28	-0	0			.875	-0	/C-1	0.0
Total	10	521	1865	215	386	68	23	3	167	147	235	.207	.265	.273	70	-58	8	0		.912	24	C-458/O-44,S321	-0.2
■ GRANT GILLIS	Gillis, Grant b: 1/24/01, Grove Hill, Ala. d: 2/4/81, Thomasville, Ala. BR/TR, 5'10", 165 lbs. Deb: 9/19/27																						
1927	Was-A	10	36	8	8	3	1	0	2	2	0	.222	.263	.361	61	-2	0	0	0	1.000	-2	S-10	-0.3
1928	Was-A	24	87	13	22	5	1	0	10	4	5	.253	.309	.333	69	-4	0	1	-1	.910	-10	S-16/2-5,3-3	-1.3
1929	Bos-A	28	73	5	18	4	0	0	11	6	8	.247	.304	.301	58	-5	0	1	-1	.956	-4	2-25	-0.7
Total	3	62	196	26	48	12	2	0	23	12	13	.245	.299	.327	63	-11	0	2	-1	.948	-16	/2-30,S-26,3-3	-2.3
■ JIM GILMAN	Gilman, James Deb: 7/10/1893																						
1893	Cle-N	2	7	1	2	0	0	0	1	0	2	.286	.286	.286	49	-1	0			.667	-1	/3-2	-0.1
■ PIT GILMAN	Gilman, Pitkin Clark b: 3/14/1864, Laporte, Ohio d: 8/17/50, Elyria, Ohio BL/TL, 170 lbs. Deb: 9/18/1884																						
1884	Cle-N	2	10	0	1	0	0	0	0	0	3	.100	.100	.100	-36	-2				1.000	0	/O-2	-0.1

YEAR	TM/L	G	AB	R	H	2B	3B	HR	RBI	BB	SO	AVG	OBP	SLG	PRO+	BR/A	SB	CS	SBR	FA	FR	G/POS	TPR
■ GROVER GILMORE	Gilmore, Ernest Grover b: 11/1/1888, Chicago, Ill. d: 11/25/19, Sioux City, Iowa BL/TL, 5'9.5", 170 lbs. Deb: 4/18/14																						
1914	KC-F	139	530	91	152	25	5	1	32	37	108	.287	.337	.358	93	-14	23			.973	3	*O-132	-1.8
1915	KC-F	119	411	53	117	22	15	1	47	26	50	.285	.347	.418	120	3	19			.979	7	*O-119	0.5
Total	2	258	941	144	269	47	20	2	79	63	158	.286	.341	.385	105	-10	42			.976	10	O-251	-1.3
■ JIM GILMORE	Gilmore, James b: 5/1853, Baltimore, Md. d: 11/18/28, Baltimore, Md. Deb: 4/26/1875																						
1875	Was-n	3	12	2	3	0	0	0	0	0	3	.250	.250	.250	77	-0	0	0	0	.667	-1	/C-2,3-1,O-1	-0.1
■ GILROY	Gilroy Deb: 9/7/1874																						
1874	Chi-n	8	38	4	8	1	0	0	7	1	3	.211	.231	.237	50	-2	0	0	0	.816	-2	/C-8	-0.3
1875	Ath-n	2	6	0	1	0	0	0	0	0	0	.167	.167	.167	15	-1	0	0	0	.800	1	/C-1,O-1	0.1
Total	2 n	10	44	4	9	1	0	0	7	1	3	.205	.222	.227	45	-3	0	0	0	.814	-1	/C-9,O-1	-0.2
■ TINSLEY GINN	Ginn, Tinsley Rucker b: 9/26/1891, Royston, Ga. d: 8/30/31, Atlanta, Ga. BL/TR, 5'9", 180 lbs. Deb: 6/27/14																						
1914	Cle-A	2	1	0	0	0	0	0	0	0	0	.000	.000	.000	-96	-0	0			.000	0	/O-2	0.0
■ JOE GINSBERG	Ginsberg, Myron Nathan b: 10/11/26, New York, N.Y. BL/TR, 5'11", 180 lbs. Deb: 9/15/48																						
1948	Det-A	11	36	7	13	0	0	0	1	3	1	.361	.410	.361	103	0	0	0	0	.943	-2	C-11	0.0
1950	Det-A	36	95	12	22	6	0	0	12	11	6	.232	.318	.295	56	-6	1	0	0	.981	-4	C-31	-0.8
1951	Det-A	102	304	44	79	10	2	8	37	43	21	.260	.355	.385	100	0	0	2	-1	.978	-1	C-95	0.2
1952	Det-A	113	307	29	68	13	2	6	36	51	21	.221	.338	.336	87	-4	1	1	-0	.984	-14	*C-101	-1.4
1953	Det-A	18	53	6	16	2	0	0	3	10	1	.302	.422	.340	109	1	0	0	0	.988	0	C-15	0.2
	Cle-A	46	109	10	31	4	0	0	10	14	4	.284	.371	.321	91	-1	0	0	0	.966	-5	C-39	-0.4
	Yr	64	162	16	47	6	0	0	13	24	5	.290	.388	.327	97	1	0	0	0	.974	-5	C-54	-0.2
1954	Cle-A	3	2	0	1	0	1	0	1	0	0	.500	.667	1.500	473	1	0	0	0	1.000	-0	/C-1	0.1
1956	KC-A	71	195	15	48	8	1	1	12	23	17	.246	.326	.313	69	-8	1	1	-0	.989	-2	C-57	-0.9
	Bal-A	15	28	0	2	0	0	0	2	2	4	.071	.133	.071	-48	-6	0	0	0	1.000	-0	/C-8	-0.6
	Yr	86	223	15	50	8	1	1	14	25	21	.224	.302	.283	56	-14	1	1	-0	.990	-3	C-65	-1.5
1957	Bal-A	85	175	15	48	8	2	1	18	18	19	.274	.349	.360	100	0	2	1	0	.986	1	C-66	0.3
1958	Bal-A	61	109	4	23	1	0	3	16	13	14	.211	.306	.303	72	-4	0	0	0	.994	3	C-39	0.1
1959	Bal-A	65	166	14	30	2	0	1	14	21	13	.181	.273	.211	35	-14	1	0	0	.993	3	C-62	-0.9
1960	Bal-A	14	30	3	8	1	0	0	6	6	1	.267	.389	.300	90	-0	0	0	0	.940	0	C-14	0.1
	Chi-A	28	75	8	19	4	0	0	9	10	8	.253	.349	.307	80	-2	1	0	0	.993	4	C-25	0.4
	Yr	42	105	11	27	5	0	0	15	16	9	.257	.361	.305	83	-2	1	0	0	.976	5	C-39	0.5
1961	Chi-A	6	3	0	0	0	0	0	0	1	2	.000	.250	.000	-27	-1	0	0	0	1.000	0	/C-2	0.0
	Bos-A	19	24	1	6	0	0	0	5	0	2	.250	.250	.250	33	-2	0	0	0	1.000	-1	/C-6	-0.3
	Yr	25	27	1	6	0	0	0	5	1	4	.222	.250	.222	27	-3	0	0	0	1.000	-1	/C-8	-0.3
1962	NY-N	2	5	0	0	0	0	0	0	0	1	.000	.000	.000	-98	-1	0	0	0	1.000	1	/C-2	0.0
Total	13	695	1716	168	414	59	8	20	182	226	135	.241	.334	.320	79	-47	7	5	-1	.983	-17	C-574	-3.9
■ AL GIONFRIDDO	Gionfriddo, Albert Francis b: 3/8/22, Dysart, Pa. BL/TL, 5'6", 165 lbs. Deb: 9/23/44																						
1944	Pit-N	4	6	0	1	0	0	0	0	1	1	.167	.286	.167	28	-1	0			1.000	0	/O-1	-0.1
1945	Pit-N	122	409	74	116	18	9	2	42	60	22	.284	.377	.386	108	6	12			.964	-8	*O-106	-0.8
1946	Pit-N	64	102	11	26	2	2	0	10	14	5	.255	.345	.314	85	-2	1			.944	-5	O-33	-0.8
1947	Pit-N	1	1	0	0	0	0	0	0	0	0	.000	.000	.000	-97	-0	0			.000	0	H	0.0
	*Bro-N	37	62	10	11	2	1	0	6	16	11	.177	.346	.242	57	-3	2			.938	-2	O-17	-0.6
	Yr	38	63	10	11	2	1	0	6	16	11	.175	.342	.238	54	-4	2			.938	-2	O-17	-0.6
Total	4	228	580	95	154	22	12	2	58	91	39	.266	.366	.355	97	0	15			.959	-15	O-157	-2.3
■ TOMMY GIORDANO	Giordano, Thomas Arthur "T-Bone" (b: Carmine Arhur Giordano) b: 10/9/25, Newark, N.J. BR/TR, 6', 175 lbs. Deb: 9/11/53																						
1953	Phi-A	11	40	6	7	2	0	2	5	5	6	.175	.267	.375	69	-2	0	1	-1	.984	1	2-11	-0.1
■ ED GIOVANOLA	Giovanola, Edward Thomas b: 3/4/69, Los Gatos, Cal. BL/TR, 5'10", 170 lbs. Deb: 9/10/95																						
1995	Atl-N	13	14	2	1	0	0	0	0	3	5	.071	.235	.071	-14	-2	0	0	0	1.000	-2	/2-7,3-3,S-1	-0.4
1996	Atl-N	43	82	10	19	2	0	0	7	8	13	.232	.308	.256	48	-6	1	0	0	.983	-2	S-25/3-6,2-5	-0.6
1997	Atl-N	14	8	0	2	0	0	0	0	2	1	.250	.400	.250	74	-0	0	0	0	1.000	1	/3-8,2-1,S-1	0.1
1998	SD-N	92	139	19	32	3	3	1	9	22	22	.230	.335	.317	78	-4	1	2	-1	.965	18	3-37,2-36/S-2	1.4
Total	4	162	243	31	54	5	3	1	16	35	41	.222	.323	.280	62	-13	2	2	-1	.971	15	/3-54,2-49,S-29	0.5
■ CHARLES GIPSON	Gipson, Charles Wells b: 12/16/72, Orange, Cal. BR/TR, 6'2", 180 lbs. Deb: 3/31/98																						
1998	Sea-A	44	51	11	12	1	0	0	2	5	9	.235	.316	.255	51	-3	2	1	0	.973	-7	O-36/3-4	-1.0
■ JOE GIRARDI	Girardi, Joseph Elliott b: 10/14/64, Peoria, Ill. BR/TR, 5'11", 195 lbs. Deb: 4/4/89																						
1989	*Chi-N	59	157	15	39	10	0	1	14	11	26	.248	.306	.331	76	-5	2	1	0	.981	13	C-59	1.2
1990	Chi-N	133	419	36	113	24	2	1	38	17	50	.270	.303	.344	72	-16	8	3	1	.985	-9	*C-133	-1.7
1991	Chi-N	21	47	3	9	2	0	0	6	6	6	.191	.283	.234	45	-3	0	0	0	.972	4	C-21	0.1
1992	Chi-N	91	270	19	73	3	1	1	12	19	38	.270	.321	.300	75	-8	0	2	-1	.991	-4	C-86	-1.0
1993	Col-N	86	310	35	90	14	5	3	31	24	41	.290	.347	.397	85	-7	6	6	-2	.989	-8	C-84	-1.2
1994	Col-N	93	330	47	91	9	4	4	34	21	48	.276	.323	.364	67	-16	3	3	-1	.992	5	C-93	-0.7
1995	*Col-N	125	462	63	121	17	2	8	55	29	76	.262	.308	.359	59	-30	3	3	-1	.988	-4	*C-122	-2.6
1996	*NY-A	124	422	55	124	22	3	2	45	30	55	.294	.348	.374	83	-10	13	4	2	.996	8	*C-120/D-2	0.5
1997	*NY-A	112	398	38	105	23	1	1	50	26	53	.264	.312	.334	69	-18	2	3	-1	.994	17	*C-111/D-1	0.5
1998	*NY-A	78	254	31	70	11	4	3	31	14	38	.276	.319	.386	84	-6	2	4	-2	.995	21	C-78	1.6
Total	10	922	3069	342	835	135	22	24	316	197	431	.272	.321	.354	73	-120	39	29	-6	.990	42	C-907/D-3	-3.3
■ TONY GIULIANI	Giuliani, Angelo John b: 11/24/12, St.Paul, Minn. BR/TR, 5'11", 175 lbs. Deb: 4/18/36																						
1936	StL-A	71	198	17	43	3	0	0	13	11	13	.217	.258	.232	21	-25	0	0	0	.966	5	C-66	-1.5
1937	StL-A	19	53	6	16	1	0	0	3	3	3	.302	.339	.321	67	-3	0	0	0	.986	-0	C-19	-0.2
1938	Was-A	46	115	10	25	4	0	0	15	8	3	.217	.268	.252	33	-12	1	0	0	1.000	-1	C-46	-1.0
1939	Was-A	54	172	20	43	6	2	0	18	4	7	.250	.267	.308	50	-13	0	1	-1	.979	1	C-50	-0.9
1940	Bro-N	1	1	0	0	0	0	0	0	0	1	.000	.000	.000	-94	-0	0			1.000	-0	/C-1	0.0
1941	Bro-N	3	2	0	0	0	0	0	0	0	0	.000	.000	.000	-96	-1	0			1.000	1	/C-3	0.0
1943	Was-A	49	133	5	30	4	1	0	20	12	14	.226	.290	.271	67	-6	0	1	-1	.962	-1	C-49	-0.5
Total	7	243	674	58	157	18	3	0	69	38	41	.233	.274	.269	42	-59	1	2		.976	6	C-234	-4.1
■ JIM GLADD	Gladd, James Walter b: 10/2/22, Ft.Gibson, Okla. d: 11/8/77, Long Beach, Cal. BR/TR, 6'2", 190 lbs. Deb: 9/9/46																						
1946	NY N	4	11	0	1	0	0	0	0	1	4	.091	.167	.091	-26	-2	0			1.000	4	/C-4	0.2
■ DAN GLADDEN	Gladden, Clinton Daniel b: 7/7/57, San Jose, Cal. BR/TR, 5'11", 180 lbs. Deb: 9/5/83																						
1983	SF-N	18	63	6	14	2	0	1	9	5	11	.222	.279	.302	63	-3	4	3	-1	1.000	2	O-18	-0.2
1984	SF-N	86	342	71	120	17	2	4	31	33	37	.351	.411	.447	146	22	31	16	-0	.988	9	O-85	2.9
1985	SF-N	142	502	64	122	15	8	7	41	40	78	.243	.308	.347	87	-9	32	15	1	.975	1	*O-124	-1.3
1986	SF-N	102	351	55	97	16	1	4	29	39	59	.276	.357	.362	104	3	27	10	2	.987	12	O-89	1.4
1987	*Min-A	121	438	69	109	21	2	8	38	38	72	.249	.313	.361	75	-15	25	9	2	.987	6	*O-111/D-4	-1.0
1988	Min-A	141	576	91	155	32	6	11	62	46	74	.269	.327	.403	100	-0	28	8	4	.991	16	*O-140/2-1,3-1,P-1	1.6
1989	Min-A	121	461	69	136	23	3	8	46	23	53	.295	.335	.410	102	1	23	7	3	.966	5	*O-117/P-1,D-2	0.6
1990	Min-A	136	534	64	147	27	6	5	40	26	67	.275	.316	.376	87	-10	25	9	2	.980	12	*O-133/D-2	0.1
1991	*Min-A	126	461	65	114	14	9	6	52	36	60	.247	.309	.356	80	-13	15	9	-1	.988	1	*O-126	-1.6
1992	Det-A	113	417	57	106	20	1	7	42	30	64	.254	.307	.357	85	-9	4	2	0	.987	0	*O-108/D-2	-1.1
1993	Det-A	91	356	52	95	16	2	13	56	21	50	.267	.313	.433	99	-2	8	5	-1	.986	8	O-86/D-5	0.4
Total	11	1197	4501	663	1215	203	40	74	446	337	625	.270	.327	.382	94	-36	222	93	11	.984	73	*O-1137/D-15,P32	1.8

YEAR	TM/L	G	AB	R	H	2B	3B	HR	RBI	BB	SO	AVG	OBP	SLG	PRO+	BR/A	SB	CS	SBR	FA	FR	G/POS	TPR
■ **BUCK GLADMAN**	Gladman, John H. b: 1864, Washington, D.C. Deb: 7/7/1883																						
1883	Phi-N	1	4	1	0	0	0	0	0	0	2	.000	.000	.000	-99	-1				1.000	-1	/3-1	-0.1
1884	Was-a	56	224	17	35	5	3	1		3		.156	.178	.219	33	-16				.796	-3	3-53/O-2,S-1	-1.7
1886	Was-N	44	152	17	21	5	3	1	15	12	30	.138	.201	.230	33	-12	5			.830	-6	3-44	-1.6
Total	3	101	380	35	56	10	6	2	15	15	32	.147	.186	.221	31	-28	5			.812	-10	/3-98,O-2,S-1	-3.4
■ **ROLAND GLADU**	Gladu, Roland Edouard b: 5/10/11, Montreal, Que., Can d: 7/26/94, Montreal, Que., Can. BL/TR, 5′8.5″, 185 lbs. Deb: 4/18/44																						
1944	Bos-N	21	66	5	16	2	1	1	7	3	8	.242	.275	.348	72	-3	0			.891	-5	3-15/O-3	-0.8
■ **DOUG GLANVILLE**	Glanville, Douglas Metunwa b: 8/25/70, Hackensack, N.J. BR/TR, 6′2″, 170 lbs. Deb: 6/9/96																						
1996	Chi-N	49	83	10	20	5	1	1	10	3	11	.241	.267	.361	62	-5	2	0	1	.973	-6	O-35	-1.0
1997	Chi-N	146	474	79	142	22	5	4	35	24	46	.300	.335	.392	87	-9	19	11	-1	.989	4	*O-138	-0.8
1998	Phi-N	158	678	106	189	28	7	8	49	42	89	.279	.326	.376	80	-19	23	6	3	.995	13	*O-158	-0.4
Total	3	353	1235	195	351	55	13	13	94	69	146	.284	.326	.381	82	-33	44	17	3	.991	12	O-331	-2.2
■ **JACK GLASSCOCK**	Glasscock, John Wesley "Pebbly Jack" b: 7/22/1859, Wheeling, W.Va. d: 2/24/47, Wheeling, W.Va. BR/TR, 5′8″, 160 lbs. Deb: 5/1/1879 M																						
1879	Cle-N	80	325	31	68	9	3	0	29	6	24	.209	.224	.255	58	-14				.919	-6	*2-66,3-14	-1.4
1880	Cle-N	77	296	37	72	13	3	0	27	2	21	.243	.248	.307	89	-3				.891	7	*S-77	0.8
1881	Cle-N	85	335	49	86	9	5	0	33	15	8	.257	.289	.313	94	-2				**.911**	9	*S-79/2-6	1.2
1882	Cle-N	84	358	66	104	27	9	4	46	13	9	.291	.315	.450	147	18				.900	**24**	*S-83/3-1	**4.1**
1883	Cle-N	96	383	67	110	19	6	0	46	13	23	.287	.311	.368	107	3				**.922**	17	*S-93/2-3	1.9
1884	Cle-N	72	281	45	70	4	4	1	22	25	16	.249	.310	.302	91	-3				.893	27	S-69/2-3,P-2	2.2
	Cin-U	38	172	48	72	9	5	2		8		.419	.444	.564	189	14				.889	1	S-36/2-2	1.3
1885	StL-N	111	446	66	125	18	3	1	40	29	10	.280	.324	.341	123	12				**.917**	19	*S-110/2-1	3.1
1886	StL-N	121	486	96	158	29	7	3	40	38	13	.325	.374	.432	154	33	38			**.906**	14	*S-120/O-1	4.2
1887	Ind-N	122	483	91	142	18	7	0	40	41	8	.294	.361	.360	105	5	62			.906	**35**	*S-122/P-1	3.5
1888	Ind-N	113	442	63	119	17	3	1	45	14	17	.269	.302	.328	99	-1	48			**.901**	11	*S-110/2-3,P-1	1.3
1889	Ind-N	134	582	128	**205**	40	3	7	85	31	10	.352	.390	.467	136	26	57			**.915**	**36**	*S-132/2-2,P-1,M	**5.9**
1890	NY-N	124	512	91	**172**	32	9	1	66	41	8	**.336**	.395	.439	143	27	54			.910	22	*S-124	**4.9**
1891	NY-N	97	369	46	89	12	6	0	55	36	11	.241	.317	.306	85	-6	29			.913	-2	*S-97	-0.3
1892	StL-N	139	566	83	151	27	5	3	72	44	19	.267	.327	.348	110	6	26			.916	6	*S-139,M	1.7
1893	StL-N	48	195	32	56	8	1	1	26	25	3	.287	.382	.354	96	-0	20			.907	-7	S-48	-0.4
	Pit-N	66	293	49	100	7	11	1	74	17	4	.341	.385	.451	124	9	16			.934	12	S-66	2.0
	Yr	114	488	81	156	15	12	2	100	42	7	.320	.384	.412	113	9	36			.923	6	*S-114	1.6
1894	Pit-N	86	332	46	93	10	7	1	63	31	4	.280	.349	.361	72	-15	18			.933	7	S-85	-0.2
1895	Lou-N	18	74	9	25	3	1	1	6	3	1	.338	.387	.446	122	2	1			.900	2	S-13/1-5	0.4
	Was-N	25	100	20	23	2	0	0	10	7	3	.230	.300	.250	43	-8	3			.895	6	S-25	-0.1
	Yr	43	174	29	48	5	1	1	16	10	4	.276	.337	.333	76	-6	4			.897	8	S-38/1-5	0.3
Total	17	1736	7030	1163	2040	313	98	27	825	439	212	.290	.337	.374	112	105	372			.910	240	*S-1628/2-86,31PO	36.1
■ **TROY GLAUS**	Glaus, Troy b: 8/3/76, Newport Beach, Cal. BR/TR, 6′5″, 220 lbs. Deb: 7/31/98																						
1998	Ana-A	48	165	19	36	9	0	1	23	15	51	.218	.283	.291	49	-12	1	0	0	.941	2	3-48	-0.9
■ **TOMMY GLAVIANO**	Glaviano, Thomas Giatano "Rabbit" b: 10/26/23, Sacramento, Cal. BR/TR, 5′9″, 175 lbs. Deb: 4/19/49																						
1949	StL-N	87	258	32	69	16	1	6	36	41	35	.267	.380	.407	106	4	0			.929	14	3-73/2-7	1.6
1950	StL-N	115	410	92	117	29	2	11	44	90	74	.285	.421	.446	122	17	6			.935	6	*3-106/2-5,S-1	2.1
1951	StL-N	54	104	20	19	4	0	1	4	26	18	.183	.356	.250	66	-4	3	0	1	.972	-3	O-17/2-9	-0.6
1952	StL-N	80	162	30	39	5	1	3	19	27	26	.241	.366	.340	97	0	0	0	0	.934	4	3-52/2-1	0.4
1953	Phi-N	53	74	17	15	1	2	3	5	24	20	.203	.410	.392	111	2	2	0	1	.892	-2	3-14,2-12/S-1	0.1
Total	5	389	1008	191	259	55	6	24	108	208	173	.257	.395	.395	108	20	11	0		.931	18	3-245/2-34,O-17,S-2	3.6
■ **HARRY GLEASON**	Gleason, Harry Gilbert b: 3/28/1875, Camden, N.J. d: 10/21/61, Camden, N.J. BR/TR, 5′6″, 160 lbs. Deb: 9/27/01 F																						
1901	Bos-A	1	1	0	1	0	0	0	0	0		1.000	1.000	1.000	464	0	1			.667	1	/3-1	0.1
1902	Bos-A	71	240	30	54	5	5	2	25	10		.225	.265	.313	58	-14	6			.930	-0	3-35,O-23/2-4	-1.5
1903	Bos-A	6	13	3	2	1	0	0	2	0		.154	.154	.231	13	-1	0			.750	-1	/3-2	-0.3
1904	StL-A	46	155	10	33	7	1	0	6	4		.213	.247	.271	68	-6	1			.908	-3	S-20,3-20/2-5,O-1	-0.9
1905	StL-A	150	535	45	116	11	5	1	57	34		.217	.269	.262	72	-17	23			.911	-15	*3-144/2-7	-2.9
Total	5	274	944	88	206	24	11	3	90	48		.218	.263	.276	67	-38	31			.914	-19	3-202/O-24,S-20,2	-5.5
■ **JACK GLEASON**	Gleason, John Day b: 7/14/1854, St.Louis, Mo. d: 9/4/44, St.Louis, Mo. BR/TR, 170 lbs. Deb: 10/2/1877 F																						
1877	StL-N	1	4	0	1	0	0	0	0	0	1	.250	.250	.250	61	-0				.000	-0	/O-1	-0.1
1882	StL-a	78	331	53	84	10	1	2		**27**		.254	.310	.308	105	2				.768	2	*3-73/O-6,2-1	0.5
1883	StL-a	9	34	2	8	0	0	0		4		.235	.316	.235	76	-1				.833	0	/O-9,3-1	0.0
	Lou-a	84	355	69	106	11	4	2		25		.299	.345	.369	140	17				.795	-33	*3-83/S-1	-1.5
	Yr	93	389	71	114	11	4	2		29		.293	.342	.357	134	16				.798	-33	3-84/O-9,S-1	-1.5
1884	StL-U	92	395	90	128	30	2	4		23		.324	.361	.441	137	7				.768	-6	*3-92	0.1
1885	StL-N	2	7	0	1	0	0	0	0	0	1	.143	.143	.143	-8	-1				.857	-0	/3-2	-0.1
1886	Phi-a	77	299	39	56	8	7	1	31	16		.187	.255	.271	64	-13	8			.797	-6	3-77	-1.4
Total	6	343	1425	253	384	59	14	9	31	95	2	.269	.320	.349	112	11	8			.781	-43	3-328/O-16,S-1,2-1	-2.5
■ **ROY GLEASON**	Gleason, Roy William b: 4/9/43, Melrose Park, Ill. BB/TR, 6′5.5″, 220 lbs. Deb: 9/3/63																						
1963	LA-N	8	1	3	1	1	0	0	0	0	0	1.000	1.000	2.000	795	1	0	0	0	.000	0	H	0.1
■ **BILL GLEASON**	Gleason, William G. "Will" b: 11/12/1858, St.Louis, Mo. d: 7/21/32, St.Louis, Mo. BR/TR, 5′8″, 170 lbs. Deb: 5/2/1882 FU																						
1882	StL-a	79	347	63	100	11	6	1		6		.288	.300	.363	118	5				.833	9	*S-79	1.7
1883	StL-a	98	425	81	122	21	9	2	42	15		.287	.311	.393	119	7				.871	-2	*S-98	0.7
1884	StL-a	110	472	97	127	21	7	1		27		.269	.325	.350	116	8				.867	-17	*S-110/3-1	-0.7
1885	*StL-a	112	472	79	119	9	5	3	53	29		.252	.316	.311	94	-3				.869	-42	*S-112	-3.9
1886	*StL-a	125	524	97	141	18	5	0	61	43		.269	.333	.323	101	-0	19			.853	-29	*S-125	-2.5
1887	*StL-a	135	598	135	172	19	1	0	76	41		.288	.342	.323	78	-21	23			.875	-10	*S-135	-2.4
1888	Phi-a	123	499	55	112	10	2	0	61	12		.224	.256	.253	63	-20	27			.858	-14	*S-121/3-1,1-1	-2.9
1889	Lou-a	16	58	6	14	2	0	0	5	4	1	.241	.302	.276	66	-2	1			.822	-3	S-16	-0.4
Total	8	798	3395	613	907	111	35	7	298	177	1	.267	.313	.327	95	-26	70			.860	-106	S-796/3-2,1-1	-10.4
■ **KID GLEASON**	Gleason, William J. b: 10/26/1866, Camden, N.J. d: 1/2/33, Philadelphia, Pa. BB/TR, 5′7″, 158 lbs. Deb: 4/20/1888 FMC																						
1888	Phi-N	24	83	4	17	2	0	0	5	3	16	.205	.233	.229	45	-5	3			.841	-3	P-24/O-1	0.0
1889	Phi-N	30	99	11	25	5	0	0	8	8	12	.253	.308	.303	65	-5	4			.862	-1	P-29/O-3,2-2	-0.1
1890	Phi-N	63	224	22	47	3	0	0	17	12	21	.210	.250	.223	37	-18	10			.937	-1	P-60/2-2	-0.1
1891	Phi-N	65	214	31	53	5	2	0	17	20	17	.248	.318	.290	75	-7	6			.896	-6	P-53/O-9,S-4	-0.4
1892	StL-N	66	233	35	50	4	2	3	25	34	23	.215	.315	.288	87	-3	7			.934	3	P-47,O-10/2-9,1-1	-0.2
1893	StL-N	59	199	25	51	6	4	0	20	19	8	.256	.327	.327	74	-8	2			.907	-0	P-48,O-11/S-1	-0.3
1894	StL-N	9	28	3	7	0	1	0	1	2	1	.250	.300	.321	50	-2	0			.885	1	/P-8,1-1	0.0
	*Bal-N	26	86	22	30	5	1	0	17	7	2	.349	.398	.430	95	-1	1			.900	-2	P-21/1-1	0.0
	Yr	35	114	25	37	5	2	0	18	9	3	.325	.374	.404	85	-3	1			.894	-0	P-29/1-2	0.0
1895	*Bal-N	112	421	90	130	14	12	0	74	33	18	.309	.366	.399	95	-4	19			.899	-17	2-85,3-12/P-9,O-4	-1.3
1896	NY-N	133	541	79	162	17	5	4	89	42	13	.299	.352	.372	93	-5	46			.938	3	*2-130/3-3,O-1	0.5
1897	NY-N	131	540	85	172	16	4	1	106	26		.319	.353	.369	93	-5	43			.930	1	*2-129/S-3	0.2
1898	NY-N	150	570	78	126	8	5	0	62	39		.221	.278	.253	54	-34	21			.938	21	*2-144/S-6	-0.3
1899	NY-N	146	576	72	152	14	4	0	59	24		.264	.293	.302	66	-28	29			.946	26	*2-146	0.5
1900	NY-N	111	420	60	104	11	3	1	29	17		.248	.280	.295	62	-22	23			.931	14	*2-111/S-1	-0.3
1901	Det-A	135	547	82	150	16	12	3	75	41		.274	.327	.364	87	-10	32			.925	6	*2-135	0.1

YEAR	TM/L	G	AB	R	H	2B	3B	HR	RBI	BB	SO	AVG	OBP	SLG	PRO+	BR/A	SB	CS	SBR	FA	FR	G/POS	TPR
1902	Det-A	118	441	42	109	11	4	1	38	25		.247	.292	.297	62	-22	17			.941	6	*2-118	-1.2
1903	Phi-N	106	412	65	117	19	6	1	49	23		.284	.326	.367	101	-1	12			.959	-4	*2-102/O-4	-0.1
1904	Phi-N	153	587	61	161	23	6	0	42	37		.274	.319	.334	106	3	17			.942	1	*2-152/3-1	0.9
1905	Phi-N	155	608	95	150	17	7	1	50	45		.247	.302	.303	83	-12	16			.947	-8	*2-155	-1.9
1906	Phi-N	135	494	47	112	17	2	0	34	36		.227	.281	.269	71	-17	17			.947	-29	*2-135	-5.1
1907	Phi-N	36	126	11	18	3	0	0	6	7		.143	.200	.167	15	-12	3			.979	-2	2-26/1-4,S-4,O-1	-1.7
1908	Phi-N	2	1	0	0	0	0	0	0	0		.000	.000	.000	-97	-0	0			1.000	0	/2-1,O-1	0.0
1912	Chi-A	1	2	0	1	0	0	0	0	0		.500	.500	.500	192	0	0			1.000	-0	/2-1	0.0
Total	22	1966	7452	1020	1944	216	80	15	823	500	131	.261	.311	.317	78	-216	328			.938	8	*2-1583,P-299/OS31	-10.8
■ BILLY GLEASON	Gleason, William Patrick b: 9/6/1894, Chicago, Ill. d: 1/9/57, Holyoke, Mass. BR/TR, 5'6.5", 157 lbs. Deb: 9/25/16																						
1916	Pit-N	1	2	0	0	0	0	0	0	0	0	.000	.000	.000	-99	-0	0			1.000	-0	/2-1	-0.1
1917	Pit-N	13	42	3	7	1	0	0	0	5	5	.167	.255	.190	36	-3	1			.978	-5	2-13	-0.9
1921	StL-A	26	74	6	19	0	1	0	8	6	6	.257	.329	.284	54	-5	0	1	-1	.960	-5	2-25	-0.9
Total	3	40	118	9	26	1	1	0	8	11	11	.220	.298	.246	47	-8	1	1		.966	-10	/2-39	-1.9
■ JIM GLEESON	Gleeson, James Joseph "Gee Gee" b: 3/5/12, Kansas City, Mo. d: 5/1/96, Kansas City, Mo. BB/TR, 6'1", 191 lbs. Deb: 4/25/36 C																						
1936	Cle-A	41	139	26	36	9	2	4	12	18	17	.259	.344	.439	91	-2	2	1	0	.958	-2	O-33	-0.5
1939	Chi-N	111	332	43	74	19	6	4	45	39	46	.223	.308	.352	76	-11	7			.957	-4	O-91	-1.9
1940	Chi-N	129	485	76	152	39	11	5	61	54	52	.313	.389	.470	139	26	4			.983	3	*O-123	2.2
1941	Cin-N	102	301	47	70	10	0	3	34	45	30	.233	.340	.296	80	-6	7			.981	-8	O-84	-2.0
1942	Cin-N	9	20	3	4	0	0	0	2	2	2	.200	.304	.200	49	-1	0			.889	-0	O/-5	-0.2
Total	5	392	1277	195	336	77	19	16	154	158	147	.263	.350	.391	101	5	20	1		.972	-11	O-336	-2.4
■ FRANK GLEICH	Gleich, Frank Elmer "Inch" b: 3/7/1894, Columbus, Ohio d: 3/27/49, Columbus, Ohio BL/TR, 5'11", 175 lbs. Deb: 9/17/19																						
1919	NY-A	5	4	0	1	0	0	0	1	1	0	.250	.400	.250	84	-0	0			.000	-2	/O-4	-0.2
1920	NY-A	24	41	6	5	0	0	0	3	6	10	.122	.234	.122	-4	-6	0	0	0	.864	-4	O-15	-1.1
Total	2	29	45	6	6	0	0	0	4	7	10	.133	.250	.133	4	-6	0	0		.826	-7	/O-19	-1.3
■ BOB GLENALVIN	Glenalvin, Robert J. (b: Robert J. Dowling) b: 1/17/1867, Indianapolis, Ind. d: 3/24/44, Detroit, Mich. TR, 5'9", 160 lbs. Deb: 7/12/1890																						
1890	Chi-N	66	250	43	67	10	3	4	26	19	31	.268	.337	.380	105	1	30			.928	-14	2-66	-0.9
1893	Chi-N	16	61	11	21	3	1	0	12	7	3	.344	.412	.426	125	2	7			.928	-5	2-16	-0.2
Total	2	82	311	54	88	13	4	4	38	26	34	.283	.352	.389	109	3	37			.928	-19	/2-82	-1.1
■ ED GLENN	Glenn, Edward C. "Mouse" b: 9/19/1860, Richmond, Va. d: 2/10/1892, Richmond, Va. BR/TR, 5'10", 160 lbs. Deb: 8/5/1884																						
1884	Ric-a	43	175	26	43	2	4	1		5		.246	.271	.320	93	-1				.833	5	O-43	0.2
1886	Pit-a	71	277	32	53	6	5	0	26	17		.191	.241	.249	54	-15	19			.865	0	O-71	-1.4
1888	KC-a	3	8	0	0	0	0	0	0	0		.000	.200	.000	-32	-1	1			.857	-0	/O-3	-0.1
	Bos-N	20	65	8	10	0	2	0	3	2	8	.154	.203	.215	33	-5	0			.957	2	O-19/3-1	-0.3
Total	3	137	525	66	106	8	11	1	29	24	8	.202	.245	.265	62	-22	20			.867	7	O-136/3-1	-1.6
■ ED GLENN	Glenn, Edward D. b: 10/1875, Ohio d: 12/6/11, Ludlow, Ky. BR/TR, Deb: 9/7/1898																						
1898	Was-N	1	4	0	0	0	0	0	0	0		.000	.000	.000	-99	-1	0			1.000	-1	/S-1	-0.2
	NY-N	2	4	1	1	0	0	0	0	3		.250	.571	.250	142	1	1			.750	-3	/S-2	-0.2
	Yr	3	8	1	1	0	0	0	0	3		.125	.364	.125	42	-0	1			.857	-3	/S-3	-0.4
1902	Chi-N	2	7	0	0	0	0	0	0	1		.000	.125	.000	-63	-1	0			1.000	-1	/S-2	-0.3
Total	2	5	15	1	1	0	0	0	0	4		.067	.263	.067	-2	-2	1			.923	-5	/S-5	-0.7
■ HARRY GLENN	Glenn, Harry Melville "Husky" b: 6/9/1890, Shelburn, Ind. d: 10/12/18, St.Paul, Minn. BR/TR, 6'1", 200 lbs. Deb: 4/14/15																						
1915	StL-N	6	16	1	5	0	0	0	1	3	0	.313	.421	.313	123	1	0			.929	-1	/C-5	0.0
■ JOHN GLENN	Glenn, John b: 7/10/28, Moultrie, Ga. BR/TR, 6'3", 180 lbs. Deb: 6/16/60																						
1960	StL-N	32	31	4	8	0	1	0	5	0	9	.258	.258	.323	53	-2	0	0	0	1.000	-7	O-28	-1.0
■ JOHN GLENN	Glenn, John W. b: 1849, Rochester, N.Y. d: 11/10/1888, Sandy Hill, N.Y. BR/TR, 5'8.5", 169 lbs. Deb: 5/13/1871																						
1871	Oly-n	26	120	25	37	3	2	0	21	3	1	.308	.325	.367	104	1	1	1	-0	.860	1	*O-26	0.2
1872	Oly-n	9	39	6	6	0	0	0	3	1	0	.154	.175	.154	2	-4	0	1	-1	.800	3	/O-9	-0.1
	Nat-n	1	4	0	2	0	0	0	0	0	0	.500	.500	.500	179	0	0	0	0	.667	-0	/O-1	0.0
	Yr	10	43	6	8	0	0	0	3	1	0	.186	.205	.186	22	-4	0	1	-1	.791	3	O-10	-0.1
1873	Was-n	39	185	39	49	8	2	1	21	3	0	.265	.277	.346	87	-3	2	1	0	.928	-2	*1-39	-0.2
1874	Chi-n	55	237	33	67	9	0	0	32	5	4	.283	.298	.321	97	-1	2	2	-1	.918	2	1-37,O-19	0.0
1875	Chi-n	69	308	46	75	8	0	0	27	3	6	.244	.251	.269	80	-6	10	2	2	.898	-2	O-44,1-29	-0.5
1876	Chi-N	66	276	55	84	9	2	0	32	12	6	.304	.333	.351	115	2				.881	-2	*O-56,1-15	0.0
1877	Chi-N	50	202	31	46	6	1	0	20	8	16	.228	.257	.267	58	-10				.948	0	O-36,1-14	-1.1
Total	5 n	199	893	149	236	28	4	1	104	15	11	.264	.276	.308	87	-12	15	7	0	.923	2	1-105/O-99	-0.6
Total	2	116	478	86	130	15	3	0	52	20	22	.272	.301	.316	90	-8				.904	-2	/O-92,1-29	-1.1
■ JOE GLENN	Glenn, Joseph Charles "Gabby" (b: Joseph Charles Gurzensky) b: 11/19/08, Dickson City, Pa. d: 5/6/85, Tunkhannock, Pa. BR/TR, 5'11", 175 lbs. Deb: 9/15/32																						
1932	NY-A	6	16	0	2	0	0	0	0	1	5	.125	.222	.125	-8	-3	0	0	0	1.000	-2	/C-5	-0.4
1933	NY-A	5	21	1	3	0	0	0	1	0	3	.143	.143	.143	-26	-4	0	0	0	1.000	-2	/C-5	-0.5
1935	NY-A	17	43	7	10	4	0	0	6	4	1	.233	.298	.326	65	-2	0	0	0	.984	0	C-16	-0.1
1936	NY-A	44	129	21	35	7	0	1	20	20	10	.271	.373	.349	82	-3	1	1	-0	.970	3	C-44	0.1
1937	NY-A	25	53	6	15	2	2	0	4	10	11	.283	.397	.396	100	0	0	0	0	.978	4	C-24	0.4
1938	NY-A	41	123	10	32	7	2	0	25	10	14	.260	.316	.350	67	-6	1	0	0	.974	0	C-40	-0.4
1939	StL-A	88	286	29	78	13	1	4	29	31	40	.273	.344	.367	80	-8	4	4	-1	.968	-13	C-82	-1.7
1940	Bos-A	22	47	3	6	1	0	0	4	5	7	.128	.212	.149	-5	-7	0	0	0	.961	-0	C-19	-0.6
Total	8	248	718	77	181	34	5	5	89	81	91	.252	.330	.334	69	-33	6	5	-1	.972	-10	C-235	-3.2
■ NORM GLOCKSON	Glockson, Norman Stanley b: 6/15/1894, Blue Island, Ill. d: 8/5/55, Maywood, Ill. BR/TR, 6'2", 200 lbs. Deb: 9/16/14																						
1914	Cin-N	7	12	0	0	0	0	0	0	1	6	.000	.077	.000	-74	-3	0			.923	-1	/C-7	-0.3
■ AL GLOSSOP	Glossop, Alban b: 7/23/15, Christopher, Ill. d: 7/2/91, Walnut Creek, Cal. BB/TR, 6', 170 lbs. Deb: 9/23/39																						
1939	NY-N	10	32	3	6	0	0	1	3	4	2	.188	.278	.281	50	-2	0			.980	0	2-10	-0.1
1940	NY-N	27	91	16	19	3	0	4	8	10	16	.209	.294	.374	82	-2	1			.952	0	2-24	0.0
	Bos-N	60	148	17	35	2	1	3	14	17	22	.236	.315	.324	81	-4	1			.938	6	2-18,3-18/S-1	0.4
	Yr	87	239	33	54	5	1	7	22	27	38	.226	.307	.343	82	-6	2			.947	7	2-42,3-18/S-1	0.4
1942	Phi-N	121	454	33	102	15	1	4	40	29	35	.225	.273	.289	68	-20	3			.961	7	*2-118/3-1	-0.6
1943	Bro-N	87	217	28	37	9	0	3	21	28	27	.171	.268	.253	51	-13	0			.927	-7	S-33,2-24,3-17,/O-1	-1.9
1946	Chi-N	4	10	2	0	0	0	0	0	1	3	.000	.231	.000	-32	-2	0			1.000	-2	/2-2,S-2	-0.3
Total	5	309	952	99	199	29	2	15	86	89	105	.209	.280	.291	66	-43	5			.954	6	2-196/S-36,3-36,O-1	-2.5
■ BILL GLYNN	Glynn, William Vincent b: 7/30/25, Sussex, N.J. BL/TL, 6', 190 lbs. Deb: 9/16/49																						
1949	Phi-N	8	10	0	2	0	0	0	1	0	3	.200	.200	.200	8	-1	0			1.000	0	/1-1	-0.1
1952	Cle-A	44	92	15	25	5	0	2	7	5	16	.272	.309	.391	101	-0	1	0	0	.973	0	1-32	-0.1
1953	Cle-A	147	411	60	100	14	2	3	30	44	65	.243	.324	.309	74	-14	1	3	-2	**.993**	6	*1-135/O-2	-1.5
1954	*Cle-A	111	171	19	43	3	2	5	18	12	21	.251	.301	.380	84	-4	3	2	-0	.987	3	1-96/O-1	-0.4
Total	4	310	684	94	170	22	4	10	56	61	105	.249	.315	.336	79	-21	5	5		.989	9	1-264/O-3	-2.1
■ JOHN GOCHNAUER	Gochnauer, John Peter b: 9/12/1875, Altoona, Pa. d: 9/27/29, Altoona, Pa. BR/TR, 5'9", 160 lbs. Deb: 9/29/01																						
1901	Bro-N	3	11	1	4	0	0	0	2	1		.364	.417	.364	124	0	1			1.000	-1	/S-3	0.0
1902	Cle-A	127	459	45	85	16	4	0	37	38		.185	.247	.237	36	-39	7			.933	-3	*S-127	-3.3

YEAR	TM/L	G	AB	R	H	2B	3B	HR	RBI	BB	SO	AVG	OBP	SLG	PRO+	BR/A	SB	CS	SBR	FA	FR	G/POS	TPR
1903	Cle-A	134	438	48	81	16	4	0	48	48		.185	.265	.240	53	-24	10			.869	-21	*S-134	-4.1
Total	3	264	908	94	170	32	8	0	87	87		.187	.258	.240	45	-63	18			.901	-24	S-264	-7.4

■ JOHN GODAR　Godar, John Michael b: 10/25/1864, Cincinnati, Ohio d: 6/23/49, Park Ridge, Ill. BR/TR, 5'9", 170 lbs. Deb: 7/8/1892

| 1892 | Bal-N | 5 | 14 | 2 | 3 | 0 | 0 | 0 | 1 | 2 | 1 | .214 | .353 | .214 | 71 | -0 | 1 | | | 1.000 | -0 | /O-5 | -0.1 |

■ DANNY GODBY　Godby, Danny Ray b: 11/4/46, Logan, W.Va. BR/TR, 6', 185 lbs. Deb: 8/10/74

| 1974 | StL-N | 13 | 13 | 2 | 2 | 0 | 0 | 0 | 1 | 3 | 4 | .154 | .313 | .154 | 34 | -1 | 0 | 0 | 0 | 1.000 | 1 | /O-4 | 0.0 |

■ JOE GODDARD　Goddard, Joseph Harold b: 7/23/50, Beckley, W.Va. BR/TR, 5'11", 181 lbs. Deb: 7/31/72

| 1972 | SD-N | 12 | 35 | 0 | 7 | 2 | 0 | 0 | 2 | 3 | 7 | .200 | .300 | .257 | 64 | -2 | 0 | 0 | 0 | .973 | -2 | C-12 | -0.4 |

■ JOHN GODWIN　Godwin, John Henry "Bunny" b: 3/10/1877, E.Liverpool, Ohio d: 5/5/56, E.Liverpool, Ohio BR/TR, 6', 190 lbs. Deb: 8/14/05

1905	Bos-A	15	43	4	14	1	0	0	10	3		.326	.408	.349	139	2	3			.950	1	/O-7,2-5	0.3
1906	Bos-A	66	193	11	36	2	1	0	15	6		.187	.215	.207	32	-15	6			.907	2	3-27,S-14,O-10,/21	-1.4
Total	2	81	236	15	50	3	1	0	25	9		.212	.253	.233	53	-13	9			.935	3	/3-27,O-17,S-14,21	-1.1

■ ED GOEBEL　Goebel, Edwin b: 9/1/1899, Brooklyn, N.Y. d: 8/12/59, Brooklyn, N.Y. BR/TR, 5'11", 170 lbs. Deb: 5/13/22

| 1922 | Was-A | 37 | 59 | 13 | 16 | 1 | 0 | 1 | 3 | 8 | 16 | .271 | .358 | .339 | 87 | -1 | 1 | 1 | -0 | 1.000 | 1 | O-16 | -0.3 |

■ BILLY GOECKEL　Goeckel, William John b: 9/3/1871, Wilkes-Barre, Pa. d: 11/1/22, Philadelphia, Pa. BR/TL, Deb: 8/10/1899

| 1899 | Phi-N | 37 | 141 | 17 | 37 | 1 | 0 | 1 | 16 | 1 | | .262 | .283 | .298 | 61 | -8 | 6 | | | .978 | -3 | 1-36 | -0.9 |

■ JERRY GOFF　Goff, Jerry Leroy b: 4/12/64, San Rafael, Cal. BL/TR, 6'3", 207 lbs. Deb: 5/15/90

1990	Mon-N	52	119	14	27	1	0	3	7	21	36	.227	.343	.311	84	-2	0	2	-1	.963	-1	C-38/1-3,3-3	-0.2
1992	Mon-N	3	3	0	0	0	0	0	0	0	3	.000	.000	.000	-99	-1	0	0	0	.000	0	/H	-0.1
1993	Pit-N	14	37	5	11	2	0	2	6	8	9	.297	.422	.514	149	3	0	0	0	.984	-2	C-14	0.1
1994	Pit-N	8	25	0	2	0	0	0	0	0	11	.080	.080	.080	-57	-6	0	0	0	.950	-1	/C-7	-0.7
1995	Hou-N	12	26	2	4	2	0	1	3	4	13	.154	.267	.346	64	-1	0	0	0	1.000	7	C-11	0.5
1996	Hou-N	1	4	1	2	0	0	1	2	0	1	.500	.500	1.250	371	1	0	0	0	1.000	0	/C-1	0.1
Total	6	90	214	22	46	5	0	7	19	33	73	.215	.320	.336	80	-5	0	2	-1	.974	2	/C-71,3-3,1-3	-0.3

■ CHUCK GOGGIN　Goggin, Charles Francis b: 7/7/45, Pompano Beach, Fla. BB/TR, 5'11", 175 lbs. Deb: 9/8/72

1972	Pit-N	5	7	0	2	0	0	0	1	1	1	.286	.375	.286	92	-0	0	0	0	1.000	0	/2-1	0.0
1973	Pit-N	1	1	1	1	0	0	0	0	0	0	1.000	1.000	1.000	468	0	0	0	0	1.000	-0	/C-1	0.0
	Atl-N	64	90	18	26	5	0	0	7	9	19	.289	.354	.344	88	-1	0	1	-1	.938	-10	2-19/O-6,S-5,C-1	-1.1
	Yr	65	91	19	27	5	0	0	7	9	19	.297	.360	.352	91	-1	0	1	-1	.938	-10	2-19/O-6,S-5,C-2	-1.1
1974	Bos-A	2	1	0	0	0	0	0	0	0	1	.000	.000	.000	-93	-0	0	0	0	.667	1	/2-2	0.0
Total	3	72	99	19	29	5	0	0	7	10	21	.293	.358	.343	91	-1	0	1	-1	.927	-9	/2-22,O-6,S-5,C-2	-1.1

■ MIKE GOLDEN　Golden, Michael Henry b: 9/11/1851, Shirley, Mass. d: 1/11/29, Rockford, Ill. BR/TR, 5'8", 168 lbs. Deb: 5/5/1875

1875	Wes-n	13	46	6	6	0	0	0	1	0	3	.130	.130	.130	-9	-5	0	0	0	.844	-1	P-13	0.0
	Chi-n	39	155	16	40	3	0	0	14	2	10	.258	.268	.277	89	-2	3	2	-0	.833	-1	O-27,P-14	-0.1
	Yr	52	201	22	46	3	0	0	15	2	13	.229	.236	.244	66	-7	3	2	-0	.833	-1	P-27,O-27	-0.1
1878	Mil-N	55	214	16	44	6	3	0	20	3	35	.206	.217	.262	53	-11				.831	-3	O-39,P-22/1-1	-1.2

■ JONAH GOLDMAN　Goldman, Jonah John b: 8/29/06, New York, N.Y. d: 8/17/80, Palm Beach, Fla. BR/TR, 5'7", 170 lbs. Deb: 9/22/28

1928	Cle-A	7	21	1	5	1	0	0	2	3	0	.238	.333	.286	63	-1	0	0	0	.878	0	/S-7	0.0
1930	Cle-A	111	306	32	74	18	0	1	44	28	25	.242	.312	.310	56	-20	3	5	-2	.945	21	S-93,3-20	0.7
1931	Cle-A	30	62	0	8	1	0	0	3	4	6	.129	.182	.145	-12	-10	1	1	-0	.947	14	S-30	0.5
Total	3	148	389	33	87	20	0	1	49	35	31	.224	.293	.283	46	-31	4	6	-2	.941	35	S-130/3-20	1.2

■ GORDON GOLDSBERRY　Goldsberry, Gordon Frederick b: 8/30/27, Sacramento, Cal. d: 2/23/96, Lake Forest, Cal. BL/TL, 6', 170 lbs. Deb: 4/20/49

1949	Chi-A	39	145	25	36	3	2	1	13	18	9	.248	.331	.317	74	-5	2	0	1	.990	-1	1-38	-0.6
1950	Chi-A	82	127	19	34	8	2	2	25	26	18	.268	.392	.409	108	2	0	2	-1	.989	3	1-40/O-3	0.4
1951	Chi-A	10	11	4	1	0	0	0	1	2	2	.091	.231	.091	-11	-2	0	0	0	1.000	1	/1-8	0.0
1952	StL-A	86	227	30	52	9	3	3	17	34	37	.229	.330	.335	83	-5	0	2	-1	.983	-3	1-72/O-2	-1.1
Total	4	217	510	78	123	20	7	6	56	80	66	.241	.344	.343	85	-10	2	4	-2	.987	1	1-158/O-5	-1.3

■ WALT GOLDSBY　Goldsby, Walton Hugh b: 12/31/1861, Louisiana d: 1/11/14, Dallas, Tex. BL , Deb: 5/28/1884

1884	StL-a	5	20	2	4	0	0	0	1	0		.200	.200	.200	30	-2				.800	-1	/O-5	-0.2
	Was-a	6	24	4	9	0	0	0	3	1		.375	.400	.375	174	2				.909	1	/O-6	0.2
	Ric-a	11	40	4	9	1	0	0	4	1		.225	.262	.250	69	-1				.737	-1	O-11	-0.2
	Yr	22	84	10	22	1	0	0	8	2		.262	.287	.274	87	-1				.800	-1	O-22	-0.2
1886	Was-N	6	18	0	4	1	0	0	1	2	3	.222	.300	.278	81	-0	0			.818	-1	/O-6	-0.1
1888	Bal-a	45	165	13	39	1	1	0	14	8		.236	.288	.255	76	-4	17			.903	-6	O-45	-1.0
Total	3	73	267	23	65	3	1	0	23	12	3	.243	.289	.262	80	-5	17			.858	-8	/O-73	-1.3

■ FRED GOLDSMITH　Goldsmith, Fred Ernest b: 5/15/1856, New Haven, Conn. d: 3/28/39, Berkley, Mich. BR/TR, 6'1", 195 lbs. Deb: 10/23/1875 U

1875	NH-n	1	4	0	2	0	0	0	1	0	0	.500	.500	.500	285	1	0	0	0	.700	0	/2-1	0.1
1879	Tro-n	9	38	6	9	1	0	0	2	1	3	.237	.256	.263	77	-1				.833	1	/P-8,O-2,1-1	0.0
1880	Chi-N	35	142	24	37	4	2	0	15	2	15	.261	.271	.317	93	-1				.968	1	P-26,O-10/1-4	-0.2
1881	Chi-N	42	158	24	38	3	4	0	16	6	17	.241	.268	.310	78	-4				.863	5	P-39/O-3	0.0
1882	Chi-N	45	183	23	42	11	1	0	19	4	29	.230	.246	.301	71	-6				.939	1	P-45/1-1	0.0
1883	Chi-N	60	235	38	52	12	3	1	16	4	35	.221	.234	.311	60	-12				.865	1	P-46,O-16/1-2	-0.3
1884	Chi-N	22	81	11	11	2	0	2	6	7	26	.136	.250	.235	35	-3				.774	-3	P-21/O-2	0.0
	Bal-a	4	14	2	2	0	0	0	0	2		.143	.250	.143	30	-1				.889	-2	/P-4,1-1	0.0
Total	6	217	851	128	191	33	10	3	74	26	125	.224	.247	.297	69	-31				.882	4	P-189/O-33,1-9	-0.5

■ WALLY GOLDSMITH　Goldsmith, Wallace b: 1849, Baltimore, Md. 5'7", 146 lbs. Deb: 5/4/1871

1871	Kek-n	19	88	8	18	1	0	0	12	4	2	.205	.239	.216	31	-8	0	0	0	.767	-10	S-14/3-8,C-2	-1.2
1872	Oly-n	9	41	4	10	2	0	0	5	0	0	.244	.244	.293	68	-1	0	0	0	.679	-1	/S-5,2-4	-0.2
1873	Mar-n	1	4	0	0	0	0	0	0	0	0	.000	.000	.000	-99	-1	0	0	0	.667	-1	/2-1	-0.1
1875	Wes-n	13	51	3	6	0	0	0	1	0	2	.118	.118	.118	-17	-6	0	0	0	.814	-1	3-13	-0.6
Total	4 n	42	184	15	34	3	0	0	18	4	4	.185	.202	.201	24	-16	0	0	0	.694	-13	/3-21,S-19,2-5,C-2	-2.1

■ LONNIE GOLDSTEIN　Goldstein, Leslie Elmer b: 5/13/18, Austin, Tex. BL/TL, 6'2.5", 190 lbs. Deb: 9/11/43

1943	Cin-N	5	5	1	1	0	0	0	0	2	1	.200	.429	.200	85	-0	0			1.000	-0	/1-2	0.0
1946	Cin-N	6	5	0	0	0	0	0	0	1	1	.000	.167	.000	-53	-1	0			.000	0	H	-0.1
Total	2	11	10	2	1	0	0	0	0	3	2	.100	.308	.100	20	-1	0			1.000	-0	/1-2	-0.1

■ PURNAL GOLDY　Goldy, Purnal William b: 11/28/37, Camden, N.J. BR/TR, 6'5", 200 lbs. Deb: 4/12/62

1962	Det-A	20	70	8	16	1	1	3	12	0	12	.229	.239	.400	66	-4	0	0	0	.964	-0	O-15	-0.5
1963	Det-A	9	8	0	2	0	0	0	0	0	4	.250	.250	.250	39	-1	0			.000	0	H	-0.1
Total	2	29	78	8	18	1	1	3	12	0	16	.231	.241	.385	64	-4	0	0	0	.964	-0	/O-15	-0.6

■ STAN GOLETZ　Goletz, Stanley "Stash" b: 5/21/18, Crescent, Ohio BL/TL, 6'3", 200 lbs. Deb: 9/9/41

| 1941 | Chi-A | 5 | 5 | 0 | 3 | 0 | 0 | 0 | 0 | 0 | 0 | .600 | .600 | .600 | 221 | 1 | 0 | 0 | 0 | .000 | 0 | H | 0.1 |

■ MIKE GOLIAT　Goliat, Mike Mitchel b: 11/5/25, Yatesboro, Pa. BR/TR, 6', 180 lbs. Deb: 8/3/49

1949	Phi-N	55	189	24	40	6	3	3	19	20	32	.212	.290	.323	66	-9	0			.969	-2	2-50/1-5	-0.9
1950	*Phi-N	145	483	49	113	13	6	13	64	53	75	.234	.314	.366	80	-15	3			.972	-18	*2-145	-2.6
1951	Phi-N	41	138	14	31	2	1	4	15	9	18	.225	.277	.341	66	-7	0	1	-1	.968	-7	2-37/3-2	-1.3

YEAR	TM/L	G	AB	R	H	2B	3B	HR	RBI	BB	SO	AVG	OBP	SLG	PRO+	BR/A	SB	CS	SBR	FA	FR	G/POS	TPR
	StL-A	5	11	0	2	0	0	0	1	0	1	.182	.182	.182	-1	-2	0	0	0	1.000	0	/2-2	-0.1
1952	StL-A	3	4	0	0	0	0	0	0	1	1	.000	.200	.000	-40	-1	0	0	0	1.000	1	/2-3	0.0
Total	4	249	825	87	186	21	10	20	99	83	127	.225	.300	.348	73	-33	3	1		.971	-26	2-237/1-5,3-2	-4.9
■ WALT GOLVIN Golvin, Walter George b: 2/1/1894, Hershey, Neb. d: 6/11/73, Gardena, Cal. BL/TL, 6', 165 lbs. Deb: 4/15/22																							
1922	Chi-N	2	2	0	0	0	0	0	1	0	0	.000	.000	.000	-98	-1	0	0	0	1.000	-0	/1-2	-0.1
■ CHRIS GOMEZ Gomez, Christopher Cory b: 6/16/71, Los Angeles, Cal. BR/TR, 6'1", 183 lbs. Deb: 7/19/93																							
1993	Det-A	46	128	11	32	7	1	0	11	9	17	.250	.304	.320	69	-6	2	2	-1	.963	11	S-29,2-17/D-1	0.6
1994	Det-A	84	296	32	76	19	0	8	53	33	64	.257	.337	.402	89	-5	5	3	-0	.981	-17	S-57,2-30	-1.5
1995	Det-A	123	431	49	96	20	2	11	50	41	96	.223	.295	.355	68	-21	4	1	1	.973	3	S-97,2-31/D-2	-0.7
1996	Det-A	48	128	21	31	5	0	1	16	18	20	.242	.340	.305	65	-6	1	1	-0	.970	3	S-47	0.0
	*SD-N	89	328	32	86	16	1	3	29	39	64	.262	.351	.345	90	-4	2	2	-1	.967	-6	S-89	-0.3
1997	SD-N	150	522	62	132	19	2	5	54	53	114	.253	.328	.326	77	-17	5	8	-3	.978	-2	*S-150	-0.9
1998	*SD-N	145	449	55	120	32	3	4	39	51	87	.267	.349	.379	98	-1	1	3	-2	**.980**	3	*S-143	1.4
Total	6	685	2282	262	573	118	9	32	252	244	462	.251	.330	.353	82	-59	20	20	-6	.975	-4	S-612/2-78,D-3	-1.4
■ CHILE GOMEZ Gomez, Jose Luis (Gonzales) b: 5/23/09, Villa Union, Mex. d: 12/1/92, Nuevo Laredo, Mex. BR/TR, 5'10", 165 lbs. Deb: 7/27/35																							
1935	Phi-N	67	222	24	51	3	0	0	16	17	34	.230	.285	.243	39	-19	2			.948	12	S-36,2-32	-0.3
1936	Phi-N	108	332	24	77	4	1	0	28	14	32	.232	.265	.250	36	-30	0			.948	18	2-71,S-40	-0.5
1942	Was-A	25	73	8	14	2	2	0	6	9	7	.192	.280	.274	57	-4	1	0	0	.973	-1	2-23/3-1	-0.4
Total	3	200	627	56	142	9	3	0	50	40	73	.226	.274	.250	39	-53	3	0		.954	29	2-126/S-76,3-1	-1.2
■ LEO GOMEZ Gomez, Leonardo (Velez) b: 3/2/66, Canovanas, P.R. BR/TR, 6', 208 lbs. Deb: 9/17/90																							
1990	Bal-A	12	39	3	9	0	0	0	1	8	7	.231	.362	.231	71	-1	0	0	0	.886	-2	3-12	-0.3
1991	Bal-A	118	391	40	91	17	2	16	45	40	82	.233	.307	.409	100	-1	1	1	-0	.972	-13	*3-105,D-10/1-3	-1.4
1992	Bal-A	137	468	62	124	24	0	17	64	63	78	.265	.362	.425	117	11	2	3	-1	.951	-13	*3-137	-0.3
1993	Bal-A	71	244	30	48	7	0	10	25	32	60	.197	.297	.348	70	-11	0	1	-1	.951	6	3-70/D-1	-0.5
1994	Bal-A	84	285	46	78	20	0	15	56	41	55	.274	.371	.502	116	7	0	0	0	.975	4	3-78/1-1,D-5	1.0
1995	Bal-A	53	127	16	30	5	0	4	12	18	23	.236	.340	.370	83	-3	0	1	-1	.978	2	3-44/1-3,D-5	-0.1
1996	Chi-N	136	362	44	86	19	0	17	56	53	94	.238	.346	.431	101	1	1	4	-2	**.972**	-5	*3-124/1-8,S-1	-0.7
Total	7	611	1916	241	466	92	2	79	259	255	399	.243	.340	.417	101	4	4	10	-5	.962	-22	3-570/D-21,1-15,S-1	-2.3
■ LUIS GOMEZ Gomez, Luis (Sanchez) b: 8/19/51, Guadalajara, Mex. BR/TR, 5'9", 150 lbs. Deb: 4/28/74																							
1974	Min-A	82	168	18	35	1	0	0	3	12	16	.208	.261	.214	37	-13	2	3	-1	.960	20	S-74/2-2,D-1	1.2
1975	Min-A	89	72	7	10	0	0	0	5	4	12	.139	.184	.139	-7	-10	0	2	-1	.975	20	S-70/2-6,D-7	1.0
1976	Min-A	38	57	5	11	1	0	0	3	3	3	.193	.233	.211	30	-5	1	0	0	.988	7	S-24/2-8,3-4,O-1,D	0.4
1977	Min-A	32	65	6	16	4	2	0	11	4	9	.246	.290	.369	79	-2	0	2	-1	.983	4	2-19/S-7,3-4,O-1,D	0.2
1978	Tor-A	153	413	39	92	7	3	0	32	34	41	.223	.282	.254	51	-26	2	10	-5	.976	-10	*S-153	-2.5
1979	Tor-A	59	163	11	39	7	0	0	11	6	17	.239	.266	.282	48	-12	1	0	0	1.000	4	3-22,2-20,S-15	-0.6
1980	Atl-N	121	278	18	53	6	0	0	24	17	27	.191	.240	.212	26	-27	0	4	-2	.968	12	*S-119	-0.8
1981	Atl-N	35	35	4	7	0	0	0	1	6	4	.200	.317	.200	48	-2	0	1	-1	.895	-3	S-21/3-9,2-3,P-1	-0.5
Total	8	609	1251	108	263	26	5	0	90	86	129	.210	.262	.239	40	-98	6	22	-11	.970	54	S-483/2-58,3DOP	-1.6
■ PRESTON GOMEZ Gomez, Pedro (Martinez) b: 4/20/23, Preston, Cuba BR/TR, 5'11", 170 lbs. Deb: 5/5/44 MC																							
1944	Was-A	8	7	2	2	1	0	0	2	0	4	.286	.286	.429	107	0	0	0	0	1.000	-1	/2-2,S-2	-0.1
■ RANDY GOMEZ Gomez, Randell Scott b: 2/4/57, San Mateo, Cal. BR/TR, 5'10", 185 lbs. Deb: 8/21/84																							
1984	SF-N	14	30	0	5	1	0	0	0	8	3	.167	.342	.200	57	-1	0	0	0	.951	3	C-14	0.3
■ JESSE GONDER Gonder, Jesse Lemar b: 1/20/36, Monticello, Ark. BL/TR, 5'10", 190 lbs. Deb: 9/23/60																							
1960	NY-A	7	7	1	2	0	0	1	3	1	1	.286	.375	.714	199	1	0	0	0	1.000	1	/C-1	0.2
1961	NY-A	15	12	2	4	1	0	0	3	3	1	.333	.467	.417	146	1	0	0	0	.000	0	H	0.1
1962	Cin-N	4	4	0	0	0	0	0	0	0	3	.000	.000	.000	-97	-1	0	0	0	.000	0	H	-0.1
1963	Cin-N	31	32	5	10	2	0	3	5	1	12	.313	.333	.656	172	3	0	0	0	1.000	1	/C-7	0.4
	NY-N	42	126	12	38	4	0	3	15	6	25	.302	.333	.405	110	1	1	2	-1	.978	-14	C-31	-1.4
	Yr	73	158	17	48	6	0	6	20	7	37	.304	.333	.456	122	4	1	2	-1	.981	-13	C-38	-1.0
1964	NY-N	131	341	28	92	11	1	7	35	29	65	.270	.331	.370	99	-0	0	0	0	.979	-1	C-97	0.3
1965	NY-N	53	105	6	25	4	0	4	9	11	20	.238	.310	.390	100	-0	0	0	0	.992	-5	C-31	-0.4
	Mil-N	31	53	2	8	2	0	1	5	4	9	.151	.211	.245	28	-5	0	0	0	.989	5	C-13	0.0
	Yr	84	158	8	33	6	0	5	14	15	29	.209	.277	.342	75	-5	0	0	0	.991	-0	C-44	-0.4
1966	Pit-N	59	160	13	36	3	1	7	16	12	39	.225	.287	.387	85	-3	0	0	0	.978	-2	C-52	-0.2
1967	Pit-N	22	36	4	5	1	0	0	3	5	9	.139	.279	.167	30	-3	0	0	0	.971	-0	C-18	-0.3
Total	8	395	876	73	220	28	2	26	94	72	184	.251	.312	.377	94	-7	1	2	-1	.981	-15	C-250	-1.4
■ DAN GONZALES Gonzales, Daniel David b: 9/30/53, Whittier, Cal. BL/TR, 6'1", 195 lbs. Deb: 4/7/79																							
1979	Det-A	7	18	1	4	1	0	0	2	0	2	.222	.222	.278	33	-2	1	0	0	1.000	-1	/O-3,D-1	-0.2
1980	Det-A	2	7	1	1	0	0	0	0	0	1	.143	.143	.143	-21	-1	0	0	0	.750	0	/O-1,D-1	-0.1
Total	2	9	25	2	5	1	0	0	2	0	3	.200	.200	.240	18	-3	1	0	0	.857	-1	/O-4,D-2	-0.3
■ LARRY GONZALES Gonzales, Lawrence Christopher b: 3/28/67, West Covina, Cal. BR/TR, 6'3", 200 lbs. Deb: 6/13/93																							
1993	Cal-A	2	2	0	1	0	0	0	1	1	0	.500	.667	.500	212	0	0	0	0	1.000	-0	/C-2	0.0
■ RENE GONZALES Gonzales, Rene Adrian b: 9/3/60, Austin, Tex. BR/TR, 6'3", 201 lbs. Deb: 7/27/84																							
1984	Mon-N	29	30	5	7	1	0	0	2	2	5	.233	.303	.267	64	-1	0	0	0	.957	1	S-27	0.0
1986	Mon-N	11	26	1	3	0	0	0	0	2	7	.115	.179	.115	-17	-4	0	2	-1	1.000	2	/S-6,3-5	-0.4
1987	Bal-A	37	60	14	16	2	1	1	7	3	11	.267	.302	.383	82	-2	1	0	0	.963	6	3-29/2-6,S-1	0.4
1988	Bal-A	92	237	13	51	6	0	2	15	13	32	.215	.265	.266	50	-16	2	0	1	.966	15	3-80,2-14/S-2,1O	-0.1
1989	Bal-A	71	166	16	36	4	0	1	11	12	30	.217	.270	.259	51	-11	5	3	-0	.978	-1	2-54,3-17/S-1	-1.1
1990	Bal-A	67	103	13	22	3	1	1	12	12	14	.214	.296	.291	67	-4	1	2	-1	.994	9	2-43,3-16/S-9,O-1	0.5
1991	*Tor-A	71	118	16	23	3	0	1	6	12	22	.195	.291	.246	48	-8	0	0	0	.973	10	S-36,3-26,2-11,/1-2	0.4
1992	Cal-A	104	329	47	91	17	1	7	38	41	46	.277	.364	.398	113	6	7	4	-0	.954	5	3-53,2-42,1-13,/S-8	1.2
1993	Cal-A	118	335	34	84	17	0	2	31	49	45	.251	.348	.319	78	-9	5	5	-2	.956	-0	3-79,1-31/S-5,2P	-1.2
1994	Cle-A	22	23	6	8	1	1	1	5	5	3	.348	.464	.609	173	3	2	0	1	.952	3	3-13/1-4,S-4,2-1	0.6
1995	Cal-A	30	18	1	6	1	0	1	3	0	4	.333	.333	.556	127	1	0	0	0	1.000	2	3-18/2-6,S-1,D-1	0.2
1996	*Tex-A	51	92	19	20	4	0	2	5	10	11	.217	.294	.326	54	-7	0	0	0	.989	6	1-23,3-15,S-10,2O	-0.1
1997	Col-N	2	2	0	1	0	0	0	1	0	0	.500	.500	.500	133	0	0	0	0	.000	0	/3-1	0.0
Total	13	705	1539	185	308	59	4	19	136	161	230	.239	.316	.320	75	-51	23	16	-3	.957	55	3-352,2-186,S/1ODP	0.4
■ ALEX GONZALEZ Gonzalez, Alexander b: 2/15/77, Cagua, Ven. BR/TR, 6', 170 lbs. Deb: 8/25/98																							
1998	Fla-N	25	86	11	13	2	0	3	7	9	30	.151	.240	.279	36	-8	0	0	0	.967	-4	S-25	-1.0
■ ALEX GONZALEZ Gonzalez, Alexander Scott b: 4/8/73, Miami, Fla. BR/TR, 6', 180 lbs. Deb: 4/4/94																							
1994	Tor-A	15	53	7	8	3	1	0	1	4	17	.151	.224	.245	21	-6	3	0	1	.918	1	S-15	-0.3
1995	Tor-A	111	367	51	89	19	4	10	42	44	114	.243	.325	.398	88	-7	4	4	-1	.957	-29	S-97/3-9,D-3	-2.7
1996	Tor-A	147	527	64	124	30	5	14	64	45	127	.235	.302	.391	74	-23	16	6	1	.973	23	*S-147	1.4
1997	Tor-A	126	426	46	102	23	2	12	35	34	94	.239	.303	.387	78	-14	15	6	1	**.986**	0	*S-125	-0.2
1998	Tor-A	158	568	70	136	28	1	13	51	28	121	.239	.282	.361	66	-29	21	6	3	.976	-11	*S-158	-2.2
Total	5	557	1941	238	459	103	13	49	193	155	473	.236	.299	.379	74	-80	59	22	5	.972	-17	S-542/3-9,D-3	-4.0
■ TONY GONZALEZ Gonzalez, Andres Antonio (Gonzalez) b: 8/28/36, Central Cunagua, Cuba BL/TR, 5'9", 170 lbs. Deb: 4/12/60																							
1960	Cin-N	39	99	10	21	5	1	3	14	4	27	.212	.250	.374	67	-5	1	0	0	.957	-4	O-31	-1.0

YEAR	TM/L	G	AB	R	H	2B	3B	HR	RBI	BB	SO	AVG	OBP	SLG	PRO+	BR/A	SB	CS	SBR	FA	FR	G/POS	TPR
	Phi-N	78	241	27	72	17	5	6	33	11	47	.299	.337	.485	122	6	2	2	-1	.981	-1	O-67	0.3
	Yr	117	340	37	93	22	6	9	47	15	74	.274	.312	.453	106	2	3	2	-0	.975	-4	O-98	-0.7
1961	Phi-N	126	426	58	118	16	8	12	58	49	66	.277	.360	.437	112	8	15	5	2	.984	-1	*O-118	0.2
1962	Phi-N	118	437	76	132	16	4	20	63	40	82	.302	.372	.494	134	21	17	8	0	**1.000**	6	*O-114	2.0
1963	Phi-N	155	555	78	170	36	12	4	66	53	68	.306	.375	.436	134	25	13	8	-1	.986	-6	*O-151	1.2
1964	Phi-N	131	421	55	117	25	3	4	40	44	74	.278	.355	.380	108	6	0	5	-3	**.996**	1	*O-119	-0.1
1965	Phi-N	108	370	48	109	19	1	13	41	31	52	.295	.354	.457	129	14	3	4	-2	.983	-6	*O-104	0.2
1966	Phi-N	132	384	53	110	20	4	6	40	26	60	.286	.337	.406	105	3	2	6	-3	.986	-1	*O-121	-0.5
1967	Phi-N	149	508	74	172	23	9	9	59	47	58	.339	.400	.472	147	32	10	9	-2	**.993**	5	*O-143	3.0
1968	Phi-N	121	416	45	110	13	4	3	38	40	42	.264	.339	.337	103	3	6	5	-1	.979	-4	*O-117	-1.0
1969	SD-N	53	182	17	41	4	0	2	8	19	24	.225	.309	.280	69	-7	1	0	0	.975	5	O-49	-0.6
	*Atl-N	89	320	51	94	15	2	10	50	27	22	.294	.358	.447	124	10	3	1	0	.989	2	O-82	0.8
	Yr	142	502	68	135	19	2	12	58	46	46	.269	.340	.386	104	3	4	1	1	.983	6	*O-131	0.2
1970	Atl-N	123	430	57	114	18	2	7	55	46	45	.265	.347	.365	86	-8	3	5	-2	.987	-3	*O-119	-1.8
	Cal-A	26	92	9	28	2	0	1	12	2	11	.304	.326	.359	92	-1	3	2	-0	.960	-1	O-24	-0.4
1971	Cal-A	111	314	32	77	9	2	3	38	28	28	.245	.313	.315	84	-7	0	1	-1	.987	-6	O-88	-1.9
Total	12	1559	5195	690	1485	238	57	103	615	467	706	.286	.353	.413	114	100	79	61	-13	.987	-12	*O-1447	0.4

■ DENNY GONZALEZ

Gonzalez, Denio Mariano (Manzueta) b: 7/22/63, Sabana Grande De Boya, D.R. BR/TR, 5'11", 185 lbs. Deb: 8/6/84

YEAR	TM/L	G	AB	R	H	2B	3B	HR	RBI	BB	SO	AVG	OBP	SLG	PRO+	BR/A	SB	CS	SBR	FA	FR	G/POS	TPR
1984	Pit-N	26	82	9	15	3	1	0	4	7	21	.183	.247	.244	38	-7	1	1	-0	1.000	1	3-11,S-10/O-3	-0.5
1985	Pit-N	35	124	11	28	4	0	4	12	13	27	.226	.299	.355	83	-3	2	4	-2	.894	-4	3-21,O-13/2-6	-1.0
1987	Pit-N	5	7	1	0	0	0	0	0	1	2	.000	.125	.000	-63	-2	0	0	0	1.000	-1	/S-1	-0.2
1988	Pit-N	24	32	5	6	1	0	0	1	6	10	.188	.316	.219	57	-2	0	0	0	1.000	0	S-14/2-4,3-2	-0.1
1989	Cle-A	8	17	3	5	1	0	0	1	0	4	.294	.333	.353	92	-0	0	0	0	.000	-0	/3-1,D-6	-0.1
Total	5	98	262	29	54	9	1	4	18	27	64	.206	.283	.294	62	-13	3	5	-2	.925	-4	/3-35,S-25,O-16,2D	-1.9

■ EUSEBIO GONZALEZ

Gonzalez, Eusebio Miguel (Lopez) "Papo" b: 7/13/1892, Havana, Cuba d: 2/14/76, Havana, Cuba BR/TR, 5'10", 165 lbs. Deb: 7/26/18

YEAR	TM/L	G	AB	R	H	2B	3B	HR	RBI	BB	SO	AVG	OBP	SLG	PRO+	BR/A	SB	CS	SBR	FA	FR	G/POS	TPR
1918	Bos-A	3	5	2	2	0	1	0	0	1	1	.400	.571	.800	319	1	0			1.000	-1	/S-2,3-1	0.1

■ FERNANDO GONZALEZ

Gonzalez, Jose Fernando (Quinones) b: 6/19/50, Arecibo, P.R. BR/TR, 5'10", 170 lbs. Deb: 9/15/72

YEAR	TM/L	G	AB	R	H	2B	3B	HR	RBI	BB	SO	AVG	OBP	SLG	PRO+	BR/A	SB	CS	SBR	FA	FR	G/POS	TPR
1972	Pit-N	3	2	0	0	0	0	0	0	0	2	.000	.000	.000	-99	-1	0	0	0	.500	0	/3-1	-0.1
1973	Pit-N	37	49	5	11	0	1	1	5	1	11	.224	.255	.327	62	-3	0	0	0	.923	-1	/3-5	-0.4
1974	KC-A	9	21	1	3	1	0	0	2	0	4	.143	.143	.190	-5	-3	1	0	0	1.000	-0	/3-8,D-1	-0.3
	NY-A	51	121	11	26	5	1	1	7	7	7	.215	.258	.298	60	-6	0	0	0	.982	2	2-42/3-7,S-3	-0.2
	Yr	60	142	12	29	6	1	1	9	7	11	.204	.242	.282	50	-9	1	0	0	.982	2	2-42,3-15/S-3,D-1	-0.5
1977	Pit-N	80	181	17	50	10	0	4	27	13	21	.276	.325	.398	90	-3	3	3	-1	.972	-8	3-37,O-16/2-6,S-2	-1.2
1978	Pit-N	9	21	2	4	1	0	0	0	1	3	.190	.227	.238	29	-2	0	0	0	.923	-4	/2-4,3-3	-0.7
	SD-N	101	320	27	80	10	2	2	29	18	32	.250	.290	.313	74	-12	4	4	-1	.982	0	2-94	-0.7
	Yr	110	341	29	84	11	2	2	29	19	35	.246	.286	.308	71	-14	4	4	-1	.981	-4	2-98/3-3	-1.4
1979	SD-N	114	323	22	70	13	3	9	34	18	34	.217	.258	.359	71	-15	0	0	0	.976	-14	*2-103/3-3	-2.3
Total	6	404	1038	85	244	40	7	17	104	58	114	.235	.276	.336	71	-44	8	7	-2	.979	-24	2-249/3-64,O-16,SD	-5.9

■ JOSE GONZALEZ

Gonzalez, Jose Rafael (Gutierrez) b: 11/23/64, Puerto Plata, D.R. BR/TR, 6'2", 196 lbs. Deb: 9/2/85

YEAR	TM/L	G	AB	R	H	2B	3B	HR	RBI	BB	SO	AVG	OBP	SLG	PRO+	BR/A	SB	CS	SBR	FA	FR	G/POS	TPR
1985	LA-N	23	11	6	3	2	0	0	0	1	3	.273	.333	.455	122	0	1	1	-0	1.000	-6	O-18	-0.6
1986	LA-N	57	93	15	20	5	1	2	6	7	29	.215	.270	.355	76	-3	4	3	-1	.924	-10	O-57	-1.6
1987	LA-N	19	16	2	3	2	0	0	1	1	2	.188	.235	.313	45	-1	5	0	2	1.000	-1	O-16	-0.1
1988	*LA-N	37	24	7	2	1	0	0	0	2	10	.083	.154	.125	-20	-4	3	0	1	.938	-8	O-24	-1.2
1989	LA-N	95	261	31	70	11	2	3	18	23	53	.268	.327	.360	98	-1	9	3	1	.968	-0	O-87	-0.2
1990	LA-N	106	99	15	23	5	3	2	8	6	27	.232	.283	.404	89	-2	3	1	0	1.000	-22	O-81	-2.5
1991	LA-N	42	28	3	0	0	0	0	0	2	9	.000	.067	.000	-82	-7	0	0	0	1.000	-7	O-27	-1.4
	Pit-N	16	20	2	2	0	0	1	3	0	6	.100	.100	.250	-5	-3	0	0	0	1.000	1	O-14	-0.5
	Yr	58	48	5	2	0	0	1	3	2	15	.042	.080	.104	-50	-10	0	0	0	1.000	-8	O-41	-1.9
	Cle-A	33	69	10	11	2	1	1	4	11	27	.159	.284	.261	51	-4	8	0	2	.981	-3	O-32	-0.6
1992	Cal-A	33	55	4	10	2	0	0	2	7	20	.182	.274	.218	39	-4	0	1	-1	1.000	-4	O-22/D-1	-0.9
Total	8	461	676	95	144	30	7	9	42	60	186	.213	.279	.318	69	-29	33	9	5	.972	-62	O-378/D-1	-9.6

■ JUAN GONZALEZ

Gonzalez, Juan Alberto (Vazquez) b: 10/20/69, Arecibo, P.R. BR/TR, 6'3", 210 lbs. Deb: 9/1/89

YEAR	TM/L	G	AB	R	H	2B	3B	HR	RBI	BB	SO	AVG	OBP	SLG	PRO+	BR/A	SB	CS	SBR	FA	FR	G/POS	TPR
1989	Tex-A	24	60	6	9	3	0	1	7	6	17	.150	.227	.250	34	-5	0	0	0	.964	-2	O-24	-0.7
1990	Tex-A	25	90	11	26	7	1	4	12	2	18	.289	.319	.522	131	3	0	1	-1	1.000	-2	O-16/D-9	0.1
1991	Tex-A	142	545	78	144	34	1	27	102	42	118	.264	.323	.479	121	13	4	4	-1	.981	-19	*O-136/D-4	-1.1
1992	Tex-A	155	584	77	152	24	2	**43**	109	35	143	.260	.308	.529	135	23	0	1	-1	.975	5	*O-148/D-4	2.4
1993	Tex-A★	140	536	105	166	33	1	**46**	118	37	99	.310	.369	**.632**	170	49	4	1	1	.985	5	*O-129,D-10	4.9
1994	Tex-A	107	422	57	116	18	4	19	85	30	66	.275	.333	.472	105	2	6	4	-1	.991	7	*O-107	0.6
1995	Tex-A	90	352	57	104	20	2	27	82	17	66	.295	.328	.594	131	13	0	0	0	1.000	0	D-83/O-5	0.7
1996	*Tex-A	134	541	89	170	33	2	47	144	45	82	.314	.370	.643	142	32	2	0	1	.988	-4	*O-102,D-32	2.1
1997	Tex-A	133	533	87	158	24	3	42	131	33	107	.296	.341	.589	130	20	0	0	0	.971	3	D-69,O-64	1.7
1998	*Tex-A★	154	606	110	193	**50**	2	45	**157**	46	126	.318	.372	.630	148	40	2	1	0	.982	0	*O-116,D-38	3.3
Total	10	1104	4269	677	1238	246	18	301	947	293	842	.290	.342	.568	135	190	18	12	-2	.982	-6	O-847,D-249	14.0

■ JULIO GONZALEZ

Gonzalez, Julio Cesar (Hernandez) b: 12/25/52, Caguas, P.R. BR/TR, 5'11", 165 lbs. Deb: 4/8/77

YEAR	TM/L	G	AB	R	H	2B	3B	HR	RBI	BB	SO	AVG	OBP	SLG	PRO+	BR/A	SB	CS	SBR	FA	FR	G/POS	TPR
1977	Hou-N	110	383	34	94	18	3	1	27	19	45	.245	.288	.316	68	-18	3	3	-1	.921	-26	S-63,2-45	-3.6
1978	Hou-N	78	223	24	52	3	1	1	16	8	31	.233	.263	.269	53	-15	6	1	1	.983	-20	2-54,S-17/3-4	-3.1
1979	Hou-N	68	181	16	45	5	2	0	10	5	14	.249	.280	.298	62	-10	2	2	0	.987	1	2-32,S-21/3-9	-0.5
1980	Hou-N	40	52	5	6	1	0	0	1	1	8	.115	.132	.135	-28	-9	1	0	0	1.000	3	S-16,3-11/2-2	-0.5
1981	StL-N	20	22	2	7	1	0	1	3	1	3	.318	.348	.500	135	1	0	0	0	1.000	1	/S-5,2-4,3-2	0.2
1982	StL-N	42	87	9	21	3	2	1	7	1	24	.241	.258	.356	70	-4	1	1	-0	.907	-1	3-21/2-9,S-1	-0.6
1983	Det-A	12	21	0	3	1	0	0	2	1	7	.143	.182	.190	3	-3	0	0	0	.889	3	/S-6,2-5,3-1	0.1
Total	7	370	969	90	228	32	8	4	66	36	132	.235	.269	.297	59	-58	13	6	0	.976	-39	2-151,S-129/3-48	-8.0

■ LUIS GONZALEZ

Gonzalez, Luis Emilio b: 9/3/67, Tampa, Fla. BL/TR, 6'2", 180 lbs. Deb: 9/4/90

YEAR	TM/L	G	AB	R	H	2B	3B	HR	RBI	BB	SO	AVG	OBP	SLG	PRO+	BR/A	SB	CS	SBR	FA	FR	G/POS	TPR
1990	Hou-N	12	21	1	4	2	0	0	0	2	5	.190	.261	.286	52	-1	0	0	0	1.000	2	/3-4,1-2	0.1
1991	Hou-N	137	473	51	120	28	9	13	69	40	101	.254	.322	.433	117	9	10	7	-1	.984	13	*O-133	1.9
1992	Hou-N	122	387	40	94	19	3	10	55	24	52	.243	.291	.385	94	-5	7	7	-2	.993	15	*O-111	0.7
1993	Hou-N	154	540	82	162	34	3	15	72	47	83	.300	.367	.457	124	18	20	9	1	.978	20	*O-149	3.5
1994	Hou-N	112	392	57	107	29	4	8	67	49	57	.273	.358	.429	110	6	15	13	-3	.991	12	*O-111	1.2
1995	Hou-N	56	209	35	54	10	4	6	35	18	30	.258	.326	.431	105	1	1	3	-2	.980	2	O-55	0.0
	Chi-N	77	262	34	76	19	4	7	34	39	33	.290	.388	.473	128	12	5	5	-2	.978	10	O-76	1.8
	Yr	133	471	69	130	29	8	13	69	57	63	.276	.361	.454	118	13	6	8	-3	.978	12	*O-131	1.8
1996	Chi-N	146	483	70	131	30	4	15	79	61	49	.271	.358	.443	107	5	9	6	-1	.988	3	*O-139/1-2	0.4
1997	*Hou-N	152	550	78	142	31	2	10	68	71	67	.258	.348	.376	93	-4	10	7	-1	.982	9	*O-146/1-1	0.0
1998	Det-A	154	547	84	146	35	5	23	71	57	62	.267	.345	.475	110	7	12	7	-1	.988	-3	*O-132,D-19	0.0
Total	9	1122	3864	532	1036	237	38	107	550	408	539	.268	.345	.432	109	48	89	64	-12	.985	83	*O-1052/D-19,1-5,3	9.6

■ MIKE GONZALEZ

Gonzalez, Miguel Angel (Cordero) b: 9/24/1890, Havana, Cuba d: 2/19/77, Havana, Cuba BR/TR, 6'1", 200 lbs. Deb: 9/28/12 MC

YEAR	TM/L	G	AB	R	H	2B	3B	HR	RBI	BB	SO	AVG	OBP	SLG	PRO+	BR/A	SB	CS	SBR	FA	FR	G/POS	TPR
1912	Bos-N	1	2	0	0	0	0	0	0	1	1	.000	.333	.000	-5	-0	0			.875	1	/C-1	0.1
1914	Cin-N	95	176	19	41	6	0	0	10	13	16	.233	.293	.267	65	-7	2			.954	10	C-83	0.8
1915	StL-N	51	97	12	22	2	2	0	10	8	9	.227	.306	.289	80	-2	4	2	0	.992	4	C-32/1-8	0.3
1916	StL-N	118	331	33	79	15	4	0	29	28	18	.239	.304	.308	89	-4	5			.981	7	C-93,1-13	1.0
1917	StL-N	106	290	28	76	8	1	1	28	22	24	.262	.316	.307	94	-2	12			.977	0	C-68,1-18/O-1	0.3
1918	StL-N	117	349	33	88	13	4	3	20	39	30	.252	.327	.338	107	3	14			.978	-1	*C-100/O-5,1-2	1.1
1919	NY-N	58	158	18	30	6	0	0	8	20	9	.190	.293	.228	58	-7	3			.962	-3	C-52/1-4	-0.7

YEAR	TM/L	G	AB	R	H	2B	3B	HR	RBI	BB	SO	AVG	OBP	SLG	PRO+	BR/A	SB	CS	SBR	FA	FR	G/POS	TPR
1920	NY-N	11	13	1	3	0	0	0	0	3	1	.231	.375	.231	77	-0	1	0	0	1.000	-1	/C-8	0.0
1921	NY-N	13	24	3	9	1	0	0	0	1	0	.375	.400	.417	116	1	0	0	0	.981	-0	/1-6,C-2	0.0
1924	StL-N	120	402	34	119	27	1	3	53	24	22	.296	.337	.391	96	-2	1	5	-3	.986	-7	*C-119	-0.4
1925	StL-N	22	71	9	22	3	0	0	4	6	2	.310	.380	.352	86	-1	1	2	-1	.982	4	C-22	0.3
	Chi-N	70	197	26	52	13	1	3	18	13	15	.264	.316	.386	77	-7	2	1	0	.989	1	C-50/1-9	-0.4
	Yr	92	268	35	74	16	1	3	22	19	17	.276	.333	.377	80	-8	3	3	-1	.987	5	C-72/1-9	-0.1
1926	Chi-N	80	253	24	63	13	3	1	23	13	17	.249	.288	.336	67	-12	3			**.989**	6	C-78	-0.1
1927	Chi-N	39	108	15	26	4	1	1	15	10	8	.241	.311	.324	70	-5	1			.994	9	C-36	0.6
1928	Chi-N	49	158	12	43	9	2	1	21	12	7	.272	.324	.373	83	-4	2			.983	8	C-45	0.8
1929	*Chi-N	60	167	15	40	3	0	0	18	18	14	.240	.317	.257	44	-14	1			.992	6	C-60	-0.3
1931	StL-N	15	19	1	2	0	0	0	3	0	3	.105	.105	.105	-42	-4	0			1.000	-0	C-12	-0.4
1932	StL-N	17	14	0	2	0	0	0	3	0	2	.143	.143	.143	-22	-2	0			1.000	2	/C-7	-0.1
Total	17	1042	2829	283	717	123	19	13	263	231	198	.253	.314	.324	81	-71	52	10		.980	45	C-868/1-60,O-6	2.9

■ ORLANDO GONZALEZ
Gonzalez, Orlando Eugene b: 11/15/51, Havana, Cuba BL/TL, 6′2″, 180 lbs. Deb: 6/7/76

YEAR	TM/L	G	AB	R	H	2B	3B	HR	RBI	BB	SO	AVG	OBP	SLG	PRO+	BR/A	SB	CS	SBR	FA	FR	G/POS	TPR
1976	Cle-A	28	68	5	17	2	0	0	4	5	7	.250	.301	.279	72	-2	1	2	-1	.992	-2	1-15/O-7,D-2	-0.7
1978	*Phi-N	26	26	1	5	0	0	0	0	1	1	.192	.222	.192	17	-3	0	0	0	1.000	-2	O-11/1-3	-0.6
1980	Oak-A	25	70	10	17	0	0	0	1	9	8	.243	.329	.243	64	-3	0	2	-1	.990	1	1-11/O-2,D-8	-0.4
Total	3	79	164	16	39	2	0	0	5	15	16	.238	.302	.250	59	-8	1	4	-2	.991	-3	/1-29,O-20,D-10	-1.7

■ PEDRO GONZALEZ
Gonzalez, Pedro (Olivares) b: 12/12/37, San Pedro De Macoris, D.R. BR/TR, 6′, 176 lbs. Deb: 4/11/63

YEAR	TM/L	G	AB	R	H	2B	3B	HR	RBI	BB	SO	AVG	OBP	SLG	PRO+	BR/A	SB	CS	SBR	FA	FR	G/POS	TPR
1963	NY-A	14	26	3	5	1	0	0	1	0	5	.192	.192	.231	18	-3	0	1	-1	.963	-1	/2-7	-0.4
1964	*NY-A	80	112	18	31	8	1	0	5	7	22	.277	.331	.366	92	-1	3	4	-2	.992	1	1-31,O-20/3-9,2-6	-0.2
1965	NY-A	7	5	0	2	1	0	0	0	0	2	.400	.400	.600	181	0	0	0	0	.000	0	H	0.1
	Cle-A	116	400	38	101	14	3	5	39	18	57	.253	.290	.340	78	-12	7	4	-0	.980	8	*2-112/O-3,3-2	0.6
	Yr	123	405	38	103	15	3	5	39	18	59	.254	.291	.343	79	-12	7	4	-0	.980	8	*2-112/O-3,3-2	0.7
1966	Cle-A	110	352	21	82	9	2	2	17	15	54	.233	.268	.287	60	-18	8	5	-1	.984	11	*2-104/3-1,O-1	-0.1
1967	Cle-A	80	189	19	43	6	0	1	8	12	36	.228	.277	.275	63	-9	4	6	-2	.971	-5	2-64/1-4,3-4,S-3	-1.4
Total	5	407	1084	99	264	39	6	8	70	52	176	.244	.283	.313	70	-43	22	20	-5	.980	14	2-293/1-35,O-24,3S	-1.4

■ CHARLIE GOOCH
Gooch, Charles Furman b: 6/5/02, Smyrna, Tenn. d: 5/30/82, Lanham, Md. BR/TR, 5′9″, 170 lbs. Deb: 4/18/29

YEAR	TM/L	G	AB	R	H	2B	3B	HR	RBI	BB	SO	AVG	OBP	SLG	PRO+	BR/A	SB	CS	SBR	FA	FR	G/POS	TPR
1929	Was-A	39	57	6	16	2	1	0	5	7	8	.281	.359	.351	83	-1	0	1	-1	.970	-2	/1-7,3-7,S-1	-0.3

■ JOHNNY GOOCH
Gooch, John Beverley b: 11/9/1897, Smyrna, Tenn. d: 5/15/75, Nashville, Tenn. BB/TR, 5′11″, 175 lbs. Deb: 9/9/21 C

YEAR	TM/L	G	AB	R	H	2B	3B	HR	RBI	BB	SO	AVG	OBP	SLG	PRO+	BR/A	SB	CS	SBR	FA	FR	G/POS	TPR
1921	Pit-N	13	38	2	9	0	0	0	3	3	3	.237	.293	.237	41	-3	1	0	0	.985	3	C-13	0.1
1922	Pit-N	105	353	45	116	15	3	1	42	39	15	.329	.403	.397	106	5	1	1	-0	.970	-3	*C-103	0.7
1923	Pit-N	66	202	16	56	10	2	1	20	17	13	.277	.336	.361	82	-5	2	1	0	.975	5	C-66	0.3
1924	Pit-N	70	224	26	65	6	5	0	25	16	12	.290	.343	.362	88	-4	1	3	-2	.988	-6	C-69	-0.7
1925	*Pit-N	79	215	24	64	8	4	0	30	20	16	.298	.357	.372	81	-6	1	0	0	.968	-5	C-76	-0.6
1926	Pit-N	86	218	19	59	15	1	1	42	20	14	.271	.340	.362	85	-4	1			.980	-5	C-80	-0.5
1927	*Pit-N	101	291	22	75	17	2	2	48	19	21	.258	.305	.351	70	-12	0			.974	3	C-91	-0.4
1928	Pit-N	31	80	7	19	2	1	0	5	3	6	.237	.265	.287	43	-7	0			.957	4	C-31	-0.1
	Bro-N	42	101	9	32	1	2	0	12	7	9	.317	.361	.366	92	-1	0			.969	-2	C-38	0.0
	Yr	73	181	16	51	3	3	0	17	10	15	.282	.319	.331	70	-8	0			.964	2	C-69	-0.1
1929	Bro-N	1	1	0	0	0	0	0	0	0	0	.000	.000	.000	-99	-0	0			.000	0	H	0.0
	Cin-N	92	287	22	86	13	5	0	34	24	10	.300	.356	.380	86	-6	4			.975	5	C-86	0.6
	Yr	93	288	22	86	13	5	0	34	24	10	.299	.355	.378	86	-6	4			.975	5	C-86	0.6
1930	Cin-N	82	276	29	67	10	3	2	30	27	15	.243	.315	.322	57	-19	0			.955	-5	C-79	-1.5
1933	Bos-A	37	77	6	14	1	1	0	2	11	7	.182	.284	.221	36	-7	0	0	0	.991	4	C-26	-0.1
Total	11	805	2363	227	662	98	29	7	293	206	141	.280	.342	.355	79	-69	11	5		.973	-2	C-758	-2.2

■ LEE GOOCH
Gooch, Lee Currin b: 2/23/1890, Oxford, N.C. d: 5/18/66, Raleigh, N.C. BR/TR, 6′, 190 lbs. Deb: 8/17/15

YEAR	TM/L	G	AB	R	H	2B	3B	HR	RBI	BB	SO	AVG	OBP	SLG	PRO+	BR/A	SB	CS	SBR	FA	FR	G/POS	TPR
1915	Cle-A	2	2	0	1	0	0	0	0	0	0	.500	.500	.500	196	0	0			.000	0	H	0.0
1917	Phi-A	17	59	4	17	2	0	1	8	4	10	.288	.333	.373	117	1	0			.893	-2	O-16	-0.2
Total	2	19	61	4	18	2	0	1	8	4	10	.295	.338	.377	120	1	0			.893	-2	/O-16	-0.2

■ GENE GOOD
Good, Eugene J. b: 12/13/1882, Roxbury, Mass. d: 8/6/47, Boston, Mass. BL/TL, 5′6″, 130 lbs. Deb: 4/12/06

YEAR	TM/L	G	AB	R	H	2B	3B	HR	RBI	BB	SO	AVG	OBP	SLG	PRO+	BR/A	SB	CS	SBR	FA	FR	G/POS	TPR
1906	Bos-N	34	119	4	18	0	0	0	0	13		.151	.246	.151	25	-10	2			.873	-2	O-34	-1.6

■ WILBUR GOOD
Good, Wilbur David "Lefty" b: 9/28/1885, Punxsutawney, Pa. d: 12/30/63, Brooksville, Fla. BL/TL, 5′6″, 165 lbs. Deb: 8/18/05

YEAR	TM/L	G	AB	R	H	2B	3B	HR	RBI	BB	SO	AVG	OBP	SLG	PRO+	BR/A	SB	CS	SBR	FA	FR	G/POS	TPR
1905	NY-A	5	8	2	3	0	0	0	0	0		.375	.375	.375	124	0	0			.889	0	/P-5	0.0
1908	Cle-A	46	154	23	43	1	3	1	14	13		.279	.351	.344	126	5	7			.845	-8	O-42	-0.6
1909	Cle-A	94	318	33	68	6	5	0	17	28		.214	.296	.264	74	-9	13			.953	2	O-80	-1.1
1910	Bos-N	23	86	15	29	5	4	0	11	6	13	.337	.394	.488	150	5	5			.969	5	O-23	0.9
1911	Bos-N	43	165	21	44	9	3	0	15	12	22	.267	.316	.358	82	-5	3			.945	8	O-43	0.1
	Chi-N	58	145	27	39	5	4	2	21	11	17	.269	.329	.400	103	0	10			.928	-5	O-40	-0.7
	Yr	101	310	48	83	14	7	2	36	23	39	.268	.322	.377	92	-4	13			.938	3	O-83	-0.6
1912	Chi-N	39	35	7	5	0	0	0	1	3	7	.143	.211	.143	-2	-5	3			1.000	-3	O-10	-0.8
1913	Chi-N	49	91	11	23	3	2	1	12	11	16	.253	.340	.363	100	0	5			.974	-3	O-26	-0.4
1914	Chi-N	154	580	70	158	24	7	2	43	53	74	.272	.341	.348	105	4	31			.930	-1	*O-154	-0.4
1915	Chi-N	128	498	66	126	18	9	2	27	34	65	.253	.307	.337	95	-4	19	17	-5	.936	-2	*O-125	-1.8
1916	Phi-N	75	136	25	34	4	3	1	15	8	13	.250	.306	.346	96	-1	7			.983	-5	O-46	-0.8
1918	Chi-A	35	148	24	37	9	4	0	11	11	16	.250	.315	.365	104	0	1			.982	4	O-35	0.3
Total	11	749	2364	324	609	84	44	9	187	190	243	.258	.322	.342	98	-7	104	17		.942	-8	O-624/P-5	-5.3

■ BILL GOODENOUGH
Goodenough, William B. b: 1863, St.Louis, Mo. d: 5/24/05, St.Louis, Mo. 6′1″, 170 lbs. Deb: 8/31/1893

YEAR	TM/L	G	AB	R	H	2B	3B	HR	RBI	BB	SO	AVG	OBP	SLG	PRO+	BR/A	SB	CS	SBR	FA	FR	G/POS	TPR
1893	StL-N	10	31	4	5	1	0	0	2	3	4	.161	.297	.194	31	-3	2			.880	-1	O-10	-0.4

■ MIKE GOODFELLOW
Goodfellow, Michael J. b: 10/3/1866, Port Jervis, N.Y. d: 2/12/20, Newark, N.J. BR/TR, 6′, 180 lbs. Deb: 6/13/1887

YEAR	TM/L	G	AB	R	H	2B	3B	HR	RBI	BB	SO	AVG	OBP	SLG	PRO+	BR/A	SB	CS	SBR	FA	FR	G/POS	TPR
1887	StL-a	1	4	0	0	0	0	0	0	0		.000	.000	.000	-90	-1	0			.800	-0	/C-1	-0.1
1888	Cle-a	68	269	24	66	7	0	0	29	11		.245	.283	.271	80	-6	7			.863	-3	O-62/C-4,1-3,S-1	-1.0
Total	2	69	273	24	66	7	0	0	29	11		.242	.279	.267	77	-7	7			.909	-3	/O-62,C-5,1-3,S-1	-1.1

■ IVAL GOODMAN
Goodman, Ival Richard "Goodie" b: 7/23/08, Northview, Mo. d: 11/25/84, Cincinnati, Ohio BL/TR, 5′11″, 170 lbs. Deb: 4/16/35

YEAR	TM/L	G	AB	R	H	2B	3B	HR	RBI	BB	SO	AVG	OBP	SLG	PRO+	BR/A	SB	CS	SBR	FA	FR	G/POS	TPR
1935	Cin-N	148	592	86	159	23	**18**	12	72	35	50	.269	.314	.429	101	-1	14			.960	8	*O-146	0.1
1936	Cin-N	136	489	81	139	15	**14**	17	71	38	53	.284	.347	.476	128	17	6			.972	3	*O-120	1.4
1937	Cin-N	147	549	86	150	25	12	12	55	55	58	.273	.347	.428	115	11	10			.974	6	*O-141	1.1
1938	Cin-N★	145	508	103	166	27	10	30	92	53	51	.292	.368	.533	149	36	3			.988	5	*O-142	3.7
1939	*Cin-N★	124	470	85	152	37	16	7	84	54	32	.323	.401	.515	144	29	2			.981	7	*O-123	3.1
1940	*Cin-N	136	519	78	134	20	6	12	63	60	54	.258	.335	.389	98	-1	9			.970	-5	*O-135	-1.4
1941	Cin-N	42	149	14	40	5	2	1	12	16	15	.268	.343	.349	95	-1	1			.966	1	O-40	-0.3
1942	Cin-N	87	226	21	55	18	1	0	15	24	32	.243	.319	.332	91	-3	0			.991	1	O-57	-0.5
1943	Chi-N	80	225	31	72	10	5	3	45	24	20	.320	.390	.449	144	13	4			.968	-7	O-61	0.4
1944	Chi-N	62	141	24	37	8	1	1	16	23	15	.262	.377	.355	107	2	0			1.000	-6	O-35	-0.5
Total	10	1107	3928	609	1104	188	85	95	525	382	380	.281	.352	.445	120	104	49			.975	12	O-1000	7.1

■ JAKE GOODMAN
Goodman, Jacob b: 9/14/1853, Lancaster, Pa. d: 3/9/1890, Reading, Pa. 6′1.5″, Deb: 5/2/1878

YEAR	TM/L	G	AB	R	H	2B	3B	HR	RBI	BB	SO	AVG	OBP	SLG	PRO+	BR/A	SB	CS	SBR	FA	FR	G/POS	TPR
1878	Mil-N	60	252	28	62	4	3	1	27	7	33	.246	.266	.298	80	-6				.944	-4	*1-60	-1.1
1882	Pit-a	10	41	5	13	2	2	0		2		.317	.349	.463	180	3				.962	1	1-10	0.3
Total	2	70	293	33	75	6	5	1	27	9	33	.256	.278	.321	92	-3				.946	-3	/1-70	-0.8

■ BILLY GOODMAN
Goodman, William Dale b: 3/22/26, Concord, N.C. d: 10/1/84, Sarasota, Fla. BL/TR, 5′11″, 165 lbs. Deb: 4/19/47 C

YEAR	TM/L	G	AB	R	H	2B	3B	HR	RBI	BB	SO	AVG	OBP	SLG	PRO+	BR/A	SB	CS	SBR	FA	FR	G/POS	TPR
1947	Bos-A	12	11	1	2	0	0	0	1	1	2	.182	.250	.182	20	-1	0	0	0	1.000	0	/O-1	-0.1
1948	Bos-A	127	445	65	138	27	2	1	66	74	44	.310	.414	.387	108	9	5	3	-0	.993	-4	*1-117/2-2,3-2	0.4
1949	Bos-A★	122	443	54	132	23	3	0	56	58	21	.298	.382	.363	91	-4	2	0	1	**.992**	-1	*1-117	-0.6
1950	Bos-A	110	424	91	150	25	3	4	68	52	25	**.354**	.427	.455	115	11	2	4	-2	.991	-2	O-45,3-27,1-21,/2S	0.4
1951	Bos-A	141	546	92	162	34	4	0	50	79	37	.297	.388	.374	97	-0	7	4	-0	.995	-2	1-62,2-44,O-38,/3-1	-0.4
1952	Bos-A	138	513	79	157	27	3	4	56	48	23	.306	.370	.394	104	4	8	2	1	.975	**20**	*2-103,1-23/3-5,O-4	3.0
1953	Bos-A★	128	514	73	161	33	5	2	41	57	11	.313	.384	.409	108	7	1	4	-2	.974	-11	*2-112,1-20	0.0
1954	Bos-A	127	489	71	148	25	4	1	36	51	15	.303	.371	.376	95	-3	3	3	-1	.979	1	2-72,1-27,O-13,3-12	0.0
1955	Bos-A	149	599	100	176	31	2	0	52	99	44	.294	.397	.352	94	-1	5	5	-2	.969	-18	*2-143/1-5,O-1	-0.9
1956	Bos-A	105	399	61	117	22	8	2	38	40	22	.293	.358	.404	90	-6	0	3	-2	.966	-11	2-95	-1.0
1957	Bos-A	18	16	1	1	1	0	0	0	2	1	.063	.167	.125	-18	-3	0	0	0	.000	0	H	-0.3
	Bal-A	73	263	36	81	10	3	3	33	21	18	.308	.366	.403	117	6	0	2	-1	.961	-10	3-54/O-9,1-8,2-5,S	-0.4
	Yr	91	279	37	82	11	3	3	33	23	19	.294	.354	.387	106	3	0	2	-1	.961	-10	3-54/O-9,1-8,2-5,S	-0.7
1958	Chi-A	116	425	41	127	15	5	0	40	37	21	.299	.358	.358	100	1	1	0	0	.954	-18	*3-111/1-3,2-1,S-1	-1.7
1959	*Chi-A	104	268	21	67	14	1	1	28	19	20	.250	.304	.321	73	-10	3	0	1	.950	-2	3-74/2-3	-1.1
1960	Chi-A	30	77	5	18	4	0	0	6	12	8	.234	.337	.286	71	-3	0	0	0	.982	3	3-20/2-7	0.1
1961	Chi-A	41	51	4	13	4	0	1	10	7	6	.255	.345	.392	98	-0	0	0	0	.944	-0	/3-7,1-2,2-1	0.0
1962	Hou-N	82	161	12	41	4	1	0	10	12	11	.255	.306	.292	66	-8	0	0	0	.972	-9	2-31,3-17/1-1	-1.5
Total	16	1623	5644	807	1691	299	44	19	591	669	329	.300	.377	.378	98	-1	37	30	-7	.972	-63	2-624,1-406,3O/S	-4.1

■ ED GOODSON
Goodson, James Edward b: 1/25/48, Pulaski, Va. BL/TR, 6′3″, 185 lbs. Deb: 9/5/70

YEAR	TM/L	G	AB	R	H	2B	3B	HR	RBI	BB	SO	AVG	OBP	SLG	PRO+	BR/A	SB	CS	SBR	FA	FR	G/POS	TPR
1970	SF-N	7	11	1	3	0	0	0	0	0	2	.273	.273	.273	47	-1	0	0	0	.941	0	/1-2	-0.1
1971	SF-N	20	42	4	8	1	0	0	1	2	4	.190	.227	.214	26	-4	0	0	0	1.000	1	1-14	-0.5
1972	SF-N	58	150	15	42	1	1	6	30	8	12	.280	.321	.420	107	1	0	0	0	.991	2	1-42	0.0
1973	SF-N	102	384	37	116	20	1	12	53	15	44	.302	.332	.453	111	4	0	1	-1	.911	-14	3-93	-1.1
1974	SF-N	98	298	25	81	15	0	6	48	18	22	.272	.320	.383	91	-4	1	0	0	.997	-4	1-73/3-8	-1.2
1975	SF-N	39	121	10	25	7	0	1	8	7	14	.207	.250	.289	47	-9	0	1	-1	.993	2	1-16,3-13	-0.9
	Atl-N	47	76	5	16	2	0	1	8	2	8	.211	.231	.276	39	-6	0	0	0	.990	0	1-13/3-1	-0.7
	Yr	86	197	15	41	9	0	2	16	9	22	.208	.243	.284	44	-15	0	1	-1	.992	2	1-29,3-14	-1.6
1976	LA-N	83	118	8	27	4	0	3	17	8	19	.229	.278	.339	76	-4	0	0	0	.833	-4	3-16/1-3,O-2,2-1	-0.9
1977	*LA-N	61	66	3	11	1	0	1	5	3	10	.167	.203	.227	15	-8	0	1	-1	1.000	1	1-13/3-4	-0.8
Total	8	515	1266	108	329	51	2	30	170	63	135	.260	.298	.374	84	-31	1	3	-2	.994	-16	1-176,3-135/O-2,2-1	-6.2

■ PEP GOODWIN
Goodwin, Claire Vernon b: 12/19/1891, Pocatello, Idaho d: 2/15/72, Oakland, Cal. BL/TR, 5′10.5″, 160 lbs. Deb: 4/16/14

YEAR	TM/L	G	AB	R	H	2B	3B	HR	RBI	BB	SO	AVG	OBP	SLG	PRO+	BR/A	SB	CS	SBR	FA	FR	G/POS	TPR
1914	KC-F	112	374	38	88	15	6	1	32	27	23	.235	.290	.316	68	-24	4			.907	-13	S-67,3-40/1-1	-3.1
1915	KC-F	81	229	22	54	5	1	0	16	15	23	.236	.291	.266	60	-16	6			.906	-8	S-42,2-23	-2.2
Total	2	193	603	60	142	20	7	1	48	42	46	.235	.291	.297	65	-39	10			.907	-20	S-109/3-40,2-23,1-1	-5.3

■ CURTIS GOODWIN
Goodwin, Curtis La Mar b: 9/30/72, Oakland, Cal. BL/TL, 5′11″, 180 lbs. Deb: 6/2/95

YEAR	TM/L	G	AB	R	H	2B	3B	HR	RBI	BB	SO	AVG	OBP	SLG	PRO+	BR/A	SB	CS	SBR	FA	FR	G/POS	TPR
1995	Bal-A	87	289	40	76	11	3	1	24	15	53	.263	.304	.332	64	-15	22	4	4	.990	1	O-84/D-3	-1.1
1996	Cin-N	49	136	20	31	3	0	0	5	19	34	.228	.323	.250	53	-9	15	6	1	.970	-5	O-42	-1.3
1997	Cin-N	85	265	27	67	11	0	1	12	24	53	.253	.317	.306	63	-14	22	13	-1	1.000	6	O-71	-1.0
1998	Col-N	119	159	27	39	7	0	1	6	16	40	.245	.314	.308	52	-11	5	1	1	.983	-18	O-91	-2.8
Total	4	340	849	114	213	32	3	3	47	74	180	.251	.313	.306	60	-49	64	24	5	.989	-15	O-288/D-3	-6.2

■ DANNY GOODWIN
Goodwin, Danny Kay b: 9/2/53, St.Louis, Mo. BL/TR, 6′1″, 195 lbs. Deb: 9/3/75

YEAR	TM/L	G	AB	R	H	2B	3B	HR	RBI	BB	SO	AVG	OBP	SLG	PRO+	BR/A	SB	CS	SBR	FA	FR	G/POS	TPR
1975	Cal-A	4	10	0	1	0	0	0	0	0	5	.100	.100	.100	-47	-2	0	0	0	.000	0	/D-3	-0.2
1977	Cal-A	35	91	5	19	6	1	1	8	5	19	.209	.250	.330	59	-5	0	0	0	.000	0	D-23	-0.6
1978	Cal-A	24	58	9	16	5	0	2	10	10	13	.276	.382	.466	143	4	0	0	0	.000	0	D-15	0.3
1979	Min-A	58	159	22	46	8	5	5	27	11	23	.289	.335	.497	117	3	0	0	0	1.000	-0	D-51/1-8	0.1
1980	Min-A	55	115	12	23	5	0	1	11	17	32	.200	.303	.270	54	-7	0	0	0	1.000	0	D-38,1-13	-0.8
1981	Min-A	59	151	18	34	6	1	2	17	16	32	.225	.299	.318	73	-5	3	1	0	.992	-2	1-40/O-1,D-5	-1.0
1982	Oak-A	17	52	6	11	2	1	2	8	2	13	.212	.241	.404	77	-2	0	0	0	.000	0	D-15	-0.3
Total	7	252	636	72	150	32	8	13	81	61	137	.236	.303	.373	84	-15	3	1	0	.994	-2	D-150/1-61,O-1	-2.5

■ TOM GOODWIN
Goodwin, Thomas Jones b: 7/27/68, Fresno, Cal. BL/TR, 6′1″, 170 lbs. Deb: 9/1/91

YEAR	TM/L	G	AB	R	H	2B	3B	HR	RBI	BB	SO	AVG	OBP	SLG	PRO+	BR/A	SB	CS	SBR	FA	FR	G/POS	TPR
1991	LA-N	16	7	3	1	0	0	0	0	0	0	.143	.143	.143	-20	-1	1	1	-0	1.000	-1	/O-5	-0.2
1992	LA-N	57	73	15	17	1	1	0	3	6	10	.233	.291	.274	62	-4	7	3	0	1.000	-9	O-45	-1.4
1993	LA-N	30	17	6	5	1	0	0	1	1	4	.294	.333	.353	89	-0	1	2	-1	1.000	-4	O-12	-0.5
1994	KC-A	2	2	0	0	0	0	0	0	0	1	.000	.000	.000	-96	-1	0	0	0	1.000	-0	/O-1,D-1	-0.1
1995	KC-A	133	480	72	138	16	3	4	28	38	72	.287	.346	.358	83	-11	50	18	4	.990	-2	*O-130/D-2	-1.2
1996	KC-A	143	524	80	148	14	4	1	35	39	79	.282	.335	.330	69	-24	66	22	7	.984	-7	*O-136/D-5	-2.5
1997	KC-A	97	367	51	100	13	4	2	22	19	51	.272	.312	.346	70	-16	34	10	4	.996	1	O-96	-1.2
	Tex-A	53	207	39	49	13	2	0	17	25	37	.237	.322	.319	65	-10	16	6	1	.986	4	O-51	-0.7
	Yr	150	574	90	149	26	6	2	39	44	88	.260	.316	.336	68	-26	50	16	5	.992	5	*O-147	-1.9
1998	*Tex-A	154	520	102	151	13	3	2	33	73	90	.290	.380	.338	85	-8	38	20	-1	.992	4	*O-150/D-1	-0.8
Total	8	685	2197	368	609	71	17	9	139	201	344	.277	.341	.337	75	-75	213	82	15	.990	-14	O-626/D-9	-8.6

■ RAY GOOLSBY
Goolsby, Raymond Daniel "Ox" b: 9/5/19, Florala, Ala. BR/TR, 6′1″, 185 lbs. Deb: 4/18/46

YEAR	TM/L	G	AB	R	H	2B	3B	HR	RBI	BB	SO	AVG	OBP	SLG	PRO+	BR/A	SB	CS	SBR	FA	FR	G/POS	TPR
1946	Was-A	3	4	0	0	0	0	0	0	1	1	.000	.200	.000	-43	-1	0	0	0	1.000	-0	/O-1	-0.1

■ GREG GOOSSEN
Goossen, Gregory Bryant b: 12/14/45, Los Angeles, Cal. BR/TR, 6′1.5″, 210 lbs. Deb: 9/3/65

YEAR	TM/L	G	AB	R	H	2B	3B	HR	RBI	BB	SO	AVG	OBP	SLG	PRO+	BR/A	SB	CS	SBR	FA	FR	G/POS	TPR
1965	NY-N	11	31	2	9	0	0	1	2	1	5	.290	.313	.387	99	-0	0	0	0	.979	-1	/C-8	-0.1
1966	NY-N	13	32	1	6	2	0	1	5	1	11	.188	.235	.344	60	-2	0	0	0	1.000	-4	C-11	-0.6
1967	NY-N	37	69	2	11	1	0	0	3	4	26	.159	.216	.174	13	-8	0	0	0	.973	-1	C-23	-0.9
1968	NY-N	38	106	4	22	7	0	0	6	10	21	.208	.288	.274	69	-4	0	0	0	.992	2	1-31/C-1	-0.5
1969	Sea-A	52	139	19	43	8	1	10	24	14	29	.309	.385	.597	174	13	1	1	-0	.993	2	1-31/O-2	1.3
1970	Mil-A	21	47	3	12	3	0	1	3	10	12	.255	.407	.383	118	2	0	0	0	.990	-1	1-15	-0.1
	Was-A	21	36	2	8	3	0	0	1	2	8	.222	.263	.306	59	-2	0	0	0	1.000	-0	/O-5,1-2	-0.3
	Yr	42	83	5	20	6	0	1	4	12	20	.241	.351	.349	96	-0	0	0	0	.992	-2	1-17/O-5	-0.4
Total	6	193	460	33	111	24	1	13	44	42	112	.241	.317	.383	99	-1	1	1	-0	.992	-5	/1-79,C-43,O-7	-1.2

■ GLEN GORBOUS
Gorbous, Glen Edward b: 7/8/30, Drumheller, Alberta, Canada d: 6/12/90, Calgary, Alberta, Canada BL/TR, 6′2″, 175 lbs. Deb: 4/11/55

YEAR	TM/L	G	AB	R	H	2B	3B	HR	RBI	BB	SO	AVG	OBP	SLG	PRO+	BR/A	SB	CS	SBR	FA	FR	G/POS	TPR
1955	Cin-N	8	18	2	6	3	0	0	4	3	1	.333	.429	.500	137	1	0	0	0	.857	-0	/O-5	0.1
	Phi-N	91	224	25	53	9	1	4	23	21	17	.237	.302	.339	71	-9	0	3	-2	.984	6	O-57	-0.7
	Yr	99	242	27	59	12	1	4	27	24	18	.244	.312	.351	77	-8	0	3	-2	.971	6	O-62	-0.6
1956	Phi-N	15	33	1	6	0	0	0	1	0	1	.182	.182	.182	-2	-5	0	0	0	1.000	-2	/O-8	-0.7
1957	Phi-N	3	2	1	1	1	0	0	1	1	0	.500	.667	1.000	351	1	0	0	0	.000	0	H	0.1
Total	3	117	277	29	66	13	1	4	29	25	19	.238	.301	.336	70	-12	0	3	-2	.973	4	/O-70	-1.2

■ JOE GORDON
Gordon, Joseph Lowell "Flash" b: 2/18/15, Los Angeles, Cal. d: 4/14/78, Sacramento, Cal. BR/TR, 5′10″, 180 lbs. Deb: 4/18/38 MC

YEAR	TM/L	G	AB	R	H	2B	3B	HR	RBI	BB	SO	AVG	OBP	SLG	PRO+	BR/A	SB	CS	SBR	FA	FR	G/POS	TPR
1938	*NY-A	127	458	83	117	24	7	25	97	56	72	.255	.340	.502	109	3	11	3	2	.960	**24**	*2-126	3.2
1939	*NY-A★	151	567	92	161	32	5	28	111	75	57	.284	.370	.506	124	19	11	10	-3	.967	6	*2-151	2.8
1940	NY-A★	155	616	112	173	32	10	30	103	52	57	.281	.340	.511	122	17	18	8	1	.975	14	*2-155	3.9
1941	*NY-A★	156	588	104	162	26	7	24	87	72	80	.276	.358	.466	118	14	10	9	-2	.958	6	*2-131,1-30	2.5
1942	*NY-A★	147	538	88	173	29	4	18	103	79	95	.322	.409	.491	156	41	12	6	0	.966	4	*2-147	5.4
1943	*NY-A☆	152	543	82	135	28	5	17	69	98	75	.249	.365	.413	126	20	4	7	-3	.969	26	*2-152	5.4
1946	NY-A★	112	376	35	79	15	0	11	47	49	72	.210	.308	.338	79	-10	2	5	-2	.974	22	*2-108	1.7
1947	Cle-A★	155	562	89	153	27	6	29	93	62	49	.272	.346	.496	136	24	7	3	0	.978	-4	*2-155	3.1
1948	*Cle-A★	144	550	96	154	21	4	32	124	77	68	.280	.371	.507	136	26	5	2	0	.971	-7	*2-144/S-2	2.7

YEAR	TM/L	G	AB	R	H	2B	3B	HR	RBI	BB	SO	AVG	OBP	SLG	PRO+	BR/A	SB	CS	SBR	FA	FR	G/POS	TPR
1949	Cle-A★	148	541	74	136	18	3	20	84	83	33	.251	.355	.407	103	2	5	6	-2	.980	-18	*2-145	-1.1
1950	Cle-A	119	368	59	87	12	1	19	57	56	44	.236	.340	.429	99	-2	4	1	1	.969	-18	*2-105	-1.4
Total	11	1566	5707	914	1530	264	52	253	975	759	702	.268	.357	.466	121	153	89	60	-9	.970	54	*2-1519/1-30,S-2	28.2

■ KEITH GORDON
Gordon, Keith Bradley b: 1/22/69, Bethesda, Md. BR/TR, 6'1", 205 lbs. Deb: 7/9/93

YEAR	TM/L	G	AB	R	H	2B	3B	HR	RBI	BB	SO	AVG	OBP	SLG	PRO+	BR/A	SB	CS	SBR	FA	FR	G/POS	TPR
1993	Cin-N	3	6	0	1	0	0	0	0	0	2	.167	.167	.167	-10	-1	0	0	0	1.000	-0	/O-2	-0.1

■ MIKE GORDON
Gordon, Michael William b: 9/11/53, Leominster, Mass. BB/TR, 6'3", 215 lbs. Deb: 4/7/77

YEAR	TM/L	G	AB	R	H	2B	3B	HR	RBI	BB	SO	AVG	OBP	SLG	PRO+	BR/A	SB	CS	SBR	FA	FR	G/POS	TPR
1977	Chi-N	8	23	0	1	0	0	0	2	2	8	.043	.120	.043	-49	-5	0	0	0	.970	-3	/C-8	-0.8
1978	Chi-N	4	5	0	1	0	0	0	0	3	2	.200	.556	.200	106	0	0	0	0	1.000	-0	/C-4	0.0
Total	2	12	28	0	2	0	0	0	2	5	10	.071	.235	.071	-11	-4	0	0	0	.979	-3	/C-12	-0.8

■ SID GORDON
Gordon, Sidney b: 8/13/17, Brooklyn, N.Y. d: 6/17/75, New York, N.Y. BR/TR, 5'10", 185 lbs. Deb: 9/11/41

YEAR	TM/L	G	AB	R	H	2B	3B	HR	RBI	BB	SO	AVG	OBP	SLG	PRO+	BR/A	SB	CS	SBR	FA	FR	G/POS	TPR
1941	NY-N	9	31	4	8	1	1	0	4	6	1	.258	.378	.355	105	0	0			1.000	-1	/O-9	-0.1
1942	NY-N	6	19	4	6	0	1	0	2	3	2	.316	.409	.421	142	1	0			.913	1	/3-6	0.3
1943	NY-N	131	474	50	119	9	11	9	63	43	32	.251	.315	.373	98	-2	2			.941	3	3-53,1-41,O-28,/2-3	-0.2
1946	NY-N	135	450	64	132	15	4	5	45	60	27	.293	.380	.378	115	11	1			.995	1	*O-101,3-30	0.8
1947	NY-N	130	437	57	119	19	8	13	57	50	21	.272	.347	.442	107	4	2			.971	1	*O-124/3-2	-0.2
1948	NY-N☆	142	521	100	156	26	4	30	107	74	39	.299	.390	.537	148	34	8			**.948**	-5	*3-115,O-23	2.7
1949	NY-N★	141	489	87	139	26	2	26	90	95	37	.284	.404	.505	142	32	1			.958	-23	*3-123,O-15/1-1	0.6
1950	Bos-N	134	481	78	146	33	4	27	103	78	31	.304	.403	.557	160	42	2			.990	6	*O-123,3-10	4.1
1951	Bos-N	150	550	96	158	28	1	29	109	80	32	.287	.383	.500	146	35	2	0	1	.984	-4	*O-122,3-34	2.7
1952	Bos-N	144	522	69	151	22	2	25	75	77	49	.289	.384	.483	144	32	0	4	-2	**.996**	2	*O-142/3-2	2.6
1953	Mil-N	140	464	67	127	22	4	19	75	71	40	.274	.372	.461	123	17	1	1	-0	.977	-1	*O-137	1.0
1954	Pit-N	131	363	38	111	12	0	12	49	67	24	.306	.414	.438	124	16	0	0	0	.977	-6	O-73,3-40	0.6
1955	Pit-N	16	47	2	8	1	0	0	1	2	6	.170	.204	.191	6	-6	0	0	0	1.000	2	/3-8,O-4	-0.5
	NY-N	66	144	19	35	6	1	7	25	25	15	.243	.355	.444	110	2	0	0	0	1.000	6	3-31,O-17	0.7
	Yr	82	191	21	43	7	1	7	26	27	21	.225	.321	.382	86	-4	0	0	0	1.000	7	3-39,O-21	0.2
Total	13	1475	4992	735	1415	220	43	202	805	731	356	.283	.377	.466	130	218	19	5		.985	-19	O-918,3-454/1-42,2	15.1

■ GEORGE GORE
Gore, George F. "Piano Legs" b: 5/3/1857, Saccarappa, Me. d: 9/16/33, Utica, N.Y. BL/TR, 5'11", 195 lbs. Deb: 5/1/1879 M

YEAR	TM/L	G	AB	R	H	2B	3B	HR	RBI	BB	SO	AVG	OBP	SLG	PRO+	BR/A	SB	CS	SBR	FA	FR	G/POS	TPR
1879	Chi-N	63	266	43	70	17	4	0	32	8	30	.263	.285	.357	104	0				.872	-2	O-54/1-9	-0.4
1880	Chi-N	77	322	70	116	23	2	2	47	21	10	**.360**	**.399**	**.463**	**180**	**26**				.879	6	*O-74/1-7	2.8
1881	Chi-N	73	309	**86**	92	18	9	1	44	27	23	.298	.354	.424	137	13				.874	2	*O-72/3-1,1-1	1.2
1882	Chi-N	84	367	**99**	117	15	7	3	51	**29**	19	.319	.369	.422	146	19				.842	6	*O-84	2.1
1883	Chi-N	92	392	105	131	30	9	2	52	27	13	.334	.377	.472	148	21				.867	11	*O-92	2.7
1884	Chi-N	103	422	104	134	18	4	5	34	**61**	26	.318	.404	.415	146	23				.868	2	*O-103	2.0
1885	*Chi-N	109	441	115	138	21	13	5	57	68	25	.313	.405	.454	156	26				.884	-3	*O-109	1.9
1886	*Chi-N	118	444	150	135	20	12	6	63	**102**	30	.304	.434	.444	146	26	23			.876	-3	*O-118	1.8
1887	NY-N	111	459	95	133	16	5	1	49	42	18	.290	.358	.353	103	4	39			.889	1	*O-111	0.3
1888	*NY-N	64	254	37	56	4	4	2	17	30	31	.220	.308	.291	93	-1	11			.836	-9	O-64	-1.2
1889	*NY-N	120	488	132	149	21	7	7	54	84	28	.305	.416	.420	134	26	28			.864	-8	*O-120	1.3
1890	NY-P	93	399	132	127	26	8	10	55	77	23	.318	.432	.499	136	20	28			.877	-12	O-93	0.4
1891	NY-N	130	528	103	150	22	7	2	48	74	34	.284	.379	.364	122	18	19			.909	-6	*O-130	0.7
1892	NY-N	53	193	47	49	11	2	0	11	49	16	.254	.412	.332	128	10	20			.932	1	O-53	0.9
	StL-N	20	73	9	15	0	1	0	4	18	6	.205	.363	.233	85	0	2			.844	-2	O-20,M	-0.2
	Yr	73	266	56	64	11	3	0	15	67	22	.241	.399	.305	116	10	22			.908	-0	O-73	0.7
Total	14	1310	5357	1327	1612	262	94	46	618	717	332	.301	.386	.411	135	232	170			.876	-14	*O-1297/1-17,3-1	16.3

■ BOB GORINSKI
Gorinski, Robert John b: 1/7/52, Latrobe, Pa. BR/TR, 6'3", 215 lbs. Deb: 4/10/77

YEAR	TM/L	G	AB	R	H	2B	3B	HR	RBI	BB	SO	AVG	OBP	SLG	PRO+	BR/A	SB	CS	SBR	FA	FR	G/POS	TPR
1977	Min-A	54	118	14	23	4	1	3	22	5	29	.195	.228	.322	49	-9	1	0	0	.936	-7	O-37/D-9	-1.6

■ HERB GORMAN
Gorman, Herbert Allen b: 12/18/24, San Francisco, Cal d: 4/5/53, San Diego, Cal. BL/TL, 5'11", 180 lbs. Deb: 4/19/52

YEAR	TM/L	G	AB	R	H	2B	3B	HR	RBI	BB	SO	AVG	OBP	SLG	PRO+	BR/A	SB	CS	SBR	FA	FR	G/POS	TPR
1952	StL-N	1	1	0	0	0	0	0	0	0	0	.000	.000	.000	-99	-0	0	0	0	.000	0	H	0.0

■ HOWIE GORMAN
Gorman, Howard Paul "Lefty" b: 5/14/13, Pittsburgh, Pa. d: 4/29/84, Harrisburg, Pa. BL/TL, 6'2", 160 lbs. Deb: 8/7/37

YEAR	TM/L	G	AB	R	H	2B	3B	HR	RBI	BB	SO	AVG	OBP	SLG	PRO+	BR/A	SB	CS	SBR	FA	FR	G/POS	TPR
1937	Phi-N	13	19	3	4	1	0	0	1	1	1	.211	.250	.263	37	-2	1			.500	-3	/O-7	-0.5
1938	Phi-N	1	1	0	0	0	0	0	0	0	0	.000	.000	.000	-99	-0	0			.000	0	H	0.0
Total	2	14	20	3	4	1	0	0	1	1	1	.200	.238	.250	30	-2	1			.500	-3	/O-7	-0.5

■ JACK GORMAN
Gorman, John F. "Stooping Jack" b: 1859, St.Louis, Mo. d: 9/9/1889, St.Louis, Mo. Deb: 7/1/1883

YEAR	TM/L	G	AB	R	H	2B	3B	HR	RBI	BB	SO	AVG	OBP	SLG	PRO+	BR/A	SB	CS	SBR	FA	FR	G/POS	TPR
1883	StL-a	1	4	0	0	0	0	0		0		.000	.000	.000	-95	-1				.667	0	/O-1	0.0
1884	KC-U	33	137	25	38	5	2	0		4		.277	.298	.343	108	-3				.954	-2	1-24/O-5,3-4	-0.7
	Pit-a	8	27	3	4	0	1	0		1		.148	.179	.222	30	-2				.750	-2	/P-3,O-3,3-2	-0.3
Total	2	42	168	28	42	5	3	0		5		.250	.272	.315	89	-6				.944	-4	/1-24,O-9,3-6,P-3	-1.0

■ JOHNNY GORYL
Goryl, John Albert b: 10/21/33, Cumberland, R.I. BR/TR, 5'10", 175 lbs. Deb: 9/20/57 MC

YEAR	TM/L	G	AB	R	H	2B	3B	HR	RBI	BB	SO	AVG	OBP	SLG	PRO+	BR/A	SB	CS	SBR	FA	FR	G/POS	TPR
1957	Chi-N	9	38	7	8	2	0	0	1	5	9	.211	.318	.263	59	-2	0	1	-1	.952	-1	/3-9	-0.4
1958	Chi-N	83	219	27	53	9	3	4	14	27	34	.242	.331	.365	85	-4	0	1	-1	.931	11	3-44,2-35	0.8
1959	Chi-N	25	48	1	9	3	1	1	6	5	3	.188	.264	.354	63	-3	1	1	-0	.973	0	2-11/3-4	-0.2
1962	Min-A	37	26	6	5	0	1	2	2	2	6	.192	.250	.500	93	-0	0	0	0	.923	-0	/2-4,S-1	-0.1
1963	Min-A	64	150	29	43	5	3	9	24	15	29	.287	.355	.540	144	9	0	0	0	.958	-9	2-34,3-11/S-7	0.3
1964	Min-A	58	114	9	16	0	2	0	1	10	25	.140	.216	.175	10	-14	1	0	0	.975	2	2-28,3-13	-1.0
Total	6	276	595	79	134	19	10	16	48	64	106	.225	.306	.371	83	-15	2	3	-1	.960	3	2-112/3-81,S-8	-0.6

■ JIM GOSGER
Gosger, James Charles b: 11/6/42, Port Huron, Mich. BL/TL, 5'11", 185 lbs. Deb: 5/4/63

YEAR	TM/L	G	AB	R	H	2B	3B	HR	RBI	BB	SO	AVG	OBP	SLG	PRO+	BR/A	SB	CS	SBR	FA	FR	G/POS	TPR
1963	Bos-A	19	16	3	1	0	0	0	0	3	5	.063	.211	.063	-19	-3	0	0	0	.818	-0	/O-4	-0.3
1965	Bos-A	81	324	45	83	15	4	9	35	29	61	.256	.321	.410	100	-0	3	1	0	.975	9	O-81	0.6
1966	Bos-A	40	126	16	32	4	0	5	17	15	20	.254	.333	.405	101	0	0	1	-1	.985	-1	O-32	-0.3
	KC-A	88	272	34	61	14	1	5	27	37	53	.224	.322	.338	93	-2	5	3	-0	.994	1	O-77	-0.5
	Yr	128	398	50	93	18	1	10	44	52	73	.234	.325	.359	96	-1	5	4	-1	.991	0	*O-109	-0.8
1967	KC-A	134	356	31	86	14	5	5	36	53	69	.242	.340	.351	108	5	5	7	-3	.981	-1	*O-113	-0.4
1968	Oak-A	88	150	7	27	1	1	0	5	17	21	.180	.263	.200	44	-10	4	0	1	1.000	-2	O-64	-1.5
1969	Sea-A	39	55	4	6	2	1	1	1	6	11	.109	.197	.236	21	-6	2	1	0	1.000	-3	O-26	-1.1
	NY-N	10	15	0	2	2	0	0	1	1	6	.133	.188	.267	25	-2	0	0	0	1.000	-1	/O-5	-0.3
1970	Mon-N	91	274	38	72	11	2	5	37	35	35	.263	.348	.372	93	-2	5	3	-0	1.000	-3	O-71,1-19	-0.9
1971	Mon-N	51	102	7	16	2	2	0	8	9	17	.157	.232	.216	27	-10	1	1	-0	.952	-2	O-23/1-6	-1.4
1973	NY-N	38	92	9	22	2	0	0	10	9	16	.239	.307	.261	60	-5	0	1	-1	1.000	-7	O-35	-1.4
1974	NY-N	26	33	3	3	0	0	0	0	3	2	.091	.167	.091	-27	-6	0	0	0	1.000	-7	O-24	-1.4
Total	10	705	1815	197	411	67	16	30	177	217	316	.226	.311	.331	83	-39	25	18	-3	.985	-17	O-555/1-25	-8.9

■ GOOSE GOSLIN
Goslin, Leon Allen b: 10/16/1900, Salem, N.J. d: 5/15/71, Bridgeton, N.J. BL/TR, 5'11.5", 185 lbs. Deb: 9/16/21 H

YEAR	TM/L	G	AB	R	H	2B	3B	HR	RBI	BB	SO	AVG	OBP	SLG	PRO+	BR/A	SB	CS	SBR	FA	FR	G/POS	TPR
1921	Was-A	14	50	8	13	1	1	1	6	6	5	.260	.351	.380	91	-1	0	0	0	1.000	0	O-14	-0.2
1922	Was-A	101	358	44	116	19	7	3	53	25	26	.324	.373	.441	117	8	4	4	-1	.932	-3	O-93	-0.2
1923	Was-A	150	600	86	180	29	**18**	9	99	40	53	.300	.347	.453	115	10	7	2	1	.957	7	*O-149	0.7
1924	*Was-A	154	579	100	199	30	17	12	**129**	68	29	.344	.421	.516	145	39	15	14	-4	.960	5	*O-154	2.9
1925	*Was-A	150	601	116	201	34	**20**	18	113	53	50	.334	.394	.547	140	33	27	8	**3**	.971	14	*O-150	3.7
1926	Was-A	147	568	105	201	26	15	17	108	63	38	.354	.425	.542	155	45	8	8	-2	.964	19	*O-147	4.9
1927	Was-A	148	581	96	194	37	15	13	120	50	28	.334	.392	.516	136	29	21	6	3	.955	2	*O-148	2.3
1928	Was-A	135	456	80	173	36	10	17	102	48	19	**.379**	.442	.614	176	50	16	3	**3**	.962	3	*O-125	4.5
1929	Was-A	145	553	82	159	28	7	18	91	66	33	.288	.366	.461	111	8	10	3	1	.968	-4	*O-142	-0.4
1930	Was-A	47	188	34	51	11	5	7	38	19	19	.271	.344	.495	110	2	3	2	-0	.937	-5	O-47	-0.6

YEAR	TM/L	G	AB	R	H	2B	3B	HR	RBI	BB	SO	AVG	OBP	SLG	PRO+	BR/A	SB	CS	SBR	FA	FR	G/POS	TPR
	StL-A	101	396	81	129	25	7	30	100	48	35	.326	.400	.652	156	32	14	9	-1	.973	12	*O-101	3.2
	Yr	148	584	115	180	36	12	37	138	67	54	.308	.382	.601	142	34	17	11	-2	.964	7	*O-148	2.6
1931	StL-A	151	591	114	194	42	10	24	105	80	41	.328	.412	.555	147	40	9	6	-1	.960	5	*O-151	3.1
1932	StL-A	150	572	88	171	28	9	17	104	92	35	.299	.398	.469	117	16	12	9	-2	.951	8	*O-149/3-1	1.2
1933	*Was-A	132	549	97	163	35	10	10	64	42	32	.297	.348	.452	112	7	5	2	0	.965	8	*O-128	0.8
1934	*Det-A	151	614	106	187	38	7	13	100	65	38	.305	.373	.453	112	10	5	4	-1	.953	2	*O-149	0.5
1935	*Det-A	147	590	88	172	34	6	9	109	56	31	.292	.355	.415	102	1	5	4	-1	.965	0	*O-144	-0.5
1936	Det-A★	147	572	122	180	33	8	24	125	85	50	.315	.403	.526	127	24	14	4	2	.955	-5	*O-144	1.4
1937	Det-A	79	181	30	43	11	1	4	35	35	18	.238	.367	.376	86	-3	0	1	-1	.954	-2	O-40/1-1	-0.7
1938	Was-A	38	57	6	9	3	0	2	8	8	5	.158	.262	.316	47	-5	0	0	0	1.000	-1	O-13	-0.6
Total	18	2287	8656	1483	2735	500	173	248	1609	949	585	.316	.387	.500	128	347	175	89	-1	.960	62	*O-2188/1-1,3-1	26.0

■ HOWIE GOSS

Goss, Howard Wayne b: 11/1/34, Wewoka, Okla. d: 7/31/96, Reno, Nev. BR/TR, 6'4", 204 lbs. Deb: 4/10/62

YEAR	TM/L	G	AB	R	H	2B	3B	HR	RBI	BB	SO	AVG	OBP	SLG	PRO+	BR/A	SB	CS	SBR	FA	FR	G/POS	TPR
1962	Pit-N	89	111	19	27	6	0	2	10	9	36	.243	.306	.351	76	-4	5	2	0	.985	-12	O-66	-1.7
1963	Hou-N	133	411	37	86	18	2	9	44	31	128	.209	.265	.328	74	-15	4	6	-2	.993	7	*O-123	-1.8
Total	2	222	522	56	113	24	2	11	54	40	164	.216	.274	.333	75	-19	9	8	-2	.991	-5	O-189	-3.5

■ DICK GOSSETT

Gossett, John Star b: 8/21/1891, Dennison, Ohio d: 10/6/62, Massillon, Ohio BR/TR, 5'11", 185 lbs. Deb: 4/30/13

YEAR	TM/L	G	AB	R	H	2B	3B	HR	RBI	BB	SO	AVG	OBP	SLG	PRO+	BR/A	SB	CS	SBR	FA	FR	G/POS	TPR
1913	NY-A	39	105	9	17	2	0	0	9	10	22	.162	.254	.181	28	-9	1			.972	-5	C-38	-1.2
1914	NY-A	10	21	3	3	0	0	0	1	5	5	.143	.333	.143	44	-1	0			.977	-1	C-10	-0.2
Total	2	49	126	12	20	2	0	0	10	15	27	.159	.269	.175	31	-10	1			.973	-6	/C-48	-1.4

■ JULIO GOTAY

Gotay, Julio Enrique (Sanchez) b: 6/9/39, Fajardo, P.R. BR/TR, 6', 180 lbs. Deb: 8/6/60

YEAR	TM/L	G	AB	R	H	2B	3B	HR	RBI	BB	SO	AVG	OBP	SLG	PRO+	BR/A	SB	CS	SBR	FA	FR	G/POS	TPR
1960	StL-N	3	8	1	3	0	0	0	0	0	2	.375	.375	.375	98	-0	1	0	0	.750	-2	/S-2,3-1	-0.1
1961	StL-N	10	45	5	11	4	0	0	5	3	5	.244	.292	.333	59	-3	0	0	0	.804	-4	S-10	-0.6
1962	StL-N	127	369	47	94	12	1	2	27	27	47	.255	.316	.309	62	-19	7	3	0	.956	5	*S-120/2-8,O-2,3-1	-0.4
1963	Pit-N	4	2	0	1	0	0	0	0	0	0	.500	.500	.500	188	0	0	0	0	.667	0	/2-1	0.0
1964	Pit-N	3	2	1	1	0	0	0	0	1	0	.500	.667	.500	235	1	0	0	0	.000	0	H	0.1
1965	Cal-A	40	77	6	19	4	0	1	3	4	9	.247	.284	.338	78	-2	0	0	0	.961	3	2-23/3-9,S-1	0.2
1966	Hou-N	4	5	0	0	0	0	0	0	0	0	.000	.000	.000	-99	-1	0	0	0	1.000	0	/3-1	-0.1
1967	Hou-N	77	234	30	66	10	2	2	15	15	30	.282	.331	.368	103	1	1	1	-0	.971	-4	2-30,S-20/3-3	0.1
1968	Hou-N	75	165	9	41	3	0	1	11	4	21	.248	.271	.285	68	-7	1	2	-1	.982	10	2-48/3-1	0.6
1969	Hou-N	46	81	7	21	5	0	0	9	7	13	.259	.318	.321	81	-2	2	1	0	.987	6	2-16/3-1	0.5
Total	10	389	988	106	257	38	3	6	70	61	127	.260	.309	.323	75	-32	12	7	-1	.944	15	S-153,2-126/3-17,O	0.3

■ CHARLIE GOULD

Gould, Charles Harvey b: 8/21/1847, Cincinnati, Ohio d: 4/10/17, Flushing, N.Y. BR/TR, 6', 172 lbs. Deb: 5/5/1871 M

YEAR	TM/L	G	AB	R	H	2B	3B	HR	RBI	BB	SO	AVG	OBP	SLG	PRO+	BR/A	SB	CS	SBR	FA	FR	G/POS	TPR
1871	Bos-n	31	151	38	43	9	2	2	32	3	1	.285	.299	.411	98	-1	6	2	1	.906	-3	*1-30/O-1	-0.1
1872	Bos-n	45	211	40	54	9	**8**	0	33	2	3	.256	.263	.374	89	-4	0	0	0	.933	0	*1-44/O-2	-0.1
1874	Bal-n	33	143	19	32	6	0	0	14	2	2	.224	.234	.266	60	-6	1	0	0	.951	1	1-32/C-1	-0.4
1875	NH-n	27	109	9	29	4	1	0	8	1	2	.266	.273	.321	121	3	0	1	-1	.946	-4	1-26/C-1,O-1,M	-0.1
1876	Cin-N	61	258	27	65	7	0	0	11	6	11	.252	.269	.279	97	1				.939	1	*1-61/P-2,M	0.0
1877	Cin-N	24	91	5	25	2	1	0	13	5	5	.275	.313	.319	112	2				.922	-1	1-24/O-1	0.1
Total	4 n	136	614	106	158	28	11	2	87	8	8	.257	.267	.349	90	-8	7	3	0	.934	-6	1-132/O-4,C-2	-0.7
Total	2	85	349	32	90	9	1	0	24	11	16	.258	.281	.289	101	2				.934	0	/1-85,P-2,O-1	0.1

■ NICK GOULISH

Goulish, Nicholas Edward b: 11/13/17, Punxsutawney, Pa. d: 5/15/84, Youngstown, Ohio BL/TL, 6'1", 179 lbs. Deb: 4/19/44

YEAR	TM/L	G	AB	R	H	2B	3B	HR	RBI	BB	SO	AVG	OBP	SLG	PRO+	BR/A	SB	CS	SBR	FA	FR	G/POS	TPR
1944	Phi-N	1	1	0	0	0	0	0	0	0	0	.000	.000	.000	-99	-0	0			.000	0	H	0.0
1945	Phi-N	13	11	4	3	0	0	0	2	1	3	.273	.333	.273	72	-0	0			1.000	-1	/O-2	-0.1
Total	2	14	12	4	3	0	0	0	2	1	3	.250	.308	.250	58	-1	0			1.000	-1	/O-2	-0.1

■ CLAUDE GOUZZIE

Gouzzie, Claude b: 1873, France d: 9/21/07, Denver, Colo. BR/TR, 5'9", 170 lbs. Deb: 7/22/03

YEAR	TM/L	G	AB	R	H	2B	3B	HR	RBI	BB	SO	AVG	OBP	SLG	PRO+	BR/A	SB	CS	SBR	FA	FR	G/POS	TPR
1903	StL-A	1	1	0	0	0	0	0	0	0		.000	.000	.000	-99	-0	0			1.000	0	/2-1	0.0

■ HANK GOWDY

Gowdy, Henry Morgan b: 8/24/1889, Columbus, Ohio d: 8/1/66, Columbus, Ohio BR/TR, 6'2", 182 lbs. Deb: 9/13/10 MC

YEAR	TM/L	G	AB	R	H	2B	3B	HR	RBI	BB	SO	AVG	OBP	SLG	PRO+	BR/A	SB	CS	SBR	FA	FR	G/POS	TPR
1910	NY-N	7	14	1	3	1	0	0	2	2	3	.214	.313	.286	75	-0	1			.943	0	/1-5	0.0
1911	NY-N	4	4	1	1	1	0	0	0	2	0	.250	.500	.500	175	1	0			1.000	-0	/1-2	0.0
	Bos-N	29	97	9	28	4	2	0	16	4	19	.289	.324	.371	87	-2	2			.966	-1	1-26/C-1	-0.3
	Yr	33	101	10	29	5	2	0	16	6	19	.287	.333	.376	92	-1	2			.969	-1	1-28/C-1	-0.3
1912	Bos-N	44	96	16	26	6	1	3	10	16	13	.271	.386	.448	126	4	3			.926	-2	C-22/1-7	0.3
1913	Bos-N	3	5	0	3	1	0	0	2	3	2	.600	.750	.800	336	2	0			1.000	-1	/C-2	0.1
1914	*Bos-N	128	366	42	89	17	6	3	46	48	40	.243	.337	.347	104	3	14			.968	-5	*C-115/1-9	0.7
1915	Bos-N	118	316	27	78	15	3	2	30	41	34	.247	.339	.332	108	4	10	4	1	.974	0	*C-114	1.5
1916	Bos-N	118	349	32	88	14	1	1	34	24	33	.252	.311	.307	94	-2	8			.980	3	*C-116	1.0
1917	Bos-N	49	154	12	33	7	0	0	14	15	13	.214	.288	.260	73	-5	2			.969	-1	C-49	-0.2
1919	Bos-N	78	219	18	61	8	1	1	22	19	16	.279	.339	.338	108	2	5			.977	5	C-74/1-1	1.4
1920	Bos-N	80	214	14	52	11	2	0	18	20	15	.243	.314	.313	84	-4	6	1	1	.980	11	C-74	1.3
1921	Bos-N	64	164	17	49	7	2	2	17	16	11	.299	.368	.402	110	3	2	0	1	.981	-1	C-53	0.4
1922	Bos-N	92	221	23	70	11	1	1	27	24	13	.317	.391	.389	107	3	2	1	0	.971	1	C-72/1-1	0.7
1923	Bos-N	23	48	5	6	1	1	0	5	15	5	.125	.354	.188	48	-3	1	1	-0	.982	-2	C-15	-0.4
	*NY-N	53	122	13	40	6	3	1	18	21	9	.328	.427	.451	133	7	2	0	1	.986	-7	C-43	0.2
	Yr	76	170	18	46	7	4	1	23	36	14	.271	.404	.376	109	4	3	1	0	.985	-10	C-58	-0.2
1924	*NY-N	87	191	25	62	9	1	4	37	26	11	.325	.411	.445	133	10	1	0	0	.982	5	C-78	1.9
1925	NY-N	47	114	14	37	4	3	3	19	12	7	.325	.389	.491	128	5	0	0	0	1.000	1	C-41	0.7
1929	Bos-N	10	16	1	7	0	0	0	3	0	2	.438	.438	.438	122	1	0			1.000	-0	/C-9	0.0
1930	Bos-N	16	25	0	5	1	0	0	2	3	1	.200	.310	.240	37	-3	0			.972	1	C-15	-0.1
Total	17	1050	2735	270	738	124	27	21	322	311	247	.270	.351	.358	105	25	59	7		.975	5	C-893/1-51	9.2

■ BILLY GRABARKEWITZ

Grabarkewitz, Billy Cordell b: 1/18/46, Lockhart, Tex. BR/TR, 5'10", 170 lbs. Deb: 4/22/69

YEAR	TM/L	G	AB	R	H	2B	3B	HR	RBI	BB	SO	AVG	OBP	SLG	PRO+	BR/A	SB	CS	SBR	FA	FR	G/POS	TPR
1969	LA-N	34	65	4	6	1	1	0	5	4	19	.092	.145	.138	-22	-11	1	0	0	.954	-2	S-18/3-6,2-3	-1.2
1970	LA-N★	156	529	92	153	20	8	17	84	95	149	.289	.403	.454	135	30	19	9	0	.959	-1	3-97,S-50,2-20	3.4
1971	LA-N	44	71	9	16	5	0	0	6	19	16	.225	.389	.296	102	1	1	2	-1	1.000	4	2-13,3-10/S-1	0.6
1972	LA-N	53	144	17	24	4	0	4	16	18	53	.167	.268	.278	57	-8	3	0	1	.902	-4	3-24,2-19/S-2	-1.1
1973	Cal-A	61	129	27	21	6	1	3	9	28	27	.163	.316	.295	79	-3	2	2	-1	.965	-6	2-18,3-12/S-1,OD	-0.9
	Phi-N	25	66	12	19	2	0	2	7	12	18	.288	.397	.409	121	2	3	1	0	.960	0	2-20/3-3,O-1	0.4
1974	Phi-N	34	30	7	4	0	0	1	2	5	10	.133	.257	.233	36	-3	3	1	0	1.000	-1	/O-5,3-1	-0.3
	Chi-N	53	125	21	31	3	2	1	12	21	28	.248	.361	.328	90	-1	1	2	-1	.954	2	2-45/S-7,3-6	0.2
	Yr	87	155	28	35	3	2	2	14	26	38	.226	.341	.310	80	-3	4	3	-1	.954	2	2-45/3-7,S-7,O-5	-0.1
1975	Oak-A	6	2	0	0	0	0	0	0	0	1	.000	.000	.000	-99	-1	0	0	0	.833	0	/2-4,D-1	0.0
Total	7	466	1161	189	274	41	12	28	141	202	321	.236	.354	.364	101	8	33	17	-0	.952	-8	3-159,2-142/SOD	1.1

■ ROD GRABER

Graber, Rodney Blaine b: 6/20/30, Massillon, Ohio BL/TL, 5'11", 175 lbs. Deb: 9/9/58

YEAR	TM/L	G	AB	R	H	2B	3B	HR	RBI	BB	SO	AVG	OBP	SLG	PRO+	BR/A	SB	CS	SBR	FA	FR	G/POS	TPR
1958	Cle-A	4	8	0	1	0	0	0	0	1	2	.125	.222	.125	-2	-1	0	0	0	1.000	-0	/O-2	-0.1

■ JOHNNY GRABOWSKI

Grabowski, John Patrick "Nig" b: 1/7/1900, Ware, Mass. d: 5/23/46, Albany, N.Y. BR/TR, 5'10", 185 lbs. Deb: 7/11/24

YEAR	TM/L	G	AB	R	H	2B	3B	HR	RBI	BB	SO	AVG	OBP	SLG	PRO+	BR/A	SB	CS	SBR	FA	FR	G/POS	TPR
1924	Chi-A	20	56	10	14	3	0	0	3	2	4	.250	.276	.304	51	-4	0	0	0	.972	1	C-19	-0.2
1925	Chi-A	21	46	5	14	4	1	0	10	2	4	.304	.333	.435	99	-0	0	1	-1	.983	0	C-21	0.0
1926	Chi-A	48	122	6	32	1	1	1	11	4	15	.262	.286	.311	58	-8	0	1	-1	.973	-2	C-38/1-1	-0.8
1927	*NY-A	70	195	29	54	2	4	0	25	20	15	.277	.350	.328	79	-5	0	0	0	.984	0	C-68	-0.1
1928	NY-A	75	202	21	48	7	1	1	21	10	21	.238	.274	.297	51	-15	0	0	0	.987	2	C-75	-0.7
1929	NY-A	22	59	4	12	1	0	0	2	3	6	.203	.242	.220	21	-7	1	0	0	.943	-0	C-22	-0.5
1931	Det-A	40	136	9	32	7	1	1	14	6	19	.235	.268	.324	53	-10	0	0	0	.984	2	C-39	-0.5
Total	7	296	816	84	206	25	8	3	86	47	84	.252	.295	.314	60	-49	1	2	-1	.979	4	C-282/1-1	-2.8

YEAR	TM/L	G	AB	R	H	2B	3B	HR	RBI	BB	SO	AVG	OBP	SLG	PRO+	BR/A	SB	CS	SBR	FA	FR	G/POS	TPR

■ JOE GRACE
Grace, Joseph Laverne b: 1/5/14, Gorham, Ill. d: 9/18/69, Murphysboro, Ill. BL/TR, 6'1", 180 lbs. Deb: 9/24/38

1938	StL-A	12	47	7	16	1	0	4	2	3		.340	.367	.362	83	-1	0	1	-1	.933	-2	O-12	-0.4
1939	StL-A	74	207	35	63	11	2	3	22	19	24	.304	.363	.420	98	-1	3	2	-0	.968	-4	O-53	-0.6
1940	StL-A	80	229	45	59	14	2	5	25	26	23	.258	.336	.402	88	-4	2	2	-1	.958	-5	O-51,C-12	-1.1
1941	StL-A	115	362	53	112	17	4	6	60	57	31	.309	.410	.428	118	12	1	3	-2	.983	-2	O-88/C-9	0.3
1946	StL-A	48	161	21	37	7	2	1	13	16	20	.230	.307	.317	71	-6	1	3	-2	.967	1	O-43	-0.9
	Was-A	77	321	39	97	17	4	2	31	24	19	.302	.358	.399	118	7	1	4	-2	.959	4	O-74	0.5
	Yr	125	482	60	134	24	6	3	44	40	39	.278	.341	.371	101	0	2	7	-4	.962	5	*O-117	-0.4
1947	Was-A	78	234	25	58	9	4	3	17	35	15	.248	.348	.359	99	0	1	2	-1	.976	2	O-67	-0.2
Total	6	484	1561	225	442	76	18	20	172	179	135	.283	.362	.393	102	7	9	17	-8	.969	-6	O-388/C-21	-2.4

■ MARK GRACE
Grace, Mark Eugene b: 6/28/64, Winston-Salem, N.C BL/TL, 6'2", 190 lbs. Deb: 5/2/88

1988	Chi-N	134	486	65	144	23	4	7	57	60	43	.296	.374	.403	118	13	3	3	-1	.987	-4	*1-133	-0.3
1989	*Chi-N	142	510	74	160	28	3	13	79	80	42	.314	.407	.457	136	27	14	7	0	.996	13	*1-142	3.0
1990	Chi-N	157	589	72	182	32	1	9	82	59	54	.309	.377	.413	109	9	15	6	1	.992	27	*1-153	2.5
1991	Chi-N	160	619	87	169	28	5	8	58	70	53	.273	.350	.373	99	0	3	4	-2	.995	20	*1-160	0.9
1992	Chi-N	158	603	72	185	37	5	9	79	72	36	.307	.384	.430	127	23	6	1	1	.998	5	*1-157	2.4
1993	Chi-N★	155	594	86	193	39	4	14	98	71	32	.325	.398	.475	135	31	8	4	0	.997	1	*1-154	1.8
1994	Chi-N	106	403	55	120	23	3	6	44	48	41	.298	.373	.414	106	5	0	1	-1	.993	1	*1-103	-0.4
1995	Chi-N★	143	552	97	180	51	3	16	92	65	46	.326	.399	.516	142	34	6	2	1	.995	4	*1-143	2.4
1996	Chi-N	142	547	88	181	39	1	9	75	62	41	.331	.400	.455	122	19	2	3	-1	.997	3	*1-141	0.7
1997	Chi-N★	151	555	87	177	32	5	13	78	88	45	.319	.414	.465	127	25	2	3	-2	.995	5	*1-148	1.2
1998	*Chi-N	158	595	92	184	39	3	17	89	93	56	.309	.405	.471	123	23	4	7	-3	.994	5	*1-156	1.1
Total	11	1606	6053	875	1875	371	37	121	831	768	489	.310	.389	.443	122	209	63	42	-6	.995	83	*1-1590	15.3

■ MIKE GRACE
Grace, Michael Lee b: 6/14/56, Pontiac, Mich. BR/TR, 6', 175 lbs. Deb: 4/18/78

| 1978 | Cin-N | 5 | 3 | 0 | 0 | 0 | 0 | 0 | 0 | 0 | 2 | .000 | .000 | .000 | -99 | -1 | 0 | 0 | 0 | 1.000 | 1 | /3-2 | 0.0 |

■ EARL GRACE
Grace, Robert Earl b: 2/24/07, Barlow, Ky. d: 12/22/80, Phoenix, Ariz. BL/TR, 6', 175 lbs. Deb: 4/23/29

1929	Chi-N	27	80	7	20	1	0	2	17	9	7	.250	.333	.338	67	-4	0			1.000	3	C-27	0.1
1931	Chi-N	7	9	2	1	0	0	0	1	4	1	.111	.385	.111	39	-1	0			1.000	-0	/C-2	0.0
	Pit-N	47	150	8	42	6	1	1	20	13	5	.280	.337	.353	87	-3	0			.974	-1	C-45	0.0
	Yr	54	159	10	43	6	1	1	21	17	6	.270	.341	.340	84	-3	0			.976	-1	C-47	0.0
1932	Pit-N	115	390	41	107	17	5	8	55	14	23	.274	.305	.405	91	-6	0			.998	-7	*C-114	-0.6
1933	Pit-N	93	291	22	84	13	1	3	44	26	23	.289	.349	.371	106	3	0			.980	1	C-88	0.9
1934	Pit-N	95	289	27	78	17	1	4	24	20	19	.270	.317	.377	83	-7	0			.982	-9	C-83/1-1	-1.2
1935	Pit-N	77	224	19	59	8	1	3	29	32	17	.263	.355	.348	87	-3	1			.990	-5	C-69	0.3
1936	Phi-N	86	221	24	55	11	0	4	32	34	20	.249	.352	.353	82	-5	0			.976	-4	C-65	-0.6
1937	Phi-N	80	223	19	47	10	1	6	29	33	15	.211	.313	.345	73	-8	0			.990	-3	C-64	-0.8
Total	8	627	1877	169	493	83	10	31	251	185	130	.263	.331	.367	86	-34	1			.987	-17	C-557/1-1	-1.9

■ JOHN GRADY
Grady, John J. b: 6/18/1860, Lowell, Mass. d: 7/15/1893, Lowell, Mass. 5'7", 150 lbs. Deb: 5/10/1884

| 1884 | Alt-U | 9 | 36 | 5 | 11 | 3 | 0 | 0 | | 2 | | .306 | .342 | .389 | 119 | -0 | | | | .909 | -1 | /1-8,O-1 | -0.2 |

■ MIKE GRADY
Grady, Michael William b: 12/23/1869, Kennett Square, Pa d: 12/3/43, Kennett Square, Pa. BR/TR, 5'11", 190 lbs. Deb: 4/24/1894

1894	Phi-N	60	190	45	69	13	8	0	40	14	13	.363	.427	.516	130	9	3			.878	-12	C-44,1-11/O-2	0.1
1895	Phi-N	46	123	21	40	3	1	1	23	14	8	.325	.407	.390	106	2	5			.926	-11	C-38/O-5,3-1,1-1	-0.5
1896	Phi-N	71	242	49	77	20	7	1	44	16	19	.318	.382	.471	126	9	10			.942	-7	C-61/3-7	0.7
1897	Phi-N	4	13	1	2	0	0	0	0	1		.154	.214	.154	-2	-2	0			1.000	1	/C-3	-0.1
	StL-N	83	322	48	90	11	3	7	45	26		.280	.352	.398	100	-0	7			.974	-1	1-83/O-1	-0.1
	Yr	87	335	49	92	11	3	7	45	27		.275	.347	.388	96	-2	7			.974	-0	1-83/C-3,O-1	-0.2
1898	NY-N	93	287	64	85	19	5	3	49	38		.296	.399	.429	142	17	20			.944	-4	C-57,O-30/1-7,S-3	1.5
1899	NY-N	86	311	47	104	18	8	2	54	29		.334	.403	.463	142	18	20			.939	-13	C-43,3-35/O-4,1-4	0.8
1900	NY-N	83	251	36	55	8	4	0	27	34		.219	.331	.283	74	-7	9			.932	-14	C-41,1-12,S/3O2	-1.6
1901	Was-A	94	347	57	99	17	10	9	56	27		.285	.351	.470	128	12	14			.975	6	1-59,C-30/O-3	1.8
1904	StL-N	101	323	44	101	15	11	5	43	31		.313	.376	.474	135	26	6			.955	-20	C-77,1-11/2-3,3-1	1.5
1905	StL-N	100	311	41	89	20	7	4	41	33		.286	.360	.434	141	15	15			.956	-11	C-71,1-20	1.2
1906	StL-N	97	280	33	70	11	3	0	27	48		.250	.369	.343	127	11	5			.983	-10	C-60,1-38	0.6
Total	11	918	3000	486	881	155	67	35	449	311	40	.294	.374	.425	127	110	114			.946	-95	C-525,1-246/3OS2	5.9

■ FRED GRAFF
Graff, Frederick Gottleib b: 8/25/1889, Canton, Ohio d: 10/4/79, Chattanooga, Tenn. BR/TR, 5'10.5", 164 lbs. Deb: 5/14/13

| 1913 | StL-A | 4 | 5 | 1 | 2 | 1 | 0 | 0 | 3 | 2 | 3 | .400 | .625 | .600 | 266 | 1 | 0 | | | 1.000 | -1 | /3-4 | 0.1 |

■ LOUIS GRAFF
Graff, Louis George "Chappie" b: 7/25/1866, Philadelphia, Pa. d: 4/16/55, Bryn Mawr, Pa. TR, Deb: 6/23/1890

| 1890 | Syr-a | 1 | 5 | 0 | 2 | 0 | 0 | 0 | | 1 | | .400 | .400 | .600 | 217 | 1 | 0 | | | .333 | -2 | /C-1 | -0.1 |

■ MILT GRAFF
Graff, Milton Edward b: 12/30/30, Jefferson Center, Pa. BL/TR, 5'7.5", 158 lbs. Deb: 4/16/57 C

1957	KC-A	56	155	16	28	4	3	0	10	15	10	.181	.262	.245	39	-13	2	5	-2	.988	1	2-53	-1.1
1958	KC-A	5	1	0	0	0	0	0	0	0	0	.000	.000	.000	-98	-0	0	0	0	1.000	0	/2-1	0.0
Total	2	61	156	16	28	4	3	0	10	15	10	.179	.260	.244	38	-13	2	5	-2	.988	2	/2-54	-1.1

■ TONY GRAFFANINO
Graffanino, Anthony Joseph b: 6/6/72, Amityville, N.Y. BR/TR, 6'1", 175 lbs. Deb: 4/19/96

1996	Atl-N	22	46	7	8	1	0	2	4	3	13	.174	.255	.239	30	-5	0	0	0	.969	4	2-18	-0.5
1997	*Atl-N	104	186	33	48	9	1	8	20	26	46	.258	.352	.446	106	2	6	4	-1	.982	12	2-75/3-2,S-2,1-1	1.6
1998	*Atl-N	105	289	32	61	14	1	5	22	24	68	.211	.276	.318	53	-20	1	4	-2	.971	13	2-93/S-2,3-1	-0.4
Total	3	231	521	72	117	24	3	13	44	54	127	.225	.302	.357	70	-23	7	8	-3	.975	29	2-186/S-4,3-3,1-1	1.2

■ MOONLIGHT GRAHAM
Graham, Archibald Wright b: 11/9/1876, Fayetteville, N.C. d: 8/25/65, Chisholm, Minn. BL/TR, 5'10.5", 170 lbs. Deb: 6/29/05

| 1905 | NY-N | 1 | 0 | 0 | 0 | 0 | 0 | 0 | 0 | 0 | | — | — | — | — | -0 | 0 | 0 | 0 | .000 | -0 | /O-1 | 0.0 |

■ SKINNY GRAHAM
Graham, Arthur William b: 8/12/09, Somerville, Mass. d: 7/10/67, Cambridge, Mass. BL/TR, 5'7", 162 lbs. Deb: 9/14/34

1934	Bos-A	13	47	7	11	2	1	0	3	6	13	.234	.321	.319	61	-3	3			1.000	-1	O-13	-0.5
1935	Bos-A	8	10	1	3	0	0	0	1	1	3	.300	.364	.300	69	-0	1	0	0	1.000	-1	/O-2	-0.1
Total	2	21	57	8	14	2	1	0	4	7	16	.246	.328	.316	62	-3	3	2	-0	1.000	-2	/O-15	-0.6

■ BARNEY GRAHAM
Graham, Barney b: Philadelphia, Pa. d: 12/31/1896, Mobile, Ala. Deb: 9/4/1889

| 1889 | Phi-a | 4 | 18 | 0 | 3 | 0 | 0 | 0 | 0 | 0 | | .167 | .167 | .167 | 5 | -2 | 0 | | | .933 | 1 | /3-4 | -0.1 |

■ BERNIE GRAHAM
Graham, Bernard W. b: 1860, Beloit, Wis. d: 10/30/1886, Mobile, Ala. BL, Deb: 7/11/1884

1884	CP-U	1	5	2	1	0	0	0		0		.200	.200	.200	22	-1				1.000	-0	/O-1	-0.1
	Bal-U	41	167	21	45	11	0	0		2		.269	.278	.335	77	-10				.814	1	O-40/1-1	-0.8
	Yr	42	172	23	46	11	0	0		2		.267	.276	.331	76	-10				.816	1	O-41/1-1	-0.9

■ BERT GRAHAM
Graham, Bert "B.G." b: 4/3/1886, Tilton, Ill. d: 6/19/71, Cottonwood, Ariz. BB/TR, 5'11.5", 187 lbs. Deb: 9/9/10

| 1910 | StL-A | 8 | 26 | 1 | 3 | 2 | 1 | 0 | | 3 | | .115 | .148 | .269 | 32 | -1 | | | | .964 | 1 | /1-5,2-2 | -0.1 |

■ CHARLIE GRAHAM
Graham, Charles Henry b: 4/24/1878, Santa Clara, Cal. d: 8/29/48, San Francisco, Cal BR/TR, 6', 190 lbs. Deb: 4/16/06

| 1906 | Bos-A | 30 | 90 | 10 | 21 | 1 | 0 | 1 | 12 | 10 | | .233 | .330 | .278 | 91 | -0 | 1 | | | .963 | 7 | C-27 | 1.0 |

■ DAN GRAHAM
Graham, Daniel Jay b: 7/19/54, Ray, Ariz. BL/TR, 6'1", 205 lbs. Deb: 6/8/79

| 1979 | Min-A | 2 | 4 | 0 | 0 | 0 | 0 | 0 | 0 | 0 | 0 | .000 | .000 | .000 | -96 | -1 | 0 | 0 | 0 | .000 | 0 | /D-1 | -0.1 |
| 1980 | Bal-A | 86 | 266 | 32 | 74 | 7 | 1 | 15 | 54 | 14 | 40 | .278 | .314 | .481 | 116 | 4 | 0 | 0 | 0 | .981 | 0 | C-73/3-9,O-1,D-2 | 0.7 |

YEAR	TM/L	G	AB	R	H	2B	3B	HR	RBI	BB	SO	AVG	OBP	SLG	PRO+	BR/A	SB	CS	SBR	FA	FR	G/POS	TPR
1981	Bal-A	55	142	7	25	3	0	2	11	13	32	.176	.245	.239	40	-11	0	0	0	.975	-4	C-40/3-4,D-6	-1.5
Total	3	143	412	39	99	10	1	17	65	27	72	.240	.287	.393	88	-7	0	0	0	.979	-4	C-113/3-13,D-9,O-1	-0.9

■ TINY GRAHAM

Graham, Dawson Francis b: 9/9/1892, Nashville, Tenn. d: 12/29/62, Nashville, Tenn. BR/TR, 6'2", 185 lbs. Deb: 8/30/14

YEAR	TM/L	G	AB	R	H	2B	3B	HR	RBI	BB	SO	AVG	OBP	SLG	PRO+	BR/A	SB	CS	SBR	FA	FR	G/POS	TPR
1914	Cin-N	25	61	5	14	1	0	0	3	3	10	.230	.266	.246	51	-4	1			.961	-2	1-25	-0.6

■ PEACHES GRAHAM

Graham, George Frederick b: 3/23/1877, Aledo, Ill. d: 7/25/39, Long Beach, Cal. BR/TR, 5'9", 180 lbs. Deb: 9/14/02 F

YEAR	TM/L	G	AB	R	H	2B	3B	HR	RBI	BB	SO	AVG	OBP	SLG	PRO+	BR/A	SB	CS	SBR	FA	FR	G/POS	TPR
1902	Cle-A	2	6	0	2	0	0	0	1	1		.333	.429	.333	118	0	0			1.000	0	/2-1	0.0
1903	Chi-N	1	2	0	0	0	0	0	0	0		.000	.000	.000	-99	-1	0			1.000	0	/P-1	0.0
1908	Bos-N	75	215	22	59	5	0	0	22	23		.274	.361	.298	112	4	4			.955	-3	C-62/2-5	0.8
1909	Bos-N	92	267	27	64	6	3	0	17	24		.240	.302	.285	79	-7	7			.948	-4	C-76/O-6,S-1,3-1	-0.4
1910	Bos-N	110	291	31	82	13	2	0	21	33	15	.282	.359	.340	100	0	5			.966	-8	C-87/3-2,1-1,O-1	0.1
1911	Bos-N	33	88	7	24	6	1	0	12	14	5	.273	.373	.364	98	0	2			.912	-5	C-26	-0.3
	Chi-N	36	71	6	17	3	0	0	8	11	8	.239	.365	.282	82	-1	2			.972	-5	C-28	-0.4
	Yr	69	159	13	41	9	1	0	20	25	13	.258	.369	.327	92	-1	4			.937	-10	C-54	-0.7
1912	Phi-N	24	59	6	17	1	0	1	4	8	5	.288	.373	.356	94	-0	1			.944	-2	C-19	0.0
Total	7	373	999	99	265	34	6	1	85	114	33	.265	.347	.314	95	-3	21			.953	-25	C-298/O-7,2-6,31SP	-0.2

■ JACK GRAHAM

Graham, John Bernard b: 12/24/16, Minneapolis, Minn. BL/TL, 6'2", 200 lbs. Deb: 4/16/46 F

YEAR	TM/L	G	AB	R	H	2B	3B	HR	RBI	BB	SO	AVG	OBP	SLG	PRO+	BR/A	SB	CS	SBR	FA	FR	G/POS	TPR
1946	Bro-N	2	5	0	1	0	0	0	0	0	0	.200	.200	.200	14	-1	0			1.000	0	/1-2	-0.1
	NY-N	100	270	34	59	6	4	14	47	23	37	.219	.282	.426	99	-2	1			.949	-1	O-62/1-7	-0.7
	Yr	102	275	34	60	6	4	14	47	23	37	.218	.281	.422	97	-3	1			.949	-1	O-62/1-9	-0.8
1949	StL-A	137	500	71	119	22	1	24	79	61	62	.238	.326	.430	95	-7	0	1	-1	.984	-6	*1-136	-1.4
Total	2	239	775	105	179	28	5	38	126	84	99	.231	.310	.427	96	-9	1	1		.985	-7	1-145/O-62	-2.2

■ LEE GRAHAM

Graham, Lee Willard b: 9/22/59, Summerfield, Fla. BL/TL, 5'10", 170 lbs. Deb: 9/3/83

YEAR	TM/L	G	AB	R	H	2B	3B	HR	RBI	BB	SO	AVG	OBP	SLG	PRO+	BR/A	SB	CS	SBR	FA	FR	G/POS	TPR
1983	Bos-A	5	6	2	0	0	0	0	1	0	0	.000	.000	.000	-93	-2	0	1	-1	1.000	1	/O-3	-0.2

■ ROY GRAHAM

Graham, Roy Vincent b: 2/22/1895, San Francisco, Cal d: 4/26/33, Manila, Philippines BR/TR, 5'10.5", 175 lbs. Deb: 5/28/22

YEAR	TM/L	G	AB	R	H	2B	3B	HR	RBI	BB	SO	AVG	OBP	SLG	PRO+	BR/A	SB	CS	SBR	FA	FR	G/POS	TPR
1922	Chi-A	5	3	0	0	0	0	0	0	0	0	.000	.400	.000	12	-0	0	0	0	1.000	-0	/C-3	0.0
1923	Chi-A	36	82	3	16	2	0	0	6	9	6	.195	.290	.220	36	-7	0	0	0	.949	-7	C-33	-1.3
Total	2	41	85	3	16	2	0	0	6	9	6	.188	.296	.212	35	-8	0	0	0	.950	-7	/C-36	-1.3

■ WAYNE GRAHAM

Graham, Wayne Leon b: 4/6/37, Yoakum, Tex. BR/TR, 6', 200 lbs. Deb: 4/10/63

YEAR	TM/L	G	AB	R	H	2B	3B	HR	RBI	BB	SO	AVG	OBP	SLG	PRO+	BR/A	SB	CS	SBR	FA	FR	G/POS	TPR
1963	Phi-N	10	22	1	4	0	0	0	0	3	1	.182	.280	.182	36	-2	0	0	0	.857	-1	/O-6	-0.3
1964	NY-N	20	33	1	3	1	0	0	0	0	5	.091	.091	.121	-42	-6	0	0	0	1.000	-2	3-11	-0.9
Total	2	30	55	2	7	1	0	0	0	3	6	.127	.172	.145	-9	-8	0	0	0	1.000	-3	/3-11,O-6	-1.2

■ ALEX GRAMMAS

Grammas, Alexander Peter b: 4/3/26, Birmingham, Ala. BR/TR, 6', 178 lbs. Deb: 4/13/54 MC

YEAR	TM/L	G	AB	R	H	2B	3B	HR	RBI	BB	SO	AVG	OBP	SLG	PRO+	BR/A	SB	CS	SBR	FA	FR	G/POS	TPR
1954	StL-N	142	401	57	106	17	4	2	29	40	29	.264	.339	.342	77	-13	6	1	1	.966	30	*S-142/3-1	2.8
1955	StL-N	128	366	32	88	19	2	3	25	33	36	.240	.308	.328	69	-16	4	1	1	.968	7	*S-126	0.1
1956	StL-N	6	12	1	3	0	0	0	1	1	1	.250	.308	.250	52	-1	0	0	0	1.000	0	/S-5	-0.1
	Cin-N	77	140	17	34	11	0	0	16	16	18	.243	.325	.321	70	-6	0	1	-1	.968	4	3-58,S-12/2-5	-0.2
	Yr	83	152	18	37	11	0	0	17	17	19	.243	.324	.316	69	-6	0	1	-1	.968	4	3-58,S-17/2-5	-0.3
1957	Cin-N	73	99	14	30	4	0	0	8	10	6	.303	.367	.343	86	-2	1	3	-2	.966	2	S-42,2-20/3-9	0.1
1958	Cin-N	105	216	25	47	8	0	0	12	34	24	.218	.329	.255	54	-13	2	2	-1	.993	-2	S-61,3-38,2-14	-1.3
1959	StL-N	131	368	43	99	14	2	3	30	38	26	.269	.339	.342	77	-11	3	3	-1	.964	12	*S-130	1.0
1960	StL-N	102	196	20	48	4	1	4	17	12	15	.245	.292	.337	66	-9	0	1	-1	.972	20	S-46,2-38,3-13	1.4
1961	StL-N	89	170	23	36	10	1	0	21	19	21	.212	.295	.282	49	-12	0	1	-1	.960	17	S-65,2-18/3-3	0.8
1962	StL-N	21	18	0	2	0	0	0	1	1	6	.111	.158	.111	-24	-3	0	0	0	.933	1	S-16/2-2	-0.1
	Chi-N	23	60	3	14	3	0	0	3	2	7	.233	.270	.283	47	-4	1	1	-0	1.000	1	S-13/2-3,3-1	-0.2
	Yr	44	78	3	16	3	0	0	4	3	13	.205	.244	.244	29	-8	1	1	-0	.978	3	S-29/2-5,3-1	-0.3
1963	Chi-N	16	27	1	5	0	0	0	0	0	3	.185	.185	.185	7	-3	0	0	0	.955	-3	S-13	-0.7
Total	10	913	2073	236	512	90	10	12	163	206	192	.247	.320	.317	67	-93	17	14	-3	.968	88	S-671,3-123,2-100	3.6

■ JACK GRANEY

Graney, John Gladstone b: 6/10/1886, St.Thomas, Ont., Can. d: 4/20/78, Louisiana, Mo. BL/TL, 5'9", 180 lbs. Deb: 4/30/08

YEAR	TM/L	G	AB	R	H	2B	3B	HR	RBI	BB	SO	AVG	OBP	SLG	PRO+	BR/A	SB	CS	SBR	FA	FR	G/POS	TPR
1908	Cle-A	2	0	0	0	0	0	0	0	0		—	—	—	—	0	0			.000	-0	/P-2	0.0
1910	Cle-A	116	454	62	107	13	9	1	31	37		.236	.293	.311	88	-7	18			.949	1	*O-114	-1.3
1911	Cle-A	146	527	84	142	25	5	1	45	66		.269	.363	.342	96	-1	21			.927	2	*O-142	-0.7
1912	Cle-A	78	264	44	64	13	2	0	20	50		.242	.367	.307	90	-1	9			.958	4	O-75	-0.1
1913	Cle-A	148	517	56	138	18	12	3	68	48	55	.267	.335	.366	102	1	27			.970	2	*O-148	-0.5
1914	Cle-A	130	460	63	122	17	10	1	39	67	46	.265	.362	.352	111	8	20	18	-5	.935	5	*O-127	0.2
1915	Cle-A	116	404	42	105	20	7	1	56	59	29	.260	.357	.351	110	6	12	15	-5	.972	5	*O-115	0.0
1916	Cle-A	155	589	106	142	**41**	14	5	54	102	72	.241	.355	.384	115	12	10			.959	3	*O-154	0.7
1917	Cle-A	146	535	87	122	29	7	3	35	**94**	49	.228	.348	.325	98	1	16			.959	-7	*O-145	-1.6
1918	Cle-A	70	177	27	42	7	4	0	9	28	13	.237	.351	.322	94	-0	3			.975	-6	O-45	-1.0
1919	Cle-A	128	461	79	108	22	8	1	30	**105**	39	.234	.380	.323	93	0	7			.961	6	*O-125	-0.3
1920	*Cle-A	62	152	31	45	11	1	0	13	27	21	.296	.412	.382	108	3	4	2	0	.941	-6	O-47	-0.6
1921	Cle-A	68	107	19	32	3	0	2	18	20	9	.299	.414	.383	103	2	1	1	-0	.933	-9	O-32	-0.9
1922	Cle-A	37	58	6	9	0	0	0	2	9	12	.155	.279	.155	16	-7	0	0	0	.862	-1	O-13	-0.9
Total	14	1402	4705	706	1178	219	79	18	420	712	345	.250	.354	.342	100	16	148	36		.953	-3	*O-1282/P-2	-7.0

■ EDDIE GRANT

Grant, Edward Leslie "Harvard Eddie" b: 5/21/1883, Franklin, Mass. d: 10/5/18, Argonne Forest, France BL/TR, 5'11.5", 168 lbs. Deb: 8/4/05

YEAR	TM/L	G	AB	R	H	2B	3B	HR	RBI	BB	SO	AVG	OBP	SLG	PRO+	BR/A	SB	CS	SBR	FA	FR	G/POS	TPR
1905	Cle-A	2	8	1	3	0	0	0	0	0		.375	.375	.375	136	0	0			.833	-2	/2-2	-0.2
1907	Phi-N	74	268	26	65	4	3	0	19	10		.243	.272	.280	74	-9	10			.916	-2	3-74	-1.0
1908	Phi-N	147	598	69	146	13	8	0	32	35		.244	.289	.293	83	-12	27			.930	2	*3-134,S-13	-0.5
1909	Phi-N	154	631	75	170	18	4	1	37	35		.269	.311	.315	94	-6	28			.957	3	*3-154	0.3
1910	Phi-N	152	579	70	155	15	5	1	67	39	54	.268	.315	.316	81	-14	25			.935	-10	*3-152	-2.2
1911	Cin-N	136	458	49	102	12	7	1	53	51	47	.223	.301	.286	67	-20	28			.953	-7	*3-122,S-11	-2.5
1912	Cin-N	96	255	37	61	6	1	2	20	18	27	.239	.292	.294	62	-13	11			.948	0	S-56,3-15	-0.9
1913	Cin-N	27	94	12	20	1	0	0	9	11	10	.213	.295	.223	49	-6	7			.929	-4	3-26	-1.0
	*NY-N	27	20	8	4	1	0	0	1	2	2	.200	.273	.250	49	-1	1			1.000	6	/3-5,2-3,S-1	0.5
	Yr	54	114	20	24	2	0	0	10	13	12	.211	.291	.228	49	-7	8			.940	2	3-31/2-3,S-1	-0.5
1914	NY-N	88	282	34	78	7	1	0	29	23	21	.277	.333	.309	94	-2	11			.948	-7	3-52,S-21,2-16	-0.6
1915	NY-N	87	192	18	40	2	1	0	10	9	20	.208	.248	.229	47	-12	5	6	-2	.970	-5	3-35/2-9,1-1,S-1	-2.0
Total	10	990	3385	399	844	79	30	5	277	233	181	.249	.300	.295	78	-95	153	6		.942	-26	3-769,S-103/2-30,1	-10.1

■ JIMMY GRANT

Grant, James Charles b: 10/6/18, Racine, Wis. d: 7/8/70, Rochester, Minn. BL/TR, 5'8", 166 lbs. Deb: 9/8/42

YEAR	TM/L	G	AB	R	H	2B	3B	HR	RBI	BB	SO	AVG	OBP	SLG	PRO+	BR/A	SB	CS	SBR	FA	FR	G/POS	TPR
1942	Chi-A	12	36	0	6	1	1	0	1	5	6	.167	.268	.250	47	-3	0	0	0	.944	1	3-10	-0.2
1943	Chi-A	58	197	23	51	9	2	4	22	18	34	.259	.321	.386	106	1	4	3	-1	.893	1	3-51	0.2
	Cle-A	15	22	3	3	2	0	0	1	4	7	.136	.269	.227	49	-1	0	0	0	.941	2	/3-5	0.0
	Yr	73	219	26	54	11	2	4	23	22	41	.247	.315	.370	101	-0	4	3	-1	.897	3	3-56	0.2
1944	Cle-A	61	99	12	27	4	3	1	12	11	20	.273	.357	.404	122	3	1	0	0	.926	-4	2-20/3-4	0.1
Total	3	146	354	38	87	16	6	5	36	38	67	.246	.322	.367	101	-0	5	3	-0	.907	-0	/3-70,2-20	0.1

■ TOM GRANT

Grant, Thomas Raymond b: 5/28/57, Worcester, Mass. BL/TR, 6'2", 190 lbs. Deb: 6/17/83

YEAR	TM/L	G	AB	R	H	2B	3B	HR	RBI	BB	SO	AVG	OBP	SLG	PRO+	BR/A	SB	CS	SBR	FA	FR	G/POS	TPR
1983	Chi-N	16	20	2	3	1	0	0	2	3	4	.150	.261	.200	28	-2	0	0	0	1.000	-2	O-10	-0.4

■ GEORGE GRANTHAM

Grantham, George Farley "Boots" b: 5/20/1900, Galena, Kan. d: 3/16/54, Kingman, Ariz. BL/TR, 5'10", 170 lbs. Deb: 9/20/22

YEAR	TM/L	G	AB	R	H	2B	3B	HR	RBI	BB	SO	AVG	OBP	SLG	PRO+	BR/A	SB	CS	SBR	FA	FR	G/POS	TPR
1922	Chi-N	7	23	3	4	1	1	0	3	1	3	.174	.208	.304	30	-2	2	0	1	1.000	-3	/3-5	-0.4
1923	Chi-N	152	570	81	160	36	8	8	70	71	92	.281	.360	.414	104	4	43	28	-4	.942	1	*2-150	0.3
1924	Chi-N	127	469	85	148	19	6	12	60	55	63	.316	.390	.458	125	18	21	21	6	.941	1	*2-118/3-6	1.4

YEAR	TM/L	G	AB	R	H	2B	3B	HR	RBI	BB	SO	AVG	OBP	SLG	PRO+	BR/A	SB	CS	SBR	FA	FR	G/POS	TPR
1925	*Pit-N	114	359	74	117	24	6	8	52	50	29	.326	.413	.493	122	13	14	4	2	.989	-4	*1-102	0.5
1926	Pit-N	141	449	66	143	27	13	8	70	60	42	.318	.400	.490	131	21	6			.990	-2	*1-132	1.0
1927	*Pit-N	151	531	96	162	33	11	8	66	74	39	.305	.396	.454	119	16	9			.953	-24	*2-124,1-29	-0.6
1928	Pit-N	124	440	93	142	24	9	10	85	59	37	.323	.408	.486	128	19	9			.986	1	*1-119/2-1,3-1	1.0
1929	Pit-N	110	349	85	107	23	10	12	90	93	38	.307	.454	.533	140	26	10			.967	-5	2-76,O-19,1-12	2.1
1930	Pit-N	146	552	120	179	34	14	18	99	81	66	.324	.413	.534	126	25	5			.958	-13	*2-141/1-4	1.6
1931	Pit-N	127	465	91	142	26	6	10	46	71	50	.305	.400	.452	130	22	5			.985	-22	1-78,2-51	-0.4
1932	Cin-N	126	493	81	144	29	6	6	39	56	40	.292	.364	.412	112	9	4			.959	-29	*2-115,1-10	-1.5
1933	Cin-N	87	260	32	53	14	3	4	28	38	21	.204	.310	.327	83	-5	4			.948	-11	2-72,1-12	-1.4
1934	NY-N	32	29	5	7	2	0	1	4	8	6	.241	.405	.414	123	1	0			1.000	0	/1-4,3-2	0.1
Total	13	1444	4989	912	1508	292	93	105	712	717	526	.302	.392	.461	121	166	132	53		.949	-108	2-848,1-502/O-19,3	3.7
■ MICKEY GRASSO	Grasso, Newton Michael b: 5/10/20, Newark, N.J. d: 10/15/75, Miami, Fla. BR/TR, 6', 195 lbs. Deb: 9/18/46																						
1946	NY-N	7	22	1	3	0	0	0	1	0	3	.136	.136	.136	-22	-4	0			.967	0	/C-7	-0.3
1950	Was-A	75	195	25	56	4	1	1	22	25	31	.287	.374	.333	86	-3	1	1	-0	.942	6	C-69	0.5
1951	Was-A	52	175	16	36	3	0	1	14	14	17	.206	.268	.240	39	-15	0	0	0	.967	-2	C-49	-1.5
1952	Was-A	115	361	22	78	9	0	0	27	29	36	.216	.276	.241	46	-26	1	0	0	.970	6	*C-114	-1.5
1953	Was-A	61	196	13	41	7	0	2	22	9	20	.209	.251	.276	43	-16	0	0	0	.984	1	C-59	-1.3
1954	*Cle-A	4	6	1	2	0	0	1	1	1	1	.333	.500	.833	256	1	0	0	0	.833	-1	/C-4	0.1
1955	NY-N	8	2	0	0	0	0	0	0	3	0	.000	.600	.000	77	0	0	0	0	.900	-0	/C-8	0.0
Total	7	322	957	78	216	23	1	5	87	81	108	.226	.291	.268	53	-62	2	1		.964	9	C-310	-4.0
■ LEW GRAULICH	Graulich, Lewis b: Camden, N.J. Deb: 9/17/1891																						
1891	Phi-N	7	26	2	8	0	0	0	3	1	2	.308	.333	.308	85	-1	0			.640	-3	/C-4,1-3	-0.3
■ FRANK GRAVES	Graves, Frank M. b: 11/2/1860, Cincinnati, Ohio 6', 163 lbs. Deb: 5/10/1886																						
1886	StL-N	43	138	7	21	2	0	0	9	7	48	.152	.193	.167	11	-14	11			.885	4	C-41/O-3,P-1	-0.5
■ JOE GRAVES	Graves, Joseph Ebenezer b: 2/26/06, Marblehead, Mass. d: 12/22/80, Salem, Mass. BR/TR, 5'10", 160 lbs. Deb: 9/26/26 F																						
1926	Chi-N	2	5	0	0	0	0	0	0	0	1	.000	.000	.000	-99	-1	0			.250	-1	/3-2	-0.3
■ SID GRAVES	Graves, Samuel Sidney "Whitey" b: 11/30/01, Marblehead, Mass. d: 12/26/83, Biddeford, Maine BR/TR, 6', 170 lbs. Deb: 7/23/27 F																						
1927	Bos N	7	20	5	5	1	1	0	2	0	1	.250	.250	.400	78	-1	1			.857	0	/O-5	-0.1
■ GARY GRAY	Gray, Gary George b: 9/21/52, New Orleans, La. BR/TR, 6', 203 lbs. Deb: 6/23/77																						
1977	Tex-A	1	2	0	0	0	0	0	0	0	1	.000	.000	.000	-99	-1	0	0	0	.000	-0	/O-1	-0.1
1978	Tex-A	17	50	4	12	1	0	2	6	1	12	.240	.255	.380	76	-2	1	0	0	.000	0	D-11	-0.2
1979	Tex-A	16	42	4	10	0	0	0	1	2	8	.238	.273	.238	40	-3	1	1	-0	.000	0	D-13	-0.4
1980	Cle-A	28	54	4	8	1	0	2	4	3	13	.148	.193	.278	27	-6	0	0	0	1.000	-2	/1-6,O-6,D-9	-0.8
1981	Sea-A	69	208	27	51	7	1	13	31	4	44	.245	.259	.476	104	-0	2	0	1	.993	-2	1-34,D-15/O-4	-0.5
1982	Sea-A	80	269	26	69	14	2	7	29	24	59	.257	.322	.401	95	-2	1	1	-0	.984	-3	1-60,D-14	-0.8
Total	6	211	625	65	150	23	3	24	71	34	137	.240	.281	.402	86	-14	5	2	0	.988	-7	1-100/D-62,O-11	-2.8
■ REDDY GRAY	Gray, James D. TR, Deb: 6/17/1890																						
1890	Pit-P	2	9	3	2	0	0	1	3	0	2	.222	.222	.556	114	0	0			.813	-1	/2-2	-0.1
	Pit-N	1	3	0	0	0	0	0	0	0	1	.000	.000	.000	-99	-1	0			.571	-1	/S-1	-0.1
1893	Pit-N	2	9	0	4	1	0	0	2	0	1	.444	.444	.556	168	1	0			.800	-3	/S-2	-0.2
Total	2	5	21	3	6	1	0	1	5	0	4	.286	.286	.476	111	0	0			.667	-4	/S-3,2-2	-0.4
■ JIM GRAY	Gray, James W. b: 8/7/1862, Pittsburgh, Pa. d: 1/31/38, Allegheny, Pa. TR, Deb: 10/9/1884																						
1884	Pit-a	1	2	0	1	0	0	0		0		.500	.500	.500	224	0				.500	-0	/3-1	0.0
■ LORENZO GRAY	Gray, Lorenzo b: 3/4/58, Mound Bayou, Miss. BR/TR, 6'1", 180 lbs. Deb: 7/8/82																						
1982	Chi-A	17	28	4	8	1	0	0	0	2	4	.286	.333	.321	81	-1	1	0	0	.864	-3	3-16	-0.4
1983	Chi-A	41	78	18	14	3	0	1	4	8	16	.179	.256	.256	40	-6	1	0	0	.940	2	3-31/D-7	-0.4
Total	2	58	106	22	22	4	0	1	4	10	20	.208	.276	.274	50	-7	2	0	1	.921	-1	/3-47,D-7	-0.8
■ MILT GRAY	Gray, Milton Marshall b: 2/21/14, Louisville, Ky. d: 6/30/69, Quincy, Fla. BR/TR, 6'1", 170 lbs. Deb: 5/27/37																						
1937	Was-A	2	6	0	0	0	0	0	0	0	1	.000	.000	.000	-99	-2	0	0	0	1.000	0	/C-2	-0.1
■ PETE GRAY	Gray, Peter J. (b: Peter Wyshner) b: 3/6/15, Nanticoke, Pa. BL/TL, 6'1", 169 lbs. Deb: 4/17/45																						
1945	StL-A	77	234	26	51	6	2	0	13	13	11	.218	.259	.261	49	-15	5	6	-2	.959	1	O-61	-2.1
■ DICK GRAY	Gray, Richard Benjamin b: 7/11/31, Jefferson, Pa. BR/TR, 5'11", 165 lbs. Deb: 4/15/58																						
1958	LA-N	58	197	25	49	5	6	9	30	19	30	.249	.327	.472	105	1	1	1	-0	.929	14	3-55	1.5
1959	LA-N	21	52	8	8	1	0	2	4	6	12	.154	.241	.288	38	-5	0	0	0	1.000	-0	3-11	-0.5
	StL-N	36	51	9	16	1	0	1	6	6	8	.314	.386	.392	101	0	3	0	1	.958	-9	S-13/3-6,2-2,O-1	-0.7
	Yr	57	103	17	24	2	0	3	10	12	20	.233	.313	.340	69	-4	3	0	1	.935	-9	3-17,S-13/2-2,O-1	-1.2
1960	StL-N	9	5	1	0	0	0	0	1	2	2	.000	.286	.000	-13	-1	0	0	0	1.000	1	/2-4,3-1	0.1
Total	3	124	305	43	73	7	6	12	41	33	52	.239	.322	.420	91	-4	4	1	1	.930	6	/3-73,S-13,2-6,O-1	0.4
■ STAN GRAY	Gray, Stanley Oscar b: 12/10/1888, Ladonia, Tex. d: 10/11/64, Snyder, Tex. BR/TR, 6'0.5", 184 lbs. Deb: 9/17/12																						
1912	Pit-N	6	20	4	5	0	1	0	2	0	3	.250	.250	.350	64	-1	0			1.000	-1	/1-4	-0.2
■ CRAIG GREBECK	Grebeck, Craig Allen b: 12/29/64, Johnstown, Pa. BR/TR, 5'7", 148 lbs. Deb: 4/13/90																						
1990	Chi-A	59	119	7	20	3	1	1	9	8	24	.168	.233	.235	32	-11	0	0	0	.987	8	3-35,S-16/2-6,D-1	-0.2
1991	Chi-A	107	224	37	63	16	3	6	31	38	40	.281	.388	.460	137	12	1	3	-2	.933	-1	3-49,2-36,S-26	1.2
1992	Chi-A	88	287	24	77	21	2	3	35	30	34	.268	.344	.387	106	2	0	3	-2	.980	-4	S-85/3-7,O-2	0.2
1993	*Chi-A	72	190	25	43	5	0	1	12	26	26	.226	.319	.268	61	-10	1	2	-1	.983	14	S-46,2-16,3-14	0.7
1994	Chi-A	35	97	17	30	5	0	0	5	12	5	.309	.391	.361	97	0	0	0	0	.982	-3	2-14,S-14/3-7	-0.1
1995	Chi-A	53	154	19	40	12	0	1	18	21	23	.260	.360	.357	91	-1	0	0	0	.961	6	S-31,3-18/2-8	0.7
1996	Fla-N	50	95	8	20	1	0	1	9	4	14	.211	.250	.253	34	-9	0	0	0	.985	10	2-29/S-2,3-1	0.2
1997	Ana-A	63	126	12	34	9	0	1	6	18	11	.270	.361	.365	90	-1	0	1	-1	1.000	-1	2-26,S-20,3-15,/OD	0.0
1998	Tor-A	102	301	33	77	17	2	2	27	29	42	.256	.329	.346	76	-10	2	2	-1	.975	14	2-91/S-6,3-4	0.8
Total	9	629	1593	182	404	89	8	16	152	186	219	.254	.337	.350	86	-27	4	11	-5	.972	42	S-246,2-226,3/OD	3.5
■ SCARBOROUGH GREEN	Green, Bertrum Scarborough b: 6/9/74, Creve Coeur, Mo. BR/TR, 5'10", 170 lbs. Deb: 8/2/97																						
1997	StL-N	20	31	5	3	0	0	0	1	2	5	.097	.152	.097	-34	-6	0	0	0	.952	-3	O-19	-0.9
■ DAVID GREEN	Green, David Alejandro (Casaya) b: 12/4/60, Managua, Nicaragua BR/TR, 6'3", 170 lbs. Deb: 9/4/81																						
1981	StL-N	21	34	6	5	1	0	0	2	6	5	.147	.275	.176	29	-3	0	1	-1	.970	-3	O-18	-0.8
1982	*StL-N	76	166	21	47	7	1	2	23	8	29	.283	.320	.373	92	-2	11	3	2	.991	-8	O-68	-1.0
1983	StL-N	146	422	52	120	14	10	8	69	26	76	.284	.327	.422	106	2	34	16	1	.970	-8	*O-136	-0.8
1984	StL-N	126	452	49	121	14	4	15	65	20	105	.268	.300	.416	102	-1	17	9	-0	.991	-5	*1-117,O-14	-1.4
1985	SF-N	106	294	36	73	10	2	5	20	22	58	.248	.303	.347	85	-6	6	5	-1	.987	-3	1-78,O-12	-1.6
1987	StL-N	14	30	4	8	2	1	1	1	2	5	.267	.313	.500	109	0	0	1	-1	.882	-1	O-10/1-3	-0.2
Total	6	489	1398	168	374	48	18	31	180	84	278	.268	.311	.394	97	-9	68	35	-1	.972	-27	O-258,1-198	-5.8
■ DANNY GREEN	Green, Edward b: 11/6/1876, Burlington, N.J. d: 11/9/14, Camden, N.J. BL/TR, Deb: 8/17/1898																						
1898	Chi-N	47	188	26	59	4	3	4	27	7		.314	.342	.431	121	4	12			.970	5	O-47	0.5
1899	Chi-N	117	475	90	140	12	11	6	56	35		.295	.352	.404	110	6	18			.947	1	*O-115	-0.1
1900	Chi-N	103	389	63	116	21	5	5	49	17		.298	.339	.416	112	5	28			.938	0	*O-102	-0.2
1901	Chi-N	133	537	82	168	16	12	6	61	40		.313	.364	.421	132	21	31			.932	8	*O-133	1.9

YEAR	TM/L	G	AB	R	H	2B	3B	HR	RBI	BB	SO	AVG	OBP	SLG	PRO+	BR/A	SB	CS	SBR	FA	FR	G/POS	TPR
1902	Chi-A	129	481	77	150	16	11	0	62	53		.312	.388	.391	122	17	35			.942	-3	*O-129	0.5
1903	Chi-A	135	499	75	154	26	7	6	62	47		.309	.375	.425	146	29	29			.933	2	*O-133	2.4
1904	Chi-A	147	536	83	142	16	10	2	62	63		.265	.352	.343	125	18	28			.964	1	*O-146	1.2
1905	Chi-A	112	379	56	92	13	6	0	44	53		.243	.345	.309	112	8	11			.914	-11	*O-107	-0.8
Total	8	923	3484	552	1021	124	65	29	423	315		.293	.359	.391	124	108	192			.941	4	O-912	5.4

■ PUMPSIE GREEN
Green, Elijah Jerry b: 10/27/33, Oakland, Cal. BB/TR, 6', 175 lbs. Deb: 7/21/59

YEAR	TM/L	G	AB	R	H	2B	3B	HR	RBI	BB	SO	AVG	OBP	SLG	PRO+	BR/A	SB	CS	SBR	FA	FR	G/POS	TPR
1959	Bos-A	50	172	30	40	6	3	1	10	29	22	.233	.350	.320	81	-3	4	2	0	.972	4	2-45/S-1	0.4
1960	Bos-A	133	260	36	63	10	3	3	21	44	47	.242	.354	.338	85	-4	3	4	-2	.982	-13	2-69,S-41	-1.3
1961	Bos-A	88	219	33	57	12	3	6	27	42	32	.260	.379	.425	112	5	4	2	0	.940	-5	S-57/2-7	0.5
1962	Bos-A	56	91	12	21	2	1	2	11	11	18	.231	.314	.341	74	-3	1	0	0	.953	-9	2-18/S-5	-1.1
1963	NY-N	17	54	8	15	1	2	1	5	12	13	.278	.409	.426	139	3	0	2	-1	.857	-1	3-16	0.1
Total	5	344	796	119	196	31	12	13	74	138	132	.246	.360	.364	94	-3	12	10	-2	.975	-24	2-139,S-104/3-16	-1.4

■ GARY GREEN
Green, Gary Allan b: 1/14/62, Pittsburgh, Pa. BR/TR, 6'3", 175 lbs. Deb: 9/14/86 F

YEAR	TM/L	G	AB	R	H	2B	3B	HR	RBI	BB	SO	AVG	OBP	SLG	PRO+	BR/A	SB	CS	SBR	FA	FR	G/POS	TPR
1986	SD-N	13	33	2	7	1	0	0	2	1	11	.212	.235	.242	33	-3	0	0	0	1.000	5	S-13	0.3
1989	SD-N	15	27	4	7	3	0	0	0	1	1	.259	.286	.370	86	-1	0	1	-1	.921	4	S-11/3-1	0.3
1990	Tex-A	62	88	10	19	3	0	0	8	6	18	.216	.266	.250	45	-6	1	1	-0	.972	21	S-58	1.6
1991	Tex-A	8	20	0	3	1	0	0	1	1	6	.150	.190	.200	8	-2	0	0	0	.968	1	/S-8	-0.2
1992	Cin-N	8	12	3	4	1	0	0	0	0	2	.333	.333	.417	108	0	0	0	0	1.000	-1	/S-6,3-1	-0.1
Total	5	106	180	19	40	9	0	0	11	9	38	.222	.259	.272	49	-12	1	2	-1	.970	29	/S-96,3-2	1.9

■ GENE GREEN
Green, Gene Leroy b: 6/26/33, Los Angeles, Cal. d: 5/23/81, St.Louis, Mo. BR/TR, 6'2", 205 lbs. Deb: 9/10/57

YEAR	TM/L	G	AB	R	H	2B	3B	HR	RBI	BB	SO	AVG	OBP	SLG	PRO+	BR/A	SB	CS	SBR	FA	FR	G/POS	TPR
1957	StL-N	6	15	0	3	1	0	0	2	0	3	.200	.200	.267	23	-2	0	0	0	1.000	-1	/O-3	-0.3
1958	StL-N	137	442	47	124	18	3	13	55	37	48	.281	.338	.423	96	-3	2	1	0	.956	9	O-75,C-48	0.5
1959	StL-N	30	74	8	14	6	0	1	3	5	18	.189	.241	.311	43	-6	0	0	0	.944	4	O-19,C-11	-0.3
1960	Bal-A	1	4	0	1	0	0	0	0	0	0	.250	.250	.250	36	-0	0	0	0	1.000	0	/O-1	0.0
1961	Was-A	110	364	52	102	16	3	18	62	35	65	.280	.345	.489	122	10	0	2	-1	.986	-22	C-79,O-21	-0.9
1962	Cle-A	66	143	16	40	4	1	11	28	8	21	.280	.318	.552	133	6	0	0	0	.964	-2	O-33/1-2	0.2
1963	Cle-A	43	78	4	16	3	0	2	7	4	22	.205	.262	.321	63	-4	0	0	0	1.000	-3	O-18	-0.8
	Cin-N	15	31	3	7	1	0	1	3	0	8	.226	.250	.355	70	-1	0	0	0	.932	-2	/C-8	-0.3
Total	7	408	1151	130	307	49	7	46	160	89	185	.267	.322	.441	101	-0	2	3	-1	.963	-16	O-170,C-146/1-2	-1.9

■ JIM GREEN
Green, James R. b: Cleveland, Ohio Deb: 7/19/1884

YEAR	TM/L	G	AB	R	H	2B	3B	HR	RBI	BB	SO	AVG	OBP	SLG	PRO+	BR/A	SB	CS	SBR	FA	FR	G/POS	TPR
1884	Was-U	10	36	4	5	1	0	0		0		.139	.139	.167	-8	-6				.818	-0	/3-9,O-1	-0.5

■ JOE GREEN
Green, Joseph Henry (a.k.a. Joseph Henry Greene) b: 9/17/1897, Philadelphia, Pa. d: 2/4/72, Bryn Mawr, Pa. BR/TR, 6'2", 170 lbs. Deb: 7/2/24

YEAR	TM/L	G	AB	R	H	2B	3B	HR	RBI	BB	SO	AVG	OBP	SLG	PRO+	BR/A	SB	CS	SBR	FA	FR	G/POS	TPR
1924	Phi-A	1	1	0	0	0	0	0	0	0	0	.000	.000	.000	-99	-0	0	0	0	.000	0	H	0.0

■ LENNY GREEN
Green, Leonard Charles b: 1/6/33, Detroit, Mich. BL/TL, 5'11", 170 lbs. Deb: 8/25/57

YEAR	TM/L	G	AB	R	H	2B	3B	HR	RBI	BB	SO	AVG	OBP	SLG	PRO+	BR/A	SB	CS	SBR	FA	FR	G/POS	TPR
1957	Bal-A	19	33	2	6	1	1	1	5	1	4	.182	.206	.364	56	-2	0	1	-1	.950	-4	O-15	-0.8
1958	Bal-A	69	91	10	21	4	0	0	4	9	10	.231	.300	.275	63	-5	0	2	-1	.965	-11	O-53	-1.8
1959	Bal-A	27	24	3	7	0	0	1	2	1	3	.292	.346	.417	111	0	0	0	0	1.000	-6	O-23	-0.7
	Was-A	88	190	29	46	6	1	2	15	20	15	.242	.314	.316	74	-7	9	5	-0	.979	-4	O-58	-1.4
	Yr	115	214	32	53	6	1	3	17	21	18	.248	.318	.327	78	-6	9	5	-0	.981	-11	O-81	-2.1
1960	Was-A	127	330	62	97	16	7	5	33	43	25	.294	.385	.430	121	11	21	8	2	.991	-6	*O-100	0.3
1961	Min-A	156	600	92	171	28	7	9	50	81	50	.285	.376	.400	102	4	17	11	-2	.978	-15	*O-153	-2.2
1962	Min-A	158	619	97	168	33	3	14	63	88	36	.271	.369	.402	104	6	8	4	0	.995	-17	*O-156	-2.1
1963	Min-A	145	280	41	67	10	1	4	27	31	21	.239	.319	.325	80	-7	11	5	0	.988	-25	*O-119	-3.8
1964	Min-A	26	15	3	0	0	0	0	0	4	6	.000	.211	.000	-35	-3	0	1	-1	1.000	-2	/O-7	-0.6
	LA-A	39	92	13	23	2	0	2	4	10	8	.250	.330	.337	96	-1	2	0	1	.977	-1	O-23	-0.2
	Bal-A	14	21	0	4	0	0	0	1	7	3	.190	.393	.190	69	-0	1	0	0	1.000	1	/O-8	0.1
	Yr	79	128	16	27	2	0	2	5	21	17	.211	.327	.273	72	-4	3	1	0	.985	-2	O-38	-0.7
1965	Bos-A	119	373	69	103	24	6	7	24	48	43	.276	.363	.429	117	9	8	2	1	.980	2	O-95	0.8
1966	Bos-A	85	133	18	32	6	0	1	12	15	19	.241	.327	.308	76	-4	0	1	-1	.978	-1	O-27	-0.7
1967	Det-A	58	151	22	42	8	1	1	13	9	17	.278	.319	.364	99	-0	1	1	-0	.983	-4	O-44	-0.7
1968	Det-A	6	4	0	1	0	0	0	0	1	0	.250	.400	.250	97	0	0	0	0	.000	-1	/O-2	-0.1
Total	12	1136	2956	461	788	138	27	47	253	368	260	.267	.353	.379	99	2	78	41	-1	.984	-95	O-883	-13.9

■ DICK GREEN
Green, Richard Larry b: 4/21/41, Sioux City, Iowa BR/TR, 5'10", 180 lbs. Deb: 9/9/63

YEAR	TM/L	G	AB	R	H	2B	3B	HR	RBI	BB	SO	AVG	OBP	SLG	PRO+	BR/A	SB	CS	SBR	FA	FR	G/POS	TPR
1963	KC-A	13	37	5	10	2	0	1	4	2	10	.270	.325	.405	98	-0	0	0	0	.941	2	/S-6,2-4	0.3
1964	KC-A	130	435	48	115	14	5	11	37	27	87	.264	.312	.395	92	-5	3	3	-1	.990	17	*2-120	2.1
1965	KC-A	133	474	64	110	15	1	15	55	50	110	.232	.309	.363	92	-5	0	2	-1	.980	-7	*2-126	-0.2
1966	KC-A	140	507	58	127	24	3	9	62	27	101	.250	.298	.363	92	-6	6	1	1	.979	-1	*2-137/3-2	0.4
1967	KC-A	122	349	26	69	12	4	5	37	30	68	.198	.261	.298	67	-15	6	3	0	.946	-2	3-59,2-50/1-1,S-1	-1.6
1968	Oak-A	76	202	19	47	6	0	6	18	21	41	.233	.308	.351	104	1	3	1	0	.974	13	2-61/C-1,3-1	1.9
1969	Oak-A	136	483	61	133	25	6	12	64	53	94	.275	.357	.427	123	15	2	3	-1	**.986**	10	*2-131	3.5
1970	Oak-A	135	384	34	73	7	0	4	29	38	73	.190	.268	.240	43	-30	3	0	1	.978	0	*2-127/3-5,C-1	-2.0
1971	*Oak-A	144	475	58	116	14	1	12	49	51	83	.244	.321	.354	93	-4	1	1	-0	.986	8	*2-143/S-1	1.6
1972	*Oak-A	26	42	1	12	1	1	0	3	3	5	.286	.348	.357	116	1	0	1	-1	.964	2	2-26	0.3
1973	*Oak-A	133	332	33	87	17	0	3	42	21	63	.262	.310	.340	88	-6	0	2	-1	.988	-9	*2-133/S-1,3-1	-0.9
1974	*Oak-A	100	287	20	61	8	2	2	22	22	50	.213	.269	.275	61	-15	2	3	-1	.983	-5	*2-100	-1.8
Total	12	1288	4007	427	960	145	23	80	422	345	785	.240	.305	.347	87	-70	26	20	-4	.983	28	*2-1158/3-68,SC1	3.6

■ SHAWN GREEN
Green, Shawn David b: 11/10/72, Des Plaines, Ill. BL/TL, 6'4", 190 lbs. Deb: 9/28/93

YEAR	TM/L	G	AB	R	H	2B	3B	HR	RBI	BB	SO	AVG	OBP	SLG	PRO+	BR/A	SB	CS	SBR	FA	FR	G/POS	TPR
1993	Tor-A	3	6	0	0	0	0	0	0	0	1	.000	.000	.000	-99	-2	0	0	0	1.000	-1	/O-2,D-1	-0.2
1994	Tor-A	14	33	1	3	1	0	0	1	1	8	.091	.118	.121	-38	-7	1	0	0	1.000	-2	O-14	-0.8
1995	Tor-A	121	379	52	109	31	4	15	54	20	68	.288	.328	.509	115	6	1	2	-1	.973	6	*O-109	0.9
1996	Tor-A	132	422	52	118	32	3	11	45	33	75	.280	.343	.448	98	-2	5	1	1	.992	7	*O-127/D-1	0.3
1997	Tor-A	135	429	57	123	22	4	16	53	36	99	.287	.343	.469	109	5	14	3	2	.984	4	O-91,D-35	0.7
1998	Tor-A	158	630	106	175	33	4	35	100	50	142	.278	.336	.510	116	13	35	12	3	.979	5	*O-157	1.7
Total	6	563	1899	268	528	119	15	77	253	140	393	.278	.333	.478	107	14	56	18	6	.982	20	O-500/D-37	2.6

■ HANK GREENBERG
Greenberg, Henry Benjamin "Hammerin' Hank" b: 1/1/11, New York, N.Y. d: 9/4/86, Beverly Hills, Cal BR/TR, 6'3.5", 210 lbs. Deb: 9/14/30 H

YEAR	TM/L	G	AB	R	H	2B	3B	HR	RBI	BB	SO	AVG	OBP	SLG	PRO+	BR/A	SB	CS	SBR	FA	FR	G/POS	TPR
1930	Det-A	1	1	0	0	0	0	0	0	0	0	.000	.000	.000	-98	-0	0	0	0	.000	0	H	0.0
1933	Det-A	117	449	59	135	33	3	12	87	46	78	.301	.367	.468	118	11	6	2	1	.988	1	*1-117	0.1
1934	*Det-A	153	593	118	201	**63**	7	26	139	63	93	.339	.404	.600	156	46	9	5	-0	.990	1	*1-153	3.2
1935	*Det-A	152	619	121	203	46	16	**36**	**170**	87	91	.328	.411	.628	171	63	4	3	-1	.992	6	*1-152	4.7
1936	Det-A	12	46	10	16	6	2	1	16	9	6	.348	.455	.630	165	5	1	0	0	.992	1	1-12	0.4
1937	Det-A☆	154	594	137	200	49	14	40	**183**	102	101	.337	.436	.668	171	64	8	3	1	.992	5	*1-154	4.7
1938	Det-A†	155	556	**144**	175	23	4	**58**	146	**119**	92	.315	.438	.683	167	57	7	5	-1	.991	7	*1-155	4.0
1939	Det-A★	138	500	112	156	42	7	33	112	91	95	.312	.420	.622	152	38	8	3	1	**.993**	-1	*1-136	2.1
1940	*Det-A★	148	573	129	195	**50**	8	**41**	**150**	93	75	.340	.433	**.670**	166	55	6	3	0	.954	1	*O-148	4.4
1941	Det-A	19	67	12	18	5	1	2	12	16	12	.269	.410	.463	118	2	1	0	0	.914	-3	O-19	-0.2
1945	*Det-A†	78	270	47	84	20	2	13	60	42	40	.311	.404	.544	164	22	3	1	0	1.000	-6	O-72	1.3
1946	Det-A	142	523	91	145	29	5	**44**	**127**	80	88	.277	.373	.604	160	40	5	1	1	.989	2	*1-140	3.5
1947	Pit-N	125	402	71	100	13	2	25	74	**104**	73	.249	.408	.478	131	21	0			.992	2	*1-119	1.8
Total	13	1394	5193	1051	1628	379	71	331	1276	852	844	.313	.412	.605	157	422	58	26		.991	15	*1-1138,O-239	30.0

■ AL GREENE
Greene, Altar Alphonse b: 11/9/54, Detroit, Mich. BL/TR, 5'11", 190 lbs. Deb: 7/23/79

YEAR	TM/L	G	AB	R	H	2B	3B	HR	RBI	BB	SO	AVG	OBP	SLG	PRO+	BR/A	SB	CS	SBR	FA	FR	G/POS	TPR
1979	Det-A	29	59	9	8	1	0	3	6	10	15	.136	.261	.305	50	-4	0	1	-1	1.000	0	D-15/O-6	-0.5

■ **CHARLIE GREENE** Greene, Charles Patrick b: 1/23/71, Miami, Fla. BR/TR, 6'1", 170 lbs. Deb: 9/15/96

YEAR	TM/L	G	AB	R	H	2B	3B	HR	RBI	BB	SO	AVG	OBP	SLG	PRO+	BR/A	SB	CS	SBR	FA	FR	G/POS	TPR
1996	NY-N	2	1	0	0	0	0	0	0	0	0	.000	.000	.000	-99	-0	0	0	0	1.000	0	/C-1	0.0
1997	Bal-A	5	2	0	0	0	0	0	1	0	1	.000	.000	.000	-99	-1	0	0	0	1.000	0	/C-4	0.0
1998	Bal-A	13	21	1	4	1	0	0	0	0	8	.190	.190	.238	11	-3	0	0	0	1.000	4	C-13	0.2
Total	3	20	24	1	4	1	0	0	1	0	9	.167	.167	.208	-3	-4	0	0	0	1.000	5	/C-18	0.2

■ **JUNE GREENE** Greene, Julius Foust b: 6/25/1899, Ramseur, N.C. d: 3/19/74, Glendora, Cal. BL/TR, 6'2.5", 185 lbs. Deb: 4/20/28

YEAR	TM/L	G	AB	R	H	2B	3B	HR	RBI	BB	SO	AVG	OBP	SLG	PRO+	BR/A	SB	CS	SBR	FA	FR	G/POS	TPR
1928	Phi-N	11	6	0	3	0	0	0	0	3	1	.500	.667	.500	202	1	0			1.000	0	/P-1	0.0
1929	Phi-N	21	19	1	4	1	0	0	0	2	4	.211	.286	.263	35	-2	0			1.000	0	/P-5	0.0
Total	2	32	25	1	7	1	0	0	0	5	5	.280	.400	.320	79	-1	0				1	/P-6	0.0

■ **PADDY GREENE** Greene, Patrick Joseph "Patsy" (a.k.a. Patrick Foley In 1902)
b: 3/20/1875, Providence, R.I. d: 10/20/34, Providence, R.I. BR/TR, 5'8", 150 lbs. Deb: 9/10/02

YEAR	TM/L	G	AB	R	H	2B	3B	HR	RBI	BB	SO	AVG	OBP	SLG	PRO+	BR/A	SB	CS	SBR	FA	FR	G/POS	TPR
1902	Phi-N	19	65	6	11	1	0	0	1	2		.169	.206	.185	21	-6	2			.912	0	3-19	-0.6
1903	NY-A	4	13	1	4	1	0	0	0	0		.308	.308	.385	100	-0	0			1.000	1	/3-2,S-1	0.1
	Det-A	1	3	0	0	0	0	0	0	0		.000	.000	.000	-99	-1	0			.750	-0	/3-1	-0.1
	Yr	5	16	1	4	1	0	0	0	0		.250	.250	.313	65	-1	0			.933	1	/3-3,S-1	0.0
Total	2	24	81	7	15	2	0	0	1	2		.185	.214	.210	30	-7	2			.916	1	/3-22,S-1	-0.6

■ **TODD GREENE** Greene, Todd Anthony b: 5/8/71, Augusta, Ga. BR/TR, 5'10", 195 lbs. Deb: 7/30/96

YEAR	TM/L	G	AB	R	H	2B	3B	HR	RBI	BB	SO	AVG	OBP	SLG	PRO+	BR/A	SB	CS	SBR	FA	FR	G/POS	TPR
1996	Cal-A	29	79	9	15	1	0	2	9	4	11	.190	.238	.278	30	-9	2	0	1	1.000	1	C-26/D-1	-0.6
1997	Ana-A	34	124	24	36	6	0	9	24	7	25	.290	.328	.556	126	4	2	0	1	1.000	-5	C-26/D-8	0.1
1998	Ana-A	29	69	3	18	4	0	1	7	2	19	.261	.282	.362	65	-4	0	0	0	1.000	-3	O-12/1-3,D-4	-0.6
Total	3	92	272	36	69	11	0	12	40	13	55	.254	.290	.426	82	-8	4	0	1	1.000	-7	/C-52,D-13,O-12,1-3	-1.1

■ **WILLIE GREENE** Greene, Willie Louis b: 9/23/71, Milledgeville, Ga. BL/TR, 5'11", 184 lbs. Deb: 9/1/92

YEAR	TM/L	G	AB	R	H	2B	3B	HR	RBI	BB	SO	AVG	OBP	SLG	PRO+	BR/A	SB	CS	SBR	FA	FR	G/POS	TPR
1992	Cin-N	29	93	10	25	5	2	2	13	10	23	.269	.340	.430	114	2	0	2	-1	.948	-1	3-25	0.0
1993	Cin-N	15	50	7	8	1	1	2	5	2	19	.160	.192	.340	39	-5	0	0	0	.978	4	S-10/3-5	0.0
1994	Cin-N	16	37	5	8	2	0	0	3	6	14	.216	.326	.270	58	-2	0	0	0	.958	0	3-13/O-1	-0.2
1995	Cin-N	8	19	1	2	0	0	0	0	3	7	.105	.227	.105	-9	-3	0	0	0	1.000	1	/3-7	-0.2
1996	Cin-N	115	287	48	70	5	5	19	63	36	88	.244	.328	.495	113	4	0	1	-1	.927	7	3-74,O-10/1-2,S-1	1.0
1997	Cin-N	151	495	62	125	22	1	26	91	78	111	.253	.355	.459	110	7	6	0	2	.934	-6	*3-103,O-39/1-7,S-3	0.2
1998	Cin-N	111	356	57	96	18	1	14	49	56	80	.270	.373	.444	109	6	6	3	0	.936	-6	3-76,O-28/S-2,D-1	0.1
	Bal-A	24	40	8	6	1	0	1	5	13	10	.150	.358	.250	67	-1	1	0	0	.941	-2	O-14/D-1	-0.3
Total	7	469	1377	198	340	54	10	64	229	204	352	.247	.346	.440	104	9	13	6	0	.937	-4	3-303/O-92,S-16,1D	0.6

■ **JIM GREENGRASS** Greengrass, James Raymond b: 10/24/27, Addison, N.Y. BR/TR, 6'1", 200 lbs. Deb: 9/9/52

YEAR	TM/L	G	AB	R	H	2B	3B	HR	RBI	BB	SO	AVG	OBP	SLG	PRO+	BR/A	SB	CS	SBR	FA	FR	G/POS	TPR
1952	Cin-N	18	68	10	21	2	1	5	24	7	12	.309	.373	.588	163	5	0	0	0	.965	2	O-17	0.6
1953	Cin-N	154	606	86	173	22	7	20	100	47	83	.285	.340	.444	102	1	6	4	-1	.983	8	*O-153	0.2
1954	Cin-N	139	542	79	152	27	4	27	95	41	81	.280	.331	.494	109	5	0	3	-2	.968	5	*O-137	0.2
1955	Cin-N	13	39	1	4	2	0	0	1	9	9	.103	.271	.154	16	-5	0	0	0	1.000	2	O-11	-0.3
	Phi-N	94	323	43	88	20	2	12	37	33	43	.272	.342	.458	112	5	0	2	-1	.988	2	O-83/3-2	0.2
	Yr	107	362	44	92	22	2	12	38	42	52	.254	.333	.425	100	0	0	2	-1	.990	4	O-94/3-2	-0.1
1956	Phi-N	86	215	24	44	9	2	5	25	28	43	.205	.296	.335	71	-9	0	0	0	.991	-2	O-62	-1.4
Total	5	504	1793	243	482	82	16	69	282	165	271	.269	.332	.448	102	2	6	9	-4	.980	17	O-463/3-2	-0.5

■ **MIKE GREENWELL** Greenwell, Michael Lewis b: 7/18/63, Louisville, Ky. BL/TR, 6', 200 lbs. Deb: 9/5/85

YEAR	TM/L	G	AB	R	H	2B	3B	HR	RBI	BB	SO	AVG	OBP	SLG	PRO+	BR/A	SB	CS	SBR	FA	FR	G/POS	TPR
1985	Bos-A	17	31	7	10	1	0	4	8	3	4	.323	.382	.742	191	4	1	0	0	1.000	-5	O-17	-0.1
1986	*Bos-A	31	35	4	11	2	0	0	4	5	7	.314	.400	.371	111	1	0	0	0	1.000	-1	O-15/D-3	-0.1
1987	Bos-A	125	412	71	135	31	6	19	89	35	40	.328	.389	.570	146	27	5	4	-1	.971	1	*O-91,D-15/C-1	2.3
1988	*Bos-A★	158	590	86	192	39	8	22	119	87	38	.325	.420	.531	158	48	16	8	0	.981	7	*O-147,D-11	4.9
1989	Bos-A★	145	578	87	178	36	0	14	95	56	44	.308	.372	.443	121	17	13	5	1	.967	-4	*O-139/D-5	1.0
1990	*Bos-A	159	610	71	181	30	6	14	73	65	43	.297	.368	.434	118	15	8	7	-2	.977	4	*O-159	1.4
1991	Bos-A	147	544	76	163	26	6	9	83	43	35	.300	.354	.419	108	6	15	5	2	.989	6	*O-143/D-1	1.0
1992	Bos-A	49	180	16	42	2	0	2	18	18	19	.233	.310	.278	62	-9	2	3	-1	1.000	1	O-41/D-6	-1.1
1993	Bos-A	146	540	77	170	38	6	13	72	54	46	.315	.381	.480	122	17	5	4	-1	.993	3	*O-134,D-10	1.5
1994	Bos-A	95	327	60	88	25	1	11	45	38	26	.269	.352	.453	101	0	2	2	-1	.993	2	O-84/D-6	0.0
1995	*Bos-A	120	481	67	143	25	4	15	76	38	35	.297	.351	.459	105	3	9	5	-0	.972	0	*O-118/D-2	0.0
1996	Bos-A	77	295	35	87	20	1	7	44	18	27	.295	.340	.441	93	-3	4	0	1	.973	4	O-76	0.0
Total	12	1269	4623	657	1400	275	38	130	726	460	364	.303	.371	.463	119	125	80	43	-2	.981	18	*O-1164/D-59,C-1	10.8

■ **BILL GREENWOOD** Greenwood, William F. b: 1857, Philadelphia, Pa. d: 5/2/02, Philadelphia, Pa. BB/TL, 5'7.5", 180 lbs. Deb: 9/16/1882

YEAR	TM/L	G	AB	R	H	2B	3B	HR	RBI	BB	SO	AVG	OBP	SLG	PRO+	BR/A	SB	CS	SBR	FA	FR	G/POS	TPR
1882	Phi-a	7	30	8	9	1	0	0	1	1		.300	.323	.333	109	0				.909	-1	/O-7,2-2	-0.1
1884	Bro-a	92	385	52	83	8	3	3		10		.216	.237	.275	66	-14				.900	-8	*2-92/S-1	-1.8
1887	Bal-a	118	495	114	130	16	6	0	65	54		.263	.336	.319	88	-5	71			**.928**	7	*2-117/O-1	0.4
1888	Bal-a	115	409	69	78	13	1	0	29	30		.191	.256	.227	57	-19	46			.913	-22	2-86,S-28/O-1	-3.5
1889	Col-a	118	414	62	93	7	10	3	49	58	71	.225	.327	.312	86	-5	37			.914	-3	*2-118	-0.2
1890	Roc-a	124	437	76	97	11	6	2	41	48		.222	.310	.288	83	-8	40			.921	2	*2-123/S-1	0.1
Total	6	574	2170	381	490	56	26	8	185	201	71	.226	.298	.287	78	-51	194			.916	-26	2-538/S-30,O-9	-5.1

■ **BRIAN GREER** Greer, Brian Keith b: 5/14/59, Lynwood, Cal. BR/TR, 6'3", 210 lbs. Deb: 9/13/77

YEAR	TM/L	G	AB	R	H	2B	3B	HR	RBI	BB	SO	AVG	OBP	SLG	PRO+	BR/A	SB	CS	SBR	FA	FR	G/POS	TPR
1977	SD-N	1	1	0	0	0	0	0	0	0	1	.000	.000	.000	-99	-0	0	0	0	.000	0	H	0.0
1979	SD-N	4	3	0	0	0	0	0	0	0	1	.000	.000	.000	-99	-1	0	0	0	1.000	-1	/O-4	-0.2
Total	2	5	4	0	0	0	0	0	0	0	2	.000	.000	.000	-99	-1	0	0	0	1.000	-1	/O-4	-0.2

■ **ED GREER** Greer, Edward C. b: 1865, Philadelphia, Pa. d: 2/4/1890, Philadelphia, Pa. BR , Deb: 6/24/1885

YEAR	TM/L	G	AB	R	H	2B	3B	HR	RBI	BB	SO	AVG	OBP	SLG	PRO+	BR/A	SB	CS	SBR	FA	FR	G/POS	TPR
1885	Bal-a	56	211	32	42	7	0	0	21	8		.199	.235	.232	49	-12				.908	-0	O-47,C-12	-1.2
1886	Bal-a	11	38	2	5	1	0	0	4	2		.132	.175	.158	5	-4	4			.875	-2	/O-9,C-2	-0.5
	Phi-a	71	264	33	51	5	3	1	20	8		.193	.223	.246	46	-17	12			.921	6	O-70/C-1	-1.1
	Yr	82	302	35	56	6	3	1	24	10		.185	.217	.235	41	-21	16			.919	4	O-79/C-3	-1.6
1887	Phi-a	3	11	1	2	0	0	0	0	0		.182	.182	.182	2	-1	2			.857	0	/O-3	-0.1
	Bro-a	91	327	49	83	13	2	2	48	25		.254	.318	.324	78	-9	33			.921	3	O-76,C-16	-0.5
	Yr	94	338	50	85	13	2	2	48	25		.251	.314	.320	76	-11	35			.918	3	O-79,C-16	-0.6
Total	3	232	851	117	183	26	5	3	93	43		.215	.261	.268	58	-44	51			.916	6	O-205/C-31	-3.4

■ **RUSTY GREER** Greer, Thurman Clyde b: 1/21/69, Fort Rucker, Ala. BL/TL, 6', 190 lbs. Deb: 5/16/94

YEAR	TM/L	G	AB	R	H	2B	3B	HR	RBI	BB	SO	AVG	OBP	SLG	PRO+	BR/A	SB	CS	SBR	FA	FR	G/POS	TPR
1994	Tex-A	80	277	36	87	16	1	10	46	46	46	.314	.415	.487	132	15	0	0	0	.976	-7	O-73/1-9	0.5
1995	Tex-A	131	417	58	113	21	2	13	61	55	66	.271	.357	.424	100	0	3	1	0	.982	-15	*O-125/1-3	-1.6
1996	*Tex-A	139	542	96	180	41	6	18	100	62	86	.332	.404	.530	127	23	9	0	3	.984	8	*O-137/1-1,D-1	2.7
1997	Tex-A	157	601	112	193	42	3	26	87	83	87	.321	.406	.531	135	32	9	5	-0	.965	-2	*O-153/D-2	2.5
1998	*Tex-A	155	598	107	183	31	5	16	108	80	93	.306	.391	.455	114	15	2	4	-2	.990	3	*O-154	1.2
Total	5	662	2435	409	756	151	17	83	402	326	378	.310	.395	.489	122	85	23	10	1	.979	-12	O-642/1-13,D-3	5.3

■ **TOMMY GREGG** Gregg, William Thomas b: 7/29/63, Boone, N.C. BL/TL, 6'1", 190 lbs. Deb: 9/14/87

YEAR	TM/L	G	AB	R	H	2B	3B	HR	RBI	BB	SO	AVG	OBP	SLG	PRO+	BR/A	SB	CS	SBR	FA	FR	G/POS	TPR
1987	Pit-N	10	8	3	2	1	0	0	0	0	2	.250	.250	.375	62	-0	0	0	0	1.000	-2	/O-4	-0.2
1988	Pit-N	14	15	4	3	1	0	1	3	1	4	.200	.250	.467	103	-0	0	1	-1	1.000	-2	/O-6	-0.3
	Atl-N	11	29	1	10	3	0	0	4	2	2	.345	.387	.448	132	1	0	0	0	1.000	2	/O-7	0.3
	Yr	25	44	5	13	4	0	1	7	3	6	.295	.340	.455	125	1	0	1	-1	1.000	0	O-13	0.0
1989	Atl-N	102	276	24	67	8	0	6	23	18	45	.243	.289	.337	76	-9	3	4	-2	.967	-10	O-48,1-37	-2.5
1990	Atl-N	124	239	18	63	13	1	5	32	20	39	.264	.323	.389	90	-3	4	3	-1	.987	-2	1-50,O-20	-0.9
1991	*Atl-N	72	107	13	20	8	1	1	4	12	24	.187	.275	.308	60	-6	2	2	-1	1.000	-2	O-14,1-13	-0.9
1992	Atl-N	18	19	1	5	0	0	1	1	1	7	.263	.300	.421	96	-0	1	0	0	1.000	-1	/O-9	-0.1

YEAR	TM/L	G	AB	R	H	2B	3B	HR	RBI	BB	SO	AVG	OBP	SLG	PRO+	BR/A	SB	CS	SBR	FA	FR	G/POS	TPR
1993	Cin-N	10	12	1	2	0	0	0	1	0	0	.167	.167	.167	-10	-2	0	0	0	1.000	-1	/O-4	-0.3
1995	Fla-N	72	156	20	37	5	0	6	20	16	33	.237	.316	.385	83	-4	3	1	0	.984	-3	O-38/1-2	-0.8
1997	*Atl-N	13	19	1	5	2	0	0	0	1	2	.263	.300	.368	73	-1	1	1	-0	1.000	-2	/O-6,1-1	-0.3
Total	9	446	880	86	214	41	2	20	88	71	158	.243	.303	.363	81	-24	14	12	-3	.981	-22	O-156,1-103	-6.0

■ ED GREMMINGER
Gremminger, Lorenzo Edward "Battleship" b: 3/30/1874, Canton, Ohio d: 5/26/42, Canton, Ohio BR/TR, 6'1", 200 lbs. Deb: 4/21/1895

YEAR	TM/L	G	AB	R	H	2B	3B	HR	RBI	BB	SO	AVG	OBP	SLG	PRO+	BR/A	SB	CS	SBR	FA	FR	G/POS	TPR
1895	Cle-N	20	78	10	21	1	0	0	15	5	13	.269	.313	.282	51	-6	0			.873	-1	3-20	-0.5
1902	Bos-N	140	522	55	134	20	12	1	65	39		.257	.314	.347	100	1	7			**.951**	3	*3-140	0.6
1903	Bos-N	140	511	57	135	24	9	5	56	31		.264	.313	.376	100	-2	12			.935	16	*3-140	1.5
1904	Det-A	83	309	18	66	13	3	1	28	14		.214	.257	.285	73	-10	3			.950	-16	3-83	-2.6
Total	4	383	1420	140	356	58	24	7	164	89	13	.251	.301	.340	92	-16	22			.940	2	3-383	-1.0

■ BUDDY GREMP
Gremp, Lewis Edward b: 8/5/19, Denver, Col. d: 1/30/95, Manteca, Cal. BR/TR, 6'1", 175 lbs. Deb: 9/13/40

YEAR	TM/L	G	AB	R	H	2B	3B	HR	RBI	BB	SO	AVG	OBP	SLG	PRO+	BR/A	SB	CS	SBR	FA	FR	G/POS	TPR
1940	Bos-N	4	9	0	2	0	0	0	2	0	0	.222	.222	.222	24	-1	0			1.000	-0	/1-3	-0.1
1941	Bos-N	37	75	7	18	3	0	0	10	5	3	.240	.287	.280	63	-4	0			.977	-3	1-21/2-6,C-3	-0.8
1942	Bos-N	72	207	12	45	11	0	3	19	13	21	.217	.267	.314	71	-8	1			.991	1	1-62/3-1	-1.1
Total	3	113	291	19	65	14	0	3	31	18	24	.223	.271	.302	67	-13	1			.988	-3	/1-86,2-6,C-3,3-1	-2.0

■ REDDY GREY
Grey, Romer Carl (b: Romer Carl Gray) b: 4/8/1875, Zanesville, Ohio d: 11/9/34, Altadena, Cal. BL/TL, 5'11", 175 lbs. Deb: 5/28/03

YEAR	TM/L	G	AB	R	H	2B	3B	HR	RBI	BB	SO	AVG	OBP	SLG	PRO+	BR/A	SB	CS	SBR	FA	FR	G/POS	TPR
1903	Pit-N	1	3	1	1	0	0	0	1	1		.333	.500	.333	135	0	0			1.000	-0	/O-1	0.0

■ BILL GREY
Grey, William Tobin b: 4/15/1871, Philadelphia, Pa. d: 12/8/32, Philadelphia, Pa. 5'11", 175 lbs. Deb: 5/14/1890

YEAR	TM/L	G	AB	R	H	2B	3B	HR	RBI	BB	SO	AVG	OBP	SLG	PRO+	BR/A	SB	CS	SBR	FA	FR	G/POS	TPR
1890	Phi-N	34	128	20	31	8	4	0	21	6	3	.242	.287	.367	88	-3	5			1.000	-11	O-10/3-8,2-8,C-7,1	-1.1
1891	Phi-N	23	75	11	18	0	0	0	7	3	10	.240	.296	.240	55	-4	3			.804	-6	C-11,O-10/S-3,3-1	-0.8
1895	Cin-N	52	181	24	55	17	4	1	29	15	8	.304	.364	.459	107	1	4			.906	-4	3-27,2-16/S-5,CO	-0.1
1896	Cin-N	46	121	15	25	2	1	0	17	19	11	.207	.314	.240	44	-10	6			.927	1	2-12,C-11/S-8,O13	-0.6
1898	Pit-N	137	528	56	121	17	5	0	67	28		.229	.283	.280	63	-26	5			.879	-20	*3-137	-4.2
Total	5	292	1033	126	250	44	14	1	141	71	32	.242	.303	.315	72	-41	23			.879	-40	3-174/2-36,COS1	-6.8

■ BOBBY GRICH
Grich, Robert Anthony b: 1/15/49, Muskegon, Mich. BR/TR, 6'2", 190 lbs. Deb: 6/29/70

YEAR	TM/L	G	AB	R	H	2B	3B	HR	RBI	BB	SO	AVG	OBP	SLG	PRO+	BR/A	SB	CS	SBR	FA	FR	G/POS	TPR
1970	Bal-A	30	95	11	20	1	3	0	8	9	21	.211	.279	.284	55	-6	1	1	-0	.915	2	S-20/2-9,3-1	-0.1
1971	Bal-A	7	30	7	9	0	0	1	6	5	8	.300	.400	.400	128	1	1	0	0	1.000	3	/S-5,2-2	0.5
1972	Bal-A★	133	460	66	128	21	3	12	50	53	96	.278	.362	.415	127	16	13	6	0	.950	-25	S-81,2-45,1-16,/3-8	0.4
1973	*Bal-A	162	581	82	146	29	7	12	50	107	91	.251	.374	.387	116	16	17	9	-0	**.995**	21	*2-162	4.7
1974	*Bal-A★	160	582	92	153	29	6	19	82	90	117	.263	.380	.431	137	31	17	11	-2	.979	9	*2-160	4.8
1975	Bal-A	150	524	81	136	26	4	13	57	107	88	.260	.393	.399	133	28	14	10	-2	.977	24	*2-150	5.8
1976	Bal-A★	144	518	93	138	31	4	13	54	86	99	.266	.374	.417	140	28	14	6	1	.985	-2	*2-140/3-2,D-2	3.9
1977	Cal-A	52	181	24	44	6	0	7	23	37	40	.243	.374	.392	114	5	6	6	-2	.983	-3	S-52	0.6
1978	Cal-A	144	487	68	122	16	2	6	42	75	83	.251	.359	.329	98	2	4	3	-1	.983	0	*2-144	1.2
1979	*Cal-A★	153	534	78	157	30	5	30	101	59	84	.294	.366	.537	145	33	1	3	-2	.984	1	*2-153	4.2
1980	Cal-A★	150	498	60	135	22	2	14	62	84	108	.271	.381	.408	119	16	3	7	-3	.989	3	*2-146/1-3	2.5
1981	Cal-A	100	352	56	107	14	2	**22**	61	40	71	.304	.381	**.543**	**164**	28	2	4	-2	.983	11	*2-100	4.5
1982	*Cal-A★	145	506	74	132	28	5	19	65	82	109	.261	.372	.449	124	19	3	3	-1	.986	11	*2-142/D-1	3.6
1983	Cal-A	120	387	65	113	17	0	16	62	76	62	.292	.417	.460	142	26	2	4	-2	.969	16	*2-118/S-1	4.5
1984	Cal-A	116	363	60	93	15	1	18	58	57	70	.256	.360	.452	124	13	2	5	-2	.982	3	2-91,1-25,3-21	1.5
1985	Cal-A	144	479	74	116	17	3	13	53	81	77	.242	.355	.372	100	2	3	5	-2	**.997**	15	*2-116,1-16,3-15,/D	1.8
1986	*Cal-A	98	313	42	84	18	0	9	30	39	54	.268	.355	.412	109	5	1	3	-2	.980	-10	2-87,1-11/3-2	-0.4
Total	17	2008	6890	1033	1833	320	47	224	864	1087	1278	.266	.373	.424	125	264	104	83	-19	.984	80	*2-1765,S-159/13D	44.0

■ TIM GRIESENBECK
Griesenbeck, Carlos Phillipe Timothy
b: 12/10/1897, San Antonio, Tex. d: 3/25/53, San Antonio, Tex. BR/TR, 5'10.5", 190 lbs. Deb: 9/11/20

YEAR	TM/L	G	AB	R	H	2B	3B	HR	RBI	BB	SO	AVG	OBP	SLG	PRO+	BR/A	SB	CS	SBR	FA	FR	G/POS	TPR
1920	StL-N	5	3	1	1	0	0	0	0	0	0	.333	.333	.333	95	-0	0	0	0	1.000	0	/C-3	0.0

■ BEN GRIEVE
Grieve, Benjamin b: 5/4/76, Arlington, Tex. BL/TR, 6'4", 220 lbs. Deb: 9/3/97 F

YEAR	TM/L	G	AB	R	H	2B	3B	HR	RBI	BB	SO	AVG	OBP	SLG	PRO+	BR/A	SB	CS	SBR	FA	FR	G/POS	TPR
1997	Oak-A	24	93	12	29	6	0	3	24	13	25	.312	.402	.473	129	4	0	0	0	1.000	-1	O-24	0.3
1998	Oak-A★	155	583	94	168	41	2	18	89	85	123	.288	.387	.458	122	22	2	2	-1	.993	-7	*O-151/D-3	1.0
Total	2	179	676	106	197	47	2	21	113	98	148	.291	.389	.460	123	26	2	2	-1	.994	-8	O-175/D-3	1.3

■ TOM GRIEVE
Grieve, Thomas Alan b: 3/4/48, Pittsfield, Mass. BR/TR, 6'2", 190 lbs. Deb: 7/5/70 F

YEAR	TM/L	G	AB	R	H	2B	3B	HR	RBI	BB	SO	AVG	OBP	SLG	PRO+	BR/A	SB	CS	SBR	FA	FR	G/POS	TPR
1970	Was-A	47	116	12	23	5	1	3	10	14	38	.198	.290	.336	76	-4	0	0	0	.939	-7	O-39	-1.3
1972	Tex-A	64	142	12	29	2	1	3	11	11	39	.204	.271	.296	72	-5	1	3	-2	.985	-4	O-49	-1.4
1973	Tex-A	66	123	22	38	6	0	7	21	7	25	.309	.351	.528	151	8	1	0	0	1.000	-12	O-59/D-1	-0.6
1974	Tex-A	84	259	30	66	10	4	9	32	20	48	.255	.313	.429	114	4	0	0	0	1.000	2	D-40,O-38/1-1	0.3
1975	Tex-A	118	369	46	102	17	1	14	61	22	74	.276	.317	.442	113	5	0	2	-1	.990	-7	O-63,D-45	-0.6
1976	Tex-A	149	546	57	139	23	3	20	81	35	119	.255	.304	.418	108	3	4	1	1	.983	2	D-96,O-52	0.1
1977	Tex-A	79	236	24	53	9	0	7	30	13	57	.225	.274	.352	68	-11	1	0	0	.976	-6	O-60,D-13	-1.9
1978	NY-N	54	101	5	21	3	0	2	8	9	23	.208	.273	.297	61	-5	0	1	-1	.979	1	O-26/1-2	-0.7
1979	StL-N	9	15	1	3	1	0	0	0	4	1	.200	.368	.267	76	-0	0	0	0	.875	-1	/O-5	-0.1
Total	9	670	1907	209	474	76	10	65	254	135	424	.249	.303	.401	100	-6	7	7	-2	.982	-31	O-391,D-195/1-3	-6.2

■ KEN GRIFFEY
Griffey, George Kenneth Jr. "Junior" b: 11/21/69, Donora, Pa. BL/TL, 6'3", 205 lbs. Deb: 4/3/89 F

YEAR	TM/L	G	AB	R	H	2B	3B	HR	RBI	BB	SO	AVG	OBP	SLG	PRO+	BR/A	SB	CS	SBR	FA	FR	G/POS	TPR
1989	Sea-A	127	455	61	120	23	0	16	61	44	83	.264	.331	.420	107	4	16	7	1	.969	5	*O-127	0.6
1990	Sea-A★	155	597	91	179	28	7	22	80	63	81	.300	.369	.481	134	27	16	11	-2	.980	1	*O-151/D-2	2.2
1991	Sea-A★	154	548	76	179	42	1	22	100	71	82	.327	.405	.527	156	42	18	6	2	.989	9	*O-152/D-1	4.9
1992	Sea-A★	142	565	83	174	39	4	27	103	44	67	.308	.363	.535	148	34	10	5	0	.997	6	*O-137/D-3	3.7
1993	Sea-A★	156	582	113	180	38	3	45	109	96	91	.309	.412	.617	170	58	17	9	-0	.991	2	*O-139,D-19/1-1	5.3
1994	Sea-A★	111	433	94	140	24	4	**40**	90	56	73	.323	.403	.674	168	43	11	3	2	.983	6	*O-103/D-9	4.2
1995	*Sea-A†	72	260	52	67	7	0	17	42	52	53	.258	.381	.481	121	9	4	2	0	.990	10	O-70/D-2	1.5
1996	Sea-A†	140	545	125	165	26	2	49	140	78	104	.303	.397	.628	153	44	16	1	4	.990	16	*O-137/D-5	5.4
1997	*Sea-A★	157	608	**125**	185	34	3	**56**	**147**	76	121	.304	.389	**.646**	165	57	15	4	2	.985	14	*O-153/D-4	**6.4**
1998	Sea-A★	161	633	120	180	33	3	**56**	146	76	121	.284	.367	.611	148	43	20	5	3	.988	15	*O-158/1-1,D-3	5.3
Total	10	1375	5226	940	1569	294	27	350	1018	656	876	.300	.382	.568	149	360	143	53	11	.986	81	*O-1327/D-48,1-2	39.5

■ KEN GRIFFEY
Griffey, George Kenneth Sr. b: 4/10/50, Donora, Pa. BL/TL, 6', 200 lbs. Deb: 8/25/73 FC

YEAR	TM/L	G	AB	R	H	2B	3B	HR	RBI	BB	SO	AVG	OBP	SLG	PRO+	BR/A	SB	CS	SBR	FA	FR	G/POS	TPR
1973	*Cin-N	25	86	19	33	5	1	3	14	6	10	.384	.424	.570	182	9	4	2	0	1.000	-3	O-21	0.5
1974	Cin-N	88	227	24	57	9	5	2	19	27	43	.251	.333	.361	96	-1	9	4	0	1.000	-4	O-70	-0.4
1975	*Cin-N	132	463	95	141	15	9	4	46	67	67	.305	.394	.402	119	14	16	7	1	.967	-5	*O-119	0.5
1976	*Cin-N★	148	562	111	189	28	9	6	74	62	65	.336	.403	.450	139	30	34	11	4	.979	-1	*O-144	2.8
1977	Cin-N☆	154	585	117	186	35	8	12	57	69	84	.318	.390	.467	126	23	17	8	0	.990	9	*O-147	2.7
1978	Cin-N	158	614	90	177	33	8	10	63	54	70	.288	.346	.417	112	9	23	5	4	.969	4	*O-154	1.1
1979	Cin-N	95	380	62	120	27	4	8	32	36	39	.316	.376	.471	129	15	12	5	1	.984	-3	O-93	0.9
1980	Cin-N★	146	544	89	160	28	10	13	85	62	77	.294	.367	.454	128	21	23	1	6	.978	-0	*O-138	2.2
1981	Cin-N	101	396	65	123	21	6	2	34	39	42	.311	.374	.409	120	11	12	4	1	.989	10	O-99	2.0
1982	NY-A	127	484	70	134	23	2	12	54	39	58	.277	.331	.407	103	2	10	4	1	.983	7	*O-125	0.6
1983	NY-A	118	458	60	140	21	3	11	46	34	45	.306	.356	.437	121	13	6	1	1	.992	-2	*1-101/O-14,D-2	0.6
1984	NY-A	120	399	44	109	20	1	7	56	29	32	.273	.324	.381	98	-1	2	2	-1	.974	-0	O-82,1-27/D-2	-0.6
1985	NY-A	127	438	68	120	28	4	10	69	41	51	.274	.336	.425	109	5	7	7	-2	.970	5	*O-110/1-1,D-7	0.4
1986	NY-A	59	198	33	60	7	0	9	26	15	24	.303	.355	.475	125	7	2	2	-1	.971	1	O-51/D-2	0.5
	Atl-N	80	292	36	90	15	3	12	32	20	43	.308	.353	.503	126	10	12	7	-1	.986	1	O-77/1-1	0.8
1987	Atl-N	122	399	65	114	24	1	14	64	46	54	.286	.361	.456	109	6	4	7	-3	.995	1	*O-107/1-3	0.0
1988	Atl-N	69	193	21	48	5	0	2	19	17	26	.249	.310	.306	74	-6	1	3	-2	.969	-4	O-42,1-11	-1.5
	Cin-N	25	50	5	14	1	0	2	4	2	5	.280	.308	.420	103	0	0	0	0	.986	-0	1-10	0.1

YEAR	TM/L	G	AB	R	H	2B	3B	HR	RBI	BB	SO	AVG	OBP	SLG	PRO+	BR/A	SB	CS	SBR	FA	FR	G/POS	TPR
	Yr	94	243	26	62	6	0	4	23	19	31	.255	.309	.329	80	-6	1	3	-2	.969	-4	O-42,1-21	-1.6
1989	Cin-N	106	236	26	62	8	3	8	30	29	42	.263	.346	.424	115	5	4	2	0	.987	-8	O-58/1-9	-0.5
1990	Cin-N	46	63	6	13	2	0	1	8	2	5	.206	.242	.286	43	-5	2	1	0	.979	0	/1-9,O-6	-0.5
	Sea-A	21	77	13	29	2	0	3	18	10	3	.377	.448	.519	168	7	0	0	0	.963	-2	O-20	0.5
1991	Sea-A	30	85	10	24	7	0	1	9	13	13	.282	.384	.400	117	2	0	0	0	1.000	-4	O-26/D-1	-0.2
Total	19	2097	7229	1129	2143	364	77	152	859	719	898	.296	.361	.431	118	175	200	83	10	.981	4	*O-1703,1-172/D-14	12.3

■ ALFREDO GRIFFIN

Griffin, Alfredo Claudino (b: Alfredo Claudino Baptist (Griffin))
b: 10/6/57, Santo Domingo, D.R. BB/TR, 5′11″, 165 lbs. Deb: 9/4/76 C

YEAR	TM/L	G	AB	R	H	2B	3B	HR	RBI	BB	SO	AVG	OBP	SLG	PRO+	BR/A	SB	CS	SBR	FA	FR	G/POS	TPR
1976	Cle-A	12	4	0	1	0	0	0	0	0	2	.250	.250	.250	47	-0	0	1	-1	.750	0	/S-6,D-4	0.0
1977	Cle-A	14	41	5	6	1	0	0	3	3	5	.146	.205	.171	4	-5	2	2	-1	.940	-1	S-13/D-1	-0.6
1978	Cle-A	5	4	1	2	1	0	0	0	2	1	.500	.667	.750	301	1	0	0	0	.917	3	/S-2	0.4
1979	Tor-A	153	624	81	179	22	10	2	31	40	59	.287	.335	.364	87	-11	21	16	-3	.956	6	*S-153	0.9
1980	Tor-A	155	653	63	166	26	**15**	2	41	24	58	.254	.285	.349	70	-28	18	23	-8	.955	2	*S-155	-1.7
1981	Tor-A	101	388	30	81	19	6	0	21	17	38	.209	.244	.289	50	-25	8	12	-5	.937	-19	S-97/3-4,2-1	-4.2
1982	Tor-A	162	539	57	130	20	8	1	48	22	48	.241	.271	.314	55	-34	10	8	-2	.968	6	*S-162	-1.4
1983	Tor-A	162	528	62	132	22	9	4	47	27	44	.250	.290	.348	71	-22	8	11	-4	.965	-4	*S-157/2-5,D-1	-1.5
1984	Tor-A★	140	419	53	101	8	2	4	30	4	33	.241	.250	.298	49	-29	11	3	2	.962	-5	*S-115,2-21/D-5	-2.2
1985	Oak-A	162	614	75	166	18	7	2	64	20	50	.270	.293	.332	77	-21	24	9	2	.960	-15	*S-162	-1.8
1986	Oak-A	162	594	74	169	23	6	4	51	35	52	.285	.326	.364	95	-5	33	16	0	.966	-11	*S-162	-0.1
1987	Oak-A	144	494	69	130	23	5	3	60	28	41	.263	.308	.348	79	-15	26	13	0	.963	0	*S-137/2-1	-0.3
1988	*LA-N	95	316	39	63	8	3	1	27	24	30	.199	.260	.253	49	-21	7	5	-1	.965	2	S-93	-1.3
1989	LA-N	136	506	49	125	27	2	0	29	29	57	.247	.288	.308	72	-19	10	7	-1	.975	-8	*S-131	-1.9
1990	LA-N	141	461	38	97	11	3	1	35	29	65	.210	.260	.254	43	-36	6	3	0	.959	10	*S-139	-1.6
1991	LA-N	109	350	27	85	6	2	0	27	22	49	.243	.290	.271	60	-18	5	4	-1	.961	19	*S-109	0.8
1992	*Tor-A	63	150	21	35	7	0	0	10	9	19	.233	.277	.280	54	-9	3	1	0	.981	-1	S-48,2-16	-0.7
1993	*Tor-A	46	95	15	20	3	0	0	3	3	13	.211	.235	.242	28	-10	0	0	0	.960	4	S-20,2-11/3-6	-0.4
Total	18	1962	6780	759	1688	245	78	24	527	338	664	.249	.287	.319	67	-306	192	134	-23	.961	-10	*S-1861/2-55,D-11,3	-17.6

■ DOUG GRIFFIN

Griffin, Douglas Lee b: 6/4/47, South Gate, Cal. BR/TR, 6′, 170 lbs. Deb: 9/11/70

YEAR	TM/L	G	AB	R	H	2B	3B	HR	RBI	BB	SO	AVG	OBP	SLG	PRO+	BR/A	SB	CS	SBR	FA	FR	G/POS	TPR
1970	Cal-A	18	55	2	7	1	0	0	4	6	5	.127	.213	.145	1	-7	0	0	0	.964	1	2-11/3-8	-0.6
1971	Bos-A	125	483	51	118	23	2	3	27	31	45	.244	.293	.319	68	-20	11	5	0	.986	7	*2-124	-0.3
1972	Bos-A	129	470	43	122	12	1	2	35	45	48	.260	.327	.302	83	-8	9	2	2	.978	2	*2-129	0.3
1973	Bos-A	113	396	43	101	14	5	1	33	21	42	.255	.298	.323	71	-16	7	5	-1	.990	-14	*2-113	-2.5
1974	Bos-A	93	312	35	83	12	4	0	33	28	21	.266	.330	.330	85	-6	2	8	-4	.979	-13	2-91/S-1	-2.0
1975	*Bos-A	100	287	21	69	6	0	1	29	18	29	.240	.290	.272	55	-17	2	2	-1	.967	-10	2-99/S-1	-2.4
1976	Bos-A	49	127	14	24	2	0	0	4	9	14	.189	.248	.205	30	-11	2	1	0	.989	-1	2-44/D-2	-1.1
1977	Bos-A	5	6	0	0	0	0	0	0	0	0	.000	.000	.000	-90	-2	0	0	0	1.000	0	/2-3	-0.1
Total	8	632	2136	209	524	70	12	7	165	158	204	.245	.301	.299	68	-87	33	23	-4	.981	-28	2-614/3-8,D-2,S-2	-8.7

■ PUG GRIFFIN

Griffin, Francis Arthur b: 4/24/1896, Lincoln, Neb. d: 10/12/51, Colorado Springs, Colo. BR/TR, 5′11.5″, 187 lbs. Deb: 7/27/17

YEAR	TM/L	G	AB	R	H	2B	3B	HR	RBI	BB	SO	AVG	OBP	SLG	PRO+	BR/A	SB	CS	SBR	FA	FR	G/POS	TPR
1917	Phi-A	18	25	4	5	1	0	1	3	1	9	.200	.231	.360	81	-1	1			1.000	1	/1-3	0.0
1920	NY-N	5	4	0	1	0	0	0	0	1	2	.250	.400	.250	90	0	0	0	0	1.000	-1	/O-2	-0.1
Total	2	23	29	4	6	1	0	1	3	2	11	.207	.258	.345	83	-1	1	0		1.000	-0	/1-3,O-2	-0.1

■ IVY GRIFFIN

Griffin, Ivy Moore b: 11/16/1896, Thomasville, Ala. d: 8/25/57, Gainesville, Fla. BL/TR, 5′11″, 180 lbs. Deb: 9/9/19

YEAR	TM/L	G	AB	R	H	2B	3B	HR	RBI	BB	SO	AVG	OBP	SLG	PRO+	BR/A	SB	CS	SBR	FA	FR	G/POS	TPR
1919	Phi-A	17	68	5	20	2	2	0	6	3	10	.294	.333	.382	99	-0	0			.989	4	1-17	0.3
1920	Phi-A	129	467	46	111	15	1	0	20	17	49	.238	.281	.274	47	-36	3	3	-1	.990	5	*1-127/2-2	-3.4
1921	Phi-A	39	103	14	33	4	2	0	13	5	6	.320	.369	.398	95	-1	1	2	-1	.973	-2	1-27	-0.4
Total	3	185	638	65	164	21	5	0	39	25	65	.257	.301	.306	60	-36	4	5		.988	7	1-171/2-2	-3.5

■ MIKE GRIFFIN

Griffin, Michael Joseph b: 3/20/1865, Utica, N.Y. d: 4/10/08, Utica, N.Y. BL/TR, 5′7″, 160 lbs. Deb: 4/16/1887 M

YEAR	TM/L	G	AB	R	H	2B	3B	HR	RBI	BB	SO	AVG	OBP	SLG	PRO+	BR/A	SB	CS	SBR	FA	FR	G/POS	TPR
1887	Bal-a	136	532	142	160	32	13	3	94	55		.301	.375	.427	131	24	94			.924	-12	*O-136	0.8
1888	Bal-a	137	542	103	139	21	11	0	46	55		.256	.331	.336	117	12	46			.938	7	*O-137	1.4
1889	Bal-a	137	531	**152**	148	21	14	4	48	91	29	.279	.387	.394	120	17	39			.910	-10	*O-109,S-25/2-5	0.4
1890	Phi-P	115	489	127	140	29	6	6	54	64	19	.286	.377	.407	107	5	30			**.954**	18	*O-115	1.5
1891	Bro-N	134	521	106	139	**36**	9	3	65	57	31	.267	.340	.388	113	8	65			**.960**	26	*O-134	2.6
1892	Bro-N	129	452	103	125	17	11	3	66	68	36	.277	.376	.383	135	21	49			**.986**	13	*O-127/S-2	2.7
1893	Bro-N	95	362	85	103	21	7	6	59	59	23	.285	.396	.431	126	15	30			**.965**	9	*O-93/2-2	1.6
1894	Bro-N	107	402	122	144	28	4	5	75	78	14	.358	.467	.485	140	32	39			.969	7	*O-106	2.4
1895	Bro-N	131	519	140	173	38	7	4	65	93	29	.333	.444	.457	144	41	27			**.969**	14	*O-131/S-1	3.6
1896	Bro-N	122	493	101	152	27	9	4	51	48	25	.308	.380	.424	118	14	23			.961	3	*O-122	0.6
1897	Bro-N	134	534	136	169	25	11	2	56	81		.316	.416	.416	127	26	16			.956	5	*O-134	1.8
1898	Bro-N	134	537	88	161	18	6	2	40	60		.300	.379	.367	114	12	15			**.974**	10	*O-134,M	1.1
Total	12	1511	5914	1405	1753	313	108	42	719	809	206	.296	.388	.407	124	228	473			.956	88	*O-1478/S-28,2-7	20.5

■ THOMAS GRIFFIN

Griffin, Thomas William b: 1/1857, Titusville, Pa. d: 4/17/33, Rockford, Ill. Deb: 9/27/1884

YEAR	TM/L	G	AB	R	H	2B	3B	HR	RBI	BB	SO	AVG	OBP	SLG	PRO+	BR/A	SB	CS	SBR	FA	FR	G/POS	TPR
1884	Mil-U	11	41	5	9	2	0	0		3		.220	.273	.268	119	-2				.918	-2	1-11	-0.4

■ SANDY GRIFFIN

Griffin, Tobias Charles b: 10/24/1858, Fayetteville, N.Y d: 6/4/26, Syracuse, N.Y. BR/TR, 5′10″, 160 lbs. Deb: 5/26/1884 M

YEAR	TM/L	G	AB	R	H	2B	3B	HR	RBI	BB	SO	AVG	OBP	SLG	PRO+	BR/A	SB	CS	SBR	FA	FR	G/POS	TPR
1884	NY-N	16	62	7	11	2	0	0	6	1	19	.177	.190	.210	25	-5				.842	-3	O-16	-0.8
1890	Roc-a	107	407	85	125	28	4	5	53	50		.307	.388	.432	153	28	21			.856	-19	*O-107/2-1	0.5
1891	Was-a	20	69	15	19	4	2	0	10	10	3	.275	.398	.391	132	4	2			.939	-3	O-20,M	0.0
1893	StL-N	23	92	9	18	1	1	0	9	16	2	.196	.315	.228	45	-7	2			.906	-2	O-23	-0.8
Total	4	166	630	116	173	35	7	5	78	77	24	.275	.361	.376	120	19	25			.873	-27	O-166/2-1	-1.1

■ BERT GRIFFITH

Griffith, Bartholomew Joseph "Buck" b: 3/30/1896, St.Louis, Mo. d: 5/5/73, Bishop, Cal. BR/TR, 5′11″, 185 lbs. Deb: 4/13/22

YEAR	TM/L	G	AB	R	H	2B	3B	HR	RBI	BB	SO	AVG	OBP	SLG	PRO+	BR/A	SB	CS	SBR	FA	FR	G/POS	TPR
1922	Bro-N	106	325	45	100	22	8	2	35	5	11	.308	.322	.443	96	-3	5	7	-3	.981	-1	O-77/1-6	-1.2
1923	Bro-N	79	248	23	73	8	4	2	37	13	16	.294	.332	.383	91	-4	1	2	-1	.949	-8	O-62	-1.5
1924	Was-A	6	8	1	1	0	0	0	0	0	1	.125	.125	.125	-37	-2	0	0	0	1.000	0	/O-2	-0.1
Total	3	191	581	69	174	30	12	4	72	18	28	.299	.324	.413	92	-8	6	9	-4	.968	-9	O-141/1-6	-2.8

■ CLARK GRIFFITH

Griffith, Clark Calvin "The Old Fox"
b: 11/20/1869, Clear Creek, Mo. d: 10/27/55, Washington, D.C. BR/TR, 5′6.5″, 156 lbs. Deb: 4/11/1891 MH

YEAR	TM/L	G	AB	R	H	2B	3B	HR	RBI	BB	SO	AVG	OBP	SLG	PRO+	BR/A	SB	CS	SBR	FA	FR	G/POS	TPR
1891	StL-a	27	77	11	12	1	0	1	8	8	15	.156	.253	.208	28	-8	2			.930	0	P-27	0.0
	Bos-a	10	23	6	4	1	1	1	3	6	5	.174	.367	.435	131	1	1			.778	-1	/P-7,O-3	0.0
	Yr	37	100	17	16	2	1	2	11	14	20	.160	.282	.260	50	-7	3			.909	1	P 34/O-3	0.0
1893	Chi-N	4	11	1	2	0	0	0	2	0	1	.182	.182	.182	-3	-2	0			1.000	1	/P-4	0.0
1894	Chi-N	46	142	27	33	5	4	0	15	23	9	.232	.339	.324	58	-10	6			.942	-3	P-36/O-7,S-1	-0.4
1895	Chi-N	43	144	20	46	3	0	1	27	16	9	.319	.391	.361	89	-2	2			.923	1	P-42/O-1	0.0
1896	Chi-N	38	135	22	36	5	2	1	16	9	7	.267	.313	.356	73	-6	3			.917	1	P-36	0.0
1897	Chi-N	46	162	27	38	8	4	0	21	18		.235	.311	.333	67	-8	2			.947	2	P-41/O-2,S-2,3-1,1	-0.1
1898	Chi-N	38	122	15	20	2	3	0	15	13		.164	.244	.230	36	-10	1			.952	1	P-38	0.0
1899	Chi-N	39	120	15	31	5	0	0	14	14		.258	.346	.300	80	-3	2			.933	6	P-38/S-1	-0.1
1900	Chi-N	30	95	16	24	4	1	1	7	8		.253	.311	.347	84	-2	2			.917	-1	P-30	0.0
1901	Chi-A	35	89	21	27	3	1	2	14	23		.303	.446	.427	147	7	0			.946	0	P-35,M	0.0
1902	Chi-A	35	92	11	20	3	0	0	8	7		.217	.273	.250	48	-6	0			**1.000**	-2	P-28/O-3,M	-0.1
1903	NY-A	25	69	5	11	4	0	1	7	11		.159	.284	.261	60	-3	1			.983	-3	P-25,M	0.0
1904	NY-A	16	42	2	6	2	0	0	1	4		.143	.217	.190	28	-3	0			.946	-1	P-16,M	0.0
1905	NY-A	26	32	2	7	1	1	0	5	3		.219	.286	.313	80	-1	0			.960	-2	P-25/O-1,M	0.0
1906	NY-A	17	18	0	2	0	0	0	1	3		.111	.238	.111	9	-2	0			1.000	1	P-17,M	0.0
1907	NY-A	5	2	0	0	0	0	0	0	0		.000	.000	.000	-93	-0	0			.800	0	/P-4,M	0.0

YEAR	TM/L	G	AB	R	H	2B	3B	HR	RBI	BB	SO	AVG	OBP	SLG	PRO+	BR/A	SB	CS	SBR	FA	FR	G/POS	TPR
1909	Cin-N	1	2	0	0	0	0	0	0	0		.000	.000	.000	-99	-0	0			1.000	1	/P-1,M	0.0
1910	Cin-N	1	0	1	0	0	0	0	0	0	0	—	—	—	—	0	0			.000	0	RM	0.0
1912	Was-A	1	1	0	0	0	0	0	0	0		.000	.000	.000	-99	-0	0			.000	1	/P-1,2-1,M	0.0
1913	Was-A	1	1	0	1	1	0	0	1	0	0	1.000	1.000	2.000	758	1	0			.000	-0	/P-1,O-1,M	0.0
1914	Was-A	1	1	0	1	1	0	0	1	0	0	1.000	1.000	2.000	769	1	0	1	-1	.000	-0	/P-1,M	0.0
Total	21	485	1380	202	321	49	17	8	166	166	46	.233	.318	.310	69	-57	22	1		.942	1	P-453/O-18,S-4,213	-0.7

■ DERRELL GRIFFITH Griffith, Robert Derrell b: 12/12/43, Anadarko, Okla. BL/TR, 6', 168 lbs. Deb: 9/26/63

YEAR	TM/L	G	AB	R	H	2B	3B	HR	RBI	BB	SO	AVG	OBP	SLG	PRO+	BR/A	SB	CS	SBR	FA	FR	G/POS	TPR
1963	LA-N	1	2	0	0	0	0	0	0	0	0	.000	.000	.000	-99	-1	0	0	0	.000	0	/2-1	-0.1
1964	LA-N	78	238	27	69	16	2	4	23	5	21	.290	.307	.424	112	2	5	1	1	.769	-12	3-35,O-29	-1.1
1965	LA-N	22	41	3	7	0	0	1	2	0	9	.171	.171	.244	16	-5	0	0	0	1.000	-0	O-11	-0.5
1966	LA-N	23	15	3	1	0	0	0	2	2	3	.067	.176	.067	-32	-3	0	0	0	1.000	-2	/O-7	-0.5
Total	4	124	296	33	77	16	2	5	27	7	33	.260	.280	.378	90	-5	5	1	1	.970	-14	/O-47,3-35,2-1	-2.2

■ TOMMY GRIFFITH Griffith, Thomas Herman b: 10/26/1889, Prospect, Ohio d: 4/13/67, Cincinnati, Ohio BL/TR, 5′10″, 175 lbs. Deb: 8/28/13

YEAR	TM/L	G	AB	R	H	2B	3B	HR	RBI	BB	SO	AVG	OBP	SLG	PRO+	BR/A	SB	CS	SBR	FA	FR	G/POS	TPR
1913	Bos-N	37	127	16	32	4	1	1	12	9	8	.252	.301	.323	77	-4	1			.886	1	O-35	-0.4
1914	Bos-N	16	48	3	5	0	0	0	1	2	6	.104	.140	.104	-27	-7	0			.931	3	O-14	-0.6
1915	Cin-N	160	583	59	179	31	16	4	85	41	34	.307	.355	.436	136	24	6	24	-13	.952	-13	*O-160	-1.0
1916	Cin-N	155	595	50	158	28	7	2	61	36	37	.266	.310	.346	104	2	16			.967	6	*O-155	-0.1
1917	Cin-N	115	363	45	98	18	7	1	45	19	23	.270	.308	.366	111	4	5			.974	6	*O-100	0.5
1918	Cin-N	118	427	47	113	10	4	2	48	39	30	.265	.326	.321	99	0	10			.969	2	*O-118	-0.5
1919	Bro-N	125	484	65	136	18	4	6	57	23	32	.281	.315	.372	104	1	8			.954	-1	*O-125	-0.9
1920	*Bro-N	93	334	41	87	9	4	2	30	15	18	.260	.292	.329	76	-11	3	3	-1	.972	-11	O-92	-3.1
1921	Bro-N	129	455	66	142	21	6	12	71	36	13	.312	.364	.464	113	8	3	3	-1	.972	7	*O-124	0.5
1922	Bro-N	99	329	44	104	17	8	4	49	23	10	.316	.361	.453	110	4	7	1	2	.952	4	O-82	0.4
1923	Bro-N	131	481	70	141	21	9	8	66	50	19	.293	.361	.424	109	7	8	2	1	.927	-7	*O-127	-0.7
1924	Bro-N	140	482	43	121	19	5	3	67	34	19	.251	.300	.330	71	-20	0	5	-3	.965	-11	*O-139	-4.3
1925	Bro-N	7	4	2	0	0	0	0	0	3	2	.000	.429	.000	20	-0	1	0	0	1.000	-1	/O-2	-0.1
	Chi-N	76	235	38	67	12	1	7	27	21	11	.285	.346	.434	97	-1	2	4	-2	.937	-3	O-60	-1.0
	Yr	83	239	40	67	12	1	7	27	24	13	.280	.348	.427	96	-2	3	4	-2	.938	-4	O-62	-1.1
Total	13	1401	4947	589	1383	208	72	52	619	351	262	.280	.328	.382	102	6	70	42		.956	-19	*O-1333	-11.3

■ ART GRIGGS Griggs, Arthur Carle b: 12/10/1883, Topeka, Kan. d: 12/19/38, Los Angeles, Cal. BR/TR, 5′11″, 185 lbs. Deb: 5/2/09

YEAR	TM/L	G	AB	R	H	2B	3B	HR	RBI	BB	SO	AVG	OBP	SLG	PRO+	BR/A	SB	CS	SBR	FA	FR	G/POS	TPR
1909	StL-A	108	364	38	102	17	5	0	43	24		.280	.330	.354	125	9	11			.982	-6	1-49,O-41/2-8,S-1	0.1
1910	StL-A	123	416	28	98	22	5	2	30	25		.236	.281	.327	96	-4	11			.878	-1	O-49,2-41,1-17,/S3	-0.8
1911	Cle-A	27	68	7	17	3	2	1	7	5		.250	.301	.397	93	-1	1			.949	-2	2-11/O-4,3-3,1-1	-0.3
1912	Cle-A	89	273	29	83	16	7	0	39	33		.304	.381	.414	123	9	10			.986	1	1-71	0.8
1914	Bro-F	40	112	10	32	6	1	1	15	5	11	.286	.328	.384	94	-3	1			.980	-3	1-27/O-1	-0.7
1915	Bro-F	27	38	4	11	1	0	1	2	3	7	.289	.372	.395	117	0	0			1.000	1	/1-5,O-1	0.1
1918	Det-A	28	99	11	36	8	0	0	16	10	5	.364	.422	.444	168	8	2			.986	-3	1-25	0.5
Total	7	442	1370	127	379	73	20	5	152	105	23	.277	.332	.370	115	19	36			.983	-13	1-195/O-96,2-60,3S	-0.3

■ DENVER GRIGSBY Grigsby, Denver Clarence b: 3/25/01, Jackson, Ky. d: 11/10/73, Sapulpa, Okla. BL/TR, 5′9″, 155 lbs. Deb: 9/1/23

YEAR	TM/L	G	AB	R	H	2B	3B	HR	RBI	BB	SO	AVG	OBP	SLG	PRO+	BR/A	SB	CS	SBR	FA	FR	G/POS	TPR
1923	Chi-N	24	72	8	21	5	2	0	5	7	5	.292	.363	.417	105	1	1	3	-2	1.000	-2	O-22	-0.4
1924	Chi-N	124	411	58	123	18	2	3	48	31	47	.299	.357	.375	95	-2	10	19	-8	.974	3	*O-121	-1.5
1925	Chi-N	51	137	20	35	5	0	0	20	19	12	.255	.346	.292	64	-7	1	1	-0	.966	-1	O-39	-1.0
Total	3	199	620	86	179	28	4	3	73	57	64	.289	.355	.361	89	-8	12	23	-10	.975	0	O-182	-2.9

■ JOHN GRIM Grim, John Helm b: 8/9/1867, Lebanon, Ky. d: 7/28/61, Indianapolis, Ind BR/TR, 6′2″, 175 lbs. Deb: 9/29/1888

YEAR	TM/L	G	AB	R	H	2B	3B	HR	RBI	BB	SO	AVG	OBP	SLG	PRO+	BR/A	SB	CS	SBR	FA	FR	G/POS	TPR
1888	Phi-N	2	7	0	1	0	0	0	0	0	0	.143	.143	.143	-8	-1	0			.000	-1	/O-1,2-1	-0.1
1890	Roc-a	50	192	30	51	6	9	2	34	7		.266	.299	.422	121	3	14			.851	-7	S-21,C-15/3-8,2O1P	0.0
1891	Mil-a	29	119	14	28	5	1	1	14	2	5	.235	.248	.319	52	-9	1			.926	3	C-16,3-10/2-3	-0.3
1892	Lou-N	97	370	40	90	16	4	1	36	13	24	.243	.280	.316	87	-7	18			.940	-10	C-69,1-11,2/OS3	-1.1
1893	Lou-N	99	415	68	111	19	8	3	54	12	10	.267	.303	.373	86	-10	15			.952	-4	*C-92/1-3,2-2,OS	-0.6
1894	Lou-N	108	410	66	122	27	7	7	70	16	15	.298	.339	.449	95	-5	14			.931	11	C-77,2-24/1-7,3-1	1.0
1895	Bro-N	93	329	54	92	17	5	0	44	13	9	.280	.321	.362	83	-9	9			.947	-0	*C-91/O-1,1-1	0.0
1896	Bro-N	81	281	32	75	13	1	2	35	12	14	.267	.311	.342	76	-10	7			.939	-1	C-77/1-5	-0.2
1897	Bro-N	80	290	26	72	10	1	0	25	1		.248	.259	.290	47	-23	3			.947	5	C-77	-0.8
1898	Bro-N	52	178	17	50	5	1	0	11	8		.281	.323	.320	85	-4	1			.950	-4	C-52	-0.3
1899	Bro-N	15	47	3	13	1	0	0	7	1		.277	.320	.298	68	-2	0			.966	1	C-12	0.0
Total	11	706	2638	350	705	119	37	16	330	85	77	.267	.302	.359	82	-76	82			.943	-7	C-578/2-44,1S3OP	-2.4

■ ROY GRIMES Grimes, Austin Roy "Bummer" b: 9/11/1893, Bergholz, Ohio d: 9/13/54, Hanover Twsp., O. BR/TR, 6′1″, 176 lbs. Deb: 7/31/20 F

YEAR	TM/L	G	AB	R	H	2B	3B	HR	RBI	BB	SO	AVG	OBP	SLG	PRO+	BR/A	SB	CS	SBR	FA	FR	G/POS	TPR
1920	NY-N	26	57	5	9	1	0	0	3	3	8	.158	.200	.175	8	-7	1	1	-0	.948	-1	2-21	-0.9

■ ED GRIMES Grimes, Edward Adelbert b: 9/8/05, Chicago, Ill. d: 10/5/74, Chicago, Ill. BR/TR, 5′10″, 165 lbs. Deb: 4/19/31

YEAR	TM/L	G	AB	R	H	2B	3B	HR	RBI	BB	SO	AVG	OBP	SLG	PRO+	BR/A	SB	CS	SBR	FA	FR	G/POS	TPR
1931	StL-A	43	57	9	15	1	2	0	5	9	3	.263	.364	.351	86	-1	1	0	0	.892	-2	3-22/2-4,S-3	-0.2
1932	StL-A	31	68	7	16	0	1	0	13	6	12	.235	.297	.265	44	-6	0	1	-1	.891	2	3-18/2-2,S-1	-0.3
Total	2	74	125	16	31	1	3	0	18	15	15	.248	.329	.304	63	-6	1	1	-0	.891	0	/3-40,2-6,S-4	-0.5

■ OSCAR GRIMES Grimes, Oscar Ray Jr. b: 4/13/15, Minerva, Ohio d: 5/19/93, Westlake, Ohio BR/TR, 5′11″, 178 lbs. Deb: 9/28/38 F

YEAR	TM/L	G	AB	R	H	2B	3B	HR	RBI	BB	SO	AVG	OBP	SLG	PRO+	BR/A	SB	CS	SBR	FA	FR	G/POS	TPR
1938	Cle-A	4	10	2	2	0	1	0	2	2	0	.200	.333	.400	85	-0	0	0	0	1.000	-1	/2-2,1-1	-0.1
1939	Cle-A	119	364	51	98	20	5	4	56	56	61	.269	.368	.385	96	-1	8	3	1	.968	-11	2-48,1-43,S-37,/3-3	-1.0
1940	Cle-A	11	13	3	0	0	0	0	0	0	5	.000	.000	.000	-99	-4	0	0	0	.958	2	/1-4,3-1	-0.2
1941	Cle-A	77	244	28	58	9	3	4	24	39	47	.238	.345	.348	88	-4	4	0	1	.995	-5	1-62,2-13/3-1	-1.1
1942	Cle-A	51	84	10	15	2	0	0	2	13	17	.179	.289	.202	42	-6	3	2	-0	.944	-3	2-24/3-8,1-1,S-1	-0.9
1943	NY-A	9	20	4	3	0	0	0	1	3	7	.150	.261	.150	21	-2	0	0	0	1.000	-1	/S-3,1-1	-0.3
1944	NY-A	116	387	44	108	17	8	5	46	59	57	.279	.377	.403	119	11	6	0	2	.945	-10	3-97,S-20	0.5
1945	NY-A†	142	480	64	127	19	7	4	45	97	73	.265	.395	.358	114	13	7	6	-2	.937	3	*3-141/1-1	1.9
1946	NY-A	14	39	1	8	1	0	0	4	1	7	.205	.225	.231	27	-4	0	1	-1	.895	0	/S-7,2-5	-0.4
	Phi-A	59	191	28	50	5	0	1	20	27	29	.262	.356	.304	86	-2	2	0	1	.958	-12	2-43/3-6,S-4	-1.1
	Yr	73	230	29	58	6	0	1	24	28	36	.252	.336	.291	76	-6	2	1	0	.957	-12	2-48,S-11/3-6	-1.5
Total	9	602	1832	235	469	73	24	18	200	297	303	.256	.363	.352	98	1	30	12	2	.940	-39	3-257,2-135,1/S	-2.7

■ RAY GRIMES Grimes, Oscar Ray Sr. b: 9/11/1893, Bergholz, Ohio d: 5/25/53, Minerva, Ohio BR/TR, 5′11″, 168 lbs. Deb: 9/24/20 F

YEAR	TM/L	G	AB	R	H	2B	3B	HR	RBI	BB	SO	AVG	OBP	SLG	PRO+	BR/A	SB	CS	SBR	FA	FR	G/POS	TPR
1920	Bos-A	1	4	1	1	0	0	0	0	1	0	.250	.400	.250	78	-0	0	0	0	1.000	-0	/1-1	0.0
1921	Chi-N	147	530	91	170	38	6	6	79	70	55	.321	.406	.449	126	22	5	8	-3	.993	-5	*1-147	1.1
1922	Chi-N	138	509	99	180	45	12	14	99	75	33	.354	.442	.572	157	45	7	7	-2	.987	-2	*1-138	3.3
1923	Chi-N	64	216	32	71	7	2	2	36	24	17	.329	.401	.407	114	5	5	0	2	.991	-1	1-62	0.3
1924	Chi-N	51	177	33	53	6	5	5	34	28	15	.299	.401	.475	132	9	4	2	0	.982	-7	1-50	-0.1
1926	Phi-N	32	101	13	30	5	0	0	15	6	13	.297	.343	.347	82	-2	0			.981	0	1-28	-0.4
Total	6	433	1537	269	505	101	25	27	263	204	133	.329	.413	.480	132	79	21	17		.989	-14	1-426	4.2

■ CHARLIE GRIMM Grimm, Charles John "Jolly Cholly" b: 8/28/1898, St.Louis, Mo. d: 11/15/83, Scottsdale, Ariz. BL/TL, 5′11.5″, 173 lbs. Deb: 7/30/16 MC

YEAR	TM/L	G	AB	R	H	2B	3B	HR	RBI	BB	SO	AVG	OBP	SLG	PRO+	BR/A	SB	CS	SBR	FA	FR	G/POS	TPR
1916	Phi-A	12	22	0	2	0	0	0	0	2	4	.091	.167	.091	-24	-3	0			.875	-2	/O-7	-0.6
1918	StL-N	50	141	11	31	7	0	0	12	6	15	.220	.262	.270	64	-6	2			.971	-3	1-42/O-2,3-1	-1.2
1919	Pit-N	14	44	6	14	1	3	0	6	2	4	.318	.348	.477	141	2	1			.968	-3	1-13	-0.1
1920	Pit-N	148	533	38	121	13	7	2	54	30	40	.227	.273	.289	60	-28	7	8	-3	**.995**	4	*1-148	-3.2
1921	Pit-N	151	562	62	154	21	17	7	71	31	38	.274	.314	.409	88	-11	6	8	-3	.994	-6	*1-150	-2.4
1922	Pit-N	154	593	64	173	28	13	0	76	43	15	.292	.343	.383	86	-12	6	10	-4	.994	-4	*1-154	-2.6
1923	Pit-N	152	563	78	194	29	13	7	99	41	43	.345	.389	.480	125	20	6	9	-4	**.995**	2	*1-152	1.0
1924	Pit-N	151	542	53	156	25	12	2	63	37	22	.288	.336	.389	92	-6	3	6	-3	**.995**	-3	*1-151	-2.1

YEAR	TM/L	G	AB	R	H	2B	3B	HR	RBI	BB	SO	AVG	OBP	SLG	PRO+	BR/A	SB	CS	SBR	FA	FR	G/POS	TPR
1925	Chi-N	141	519	73	159	29	5	10	76	38	25	.306	.354	.439	100	-1	4	3	-1	.989	0	*1-139	-0.8
1926	Chi-N	147	524	58	145	30	6	8	82	49	25	.277	.342	.403	99	-1	3			.988	-6	*1-147	-1.6
1927	Chi-N	147	543	68	169	29	6	2	74	45	21	.311	.367	.398	105	4	3			.990	3	*1-147	-0.3
1928	Chi-N	147	547	67	161	25	5	5	62	39	20	.294	.342	.386	91	-7	7			**.993**	-2	*1-147	-2.2
1929	*Chi-N	120	463	66	138	28	3	10	91	42	25	.298	.358	.436	95	-4	3			.992	0	*1-120	-1.4
1930	Chi-N	114	429	58	124	27	2	6	66	41	26	.289	.359	.403	83	-11	1			**.995**	1	*1-113	-1.9
1931	Chi-N	146	531	65	176	33	11	4	66	53	29	.331	.393	.458	126	20	1			**.993**	2	*1-144	0.8
1932	*Chi-N	149	570	66	175	42	2	7	80	35	22	.307	.349	.425	108	6	2			.993	10	*1-149,M	0.5
1933	Chi-N	107	384	38	95	15	2	3	37	23	15	.247	.290	.320	74	-13	1			**.996**	9	*1-104,M	-1.4
1934	Chi-N	75	267	24	79	8	1	5	47	16	12	.296	.338	.390	96	-2	1			.995	1	1-74,M	-0.6
1935	Chi-N	2	8	0	0	0	0	0	0	0	1	.000	.000	.000	-99	-2	0			1.000	-0	/1-2,M	-0.3
1936	Chi-N	39	132	13	33	4	0	1	16	5	8	.250	.277	.303	55	-8	0			1.000	5	1-35,M	-0.6
Total	20	2166	7917	908	2299	394	108	79	1078	578	410	.290	.341	.397	95	-63	57	44		.993	10	*1-2131/O-9,3-1	-21.0

■ MYRON GRIMSHAW Grimshaw, Myron Frederick b: 11/30/1875, St.Johnsville, N.Y d: 12/11/36, Canajoharie, N.Y. BB/TR, 6'1", 173 lbs. Deb: 4/25/05

YEAR	TM/L	G	AB	R	H	2B	3B	HR	RBI	BB	SO	AVG	OBP	SLG	PRO+	BR/A	SB	CS	SBR	FA	FR	G/POS	TPR
1905	Bos-A	85	285	39	68	8	2	4	35	21		.239	.293	.323	94	-2	4			.980	-5	1-74	-1.1
1906	Bos-A	110	428	46	124	16	12	0	48	23		.290	.332	.383	124	11	5			.987	-1	*1-110	0.7
1907	Bos-A	64	181	19	37	7	2	0	33	16		.204	.273	.265	72	-5	6			.980	-6	1-20,O-18/S-2	-1.4
Total	3	259	894	104	229	31	16	4	116	60		.256	.307	.340	104	3	15			.984	-12	1-204/O-18,S-2	-1.8

■ MARQUIS GRISSOM Grissom, Marquis Deon b: 4/17/67, Atlanta, Ga. BR/TR, 5'11", 190 lbs. Deb: 8/22/89

YEAR	TM/L	G	AB	R	H	2B	3B	HR	RBI	BB	SO	AVG	OBP	SLG	PRO+	BR/A	SB	CS	SBR	FA	FR	G/POS	TPR
1989	Mon-N	26	74	16	19	2	0	1	2	12	21	.257	.360	.324	96	0	1	0	0	.943	-4	O-23	-0.5
1990	Mon-N	98	288	42	74	14	2	3	29	27	40	.257	.321	.351	88	-5	22	2	5	.988	-4	O-87	-0.5
1991	Mon-N	148	558	73	149	23	9	6	39	34	89	.267	.310	.373	93	-6	**76**	17	**13**	.984	20	*O-138	2.4
1992	Mon-N	159	653	99	180	39	6	14	66	42	81	.276	.324	.418	110	7	**78**	13	**16**	.983	7	*O-157	2.8
1993	Mon-N★	157	630	104	188	27	2	19	95	52	76	.298	.355	.438	106	6	53	10	**10**	.984	11	*O-157	2.3
1994	Mon-N★	110	475	96	137	25	4	11	45	41	66	.288	.346	.427	99	-1	36	6	7	.985	16	*O-109	2.0
1995	*Atl-N	139	551	80	142	23	3	12	42	47	61	.258	.319	.376	80	-16	29	9	3	.994	11	*O-136	-0.5
1996	*Atl-N	158	671	106	207	32	10	23	74	41	73	.308	.351	.489	112	11	28	11	2	.997	9	*O-158	1.7
1997	*Cle-A	144	558	74	146	27	6	12	66	43	89	.262	.321	.396	83	-14	22	13	-1	.992	8	*O-144	-1.0
1998	Mil-N	142	542	57	147	28	1	10	60	24	78	.271	.305	.382	76	-20	13	8	-1	.991	8	*O-137	-1.4
Total	10	1281	5000	747	1389	240	43	111	518	363	674	.278	.330	.410	95	-39	358	89	54	.988	83	*O-1246	7.3

■ DICK GROAT Groat, Richard Morrow b: 11/4/30, Wilkinsburg, Pa. BR/TR, 5'11.5", 180 lbs. Deb: 6/19/52

YEAR	TM/L	G	AB	R	H	2B	3B	HR	RBI	BB	SO	AVG	OBP	SLG	PRO+	BR/A	SB	CS	SBR	FA	FR	G/POS	TPR
1952	Pit-N	95	384	38	109	6	1	1	29	19	27	.284	.319	.313	74	-13	2	4	-2	.952	1	S-94	-0.7
1955	Pit-N	151	521	45	139	28	2	4	51	38	26	.267	.318	.351	78	-16	0	2	-1	.961	15	*S-149	1.1
1956	Pit-N	142	520	40	142	19	3	0	37	35	25	.273	.319	.321	74	-18	0	3	-2	.954	0	*S-141/3-2	-0.8
1957	Pit-N	125	501	58	158	30	5	7	54	27	28	.315	.354	.437	114	10	0	1	-1	.968	-1	*S-123/3-2	2.0
1958	Pit-N	151	584	67	175	36	9	3	66	23	32	.300	.331	.408	97	-4	2	2	-1	.975	3	*S-149	1.2
1959	Pit-N★	147	593	74	163	22	7	5	51	32	35	.275	.314	.361	80	-17	0	2	-1	.964	3	*S-145	-0.3
1960	*Pit-N★	138	573	85	186	26	4	2	50	39	35	**.325**	.372	.394	109	8	0	2	-1	.966	11	*S-136	2.9
1961	Pit-N	148	596	71	164	25	6	6	55	40	44	.275	.322	.367	82	-15	0	4	-2	.957	9	*S-144/3-1	0.4
1962	Pit-N★	161	678	76	199	34	3	2	61	31	61	.294	.327	.361	85	-15	2	1	0	.956	14	*S-161	1.4
1963	StL-N★	158	631	85	201	**43**	11	6	73	56	58	.319	.380	.450	126	22	3	1	0	.964	-13	*S-158	2.2
1964	*StL-N★	161	636	70	186	35	6	1	70	44	42	.292	.338	.371	92	-6	2	3	-1	.949	-12	*S-160	-0.9
1965	StL-N	153	587	55	149	26	5	0	52	56	50	.254	.320	.315	73	-20	1	1	-0	.962	-8	*S-148/3-2	-2.0
1966	Phi-N	155	584	58	152	21	4	2	53	40	38	.260	.313	.320	77	-18	2	1	0	.974	11	*S-139,3-20/1-1	0.6
1967	Phi-N	10	26	3	3	0	0	0	1	4	4	.115	.233	.115	3	-3	0	0	0	.947	2	/S-6	0.0
	SF-N	34	70	4	12	1	1	0	4	6	7	.171	.237	.214	30	-6	0	0	0	.912	-8	S-24/2-1	-1.4
	Yr	44	96	7	15	1	1	0	5	10	11	.156	.236	.188	23	-9	0	0	0	.925	-5	S-30/2-1	-1.4
Total	14	1929	7484	829	2138	352	67	39	707	490	512	.286	.332	.366	89	-112	14	27	-12	.961	28	*S-1877/3-27,2-1,1	5.7

■ HEINIE GROH Groh, Henry Knight b: 9/18/1889, Rochester, N.Y. d: 8/22/68, Cincinnati, Ohio BR/TR, 5'8", 158 lbs. Deb: 4/12/12 FM

YEAR	TM/L	G	AB	R	H	2B	3B	HR	RBI	BB	SO	AVG	OBP	SLG	PRO+	BR/A	SB	CS	SBR	FA	FR	G/POS	TPR
1912	NY-N	27	48	8	13	2	1	0	3	8	7	.271	.375	.354	97	0	6			.887	3	2-12/S-7,3-6	0.3
1913	NY-N	4	2	0	0	0	0	0	0	0	1	.000	.000	.000	-99	-1	0			1.000	1	/3-2,S-1	0.0
	Cin-N	117	397	51	112	19	5	3	48	38	36	.282	.351	.378	109	5	24			.963	10	*2-113/S-4	1.3
	Yr	121	399	51	112	19	5	3	48	38	37	.281	.349	.376	107	4	24			.963	10	*2-113/S-5,3-2	1.3
1914	Cin-N	139	455	59	131	18	4	2	32	64	28	.288	.391	.358	120	15	24			.936	-7	*2-134/S-2	0.7
1915	Cin-N	160	587	72	170	32	9	3	50	50	33	.290	.354	.390	123	17	12	17	-7	.969	11	*3-131,2-29	2.9
1916	Cin-N	149	553	85	149	24	14	2	28	**84**	34	.269	.370	.374	132	24	13			.957	19	*3-110,2-33/S-5	**5.4**
1917	Cin-N	156	599	91	**182**	**39**	11	1	53	71	30	.304	**.385**	.411	150	38	15			**.966**	8	*3-154/2-2	5.3
1918	Cin-N	126	493	**86**	158	**28**	3	1	37	54	24	.320	**.395**	.396	144	**28**	11			**.969**	2	*3-126,M	**3.6**
1919	*Cin-N	122	448	79	139	17	11	5	63	56	26	.310	.392	.431	151	29	21			.971	-2	*3-121	3.5
1920	Cin-N	145	550	86	164	28	12	0	49	60	29	.298	.375	.393	122	18	16	19	-7	.969	-6	*3-144/S-1	1.3
1921	Cin-N	97	357	54	118	19	6	0	48	36	17	.331	.398	.417	122	13	22	14	-2	.950	1	3-97	1.8
1922	*NY-N	115	426	63	113	21	3	3	51	53	21	.265	.353	.350	81	-10	5	6	-2	**.965**	1	*3-110	-0.3
1923	*NY-N	123	465	91	135	22	5	4	48	60	22	.290	.379	.385	103	4	3	4	-2	**.975**	4	*3-118	1.6
1924	*NY-N	145	559	82	157	32	3	2	46	52	29	.281	.354	.360	94	-3	8	6	-1	**.983**	5	*3-145	1.2
1925	NY-N	25	65	7	15	4	0	0	4	6	3	.231	.296	.292	53	-5	0	0	0	.909	-6	3-16/2-2	-0.9
1926	NY-N	12	35	2	8	2	0	0	3	2	3	.229	.270	.286	50	-2	0			.950	-1	/3-7	-0.3
1927	*Pit-N	14	35	2	10	1	0	0	3	2	2	.286	.324	.314	67	-2	0			.958	-1	3-12	-0.2
Total	16	1676	6074	918	1774	308	87	26	566	696	345	.292	.373	.384	119	167	180	66		.967	41	*3-1299,2-325/S-20	27.2

■ LEW GROH Groh, Lewis Carl "Silver" b: 10/16/1883, Rochester, N.Y. d: 10/20/60, Rochester, N.Y. BR/TR, Deb: 8/2/19 F

YEAR	TM/L	G	AB	R	H	2B	3B	HR	RBI	BB	SO	AVG	OBP	SLG	PRO+	BR/A	SB	CS	SBR	FA	FR	G/POS	TPR
1919	Phi-A	2	4	0	0	0	0	0	0	0	2	.000	.000	.000	-99	-1	0			1.000	-0	/3-1	-0.1

■ HOWDY GROSKLOSS Groskloss, Howard Hoffman b: 4/9/07, Pittsburgh, Pa. BR/TR, 5'9", 176 lbs. Deb: 6/23/30

YEAR	TM/L	G	AB	R	H	2B	3B	HR	RBI	BB	SO	AVG	OBP	SLG	PRO+	BR/A	SB	CS	SBR	FA	FR	G/POS	TPR
1930	Pit-N	2	3	0	1	0	0	0	1	0	0	.333	.333	.333	62	-0	0			.000	-1	/S-1	-0.1
1931	Pit-N	53	161	13	45	7	2	0	20	11	16	.280	.326	.348	82	-4	1			.981	-1	2-39/S-3	-0.3
1932	Pit-N	17	20	1	2	0	0	0	0	0	3	.100	.100	.100	-47	-4	0			.800	-1	/S-1	-0.5
Total	3	72	184	14	48	7	2	0	21	11	19	.261	.303	.321	68	-8	1			.700	-3	/2-39,S-5	-0.9

■ EMIL GROSS Gross, Emil Michael b: 3/3/1858, Chicago, Ill. d: 8/24/21, Eagle River, Wis. BR/TR, 6', 190 lbs. Deb: 8/13/1879

YEAR	TM/L	G	AB	R	H	2B	3B	HR	RBI	BB	SO	AVG	OBP	SLG	PRO+	BR/A	SB	CS	SBR	FA	FR	G/POS	TPR
1879	Pro-N	30	132	31	46	9	5	0	24	4	8	.348	.368	.492	183	12				.897	-5	C-30	0.7
1880	Pro-N	87	347	43	90	18	3	1	34	16	15	.259	.292	.337	116	6				.866	-14	*C-87	-0.6
1881	Pro-N	51	182	15	50	9	4	1	24	13	11	.275	.323	.385	124	5				.893	-4	C-50/O-1	0.3
1883	Phi-N	57	231	39	71	25	7	1	25	12	18	.307	.342	.489	163	18				.789	-24	C-55/O-2	-0.3
1884	CP-U	23	95	13	34	6	2	4		6		.358	.396	.589	196	8				.860	-3	C-15/O-9	0.6
Total	5	248	987	141	291	67	21	7	107	51	52	.295	.329	.427	146	49				.859	-50	C-237/O-12	0.7

■ TURKEY GROSS Gross, Ewell b: 2/21/1896, Mesquite, Tex. d: 1/11/36, Dallas, Tex. BR/TR, 6', 165 lbs. Deb: 4/14/25

YEAR	TM/L	G	AB	R	H	2B	3B	HR	RBI	BB	SO	AVG	OBP	SLG	PRO+	BR/A	SB	CS	SBR	FA	FR	G/POS	TPR
1925	Bos-A	9	32	2	3	0	1	0	2	2	2	.094	.171	.156	-16	-6	0	0	0	.976	-1	/S-9	-0.5

■ GREG GROSS Gross, Gregory Eugene b: 8/1/52, York, Pa. BL/TL, 5'11", 175 lbs. Deb: 9/5/73

YEAR	TM/L	G	AB	R	H	2B	3B	HR	RBI	BB	SO	AVG	OBP	SLG	PRO+	BR/A	SB	CS	SBR	FA	FR	G/POS	TPR
1973	Hou-N	14	39	5	9	2	1	0	1	4	4	.231	.302	.333	76	-1	2	1	0	1.000	1	/O-9	-0.1
1974	Hou-N	156	589	78	185	21	8	0	36	76	39	.314	.393	.377	121	20	12	20	-8	.994	-9	*O-151	-0.5
1975	Hou-N	132	483	67	142	14	10	0	41	63	37	.294	.375	.364	114	11	2	2	-1	.958	5	*O-121	1.0
1976	Hou-N	128	426	52	122	12	3	0	27	64	39	.286	.380	.329	112	10	2	6	-3	.978	3	*O-115	0.5
1977	Chi-N	115	239	43	77	10	4	5	32	33	19	.322	.404	.460	118	7	0	1	-1	.991	-8	O-71	-0.4
1978	Chi-N	124	347	34	92	12	7	1	39	33	19	.265	.329	.349	80	-9	3	1	0	.979	-14	*O-111	-2.8
1979	Phi-N	111	174	21	58	6	3	0	15	29	5	.333	.429	.402	124	7	5	2	0	.978	-12	O-73	-0.6

YEAR	TM/L	G	AB	R	H	2B	3B	HR	RBI	BB	SO	AVG	OBP	SLG	PRO+	BR/A	SB	CS	SBR	FA	FR	G/POS	TPR
1980	*Phi-N	127	154	19	37	7	2	0	12	24	7	.240	.346	.312	80	-3	1	1	-0	.973	-22	O-91/1-1	-2.9
1981	*Phi-N	83	102	14	23	6	1	0	7	15	5	.225	.325	.304	76	-3	2	2	-1	.982	-7	O-55	-1.2
1982	Phi-N	119	134	14	40	4	0	0	10	19	8	.299	.386	.328	99	1	4	3	-1	.983	-18	O-71	-1.9
1983	*Phi-N	136	245	25	74	12	3	0	29	34	16	.302	.389	.376	114	6	3	5	-2	.991	-28	*O-110/1-1	-2.7
1984	Phi-N	112	202	19	65	9	1	0	16	24	11	.322	.396	.376	116	5	1	0	0	.986	-4	O-48,1-28	0.0
1985	Phi-N	93	169	21	44	5	2	0	14	32	9	.260	.378	.314	93	-0	1	0	0	1.000	-7	O-52/1-8	-0.8
1986	Phi-N	87	101	11	25	5	0	0	8	21	11	.248	.382	.297	87	-1	1	0	0	1.000	-3	O-27/1-5,P-1	-0.4
1987	Phi-N	114	133	14	38	4	1	1	12	25	12	.286	.403	.353	99	1	0	0	0	1.000	-12	O-50,1-11	-1.2
1988	Phi-N	98	133	10	27	1	0	0	5	16	3	.203	.293	.211	46	-9	0	0	0	1.000	-11	O-37,1-14	-2.3
1989	Hou-N	60	75	2	15	0	0	0	4	11	6	.200	.310	.200	51	-4	0	0	0	.929	-3	O-12/1-6,P-1	-0.8
Total	17	1809	3745	449	1073	130	46	7	308	523	250	.287	.375	.351	103	38	39	44	-15	.982	-148	*O-1204/1-74,P-2	-17.1
■ **WAYNE GROSS**	Gross, Wayne Dale b: 1/14/52, Riverside, Cal. BL/TR, 6'2", 210 lbs. Deb: 8/21/76																						
1976	Oak-A	10	18	0	4	0	0	0	1	2	1	.222	.300	.222	57	-1	0	0	0	.966	-1	/1-3,O-2,D-3	-0.2
1977	Oak-A☆	146	485	66	113	21	1	22	63	86	84	.233	.354	.416	111	9	5	4	-1	.932	-23	*3-145/1-1	-1.7
1978	Oak-A	118	285	18	57	10	2	7	23	40	63	.200	.309	.323	82	-6	0	2	-1	.917	-8	*3-106,1-15	-1.7
1979	Oak-A	138	442	54	99	19	1	14	50	72	62	.224	.334	.367	94	-3	4	3	-1	.943	-10	*3-120,1-18/O-2	-1.5
1980	Oak-A	113	366	45	103	20	3	14	61	44	39	.281	.360	.467	134	17	5	3	-0	.948	-28	3-99,1-10/D-1	-1.3
1981	*Oak-A	82	243	29	50	7	1	10	31	34	28	.206	.308	.366	98	-0	2	1	0	.946	-9	3-73/1-2,D-1	-1.2
1982	Oak-A	129	386	43	97	14	0	9	41	53	50	.251	.345	.358	98	-0	3	1	0	.970	-7	*3-108,1-16/D-1	-1.0
1983	Oak-A	137	339	34	79	18	0	12	44	36	52	.233	.312	.392	98	-1	3	5	-2	.996	-5	1-74,3-67/P-1,D-1	-1.2
1984	Bal-A	127	342	53	74	9	1	22	64	68	69	.216	.348	.442	119	10	1	2	-1	.937	-5	*3-117/1-3,D-1	0.3
1985	Bal-A	103	217	31	51	8	0	11	18	46	48	.235	.369	.424	120	7	1	1	-0	.933	-0	3-67,D-10/1-9	0.5
1986	Oak-A	3	2	0	0	0	0	0	0	1	0	.000	.333	.000	0	-0	0	0	0	.000	-0	/3-1	-0.1
Total	11	1106	3125	373	727	126	9	121	396	482	496	.233	.339	.395	106	31	24	22	-6	.941	-96	3-903,1-151/DOP	-9.1
■ **GEORGE GROSSART**	Grossart, George Albert b: 4/11/1880, Meadville, Pa. d: 4/18/02, Pittsburgh, Pa. Deb: 6/7/01																						
1901	Bos-N	7	26	4	3	0	0	0	1	0		.115	.115	.115	-30	-4	0			1.000	0	/O-7	-0.5
■ **JERRY GROTE**	Grote, Gerald Wayne b: 10/6/42, San Antonio, Tex. BR/TR, 5'10", 190 lbs. Deb: 9/21/63																						
1963	Hou-N	3	5	0	1	0	0	0	1	1	3	.200	.333	.200	61	-0	0	0	0	1.000	-1	/C-3	-0.1
1964	Hou-N	100	298	26	54	9	3	3	24	20	75	.181	.242	.262	44	-22	0	2	-1	.985	2	C-98	-1.8
1966	NY-N	120	317	26	75	12	2	3	31	40	81	.237	.328	.315	82	-7	4	3	-1	.981	0	*C-115/3-2	-0.1
1967	NY-N	120	344	25	67	8	0	4	23	14	65	.195	.228	.253	38	-28	2	2	-1	.990	2	*C-119	-2.3
1968	NY-N★	124	404	29	114	18	0	3	31	44	81	.282	.357	.349	112	7	1	5	-3	.994	7	*C-115	2.3
1969	*NY-N	113	365	38	92	12	3	6	40	32	59	.252	.314	.351	84	-8	2	2	1	-0	.991	19	*C-112	1.8
1970	NY-N	126	415	38	106	14	1	2	34	36	39	.255	.316	.308	68	-18	2	1	0	.991	10	*C-125	-0.2
1971	NY-N	125	403	35	109	25	0	2	35	40	47	.270	.339	.347	96	-1	1	4	-2	.990	5	*C-122	0.7
1972	NY-N	64	205	15	43	5	1	3	21	26	27	.210	.308	.288	72	-7	1	0	0	.998	3	C-59/3-3,O-1	-0.1
1973	*NY-N	84	285	17	73	10	2	1	32	13	23	.256	.291	.316	69	-12	0	0	0	.995	9	C-81/3-2	0.0
1974	NY-N★	97	319	25	82	8	1	5	36	33	33	.257	.331	.335	88	-5	0	1	-1	.988	-3	C-94	-0.5
1975	NY-N	119	386	28	114	14	5	2	39	38	23	.295	.360	.373	109	5	0	1	-1	**.995**	6	*C-111	1.6
1976	NY-N	101	323	30	88	14	2	4	28	38	19	.272	.351	.365	110	5	1	2	-1	.993	12	C-95/O-2	1.9
1977	NY-N	42	115	8	31	3	1	0	7	9	12	.270	.333	.313	78	-3	0	0	0	1.000	-2	C-28,3-11	-0.5
	*LA-N	18	27	3	7	0	0	0	4	2	5	.259	.310	.259	55	-2	0	1	-1	1.000	4	C-16/3-2	0.2
	Yr	60	142	11	38	3	1	0	11	11	17	.268	.329	.303	73	-5	0	1	-1	1.000	2	C-44,3-13	-0.3
1978	*LA-N	41	70	5	19	5	0	0	9	10	5	.271	.363	.343	98	0	0	0	0	.985	8	C-32/3-7	0.9
1981	KC-A	22	56	4	17	3	1	1	9	3	2	.304	.350	.446	129	2	1	0	0	1.000	4	C-22	0.7
	LA-N	2	2	0	0	0	0	0	0	0	1	.000	.000	.000	-99	-1	0	0	0	1.000	0	/C-1	0.0
Total	16	1421	4339	352	1092	160	22	39	404	399	600	.252	.318	.326	83	-95	15	23	-9	.991	85	*C-1348/3-27,O-3	4.5
■ **JEFF GROTEWOLD**	Grotewold, Jeffrey Scott b: 12/8/65, Madera, Cal. BL/TR, 6', 215 lbs. Deb: 4/12/92																						
1992	Phi-N	72	65	7	13	2	0	3	5	9	16	.200	.307	.369	91	-1	0	0	0	1.000	-1	/C-2,O-2,1-1	-0.2
1995	KC-A	15	36	4	10	1	0	1	6	9	7	.278	.422	.389	111	1	0	0	0	.750	-0	D-11/1-1	0.0
Total	2	87	101	11	23	3	0	4	11	18	23	.228	.350	.376	99	0	0	0	0	.833	-2	/D-11,1-2,O-2,C-2	-0.2
■ **JOHNNY GROTH**	Groth, John Thomas b: 7/23/26, Chicago, Ill. BR/TR, 6', 182 lbs. Deb: 9/5/46																						
1946	Det-A	4	9	1	0	0	0	0	0	0	3	.000	.000	.000	-94	-2	0	0	0	1.000	-1	/O-4	-0.4
1947	Det-A	2	4	1	1	0	0	0	0	2	1	.250	.500	.250	109	0	0	0	0	1.000	1	/O-1	0.1
1948	Det-A	6	17	3	8	3	0	1	5	1	1	.471	.500	.824	242	3	0	0	0	.900	0	/O-4	0.3
1949	Det-A	103	348	60	102	19	5	11	73	65	27	.293	.407	.471	132	17	3	7	-3	.966	1	O-99	0.9
1950	Det-A	157	566	95	173	30	8	12	85	95	27	.306	.407	.451	116	16	1	5	-3	.985	-12	*O-157	-0.6
1951	Det-A	118	428	41	128	29	1	3	49	31	32	.299	.349	.393	100	-1	1	1	-0	**.993**	-1	*O-112	-0.5
1952	Det-A	141	524	56	149	22	2	4	51	51	39	.284	.348	.357	96	-3	2	10	-5	.986	0	*O-139	-1.4
1953	StL-A	141	557	65	141	27	4	10	57	42	53	.253	.308	.370	81	-16	5	6	-2	.991	17	*O-141	-0.7
1954	Chi-A	125	422	41	116	20	0	7	60	42	37	.275	.343	.372	93	-4	3	9	-5	.988	-1	*O-125	-1.5
1955	Chi-A	32	77	13	26	7	0	2	11	6	13	.338	.386	.506	135	3	1	0	0	1.000	-0	O-26	0.2
	Was-A	63	183	22	40	4	5	2	17	18	18	.219	.289	.328	69	-9	2	0	1	.984	-1	O-48	-1.1
	Yr	95	260	35	66	11	5	4	28	24	31	.254	.317	.381	89	-5	3	0	1	.989	-1	O-74	-0.9
1956	KC-A	95	244	22	63	13	3	5	37	30	31	.258	.339	.398	94	-2	1	2	-1	1.000	-7	O-84	-1.4
1957	KC-A	55	59	10	15	0	0	0	2	7	6	.254	.333	.254	62	-3	0	0	0	.974	-13	O-50	-1.7
	Det-A	38	103	11	30	10	0	0	16	6	7	.291	.336	.388	95	-1	0	0	0	1.000	-3	O-36	-0.5
	Yr	93	162	21	45	10	0	0	18	13	13	.278	.335	.340	83	-4	0	0	0	.991	-16	O-86	-2.2
1958	Det-A	88	146	24	41	5	2	2	11	13	19	.281	.340	.384	92	-2	0	1	-1	.990	-11	O-80	-1.6
1959	Det-A	55	102	12	24	7	1	1	10	7	14	.235	.284	.353	70	-4	0	0	0	.983	-6	O-41	-1.2
1960	Det-A	25	19	3	7	1	0	0	2	3	1	.368	.455	.421	135	1	0	1	-1	1.000	-3	/O-8	-0.2
Total	15	1248	3808	480	1064	197	31	60	486	419	329	.279	.353	.395	99	-5	19	42	-20	.987	-40	*O-1155	-11.3
■ **ROY GROVER**	Grover, Roy Arthur b: 1/17/1892, Snohomish, Wash. d: 2/7/78, Milwaukie, Ore. BR/TR, 5'8", 150 lbs. Deb: 9/13/16																						
1916	Phi-A	20	77	8	21	1	2	0	7	6	10	.273	.325	.338	104	0	5			.952	-7	2-20	-0.7
1917	Phi-A	141	482	45	108	15	7	0	34	43	53	.224	.292	.284	77	-14	12			.960	5	*2-139	-0.2
1919	Phi-A	22	56	8	13	1	0	0	2	5	6	.232	.295	.250	53	-3	0			.915	-6	2-12/3-3	-0.9
	Was-A	24	75	6	14	0	0	0	7	6	10	.187	.256	.187	25	-7	2			.947	-4	2-24	-1.1
	Yr	46	131	14	27	1	0	0	9	11	16	.206	.273	.214	37	-11	2			.936	-10	2-36/3-3	-2.0
Total	3	207	690	67	156	17	9	0	50	60	79	.226	.292	.277	72	-24	19			.956	-12	2-195/3-3	-2.9
■ **HARVEY GRUBB**	Grubb, Harvey Harrison b: 9/18/1890, Lexington, N.C. d: 1/25/70, Corpus Christi, Tex. BR/TR, 6', 165 lbs. Deb: 9/27/12																						
1912	Cle-A	1	0	0	0	0	0	0	0	0		—	1.000	—	187	0	0			1.000	0	/3-1	0.0
■ **JOHNNY GRUBB**	Grubb, John Maywood b: 8/4/48, Richmond, Va. BL/TR, 6'3", 188 lbs. Deb: 9/10/72																						
1972	SD-N	7	21	4	7	1	1	0	1	1	3	.333	.364	.476	147	1	0	1	-1	1.000	0	/O-6	0.1
1973	SD-N	113	389	52	121	22	3	8	37	37	50	.311	.374	.445	137	19	9	3	1	.988	7	*O-102/3-2	2.2
1974	SD-N★	140	444	53	127	20	4	8	42	46	47	.286	.358	.403	118	10	4	0	1	.976	12	*O-122/3-2	1.9
1975	SD-N	144	553	72	149	36	2	4	38	59	59	.269	.345	.363	103	2	2	7	-4	.991	-4	*O-139	-1.1
1976	SD-N	109	384	54	109	22	1	5	27	65	53	.284	.393	.385	132	19	1	2	-1	.974	-9	O-98/1-9,3-3	0.4
1977	Cle-A	34	93	8	28	3	3	2	14	19	18	.301	.425	.462	146	7	0	3	-2	1.000	-0	O-28/D-4	0.4
1978	Cle-A	113	378	54	100	16	6	14	61	59	60	.265	.367	.450	130	16	5	1	1	.973	5	*O-110	1.8
	Tex-A	21	33	8	13	3	0	1	6	11	5	.394	.545	.576	215	6	1	1	-0	1.000	-1	O-13/D-3	0.5
	Yr	134	411	62	113	19	6	15	67	70	65	.275	.383	.460	137	22	6	2	1	.974	5	*O-123/D-3	2.3
1979	Tex-A	102	289	42	79	14	0	10	37	34	44	.273	.352	.426	110	4	2	4	-2	.986	-8	O-82	-0.8
1980	Tex-A	110	274	40	76	12	1	9	32	42	35	.277	.377	.427	124	10	2	3	-1	.952	-7	O-77/D-8	0.0

YEAR	TM/L	G	AB	R	H	2B	3B	HR	RBI	BB	SO	AVG	OBP	SLG	PRO+	BR/A	SB	CS	SBR	FA	FR	G/POS	TPR
1981	Tex-A	67	199	26	46	9	1	3	26	23	25	.231	.317	.332	92	-2	0	3	-2	.990	-4	O-58	-1.0
1982	Tex-A	103	308	35	86	13	3	3	26	39	37	.279	.371	.370	110	6	0	3	-2	.965	-6	O-77,D-18	-0.4
1983	Det-A	57	134	20	34	5	2	4	22	28	17	.254	.390	.410	124	6	0	0	0	1.000	-3	O-26,D-18	0.1
1984	*Det-A	86	176	25	47	5	0	8	17	36	36	.267	.397	.432	130	9	1	0	0	1.000	-6	O-36,D-33	0.2
1985	Det-A	78	155	19	38	7	1	5	25	24	25	.245	.350	.400	106	2	0	1	-1	1.000	-3	D-33,O-18	-0.2
1986	Det-A	81	210	32	70	13	1	13	51	28	28	.333	.417	.590	171	21	0	1	-1	1.000	-2	D-52,O-19	1.6
1987	*Det-A	59	114	9	23	6	0	2	13	15	16	.202	.295	.307	63	-6	0	0	0	1.000	-4	O-31,D-16/3-1	-1.0
Total	16	1424	4154	553	1153	207	29	99	475	566	558	.278	.369	.413	121	130	27	33	-12	.981	-31	*O-1042,D-185/1-9,3	4.7

■ FRANK GRUBE Grube, Franklin Thomas "Hans" b: 1/7/05, Easton, Pa. d: 7/2/45, New York, N.Y. BR/TR, 5'9", 190 lbs. Deb: 5/12/31

YEAR	TM/L	G	AB	R	H	2B	3B	HR	RBI	BB	SO	AVG	OBP	SLG	PRO+	BR/A	SB	CS	SBR	FA	FR	G/POS	TPR
1931	Chi-A	88	265	29	58	13	2	1	24	22	22	.219	.284	.294	55	-18	2	2	-1	.977	-10	C-81	-2.2
1932	Chi-A	93	277	36	78	16	2	0	31	33	13	.282	.362	.354	92	-2	6	1	1	.957	-2	C-92	0.2
1933	Chi-A	85	256	23	59	13	0	0	23	38	20	.230	.334	.281	67	-11	1	1	-0	.984	-7	C-83	-1.3
1934	StL-A	65	170	22	49	10	0	0	11	24	11	.288	.379	.347	82	-4	2	1	0	.963	-0	C-55	-0.2
1935	StL-A	3	6	3	2	1	0	0	0	0	1	.333	.333	.500	108	0	0	0	0	1.000	0	/C-3	0.0
	Chi-A	9	19	1	7	2	0	0	6	3	2	.368	.455	.474	137	1	0	0	0	.944	3	/C-9	0.4
	Yr	12	25	4	9	3	0	0	6	3	3	.360	.429	.480	131	1	0	0	0	.955	3	C-12	0.4
1936	Chi-A	33	93	6	15	2	1	0	11	9	15	.161	.235	.204	9	-14	1	0	0	.991	2	C-32	-0.9
1941	StL-A	18	39	1	6	2	0	0	1	2	4	.154	.195	.205	6	-5	0	0	0	.951	3	C-18	-0.2
Total	7	394	1125	121	274	59	5	1	107	131	88	.244	.326	.308	67	-52	12	5	1	.970	-13	C-373	-4.2

■ KELLY GRUBER Gruber, Kelly Wayne b: 2/26/62, Houston, Tex. BR/TR, 6', 185 lbs. Deb: 4/20/84

YEAR	TM/L	G	AB	R	H	2B	3B	HR	RBI	BB	SO	AVG	OBP	SLG	PRO+	BR/A	SB	CS	SBR	FA	FR	G/POS	TPR
1984	Tor-A	15	16	1	1	0	0	1	2	0	5	.063	.063	.250	-18	-3	0	0	0	.933	1	3-12/O-2,S-1	-0.1
1985	Tor-A	5	13	0	3	0	0	0	1	0	3	.231	.231	.231	26	-1	0	0	0	1.000	-1	/3-5,2-1	-0.2
1986	Tor-A	87	143	20	28	4	1	5	15	5	27	.196	.223	.343	50	-10	2	5	-2	.940	7	3-42,2-14,D-14,/OS	-0.6
1987	Tor-A	138	341	50	80	14	3	12	36	17	70	.235	.285	.399	77	-12	12	2	2	.948	8	*3-119,S-21/2-7,OD	-0.2
1988	Tor-A	158	569	75	158	33	5	16	81	38	92	.278	.331	.438	113	9	23	5	4	.971	25	*3-156/2-7,O-2,SD	3.7
1989	*Tor-A☆	135	545	83	158	24	4	18	73	30	60	.290	.330	.448	120	12	10	5	0	.945	19	*3-119,O-16/S-1,D-1	3.2
1990	Tor-A★	150	592	92	162	36	6	31	118	48	94	.274	.336	.512	132	23	14	2	3	.955	-3	*3-145/O-6,D-1	2.3
1991	*Tor-A	113	429	58	108	18	2	20	65	31	70	.252	.311	.443	102	0	12	7	-1	.962	4	*3-111/D-2	0.4
1992	*Tor-A	120	446	42	102	16	3	11	43	26	72	.229	.277	.352	72	-18	7	7	-2	.949	-4	*3-120	-2.4
1993	Cal-A	18	65	10	18	3	0	3	9	2	11	.277	.309	.462	101	-0	0	0	0	.938	6	3-17/O-1,D-1	0.6
Total	10	939	3159	431	818	148	24	117	443	197	504	.259	.310	.432	102	-1	80	33	4	.955	64	3-846/O-38,2-29,SD	6.7

■ MARK GRUDZIELANEK Grudzielanek, Mark James b: 6/30/70, Milwaukee, Wis. BR/TR, 6'1", 185 lbs. Deb: 4/28/95

YEAR	TM/L	G	AB	R	H	2B	3B	HR	RBI	BB	SO	AVG	OBP	SLG	PRO+	BR/A	SB	CS	SBR	FA	FR	G/POS	TPR
1995	Mon-N	78	269	27	66	12	2	1	20	14	47	.245	.300	.316	60	-15	8	3	1	.987	7	S-34,3-31,2-13	-0.4
1996	Mon-N★	153	657	99	201	34	4	6	49	26	83	.306	.341	.397	92	-8	33	7	6	.959	-11	*S-153	0.1
1997	Mon-N	156	649	76	177	**54**	3	4	51	23	76	.273	.308	.384	80	-20	25	9	2	.955	-7	*S-156	-1.1
1998	Mon-N	105	396	51	109	15	1	8	41	21	50	.275	.326	.379	86	-9	11	5	0	.950	-16	*S-105	-1.3
	LA-N	51	193	11	51	6	0	2	21	5	23	.264	.290	.326	64	-11	7	0	2	.962	13	S-51	1.0
	Yr	156	589	62	160	21	1	10	62	26	73	.272	.315	.362	79	-19	18	5	2	.954	-3	*S-156	-0.3
Total	4	543	2164	264	604	121	10	21	182	89	279	.279	.319	.373	81	-62	84	24	11	.958	-14	S-499/3-31,2-13	-1.7

■ SIG GRYSKA Gryska, Sigmund Stanley b: 11/4/14, Chicago, Ill. d: 8/27/94, Hines, Ill. BR/TR, 5'11.5", 173 lbs. Deb: 9/28/38

YEAR	TM/L	G	AB	R	H	2B	3B	HR	RBI	BB	SO	AVG	OBP	SLG	PRO+	BR/A	SB	CS	SBR	FA	FR	G/POS	TPR
1938	StL-A	7	21	3	10	2	1	0	4	3	3	.476	.542	.667	202	3	0	0	0	.912	1	/S-7	0.4
1939	StL-A	18	49	4	13	2	0	0	8	6	10	.265	.345	.306	66	-2	3	1	0	.873	-4	S-14	-0.5
Total	2	25	70	7	23	4	1	0	12	9	13	.329	.405	.414	107	1	3	1	0	.887	-4	/S-21	-0.1

■ MARV GUDAT Gudat, Marvin John b: 8/27/05, Goliad, Tex. d: 3/1/54, Los Angeles, Cal. BL/TL, 5'11", 162 lbs. Deb: 5/21/29

YEAR	TM/L	G	AB	R	H	2B	3B	HR	RBI	BB	SO	AVG	OBP	SLG	PRO+	BR/A	SB	CS	SBR	FA	FR	G/POS	TPR
1929	Cin-N	9	10	0	2	0	0	0	0	0	0	.200	.200	.200	-1	-2	0			.800	-1	/P-7	0.0
1932	*Chi-N	60	94	15	24	4	1	1	15	16	10	.255	.369	.351	96	0	0			.933	-6	O-14/1-8,P-1	-0.7
Total	2	69	104	15	26	4	1	1	15	16	10	.250	.355	.337	87	-1	0			.800	6	/O-14,1-8,P-8	-0.7

■ MIKE GUERRA Guerra, Fermin (Romero) b: 10/11/12, Havana, Cuba d: 10/9/92, Miami Beach, Fla. BR/TR, 5'9", 162 lbs. Deb: 9/19/37

YEAR	TM/L	G	AB	R	H	2B	3B	HR	RBI	BB	SO	AVG	OBP	SLG	PRO+	BR/A	SB	CS	SBR	FA	FR	G/POS	TPR
1937	Was-A	1	3	0	0	0	0	0	0	0	2	.000	.000	.000	-99	-1	0	0	0	.750	-1	/C-1	-0.1
1944	Was-A	75	210	29	59	7	2	1	29	13	14	.281	.323	.348	96	-2	8	2	1	.960	-5	C-58/O-1	-0.2
1945	Was-A	56	138	11	29	1	1	1	15	10	12	.210	.268	.254	57	-8	4	1	1	.990	5	C-38	0.0
1946	Was-A	41	83	3	21	2	1	0	4	5	6	.253	.295	.301	71	-3	1	0	0	.938	-2	C-27	-0.4
1947	Phi-A	72	209	20	45	2	2	0	18	10	15	.215	.251	.244	37	-18	1	2	-1	.964	3	C-62	-1.3
1948	Phi-A	53	142	18	30	4	2	1	23	18	13	.211	.300	.289	57	-9	2	3	-1	.973	-0	C-47	-0.7
1949	Phi-A	98	298	41	79	14	1	3	31	37	26	.265	.346	.349	87	-6	3	0	1	.982	-3	C-95	-0.2
1950	Phi-A	87	252	25	71	10	4	2	26	16	12	.282	.325	.377	81	-8	1	0	0	.990	-6	C-78	-1.0
1951	Bos-A	10	32	1	5	0	0	0	2	6	5	.156	.289	.156	21	-3	1	0	0	1.000	-1	C-10	-0.3
	Was-A	72	214	20	43	2	1	1	20	16	18	.201	.257	.234	34	-20	4	4	-1	.977	-11	C-66	-2.9
	Yr	82	246	21	48	2	1	1	22	22	23	.195	.261	.224	32	-23	5	4	-1	.982	-11	C-76	-3.2
Total	9	565	1581	168	382	42	14	9	168	131	123	.242	.300	.303	65	-77	25	12	0	.975	-20	C-482/O-1	-7.1

■ JUAN GUERRERO Guerrero, Juan Antonio b: 2/1/67, Los Llanos, D.R. BR/TR, 5'11", 160 lbs. Deb: 4/9/92

YEAR	TM/L	G	AB	R	H	2B	3B	HR	RBI	BB	SO	AVG	OBP	SLG	PRO+	BR/A	SB	CS	SBR	FA	FR	G/POS	TPR
1992	Hou-N	79	125	8	25	4	2	1	14	10	32	.200	.265	.288	59	-7	1	0	0	.980	-7	S-19,3-12/O-3,2-2	-1.4

■ MARIO GUERRERO Guerrero, Mario Miguel (Abud) b: 9/28/49, Santo Domingo, D.R. BR/TR, 5'10", 155 lbs. Deb: 4/8/73

YEAR	TM/L	G	AB	R	H	2B	3B	HR	RBI	BB	SO	AVG	OBP	SLG	PRO+	BR/A	SB	CS	SBR	FA	FR	G/POS	TPR
1973	Bos-A	66	219	19	51	5	2	0	11	10	21	.233	.273	.274	51	-14	2	2	-1	.974	1	S-46,2-24	-0.8
1974	Bos-A	93	284	18	70	6	2	0	23	13	22	.246	.284	.282	59	-15	3	1	0	.969	-0	S-93	-0.4
1975	StL-N	64	184	17	44	9	0	0	11	10	7	.239	.286	.288	57	-11	0	0	0	.955	6	S-64	0.1
1976	Cal-A	83	268	24	76	12	0	1	18	7	12	.284	.309	.340	96	-2	0	0	0	.973	-12	2-41,S-41/D-7	-0.9
1977	Cal-A	86	244	17	69	8	2	1	28	4	16	.283	.294	.344	76	-8	0	0	0	.985	-2	S-31,D-19,2-12	-0.7
1978	Oak-A	143	505	27	139	18	4	3	38	15	35	.275	.304	.345	87	-10	0	5	-3	.958	-40	*S-142	-3.7
1979	Oak-A	46	166	12	38	5	0	0	18	6	7	.229	.256	.259	42	-14	0	1	-1	.952	-4	S-43	-1.4
1980	Oak-A	116	381	32	91	16	2	2	23	19	32	.239	.277	.307	64	-19	3	3	-1	.962	-42	*S-116	-5.0
Total	8	697	2251	166	578	79	12	7	170	84	152	.257	.288	.312	69	-93	8	12	-5	.961	-95	S-576/2-77,D-26	-12.8

■ PEDRO GUERRERO Guerrero, Pedro b: 6/29/56, San Pedro De Macoris, D.R. BR/TR, 6', 195 lbs. Deb: 9/22/78

YEAR	TM/L	G	AB	R	H	2B	3B	HR	RBI	BB	SO	AVG	OBP	SLG	PRO+	BR/A	SB	CS	SBR	FA	FR	G/POS	TPR
1978	LA-N	5	8	3	5	0	1	0	1	0	0	.625	.625	.875	316	2	0	0	0	1.000	0	/1-4	0.2
1979	LA-N	25	62	7	15	2	0	2	9	1	14	.242	.254	.371	69	-3	2	0	1	1.000	-3	O-12/1-8,3-3	-0.6
1980	LA-N	75	183	27	59	9	1	7	31	12	31	.322	.364	.497	141	9	2	1	0	.987	-3	O-40,2-12/3-3,1-2	0.6
1981	*LA-N★	98	347	46	104	17	2	12	48	34	57	.300	.366	.464	139	17	5	9	-4	.974	3	O-75,3-21/1-1	1.4
1982	LA-N	150	575	87	175	27	5	32	100	65	89	.304	.380	.536	157	43	22	5	4	.976	2	*O-137,3-24	4.6
1983	*LA-N★	160	584	87	174	28	6	32	103	72	110	.298	.377	.531	150	38	23	7	3	.934	6	*3-157/1-2	4.6
1984	LA-N	144	535	85	162	29	4	16	72	49	105	.303	.362	.462	132	22	9	8	-2	.917	-8	3-76,O-58,1-16	0.8
1985	*LA-N†	137	487	99	156	22	2	33	87	83	68	.320	**.425**	**.577**	**183**	**56**	12	4	1	.974	8	O-81,3-44,1-12	6.3
1986	LA-N	31	61	7	15	3	0	5	10	2	19	.246	.281	.541	131	2	0	0	0	1.000	-2	O-10/1-4	-0.1
1987	LA-N★	152	545	89	184	25	2	27	89	74	85	.338	.421	.539	156	46	9	7	-2	.971	1	*O-109,1-40	3.8
1988	LA-N	59	215	24	64	7	1	5	35	25	33	.298	.379	.409	130	9	2	1	0	.895	-13	3-45,1-15/O-2	-0.6
	StL-N	44	149	16	40	7	1	5	30	21	26	.268	.366	.430	126	6	2	0	1	1.000	-2	1-37/O-7	0.1
	Yr	103	364	40	104	14	2	10	65	46	59	.286	.373	.418	128	15	4	1	1	.998	-15	1-52,3-45/O-9	-0.5
1989	StL-N★	162	570	60	177	**42**	1	17	117	79	84	.311	.398	.477	145	35	2	0	1	.990	-14	*1-160	0.9
1990	StL-N	136	498	42	140	31	1	13	80	44	70	.281	.341	.426	109	6	1	1	-0	.989	-10	*1-132	-1.5
1991	StL-N	115	427	41	116	12	1	8	70	37	46	.272	.331	.361	94	-3	4	2	0	.985	-8	*1-112	-1.9
1992	StL-N	43	146	10	32	6	1	1	16	11	25	.219	.274	.295	63	-7	2	2	-1	.988	-7	1-28,O-10	-1.9
Total	15	1536	5392	730	1618	267	29	215	898	609	862	.300	.374	.480	138	277	97	47	1	.988	-49	1-573,O-541,3/2	16.7

YEAR	TM/L	G	AB	R	H	2B	3B	HR	RBI	BB	SO	AVG	OBP	SLG	PRO+	BR/A	SB	CS	SBR	FA	FR	G/POS	TPR
■ **VLADIMIR GUERRERO**	Guerrero, Vladimir b: 2/9/76, Nizao Bani, D.R. BR/TR, 6'2", 158 lbs. Deb: 9/19/96																						
1996	Mon-N	9	27	2	5	0	0	1	1	0	3	.185	.185	.296	24	-3	0	0	0	1.000	-1	/O-8	-0.4
1997	Mon-N	90	325	44	98	22	2	11	40	19	39	.302	.353	.483	117	7	3	4	-2	.929	4	O-85	0.8
1998	Mon-N	159	623	108	202	37	7	38	109	42	95	.324	.374	.589	150	43	11	9	-2	.952	11	*O-157	4.9
Total	3	258	975	154	305	59	9	50	150	61	137	.313	.362	.546	135	48	14	13	-4	.945	14	O-250	5.3
■ **WILTON GUERRERO**	Guerrero, Wilton b: 10/24/74, Don Gregorio, D.R. BB/TR, 5'11", 145 lbs. Deb: 9/3/96																						
1996	LA-N	5	2	1	0	0	0	0	0	0	2	.000	.000	.000	-99	-1	0	0	0	.000	0	/H	-0.1
1997	LA-N	111	357	39	104	10	9	4	32	8	52	.291	.307	.403	91	-6	6	5	-1	.989	-22	2-90/S-5	-2.4
1998	LA-N	64	180	21	51	4	3	0	7	4	33	.283	.303	.339	72	-8	5	2	0	.968	-12	2-32,S-14/O-7	-1.7
	Mon-N	52	222	29	63	10	6	2	20	10	30	.284	.315	.410	89	-4	3	0	1	.975	-8	2-52	-0.8
	Yr	116	402	50	114	14	9	2	27	14	63	.284	.309	.378	82	-12	8	2	1	.972	-21	2-84,S-14/O-7	-2.5
Total	3	232	761	90	218	24	18	6	59	22	117	.286	.307	.389	85	-19	14	7	0	.981	-43	2-174/S-19,O-7	-5.0
■ **GIOMAR GUEVARA**	Guevara, Giomar Antonio (Diaz) b: 10/23/72, Miranda, Venez. BB/TR, 5'8", 150 lbs. Deb: 9/19/97																						
1997	Sea-A	5	4	0	0	0	0	0	0	0	2	.000	.000	.000	-99	-1	1	0	0	.875	2	/2-2,S-1,D-2	0.1
1998	Sea-A	11	13	4	3	2	0	0	0	4	4	.231	.444	.385	118	1	0	0	0	1.000	2	/2-5,S-5	0.2
Total	2	16	17	4	3	2	0	0	0	4	6	.176	.364	.294	74	-0	1	0	0	.957	3	/2-7,S-6,D-2	0.3
■ **CARLOS GUILLEN**	Guillen, Carlos Alfonso b: 9/30/75, Maracay, Venez. BB/TR, 6'1", 180 lbs. Deb: 9/6/98																						
1998	Sea-A	10	39	9	13	1	1	0	5	3	9	.333	.381	.410	106	0	2	0	1	1.000	2	2-10	0.3
■ **JOSE GUILLEN**	Guillen, Jose Manuel b: 5/17/76, San Cristobal, D.R. BR/TR, 5'11", 165 lbs. Deb: 4/1/97																						
1997	Pit-N	143	498	58	133	20	5	14	70	17	88	.267	.302	.412	83	-13	1	2	-1	.963	-1	*O-136	-1.7
1998	Pit-N	153	573	60	153	38	2	14	84	21	100	.267	.300	.414	81	-17	3	5	-2	.968	12	*O-151	-0.8
Total	2	296	1071	118	286	58	7	28	154	38	188	.267	.301	.413	82	-30	4	7	-3	.966	12	O-287	-2.5
■ **OZZIE GUILLEN**	Guillen, Oswaldo Jose (Barrios) b: 1/20/64, Oculare Del Tuy, Venezuela BL/TR, 5'11", 150 lbs. Deb: 4/9/85																						
1985	Chi-A	150	491	71	134	21	9	1	33	12	36	.273	.292	.358	74	-18	7	4	-0	**.980**	12	*S-150	0.6
1986	Chi-A	159	547	58	137	19	4	2	47	12	52	.250	.268	.311	55	-34	8	4	0	.970	14	*S-157/D-1	-0.5
1987	Chi-A	149	560	64	156	22	7	2	51	22	52	.279	.307	.354	73	-22	25	8	3	.975	13	*S-149	0.6
1988	Chi-A†	156	566	58	148	16	7	0	39	25	40	.261	.295	.314	71	-22	25	13	-0	.977	**43**	*S-156	3.3
1989	Chi-A	155	597	63	151	20	8	1	54	15	48	.253	.271	.318	67	-27	36	17	1	.973	14	*S-155	0.0
1990	Chi-A★	160	516	61	144	21	4	1	58	26	37	.279	.315	.341	85	-11	13	17	-6	.977	3	*S-159	-0.1
1991	Chi-A★	154	524	52	143	20	3	3	49	11	38	.273	.288	.340	75	-19	21	15	-3	.970	-3	*S-149	-1.4
1992	Chi-A	12	40	5	8	4	0	0	7	1	5	.200	.220	.300	45	-3	1	0	0	1.000	1	S-12	-0.1
1993	*Chi-A	134	457	44	128	23	4	4	50	10	41	.280	.296	.374	80	-14	5	4	-1	.972	-12	*S-133	-1.6
1994	Chi-A	100	365	46	105	9	5	1	39	14	35	.288	.314	.348	72	-15	5	4	-1	.959	-23	S-99	-2.9
1995	Chi-A	122	415	50	103	20	3	1	41	13	25	.248	.271	.318	55	-28	6	7	-2	.976	-1	*S-120/D-1	-2.0
1996	Chi-A	150	499	62	131	24	8	4	45	10	27	.263	.277	.367	64	-29	6	5	-1	.981	-24	*S-146/O-2	-3.8
1997	Chi-A	142	490	59	120	21	6	4	52	22	24	.245	.277	.337	62	-28	5	3	-0	.974	-25	*S-139	-3.9
1998	Bal-A	12	16	2	1	0	0	0	0	1	2	.063	.118	.063	-52	-4	0	1	-1	.933	-1	/S-6,3-1	-0.4
	*Atl-N	83	264	35	73	15	1	1	22	24	25	.277	.339	.352	78	-8	1	4	-2	.977	-4	S-71/2-2,1-1,3-1	-0.8
Total	14	1838	6347	730	1682	255	69	25	587	218	487	.265	.290	.339	69	-281	164	106	-14	.974	8	*S-1801/2-2,3OD1	-13.0
■ **BOBBY GUINDON**	Guindon, Robert Joseph b: 9/4/43, Brookline, Mass. BL/TL, 6'2", 185 lbs. Deb: 9/19/64																						
1964	Bos-A	5	8	0	1	1	0	0	0	1	4	.125	.222	.250	30	-1	0	0	0	1.000	-0	/1-1,O-1	-0.1
■ **BEN GUINEY**	Guiney, Benjamin Franklin b: 11/16/1858, Detroit, Mich. d: 12/5/30, Detroit, Mich. BB/TR, 6', 170 lbs. Deb: 9/4/1883																						
1883	Det-N	1	5	1	1	0	0	0	0	0	1	.200	.200	.200	23	-0				.000	-1	/O-1	-0.1
1884	Det-N	2	7	0	0	0	0	0	0	0	3	.000	.000	.000	-99	-2				.750	-2	/C-2	-0.3
Total	2	3	12	1	1	0	0	0	0	0	4	.083	.083	.083	-51	-2				.750	-2	/C-2,O-1	-0.4
■ **BEN GUINTINI**	Guintini, Benjamin John b: 1/13/20, Los Banos, Cal. BR/TR, 6'1.5", 190 lbs. Deb: 4/21/46																						
1946	Pit-N	2	3	0	0	0	0	0	0	0	0	.000	.000	.000	-98	-1	0			1.000	-0	/O-1	-0.1
1950	Phi-A	3	4	0	0	0	0	0	0	0	1	.000	.000	.000	-99	-1	0	0	0	1.000	0	/O-1	-0.1
Total	2	5	7	0	0	0	0	0	0	0	1	.000	.000	.000	-99	-2	0	0		1.000	0	/O-2	-0.2
■ **LOU GUISTO**	Guisto, Louis Joseph b: 1/16/1895, Napa, Cal. d: 10/15/89, Napa, Cal. BR/TR, 5'11", 193 lbs. Deb: 9/10/16																						
1916	Cle-A	6	19	2	3	0	0	0	2	4	3	.158	.304	.158	37	-1	1			1.000	0	/1-6	-0.2
1917	Cle-A	73	200	9	37	4	2	0	29	25	18	.185	.282	.225	51	-11	3			.989	-1	1-59	-1.6
1921	Cle-A	2	2	0	1	0	0	0	1	0	1	.500	.500	.500	153	0	0	0	0	1.000	0	/1-1	0.0
1922	Cle-A	35	84	7	21	10	1	0	9	2	7	.250	.276	.393	72	-4	0	0	0	.995	1	1-24	-0.4
1923	Cle-A	40	144	17	26	5	0	0	18	15	15	.181	.262	.215	27	-15	1	1	-0	.988	1	1-40	-1.6
Total	5	156	449	35	88	19	3	0	59	46	44	.196	.277	.252	47	-31	5	1		.990	1	1-130	-3.8
■ **MIKE GULAN**	Gulan, Michael Watts b: 12/18/70, Steubenville, O. BR/TR, 6'1", 192 lbs. Deb: 5/14/97																						
1997	StL-N	5	9	2	0	0	0	0	1	1	5	.000	.100	.000	-72	-2	0	0	0	1.000	-1	/3-3	-0.3
■ **BRAD GULDEN**	Gulden, Bradley Lee b: 6/10/56, New Ulm, Minn. BL/TR, 5'11", 180 lbs. Deb: 9/22/78																						
1978	LA-N	3	4	0	0	0	0	0	0	0	2	.000	.000	.000	-99	-1	0	0	0	1.000	1	/C-3	0.0
1979	NY-A	40	92	10	15	4	0	0	6	9	16	.163	.238	.207	21	-10	0	1	-1	.995	11	C-40	0.2
1980	NY-A	2	3	1	1	0	0	1	2	0	0	.333	.333	1.333	340	1	0	0	0	1.000	-1	/C-2	0.0
1981	Sea-A	8	16	0	3	2	0	0	1	0	2	.188	.188	.313	40	-1	0	0	0	1.000	2	/C-6	0.1
1982	Mon-N	5	6	1	0	0	0	0	0	1	1	.000	.143	.000	-56	-1	0	0	0	1.000	1	/C-2	0.0
1984	Cin-N	107	292	31	66	8	2	4	33	33	35	.226	.309	.308	71	-11	2	2	-1	.975	-4	*C-100	-1.2
1986	SF-N	17	22	2	2	0	0	0	1	2	5	.091	.167	.091	-28	-4	0	0	0	1.000	-1	C-10	-0.5
Total	7	182	435	45	87	14	2	5	43	45	61	.200	.278	.276	53	-27	2	3	-1	.982	9	C-163	-1.4
■ **TOM GULLEY**	Gulley, Thomas Jefferson b: 12/25/1899, Garner, N.C. d: 11/24/66, St.Charles, Ark. BL/TR, 5'11", 178 lbs. Deb: 8/24/23																						
1923	Cle-A	2	3	1	1	1	0	0	0	0	0	.333	.333	.667	159	0	0	0	0	1.000	-0	/O-1	0.0
1924	Cle-A	8	20	4	3	0	1	0	1	3	2	.150	.261	.250	32	-2	0	0	0	.933	0	/O-5	-0.2
1926	Chi-A	16	35	5	8	3	1	0	8	5	2	.229	.325	.371	84	-1	0	0	0	1.000	-2	O-12	-0.3
Total	3	26	58	10	12	4	2	0	9	8	4	.207	.303	.345	69	-3	0	0	0	.971	-2	/O-18	-0.5
■ **TED GULLIC**	Gullic, Tedd Jasper b: 1/2/07, Koshkonong, Mo. BR/TR, 6'2", 175 lbs. Deb: 4/15/30																						
1930	StL-A	92	308	39	77	7	5	4	44	27	43	.250	.310	.344	64	-17	4	0	1	.967	3	O-82/1-3	-1.8
1933	StL-A	104	304	34	74	18	3	5	35	15	38	.243	.281	.372	67	-15	3	1	0	.988	10	O-36,3-33,1-14	-0.6
Total	2	196	612	73	151	25	8	9	79	42	81	.247	.296	.358	65	-33	7	1	2	.975	12	O-118/3-33,1-17	-2.4
■ **GLENN GULLIVER**	Gulliver, Glenn James b: 10/15/54, Detroit, Mich. BL/TR, 5'11", 175 lbs. Deb: 7/17/82																						
1982	Bal-A	50	145	24	29	7	0	1	5	37	18	.200	.363	.269	77	-3	0	0	0	.970	-4	3-50	-0.8
1983	Bal-A	23	47	5	10	3	0	0	2	9	5	.213	.339	.277	73	-1	0	1	-1	1.000	0	3-21	-0.2
Total	2	73	192	29	39	10	0	1	7	46	23	.203	.357	.271	76	-4	0	1	-1	.978	-4	/3-71	-1.0
■ **FRED GUNKLE**	Gunkle, Frederick W. b: Reading, Pa. Deb: 5/17/1879																						
1879	Cle-N	1	3	1	0	0	0	0	0	0	1	.000	.000	.000	-99	-1				1.000	-2	/O-1,C-1	-0.3
■ **HY GUNNING**	Gunning, Hyland b: 8/6/1888, Maplewood, N.J. d: 3/28/75, Togus, Me. BL/TR, 6'1.5", 189 lbs. Deb: 8/8/11																						
1911	Bos-A	4	9	0	1	0	0	0	2	2		.111	.273	.111	9	-1	0			1.000	-1	/1-4	-0.2
■ **TOM GUNNING**	Gunning, Thomas Francis b: 3/4/1862, Newmarket, N.H. d: 3/17/31, Fall River, Mass. BR/TR, 5'10", 160 lbs. Deb: 7/26/1884 U																						
1884	Bos-N	12	45	4	5	1	1	0	2	1	12	.111	.130	.178	-4	-5				.914	-5	C-12	-0.9

YEAR	TM/L	G	AB	R	H	2B	3B	HR	RBI	BB	SO	AVG	OBP	SLG	PRO+	BR/A	SB	CS	SBR	FA	FR	G/POS	TPR
1885	Bos-N	48	174	17	32	3	0	0	15	5	29	.184	.207	.201	34	-12				.877	-7	C-48	-1.5
1886	Bos-N	27	98	15	22	2	1	0	7	3	19	.224	.248	.265	58	-5	3			.892	-5	C-27	-0.6
1887	Phi-N	28	104	22	27	6	1	1	16	5	6	.260	.306	.365	81	-3	18			.895	6	C-28	0.5
1888	Phi-a	23	92	18	18	0	0	0	5	2		.196	.237	.196	40	-6	14			.894	-1	C-23	-0.5
1889	Phi-a	8	24	3	6	0	1	1	1	0	4	.250	.250	.458	101	-0	3			.838	-2	/C-8	-0.1
Total	6	146	537	79	110	12	4	2	46	16	70	.205	.235	.253	50	-32	38			.887	-15	C-146	-3.1

■ JOE GUNSON

Gunson, Joseph Brook b: 3/23/1863, Philadelphia, Pa. d: 11/15/42, Philadelphia, Pa. BR/TR, 5'6", 160 lbs. Deb: 6/14/1884

YEAR	TM/L	G	AB	R	H	2B	3B	HR	RBI	BB	SO	AVG	OBP	SLG	PRO+	BR/A	SB	CS	SBR	FA	FR	G/POS	TPR
1884	Was-U	45	166	15	23	2	0	0		3		.139	.154	.151	-8	-27				.915	10	C-33,O-18	-1.3
1889	KC-a	34	122	15	24	3	1	0	12	3	17	.197	.228	.238	31	-11	2			.862	-6	C-32/O-1,3-1	-1.3
1892	Bal-N	89	314	35	67	10	5	0	32	16	17	.213	.267	.277	63	-15	2			.921	-1	C-67,O-20/1-2,2-1	-1.1
1893	StL-N	40	151	20	41	5	0	0	15	6	6	.272	.321	.305	66	-7	0			.927	3	C-35/O-5	-0.1
	Cle-N	21	73	11	19	1	0	0	9	6	0	.260	.316	.274	54	-5	0			.942	2	C-20	-0.1
	Yr	61	224	31	60	6	0	0	24	12	6	.268	.320	.295	62	-12	0			.932	5	C-55/O-5	-0.2
Total	4	229	826	96	174	21	6	0	68	34	40	.211	.254	.251	45	-65	4			.912	8	C-187/O-44,1-2,2-3	-3.9

■ ERNIE GUST

Gust, Ernest Herman Frank "Red" b: 1/24/1888, Bay City, Mich. d: 10/26/45, Maupin, Ore. BR/TR, 6', 170 lbs. Deb: 8/17/11

YEAR	TM/L	G	AB	R	H	2B	3B	HR	RBI	BB	SO	AVG	OBP	SLG	PRO+	BR/A	SB	CS	SBR	FA	FR	G/POS	TPR
1911	StL-A	3	12	0	0	0	0	0	0	0	0	.000	.000	.000	-99	-3	0			.974	-0	/1-3	-0.4

■ FRANKIE GUSTINE

Gustine, Frank William b: 2/20/20, Hoopeston, Ill. d: 4/1/91, Davenport, Iowa BR/TR, 6', 180 lbs. Deb: 9/13/39 C

YEAR	TM/L	G	AB	R	H	2B	3B	HR	RBI	BB	SO	AVG	OBP	SLG	PRO+	BR/A	SB	CS	SBR	FA	FR	G/POS	TPR
1939	Pit-N	22	70	5	13	3	0	0	3	9	4	.186	.278	.229	38	-6	0			.896	4	3-22	-0.2
1940	Pit-N	133	524	59	147	32	7	1	55	35	39	.281	.328	.374	94	-5	7			.941	-8	*2-130	-0.4
1941	Pit-N	121	463	46	125	24	7	1	46	28	38	.270	.313	.359	89	-8	5			.954	-1	*2-104,3-15	-0.1
1942	Pit-N	115	388	34	89	11	4	2	35	29	27	.229	.286	.294	68	-16	5			.954	-10	*2-108/S-2,3-2,C-1	-2.1
1943	Pit-N	112	414	40	120	21	3	0	43	32	36	.290	.341	.355	98	-1	12			.938	-6	S-68,2-40/1-1	0.0
1944	Pit-N	127	405	42	93	18	3	2	42	33	41	.230	.288	.304	64	-19	8			.938	-27	*S-116,2-11/3-1	-3.9
1945	Pit-N	128	478	67	134	27	5	2	66	37	33	.280	.335	.370	92	-5	8			.930	-19	*S-104,2-29/C-1	-1.5
1946	Pit-N★	131	495	60	128	23	6	8	52	40	52	.259	.318	.378	95	-5	2			.967	8	*2-113,S-13/3-7	1.2
1947	Pit-N★	156	616	102	183	30	6	9	67	63	65	.297	.364	.409	102	2	5			.944	15	*3-156	1.8
1948	Pit-N★	131	449	68	120	19	2	9	42	42	62	.267	.333	.379	90	-6	5			.947	9	*3-118	0.2
1949	Chi-N	76	261	29	59	13	4	4	27	18	22	.226	.279	.352	70	-12	3			.931	1	3-55,2-16	-1.1
1950	StL-A	9	19	1	3	1	0	0	2	3	8	.158	.273	.211	24	-2	0	1	-1	.857	-0	/3-6	-0.3
Total	12	1261	4582	553	1214	222	47	38	480	369	427	.265	.322	.359	87	-82	60	1		.955	-35	2-551,3-382,S/C1	-6.4

■ BUCKY GUTH

Guth, Charles Henry b: 8/18/47, Baltimore, Md. BR/TR, 6'1", 180 lbs. Deb: 9/12/72

YEAR	TM/L	G	AB	R	H	2B	3B	HR	RBI	BB	SO	AVG	OBP	SLG	PRO+	BR/A	SB	CS	SBR	FA	FR	G/POS	TPR
1972	Min-A	3	3	1	0	0	0	0	0	0	0	.000	.000	.000	-95	-1	0	0	0	1.000	1	/S-1	0.0

■ CESAR GUTIERREZ

Gutierrez, Cesar Dario "Coca" b: 1/26/43, Coro, Venez. BR/TR, 5'9", 155 lbs. Deb: 4/16/67

YEAR	TM/L	G	AB	R	H	2B	3B	HR	RBI	BB	SO	AVG	OBP	SLG	PRO+	BR/A	SB	CS	SBR	FA	FR	G/POS	TPR
1967	SF-N	18	21	4	3	0	0	0	0	1	4	.143	.217	.143	5	-3	1	0	0	.946	3	S-15/2-1	0.1
1969	SF-N	15	23	4	5	1	0	0	0	6	2	.217	.379	.261	84	-0	0	0	0	.882	-0	/3-7,S-4	0.0
	Det-A	17	49	5	12	1	0	0	0	5	3	.245	.315	.265	61	-2	1	2	-1	.946	1	S-16	0.0
1970	Det-A	135	415	40	101	11	6	0	22	18	39	.243	.276	.299	58	-24	4	3	-1	.957	-18	*S-135	-2.9
1971	Det-A	38	37	8	7	0	0	0	4	0	3	.189	.211	.189	13	-4	0	0	0	.971	5	S-14/3-5,2-2	0.2
Total	4	223	545	61	128	13	6	0	26	30	51	.235	.279	.281	55	-33	7	5	-1	.955	-9	S-184/3-12,2-3	-2.6

■ JACKIE GUTIERREZ

Gutierrez, Joaquin Fernando b: 6/27/60, Cartagena, Colombia BR/TR, 5'11", 175 lbs. Deb: 9/6/83

YEAR	TM/L	G	AB	R	H	2B	3B	HR	RBI	BB	SO	AVG	OBP	SLG	PRO+	BR/A	SB	CS	SBR	FA	FR	G/POS	TPR
1983	Bos-A	5	10	2	3	0	0	0	0	1	1	.300	.364	.300	79	-0	0	1	-1	.938	-0	/S-4	-0.1
1984	Bos-A	151	449	55	118	12	3	2	29	15	49	.263	.287	.316	64	-22	12	5	1	.949	-33	*S-150	-4.2
1985	Bos-A	103	275	33	60	5	2	2	21	12	37	.218	.251	.273	42	-22	10	2	2	.943	5	S-99	-0.7
1986	Bal-A	61	145	8	27	3	0	0	4	3	27	.186	.208	.207	14	-17	3	1	0	.990	7	2-53/3-6,D-1	-0.8
1987	Bal-A	3	1	0	0	0	0	0	0	0	0	.000	.000	.000	-99	-0	0	0	0	.000	0	/2-1,3-1	0.0
1988	Phi-N	33	77	8	19	4	0	0	9	2	9	.247	.266	.299	61	-4	0	0	0	.919	-2	S-22,3-13	-0.6
Total	6	356	957	106	227	24	5	4	63	33	123	.237	.263	.285	50	-66	25	9	2	.945	-23	S-275/2-54,3-20,D-1	-6.4

■ RICKY GUTIERREZ

Gutierrez, Ricardo b: 5/23/70, Miami, Fla. BR/TR, 6'1", 175 lbs. Deb: 4/13/93

YEAR	TM/L	G	AB	R	H	2B	3B	HR	RBI	BB	SO	AVG	OBP	SLG	PRO+	BR/A	SB	CS	SBR	FA	FR	G/POS	TPR
1993	SD-N	133	438	76	110	10	5	5	26	50	97	.251	.335	.331	78	-13	4	3	-1	.971	-15	*S-117/2-6,O-5,3-4	-1.9
1994	SD-N	90	275	27	66	11	2	1	28	32	54	.240	.324	.305	67	-13	2	6	-3	.925	-8	S-78/2-7	-1.7
1995	Hou-N	52	156	22	43	6	0	0	12	10	33	.276	.323	.314	74	-6	5	0	2	.956	-6	S-44/3-2	-0.6
1996	Hou-N	89	218	28	62	8	1	1	15	23	42	.284	.361	.344	94	-1	6	1	2	.953	-10	S-74/3-6,2-5	-0.4
1997	*Hou-N	102	303	33	79	14	4	3	34	21	50	.261	.315	.363	80	-9	5	2	0	.967	-6	S-64,3-22/2-9	-0.9
1998	*Hou-N	141	491	55	128	24	3	2	46	54	84	.261	.341	.334	78	-14	13	7	-0	.976	9	*S-141	0.8
Total	6	607	1881	241	488	73	15	12	161	190	360	.259	.334	.333	78	-56	35	19	-1	.962	-34	S-518/3-34,2-27,O-5	-4.7

■ DON GUTTERIDGE

Gutteridge, Donald Joseph b: 6/19/12, Pittsburg, Kan. BR/TR, 5'10.5", 165 lbs. Deb: 9/7/36 MC

YEAR	TM/L	G	AB	R	H	2B	3B	HR	RBI	BB	SO	AVG	OBP	SLG	PRO+	BR/A	SB	CS	SBR	FA	FR	G/POS	TPR
1936	StL-N	23	91	13	29	3	4	3	16	1	14	.319	.326	.538	130	3	3			.967	0	3-23	0.4
1937	StL-N	119	447	66	121	26	10	7	61	25	66	.271	.311	.421	95	-4	12			.978	2	*3-105/S-8	0.0
1938	StL-N	142	552	61	141	21	15	9	64	29	49	.255	.293	.397	83	-14	14			.945	0	3-73,S-68	-0.8
1939	StL-N	148	524	71	141	27	4	7	54	27	70	.269	.309	.376	78	-17	5			.934	-18	*3-143/S-2	-3.4
1940	StL-N	69	108	19	29	5	0	3	14	5	15	.269	.301	.398	86	-2	3			.877	-2	3-39	-0.3
1942	StL-A	147	616	90	157	27	11	1	50	59	54	.255	.320	.339	84	-13	16	13	-3	.973	3	*2-145/3-2	-0.5
1943	StL-A	132	538	77	147	35	6	1	36	50	46	.273	.335	.366	103	2	10	9	-2	.958	-31	*2-132	-2.6
1944	*StL-A	148	603	89	148	27	11	3	36	51	63	.245	.304	.342	80	-17	20	8	1	.957	-8	*2-146	-1.6
1945	StL-A	143	543	72	129	24	3	2	49	43	46	.238	.295	.304	70	-21	9	6	-1	.970	-20	*2-128,O-14	-3.7
1946	*Bos-A	22	47	8	11	3	0	1	6	2	7	.234	.265	.362	70	-2	0	0	0	1.000	-1	/2-9,3-8	-0.3
1947	Bos-A	54	131	20	22	3	0	2	5	17	13	.168	.264	.229	35	-11	3	1	0	.938	-1	2-20,3-19	-1.2
1948	Pit-N	4	2	0	0	0	0	0	0	0	1	.000	.000	.000	-98	-1	0			.000	0	H	-0.1
Total	12	1151	4202	586	1075	200	64	39	391	309	444	.256	.308	.362	84	-98	95	37		.964	-76	2-580,3-412/S-78,O	-14.1

■ DOUG GWOSDZ

Gwosdz, Douglas Wayne "Eye Chart" b: 6/20/60, Houston, Tex. BR/TR, 5'11", 185 lbs. Deb: 8/17/81

YEAR	TM/L	G	AB	R	H	2B	3B	HR	RBI	BB	SO	AVG	OBP	SLG	PRO+	BR/A	SB	CS	SBR	FA	FR	G/POS	TPR
1981	SD-N	16	24	1	4	2	0	0	3	3	6	.167	.259	.250	48	-2	0	0	0	1.000	2	C-13	0.1
1982	SD-N	7	17	1	3	0	0	0	0	2	7	.176	.263	.176	27	-2	0	0	0	1.000	2	/C-7	0.0
1983	SD-N	39	55	7	6	1	0	1	4	7	19	.109	.210	.182	10	-7	0	0	0	.971	2	C-32	-0.5
1984	SD-N	7	8	0	2	0	0	0	1	2	5	.250	.400	.250	86	-0	0	0	0	.963	2	/C-6	0.2
Total	4	69	104	9	15	3	0	1	8	14	37	.144	.246	.202	27	-10	0	0	0	.981	8	/C-58	-0.2

■ TONY GWYNN

Gwynn, Anthony Keith b: 5/9/60, Los Angeles, Cal. BL/TL, 5'11", 199 lbs. Deb: 7/19/82 F

YEAR	TM/L	G	AB	R	H	2B	3B	HR	RBI	BB	SO	AVG	OBP	SLG	PRO+	BR/A	SB	CS	SBR	FA	FR	G/POS	TPR
1982	SD-N	54	190	33	55	12	2	1	17	14	16	.289	.338	.389	109	2	8	3	1	.991	-6	O-52	-0.5
1983	SD-N	86	304	34	94	12	2	1	37	23	21	.309	.358	.372	106	3	7	4	-0	.994	6	O-81	0.6
1984	*SD-N★	158	606	88	**213**	21	10	5	71	59	23	**.351**	.411	.444	140	34	33	18	-1	.989	16	*O-156	4.5
1985	SD-N★	154	622	90	197	29	5	6	46	45	33	.317	.365	.408	118	15	14	11	-2	.989	17	*O-152	2.5
1986	SD-N★	160	642	**107**	**211**	33	7	14	59	52	35	.329	.382	.467	136	31	37	9	6	.989	20	*O-160	5.2
1987	SD-N★	157	589	119	**218**	36	13	7	54	82	35	**.370**	.450	.511	160	**54**	56	12	10	.981	9	*O-156	6.6
1988	SD-N	133	521	64	163	22	5	7	70	51	40	**.313**	.374	.415	128	20	26	11	1	.982	3	*O-133	2.1
1989	SD-N★	158	604	82	**203**	27	7	4	62	56	30	**.336**	.393	.424	133	27	40	16	2	.984	11	*O-157	3.9
1990	SD-N★	141	573	79	177	29	10	4	72	44	23	.309	.359	.415	112	9	17	8	0	.985	15	*O-141	2.2
1991	SD-N★	134	530	69	168	27	11	4	62	34	19	.317	.358	.432	118	12	8	8	-2	.990	11	*O-134	1.8
1992	SD-N★	128	520	77	165	27	3	6	41	46	16	.317	.373	.415	121	15	3	6	-3	.982	12	*O-127	2.3
1993	SD-N★	122	489	70	175	41	3	7	59	36	19	.358	.403	.497	137	26	14	1	4	.981	4	*O-121	3.0
1994	SD-N★	110	419	79	**165**	35	1	12	64	48	19	**.394**	.458	.568	171	45	5	0	2	.985	2	*O-106	4.5
1995	SD-N★	135	535	82	**197**	33	1	9	90	35	15	**.368**	.408	.484	139	30	17	5	2	.992	4	*O-133	3.2
1996	*SD-N†	116	451	67	159	27	2	3	50	39	17	**.353**	.405	.441	131	21	11	4	1	.989	-5	*O-111	1.4

YEAR	TM/L	G	AB	R	H	2B	3B	HR	RBI	BB	SO	AVG	OBP	SLG	PRO+	BR/A	SB	CS	SBR	FA	FR	G/POS	TPR
1997	SD-N★	149	592	97	**220**	49	2	17	119	43	28	**.372**	.417	.547	162	52	12	5	1	.983	-5	*O-143/D-3	4.3
1998	*SD-N★	127	461	65	148	35	0	16	69	35	18	.321	.370	.501	136	23	3	1	0	.993	-10	*O-116/D-3	1.2
Total	17	2222	8648	1302	2928	495	84	123	1042	742	407	.339	.392	.458	134	418	311	122	20	.987	105	*O-2179/D-6	48.8

■ CHRIS GWYNN Gwynn, Christopher Karlton b: 10/13/64, Los Angeles, Cal. BL/TL, 6', 210 lbs. Deb: 8/14/87 F

YEAR	TM/L	G	AB	R	H	2B	3B	HR	RBI	BB	SO	AVG	OBP	SLG	PRO+	BR/A	SB	CS	SBR	FA	FR	G/POS	TPR
1987	LA-N	17	32	2	7	1	0	0	2	1	7	.219	.242	.250	32	-3	0	0	0	1.000	-1	O-10	-0.5
1988	LA-N	12	11	1	2	0	0	0	0	1	2	.182	.250	.182	27	-1	0	0	0	.000	-2	/O-4	-0.3
1989	LA-N	32	68	8	16	4	1	0	7	2	9	.235	.257	.324	66	-3	1	0	0	1.000	-2	O-19	-0.6
1990	LA-N	101	141	19	40	2	1	5	22	7	28	.284	.318	.418	104	0	0	1	-1	1.000	-9	O-44	-1.1
1991	LA-N	94	139	18	35	5	1	5	22	10	23	.252	.307	.410	102	-0	1	0	0	1.000	-9	O-41	-1.0
1992	KC-A	34	84	10	24	3	2	1	7	3	10	.286	.310	.405	96	-1	0	0	0	1.000	-2	O-19/D-2	-0.3
1993	KC-A	103	287	36	86	14	4	1	25	24	34	.300	.356	.387	94	-2	0	1	-1	.994	0	O-83/1-1,D-5	-0.4
1994	LA-N	58	71	9	19	0	0	3	13	7	7	.268	.333	.394	95	-1	0	2	-1	1.000	-4	O-20	-0.6
1995	*LA-N	67	84	8	18	3	2	1	10	6	23	.214	.275	.333	65	-5	0	0	0	1.000	-1	O-17/1-2	-0.6
1996	*SD-N	81	90	8	16	4	0	1	10	10	28	.178	.260	.256	39	-8	0	0	0	1.000	-7	O-29/1-1	-1.5
Total	10	599	1007	119	263	36	11	17	118	71	171	.261	.312	.369	85	-23	2	4	-2	.997	-36	O-286/D-7,1-4	-6.9

■ DICK GYSELMAN Gyselman, Richard Renald b: 4/6/08, San Francisco, Cal. d: 9/20/90, Seattle, Wash. BR/TR, 6'2", 170 lbs. Deb: 4/20/33

YEAR	TM/L	G	AB	R	H	2B	3B	HR	RBI	BB	SO	AVG	OBP	SLG	PRO+	BR/A	SB	CS	SBR	FA	FR	G/POS	TPR
1933	Bos-N	58	155	10	37	6	2	0	12	7	21	.239	.272	.303	70	-7	0			.926	6	3-42/2-5,S-1	0.2
1934	Bos-N	24	36	7	6	1	1	0	4	2	11	.167	.211	.250	25	-4	0			.739	-2	3-15/2-2	-0.5
Total	2	82	191	17	43	7	3	0	16	9	32	.225	.260	.293	61	-11	0			.901	4	/3-57,2-7,S-1	-0.3

■ BERT HAAS Haas, Berthold John b: 2/8/14, Naperville, Ill. BR/TR, 5'11", 180 lbs. Deb: 9/9/37

YEAR	TM/L	G	AB	R	H	2B	3B	HR	RBI	BB	SO	AVG	OBP	SLG	PRO+	BR/A	SB	CS	SBR	FA	FR	G/POS	TPR
1937	Bro-N	16	25	2	10	3	0	0	2	1	1	.400	.423	.520	152	2	0			1.000	-1	/O-4,1-3	0.1
1938	Bro-N	1	0	0	0	0	0	0	0	0	0	—	—	—	—	0	0			.000	0	H	0.0
1942	Cin-N	154	585	59	140	21	6	6	54	59	54	.239	.310	.326	86	-10	6			.925	-10	*3-146/1-6,O-2	-2.0
1943	Cin-N	101	332	39	87	17	6	4	44	22	26	.262	.308	.386	101	-1	6			.993	9	1-44,3-23,O-18	0.5
1946	Cin-N	140	535	57	141	24	7	3	50	33	42	.264	.310	.351	91	-8	22			.994	0	*1-140/3-6	-1.7
1947	Cin-N★	135	482	58	138	17	7	3	67	42	27	.286	.346	.369	91	-6	9			.956	-4	O-69,1-53	-1.6
1948	Phi-N	95	333	35	94	9	2	4	34	36	25	.282	.354	.357	95	-2	8			.892	-8	3-54,1-35	-1.1
1949	Phi-N	2	1	0	0	0	0	0	0	1	1	.000	.500	.000	47	0	0			.000	0	H	0.0
	NY-N	54	104	12	27	2	3	1	10	5	8	.260	.294	.365	76	-4	0			.983	-1	1-23,3-11	-0.5
	Yr	56	105	12	27	2	3	1	10	6	9	.257	.297	.362	76	-4	0			.983	-1	1-23,3-11	-0.5
1951	Chi-A	23	43	1	7	0	1	1	2	5	4	.163	.250	.279	44	-4	0	0	0	1.000	-1	/1-7,O-4,3-1	-0.5
Total	9	721	2440	263	644	93	32	22	263	204	188	.264	.323	.355	91	-33	51	0		.991	-17	1-311,3-241/O-97	-6.8

■ BRUNO HAAS Haas, Bruno Philip "Boon" b: 5/5/1891, Worcester, Mass. d: 6/5/52, Sarasota, Fla. BB/TL, 5'10", 180 lbs. Deb: 6/23/15

YEAR	TM/L	G	AB	R	H	2B	3B	HR	RBI	BB	SO	AVG	OBP	SLG	PRO+	BR/A	SB	CS	SBR	FA	FR	G/POS	TPR
1915	Phi-A	12	18	1	1	0	0	0	0	1	7	.056	.105	.056	-54	-3	0			.875	1	/P-6,O-3	-0.2

■ EDDIE HAAS Haas, George Edwin b: 5/26/35, Paducah, Ky. BL/TR, 5'11", 178 lbs. Deb: 9/8/57 MC

YEAR	TM/L	G	AB	R	H	2B	3B	HR	RBI	BB	SO	AVG	OBP	SLG	PRO+	BR/A	SB	CS	SBR	FA	FR	G/POS	TPR
1957	Chi-N	14	24	1	5	1	0	0	4	1	5	.208	.240	.250	32	-2	0	0	0	1.000	-1	/O-4	-0.3
1958	Mil-N	9	14	2	5	0	0	0	1	2	1	.357	.438	.357	124	1	0	0	0	1.000	-0	/O-3	0.0
1960	Mil-N	32	32	4	7	2	0	1	5	5	14	.219	.324	.375	98	-0	0	0	0	1.000	-0	/O-2	-0.1
Total	3	55	70	7	17	3	0	1	10	8	20	.243	.321	.329	80	-2	0	0	0	1.000	-2	/O-9	-0.4

■ MULE HAAS Haas, George William b: 10/15/03, Montclair, N.J. d: 6/30/74, New Orleans, La. BL/TR, 6'1", 175 lbs. Deb: 8/15/25 C

YEAR	TM/L	G	AB	R	H	2B	3B	HR	RBI	BB	SO	AVG	OBP	SLG	PRO+	BR/A	SB	CS	SBR	FA	FR	G/POS	TPR
1925	Pit-N	4	3	1	0	0	0	0	0	0	1	.000	.000	.000	-94	-1	0	0	0	1.000	-1	/O-2	-0.2
1928	Phi-A	91	332	41	93	21	4	6	39	23	20	.280	.331	.422	94	-4	2	3	-1	.974	-3	O-82	-1.3
1929	*Phi-A	139	578	115	181	41	9	16	82	34	38	.313	.356	.498	113	9	0	4	-2	.982	2	*O-139	-0.1
1930	*Phi-A	132	532	91	159	33	7	2	68	43	33	.299	.352	.398	86	-11	2	2	-1	.976	12	*O-131	-0.8
1931	*Phi-A	102	440	82	142	29	7	8	56	30	29	.323	.366	.475	113	7	0	0	0	.989	4	*O-102	0.3
1932	Phi-A	143	558	91	170	28	5	6	65	62	49	.305	.376	.405	99	0	1	0	0	.987	7	*O-137	-0.2
1933	Chi-A	146	585	97	168	33	4	1	51	65	41	.287	.360	.362	96	-2	0	5	-3	.983	-5	*O-146	-1.6
1934	Chi-A	106	351	54	94	16	3	2	22	47	22	.268	.354	.348	79	-10	1	0	0	.991	-2	O-89	-1.5
1935	Chi-A	92	327	44	95	22	1	2	40	37	17	.291	.363	.382	90	-4	4	1	1	.989	-1	O-84	-0.7
1936	Chi-A	119	408	75	116	26	2	0	46	64	29	.284	.383	.358	81	-10	1	1	-0	.989	-6	O-96/1-7	-1.9
1937	Chi-A	54	111	8	23	3	3	0	15	16	10	.207	.313	.288	52	-8	1	0	0	.975	0	1-32/O-2	-1.0
1938	Phi-A	40	78	7	16	2	0	0	12	12	10	.205	.311	.231	39	-7	0	0	0	1.000	-2	O-12/1-6	-1.0
Total	12	1168	4303	706	1257	254	45	43	496	433	299	.292	.359	.402	93	-41	12	16	-6	.984	5	*O-1022/1-45	-10.0

■ EMIL HABERER Haberer, Emil Karl b: 2/2/1878, Cincinnati, Ohio d: 10/19/51, Louisville, Ky. BR/TR, 6'1", 204 lbs. Deb: 7/9/01

YEAR	TM/L	G	AB	R	H	2B	3B	HR	RBI	BB	SO	AVG	OBP	SLG	PRO+	BR/A	SB	CS	SBR	FA	FR	G/POS	TPR
1901	Cin-N	6	18	2	3	0	1	0	1	3		.167	.286	.278	68	-1	0			.545	-2	/3-3,1-2	-0.2
1903	Cin-N	5	13	1	1	0	0	0	0	2		.077	.200	.077	-18	-2	0			.933	-2	/C-4	-0.4
1909	Cin-N	5	16	1	3	1	0	0	2	0		.188	.188	.250	36	-1	0			.895	-2	/C-4	-0.3
Total	3	16	47	4	7	1	1	0	3	5		.149	.231	.213	31	-4	0			.912	-6	/C-8,3-3,1-2	-0.9

■ IRV HACH Hach, Irvin William "Major" b: 6/6/1873, Louisville, Ky. d: 8/13/36, Louisville, Ky. BR/TR, Deb: 7/1/1897

YEAR	TM/L	G	AB	R	H	2B	3B	HR	RBI	BB	SO	AVG	OBP	SLG	PRO+	BR/A	SB	CS	SBR	FA	FR	G/POS	TPR
1897	Lou-N	16	51	5	11	2	0	0	3	5		.216	.322	.255	55	-3	1			.889	-2	/2-9,3-7	-0.3

■ STAN HACK Hack, Stanley Camfield "Smiling Stan" b: 12/6/09, Sacramento, Cal d: 12/15/79, Dixon, Ill. BL/TR, 6', 170 lbs. Deb: 4/12/32 MC

YEAR	TM/L	G	AB	R	H	2B	3B	HR	RBI	BB	SO	AVG	OBP	SLG	PRO+	BR/A	SB	CS	SBR	FA	FR	G/POS	TPR
1932	*Chi-N	72	178	32	42	5	6	2	19	17	16	.236	.306	.365	80	-5	5			.913	-5	3-51	-0.7
1933	Chi-N	20	60	10	21	3	1	1	2	8	3	.350	.451	.483	167	6	4			.983	6	3-17	1.3
1934	Chi-N	111	402	54	116	16	6	1	21	45	42	.289	.363	.366	98	0	11			.949	0	*3-109	0.5
1935	*Chi-N	124	427	75	133	23	9	4	64	65	17	.311	.406	.436	125	18	14			.942	11	*3-111/1-7	3.1
1936	Chi-N	149	561	102	167	27	4	6	78	89	39	.298	.396	.392	110	12	17			.950	-12	*3-140,1-11	0.4
1937	Chi-N	154	582	106	173	27	6	2	63	83	42	.297	.388	.375	104	6	16			.968	-9	*3-150/1-4	0.1
1938	*Chi-N★	152	609	109	195	34	11	4	67	94	39	.320	.411	.432	128	28	**16**			.954	7	*3-152	3.6
1939	Chi-N★	156	641	112	191	28	6	8	56	65	35	.298	.364	.398	103	4	**17**			.956	-7	*3-156	-0.1
1940	Chi-N	149	603	101	**191**	38	6	8	40	75	24	.317	.395	.439	132	29	21			.954	14	*3-148/1-1	4.5
1941	Chi-N★	151	586	111	**186**	33	5	7	45	99	40	.317	.417	.427	143	38	10			.954	-16	*3-150/1-1	2.6
1942	Chi-N	140	553	91	166	36	3	6	39	94	40	.300	.402	.409	143	34	9			**.965**	-10	*3-139	2.7
1943	Chi-N★	144	533	78	154	24	4	3	35	82	27	.289	.384	.366	119	16	5			.960	-7	*3-136	1.1
1944	Chi-N	98	383	65	108	16	1	3	32	53	21	.282	.369	.352	104	4	5			.939	2	3-75,1-18	0.6
1945	*Chi-N†	150	597	110	193	29	7	2	43	99	30	.323	.420	.405	133	32	12			**.975**	18	*3-146/1-5	5.2
1946	Chi-N	92	323	55	92	13	4	0	26	83	32	.285	.431	.350	125	17	3			.968	-3	3-90	1.6
1947	Chi-N	76	240	28	65	11	2	0	12	41	19	.271	.377	.333	94	-0	0			.962	7	3-66	0.7
Total	16	1938	7278	1239	2193	363	81	57	642	1092	466	.301	.394	.397	120	238	165			.957	-4	*3-1836/1-47	27.2

■ RICH HACKER Hacker, Richard Warren b: 10/6/47, Belleville, Ill. BB/TR, 6', 160 lbs. Deb: 7/2/71 C

YEAR	TM/L	G	AB	R	H	2B	3B	HR	RBI	BB	SO	AVG	OBP	SLG	PRO+	BR/A	SB	CS	SBR	FA	FR	G/POS	TPR
1971	Mon-N	16	33	2	4	1	0	0	2	3	12	.121	.194	.152	-1	-4	0	0	0	.984	5	S-16	0.2

■ JIM HACKETT Hackett, James Joseph "Sunny Jim" b: 10/1/1877, Jacksonville, Ill. d: 3/28/61, Douglas, Mich. BR/TR, 6'2", 185 lbs. Deb: 9/14/02

YEAR	TM/L	G	AB	R	H	2B	3B	HR	RBI	BB	SO	AVG	OBP	SLG	PRO+	BR/A	SB	CS	SBR	FA	FR	G/POS	TPR
1902	StL-N	6	21	2	6	1	0	0	4	2		.286	.348	.333	115	0	1			.833	-1	/P-4,O-2	0.0
1903	StL-N	99	351	24	80	13	8	0	36	19		.228	.272	.311	68	-16	2			.972	-6	1-89/P-7	-2.2
Total	2	105	372	26	86	14	8	0	40	21		.231	.276	.312	70	-15	3			.893	-7	/1-89,P-11,O-2	-2.2

■ MERT HACKETT Hackett, Mortimer Martin b: 11/11/1859, Cambridge, Mass. d: 2/22/38, Cambridge, Mass. BR/TR, 5'10.5", 175 lbs. Deb: 5/2/1883 F

YEAR	TM/L	G	AB	R	H	2B	3B	HR	RBI	BB	SO	AVG	OBP	SLG	PRO+	BR/A	SB	CS	SBR	FA	FR	G/POS	TPR
1883	Bos-N	46	179	20	42	8	6	2	24	1	48	.235	.239	.380	82	-4				.909	-6	C-44/O-4	-0.7
1884	Bos-N	72	268	28	55	13	2	1	20	2	66	.205	.211	.280	53	-14				.928	12	C-71/3-1	0.3
1885	Bos-N	34	115	9	21	7	1	0	4	2	28	.183	.197	.261	49	-6				.901	5	C-34	0.2
1886	KC-N	62	230	18	50	8	3	3	25	4	59	.217	.231	.317	61	-11	1			.926	-17	C-53,O-13	-2.1

YEAR	TM/L	G	AB	R	H	2B	3B	HR	RBI	BB	SO	AVG	OBP	SLG	PRO+	BR/A	SB	CS	SBR	FA	FR	G/POS	TPR
1887	Ind-N	42	147	12	35	6	3	2	10	7	24	.238	.282	.361	80	-4	4			.938	-9	C-40/O-2,1-1	-0.8
Total	5	256	939	87	203	42	15	8	83	16	225	.216	.231	.318	65	-40	5			.921	-15	C-242/O-19,1-1,3-1	-3.1

■ WALTER HACKETT Hackett, Walter Henry b: 8/15/1857, Cambridge, Mass. d: 10/2/20, Cambridge, Mass. Deb: 4/17/1884 F

YEAR	TM/L	G	AB	R	H	2B	3B	HR	RBI	BB	SO	AVG	OBP	SLG	PRO+	BR/A	SB	CS	SBR	FA	FR	G/POS	TPR
1884	Bos-U	103	415	71	101	19	0	1		7		.243	.256	.296	68	-28				**.855**	12	*S-103	-1.3
1885	Bos-N	35	125	8	23	3	0	0	9	3	22	.184	.203	.208	34	-9				.893	-12	2-20,S-15	-1.9
Total	2	138	540	79	124	22	0	1	9	10	22	.230	.244	.276	61	-37				.852	1	S-118/2-20	-3.2

■ KENT HADLEY Hadley, Kent William b: 12/17/34, Pocatello, Idaho BL/TL, 6'3", 190 lbs. Deb: 9/14/58

YEAR	TM/L	G	AB	R	H	2B	3B	HR	RBI	BB	SO	AVG	OBP	SLG	PRO+	BR/A	SB	CS	SBR	FA	FR	G/POS	TPR
1958	KC-A	3	11	1	2	0	0	0	0	0	4	.182	.182	.182	0	-1	0	0	0	1.000	-1	/1-2	-0.2
1959	KC-A	113	288	40	73	11	1	10	39	24	74	.253	.313	.403	93	-3	1	2	-1	.989	-2	1-95	-1.1
1960	NY-A	55	64	8	13	2	0	4	11	6	19	.203	.271	.422	90	-1	0	0	0	.991	-0	1-24	-0.2
Total	3	171	363	49	88	13	1	14	50	30	97	.242	.302	.399	90	-6	1	2	-1	.989	-2	1-121	-1.5

■ BILL HAEFFNER Haeffner, William Bernhard b: 7/8/1894, Philadelphia, Pa. d: 1/27/82, Springfield, Pa. BR/TR, 5'9", 165 lbs. Deb: 6/29/15

YEAR	TM/L	G	AB	R	H	2B	3B	HR	RBI	BB	SO	AVG	OBP	SLG	PRO+	BR/A	SB	CS	SBR	FA	FR	G/POS	TPR
1915	Phi-A	3	4	0	1	0	0	0	0	0	1	.250	.250	.250	51	-0	0			1.000	-1	/C-3	-0.2
1920	Pit-N	54	175	8	34	4	1	0	14	8	14	.194	.230	.229	31	-15	1	1	-0	.972	-3	C-52	-1.7
1928	NY-N	2	1	0	0	0	0	0	0	0	0	.000	.000	.000	-99	-0	0			.750	0	/C-2	0.0
Total	3	59	180	8	35	4	1	0	14	8	15	.194	.229	.228	30	-16	1	1		.968	-5	/C-57	-1.9

■ CHICK HAFEY Hafey, Charles James b: 2/12/03, Berkeley, Cal. d: 7/2/73, Calistoga, Cal. BR/TR, 6', 185 lbs. Deb: 8/28/24 H

YEAR	TM/L	G	AB	R	H	2B	3B	HR	RBI	BB	SO	AVG	OBP	SLG	PRO+	BR/A	SB	CS	SBR	FA	FR	G/POS	TPR
1924	StL-N	24	91	10	23	5	2	2	22	4	8	.253	.292	.418	90	-2	1	0	0	.927	-1	O-24	-0.4
1925	StL-N	93	358	36	108	25	2	5	57	10	29	.302	.321	.425	87	-8	3	7	-3	.955	-1	O-88	-1.7
1926	*StL-N	78	225	30	61	19	2	4	38	11	36	.271	.311	.427	93	-3	2			.974	-6	O-64	-1.2
1927	StL-N	103	346	62	114	26	5	18	63	36	41	.329	.401	**.590**	157	27	12			.980	5	O-94	2.6
1928	*StL-N	138	520	101	175	46	6	27	111	40	53	.337	.386	.604	152	37	8			.965	3	*O-133	2.9
1929	StL-N	134	517	101	175	47	9	29	125	45	42	.338	.394	.632	148	36	7			.966	3	*O-130	2.7
1930	*StL-N	120	446	108	150	39	12	26	107	46	51	.336	.407	.652	146	31	12			.976	-3	*O-116	1.8
1931	*StL-N	122	450	94	157	35	8	16	95	39	43	**.349**	**.404**	.569	153	33	11			.983	-4	*O-118	2.0
1932	Cin-N	83	253	34	87	19	3	2	36	22	20	.344	.403	.466	137	14	4			.965	-3	O-65	0.7
1933	Cin-N★	144	568	77	172	34	6	7	62	40	44	.303	.351	.421	121	15	3			.987	8	*O-144	1.6
1934	Cin-N	140	535	75	157	29	6	18	67	52	63	.293	.359	.471	123	17	4			.967	4	*O-140	1.5
1935	Cin-N	15	59	10	20	6	1	1	9	4	5	.339	.400	.525	151	4	1			.912	-3	O-15	0.1
1937	Cin-N	89	257	39	67	11	5	9	41	23	42	.261	.324	.447	113	4	2			.971	-2	O-64	0.0
Total	13	1283	4625	777	1466	341	67	164	833	372	477	.317	.372	.526	133	205	70	7		.971	1	*O-1195	12.6

■ BUD HAFEY Hafey, Daniel Albert b: 8/6/12, Berkeley, Cal. d: 7/27/86, Sacramento, Cal. BR/TR, 6', 185 lbs. Deb: 4/21/35 F

YEAR	TM/L	G	AB	R	H	2B	3B	HR	RBI	BB	SO	AVG	OBP	SLG	PRO+	BR/A	SB	CS	SBR	FA	FR	G/POS	TPR
1935	Chi-A	2	0	1	0	0	0	0	0	0	0	—	—	—	—	0	0	0	0	.000	0	R	0.0
	Pit-N	58	184	29	42	11	2	6	16	16	48	.228	.290	.408	83	-5	0			.970	4	O-47	-0.3
1936	Pit-N	39	118	19	25	6	1	4	13	10	27	.212	.273	.381	73	-5	0			.932	0	O-29	-0.6
1939	Cin-N	6	13	1	2	1	0	0	1	1	4	.154	.214	.231	19	-1	1			1.000	-0	/O-4	-0.2
	Phi-N	18	51	3	9	1	0	0	3	3	12	.176	.222	.196	14	-6	1			1.000	1	O-13/P-2	-0.6
	Yr	24	64	4	11	2	0	0	4	4	16	.172	.221	.203	15	-8	2			1.000	1	O-17/P-2	-0.8
Total	3	123	366	53	78	19	3	10	33	30	91	.213	.273	.363	68	-18	2	0		.963	4	/O-93,P-2	-1.7

■ TOM HAFEY Hafey, Thomas Francis "Heave-O" or "The Arm" b: 7/12/13, Berkeley, Cal. d: 10/2/96, ElCerrito, Cal. BR/TR, 6'1", 180 lbs. Deb: 7/21/39 F

YEAR	TM/L	G	AB	R	H	2B	3B	HR	RBI	BB	SO	AVG	OBP	SLG	PRO+	BR/A	SB	CS	SBR	FA	FR	G/POS	TPR
1939	NY-N	70	256	37	62	10	1	6	26	10	44	.242	.271	.359	67	-13	1			.960	-0	3-70	-1.2
1944	StL-A	8	14	1	5	2	0	0	2	1	4	.357	.400	.500	148	1	0	0	0	1.000	-0	/O-4,1-1	0.1
Total	2	78	270	38	67	12	1	6	28	11	48	.248	.278	.367	72	-12	1	0		.960	-0	/3-70,O-4,1-1	-1.1

■ JOE HAGUE Hague, Joe Clarence b: 4/25/44, Huntington, W.Va. d: 11/5/94, San Antonio, Tex. BL/TL, 6', 198 lbs. Deb: 9/19/68

YEAR	TM/L	G	AB	R	H	2B	3B	HR	RBI	BB	SO	AVG	OBP	SLG	PRO+	BR/A	SB	CS	SBR	FA	FR	G/POS	TPR
1968	StL-N	7	17	2	4	0	0	1	1	2	2	.235	.316	.412	119	0	0	0	0	.800	-1	/O-3,1-2	-0.1
1969	StL-N	40	100	8	17	2	1	2	8	12	23	.170	.259	.270	48	-7	0	2	-1	.939	-0	O-17/1-9	-1.1
1970	StL-N	139	451	58	122	16	4	14	68	63	87	.271	.361	.417	106	4	2	1	0	.994	-4	1-82,O-52	-0.9
1971	StL-N	129	380	46	86	9	3	16	54	58	69	.226	.332	.392	100	1	0	3	-2	.996	-3	1-91,O-36	-1.3
1972	StL-N	27	76	8	18	5	1	3	11	17	18	.237	.376	.447	135	4	0	1	-1	1.000	-0	1-22/O-3	0.1
	*Cin-N	69	138	17	34	7	1	4	20	20	18	.246	.342	.399	116	3	1	1	-0	1.000	-2	1-22,O-19	-0.1
	Yr	96	214	25	52	12	2	7	31	37	36	.243	.355	.416	124	7	1	2	-1	1.000	-2	1-44,O-22	0.0
1973	Cin-N	19	33	2	5	2	0	0	1	5	5	.152	.263	.212	35	-3	1	0	0	1.000	-1	/O-5,1-4	-0.4
Total	6	430	1195	141	286	41	10	40	163	177	222	.239	.339	.391	101	3	4	8	-4	.996	-11	1-232,O-135	-3.8

■ BILL HAGUE Hague, William L. (b: William L. Haug) b: 1852, Philadelphia, Pa. BR/TR, 5'9", 164 lbs. Deb: 5/4/1875

YEAR	TM/L	G	AB	R	H	2B	3B	HR	RBI	BB	SO	AVG	OBP	SLG	PRO+	BR/A	SB	CS	SBR	FA	FR	G/POS	TPR
1875	StL-n	62	260	24	57	2	0	0	22	2	9	.219	.225	.227	63	-8	3	4	-2	.781	3	*3-62/1-1	-0.6
1876	Lou-N	67	294	31	78	8	0	1	22	2	10	.265	.270	.303	77	-10				.754	-26	*3-67/S-1	-3.1
1877	Lou-N	59	263	38	70	7	1	1	24	7	18	.266	.285	.312	75	-10				.843	-19	*3-59	-2.5
1878	Pro-N	62	250	21	51	3	0	0	25	5	34	.204	.220	.216	44	-15				**.925**	19	*3-62	0.7
1879	Pro-N	51	209	20	47	3	1	0	21	3	19	.225	.236	.249	61	-8				.822	5	3-51	-0.3
Total	4	239	1016	110	246	21	2	2	92	17	81	.242	.255	.273	66	-43				.843	-22	3-239/S-1	-5.2

■ DON HAHN Hahn, Donald Antone b: 11/16/48, San Francisco, Cal. BR/TR, 6'1", 185 lbs. Deb: 4/8/69

YEAR	TM/L	G	AB	R	H	2B	3B	HR	RBI	BB	SO	AVG	OBP	SLG	PRO+	BR/A	SB	CS	SBR	FA	FR	G/POS	TPR
1969	Mon-N	4	9	0	1	0	0	0	2	0	5	.111	.111	.111	-37	-2	0	0	0	1.000	0	/O-3	-0.2
1970	Mon-N	82	149	22	38	8	0	0	8	27	27	.255	.376	.309	86	-2	4	2	0	.986	-7	O-61	-1.0
1971	NY-N	98	178	16	42	5	1	1	11	21	32	.236	.320	.292	76	-5	2	3	-1	.973	-6	O-80	-1.5
1972	NY-N	17	37	0	6	0	0	0	1	4	12	.162	.244	.162	18	-4	0	0	0	1.000	-2	O-10	-0.7
1973	*NY-N	93	262	22	60	10	0	2	21	22	43	.229	.289	.290	62	-13	2	1	0	.989	-3	O-87	-2.1
1974	NY-N	110	323	34	81	14	1	4	28	37	34	.251	.330	.337	88	-5	2	0	1	.987	-1	*O-106	-1.0
1975	Phi-N	9	5	0	0	0	0	0	0	0	2	.000	.000	.000	-96	-1	0	0	0	1.000	-2	/O-7	-0.3
	StL-N	7	8	3	1	0	0	0	0	1	1	.125	.222	.125	-2	-1	0	0	0	1.000	-1	/O-4	-0.2
	SD-N	34	26	7	6	1	2	0	3	10	2	.231	.444	.423	151	3	1	0	0	1.000	-7	O-26	-0.5
	Yr	50	39	10	7	1	2	0	3	11	5	.179	.360	.308	89	-0	1	0	0	1.000	-10	O-37	-1.0
Total	7	454	997	104	235	38	4	7	74	122	158	.236	.321	.303	75	-30	11	6	-0	.985	-29	O-384	-7.5

■ DICK HAHN Hahn, Richard Frederick b: 7/24/16, Canton, Ohio d: 11/5/92, Orlando, Fla. BR/TR, 5'11", 176 lbs. Deb: 9/7/40

YEAR	TM/L	G	AB	R	H	2B	3B	HR	RBI	BB	SO	AVG	OBP	SLG	PRO+	BR/A	SB	CS	SBR	FA	FR	G/POS	TPR
1940	Was-A	1	3	0	0	0	0	0	0	0	0	.000	.000	.000	-99	-1	0	0	0	1.000	0	/C-1	-0.1

■ ED HAHN Hahn, William Edgar b: 8/27/1875, Nevada, Ohio d: 11/29/41, Des Moines, Iowa BL/TR, 160 lbs. Deb: 8/31/05

YEAR	TM/L	G	AB	R	H	2B	3B	HR	RBI	BB	SO	AVG	OBP	SLG	PRO+	BR/A	SB	CS	SBR	FA	FR	G/POS	TPR
1905	NY-A	43	160	32	51	5	0	0	11	25		.319	.426	.350	132	7	1			.957	2	O-43	0.8
1906	NY-A	11	22	2	2	1	0	0	1	3		.091	.259	.136	23	-2	2			1.000	-1	/O-7	-0.3
	*Chi-A	130	484	80	110	7	5	0	27	69		.227	.335	.262	90	-2	19			.949	-6	*O-130	-1.5
	Yr	141	506	82	112	8	5	0	28	72		.221	.331	.257	86	-4	21			.952	-6	*O-137	-1.8
1907	Chi-A	156	592	87	151	9	7	0	45	84		.255	.359	.294	112	14	17			**.990**	-5	*O-156	0.3
1908	Chi-A	122	447	58	112	12	8	0	21	39		.251	.329	.313	111	7	11			.965	-11	*O-118	-1.1
1909	Chi-A	76	287	30	52	6	0	1	16	31		.181	.268	.213	54	-14	9			.990	-7	O-76	-2.8
1910	Chi-A	15	53	2	6	2	0	0	1	7		.113	.217	.151	16	-5	0			.933	-3	O-15	-1.0
Total	6	553	2045	291	484	42	20	1	122	258		.237	.335	.278	97	5	59			.970	-30	O-545	-5.6

■ ED HAIGH Haigh, Edward E. b: 2/7/1867, Philadelphia, Pa. d: 2/13/53, Atlantic City, N.J Deb: 8/14/1892

YEAR	TM/L	G	AB	R	H	2B	3B	HR	RBI	BB	SO	AVG	OBP	SLG	PRO+	BR/A	SB	CS	SBR	FA	FR	G/POS	TPR
1892	StL-N	1	4	0	1	0	0	0	0	0	2	.250	.250	.250	54	-0	0			1.000	1	/O-1	0.0

■ HINKEY HAINES Haines, Henry Luther b: 12/23/1898, Red Lion, Pa. d: 1/9/79, Sharon Hill, Pa. BR/TR, 5'10", 170 lbs. Deb: 4/20/23

YEAR	TM/L	G	AB	R	H	2B	3B	HR	RBI	BB	SO	AVG	OBP	SLG	PRO+	BR/A	SB	CS	SBR	FA	FR	G/POS	TPR
1923	*NY-A	28	25	9	4	2	0	0	3	4	5	.160	.276	.240	36	-2	3	1	0	1.000	-3	O-14	-0.5

YEAR	TM/L	G	AB	R	H	2B	3B	HR	RBI	BB	SO	AVG	OBP	SLG	PRO+	BR/A	SB	CS	SBR	FA	FR	G/POS	TPR
■ JERRY HAIRSTON Hairston, Jerry Wayne Jr. b: 5/29/76, Naperville, Ill. BR/TR, 5'10", 172 lbs. Deb: 9/11/98 F																							
1998	Bal-A	6	7	2	0	0	0	0	0	0	1	.000	.000	.000	-99	-2	0	0	0	.750	-0	/2-4	-0.2
■ JERRY HAIRSTON Hairston, Jerry Wayne Sr. b: 2/16/52, Birmingham, Ala. BB/TR, 5'10", 180 lbs. Deb: 7/26/73 F																							
1973	Chi-A	60	210	25	57	11	1	0	23	33	30	.271	.373	.333	97	1	0	0	0	.944	2	O-33,1-19/D-8	-0.1
1974	Chi-A	45	109	8	25	7	0	0	8	13	18	.229	.311	.294	73	-4	0	2	-1	.926	-4	O-22,D-10	-1.0
1975	Chi-A	69	219	26	62	8	0	0	23	46	23	.283	.410	.320	107	5	1	0	0	.951	1	O-59/D-8	0.4
1976	Chi-A	44	119	20	27	2	2	0	10	24	19	.227	.357	.277	87	-1	1	1	-0	.973	-3	O-40	-0.6
1977	Chi-A	13	26	3	8	2	0	0	4	5	7	.308	.419	.385	121	1	0	0	0	1.000	-2	O-11	-0.1
	Pit-N	51	52	5	10	2	0	2	6	6	10	.192	.276	.346	64	-3	0	0	0	.923	-4	O-14/2-1	-0.7
1981	Chi-A	9	25	5	7	1	0	1	6	2	4	.280	.357	.440	131	1	0	0	0	.933	-1	/O-7	0.0
1982	Chi-A	85	90	11	21	5	0	5	18	9	15	.233	.303	.456	105	0	0	0	0	1.000	-8	O-36/D-2	-0.8
1983	*Chi-A	101	126	17	37	9	1	5	22	23	16	.294	.403	.500	141	8	0	1	-1	.968	-9	O-32/D-4	-0.2
1984	Chi-A	115	227	41	59	13	2	5	19	41	29	.260	.375	.401	110	4	2	1	0	.967	-5	O-37,D-20	-0.2
1985	Chi-A	95	140	9	34	8	0	2	20	29	18	.243	.380	.343	96	1	0	0	0	1.000	-1	D-29/O-5	-0.1
1986	Chi-A	101	225	32	61	15	0	5	26	26	26	.271	.349	.404	101	1	0	0	0	1.000	-3	D-29,1-19,O-11	-0.4
1987	Chi-A	66	126	14	29	8	0	5	20	25	25	.230	.362	.413	102	1	0	0	0	1.000	-0	O-13,D-13/1-7	0.0
1988	Chi-A	2	2	0	0	0	0	0	0	0	0	.000	.000	.000	-99	-1	0	0	0	.000	0	/H	-0.1
1989	Chi-A	3	3	0	1	0	0	0	0	0	0	.333	.333	.333	91	-0	0	0	0	.000	0	/D-2	0.0
Total	14	859	1699	216	438	91	6	30	205	282	240	.258	.366	.371	103	15	4	5	-2	.963	-35	O-320,D-125/1-45,2	-3.9
■ JOHNNY HAIRSTON Hairston, John Louis b: 8/27/44, Birmingham, Ala. BR/TR, 6'2", 200 lbs. Deb: 9/6/69 F																							
1969	Chi-N	3	4	0	1	0	0	0	0	0	2	.250	.250	.250	36	-0	0	0	0	1.000	-1	/C-1,O-1	-0.1
■ SAMMY HAIRSTON Hairston, Samuel Harding b: 1/20/20, Crawford, Miss. d: 10/31/97, Birmingham, Ala. BR/TR, 5'10.5", 187 lbs. Deb: 7/21/51 FC																							
1951	Chi-A	4	5	1	2	1	0	0	1	2	0	.400	.571	.600	222	1	0	0	0	1.000	-1	/C-2	0.0
■ CHET HAJDUK Hajduk, Chester b: 7/21/18, Chicago, Ill. BR/TR, 6', 195 lbs. Deb: 4/16/41																							
1941	Chi-A	1	1	0	0	0	0	0	0	0	0	.000	.000	.000	-99	-0	0	0	0	.000	0	H	0.0
■ DAVE HAJEK Hajek, David Vincent b: 10/14/67, Roseville, Cal. BR/TR, 5'10", 165 lbs. Deb: 9/15/95																							
1995	Hou-N	5	2	0	0	0	0	0	0	1	1	.000	.333	.000	-3	-0	1	0	0	.000	0	-0,-0	0.0
1996	Hou-N	8	10	3	3	1	0	0	0	2	0	.300	.417	.400	127	0	0	0	0	1.000	1	/3-3,2-2	0.2
Total	2	13	12	3	3	1	0	0	0	3	1	.250	.400	.333	104	0	1	0	0	1.000	1	/3-3,2-2	0.2
■ GEORGE HALAS Halas, George Stanley b: 2/2/1895, Chicago, Ill. d: 10/31/83, Chicago, Ill. BB/TR, 6', 164 lbs. Deb: 5/6/19																							
1919	NY-A	12	22	0	2	0	0	0	0	0	8	.091	.091	.091	-49	-4	0			1.000	-1	/O-6	-0.6
■ JOHN HALDEMAN Haldeman, John Avery b: 12/2/1855, Pewee Valley, Ky. d: 9/17/1899, Louisville, Ky. BL/TR, 5'10", 175 lbs. Deb: 7/3/1877																							
1877	Lou-N	1	4	0	0	0	0	0	0	0	0	.000	.000	.000	-85	-1				.571	-1	/2-1	-0.2
■ ODELL HALE Hale, Arvel Odell "Bad News" b: 8/10/08, Hosston, La. d: 6/9/80, ElDorado, Ark. BR/TR, 5'10", 175 lbs. Deb: 8/1/31																							
1931	Cle-A	25	92	14	26	2	4	1	5	8	8	.283	.340	.424	94	-1	2	0	1	.918	-4	3-15,2-10/S-1	-0.3
1933	Cle-A	98	351	49	97	19	8	10	64	30	37	.276	.333	.462	104	0	2	3	-1	.954	3	2-73,3-21	0.8
1934	Cle-A	143	563	82	170	44	6	13	101	48	50	.302	.357	.471	110	7	8	12	-5	.956	**26**	*2-137/3-5	3.3
1935	Cle-A	150	589	80	179	37	11	16	101	52	55	.304	.361	.486	115	11	15	13	-3	.938	7	*3-149/2-1	1.9
1936	Cle-A	153	620	126	196	50	13	14	87	64	43	.316	.380	.506	116	14	8	5	-1	.946	17	*3-148/2-3	3.1
1937	Cle-A	154	561	74	150	32	4	6	82	56	41	.267	.335	.371	77	-20	9	6	-1	.964	26	3-90,2-64	1.1
1938	Cle-A	130	496	69	138	32	2	8	69	44	39	.278	.338	.399	86	-12	8	1	2	.963	-13	*2-127	-1.4
1939	Cle-A	108	253	36	79	16	2	4	48	25	18	.312	.374	.439	111	4	4	5	-2	.966	-16	2-73/3-2	-0.9
1940	Cle-A	48	50	3	11	3	1	0	6	5	7	.220	.291	.320	60	-3	0	0	0	.700	-1	/3-3	-0.4
1941	Bos-A	12	24	5	5	2	0	1	1	3	4	.208	.296	.417	85	-1	0	0	0	.857	-3	/3-6,2-1	-0.4
	NY-N	41	102	13	20	3	0	0	9	18	13	.196	.317	.225	53	-6	1			.964	1	2-29	-0.3
Total	10	1062	3701	551	1071	240	51	73	573	353	315	.289	.352	.441	100	-6	57	45		.959	42	2-518,3-439/S-1	6.5
■ GEORGE HALE Hale, George Wagner "Ducky" b: 8/3/1894, Dexter, Kan. d: 11/1/45, Wichita, Kan. BR/TR, 5'10", 160 lbs. Deb: 8/24/14																							
1914	StL-A	6	11	1	2	0	0	0	0	0	3	.182	.182	.182	10	-1	0			.895	-0	/C-6	-0.1
1916	StL-A	4	1	0	0	0	0	0	0	0	1	.000	.500	.000	54	0	0			1.000	0	/C-3	0.0
1917	StL-A	38	61	4	12	2	1	0	8	10	12	.197	.310	.262	78	-1	0			.927	3	C-28	0.3
1918	StL-A	12	30	0	4	1	0	0	1	1	5	.133	.161	.167	-1	-4	0			.981	2	C-11	-0.1
Total	4	60	103	5	18	3	1	0	9	11	21	.175	.261	.223	49	-6	0			.940	5	/C-48	0.1
■ JOHN HALE Hale, John Steven b: 8/5/53, Fresno, Cal. BL/TR, 6'2", 195 lbs. Deb: 9/8/74																							
1974	LA-N	4	4	2	4	1	0	0	2	0	0	1.000	1.000	1.250	549	2	0	0	0	.000	-1	/O-3	0.1
1975	LA-N	71	204	20	43	7	0	6	22	26	51	.211	.306	.333	81	-5	1	2	-1	.977	-7	O-68	-1.7
1976	LA-N	44	91	4	14	2	1	0	8	16	14	.154	.294	.198	42	-6	4	1	1	.983	-4	O-37	-1.2
1977	LA-N	79	108	10	26	4	1	2	11	15	28	.241	.333	.352	84	-2	2	1	0	.986	-16	O-73	-2.0
1978	Sea-A	107	211	24	36	8	0	4	22	34	64	.171	.286	.265	56	-12	3	4	-2	.988	-13	O-98/D-3	-3.0
1979	Sea-A	54	63	6	14	3	0	2	7	12	26	.222	.347	.365	91	-1	0	0	0	1.000	-11	O-42/D-2	-1.2
Total	6	359	681	66	137	25	2	14	72	103	183	.201	.310	.305	72	-24	10	8	-2	.985	-52	O-321/D-5	-9.0
■ BOB HALE Hale, Robert Houston b: 11/7/33, Sarasota, Fla. BL/TL, 5'10", 195 lbs. Deb: 7/4/55																							
1955	Bal-A	67	182	13	65	7	1	0	29	5	19	.357	.378	.407	119	4	0	2	-1	.974	2	1-44	0.3
1956	Bal-A	85	207	18	49	10	1	1	24	11	10	.237	.279	.309	60	-13	0	2	-1	.975	-0	1-51	-1.7
1957	Bal-A	42	44	2	11	0	0	0	7	2	2	.250	.283	.250	50	-3	0	0	0	1.000	-0	/1-5	-0.4
1958	Bal-A	19	20	2	7	2	0	0	3	2	1	.350	.409	.450	144	1	0	0	0	1.000	1	/1-2	0.2
1959	Bal-A	40	54	2	10	3	0	0	7	2	6	.185	.214	.241	25	-6	0	0	0	1.000	-1	/1-8	-0.7
1960	Cle-A	70	70	2	21	7	0	0	12	3	6	.300	.329	.400	99	-0	0	0	0	.944	0	/1-5	0.0
1961	Cle-A	42	36	0	6	0	0	0	6	1	7	.167	.211	.167	2	-5	0	0	0	.000	0	H	-0.5
	NY-A	11	13	2	2	0	0	1	1	0	0	.154	.154	.385	41	-1	0	0	0	1.000	-0	/1-5	-0.1
	Yr	53	49	2	8	0	0	1	7	1	7	.163	.196	.224	12	-6	0	0	0	1.000	-0	/1-5	-0.6
Total	7	376	626	41	171	29	2	2	89	26	51	.273	.305	.335	76	-22	0	4	-2	.977	2	1-120	-2.9
■ SAMMY HALE Hale, Samuel Douglas b: 9/10/1896, Glen Rose, Tex. d: 9/6/74, Wheeler, Tex. BR/TR, 5'8.5", 160 lbs. Deb: 4/20/20																							
1920	Det-A	76	116	13	34	3	3	1	14	5	15	.293	.322	.397	92	-2	2	0	1	.886	-3	3-16/O-4,2-1	-0.3
1921	Det-A	9	2	2	0	0	0	0	0	0	1	.000	.000	.000	-99	-1	0	1	-1	.000	0	H	-0.1
1923	Phi-A	115	434	68	125	22	8	3	51	17	31	.288	.327	.396	89	-9	8	3	1	.916	-19	*3-107	-1.7
1924	Phi-A	80	261	41	83	14	2	2	17	17	19	.318	.367	.410	99	-1	3	2	-0	.948	-8	3-55/O-5,S-1	-0.4
1925	Phi-A	110	391	62	135	30	11	8	63	17	27	.345	.376	.540	122	11	7	4	-0	.919	-4	3-96/2-1	1.2
1926	Phi-A	111	327	49	92	22	9	4	43	13	36	.281	.311	.440	89	-7	1	4	-2	.947	-2	3-77/O-1	-0.6
1927	Phi-A	131	501	77	157	24	8	5	81	32	32	.313	.358	.423	97	-3	11	3	2	.961	1	*3-128	0.5
1928	Phi-A	88	314	38	97	20	9	4	58	9	21	.309	.334	.468	106	1	2	0	1	.932	12	3-79	1.7
1929	Phi-A	101	379	51	105	14	3	1	40	12	18	.277	.303	.338	62	-21	6	2	1	.956	-7	3-99/2-1	-2.3
1930	StL-A	62	190	21	52	8	1	2	25	8	18	.274	.303	.358	65	-10	1	1	-0	.947	-3	3-47	-1.0
Total	10	883	2915	422	880	157	54	30	392	130	218	.302	.336	.424	93	-42	41	20	0	.939	-33	3-704/O-10,2-3,S-1	-3.0
■ CHIP HALE Hale, Walter William b: 12/2/64, San Jose, Cal. BL/TR, 5'11", 191 lbs. Deb: 8/27/89																							
1989	Min-A	28	67	6	14	3	0	0	4	1	6	.209	.221	.254	31	-6	0	0	0	.980	-3	2-16/3-9,D-2	-0.9
1990	Min-A	1	2	0	0	0	0	0	2	0	1	.000	.000	.000	-94	-1	0	0	0	1.000	1	/2-1	0.1
1993	Min-A	69	186	25	62	6	1	3	27	18	17	.333	.410	.425	124	7	2	1	0	.952	-3	2-21,3-19,D-19,/1S	0.4
1994	Min-A	67	118	13	31	9	0	1	11	16	14	.263	.356	.364	86	-2	0	2	-1	.964	5	3-21,D-10/1-7,2O	0.1
1995	Min-A	69	103	10	27	4	0	2	18	11	20	.262	.333	.359	80	-3	0	0	0	1.000	1	D-27/2-7,3-5,1-3	-0.4

YEAR	TM/L	G	AB	R	H	2B	3B	HR	RBI	BB	SO	AVG	OBP	SLG	PRO+	BR/A	SB	CS	SBR	FA	FR	G/POS	TPR
1996	Min-A	85	87	8	24	5	0	1	16	10	6	.276	.351	.368	81	-2	0	0	0	1.000	1	2-14,D-10/1-6,3O	-0.1
1997	LA-N	14	12	0	1	0	0	0	0	2	4	.083	.214	.083	-20	-2	0	0	0	1.000	-0	/3-2	-0.2
Total	7	333	575	62	159	27	1	7	78	58	68	.277	.350	.363	88	-9	2	3	-1	.969	2	/D-68,2-64,31OS	-1.0

■ FRED HALEY Haley, Frederick b: 6/18/1853, Wheeling, W.Va. TR , Deb: 6/22/1880

YEAR	TM/L	G	AB	R	H	2B	3B	HR	RBI	BB	SO	AVG	OBP	SLG	PRO+	BR/A	SB	CS	SBR	FA	FR	G/POS	TPR
1880	Tro-N	2	7	0	0	0	0	0	0	1	2	.000	.125	.000	-51	-1				.750	-2	/C-2	-0.3

■ RAY HALEY Haley, Raymond Timothy "Pat" b: 1/23/1891, Danbury, Iowa d: 10/8/73, Bradenton, Fla. BR/TR, 5'11", 180 lbs. Deb: 4/21/15

YEAR	TM/L	G	AB	R	H	2B	3B	HR	RBI	BB	SO	AVG	OBP	SLG	PRO+	BR/A	SB	CS	SBR	FA	FR	G/POS	TPR
1915	Bos-A	5	7	2	1	1	0	0	0	1	0	.143	.250	.286	62	-0	0			1.000	0	/C-4	0.0
1916	Bos-A	1	1	0	0	0	0	0	0	0	1	.000	.000	.000	-99	-0	0			.000	0	H	0.0
	Phi-A	34	108	8	25	5	0	0	4	6	19	.231	.278	.278	70	-4	0			.982	6	C-33	0.5
	Yr	35	109	8	25	5	0	0	4	6	20	.229	.276	.275	69	-4	0			.982	6	C-33	0.5
1917	Phi-A	41	98	7	27	2	1	0	11	4	12	.276	.311	.316	93	-1	2			.947	-6	C-34	-0.6
Total	3	81	214	17	53	8	1	0	15	11	32	.248	.291	.294	80	-6	2			.970	1	/C-71	-0.1

■ ALBERT HALL Hall, Albert b: 3/7/58, Birmingham, Ala. BB/TR, 5'11", 155 lbs. Deb: 9/12/81

YEAR	TM/L	G	AB	R	H	2B	3B	HR	RBI	BB	SO	AVG	OBP	SLG	PRO+	BR/A	SB	CS	SBR	FA	FR	G/POS	TPR
1981	Atl-N	6	2	1	0	0	0	0	0	1	1	.000	.333	.000	1	-0	0	0	0	.000	-1	/O-2	-0.1
1982	Atl-N	5	0	1	0	0	0	0	0	0	0	—	—	—	—	0	0	0	0	.000	0	/R	0.0
1983	Atl-N	10	8	2	0	0	0	0	0	2	2	.000	.200	.000	-37	-1	1	1	-0	.750	-2	/O-4	-0.4
1984	Atl-N	87	142	25	37	6	1	1	9	10	18	.261	.309	.338	76	-4	6	4	-1	.932	-10	O-66	-1.7
1985	Atl-N	54	47	5	7	0	1	0	3	9	12	.149	.286	.191	34	-4	1	1	-0	.900	-4	O-13	-0.8
1986	Atl-N	16	50	6	12	2	0	0	1	5	6	.240	.309	.280	60	-3	8	3	1	.900	0	O-14	-0.3
1987	Atl-N	92	292	54	83	20	4	3	24	38	36	.284	.370	.411	102	2	33	10	4	.981	3	O-69	0.6
1988	Atl-N	85	231	27	57	7	1	1	15	21	35	.247	.315	.299	73	-7	15	10	-2	.973	2	O-63	-1.0
1989	Pit-N	20	33	4	6	2	1	0	1	3	5	.182	.250	.303	59	-2	3	0	1	.909	-3	O-12	-0.5
Total	9	375	805	125	202	37	8	5	53	89	115	.251	.329	.335	80	-20	67	29	3	.958	-15	O-243	-4.2

■ AL HALL Hall, Archibald W. b: Worcester, Mass. d: 2/10/1885, Warren, Pa. Deb: 5/1/1879

YEAR	TM/L	G	AB	R	H	2B	3B	HR	RBI	BB	SO	AVG	OBP	SLG	PRO+	BR/A	SB	CS	SBR	FA	FR	G/POS	TPR
1879	Tro-N	67	306	30	79	7	3	0	14	3	13	.258	.265	.301	92	-2				.842	5	*O-67	-0.1
1880	Cle-N	3	8	1	1	0	0	0	0	0	0	.125	.125	.125	-15	-1				1.000	-1	/O-3	-0.2
Total	2	70	314	31	80	7	3	0	14	3	13	.255	.262	.296	90	-3				.843	4	/O-70	-0.3

■ CHARLIE HALL Hall, Charles Walter "Doc" b: 8/24/1863, Toulon, Ill. d: 6/24/21, Tacoma, Wash. Deb: 5/3/1887

YEAR	TM/L	G	AB	R	H	2B	3B	HR	RBI	BB	SO	AVG	OBP	SLG	PRO+	BR/A	SB	CS	SBR	FA	FR	G/POS	TPR
1887	NY-a	3	12	1	1	0	0	0	0	2		.083	.214	.083	-16	-2	1			1.000	0	/O-3	-0.1

■ GEORGE HALL Hall, George William b: 3/29/1849, Stepney, England d: 6/11/23, Ridgewood, N.J. BL , 5'7", 142 lbs. Deb: 5/5/1871

YEAR	TM/L	G	AB	R	H	2B	3B	HR	RBI	BB	SO	AVG	OBP	SLG	PRO+	BR/A	SB	CS	SBR	FA	FR	G/POS	TPR
1871	Oly-n	32	136	31	40	3	3	2	17	8	0	.294	.333	.404	117	4	2	1	0	.913	7	*O-32	0.8
1872	Bal-n	53	250	69	84	17	6	1	37	3	1	.336	.344	.464	140	10	6	1	1	.836	-3	*O-52/1-1	0.7
1873	Bal-n	35	168	44	58	6	3	0	30	2	0	.345	.353	.417	128	6	0	0	0	.840	2	*O-35	0.6
1874	Bos-n	47	222	58	64	10	8	1	34	1	0	.288	.291	.419	118	3	2	0	1	.811	-3	*O-47	0.2
1875	Ath-n	77	358	71	107	10	12	4	62	3	4	.299	.305	.427	136	10	8	5	-1	.887	4	*O-77/1-1	1.2
1876	Phi-N	60	268	51	98	7	13	**5**	45	8	4	.366	.384	.545	208	30				.801	-2	*O-60	2.4
1877	Lou-N	61	269	53	87	15	8	0	26	12	19	.323	.352	.439	125	5				**.900**	-6	*O-61	-0.3
Total	5 n	244	1134	273	353	46	32	8	180	17	5	.311	.321	.429	130	32	18	7	1	.861	7	O-243/1-2	3.5
Total	2	121	537	104	185	22	21	5	71	20	23	.345	.368	.492	162	35				.837	-7	O-121	2.1

■ IRV HALL Hall, Irvin Gladstone b: 10/7/18, Alberton, Md. BR/TR, 5'10.5", 160 lbs. Deb: 4/20/43

YEAR	TM/L	G	AB	R	H	2B	3B	HR	RBI	BB	SO	AVG	OBP	SLG	PRO+	BR/A	SB	CS	SBR	FA	FR	G/POS	TPR
1943	Phi-A	151	544	37	139	15	4	0	54	22	42	.256	.292	.298	73	-19	10	7	-1	.948	-11	*S-148/2-1,3-1	-2.2
1944	Phi-A	143	559	60	150	20	8	0	45	31	46	.268	.309	.333	85	-12	2	5	-2	.980	-5	2-97,S-40/1-4	-1.2
1945	Phi-A	151	616	62	161	17	5	0	50	35	42	.261	.307	.305	78	-17	3	10	-5	.978	**26**	*2-151	1.4
1946	Phi-A	63	185	19	46	6	2	0	19	9	18	.249	.287	.303	65	-9	1	1	-0	.973	-4	2-40/S-7	-1.1
Total	4	508	1904	178	496	58	19	0	168	97	148	.261	.302	.311	77	-58	16	23	-9	.977	6	2-289,S-195/1-4,3-1	-3.1

■ JIM HALL Hall, James d: 1/30/1886, Brooklyn, N.Y. Deb: 5/20/1872

YEAR	TM/L	G	AB	R	H	2B	3B	HR	RBI	BB	SO	AVG	OBP	SLG	PRO+	BR/A	SB	CS	SBR	FA	FR	G/POS	TPR
1872	Atl-n	13	57	9	18	0	1	0	6	1	0	.316	.328	.351	93	-2	0	0	0	.750	-3	2-13	-0.4
1874	Atl-n	2	9	0	1	0	0	0	0	0	0	.111	.111	.111	-32	-1	0	0	0	.857	-1	/2-2,O-1	-0.2
1875	Wes-n	1	3	0	1	0	1	0	1	0	0	.333	.333	1.000	327	1	0	0	0	.000	-1	/O-1	0.0
Total	3 n	16	69	9	20	0	2	0	7	1	0	.290	.300	.348	89	-2	0	0	0	.758	-5	/2-15,O-2	-0.6

■ JIMMIE HALL Hall, Jimmie Randolph b: 3/17/38, Mt.Holly, N.C. BL/TR, 6', 175 lbs. Deb: 4/9/63

YEAR	TM/L	G	AB	R	H	2B	3B	HR	RBI	BB	SO	AVG	OBP	SLG	PRO+	BR/A	SB	CS	SBR	FA	FR	G/POS	TPR
1963	Min-A	156	497	88	129	21	5	33	80	63	101	.260	.343	.521	136	23	3	3	-1	.982	-10	*O-143	0.5
1964	Min-A★	149	510	61	144	20	3	25	75	44	112	.282	.341	.480	125	16	5	2	0	.985	13	*O-137	2.4
1965	*Min-A★	148	522	81	149	25	4	20	86	51	79	.285	.350	.464	124	16	14	7	0	.976	-2	*O-141	0.8
1966	Min-A	120	356	52	85	7	4	20	47	33	66	.239	.303	.449	106	2	1	2	-1	.978	-1	*O-103	-0.4
1967	Cal-A	129	401	54	100	8	3	16	55	42	65	.249	.321	.404	117	8	4	1	1	.990	-2	*O-120	0.1
1968	Cal-A	46	126	15	27	3	0	1	8	16	19	.214	.303	.262	75	-3	1	0	0	.981	-4	O-39	-1.0
	Cle-A	53	111	4	22	4	0	1	8	10	19	.198	.264	.261	61	-5	1	0	0	.983	2	O-29	-0.5
	Yr	99	237	19	49	7	0	2	16	26	38	.207	.285	.262	68	-9	2	0	1	.982	-2	O-68	-1.5
1969	Cle-A	4	10	1	0	0	0	0	0	2	3	.000	.167	.000	-48	-2	1	0	0	1.000	-0	/O-3	-0.2
	NY-A	80	212	21	50	8	5	3	26	19	34	.236	.299	.363	88	-4	8	3	1	.963	-5	O-50/1-7	-1.2
	Yr	84	222	22	50	8	5	3	26	21	37	.225	.292	.347	81	-6	9	3	1	.966	-5	O-53/1-7	-1.4
	Chi-N	11	24	1	5	1	0	0	1	1	5	.208	.240	.250	33	-2	0	0	0	1.000	-1	/O-5	-0.4
1970	Chi-N	28	32	2	3	1	0	0	1	4	12	.094	.194	.125	-11	-5	0	0	0	1.000	-2	/O-8	-0.7
	Atl-N	39	47	7	10	2	0	2	4	2	14	.213	.245	.383	62	-3	0	0	0	1.000	-6	O-28	-0.9
	Yr	67	79	9	13	3	0	2	5	6	26	.165	.224	.278	31	-8	0	0	0	1.000	-7	O-36	-1.6
Total	8	963	2848	387	724	100	24	121	391	287	529	.254	.323	.434	112	40	38	18	1	.982	-17	O-806/1-7	-1.5

■ JOE HALL Hall, Joseph Geroy b: 3/6/66, Paducah, Ky. BR/TR, 6', 180 lbs. Deb: 4/5/94

YEAR	TM/L	G	AB	R	H	2B	3B	HR	RBI	BB	SO	AVG	OBP	SLG	PRO+	BR/A	SB	CS	SBR	FA	FR	G/POS	TPR
1994	Chi-A	17	28	6	11	3	0	1	5	2	4	.393	.452	.607	173	3	0	0	0	.917	-2	/O-9,D-2	0.1
1995	Det-A	7	15	2	2	0	0	0	0	2	3	.133	.235	.133	-1	-2	0	0	0	1.000	1	/O-5,D-2	-0.1
1997	Det-A	2	4	1	2	1	0	0	3	0	0	.500	.500	.750	222	1	0	0	0	1.000	-0	/O-1	0.0
Total	3	26	47	9	15	4	0	1	8	4	7	.319	.385	.468	121	2	0	0	0	.960	-1	/O-15,D-4	0.0

■ MEL HALL Hall, Melvin b: 9/16/60, Lyons, N.Y. BL/TL, 6'1", 205 lbs. Deb: 9/3/81

YEAR	TM/L	G	AB	R	H	2B	3B	HR	RBI	BB	SO	AVG	OBP	SLG	PRO+	BR/A	SB	CS	SBR	FA	FR	G/POS	TPR
1981	Chi-N	10	11	1	1	0	0	1	2	1	4	.091	.167	.364	45	-1	0	0	0	.000	-2	/O-3	-0.3
1982	Chi-N	24	80	6	21	3	2	0	4	5	17	.262	.322	.350	86	-1	0	1	-1	.939	1	O-22	-0.2
1983	Chi-N	112	410	60	116	23	5	17	56	42	101	.283	.354	.488	125	13	6	6	-2	.988	0	*O-112	0.8
1984	Chi-N	48	150	25	42	11	3	4	22	12	23	.280	.333	.473	114	2	2	1	0	.961	-2	O-46	-0.1
	Cle-A	83	257	43	66	13	1	7	30	35	55	.257	.350	.397	104	2	1	1	-0	.993	0	O-69/D-9	0.0
1985	Cle-A	23	66	7	21	6	0	0	12	8	12	.318	.392	.409	121	2	0	1	-1	1.000	-3	O-15/D-5	-0.2
1986	Cle-A	140	442	68	131	29	2	18	77	33	65	.296	.348	.493	128	16	6	2	1	.972	-7	*O-126/D-7	0.6
1987	Cle-A	142	485	57	136	21	1	18	76	20	68	.280	.310	.439	95	-5	5	4	-1	.989	6	*O-122,D-14	-0.4
1988	Cle-A	150	515	69	144	32	4	6	71	28	50	.280	.317	.392	95	-4	7	3	0	.967	-3	*O-141/D-6	-1.1
1989	NY-A	113	361	54	94	9	0	17	58	21	37	.260	.301	.427	104	1	0	0	0	.993	-2	O-75,D-34	-0.4
1990	NY-A	113	360	41	93	23	2	12	46	6	46	.258	.274	.433	95	-5	0	0	0	.973	-6	D-54,O-50	-1.3
1991	NY-A	141	492	67	140	23	2	19	80	26	40	.285	.324	.455	113	7	0	1	-1	.987	-0	*O-120,D-10	0.3
1992	NY-A	152	583	67	163	36	3	15	81	29	53	.280	.315	.429	107	3	4	2	0	.990	6	*O-136,D-11	0.6
1996	SF-N	25	25	3	3	0	0	0	5	1	4	.120	.154	.120	-28	-5	0	0	0	.000	-1	/O-4	-0.6
Total	13	1276	4237	568	1171	229	25	134	620	267	575	.276	.322	.437	107	26	31	22	-4	.981	-13	*O-1041,D-150	-2.3

■ DICK HALL Hall, Richard Wallace b: 9/27/30, St.Louis, Mo. BR/TR, 6'6", 200 lbs. Deb: 4/15/52

YEAR	TM/L	G	AB	R	H	2B	3B	HR	RBI	BB	SO	AVG	OBP	SLG	PRO+	BR/A	SB	CS	SBR	FA	FR	G/POS	TPR
1952	Pit-N	26	80	6	11	1	0	0	2	2	17	.138	.159	.150	-14	-12	0	1	-1	.972	0	O-14/3-5	-1.4

YEAR	TM/L	G	AB	R	H	2B	3B	HR	RBI	BB	SO	AVG	OBP	SLG	PRO+	BR/A	SB	CS	SBR	FA	FR	G/POS	TPR
1953	Pit-N	7	24	2	4	0	0	0	1	1	3	.167	.200	.167	-3	-4	1	1	-0	.978	11	/2-7	0.6
1954	Pit-N	112	310	38	74	8	4	2	27	33	46	.239	.312	.310	64	-16	3	0	1	.956	-2	*O-102	-2.1
1955	Pit-N	21	40	3	7	1	0	1	3	6	5	.175	.283	.275	50	-3	0	0	0	1.000	-3	P-15/O-3	-0.2
1956	Pit-N	33	29	5	10	0	0	0	1	5	7	.345	.441	.345	118	1	0	0	0	1.000	-1	P-19/1-1	0.0
1957	Pit-N	10	1	0	0	0	0	0	0	0	1	.000	.000	.000	-99	-0	0	0	0	.000	-0	/P-8	0.0
1959	Pit-N	2	2	0	0	0	0	0	0	0	0	.000	.000	.000	-99	-1	0	0	0	1.000	-0	/P-2	0.0
1960	KC-A	32	56	5	6	0	0	0	4	4	15	.107	.167	.107	-24	-10	1	0	0	.925	-1	P-29	0.0
1961	Bal-A	30	36	4	5	0	0	0	1	3	13	.139	.205	.139	-6	-5	0	0	0	.970	1	P-29	0.0
1962	Bal-A	44	24	3	4	1	0	0	1	4	9	.167	.286	.208	38	-2	0	0	0	1.000	-0	P-43	0.0
1963	Bal-A	48	28	7	13	1	0	1	4	0	8	.464	.464	.607	205	4	0	0	0	1.000	1	P-47	0.0
1964	Bal-A	45	16	1	2	0	0	0	3	1	3	.125	.176	.125	-14	-2	0	0	0	1.000	-0	P-45	0.0
1965	Bal-A	49	15	1	5	2	0	0	4	1	4	.333	.412	.467	146	1	0	0	0	.923	-1	P-48	0.0
1966	Bal-A	32	12	0	2	0	0	0	2	0	5	.167	.231	.167	17	-1	0	0	0	1.000	-0	P-32	0.0
1967	Phi-N	48	14	1	1	0	0	0	0	0	5	.071	.071	.071	-58	-3	0	0	0	1.000	1	P-48	0.0
1968	Phi-N	32	3	0	1	0	0	0	0	0	1	.333	.333	.333	101	-0	0	0	0	1.000	-0	P-32	0.0
1969	*Bal-A	39	7	1	2	0	0	0	2	1	1	.286	.375	.286	86	-0	1	0	0	1.000	-1	P-39	0.0
1970	*Bal-A	32	12	2	1	0	0	0	1	0	3	.083	.083	.083	-53	-2	0	0	0	1.000	-1	P-32	0.0
1971	*Bal-A	27	5	0	2	1	0	0	0	0	1	.400	.400	.600	182	0	0	0	0	.800	-1	P-27	0.0
Total	19	669	714	79	150	15	4	4	56	61	147	.210	.274	.259	44	-56	6	2	1	.976	2	P-495,O-119/2-7,31	-3.1

■ BOB HALL Hall, Robert Prill b: 12/20/1878, Baltimore, Md. d: 12/1/50, Wellesley, Mass. TR , 5'10", 158 lbs. Deb: 4/18/04

YEAR	TM/L	G	AB	R	H	2B	3B	HR	RBI	BB	SO	AVG	OBP	SLG	PRO+	BR/A	SB	CS	SBR	FA	FR	G/POS	TPR
1904	Phi-N	46	163	11	26	4	0	0	17	14		.160	.226	.184	28	-13	5			.843	-10	3-20,S-15,1-11	-2.5
1905	NY-N	1	3	1	1	0	0	0	0	0		.333	.333	.333	97	-0	0			.000	-0	/O-1	0.0
	Bro-N	56	203	21	48	4	1	2	15	11		.236	.279	.296	77	-6	8			.939	6	O-42/2-7,1-3	-0.3
	Yr	57	206	22	49	4	1	2	15	11		.238	.280	.296	77	-6	8			.939	5	O-43/2-7,1-3	-0.3
Total	2	103	369	33	75	8	1	2	32	25		.203	.256	.247	55	-20	13			.968	-5	/O-43,3-20,S-15,12	-2.8

■ RUSS HALL Hall, Robert Russell b: 9/29/1871, Shelbyville, Ky. d: 7/1/37, Los Angeles, Cal. TL , 5'10", 170 lbs. Deb: 4/15/1898

YEAR	TM/L	G	AB	R	H	2B	3B	HR	RBI	BB	SO	AVG	OBP	SLG	PRO+	BR/A	SB	CS	SBR	FA	FR	G/POS	TPR
1898	StL-N	39	143	13	35	2	1	0	10	7		.245	.285	.273	59	-8	1			.835	-14	S-35/3-3,O-1	-2.0
1901	Cle-A	1	4	2	2	0	0	0	0	0		.500	.500	.500	185	0	0			.500	-1	/S-1	-0.1
Total	2	40	147	15	37	2	1	0	10	7		.252	.290	.279	62	-7	1			.824	-16	/S-36,3-3,O-1	-2.1

■ BILL HALL Hall, William Lemuel b: 7/30/28, Moultrie, Ga. d: 1/1/86, Moultrie, Ga. BL/TR, 5'11", 165 lbs. Deb: 4/18/54

YEAR	TM/L	G	AB	R	H	2B	3B	HR	RBI	BB	SO	AVG	OBP	SLG	PRO+	BR/A	SB	CS	SBR	FA	FR	G/POS	TPR
1954	Pit-N	5	7	0	0	0	0	0	0	0	0	.000	.000	.000	-99	-2	0	0	0	1.000	-0	/C-1	-0.2
1956	Pit-N	1	3	0	0	0	0	0	0	0	1	.000	.000	.000	-99	-1	0	0	0	1.000	1	/C-1	0.0
1958	Pit-N	51	116	15	33	6	0	1	15	15	13	.284	.366	.362	96	-0	0	0	0	.982	7	C-51	0.9
Total	3	57	126	15	33	6	0	1	15	15	14	.262	.340	.333	81	-3	0	0	0	.983	8	/C-53	0.7

■ TOM HALLER Haller, Thomas Frank b: 6/23/37, Lockport, Ill. BL/TR, 6'4", 195 lbs. Deb: 4/11/61 C

YEAR	TM/L	G	AB	R	H	2B	3B	HR	RBI	BB	SO	AVG	OBP	SLG	PRO+	BR/A	SB	CS	SBR	FA	FR	G/POS	TPR
1961	SF-N	30	62	5	9	1	0	2	8	9	23	.145	.264	.258	41	-5	0	1	-1	1.000	2	C-25	-0.3
1962	*SF-N	99	272	53	71	13	1	18	55	51	59	.261	.385	.515	142	17	1	4	-2	.992	-2	C-91	1.6
1963	SF-N	98	298	32	76	8	1	14	44	34	45	.255	.335	.430	120	8	4	6	-2	.994	-4	C-85/O-7	0.4
1964	SF-N	117	388	43	98	14	3	16	48	55	51	.253	.348	.428	115	9	4	2	0	.989	-1	*C-113/O-3	1.3
1965	SF-N	134	422	40	106	4	3	16	49	47	67	.251	.338	.389	101	1	0	0	0	.987	-5	*C-133	0.4
1966	SF-N☆	142	471	74	113	19	2	27	67	53	74	.240	.325	.461	112	7	1	3	-2	.991	-7	*C-136/1-4	0.8
1967	SF-N★	141	455	54	114	23	5	14	49	62	61	.251	.345	.415	118	12	0	4	-2	.997	-1	*C-136/O-1	1.7
1968	LA-N★	144	474	37	135	27	5	4	53	46	76	.285	.351	.388	132	18	1	4	-2	.994	3	*C-139	3.2
1969	LA-N	134	445	46	117	18	3	6	39	48	58	.263	.337	.357	102	1	0	3	-2	.992	-9	*C-132	-0.3
1970	LA-N	112	325	47	93	16	6	10	47	32	35	.286	.354	.465	123	10	3	0	1	.993	-8	*C-106	0.7
1971	LA-N	84	202	23	54	5	0	5	32	25	30	.267	.354	.366	111	3	0	2	-1	.978	4	C-67	0.9
1972	*Det-A	59	121	7	25	5	2	2	13	15	14	.207	.294	.331	83	-2	0	1	-1	1.000	8	C-36	0.7
Total	12	1294	3935	461	1011	153	31	134	504	477	593	.257	.342	.414	114	78	14	30	-14	.992	-20	*C-1199/O-11,1-4	11.1

■ NEWT HALLIDAY Halliday, Newton Reese b: 6/18/1896, Chicago, Ill. d: 4/6/18, Great Lakes, Ill. BR/TR, 6'1", 175 lbs. Deb: 8/19/16

YEAR	TM/L	G	AB	R	H	2B	3B	HR	RBI	BB	SO	AVG	OBP	SLG	PRO+	BR/A	SB	CS	SBR	FA	FR	G/POS	TPR
1916	Pit-N	1	1	0	0	0	0	0	0	0	1	.000	.000	.000	-99	-0	0			1.000	0	/1-1	0.0

■ JOCKO HALLIGAN Halligan, William E. b: 12/8/1868, Avon, N.Y. d: 2/13/45, Buffalo, N.Y. BL , 5'9", 166 lbs. Deb: 5/13/1890

YEAR	TM/L	G	AB	R	H	2B	3B	HR	RBI	BB	SO	AVG	OBP	SLG	PRO+	BR/A	SB	CS	SBR	FA	FR	G/POS	TPR
1890	Buf-P	57	211	28	53	9	2	3	33	20	19	.251	.319	.355	87	-4	7			.824	-5	O-43,C-16	-0.7
1891	Cin-N	61	247	43	77	13	6	3	44	24	25	.312	.375	.449	139	12	5			.856	-3	O-61	0.6
1892	Cin-N	26	101	14	29	4	0	2	12	12	9	.287	.363	.386	128	4	3			.875	-1	O-26	0.2
	Bal-N	46	178	38	48	4	7	2	43	30	24	.270	.381	.404	134	8	8			.861	-7	O-22,1-19/C-5	-0.1
	Yr	72	279	52	77	8	7	4	55	42	33	.276	.375	.398	132	12	11			.869	-8	O-48,1-19/C-5	0.1
Total	3	190	737	123	207	30	15	10	132	86	77	.281	.359	.403	121	19	23			.848	-16	O-152/C-21,1-19	0.0

■ ED HALLINAN Hallinan, Edward S. b: 8/23/1888, San Francisco, Cal d: 8/24/40, San Francisco, Cal BR/TR, 5'9", 168 lbs. Deb: 5/13/11

YEAR	TM/L	G	AB	R	H	2B	3B	HR	RBI	BB	SO	AVG	OBP	SLG	PRO+	BR/A	SB	CS	SBR	FA	FR	G/POS	TPR
1911	StL-A	52	169	13	35	3	1	0	14	14		.207	.268	.237	43	-13	4			.902	-6	S-34,2-15/3-3	-1.7
1912	StL-A	29	86	11	19	2	0	0	1	5		.221	.272	.244	50	-6	3			.866	-7	S-26	-1.1
Total	2	81	255	24	54	5	1	0	15	19		.212	.269	.239	45	-19	7			.887	-12	/S-60,2-15,3-3	-2.8

■ JIMMY HALLINAN Hallinan, James H. b: 5/27/1849, Ireland d: 10/28/1879, Chicago, Ill. BL/TL, 5'9", 172 lbs. Deb: 7/26/1871

YEAR	TM/L	G	AB	R	H	2B	3B	HR	RBI	BB	SO	AVG	OBP	SLG	PRO+	BR/A	SB	CS	SBR	FA	FR	G/POS	TPR
1871	Kek-n	5	25	7	5	0	0	0	2	2	0	.200	.259	.200	34	-2	1	1	-0	.475	-6	/S-5	-0.6
1875	Wes-n	13	51	12	14	2	1	0	3	0	1	.275	.275	.353	110	0	2	2	-1	.742	-5	S-13	-0.5
	Mut-n	44	203	29	58	6	3	3	21	1	2	.286	.289	.389	127	4	2	2	-1	.765	-10	S-43/3-1,O-1	-0.7
	Yr	57	254	41	72	8	4	3	24	1	3	.283	.286	.382	123	5	4	4	-1	.761	-15	S-56/3-1,O-1	-1.2
1876	NY-N	54	240	45	67	7	6	2	36	2	4	.279	.285	.383	139	10				.764	-15	*S-50/2-4,O-2	-0.5
1877	Cin-N	16	73	18	27	1	1	0	7	1	1	.370	.378	.411	167	6				.854	-6	2-16	0.0
	Chi-N	19	89	17	25	4	1	0	11	4	2	.281	.312	.348	96	-1				.800	-2	O-19	-0.3
	Yr	35	162	35	52	5	2	0	18	5	3	.321	.341	.377	124	4				.800	-8	O-19,2-16	-0.3
1878	Chi-N	16	67	14	19	3	0	0	2	5	6	.284	.333	.328	111	1				.789	-4	O-11/2-5	-0.3
	Ind-N	3	12	0	3	2	0	0	1	0	2	.250	.250	.417	134	0				.667	-1	/O-3	0.0
	Yr	19	79	14	22	5	0	0	3	5	8	.278	.321	.342	114	1				.760	-5	O-14/2-5	-0.3
Total	2 n	62	279	48	77	8	4	3	26	3	3	.276	.284	.366	114	3	5	5	-2	.728	-22	/S-61,O-1,3-1	-1.8
Total	3	108	481	94	141	17	8	2	57	12	15	.293	.310	.374	129	16				.783	-28	/S-50,O-35,2-25	-1.1

■ BILL HALLMAN Hallman, William Harry b: 3/15/1876, Philadelphia, Pa. d: 4/23/50, Philadelphia, Pa. BL/TL, Deb: 4/25/01

YEAR	TM/L	G	AB	R	H	2B	3B	HR	RBI	BB	SO	AVG	OBP	SLG	PRO+	BR/A	SB	CS	SBR	FA	FR	G/POS	TPR
1901	Mil-A	139	549	70	135	27	6	2	47	41		.246	.301	.328	78	-16	12			.905	-2	*O-139	-2.7
1903	Chi-A	63	207	29	43	7	4	0	18	31		.208	.320	.280	85	-2	11			.953	2	O-57	-0.4
1906	Pit-N	23	89	12	24	3	1	1	6	15		.270	.375	.360	124	3	3			.935	-1	O-23	0.1
1907	Pit-N	94	302	39	67	6	2	0	15	33		.222	.305	.255	74	-8	21			.966	-6	O-84	-1.9
Total	4	319	1147	150	269	43	13	3	86	120		.235	.311	.303	82	-24	47			.933	-7	O-303	-4.9

■ BILL HALLMAN Hallman, William Wilson b: 3/31/1867, Pittsburgh, Pa. d: 9/11/20, Philadelphia, Pa. BR/TR, 5'8", 160 lbs. Deb: 4/23/1888 M

YEAR	TM/L	G	AB	R	H	2B	3B	HR	RBI	BB	SO	AVG	OBP	SLG	PRO+	BR/A	SB	CS	SBR	FA	FR	G/POS	TPR
1888	Phi-N	18	63	5	13	4	1	0	6	1	12	.206	.219	.302	61	-3	1			.898	-7	C-10/2-4,O-3,S-1,3	-0.9
1889	Phi-N	119	462	67	117	21	8	2	60	36	54	.253	.313	.346	77	-16	20			.895	7	*S-106,2-13/C-1	-0.2
1890	Phi-P	84	356	59	95	16	7	1	37	33	24	.267	.338	.360	84	-9	6			.885	-8	O-34,C-26,2-14,3/S	-1.1
1891	Phi-a	141	587	112	166	21	13	6	69	38	56	.283	.332	.394	104	-0	18			.930	-5	*2-141	0.1
1892	Phi-N	138	586	106	171	27	10	2	84	32	52	.292	.335	.382	117	10	19			.936	-24	*2-138	-1.0
1893	Phi-N	132	596	119	183	28	7	5	76	51	27	.307	.367	.403	105	3	22			.950	-15	*2-120,1-12	-0.7
1894	Phi-N	119	505	107	156	19	7	0	66	36	15	.309	.360	.374	79	-16	36			.930	-19	*2-119	-2.3
1895	Phi-N	124	539	94	169	26	5	1	91	34	20	.314	.359	.386	92	-7	16			.943	6	*2-122/S-3	0.4
1896	Phi-N	120	469	82	150	21	3	2	83	45	23	.320	.382	.390	105	5	16			.945	3	*2-120/P-1	1.2
1897	Phi-N	31	126	16	33	3	0	0	15	8		.262	.326	.286	64	-6	1			.958	-10	2-31	-1.2

YEAR	TM/L	G	AB	R	H	2B	3B	HR	RBI	BB	SO	AVG	OBP	SLG	PRO+	BR/A	SB	CS	SBR	FA	FR	G/POS	TPR
	StL-N	79	298	31	66	6	2	0	26	24		.221	.288	.255	45	-23	12			.939	3	2-77/1-3,M	-1.4
	Yr	110	424	47	99	9	2	0	41	32		.233	.300	.264	51	-29	13			.944	-7	*2-108/1-3	-2.6
1898	Bro-N	134	509	57	124	10	7	2	63	29		.244	.291	.303	70	-20	9			.944	-3	*2-124,3-10	-1.4
1901	Cle-A	5	19	2	4	0	0	0	3	2		.211	.286	.211	41	-1	0			.815	-3	/S-5	-0.4
	Phi-N	123	445	46	82	13	5	0	38	26		.184	.236	.236	36	-36	13			.971	-5	2-90,3-33	-3.7
1902	Phi-N	73	254	14	63	8	4	0	35	14		.248	.287	.311	84	-5	9			.932	-6	3-72	-1.1
1903	Phi-N	63	198	20	42	11	2	0	17	16		.212	.271	.288	61	-10	2			.932	-3	2-22,3-19/1-9,OS	-1.2
Total	14	1503	6012	937	1634	234	81	21	769	425	283	.272	.325	.348	84	-136	200			.940	-88	*2-1135,3-145,S/OC1P	-14.9

■ JIM HALPIN Halpin, James Nathaniel b: 10/4/1863, England d: 1/4/1893, Boston, Mass. Deb: 6/15/1882

YEAR	TM/L	G	AB	R	H	2B	3B	HR	RBI	BB	SO	AVG	OBP	SLG	PRO+	BR/A	SB	CS	SBR	FA	FR	G/POS	TPR
1882	Wor-N	2	8	0	0	0	0	0	0	0	2	.000	.000	.000	-98	-2				.625	-1	/3-2	-0.3
1884	Was-U	46	168	24	31	3	0	0		2		.185	.194	.202	21	-21				.809	-7	S-39/3-7	-2.5
1885	Det-N	15	54	3	7	2	0	0	1	1	12	.130	.145	.167	1	-6				.846	1	S-15	-0.5
Total	3	63	230	27	38	5	0	0	1	3	14	.165	.176	.187	12	-28				.821	-8	/S-54,3-9	-3.3

■ AL HALT Halt, Alva William b: 11/23/1890, Sandusky, Ohio d: 1/22/73, Sandusky, Ohio BR/TR, 6', 180 lbs. Deb: 5/29/14

YEAR	TM/L	G	AB	R	H	2B	3B	HR	RBI	BB	SO	AVG	OBP	SLG	PRO+	BR/A	SB	CS	SBR	FA	FR	G/POS	TPR
1914	Bro-F	80	261	26	61	6	2	3	25	13	39	.234	.270	.307	57	-20	11			.890	-11	S-71/2-3,O-1	-2.7
1915	Bro-F	151	524	41	131	22	7	3	64	39	79	.250	.307	.336	81	-21	20			.930	3	*3-111,S-40	-1.2
1918	Cle-A	26	69	9	12	2	0	0	1	9	12	.174	.269	.203	39	-5	4			.971	-1	3-14/2-4,S-4,1-2	-0.6
Total	3	257	854	76	204	30	9	6	90	61	130	.239	.293	.316	70	-47	35			.933	-9	3-125,S-115/2-7,1O	-4.5

■ SHANE HALTER Halter, Shane David b: 11/8/69, LaPlata, Md. BR/TR, 5'10", 160 lbs. Deb: 4/6/97

YEAR	TM/L	G	AB	R	H	2B	3B	HR	RBI	BB	SO	AVG	OBP	SLG	PRO+	BR/A	SB	CS	SBR	FA	FR	G/POS	TPR
1997	KC-A	74	123	16	34	5	1	2	10	10	28	.276	.341	.382	86	-2	4	3	-1	1.000	-9	O-32,2-18,3-12,/SD	-1.0
1998	KC-A	86	204	17	45	12	0	2	13	12	38	.221	.267	.309	47	-16	2	5	-2	.964	-1	S-66/O-9,3-8,21P	-1.4
Total	2	160	327	33	79	17	1	4	23	22	66	.242	.295	.336	62	-18	6	8	-3	.963	-9	/S-71,O-41,23DP1	-2.4

■ RALPH HAM Ham, Ralph A. b: 3/1849, Troy, N.Y. d: 2/13/05, Troy, N.Y. 5'8", 158 lbs. Deb: 5/6/1871

YEAR	TM/L	G	AB	R	H	2B	3B	HR	RBI	BB	SO	AVG	OBP	SLG	PRO+	BR/A	SB	CS	SBR	FA	FR	G/POS	TPR
1871	Rok-n	25	113	25	28	4	0	0	12	1	7	.248	.254	.283	57	-6	6	2	1	.723	-5	O-19/3-7,S-2	-0.6

■ CHARLIE HAMBURG Hamburg, Charles M. (b: Charles M. Hambrick) b: 11/22/1863, Louisville, Ky. d: 5/18/31, Union, N.J. 6', 175 lbs. Deb: 4/18/1890

YEAR	TM/L	G	AB	R	H	2B	3B	HR	RBI	BB	SO	AVG	OBP	SLG	PRO+	BR/A	SB	CS	SBR	FA	FR	G/POS	TPR
1890	*Lou-a	133	485	93	132	22	2	3	77	69		.272	.370	.344	113	11	46			.946	-2	*O-133	0.4

■ JIM HAMBY Hamby, James Sanford "Cracker" b: 7/29/1897, Wilkesboro, N.C. d: 10/21/91, Springfield, Ill. BR/TR, 6', 170 lbs. Deb: 9/20/26

YEAR	TM/L	G	AB	R	H	2B	3B	HR	RBI	BB	SO	AVG	OBP	SLG	PRO+	BR/A	SB	CS	SBR	FA	FR	G/POS	TPR
1926	NY-N	1	3	0	0	0	0	0	0	0	0	.000	.000	.000	-99	-1	0			.600	-1	/C-1	-0.2
1927	NY-N	21	52	6	10	0	1	0	5	7	7	.192	.288	.231	40	-4	1			.904	-0	C-19	-0.3
Total	2	22	55	6	10	0	1	0	5	7	7	.182	.274	.218	33	-5	1			.885	-1	/C-20	-0.5

■ BOB HAMELIN Hamelin, Robert James b: 11/29/67, Elizabeth, N.J. BL/TL, 6', 235 lbs. Deb: 9/12/93

YEAR	TM/L	G	AB	R	H	2B	3B	HR	RBI	BB	SO	AVG	OBP	SLG	PRO+	BR/A	SB	CS	SBR	FA	FR	G/POS	TPR
1993	KC-A	16	49	2	11	3	0	2	5	6	15	.224	.309	.408	86	-1	0	0	0	.986	-0	1-15	-0.2
1994	KC-A	101	312	64	88	25	1	24	65	56	62	.282	.393	.599	145	21	4	3	-1	.992	1	D-70,1-24	1.4
1995	KC-A	72	208	20	35	7	1	7	25	26	56	.168	.279	.313	53	-15	0	1	-1	1.000	1	D-56/1-8	-1.8
1996	KC-A	89	239	31	61	14	1	9	40	54	58	.255	.397	.435	110	6	5	2	0	.984	0	D-47,1-33	0.1
1997	Det-A	110	318	47	86	15	0	18	52	48	72	.270	.368	.487	122	10	2	1	0	1.000	-1	D-95/1-7	0.4
1998	Mil-N	109	146	15	32	6	0	7	22	16	30	.219	.301	.404	80	-5	0	1	-1	.992	-4	1-51/D-1	-1.1
Total	6	497	1272	179	313	70	3	67	209	206	293	.246	.356	.464	108	16	11	8	-2	.990	-3	D-269,1-138	-1.2

■ DARRYL HAMILTON Hamilton, Darryl Quinn b: 12/3/64, Baton Rouge, La. BL/TR, 6'1", 180 lbs. Deb: 6/3/88

YEAR	TM/L	G	AB	R	H	2B	3B	HR	RBI	BB	SO	AVG	OBP	SLG	PRO+	BR/A	SB	CS	SBR	FA	FR	G/POS	TPR
1988	Mil-A	44	103	14	19	4	0	1	11	12	9	.184	.276	.252	49	-7	7	3	0	1.000	-1	O-37/D-3	-0.8
1990	Mil-A	89	156	27	46	5	0	1	18	9	12	.295	.333	.346	91	-2	10	3	1	.992	-6	O-72/D-9	-0.8
1991	Mil-A	122	405	64	126	15	6	1	57	33	38	.311	.363	.385	110	6	16	6	1	.996	-10	*O-117	-0.5
1992	Mil-A	128	470	67	140	19	7	5	62	45	42	.298	.360	.400	115	10	41	14	4	**1.000**	1	*O-124	1.2
1993	Mil-A	135	520	74	161	21	1	9	48	45	62	.310	.368	.406	109	8	21	13	-2	.992	6	*O-129/D-1	0.9
1994	Mil-A	36	141	23	37	10	1	1	13	15	17	.262	.333	.369	77	-5	3	0	1	1.000	-4	O-32/D-4	-0.8
1995	Mil-A	112	398	54	108	20	6	5	44	47	35	.271	.353	.389	88	-7	11	1	3	.989	-2	*O-109/D-2	-0.8
1996	*Tex-A	148	627	94	184	29	4	6	51	54	66	.293	.351	.381	81	-17	15	5	2	**1.000**	7	*O-147	-1.2
1997	*SF-N	125	460	78	124	23	3	5	43	61	61	.270	.355	.365	91	-5	15	10	-2	.980	-2	*O-118	-1.0
1998	SF-N	97	367	65	108	19	2	1	26	59	53	.294	.395	.365	103	4	9	8	-2	1.000	-2	O-96	0.0
	Col-N	51	194	30	65	9	1	5	25	23	20	.335	.408	.469	106	2	4	1	1	.990	-1	O-48	0.1
	Yr	148	561	95	173	28	3	6	51	82	73	.308	.399	.401	104	7	13	9	-2	.997	-3	*O-144	0.1
Total	10	1087	3841	590	1118	174	31	40	398	403	415	.291	.360	.384	96	-12	152	64	7	.994	-13	*O-1029/D-19	-3.7

■ JEFF HAMILTON Hamilton, Jeffrey Robert b: 3/19/64, Flint, Mich. BR/TR, 6'3", 207 lbs. Deb: 6/28/86

YEAR	TM/L	G	AB	R	H	2B	3B	HR	RBI	BB	SO	AVG	OBP	SLG	PRO+	BR/A	SB	CS	SBR	FA	FR	G/POS	TPR
1986	LA-N	71	147	22	33	5	0	5	19	2	43	.224	.235	.361	66	-8	0	0	0	.968	11	3-66/S-2	0.3
1987	LA-N	35	83	5	18	3	0	0	1	7	22	.217	.286	.253	45	-6	0	1	-1	.935	9	3-31/S-1	0.2
1988	*LA-N	111	309	34	73	14	2	6	33	10	51	.236	.269	.353	80	-9	0	2	-1	.941	-0	*3-105/S-2,1-1	-1.2
1989	LA-N	151	548	45	134	35	1	12	56	20	71	.245	.275	.378	86	-12	0	0	0	.951	-6	*3-147/P-1,2-1,S-1	-1.8
1990	LA-N	7	24	1	3	0	0	0	1	0	3	.125	.125	.125	-32	-4	0	0	0	1.000	1	/3-7	-0.4
1991	LA-N	41	94	4	21	4	0	1	14	4	21	.223	.255	.298	56	-6	0	0	0	.928	0	3-33/S-1	-0.6
Total	6	416	1205	111	282	61	3	24	124	43	211	.234	.265	.349	74	-45	0	3	-2	.948	15	3-389/S-7,2-1,P1	-3.5

■ TOM HAMILTON Hamilton, Thomas Ball "Ham" b: 9/29/25, Altoona, Kan. d: 11/29/73, Tyler, Tex. BL/TR, 6'4", 213 lbs. Deb: 9/4/52

YEAR	TM/L	G	AB	R	H	2B	3B	HR	RBI	BB	SO	AVG	OBP	SLG	PRO+	BR/A	SB	CS	SBR	FA	FR	G/POS	TPR
1952	Phi-A	9	10	1	2	1	0	0	1	1	1	.200	.273	.300	56	-1	0	0	0	1.000	-0	/1-5	-0.1
1953	Phi-A	58	56	8	11	2	0	0	5	7	11	.196	.286	.232	40	-5	0	0	0	1.000	-1	/1-7,O-2	-0.6
Total	2	67	66	9	13	3	0	0	6	8	12	.197	.284	.242	42	-5	0	0	0	1.000	-1	/1-12,O-2	-0.7

■ BILLY HAMILTON Hamilton, William Robert "Sliding Billy" b: 2/16/1866, Newark, N.J. d: 12/16/40, Worcester, Mass. BL/TR, 5'6", 165 lbs. Deb: 7/31/1888 H

YEAR	TM/L	G	AB	R	H	2B	3B	HR	RBI	BB	SO	AVG	OBP	SLG	PRO+	BR/A	SB	CS	SBR	FA	FR	G/POS	TPR
1888	KC-a	35	129	21	34	4	4	0	11	4		.264	.307	.357	106	0	19			.961	-2	O-35	-0.3
1889	KC-a	137	534	144	161	17	12	3	77	87	41	.301	.413	.395	123	19	**111**			.857	-7	*O-137	0.7
1890	Phi-N	123	496	133	161	13	9	2	49	83	37	.325	.430	.399	139	29	**102**			.882	4	*O-123	2.5
1891	Phi-N	133	527	**141**	**179**	23	7	2	60	**102**	28	**.340**	**.453**	.421	151	41	**111**			.907	5	*O-133	3.7
1892	Phi-N	139	554	132	183	21	7	3	53	81	29	.330	.423	.410	153	39	57			.919	14	*O-139	4.3
1893	Phi-N	82	355	110	135	22	7	5	44	63	7	.380	**.490**	.524	**170**	40	43			.937	4	O-82	3.3
1894	Phi-N	129	544	**192**	220	25	15	4	87	**126**	17	.404	**.523**	.528	158	**65**	**98**			.964	5	*O-129	4.6
1895	Phi-N	123	517	**166**	201	22	6	7	74	**96**	30	.389	.490	.495	154	49	**97**			.913	-1	*O-123	3.1
1896	Bos-N	131	524	153	192	24	10	3	55	**110**	29	.366	**.478**	.468	141	37	83			.934	-11	*O-131	1.3
1897	*Bos-N	127	507	**152**	174	17	5	3	61	**105**		.343	.461	.414	124	24	66			.962	-3	*O-126	1.0
1898	Bos-N	110	417	110	154	16	5	3	50	87		.369	**.480**	.453	**159**	38	54			.904	-15	*O-110	1.4
1899	Bos-N	84	297	63	92	7	1	1	33	72		.310	.446	.350	109	8	19			.952	-2	O-81	-0.1
1900	Bos-N	136	520	103	173	20	5	1	47	107		.333	.449	.396	119	18	32			.947	2	*O-136	0.9
1901	Bos-N	102	348	71	100	11	2	3	38	64		.287	.404	.356	111	8	20			.945	1	O-99	0.1
Total	14	1591	6269	1691	2159	242	95	40	739	1187	218	.344	.455	.432	139	415	912			.926	-5	*O-1584	26.5

■ KEN HAMLIN Hamlin, Kenneth Lee b: 5/18/35, Detroit, Mich. BR/TR, 5'10", 170 lbs. Deb: 6/17/57

YEAR	TM/L	G	AB	R	H	2B	3B	HR	RBI	BB	SO	AVG	OBP	SLG	PRO+	BR/A	SB	CS	SBR	FA	FR	G/POS	TPR
1957	Pit-N	2	1	0	0	0	0	0	0	0	0	.000	.000	.000	-99	-0	0	0	0	1.000	0	/S-1	0.0
1959	Pit-N	3	8	1	1	0	0	0	0	2	1	.125	.300	.125	19	-1	0	0	0	1.000	-1	/S-3	-0.2
1960	KC-A	140	428	51	96	10	2	2	24	44	48	.224	.298	.271	55	-26	1	1	-0	.955	-41	*S-139	-5.9
1961	LA-A	42	91	4	19	3	0	1	5	11	9	.209	.301	.275	49	-6	0	1	-1	.963	13	S-39	0.8
1962	Was-A	98	292	29	74	12	0	3	22	22	22	.253	.306	.325	70	-12	7	7	-2	.963	-11	S-87/2-2	-1.9
1965	Was-A	117	362	45	99	21	1	4	22	33	45	.273	.336	.370	102	1	8	2	1	.976	-29	2-77,S-47/3-1	-2.0
1966	Was-A	66	158	13	34	7	1	1	16	13	21	.215	.275	.291	63	-7	1	0	0	.963	6	2-50/3-1	0.2
Total	7	468	1340	143	323	53	4	11	89	125	146	.241	.307	.311	71	-52	17	11	-2	.959	-63	S-316,2-129/3-2	-9.0

YEAR	TM/L	G	AB	R	H	2B	3B	HR	RBI	BB	SO	AVG	OBP	SLG	PRO+	BR/A	SB	CS	SBR	FA	FR	G/POS	TPR
■ **STEVE HAMMOND**	Hammond, Steven Benjamin b: 5/9/57, Atlanta, Ga. BL/TR, 6'2", 190 lbs. Deb: 6/28/82 F																						
1982	KC-A	46	126	14	29	5	1	1	11	4	18	.230	.254	.310	54	-8	0	1	-1	1.000	3	O-37/D-1	-0.7
■ **JACK HAMMOND**	Hammond, Walter Charles "Wobby" b: 2/26/1891, Amsterdam, N.Y. d: 3/4/42, Kenosha, Wis. BR/TR, 5'11", 170 lbs. Deb: 4/15/15																						
1915	Cle-A	35	84	9	18	2	1	0	4	1	19	.214	.224	.262	44	-6	0	1	-1	.957	-8	2-19	-1.6
1922	Cle-A	1	4	1	1	0	0	0	0	0	0	.250	.250	.250	30	-0	0	0	0	.333	-2	/2-1	-0.2
	Pit-N	9	11	3	3	0	0	0	0	1	0	.273	.333	.273	57	-1	0	0	0	1.000	2	/2-4	0.1
Total	2	45	99	13	22	2	1	0	4	2	19	.222	.238	.263	45	-7	0	1	-1	.943	-8	/2-24	-1.7
■ **JEFFREY HAMMONDS**	Hammonds, Jeffrey Bryan b: 3/5/71, Plainfield, N.J. BR/TR, 6', 195 lbs. Deb: 6/25/93																						
1993	Bal-A	33	105	10	32	8	0	3	19	2	16	.305	.318	.467	104	0	4	0	1	.961	1	O-23/D-8	0.1
1994	Bal-A	68	250	45	74	18	2	8	31	17	39	.296	.346	.480	105	1	5	0	2	.962	4	O-66	0.5
1995	Bal-A	57	178	18	43	9	1	4	23	9	30	.242	.282	.371	67	-9	4	2	0	.989	1	O-46/D-5	-0.8
1996	Bal-A	71	248	38	56	10	1	9	27	23	53	.226	.302	.383	72	-11	3	3	-1	.980	-0	O-70/D-1	-1.3
1997	*Bal-A	118	397	71	105	19	3	21	55	32	73	.264	.324	.486	111	5	15	1	4	.980	-3	*O-114/D-4	0.4
1998	Bal-A	63	171	36	46	12	1	6	28	26	38	.269	.375	.456	117	5	7	2	1	.980	-6	O-53/D-7	-0.1
	Cin-N	26	86	14	26	4	1	0	11	13	18	.302	.394	.372	99	0	1	1	-0	.985	4	O-25	0.4
Total	6	436	1435	232	382	80	9	51	194	122	267	.266	.329	.441	97	-9	39	9	6	.977	1	O-397/D-25	-0.8
■ **GRANNY HAMNER**	Hamner, Granville Wilbur b: 4/26/27, Richmond, Va. d: 9/12/93, Philadelphia, Pa. BR/TR, 5'10", 163 lbs. Deb: 9/14/44 F																						
1944	Phi-N	21	77	6	19	1	0	0	5	3	7	.247	.275	.260	53	-5	0			.933	6	S-21	0.3
1945	Phi-N	14	41	3	7	2	0	0	6	1	3	.171	.190	.220	14	-5	0			.861	3	S-13	-0.1
1946	Phi-N	2	7	0	1	0	0	0	0	0	3	.143	.143	.143	-19	-1	0			.857	-1	/S-2	-0.2
1947	Phi-N	2	7	1	2	0	0	0	0	1	0	.286	.375	.286	81	-0	0			1.000	0	/S-2	0.0
1948	Phi-N	129	446	42	116	21	5	3	48	22	39	.260	.298	.350	76	-16	2			.967	-8	2-87,S-37/3-3	-1.7
1949	Phi-N	154	662	83	174	32	5	6	53	25	47	.263	.290	.353	74	-27	6			.961	-0	*S-154	-1.6
1950	*Phi-N	157	637	78	172	27	5	11	82	39	35	.270	.314	.380	83	-17	2			.944	-5	*S-157	-0.9
1951	Phi-N	150	589	61	150	23	7	9	72	29	32	.255	.290	.363	76	-22	10	5	0	.958	-2	*S-150	-1.3
1952	Phi-N★	151	596	74	164	30	5	17	87	27	51	.275	.307	.428	103	-0	7	3	0	.951	-4	*S-151	0.7
1953	Phi-N★	154	609	90	168	30	8	21	92	32	28	.276	.313	.455	98	-4	2	1	0	.970	-8	2-93,S-71	-0.3
1954	Phi-N★	152	596	83	178	39	11	13	89	53	44	.299	.356	.466	112	10	1	2	-1	.978	-23	*2-152/S-1	-0.3
1955	Phi-N	104	405	57	104	12	4	5	43	41	30	.257	.327	.343	79	-11	0	1	-1	.960	-36	2-82,S-32	-3.9
1956	Phi-N	122	401	42	90	24	3	4	42	30	42	.224	.278	.329	64	-21	2	0	1	.937	-13	*S-110,2-11/P-3	-2.4
1957	Phi-N	133	502	59	114	19	5	10	62	34	42	.227	.276	.345	68	-24	3	1	0	.963	-39	*2-125/S-5,P-1	-5.5
1958	Phi-N	35	133	18	40	7	3	2	18	8	16	.301	.340	.444	107	1	0	0	0	.984	-3	3-22,2-11/S-3	-0.1
1959	Phi-N	21	64	10	19	4	0	2	6	5	5	.297	.348	.453	109	1	0	1	-1	.947	-7	S-15/3-1	-0.6
	Cle-A	27	67	4	11	1	1	1	3	1	8	.164	.176	.254	17	-8	0	0	0	.960	-2	S-10/2-7,3-5	-0.9
1962	KC-A	3	0	0	0	0	0	0	0	0	0	—	—	—	—	0	0	0	0	1.000	0	/P-3	0.0
Total	17	1531	5839	711	1529	272	62	104	708	351	432	.262	.304	.383	84	-149	35	14		.946	-139	S-934,2-568/3-31,P	-18.8
■ **GARVIN HAMNER**	Hamner, Wesley Garvin b: 3/18/24, Richmond, Va. BR/TR, 5'11", 172 lbs. Deb: 4/17/45 F																						
1945	Phi-N	32	101	12	20	3	0	0	5	7	9	.198	.250	.228	34	-9	2			.962	-4	2-21/S-9,3-1	-1.1
■ **IKE HAMPTON**	Hampton, Isaac Bernard b: 8/22/51, Camden, S.C. BB/TR, 6'1", 185 lbs. Deb: 9/12/74																						
1974	NY-N	4	4	0	0	0	0	0	1	0	1	.000	.000	.000	-99	-1	0	0	0	1.000	-0	/C-1	-0.1
1975	Cal-A	31	66	8	10	3	0	0	4	7	19	.152	.243	.197	28	-6	0	0	0	.947	-5	C-28/S-2,3-1	-1.0
1976	Cal-A	3	2	0	0	0	0	0	0	0	0	.000	.000	.000	-99	-1	0	0	0	1.000	1	/C-2,S-1	0.0
1977	Cal-A	52	44	5	13	1	0	3	9	2	10	.295	.340	.523	137	2	0	0	0	.968	1	C-47/D-2	0.3
1978	Cal-A	19	14	2	3	0	1	1	4	2	7	.214	.313	.571	149	1	1	0	0	.905	1	C-13/1-1,D-4	0.2
1979	Cal-A	4	5	0	2	0	0	0	0	0	1	.400	.400	.400	121	0	0	0	0	1.000	1	/1-2	0.1
Total	6	113	135	15	28	4	1	4	18	11	38	.207	.277	.341	75	-5	1	0	0	.953	-2	/C-91,D-6,1-3,S3	-0.5
■ **BERT HAMRIC**	Hamric, Odbert Herman b: 3/1/28, Clarksburg, W.Va. d: 8/8/84, Springboro, Ohio BL/TR, 6', 165 lbs. Deb: 4/24/55																						
1955	Bro-N	2	1	0	0	0	0	0	0	0	1	.000	.000	.000	-97	-0	0	0	0	.000	0	H	0.0
1958	Bal-A	8	8	0	1	0	0	0	0	0	6	.125	.125	.125	-33	-1	0	0	0	.000	0	H	-0.2
Total	2	10	9	0	1	0	0	0	0	0	7	.111	.111	.111	-41	-2	0	0	0		0	-0,-0	-0.2
■ **RAY HAMRICK**	Hamrick, Raymond Bernard b: 8/1/21, Nashville, Tenn. BR/TR, 5'11.5", 160 lbs. Deb: 8/14/43																						
1943	Phi-N	44	160	12	32	3	1	0	9	8	28	.200	.238	.231	37	-13	0			.960	-11	2-31,S-12	-2.4
1944	Phi-N	74	292	22	60	10	1	1	23	23	34	.205	.268	.257	50	-19	1			.948	20	S-74	0.7
Total	2	118	452	34	92	13	2	1	32	31	62	.204	.258	.248	46	-33	1			.946	9	/S-86,2-31	-1.7
■ **BUDDY HANCKEN**	Hancken, Morris Medlock b: 8/30/14, Birmingham, Ala. BR/TR, 6'1", 175 lbs. Deb: 5/14/40 C																						
1940	Phi-A	1	0	0	0	0	0	0	0	0	0	—	—	—	—	0	0	0	0	1.000	-0	/C-1	0.0
■ **FRED HANCOCK**	Hancock, Fred James b: 3/28/20, Allenport, Pa. d: 3/12/86, Clearwater, Fla. BR/TR, 5'8", 170 lbs. Deb: 4/26/49																						
1949	Chi-A	39	52	7	7	2	1	0	9	8	9	.135	.262	.212	27	-6	0	1	-1	.978	-3	S-27/3-3,O-1	-0.9
■ **GARRY HANCOCK**	Hancock, Ronald Garry b: 1/23/54, Tampa, Fla. BL/TL, 6', 175 lbs. Deb: 7/16/78																						
1978	Bos-A	38	80	10	18	3	0	0	4	1	12	.225	.235	.262	36	-7	0	0	0	1.000	-0	O-19,D-13	-0.8
1980	Bos-A	46	115	9	33	6	0	4	19	3	11	.287	.305	.443	97	-1	0	3	-2	.963	-2	O-27,D-12	-0.6
1981	Bos-A	26	45	4	7	3	0	0	3	2	4	.156	.191	.222	18	-5	0	0	0	1.000	-0	/O-8,D-4	-0.5
1982	Bos-A	11	14	3	0	0	0	0	0	1	1	.000	.067	.000	-75	-3	0	0	0	1.000	-2	/O-7	-0.6
1983	Oak-A	101	256	29	70	7	3	8	30	5	13	.273	.290	.418	98	-2	2	0	1	.981	-9	O-67,1-27/D-9	-1.3
1984	Oak-A	51	60	2	13	2	0	0	8	0	1	.217	.217	.250	31	-6	0	0	0	1.000	-5	O-18/1-4,P-1,D-5	-1.1
Total	6	273	570	57	141	21	3	12	64	12	42	.247	.264	.358	71	-23	2	3	-1	.982	-19	O-146/D-43,1-31,P-1	-4.9
■ **MIKE HANDIBOE**	Handiboe, Aloysius James "Coalyard Mike" b: 7/21/1887, Washington, D.C. d: 1/31/53, Savannah, Ga. BL/TL, 5'10", 155 lbs. Deb: 9/8/11																						
1911	NY-A	5	15	0	1	0	0	0	0	2		.067	.176	.067	-29	-3	0			1.000	-0	/O-4	-0.3
■ **GENE HANDLEY**	Handley, Eugene Louis b: 11/25/14, Kennett, Mo. BR/TR, 5'10.5", 165 lbs. Deb: 4/16/46 F																						
1946	Phi-A	89	251	31	63	8	5	0	21	22	25	.251	.311	.323	78	-8	8	3	1	.947	-17	2-68/3-4,S-1	-2.1
1947	Phi-A	36	90	10	23	2	1	0	8	10	2	.256	.330	.300	74	-3	1	0	0	.973	-5	2-17,3-10/S-1	-0.7
Total	2	125	341	41	86	10	6	0	29	32	27	.252	.316	.317	77	-10	9	3	1	.952	-23	/2-85,3-14,S-2	-2.8
■ **LEE HANDLEY**	Handley, Lee Elmer "Jeep" b: 7/31/13, Clarion, Iowa d: 4/8/70, Pittsburgh, Pa. BR/TR, 5'7", 160 lbs. Deb: 4/15/36 F																						
1936	Cin-N	24	78	10	24	1	0	2	8	7	16	.308	.365	.397	112	1	3			.926	-0	2-16/3-7	0.2
1937	Pit-N	127	480	59	120	21	12	3	37	37	40	.250	.305	.363	81	-14	5			.950	-14	*2-126/3-1	-1.9
1938	Pit-N	139	570	91	153	25	8	6	51	53	31	.268	.332	.372	93	-6	7			.948	9	*3-136	0.5
1939	Pit-N	101	376	43	107	14	5	1	42	32	20	.285	.341	.356	89	-6	**17**			.936	-10	*3-100	-1.5
1940	Pit-N	98	302	50	85	7	4	1	19	27	16	.281	.340	.341	89	-4	7			.925	1	3-80/2-2	-0.2
1941	Pit-N	124	459	59	132	18	4	0	33	35	22	.288	.338	.344	93	-4	16			.947	-1	*3-114	-0.2
1944	Pit-N	40	86	7	19	2	0	0	5	3	5	.221	.247	.244	37	-7	1			.947	2	2-19,3-11/S-3	-0.4
1945	Pit-N	98	312	39	93	16	2	1	32	20	16	.298	.340	.372	94	-3	7			.947	15	3-79	1.4
1946	Pit-N	116	416	43	99	8	7	1	28	29	20	.238	.289	.298	65	-19	4			.958	13	*3-102/2-3	-0.5
1947	Phi-N	101	277	17	70	10	3	0	42	24	18	.253	.312	.310	68	-12	1			.975	2	3-83/2-3,S-1	-1.0
Total	10	968	3356	418	902	122	45	15	297	267	204	.269	.323	.345	84	-73	68			.949	16	3-713,2-169/S-4	-3.6
■ **HARRY HANEBRINK**	Hanebrink, Harry Aloysius b: 11/12/27, St.Louis, Mo. d: 9/9/96, Bridgeton, Mo. BL/TR, 6', 165 lbs. Deb: 5/3/53																						
1953	Mil-N	51	80	8	19	1	1	1	8	6	8	.237	.291	.313	61	-5	1	0	0	.979	4	2-21/3-1	0.0
1957	Mil-N	6	7	0	2	0	0	0	0	1	2	.286	.375	.286	87	-0	0	0	0	1.000	1	/3-2	0.1
1958	*Mil-N	63	133	14	25	3	0	4	10	13	9	.188	.270	.301	56	-9	0	1	-1	.982	-0	O-33/3-7	-1.1

YEAR	TM/L	G	AB	R	H	2B	3B	HR	RBI	BB	SO	AVG	OBP	SLG	PRO+	BR/A	SB	CS	SBR	FA	FR	G/POS	TPR
1959	Phi-N	57	97	10	25	3	1	1	7	2	12	.258	.273	.340	61	-5	0	0	0	.889	-6	2-15/3-9,O-1	-1.1
Total	4	177	317	32	71	7	2	6	25	22	31	.224	.279	.315	60	-19	1	1	-0	.959	-2	/2-36,O-34,3-19	-2.1

■ FRED HANEY Haney, Fred Girard "Pudge" b: 4/25/1898, Albuquerque, N.Mex d: 11/9/77, Beverly Hills, Cal. BR/TR, 5'6", 170 lbs. Deb: 4/18/22 MC

YEAR	TM/L	G	AB	R	H	2B	3B	HR	RBI	BB	SO	AVG	OBP	SLG	PRO+	BR/A	SB	CS	SBR	FA	FR	G/POS	TPR
1922	Det-A	81	213	41	75	7	4	0	25	32	14	.352	.439	.423	129	11	3	8	-4	.937	2	3-53,1-11/S-2	1.2
1923	Det-A	142	503	85	142	13	4	4	67	45	23	.282	.347	.348	85	-10	13	5	1	.955	-2	2-69,3-55,S-16	-0.5
1924	Det-A	86	256	54	79	11	1	1	30	39	13	.309	.400	.371	101	2	7	4	-0	.933	4	3-59/S-4,2-3	1.0
1925	Det-A	114	398	84	111	15	3	0	40	66	29	.279	.384	.332	84	-7	11	1	3	.953	-2	*3-106	0.2
1926	Bos-A	138	462	47	102	15	7	0	52	74	28	.221	.330	.284	63	-23	13	6	0	.957	6	*3-137	-0.8
1927	Bos-A	47	116	23	32	4	1	3	12	25	14	.276	.404	.405	113	3	4	1	1	.936	-2	3-34/O-1	0.3
	Chi-N	4	3	0	0	0	0	0	0	0	0	.000	.000	.000	-99	-1	0			.000	0	H	-0.1
1929	StL-N	10	26	4	3	1	1	0	2	1	2	.115	.179	.231	1	-4	0			.958	3	/3-6	-0.1
Total	7	622	1977	338	544	66	21	8	228	282	123	.275	.368	.342	87	-29	51	25		.949	9	3-450/2-72,S-22,1O	1.2

■ TODD HANEY Haney, Todd Michael b: 7/30/65, Waco, Tex. BR/TR, 5'9", 165 lbs. Deb: 9/9/92

YEAR	TM/L	G	AB	R	H	2B	3B	HR	RBI	BB	SO	AVG	OBP	SLG	PRO+	BR/A	SB	CS	SBR	FA	FR	G/POS	TPR
1992	Mon-N	7	10	0	3	1	0	0	1	0	0	.300	.300	.400	97	-0	0	0	0	1.000	-0	/2-5	-0.1
1994	Chi-N	17	37	6	6	0	0	1	2	3	3	.162	.244	.243	28	-4	2	1	0	.979	-0	2-11/3-3	-0.4
1995	Chi-N	25	73	11	30	8	0	2	6	7	11	.411	.463	.603	182	9	0	0	0	.978	3	2-17/3-4	1.2
1996	Chi-N	49	82	11	11	1	0	0	3	7	15	.134	.202	.146	-6	-13	1	0	0	.978	7	2-23/3-4,S-3	-0.4
1998	NY-N	3	3	0	0	0	0	0	0	1	0	.000	.250	.000	-27	-1	0	0	0	.000	-1	/2-1,O-1	-0.2
Total	5	101	205	28	50	10	0	3	12	18	29	.244	.308	.337	70	-8	3	1	0	.979	9	/2-57,3-11,S-3,O-1	0.1

■ LARRY HANEY Haney, Wallace Larry b: 11/19/42, Charlottesville, Va BR/TR, 6'2", 195 lbs. Deb: 7/27/66 FC

YEAR	TM/L	G	AB	R	H	2B	3B	HR	RBI	BB	SO	AVG	OBP	SLG	PRO+	BR/A	SB	CS	SBR	FA	FR	G/POS	TPR
1966	Bal-A	20	56	3	9	1	0	1	3	1	15	.161	.190	.232	21	-6	0	0	0	.985	3	C-20	-0.2
1967	Bal-A	58	164	13	44	11	0	3	20	6	28	.268	.294	.390	101	-0	1	0	0	.991	2	C-57	0.5
1968	Bal-A	38	89	5	21	3	1	1	5	0	19	.236	.236	.326	69	-4	0	0	0	.994	4	C-32	0.2
1969	Sea-A	22	59	3	15	3	0	2	7	6	12	.254	.323	.407	105	0	1	1	-0	.956	-2	C-20	-0.1
	Oak-A	53	86	8	13	4	0	2	12	7	19	.151	.223	.267	38	-7	0	0	0	.994	-0	C-53	-0.7
	Yr	75	145	11	28	7	0	4	19	13	31	.193	.264	.324	66	-7	1	1	-0	.979	-2	C-73	-0.8
1970	Oak-A	2	2	2	0	0	0	0	0	2	1	.000	.500	.000	51	0	0	0	0	1.000	0	/C-1	0.0
1972	Oak-A	5	4	0	0	0	0	0	0	0	1	.000	.000	.000	-99	-1	0	0	0	.800	-1	/C-4,2-1	-0.3
1973	Oak-A	2	2	0	1	0	0	0	0	0	0	.500	.500	.500	192	0	0	0	0	1.000	-0	/C-2	0.0
	StL-N	2	1	0	0	0	0	0	0	0	1	.000	.000	.000	-99	-0	0	0	0	1.000	0	/C-2	0.0
1974	*Oak-A	76	121	12	20	4	0	2	3	3	18	.165	.185	.248	25	-12	1	0	0	.992	10	C-73/3-3,1-2	0.0
1975	Oak-A	47	26	3	5	0	0	1	2	1	4	.192	.222	.308	50	-2	0	0	0	1.000	7	C-43/3-4	0.6
1976	Oak-A	88	177	12	40	2	0	0	10	13	26	.226	.283	.237	56	-10	0	1	-1	.974	9	C-87	0.1
1977	Mil-A	63	127	7	29	2	0	0	10	5	30	.228	.258	.244	38	-11	0	0	0	.985	8	C-63	-0.2
1978	Mil-A	4	5	0	1	0	0	0	1	0	1	.200	.200	.200	13	-1	0	0	0	1.000	-0	/C-4	-0.1
Total	12	480	919	68	198	30	1	12	73	44	175	.215	.254	.289	57	-53	3	2	-0	.985	40	C-461/3-7,1-2,2-1	-0.2

■ CHARLIE HANFORD Hanford, Charles Joseph b: 6/3/1881, Tunstall, England d: 7/19/63, Trenton, N.J. BR/TR, 5'6.5", 145 lbs. Deb: 4/13/14

YEAR	TM/L	G	AB	R	H	2B	3B	HR	RBI	BB	SO	AVG	OBP	SLG	PRO+	BR/A	SB	CS	SBR	FA	FR	G/POS	TPR
1914	Buf-F	155	597	83	174	28	13	12	90	32	81	.291	.332	.442	107	-5	37			.973	10	*O-155	-0.3
1915	Chi-F	77	179	27	43	4	5	0	22	12	28	.240	.295	.318	77	-9	10			.971	-4	O-43	-1.6
Total	2	232	776	110	217	32	18	12	112	44	109	.280	.323	.414	101	-14	47			.972	6	O-198	-1.9

■ JAY HANKINS Hankins, Jay Nelson b: 11/7/35, St.Louis Co., Mo. BL/TR, 5'7", 170 lbs. Deb: 4/15/61

YEAR	TM/L	G	AB	R	H	2B	3B	HR	RBI	BB	SO	AVG	OBP	SLG	PRO+	BR/A	SB	CS	SBR	FA	FR	G/POS	TPR
1961	KC-A	76	173	23	32	0	3	3	6	8	17	.185	.225	.272	32	-17	2	0	1	.970	-10	O-65	-2.9
1963	KC-A	10	34	2	6	0	1	1	4	0	3	.176	.176	.324	35	-3	0	1	-1	.952	1	/O-9	-0.4
Total	2	86	207	25	38	0	4	4	10	8	20	.184	.218	.280	32	-20	2	1	0	.967	-10	/O-74	-3.3

■ FRANK HANKINSON Hankinson, Frank Edward b: 4/29/1856, New York, N.Y. d: 4/5/11, Palisades Park, N.J BR/TR, 5'11", 168 lbs. Deb: 5/1/1878

YEAR	TM/L	G	AB	R	H	2B	3B	HR	RBI	BB	SO	AVG	OBP	SLG	PRO+	BR/A	SB	CS	SBR	FA	FR	G/POS	TPR
1878	Chi-N	58	240	38	64	8	3	1	27	5	36	.267	.282	.338	96	-2				.875	8	*3-57/P-1	0.8
1879	Chi-N	44	171	14	31	4	0	0	8	2	14	.181	.191	.205	29	-13				.933	6	P-26,O-14/3-5	-0.4
1880	Cle-N	69	263	32	55	7	4	1	19	1	23	.209	.212	.278	66	-9				.844	-12	*3-56,O-12/P-4	-2.0
1881	Tro-N	85	321	34	62	15	0	1	19	10	41	.193	.218	.249	44	-21				.907	7	*3-84/S-1	-1.1
1883	NY-N	94	337	40	74	13	6	2	30	19	38	.220	.261	.312	74	-10				.870	-4	*3-93/O-1	-1.3
1884	NY-N	105	389	44	90	16	7	2	43	23	59	.231	.274	.324	85	-7				.871	-1	*3-105/O-1	-0.6
1885	NY-a	94	362	43	81	12	2	2	44	12		.224	.251	.285	75	-10				**.906**	18	*3-94/P-1	0.9
1886	NY-a	136	522	66	126	14	5	2	63	49		.241	.306	.299	94	-2	10			.873	25	*3-136	2.3
1887	NY-a	127	512	79	137	29	11	1	71	38		.268	.318	.373	97	-3	19			.864	8	*3-127	0.6
1888	KC-a	37	155	20	27	4	1	1	20	11		.174	.229	.232	45	-10	2			.947	-5	2-13/S-9,O-7,3-7,1	-1.3
Total	10	849	3272	410	747	122	39	13	344	170	211	.228	.267	.301	77	-85	31			.875	50	3-764/O-35,P2S1	-2.1

■ NED HANLON Hanlon, Edward Hugh b: 8/22/1857, Montville, Conn. d: 4/14/37, Baltimore, Md. BL/TR, 5'9.5", 170 lbs. Deb: 5/1/1880 MH

YEAR	TM/L	G	AB	R	H	2B	3B	HR	RBI	BB	SO	AVG	OBP	SLG	PRO+	BR/A	SB	CS	SBR	FA	FR	G/POS	TPR
1880	Cle-N	73	280	30	69	10	3	0	32	11	30	.246	.275	.304	98	-0				.804	-3	*O-69/S-4	-0.4
1881	Det-N	76	305	63	85	14	8	2	28	22	11	.279	.327	.397	122	7				.897	-5	*O-74/S-2	0.1
1882	Det-N	82	347	68	80	18	6	5	38	26	25	.231	.284	.360	105	3				.887	14	*O-82/2-1	1.4
1883	Det-N	100	413	65	100	13	2	1	40	34	44	.242	.300	.291	84	-6				.884	2	*O-90,2-11	-0.4
1884	Det-N	114	450	86	119	18	6	5	39	40	52	.264	.324	.364	124	14				.874	13	*O-114	2.2
1885	Det-N	105	424	93	128	18	8	1	29	47	18	.302	.372	.389	146	23				.863	4	*O-105	2.2
1886	Det-N	126	494	105	116	6	6	4	60	57	39	.235	.314	.296	84	-8	50			.929	-4	*O-126/2-1	-1.4
1887	*Det-N	118	471	79	129	13	7	4	69	30	24	.274	.320	.357	85	-10	69			.904	3	*O-118	-0.8
1888	Det-N	109	459	64	122	6	8	5	39	15	32	.266	.295	.346	104	1	38			.919	-6	*O-109	-0.7
1889	Pit-N	116	461	81	110	14	10	2	37	58	25	.239	.326	.325	91	-4	53			.919	-3	*O-116,M	-0.8
1890	Pit-P	118	472	106	131	16	6	1	44	80	24	.278	.389	.343	105	9	65			.911	-2	*O-118,M	0.3
1891	Pit-N	119	455	87	121	12	8	0	60	48	30	.266	.341	.327	97	-0	54			.881	0	*O-119/S-1,M	-0.3
1892	Bal-N	11	43	3	7	1	1	0	2	3	3	.163	.217	.233	35	-3	0			.786	-0	O-11,M	-0.4
Total	13	1267	5074	930	1317	159	79	30	517	471	357	.260	.325	.340	102	25	329			.891	14	*O-1251/2-13,S-7	1.0

■ BILL HANLON Hanlon, William Joseph "Big Bill" b: 6/24/1876, Los Angeles, Cal. d: 11/23/05, Los Angeles, Cal. 6', Deb: 4/16/03

YEAR	TM/L	G	AB	R	H	2B	3B	HR	RBI	BB	SO	AVG	OBP	SLG	PRO+	BR/A	SB	CS	SBR	FA	FR	G/POS	TPR
1903	Chi-N	8	21	4	2	0	0	0	2	6		.095	.296	.095	14	-2	1			.980	-0	/1-8	-0.2

■ JOHN HANNA Hanna, John b: 11/3/1863, Philadelphia, Pa. d: 11/7/30, Philadelphia, Pa. Deb: 5/23/1884

YEAR	TM/L	G	AB	R	H	2B	3B	HR	RBI	BB	SO	AVG	OBP	SLG	PRO+	BR/A	SB	CS	SBR	FA	FR	G/POS	TPR
1884	Was-a	23	76	8	5	0	0	0		6		.066	.134	.066	-37	-11				.874	0	C-18/O-6	-0.9
	Ric-a	22	67	6	13	2	1	0		0		.194	.206	.254	50	-4				.924	4	C-21/S-1	0.2
	Yr	45	143	14	18	2	1	0		6		.126	.167	.154	6	-14				.900	4	C-39/O-6,S-1	-0.7

■ TRUCK HANNAH Hannah, James Harrison b: 6/5/1889, Larimore, N.D. d: 4/27/82, Fountain Valley, Cal. BR/TR, 6'1", 190 lbs. Deb: 4/15/18

YEAR	TM/L	G	AB	R	H	2B	3B	HR	RBI	BB	SO	AVG	OBP	SLG	PRO+	BR/A	SB	CS	SBR	FA	FR	G/POS	TPR
1918	NY-A	90	250	24	55	6	0	2	21	51	25	.220	.361	.268	88	-1	5			.974	3	C-88	1.0
1919	NY-A	75	227	14	54	8	3	1	20	22	19	.238	.313	.313	76	-7	0			**.984**	-9	C-73/1-1	-1.0
1920	NY-A	79	259	24	64	11	1	2	25	24	35	.247	.313	.320	66	-13	2	0	1	.961	-6	C-78	-1.2
Total	3	244	736	62	173	25	4	5	66	97	79	.235	.331	.300	76	-21	7	0		.973	-11	C-239/1-1	-1.2

■ PAT HANNIFAN Hannifan, Patrick James b: 4/20/1866, Halifax, N.S., Can. d: 11/5/08, Springfield, Mass. TL, Deb: 4/29/1897

YEAR	TM/L	G	AB	R	H	2B	3B	HR	RBI	BB	SO	AVG	OBP	SLG	PRO+	BR/A	SB	CS	SBR	FA	FR	G/POS	TPR
1897	Bro-N	10	20	4	5	0	0	0	2	1		.250	.375	.250	71	-1	4			.867	2	/O-3,2-2	0.1

■ JACK HANNIFIN Hannifin, John Joseph b: 2/25/1883, Holyoke, Mass. d: 10/27/45, Northampton, Mass. BR/TR, 5'11", 167 lbs. Deb: 4/19/06

YEAR	TM/L	G	AB	R	H	2B	3B	HR	RBI	BB	SO	AVG	OBP	SLG	PRO+	BR/A	SB	CS	SBR	FA	FR	G/POS	TPR
1906	Phi-A	1	1	0	1	0	0	0	0	0		1.000	1.000	1.000	511	0	0			.000	0	H	0.0
	NY-N	10	30	4	6	0	1	0	3	2		.200	.250	.267	60	-1	1			.903	-1	/S-6,3-3,2-1	-0.2
1907	NY-N	56	149	16	34	7	3	1	15	15		.228	.303	.336	97	-1	6			.996	-4	1-29,3-10/S-9,O-2	-0.5
1908	NY-N	1	2	0	0	0	0	0	0	0		.000	.000	.000	-95	-0	0			.000	-0	/O-1	-0.1
	Bos-N	90	257	30	53	6	2	2	22	28		.206	.284	.268	78	-6	7			.930	5	3-35,2-22,S-15,/O-7	0.0

YEAR	TM/L	G	AB	R	H	2B	3B	HR	RBI	BB	SO	AVG	OBP	SLG	PRO+	BR/A	SB	CS	SBR	FA	FR	G/POS	TPR
	Yr	91	259	30	53	6	2	2	22	28		.205	.282	.266	77	-6	7			.930	5	3-35,2-22,S-15,/O-8	-0.1
Total	3	158	439	50	94	13	6	3	40	45		.214	.289	.292	84	-8	14			.937	0	/3-48,S-30,1-29,2O	-0.8
■ DAVE HANSEN	Hansen, David Andrew b: 11/24/68, Long Beach, Cal. BL/TR, 6', 195 lbs. Deb: 9/16/90																						
1990	LA-N	5	7	0	1	0	0	0	1	0	3	.143	.143	.143	-22	-1	0	0	0	.500	-1	/3-2	-0.2
1991	LA-N	53	56	3	15	4	0	1	5	2	12	.268	.293	.393	93	-1	1	0	0	1.000	2	3-21/S-1	0.1
1992	LA-N	132	341	30	73	11	0	6	22	34	49	.214	.287	.299	67	-15	0	2	-1	**.968**	7	*3-108	-1.0
1993	LA-N	84	105	13	38	3	0	4	30	21	13	.362	.468	.505	170	12	0	1	-1	.927	-1	3-18	1.0
1994	LA-N	40	44	3	15	3	0	0	5	5	5	.341	.408	.409	122	2	0	0	0	.857	-1	/3-7	0.0
1995	*LA-N	100	181	19	52	10	0	1	14	28	28	.287	.386	.359	107	3	0	0	0	.933	-6	3-58	-0.3
1996	*LA-N	80	104	7	23	1	0	0	6	11	22	.221	.296	.231	45	-8	0	0	0	.962	-0	3-19/1-8	-0.9
1997	Chi-N	90	151	19	47	8	2	3	21	31	32	.311	.432	.450	128	8	1	2	-1	.922	-9	3-51/1-4,2-1	-0.2
Total	8	584	989	94	264	40	2	15	104	132	164	.267	.355	.357	97	-0	2	5	-2	.949	-10	3-284/1-12,2-1,S-1	-1.5
■ DOUG HANSEN	Hansen, Douglas William b: 12/16/28, Los Angeles, Cal. BR/TR, 6', 180 lbs. Deb: 9/4/51																						
1951	Cle-A	3	0	2	0	0	0	0	0	0	0	—	—	—	—	0	0	0	0	.000	0	R	0.0
■ JED HANSEN	Hansen, Jed Ramon b: 8/19/72, Tacoma, Wash. BR/TR, 6'1", 195 lbs. Deb: 7/29/97																						
1997	KC-A	34	94	11	29	6	1	1	14	13	29	.309	.398	.426	112	2	3	2	-0	.993	-2	2-31	0.2
1998	KC-A	4	3	0	0	0	0	0	0	0	3	.000	.000	.000	-96	-1	0	0	0	1.000	-0	/2-2	-0.1
Total	2	38	97	11	29	6	1	1	14	13	32	.299	.387	.412	106	1	3	2	-0	.993	-2	/2-33	0.1
■ BOB HANSEN	Hansen, Robert Joseph b: 5/26/48, Boston, Mass. BL/TL, 6', 195 lbs. Deb: 5/10/74																						
1974	Mil-A	58	88	8	26	4	1	2	9	3	16	.295	.319	.432	115	1	2	1	0	1.000	-0	D-18/1-3	0.1
1976	Mil-A	24	61	4	10	1	0	0	4	6	8	.164	.239	.180	24	-6	0	0	0	.000	-0	D-14/1-1	-0.7
Total	2	82	149	12	36	5	1	2	13	9	24	.242	.285	.329	78	-4	2	1	0	1.000	-0	/D-32,1-4	-0.6
■ RON HANSEN	Hansen, Ronald Lavern b: 4/5/38, Oxford, Neb. BR/TR, 6'3", 200 lbs. Deb: 4/15/58 C																						
1958	Bal-A	12	19	1	0	0	0	0	1	0	7	.000	.050	.000	-90	-5	0	0	0	.943	-0	S-12	-0.5
1959	Bal-A	2	4	0	0	0	0	0	0	1	1	.000	.200	.000	-41	-1	0	0	0	.889	1	/S-2	0.0
1960	Bal-A★	153	530	72	135	22	5	22	86	69	94	.255	.343	.440	111	8	3	3	-1	.964	6	*S-153	2.5
1961	Bal-A	155	533	51	132	13	2	12	51	66	96	.248	.332	.347	85	-11	1	3	-2	.959	12	*S-149/2-7	1.3
1962	Bal-A	71	196	12	34	7	0	3	17	30	36	.173	.289	.255	51	-13	0	1	-1	.965	4	S-64	-0.5
1963	Chi-A	144	482	55	109	17	2	13	67	78	74	.226	.334	.351	94	-2	1	1	-0	.983	**27**	*S-144	3.6
1964	Chi-A	158	575	85	150	25	3	20	68	73	73	.261	.350	.419	116	13	1	0	0	.975	16	*S-158	4.3
1965	Chi-A	162	587	61	138	23	4	11	66	60	73	.235	.308	.344	91	-8	1	1	-0	.969	17	*S-161/2-1	2.1
1966	Chi-A	23	74	3	13	1	0	0	4	15	10	.176	.322	.189	55	-4	0	1	-1	.946	3	S-23	0.0
1967	Chi-A	157	498	35	116	20	0	8	51	64	51	.233	.320	.321	94	-3	0	3	-2	.964	2	*S-157	1.4
1968	Was-A	86	275	28	51	12	0	8	28	35	49	.185	.282	.316	84	-5	0	0	0	.963	2	S-81/3-5	0.5
	Chi-A	40	87	7	20	3	0	1	4	11	12	.230	.316	.299	86	-1	0	0	0	.959	6	3-29/S-7,2-2	0.6
	Yr	126	362	35	71	15	0	9	32	46	61	.196	.290	.312	84	-7	0	0	0	.963	7	S-88,3-34/2-2	1.1
1969	Chi-A	85	185	15	48	6	1	2	22	18	25	.259	.328	.335	82	-4	2	0	1	.967	-1	2-26,1-21/S-8,3-7	-0.4
1970	NY-A	59	91	13	27	4	0	4	14	19	9	.297	.423	.473	155	8	0	1	-1	.983	-3	S-15,3-11/2-1	0.6
1971	NY-A	61	145	6	30	3	0	2	20	9	27	.207	.253	.269	51	-10	0	0	0	.918	-3	3-30/2-9,S-3	-1.3
1972	KC-A	16	30	2	4	0	0	0	2	3	6	.133	.212	.133	4	-3	0	0	0	.944	3	/S-6,3-4,2-1	0.0
Total	15	1384	4311	446	1007	156	17	106	501	551	643	.234	.323	.351	92	-42	9	14	-6	.968	90	*S-1143/3-86,2-47,1	14.2
■ DON HANSKI	Hanski, Donald Thomas (b: Donald Thomas Hanyzewski) b: 2/27/16, LaPorte, Ind. d: 9/2/57, Worth, Ill. BL/TL, 5'11", 180 lbs. Deb: 5/6/43																						
1943	Chi-A	9	21	1	5	1	0	0	2	0	5	.238	.238	.286	53	-1	0	1	-1	.952	-0	/1-5,P-1	-0.3
1944	Chi-A	2	1	0	0	0	0	0	0	0	0	.000	.000	.000	-99	-0	0	0	0	.000	-0	/P-2	0.0
Total	2	11	22	1	5	1	0	0	2	0	5	.227	.227	.273	46	-2	0	1	-1	—	-1	/1-5,P-3	-0.3
■ HARRY HANSON	Hanson, Harry Francis b: 1/17/1896, Elgin, Ill. d: 10/5/66, Savannah, Ga. BR/TR, 5'11", Deb: 7/14/13																						
1913	NY-A	1	2	0	0	0	0	0	0	0	0	.000	.000	.000	-99	-0	0			1.000	-0	/C-1	-0.1
■ JOHN HAPPENNY	Happenny, John Clifford "Cliff" b: 5/18/01, Waltham, Mass. d: 12/29/88, Coral Springs, Fla BR/TR, 5'11", 165 lbs. Deb: 7/2/23																						
1923	Chi-A	32	86	7	19	5	0	0	10	3	13	.221	.256	.279	41	-8	0	0	0	.947	0	2-19/S-9,3-2	-0.6
■ BILL HARBIDGE	Harbidge, William Arthur "Yaller Bill" b: 3/29/1855, Philadelphia, Pa. d: 3/17/24, Philadelphia, Pa. BL/TL, 162 lbs. Deb: 5/15/1875																						
1875	Har-n	53	208	32	50	3	3	0	26	9	3	.240	.272	.284	89	-3	2	4	-2	.871	-0	C-31,O-13,2-11,/1S	-0.3
1876	Har-N	30	106	11	23	2	1	0	6	3	2	.217	.239	.255	59	-5				.799	1	C-24/O-6,1-2	-0.3
1877	Har-N	41	167	18	37	5	2	0	8	3	6	.222	.235	.275	68	-6				.881	-4	C-32/O-5,2-4,3-1	-0.8
1878	Chi-N	54	240	32	71	12	0	0	37	6	13	.296	.313	.346	109	2				.878	-8	*C-53/O-8	-0.6
1879	Chi-N	4	18	2	2	0	0	0	1	0	5	.111	.111	.111	-25	-2				.571	-1	/O-4	-0.3
1880	Tro-N	9	27	3	10	0	1	0	2	0	3	.370	.370	.444	166	2				.887	0	/C-9,O-1	0.2
1882	Tro-N	32	123	11	23	1	1	0	13	10	17	.187	.248	.211	52	-6				.836	-4	O-23/1-6,C-3	-0.9
1883	Phi-N	73	280	32	62	12	3	0	21	24	20	.221	.283	.286	81	-5				.796	-11	O-44,S-11/2-9,C3	-1.4
1884	Cin-U	82	341	59	95	12	5	2		25		.279	.328	.361	101	-10				.906	5	*O-80/S-3,1-2	-0.6
Total	8	325	1302	168	323	44	13	2	88	71	66	.248	.287	.306	86	-30				.849	-21	O-171,C-128/S213	-4.7
■ SCOTT HARDESTY	Hardesty, Scott Durbin b: 1/26/1870, Bellville, Ohio d: 10/29/44, Fostoria, Ohio Deb: 8/17/1899																						
1899	NY-N	22	72	4	16	0	0	0	4	1		.222	.243	.222	29	-7	2			.895	2	S-20/1-2	-0.3
■ PAT HARDGROVE	Hardgrove, William Henry b: 5/10/1895, Palmyra, Kan. d: 1/26/73, Jackson, Miss. BR/TR, 5'10", 158 lbs. Deb: 6/8/18																						
1918	Chi-A	2	2	0	0	0	0	0	0	0	0	.000	.000	.000	-99	-0	0			.000	0	H	-0.1
■ LOU HARDIE	Hardie, Louis W. b: 8/24/1864, New York, N.Y. d: 3/5/29, Oakland, Cal. 5'11", 180 lbs. Deb: 5/22/1884																						
1884	Phi-N	3	8	0	3	2	0	0	0	0	2	.375	.375	.625	219	1				.857	-3	/C-3	-0.1
1886	Chi-N	16	51	4	9	0	0	0	3	4	10	.176	.236	.176	24	-5	1			.964	-0	C-13/O-2,3-1	-0.4
1890	Bos-N	47	185	17	42	8	0	3	17	18	36	.227	.296	.319	73	-7	4			.886	-0	C-25,O-15/3-7,S1	-0.5
1891	Bal-a	15	56	7	13	0	3	0	1	8	8	.232	.328	.339	90	-1	3			1.000	1	O-15	0.0
Total	4	81	300	28	67	10	3	3	21	30	56	.223	.294	.307	71	-12	8			.910	-2	/C-41,O-32,3-8,1S	-1.0
■ BUD HARDIN	Hardin, William Edgar b: 6/14/22, Shelby, N.C. d: 7/28/97, Rancho Santa Fe, Cal. BR/TR, 5'10", 165 lbs. Deb: 4/15/52																						
1952	Chi-N	3	7	1	1	0	0	0	0	0	0	.143	.143	.143	-20	-1	0	0	0	1.000	0	/S-2,2-1	-0.1
■ LOU HARDING	Harding, Louis Edward "Jumbo" b: 1865, San Francisco, Cal. 5'9.5", 213 lbs. Deb: 10/5/1886																						
1886	StL-a	1	3	0	1	1	0	0	1	0		.333	.333	.667	201	0	0			.889	1	/C-1	0.1
■ JASON HARDTKE	Hardtke, Jason Robert b: 9/15/71, Milwaukee, Wis. BB/TR, 5'10", 175 lbs. Deb: 9/8/96																						
1996	NY-N	19	57	3	11	5	0	0	6	2	12	.193	.233	.281	36	-5	0	0	0	1.000	-2	2-18	-0.6
1997	NY-N	30	56	9	15	2	0	2	8	4	6	.268	.328	.411	95	-0	1	1	-0	.981	-6	2-21/3-1	-0.6
1998	Chi-N	18	21	2	5	0	0	0	2	2	6	.238	.304	.238	42	-2	0	0	0	1.000	-2	/3-7,O-1,D-1	-0.3
Total	3	67	134	14	31	7	0	2	16	8	24	.231	.285	.328	62	-8	1	1	-0	.991	-10	/2-39,3-8,D-1,O-1	-1.5
■ CARROLL HARDY	Hardy, Carroll William b: 5/18/33, Sturgis, S.Dak. BR/TR, 6', 185 lbs. Deb: 4/15/58																						
1958	Cle-A	27	49	10	10	3	0	1	6	6	14	.204	.304	.327	75	-2	1	2	-1	1.000	1	O-17	-0.3
1959	Cle-A	32	53	12	11	1	0	0	2	3	7	.208	.250	.226	33	-5	1	1	-0	1.000	1	O-15	-0.5
1960	Cle-A	29	18	7	2	1	0	0	1	2	2	.111	.200	.167	0	-3	0	0	0	1.000	-4	O-17	-0.7
	Bos-A	73	145	26	34	5	2	2	15	17	40	.234	.315	.338	74	-5	3	2	-0	.968	-6	O-59	-1.4
	Yr	102	163	33	36	6	2	2	16	19	42	.221	.302	.319	67	-7	3	2	-0	.973	-11	O-76	-2.1
1961	Bos-A	85	281	46	74	20	2	3	36	26	53	.263	.330	.381	87	-5	4	2	0	.961	-1	O-76	-1.0
1962	Bos-A	115	362	52	78	13	5	8	36	54	68	.215	.321	.345	77	-11	3	7	-3	.991	1	*O-105	-1.9

YEAR	TM/L	G	AB	R	H	2B	3B	HR	RBI	BB	SO	AVG	OBP	SLG	PRO+	BR/A	SB	CS	SBR	FA	FR	G/POS	TPR
1963	Hou-N	15	44	5	10	3	0	0	3	3	7	.227	.277	.295	69	-2	1	0	0	.947	1	O-10	-0.1
1964	Hou-N	46	157	13	29	1	1	2	12	8	30	.185	.234	.242	36	-13	0	0	0	.990	5	O-41	-1.2
1967	Min-A	11	8	1	3	0	0	1	2	1	1	.375	.444	.750	229	1	0	0	0	.000	-1	/O-4	0.0
Total	8	433	1117	172	251	47	10	17	113	120	222	.225	.304	.330	72	-45	13	14	-5	.981	-5	O-344	-7.1

■ JACK HARDY Hardy, John Doolittle b: 6/23/1877, Cleveland, Ohio d: 10/20/21, Cleveland, Ohio BR/TR, 6', 185 lbs. Deb: 8/29/03

YEAR	TM/L	G	AB	R	H	2B	3B	HR	RBI	BB	SO	AVG	OBP	SLG	PRO+	BR/A	SB	CS	SBR	FA	FR	G/POS	TPR
1903	Cle-A	5	19	1	3	1	0	0	1	1		.158	.200	.211	24	-2	1			1.000	-1	/O-5	-0.3
1907	Chi-N	1	4	0	1	0	0	0	0	0		.250	.250	.250	53	-0	0			.909	0	/C-1	0.0
1909	Was-A	10	24	3	4	0	0	0	4	1		.167	.200	.167	17	-2	0			.974	-2	/C-9,2-1	-0.4
1910	Was-A	7	8	1	2	0	0	0	0	0		.250	.250	.250	59	-0	0			.933	1	/C-4,O-1	0.0
Total	4	23	55	5	10	1	0	0	5	2		.182	.211	.200	28	-5	1			.953	-2	/C-14,O-6,2-1	-0.7

■ SHAWN HARE Hare, Shawn Robert b: 3/26/67, St.Louis, Mo. BL/TL, 6'2", 190 lbs. Deb: 9/6/91

YEAR	TM/L	G	AB	R	H	2B	3B	HR	RBI	BB	SO	AVG	OBP	SLG	PRO+	BR/A	SB	CS	SBR	FA	FR	G/POS	TPR
1991	Det-A	9	19	0	1	1	0	0	0	2	1	.053	.143	.105	-30	-3	0	0	0	1.000	0	/O-6,D-2	-0.4
1992	Det-A	15	26	0	3	1	0	0	5	2	4	.115	.179	.154	-6	-4	0	0	0	1.000	-2	/O-9,1-4	-0.6
1994	NY-N	22	40	7	9	1	1	0	2	4	11	.225	.295	.300	56	-3	0	0	0	1.000	-0	O-14	-0.3
1995	Tex-A	18	24	2	6	1	0	0	2	4	6	.250	.357	.292	70	-1	0	0	0	1.000	-1	/O-9,1-1,D-3	-0.2
Total	4	64	109	9	19	4	1	0	9	12	22	.174	.256	.229	31	-11	0	0	0	1.000	-3	/O-38,1-5,D-5	-1.5

■ GARY HARGIS Hargis, Gary Lynn b: 11/2/56, Minneapolis, Minn. BR/TR, 5'11", 165 lbs. Deb: 9/29/79

YEAR	TM/L	G	AB	R	H	2B	3B	HR	RBI	BB	SO	AVG	OBP	SLG	PRO+	BR/A	SB	CS	SBR	FA	FR	G/POS	TPR
1979	Pit-N	1	0	0	0	0	0	0	0	0	0	—	—	—	—	0	0	0	0	.000	0	/R	0.0

■ BUBBLES HARGRAVE Hargrave, Eugene Franklin b: 7/15/1892, New Haven, Ind. d: 2/23/69, Cincinnati, Ohio BR/TR, 5'10.5", 174 lbs. Deb: 9/18/13 F

YEAR	TM/L	G	AB	R	H	2B	3B	HR	RBI	BB	SO	AVG	OBP	SLG	PRO+	BR/A	SB	CS	SBR	FA	FR	G/POS	TPR
1913	Chi-N	3	3	0	1	0	0	0	1	0	0	.333	.333	.333	91	-0	0			1.000	0	/C-2	0.0
1914	Chi-N	23	36	3	8	2	0	0	2	0	4	.222	.222	.278	48	-2	2			.930	-4	C-16	-0.6
1915	Chi-N	15	19	2	3	0	1	0	2	1	5	.158	.200	.263	40	-1	0			1.000	-1	/C-9	-0.2
1921	Cin-N	93	263	28	76	17	8	1	38	12	15	.289	.327	.426	102	0	4	2	0	.973	-7	C-73	-0.3
1922	Cin-N	98	320	49	101	22	10	7	57	26	18	.316	.371	.512	128	12	7	4	-0	.982	-9	C-87	0.7
1923	Cin-N	118	378	54	126	23	9	10	78	44	22	.333	.419	.521	150	28	4	5	-2	.988	3	*C-109	3.3
1924	Cin-N	98	312	42	94	19	10	3	33	30	20	.301	.370	.455	122	10	2	2	-1	.983	-1	C-91	1.4
1925	Cin-N	87	273	28	82	13	6	2	33	25	23	.300	.361	.414	100	0	4	3	-1	.979	-6	C-84	-0.2
1926	Cin-N	105	326	42	115	22	8	6	62	25	17	**.353**	.406	.525	153	24	2			.988	-12	C-93	1.8
1927	Cin-N	102	305	36	94	18	3	0	35	31	18	.308	.376	.387	108	4	0			**.988**	-10	C-92	0.1
1928	Cin-N	65	190	19	56	12	3	0	23	13	14	.295	.353	.389	95	-1	4			.991	2	C-57	0.5
1930	NY-A	45	108	11	30	7	0	0	12	10	9	.278	.339	.343	77	-4	0	0	0	.992	-5	C-34	-0.6
Total	12	852	2533	314	786	155	58	29	376	217	165	.310	.372	.452	119	70	29	16		.983	-50	C-747	5.9

■ PINKY HARGRAVE Hargrave, William McKinley b: 1/31/1896, New Haven, Ind. d: 10/3/42, Ft.Wayne, Ind. BB/TR, 5'8.5", 180 lbs. Deb: 5/18/23 F

YEAR	TM/L	G	AB	R	H	2B	3B	HR	RBI	BB	SO	AVG	OBP	SLG	PRO+	BR/A	SB	CS	SBR	FA	FR	G/POS	TPR
1923	Was-A	33	59	4	17	2	0	0	8	2	6	.288	.311	.322	70	-3	0	0	0	.917	-4	/3-8,C-5,O-1	-0.6
1924	Was-A	24	33	3	5	1	1	0	5	1	4	.152	.176	.242	8	-5	0	0	0	1.000	-1	/C-8	-0.5
1925	Was-A	5	6	0	3	0	0	0	0	1	2	.500	.571	.500	177	1	0	0	0	1.000	1	/C-1	0.2
	StL-A	67	225	34	64	15	2	8	43	13	13	.284	.326	.476	97	-3	2	0	1	.981	-6	C-62	-0.5
	Yr	72	231	34	67	15	2	8	43	14	15	.290	.333	.476	99	-2	2	0	1	.981	-5	C-63	-0.3
1926	StL-A	92	235	20	66	16	3	7	37	10	38	.281	.319	.464	98	-2	3	0	1	.977	-2	C-58	0.0
1928	Det-A	121	320	38	88	13	5	10	63	32	28	.275	.343	.441	103	1	4	1	1	.977	-14	C-88	-0.5
1929	Det-A	76	185	26	61	12	0	3	26	20	24	.330	.401	.443	117	5	2	2	-1	.973	-1	C-48	0.7
1930	Det-A	55	137	18	39	8	0	5	18	20	12	.285	.380	.453	108	2	2	0	1	.984	-4	C-40	0.2
	Was-A	10	31	3	6	2	2	1	7	3	1	.194	.265	.484	85	-1	1	0	0	1.000	1	/C-9	0.1
	Yr	65	168	21	45	10	2	6	25	23	13	.268	.359	.458	104	1	3	0	1	.987	-3	C-49	0.3
1931	Was-A	40	80	6	26	8	0	1	19	9	12	.325	.393	.463	124	3	1	0	0	.978	-2	C-25	0.2
1932	Bos-N	82	217	20	57	14	3	4	33	24	18	.263	.336	.410	103	1	1			.968	-4	C-73	0.1
1933	Bos-N	45	73	5	13	0	0	0	6	5	7	.178	.241	.178	23	-7	1			.957	1	C-25	-0.6
Total	10	650	1601	177	445	91	16	39	265	140	165	.278	.339	.428	98	-8	17	3		.976	-35	C-442/3-8,O-1	-1.2

■ CHARLIE HARGREAVES Hargreaves, Charles Russell b: 12/14/1896, Trenton, N.J. d: 5/9/79, Neptune, N.J. BR/TR, 6', 170 lbs. Deb: 7/15/23

YEAR	TM/L	G	AB	R	H	2B	3B	HR	RBI	BB	SO	AVG	OBP	SLG	PRO+	BR/A	SB	CS	SBR	FA	FR	G/POS	TPR
1923	Bro-N	20	57	5	16	0	0	0	4	1	2	.281	.293	.281	54	-4	0	0	0	.921	-4	C-15	-0.7
1924	Bro-N	15	27	4	11	2	0	0	5	1	1	.407	.429	.481	148	2	0	1	-1	1.000	-1	/C-9	0.0
1925	Bro-N	45	83	9	23	3	1	0	13	6	1	.277	.326	.337	72	-3	1	1	-0	.986	2	C-18/1-2	-0.1
1926	Bro-N	85	208	14	52	13	2	2	23	19	10	.250	.316	.361	83	-5	1			.986	4	C-70	0.2
1927	Bro-N	46	133	9	38	3	1	0	11	14	7	.286	.362	.323	85	-2	1			.985	-1	C-44	0.0
1928	Bro-N	20	61	3	12	2	0	0	5	6	6	.197	.269	.230	32	-6	1			.979	2	C-20	-0.3
	Pit-N	79	260	15	74	8	2	1	32	12	9	.285	.319	.342	70	-11	1			.962	-5	C-77	-1.0
	Yr	99	321	18	86	10	2	1	37	18	15	.268	.309	.321	63	-17	2			.966	-3	C-97	-1.3
1929	Pit-N	102	328	33	88	12	5	1	44	16	12	.268	.306	.345	60	-21	1			.981	2	*C-101	-0.9
1930	Pit-N	11	31	4	7	1	0	0	2	2	1	.226	.273	.258	29	-4	0			1.000	6	C-11	0.3
Total	8	423	1188	96	321	44	11	4	139	77	49	.270	.318	.336	69	-55	6	2		.977	4	C-365/1-2	-2.5

■ MIKE HARGROVE Hargrove, Dudley Michael b: 10/26/49, Perryton, Tex. BL/TL, 6', 195 lbs. Deb: 4/7/74 MC

YEAR	TM/L	G	AB	R	H	2B	3B	HR	RBI	BB	SO	AVG	OBP	SLG	PRO+	BR/A	SB	CS	SBR	FA	FR	G/POS	TPR
1974	Tex-A	131	415	57	134	18	6	4	66	49	42	.323	.400	.424	141	23	0	0	0	.987	9	1-91,D-32/O-6	2.7
1975	Tex-A★	145	519	82	157	22	2	11	62	79	66	.303	.399	.416	132	25	4	3	-1	.964	3	O-96,1-48,D-12	2.1
1976	Tex-A	151	541	80	155	30	1	7	58	**97**	64	.287	.401	.384	128	24	2	3	-1	.984	1	*1-141/D-5	1.5
1977	Tex-A	153	525	98	160	28	4	18	69	103	59	.305	.424	.476	143	37	2	5	-2	.993	-0	*1-152	2.5
1978	Tex-A	146	494	63	124	24	1	7	40	**107**	47	.251	.391	.346	109	12	2	5	-2	.987	7	*1-140/D-4	0.8
1979	SD-N	52	125	15	24	5	0	0	8	25	15	.192	.327	.232	59	-6	0	2	-1	.986	-2	1-37	-1.2
	Cle-A	100	338	60	110	21	4	10	56	63	40	.325	.438	.500	152	28	2	3	-1	.993	0	O-65,1-28/D-7	2.2
1980	Cle-A	160	589	86	179	22	2	11	85	111	36	.304	.421	.404	127	28	4	2	0	.993	-5	*1-160	1.3
1981	Cle-A	94	322	43	102	21	0	2	49	60	16	.317	**.432**	.401	143	22	5	4	-1	.989	6	1-88/D-4	2.3
1982	Cle-A	160	591	67	160	26	1	4	65	101	58	.271	.380	.338	100	5	2	2	-1	.996	11	*1-153/D-5	0.7
1983	Cle-A	134	469	57	134	21	4	3	57	78	40	.286	.393	.367	107	8	0	6	-4	.994	12	*1-131/D-1	0.9
1984	Cle-A	133	352	44	94	14	2	2	44	53	38	.267	.363	.335	93	-1	0	2	-1	.991	6	*1-124	-0.3
1985	Cle-A	107	284	31	81	14	1	1	27	39	29	.285	.372	.352	100	2	1	0	0	.991	5	1-85	0.2
Total	12	1666	5564	783	1614	266	28	80	686	965	550	.290	.400	.391	121	205	24	37	-15	.991	52	*1-1378,O-167/D-70	15.7

■ TIM HARKNESS Harkness, Thomas William b: 12/23/37, Lachine, Que., Can. BL/TL, 6'2", 182 lbs. Deb: 9/12/61

YEAR	TM/L	G	AB	R	H	2B	3B	HR	RBI	BB	SO	AVG	OBP	SLG	PRO+	BR/A	SB	CS	SBR	FA	FR	G/POS	TPR
1961	LA-N	5	8	4	4	2	0	0	0	3	1	.500	.636	.750	245	2	1	0	0	1.000	-0	/1-2	0.2
1962	LA-N	92	62	9	16	2	0	2	7	10	20	.258	.370	.387	110	1	1	0	0	1.000	1	1-59	0.2
1963	NY-N	123	375	35	79	12	3	10	41	36	79	.211	.292	.339	80	-10	4	3	-1	.986	16	*1-106	0.2
1964	NY-N	39	117	11	33	2	1	2	13	9	18	.282	.339	.368	101	0	1	1	-0	.993	3	1-32	0.2
Total	4	259	562	59	132	18	4	14	61	58	118	.235	.316	.356	90	-6	7	4	-0	.989	21	1-199	0.8

■ DICK HARLEY Harley, Richard Joseph b: 9/25/1872, Philadelphia, Pa. d: 4/3/52, Philadelphia, Pa. BL/TR, 5'10.5", 165 lbs. Deb: 6/2/1897

YEAR	TM/L	G	AB	R	H	2B	3B	HR	RBI	BB	SO	AVG	OBP	SLG	PRO+	BR/A	SB	CS	SBR	FA	FR	G/POS	TPR
1897	StL-N	89	330	43	96	6	4	3	35	36		.291	.379	.361	98	1	23			.899	1	*O-89	-0.4
1898	StL-N	142	549	74	135	6	5	0	42	34		.246	.316	.275	68	-22	13			.926	9	*O-141	-2.2
1899	Cle-N	142	567	70	142	15	7	1	50	40		.250	.315	.307	76	-18	15			.924	5	*O-142	-2.2
1900	Cin-N	5	21	2	9	1	0	0	5	1		.429	.455	.476	161	2	4			1.000	-1	/O-5	0.0
1901	Cin-N	133	535	69	146	13	2	4	27	31		.273	.323	.327	95	-3	37			.898	-5	*O-133	-1.7
1902	Det-A	125	491	59	138	9	8	2	44	36		.281	.345	.344	90	-6	20			.930	-2	*O-125	-1.5
1903	Chi-N	104	386	72	89	9	1	0	33	45		.231	.328	.259	70	-13	27			.923	3	*O-103	-1.5
Total	7	740	2879	389	755	59	27	10	236	223		.262	.332	.312	83	-58	139			.918	10	O-738	-9.5

■ LARRY HARLOW Harlow, Larry Duane b: 11/13/51, Colorado Springs, Colo. BL/TL, 6'2", 185 lbs. Deb: 9/20/75

YEAR	TM/L	G	AB	R	H	2B	3B	HR	RBI	BB	SO	AVG	OBP	SLG	PRO+	BR/A	SB	CS	SBR	FA	FR	G/POS	TPR
1975	Bal-A	4	3	1	1	0	0	0	0	0	1	.333	.333	.333	95	-0	0	0	0	1.000	-2	/O-4	-0.2

YEAR	TM/L	G	AB	R	H	2B	3B	HR	RBI	BB	SO	AVG	OBP	SLG	PRO+	BR/A	SB	CS	SBR	FA	FR	G/POS	TPR
1977	Bal-A	46	48	4	10	0	1	0	0	5	8	.208	.283	.250	50	-3	6	1	1	.887	-12	O-38	-1.4
1978	Bal-A	147	460	67	112	25	1	8	26	55	72	.243	.326	.354	97	-2	14	11	-2	.979	-5	*O-138/P-1	-1.5
1979	Bal-A	38	41	5	11	1	0	0	1	7	4	.268	.375	.293	86	-0	1	3	-2	.970	-10	O-31/D-1	-1.2
	*Cal-A	62	159	22	37	8	2	0	14	25	34	.233	.344	.308	80	-4	1	3	-2	.975	-2	O-58	-0.9
	Yr	100	200	27	48	9	2	0	15	32	38	.240	.350	.305	81	-4	2	6	-3	.974	-12	O-89/D-1	-2.1
1980	Cal-A	109	301	47	83	13	4	4	27	48	61	.276	.377	.385	112	7	3	2	-0	.976	12	O-94/1-1,D-1	1.5
1981	Cal-A	43	82	13	17	1	0	0	4	16	25	.207	.337	.220	63	-3	1	1	-0	.981	-8	O-39	-1.3
Total	6	449	1094	159	271	48	8	12	72	156	205	.248	.344	.339	94	-5	26	21	-5	.971	-26	O-402/D-2,1-1,P-1	-5.0

■ BILL HARMAN

Harman, William Bell b: 1/2/19, Bridgewater, Va. BR/TR, 6'4", 200 lbs. Deb: 6/17/41

YEAR	TM/L	G	AB	R	H	2B	3B	HR	RBI	BB	SO	AVG	OBP	SLG	PRO+	BR/A	SB	CS	SBR	FA	FR	G/POS	TPR
1941	Phi-N	15	14	1	1	0	0	0	0	0	3	.071	.071	.071	-62	-3	0			1.000	-1	/P-5,C-5	-0.2

■ CHUCK HARMON

Harmon, Charles Byron b: 4/23/24, Washington, Ind. BR/TR, 6'2", 175 lbs. Deb: 4/17/54

YEAR	TM/L	G	AB	R	H	2B	3B	HR	RBI	BB	SO	AVG	OBP	SLG	PRO+	BR/A	SB	CS	SBR	FA	FR	G/POS	TPR
1954	Cin-N	94	286	39	68	7	3	2	25	17	27	.238	.283	.304	52	-20	7	3	0	.961	4	3-67/1-3	-1.7
1955	Cin-N	96	198	31	50	6	3	5	28	26	24	.253	.348	.389	90	-2	9	9	-3	.935	4	3-39,O-32/1-4	-0.3
1956	Cin-N	13	4	2	0	0	0	0	0	0	0	.000	.000	.000	-94	-1	1	0	0	1.000	-2	/O-6,1-2	-0.3
	StL-N	20	15	2	0	0	0	0	0	2	2	.000	.118	.000	-65	-4	0	0	0	1.000	-4	O-11/1-2,3-1	-0.8
	Yr	33	19	4	0	0	0	0	0	2	2	.000	.095	.000	-70	-5	1	0	0	1.000	-6	O-17/1-4,3-1	-1.1
1957	StL-N	9	3	2	1	0	1	0	1	0	0	.333	.333	1.000	236	1	1	0	0	1.000	-3	/O-8	-0.2
	Phi-N	57	86	14	22	2	1	0	5	1	4	.256	.264	.302	53	-6	7	2	1	1.000	-2	O-25/3-5,1-2	-0.7
	Yr	66	89	16	23	2	2	0	6	1	4	.258	.267	.326	60	-5	8	2	1	1.000	-5	O-33/3-5,1-2	-0.9
Total	4	289	592	90	141	15	8	7	59	46	57	.238	.298	.326	62	-33	25	14	-1	.952	-3	3-112/O-82,1-13	-4.0

■ TERRY HARMON

Harmon, Terry Walter b: 4/12/44, Toledo, Ohio BR/TR, 6'2", 180 lbs. Deb: 7/23/67

YEAR	TM/L	G	AB	R	H	2B	3B	HR	RBI	BB	SO	AVG	OBP	SLG	PRO+	BR/A	SB	CS	SBR	FA	FR	G/POS	TPR
1967	Phi-N	2	0	0	0	0	0	0	0	0	0	—	—	—	—	0	0	0	0	.000	0	R	0.0
1969	Phi-N	87	201	25	48	8	1	0	16	22	31	.239	.323	.289	74	-6	1	2	-1	.968	8	S-38,2-19/3-2	0.7
1970	Phi-N	71	129	16	32	2	4	0	7	12	22	.248	.317	.326	75	-5	6	3	0	.989	-3	S-35,2-14/3-2	-0.4
1971	Phi-N	79	221	27	45	4	2	0	12	20	45	.204	.282	.240	49	-14	3	2	-0	.986	8	2-58/S-9,3-3,1-2	-0.1
1972	Phi-N	73	218	35	62	8	2	2	13	29	28	.284	.373	.367	108	4	3	2	-0	.996	-1	2-50,S-15/3-5	0.6
1973	Phi-N	72	148	17	31	3	0	0	8	13	14	.209	.278	.230	41	-11	1	0	0	.988	2	2-43,S-19/3-1	-0.7
1974	Phi-N	27	15	5	2	0	0	0	0	3	3	.133	.278	.133	17	-2	0	0	0	1.000	3	/S-7,2-5	0.1
1975	Phi-N	48	72	14	13	1	2	0	5	9	13	.181	.280	.250	46	-5	0	0	0	.989	1	S-25/2-7,3-1	-0.2
1976	*Phi-N	42	61	12	18	4	1	0	6	3	10	.295	.328	.393	101	-0	3	0	1	.960	3	S-19,2-13/3-5	0.6
1977	Phi-N	46	60	13	11	1	0	2	5	6	9	.183	.269	.300	50	-4	0	2	-1	.982	8	2-28,S-16/3-3	0.4
Total	10	547	1125	164	262	31	12	4	72	117	175	.233	.312	.292	69	-44	17	11	-2	.989	29	2-237,S-183/3-22,1	1.0

■ BRIAN HARPER

Harper, Brian David b: 10/16/59, Los Angeles, Cal. BR/TR, 6'2", 195 lbs. Deb: 9/29/79

YEAR	TM/L	G	AB	R	H	2B	3B	HR	RBI	BB	SO	AVG	OBP	SLG	PRO+	BR/A	SB	CS	SBR	FA	FR	G/POS	TPR
1979	Cal-A	1	2	0	0	0	0	0	0	0	1	.000	.000	.000	-99	-1	0	0	0	.000	0	/D-1	-0.1
1981	Cal-A	4	11	1	3	0	0	0	1	0	0	.273	.273	.273	58	-1	1	0	0	.833	-0	/O-2,D-1	0.0
1982	Pit-N	20	29	4	8	1	0	2	4	1	4	.276	.300	.517	121	1	0	0	0	1.000	-1	/O-8	-0.1
1983	Pit-N	61	131	16	29	4	1	7	20	2	15	.221	.239	.427	79	-4	0	0	0	1.000	-5	O-35/1-1	-1.1
1984	Pit-N	46	112	4	29	4	0	2	11	5	11	.259	.303	.348	82	-3	0	0	0	.981	-2	O-37/C-2	-0.6
1985	*StL-N	43	52	5	13	4	0	0	8	2	3	.250	.278	.327	69	-2	0	0	0	1.000	-4	O-13/3-6,C-2,1-1	-0.7
1986	Det-A	19	36	2	5	1	0	0	3	3	3	.139	.205	.167	3	-5	0	0	0	.929	-2	O-11/C-2,1-2,D-6	-0.7
1987	Oak-A	11	17	1	4	1	0	0	3	0	4	.235	.235	.294	42	-1	0	0	0	.000	-0	/O-1,D-7	-0.2
1988	Min-A	60	166	15	49	11	1	3	20	10	12	.295	.346	.428	112	3	0	3	-2	.991	-7	C-48/3-2,D-5	-0.3
1989	Min-A	126	385	43	125	24	0	8	57	13	16	.325	.356	.449	118	8	2	4	-2	.978	-14	*C-101,D-19/O-3,13	-0.3
1990	Min-A	134	479	61	141	42	3	6	54	19	27	.294	.331	.432	105	2	3	2	-0	.985	2	*C-120,D-11/3-3,1-2	1.1
1991	*Min-A	123	441	54	137	28	1	10	69	14	22	.311	.341	.447	111	5	1	2	-1	.988	-6	*C-119/1-1,O-1,D-2	0.5
1992	Min-A	140	502	58	154	25	0	9	73	26	22	.307	.350	.410	109	5	0	1	-1	.984	-7	*C-133/D-2	0.6
1993	Min-A	147	530	52	161	26	1	12	73	29	29	.304	.350	.425	107	5	1	3	-2	.988	-14	*C-134/D-7	-0.3
1994	Mil-A	64	251	23	73	15	0	4	32	9	18	.291	.323	.398	81	-7	0	2	-1	.981	2	D-36,C-25/O-3	-0.7
1995	Oak-A	2	7	0	0	0	0	0	0	0	1	.000	.000	.000	-99	-2	0	0	0	1.000	-1	/C-2	-0.3
Total	16	1001	3151	339	931	186	7	63	428	133	188	.295	.333	.419	102	2	8	17	-8	.985	-60	C-688,O-114/D31	-3.2

■ GEORGE HARPER

Harper, George Washington b: 6/24/1892, Arlington, Ky. d: 8/18/78, Magnolia, Ark. BL/TR, 5'8", 167 lbs. Deb: 4/15/16

YEAR	TM/L	G	AB	R	H	2B	3B	HR	RBI	BB	SO	AVG	OBP	SLG	PRO+	BR/A	SB	CS	SBR	FA	FR	G/POS	TPR
1916	Det-A	44	56	4	9	1	0	0	3	5	8	.161	.230	.179	22	-5	0			.938	-4	O-14	-1.0
1917	Det-A	47	117	6	24	3	0	0	12	11	15	.205	.290	.231	59	-5	2			.980	-3	O-31	-1.1
1918	Det-A	69	227	19	55	5	2	0	16	18	14	.242	.301	.282	79	-6	3			.956	-1	O-64	-1.2
1922	Cin-N	128	430	67	146	22	8	2	68	35	22	.340	.397	.442	118	13	11	10	-3	.955	1	*O-109	0.3
1923	Cin-N	61	125	14	32	4	2	3	16	11	9	.256	.316	.392	88	-3	0	2	-1	.967	-2	O-29	-0.7
1924	Cin-N	28	74	7	20	3	0	0	3	13	5	.270	.393	.311	92	0	1	3	-2	.964	1	O-22	-0.2
	Phi-N	109	411	68	121	26	6	16	55	38	23	.294	.361	.504	115	8	10	11	-4	.991	3	*O-109	0.0
	Yr	137	485	75	141	29	6	16	58	51	28	.291	.366	.474	113	8	11	14	-5	.986	4	*O-131	-0.2
1925	Phi-N	132	495	86	173	35	7	18	97	28	32	.349	.391	.558	128	19	10	8	-2	.971	6	*O-126	1.5
1926	Phi-N	56	194	32	61	6	5	7	38	16	7	.314	.367	.505	126	6	6			.942	-6	O-55	-0.3
1927	NY-N	145	483	85	160	19	6	16	87	84	27	.331	.435	.495	149	37	7			.975	-2	*O-142	2.7
1928	NY-N	19	57	11	13	1	0	2	7	10	4	.228	.353	.351	84	-1	0			.957	2	O-18	0.0
	*StL-N	99	272	41	83	8	2	17	58	51	15	.305	.418	.537	145	19	2			.988	1	O-84	1.4
	Yr	118	329	52	96	9	2	19	65	61	19	.292	.407	.505	135	18	3			.982	3	*O-102	1.4
1929	Bos-N	136	457	65	133	25	5	10	68	69	27	.291	.389	.433	108	7	5			.972	-1	*O-130	-0.3
Total	11	1073	3398	505	1030	158	43	91	528	389	208	.303	.380	.455	118	90	58	34		.970	-5	O-933	1.1

■ TERRY HARPER

Harper, Terry Joe b: 8/19/55, Douglasville, Ga. BR/TR, 6'4", 195 lbs. Deb: 9/12/80

YEAR	TM/L	G	AB	R	H	2B	3B	HR	RBI	BB	SO	AVG	OBP	SLG	PRO+	BR/A	SB	CS	SBR	FA	FR	G/POS	TPR
1980	Atl-N	21	54	3	10	2	1	0	3	6	5	.185	.279	.259	49	-4	2	1	0	.968	-2	O-18	-0.6
1981	Atl-N	40	73	9	19	1	0	2	8	11	17	.260	.357	.356	100	0	5	1	1	.976	-2	O-27	-0.1
1982	*Atl-N	48	150	16	43	3	0	2	16	14	28	.287	.352	.347	92	-1	7	4	-0	.987	-0	O-41	-0.3
1983	Atl-N	80	201	19	53	13	1	3	26	20	43	.264	.333	.383	91	-2	6	5	-1	.952	-1	O-60	-0.7
1984	Atl-N	40	102	4	16	3	1	0	8	4	21	.157	.196	.206	12	-12	4	1	1	1.000	4	O-29	-0.9
1985	Atl-N	138	492	58	130	15	2	17	72	44	76	.264	.328	.407	98	-1	9	9	-3	.978	1	*O-131	-0.7
1986	Atl-N	106	265	26	68	12	0	8	30	29	39	.257	.332	.392	94	-2	3	6	-3	.970	-11	O-83	-1.9
1987	Det-A	31	64	4	13	3	0	3	10	9	8	.203	.301	.391	85	-1	1	0	0	.952	-2	D-15,O-14	-0.3
	Pit-N	36	66	8	19	3	0	1	7	7	11	.288	.356	.379	94	-0	0	1	-1	1.000	-3	O-20	-0.4
Total	8	540	1467	147	371	55	5	36	180	144	248	.253	.323	.371	88	-24	37	28	-6	.976	-16	O-423/D-15	-5.9

■ TOMMY HARPER

Harper, Tommy b: 10/14/40, Oak Grove, La. BR/TR, 5'10", 168 lbs. Deb: 4/9/62 C

YEAR	TM/L	G	AB	R	H	2B	3B	HR	RBI	BB	SO	AVG	OBP	SLG	PRO+	BR/A	SB	CS	SBR	FA	FR	G/POS	TPR
1962	Cin-N	6	23	1	4	0	0	0	1	2	6	.174	.240	.174	13	-3	1	0	0	.929	-1	/3-6	-0.4
1963	Cin-N	129	408	67	106	12	3	10	37	44	72	.260	.336	.377	102	2	12	1	3	.983	6	*O-118/3-1	0.5
1964	Cin-N	102	317	42	77	5	2	4	22	39	56	.243	.328	.309	78	-8	24	3	5	.994	5	O-92/3-2	-0.2
1965	Cin-N	159	646	**126**	166	28	3	18	64	78	127	.257	.342	.393	99	1	35	6	7	.983	7	*O-159/3-2,2-1	0.8
1966	Cin-N	149	553	85	154	22	5	5	31	57	85	.278	.349	.363	91	-6	29	10	3	.996	-13	*O-147	-2.4
1967	Cin-N	103	365	55	82	17	3	7	22	43	51	.225	.306	.345	77	-10	23	8	2	.995	7	*O-100	-0.7
1968	Cle-A	130	235	26	51	15	2	6	26	26	56	.217	.298	.374	104	1	11	7	-1	.984	-16	*O-115/2-2	-2.3
1969	Sea-A	148	537	78	126	10	2	9	41	95	90	.235	.351	.311	88	-5	**73**	18	11	.959	-15	2-59,3-59,O-26	-0.6
1970	Mil-A★	154	604	104	179	35	4	31	82	77	107	.296	.380	.522	145	37	38	16	2	.943	-3	*3-128,2-22,O-13	3.6
1971	Mil-A	152	585	79	151	26	3	14	52	65	92	.258	.333	.385	104	3	25	3	6	.975	-19	O-90,3-70/2-1	-1.6
1972	Bos-A	144	556	92	141	29	2	14	49	67	104	.254	.343	.388	111	9	25	7	3	.985	3	*O-144	0.8
1973	Bos-A	147	566	92	159	23	3	17	71	61	93	.281	.352	.422	111	8	**54**	14	**8**	.985	3	*O-143/D-1	1.2
1974	Bos-A	118	443	66	105	15	3	5	24	46	65	.237	.313	.318	77	-13	28	12	1	.982	-3	O-61,D-51	-1.9
1975	Cal-A	89	285	40	68	10	1	3	31	38	51	.239	.332	.312	89	-3	19	8	1	.992	-2	D-57,1-19/O-9	-0.7
	*Oak-A	34	69	11	22	4	0	2	7	5	9	.319	.373	.464	139	3	7	0	2	.963	-3	1-16/O-9,3-2,D-3	0.1

YEAR	TM/L	G	AB	R	H	2B	3B	HR	RBI	BB	SO	AVG	OBP	SLG	PRO+	BR/A	SB	CS	SBR	FA	FR	G/POS	TPR
	Yr	123	354	51	90	14	1	5	38	43	60	.254	.340	.342	99	0	26	8	3	.978	-5	D-60,1-35,O-18,/3-2	-0.6
1976	Bal-A	46	77	8	18	5	0	1	7	10	16	.234	.322	.338	99	0	4	3	-1	1.000	-1	D-27/1-1,O-1	-0.2
Total	15	1810	6269	972	1609	256	36	146	567	753	1080	.257	.340	.379	100	15	408	116	53	.986	-47	*O-1227,3-270,D/21	-4.0

■ TOBY HARRAH
Harrah, Colbert Dale b: 10/26/48, Sissonville, W.Va. BR/TR, 6', 180 lbs. Deb: 9/5/69 MC

YEAR	TM/L	G	AB	R	H	2B	3B	HR	RBI	BB	SO	AVG	OBP	SLG	PRO+	BR/A	SB	CS	SBR	FA	FR	G/POS	TPR
1969	Was-A	8	1	4	0	0	0	0	0	0	0	.000	.000	.000	-99	-0	0	0	0	.000	0	/S-1	0.0
1971	Was-A	127	383	45	88	11	3	2	22	40	48	.230	.303	.290	73	-14	10	9	-2	.955	-7	*S-116/3-7	-1.0
1972	Tex-A†	116	374	47	97	14	3	1	31	34	31	.259	.321	.321	95	-2	16	7	1	.960	-9	*S-106	0.5
1973	Tex-A	118	461	64	120	16	1	10	50	46	49	.260	.330	.364	100	-0	10	3	1	.951	-13	S-76,3-52	-0.2
1974	Tex-A	161	573	79	149	23	2	21	74	50	65	.260	.322	.417	114	9	15	14	-4	.963	-2	*S-158/3-3	2.5
1975	Tex-A☆	151	522	81	153	24	1	20	93	98	71	.293	.406	.458	145	34	23	9	2	.963	14	*S-118,3-28,2-21	**6.2**
1976	Tex-A★	155	584	64	152	21	1	15	67	91	59	.260	.363	.377	114	13	8	5	-1	.955	-0	*S-146/3-5,D-4	3.2
1977	Tex-A	159	539	90	142	25	5	27	87	**109**	73	.263	.397	.479	136	31	27	5	5	.963	-24	*3-159/S-1	1.0
1978	Tex-A	139	450	56	103	17	3	12	59	83	66	.229	.351	.360	100	3	31	8	5	.965	-8	*3-91,S-49	0.4
1979	Cle-A	149	527	99	147	25	1	20	77	89	60	.279	.391	.444	124	21	20	9	1	.940	-49	*3-127,S-33/D-9	-2.6
1980	Cle-A	160	561	100	150	22	4	11	72	98	60	.267	.383	.380	109	11	17	2	4	.971	2	*3-156/S-2,D-3	1.5
1981	Cle-A	103	361	64	105	12	4	5	44	57	44	.291	.389	.388	126	15	12	1	3	.949	-12	*3-101/S-3,D-1	0.4
1982	Cle-A☆	162	602	100	183	29	4	25	78	84	52	.304	.400	.490	144	39	17	3	3	.971	-19	*3-159/2-3,S-2	1.9
1983	Cle-A	138	526	81	140	23	1	9	53	75	49	.266	.365	.365	98	1	16	10	-1	**.971**	-11	*3-137/2-1,D-1	-1.3
1984	NY-A	88	253	40	55	9	4	1	26	42	28	.217	.333	.296	79	-6	3	0	1	.968	3	3-74/2-4,O-1,D-2	-0.3
1985	Tex-A	126	396	65	107	18	1	9	44	113	60	.270	.437	.389	127	22	11	4	1	.989	-14	*2-122/S-2,D-1	1.4
1986	Tex-A	95	289	36	63	18	2	7	41	44	53	.218	.325	.367	86	-5	2	5	-2	.982	-20	2-93	-2.4
Total	17	2155	7402	1115	1954	307	40	195	918	1153	868	.264	.368	.395	114	171	238	94	15	.963	-167	*3-1099,S-813,2/DO	11.2

■ JOHN HARRELL
Harrell, John Robert b: 11/27/47, Long Beach, Cal. BR/TR, 6'2", 190 lbs. Deb: 10/1/69

YEAR	TM/L	G	AB	R	H	2B	3B	HR	RBI	BB	SO	AVG	OBP	SLG	PRO+	BR/A	SB	CS	SBR	FA	FR	G/POS	TPR
1969	SF-N	2	6	0	3	0	0	0	2	2	1	.500	.625	.500	223	1	0	0	0	1.000	-0	/C-2	0.1

■ BILLY HARRELL
Harrell, William b: 7/18/28, Norristown, Pa. BR/TR, 6'1.5", 180 lbs. Deb: 9/2/55

YEAR	TM/L	G	AB	R	H	2B	3B	HR	RBI	BB	SO	AVG	OBP	SLG	PRO+	BR/A	SB	CS	SBR	FA	FR	G/POS	TPR
1955	Cle-A	13	19	2	8	0	0	0	1	3	3	.421	.500	.421	144	1	1	0	0	.926	-0	S-11	0.2
1957	Cle-A	22	57	6	15	1	1	1	5	4	7	.263	.311	.368	86	-1	3	1	0	.893	-4	S-14/3-6,2-1	-0.4
1958	Cle-A	101	229	36	50	4	0	7	19	15	36	.218	.272	.328	66	-11	12	2	2	.986	-7	3-46,S-45/2-7,O-1	-1.2
1961	Bos-A	37	37	10	6	2	0	0	1	1	8	.162	.184	.216	6	-5	1	0	0	1.000	7	3-10/S-7,1-3	0.2
Total	4	173	342	54	79	7	1	8	26	23	54	.231	.283	.327	68	-16	17	3	3	.933	-5	/S-77,3-62,2-8,1O	-1.2

■ BUD HARRELSON
Harrelson, Derrel McKinley b: 6/6/44, Niles, Cal. BB/TR, 5'11", 160 lbs. Deb: 9/2/65 MC

YEAR	TM/L	G	AB	R	H	2B	3B	HR	RBI	BB	SO	AVG	OBP	SLG	PRO+	BR/A	SB	CS	SBR	FA	FR	G/POS	TPR
1965	NY-N	19	37	3	4	1	1	0	0	2	11	.108	.154	.189	-4	-5	0	0	0	.955	4	S-18	-0.1
1966	NY-N	33	99	20	22	2	4	0	4	13	23	.222	.313	.323	79	-3	7	3	0	.993	5	S-29	0.5
1967	NY-N	151	540	59	137	16	4	1	28	48	64	.254	.319	.304	80	-13	12	13	-4	.958	7	*S-149	0.4
1968	NY-N	111	402	38	88	7	3	0	14	29	68	.219	.273	.251	58	-20	4	5	-2	.972	-5	*S-106	-1.8
1969	*NY-N	123	395	42	98	11	6	0	24	54	54	.248	.341	.306	81	-8	1	3	-2	.969	-5	*S-119	-0.2
1970	NY-N★	157	564	72	137	18	8	1	42	95	74	.243	.355	.309	79	-13	23	4	5	.971	-28	*S-156	-1.8
1971	NY-N★	142	547	55	138	16	6	0	32	53	59	.252	.321	.303	79	-14	28	7	4	.978	11	*S-140	2.0
1972	NY-N	115	418	54	90	10	4	1	24	58	57	.215	.315	.266	68	-16	12	4	1	.970	-12	*S-115	-1.0
1973	*NY-N	106	356	35	92	12	3	0	20	48	49	.258	.348	.309	85	-6	5	1	1	.979	-3	*S-103	0.6
1974	NY-N	106	331	48	75	10	0	1	13	71	39	.227	.366	.266	80	-5	9	4	0	.968	16	S-97	2.4
1975	NY-N	34	73	5	16	2	0	0	3	12	13	.219	.329	.247	65	-3	0	0	0	.941	1	S-34	0.0
1976	NY-N	118	359	34	84	12	4	1	26	63	56	.234	.351	.298	91	-2	9	3	1	.962	-5	*S-117	0.8
1977	NY-N	107	269	25	48	6	2	1	12	27	28	.178	.256	.227	32	-26	5	4	-1	.984	-2	S-98	-2.0
1978	Phi-N	71	103	16	22	1	0	0	9	18	21	.214	.331	.223	57	-5	5	2	0	.972	15	2-43,S-15	1.3
1979	Phi-N	53	71	7	20	6	0	0	7	13	14	.282	.400	.366	107	1	3	3	-1	.990	6	2-25,S-17/3-9,O-1	0.8
1980	Tex-A	87	180	26	49	6	0	1	9	29	23	.272	.373	.322	95	0	4	4	-1	.952	11	S-87/2-2	1.7
Total	16	1533	4744	539	1120	136	45	7	267	633	653	.236	.329	.288	75	-136	127	60	2	.969	16	*S-1400/2-70,3-9,O	3.6

■ KEN HARRELSON
Harrelson, Kenneth Smith "Hawk" b: 9/4/41, Woodruff, S.C. BR/TR, 6'2", 190 lbs. Deb: 6/9/63

YEAR	TM/L	G	AB	R	H	2B	3B	HR	RBI	BB	SO	AVG	OBP	SLG	PRO+	BR/A	SB	CS	SBR	FA	FR	G/POS	TPR
1963	KC-A	79	226	16	52	10	1	6	23	23	58	.230	.301	.363	81	-6	1	1	-0	.980	-5	1-34,O-28	-1.5
1964	KC-A	49	139	15	27	5	0	7	12	13	34	.194	.263	.381	74	-5	0	1	-1	.977	3	O-24,1-15	-0.4
1965	KC-A	150	483	61	115	17	3	23	66	66	112	.238	.331	.429	116	10	9	7	-2	.992	-4	*1-125/O-4	-0.2
1966	KC-A	63	210	24	47	5	0	5	22	27	59	.224	.312	.319	85	-4	9	2	2	.985	2	1-58/O-3	-0.4
	Was-A	71	250	25	62	8	1	7	28	26	53	.248	.321	.372	100	-0	4	1	1	.991	-4	1-70	-0.9
	Yr	134	460	49	109	13	1	12	50	53	112	.237	.317	.348	93	-4	13	3	2	.989	-2	*1-128/O-3	-1.3
1967	Was-A	26	79	10	16	0	0	3	10	7	15	.203	.267	.316	75	-3	1	0	0	.996	0	1-23	-0.4
	KC-A	61	174	23	53	11	0	6	30	17	17	.305	.366	.471	151	11	8	2	1	.992	-1	1-45	0.9
	*Bos-A	23	80	9	16	4	1	3	14	5	12	.200	.247	.387	79	-2	1	1	-0	.929	-3	O-23/1-1	-0.8
	Yr	110	333	42	85	15	1	12	54	29	44	.255	.315	.414	115	5	10	3	1	.993	-4	1-69,O-23	-0.3
1968	Bos-A★	150	535	79	147	17	4	35	**109**	69	90	.275	.360	.518	153	34	2	6	-3	**1.000**	8	*O-132,1-19	3.5
1969	Bos-A	10	46	6	10	1	0	3	8	4	6	.217	.280	.435	92	-1	0	1	-1	.991	2	1-10	-0.1
	Cle-A	149	519	83	115	13	4	27	84	95	96	.222	.344	.418	109	7	17	8	0	.985	5	*O-144,1-16	0.3
	Yr	159	565	89	125	14	4	30	92	99	102	.221	.339	.419	107	6	17	9	-0	.985	6	*O-144,1-26	0.2
1970	Cle-A	17	39	3	11	1	0	1	1	6	4	.282	.378	.385	106	0	0	0	0	1.000	1	1-13	0.0
1971	Cle-A	52	161	20	32	2	0	5	14	24	21	.199	.303	.304	66	-7	1	0	0	.988	-1	1-40/O-7	-1.3
Total	9	900	2941	374	703	94	14	131	421	382	577	.239	.328	.414	109	35	53	30	-2	.990	2	1-469,O-365	-1.3

■ ANDY HARRINGTON
Harrington, Andrew Matthew b: 2/12/03, Mountain View, Cal d: 1/26/79, Boise, Idaho BR/TR, 5'11", 170 lbs. Deb: 4/18/25

YEAR	TM/L	G	AB	R	H	2B	3B	HR	RBI	BB	SO	AVG	OBP	SLG	PRO+	BR/A	SB	CS	SBR	FA	FR	G/POS	TPR
1925	Det-A	1	1	0	0	0	0	0	0	0	0	.000	.000	.000	-99	-0	0	0	0	.000	0	H	0.0

■ MICKEY HARRINGTON
Harrington, Charles Michael b: 10/8/34, Hattiesburg, Miss. BR/TR, 6'4", 205 lbs. Deb: 7/10/63

YEAR	TM/L	G	AB	R	H	2B	3B	HR	RBI	BB	SO	AVG	OBP	SLG	PRO+	BR/A	SB	CS	SBR	FA	FR	G/POS	TPR
1963	Phi-N	1	0	0	0	0	0	0	0	0	0	—	—	—	—	0	0	0	0	.000	0	R	0.0

■ JERRY HARRINGTON
Harrington, Jeremiah Peter b: 8/12/1869, Keokuk, Iowa d: 4/16/13, Keokuk, Iowa BR/TR, 5'11", 220 lbs. Deb: 4/30/1890

YEAR	TM/L	G	AB	R	H	2B	3B	HR	RBI	BB	SO	AVG	OBP	SLG	PRO+	BR/A	SB	CS	SBR	FA	FR	G/POS	TPR
1890	Cin-N	65	236	25	58	7	1	1	23	15	29	.246	.299	.297	74	-8	4			.957	5	C-65	0.3
1891	Cin-N	92	333	25	76	10	5	2	41	19	34	.228	.272	.306	68	-15	4			.908	-3	C-92/3-1	-0.8
1892	Cin-N	22	61	6	13	1	0	0	3	6	1	.213	.284	.230	56	-3	0			.989	1	C-22/1-1	-0.1
1893	Lou-N	10	36	4	4	1	0	0	6	3	9	.111	.179	.139	-16	-6	0			.853	-4	C-10	-0.8
Total	4	189	666	60	151	19	6	3	73	43	73	.227	.278	.287	64	-32	8			.932	-1	C-189/1-1,3-1	-1.4

■ JOE HARRINGTON
Harrington, Joseph C. b: 12/21/1869, Fall River, Mass. d: 9/13/33, Fall River, Mass. BR/TR, 5'8.5", 162 lbs. Deb: 9/10/1895

YEAR	TM/L	G	AB	R	H	2B	3B	HR	RBI	BB	SO	AVG	OBP	SLG	PRO+	BR/A	SB	CS	SBR	FA	FR	G/POS	TPR
1895	Bos-N	18	65	21	18	0	2	2	13	7	5	.277	.356	.431	95	-1	3			.912	0	2-18	0.0
1896	Bos-N	54	199	26	40	5	3	1	25	19	17	.201	.274	.271	42	-18	2			.816	-10	3-49/S-4,2-1	-2.3
Total	2	72	264	47	58	5	5	3	38	26	22	.220	.295	.311	55	-18	5			.901	-10	/3-49,2-19,S-4	-2.3

■ CANDY HARRIS
Harris, Alonzo b: 9/17/47, Selma, Ala. BB/TR, 6', 160 lbs. Deb: 4/13/67

YEAR	TM/L	G	AB	R	H	2B	3B	HR	RBI	BB	SO	AVG	OBP	SLG	PRO+	BR/A	SB	CS	SBR	FA	FR	G/POS	TPR
1967	Hou-N	6	1	0	0	0	0	0	0	0	1	.000	.000	.000	-99	-0	0	0	0	.000	0	H	0.0

■ SPENCER HARRIS
Harris, Anthony Spencer b: 8/12/1900, Duluth, Minn. d: 7/3/82, Minneapolis, Minn. BL/TL, 5'9", 145 lbs. Deb: 4/14/25

YEAR	TM/L	G	AB	R	H	2B	3B	HR	RBI	BB	SO	AVG	OBP	SLG	PRO+	BR/A	SB	CS	SBR	FA	FR	G/POS	TPR
1925	Chi-A	56	92	12	26	2	0	1	13	14	13	.283	.383	.337	89	-1	1	3	-2	.957	-5	O-27	-0.8
1926	Chi-A	80	222	36	56	11	3	2	27	20	15	.252	.317	.356	78	-8	8	3	1	.949	-6	O-63	-1.6
1929	Was-A	6	14	1	3	1	0	0	1	0	3	.214	.214	.286	27	-2	1	0	0	1.000	-1	/O-4	-0.2
1930	Phi-A	22	49	4	9	1	0	0	5	5	2	.184	.259	.204	18	-6	0	0	0	.958	0	O-13	-0.6
Total	4	164	377	53	94	15	3	3	46	39	33	.249	.323	.329	70	-16	10	6	-1	.954	-11	O-107	-3.2

■ GAIL HARRIS
Harris, Boyd Gail b: 10/15/31, Abingdon, Va. BL/TL, 6', 195 lbs. Deb: 6/3/55

YEAR	TM/L	G	AB	R	H	2B	3B	HR	RBI	BB	SO	AVG	OBP	SLG	PRO+	BR/A	SB	CS	SBR	FA	FR	G/POS	TPR
1955	NY-N	79	263	27	61	9	0	12	36	20	46	.232	.291	.403	82	-8	0	0	0	.982	0	1-75	-1.1

YEAR	TM/L	G	AB	R	H	2B	3B	HR	RBI	BB	SO	AVG	OBP	SLG	PRO+	BR/A	SB	CS	SBR	FA	FR	G/POS	TPR
1956	NY-N	12	38	2	5	0	1	1	1	3	10	.132	.233	.263	33	-4	0	0	0	.975	0	1-11	-0.4
1957	NY-N	90	225	28	54	7	3	9	31	16	28	.240	.308	.418	93	-3	1	0	0	.985	-2	1-61	-0.8
1958	Det-A	134	451	63	123	18	8	20	83	36	60	.273	.332	.481	113	7	1	2	-1	.986	3	*1-122	0.1
1959	Det-A	114	349	39	77	4	3	9	39	29	49	.221	.292	.327	66	-16	0	1	-1	.992	3	1-93	-2.1
1960	Det-A	8	5	0	0	0	0	0	0	2	1	.000	.286	.000	-15	-1	0	0	0	1.000	0	/1-5	-0.1
Total	6	437	1331	159	320	38	15	51	190	106	194	.240	.306	.406	88	-25	2	3	-1	.986	4	1-367	-4.4

■ CHARLIE HARRIS
Harris, Charles Jenkins b: 10/21/1877, Macon, Ga. d: 3/14/63, Gainesville, Fla. BR/TR, 5'8", 200 lbs. Deb: 5/25/1899

YEAR	TM/L	G	AB	R	H	2B	3B	HR	RBI	BB	SO	AVG	OBP	SLG	PRO+	BR/A	SB	CS	SBR	FA	FR	G/POS	TPR
1899	Bal-N	30	68	16	19	3	0	0	1	3		.279	.319	.324	73	-3	4			.872	-5	3-21/O-3,2-2,S-1	-0.7

■ DAVE HARRIS
Harris, David Stanley "Sheriff" b: 7/14/1900, Summerfield, N.C. d: 9/18/73, Atlanta, Ga. BR/TR, 5'11", 170 lbs. Deb: 4/14/25

YEAR	TM/L	G	AB	R	H	2B	3B	HR	RBI	BB	SO	AVG	OBP	SLG	PRO+	BR/A	SB	CS	SBR	FA	FR	G/POS	TPR
1925	Bos-N	92	340	49	90	8	7	5	36	27	44	.265	.321	.374	84	-9	6	4	-1	.962	8	O-90	-0.7
1928	Bos-N	7	17	2	2	1	0	0	0	2	6	.118	.211	.176	2	-2	0			.833	-1	/O-6	-0.4
1930	Chi-A	33	86	16	21	2	1	5	13	7	22	.244	.309	.465	96	-1	0	0	0	1.000	-0	O-23/2-1	-0.3
	Was-A	73	205	40	65	19	8	4	44	28	35	.317	.399	.546	137	11	6	3	0	.983	1	O-59	0.8
	Yr	106	291	56	86	21	9	9	57	35	57	.296	.373	.522	125	11	6	3	0	.988	1	O-82/2-1	0.5
1931	Was-A	77	231	49	72	14	8	5	50	49	38	.312	.434	.506	146	17	7	6	-2	.950	-2	O-60	0.9
1932	Was-A	81	156	26	51	7	4	6	29	19	34	.327	.400	.538	143	10	4	4	-1	.932	-2	O-34	0.4
1933	*Was-A	82	177	33	46	9	2	5	38	25	26	.260	.358	.418	106	2	3	1	0	.964	-7	O-45/1-6,3-2	-0.7
1934	Was-A	97	235	28	59	14	3	2	37	39	40	.251	.358	.362	89	-3	2	3	-1	.973	-4	O-64/3-5	-0.9
Total	7	542	1447	243	406	74	33	32	247	196	245	.281	.368	.444	112	25	28	21		.963	-8	O-381/3-7,1-6,2-1	-0.9

■ DONALD HARRIS
Harris, Donald b: 11/12/67, Waco, Tex. BR/TR, 6'1", 185 lbs. Deb: 9/4/91

YEAR	TM/L	G	AB	R	H	2B	3B	HR	RBI	BB	SO	AVG	OBP	SLG	PRO+	BR/A	SB	CS	SBR	FA	FR	G/POS	TPR
1991	Tex-A	18	8	4	3	0	0	1	2	1	3	.375	.444	.750	228	1	1	0	0	1.000	-5	O-12/D-3	-0.3
1992	Tex-A	24	33	3	6	1	0	0	1	0	15	.182	.182	.212	10	-4	1	0	0	.974	-4	O-24	-0.8
1993	Tex-A	40	76	10	15	2	0	1	8	5	18	.197	.256	.263	41	-6	0	1	-1	.943	-7	O-38/D-3	-1.5
Total	3	82	117	17	24	3	0	2	11	6	36	.205	.250	.282	46	-9	2	1	0	.959	-16	/O-74,D-6	-2.6

■ FRANK HARRIS
Harris, Frank W. b: 11/2/1858, Pittsburgh, Pa. d: 11/26/39, E.Moline, Ill. BR/TR, Deb: 4/17/1884

YEAR	TM/L	G	AB	R	H	2B	3B	HR	RBI	BB	SO	AVG	OBP	SLG	PRO+	BR/A	SB	CS	SBR	FA	FR	G/POS	TPR
1884	Alt-U	24	95	10	25	2	1	0		3		.263	.286	.305	78	-5				.941	-1	1-17/O-7	-0.7

■ BILLY HARRIS
Harris, James William b: 11/24/43, Hamlet, N.C. BL/TR, 6', 175 lbs. Deb: 6/16/68

YEAR	TM/L	G	AB	R	H	2B	3B	HR	RBI	BB	SO	AVG	OBP	SLG	PRO+	BR/A	SB	CS	SBR	FA	FR	G/POS	TPR
1968	Cle-A	38	94	10	20	5	1	0	3	8	22	.213	.275	.287	71	-3	2	0	1	.970	-1	2-27,3-10/S-1	-0.3
1969	KC-A	5	7	1	2	1	0	0	0	0	1	.286	.286	.429	97	-0	0	0	0	1.000	-0	/2-1	0.0
Total	2	43	101	11	22	6	1	0	3	8	23	.218	.275	.297	73	-3	2	0	1	.971	-1	/2-28,3-10,S-1	-0.3

■ JOHN HARRIS
Harris, John Thomas b: 9/13/54, Portland, Ore. BL/TL, 6'3", 205 lbs. Deb: 9/26/79

YEAR	TM/L	G	AB	R	H	2B	3B	HR	RBI	BB	SO	AVG	OBP	SLG	PRO+	BR/A	SB	CS	SBR	FA	FR	G/POS	TPR
1979	Cal-A	1	2	0	0	0	0	0	0	0	0	.000	.000	.000	-99	-1	0	0	0	1.000	-0	/1-1	-0.1
1980	Cal-A	19	41	8	12	5	0	2	7	7	4	.293	.396	.561	163	4	0	1	-1	1.000	-0	1-10/O-3	0.2
1981	Cal-A	36	77	5	19	3	0	3	9	3	11	.247	.275	.403	93	-1	0	0	0	.976	-4	1-11,O-10/D-1	-0.6
Total	3	56	120	13	31	8	0	5	16	10	15	.258	.315	.450	115	2	0	1	-1	.987	-4	/1-22,O-13,D-1	-0.5

■ JOE HARRIS
Harris, Joseph "Moon" b: 5/20/1891, Coulters, Pa. d: 12/10/59, Renton, Pa. BR/TR, 5'9", 170 lbs. Deb: 6/9/14

YEAR	TM/L	G	AB	R	H	2B	3B	HR	RBI	BB	SO	AVG	OBP	SLG	PRO+	BR/A	SB	CS	SBR	FA	FR	G/POS	TPR
1914	NY-A	2	1	0	0	0	0	0	0	3	1	.000	.800	.000	143	1	0			1.000	-1	/1-1,O-1	0.0
1917	Cle-A	112	369	40	112	22	4	0	65	55	32	.304	.398	.385	129	15	11			.985	10	1-95/O-5,3-2	2.3
1919	Cle-A	62	184	30	69	16	1	1	46	33	21	.375	.472	.489	160	17	2			.988	2	1-46/S-4	1.8
1922	Bos-A	119	408	53	129	30	9	6	54	30	15	.316	.364	.478	119	10	2	6	-3	.953	7	O-83,1-21	0.7
1923	Bos-A	142	483	82	162	28	11	13	76	52	27	.335	.406	.520	142	28	7	3	0	.968	-2	*O-132/1-9	1.7
1924	Bos-A	133	491	82	148	36	9	3	77	81	25	.301	.406	.430	115	14	6	1	1	.993	6	*1-128/O-3	1.2
1925	Bos-A	8	19	4	3	0	1	1	2	5	5	.158	.333	.421	90	-0	0	0	0	1.000	-1	/1-6	-0.1
	*Was-A	100	300	60	97	21	9	12	59	51	28	.323	.430	.573	156	26	6	3	0	.989	-0	1-58,O-41	1.9
	Yr	108	319	64	100	21	10	13	61	56	33	.313	.424	.564	152	26	6	3	0	.990	-1	1-64,O-41	1.8
1926	Was-A	92	257	43	79	13	9	5	55	37	9	.307	.405	.486	135	14	2	3	-1	.994	-3	1-36,O-35	0.5
1927	*Pit-N	129	411	57	134	27	9	5	73	48	19	.326	.402	.472	125	15	2			.990	2	*1-116/O-3	0.9
1928	Pit-N	16	23	2	9	2	1	0	2	4	2	.391	.500	.565	171	3	0			1.000	1	/1-6	0.3
	Bro-N	55	89	8	21	6	1	1	8	14	4	.236	.340	.360	84	-2	0			.958	-2	O-16	-0.4
	Yr	71	112	10	30	8	2	1	10	18	6	.268	.374	.402	103	1	0			.958	-0	O-16/1-6	-0.1
Total	10	970	3035	461	963	201	64	47	517	413	188	.317	.404	.472	131	140	36	16		.989	20	1-522,O-319/S-4,3-2	10.8

■ LENNY HARRIS
Harris, Leonard Anthony b: 10/28/64, Miami, Fla. BL/TR, 5'10", 205 lbs. Deb: 9/7/88

YEAR	TM/L	G	AB	R	H	2B	3B	HR	RBI	BB	SO	AVG	OBP	SLG	PRO+	BR/A	SB	CS	SBR	FA	FR	G/POS	TPR
1988	Cin-N	16	43	7	16	1	0	0	8	5	4	.372	.438	.395	135	2	4	1	1	1.000	1	3-10/2-6	0.4
1989	Cin-N	61	188	17	42	4	0	2	11	9	20	.223	.263	.277	52	-12	10	6	-1	.980	1	2-32,S-17,3-16	-1.0
	LA-N	54	147	19	37	6	1	1	15	11	13	.252	.308	.327	83	-3	4	3	-1	1.000	-7	O-21,2-14/3-8,S-1	-1.1
	Yr	115	335	36	79	10	1	3	26	20	33	.236	.283	.299	66	-15	14	9	-1	.975	-5	2-46,3-24,O-21,S-18	-2.1
1990	LA-N	137	431	61	131	16	4	2	29	29	31	.304	.349	.374	102	1	15	10	-2	.959	-8	3-94,2-44/O-2,S-1	-0.7
1991	LA-N	145	429	59	123	16	1	3	38	37	32	.287	.350	.350	100	1	12	3	2	.943	-1	*3-113,2-27,S-20,/O	0.3
1992	LA-N	135	347	28	94	11	0	0	30	24	24	.271	.320	.303	78	-9	19	7	2	.963	17	2-81,3-33,O-15,S-10	1.1
1993	LA-N	107	160	20	38	6	1	2	11	15	15	.237	.303	.325	72	-6	3	1	0	.987	2	2-35,3-17/S-3,O-2	-0.3
1994	Cin-N	66	100	13	31	3	1	0	14	5	13	.310	.343	.360	84	-2	7	2	1	.846	-0	3-15/1-4,O-3,2-2	-0.2
1995	*Cin-N	101	197	32	41	8	3	2	16	14	20	.208	.261	.310	50	-15	10	1	2	.939	-2	3-24,1-23/O-8,2-1	-1.7
1996	Cin-N	125	302	33	86	17	2	5	32	21	31	.285	.333	.404	93	-3	14	6	1	1.000	-6	O-37,3-24,1-16,/2-8	-1.1
1997	Cin-N	120	238	32	65	13	1	3	28	18	18	.273	.329	.374	83	-6	4	3	-1	.977	-14	O-42,2-20,3-13,1-11	-2.0
1998	Cin-N	57	122	12	36	8	0	0	10	8	9	.295	.344	.361	82	-3	1	3	-2	.929	-3	O-32/P-1	-0.8
	NY-N	75	168	18	39	7	0	6	17	9	12	.232	.275	.381	69	-8	5	2	0	.988	-11	O-65,3-10/2-2,1D	-1.9
	Yr	132	290	30	75	15	0	6	27	17	21	.259	.304	.372	74	-11	6	5	-1	.968	-15	O-97,3-10/2-2,P1D	-2.7
Total	11	1199	2872	351	779	116	14	26	259	205	242	.271	.323	.349	84	-64	108	48	4	.941	-32	3-377,2-272,O/1SDP	-9.0

■ NED HARRIS
Harris, Robert Ned b: 7/9/16, Ames, Iowa d: 12/18/76, W.Palm Beach, Fla. BL/TL, 5'11", 175 lbs. Deb: 4/20/41

YEAR	TM/L	G	AB	R	H	2B	3B	HR	RBI	BB	SO	AVG	OBP	SLG	PRO+	BR/A	SB	CS	SBR	FA	FR	G/POS	TPR
1941	Det-A	26	61	11	13	3	1	1	4	6	13	.213	.284	.344	59	-4	1	0	0	1.000	-2	O-12	-0.6
1942	Det-A	121	398	53	108	16	10	9	45	49	35	.271	.351	.430	110	5	5	4	-1	.944	-10	*O-104	-1.1
1943	Det-A	114	354	43	90	14	3	6	32	47	29	.254	.343	.362	99	-0	6	8	-3	.961	-3	O-96	-1.2
1946	Det-A	1	1	0	0	0	0	0	0	0	0	.000	.000	.000	-94	-0	0	0	0	.000	0	H	0.0
Total	4	262	814	107	211	33	14	16	81	102	77	.259	.342	.393	101	1	12	12	-4	.955	-15	O-212	-2.9

■ BUCKY HARRIS
Harris, Stanley Raymond b: 11/8/1896, Port Jervis, N.Y. d: 11/8/77, Bethesda, Md. BR/TR, 5'9.5", 156 lbs. Deb: 8/28/19 MH

YEAR	TM/L	G	AB	R	H	2B	3B	HR	RBI	BB	SO	AVG	OBP	SLG	PRO+	BR/A	SB	CS	SBR	FA	FR	G/POS	TPR
1919	Was-A	8	28	0	6	2	0	0	4	1	3	.214	.267	.286	56	-2	0			.925	2	/2-8	0.1
1920	Was-A	136	506	76	152	26	6	1	68	41	36	.300	.377	.381	104	5	16	17	-5	.958	-10	*2-134	-0.6
1921	Was-A	154	584	82	169	22	8	0	54	54	39	.289	.367	.354	89	-7	29	9	3	.959	12	*2-154	1.1
1922	Was-A	154	602	95	162	24	8	2	40	52	38	.269	.341	.346	84	-14	25	11	1	.970	**26**	*2-154	1.7
1923	Was-A	145	532	60	150	21	13	2	70	50	29	.282	.358	.382	100	0	23	16	-3	.961	19	*2-144/S-1	1.8
1924	*Was-A	143	544	88	146	28	9	1	58	56	41	.268	.344	.358	84	-13	20	10	0	.968	-13	*2-143,M	-2.3
1925	*Was-A	144	551	91	158	30	3	1	66	64	21	.287	.370	.354	87	-9	14	12	-3	.970	3	*2-144,M	-0.6
1926	Was-A	141	537	94	152	39	9	1	63	58	41	.283	.363	.395	100	0	16	11	-2	.963	-11	*2-141,M	-0.8
1927	Was-A	128	475	98	127	20	3	1	55	66	33	.267	.363	.328	81	-11	18	3	4	**.972**	1	*2-128,M	-0.1
1928	Was-A	99	358	34	73	11	5	0	28	27	26	.204	.264	.263	39	-32	5	2	0	.970	11	2-96/3-1,O-1,M	-1.8
1929	Det-A	7	11	3	1	0	0	0	0	2	2	.091	.231	.091	-14	-2	1	0	0	.900	0	/2-4,S-1,M	-0.1
1931	Det-A	4	8	1	1	1	0	0	0	1	1	.125	.222	.250	23	-1	0	0	0	1.000	0	/2-3,M	-0.1
Total	12	1263	4736	722	1297	224	64	9	506	472	310	.274	.352	.354	86	-85	167	91		.965	43	*2-1253/S-2,O-1,3-1	-1.7

■ VIC HARRIS
Harris, Victor Lanier b: 3/27/50, Los Angeles, Cal. BB/TR, 6', 170 lbs. Deb: 7/21/72

YEAR	TM/L	G	AB	R	H	2B	3B	HR	RBI	BB	SO	AVG	OBP	SLG	PRO+	BR/A	SB	CS	SBR	FA	FR	G/POS	TPR
1972	Tex-A	61	186	8	26	5	1	0	10	12	39	.140	.192	.177	11	-21	7	3	0	.960	0	2-58/S-1	-2.0
1973	Tex-A	152	555	71	138	14	7	8	44	55	81	.249	.319	.342	90	-7	13	12	-3	.977	2	*O-113,3-25,2-18	-1.4

YEAR	TM/L	G	AB	R	H	2B	3B	HR	RBI	BB	SO	AVG	OBP	SLG	PRO+	BR/A	SB	CS	SBR	FA	FR	G/POS	TPR
1974	Chi-N	62	200	18	39	6	3	0	11	29	26	.195	.297	.255	53	-12	9	3	1	.943	-17	2-56	-2.7
1975	Chi-N	51	56	6	10	0	0	0	5	6	7	.179	.258	.179	22	-6	0	0	0	.900	-2	O-11/3-7,2-5	-0.8
1976	StL-N	97	259	21	59	12	3	1	19	16	55	.228	.275	.309	65	-12	1	2	-1	.945	-8	2-37,O-35,3-12,/S-1	-2.1
1977	SF-N	69	165	28	43	12	0	2	14	19	36	.261	.337	.370	90	-2	2	1	0	.973	-10	2-27,S-11/3-9,O-3	-0.9
1978	SF-N	53	100	8	15	4	0	1	11	11	24	.150	.234	.220	29	-10	0	0	0	.934	-7	S-22,2-10/O-6	-1.5
1980	Mil-A	34	89	8	19	4	1	1	7	12	13	.213	.307	.315	73	-3	4	1	1	.967	-2	O-31/3-2,2-1	-0.6
Total	8	579	1610	168	349	57	15	13	121	160	281	.217	.289	.295	65	-73	36	22	-2	.954	-43	2-212,O-199/3-55,S	-12.0

■ CHUCK HARRISON
Harrison, Charles William b: 4/25/41, Abilene, Tex. BR/TR, 5'10", 190 lbs. Deb: 9/15/65

YEAR	TM/L	G	AB	R	H	2B	3B	HR	RBI	BB	SO	AVG	OBP	SLG	PRO+	BR/A	SB	CS	SBR	FA	FR	G/POS	TPR
1965	Hou-N	15	45	2	9	4	0	1	9	8	9	.200	.321	.356	97	-0	0	0	0	.983	0	1-12	-0.1
1966	Hou-N	119	434	52	111	23	2	9	52	37	69	.256	.317	.380	100	-1	2	0	1	.992	4	*1-114	-0.5
1967	Hou-N	70	177	13	43	7	3	2	26	13	30	.243	.295	.350	87	-3	0	0	0	.987	-0	1-59	-0.7
1969	KC-A	75	213	18	47	5	1	3	18	16	20	.221	.278	.296	60	-11	1	2	-1	.993	2	1-55	-1.6
1971	KC-A	49	143	9	31	4	0	2	21	11	19	.217	.273	.287	59	-8	0	0	0	.992	0	1-39	-1.2
Total	5	328	1012	94	241	43	6	17	126	85	147	.238	.299	.343	83	-24	3	2	-0	.991	5	1-279	-4.1

■ BEN HARRISON
Harrison, Leo J. BR , Deb: 9/27/01

YEAR	TM/L	G	AB	R	H	2B	3B	HR	RBI	BB	SO	AVG	OBP	SLG	PRO+	BR/A	SB	CS	SBR	FA	FR	G/POS	TPR
1901	Was-A	1	2	0	0	0	0	0	0	1		.000	.333	.000	-2	-0	0			.000	-0	/O-1	-0.1

■ TOM HARRISON
Harrison, Thomas James b: 1/18/45, Trail, B.C., Canada BR/TR, 6'3", 200 lbs. Deb: 5/7/65

YEAR	TM/L	G	AB	R	H	2B	3B	HR	RBI	BB	SO	AVG	OBP	SLG	PRO+	BR/A	SB	CS	SBR	FA	FR	G/POS	TPR
1965	KC-A	2	0	0	0	0	0	0	0	0	0	—	—	—	—	0	0	0	0	.000	-0	/P-1	0.0

■ RIT HARRISON
Harrison, Washington Ritter b: 9/16/1849, Waterbury, Conn. d: 11/7/1888, Bridgeport, Conn. Deb: 5/20/1875

YEAR	TM/L	G	AB	R	H	2B	3B	HR	RBI	BB	SO	AVG	OBP	SLG	PRO+	BR/A	SB	CS	SBR	FA	FR	G/POS	TPR
1875	NH-n	1	4	0	2	1	0	0	1	0	0	.500	.500	.750	376	1	0	1	-1	.333	-2	/C-1,S-1	-0.2

■ SAM HARSHANEY
Harshaney, Samuel b: 4/24/10, Madison, Ill. BR/TR, 6', 180 lbs. Deb: 9/28/37

YEAR	TM/L	G	AB	R	H	2B	3B	HR	RBI	BB	SO	AVG	OBP	SLG	PRO+	BR/A	SB	CS	SBR	FA	FR	G/POS	TPR
1937	StL-A	5	11	0	1	1	0	0	0	3	0	.091	.286	.182	20	-1	0	0	0	.905	1	/C-4	-0.1
1938	StL-A	11	24	2	7	0	0	0	0	3	2	.292	.370	.292	68	-1	0	0	0	.975	-0	C-10	-0.1
1939	StL-A	42	145	15	35	2	0	0	15	9	8	.241	.290	.255	40	-13	0	1	-1	.994	-2	C-36	-1.2
1940	StL-A	3	1	0	0	0	0	0	0	1	0	.000	.500	.000	41	0	0	0	0	.000	0	/C-2	0.0
Total	4	61	181	17	43	3	0	0	15	16	10	.238	.303	.254	43	-15	0	1	-1	.983	-2	/C-52	-1.4

■ JACK HARSHMAN
Harshman, John Elvin b: 7/12/27, San Diego, Cal. BL/TL, 6'2", 185 lbs. Deb: 9/16/48

YEAR	TM/L	G	AB	R	H	2B	3B	HR	RBI	BB	SO	AVG	OBP	SLG	PRO+	BR/A	SB	CS	SBR	FA	FR	G/POS	TPR
1948	NY-N	5	8	0	2	0	0	0	1	1	3	.250	.333	.250	60	-0	0			1.000	0	/1-3	0.0
1950	NY-N	9	32	3	4	0	0	2	4	3	6	.125	.200	.313	32	-3	0			.989	0	/1-9	-0.3
1952	NY-N	3	2	0	0	0	0	0	0	0	0	.000	.000	.000	-99	-1	0	0	0	1.000	0	/P-2	0.0
1954	Chi-A	36	56	6	8	1	0	2	5	12	21	.143	.294	.268	53	-4	0	0	0	.967	-1	P-35/1-1	0.0
1955	Chi-A	32	60	6	11	1	0	2	8	9	17	.183	.290	.300	57	-4	0	0	0	.970	-0	P-32	0.0
1956	Chi-A	36	71	8	12	1	0	6	19	11	21	.169	.280	.437	86	-2	0	0	0	.886	-2	P-34	0.0
1957	Chi-A	30	45	5	10	1	0	2	5	10	17	.222	.364	.378	102	0	0	0	0	.947	-3	P-30	0.0
1958	Bal-A	47	82	11	16	1	0	6	14	17	22	.195	.333	.427	114	2	0	0	0	.980	0	P-34/O-1	0.0
1959	Bal-A	15	10	3	2	0	0	1	1	2	2	.200	.333	.500	128	0	0	0	0	1.000	1	P-14	0.0
	Bos-A	9	7	1	1	0	0	0	2	2	2	.143	.333	.143	34	-1	0	0	0	1.000	-1	/P-8	0.0
	Cle-A	21	34	3	7	1	0	0	5	5	4	.206	.308	.235	53	-2	0	0	0	1.000	-0	P-13	0.0
	Yr	45	51	7	10	1	0	1	8	9	8	.196	.317	.275	65	-2	0	0	0	1.000	1	P-35	0.0
1960	Cle-A	15	17	0	3	1	0	0	1	0	4	.176	.176	.235	11	-2	0	0	0	1.000	-1	P-15	0.0
Total	10	258	424	46	76	7	0	21	65	72	119	.179	.298	.344	74	-16	0	0		.962	-5	P-217/1-13,O-1	-0.3

■ BURT HART
Hart, James Burton b: 6/28/1870, Brown Co., Minn. d: 1/29/21, Sacramento, Cal. BB , 6'3", 200 lbs. Deb: 6/6/01

YEAR	TM/L	G	AB	R	H	2B	3B	HR	RBI	BB	SO	AVG	OBP	SLG	PRO+	BR/A	SB	CS	SBR	FA	FR	G/POS	TPR
1901	Bal-A	58	206	33	64	3	5	0	23	20		.311	.383	.374	106	2	7			.976	-8	1-58	-0.6

■ HUB HART
Hart, James Henry b: 2/2/1878, Everett, Mass. d: 10/10/60, Fort Wayne, Ind. BL/TR, 5'11", 170 lbs. Deb: 7/16/05

YEAR	TM/L	G	AB	R	H	2B	3B	HR	RBI	BB	SO	AVG	OBP	SLG	PRO+	BR/A	SB	CS	SBR	FA	FR	G/POS	TPR
1905	Chi-A	11	20	3	2	0	0	0	4	3		.100	.217	.100	2	-2	0			1.000	-2	/C-7	-0.4
1906	Chi-A	17	37	1	6	0	0	0	0	2		.162	.205	.162	16	-4	0			.935	-4	C-15	-0.7
1907	Chi-A	29	70	6	19	1	0	0	7	5		.271	.329	.286	100	0	1			.956	-5	C-25	-0.3
Total	3	57	127	10	27	1	0	0	11	10		.213	.275	.220	59	-5	1			.957	-11	/C-47	-1.4

■ MIKE HART
Hart, James Michael b: 12/20/51, Kalamazoo, Mich. BB/TR, 6'3", 185 lbs. Deb: 6/12/80

YEAR	TM/L	G	AB	R	H	2B	3B	HR	RBI	BB	SO	AVG	OBP	SLG	PRO+	BR/A	SB	CS	SBR	FA	FR	G/POS	TPR
1980	Tex-A	5	4	1	1	0	0	0	0	1	1	.250	.400	.250	85	-0	0	0	0	1.000	-1	/O-2	-0.1

■ JIM RAY HART
Hart, James Ray b: 10/30/41, Hookerton, N.C. BR/TR, 5'11", 185 lbs. Deb: 7/7/63

YEAR	TM/L	G	AB	R	H	2B	3B	HR	RBI	BB	SO	AVG	OBP	SLG	PRO+	BR/A	SB	CS	SBR	FA	FR	G/POS	TPR
1963	SF-N	7	20	1	4	1	0	0	2	3	6	.200	.360	.250	80	-0	0	0	0	1.000	0	/3-7	0.0
1964	SF-N	153	566	71	162	15	6	31	81	47	94	.286	.345	.498	132	23	5	2	0	.937	4	*3-149/O-6	2.7
1965	SF-N	160	591	91	177	30	6	23	96	47	75	.299	.353	.487	130	23	6	4	-1	.919	-13	*3-144,O-15	0.6
1966	SF-N★	156	578	88	165	23	4	33	93	48	75	.285	.344	.510	130	22	2	5	-2	.941	-5	*3-139,O-17	1.2
1967	SF-N	158	578	98	167	26	7	29	99	77	100	.289	.376	.509	153	40	1	1	-0	.937	-15	3-89,O-72	2.2
1968	SF-N	136	480	67	124	14	3	23	78	46	74	.258	.327	.444	130	17	3	1	0	.925	-12	3-72,O-65	0.2
1969	SF-N	95	236	27	60	9	0	3	26	28	49	.254	.346	.331	92	-2	0	0	0	.943	-7	O-68/3-3	-1.2
1970	SF-N	76	255	30	72	12	1	8	37	30	29	.282	.365	.431	114	5	0	0	0	.908	-17	3-56,O-18	-1.3
1971	*SF-N	31	39	5	10	0	0	2	5	6	8	.256	.356	.410	118	1	0	1	-1	.833	-1	/3-3,O-3	-0.1
1972	SF-N	24	79	10	24	5	0	5	8	6	10	.304	.360	.557	155	5	0	1	-1	.886	-9	3-20	-0.5
1973	SF-N	5	3	0	0	0	0	0	1	3	1	.000	.500	.000	48	0	0	0	0	.600	0	/3-1	0.0
	NY-A	114	339	29	86	13	2	13	52	36	45	.254	.325	.419	112	5	0	2	-1	.000	0	*D-106	0.1
1974	NY-A	10	19	1	1	0	0	0	0	3	7	.053	.182	.053	-30	-3	0	0	0	.000	0	/D-4	-0.3
Total	12	1125	3783	518	1052	148	29	170	578	380	573	.278	.348	.467	128	136	17	17	-5	.929	-73	3-683,O-264,D-110	3.6

■ MIKE HART
Hart, Michael Lawrence b: 2/17/58, Milwaukee, Wis. BL/TL, 5'11", 185 lbs. Deb: 5/8/84

YEAR	TM/L	G	AB	R	H	2B	3B	HR	RBI	BB	SO	AVG	OBP	SLG	PRO+	BR/A	SB	CS	SBR	FA	FR	G/POS	TPR
1984	Min-A	13	29	0	5	0	0	0	5	1	2	.172	.200	.172	4	-4	0	1	-1	1.000	1	O-11	-0.4
1987	Bal-A	34	76	7	12	2	0	4	12	6	19	.158	.220	.342	47	-6	1	4	-2	1.000	-2	O-32	-1.0
Total	2	47	105	7	17	2	0	4	17	7	21	.162	.214	.295	35	-10	1	5	-3	1.000	-1	/O-43	-1.4

■ TOM HART
Hart, Thomas Henry "Bushy" b: 6/15/1869, Canaan, N.Y. d: 9/17/39, Gardner, Mass. 5'7", 160 lbs. Deb: 4/15/1891

YEAR	TM/L	G	AB	R	H	2B	3B	HR	RBI	BB	SO	AVG	OBP	SLG	PRO+	BR/A	SB	CS	SBR	FA	FR	G/POS	TPR
1891	Was-a	8	24	1	3	0	0	0	2	2	1	.125	.192	.125	-9	-3	1			1.000	1	/C-5,O-3	-0.2

■ BILL HART
Hart, William Woodrow b: 3/4/13, Wiconisco, Pa. d: 7/29/68, Lykens, Pa. BR/TR, 6', 175 lbs. Deb: 9/18/43

YEAR	TM/L	G	AB	R	H	2B	3B	HR	RBI	BB	SO	AVG	OBP	SLG	PRO+	BR/A	SB	CS	SBR	FA	FR	G/POS	TPR
1943	Bro-N	8	19	0	3	0	0	0	1	1	2	.158	.200	.158	4	-2	0			1.000	4	/3-6,S-1	0.2
1944	Bro-N	29	90	8	16	4	2	0	4	9	7	.178	.253	.267	47	-6	1			.941	-8	S-25/3-2	-1.3
1945	Bro-N	58	161	27	37	6	2	3	27	14	21	.230	.291	.348	78	-5	7			.913	-2	3-39/S-8	-0.6
Total	3	95	270	35	56	10	4	3	32	24	30	.207	.272	.307	63	-14	8			.924	-6	/3-47,S-34	-1.7

■ CHUCK HARTENSTEIN
Hartenstein, Charles Oscar "Twiggy" b: 5/26/42, Seguin, Tex. BR/TR, 5'11", 165 lbs. Deb: 9/11/65 C

YEAR	TM/L	G	AB	R	H	2B	3B	HR	RBI	BB	SO	AVG	OBP	SLG	PRO+	BR/A	SB	CS	SBR	FA	FR	G/POS	TPR
1965	Chi-N	1	0	0	0	0	0	0	0	0	0	—	—	—	—	0	0	0	0	.000	0	R	0.0
1966	Chi-N	5	0	0	0	0	0	0	0	0	0	—	—	—	—	0	0	0	0	1.000	0	/P-5	0.0
1967	Chi-N	45	16	0	1	0	0	0	1	0	9	.063	.063	.063	-61	-3	0	0	0	.950	-0	P-45	0.0
1968	Chi-N	28	2	0	0	0	0	0	0	0	0	.000	.000	.000	-94	-0	0	0	0	.818	-0	P-28	0.0
1969	Pit-N	56	14	0	1	0	0	0	0	1	8	.071	.133	.071	-42	-3	0	0	0	1.000	1	P-56	0.0
1970	Pit-N	17	1	1	0	0	0	0	0	0	0	.000	.000	.000	-99	-0	0	0	0	.900	1	P-17	0.0
	StL-N	6	2	0	0	0	0	0	0	1	2	.000	.333	.000	-3	-0	0	0	0	1.000	0	/P-6	0.0
	Yr	23	3	1	0	0	0	0	0	1	2	.000	.250	.000	-27	-1	0	0	0	.923	1	P-23	0.0
	Bos-A	17	2	0	0	0	0	0	0	1	2	.000	.333	.000	-0	-0	0	0	0	1.000	-1	P-17	0.0
1977	Tor-A	13	0	0	0	0	0	0	0	0	0	—	—	—	—	0	0	0	0	1.000	-0	P-13	0.0
Total	7	188	37	1	2	0	0	0	1	3	21	.054	.125	.054	-47	-7	0	0	0	.952	2	P-187	0.0

YEAR	TM/L	G	AB	R	H	2B	3B	HR	RBI	BB	SO	AVG	OBP	SLG	PRO+	BR/A	SB	CS	SBR	FA	FR	G/POS	TPR
■ BRUCE HARTFORD Hartford, Bruce Daniel b: 5/14/1892, Chicago, Ill. d: 5/25/75, Los Angeles, Cal. BR/TR, 6'0.5", 190 lbs. Deb: 6/3/14																							
1914	Cle-A	8	22	5	4	1	0	0	0	4	9	.182	.308	.227	59	-1	0			.913	-3	/S-8	-0.4
■ CHRIS HARTJE Hartje, Christian Henry b: 3/25/15, San Francisco, Cal d: 6/26/46, Seattle, Wash. BR/TR, 5'10.5", 165 lbs. Deb: 9/9/39																							
1939	Bro-N	9	16	2	5	1	0	0	5	1	0	.313	.353	.375	92	-0	0			.909	-2	/C-8	-0.2
■ GROVER HARTLEY Hartley, Grover Allen "Slick" b: 7/2/1888, Osgood, Ind. d: 10/19/64, Daytona Beach, Fla BR/TR, 5'11", 175 lbs. Deb: 5/13/11 C																							
1911	NY-N	11	18	1	4	2	0	0	1	1	1	.222	.263	.333	64	-1	1			.962	3	C-10	0.2
1912	NY-N	25	34	3	8	2	1	0	7	0	4	.235	.257	.353	64	-2	2			.960	2	C-25	0.1
1913	NY-N	23	19	4	6	0	0	0	0	1	2	.316	.350	.316	90	-0	4			.978	2	C-21/1-1	0.2
1914	StL-F	86	212	24	61	13	2	1	25	12	26	.288	.329	.382	89	-7	4			.956	-9	C-32,2-13/1-9,30	-1.4
1915	StL-F	120	394	47	108	21	6	1	50	42	21	.274	.356	.365	98	-5	10			.972	-7	*C-113/1-1	-0.4
1916	StL-A	89	222	19	50	8	0	0	12	30	24	.225	.325	.261	80	-4	4			.968	1	C-75	0.1
1917	StL-A	19	13	2	3	0	0	0	0	2	1	.231	.333	.231	75	-0	0			.875	1	/C-4,S-1,3-1	0.1
1924	NY-N	4	7	1	2	1	0	0	1	1	0	.286	.375	.429	118	0	1	0	0	1.000	-0	/C-3	0.1
1925	NY-N	46	95	9	30	1	1	0	8	8	3	.316	.375	.347	89	-1	2	0	1	.974	4	C-37/1-8	0.4
1926	NY-N	13	21	0	1	0	0	0	0	5	0	.048	.231	.048	-22	-4	0			1.000	0	C-13	-0.3
1927	Bos-A	103	244	23	67	11	0	1	31	22	14	.275	.337	.332	76	-8	1	0	0	.967	-13	C-86	-1.5
1929	Cle-A	24	33	2	9	0	1	0	8	2	1	.273	.314	.333	64	-2	0	0	0	1.000	-3	C-13	-0.4
1930	Cle-A	1	4	0	3	0	0	0	1	0	0	.750	.750	.750	271	1	0	0	0	.750	-0	/C-1	0.1
1934	StL-A	5	3	0	1	1	0	0	0	1	0	.333	.500	.667	183	0	0	0	0	1.000	0	/C-2	0.1
Total	14	569	1319	135	353	60	11	3	144	127	97	.268	.339	.337	85	-33	29	0		.968	-19	C-435/1-19,23OS	-2.6
■ CHICK HARTLEY Hartley, Walter Scott b: 8/22/1880, Philadelphia, Pa. d: 7/18/48, Philadelphia, Pa. BR/TR, 5'8", 180 lbs. Deb: 6/4/02																							
1902	NY-N	1	4	0	0	0	0	0	0	0		.000	.000	.000	-99	-1	0			1.000	-0	/O-1	-0.1
■ FRED HARTMAN Hartman, Frederick Orrin "Dutch" b: 4/25/1868, Allegheny, Pa. d: 11/11/38, McKeesport, Pa. BR/TR, 5'8", 170 lbs. Deb: 7/26/1894																							
1894	Pit-N	49	182	41	58	4	7	2	20	16	11	.319	.389	.451	103	1	12			.876	-4	3-49	-0.2
1897	StL-N	124	516	67	158	21	8	2	67	26		.306	.350	.390	97	-3	18			.867	-4	*3-124	-0.3
1898	NY-N	123	475	57	129	16	11	2	88	25		.272	.313	.364	97	-3	11			.882	9	*3-123	0.6
1899	NY-N	50	174	25	41	3	5	1	16	12		.236	.318	.328	80	-5	2			.886	-4	3-50	-0.7
1901	Chi-A	120	473	77	146	23	13	3	89	25		.309	.355	.431	120	12	31			.894	-6	*3-119	0.7
1902	StL-N	114	416	30	90	10	3	0	52	14		.216	.251	.255	58	-21	14			.908	-4	*3-105/S-4,1-3	-2.5
Total	6	580	2236	297	622	77	47	10	332	118	11	.278	.326	.368	95	-19	88			.886	-12	3-570/S-4,1-3	-2.4
■ J C HARTMAN Hartman, J C b: 4/15/34, Cottonton, Ala. BR/TR, 6', 175 lbs. Deb: 7/21/62																							
1962	Hou-N	51	148	11	33	5	0	0	5	4	16	.223	.248	.257	39	-13	1	1	-0	.972	7	S-48	-0.3
1963	Hou-N	39	90	2	11	1	0	0	3	2	13	.122	.151	.133	-19	-14	1	0	0	.950	0	S-32	-1.3
Total	2	90	238	13	44	6	0	0	8	6	29	.185	.211	.210	18	-27	2	1	0	.964	7	/S-80	-1.6
■ GABBY HARTNETT Hartnett, Charles Leo b: 12/20/1900, Woonsocket, R.I. d: 12/20/72, Park Ridge, Ill. BR/TR, 6'1", 195 lbs. Deb: 4/12/22 MCH																							
1922	Chi-N	31	72	4	14	1	1	0	4	6	8	.194	.256	.236	27	-8	1	0	0	.982	6	C-27	-0.1
1923	Chi-N	85	231	28	62	12	2	8	39	25	22	.268	.347	.442	107	2	4	0	1	.994	4	C-39,1-31	0.7
1924	Chi-N	111	354	56	106	17	7	16	67	39	37	.299	.377	.523	137	18	10	2	2	.963	-4	*C-105	2.3
1925	Chi-N	117	398	61	115	28	3	24	67	36	77	.289	.351	.555	126	13	1	5	-3	.958	10	*C-110	2.5
1926	Chi-N	93	284	35	78	25	3	8	41	32	37	.275	.352	.468	118	7	0			.978	5	C-88	1.7
1927	Chi-N	127	449	56	132	32	5	10	80	44	42	.294	.361	.454	117	10	2			.973	4	*C-126	2.3
1928	Chi-N	120	388	61	117	26	9	14	57	65	32	.302	.404	.523	143	25	3			**.989**	9	*C-118	4.2
1929	*Chi-N	25	22	2	6	2	1	1	9	5	5	.273	.407	.591	144	2	1			1.000	-0	/C-1	0.1
1930	Chi-N	141	508	84	172	31	3	37	122	55	62	.339	.404	.630	144	35	0			**.989**	3	*C-136	4.4
1931	Chi-N	116	380	53	107	32	1	8	70	52	48	.282	.370	.434	113	8	3			.981	2	*C-105	1.7
1932	*Chi-N	121	406	52	110	25	3	12	52	51	59	.271	.354	.436	112	7	0			.982	6	*C-117/1-1	2.0
1933	Chi-N★	140	490	55	135	21	4	16	88	37	51	.276	.326	.433	115	9	1			.989	7	*C-140	2.6
1934	Chi-N★	130	438	58	131	21	1	22	90	37	46	.299	.358	.502	130	18	0			**.996**	14	*C-129	3.5
1935	*Chi-N★	116	413	67	142	32	6	13	91	41	46	.344	.404	.545	152	30	1			.984	15	*C-110	4.8
1936	Chi-N★	121	424	49	130	25	6	7	64	30	36	.307	.361	.443	113	7	0			**.991**	9	*C-114	2.1
1937	Chi-N★	110	356	47	126	21	6	12	82	43	19	.354	.424	.548	156	28	0			**.996**	1	*C-103	3.3
1938	*Chi-N☆	88	299	40	82	19	1	10	59	48	17	.274	.380	.445	123	10	1			**.995**	-4	C-83,M	1.1
1939	Chi-N	97	306	36	85	18	2	12	59	37	32	.278	.358	.467	118	7	0			.992	-8	C-86,M	0.4
1940	Chi-N	37	64	3	17	3	0	1	12	8	7	.266	.347	.359	97	-0	0			.951	1	C-22/1-1,M	0.2
1941	NY-N	64	150	20	45	5	0	5	26	12	14	.300	.356	.433	119	4	0			.994	-3	C-34	0.3
Total	20	1990	6432	867	1912	396	64	236	1179	703	697	.297	.370	.489	126	232	28	7		.984	74	*C-1793/1-33	40.1
■ PAT HARTNETT Hartnett, Patrick J. "Happy" b: 10/20/1863, Boston, Mass. d: 4/10/35, Boston, Mass. 6'1", 175 lbs. Deb: 4/18/1890																							
1890	StL-a	14	53	6	10	2	1	0	4	6		.189	.283	.264	54	-3	1			.954	-1	1-14	-0.4
■ GREG HARTS Harts, Gregory Rudolph b: 4/21/50, Atlanta, Ga. BL/TL, 6', 168 lbs. Deb: 9/15/73																							
1973	NY-N	3	2	0	1	0	0	0	0	0	0	.500	.500	.500	181	0	0	0	0	.000	0	H	0.0
■ TOPSY HARTSEL Hartsel, Tully Frederick b: 6/26/1874, Polk, Ohio d: 10/14/44, Toledo, Ohio BL/TL, 5'5", 155 lbs. Deb: 9/14/1898																							
1898	Lou-N	22	71	11	23	0	0	0	9	11		.324	.422	.324	116	2	2			.931	-2	O-21	-0.1
1899	Lou-N	30	75	8	18	1	1	1	7	11		.240	.345	.320	83	-1	1			.927	-2	O-22	-0.4
1900	Cin-N	18	64	10	21	2	1	2	5	8		.328	.403	.484	148	4	7			.957	-5	O-18	-0.2
1901	Chi-N	140	558	111	187	25	16	7	54	74		.335	.414	.475	164	47	41			.951	-1	*O-140	3.5
1902	Phi-A	137	545	**109**	154	20	12	5	58	**87**		.283	.383	.391	110	10	**47**			.955	-1	*O-137	0.0
1903	Phi-A	98	373	65	116	19	14	5	26	49		.311	.391	.477	152	25	13			.968	-6	O-96	1.4
1904	Phi-A	147	534	79	135	17	12	2	25	75		.253	.347	.341	112	10	19			.959	-4	*O-147	-0.3
1905	*Phi-A	150	538	88	148	22	8	0	28	**121**		.275	**.409**	.346	138	31	37			.939	-7	*O-149	1.8
1906	Phi-A	144	533	96	136	21	9	1	30	**88**		.255	.363	.334	115	13	31			.969	0	*O-144	0.7
1907	Phi-A	143	507	93	142	23	6	3	29	**106**		.280	**.405**	.367	143	31	20			.967	-11	*O-143	1.6
1908	Phi-A	129	460	73	112	16	6	4	29	**93**		.243	.371	.330	120	14	15			.960	-5	*O-129	0.5
1909	Phi-A	83	267	30	72	4	4	1	18	48		.270	.381	.326	121	9	3			.966	-4	O-74	0.3
1910	*Phi-A	90	285	45	63	10	3	0	22	58		.221	.353	.277	99	3	11			.945	-6	O-83	-0.8
1911	Phi-A	25	38	8	9	2	0	0	1	8		.237	.396	.289	94	0	0			.941	1	/O-9	0.1
Total	14	1356	4848	826	1336	182	92	31	341	837		.276	.384	.370	128	199	247			.956	-53	*O-1312	8.1
■ ROY HARTSFIELD Hartsfield, Roy Thomas "Spec" b: 10/25/25, Chattahoochee, Ga. BR/TR, 5'9", 165 lbs. Deb: 4/28/50 MC																							
1950	Bos-N	107	419	62	116	15	2	7	24	27	61	.277	.322	.372	88	-8	7			.949	-24	2-96	-2.8
1951	Bos-N	120	450	63	122	11	2	6	31	41	73	.271	.333	.344	89	-7	7	2	1	.969	-5	*2-114	-0.5
1952	Bos-N	38	107	13	28	4	3	0	4	5	12	.262	.295	.355	82	-3	0	0	0	.950	-6	2-29	-0.7
Total	3	265	976	138	266	30	7	13	59	73	146	.273	.324	.358	88	-18	14	2		.959	-34	2-239	-4.0
■ CLINT HARTUNG Hartung, Clinton Clarence "Floppy" or "The Hondo Hurricane" b: 8/10/22, Hondo, Tex. BR/TR, 6'4", 215 lbs. Deb: 4/15/47																							
1947	NY-N	34	94	13	29	4	3	4	13	3	21	.309	.330	.543	127	3	0			1.000	-2	P-23/O-7	-0.1
1948	NY-N	43	56	5	10	1	1	0	3	7	24	.179	.270	.232	37	-5	0			1.000	-0	P-36	0.0
1949	NY-N	38	63	7	12	0	0	4	7	4	21	.190	.239	.381	64	-4	0			.957	2	P-33	0.0
1950	NY-N	32	43	7	13	2	1	3	10	1	13	.302	.318	.605	136	2	0			.939	3	P-20/O-2,1-1	0.0
1951	*NY-N	21	44	4	9	1	0	0	2	1	9	.205	.222	.227	21	-5	0	0	0	1.000	-2	O-12	-0.8
1952	NY-N	28	78	6	17	2	1	3	8	9	24	.218	.299	.385	88	-1	0	0	0	.932	-1	O-24	-0.3
Total	6	196	378	42	90	10	6	14	43	25	112	.238	.285	.407	84	-10	0	0		.972	-2	P-112/O-45,1-1	-1.2

YEAR	TM/L	G	AB	R	H	2B	3B	HR	RBI	BB	SO	AVG	OBP	SLG	PRO+	BR/A	SB	CS	SBR	FA	FR	G/POS	TPR
■ **ROY HARTZELL** Hartzell, Roy Allen b: 7/6/1881, Golden, Colo. d: 11/6/61, Golden, Colo. BL/TR, 5′8.5″, 155 lbs. Deb: 4/17/06																							
1906	StL-A	113	404	43	86	7	0	0	24	19		.213	.266	.230	58	-19	21			.889	-3	*3-103/S-6,2-2	-2.0
1907	StL-A	60	220	20	52	3	5	0	13	11		.236	.285	.295	85	-4	7			.911	0	3-38,2-12/S-2,O-2	-0.3
1908	StL-A	115	422	41	112	5	6	2	32	19		.265	.302	.320	101	-0	24			.943	-6	O-82,S-18/3-7,2-4	-1.0
1909	StL-A	152	595	64	161	12	5	0	32	29		.271	.312	.308	103	1	14			.940	4	O-85,S-65/2-1	0.3
1910	StL-A	151	542	52	118	13	5	2	30	49		.218	.290	.271	81	-12	18			.929	1	3-89,S-38,O-23	-0.9
1911	NY-A	144	527	67	156	17	11	3	91	63		.296	.375	.387	106	5	22			.936	-12	*3-124,S-12/O-8	-0.5
1912	NY-A	125	416	50	113	10	11	1	38	64		.272	.370	.356	102	2	20			.906	-0	3-56,O-56,S-10,/2-2	0.1
1913	NY-A	141	490	60	127	18	1	0	38	67	40	.259	.353	.300	91	-3	26			.942	-0	2-81,O-31,3-21,/S-4	-0.5
1914	NY-A	137	481	55	112	15	9	1	32	68	38	.233	.335	.308	94	-2	22	25	-8	.973	0	*O-128/2-5	-1.8
1915	NY-A	119	387	39	97	11	2	3	60	57	37	.251	.351	.313	99	1	7	19	-9	.963	-3	*O-107/2-5,3-2	-1.8
1916	NY-A	33	64	12	12	1	0	0	7	9	3	.188	.297	.203	49	-4	1			1.000	-6	O-28	-1.2
Total	11	1290	4548	503	1146	112	55	12	397	455	118	.252	.327	.309	93	-33	182	44		.959	-26	O-550,3-440,S2	-9.6
■ **LUTHER HARVEL** Harvel, Luther Raymond "Red" b: 9/30/05, Cambria, Ill. d: 4/10/86, Kansas City, Mo. BR/TR, 5′11″, 180 lbs. Deb: 7/31/28																							
1928	Cle-A	40	136	12	30	6	1	0	12	4	17	.221	.264	.279	42	-11	1	1	-0	.948	-2	O-39	-1.5
■ **ZAZA HARVEY** Harvey, Ervin King b: 1/5/1879, Saratoga, Cal. d: 6/3/54, Santa Monica, Cal. BL/TL, 6′, 190 lbs. Deb: 5/3/00																							
1900	Chi-N	2	3	0	0	0	0	0	0	0		.000	.000	.000	-99	-1	0			1.000	-0	/P-1	0.0
1901	Chi-A	17	40	11	10	3	1	0	3	2		.250	.302	.375	89	-1	1			.930	2	P-16	0.0
	Cle-A	45	170	21	60	5	5	1	24	9		.353	.392	.459	141	9	15			.890	2	O-45	0.7
	Yr	62	210	32	70	8	6	1	27	11		.333	.375	.443	131	9	16			.890	3	O-45,P-16	0.7
1902	Cle-A	12	46	5	16	2	0	0	5	3		.348	.388	.391	121	1	1			1.000	0	O-12	0.1
Total	3	76	259	37	86	10	6	1	32	14		.332	.373	.429	127	9	17			.907	4	/O-57,P-17	0.8
■ **ZIGGY HASBROOK** Hasbrook, Robert Lyndon "Ziggy" b: 11/21/1893, Grundy Center, Ia. d: 2/9/76, Garland, Tex. BR/TR, 6′1″, 180 lbs. Deb: 9/6/16																							
1916	Chi-A	9	8	1	1	0	0	0	0	1	2	.125	.222	.125	4	-1	0			1.000	1	/1-7	0.0
1917	Chi-A	2	1	1	0	0	0	0	0	0	0	.000	.000	.000	-98	-0	0			1.000	1	/2-1	0.0
Total	2	11	9	2	1	0	0	0	0	1	2	.111	.200	.111	-6	-1	0			1.000	1	/1-7,2-1	0.0
■ **BILL HASELMAN** Haselman, William Joseph b: 5/25/66, Long Branch, N.J. BR/TR, 6′3″, 220 lbs. Deb: 9/3/90																							
1990	Tex-A	7	13	0	2	0	0	0	3	1	5	.154	.214	.154	5	-2	0	0	0	1.000	0	/C-1,D-3	-0.1
1992	Sea-A	8	19	1	5	0	0	0	0	0	7	.263	.263	.263	48	-1	0	0	0	1.000	-2	/C-5,O-2	-0.3
1993	Sea-A	58	137	21	35	8	0	5	16	12	19	.255	.320	.423	97	-1	2	1	0	.992	-2	C-49/O-2,D-4	-0.1
1994	Sea-A	38	83	11	16	7	1	1	8	3	11	.193	.230	.337	43	-7	1	0	0	.982	-1	C-33/O-2,D-3	-0.6
1995	*Bos-A	64	152	22	37	6	1	5	23	17	30	.243	.327	.395	84	-4	0	2	-1	.989	7	C-48,D-11/1-1,3-1	0.4
1996	Bos-A	77	237	33	65	13	1	8	34	19	52	.274	.331	.439	91	-4	4	2	0	.994	20	C-69/1-2,D-2	1.7
1997	Bos-A	67	212	22	50	15	0	6	26	15	44	.236	.293	.392	75	-8	0	2	-1	.983	4	C-66	-0.2
1998	Tex-A	40	105	11	33	6	0	6	17	3	17	.314	.333	.543	118	2	0	0	0	.995	3	C-36/D-2	0.7
Total	8	359	958	121	243	55	3	31	127	70	185	.254	.309	.414	84	-25	7	7	-2	.990	30	C-307/D-25,O-6,13	1.5
■ **DON HASENMAYER** Hasenmayer, Donald Irvin b: 4/4/27, Roslyn, Pa. BR/TR, 5′10.5″, 180 lbs. Deb: 5/2/45																							
1945	Phi-N	5	18	1	2	0	0	0	1	2	1	.111	.200	.111	-13	-3	0			.920	3	/2-4,3-1	0.0
1946	Phi-N	6	12	0	1	1	0	0	0	0	2	.083	.083	.167	-31	-2	0			1.000	2	/3-3	0.0
Total	2	11	30	1	3	1	0	0	1	2	3	.100	.156	.133	-19	-5	0			1.000	5	/3-4,2-4	0.0
■ **MICKEY HASLIN** Haslin, Michael Joseph b: 10/31/10, Wilkes-Barre, Pa. BR/TR, 5′8″, 165 lbs. Deb: 9/7/33																							
1933	Phi-N	26	89	3	21	2	0	0	9	3	5	.236	.261	.258	43	-6	1			.956	-4	2-26	-1.0
1934	Phi-N	72	166	28	44	8	2	1	11	16	13	.265	.330	.355	74	-6	1			.941	-3	3-26,2-21/S-4	-0.7
1935	Phi-N	110	407	53	108	17	3	3	52	19	25	.265	.300	.344	66	-20	5			.931	-3	S-87,3-11/2-9	-1.7
1936	Phi-N	16	64	6	22	1	1	0	6	3	5	.344	.373	.391	96	-0	0			.938	-5	2-12/3-5	-0.4
	Bos-N	36	104	14	29	1	2	2	11	5	9	.279	.312	.385	93	-1	0			.892	-5	3-17/2-7	-0.5
	Yr	52	168	20	51	2	3	2	17	8	14	.304	.335	.387	95	-1	0			.854	-10	3-22,2-19	-0.9
1937	NY-N	27	42	8	8	1	0	0	5	9	3	.190	.333	.214	51	-2	1			.920	6	/S-9,2-4,3-4	0.4
1938	NY-N	31	102	13	33	3	0	3	15	4	4	.324	.361	.441	119	2	0			.902	-2	3-15,2-13	0.1
Total	6	318	974	125	265	33	8	9	109	59	64	.272	.316	.350	74	-34	8			.927	-15	S-100/2-92,3-78	-3.8
■ **PETE HASNEY** Hasney, Peter James b: 5/26/1865, England d: 5/24/08, Philadelphia, Pa. Deb: 9/13/1890																							
1890	Phi-a	2	7	1	1	0	0	0	0	1		.143	.250	.143	16	-1	0			.000	-1	/O-2	-0.2
■ **BILL HASSAMAER** Hassamaer, William Louis "Roaring Bill" b: 7/26/1864, St.Louis, Mo. d: 5/29/10, St.Louis, Mo. 6′, 180 lbs. Deb: 4/19/1894																							
1894	Was-N	118	494	106	159	33	17	4	90	41	20	.322	.375	.482	109	6	16			.916	5	O-68,3-31,2-14,/S-4	0.5
1895	Was-N	85	358	42	100	18	4	1	60	26	13	.279	.328	.360	78	-12	8			.964	-7	O-75/1-9,S-1,3-1	-2.0
	Lou-N	23	96	7	20	2	2	0	14	3	4	.208	.232	.271	31	-10	0			.980	3	1-21/2-1,S-1	-0.5
	Yr	108	454	49	120	20	6	1	74	29	17	.264	.308	.341	69	-22	8			.964	-4	O-75,1-30/S-2,32	-2.5
1896	Lou-N	30	106	8	26	5	0	2	14	14	7	.245	.333	.349	83	-2	1			.976	6	1-29	0.4
Total	3	256	1054	163	305	58	23	7	178	84	44	.289	.342	.408	90	-19	25			.938	7	O-143/1-59,3-32,2S	-1.6
■ **BUDDY HASSETT** Hassett, John Aloysius b: 9/5/11, New York, N.Y. d: 8/23/97, Westwood, N.J. BL/TL, 5′11″, 180 lbs. Deb: 4/14/36																							
1936	Bro-N	156	635	79	197	29	11	3	82	35	17	.310	.350	.405	102	1	5			.983	5	*1-156	-0.9
1937	Bro-N	137	556	71	169	31	6	1	53	20	19	.304	.334	.387	94	-5	13			.984	9	*1-131/O-7	-1.2
1938	Bro-N	115	335	49	98	11	6	0	40	32	19	.293	.356	.361	95	-1	3			.945	-2	O-71/1-8	-0.7
1939	Bos-N	147	590	72	182	15	3	2	60	29	14	.308	.342	.354	94	-6	13			.985	9	*1-123,O-23	-1.1
1940	Bos-N	124	458	59	107	19	4	0	27	25	16	.234	.273	.293	59	-26	4			.979	7	1-98,O-13	-2.9
1941	Bos-N	118	405	59	120	9	4	1	33	36	15	.296	.354	.346	102	1	10			.991	7	1-99	0.1
1942	*NY-A	132	538	80	153	16	6	5	48	32	16	.284	.325	.364	95	-5	5	5	-2	.991	11	*1-132	-0.3
Total	7	929	3517	469	1026	130	40	12	343	209	116	.292	.333	.362	92	-40	53	5		.985	45	1-747,O-114	-7.0
■ **RON HASSEY** Hassey, Ronald William b: 2/27/53, Tucson, Ariz. BL/TR, 6′2″, 200 lbs. Deb: 4/23/78 C																							
1978	Cle-A	25	74	5	15	0	0	2	9	5	7	.203	.262	.284	54	-5	2	0	1	.993	5	C-24	0.2
1979	Cle-A	75	223	20	64	14	0	4	32	19	19	.287	.343	.404	100	0	1	0	0	.992	7	C-68/1-2,D-1	0.9
1980	Cle-A	130	390	43	124	18	4	8	65	49	51	.318	.395	.446	130	17	0	2	-1	.993	-7	*C-113/1-3,D-7	1.3
1981	Cle-A	61	190	8	44	4	0	1	25	17	11	.232	.301	.268	66	-8	0	1	-1	.991	8	C-56/1-5,D-1	0.2
1982	Cle-A	113	323	33	81	18	0	5	34	53	32	.251	.358	.353	97	0	3	2	-0	.993	8	*C-105/1-2,D-2	1.2
1983	Cle-A	117	341	48	92	21	0	6	42	38	35	.270	.346	.384	97	-1	2	2	-1	.995	-3	*C-113/D-1	0.0
1984	Cle-A	48	149	11	38	5	1	0	19	15	26	.255	.323	.302	73	-5	1	0	0	1.000	-1	C-44/1-1,D-1	-0.4
	Chi-N	19	33	5	11	0	0	2	5	4	6	.333	.405	.515	144	2	0	1	-1	1.000	-0	/C-6,1-4	0.1
1985	NY-A	92	267	31	79	16	1	13	42	28	21	.296	.369	.509	141	15	0	0	0	.984	-2	C-69/1-2,D-2	1.6
1986	NY-A	64	191	23	57	14	0	6	29	24	16	.298	.382	.466	131	9	1	1	-0	.985	-13	C-51/D-3	-0.2
	Chi-A	49	150	22	53	11	1	3	20	22	11	.353	.439	.500	150	11	0	0	0	1.000	1	D-34,C-11	1.2
	Yr	113	341	45	110	25	1	9	49	46	27	.323	.408	.481	140	20	1	1	-0	.988	-12	C-62,D-37	1.0
1987	Chi-A	49	145	15	31	9	0	3	12	17	11	.214	.305	.338	69	-6	0	0	0	1.000	1	C-24,D-18	-0.4
1988	*Oak-A	107	323	32	83	15	0	7	45	30	42	.257	.328	.368	98	-1	2	0	1	.994	-1	C-91/D-9	0.4
1989	*Oak-A	97	268	29	61	12	0	5	23	24	45	.228	.294	.328	78	-8	1	0	0	.991	7	C-78/1-1,D-2	0.3
1990	*Oak-A	94	254	18	54	7	0	5	22	27	29	.213	.291	.299	68	-11	0	0	0	.997	3	C-59,D-15/1-3	-0.5
1991	Mon-N	52	119	5	27	8	0	1	14	13	16	.227	.303	.319	76	-4	1	1	-0	.989	-4	C-34	-0.7
Total	14	1192	3440	348	914	172	7	71	438	385	378	.266	.343	.382	100	7	14	10	-2	.993	10	C-946/D-96,1-23	5.2
■ **JOE HASSLER** Hassler, Joseph Frederick b: 4/7/05, Ft.Smith, Ark. d: 9/4/71, Duncan, Okla. BR/TR, 6′, 165 lbs. Deb: 5/26/28																							
1928	Phi-A	28	34	5	9	2	0	0	3	2	4	.265	.306	.324	64	-2	0	1	-1	.879	1	S-28	0.0
1929	Phi-A	4	4	1	0	0	0	0	0	0	2	.000	.000	.000	-97	-1	0	0	0	.600	-0	/S-2	-0.1

YEAR	TM/L	G	AB	R	H	2B	3B	HR	RBI	BB	SO	AVG	OBP	SLG	PRO+	BR/A	SB	CS	SBR	FA	FR	G/POS	TPR
1930	StL-A	5	8	3	2	0	0	0	1	0	1	.250	.250	.250	26	-1	0	0	0	1.000	1	/S-3	0.1
Total	3	37	46	9	11	2	0	0	4	2	7	.239	.271	.283	43	-4	0	1	-1	.875	2	/S-33	0.0

■ GENE HASSON
Hasson, Charles Eugene b: 7/20/15, Connellsville, Pa BL/TL, 6′, 197 lbs. Deb: 9/9/37

YEAR	TM/L	G	AB	R	H	2B	3B	HR	RBI	BB	SO	AVG	OBP	SLG	PRO+	BR/A	SB	CS	SBR	FA	FR	G/POS	TPR
1937	Phi-A	28	98	12	30	6	3	3	14	13	14	.306	.387	.520	129	4	0	0	0	1.000	-2	1-28	-0.1
1938	Phi-A	19	69	10	19	6	2	1	12	12	7	.275	.383	.464	114	2	0	0	0	.958	-4	1-19	-0.4
Total	2	47	167	22	49	12	5	4	26	25	21	.293	.385	.497	123	6	0	0	0	.985	-6	/1-47	-0.5

■ SCOTT HASTINGS
Hastings, Winfield Scott b: 8/10/1847, Hillsboro, Ohio d: 8/14/07, Sawtelle, Cal. BR/TR, 5′8″, 161 lbs. Deb: 5/6/1871 M

YEAR	TM/L	G	AB	R	H	2B	3B	HR	RBI	BB	SO	AVG	OBP	SLG	PRO+	BR/A	SB	CS	SBR	FA	FR	G/POS	TPR
1871	Rok-n	25	118	27	30	6	4	0	20	2	4	.254	.267	.373	85	-2	11	2	2	.856	-1	*C-23/2-2,O-2,1M	-0.1
1872	Cle-n	22	115	34	45	4	0	0	16	3	2	.391	.407	.426	165	9	5	1	1	.797	-7	C-12/O-8,2-6,M	0.2
	Bal-n	13	62	16	19	3	1	0	4	1	2	.306	.317	.387	111	0	0	1	-1	.900	4	C-12/2-2,O-1	0.2
	Yr	35	177	50	64	7	1	0	20	4	4	.362	.376	.412	145	9	5	2	0	.851	-3	C-24/O-9,2-8	0.4
1873	Bal-n	30	146	41	41	4	0	0	15	4	1	.281	.300	.308	81	-3	4	2	0	.892	-3	C-19,O-12/2-1	-0.4
1874	Har-n	52	247	60	80	11	2	0	30	4	3	.324	.335	.385	124	5	10	5	0	.753	-14	C-39,O-26/2-1,S-1	-0.6
1875	Chi-n	65	287	43	73	9	0	0	30	9	14	.254	.277	.286	95	-1	13	11	-3	.815	3	C-46,O-29/2-3	0.0
1876	Lou-N	67	283	36	73	6	1	0	21	5	11	.258	.271	.286	73	-11				.872	-7	*O-65/C-5	-1.7
1877	Cin-N	20	71	7	10	1	0	0	3	3	6	.141	.176	.155	6	-7				.791	-9	C-20/O-1	-1.4
Total	5 n	207	975	221	288	37	7	0	115	23	26	.295	.312	.348	108	9	43	22	-0	.822	-19	C-151/O-78,2-15,S1	-0.7
Total	2	87	354	43	83	7	1	0	24	8	17	.234	.251	.260	61	-18				.872	-17	/O-66,C-25	-3.1

■ CHRIS HATCHER
Hatcher, Christopher Kenneth b: 1/7/69, Anaheim, Cal. BR/TR, 6′3″, 220 lbs. Deb: 9/6/98

YEAR	TM/L	G	AB	R	H	2B	3B	HR	RBI	BB	SO	AVG	OBP	SLG	PRO+	BR/A	SB	CS	SBR	FA	FR	G/POS	TPR
1998	KC-A	8	15	0	1	0	0	0	1	1	7	.067	.125	.067	-46	-3	0	0	0	1.000	-1	/O-5	-0.4

■ MICKEY HATCHER
Hatcher, Michael Vaughn b: 3/15/55, Cleveland, Ohio BR/TR, 6′2″, 200 lbs. Deb: 8/3/79 C

YEAR	TM/L	G	AB	R	H	2B	3B	HR	RBI	BB	SO	AVG	OBP	SLG	PRO+	BR/A	SB	CS	SBR	FA	FR	G/POS	TPR
1979	LA-N	33	93	9	25	4	1	1	5	7	12	.269	.327	.366	90	-1	1	3	-2	.974	-1	O-19,3-17	-0.5
1980	LA-N	57	84	4	19	2	0	1	5	2	12	.226	.244	.286	48	-6	0	2	-1	1.000	-5	O-25,3-18	-1.4
1981	Min-A	99	377	36	96	23	2	3	37	15	29	.255	.287	.350	77	-11	3	1	0	.992	4	O-91/1-7,3-2,D-1	-1.2
1982	Min-A	84	277	23	69	13	2	3	26	8	27	.249	.270	.343	65	-13	0	2	-1	.988	0	O-47,D-29/3-5	-1.7
1983	Min-A	106	375	50	119	15	3	9	47	14	19	.317	.344	.445	111	5	2	0	1	.979	6	O-56,D-39/1-7,3-1	0.8
1984	Min-A	152	576	61	174	35	5	5	69	37	34	.302	.346	.406	103	2	0	1	-1	.974	13	*O-100,D-37,1-17,/3	1.0
1985	Min-A	116	444	46	125	28	0	3	49	16	23	.282	.310	.365	79	-13	0	0	0	.991	8	O-97,D-11/1-4	-0.9
1986	Min-A	115	317	40	88	13	3	3	32	19	26	.278	.318	.366	84	-7	2	1	0	.971	-3	O-46,D-28,1-22,/3-3	-1.3
1987	LA-N	101	287	27	81	19	1	7	42	20	19	.282	.331	.429	102	0	2	3	-1	.929	0	3-49,1-37/O-7	-0.4
1988	*LA-N	88	191	22	56	8	0	1	25	7	7	.293	.325	.351	97	-1	0	0	0	1.000	-2	O-29,1-25/3-3	-0.6
1989	LA-N	94	224	18	66	9	2	2	25	13	16	.295	.336	.379	106	1	1	2	-1	.961	-3	O-48,3-16/1-5,P-1	-0.4
1990	LA-N	85	132	12	28	3	1	0	13	6	22	.212	.252	.250	40	-11	0	0	0	1.000	-4	1-25,3-10,O-10	-1.7
Total	12	1130	3377	348	946	172	20	38	375	164	246	.280	.316	.377	89	-55	11	15	-6	.983	13	O-575,1-149,D3/P	-8.3

■ BILLY HATCHER
Hatcher, William Augustus b: 10/4/60, Williams, Ariz. BR/TR, 5′9″, 175 lbs. Deb: 9/10/84 C

YEAR	TM/L	G	AB	R	H	2B	3B	HR	RBI	BB	SO	AVG	OBP	SLG	PRO+	BR/A	SB	CS	SBR	FA	FR	G/POS	TPR
1984	Chi-N	8	9	1	1	0	0	0	0	1	0	.111	.200	.111	-10	-1	2	0	1	1.000	-0	/O-4	-0.1
1985	Chi-N	53	163	24	40	12	1	2	10	8	12	.245	.293	.368	75	-6	2	4	-2	.988	-3	O-44	-1.2
1986	*Hou-N	127	419	55	108	15	4	6	36	22	52	.258	.303	.356	83	-10	38	14	3	.983	-5	*O-121	-1.7
1987	Hou-N	141	564	96	167	28	3	11	63	42	70	.296	.354	.415	107	6	53	9	11	.986	10	*O-140	2.2
1988	Hou-N	145	530	79	142	25	4	7	52	37	56	.268	.325	.370	103	2	32	13	2	.983	2	*O-142	0.1
1989	Hou-N	108	395	49	90	15	3	3	44	30	53	.228	.284	.304	71	-15	22	6	3	.991	2	*O-104	-1.4
	Pit-N	27	86	10	21	4	0	1	7	0	9	.244	.253	.326	67	-4	2	1	0	1.000	-4	O-20	-0.9
	Yr	135	481	59	111	19	3	4	51	30	62	.231	.279	.308	70	-19	24	7	3	.992	-2	*O-124	-2.3
1990	*Cin-N	139	504	68	139	28	5	5	25	33	42	.276	.328	.381	91	-6	30	10	3	**.997**	8	*O-131	0.1
1991	Cin-N	138	442	45	116	25	3	4	41	26	55	.262	.314	.360	86	-9	11	9	-2	.981	-2	*O-121	-1.6
1992	Cin-N	43	94	10	27	3	0	2	10	5	11	.287	.323	.383	97	-1	0	2	-1	.967	-3	O-23	-0.5
	Bos-A	75	315	37	75	16	2	1	23	17	41	.238	.284	.311	62	-16	4	6	-2	.968	-1	O-75	-2.2
1993	Bos-A	136	508	71	146	24	3	9	57	28	46	.287	.338	.400	92	-6	14	7	0	.993	-4	*O-130/2-2	-1.3
1994	Bos-A	44	164	24	40	9	1	1	18	11	14	.244	.295	.329	58	-10	4	5	-2	.968	1	O-43/D-1	-1.1
	Phi-N	43	134	15	33	5	1	2	13	6	14	.246	.279	.343	60	-8	4	1	1	1.000	-3	O-40	-1.1
1995	Tex-A	6	12	2	1	1	0	0	0	1	1	.083	.154	.167	-16	-2	0	0	0	1.000	1	/O-5,D-1	-0.1
Total	12	1233	4339	586	1146	210	30	54	399	267	476	.264	.315	.364	85	-88	218	87	13	.986	-1	*O-1143/D-2,2-2	-10.8

■ FRED HATFIELD
Hatfield, Fred James b: 3/18/25, Lanett, Ala. d: 5/22/98, Tallahassee, Fla. BL/TR, 6′1″, 171 lbs. Deb: 8/31/50 C

YEAR	TM/L	G	AB	R	H	2B	3B	HR	RBI	BB	SO	AVG	OBP	SLG	PRO+	BR/A	SB	CS	SBR	FA	FR	G/POS	TPR
1950	Bos-A	10	12	3	3	0	0	0	2	3	1	.250	.400	.250	63	-1	0	0	0	1.000	3	/3-3	0.2
1951	Bos-A	80	163	23	28	4	2	2	14	22	27	.172	.274	.258	40	-14	1	0	0	.959	21	3-49	0.6
1952	Bos-A	19	25	6	8	1	1	1	3	4	2	.320	.433	.560	162	2	0	3	-2	1.000	4	3-17	0.4
	Det-A	112	441	42	104	12	2	2	25	35	52	.236	.301	.286	63	-21	2	2	-1	.968	14	*3-107/S-9	-1.0
	Yr	131	466	48	112	13	3	3	28	39	54	.240	.309	.300	69	-19	2	5	-2	**.971**	18	*3-124/S-9	-0.6
1953	Det-A	109	311	41	79	11	1	3	19	40	34	.254	.341	.325	81	-7	3	5	-2	.978	9	3-54,2-28/S-1	0.0
1954	Det-A	81	218	31	64	12	0	2	25	28	24	.294	.386	.376	112	5	4	2	0	.972	-7	2-54,3-15	0.0
1955	Det-A	122	413	51	96	15	3	8	33	61	49	.232	.338	.341	85	-8	3	2	-0	.975	-6	2-92,3-16,S-14	-0.6
1956	Det-A	8	12	2	3	0	0	0	2	2	1	.250	.400	.250	75	-0	0	0	0	1.000	-1	/2-4	-0.1
	Chi-A	106	321	46	84	9	1	7	33	37	36	.262	.352	.361	88	-5	1	0	0	.961	5	*3-100/S-3	0.1
	Yr	114	333	48	87	9	1	7	35	39	37	.261	.354	.357	87	-5	1	0	0	.961	4	*3-100/2-4,S-3	0.0
1957	Chi-A	69	114	14	23	3	0	0	8	15	20	.202	.321	.228	52	-7	1	0	0	.951	2	3-44	-0.4
1958	Cle-A	3	8	0	1	0	0	0	1	1	1	.125	.222	.125	-2	-1	0	0	0	1.000	1	/3-2	0.0
	Cin-N	3	1	0	0	0	0	0	0	0	0	.000	.000	.000	-95	-0	0	0	0	.000	0	/2-1,3-1	0.0
Total	9	722	2039	259	493	67	10	25	165	248	247	.242	.334	.321	78	-57	15	14	-4	.962	43	3-408,2-179/S-27	-0.8

■ GIL HATFIELD
Hatfield, Gilbert "Colonel" b: 1/27/1855, Hoboken, N.J. d: 5/27/21, Hoboken, N.J. TR , 5′9.5″, 168 lbs. Deb: 9/24/1885 F

YEAR	TM/L	G	AB	R	H	2B	3B	HR	RBI	BB	SO	AVG	OBP	SLG	PRO+	BR/A	SB	CS	SBR	FA	FR	G/POS	TPR
1885	Buf-N	11	30	1	4	0	1	0	0	0	11	.133	.133	.200	6	-3				.913	-0	/3-8,2-3	-0.3
1887	NY-N	2	7	2	3	1	0	0	3	0	1	.429	.429	.571	184	1	0			1.000	0	/3-2	0.1
1888	*NY-N	28	105	7	19	1	0	0	9	2	18	.181	.211	.190	29	-8	8			.813	-1	3-14,S-13/O-1,2-1	-0.9
1889	NY-N	32	125	21	23	2	0	1	12	9	15	.184	.250	.224	33	-11	9			.858	1	S-24/P-6,3-2	-0.6
1890	NY-P	71	287	32	80	13	6	2	37	17	19	.279	.328	.387	83	-9	12			.842	-19	3-42,S-27/P-3,O-1	-2.0
1891	Was-a	134	500	83	128	11	8	1	48	50	39	.256	.335	.316	90	-5	43			.869	9	*S-105,3-27/P-4,O-3	1.0
1893	Bro-N	34	120	24	35	3	3	2	19	17	5	.292	.388	.417	119	4	9			.875	-7	3-34	-0.2
1895	Lou-N	5	16	3	3	0	0	0	1	1	1	.188	.278	.188	23	-2	0			.889	-1	/3-3,S-2	-0.2
Total	8	317	1190	173	295	31	18	6	129	96	109	.248	.315	.319	79	-34	81			.850	-17	S-171,3-132/PO2	-3.1

■ JOHN HATFIELD
Hatfield, John Van Buskirk b: 7/20/1847, New Jersey d: 2/20/09, Long Island City, N.Y. 5′10″, 165 lbs. Deb: 5/18/1871 FM

YEAR	TM/L	G	AB	R	H	2B	3B	HR	RBI	BB	SO	AVG	OBP	SLG	PRO+	BR/A	SB	CS	SBR	FA	FR	G/POS	TPR
1871	Mut-n	33	168	41	43	3	2	0	22	4	0	.256	.273	.298	70	-5	10	3	1	.853	5	*O-24/2-7,3-2	0.1
1872	Mut-n	56	288	76	92	15	1	1	45	9	6	.319	.340	.389	132	13	12	5	1	.847	7	*2-56,M	1.0
1873	Mut-n	52	255	54	78	5	6	2	45	3	2	.306	.314	.396	110	3	2	0	1	.744	-8	*3-45,2-11/O-1,M	-0.5
1874	Mut-n	63	292	47	66	12	1	0	29	7	12	.226	.244	.274	64	-12	4	0	1	.874	7	*O-58/3-7,P-3,1S	-0.2
1875	Mut-n	1	4	1	2	1	0	0	1	0	0	.500	.500	.750	312	1	0	0	0	1.000	0	/O-1	0.1
1876	NY-N	1	4	0	1	0	0	0	1	0	0	.250	.250	.250	77	-0				.833	-0	/2-1	0.0
Total	5 n	205	1007	219	281	36	10	3	142	23	20	.279	.295	.344	97	-0	28	8	4	.868	11	/O-84,2-74,3PS1	0.5

■ SCOTT HATTEBERG
Hatteberg, Scott Allen b: 12/14/69, Salem, Ore. BL/TR, 6′1″, 185 lbs. Deb: 9/8/95

YEAR	TM/L	G	AB	R	H	2B	3B	HR	RBI	BB	SO	AVG	OBP	SLG	PRO+	BR/A	SB	CS	SBR	FA	FR	G/POS	TPR
1995	Bos-A	2	2	1	1	0	0	0	0	0	0	.500	.500	.500	156	0	0	0	0	1.000	0	/C-2	0.0
1996	Bos-A	10	11	3	2	1	0	0	0	3	2	.182	.357	.273	61	-1	0	0	0	1.000	2	C-10	0.1
1997	Bos-A	114	350	46	97	23	1	10	44	40	70	.277	.355	.434	102	2	0	1	-1	.983	-8	*C-106/D-1	-0.1
1998	*Bos-A	112	359	46	99	23	1	12	43	43	58	.276	.361	.446	108	5	0	0	0	.993	8	*C-108	1.8
Total	4	238	722	96	199	47	2	22	87	86	130	.276	.358	.438	105	6	0	1	-1	.989	2	C-226/D-1	1.8

■ **GRADY HATTON** Hatton, Grady Edgebert b: 10/7/22, Beaumont, Tex. BL/TR, 5'9", 175 lbs. Deb: 4/16/46 MC

YEAR	TM/L	G	AB	R	H	2B	3B	HR	RBI	BB	SO	AVG	OBP	SLG	PRO+	BR/A	SB	CS	SBR	FA	FR	G/POS	TPR
1946	Cin-N	116	436	56	118	18	3	14	69	66	53	.271	.369	.422	129	17	6			.941	-19	*3-116/O-2	-0.1
1947	Cin-N	146	524	91	147	24	8	16	77	81	50	.281	.377	.448	119	15	7			.938	-8	*3-136	0.7
1948	Cin-N	133	458	58	110	17	2	9	44	72	50	.240	.343	.345	90	-5	7			.932	4	*3-123/2-3,S-2,O-1	-0.2
1949	Cin-N	137	537	71	141	38	5	11	69	62	48	.263	.342	.413	101	0	4			**.975**	-1	*3-136	-0.3
1950	Cin-N	130	438	67	114	17	1	11	54	70	39	.260	.366	.379	96	-1	6			.954	-3	*3-126/2-1,S-1	-0.5
1951	Cin-N	96	331	41	84	9	3	4	37	33	32	.254	.321	.335	76	-11	4	2	0	.972	3	3-87/O-2	-0.9
1952	Cin-N☆	128	433	48	92	14	1	9	57	66	60	.212	.319	.312	76	-13	5	4	-1	**.990**	-17	*2-120	-2.6
1953	Cin-N	83	159	22	37	3	1	7	22	29	24	.233	.351	.396	94	-1	0	1	-1	.991	-11	2-35,1-10/3-5	-1.1
1954	Cin-N	1	1	0	0	0	0	0	0	0	0	.000	.000	.000	-97	-0	0	0	0	.000	0	H	0.0
	Chi-A	13	30	3	5	1	0	0	3	5	3	.167	.286	.200	34	-3	1	0	0	1.000	-1	3-10/1-3	-0.4
	Bos-A	99	302	40	85	12	3	5	33	58	25	.281	.401	.391	106	4	1	1	-0	.966	6	3-93/1-1,S-1	0.9
	Yr	112	332	43	90	13	3	5	36	63	28	.271	.390	.373	100	2	2	1	0	**.969**	5	*3-103/1-4,S-1	0.5
1955	Bos-A	126	380	48	93	11	4	4	49	76	28	.245	.371	.326	81	-8	0	1	-1	.976	-2	*3-111/2-1	-1.1
1956	Bos-A	5	5	0	2	0	0	0	2	0	0	.400	.400	.400	100	0	0	0	0	.000	0	H	0.0
	StL-N	44	73	10	18	1	2	0	7	13	7	.247	.360	.315	84	-1	1	0	0	.951	-4	2-13/3-1	-0.4
	Bal-A	27	61	4	9	1	0	1	3	13	6	.148	.297	.213	40	-5	0	0	0	1.000	-5	2-15,3-12	-0.9
1960	Chi-N	28	38	3	13	0	0	0	7	2	5	.342	.390	.342	104	0	0	0	0	.931	-2	/2-8	-0.1
Total	12	1312	4206	562	1068	166	33	91	533	646	430	.254	.355	.374	96	-10	42	9		.956	-60	3-956,2-196/1OS	-7.0

■ **ARTHUR HAUGER** Hauger, John Arthur b: 11/18/1893, Delhi, Ohio d: 8/2/44, Redwood City, Cal BL/TR, 5'11", 168 lbs. Deb: 7/17/12

YEAR	TM/L	G	AB	R	H	2B	3B	HR	RBI	BB	SO	AVG	OBP	SLG	PRO+	BR/A	SB	CS	SBR	FA	FR	G/POS	TPR
1912	Cle-A	15	18	0	1	0	0	0	0	1		.056	.105	.056	-52	-4	0			1.000	-2	/O-5	-0.5

■ **ARNOLD HAUSER** Hauser, Arnold George "Peewee" or "Stub" b: 9/25/1888, Chicago, Ill. d: 5/22/66, Aurora, Ill. BR/TR, 5'6", 145 lbs. Deb: 4/21/10

YEAR	TM/L	G	AB	R	H	2B	3B	HR	RBI	BB	SO	AVG	OBP	SLG	PRO+	BR/A	SB	CS	SBR	FA	FR	G/POS	TPR
1910	StL-N	119	375	37	77	7	2	2	36	49	39	.205	.312	.251	67	-14	15			.931	-8	*S-117/3-1	-1.9
1911	StL-N	136	515	61	124	11	8	3	46	26	67	.241	.286	.311	69	-23	24			.918	-15	*S-134/3-2	-2.9
1912	StL-N	133	479	73	124	14	7	1	42	39	69	.259	.319	.324	78	-15	26			.934	10	*S-132	0.6
1913	StL-N	22	45	3	13	0	3	0	9	2	2	.289	.347	.422	121	1	1			.848	-3	/S-8,2-4	-0.2
1915	Chi-F	23	54	6	11	1	0	0	4	5	7	.204	.283	.222	46	-5	2			.851	-3	S-16/3-6	-0.7
Total	5	433	1468	180	349	33	20	6	137	121	184	.238	.305	.300	72	-55	68			.924	-19	S-407/3-9,2-4	-5.1

■ **JOE HAUSER** Hauser, Joseph John "Unser Choe" b: 1/12/1899, Milwaukee, Wis. d: 7/11/97, Sheboygan, Wis. BL/TL, 5'10.5", 175 lbs. Deb: 4/18/22

YEAR	TM/L	G	AB	R	H	2B	3B	HR	RBI	BB	SO	AVG	OBP	SLG	PRO+	BR/A	SB	CS	SBR	FA	FR	G/POS	TPR
1922	Phi-A	111	368	61	119	21	5	9	43	30	37	.323	.378	.481	119	10	1	5	-3	.986	-3	1-94	0.0
1923	Phi-A	146	537	93	165	21	9	17	94	69	52	.307	.398	.475	127	22	6	6	-2	.990	-3	*1-146	0.9
1924	Phi-A	149	562	97	162	31	8	27	115	56	52	.288	.358	.516	123	15	7	5	-1	.993	-3	*1-146	0.2
1926	Phi-A	91	229	31	44	10	0	8	36	39	35	.192	.312	.341	66	-12	1	1	-0	.996	0	1-65	-1.5
1928	Phi-A	95	300	61	78	19	5	16	59	52	45	.260	.369	.517	127	11	4	2	0	.986	-6	1-88	-0.2
1929	Cle-A	37	48	8	12	1	1	3	9	4	8	.250	.321	.500	104	0	0	0	0	.986	1	/1-8	0.0
Total	6	629	2044	351	580	103	28	80	356	250	229	.284	.368	.479	117	46	19	19	-6	.990	-14	1-547	-0.6

■ **GEORGE HAUSMANN** Hausmann, George John b: 2/11/16, St.Louis, Mo. BR/TR, 5'5", 145 lbs. Deb: 4/18/44

YEAR	TM/L	G	AB	R	H	2B	3B	HR	RBI	BB	SO	AVG	OBP	SLG	PRO+	BR/A	SB	CS	SBR	FA	FR	G/POS	TPR
1944	NY-N	131	466	70	124	20	4	1	30	40	25	.266	.324	.333	85	-9	3			.960	-7	*2-122	-0.9
1945	NY-N	154	623	98	174	15	8	2	45	73	46	.279	.356	.339	92	-5	7			.968	5	*2-154	1.0
1949	NY-N	16	47	5	6	0	1	0	3	7	6	.128	.241	.170	12	-6	0			.984	-0	2-13	-0.6
Total	3	301	1136	173	304	35	13	3	78	120	77	.268	.338	.329	86	-19	10			.965	-3	2-289	-0.5

■ **CHARLIE HAUTZ** Hautz, Charles A. b: 2/5/1852, St.Louis, Mo. d: 1/24/29, St.Louis, Mo. BR, 5'7", 150 lbs. Deb: 5/4/1875

YEAR	TM/L	G	AB	R	H	2B	3B	HR	RBI	BB	SO	AVG	OBP	SLG	PRO+	BR/A	SB	CS	SBR	FA	FR	G/POS	TPR
1875	RS-n	19	83	5	25	3	0	0	4	0	9	.301	.301	.337	134	3	5	1	1	.921	-1	1-19	0.2
1884	Pit-a	7	24	0	5	0	0	0		3		.208	.296	.208	66	-1				.980	0	/1-5,O-2	-0.1

■ **ROY HAWES** Hawes, Roy Lee b: 7/5/26, Shiloh, Ill. BL/TL, 6'2", 190 lbs. Deb: 9/23/51

YEAR	TM/L	G	AB	R	H	2B	3B	HR	RBI	BB	SO	AVG	OBP	SLG	PRO+	BR/A	SB	CS	SBR	FA	FR	G/POS	TPR
1951	Was-A	3	6	0	1	0	0	0	0	0	1	.167	.167	.167	-10	-1	0	0	0	1.000	-0	/1-1	-0.1

■ **BILL HAWES** Hawes, William Hildreth b: 11/17/1853, Nashua, N.H. d: 6/16/40, Lowell, Mass. BR/TR, 5'10", 155 lbs. Deb: 5/1/1879

YEAR	TM/L	G	AB	R	H	2B	3B	HR	RBI	BB	SO	AVG	OBP	SLG	PRO+	BR/A	SB	CS	SBR	FA	FR	G/POS	TPR
1879	Bos-N	38	155	19	31	3	3	0	9	2	13	.200	.210	.258	52	-8				.828	-3	O-34/C-5	-1.2
1884	Cin-U	79	349	80	97	7	4	4		5		.278	.288	.355	87	-16				.827	-7	O-58,1-21	-2.4
Total	2	117	504	99	128	10	7	4	9	7	13	.254	.264	.325	77	-24				.827	-10	/O-92,1-21,C-5	-3.6

■ **THORNY HAWKES** Hawkes, Thorndike Proctor b: 10/15/1852, Danvers, Mass. d: 2/3/29, Danvers, Mass. BR/TR, 5'8", 135 lbs. Deb: 5/1/1879

YEAR	TM/L	G	AB	R	H	2B	3B	HR	RBI	BB	SO	AVG	OBP	SLG	PRO+	BR/A	SB	CS	SBR	FA	FR	G/POS	TPR
1879	Tro-N	64	250	24	52	6	1	0	20	4	14	.208	.220	.240	55	-11				.896	16	*2-64	0.8
1884	Was-a	38	151	16	42	4	2	0		4		.278	.297	.331	118	3				.917	3	2-38/O-2	0.6
Total	2	102	401	40	94	10	3	0	20	8	14	.234	.249	.274	79	-8				.903	19	2-102/O-2	1.4

■ **CHICKEN HAWKS** Hawks, Nelson Louis b: 2/3/1896, San Francisco, Cal. d: 5/26/73, San Rafael, Cal. BL/TL, 5'11", 167 lbs. Deb: 4/14/21

YEAR	TM/L	G	AB	R	H	2B	3B	HR	RBI	BB	SO	AVG	OBP	SLG	PRO+	BR/A	SB	CS	SBR	FA	FR	G/POS	TPR
1921	NY-A	41	73	16	21	2	3	2	15	5	12	.288	.333	.479	103	-0	0	1	-1	.970	-2	O-15	-0.3
1925	Phi-N	105	320	52	103	15	5	5	45	32	33	.322	.387	.447	103	2	3	6	-3	.986	-0	1-90	-0.5
Total	2	146	393	68	124	17	8	7	60	37	45	.316	.377	.453	103	2	3	7	-3	.986	-2	/1-90,O-15	-0.8

■ **HOWIE HAWORTH** Haworth, Homer Howard "Cully" b: 8/27/1893, Newberg, Ore. d: 1/28/53, Troutdale, Ore. BL/TR, 5'10.5", 165 lbs. Deb: 8/14/15

YEAR	TM/L	G	AB	R	H	2B	3B	HR	RBI	BB	SO	AVG	OBP	SLG	PRO+	BR/A	SB	CS	SBR	FA	FR	G/POS	TPR
1915	Cle-A	7	7	0	1	0	0	0	1	2	2	.143	.333	.143	42	-0	0			.917	-1	/C-5	-0.1

■ **JACK HAYDEN** Hayden, John Francis b: 10/21/1880, Bryn Mawr, Pa. d: 8/3/42, Haverford, Pa. BL/TL, 5'9", Deb: 4/26/01

YEAR	TM/L	G	AB	R	H	2B	3B	HR	RBI	BB	SO	AVG	OBP	SLG	PRO+	BR/A	SB	CS	SBR	FA	FR	G/POS	TPR
1901	Phi-A	51	211	35	56	6	4	0	17	18		.265	.323	.332	78	-6	4			.841	-4	O-50	-1.2
1906	Bos-A	85	322	22	80	6	4	1	14	17		.248	.292	.301	86	-5	6			.973	-1	O-85	-1.2
1908	Chi-N	11	45	3	9	2	0	0	2	1		.200	.217	.244	45	-3	1			1.000	-1	O-11	-0.5
Total	3	147	578	60	145	14	8	1	33	36		.251	.298	.308	80	-14	11			.929	-5	O-146	-2.9

■ **CHARLIE HAYES** Hayes, Charles Dewayne b: 5/29/65, Hattiesburg, Miss. BR/TR, 6', 207 lbs. Deb: 9/11/88

YEAR	TM/L	G	AB	R	H	2B	3B	HR	RBI	BB	SO	AVG	OBP	SLG	PRO+	BR/A	SB	CS	SBR	FA	FR	G/POS	TPR
1988	SF-N	7	11	0	1	0	0	0	0	0	3	.091	.091	.091	-50	-2	0	0	0	1.000	-1	/O-4,3-3	-0.3
1989	SF-N	3	5	0	1	0	0	0	0	0	1	.200	.200	.200	15	-1	0	0	0	1.000	-0	/3-3	-0.1
	Phi-N	84	299	26	77	15	1	8	43	11	49	.258	.284	.395	92	-4	3	1	0	.910	10	3-82	0.7
	Yr	87	304	26	78	15	1	8	43	11	50	.257	.283	.391	91	-5	3	1	0	.911	10	3-85	0.6
1990	Phi-N	152	561	56	145	20	0	10	57	28	91	.258	.296	.348	77	-19	4	4	-1	.957	24	*3-146/1-4,2-1	0.5
1991	Phi-N	142	460	34	106	23	1	12	53	16	75	.230	.258	.363	74	-18	3	3	-1	.958	7	*3-138/S-2	-1.1
1992	NY-A	142	509	52	131	19	2	18	66	28	100	.257	.300	.409	98	-4	3	5	-2	.963	-11	*3-139/1-4	-1.8
1993	Col-N	157	573	89	175	**45**	2	25	98	43	82	.305	.359	.522	114	9	11	6	-0	.954	4	*3-154/S-1	1.3
1994	Col-N	113	423	46	122	23	4	10	50	36	71	.288	.348	.433	88	-8	3	6	-3	.944	1	*3-110	-1.0
1995	Phi-N	141	529	58	146	30	3	11	85	50	88	.276	.343	.406	96	-3	5	1	1	**.963**	-6	*3-141	-0.7
1996	Pit-N	128	459	51	114	21	2	10	62	36	78	.248	.303	.368	74	-18	6	0	2	.950	17	*3-124	0.0
	*NY-A	20	67	7	19	3	0	2	13	1	12	.284	.294	.418	77	-2	0	0	0	1.000	3	3-19	0.0
1997	*NY-A	100	353	39	91	16	0	11	53	40	66	.258	.335	.397	91	-5	3	2	-0	.947	3	3-98/2-5	-0.2
1998	SF-N	111	329	39	94	8	0	12	62	34	61	.286	.353	.419	103	2	2	1	0	.989	-2	3-46,1-45/D-2	-0.2
Total	11	1300	4578	497	1222	223	15	129	642	323	777	.267	.318	.407	91	-72	43	29	-5	.953	49	*3-1203/1-53,2OSD	-2.9

■ **FRANKIE HAYES** Hayes, Franklin Witman "Blimp" b: 10/13/14, Jamesburg, N.J. d: 6/22/55, Point Pleasant, N.J. BR/TR, 6', 185 lbs. Deb: 9/21/33

YEAR	TM/L	G	AB	R	H	2B	3B	HR	RBI	BB	SO	AVG	OBP	SLG	PRO+	BR/A	SB	CS	SBR	FA	FR	G/POS	TPR
1933	Phi-A	3	5	0	0	0	0	0	0	0	2	.000	.000	.000	-99	-1	0	0	0	.889	0	/C-3	-0.1
1934	Phi-A	92	248	24	56	10	0	6	30	20	44	.226	.286	.339	63	-15	2	1	0	.955	-11	C-89	-2.1
1936	Phi-A	144	505	59	137	25	2	10	67	46	58	.271	.335	.388	79	-17	3	5	-2	.972	-22	*C-143	-3.1
1937	Phi-A	60	188	24	49	11	1	10	38	29	34	.261	.359	.489	114	3	0	0	0	.971	-4	C-56	0.2
1938	Phi-A	99	316	56	92	19	3	11	55	54	51	.291	.396	.475	120	11	2	3	-1	.975	-16	C-90	-0.2
1939	Phi-A☆	124	431	66	122	28	5	20	83	40	55	.283	.348	.510	119	10	4	1	1	.978	-12	*C-114	0.5
1940	Phi-A★	136	465	73	143	23	4	16	70	61	59	.308	.389	.477	126	19	9	3	1	.971	-13	*C-134/1-2	1.5

YEAR	TM/L	G	AB	R	H	2B	3B	HR	RBI	BB	SO	AVG	OBP	SLG	PRO+	BR/A	SB	CS	SBR	FA	FR	G/POS	TPR
1941	Phi-A★	126	439	66	123	27	4	12	63	62	56	.280	.369	.442	117	11	2	0	1	.983	-11	*C-123	1.0
1942	Phi-A	21	63	8	15	4	0	0	5	9	8	.238	.333	.302	80	-1	1	1	-0	1.000	-4	C-20	-0.5
	StL-A	56	159	14	40	6	0	2	17	28	39	.252	.364	.327	94	-0	0	0	0	.971	-8	C-51	-0.4
	Yr	77	222	22	55	10	0	2	22	37	47	.248	.355	.320	90	-2	1	1	-0	.979	-12	C-71	-0.9
1943	StL-A	88	250	16	47	7	0	5	30	37	36	.188	.295	.276	66	-10	1	0	0	.983	-9	C-76/1-1	-1.5
1944	Phi-A★	155	581	62	144	18	6	13	78	57	59	.248	.315	.367	96	-4	2	1	0	.982	3	*C-155/1-1	0.9
1945	Phi-A	32	110	12	25	2	1	3	14	18	14	.227	.336	.345	98	0	1	0	0	.994	2	C-32	0.4
	Cle-A†	119	385	39	91	15	6	6	43	53	52	.236	.335	.353	104	2	1	1	-0	.988	2	*C-119	1.2
	Yr	151	495	51	116	17	7	9	57	71	66	.234	.335	.352	103	3	2	1	0	.989	3	*C-151	1.6
1946	Cle-A★	51	156	11	40	12	0	3	18	21	26	.256	.345	.391	112	3	1	3	-2	.981	-1	C-50	0.3
	Chi-A	53	179	15	38	6	0	2	16	29	33	.212	.322	.279	72	-6	1	1	-0	.979	-3	C-52	-0.7
	Yr	104	335	26	78	18	0	5	34	50	59	.233	.332	.331	90	-4	2	4	-2	.980	-4	*C-102	-0.4
1947	Bos-A	5	13	0	2	0	0	0	1	0	1	.154	.154	.154	-13	-2	0	0	0	.917	1	/C-4	0.0
Total	14	1364	4493	545	1164	213	32	119	628	564	627	.259	.343	.400	100	1	30	20	-3	.977	-106	*C-1311/1-4	-2.6
■ **JACKIE HAYES**	Hayes, John J. b: 6/27/1861, Brooklyn, N.Y. TR , Deb: 5/2/1882																						
1882	Wor-N	78	326	27	88	22	4	4	54	6	26	.270	.283	.399	113	4				.855	-10	*O-58,C-15/3-5,S-1	-0.5
1883	Pit-a	85	351	41	92	23	5	3		15		.262	.292	.382	121	8				.911	-18	C-62,O-18/S-5,12	-0.5
1884	Pit-a	33	124	11	28	6	1	0		4		.226	.256	.290	77	-3				.912	-1	C-24/1-5,O-3,2-1	-0.2
	Bro-a	16	51	4	12	3	0	0		3		.235	.278	.294	86	-1				.946	6	C-14/O-2	0.6
	Yr	49	175	15	40	9	1	0		7		.229	.262	.291	79	-4				.925	6	C-38/1-5,O-5,2-1	0.4
1885	Bro-a	42	137	10	18	3	0	0	10	5		.131	.179	.153	6	-14				.900	-2	C-42	-1.2
1886	Was-N	26	89	8	17	3	0	3	9	4	23	.191	.226	.326	70	-3	0			.926	-4	C-14,O-12/2-1	-0.6
1887	Bal-a	8	28	2	4	3	0	0	3	0		.143	.143	.250	9	-3	0			.250	-4	/O-4,3-3,C-1	-0.6
1890	Bro-P	12	42	3	8	0	0	0	5	2	4	.190	.227	.190	11	-5	0			.867	-3	/O-6,S-3,C-2,2-1	-0.7
Total	7	300	1148	106	267	63	10	10	81	39	53	.233	.260	.331	87	-18	0			.906	-36	C-174,O-103/1S32	-3.7
■ **MIKE HAYES**	Hayes, Michael b: 1853, Cleveland, Ohio 5′7.5″, 170 lbs. Deb: 9/9/1876																						
1876	NY-N	5	21	1	3	0	2	0	2	0	0	.143	.143	.333	63	-1				.882	0	/O-5	-0.1
■ **JACKIE HAYES**	Hayes, Minter Carney b: 7/19/06, Clanton, Ala. d: 2/9/83, Birmingham, Ala. BR/TR, 5′10.5″, 165 lbs. Deb: 8/5/27																						
1927	Was-A	10	29	2	7	0	0	0	2	1	2	.241	.267	.241	33	-3	0	0	0	.969	-1	/S-8,3-1	-0.3
1928	Was-A	60	210	30	54	7	3	0	22	5	10	.257	.274	.319	56	-14	3	0	1	.974	8	2-41,S-15/3-2	-0.2
1929	Was-A	123	424	52	117	20	3	2	57	24	29	.276	.316	.351	71	-18	4	5	-2	.945	3	3-63,2-57/S-2	-1.1
1930	Was-A	51	166	25	47	7	2	1	20	7	8	.283	.312	.367	71	-7	2	3	-1	.981	8	2-29/3-9,1-8	0.1
1931	Was-A	38	108	11	24	2	1	0	8	6	4	.222	.263	.259	38	-10	2	0	1	.962	-4	2-19/3-8,S-3	-1.1
1932	Chi-A	117	475	53	122	20	5	2	54	30	28	.257	.302	.333	69	-23	7	4	-0	.967	1	2-97,S-10,3-10	-1.5
1933	Chi-A	138	535	65	138	23	5	2	47	55	36	.258	.331	.331	79	-16	2	3	-1	.981	10	*2-138	0.1
1934	Chi-A	62	226	19	58	9	1	1	31	23	20	.257	.325	.319	65	-12	3	2	-0	.980	-9	2-61	-1.6
1935	Chi-A	89	329	45	88	14	0	4	45	29	15	.267	.327	.347	72	-13	3	1	0	.966	-6	2-85	-1.2
1936	Chi-A	108	417	53	130	34	3	5	84	35	25	.312	.366	.444	96	-4	4	2	0	.979	**17**	2-89,S-13/3-2	1.8
1937	Chi-A	143	573	63	131	27	4	2	79	41	37	.229	.282	.300	47	-47	1	6	-3	.984	21	*2-143	-1.9
1938	Chi-A	62	238	40	78	21	2	1	20	24	6	.328	.389	.445	106	2	3	2	-0	.976	-3	2-61	0.2
1939	Chi-A	72	269	34	67	12	3	0	23	27	10	.249	.320	.316	62	-15	0	3	-2	.974	5	2-69	-0.8
1940	Chi-A	18	41	2	8	0	1	0	1	2	11	.195	.233	.244	23	-5	0	0	0	.981	-0	2-15	-0.4
Total	14	1091	4040	494	1069	196	33	20	493	309	241	.265	.318	.344	70	-184	34	31	-8	.976	52	2-904/3-95,S-51,1-8	-7.9
■ **VON HAYES**	Hayes, Von Francis b: 8/31/58, Stockton, Cal. BL/TR, 6′5″, 185 lbs. Deb: 4/14/81																						
1981	Cle-A	43	109	21	28	8	2	1	17	14	10	.257	.352	.394	116	3	8	1	2	.939	1	D-21,O-13/3-5	0.4
1982	Cle-A	150	527	65	132	25	3	14	82	42	63	.250	.311	.389	91	-7	32	13	2	.981	6	*O-139/3-5,1-4	-0.3
1983	*Phi-N	124	351	45	93	9	5	6	32	36	55	.265	.338	.370	97	-1	20	12	-1	.972	-19	*O-103	-2.5
1984	Phi-N	152	561	85	164	27	6	16	67	59	84	.292	.360	.447	124	17	48	13	7	.988	-8	*O-148	1.3
1985	Phi-N	152	570	76	150	30	4	13	70	61	99	.263	.334	.398	101	1	21	8	2	.984	-6	*O-146	-0.8
1986	Phi-N	158	610	**107**	186	**46**	2	19	98	74	77	.305	.381	.480	131	27	24	12	0	.990	2	*1-134,O-31	1.9
1987	Phi-N	158	556	84	154	36	5	21	84	121	77	.277	.406	.473	128	26	16	7	1	.990	-13	*1-144,O-32	0.3
1988	Phi-N	104	367	43	100	28	2	6	45	49	59	.272	.360	.409	118	9	20	9	1	.990	-1	1-85,O-16/3-3	0.1
1989	Phi-N★	154	540	93	140	27	2	26	78	101	103	.259	.380	.461	139	30	28	7	4	.980	3	*O-128,1-30,3-10	3.4
1990	Phi-N	129	467	70	122	14	3	17	73	87	81	.261	.382	.413	119	15	16	7	1	.979	5	*O-127	1.8
1991	Phi-N	77	284	43	64	15	1	0	21	31	42	.225	.308	.285	69	-11	9	2	2	.990	11	O-72	0.0
1992	Cal-A	94	307	35	69	17	1	4	29	37	54	.225	.308	.326	77	-9	11	6	-0	.983	-1	O-85/1-4,D-5	-1.3
Total	12	1495	5249	767	1402	282	36	143	696	712	804	.267	.357	.416	113	101	253	97	18	.983	-20	*O-1040,1-401/D3	4.3
■ **BILL HAYES**	Hayes, William Ernest b: 10/24/57, Cheverly, Md. BR/TR, 6′, 195 lbs. Deb: 9/30/80 C																						
1980	Chi-N	4	9	0	2	1	0	0	0	0	3	.222	.222	.333	49	-1	0	0	0	1.000	-0	/C-3	-0.1
1981	Chi-N	1	0	0	0	0	0	0	0	0	0	—	—	—	—	0	0	0	0	.000	0	/C-1	0.0
Total	2	5	9	0	2	1	0	0	0	0	3	.222	.222	.333	49	-1	0	0	0	1.000	-0	/C-4	-0.1
■ **RED HAYWORTH**	Hayworth, Myron Claude b: 5/14/15, High Point, N.C. BR/TR, 6′1.5″, 200 lbs. Deb: 4/21/44 F																						
1944	*StL-A	90	270	20	60	11	1	1	25	10	13	.222	.253	.281	50	-18	0	0	0	.967	1	C-87	-1.4
1945	StL-A	56	160	7	31	4	0	0	17	7	6	.194	.228	.219	28	-15	0	2	-1	.992	4	C-55	-1.0
Total	2	146	430	27	91	15	1	1	42	17	19	.212	.243	.258	42	-33	0	2	-1	.976	4	C-142	-2.4
■ **RAY HAYWORTH**	Hayworth, Raymond Hall b: 1/29/04, High Point, N.C. BR/TR, 6′, 180 lbs. Deb: 6/27/26 FC																						
1926	Det-A	12	11	1	3	0	0	0	5	1	1	.273	.333	.273	59	-1	0	0	0	1.000	-1	/C-8	-0.1
1929	Det-A	14	43	5	11	0	0	0	4	3	8	.256	.304	.256	45	-3	0	0	0	.951	0	C-14	-0.2
1930	Det-A	77	227	24	63	15	4	0	22	20	19	.278	.336	.379	79	-7	0	2	-1	.977	-13	C-76	-1.3
1931	Det-A	88	273	28	70	10	3	0	25	19	27	.256	.307	.315	62	-15	0	1	-1	.973	4	C-88	-0.6
1932	Det-A	109	338	41	99	20	2	2	44	31	22	.293	.354	.382	87	-6	1	1	-0	.991	3	*C-106	0.2
1933	Det-A	134	425	37	104	14	3	1	45	35	28	.245	.302	.299	59	-25	0	0	0	.994	2	*C-133	-1.5
1934	*Det-A	54	167	20	49	5	2	0	27	16	22	.293	.355	.347	82	-4	0	2	-1	.984	7	C-54	0.3
1935	Det-A	51	175	22	54	14	2	0	22	9	14	.309	.342	.411	98	-1	0	0	0	.996	11	C-48	1.1
1936	Det-A	81	250	31	60	10	0	1	30	39	18	.240	.347	.292	59	-15	0	0	0	**.988**	-4	C-81	-1.4
1937	Det-A	30	78	9	21	2	0	1	8	14	15	.269	.394	.333	83	-1	0	0	0	.992	6	C-28	0.5
1938	Det-A	8	19	1	4	0	0	0	5	3	4	.211	.318	.211	33	-2	1	0	0	.971	2	/C-7	0.1
	Bro-N	5	4	0	0	0	0	0	0	1	1	.000	.200	.000	-40	-1	0			1.000	0	/C-3	-0.1
1939	Bro-N	21	26	0	4	2	0	0	1	4	7	.154	.267	.231	34	-2	0			1.000	1	C-18	-0.1
	NY-N	5	13	1	3	0	0	0	0	0	1	.231	.231	.231	24	-1	0			1.000	1	/C-5	0.0
	Yr	26	39	1	7	2	0	0	1	4	8	.179	.256	.231	31	-4	0			1.000	2	C-23	-0.1
1942	StL-A	1	1	0	1	0	0	0	0	0	0	1.000	1.000	1.000	456	0	0	0	0	.000	0	H	0.0
1944	Bro-N	7	10	0	0	0	0	0	0	2	1	.000	.167	.000	-51	-2	0			1.000	2	/C-6	0.0
1945	Bro-N	2	2	0	0	0	0	0	0	1	0	.000	.333	.000	-3	-0	0			1.000	0	/C-2	0.0
Total	15	699	2062	220	546	92	16	5	238	198	188	.265	.331	.332	71	-87	2	6		.987	20	C-677	-3.1
■ **DRUNGO HAZEWOOD**	Hazewood, Drungo La Rue b: 9/2/59, Mobile, Ala. BR/TR, 6′3″, 210 lbs. Deb: 9/19/80																						
1980	Bal-A	6	5	1	0	0	0	0	0	0	4	.000	.000	.000	-99	-1	0	0	0	1.000	-1	/O-3	-0.2
■ **BOB HAZLE**	Hazle, Robert Sidney "Hurricane" b: 12/9/30, Laurens, S.C. d: 4/25/92, Columbia, S.C. BL/TR, 6′, 190 lbs. Deb: 9/8/55																						
1955	Cin-N	6	13	0	3	0	0	0	0	0	3	.231	.231	.231	22	-1	0	0	0	1.000	2	/O-3	0.0
1957	*Mil-N	41	134	26	54	12	0	7	27	18	15	.403	.477	.649	214	22	1	3	-2	.906	-5	O-40	1.3
1958	Mil-N	20	56	6	10	0	0	0	5	9	4	.179	.303	.179	34	-5	0	0	0	1.000	-1	O-20	-0.7

YEAR	TM/L	G	AB	R	H	2B	3B	HR	RBI	BB	SO	AVG	OBP	SLG	PRO+	BR/A	SB	CS	SBR	FA	FR	G/POS	TPR
	Det-A	43	58	5	14	2	0	2	5	5	13	.241	.302	.379	80	-2	0	0	0	1.000	-2	O-12	-0.4
Total	3	110	261	37	81	14	0	9	37	32	35	.310	.390	.467	135	14	1	3	-2	.951	-7	/O-75	0.2
■ DOC HAZLETON	Hazleton, Willard Carpenter b: 8/28/1876, Strafford, Vt. d: 3/10/41, Burlington, Vt. Deb: 4/17/02																						
1902	StL-N	7	23	0	3	0	0	0	0	2		.130	.231	.130	12	-2	0			.973	0	/1-7	-0.3
■ FRAN HEALY	Healy, Francis Xavier b: 9/6/46, Holyoke, Mass. BR/TR, 6'5", 220 lbs. Deb: 9/3/69																						
1969	KC-A	6	10	0	4	1	0	0	0	0	5	.400	.400	.500	149	1	0	0	0	1.000	0	/C-5	0.1
1971	SF-N	47	93	10	26	3	0	2	11	15	24	.280	.380	.376	117	3	1	0	0	.966	-2	C-22	0.2
1972	SF-N	45	99	12	15	4	0	1	8	13	24	.152	.257	.222	37	-8	0	1	-1	.995	7	C-43	-0.1
1973	KC-A	95	279	25	77	15	2	6	34	31	56	.276	.348	.409	104	2	3	4	-2	.979	-3	C-92/D-1	0.1
1974	KC-A	139	445	59	112	24	2	9	53	62	73	.252	.344	.375	101	2	16	8	0	.977	-7	*C-138	0.1
1975	KC-A	56	188	16	48	5	2	2	18	14	19	.255	.307	.335	79	-5	4	3	-1	.982	-7	C-51/D-4	-1.1
1976	KC-A	8	24	2	3	0	0	0	1	4	10	.125	.250	.125	12	-3	2	0	1	1.000	0	/C-6,D-1	-0.2
	NY-A	46	120	10	32	3	0	0	9	9	17	.267	.318	.292	80	-3	3	1	0	.983	3	C-31/D-9	0.1
	Yr	54	144	12	35	3	0	0	10	13	27	.243	.306	.264	68	-5	5	1	1	.987	3	C-37,D-10	-0.1
1977	NY-A	27	67	10	15	5	0	0	7	6	13	.224	.288	.299	61	-4	1	0	0	.971	-0	C-26	-0.3
1978	NY-A	1	1	0	0	0	0	0	0	0	1	.000	.000	.000	-99	-0	0	0	0	.000	0	/C-1	0.0
Total	9	470	1326	144	332	60	6	20	141	154	242	.250	.329	.350	90	-16	30	17	-1	.980	-8	C-415/D-15	-1.1
■ FRANCIS HEALY	Healy, Francis Xavier Paul b: 6/29/10, Holyoke, Mass. BR/TR, 5'9.5", 175 lbs. Deb: 4/29/30																						
1930	NY-N	7	2	2	0	0	0	0	0	0	0	.000	.000	.000	-99	-1	0			.000	0	/C-1	-0.1
1931	NY-N	6	7	1	1	0	0	0	0	0	0	.143	.143	.143	-24	-1	0			1.000	0	/C-4	-0.1
1932	NY-N	14	32	5	8	2	0	0	4	2	8	.250	.294	.313	65	-2	0			.960	2	C-11	0.1
1934	StL-N	15	13	1	4	1	0	0	1	0	2	.308	.308	.385	79	-0	0			1.000	1	/C-2,3-1,O-1	0.0
Total	4	42	54	9	13	3	0	0	5	2	10	.241	.268	.296	51	-4	0			.969	3	/C-18,O-1,3-1	-0.1
■ THOMAS HEALY	Healy, Thomas Fitzgerald b: 10/30/1895, Altoona, Pa. d: 1/15/74, Cleveland, Ohio BR/TR, 6', 172 lbs. Deb: 7/13/15																						
1915	Phi-A	23	77	11	17	1	0	0	5	6	4	.221	.310	.234	65	-3	0	4	-2	.933	5	3-17/S-1	0.0
1916	Phi-A	6	23	4	6	1	1	0	2	1	2	.261	.320	.391	119	0	1			.947	-1	/3-6	0.0
Total	2	29	100	15	23	2	1	0	7	7	6	.230	.313	.270	77	-3	1	4		.936	4	/3-23,S-1	0.0
■ CHARLIE HEARD	Heard, Charles b: 1/30/1872, Philadelphia, Pa. d: 2/20/45, Philadelphia, Pa. BR/TR, 6'2", 190 lbs. Deb: 7/14/1890																						
1890	Pit-N	12	43	2	8	2	0	0	0	1	15	.186	.205	.233	31	-4	0			.600	-3	/O-6,P-6	-0.4
■ ED HEARN	Hearn, Edmund b: 9/17/1888, Ventura, Cal. d: 9/8/52, Sawtelle, Cal. BR/TR, 5'9", 160 lbs. Deb: 6/9/10																						
1910	Bos-A	2	2	0	0	0	0	0	0	0		.000	.000	.000	-98	-0	0			1.000	2	/S-2	0.1
■ ED HEARN	Hearn, Edward John b: 8/23/60, Stuart, Fla. BR/TR, 6'3", 215 lbs. Deb: 5/17/86																						
1986	NY-N	49	136	16	36	5	0	4	10	12	19	.265	.324	.390	99	-0	0	1	-1	.987	-6	C-45	-0.5
1987	KC-A	6	17	2	5	2	0	0	3	4	2	.294	.429	.412	121	1	0	0	0	1.000	-2	/C-5	-0.1
1988	KC-A	7	18	1	4	2	0	0	1	0	1	.222	.222	.333	53	-1	0	0	0	1.000	-0	/C-4,D-2	-0.1
Total	3	62	171	19	45	9	0	4	14	16	22	.263	.326	.386	97	-1	0	1	-1	.989	-8	/C-54,D-2	-0.7
■ HUGHIE HEARNE	Hearne, Hugh Joseph b: 4/18/1873, Troy, N.Y. d: 9/22/32, Troy, N.Y. BR/TR, 5'8", 182 lbs. Deb: 8/29/01																						
1901	Bro-N	2	5	1	2	0	0	0	3	0		.400	.400	.400	129	0	0			1.000	0	/C-2	0.0
1902	Bro-N	66	231	22	65	10	0	0	28	16		.281	.336	.325	103	1	3			.966	-10	C-65	-0.2
1903	Bro-N	26	57	8	16	3	2	0	4	3		.281	.328	.404	111	1	2			.960	3	C-17/1-2	0.5
Total	3	94	293	31	83	13	2	0	35	19		.283	.335	.341	105	2	5			.965	-7	/C-84,1-2	0.3
■ JEFF HEARRON	Hearron, Jeffrey Vernon b: 11/19/61, Long Beach, Cal. BR/TR, 6'1", 195 lbs. Deb: 8/25/85																						
1985	*Tor-A	4	7	0	1	0	0	0	0	0	2	.143	.143	.143	-21	-1	0	0	0	1.000	2	/C-4	0.0
1986	Tor-A	12	23	2	5	1	0	0	4	3	7	.217	.308	.261	55	-1	0	0	0	.980	1	C-12	0.0
Total	2	16	30	2	6	1	0	0	4	3	9	.200	.273	.233	39	-2	0	0	0	.985	2	/C-16	0.0
■ JEFF HEATH	Heath, John Geoffrey b: 4/1/15, Ft.William, Ont., Canada d: 12/9/75, Seattle, Wash. BL/TR, 5'11.5", 200 lbs. Deb: 9/13/36																						
1936	Cle-A	12	41	6	14	3	3	1	8	3	4	.341	.386	.634	147	3	1	0	0	1.000	-3	O-12	0.0
1937	Cle-A	20	61	8	14	1	4	0	8	0	9	.230	.230	.377	50	-5	0	1	-1	1.000	-1	O-14	-0.6
1938	Cle-A	126	502	104	172	31	**18**	21	112	33	55	.343	.383	.602	146	32	3	1	0	.974	1	*O-122	2.6
1939	Cle-A	121	431	64	126	31	7	14	69	41	64	.292	.354	.494	119	10	8	4	0	.964	6	*O-108	1.1
1940	Cle-A	100	356	55	78	16	3	14	50	40	62	.219	.298	.399	81	-11	5	3	-0	.971	2	O-90	-1.4
1941	Cle-A★	151	585	89	199	32	**20**	24	123	50	69	.340	.396	.586	165	51	18	12	-2	.949	-4	*O-151	3.4
1942	Cle-A	147	568	82	158	37	13	10	76	62	66	.278	.350	.442	130	20	9	9	-3	.980	2	*O-146	1.2
1943	Cle-A★	118	424	58	116	22	6	18	79	63	58	.274	.369	.481	157	30	5	8	-3	.968	-4	*O-111	1.8
1944	Cle-A†	60	151	20	50	5	2	5	33	18	12	.331	.402	.490	160	12	0	1	-1	.952	-1	O-37	0.9
1945	Cle-A†	102	370	60	113	16	7	15	61	56	39	.305	.398	.508	169	33	3	1	0	.973	-4	*O-101	2.5
1946	Was-A	48	166	23	47	12	3	4	27	36	36	.283	.411	.464	153	13	0	4	-2	.969	-2	O-47	0.6
	StL-A	86	316	46	87	20	4	12	57	37	37	.275	.353	.478	124	10	0	2	-1	.962	-6	O-83	-0.2
	Yr	134	482	69	134	32	7	16	84	73	73	.278	.374	.473	134	22	0	6	-4	.965	-9	*O-130	0.4
1947	StL-A	141	491	81	123	20	7	27	85	88	87	.251	.366	.485	133	21	2	1	0	.987	-3	*O-140	1.1
1948	Bos-N	115	364	64	116	26	5	20	76	51	46	.319	.404	.582	167	33	2			**.991**	-2	*O-106	2.6
1949	Bos-N	36	111	17	34	7	0	9	23	15	26	.306	.389	.613	174	11	0			.983	-2	O-31	0.8
Total	14	1383	4937	777	1447	279	102	194	887	593	670	.293	.370	.509	140	262	56	47		.972	-20	*O-1299	16.4
■ KELLY HEATH	Heath, Kelly Mark b: 9/4/57, Plattsburgh, N.Y. BR/TR, 5'7", 155 lbs. Deb: 4/20/82																						
1982	KC-A	1	1	0	0	0	0	0	0	0	0	.000	.000	.000	-99	-0	0	0	0	1.000	1	/2-1	0.1
■ MIKE HEATH	Heath, Michael Thomas b: 2/5/55, Tampa, Fla. BR/TR, 5'11", 190 lbs. Deb: 6/3/78																						
1978	*NY-A	33	92	6	21	3	1	0	8	4	9	.228	.268	.283	56	-5	0	0	0	.970	3	C-33	-0.2
1979	Oak-A	74	258	19	66	8	0	3	27	17	18	.256	.309	.322	75	-9	1	0	0	.978	-1	O-46,C-22/3-7,D-3	-1.1
1980	Oak-A	92	305	27	74	10	2	1	33	16	28	.243	.280	.298	63	-16	3	3	-1	.986	8	C-47,D-31/O-8	-0.8
1981	*Oak-A	84	301	26	71	7	1	8	30	13	36	.236	.270	.346	80	-9	3	3	-1	.978	4	C-78/O-6	-0.3
1982	Oak-A	101	318	43	77	18	4	3	39	27	36	.242	.301	.352	82	-8	8	3	1	.973	-8	C-90,O-10/3-5	-1.2
1983	Oak-A	96	345	45	97	17	0	6	33	18	59	.281	.319	.383	98	-2	3	4	-2	.973	-10	C-80,O-24/3-2,D-2	-1.1
1984	Oak-A	140	475	49	118	21	5	13	64	26	72	.248	.289	.396	94	-6	7	4	-0	.986	-19	*C-108,O-45/3-2,S-1	-2.1
1985	Oak-A	138	436	71	109	18	6	13	55	41	63	.250	.316	.408	104	2	7	7	-2	.981	-13	*C-112,O-35,3-13	-0.9
1986	StL-N	65	190	19	39	8	1	4	25	23	36	.205	.294	.321	70	-8	2	3	-1	.967	-7	C-63/O-2	-1.2
	Det-A	30	98	11	26	3	0	4	11	4	17	.265	.294	.418	92	-1	4	1	1	.987	-2	C-29/3-1	-0.1
1987	*Det-A	93	270	34	76	16	0	8	33	21	42	.281	.340	.430	107	3	1	5	-3	.989	2	C-67,O-24/1-4,3S2	0.5
1988	Det-A	86	219	24	54	7	2	5	18	18	32	.247	.307	.365	91	-3	1	0	0	.984	-1	C-75/O-9	0.1
1989	Det-A	122	396	38	104	16	2	10	43	24	71	.263	.311	.389	98	-2	7	1	2	.986	0	*C-117/3-4,O-3,D-1	0.6
1990	Det-A	122	370	46	100	18	2	7	38	19	71	.270	.313	.386	94	-4	7	6	-2	.980	-2	*C-117/O-3,S-1,D-2	0.0
1991	Atl-N	49	139	4	29	3	1	1	12	7	26	.209	.252	.266	43	-10	0	0	0	.991	-0	C-45	-0.9
Total	14	1325	4212	462	1061	173	27	86	469	278	616	.252	.302	.367	87	-79	54	40	-8	.981	-46	*C-1083,O-215/D31S2	-8.7
■ MICKEY HEATH	Heath, Minor Wilson b: 10/30/03, Toledo, Ohio d: 7/30/86, Dallas, Tex. BL/TL, 6', 175 lbs. Deb: 4/18/31																						
1931	Cin-N	7	26	2	7	0	0	0	3	2	5	.269	.321	.269	64	-1	0			1.000	-0	/1-7	-0.2
1932	Cin-N	39	134	14	27	1	3	0	15	20	23	.201	.310	.254	55	-8	0			.991	2	1-39	-0.9
Total	2	46	160	16	34	1	3	0	18	22	28	.213	.311	.256	57	-9	0			.992	2	/1-46	-1.1
■ TOMMY HEATH	Heath, Thomas George b: 8/18/13, Akron, Col. d: 2/26/67, Los Gatos, Cal. BR/TR, 5'10", 185 lbs. Deb: 4/23/35																						
1935	StL-A	47	93	10	22	3	0	0	9	20	13	.237	.372	.269	65	-4	0	0	0	.982	-2	C-37	-0.4

YEAR	TM/L	G	AB	R	H	2B	3B	HR	RBI	BB	SO	AVG	OBP	SLG	PRO+	BR/A	SB	CS	SBR	FA	FR	G/POS	TPR
1937	StL-A	17	43	4	10	0	2	1	3	10	3	.233	.377	.395	94	-0	0	0	0	1.000	-0	C-14	0.0
1938	StL-A	70	194	22	44	13	0	2	22	35	24	.227	.345	.325	69	-9	0	1	-1	.986	7	C-65	0.0
Total	3	134	330	36	76	16	2	3	34	65	40	.230	.357	.318	71	-13	0	1	-1	.987	5	C-116	-0.4

■ BILL HEATH

Heath, William Chris b: 3/10/39, Yuba City, Cal. BL/TR, 5'8", 175 lbs. Deb: 10/3/65

YEAR	TM/L	G	AB	R	H	2B	3B	HR	RBI	BB	SO	AVG	OBP	SLG	PRO+	BR/A	SB	CS	SBR	FA	FR	G/POS	TPR
1965	Chi-A	1	1	0	0	0	0	0	0	0	0	.000	.000	.000	-99	-0	0	0	0	.000	0	H	0.0
1966	Hou-N	55	123	12	37	6	0	0	8	9	11	.301	.353	.350	103	1	1	0	0	.995	-1	C-37	0.2
1967	Hou-N	9	11	0	1	0	0	0	0	4	3	.091	.333	.091	28	-1	0	0	0	1.000	1	/C-5	0.0
	Det-A	20	32	0	4	0	0	0	4	1	4	.125	.152	.125	-17	-5	0	0	0	1.000	1	/C-7	-0.3
1969	Chi-N	27	32	1	5	0	1	0	1	12	4	.156	.386	.219	65	-1	0	0	0	.979	0	/C-9	-0.1
Total	4	112	199	13	47	6	1	0	13	26	22	.236	.327	.276	73	-6	1	0	0	.993	1	/C-58	-0.2

■ CLIFF HEATHCOTE

Heathcote, Clifton Earl b: 1/24/1898, Glen Rock, Pa. d: 1/19/39, York, Pa. BL/TL, 5'10.5", 160 lbs. Deb: 6/4/18

YEAR	TM/L	G	AB	R	H	2B	3B	HR	RBI	BB	SO	AVG	OBP	SLG	PRO+	BR/A	SB	CS	SBR	FA	FR	G/POS	TPR
1918	StL-N	88	348	37	90	12	3	4	32	20	40	.259	.301	.345	100	-1	12			.934	-4	O-87	-1.1
1919	StL-N	114	401	53	112	13	4	1	29	20	41	.279	.315	.339	103	1	27			.967	-3	*O-101/1-2	-1.0
1920	StL-N	133	489	55	139	18	8	3	56	25	31	.284	.320	.372	102	0	21	14	-2	.964	10	*O-129	-0.1
1921	StL-N	62	156	18	38	6	2	0	9	10	9	.244	.293	.308	61	-9	7	5	-1	.926	-8	O-51	-2.1
1922	StL-N	34	98	11	24	5	2	0	14	9	4	.245	.315	.337	71	-4	0	2	-1	.950	2	O-32	-0.5
	Chi-N	76	243	37	68	8	7	1	34	18	15	.280	.330	.383	82	-7	5	2	0	.986	-1	O-60	-1.2
	Yr	110	341	48	92	13	9	1	48	27	19	.270	.325	.370	79	-11	5	4	-1	.971	0	O-92	-1.7
1923	Chi-N	117	393	48	98	14	3	1	27	25	22	.249	.298	.308	60	-23	32	17	-1	.980	4	*O-112	-2.5
1924	Chi-N	113	392	66	121	19	7	0	30	28	28	.309	.356	.393	100	0	26	24	-7	.979	-2	*O-111	-1.6
1925	Chi-N	109	380	57	100	14	5	5	39	39	26	.263	.343	.366	80	-11	15	11	-2	.970	14	O-99	-0.5
1926	Chi-N	139	510	98	141	33	3	10	53	58	30	.276	.353	.412	104	3	18			**.985**	13	*O-133	0.7
1927	Chi-N	83	228	28	67	12	4	2	25	20	16	.294	.359	.408	105	2	6			.987	8	O-57	0.7
1928	Chi-N	67	137	26	39	8	0	3	18	17	12	.285	.364	.409	103	1	6			.973	-2	O-39	-0.4
1929	*Chi-N	82	224	45	70	17	0	2	31	25	17	.313	.384	.415	98	-0	9			.985	3	O-52	-0.1
1930	Chi-N	70	150	30	39	10	1	9	18	18	15	.260	.343	.520	104	0	4			.986	-2	O-35	-0.3
1931	Cin-N	90	252	24	65	15	6	0	28	32	16	.258	.342	.365	96	-1	3			.989	12	O-59	0.7
1932	Cin-N	8	3	3	0	0	0	0	0	0	0	.000	.000	.000	-99	-1	0			.000	0	H	-0.1
	Phi-N	30	39	7	11	2	0	1	5	3	3	.282	.333	.410	88	-1	0			.962	-0	/1-7	-0.1
	Yr	38	42	10	11	2	0	1	5	3	3	.262	.311	.381	78	-1	0			.962	-0	/1-7	-0.2
Total	15	1415	4443	643	1222	206	55	42	448	367	325	.275	.333	.375	92	-51	191	75		.971	43	*O-1157/1-9	-9.5

■ RICHIE HEBNER

Hebner, Richard Joseph b: 11/26/47, Boston, Mass. BL/TR, 6'1", 197 lbs. Deb: 9/23/68 C

YEAR	TM/L	G	AB	R	H	2B	3B	HR	RBI	BB	SO	AVG	OBP	SLG	PRO+	BR/A	SB	CS	SBR	FA	FR	G/POS	TPR
1968	Pit-N	2	1	0	0	0	0	0	0	0	0	.000	.000	.000	-99	-0	0	0	0	.000	0	H	0.0
1969	Pit-N	129	459	72	138	23	4	8	47	53	53	.301	.383	.420	127	18	4	1	1	.944	3	*3-124/1-1	2.3
1970	*Pit-N	120	420	60	122	24	8	11	46	42	48	.290	.365	.464	123	13	2	3	-1	.940	1	*3-117	1.2
1971	*Pit-N	112	388	50	105	17	8	17	67	32	68	.271	.331	.487	130	14	2	2	-1	.949	-8	*3-108	0.4
1972	*Pit-N	124	427	63	128	24	4	19	72	52	54	.300	.384	.508	155	31	0	0	0	.969	-15	*3-121	1.5
1973	Pit-N	144	509	73	138	28	1	25	74	56	60	.271	.348	.477	130	19	0	1	-1	.939	-14	*3-139	0.4
1974	*Pit-N	146	550	97	160	21	6	18	68	60	53	.291	.367	.449	132	23	0	3	-2	.937	-6	*3-141	1.5
1975	*Pit-N	128	472	65	116	16	4	15	57	43	48	.246	.322	.392	98	-2	0	1	-1	.946	-15	*3-126	-1.9
1976	Pit-N	132	434	60	108	21	3	8	51	47	39	.249	.328	.366	96	-2	0	3	-2	.953	-10	*3-126	-1.5
1977	*Phi-N	118	397	67	113	17	4	18	62	61	46	.285	.384	.484	125	15	7	8	-3	.991	2	*1-103,3-13/2-1	0.9
1978	*Phi-N	137	435	61	123	22	3	17	71	53	58	.283	.372	.464	131	19	4	7	-3	.994	-2	*1-117,3-19/2-1	0.8
1979	NY-N	136	473	54	127	25	2	10	79	59	59	.268	.359	.393	109	7	3	1	0	.940	-7	*3-134/1-6	-0.1
1980	Det-A	104	341	48	99	10	7	12	82	38	45	.290	.365	.466	123	11	0	3	-2	.998	-5	1-61,3-32/D-5	0.0
1981	Det-A	78	226	19	51	8	2	5	28	27	28	.226	.314	.345	87	-4	1	2	-1	.995	-3	1-61,D-11	-1.2
1982	Det-A	68	179	25	49	6	0	8	18	25	21	.274	.363	.441	119	5	1	1	-0	.990	2	1-40,D-20	0.4
	Pit-N	25	70	6	21	2	0	2	12	5	3	.300	.347	.414	109	1	4	0	1	.964	-2	O-21/1-4,3-1	-0.1
1983	Pit-N	78	162	23	43	4	1	5	26	17	28	.265	.339	.395	100	0	8	3	1	.967	-6	3-40/1-7,O-7	-0.6
1984	*Chi-N	44	81	12	27	3	0	2	8	10	15	.333	.407	.444	127	3	1	0	0	.963	-2	3-14/1-3,O-3	0.2
1985	Chi-N	83	120	10	26	2	0	3	22	7	15	.217	.266	.308	54	-7	0	1	-1	.991	-0	1-12/3-7,O-1	-0.9
Total	18	1908	6144	865	1694	273	57	203	890	687	741	.276	.356	.438	120	164	38	40	-13	.946	-85	*3-1262,1-415/DO2	3.3

■ MIKE HECHINGER

Hechinger, Michael Vincent b: 2/14/1890, Chicago, Ill. d: 8/13/67, Chicago, Ill. BR/TR, 6', 175 lbs. Deb: 9/27/12

YEAR	TM/L	G	AB	R	H	2B	3B	HR	RBI	BB	SO	AVG	OBP	SLG	PRO+	BR/A	SB	CS	SBR	FA	FR	G/POS	TPR
1912	Chi-N	2	3	0	0	0	0	0	0	2	0	.000	.400	.000	14	-0	0			1.000	0	/C-2	0.0
1913	Chi-N	2	2	0	0	0	0	0	0	0	0	.000	.000	.000	-99	-1	0			.000	0	H	-0.1
	Bro-N	9	11	1	2	1	0	0	0	0	2	.182	.182	.273	28	-1	0			1.000	-1	/C-4	-0.2
	Yr	11	13	1	2	1	0	0	0	0	2	.154	.154	.231	9	-2	0			1.000	-1	/C-4	-0.3
Total	2	13	16	1	2	1	0	0	0	2	2	.125	.222	.188	16	-2	0			1.000	-1	/C-6	-0.3

■ GUY HECKER

Hecker, Guy Jackson b: 4/3/1856, Youngsville, Pa. d: 12/3/38, Wooster, Ohio BR/TR, 6', 190 lbs. Deb: 5/2/1882 MU

YEAR	TM/L	G	AB	R	H	2B	3B	HR	RBI	BB	SO	AVG	OBP	SLG	PRO+	BR/A	SB	CS	SBR	FA	FR	G/POS	TPR
1882	Lou-a	78	340	62	94	14	4	3		5		.276	.287	.368	126	9				.958	5	*1-66,P-13/O-2	0.2
1883	Lou-a	81	332	59	90	6	6	1		12		.271	.297	.334	111	5				.933	4	P-53,O-23,1-10	0.0
1884	Lou-a	78	316	53	94	14	8	4	42	10		.297	.323	.430	150	17				.951	6	*P-75/O-5	0.0
1885	Lou-a	70	297	48	81	9	2	2	35	5		.273	.287	.337	97	-2				.927	3	P-53,1-17/O-3	-0.4
1886	Lou-a	84	343	76	117	14	5	4	48	32		**.341**	.402	.446	157	21	25			.875	-6	P-49,1-22,O-17	0.0
1887	Lou-a	91	370	89	118	21	6	4	50	31		.319	.381	.441	126	13	48			.954	-4	1-43,P-34,O-16	-0.4
1888	Lou-a	56	211	32	48	9	2	0	29	11		.227	.285	.289	86	-3	20			.936	-4	1-30,P-26/O-1	-0.9
1889	Lou-a	81	327	42	93	17	5	1	36	18	27	.284	.333	.376	104	1	17			.969	-0	1-65,P-19/O-1	-0.4
1890	Pit-N	86	340	43	77	13	9	0	38	19	17	.226	.285	.318	86	-7	13			.962	1	1-69,P-14/O-7,M	-0.7
Total	9	705	2876	504	812	117	47	19	278	143	44	.282	.324	.376	118	55	123			.934	5	P-336,1-322/O-75	-2.6

■ DANNY HEEP

Heep, Daniel William b: 7/3/57, San Antonio, Tex. BL/TL, 5'11", 185 lbs. Deb: 8/31/79

YEAR	TM/L	G	AB	R	H	2B	3B	HR	RBI	BB	SO	AVG	OBP	SLG	PRO+	BR/A	SB	CS	SBR	FA	FR	G/POS	TPR
1979	Hou-N	14	14	0	2	0	0	0	2	1	4	.143	.200	.143	-5	-2	0	0	0	1.000	1	/O-2	-0.1
1980	*Hou-N	33	87	6	24	8	0	0	6	8	9	.276	.344	.368	107	1	0	0	0	.990	-2	1-22	-0.2
1981	Hou-N	33	96	6	24	3	0	0	11	10	11	.250	.321	.281	76	-3	0	0	0	.990	-3	1-22/O-1	-0.8
1982	Hou-N	85	198	16	47	14	1	4	22	21	31	.237	.314	.379	100	-0	0	2	-1	1.000	-3	O-39,1-16	-0.7
1983	NY-N	115	253	30	64	12	0	8	21	29	40	.253	.332	.395	102	1	3	3	-1	1.000	-5	O-61,1-14	-0.7
1984	NY-N	99	199	36	46	9	2	1	12	27	22	.231	.326	.312	81	-4	3	1	0	.967	1	O-48,1-10	-0.5
1985	NY-N	95	271	26	76	17	0	7	42	27	27	.280	.348	.421	117	6	2	2	-1	.977	-5	O-78/1-4	-0.2
1986	*NY-N	86	195	24	55	8	2	5	33	30	31	.282	.381	.421	124	7	1	4	-2	.988	-2	O-56	0.1
1987	LA-N	60	98	7	16	4	0	0	9	8	10	.163	.226	.204	16	-12	1	0	0	.962	-1	O-22/1-6	-1.4
1988	*LA-N	95	149	14	36	2	0	0	11	22	13	.242	.343	.255	76	-3	2	0	1	1.000	-2	O-32,1-12/P-1	-0.7
1989	Bos-A	113	320	36	96	17	0	5	49	29	26	.300	.360	.400	107	3	0	1	-1	.989	-12	O-75,1-19/D-9	-1.2
1990	*Bos-A	41	69	3	12	1	1	0	8	7	14	.174	.260	.217	33	-6	0	0	0	1.000	-0	O-14/1-5,P-1,D-6	-0.7
1991	Atl-N	14	12	4	5	1	0	0	3	1	4	.417	.462	.500	161	1	0	1	-1	1.000	-0	/1-1,O-1	0.0
Total	13	883	1961	208	503	96	6	30	229	220	242	.257	.334	.357	95	-12	12	14	-5	.986	-34	O-429,1-131/D-15,P	-7.1

■ BERT HEFFERNAN

Heffernan, Bertram Alexander b: 3/3/65, Centereach, N.Y. BL/TR, 5'10", 185 lbs. Deb: 5/13/92

YEAR	TM/L	G	AB	R	H	2B	3B	HR	RBI	BB	SO	AVG	OBP	SLG	PRO+	BR/A	SB	CS	SBR	FA	FR	G/POS	TPR
1992	Sea-A	8	11	0	1	1	0	0	1	0	1	.091	.091	.182	-25	-2	0	0	0	1.000	1	/C-5,D-1	-0.1

■ DON HEFFNER

Heffner, Donald Henry "Jeep" b: 2/8/11, Rouzerville, Pa. d: 8/1/89, Pasadena, Cal. BR/TR, 5'10", 155 lbs. Deb: 4/17/34 MC

YEAR	TM/L	G	AB	R	H	2B	3B	HR	RBI	BB	SO	AVG	OBP	SLG	PRO+	BR/A	SB	CS	SBR	FA	FR	G/POS	TPR
1934	NY-A	72	241	29	63	8	3	0	25	25	18	.261	.331	.320	73	-9	1	1	-0	.971	-8	2-68	-1.3
1935	NY-A	10	36	3	11	3	1	0	8	4	1	.306	.375	.444	118	1	0	0	0	.980	-1	2-10	0.1
1936	NY-A	19	48	7	11	2	1	0	6	6	5	.229	.315	.313	57	-3	0	0	0	.971	4	/3-8,2-5,S-3	0.1
1937	NY-A	60	201	23	50	6	5	0	21	19	19	.249	.314	.328	62	-12	1	4	-2	.980	-8	2-38,S-13/3-3,10	-1.7
1938	StL-A	141	473	47	116	23	3	2	69	65	53	.245	.341	.319	67	-23	1	1	-0	.971	-9	*2-141	-2.2
1939	StL-A	110	375	45	100	10	2	1	35	48	39	.267	.350	.312	69	-16	1	7	-4	.944	-4	S-73,2-32	-1.5

YEAR	TM/L	G	AB	R	H	2B	3B	HR	RBI	BB	SO	AVG	OBP	SLG	PRO+	BR/A	SB	CS	SBR	FA	FR	G/POS	TPR
1940	StL-A	126	487	52	115	23	2	3	53	39	37	.236	.295	.310	56	-32	5	5	-2	**.977**	**19**	*2-125	-0.5
1941	StL-A	110	399	48	93	14	2	0	17	38	27	.233	.303	.278	53	-27	5	6	-2	.974	3	*2-105	-1.9
1942	StL-A	19	36	2	6	2	0	0	3	1	4	.167	.189	.222	15	-4	1	0	0	.906	1	/2-6,1-4	-0.2
1943	StL-A	18	33	2	4	1	0	0	2	2	2	.121	.171	.152	-5	-4	0	0	0	.974	-0	2-13/1-1	-0.5
	Phi-A	52	178	17	37	6	0	0	8	18	12	.208	.284	.242	55	-10	3	2	-0	.978	-10	2-47/1-1	-1.9
	Yr	70	211	19	41	7	0	0	10	20	14	.194	.267	.227	45	-14	3	2	-0	.978	-10	2-60/1-2	-2.4
1944	Det-A	6	19	0	4	1	0	0	1	5	1	.211	.375	.263	80	-0	0	0	0	.962	-1	/2-5	-0.1
Total	11	743	2526	275	610	99	19	6	248	270	218	.241	.317	.303	61	-140	18	26	-10	.973	-13	2-595/S-89,3-11,10	-11.6

■ JIM HEGAN

Hegan, James Edward b: 8/3/20, Lynn, Mass. d: 6/17/84, Swampscott, Mass. BR/TR, 6′2″, 195 lbs. Deb: 9/9/41 FC

YEAR	TM/L	G	AB	R	H	2B	3B	HR	RBI	BB	SO	AVG	OBP	SLG	PRO+	BR/A	SB	CS	SBR	FA	FR	G/POS	TPR
1941	Cle-A	16	47	4	15	2	0	1	5	4	7	.319	.373	.426	116	1	0	0	0	.973	-0	C-16	0.2
1942	Cle-A	68	170	10	33	5	0	0	11	11	31	.194	.243	.224	34	-15	1	3	-2	.977	8	C-66	-0.5
1946	Cle-A	88	271	29	64	11	5	0	17	17	44	.236	.284	.314	71	-11	1	4	-2	.991	9	C-87	0.0
1947	Cle-A☆	135	378	38	94	14	5	4	42	41	49	.249	.324	.344	88	-6	3	1	0	.989	7	*C-133	0.9
1948	*Cle-A	144	472	60	117	21	6	14	61	48	74	.248	.317	.407	94	-7	6	3	0	.990	21	*C-142	2.3
1949	Cle-A☆	152	468	54	105	19	5	8	55	49	89	.224	.298	.338	69	-23	1	0	0	.990	10	*C-152	-0.3
1950	Cle-A★	131	415	53	91	16	5	14	58	42	52	.219	.291	.383	74	-19	1	0	0	.993	24	*C-129	1.0
1951	Cle-A★	133	416	60	99	17	5	6	43	38	72	.238	.302	.346	79	-13	0	3	-2	.991	11	*C-129	0.1
1952	Cle-A☆	112	333	39	75	17	2	4	41	29	47	.225	.287	.324	75	-13	0	2	-1	.987	7	*C-107	-0.2
1953	Cle-A	112	299	37	65	10	1	9	37	25	41	.217	.280	.348	71	-13	1	2	-1	.976	3	*C-106	-0.7
1954	*Cle-A	139	423	56	99	12	7	11	40	34	48	.234	.291	.374	80	-13	0	1	-1	**.994**	13	*C-137	0.5
1955	Cle-A	116	304	30	67	5	2	9	40	34	33	.220	.299	.339	69	-14	0	1	-1	**.997**	7	*C-111	-0.4
1956	Cle-A	122	315	42	70	15	2	6	34	49	54	.222	.327	.340	75	-11	1	1	-0	.985	16	*C-118	0.8
1957	Cle-A	58	148	14	32	7	0	4	15	16	23	.216	.293	.345	74	-5	0	1	-1	1.000	3	C-58	-0.2
1958	Det-A	45	130	14	25	6	0	1	7	10	32	.192	.250	.262	38	-11	0	0	0	.996	1	C-45	-0.8
	Phi-N	25	59	5	13	6	0	0	6	4	16	.220	.270	.322	57	-4	0	0	0	.991	4	C-25	0.1
1959	Phi-N	25	51	1	10	1	0	0	8	3	10	.196	.241	.216	22	-6	0	1	-1	.990	1	C-25	-0.5
	SF-N	21	30	0	4	1	0	0	0	1	10	.133	.161	.167	-13	-5	0	1	-1	.975	5	C-21	0.0
	Yr	46	81	1	14	2	0	0	8	4	20	.173	.212	.198	10	-10	0	2	-1	.983	5	C-46	-0.5
1960	Chi-N	24	43	4	9	2	1	1	5	1	10	.209	.244	.372	67	-2	0	0	0	.977	2	C-22	0.1
Total	17	1666	4772	550	1087	187	46	92	525	456	742	.228	.296	.344	74	-191	15	24	-10	.990	149	*C-1629	2.4

■ MIKE HEGAN

Hegan, James Michael b: 7/21/42, Cleveland, Ohio BL/TL, 6′1″, 190 lbs. Deb: 9/13/64 F

YEAR	TM/L	G	AB	R	H	2B	3B	HR	RBI	BB	SO	AVG	OBP	SLG	PRO+	BR/A	SB	CS	SBR	FA	FR	G/POS	TPR
1964	*NY-A	5	5	0	0	0	0	0	0	1	2	.000	.167	.000	-48	-1	0	0	0	1.000	1	/1-2	0.0
1966	NY-A	13	39	7	8	0	1	0	2	7	11	.205	.326	.256	73	-1	1	1	-0	.991	-0	1-13	-0.3
1967	NY-A	68	118	12	16	4	1	1	3	20	40	.136	.266	.212	44	-8	7	1	2	1.000	1	1-54,O-10	-0.8
1969	Sea-A†	95	267	54	78	9	6	8	37	62	61	.292	.427	.461	151	21	6	5	-1	.955	2	O-64,1-19	1.8
1970	Mil-A	148	476	70	116	21	2	11	52	67	116	.244	.338	.366	93	-3	9	7	-2	.994	11	*1-139/O-8	-0.6
1971	Mil-A	46	122	19	27	4	1	4	11	26	19	.221	.358	.369	107	2	1	1	-0	1.000	4	1-45	0.3
	*Oak-A	65	55	5	13	3	0	0	3	5	13	.236	.300	.291	69	-2	1	0	0	1.000	2	1-47/O-2	-0.1
	Yr	111	177	24	40	7	1	4	14	31	32	.226	.341	.345	96	-0	2	1	0	1.000	6	1-92/O-2	0.2
1972	*Oak-A	98	79	13	26	3	1	1	5	7	20	.329	.384	.430	150	5	1	0	0	1.000	2	1-64/O-3	0.6
1973	Oak-A	75	71	8	13	2	0	1	5	5	17	.183	.237	.254	40	-6	0	0	0	.988	-3	1-56/O-3,D-3	-1.0
	NY-A	37	131	12	36	3	2	6	14	7	34	.275	.312	.466	121	3	0	0	0	.992	2	1-37	0.2
	Yr	112	202	20	49	5	2	7	19	12	51	.243	.285	.391	93	-3	0	0	0	.991	-1	1-93/O-3,D-3	-0.8
1974	NY-A	18	53	3	12	2	0	2	9	5	9	.226	.317	.377	101	0	1	1	-0	1.000	-0	1-17	-0.1
	Mil-A	89	190	21	45	7	1	7	32	33	34	.237	.350	.395	114	4	0	4	-2	.991	-2	D-37,1-17,O-17	-0.2
	Yr	107	243	24	57	9	1	9	41	38	43	.235	.343	.391	111	4	1	5	-3	.996	-2	D-37,1-34,O-17	-0.3
1975	Mil-A	93	203	19	51	11	0	5	22	31	42	.251	.350	.379	106	2	1	1	-0	.984	-4	O-42,1-27/D-5	-0.4
1976	Mil-A	80	218	30	54	4	3	5	31	25	54	.248	.328	.362	104	1	0	0	0	1.000	-3	D-40,O-20,1-10	-0.4
1977	Mil-A	35	53	8	9	0	0	2	3	10	17	.170	.313	.283	64	-2	0	0	0	1.000	-3	/O-8,1-6,D-7	-0.6
Total	12	965	2080	281	504	73	18	53	229	311	489	.242	.343	.371	103	15	28	21	-4	.995	11	1-553,O-177/D-92	-1.6

■ BOB HEGMAN

Hegman, Robert Hilmer b: 2/26/58, Springfield, Minn. BR/TR, 6′1″, 180 lbs. Deb: 8/8/85

YEAR	TM/L	G	AB	R	H	2B	3B	HR	RBI	BB	SO	AVG	OBP	SLG	PRO+	BR/A	SB	CS	SBR	FA	FR	G/POS	TPR
1985	KC-A	1	0	0	0	0	0	0	0	0	0	—	—	—	—	0	0	0	0	.000	0	/2-1	0.0

■ JACK HEIDEMANN

Heidemann, Jack Seale b: 7/11/49, Brenham, Tex. BR/TR, 6′, 178 lbs. Deb: 5/2/69

YEAR	TM/L	G	AB	R	H	2B	3B	HR	RBI	BB	SO	AVG	OBP	SLG	PRO+	BR/A	SB	CS	SBR	FA	FR	G/POS	TPR
1969	Cle-A	3	3	0	0	0	0	0	0	0	2	.000	.250	.000	-24	-0	0	0	0	1.000	1	/S-3	0.0
1970	Cle-A	133	445	44	94	14	2	6	37	34	88	.211	.270	.292	52	-29	2	4	-2	.961	-2	*S-132	-1.9
1971	Cle-A	81	240	16	50	7	0	0	9	12	46	.208	.252	.237	36	-20	1	3	-2	.977	-9	S-81	-2.4
1972	Cle-A	10	20	0	3	0	0	0	0	2	3	.150	.261	.150	24	-2	0	0	0	.964	-1	S-10	-0.3
1974	Cle-A	12	11	2	1	0	0	0	0	0	2	.091	.091	.091	-48	-2	0	0	0	1.000	-1	/3-6,S-4,1-1,2-1	-0.3
	StL-N	47	70	8	19	1	0	0	3	5	10	.271	.320	.286	71	-3	0	0	0	.967	-10	S-45/3-1	-1.0
1975	NY-N	61	145	12	31	4	2	1	16	17	28	.214	.296	.290	66	-7	1	0	0	.951	-12	S-44/3-4,2-1	-1.6
1976	NY-N	5	12	0	1	0	0	0	0	0	0	.083	.083	.083	-56	-2	0	0	0	1.000	0	/S-3,2-1	-0.2
	Mil-A	69	146	11	32	1	0	2	10	7	24	.219	.255	.267	54	-9	1	3	-2	.962	-7	3-40,2-24/D-1	-1.7
1977	Mil-A	5	1	1	0	0	0	0	0	1	0	.000	.500	.000	50	0	0	0	0	1.000	1	/2-1,D-3	0.1
Total	8	426	1093	94	231	27	4	9	75	78	203	.211	.268	.268	49	-73	5	10	-5	.965	-42	S-322/3-51,2-28,D1	-9.3

■ EMMET HEIDRICK

Heidrick, R. Emmet "Snags" b: 7/9/1876, Queenstown, Pa. d: 1/20/16, Clarion, Pa. BL/TR, 6′, 185 lbs. Deb: 9/14/1898

YEAR	TM/L	G	AB	R	H	2B	3B	HR	RBI	BB	SO	AVG	OBP	SLG	PRO+	BR/A	SB	CS	SBR	FA	FR	G/POS	TPR
1898	Cle-N	19	76	10	23	2	2	0	8	3		.303	.329	.382	105	0	3			.850	-1	O-19	-0.2
1899	StL-N	146	591	109	194	21	14	2	82	34		.328	.368	.421	114	9	55			.925	4	*O-145	0.2
1900	StL-N	85	339	51	102	6	8	2	45	18		.301	.338	.383	100	-1	22			.959	15	O-83	0.7
1901	StL-N	118	502	94	170	24	12	6	67	21		.339	.366	.470	149	29	32			.945	1	*O-118	2.0
1902	StL-A	110	447	75	129	19	10	3	56	34		.289	.339	.396	105	2	17			.940	2	*O-109/P-1,S-1,3-1	-0.2
1903	StL-A	120	461	55	129	20	15	1	42	19		.280	.310	.395	113	6	19			.954	2	*O-119/C-1	0.1
1904	StL-A	133	538	66	147	14	10	1	36	16		.273	.294	.342	107	3	35			.963	11	*O-130	0.7
1908	StL-A	26	93	8	20	2	2	1	6	1		.215	.223	.312	73	-3	3			.957	-1	O-25	-0.6
Total	8	757	3047	468	914	108	73	16	342	146		.300	.333	.399	114	45	186			.946	33	O-748/C-1,3-1,SP	2.7

■ FRANK HEIFER

Heifer, Franklin "Heck" b: 1/18/1854, Reading, Pa. d: 8/29/1893, Reading, Pa. 5′10.5″, 175 lbs. Deb: 6/4/1875

YEAR	TM/L	G	AB	R	H	2B	3B	HR	RBI	BB	SO	AVG	OBP	SLG	PRO+	BR/A	SB	CS	SBR	FA	FR	G/POS	TPR
1875	Bos-n	11	50	11	14	0	3	0	5	0	0	.280	.280	.400	129	1	0	0	0	.885	-2	/1-9,O-6,P-2	0.0

■ CHINK HEILEMAN

Heileman, John George b: 8/10/1872, Cincinnati, Ohio d: 7/19/40, Cincinnati, Ohio BR/TR, 5′8″, 155 lbs. Deb: 7/8/01

YEAR	TM/L	G	AB	R	H	2B	3B	HR	RBI	BB	SO	AVG	OBP	SLG	PRO+	BR/A	SB	CS	SBR	FA	FR	G/POS	TPR
1901	Cin-N	5	15	1	2	1	0	0	1	0		.133	.133	.200	-4	-2	0			.667	-1	/3-4,2-1	-0.3

■ HARRY HEILMANN

Heilmann, Harry Edwin "Slug" b: 8/3/1894, San Francisco, Cal. d: 7/9/51, Southfield, Mich. BR/TR, 6′1″, 195 lbs. Deb: 5/16/14 CH

YEAR	TM/L	G	AB	R	H	2B	3B	HR	RBI	BB	SO	AVG	OBP	SLG	PRO+	BR/A	SB	CS	SBR	FA	FR	G/POS	TPR
1914	Det-A	69	182	25	41	8	1	2	18	22	29	.225	.316	.313	86	-3	1	8	-5	.870	-6	O-31,1-16/2-6	-1.6
1916	Det-A	136	451	57	127	30	11	2	73	42	40	.282	.349	.410	124	12	9			.952	-10	O-77,1-30/2-9	-0.3
1917	Det-A	150	556	57	156	22	11	5	86	41	54	.281	.333	.387	120	11	11			.960	-2	*O-123,1-27	0.2
1918	Det-A	79	286	34	79	10	6	5	39	35	10	.276	.359	.406	136	12	13			.957	-4	O-40,1-37/2-2	0.5
1919	Det-A	140	537	74	172	30	15	8	93	37	41	.320	.366	.477	139	25	7			.979	-10	*1-140	1.1
1920	Det-A	145	543	66	168	28	5	9	89	39	32	.309	.358	.429	111	7	3	7	-3	.985	-1	*1-122,O-22	-0.1
1921	Det-A	149	602	114	**237**	43	14	19	139	53	37	**.394**	.444	.606	167	60	2	6	-3	.962	-11	*O-147/1-3	3.2
1922	Det-A	118	455	92	162	27	10	21	92	58	28	.356	.432	.598	172	47	8	4	0	.948	-10	*O-115/1-5	2.7
1923	Det-A	144	524	121	211	44	11	18	115	74	40	**.403**	.481	.632	195	74	9	7	-2	.960	2	*O-130,1-12	6.2
1924	Det-A	153	570	107	197	**45**	16	10	114	78	41	.346	.428	.533	149	42	13	5	1	.970	9	*O-147/1-4	3.9
1925	Det-A	150	573	97	225	40	11	13	134	67	27	**.393**	.457	.569	161	**55**	6	6	-2	.970	-3	*O-148	3.7
1926	Det-A	141	502	90	184	41	8	9	103	67	19	.367	.445	.534	152	40	6	7	-2	.972	-2	*O-134	2.6
1927	Det-A	141	505	106	201	50	9	14	120	72	16	**.398**	.475	.616	179	60	11	5	0	.966	-8	*O-135	4.2
1928	Det-A	151	558	83	183	38	10	14	107	57	45	.328	.390	.507	132	25	7	3	0	.971	1	*O-125,1-25	1.6

YEAR	TM/L	G	AB	R	H	2B	3B	HR	RBI	BB	SO	AVG	OBP	SLG	PRO+	BR/A	SB	CS	SBR	FA	FR	G/POS	TPR
1929	Det-A	125	453	86	156	41	7	15	120	50	39	.344	.412	.565	148	32	5	6	-2	.966	-6	*O-114/1-2	1.6
1930	Cin-N	142	459	79	153	43	6	19	91	64	50	.333	.416	.577	144	33	2			.955	12	*O-106,1-19	3.1
1932	Cin-N	15	31	3	8	2	0	0	6	0	2	.258	.258	.323	57	-2	0			.981	-0	/1-6	-0.3
Total	17	2148	7787	1291	2660	542	151	183	1539	856	550	.342	.410	.520	148	532	113	64		.962	-48	*O-1594,1-448/2-17	32.3
■ VAL HEIM	Heim, Val Raymond b: 11/4/20, Plymouth, Wis. BL/TR, 5'11", 170 lbs. Deb: 8/31/42																						
1942	Chi-A	13	45	6	9	1	1	0	7	5	3	.200	.294	.267	60	-2	1	0	0	.958	-1	O-12	-0.4
■ BUD HEINE	Heine, William Henry b: 9/22/1900, Elmira, N.Y. d: 9/2/76, Ft.Lauderdale, Fla BL/TR, 5'8", 145 lbs. Deb: 10/1/21																						
1921	NY-N	1	2	0	0	0	0	0	0	0	0	.000	.000	.000	-99	-1	0	0	0	1.000	-0	/2-1	-0.1
■ TOM HEINTZELMAN	Heintzelman, Thomas Kenneth b: 11/3/46, St.Charles, Mo. BR/TR, 6'1", 180 lbs. Deb: 8/12/73 F																						
1973	StL-N	23	29	5	9	0	0	0	0	3	3	.310	.375	.310	92	-0	0	0	0	1.000	1	/2-6	0.1
1974	StL-N	38	74	10	17	4	0	1	6	9	14	.230	.313	.324	79	-2	0	0	0	.978	0	2-28/3-2,S-1	-0.1
1977	SF-N	2	2	0	0	0	0	0	0	0	0	.000	.000	.000	-99	-1	0	0	0	.000	0	H	-0.1
1978	SF-N	27	35	2	8	1	0	2	6	2	5	.229	.270	.429	96	-0	0	0	0	1.000	2	/2-5,3-3,1-2	0.2
Total	4	90	140	17	34	5	0	3	12	14	22	.243	.312	.343	84	-3	0	0	0	.984	4	/2-39,3-5,1-2,S-1	0.1
■ JACK HEINZMAN	Heinzman, John Peter b: 9/27/1863, New Albany, Ind. d: 11/10/14, Louisville, Ky. BR/TR, Deb: 10/2/1886																						
1886	Lou-a	1	5	1	0	0	0	0	0	0		.000	.000	.000	-95	-1	0			1.000	-0	/1-1	-0.1
■ BOB HEISE	Heise, Robert Lowell b: 5/12/47, San Antonio, Tex. BR/TR, 6', 175 lbs. Deb: 9/12/67																						
1967	NY-N	16	62	7	20	4	0	0	3	3	1	.323	.354	.387	114	1	0	1	-1	.973	2	2-12/S-3,3-2	0.3
1968	NY-N	6	23	3	5	0	0	0	1	1	1	.217	.250	.217	41	-2	0	0	0	.929	-5	/S-6,2-1	-0.8
1969	NY-N	4	10	1	3	1	0	0	0	3	2	.300	.462	.400	140	1	0	0	0	1.000	-3	/S-3	-0.2
1970	SF-N	67	154	15	36	5	1	1	22	5	13	.234	.258	.299	49	-11	0	1	-1	.915	-1	S-33,2-28/3-2	-0.9
1971	SF-N	13	11	2	0	0	0	0	0	0	1	.000	.000	.000	-99	-3	0	0	0	.833	0	/S-3,3-2,2-1	-0.3
	Mil-A	68	189	10	48	7	0	0	7	7	15	.254	.281	.291	63	-9	1	1	-0	.961	7	S-51,3-11/2-3,O-1	0.3
1972	Mil-A	95	271	23	72	10	1	0	12	12	14	.266	.302	.310	84	-6	1	1	-0	.990	-3	2-49,3-24/S-9	-0.7
1973	Mil-A	49	98	8	20	2	0	0	4	4	4	.204	.235	.224	31	-9	1	0	0	.956	-1	S-29/3-9,1-4,2-4,D	-0.7
1974	StL-N	3	7	0	1	0	0	0	0	0	0	.143	.143	.143	-20	-1	0	0	0	1.000	2	/2-3	0.1
	Cal-A	29	75	7	20	7	0	0	6	5	10	.267	.313	.360	99	-0	0	1	-1	1.000	2	2-17/3-6,S-3	0.2
1975	Bos-A	63	126	12	27	3	0	0	21	4	6	.214	.250	.238	35	-11	0	0	0	.940	11	3-45,2-14/S-4,1-1	0.1
1976	Bos-A	32	56	5	15	2	0	0	5	1	2	.268	.293	.304	67	-2	0	1	-1	.968	2	3-22/S-9,2-1	0.0
1977	KC-A	54	62	11	16	2	1	0	5	2	8	.258	.292	.323	67	-3	0	1	-1	1.000	10	2-21,S-21,3-12,/1-1	0.8
Total	11	499	1144	104	283	43	3	1	86	47	77	.247	.281	.293	63	-55	3	7	-3	.945	23	S-174,2-154,3/1DO	-1.8
■ AL HEIST	Heist, Alfred Michael b: 10/5/27, Brooklyn, N.Y. BR/TR, 6'2", 185 lbs. Deb: 7/17/60 C																						
1960	Chi-N	41	102	11	28	5	3	1	6	10	12	.275	.339	.412	106	1	3	1	0	.985	-2	O-33	-0.2
1961	Chi-N	109	321	48	82	14	3	7	37	39	51	.255	.338	.383	90	-4	3	3	-1	.978	0	O-99	-1.0
1962	Hou-N	27	72	4	16	1	0	0	3	3	9	.222	.263	.236	38	-6	0	0	0	.974	-3	O-23	-1.0
Total	3	177	495	63	126	20	6	8	46	52	72	.255	.328	.368	86	-10	6	4	-1	.979	-4	O-155	-2.2
■ HEINIE HEITMULLER	Heitmuller, William Frederick b: 5/25/1883, San Francisco, Cal d: 10/8/12, Los Angeles, Cal. BR/TR, 6'2", 215 lbs. Deb: 4/26/09																						
1909	Phi-A	64	210	36	60	9	8	0	15	18		.286	.351	.405	136	8	7			.927	-2	O-61	0.5
1910	Phi-A	31	111	11	27	2	2	0	7	7		.243	.288	.297	84	-2	6			.981	-0	O-28	-0.4
Total	2	95	321	47	87	11	10	0	22	25		.271	.330	.368	118	6	13			.943	-2	/O-89	0.1
■ WOODIE HELD	Held, Woodson George b: 3/25/32, Sacramento, Cal. BR/TR, 5'11", 180 lbs. Deb: 9/5/54																						
1954	NY-A	4	3	2	0	0	0	0	0	2	1	.000	.400	.000	17	-0	0	0	0	1.000	-1	/S-4,3-1	-0.1
1957	NY-A	1	1	0	0	0	0	0	0	0	0	.000	.000	.000	-99	-0	0	0	0	.000	0	H	0.0
	KC-A	92	326	48	78	14	3	20	50	37	81	.239	.322	.485	116	6	4	0	1	.996	17	O-92	1.8
	Yr	93	327	48	78	14	3	20	50	37	81	.239	.322	.483	115	5	4	0	1	.996	17	O-92	1.8
1958	KC-A	47	131	13	28	2	0	4	16	10	28	.214	.280	.321	64	-7	0	1	-1	1.000	-3	O-41/3-4,S-1	-1.3
	Cle-A	67	144	12	28	4	1	3	17	15	36	.194	.288	.299	63	-7	1	2	-1	.966	-0	O-43,S-14/3-4	-0.9
	Yr	114	275	25	56	6	1	7	33	25	64	.204	.284	.309	64	-14	1	3	-2	.982	-4	O-84,S-15/3-8	-2.2
1959	Cle-A	143	525	82	132	19	3	29	71	46	118	.251	.314	.465	115	8	1	2	-1	.962	-9	*S-103,3-40/O-6,2-3	0.7
1960	Cle-A	109	376	45	97	15	1	21	67	44	73	.258	.344	.471	122	11	0	1	-1	.967	9	*S-109	2.7
1961	Cle-A	146	509	67	136	23	5	23	78	69	111	.267	.358	.468	122	16	0	0	0	.960	-14	*S-144	1.4
1962	Cle-A	139	466	55	116	12	2	19	58	73	107	.249	.364	.406	110	8	5	1	1	.956	-14	*S-133/3-5,O-1	0.7
1963	Cle-A	133	416	61	103	19	4	17	61	61	96	.248	.355	.435	121	13	2	2	-1	.982	-3	2-96,O-35/S-5,3-3	1.7
1964	Cle-A	118	364	50	86	13	0	18	49	43	88	.236	.329	.420	107	4	1	0	0	.966	0	2-52,O-41,3-30	0.6
1965	Was-A	122	332	46	82	16	2	16	54	49	74	.247	.349	.452	128	12	0	0	0	.963	-19	*O-106/3-5,2-4,S-2	-1.1
1966	Bal-A	56	82	6	17	3	1	1	7	12	30	.207	.309	.305	78	-2	0	0	0	1.000	-4	O-10/2-5,S-3,3-3	-0.6
1967	Bal-A	26	41	4	6	3	0	1	6	6	12	.146	.286	.293	72	-1	0	0	0	.974	1	/2-9,3-5,O-2	0.0
	Cal-A	58	141	15	31	3	0	4	17	18	41	.220	.317	.326	94	-1	0	2	-1	.979	-4	3-19,O-17,S-13,/2-3	-0.7
	Yr	84	182	19	37	6	0	5	23	24	53	.203	.310	.319	88	-2	0	2	-1	.962	-3	3-24,O-19,S-13,2-12	-0.7
1968	Cal-A	33	45	4	5	1	0	0	0	5	15	.111	.231	.133	13	-5	0	0	0	1.000	-3	/2-5,S-5,3-5,O-3	-0.9
	Chi-A	40	54	5	9	1	0	0	2	5	14	.167	.250	.185	33	-4	0	0	0	1.000	-6	O-33/3-5,2-1	-1.2
	Yr	73	99	9	14	2	0	0	2	10	29	.141	.241	.162	24	-9	0	0	0	1.000	-9	O-36,3-10/2-6,S-5	-2.1
1969	Chi-A	56	63	9	9	2	0	3	6	13	19	.143	.299	.317	69	-3	0	0	0	1.000	-3	O-18/S-3,3-3,2-1	-0.6
Total	14	1390	4019	524	963	150	22	179	559	508	944	.240	.333	.421	109	48	14	11	-2	.960	-56	S-539,O-448,23	2.2
■ HANK HELF	Helf, Henry Hartz b: 8/26/13, Austin, Tex. d: 10/27/84, Austin, Tex. BR/TR, 6'1", 196 lbs. Deb: 5/5/38																						
1938	Cle-A	6	13	1	1	0	0	0	1	1	1	.077	.143	.077	-44	-3	0	0	0	.947	0	/C-5	-0.2
1940	Cle-A	1	1	0	0	0	0	0	0	0	0	.000	.000	.000	-99	-0	0	0	0	1.000	-0	/C-1	0.0
1946	StL-A	71	182	17	35	11	0	6	21	9	40	.192	.234	.352	59	-11	0	1	-1	.965	12	C-69	0.4
Total	3	78	196	18	36	11	0	6	22	10	41	.184	.227	.332	51	-14	0	1	-1	.964	12	/C-75	0.2
■ ERIC HELFAND	Helfand, Eric James b: 3/25/69, Erie, Pa. BL/TR, 6', 195 lbs. Deb: 9/4/93																						
1993	Oak-A	8	13	1	3	0	0	0	1	0	1	.231	.231	.231	26	-1	0	0	0	1.000	4	/C-5	0.2
1994	Oak-A	7	6	1	1	0	0	0	1	0	1	.167	.167	.167	-15	-1	0	0	0	1.000	1	/C-6	0.0
1995	Oak-A	38	86	9	14	2	1	0	7	11	25	.163	.265	.209	27	-9	0	0	0	.994	3	C-36	-0.5
Total	3	53	105	11	18	2	1	0	9	11	27	.171	.256	.210	25	-12	0	0	0	.996	7	/C-47	-0.3
■ TY HELFRICH	Helfrich, Emory Wilbur b: 10/9/1890, Pleasantville, N.J. d: 3/18/55, Pleasantville, N.J BR/TR, 5'10", 178 lbs. Deb: 6/30/15																						
1915	Bro-F	43	104	12	25	6	0	0	5	15	21	.240	.336	.298	80	-4	2			.912	-4	2-34/O-1	-0.8
■ HELLINGS	Hellings b: Philadelphia, Pa. Deb: 7/19/1875																						
1875	Atl-n	1	4	0	1	0	0	0	0	0	0	.250	.250	.250	85	-0	0	0	0	.750	-0	/2-1	0.0
■ TONY HELLMAN	Hellman, Anthony J. b: 1861, Cincinnati, Ohio d: 3/29/1898, Cincinnati, Ohio Deb: 10/10/1886																						
1886	Bal-a	1	3	0	0	0	0	0	0	0		.000	.000	.000	-99	-1	0			1.000	1	/C-1	0.0
■ TOMMY HELMS	Helms, Tommy Vann b: 5/5/41, Charlotte, N.C. BR/TR, 5'10", 175 lbs. Deb: 9/23/64 MC																						
1964	Cin-N	2	1	0	0	0	0	0	0	0	1	.000	.000	.000	-97	-0	0	0	0	.000	0	H	0.0
1965	Cin-N	21	42	4	16	2	2	0	6	3	7	.381	.435	.524	158	3	1	0	0	.973	-2	/S-8,3-2,2-1	0.3
1966	Cin-N	138	542	72	154	23	1	9	49	24	31	.284	.317	.380	85	-11	3	4	-2	.961	-13	*3-113,2-20	-2.8
1967	Cin-N★	137	497	40	136	27	4	2	35	24	41	.274	.307	.356	80	-13	5	10	-5	.978	-9	2-88,S-46	-1.8
1968	Cin-N★	127	507	35	146	28	2	2	47	12	27	.288	.307	.363	94	-4	5	6	-2	.979	8	*2-127/S-2,3-1	1.1
1969	Cin-N	126	480	38	129	18	1	1	40	18	33	.269	.297	.317	68	-20	4	6	-2	.975	-3	*2-125/S-4	-1.6
1970	★Cin-N	150	575	42	136	21	1	1	45	21	33	.237	.263	.282	46	-44	2	2	-1	**.983**	1	*2-148,S-12	-3.2

YEAR	TM/L	G	AB	R	H	2B	3B	HR	RBI	BB	SO	AVG	OBP	SLG	PRO+	BR/A	SB	CS	SBR	FA	FR	G/POS	TPR
1971	Cin-N	150	547	40	141	26	1	3	52	26	33	.258	.293	.325	76	-18	3	4	-2	**.990**	14	*2-149	0.8
1972	Hou-N	139	518	45	134	20	5	5	60	24	27	.259	.297	.346	84	-12	4	3	-1	.979	**27**	*2-139	2.3
1973	Hou-N	146	543	44	156	28	2	4	61	32	21	.287	.327	.368	93	-6	1	1	-0	.988	-1	*2-145	0.1
1974	Hou-N	137	452	32	126	21	1	5	50	23	27	.279	.315	.363	93	-6	5	4	-1	**.985**	-11	*2-133	-1.2
1975	Hou-N	64	135	7	28	2	0	0	14	10	8	.207	.267	.222	40	-11	0	0	0	.988	-0	2-42/3-3,S-1	-1.0
1976	Pit-N	62	87	10	24	5	1	1	13	10	5	.276	.357	.391	111	1	0	0	0	.921	2	3-22,2-11/S-1	0.4
1977	Pit-N	15	12	0	0	0	0	0	0	0	3	.000	.000	.000	-97	-3	0	0	0	.000	0	H	-0.4
	Bos-A	21	59	5	16	2	0	1	5	4	4	.271	.328	.356	77	-2	0	0	0	1.000	-2	D-13/3-2,2-1	-0.4
Total	14	1435	4997	414	1342	223	21	34	477	231	301	.269	.303	.342	79	-145	33	40	-14	.983	11	*2-1129,3-143/SD	-7.4

■ WES HELMS Helms, Wesley Ray b: 5/12/76, Gastonia, N.C. BR/TR, 6′4″, 230 lbs. Deb: 9/5/98

YEAR	TM/L	G	AB	R	H	2B	3B	HR	RBI	BB	SO	AVG	OBP	SLG	PRO+	BR/A	SB	CS	SBR	FA	FR	G/POS	TPR
1998	Atl-N	7	13	2	4	1	0	1	2	0	4	.308	.308	.615	129	0	0	0	0	.750	-1	/3-4	-0.1

■ TODD HELTON Helton, Todd Lynn b: 8/20/73, Knoxville, Tenn. BL/TL, 6′2″, 195 lbs. Deb: 8/2/97

YEAR	TM/L	G	AB	R	H	2B	3B	HR	RBI	BB	SO	AVG	OBP	SLG	PRO+	BR/A	SB	CS	SBR	FA	FR	G/POS	TPR
1997	Col-N	35	93	13	26	2	1	5	11	8	11	.280	.337	.484	91	-2	0	1	-1	1.000	1	O-15/1-8	-0.3
1998	Col-N	152	530	78	167	37	1	25	97	53	54	.315	.384	.530	112	8	3	3	-1	.995	16	*1-146	1.1
Total	2	187	623	91	193	39	2	30	108	61	65	.310	.377	.523	109	7	3	4	-2	.995	17	1-154/O-15	0.8

■ HEINIE HELTZEL Heltzel, William Wade b: 12/21/13, York, Pa. BR/TR, 5′10″, 150 lbs. Deb: 7/27/43

YEAR	TM/L	G	AB	R	H	2B	3B	HR	RBI	BB	SO	AVG	OBP	SLG	PRO+	BR/A	SB	CS	SBR	FA	FR	G/POS	TPR
1943	Bos-N	29	86	6	13	3	0	0	5	7	13	.151	.215	.186	17	-9	0			.880	-3	3-29	-1.3
1944	Phi-N	11	22	1	4	1	0	0	0	2	3	.182	.280	.227	45	-2	0			.919	-2	S-10	-0.3
Total	2	40	108	7	17	4	0	0	5	9	16	.157	.229	.194	23	-11	0			.880	-5	/3-29,S-10	-1.6

■ ED HEMINGWAY Hemingway, Edson Marshall b: 5/8/1893, Sheridan, Mich. d: 7/5/69, Grand Rapids, Mich BB/TR, 5′11.5″, 165 lbs. Deb: 9/17/14

YEAR	TM/L	G	AB	R	H	2B	3B	HR	RBI	BB	SO	AVG	OBP	SLG	PRO+	BR/A	SB	CS	SBR	FA	FR	G/POS	TPR
1914	StL-A	3	5	0	0	0	0	0	0	1	1	.000	.167	.000	-51	-1	1			1.000	0	/3-3	-0.1
1917	NY-N	7	25	3	8	1	1	0	1	2	1	.320	.370	.440	153	2	2			.958	1	/3-7	0.3
1918	Phi-N	33	108	7	23	4	1	0	12	7	9	.213	.267	.269	59	-5	4			.955	2	2-25/3-3,1-1	-0.2
Total	3	43	138	10	31	5	2	0	13	10	11	.225	.282	.290	71	-5	7			.952	3	/2-25,3-13,1-1	0.0

■ SCOTT HEMOND Hemond, Scott Mathew b: 11/18/65, Taunton, Mass. BR/TR, 6′, 205 lbs. Deb: 9/9/89

YEAR	TM/L	G	AB	R	H	2B	3B	HR	RBI	BB	SO	AVG	OBP	SLG	PRO+	BR/A	SB	CS	SBR	FA	FR	G/POS	TPR
1989	Oak-A	4	0	2	0	0	0	0	0	0	0	—	—	—	—	0	0	0	0	.000	0	R	0.0
1990	Oak-A	7	13	0	2	0	0	0	1	0	5	.154	.154	.154	-14	-2	0	0	0	1.000	-1	/3-7,2-1	-0.3
1991	Oak-A	23	23	4	5	0	0	0	0	1	7	.217	.250	.217	32	-2	1	2	-1	.947	5	/C-8,2-7,3-2,S-1,D	0.2
1992	Oak-A	17	27	7	6	1	0	0	1	3	7	.222	.300	.259	61	-1	1	0	0	1.000	-0	/C-8,S-3,3-2,O-2,D	-0.1
	Chi-A	8	13	1	3	1	0	0	1	1	6	.231	.286	.308	67	-1	0	0	0	1.000	-0	/O-2,C-1,3-1,D-4	-0.1
	Yr	25	40	8	9	2	0	0	2	4	13	.225	.295	.275	63	-2	1	0	0	1.000	-1	/C-9,D-5,O-4,S-3,3	-0.2
1993	Oak-A	91	215	31	55	16	0	6	26	32	55	.256	.355	.414	113	4	14	5	1	.991	4	C-75/O-6,1-1,2-1,D	1.3
1994	Oak-A	91	198	23	44	11	0	3	20	16	51	.222	.280	.323	60	-12	7	6	-2	1.000	7	C-39,2-25,3/1OD	-0.4
1995	StL-N	57	118	11	17	1	0	3	9	12	31	.144	.235	.229	23	-13	0	0	0	.985	1	C-38/2-6	-1.1
Total	7	298	607	79	132	30	0	12	58	65	162	.217	.296	.326	69	-27	23	13	-1	.991	16	C-169/2-40,3DO1S	-0.5

■ DUCKY HEMP Hemp, William H. b: 12/27/1867, St.Louis, Mo. d: 3/6/23, St.Louis, Mo. Deb: 10/6/1887

YEAR	TM/L	G	AB	R	H	2B	3B	HR	RBI	BB	SO	AVG	OBP	SLG	PRO+	BR/A	SB	CS	SBR	FA	FR	G/POS	TPR
1887	Lou-a	1	3	1	1	1	0	0	0	1		.333	.500	.667	219	1	0			.000	-1	/O-1	0.0
1890	Pit-N	21	81	9	19	0	2	0	4	8	12	.235	.311	.284	83	-1	3			.867	0	O-21	-0.2
	Syr-a	9	33	1	5	1	0	0	1	0		.152	.176	.182	6	-4	1			.947	2	/O-9	-0.2
Total	2	31	117	11	25	2	2	0	5	9	12	.214	.281	.265	67	-5	4			.877	2	/O-31	-0.4

■ CHARLIE HEMPHILL Hemphill, Charles Judson "Eagle Eye" b: 4/20/1876, Greenville, Mich. d: 6/22/53, Detroit, Mich. BL/TL, 5′9″, 160 lbs. Deb: 6/27/1899 F

YEAR	TM/L	G	AB	R	H	2B	3B	HR	RBI	BB	SO	AVG	OBP	SLG	PRO+	BR/A	SB	CS	SBR	FA	FR	G/POS	TPR
1899	StL-N	11	37	4	9	0	0	1	3	6		.243	.364	.324	87	-0	0			.750	-2	O-10	-0.3
	Cle-N	55	202	23	56	3	5	2	23	6		.277	.301	.371	91	-4	3			.859	-8	O-54	-1.4
	Yr	66	239	27	65	3	5	3	26	12		.272	.312	.364	90	-4	3			.837	-10	O-64	-1.7
1901	Bos-A	136	545	71	142	10	10	3	62	39		.261	.312	.332	80	-14	11			.925	-4	*O-136	-2.6
1902	Cle-A	25	94	14	25	2	0	0	11	5		.266	.303	.287	67	-4	4			.860	-1	O-19	-0.6
	StL-A	103	416	67	132	14	11	6	58	44		.317	.383	.447	131	18	23			.952	-3	*O-101/2-2	0.8
	Yr	128	510	81	157	16	11	6	69	49		.308	.369	.418	120	14	27			.935	-3	*O-120/2-2	0.2
1903	StL-A	105	383	36	94	6	3	3	29	23		.245	.292	.300	80	-9	16			.961	2	*O-104	-1.3
1904	StL-A	114	438	47	112	13	2	2	45	35		.256	.311	.308	102	1	23			.926	-2	*O-108/2-1	-0.8
1906	StL-A	154	585	90	169	19	12	4	62	43		.289	.338	.383	131	20	33			.961	1	*O-154	1.4
1907	StL-A	153	603	66	156	20	9	0	38	51		.259	.319	.322	105	3	14			.957	-2	*O-153	-0.5
1908	NY-A	142	505	62	150	12	9	0	44	59		.297	.374	.356	136	22	42			.937	-2	*O-142	1.7
1909	NY-A	73	181	23	44	5	1	0	10	32		.243	.357	.282	101	2	10			.976	-1	O-45	-0.1
1910	NY-A	102	351	45	84	9	4	0	21	55		.239	.350	.288	95	0	19			.971	-2	O-94	-0.7
1911	NY-A	69	201	32	57	4	2	1	15	37		.284	.397	.338	99	2	9			.952	-7	O-55	-0.8
Total	11	1242	4541	580	1230	117	68	22	421	435		.271	.337	.341	106	37	207			.944	-29	*O-1175/2-3	-5.2

■ FRANK HEMPHILL Hemphill, Frank Vernon b: 5/13/1878, Greenville, Mich. d: 11/16/50, Chicago, Ill. BR/TR, 5′11″, 165 lbs. Deb: 4/17/06 F

YEAR	TM/L	G	AB	R	H	2B	3B	HR	RBI	BB	SO	AVG	OBP	SLG	PRO+	BR/A	SB	CS	SBR	FA	FR	G/POS	TPR
1906	Chi-A	13	40	0	3	0	0	0	2	9		.075	.275	.075	11	-3	1			.970	1	O-13	-0.3
1909	Was-A	1	3	0	0	0	0	0	0	0		.000	.000	.000	-99	-1	0			1.000	0	/O-1	-0.1
Total	2	14	43	0	3	0	0	0	2	9		.070	.259	.070	5	-4	1			.971	1	/O-14	-0.4

■ ROLLIE HEMSLEY Hemsley, Ralston Burdett b: 6/24/07, Syracuse, Ohio d: 7/31/72, Washington, D.C. BR/TR, 5′10″, 170 lbs. Deb: 4/13/28 C

YEAR	TM/L	G	AB	R	H	2B	3B	HR	RBI	BB	SO	AVG	OBP	SLG	PRO+	BR/A	SB	CS	SBR	FA	FR	G/POS	TPR
1928	Pit-N	50	133	14	36	2	3	0	18	4	10	.271	.292	.331	60	-8	1			.962	1	C-49	-0.4
1929	Pit-N	88	235	31	68	13	7	0	37	11	22	.289	.321	.404	77	-9	1			.954	8	C-80	0.4
1930	Pit-N	104	324	45	82	19	6	2	45	22	21	.253	.301	.367	60	-21	3			.979	3	C-98	-0.9
1931	Pit-N	10	35	3	6	3	0	0	1	3	3	.171	.237	.257	33	-3	0			1.000	1	/C-9	-0.2
	Chi-N	66	204	28	63	17	4	3	31	17	30	.309	.362	.475	121	6	4			.975	5	C-53	1.5
	Yr	76	239	31	69	20	4	3	32	20	33	.289	.344	.444	109	3	4			.978	6	C-62	1.3
1932	*Chi-N	60	151	27	36	10	3	4	20	10	16	.238	.286	.424	89	-3	2			.974	2	C-47/O-1	0.1
1933	Cin-N	49	116	9	22	8	0	0	7	6	8	.190	.230	.259	40	-9	0			.970	5	C-41	-0.3
	StL-A	32	95	7	23	2	1	1	15	11	12	.242	.321	.316	65	-5	0	0	0	.965	-3	C-27	-0.5
1934	StL-A	123	431	47	133	31	7	2	52	29	37	.309	.355	.427	93	-5	6	2	1	.973	23	*C-114/O-6	2.2
1935	StL-A★	144	504	57	146	32	7	0	48	44	41	.290	.349	.381	85	-11	3	2	-0	.979	10	*C-141	0.5
1936	StL-A☆	116	377	43	99	24	2	2	39	46	30	.263	.343	.353	70	-18	2	3	-1	.969	-11	*C-114	-2.1
1937	StL-A	100	334	30	74	12	3	3	28	25	29	.222	.276	.302	45	-29	0	0	0	.969	-5	C-94/1-2	-2.6
1938	Cle-A	66	203	27	60	11	3	2	28	23	14	.296	.367	.409	96	-1	1	1	-0	.980	15	C-58	1.4
1939	Cle-A☆	107	395	58	104	17	4	2	36	26	26	.263	.309	.342	69	-19	2	4	-2	.984	6	*C-106	-0.8
1940	Cle-A★	119	416	46	111	20	5	4	42	22	25	.267	.301	.368	75	-16	1	3	-2	**.994**	9	*C-117	0.0
1941	Cle-A	98	288	29	69	10	5	2	24	18	19	.240	.284	.330	65	-15	2	0	1	.980	-2	C-96	-0.9
1942	Cin-N	36	115	7	13	1	2	0	7	4	11	.113	.143	.157	-12	-16	0			.982	11	C-34	-0.3
	NY-A	31	85	12	25	3	1	0	15	5	9	.294	.333	.353	95	-1	1	0	0	.991	1	C-29	0.3
1943	NY-A	62	180	12	43	6	3	2	24	13	9	.239	.290	.339	83	-4	0	1	-1	.981	2	C-52	0.0
1944	NY-A★	81	284	23	76	12	5	2	26	9	13	.268	.290	.366	84	-7	0	2	-1	.983	-2	C-76	-0.6
1946	Phi-N	49	139	7	31	4	1	0	11	9	10	.223	.270	.266	54	-9	0			.977	11	C-45	0.4
1947	Phi-N	2	3	0	1	0	0	0	1	0	0	.333	.333	.333	80	-0	0			1.000	-0	/C-2	0.0
Total	19	1593	5047	562	1321	257	72	31	555	357	395	.262	.311	.360	74	-205	29	18		.978	90	*C-1482/O-7,1-2	-2.8

■ SOLLY HEMUS Hemus, Solomon Joseph b: 4/17/23, Phoenix, Ariz. BL/TR, 5′9″, 175 lbs. Deb: 4/27/49 MC

YEAR	TM/L	G	AB	R	H	2B	3B	HR	RBI	BB	SO	AVG	OBP	SLG	PRO+	BR/A	SB	CS	SBR	FA	FR	G/POS	TPR
1949	StL-N	20	33	8	11	1	0	0	2	7	3	.333	.450	.364	115	1	0			.981	2	2-16	0.3
1950	StL-N	11	15	1	2	1	0	0	0	2	4	.133	.235	.200	15	-2	0			1.000	1	/3-5	-0.1
1951	StL-N	120	420	68	118	18	9	2	32	75	31	.281	.395	.381	109	9	7	7	-2	.965	13	*S-105,2-12	2.8
1952	StL-N	151	570	**105**	153	28	8	15	52	96	55	.268	.392	.425	126	24	1	5	-3	.960	4	*S-148/3-2	3.8
1953	StL-N	154	585	110	163	32	11	14	61	86	40	.279	.382	.443	114	15	2	1	0	.964	7	*S-150/2-3	3.1

YEAR	TM/L	G	AB	R	H	2B	3B	HR	RBI	BB	SO	AVG	OBP	SLG	PRO+	BR/A	SB	CS	SBR	FA	FR	G/POS	TPR
1954	StL-N	124	214	43	65	15	3	2	27	55	27	.304	.456	.430	131	14	5	1	1	.944	-20	S-66,3-27,2-12	-0.1
1955	StL-N	96	206	36	50	10	2	5	21	27	22	.243	.336	.383	91	-3	1	1	-0	.956	-4	3-43,2-10/S-2	-0.6
1956	StL-N	8	5	1	1	0	0	0	2	1	1	.200	.429	.200	77	-0	0	0	0	.000	0	H	0.0
	Phi-N	78	187	24	54	10	4	5	24	28	21	.289	.401	.465	134	10	1	1	-0	.974	-25	2-49/3-1	-1.1
	Yr	86	192	25	55	10	4	5	26	29	22	.286	.402	.458	133	10	1	1	-0	.974	-25	2-49/3-1	-1.1
1957	Phi-N	70	108	8	20	6	1	0	5	20	8	.185	.323	.259	61	-5	1	1	-0	.980	-3	2-24	-0.8
1958	Phi-N	105	334	53	95	14	3	8	36	51	34	.284	.392	.416	116	10	3	1	0	.969	-14	2-85/3-1	0.2
1959	StL-N	24	17	2	4	2	0	0	1	8	2	.235	.500	.353	124	1	0	0	0	1.000	1	/2-1,3-1,M	0.2
Total	11	961	2694	459	736	137	41	51	263	456	248	.273	.390	.411	115	75	21	18		.962	-38	S-471,2-212/3-80	7.7

■ DAVE HENDERSON

Henderson, David Lee b: 7/21/58, Merced, Cal. BR/TR, 6'2", 220 lbs. Deb: 4/9/81

YEAR	TM/L	G	AB	R	H	2B	3B	HR	RBI	BB	SO	AVG	OBP	SLG	PRO+	BR/A	SB	CS	SBR	FA	FR	G/POS	TPR
1981	Sea-A	59	126	17	21	3	0	6	13	16	24	.167	.266	.333	69	-5	2	1	0	1.000	-7	O-58	-1.5
1982	Sea-A	104	324	47	82	17	1	14	48	36	67	.253	.328	.441	106	2	2	5	-2	.985	7	*O-101	0.5
1983	Sea-A	137	484	50	130	24	5	17	55	28	93	.269	.310	.444	101	-1	9	3	1	.982	12	*O-133/D-3	0.8
1984	Sea-A	112	350	42	98	23	0	14	43	19	56	.280	.321	.466	116	6	5	5	-2	.988	8	*O-97,D-10	1.0
1985	Sea-A	139	502	70	121	28	2	14	68	48	104	.241	.311	.388	90	-7	6	1	1	.986	-4	*O-138	-1.5
1986	Sea-A	103	337	51	93	19	4	14	44	37	95	.276	.351	.481	123	10	1	3	-2	.979	5	O-80,D-22	1.0
	*Bos-A	36	51	8	10	3	0	1	3	2	15	.196	.226	.314	45	-4	1	0	0	.981	-5	O-32	-0.9
	Yr	139	388	59	103	22	4	15	47	39	110	.265	.336	.459	113	6	2	3	-1	.980	0	*O-112,D-22	0.1
1987	Bos-A	75	184	30	43	10	0	8	25	22	48	.234	.316	.418	90	-3	1	1	-0	.958	-5	O-64/D-1	-1.0
	SF-N	15	21	2	5	2	0	0	1	8	5	.238	.448	.333	117	1	2	0	1	1.000	-1	/O-9	0.0
1988	*Oak-A	146	507	100	154	38	1	24	94	47	92	.304	.367	.525	152	34	2	4	-2	.982	5	*O-143	3.3
1989	*Oak-A	152	579	77	145	24	3	15	80	54	131	.250	.318	.380	99	-1	8	5	-1	.977	5	*O-149/D-2	-0.1
1990	*Oak-A	127	450	65	122	28	0	20	63	40	105	.271	.332	.467	126	14	3	1	0	.988	9	*O-116/D-6	2.1
1991	Oak-A★	150	572	86	158	33	0	25	85	58	113	.276	.347	.465	130	22	6	6	-2	.997	11	*O-140/2-1,D-7	2.7
1992	Oak-A	20	63	1	9	1	0	0	2	2	16	.143	.169	.159	-8	-9	0	0	0	.950	-3	O-12/D-4	-1.2
1993	Oak-A	107	382	37	84	19	0	20	53	32	113	.220	.280	.427	93	-6	0	3	-2	.991	9	O-76,D-28	-0.2
1994	KC-A	56	198	27	49	14	1	5	31	16	28	.247	.307	.404	78	-7	2	0	1	.962	-0	O-40,D-16	-0.8
Total	14	1538	5130	710	1324	286	17	197	708	465	1105	.258	.322	.436	108	47	50	38	-8	.984	44	*O-1388/D-99,2-1	4.2

■ KEN HENDERSON

Henderson, Kenneth Joseph b: 6/15/46, Carroll, Iowa BB/TR, 6'2", 180 lbs. Deb: 4/23/65

YEAR	TM/L	G	AB	R	H	2B	3B	HR	RBI	BB	SO	AVG	OBP	SLG	PRO+	BR/A	SB	CS	SBR	FA	FR	G/POS	TPR
1965	SF-N	63	73	10	14	1	1	0	7	9	19	.192	.280	.233	45	-5	1	1	-0	.980	-9	O-48	-1.6
1966	SF-N	11	29	4	9	1	1	1	1	2	3	.310	.375	.517	141	2	0	0	0	.917	-3	O-10	-0.2
1967	SF-N	65	179	15	34	3	0	4	14	19	52	.190	.275	.274	58	-9	0	1	-1	.947	-5	O-52	-1.9
1968	SF-N	3	3	1	1	0	0	0	0	2	1	.333	.600	.333	186	1	0	0	0	1.000	-0	/O-2	0.0
1969	SF-N	113	374	42	84	14	4	6	44	42	64	.225	.311	.332	82	-9	6	4	-1	.969	-3	*O-111/3-3	-2.0
1970	SF-N	148	554	104	163	35	3	17	88	87	78	.294	.395	.460	130	26	20	3	4	.966	2	*O-146	2.4
1971	*SF-N	141	504	80	133	26	6	15	65	84	76	.264	.372	.429	128	21	18	3	4	.966	-1	*O-138/1-1	1.7
1972	SF-N	130	439	60	113	21	2	18	51	38	66	.257	.319	.437	112	5	14	7	0	.974	9	*O-123	0.9
1973	Chi-A	73	262	32	68	13	0	6	32	27	49	.260	.331	.378	96	-1	3	4	-2	.972	-1	O-44,D-26	-0.7
1974	Chi-A	162	602	76	176	35	5	20	95	66	112	.292	.364	.467	134	26	12	7	-1	.987	9	*O-162	2.8
1975	Chi-A	140	513	65	129	20	3	9	53	74	65	.251	.350	.355	98	1	5	3	-0	.990	13	*O-137/D-1	0.8
1976	Atl-N	133	435	52	114	19	0	13	61	62	68	.262	.355	.395	106	5	5	7	-3	.987	-12	*O-122	-1.6
1977	Tex-A	75	244	23	63	14	0	5	23	18	37	.258	.317	.377	87	-4	2	1	0	.983	-6	O-65/D-3	-1.3
1978	NY-N	7	22	2	5	2	0	1	4	4	4	.227	.346	.455	127	1	0	1	-1	1.000	0	/O-7	0.0
	Cin-N	64	144	10	24	6	1	3	19	23	32	.167	.281	.285	59	-8	0	0	0	1.000	-2	O-38	-1.2
	Yr	71	166	12	29	8	1	4	23	27	36	.175	.290	.307	67	-7	0	1	-1	1.000	-2	O-45	-1.2
1979	Cin-N	10	13	1	3	1	0	0	2	0	2	.231	.231	.308	45	-1	0	0	0	1.000	-0	/O-2	-0.2
	Chi-N	62	81	11	19	2	0	2	8	15	16	.235	.361	.333	83	-1	0	0	0	.950	-6	O-23	-0.8
	Yr	72	94	12	22	3	0	2	10	15	18	.234	.345	.330	79	-2	0	0	0	.955	-6	O-25	-1.0
1980	Chi-N	44	82	7	16	3	0	2	9	17	19	.195	.333	.305	74	-2	0	0	0	.944	-1	O-22	-0.4
Total	16	1444	4553	595	1168	216	26	122	576	589	763	.257	.346	.396	106	45	86	42	1	.977	-19	*O-1252/D-30,3-3,1	-3.3

■ RICKEY HENDERSON

Henderson, Rickey Henley b: 12/25/58, Chicago, Ill. BR/TL, 5'10", 195 lbs. Deb: 6/24/79

YEAR	TM/L	G	AB	R	H	2B	3B	HR	RBI	BB	SO	AVG	OBP	SLG	PRO+	BR/A	SB	CS	SBR	FA	FR	G/POS	TPR
1979	Oak-A	89	351	49	96	13	3	1	26	34	39	.274	.341	.336	88	-5	33	11	3	.973	3	O-88	-0.3
1980	Oak-A★	158	591	111	179	22	4	9	53	117	54	.303	.422	.399	136	37	**100**	26	14	.984	23	*O-157/D-1	**6.6**
1981	*Oak-A	108	423	**89**	**135**	18	7	6	35	64	68	.319	.411	.437	152	31	**56**	22	4	.979	20	*O-107	**5.2**
1982	Oak-A★	149	536	119	143	24	4	10	51	**116**	94	.267	.399	.382	121	22	**130**	42	**14**	.977	9	*O-144/D-4	4.0
1983	Oak-A★	145	513	105	150	25	7	9	48	**103**	80	.292	.415	.421	139	33	**108**	19	**21**	.992	9	*O-142/D-1	5.7
1984	Oak-A★	142	502	113	147	27	4	16	58	86	81	.293	.401	.458	147	35	**66**	18	9	.969	8	*O-140	4.7
1985	NY-A★	143	547	**146**	172	28	5	24	72	99	65	.314	.422	.516	159	48	**80**	10	**18**	.980	16	*O-141/D-1	**7.4**
1986	NY-A★	153	608	**130**	160	31	5	28	74	89	81	.263	.359	.469	125	21	**87**	18	**15**	.986	12	*O-146/D-5	4.2
1987	NY-A★	95	358	78	104	17	3	17	37	80	52	.291	.423	.497	144	27	41	8	8	.980	7	O-69,D-24	3.5
1988	NY-A★	140	554	118	169	30	2	6	50	82	54	.305	.397	.399	125	22	**93**	13	**20**	.965	10	*O-136/D-3	4.7
1989	NY-A	65	235	41	58	13	1	3	22	56	29	.247	.394	.349	112	7	25	8	3	.993	4	O-65	1.2
	*Oak-A	85	306	72	90	13	2	9	35	70	39	.294	.429	.438	150	25	52	6	12	.985	7	O-82/D-3	4.1
	Yr	150	541	**113**	148	26	3	12	57	**126**	68	.274	.413	.399	133	31	**77**	14	**15**	.988	11	*O-147/D-3	**5.3**
1990	*Oak-A★	136	489	**119**	159	33	3	28	61	97	60	.325	**.441**	.577	**190**	**63**	**65**	10	**14**	.983	11	*O-118,D-15	**8.2**
1991	Oak-A★	134	470	105	126	17	1	18	57	98	73	.268	.402	.423	136	28	**58**	18	7	.970	10	*O-119,D-10	4.1
1992	*Oak-A	117	396	77	112	18	3	15	46	95	56	.283	.429	.457	156	36	48	11	8	.984	6	*O-108/D-6	**4.7**
1993	Oak-A	90	318	77	104	19	1	17	47	85	46	.327	.472	.553	186	44	31	6	6	.974	9	O-74,D-16	5.3
	*Tor-A	44	163	37	35	3	1	4	12	35	19	.215	.360	.319	84	-2	22	2	5	.975	-2	O-44	0.0
	Yr	134	481	114	139	22	2	21	59	120	65	.289	.435	.474	150	41	53	8	11	.974	7	*O-118,D-16	5.3
1994	Oak-A	87	296	66	77	13	0	6	20	72	45	.260	.413	.365	112	10	22	7	2	.977	4	O-71,D-13	1.3
1995	Oak-A	112	407	67	122	31	1	9	54	72	66	.300	.410	.447	130	21	32	10	4	.988	1	O-90,D-19	2.0
1996	*SD-N	148	465	110	112	17	2	9	29	125	90	.241	.412	.344	108	14	37	15	2	.975	-3	*O-134	1.0
1997	SD-N	88	288	63	79	11	0	6	27	71	62	.274	.424	.375	120	13	29	4	6	.959	4	O-78/D-2	2.1
	Ana-A	32	115	21	21	3	0	2	7	26	23	.183	.343	.261	61	-6	16	4	2	1.000	-0	D-19,O-13	-0.5
1998	Oak-A	152	542	101	128	16	1	14	57	**118**	114	.236	.377	.347	93	-1	**66**	13	**12**	.988	-2	*O-151	0.5
Total	20	2612	9473	2014	2678	442	60	266	978	1890	1390	.283	.406	.426	133	522	1297	301	209	.979	164	*O-2417,D-142	79.7

■ STEVE HENDERSON

Henderson, Stephen Curtis b: 11/18/52, Houston, Tex. BR/TR, 6'2", 190 lbs. Deb: 6/16/77 C

YEAR	TM/L	G	AB	R	H	2B	3B	HR	RBI	BB	SO	AVG	OBP	SLG	PRO+	BR/A	SB	CS	SBR	FA	FR	G/POS	TPR
1977	NY-N	99	350	67	104	16	6	12	65	43	79	.297	.376	.480	134	17	6	3	0	.980	6	O-97	1.9
1978	NY-N	157	587	83	156	30	9	10	65	60	109	.266	.336	.399	108	6	13	7	-0	.968	16	*O-155	1.6
1979	NY-N	98	350	42	107	16	8	5	39	38	58	.306	.380	.440	128	14	13	5	1	.990	9	O-94	2.1
1980	NY-N	143	513	75	149	17	8	8	58	62	90	.290	.370	.402	119	14	23	12	-0	.981	13	*O-136	2.3
1981	Chi-N	82	287	32	84	9	5	5	35	42	61	.293	.387	.411	121	9	5	7	-3	.951	1	O-77	0.5
1982	Chi-N	92	257	23	60	12	4	2	29	22	64	.233	.294	.335	73	-9	6	5	-1	.956	0	O-70	-1.2
1983	Sea-A	121	436	50	128	32	3	10	54	44	82	.294	.358	.450	116	10	10	14	-5	.970	1	*O-112/D-6	0.2
1984	Sea-A	109	325	42	85	12	3	10	35	38	62	.262	.341	.409	108	4	2	4	-2	.936	-2	O-53,D-51	-0.3
1985	Oak-A	85	193	25	58	8	3	3	31	18	34	.301	.360	.420	122	6	0	0	0	.953	-7	O-58/D-1	-0.2
1986	Oak-A	11	26	2	2	1	0	0	3	0	5	.077	.077	.115	-52	-5	0	0	0	.800	-2	/O-7,D-1	-0.7
1987	Oak-A	46	114	14	33	7	0	3	9	12	19	.289	.357	.430	115	3	0	0	0	.943	-7	O-31/D-9	-0.5
1988	Hou-N	42	46	4	10	2	0	0	5	7	14	.217	.321	.261	72	-1	1	1	-0	1.000	0	/O-8,1-1	-0.2
Total	12	1085	3484	459	976	162	49	68	428	386	677	.280	.354	.413	113	66	79	58	-11	.968	29	O-898/D-68,1-1	5.5

■ GEORGE HENDRICK

Hendrick, George Andrew b: 10/18/49, Los Angeles, Cal. BR/TR, 6'3", 195 lbs. Deb: 6/4/71 C

YEAR	TM/L	G	AB	R	H	2B	3B	HR	RBI	BB	SO	AVG	OBP	SLG	PRO+	BR/A	SB	CS	SBR	FA	FR	G/POS	TPR
1971	Oak-A	42	114	8	27	4	1	0	8	3	20	.237	.256	.289	55	-7	0	1	-1	.981	-7	O-36	-1.8
1972	*Oak-A	58	121	10	22	1	1	4	15	3	22	.182	.208	.306	54	-7	3	2	-0	1.000	-7	O-41	-1.8
1973	Cle-A	113	440	64	118	18	0	21	61	25	71	.268	.310	.452	111	4	7	6	-2	.988	-3	*O-110	-0.6

YEAR	TM/L	G	AB	R	H	2B	3B	HR	RBI	BB	SO	AVG	OBP	SLG	PRO+	BR/A	SB	CS	SBR	FA	FR	G/POS	TPR
1974	Cle-A★	139	495	65	138	23	1	19	67	33	73	.279	.325	.444	121	11	6	4	-1	.989	3	*O-133/D-1	0.8
1975	Cle-A★	145	561	82	145	21	2	24	86	40	78	.258	.308	.431	107	3	6	7	-2	.983	1	*O-143	-0.5
1976	Cle-A	149	551	72	146	20	3	25	81	51	82	.265	.327	.448	127	17	4	4	-1	.987	3	*O-146/D-3	1.3
1977	SD-N	152	541	75	168	25	2	23	81	61	74	.311	.382	.492	148	35	11	6	-0	.983	8	*O-142	3.8
1978	SD-N	36	111	9	27	4	0	3	8	12	16	.243	.317	.360	96	-1	1	1	-0	.986	-0	O-33	-0.3
	StL-N	102	382	55	110	27	1	17	67	28	44	.288	.340	.497	133	15	1	0	0	.996	6	*O-101	1.8
	Yr	138	493	64	137	31	1	20	75	40	60	.278	.335	.467	126	15	2	1	0	.994	6	*O-134	1.5
1979	StL-N	140	493	67	148	27	1	16	75	49	62	.300	.363	.456	121	14	2	3	-1	.993	6	*O-138	1.4
1980	StL-N★	150	572	73	173	33	2	25	109	32	67	.302	.344	.498	128	20	6	1	1	.994	-6	*O-149	0.9
1981	StL-N	101	394	67	112	19	3	18	61	41	44	.284	.358	.485	134	17	4	2	0	.983	-4	*O-101	1.0
1982	*StL-N	136	515	65	145	20	5	19	104	37	80	.282	.331	.450	115	9	3	2	-0	.980	-2	*O-134	0.3
1983	StL-N☆	144	529	73	168	33	3	18	97	51	76	.318	.380	.493	140	28	3	4	-2	.992	1	1-92,O-51	2.1
1984	StL-N	120	441	57	122	28	1	9	69	32	75	.277	.327	.406	108	3	0	2	-1	.990	-1	*O-116/1-1	-0.2
1985	Pit-N	69	256	23	59	15	0	2	25	18	42	.230	.281	.313	66	-12	1	0	0	.971	3	O-65	-1.1
	Cal-A	16	41	5	5	1	0	2	6	4	8	.122	.200	.293	33	-4	0	0	0	1.000	-1	O-12/D-1	-0.5
1986	*Cal-A	102	283	45	77	13	1	14	47	26	41	.272	.335	.473	119	7	1	1	-0	.968	-6	O-93/1-7,D-4	-0.2
1987	Cal-A	65	162	14	39	10	0	5	25	14	18	.241	.301	.395	85	-4	0	0	0	.967	-8	O-45/1-9,D-5	-1.3
1988	Cal-A	69	127	12	31	1	0	3	19	7	20	.244	.289	.323	73	-5	0	1	-1	.933	-1	O-24,1-12/D-3	-0.8
Total	18	2048	7129	941	1980	343	27	267	1111	567	1013	.278	.333	.446	117	144	59	47	-11	.985	-17	*O-1813,1-121/D-17	4.3

■ HARVEY HENDRICK

Hendrick, Harvey "Gink" b: 11/9/1897, Mason, Tenn. d: 10/29/41, Covington, Tenn. BL/TR, 6'2", 190 lbs. Deb: 4/20/23

YEAR	TM/L	G	AB	R	H	2B	3B	HR	RBI	BB	SO	AVG	OBP	SLG	PRO+	BR/A	SB	CS	SBR	FA	FR	G/POS	TPR
1923	*NY-A	37	66	9	18	3	1	3	12	2	8	.273	.294	.485	101	-1	3	0	1	.947	-2	O-13	-0.2
1924	NY-A	40	76	7	20	0	0	1	11	2	7	.263	.291	.303	53	-5	1	0	0	.975	0	O-17	-0.6
1925	Cle-A	25	28	2	8	1	2	0	9	3	5	.286	.355	.464	106	0	0	0	0	1.000	0	/1-3	0.0
1927	Bro-N	128	458	55	142	18	11	4	50	24	40	.310	.350	.424	106	3	29			.969	-16	O-64,1-53/2-1	-2.0
1928	Bro-N	126	425	83	135	15	10	11	59	54	34	.318	.397	.478	129	19	16			.913	3	3-91,O-17	2.5
1929	Bro-N	110	384	69	136	25	6	14	82	31	20	.354	.404	.560	139	22	14			.975	0	O-42,1-39/3-7,S-4	1.5
1930	Bro-N	68	167	29	43	10	1	5	28	20	19	.257	.344	.419	84	-4	2			.947	-3	O-42/1-7	-0.9
1931	Bro-N	1	1	0	0	0	0	0	0	0	0	.000	.000	.000	-99	-0	0			.000	0	H	0.0
	Cin-N	137	530	74	167	32	9	1	75	53	40	.315	.379	.415	121	16	3			.987	-5	*1-137	-0.2
	Yr	138	531	74	167	32	9	1	75	53	40	.315	.379	.414	120	16	3			.987	-5	*1-137	-0.2
1932	StL-N	28	72	8	18	2	0	1	5	5	9	.250	.299	.319	64	-4	0			.862	-3	3-12/O-5	-0.6
	Cin-N	94	398	56	120	30	3	4	40	23	29	.302	.341	.422	107	4	3			.986	-4	1-94	-0.8
	Yr	122	470	64	138	32	3	5	45	28	38	.294	.335	.406	100	-0	3			.986	-7	1-94,3-12/O-5	-1.4
1933	Chi-N	69	189	30	55	13	3	4	23	13	17	.291	.346	.455	128	6	4			.983	-1	1-38/O-8,3-1	0.2
1934	Phi-N	59	116	12	34	8	0	0	19	9	15	.293	.344	.362	79	-3	0			.962	-3	O-12/1-7,3-7	-0.7
Total	11	922	2910	434	896	157	46	48	413	239	243	.308	.364	.443	113	53	75	0		.986	-32	1-378,O-220,3/S2	-1.8

■ ELLIE HENDRICKS

Hendricks, Elrod Jerome b: 12/22/40, Charlotte Amalie, V.I. BL/TR, 6'1", 175 lbs. Deb: 4/13/68 C

YEAR	TM/L	G	AB	R	H	2B	3B	HR	RBI	BB	SO	AVG	OBP	SLG	PRO+	BR/A	SB	CS	SBR	FA	FR	G/POS	TPR
1968	Bal-A	79	183	19	37	8	1	7	23	19	51	.202	.281	.372	96	-1	0	0	0	.991	-5	C-53	-0.3
1969	*Bal-A	105	295	36	72	5	0	12	38	39	44	.244	.336	.383	100	0	0	1	-1	**.998**	5	C-87/1-4	1.0
1970	*Bal-A	106	322	32	78	9	0	12	41	33	44	.242	.320	.382	92	-4	1	0	0	.986	-8	C-95	-0.7
1971	*Bal-A	101	316	33	79	14	1	9	42	39	38	.250	.336	.386	105	2	0	0	0	.985	-8	C-90/1-3	-0.2
1972	Bal-A	33	84	6	13	4	0	0	4	12	19	.155	.260	.202	38	-6	0	1	-1	.986	2	C-28	-0.5
	Chi-N	17	43	7	5	1	0	2	6	13	8	.116	.321	.279	65	-2	0	1	-1	.978	1	C-16	-0.1
1973	Bal-A	41	101	9	18	5	1	3	15	10	22	.178	.259	.337	67	-5	0	0	0	.994	4	C-38/D-1	0.1
1974	*Bal-A	66	159	18	33	8	2	3	8	17	25	.208	.288	.340	83	-4	0	0	0	1.000	-4	C-54/1-1,D-1	-0.7
1975	Bal-A	85	223	32	48	8	2	8	38	34	40	.215	.322	.377	103	1	0	1	-1	**.995**	-1	C-83	0.3
1976	Bal-A	28	79	2	11	1	0	1	4	7	13	.139	.209	.190	19	-8	0	1	-1	.971	-5	C-27	-1.4
	*NY-A	26	53	6	12	1	0	3	5	3	10	.226	.268	.415	99	-0	0	0	0	1.000	1	C-18	0.1
	Yr	54	132	8	23	2	0	4	9	10	23	.174	.232	.280	52	-8	0	1	-1	.982	-4	C-45	-1.3
1977	NY-A	10	11	1	3	1	0	1	5	0	2	.273	.273	.636	140	0	0	0	0	1.000	0	/C-6	0.1
1978	Bal-A	13	18	4	6	1	0	1	1	3	3	.333	.429	.556	186	2	0	0	0	.955	0	/C-6,P-1,D-1	0.2
1979	Bal-A	1	1	0	0	0	0	0	0	0	0	.000	.000	.000	-99	-0	0	0	0	.500	-1	/C-1	-0.1
Total	12	711	1888	205	415	66	7	62	230	229	319	.220	.308	.361	90	-24	1	5	-3	.990	-17	C-602/1-8,D-3,P-1	-2.2

■ JACK HENDRICKS

Hendricks, John Charles b: 4/9/1875, Joliet, Ill. d: 5/13/43, Chicago, Ill. BL/TL, 5'11.5", 160 lbs. Deb: 6/12/02 M

YEAR	TM/L	G	AB	R	H	2B	3B	HR	RBI	BB	SO	AVG	OBP	SLG	PRO+	BR/A	SB	CS	SBR	FA	FR	G/POS	TPR
1902	NY-N	8	26	1	6	2	0	0	0	2		.231	.286	.308	84	-1	2			.929	0	/O-7	-0.1
	Chi-N	2	7	0	4	0	1	0	0	0		.571	.571	.857	350	2	0			1.000	0	/O-2	0.2
	Yr	10	33	1	10	2	1	0	0	2		.303	.343	.424	138	1	2			.950	1	/O-9	0.1
1903	Was-A	32	112	10	20	1	3	0	4	13		.179	.264	.241	51	-6	3			.891	-4	O-32	-1.3
Total	2	42	145	11	30	3	4	0	4	15		.207	.281	.283	70	-5	5			.909	-3	/O-41	-1.2

■ TIM HENDRYX

Hendryx, Timothy Green b: 1/31/1891, LeRoy, Ill. d: 8/14/57, Corpus Christi, Tex. BR/TR, 5'9", 170 lbs. Deb: 9/4/11

YEAR	TM/L	G	AB	R	H	2B	3B	HR	RBI	BB	SO	AVG	OBP	SLG	PRO+	BR/A	SB	CS	SBR	FA	FR	G/POS	TPR
1911	Cle-A	4	7	0	2	0	0	0	0	0		.286	.286	.286	59	-0	0			1.000	-1	/3-3	-0.1
1912	Cle-A	23	70	9	17	2	4	1	14	8		.243	.329	.429	113	1	3			1.000	-2	O-22	-0.2
1915	NY-A	13	40	4	8	2	0	0	1	4	2	.200	.289	.250	61	-2	0	3	-2	.968	1	O-12	-0.4
1916	NY-A	15	62	10	18	7	1	0	5	8	6	.290	.380	.435	142	3	4			1.000	-2	O-15	0.1
1917	NY-A	125	393	43	98	14	7	5	44	62	45	.249	.359	.359	118	10	6			.955	5	*O-107	1.0
1918	StL-A	88	219	22	61	14	3	0	33	37	35	.279	.388	.370	133	10	5			.982	-9	O-65	-0.2
1920	Bos-A	99	363	54	119	21	5	0	73	42	27	.328	.400	.413	121	12	7	9	-3	.964	-10	O-98	-0.7
1921	Bos-A	49	137	10	33	8	2	0	22	24	13	.241	.362	.328	79	-3	1	1	-0	.958	-4	O-41	-1.0
Total	8	416	1291	152	356	68	22	6	192	185	128	.276	.372	.376	115	31	26	13		.966	-22	O-360/3-3	-1.5

■ DAVE HENGEL

Hengel, David Lee b: 12/18/61, Oakland, Cal. BR/TR, 6', 185 lbs. Deb: 9/3/86

YEAR	TM/L	G	AB	R	H	2B	3B	HR	RBI	BB	SO	AVG	OBP	SLG	PRO+	BR/A	SB	CS	SBR	FA	FR	G/POS	TPR
1986	Sea-A	21	63	3	12	1	0	1	6	1	13	.190	.215	.254	27	-6	0	0	0	1.000	-1	D-11/O-8	-0.7
1987	Sea-A	10	19	2	6	0	0	1	4	0	4	.316	.316	.474	100	-0	0	0	0	.875	-2	/O-7,D-1	-0.2
1988	Sea-A	26	60	3	10	1	0	2	7	1	15	.167	.180	.283	27	-6	0	0	0	.952	-1	O-12,D-12	-0.8
1989	Cle-A	12	25	2	3	1	0	0	1	2	4	.120	.185	.160	-2	-3	0	0	0	1.000	-1	/O-9,D-3	-0.4
Total	4	69	167	10	31	3	0	4	18	4	36	.186	.209	.275	31	-16	0	0	0	.962	-5	/O-36,D-27	-2.1

■ MOXIE HENGLE

Hengle, Emery J. b: 10/7/1857, Chicago, Ill. d: 12/11/24, River Forest, Ill. BR, 5'8", 144 lbs. Deb: 4/20/1884

YEAR	TM/L	G	AB	R	H	2B	3B	HR	RBI	BB	SO	AVG	OBP	SLG	PRO+	BR/A	SB	CS	SBR	FA	FR	G/POS	TPR
1884	CP-U	19	74	9	15	2	1	0		3		.203	.234	.257	49	-7				.840	-7	2-19	-1.2
	StP-U	9	33	2	5	1	1	0		0		.152	.152	.242	32	-6				.923	1	/2-9	-0.4
	Yr	28	107	11	20	3	2	0		3		.187	.209	.252	46	-11				.870	-6	2-28	-1.6
1885	Buf-N	7	26	2	4	0	0	0	0	1	2	.154	.185	.154	10	-3				.864	-3	/2-5,O-3	-0.5
Total	2	35	133	13	24	3	2	0	0	4	2	.180	.204	.233	38	-15				.869	-9	/2-33,O-3	-2.1

■ GAIL HENLEY

Henley, Gail Curtice b: 10/15/28, Wichita, Kan. BL/TR, 5'9", 180 lbs. Deb: 4/13/54

YEAR	TM/L	G	AB	R	H	2B	3B	HR	RBI	BB	SO	AVG	OBP	SLG	PRO+	BR/A	SB	CS	SBR	FA	FR	G/POS	TPR
1954	Pit-N	14	30	7	9	1	0	1	2	4	4	.300	.382	.433	114	1	0	0	0	1.000	-0	/O-9	0.0

■ BOB HENLEY

Henley, Robert Clifton b: 1/30/73, Mobile, Ala. BR/TR, 6'2", 190 lbs. Deb: 7/19/98

YEAR	TM/L	G	AB	R	H	2B	3B	HR	RBI	BB	SO	AVG	OBP	SLG	PRO+	BR/A	SB	CS	SBR	FA	FR	G/POS	TPR
1998	Mon-N	41	115	16	35	8	1	3	18	11	26	.304	.380	.470	123	4	3	0	1	.995	-6	C-35	0.2

■ BUTCH HENLINE

Henline, Walter John b: 12/20/1894, Ft.Wayne, Ind. d: 10/9/57, Sarasota, Fla. BR/TR, 5'10", 175 lbs. Deb: 4/13/21 U

YEAR	TM/L	G	AB	R	H	2B	3B	HR	RBI	BB	SO	AVG	OBP	SLG	PRO+	BR/A	SB	CS	SBR	FA	FR	G/POS	TPR
1921	NY-N	1	1	0	0	0	0	0	0	0	1	.000	.000	.000	-99	-0	0	0	0	.000	0	H	0.0
	Phi-N	33	111	8	34	2	0	0	8	2	6	.306	.319	.324	65	-5	1	0	0	.987	9	C-32	0.5
	Yr	34	112	8	34	2	0	0	8	2	7	.304	.316	.321	64	-6	1	0	0	.987	9	C-32	0.5
1922	Phi-N	125	430	57	136	20	4	14	64	36	33	.316	.380	.479	110	6	2	2	-1	**.983**	2	*C-119	1.2
1923	Phi-N	111	330	45	107	14	3	7	46	37	33	.324	.407	.448	112	7	7	5	-1	.978	-16	C-96/O-1	-0.5
1924	Phi-N	115	289	41	82	18	4	5	35	27	15	.284	.361	.426	98	-1	1	2	-1	.973	-1	C-83/O-2	0.2

YEAR	TM/L	G	AB	R	H	2B	3B	HR	RBI	BB	SO	AVG	OBP	SLG	PRO+	BR/A	SB	CS	SBR	FA	FR	G/POS	TPR
1925	Phi-N	93	263	43	80	12	5	8	48	24	16	.304	.380	.479	108	3	3	1	0	.956	-2	C-68/O-1	0.5
1926	Phi-N	99	283	32	80	14	1	2	30	21	18	.283	.339	.360	84	-6	1			.970	-10	C-77/1-4,O-2	-1.1
1927	Bro-N	67	177	12	47	10	3	1	18	17	10	.266	.337	.373	90	-3	1			.947	1	C-60	0.2
1928	Bro-N	55	132	12	28	3	1	2	8	17	8	.212	.302	.295	58	-8	2			.976	-4	C-45	-0.8
1929	Bro-N	27	62	5	15	2	0	1	7	9	9	.242	.338	.323	66	-3	0			.967	1	C-21	-0.1
1930	Chi-A	3	8	1	1	0	0	0	2	0	3	.125	.125	.125	-38	-2	0	0	0	1.000	0	/C-3	-0.1
1931	Chi-A	11	15	2	1	1	0	0	2	2	4	.067	.176	.133	-19	-3	0	0	0	.889	0	/C-4	-0.2
Total	11	740	2101	258	611	96	21	40	268	192	156	.291	.361	.414	96	-15	18	10		.971	-20	C-608/O-6,1-4	-0.2

■ LES HENNESSEY Hennessey, Lester Baker b: 12/12/1893, Lynn, Mass. d: 11/20/76, New York, N.Y. BR/TR, 6′, 190 lbs. Deb: 6/4/13

YEAR	TM/L	G	AB	R	H	2B	3B	HR	RBI	BB	SO	AVG	OBP	SLG	PRO+	BR/A	SB	CS	SBR	FA	FR	G/POS	TPR
1913	Det-A	14	22	2	3	0	0	0	0	3	6	.136	.240	.136	11	-2	2			.880	-2	2-10	-0.5

■ FRITZ HENRICH Henrich, Frank Wilde b: 5/8/1899, Cincinnati, Ohio d: 5/1/59, Philadelphia, Pa. BL/TL, 5′10″, 160 lbs. Deb: 4/21/24

YEAR	TM/L	G	AB	R	H	2B	3B	HR	RBI	BB	SO	AVG	OBP	SLG	PRO+	BR/A	SB	CS	SBR	FA	FR	G/POS	TPR
1924	Phi-N	36	90	4	19	4	0	0	4	2	12	.211	.228	.256	26	-9	0	0	0	.978	-9	O-32	-2.0

■ BOBBY HENRICH Henrich, Robert Edward b: 12/24/38, Lawrence, Kan. BR/TR, 6′1″, 185 lbs. Deb: 5/3/57

YEAR	TM/L	G	AB	R	H	2B	3B	HR	RBI	BB	SO	AVG	OBP	SLG	PRO+	BR/A	SB	CS	SBR	FA	FR	G/POS	TPR
1957	Cin-N	29	10	8	2	0	0	0	1	1	4	.200	.273	.200	28	-1	0	0	0	.875	0	/S-7,O-6,3-2,2-1	-0.1
1958	Cin-N	5	3	2	0	0	0	0	0	0	2	.000	.000	.000	-95	-1	0	0	0	1.000	1	/S-2	0.0
1959	Cin-N	14	3	3	0	0	0	0	0	0	1	.000	.000	.000	-97	-1	0	0	0	1.000	0	/S-5,3-1	-0.1
Total	3	48	16	13	2	0	0	0	1	1	7	.125	.176	.125	-17	-3	0	0	0	.929	1	/S-14,O-6,3-3,2-1	-0.2

■ TOMMY HENRICH Henrich, Thomas David "The Clutch" or "Old Reliable" b: 2/20/13, Massillon, Ohio BL/TL, 6′, 180 lbs. Deb: 5/11/37 C

YEAR	TM/L	G	AB	R	H	2B	3B	HR	RBI	BB	SO	AVG	OBP	SLG	PRO+	BR/A	SB	CS	SBR	FA	FR	G/POS	TPR
1937	NY-A	67	206	39	66	14	5	8	42	35	17	.320	.419	.553	142	14	4	0	1	.970	-4	O-59	0.8
1938	*NY-A	131	471	109	127	24	7	22	91	92	32	.270	.391	.490	120	15	6	2	1	.984	-1	*O-130	1.0
1939	NY-A	99	347	64	96	18	4	9	57	51	23	.277	.371	.429	106	3	7	0	2	.991	2	O-88/1-1	0.4
1940	NY-A	90	293	57	90	28	5	10	53	48	30	.307	.408	.539	149	22	1	2	-1	.969	-1	O-76/1-2	1.5
1941	*NY-A	144	538	106	149	27	5	31	85	81	40	.277	.377	.519	137	27	3	1	0	.980	-1	*O-139	1.8
1942	NY-A★	127	483	77	129	30	5	13	67	58	42	.267	.352	.431	122	13	4	4	-1	.987	-1	*O-119/1-7	0.4
1946	NY-A	150	565	92	142	25	4	19	83	87	63	.251	.358	.411	113	11	5	2	0	.992	2	*O-111,1-41	0.6
1947	*NY-A★	142	550	109	158	35	**13**	16	98	71	54	.287	.372	.485	139	27	3	2	-0	.983	6	*O-132/1-6	2.7
1948	NY-A★	146	588	**138**	181	42	**14**	25	100	76	42	.308	.391	.554	151	40	2	3	-1	.978	-0	*O-102,1-46	3.1
1949	*NY-A☆	115	411	90	118	20	3	24	85	86	34	.287	.416	.526	148	30	2	2	-1	.958	-4	O-61,1-52	2.1
1950	NY-A★	73	151	20	41	6	8	6	34	27	6	.272	.382	.536	137	8	0	1	-1	.987	-5	1-34	0.1
Total	11	1284	4603	901	1297	269	73	183	795	712	383	.282	.382	.491	132	211	37	19	-0	.981	-7	*O-1017,1-189	14.5

■ OLAF HENRIKSEN Henriksen, Olaf "Swede" b: 4/26/1888, Kirkerup, Denmark d: 10/17/62, Norwood, Mass. BL/TL, 5′7.5″, 158 lbs. Deb: 8/11/11

YEAR	TM/L	G	AB	R	H	2B	3B	HR	RBI	BB	SO	AVG	OBP	SLG	PRO+	BR/A	SB	CS	SBR	FA	FR	G/POS	TPR
1911	Bos-A	27	93	17	34	2	1	0	8	14		.366	.449	.409	141	6	4			.953	-0	O-25	0.4
1912	*Bos-A	44	56	20	18	3	1	0	8	14		.321	.457	.411	142	4	0			.909	-2	O-11	0.1
1913	Bos-A	31	40	8	15	1	0	0	2	7	5	.375	.468	.400	151	3	3			1.000	-1	/O-7	0.2
1914	Bos-A	63	95	16	25	2	1	1	5	22	12	.263	.407	.337	124	4	5	4	-1	.947	-5	O-29	-0.3
1915	*Bos-A	73	92	9	18	2	2	0	13	18	7	.196	.333	.261	80	-1	1	5	-3	.967	-4	O-25	-0.9
1916	*Bos-A	68	99	13	20	2	2	0	11	19	15	.202	.331	.263	78	-2	2			1.000	-4	O-31	-0.8
1917	Bos-A	15	12	1	1	0	0	0	1	3	4	.083	.267	.083	7	-1	0			.000	0	H	-0.1
Total	7	321	487	84	131	12	7	1	48	97	43	.269	.392	.329	112	13	15	9		.966	-17	O-128	-1.4

■ SNAKE HENRY Henry, Frederick Marshall b: 7/19/1895, Waynesville, N.C. d: 10/12/87, Wendell, N.C. BL/TL, 6′, 170 lbs. Deb: 9/15/22

YEAR	TM/L	G	AB	R	H	2B	3B	HR	RBI	BB	SO	AVG	OBP	SLG	PRO+	BR/A	SB	CS	SBR	FA	FR	G/POS	TPR
1922	Bos-N	18	66	5	13	4	1	0	5	2	8	.197	.221	.288	32	-7	2	2	-1	.995	1	1-18	-0.7
1923	Bos-N	11	9	1	1	0	0	0	2	1	1	.111	.200	.111	-17	-2	0	0	0	.000	0	H	-0.1
Total	2	29	75	6	14	4	1	0	7	3	9	.187	.218	.267	26	-8	2	2	-1	.995	1	/1-18	-0.8

■ GEORGE HENRY Henry, George Washington b: 8/10/1863, Philadelphia, Pa. d: 12/30/34, Lynn, Mass. BR/TR, 5′9″, 180 lbs. Deb: 4/27/1893

YEAR	TM/L	G	AB	R	H	2B	3B	HR	RBI	BB	SO	AVG	OBP	SLG	PRO+	BR/A	SB	CS	SBR	FA	FR	G/POS	TPR
1893	Cin-N	21	83	11	23	3	0	0	13	11	12	.277	.375	.313	82	-2	2			.965	5	O-21	0.1

■ JOHN HENRY Henry, John Michael b: 9/2/1863, Springfield, Mass. d: 6/11/39, Hartford, Conn. TL , Deb: 8/13/1884

YEAR	TM/L	G	AB	R	H	2B	3B	HR	RBI	BB	SO	AVG	OBP	SLG	PRO+	BR/A	SB	CS	SBR	FA	FR	G/POS	TPR
1884	Cle-N	9	26	2	4	0	0	0	0	0	12	.154	.154	.154	-3	-3				1.000	0	/P-5,O-4	-0.1
1885	Bal-a	10	34	4	9	3	0	0	3	1		.265	.286	.353	102	0				.931	2	/P-9,O-1	0.0
1886	Was-N	4	14	3	5	0	0	0	0	0	3	.357	.357	.357	125	0	0			.833	-0	/P-4	0.0
1890	NY-N	37	144	19	35	6	0	0	16	7	12	.243	.283	.285	65	-7	12			.870	-3	O-37	-0.9
Total	4	60	218	28	53	9	0	0	19	8	27	.243	.273	.284	66	-9	12			.867	-1	/O-42,P-18	-1.0

■ JOHN HENRY Henry, John Park "Bull" b: 12/26/1889, Amherst, Mass. d: 11/24/41, Fort Huachuca, Ariz. BR/TR, 6′, 180 lbs. Deb: 7/8/10

YEAR	TM/L	G	AB	R	H	2B	3B	HR	RBI	BB	SO	AVG	OBP	SLG	PRO+	BR/A	SB	CS	SBR	FA	FR	G/POS	TPR
1910	Was-A	29	87	2	13	1	1	0	5	2		.149	.169	.184	11	-9	2			.989	2	C-18,1-10	-0.7
1911	Was-A	85	261	24	53	5	0	0	21	25		.203	.273	.222	39	-21	8			.969	9	C-51,1-30	-0.7
1912	Was-A	66	191	23	37	4	1	0	9	31		.194	.309	.225	53	-11	10			.977	8	C-65	0.4
1913	Was-A	96	273	26	61	8	4	1	26	30	43	.223	.309	.293	75	-8	5			**.982**	3	C-96	0.3
1914	Was-A	92	261	22	44	7	4	0	20	37	47	.169	.274	.226	49	-16	7	3	0	.980	6	C-92	-0.2
1915	Was-A	95	277	20	61	9	2	1	22	36	28	.220	.323	.278	78	-6	10	2	2	.972	4	C-94	0.7
1916	Was-A	117	305	28	76	12	3	0	46	49	40	.249	.364	.308	103	4	12			.981	-4	*C-116	0.8
1917	Was-A	65	163	10	31	6	0	0	18	24	16	.190	.302	.227	62	-6	1			.988	1	C-59	-0.1
1918	Bos-N	43	102	6	21	2	0	0	4	10	15	.206	.283	.225	58	-5	0			.964	1	C-38	-0.1
Total	9	688	1920	161	397	54	15	2	171	244	189	.207	.303	.254	65	-79	55	5		.978	31	C-629/1-40	0.4

■ RON HENRY Henry, Ronald Baxter b: 8/7/36, Chester, Pa. BR/TR, 6′1″, 180 lbs. Deb: 4/15/61

YEAR	TM/L	G	AB	R	H	2B	3B	HR	RBI	BB	SO	AVG	OBP	SLG	PRO+	BR/A	SB	CS	SBR	FA	FR	G/POS	TPR
1961	Min-A	20	28	1	4	0	0	0	3	2	7	.143	.200	.143	-6	-4	0	0	0	1.000	-1	/C-5,1-1	-0.5
1964	Min-A	22	41	4	5	1	1	2	5	2	17	.122	.163	.341	36	-4	0	0	0	.984	-0	C-13	-0.4
Total	2	42	69	5	9	1	1	2	8	4	24	.130	.178	.261	18	-8	0	0	0	.988	-1	/C-18,1-1	-0.9

■ BABE HERMAN Herman, Floyd Caves b: 6/26/03, Buffalo, N.Y. d: 11/27/87, Glendale, Cal. BL/TL, 6′4″, 190 lbs. Deb: 4/14/26 C

YEAR	TM/L	G	AB	R	H	2B	3B	HR	RBI	BB	SO	AVG	OBP	SLG	PRO+	BR/A	SB	CS	SBR	FA	FR	G/POS	TPR
1926	Bro-N	137	496	64	158	35	11	11	81	44	53	.319	.375	.500	136	24	8			.986	0	*1-101,O-35	1.5
1927	Bro-N	130	412	65	112	26	9	14	73	39	41	.272	.336	.481	116	8	4			.980	0	*1-105/O-1	0.1
1928	Bro-N	134	486	64	165	37	6	12	91	38	36	.340	.390	.514	136	25	1			.937	-7	*O-127	1.0
1929	Bro-N	146	569	105	217	42	13	21	113	55	45	.381	.436	.612	160	52	21			.941	-17	*O-141/1-2	2.3
1930	Bro-N	153	614	143	241	48	11	35	130	66	56	.393	.455	.678	171	71	18			.978	-20	*O-153	3.4
1931	Bro-N	151	610	93	191	43	16	18	97	50	65	.313	.365	.525	137	30	17			.960	-1	*O-150	1.9
1932	Cin-N	148	577	87	188	38	**19**	16	87	60	45	.326	.389	.541	152	42	7			.969	16	*O-146	4.7
1933	Chi-N	137	508	77	147	36	12	16	93	50	57	.289	.353	.502	142	27	6			.957	-5	*O-131	1.5
1934	Chi-N	125	467	65	142	34	5	14	84	35	71	.304	.353	.488	125	15	1			.971	-10	*O-113/1-7	0.0
1935	Pit-N	26	81	8	19	8	1	0	7	3	10	.235	.271	.358	65	-4	0			.958	-3	O-15/1-3	-0.8
	Cin-N	92	349	44	117	23	5	10	58	35	25	.335	.396	.516	147	23	5			.976	-1	O-76,1-14	1.7
	Yr	118	430	52	136	31	6	10	65	38	35	.316	.373	.486	131	19	5			.974	-4	O-91,1-17	0.9
1936	Cin-N	119	380	59	106	25	2	13	71	39	36	.279	.348	.458	123	11	4			.967	-7	O-92/1-4	0.1
1937	Det-A	17	20	2	6	3	0	0	3	1	6	.300	.364	.450	102	0	2	0	1	1.000	-0	/O-2	0.0
1945	Bro-N	37	34	6	9	1	0	1	9	5	7	.265	.359	.382	107	0	0			.000	-1	/O-3	-0.1
Total	13	1552	5603	882	1818	399	110	181	997	520	553	.324	.383	.532	141	323	94	0		.961	-55	*O-1185,1-236	17.3

■ BILLY HERMAN Herman, William Jennings Bryan b: 7/7/09, New Albany, Ind. d: 9/5/92, W.Palm Beach, Fla. BR/TR, 5′11″, 180 lbs. Deb: 8/29/31 MCH

YEAR	TM/L	G	AB	R	H	2B	3B	HR	RBI	BB	SO	AVG	OBP	SLG	PRO+	BR/A	SB	CS	SBR	FA	FR	G/POS	TPR
1931	Chi-N	25	98	14	32	7	0	0	16	13	6	.327	.405	.398	115	3	2			.939	3	2-25	0.7
1932	*Chi-N	154	656	102	206	42	7	1	51	40	33	.314	.358	.404	105	6	14			.961	17	*2-154	3.0
1933	Chi-N	153	619	82	173	35	2	0	44	45	34	.279	.332	.342	93	-5	5			.956	29	*2-153	3.5
1934	Chi-N★	113	456	79	138	21	6	3	42	34	31	.303	.355	.395	102	2	6			.975	16	*2-111	2.3
1935	*Chi-N★	154	666	113	**227**	**57**	6	7	83	42	29	.341	.383	.476	128	26	6			**.964**	19	*2-154	5.4
1936	Chi-N★	153	632	101	211	57	7	5	93	59	30	.334	.392	.470	128	25	5			**.975**	15	*2-153	5.0

YEAR	TM/L	G	AB	R	H	2B	3B	HR	RBI	BB	SO	AVG	OBP	SLG	PRO+	BR/A	SB	CS	SBR	FA	FR	G/POS	TPR
1937	Chi-N★	138	564	106	189	35	11	8	65	56	22	.335	.396	.479	131	25	2			.954	19	*2-137	5.2
1938	*Chi-N★	152	624	86	173	34	7	1	56	59	31	.277	.342	.359	90	-7	3			**.981**	25	*2-151	2.6
1939	Chi-N★	156	623	111	191	34	**18**	7	70	66	31	.307	.378	.453	120	18	9			.967	-3	*2-156	2.3
1940	Chi-N★	135	558	77	163	24	4	5	57	47	30	.292	.347	.376	101	1	1			.974	19	*2-135	2.9
1941	Chi-N	11	36	4	7	0	1	0	0	9	5	.194	.356	.250	75	-1	0			.898	-5	2-11	-0.5
	*Bro-N★	133	536	77	156	30	4	3	41	58	38	.291	.361	.379	104	4	1			.970	-27	*2-133	-1.4
	Yr	144	572	81	163	30	5	3	41	67	43	.285	.361	.371	103	3	1			.964	-32	*2-144	-1.9
1942	Bro-N★	155	571	76	146	34	2	2	65	72	52	.256	.339	.333	95	-2	6			.973	-11	*2-153/1-3	-0.4
1943	Bro-N★	153	585	76	193	41	2	2	100	66	26	.330	.398	.417	135	28	4			.971	-17	*2-117,3-37	1.9
1946	Bro-N	47	184	24	53	8	4	0	28	26	10	.288	.376	.375	112	4	2			.945	-2	3-29,2-16	0.4
	Bos-N	75	252	32	77	23	1	3	22	43	13	.306	.409	.440	139	14	1			.956	-16	2-44,1-22/3-5	0.0
	Yr	122	436	56	130	31	5	3	50	69	23	.298	.395	.413	128	18	3			.968	-18	2-60,3-34,1-22	0.4
1947	Pit-N	15	47	3	10	4	0	0	6	2	7	.213	.245	.298	42	-4	0			1.000	-9	2-10/1-2,M	-1.2
Total	15	1922	7707	1163	2345	486	82	47	839	737	428	.304	.367	.407	112	138	67			.967	71	*2-1813/3-71,1-27	31.7
■ **AL HERMANN**	Hermann, Albert Bartel b: 3/28/1899, Milltown, N.J. d: 8/20/80, Lewes, Del. BR/TR, 6′, 180 lbs. Deb: 7/17/23																						
1923	Bos-N	31	93	2	22	4	0	0	11	0	7	.237	.237	.280	37	-9	3	2	-0	.957	-6	2-15/3-5,1-4	-1.4
1924	Bos-N	1	1	0	0	0	0	0	0	0	1	.000	.000	.000	-99	-0	0	0	0	.000	0	H	0.0
Total	2	32	94	2	22	4	0	0	11	0	8	.234	.234	.277	36	-9	3	2	-0	.957	-6	/2-15,3-5,1-4	-1.4
■ **GENE HERMANSKI**	Hermanski, Eugene Victor b: 5/11/20, Pittsfield, Mass. BL/TR, 5′11.5″, 185 lbs. Deb: 8/15/43																						
1943	Bro-N	18	60	6	18	2	1	0	12	11	7	.300	.417	.367	127	3	1			.976	3	O-17	0.5
1946	Bro-N	64	110	15	22	2	2	0	8	17	10	.200	.313	.255	61	-5	2			.938	-7	O-34	-1.4
1947	*Bro-N	79	189	36	52	7	1	7	39	28	7	.275	.377	.434	111	3	5			.982	-7	O-66	-0.6
1948	Bro-N	133	400	63	116	22	7	15	60	64	46	.290	.391	.493	133	19	15			.971	4	*O-119	1.7
1949	*Bro-N	87	224	48	67	12	3	8	42	47	21	.299	.431	.487	140	15	12			.980	-4	O-77	0.8
1950	Bro-N	94	289	36	86	17	3	7	34	36	26	.298	.381	.450	115	7	2			.989	3	O-78	0.7
1951	Bro-N	31	80	8	20	4	0	1	5	10	12	.250	.333	.338	79	-2	0	2	-1	.977	1	O-19	-0.3
	Chi-N	75	231	28	65	12	1	3	20	35	30	.281	.385	.381	105	3	3	0	1	.966	5	O-63	0.6
	Yr	106	311	36	85	16	1	4	25	45	42	.273	.372	.370	98	1	3	2	-0	.969	6	O-82	0.3
1952	Chi-N	99	275	28	70	6	0	4	34	29	32	.255	.330	.320	80	-7	2	0	1	.981	2	O-76	-0.7
1953	Chi-N	18	40	1	6	1	0	0	1	4	7	.150	.227	.175	7	-5	1	0	0	1.000	-2	O-13	-0.7
	Pit-N	41	62	7	11	0	0	1	4	8	14	.177	.282	.226	35	-6	0	0	0	1.000	-0	O-13	-0.6
	Yr	59	102	8	17	1	0	1	5	12	21	.167	.261	.206	24	-11	1	0	0	1.000	-2	O-26	-1.3
Total	9	739	1960	276	533	85	18	46	259	289	212	.272	.372	.404	107	25	43	2		.977	-1	O-575	-0.0
■ **REMY HERMOSO**	Hermoso, Angel Remigio b: 10/1/46, Carabobo, Venezuela BR/TR, 5′8″, 155 lbs. Deb: 9/14/67																						
1967	Atl-N	11	26	3	8	0	0	0	0	2	4	.308	.357	.308	93	-0	1	0	0	.952	1	/S-9,2-2	0.2
1969	Mon-N	28	74	6	12	0	0	0	3	5	10	.162	.225	.162	10	-9	3	1	0	.968	4	2-18/S-6	-0.3
1970	Mon-N	4	1	1	0	0	0	0	0	0	0	.000	.000	.000	-99	-0	0	0	0	1.000	0	/2-1,3-1	0.0
1974	Cle-A	48	122	15	27	3	1	0	5	7	7	.221	.264	.262	52	-8	2	2	-1	.967	7	2-45	0.1
Total	4	91	223	25	47	3	1	0	8	14	21	.211	.261	.233	42	-17	6	3	0	.968	12	/2-66,S-15,3-1	-0.0
■ **CARLOS HERNANDEZ**	Hernandez, Carlos Alberto (Almeida) b: 5/24/67, San Felix, Venez. BR/TR, 5′11″, 218 lbs. Deb: 4/20/90																						
1990	LA-N	10	20	2	4	1	0	0	1	0	2	.200	.200	.250	24	-2	0	0	0	1.000	1	C-10	-0.1
1991	LA-N	15	14	1	3	1	0	0	1	0	5	.214	.267	.286	57	-1	1	0	0	.966	1	C-13/3-1	0.0
1992	LA-N	69	173	11	45	4	0	3	17	11	21	.260	.319	.335	87	-3	0	1	-1	.979	2	C-63	0.2
1993	LA-N	50	99	6	25	5	0	2	7	2	11	.253	.267	.364	71	-4	0	0	0	.966	7	C-43	0.4
1994	LA-N	32	64	6	14	2	0	2	6	1	14	.219	.231	.344	51	-5	0	0	0	1.000	5	C-27	0.1
1995	LA-N	45	94	3	14	1	0	2	8	7	25	.149	.216	.223	18	-12	0	0	0	.983	12	C-41	0.2
1996	LA-N	13	14	1	4	0	0	0	0	2	2	.286	.375	.286	84	-0	0	0	0	1.000	2	/C-9	0.2
1997	SD-N	50	134	15	42	7	1	3	14	3	27	.313	.328	.448	109	1	0	2	-1	.989	3	C-44/1-4	0.5
1998	*SD-N	129	390	34	102	15	0	9	52	16	54	.262	.306	.369	82	-12	2	2	-1	.992	10	*C-122/1-1	0.6
Total	9	413	1002	79	253	36	1	21	106	42	161	.252	.293	.353	76	-38	3	5	-2	.986	43	C-372/1-5,3-1	2.1
■ **CESAR HERNANDEZ**	Hernandez, Cesar Dario (Perez) b: 9/28/66, Yamasa, D.R. BR/TR, 6′, 160 lbs. Deb: 7/19/92																						
1992	Cin-N	34	51	6	14	4	0	0	4	0	10	.275	.275	.353	74	-2	3	1	0	.952	-2	O-18	-0.4
1993	Cin-N	27	24	3	2	0	0	0	1	1	8	.083	.120	.083	-44	-5	1	2	-1	.970	-2	O-23	-0.8
Total	2	61	75	9	16	4	0	0	5	1	18	.213	.224	.267	35	-7	4	3	-1	.963	-5	/O-41	-1.2
■ **ENZO HERNANDEZ**	Hernandez, Enzo Octavio b: 2/12/49, Valle De Guanape, Venez. BR/TR, 5′8″, 155 lbs. Deb: 4/17/71																						
1971	SD-N	143	549	58	122	9	3	0	12	54	34	.222	.295	.250	60	-28	21	5	3	.955	-11	*S-143	-1.9
1972	SD-N	114	329	33	64	11	2	1	15	22	25	.195	.245	.249	44	-25	24	3	5	.963	5	*S-107/O-3	-0.1
1973	SD-N	70	247	26	55	2	1	0	9	17	14	.223	.273	.239	47	-18	15	4	2	.977	-1	S-67	-0.9
1974	SD-N	147	512	55	119	19	2	0	34	38	36	.232	.285	.277	60	-27	37	10	5	.966	-8	*S-145	-1.2
1975	SD-N	116	344	37	75	12	2	0	19	26	25	.218	.277	.265	54	-22	20	4	4	.965	8	*S-111	0.0
1976	SD-N	113	340	31	87	13	3	1	24	32	16	.256	.320	.321	89	-5	12	7	-1	.964	4	*S-101	1.1
1977	SD-N	7	3	1	0	0	0	0	0	0	0	.000	.000	.000	-99	-1	0	0	0	1.000	2	/S-7	0.1
1978	LA-N	4	3	0	0	0	0	0	0	0	1	.000	.000	.000	-99	-1	0	0	0	.000	0	/S-2	-0.1
Total	8	714	2327	241	522	66	13	2	113	189	151	.224	.284	.266	59	-127	129	33	19	.964	-1	S-683/O-3	-3.0
■ **JACKIE HERNANDEZ**	Hernandez, Jacinto (Zulueta) b: 9/11/40, Central Tinguaro, Cuba BR/TR, 6′, 175 lbs. Deb: 9/14/65																						
1965	Cal-A	6	6	2	2	1	0	0	1	0	1	.333	.333	.500	137	0	1	0	0	1.000	-0	/S-2,3-1	0.0
1966	Cal-A	58	23	19	1	0	0	0	2	1	4	.043	.083	.043	-64	-5	1	1	-0	.857	13	3-11/2-8,S-8,O-3	0.9
1967	Min-A	29	28	1	4	0	0	0	3	0	6	.143	.143	.143	-14	-4	0	0	0	.974	6	S-15,3-13	0.3
1968	Min-A	83	199	13	35	3	0	2	17	9	52	.176	.219	.221	32	-16	5	2	0	.927	9	S-79/1-1	-0.1
1969	KC-A	145	504	54	112	14	2	4	40	38	111	.222	.279	.282	57	-29	17	7	1	.954	-15	*S-144	-3.0
1970	KC-A	83	238	14	55	4	1	2	10	15	50	.231	.282	.282	56	-14	1	3	-2	.951	-5	S-77	-1.4
1971	*Pit-N	88	233	30	48	7	3	3	26	17	45	.206	.260	.300	59	-13	0	2	-1	.950	12	S-75/3-9	0.6
1972	Pit-N	72	176	12	33	7	1	1	14	9	43	.188	.227	.256	38	-15	0	0	0	.929	17	S-68/3-4	0.9
1973	Pit-N	54	73	8	18	1	2	0	8	4	12	.247	.286	.315	68	-3	0	0	0	.940	17	S-49	1.6
Total	9	618	1480	153	308	37	9	12	121	93	324	.208	.258	.270	49	-99	25	15	-1	.945	53	S-517/3-38,2-8,O1	-0.2
■ **JOSE HERNANDEZ**	Hernandez, Jose Antonio (Figueroa) b: 7/14/69, Rio Piedras, P.R. BR/TR, 6′1″, 180 lbs. Deb: 8/9/91																						
1991	Tex-A	45	98	8	18	2	1	0	4	3	31	.184	.208	.224	20	-11	0	1	-1	.975	9	S-44/3-1	0.0
1992	Cle-A	3	4	0	0	0	0	0	0	0	2	.000	.000	.000	-99	-1	0	0	0	.857	-0	/S-3	-0.1
1994	Chi-N	56	132	18	32	2	3	1	9	8	29	.242	.291	.326	61	-8	2	2	-1	.938	0	3-28,S-21/2-8,O-1	-0.6
1995	Chi-N	93	245	37	60	11	4	13	40	13	69	.245	.283	.482	99	-2	1	0	0	.961	10	S-43,2-29,3-20	1.2
1996	Chi-N	131	331	52	80	14	1	10	41	24	97	.242	.295	.381	75	-13	4	0	1	.948	-7	S-87,3-43/2-1,O-1	-1.1
1997	Chi-N	121	183	33	50	8	5	7	26	14	42	.273	.325	.486	106	1	2	5	-2	.922	-3	3-47,S-21,2/O1D	-0.3
1998	*Chi-N	149	488	76	124	23	7	23	75	40	140	.254	.312	.471	97	-4	4	6	-2	.958	3	3-72,O-54,S-45,/12	0.1
Total	7	598	1481	224	364	60	21	54	195	102	410	.246	.296	.424	85	-37	13	14	-5	.960	12	S-264,3-211/O21D	-0.8
■ **KEITH HERNANDEZ**	Hernandez, Keith b: 10/20/53, San Francisco, Cal. BL/TL, 6′, 195 lbs. Deb: 8/30/74																						
1974	StL-N	14	34	3	10	1	2	0	2	7	8	.294	.415	.441	141	2	0	0	0	.973	-2	/1-9	0.0
1975	StL-N	64	188	20	47	8	2	3	20	17	26	.250	.312	.362	84	-4	0	1	-1	.996	3	1-56	-0.5
1976	StL-N	129	374	54	108	21	5	7	46	49	53	.289	.376	.428	126	14	4	2	0	.990	16	*1-110	2.4
1977	StL-N	161	560	90	163	41	4	15	91	79	88	.291	.380	.459	126	22	7	7	-2	.992	5	*1-158	1.5
1978	StL-N	159	542	90	138	32	4	11	64	82	68	.255	.355	.389	109	8	13	5	1	.994	3	*1-158	0.3
1979	StL-N★	161	610	**116**	210	**48**	11	11	105	80	78	**.344**	**.421**	.513	152	46	11	6	-0	.995	19	*1-160	5.6
1980	StL-N★	159	595	**111**	191	39	8	16	99	86	73	.321	**.410**	.494	147	40	14	8	-1	.995	5	*1-157	3.6

YEAR	TM/L	G	AB	R	H	2B	3B	HR	RBI	BB	SO	AVG	OBP	SLG	PRO+	BR/A	SB	CS	SBR	FA	FR	G/POS	TPR
1981	StL-N	103	376	65	115	27	4	8	48	61	45	.306	.405	.463	142	23	12	5	1	.997	6	1-98/O-3	2.5
1982	*StL-N	160	579	79	173	33	6	7	94	100	67	.299	.404	.413	128	26	19	11	-1	.994	6	*1-158/O-4	2.4
1983	StL-N	55	218	34	62	15	4	3	26	24	30	.284	.355	.431	117	5	1	1	-0	.991	3	1-54	0.5
	NY-N	95	320	43	98	8	3	9	37	64	42	.306	.425	.434	140	21	8	4	0	.993	11	1-90	2.7
	Yr	150	538	77	160	23	7	12	63	88	72	.297	.398	.433	131	26	9	5	-0	.992	14	*1-144	3.2
1984	NY-N★	154	550	83	171	31	0	15	94	97	89	.311	.415	.449	145	37	2	3	-1	.994	18	*1-153	4.6
1985	NY-N	158	593	87	183	34	4	10	91	77	59	.309	.390	.430	132	28	3	3	-1	**.997**	16	*1-157	3.4
1986	*NY-N★	149	551	94	171	34	1	13	83	**94**	69	.310	.414	.446	141	35	2	1	0	**.996**	18	*1-149	4.4
1987	NY-N★	154	587	87	170	28	2	18	89	81	104	.290	.379	.436	122	20	0	2	-1	.993	18	*1-154	2.5
1988	*NY-N	95	348	43	96	16	0	11	55	31	57	.276	.337	.417	121	9	2	1	0	.998	8	1-93	1.0
1989	NY-N	75	215	18	50	8	0	4	19	27	39	.233	.324	.326	90	-2	0	3	-2	.991	-2	1-58	-1.1
1990	Cle-A	43	130	7	26	2	0	1	8	14	17	.200	.283	.238	47	-9	0	0	0	.994	-2	1-42	-1.4
Total	17	2088	7370	1124	2182	426	60	162	1071	1070	1012	.296	.388	.436	129	320	98	63	-8	.994	148	*1-2014/O-7	34.4

■ LEO HERNANDEZ

Hernandez, Leonardo Jesus b: 11/6/59, Santa Lucia, Venez. BR/TR, 5'11", 170 lbs. Deb: 9/19/82

YEAR	TM/L	G	AB	R	H	2B	3B	HR	RBI	BB	SO	AVG	OBP	SLG	PRO+	BR/A	SB	CS	SBR	FA	FR	G/POS	TPR
1982	Bal-A	2	2	0	0	0	0	0	0	0	2	.000	.000	.000	-99	-1	0	0	0	.000	0	/H	-0.1
1983	Bal-A	64	203	21	50	6	1	6	26	12	19	.246	.288	.374	82	-5	1	0	0	.922	-12	3-64	-1.8
1985	Bal-A	12	21	0	1	0	0	0	0	0	4	.048	.048	.048	-76	-5	0	0	0	1.000	-1	/1-1,O-1,D-8	-0.6
1986	NY-A	7	22	2	5	2	0	1	4	1	8	.227	.261	.455	91	-0	0	0	0	1.000	-1	/3-7,2-1	-0.1
Total	4	85	248	23	56	8	1	7	30	13	33	.226	.264	.351	69	-11	1	0	0	.927	-13	/3-71,D-8,2-1,O1	-2.6

■ PEDRO HERNANDEZ

Hernandez, Pedro Julio (b: Pedro Julio Montas (Hernandez)) b: 4/4/59, LaRomana, D.R. BR/TR, 6'1", 160 lbs. Deb: 9/8/79

YEAR	TM/L	G	AB	R	H	2B	3B	HR	RBI	BB	SO	AVG	OBP	SLG	PRO+	BR/A	SB	CS	SBR	FA	FR	G/POS	TPR
1979	Tor-A	3	0	1	0	0	0	0	0	0	0	—	—	—	—	0	0	0	0	.000	0	/R	0.0
1982	Tor-A	8	9	1	0	0	0	0	0	0	3	.000	.000	.000	-92	-2	0	0	0	.000	-1	/3-2,O-1,D-3	-0.3
Total	2	11	9	2	0	0	0	0	0	0	3	.000	.000	.000	-92	-2	0	0	0	—	-1	/D-3,3-2,O-1	-0.3

■ TOBY HERNANDEZ

Hernandez, Rafael Tobias (Alvarado) b: 11/30/58, Calabozo, Venez. BR/TR, 6'1", 160 lbs. Deb: 6/22/84

YEAR	TM/L	G	AB	R	H	2B	3B	HR	RBI	BB	SO	AVG	OBP	SLG	PRO+	BR/A	SB	CS	SBR	FA	FR	G/POS	TPR
1984	Tor-A	3	2	1	1	0	0	0	0	0	0	.500	.500	.500	171	0	0	0	0	1.000	-1	/C-3	0.0

■ RUDY HERNANDEZ

Hernandez, Rodolfo (Acosta) b: 10/18/51, Empalme, Mexico BR/TR, 5'9", 150 lbs. Deb: 9/6/72

YEAR	TM/L	G	AB	R	H	2B	3B	HR	RBI	BB	SO	AVG	OBP	SLG	PRO+	BR/A	SB	CS	SBR	FA	FR	G/POS	TPR
1972	Chi-A	8	21	0	4	0	0	0	1	0	3	.190	.190	.190	13	-2	0	0	0	1.000	1	/S-6	-0.1

■ CHICO HERNANDEZ

Hernandez, Salvador Jose (Ramos) b: 1/3/16, Havana, Cuba d: 1/3/86, Havana, Cuba BR/TR, 6', 195 lbs. Deb: 4/16/42

YEAR	TM/L	G	AB	R	H	2B	3B	HR	RBI	BB	SO	AVG	OBP	SLG	PRO+	BR/A	SB	CS	SBR	FA	FR	G/POS	TPR
1942	Chi-N	47	118	6	27	5	0	0	7	11	13	.229	.295	.271	69	-5	0			.975	-2	C-43	-0.4
1943	Chi-N	43	126	10	34	4	0	0	9	9	9	.270	.324	.302	82	-3	0			.981	-3	C-41	-0.3
Total	2	90	244	16	61	9	0	0	16	20	22	.250	.309	.287	76	-7	0			.978	-5	/C-84	-0.7

■ LARRY HERNDON

Herndon, Larry Darnell b: 11/3/53, Sunflower, Miss. BR/TR, 6'3", 195 lbs. Deb: 9/4/74 C

YEAR	TM/L	G	AB	R	H	2B	3B	HR	RBI	BB	SO	AVG	OBP	SLG	PRO+	BR/A	SB	CS	SBR	FA	FR	G/POS	TPR
1974	StL-N	12	1	3	1	0	0	0	0	0	0	1.000	1.000	1.000	465	0	0	0	0	1.000	-0	/O-1	0.0
1976	SF-N	115	337	42	97	11	3	2	23	23	45	.288	.337	.356	94	-2	12	10	-2	.967	-6	*O-110	-1.5
1977	SF-N	49	109	13	26	4	3	1	5	5	20	.239	.278	.358	69	-5	4	2	0	.957	-3	O-44	-0.9
1978	SF-N	151	471	52	122	15	9	1	32	35	71	.259	.312	.335	84	-11	13	8	-1	.974	4	*O-149	-1.4
1979	SF-N	132	354	35	91	14	5	7	36	29	70	.257	.315	.384	96	-3	8	6	-1	.963	-15	*O-122	-2.3
1980	SF-N	139	493	54	127	17	11	8	49	19	91	.258	.287	.385	88	-10	8	8	-2	.959	-4	*O-122	-2.3
1981	SF-N	96	364	48	105	15	8	5	41	20	55	.288	.327	.415	111	4	15	6	1	.977	5	O-93	0.8
1982	Det-A	157	614	92	179	21	13	23	88	38	92	.292	.334	.480	120	15	12	9	-2	.983	6	*O-155/D-3	1.5
1983	Det-A	153	603	88	182	28	9	20	92	46	95	.302	.354	.478	130	23	9	3	1	.951	1	*O-133,D-19	2.0
1984	*Det-A	125	407	52	114	18	5	7	43	32	63	.280	.336	.400	103	2	6	2	1	.986	-5	*O-117/D-4	-0.5
1985	Det-A	137	442	45	108	12	7	12	37	33	79	.244	.298	.385	86	-9	2	1	0	.976	5	*O-136	-0.8
1986	Det-A	106	283	33	70	13	1	8	37	27	40	.247	.315	.385	90	-4	2	1	0	.988	-1	O-83,D-18	-0.8
1987	*Det-A	89	225	32	73	13	2	9	47	23	35	.324	.387	.520	144	14	1	0	0	.989	-4	O-57,D-23	0.8
1988	Det-A	76	174	16	39	5	0	4	20	23	37	.224	.318	.322	83	-4	0	1	-1	1.000	-2	D-53,O-15	-0.8
Total	14	1537	4877	605	1334	186	76	107	550	353	793	.274	.325	.409	103	11	92	57	-7	.972	-19	*O-1337,D-120	-6.2

■ TOM HERNON

Hernon, Thomas H. b: 11/4/1866, E.Bridgewater, Mass d: 2/4/02, New Bedford, Mass. BR/TR, Deb: 9/13/1897

YEAR	TM/L	G	AB	R	H	2B	3B	HR	RBI	BB	SO	AVG	OBP	SLG	PRO+	BR/A	SB	CS	SBR	FA	FR	G/POS	TPR
1897	Chi-N	4	16	2	1	0	0	0	2	0		.063	.063	.063	-65	-4	1			1.000	0	/O-4	-0.4

■ ED HERR

Herr, Edward Joseph b: 5/18/1862, St.Louis, Mo. d: 7/18/43, St.Louis, Mo. BR/TR, 5'9.5", 179 lbs. Deb: 4/16/1887

YEAR	TM/L	G	AB	R	H	2B	3B	HR	RBI	BB	SO	AVG	OBP	SLG	PRO+	BR/A	SB	CS	SBR	FA	FR	G/POS	TPR
1887	Cle-a	11	44	6	12	2	0	0	6	6		.273	.360	.318	93	-0	2			.729	-3	3-11	-0.2
1888	*StL-a	43	172	21	46	7	1	3	43	11		.267	.323	.372	110	1	9			.872	-9	S-28,O-11/3-4	-0.7
1890	StL-a	12	41	5	9	2	1	0	1	5		.220	.347	.317	84	-1	2			.793	-7	/2-7,O-4,3-1	-0.7
Total	3	66	257	32	67	11	2	3	50	22		.261	.333	.354	102	-0	13			.762	-18	/S-28,3-16,O-15,2-7	-1.6

■ TOM HERR

Herr, Thomas Mitchell b: 4/4/56, Lancaster, Pa. BB/TR, 6', 185 lbs. Deb: 8/13/79

YEAR	TM/L	G	AB	R	H	2B	3B	HR	RBI	BB	SO	AVG	OBP	SLG	PRO+	BR/A	SB	CS	SBR	FA	FR	G/POS	TPR
1979	StL-N	14	10	4	2	0	0	0	1	2	2	.200	.333	.200	49	-1	1	0	0	1.000	6	/2-6	0.5
1980	StL-N	76	222	29	55	12	5	0	15	16	21	.248	.301	.347	78	-7	9	2	2	.984	2	2-58,S-14	0.1
1981	StL-N	103	411	50	110	14	9	0	46	39	30	.268	.333	.345	90	-5	23	7	3	**.992**	4	*2-103	0.9
1982	*StL-N	135	493	83	131	19	4	0	36	57	56	.266	.344	.320	86	-7	25	12	0	.987	4	*2-128	0.3
1983	StL-N	89	313	43	101	14	4	2	31	43	27	.323	.406	.412	127	13	6	8	-3	.986	-19	2-86	-0.4
1984	StL-N	145	558	67	154	23	2	4	49	49	56	.276	.337	.346	94	-3	13	7	-0	.992	-1	*2-144	0.1
1985	*StL-N★	159	596	97	180	38	3	8	110	80	55	.302	.386	.416	126	23	31	3	8	.985	-31	*2-158	0.6
1986	StL-N	152	559	48	141	30	4	2	61	73	75	.252	.344	.331	88	-7	22	8	2	.988	-22	*2-152	-2.2
1987	*StL-N	141	510	73	134	29	0	2	83	68	62	.263	.353	.331	81	-12	19	4	3	.989	-17	*2-137	-1.9
1988	StL-N	15	50	4	13	0	0	1	3	11	4	.260	.393	.320	106	1	3	0	1	.984	-6	2-15	-0.4
	Min-A	86	304	42	80	16	0	1	21	40	47	.263	.349	.326	88	-4	10	3	1	.988	-8	2-73/S-2,D-3	-0.8
1989	Phi-N	151	561	65	161	25	6	2	37	54	63	.287	.353	.364	105	5	10	7	-1	.990	2	*2-144	1.1
1990	Phi-N	119	447	39	118	21	3	4	50	36	47	.264	.322	.351	85	-9	7	1	2	.991	-3	*2-114	-0.8
	NY-N	27	100	9	25	5	0	1	10	14	11	.250	.342	.330	86	-2	0	0	0	.979	-5	2-26	-0.6
	Yr	146	547	48	143	26	3	5	60	50	58	.261	.326	.347	85	-10	7	1	2	.989	-8	*2-140	-1.4
1991	NY-N	70	155	17	30	7	0	1	14	32	21	.194	.332	.258	68	-5	7	2	1	1.000	7	2-57/O-1	0.3
	SF-N	32	60	6	15	1	1	0	7	13	7	.250	.384	.300	98	1	2	0	1	1.000	-6	2-15/3-3	-0.5
	Yr	102	215	23	45	8	1	1	21	45	28	.209	.346	.270	77	-5	9	2	2	1.000	1	2-72/3-3,O-1	-0.2
Total	13	1514	5349	676	1450	254	41	28	574	627	584	.271	.350	.350	95	-18	188	64	18	.989	-94	*2-1416/S-16,3DO	-3.7

■ JOSE HERRERA

Herrera, Jose Concepcion (Ontiveros) "Loco" b: 4/8/42, San Lorenzo, Venez. BR/TR, 5'8", 165 lbs. Deb: 6/3/67

YEAR	TM/L	G	AB	R	H	2B	3B	HR	RBI	BB	SO	AVG	OBP	SLG	PRO+	BR/A	SB	CS	SBR	FA	FR	G/POS	TPR
1967	Hou-N	5	4	0	1	0	0	0	1	0	1	.250	.250	.250	45	-0	0	0	0	.000	0	H	0.0
1968	Hou-N	27	100	9	24	5	0	0	7	4	12	.240	.269	.290	69	-4	0	2	-1	.958	-2	O-17/2-7	-0.9
1969	Mon-N	47	126	7	36	5	0	2	12	3	14	.286	.302	.373	88	-2	1	2	-1	.980	-2	O-31/2-2,3-1	-0.7
1970	Mon-N	1	1	0	0	0	0	0	0	0	1	.000	.000	.000	-99	-0	0	0	0	.000	0	H	0.0
Total	4	80	231	16	61	10	0	2	20	7	28	.264	.286	.333	79	-7	1	4	-2	.973	-4	/O-48,2-9,3-1	-1.6

■ JOSE HERRERA

Herrera, Jose Ramon (Catalino) b: 8/30/72, Santo Domingo, D.R. BL/TL, 6', 165 lbs. Deb: 8/12/95

YEAR	TM/L	G	AB	R	H	2B	3B	HR	RBI	BB	SO	AVG	OBP	SLG	PRO+	BR/A	SB	CS	SBR	FA	FR	G/POS	TPR
1995	Oak-A	33	70	9	17	1	2	0	2	6	11	.243	.303	.314	64	-4	1	3	-2	.956	-3	O-25/D-5	-0.8
1996	Oak-A	108	320	44	86	15	1	6	30	20	59	.269	.318	.378	77	-12	8	2	1	.970	-10	*O-100/D-1	-2.0
Total	2	141	390	53	103	16	3	6	32	26	70	.264	.315	.367	74	-15	9	5	-0	.967	-13	O-125/D-6	-2.8

■ PANCHO HERRERA

Herrera, Juan Francisco (Willavicencio) b: 6/16/34, Santiago De Cuba, Cuba BR/TR, 6'3", 220 lbs. Deb: 4/15/58

YEAR	TM/L	G	AB	R	H	2B	3B	HR	RBI	BB	SO	AVG	OBP	SLG	PRO+	BR/A	SB	CS	SBR	FA	FR	G/POS	TPR
1958	Phi-N	29	63	5	17	3	0	1	6	7	15	.270	.352	.365	92	-1	1	2	-1	.980	2	3-16,1-11	0.0
1960	Phi-N	145	512	61	144	26	6	17	71	51	136	.281	.352	.455	119	13	2	3	-1	.988	10	*1-134,2-17	1.4
1961	Phi-N	126	400	56	103	17	2	13	51	55	120	.257	.353	.408	102	2	5	1	1	.993	6	*1-115	0.0
Total	3	300	975	122	264	46	8	31	128	113	271	.271	.352	.430	110	15	8	6	-1	.990	18	1-260/2-17,3-16	1.4

YEAR	TM/L	G	AB	R	H	2B	3B	HR	RBI	BB	SO	AVG	OBP	SLG	PRO+	BR/A	SB	CS	SBR	FA	FR	G/POS	TPR
■ MIKE HERRERA	Herrera, Ramon b: 12/19/1897, Havana, Cuba d: 2/3/78, Havana, Cuba BR/TR, 5'6", 147 lbs. Deb: 9/22/25																						
1925	Bos-A	10	39	2	15	0	0	0	8	2	2	.385	.415	.385	104	0	1	0	0	.958	3	2-10	0.4
1926	Bos-A	74	237	20	61	14	1	0	19	15	13	.257	.304	.325	66	-12	0	5	-3	.962	5	2-48,3-16/S-4	-0.8
Total	2	84	276	22	76	14	1	0	27	17	15	.275	.320	.333	72	-12	1	5	-3	.961	8	/2-58,3-16,S-4	-0.4
■ LEFTY HERRING	Herring, Silas Clarke b: 3/4/1880, Philadelphia, Pa. d: 2/11/65, Massapequa, N.Y. BL/TL, 5'11", 160 lbs. Deb: 5/16/1899																						
1899	Was-N	2	1	1	1	0	0	0	0	1		1.000	1.000	1.000	454	1	0			1.000	0	/P-2	0.0
1904	Was-A	15	46	3	8	1	0	0	2	7		.174	.283	.196	54	-2	0			.991	1	1-10/O-5	-0.2
Total	2	17	47	4	9	1	0	0	2	8		.191	.309	.213	67	-1	0			.991	1	/1-10,O-5,P-2	-0.2
■ ED HERRMANN	Herrmann, Edward Martin b: 8/27/46, San Diego, Cal. BL/TR, 6'1", 210 lbs. Deb: 9/1/67 F																						
1967	Chi-A	2	3	1	2	1	0	0	1	1	0	.667	.750	1.000	429	1	0	0	0	1.000	1	/C-2	0.3
1969	Chi-A	102	290	31	67	8	0	8	31	30	35	.231	.320	.341	81	-7	0	2	-1	.983	-3	C-92	-0.7
1970	Chi-A	96	297	42	84	9	0	19	52	31	41	.283	.356	.505	130	12	0	1	-1	.988	5	C-88	2.0
1971	Chi-A	101	294	32	63	6	0	11	35	44	48	.214	.321	.347	86	-5	2	0	1	.995	9	C-97	0.9
1972	Chi-A	116	354	23	88	9	0	10	40	43	37	.249	.337	.359	105	3	0	0	0	.989	0	*C-112	0.9
1973	Chi-A	119	379	42	85	17	1	10	39	31	55	.224	.295	.354	79	-11	2	4	-2	.984	5	*C-114/D-2	-0.3
1974	Chi-A†	107	367	32	95	13	1	10	39	16	49	.259	.290	.381	90	-6	1	0	0	.987	3	*C-107	0.2
1975	NY-A	80	200	16	51	9	2	6	30	16	23	.255	.310	.410	104	0	0	0	0	.979	7	D-35,C-24	0.8
1976	Cal-A	29	46	5	8	3	0	2	8	7	8	.174	.283	.370	96	-0	0	0	0	.954	-6	C-27	-0.6
	Hou-N	79	265	14	54	8	0	3	25	22	40	.204	.275	.268	60	-14	0	0	0	.987	0	C-79	-1.3
1977	Hou-N	56	158	7	46	7	0	1	17	15	18	.291	.356	.354	100	0	1	1	-0	.990	9	C-49	1.0
1978	Hou-N	16	36	1	4	1	0	0	0	3	3	.111	.179	.139	-11	-5	0	0	0	1.000	-1	C-14	-0.6
	Mon-N	19	40	1	7	1	0	0	3	1	4	.175	.195	.200	11	-5	0	0	0	.977	-1	C-12	-0.6
	Yr	35	76	2	11	2	0	0	3	4	7	.145	.188	.171	1	-10	0	0	0	.991	-2	C-26	-1.2
Total	11	922	2729	247	654	92	4	80	320	260	361	.240	.312	.364	91	-37	6	8	-3	.987	29	C-817/D-37	2.0
■ JOHN HERRNSTEIN	Herrnstein, John Ellett b: 3/31/38, Hampton, Va. BL/TL, 6'3", 215 lbs. Deb: 9/15/62																						
1962	Phi-N	6	5	0	1	0	0	0	1	1	3	.200	.333	.200	48	-0	0	0	0	.000	-0	/O-1	-0.1
1963	Phi-N	15	12	1	2	0	0	1	1	1	5	.167	.231	.417	83	-0	0	0	0	1.000	-1	/O-2,1-1	-0.1
1964	Phi-N	125	303	38	71	12	4	6	25	22	67	.234	.291	.360	83	-7	1	2	-1	.977	-20	O-69,1-68	-3.4
1965	Phi-N	63	85	8	17	2	0	1	5	2	18	.200	.227	.259	37	-7	0	0	0	.984	-3	1-18,O-14	-1.1
1966	Phi-N	4	10	0	1	0	0	0	1	0	7	.100	.100	.100	44	2	0	0	0	1.000	-0	/O 2	-0.2
	Chi-N	9	17	3	3	0	0	0	0	3	8	.176	.300	.176	36	-1	0	0	0	.975	-1	/1-4,O-1	-0.3
	Atl-N	17	18	2	4	0	0	0	1	0	7	.222	.222	.222	24	-2	0	0	0	1.000	-1	/O-5	-0.3
	Yr	30	45	5	8	0	0	0	2	3	22	.178	.229	.178	15	-5	0	0	0	1.000	-2	/O-8,1-4	-0.8
Total	5	239	450	52	99	14	4	8	34	29	115	.220	.272	.322	67	-20	1	2	-1	.983	-26	/O-94,1-91	-5.5
■ RICK HERRSCHER	Herrscher, Richard Franklin b: 11/3/36, St.Louis, Mo. BR/TR, 6'2.5", 187 lbs. Deb: 8/1/62																						
1962	NY-N	35	50	5	11	3	0	1	6	5	11	.220	.291	.340	68	-2	0	0	0	1.000	2	1-10/3-6,O-4,S-3	0.0
■ EARL HERSH	Hersh, Earl Walter b: 5/21/32, Ebbvale, Md. BL/TL, 6', 205 lbs. Deb: 9/4/56																						
1956	Mil-N	7	13	0	3	3	0	0	0	0	5	.231	.231	.462	85	-0	0	0	0	.000	-1	/O-2	-0.2
■ MIKE HERSHBERGER	Hershberger, Norman Michael b: 10/9/39, Massillon, Ohio BR/TR, 5'10", 175 lbs. Deb: 9/5/61																						
1961	Chi-A	15	55	9	17	3	0	0	5	2	2	.309	.333	.364	88	-1	1	1	-0	1.000	2	O-13	-0.1
1962	Chi-A	148	427	54	112	14	2	4	46	37	36	.262	.325	.333	78	-13	10	6	-1	.984	-7	*O-135	-2.7
1963	Chi-A	135	476	64	133	26	2	3	45	39	39	.279	.339	.361	98	-1	9	3	1	.976	-5	*O-119	-1.2
1964	Chi-A	141	452	55	104	15	3	2	31	48	47	.230	.310	.290	70	-18	8	6	-1	.984	-8	*O-134	-3.4
1965	KC-A	150	494	43	114	15	5	5	48	37	42	.231	.291	.312	72	-18	7	3	0	.988	4	*O-144	-2.1
1966	KC-A	146	538	55	136	27	7	2	57	47	37	.253	.316	.340	92	-6	13	5	1	.977	12	*O-143	0.1
1967	KC-A	142	480	55	122	25	1	1	49	38	40	.254	.318	.317	91	-5	10	3	1	.982	7	*O-130	-0.3
1968	Oak-A	99	246	23	67	9	2	5	32	21	22	.272	.332	.386	123	6	8	3	1	.978	-7	O-90	-0.4
1969	Oak-A	51	129	11	26	2	0	1	10	10	15	.202	.259	.240	42	-10	1	2	-1	.980	-5	O-35	-1.9
1970	Mil-A	49	98	7	23	5	0	1	6	10	8	.235	.306	.316	71	-4	1	2	-1	.946	-6	O-35	-1.2
1971	Chi-A	74	177	22	46	9	0	2	15	30	23	.260	.379	.345	103	2	6	2	1	.960	-8	O-59	-0.9
Total	11	1150	3572	398	900	150	22	26	344	319	311	.252	.319	.328	85	-66	74	36	1	.980	-21	*O-1037	-14.1
■ WILLARD HERSHBERGER	Hershberger, Willard McKee "Bill" b: 5/28/10, Lemoncove, Cal. d: 8/3/40, Boston, Mass. BR/TR, 5'10.5", 167 lbs. Deb: 4/19/38																						
1938	Cin-N	49	105	12	29	3	1	0	12	5	6	.276	.315	.324	78	-3	1			.960	-1	C-39/2-1	-0.2
1939	*Cin-N	63	174	23	60	9	2	0	32	9	4	.345	.384	.420	115	4	1			.987	-2	C-60	0.5
1940	Cin-N	48	123	6	38	4	2	0	26	6	6	.309	.351	.374	99	-0	0			.985	-2	C-37	0.0
Total	3	160	402	41	127	16	5	0	70	20	16	.316	.356	.381	101	1	2			.980	-5	C-136/2-1	0.3
■ NEAL HERTWECK	Hertweck, Neal Charles b: 11/22/31, St.Louis, Mo. BL/TL, 6'1.5", 175 lbs. Deb: 9/27/52																						
1952	StL-N	2	6	0	0	0	0	0	0	1	1	.000	.143	.000	-57	-1	0	0	0	1.000	-0	/1-2	-0.2
■ STEVE HERTZ	Hertz, Stephen Allan b: 2/26/45, Fairfield, Ohio BR/TR, 6'1", 195 lbs. Deb: 4/21/64																						
1964	Hou-N	5	4	2	0	0	0	0	0	0	3	.000	.000	.000	-99	-1	0	0	0	1.000	0	/3-2	-0.1
■ BUCK HERZOG	Herzog, Charles Lincoln b: 7/9/1885, Baltimore, Md. d: 9/4/53, Baltimore, Md. BR/TR, 5'11", 160 lbs. Deb: 4/17/08 M																						
1908	NY-N	64	160	38	48	6	2	0	11	36		.300	.448	.363	152	13	16			.921	1	2-42,S-12/3-4,O-1	1.6
1909	NY-N	42	130	16	24	2	0	0	8	13		.185	.264	.200	43	-8	2			.914	-2	O-29/2-6,3-4,S-1	-1.3
1910	Bos-N	106	380	51	95	20	3	3	32	30	34	.250	.329	.342	92	-4	13			.915	4	*3-105	0.3
1911	Bos-N	79	294	53	91	19	5	5	41	33	21	.310	.398	.459	129	11	26			.934	8	S-74/3-4	2.4
	*NY-N	69	247	37	66	14	4	1	26	14	19	.267	.325	.368	91	-4	22			.926	10	3-65/2-3,S-1	0.7
	Yr	148	541	90	157	33	9	6	67	47	40	.290	.365	.418	112	8	48			.935	18	S-75,3-69/2-3	3.1
1912	*NY-N	140	482	72	127	20	9	2	47	57	34	.263	.350	.355	90	-6	37			.942	19	*3-140	1.4
1913	*NY-N	96	290	46	83	15	3	3	31	22	12	.286	.349	.390	110	4	23			.947	1	3-84/2-2	0.6
1914	Cin-N	138	498	54	140	14	8	1	40	42	27	.281	.348	.347	104	3	46			.939	31	*S-137/1-2,M	4.7
1915	Cin-N	155	579	61	153	14	10	1	42	34	21	.264	.314	.328	93	-5	35	16	1	.945	31	*S-153/1-2,M	4.2
1916	Cin-N	79	281	30	75	14	2	1	24	21	12	.267	.329	.342	109	3	15	12	-3	.931	-2	S-65,3-12/O-1,M	0.5
	NY-N	77	280	40	73	10	4	0	25	22	24	.261	.326	.325	106	2	19	16	-4	.978	14	2-44,3-27/S-9	2.1
	Yr	156	561	70	148	24	6	1	49	43	36	.264	.327	.333	107	5	34	28	-7	.926	12	S-74,2-44,3-39,/O-1	2.6
1917	*NY-N	114	417	69	98	10	8	2	31	31	36	.235	.308	.312	93	-3	12			.948	-9	*2-113	-0.6
1918	Bos-N	118	473	57	108	12	6	0	26	29	28	.228	.280	.279	74	-15	10			.961	4	2-99,1-12/S-7	-0.6
1919	Bos-N	73	275	27	77	8	5	1	25	13	11	.280	.327	.356	110	3	16			.953	-14	2-70/1-1	-0.9
	Chi-N	52	193	15	53	4	4	0	17	10	7	.275	.336	.337	102	1	12			.987	-11	2-52	-0.8
	Yr	125	468	42	130	12	9	1	42	23	18	.278	.331	.348	106	4	28			.967	-25	*2-122/1-1	-1.7
1920	Chi-N	91	305	39	59	9	2	0	19	20	21	.193	.261	.236	43	-22	8	9	-3	.938	-6	2-59,3-28/1-1	-3.0
Total	13	1493	5284	705	1370	191	75	20	445	427	307	.259	.329	.335	96	-27	312	53		.954	77	2-490,3-473,S/O1	11.3
■ WHITEY HERZOG	Herzog, Dorrel Norman Elvert b: 11/9/31, New Athens, Ill. BL/TL, 5'11", 182 lbs. Deb: 4/17/56 MC																						
1956	Was-A	117	421	49	103	13	7	4	35	35	74	.245	.303	.337	69	-20	8	5	-1	.980	1	*O-103/1-5	-2.4
1957	Was-A	36	78	7	13	3	0	0	4	13	12	.167	.301	.205	41	-6	1	1	-0	.981	-3	O-28	-1.2
1958	Was-A	8	5	0	0	0	0	0	0	1	5	.000	.167	.000	-51	-1	0	0	0	1.000	-2	/O-7	-0.3
	KC-A	88	96	11	23	1	2	0	9	16	21	.240	.348	.292	77	-2	0	3	-2	.968	-10	O-37,1-22	-1.6
	Yr	96	101	11	23	1	2	0	9	17	26	.228	.339	.277	71	-3	0	3	-2	.972	-12	O-44,1-22	-1.9
1959	KC-A	38	123	25	36	7	1	1	9	34	23	.293	.446	.390	129	7	1	0	0	.963	2	O-34/1-1	0.8
1960	KC-A	83	252	43	67	10	2	8	38	40	32	.266	.366	.417	111	4	0	1	-1	.985	1	O-69/1-2	0.1
1961	Bal-A	113	323	39	94	11	6	5	35	50	41	.291	.388	.409	117	9	1	4	-2	1.000	-11	O-98	-0.8

YEAR	TM/L	G	AB	R	H	2B	3B	HR	RBI	BB	SO	AVG	OBP	SLG	PRO+	BR/A	SB	CS	SBR	FA	FR	G/POS	TPR
1962	Bal-A	99	263	34	70	13	1	7	35	41	36	.266	.371	.403	116	7	2	3	-1	.978	0	O-70	0.2
1963	Det-A	52	53	5	8	2	1	0	7	11	17	.151	.308	.226	51	-3	0	0	0	.976	-2	/1-7,O-4	-0.5
Total	8	634	1614	213	414	60	20	25	172	241	261	.257	.356	.365	96	-4	13	18	-7	.982	-23	O-450/1-37	-5.7
■ **OTTO HESS**	Hess, Otto C. b: 10/10/1878, Bern, Switzerland d: 2/25/26, Tucson, Ariz. BL/TL, 6'1", 170 lbs. Deb: 8/3/02																						
1902	Cle-A	7	14	2	1	0	0	0	1	2		.071	.188	.071	-27	-2	0			.870	1	/P-7	0.0
1904	Cle-A	34	100	4	12	2	1	0	5	3		.120	.146	.160	-3	-12	0			.951	-1	P-21,O-12	-0.5
1905	Cle-A	54	173	15	44	8	1	2	13	7		.254	.291	.347	101	-0	2			.950	3	O-28,P-26	0.1
1906	Cle-A	53	154	13	31	5	2	0	11	2		.201	.212	.260	48	-10	1			.949	-3	P-43/O-5	-0.2
1907	Cle-A	19	30	4	4	0	0	0	0	4		.133	.278	.133	31	-2	1			.941	-1	P-17/O-2	-0.1
1908	Cle-A	9	14	0	0	0	0	0	0	1		.000	.067	.000	-78	-3	0			1.000	-1	/P-4,O-4	-0.4
1912	Bos-N	33	94	10	23	4	4	0	10	0	26	.245	.245	.372	66	-5	0			.951	-4	P-33	0.0
1913	Bos-N	35	83	9	26	0	1	2	11	7	15	.313	.367	.410	119	2	0			.945	1	P-29	0.0
1914	Bos-N	31	47	5	11	1	0	1	6	1	11	.234	.250	.319	69	-2	0			.947	1	P-14/1-5	-0.1
1915	Bos-N	5	5	1	2	1	0	0	1	0	2	.400	.400	.600	210	1	0			.800	-0	/P-4,1-1	0.0
Total	10	280	714	63	154	21	9	5	58	27	54	.216	.248	.291	63	-33	4			.941	-3	P-198/O-51,1-6	-1.2
■ **TOM HESS**	Hess, Thomas (b: Thomas Heslin) b: 8/15/1875, Brooklyn, N.Y. d: 12/15/45, Albany, N.Y. Deb: 6/6/1892																						
1892	Bal-N	1	2	0	0	0	0	0	0	0	0	.000	.000	.000	-97	-0	0			.000	0	/C-1	0.0
■ **GUS HETLING**	Hetling, August Julius b: 11/21/1885, St.Louis, Mo. d: 10/13/62, Wichita, Kan. BR/TR, 5'10", 165 lbs. Deb: 10/6/06																						
1906	Det-A	2	7	0	1	0	0	0	0	0		.143	.143	.143	-10	-1	0			1.000	-0	/3-2	-0.1
■ **GEORGE HEUBEL**	Heubel, George A. b: 1849, Paterson, N.J. d: 1/22/1896, Philadelphia, Pa. 5'11.5", 178 lbs. Deb: 5/20/1871 U																						
1871	Ath-n	17	75	18	23	4	2	0	13	2	0	.307	.325	.413	112	1	1	0	0	.758	1	O-16/1-1	0.2
1872	Oly-n	5	23	2	3	0	0	0	1	0	0	.130	.130	.130	-21	-3	0	0	0	.800	-1	/O-5	-0.3
1876	NY-N	1	4	0	0	0	0	0	0	0	0	.000	.000	.000	-99	-1				.750	-0	/1-1	-0.1
Total	2 n	22	98	20	26	4	2	0	14	2	0	.265	.280	.347	83	-2	1	0	0	.767	0	/O-21,1-1	-0.1
■ **JOHNNIE HEVING**	Heving, John Aloysius b: 4/29/1896, Covington, Ky. d: 12/24/68, Salisbury, N.C. BR/TR, 6', 175 lbs. Deb: 9/24/20 F																						
1920	StL-A	1	1	0	0	0	0	0	0	0	0	.000	.000	.000	-97	-0	0	0	0	.000	0	H	0.0
1924	Bos-A	45	109	15	31	5	1	0	11	10	7	.284	.345	.349	79	-3	0	0	0	.969	4	C-29	0.2
1925	Bos-A	45	119	14	20	7	0	0	6	12	7	.168	.244	.227	20	-15	0	1	-1	.958	3	C-34	-1.0
1928	Bos-A	82	158	11	41	7	2	0	11	11	10	.259	.308	.329	69	-7	1	1	-0	.967	-4	C-62	-0.7
1929	Bos-A	76	188	26	60	4	3	0	23	8	7	.319	.354	.372	89	-3	1	2	-1	.988	5	C-55	0.6
1930	Bos-A	75	220	15	61	5	3	0	17	11	14	.277	.312	.327	65	-12	2	0	1	.987	-4	C-71	-0.9
1931	*Phi-A	42	113	8	27	3	2	1	12	6	8	.239	.277	.327	55	-8	0	0	0	.993	2	C-40	-0.3
1932	Phi-A	33	77	14	21	6	1	0	10	7	6	.273	.333	.377	81	-2	0	0	0	1.000	-1	C-28	-0.2
Total	8	399	985	103	261	37	12	1	90	65	59	.265	.312	.330	66	-50	4	4	-1	.981	4	C-319	-2.3
■ **MIKE HEYDON**	Heydon, Michael Edward "Ed" b: 7/15/1874, Missouri d: 10/13/13, Indianapolis, Ind. BL/TR, 6', Deb: 10/12/1898																						
1898	Bal-N	3	9	2	1	0	0	0	1	2		.111	.333	.111	28	-1	0			.917	-1	/C-3	-0.1
1899	Was-N	3	3	0	0	0	0	0	0	2		.000	.400	.000	14	-0	0			.833	-0	/C-2	0.0
1901	StL-N	16	43	2	9	1	1	1	6	5		.209	.292	.349	90	-1	2			.941	-3	C-13/O-1	-0.2
1904	Chi-A	4	10	0	1	1	0	0	1	1		.100	.250	.200	45	-1	0			1.000	1	/C-4	0.1
1905	Was-A	77	245	20	47	7	4	1	26	21		.192	.261	.265	70	-8	5			.955	12	C-77	1.2
1906	Was-A	49	145	14	23	7	1	0	10	14		.159	.237	.221	46	-9	2			.937	-2	C-49	-0.7
1907	Was-A	62	164	14	30	3	0	0	9	25		.183	.302	.201	66	-5	3			.961	-8	C-57	-0.9
Total	7	214	619	52	111	19	6	2	53	70		.179	.271	.239	64	-24	12			.952	-0	C-205/O-1	-0.6
■ **JACK HIATT**	Hiatt, Jack E b: 7/27/42, Bakersfield, Cal. BR/TR, 6'2", 190 lbs. Deb: 9/7/64 C																						
1964	LA-A	9	16	2	6	0	0	0	2	2	3	.375	.444	.375	145	1	0	0	0	.889	-1	/C-3,1-2	0.0
1965	SF-N	40	67	5	19	4	0	1	7	12	14	.284	.392	.388	118	2	0	0	0	.987	-2	C-21/1-7	0.0
1966	SF-N	18	23	2	7	2	0	0	1	4	5	.304	.407	.391	120	1	0	0	0	.982	1	/1-7	0.2
1967	SF-N	73	153	24	42	6	0	6	26	27	37	.275	.387	.431	136	8	0	0	0	.990	-3	1-36/C-3,O-2	0.4
1968	SF-N	90	224	14	52	10	2	4	34	41	61	.232	.353	.348	111	5	0	0	0	.994	-1	C-58,1-10	0.8
1969	SF-N	69	194	18	38	4	0	7	34	48	58	.196	.355	.325	93	0	0	0	0	.992	0	C-60/1-3	0.3
1970	Mon-N	17	43	4	14	2	0	0	7	14	14	.326	.491	.372	135	3	0	0	0	.961	-4	C-12/1-2	0.1
	Chi-N	66	178	19	43	12	1	2	22	31	48	.242	.354	.354	81	-5	0	0	0	.990	5	C-63/1-2	0.3
	Yr	83	221	23	57	14	1	2	29	45	62	.258	.383	.357	91	-1	0	0	0	.986	2	C-75/1-4	0.4
1971	Hou-N	69	174	16	48	8	1	1	16	35	39	.276	.403	.351	118	6	0	1	-1	.991	-1	C-65/1-1	0.7
1972	Hou-N	10	25	2	5	3	0	0	0	5	5	.200	.333	.320	88	-0	0	0	0	1.000	-3	C-10	-0.3
	Cal-A	22	45	4	13	0	1	1	5	5	11	.289	.360	.400	133	2	0	0	0	1.000	-8	C-17	-0.7
Total	9	483	1142	110	287	51	5	22	154	224	295	.251	.376	.363	109	24	0	1	-1	.990	-16	C-312/1-70,O-2	1.8
■ **PHIL HIATT**	Hiatt, Philip Farrell b: 5/1/69, Pensacola, Fla. BR/TR, 6'3", 200 lbs. Deb: 4/7/93																						
1993	KC-A	81	238	30	52	12	1	7	36	16	82	.218	.287	.366	70	-11	6	3	0	.909	-1	3-70/D-9	-1.1
1995	KC-A	52	113	11	23	6	0	4	12	9	37	.204	.262	.363	60	-7	1	0	0	.957	-4	O-47/D-2	-1.1
1996	Det-A	7	21	3	4	0	1	0	1	2	11	.190	.261	.286	38	-2	0	0	0	1.000	1	/3-3,O-2,D-1	-0.1
Total	3	140	372	44	79	18	2	11	49	27	130	.212	.278	.360	65	-20	7	3	0	.913	-5	/3-73,O-49,D-12	-2.3
■ **JIM HIBBS**	Hibbs, James Kerr b: 9/10/44, Klamath Falls, Ore. BR/TR, 6', 190 lbs. Deb: 4/12/67																						
1967	Cal-A	3	3	0	0	0	0	0	0	0	2	.000	.000	.000	-99	-1	0	0	0	.000	0	H	-0.1
■ **EDDIE HICKEY**	Hickey, Edward A. b: 8/18/1872, Cleveland, Ohio d: 3/25/41, Tacoma, Wash. Deb: 9/3/01																						
1901	Chi-N	10	37	4	6	0	0	0	3	2		.162	.225	.162	14	-4	1			.743	-2	3-10	-0.6
■ **MIKE HICKEY**	Hickey, Michael Francis b: 12/25/1871, Chicopee, Mass. d: 6/11/18, Springfield, Mass BR/TR, 5'10.5", 150 lbs. Deb: 9/14/1899																						
1899	Bos-N	1	3	0	1	0	0	0	0	0		.333	.333	.333	76	-0	0			.889	1	/2-1	0.1
■ **CHARLIE HICKMAN**	Hickman, Charles Taylor "Cheerful Charlie" or "Piano Legs" b: 3/4/1876, Taylortown, Dunkard Township, Pa. d: 4/19/34, Morgantown, W.Va. BR/TR, 5'11.5", 215 lbs. Deb: 9/8/1897																						
1897	*Bos-N	2	3	1	2	0	0	1	2	0		.667	.667	1.667	475	1	0			1.000	0	/P-2	0.0
1898	Bos-N	19	58	4	15	2	0	0	7	1		.259	.283	.293	62	-3	0			1.000	-1	/O-7,1-6,P-6	-0.3
1899	Bos-N	19	63	15	25	2	7	0	15	2		.397	.433	.651	178	6	1			.941	-2	P-11/O-7,1-1	0.1
1900	NY-N	127	473	65	148	19	17	9	91	17		.313	.359	.482	137	21	10			.842	-4	*3-120/O-7	1.6
1901	NY-N	112	406	44	113	20	6	4	62	15		.278	.315	.387	107	2	5			.904	-7	O-50,S-23,3/P21	-0.6
1902	Bos-A	28	108	13	32	5	2	3	16	3		.296	.339	.463	118	2	1			.939	1	O-27	0.1
	Cle-A	102	426	61	161	31	11	8	94	12		.378	.399	.559	170	37	8			.966	-7	1-98/2-3,P-1	2.7
	Yr	130	534	74	**193**	36	13	11	110	15		.361	.387	.539	159	39	9			.966	-6	1-98,O-27/2-3,P-1	2.8
1903	Cle-A	131	522	64	154	31	11	12	97	17		.295	.325	.466	137	21	14			.972	-7	*1-125/2-7	1.3
1904	Cle-A	86	337	34	97	22	10	4	45	13		.288	.318	.448	142	14	9			.943	-0	2-45,1-40/O-1	1.6
	Det-A	42	144	18	35	6	6	2	22	11		.243	.297	.410	126	4	3			.970	-2	1-39	0.1
	Yr	128	481	52	132	28	16	6	67	24		.274	.312	.437	137	18	12			.969	-3	1-79,2-45/O-1	1.7
1905	Det-A	59	213	21	47	12	3	2	20	12		.221	.278	.333	93	-2	3			.940	3	O-47,1-12	-0.2
	Was-A	88	360	48	112	25	9	2	46	9		.311	.332	.447	152	19	3			.922	8	2-85/1-3	2.9
	Yr	147	573	69	159	37	12	4	66	21		.277	.311	.405	129	16	6			.922	10	2-85,O-47,1-15	2.7
1906	Was-A	120	451	53	128	25	5	9	57	14		.284	.311	.421	135	15	9			.955	-1	O-95,1-18/3-5,2-1	1.0
1907	Was-A	60	198	20	55	9	3	1	23	14		.278	.338	.369	136	8	4			.965	-4	1-30,O-18/2-3,P-1	0.2
	Chi-A	21	23	1	6	2	0	0	1	4		.261	.370	.348	134	1	0			.667	-1	/O-3	0.0
	Yr	81	221	21	61	11	3	1	24	18		.276	.342	.367	135	9	4			.965	-5	1-30,O-21/2-3,P-1	0.2

YEAR	TM/L	G	AB	R	H	2B	3B	HR	RBI	BB	SO	AVG	OBP	SLG	PRO+	BR/A	SB	CS	SBR	FA	FR	G/POS	TPR
1908	Cle-A	65	197	16	46	6	1	2	16	9		.234	.271	.305	86	-3	2			.907	-0	O-28,1-20/2-1	-0.6
Total	12	1081	3982	478	1176	217	91	59	614	153		.295	.331	.440	133	144	72			.968	-25	1-394,O-290,23/PS	9.9

■ JIM HICKMAN Hickman, David James b: 5/19/1892, Johnson City, Tenn d: 12/30/58, Brooklyn, N.Y. BR/TR, 5'7.5", 170 lbs. Deb: 9/17/15

YEAR	TM/L	G	AB	R	H	2B	3B	HR	RBI	BB	SO	AVG	OBP	SLG	PRO+	BR/A	SB	CS	SBR	FA	FR	G/POS	TPR
1915	Bal-F	20	81	7	17	4	1	1	7	4	14	.210	.256	.321	60	-6	5			.963	4	O-20	-0.3
1916	Bro-N	9	5	3	1	0	0	0	0	2	0	.200	.429	.200	94	0	1			1.000	-1	/O-3	-0.1
1917	Bro-N	114	370	46	81	15	4	6	36	17	66	.219	.253	.330	76	-12	14			.942	7	*O-101	-1.0
1918	Bro-N	53	167	14	39	4	7	1	16	8	31	.234	.281	.359	95	-2	5			.914	-3	O-46	-0.8
1919	Bro-N	57	104	14	20	3	1	0	11	6	17	.192	.236	.240	43	-7	2			.962	-4	O-29	-1.4
Total	5	253	727	84	158	26	13	8	70	37	128	.217	.259	.322	74	-26	27			.941	4	O-199	-3.6

■ JIM HICKMAN Hickman, James Lucius b: 5/10/37, Henning, Tenn. BR/TR, 6'4", 205 lbs. Deb: 4/14/62

YEAR	TM/L	G	AB	R	H	2B	3B	HR	RBI	BB	SO	AVG	OBP	SLG	PRO+	BR/A	SB	CS	SBR	FA	FR	G/POS	TPR
1962	NY-N	140	392	54	96	18	2	13	46	47	96	.245	.330	.401	94	-4	4	4	-1	.971	1	*O-124	-1.0
1963	NY-N	146	494	53	113	21	6	17	51	44	120	.229	.293	.399	96	-3	0	5	-3	.963	-0	O-82,3-59	-1.2
1964	NY-N	139	409	48	105	14	1	11	57	36	90	.257	.320	.377	98	-1	0	1	-1	.976	-9	*O-113/3-1	-1.6
1965	NY-N	141	369	32	87	18	0	15	40	27	76	.236	.291	.407	98	-2	3	1	0	.965	-8	O-91,1-30,3-14	-1.6
1966	NY-N	58	160	15	38	7	0	4	16	13	34	.237	.299	.356	83	-4	2	1	0	.986	1	O-45,1-17	-0.6
1967	LA-N	65	98	7	16	6	1	0	10	14	28	.163	.268	.245	52	-6	1	1	-0	1.000	-3	O-37/1-2,3-2,P-1	-1.1
1968	Chi-N	75	188	22	42	6	3	5	23	18	38	.223	.295	.367	91	-2	1	1	-0	.975	-4	O-66	-1.1
1969	Chi-N	134	338	38	80	11	2	21	54	47	74	.237	.330	.467	107	2	2	1	0	.981	-14	*O-125	-1.8
1970	Chi-N★	149	514	102	162	33	4	32	115	93	99	.315	.421	.582	148	35	0	1	-1	.974	6	O-79,1-74	3.0
1971	Chi-N	117	383	50	98	13	2	19	60	50	61	.256	.346	.449	108	4	0	1	-1	.982	-4	O-69,1-44	-0.9
1972	Chi-N	115	368	65	100	15	2	17	64	52	64	.272	.365	.462	121	10	3	1	0	.992	7	1-77,O-27	1.1
1973	Chi-N	92	201	27	49	1	2	3	20	42	42	.244	.374	.313	86	-2	1	1	-0	.988	-2	1-51,O-13	-0.9
1974	StL-N	50	60	5	16	0	0	2	4	8	10	.267	.353	.367	102	0	0	0	0	.986	1	1-14/3-1	0.1
Total	13	1421	3974	518	1002	163	25	159	560	491	832	.252	.337	.426	106	28	17	19	-6	.976	-29	O-871,1-309/3-77,P	-7.6

■ BUDDY HICKS Hicks, Clarence Walter b: 2/15/27, Belvedere, Cal. BB/TR, 5'10", 170 lbs. Deb: 4/17/56

YEAR	TM/L	G	AB	R	H	2B	3B	HR	RBI	BB	SO	AVG	OBP	SLG	PRO+	BR/A	SB	CS	SBR	FA	FR	G/POS	TPR
1956	Det-A	26	47	5	10	2	0	0	5	3	2	.213	.260	.255	36	-4	0	1	-1	1.000	-1	S-16/2-6,3-1	-0.5

■ JIM HICKS Hicks, James Edward b: 5/18/40, East Chicago, Ind. BR/TR, 6'3", 205 lbs. Deb: 10/2/64

YEAR	TM/L	G	AB	R	H	2B	3B	HR	RBI	BB	SO	AVG	OBP	SLG	PRO+	BR/A	SB	CS	SBR	FA	FR	G/POS	TPR
1964	Chi-A	2	0	0	0	0	0	0	0	0	0	—	—	—	—	0	0	0	0	.000	0	R	0.0
1965	Chi-A	13	19	2	5	1	0	1	2	0	9	.263	.263	.474	112	0	0	0	0	.750	-2	/O-5	-0.2
1966	Chi-A	18	26	3	5	0	1	0	1	1	5	.192	.222	.269	43	-2	0	0	0	1.000	-1	O-10/1-2	-0.4
1969	StL-N	19	44	5	8	0	2	1	3	4	14	.182	.250	.341	64	-2	0	0	0	1.000	1	O-15	-0.2
	Cal-A	37	48	6	4	0	0	3	8	13	18	.083	.279	.271	57	-3	0	1	-1	1.000	-3	O-10/1-8	-0.8
1970	Cal-A	4	4	0	1	0	0	0	0	0	2	.250	.250	.250	40	-0	0	0	0	.000	0	H	0.0
Total	5	93	141	16	23	1	3	5	14	18	48	.163	.258	.319	64	-7	0	1	-1	.981	-6	/O-40,1-10	-1.6

■ NAT HICKS Hicks, Nathaniel Woodhull b: 4/19/1845, Hempstead, N.Y. d: 4/21/07, Hoboken, N.J. BR/TR, 6'1", 186 lbs. Deb: 4/22/1872 M

YEAR	TM/L	G	AB	R	H	2B	3B	HR	RBI	BB	SO	AVG	OBP	SLG	PRO+	BR/A	SB	CS	SBR	FA	FR	G/POS	TPR
1872	Mut-n	56	268	55	82	12	2	0	33	5	3	.306	.319	.366	117	7	3	0	1	.875	5	*C-54/O-3	0.9
1873	Mut-n	28	121	12	29	1	2	1	14	7	0	.240	.281	.306	75	-3	2	0	1	.788	4	C-28	0.1
1874	Phi-n	58	266	51	73	8	1	0	30	5	4	.274	.288	.312	89	-4	3	2	-0	.823	6	*C-57/O-4,2-1,M	0.3
1875	Mut-n	62	269	32	67	10	0	0	22	2	10	.249	.255	.286	83	-5	1	0	0	.819	6	*C-60/O-5,M	0.2
1876	NY-N	45	188	20	44	4	1	0	15	3	4	.234	.246	.266	81	-3				.741	-6	C-45	-0.6
1877	Cin-N	8	32	3	6	0	0	0	3	1	2	.188	.212	.188	30	-2				.868	0	/C-8	-0.2
Total	4 n	204	924	150	251	31	5	1	99	19	17	.272	.286	.319	93	-5	9	2	2	.829	22	C-199/O-12,2-1	1.5
Total	2	53	220	23	50	4	1	0	18	4	6	.227	.241	.255	73	-5				.757	-5	/C-53	-0.8

■ JOE HICKS Hicks, William Joseph b: 4/7/33, Ivy, Va. BL/TR, 6', 180 lbs. Deb: 9/18/59

YEAR	TM/L	G	AB	R	H	2B	3B	HR	RBI	BB	SO	AVG	OBP	SLG	PRO+	BR/A	SB	CS	SBR	FA	FR	G/POS	TPR
1959	Chi-A	6	7	0	3	0	0	0	0	1	1	.429	.500	.429	160	1	0	1	-1	1.000	-0	/O-4	0.0
1960	Chi-A	36	47	3	9	1	0	0	2	6	3	.191	.296	.213	40	-4	0	1	-1	1.000	-4	O-14	-0.9
1961	Was-A	12	29	2	5	0	0	1	1	0	4	.172	.172	.276	18	-3	0	1	-1	1.000	1	/O-7	-0.4
1962	Was-A	102	174	20	39	4	2	6	14	15	34	.224	.286	.374	76	-6	3	1	0	.962	-3	O-42	-1.1
1963	NY-N	56	159	16	36	6	1	5	22	7	31	.226	.272	.371	82	-4	0	2	-1	.966	-2	O-41	-1.0
Total	5	212	416	41	92	11	3	12	39	29	73	.221	.278	.349	72	-17	3	6	-3	.970	-8	O-108	-3.4

■ RICHARD HIDALGO Hidalgo, Richard Jose b: 7/2/75, Caracas, Venez. BR/TR, 6'3", 190 lbs. Deb: 9/1/97

YEAR	TM/L	G	AB	R	H	2B	3B	HR	RBI	BB	SO	AVG	OBP	SLG	PRO+	BR/A	SB	CS	SBR	FA	FR	G/POS	TPR
1997	*Hou-N	19	62	8	19	5	0	2	6	4	18	.306	.358	.484	123	2	1	0	0	1.000	-2	O-19	0.0
1998	*Hou-N	74	211	31	64	15	0	7	35	17	37	.303	.361	.474	117	5	3	3	-1	.978	-5	O-72	-0.1
Total	2	93	273	39	83	20	0	9	41	21	55	.304	.360	.476	118	7	4	3	-1	.982	-8	/O-91	-0.1

■ MAHLON HIGBEE Higbee, Mahlon Jesse b: 8/16/01, Louisville, Ky. d: 4/7/68, Depauw, Ind. BR/TR, 5'11", 165 lbs. Deb: 9/27/22

YEAR	TM/L	G	AB	R	H	2B	3B	HR	RBI	BB	SO	AVG	OBP	SLG	PRO+	BR/A	SB	CS	SBR	FA	FR	G/POS	TPR
1922	NY-N	3	10	2	4	0	0	1	5	0	2	.400	.400	.700	177	1	0	0	0	1.000	-1	/O-3	0.0

■ HIGBY Higby Deb: 9/18/1872

YEAR	TM/L	G	AB	R	H	2B	3B	HR	RBI	BB	SO	AVG	OBP	SLG	PRO+	BR/A	SB	CS	SBR	FA	FR	G/POS	TPR
1872	Atl-n	1	4	0	0	0	0	0	0	0	0	.000	.000	.000	-85	-1	0	0	0	.667	0	/O-1	-0.1

■ BILL HIGDON Higdon, William Travis b: 4/27/24, Camp Hill, Ala. d: 8/30/86, Pascagoula, Miss. BL/TR, 6'1", 193 lbs. Deb: 9/10/49

YEAR	TM/L	G	AB	R	H	2B	3B	HR	RBI	BB	SO	AVG	OBP	SLG	PRO+	BR/A	SB	CS	SBR	FA	FR	G/POS	TPR
1949	Chi-A	11	23	3	7	3	0	0	1	6	3	.304	.448	.435	139	2	1	0	0	1.000	-1	/O-6	0.1

■ KEVIN HIGGINS Higgins, Kevin Wayne b: 1/22/67, San Gabriel, Cal. BL/TR, 5'11", 170 lbs. Deb: 5/29/93

YEAR	TM/L	G	AB	R	H	2B	3B	HR	RBI	BB	SO	AVG	OBP	SLG	PRO+	BR/A	SB	CS	SBR	FA	FR	G/POS	TPR
1993	SD-N	71	181	17	40	4	1	0	13	16	17	.221	.295	.254	48	-13	0	1	-1	.983	-3	C-59/3-4,1-3,O-3,2	-1.3

■ MARK HIGGINS Higgins, Mark Douglas b: 7/9/63, Miami, Fla. BR/TR, 6'2", 210 lbs. Deb: 9/7/89

YEAR	TM/L	G	AB	R	H	2B	3B	HR	RBI	BB	SO	AVG	OBP	SLG	PRO+	BR/A	SB	CS	SBR	FA	FR	G/POS	TPR
1989	Cle-A	6	10	1	1	0	0	0	0	1	6	.100	.182	.100	-18	-2	0	0	0	1.000	1	/1-5	-0.1

■ PINKY HIGGINS Higgins, Michael Franklin "Mike" b: 5/27/09, Red Oak, Tex. d: 3/21/69, Dallas, Tex. BR/TR, 6'1", 185 lbs. Deb: 6/25/30 M

YEAR	TM/L	G	AB	R	H	2B	3B	HR	RBI	BB	SO	AVG	OBP	SLG	PRO+	BR/A	SB	CS	SBR	FA	FR	G/POS	TPR
1930	Phi-A	14	24	1	6	2	0	0	0	4	5	.250	.357	.333	73	-1	0	0	0	1.000	-2	/3-5,2-2,S-1	-0.3
1933	Phi-A	152	567	85	178	34	12	13	99	61	53	.314	.383	.485	127	22	2	7	-4	.947	-6	*3-152	2.0
1934	Phi-A☆	144	543	89	179	37	6	16	90	56	70	.330	.392	.508	136	28	9	2	2	.914	-19	*3-144	1.5
1935	Phi-A	133	524	69	155	32	4	23	94	42	62	.296	.350	.504	120	12	6	2	1	.947	-14	*3-131	0.4
1936	Phi-A★	146	550	89	159	32	2	12	80	67	61	.289	.366	.420	96	-4	7	4	-0	.941	-14	*3-145	-1.2
1937	Bos-A	153	570	88	172	33	5	9	106	76	51	.302	.385	.425	100	1	2	6	-3	.935	-17	*3-152	-1.3
1938	Bos-A	139	524	77	159	29	5	5	106	71	55	.303	.388	.406	95	-3	10	9	-2	.914	-10	*3-138	-1.2
1939	Det-A	132	489	57	135	23	2	8	76	56	41	.276	.353	.380	81	-14	7	4	-0	.914	-11	*3-130	-2.1
1940	*Det-A	131	480	70	130	24	3	13	76	61	31	.271	.357	.415	91	-7	4	2	0	.928	-11	*3-129	-1.4
1941	Det-A	147	540	79	161	28	3	11	73	67	45	.298	.378	.422	101	1	5	4	-1	.946	1	*3-145	0.5
1942	Det-A	143	499	65	133	34	2	11	79	72	21	.267	.362	.409	108	6	3	7	-3	.926	-14	*3-137	-0.9
1943	Det-A	138	523	62	145	20	1	10	84	57	31	.277	.349	.377	104	3	2	5	-2	.940	-7	*3-138	-0.5
1944	Det-A★	148	543	79	161	32	4	7	76	81	34	.297	.392	.409	122	18	4	4	-1	.954	-7	*3-146	1.2
1946	Det-A	18	60	2	13	3	1	0	8	5	6	.217	.277	.300	58	-3	0	1	-1	.949	-2	3-17	-0.6
	*Bos-A	64	200	18	55	11	1	2	28	24	24	.275	.356	.370	97	-0	0	2	-1	.947	0	3-59	0.0
	Yr	82	260	20	68	14	2	2	36	29	30	.262	.338	.354	88	-4	0	3	-2	.947	-2	3-76	-0.6
Total	14	1802	6636	930	1941	374	51	140	1075	800	590	.292	.370	.428	106	60	61	59	-17	.935	-131	*3-1768/2-2,S-1	-3.9

■ BOB HIGGINS Higgins, Robert Stone b: 9/23/1886, Fayetteville, Tenn. d: 5/25/41, Chattanooga, Tenn. BR/TR, 5'8", 176 lbs. Deb: 9/13/09

YEAR	TM/L	G	AB	R	H	2B	3B	HR	RBI	BB	SO	AVG	OBP	SLG	PRO+	BR/A	SB	CS	SBR	FA	FR	G/POS	TPR
1909	Cle-A	8	23	0	2	0	0	0	0	0		.087	.087	.087	-43	-4	0			1.000	3	/C-8	0.0
1911	Bro-N	4	10	1	3	0	0	0	2	1	0	.300	.364	.300	90	-0	1			.933	0	/C-2,3-1	0.0
1912	Bro-N	1	2	0	0	0	0	0	0	0	1	.000	.000	.000	-99	-1	0			.750	-0	/C-1	-0.1
Total	3	13	35	1	5	0	0	0	2	1	1	.143	.167	.143	-6	-4	1			.970	3	/C-11,3-1	-0.1

YEAR	TM/L	G	AB	R	H	2B	3B	HR	RBI	BB	SO	AVG	OBP	SLG	PRO+	BR/A	SB	CS	SBR	FA	FR	G/POS	TPR
■ BILL HIGGINS	Higgins, William Edward b: 9/8/1861, Wilmington, Del. d: 4/25/19, Wilmington, Del. TR, 5'9", 155 lbs. Deb: 8/9/1888																						
1888	Bos-N	14	54	5	10	1	0	0	4	1	3	.185	.200	.204	28	-4	1			.906	5	2-14	0.2
1890	StL-a	67	258	39	65	6	2	0	35	24		.252	.316	.291	69	-12	7			.951	13	2-67	0.5
	Syr-a	1	4	1	1	1	0	0	1	0		.250	.250	.500	135	0	0			1.000	1	/2-1	0.1
	Yr	68	262	40	66	7	2	0	36	24		.252	.315	.294	70	-12	7			.952	14	2-68	0.6
Total	2	82	316	45	76	8	2	0	40	25	3	.241	.296	.278	64	-16	8			.943	20	/2-82	0.8
■ BOBBY HIGGINSON	Higginson, Robert Leigh b: 8/18/70, Philadelphia, Pa. BL/TR, 5'11", 180 lbs. Deb: 4/26/95																						
1995	Det-A	131	410	61	92	17	5	14	43	62	107	.224	.333	.393	89	-7	6	4	-1	.985	6	*O-123/D-2	-0.5
1996	Det-A	130	440	75	141	35	0	26	81	65	66	.320	.409	.577	146	32	6	3	0	.963	-7	*O-123/D-4	1.9
1997	Det-A	146	546	94	163	30	5	27	101	70	85	.299	.381	.520	133	27	12	7	-1	.972	6	*O-143/D-2	2.7
1998	Det-A	157	612	92	174	37	4	25	85	63	101	.284	.357	.480	114	13	3	3	-1	.982	9	*O-153/D-2	1.6
Total	4	564	2008	322	570	119	14	92	310	260	359	.284	.370	.495	121	65	27	17	-2	.976	14	O-542/D-10	5.7
■ ANDY HIGH	High, Andrew Aird "Handy Andy" b: 11/21/1897, Ava, Ill. d: 2/22/81, Sylvania, Ohio BL/TR, 5'6", 155 lbs. Deb: 4/12/22 FC																						
1922	Bro-N	153	579	82	164	27	10	6	65	59	26	.283	.354	.396	94	-5	3	12	-6	.958	-5	*3-130,S-22/2-1	-0.4
1923	Bro-N	123	426	51	115	23	9	3	37	47	13	.270	.344	.387	95	-3	4	1	1	.969	-9	3-80,S-45/2-5	0.0
1924	Bro-N	144	582	98	191	26	13	6	61	57	16	.328	.390	.448	128	24	3	6	-3	.964	-10	*2-133,S-17/3-1	1.3
1925	Bro-N	44	115	11	23	4	1	0	6	14	5	.200	.287	.252	40	-10	0	1	-1	.938	-5	2-11,3-11/S-3	-1.4
	Bos-N	60	219	31	63	11	1	4	28	24	2	.288	.361	.402	104	1	3	5	-2	.979	-9	3-60/2-1	-0.6
	Yr	104	334	42	86	15	2	4	34	38	7	.257	.335	.350	80	-10	3	6	-3	.963	-14	3-71,2-12/S-3	-2.0
1926	Bos-N	130	476	55	141	17	10	2	66	39	9	.296	.351	.387	108	5	4			.962	-6	3-81,2-49	0.5
1927	Bos-N	113	384	59	116	15	9	4	46	26	11	.302	.350	.419	114	6	4			.915	-20	3-89/2-8,S-2	-0.9
1928	*StL-N	111	368	58	105	14	3	6	37	37	10	.285	.355	.389	93	-3	2			.935	-19	3-73,2-19	-1.8
1929	StL-N	146	603	95	178	32	4	10	63	38	18	.295	.340	.411	84	-15	7			**.967**	-19	*3-123,2-22	-2.6
1930	*StL-N	72	215	34	60	12	2	2	29	23	6	.279	.349	.381	74	-9	1			.990	-7	3-48/2-3	-1.1
1931	*StL-N	63	131	20	35	6	1	0	19	24	4	.267	.389	.328	91	-0	0			1.000	-5	3-23,2-19	-0.3
1932	Cin-N	84	191	16	36	4	2	0	12	23	6	.188	.276	.230	39	-16	1			.950	-10	3-46,2-12	-2.3
1933	Cin-N	24	43	4	9	2	0	1	6	5	1	.209	.292	.326	77	-1	0			.966	1	3-11/2-2	0.0
1934	Phi-N	47	68	4	14	2	0	0	7	9	3	.206	.299	.235	40	-6	1			.906	-2	3-14/2-2	-0.7
Total	13	1314	4400	618	1250	195	65	44	482	425	130	.284	.350	.388	94	-33	33	25		.956	-125	3-790,2-287/S-89	-10.3
■ CHARLIE HIGH	High, Charles Edwin b: 12/1/1898, Ava, Ill. d: 9/11/60, Oak Grove, Ore. BL/TR, 5'9", 170 lbs. Deb: 9/5/19 F																						
1919	Phi-A	11	29	2	2	0	0	0	1	3	4	.069	.182	.069	-28	-5	2			.944	-0	/O-9	-0.6
1920	Phi-A	17	65	7	20	2	1	1	6	3	6	.308	.375	.415	108	1	0	2	-1	.882	-1	O-17	-0.2
Total	2	28	94	9	22	2	1	1	7	6	10	.234	.314	.309	68	-4	2	2		.904	-1	/O-26	-0.8
■ HUGH HIGH	High, Hugh Jenken "Bunny" b: 10/24/1887, Pottstown, Pa. d: 11/16/62, St.Louis, Mo. BL/TL, 5'7.5", 155 lbs. Deb: 4/11/13 F																						
1913	Det-A	87	183	18	42	6	1	0	16	28	24	.230	.335	.273	80	-4	6			.982	1	O-52	-0.5
1914	Det-A	84	184	25	49	5	3	0	17	26	21	.266	.363	.326	104	2	7	6	-2	.959	-7	O-53	-1.0
1915	NY-A	119	427	51	110	19	7	1	43	62	47	.258	.356	.342	109	6	22	13	-1	**.981**	-1	*O-117	-0.2
1916	NY-A	116	377	44	99	13	4	1	28	47	44	.263	.349	.326	101	1	13			.950	-1	*O-110	-0.6
1917	NY-A	103	365	37	86	11	6	1	19	48	31	.236	.329	.307	93	-2	8			.986	0	*O-100	-0.8
1918	NY-A	7	10	1	0	0	0	0	0	1	1	.000	.091	.000	-71	-2	0			1.000	0	/O-4	-0.2
Total	6	516	1546	176	386	54	21	3	123	212	168	.250	.345	.318	98	2	56	19		.972	-8	O-436	-3.3
■ DICK HIGHAM	Higham, Richard b: 1852, Ipswich, England d: 3/18/05, Chicago, Ill. BL/TR, 5'8.5", 171 lbs. Deb: 6/1/1871 MU																						
1871	Mut-n	21	94	21	34	3	1	0	9	2	0	.362	.375	.415	139	6	3	2	-0	.747	-5	2-12/O-8,C-1	0.0
1872	Bal-n	50	245	72	84	10	1	2	38	2	3	.343	.348	.416	128	7	3	5	-2	.847	-3	C-25,O-24/2-5,31	0.2
1873	Mut-n	49	245	57	77	5	4	0	34	2	1	.314	.320	.367	104	1	1	3	-2	.714	-14	O-19,2-18,C-17	-1.1
1874	Mut-n	65	333	58	87	14	3	1	38	4	0	.261	.270	.330	89	-5	5	3	-0	**.852**	8	*C-48,O-33/2-1,M	0.3
1875	Chi-n	42	208	44	49	5	3	0	12	0	0	.236	.236	.288	80	-4	6	2	1	.821	-7	C-24,O-14,2-13	-0.8
	Mut-n	15	64	12	25	5	0	0	10	0	1	.391	.391	.469	187	5	0	0	0	.739	-3	/C-8,2-6,O-3,1-2	0.2
	Yr	57	272	56	74	10	3	0	22	0	1	.272	.272	.331	106	1	6	2	1	.802	-10	C-32,2-19,O-17,/1-2	-0.6
1876	Har-N	67	312	59	102	**21**	2	0	35	2	7	.327	.331	.407	134	9				.869	-2	*O-59,C-13/S-1,2-1	0.6
1878	Pro-N	62	281	**60**	90	**22**	1	1	29	5	16	.320	.332	.416	145	13				.811	3	*O-62/C-1	1.2
1880	Tro-N	1	5	1	1	0	0	0	0	0	0	.200	.200	.200	34	-0				.000	-2	/O-1,C-1	-0.3
Total	5 n	242	1189	264	356	42	12	3	141	10	5	.299	.305	.362	108	10	18	15	-4	.837	-24	C-123,O-101/213	-1.2
Total	3	130	598	120	193	43	3	1	64	7	23	.323	.331	.410	138	22				.834	-2	O-122/C-15,2-1,S-1	1.5
■ JOHN HILAND	Hiland, John William b: 9/1860, Baltic, R.I. d: 4/10/01, Philadelphia, Pa. BL/TL, 5'8.5", 165 lbs. Deb: 8/20/1885																						
1885	Phi-N	3	9	0	0	0	0	0	0	0	4	.000	.000	.000	-99	-2				.833	-2	/2-3	-0.4
■ GEORGE HILDEBRAND	Hildebrand, George Albert b: 9/6/1878, San Francisco, Cal d: 5/30/60, Reseda, Cal. BR/TR, 5'8", 170 lbs. Deb: 4/17/02 U																						
1902	Bro-N	11	41	3	9	1	0	0	5	3		.220	.289	.244	64	-2	0			1.000	2	O-11	0.0
■ PALMER HILDEBRAND	Hildebrand, Palmer Marion "Pete" b: 12/23/1884, Shauck, Ohio d: 1/25/60, N.Canton, Ohio BR/TR, 5'10", 170 lbs. Deb: 5/14/13																						
1913	StL-N	26	55	3	9	2	0	0	1	1	10	.164	.207	.200	17	-6	1			.968	0	C-22/O-1	-0.5
■ HILDEBRAND	Hildebrand Deb: 8/29/02																						
1902	Chi-N	1	4	1	0	0	0	0	0	1		.000	.200	.000	-39	-1	0			1.000	-0	/O-1	-0.1
■ BELDEN HILL	Hill, Belden L. b: 8/24/1864, Kewanee, Ill. d: 10/22/34, Cedar Rapids, Iowa BR/TR, 6', Deb: 8/27/1890																						
1890	Bal-a	9	30	3	5	2	0	0	2	3		.167	.306	.233	56	-2	6			.857	1	/3-9	0.0
■ DONNIE HILL	Hill, Donald Earl b: 11/12/60, Pomona, Cal. BB/TR, 5'10", 160 lbs. Deb: 7/25/83																						
1983	Oak-A	53	158	20	42	7	0	2	15	4	21	.266	.284	.348	77	-5	1	1	-0	.961	0	S-53	-0.1
1984	Oak-A	73	174	21	40	6	0	2	16	5	12	.230	.251	.299	55	-11	1	1	-0	.949	-12	S-66/2-4,3-2,D-2	-1.8
1985	Oak-A	123	393	45	112	13	2	3	48	23	33	.285	.325	.351	92	-5	9	4	0	.973	-41	*2-122	-4.1
1986	Oak-A	108	339	37	96	16	2	4	29	23	38	.283	.329	.378	99	-1	5	2	0	.984	-12	2-68,3-33/S-2,D-3	-1.1
1987	Chi-A	111	410	57	98	14	6	9	46	30	35	.239	.293	.368	72	-17	1	0	0	.987	-29	2-84,3-32/D-1	-4.1
1988	Chi-A	83	221	17	48	6	1	2	20	26	32	.217	.300	.281	64	-10	3	1	0	.975	-11	2-59,3-12/D-5	-1.9
1990	Cal-A	103	352	36	93	18	2	3	32	29	27	.264	.322	.352	90	-5	1	2	-1	.990	3	2-60,S-24,3/1PD	0.0
1991	Cal-A	77	209	36	50	8	1	1	20	30	21	.239	.335	.301	77	-5	1	0	0	.971	-3	2-39,S-29/1-3	-0.5
1992	Min-A	25	51	7	15	3	0	0	2	5	6	.294	.368	.353	100	0	0	0	0	.944	-3	S-10/2-7,3-5,O-1	-0.2
Total	9	756	2307	276	594	91	14	26	228	175	225	.257	.311	.343	81	-59	22	11	0	.980	-107	2-443,S-184,3/D1OP	-13.8
■ GLENALLEN HILL	Hill, Glenallen b: 3/22/65, Santa Cruz, Cal. BR/TR, 6'2", 210 lbs. Deb: 9/1/89																						
1989	Tor-A	19	52	4	15	0	0	1	7	3	12	.288	.327	.346	92	-1	2	1	0	.964	-2	O-16/D-3	-0.3
1990	Tor-A	84	260	47	60	11	3	12	32	18	62	.231	.281	.435	95	-3	8	3	1	.983	0	O-60,D-20	-0.4
1991	Tor-A	35	99	14	25	5	2	3	11	7	24	.253	.302	.434	97	-1	2	2	-1	.967	1	D-16,O-13	-0.2
	Cle-A	37	122	15	32	3	0	5	14	16	30	.262	.348	.410	108	1	4	2	0	.978	-1	O-33/D-1	0.0
	Yr	72	221	29	57	8	2	8	25	23	54	.258	.328	.421	103	1	6	4	-1	.975	-0	O-46,D-17	-0.2
1992	Cle-A	102	369	38	89	16	1	18	49	20	73	.241	.288	.436	102	-1	9	6	-1	.956	2	O-59,D-34	-0.2
1993	Cle-A	66	174	19	39	7	2	5	25	11	50	.224	.274	.374	73	-7	7	3	0	.940	-4	O-39,D-18	-1.2
	Chi-N	31	87	14	30	7	0	10	22	6	21	.345	.387	.770	204	12	1	0	0	.957	1	O-21	1.3
1994	Chi-N	89	269	48	80	12	1	10	38	29	57	.297	.366	.461	115	6	19	6	2	.987	-6	O-78	0.1
1995	SF-N	132	497	71	131	29	4	24	86	39	98	.264	.318	.483	111	6	25	5	5	.959	-1	*O-125	0.5
1996	SF-N	98	379	56	106	26	0	19	67	33	95	.280	.347	.499	125	12	6	3	0	.960	-2	O-98	0.7
1997	*SF-N	128	398	47	104	28	4	11	64	19	87	.261	.302	.435	92	-6	7	4	-0	.947	-6	O-97/D-7	-1.4
1998	Sea-A	74	259	37	75	20	2	12	33	14	45	.290	.333	.521	118	6	1	1	-0	.965	-4	O-71	0.0

YEAR	TM/L	G	AB	R	H	2B	3B	HR	RBI	BB	SO	AVG	OBP	SLG	PRO+	BR/A	SB	CS	SBR	FA	FR	G/POS	TPR
	*Chi-N	48	131	26	46	5	0	8	23	14	34	.351	.414	.573	148	9	0	0	0	.984	2	O-34	1.1
Total	10	943	3096	436	832	169	19	138	471	229	688	.269	.323	.469	110	34	91	36	6	.964	-20	O-744/D-99	-0.0

■ HERMAN HILL
Hill, Herman Alexander b: 10/12/45, Tuskegee, Ala. d: 12/14/70, Valencia, Venez. BL/TR, 6'2", 190 lbs. Deb: 9/2/69

YEAR	TM/L	G	AB	R	H	2B	3B	HR	RBI	BB	SO	AVG	OBP	SLG	PRO+	BR/A	SB	CS	SBR	FA	FR	G/POS	TPR
1969	Min-A	16	2	4	0	0	0	0	0	0	1	.000	.000	.000	-98	-1	1	2	-1	.000	-1	/O-2	-0.2
1970	Min-A	27	22	8	2	0	0	0	0	0	6	.091	.091	.091	-49	-4	0	0	0	1.000	-2	O-14	-0.7
Total	2	43	24	12	2	0	0	0	0	0	7	.083	.083	.083	-53	-5	1	2	-1	1.000	-3	/O-16	-0.9

■ HUGH HILL
Hill, Hugh Ellis b: 7/21/1879, Ringgold, Ga. d: 9/6/58, Cincinnati, Ohio BL/TR, 5'11.5", 168 lbs. Deb: 5/1/03 F

YEAR	TM/L	G	AB	R	H	2B	3B	HR	RBI	BB	SO	AVG	OBP	SLG	PRO+	BR/A	SB	CS	SBR	FA	FR	G/POS	TPR
1903	Cle-A	1	1	0	0	0	0	0	0	0		.000	.000	.000	-99	-0	0			.000	0	H	0.0
1904	StL-N	23	93	13	21	2	1	3	4	2		.226	.242	.366	91	-2	3			1.000	0	O-23	-0.3
Total	2	24	94	13	21	2	1	3	4	2		.223	.240	.362	89	-2	3			1.000	0	/O-23	-0.3

■ HUNTER HILL
Hill, Hunter Benjamin b: 6/21/1879, Austin, Tex. d: 2/22/59, Austin, Tex. BR/TR, Deb: 7/1/03

YEAR	TM/L	G	AB	R	H	2B	3B	HR	RBI	BB	SO	AVG	OBP	SLG	PRO+	BR/A	SB	CS	SBR	FA	FR	G/POS	TPR
1903	StL-A	86	317	30	77	11	3	0	25	8		.243	.264	.297	70	-12	2			.923	-1	3-86	-1.2
1904	StL-A	58	219	19	47	3	0	0	14	6		.215	.246	.228	54	-12	4			.826	-16	3-56/O-1	-3.0
	Was-A	77	290	18	57	6	1	0	17	11		.197	.228	.224	44	-18	10			.895	-6	3-71/O-5	-2.6
	Yr	135	509	37	104	9	1	0	31	17		.204	.236	.226	48	-30	14			.864	-23	*3-127/O-6	-5.6
1905	Was-A	104	374	37	78	12	1	1	24	32		.209	.278	.254	72	-11	10			.908	-1	*3-103	-0.9
Total	3	325	1200	104	259	32	5	1	80	57		.216	.257	.253	62	-53	26			.895	-24	3-316/O-6	-7.7

■ JESSE HILL
Hill, Jesse Terrill b: 1/20/07, Yates, Mo. d: 8/31/93, Pasadena, Cal. BR/TR, 5'9", 165 lbs. Deb: 4/17/35

YEAR	TM/L	G	AB	R	H	2B	3B	HR	RBI	BB	SO	AVG	OBP	SLG	PRO+	BR/A	SB	CS	SBR	FA	FR	G/POS	TPR
1935	NY-A	107	392	69	115	20	3	4	33	42	32	.293	.362	.390	100	0	14	4	2	.951	2	O-94	0.1
1936	Was-A	85	233	50	71	19	5	0	34	29	23	.305	.384	.429	106	3	11	0	3	.967	-8	O-60	-0.3
1937	Was-A	33	92	24	20	2	1	1	4	13	16	.217	.314	.293	57	-6	2	1	0	.986	2	O-21	-0.4
	Phi-A	70	242	32	71	12	3	1	37	31	20	.293	.374	.380	92	-2	16	3	3	.954	-5	O-68	-0.6
	Yr	103	334	56	91	14	4	2	41	44	36	.272	.357	.356	82	-8	18	4	3	.964	-3	O-89	-1.0
Total	3	295	959	175	277	53	12	6	108	115	91	.289	.366	.388	95	-5	43	8	8	.959	-8	O-243	-1.2

■ MARC HILL
Hill, Marc Kevin b: 2/18/52, Elsberry, Mo. BR/TR, 6'3", 210 lbs. Deb: 9/28/73 C

YEAR	TM/L	G	AB	R	H	2B	3B	HR	RBI	BB	SO	AVG	OBP	SLG	PRO+	BR/A	SB	CS	SBR	FA	FR	G/POS	TPR
1973	StL-N	1	3	0	0	0	0	0	0	0	1	.000	.000	.000	-99	-1	0	0	0	1.000	0	/C-1	-0.1
1974	StL-N	10	21	2	5	1	0	0	2	4	5	.238	.360	.286	83	-0	0	0	0	1.000	3	/C-9	0.3
1975	SF-N	72	182	14	39	4	0	5	23	25	27	.214	.309	.319	71	-7	0	0	0	.994	1	C-60/3-1	-0.4
1976	SF-N	54	131	11	24	5	0	3	15	10	19	.183	.246	.290	50	-9	0	1	-1	.995	1	C-49/1-1	-0.8
1977	SF-N	108	320	28	80	10	0	9	50	34	34	.250	.322	.366	84	-7	0	1	-1	.989	-3	*C-102	-0.7
1978	SF-N	117	358	20	87	15	1	3	36	45	39	.243	.329	.316	84	-7	1	2	-1	.986	0	*C-116/1-2	-0.5
1979	SF-N	63	169	20	35	3	0	3	15	26	25	.207	.313	.278	67	-7	0	1	-1	.991	-6	C-58/1-1	-1.2
1980	SF-N	17	41	1	7	2	0	0	0	1	7	.171	.190	.220	14	-5	0	0	0	.972	2	C-14	-0.3
	Sea-A	29	70	8	16	2	1	2	9	3	10	.229	.260	.371	70	-3	0	0	0	.991	-0	C-29	-0.3
1981	Chi-A	16	6	0	0	0	0	0	0	0	1	.000	.000	.000	-99	-2	0	0	0	1.000	0	C-14/1-1,3-1	-0.1
1982	Chi-A	53	88	9	23	2	0	3	13	6	13	.261	.316	.386	92	-1	0	0	0	.993	6	C-49/1-1,3-1	0.5
1983	Chi-A	58	133	11	30	6	0	1	11	9	24	.226	.275	.293	54	-8	0	1	-1	.991	5	C-55/1-1,D-2	-0.2
1984	Chi-A	77	193	15	45	10	1	5	20	9	26	.233	.275	.373	74	-7	0	1	-1	.991	4	C-72/1-2	-0.1
1985	Chi-A	40	75	5	10	2	0	0	4	12	9	.133	.253	.160	16	-9	0	0	0	.985	9	C-37/3-1	0.1
1986	Chi-A	22	19	2	3	0	0	0	0	1	3	.158	.238	.158	10	-2	0	0	0	1.000	7	C-22	0.5
Total	14	737	1809	146	404	62	3	34	198	185	243	.223	.298	.317	69	-74	1	7	-4	.990	30	C-687/1-9,3-4,D-2	-3.3

■ OLIVER HILL
Hill, Oliver Clinton b: 10/16/09, Powder Springs, Ga d: 9/20/70, Decatur, Ga. BL/TR, 5'11", 178 lbs. Deb: 4/19/39

YEAR	TM/L	G	AB	R	H	2B	3B	HR	RBI	BB	SO	AVG	OBP	SLG	PRO+	BR/A	SB	CS	SBR	FA	FR	G/POS	TPR
1939	Bos-N	2	2	1	1	1	0	0	0	0	0	.500	.500	1.000	317	1	0			.000	0	H	0.1

■ HOMER HILLEBRAND
Hillebrand, Homer Hiller Henry b: 10/10/1879, Freeport, Ill. d: 1/20/74, Elsinore, Cal. BR/TL, 5'8", 165 lbs. Deb: 4/24/05

YEAR	TM/L	G	AB	R	H	2B	3B	HR	RBI	BB	SO	AVG	OBP	SLG	PRO+	BR/A	SB	CS	SBR	FA	FR	G/POS	TPR
1905	Pit-N	39	110	9	26	3	2	0	7	6		.236	.282	.300	72	-4	1			.978	-3	1-16,P-10/O-7,C-3	-0.6
1906	Pit-N	7	21	1	5	1	0	0	3	1		.238	.273	.286	71	-1	0			1.000	1	/P-7	0.0
1908	Pit-N	1	0	0	0	0	0	0	0	0		—	—	—	—	0	0			.000	-0	/P-1	0.0
Total	3	47	131	10	31	4	2	0	10	7		.237	.281	.298	71	-5	1			1.000	-1	/P-18,1-16,O-7,C-3	-0.6

■ CHUCK HILLER
Hiller, Charles Joseph b: 10/1/34, Johnsburg, Ill. BL/TR, 5'11", 170 lbs. Deb: 4/11/61 C

YEAR	TM/L	G	AB	R	H	2B	3B	HR	RBI	BB	SO	AVG	OBP	SLG	PRO+	BR/A	SB	CS	SBR	FA	FR	G/POS	TPR
1961	SF-N	70	240	38	57	12	1	2	12	32	30	.237	.330	.321	76	-7	4	4	-1	.973	-14	2-67	-1.6
1962	*SF-N	161	602	94	166	22	2	3	48	55	49	.276	.344	.334	84	-12	5	4	-1	.964	-18	*2-161	-1.4
1963	SF-N	111	417	44	93	10	2	6	33	20	23	.223	.262	.300	62	-21	3	2	-0	.963	-15	*2-109	-2.9
1964	SF-N	80	205	21	37	8	1	1	17	17	23	.180	.247	.244	38	-17	1	1	-0	.977	2	2-60/3-1	-1.2
1965	SF-N	7	7	1	1	0	0	1	1	0	1	.143	.143	.571	88	-0	0	0	0	1.000	-1	/2-2	-0.1
	NY-N	100	286	24	68	11	1	5	21	14	24	.238	.276	.336	74	-10	1	1	-0	.959	-12	2-80/O-4,3-2	-1.8
	Yr	107	293	25	69	11	1	6	22	14	25	.235	.273	.341	74	-11	1	1	-0	.959	-13	2-82/O-4,3-2	-1.9
1966	NY-N	108	254	25	71	8	2	2	14	15	22	.280	.332	.350	92	-2	0	0	0	.981	11	2-45,3-14/O-9	1.1
1967	NY-N	25	54	0	5	3	0	0	3	2	11	.093	.125	.148	-22	-9	0	0	0	.968	2	2-14	-0.6
	Phi-N	31	43	4	13	1	0	0	2	2	4	.302	.333	.326	88	-1	0	2	-1	.947	-3	/2-6	-0.4
	Yr	56	97	4	18	4	0	0	5	4	15	.186	.218	.227	27	-9	0	2	-1	.963	-0	2-20	-1.0
1968	Pit-N	11	13	2	5	1	0	0	1	0	0	.385	.385	.462	155	1	0	0	0	.857	-0	/2-2	0.1
Total	8	704	2121	253	516	76	9	20	152	157	187	.243	.301	.316	72	-78	14	14	-4	.967	-49	2-546/3-17,O-13	-8.8

■ HOB HILLER
Hiller, Harvey Max b: 5/12/1893, E.Mauch Chunk, Pa. d: 12/27/56, Lehighton, Pa. BR/TR, 5'8", 162 lbs. Deb: 4/22/20

YEAR	TM/L	G	AB	R	H	2B	3B	HR	RBI	BB	SO	AVG	OBP	SLG	PRO+	BR/A	SB	CS	SBR	FA	FR	G/POS	TPR
1920	Bos-A	17	29	4	5	1	1	0	2	2	5	.172	.226	.276	34	-3	0	3	-2	.905	1	/3-6,S-5,2-2,O-1	-0.4
1921	Bos-A	1	1	0	0	0	0	0	0	0	0	.000	.000	.000	-99	-0	0	0	0	.000	0	H	0.0
Total	2	18	30	4	5	1	1	0	2	2	5	.167	.219	.267	29	-3	0	3	-2	.905	1	/3-6,S-5,2-2,O-1	-0.4

■ ED HILLEY
Hilley, Edward Garfield "Whitey" b: 6/17/1879, Cleveland, Ohio d: 11/14/56, Cleveland, Ohio BR/TR, 5'10.5", 170 lbs. Deb: 9/29/03

YEAR	TM/L	G	AB	R	H	2B	3B	HR	RBI	BB	SO	AVG	OBP	SLG	PRO+	BR/A	SB	CS	SBR	FA	FR	G/POS	TPR
1903	Phi-A	1	3	1	1	0	0	0	0	1		.333	.500	.333	147	0	0			.800	-0	/3-1	0.0

■ MACK HILLIS
Hillis, Malcolm David b: 7/23/01, Cambridge, Mass. d: 6/16/61, Cambridge, Mass. BR/TR, 5'10", 165 lbs. Deb: 9/13/24

YEAR	TM/L	G	AB	R	H	2B	3B	HR	RBI	BB	SO	AVG	OBP	SLG	PRO+	BR/A	SB	CS	SBR	FA	FR	G/POS	TPR
1924	NY-A	1	1	1	0	0	0	0	0	0	0	.000	.000	.000	-99	-0	0	0	0	.000	0	/2-1	0.0
1928	Pit-N	11	36	6	9	2	3	1	7	0	6	.250	.250	.556	101	-0	1			.973	-1	/2-8,3-1	-0.1
Total	2	12	37	7	9	2	3	1	7	0	6	.243	.243	.541	96	-1	1	0		.973	-1	/2-9,3-1	-0.1

■ PAT HILLY
Hilly, William Edward (b: William Edward Hilgerink) b: 2/24/1887, Fostoria, Ohio d: 7/25/53, Eureka, Mo. BR/TR, 5'11", 180 lbs. Deb: 5/7/14

YEAR	TM/L	G	AB	R	H	2B	3B	HR	RBI	BB	SO	AVG	OBP	SLG	PRO+	BR/A	SB	CS	SBR	FA	FR	G/POS	TPR
1914	Phi-N	8	10	2	3	0	0	0	1	1	5	.300	.364	.300	92	-0	0			1.000	-1	/O-4	-0.1

■ CHARLIE HILSEY
Hilsey, Charles T. b: 3/23/1864, Philadelphia, Pa. d: 10/31/18, Philadelphia, Pa. 5'7", 180 lbs. Deb: 9/27/1883

YEAR	TM/L	G	AB	R	H	2B	3B	HR	RBI	BB	SO	AVG	OBP	SLG	PRO+	BR/A	SB	CS	SBR	FA	FR	G/POS	TPR
1883	Phi-N	3	10	0	1	0	0	0	1	0	4	.100	.100	.100	-43	-2				.714	-0	/P-3	0.0
1884	Phi-a	6	24	5	5	1	1	0		0		.208	.208	.333	69	-1				.250	-0	/O-3,P-3	-0.1
Total	2	9	34	5	6	1	1	0	1	0	4	.176	.176	.265	38	-3				.824	-1	/P-6,O-3	-0.1

■ DAVE HILTON
Hilton, John David b: 9/15/50, Uvalde, Tex. BR/TR, 5'11", 191 lbs. Deb: 9/10/72 C

YEAR	TM/L	G	AB	R	H	2B	3B	HR	RBI	BB	SO	AVG	OBP	SLG	PRO+	BR/A	SB	CS	SBR	FA	FR	G/POS	TPR
1972	SD-N	13	47	2	10	2	1	0	5	3	6	.213	.260	.298	63	-2	1	0	0	.939	-3	3-13	-0.5
1973	SD-N	70	234	21	46	9	0	5	16	19	35	.197	.260	.299	59	-14	2	1	0	.970	-4	3-47,2-23	-1.8
1974	SD-N	74	217	17	52	8	2	1	12	13	28	.240	.283	.309	68	-10	3	5	-2	.948	-5	3-55,2-15	-1.8
1975	SD-N	4	8	0	0	0	0	0	0	0	0	.000	.000	.000	-99	-2	0	0	0	.900	1	/3-4	-0.1
Total	4	161	506	40	108	19	3	6	33	35	69	.213	.266	.298	61	-28	6	6	-2	.954	-11	3-119/2-38	-4.2

■ JACK HIMES
Himes, John Herb b: 9/22/1878, Bryan, Ohio d: 12/16/49, Joliet, Ill. BL/TR, 6'2", 180 lbs. Deb: 9/18/05

YEAR	TM/L	G	AB	R	H	2B	3B	HR	RBI	BB	SO	AVG	OBP	SLG	PRO+	BR/A	SB	CS	SBR	FA	FR	G/POS	TPR
1905	StL-N	12	41	3	6	0	0	0	0	1		.146	.167	.146	-7	-5	0			1.000	-1	O-11	-0.7
1906	StL-N	40	155	10	42	5	2	0	14	7		.271	.307	.329	102	-0	4			.977	5	O-40	0.3
Total	2	52	196	13	48	5	2	0	14	8		.245	.278	.291	79	-5	4			.981	4	/O-51	-0.4

YEAR	TM/L	G	AB	R	H	2B	3B	HR	RBI	BB	SO	AVG	OBP	SLG	PRO+	BR/A	SB	CS	SBR	FA	FR	G/POS	TPR
■ **A.J. HINCH** Hinch, Andrew Jay b: 5/15/74, Waverly, Iowa BR/TR, 6'1", 195 lbs. Deb: 4/1/98																							
1998	Oak-A	120	337	34	78	10	0	9	35	30	89	.231	.302	.341	69	-15	3	0	1	.986	-7	*C-118	-1.3
■ **HARRY HINCHMAN** Hinchman, Harry Sibley b: 8/4/1878, Philadelphia, Pa. d: 1/19/33, Toledo, Ohio BB/TR, 5'11", 165 lbs. Deb: 7/29/07 F																							
1907	Cle-A	15	51	3	11	3	1	0	9	5		.216	.286	.314	90	-1	2			.904	4	2-15	0.4
■ **BILL HINCHMAN** Hinchman, William White b: 4/4/1883, Philadelphia, Pa. d: 2/20/63, Columbus, Ohio BR/TR, 5'11", 190 lbs. Deb: 9/24/05 FC																							
1905	Cin-N	17	51	10	13	4	1	0	10	13		.255	.415	.373	122	2	4			.905	-3	O-12/3-4,1-1	-0.1
1906	Cin-N	18	54	7	11	1	1	0	1	8		.204	.306	.259	73	-1	2			.963	1	O-16	-0.2
1907	Cle-A	152	514	62	117	19	9	1	50	47		.228	.311	.305	96	-1	15			.958	-5	*O-148/1-4,2-1	-1.3
1908	Cle-A	137	464	55	107	23	8	6	59	38		.231	.301	.353	112	6	9			.975	-6	O-75,S-51/1-4	-0.3
1909	Cle-A	139	457	57	118	20	13	2	53	41		.258	.331	.372	117	9	22			.918	1	*O-131/S-6	0.6
1915	Pit-N	156	577	72	177	33	14	5	77	48	75	.307	.368	.438	146	31	17	17	-5	.969	4	*O-156	2.4
1916	Pit-N	152	555	64	175	18	**16**	4	76	54	61	.315	.378	.427	146	30	10			.962	-4	*O-124,1-31	2.2
1917	Pit-N	69	244	27	46	5	5	2	29	33	27	.189	.288	.275	71	-8	5			.945	-1	O-48,1-20	-1.4
1918	Pit-N	50	111	10	26	5	2	0	13	15	8	.234	.336	.315	96	-0	1			1.000	-4	O-40/1-3	-0.6
1920	Pit-N	18	16	0	3	0	0	0	1	1	3	.188	.278	.188	34	-1	0	0	0	.000	0	H	-0.1
Total	10	908	3043	364	793	128	69	20	369	298	174	.261	.336	.368	118	66	85	17		.954	-17	O-750/1-63,S-57,32	1.2
■ **HUNKEY HINES** Hines, Henry Fred b: 9/29/1867, Elgin, Ill. d: 1/2/28, Rockford, Ill. BR/TR, 5'7", 165 lbs. Deb: 5/16/1895																							
1895	Bro-N	2	8	3	2	0	0	0	1	2	0	.250	.400	.250	76	-0	0			1.000	0	/O-2	0.0
■ **MIKE HINES** Hines, Michael P. b: 9/1862, Ireland d: 3/14/10, New Bedford, Mass. BR/TL, 5'10", 176 lbs. Deb: 5/1/1883																							
1883	Bos-N	63	231	38	52	13	1	0	16	7	36	.225	.248	.290	61	-11				.887	8	C-59/O-7	0.1
1884	Bos-N	35	132	16	23	3	0	0	3	3	24	.174	.193	.197	23	-11				.919	6	C-35	-0.2
1885	Bos-N	14	56	11	13	4	0	0	4	4	5	.232	.283	.304	93	-0				.857	-3	O-14	-0.4
	Bro-a	3	13	1	1	0	1	0	1	0		.077	.077	.231	-6	-2				1.000	-1	/C-3	-0.2
	Pro-N	1	3	0	0	0	0	0	0	0	2	.000	.000	.000	-99	-1				.636	-0	/C-1	-0.1
1888	Bos-N	4	16	3	2	0	1	0	2	2	0	.125	.222	.250	49	-1	0			1.000	-0	/O-3,C-1	-0.1
Total	4	120	451	69	91	20	3	0	26	16	67	.202	.229	.259	51	-25	0			.896	9	/C-99,O-24	-0.9
■ **PAUL HINES** Hines, Paul A. b: 3/1/1852, Washington, D.C. d: 7/10/35, Hyattsville, Md. BR/TR, 5'9.5", 173 lbs. Deb: 4/20/1872																							
1872	Nat-n	11	49	9	12	1	0	0	5	0	0	.245	.245	.265	49	-4	0	0	0	.862	-3	/1-9,3-2,C-1	-0.5
1873	Was-n	39	181	33	60	6	3	1	29	1	1	.331	.335	.414	125	6	0	1	-1	.798	-0	*O-36/2-2,C-1	0.4
1874	Chi-n	59	271	47	80	10	2	0	34	4	4	.295	.305	.347	108	2	4	1	1	.877	5	*O-50,2-11/S-2	0.7
1875	Chi-n	69	308	45	101	14	4	0	36	1	0	.328	.330	.399	151	15	6	9	-4	.889	9	O-39,2-30/C-1,S-1	1.7
1876	Chi-N	64	305	62	101	**21**	3	2	59	1	3	.331	.333	.439	139	10				**.923**	5	*O-64/2-1	1.2
1877	Chi-N	60	261	44	73	11	7	0	23	1	8	.280	.282	.375	94	-3				.806	-10	*O-49,2-11	-1.3
1878	Pro-N	62	257	42	92	13	4	**4**	**50**	2	10	.358	.363	**.486**	178	20				.849	3	*O-61/S-1	1.8
1879	Pro-N	85	409	81	**146**	25	10	2	52	8	16	.357	.369	.482	181	**34**				.867	7	*O-85	3.3
1880	Pro-N	85	374	64	115	20	2	3	35	13	17	.307	.331	.396	150	19				**.927**	8	*O-75/2-6,1-4	2.4
1881	Pro-N	80	361	65	103	**27**	5	2	31	13	12	.285	.310	.404	125	10				.897	-1	*O-78/2-4,1-1	0.7
1882	Pro-N	84	379	73	117	28	10	4	34	10	14	.309	.326	.467	151	21				.861	1	*O-82/1-2	1.9
1883	Pro-N	97	442	94	132	32	4	4	45	18	23	.299	.326	.416	120	10				.905	7	*O-89/1-9	1.3
1884	*Pro-N	114	490	94	148	**36**	10	3	41	44	28	.302	.360	.435	151	30				.895	2	*O-108/1-7,P-1	2.5
1885	Pro-N	98	411	63	111	20	4	1	35	19	18	.270	.302	.345	112	6				.865	4	*O-92/1-4,S-1,32	0.6
1886	Was-N	121	487	80	152	30	8	9	56	35	21	.312	.358	.462	157	33	21			.899	3	*O-92,3-15,1/S2	3.0
1887	Was-N	123	478	83	147	32	5	10	72	48	24	.308	.380	.458	139	27	46			.886	-14	*O-109/1-7,2-5,S-4	0.9
1888	Ind-N	133	513	84	144	26	3	4	58	41	45	.281	.343	.366	124	15	31			.912	-7	*O-125/1-6,S-2	0.4
1889	Ind-N	121	486	77	148	27	1	6	72	49	22	.305	.374	.401	114	10	34			.964	4	*1-109,O-12	0.5
1890	Pit-N	31	121	11	22	1	0	0	9	11	7	.182	.256	.190	34	-10	6			.973	2	1-17,O-14	-0.8
	Bos-N	69	273	41	72	12	3	2	48	32	20	.264	.350	.352	97	-2	9			.881	-12	O-69/1-1	-1.4
	Yr	100	394	52	94	13	3	2	57	43	27	.239	.321	.302	80	-9	15			.871	-10	O-83,1-18	-2.2
1891	Was-a	54	206	25	58	7	5	0	31	21	16	.282	.376	.364	117	6	6			.856	-3	O-47/1-8	0.0
Total	4 n	178	809	134	253	31	9	1	104	6	5	.313	.318	.377	123	19	10	11	-4	.857	11	O-125/2-43,1-9,SC3	2.3
Total	16	1481	6253	1083	1881	368	84	56	751	366	304	.301	.343	.413	133	234	153			.887	-3	*O-1251,1-185/23SP	17.0
■ **GORDIE HINKLE** Hinkle, Daniel Gordon b: 4/3/05, Toronto, Ohio d: 3/19/72, Houston, Tex. BR/TR, 6', 185 lbs. Deb: 4/19/34																							
1934	Bos-A	27	75	7	13	6	1	0	9	7	23	.173	.244	.280	33	-8	0	0	0	.992	4	C-26	-0.2
■ **GEORGE HINSHAW** Hinshaw, George Addison b: 10/23/59, Los Angeles, Cal. BR/TR, 6', 185 lbs. Deb: 9/19/82																							
1982	SD-N	6	15	1	4	0	0	0	1	3	5	.267	.389	.267	91	0	0	0	0	1.000	0	/O-6	0.0
1983	SD-N	7	16	1	7	1	0	0	4	0	4	.438	.438	.500	165	1	1	0	0	1.000	-0	/3-5	0.1
Total	2	13	31	2	11	1	0	0	5	3	9	.355	.412	.387	129	1	1	0	0	1.000	0	/O-6,3-5	0.1
■ **PAUL HINSON** Hinson, James Paul b: 5/9/04, Vanleer, Tenn. d: 9/23/60, Muskogee, Okla. BR/TR, 5'10", 150 lbs. Deb: 4/19/28																							
1928	Bos-A	3	0	1	0	0	0	0	0	0	0	—	—	—	—	0	0	0	0	.000	0	R	0.0
■ **CHUCK HINTON** Hinton, Charles Edward b: 5/3/34, Rocky Mount, N.C. BR/TR, 6'1", 197 lbs. Deb: 5/14/61																							
1961	Was-A	106	339	51	88	13	5	6	34	40	81	.260	.339	.381	93	-3	22	5	4	.963	0	O-92	-0.4
1962	Was-A	151	542	73	168	25	6	17	75	47	66	.310	.365	.472	124	18	28	10	2	.988	-10	*O-136,2-12/S-1	0.4
1963	Was-A	150	566	80	152	20	12	15	55	64	79	.269	.344	.426	115	11	25	9	2	.989	-1	*O-125,3-19/1-6,S-2	0.6
1964	Was-A★	138	514	71	141	25	7	11	53	57	77	.274	.348	.414	112	8	17	6	2	.985	10	*O-131/3-2	1.4
1965	Cle-A	133	431	59	110	17	6	18	54	53	65	.255	.338	.448	120	11	17	3	3	.966	-9	O-72,1-40,2-23,/3-1	0.3
1966	Cle-A	123	348	46	89	9	3	12	50	35	66	.256	.326	.402	108	3	10	6	-1	.973	-8	*O-104/1-6,2-2	-1.0
1967	Cle-A	147	498	55	122	19	3	10	37	43	100	.245	.306	.355	94	-4	6	8	-3	.976	-13	*O-136/2-5	-2.8
1968	Cal-A	116	267	28	52	10	3	7	23	24	61	.195	.261	.333	82	-6	3	1	0	.987	-6	1-48,O-37,3-13,/2-9	-1.8
1969	Cle-A	94	121	18	31	3	2	3	19	8	22	.256	.308	.388	91	-2	2	0	1	.941	-10	O-40,3-14	-1.2
1970	Cle-A	107	195	24	62	4	0	9	29	25	34	.318	.395	.477	133	9	0	2	-1	.994	-6	1-40,O-35/C-4,23	-0.1
1971	Cle-A	88	147	13	33	7	0	5	14	20	34	.224	.317	.374	87	-2	0	0	0	1.000	-7	1-20,O-20/C-5	-1.2
Total	11	1353	3968	518	1048	152	47	113	443	416	685	.264	.335	.412	108	44	130	50	9	.979	-59	O-928,1-160/23CS	-5.8
■ **JOHN HINTON** Hinton, John Robert "Red" b: 6/20/1876, Pittsburgh, Pa. d: 7/19/20, Braddock, Pa. BR/TR, 6', 200 lbs. Deb: 6/3/01																							
1901	Bos-N	4	13	0	1	0	0	0	0	2		.077	.200	.077	-17	-2	0			.750	-2	/3-4	-0.4
■ **TOMMY HINZO** Hinzo, Thomas Lee b: 6/18/64, San Diego, Cal. BB/TR, 5'10", 170 lbs. Deb: 7/16/87																							
1987	Cle-A	67	257	31	68	9	3	3	21	10	47	.265	.297	.358	72	-10	9	4	0	.973	-4	2-67	-1.0
1989	Cle-A	18	17	4	0	0	0	0	0	2	6	.000	.105	.000	-67	-4	1	2	-1	.867	0	/2-6,S-1,D-1	-0.4
Total	2	85	274	35	68	9	3	3	21	12	53	.248	.285	.336	64	-14	10	6	-1	.968	-4	/2-73,D-1,S-1	-1.4
■ **GENE HISER** Hiser, Gene Taylor b: 12/11/48, Baltimore, Md. BL/TL, 5'11", 175 lbs. Deb: 8/20/71																							
1971	Chi-N	17	29	4	6	0	0	0	1	4	8	.207	.303	.207	41	-2	1	0	0	1.000	-0	/O-9	-0.2
1972	Chi-N	32	46	2	9	0	0	0	4	6	8	.196	.288	.196	36	-4	1	0	0	1.000	-0	O-15	-0.4
1973	Chi-N	100	109	15	19	3	0	1	6	11	17	.174	.256	.229	33	-10	4	5	-2	.980	-18	O-64	-3.2
1974	Chi-N	12	17	2	4	1	0	0	1	0	3	.235	.235	.294	46	-1	0	0	0	1.000	-2	/O-8	-0.3
1975	Chi-N	45	62	11	15	3	0	0	6	11	7	.242	.356	.290	77	-1	0	1	-1	1.000	-3	O-18/1-1	-0.5
Total	5	206	263	34	53	7	0	1	18	32	43	.202	.291	.240	46	-18	6	6	-2	.992	-22	O-114/1-1	-4.6
■ **LARRY HISLE** Hisle, Larry Eugene b: 5/5/47, Portsmouth, Ohio BR/TR, 6'2", 195 lbs. Deb: 4/10/68 C																							
1968	Phi-N	7	11	1	4	1	0	0	1	1	4	.364	.417	.455	161	1	0	0	0	1.000	-1	/O-6	0.0
1969	Phi-N	145	482	75	128	23	5	20	56	48	152	.266	.338	.459	125	14	18	8	1	.977	11	*O-140	1.9
1970	Phi-N	126	405	52	83	22	4	10	44	53	139	.205	.302	.353	77	-14	5	5	-2	.978	5	*O-121	-1.6

YEAR	TM/L	G	AB	R	H	2B	3B	HR	RBI	BB	SO	AVG	OBP	SLG	PRO+	BR/A	SB	CS	SBR	FA	FR	G/POS	TPR
1971	Phi-N	36	76	7	15	3	0	0	3	6	22	.197	.256	.237	40	-6	1	0	0	.962	-0	O-27	-0.7
1973	Min-A	143	545	88	148	25	6	15	64	64	128	.272	.352	.422	113	10	11	4	1	.975	6	*O-143	1.0
1974	Min-A	143	510	68	146	20	7	19	79	48	112	.286	.357	.465	131	20	12	6	0	.979	-8	*O-137	0.6
1975	Min-A	80	255	37	80	9	2	11	51	27	39	.314	.382	.494	144	15	17	3	3	.976	-7	O-58,D-14	0.8
1976	Min-A	155	581	81	158	19	5	14	96	56	93	.272	.340	.394	112	9	31	18	-2	.984	14	*O-154	1.6
1977	Min-A★	141	546	95	165	36	3	28	**119**	56	106	.302	.373	.533	146	34	21	10	0	.974	1	*O-134/D-6	2.9
1978	Mil-A★	142	520	96	151	24	0	34	115	67	90	.290	.377	.533	153	36	10	6	-1	.978	-2	O-87,D-51	2.9
1979	Mil-A	26	96	18	27	7	0	3	14	11	19	.281	.355	.448	115	2	1	0	0	1.000	1	D-15,O-10	0.2
1980	Mil-A	17	60	16	17	0	0	6	16	14	7	.283	.427	.583	180	7	1	1	-0	.000	0	D-17	0.6
1981	Mil-A	27	87	11	20	4	0	4	11	6	17	.230	.295	.414	108	1	0	0	0	.000	0	D-24	0.0
1982	Mil-A	9	31	7	4	0	0	2	5	5	13	.129	.250	.323	60	-2	0	0	0	.000	0	/D-8	-0.2
Total	14	1197	4205	652	1146	193	32	166	674	462	941	.273	.350	.452	123	126	128	61	2	.978	19	*O-1017,D-135	10.0

■ JIM HITCHCOCK

Hitchcock, James Franklin b: 6/28/11, Inverness, Ala. d: 6/23/59, Montgomery, Ala. BR/TR, 5′11″, 175 lbs. Deb: 8/24/38 F

YEAR	TM/L	G	AB	R	H	2B	3B	HR	RBI	BB	SO	AVG	OBP	SLG	PRO+	BR/A	SB	CS	SBR	FA	FR	G/POS	TPR
1938	Bos-N	28	76	2	13	0	0	0	7	2	11	.171	.192	.171	1	-10	1			.881	-2	S-24/3-2	-1.1

■ BILLY HITCHCOCK

Hitchcock, William Clyde b: 7/31/16, Inverness, Ala. BR/TR, 6′1.5″, 185 lbs. Deb: 4/14/42 FMC

YEAR	TM/L	G	AB	R	H	2B	3B	HR	RBI	BB	SO	AVG	OBP	SLG	PRO+	BR/A	SB	CS	SBR	FA	FR	G/POS	TPR
1942	Det-A	85	280	27	59	8	1	0	29	26	21	.211	.280	.246	45	-20	2	2	-1	.944	-3	S-80/3-1	-2.0
1946	Det-A	3	3	0	0	0	0	0	0	1	0	.000	.250	.000	-25	-0	0	0	0	1.000	0	/2-1	0.0
	Was-A	98	354	27	75	8	3	0	25	26	52	.212	.268	.251	48	-25	2	4	-2	.966	-4	S-53,3-46	-2.8
	Yr	101	357	27	75	8	3	0	25	27	52	.210	.268	.249	48	-25	2	4	-2	.966	-3	S-53,3-46/2-1	-2.8
1947	StL-A	80	275	25	61	2	2	1	28	21	34	.222	.277	.255	47	-19	3	0	1	.977	11	2-46,3-17/S-7,1-5	-0.4
1948	Bos-A	49	124	15	37	3	2	1	20	7	9	.298	.341	.379	87	-3	0	0	0	.951	6	2-15,3-15	0.4
1949	Bos-A	55	147	22	30	6	1	0	9	17	11	.204	.291	.259	43	-12	2	3	-1	.993	-8	1-29/2-8	-2.1
1950	Phi-A	115	399	35	109	22	5	1	54	45	32	.273	.347	.361	83	-10	3	1	0	.967	-3	*2-107/S-1	-0.7
1951	Phi-A	77	222	27	68	10	4	1	36	21	23	.306	.371	.401	107	2	2	0	1	.929	7	3-45,2-23/1-1	1.0
1952	Phi-A	119	407	45	100	8	4	1	56	39	45	.246	.318	.292	66	-18	1	1	-0	.942	-1	*3-104,1-13	-2.2
1953	Det-A	22	38	8	8	0	0	0	0	3	3	.211	.268	.211	31	-4	0	0	0	.929	0	3-12/2-1,S-1	-0.4
Total	9	703	2249	231	547	67	22	5	257	206	230	.243	.310	.299	65	-109	15	11	-2	.938	7	3-240,2-201,S/1	-9.2

■ MYRIL HOAG

Hoag, Myril Oliver b: 3/9/08, Davis, Cal. d: 7/28/71, High Springs, Fla BR/TR, 5′11″, 180 lbs. Deb: 4/15/31

YEAR	TM/L	G	AB	R	H	2B	3B	HR	RBI	BB	SO	AVG	OBP	SLG	PRO+	BR/A	SB	CS	SBR	FA	FR	G/POS	TPR
1931	NY-A	44	28	6	4	2	0	0	3	1	8	.143	.172	.214	1	-4	0	0	0	1.000	-7	O-23/3-1	-1.0
1932	*NY-A	46	54	18	20	5	0	1	7	7	13	.370	.443	.519	156	5	1	1	-0	.962	-10	O-35/1-1	-0.6
1934	NY-A	97	251	45	67	8	2	3	34	21	21	.267	.324	.351	79	-8	1	3	-2	.974	-9	O-86	-2.0
1935	NY-A	48	110	13	28	4	1	1	13	12	19	.255	.328	.336	76	-4	4	2	0	.986	-2	O-37/3-1	-0.6
1936	NY-A	45	156	23	47	9	4	3	34	7	16	.301	.343	.468	102	-0	3	1	0	.955	-4	O-39	-0.5
1937	*NY-A	106	362	48	109	19	8	3	46	33	33	.301	.364	.423	97	-2	4	7	-3	.955	-6	O-99	-1.3
1938	*NY-A	85	267	28	74	14	3	0	48	25	31	.277	.344	.352	75	-10	4	3	-1	.965	-4	O-70	-1.6
1939	StL-A★	129	482	58	142	23	4	10	75	24	35	.295	.329	.421	89	-10	9	5	-0	.971	-8	*O-117/P-1	-2.0
1940	StL-A	76	191	20	50	11	0	3	26	13	30	.262	.309	.366	73	-8	2	0	1	.971	-6	O-46	-1.5
1941	StL-A	1	1	0	0	0	0	0	0	0	0	.000	.000	.000	-97	-0	0	0	0	.000	0	H	0.0
	Chi-A	106	380	30	97	13	3	1	44	27	29	.255	.306	.313	65	-19	6	10	-4	.957	-6	O-99	-3.4
	Yr	107	381	30	97	13	3	1	44	27	29	.255	.306	.312	65	-20	6	10	-4	.957	-6	O-99	-3.4
1942	Chi-A	113	412	47	99	18	2	2	37	36	21	.240	.301	.308	73	-15	17	8	0	.972	-4	*O-112	-2.6
1944	Chi-A	17	48	5	11	1	0	0	4	10	1	.229	.362	.250	77	-1	1	3	-2	.969	-1	O-14	-0.4
	Cle-A	67	277	33	79	9	3	1	27	25	23	.285	.347	.350	103	1	6	4	-1	.947	-1	O-66	-0.4
	Yr	84	325	38	90	10	3	1	31	35	24	.277	.349	.335	99	0	7	7	-2	.950	-2	O-80	-0.8
1945	Cle-A	40	128	10	27	5	3	0	3	11	18	.211	.279	.297	70	-5	1	2	-1	.987	0	O-33/P-2	-0.8
Total	13	1020	3147	384	854	141	33	28	401	252	298	.271	.328	.364	83	-80	59	49	-12	.965	-67	O-876/P-3,3-2,1-1	-18.7

■ DON HOAK

Hoak, Donald Albert "Tiger" b: 2/5/28, Roulette, Pa. d: 10/9/69, Pittsburgh, Pa. BR/TR, 6′, 175 lbs. Deb: 4/18/54 C

YEAR	TM/L	G	AB	R	H	2B	3B	HR	RBI	BB	SO	AVG	OBP	SLG	PRO+	BR/A	SB	CS	SBR	FA	FR	G/POS	TPR
1954	Bro-N	88	261	41	64	9	5	7	26	25	39	.245	.321	.398	83	-7	8	3	1	.950	4	3-75	-0.3
1955	*Bro-N	94	279	50	67	13	3	5	19	46	50	.240	.350	.362	87	-4	9	5	-0	.960	17	3-78	1.2
1956	Chi-N	121	424	51	91	18	4	5	37	41	46	.215	.285	.311	61	-23	8	3	1	.949	-18	*3-110	-4.1
1957	Cin-N★	149	529	78	155	**39**	2	19	89	74	54	.293	.384	.482	122	18	8	15	-7	**.971**	-0	*3-149/2-1	1.4
1958	Cin-N	114	417	51	109	30	0	6	50	43	36	.261	.333	.376	83	-10	6	8	-3	.964	4	*3-112/S-1	-0.8
1959	Pit-N	155	564	60	166	29	3	8	65	71	75	.294	.377	.399	108	9	9	2	2	.961	9	*3-155	2.0
1960	*Pit-N	155	553	97	156	24	9	16	79	74	74	.282	.368	.445	120	17	3	2	-0	.948	4	*3-155	2.0
1961	Pit-N	145	503	72	150	27	7	12	61	73	53	.298	.390	.451	122	18	4	2	0	.953	-3	*3-143	1.6
1962	Pit-N	121	411	63	99	14	8	5	48	49	49	.241	.323	.350	81	-11	4	2	0	**.969**	-3	*3-116	-1.2
1963	Phi-N	115	377	35	87	11	3	6	24	27	52	.231	.284	.324	75	-12	5	5	-2	.958	6	*3-106	-0.8
1964	Phi-N	6	4	0	0	0	0	0	0	0	2	.000	.000	.000	-99	-1	0	0	0	.000	0	H	-0.1
Total	11	1263	4322	598	1144	214	44	89	498	523	530	.265	.347	.396	98	-6	64	47	-9	.959	20	*3-1199/S-1,2-1	0.9

■ BILL HOBBS

Hobbs, William Lee "Smokey" b: 5/7/1893, Grants Lick, Ky. d: 1/5/45, Hamilton, Ohio BR/TR, 5′9.5″, 155 lbs. Deb: 8/9/13

YEAR	TM/L	G	AB	R	H	2B	3B	HR	RBI	BB	SO	AVG	OBP	SLG	PRO+	BR/A	SB	CS	SBR	FA	FR	G/POS	TPR
1913	Cin-N	4	4	0	0	0	0	0	0	0	3	.000	.000	.000	-99	-1	0			1.000	1	/2-1,3-1	0.0
1916	Cin-N	6	11	1	2	1	0	0	1	2	0	.182	.308	.273	81	-0	1			.947	6	/S-6	0.6
Total	2	10	15	1	2	1	0	0	1	2	3	.133	.235	.200	32	-1	1			.947	6	/S-6,3-1,2-1	0.6

■ DICK HOBLITZEL

Hoblitzel, Richard Carleton "Doc" (b: Richard Carleton Hoblitzell)
b: 10/26/1888, Waverly, W.Va. d: 11/14/62, Parkersburg, W.Va. BL/TL, 6′, 172 lbs. Deb: 9/5/08

YEAR	TM/L	G	AB	R	H	2B	3B	HR	RBI	BB	SO	AVG	OBP	SLG	PRO+	BR/A	SB	CS	SBR	FA	FR	G/POS	TPR
1908	Cin-N	32	114	8	29	3	2	0	8	7		.254	.309	.316	102	0	2			.985	2	1-32	0.1
1909	Cin-N	142	517	59	159	23	11	4	67	44		.308	.364	.418	144	25	17			.982	-3	*1-142	2.3
1910	Cin-N	155	611	85	170	24	13	4	70	47	32	.278	.332	.380	112	7	28			.984	-8	*1-148/2-7	-0.1
1911	Cin-N	158	622	81	180	19	13	11	91	42	44	.289	.342	.415	116	10	32			.990	2	*1-158	1.2
1912	Cin-N	148	558	73	164	32	12	2	85	48	28	.294	.352	.405	110	7	23			.985	2	*1-147	0.6
1913	Cin-N	137	502	59	143	23	7	3	62	35	26	.285	.334	.376	103	1	18			.988	-5	*1-134	-0.6
1914	Cin-N	78	248	31	52	8	7	0	26	26	26	.210	.287	.298	72	-9	7			.988	-4	1-75	-1.6
	Bos-A	69	229	31	73	10	3	0	33	19	21	.319	.386	.389	133	9	12	12	-4	.979	-5	1-68	-0.1
1915	*Bos-A	124	399	54	113	15	12	2	61	38	26	.283	.351	.396	128	13	9	14	-6	.987	-1	*1-117	0.3
1916	*Bos-A	130	417	57	108	17	1	0	39	47	28	.259	.338	.305	93	-3	10			.989	-1	*1-126	-0.9
1917	Bos-A	120	420	49	108	19	7	1	47	46	22	.257	.336	.343	108	4	12			.990	-8	*1-118	-0.9
1918	Bos-A	25	69	4	11	1	0	0	4	8	3	.159	.266	.174	33	-5	3			.996	1	1-19	-0.6
Total	11	1318	4706	591	1310	194	88	27	593	407	256	.278	.341	.374	111	61	173	26		.987	-29	*1-1284/2-7	-0.3

■ BUTCH HOBSON

Hobson, Clell Lavern b: 8/17/51, Tuscaloosa, Ala. BR/TR, 6′1″, 193 lbs. Deb: 9/7/75 M

YEAR	TM/L	G	AB	R	H	2B	3B	HR	RBI	BB	SO	AVG	OBP	SLG	PRO+	BR/A	SB	CS	SBR	FA	FR	G/POS	TPR
1975	Bos-A	2	4	0	1	0	0	0	0	0	2	.250	.250	.250	38	-0	0	0	0	1.000	1	/3-1	0.0
1976	Bos-A	76	269	34	63	7	5	8	34	15	62	.234	.275	.387	82	-7	0	1	-1	.936	-7	3-76	-1.7
1977	Bos-A	159	593	77	157	33	5	30	112	27	162	.265	.301	.489	100	-3	5	4	-1	.946	-28	*3-159	-3.4
1978	Bos-A	147	512	65	128	26	2	17	80	50	122	.250	.317	.408	92	-6	1	0	0	.899	-14	*3-133,D-14	-2.3
1979	Bos-A	146	528	74	138	26	7	28	93	30	78	.261	.301	.496	105	1	3	2	-0	.935	-21	*3-142/2-1	-2.1
1980	Bos-A	93	324	35	74	6	0	11	39	25	69	.228	.284	.349	69	-14	1	1	-0	.910	-9	3-57,D-36	-2.6
1981	Cal-A	85	268	27	63	7	4	4	36	35	60	.235	.326	.336	91	-2	1	1	-0	.929	-11	3-83/D-2	-1.7
1982	NY-A	30	58	2	10	2	0	0	3	1	14	.172	.186	.207	8	-7	0	0	0	.951	-1	D-15,1-11	-0.9
Total	8	738	2556	314	634	107	23	98	397	183	569	.248	.300	.423	91	-40	11	9	-2	.926	-90	3-651/D-67,1-11,2-1	-14.7

■ ED HOCK

Hock, Edward Francis b: 3/27/1899, Franklin Furnace, Ohio d: 11/21/63, Portsmouth, Ohio BL/TL, 5′10.5″, 165 lbs. Deb: 7/8/20

YEAR	TM/L	G	AB	R	H	2B	3B	HR	RBI	BB	SO	AVG	OBP	SLG	PRO+	BR/A	SB	CS	SBR	FA	FR	G/POS	TPR
1920	StL-N	1	0	0	0	0	0	0	0	0	0	—	—	—	—	0	0	0	0	.000	-1	/O-1	-0.1
1923	Cin-N	2	0	0	0	0	0	0	0	0	0	—	—	—	—	0	0	0	0	.000	0	R	0.0
1924	Cin-N	16	10	7	1	0	0	0	0	0	2	.100	.182	.100	-23	-2	0	0	0	1.000	-0	/O-2	-0.2
Total	3	19	10	7	1	0	0	0	0	0	2	.100	.182	.100	-23	-2	0	0	0	1.000	-1	/O-3	-0.3

YEAR	TM/L	G	AB	R	H	2B	3B	HR	RBI	BB	SO	AVG	OBP	SLG	PRO+	BR/A	SB	CS	SBR	FA	FR	G/POS	TPR
■ ORIS HOCKETT Hockett, Oris Leon "Brown" b: 9/29/09, Amboy, Ind. d: 3/23/69, Torrance, Cal. BL/TR, 5'9", 182 lbs. Deb: 9/4/38																							
1938	Bro-N	21	70	8	23	5	1	1	8	4	9	.329	.365	.471	126	2	0			.893	-4	O-17	-0.2
1939	Bro-N	9	13	3	3	0	0	0	1	1	1	.231	.286	.231	39	-1	0			1.000	1	/O-1	-0.1
1941	Cle-A	2	6	0	2	0	0	0	1	2	0	.333	.500	.333	131	0	0	0	0	1.000	-1	/O-2	0.0
1942	Cle-A	148	601	85	150	22	7	7	48	45	45	.250	.305	.344	88	-12	12	12	-4	.980	-2	*O-145	-2.6
1943	Cle-A	141	601	70	166	33	4	2	51	45	45	.276	.331	.354	107	4	13	18	-7	.960	1	*O-139	-1.0
1944	Cle-A☆	124	457	47	132	29	5	1	50	35	27	.289	.339	.381	110	5	8	9	-3	.986	-4	*O-110	-0.8
1945	Chi-A	106	417	46	122	23	4	2	55	27	30	.293	.340	.381	112	5	10	9	-2	.982	1	*O-106	-0.1
Total	7	551	2165	259	598	112	21	13	214	159	157	.276	.329	.365	103	3	43	48		.974	-6	O-520	-4.8
■ DENNIS HOCKING Hocking, Dennis Lee b: 4/2/70, Torrance, Cal. BB/TR, 5'10", 176 lbs. Deb: 9/10/93																							
1993	Min-A	15	36	7	5	1	0	0	0	6	8	.139	.262	.167	18	-4	1	0	0	.971	-2	S-12/2-1	-0.5
1994	Min-A	11	31	3	10	3	0	0	2	0	4	.323	.323	.419	89	-1	2	0	1	1.000	1	S-10	0.1
1995	Min-A	9	25	4	5	0	2	0	3	2	2	.200	.259	.360	59	-2	1	0	0	.971	1	/S-6	0.0
1996	Min-A	49	127	16	25	6	0	1	10	8	24	.197	.244	.268	29	-14	3	3	-1	.985	1	O-33/S-6,2-2,1-1,D	-1.3
1997	Min-A	115	253	28	65	12	4	2	25	18	51	.257	.309	.360	73	-10	3	5	-2	.975	3	S-44,3-39,O2/1D	-0.6
1998	Min-A	110	198	32	40	6	1	3	15	16	44	.202	.262	.288	43	-17	2	1	0	1.000	4	2-48,S-28,O3/1D	-1.1
Total	6	309	670	90	150	28	7	6	55	50	133	.224	.279	.313	53	-47	12	9	-2	.974	7	S-106/O-77,23D1	-3.4
■ JOHNNY HODAPP Hodapp, Urban John b: 9/26/05, Cincinnati, Ohio d: 6/14/80, Cincinnati, Ohio BR/TR, 6', 185 lbs. Deb: 8/19/25																							
1925	Cle-A	37	130	12	31	5	1	0	14	11	7	.238	.298	.292	50	-10	2	3	-1	.960	3	3-37	-0.5
1926	Cle-A	3	5	0	1	0	0	0	0	0	1	.200	.200	.200	4	-1	0	0	0	.750	-1	/3-3	-0.1
1927	Cle-A	79	240	25	73	15	3	5	40	14	23	.304	.343	.454	105	1	2	2	-1	.935	1	3-67/1-4	0.3
1928	Cle-A	116	449	51	145	31	6	2	73	20	20	.323	.352	.432	104	2	2	1	0	.944	-2	*3-101,1-13	0.4
1929	Cle-A	90	294	30	96	12	7	4	51	15	14	.327	.361	.456	105	2	3	3	-1	.977	5	2-72	0.8
1930	Cle-A	154	635	111	**225**	**51**	8	9	121	32	29	.354	.386	.502	119	17	6	5	-1	.970	12	*2-154	3.2
1931	Cle-A	122	468	71	138	19	4	2	56	27	23	.295	.336	.365	80	-14	1	5	-3	.969	16	*2-121	0.7
1932	Cle-A	7	16	2	2	1	0	0	0	0	2	.125	.125	.188	-19	-3	0	0	0	1.000	-2	/2-7	-0.4
	Chi-A	68	176	21	40	8	0	3	20	11	3	.227	.273	.324	58	-12	1	0	0	.967	-5	O-31/2-5,3-4	-1.7
	Yr	75	192	23	42	9	0	3	20	11	5	.219	.261	.313	51	-15	1	0	0	.967	-7	O-31,2-12/3-4	-2.1
1933	Bos-A	115	413	55	129	27	5	3	54	33	14	.312	.365	.424	109	5	1	1	-0	.960	3	*2-101,1-10	1.2
Total	9	791	2826	378	880	169	34	28	429	163	136	.311	.350	.425	98	-13	18	20	-7	.967	30	2-460,3-212/O-31,1	3.9
■ MEL HODERLEIN Hoderlein, Melvin Anthony b: 6/24/23, Mt.Carmel, Ohio BB/TR, 5'10", 185 lbs. Deb: 8/16/51																							
1951	Bos-A	9	14	1	5	1	1	0	1	6	2	.357	.550	.571	185	2	0	1	-1	1.000	1	/2-3,3-3	0.2
1952	Was-A	72	208	16	56	8	2	0	17	18	22	.269	.333	.327	87	-3	2	0	1	.978	-2	2-58	-0.2
1953	Was-A	23	47	5	9	0	0	0	5	6	9	.191	.283	.191	31	-4	0	0	0	.953	-3	2-11/S-2	-0.7
1954	Was-A	14	25	0	4	1	0	0	1	1	4	.160	.192	.200	8	-3	0	0	0	.939	1	/S-6,2-5	-0.1
Total	4	118	294	22	74	10	3	0	24	31	37	.252	.327	.306	78	-9	2	1	0	.973	-3	/2-77,S-8,3-3	-0.8
■ CHARLIE HODES Hodes, Charles b: 1848, New York, N.Y. d: 2/14/1875, Brooklyn, N.Y. TR, 5'11.5", 175 lbs. Deb: 5/8/1871																							
1871	Chi-n	28	130	32	36	4	1	2	25	7	0	.277	.314	.369	86	-4	3	0	1	.796	3	*C-20,3-10/O-4,S-1	0.0
1872	Tro-n	13	61	17	15	3	0	0	12	1	0	.246	.258	.295	69	-2	0	0	0	.759	0	/S-5,O-4,C-3,3-1	-0.2
1874	Atl-n	21	81	8	12	3	0	0	7	0	2	.148	.148	.185	7	-7	0	0	0	.825	-4	O-18/C-3,2-3,1-1	-0.9
Total	3 n	62	272	57	63	10	1	2	44	8	2	.232	.254	.298	64	-14	3	0	1	.820	-0	/O-26,C-26,3S21	-1.1
■ BERT HODGE Hodge, Edward Burton b: 5/25/17, Knoxville, Tenn. BL/TR, 5'11", 170 lbs. Deb: 4/14/42																							
1942	Phi-N	8	11	0	2	0	0	0	0	1	0	.182	.250	.182	29	-1	0			1.000	-1	/3-2	-0.2
■ GOMER HODGE Hodge, Harold Morris b: 4/3/44, Rutherfordton, N.C. BB/TR, 6'2", 185 lbs. Deb: 4/6/71																							
1971	Cle-A	80	83	3	17	3	0	1	9	4	19	.205	.258	.277	47	-6	0	0	0	1.000	-2	/1-3,3-3,2-2	-0.8
■ GIL HODGES Hodges, Gilbert Raymond (b: Gilbert Ray Hodge) b: 4/4/24, Princeton, Ind. d: 4/2/72, West Palm Beach, Fla BR/TR, 6'1.5", 200 lbs. Deb: 10/3/43 M																							
1943	Bro-N	1	2	0	0	0	0	0	0	1	2	.000	.333	.000	0	-0	1			.600	0	/3-1	0.0
1947	*Bro-N	28	77	9	12	3	1	1	7	14	19	.156	.286	.260	44	-6	0			.958	-2	C-24	-0.7
1948	Bro-N	134	481	48	120	18	5	11	70	43	61	.249	.311	.376	82	-13	7			.986	-1	1-96,C-38	-1.2
1949	*Bro-N★	156	596	94	170	23	4	23	115	66	64	.285	.360	.453	112	10	10			**.995**	-4	*1-156	0.5
1950	Bro-N☆	153	561	98	159	26	2	32	113	73	73	.283	.367	.508	125	20	6			**.994**	1	*1-153	1.6
1951	Bro-N★	158	582	118	156	25	3	40	103	93	99	.268	.374	.527	137	30	9	7	-2	.992	7	*1-158	2.9
1952	*Bro-N☆	153	508	87	129	27	1	32	102	107	90	.254	.386	.500	142	31	2	4	-2	.992	5	*1-153	3.0
1953	*Bro-N★	141	520	101	157	22	7	31	122	75	84	.302	.393	.550	139	31	1	4	-2	.993	8	*1-127,O-24	2.9
1954	Bro-N★	154	579	106	176	23	5	42	130	74	84	.304	.384	.579	142	35	3	3	-1	.995	9	*1-154	3.4
1955	*Bro-N★	150	546	75	158	24	5	27	102	80	91	.289	.383	.500	128	23	2	1	0	.991	1	*1-139,O-16	1.6
1956	*Bro-N	153	550	86	146	29	4	32	87	76	91	.265	.355	.507	119	15	3	3	-1	.992	1	*1-138,O-30/C-1	0.6
1957	Bro-N★	150	579	94	173	28	7	27	98	63	91	.299	.370	.511	122	18	5	3	-0	.990	2	*1-150/3-2,2-1	1.0
1958	LA-N	141	475	68	123	15	1	22	64	52	87	.259	.332	.434	98	-2	8	2	1	.992	1	*1-122,3-15/O-9,C-1	-0.7
1959	*LA-N	124	413	57	114	19	2	25	80	58	92	.276	.369	.513	123	14	3	2	-0	**.992**	0	*1-113/3-4	0.6
1960	LA-N	101	197	22	39	8	1	8	30	26	37	.198	.295	.371	76	-7	0	1	-1	.995	1	1-92,3-10	-1.0
1961	LA-N	109	215	25	52	4	0	8	31	24	43	.242	.318	.372	76	-7	3	1	0	.998	0	*1-100	-1.1
1962	NY-N	54	127	15	32	1	0	9	17	15	27	.252	.331	.472	111	2	0	0	0	.986	3	1-47	0.3
1963	NY-N	11	22	2	5	0	0	0	3	3	2	.227	.320	.227	60	-1	0	0	0	1.000	2	1-10	0.0
Total	18	2071	7030	1105	1921	295	48	370	1274	943	1137	.273	.361	.487	119	191	63	31		.992	34	*1-1908/O-79,C32	13.7
■ RON HODGES Hodges, Ronald Wray b: 6/22/49, Rocky Mount, Va. BL/TR, 6'1", 185 lbs. Deb: 6/13/73																							
1973	*NY-N	45	127	5	33	2	0	1	18	11	19	.260	.319	.299	73	-4	0	1	-1	.992	2	C-40	-0.1
1974	NY-N	59	136	16	30	4	0	4	14	19	11	.221	.316	.338	84	-3	0	0	0	.953	-2	C-44	-0.3
1975	NY-N	9	34	3	7	1	0	2	4	1	6	.206	.229	.412	79	-1	0	0	0	1.000	0	/C-9	-0.1
1976	NY-N	56	155	21	35	6	0	4	24	27	16	.226	.341	.342	100	1	2	0	1	.976	-9	C-52	-0.7
1977	NY-N	66	117	6	31	4	0	1	5	9	17	.265	.317	.325	76	-4	0	2	-1	.992	-0	C-27	-0.5
1978	NY-N	47	102	4	26	4	1	0	7	10	11	.255	.327	.314	83	-2	1	2	-1	.982	6	C-30	0.4
1979	NY-N	59	86	4	14	4	0	0	5	19	16	.163	.314	.209	47	-6	0	0	0	.980	1	C-22	-0.4
1980	NY-N	36	42	4	10	2	0	0	5	10	13	.238	.385	.286	92	0	1	1	-0	.982	4	/C-9	0.4
1981	NY-N	35	43	5	13	2	0	1	6	5	8	.302	.375	.419	127	2	1	0	0	1.000	-1	/C-7	0.1
1982	NY-N	80	228	26	56	12	1	5	27	41	40	.246	.361	.373	106	3	4	3	-1	.980	-0	C-74	0.5
1983	NY-N	110	250	20	65	12	0	0	21	49	42	.260	.385	.308	95	1	0	3	-2	.971	-10	C-96	-0.7
1984	NY-N	64	106	5	22	3	0	1	11	23	18	.208	.354	.264	77	-2	1	1	-0	.979	-1	C-35	-0.2
Total	12	666	1426	119	342	56	2	19	147	224	217	.240	.345	.322	88	-16	10	13	-5	.978	-9	C-445	-1.6
■ RALPH HODGIN Hodgin, Elmer Ralph b: 2/10/16, Greensboro, N.C. BL/TR, 5'10", 170 lbs. Deb: 4/19/39																							
1939	Bos-N	32	48	4	10	1	0	0	4	3	4	.208	.255	.229	33	-5	0			1.000	-1	/O-9	-0.6
1943	Chi-A	117	407	52	128	22	8	1	50	20	24	.314	.356	.415	125	12	3	5	-2	.945	-7	3-56,O-42	0.2
1944	Chi-A	121	465	56	137	25	7	1	51	21	14	.295	.333	.385	106	2	3	1	0	.942	12	3-82,O-33	1.5
1946	Chi-A	87	258	32	65	10	1	0	25	19	6	.252	.308	.298	73	-9	0	1	-1	.983	-2	O-57	-1.6
1947	Chi-A	59	180	26	53	10	3	1	24	13	4	.294	.352	.400	113	3	1	0	0	.990	1	O-41	0.2
1948	Chi-A	114	331	28	88	11	5	1	34	21	11	.266	.310	.338	75	-13	0	3	-2	.970	5	O-79	-1.4
Total	6	530	1689	198	481	79	24	4	188	97	63	.285	.330	.367	98	-10	7	10		.985	7	O-261,3-138	-1.7
■ PAUL HODGSON Hodgson, Paul Joseph Denis b: 4/14/60, Montreal, Que., Can. BR/TR, 6'2", 190 lbs. Deb: 8/31/80																							
1980	Tor-A	20	41	5	9	0	1	1	5	3	12	.220	.273	.341	64	-2	0	1	-1	1.000	-0	O-11/D-3	-0.3

YEAR	TM/L	G	AB	R	H	2B	3B	HR	RBI	BB	SO	AVG	OBP	SLG	PRO+	BR/A	SB	CS	SBR	FA	FR	G/POS	TPR

■ ART HOELSKOETTER Hoelskoetter, Arthur "Holley" or "Hoss" (a.k.a. Arthur H. Hostetter) b: 9/30/1882, St.Louis, Mo. d: 8/3/54, St.Louis, Mo. BR/TR, 6'2", Deb: 9/10/05

1905	StL-N	24	83	7	20	2	1	0	5	3		.241	.267	.289	68	-3	1			.972	1	3-20/2-3,P-1	-0.2
1906	StL-N	94	317	21	71	6	3	0	14	4		.224	.238	.262	58	-17	2			.943	-6	3-53,S-16,P-12,O/2	-2.1
1907	StL-N	119	397	21	98	6	3	2	28	27		.247	.298	.292	88	-6	5			.927	10	2-73,1-27/C-8,OP3	0.4
1908	StL-N	62	155	10	36	7	1	0	6	6		.232	.265	.290	81	-4	1			.948	1	C-41/3-2,1-1,2-1	0.0
Total	4	299	952	59	225	21	8	2	53	40		.236	.271	.282	75	-30	9			.924	5	/2-78,3-77,C1OSP	-1.9

■ JACK HOEY Hoey, John Bernard b: 11/10/1881, Watertown, Mass. d: 11/14/47, Waterbury, Conn. BL/TR, 5'9", 185 lbs. Deb: 6/27/06

1906	Bos-A	94	361	27	88	8	4	0	24	14		.244	.274	.288	76	-10	10			.915	-8	O-94	-2.5
1907	Bos-A	39	96	7	21	2	1	0	8	1		.219	.227	.260	56	-5	2			.857	-5	O-21	-1.3
1908	Bos-A	13	43	5	7	0	0	0	3	0		.163	.163	.163	6	-4	1			1.000	-0	O-11	-0.6
Total	3	146	500	39	116	10	5	0	35	15		.232	.256	.272	66	-20	13			.913	-13	O-126	-4.4

■ STEW HOFFERTH Hofferth, Stewart Edward b: 1/27/13, Logansport, Ind. d: 3/7/94, Valparaiso, Ind. BR/TR, 6'2", 195 lbs. Deb: 4/19/44

1944	Bos-N	66	180	14	36	8	0	1	26	11	5	.200	.246	.261	41	-14	0			.984	0	C-47	-1.2
1945	Bos-N	50	170	13	40	2	0	3	15	14	11	.235	.297	.300	66	-8	1			.980	6	C-45	0.1
1946	Bos-N	20	58	3	12	1	1	0	10	3	6	.207	.246	.259	43	-4	0			1.000	-1	C-15	-0.5
Total	3	136	408	30	88	11	1	4	51	28	22	.216	.268	.277	52	-26	1			.985	6	C-107	-1.6

■ DUTCH HOFFMAN Hoffman, Clarence Casper "Red" b: 1/28/04, Freeburg, Ill. d: 12/6/62, Belleville, Ill. BR/TR, 6', 175 lbs. Deb: 4/23/29

| 1929 | Chi-A | 107 | 337 | 27 | 87 | 16 | 5 | 3 | 37 | 24 | 28 | .258 | .307 | .362 | 73 | -14 | 6 | 3 | 0 | .984 | -1 | O-88 | -2.0 |

■ DANNY HOFFMAN Hoffman, Daniel John b: 3/2/1880, Canton, Conn. d: 3/14/22, Manchester, Conn. BL/TL, 5'9", 175 lbs. Deb: 4/20/03

1903	Phi-A	74	248	29	61	5	7	2	22	6		.246	.267	.347	79	-7	7			.950	0	O-62/P-1	-1.0
1904	Phi-A	53	204	31	61	7	5	3	24	5		.299	.329	.426	131	6	9			.936	0	O-51	0.4
1905	*Phi-A	120	459	66	120	10	10	1	35	33		.261	.312	.333	103	1	46			.942	-2	*O-118	-0.7
1906	Phi-A	7	22	4	5	0	0	0	0	3		.227	.320	.227	70	-1	1			1.000	1	/O-7	-1.8
	NY-A	100	320	34	82	10	6	0	23	27		.256	.318	.325	92	-3	32			.938	-9	O-98	-1.8
	Yr	107	342	38	87	10	6	0	23	30		.254	.318	.319	91	-4	33			.943	-8	*O-105	-1.8
1907	NY-A	136	517	81	131	8	3	5	46	42		.253	.325	.313	96	-2	30			.953	8	O-135	0.1
1908	StL-A	99	363	41	91	9	7	1	25	23		.251	.304	.322	103	1	17			.962	11	O-99	0.9
1909	StL-A	110	387	44	104	6	7	2	26	41		.269	.340	.336	125	12	24			.968	2	*O-110	1.1
1910	StL-A	106	380	20	90	11	5	0	27	34		.237	.306	.292	93	-3	16			.960	1	O-106	-0.8
1911	StL-A	24	81	11	17	3	2	0	7	12		.210	.326	.296	77	-2	3			.908	3	O-23	0.0
Total	9	829	2981	361	762	71	52	14	235	226		.256	.316	.328	101	4	185			.951	15	O-809/P-1	-1.8

■ TEX HOFFMAN Hoffman, Edward Adolph b: 11/30/1893, San Antonio, Tex. d: 5/19/47, New Orleans, La. BL/TR, 5'9", 195 lbs. Deb: 7/11/15

| 1915 | Cle-A | 9 | 13 | 1 | 2 | 0 | 0 | 0 | 2 | 1 | 5 | .154 | .214 | .154 | 10 | -1 | 0 | | | .750 | -2 | /3-3 | -0.3 |

■ GLENN HOFFMAN Hoffman, Glenn Edward b: 7/7/58, Orange, Cal. BR/TR, 6'2", 190 lbs. FM

1980	Bos-A	114	312	37	89	15	4	4	42	19	41	.285	.330	.397	94	-3	2	4	-2	.946	-0	*3-110/S-5,2-2	-0.6
1981	Bos-A	78	242	28	56	10	4	1	20	12	25	.231	.271	.285	57	-13	0	1	-1	.960	5	S-78/3-1	-0.1
1982	Bos-A	150	469	53	98	23	2	7	49	30	69	.209	.264	.311	54	-30	0	4	-2	.972	13	*S-150	-0.6
1983	Bos-A	143	473	56	123	24	1	4	41	30	76	.260	.307	.340	73	-18	1	1	-0	.962	-6	*S-143	-1.0
1984	Bos-A	64	74	8	14	4	0	0	4	5	10	.189	.241	.243	33	-7	0	1	-1	.957	5	S-56/3-4,2-2	0.0
1985	Bos-A	96	279	40	77	17	2	6	34	25	40	.276	.346	.416	103	1	2	2	-1	.975	-1	S-93/2-3,3-3	0.8
1986	Bos-A	12	23	1	5	2	0	0	1	2	3	.217	.280	.304	59	-1	0	0	0	.923	-2	S-11/3-1	-0.3
1987	Bos-A	21	55	5	11	3	0	0	6	3	9	.200	.267	.255	38	-5	0	0	0	.984	2	S-16/3-3,2-2	-0.1
	LA-N	40	132	10	29	5	0	0	10	7	23	.220	.270	.258	42	-11	0	1	-1	.966	1	S-40	-0.5
1989	Cal-A	48	104	9	22	3	0	1	10	3	23	.212	.241	.269	44	-8	0	2	-1	.982	5	S-23,3-18/2-4,1D	-0.5
Total	9	766	2163	247	524	106	9	23	210	136	309	.242	.293	.331	68	-94	5	16	-8	.966	21	S-615,3-140/2D1	-3.1

■ IZZY HOFFMAN Hoffman, Harry C. b: 1/5/1875, Bridgeport, N.J. d: 11/13/42, Philadelphia, Pa. BL/TL, 5'9", 160 lbs. Deb: 4/14/04

1904	Was-A	10	30	1	3	1	0	0	0	1		.100	.156	.133	-8	-4	0			1.000	1	/O-9	-0.4
1907	Bos-N	19	86	17	24	3	1	0	3	6		.279	.324	.337	108	1	2			.897	-2	O-19	-0.2
Total	2	29	116	18	27	4	1	0	4	8		.233	.282	.284	79	-3	2			.939	-1	/O-28	-0.6

■ JOHN HOFFMAN Hoffman, John Edward "Pork Chop" b: 10/31/43, Aberdeen, S.D. BL/TR, 6', 190 lbs. Deb: 7/30/64

1964	Hou-N	6	15	1	1	0	0	0	1	0	7	.067	.125	.067	-47	-3	0	0	0	1.000	-2	/C-5	-0.5
1965	Hou-N	2	6	1	2	0	0	0	0	1	3	.333	.333	.333	95	-0	0	0	0	1.000	-1	/C-2	-0.1
Total	2	8	21	2	3	0	0	0	1	1	10	.143	.182	.143	-8	-3	0	0	0	1.000	-2	/C-7	-0.6

■ LARRY HOFFMAN Hoffman, Lawrence Charles b: 7/18/1878, Chicago, Ill. d: 12/29/48, Chicago, Ill. BR/TR, Deb: 7/9/01

| 1901 | Chi-N | 6 | 22 | 2 | 7 | 1 | 0 | 0 | 6 | 0 | | .318 | .348 | .364 | 111 | -0 | 2 | | | .800 | -2 | /3-5,2-1 | -0.1 |

■ HICKEY HOFFMAN Hoffman, Otto Charles b: 10/27/1856, Cleveland, Ohio d: 10/27/15, Peoria, Ill. Deb: 5/10/1879

| 1879 | Cle-N | 2 | 6 | 0 | 0 | 0 | 0 | 0 | | 0 | 3 | .000 | .000 | .000 | -99 | -1 | | | | .857 | 0 | /C-2,O-1 | -0.1 |

■ RAY HOFFMAN Hoffman, Raymond Lamont b: 6/14/17, Detroit, Mich. BL/TR, 6'0.5", 175 lbs. Deb: 8/30/42

| 1942 | Was-A | 7 | 19 | 2 | 1 | 0 | 0 | 0 | 2 | 1 | 1 | .053 | .100 | .053 | -57 | -4 | 0 | 0 | 0 | .815 | 2 | /3-6 | -0.2 |

■ JESSE HOFFMEISTER Hoffmeister, Jesse H. b: Toledo, Ohio TR, Deb: 7/24/1897

| 1897 | Pit-N | 48 | 188 | 33 | 58 | 6 | 9 | 3 | 36 | 8 | | .309 | .337 | .484 | 120 | 4 | 6 | | | .792 | -12 | 3-48 | -0.6 |

■ SOLLY HOFMAN Hofman, Arthur Frederick "Circus Solly" b: 10/29/1882, St.Louis, Mo. d: 3/10/56, St.Louis, Mo. BR/TR, 6', 160 lbs. Deb: 7/28/03

1903	Pit-N	3	2	1	0	0	0	0	0	0		.000	.000	.000	-97	-1	0			.000	-1	/O-2	-0.1
1904	Chi-N	7	26	7	7	0	0	1	4	1		.269	.296	.385	110	-0	2			1.000	0	/O-6,S-1	0.0
1905	Chi-N	86	287	43	68	14	4	1	38	20		.237	.289	.324	79	-8	15			.955	4	2-59/1-9,S-9,3-3,O	-0.4
1906	*Chi-N	64	195	30	50	2	3	2	20	20		.256	.326	.328	98	-0	13			.976	-1	O-23,1-21/S-9,23	-0.3
1907	Chi-N	134	470	67	126	11	3	1	36	41		.268	.328	.311	94	-3	29			.938	2	O-69,S-42,1-18/32	-0.4
1908	*Chi-N	120	411	55	100	15	5	2	42	33		.243	.309	.319	96	-2	15			.955	5	O-50,1-37,2-22/3-9	0.2
1909	Chi-N	153	527	60	150	21	4	2	58	53		.285	.351	.351	115	10	20			.965	5	*O-153	1.0
1910	*Chi-N	136	477	83	155	24	16	3	86	65	34	.325	.406	.461	154	33	29			.975	5	*O-110,1-24/3-1	3.4
1911	Chi-N	143	512	66	129	17	2	2	70	66	40	.252	.341	.305	81	-11	30			.968	-6	O-107,1-36	-2.3
1912	Chi-N	36	125	28	34	11	0	0	18	22	13	.272	.385	.360	105	2	5			.987	4	O-27/1-9	0.4
	Pit-N	17	53	7	15	4	1	0	2	5	6	.283	.345	.396	104	0	0			1.000	2	O-15	0.6
	Yr	53	178	35	49	15	1	0	20	27	19	.275	.374	.371	105	2	5			.991	6	O-42/1-9	1.0
1913	Pit-N	28	83	11	19	5	2	0	7	8	6	.229	.297	.337	84	-2	3			.964	-1	O-24	-0.4
1914	Bro-F	147	515	65	148	25	12	5	83	54	41	.287	.357	.412	110	-1	34			.951	5	*2-108,1-22,O-21,/S	0.2
1915	Buf-F	109	346	29	81	10	6	0	27	30	28	.234	.295	.298	66	-21	12			.961	1	O-82,1-11/3-4,2S	-2.6
1916	NY-A	6	27	0	8	1	1	0	2	1	1	.296	.321	.407	116	0	1			1.000	2	/O-6	0.2
	Chi-N	5	16	2	5	1	0	0	3	1	1	.313	.389	.563	172	1	0			1.000	0	/O-4	0.2
Total	14	1194	4072	554	1095	162	60	19	495	421	171	.269	.340	.352	102	-1	208			.967	26	O-702,2-198,1/S3	-0.7

■ BOBBY HOFMAN Hofman, Robert George b: 10/5/25, St.Louis, Mo. d: 4/5/94, Chesterfield, Mo. BR/TR, 5'11", 175 lbs. Deb: 4/19/49 C

1949	NY-N	19	48	4	10	3	5	3	5	6		.208	.296	.208	38	-4	0			.939	-0	2-16	-0.4
1952	NY-N	32	63	11	18	2	2	2	4	8	7	.286	.375	.476	134	3	2			.964	3	2-21/3-2,1-1	0.7
1953	NY-N	74	169	21	45	7	2	12	34	12	20	.266	.315	.544	117	7	0			.918	2	3-23,2-17	0.5
1954	NY-N	71	125	12	28	5	0	8	30	7	15	.224	.322	.456	99	-1	0			.994	-4	1-21,2-10/3-8	-0.5
1955	NY-N	96	207	32	55	3	2	10	28	22	31	.266	.339	.464	110	3	0			1.000	-5	1-24,C-19,2-19,/3-5	-0.4
1956	NY-N	47	56	1	10	1	0	0	4	9	8	.179	.270	.196	28	-6	0			1.000	0	/C-7,3-7,1-3,2-2	-0.4

YEAR	TM/L	G	AB	R	H	2B	3B	HR	RBI	BB	SO	AVG	OBP	SLG	PRO+	BR/A	SB	CS	SBR	FA	FR	G/POS	TPR
1957	NY-N	2	2	0	0	0	0	0	0	0	1	.000	.000	.000	-99	-1	0	0	0	.000	0	H	-0.1
Total	7	341	670	81	166	22	6	32	101	70	94	.248	.323	.442	100	-2	1	3		.969	-3	/2-85,1-49,3-45,C	-0.6

■ FRED HOFMANN

Hofmann, Fred "Bootnose" b: 6/10/1894, St.Louis, Mo. d: 11/19/64, St.Helena, Cal. BR/TR, 5'11.5", 175 lbs. Deb: 9/26/19 C

YEAR	TM/L	G	AB	R	H	2B	3B	HR	RBI	BB	SO	AVG	OBP	SLG	PRO+	BR/A	SB	CS	SBR	FA	FR	G/POS	TPR
1919	NY-A	1	1	0	0	0	0	0	0	0	0	.000	.000	.000	-99	-0	0			1.000	0	/C-1	0.0
1920	NY-A	15	24	3	7	0	0	0	1	1	2	.292	.346	.292	68	-1	0	0	0	.905	-4	C-14	-0.4
1921	NY-A	23	62	7	11	1	1	1	5	5	13	.177	.250	.274	33	-6	0	0	0	.952	-0	C-18/1-1	-0.6
1922	NY-A	37	91	13	27	5	3	2	10	9	12	.297	.360	.484	116	2	0	0	0	.962	-4	C-29	-0.1
1923	*NY-A	72	238	24	69	10	4	3	26	18	27	.290	.350	.403	96	-2	2	1	0	.979	-3	C-70	-0.2
1924	NY-A	62	166	17	29	6	1	1	11	12	15	.175	.239	.241	24	-19	2	1	0	.991	2	C-54	-1.4
1925	NY-A	3	2	0	0	0	0	0	0	0	0	.000	.000	.000	-99	-1	0	0	0	1.000	0	/C-1	0.0
1927	Bos-A	87	217	20	59	19	1	0	24	21	26	.272	.342	.369	86	-4	2	0	1	.943	-2	C-81	-0.1
1928	Bos-A	78	199	14	45	8	1	0	16	11	25	.226	.270	.276	45	-16	0	1	-1	.982	4	C-71	-0.7
Total	9	378	1000	98	247	49	11	7	93	77	120	.247	.308	.339	68	-48	6	3		.969	-7	C-339/1-1	-3.5

■ HARRY HOGAN

Hogan, Harry S. b: 11/1/1875, Syracuse, N.Y. d: 1/24/34, Syracuse, N.Y. Deb: 8/13/01

YEAR	TM/L	G	AB	R	H	2B	3B	HR	RBI	BB	SO	AVG	OBP	SLG	PRO+	BR/A	SB	CS	SBR	FA	FR	G/POS	TPR
1901	Cle-A	1	4	0	0	0	0	0	0	0		.000	.000	.000	-99	-1	0			.000	-0	/O-1	-0.1

■ SHANTY HOGAN

Hogan, James Francis b: 3/21/06, Somerville, Mass. d: 4/7/67, Boston, Mass. BR/TR, 6'1", 240 lbs. Deb: 6/23/25

YEAR	TM/L	G	AB	R	H	2B	3B	HR	RBI	BB	SO	AVG	OBP	SLG	PRO+	BR/A	SB	CS	SBR	FA	FR	G/POS	TPR
1925	Bos-N	9	21	2	6	1	1	0	3	1	3	.286	.318	.429	97	-0	0	0	0	1.000	-1	/O-5	-0.1
1926	Bos-N	4	14	1	4	1	1	0	5	0	0	.286	.286	.500	119	0	0			.852	1	/C-4	0.1
1927	Bos-N	71	229	24	66	17	1	3	32	9	23	.288	.324	.410	104	-0	2			.985	2	C-61	0.6
1928	NY-N	131	411	48	137	25	2	10	71	42	25	.333	.406	.477	129	19	0			.978	-10	*C-124	1.9
1929	NY-N	102	317	19	95	13	0	5	45	25	22	.300	.362	.388	86	-6	1			.979	-4	C-93	-0.2
1930	NY-N	122	389	60	132	26	2	13	75	21	24	.339	.378	.517	116	9	2			.982	-3	C-96	1.3
1931	NY-N	123	396	42	119	17	1	12	65	29	29	.301	.354	.439	115	8	1			**.996**	-0	*C-113	1.5
1932	NY-N	140	502	36	144	18	2	8	77	26	22	.287	.323	.378	90	-7	0			.983	-8	*C-136	-0.7
1933	Bos-N	96	328	15	83	7	0	3	30	13	9	.253	.288	.302	75	-12	0			**.997**	-1	C-95	-0.7
1934	Bos-N	92	279	20	73	5	2	4	34	16	13	.262	.316	.337	81	-8	0			.986	-2	C-90	-0.6
1935	Bos-N	59	163	9	49	8	0	2	25	21	8	.301	.394	.387	120	6	0			.990	-4	C-56	0.4
1936	Was-A	19	65	8	21	4	0	1	7	11	2	.323	.421	.431	117	2	0	1	-1	.989	2	C-19	0.4
1937	Was-A	21	66	4	10	4	0	0	5	6	8	.152	.222	.212	10	-9	0	1	-1	.979	2	C-21	-0.7
Total	13	989	3180	288	939	146	12	61	474	220	188	.295	.348	.406	101	1	6	2		.985	-26	C-908/O-5	3.2

■ KENNY HOGAN

Hogan, Kenneth Sylvester b: 10/9/02, Cleveland, Ohio d: 1/2/80, Cleveland, Ohio BL/TR, 5'9", 145 lbs. Deb: 10/2/21

YEAR	TM/L	G	AB	R	H	2B	3B	HR	RBI	BB	SO	AVG	OBP	SLG	PRO+	BR/A	SB	CS	SBR	FA	FR	G/POS	TPR
1921	Cin-N	1	2	0	0	0	0	0	0	0	1	.000	.000	.000	-99	-1	0	0	0	.000	-1	/O-1	-0.1
1923	Cle-A	1	0	0	0	0	0	0	0	0	0	—	—	—	—	0	0	0	0	.000	0	R	0.0
1924	Cle-A	2	1	0	0	0	0	0	0	0	0	.000	.000	.000	-99	-0	0	0	0	.000	0	H	0.0
Total	3	4	3	0	0	0	0	0	0	0	1	.000	.000	.000	-99	-1	0	0	0	—	-1	/O-1	-0.1

■ MARTY HOGAN

Hogan, Martin F. b: 10/15/1869, Wensbury, England d: 8/15/23, Youngstown, Ohio BR , 5'8", 145 lbs. Deb: 8/6/1894

YEAR	TM/L	G	AB	R	H	2B	3B	HR	RBI	BB	SO	AVG	OBP	SLG	PRO+	BR/A	SB	CS	SBR	FA	FR	G/POS	TPR
1894	Cin-N	6	23	4	3	0	0	0	3	1	4	.130	.167	.130	-27	-5	2			.846	-0	/O-6	-0.4
	StL-N	29	100	11	28	3	4	0	13	3	13	.280	.308	.390	67	-6	7			.887	-1	O-29	-0.7
	Yr	35	123	15	31	3	4	0	16	4	17	.252	.281	.341	49	-11	9			.879	-2	O-35	-1.1
1895	StL-N	5	18	2	3	1	0	0	2	3	0	.167	.286	.222	32	-2	2			.833	1	/O-5	-0.1
Total	2	40	141	17	34	4	4	0	18	7	17	.241	.282	.326	47	-12	11			.869	-1	/O-40	-1.2

■ EDDIE HOGAN

Hogan, Robert Edward b: 4/1860, St.Louis, Mo. BR , 5'7", 153 lbs. Deb: 7/5/1882

YEAR	TM/L	G	AB	R	H	2B	3B	HR	RBI	BB	SO	AVG	OBP	SLG	PRO+	BR/A	SB	CS	SBR	FA	FR	G/POS	TPR
1882	StL-a	1	3	1	1	0	0	0		0		.333	.333	.333	121	0				.333	-1	/P-1	0.0
1884	Mil-U	11	37	6	3	1	0	0		7		.081	.227	.108	9	-7				.806	7	O-11	0.0
1887	NY-a	32	120	22	24	6	1	0	5	30		.200	.373	.267	84	-0	12			.750	-7	O-29/S-4,3-1	-0.6
1888	Cle-a	78	269	60	61	16	6	0	24	50		.227	.368	.331	128	12	30			.896	-5	O-78	0.5
Total	4	122	429	89	89	23	7	0	29	87		.207	.357	.294	108	5	42			.844	-6	O-118/S-4,3-1,P-1	-0.1

■ WILLIE HOGAN

Hogan, William Henry b: 9/14/1884, N.San Juan, Cal. d: 9/28/74, San Jose, Cal. BR/TR, 5'10", 175 lbs. Deb: 4/12/11 F

YEAR	TM/L	G	AB	R	H	2B	3B	HR	RBI	BB	SO	AVG	OBP	SLG	PRO+	BR/A	SB	CS	SBR	FA	FR	G/POS	TPR
1911	Phi-A	7	19	1	2	1	0	0	2	0		.105	.105	.158	-27	-3	0			.900	0	/O-6	-0.3
	StL-A	123	443	53	115	17	8	2	62	43		.260	.328	.348	92	-5	18			.929	13	*O-117/1-5	0.2
	Yr	130	462	54	117	18	8	2	64	43		.253	.320	.340	87	-8	18			.928	13	*O-123/1-5	-0.1
1912	StL-A	108	360	32	77	10	2	1	36	34		.214	.284	.261	58	-19	17			.972	11	*O-100	-1.4
Total	2	238	822	86	194	28	10	3	100	77		.236	.304	.305	75	-28	35			.947	24	O-223/1-5	-1.5

■ BERT HOGG

Hogg, Wilbert George "Sonny" b: 4/21/13, Detroit, Mich. d: 11/5/73, Detroit, Mich. BR/TR, 5'11.5", 162 lbs. Deb: 6/1/34

YEAR	TM/L	G	AB	R	H	2B	3B	HR	RBI	BB	SO	AVG	OBP	SLG	PRO+	BR/A	SB	CS	SBR	FA	FR	G/POS	TPR
1934	Bro-N	2	1	0	0	0	0	0	0	0	0	.000	.000	.000	-99	-0	0			.000	0	/3-1	0.0

■ GEORGE HOGRIEVER

Hogriever, George C. b: 3/17/1869, Cincinnati, Ohio d: 1/26/61, Appleton, Wis. BR/TR, 5'8", 160 lbs. Deb: 4/24/1895

YEAR	TM/L	G	AB	R	H	2B	3B	HR	RBI	BB	SO	AVG	OBP	SLG	PRO+	BR/A	SB	CS	SBR	FA	FR	G/POS	TPR
1895	Cin-N	69	239	61	65	8	7	2	34	36	17	.272	.374	.389	93	-2	41			.934	2	O-66/2-3	-0.4
1901	Mil-A	54	221	25	52	10	2	0	16	30		.235	.329	.299	79	-5	7			.901	2	O-54	-0.7
Total	2	123	460	86	117	18	9	2	50	66	17	.254	.353	.346	87	-7	48			.920	4	O-120/2-3	-1.1

■ BILL HOHMAN

Hohman, William Henry b: 11/27/03, Brooklyn, Md. d: 10/29/68, Baltimore, Md. BR/TR, 6', 178 lbs. Deb: 8/24/27

YEAR	TM/L	G	AB	R	H	2B	3B	HR	RBI	BB	SO	AVG	OBP	SLG	PRO+	BR/A	SB	CS	SBR	FA	FR	G/POS	TPR
1927	Phi-N	7	18	1	5	0	0	0	0	2	3	.278	.350	.278	69	-1	0			.917	-0	/O-6	-0.1

■ EDDIE HOHNHORST

Hohnhorst, Edward Hicks b: 1/31/1885, Covington, Ky. d: 3/28/16, Covington, Ky. BL/TL, 6'1", 175 lbs. Deb: 9/10/10

YEAR	TM/L	G	AB	R	H	2B	3B	HR	RBI	BB	SO	AVG	OBP	SLG	PRO+	BR/A	SB	CS	SBR	FA	FR	G/POS	TPR
1910	Cle-A	18	63	8	20	3	1	0	6	4		.317	.358	.397	135	2	3			.972	-1	1-18	0.1
1912	Cle-A	15	54	5	11	1	0	0	2	2		.204	.232	.222	29	-5	5			.963	-1	1-15	-0.6
Total	2	33	117	13	31	4	1	0	8	6		.265	.301	.316	83	-3	8			.968	-2	/1-33	-0.5

■ CHRIS HOILES

Hoiles, Christopher Allen b: 3/20/65, Bowling Green, O. BR/TR, 6', 213 lbs. Deb: 4/25/89

YEAR	TM/L	G	AB	R	H	2B	3B	HR	RBI	BB	SO	AVG	OBP	SLG	PRO+	BR/A	SB	CS	SBR	FA	FR	G/POS	TPR
1989	Bal-A	6	9	0	1	1	0	0	1	1	3	.111	.200	.222	19	-1	0	0	0	1.000	1	/C-3,D-3	0.0
1990	Bal-A	23	63	7	12	3	0	1	6	5	12	.190	.250	.286	51	-4	0	0	0	1.000	-1	/C-7,1-6,D-7	-0.5
1991	Bal-A	107	341	36	83	15	0	11	31	29	61	.243	.305	.384	93	-4	0	2	-1	**.998**	-14	C-89,D-13/1-2	-1.4
1992	Bal-A	96	310	49	85	10	1	20	40	55	60	.274	.387	.506	145	19	0	2	-1	.994	-10	C-95/D-1	1.4
1993	Bal-A	126	419	80	130	28	0	29	82	69	94	.310	.419	.585	160	37	1	1	-0	.993	-0	*C-124/D-2	4.1
1994	Bal-A	99	332	45	82	10	0	19	53	63	73	.247	.375	.449	106	4	2	0	1	.989	5	C-98	1.4
1995	Bal-A	114	352	53	88	15	1	19	58	67	80	.250	.376	.460	114	9	1	0	0	**.996**	-2	*C-107/D-6	1.3
1996	*Bal-A	127	407	64	105	13	0	25	73	57	97	.258	.362	.474	110	6	0	1	-1	.992	-11	*C-126/1-1	0.2
1997	*Bal-A	99	320	45	83	15	0	12	49	51	86	.259	.378	.419	111	7	1	0	0	**1.000**	-3	C-87/1-4,3-1,D-8	0.9
1998	Bal-A	97	267	36	70	12	0	15	56	38	50	.262	.362	.476	118	7	0	1	-1	**.995**	1	C-83/1-6,D-6	1.2
Total	10	894	2820	415	739	122	2	151	449	435	616	.262	.369	.467	119	80	5	7	-3	.994	-33	C-819/D-46,1-19,3-1	8.6

■ AARON HOLBERT

Holbert, Aaron Keith b: 1/9/73, Torrance, Cal. BR/TR, 6', 160 lbs. Deb: 4/14/96 F

YEAR	TM/L	G	AB	R	H	2B	3B	HR	RBI	BB	SO	AVG	OBP	SLG	PRO+	BR/A	SB	CS	SBR	FA	FR	G/POS	TPR
1996	StL-N	1	3	0	0	0	0	0	0	0	0	.000	.000	.000	-99	-1	0	0	0	1.000	-1	/2-1	-0.2

■ RAY HOLBERT

Holbert, Ray Arthur b: 9/25/70, Torrance, Cal. BR/TR, 6', 170 lbs. Deb: 5/2/94 F

YEAR	TM/L	G	AB	R	H	2B	3B	HR	RBI	BB	SO	AVG	OBP	SLG	PRO+	BR/A	SB	CS	SBR	FA	FR	G/POS	TPR
1994	SD-N	5	5	1	1	0	0	0	0	0	4	.200	.200	.200	5	-1	0	0	0	.000	0	/S-1	-0.1
1995	SD-N	63	73	11	13	2	1	2	5	8	20	.178	.277	.315	58	-5	4	0	1	.940	6	S-30/2-7,O-1	0.4
1998	Atl-N	8	15	2	2	0	0	0	1	2	4	.133	.235	.133	-1	-2	0	0	0	.952	2	/S-7	0.0
	Mon-N	2	5	0	0	0	0	0	0	0	1	.000	.000	.000	-99	-1	0	0	0	1.000	-0	/2-1	-0.2
	Yr	10	20	2	2	0	0	0	1	2	5	.100	.182	.100	-24	-4	0	0	0	.952	2	/S-7,2-1	-0.2
Total	3	78	98	14	16	2	1	2	6	10	29	.163	.255	.265	38	-9	4	0	1	.943	8	/S-38,2-8,O-1	0.1

■ BILL HOLBERT

Holbert, William Henry b: 3/14/1855, Baltimore, Md. d: 3/20/35, Laurel, Md. BR/TR, 197 lbs. Deb: 9/5/1876 MU

YEAR	TM/L	G	AB	R	H	2B	3B	HR	RBI	BB	SO	AVG	OBP	SLG	PRO+	BR/A	SB	CS	SBR	FA	FR	G/POS	TPR
1876	Lou-N	12	43	3	11	0	0	0	5	0	3	.256	.256	.256	60	-2				.843	7	C-12	0.5

YEAR	TM/L	G	AB	R	H	2B	3B	HR	RBI	BB	SO	AVG	OBP	SLG	PRO+	BR/A	SB	CS	SBR	FA	FR	G/POS	TPR
1878	Mil-N	45	173	10	32	2	0	0	12	3	14	.185	.199	.197	28	-13				.818	7	O-30,C-21	-0.7
1879	Syr-N	59	229	11	46	0	0	0	21	1	20	.201	.204	.201	39	-14				.897	-1	*C-56/O-4,M	-1.2
	Tro-N	4	15	1	4	0	0	0	2	0	1	.267	.267	.267	82	-0				.893	1	/C-4	0.0
	Yr	63	244	12	50	0	0	0	23	1	21	.205	.208	.205	41	-14				.897	0	C-60/O-4	-1.2
1880	Tro-N	60	212	18	40	5	1	0	8	9	18	.189	.222	.222	48	-11				.911	12	*C-58/O-3	0.1
1881	Tro-N	46	180	16	49	3	0	0	14	3	13	.272	.284	.289	77	-5				.918	7	C-43/O-3	0.3
1882	Tro-N	71	251	24	46	5	0	0	23	11	22	.183	.218	.203	38	-16				.892	16	*C-58,3-12/O-3	0.1
1883	NY-a	73	299	26	71	9	1	0		1		.237	.240	.274	62	-13				.920	**34**	*C-68/O-5,2-1	2.2
1884	*NY-a	65	255	28	53	5	0	0		7		.208	.235	.227	53	-13				.920	21	C-59/O-5,S-1	1.2
1885	NY-a	56	202	13	35	3	0	0	13	8		.173	.205	.188	27	-16				.900	12	C-39,O-13/3-5	0.0
1886	NY-a	48	171	8	35	4	2	0	13	6		.205	.232	.251	54	-9	4			.922	19	C-45/O-3,S-1	1.3
1887	NY-a	69	255	20	58	4	3	0	32	7		.227	.248	.267	46	-19	12			.894	2	C-60/1-8,S-2,2-1	-1.0
1888	Bro-a	15	50	4	6	1	0	0	1	2		.120	.170	.140	-0	-6	0			.926	2	C-15	-0.2
Total	12	623	2335	182	486	41	7	0	144	58	91	.208	.228	.232	47	-138	16			.907	139	C-538/O-69,31S2	2.6

■ **SAMMY HOLBROOK** Holbrook, James Marbury b: 7/17/10, Meridian, Miss. d: 4/10/91, Jackson, Miss. BR/TR, 5′11″, 189 lbs. Deb: 4/25/35

YEAR	TM/L	G	AB	R	H	2B	3B	HR	RBI	BB	SO	AVG	OBP	SLG	PRO+	BR/A	SB	CS	SBR	FA	FR	G/POS	TPR
1935	Was-A	52	135	20	35	2	2	2	25	30	16	.259	.408	.348	101	2	0	0	0	.952	-11	C-47	-0.7

■ **JOE HOLDEN** Holden, Joseph Francis "Socks" b: 6/4/13, St.Clair, Pa. d: 5/10/96, St.Clair, Pa. BL/TR, 5′8″, 175 lbs. Deb: 6/14/34

YEAR	TM/L	G	AB	R	H	2B	3B	HR	RBI	BB	SO	AVG	OBP	SLG	PRO+	BR/A	SB	CS	SBR	FA	FR	G/POS	TPR
1934	Phi-N	10	14	1	1	0	0	0	0	0	2	.071	.071	.071	-54	-3	0			1.000	2	/C-6	-0.1
1935	Phi-N	6	9	0	1	0	0	0	0	0	3	.111	.111	.111	-36	-2	1			1.000	-1	/C-4	-0.2
1936	Phi-N	1	1	0	0	0	0	0	0	0	0	.000	.000	.000	-91	-0	0			.000	0	H	0.0
Total	3	17	24	1	2	0	0	0	0	0	5	.083	.083	.083	-49	-5	1			1.000	2	/C-10	-0.3

■ **BILL HOLDEN** Holden, William Paul b: 9/7/1889, Birmingham, Ala. d: 9/14/71, Pensacola, Fla. BR/TR, 6′, 170 lbs. Deb: 9/11/13

YEAR	TM/L	G	AB	R	H	2B	3B	HR	RBI	BB	SO	AVG	OBP	SLG	PRO+	BR/A	SB	CS	SBR	FA	FR	G/POS	TPR
1913	NY-A	18	53	6	16	3	1	0	8	8	5	.302	.393	.396	131	2	0			.977	3	O-16	0.4
1914	NY-A	50	165	12	30	3	2	0	12	16	26	.182	.254	.224	44	-11	2	4	-2	.981	-1	O-45	-1.8
	Cin-N	11	28	2	6	0	0	0	1	3	5	.214	.290	.214	49	-2	0			1.000	-2	O-10	-0.4
Total	2	79	246	20	52	6	3	0	21	27	36	.211	.289	.260	64	-11	2	4		.981	0	/O-71	-1.8

■ **JIM HOLDSWORTH** Holdsworth, James "Long Jim" b: 7/14/1850, New York, N.Y. d: 3/22/18, New York, N.Y. BR/TR, Deb: 5/14/1872

YEAR	TM/L	G	AB	R	H	2B	3B	HR	RBI	BB	SO	AVG	OBP	SLG	PRO+	BR/A	SB	CS	SBR	FA	FR	G/POS	TPR
1872	Cle-n	22	110	19	33	5	0	0	11	1	2	.300	.306	.345	106	1	3	2	-0	.765	-1	S-22	0.0
	Eck-n	2	7	1	2	0	0	0	0	0	0	.286	.286	.286	90	0	0	0	0	.933	2	/S-2	0.1
	Yr	24	117	20	35	5	0	0	11	1	2	.299	.305	.342	105	1	3	2	-0	.780	1	S-24	0.1
1873	Mut-n	53	233	46	75	4	8	0	28	0	3	.322	.322	.408	116	4	1	0	0	.775	-14	*S-53	-0.8
1874	Phi-n	57	285	60	97	8	9	0	37	1	0	.340	.343	.432	142	12	1	2	-1	.694	-25	3-31,S-21/O-6,21	-1.2
1875	Mut-n	71	324	45	92	12	1	0	23	1	3	.284	.286	.327	107	1	3	3	-1	.780	1	O-45,S-26	0.0
1876	NY-N	52	241	23	64	3	2	0	19	1	2	.266	.269	.295	101	1				.902	1	*O-49/2-3	0.1
1877	Har-N	55	260	26	66	5	2	0	20	2	8	.254	.260	.288	81	-5				.833	-3	*O-55	-0.9
1882	Tro-N	1	3	0	0	0	0	0	0	0	1	.000	.000	.000	-99	-1				1.000	1	/O-1	0.0
1884	Ind-a	5	18	1	2	0	0	0		2		.111	.200	.111	4	-2				.929	1	/O-5	0.0
Total	4 n	205	959	171	299	29	18	0	99	3	8	.312	.314	.380	119	18	8	7	-2	.750	-38	S-124/O-51,3-31,21	-1.9
Total	4	113	522	50	132	8	4	0	39	5	11	.253	.260	.284	85	-6				.875	0	O-110/2-3	-0.8

■ **WALTER HOLKE** Holke, Walter Henry "Union Man" b: 12/25/1892, St.Louis, Mo. d: 10/12/54, St.Louis, Mo. BB/TL, 6′1.5″, 185 lbs. Deb: 10/6/14 C

YEAR	TM/L	G	AB	R	H	2B	3B	HR	RBI	BB	SO	AVG	OBP	SLG	PRO+	BR/A	SB	CS	SBR	FA	FR	G/POS	TPR
1914	NY-N	2	6	0	2	0	0	0	0	0	0	.333	.333	.333	102	-0	0			.950	0	/1-2	0.0
1916	NY-N	34	111	16	39	4	2	0	13	6	16	.351	.390	.423	158	7	10			.997	-0	1-34	0.7
1917	*NY-N	153	527	55	146	12	7	2	55	34	54	.277	.327	.338	107	4	13			.989	-5	*1-153	-0.7
1918	NY-N	88	326	38	82	17	4	1	27	10	26	.252	.276	.337	88	-6	10			.990	5	1-88	-0.5
1919	Bos-N	137	518	48	151	14	6	0	48	21	25	.292	.325	.342	105	2	19			.993	6	*1-136	0.4
1920	Bos-N	144	551	53	162	15	11	3	64	28	31	.294	.329	.377	107	4	4	11	-5	.991	-3	*1-143	-0.8
1921	Bos-N	150	579	60	151	15	10	3	63	17	41	.261	.284	.337	67	-28	8	11	-4	**.997**	3	*1-150	-3.4
1922	Bos-N	105	395	35	115	9	4	0	46	14	23	.291	.317	.334	71	-17	6	8	-3	.993	-4	*1-105	-2.7
1923	Phi-N	147	562	64	175	31	4	7	70	16	37	.311	.330	.418	86	-13	7	9	-3	.991	-1	*1-146/P-1	-2.4
1924	Phi-N	148	563	60	169	23	6	6	64	25	33	.300	.330	.394	83	-14	3	8	-4	.993	4	*1-148	-2.4
1925	Phi-N	39	86	11	21	5	0	1	17	3	6	.244	.270	.337	50	-7	0	0	0	.994	1	1-23	-0.6
	Cin-N	65	232	24	65	8	4	1	20	17	12	.280	.329	.362	78	-8	1	3	-2	.997	1	1-65	-1.1
	Yr	104	318	35	86	13	4	2	37	20	18	.270	.314	.355	69	-15	1	3	-2	.996	2	1-88	-1.7
Total	11	1212	4456	464	1278	153	58	24	487	191	304	.287	.318	.363	89	-74	81	50		.993	7	*1-1193/P-1	-13.5

■ **BILL HOLLAHAN** Hollahan, William James "Happy" b: 11/22/1896, New York, N.Y. d: 11/27/65, New York, N.Y. BR/TR, 5′8″, 165 lbs. Deb: 9/27/20

YEAR	TM/L	G	AB	R	H	2B	3B	HR	RBI	BB	SO	AVG	OBP	SLG	PRO+	BR/A	SB	CS	SBR	FA	FR	G/POS	TPR
1920	Was-A	3	4	0	1	0	0	0	1	1	2	.250	.400	.250	77	-0	1	0	0	1.000	0	/3-3	0.1

■ **DUTCH HOLLAND** Holland, Robert Clyde b: 10/12/03, Middlesex, N.C. d: 6/16/67, Lumberton, N.C. BR/TR, 6′1″, 190 lbs. Deb: 8/16/32

YEAR	TM/L	G	AB	R	H	2B	3B	HR	RBI	BB	SO	AVG	OBP	SLG	PRO+	BR/A	SB	CS	SBR	FA	FR	G/POS	TPR
1932	Bos-N	39	156	15	46	11	1	1	18	12	20	.295	.345	.397	103	1	0			.990	2	O-39	0.0
1933	Bos-N	13	31	3	8	3	0	0	3	3	8	.258	.324	.355	102	0	1			.867	-1	/O-7	-0.2
1934	Cle-A	50	128	19	32	12	1	2	13	13	11	.250	.319	.406	85	-3	0	0	0	.957	-4	O-31	-0.8
Total	3	102	315	37	86	26	2	3	34	28	39	.273	.332	.397	95	-3	1	0		.969	-3	/O-77	-1.0

■ **WILL HOLLAND** Holland, Willard A. b: Georgetown, Del. d: 7/19/30, Philadelphia, Pa. 5′10″, 180 lbs. Deb: 7/10/1889

YEAR	TM/L	G	AB	R	H	2B	3B	HR	RBI	BB	SO	AVG	OBP	SLG	PRO+	BR/A	SB	CS	SBR	FA	FR	G/POS	TPR
1889	Bal-a	40	143	13	27	1	2	0	16	9	28	.189	.247	.224	34	-13	4			.853	-15	S-39/O-1	-2.2

■ **TODD HOLLANDSWORTH** Hollandsworth, Todd Mathew b: 4/20/73, Dayton, Ohio BL/TL, 6′2″, 195 lbs. Deb: 4/25/95

YEAR	TM/L	G	AB	R	H	2B	3B	HR	RBI	BB	SO	AVG	OBP	SLG	PRO+	BR/A	SB	CS	SBR	FA	FR	G/POS	TPR
1995	*LA-N	41	103	16	24	2	0	5	13	10	29	.233	.307	.398	92	-2	2	1	0	.938	-3	O-37	-0.5
1996	*LA-N	149	478	64	139	26	4	12	59	41	93	.291	.349	.437	115	9	21	6	3	.978	-3	*O-142	0.6
1997	LA-N	106	296	39	73	20	2	4	31	17	60	.247	.288	.368	76	-12	5	5	-2	.984	-3	O-99	-1.8
1998	LA-N	55	175	23	47	6	4	3	20	9	42	.269	.308	.400	88	-4	4	3	-1	.957	-3	O-51	-0.7
Total	4	351	1052	142	283	54	10	24	123	77	224	.269	.321	.408	97	-8	32	15	1	.972	-11	O-329	-2.4

■ **GARY HOLLE** Holle, Gary Charles b: 8/11/54, Albany, N.Y. BR/TL, 6′6″, 210 lbs. Deb: 6/2/79

YEAR	TM/L	G	AB	R	H	2B	3B	HR	RBI	BB	SO	AVG	OBP	SLG	PRO+	BR/A	SB	CS	SBR	FA	FR	G/POS	TPR
1979	Tex-A	5	6	0	1	1	0	0	0	1	0	.167	.286	.333	67	-0	0	0	0	1.000	-0	/1-1	-0.1

■ **BUG HOLLIDAY** Holliday, James Wear b: 2/8/1867, St.Louis, Mo. d: 2/15/10, Cincinnati, Ohio BR/TR, 5′11″, 151 lbs. Deb: 4/17/1889 U

YEAR	TM/L	G	AB	R	H	2B	3B	HR	RBI	BB	SO	AVG	OBP	SLG	PRO+	BR/A	SB	CS	SBR	FA	FR	G/POS	TPR
1889	Cin-a	135	563	107	181	28	7	**19**	104	43	59	.321	.372	.497	142	27	46			.923	-7	*O-135	1.4
1890	Cin-N	131	518	93	140	18	14	4	75	49	36	.270	.341	.382	111	7	50			.948	-2	*O-131	0.0
1891	Cin-N	111	442	74	141	21	10	9	84	37	28	.319	.376	.473	145	24	30			.939	-8	*O-111	1.1
1892	Cin-N	152	602	114	176	23	16	**13**	91	57	39	.292	.355	.449	145	30	43			.933	-4	*O-152/P-1	1.8
1893	Cin-N	126	500	108	155	24	10	5	89	73	22	.310	.401	.428	117	13	32			.944	-10	*O-125/1-1	-0.3
1894	Cin-N	121	511	119	190	24	7	13	119	40	20	.372	.420	.523	121	16	29			.914	0	*O-119/1-1	0.6
1895	Cin-N	32	127	25	38	9	2	0	20	10	3	.299	.350	.402	90	-2	6			.940	-4	O-32	-0.7
1896	Cin-N	29	84	17	27	4	0	0	8	9	4	.321	.394	.369	95	-0	1			.925	-2	O-16/1-5,S-1,P-1	-0.3
1897	Cin-N	61	195	50	61	9	4	2	20	27		.313	.399	.431	112	3	6			.940	-6	O-42/S-4,2-3,1-3	-0.5
1898	Cin-N	30	106	21	25	2	1	0	7	14		.236	.325	.274	67	-4	5			.969	-2	O-28	-0.8
Total	10	928	3648	728	1134	162	71	65	617	359	211	.311	.376	.448	125	114	248			.935	-45	O-891/1-10,S-5,2P	2.3

■ **HOLLY HOLLINGSHEAD** Hollingshead, John Samuel (a.k.a. Samuel John Holly) b: 1/17/1853, Washington, D.C. d: 10/6/26, Washington, D.C. Deb: 4/20/1872 M

YEAR	TM/L	G	AB	R	H	2B	3B	HR	RBI	BB	SO	AVG	OBP	SLG	PRO+	BR/A	SB	CS	SBR	FA	FR	G/POS	TPR
1872	Nat-n	9	44	12	15	1	1	0	6	1	0	.341	.356	.409	115	-0	0	0	0	.778	-3	/2-9	-0.3
1873	Was-n	30	136	25	35	2	2	0	22	0	6	.257	.257	.301	68	-5	0	0	0	.833	2	O-30/2-2	-0.2
1875	Was-n	19	81	8	20	1	1	0	5	1	2	.247	.256	.284	91	-1	2	1	0	.826	2	O-19,M	0.1
Total	3 n	58	261	45	70	4	4	0	33	2	8	.268	.274	.314	83	-6	2	1	0	.831	1	/O-49,2-11	-0.4

YEAR	TM/L	G	AB	R	H	2B	3B	HR	RBI	BB	SO	AVG	OBP	SLG	PRO+	BR/A	SB	CS	SBR	FA	FR	G/POS	TPR
■ **DAMON HOLLINS**	Hollins, Damon Jamall b: 6/12/74, Fairfield, Cal. BR/TL, 5'11", 180 lbs. Deb: 4/24/98																						
1998	Atl-N	3	6	0	1	0	0	0	0	0	1	.167	.167	.167	-13	-1	0	0	0	1.000	-1	/O-3	-0.2
	LA-N	5	9	1	2	0	0	0	2	0	2	.222	.222	.222	17	-1	0	1	-1	1.000	-0	/O-4	-0.2
	Yr	8	15	1	3	0	0	0	2	0	3	.200	.200	.200	5	-2	0	1	-1	1.000	-1	/O-7	-0.4
■ **DAVE HOLLINS**	Hollins, David Michael b: 5/25/66, Buffalo, N.Y. BB/TR, 6'1", 207 lbs. Deb: 4/12/90																						
1990	Phi-N	72	114	14	21	0	0	5	15	10	28	.184	.256	.316	57	-7	0	0	0	.932	-1	3-30/1-1	-0.9
1991	Phi-N	56	151	18	45	10	2	6	21	17	26	.298	.380	.510	150	10	1	1	-0	.922	-3	3-36/1-6	0.6
1992	Phi-N	156	586	104	158	28	4	27	93	76	110	.270	.372	.469	137	30	9	6	-1	.954	-20	*3-156/1-1	0.9
1993	*Phi-N★	143	543	104	148	30	4	18	93	85	109	.273	.376	.442	120	17	2	3	-1	.914	-29	*3-143	-1.2
1994	Phi-N	44	162	28	36	7	1	4	26	23	32	.222	.333	.352	77	-5	1	0	0	.887	-15	3-43/O-1	-2.0
1995	Phi-N	65	205	46	47	12	2	7	25	53	38	.229	.399	.410	113	6	1	1	-0	.988	-6	1-61	-0.5
	Bos-A	5	13	2	2	0	0	0	1	4	7	.154	.353	.154	37	-1	0	0	0	1.000	-0	/O-2,D-3	-0.1
1996	Min-A	121	422	71	102	26	0	13	53	71	102	.242	.364	.396	91	-5	6	4	-1	.953	-4	*3-116/S-1,D-3	-0.9
	Sea-A	28	94	17	33	3	0	3	25	13	15	.351	.445	.479	134	6	0	2	-1	.961	2	3-28/1-1	0.6
	Yr	149	516	88	135	29	0	16	78	84	117	.262	.378	.411	98	1	6	6	-2	.955	-2	*3-144/D-3,S-1,1-1	-0.3
1997	Ana-A	149	572	101	165	29	2	16	85	62	124	.288	.366	.430	107	7	16	6	1	.922	-11	*3-135,1-14	-0.3
1998	Ana-A	101	363	60	88	16	2	11	39	44	69	.242	.336	.388	87	-7	11	3	2	.929	-7	3-91/1-7,D-2	-1.2
Total	9	940	3225	565	845	161	17	110	476	458	660	.262	.365	.425	109	52	47	26	-2	.933	-93	3-778/1-91,D-8,OS	-5.0
■ **STAN HOLLMIG**	Hollmig, Stanley Ernest "Hondo" b: 1/2/26, Fredericksburg, Tex d: 12/4/81, San Antonio, Tex. BR/TR, 6'2.5", 190 lbs. Deb: 4/19/49																						
1949	Phi-N	81	251	28	64	11	6	2	26	20	43	.255	.315	.371	85	-6	1			.958	-6	O-66	-1.4
1950	Phi-N	11	12	1	3	2	0	0	1	0	3	.250	.250	.417	73	-1	0			1.000	-1	/O-3	-0.1
1951	Phi-N	2	2	0	0	0	0	0	0	0	0	.000	.000	.000	-99	-1	0	0	0	.000	0	H	-0.1
Total	3	94	265	29	67	13	6	2	27	20	46	.253	.310	.370	84	-7	1	0		.959	-6	/O-69	-1.6
■ **CHARLIE HOLLOCHER**	Hollocher, Charles Jacob b: 6/11/1896, St.Louis, Mo. d: 8/14/40, Frontenac, Mo. BL/TR, 5'7", 154 lbs. Deb: 4/16/18																						
1918	*Chi-N	131	509	72	**161**	23	6	2	38	47	30	.316	.379	.397	133	21	26			.929	-19	*S-131	0.8
1919	Chi-N	115	430	51	116	14	5	3	26	44	19	.270	.347	.347	108	6	16			.941	6	*S-115	2.0
1920	Chi-N	80	301	53	96	17	2	0	22	41	15	.319	.406	.389	126	12	20	14	-2	.954	9	S-80	2.7
1921	Chi-N	140	558	71	161	28	8	3	37	43	13	.289	.342	.384	91	-6	5	16	-8	**.963**	3	*S-137	0.2
1922	Chi-N	152	592	90	201	37	8	3	69	58	5	.340	.403	.444	116	16	19	29	-12	**.965**	-5	*S-152	1.3
1923	Chi-N	66	260	46	89	14	2	1	28	26	5	.342	.410	.423	120	9	9	10	-3	.963	-9	S-65	0.3
1924	Chi-N	76	286	28	70	12	4	2	21	18	7	.245	.292	.336	67	-14	4	11	-5	.969	4	S-71	-0.8
Total	7	760	2936	411	894	145	35	14	241	277	94	.304	.370	.392	110	44	99	80		.954	-13	S-751	6.5
■ **ED HOLLY**	Holly, Edward William (b: Edward William Ruthlavy) b: 7/6/1879, Chicago, Ill. d: 11/27/73, Williamsport, Pa. BR/TR, 5'10", 165 lbs. Deb: 7/18/06																						
1906	StL-N	10	34	1	2	0	0	0	7	5		.059	.179	.059	-27	-5	0			.939	-3	S-10	-0.8
1907	StL-N	150	545	55	125	18	3	1	40	36		.229	.283	.279	79	-14	16			.927	11	*S-147/2-3	0.0
1914	Pit-F	100	350	28	86	9	4	0	26	17	52	.246	.281	.294	57	-27	14			.942	-2	S-94/O-2,2-1	-2.3
1915	Pit-F	16	42	8	11	2	0	0	5	5	6	.262	.354	.310	88	-1	3			.865	-4	S-11/3-3	-0.5
Total	4	276	971	92	224	29	7	1	78	63	58	.231	.282	.278	67	-47	33			.931	1	S-262/2-4,3-3,O-2	-3.6
■ **WATTIE HOLM**	Holm, Roscoe Albert b: 12/28/01, Peterson, Iowa d: 5/19/50, Everly, Iowa BR/TR, 5'9.5", 160 lbs. Deb: 4/15/24																						
1924	StL-N	81	293	40	86	10	4	0	23	8	16	.294	.317	.355	81	-8	1	4	-2	.988	2	O-64/C-9,3-4	-1.3
1925	StL-N	13	58	10	12	1	1	0	2	3	1	.207	.246	.259	28	-6	1	0	0	.976	2	O-13	-0.5
1926	*StL-N	55	144	18	41	5	1	0	21	18	14	.285	.364	.333	85	-2	3			.962	-3	O-39	-0.8
1927	StL-N	110	419	55	120	27	8	3	66	24	29	.286	.327	.411	93	-5	4			.967	-8	O-97/3-9	-1.8
1928	*StL-N	102	386	61	107	24	6	3	47	32	17	.277	.334	.394	88	-7	1			.918	-10	3-83/O-7	-1.3
1929	StL-N	64	176	21	41	5	6	0	14	12	8	.233	.282	.330	50	-14	1			.944	3	O-44/3-1	-1.3
1932	StL-N	11	17	2	3	1	0	0	1	3	1	.176	.333	.235	55	-1	0			1.000	0	/O-4	-0.1
Total	7	436	1493	207	410	73	26	6	174	100	86	.275	.322	.370	81	-44	11	4		.970	-15	O-268/3-97,C-9	-7.1
■ **BILLY HOLM**	Holm, William Frederick Henry b: 7/21/12, Chicago, Ill. d: 7/27/77, East Chicago, Ind BR/TR, 5'10.5", 168 lbs. Deb: 9/24/43																						
1943	Chi-N	7	15	0	1	0	0	0	0	2	4	.067	.176	.067	-29	-2	0			1.000	1	/C-7	-0.1
1944	Chi-N	54	132	10	18	2	0	0	6	16	19	.136	.235	.152	10	-15	1			.979	-2	C-50	-1.6
1945	Bos-A	58	135	12	25	2	1	0	9	23	17	.185	.317	.215	54	-7	1	1	-0	.980	-4	C-57	-0.9
Total	3	119	282	22	44	4	1	0	15	41	40	.156	.272	.177	30	-25	2	1		.981	-4	C-114	-2.6
■ **GARY HOLMAN**	Holman, Gary Richard b: 1/25/44, Long Beach, Cal. BL/TL, 6'1", 200 lbs. Deb: 6/26/68																						
1968	Was-A	75	85	10	25	5	1	0	7	13	15	.294	.388	.376	137	4	0	0	0	1.000	2	1-33,O-10	0.6
1969	Was-A	41	31	1	5	1	0	0	2	4	7	.161	.257	.194	29	-3	0	0	0	1.000	-1	1-11/O-3	-0.5
Total	2	116	116	11	30	6	1	0	9	17	22	.259	.353	.328	107	1	0	0	0	1.000	1	/1-44,O-13	0.1
■ **FRED HOLMES**	Holmes, Frederick C. b: 7/1/1878, Chicago, Ill. d: 2/13/56, Norwood Park, Ill. BR/TR, Deb: 8/23/03																						
1903	NY-A	1	0	0	0	0	0	0	0	1		—	1.000	—	207	0	0			.833	-0	/1-1	0.0
1904	Chi-N	1	3	1	1	1	0	0	0	0		.333	.333	.667	206	0	0			1.000	0	/C-1	0.0
Total	2	2	3	1	1	1	0	0	0	1		.333	.500	.667	255	1	0			1.000	-0	/C-1,1-1	0.0
■ **DUCKY HOLMES**	Holmes, Howard Elbert b: 7/8/1883, Dayton, Ohio d: 9/18/45, Dayton, Ohio BR/TR, 5'10", 160 lbs. Deb: 4/18/06 U																						
1906	StL-N	9	27	2	5	0	0	0	2	2		.185	.267	.185	43	-2	0			.979	-0	/C-9	-0.2
■ **DUCKY HOLMES**	Holmes, James William b: 1/28/1869, Des Moines, Iowa d: 8/6/32, Truro, Iowa BL/TR, 5'6", 170 lbs. Deb: 8/8/1895																						
1895	Lou-N	40	161	33	60	10	2	3	20	12	9	.373	.426	.516	152	13	9			.780	-11	O-29/S-8,3-4,P-2	0.0
1896	Lou-N	47	141	22	38	3	2	0	18	13	5	.270	.360	.319	83	-3	8			.790	-7	O-33/P-2,S-1,2-1	-1.0
1897	Lou-N	2	4	0	0	0	0	0	0	1		.000	.200	.000	-46	-1	0			1.000	1	/S-1	0.0
	NY-N	79	306	51	82	8	6	1	44	18		.268	.317	.343	76	-11	30			.904	-7	O-77/S-1	-2.1
	Yr	81	310	51	82	8	6	1	44	19		.265	.315	.339	75	-12	30			.904	-6	O-77/S-2	-2.1
1898	StL-N	23	101	9	24	1	1	0	0	2		.238	.260	.267	50	-7	4			.900	2	O-22	-0.6
	Bal-N	113	442	54	126	10	9	1	64	23		.285	.333	.355	96	-3	25			.935	4	*O-113	-0.7
	Yr	136	543	63	150	11	10	1	64	25		.276	.320	.339	87	-10	29			.930	6	*O-135	-1.3
1899	Bal-N	138	553	80	177	31	7	4	66	39		.320	.381	.423	114	10	50			.927	6	*O-138	0.5
1901	Det-A	131	537	90	158	28	10	4	62	37		.294	.347	.406	103	1	35			.907	-2	*O-131	-0.9
1902	Det-A	92	362	50	93	15	4	2	33	28		.257	.319	.337	80	-9	16			.950	6	O-92	-0.9
1903	Was-A	21	71	13	16	3	1	1	8	5		.225	.286	.338	85	-1	10			.912	1	O-14/3-4,2-2	-0.1
	Chi-A	86	344	53	96	7	5	0	18	25		.279	.335	.328	104	3	25			.965	2	O-82/3-3	0.0
	Yr	107	415	66	112	10	6	1	26	30		.270	.327	.330	101	1	35			.956	3	O-96/3-7,2-2	-0.1
1904	Chi-A	68	251	42	78	11	9	1	19	14		.311	.354	.438	156	15	13			.975	2	O-63	1.5
1905	Chi-A	92	328	42	66	15	2	0	22	19		.201	.258	.259	67	-12	11			.936	-1	O-89	-2.0
Total	10	932	3601	539	1014	142	58	17	374	236	14	.282	.337	.367	99	-5	236			.924	-5	O-883/3-11,S-11,P2	-6.3
■ **TOMMY HOLMES**	Holmes, Thomas Francis "Kelly" b: 3/29/17, Brooklyn, N.Y. BL/TL, 5'10", 180 lbs. Deb: 4/14/42 M																						
1942	Bos-N	141	558	56	155	24	4	4	41	64	10	.278	.353	.357	110	8	2			.990	15	*O-140	1.7
1943	Bos-N	152	629	75	170	33	10	5	41	58	20	.270	.334	.378	107	5	7			.993	8	*O-152	0.5
1944	Bos-N	155	631	93	195	42	6	13	73	61	11	.309	.372	.456	127	22	4			.991	6	*O-155	2.0
1945	Bos-N†	154	636	125	**224**	**47**	6	**28**	117	70	9	.352	.420	**.577**	**175**	**62**	15			.983	1	*O-154	**5.4**
1946	Bos-N	149	568	80	176	35	6	6	79	58	14	.310	.377	.424	126	19	7			.987	8	*O-146	2.1
1947	Bos-N	150	618	90	**191**	33	3	9	53	44	16	.309	.360	.416	108	7	3			.989	10	*O-147	0.8
1948	*Bos-N★	139	585	85	190	35	7	6	61	46	20	.325	.375	.439	122	17	1			.983	3	*O-137	1.3
1949	Bos-N	117	380	47	101	20	4	8	59	39	6	.266	.337	.403	103	1	1			.987	5	*O-103	0.1
1950	Bos-N	105	322	44	96	20	1	9	51	33	8	.298	.370	.450	122	10	0			1.000	-0	O-88	0.6

YEAR	TM/L	G	AB	R	H	2B	3B	HR	RBI	BB	SO	AVG	OBP	SLG	PRO+	BR/A	SB	CS	SBR	FA	FR	G/POS	TPR
1951	Bos-N	27	29	1	5	2	0	0	5	3	4	.172	.250	.241	35	-3	0	0	0	1.000	-1	/O-3,M	-0.4
1952	*Bro-N	31	36	2	4	1	0	0	1	4	4	.111	.200	.139	-4	-5	0	0	0	1.000	-1	/O-6	-0.6
Total	11	1320	4992	698	1507	292	47	88	581	480	122	.302	.366	.432	122	144	40	0		.989	53	*O-1231	13.5

■ RED HOLT Holt, James Emmett Madison b: 7/25/1894, Dayton, Tenn. d: 2/2/61, Birmingham, Ala. BL/TL, 5'11", 175 lbs. Deb: 9/5/25

YEAR	TM/L	G	AB	R	H	2B	3B	HR	RBI	BB	SO	AVG	OBP	SLG	PRO+	BR/A	SB	CS	SBR	FA	FR	G/POS	TPR
1925	Phi-A	27	88	13	24	7	0	1	8	12	9	.273	.360	.386	84	-2	0	0	0	.986	0	1-25	-0.3

■ JIM HOLT Holt, James William b: 5/27/44, Graham, N.C. BL/TR, 6', 195 lbs. Deb: 4/17/68

YEAR	TM/L	G	AB	R	H	2B	3B	HR	RBI	BB	SO	AVG	OBP	SLG	PRO+	BR/A	SB	CS	SBR	FA	FR	G/POS	TPR
1968	Min-A	70	106	9	22	2	1	0	8	4	20	.208	.236	.245	44	-7	0	1	-1	.973	-5	O-38/1-1	-1.6
1969	Min-A	12	14	3	5	0	0	1	2	0	4	.357	.357	.571	153	1	0	0	0	1.000	-2	/O-5,1-1	-0.1
1970	*Min-A	142	319	37	85	9	3	3	40	17	32	.266	.304	.342	77	-10	3	1	0	.995	-11	*O-130/1-2	-2.6
1971	Min-A	126	340	35	88	11	3	1	29	16	28	.259	.294	.318	71	-13	5	1	1	.986	-5	*O-106/1-3	-2.3
1972	Min-A	10	27	6	12	1	0	1	6	0	1	.444	.444	.593	197	3	0	0	0	.917	0	/O-7,1-1	0.3
1973	Min-A	132	441	52	131	25	3	11	58	29	43	.297	.343	.442	115	8	0	3	-2	.990	5	*O-102,1-33	0.4
1974	Min-A	79	197	24	50	11	0	0	16	14	16	.254	.307	.310	75	-6	0	0	0	.996	5	1-67/O-5	-0.5
	*Oak-A	30	42	1	6	0	0	0	0	1	9	.143	.182	.143	-6	-6	0	0	0	1.000	1	1-17/D-3	-0.5
	Yr	109	239	25	56	11	0	0	16	15	25	.234	.285	.280	63	-11	0	0	0	.996	6	1-84/O-5,D-3	-1.0
1975	*Oak-A	102	123	7	27	3	0	2	16	11	11	.220	.294	.293	68	-5	0	0	0	.991	1	1-52/O-2,C-1,D-4	-0.6
1976	Oak-A	4	7	0	2	2	0	0	2	1	2	.286	.375	.571	182	1	0	0	0	.000	0	/D-2	0.1
Total	9	707	1616	174	428	64	10	19	177	93	166	.265	.308	.352	84	-35	8	6	-1	.988	-11	O-395,1-177/D-9,C-1	-7.4

■ ROGER HOLT Holt, Roger Boyd b: 4/8/56, Daytona Beach, Fla. BB/TR, 5'11", 165 lbs. Deb: 10/4/80

YEAR	TM/L	G	AB	R	H	2B	3B	HR	RBI	BB	SO	AVG	OBP	SLG	PRO+	BR/A	SB	CS	SBR	FA	FR	G/POS	TPR
1980	NY-A	2	6	0	1	0	0	0	1	1	2	.167	.286	.167	28	-1	0	0	0	1.000	1	/2-2	0.0

■ MARTY HONAN Honan, Martin Weldon b: 4/1871, Chicago, Ill. d: 8/20/08, Chicago, Ill. Deb: 10/3/1890

YEAR	TM/L	G	AB	R	H	2B	3B	HR	RBI	BB	SO	AVG	OBP	SLG	PRO+	BR/A	SB	CS	SBR	FA	FR	G/POS	TPR
1890	Chi-N	1	3	0	0	0	0	0	1	0	2	.000	.000	.000	-96	-1	0			.857	-0	/C-1	-0.1
1891	Chi-N	5	12	1	2	0	1	0	3	1	3	.167	.231	.333	64	-1	0			.963	2	/C-5	0.1
Total	2	6	15	1	2	0	1	0	4	1	5	.133	.188	.267	32	-1	0			.941	1	/C-6	0.0

■ ABIE HOOD Hood, Albie Larrison b: 1/31/03, Sanford, N.C. d: 10/14/88, Chesapeake, Va. BL/TR, 5'7", 152 lbs. Deb: 7/15/25

YEAR	TM/L	G	AB	R	H	2B	3B	HR	RBI	BB	SO	AVG	OBP	SLG	PRO+	BR/A	SB	CS	SBR	FA	FR	G/POS	TPR
1925	Bos-N	5	21	2	6	2	0	1	2	1	0	.286	.318	.524	122	0	0	0	0	.920	-4	/2-5	-0.3

■ WALLY HOOD Hood, Wallace James Sr. b: 2/9/1895, Whittier, Cal. d: 5/2/65, Hollywood, Cal. BR/TR, 5'11.5", 160 lbs. Deb: 4/15/20 F

YEAR	TM/L	G	AB	R	H	2B	3B	HR	RBI	BB	SO	AVG	OBP	SLG	PRO+	BR/A	SB	CS	SBR	FA	FR	G/POS	TPR
1920	Bro-N	7	14	4	2	1	0	0	1	4	4	.143	.333	.214	58	-1	2	0	1	.944	1	/O-5	0.1
	Pit-N	2	1	1	0	0	0	0	0	1	0	.000	.500	.000	50	0	1	0	0	.000	0	H	0.0
	Yr	9	15	5	2	1	0	0	1	5	4	.133	.350	.200	59	-1	3	0	1	.944	1	/O-5	0.1
1921	Bro-N	56	65	16	17	1	2	1	4	9	14	.262	.360	.385	94	-0	2	2	-1	.957	-6	O-20	-0.7
1922	Bro-N	2	0	2	0	0	0	0	0	0	0	—	—	—	—	0	0	0	0	.000	0	R	0.0
Total	3	67	80	23	19	2	2	1	5	14	18	.237	.358	.350	88	-1	5	2	0	.951	-4	/O-25	-0.6

■ ALEX HOOKS Hooks, Alexander Marcus b: 8/29/06, Edgewood, Tex. d: 6/19/93, Edgewood, Tex. BL/TL, 6'1", 183 lbs. Deb: 4/17/35

YEAR	TM/L	G	AB	R	H	2B	3B	HR	RBI	BB	SO	AVG	OBP	SLG	PRO+	BR/A	SB	CS	SBR	FA	FR	G/POS	TPR
1935	Phi-A	15	44	4	10	3	0	0	4	3	10	.227	.277	.295	48	-3	0	0	0	1.000	0	1-10	-0.4

■ HARRY HOOPER Hooper, Harry Bartholomew b: 8/24/1887, Bell Station, Cal. d: 12/18/74, Santa Cruz, Cal. BL/TR, 5'10", 168 lbs. Deb: 4/16/09 H

YEAR	TM/L	G	AB	R	H	2B	3B	HR	RBI	BB	SO	AVG	OBP	SLG	PRO+	BR/A	SB	CS	SBR	FA	FR	G/POS	TPR
1909	Bos-A	81	255	29	72	3	4	0	12	16		.282	.337	.325	107	2	15			.952	4	O-74	0.4
1910	Bos-A	155	584	81	156	9	10	2	27	62		.267	.346	.327	108	7	40			.938	11	*O-155	1.1
1911	Bos-A	130	524	93	163	20	6	4	45	73		.311	.399	.395	123	19	38			.954	6	*O-130	1.7
1912	*Bos-A	147	590	98	143	20	12	2	53	66		.242	.326	.327	83	-13	29			.964	2	*O-147	-1.9
1913	Bos-A	148	586	100	169	29	12	4	40	60	51	.288	.359	.399	119	14	26			.968	9	*O-147/P-1	1.7
1914	Bos-A	142	530	85	137	23	15	1	41	58	47	.258	.336	.364	110	6	19	14	-3	.973	11	*O-140	0.9
1915	*Bos-A	149	566	90	133	20	13	2	51	89	36	.235	.342	.327	103	4	22	20	-5	.972	11	*O-149	0.2
1916	*Bos-A	151	575	75	156	20	11	1	37	80	35	.271	.361	.350	113	11	27	11	2	.966	8	*O-151	1.4
1917	Bos-A	151	559	89	143	21	11	3	45	80	40	.256	.355	.349	116	13	21			.971	-1	*O-151	0.4
1918	*Bos-A	126	474	81	137	26	13	1	44	75	25	.289	.391	.405	143	26	24			.963	-0	*O-126	2.1
1919	Bos-A	128	491	76	131	25	6	3	49	79	28	.267	.374	.360	113	12	23			.979	10	*O-128	1.3
1920	Bos-A	139	536	91	167	30	17	7	53	88	27	.312	.411	.470	139	32	16	18	-6	.963	7	*O-139	2.2
1921	Chi-A	108	419	74	137	26	5	8	58	55	21	.327	.406	.470	125	17	13	7	-0	.975	-3	*O-108	0.5
1922	Chi-A	152	602	111	183	35	8	11	80	68	33	.304	.379	.444	114	13	16	12	-2	.962	7	*O-149	0.7
1923	Chi-A	145	576	87	166	32	4	10	65	68	22	.288	.370	.410	106	6	18	18	-5	.960	-4	*O-143	-1.3
1924	Chi-A	130	476	107	156	27	8	10	62	65	26	.328	.413	.481	134	25	16	13	-3	.986	11	*O-123	2.3
1925	Chi-A	127	442	62	117	23	5	6	55	54	21	.265	.351	.380	90	-7	12	8	-1	.976	4	*O-124	-1.1
Total	17	2309	8785	1429	2466	389	160	75	817	1136	412	.281	.368	.387	114	188	375	121		.966	91	*O-2284/P-1	12.6

■ MIKE HOOPER Hooper, Michael H. b: 2/7/1850, Baltimore, Md. d: 12/1/17, Baltimore, Md. 5'6", 165 lbs. Deb: 6/27/1873

YEAR	TM/L	G	AB	R	H	2B	3B	HR	RBI	BB	SO	AVG	OBP	SLG	PRO+	BR/A	SB	CS	SBR	FA	FR	G/POS	TPR
1873	Mar-n	3	14	3	3	1	0	0	2	0	0	.214	.214	.286	62	-0	0	0	0	.833	-1	/O-2,C-1	-0.1

■ CHARLIE HOOVER Hoover, Charles E. b: 9/21/1865, Mound City, Ill. BL/TR, 5'8", Deb: 10/9/1888

YEAR	TM/L	G	AB	R	H	2B	3B	HR	RBI	BB	SO	AVG	OBP	SLG	PRO+	BR/A	SB	CS	SBR	FA	FR	G/POS	TPR
1888	KC-a	3	10	0	3	0	0	0	1	0		.300	.300	.300	87	-0	0			.857	0	/C-3	0.0
1889	KC-a	71	258	44	64	2	5	1	25	29	38	.248	.329	.306	77	-8	9			.916	-4	C-66/3-4,O-3	-0.5
Total	2	74	268	44	67	2	5	1	26	29	38	.250	.328	.306	77	-8	9			.913	-4	/C-69,3-4,O-3	-0.5

■ JOE HOOVER Hoover, Robert Joseph b: 4/15/15, Brawley, Cal. d: 9/2/65, Los Angeles, Cal. BR/TR, 5'11", 175 lbs. Deb: 4/21/43

YEAR	TM/L	G	AB	R	H	2B	3B	HR	RBI	BB	SO	AVG	OBP	SLG	PRO+	BR/A	SB	CS	SBR	FA	FR	G/POS	TPR
1943	Det-A	144	575	78	140	15	8	4	38	36	101	.243	.289	.318	72	-21	6	5	-1	.944	-6	*S-144	-1.9
1944	Det-A	120	441	67	104	20	2	0	29	35	66	.236	.301	.290	66	-19	7	10	-4	.932	15	*S-119/2-1	0.2
1945	*Det-A	74	222	33	57	10	5	1	17	21	35	.257	.324	.360	92	-2	6	2	1	.944	-7	S-68	-0.4
Total	3	338	1238	178	301	45	15	5	84	92	202	.243	.300	.316	73	-43	19	17	-5	.939	3	S-331/2-1	-2.1

■ BUSTER HOOVER Hoover, William J. b: 1863, Philadelphia, Pa. BR/TR, 6'1", 178 lbs. Deb: 4/17/1884

YEAR	TM/L	G	AB	R	H	2B	3B	HR	RBI	BB	SO	AVG	OBP	SLG	PRO+	BR/A	SB	CS	SBR	FA	FR	G/POS	TPR
1884	Phi-U	63	275	76	100	20	8	0		12		.364	.390	.495	180	19				.780	-1	O-37,S-15/1-6,23	1.5
	Phi-N	10	42	6	8	1	0	1	4	4	9	.190	.261	.286	75	-1				.929	-1	O-10	-0.2
1886	Bal-a	40	157	25	34	2	6	0	10	16		.217	.297	.306	91	-1	15			.839	-1	O-40	-0.3
1892	Cin-N	14	51	7	9	0	0	0	2	5	4	.176	.250	.176	30	-4	1			.966	1	O-14	-0.4
Total	3	127	525	114	151	23	14	1	16	37	13	.288	.337	.390	129	12	16			.840	-3	O-101/S-15,2-6,13	0.6

■ DON HOPKINS Hopkins, Donald b: 1/9/52, West Point, Miss. BL/TR, 6', 175 lbs. Deb: 4/8/75

YEAR	TM/L	G	AB	R	H	2B	3B	HR	RBI	BB	SO	AVG	OBP	SLG	PRO+	BR/A	SB	CS	SBR	FA	FR	G/POS	TPR
1975	*Oak-A	82	6	25	1	0	0	0	0	2	0	.167	.375	.167	59	-0	21	9	1	1.000	-2	D-20/O-5R-0	-0.2
1976	Oak-A	3	0	0	0	0	0	0	0	0	0	—	—	—	—	0	0	1	-1	.000	0	R	-0.1
Total	2	85	6	25	1	0	0	0	0	2	0	.167	.375	.167	59	-0	21	10	0	1.000	-2	/D-20,O-5	-0.3

■ GAIL HOPKINS Hopkins, Gail Eason b: 2/19/43, Tulsa, Okla. BL/TR, 5'10", 200 lbs. Deb: 6/29/68

YEAR	TM/L	G	AB	R	H	2B	3B	HR	RBI	BB	SO	AVG	OBP	SLG	PRO+	BR/A	SB	CS	SBR	FA	FR	G/POS	TPR
1968	Chi-A	29	37	4	8	2	0	0	2	6	3	.216	.326	.270	81	-1	0	0	0	1.000	-1	/1-7	-0.2
1969	Chi-A	124	373	52	99	13	3	8	46	50	28	.265	.354	.381	100	1	2	1	0	.994	-3	*1-101	-1.0
1970	Chi-A	116	287	32	82	8	1	6	29	28	19	.286	.351	.383	99	-0	0	0	0	.987	-2	1-77/C-8	-0.8
1971	KC-A	103	295	35	82	16	1	9	47	37	13	.278	.366	.431	126	11	3	1	0	.990	3	1-83	0.6
1972	KC-A	53	71	1	15	2	0	0	5	7	4	.211	.282	.239	56	-4	0	0	0	.990	-2	1-13/3-1	-0.7
1973	KC-A	74	138	17	34	6	1	2	16	29	15	.246	.385	.348	100	1	1	2	-1	1.000	0	D-36,1-10	0.0
1974	LA-N	15	18	1	4	0	0	0	0	3	1	.222	.333	.222	60	-1	0	0	0	1.000	1	/C-2,1-2	0.0
Total	7	514	1219	142	324	47	6	25	145	160	83	.266	.355	.376	103	8	6	4	-1	.991	-4	1-293/D-36,C-10,3-1	-2.1

■ BUCK HOPKINS Hopkins, John Winton "Sis" b: 1/3/1883, Grafton, Va. d: 10/2/29, Phoebus, Va. BL/TL, 5'10", 165 lbs. Deb: 7/22/07

YEAR	TM/L	G	AB	R	H	2B	3B	HR	RBI	BB	SO	AVG	OBP	SLG	PRO+	BR/A	SB	CS	SBR	FA	FR	G/POS	TPR
1907	StL-N	15	44	7	6	3	0	0	3	10		.136	.333	.205	71	-1	2			.875	-4	O-15	-0.6

YEAR	TM/L	G	AB	R	H	2B	3B	HR	RBI	BB	SO	AVG	OBP	SLG	PRO+	BR/A	SB	CS	SBR	FA	FR	G/POS	TPR
■ MARTY HOPKINS Hopkins, Meredith Hilliard b: 2/22/07, Wolfe City, Tex. d: 11/20/63, Dallas, Tex. BR/TR, 5'11", 175 lbs. Deb: 4/17/34																							
1934	Phi-N	10	25	6	3	2	0	0	3	7	5	.120	.313	.200	36	-2	0			1.000	-1	/3-9	-0.3
	Chi-A	67	210	22	45	7	0	2	28	42	26	.214	.348	.276	61	-11	0	3	-2	.957	4	3-63	-0.6
1935	Chi-A	59	144	20	32	3	0	2	17	36	23	.222	.378	.285	72	-5	1	0	0	.960	-7	3-49/2-5	-0.9
Total	2	136	379	48	80	12	0	4	48	85	54	.211	.357	.274	63	-18	1	3		.960	-4	3-121/2-5	-1.8
■ MIKE HOPKINS Hopkins, Michael Joseph "Skinner" b: 11/1/1872, Glasgow, Scotland d: 2/5/52, Pittsburgh, Pa. BR/TR, 5'8", 160 lbs. Deb: 8/24/02																							
1902	Pit-N	1	2	0	2	1	0	0	0	0		1.000	1.000	1.500	647	1	0			1.000	0	/C-1	0.1
■ JOHNNY HOPP Hopp, John Leonard "Hippity" b: 7/18/16, Hastings, Neb. BL/TL, 5'10", 175 lbs. Deb: 9/18/39 C																							
1939	StL-N	6	4	1	2	1	0	0	2	1	1	.500	.600	.750	246	1	0			1.000	0	/1-2	0.1
1940	StL-N	80	152	24	41	7	4	1	14	9	21	.270	.315	.388	88	-3	3			.967	-2	O-39,1-10	-0.6
1941	StL-N	134	445	83	135	25	11	4	50	50	63	.303	.378	.436	121	12	15			.982	1	O-91,1-39	0.6
1942	*StL-N	95	314	41	81	16	7	3	37	36	40	.258	.334	.382	102	1	14			.983	-4	1-88	-0.9
1943	*StL-N	91	241	33	54	10	2	2	25	24	22	.224	.297	.307	71	-9	8			.950	-2	O-52,1-27	-1.5
1944	*StL-N	139	527	106	177	35	9	11	72	58	47	.336	.404	.499	150	35	15			**.997**	-10	*O-131/1-6	1.9
1945	StL-N	124	446	67	129	22	8	3	44	49	24	.289	.363	.395	108	5	14			.980	-7	*O-104,1-15	-0.7
1946	Bos-N★	129	445	71	148	23	8	3	48	34	34	.333	.386	.440	133	19	21			.981	-1	1-68,O-58	1.2
1947	Bos-N	134	430	74	124	20	2	2	32	58	30	.288	.376	.358	98	1	13			.980	-6	*O-125	-1.1
1948	Pit-N	120	392	64	109	15	12	1	31	40	25	.278	.345	.385	95	-2	5			1.000	1	O-80,1-25	-0.6
1949	Pit-N	20	55	5	12	3	1	0	3	7	3	.218	.306	.309	64	-3	0			.929	-1	/O-7,1-6	-0.4
	Bro-N	8	14	0	0	0	0	0	0	0	3	.000	.000	.000	-96	-4	0			1.000	1	/O-4,1-2	-0.3
	Pit-N	85	316	50	106	11	4	5	36	30	26	.335	.393	.443	121	10	9			.994	-0	1-71/O-9	0.8
	Yr	113	385	55	118	14	5	5	39	37	32	.306	.367	.408	105	3	9			.990	-0	1-79,O-20	0.1
1950	Pit-N	106	318	51	108	24	5	8	47	43	17	.340	.420	.522	141	20	7			.990	-6	1-70/O-7	1.2
	*NY-A	19	27	9	9	2	1	1	8	8	1	.333	.486	.593	180	4	0	1	-1	1.000	-1	1-12/O-6	0.2
1951	*NY-A	46	63	10	13	1	0	2	4	9	11	.206	.306	.317	71	-3	2	0	1	.992	-1	1-25	-0.4
1952	NY-A	15	25	4	4	0	0	0	2	2	3	.160	.250	.160	17	-3	2	0	1	1.000	1	1-12	-0.2
	Det-A	42	46	5	10	1	0	0	3	6	7	.217	.308	.239	53	-3	0	0	0	1.000	-1	/O-4,1-1	-0.4
	Yr	57	71	9	14	1	0	0	5	8	10	.197	.287	.211	41	-5	2	0	1	1.000	-0	1-13/O-4	-0.6
Total	14	1393	4260	698	1262	216	74	46	458	464	378	.296	.368	.414	113	79	128	1		.985	-36	O-717,1-479	-1.1
■ SHAGS HORAN Horan, Joseph Patrick b: 9/6/1895, St.Louis, Mo. d: 2/13/69, Torrance, Cal. BR/TR, 5'10", 170 lbs. Deb: 7/14/24																							
1924	NY-A	22	31	4	9	1	0	0	7	1	5	.290	.313	.323	64	-2	0	0	0	1.000	-4	O-14	-0.6
■ SAM HORN Horn, Samuel Lee b: 11/2/63, Dallas, Tex. BL/TL, 6'5", 250 lbs. Deb: 7/25/87																							
1987	Bos-A	46	158	31	44	7	0	14	34	17	55	.278	.356	.589	141	9	0	1	-1	.000	0	D-40	0.7
1988	Bos-A	24	61	4	9	0	0	2	8	11	20	.148	.278	.246	46	-4	0	0	0	.000	0	D-16	-0.5
1989	Bos-A	33	54	1	8	2	0	0	4	8	16	.148	.258	.185	25	-5	0	0	0	1.000	-0	D-14/1-2	-0.6
1990	Bal-A	79	246	30	61	13	0	14	45	32	62	.248	.335	.472	127	8	0	0	0	.970	-0	D-63,1-10	0.5
1991	Bal-A	121	317	45	74	16	0	23	61	41	99	.233	.327	.502	131	12	0	0	0	.000	0	*D-102	0.8
1992	Bal-A	63	162	13	38	10	1	5	19	21	60	.235	.326	.401	100	0	0	0	0	.000	0	D-46	-0.2
1993	Cle-A	12	33	8	15	1	0	4	8	1	5	.455	.486	.848	252	7	0	0	0	.000	0	D-11	0.6
1995	Tex-A	11	9	0	1	0	0	0	0	1	6	.111	.200	.111	-16	-2	0	0	0	.000	0	/D-1	-0.2
Total	8	389	1040	132	250	49	1	62	179	132	323	.240	.330	.468	118	25	0	1	-1	.972	-0	D-293/1-12	1.1
■ BOB HORNER Horner, James Robert b: 8/6/57, Junction City, Kan. BR/TR, 6'1", 210 lbs. Deb: 6/16/78																							
1978	Atl-N	89	323	50	86	17	1	23	63	24	42	.266	.321	.539	123	8	0	0	0	.956	6	3-89	1.3
1979	Atl-N	121	487	66	153	15	1	33	98	22	74	.314	.348	.552	132	19	0	2	-1	.930	-7	3-82,1-45	0.8
1980	Atl-N	124	463	81	124	14	1	35	89	27	50	.268	.310	.529	126	13	3	1	0	.935	5	*3-121/1-1	1.7
1981	Atl-N	79	300	42	83	10	0	15	42	32	39	.277	.348	.460	125	9	2	3	-1	.938	-15	3-79	-0.9
1982	*Atl-N★	140	499	85	130	24	0	32	97	66	75	.261	.351	.501	131	20	3	5	-2	.970	-17	*3-137	-0.3
1983	Atl-N	104	386	75	117	25	1	20	68	50	63	.303	.384	.528	140	21	4	2	0	.958	-13	*3-104/1-1	0.7
1984	Atl-N	32	113	15	31	8	0	3	19	14	17	.274	.354	.425	110	2	0	0	0	.965	-1	3-32	0.1
1985	Atl-N	130	483	61	129	25	3	27	89	50	57	.267	.337	.499	123	14	1	1	-0	1.000	-10	1-87,3-40	-0.3
1986	Atl-N	141	517	70	141	22	0	27	87	52	72	.273	.342	.472	116	10	1	4	-2	.995	2	*1-139	0.0
1988	StL-N	60	206	15	53	9	1	3	33	32	23	.257	.360	.354	105	2	0	0	0	.990	-1	1-57	-0.3
Total	10	1020	3777	560	1047	169	8	218	685	369	512	.277	.344	.499	125	117	14	18	-7	.946	-50	3-684,1-330	2.8
■ ROGERS HORNSBY Hornsby, Rogers "Rajah" b: 4/27/1896, Winters, Tex. d: 1/5/63, Chicago, Ill. BR/TR, 5'11", 175 lbs. Deb: 9/10/15 MCH																							
1915	StL-N	18	57	5	14	2	0	0	4	2	6	.246	.271	.281	67	-2	0	2	-1	.922	1	S-18	-0.2
1916	StL-N	139	495	63	155	17	15	6	65	40	63	.313	.369	.444	150	29	17			.928	-2	3-83,S-45,1-15,/2-1	3.5
1917	StL-N	145	523	86	171	24	**17**	8	66	45	34	.327	.385	**.484**	**170**	**42**	17			.939	21	*S-144	**7.7**
1918	StL-N	115	416	51	117	19	11	5	60	40	43	.281	.349	.416	138	18	8			.933	10	*S-109/O-3	3.6
1919	StL-N	138	512	68	163	15	9	8	71	48	41	.318	.384	.430	**154**	**34**	17			.933	2	3-72,S-37,2-25,/1-5	4.5
1920	StL-N	149	589	96	**218**	**44**	20	9	**94**	60	50	**.370**	**.431**	**.559**	**190**	**68**	12	15	-5	.962	11	*2-149	**8.1**
1921	StL-N	154	592	**131**	**235**	**44**	**18**	21	**126**	60	48	**.397**	**.458**	**.639**	**191**	**78**	13	13	-4	.969	-3	*2-142/O-6,S-3,31	7.1
1922	StL-N	154	623	**141**	**250**	**46**	14	**42**	**152**	65	50	**.401**	**.459**	**.722**	**210**	**99**	17	12	-2	**.967**	-7	*2-154	**8.5**
1923	StL-N	107	424	89	163	32	10	17	83	55	29	**.384**	**.459**	**.627**	**188**	**54**	3	7	-3	.962	-17	2-96,1-10	3.3
1924	StL-N	143	536	**121**	**227**	**43**	14	25	94	**89**	32	**.424**	**.507**	**.696**	**223**	**97**	5	12	-6	.965	-4	*2-143	**8.6**
1925	StL-N	138	504	133	203	41	10	**39**	**143**	83	39	**.403**	**.489**	**.756**	**208**	**83**	5	3	-0	.954	-20	*2-136,M	**6.0**
1926	*StL-N	134	527	96	167	34	5	11	93	61	39	.317	.388	.463	123	18	3			.962	-29	*2-134,M	-0.8
1927	NY-N	155	568	**133**	205	32	9	26	125	**86**	38	.361	**.448**	.586	**176**	**63**	9			.972	3	*2-155,M	6.9
1928	Bos-N	140	486	99	188	42	7	21	94	**107**	41	**.387**	**.498**	**.632**	**204**	**80**	5			.973	-24	*2-140,M	**5.8**
1929	*Chi-N	156	602	**156**	229	47	8	39	149	87	65	.380	.459	**.679**	**178**	**74**	2			.973	1	*2-156	**7.2**
1930	Chi-N	42	104	15	32	5	1	2	18	12	12	.308	.385	.433	96	-0	0			.916	-3	2-25,M	-0.2
1931	Chi-N	100	357	64	118	37	1	16	90	56	23	.331	.421	.574	162	32	1			.951	-15	2-69,3-26,M	2.3
1932	Chi-N	19	58	10	13	2	0	1	7	10	4	.224	.357	.310	82	-1	0			1.000	-4	O-10/3-6,M	-0.5
1933	StL-N	46	83	9	27	6	0	2	21	12	6	.325	.423	.470	147	6	1			.967	-7	2-17	-0.1
	StL-A	11	9	2	3	1	0	1	2	2	1	.333	.455	.778	208	1	0	0	0	.000	0	HM	0.1
1934	StL-A	24	23	2	7	2	0	1	11	7	4	.304	.484	.522	147	2	0	0	0	1.000	0	/3-1,O-1,M	0.2
1935	StL-A	10	24	1	5	3	0	0	3	3	6	.208	.296	.333	60	-1	0	0	0	1.000	0	/1-3,2-2,3-1,M	-0.2
1936	StL-A	2	5	1	2	0	0	0	2	1	0	.400	.500	.400	121	0	0	0	0	1.000	-0	/1-1,M	0.0
1937	StL-A	20	56	7	18	3	0	1	11	7	5	.321	.397	.429	107	1	0	0	0	.947	-5	2-17,M	-0.2
Total	23	2259	8173	1579	2930	541	169	301	1584	1038	679	.358	.434	.577	176	874	135	64		.965	-91	*2-1561,S-356,3/10	81.2
■ JOE HORNUNG Hornung, Michael Joseph "Ubbo Ubbo" b: 6/12/1857, Carthage, N.Y. d: 10/30/31, Howard Beach, N.Y. BR/TR, 5'8.5", 164 lbs. Deb: 5/1/1879 U																							
1879	Buf-N	78	319	46	85	18	7	0	38	2	27	.266	.271	.367	105	1				.844	-2	*O-77/1-1	-0.4
1880	Buf-N	85	342	47	91	8	11	1	42	8	29	.266	.283	.363	115	5				.874	-0	*O-67,1-18/2-5,P-1	0.1
1881	Bos-N	83	324	40	78	12	8	2	25	5	25	.241	.252	.346	90	-4				**.948**	12	*O-83	0.6
1882	Bos-N	85	388	67	117	14	11	1	50	2	25	.302	.305	.402	124	10				**.932**	11	*O-84/1-1	1.8
1883	Bos-N	98	446	**107**	124	25	13	8	66	8	54	.278	.291	.446	117	8				**.936**	7	*O-98/3-1	1.2
1884	Bos-N	115	518	119	139	27	10	7	51	17	80	.268	.292	.400	116	8				.916	3	*O-110/1-6	0.8
1885	Bos-N	25	109	14	22	4	1	1	7	1	20	.202	.209	.284	61	-5				.919	-3	O-25	-0.8
1886	Bos-N	94	424	67	109	12	2	2	40	10	62	.257	.274	.309	80	-10	16			**.948**	7	*O-94	-0.5
1887	Bos-N	98	437	85	118	10	6	5	49	17	28	.270	.302	.355	82	-11	41			**.935**	13	*O-98	0.0
1888	Bos-N	107	431	61	103	11	7	3	53	16	39	.239	.269	.318	85	-8	29			.947	-8	*O-107	-1.9
1889	Bal-a	135	533	73	122	13	9	1	78	22	72	.229	.269	.293	59	-30	34			.913	11	*O-134/3-1	-1.9
1890	NY-N	120	513	62	122	18	5	0	65	12	37	.238	.258	.292	60	-28	39			.931	-3	O-77,1-36/3-5,S-2	-3.1
Total	12	1123	4784	788	1230	172	90	31	564	120	498	.257	.277	.350	91	-64	159			.922	49	*O-1054/1-62,32SP	-4.1

■ TONY HORTON
Horton, Anthony Darrin b: 12/6/44, Santa Monica, Cal. BR/TR, 6'3", 210 lbs. Deb: 7/31/64

YEAR	TM/L	G	AB	R	H	2B	3B	HR	RBI	BB	SO	AVG	OBP	SLG	PRO+	BR/A	SB	CS	SBR	FA	FR	G/POS	TPR
1964	Bos-A	36	126	9	28	5	0	1	8	3	20	.222	.240	.286	44	-10	0	0	0	1.000	1	O-24/1-8	-1.1
1965	Bos-A	60	163	23	48	8	1	7	23	18	36	.294	.365	.485	131	7	0	2	-1	.980	-1	1-44	0.2
1966	Bos-A	6	22	0	3	0	0	0	2	0	5	.136	.136	.136	-19	-3	0	0	0	1.000	1	/1-6	-0.3
1967	Bos-A	21	39	2	12	3	0	0	9	0	5	.308	.308	.385	96	-0	0	0	0	.929	-1	/1-6	-0.2
	Cle-A	106	363	35	102	13	4	10	44	18	52	.281	.322	.421	117	7	3	0	1	.991	-6	1-94	-0.4
	Yr	127	402	37	114	16	4	10	53	18	57	.284	.321	.418	114	6	3	0	1	.987	-6	*1-100	-0.6
1968	Cle-A	133	477	57	119	29	3	14	59	34	56	.249	.304	.411	117	8	3	1	0	.992	-4	*1-128	-0.6
1969	Cle-A	159	625	77	174	25	4	27	93	37	91	.278	.321	.461	113	8	3	3	-1	.989	-0	*1-157	-0.6
1970	Cle-A	115	413	48	111	19	3	17	59	30	54	.269	.324	.453	107	3	3	2	-0	.994	3	*1-112	-0.4
Total	7	636	2228	251	597	102	15	76	297	140	319	.268	.315	.430	109	18	12	8	-1	.990	-7	1-555/O-24	-3.4

■ WILLIE HORTON
Horton, Willie Watterson b: 10/18/42, Arno, Va. BR/TR, 5'11", 209 lbs. Deb: 9/10/63 C

YEAR	TM/L	G	AB	R	H	2B	3B	HR	RBI	BB	SO	AVG	OBP	SLG	PRO+	BR/A	SB	CS	SBR	FA	FR	G/POS	TPR
1963	Det-A	15	43	6	14	2	1	1	4	0	8	.326	.326	.488	120	1	2	0	1	1.000	-1	/O-9	0.0
1964	Det-A	25	80	6	13	1	3	1	10	11	20	.162	.272	.287	55	-5	0	0	0	.943	-2	O-23	-0.8
1965	Det-A★	143	512	69	140	20	2	29	104	48	101	.273	.343	.490	132	21	5	9	-4	.988	5	*O-141/3-1	1.6
1966	Det-A	146	526	72	138	22	6	27	100	44	103	.262	.323	.481	125	15	1	1	-0	.979	-4	*O-137	0.6
1967	Det-A	122	401	47	110	20	3	19	67	36	80	.274	.340	.481	137	17	0	0	0	.971	-0	*O-110	1.3
1968	*Det-A★	143	512	68	146	20	2	36	85	49	110	.285	.357	.543	165	38	0	3	-2	.973	0	*O-139	3.4
1969	Det-A	141	508	66	133	17	1	28	91	52	93	.262	.334	.465	116	10	3	3	-1	.972	9	*O-136	1.0
1970	Det-A★	96	371	53	113	18	2	17	69	28	43	.305	.357	.501	133	15	0	1	-1	.982	5	O-96	1.6
1971	Det-A	119	450	64	130	25	1	22	72	37	75	.289	.352	.496	133	18	1	5	-3	.963	-10	*O-118	-0.1
1972	*Det-A	108	333	44	77	9	5	11	36	27	47	.231	.295	.387	99	-1	0	0	0	1.000	-10	O-98	-1.8
1973	Det-A★	111	411	42	130	19	3	17	53	23	57	.316	.363	.501	132	16	1	4	-2	.942	-10	*O-107/D-1	0.0
1974	Det-A	72	238	32	71	8	1	15	47	21	36	.298	.363	.529	149	14	0	1	-1	.947	-4	O-64/D-1	0.8
1975	Det-A	159	615	62	169	13	1	25	92	44	109	.275	.323	.421	104	2	1	2	-1	.000	0	*D-159	-0.3
1976	Det-A	114	401	40	105	17	0	14	56	49	63	.262	.345	.409	116	8	0	0	0	.000	0	*D-105	0.6
1977	Det-A	1	4	0	1	0	0	0	0	0	0	.250	.250	.250	35	-0	0	0	0	1.000	-0	/O-1	-0.1
	Tex-A	139	519	55	150	23	3	15	75	42	117	.289	.342	.432	108	6	2	3	-1	.938	-1	*D-128,O-10	-0.1
	Yr	140	523	55	151	23	3	15	75	42	117	.289	.342	.430	108	5	2	3	-1	.941	-2	*D-128,O-11	-0.2
1978	Cle-A	50	169	15	42	7	0	5	22	15	25	.249	.314	.379	95	-1	3	0	1	.000	0	D-48	-0.2
	Oak-A	32	102	11	32	8	0	3	19	9	15	.314	.369	.480	145	6	0	1	-1	.333	-1	D-27/O-1	0.4
	Tor-A	33	122	12	25	6	0	3	19	4	29	.205	.230	.328	54	-8	0	0	0	.000	0	D-30	-0.9
	Yr	115	393	38	99	21	0	11	60	28	69	.252	.303	.389	95	-4	3	1	0	.333	-1	*D-105/O-1	-0.7
1979	Sea-A	162	646	77	180	19	5	29	106	42	112	.279	.327	.458	107	5	1	1	-0	.000	0	*D-162	-0.1
1980	Sea-A	97	335	32	74	10	1	8	36	39	70	.221	.310	.328	74	-11	0	4	-2	.000	0	D-92	-1.7
Total	18	2028	7298	873	1993	284	40	325	1163	620	1313	.273	.335	.457	119	166	20	38	-17	.972	-24	*O-1190,D-753/3-1	5.2

■ DWAYNE HOSEY
Hosey, Dwayne Samuel b: 3/11/67, Sharon, Pa. BB/TR, 5'10", 175 lbs. Deb: 9/1/95

YEAR	TM/L	G	AB	R	H	2B	3B	HR	RBI	BB	SO	AVG	OBP	SLG	PRO+	BR/A	SB	CS	SBR	FA	FR	G/POS	TPR
1995	*Bos-A	24	68	20	23	8	1	3	7	8	16	.338	.408	.618	157	6	6	0	2	1.000	-1	O-21/D-1	0.6
1996	Bos-A	28	78	13	17	2	2	1	3	7	17	.218	.282	.333	54	-6	6	3	0	.984	1	O-26/D-2	-0.4
Total	2	52	146	33	40	10	3	4	10	15	33	.274	.342	.466	102	-0	12	3	2	.991	1	/O-47,D-3	0.2

■ STEVE HOSEY
Hosey, Steven Bernard b: 4/2/69, Oakland, Cal. BR/TR, 6'3", 215 lbs. Deb: 8/29/92

YEAR	TM/L	G	AB	R	H	2B	3B	HR	RBI	BB	SO	AVG	OBP	SLG	PRO+	BR/A	SB	CS	SBR	FA	FR	G/POS	TPR
1992	SF-N	21	56	6	14	1	0	1	6	0	15	.250	.250	.321	64	-3	1	1	-0	.960	-2	O-18	-0.6
1993	SF-N	3	2	0	1	1	0	0	1	1	1	.500	.667	1.000	350	1	0	0	0	.000	-0	/O-1	0.0
Total	2	24	58	6	15	2	0	1	7	1	16	.259	.271	.345	77	-2	1	1	-0	.960	-3	/O-19	-0.6

■ TIM HOSLEY
Hosley, Timothy Kenneth b: 5/10/47, Spartanburg, S.C. BR/TR, 5'10", 195 lbs. Deb: 9/8/70

YEAR	TM/L	G	AB	R	H	2B	3B	HR	RBI	BB	SO	AVG	OBP	SLG	PRO+	BR/A	SB	CS	SBR	FA	FR	G/POS	TPR
1970	Det-A	7	12	1	2	0	0	1	2	0	6	.167	.167	.417	55	-1	0	0	0	1.000	2	/C-4	0.1
1971	Det-A	7	16	2	3	0	0	2	6	0	1	.188	.188	.563	102	-0	0	0	0	1.000	-0	/C-4,1-1	0.0
1973	Oak-A	13	14	3	3	0	0	0	2	2	3	.214	.313	.214	53	-1	0	0	0	.952	-1	C-13	-0.2
1974	Oak-A	11	7	3	2	0	0	0	1	1	2	.286	.375	.286	99	0	0	0	0	1.000	0	/C-8,1-1	0.0
1975	Chi-N	62	141	22	36	7	0	6	20	27	25	.255	.382	.433	120	5	1	1	-0	.968	-2	C-53	0.4
1976	Oak-A	37	55	4	9	2	0	1	4	8	12	.164	.270	.255	56	-3	0	0	0	.968	-1	C-37	-0.3
	Chi-N	1	1	0	0	0	0	0	0	0	0	.000	.000	.000	-92	-0	0	0	0	.000	0	H	0.0
1977	Oak-A	39	78	5	15	0	0	1	10	16	13	.192	.337	.231	59	-4	0	0	0	.955	3	C-19,D-12/1-3	-0.1
1978	Oak-A	13	23	1	7	2	0	0	3	1	6	.304	.360	.391	117	1	0	0	0	.962	0	/C-6,D-1	0.1
1981	Oak-A	18	21	2	2	0	0	1	5	2	5	.095	.174	.238	19	-2	0	0	0	.750	-0	/1-1,D-4	-0.3
Total	9	208	368	43	79	11	0	12	53	57	73	.215	.326	.342	87	-6	1	1	-0	.968	0	C-144/D-17,1-6	-0.3

■ CHUCK HOSTETLER
Hostetler, Charles Cloyd b: 9/22/03, McClellandtown, Pa. d: 2/18/71, Fort Collins, Colo BL/TR, 6', 175 lbs. Deb: 4/18/44

YEAR	TM/L	G	AB	R	H	2B	3B	HR	RBI	BB	SO	AVG	OBP	SLG	PRO+	BR/A	SB	CS	SBR	FA	FR	G/POS	TPR
1944	Det-A	90	265	42	79	9	2	0	20	21	31	.298	.350	.347	94	-2	4	4	-1	.985	0	O-65	-0.6
1945	*Det-A	42	44	3	7	3	0	0	2	7	8	.159	.275	.227	43	-3	0	0	0	.889	-3	/O-8	-0.6
Total	2	132	309	45	86	12	2	0	22	28	39	.278	.338	.330	87	-5	4	4	-1	.979	-2	/O-73	-1.2

■ DAVE HOSTETLER
Hostetler, David Alan b: 3/27/56, Pasadena, Cal. BR/TR, 6'4", 215 lbs. Deb: 9/15/81

YEAR	TM/L	G	AB	R	H	2B	3B	HR	RBI	BB	SO	AVG	OBP	SLG	PRO+	BR/A	SB	CS	SBR	FA	FR	G/POS	TPR
1981	Mon-N	5	6	1	3	0	0	1	1	0	2	.500	.500	1.000	314	2	0	0	0	1.000	-0	/1-2	0.1
1982	Tex-A	113	418	53	97	12	3	22	67	42	113	.232	.304	.433	105	1	2	2	-1	.990	-11	*1-109/D-3	-1.6
1983	Tex-A	94	304	31	67	9	2	11	46	42	103	.220	.325	.372	93	-2	0	2	-1	1.000	-0	D-88/1-2	-0.7
1984	Tex-A	37	82	7	18	2	1	3	10	13	27	.220	.326	.378	91	-1	0	0	0	1.000	1	1-14,D-13	-0.1
1988	Pit-N	6	8	0	2	0	0	0	0	0	3	.250	.250	.250	45	-1	0	0	0	.944	-0	/1-4,C-1	-0.1
Total	5	255	818	92	187	23	6	37	124	97	248	.229	.315	.407	100	-1	2	4	-2	.990	-11	1-131,D-104/C-1	-2.4

■ PETE HOTALING
Hotaling, Peter James "Monkey" b: 12/16/1856, Mohawk, N.Y. d: 7/3/28, Cleveland, Ohio BL/TR, 5'8", 166 lbs. Deb: 5/1/1879

YEAR	TM/L	G	AB	R	H	2B	3B	HR	RBI	BB	SO	AVG	OBP	SLG	PRO+	BR/A	SB	CS	SBR	FA	FR	G/POS	TPR
1879	Cin-N	81	369	64	103	20	9	1	27	12	17	.279	.302	.390	133	13				.843	-0	*O-69/C-8,2-6,3-3	0.9
1880	Cle-N	78	325	40	78	17	8	0	41	10	30	.240	.263	.342	105	2				.896	-2	*O-78/C-2	-0.2
1881	Wor-N	77	317	51	98	15	3	1	35	18	12	.309	.346	.385	123	8				.862	-3	*O-74/C-3	0.3
1882	Bos-N	84	378	64	98	16	5	0	28	16	21	.259	.289	.328	97	-1				.865	2	*O-84	0.1
1883	Cle-N	100	417	54	108	20	8	0	30	12	31	.259	.280	.345	90	-5				.829	1	*O-100	-0.4
1884	Cle-N	102	408	69	99	16	6	3	27	28	50	.243	.291	.333	93	-4				.849	-1	*O-102/2-1	-0.6
1885	Bro-a	94	370	73	95	9	5	1	34	49		.257	.350	.316	111	7				.893	0	*O-94	0.4
1887	Cle-a	126	505	108	151	28	13	3	94	53		.299	.373	.424	126	19	43			.903	1	*O-126	1.4
1888	Cle-a	98	403	67	101	7	6	0	55	26		.251	.307	.298	97	-1	35			.878	-9	*O-98	-1.1
Total	9	840	3492	590	931	148	63	9	371	224	161	.267	.314	.353	108	38	78			.869	-11	O-825/C-13,2-7,3-3	0.8

■ KEN HOTTMAN
Hottman, Kenneth Roger b: 6/7/48, Stockton, Cal. BR/TR, 5'11", 190 lbs. Deb: 9/11/71

YEAR	TM/L	G	AB	R	H	2B	3B	HR	RBI	BB	SO	AVG	OBP	SLG	PRO+	BR/A	SB	CS	SBR	FA	FR	G/POS	TPR
1971	Chi-A	6	16	1	2	0	0	0	0	1	2	.125	.176	.125	-13	-2	0	0	0	1.000	-1	/O-5	-0.4

■ SADIE HOUCK
Houck, Sargent Perry b: 3/1856, Washington, D.C. d: 5/26/19, Washington, D.C. BR/TR, 5'7", 151 lbs. Deb: 5/1/1879

YEAR	TM/L	G	AB	R	H	2B	3B	HR	RBI	BB	SO	AVG	OBP	SLG	PRO+	BR/A	SB	CS	SBR	FA	FR	G/POS	TPR
1879	Bos-N	80	356	69	95	24	9	2	49	4	11	.267	.275	.402	117	6				.814	-8	O-47,S-33	-0.2
1880	Bos-N	12	47	2	7	0	0	0	2	0	6	.149	.149	.149	1	-5				.786	-1	O-12	-0.6
	Pro-N	49	184	27	37	7	7	1	22	3	6	.201	.214	.332	85	-3				.873	-1	O-49	-0.5
	Yr	61	231	29	44	7	7	1	24	3	12	.190	.201	.294	68	-7				.855	-3	O-61	-1.1
1881	Det-N	75	308	43	86	16	6	1	36	6	6	.279	.293	.380	106	1				.868	1	*S-75	0.6
1883	Det-N	101	416	52	105	18	12	0	40	9	18	.252	.268	.353	91	-4				.852	5	*S-101	0.3
1884	Phi-a	108	472	93	140	19	14	0		7		.297	.318	.396	124	10				**.893**	23	*S-108/2-1	3.1
1885	Phi-a	93	388	74	99	10	9	0	54	10		.255	.286	.327	88	-7				.863	22	*S-93	1.5
1886	Bal-a	61	260	29	50	8	1	0	17	4		.192	.216	.231	41	-18	25			.849	-5	S-55/2-5,O-1	-2.0
	Was-N	52	195	14	42	3	0	0	14	2	28	.215	.223	.231	41	-14	4			.858	0	S-51/2-1	-1.2

YEAR	TM/L	G	AB	R	H	2B	3B	HR	RBI	BB	SO	AVG	OBP	SLG	PRO+	BR/A	SB	CS	SBR	FA	FR	G/POS	TPR
1887	NY-a	10	33	3	5	1	0	0	0	3		.152	.243	.182	20	-3	2			.831	4	S-10/2-1	0.1
Total	8	641	2659	406	666	106	58	4	234	48	75	.250	.269	.338	91	-35	31			.863	39	S-526,O-109/2-8	1.1

■ RALPH HOUK

Houk, Ralph George "Major" b: 8/9/19, Lawrence, Kan. BR/TR, 5'11", 193 lbs. Deb: 4/26/47 MC

YEAR	TM/L	G	AB	R	H	2B	3B	HR	RBI	BB	SO	AVG	OBP	SLG	PRO+	BR/A	SB	CS	SBR	FA	FR	G/POS	TPR
1947	*NY-A	41	92	7	25	3	1	0	12	11	5	.272	.356	.326	91	-1	0	0	0	.987	2	C-41	0.3
1948	NY-A	14	29	3	8	2	0	0	3	0	0	.276	.276	.345	65	-2	0	0	0	1.000	5	C-14	0.3
1949	NY-A	5	7	0	4	0	0	0	1	0	1	.571	.571	.571	203	1	0	0	0	.889	-1	/C-5	0.1
1950	NY-A	10	9	0	1	1	0	0	1	0	2	.111	.111	.222	-17	-2	0	0	0	.929	1	/C-9	-0.1
1951	NY-A	3	5	0	1	0	0	0	2	0	1	.200	.200	.200	9	-1	0	0	0	1.000	-1	/C-3	-0.1
1952	*NY-A	9	6	0	2	0	0	0	0	1	0	.333	.429	.333	121	0	0	0	0	.917	1	/C-9	0.1
1953	NY-A	8	9	2	2	0	0	0	1	0	1	.222	.222	.222	21	-1	0	0	0	1.000	-0	/C-8	-0.1
1954	NY-A	1	1	0	0	0	0	0	0	0	0	.000	.000	.000	-99	-0	0	0	0	.000	0	H	0.0
Total	8	91	158	12	43	6	1	0	20	12	10	.272	.327	.323	79	-5	0	0	0	.981	6	/C-89	0.5

■ FRANK HOUSE

House, Henry Franklin "Pig" b: 2/18/30, Bessemer, Ala. BL/TR, 6'2", 190 lbs. Deb: 7/21/50

YEAR	TM/L	G	AB	R	H	2B	3B	HR	RBI	BB	SO	AVG	OBP	SLG	PRO+	BR/A	SB	CS	SBR	FA	FR	G/POS	TPR
1950	Det-A	5	5	1	2	1	0	0	0	0	1	.400	.400	.600	148	0	0	0	0	1.000	0	/C-5	0.0
1951	Det-A	18	41	3	9	2	0	1	4	6	2	.220	.319	.341	78	-1	1	1	-0	.957	1	C-18	0.0
1954	Det-A	114	352	35	88	12	1	9	38	31	34	.250	.313	.366	87	-7	2	1	0	.992	-1	*C-107	-0.3
1955	Det-A	102	328	37	85	11	1	15	53	22	25	.259	.312	.436	102	-1	0	0	0	.987	2	C-93	0.4
1956	Det-A	94	321	44	77	6	2	10	44	21	19	.240	.293	.364	72	-14	1	1	-0	.986	-6	C-88	-1.7
1957	Det-A	106	348	31	90	9	0	7	36	35	26	.259	.328	.345	82	-8	1	1	-0	.997	9	C-97	0.4
1958	KC-A	76	202	16	51	6	3	4	24	12	13	.252	.298	.371	81	-5	1	0	0	.992	-7	C-55	-1.0
1959	KC-A	98	347	32	82	14	3	1	30	20	23	.236	.282	.303	59	-19	0	3	-2	.982	-8	C-95	-2.5
1960	Cin-N	23	28	0	5	2	0	0	3	0	2	.179	.179	.250	16	-3	0	0	0	1.000	1	/C-8	-0.2
1961	Det-A	17	22	3	5	1	1	0	3	4	2	.227	.346	.364	87	-0	0	0	0	.974	-1	C-14	-0.1
Total	10	653	1994	202	494	64	11	47	235	151	147	.248	.304	.362	80	-60	6	7	-2	.988	-10	C-580	-5.0

■ CHARLIE HOUSEHOLDER

Householder, Charles F. b: 1856, Harrisburg, Pa. BR/TR, 5'7", 150 lbs. Deb: 4/20/1884

YEAR	TM/L	G	AB	R	H	2B	3B	HR	RBI	BB	SO	AVG	OBP	SLG	PRO+	BR/A	SB	CS	SBR	FA	FR	G/POS	TPR
1884	CP-U	83	310	32	74	12	5	1		12		.239	.267	.319	77	-18				.796	-6	3-41,O-40/S-3,P-2	-2.1

■ CHARLIE HOUSEHOLDER

Householder, Charles W. b: 1856, Harrisburg, Pa. d: 12/26/08, Harrisburg, Pa. BL/TL, 5'11", 158 lbs. Deb: 5/2/1882

YEAR	TM/L	G	AB	R	H	2B	3B	HR	RBI	BB	SO	AVG	OBP	SLG	PRO+	BR/A	SB	CS	SBR	FA	FR	G/POS	TPR
1882	Bal-a	74	307	42	78	10	7	1		4		.254	.264	.342	111	4				.971	3	*1-74/C-3	-0.2
1884	Bro-a	76	273	28	66	15	3	3		12		.242	.279	.352	104	1				.959	-5	1-40,C-31/O-6,2-1	-0.5
Total	2	150	580	70	144	25	10	4		16		.248	.271	.347	108	5				.967	-2	1-114/C-34,O-6,2-1	-0.7

■ ED HOUSEHOLDER

Householder, Edward H. b: 10/12/1869, Pittsburgh, Pa. d: 7/3/24, Los Angeles, Cal. BL/TL, Deb: 4/17/03

YEAR	TM/L	G	AB	R	H	2B	3B	HR	RBI	BB	SO	AVG	OBP	SLG	PRO+	BR/A	SB	CS	SBR	FA	FR	G/POS	TPR
1903	Bro-N	12	43	5	9	0	0	0	9	2		.209	.244	.209	31	-4	3			.967	1	O-12	-0.4

■ PAUL HOUSEHOLDER

Householder, Paul Wesley b: 9/4/58, Columbus, Ohio BB/TR, 6', 180 lbs. Deb: 8/26/80

YEAR	TM/L	G	AB	R	H	2B	3B	HR	RBI	BB	SO	AVG	OBP	SLG	PRO+	BR/A	SB	CS	SBR	FA	FR	G/POS	TPR
1980	Cin-N	20	45	3	11	1	1	0	7	1	13	.244	.261	.311	59	-3	1	0	0	1.000	-1	O-14	-0.4
1981	Cin-N	23	69	12	19	4	0	2	9	10	16	.275	.367	.420	121	2	3	1	0	1.000	-1	O-19	0.1
1982	Cin-N	138	417	40	88	11	5	9	34	30	77	.211	.267	.326	64	-21	17	11	-2	.992	6	*O-131	-2.0
1983	Cin-N	123	380	40	97	24	4	6	43	44	60	.255	.336	.387	96	-2	12	12	-4	**.991**	-1	*O-112	-0.9
1984	Cin-N	14	12	3	1	1	0	0	0	3	3	.083	.267	.167	23	-1	1	1	-0	1.000	-2	O-10	-0.4
	StL-N	13	14	1	2	0	0	0	0	0	3	.143	.143	.143	-20	-2	0	0	0	1.000	-3	/O-8	-0.6
	Yr	27	26	4	3	1	0	0	0	3	6	.115	.207	.154	3	-3	1	1	-0	1.000	-5	O-18	-1.0
1985	Mil-A	95	299	41	77	15	0	11	34	27	60	.258	.321	.418	101	0	1	2	-1	.986	-1	O-91/D-3	-0.5
1986	Mil-A	26	78	4	17	3	1	1	16	7	16	.218	.291	.321	64	-4	1	2	-1	1.000	-3	O-22/D-3	-0.8
1987	Hou-N	14	12	2	1	1	0	0	1	4	2	.083	.313	.167	33	-1	0	0	0	1.000	-2	/O-7	-0.3
Total	8	466	1326	146	313	60	11	29	144	126	250	.236	.305	.363	83	-31	36	29	-7	.991	-7	O-414/D-6	-5.8

■ JOHN HOUSEMAN

Houseman, John Franklin b: 1/10/1870, Holland d: 11/4/22, Chicago, Ill. 160 lbs. Deb: 9/11/1894

YEAR	TM/L	G	AB	R	H	2B	3B	HR	RBI	BB	SO	AVG	OBP	SLG	PRO+	BR/A	SB	CS	SBR	FA	FR	G/POS	TPR
1894	Chi-N	4	15	5	6	3	1	0	4	5	3	.400	.571	.733	202	3	2			.950	-0	/S-3,2-1	0.2
1897	StL-N	80	278	34	68	6	6	0	21	28		.245	.329	.309	70	-11	16			.918	-2	2-41,O-33/S-5,3-3	-1.2
Total	2	84	293	39	74	9	7	0	25	33	3	.253	.344	.331	79	-8	18			.916	-3	/2-42,O-33,S-8,3-3	-1.0

■ BEN HOUSER

Houser, Benjamin Franklin b: 11/30/1883, Shenandoah, Pa. d: 1/15/52, Augusta, Maine BL/TL, 6'1", 185 lbs. Deb: 5/2/10

YEAR	TM/L	G	AB	R	H	2B	3B	HR	RBI	BB	SO	AVG	OBP	SLG	PRO+	BR/A	SB	CS	SBR	FA	FR	G/POS	TPR
1910	Phi-A	34	69	9	13	3	2	0	7	7		.188	.263	.290	74	-2	0			1.000	-0	1-26	-0.3
1911	Bos-N	20	71	11	18	1	0	1	9	8	6	.254	.329	.310	73	-2	2			.988	0	1-20	-0.2
1912	Bos-N	108	332	38	95	17	3	8	52	22	29	.286	.332	.428	105	1	1			.986	-3	1-83	-0.3
Total	3	162	472	58	126	21	5	9	68	37	35	.267	.322	.390	96	-4	3			.989	-3	1-129	-0.8

■ WAYNE HOUSIE

Housie, Wayne Tyrone b: 5/20/65, Hampton, Va. BB/TR, 5'9", 165 lbs. Deb: 9/17/91

YEAR	TM/L	G	AB	R	H	2B	3B	HR	RBI	BB	SO	AVG	OBP	SLG	PRO+	BR/A	SB	CS	SBR	FA	FR	G/POS	TPR
1991	Bos-A	11	8	2	2	1	0	0	0	1	3	.250	.333	.375	91	-0	1	0	0	1.000	-1	/O-4,D-2	-0.1
1993	NY-N	18	16	2	3	1	0	0	1	1	1	.188	.235	.250	30	-2	0	0	0	.000	-1	/O-2	-0.2
Total	2	29	24	4	5	2	0	0	1	2	4	.208	.269	.292	51	-2	1	0	0	1.000	-2	/O-6,D-2	-0.3

■ TYLER HOUSTON

Houston, Tyler Sam b: 1/17/71, Las Vegas, Nev. BL/TR, 6'2", 210 lbs. Deb: 4/3/96

YEAR	TM/L	G	AB	R	H	2B	3B	HR	RBI	BB	SO	AVG	OBP	SLG	PRO+	BR/A	SB	CS	SBR	FA	FR	G/POS	TPR
1996	Atl-N	33	27	3	6	2	1	1	8	1	9	.222	.250	.481	83	-1	0	0	0	1.000	0	1-11	-0.1
	Chi-N	46	115	18	39	7	0	2	19	8	18	.339	.382	.452	116	3	3	2	-0	.986	-3	C-27/3-9,2-2,1-1,O	0.1
	Yr	79	142	21	45	9	1	3	27	9	27	.317	.358	.458	109	2	3	2	-0	.986	-3	C-27,1-12/3-9,2O	0.0
1997	Chi-N	72	196	15	51	10	0	2	28	9	35	.260	.293	.342	64	-10	1	0	0	.986	-3	C-41,3-12/1-2,2S	-1.1
1998	*Chi-N	95	255	26	65	7	1	9	33	13	53	.255	.291	.396	74	-10	2	2	-1	.993	2	C-63,3-12/1-7	-0.5
Total	3	246	593	62	161	26	2	14	88	31	115	.272	.308	.393	79	-19	6	4	-1	.990	-5	C-131/3-33,12SO	-1.6

■ LEFTY HOUTZ

Houtz, Fred Fritz b: 9/4/1875, Connersville, Ind. d: 2/15/59, St.Marys, Ohio BL/TL, 5'10", 170 lbs. Deb: 7/23/1899

YEAR	TM/L	G	AB	R	H	2B	3B	HR	RBI	BB	SO	AVG	OBP	SLG	PRO+	BR/A	SB	CS	SBR	FA	FR	G/POS	TPR
1899	Cin-N	5	17	1	4	0	1	0	0	4		.235	.381	.353	100	0	1			1.000	4	/O-5	0.4

■ STEVE HOVLEY

Hovley, Stephen Eugene b: 12/18/44, Ventura, Cal. BL/TL, 5'10", 188 lbs. Deb: 6/26/69

YEAR	TM/L	G	AB	R	H	2B	3B	HR	RBI	BB	SO	AVG	OBP	SLG	PRO+	BR/A	SB	CS	SBR	FA	FR	G/POS	TPR
1969	Sea-A	91	329	41	91	14	3	3	20	30	34	.277	.339	.365	98	-1	10	4	1	.989	7	O-84	0.2
1970	Mil-A	40	135	17	38	9	0	0	16	17	11	.281	.366	.348	97	0	5	1	1	.958	-2	O-38	-0.3
	Oak-A	72	100	8	19	1	0	0	1	5	11	.190	.229	.200	20	-11	3	0	1	1.000	-6	O-42	-1.8
	Yr	112	235	25	57	10	0	0	17	22	22	.243	.310	.285	67	-10	8	1	2	.977	-8	O-80	-2.1
1971	Oak-A	24	27	3	3	2	0	0	3	7	9	.111	.314	.185	45	-2	2	0	1	1.000	-1	O-11	-0.2
1972	KC-A	105	196	24	53	5	1	3	24	24	29	.270	.353	.352	111	3	3	3	-1	.982	-5	O-68	-0.5
1973	KC-A	104	232	29	59	8	1	2	24	33	34	.254	.347	.323	83	-4	6	4	-1	.975	-10	O-79,D-15	-1.8
Total	5	436	1019	122	263	39	5	8	88	116	128	.258	.336	.330	88	-14	29	12	2	.982	-16	O-322/D-15	-4.4

■ CHRIS HOWARD

Howard, Christopher Hugh b: 2/27/66, San Diego, Cal. BR/TR, 6'2", 200 lbs. Deb: 9/15/91

YEAR	TM/L	G	AB	R	H	2B	3B	HR	RBI	BB	SO	AVG	OBP	SLG	PRO+	BR/A	SB	CS	SBR	FA	FR	G/POS	TPR
1991	Sea-A	9	6	1	1	1	0	0	0	1	2	.167	.286	.333	71	-0	0	0	0	1.000	1	/C-9	0.1
1993	Sea-A	4	1	0	0	0	0	0	0	0	0	.000	.000	.000	-99	-0	0	0	0	1.000	1	/C-4	0.0
1994	Sea-A	9	25	2	5	1	0	0	2	1	6	.200	.259	.240	29	-3	0	0	0	1.000	-3	/C-9	-0.5
Total	3	22	32	3	6	2	0	0	2	2	8	.188	.257	.250	33	-3	0	0	0	1.000	-1	/C-22	-0.4

■ DAVE HOWARD

Howard, David Austin "Del" b: 5/1/1889, Washington, D.C. d: 1/26/56, Dallas, Tex. BR/TR, 5'11", 165 lbs. Deb: 5/8/12

YEAR	TM/L	G	AB	R	H	2B	3B	HR	RBI	BB	SO	AVG	OBP	SLG	PRO+	BR/A	SB	CS	SBR	FA	FR	G/POS	TPR
1912	Was-A	1	0	1	0	0	0	0	0	0		—	—	—	—	0	0			.000	-0	R	0.0
1915	Bro-F	24	36	5	8	1	0	0	1	1	8	.222	.243	.250	39	-4	0			.925	3	2-12/O-2,S-1,3-1	-0.1
Total	2	25	36	6	8	1	0	0	1	1	8	.222	.243	.250	39	-4	0			.925	3	/2-12,O-2,3-1,S-1	-0.1

■ DAVID HOWARD

Howard, David Wayne b: 2/26/67, Sarasota, Fla. BB/TR, 6', 175 lbs. Deb: 4/14/91 F

YEAR	TM/L	G	AB	R	H	2B	3B	HR	RBI	BB	SO	AVG	OBP	SLG	PRO+	BR/A	SB	CS	SBR	FA	FR	G/POS	TPR
1991	KC-A	94	236	20	51	7	0	1	17	16	45	.216	.269	.258	46	-17	3	2	-0	.962	19	S-63,2-26/3-1,OD	0.6
1992	KC-A	74	219	19	49	6	2	1	18	15	43	.224	.274	.283	55	-13	3	4	-2	.976	-3	S-74/O-2	-1.3
1993	KC-A	15	24	5	8	0	1	0	2	2	5	.333	.385	.417	109	0	1	0	0	.927	2	/2-7,S-3,3-2,O-1	0.2

YEAR	TM/L	G	AB	R	H	2B	3B	HR	RBI	BB	SO	AVG	OBP	SLG	PRO+	BR/A	SB	CS	SBR	FA	FR	G/POS	TPR
1994	KC-A	46	83	9	19	4	0	1	13	11	23	.229	.319	.313	61	-5	3	2	-0	1.000	8	3-25,S-15/2-3,OPD	0.4
1995	KC-A	95	255	23	62	13	4	0	19	24	41	.243	.311	.325	65	-13	6	1	1	.994	15	2-41,S-33,O-30,/1D	0.6
1996	KC-A	143	420	51	92	14	5	4	48	40	74	.219	.293	.305	52	-31	5	6	-2	**.982**	19	*S-135/2-3,1-2,O-1	-0.3
1997	KC-A	80	162	24	39	8	1	1	13	10	31	.241	.289	.321	58	-10	2	2	-1	.973	7	2-34,O-23/S-9,3D	-0.2
1998	StL-N	46	102	15	25	1	1	2	12	12	22	.245	.325	.333	72	-4	0	0	0	1.000	4	2-19,S-16,3-14,/O-2	0.1
Total	8	593	1501	166	345	53	14	10	142	130	284	.230	.294	.304	57	-93	23	17	-3	.976	70	S-348,2-133/O3D1P	0.1

■ DOUG HOWARD

Howard, Douglas Lynn b: 2/6/48, Salt Lake City, Utah BR/TR, 6'3", 185 lbs. Deb: 9/6/72

YEAR	TM/L	G	AB	R	H	2B	3B	HR	RBI	BB	SO	AVG	OBP	SLG	PRO+	BR/A	SB	CS	SBR	FA	FR	G/POS	TPR
1972	Cal-A	11	38	4	10	1	0	0	2	1	3	.263	.300	.289	81	-1	0	0	0	1.000	-1	/O-8,1-1,3-1	-0.2
1973	Cal-A	8	21	2	2	0	0	0	1	1	6	.095	.136	.095	-37	-4	0	0	0	1.000	-1	/O-6,1-1,3-1	-0.5
1974	Cal-A	22	39	5	9	0	1	0	5	2	1	.231	.268	.282	62	-2	1	0	0	1.000	-2	/O-8,1-5,D-3	-0.4
1975	StL-N	17	29	1	6	1	0	1	1	0	7	.207	.207	.310	41	-2	0	0	0	1.000	2	/1-7	-0.1
1976	Cle-A	39	90	7	19	4	0	0	13	3	13	.211	.245	.256	47	-6	1	1	-0	.991	1	1-32/O-2,D-4	-0.7
Total	5	97	217	19	46	5	1	1	22	7	30	.212	.243	.258	46	-15	2	1	0	.994	-1	/1-46,O-24,D-7,3-2	-1.9

■ ELSTON HOWARD

Howard, Elston Gene b: 2/23/29, St.Louis, Mo. d: 12/14/80, New York, N.Y. BR/TR, 6'2", 200 lbs. Deb: 4/14/55 C

YEAR	TM/L	G	AB	R	H	2B	3B	HR	RBI	BB	SO	AVG	OBP	SLG	PRO+	BR/A	SB	CS	SBR	FA	FR	G/POS	TPR
1955	*NY-A	97	279	33	81	8	7	10	43	20	36	.290	.340	.477	120	6	0	0	0	.978	2	O-75/C-9	0.5
1956	*NY-A	98	290	35	76	8	3	5	34	21	30	.262	.314	.362	81	-9	0	0	-1	.990	-5	O-65,C-26	-1.5
1957	*NY-A☆	110	356	33	90	13	4	8	44	16	43	.253	.285	.379	81	-11	2	5	-2	.961	-12	O-71,C-32/1-2	-2.8
1958	*NY-A☆	103	376	45	118	19	5	11	66	22	60	.314	.352	.479	131	14	1	1	-0	.997	2	C-67,O-24/1-5	1.9
1959	NY-A☆	125	443	59	121	24	6	18	73	20	57	.273	.309	.476	116	7	0	1	-1	.985	-2	1-50,C-43,O-28	0.2
1960	*NY-A★	107	323	29	79	11	3	6	39	28	43	.245	.305	.353	82	-9	3	0	1	.987	2	C-91/O-1	-0.1
1961	*NY-A★	129	446	64	155	17	5	21	77	28	65	.348	.390	.549	156	33	0	3	-2	.993	7	*C-111/1-9	4.2
1962	*NY-A★	136	494	63	138	23	5	21	91	31	76	.279	.323	.474	115	8	1	1	-0	.995	-1	*C-129	1.2
1963	*NY-A★	135	487	75	140	21	6	28	85	35	68	.287	.343	.528	141	25	0	0	0	.994	-3	*C-132	2.7
1964	*NY-A★	150	550	63	172	27	3	15	84	48	73	.313	.373	.455	127	20	1	1	-0	**.998**	11	*C-146	3.9
1965	*NY-A☆	110	391	38	91	15	1	9	45	24	65	.233	.279	.345	77	-13	0	0	0	.991	-5	C-95/1-5,O-1	-1.3
1966	NY-A	126	410	38	105	19	2	6	35	37	65	.256	.319	.356	97	-1	0	0	0	.985	-4	*C-100,1-13	0.0
1967	NY-A	66	199	13	39	6	0	3	17	12	36	.196	.249	.271	56	-11	0	0	0	.984	-1	C-48/1-1	-1.0
	*Bos-A	42	116	9	17	3	0	1	11	9	24	.147	.214	.198	21	-11	0	0	0	.996	2	C-41	-0.8
	Yr	108	315	22	56	9	0	4	28	21	60	.178	.236	.244	42	-23	0	0	0	.990	1	C-89/1-1	-1.8
1968	Bos-A	71	203	22	49	4	0	5	18	22	45	.241	.319	.335	92	-2	1	1	-0	.995	-3	C-68	-0.1
Total	14	1605	5363	619	1471	218	50	167	762	373	786	.274	.325	.427	108	48	9	14	-6	.993	-9	*C-1138,O-265/1-85	7.0

■ FRANK HOWARD

Howard, Frank Oliver "Hondo" or "The Capital Punisher" b: 8/8/36, Columbus, Ohio BR/TR, 6'7", 255 lbs. Deb: 9/10/58 MC

YEAR	TM/L	G	AB	R	H	2B	3B	HR	RBI	BB	SO	AVG	OBP	SLG	PRO+	BR/A	SB	CS	SBR	FA	FR	G/POS	TPR
1958	LA-N	8	29	3	7	1	0	1	2	1	11	.241	.267	.379	66	-1	0	0	0	1.000	0	/O-8	-0.2
1959	LA-N	9	21	2	3	0	1	1	6	2	9	.143	.217	.381	52	-2	0	0	0	1.000	-0	/O-6	-0.2
1960	LA-N	117	448	54	120	15	2	23	77	32	108	.268	.321	.464	105	2	0	1	-1	.984	-2	*O-115/1-4	-0.7
1961	LA-N	92	267	36	79	10	2	15	45	21	50	.296	.349	.517	116	5	0	1	-1	.934	-4	O-65/1-7	-0.3
1962	LA-N	141	493	80	146	25	6	31	119	39	108	.296	.349	.560	148	30	1	0	0	.972	2	*O-131	2.5
1963	*LA-N	123	417	58	114	16	1	28	64	33	116	.273	.333	.518	151	25	1	2	-1	.960	-1	*O-111	1.9
1964	LA-N	134	433	60	98	13	2	24	69	51	113	.226	.308	.432	114	7	1	0	0	.979	-7	*O-122	-0.5
1965	Was-A	149	516	53	149	22	6	21	84	55	112	.289	.360	.477	138	25	0	0	0	.981	-8	*O-138	1.2
1966	Was-A	146	493	52	137	19	4	18	71	53	104	.278	.349	.442	127	17	1	1	-0	.982	-2	*O-135	0.9
1967	Was-A	149	519	71	133	20	2	36	89	60	155	.256	.339	.511	154	33	0	1	-1	.986	-7	*O-141/1-4	2.1
1968	Was-A★	158	598	79	164	28	3	**44**	106	54	141	.274	.340	**.552**	**172**	49	0	0	0	.955	2	*O-107,1-55	4.6
1969	Was-A★	161	592	111	175	17	2	48	111	102	96	.296	.403	.574	180	64	1	0	0	.974	-18	*O-114,1-70	3.7
1970	Was-A★	161	566	90	160	15	1	**44**	**126**	**132**	125	.283	.420	.546	173	61	1	2	-1	.973	-9	*O-120,1-48	4.2
1971	Was-A★	153	549	60	153	25	2	26	83	77	121	.279	.369	.474	146	33	1	0	0	.993	3	*O-100,1-68	2.8
1972	Tex-A	95	287	28	70	9	0	9	31	42	55	.244	.342	.369	117	7	1	0	0	.981	-6	1-66,O-21	-0.6
	Det-A	14	33	1	8	1	0	1	7	4	8	.242	.324	.364	101	0	0	0	0	.952	-1	1-10/O-1	-0.1
	Yr	109	320	29	78	10	0	10	38	46	63	.244	.341	.369	115	7	1	0	0	.978	-7	1-76,O-22	-0.7
1973	Det-A	85	227	26	58	9	1	12	29	24	28	.256	.327	.463	113	3	0	1	-1	.923	-1	D-76/1-2	0.0
Total	16	1895	6488	864	1774	245	35	382	1119	782	1460	.273	.355	.499	143	357	8	9	-3	.975	-57	*O-1435,1-334/D-76	21.3

■ DEL HOWARD

Howard, George Elmer b: 12/24/1877, Kenney, Ill. d: 12/24/56, Seattle, Wash. BL/TR, 6', 180 lbs. Deb: 4/15/05 F

YEAR	TM/L	G	AB	R	H	2B	3B	HR	RBI	BB	SO	AVG	OBP	SLG	PRO+	BR/A	SB	CS	SBR	FA	FR	G/POS	TPR
1905	Pit-N	123	435	56	127	18	5	2	63	27		.292	.345	.370	110	5	19			.978	-7	1-90,O-28/P-1	-0.6
1906	Bos-N	147	545	46	142	19	8	1	54	26		.261	.306	.330	101	-1	17			.911	-12	O-87,2-45,S-14,/1-2	-1.8
1907	Bos-N	50	187	20	51	4	2	1	13	11		.273	.330	.332	108	2	11			.969	-3	O-45/2-3	-0.3
	*Chi-N	51	148	10	34	2	2	0	13	6		.230	.269	.270	65	-6	3			.972	-4	1-33/O-8	-1.2
	Yr	101	335	30	85	6	4	1	26	17		.254	.304	.304	88	-5	14			.961	-6	O-53,1-33/2-3	-1.5
1908	*Chi-N	96	315	42	88	7	3	1	26	23		.279	.338	.330	109	3	11			.965	-5	O-81/1-5	-0.6
1909	Chi-N	69	203	25	40	4	2	1	24	18		.197	.282	.251	64	-8	6			.980	0	1-57	-1.0
Total	5	536	1833	199	482	54	22	6	193	111		.263	.318	.326	98	-5	67			.946	-30	O-249,1-187/2SP	-5.5

■ IVAN HOWARD

Howard, Ivan Chester b: 10/12/1882, Kenney, Ill. d: 3/30/67, Medford, Ore. BB/TR, 5'10", 170 lbs. Deb: 4/25/14 F

YEAR	TM/L	G	AB	R	H	2B	3B	HR	RBI	BB	SO	AVG	OBP	SLG	PRO+	BR/A	SB	CS	SBR	FA	FR	G/POS	TPR
1914	StL-A	81	209	21	51	6	2	0	20	28	42	.244	.342	.292	94	-0	14	10	-2	.936	-7	3-34,1-28/O-3,S-1	-1.0
1915	StL-A	113	324	43	90	10	7	2	43	43	48	.278	.368	.370	126	11	29	12	2	.992	5	1-48,3-23,O-17,/2S	1.7
1916	Cle-A	81	246	20	46	11	5	0	23	30	34	.187	.298	.272	68	-9	9			.970	7	2-65/1-7	-0.1
1917	Cle-A	27	39	7	4	0	0	0	0	3	5	.103	.167	.103	-17	-5	1			.833	2	/3-6,2-4,O-4	-0.4
Total	4	302	818	91	191	27	14	2	86	104	129	.233	.331	.308	92	-4	53	22		.990	6	/1-83,2-71,3-63,OS	0.2

■ LARRY HOWARD

Howard, Lawrence Rayford b: 6/6/45, Columbus, Ohio BR/TR, 6'3", 200 lbs. Deb: 8/9/70

YEAR	TM/L	G	AB	R	H	2B	3B	HR	RBI	BB	SO	AVG	OBP	SLG	PRO+	BR/A	SB	CS	SBR	FA	FR	G/POS	TPR
1970	Hou-N	31	88	11	27	6	0	2	16	10	23	.307	.378	.443	124	3	0	0	0	.993	-5	C-26/1-2,O-1	-0.1
1971	Hou-N	24	64	6	15	3	0	2	14	3	17	.234	.269	.375	83	-2	0	1	-1	.992	2	C-22	0.1
1972	Hou-N	54	157	16	35	7	0	2	13	17	30	.223	.299	.306	74	-5	0	0	0	.980	0	C-53/O-1	-0.4
1973	Hou-N	20	48	3	8	3	0	0	4	5	12	.167	.245	.229	32	-4	0	0	0	.989	-1	C-20	-0.5
	Atl-N	4	8	0	1	0	0	0	0	2	3	.125	.300	.125	20	-1	0	0	0	1.000	-0	/C-2	-0.1
	Yr	24	56	3	9	3	0	0	4	7	15	.161	.254	.214	31	-5	0	0	0	.990	-1	C-22	-0.6
Total	4	133	365	36	86	19	0	6	47	37	85	.236	.306	.337	81	-9	0	1	-1	.986	-4	C-123/O-2,1-2	-1.0

■ MATT HOWARD

Howard, Matthew Christopher b: 9/22/67, Fall River, Mass. BR/TR, 5'10", 170 lbs. Deb: 5/17/96

YEAR	TM/L	G	AB	R	H	2B	3B	HR	RBI	BB	SO	AVG	OBP	SLG	PRO+	BR/A	SB	CS	SBR	FA	FR	G/POS	TPR
1996	NY-A	35	54	9	11	1	0	1	9	2	8	.204	.232	.278	28	-6	1	0	0	.976	-5	2-30/3-6	-0.9

■ MIKE HOWARD

Howard, Michael Fredric b: 4/2/58, Seattle, Wash. BB/TR, 6'2", 185 lbs. Deb: 9/12/81

YEAR	TM/L	G	AB	R	H	2B	3B	HR	RBI	BB	SO	AVG	OBP	SLG	PRO+	BR/A	SB	CS	SBR	FA	FR	G/POS	TPR
1981	NY-N	14	24	4	4	1	0	0	3	4	6	.167	.286	.208	43	-2	2	0	1	.952	-1	O-14	-0.2
1982	NY-N	33	39	5	7	0	0	1	3	6	7	.179	.304	.256	59	-2	2	0	1	1.000	-3	O-22/2-3	-0.4
1983	NY-N	1	3	0	1	0	0	0	0	0	0	.333	.333	.333	86	-0	0	0	0	.000	0	/O-1	0.0
Total	3	48	66	9	12	1	0	1	7	10	14	.182	.299	.242	54	-4	4	0	1	.980	-4	/O-37,2-3	-0.6

■ PAUL HOWARD

Howard, Paul Joseph "Del" b: 5/20/1884, Boston, Mass. d: 8/29/68, Miami, Fla. BR/TR, 5'8", 170 lbs. Deb: 9/16/09

YEAR	TM/L	G	AB	R	H	2B	3B	HR	RBI	BB	SO	AVG	OBP	SLG	PRO+	BR/A	SB	CS	SBR	FA	FR	G/POS	TPR
1909	Bos-A	6	15	2	3	1	0	0	2	3		.200	.368	.267	99	0	0			1.000	-1	/O-6	-0.1

■ STEVE HOWARD

Howard, Steven Bernard b: 12/7/63, Oakland, Cal. BR/TR, 6'2", 205 lbs. Deb: 6/16/90

YEAR	TM/L	G	AB	R	H	2B	3B	HR	RBI	BB	SO	AVG	OBP	SLG	PRO+	BR/A	SB	CS	SBR	FA	FR	G/POS	TPR
1990	Oak-A	21	52	5	12	4	0	0	1	4	17	.231	.286	.308	69	-2	0	0	0	.933	-4	O-14/D-7	-0.7

■ THOMAS HOWARD

Howard, Thomas Sylvester b: 12/11/64, Middletown, Ohio BB/TR, 6'2", 205 lbs. Deb: 7/3/90

YEAR	TM/L	G	AB	R	H	2B	3B	HR	RBI	BB	SO	AVG	OBP	SLG	PRO+	BR/A	SB	CS	SBR	FA	FR	G/POS	TPR
1990	SD-N	20	44	4	12	2	0	0	0	0	11	.273	.273	.318	61	-2	0	1	-1	.950	-2	O-13	-0.5
1991	SD-N	106	281	30	70	12	3	4	22	24	57	.249	.310	.356	84	-6	10	7	-1	.995	3	O-86	-0.6
1992	SD-N	5	3	1	1	0	0	0	0	0	0	.333	.333	.333	88	-0	0	0	0	.000	0	/H	0.0
	Cle-A	117	358	36	99	15	2	2	32	17	60	.277	.309	.346	85	-8	15	8	-0	.990	-7	O-97/D-2	-1.7
1993	Cle-A	74	178	26	42	7	0	3	23	12	42	.236	.284	.326	64	-9	5	1	1	.977	-3	O-47/D-7	-1.2

YEAR	TM/L	G	AB	R	H	2B	3B	HR	RBI	BB	SO	AVG	OBP	SLG	PRO+	BR/A	SB	CS	SBR	FA	FR	G/POS	TPR
	Cin-N	38	141	22	39	8	3	4	13	12	21	.277	.333	.461	110	2	5	6	-2	.987	2	O-37	0.1
1994	Cin-N	83	178	24	47	11	0	5	24	10	30	.264	.303	.410	85	-4	4	2	0	.965	-5	O-57	-1.0
1995	*Cin-N	113	281	42	85	15	2	3	26	20	37	.302	.351	.402	98	-1	17	8	0	.985	-9	O-82	-1.0
1996	Cin-N	121	360	50	98	19	10	6	42	17	51	.272	.311	.431	93	-5	6	5	-1	.982	-9	*O-103	-1.7
1997	*Hou-N	107	255	24	63	16	1	3	22	26	48	.247	.324	.353	80	-7	1	2	-1	1.000	-2	O-62	-1.1
1998	LA-N	47	76	9	14	4	0	2	4	3	15	.184	.215	.316	38	-7	1	0	0	1.000	-3	O-29/D-1	-1.0
Total	9	831	2155	268	570	109	21	32	208	141	372	.265	.312	.379	85	-48	64	40	-5	.986	-35	O-613/D-10	-9.7

■ WILBUR HOWARD

Howard, Wilbur Leon b: 1/8/49, Lowell, N.C. BB/TR, 6′2″, 175 lbs. Deb: 9/4/73

1973	Mil-A	16	39	3	8	0	0	0	1	2	10	.205	.244	.205	28	-4	0	1	-1	.969	2	O-12/D-1	-0.2
1974	Hou-N	64	111	19	24	4	0	2	5	5	18	.216	.250	.306	57	-7	4	5	-2	1.000	-4	O-50	-1.5
1975	Hou-N	121	392	62	111	16	8	0	21	21	67	.283	.325	.365	98	-3	32	11	3	.995	1	O-95	-0.2
1976	Hou-N	94	191	26	42	7	2	1	18	7	28	.220	.247	.293	58	-11	7	5	-1	.961	-8	O-63/2-2	-2.3
1977	Hou-N	87	187	22	48	6	0	2	13	5	30	.257	.276	.321	65	-10	11	1	3	.990	-4	O-62/2-4	-1.3
1978	Hou-N	84	148	17	34	4	1	1	13	5	22	.230	.269	.291	61	-8	6	2	1	1.000	-7	O-38/C-3,2-1	-1.7
Total	6	466	1068	149	267	37	11	6	71	45	175	.250	.284	.322	73	-42	60	25	3	.987	-20	O-320/2-7,C-3,D-1	-7.2

■ JIM HOWARTH

Howarth, James Eugene b: 3/7/47, Biloxi, Miss. BL/TL, 5′11″, 175 lbs. Deb: 9/5/71

1971	SF-N	7	13	3	3	1	0	0	2	3	3	.231	.375	.308	97	0	0	0	0	1.000	-1	/O-6	-0.1
1972	SF-N	74	119	16	28	4	0	1	7	16	18	.235	.326	.294	76	-3	3	2	-0	1.000	-3	O-25/1-4	-0.9
1973	SF-N	65	90	8	18	1	1	0	7	7	8	.200	.258	.233	36	-8	0	0	0	1.000	-5	O-33/1-1	-1.4
1974	SF-N	6	4	0	0	0	0	0	0	0	0	.000	.000	.000	-96	-1	0	0	0	.000	-0	/O-1	-0.1
Total	4	152	226	27	49	6	1	1	16	26	29	.217	.298	.265	58	-12	3	2	-0	1.000	-9	/O-65,1-5	-2.5

■ ART HOWE

Howe, Arthur Henry b: 12/15/46, Pittsburgh, Pa. BR/TR, 6′2″, 190 lbs. Deb: 7/10/74 MC

1974	*Pit-N	29	74	10	18	4	1	1	5	9	13	.243	.325	.365	96	-0	0	0	0	.937	4	3-20/S-2	0.3
1975	Pit-N	63	146	13	25	9	0	1	10	15	15	.171	.248	.253	40	-12	1	0	0	.938	3	3-42/S-3	-0.9
1976	Hou-N	21	29	0	4	1	0	0	0	6	6	.138	.286	.172	35	-2	0	0	0	.938	2	/3-8,2-2	-0.1
1977	Hou-N	125	413	44	109	23	7	8	58	41	60	.264	.338	.412	110	5	0	1	-1	.985	6	2-96,3-19,S-11	1.7
1978	Hou-N	119	420	46	123	33	3	7	55	34	41	.293	.347	.436	127	14	2	3	-1	.977	-4	*2-107,3-11/1-1	1.7
1979	Hou-N	118	355	32	88	15	2	6	33	36	37	.248	.319	.352	88	-6	3	1	0	.991	6	2-68,3-59/1-3	0.3
1980	*Hou-N	110	321	34	91	12	5	10	46	34	29	.283	.354	.445	132	13	1	0	0	.986	1	1-77,3-25/S-5,2-3	1.1
1981	*Hou-N	103	361	43	107	22	4	3	36	41	23	.296	.368	.404	125	12	1	3	-2	.966	5	3-98/1-2	1.5
1982	Hou-N	110	365	29	87	15	1	5	38	41	45	.238	.317	.326	87	-6	2	0	1	.972	8	3-72,1-35	-0.2
1984	StL-N	89	139	17	30	5	0	2	12	18	18	.216	.306	.295	71	-5	0	2	-1	.979	8	3-45,1-11/2-8,S-5	0.1
1985	StL-N	4	3	0	0	0	0	0	0	0	0	.000	.000	.000	-99	-1	0	0	0	1.000	0	/1-1,3-1	-0.1
Total	11	891	2626	268	682	139	23	43	293	275	287	.260	.332	.379	103	10	10	10	-3	.965	38	3-400,2-284,1/S	5.4

■ SHORTY HOWE

Howe, John b: New York, N.Y. Deb: 6/17/1890

1890	NY-N	19	64	4	11	0	0	0	4	3	2	.172	.221	.172	15	-7	3			.887	3	2-18/3-1	-0.2
1893	NY-N	1	5	1	3	0	0	0	2	0	0	.600	.600	.600	219	1	1			.400	-1	/3-1	0.0
Total	2	20	69	5	14	0	0	0	6	3	2	.203	.247	.203	30	-6	4			.400	2	/2-18,3-2	-0.2

■ HARRY HOWELL

Howell, Henry Harry b: 11/14/1876, New Jersey d: 5/22/56, Spokane, Wash. BR/TR, 5′9″, Deb: 10/10/1898 U

1898	Bro-N	2	8	1	2	0	0	0	1	1		.250	.333	.250	68	-0	0			1.000	0	/P-2	0.0
1899	Bal-N	28	82	4	12	2	2	0	3	3		.146	.195	.220	13	-10	0			.940	1	P-28	0.0
1900	*Bro-N	22	42	6	12	2	0	1	6	6		.286	.388	.405	112	1	1			.949	1	P-21	0.0
1901	Bal-A	53	188	26	41	10	5	2	26	5		.218	.242	.356	62	-11	6			.905	-3	P-37/O-9,S-6,1-2,2	-0.5
1902	Bal-A	96	347	42	93	16	11	2	42	18		.268	.312	.395	91	-5	7			.951	-9	P-26,2-26,O3S/1	-1.6
1903	NY-A	40	106	14	23	3	2	1	12	5		.217	.259	.311	66	-4	1			**1.000**	1	P-25/3-7,S-5,1-1,2	-0.4
1904	StL-A	36	113	9	25	5	2	1	6	4		.221	.261	.327	91	-2	0			.971	9	P-34	0.0
1905	StL-A	42	135	9	26	6	2	1	10	3		.193	.216	.289	63	-6	0			.966	18	P-38/O-3	-0.1
1906	StL-A	35	103	5	13	3	1	0	6	6		.126	.174	.175	10	-11	2			.934	8	P-35	0.0
1907	StL-A	44	114	12	27	5	0	2	7	7		.237	.281	.333	96	-1	2			.982	9	P-42/O-2	0.1
1908	StL-A	41	120	10	22	7	0	1	9	4		.183	.210	.267	54	-6	0			.961	0	P-41	0.0
1909	StL-A	18	34	5	6	1	0	0	3	2		.176	.222	.206	38	-2	0			.938	1	P-10/3-7,O-1	0.0
1910	StL-A	1	2	0	0	0	0	0	0	0		.000	.000	.000	-99	-0	0			1.000	0	/P-1	0.0
Total	13	458	1394	143	302	60	25	11	131	64		.217	.257	.319	69	-59	19			.958	36	P-340/O-33,32S1	-2.5

■ DIXIE HOWELL

Howell, Homer Elliott b: 4/24/20, Louisville, Ky. d: 10/5/90, Binghamton, N.Y. BR/TR, 5′11″, 195 lbs. Deb: 5/6/47

1947	Pit-N	76	214	23	59	11	0	4	25	27	34	.276	.357	.383	94	-1	1			.974	-3	C-74	0.0
1949	Cin-N	64	172	17	42	6	1	2	18	8	21	.244	.286	.326	63	-9	0			.987	5	C-56	-0.1
1950	Cin-N	82	224	30	50	9	1	2	22	32	31	.223	.326	.299	65	-11	0			.986	-4	C-81	-1.1
1951	Cin-N	77	207	22	52	6	1	2	18	15	34	.251	.302	.319	66	-10	0	2	-1	.987	4	C-73	-0.5
1952	Cin-N	17	37	4	7	1	1	2	4	3	9	.189	.250	.432	86	-1	0	0	0	.981	1	C-16	0.0
1953	Bro-N	1	1	0	0	0	0	0	0	0	1	.000	.000	.000	-98	-0	0	0	0	.000	0	H	0.0
1955	Bro-N	16	42	2	11	4	0	0	5	1	7	.262	.279	.357	66	-2	0	0	0	.981	-2	C-13	-0.3
1956	Bro-N	7	13	0	3	2	0	0	1	1	3	.231	.286	.385	72	-1	0	0	0	1.000	-0	/C-6	-0.1
Total	8	340	910	98	224	39	4	12	93	87	140	.246	.315	.337	73	-35	1	2		.984	2	C-319	-2.1

■ JACK HOWELL

Howell, Jack Robert b: 8/18/61, Tucson, Ariz. BL/TR, 6′, 201 lbs. Deb: 5/20/85

1985	Cal-A	43	137	19	27	4	0	5	18	16	33	.197	.281	.336	68	-6	1	1	-0	.931	-1	3-42	-0.8
1986	*Cal-A	63	151	26	41	14	2	4	21	19	28	.272	.353	.470	123	5	2	0	1	.977	-1	3-39/O-8,D-2	0.4
1987	Cal-A	138	449	64	110	18	5	23	64	57	118	.245	.333	.461	111	7	4	3	-1	.987	-8	O-89,3-48,2-13	-0.5
1988	Cal-A	154	500	59	127	32	2	16	63	46	130	.254	.324	.422	110	6	2	6	-3	.953	-20	*3-152/O-2	-1.8
1989	Cal-A	144	474	56	108	19	4	20	52	52	125	.228	.308	.411	103	1	0	3	-2	**.974**	23	*3-142/O-4	2.3
1990	Cal-A	105	316	35	72	19	1	8	33	46	61	.228	.328	.370	97	-1	3	0	1	.939	7	*3-102/1-1,S-1	0.8
1991	Cal-A	32	81	11	17	2	0	2	7	11	11	.210	.304	.309	70	-3	1	1	-0	.968	2	2-12/3-8,O-5,1-3,D	-0.2
	SD-N	58	160	24	33	3	1	6	16	18	33	.206	.287	.350	76	-5	0	0	0	.985	6	3-54	0.1
1996	Cal-A	66	126	20	34	4	1	8	21	10	30	.270	.324	.508	106	0	0	1	-1	.884	-2	3-43/1-2,2-1,D-4	-0.2
1997	Ana-A	77	174	25	45	7	0	14	34	13	36	.259	.310	.540	117	3	1	0	0	.976	1	3-24,D-22,1-12	0.3
1998	Hou-N	24	38	4	11	5	0	1	7	4	12	.289	.357	.500	122	1	0	0	0	1.000	2	1-10/3-2	0.3
Total	10	904	2606	343	625	127	16	107	336	292	617	.240	.319	.424	103	8	14	15	-5	.958	8	3-656,O-108/D12S	0.7

■ RED HOWELL

Howell, Murray Donald "Porky" b: 1/29/09, Atlanta, Ga. d: 10/1/50, Travelers Rest, S.C BR/TR, 6′, 215 lbs. Deb: 4/24/41

1941	Cle-A	11	7	0	2	0	0	0	2	4	2	.286	.545	.286	132	1	0	0	0	.000	0	H	0.1

■ PAT HOWELL

Howell, Patrick O'Neal b: 8/31/68, Mobile, Ala. BB/TR, 5′11″, 155 lbs. Deb: 7/10/92

1992	NY-N	31	75	9	14	1	0	0	1	2	15	.187	.218	.200	19	-8	4	2	0	1.000	-0	O-28	-1.0

■ ROY HOWELL

Howell, Roy Lee b: 12/18/53, Lompoc, Cal. BL/TR, 6′1″, 190 lbs. Deb: 9/9/74

1974	Tex-A	13	44	2	11	1	0	1	3	2	10	.250	.283	.341	81	-1	0	0	0	.906	-2	3-12	-0.3
1975	Tex-A	125	383	43	96	15	2	10	51	39	79	.251	.325	.379	99	-1	2	2	-1	.933	-7	*3-115/D-5	-0.8
1976	Tex-A	140	491	55	124	28	2	8	53	30	106	.253	.297	.367	92	-6	1	0	0	.926	-8	*3-130/D-8	-1.5
1977	Tex-A	7	17	0	0	0	0	0	0	2	4	.000	.105	.000	-68	-4	0	0	0	1.000	-0	/O-2,1-1,3-1,D-2	-0.4
	Tor-A	96	364	41	115	17	1	10	44	42	76	.316	.388	.451	126	14	4	1	1	.953	-7	3-87/D-8	0.7
	Yr	103	381	41	115	17	1	10	44	44	80	.302	.376	.430	117	10	4	1	1	.954	-7	3-88,D-10/O-2,1-1	0.3
1978	Tor-A★	140	551	67	149	28	3	8	61	44	78	.270	.326	.376	95	-4	0	1	-1	.950	11	*3-131/O-5,D-1	0.4
1979	Tor-A	138	511	60	126	28	4	15	72	42	91	.247	.311	.405	90	-8	1	4	-2	.952	-1	*3-133/D-4	-1.2
1980	Tor-A	142	528	51	142	28	9	10	57	50	92	.269	.338	.413	100	-0	0	0	0	.958	-18	*3-138/D-2	-2.0
1981	*Mil-A	76	244	37	58	13	1	6	33	23	39	.238	.309	.373	101	-0	0	0	0	.958	-6	3-53,D-13/1-3,O-1	-0.8
1982	*Mil-A	98	300	31	78	11	2	4	38	21	39	.260	.308	.350	86	-6	0	2	-1	.933	-1	D-84/1-4,O-2	-1.2

YEAR	TM/L	G	AB	R	H	2B	3B	HR	RBI	BB	SO	AVG	OBP	SLG	PRO+	BR/A	SB	CS	SBR	FA	FR	G/POS	TPR
1983	Mil-A	69	194	23	54	9	6	4	25	15	29	.278	.330	.448	121	5	1	3	-2	.960	1	D-54/1-2	0.2
1984	Mil-A	68	164	12	38	5	1	4	17	8	32	.232	.284	.348	77	-5	0	1	-1	.907	1	3-46/1-4,D-8	-0.5
Total	11	1112	3791	422	991	183	31	80	454	318	675	.261	.322	.389	97	-17	9	14	-6	.944	-35	3-846,D-189/1-14,O	-7.4
■ **BILL HOWERTON**	Howerton, William Ray "Hopalong" b: 12/12/21, Lompoc, Cal. BL/TR, 5'11", 185 lbs. Deb: 9/11/49																						
1949	StL-N	9	13	1	4	1	0	0	1	0	2	.308	.308	.385	81	-0	0			.900	-1	/O-6	-0.2
1950	StL-N	110	313	50	88	20	8	10	59	47	60	.281	.375	.492	120	9	0			.969	-11	O-94	-0.5
1951	StL-N	24	65	10	17	4	1	1	4	10	12	.262	.360	.400	104	1	0	1	-1	.949	1	O-17	0.0
	Pit-N	80	219	29	60	12	2	11	37	26	44	.274	.351	.498	122	6	1	0	0	.950	-8	O-53/3-4	-0.3
	Yr	104	284	39	77	16	3	12	41	36	56	.271	.353	.475	118	7	1	1	-0	.950	-8	O-70/3-4	-0.3
1952	Pit-N	13	25	3	8	1	1	0	4	6	5	.320	.452	.440	144	2	0	0	0	.900	-2	/O-5,3-1	0.0
	NY-N	11	15	2	1	1	0	0	1	3	2	.067	.222	.133	1	-2	0	0	0	1.000	-0	/O-3	-0.2
	Yr	24	40	5	9	2	1	0	5	9	7	.225	.367	.325	92	-0	0	0	0	.938	-2	/O-8,3-1	-0.2
Total	4	247	650	95	178	39	12	22	106	92	125	.274	.364	.472	117	16	1	1		.958	-22	O-178/3-5	-1.2
■ **DANN HOWITT**	Howitt, Dann Paul John b: 2/13/64, Battle Creek, Mich. BL/TR, 6'5", 205 lbs. Deb: 9/15/89																						
1989	Oak-A	3	3	0	0	0	0	0	0	0	2	.000	.000	.000	-99	-1	0	0	0	1.000	-1	/1-1,O-1	-0.1
1990	Oak-A	14	22	3	3	0	1	0	1	3	12	.136	.240	.227	33	-2	0	0	0	1.000	-2	O-11/1-5,3-1	-0.4
1991	Oak-A	21	42	5	7	1	0	1	3	1	12	.167	.186	.262	24	-4	0	0	0	1.000	-4	O-20/1-1	-0.9
1992	Oak-A	22	48	1	6	0	0	1	2	5	4	.125	.208	.188	12	-6	0	0	0	.951	1	O-19/1-4,D-1	-0.6
	Sea-A	13	37	6	10	4	1	1	8	3	5	.270	.325	.514	131	1	1	1	-0	1.000	1	O-11	0.2
	Yr	35	85	7	16	4	1	2	10	8	9	.188	.258	.329	66	-4	1	1	-0	.970	2	O-30/1-4,D-1	-0.4
1993	Sea-A	32	76	6	16	3	1	2	8	4	18	.211	.250	.355	60	-5	0	0	0	1.000	-5	O-29/D-2	-1.0
1994	Chi-A	10	14	4	5	3	0	0	0	1	7	.357	.400	.571	149	1	0	0	0	1.000	-2	/O-7,1-4	-0.1
Total	6	115	242	25	47	11	3	5	22	17	60	.194	.247	.326	57	-15	1	1	-0	.987	-12	/O-98,1-15,D-3,3-1	-2.9
■ **DAN HOWLEY**	Howley, Daniel Philip "Howling Dan" or "Dapper Dan" b: 10/16/1885, Weymouth, Mass. d: 3/10/44, Weymouth, Mass. BR/TR, 6', 187 lbs. Deb: 5/15/13 MC																						
1913	Phi-N	26	32	5	4	2	0	0	2	4	4	.125	.222	.188	17	-3	3			.954	1	C-22	-0.2
■ **DICK HOWSER**	Howser, Richard Dalton b: 5/14/36, Miami, Fla. d: 6/17/87, Kansas City, Mo. BR/TR, 5'8", 155 lbs. Deb: 4/11/61 MC																						
1961	KC-A★	158	611	108	171	29	6	3	45	92	38	.280	.379	.362	97	1	37	9	6	.950	-17	*S-157	0.3
1962	KC-A	83	286	53	68	8	3	6	34	38	8	.238	.329	.350	79	-8	19	2	5	.962	-8	S-72	-0.5
1963	KC-A	15	41	4	8	0	0	0	1	7	3	.195	.313	.195	44	-3	0	0	0	.957	-4	S-10	-0.6
	Cle-A	49	162	25	40	5	0	1	10	22	18	.247	.337	.296	80	-4	9	3	1	.950	-17	S-44	-1.7
	Yr	64	203	29	48	5	0	1	11	29	21	.236	.332	.276	72	-7	9	3	1	.951	-20	S-54	-2.3
1964	Cle-A	162	637	101	163	23	4	3	52	76	39	.256	.337	.319	84	-11	20	7	2	.974	3	*S-162	0.6
1965	Cle-A	107	307	47	72	8	2	1	6	57	25	.235	.356	.283	83	-4	17	4	3	.977	-6	S-73,2-17	-0.1
1966	Cle-A	67	140	18	32	9	1	2	4	15	23	.229	.303	.350	87	-2	2	4	-2	.986	-7	2-26,S-26	-0.8
1967	NY-A	63	149	18	40	6	0	0	10	25	15	.268	.381	.309	110	3	1	4	-2	.990	-6	2-22,3-12/S-3	-0.4
1968	NY-A	85	150	24	23	2	1	0	3	35	17	.153	.321	.180	57	-6	0	1	-1	.982	5	2-29/3-2,S-1	0.0
Total	8	789	2483	398	617	90	17	16	165	367	186	.248	.348	.318	86	-34	105	34	11	.963	-56	S-548/2-94,3-14	-3.2
■ **DUMMY HOY**	Hoy, William Ellsworth b: 5/23/1862, Houcktown, Ohio d: 12/15/61, Cincinnati, Ohio BL/TR, 5'6", 160 lbs. Deb: 4/20/1888																						
1888	Was-N	136	503	77	138	10	8	2	29	69	48	.274	.374	.338	136	25	**82**			.897	7	*O-136	2.7
1889	Was-N	127	507	98	139	11	6	0	39	75	30	.274	.374	.320	101	6	35			.890	-4	*O-127	-0.1
1890	Buf-P	122	493	107	147	17	8	1	53	94	36	.298	.418	.371	122	24	39			.912	6	*O-122/2-1	2.0
1891	StL-a	141	567	136	165	14	5	5	66	**119**	25	.291	.424	.360	108	7	59			.909	-1	*O-141	0.1
1892	Was-N	152	593	108	166	19	8	3	75	86	23	.280	.375	.354	124	21	60			.884	-12	*O-152	0.2
1893	Was-N	130	564	106	138	12	6	0	45	66	9	.245	.337	.287	68	-23	48			.892	-1	*O-130	-2.5
1894	Cin-N	126	495	114	148	22	13	5	70	87	18	.299	.416	.426	100	2	27			.896	3	*O-126	-0.3
1895	Cin-N	107	429	93	119	21	12	3	55	52	8	.277	.363	.403	94	-5	50			.883	-3	*O-107	-1.3
1896	Cin-N	121	443	120	132	23	7	4	57	65	13	.298	.403	.409	107	6	50			.946	5	*O-120	0.1
1897	Cin-N	128	497	87	145	24	6	2	42	54		.292	.375	.376	92	-5	37			.934	7	*O-128	-0.6
1898	Lou-N	148	582	104	177	15	16	6	66	49		.304	.367	.416	126	19	37			.946	6	*O-148	1.3
1899	Lou-N	154	633	116	194	17	13	5	49	61		.306	.376	.398	113	12	32			.927	-6	*O-154	-0.5
1901	Chi-A	132	527	112	155	28	11	2	60	**86**		.294	.407	.400	128	25	27			.958	2	*O-132	1.5
1902	Cin-N	72	279	48	81	15	2	2	20	41		.290	.389	.380	125	10	11			.933	-5	O-72	0.0
Total	14	1796	7112	1426	2044	248	121	40	726	1004	210	.287	.386	.373	109	123	594			.915	2	*O-1795/2-1	2.6
■ **KENT HRBEK**	Hrbek, Kent Alan b: 5/21/60, Minneapolis, Minn. BL/TR, 6'4", 235 lbs. Deb: 8/24/81																						
1981	Min-A	24	67	5	16	5	0	1	7	5	9	.239	.301	.358	84	-1	0	0	0	1.000	-2	1-13/D-8	-0.4
1982	Min-A★	140	532	82	160	21	4	23	92	54	80	.301	.365	.485	128	20	3	1	0	.993	-0	*1-138/D-2	1.2
1983	Min-A	141	515	75	153	41	5	16	84	57	71	.297	.370	.489	130	21	4	6	-2	.990	-2	*1-137/D-2	0.8
1984	Min-A	149	559	80	174	31	3	27	107	65	87	.311	.387	.522	142	32	1	1	-0	.990	-6	*1-148/D-1	1.7
1985	Min-A	158	593	78	165	31	2	21	93	67	87	.278	.353	.444	110	9	1	1	-0	.995	1	*1-156/D-2	0.0
1986	Min-A	149	550	85	147	27	1	29	91	71	81	.267	.357	.478	122	17	2	2	-1	.992	-2	*1-147/D-1	0.3
1987	*Min-A	143	477	85	136	20	1	34	90	84	60	.285	.392	.545	140	29	5	2	0	.996	-10	*1-137/D-1	0.9
1988	Min-A	143	510	75	159	31	0	25	76	67	54	.312	.392	.520	149	34	0	3	-2	.997	-6	*1-105,D-37	1.6
1989	Min-A	109	375	59	102	17	0	25	84	53	35	.272	.364	.517	136	18	3	0	1	.995	1	1-89,D-18	1.2
1990	Min-A	143	492	61	141	26	0	22	79	69	45	.287	.382	.474	129	20	5	2	0	**.997**	1	*1-120,D-20/3-1	1.2
1991	*Min-A	132	462	72	131	20	1	20	89	67	48	.284	.374	.461	124	16	4	4	-1	.994	4	*1-128	1.0
1992	Min-A	112	394	52	96	20	0	15	58	71	56	.244	.359	.409	111	7	5	2	0	.997	-1	*1-104/D-8	0.0
1993	Min-A	123	392	60	95	11	1	25	83	71	57	.242	.360	.467	120	12	4	2	0	.995	3	*1-115/D-2	0.5
1994	Min-A	81	274	34	74	11	0	10	53	37	28	.270	.359	.420	100	0	0	0	0	.997	-2	1-72/D-4	-0.7
Total	14	1747	6192	903	1749	312	18	293	1086	838	798	.282	.370	.481	127	233	37	26	-5	.994	-21	*1-1609,D-106/3-1	9.3
■ **WALT HRINIAK**	Hriniak, Walter John b: 5/22/43, Natick, Mass. BL/TR, 5'11", 180 lbs. Deb: 9/10/68 C																						
1968	Atl-N	9	26	0	9	0	0	0	3	0	3	.346	.346	.346	108	0	0	0	0	.967	3	/C-9	0.4
1969	Atl-N	7	7	0	1	0	0	0	0	2	1	.143	.333	.143	38	-0	0	0	0	1.000	-1	/C-6	-0.1
	SD-N	31	66	4	15	0	0	0	1	8	11	.227	.329	.227	61	-3	0	0	0	.981	-2	C-19	-0.4
	Yr	38	73	4	16	0	0	0	1	10	12	.219	.329	.219	58	-4	0	0	0	.982	-3	C-25	-0.5
Total	2	47	99	4	25	0	0	0	4	10	15	.253	.333	.253	71	-3	0	0	0	.977	-0	/C-34	-0.1
■ **AL HUBBARD**	Hubbard, Allen (a.k.a. Al West For 1 Game In 1883) b: 12/9/1860, Westfield, Mass. d: 12/14/30, Newton, Mass. Deb: 9/13/1883																						
1883	Phi-a	2	6	2	2	0	0	0	2	1		.333	.429	.333	138	0				.750	-0	/S-1,C-1	0.0
■ **GLENN HUBBARD**	Hubbard, Glenn Dee b: 9/25/57, Hahn Air Force Base, W.Germany BR/TR, 5'7", 180 lbs. Deb: 7/14/78																						
1978	Atl-N	44	163	15	42	4	0	2	13	10	20	.258	.309	.319	68	-7	2	1	0	.979	3	2-44	0.0
1979	Atl-N	97	325	34	75	12	0	3	29	27	43	.231	.292	.295	56	-19	0	6	-4	.968	5	2-91	-1.3
1980	Atl-N	117	431	55	107	21	3	9	43	49	69	.248	.325	.374	91	-5	7	5	-1	.978	19	*2-117	2.2
1981	Atl-N	99	361	39	85	13	5	6	33	33	59	.235	.303	.349	82	-8	4	2	0	.991	-4	2-98	-0.7
1982	*Atl-N	145	532	75	132	25	1	9	59	59	62	.248	.327	.350	86	-9	4	3	-1	.983	20	*2-144	1.8
1983	Atl-N★	148	517	65	136	24	6	12	70	55	71	.263	.339	.402	97	-2	3	8	-4	.985	22	*2-148	2.4
1984	Atl-N	120	397	53	93	27	2	9	43	55	61	.234	.333	.380	93	-3	4	1	1	.988	20	*2-117	2.2
1985	Atl-N	142	439	51	102	21	0	5	39	56	54	.232	.325	.314	75	-13	4	3	-1	.989	**62**	*2-140	5.4
1986	Atl-N	143	408	42	94	16	1	4	36	66	74	.230	.343	.304	76	-11	3	2	-0	.976	**41**	*2-142	3.5
1987	Atl-N	141	443	69	117	33	2	5	38	77	57	.264	.380	.381	98	1	1	1	-0	.986	**28**	*2-139	3.5
1988	*Oak-A	105	294	35	75	12	2	3	33	33	50	.255	.336	.340	93	-2	1	3	-2	.987	4	*2-104/D-1	0.4
1989	Oak-A	53	131	12	26	6	0	3	12	19	20	.198	.300	.313	76	-4	2	0	1	.968	10	2-48/D-3	0.8
Total	12	1354	4441	545	1084	214	22	70	448	539	640	.244	.330	.349	85	-83	35	35	-11	.983	229	*2-1332/D-4	20.2

■ MIKE HUBBARD
Hubbard, Michael Wayne b: 2/16/71, Lynchburg, Va. BR/TR, 6'1", 180 lbs. Deb: 7/13/95

YEAR	TM/L	G	AB	R	H	2B	3B	HR	RBI	BB	SO	AVG	OBP	SLG	PRO+	BR/A	SB	CS	SBR	FA	FR	G/POS	TPR
1995	Chi-N	15	23	2	4	0	0	0	1	2	2	.174	.240	.174	12	-3	0	0	0	.971	-1	/C-9	-0.4
1996	Chi-N	21	38	1	4	0	0	1	4	0	15	.105	.105	.184	-25	-7	0	0	0	1.000	-0	C-14	-0.6
1997	Chi-N	29	64	4	13	0	0	1	2	2	21	.203	.227	.250	24	-7	0	0	0	.992	3	C-20/3-1	-0.3
1998	Mon-N	32	55	3	8	1	0	1	3	0	17	.145	.161	.218	-3	-8	0	0	0	1.000	-1	C-24/2-1	-0.8
Total	4	97	180	10	29	1	0	3	10	4	55	.161	.184	.217	4	-25	0	0	0	.993	1	/C-67,2-1,3-1	-2.1

■ TRENIDAD HUBBARD
Hubbard, Trenidad Aviel (b: Trent Hubbard) b: 5/11/64, Chicago, Ill. BR/TR, 5'8", 180 lbs. Deb: 7/7/94

YEAR	TM/L	G	AB	R	H	2B	3B	HR	RBI	BB	SO	AVG	OBP	SLG	PRO+	BR/A	SB	CS	SBR	FA	FR	G/POS	TPR
1994	Col-N	18	25	3	7	1	1	1	3	3	4	.280	.357	.520	107	0	0	0	0	1.000	-1	/O-5	-0.1
1995	*Col-N	24	58	13	18	4	0	3	9	8	6	.310	.394	.534	110	0	2	1	0	1.000	-4	O-16	-0.4
1996	Col-N	45	60	12	13	5	1	1	12	9	22	.217	.329	.383	70	-3	2	0	1	1.000	-2	O-19	-0.4
	SF-N	10	29	3	6	0	1	1	2	2	5	.207	.258	.379	68	-1	0	0	0	1.000	1	/O-9	0.0
	Yr	55	89	15	19	5	2	2	14	11	27	.213	.307	.382	68	-4	2	0	1	1.000	-0	O-28	-0.4
1997	Cle-A	7	12	3	3	1	0	0	0	1	3	.250	.308	.333	65	-1	2	0	1	1.000	-2	/O-6	-0.2
1998	LA-N	94	208	29	62	9	1	7	18	18	46	.298	.362	.452	118	5	9	5	-0	.991	-9	O-81/3-1	-0.4
Total	5	198	392	63	109	20	4	13	44	41	86	.278	.352	.449	102	1	15	6	1	.995	-16	O-136/3-1	-1.5

■ KEN HUBBS
Hubbs, Kenneth Douglas b: 12/23/41, Riverside, Cal. d: 2/13/64, Provo, Utah BR/TR, 6'2", 175 lbs. Deb: 9/10/61

YEAR	TM/L	G	AB	R	H	2B	3B	HR	RBI	BB	SO	AVG	OBP	SLG	PRO+	BR/A	SB	CS	SBR	FA	FR	G/POS	TPR
1961	Chi-N	10	28	4	5	1	1	1	2	0	8	.179	.179	.393	46	-2	0	0	0	1.000	-2	/2-8	-0.3
1962	Chi-N	160	661	90	172	24	9	5	49	35	129	.260	.300	.346	71	-28	3	7	-3	.983	4	*2-159	-1.0
1963	Chi-N	154	566	54	133	19	3	8	47	39	93	.235	.287	.322	71	-21	8	9	-3	.974	20	*2-152	1.1
Total	3	324	1255	148	310	44	13	14	98	74	230	.247	.292	.336	70	-51	11	16	-6	.979	23	2-319	-0.2

■ CLARENCE HUBER
Huber, Clarence Bill "Gilly" b: 10/27/1896, Tyler, Tex. d: 2/22/65, Laredo, Tex. BR/TR, 5'10", 165 lbs. Deb: 9/17/20

YEAR	TM/L	G	AB	R	H	2B	3B	HR	RBI	BB	SO	AVG	OBP	SLG	PRO+	BR/A	SB	CS	SBR	FA	FR	G/POS	TPR
1920	Det-A	11	42	4	9	2	1	0	5	0	5	.214	.214	.310	39	-4	0	0	0	.907	2	3-11	-0.1
1921	Det-A	1	0	0	0	0	0	0	0	0	0	—	—	—	—	0	0	0	0	1.000	-0	/3-1	0.0
1925	Phi-N	124	436	46	124	28	5	5	54	17	33	.284	.311	.406	75	-17	3	5	-2	.947	-9	*3-120	-1.9
1926	Phi-N	118	376	45	92	17	7	1	34	42	29	.245	.324	.335	74	-13	9			.956	8	*3-115	0.1
Total	4	254	854	95	225	47	13	6	93	59	67	.263	.313	.370	73	-35	12	5		.948	1	3-247	-1.9

■ OTTO HUBER
Huber, Otto b: 3/12/14, Garfield, N.J. d: 4/9/89, Passaic, N.J. BR/TR, 5'10", 165 lbs. Deb: 6/10/39

YEAR	TM/L	G	AB	R	H	2B	3B	HR	RBI	BB	SO	AVG	OBP	SLG	PRO+	BR/A	SB	CS	SBR	FA	FR	G/POS	TPR
1939	Bos-N	11	22	2	6	1	0	0	3	0	1	.273	.273	.318	63	-1	0			1.000	-0	/2-4,3-4	-0.1

■ DAVE HUDGENS
Hudgens, David Mark b: 12/5/56, Oroville, Cal. BL/TL, 6'2", 210 lbs. Deb: 9/4/83

YEAR	TM/L	G	AB	R	H	2B	3B	HR	RBI	BB	SO	AVG	OBP	SLG	PRO+	BR/A	SB	CS	SBR	FA	FR	G/POS	TPR
1983	Oak-A	6	7	0	1	0	0	0	0	0	3	.143	.143	.143	-22	-1	0	0	0	1.000	-0	/1-3,D-1	-0.1

■ JIMMY HUDGENS
Hudgens, James Price b: 8/24/02, Newburg, Mo. d: 8/26/55, St.Louis, Mo. BL/TR, 6', 180 lbs. Deb: 9/14/23

YEAR	TM/L	G	AB	R	H	2B	3B	HR	RBI	BB	SO	AVG	OBP	SLG	PRO+	BR/A	SB	CS	SBR	FA	FR	G/POS	TPR
1923	StL-N	6	12	2	3	1	0	0	0	3	3	.250	.400	.333	97	0	0	0	0	1.000	1	/1-3,2-1	0.1
1925	Cin-N	3	7	0	3	1	1	0	0	1	1	.429	.500	.857	245	2	0	0	0	1.000	0	/1-3	0.1
1926	Cin-N	17	20	2	5	1	0	0	1	1	0	.250	.286	.300	59	-1	0			1.000	0	/1-6	-0.1
Total	3	26	39	4	11	3	1	0	1	5	4	.282	.364	.410	107	0	0	0		1.000	1	/1-12,2-1	0.1

■ REX HUDLER
Hudler, Rex Allen b: 9/2/60, Tempe, Ariz. BR/TR, 6', 180 lbs. Deb: 9/9/84

YEAR	TM/L	G	AB	R	H	2B	3B	HR	RBI	BB	SO	AVG	OBP	SLG	PRO+	BR/A	SB	CS	SBR	FA	FR	G/POS	TPR
1984	NY-A	9	7	2	1	1	0	0	0	1	5	.143	.333	.286	76	-0	0	0	0	1.000	0	/2-9	0.0
1985	NY-A	20	51	4	8	0	1	0	1	1	9	.157	.173	.196	1	-7	0	1	-1	.977	7	2-16/1-1,S-1	0.0
1986	Bal-A	14	1	1	0	0	0	0	0	0	0	.000	.000	.000	-99	-0	1	0	1	.800	1	2-13/3-1	0.1
1988	Mon-N	77	216	38	59	14	2	4	14	10	34	.273	.305	.412	100	-1	29	7	5	.978	-1	2-41,S-27/O-4	0.6
1989	Mon-N	92	155	21	38	7	0	6	13	6	23	.245	.278	.406	92	-2	15	4	2	.958	-14	2-38,O-23,S-18	-1.4
1990	Mon-N	4	3	1	1	0	0	0	0	0	1	.333	.333	.333	87	-0	0	0	0	.000	0	/H	0.0
	StL-N	89	217	30	61	11	2	7	22	12	31	.281	.325	.447	110	2	18	10	-1	.979	0	O-45,2-10/1-6,3S	0.1
	Yr	93	220	31	62	11	2	7	22	12	32	.282	.325	.445	109	2	18	10	-1	.979	0	O-45,2-10/1-6,3S	0.1
1991	StL-N	101	207	21	47	10	2	1	15	10	29	.227	.263	.309	60	-11	12	8	-1	.981	-3	O-58,1-12/2-5	-1.8
1992	StL-N	61	98	17	24	4	0	3	5	2	23	.245	.267	.378	83	-3	2	6	-3	.957	-8	2-16,O-12/1-8	-1.4
1994	Cal-A	56	124	17	37	8	0	8	20	6	28	.298	.331	.556	122	3	2	2	-1	.971	-2	2-22,O-18/3-4,1D	0.1
1995	Cal-A	84	223	30	59	16	0	6	27	10	48	.265	.311	.417	88	-4	13	0	4	.986	-12	2-52,O-22/1-2,D-3	-1.0
1996	Cal-A	92	302	60	94	20	3	16	40	9	54	.311	.338	.556	120	8	14	5	1	.982	-7	2-53,O-21/1-7,D-8	0.4
1997	Phi-N	50	122	17	27	4	0	5	10	6	28	.221	.264	.377	65	-7	1	0	0	.962	-3	O-35/2-6	-1.0
1998	Phi-N	25	41	2	5	1	0	0	2	4	12	.122	.200	.146	-8	-7	0	0	0	1.000	1	/O-9,1-1	-0.6
Total	13	774	1767	261	461	96	10	56	169	77	325	.261	.297	.422	91	-29	107	43	6	.975	-42	2-281,O-247/S1D3	-5.9

■ JOHNNY HUDSON
Hudson, John Wilson "Mr. Chips" b: 6/30/12, Bryan, Tex. d: 11/7/70, Bryan, Tex. BR/TR, 5'10", 160 lbs. Deb: 6/20/36

YEAR	TM/L	G	AB	R	H	2B	3B	HR	RBI	BB	SO	AVG	OBP	SLG	PRO+	BR/A	SB	CS	SBR	FA	FR	G/POS	TPR
1936	Bro-N	6	12	1	2	0	0	0	0	2	1	.167	.286	.167	24	-1	0			.889	-1	/S-4,2-1	-0.2
1937	Bro-N	13	27	3	5	4	0	0	2	3	9	.185	.267	.333	61	-2	0			.867	-4	S-11/2-1	-0.5
1938	Bro-N	135	498	59	130	21	5	2	37	39	76	.261	.315	.335	77	-15	7			.963	-4	*2-132/S-3	-1.2
1939	Bro-N	109	343	46	87	17	3	2	32	30	36	.254	.317	.338	74	-13	5			.959	-18	S-50,2-45/3-1	-2.4
1940	Bro-N	85	179	13	39	4	3	0	19	9	26	.218	.255	.274	43	-14	2			.921	0	S-38,2-27/3-1	-1.0
1941	Chi-N	50	99	8	20	4	0	0	6	3	15	.202	.225	.242	33	-9	3			.907	-1	S-17,2-13,3-10	-0.8
1945	NY-N	28	11	8	0	0	0	0	0	1	1	.000	.083	.000	-75	-3	0			.875	3	/3-5,2-2	0.0
Total	7	426	1169	138	283	50	11	4	96	87	164	.242	.296	.314	65	-56	17			.962	-25	2-221,S-123/3-17	-6.1

■ FRANK HUELSMAN
Huelsman, Frank Elmer b: 6/5/1874, St.Louis, Mo. d: 6/9/59, Affton, Mo. BR/TR, 6'2", 210 lbs. Deb: 10/3/1897

YEAR	TM/L	G	AB	R	H	2B	3B	HR	RBI	BB	SO	AVG	OBP	SLG	PRO+	BR/A	SB	CS	SBR	FA	FR	G/POS	TPR
1897	StL-N	2	7	0	2	1	0	0	0	0		.286	.286	.429	89	-0	0			.000	-1	/O-2	-0.1
1904	Chi-A	3	6	0	1	1	0	0	0	0		.167	.167	.333	58	-0	0			.000	-1	/O-1	-0.1
	Det-A	4	18	1	6	1	0	0	4	1		.333	.368	.389	144	1	1			1.000	-1	/O-4	0.0
	Chi-A	1	1	0	0	0	0	0	0	0		.000	.000	.000	-99	-0	0			.000	0	H	0.0
	StL-A	20	68	6	15	2	1	0	1	6		.221	.303	.279	90	-1	0			1.000	-3	O-18	-0.5
	Was-A	84	303	21	75	19	4	2	30	24		.248	.313	.356	113	5	6			.960	-3	O-84	-0.4
	Yr	112	396	28	97	23	5	2	35	31		.245	.311	.343	110	5	7			.960	-8	*O-107	-1.0
1905	Was-A	121	421	48	114	28	8	3	62	31		.271	.333	.397	136	17	11			.929	-9	*O-116	0.3
Total	3	235	824	76	213	52	13	5	97	62		.258	.322	.371	123	21	18			.941	-17	O-225	-0.8

■ MIKE HUFF
Huff, Michael Kale b: 8/11/63, Honolulu, Hawaii BR/TR, 6'1", 190 lbs. Deb: 8/7/89

YEAR	TM/L	G	AB	R	H	2B	3B	HR	RBI	BB	SO	AVG	OBP	SLG	PRO+	BR/A	SB	CS	SBR	FA	FR	G/POS	TPR
1989	LA-N	12	25	4	5	1	0	1	2	3	6	.200	.310	.360	93	-0	0	1	-1	1.000	-0	/O-9	-0.1
1991	Cle-A	51	146	28	35	6	1	2	10	25	30	.240	.366	.336	95	0	11	2	2	.990	-3	O-48/2-2	-0.2
	Chi-A	51	97	14	26	4	1	1	15	12	18	.268	.360	.361	103	1	3	2	-0	.986	-11	O-48/2-2,D-2	-1.1
	Yr	102	243	42	61	10	2	3	25	37	48	.251	.364	.346	98	1	14	4	2	.988	-14	O-96/2-4,D-2	-1.3
1992	Chi-A	60	115	13	24	5	0	0	8	10	24	.209	.278	.252	50	-8	1	2	-1	1.000	-10	O-56/D-1	-2.0
1993	Chi-A	43	44	4	8	2	0	1	6	9	15	.182	.333	.295	72	-1	1	0	0	1.000	-12	O-43	-1.3
1994	Tor-A	80	207	31	63	15	3	3	25	27	27	.304	.392	.449	116	6	2	1	0	.992	-6	O-76	-0.2
1995	Tor-A	61	138	14	32	9	1	1	9	22	21	.232	.342	.333	77	-4	1	1	-0	.980	-5	O-55	-1.0
1996	Tor-A	11	29	5	5	0	1	0	0	1	5	.172	.200	.241	11	-4	0	0	0	1.000	-2	/O-9,3-3	-0.5
Total	7	369	801	113	198	42	7	9	75	109	146	.247	.347	.351	88	-11	19	9	0	.991	-48	O-344/2-4,3-3,D-3	-6.4

■ BEN HUFFMAN
Huffman, Bennie F b: 7/18/14, Rileyville, Va. BL/TR, 5'11.5", 175 lbs. Deb: 4/23/37

YEAR	TM/L	G	AB	R	H	2B	3B	HR	RBI	BB	SO	AVG	OBP	SLG	PRO+	BR/A	SB	CS	SBR	FA	FR	G/POS	TPR
1937	StL-A	76	176	18	48	9	0	1	24	10	7	.273	.323	.341	67	-9	1	0	0	.970	-8	C-42	-1.3

■ ED HUG
Hug, Edward Ambrose b: 7/14/1880, Fayetteville, O. d: 5/11/53, Cincinnati, Ohio BR/TR, Deb: 7/6/03

YEAR	TM/L	G	AB	R	H	2B	3B	HR	RBI	BB	SO	AVG	OBP	SLG	PRO+	BR/A	SB	CS	SBR	FA	FR	G/POS	TPR
1903	Bro-N	1	0	0	0	0	0	0	0	1		—	1.000	—	199	0	0			.000	0	/C-1	0.0

■ MILLER HUGGINS
Huggins, Miller James "Hug" or "Mighty Mite"
b: 3/27/1879, Cincinnati, Ohio d: 9/25/29, New York, N.Y. BB/TR, 5'6.5", 140 lbs. Deb: 4/15/04 MH

YEAR	TM/L	G	AB	R	H	2B	3B	HR	RBI	BB	SO	AVG	OBP	SLG	PRO+	BR/A	SB	CS	SBR	FA	FR	G/POS	TPR
1904	Cin-N	140	491	96	129	12	7	2	30	88		.263	.377	.328	108	8	13			.945	1	*2-140	1.4

YEAR	TM/L	G	AB	R	H	2B	3B	HR	RBI	BB	SO	AVG	OBP	SLG	PRO+	BR/A	SB	CS	SBR	FA	FR	G/POS	TPR
1905	Cin-N	149	564	117	154	11	8	1	38	**103**		.273	.392	.326	103	7	27			.945	**36**	*2-149	4.5
1906	Cin-N	146	545	81	159	11	7	0	26	71		.292	.376	.338	118	14	41			.948	22	*2-146	4.0
1907	Cin-N	156	561	64	139	12	4	1	31	**83**		.248	.346	.289	95	0	28			.961	0	*2-156	-0.1
1908	Cin-N	135	498	65	119	14	5	0	23	58		.239	.321	.287	97	0	30			.959	4	*2-135	0.3
1909	Cin-N	57	159	18	34	3	1	0	6	28		.214	.335	.245	81	-2	11			.933	4	2-31,3-15	0.2
1910	StL-N	151	547	101	145	15	6	1	36	**116**	46	.265	.399	.320	114	18	34			.963	3	*2-151	1.8
1911	StL-N	138	509	106	133	19	2	1	24	96	52	.261	.385	.312	99	5	37			.961	11	*2-136	1.3
1912	StL-N	120	431	82	131	15	4	0	29	87	31	.304	.422	.357	117	16	35			.943	-7	*2-114	0.6
1913	StL-N	121	382	74	109	12	0	0	27	92	49	.285	**.432**	.317	117	17	23			**.977**	0	*2-113,M	1.6
1914	StL-N	148	509	85	134	17	4	1	24	**105**	63	.263	.396	.318	115	16	32			.964	-5	*2-147,M	1.1
1915	StL-N	107	353	57	85	5	2	2	24	74	68	.241	.377	.283	101	5	13	12	-3	.957	4	*2-105,M	0.7
1916	StL-N	18	9	2	3	0	0	0	0	2	3	.333	.500	.333	159	1	0			1.000	4	/2-7,M	0.6
Total	13	1586	5558	948	1474	146	50	9	318	1003	312	.265	.382	.314	107	105	324	12		.956	78	*2-1530/3-15	18.0

■ **ED HUGHES** Hughes, Edward J. b: 10/5/1880, Chicago, Ill. d: 10/11/27, McHenry, Ill. BR/TR, 6'1", 180 lbs. Deb: 8/29/02 F

YEAR	TM/L	G	AB	R	H	2B	3B	HR	RBI	BB	SO	AVG	OBP	SLG	PRO+	BR/A	SB	CS	SBR	FA	FR	G/POS	TPR
1902	Chi-A	1	4	0	1	0	0	0	0	0		.250	.250	.250	41	-0	0			.778	0	/C-1	0.0
1905	Bos-A	6	14	2	3	0	0	0	2	0		.214	.214	.214	36	-1	0			.500	-2	/P-6	0.0
1906	Bos-A	2	3	0	0	0	0	0	0	0		.000	.000	.000	-99	-1	0			.750	-0	/P-2	0.0
Total	3	9	21	2	4	0	0	0	2	0		.190	.190	.190	17	-2	0			.571	-2	/P-8,C-1	0.0

■ **JOE HUGHES** Hughes, Joseph Thompson b: 2/21/1880, Pardoe, Pa. d: 3/13/51, Cleveland, Ohio BR/TR, 5'10", 165 lbs. Deb: 8/30/02

YEAR	TM/L	G	AB	R	H	2B	3B	HR	RBI	BB	SO	AVG	OBP	SLG	PRO+	BR/A	SB	CS	SBR	FA	FR	G/POS	TPR
1902	Chi-N	1	3	0	0	0	0	0	0	0		.000	.000	.000	-99	-1	0			.000	-0	/O-1	-0.1

■ **KEITH HUGHES** Hughes, Keith Wills b: 9/12/63, Bryn Mawr, Pa. BL/TL, 6'3", 210 lbs. Deb: 5/19/87

YEAR	TM/L	G	AB	R	H	2B	3B	HR	RBI	BB	SO	AVG	OBP	SLG	PRO+	BR/A	SB	CS	SBR	FA	FR	G/POS	TPR
1987	NY-A	4	4	0	0	0	0	0	0	0	2	.000	.000	.000	-99	-1	0	0	0	.000	0	/H	-0.1
	Phi-N	37	76	8	20	2	0	0	10	7	11	.263	.333	.289	65	-4	0	0	0	.963	-2	O-19	-0.6
1988	Bal-A	41	108	10	21	4	2	2	14	16	27	.194	.298	.324	76	-3	1	0	0	.969	2	O-31/D-1	-0.2
1990	NY-N	8	9	0	0	0	0	0	0	0	4	.000	.000	.000	-99	-2	0	0	0	1.000	-1	/O-5	-0.4
1993	Cin-N	3	4	0	0	0	0	0	0	0	0	.000	.000	.000	-99	-1	0	0	0	.000	-1	/O-2	-0.2
Total	4	93	201	18	41	6	2	2	24	23	44	.204	.289	.284	57	-12	1	0	0	.969	-2	/O-57,D-1	-1.5

■ **BOBBY HUGHES** Hughes, Robert E. b: 3/10/71, Burbank, Cal. BR/TR, 6'4", 237 lbs. Deb: 4/2/98

YEAR	TM/L	G	AB	R	H	2B	3B	HR	RBI	BB	SO	AVG	OBP	SLG	PRO+	BR/A	SB	CS	SBR	FA	FR	G/POS	TPR
1998	Mil-N	85	218	28	50	7	2	9	29	16	53	.229	.285	.404	76	-8	1	2	-1	.995	2	C-72/O-3	-0.3

■ **ROY HUGHES** Hughes, Roy John "Jeep" or "Sage" b: 1/11/11, Cincinnati, Ohio d: 3/5/95, Asheville, N.C. BR/TR, 5'10.5", 167 lbs. Deb: 4/16/35

YEAR	TM/L	G	AB	R	H	2B	3B	HR	RBI	BB	SO	AVG	OBP	SLG	PRO+	BR/A	SB	CS	SBR	FA	FR	G/POS	TPR
1935	Cle-A	82	266	40	78	15	3	0	14	18	17	.293	.340	.372	83	-7	13	3	2	.987	-1	2-40,S-29/3-1	-0.1
1936	Cle-A	152	638	112	188	35	9	0	63	57	40	.295	.356	.378	81	-19	20	9	1	.973	5	*2-152	-0.2
1937	Cle-A	104	346	57	96	12	6	1	40	40	22	.277	.352	.355	78	-11	11	6	-0	.939	12	3-58,2-32	0.4
1938	StL-A	58	96	16	27	3	0	2	13	12	11	.281	.361	.375	85	-2	3	0	1	.957	4	2-21/3-5,S-2	0.4
1939	StL-A	17	23	6	2	0	0	0	1	4	4	.087	.222	.087	-18	-4	0	0	0	1.000	1	/2-6,S-1	-0.3
	Phi-N	65	237	22	54	5	1	1	16	21	18	.228	.291	.270	53	-15	4			.984	0	2-65	-1.2
1940	Phi-N	1	0	0	0	0	0	0	0	0	0	—	—	—	—	0	0			1.000	-0	/2-1	0.0
1944	Chi-N	126	478	86	137	16	6	1	28	35	30	.287	.337	.351	94	-3	16			.951	11	3-66,S-52	1.3
1945	*Chi-N	69	222	34	58	8	1	0	8	16	18	.261	.311	.306	73	-8	6			.931	-8	S-36,2-21/3-9,1-2	-1.2
1946	Phi-N	89	276	23	65	11	1	0	22	19	15	.236	.287	.283	64	-13	7			.942	-12	S-34,3-31/2-7,1-1	-2.5
Total	9	763	2582	396	705	105	27	5	205	222	175	.273	.332	.340	78	-83	80	18		.980	12	2-345,3-170,S/1	-3.4

■ **TERRY HUGHES** Hughes, Terry Wayne b: 5/13/49, Spartanburg, S.C. BR/TR, 6'1", 185 lbs. Deb: 9/2/70

YEAR	TM/L	G	AB	R	H	2B	3B	HR	RBI	BB	SO	AVG	OBP	SLG	PRO+	BR/A	SB	CS	SBR	FA	FR	G/POS	TPR
1970	Chi-N	2	3	0	1	0	0	0	0	0	0	.333	.333	.333	71	-0	0	0	0	.000	-0	/3-1,O-1	0.0
1973	StL-N	11	14	1	3	1	0	0	1	1	4	.214	.267	.286	53	-1	0	0	0	1.000	0	/3-5,1-1	-0.1
1974	Bos-A	41	69	5	14	2	0	1	6	6	18	.203	.286	.275	58	-4	0	0	0	.958	4	3-36/D-1	0.0
Total	3	54	86	6	18	3	0	1	7	7	22	.209	.284	.279	58	-5	0	0	0	.961	3	/3-42,D-1,1-1,O-1	-0.1

■ **TOM HUGHES** Hughes, Thomas Franklin b: 8/6/07, Emmet, Ark. d: 8/10/89, Beaumont, Tex. BL/TR, 6'1", 190 lbs. Deb: 9/9/30

YEAR	TM/L	G	AB	R	H	2B	3B	HR	RBI	BB	SO	AVG	OBP	SLG	PRO+	BR/A	SB	CS	SBR	FA	FR	G/POS	TPR
1930	Det-A	17	59	8	22	2	3	0	5	4	8	.373	.413	.508	130	3	0	1	-1	.897	-3	O-16	-0.2

■ **BILL HUGHES** Hughes, William R. b: 11/25/1866, Blandinsville, Ill. d: 8/25/43, Santa Ana, Cal. BL/TL, Deb: 9/28/1884

YEAR	TM/L	G	AB	R	H	2B	3B	HR	RBI	BB	SO	AVG	OBP	SLG	PRO+	BR/A	SB	CS	SBR	FA	FR	G/POS	TPR
1884	Was-U	14	49	5	6	0	0	0		2		.122	.157	.122	-15	-8				.955	0	/1-9,O-6	-0.8
1885	Phi-a	4	16	3	3	1	1	0	1	1		.188	.278	.375	99	-0				1.000	-0	/O-2,P-2	0.0
Total	2	18	65	8	9	1	1	0	1	3		.138	.188	.185	15	-8				.813	-0	/1-9,O-8,P-2	-0.8

■ **EMIL HUHN** Huhn, Emil Hugo "Hap" b: 3/10/1892, North Vernon, Ind. d: 9/5/25, Camden, S.C. BR/TR, 6', 180 lbs. Deb: 4/10/15

YEAR	TM/L	G	AB	R	H	2B	3B	HR	RBI	BB	SO	AVG	OBP	SLG	PRO+	BR/A	SB	CS	SBR	FA	FR	G/POS	TPR
1915	New-F	124	415	34	94	18	1	1	41	28	40	.227	.279	.282	61	-29	13			.985	-2	*1-101,C-16	-3.6
1916	Cin-N	37	94	4	24	3	2	0	3	2	11	.255	.271	.330	86	-2	0			.989	1	C-18,1-14/O-1	-0.1
1917	Cin-N	23	51	2	10	1	2	0	3	2	5	.196	.226	.294	62	-3	1			.969	-2	C-15/1-1	-0.4
Total	3	184	560	40	128	22	5	1	47	32	56	.229	.273	.291	65	-33	14			.986	-3	1-116/C-49,O-1	-4.1

■ **BILLY HULEN** Hulen, William Franklin b: 3/12/1870, Dixon, Cal. d: 10/2/47, Santa Rosa, Cal. BL/TL, 5'8", 148 lbs. Deb: 5/2/1896

YEAR	TM/L	G	AB	R	H	2B	3B	HR	RBI	BB	SO	AVG	OBP	SLG	PRO+	BR/A	SB	CS	SBR	FA	FR	G/POS	TPR
1896	Phi-N	88	339	87	90	18	7	0	38	55	20	.265	.368	.360	93	-2	23			.874	-21	S-73,O-12/2-2	-1.8
1899	Was-N	19	68	10	10	1	0	0	3	10		.147	.256	.162	16	-8	5			.902	-4	S-19	-0.9
Total	2	107	407	97	100	19	7	0	41	65	20	.246	.350	.327	81	-9	28			.880	-25	/S-92,O-12,2-2	-2.7

■ **TIM HULETT** Hulett, Timothy Craig b: 1/12/60, Springfield, Ill. BR/TR, 6', 195 lbs. Deb: 9/15/83

YEAR	TM/L	G	AB	R	H	2B	3B	HR	RBI	BB	SO	AVG	OBP	SLG	PRO+	BR/A	SB	CS	SBR	FA	FR	G/POS	TPR
1983	Chi-A	6	5	0	1	0	0	0	0	0	0	.200	.200	.200	10	-1	1	0	0	.875	2	/2-6	0.1
1984	Chi-A	8	7	1	0	0	0	0	0	1	4	.000	.125	.000	-59	-2	1	0	0	1.000	4	/3-4,2-3	0.3
1985	Chi-A	141	395	52	106	19	4	5	37	30	81	.268	.326	.375	88	-6	6	4	-1	.924	8	*3-115,2-28/O-1	0.1
1986	Chi-A	150	520	53	120	16	5	17	44	21	91	.231	.262	.379	70	-23	4	1	1	.951	-6	3-89,2-66	-2.7
1987	Chi-A	68	240	20	52	10	0	7	28	10	41	.217	.248	.346	54	-16	0	2	-1	.953	-3	3-61/2-8	-2.0
1989	Bal-A	33	97	12	27	5	0	3	18	10	17	.278	.346	.423	119	2	0	0	0	.976	-5	2-23,3-11	-0.2
1990	Bal-A	53	153	16	39	7	1	3	16	15	41	.255	.321	.373	97	-1	1	0	0	.961	6	3-24,2-16/D-8	0.6
1991	Bal-A	79	206	29	42	9	0	7	18	13	49	.204	.255	.350	68	-10	0	1	-1	.976	-8	3-39,2-26,D-15,/S-1	-1.8
1992	Bal-A	57	142	11	41	7	2	2	21	10	31	.289	.340	.408	106	1	0	1	-1	.935	10	3-27,D-13,2-10,/S-5	1.0
1993	Bal-A	85	260	40	78	15	0	2	23	23	56	.300	.364	.381	96	-1	1	2	-1	.963	19	3-75/S-8,2-4,D-2	1.7
1994	Bal-A	36	92	11	21	2	1	2	15	12	24	.228	.317	.337	66	-5	0	0	0	.992	13	2-23/3-9,S-6	0.9
1995	StL-N	4	11	0	2	0	0	0	0	0	3	.182	.182	.182	-4	-2	0	0	0	.941	2	/2-2,S-1	0.1
Total	12	720	2128	245	529	90	13	48	220	145	438	.249	.300	.371	80	-62	14	11	-2	.947	43	3-454,2-215/DSO	-1.9

■ **DAVID HULSE** Hulse, David Lindsey b: 2/25/68, San Angelo, Tex. BL/TL, 5'11", 170 lbs. Deb: 8/11/92

YEAR	TM/L	G	AB	R	H	2B	3B	HR	RBI	BB	SO	AVG	OBP	SLG	PRO+	BR/A	SB	CS	SBR	FA	FR	G/POS	TPR
1992	Tex-A	32	92	14	28	4	0	0	2	3	18	.304	.326	.348	92	-1	3	1	0	.984	-4	O-31/D-1	-0.5
1993	Tex-A	114	407	71	118	9	10	1	29	26	57	.290	.334	.369	92	-5	29	9	3	.988	-6	*O-112/D-2	-0.9
1994	Tex-A	77	310	58	79	8	4	1	19	21	53	.255	.306	.316	61	-18	18	2	4	.978	-4	O-76/D-1	-1.8
1995	Mil-A	119	339	46	85	11	6	3	47	18	60	.251	.289	.345	61	-20	15	3	3	.984	-26	*O-115	-4.3
1996	Mil-A	81	117	18	26	3	0	0	6	8	16	.222	.272	.248	32	-12	4	1	1	.990	-14	O-68/D-4	-2.4
Total	5	423	1265	207	336	35	20	5	103	76	204	.266	.309	.337	69	-56	69	16	11	.985	-53	O-402/D-8	-9.9

■ **RUDY HULSWITT** Hulswitt, Rudolph Edward b: 2/23/1877, Newport, Ky. d: 1/16/50, Louisville, Ky. BR/TR, 5'8.5", 165 lbs. Deb: 6/16/1899 C

YEAR	TM/L	G	AB	R	H	2B	3B	HR	RBI	BB	SO	AVG	OBP	SLG	PRO+	BR/A	SB	CS	SBR	FA	FR	G/POS	TPR
1899	Lou-N	1	0	0	0	0	0	0	0	0		—	—	—	—	0	0			.333	-1	/S-1	-0.1
1902	Phi-N	128	497	59	135	11	7	0	38	30		.272	.316	.322	97	-2	12			.917	8	*S-125/3-3	1.4
1903	Phi-N	138	519	56	128	22	9	1	58	28		.247	.288	.329	78	-16	10			.906	-3	*S-138	-1.3
1904	Phi-N	113	406	36	99	11	4	1	36	16		.244	.276	.298	80	-10	8			.912	-13	*S-113	-2.1
1908	Cin-N	119	386	27	88	5	7	1	28	30		.228	.287	.285	85	-7	7			.936	-6	*S-118/2-1	-1.2
1909	StL-N	82	289	21	81	8	3	0	29	19		.280	.329	.329	111	3	7			.930	-6	S-65,2-12	-0.2

YEAR	TM/L	G	AB	R	H	2B	3B	HR	RBI	BB	SO	AVG	OBP	SLG	PRO+	BR/A	SB	CS	SBR	FA	FR	G/POS	TPR
1910	StL-N	63	133	9	33	7	2	0	14	13	10	.248	.320	.331	93	-1	5			.854	-13	S-30/2-2	-1.4
Total	7	644	2230	208	564	64	32	3	203	136	10	.253	.299	.314	89	-33	49			.915	-32	S-590/2-15,3-3	-4.9

■ JOHN HUMMEL Hummel, John Edwin "Silent John" b: 4/4/1883, Bloomsburg, Pa. d: 5/18/59, Springfield, Mass. BR/TR, 5′11″, 160 lbs. Deb: 9/12/05

YEAR	TM/L	G	AB	R	H	2B	3B	HR	RBI	BB	SO	AVG	OBP	SLG	PRO+	BR/A	SB	CS	SBR	FA	FR	G/POS	TPR
1905	Bro-N	30	109	19	29	3	4	0	7	9		.266	.322	.367	114	2	6			.962	0	2-30	0.2
1906	Bro-N	97	286	20	57	6	4	1	21	36		.199	.289	.259	77	-7	10			.953	1	2-50,O-21,1-15	-0.8
1907	Bro-N	107	342	41	80	12	3	3	31	26		.234	.294	.313	98	-2	8			.951	13	2-44,O-33,1-12,/S-8	1.0
1908	Bro-N	154	594	51	143	11	12	4	41	34		.241	.284	.320	97	-4	20			.973	8	O-95,2-43/S-9,1-8	0.0
1909	Bro-N	146	542	54	152	15	9	4	52	22		.280	.311	.363	113	5	16			.987	-17	1-54,2-38,S-36,O-17	-1.5
1910	Bro-N	153	578	67	141	21	13	5	74	57	81	.244	.314	.351	97	-4	21			**.965**	-14	*2-153	-2.2
1911	Bro-N	137	477	54	129	21	11	5	58	67	66	.270	.360	.392	115	10	16			**.972**	-5	*2-127/1-4,S-2	0.2
1912	Bro-N	122	411	55	116	21	7	5	54	49	55	.282	.359	.404	113	7	7			.969	-15	2-58,O-44,1-11	-1.1
1913	Bro-N	67	198	20	48	7	7	2	24	13	23	.242	.292	.379	88	-4	4			.938	-1	O-28,S-17/1-6,2-3	-0.4
1914	Bro-N	73	208	25	55	8	9	0	20	16	25	.264	.317	.389	107	1	5			.982	-2	1-36,O-19/2-1,S-1	-0.2
1915	Bro-N	53	100	6	23	2	3	0	8	6	11	.230	.274	.310	75	-3	1	1	-0	1.000	-4	O-21,1-11/S-1	-0.9
1918	NY-A	22	61	9	18	1	2	0	4	11	8	.295	.411	.377	135	3	3			.960	-3	O-15/1-3,2-1	-0.1
Total	12	1161	3906	421	991	128	84	29	394	346	269	.254	.316	.352	103	5	117	1		.963	-40	2-548,O-293,1/S	-5.8

■ AL HUMPHREY Humphrey, Albert b: 2/28/1886, Ashtabula, Ohio d: 5/13/61, Ashtabula, Ohio BL/TR, 5′11″, 180 lbs. Deb: 9/1/11

YEAR	TM/L	G	AB	R	H	2B	3B	HR	RBI	BB	SO	AVG	OBP	SLG	PRO+	BR/A	SB	CS	SBR	FA	FR	G/POS	TPR
1911	Bro-N	8	27	4	5	0	0	0	0	3	7	.185	.267	.185	29	-3	0			.923	-2	/O-8	-0.5

■ TERRY HUMPHREY Humphrey, Terryal Gene b: 8/4/49, Chickasha, Okla. BR/TR, 6′3″, 190 lbs. Deb: 9/5/71

YEAR	TM/L	G	AB	R	H	2B	3B	HR	RBI	BB	SO	AVG	OBP	SLG	PRO+	BR/A	SB	CS	SBR	FA	FR	G/POS	TPR
1971	Mon-N	9	26	1	5	1	0	0	1	0	4	.192	.192	.231	19	-3	0	0	0	.981	2	/C-9	0.0
1972	Mon-N	69	215	13	40	8	0	1	9	16	38	.186	.249	.237	38	-17	4	1	1	.986	-3	C-65	-1.9
1973	Mon-N	43	90	5	15	2	0	1	9	5	16	.167	.211	.222	19	-10	0	1	-1	1.000	5	C-35	-0.5
1974	Mon-N	20	52	3	10	3	0	0	3	4	9	.192	.250	.250	38	-4	0	0	0	.990	6	C-17	0.2
1975	Det-A	18	41	0	10	0	0	0	1	2	6	.244	.279	.244	47	-3	0	0	0	1.000	1	C-18	-0.1
1976	Cal-A	71	196	17	48	10	0	1	19	13	30	.245	.308	.311	87	-3	0	1	-1	.980	1	C-71	-0.1
1977	Cal-A	123	304	17	69	11	0	2	34	21	58	.227	.286	.283	58	-18	1	1	-0	.989	-0	*C-123	-1.5
1978	Cal-A	53	114	11	25	4	1	1	9	6	12	.219	.270	.298	62	-6	0	1	-1	.978	11	C-52/2-1,3-1	0.5
1979	Cal-A	9	17	2	1	0	0	0	0	1	2	.059	.111	.059	-55	-4	0	0	0	.983	6	/C-9	0.2
Total	9	415	1055	69	223	39	1	6	85	68	175	.211	.268	.267	51	-67	5	5	-2	.986	28	C-399/3-1,2-1	-3.2

■ MIKE HUMPHREYS Humphreys, Michael Butler b: 4/10/67, Dallas, Tex. BR/TR, 6′, 185 lbs. Deb: 7/29/91

YEAR	TM/L	G	AB	R	H	2B	3B	HR	RBI	BB	SO	AVG	OBP	SLG	PRO+	BR/A	SB	CS	SBR	FA	FR	G/POS	TPR
1991	NY-A	25	40	9	8	0	0	0	3	9	7	.200	.347	.200	55	-2	2	0	1	1.000	-2	/O-9,3-6,D-7	-0.3
1992	NY-A	4	10	0	1	0	0	0	0	0	1	.100	.100	.100	-44	-2	0	0	0	1.000	1	/O-2,D-1	-0.1
1993	NY-A	25	35	6	6	2	1	1	6	4	11	.171	.256	.371	69	-2	2	1	0	1.000	-7	O-21/D-3	-0.9
Total	3	54	85	15	15	2	1	1	9	13	19	.176	.286	.259	51	-6	4	1	1	1.000	-8	/O-32,D-11,3-6	-1.3

■ JOHN HUMPHRIES Humphries, John Henry b: 11/12/1861, N.Gower, Ont., Can. d: 11/29/33, Salinas, Cal. BL/TL, 6′, 185 lbs. Deb: 7/7/1883

YEAR	TM/L	G	AB	R	H	2B	3B	HR	RBI	BB	SO	AVG	OBP	SLG	PRO+	BR/A	SB	CS	SBR	FA	FR	G/POS	TPR
1883	NY-N	29	107	5	12	1	0	0	4	1	22	.112	.120	.121	-26	-16				.815	-5	C-20,O-12	-1.8
1884	Was-a	49	193	23	34	2	0	0		9		.176	.217	.187	37	-12				.890	-6	C-35,O-12/1-4	-1.4
	NY-N	20	64	6	6	0	0	0	2	9	19	.094	.205	.094	-2	-7				.896	11	C-20	0.4
Total	2	98	364	34	52	3	0	0	6	19	41	.143	.188	.151	9	-35				.876	-0	/C-75,O-24,1-4	-2.8

■ RANDY HUNDLEY Hundley, Cecil Randolph b: 6/1/42, Martinsville, Va. BR/TR, 6′, 175 lbs. Deb: 9/27/64 FC

YEAR	TM/L	G	AB	R	H	2B	3B	HR	RBI	BB	SO	AVG	OBP	SLG	PRO+	BR/A	SB	CS	SBR	FA	FR	G/POS	TPR
1964	SF-N	2	1	1	0	0	0	0	0	0	1	.000	.000	.000	-98	-0	0	0	0	.000	0	/C-2	0.0
1965	SF-N	6	15	0	1	0	0	0	0	0	4	.067	.067	.067	-61	-3	0	0	0	1.000	4	/C-6	0.1
1966	Chi-N	149	526	50	124	22	3	19	63	35	113	.236	.287	.397	87	-10	1	3	-2	.986	-11	*C-149	-1.4
1967	Chi-N	152	539	68	144	25	3	14	60	44	75	.267	.325	.403	102	1	2	4	-2	.996	-12	*C-152	-0.4
1968	Chi-N	160	553	41	125	18	4	7	65	39	69	.226	.282	.311	73	-18	1	0	0	.995	-13	*C-160	-2.3
1969	Chi-N★	151	522	67	133	15	1	18	64	61	90	.255	.336	.391	91	-6	2	3	-1	.992	12	*C-151	1.3
1970	Chi-N	73	250	13	61	5	0	7	36	16	52	.244	.289	.348	62	-14	0	1	-1	.990	-1	C-73	-1.1
1971	Chi-N	9	21	1	7	1	0	0	2	0	2	.333	.333	.381	89	-0	0	0	0	.979	3	/C-8	0.3
1972	Chi-N	114	357	23	78	12	0	5	30	22	62	.218	.264	.294	53	-22	1	0	0	**.995**	7	*C-113	-1.1
1973	Chi-N	124	368	35	83	11	1	10	43	30	51	.226	.284	.342	68	-16	5	6	-2	.993	11	*C-122	-0.3
1974	Min-A	32	88	2	17	2	0	0	3	4	12	.193	.228	.216	27	-8	0	0	0	.965	1	C-28	-0.6
1975	SD-N	74	180	7	37	5	1	2	14	19	29	.206	.285	.278	60	-10	0	0	0	.970	1	C-51	-0.8
1976	Chi-N	13	18	3	3	2	0	0	1	1	4	.167	.211	.278	35	-2	0	0	0	.923	-0	/C-9	-0.2
1977	Chi-N	2	4	0	0	0	0	0	0	0	1	.000	.000	.000	-90	-1	0	0	0	1.000	0	/C-2	-0.1
Total	14	1061	3442	311	813	118	13	82	381	271	565	.236	.294	.350	76	-109	12	17	-7	.990	2	*C-1026	-6.6

■ TODD HUNDLEY Hundley, Todd Randolph b: 5/27/69, Martinsville, Va. BB/TR, 5′11″, 185 lbs. Deb: 5/18/90 F

YEAR	TM/L	G	AB	R	H	2B	3B	HR	RBI	BB	SO	AVG	OBP	SLG	PRO+	BR/A	SB	CS	SBR	FA	FR	G/POS	TPR
1990	NY-N	36	67	8	14	6	0	0	2	6	18	.209	.274	.299	58	-4	0	0	0	.988	2	C-36	-0.1
1991	NY-N	21	60	5	8	0	1	1	7	6	14	.133	.224	.217	25	-6	0	0	0	1.000	-6	C-20	-1.2
1992	NY-N	123	358	32	75	17	0	7	32	19	76	.209	.257	.316	62	-19	3	0	1	.996	2	*C-121	-1.0
1993	NY-N	130	417	40	95	17	2	11	53	23	62	.228	.271	.357	68	-20	1	1	-0	.988	-6	*C-123	-2.0
1994	NY-N	91	291	45	69	10	1	16	42	25	73	.237	.304	.443	93	-4	2	1	0	.990	-4	C-82	-0.3
1995	NY-N	90	275	39	77	11	0	15	51	42	64	.280	.385	.484	131	13	1	0	0	.987	-11	C-89	0.8
1996	NY-N★	153	540	85	140	32	1	41	112	79	146	.259	.357	.550	141	31	1	3	-2	.992	-8	*C-150	2.9
1997	NY-N†	132	417	78	114	21	2	30	86	83	116	.273	.398	.549	150	32	2	3	-1	.987	-20	*C-122/D-1	1.9
1998	NY-N	53	124	8	20	4	0	3	12	16	55	.161	.262	.266	38	-11	1	1	-0	.898	-1	O-34/C-2	-1.2
Total	9	829	2549	340	612	118	7	124	397	299	624	.240	.325	.438	104	12	11	9	-2	.990	-50	C-745/O-34,D-1	-0.2

■ BERNIE HUNGLING Hungling, Bernard Herman "Bud" b: 3/5/1896, Dayton, Ohio d: 3/30/68, Dayton, Ohio BR/TR, 6′2″, 180 lbs. Deb: 4/14/22

YEAR	TM/L	G	AB	R	H	2B	3B	HR	RBI	BB	SO	AVG	OBP	SLG	PRO+	BR/A	SB	CS	SBR	FA	FR	G/POS	TPR
1922	Bro-N	39	102	9	23	1	2	1	13	6	20	.225	.269	.304	48	-8	2	0	1	.968	1	C-36	-0.4
1923	Bro-N	2	4	0	0	0	0	0	0	0	2	.000	.000	.000	-99	-1	0	1	-1	.667	-1	/C-1	-0.2
1930	StL-A	10	31	4	10	2	0	0	2	5	3	.323	.417	.387	102	0	0	1	-1	1.000	-4	C-10	-0.3
Total	3	51	137	13	33	3	2	1	15	11	25	.241	.297	.314	57	-9	2	2	-1	.968	-3	/C-47	-0.9

■ BILL HUNNEFIELD Hunnefield, William Fenton "Wild Bill" b: 1/5/1899, Dedham, Mass. d: 8/28/76, Nantucket, Mass. BB/TR, 5′10″, 165 lbs. Deb: 4/17/26

YEAR	TM/L	G	AB	R	H	2B	3B	HR	RBI	BB	SO	AVG	OBP	SLG	PRO+	BR/A	SB	CS	SBR	FA	FR	G/POS	TPR
1926	Chi-A	131	470	81	129	26	4	3	48	37	28	.274	.329	.366	84	-12	24	9	2	.931	-8	S-98,3-17,2-15	-0.7
1927	Chi-A	112	365	45	104	25	1	2	36	25	24	.285	.332	.375	85	-8	15	13	-3	.933	-20	S-79,2-17/3-1	-2.3
1928	Chi-A	94	333	42	98	8	3	2	24	26	24	.294	.351	.354	87	-6	16	6	1	.967	-12	2-82/S-3,3-1	-1.4
1929	Chi-A	47	127	13	23	5	0	0	9	7	3	.181	.224	.220	15	-16	5	2	0	.969	-4	2-29/3-4,S-2	-1.8
1930	Chi-A	31	81	11	22	2	0	1	5	4	10	.272	.314	.333	67	-4	1	1	-0	.932	-11	S-22/1-1	-1.2
1931	Cle-A	21	71	13	17	4	1	0	4	9	4	.239	.325	.324	67	-3	3	1	0	.853	-10	S-21/2-1	-1.0
	Bos-N	11	21	2	6	0	0	0	1	0	2	.286	.286	.286	56	-1	0			.864	2	/3-5,2-4	0.1
	NY-N	64	196	23	53	5	0	1	17	9	16	.270	.302	.311	67	-9	3			.951	-5	2-56/S-5	-1.1
	Yr	75	217	25	59	5	0	1	18	9	18	.272	.301	.309	66	-10	3			.951	-3	2-60/3-5,S-5	-1.0
Total	6	511	1664	230	452	75	9	9	144	117	111	.272	.322	.344	76	-60	67	32		.925	-67	S-230,2-204/3-28,1	-9.4

■ RANDY HUNT Hunt, James Randall b: 1/3/60, Prattville, Ala. BR/TR, 6′, 185 lbs. Deb: 6/4/85

YEAR	TM/L	G	AB	R	H	2B	3B	HR	RBI	BB	SO	AVG	OBP	SLG	PRO+	BR/A	SB	CS	SBR	FA	FR	G/POS	TPR
1985	StL-N	14	19	1	3	0	0	0	1	0	5	.158	.158	.158	-12	-3	0	1	-1	1.000	1	C-13	-0.2
1986	Mon-N	21	48	4	10	0	0	2	5	5	16	.208	.283	.333	70	-2	0	0	0	.960	6	C-21	0.5
Total	2	35	67	5	13	0	0	2	6	5	21	.194	.250	.284	48	-5	0	1	-1	.967	7	/C-34	0.3

■ KEN HUNT Hunt, Kenneth Lawrence b: 7/13/34, Grand Forks, N.Dak d: 6/8/97, Gardena, Cal. BR/TR, 6′1″, 205 lbs. Deb: 9/10/59

YEAR	TM/L	G	AB	R	H	2B	3B	HR	RBI	BB	SO	AVG	OBP	SLG	PRO+	BR/A	SB	CS	SBR	FA	FR	G/POS	TPR
1959	NY-A	6	12	2	4	1	0	0	1	0	3	.333	.333	.417	108	0	0	0	0	1.000	0	/O-5	0.0
1960	NY-A	25	22	4	6	2	0	0	1	4	4	.273	.407	.364	117	1	0	0	0	.957	-6	O-24	-0.5
1961	LA-A	149	479	70	122	29	3	25	84	49	120	.255	.329	.484	103	-0	8	2	1	.950	-6	*O-134/2-1	-1.2
1962	LA-A	13	11	4	2	0	0	1	1	1	5	.182	.250	.455	88	-0	1	0	0	.867	-1	/1-3	-0.1

YEAR	TM/L	G	AB	R	H	2B	3B	HR	RBI	BB	SO	AVG	OBP	SLG	PRO+	BR/A	SB	CS	SBR	FA	FR	G/POS	TPR
1963	LA-A	59	142	17	26	6	1	5	16	15	49	.183	.261	.345	72	-6	0	1	-1	.972	-6	O-50	-1.6
	Was-A	7	20	1	4	0	0	1	4	2	6	.200	.273	.350	73	-1	0	0	0	1.000	0	/O-5	-0.1
	Yr	66	162	18	30	6	1	6	20	17	55	.185	.263	.346	73	-6	0	1	-1	.976	-6	O-55	-1.7
1964	Was-A	51	96	9	13	4	0	1	4	14	35	.135	.245	.208	28	-9	0	1	-1	1.000	-2	O-37	-1.4
Total	6	310	782	107	177	42	4	33	111	85	222	.226	.306	.417	89	-15	9	4	0	.964	-21	O-255/1-3,2-1	-4.9

■ JOEL HUNT Hunt, Oliver Joel "Jodie" b: 10/11/05, Texico, N.Mex. d: 7/24/78, Teague, Tex. BR/TR, 5'10", 165 lbs. Deb: 4/27/31

YEAR	TM/L	G	AB	R	H	2B	3B	HR	RBI	BB	SO	AVG	OBP	SLG	PRO+	BR/A	SB	CS	SBR	FA	FR	G/POS	TPR
1931	StL-N	4	1	2	0	0	0	0	0	0	1	.000	.000	.000	-96	-0	0			.000	-1	/O-1	-0.1
1932	StL-N	12	21	0	4	1	0	0	3	4	3	.190	.320	.238	51	-1	0			1.000	0	/O-5	-0.1
Total	2	16	22	2	4	1	0	0	3	4	4	.182	.308	.227	45	-2	0			1.000	-0	/O-6	-0.2

■ DICK HUNT Hunt, Richard M. b: 1847, New York d: 11/20/1895, Brooklyn, N.Y. 5'9", 145 lbs. Deb: 5/7/1872

YEAR	TM/L	G	AB	R	H	2B	3B	HR	RBI	BB	SO	AVG	OBP	SLG	PRO+	BR/A	SB	CS	SBR	FA	FR	G/POS	TPR
1872	Eck-n	11	48	11	15	1	1	0	5	1	0	.313	.327	.375	136	3	0	1	-1	.636	-3	/O-8,2-3	-0.1

■ RON HUNT Hunt, Ronald Kenneth b: 2/23/41, St.Louis, Mo. BR/TR, 6', 186 lbs. Deb: 4/16/63

YEAR	TM/L	G	AB	R	H	2B	3B	HR	RBI	BB	SO	AVG	OBP	SLG	PRO+	BR/A	SB	CS	SBR	FA	FR	G/POS	TPR
1963	NY-N	143	533	64	145	28	4	10	42	40	50	.272	.338	.396	109	6	5	4	-1	.967	2	*2-142/3-1	2.3
1964	NY-N★	127	475	59	144	19	6	6	42	29	30	.303	.357	.406	117	11	6	2	1	.979	-8	*2-109,3-12	1.4
1965	NY-N	57	196	21	47	12	1	1	10	14	19	.240	.310	.327	82	-4	2	7	-4	.979	-5	2-46/3-6	-0.9
1966	NY-N★	132	479	63	138	19	2	3	33	41	34	.288	.358	.355	101	2	8	10	-4	.970	7	*2-123/S-1,3-1	1.5
1967	LA-N	110	388	44	102	17	3	3	33	39	24	.263	.346	.345	107	4	2	1	0	.980	-16	2-90/3-8	-0.6
1968	SF-N	148	529	79	132	19	0	2	28	78	41	.250	.372	.297	103	7	6	6	-2	.972	-17	*2-147	-0.3
1969	SF-N	128	478	72	125	23	3	3	41	51	47	.262	.363	.341	100	3	9	2	2	.979	-9	*2-125/3-1	0.6
1970	SF-N	117	367	70	103	17	1	6	41	44	29	.281	.396	.381	111	9	1	2	-1	.968	-28	2-85,3-16	-1.4
1971	Mon-N	152	520	89	145	20	3	5	38	58	41	.279	.403	.358	116	17	5	7	-3	.979	-9	*2-133,3-19	1.7
1972	Mon-N	129	443	56	112	20	0	0	18	51	29	.253	.363	.298	88	-3	9	2	2	.982	-7	*2-122/3-5	-0.2
1973	Mon-N	113	401	61	124	14	0	0	18	52	19	.309	.419	.344	110	10	10	7	-1	.982	-21	*2-102,3-14	-0.7
1974	Mon-N	115	403	66	108	15	0	0	26	55	17	.268	.375	.305	87	-4	2	5	-2	.941	-14	3-75,2-31/S-1	-2.0
	StL-N	12	23	1	4	0	0	0	0	3	2	.174	.321	.174	42	-2	0	0	0	1.000	-1	/2-5	-0.3
	Yr	127	426	67	112	15	0	0	26	58	19	.263	.372	.298	85	-5	2	5	-2	.941	-16	3-75,2-36/S-1	-2.3
Total	12	1483	5235	745	1429	223	23	39	370	555	382	.273	.369	.347	104	57	65	55	-14	.976	-126	*2-1260,3-158/S-2	1.1

■ BRIAN HUNTER Hunter, Brian Lee b: 3/5/71, Portland, Ore. BR/TR, 6'4", 180 lbs. Deb: 6/27/94

YEAR	TM/L	G	AB	R	H	2B	3B	HR	RBI	BB	SO	AVG	OBP	SLG	PRO+	BR/A	SB	CS	SBR	FA	FR	G/POS	TPR
1994	Hou-N	6	24	2	6	1	0	0	0	1	6	.250	.280	.292	52	-2	2	1	0	.938	1	/O-6	-0.1
1995	Hou-N	78	321	52	97	14	5	2	28	21	52	.302	.349	.396	103	1	24	7	3	.955	9	O-74	1.1
1996	Hou-N	132	526	74	145	27	2	5	35	17	92	.276	.301	.363	80	-17	35	9	5	.960	9	*O-127	-0.6
1997	Det-A	162	658	112	177	29	7	4	45	66	121	.269	.337	.353	81	-17	**74**	18	11	.990	8	*O-162	-0.2
1998	Det-A	142	595	67	151	29	3	4	36	36	94	.254	.299	.333	64	-32	42	12	5	.988	14	*O-139	-1.5
Total	5	520	2124	307	576	100	17	15	144	141	365	.271	.319	.355	79	-66	177	47	25	.977	40	O-508	-1.3

■ BRIAN HUNTER Hunter, Brian Ronald b: 3/4/68, Torrance, Cal. BR/TL, 6', 195 lbs. Deb: 5/31/91

YEAR	TM/L	G	AB	R	H	2B	3B	HR	RBI	BB	SO	AVG	OBP	SLG	PRO+	BR/A	SB	CS	SBR	FA	FR	G/POS	TPR
1991	*Atl-N	97	271	32	68	16	1	12	50	17	48	.251	.298	.450	101	-1	0	2	-1	.988	-4	1-85/O-6	-1.1
1992	*Atl-N	102	238	34	57	13	2	14	41	21	50	.239	.301	.487	113	3	1	2	-1	.997	3	1-92/O-6	0.1
1993	Atl-N	37	80	4	11	3	1	0	8	2	15	.138	.159	.200	-5	-12	0	0	0	.994	0	1-29/O-2	-1.3
1994	Pit-N	76	233	28	53	15	1	11	47	15	55	.227	.274	.442	82	-7	0	0	0	.991	-1	1-59/O-5	-1.3
	Cin-N	9	23	6	7	1	0	4	10	2	1	.304	.360	.870	209	3	0	0	0	1.000	-0	/O-5,1-1	0.3
	Yr	85	256	34	60	16	1	15	57	17	56	.234	.282	.480	93	-4	0	0	0	.991	-1	1-60,O-10	-1.0
1995	Cin-N	40	79	9	17	6	0	1	9	11	21	.215	.319	.329	72	-3	2	1	0	.983	0	1-23/O-4	-0.4
1996	Sea-A	75	198	21	53	10	0	7	28	15	43	.268	.332	.424	89	-3	0	1	-1	.991	-2	1-41,O-29/D-2	-0.9
1998	StL-N	62	112	11	23	9	1	4	13	7	23	.205	.258	.411	71	-5	1	1	-0	.938	-1	O-25,1-10/D-1	-0.7
Total	7	498	1234	145	289	73	6	53	206	90	256	.234	.290	.432	88	-25	4	7	-3	.991	-5	1-340/O-82,D-3	-5.3

■ EDDIE HUNTER Hunter, Edison Franklin b: 2/6/05, Bellevue, Ky. d: 3/14/67, Colerain, Ohio BR/TR, 5'7.5", 150 lbs. Deb: 8/5/33

YEAR	TM/L	G	AB	R	H	2B	3B	HR	RBI	BB	SO	AVG	OBP	SLG	PRO+	BR/A	SB	CS	SBR	FA	FR	G/POS	TPR
1933	Cin-N	1	0	0	0	0	0	0	0	0	0	—	—	—	—	0	0			.000	0	/3-1	0.0

■ NEWT HUNTER Hunter, Frederick Creighton b: 1/5/1880, Chillicothe, Ohio d: 10/26/63, Columbus, Ohio BR/TR, 6', 180 lbs. Deb: 4/12/11 C

YEAR	TM/L	G	AB	R	H	2B	3B	HR	RBI	BB	SO	AVG	OBP	SLG	PRO+	BR/A	SB	CS	SBR	FA	FR	G/POS	TPR
1911	Pit-N	65	209	35	53	10	6	2	24	25	43	.254	.345	.388	101	0	9			.989	-2	1-61	-0.2

■ GEORGE HUNTER Hunter, George Henry b: 7/8/1887, Buffalo, N.Y. d: 1/11/68, Harrisburg, Pa. BB/TL, 5'8.5", 165 lbs. Deb: 5/4/09 F

YEAR	TM/L	G	AB	R	H	2B	3B	HR	RBI	BB	SO	AVG	OBP	SLG	PRO+	BR/A	SB	CS	SBR	FA	FR	G/POS	TPR
1909	Bro-N	44	123	8	28	7	0	0	8	9		.228	.286	.285	80	-3	1			.871	-4	O-23,P-16	-0.8
1910	Bro-N	1	0	0	0	0	0	0	0	0	0	—	—	—	—	0	0			.000	-0	/O-1	0.0
Total	2	45	123	8	28	7	0	0	8	9	0	.228	.286	.285	80	-3	1			.871	-5	/O-24,P-16	-0.8

■ BILLY HUNTER Hunter, Gordon William b: 6/4/28, Punxsutawney, Pa. BR/TR, 6', 180 lbs. Deb: 4/14/53 MC

YEAR	TM/L	G	AB	R	H	2B	3B	HR	RBI	BB	SO	AVG	OBP	SLG	PRO+	BR/A	SB	CS	SBR	FA	FR	G/POS	TPR
1953	StL-A★	154	567	50	124	18	1	1	37	24	45	.219	.253	.259	38	-50	3	1	0	.970	15	*S-152	-2.4
1954	Bal-A	125	411	28	100	9	5	2	27	21	38	.243	.283	.304	66	-21	5	4	-1	.948	1	*S-124	-1.2
1955	NY-A	98	255	14	58	7	1	3	20	15	18	.227	.270	.298	54	-17	9	2	2	.958	1	S-98	-0.8
1956	NY-A	39	75	8	21	3	4	0	11	2	4	.280	.299	.427	93	-1	0	1	-1	1.000	10	S-32/3-4	0.9
1957	KC-A	116	319	39	61	10	4	8	29	27	43	.191	.261	.323	58	-19	1	2	-1	.974	-5	2-64,S-35,3-17	-1.9
1958	KC-A	22	58	6	9	1	1	2	11	5	7	.155	.222	.310	44	-5	1	1	-0	.933	-3	S-12/2-8,3-1	-0.6
	Cle-A	76	190	21	37	10	2	0	9	17	37	.195	.264	.268	48	-14	4	1	1	.948	1	S-75/3-2	-0.7
	Yr	98	248	27	46	11	3	2	20	22	44	.185	.255	.278	47	-18	5	2	0	.946	-1	S-87/2-8,3-3	-1.3
Total	6	630	1875	166	410	58	18	16	144	111	192	.219	.265	.294	53	-126	23	12	-0	.958	19	S-528/2-72,3-24	-6.7

■ BUDDY HUNTER Hunter, Harold James b: 8/9/47, Omaha, Neb. BR/TR, 5'10", 170 lbs. Deb: 7/1/71

YEAR	TM/L	G	AB	R	H	2B	3B	HR	RBI	BB	SO	AVG	OBP	SLG	PRO+	BR/A	SB	CS	SBR	FA	FR	G/POS	TPR
1971	Bos-A	8	9	2	2	1	0	0	0	2	1	.222	.364	.333	92	-0	0	0	0	1.000	1	/2-6	0.1
1973	Bos-A	13	7	3	3	1	0	0	2	3	1	.429	.636	.571	229	2	0	0	0	1.000	3	/3-3,2-2,D-1	0.5
1975	Bos-A	1	1	0	0	0	0	0	0	0	0	.000	.000	.000	-92	-0	0	0	0	.750	0	/2-1	0.0
Total	3	22	17	5	5	2	0	0	2	5	2	.294	.478	.412	144	1	0	0	0	.968	5	/2-9,3-3,D-1	0.6

■ HERB HUNTER Hunter, Herbert Harrison b: 12/25/1896, Boston, Mass. d: 7/25/70, Orlando, Fla. BL/TR, 6'0.5", 165 lbs. Deb: 4/29/16

YEAR	TM/L	G	AB	R	H	2B	3B	HR	RBI	BB	SO	AVG	OBP	SLG	PRO+	BR/A	SB	CS	SBR	FA	FR	G/POS	TPR
1916	NY-N	21	28	3	7	0	0	1	4	0	5	.250	.250	.357	90	-1	0			1.000	0	/3-6,1-2	0.0
	Chi-N	2	4	0	0	0	0	0	0	0	0	.000	.000	.000	-90	-1	0			.750	0	/3-1	-0.1
	Yr	23	32	3	7	0	0	1	4	0	5	.219	.219	.313	65	-1	0			.941	1	/3-7,1-2	-0.1
1917	Chi-N	3	3	0	0	0	0	0	0	0	0	.000	.000	.000	-93	-1	0			1.000	0	/2-1,3-1	0.0
1920	Bos-A	4	12	2	1	0	0	0	0	1	1	.083	.154	.083	-38	-2	0	0	0	.857	-1	/O-4	-0.3
1921	StL-N	9	2	3	0	0	0	0	0	1	0	.000	.333	.000	-4	-0	0	3	-2	1.000	0	/1-1	-0.2
Total	4	39	49	8	8	0	0	1	4	2	6	.163	.196	.224	24	-5	0	3		.905	0	/3-8,O-4,1-3,2-1	-0.6

■ LEM HUNTER Hunter, Robert Lemuel b: 1/16/1863, Warren, Ohio d: 11/9/56, W.Lafayette, Ohio Deb: 9/1/1883

YEAR	TM/L	G	AB	R	H	2B	3B	HR	RBI	BB	SO	AVG	OBP	SLG	PRO+	BR/A	SB	CS	SBR	FA	FR	G/POS	TPR
1883	Cle-N	1	4	1	1	0	0	0	0	0	2	.250	.250	.250	53	-0				.000	-1	/O-1,P-1	0.0

■ TORII HUNTER Hunter, Torii Kedar b: 7/18/75, Pine Bluff, Ark. BR/TR, 6'2", 205 lbs. Deb: 8/22/97

YEAR	TM/L	G	AB	R	H	2B	3B	HR	RBI	BB	SO	AVG	OBP	SLG	PRO+	BR/A	SB	CS	SBR	FA	FR	G/POS	TPR
1997	Min-A	1	0	0	0	0	0	0	0	0	0	—	—	—	—	0	0	0	0	.000	0	/R	0.0
1998	Min-A	6	17	0	4	1	0	0	2	2	6	.235	.316	.294	60	-1	0	1	-1	1.000	-2	/O-6	-0.3
Total	2	7	17	0	4	1	0	0	2	2	6	.235	.316	.294	60	-1	0	1	-1	1.000	-2	/O-6	-0.3

■ BILL HUNTER Hunter, William Ellsworth b: 7/8/1887, Buffalo, N.Y. d: 4/10/34, Buffalo, N.Y. BL/TL, 5'7.5", 155 lbs. Deb: 8/6/12 F

YEAR	TM/L	G	AB	R	H	2B	3B	HR	RBI	BB	SO	AVG	OBP	SLG	PRO+	BR/A	SB	CS	SBR	FA	FR	G/POS	TPR
1912	Cle-A	21	55	6	9	2	0	0	2	10		.164	.303	.200	43	-4	0			1.000	-0	O-16	-0.5

■ BILL HUNTER Hunter, William Robert b: 1855, St.Thomas, Ont., Can. 5'7.5", 160 lbs. Deb: 5/2/1884

YEAR	TM/L	G	AB	R	H	2B	3B	HR	RBI	BB	SO	AVG	OBP	SLG	PRO+	BR/A	SB	CS	SBR	FA	FR	G/POS	TPR
1884	Lou-a	2	7	1	1	0	0	0		0		.143	.143	.143	-7	-1				.667	-2	/C-2	-0.3

YEAR	TM/L	G	AB	R	H	2B	3B	HR	RBI	BB	SO	AVG	OBP	SLG	PRO+	BR/A	SB	CS	SBR	FA	FR	G/POS	TPR

■ STEVE HUNTZ
Huntz, Stephen Michael b: 12/3/45, Cleveland, Ohio BB/TR, 6'1", 204 lbs. Deb: 9/19/67

1967	StL-N	3	6	1	1	0	0	0	1	2		.167	.286	.167	33	-0	0	0	0	1.000	-1	/2-2	-0.2
1969	StL-N	71	139	13	27	4	0	3	13	27	34	.194	.325	.288	73	-4	0	0	0	.945	-6	S-52,2-12/3-6	-0.6
1970	SD-N	106	352	54	77	8	0	11	37	66	69	.219	.344	.335	86	-5	0	3	-2	.958	-12	S-57,3-51	-1.3
1971	Chi-A	35	86	10	18	3	1	2	6	7	9	.209	.269	.337	69	-4	1	0	0	1.000	-1	2-14/S-7,3-6	-0.3
1975	SD-N	22	53	3	8	4	0	0	4	7	8	.151	.250	.226	35	-5	0	0	0	.939	1	3-16/2-2	-0.4
Total	5	237	636	81	131	19	1	16	60	108	122	.206	.322	.314	76	-19	1	3	-2	.955	-18	S-116/3-79,2-30	-2.8

■ DAVE HUPPERT
Huppert, David Blain b: 4/17/57, South Gate, Cal. BR/TR, 6'1", 190 lbs. Deb: 9/15/83

1983	Bal-A	2	0	0	0	0	0	0	0	0	0	—	—	—			0	0	0	1.000	0	/C-2	0.0
1985	Mil-A	15	21	1	1	0	0	0	0	2	7	.048	.130	.048	-49	-4	0	0	0	.960	2	C-15	-0.2
Total	2	17	21	1	1	0	0	0	0	2	7	.048	.130	.048	-49	-4	0	0	0	.962	3	/C-17	-0.2

■ CLINT HURDLE
Hurdle, Clinton Merrick b: 7/30/57, Big Rapids, Mich. BL/TR, 6'3", 195 lbs. Deb: 9/18/77 C

1977	KC-A	9	26	5	8	0	0	2	7	2	7	.308	.357	.538	139	1	0	0	0	1.000	-0	/O-9	0.1
1978	*KC-A	133	417	48	110	25	5	7	56	56	84	.264	.352	.398	108	5	1	3	-2	.958	-11	O-78,1-52/3-1,D-1	-1.3
1979	KC-A	59	171	16	41	10	3	3	30	28	24	.240	.350	.386	96	-0	0	1	-1	.968	-3	O-50/3-1,D-4	-0.6
1980	*KC-A	130	395	50	116	31	2	10	60	34	61	.294	.353	.458	119	10	0	0	0	.960	-3	*O-126	0.3
1981	*KC-A	28	76	12	25	3	1	4	15	13	10	.329	.427	.553	182	8	0	0	0	1.000	1	O-28	0.8
1982	Cin-N	19	34	2	7	1	0	0	1	2	6	.206	.270	.235	42	-3	0	1	-1	.950	-2	O-17	-0.6
1983	NY-N	13	33	3	6	2	0	0	2	2	10	.182	.229	.242	31	-3	0	0	0	.800	-2	/3-9,O-1	-0.5
1985	NY-N	43	82	7	16	4	0	3	7	13	20	.195	.313	.354	88	-1	0	1	-1	1.000	-2	C-17,O-10	-0.3
1986	StL-N	78	154	18	30	5	1	3	15	26	38	.195	.315	.299	71	-6	0	0	0	.994	-6	1-39,O-10/C-5,3-4	-1.0
1987	NY-N	3	3	1	1	0	0	0	0	1	1	.333	.333	.333	82	-0	0	0	0	1.000	-0	/1-1	-0.0
Total	10	515	1391	162	360	81	12	32	193	176	261	.259	.345	.403	106	12	1	6	-3	.965	-23	O-329/1-92,C-22,3D	-3.1

■ JERRY HURLEY
Hurley, Jeremiah b: 4/1875, New York, N.Y. d: 12/27/19, New York, N.Y. BR/TR Deb: 9/23/01

1901	Cin-N	9	21	1	1	0	0	0	0	0	1	.048	.130	.048	-51	-4	1			.938	1	/C-7	-0.3
1907	Bro-N	1	2	0	0	0	0	0	0	0	1	.000	.333	.000	5	-0	0			1.000	-0	/C-1	0.0
Total	2	10	23	1	1	0	0	0	0	0	2	.043	.154	.043	-44	-4	1			.943	1	/C-8	-0.3

■ JERRY HURLEY
Hurley, Jeremiah Joseph b: 6/15/1863, Boston, Mass. d: 9/17/50, Boston, Mass. BR/TR, 6', 190 lbs. Deb: 5/1/1889

1889	Bos-N	1	4	0	0	0	0	0	0	0	0	.000	.000	.000	-94	-1	0			.000	-1	/O-1,C-1	-0.2
1890	Pit-P	8	22	5	6	1	0	0	2	2	5	.273	.333	.318	81	-1	0			.906	-0	/C-7,O-1	0.0
1891	Cin-a	24	66	10	14	3	2	0	6	12	13	.212	.333	.318	80	-2	2			.862	-3	C-24/O-1,1-1	-0.3
Total	3	33	92	15	20	4	2	0	8	14	18	.217	.321	.304	72	-3	2			.870	-5	/C-32,O-3,1-1	-0.5

■ DICK HURLEY
Hurley, William H. b: 1847, Honesdale, Pa. 5'7", 160 lbs. Deb: 4/18/1872

| 1872 | Oly-n | 2 | 7 | 0 | 0 | 0 | 0 | 0 | 0 | 0 | 0 | .000 | .000 | .000 | -99 | -2 | 0 | | | .667 | -0 | /O-2 | -0.1 |

■ DON HURST
Hurst, Frank O'Donnell b: 8/12/05, Maysville, Ky. d: 12/6/52, Los Angeles, Cal. BL/TL, 6', 215 lbs. Deb: 5/13/28

1928	Phi-N	107	396	73	113	23	4	19	64	68	40	.285	.391	.508	129	17	3			.989	4	*1-104	1.2
1929	Phi-N	154	589	100	179	29	4	31	125	80	36	.304	.390	.525	117	15	10			.985	5	*1-154	0.4
1930	Phi-N	119	391	78	128	19	3	17	78	46	22	.327	.401	.522	113	8	6			.984	-3	1-96/O-7	-0.4
1931	Phi-N	137	489	63	149	37	5	11	91	64	28	.305	.386	.468	119	14	8			.986	11	*1-135	1.2
1932	Phi-N	150	579	109	196	41	4	24	**143**	65	27	.339	.412	.547	139	32	10			**.993**	-3	*1-150	1.7
1933	Phi-N	147	550	58	147	27	8	8	76	60	32	.267	.327	.389	92	-6	3			.985	7	*1-142	-1.3
1934	Phi-N	40	130	16	34	9	0	2	21	12	7	.262	.324	.377	77	-4	1			.994	-1	1-34	-0.8
	Chi-N	51	151	13	30	5	0	3	12	8	18	.199	.239	.291	42	-13	0			.986	-2	1-48	-1.8
	Yr	91	281	29	64	14	0	5	33	20	25	.228	.279	.331	60	-16	1			.990	-3	1-82	-2.6
Total	7	905	3275	510	976	190	28	115	610	391	210	.298	.375	.478	113	63	41			.987	19	1-863/O-7	0.2

■ JIMMY HURST
Hurst, Jimmy O'Neal b: 3/1/72, Tuscaloosa, Ala. BR/TR, 6'6", 225 lbs. Deb: 9/10/97

| 1997 | Det-A | 13 | 17 | 1 | 3 | 1 | 0 | 1 | 1 | 2 | 6 | .176 | .263 | .412 | 73 | -1 | 0 | 0 | 0 | 1.000 | -3 | O-12/D-1 | -0.3 |

■ BUTCH HUSKEY
Huskey, Robert Leon b: 11/10/71, Anadarko, Okla. BR/TR, 6'3", 244 lbs. Deb: 9/8/93

1993	NY-N	13	41	2	6	1	0	0	3	1	13	.146	.171	.171	-10	-6	0	0	0	.923	3	3-13	-0.3
1995	NY-N	28	90	8	17	1	0	3	11	10	16	.189	.270	.300	52	-6	1	0	0	.925	5	3-27/O-1	-0.1
1996	NY-N	118	414	43	115	16	2	15	60	27	77	.278	.322	.435	102	-0	1	2	-1	.984	-6	1-75,O-40/3-6	-1.4
1997	NY-N	142	471	61	135	26	1	24	81	25	84	.287	.344	.503	117	9	8	5	-1	.968	-3	O-92,1-22,3-15/D-4	0.2
1998	NY-N	113	369	43	93	18	0	13	59	26	66	.252	.303	.407	83	-10	7	6	-2	.978	1	*O-103/D-1	-1.2
Total	5	414	1385	157	366	62	4	55	214	89	256	.264	.310	.434	95	-14	17	13	-3	.968	-0	O-236/1-97,3-61,D-5	-2.8

■ JEFF HUSON
Huson, Jeffrey Kent b: 8/15/64, Scottsdale, Ariz. BL/TR, 6'3", 180 lbs. Deb: 9/2/88

1988	Mon-N	20	42	7	13	0	3	0	4	3	4	.310	.370	.357	105	0	2	1	0	.932	1	S-15/2-2,3-1,O-1	0.2
1989	Mon-N	32	74	1	12	5	0	0	2	6	6	.162	.225	.230	30	-7	3	0	1	.886	4	S-20/2-9,3-1	-0.1
1990	Tex-A	145	396	57	95	12	2	0	28	46	54	.240	.322	.280	70	-15	12	4	1	.960	-13	*S-119,3-36,2-12	-1.9
1991	Tex-A	119	268	36	57	8	3	2	26	39	32	.213	.313	.287	68	-11	8	3	1	.965	-0	*S-116/2-2,3-1	-0.3
1992	Tex-A	123	318	49	83	14	3	4	24	41	43	.261	.347	.362	102	2	18	6	2	.968	-9	S-82,2-47/O-2,D-1	0.0
1993	Tex-A	23	45	3	6	1	1	0	2	0	6	.133	.133	.200	-12	-7	0	0	0	.909	5	S-12/2-5,3-2,D-2	-0.1
1995	Bal-A	66	161	24	40	4	2	1	19	15	20	.248	.316	.317	64	-8	5	4	-1	1.000	5	3-33,2-21/S-1,D-3	-0.6
1996	Bal-A	17	28	5	9	1	0	0	2	1	3	.321	.345	.357	78	-1	0	0	0	.973	1	2-12/3-3,O-1	0.1
1997	Mil-A	84	143	12	29	3	0	0	11	5	15	.203	.240	.224	22	-16	3	0	1	.989	-2	2-32,1-21/O-9,3D	-1.7
1998	Sea-A	31	49	8	8	1	0	1	4	5	6	.163	.241	.245	27	-5	1	1	-0	1.000	-2	/2-8,3-8,1-7,SOD	-0.8
Total	10	660	1524	202	352	51	14	8	121	162	192	.231	.307	.295	66	-68	52	19	4	.955	-13	S-366,2-150/310D	-5.2

■ CARL HUSTA
Husta, Carl Lawrence "Sox" b: 4/8/02, Egg Harbor City, N.J. d: 11/6/51, Kingston, N.Y. BR/TR, 5'11", 176 lbs. Deb: 9/24/25

| 1925 | Phi-A | 6 | 22 | 2 | 3 | 0 | 0 | 0 | 2 | 2 | 3 | .136 | .208 | .136 | -11 | -4 | 0 | 0 | 0 | .976 | 2 | /S-6 | -0.1 |

■ HARRY HUSTON
Huston, Harry Emanuel Kress b: 10/14/1883, Bellefontaine, O. d: 10/13/69, Blackwell, Okla. BR/TR, 5'9", 168 lbs. Deb: 9/3/06

| 1906 | Phi-N | 2 | 4 | 0 | 0 | 0 | 0 | 0 | 0 | 0 | | .000 | .200 | .000 | -37 | -1 | 0 | | | 1.000 | -0 | /C-2 | -0.1 |

■ WARREN HUSTON
Huston, Warren Llewellyn b: 10/31/13, Newtonville, Mass. BR/TR, 6', 170 lbs. Deb: 6/24/37

1937	Phi-A	38	54	5	7	0	0	0	2	9		.130	.161	.185	-13	-10	0	1	-1	.918	8	2-16,S-15/3-2	-0.1
1944	Bos-N	33	55	7	11	1	0	0	8	5		.200	.313	.218	49	-3	0			.979	3	3-20/2-5,S-4	0.0
Total	2	71	109	12	18	1	0	0	4	10	14	.165	.242	.202	19	-13	0			.964	11	/3-22,2-21,S-19	-0.1

■ JOE HUTCHESON
Hutcheson, Joseph Johnson "Slug" or "Poodles" b: 2/5/05, Springtown, Tex. d: 2/23/93, Tyler, Tex. BL/TR, 6'2", 200 lbs. Deb: 7/8/33

| 1933 | Bro-N | 55 | 184 | 19 | 43 | 4 | 1 | 6 | 21 | 15 | 13 | .234 | .295 | .364 | 94 | -1 | 1 | | | .989 | 1 | O-45 | -0.4 |

■ ED HUTCHINSON
Hutchinson, Edwin Forrest b: 5/19/1867, Pittsburgh, Pa. d: 7/19/34, Colfax, Cal. BL/TR, 5'11", 175 lbs. Deb: 6/17/1890

| 1890 | Chi-N | 4 | 17 | 0 | 1 | 0 | 0 | 0 | 0 | 0 | 0 | .059 | .059 | .118 | -47 | -3 | 0 | | | 1.000 | 6 | /2-4 | 0.2 |

■ FRED HUTCHINSON
Hutchinson, Frederick Charles b: 8/12/19, Seattle, Wash. d: 11/12/64, Bradenton, Fla. BL/TR, 6'2", 200 lbs. Deb: 5/2/39 M

1939	Det-A	13	34	5	13	1	0	0	6	2	0	.382	.417	.412	105	0	0	0	0	1.000	-0	P-13	0.0
1940	*Det-A	17	30	1	8	1	0	0	3	0	3	.267	.267	.300	43	-3	0	0	0	.900	4	P-17	0.0
1941	Det-A	2	0	0	0	0	0	0	0	0	0	.000	.000	.000	-91	-0	0	0	0	.000	-0	H	-0.1
1946	Det-A	40	89	11	28	4	0	0	13	6	1	.315	.358	.360	95	-0	0	0	0	.983	3	P-28	0.0
1947	Det-A	56	106	8	32	5	2	1	6	3	1	.302	.339	.443	113	4	1	2	0	.982	3	P-33	0.0
1948	Det-A	76	112	11	23	2	0	0	22	6	9	.205	.341	.241	55	-6	3	0	1	**1.000**	3	P-33	0.0
1949	Det-A	38	73	12	18	2	0	0	7	8	5	.247	.329	.301	67	-3	0	0	0	.983	-0	P-33	0.0
1950	Det-A	44	95	15	31	7	0	0	20	12	3	.326	.407	.400	104	1	0	0	0	.944	-2	P-39	0.0

YEAR	TM/L	G	AB	R	H	2B	3B	HR	RBI	BB	SO	AVG	OBP	SLG	PRO+	BR/A	SB	CS	SBR	FA	FR	G/POS	TPR
1951	Det-A★	47	85	7	16	2	0	0	7	7	4	.188	.250	.212	26	-9	0	1	-1	.939	2	P-31	0.0
1952	Det-A	17	18	0	1	0	0	0	0	3	0	.056	.190	.056	-29	-3	0	0	0	1.000	2	P-12,M	0.0
1953	Det-A	4	6	1	1	0	0	1	1	0	0	.167	.167	.667	118	0	0	0	0	1.000	-0	/P-3,1-1,M	0.0
Total	11	354	650	71	171	23	3	4	83	66	30	.263	.334	.326	75	-22	6	1	1	.970	15	P-242/1-1	-0.1
■ **ROY HUTSON** Hutson, Roy Lee b: 2/27/02, Luray, Mo. d: 5/20/57, LaMesa, Cal. BL/TR, 5'9", 165 lbs. Deb: 9/20/25																							
1925	Bro-N	7	8	1	4	0	0	0	1	1	1	.500	.556	.500	177	1	0	0	0	1.000	-1	/O-4	0.0
■ **JIM HUTTO** Hutto, James Neamon b: 10/17/47, Norfolk, Va. BR/TR, 5'11", 195 lbs. Deb: 4/17/70																							
1970	Phi-N	57	92	7	17	2	0	3	12	5	20	.185	.227	.304	42	-8	0	0	0	1.000	-3	O-22,1-12/C-5,3-1	-1.2
1975	Bal-A	4	5	0	0	0	0	0	0	0	2	.000	.000	.000	-99	-1	0	0	0	1.000	-0	/C-3	-0.1
Total	2	61	97	7	17	2	0	3	12	5	22	.175	.216	.289	35	-9	0	0	0	1.000	-3	/O-22,1-12,C-8,3-1	-1.3
■ **TOM HUTTON** Hutton, Thomas George b: 4/20/46, Los Angeles, Cal. BL/TL, 5'11", 180 lbs. Deb: 9/16/66																							
1966	LA-N	3	2	0	0	0	0	0	0	0	0	.000	.000	.000	-99	-1	0	0	0	1.000	-0	/1-3	-0.1
1969	LA-N	16	48	2	13	0	0	0	4	5	7	.271	.340	.271	78	-1	0	0	0	.993	4	1-16	0.2
1972	Phi-N	134	381	40	99	16	2	4	38	56	24	.260	.355	.344	97	0	5	8	-3	.992	1	1-87,O-48	-1.1
1973	Phi-N	106	247	31	65	11	0	5	29	32	31	.263	.348	.368	96	-1	3	1	0	.998	4	1-71	0.0
1974	Phi-N	96	208	32	50	6	3	4	33	30	13	.240	.336	.356	90	-2	2	2	-1	.996	-3	1-39,O-33	-0.9
1975	Phi-N	113	165	24	41	6	0	3	24	27	10	.248	.354	.339	90	-2	2	5	-2	.994	3	1-71,O-12	-0.4
1976	*Phi-N	95	124	15	25	5	1	1	13	27	11	.202	.344	.282	77	-3	1	2	-1	1.000	4	1-72/O-1	-0.2
1977	*Phi-N	107	81	12	25	3	0	2	11	12	10	.309	.398	.420	114	2	1	1	-0	.993	1	1-73/O-9	0.2
1978	Tor-A	64	173	19	44	9	0	2	9	19	11	.254	.328	.341	87	-3	1	2	-1	1.000	-5	O-55/1-9	-1.1
	Mon-N	39	59	4	12	3	0	0	5	10	5	.203	.319	.254	63	-3	0	0	0	1.000	-3	1-17/O-5	-0.7
1979	Mon-N	86	83	14	21	2	1	1	13	10	7	.253	.333	.337	84	-2	0	0	0	1.000	1	1-25/O-9	-0.1
1980	Mon-N	62	55	2	12	2	0	0	5	4	10	.218	.271	.255	47	-4	0	0	0	1.000	-2	/1-7,O-4,P-1	-0.6
1981	Mon-N	31	29	1	3	0	0	0	2	2	1	.103	.161	.103	-23	-5	0	0	0	1.000	-0	/1-9,O-2	-0.6
Total	12	952	1655	196	410	63	7	22	186	234	140	.248	.341	.334	87	-22	15	21	-8	.995	5	1-499,O-178/P-1	-5.4
■ **HAM HYATT** Hyatt, Robert Hamilton b: 11/1/1884, Buncombe Co., N.C. d: 9/11/63, Liberty Lake, Wash. BL/TR, 6'1", 185 lbs. Deb: 4/15/09																							
1909	*Pit-N	49	67	9	20	3	4	0	7	3		.299	.329	.463	134	2	1			.933	3	/O-6,1-2	0.5
1910	Pit-N	74	175	19	46	5	6	1	30	8	14	.263	.306	.377	94	-2	3			.986	-2	1-38/O-4	-0.4
1912	Pit-N	46	97	13	28	3	1	0	22	6	8	.289	.330	.340	85	-2	2			.955	-2	O-15/1-3	-0.5
1913	Pit-N	63	81	8	27	6	2	4	16	3	8	.333	.372	.605	184	8	0			1.000	-2	/1-5,O-5	0.6
1914	Pit-N	74	79	2	17	3	1	1	15	7	14	.215	.295	.316	86	-1	1			.980	-2	/1-7,C-1	-0.4
1915	StL-N	106	295	23	79	8	9	2	46	28	24	.268	.337	.376	116	6	3	3	-1	.991	-6	1-64,O-25	-0.4
1918	NY-A	53	131	11	30	8	0	2	10	8	8	.229	.273	.336	82	-4	1			1.000	-1	O-25/1-5	-0.7
Total	7	465	925	85	247	36	23	10	146	63	76	.267	.321	.388	108	6	11	3		.989	-11	1-124/O-80,C-1	-1.3
■ **TIM HYERS** Hyers, Timothy James b: 10/3/71, Atlanta, Ga. BL/TL, 6'1", 185 lbs. Deb: 4/4/94																							
1994	SD-N	52	118	13	30	3	0	0	7	9	15	.254	.307	.280	56	-7	3	0	1	.986	0	1-41/O-2	-0.9
1995	SD-N	6	5	0	0	0	0	0	0	0	1	.000	.000	.000	-99	-1	0	0	0	1.000	0	/1-1	-0.1
1996	Det-A	17	26	1	2	1	0	0	0	4	5	.077	.200	.115	-18	-5	0	0	0	1.000	-0	/1-9,O-1,D-2	-0.5
Total	3	75	149	14	32	4	0	0	7	13	21	.215	.278	.242	37	-14	3	0	1	.987	0	/1-51,O-3,D-2	-1.5
■ **JIM HYNDMAN** Hyndman, James William b: 7/1865, Ontario, Canada Deb: 7/23/1886																							
1886	Phi-a	1	4	0	0	0	0	0	0	0		.000	.000	.000	-99	-1	0			1.000	0	/O-1,P-1	-0.1
■ **PAT HYNES** Hynes, Patrick J. b: 3/12/1884, St.Louis, Mo. d: 3/12/07, St.Louis, Mo. TL , Deb: 9/27/03																							
1903	StL-N	1	3	0	0	0	0	0	0	0		.000	.000	.000	-99	-1	0			.500	-1	/P-1	0.0
1904	StL-A	66	254	23	60	7	3	0	15	3		.236	.248	.287	74	-8	3			.901	-12	O-63/P-5	-2.5
Total	2	67	257	23	60	7	3	0	15	3		.233	.245	.284	71	-9	3			.857	-12	/O-63,P-6	-2.5
■ **RAUL IBANEZ** Ibanez, Raul Javier b: 6/2/72, New York, N.Y. BL/TR, 6'2", 210 lbs. Deb: 8/1/96																							
1996	Sea-A	4	5	0	0	0	0	0	0	0	1	.000	.167	.000	-53	-1	0	0	0	.000	0	/D-2	-0.1
1997	Sea-A	11	26	3	4	0	1	1	4	0	6	.154	.154	.346	26	-3	0	0	0	1.000	-1	/O-8,D-1	-0.4
1998	Sea-A	37	98	12	25	7	1	2	12	5	22	.255	.291	.408	79	-3	0	0	0	1.000	-5	O-17,1-16/D-1	-1.0
Total	3	52	129	15	29	7	2	3	16	5	29	.225	.259	.380	63	-7	0	0	0	1.000	-6	/O-25,1-16,D-4	-1.5
■ **PETE INCAVIGLIA** Incaviglia, Peter Joseph b: 4/2/64, Pebble Beach, Cal. BR/TR, 6'1", 230 lbs. Deb: 4/8/86																							
1986	Tex-A	153	540	82	135	21	2	30	88	55	185	.250	.324	.463	108	5	3	2	-0	.921	-11	*O-114,D-36	-1.0
1987	Tex-A	139	509	85	138	26	4	27	80	48	168	.271	.335	.497	116	11	9	3	1	.945	-3	*O-132/D-6	0.4
1988	Tex-A	116	418	59	104	19	3	22	54	39	153	.249	.323	.467	116	8	6	4	-1	.989	6	O-93,D-21	1.0
1989	Tex-A	133	453	48	107	27	4	21	81	32	136	.236	.295	.453	106	2	5	7	-3	.973	-3	*O-125/D-5	-0.7
1990	Tex-A	153	529	59	123	27	0	24	85	45	146	.233	.304	.420	100	-1	3	4	-2	.974	-0	*O-145/D-2	-0.7
1991	Det-A	97	337	38	72	12	1	11	38	36	92	.214	.291	.353	76	-11	1	3	-2	.973	2	O-54,D-41	-1.4
1992	Hou-N	113	349	31	93	22	1	11	44	25	99	.266	.321	.430	116	6	2	2	-1	.970	4	O-98	0.8
1993	*Phi-N	116	368	60	101	16	3	24	89	21	82	.274	.324	.530	126	11	1	1	-0	.971	-2	O-97	0.7
1994	Phi-N	80	244	28	56	10	1	13	32	16	71	.230	.280	.439	82	-8	1	0	0	.979	-2	O-63	-1.1
1996	Phi-N	99	269	33	63	7	2	16	42	30	82	.234	.318	.454	99	-1	2	0	1	.969	-3	O-71	-0.5
	*Bal-A	12	33	4	10	2	0	2	8	0	7	.303	.324	.545	115	1	0	0	0	1.000	-0	/O-7,D-4	0.0
1997	Bal-A	48	138	18	34	4	0	5	12	11	43	.246	.316	.384	84	-3	0	0	0	.952	-3	D-26,O-18	-0.8
	NY-A	5	16	1	4	0	0	0	0	0	3	.250	.250	.250	31	-2	0	0	0	.000	0	/D-5	-0.2
	Yr	53	154	19	38	4	0	5	12	11	46	.247	.310	.370	79	-5	0	0	0	.952	-3	D-31,O-18	-1.0
1998	Det-A	7	14	0	1	0	0	0	0	1	6	.071	.133	.071	-44	-3	0	0	0	.000	0	/D-4	-0.3
	*Hou-N	13	16	0	2	1	0	0	2	1	4	.125	.176	.188	-6	-3	0	0	0	1.000	-0	/O-3	-0.3
Total	12	1284	4233	546	1043	194	21	206	655	360	1277	.246	.312	.448	104	12	33	26	-6	.966	-18	*O-1020,D-150	-4.1
■ **ALEXIS INFANTE** Infante, Fermin Alexis (Carpio) b: 12/4/61, Barquisimeto, Venez. BR/TR, 5'10", 175 lbs. Deb: 9/27/87																							
1987	Tor-A	1	0	0	0	0	0	0	0	0	0	—	—	—	—	0	0	0	0	.000	0	/R	0.0
1988	Tor-A	19	15	7	3	0	0	0	0	2	4	.200	.294	.200	41	-1	0	0	0	.909	1	/3-9,S-2,D-7	0.0
1989	Tor-A	20	12	1	2	0	0	0	0	0	1	.167	.167	.167	-6	-2	1	0	0	1.000	4	/S-9,3-4,2-1,D-4	0.3
1990	Atl-N	20	28	3	1	1	0	0	0	0	7	.036	.069	.071	-58	-6	0	0	0	.964	4	2-10/3-4,S-3	-0.2
Total	4	60	55	11	6	1	0	0	0	2	12	.109	.155	.127	-20	-9	1	0	0	.933	9	/3-17,S-14,2-11,D	0.1
■ **SCOTTY INGERTON** Ingerton, William John b: 4/19/1886, Peninsula, Ohio d: 6/15/56, Cleveland, Ohio BR/TR, 6'1", 172 lbs. Deb: 4/12/11																							
1911	Bos-N	136	521	63	130	24	4	5	61	39	68	.250	.304	.340	74	-20	6			.942	18	3-58,O-43,1-17,2/S	-0.3
■ **CHARLIE INGRAHAM** Ingraham, Charles W. b: 4/8/1860, Illinois d: 2/18/06, Chicago, Ill. 5'11", 170 lbs. Deb: 7/4/1883																							
1883	Bal-a	1	4	0	1	0	0	0	0			.250	.250	.250	60	-0				.833	-1	/C-1	-0.1
■ **GAREY INGRAM** Ingram, Garey Lamar b: 7/25/70, Columbus, Ga. BR/TR, 5'11", 180 lbs. Deb: 5/15/94																							
1994	LA-N	26	78	10	22	1	0	3	8	7	22	.282	.341	.410	101	0	0	0	0	.982	6	2-23	0.7
1995	LA-N	44	55	5	11	2	0	0	3	9	8	.200	.313	.236	52	-4	3	0	1	.750	0	3-12/2-7,O-4	-0.2
1997	LA-N	12	9	2	4	0	0	0	1	1	3	.444	.500	.444	162	1	1	0	0	1.000	-2	/O-7	0.0
Total	3	82	142	17	37	3	0	3	12	17	33	.261	.340	.345	87	-3	4	0	1	.985	5	/2-30,3-12,O-11	0.5
■ **MEL INGRAM** Ingram, Melvin David b: 7/4/04, Asheville, N.C. d: 10/28/79, Medford, Ore. BR/TR, 5'11.5", 175 lbs. Deb: 7/24/29																							
1929	Pit-N	3	0	1	0	0	0	0	0	0	0	—	—	—	—	0	0			.000	0	R	0.0
■ **RICCARDO INGRAM** Ingram, Riccardo Benay b: 9/10/66, Douglas, Ga. BR/TR, 6', 205 lbs. Deb: 6/26/94																							
1994	Det-A	12	23	3	5	0	0	0	2	1	2	.217	.250	.217	22	-3	0	1	-1	1.000	-0	/O-8,D-1	-0.3

YEAR	TM/L	G	AB	R	H	2B	3B	HR	RBI	BB	SO	AVG	OBP	SLG	PRO+	BR/A	SB	CS	SBR	FA	FR	G/POS	TPR
1995	Min-A	4	8	0	1	0	0	0	1	2	1	.125	.300	.125	16	-1	0	0	0	.000	0	/D-3	-0.1
Total	2	16	31	3	6	0	0	0	3	3	3	.194	.265	.194	21	-4	0	1	-1	1.000	-0	/O-8,D-4	-0.4

■ DANE IORG Iorg, Dane Charles b: 5/11/50, Eureka, Cal. BL/TR, 6′, 180 lbs. Deb: 4/9/77 F

YEAR	TM/L	G	AB	R	H	2B	3B	HR	RBI	BB	SO	AVG	OBP	SLG	PRO+	BR/A	SB	CS	SBR	FA	FR	G/POS	TPR
1977	Phi-N	12	30	3	5	1	0	0	2	1	3	.167	.194	.200	6	-4	0	0	0	.986	-0	/1-9	-0.5
	StL-N	30	32	2	10	1	0	0	4	5	4	.313	.405	.344	105	1	0	1	-1	.875	-2	/O-7	-0.2
	Yr	42	62	5	15	2	0	0	6	6	7	.242	.309	.274	58	-4	0	1	-1	.986	-2	/1-9,O-7	-0.7
1978	StL-N	35	85	6	23	4	1	0	4	4	10	.271	.303	.341	81	-2	0	0	0	1.000	0	O-25	-0.3
1979	StL-N	79	179	12	52	11	1	1	21	12	28	.291	.339	.380	95	-1	1	2	-1	.964	-6	O-39,1-10	-1.0
1980	StL-N	105	251	33	76	23	1	3	36	20	34	.303	.354	.438	116	5	1	1	-0	.991	-3	O-63/1-5,3-1	-0.1
1981	StL-N	75	217	23	71	11	2	2	39	7	9	.327	.348	.424	115	4	2	0	1	.963	-11	O-57/1-8,3-2	-0.9
1982	*StL-N	102	238	17	70	14	1	0	34	23	23	.294	.356	.361	100	1	0	1	-1	.971	-5	O-63,1-10/3-2	-0.7
1983	StL-N	58	116	6	31	9	1	0	11	10	11	.267	.331	.362	92	-1	1	0	0	.974	-3	O-22,1-11	-0.5
1984	StL-N	15	28	3	4	2	0	0	3	2	6	.143	.200	.214	17	-3	0	0	0	1.000	-1	/1-6,O-5	-0.4
	*KC-A	78	235	27	60	16	2	5	30	13	15	.255	.294	.404	90	-4	0	1	-1	.995	-4	1-43,O-22/3-1,D-5	-1.1
1985	*KC-A	64	130	7	29	9	1	1	21	8	16	.223	.268	.331	63	-7	0	1	-1	1.000	-5	O-32/1-2,3-1,D-2	-1.3
1986	SD-N	90	106	10	24	2	1	2	11	2	21	.226	.241	.321	55	-7	0	0	0	1.000	-2	1-10/3-6,O-3,P-2	-0.9
Total	10	743	1647	149	455	103	11	14	216	107	180	.276	.321	.378	92	-19	5	7	-3	.977	-41	O-338,1-114/3DP	-7.9

■ GARTH IORG Iorg, Garth Ray b: 10/12/54, Arcata, Cal. BR/TR, 5′11″, 170 lbs. Deb: 4/9/78 F

YEAR	TM/L	G	AB	R	H	2B	3B	HR	RBI	BB	SO	AVG	OBP	SLG	PRO+	BR/A	SB	CS	SBR	FA	FR	G/POS	TPR
1978	Tor-A	19	49	3	8	0	0	0	3	3	4	.163	.226	.163	11	-6	0	0	0	.966	4	2-18	-0.1
1980	Tor-A	80	222	24	55	10	1	2	14	12	39	.248	.286	.329	65	-11	2	1	0	.988	8	2-32,3-20,O1/SD	-0.2
1981	Tor-A	70	215	17	52	11	0	0	10	7	31	.242	.269	.293	58	-12	2	3	-1	.963	-0	2-46,3-17/S-2,1D	-1.1
1982	Tor-A	129	417	45	119	20	5	1	36	12	38	.285	.312	.365	78	-13	3	2	-0	.946	-4	*3-100,2-30/D-1	-1.8
1983	Tor-A	122	375	40	103	22	5	2	39	13	45	.275	.301	.376	80	-11	7	0	2	.976	-3	3-85,2-39/S-1	-1.1
1984	Tor-A	121	247	24	56	10	3	1	25	5	16	.227	.245	.304	49	-17	1	3	-2	.945	1	*3-112/2-7,S-2,D-1	-1.8
1985	*Tor-A	131	288	33	90	22	1	7	37	21	26	.313	.359	.469	122	8	3	6	-3	.951	11	*3-104,2-23	1.6
1986	Tor-A	137	327	30	85	19	1	3	44	20	47	.260	.305	.352	76	-11	3	0	1	.955	-15	3-90,2-52/S-2	-2.4
1987	Tor-A	122	310	35	65	11	0	4	30	21	52	.210	.264	.284	45	-25	2	2	-1	.982	-13	2-91,3-28/D-5	-3.4
Total	9	931	2450	251	633	125	16	20	238	114	298	.258	.294	.347	72	-96	23	17	-3	.955	-12	3-556,2-338/O1DS	-10.3

■ HAPPY IOTT Iott, Frederick "Happy Jack" or "Biddo" (b: Frederick Hoyot)
b: 7/7/1876, Houlton, Me. d: 2/17/41, Island Falls, Me. BR/TR, 5′10″, 175 lbs. Deb: 9/16/03

YEAR	TM/L	G	AB	R	H	2B	3B	HR	RBI	BB	SO	AVG	OBP	SLG	PRO+	BR/A	SB	CS	SBR	FA	FR	G/POS	TPR
1903	Cle-A	3	10	1	2	0	0	0	0	2		.200	.333	.200	64	-0	1			.875	-0	/O-3	-0.1

■ HAL IRELAN Irelan, Harold "Grump" b: 8/5/1890, Burnettsville, Ind. d: 7/16/44, Carmel, Ind. BB/TR, 5′7″, 165 lbs. Deb: 4/23/14

YEAR	TM/L	G	AB	R	H	2B	3B	HR	RBI	BB	SO	AVG	OBP	SLG	PRO+	BR/A	SB	CS	SBR	FA	FR	G/POS	TPR
1914	Phi-N	67	165	16	39	8	0	1	16	21	22	.236	.326	.303	82	-3	3			.909	11	2-44/S-3,1-2,3-2	0.8

■ TIM IRELAND Ireland, Timothy Neal b: 3/14/53, Oakland, Cal. BR/TR, 6′, 180 lbs. Deb: 9/20/81

YEAR	TM/L	G	AB	R	H	2B	3B	HR	RBI	BB	SO	AVG	OBP	SLG	PRO+	BR/A	SB	CS	SBR	FA	FR	G/POS	TPR
1981	KC-A	4	0	1	0	0	0	0	0	0	0	—	—	—	—	0	0	1	-1	1.000	-0	/1-4	-0.1
1982	KC-A	7	7	2	1	0	0	0	0	1	1	.143	.250	.143	11	-1	0	0	0	1.000	0	/2-4,O-2,3-1	-0.1
Total	2	11	7	3	1	0	0	0	0	1	1	.143	.250	.143	11	-1	0	1	-1	1.000	0	/2-4,1-4,O-2,3-1	-0.2

■ MONTE IRVIN Irvin, Monford b: 2/25/19, Columbia, Ala. BR/TR, 6′1″, 195 lbs. Deb: 7/8/49 H

YEAR	TM/L	G	AB	R	H	2B	3B	HR	RBI	BB	SO	AVG	OBP	SLG	PRO+	BR/A	SB	CS	SBR	FA	FR	G/POS	TPR
1949	NY-N	36	76	7	17	3	2	0	7	17	11	.224	.366	.316	84	-1	0			1.000	0	O-10/1-5,3-5	-0.1
1950	NY-N	110	374	61	112	19	5	15	66	52	41	.299	.392	.497	131	18	3			.979	5	1-59,O-49/3-1	1.8
1951	*NY-N	151	558	94	174	19	11	24	**121**	89	44	.312	.415	.514	147	40	12	2	2	.996	11	*O-112,1-39	4.6
1952	NY-N†	46	126	10	39	2	1	4	21	10	11	.310	.365	.437	120	3	0	1	-1	1.000	-2	O-32	0.0
1953	NY-N	124	444	72	146	21	5	21	97	55	34	.329	.406	.541	142	28	2	0	1	.973	8	*O-113	3.0
1954	*NY-N	135	432	62	113	13	3	19	64	70	23	.262	.367	.438	108	6	7	4	-0	.976	4	*O-128/1-1,3-1	0.5
1955	NY-N	51	150	16	38	7	1	1	17	17	15	.253	.341	.333	80	-4	3	0	1	.961	1	O-45	-0.4
1956	Chi-N	111	339	44	92	13	3	15	50	41	41	.271	.350	.460	118	8	1	0	0	.991	11	O-96	1.5
Total	8	764	2499	366	731	97	31	99	443	351	220	.293	.385	.475	126	98	28	7		.983	38	O-585,1-104/3-7	10.9

■ ED IRVIN Irvin, William Edward b: 1882, Philadelphia, Pa. d: 2/18/16, Philadelphia, Pa. BR/TR, Deb: 5/18/12

YEAR	TM/L	G	AB	R	H	2B	3B	HR	RBI	BB	SO	AVG	OBP	SLG	PRO+	BR/A	SB	CS	SBR	FA	FR	G/POS	TPR
1912	Det-A	1	3	0	2	0	2	0	0	0		.667	.667	2.000	675	2	0			.500	-1	/3-1	0.1

■ ARTHUR IRWIN Irwin, Arthur Albert "Doc" or "Sandy"
b: 2/14/1858, Toronto, Ont., Can. d: 7/16/21, AtSea Atlantic Ocean N.Y. To Boston BL/TR, 5′8.5″, 158 lbs. Deb: 5/1/1880 FMU

YEAR	TM/L	G	AB	R	H	2B	3B	HR	RBI	BB	SO	AVG	OBP	SLG	PRO+	BR/A	SB	CS	SBR	FA	FR	G/POS	TPR
1880	Wor-N	85	352	53	91	19	4	1	35	11	27	.259	.281	.344	102	-1				.895	**31**	*S-82/3-3,C-1	**3.4**
1881	Wor-N	50	206	27	55	8	2	0	24	7	4	.267	.291	.325	88	-3				.851	-8	S-50	-0.7
1882	Wor-N	84	333	30	73	12	4	0	30	14	34	.219	.251	.279	68	-12				.837	21	3-51,S-33	1.0
1883	Pro-N	98	406	67	116	22	7	0	44	12	38	.286	.306	.374	103	1				.856	-7	*S-94/2-4	-0.4
1884	*Pro-N	102	404	73	97	14	3	2	44	28	52	.240	.289	.304	89	-4				.881	-6	*S-102/P-1	-0.8
1885	Pro-N	59	218	16	39	2	1	0	14	14	29	.179	.228	.197	40	-14				.875	4	S-58/3-1,2-1	-0.8
1886	Phi-N	101	373	51	87	6	6	0	34	35	39	.233	.299	.282	77	-10	24			.891	4	*S-100/3-1	-0.4
1887	Phi-N	100	374	65	95	14	8	2	56	48	26	.254	.344	.350	88	-6	19			.892	-10	*S-100	-1.2
1888	Phi-N	125	448	51	98	12	4	0	28	33	56	.219	.277	.263	69	-15	19			.900	12	*S-122/2-3	-0.1
1889	Phi-N	18	73	9	16	5	0	0	10	6	6	.219	.278	.288	54	-5	6			.845	-6	S-18	-0.9
	Was-N	85	313	49	73	10	5	0	32	42	37	.233	.326	.297	80	-7	9			.895	12	S-85/P-1,2-1,M	0.8
	Yr	103	386	58	89	15	5	0	42	48	43	.231	.317	.295	74	-12	15			.888	6	*S-103/P-1,2-1	-0.1
1890	Bos-P	96	354	60	92	17	1	0	45	57	29	.260	.364	.314	77	-11	16			.878	3	*S-96	-0.3
1891	Bos-a	6	17	1	2	0	0	0	0	2	1	.118	.286	.118	16	-2	0			.778	-1	/S-6,M	-0.2
1894	Phi-N	1	0	0	0	0	0	0	0	0	0	—	—	—	—	0	0			.000	0	/S-1,M	0.0
Total	13	1010	3871	552	934	141	45	5	396	309	378	.241	.299	.305	81	-89	93			.881	49	S-947/3-56,2-9,PC	-0.6

■ CHARLIE IRWIN Irwin, Charles Edwin b: 2/15/1869, Clinton, Ill. d: 9/21/25, Chicago, Ill. BL/TR, 5′10″, 160 lbs. Deb: 9/3/1893

YEAR	TM/L	G	AB	R	H	2B	3B	HR	RBI	BB	SO	AVG	OBP	SLG	PRO+	BR/A	SB	CS	SBR	FA	FR	G/POS	TPR
1893	Chi-N	21	82	14	25	6	2	0	13	10	1	.305	.394	.427	120	3	4			.910	-1	S-21	0.2
1894	Chi-N	128	498	84	144	24	9	8	95	63	23	.289	.379	.422	88	-11	35			.822	-11	3-67,S-61	-1.4
1895	Chi-N	3	10	4	2	0	0	0	0	2	1	.200	.333	.200	37	-1	0			.900	-2	/S-3	-0.2
1896	Cin-N	127	476	77	141	16	6	1	67	26	17	.296	.338	.361	79	-16	31			**.931**	7	*3-127	-0.6
1897	Cin-N	134	505	89	146	26	6	0	74	47		.289	.360	.364	86	-11	27			.940	-7	*3-134	-1.2
1898	Cin-N	136	501	77	120	14	5	3	55	31		.240	.297	.305	68	-22	18			.940	14	*3-136	-0.7
1899	Cin-N	90	314	42	73	4	8	1	52	26		.232	.295	.306	64	-16	26			.909	-13	3-78/S-6,2-3,1-1	-2.6
1900	Cin-N	87	333	59	91	15	6	1	44	14		.273	.314	.363	89	-6	9			.931	-11	3-61,S-16/O-6,2-3	-1.4
1901	Cin-N	67	260	25	62	12	2	0	25	14		.238	.285	.300	75	-9	13			.893	4	3-67	-0.4
	Bro-N	65	242	25	52	13	2	0	20	14		.215	.269	.285	59	-13	4			.956	-2	3-65	-1.4
	Yr	132	502	50	114	25	4	0	45	28		.227	.277	.293	67	-21	17			.921	2	*3-132	-1.8
1902	Bro-N	131	458	59	125	14	0	2	43	39		.273	.346	.317	104	4	13			.927	-10	*3-130/S-1	-0.6
Total	10	989	3679	555	981	144	46	16	488	286	42	.267	.330	.344	82	-97	180			.921	-32	3-865,S-108/O-6,21	-10.3

■ JOHN IRWIN Irwin, John b: 7/21/1861, Toronto, Ont., Can d: 2/28/34, Boston, Mass. BL/TR, 5′10″, 168 lbs. Deb: 5/31/1882 F

YEAR	TM/L	G	AB	R	H	2B	3B	HR	RBI	BB	SO	AVG	OBP	SLG	PRO+	BR/A	SB	CS	SBR	FA	FR	G/POS	TPR
1882	Wor-N	1	4	0	0	0	0	0	0	0	2	.000	.000	.000	-98	-1				.636	-1	/1-1	-0.2
1884	Bos-U	105	432	81	101	22	6	1		15		.234	.260	.319	76	-26				.780	4	*3-105	-1.9
1886	Phi-a	3	13	4	3	1	0	0	1	0		.231	.231	.308	67	-1	0			.714	-1	/S-2,3-1	-0.2
1887	Was-N	8	31	6	11	2	0	2	3	3	6	.355	.429	.613	196	4	6			.875	-2	/S-5,3-4	0.2
1888	Was-N	37	126	14	28	5	2	0	8	5	18	.222	.263	.294	82	-2	15			.860	-1	S-27,3-10	-0.3
1889	Was-N	58	228	42	66	11	4	0	25	25	14	.289	.370	.373	115	6	10			.868	0	3-58	0.7
1890	Buf-P	77	308	62	72	11	4	0	34	43	19	.234	.335	.295	75	-9	18			.883	4	3-64,1-12/2-1	-0.2
1891	Bos-a	19	72	6	16	2	2	0	15	6	9	.222	.282	.306	69	-3	6			.882	0	O-17/3-2,S-1	-0.3
	Lou-a	14	55	7	15	1	1	0	7	5	6	.273	.344	.327	93	-0	1			.795	-7	3-14	-0.6

YEAR	TM/L	G	AB	R	H	2B	3B	HR	RBI	BB	SO	AVG	OBP	SLG	PRO+	BR/A	SB	CS	SBR	FA	FR	G/POS	TPR
	Yr	33	127	13	31	3	3	0	22	11	15	.244	.309	.315	80	-4	7			.882	-6	O-17,3-16/S-1	-0.9
Total	8	322	1269	222	312	55	19	3	93	102	74	.246	.308	.326	87	-32	56			.829	-4	3-258/S-35,O-17,12	-2.8

■ TOMMY IRWIN Irwin, Thomas Andrew b: 12/20/12, Altoona, Pa. d: 4/25/96, Altoona, Pa. BR/TR, 5'11", 165 lbs. Deb: 10/1/38

YEAR	TM/L	G	AB	R	H	2B	3B	HR	RBI	BB	SO	AVG	OBP	SLG	PRO+	BR/A	SB	CS	SBR	FA	FR	G/POS	TPR
1938	Cle-A	3	9	1	1	0	0	0	0	3	1	.111	.333	.111	16	-1	0	0	0	1.000	0	/S-3	-0.1

■ WALT IRWIN Irwin, Walter Kingsley b: 9/23/1897, Henrietta, Pa. d: 8/18/76, Spring Lake, Mich. BR/TR, 5'10.5", 170 lbs. Deb: 4/24/21

YEAR	TM/L	G	AB	R	H	2B	3B	HR	RBI	BB	SO	AVG	OBP	SLG	PRO+	BR/A	SB	CS	SBR	FA	FR	G/POS	TPR
1921	StL-N	4	1	1	0	0	0	0	0	0	1	.000	.000	.000	-99	-0	0	0	0	.000	0	H	0.0

■ ORLANDO ISALES Isales, Orlando (Pizarro) b: 12/22/59, Santurce, P.R. BR/TR, 5'9", 175 lbs. Deb: 9/11/80

YEAR	TM/L	G	AB	R	H	2B	3B	HR	RBI	BB	SO	AVG	OBP	SLG	PRO+	BR/A	SB	CS	SBR	FA	FR	G/POS	TPR
1980	Phi-N	3	5	1	2	0	1	0	3	1	0	.400	.500	.800	244	1	0	0	0	1.000	-0	/O-2	0.1

■ FRANK ISBELL Isbell, William Frank "Bald Eagle" b: 8/21/1875, Delevan, N.Y. d: 7/15/41, Wichita, Kan. BL/TR, 5'11", 190 lbs. Deb: 5/1/1898

YEAR	TM/L	G	AB	R	H	2B	3B	HR	RBI	BB	SO	AVG	OBP	SLG	PRO+	BR/A	SB	CS	SBR	FA	FR	G/POS	TPR
1898	Chi-N	45	159	17	37	4	0	0	8	3		.233	.252	.258	46	-11	3			.956	-7	O-28,P-13/3-3,2S	-1.6
1901	Chi-A	137	556	93	143	15	8	3	70	36		.257	.311	.329	79	-15	**52**			.980	13	*1-137/2-2,P-1,S3	-0.3
1902	Chi-A	137	515	62	130	14	4	4	59	14		.252	.276	.318	68	-23	38			.986	10	*1-133/S-4,P-1,C-1	-1.6
1903	Chi-A	138	546	52	132	25	9	2	59	12		.242	.266	.332	82	-13	26			.984	7	*1-117,3-19/2-2,SO	-0.8
1904	Chi-A	96	314	27	66	10	3	1	34	16		.210	.255	.271	69	-11	19			.986	0	1-57,2-27/O-5,S-4	-1.3
1905	Chi-A	94	341	55	101	21	11	2	45	15		.296	.335	.440	151	18	15			.964	-1	2-43,O-41/1-9,S-2	1.6
1906	*Chi-A	143	549	71	153	18	11	0	57	30		.279	.324	.352	115	8	37			.949	-22	*2-132,O-14/P-1,C-1	-1.4
1907	Chi-A	125	486	60	118	19	7	0	41	22		.243	.281	.311	92	-6	22			.957	10	*2-119/O-5,P-1,S-1	0.3
1908	Chi-A	84	320	31	79	15	3	1	49	19		.247	.297	.322	103	1	18			.990	2	1-65,2-18	0.1
1909	Chi-A	120	433	33	97	17	6	0	33	23		.224	.265	.291	79	-12	23			.994	1	*1-101/O-9,2-5	-1.3
Total	10	1119	4219	501	1056	158	62	13	455	190		.250	.289	.326	89	-64	253			.986	13	1-619,2-351,O/3PSC	-6.3

■ MIKE IVIE Ivie, Michael Wilson b: 8/8/52, Atlanta, Ga. BR/TR, 6'3", 205 lbs. Deb: 9/4/71

YEAR	TM/L	G	AB	R	H	2B	3B	HR	RBI	BB	SO	AVG	OBP	SLG	PRO+	BR/A	SB	CS	SBR	FA	FR	G/POS	TPR
1971	SD-N	6	17	0	8	0	0	0	3	1	1	.471	.526	.471	198	2	0	0	0	1.000	-2	/C-6	0.1
1974	SD-N	12	34	1	3	0	0	1	3	2	8	.088	.139	.176	-13	-5	0	0	0	.986	-0	1-11	-0.6
1975	SD-N	111	377	36	94	16	2	8	46	20	63	.249	.294	.366	88	-8	4	4	-1	.989	-5	1-78,3-61/C-1	-1.9
1976	SD-N	140	405	51	118	19	5	7	70	30	41	.291	.348	.415	126	12	6	6	-2	.995	1	*1-135/C-2,3-2	0.4
1977	SD-N	134	489	66	133	29	2	9	66	39	57	.272	.328	.395	104	1	3	2	-0	.992	-5	*1-105,3-25	-1.1
1978	SF-N	117	318	34	98	14	3	11	55	27	45	.308	.366	.475	139	16	3	0	1	.995	-10	1-76,O-22	0.2
1979	SF-N	133	402	58	115	18	3	27	89	47	80	.286	.362	.547	155	29	5	1	1	.995	-6	1-98,O-24/3-4,2-1	1.9
1980	SF-N	79	286	21	69	16	1	4	25	19	40	.241	.289	.346	78	-9	1	2	-1	.993	-6	1-72	-2.2
1981	SF-N	7	17	1	5	2	0	0	3	0	1	.294	.294	.412	100	-0	0	0	0	1.000	1	/1-5	0.0
	Hou-N	19	42	2	10	3	0	0	6	2	11	.238	.273	.310	68	-2	0	1	-1	.989	2	1-10	-0.1
	Yr	26	59	3	15	5	0	0	9	2	12	.254	.279	.339	78	-2	0	1	-1	.992	3	1-15	-0.1
1982	Hou-N	7	6	0	2	0	0	0	0	1	0	.333	.429	.333	125	0	0	0	0	.000	0	/H	0.0
	Det-A	80	259	35	60	12	1	14	38	24	51	.232	.302	.448	102	0	0	0	0	.000	0	D-79	-0.3
1983	Det-A	12	42	4	9	4	0	0	7	2	4	.214	.250	.310	54	-3	0	0	0	1.000	-0	1-12	-0.4
Total	11	857	2694	309	724	133	17	81	411	214	402	.269	.326	.421	112	33	22	16	-3	.993	-31	1-602/3-92,DOC2	-4.0

■ HANK IZQUIERDO Izquierdo, Enrique Roberto (Valdes) b: 3/20/31, Matanzas, Cuba BR/TR, 5'11", 175 lbs. Deb: 8/9/67

YEAR	TM/L	G	AB	R	H	2B	3B	HR	RBI	BB	SO	AVG	OBP	SLG	PRO+	BR/A	SB	CS	SBR	FA	FR	G/POS	TPR
1967	Min-A	16	26	4	7	2	0	0	2	1	2	.269	.296	.346	83	-1	0	0	0	.986	3	C-16	0.3

■ RAY JABLONSKI Jablonski, Raymond Leo "Jabbo" b: 12/17/26, Chicago, Ill. d: 11/25/85, Chicago, Ill. BR/TR, 5'10", 183 lbs. Deb: 4/14/53

YEAR	TM/L	G	AB	R	H	2B	3B	HR	RBI	BB	SO	AVG	OBP	SLG	PRO+	BR/A	SB	CS	SBR	FA	FR	G/POS	TPR
1953	StL-N	157	604	64	162	23	5	21	112	34	61	.268	.308	.427	89	-11	2	2	-1	.932	-16	*3-157	-3.0
1954	StL-N★	152	611	80	181	33	3	12	104	49	42	.296	.350	.419	99	-1	9	4	0	.925	-7	*3-149/1-1	-1.1
1955	Cin-N	74	221	28	53	9	0	9	28	13	35	.240	.291	.403	77	-8	0	1	-1	.872	-10	3-28,O-28	-2.0
1956	Cin-N	130	407	42	104	25	1	15	66	37	57	.256	.328	.432	96	-2	2	4	-2	.970	-25	*3-127/2-1	-2.9
1957	NY-N	107	305	37	88	15	1	9	57	31	47	.289	.354	.433	110	5	0	2	-1	.941	-3	3-70/1-6,O-1	0.2
1958	SF-N	82	230	28	53	15	1	12	46	17	50	.230	.289	.461	97	-2	2	0	1	.946	-8	3-57	-0.9
1959	StL-N	60	87	11	22	4	0	3	14	8	19	.253	.316	.402	84	-2	1	0	0	.900	-3	3-19/S-1	-0.5
	KC-A	25	65	4	17	1	0	2	8	3	11	.262	.294	.369	79	-2	0	0	0	.947	-3	3-17	-0.5
1960	KC-A	21	32	3	7	1	0	0	3	4	8	.219	.306	.250	52	-2	0	0	0	.944	0	/3-6	-0.2
Total	8	808	2562	297	687	126	11	83	438	196	330	.268	.324	.423	94	-26	16	13	-3	.936	-75	3-630/O-29,1-7,S2	-10.9

■ FRED JACKLITSCH Jacklitsch, Frederick Lawrence b: 5/24/1876, Brooklyn, N.Y. d: 7/18/37, Brooklyn, N.Y. BR/TR, 5'9", 180 lbs. Deb: 6/6/00

YEAR	TM/L	G	AB	R	H	2B	3B	HR	RBI	BB	SO	AVG	OBP	SLG	PRO+	BR/A	SB	CS	SBR	FA	FR	G/POS	TPR
1900	Phi-N	5	11	0	2	1	0	0	3	0		.182	.182	.273	25	-1	0			1.000	-2	/C-3	-0.2
1901	Phi-N	33	120	14	30	4	3	0	24	12		.250	.328	.333	90	-1	2			.971	-1	C-30/3-1	0.1
1902	Phi-N	38	114	8	23	4	0	0	8	9		.202	.278	.237	59	-5	2			.927	-9	C-29/O-1	-1.2
1903	Bro-N	60	176	31	47	8	3	1	21	33		.267	.389	.364	118	6	4			.975	-9	C-53/2-1,O-1	0.3
1904	Bro-N	26	77	8	18	3	1	0	8	7		.234	.322	.299	94	-0	7			.957	-7	1-11/2-8,C-5	-0.7
1905	NY-A	1	3	1	0	0	0	0	1	1		.000	.250	.000	-17	-0	0			1.000	-0	/C-1	0.0
1907	Phi-N	73	202	19	43	7	0	0	17	27		.213	.312	.248	76	-4	7			.984	11	C-58/1-6,O-1	1.3
1908	Phi-N	37	86	6	19	3	0	0	7	14		.221	.337	.256	87	-1	3			.976	3	C-30	0.6
1909	Phi-N	20	32	6	10	1	1	0	1	10		.313	.476	.406	173	4	1			.964	-2	C-11/2-1	0.3
1910	Phi-N	25	51	7	10	3	0	0	2	5	9	.196	.268	.255	51	-3	0			.989	5	C-13/1-2,2-1,3-1	0.3
1914	Bal-F	122	337	40	93	21	4	2	48	52	66	.276	.376	.380	103	-2	7			**.988**	2	*C-118	1.0
1915	Bal-F	49	135	20	32	9	0	2	13	31	25	.237	.387	.348	104	0	2			.992	-7	C-45/S-1	-0.3
1917	Bos-N	1	0	0	0	0	0	0	0	0	0	—	—	—	—	0	0			1.000	-0	/C-1	0.0
Total	13	490	1344	160	327	64	12	5	153	201	100	.243	.349	.320	95	-8	35			.978	-14	C-397/1-19,2O3S	1.5

■ CHARLIE JACKSON Jackson, Charles Herbert "Lefty" b: 2/7/1894, Granite City, Ill. d: 5/27/68, Radford, Va. BL/TL, 5'9", 150 lbs. Deb: 8/20/15

YEAR	TM/L	G	AB	R	H	2B	3B	HR	RBI	BB	SO	AVG	OBP	SLG	PRO+	BR/A	SB	CS	SBR	FA	FR	G/POS	TPR
1915	Chi-A	1	1	0	0	0	0	0	0	0	1	.000	.000	.000	-97	-0	0			.000	0	H	0.0
1917	Pit-N	41	121	7	29	3	2	0	1	10	22	.240	.303	.298	82	-2	4			.986	0	O-36	-0.4
Total	2	42	122	7	29	3	2	0	1	10	23	.238	.301	.295	80	-3	4			.986	0	/O-36	-0.4

■ CHUCK JACKSON Jackson, Charles Leo b: 3/19/63, Seattle, Wash. BR/TR, 6', 185 lbs. Deb: 5/26/87

YEAR	TM/L	G	AB	R	H	2B	3B	HR	RBI	BB	SO	AVG	OBP	SLG	PRO+	BR/A	SB	CS	SBR	FA	FR	G/POS	TPR
1987	Hou-N	35	71	3	15	3	0	1	6	7	19	.211	.282	.296	55	-5	1	1	-0	.957	-1	3-16,O-13/S-1	-0.6
1988	Hou-N	46	83	7	19	5	1	1	8	7	16	.229	.289	.349	86	-2	1	1	-0	.908	1	3-32/S-3,O-3	-0.1
1994	Tex-A	1	2	0	0	0	0	0	0	0	0	.000	.000	.000	-99	-1	0	0	0	.000	0	/3-1	-0.1
Total	3	82	156	10	34	8	1	2	14	14	35	.218	.282	.321	69	-7	2	2	-1	.928	1	/3-49,O-16,S-4	-0.8

■ DAMIAN JACKSON Jackson, Damian Jacques b: 8/16/73, Los Angeles, Cal. BR/TR, 5'10", 160 lbs. Deb: 9/12/96

YEAR	TM/L	G	AB	R	H	2B	3B	HR	RBI	BB	SO	AVG	OBP	SLG	PRO+	BR/A	SB	CS	SBR	FA	FR	G/POS	TPR
1996	Cle-A	5	10	2	3	2	0	0	1	1	4	.300	.364	.500	116	0	0	0	0	1.000	2	/S-5	0.3
1997	Cle-A	8	9	2	1	0	0	0	0	0	1	.111	.200	.111	-16	-2	1	0	0	1.000	1	/S-5,2-1	0.0
	Cin-N	12	27	6	6	2	1	1	2	4	7	.222	.323	.481	106	0	1	1	-0	1.000	0	/S-6,2-3	0.1
1998	Cin-N	13	38	4	12	5	0	0	7	6	4	.316	.409	.447	120	1	2	0	1	.971	-1	S-10/O-3	0.2
Total	3	38	84	14	22	9	1	1	10	11	16	.262	.354	.429	100	0	4	1	1	.988	3	/S-26,2-4,O-3	0.6

■ DARRIN JACKSON Jackson, Darrin Jay b: 8/22/62, Los Angeles, Cal. BR/TR, 6', 185 lbs. Deb: 6/17/85

YEAR	TM/L	G	AB	R	H	2B	3B	HR	RBI	BB	SO	AVG	OBP	SLG	PRO+	BR/A	SB	CS	SBR	FA	FR	G/POS	TPR
1985	Chi-N	5	11	0	1	0	0	0	0	0	3	.091	.091	.091	-44	-2	0	0	0	1.000	-1	/O-4	-0.3
1987	Chi-N	7	5	2	4	1	0	0	0	0	0	.800	.800	1.000	359	2	0	0	0	1.000	-2	/O-5	0.0
1988	Chi-N	100	188	29	50	11	3	6	20	5	28	.266	.289	.452	105	0	4	1	1	.983	-10	O-74	-1.1
1989	Chi-N	45	83	7	19	4	0	1	8	6	17	.229	.281	.313	65	-4	1	2	-1	.970	-1	O-39	-0.7
	SD-N	25	87	10	18	3	0	3	12	7	17	.207	.266	.345	73	-3	0	2	-1	.954	2	O-24	-0.3
	Yr	70	170	17	37	7	0	4	20	13	34	.218	.273	.329	68	-7	1	4	-2	.962	1	O-63	-1.0
1990	SD-N	58	113	10	29	3	0	3	9	5	24	.257	.288	.363	77	-4	3	0	1	.985	-5	O-39	-0.9
1991	SD-N	122	359	51	94	12	1	21	49	27	66	.262	.317	.476	117	7	5	3	-0	.992	7	O-98/P-1	1.2
1992	SD-N	155	587	72	146	23	5	17	70	26	106	.249	.285	.392	88	-11	14	3	2	.996	24	*O-153	1.4
1993	Tor-A	46	176	15	38	8	0	5	19	8	53	.216	.250	.347	58	-11	0	2	-1	.989	-2	O-46	-1.4

YEAR	TM/L	G	AB	R	H	2B	3B	HR	RBI	BB	SO	AVG	OBP	SLG	PRO+	BR/A	SB	CS	SBR	FA	FR	G/POS	TPR
	NY-N	31	87	4	17	1	0	1	7	2	22	.195	.213	.241	22	-10	0	0	0	1.000	2	O-26	-0.8
1994	Chi-A	104	369	43	115	17	3	10	51	27	56	.312	.363	.455	111	6	7	1	2	.996	0	*O-102	0.5
1997	Min-A	49	130	19	33	2	1	3	21	4	21	.254	.276	.354	62	-7	2	0	1	.990	0	O-44	-0.7
	Mil-A	26	81	7	22	7	0	2	15	2	10	.272	.289	.432	84	-2	2	1	0	1.000	-1	O-26	-0.4
	Yr	75	211	26	55	9	1	5	36	6	31	.261	.281	.384	70	-10	4	1	1	.994	-1	O-70	-1.1
1998	Mil-N	114	204	20	49	13	1	4	20	9	37	.240	.276	.373	66	-11	1	1	-0	.982	-17	O-94/D-2	-2.8
Total	11	887	2480	289	635	105	14	76	301	128	460	.256	.296	.402	87	-49	39	16	2	.990	-3	O-774/D-2,P-1	-6.3

■ GEORGE JACKSON
Jackson, George Christopher "Hickory" b: 10/14/1882, Springfield, Mo. d: 11/25/72, Cleburne, Tex. BR/TR, 6'0.5", 180 lbs. Deb: 8/2/11

YEAR	TM/L	G	AB	R	H	2B	3B	HR	RBI	BB	SO	AVG	OBP	SLG	PRO+	BR/A	SB	CS	SBR	FA	FR	G/POS	TPR
1911	Bos-N	39	147	28	51	11	2	0	25	12	21	.347	.404	.449	128	5	12			.929	-2	O-39	0.1
1912	Bos-N	110	397	55	104	13	5	4	48	38	72	.262	.342	.350	88	-6	22			.943	2	*O-107	-1.0
1913	Bos-N	3	10	2	3	0	0	0	0	0	2	.300	.300	.300	70	-0	0			.875	0	/O-3	0.0
Total	3	152	554	85	158	24	7	4	73	50	95	.285	.357	.375	98	-1	34			.938	-0	O-149	-0.9

■ HENRY JACKSON
Jackson, Henry Everett b: 6/23/1861, Union City, Ind. d: 9/14/32, Chicago, Ill. BR/TR, 6'2", 185 lbs. Deb: 9/13/1887

YEAR	TM/L	G	AB	R	H	2B	3B	HR	RBI	BB	SO	AVG	OBP	SLG	PRO+	BR/A	SB	CS	SBR	FA	FR	G/POS	TPR
1887	Ind-N	10	38	1	10	1	0	0	3	0	12	.263	.263	.289	55	-2	2			.933	-1	1-10	-0.4

■ JIM JACKSON
Jackson, James Benner b: 11/28/1877, Philadelphia, Pa. d: 10/9/55, Philadelphia, Pa. BR/TR, Deb: 4/26/01

YEAR	TM/L	G	AB	R	H	2B	3B	HR	RBI	BB	SO	AVG	OBP	SLG	PRO+	BR/A	SB	CS	SBR	FA	FR	G/POS	TPR
1901	Bal-A	99	364	42	91	17	3	2	50	20		.250	.291	.330	69	-16	11			**.971**	3	O-96	-1.9
1902	NY-N	35	110	14	20	5	1	0	13	15		.182	.280	.245	63	-4	6			.897	-2	O-34	-1.0
1905	Cle-A	109	426	59	109	12	4	2	31	34		.256	.317	.317	100	0	15			.951	5	*O-106/3-3	0.0
1906	Cle-A	105	374	44	80	13	2	0	38	38		.214	.290	.259	73	-10	25			.975	-6	*O-104	-2.3
Total	4	348	1274	159	300	47	10	4	132	107		.235	.298	.297	80	-31	57			.959	-1	O-340/3-3	-5.2

■ JOE JACKSON
Jackson, Joseph Jefferson "Shoeless Joe" b: 7/16/1889, Pickens Co., S.C. d: 12/5/51, Greenville, S.C. BL/TR, 6'1", 200 lbs. Deb: 8/25/08

YEAR	TM/L	G	AB	R	H	2B	3B	HR	RBI	BB	SO	AVG	OBP	SLG	PRO+	BR/A	SB	CS	SBR	FA	FR	G/POS	TPR
1908	Phi-A	5	23	0	3	0	0	0	3	0		.130	.130	.130	-14	-3	0			.875	-1	/O-5	-0.4
1909	Phi-A	5	17	3	3	0	0	0	3	1		.176	.222	.176	26	-1	0			.833	-0	/O-4	-0.2
1910	Cle-A	20	75	15	29	2	5	1	11	8		.387	.446	.587	220	10	4			.977	0	O-20	1.0
1911	Cle-A	147	571	126	233	45	19	7	83	56		.408	**.468**	.590	192	70	41			.958	8	*O-147	6.8
1912	Cle-A	154	572	121	**226**	44	**26**	3	90	54		.395	.458	.579	190	66	35			.950	13	*O-150	6.9
1913	Cle-A	148	528	109	**197**	**39**	17	7	71	80	26	.373	.460	**.551**	190	**62**	26			.930	2	*O-148	6.0
1914	Cle-A	122	453	61	153	22	13	3	53	41	34	.338	.399	.464	153	28	22	15	-2	.967	2	*O-119	2.4
1915	Cle-A	83	303	42	99	16	9	3	45	28	11	.327	.389	.469	154	19	10	10	-3	.961	-3	O-50,1-30	1.0
	Chi-A	45	158	21	43	4	5	2	36	24	12	.272	.378	.399	129	6	6	10	-4	.947	-2	O-45	-0.2
	Yr	128	461	63	142	20	14	5	81	52	23	.308	.385	.445	145	25	16	20	-7	.953	-5	O-95,1-30	0.8
1916	Chi-A	155	592	91	202	40	**21**	3	78	46	25	.341	.393	.495	165	44	24	14	-1	.975	-1	*O-155	3.6
1917	*Chi-A	146	538	91	162	20	17	5	75	57	25	.301	.375	.429	142	27	13			.984	9	*O-145	3.1
1918	Chi-A	17	65	9	23	2	2	1	20	8	1	.354	.425	.492	175	6	3			1.000	-0	O-17	0.5
1919	*Chi-A	139	516	79	181	31	14	7	96	60	10	.351	.422	.506	159	41	9			.967	-4	*O-139	2.9
1920	Chi-A	146	570	105	218	42	**20**	12	121	56	14	.382	.444	.589	172	58	9	12	-5	.965	-1	*O-145	4.1
Total	13	1332	4981	873	1772	307	168	54	785	519	158	.356	.423	.517	169	433	202	61		.962	23	*O-1289/1-30	37.5

■ KEN JACKSON
Jackson, Kenneth Bernard b: 8/21/63, Shreveport, La. BR/TR, 5'9", 170 lbs. Deb: 9/12/87

YEAR	TM/L	G	AB	R	H	2B	3B	HR	RBI	BB	SO	AVG	OBP	SLG	PRO+	BR/A	SB	CS	SBR	FA	FR	G/POS	TPR
1987	Phi-N	8	16	1	4	2	0	0	2	1	4	.250	.333	.375	85	-0	0	0	0	.955	-1	/S-8	-0.1

■ LOU JACKSON
Jackson, Louis Clarence b: 7/26/35, Riverton, La. d: 5/27/69, Tokyo, Japan BL/TR, 5'10", 168 lbs. Deb: 7/23/58

YEAR	TM/L	G	AB	R	H	2B	3B	HR	RBI	BB	SO	AVG	OBP	SLG	PRO+	BR/A	SB	CS	SBR	FA	FR	G/POS	TPR
1958	Chi-N	24	35	5	6	2	1	1	6	1	9	.171	.194	.371	46	-3	0	1	-1	1.000	-4	O-12	-0.8
1959	Chi-N	6	4	2	1	0	0	0	1	0	2	.250	.250	.250	34	-0	0	0	0	.000	0	H	0.0
1964	Bal-A	4	8	0	3	0	0	0	0	0	2	.375	.375	.375	110	0	0	0	0	1.000	1	/O-1	0.1
Total	3	34	47	7	10	2	1	1	7	1	13	.213	.229	.362	55	-3	0	1	-1	1.000	-4	/O-13	-0.7

■ RANDY JACKSON
Jackson, Ransom Joseph "Handsome Ransom" b: 2/10/26, Little Rock, Ark. BR/TR, 6'1.5", 180 lbs. Deb: 5/2/50

YEAR	TM/L	G	AB	R	H	2B	3B	HR	RBI	BB	SO	AVG	OBP	SLG	PRO+	BR/A	SB	CS	SBR	FA	FR	G/POS	TPR
1950	Chi-N	34	111	13	25	4	3	3	6	7	25	.225	.271	.396	74	-5	4			.911	-4	3-27	-0.9
1951	Chi-N	145	557	78	153	24	6	16	76	47	44	.275	.332	.425	101	-1	14	3	2	.956	8	*3-143	0.8
1952	Chi-N	116	379	44	88	8	5	9	34	27	42	.232	.285	.351	75	-14	6	5	-1	.958	-8	*3-104/O-1	-2.0
1953	Chi-N	139	498	61	142	22	8	19	66	42	61	.285	.341	.476	108	5	8	4	0	.949	3	*3-133	0.5
1954	Chi-N★	126	484	77	132	17	6	19	67	44	55	.273	.336	.450	102	0	2	1	0	.955	-1	*3-124	-0.3
1955	Chi-N★	138	499	73	132	13	7	21	70	58	58	.265	.342	.445	107	5	0	2	-1	.949	13	*3-134	1.0
1956	*Bro-N	101	307	37	84	15	7	8	53	28	38	.274	.338	.446	101	0	2	1	0	.993	21	3-80	2.3
1957	Bro-N	48	131	7	26	1	0	2	16	9	20	.198	.250	.252	32	-12	0	0	0	.976	-2	3-34	-1.5
1958	LA-N	35	65	8	12	3	0	1	4	5	10	.185	.243	.277	36	-6	0	0	0	.964	7	3-17	0.1
	Cle-A	29	91	7	22	3	1	4	13	3	18	.242	.266	.429	90	-2	0	0	0	.901	5	3-24	0.4
1959	Cle-A	3	7	0	1	0	0	0	0	0	1	.143	.143	.143	-22	-1	0	0	0	1.000	-1	/3-2	-0.2
	Chi-N	41	74	7	18	5	1	1	10	11	10	.243	.341	.378	92	-1	0	0	0	.941	-3	3-22/O-1	-0.3
Total	10	955	3203	412	835	115	44	103	415	281	382	.261	.322	.421	94	-31	36	16		.955	18	3-844/O-2	-2.1

■ REGGIE JACKSON
Jackson, Reginald Martinez b: 5/18/46, Wyncote, Pa. BL/TL, 6', 200 lbs. Deb: 6/9/67 H

YEAR	TM/L	G	AB	R	H	2B	3B	HR	RBI	BB	SO	AVG	OBP	SLG	PRO+	BR/A	SB	CS	SBR	FA	FR	G/POS	TPR
1967	KC-A	35	118	13	21	4	4	1	6	10	46	.178	.271	.305	72	-4	1	1	-0	.933	-2	O-34	-0.9
1968	Oak-A	154	553	82	138	13	6	29	74	50	171	.250	.317	.452	138	23	14	4	2	.959	8	*O-151	2.8
1969	Oak-A★	152	549	**123**	151	36	3	47	118	114	142	.275	.410	**.608**	**190**	**68**	13	5	1	.964	5	*O-150	6.6
1970	Oak-A	149	426	57	101	21	2	23	66	75	135	.237	.361	.458	129	18	26	17	-2	.956	-11	*O-142	-0.2
1971	*Oak-A★	150	567	87	157	29	3	32	80	63	161	.277	.355	.508	145	32	16	10	-1	.977	9	*O-145	3.4
1972	*Oak-A★	135	499	72	132	25	2	25	75	59	125	.265	.352	.473	152	31	9	8	-2	.971	2	*O-135	2.7
1973	*Oak-A★	151	539	**99**	158	28	2	**32**	**117**	76	111	.293	.387	**.531**	**165**	**46**	22	8	2	.971	4	*O-145/D-3	4.6
1974	*Oak-A★	148	506	90	146	25	1	29	93	86	105	.289	.396	.514	**171**	48	25	5	**5**	.968	9	*O-127,D-19	5.6
1975	*Oak-A★	157	593	91	150	39	3	**36**	104	67	133	.253	.332	.511	138	27	17	8	0	.965	9	*O-147/D-9	3.0
1976	Bal-A	134	498	84	138	27	2	27	91	54	108	.277	.353	**.502**	**158**	34	28	7	4	.964	2	*O-121,D-11	3.7
1977	*NY-A★	146	525	93	150	39	2	32	110	74	129	.286	.377	.550	151	37	17	3	3	.949	-1	*O-127,D-18	3.3
1978	*NY-A†	139	511	82	140	13	5	27	97	58	133	.274	.358	.477	136	24	14	11	-2	.986	3	*O-104,D-35	1.9
1979	NY-A★	131	465	78	138	24	2	29	89	65	107	.297	.385	.544	151	33	9	8	-2	.986	7	*O-125/D-3	3.1
1980	*NY-A★	143	514	94	154	22	4	**41**	111	83	122	.300	.399	.597	172	51	1	2	-1	.962	-2	O-94,D-46	4.2
1981	*NY-A★	94	334	33	79	17	1	15	54	46	82	.237	.331	.428	119	8	0	3	-2	.974	0	O-61,D-33	0.3
1982	*Cal-A★	153	530	92	146	17	1	**39**	101	85	156	.275	.378	.532	147	35	4	5	-2	.972	-18	*O-139/D-5	1.2
1983	Cal-A†	116	397	43	77	14	1	14	49	52	140	.194	.294	.340	74	-14	0	2	-1	.986	-5	D-62,O-47	-2.3
1984	Cal-A★	143	525	67	117	17	2	25	81	55	141	.223	.300	.406	94	-5	8	4	0	1.000	0	*D-134/O-3	-0.9
1985	Cal-A	143	460	64	116	27	0	27	85	78	138	.252	.362	.487	130	20	1	2	-1	.944	-9	O-81,D-52	0.7
1986	*Cal-A	132	419	65	101	12	2	18	58	92	115	.241	.381	.408	116	13	1	1	-0	.833	-0	*D-121/O-4	1.0
1987	Oak-A	115	336	42	74	14	1	15	43	33	97	.220	.298	.402	89	-6	2	1	0	1.000	-2	D-79,O-20	-1.0
Total	21	2820	9864	1551	2584	463	49	563	1702	1375	2597	.262	.358	.490	140	519	228	115	-1	.967	8	*O-2102,D-630	42.8

■ SONNY JACKSON
Jackson, Roland Thomas b: 7/9/44, Washington, D.C. BL/TR, 5'9", 155 lbs. Deb: 9/27/63 C

YEAR	TM/L	G	AB	R	H	2B	3B	HR	RBI	BB	SO	AVG	OBP	SLG	PRO+	BR/A	SB	CS	SBR	FA	FR	G/POS	TPR
1963	Hou-N	1	3	0	0	0	0	0	0	0	1	.000	.000	.000	-99	-1	0	0	0	.833	1	/S-1	0.0
1964	Hou-N	9	23	3	8	1	0	0	1	2	3	.348	.400	.391	131	1	1	0	0	.870	-4	/S-7	-0.2
1965	Hou-N	10	23	1	3	0	0	0	0	1	3	.130	.167	.130	-16	-2	1	0	0	.969	-1	/S-8,3-1	-0.4
1966	Hou-N	150	596	80	174	6	5	3	25	42	53	.292	.342	.334	95	-3	49	14	6	.951	-13	*S-150	0.4
1967	Hou-N	129	520	67	123	18	3	0	25	36	45	.237	.286	.283	66	-23	22	9	1	.943	-8	*S-128	-1.9
1968	Atl-N	105	358	37	81	8	2	1	19	25	35	.226	.282	.268	66	-14	16	6	1	.952	-17	S-99	-2.4
1969	*Atl-N	98	318	41	76	3	5	1	27	35	33	.239	.318	.289	71	-11	12	7	-1	.961	-23	S-97	-2.6
1970	Atl-N	103	328	60	85	14	3	0	20	45	27	.259	.350	.320	76	-10	11	4	1	.933	-23	S-87	-2.1
1971	Atl-N	149	547	58	141	20	5	2	25	35	45	.258	.304	.324	73	-19	7	6	-2	.980	3	*O-145	-2.7
1972	Atl-N	60	126	20	30	6	3	0	8	7	9	.238	.278	.333	67	-6	1	0	0	.976	-6	S-17,O-10/3-6	-1.0

YEAR	TM/L	G	AB	R	H	2B	3B	HR	RBI	BB	SO	AVG	OBP	SLG	PRO+	BR/A	SB	CS	SBR	FA	FR	G/POS	TPR
1973	Atl-N	117	206	29	43	5	2	0	12	22	13	.209	.288	.252	47	-14	6	3	0	.981	-14	O-56,S-36	-2.7
1974	Atl-N	5	7	0	3	0	0	0	0	0	0	.429	.429	.429	134	0	0	1	-1	1.000	0	/O-1	0.0
Total	12	936	3055	396	767	81	28	7	162	250	265	.251	.310	.303	73	-104	126	51	7	.949	-104	S-630,O-212/3-7	-15.6

■ RON JACKSON Jackson, Ronald Harris b: 10/22/33, Kalamazoo, Mich. BR/TR, 6'7", 225 lbs. Deb: 6/15/54

YEAR	TM/L	G	AB	R	H	2B	3B	HR	RBI	BB	SO	AVG	OBP	SLG	PRO+	BR/A	SB	CS	SBR	FA	FR	G/POS	TPR
1954	Chi-A	40	93	10	26	4	0	4	10	6	20	.280	.337	.452	111	1	2	1	0	.988	-3	1-35	-0.3
1955	Chi-A	40	74	10	15	1	1	2	7	8	22	.203	.280	.324	61	-4	1	0	0	.988	-1	1-29	-0.6
1956	Chi-A	22	56	7	12	3	0	1	4	10	13	.214	.333	.321	73	-2	1	0	0	1.000	1	1-19	-0.2
1957	Chi-A	13	60	4	19	3	0	2	8	1	12	.317	.328	.467	114	1	0	0	0	.992	-1	1-13	-0.1
1958	Chi-A	61	146	19	34	4	0	7	21	18	46	.233	.325	.404	101	0	2	0	1	.997	-2	1-38	-0.3
1959	Chi-A	10	14	3	3	1	0	1	2	1	0	.214	.313	.500	121	0	0	0	0	1.000	-0	/1-5	0.0
1960	Bos-A	10	31	1	7	2	0	0	0	1	6	.226	.250	.290	44	-2	0	0	0	.973	-0	/1-9	-0.3
Total	7	196	474	54	116	18	1	17	52	45	119	.245	.317	.395	92	-6	6	1	1	.992	-6	1-148	-1.8

■ RON JACKSON Jackson, Ronnie Damien b: 5/9/53, Birmingham, Ala. BR/TR, 6', 205 lbs. Deb: 9/12/75 C

YEAR	TM/L	G	AB	R	H	2B	3B	HR	RBI	BB	SO	AVG	OBP	SLG	PRO+	BR/A	SB	CS	SBR	FA	FR	G/POS	TPR
1975	Cal-A	13	39	2	9	2	0	0	2	2	10	.231	.268	.282	60	-2	1	1	-0	.947	-0	/O-9,3-3,D-1	-0.3
1976	Cal-A	127	410	44	93	18	3	8	40	30	58	.227	.291	.344	91	-6	5	4	-1	.950	1	*3-114/2-7,O-4,D-6	-0.7
1977	Cal-A	106	292	38	71	15	2	8	28	24	42	.243	.303	.390	91	-4	3	2	-0	.990	2	1-43,3-30,D-20,/OS	-0.6
1978	Cal-A	105	387	49	115	18	6	6	57	16	31	.297	.340	.421	117	8	2	3	-1	.994	-3	1-75,3-31/O-1,D-1	-0.1
1979	Min-A	159	583	85	158	40	5	14	68	51	59	.271	.339	.429	102	1	3	1	0	.994	11	*1-157/S-1,3-1,O-1	0.3
1980	Min-A	131	396	48	105	29	3	5	42	28	41	.265	.319	.391	87	-7	1	8	-5	.991	-1	*1-119,O-15/3-2,D-1	-1.9
1981	Min-A	54	175	17	46	9	0	4	28	10	15	.263	.306	.383	91	-2	2	2	-1	.988	1	1-36/O-7,3-3,D-6	-0.4
	Det-A	31	95	12	27	8	1	1	12	8	11	.284	.340	.421	114	2	4	1	1	1.000	-1	1-29	0.0
	Yr	85	270	29	73	17	1	5	40	18	26	.270	.318	.396	99	-1	6	3	0	.993	1	1-65/O-7,D-6,3-3	-0.4
1982	*Cal-A	53	142	15	47	6	0	2	19	10	12	.331	.383	.415	119	4	0	1	-1	.994	0	1-37/3-9	0.2
1983	Cal-A	102	348	41	80	16	1	8	39	27	33	.230	.291	.351	76	-12	2	2	-1	.957	2	3-38,1-35,D-16,O-15	-1.4
1984	Cal-A	33	91	5	15	2	1	0	5	7	13	.165	.224	.209	21	-10	0	0	0	.990	-0	1-21/3-9,O-1	-1.1
	Bal-A	12	28	0	8	2	0	0	2	0	4	.286	.286	.357	78	-1	0	2	-1	.960	2	3-10	-0.1
	Yr	45	119	5	23	4	1	0	7	7	17	.193	.238	.244	34	-11	0	2	-1	.990	1	1-21,3-19/O-1	-1.2
Total	10	926	2986	356	774	165	22	56	342	213	329	.259	.316	.385	94	-29	23	27	-9	.993	14	1-552,3-250/OD2S	-6.1

■ RYAN JACKSON Jackson, Ryan Dewitte b: 11/15/71, Orlando, Fla. BL/TL, 6'2", 195 lbs. Deb: 3/31/98

YEAR	TM/L	G	AB	R	H	2B	3B	HR	RBI	BB	SO	AVG	OBP	SLG	PRO+	BR/A	SB	CS	SBR	FA	FR	G/POS	TPR
1998	Fla-N	111	260	26	65	15	1	5	31	20	73	.250	.306	.373	78	-9	1	1	-0	.973	-7	1-44,O-32/D-5	-1.9

■ SAM JACKSON Jackson, Samuel b: 3/24/1849, Ripon, England d: 8/4/1893, Clifton Springs, N.Y. BR/TR, 5'5.5", 160 lbs. Deb: 5/16/1871

YEAR	TM/L	G	AB	R	H	2B	3B	HR	RBI	BB	SO	AVG	OBP	SLG	PRO+	BR/A	SB	CS	SBR	FA	FR	G/POS	TPR
1871	Bos-n	16	76	17	17	5	3	0	11	1	4	.224	.234	.368	68	-3	0	1	-1	.818	-1	2-14/S-1,O-1	-0.4
1872	Atl-n	4	12	0	2	0	0	0	0	0	0	.167	.167	.167	2	-2	0	0	0	.667	-3	/O-3,2-1,3-1	-0.3
Total	2 n	20	88	17	19	5	3	0	11	1	4	.216	.225	.341	58	-5	0	1	-1	.810	-5	/2-15,O-4,3-1,S-1	-0.7

■ TRAVIS JACKSON Jackson, Travis Calvin "Stonewall" b: 11/2/03, Waldo, Ark. d: 7/27/87, Waldo, Ark. BR/TR, 5'10.5", 160 lbs. Deb: 9/27/22 CH

YEAR	TM/L	G	AB	R	H	2B	3B	HR	RBI	BB	SO	AVG	OBP	SLG	PRO+	BR/A	SB	CS	SBR	FA	FR	G/POS	TPR
1922	NY-N	3	8	1	0	0	0	0	0	0	2	.000	.000	.000	-99	-2	0	0	0	.909	0	/S-3	-0.2
1923	*NY-N	96	327	45	90	12	7	4	37	22	40	.275	.321	.391	88	-6	3	3	-1	.943	-3	S-60,3-31/2-1	-0.3
1924	*NY-N	151	596	81	180	26	8	11	76	21	56	.302	.326	.428	103	1	6	7	-2	.937	-0	*S-151	1.5
1925	NY-N	112	411	51	117	15	2	9	59	24	43	.285	.327	.397	87	-9	8	3	1	.942	3	*S-110	0.6
1926	NY-N	111	385	64	126	24	8	8	51	20	26	.327	.362	.494	130	14	2			.962	1	*S-108/O-1	2.6
1927	NY-N	127	469	67	149	29	4	14	98	32	30	.318	.363	.486	126	16	8			.952	28	*S-124/3-2	5.4
1928	NY-N	150	537	73	145	35	6	14	77	56	46	.270	.339	.436	101	-1	8			.952	28	*S-149	4.3
1929	NY-N	149	551	92	162	21	12	21	94	64	56	.294	.367	.490	111	8	10			**.969**	19	*S-149	4.1
1930	NY-N	116	431	70	146	27	8	13	82	32	25	.339	.386	.529	121	14	6			.956	11	*S-115	3.3
1931	NY-N	145	555	65	172	26	10	5	71	36	23	.310	.353	.420	110	7	13			**.970**	10	*S-145	3.1
1932	NY-N	52	195	23	50	17	1	4	38	13	16	.256	.310	.415	95	-2	1			.925	-5	S-52	-0.2
1933	*NY-N	53	122	11	30	5	0	0	12	8	11	.246	.292	.287	67	-5	2			.890	7	S-21,3-21	0.4
1934	NY-N★	137	523	75	140	26	7	16	101	37	71	.268	.316	.436	102	-0	1			.945	12	*S-130/3-9	1.9
1935	NY-N	128	511	74	154	20	12	9	80	29	64	.301	.340	.440	110	6	3			.947	-7	*3-128	0.4
1936	*NY-N	126	465	41	107	8	1	7	53	18	56	.230	.260	.297	50	-33	0			.952	-1	*3-116/S-9	-2.9
Total	15	1656	6086	833	1768	291	86	135	929	412	565	.291	.337	.433	102	7	71	13		.952	103	*S-1326,3-307/O-1,2	24.0

■ BO JACKSON Jackson, Vincent Edward b: 11/30/62, Bessemer, Ala. BR/TR, 6'1", 225 lbs. Deb: 9/2/86

YEAR	TM/L	G	AB	R	H	2B	3B	HR	RBI	BB	SO	AVG	OBP	SLG	PRO+	BR/A	SB	CS	SBR	FA	FR	G/POS	TPR
1986	KC-A	25	82	9	17	2	1	2	9	7	34	.207	.286	.329	66	-4	3	1	0	.886	-3	O-23/D-1	-0.7
1987	KC-A	116	396	46	93	17	2	22	53	30	158	.235	.297	.455	93	-5	10	4	1	.955	-7	*O-113/D-1	-1.5
1988	KC-A	124	439	63	108	16	4	25	68	25	146	.246	.288	.472	108	2	27	6	5	.973	6	*O-121/D-2	1.0
1989	KC-A★	135	515	86	132	15	6	32	105	39	172	.256	.312	.495	125	14	26	9	2	.967	7	*O-110,D-24	2.1
1990	KC-A	111	405	74	110	16	1	28	78	44	128	.272	.346	.523	142	21	15	9	-1	.952	8	O-97,D-10	2.6
1991	Chi-A	23	71	8	16	4	0	3	14	12	25	.225	.337	.408	108	1	0	1	-1	.000	0	D-21	-0.1
1993	*Chi-A	85	284	32	66	9	0	16	45	23	106	.232	.290	.433	94	-4	0	2	-1	.989	3	O-47,D-36	-0.5
1994	Cal-A	75	201	23	56	7	0	13	43	20	72	.279	.347	.507	115	4	1	0	0	.964	-2	O-46/D-9	0.1
Total	8	694	2393	341	598	86	14	141	415	200	841	.250	.311	.474	112	30	82	32	5	.962	12	O-557,D-104	3.0

■ BILL JACKSON Jackson, William Riley b: 4/4/1881, Pittsburgh, Pa. d: 9/24/58, Peoria, Ill. BL/TL, 5'11.5", 160 lbs. Deb: 4/30/14

YEAR	TM/L	G	AB	R	H	2B	3B	HR	RBI	BB	SO	AVG	OBP	SLG	PRO+	BR/A	SB	CS	SBR	FA	FR	G/POS	TPR
1914	Chi-F	26	25	2	1	0	0	0	1	3	5	.040	.143	.040	-52	-6	0			.917	0	/O-6,1-4	-0.6
1915	Chi-F	50	98	15	16	1	0	1	12	14	15	.163	.268	.204	36	-10	3			.983	0	1-36/O-1	-1.2
Total	2	76	123	17	17	1	0	1	13	17	20	.138	.243	.171	18	-16	3			.984	0	/1-40,O-7	-1.8

■ SPOOK JACOBS Jacobs, Forrest Vandergrift b: 11/4/25, Cheswold, Del. BR/TR, 5'8.5", 155 lbs. Deb: 4/13/54

YEAR	TM/L	G	AB	R	H	2B	3B	HR	RBI	BB	SO	AVG	OBP	SLG	PRO+	BR/A	SB	CS	SBR	FA	FR	G/POS	TPR
1954	Phi-A	132	508	63	131	11	1	0	26	60	22	.258	.336	.283	71	-18	17	3	3	.974	-19	*2-131	-2.7
1955	KC-A	13	23	7	6	0	0	0	1	3	0	.261	.370	.261	71	-1	1	2	-1	1.000	-3	/2-7	-0.4
1956	KC-A	32	97	13	21	3	0	0	5	15	5	.216	.321	.247	52	-6	4	1	1	.968	-4	2-31	-0.7
	Pit-N	11	37	4	6	2	0	0	1	2	5	.162	.225	.216	20	-4	0	2	-1	.926	-4	2-11	-0.9
Total	3	188	665	87	164	16	1	0	33	80	32	.247	.329	.274	65	-30	22	8	2	.971	-29	2-180	-4.7

■ JAKE JACOBS Jacobs, Lamar Gary b: 6/9/37, Youngstown, Ohio BR/TR, 6', 175 lbs. Deb: 9/13/60

YEAR	TM/L	G	AB	R	H	2B	3B	HR	RBI	BB	SO	AVG	OBP	SLG	PRO+	BR/A	SB	CS	SBR	FA	FR	G/POS	TPR
1960	Was-A	6	2	0	0	0	0	0	0	0	0	.000	.000	.000	-99	-1	0	0	0	.000	0	H	-0.1
1961	Min-A	4	8	0	2	0	0	0	0	0	2	.250	.250	.250	32	-1	0	0	0	1.000	-1	/O-3	-0.2
Total	2	10	10	0	2	0	0	0	0	0	2	.200	.200	.200	7	-1	0	0	0	1.000	-1	/O-3	-0.3

■ MIKE JACOBS Jacobs, Morris Elmore b: 12/1877, Louisville, Ky. d: 3/21/49, Louisville, Ky. Deb: 7/16/02

YEAR	TM/L	G	AB	R	H	2B	3B	HR	RBI	BB	SO	AVG	OBP	SLG	PRO+	BR/A	SB	CS	SBR	FA	FR	G/POS	TPR
1902	Chi-N	5	19	1	4	0	0	0	2	0		.211	.211	.211	31	-2	0			.880	-2	/S-5	-0.3

■ OTTO JACOBS Jacobs, Otto Albert b: 4/19/1889, Chicago, Ill. d: 11/19/55, Chicago, Ill. BR/TR, 5'9", 180 lbs. Deb: 6/13/18

YEAR	TM/L	G	AB	R	H	2B	3B	HR	RBI	BB	SO	AVG	OBP	SLG	PRO+	BR/A	SB	CS	SBR	FA	FR	G/POS	TPR
1918	Chi-A	29	73	4	15	3	1	0	3	5	8	.205	.256	.274	59	-4	0			.955	-4	C-21	-0.7

■ RAY JACOBS Jacobs, Raymond F. b: 1/2/02, Salt Lake City, Utah d: 4/5/52, Los Angeles, Cal. BR/TR, 6', 160 lbs. Deb: 4/20/28

YEAR	TM/L	G	AB	R	H	2B	3B	HR	RBI	BB	SO	AVG	OBP	SLG	PRO+	BR/A	SB	CS	SBR	FA	FR	G/POS	TPR
1928	Chi-N	2	2	0	0	0	0	0	0	0	1	.000	.000	.000	-99	-1	0			.000	0	H	-0.1

■ MERWIN JACOBSON Jacobson, Merwin John William "Jake" b: 3/7/1894, New Britain, Conn. d: 1/13/78, Baltimore, Md. BL/TL, 5'11.5", 165 lbs. Deb: 9/8/15

YEAR	TM/L	G	AB	R	H	2B	3B	HR	RBI	BB	SO	AVG	OBP	SLG	PRO+	BR/A	SB	CS	SBR	FA	FR	G/POS	TPR
1915	NY-N	8	24	0	2	0	0	0	0	1	5	.083	.120	.083	-40	-4	0			.909	0	/O-5	-0.5
1916	Chi-N	4	13	2	3	0	0	0	0	1	4	.231	.286	.231	54	-1	2			1.000	0	/O-4	-0.1
1926	Bro-N	110	288	41	71	9	2	0	23	36	24	.247	.330	.292	70	-11	5			.975	-3	O-86	-1.9
1927	Bro-N	11	6	4	0	0	0	0	1	0	1	.000	.000	.000	-99	-2	0			1.000	-1	/O-3	-0.3
Total	4	133	331	47	76	9	2	0	24	38	34	.230	.309	.269	59	-18	7			.973	-4	/O-98	-2.8

YEAR	TM/L	G	AB	R	H	2B	3B	HR	RBI	BB	SO	AVG	OBP	SLG	PRO+	BR/A	SB	CS	SBR	FA	FR	G/POS	TPR
■ **BABY DOLL JACOBSON**	Jacobson, William Chester b: 8/16/1890, Cable, Ill. d: 1/16/77, Orion, Ill. BR/TR, 6'3", 215 lbs. Deb: 4/14/15																						
1915	Det-A	37	65	5	14	6	2	0	4	5	14	.215	.282	.369	90	-1	0	2	-1	.983	-2	1-10/O-7	-0.6
	StL-A	34	115	13	24	6	1	1	9	10	26	.209	.295	.304	82	-3	3	3	-1	.981	-1	O-32	-0.7
	Yr	71	180	18	38	12	3	1	13	15	40	.211	.290	.328	84	-4	3	5	-2	.984	-4	O-39,1-10	-1.3
1917	StL-A	148	529	53	131	23	7	4	55	31	67	.248	.294	.340	97	-4	10			.975	7	*O-131,1-11	-0.5
1919	StL-A	120	455	70	147	31	8	4	51	24	47	.323	.362	.453	125	13	9			.949	1	*O-106/1-8	0.7
1920	StL-A	154	609	97	216	34	14	9	122	46	37	.355	.402	.501	134	29	11	7	-1	.979	11	*O-154/1-1	2.6
1921	StL-A	151	599	90	211	38	14	5	90	42	30	.352	.398	.487	118	15	8	8	-2	.982	3	*O-142,1-10	0.5
1922	StL-A	145	555	88	176	22	16	9	102	46	36	.317	.379	.463	114	11	19	6	2	.969	4	*O-137/1-7	0.7
1923	StL-A	147	592	76	183	29	6	8	81	29	27	.309	.343	.419	95	-6	6	6	-2	.974	9	*O-146	-0.9
1924	StL-A	152	579	103	184	41	12	19	97	35	45	.318	.361	.528	120	13	6	8	-3	.986	16	*O-152	1.5
1925	StL-A	142	540	103	184	30	9	15	76	45	26	.341	.392	.513	122	16	8	11	-4	.965	1	*O-139	0.4
1926	StL-A	50	182	18	52	15	1	2	21	9	14	.286	.319	.412	86	-5	1	2	-1	.964	-6	O-50	-1.5
	Bos-A	98	394	44	120	36	1	6	69	22	22	.305	.344	.447	109	3	4	1	1	.980	-8	O-98	-1.1
	Yr	148	576	62	172	51	2	8	90	31	36	.299	.337	.436	101	-2	5	3	-0	.975	-15	*O-148	-2.6
1927	Bos-A	45	155	11	38	9	3	0	24	5	12	.245	.278	.342	61	-9	1	0	0	.979	1	O-39	-1.0
	Cle-A	32	103	13	26	5	0	0	13	6	4	.252	.300	.301	56	-7	0	0	0	.932	-1	O-31	-0.9
	Phi-A	17	35	3	8	3	0	1	5	0	3	.229	.229	.400	57	-2	0	0	0	1.000	-5	O-14	-0.8
	Yr	94	293	27	72	17	3	1	42	11	19	.246	.280	.334	59	-19	1	0	0	.959	-5	O-84	-2.7
Total	11	1472	5507	787	1714	328	94	83	819	355	410	.311	.357	.450	111	63	86	54		.973	28	*O-1378/1-47	-1.6
■ **BROOK JACOBY**	Jacoby, Brook Wallace b: 11/23/59, Philadelphia, Pa. BR/TR, 5'11", 195 lbs. Deb: 9/13/81																						
1981	Atl-N	11	10	0	2	0	0	0	1	0	3	.200	.200	.200	13	-1	0	0	0	1.000	2	/3-3	0.1
1983	Atl-N	4	8	0	0	0	0	0	0	0	1	.000	.000	.000	-93	-2	0	0	0	1.000	-1	/3-2	-0.3
1984	Cle-A	126	439	64	116	19	3	7	40	32	73	.264	.319	.369	88	-7	3	2	-0	.951	-20	*3-126/S-1	-2.9
1985	Cle-A	161	606	72	166	26	3	20	87	48	120	.274	.327	.426	105	3	2	3	-1	.958	-7	*3-161/2-1	-0.7
1986	Cle-A★	158	583	83	168	30	4	17	80	56	137	.288	.351	.441	116	13	2	1	0	.941	-13	*3-158	-0.3
1987	Cle-A	155	540	73	162	26	4	32	69	75	73	.300	.388	.541	142	33	2	3	-1	.946	-7	*3-144/1-7,D-4	2.1
1988	Cle-A	152	552	59	133	25	0	9	49	48	101	.241	.303	.335	76	-17	2	3	-1	.975	1	*3-151	-1.9
1989	Cle-A	147	519	49	141	26	5	13	64	62	90	.272	.353	.416	114	10	2	5	-2	.955	-10	*3-144/D-3	-0.1
1990	Cle-A★	155	553	77	162	24	4	14	75	63	58	.293	.367	.427	122	17	1	4	-2	.981	-12	3-99,1-78	-0.2
1991	Cle-A	66	231	14	54	9	1	4	24	16	32	.234	.289	.333	71	-9	0	1	-1	.988	-0	1-55,3-15	-1.3
	Oak-A	56	188	14	40	12	0	0	20	11	22	.213	.260	.277	51	-13	2	0	1	.982	-8	3-52/1-3	-2.1
	Yr	122	419	28	94	21	1	4	44	27	54	.224	.276	.308	63	-22	2	1	0	.987	-8	3-67,1-58	-3.4
1992	Cle-A	120	291	30	76	7	0	4	36	28	54	.261	.328	.326	85	-5	0	3	-2	.957	3	*3-111,1-10	-0.5
Total	11	1311	4520	535	1220	204	24	120	545	439	764	.270	.337	.405	104	22	16	25	-10	.958	-71	*3-1166,1-153/D2S	-8.1
■ **HARRY JACOBY**	Jacoby, Harry b: Philadelphia, Pa. Deb: 5/2/1882																						
1882	Bal-a	31	121	17	21	1	1	1		7		.174	.219	.223	53	-5				.776	8	3-19,O-13	0.3
1885	Bal-a	11	43	4	6	2	0	0	1	2		.140	.178	.186	15	-4				.896	-8	2-11	-1.1
Total	2	42	164	21	27	3	1	1	1	9		.165	.208	.213	43	-9				.776	-0	/3-19,O-13,2-11	-0.8
■ **JOHN JAHA**	Jaha, John Emil b: 5/27/66, Portland, Ore. BR/TR, 6'1", 205 lbs. Deb: 7/9/92																						
1992	Mil-A	47	133	17	30	3	1	2	10	12	30	.226	.299	.308	72	-5	10	0	3	1.000	-0	1-38/O-1,D-8	-0.4
1993	Mil-A	153	515	78	136	21	0	19	70	51	109	.264	.340	.416	103	2	13	9	-2	.992	9	*1-150/2-1,3-1	-0.3
1994	Mil-A	84	291	45	70	14	0	12	39	32	75	.241	.336	.412	88	-5	3	3	-1	.989	-1	1-73,D-11	-1.3
1995	Mil-A	88	316	59	99	20	2	20	65	36	66	.313	.390	.579	140	18	2	1	0	.997	3	1-81/D-6	1.3
1996	Mil-A	148	543	108	163	28	1	34	118	85	118	.300	.400	.543	130	26	3	1	0	.992	1	1-85,D-63	1.4
1997	Mil-A	46	162	25	40	7	0	11	26	25	40	.247	.358	.494	118	4	1	0	0	.992	-1	1-27,D-20	0.0
1998	Mil-N	73	216	29	45	6	1	7	38	49	66	.208	.369	.343	86	-3	1	3	-2	.994	-6	1-57/D-8	-1.4
Total	7	639	2176	361	583	99	5	105	366	290	504	.268	.364	.463	112	38	33	17	-0	.993	3	1-511,D-116/3-1,2O	-0.7
■ **ART JAHN**	Jahn, Arthur Charles b: 12/2/1895, Struble, Iowa d: 1/9/48, Little Rock, Ark. BR/TR, 6', 180 lbs. Deb: 7/2/25																						
1925	Chi-N	58	226	30	68	10	8	0	37	11	20	.301	.336	.416	90	-4	2	2	-1	.985	2	O-58	-0.6
1928	NY-N	10	29	7	8	1	0	1	7	2	5	.276	.323	.414	91	-0	0			1.000	1	/O-8	0.0
	Phi-N	36	94	8	21	4	0	0	11	4	11	.223	.270	.266	39	-8	0			.978	-4	O-29	-1.4
	Yr	46	123	15	29	5	0	1	18	6	16	.236	.282	.301	51	-9	0			.985	-3	O-37	-1.4
Total	2	104	349	45	97	15	8	1	55	17	36	.278	.317	.375	76	-13	2	2		.985	-1	/O-95	-2.0
■ **ART JAMES**	James, Arthur b: 8/2/52, Detroit, Mich. BL/TL, 6', 170 lbs. Deb: 4/10/75																						
1975	Det-A	11	40	2	9	2	0	0	1	1	3	.225	.244	.275	44	-3	1	2	-1	1.000	2	O-11	-0.3
■ **BERT JAMES**	James, Berton Hulon "Jesse" b: 7/7/1886, Coopertown, Tenn. d: 1/2/59, Adairville, Ky. BL/TR, 5'11", 175 lbs. Deb: 9/18/09																						
1909	StL-N	6	21	1	6	0	0	0	0	4		.286	.400	.286	120	1	1			.909	0	/O-6	0.1
■ **CHARLIE JAMES**	James, Charles Wesley b: 12/22/37, St.Louis, Mo. BR/TR, 6'1", 195 lbs. Deb: 8/2/60																						
1960	StL-N	43	50	5	9	1	0	2	5	1	12	.180	.196	.320	35	-5	0	0	0	.917	-10	O-37	-1.6
1961	StL-N	108	349	43	89	19	2	4	44	15	59	.255	.292	.355	64	-18	2	2	-1	.962	-6	O-90	-3.0
1962	StL-N	129	388	50	107	13	4	8	59	10	58	.276	.301	.392	77	-13	3	4	-2	.988	-10	*O-116	-3.0
1963	StL-N	116	347	34	93	14	2	10	45	10	64	.268	.292	.406	91	-5	2	1	0	.994	1	*O-101	-1.0
1964	*StL-N	88	233	24	52	9	1	5	17	11	58	.223	.261	.335	61	-12	0	0	0	.963	-3	O-60	-1.9
1965	Cin-N	26	39	2	8	0	0	0	2	1	9	.205	.225	.205	21	-4	0	0	0	.909	-1	/O-7	-0.5
Total	6	510	1406	158	358	56	9	29	172	48	260	.255	.284	.369	71	-57	7	7	-2	.976	-29	O-411	-11.0
■ **CLEO JAMES**	James, Cleo Joel b: 8/31/40, Clarksdale, Miss. BR/TR, 5'10", 176 lbs. Deb: 4/15/68																						
1968	LA-N	10	10	2	2	1	0	0	0	0	6	.200	.200	.300	52	-1	0	0	0	1.000	-0	/O-2	-0.1
1970	Chi-N	100	176	33	37	7	2	3	14	17	24	.210	.298	.324	59	-10	5	0	2	1.000	-10	O-90	-2.1
1971	Chi-N	54	150	25	43	7	0	2	13	10	16	.287	.355	.373	93	-1	6	2	1	.979	-1	O-48/3-2	-0.4
1973	Chi-N	44	45	9	5	0	0	0	0	1	6	.111	.130	.111	-30	-8	5	0	2	.960	-4	O-22	-1.1
Total	4	208	381	69	87	15	2	5	27	28	52	.228	.300	.318	63	-20	16	2	4	.988	-15	O-162/3-2	-3.7
■ **DION JAMES**	James, Dion b: 11/9/62, Philadelphia, Pa. BL/TL, 6'1", 170 lbs. Deb: 9/16/83																						
1983	Mil-A	11	20	1	2	0	0	0	1	2	2	.100	.182	.100	-22	-3	1	0	0	1.000	-3	/O-9,D-2	-0.7
1984	Mil-A	128	387	52	114	19	5	1	30	32	41	.295	.353	.377	106	4	10	10	-3	.989	-1	*O-118	-0.4
1985	Mil-A	18	49	5	11	1	0	0	3	6	6	.224	.309	.245	54	-3	0	0	0	1.000	-2	O-11/D-3	-0.5
1987	Atl-N	134	494	80	154	37	6	10	61	70	63	.312	.399	.472	124	19	10	8	-2	**.996**	1	*O-126	1.3
1988	Atl-N	132	386	46	99	17	5	3	30	58	59	.256	.355	.350	98	1	9	9	-3	.987	-12	*O-120	-1.9
1989	Atl-N	63	170	15	44	7	0	1	11	25	23	.259	.357	.318	92	-1	1	3	-2	1.000	-0	O-46/1-8	-0.4
	Cle-A	71	245	26	75	11	0	4	29	24	26	.306	.368	.400	114	5	1	4	-2	.976	0	O-37,D-27/1-2	0.2
1990	Cle-A	87	248	28	68	15	2	1	22	27	23	.274	.348	.363	99	0	5	3	-0	.996	-5	1-35,O-33,D-10	-0.8
1992	NY-A	67	145	24	38	8	0	3	17	22	15	.262	.363	.379	109	2	1	0	0	1.000	-8	O-46/D-5	-0.6
1993	NY-A	115	343	62	114	21	2	7	36	31	31	.332	.391	.466	134	17	0	0	0	.966	-14	*O-103/1-1,D-1	0.0
1995	*NY-A	85	209	22	60	6	1	2	26	20	16	.287	.349	.354	85	-4	4	1	1	.968	-5	O-29,D-27/1-6	-1.1
1996	NY-A	6	12	1	2	0	0	0	0	1	2	.167	.231	.167	3	-2	1	0	0	1.000	-1	/O-4,D-1	-0.2
Total	11	917	2708	362	781	142	21	32	266	318	307	.288	.365	.392	107	35	43	38	-10	.986	-51	O-682/D-76,1-52	-5.1
■ **CHRIS JAMES**	James, Donald Chris b: 10/4/62, Rusk, Tex. BR/TR, 6'1", 190 lbs. Deb: 4/23/86																						
1986	Phi-N	16	46	5	13	3	0	1	5	1	13	.283	.298	.413	91	-1	0	0	0	1.000	-1	O-11	-0.2
1987	Phi-N	115	358	48	105	20	6	17	54	27	67	.293	.346	.525	123	11	3	1	0	.990	-2	*O-108	0.6
1988	Phi-N	150	566	57	137	24	1	19	66	31	73	.242	.285	.389	90	-9	7	4	-0	.989	-4	*O-116/3-31	-1.8
1989	Phi-N	45	179	14	37	4	0	2	19	4	23	.207	.224	.263	39	-14	3	1	0	.985	-1	O-37,3-11	-1.8

YEAR	TM/L	G	AB	R	H	2B	3B	HR	RBI	BB	SO	AVG	OBP	SLG	PRO+	BR/A	SB	CS	SBR	FA	FR	G/POS	TPR
	SD-N	87	303	41	80	13	2	11	46	22	45	.264	.316	.429	111	3	2	1	0	.987	-0	O-79/3-6	0.1
	Yr	132	482	55	117	17	2	13	65	26	68	.243	.283	.367	84	-11	5	2	0	.986	-1	*O-116,3-17	-1.7
1990	Cle-A	140	528	62	158	32	4	12	70	31	71	.299	.343	.443	119	12	4	3	-1	1.000	0	*D-124,O-14	0.7
1991	Cle-A	115	437	31	104	16	2	5	41	18	61	.238	.275	.318	63	-22	3	4	-2	1.000	0	D-60,O-39,1-15	-2.8
1992	SF-N	111	248	25	60	10	4	5	32	14	45	.242	.288	.375	91	-4	2	3	-1	.974	1	O-62	-0.6
1993	Hou-N	65	129	19	33	10	1	6	19	15	34	.256	.338	.488	122	4	2	0	1	.958	3	O-34	0.6
	Tex-A	8	31	5	11	1	0	3	7	3	6	.355	.412	.677	195	4	0	0	0	1.000	-1	/O-7	0.3
1994	Tex-A	52	133	28	34	8	4	7	19	20	38	.256	.365	.534	128	6	0	0	0	1.000	-6	O-48	-0.1
1995	KC-A	26	58	6	18	3	0	2	7	6	10	.310	.385	.466	118	2	1	0	0	1.000	-0	D-14/O-5	0.1
	Bos-A	16	24	2	4	1	0	0	1	1	4	.167	.200	.208	6	-3	0	0	0	1.000	-0	/O-8,D-6	-0.4
	Yr	42	82	8	22	4	0	2	8	7	14	.268	.333	.390	86	-2	1	0	0	1.000	-1	D-20,O-13	-0.3
Total	10	946	3040	343	794	145	24	90	386	193	490	.261	.310	.413	99	-13	27	17	-2	.987	-12	O-568,D-204/3-48,1	-5.3
■ **SKIP JAMES**	James, Philip Robert b: 10/21/49, Elmhurst, Ill. BL/TL, 6', 185 lbs. Deb: 9/12/77																						
1977	SF-N	10	15	3	4	1	0	0	3	2	3	.267	.353	.333	86	-0	0	0	0	1.000	1	/1-9	0.0
1978	SF-N	41	21	5	2	1	0	0	3	4	5	.095	.240	.143	10	-3	1	0	0	1.000	2	1-27	-0.1
Total	2	51	36	8	6	2	0	0	6	6	8	.167	.286	.222	42	-3	1	0	0	1.000	3	/1-36	-0.1
■ **BERNIE JAMES**	James, Robert Byrne b: 9/2/05, Angleton, Tex. d: 8/1/94, San Antonio, Tex. BB/TR, 5'9.5", 150 lbs. Deb: 5/6/29																						
1929	Bos-N	46	101	12	31	3	2	0	9	9	13	.307	.369	.376	89	-2	3			.940	-9	2-32/O-1	-0.9
1930	Bos-N	8	11	1	2	1	0	0	1	0	1	.182	.182	.273	8	-2	0			.941	0	/2-7	-0.1
1933	NY-N	60	125	22	28	2	1	1	10	8	12	.224	.271	.280	58	-7	5			.948	2	2-26/S-6,3-5	-0.3
Total	3	114	237	35	61	6	3	1	20	17	26	.257	.310	.321	70	-10	8			.944	-7	/2-65,S-6,3-5,O-1	-1.3
■ **CHARLIE JAMIESON**	Jamieson, Charles Devine "Cuckoo" b: 2/7/1893, Paterson, N.J. d: 10/27/69, Paterson, N.J. BL/TL, 5'8.5", 165 lbs. Deb: 9/20/15																						
1915	Was-A	17	68	9	19	3	2	0	7	6	9	.279	.338	.382	113	1	0			1.000	4	O-17	0.4
1916	Was-A	64	145	16	36	4	0	0	13	18	18	.248	.331	.276	83	-2	5			.913	-4	O-41/1-4,P-1	-0.9
1917	Was-A	20	35	4	6	2	0	0	2	6	5	.171	.293	.229	60	-2	0			.875	-2	/O-9,P-1	-0.4
	Phi-A	85	345	41	92	6	2	0	27	37	36	.267	.341	.296	96	-1	8			.937	-2	O-83	-0.8
	Yr	105	380	45	98	8	2	0	29	43	41	.258	.336	.289	92	-2	8			.930	-4	O-92/P-1	-1.2
1918	Phi-A	110	416	50	84	11	2	0	11	54	30	.202	.297	.238	61	-18	11			.970	-0	*O-102/P-5	-2.7
1919	Cle-A	26	17	3	6	2	1	0	2	0	2	.353	.353	.588	153	1	2			.750	-1	/P-4,O-3	0.0
1920	*Cle-A	108	370	69	118	17	7	1	40	41	26	.319	.388	.411	108	5	2	9	-5	.966	-2	O-98/1-4	-0.8
1921	Cle-A	140	536	94	166	33	10	1	46	67	27	.310	.387	.414	103	4	8	4	0	.974	-6	*O-137	-1.1
1922	Cle-A	145	567	87	183	29	11	3	57	54	22	.323	.388	.429	112	11	15	9	-1	.978	-2	*O-144/P-2	-0.2
1923	Cle-A	152	644	130	**222**	36	12	2	51	80	37	.345	.422	.447	129	30	18	14	-3	.974	7	*O-152	2.3
1924	Cle-A	143	594	98	213	34	8	3	54	47	15	.359	.407	.458	121	19	21	12	-1	.974	4	*O-139	1.2
1925	Cle-A	138	557	109	165	24	5	4	42	72	26	.296	.380	.379	92	-5	14	18	-7	.955	7	*O-135	-1.2
1926	Cle-A	143	555	89	166	33	7	2	45	53	22	.299	.361	.395	96	-3	9	7	-2	.960	-0	*O-143	-1.4
1927	Cle-A	127	489	73	151	23	6	0	36	64	14	.309	.394	.380	101	4	7	9	-3	.969	5	*O-127	-0.3
1928	Cle-A	112	433	63	133	18	4	1	37	56	20	.307	.388	.374	100	2	3	12	-6	.984	20	*O-111	0.8
1929	Cle-A	102	364	56	106	22	1	0	26	50	12	.291	.378	.357	87	-5	2	13	-7	.980	-2	O-93	-1.9
1930	Cle-A	103	366	64	110	22	1	1	52	36	20	.301	.368	.374	85	-7	5	2	0	.955	-5	O-95	-1.7
1931	Cle-A	28	43	7	13	2	1	0	4	5	1	.302	.375	.395	97	-0	1	1	-0	.833	-2	/O-7	-0.2
1932	Cle-A	16	16	0	1	1	0	0	0	2	3	.063	.211	.125	-10	-3	0	0	0	1.000	1	/O-2	-0.2
Total	18	1779	6560	1062	1990	322	80	18	552	748	345	.303	.378	.385	101	31	131	110		.967	19	*O-1638/P-13,1-8	-9.1
■ **VIC JANOWICZ**	Janowicz, Victor Felix b: 2/26/30, Elyria, Ohio d: 2/27/96, Columbus, Ohio BR/TR, 5'9", 185 lbs. Deb: 5/31/53																						
1953	Pit-N	42	123	10	31	3	1	2	8	5	31	.252	.287	.341	63	-7	0	1	-1	.937	-12	C-35	-1.7
1954	Pit-N	41	73	10	11	3	0	0	2	7	23	.151	.235	.192	13	-9	0	0	0	.904	1	3-18/O-1	-0.9
Total	2	83	196	20	42	6	1	2	10	12	54	.214	.267	.286	44	-16	0	1	-1	.937	-11	/C-35,3-18,O-1	-2.6
■ **RAY JANSEN**	Jansen, Raymond William b: 1/16/1889, St.Louis, Mo. d: 3/19/34, St.Louis, Mo. BR/TR, 5'11", 155 lbs. Deb: 9/30/10																						
1910	StL-A	1	5	0	4	0	0	0	0	0		.800	.800	.800	428	2	0			.700	0	/3-1	0.2
■ **HEINIE JANTZEN**	Jantzen, Walter C. b: 4/9/1890, Chicago, Ill. d: 4/1/48, Hines, Ill. BR/TR, 5'11.5", 170 lbs. Deb: 6/29/12																						
1912	StL-A	31	119	10	22	0	1	1	8	4		.185	.218	.227	28	-11	3			1.000	3	O-31	-1.0
■ **HAL JANVRIN**	Janvrin, Harold Chandler "Childe Harold" b: 8/27/1892, Haverhill, Mass. d: 3/1/62, Boston, Mass. BR/TR, 5'11.5", 168 lbs. Deb: 7/9/11																						
1911	Bos-A	9	27	2	4	1	0	0	1	3		.148	.258	.185	25	-3	0			.733	-2	/3-5,1-4	-0.5
1913	Bos-A	87	276	18	57	5	1	3	25	23	27	.207	.272	.264	56	-16	17			.923	-10	S-48,3-19/2-8,1-6	-2.4
1914	Bos-A	145	492	65	117	18	6	1	51	38	50	.238	.296	.305	81	-12	29	20	-3	.919	-22	2-59,1-57,S-20,/3-6	-4.3
1915	*Bos-A	99	316	41	85	9	1	0	37	14	27	.269	.317	.304	88	-5	8	14	-6	.917	-20	S-64,3-20/2-8	-2.8
1916	*Bos-A	117	310	32	69	11	4	0	26	32	32	.223	.299	.284	75	-9	6			.921	-19	S-59,2-39/1-4,3-4	-2.7
1917	Bos-A	55	127	21	25	3	0	0	8	11	13	.197	.266	.220	49	-8	2			.940	1	2-38,S-10/1-1	-0.5
1919	Was-A	61	208	17	37	4	1	1	13	19	17	.178	.253	.221	34	-18	8			.927	-27	2-56/S-2	-4.6
	StL-N	7	14	1	3	1	0	0	1	2	2	.214	.313	.286	86	-0	0			1.000	-2	/2-2,S-1,3-1	-0.2
1920	StL-N	87	270	33	74	8	4	1	28	17	19	.274	.317	.344	93	-3	5	6	-2	.926	-2	S-27,1-25,O-20,/2-6	-0.8
1921	StL-N	18	32	5	9	1	0	0	5	1	0	.281	.303	.313	65	-2	1	0	0	.968	0	/1-9,2-1	-0.1
	Bro-N	44	92	8	18	4	0	0	14	7	6	.196	.253	.239	30	-9	3	1	0	.922	-4	S-17,2-10/1-8,3O	-1.2
	Yr	62	124	13	27	5	0	0	19	8	6	.218	.265	.258	38	-11	4	1	1	.922	-3	1-17,S-17,2-11,/3O	-1.3
1922	Bro-N	30	57	7	17	3	1	0	1	4	4	.298	.344	.386	89	-1	0	0	0	.889	-4	2-15/S-4,3-2,1-1,O	-0.4
Total	10	759	2221	250	515	68	18	6	210	171	197	.232	.292	.287	70	-85	79	41		.907	-110	S-252,2-242,1/3O	-20.5
■ **ROY JARVIS**	Jarvis, Leroy Gilbert b: 6/27/26, Shawnee, Okla. d: 1/13/90, Oklahoma City, Okla. BR/TR, 5'9", 160 lbs. Deb: 4/30/44																						
1944	Bro-N	1	1	0	0	0	0	0	0	0	1	.000	.000	.000	-99	-0	0			1.000	-0	/C-1	0.0
1946	Pit-N	2	4	0	1	0	0	0	0	1	1	.250	.400	.250	84	-0	0			.800	-0	/C-1	0.0
1947	Pit-N	18	45	4	7	1	0	1	4	6	5	.156	.255	.244	32	-4	0			.967	-0	C-15	-0.4
Total	3	21	50	4	8	1	0	1	4	7	7	.160	.263	.240	34	-5	0			.955	-1	/C-17	-0.4
■ **PAUL JATA**	Jata, Paul b: 9/4/49, Astoria, N.Y. BR/TR, 6'1", 190 lbs. Deb: 4/19/72																						
1972	Det-A	32	74	8	17	2	0	0	3	7	14	.230	.296	.257	64	-3	0	1	-1	.991	-1	1-12,O-10/C-1	-0.7
■ **AL JAVIER**	Javier, Ignacio Alfredo (b: Ignacio Alfredo Wilkes (Javier)) b: 2/4/54, San Pedro De Macoris, D.R. BR/TR, 5'11", 170 lbs. Deb: 9/9/76																						
1976	Hou-N	8	24	1	5	0	0	0	0	2	5	.208	.269	.208	41	-2	0	0	0	1.000	-2	/O-7	-0.4
■ **JULIAN JAVIER**	Javier, Manuel Julian (Liranzo) b: 8/9/36, San Francisco De Macoris, D.R. BR/TR, 6'1", 175 lbs. Deb: 5/28/60 F																						
1960	StL-N	119	451	55	107	19	8	4	21	21	72	.237	.273	.341	62	-24	19	4	3	.962	5	*2-119	-0.5
1961	StL-N	113	445	58	124	14	3	2	41	30	51	.279	.327	.337	70	-19	11	4	1	.966	-0	*2-113	-0.6
1962	StL-N	155	598	97	157	25	5	7	39	47	73	.263	.317	.356	73	-22	26	9	2	.977	1	*2-151/S-4	-0.4
1963	StL-N★	161	609	82	160	27	9	9	46	24	86	.263	.297	.381	86	-12	18	10	-1	.969	-14	*2-161	-1.2
1964	*StL-N	155	535	66	129	19	5	12	65	30	82	.241	.283	.363	74	-19	9	7	-2	.966	-7	*2-154	-1.6
1965	StL-N	77	229	34	52	6	4	2	23	8	44	.227	.262	.314	56	-13	5	5	-2	.975	-6	2-69	-1.6
1966	StL-N	147	460	52	105	13	5	7	31	26	63	.228	.271	.324	64	-22	11	5	0	.981	2	*2-145	-1.2
1967	*StL-N	140	520	68	146	16	3	14	64	25	92	.281	.315	.404	106	2	6	7	-2	.965	-19	*2-138	-1.1
1968	*StL-N★	139	519	54	135	25	4	4	52	24	61	.260	.294	.347	93	-5	10	3	1	.976	-24	*2-139	-2.3
1969	StL-N	143	493	59	139	28	2	10	42	40	74	.282	.337	.408	107	4	8	4	0	.967	-18	*2-141	-0.2
1970	StL-N	139	513	62	129	16	3	2	42	24	70	.251	.286	.306	58	-31	6	4	-1	.980	13	*2-137	-0.8
1971	StL-N	90	259	32	67	6	4	3	28	9	33	.259	.289	.347	76	-8	5	1	1	.978	2	2-80/3-1	-0.1
1972	*Cin-N	44	91	3	19	2	0	2	12	6	11	.209	.258	.297	61	-5	1	0	0	.896	-3	3-19/2-5,1-1	-0.8
Total	13	1622	5722	722	1469	216	55	78	506	314	812	.257	.298	.355	78	-174	135	63	3	.972	-68	*2-1552/3-20,S-4,1	-12.4

■ STAN JAVIER Javier, Stanley Julian Antonio (De Javier) b: 1/9/64, San Francisco De Macoris, D.R. BB/TR, 6', 185 lbs. Deb: 4/15/84 F

YEAR	TM/L	G	AB	R	H	2B	3B	HR	RBI	BB	SO	AVG	OBP	SLG	PRO+	BR/A	SB	CS	SBR	FA	FR	G/POS	TPR
1984	NY-A	7	7	1	1	0	0	0	0	0	1	.143	.143	.143	-22	-1	0	0	0	1.000	-2	/O-5	-0.3
1986	Oak-A	59	114	13	23	8	0	0	8	16	27	.202	.305	.272	63	-6	8	0	2	1.000	-1	O-51/D-2	-0.5
1987	Oak-A	81	151	22	28	3	1	2	9	19	33	.185	.276	.258	46	-12	3	2	-0	.983	-9	O-71/1-6,D-1	-2.2
1988	*Oak-A	125	397	49	102	13	3	2	35	32	63	.257	.316	.320	81	-10	20	1	5	.980	-13	*O-115/1-4,D-2	-2.1
1989	*Oak-A	112	310	42	77	12	3	1	28	31	45	.248	.319	.316	82	-7	12	2	2	.991	-8	*O-107/1-1,2-1	-1.5
1990	Oak-A	19	33	4	8	0	2	0	3	3	6	.242	.306	.364	90	-0	0	0	0	1.000	-2	O-13/D-2	-0.3
	LA-N	104	276	56	84	9	4	3	24	37	44	.304	.387	.399	120	9	15	7	0	1.000	2	O-87	0.9
1991	LA-N	121	176	21	36	5	3	1	11	16	36	.205	.271	.284	57	-10	7	1	2	.986	-14	O-69/1-2	-2.4
1992	LA-N	56	58	6	11	3	0	1	5	6	11	.190	.277	.293	63	-3	1	2	-1	1.000	-7	O-27	-1.2
	Phi-N	74	276	36	72	14	1	0	24	31	43	.261	.340	.319	88	-3	17	1	5	.986	13	O-74	1.3
	Yr	130	334	42	83	17	1	1	29	37	54	.249	.329	.314	84	-6	18	3	4	.987	5	*O-101	0.1
1993	Cal-A	92	237	33	69	10	4	3	28	27	33	.291	.366	.405	104	2	12	2	2	.981	-11	O-64,1-12/2-2,D-1	-0.9
1994	Oak-A	109	419	75	114	23	0	10	44	49	76	.272	.351	.399	101	1	24	7	3	.986	0	*O-108/1-1,3-1	0.2
1995	Oak-A	130	442	81	123	20	2	8	56	49	63	.278	.356	.387	98	-0	36	5	8	**1.000**	7	*O-124/3-1	1.0
1996	SF-N	71	274	44	74	25	0	2	22	25	51	.270	.336	.383	93	-3	14	2	3	.984	7	O-71	0.5
1997	*SF-N	142	440	69	126	16	4	8	50	56	70	.286	.373	.395	104	4	25	3	6	.977	-6	*O-130/1-3	0.1
1998	SF-N	135	417	63	121	13	5	4	49	65	63	.290	.387	.374	103	4	21	5	3	.986	-9	*O-121	-0.2
Total	14	1437	4027	615	1069	174	32	45	396	462	665	.265	.344	.358	92	-35	215	40	41	.988	-53	*O-1237/1-29,D23	-7.6

■ TEX JEANES Jeanes, Ernest Lee b: 12/19/1900, Maypearl, Tex. d: 4/5/73, Longview, Tex. BR/TR, 6', 176 lbs. Deb: 4/20/21

YEAR	TM/L	G	AB	R	H	2B	3B	HR	RBI	BB	SO	AVG	OBP	SLG	PRO+	BR/A	SB	CS	SBR	FA	FR	G/POS	TPR
1921	Cle-A	5	3	2	2	1	0	0	4	1	0	.667	.750	1.000	338	1	0	0	0	1.000	-1	/O-5	0.0
1922	Cle-A	1	1	0	0	0	0	0	0	1	0	.000	.500	.000	39	0	0	0	0	.000	-1	/P-1,O-1	0.0
1925	Was-A	15	19	2	5	1	0	1	4	3	2	.263	.364	.474	113	0	1	0	0	1.000	-5	O-13	-0.5
1926	Was-A	21	30	6	7	2	0	0	3	0	3	.233	.233	.300	39	-3	0	0	0	1.000	-3	O-14	-0.6
1927	NY-N	11	20	5	6	0	0	0	0	2	2	.300	.364	.300	79	-0	0	0	0	1.000	1	/O-6,P-1	0.0
Total	5	53	73	15	20	4	0	1	11	7	7	.274	.338	.370	85	-2	1	0		1.000	-9	/O-39,P-2	-1.1

■ HAL JEFFCOAT Jeffcoat, Harold Bentley b: 9/6/24, W.Columbia, S.C. BR/TR, 5'10.5", 185 lbs. Deb: 4/20/48 F

YEAR	TM/L	G	AB	R	H	2B	3B	HR	RBI	BB	SO	AVG	OBP	SLG	PRO+	BR/A	SB	CS	SBR	FA	FR	G/POS	TPR
1948	Chi-N	134	473	53	132	16	4	4	42	24	68	.279	.315	.355	85	-11	8			.976	9	*O-119	-0.9
1949	Chi-N	108	363	43	89	18	6	2	26	20	48	.245	.286	.344	70	-16	12			.963	7	*O-101	-1.4
1950	Chi-N	66	179	21	42	13	1	2	18	6	23	.235	.259	.352	60	-11	7			.967	-3	O-53	-1.6
1951	Chi-N	113	278	44	76	20	2	4	27	16	23	.273	.315	.403	90	-4	8	4	0	.989	-2	O-87	-0.8
1952	Chi-N	102	297	29	65	17	2	4	30	15	40	.219	.259	.330	61	-16	7	2	1	.996	3	O-95	-1.6
1953	Chi-N	106	183	22	43	3	1	4	22	21	26	.235	.314	.328	66	-9	5	0	2	.973	-17	*O-100	-2.6
1954	Chi-N	56	31	13	8	2	1	1	6	1	7	.258	.281	.484	94	-0	2	0	1	.889	-1	P-43/O-3	-0.1
1955	Chi-N	52	23	3	4	0	0	1	1	2	9	.174	.240	.304	43	-2	0	0	0	.903	1	P-50	0.0
1956	Cin-N	49	54	5	8	2	0	0	5	3	20	.148	.193	.185	2	-7	0	1	-1	.969	3	P-38	0.0
1957	Cin-N	53	69	13	14	3	1	4	11	5	20	.203	.267	.449	82	-2	0	0	0	.958	-1	P-37	0.0
1958	Cin-N	50	9	2	5	0	0	0	0	1	2	.556	.600	.556	198	1	0	0	0	1.000	2	P-49/O-1	0.0
1959	Cin-N	17	1	1	1	1	0	0	0	0	0	1.000	1.000	2.000	655	1	0	0	0	1.000	0	P-17	0.0
	StL-N	12	3	0	0	0	0	0	0	0	3	.000	.000	.000	-94	-1	0	0	0	1.000	0	P-11	0.0
	Yr	29	4	1	1	1	0	0	0	0	3	.250	.250	.500	90	-0	0	0	0	1.000	0	P-28	0.0
Total	12	918	1963	249	487	95	18	26	188	114	289	.248	.291	.355	73	-78	49	7		.978	0	O-559,P-245	-9.0

■ GREGG JEFFERIES Jefferies, Gregory Scott b: 8/1/67, Burlingame, Cal. BB/TR, 5'10", 185 lbs. Deb: 9/6/87

YEAR	TM/L	G	AB	R	H	2B	3B	HR	RBI	BB	SO	AVG	OBP	SLG	PRO+	BR/A	SB	CS	SBR	FA	FR	G/POS	TPR
1987	NY-N	6	6	0	3	1	0	0	2	0	0	.500	.500	.667	217	1	0	0	0	.000	0	/H	0.1
1988	*NY-N	29	109	19	35	8	2	6	17	8	10	.321	.368	.596	181	11	5	1	1	.979	-3	3-20,2-10	0.9
1989	NY-N	141	508	72	131	28	2	12	56	39	46	.258	.317	.392	107	3	21	6	3	.975	-31	*2-123,3-20	-2.3
1990	NY-N	153	604	96	171	**40**	3	15	68	46	40	.283	.339	.434	111	8	11	2	2	.976	-9	*2-118,3-34	0.4
1991	NY-N	136	486	59	132	19	2	9	62	47	38	.272	.338	.374	101	1	26	5	5	.982	-16	2-77,3-51	-0.9
1992	KC-A	152	604	66	172	36	3	10	75	43	29	.285	.333	.404	103	1	19	9	0	.939	-2	*3-146/2-1,D-1	0.0
1993	StL-N★	142	544	89	186	24	3	16	83	62	32	.342	.411	.485	142	34	46	9	8	.993	-11	*1-140/2-1	1.9
1994	StL-N★	103	397	52	129	27	1	12	55	45	26	.325	.395	.489	131	19	12	5	1	.993	-9	*1-102	0.1
1995	Phi-N	114	480	69	147	31	2	11	56	35	26	.306	.353	.448	109	6	9	5	-0	.994	-2	1-59,O-55	-0.4
1996	Phi-N	104	404	59	118	17	3	7	51	36	21	.292	.351	.401	97	-1	20	6	2	.998	6	1-53,O-51	0.1
1997	Phi-N	130	476	68	122	25	3	11	48	53	27	.256	.333	.391	89	-8	12	6	0	.986	5	*O-124	-0.5
1998	Phi-N	125	483	65	142	22	3	8	48	29	27	.294	.335	.402	89	-8	11	3	2	.994	-1	*O-121	-0.8
	Ana-A	19	72	7	25	6	0	1	10	0	5	.347	.347	.472	109	1	1	0	0	1.000	-1	O-15/1-3	0.0
Total	12	1354	5173	721	1513	284	27	118	631	443	327	.292	.351	.426	109	68	193	57	24	.994	-74	O-366,1-357,23/D	-1.4

■ REGGIE JEFFERSON Jefferson, Reginald Jirod b: 9/25/68, Tallahassee, Fla. BL/TL, 6'4", 215 lbs. Deb: 5/18/91

YEAR	TM/L	G	AB	R	H	2B	3B	HR	RBI	BB	SO	AVG	OBP	SLG	PRO+	BR/A	SB	CS	SBR	FA	FR	G/POS	TPR
1991	Cin-N	5	7	1	1	0	0	1	1	1	2	.143	.250	.571	120	0	0	0	0	1.000	0	/1-2	0.0
	Cle-A	26	101	10	20	3	0	2	12	3	22	.198	.221	.287	39	-8	0	0	0	.993	2	1-26	-0.8
1992	Cle-A	24	89	8	30	6	2	1	6	1	17	.337	.352	.483	134	4	0	0	0	.993	1	1-15/D-7	0.3
1993	Cle-A	113	366	35	91	11	2	10	34	28	78	.249	.311	.372	83	-9	1	3	-2	.976	-0	D-88,1-15	-1.6
1994	Sea-A	63	162	24	53	11	0	8	32	17	32	.327	.394	.543	136	9	0	0	0	.981	1	D-32,1-13/O-2	0.6
1995	*Bos-A	46	121	21	35	8	0	5	26	9	24	.289	.338	.479	106	1	0	0	0	1.000	2	D-32/1-7,O-2	-0.1
1996	Bos-A	122	386	67	134	30	4	19	74	25	89	.347	.391	.593	141	23	0	0	0	.969	-3	D-49,O-45,1-16	1.4
1997	Bos-A	136	489	74	156	33	1	13	67	24	93	.319	.360	.470	112	8	1	2	-1	.975	-1	*D-119,1-12	-0.1
1998	Bos-A	62	196	24	60	16	1	8	31	21	40	.306	.376	.520	130	9	0	0	0	.953	-0	D-48/1-7	0.5
Total	8	597	1917	264	580	118	10	67	283	129	397	.303	.352	.479	114	35	2	5	-2	.986	-0	D-375,1-113/O-49	0.2

■ STAN JEFFERSON Jefferson, Stanley b: 12/4/62, New York, N.Y. BB/TR, 5'11", 175 lbs. Deb: 9/7/86

YEAR	TM/L	G	AB	R	H	2B	3B	HR	RBI	BB	SO	AVG	OBP	SLG	PRO+	BR/A	SB	CS	SBR	FA	FR	G/POS	TPR
1986	NY-N	14	24	6	5	1	0	1	3	2	8	.208	.296	.375	86	-0	0	0	0	1.000	-1	/O-7	-0.1
1987	SD-N	116	422	59	97	8	7	8	29	39	92	.230	.298	.339	71	-18	34	11	4	.987	-10	*O-107	-2.8
1988	SD-N	49	111	16	16	1	2	1	4	9	22	.144	.215	.216	25	-11	5	1	1	1.000	-4	O-38	-1.7
1989	NY-A	10	12	1	1	0	0	0	1	0	4	.083	.083	.083	-54	-2	1	1	-0	1.000	-3	/O-7,D-1	-0.6
	Bal-A	35	127	19	33	7	0	4	20	4	22	.260	.288	.409	97	-1	9	3	1	.988	2	O-32/D-2	0.1
	Yr	45	139	20	34	7	0	4	21	4	26	.245	.271	.381	84	-4	10	4	1	.988	-2	O-39/D-3	-0.5
1990	Bal-A	10	19	1	0	0	0	0	0	2	8	.000	.095	.000	-74	-4	1	0	0	1.000	-2	/O-5,D-1	-0.6
	Cle-A	49	98	21	27	8	0	2	10	8	18	.276	.343	.418	112	2	8	4	0	.985	0	O-34/D-5	0.1
	Yr	59	117	22	27	8	0	2	10	10	26	.231	.302	.350	83	-3	9	4	0	.987	-2	O-39/D-6	-0.5
1991	Cin-N	13	19	2	1	0	0	0	0	1	3	.053	.100	.053	-54	-4	2	0	1	1.000	-2	/O-5	-0.5
Total	6	296	832	125	180	25	9	16	67	65	177	.216	.279	.326	66	-40	60	20	6	.990	-20	O-235/D-9	-6.1

■ IRV JEFFRIES Jeffries, Irvine Franklin b: 9/10/05, Louisville, Ky. d: 6/8/82, Louisville, Ky. BR/TR, 5'10", 175 lbs. Deb: 4/30/30

YEAR	TM/L	G	AB	R	H	2B	3B	HR	RBI	BB	SO	AVG	OBP	SLG	PRO+	BR/A	SB	CS	SBR	FA	FR	G/POS	TPR
1930	Chi-A	40	97	14	23	3	0	2	11	3	2	.237	.275	.330	54	-7	1	2	-1	.976	-3	3-20,S-13	-0.8
1931	Chi-A	79	223	29	50	10	0	2	16	14	9	.224	.270	.296	52	-16	3	0	1	.949	2	3-61/2-6,S-5,O-1	-0.9
1934	Phi-N	56	175	28	43	6	0	4	19	15	10	.246	.305	.349	66	-9	2			.962	4	2-52/3-1	-0.2
Total	3	175	495	71	116	19	0	8	46	32	21	.234	.284	.321	58	-32	6	2		.955	3	/3-82,2-58,S-18,O-1	-1.9

■ CHRIS JELIC Jelic, Christopher John b: 12/16/63, Bethlehem, Pa. BR/TR, 5'11", 180 lbs. Deb: 9/30/90

YEAR	TM/L	G	AB	R	H	2B	3B	HR	RBI	BB	SO	AVG	OBP	SLG	PRO+	BR/A	SB	CS	SBR	FA	FR	G/POS	TPR
1990	NY-N	4	11	2	1	0	0	1	1	0	3	.091	.091	.364	19	-1	0	0	0	1.000	-1	/O-4	-0.3

■ FRANK JELINCICH Jelincich, Frank Anthony "Jelly" b: 9/3/19, San Jose, Cal. d: 6/27/92, Rochester, Minn. BR/TR, 6'2", 198 lbs. Deb: 9/6/41

YEAR	TM/L	G	AB	R	H	2B	3B	HR	RBI	BB	SO	AVG	OBP	SLG	PRO+	BR/A	SB	CS	SBR	FA	FR	G/POS	TPR
1941	Chi-N	4	8	0	1	0	0	0	2	1	2	.125	.222	.125	-1	-1	0			1.000	-1	/O-2	-0.2

■ GREG JELKS Jelks, Gregory Dion b: 8/16/61, Cherokee, Ala. BR/TR, 6'2", 190 lbs. Deb: 8/20/87

YEAR	TM/L	G	AB	R	H	2B	3B	HR	RBI	BB	SO	AVG	OBP	SLG	PRO+	BR/A	SB	CS	SBR	FA	FR	G/POS	TPR
1987	Phi-N	10	11	2	1	1	0	0	0	3	4	.091	.286	.182	26	-1	0	0	0	.750	0	/3-4,1-2,O-1	-0.1

■ STEVE JELTZ
Jeltz, Larry Steven b: 5/28/59, Paris, France BB/TR, 5′11″, 180 lbs. Deb: 7/17/83

YEAR	TM/L	G	AB	R	H	2B	3B	HR	RBI	BB	SO	AVG	OBP	SLG	PRO+	BR/A	SB	CS	SBR	FA	FR	G/POS	TPR
1983	Phi-N	13	8	0	1	0	1	0	1	1	2	.125	.222	.375	63	-0	0	0	0	1.000	1	/2-4,S-2,3-2	0.0
1984	Phi-N	28	68	7	14	0	1	1	7	7	11	.206	.280	.279	57	-4	2	1	0	.992	11	S-27/3-1	1.0
1985	Phi-N	89	196	17	37	4	1	0	12	26	55	.189	.284	.219	41	-15	1	1	-0	.958	6	S-86	-0.3
1986	Phi-N	145	439	44	96	11	4	0	36	65	97	.219	.321	.262	60	-22	6	3	0	.967	-2	*S-141	-1.1
1987	Phi-N	114	293	37	68	9	6	0	12	39	54	.232	.324	.304	66	-14	1	2	-1	.971	3	*S-114/O-1	-0.3
1988	Phi-N	148	379	39	71	11	4	0	27	59	58	.187	.297	.237	54	-21	3	0	1	.976	-1	*S-148	-1.1
1989	Phi-N	116	263	28	64	7	3	4	25	45	44	.243	.356	.338	99	1	4	2	0	.985	1	S-63,3-30,2-23,/O-1	0.7
1990	KC-A	74	103	11	16	4	0	0	10	6	21	.155	.202	.194	11	-12	1	1	-0	.977	9	2-34,S-23,O-13,/3D	-0.3
Total	8	727	1749	183	367	46	20	5	130	248	342	.210	.309	.268	61	-86	18	10	-1	.971	28	S-604/2-61,3-36,OD	-1.4

■ GEOFF JENKINS
Jenkins, Geoffrey Scott b: 7/21/74, Olympia, Wash. BL/TR, 6′1″, 205 lbs. Deb: 4/24/98

YEAR	TM/L	G	AB	R	H	2B	3B	HR	RBI	BB	SO	AVG	OBP	SLG	PRO+	BR/A	SB	CS	SBR	FA	FR	G/POS	TPR
1998	Mil-N	84	262	33	60	12	1	9	28	20	61	.229	.289	.385	72	-11	1	3	-2	.968	0	O-81	-1.3

■ JOHN JENKINS
Jenkins, John Robert b: 7/7/1896, Bosworth, Mo. d: 8/3/68, Columbia, Mo. BR/TR, 5′8″, 160 lbs. Deb: 8/5/22

YEAR	TM/L	G	AB	R	H	2B	3B	HR	RBI	BB	SO	AVG	OBP	SLG	PRO+	BR/A	SB	CS	SBR	FA	FR	G/POS	TPR
1922	Chi-A	5	3	0	0	0	0	0	1	0	2	.000	.000	.000	-99	-1	0	0	0	.000	-0	/2-1,S-1	-0.1

■ JOE JENKINS
Jenkins, Joseph Daniel b: 10/12/1890, Shelbyville, Tenn. d: 6/21/74, Fresno, Cal. BR/TR, 5′11″, 170 lbs. Deb: 4/30/14

YEAR	TM/L	G	AB	R	H	2B	3B	HR	RBI	BB	SO	AVG	OBP	SLG	PRO+	BR/A	SB	CS	SBR	FA	FR	G/POS	TPR
1914	StL-A	19	32	0	4	1	1	0	0	1	11	.125	.152	.219	12	-4	2			.931	-4	/C-9	-0.8
1917	Chi-A	10	9	0	1	0	0	0	2	0	5	.111	.111	.111	-32	-1	0			.000	0	/C-1	-0.2
1919	Chi-A	11	19	0	3	1	0	0	1	1	1	.158	.200	.211	15	-2	1			.824	-2	/C-4	-0.4
Total	3	40	60	0	8	2	1	0	3	2	17	.133	.161	.200	6	-7	3			.891	-6	/C-14	-1.4

■ TOM JENKINS
Jenkins, Thomas Griffith "Tut" b: 4/10/1898, Camden, Ala. d: 5/3/79, Weymouth, Mass. BL/TR, 6′1.5″, 174 lbs. Deb: 9/15/25

YEAR	TM/L	G	AB	R	H	2B	3B	HR	RBI	BB	SO	AVG	OBP	SLG	PRO+	BR/A	SB	CS	SBR	FA	FR	G/POS	TPR
1925	Bos-A	15	64	9	19	2	1	0	5	3	4	.297	.338	.359	77	-2	0	0	0	.938	-2	O-15	-0.5
1926	Bos-A	21	50	3	9	1	1	0	6	3	7	.180	.226	.240	22	-6	0	0	0	1.000	-1	O-13	-0.8
	Phi-A	6	23	3	4	2	0	0	0	0	2	.174	.174	.261	12	-3	0	0	0	1.000	0	/O-6	-0.3
	Yr	27	73	6	13	3	1	0	6	3	9	.178	.211	.247	19	-9	0	0	0	1.000	-1	O-19	-1.1
1929	StL-A	21	22	1	4	0	1	0	0	4	8	.182	.308	.273	49	-2	0	0	0	1.000	-1	/O-3	-0.3
1930	StL-A	2	8	1	2	1	1	0	3	0	1	.250	.250	.625	110	0	0	0	0	1.000	-0	/O-2	0.0
1931	StL-A	81	230	20	61	7	2	3	25	17	25	.265	.316	.352	73	-9	1	3	-2	.952	-4	O-58	-1.7
1932	StL-A	25	62	5	20	1	0	0	5	1	6	.323	.333	.339	70	-3	0	0	0	.939	2	O 12	-0.2
Total	6	171	459	42	119	14	6	3	44	28	53	.259	.303	.336	64	-25	1	3	-2	.958	-6	O-109	-3.8

■ ALAMAZOO JENNINGS
Jennings, Alfred Gorden b: 11/30/1850, Newport, Ky. d: 11/2/1894, Cincinnati, Ohio Deb: 8/15/1878 U

YEAR	TM/L	G	AB	R	H	2B	3B	HR	RBI	BB	SO	AVG	OBP	SLG	PRO+	BR/A	SB	CS	SBR	FA	FR	G/POS	TPR
1878	Mil-N	1	2	0	0	0	0	0	0	1	0	.000	.333	.000	16	-0				.429	-2	/C-1	-0.2

■ HUGHIE JENNINGS
Jennings, Hugh Ambrose "Ee-Yah" b: 4/2/1869, Pittston, Pa. d: 2/1/28, Scranton, Pa. BR/TR, 5′8.5″, 165 lbs. Deb: 6/1/1891 MCH

YEAR	TM/L	G	AB	R	H	2B	3B	HR	RBI	BB	SO	AVG	OBP	SLG	PRO+	BR/A	SB	CS	SBR	FA	FR	G/POS	TPR
1891	Lou-a	90	360	53	105	10	8	1	58	17	36	.292	.339	.372	105	1	12			.894	7	S-70,1-17/3-3	1.0
1892	Lou-N	152	594	65	132	16	4	2	61	30	30	.222	.270	.273	70	-22	28			.907	15	*S-152	0.0
1893	Lou-N	23	88	6	12	3	0	0	9	3	3	.136	.174	.170	-9	-14	0			.899	6	S-23	-0.6
	Bal-N	16	55	6	14	0	0	1	6	4	3	.255	.339	.309	71	-2	0			.886	-2	S-15/O-1	-0.3
	Yr	39	143	12	26	3	0	1	15	7	6	.182	.240	.224	25	-16	0			.895	4	S-38/O-1	-0.9
1894	*Bal-N	128	501	134	168	28	16	4	109	37	17	.335	.411	.479	109	7	37			**.928**	**33**	*S-128	3.6
1895	*Bal-N	131	529	159	204	41	7	4	125	24	17	.386	.444	.512	142	34	53			**.940**	**36**	*S-131	**6.0**
1896	*Bal-N	130	521	125	209	27	9	0	121	19	11	.401	.472	.488	151	42	70			**.928**	34	*S-130	**6.7**
1897	*Bal-N	117	439	133	156	26	9	2	79	42		.355	.463	.469	146	35	60			**.933**	27	*S-116	**5.4**
1898	Bal-N	143	534	135	175	25	11	1	87	78		.328	.454	.421	149	42	28			.929	-0	*S-115,2-27/O-1	4.5
1899	Bro-N	16	41	7	7	0	2	0	6	9		.171	.346	.268	68	-1	4			.825	-6	S-11/1-4	-0.6
	Bal-N	2	8	2	3	0	2	0	2	0		.375	.375	.875	227	1	0			1.000	-1	/2-2	0.0
	Bro-N	51	175	35	57	3	8	0	34	13		.326	.424	.434	133	9	14			.987	-1	1-46/2-1,S-1	0.7
	Yr	69	224	44	67	3	12	0	42	22		.299	.408	.420	124	9	18			.985	-8	1-50,S-12/2-3	0.1
1900	*Bro-N	115	441	61	120	18	6	1	69	31		.272	.348	.347	87	-8	31			.982	5	*1-112/2-2	-0.3
1901	Phi-N	82	302	38	79	21	2	1	39	25		.262	.342	.354	100	1	13			.979	-3	1-80/2-1,S-1	-0.3
1902	Phi-N	78	290	32	79	13	4	1	32	14		.272	.330	.355	111	4	8			.983	2	1-69/S-5,2-4	0.5
1903	Bro-N	6	17	2	4	0	0	0	1	1		.235	.316	.235	60	-1	1			1.000	-0	/O-4	-0.1
1907	Det-A	1	4	0	1	1	0	0	0	0		.250	.250	.500	133	0	0			.750	-1	/2-1,S-1,M	-0.1
1909	Det-A	2	4	1	2	0	0	0	2	0		.500	.500	.500	207	0	0			1.000	0	/1-2,M	0.1
1912	Det-A	1	1	0	0	0	0	0	0	0		.000	.000	.000	-99	-0	0			.000	0	HM	0.0
1918	Det-A	1	0	0	0	0	0	0	0	0	0	—	—	—	—	0	0			1.000	-0	/1-1,M	0.0
Total	17	1285	4904	994	1527	232	88	18	840	347	117	.311	.390	.406	117	127	359			.922	150	S-899,1-331/2O3	26.2

■ DOUG JENNINGS
Jennings, James Douglas b: 9/30/64, Atlanta, Ga. BL/TL, 5′10″, 170 lbs. Deb: 4/8/88

YEAR	TM/L	G	AB	R	H	2B	3B	HR	RBI	BB	SO	AVG	OBP	SLG	PRO+	BR/A	SB	CS	SBR	FA	FR	G/POS	TPR
1988	Oak-A	71	101	9	21	6	0	1	15	21	28	.208	.355	.297	88	-1	0	1	-1	1.000	-3	O-23,1-14/D-2	-0.5
1989	Oak-A	4	4	0	0	0	0	0	0	0	2	.000	.000	.000	-99	-1	0	0	0	1.000	-1	/O-3	-0.2
1990	*Oak-A	64	156	19	30	7	2	2	14	17	48	.192	.280	.301	65	-7	0	3	-2	.984	-8	O-45/1-4,D-8	-1.9
1991	Oak-A	8	9	0	1	0	0	0	0	2	2	.111	.273	.111	11	-1	0	1	-1	1.000	-1	/O-6	-0.2
1993	Chi-N	42	52	8	13	3	1	2	8	3	10	.250	.316	.462	107	0	0	0	0	1.000	-1	1-10	-0.1
Total	5	189	322	36	65	16	3	5	37	43	90	.202	.307	.317	76	-10	0	5	-3	.991	-13	/O-77,1-28,D-10	-2.9

■ ROBIN JENNINGS
Jennings, Robin Christopher b: 4/11/72, Singapore, Singapore BL/TL, 6′2″, 205 lbs. Deb: 4/18/96

YEAR	TM/L	G	AB	R	H	2B	3B	HR	RBI	BB	SO	AVG	OBP	SLG	PRO+	BR/A	SB	CS	SBR	FA	FR	G/POS	TPR
1996	Chi-N	31	58	7	13	5	0	0	4	3	9	.224	.274	.310	52	-4	1	0	0	1.000	1	O-11	-0.3
1997	Chi-N	9	18	1	3	1	0	0	2	0	2	.167	.167	.222	1	-3	0	0	0	1.000	-1	/O-5	-0.4
Total	2	40	76	8	16	6	0	0	6	3	11	.211	.250	.289	40	-7	1	0	0	1.000	-0	/O-16	-0.7

■ BILL JENNINGS
Jennings, William Lee b: 9/28/25, St.Louis, Mo. BR/TR, 6′2″, 175 lbs. Deb: 7/19/51

YEAR	TM/L	G	AB	R	H	2B	3B	HR	RBI	BB	SO	AVG	OBP	SLG	PRO+	BR/A	SB	CS	SBR	FA	FR	G/POS	TPR
1951	StL-A	64	195	20	35	10	2	0	13	26	42	.179	.276	.251	42	-16	1	0	0	.953	-5	S-64	-1.6

■ WOODY JENSEN
Jensen, Forrest Docenus b: 8/11/07, Bremerton, Wash. BL/TL, 5′10.5″, 160 lbs. Deb: 4/20/31

YEAR	TM/L	G	AB	R	H	2B	3B	HR	RBI	BB	SO	AVG	OBP	SLG	PRO+	BR/A	SB	CS	SBR	FA	FR	G/POS	TPR
1931	Pit-N	73	267	43	65	5	4	3	17	10	18	.243	.276	.326	62	-15	4			.974	5	O-67	-1.4
1932	Pit-N	7	5	2	0	0	0	0	0	0	2	.000	.000	.000	-99	-1	0			.000	-1	/O-1	-0.2
1933	Pit-N	70	196	29	58	7	3	0	15	8	2	.296	.330	.362	98	-1	1			.980	-0	O-40	-0.3
1934	Pit-N	88	283	34	82	13	4	0	27	4	13	.290	.304	.364	76	-10	2			.993	-3	O-66	-1.4
1935	Pit-N	143	627	97	203	28	7	8	62	15	14	.324	.344	.429	103	2	9			.977	-4	*O-140	-0.7
1936	Pit-N	153	696	98	197	34	10	10	58	16	19	.283	.305	.404	87	-14	2			.975	1	*O-153	-2.0
1937	Pit-N	124	509	77	142	23	9	5	45	15	29	.279	.301	.389	86	-11	2			.963	-0	*O-120	-1.6
1938	Pit-N	68	125	12	25	4	0	0	10	1	3	.200	.213	.232	22	-13	0			.900	-11	O-38	-2.6
1939	Pit-N	12	12	0	2	0	0	0	1	0	0	.167	.167	.167	-10	-2	0			1.000	-1	/O-3	-0.3
Total	9	738	2720	392	774	114	37	26	235	69	100	.285	.307	.382	84	-66	20			.972	-13	O-628	-10.5

■ JACKIE JENSEN
Jensen, Jack Eugene b: 3/9/27, San Francisco, Cal. d: 7/14/82, Charlottesville, Va. BR/TR, 5′11″, 190 lbs. Deb: 4/18/50

YEAR	TM/L	G	AB	R	H	2B	3B	HR	RBI	BB	SO	AVG	OBP	SLG	PRO+	BR/A	SB	CS	SBR	FA	FR	G/POS	TPR
1950	*NY-A	45	70	13	12	2	2	1	5	7	8	.171	.247	.300	41	-7	4	0	1	.947	-4	O-23	-1.0
1951	NY-A	56	168	30	50	8	1	8	25	18	18	.298	.369	.500	138	8	8	2	1	.974	1	O-48	0.8
1952	NY-A	7	19	3	2	1	1	0	2	4	4	.105	.261	.263	49	-1	1	0	0	1.000	-1	/O-5	-0.3
	Was-A★	144	570	80	163	29	5	10	80	63	40	.286	.360	.407	117	13	17	6	2	.977	6	*O-143	1.5
	Yr	151	589	83	165	30	6	10	82	67	44	.280	.357	.402	115	12	18	6	**2**	.978	5	*O-148	1.2
1953	Was-A	147	552	87	147	32	8	10	84	73	51	.266	.357	.408	109	7	18	8	1	.983	-4	*O-146	-0.2
1954	Bos-A	152	580	92	160	25	7	25	117	79	52	.276	.365	.472	115	11	**22**	7	2	.986	-7	*O-151	0.0
1955	Bos-A★	152	574	95	158	27	6	26	**116**	89	63	.275	.375	.479	118	14	16	7	1	.977	1	*O-150	0.9
1956	Bos-A	151	578	80	182	23	**11**	20	97	89	43	.315	.407	.497	123	19	11	3	2	.962	2	*O-151	1.4
1957	Bos-A	145	544	82	153	29	2	23	103	75	66	.281	.370	.469	121	16	8	5	-1	.960	4	*O-144	1.2

YEAR	TM/L	G	AB	R	H	2B	3B	HR	RBI	BB	SO	AVG	OBP	SLG	PRO+	BR/A	SB	CS	SBR	FA	FR	G/POS	TPR
1958	Bos-A★	154	548	83	157	31	0	35	**122**	99	65	.286	.398	.535	144	35	9	4	0	.981	3	*O-153	3.1
1959	Bos-A	148	535	101	148	31	0	28	**112**	88	67	.277	.379	.492	131	24	20	5	3	.982	15	*O-146	3.4
1961	Bos-A	137	498	64	131	21	2	13	66	66	69	.263	.353	.392	96	-2	9	8	-2	.986	11	*O-131	0.0
Total	11	1438	5236	810	1463	259	45	199	929	750	546	.279	.372	.460	119	138	143	55	10	.977	28	*O-1391	10.8

■ MARCUS JENSEN
Jensen, Marcus C. b: 12/14/72, Oakland, Cal. BB/TR, 6'4", 195 lbs. Deb: 4/14/96

YEAR	TM/L	G	AB	R	H	2B	3B	HR	RBI	BB	SO	AVG	OBP	SLG	PRO+	BR/A	SB	CS	SBR	FA	FR	G/POS	TPR
1996	SF-N	9	19	4	4	1	0	0	4	8	7	.211	.444	.263	96	1	0	0	0	.955	-0	/C-7	0.1
1997	SF-N	30	74	5	11	2	0	1	3	7	23	.149	.222	.216	16	-9	0	0	0	.983	-7	C-28	-1.5
	Det-A	8	11	1	2	0	0	0	1	1	5	.182	.250	.182	15	-1	0	0	0	.964	1	/C-8	0.0
1998	Mil-N	2	2	0	0	0	0	0	0	0	2	.000	.000	.000	-99	-1	0	0	0	1.000	-0	/C-1	-0.1
Total	3	49	106	10	17	3	0	1	8	16	37	.160	.270	.217	30	-11	0	0	0	.974	-6	/C-44	-1.5

■ DAN JESSEE
Jessee, Daniel Edward b: 2/22/01, Olive Hill, Ky. d: 4/30/70, Venice, Fla. BL/TR, 5'10", 165 lbs. Deb: 8/14/29

YEAR	TM/L	G	AB	R	H	2B	3B	HR	RBI	BB	SO	AVG	OBP	SLG	PRO+	BR/A	SB	CS	SBR	FA	FR	G/POS	TPR
1929	Cle-A	1	0	0	0	0	0	0	0	0	0	—	—	—	—	0	0	0	0	.000	0	R	0.0

■ GARRY JESTADT
Jestadt, Garry Arthur b: 3/19/47, Chicago, Ill. BR/TR, 6'2", 188 lbs. Deb: 9/17/69

YEAR	TM/L	G	AB	R	H	2B	3B	HR	RBI	BB	SO	AVG	OBP	SLG	PRO+	BR/A	SB	CS	SBR	FA	FR	G/POS	TPR
1969	Mon-N	6	6	1	0	0	0	0	1	0	0	.000	.000	.000	-99	-2	0	0	0	.667	-0	/S-1	-0.2
1971	Chi-N	3	3	0	0	0	0	0	0	0	0	.000	.000	.000	-87	-1	0	0	0	.000	0	/3-1	-0.1
	SD-N	75	189	17	55	13	0	0	13	11	24	.291	.330	.360	102	0	1	3	-2	.935	11	3-49,2-23/S-1	1.1
	Yr	78	192	17	55	13	0	0	13	11	24	.286	.325	.354	98	-1	1	3	-2	.935	11	3-50,2-23/S-1	1.0
1972	SD-N	92	256	15	63	5	1	6	22	13	21	.246	.283	.344	83	-7	0	0	0	.944	-17	2-48,3-25/S-3	-2.4
Total	3	176	454	33	118	18	1	6	36	24	45	.260	.297	.344	87	-9	1	3	-2	.942	-7	/3-75,2-71,S-5	-1.6

■ DEREK JETER
Jeter, Derek Sanderson b: 6/26/74, Pequannock, N.J. BR/TR, 6'3", 175 lbs. Deb: 5/29/95

YEAR	TM/L	G	AB	R	H	2B	3B	HR	RBI	BB	SO	AVG	OBP	SLG	PRO+	BR/A	SB	CS	SBR	FA	FR	G/POS	TPR
1995	NY-A	15	48	5	12	4	1	0	7	3	11	.250	.294	.375	73	-2	0	0	0	.962	-1	S-15	-0.2
1996	*NY-A	157	582	104	183	25	6	10	78	48	102	.314	.376	.430	103	4	14	7	0	.969	-3	*S-157	1.4
1997	*NY-A	159	654	116	190	31	7	10	70	74	125	.291	.371	.405	103	5	23	12	-0	.975	-0	*S-159	1.8
1998	*NY-A★	149	626	**127**	203	25	8	19	84	57	119	.324	.385	.481	126	25	30	6	5	.986	-24	*S-148	1.9
Total	4	480	1910	352	588	85	22	39	239	182	357	.308	.375	.437	110	32	67	25	5	.976	-28	S-479	4.9

■ JOHNNY JETER
Jeter, John b: 10/24/44, Shreveport, La. BR/TR, 6'1", 180 lbs. Deb: 6/14/69 F

YEAR	TM/L	G	AB	R	H	2B	3B	HR	RBI	BB	SO	AVG	OBP	SLG	PRO+	BR/A	SB	CS	SBR	FA	FR	G/POS	TPR
1969	Pit-N	28	29	7	9	1	1	1	6	3	15	.310	.375	.517	151	2	1	1	-0	1.000	-4	O-20	-0.2
1970	*Pit-N	85	126	27	30	3	2	2	12	13	34	.238	.314	.341	77	-4	9	5	-0	1.000	-8	O-56	-1.4
1971	SD-N	18	75	8	24	4	0	1	3	2	16	.320	.338	.413	120	2	2	0	1	.967	4	O-17	0.6
1972	SD-N	110	326	25	72	4	3	7	21	18	92	.221	.266	.316	70	-14	11	5	0	.987	1	O-91	-1.8
1973	Chi-A	89	300	38	72	14	4	7	26	9	74	.240	.262	.383	77	-10	4	3	-1	.955	-3	O-72/D-3	-1.8
1974	Cle-A	6	17	3	6	1	0	0	1	1	6	.353	.389	.412	132	1	1	2	-1	.833	-2	/O-6	-0.2
Total	6	336	873	108	213	27	10	18	69	46	237	.244	.284	.360	82	-24	28	16	-1	.975	-11	O-262/D-3	-4.8

■ SHAWN JETER
Jeter, Shawn Darrell b: 6/28/66, Shreveport, La. BL/TR, 6'2", 185 lbs. Deb: 6/13/92 F

YEAR	TM/L	G	AB	R	H	2B	3B	HR	RBI	BB	SO	AVG	OBP	SLG	PRO+	BR/A	SB	CS	SBR	FA	FR	G/POS	TPR
1992	Chi-A	13	18	1	2	0	0	0	0	0	7	.111	.111	.111	-38	-3	0	0	0	.909	-2	/O-8,D-3	-0.5

■ SAM JETHROE
Jethroe, Samuel "Jet" b: 1/20/18, E.St.Louis, Ill. BB/TR, 6'1", 178 lbs. Deb: 4/18/50

YEAR	TM/L	G	AB	R	H	2B	3B	HR	RBI	BB	SO	AVG	OBP	SLG	PRO+	BR/A	SB	CS	SBR	FA	FR	G/POS	TPR
1950	Bos-N	141	582	100	159	28	8	18	58	52	93	.273	.338	.442	110	7	**35**			.969	8	*O-141	0.9
1951	Bos-N	148	572	101	160	29	10	18	65	57	88	.280	.356	.460	127	20	**35**	5	**8**	.974	7	*O-140	2.9
1952	Bos-N	151	608	79	141	23	7	13	58	68	112	.232	.318	.357	90	-8	28	9	3	.970	4	*O-151	-0.8
1954	Pit-N	2	1	0	0	0	0	0	0	0	0	.000	.000	.000	-99	-0	0	0	0	1.000	-0	/O-1	-0.1
Total	4	442	1763	280	460	80	25	49	181	177	293	.261	.337	.418	108	18	98	14		.971	19	O-433	2.9

■ NAT JEWETT
Jewett, Nathan W. b: 12/25/1842, New York, N.Y. d: 2/23/14, Bronx, N.Y. 5'6", 137 lbs. Deb: 7/4/1872

YEAR	TM/L	G	AB	R	H	2B	3B	HR	RBI	BB	SO	AVG	OBP	SLG	PRO+	BR/A	SB	CS	SBR	FA	FR	G/POS	TPR
1872	Eck-n	2	8	1	1	0	0	0	0	0	0	.125	.125	.125	-27	-1	0	0	0	.700	-2	/C-2	-0.2

■ HOUSTON JIMENEZ
Jimenez, Alfonso (Gonzales) b: 10/30/57, Navojoa, Mexico BR/TR, 5'8", 144 lbs. Deb: 6/13/83

YEAR	TM/L	G	AB	R	H	2B	3B	HR	RBI	BB	SO	AVG	OBP	SLG	PRO+	BR/A	SB	CS	SBR	FA	FR	G/POS	TPR
1983	Min-A	36	86	5	15	5	1	0	9	4	11	.174	.211	.256	27	-9	0	1	-1	.969	4	S-36	-0.3
1984	Min-A	108	298	28	60	11	1	0	19	15	34	.201	.240	.245	33	-27	0	1	-1	.959	-5	*S-107	-2.4
1987	Pit-N	5	6	0	0	0	0	0	0	1	2	.000	.143	.000	-58	-1	0	0	0	1.000	1	/2-2,S-2	0.0
1988	Cle-A	9	21	1	1	0	0	0	1	0	2	.048	.048	.048	-71	-5	0	0	0	.973	6	/2-7,S-2	0.1
Total	4	158	411	34	76	16	2	0	29	20	49	.185	.223	.234	25	-42	0	2	-1	.962	7	S-147/2-9	-2.6

■ ELVIO JIMENEZ
Jimenez, Felix Elvio (Rivera) b: 1/6/40, San Pedro De Macoris, D.R. BR/TR, 5'9", 170 lbs. Deb: 10/4/64 F

YEAR	TM/L	G	AB	R	H	2B	3B	HR	RBI	BB	SO	AVG	OBP	SLG	PRO+	BR/A	SB	CS	SBR	FA	FR	G/POS	TPR
1964	NY-A	1	6	0	2	0	0	0	0	0	0	.333	.333	.333	85	-0	0	0	0	1.000	0	/O-1	0.0

■ MANNY JIMENEZ
Jimenez, Manuel Emilio (Rivera) b: 11/19/38, San Pedro De Macoris, D.R. BL/TR, 6'1", 195 lbs. Deb: 4/11/62 F

YEAR	TM/L	G	AB	R	H	2B	3B	HR	RBI	BB	SO	AVG	OBP	SLG	PRO+	BR/A	SB	CS	SBR	FA	FR	G/POS	TPR
1962	KC-A	139	479	48	144	24	2	11	69	31	34	.301	.357	.428	105	4	0	1	-1	.985	-5	*O-122	-0.9
1963	KC-A	60	157	12	44	9	0	0	15	16	14	.280	.365	.338	93	-1	0	1	-1	.960	1	O-40	-0.2
1964	KC-A	95	204	19	46	7	0	12	38	15	24	.225	.295	.436	97	-1	0	0	0	.939	-4	O-49	-0.7
1966	KC-A	13	35	1	4	0	1	0	1	6	4	.114	.244	.171	22	-3	0	0	0	.909	-2	O-12	-0.7
1967	Pit-N	50	56	3	14	2	0	2	10	1	4	.250	.276	.393	89	-1	0	0	0	1.000	-1	/O-6	-0.3
1968	Pit-N	66	66	7	20	1	1	1	11	6	15	.303	.403	.394	142	4	0	0	0	.857	-1	/O-5	0.3
1969	Chi-N	6	6	0	1	0	0	0	0	0	2	.167	.167	.167	-6	-1	0	0	0	.000	0	H	-0.1
Total	7	429	1003	90	273	43	4	26	144	75	97	.272	.339	.401	100	0	0	2	-1	.966	-11	O-234	-2.6

■ KEITH JOHNS
Johns, Robert Keith b: 7/19/71, Callahan, Fla. BR/TR, 6'1", 175 lbs. Deb: 5/23/98

YEAR	TM/L	G	AB	R	H	2B	3B	HR	RBI	BB	SO	AVG	OBP	SLG	PRO+	BR/A	SB	CS	SBR	FA	FR	G/POS	TPR
1998	Bos-A	2	0	0	0	0	0	0	0	1	0	—	1.000	—	191	0	0	0	0	1.000	0	/2-1,D-1	0.1

■ TOMMY JOHNS
Johns, Thomas Pearce b: 9/7/1851, Baltimore, Md. d: 4/13/27, Baltimore, Md. Deb: 5/14/1873

YEAR	TM/L	G	AB	R	H	2B	3B	HR	RBI	BB	SO	AVG	OBP	SLG	PRO+	BR/A	SB	CS	SBR	FA	FR	G/POS	TPR
1873	Mar-n	1	4	0	0	0	0	0	0	0	0	.000	.000	.000	-99	-1	0	0	0	.000	-1	/O-1	-0.1

■ PETE JOHNS
Johns, William R. b: 1/17/1889, Cleveland, Ohio d: 8/9/64, Cleveland, Ohio BR/TR, 5'10", 165 lbs. Deb: 8/25/15

YEAR	TM/L	G	AB	R	H	2B	3B	HR	RBI	BB	SO	AVG	OBP	SLG	PRO+	BR/A	SB	CS	SBR	FA	FR	G/POS	TPR
1915	Chi-A	28	100	7	21	2	1	0	11	8	11	.210	.275	.250	56	-6	2	7	-4	.943	4	3-28	-0.5
1918	StL-A	46	89	5	16	1	1	0	11	4	6	.180	.215	.213	30	-8	0			.990	-1	1-10/S-4,3-4,O-4,2	-1.1
Total	2	74	189	12	37	3	2	0	22	12	17	.196	.248	.233	44	-13	2	7		.929	2	/3-32,1-10,O-4,S2	-1.6

■ ABBIE JOHNSON
Johnson, Albert L. b: 1875, Chicago, Ill. d: 11/28/60, Detroit, Mich. 5'9.5", 165 lbs. Deb: 9/1/1896

YEAR	TM/L	G	AB	R	H	2B	3B	HR	RBI	BB	SO	AVG	OBP	SLG	PRO+	BR/A	SB	CS	SBR	FA	FR	G/POS	TPR
1896	Lou-N	25	87	10	20	2	1	0	14	4	6	.230	.264	.276	44	-7	0			.937	-5	2-25	-0.9
1897	Lou-N	48	161	16	39	6	1	0	23	13		.242	.303	.292	59	-9	2			.879	-11	2-33,S-12	-1.6
Total	2	73	248	26	59	8	2	0	37	17	6	.238	.289	.286	54	-16	2			.903	-15	/2-58,S-12	-2.5

■ ALEX JOHNSON
Johnson, Alexander b: 12/7/42, Helena, Ark. BR/TR, 6', 205 lbs. Deb: 7/25/64

YEAR	TM/L	G	AB	R	H	2B	3B	HR	RBI	BB	SO	AVG	OBP	SLG	PRO+	BR/A	SB	CS	SBR	FA	FR	G/POS	TPR
1964	Phi-N	43	109	18	33	7	1	4	18	6	26	.303	.345	.495	135	5	1	2	-1	.980	-1	O-35	0.2
1965	Phi-N	97	262	27	77	9	3	8	28	15	60	.294	.337	.443	120	6	4	4	-1	.966	-5	O-82	-0.2
1966	StL-N	25	86	7	16	0	1	2	6	5	18	.186	.231	.279	41	-7	1	1	-0	.962	-1	O-22	-1.0
1967	StL-N	81	175	20	39	9	2	1	12	9	26	.223	.273	.314	68	-7	6	3	0	.970	0	O-57	-1.0
1968	Cin-N	149	603	79	188	32	6	2	58	26	71	.312	.343	.395	114	10	16	6	1	.947	5	*O-140	0.9
1969	Cin-N	139	523	86	165	18	4	17	88	25	69	.315	.357	.463	122	14	11	8	-2	.927	1	*O-132	0.7
1970	Cal-A★	156	614	85	202	26	6	14	86	35	68	**.329**	.372	.459	133	26	17	2	4	.959	5	*O-156	2.7
1971	Cal-A	65	242	19	63	8	0	2	21	15	34	.260	.309	.318	84	-6	5	2	0	.926	-6	O-61	-1.5
1972	Cle-A	108	356	31	85	10	1	8	37	22	40	.239	.285	.340	83	-8	6	8	-3	.955	-5	O-95	-2.4
1973	Tex-A	158	624	62	179	26	3	8	68	32	82	.287	.324	.377	101	-1	10	5	0	.987	1	*D-116,O-41	-0.4
1974	Tex-A	114	453	57	132	14	3	4	41	28	59	.291	.338	.362	104	2	20	9	1	.956	6	O-81,D-32	0.4
	NY-A	10	28	3	6	1	0	1	2	0	3	.214	.214	.357	63	-1	0	0	0	.000	-0	/O-1,D-4	-0.2
	Yr	124	481	60	138	15	3	5	43	28	62	.287	.331	.362	102	1	20	9	1	.956	5	O-82,D-36	0.2
1975	NY-A	52	119	15	31	5	1	1	15	7	21	.261	.302	.345	84	-3	2	3	-1	1.000	-1	D-28/O-7	-0.6

YEAR	TM/L	G	AB	R	H	2B	3B	HR	RBI	BB	SO	AVG	OBP	SLG	PRO+	BR/A	SB	CS	SBR	FA	FR	G/POS	TPR
1976	Det-A	125	429	41	115	15	2	6	45	19	49	.268	.302	.354	88	-7	14	10	-2	.954	-3	O-90,D-19	-1.8
Total	13	1322	4623	550	1331	180	33	78	525	244	626	.288	.329	.392	105	22	113	63	-4	.953	-5	O-1000,D-199	-4.2

■ **TONY JOHNSON** Johnson, Anthony Clair b: 6/23/56, Memphis, Tenn. BR/TR, 6'3", 145 lbs. Deb: 9/28/81

YEAR	TM/L	G	AB	R	H	2B	3B	HR	RBI	BB	SO	AVG	OBP	SLG	PRO+	BR/A	SB	CS	SBR	FA	FR	G/POS	TPR
1981	Mon-N	2	1	0	0	0	0	0	0	0	0	.000	.000	.000	-99	-0	0	0	0	.000	-0	/O-1	-0.1
1982	Tor-A	70	98	17	23	2	1	3	14	11	26	.235	.312	.367	79	-3	3	13	-7	.979	-2	O-28,D-28	-1.4
Total	2	72	99	17	23	2	1	3	14	11	26	.232	.309	.364	77	-3	3	13	-7	.979	-3	/O-29,D-28	-1.5

■ **BOB JOHNSON** Johnson, Bobby Earl b: 7/31/59, Dallas, Tex. BR/TR, 6'3", 195 lbs. Deb: 9/1/81

YEAR	TM/L	G	AB	R	H	2B	3B	HR	RBI	BB	SO	AVG	OBP	SLG	PRO+	BR/A	SB	CS	SBR	FA	FR	G/POS	TPR
1981	Tex-A	6	18	2	5	0	0	2	4	1	3	.278	.316	.611	171	1	0	0	0	1.000	-1	/C-5,1-1	0.1
1982	Tex-A	20	56	4	7	2	0	2	7	3	22	.125	.183	.268	23	-6	0	1	-1	1.000	0	C-14/1-3	-0.6
1983	Tex-A	72	175	18	37	6	1	5	16	16	55	.211	.281	.343	72	-7	3	0	1	1.000	3	C-62,1-10	-0.1
Total	3	98	249	24	49	8	1	9	27	20	80	.197	.262	.345	68	-12	3	1	0	1.000	3	/C-81,1-14	-0.6

■ **BRIAN JOHNSON** Johnson, Brian David b: 1/8/68, Oakland, Cal. BR/TR, 6'2", 210 lbs. Deb: 4/5/94

YEAR	TM/L	G	AB	R	H	2B	3B	HR	RBI	BB	SO	AVG	OBP	SLG	PRO+	BR/A	SB	CS	SBR	FA	FR	G/POS	TPR
1994	SD-N	36	93	7	23	4	1	3	16	5	21	.247	.286	.409	81	-3	0	0	0	1.000	2	C-24/1-5	0.1
1995	SD-N	68	207	20	52	9	0	3	29	11	39	.251	.292	.338	68	-10	0	0	0	.993	1	C-55/1-2	-0.5
1996	*SD-N	82	243	18	66	13	1	8	35	4	36	.272	.295	.432	94	-3	0	0	0	.989	1	C-66/1-1,3-1	0.1
1997	Det-A	45	139	13	33	6	1	2	18	5	19	.237	.264	.338	56	-9	1	0	0	.987	-6	C-43/D-2	-1.2
	*SF-N	56	179	19	50	7	2	11	27	14	26	.279	.338	.525	125	6	0	1	-1	.995	0	C-55/1-2	0.8
1998	SF-N	99	308	34	73	8	1	13	34	28	67	.237	.311	.396	85	-7	0	2	-1	.994	-1	C-95/O-1	-0.3
Total	5	386	1169	111	297	47	6	40	159	67	208	.254	.301	.407	86	-27	1	3	-2	.993	-3	C-338/1-10,D-2,O3	-1.0

■ **CALEB JOHNSON** Johnson, Caleb Clark b: 5/23/1844, Fulton, Ill. d: 3/7/25, Sterling, Ill. Deb: 5/24/1871

YEAR	TM/L	G	AB	R	H	2B	3B	HR	RBI	BB	SO	AVG	OBP	SLG	PRO+	BR/A	SB	CS	SBR	FA	FR	G/POS	TPR
1871	Cle-n	16	67	10	15	1	0	0	7	0	1	.224	.224	.239	35	-5	1	0	0	.736	-5	2-10/O-6	-0.7

■ **CHARLIE JOHNSON** Johnson, Charles Cleveland "Home Run" b: 3/12/1885, Slatington, Pa. d: 8/28/40, Marcus Hook, Pa. BL/TL, 5'9", 150 lbs. Deb: 9/21/08

YEAR	TM/L	G	AB	R	H	2B	3B	HR	RBI	BB	SO	AVG	OBP	SLG	PRO+	BR/A	SB	CS	SBR	FA	FR	G/POS	TPR
1908	Phi-N	6	16	2	4	0	1	0	2	1		.250	.333	.375	122	0	0			1.000	-0	/O-4	0.0

■ **CHARLES JOHNSON** Johnson, Charles Edward b: 7/20/71, Fort Pierce, Fla. BR/TR, 6'2", 215 lbs. Deb: 5/6/94

YEAR	TM/L	G	AB	R	H	2B	3B	HR	RBI	BB	SO	AVG	OBP	SLG	PRO+	BR/A	SB	CS	SBR	FA	FR	G/POS	TPR
1994	Fla-N	4	11	5	5	1	0	1	4	1	4	.455	.500	.818	229	2	0	0	0	1.000	0	/C-4	0.2
1995	Fla-N	97	315	40	79	15	1	11	39	46	71	.251	.353	.410	100	1	0	2	-1	.992	-0	C-97	0.6
1996	Fla-N	120	386	34	84	13	1	13	37	40	91	.218	.294	.358	73	-16	1	0	0	**.995**	6	*C-120	-0.2
1997	*Fla-N★	124	416	43	104	26	1	19	63	60	109	.250	.349	.454	113	8	0	2	-1	**1.000**	8	*C-123	2.2
1998	Fla-N	31	113	13	25	5	0	7	23	16	30	.221	.318	.451	101	-0	0	1	-1	.990	-7	C-31	-0.6
	LA-N	102	346	31	75	13	0	12	35	29	99	.217	.279	.358	69	-17	0	1	-1	.992	1	*C-100	-0.9
	Yr	133	459	44	100	18	0	19	58	45	129	.218	.289	.381	77	-17	0	2	-1	.992	-6	*C-131	-1.5
Total	5	478	1587	166	372	73	3	63	201	192	404	.234	.321	.403	92	-22	1	6	-3	.995	8	C-475	1.3

■ **CLIFF JOHNSON** Johnson, Clifford b: 7/22/47, San Antonio, Tex. BR/TR, 6'4", 225 lbs. Deb: 9/13/72

YEAR	TM/L	G	AB	R	H	2B	3B	HR	RBI	BB	SO	AVG	OBP	SLG	PRO+	BR/A	SB	CS	SBR	FA	FR	G/POS	TPR
1972	Hou-N	5	4	0	1	0	0	0	0	2	0	.250	.500	.250	121	0	0	0	0	1.000	1	/C-1	0.1
1973	Hou-N	7	20	6	6	2	0	2	6	1	7	.300	.364	.700	189	2	0	0	0	1.000	-0	/1-5	0.2
1974	Hou-N	83	171	26	39	4	1	10	29	33	45	.228	.362	.439	129	7	0	1	-1	.978	-4	C-28,1-21	0.3
1975	Hou-N	122	340	52	94	16	1	20	65	46	64	.276	.371	.506	152	23	1	0	0	.991	-12	1-47,C-41/O-1	1.0
1976	Hou-N	108	318	36	72	21	2	10	49	62	59	.226	.359	.399	126	12	0	0	0	.977	-12	C-66,O-20,1-16	0.1
1977	Hou-N	51	144	22	43	8	0	10	23	23	30	.299	.409	.563	173	15	0	1	-1	.946	-0	O-34,1-10	1.2
	*NY-A	56	142	24	42	8	0	12	31	20	23	.296	.405	.606	173	15	0	1	-1	1.000	3	D-25,C-15,1-11	1.5
1978	*NY-A	76	174	20	32	9	1	6	19	30	32	.184	.307	.351	87	-3	0	0	0	.975	0	D-39,C-22/1-1	-0.3
1979	NY-A	28	64	11	17	6	0	2	6	10	7	.266	.365	.453	122	2	0	0	0	1.000	-0	D-22/C-4	0.1
	Cle-A	72	240	37	65	10	0	18	61	24	39	.271	.349	.538	135	11	2	0	1	.000	-0	D-62/C-1	0.9
	Yr	100	304	48	82	16	0	20	67	34	46	.270	.353	.520	132	13	2	0	1	1.000	-1	D-84/C-5	1.0
1980	Cle-A	54	174	25	40	3	1	6	28	25	30	.230	.327	.362	88	-3	0	1	-1	.000	0	D-45	-0.5
	Chi-N	68	196	28	46	8	0	10	34	29	35	.235	.336	.429	104	1	0	0	0	.992	-6	1-46/O-3,C-1	-0.8
1981	*Oak-A	84	273	40	71	8	0	17	59	28	60	.260	.336	.476	138	13	5	3	-0	1.000	-1	D-68/1-9	0.9
1982	Oak-A	73	214	19	51	10	0	7	31	26	41	.238	.326	.383	98	-0	1	2	-1	.987	1	D-48,1-11	-0.3
1983	Tor-A	142	407	59	108	23	1	22	76	67	69	.265	.376	.489	128	17	0	1	-1	1.000	0	*D-130/1-6	1.1
1984	Tor-A	127	359	51	109	23	1	16	61	50	62	.304	.393	.507	142	21	0	1	-1	1.000	-1	*D-109/1-2	1.7
1985	Tex-A	82	296	31	76	17	1	12	56	31	44	.257	.333	.443	109	3	0	0	0	.000	0	D-82	0.2
	*Tor-A	24	73	4	20	0	0	1	10	9	15	.274	.354	.315	83	-1	0	0	0	.947	-1	D-21/1-3	-0.2
	Yr	106	369	35	96	17	1	13	66	40	59	.260	.337	.417	104	2	0	0	0	.947	-1	*D-103/1-3	0.0
1986	Tor-A	107	336	48	84	12	1	15	55	52	57	.250	.357	.426	109	5	0	1	-1	1.000	0	D-95/1-1	0.3
Total	15	1369	3945	539	1016	188	10	196	699	568	719	.258	.358	.459	125	141	9	12	-5	.993	-33	D-746,1-189,C/O	7.5

■ **DARRELL JOHNSON** Johnson, Darrell Dean b: 8/25/28, Horace, Neb. BR/TR, 6'1", 180 lbs. Deb: 4/20/52 MC

YEAR	TM/L	G	AB	R	H	2B	3B	HR	RBI	BB	SO	AVG	OBP	SLG	PRO+	BR/A	SB	CS	SBR	FA	FR	G/POS	TPR
1952	StL-A	29	78	9	22	2	1	0	9	11	4	.282	.371	.333	94	-0	0	0	0	.990	1	C-22	0.2
	Chi-A	22	37	3	4	0	0	0	1	5	9	.108	.214	.108	-8	-5	1	0	0	.955	5	C-21	0.0
	Yr	51	115	12	26	2	1	0	10	16	13	.226	.321	.261	62	-5	1	0	0	.974	6	C-43	0.2
1957	NY-A	21	46	4	10	1	0	1	8	3	10	.217	.280	.304	61	-3	0	0	0	1.000	4	C-20	0.2
1958	NY-A	5	16	1	4	0	0	0	0	0	2	.250	.250	.250	39	-1	0	0	0	1.000	1	/C-4	0.0
1960	StL-N	8	2	0	0	0	0	0	0	1	0	.000	.333	.000	1	-0	0	0	0	1.000	1	/C-8	0.1
1961	Phi-N	21	61	4	14	1	0	0	3	3	8	.230	.277	.246	41	-5	0	0	0	.982	2	C-21	-0.2
	*Cin-N	20	54	3	17	2	0	1	6	1	2	.315	.327	.407	92	-1	0	0	0	1.000	4	C-20	0.4
	Yr	41	115	7	31	3	0	1	9	4	10	.270	.300	.322	65	-6	0	0	0	.991	6	C-41	0.2
1962	Cin-N	2	4	0	0	0	0	0	0	2	0	.000	.333	.000	-2	-0	0	0	0	1.000	2	/C-2	0.1
	Bal-A	6	22	0	4	0	0	0	1	0	4	.182	.182	.182	-2	-3	0	0	0	1.000	-1	/C-6	-0.4
Total	6	134	320	24	75	6	1	2	28	26	39	.234	.296	.278	57	-19	1	0	0	.988	20	C-124	0.4

■ **DAVEY JOHNSON** Johnson, David Allen b: 1/30/43, Orlando, Fla. BR/TR, 6'1", 180 lbs. Deb: 4/13/65 M

YEAR	TM/L	G	AB	R	H	2B	3B	HR	RBI	BB	SO	AVG	OBP	SLG	PRO+	BR/A	SB	CS	SBR	FA	FR	G/POS	TPR
1965	Bal-A	20	47	5	8	3	0	0	1	5	6	.170	.250	.234	38	-4	3	0	1	.929	3	/3-9,2-3,S-2	0.0
1966	*Bal-A	131	501	47	129	20	3	7	56	31	64	.257	.302	.351	88	-8	3	4	-2	.971	2	*2-126/S-3	0.2
1967	Bal-A	148	510	62	126	30	3	10	64	59	82	.247	.330	.376	109	6	4	5	-2	.981	0	*2-144/3-3	1.6
1968	Bal-A★	145	504	50	122	24	4	9	56	44	80	.242	.309	.359	102	1	7	3	0	.978	4	*2-127,S-34	1.6
1969	*Bal-A†	142	511	52	143	34	1	7	57	57	52	.280	.356	.391	108	6	3	4	-2	.984	-3	*2-142/S-2	1.3
1970	*Bal-A★	149	530	68	149	27	1	10	53	66	68	.281	.361	.392	106	6	2	1	0	.990	1	*2-149/S-2	1.9
1971	*Bal-A	142	510	67	144	26	1	18	72	51	55	.282	.353	.443	125	17	3	1	0	.984	-1	*2-140	3.0
1972	Bal-A	118	376	31	83	22	3	5	32	52	68	.221	.322	.335	93	-2	1	1	-0	**.990**	10	*2-116	1.6
1973	Atl-N★	157	559	84	151	25	0	43	99	81	93	.270	.371	.546	140	30	5	3	-0	.966	-3	*2-156	3.7
1974	Atl-N	136	454	56	114	18	0	15	62	75	59	.251	.361	.390	105	5	1	2	-1	.993	7	1-73,2 71	1.0
1975	Atl-N	1	1	0	1	1	0	0	1	0	0	1.000	1.000	2.000	691	1	0	0	0	.000	0	H	0.1
1977	*Phi-N	78	156	23	50	9	1	8	36	23	20	.321	.414	.545	148	11	1	1	-0	1.000	-2	1-43/2-9,3-6	0.8
1978	Phi-N	44	89	14	17	2	0	2	14	10	19	.191	.287	.281	59	-5	0	0	0	.930	-6	2-15/3-9,1-7	-1.1
	Chi-N	24	49	5	15	1	1	2	6	5	9	.306	.393	.490	130	2	0	0	0	.839	-3	3-12	-0.1
	Yr	68	138	19	32	3	1	4	20	15	28	.232	.325	.355	86	-2	0	0	0	.844	-9	3-21,2-15/1-7	-1.2
Total	13	1435	4797	564	1252	242	18	136	609	559	675	.261	.343	.404	110	66	33	25	-5	.980	10	*2-1198,1-123/S3	15.6

■ **DERON JOHNSON** Johnson, Deron Roger b: 7/17/38, San Diego, Cal. d: 4/23/92, Poway, Cal. BR/TR, 6'2", 209 lbs. Deb: 9/20/60 C

YEAR	TM/L	G	AB	R	H	2B	3B	HR	RBI	BB	SO	AVG	OBP	SLG	PRO+	BR/A	SB	CS	SBR	FA	FR	G/POS	TPR
1960	NY-A	6	4	0	2	1	0	0	0	0	0	.500	.500	.750	247	1	0	0	0	.750	0	/3-5	0.1
1961	NY-A	13	19	1	2	0	0	0	2	2	5	.105	.190	.105	-20	-3	0	0	0	1.000	2	/3-8	-0.1
	KC-A	83	283	31	61	11	3	8	42	14	44	.216	.255	.360	61	-16	0	1	-1	.948	3	O-59,3-19/1-3	-1.8
	Yr	96	302	32	63	11	3	8	44	16	49	.209	.251	.344	57	-19	0	1	-1	.948	5	O-59,3-27/1-3	-1.9
1962	KC-A	17	19	1	2	1	0	0	0	3	8	.105	.227	.158	6	-3	0	0	0	1.000	-1	/1-2,3-2,O-2	-0.4
1964	Cin-N	140	477	63	130	24	4	21	79	37	98	.273	.328	.472	118	10	4	3	-1	.990	3	*1-131,O-10/3-1	0.7

YEAR	TM/L	G	AB	R	H	2B	3B	HR	RBI	BB	SO	AVG	OBP	SLG	PRO+	BR/A	SB	CS	SBR	FA	FR	G/POS	TPR
1965	Cin-N	159	616	92	177	30	7	32	**130**	52	97	.287	.345	.515	129	23	0	4	-2	.948	-12	*3-159	0.5
1966	Cin-N	142	505	75	130	25	3	24	81	39	87	.257	.313	.461	103	1	1	2	-1	.980	-8	*O-106,1-71,3-18	-1.5
1967	Cin-N	108	361	39	81	18	1	13	53	22	104	.224	.273	.388	78	-11	0	1	-1	.997	-4	1-81,3-24	-2.2
1968	Atl-N	127	342	29	71	11	1	8	33	35	79	.208	.287	.316	81	-8	0	1	-1	.996	-1	1-97,3-21	-1.8
1969	Phi-N	138	475	51	121	19	4	17	80	60	111	.255	.338	.419	114	9	4	2	0	1.000	-14	O-72,3-50,1-18	-1.0
1970	Phi-N	159	574	66	147	28	3	27	93	72	132	.256	.339	.456	114	10	0	0	0	.995	-11	*1-154/3-3	-1.3
1971	Phi-N	158	582	74	154	29	0	34	95	72	146	.265	.348	.490	135	26	0	1	-1	.995	-4	*1-136,3-22	0.9
1972	Phi-N	96	230	19	49	4	1	9	31	26	69	.213	.301	.357	84	-5	0	1	-1	.982	-4	1-62	-1.5
1973	Phi-N	12	36	3	6	2	0	1	5	5	10	.167	.286	.306	62	-2	0	0	0	.976	-0	1-10	-0.3
	*Oak-A	131	464	61	114	14	2	19	81	59	116	.246	.332	.407	113	8	0	1	-1	.994	-3	*D-107,1-23	0.0
1974	Oak-A	50	174	16	34	1	2	7	23	11	37	.195	.243	.345	72	-7	1	0	0	.991	-2	1-28,D-23	-1.2
	Mil-A	49	152	14	23	3	0	6	18	21	41	.151	.254	.289	56	-9	1	0	0	.833	-0	D-46/1-2	-1.1
	Bos-A	11	25	0	3	0	0	0	2	0	6	.120	.120	.120	-29	-4	0	0	0	.000	0	/D-8	-0.5
	Yr	110	351	30	60	4	2	13	43	32	84	.171	.240	.305	57	-20	2	0	1	.983	-3	D-77,1-30	-2.8
1975	Chi-A	148	555	66	129	25	1	18	72	48	117	.232	.295	.378	88	-10	0	1	-1	.994	-4	D-93,1-55	-2.2
	Bos-A	3	10	2	6	0	0	1	3	2	0	.600	.667	.900	313	3	0	0	0	1.000	-1	/1-2,D-1	0.2
	Yr	151	565	68	135	25	1	19	75	50	117	.239	.302	.388	92	-7	0	1	-1	.994	-5	D-94,1-57	-2.0
1976	Bos-A	15	38	3	5	1	1	0	0	5	11	.132	.233	.211	27	-4	0	0	0	1.000	-0	/1-5,D-9	-0.4
Total	16	1765	5941	706	1447	247	33	245	923	585	1318	.244	.313	.420	102	9	11	18	-8	.993	-63	1-880,3-332,DO	-14.9
■ **DON JOHNSON**	Johnson, Donald Spore "Pep" b: 12/7/11, Chicago, Ill. BR/TR, 6', 170 lbs. Deb: 9/26/43 F																						
1943	Chi-N	10	42	5	8	2	0	0	1	2	4	.190	.227	.238	35	-4	0			.957	3	2-10	0.0
1944	Chi-N☆	154	608	50	169	37	1	2	71	28	48	.278	.311	.352	87	-12	8			.947	1	*2-154	-0.3
1945	*Chi-N†	138	557	94	168	23	2	2	58	32	34	.302	.343	.361	98	-2	9			.975	10	*2-138	1.7
1946	Chi-N	83	314	37	76	10	1	1	19	26	39	.242	.306	.290	71	-12	6			.981	-10	2-83	-1.7
1947	Chi-N	120	402	33	104	17	2	3	26	24	45	.259	.302	.333	71	-17	2			.970	-4	*2-108/3-6	-1.4
1948	Chi-N	6	12	0	3	0	0	0	0	0	1	.250	.250	.250	37	-1	1			1.000	-2	/2-2,3-2	-0.3
Total	6	511	1935	219	528	89	6	8	175	112	171	.273	.315	.337	83	-48	26			.966	-2	2-495/3-8	-2.0
■ **ED JOHNSON**	Johnson, Edwin Cyril b: 3/31/1899, Morganfield, Ky. d: 7/3/75, Morganfield, Ky. BL/TR, 5'9", 160 lbs. Deb: 9/26/20																						
1920	Was-A	4	13	1	3	0	0	0	2	3	2	.231	.375	.231	65	-0	0	0	0	.625	-1	/O-4	-0.1
■ **ELMER JOHNSON**	Johnson, Elmer Ellsworth "Hickory" b: 6/12/1884, Beard, Ind. d: 10/31/66, Hollywood, Fla. BR/TR, 5'9", 185 lbs. Deb: 4/24/14																						
1914	NY-N	11	12	0	2	1	0	0	0	1	3	.167	.231	.250	44	-1	0			.947	-1	C-11	-0.2
■ **ERIK JOHNSON**	Johnson, Erik Anthony b: 10/11/65, Oakland, Cal. BR/TR, 5'11", 175 lbs. Deb: 7/8/93																						
1993	SF-N	4	5	1	2	2	0	0	0	0	1	.400	.400	.800	219	1	0	0	0	1.000	-1	/2-2,3-1,S-1	0.0
1994	SF-N	5	13	0	2	0	0	0	0	0	4	.154	.154	.154	-20	-2	0	0	0	1.000	1	/2-2,S-1	-0.1
Total	2	9	18	1	4	2	0	0	0	0	5	.222	.222	.333	45	-2	0	0	0	1.000	-0	/2-4,S-2,3-1	-0.1
■ **ERNIE JOHNSON**	Johnson, Ernest Rudolph b: 4/29/1888, Chicago, Ill. d: 5/1/52, Monrovia, Cal. BL/TR, 5'9", 151 lbs. Deb: 8/5/12 F																						
1912	Chi-A	21	42	7	11	0	1	0	5	1		.262	.279	.310	70	-2	0			.984	3	S-16	0.2
1915	StL-F	152	512	58	123	18	10	7	67	46	35	.240	.305	.355	81	-21	32			.942	18	*S-152	0.9
1916	StL-A	74	236	29	54	9	3	0	19	30	23	.229	.323	.292	89	-2	13			.936	-8	S-60,3-12	-0.8
1917	StL-A	80	199	28	49	6	2	2	20	12	16	.246	.296	.327	93	-2	13			.924	11	S-39,2-18,3-14	1.2
1918	StL-A	29	34	7	9	1	0	0	0	0	2	.265	.286	.294	77	-1	4			.821	-2	S-11/3-1	-0.3
1921	Chi-A	142	613	93	181	28	7	1	51	29	24	.295	.328	.369	78	-21	22	13	-1	.947	18	*S-141	0.9
1922	Chi-A	144	603	85	153	17	3	0	56	40	30	.254	.304	.292	56	-38	21	18	-5	.952	2	*S-141	-2.6
1923	Chi-A	12	53	5	10	2	0	0	1	3	5	.189	.246	.226	25	-6	2	1	0	.922	-0	S-12	-0.5
	*NY-A	19	38	6	17	1	1	1	8	1	1	.447	.462	.605	176	4	0	0	0	.977	-1	S-15/3-1	0.4
	Yr	31	91	11	27	3	1	1	9	4	6	.297	.333	.385	88	-2	2	1	0	.944	-1	S-27/3-1	-0.1
1924	NY-A	64	119	24	42	4	8	3	12	11	7	.353	.412	.597	158	10	1	6	-3	.955	-1	2-27/S-9,3-2	0.5
1925	NY-A	76	170	30	48	5	1	5	17	8	10	.282	.315	.412	85	-5	6	3	0	.955	-10	2-34,S-28/3-2	-1.2
Total	10	813	2619	372	697	91	36	19	256	181	153	.266	.317	.350	80	-84	114	41		.944	29	S-624/2-79,3-32	-1.3
■ **FRANK JOHNSON**	Johnson, Frank Herbert b: 7/22/42, ElPaso, Tex. BR/TR, 6'1", 155 lbs. Deb: 9/7/66																						
1966	SF-N	15	32	2	7	0	0	0	0	2	7	.219	.265	.219	35	-3	0	1	-1	1.000	-3	O-13	-0.8
1967	SF-N	8	10	3	3	0	0	0	0	1	2	.300	.364	.300	93	-0	0	0	0	.889	-0	/O-3	0.0
1968	SF-N	67	174	11	33	2	0	1	7	12	23	.190	.246	.218	40	-12	1	0	0	.944	3	3-36/O-8,S-5,2-3	-1.0
1969	SF-N	7	10	2	1	0	0	0	0	0	1	.100	.100	.100	-45	-2	0	0	0	1.000	-1	/O-7	-0.3
1970	SF-N	67	161	25	44	1	2	3	31	19	18	.273	.357	.360	94	-1	1	1	-0	.979	-2	O-33,1-27	-0.6
1971	SF-N	32	49	4	4	1	0	0	5	3	9	.082	.135	.102	-33	-9	0	0	0	.975	-3	/1-9,O-4	-1.3
Total	6	196	436	47	92	4	2	4	43	37	60	.211	.277	.257	52	-26	2	2	-1	.979	-6	/O-68,1-36,3-36,S2	-4.0
■ **HOWARD JOHNSON**	Johnson, Howard Michael b: 11/29/60, Clearwater, Fla. BB/TR, 5'11", 178 lbs. Deb: 4/14/82																						
1982	Det-A	54	155	23	49	5	0	4	14	16	30	.316	.384	.426	122	5	7	4	-0	.901	-9	3-33,D-10/O-9	-0.5
1983	Det-A	27	66	11	14	0	0	3	5	7	10	.212	.297	.348	79	-2	0	0	0	.851	-6	3-21/D-2	-0.8
1984	*Det-A	116	355	43	88	14	1	12	50	40	67	.248	.326	.394	99	-0	10	6	-1	.944	-18	*3-108/S-9,1-1,OD	-2.0
1985	NY-N	126	389	38	94	18	4	11	46	34	78	.242	.303	.393	96	-3	6	4	-1	.941	-13	*3-113/S-7,O-1	-1.8
1986	*NY-N	88	220	30	54	14	0	10	39	31	64	.245	.341	.445	119	5	8	1	2	.903	-2	3-45,S-34/O-1	0.7
1987	NY-N	157	554	93	147	22	1	36	99	83	113	.265	.366	.504	135	27	32	10	4	.938	-18	*3-140,S-38/O-2	1.3
1988	*NY-N	148	495	85	114	21	1	24	68	86	104	.230	.348	.422	126	18	23	7	3	.951	-14	*3-131/S-52	1.0
1989	NY-N★	153	571	**104**	164	41	3	36	101	77	126	.287	.373	.559	171	51	41	8	8	.910	-33	*3-143,S-31	3.0
1990	NY-N	154	590	89	144	37	3	23	90	69	100	.244	.323	.434	107	4	34	8	5	.913	-5	3-92,S-73	1.1
1991	NY-N★	156	564	108	146	34	4	**38**	**117**	78	120	.259	.350	.535	147	33	30	16	-1	.927	-4	*3-104,O-30,S-28	3.2
1992	NY-N	100	350	48	78	19	0	7	43	55	79	.223	.332	.337	91	-3	22	5	4	.981	-4	O-98	-0.6
1993	NY-N	72	235	32	56	8	2	7	26	43	43	.238	.356	.379	98	0	6	4	-1	.944	5	3-67	0.5
1994	Col-N	93	227	30	48	10	2	10	40	39	73	.211	.327	.405	77	-8	11	3	2	.979	-2	O-62/1-1	-1.0
1995	Chi-N	87	169	26	33	4	1	7	22	34	46	.195	.333	.355	83	-4	1	1	-0	.926	-8	3-34,O-13/2-8,1S	-1.2
Total	14	1531	4940	760	1229	247	22	228	760	692	1053	.249	.343	.446	118	125	231	77	23	.929	-129	*3-1031,S-273,O/D21	2.9
■ **SPUD JOHNSON**	Johnson, John Ralph b: 1860, Canada BL/TL, 5'9", 175 lbs. Deb: 4/18/1889																						
1889	Col-a	116	459	91	130	14	10	2	79	39	47	.283	.355	.370	112	9	34			.879	-11	O-69,3-44/1-2,S-1	-0.2
1890	Col-a	135	538	106	186	23	18	1	**113**	48		.346	.409	.461	168	46	43			.926	-16	*O-135	2.2
1891	Cle-N	80	327	49	84	8	3	1	46	22	23	.257	.319	.309	80	-9	16			.872	-5	O-79/1-1	-1.4
Total	3	331	1324	246	400	45	31	4	238	109	70	.302	.368	.392	125	46	93			.899	-32	O-283/3-44,1-3,S-1	0.6
■ **LANCE JOHNSON**	Johnson, Kenneth Lance b: 7/6/63, Cincinnati, Ohio BL/TL, 5'11", 160 lbs. Deb: 7/10/87																						
1987	*StL-N	33	59	4	13	2	1	0	7	4	6	.220	.270	.288	47	-4	6	1	1	.931	-6	O-25	-0.9
1988	Chi-A	33	124	11	23	4	1	0	6	6	11	.185	.223	.234	28	-12	6	2	1	.970	-4	O-31/D-1	-1.7
1989	Chi-A	50	180	28	54	8	2	0	16	17	24	.300	.360	.367	108	2	16	3	3	.983	0	O-45/D-1	0.4
1990	Chi-A	151	541	76	154	18	9	1	51	33	45	.285	.327	.357	93	-5	36	22	-2	.973	-2	*O-148/D-1	-1.3
1991	Chi-A	159	588	72	161	14	**13**	0	49	26	58	.274	.306	.342	81	-16	26	11	1	.995	13	*O-157	-0.5
1992	Chi-A	157	567	67	158	15	**12**	3	47	34	33	.279	.321	.363	92	-6	41	14	4	.987	8	*O-157	0.3
1993	*Chi-A	147	540	75	168	18	**14**	0	47	36	33	.311	.354	.396	104	3	35	7	6	.980	16	*O-146	2.1
1994	Chi-A	106	412	56	114	11	**14**	3	54	26	23	.277	.323	.393	85	-10	26	6	4	**1.000**	13	*O-103/D-1	0.5
1995	Chi-A	142	607	98	**186**	18	12	10	57	32	31	.306	.342	.425	103	1	40	6	**8**	.991	6	*O-140/D-1	1.1
1996	NY-N★	160	682	117	**227**	31	**21**	9	69	33	40	.333	.365	.479	126	24	50	12	**8**	.971	14	*O-157	4.0
1997	NY-N	72	265	43	82	10	6	1	24	33	21	.309	.386	.404	111	5	15	10	-2	.975	4	O-66	0.6
	Chi-N	39	145	17	44	6	2	4	15	9	10	.303	.344	.455	105	1	5	2	0	.963	-1	O-39/D-1	-0.1
	Yr	111	410	60	126	16	8	5	39	42	31	.307	.372	.422	109	6	20	12	-1	.971	3	*O-105/D-1	0.5

YEAR	TM/L	G	AB	R	H	2B	3B	HR	RBI	BB	SO	AVG	OBP	SLG	PRO+	BR/A	SB	CS	SBR	FA	FR	G/POS	TPR
1998	*Chi-N	85	304	51	85	8	4	2	21	26	22	.280	.336	.352	77	-10	10	6	-1	.975	-0	O-78	-1.1
Total	12	1334	5014	715	1469	163	111	33	463	315	357	.293	.336	.390	96	-27	312	102	32	.983	62	*O-1292/D-6	3.4

■ LAMAR JOHNSON Johnson, Lamar b: 9/2/50, Bessemer, Ala. BR/TR, 6'2", 225 lbs. Deb: 5/18/74

YEAR	TM/L	G	AB	R	H	2B	3B	HR	RBI	BB	SO	AVG	OBP	SLG	PRO+	BR/A	SB	CS	SBR	FA	FR	G/POS	TPR
1974	Chi-A	10	29	1	10	0	0	0	2	0	3	.345	.345	.345	97	-0	0	0	0	1.000	-0	/1-7,D-3	-0.1
1975	Chi-A	8	30	2	6	3	0	1	1	1	5	.200	.226	.400	73	-1	0	0	0	.960	-1	/1-6,D-2	-0.3
1976	Chi-A	82	222	29	71	11	1	4	33	19	37	.320	.379	.432	136	10	2	1	0	.983	-1	D-35,1-34/O-1	0.7
1977	Chi-A	118	374	52	113	12	5	18	65	24	53	.302	.344	.505	128	13	1	1	-0	.990	1	D-68,1-45	1.0
1978	Chi-A	148	498	52	136	23	2	8	72	43	46	.273	.333	.376	98	-1	6	5	-1	.992	2	*1-108,D-36	-0.8
1979	Chi-A	133	479	60	148	29	1	12	74	41	56	.309	.366	.449	118	12	8	2	1	.987	-1	1-94,D-37	0.6
1980	Chi-A	147	541	51	150	26	3	13	81	47	53	.277	.335	.409	103	2	2	3	-1	.990	2	1-80,D-66	-0.4
1981	Chi-A	41	134	10	37	7	0	1	15	5	14	.276	.302	.351	89	-2	0	2	-1	.989	-2	1-36/D-2	-0.8
1982	Tex-A	105	324	37	84	11	0	7	38	31	40	.259	.326	.358	92	-3	3	5	-2	.982	-2	D-77,1-12	-1.1
Total	9	792	2631	294	755	122	12	64	381	211	307	.287	.342	.415	109	30	22	19	-5	.989	-1	1-422,D-326/O-1	-1.2

■ LARRY JOHNSON Johnson, Larry Doby b: 8/17/50, Cleveland, Ohio BR/TR, 6', 185 lbs. Deb: 10/3/72

YEAR	TM/L	G	AB	R	H	2B	3B	HR	RBI	BB	SO	AVG	OBP	SLG	PRO+	BR/A	SB	CS	SBR	FA	FR	G/POS	TPR
1972	Cle-A	1	2	0	1	0	0	0	0	0	1	.500	.500	.500	192	0	0	0	0	1.000	0	/C-1	0.1
1974	Cle-A	1	0	1	0	0	0	0	0	0	0	—	—	—	—	0	0	0	0	.000	0	R	0.0
1975	Mon-N	1	3	0	1	1	0	0	1	1	1	.333	.500	.667	212	1	0	0	0	1.000	-0	/C-1	0.0
1976	Mon-N	6	13	0	2	1	0	0	0	0	2	.154	.154	.231	8	-2	0	0	0	1.000	1	/C-5	-0.1
1978	Chi-A	3	8	0	1	0	0	0	0	1	4	.125	.222	.125	0	-1	0	0	0	.857	-0	/C-2,D-1	-0.2
Total	5	12	26	1	5	2	0	0	1	2	8	.192	.250	.269	46	-2	0	0	0	.975	1	/C-9,D-1	-0.2

■ LOU JOHNSON Johnson, Louis Brown "Slick" b: 9/22/34, Lexington, Ky. BR/TR, 5'11", 175 lbs. Deb: 4/17/60

YEAR	TM/L	G	AB	R	H	2B	3B	HR	RBI	BB	SO	AVG	OBP	SLG	PRO+	BR/A	SB	CS	SBR	FA	FR	G/POS	TPR
1960	Chi-N	34	68	6	14	2	1	0	1	5	19	.206	.270	.265	48	-5	3	1	0	1.000	1	O-25	-0.4
1961	LA-A	1	0	0	0	0	0	0	0	0	0	—	—	—	—	0	0	0	0	.000	-0	/O-1	0.0
1962	Mil-N	61	117	22	33	4	5	2	13	11	27	.282	.349	.453	116	3	6	1	1	1.000	-9	O-55	-0.7
1965	*LA-N	131	468	57	121	24	1	12	58	24	81	.259	.317	.391	105	2	15	6	1	.985	-3	*O-128	-0.6
1966	*LA-N	152	526	71	143	20	2	17	73	21	75	.272	.317	.414	110	5	8	10	-4	.985	-2	*O-148	-0.7
1967	LA-N	104	330	39	89	14	1	11	41	24	52	.270	.332	.418	124	9	4	3	-1	.976	2	O-91	0.7
1968	Chi-N	62	205	14	50	14	3	1	14	6	23	.244	.289	.356	87	-3	3	1	0	.970	-4	O-57	-1.2
	Cle-A	65	202	25	52	11	1	5	23	9	24	.257	.302	.396	112	2	6	1	1	.989	1	O-57	0.2
1969	Cal-A	67	133	10	27	8	0	0	9	10	19	.203	.274	.263	53	-8	5	1	1	.935	-5	O-44	-1.5
Total	8	677	2049	244	529	97	14	48	232	110	320	.258	.313	.389	103	5	50	24	1	.981	-19	O-606	-4.2

■ MARK JOHNSON Johnson, Mark Landon b: 9/12/75, Wheat Ridge, Colo. BL/TR, 6', 185 lbs. Deb: 9/14/98

YEAR	TM/L	G	AB	R	H	2B	3B	HR	RBI	BB	SO	AVG	OBP	SLG	PRO+	BR/A	SB	CS	SBR	FA	FR	G/POS	TPR
1998	Chi-A	7	23	2	2	0	2	0	1	1	8	.087	.125	.261	-3	-4	0	0	0	1.000	-1	/C-7	-0.4

■ MARK JOHNSON Johnson, Mark Patrick b: 10/17/67, Worcester, Mass. BL/TL, 6'4", 230 lbs. Deb: 4/26/95

YEAR	TM/L	G	AB	R	H	2B	3B	HR	RBI	BB	SO	AVG	OBP	SLG	PRO+	BR/A	SB	CS	SBR	FA	FR	G/POS	TPR
1995	Pit-N	79	221	32	46	6	1	13	28	37	66	.208	.327	.421	94	-2	5	2	0	.986	-4	1-70	-1.1
1996	Pit-N	127	343	55	94	24	0	13	47	44	64	.274	.365	.458	112	7	6	4	-1	.994	5	*1-100/O-1	0.3
1997	Pit-N	78	219	30	47	10	0	4	29	43	78	.215	.348	.315	74	-7	1	1	-0	.992	1	1-63/D-1	-1.2
1998	Ana-A	10	14	1	1	0	0	0	0	0	6	.071	.071	.071	-62	-3	0	0	0	1.000	0	/1-5,D-2	-0.3
Total	4	294	797	118	188	40	1	30	104	124	214	.236	.345	.402	94	-6	12	7	-1	.991	2	1-238/D-3,O-1	-2.3

■ OTIS JOHNSON Johnson, Otis L. b: 11/5/1883, Fowler, Ind. d: 11/9/15, Johnson City, N.Y. BB/TR, 5'9", 185 lbs. Deb: 4/12/11

YEAR	TM/L	G	AB	R	H	2B	3B	HR	RBI	BB	SO	AVG	OBP	SLG	PRO+	BR/A	SB	CS	SBR	FA	FR	G/POS	TPR
1911	NY-A	71	209	21	49	9	6	3	36	39		.234	.363	.378	100	1	12			.907	-9	S-47,2-15/3-3	-0.6

■ PAUL JOHNSON Johnson, Paul Oscar b: 9/2/1896, N.Grosvenor Dale, Conn. d: 2/14/73, McAllen, Tex. BR/TR, 5'8", 160 lbs. Deb: 9/13/20

YEAR	TM/L	G	AB	R	H	2B	3B	HR	RBI	BB	SO	AVG	OBP	SLG	PRO+	BR/A	SB	CS	SBR	FA	FR	G/POS	TPR
1920	Phi-A	18	72	6	15	0	0	0	5	4	8	.208	.250	.208	22	-8	1	1	-0	.933	-3	O-18	-1.2
1921	Phi-A	48	127	17	40	6	2	1	10	9	17	.315	.360	.417	97	-1	0	2	-1	.969	-5	O-32	-0.8
Total	2	66	199	23	55	6	2	1	15	13	25	.276	.321	.342	71	-9	1	3	-2	.958	-7	/O-50	-2.0

■ RANDY JOHNSON Johnson, Randall Glenn b: 6/10/56, Escondido, Cal. BR/TR, 6'1", 190 lbs. Deb: 4/27/82

YEAR	TM/L	G	AB	R	H	2B	3B	HR	RBI	BB	SO	AVG	OBP	SLG	PRO+	BR/A	SB	CS	SBR	FA	FR	G/POS	TPR
1982	Atl-N	27	46	5	11	5	0	0	6	6	4	.239	.352	.348	93	-0	0	1	-1	.955	5	2-13/3-4	0.5
1983	Atl-N	86	144	22	36	3	0	1	17	20	27	.250	.345	.292	73	-5	1	3	-2	.991	10	3-53/2-4	0.4
1984	Atl-N	91	294	28	82	13	0	5	30	21	21	.279	.329	.374	91	-4	4	7	-3	.939	5	3-81	-0.3
Total	3	204	484	55	129	21	0	6	53	47	52	.267	.336	.347	85	-8	5	11	-5	.956	20	3-138/2-17	0.6

■ RANDY JOHNSON Johnson, Randall Stuart b: 8/15/58, Miami, Fla. BL/TL, 6'2", 195 lbs. Deb: 7/5/80

YEAR	TM/L	G	AB	R	H	2B	3B	HR	RBI	BB	SO	AVG	OBP	SLG	PRO+	BR/A	SB	CS	SBR	FA	FR	G/POS	TPR
1980	Chi-A	12	20	0	4	0	0	0	3	2	4	.200	.304	.200	41	-1	0	0	0	.000	-0	/1-1,O-1,D-4	-0.2
1982	Min-A	89	234	26	58	10	0	10	33	30	46	.248	.333	.419	102	1	0	0	0	1.000	-0	D-67/O-2	-0.2
Total	2	101	254	26	62	10	0	10	36	32	50	.244	.331	.402	98	-1	0	0	0	1.000	-1	/D-71,O-3,1-1	-0.4

■ FOOTER JOHNSON Johnson, Richard Allan "Treads" b: 2/15/32, Dayton, Ohio BL/TL, 5'11", 175 lbs. Deb: 6/22/58

YEAR	TM/L	G	AB	R	H	2B	3B	HR	RBI	BB	SO	AVG	OBP	SLG	PRO+	BR/A	SB	CS	SBR	FA	FR	G/POS	TPR
1958	Chi-N	8	5	1	0	0	0	0	0	0	1	.000	.000	.000	-99	-1	0	0	0	.000	0	H	-0.1

■ BOB JOHNSON Johnson, Robert Lee "Indian Bob" b: 11/26/06, Pryor, Okla. d: 7/6/82, Tacoma, Wash. BR/TR, 6', 180 lbs. Deb: 4/12/33 F

YEAR	TM/L	G	AB	R	H	2B	3B	HR	RBI	BB	SO	AVG	OBP	SLG	PRO+	BR/A	SB	CS	SBR	FA	FR	G/POS	TPR
1933	Phi-A	142	535	103	155	44	4	21	93	85	74	.290	.387	.505	133	26	8	3	1	.952	2	*O-142	1.9
1934	Phi-A	141	547	111	168	26	6	34	92	58	60	.307	.375	.563	144	33	12	8	-1	.967	10	*O-139	3.3
1935	Phi-A★	147	582	103	174	29	5	28	109	78	76	.299	.384	.510	130	25	2	4	-2	.946	4	*O-147	2.1
1936	Phi-A	153	566	91	165	29	14	25	121	88	71	.292	.389	.525	126	22	6	6	-2	.962	3	*O-131,2-22/1-1	1.7
1937	Phi-A	138	477	91	146	32	6	25	108	98	65	.306	.425	.556	148	37	9	7	-2	.976	9	*O-133/2-2	3.6
1938	Phi-A★	152	563	114	176	27	9	30	113	87	73	.313	.406	.552	142	36	9	8	-2	.963	10	*O-150/2-3,3-1	3.5
1939	Phi-A☆	150	544	115	184	30	9	23	114	99	59	.338	.440	.553	156	49	15	5	2	.967	7	*O-150/2-1	4.7
1940	Phi-A☆	138	512	93	137	25	4	31	103	83	64	.268	.374	.514	130	23	8	2	1	.962	5	*O-136	2.1
1941	Phi-A	149	552	98	152	30	8	22	107	95	75	.275	.385	.478	130	25	6	4	-1	.990	7	*O-122,1-28	2.1
1942	Phi-A★	149	550	78	160	35	7	13	80	82	61	.291	.384	.451	135	26	3	2	-0	.963	5	*O-149	2.4
1943	Was-A★	117	438	65	116	22	8	7	63	64	50	.265	.362	.400	127	16	11	5	0	.996	9	O-88,3-19,1-10	2.2
1944	Bos-A★	144	525	106	170	40	8	17	106	95	67	.324	**.431**	.528	**175**	**54**	2	7	-4	.977	4	*O-142	4.9
1945	Bos-A†	143	529	71	148	27	7	12	74	63	56	.280	.358	.425	124	16	5	3	-0	.975	3	*O-140	1.1
Total	13	1863	6920	1239	2051	396	95	288	1283	1075	851	.296	.393	.506	139	387	96	64	-10	.968	79	*O-1769/1-39,2-28,3	35.6

■ BOB JOHNSON Johnson, Robert Wallace b: 3/4/36, Omaha, Neb. BR/TR, 5'10", 175 lbs. Deb: 4/19/60

YEAR	TM/L	G	AB	R	H	2B	3B	HR	RBI	BB	SO	AVG	OBP	SLG	PRO+	BR/A	SB	CS	SBR	FA	FR	G/POS	TPR
1960	KC-A	76	146	12	30	4	0	1	9	19	23	.205	.301	.253	51	-10	2	0	1	.947	12	S-30,2-27,3-11	0.6
1961	Was-A	61	224	27	66	13	1	6	28	19	26	.295	.352	.442	113	4	4	2	0	.956	-2	S-57/2-2,3-2	0.6
1962	Was-A	135	466	58	134	20	2	12	43	32	50	.288	.335	.416	102	0	9	6	-1	.944	4	3-72,S-50/2-3,O-1	0.1
1963	Bal-A	82	254	34	75	10	0	8	32	18	35	.295	.347	.429	120	7	5	1	1	.987	-2	2-50/1-8,S-7,3-5	1.0
1964	Bal-A	93	210	18	52	8	2	3	29	9	37	.248	.282	.348	74	-8	0	0	0	.964	-12	S-18,1-15,2-15,/3O	-1.9
1965	Bal-A	87	273	36	66	13	2	5	27	15	34	.242	.284	.359	80	-8	1	0	0	.996	-11	1-34,S-23,3-13,/2-5	-1.9
1966	Bal-A	71	157	13	34	5	0	1	10	12	24	.217	.276	.268	58	-8	0	1	-1	.966	0	2-20,1-17/3-3	-0.9
1967	Bal-A	4	3	1	1	0	0	0	0	1	1	.333	.500	.333	152	0	0	0	0	.000	0	H	0.0
	NY-N	90	230	26	80	8	3	5	27	12	29	.348	.380	.474	145	13	1	1	-0	.987	-7	2-39,1-23,S-14,/3-1	0.8
1968	Cin-N	16	15	2	4	0	0	0	1	1	2	.267	.313	.267	71	-0	0	0	0	.500	-1	/S-2,1-1	-0.1
	Atl-N	59	187	15	49	5	1	0	11	10	20	.262	.299	.299	80	-5	0	0	0	.948	1	3-48/2-4	-0.3
	Yr	75	202	17	53	5	1	0	12	11	22	.262	.300	.297	79	-5	0	0	0	.948	1	3-48/2-4,S-2,1-1	-0.4
1969	StL-N	19	29	1	6	0	0	1	2	2	4	.207	.258	.310	58	-2	0	0	0	.833	-1	/3-4,1-1	-0.3
	Oak-A	51	67	5	23	1	0	1	9	3	4	.343	.380	.403	125	2	0	0	0	1.000	0	/1-7,2-2	0.2
1970	Oak-A	30	46	6	8	1	0	1	2	3	2	.174	.240	.261	39	-4	2	1	0	.952	1	/3-6,1-1	-0.3
Total	11	874	2307	254	628	88	11	44	230	156	291	.272	.321	.377	95	-18	24	12	0	.956	-26	S-201,2-167,31/O	-2.4

YEAR	TM/L	G	AB	R	H	2B	3B	HR	RBI	BB	SO	AVG	OBP	SLG	PRO+	BR/A	SB	CS	SBR	FA	FR	G/POS	TPR
■ **RON JOHNSON**	Johnson, Ronald David b: 3/23/56, Long Beach, Cal. BR/TR, 6'3", 215 lbs. Deb: 9/12/82																						
1982	KC-A	8	14	2	4	2	0	0	0	4	3	.286	.444	.429	141	1	0	0	0	.976	-0	/1-7	0.0
1983	KC-A	9	27	2	7	0	0	0	1	3	1	.259	.333	.259	66	-1	0	0	0	.971	-1	/1-7,C-2	-0.3
1984	Mon-N	5	5	0	1	0	0	0	1	0	2	.200	.200	.200	13	-1	0	0	0	1.000	-1	/1-2,O-1	-0.1
Total	3	22	46	4	12	2	0	0	2	7	6	.261	.358	.304	85	-1	0	0	0	.974	-2	/1-16,C-2,O-1	-0.4
■ **RONDIN JOHNSON**	Johnson, Rondin Allen b: 12/16/58, Bremerton, Wash. BB/TR, 5'10", 160 lbs. Deb: 9/3/86																						
1986	KC-A	11	31	1	8	0	1	0	2	0	3	.258	.258	.323	56	-2	0	0	0	1.000	4	2-11	0.2
■ **ROY JOHNSON**	Johnson, Roy Cleveland b: 2/23/03, Pryor, Okla. d: 9/10/73, Tacoma, Wash. BL/TR, 5'9", 175 lbs. Deb: 4/18/29 F																						
1929	Det-A	148	640	128	201	**45**	14	10	69	67	60	.314	.379	.475	118	17	20	15	-3	.928	14	*O-146	1.7
1930	Det-A	125	462	84	127	30	13	2	35	40	46	.275	.333	.409	85	-11	17	10	-1	.936	4	*O-118	-1.4
1931	Det-A	151	621	107	173	37	**19**	8	55	72	51	.279	.355	.438	104	3	33	21	-3	.960	15	*O-150	0.5
1932	Det-A	49	195	33	49	14	2	3	22	20	26	.251	.324	.390	81	-6	7	2	1	.929	0	O-48	-0.7
	Bos-A	94	349	70	104	24	4	11	47	44	41	.298	.378	.484	125	13	13	4	2	.930	-6	O-85	0.3
	Yr	143	544	103	153	38	6	14	69	64	67	.281	.359	.450	109	7	20	6	2	.930	-5	*O-133	-0.4
1933	Bos-A	133	483	88	151	30	7	10	95	55	36	.313	.387	.466	126	19	13	10	-2	.922	4	*O-125	1.3
1934	Bos-A	143	569	85	182	43	10	7	119	54	36	.320	.379	.467	109	7	11	5	0	.948	-3	*O-137	-0.2
1935	Bos-A	145	553	70	174	33	9	3	66	74	34	.315	.398	.423	105	6	11	12	-4	.944	-2	*O-142	-0.4
1936	*NY-A	63	147	21	39	8	2	1	19	21	14	.265	.361	.367	83	-4	3	1	0	.944	0	O-33	-0.4
1937	NY-A	12	51	5	15	3	0	0	6	3	2	.294	.333	.353	73	-2	1	0	0	.840	-2	O-12	-0.4
	Bos-N	85	260	24	72	8	3	3	22	38	29	.277	.369	.365	110	5	5			.965	-1	O-63/3-1	0.2
1938	Bos-N	7	29	2	5	0	0	0	1	1	5	.172	.200	.172	4	-4	1			.769	-2	/O-7	-0.6
Total	10	1155	4359	717	1292	275	83	58	556	489	380	.296	.369	.437	107	43	135	80		.938	22	*O-1066/3-1	-0.1
■ **ROY JOHNSON**	Johnson, Roy Edward b: 6/27/59, Parkin, Ark. BL/TL, 6'4", 205 lbs. Deb: 7/3/82																						
1982	Mon-N	17	32	2	7	2	0	0	2	1	6	.219	.242	.281	45	-2	0	0	0	1.000	-2	O-11	-0.5
1984	Mon-N	16	33	2	5	2	0	1	2	7	10	.152	.300	.303	73	-1	1	0	0	.938	-1	O-10	-0.2
1985	Mon-N	3	5	0	0	0	0	0	0	0	3	.000	.000	.000	-99	-1	0	0	0	.000	-1	/O-3	-0.3
Total	3	36	70	4	12	4	0	1	4	8	19	.171	.256	.271	49	-5	1	0	0	.971	-4	/O-24	-1.0
■ **STAN JOHNSON**	Johnson, Stanley Lucius b: 2/12/37, Dallas, Tex. BL/TL, 5'10", 180 lbs. Deb: 9/18/60																						
1960	Chi-A	5	6	1	1	0	0	1	1	0	1	.167	.167	.667	116	0	0	1	-1	1.000	-1	/O-2	-0.1
1961	KC-A	3	3	1	0	0	0	0	0	2	1	.000	.400	.000	17	-0	0	0	0	.000	-1	/O-2	-0.1
Total	2	8	9	2	1	0	0	1	1	2	2	.111	.273	.444	89	-0	0	1	-1	1.000	-2	/O-4	-0.2
■ **TIM JOHNSON**	Johnson, Timothy Evald b: 7/22/49, Grand Forks, N.D. BL/TR, 6'1", 170 lbs. Deb: 4/24/73 MC																						
1973	Mil-A	136	465	39	99	10	2	0	32	29	93	.213	.261	.243	44	-35	6	3	0	.962	-18	*S-135	-3.7
1974	Mil-A	93	245	25	60	7	7	0	25	11	48	.245	.280	.331	76	-8	4	3	-1	.970	-2	S-64,2-26/3-1,OD	-0.3
1975	Mil-A	38	85	6	12	1	0	0	2	6	17	.141	.198	.153	0	-11	3	0	1	1.000	1	2-11,3-11,S-10,/1D	-0.8
1976	Mil-A	105	273	25	75	4	3	0	14	19	32	.275	.327	.311	89	-3	4	1	1	.980	-18	*2-100,3-17/1-1,S-1	-1.7
1977	Mil-A	30	33	5	2	1	0	0	2	5	10	.061	.184	.091	-22	-6	1	0	0	.929	3	2-10/S-6,3-4,O-1,D	-0.2
1978	Mil-A	3	3	1	0	0	0	0	0	2	0	.000	.400	.000	22	-0	0	0	0	1.000	-1	/S-2	-0.1
	Tor-A	68	79	9	19	2	0	0	3	8	16	.241	.318	.266	65	-3	0	1	-1	.975	5	S-49,2-13	0.4
	Yr	71	82	10	19	2	0	0	3	10	16	.232	.323	.256	63	-4	0	1	-1	.975	4	S-51,2-13	0.3
1979	Tor-A	43	86	6	16	2	1	0	6	8	15	.186	.255	.233	32	-8	0	1	-1	.958	6	2-25/3-9,1-7	-0.2
Total	7	516	1269	116	283	27	13	0	84	88	231	.223	.276	.265	55	-75	18	9	0	.965	-25	S-267,2-185/31DO	-6.6
■ **WALLACE JOHNSON**	Johnson, Wallace Darnell b: 12/25/56, Gary, Ind. BB/TR, 5'11", 185 lbs. Deb: 9/8/81 C																						
1981	*Mon-N	11	9	1	2	0	1	0	3	1	1	.222	.300	.444	108	0	1	1	-0	1.000	1	/2-1	0.1
1982	Mon-N	36	57	5	11	0	2	0	2	5	5	.193	.258	.263	45	-4	4	1	1	.952	-6	2-13	-0.9
1983	Mon-N	3	2	1	1	0	0	0	0	1	0	.500	.667	.500	229	1	1	0	0	.000	0	/H	0.1
	SF-N	7	8	0	1	0	0	0	1	0	0	.125	.125	.125	-32	-1	0	0	0	1.000	1	/2-1	-0.1
	Yr	10	10	1	2	0	0	0	1	1	0	.200	.273	.200	34	-1	1	0	0	1.000	1	/2-1	0.0
1984	Mon-N	17	24	3	5	0	0	0	4	5	4	.208	.345	.208	61	-1	0	0	0	.968	0	/1-4	-0.1
1986	Mon-N	61	127	13	36	3	1	1	10	7	9	.283	.321	.346	85	-3	6	3	0	.991	-0	1-27	-0.5
1987	Mon-N	75	85	7	21	5	0	1	14	7	6	.247	.304	.341	69	-4	5	0	2	.972	-1	/1-9	-0.4
1988	Mon-N	86	94	7	29	5	1	0	3	12	15	.309	.387	.383	116	2	0	2	-1	.989	1	1-13/2-1	0.2
1989	Mon-N	85	114	9	31	3	1	2	17	7	12	.272	.314	.368	93	-1	1	0	0	.972	-1	1-18	-0.4
1990	Mon-N	47	49	6	8	1	0	1	5	7	6	.163	.281	.245	48	-3	1	0	0	1.000	-1	/1-7	-0.5
Total	9	428	569	52	145	17	6	5	59	52	58	.255	.318	.332	81	-15	19	7	2	.983	-7	/1-78,2-16	-2.5
■ **WALTER JOHNSON**	Johnson, Walter Perry "Barney" or "The Big Train" b: 11/6/1887, Humboldt, Kan. d: 12/10/46, Washington, D.C. BR/TR, 6'1", 200 lbs. Deb: 8/2/07 MH																						
1907	Was-A	14	36	3	4	0	1	0	1	1		.111	.135	.167	-4	-4	0			.893	-2	P-14	0.0
1908	Was-A	36	79	7	13	3	2	0	5	6		.165	.250	.253	69	-3	0			.938	-4	P-36	0.0
1909	Was-A	40	101	6	13	3	0	1	6	1		.129	.137	.188	3	-11	0			.926	-2	P-40	0.0
1910	Was-A	45	137	14	24	6	1	2	12	4		.175	.199	.277	51	-8	2			.950	-1	P-45	0.0
1911	Was-A	42	128	18	30	5	3	1	15	0		.234	.234	.344	62	-7	1			.965	4	P-40	0.0
1912	Was-A	55	144	16	38	6	4	2	20	7		.264	.298	.403	99	-1	2			.964	1	P-50	0.0
1913	Was-A	54	134	12	35	5	6	2	14	5	14	.261	.293	.433	109	0	2			**1.000**	-0	P-48/O-1	0.0
1914	Was-A	55	136	23	30	4	1	3	16	10	27	.221	.274	.331	79	-4	2	1	0	.964	2	P-51/O-1	-0.1
1915	Was-A	64	147	14	34	7	4	2	17	8	34	.231	.276	.374	93	-2	0	2	-1	.951	0	P-47/O-4	-0.2
1916	Was-A	58	142	13	32	2	4	1	7	11	28	.225	.286	.317	82	-4	0			.937	-5	P-48	0.0
1917	Was-A	57	130	15	33	12	1	0	15	9	30	.254	.312	.362	107	1	1			**1.000**	-1	P-47	0.0
1918	Was-A	65	150	10	40	4	4	1	18	9	18	.267	.321	.367	109	1	2			.988	-3	P-39/O-4	0.0
1919	Was-A	56	125	13	24	1	3	1	8	12	17	.192	.263	.272	51	-8	1			.988	-0	P-39/O-3	-0.1
1920	Was-A	33	64	6	17	1	3	1	7	3	10	.266	.299	.422	92	-1	0	0	0	.971	-1	P-21	0.0
1921	Was-A	38	111	10	30	7	0	0	10	6	14	.270	.308	.333	67	-6	0	0	0	.982	-3	P-35	0.0
1922	Was-A	43	108	8	22	3	0	1	15	2	12	.204	.218	.259	25	-12	0	0	0	**1.000**	1	P-41	0.0
1923	Was-A	42	93	11	18	3	3	0	13	4	15	.194	.227	.290	37	-9	0	0	0	.970	-2	P-42	0.0
1924	*Was-A	39	113	18	32	9	0	1	14	3	11	.283	.308	.389	82	-4	0	0	0	**1.000**	-1	P-38	0.0
1925	*Was-A	36	97	12	42	6	1	2	20	3	6	.433	.455	.577	164	9	0	1	-1	**1.000**	-4	P-30	0.0
1926	Was-A	35	103	6	20	5	0	1	12	3	11	.194	.217	.272	28	-11	0	0	0	.980	-5	P-33	0.0
1927	Was-A	26	46	6	16	2	0	2	10	3	4	.348	.388	.522	136	2	0	0	0	1.000	0	P-18	0.0
Total	21	933	2324	241	547	94	41	24	255	110	251	.235	.274	.342	76	-84	13	4		.969	-25	P-802/O-13	-0.4
■ **BILL JOHNSON**	Johnson, William F. "Sleepy Bill" b: 9/1862, New Jersey d: 7/17/42, Chester, Pa. BL/TL, 140 lbs. Deb: 6/27/1884																						
1884	Phi-U	1	4	0	0	0	0	0		0		.000	.000	.000	-99	-1				.000	-0	/O-1	-0.1
1887	Ind-N	11	42	3	8	0	0	0	3	0	6	.190	.209	.190	12	-5	5			.765	-2	O-11	-0.6
1890	Bal-a	24	95	15	28	2	3	0	6	7		.295	.350	.379	110	1	8			.865	2	O-24	0.2
1891	Bal-a	129	480	101	130	13	14	2	79	89	55	.271	.389	.369	116	13	32			.877	6	*O-129	1.2
1892	Bal-N	4	15	2	2	0	0	0	2	2	0	.133	.235	.133	12	-2	0			.667	-1	/O-4	-0.3
Total	5	169	636	121	168	15	17	2	90	98	61	.264	.368	.351	105	6	45			.867	5	O-169	0.4
■ **BILL JOHNSON**	Johnson, William Lawrence b: 10/18/1892, Chicago, Ill. d: 11/3/50, Los Angeles, Cal. BL/TR, 5'11", 170 lbs. Deb: 9/22/16																						
1916	Phi-A	4	15	1	4	1	0	0	1	0	4	.267	.267	.333	84	-0	0			1.000	-1	/O-4	-0.2
1917	Phi-A	48	109	7	19	2	2	1	8	8	14	.174	.237	.257	51	-7	4			.900	-3	O-30	-1.2
Total	2	52	124	8	23	3	2	1	9	8	18	.185	.241	.266	55	-7	4			.909	-4	/O-34	-1.4

YEAR	TM/L	G	AB	R	H	2B	3B	HR	RBI	BB	SO	AVG	OBP	SLG	PRO+	BR/A	SB	CS	SBR	FA	FR	G/POS	TPR
■ **BILLY JOHNSON**	Johnson, William Russell "Bull" b: 8/30/18, Montclair, N.J. BR/TR, 5'10", 180 lbs. Deb: 4/22/43																						
1943	*NY-A	155	592	70	166	24	6	5	94	53	30	.280	.344	.367	107	5	3	5	-2	.966	12	*3-155	1.8
1946	NY-A	85	296	51	77	14	5	4	35	31	42	.260	.334	.382	98	-1	1	0	0	.955	7	3-74	0.8
1947	*NY-A★	132	494	67	141	19	8	10	95	44	43	.285	.351	.417	114	8	1	2	-1	.952	-17	*3-132	-0.9
1948	NY-A	127	446	59	131	20	6	12	64	41	30	.294	.358	.446	114	8	0	0	0	.947	6	*3-118	1.2
1949	*NY-A	113	329	48	82	11	3	8	56	48	44	.249	.348	.374	91	-4	1	0	0	.951	-2	3-81,1-21/2-1	-0.8
1950	*NY-A	108	327	44	85	16	2	6	40	42	30	.260	.346	.376	87	-6	1	0	0	.958	-1	*3-100/1-5	-0.8
1951	NY-A	15	40	5	12	3	0	0	4	7	0	.300	.404	.375	116	1	0	1	-1	.960	-3	3-13	-0.2
	StL-N	124	442	52	116	23	1	14	64	46	49	.262	.340	.414	101	1	5	3	-0	**.976**	11	*3-124	1.0
1952	StL-N	94	282	23	71	10	2	2	34	34	21	.252	.339	.323	84	-5	1	0	0	.951	2	3-89	-0.5
1953	StL-N	11	5	0	1	1	0	0	1	1	1	.200	.333	.400	90	-0	0	0	0	1.000	2	3-11	0.2
Total	9	964	3253	419	882	141	33	61	487	347	290	.271	.346	.391	102	6	13	11	-3	.959	18	3-897/1-26,2-1	1.8
■ **RUSS JOHNSON**	Johnson, William Russell b: 2/22/73, Baton Rouge, La. BR/TR, 5'10", 185 lbs. Deb: 4/8/97																						
1997	*Hou-N	21	60	7	18	1	0	2	9	6	14	.300	.364	.417	108	1	1	1	-0	.963	-2	3-14/2-3	-0.2
1998	Hou-N	8	13	2	3	1	0	0	0	1	5	.231	.333	.308	70	-1	1	0	0	1.000	4	/3-5,2-1	0.4
Total	2	29	73	9	21	2	0	2	9	7	19	.288	.358	.397	101	0	2	1	0	.971	2	/3-19,2-4	0.2
■ **GREG JOHNSTON**	Johnston, Gregory Bernard b: 2/12/55, Los Angeles, Cal. BL/TL, 6', 175 lbs. Deb: 7/27/79																						
1979	SF-N	42	74	5	15	2	0	1	7	2	17	.203	.224	.270	37	-7	0	0	0	.966	-1	O-17	-0.9
1980	Min-A	14	27	3	5	3	0	0	1	2	4	.185	.241	.296	43	-2	0	0	0	1.000	-3	O-14	-0.5
1981	Min-A	7	16	2	2	0	0	0	0	2	5	.125	.222	.125	2	-2	0	0	0	1.000	0	/O-6	-0.2
Total	3	63	117	10	22	5	0	1	8	6	26	.188	.228	.256	33	-11	0	0	0	.985	-4	/O-37	-1.6
■ **JIMMY JOHNSTON**	Johnston, James Harle b: 12/10/1889, Cleveland, Tenn. d: 2/14/67, Chattanooga, Tenn. BR/TR, 5'10", 160 lbs. Deb: 5/3/11 FC																						
1911	Chi-A	1	2	0	0	0	0	0	2	0		.000	.000	.000	-99	-1	0			1.000	-0	/O-1	-0.1
1914	Chi-N	50	101	9	23	3	2	1	8	4	9	.228	.264	.327	76	-3	3			.929	4	O-28/2-4	0.0
1916	*Bro-N	118	425	58	107	13	8	1	26	35	38	.252	.313	.327	94	-3	22	19	-5	.964	7	*O-106	-0.7
1917	Bro-N	103	330	33	89	10	4	0	25	23	28	.270	.321	.324	96	-1	16			.958	4	O-66,1-14/S-4,23	-0.2
1918	Bro-N	123	484	54	136	16	8	0	27	33	31	.281	.328	.347	106	3	22			.956	8	O-96,1-21/3-4,2-1	0.5
1919	Bro-N	117	405	56	114	11	4	1	23	29	26	.281	.334	.336	100	0	11			.960	-6	2-87,O-14/1-2,S-1	-0.2
1920	*Bro-N	155	635	87	185	17	12	1	52	43	23	.291	.338	.361	98	-2	19	15	-3	.934	-6	*3-146/O-7,S-3	-0.4
1921	Bro-N	152	624	104	203	41	14	5	56	45	26	.325	.372	.460	115	13	28	16	-1	.935	8	*3-150/S-3	3.0
1922	Bro-N	138	567	110	181	20	7	4	49	38	17	.319	.364	.400	98	-1	18	9	0	.947	7	2-62,S-50,3-26	1.3
1923	Bro-N	151	625	111	203	29	11	4	60	53	15	.325	.378	.426	115	14	16	13	-3	.948	19	2-84,S-52,3-14	3.6
1924	Bro-N	86	315	51	94	11	2	2	29	27	10	.298	.356	.365	97	-1	5	6	-2	.939	-4	S-63,3-10/1-4,O-1	0.1
1925	Bro-N	123	431	63	128	13	3	2	43	45	15	.297	.369	.355	88	-6	7	5	-1	.886	-23	3-81,O-20/1-8,S-2	-2.4
1926	Bos-N	23	57	7	14	1	0	1	5	10	3	.246	.358	.316	91	-0	2			.865	-4	3-14/2-2,O-1	-0.3
	NY-N	37	69	11	16	0	0	0	5	6	5	.232	.293	.232	43	-5	0			1.000	-5	O-14	-1.1
	Yr	60	126	18	30	1	0	1	10	16	8	.238	.324	.270	64	-6	2			1.000	-8	O-15,3-14/2-2	-1.4
Total	13	1377	5070	754	1493	185	75	22	410	391	246	.294	.347	.374	100	7	169	83		.926	10	3-448,O-354,2S/1	3.1
■ **JOHNNY JOHNSTON**	Johnston, John Thomas b: 3/28/1890, Longview, Tex. d: 3/7/40, San Diego, Cal. BL/TR, 5'11", 172 lbs. Deb: 4/10/13																						
1913	StL-A	111	380	37	85	14	4	2	27	42	51	.224	.308	.297	79	-10	11			.965	12	*O-107	-0.3
■ **REX JOHNSTON**	Johnston, Rex David b: 11/8/37, Colton, Cal. BB/TR, 6'1.5", 202 lbs. Deb: 4/15/64																						
1964	Pit-N	14	7	1	0	0	0	0	0	3	0	.000	.300	.000	-7	-1	0	0	0	1.000	-2	/O-8	-0.3
■ **DICK JOHNSTON**	Johnston, Richard Frederick b: 4/6/1863, Kingston, N.Y. d: 4/4/34, Detroit, Mich. BR/TR, 5'8", 155 lbs. Deb: 8/12/1884																						
1884	Ric-a	39	146	23	41	5	5	2		2		.281	.291	.425	132	5				.865	9	O-37/S-2	1.1
1885	Bos-N	26	111	17	26	6	3	1	23	0	15	.234	.234	.369	96	-1				.842	1	O-26	0.0
1886	Bos-N	109	413	48	99	18	9	1	57	3	70	.240	.245	.334	78	-12	11			.892	17	*O-109	0.2
1887	Bos-N	127	507	87	131	13	20	5	77	16	35	.258	.281	.393	85	-12	52			.933	25	*O-127	0.9
1888	Bos-N	135	585	102	173	31	**18**	12	68	15	33	.296	.314	.472	145	27	35			.898	7	*O-135	2.9
1889	Bos-N	132	539	80	123	16	4	5	67	41	60	.228	.285	.301	60	-31	34			.917	-7	*O-132	-3.6
1890	Bos-P	2	9	0	1	0	0	0	0	0	1	.111	.111	.111	-38	-2	0			.800	0	/O-2	-0.1
	NY-P	77	306	37	74	9	7	1	43	18	25	.242	.288	.327	59	-20	7			.897	3	O-76/S-2	-1.6
	Yr	79	315	37	75	9	7	1	43	18	26	.238	.284	.321	56	-22	7			.894	3	O-78/S-2	-1.7
1891	Cin-a	99	376	59	83	11	2	6	51	38	44	.221	.301	.309	68	-18	12			.895	-1	*O-99	-1.9
Total	8	746	2992	453	751	109	68	33	386	133	283	.251	.285	.366	87	-63	151			.903	54	O-743/S-4	-2.1
■ **DOC JOHNSTON**	Johnston, Wheeler Roger b: 9/9/1887, Cleveland, Tenn. d: 2/17/61, Chattanooga, Tenn. BL/TL, 6', 170 lbs. Deb: 10/3/09 F																						
1909	Cin-N	3	10	1	0	0	0	0	1	0		.000	.000	.000	-99	-2	0			1.000	0	/1-3	-0.2
1912	Cle-A	43	164	22	46	7	4	1	11	11		.280	.326	.390	101	-0	8			.991	-2	1-41	-0.3
1913	Cle-A	133	530	74	135	19	12	2	39	35	65	.255	.309	.347	89	-8	19			.989	-1	*1-133	-1.2
1914	Cle-A	103	340	43	83	15	1	0	23	28	46	.244	.311	.294	79	-9	14	9	-1	.987	-7	1-90/O-2	-2.1
1915	Pit-N	147	543	71	144	19	12	5	64	38	40	.265	.328	.372	113	8	26	17	-2	.991	-12	*1-147	-1.1
1916	Pit-N	114	404	33	86	10	10	0	39	20	42	.213	.262	.287	68	-16	17			.987	-2	*1-110	-2.5
1918	Cle-A	74	273	30	62	12	2	0	25	26	19	.227	.301	.286	70	-10	12			.989	-3	1-73	-1.8
1919	Cle-A	102	331	42	101	17	3	1	33	25	18	.305	.359	.384	102	1	21			.984	-3	1-98	-0.6
1920	*Cle-A	147	535	68	156	24	10	2	71	28	32	.292	.333	.385	87	-11	13	7	-0	.992	-1	*1-147	-1.5
1921	Cle-A	118	384	53	114	20	7	2	46	29	15	.297	.353	.401	90	-6	2	9	-5	.988	-1	*1-116	-1.3
1922	Phi-A	71	260	41	65	11	7	1	29	24	15	.250	.316	.358	73	-10	7	6	-2	.990	-5	1-65	-2.0
Total	11	1055	3774	478	992	154	68	14	381	264	292	.263	.319	.351	88	-63	139	48		.989	-37	*1-1023/O-2	-14.6
■ **FRED JOHNSTON**	Johnston, Wilfred Ivy b: 7/9/1899, Charlotte, N.C. d: 7/14/59, Tyler, Tex. BR/TR, 5'11.5", 170 lbs. Deb: 6/29/24																						
1924	Bro-N	4	4	1	1	0	0	0	0	0	1	.250	.250	.250	35	-0	0	0	0	.667	0	/2-1,3-1	0.0
■ **JAY JOHNSTONE**	Johnstone, John William b: 11/20/45, Manchester, Conn. BL/TR, 6'1", 175 lbs. Deb: 7/30/66																						
1966	Cal-A	61	254	35	67	12	4	3	17	11	36	.264	.297	.378	95	-2	3	3	-1	.975	-2	O-61	-0.8
1967	Cal-A	79	230	18	48	7	1	2	10	5	37	.209	.226	.274	49	-15	3	2	-0	.973	2	O-63	-1.8
1968	Cal-A	41	115	11	30	4	1	0	3	7	15	.261	.303	.313	90	-2	2	1	0	.984	2	O-29	-0.1
1969	Cal-A	148	540	64	146	20	5	10	59	38	75	.270	.324	.381	102	-0	3	9	-5	.983	12	*O-144	0.0
1970	Cal-A	119	320	34	76	10	5	11	39	24	53	.237	.293	.403	93	-4	1	0	0	.981	-1	*O-100	-1.0
1971	Chi-A	124	388	53	101	14	1	16	40	38	50	.260	.331	.425	109	4	10	5	0	.968	-3	*O-119	-0.4
1972	Chi-A	113	261	27	49	9	0	4	17	25	42	.188	.259	.268	56	-14	2	1	0	.988	-12	O-97	-3.3
1973	Oak-A	23	28	1	3	1	0	0	3	2	4	.107	.167	.143	-13	-4	0	1	-1	1.000	-2	/O-7,2-2,D-4	-0.7
1974	Phi-N	64	200	30	59	10	4	6	30	24	28	.295	.371	.475	130	8	5	5	-2	.968	-7	O-59	-0.3
1975	Phi-N	122	350	50	115	19	2	7	54	42	39	.329	.401	.454	132	16	7	3	0	.976	-2	*O-101	1.1
1976	*Phi-N	129	440	62	140	38	4	5	53	41	39	.318	.379	.457	132	19	5	5	-2	.982	8	*O-122/1-6	2.1
1977	*Phi-N	112	363	64	103	18	4	15	59	38	38	.284	.355	.479	116	8	3	7	-3	1.000	3	O-91,1-19	0.3
1978	Phi-N	35	56	3	10	2	0	0	4	6	9	.179	.258	.214	33	-5	0	2	-1	.988	-1	/1-8,O-7	-0.9
	*NY-A	36	65	6	17	0	0	1	6	4	10	.262	.333	.308	83	-1	0	1	-1	1.000	-3	O-22/D-5	-0.5
1979	NY-A	23	48	7	10	1	0	1	7	2	7	.208	.240	.292	44	-4	1	0	0	1.000	-2	O-19/D-3	-0.6
	SD-N	75	201	10	59	8	2	0	32	18	21	.294	.352	.353	99	-0	1	3	-2	.985	-3	O-45,1-22	-0.7
1980	LA-N	109	251	31	77	15	2	2	20	24	29	.307	.372	.406	119	7	3	2	-0	.965	1	O-61	0.6
1981	*LA-N	61	83	8	17	3	0	3	6	7	13	.205	.267	.349	76	-3	0	1	-1	.957	-0	O-16/1-2	-0.4
1982	LA-N	21	13	1	1	1	0	0	2	5	2	.077	.333	.154	41	-1	0	0	0	.000	0	H	-0.2
	Chi-N	98	269	39	67	13	1	10	43	40	41	.249	.346	.416	109	4	0	2	-1	.982	1	O-86	0.1
	Yr	119	282	40	68	14	1	10	45	45	43	.241	.346	.404	107	3	0	2	-1	.982	1	O-86	-0.1
1983	Chi-N	86	140	16	36	7	0	6	22	20	24	.257	.362	.436	115	3	1	1	-0	.935	-4	O-44	-0.2

YEAR	TM/L	G	AB	R	H	2B	3B	HR	RBI	BB	SO	AVG	OBP	SLG	PRO+	BR/A	SB	CS	SBR	FA	FR	G/POS	TPR
1984	Chi-N	52	73	8	21	2	2	0	3	7	18	.288	.350	.370	94	-0	0	0	0	1.000	-4	O-15	-0.5
1985	*LA-N	17	15	0	2	1	0	0	2	1	2	.133	.188	.200	9	-2	0	0	0	.000	0	H	-0.2
Total	20	1748	4703	578	1254	215	38	102	531	429	632	.267	.331	.394	103	10	50	54	-17	.979	-17	*O-1308/1-57,D-12,2	-8.4
■ **STAN JOK**	Jok, Stanley Edward "Tucker" b: 5/3/26, Buffalo, N.Y. d: 3/6/72, Buffalo, N.Y. BR/TR, 6′, 190 lbs. Deb: 4/13/54																						
1954	Phi-N	3	3	0	0	0	0	0	0	0	2	.000	.000	.000	-99	-1	0	0	0	.000	0	H	-0.1
	Chi-A	3	12	1	2	0	0	0	2	1	2	.167	.231	.167	10	-1	0	0	0	1.000	-0	/3-3	-0.2
1955	Chi-A	6	4	3	1	0	0	1	2	1	1	.250	.400	1.000	260	1	0	0	0	.857	1	/3-3,O-1	0.1
Total	2	12	19	4	3	0	0	1	4	2	5	.158	.238	.316	47	-2	0	0	0	.941	0	/3-6,O-1	-0.2
■ **SMEAD JOLLEY**	Jolley, Smead Powell "Guinea" or "Smudge" b: 1/14/02, Wesson, Ark. d: 11/17/91, Alameda, Cal. BL/TR, 6′3.5″, 210 lbs. Deb: 4/17/30																						
1930	Chi-A	152	616	76	193	38	12	16	114	28	52	.313	.346	.492	114	10	3	1	0	.950	-3	*O-151	-0.3
1931	Chi-A	54	110	5	33	11	0	3	28	7	4	.300	.353	.482	125	3	0	0	0	.857	-5	O-23	-0.2
1932	Chi-A	12	42	3	15	3	0	0	7	3	0	.357	.413	.429	127	2	1	0	0	.923	-2	O-11	-0.1
	Bos-A	137	531	57	164	27	5	18	99	27	29	.309	.345	.480	115	9	0	5	-3	.943	-5	*O-126/C-5	-0.6
	Yr	149	573	60	179	30	5	18	106	30	29	.312	.350	.476	116	11	1	5	-3	.942	-8	*O-137/C-5	-0.7
1933	Bos-A	118	411	47	116	32	4	9	65	24	20	.282	.325	.445	103	-0	1	1	-0	.955	-4	*O-102	-0.9
Total	4	473	1710	188	521	111	21	46	313	89	105	.305	.343	.475	112	24	5	7	-3	.944	-19	O-413/C-5	-2.1
■ **JONES**	Jones Deb: 5/14/1873																						
1873	Mar-n	1	4	0	3	0	0	0	1	0	0	.750	.750	.750	452	2	0	0	0	.800	0	/O-1	0.1
1874	Bal-n	2	7	0	1	0	0	0	1	0	0	.143	.143	.143	-8	-1	0	0	0	.875	-1	/C-1,O-1	-0.1
Total	2 n	3	11	0	4	0	0	0	2	0	0	.364	.364	.364	140	1	0	0	0	.800	-0	/O-2,C-1	0.0
■ **JONES**	Jones b: Johnstown, Pa. Deb: 7/14/1884																						
1884	Was-a	4	17	2	5	0	0	0		1		.294	.333	.294	120	0				1.000	-0	/O-4	0.0
■ **JONES**	Jones Deb: 4/30/1885																						
1885	NY-a	1	4	0	1	0	0	0	0	0		.250	.250	.250	63	-0				1.000	1	/3-1	0.1
■ **ANDRUW JONES**	Jones, Andruw Rudolf b: 4/23/77, Willemstad, Curacao BR/TR, 6′1″, 170 lbs. Deb: 8/15/96																						
1996	*Atl-N	31	106	11	23	7	1	5	13	7	29	.217	.265	.443	78	-4	3	0	1	.975	5	O-29	0.1
1997	*Atl-N	153	399	60	92	18	1	18	70	56	107	.231	.331	.416	93	-4	20	11	-1	.977	8	*O-147	0.1
1998	*Atl-N	159	582	89	158	33	8	31	90	40	129	.271	.323	.515	110	7	27	4	6	.995	**32**	*O-159	4.2
Total	3	343	1087	160	273	58	10	54	173	103	265	.251	.321	.472	101	-1	50	15	6	.987	45	O-335	4.4
■ **CHARLIE JONES**	Jones, Charles Claude "Casey" b: 6/2/1876, Butler, Pa. d: 4/2/47, Two Harbors, Minn. BR/TR, 6′1″, Deb: 5/2/01																						
1901	Bos-A	10	41	6	6	2	0	0	6	1		.146	.167	.195	0	-6	2			.929	-2	O-10	-0.8
1904	Chi-A	5	17	2	4	0	1	0	1	1		.235	.278	.353	103	0	0			1.000	1	/O-5	0.1
1905	Was-A	142	544	68	113	18	4	2	41	31		.208	.254	.267	68	-20	24			.971	17	*O-142	-1.2
1906	Was-A	131	497	56	120	11	11	3	42	24		.241	.283	.326	95	-4	34			.961	8	*O-128/2-1	-0.2
1907	Was-A	121	437	48	116	14	10	0	37	22		.265	.304	.343	115	6	26			.967	-1	*O-111/2-5,1-4,S-2	0.1
1908	StL-A	74	263	37	61	11	2	0	17	14		.232	.279	.289	84	-5	14			.963	-1	O-72	-1.0
Total	6	483	1799	217	420	56	28	5	144	93		.233	.276	.304	87	-29	100			.966	21	O-468/2-6,1-4,S-2	-3.0
■ **CHARLIE JONES**	Jones, Charles F. b: New York, N.Y. Deb: 6/28/1884																						
1884	Bro-a	25	90	10	16	1	0	0		5		.178	.221	.189	35	-6				.871	-7	2-13,3-11/O-2	-1.2
■ **CHARLEY JONES**	Jones, Charles Wesley "Baby" (b: Benjamin Wesley Rippay) b: 4/30/1850, Alamance Co., N.C. BR/TR, 5′11.5″, 202 lbs. Deb: 5/4/1875 U																						
1875	Wes-n	12	47	4	13	2	4	0	10	0	5	.277	.277	.489	152	2	1	1	-0	.800	-2	O-12	0.0
	Har-n	1	4	1	0	0	0	0	0	0	1	.000	.000	.000	-95	-1	0	0	0	.667	-0	/O-1	-0.1
	Yr	13	51	5	13	2	4	0	10	0	6	.255	.255	.451	133	1	1	1	-0	.778	-2	O-13	-0.1
1876	Cin-N	64	276	40	79	17	4	4	38	7	17	.286	.304	.420	162	19				.857	3	*O-64	1.8
1877	Cin-N	17	69	16	21	3	3	1	10	4	8	.304	.342	.478	175	6				.920	1	1-10/O-8	0.6
	Chi-N	2	8	1	3	1	0	0	2	1	0	.375	.444	.500	176	1				1.000	1	/O-2	0.1
	Cin-N	38	163	36	51	8	7	1	26	10	17	.313	.353	.466	175	14				.838	10	O-38	2.0
	Yr	57	240	53	75	12	10	2	38	15	25	.313	.353	.471	175	21				.845	12	O-48,1-10	**2.7**
1878	Cin-N	61	261	50	81	11	7	3	39	4	17	.310	.321	.441	163	17				.896	6	*O-61	1.9
1879	Bos-N	83	355	**85**	112	22	10	**9**	**62**	**29**	38	.315	.367	.510	182	31				**.933**	12	*O-83	3.5
1880	Bos-N	66	280	44	84	15	3	5	37	11	27	.300	.326	.429	159	17				.826	-4	*O-66	1.0
1883	Cin-a	90	391	84	115	15	12	10	80	20		.294	.328	.471	146	18				.876	2	*O-90	1.7
1884	Cin-a	112	472	117	148	19	17	7	71	37		.314	**.376**	.470	166	34				.887	3	*O-112	3.1
1885	Cin-a	112	487	108	157	19	17	5	35	21		.322	.362	.462	156	29				.891	12	*O-112	3.4
1886	Cin-a	127	500	87	135	22	10	6	68	61		.270	.356	.390	130	17	3			.879	3	*O-127	1.5
1887	Cin-a	41	153	28	48	7	4	2	40	19		.314	.400	.451	134	7	7			.900	-0	O-41	0.5
	NY-a	62	247	30	63	11	3	3	29	12		.255	.306	.360	89	-4	8			.917	4	O-62/P-2,1-1	-0.1
	Yr	103	400	58	111	18	7	5	69	31		.278	.343	.395	107	4	15			.910	4	*O-103/P-2,1-1	0.4
1888	KC-a	6	25	2	4	0	1	0	5	1		.160	.192	.240	36	-2	1			.750	-1	/O-6	-0.3
Total	11	881	3687	728	1101	170	98	56	542	237	124	.299	.347	.443	150	206	19	0		.882	51	O-872/1-11,P-2	20.7
■ **CHRIS JONES**	Jones, Christopher Carlos b: 12/16/65, Utica, N.Y. BR/TR, 6′2″, 205 lbs. Deb: 4/21/91																						
1991	Cin-N	52	89	14	26	1	2	2	6	2	31	.292	.308	.416	98	-1	2	1	0	1.000	-5	O-26	-0.6
1992	Hou-N	54	63	7	12	2	1	1	4	7	21	.190	.271	.302	65	-3	3	0	1	.931	-13	O-43	-1.7
1993	Col-N	86	209	29	57	11	4	6	31	10	48	.273	.306	.450	85	-5	9	4	0	.983	-9	O-70	-1.5
1994	Col-N	21	40	6	12	2	1	0	2	2	14	.300	.333	.400	77	-1	0	1	-1	.941	-5	O-14	-0.7
1995	NY-N	79	182	33	51	6	2	8	31	13	45	.280	.332	.467	111	2	2	1	0	.976	-2	O-52/1-5	-0.1
1996	NY-N	89	149	22	36	7	0	4	18	12	42	.242	.307	.369	81	-4	1	0	0	.957	-14	O-66/1-5	-1.9
1997	SD-N	92	152	24	37	9	0	7	25	16	45	.243	.324	.441	105	1	7	2	1	.951	-9	O-61	-0.8
1998	Ari-N	20	31	3	6	1	0	0	3	3	9	.194	.265	.226	29	-3	0	0	0	1.000	-1	/O-8	-0.4
	SF-N	43	90	14	17	2	1	2	10	8	28	.189	.255	.300	45	-8	2	1	0	.941	-4	O-29/D-2	-1.2
	Yr	63	121	17	23	3	1	2	13	11	37	.190	.258	.281	41	-11	2	1	0	.956	-5	O-37/D-2	-1.6
Total	8	536	1005	152	254	41	11	30	130	73	283	.253	.307	.405	86	-22	26	10	2	.966	-62	O-369/1-10,D-2	-8.9
■ **CHRIS JONES**	Jones, Christopher Dale b: 7/13/57, Los Angeles, Cal. BL/TL, 6′, 183 lbs. Deb: 6/8/85																						
1985	Hou-N	31	25	0	5	0	0	0	1	3	7	.200	.286	.200	39	-2	0	0	0	1.000	-3	O-15	-0.6
1986	SF-N	3	1	0	0	0	0	0	0	0	0	.000	.000	.000	-99	-0	1	0	0	.000	0	/H	0.0
Total	2	34	26	0	5	0	0	0	1	3	7	.192	.276	.192	34	-2	1	0	0	1.000	-3	/O-15	-0.6
■ **CLARENCE JONES**	Jones, Clarence Woodrow b: 11/7/41, Zanesville, Ohio BL/TL, 6′2″, 185 lbs. Deb: 4/20/67 C																						
1967	Chi-N	53	135	13	34	7	0	2	16	14	33	.252	.322	.348	88	-2	0	0	0	.978	-4	O-31,1-13	-0.9
1968	Chi-N	5	2	0	0	0	0	0	0	2	1	.000	.500	.000	56	0	0	0	0	1.000	-0	/1-1	0.0
Total	2	58	137	13	34	7	0	2	16	16	34	.248	.327	.343	88	-2	0	0	0	.979	-4	/O-31,1-14	-0.9
■ **CLEON JONES**	Jones, Cleon Joseph b: 8/4/42, Plateau, Ala. BR/TL, 6′, 200 lbs. Deb: 9/14/63																						
1963	NY-N	6	15	1	2	0	0	0	1	0	4	.133	.133	.133	-23	-2	0	0	0	1.000	-1	/O-5	-0.4
1965	NY-N	30	74	2	11	1	0	1	9	2	23	.149	.171	.203	5	-9	1	0	0	1.000	-1	O-23	-1.2
1966	NY-N	139	495	74	136	16	4	8	57	30	62	.275	.320	.372	94	-4	16	8	0	.979	-2	*O-129	-1.3
1967	NY-N	129	411	46	101	10	5	5	30	19	57	.246	.286	.331	77	-13	12	2	2	.977	-6	*O-115	-2.4
1968	NY-N	147	509	63	151	29	4	14	55	31	98	.297	.343	.452	136	21	23	12	-0	.963	-10	*O-139	0.5
1969	*NY-N★	137	483	92	164	25	4	12	75	64	60	.340	.424	.482	150	35	16	8	0	.991	8	*O-122,1-15	3.7
1970	NY-N	134	506	71	140	25	8	10	63	57	87	.277	.356	.417	106	5	12	3	2	.981	12	*O-130	1.2
1971	NY-N	136	505	63	161	24	6	14	69	53	87	.319	.386	.473	144	29	6	5	-1	.981	7	*O-132	3.0

YEAR	TM/L	G	AB	R	H	2B	3B	HR	RBI	BB	SO	AVG	OBP	SLG	PRO+	BR/A	SB	CS	SBR	FA	FR	G/POS	TPR
1972	NY-N	106	375	39	92	15	1	5	52	30	83	.245	.308	.331	84	-8	1	6	-3	.986	-1	O-84,1-20	-1.9
1973	*NY-N	92	339	48	88	13	0	11	48	28	51	.260	.322	.395	99	-1	1	1	-0	.967	1	O-92	-0.5
1974	NY-N	124	461	62	130	23	1	13	60	38	79	.282	.345	.421	115	8	3	3	-1	.970	3	*O-120	0.5
1975	NY-N	21	50	2	12	1	0	0	2	3	6	.240	.283	.260	54	-3	0	0	0	1.000	-3	O-12	-0.7
1976	Chi-A	12	40	2	8	1	0	0	3	5	5	.200	.304	.225	56	-2	0	0	0	1.000	-2	/O-8,D-3	-0.5
Total	13	1213	4263	565	1196	183	33	93	524	360	702	.281	.342	.404	111	56	91	48	-2	.978	6	*O-1111/1-35,D-3	-0.0
■ **COBE JONES**	Jones, Coburn Dyas b: 8/21/07, Denver, Colo. d: 6/3/69, Denver, Colo. BB/TR, 5'7", 155 lbs. Deb: 9/27/28																						
1928	Pit-N	1	2	0	1	0	0	0	0	0	0	.500	.500	.500	156	0	0			1.000	-0	/S-1	0.0
1929	Pit-N	25	63	6	16	5	1	0	4	1	5	.254	.266	.365	53	-5	1			.919	-8	S-15	-1.0
Total	2	26	65	6	17	5	1	0	4	1	5	.262	.273	.369	56	-5	1			.921	-8	/S-16	-1.0
■ **DARRYL JONES**	Jones, Darryl Lee b: 6/5/51, Meadville, Pa. BR/TR, 5'10", 175 lbs. Deb: 6/6/79 F																						
1979	NY-A	18	47	6	12	5	1	0	6	2	7	.255	.286	.404	86	-1	0	0	0	1.000	-1	D-15/O-2	-0.2
■ **DAVY JONES**	Jones, David Jefferson "Kangaroo" b: 6/30/1880, Cambria, Wis. d: 3/31/72, Mankato, Minn. BL/TR, 5'10", 165 lbs. Deb: 9/15/01																						
1901	Mil-A	14	52	12	9	0	0	3	5	11		.173	.328	.346	91	-0	4			.911	1	O-14	0.0
1902	StL-A	15	49	4	11	1	1	0	3	6		.224	.309	.286	67	-2	5			.973	5	O-15	0.1
	Chi-N	64	243	41	74	12	3	0	14	38		.305	.399	.379	144	15	12			.955	-1	O-64	1.0
1903	Chi-N	130	497	64	140	18	3	1	62	53		.282	.352	.336	99	1	15			.970	0	*O-130	-0.6
1904	Chi-N	98	336	44	82	11	5	3	39	41		.244	.330	.333	105	3	14			.932	-10	O-97	-1.3
1906	Det-A	84	323	41	84	12	2	0	24	41		.260	.347	.310	103	3	21			.981	4	O-83	0.3
1907	*Det-A	126	491	101	134	10	6	0	27	60		.273	.357	.318	111	9	30			.971	13	*O-125	1.9
1908	*Det-A	56	121	17	25	2	1	0	10	13		.207	.284	.240	68	-4	11			.960	2	O-32	-0.3
1909	*Det-A	69	204	44	57	2	2	0	10	28		.279	.369	.309	110	4	12			.982	-2	O-57	-0.1
1910	Det-A	113	377	77	100	6	6	0	24	51		.265	.362	.313	104	4	25			.956	1	*O-101	0.0
1911	Det-A	98	341	78	93	10	0	0	19	41		.273	.354	.302	80	-8	25			.950	-1	O-92	-1.4
1912	Det-A	99	316	54	93	5	2	0	24	38		.294	.370	.323	102	2	16			.962	-1	O-81	-0.2
1913	Chi-A	12	21	2	6	0	0	0	0	9	0	.286	.500	.286	132	2	1			.867	-1	/O-9	0.1
1914	Pit-F	97	352	58	96	9	8	2	24	42	16	.273	.355	.361	96	-6	15			.970	8	O-93	-0.3
1915	Pit-F	14	49	6	16	0	1	0	4	6	0	.327	.400	.367	118	1	1			.926	-1	O-13	-0.1
Total	14	1089	3772	643	1020	98	40	9	289	478	16	.270	.356	.325	102	22	207			.962	18	*O-1006	-0.9
■ **DAX JONES**	Jones, Dax Xenos b: 8/4/70, Pittsburgh, Pa. BR/TR, 6', 170 lbs. Deb: 7/11/96																						
1996	SF-N	34	58	7	10	0	2	1	7	8	12	.172	.273	.293	51	-4	2	2	-1	1.000	-4	O-33	-0.9
■ **FIELDER JONES**	Jones, Fielder Allison b: 8/13/1871, Shinglehouse, Pa. d: 3/13/34, Portland, Ore. BL/TR, 5'11", 180 lbs. Deb: 4/18/1896 M																						
1896	Bro-N	104	395	82	140	10	8	3	46	48	15	.354	.427	.443	137	24	18			.928	-4	*O-103	1.0
1897	Bro-N	135	548	134	172	15	10	1	49	61		.314	.392	.383	111	12	48			.941	4	*O-135	0.5
1898	Bro-N	146	596	89	181	15	9	1	69	46		.304	.362	.364	108	7	36			.946	-7	*O-144/S-2	1.0
1899	Bro-N	102	365	75	104	8	2	2	38	54		.285	.390	.334	97	2	18			.946	-3	O-96	-0.8
1900	*Bro-N	136	552	106	171	26	4	4	54	57		.310	.383	.393	108	7	33			.957	0	*O-136	-0.3
1901	Chi-A	133	521	120	162	16	3	2	65	84		.311	.412	.365	120	20	38			.937	1	*O-133	1.0
1902	Chi-A	135	532	98	171	16	5	0	54	57		.321	.390	.370	117	15	33			.972	13	*O-135	1.8
1903	Chi-A	136	530	71	152	18	5	0	45	47		.287	.348	.340	112	9	21			**.985**	0	*O-136	0.1
1904	Chi-A	149	547	72	133	14	5	3	42	53		.243	.316	.303	100	2	25			.977	5	*O-149,M	-0.2
1905	Chi-A	153	568	91	139	17	12	2	38	73		.245	.335	.327	115	12	20			.970	8	*O-153,M	1.4
1906	*Chi-A	144	496	77	114	22	4	2	34	83		.230	.346	.302	106	8	26			**.988**	8	*O-144,M	1.0
1907	Chi-A	154	559	72	146	18	1	0	47	67		.261	.345	.297	109	9	17			.973	3	*O-154,M	0.6
1908	Chi-A	149	529	92	134	11	7	1	50	86		.253	.366	.306	121	17	26			.968	-2	*O-149,M	1.1
1914	StL-F	5	3	0	1	0	0	0	0	1	0	.333	.500	.333	123	0	0			.000	0	HM	0.0
1915	StL-F	7	6	1	0	0	0	0	0	0	0	.000	.000	.000	-95	-2	0			1.000	-1	/O-3,M	-0.3
Total	15	1788	6747	1180	1920	206	75	21	631	817	15	.285	.368	.347	112	142	359			.964	25	*O-1770/S-2	5.9
■ **FRANK JONES**	Jones, Frank M. b: 8/25/1858, Princeton, Ill. d: 2/4/36, Marietta, Ohio BL , Deb: 7/2/1884																						
1884	Det-N	2	8	0	1	0	0	0	0	0	1	.125	.125	.125	-22	-1				.667	-1	/S-1,O-1	-0.2
■ **DEACON JONES**	Jones, Grover William b: 4/18/34, White Plains, N.Y. BL/TR, 5'10", 185 lbs. Deb: 9/8/62 C																						
1962	Chi-A	18	28	3	9	2	0	0	8	4	6	.321	.406	.393	117	1	0	0	0	.962	-0	/1-6	0.0
1963	Chi-A	17	16	4	3	0	1	1	2	2	2	.188	.316	.500	127	1	0	0	0	1.000	0	/1-1	0.1
1966	Chi-A	5	5	0	2	0	0	0	0	0	0	.400	.400	.400	140	0	0	0	0	.000	0	H	0.0
Total	3	40	49	7	14	2	1	1	10	6	8	.286	.375	.429	122	2	0	0	0	.966	-0	/1-7	0.1
■ **HAL JONES**	Jones, Harold Marion b: 4/9/36, Louisiana, Mo. BR/TR, 6'2", 194 lbs. Deb: 4/25/61																						
1961	Cle-A	12	35	2	6	0	0	2	4	2	12	.171	.216	.343	48	-3	0	0	0	.974	-2	1-10	-0.5
1962	Cle-A	5	16	2	5	1	0	0	1	0	4	.313	.353	.375	99	-0	0	0	0	.969	0	/1-4	0.0
Total	2	17	51	4	11	1	0	2	5	2	16	.216	.259	.353	64	-3	0	0	0	.973	-2	/1-14	-0.5
■ **HENRY JONES**	Jones, Henry Monroe "Baldy" b: 5/10/1857, New York d: 5/31/55, Manistee, Mich. BB , 5'6", 149 lbs. Deb: 8/20/1884																						
1884	Det-N	34	127	24	28	3	1	0	3	16	18	.220	.308	.260	86	-1				.897	-2	2-16,O-11/S-7	-0.3
■ **HOWIE JONES**	Jones, Howard "Cotton" (b: Howard Painter) b: 3/1/1897, Irwin, Pa. d: 7/15/72, Jeannette, Pa. BL/TL, 5'11", 165 lbs. Deb: 9/5/21																						
1921	StL-N	3	2	0	0	0	0	0	0	0	1	.000	.000	.000	-99	-1	0	0	0	.000	-1	/O-1	-0.1
■ **DALTON JONES**	Jones, James Dalton b: 12/10/43, McComb, Miss. BL/TR, 6'1", 180 lbs. Deb: 4/17/64																						
1964	Bos-A	118	374	37	86	16	4	6	39	22	38	.230	.275	.342	67	-17	6	3	0	.959	-8	2-85/S-1,3-1	-1.9
1965	Bos-A	112	367	41	99	13	5	5	37	28	45	.270	.325	.373	92	-4	8	1	2	.930	-3	3-81/2-8	-0.7
1966	Bos-A	115	252	26	59	11	5	4	23	22	27	.234	.303	.365	83	-6	1	2	-1	.962	-15	2-70/3-3	-1.9
1967	*Bos-A	89	159	18	46	6	2	3	25	11	23	.289	.335	.409	110	2	0	1	-1	.912	-4	3-30,2-19/1-1	-0.3
1968	Bos-A	111	354	38	83	13	0	5	29	17	53	.234	.272	.314	72	-12	1	1	-0	.996	-6	1-56,2-26/3-8	-2.5
1969	Bos-A	111	336	50	74	18	3	3	33	39	36	.220	.305	.318	71	-13	1	1	-0	.992	-1	1-81/3-9,2-1	-2.1
1970	Det-A	89	191	29	42	7	0	6	21	33	33	.220	.338	.351	90	-2	1	1	-0	.985	-3	2-35,3-18,1-10	-0.4
1971	Det-A	83	138	15	35	5	0	5	11	9	21	.254	.304	.399	94	-1	1	3	-2	1.000	-7	O-16,3-13/1-3,2-1	-1.1
1972	Det-A	7	7	0	0	0	0	0	0	0	2	.000	.000	.000	-97	-2	0	0	0	.000	0	H	-0.2
	Tex-A	72	151	14	24	2	0	4	19	10	31	.159	.211	.252	39	-12	1	0	0	.979	-7	3-23,2-17/1-7,O-2	-2.1
	Yr	79	158	14	24	2	0	4	19	10	33	.152	.202	.241	33	-14	1	0	0	.979	-7	3-23,2-17/1-7,O-2	-2.3
Total	9	907	2329	268	548	91	19	41	237	191	309	.235	.296	.343	79	-66	20	13	-2	.967	-54	2-262,3-186,1/OS	-13.2
■ **JAKE JONES**	Jones, James Murrell b: 11/23/20, Epps, La. BR/TR, 6'3", 197 lbs. Deb: 9/20/41																						
1941	Chi-A	3	11	0	0	0	0	0	0	0	4	.000	.000	.000	-99	-3	0	0	0	1.000	-1	/1-3	-0.4
1942	Chi-A	7	20	2	3	1	0	0	0	2	2	.150	.227	.200	21	-2	1	0	0	.961	-1	/1-5	-0.3
1946	Chi-A	24	79	10	21	5	1	3	13	2	13	.266	.284	.468	112	0	0	0	0	.986	-3	1-20	-0.4
1947	Chi-A	45	171	15	41	7	1	3	20	13	25	.240	.297	.345	81	-5	1	0	0	.988	-1	1-43	-0.7
	Bos-A	109	404	50	95	14	3	16	76	41	60	.235	.310	.403	91	-6	5	4	-1	.991	-2	*1-109	-1.4
	Yr	154	575	65	136	21	4	19	96	54	85	.237	.306	.386	88	-11	6	4	-1	.990	-3	*1-152	-2.1
1948	Bos-A	36	105	3	21	4	0	1	8	11	26	.200	.276	.267	43	-9	1	0	0	.993	2	1-31	-0.6
Total	5	224	790	80	181	31	5	23	117	69	130	.229	.294	.368	80	-25	8	4	0	.989	-6	1-211	-3.8
■ **JIM JONES**	Jones, James Tilford "Sheriff" b: 12/25/1876, London, Ky. d: 5/6/53, London, Ky. BR/TR, 5'10", 162 lbs. Deb: 6/29/1897																						
1897	Lou-N	2	4	2	1	1	0	0	0	1		.250	.400	.500	141	0	0			.000	-0	/P-1	0.0
1901	NY-N	21	91	10	19	4	3	0	5	4		.209	.250	.319	67	-4	2			.900	1	O-20/P-1	-0.5

YEAR	TM/L	G	AB	R	H	2B	3B	HR	RBI	BB	SO	AVG	OBP	SLG	PRO+	BR/A	SB	CS	SBR	FA	FR	G/POS	TPR
1902	NY-N	67	249	16	59	11	1	0	19	13		.237	.275	.289	75	-8	7			.897	-1	O-67	-1.4
Total	3	90	344	28	79	16	4	0	24	18		.230	.270	.299	73	-12	9			.898	-0	/O-87,P-2	-1.9
■ JEFF JONES Jones, Jeffrey Raymond b: 10/22/57, Philadelphia, Pa. BR/TR, 6'2", 200 lbs. Deb: 4/4/83																							
1983	Cin-N	16	44	6	10	3	0	0	5	11	13	.227	.393	.295	90	0	2	0	1	1.000	1	O-13/1-1	0.1
■ BINKY JONES Jones, John Joseph b: 7/11/1899, St.Louis, Mo. d: 5/13/61, St.Louis, Mo. BR/TR, 5'9", 154 lbs. Deb: 4/15/24																							
1924	Bro-N	10	37	0	4	1	0	0	2	0	3	.108	.108	.135	-36	-7	0	0	0	.898	-1	S-10	-0.7
■ JOHN JONES Jones, John William "Skins" b: 5/13/01, Coatesville, Pa. d: 11/3/56, Baltimore, Md. BL/TL, 5'11", 185 lbs. Deb: 9/26/23																							
1923	Phi-A	1	4	0	1	0	0	0	1	0	1	.250	.250	.250	31	-0	0	0	0	1.000	0	/O-1	0.0
1932	Phi-A	4	6	0	1	0	0	0	0	0	3	.167	.167	.167	-13	-1	0	0	0	1.000	-0	/O-1	-0.1
Total	2	5	10	0	2	0	0	0	1	0	4	.200	.200	.200	4	-1	0	0	0	1.000	0	/O-2	-0.1
■ CHIPPER JONES Jones, Larry Wayne b: 4/24/72, DeLand, Fla. BB/TR, 6'3", 185 lbs. Deb: 9/11/93																							
1993	Atl-N	8	3	2	2	1	0	0	0	1	1	.667	.750	1.000	360	1	0	0	0	1.000	1	/S-3	0.2
1995	*Atl-N	140	524	87	139	22	3	23	86	73	99	.265	.355	.450	107	6	8	4	0	.931	3	*3-123,O-20	0.8
1996	*Atl-N★	157	598	114	185	32	5	30	110	87	88	.309	.397	.530	134	31	14	1	4	.947	-24	*3-118,S-38/O-1	1.3
1997	*Atl-N★	157	597	100	176	41	3	21	111	76	88	.295	.374	.479	120	18	20	5	3	.955	-21	*3-152/O-5	0.1
1998	*Atl-N★	160	601	123	188	29	5	34	107	96	93	.313	.408	.547	142	40	16	6	1	.971	-2	*3-158	4.0
Total	5	622	2323	426	690	125	16	108	414	333	369	.297	.385	.504	127	95	58	16	8	.952	-43	3-551/S-41,O-26	6.4
■ LYNN JONES Jones, Lynn Morris b: 1/1/53, Meadville, Pa. BR/TR, 5'9", 175 lbs. Deb: 4/13/79 FC																							
1979	Det-A	95	213	33	63	8	0	4	26	17	22	.296	.351	.390	96	-1	9	6	-1	.980	-10	O-84/D-6	-1.4
1980	Det-A	30	55	9	14	2	2	0	6	10	5	.255	.369	.364	99	0	1	0	0	1.000	-2	O-17/D-6	-0.1
1981	Det-A	71	174	19	45	5	0	2	19	18	10	.259	.332	.322	86	-3	1	2	-1	.989	-4	O-60/D-4	-1.0
1982	Det-A	58	139	15	31	3	1	0	14	7	14	.223	.260	.259	43	-11	0	2	-1	1.000	-5	O-56/D-1	-1.8
1983	Det-A	49	64	9	17	1	2	0	6	3	6	.266	.299	.344	78	-2	1	0	0	.968	-7	O-31/D-6	-0.9
1984	*KC-A	47	103	11	31	6	0	1	10	4	9	.301	.333	.388	98	-0	1	3	-2	.962	-12	O-45	-1.5
1985	*KC-A	110	152	12	32	7	0	0	9	8	15	.211	.264	.257	43	-12	0	1	-1	.983	-24	*O-100/D-2	-3.8
1986	KC-A	67	47	1	6	2	0	0	1	6	5	.128	.226	.170	10	-6	0	0	0	.971	-21	O-62/2-1,D-3	-2.7
Total	8	527	947	109	239	34	5	7	91	73	86	.252	.310	.321	73	-34	13	14	-5	.983	-84	O-455/D-28,2-1	-13.2
■ MACK JONES Jones, Mack "Mack The Knife" b: 11/6/38, Atlanta, Ga. BL/TR, 6'1", 180 lbs. Deb: 7/13/61																							
1961	Mil-N	28	104	13	24	3	2	0	12	12	28	.231	.322	.298	70	-4	4	4	-1	1.000	-2	O-26	-0.9
1962	Mil-N	91	333	51	85	17	4	10	36	44	100	.255	.354	.420	110	5	5	1	1	.973	-8	O-91	-0.7
1963	Mil-N	93	228	36	50	11	4	3	22	26	59	.219	.318	.342	91	-2	8	4	0	.978	-8	O-80	-1.4
1965	Mil-N	143	504	78	132	18	7	31	75	29	122	.262	.314	.510	127	16	8	2	1	.980	-10	*O-133	0.1
1966	Atl-N	118	417	60	110	14	1	23	66	39	85	.264	.338	.468	120	11	16	10	-1	.981	-3	*O-112/1-1	0.2
1967	Atl-N	140	454	72	115	23	4	17	50	64	108	.253	.357	.434	127	17	10	6	-1	.985	2	*O-126	1.3
1968	Cin-N	103	234	40	59	9	1	10	34	28	46	.252	.345	.427	123	7	2	3	-1	.988	-8	O-60	-0.6
1969	Mon-N	135	455	73	123	23	5	22	79	67	110	.270	.382	.488	142	27	6	7	-2	.959	7	*O-129	2.5
1970	Mon-N	108	271	51	65	11	3	14	32	59	74	.240	.399	.458	129	14	5	3	-0	.968	-4	O-87	0.5
1971	Mon-N	43	91	11	15	3	0	3	9	15	24	.165	.296	.297	68	-4	1	0	0	.952	-2	O-27	-0.6
Total	10	1002	3091	485	778	132	31	133	415	383	756	.252	.349	.444	120	86	65	40	-5	.976	-35	O-871/1-1	0.4
■ RED JONES Jones, Maurice Morris b: 11/2/14, Timpson, Tex. d: 6/30/75, Lincoln, Cal. BL/TR, 6'3", 190 lbs. Deb: 4/16/40																							
1940	StL-N	12	11	0	1	0	0	0	1	1	2	.091	.167	.091	-26	-2	0			1.000	-0	/O-1	-0.2
■ RICKY JONES Jones, Ricky Miron b: 6/4/58, Tupelo, Miss. BR/TR, 6'3", 186 lbs. Deb: 9/3/86																							
1986	Bal-A	16	33	2	6	2	0	0	4	6	8	.182	.308	.242	53	-2	0	0	0	1.000	7	2-11/3-6	0.5
■ BOB JONES Jones, Robert Oliver b: 10/11/49, Elkton, Md. BL/TL, 6'2", 195 lbs. Deb: 10/1/74																							
1974	Tex-A	2	5	0	0	0	0	0	0	0	1	.000	.000	.000	-99	-1	0	0	0	1.000	0	/O-2	-0.1
1975	Tex-A	9	11	2	1	0	0	0	0	3	3	.091	.286	.091	11	-1	0	0	0	1.000	-1	/O-5,D-1	-0.2
1976	Cal-A	78	166	22	35	6	0	6	17	14	30	.211	.276	.355	90	-3	3	0	1	.990	-5	O-62/D-2	-0.9
1977	Cal-A	14	17	3	3	0	0	1	3	4	5	.176	.333	.353	91	-0	0	0	0	.000	0	/D-6	0.0
1981	Tex-A	10	34	4	9	1	0	3	7	1	7	.265	.286	.559	146	2	0	1	-1	1.000	3	O-10	0.4
1983	Tex-A	41	72	5	16	4	0	1	11	5	17	.222	.291	.319	69	-3	0	2	-1	1.000	0	O-11,D-11/1-1	-0.5
1984	Tex-A	64	143	14	37	4	0	4	22	10	19	.259	.312	.371	85	-3	1	1	-0	1.000	-0	O-22,1-15/D-4	-0.5
1985	Tex-A	83	134	14	30	2	0	5	23	11	30	.224	.288	.351	73	-5	1	0	0	1.000	-7	O-30,D-10/1-4	-1.3
1986	Tex-A	13	21	1	2	0	0	0	3	2	5	.095	.174	.095	-24	-4	0	0	0	.909	-2	/O-9,1-2	-0.6
Total	9	314	603	65	133	17	0	20	86	50	117	.221	.286	.348	78	-18	5	4	-1	.992	-11	O-151/D-34,1-22	-3.7
■ BOB JONES Jones, Robert Walter "Ducky" b: 12/2/1889, Clayton, Cal. d: 8/30/64, San Diego, Cal. BL/TR, 6', 170 lbs. Deb: 4/11/17																							
1917	Det-A	46	77	16	12	1	2	0	2	4	8	.156	.198	.221	28	-7	3			.938	-1	2-18/3-8	-0.8
1918	Det-A	74	287	43	79	14	4	0	21	17	16	.275	.320	.352	107	1	7			.947	-8	3-63/1-6,O-1	-0.7
1919	Det-A	127	439	37	114	18	6	1	57	34	39	.260	.314	.335	84	-10	11			.944	-24	*3-127	-3.0
1920	Det-A	81	265	35	66	6	3	1	18	22	13	.249	.309	.306	65	-13	3	4	-2	.942	-5	3-67/2-5,S-1	-1.6
1921	Det-A	141	554	82	168	23	9	1	72	37	24	.303	.348	.383	87	-11	8	9	-3	.950	10	*3-141	0.6
1922	Det-A	124	455	65	117	10	6	3	44	36	18	.257	.314	.325	69	-21	8	5	-1	**.962**	11	*3-119	-0.2
1923	Det-A	100	372	51	93	15	4	1	40	29	13	.250	.306	.320	66	-19	7	6	-2	.954	5	3-97	-0.6
1924	Det-A	110	393	52	107	27	4	0	47	20	20	.272	.308	.361	73	-17	1	5	-3	.956	-2	*3-106	-1.3
1925	Det-A	50	148	18	35	6	0	0	15	9	5	.236	.280	.277	42	-13	1	1	-0	.985	9	3-46	-0.2
Total	9	853	2990	399	791	120	38	7	316	208	156	.265	.314	.337	75	-109	49	30		.953	-4	3-774/2-23,1-6,SO	-7.8
■ RON JONES Jones, Ronald Glen b: 6/11/64, Seguin, Tex. BL/TR, 5'10", 195 lbs. Deb: 8/26/88																							
1988	Phi-N	33	124	15	36	6	1	8	26	2	14	.290	.302	.548	136	5	0	0	0	1.000	2	O-32	0.7
1989	Phi-N	12	31	7	9	0	0	2	4	9	1	.290	.450	.484	167	3	1	0	0	1.000	2	O-12	0.5
1990	Phi-N	24	58	5	16	2	0	3	7	9	9	.276	.373	.466	130	2	0	1	-1	1.000	-1	O-16	0.1
1991	Phi-N	28	26	0	4	2	0	0	3	2	9	.154	.214	.231	25	-3	0	0	0	.000	0	H	-0.4
Total	4	97	239	27	65	10	1	13	40	22	33	.272	.333	.485	128	8	1	1	-0	1.000	3	/O-60	0.9
■ ROSS JONES Jones, Ross A. b: 1/14/60, Miami, Fla. BR/TR, 6'2", 185 lbs. Deb: 4/2/84																							
1984	NY-N	17	10	2	1	1	0	0	1	3	4	.100	.308	.200	46	-1	0	0	0	.833	1	/S-6,2-1,3-1	0.1
1986	Sea-A	11	21	0	2	0	0	0	0	0	4	.095	.095	.095	-48	-4	0	1	-1	1.000	1	/S-4,2-3,3-2,D-1	-0.4
1987	KC-A	39	114	10	29	4	2	0	10	5	15	.254	.292	.325	62	-6	1	0	0	.974	1	S-36/2-3	-0.2
Total	3	67	145	12	32	5	2	0	11	8	23	.221	.266	.283	46	-11	1	1	-0	.971	3	/S-46,2-7,3-3,D-1	-0.5
■ RUPPERT JONES Jones, Ruppert Sanderson b: 3/12/55, Dallas, Tex. BL/TL, 5'10", 175 lbs. Deb: 8/1/76																							
1976	KC-A	28	51	9	11	1	1	1	7	3	16	.216	.259	.333	72	-2	0	2	-1	1.000	-5	O-17/D-3	-0.9
1977	Sea-A★	160	597	85	157	26	8	24	76	55	120	.263	.327	.454	111	8	13	9	-2	.981	22	*O-155/D-4	2.2
1978	Sea-A	129	472	48	111	24	3	6	46	55	85	.235	.315	.337	84	-10	22	6	3	.985	16	*O-128	0.4
1979	Sea-A	162	622	109	166	29	9	21	78	85	78	.267	.358	.444	113	12	33	12	3	.989	14	*O-161	2.1
1980	NY-A	83	328	38	73	11	3	9	42	34	50	.223	.301	.357	81	-9	18	8	1	.988	8	O-82	-0.3
1981	SD-N	105	397	53	99	34	1	4	39	43	66	.249	.323	.370	104	1	7	9	-3	.993	10	*O-104	0.5
1982	SD-N★	116	424	69	120	20	2	12	61	62	90	.283	.376	.425	130	18	18	15	-4	.984	8	*O-114	2.1
1983	SD-N	133	335	42	78	12	3	12	49	35	58	.233	.305	.394	96	-3	11	11	-3	.981	-2	*O-111/1-5	-1.2
1984	*Det-A	79	215	26	61	12	1	12	37	21	47	.284	.347	.516	136	10	2	4	-2	1.000	-5	O-73/D-2	0.2
1985	Cal-A	125	389	66	90	17	2	21	67	57	82	.231	.330	.447	111	6	7	4	-0	.995	10	O-73,D-43	1.2
1986	*Cal-A	126	393	73	90	21	3	17	49	64	87	.229	.341	.427	109	6	10	3	1	.981	-12	*O-121	-0.9

YEAR	TM/L	G	AB	R	H	2B	3B	HR	RBI	BB	SO	AVG	OBP	SLG	PRO+	BR/A	SB	CS	SBR	FA	FR	G/POS	TPR
1987	Cal-A	85	192	25	47	8	2	8	28	20	38	.245	.316	.432	99	-1	2	1	0	.965	-15	O-66/D-3	-1.6
Total	12	1331	4415	643	1103	215	38	147	579	534	817	.250	.332	.416	106	37	143	84	-8	.986	51	*O-1205/D-55,1-5	3.8

■ JACK JONES Jones, Ryerson L. "Ri" or "Angel Sleeves" b: Cincinnati, Ohio TR , Deb: 8/13/1883

YEAR	TM/L	G	AB	R	H	2B	3B	HR	RBI	BB	SO	AVG	OBP	SLG	PRO+	BR/A	SB	CS	SBR	FA	FR	G/POS	TPR
1883	Lou-a	2	7	1	0	0	0	0		0		.000	.000	.000	-99	-2				.500	-1	/O-2,S-1	-0.2
1884	Cin-U	69	272	36	71	5	1	2		12		.261	.292	.309	76	-16				.858	2	S-41,2-19,3-10	-1.2
Total	2	71	279	37	71	5	1	2		12		.254	.285	.301	73	-17				.857	1	/S-42,2-19,3-10,O-2	-1.4

■ TERRY JONES Jones, Terry Lee b: 2/15/71, Birmingham, Ala. BB/TR, 5'10", 160 lbs. Deb: 9/9/96

YEAR	TM/L	G	AB	R	H	2B	3B	HR	RBI	BB	SO	AVG	OBP	SLG	PRO+	BR/A	SB	CS	SBR	FA	FR	G/POS	TPR
1996	Col-N	12	10	6	3	0	0	0	1	0	3	.300	.300	.300	48	-1	0	0	0	1.000	-1	/O-4	-0.2
1998	Mon-N	60	212	30	46	7	2	1	15	21	46	.217	.288	.283	51	-15	16	4	2	.988	9	O-60	-0.5
Total	2	72	222	36	49	7	2	1	16	21	49	.221	.288	.284	51	-16	16	4	2	.988	8	/O-64	-0.7

■ TOM JONES Jones, Thomas b: 1/22/1877, Honesdale, Pa. d: 6/21/23, Danville, Pa. BR/TR, 6'1", 195 lbs. Deb: 8/25/02

YEAR	TM/L	G	AB	R	H	2B	3B	HR	RBI	BB	SO	AVG	OBP	SLG	PRO+	BR/A	SB	CS	SBR	FA	FR	G/POS	TPR
1902	Bal-A	37	159	22	45	8	4	0	14	2		.283	.292	.384	83	-4	1			.955	-2	1-37/2-1	-0.6
1904	StL-A	156	625	53	152	15	10	2	68	15		.243	.270	.309	88	-10	16			.988	0	*1-134,2-23/O-4	-1.4
1905	StL-A	135	504	44	122	16	2	0	48	30		.242	.290	.282	86	-8	5			.985	7	*1-135	-0.6
1906	StL-A	144	539	51	136	22	6	0	30	24		.252	.290	.315	94	-5	27			.985	11	*1-143	0.2
1907	StL-A	155	549	53	137	17	3	0	34	34		.250	.298	.291	88	-7	24			.983	2	*1-155	-1.1
1908	StL-A	155	549	43	135	14	2	1	50	30		.246	.290	.284	86	-8	18			.986	-2	*1-155	-1.5
1909	StL-A	97	337	30	84	9	3	0	29	18		.249	.299	.294	94	-3	13			.989	7	1-95/3-2	0.4
	*Det-A	44	153	13	43	9	0	0	18	5		.281	.317	.340	103	0	9			.984	2	1-44	0.2
	Yr	141	490	43	127	18	3	0	47	23		.259	.305	.308	97	-2	22			.988	9	*1-139/3-2	0.6
1910	Det-A	135	432	32	110	12	4	1	45	35		.255	.325	.308	92	-4	22			.985	-4	*1-135	-0.8
Total	8	1058	3847	341	964	122	34	4	336	193		.251	.294	.303	90	-49	135			.984	22	*1-1033/2-24,O-4,3	-5.2

■ TRACY JONES Jones, Tracy Donald b: 3/31/61, Hawthorne, Cal. BR/TR, 6'3", 220 lbs. Deb: 4/7/86

YEAR	TM/L	G	AB	R	H	2B	3B	HR	RBI	BB	SO	AVG	OBP	SLG	PRO+	BR/A	SB	CS	SBR	FA	FR	G/POS	TPR
1986	Cin-N	46	86	16	30	3	0	2	10	9	5	.349	.411	.453	132	4	7	1	2	1.000	-0	O-24/1-2	0.5
1987	Cin-N	117	359	53	104	17	3	10	44	23	40	.290	.338	.437	99	-1	31	8	5	.990	-3	O-95	-0.3
1988	Cin-N	37	83	9	19	1	0	1	9	8	6	.229	.304	.277	65	-3	9	0	3	.955	-2	O-25	-0.4
	Mon-N	53	141	20	47	5	1	2	15	12	12	.333	.390	.426	128	5	9	6	-1	1.000	-8	O-43	-0.5
	Yr	90	224	29	66	6	1	3	24	20	18	.295	.358	.371	105	2	18	6	2	.980	-10	O-68	-0.9
1989	SF-N	40	97	5	18	4	0	0	12	5	14	.186	.233	.227	33	-8	2	1	0	1.000	-8	O-30	-1.9
	Det-A	46	158	17	41	10	0	3	26	16	16	.259	.331	.380	102	1	1	1	-0	.986	-1	O-36/D-8	-0.2
1990	Det-A	50	118	15	27	4	1	4	9	6	13	.229	.283	.381	84	-3	1	1	-0	.952	-2	O-27,D-20	-0.6
	Sea-A	25	86	8	26	4	0	2	15	3	12	.302	.341	.419	110	1	0	1	-1	1.000	-1	O-18/D-5	-0.1
	Yr	75	204	23	53	8	1	6	24	9	25	.260	.307	.397	95	-2	1	2	-1	.973	-3	O-45,D-25	-0.7
1991	Sea-A	79	175	30	44	8	1	3	24	18	22	.251	.325	.360	89	-2	2	0	1	1.000	-5	D-37,O-36	-0.9
Total	6	493	1303	173	356	56	6	27	164	100	140	.273	.331	.388	96	-7	62	19	7	.988	-31	O-334/D-70,1-2	-4.4

■ NIPPY JONES Jones, Vernal Leroy b: 6/29/25, Los Angeles, Cal. d: 10/3/95, Sacramento, Cal. BR/TR, 6'1", 185 lbs. Deb: 6/8/46

YEAR	TM/L	G	AB	R	H	2B	3B	HR	RBI	BB	SO	AVG	OBP	SLG	PRO+	BR/A	SB	CS	SBR	FA	FR	G/POS	TPR
1946	*StL-N	16	12	3	4	0	0	0	1	2	2	.333	.429	.333	113	0	0			.800	1	/2-3	0.1
1947	StL-N	23	73	6	18	4	0	1	5	2	10	.247	.267	.342	58	-5	0			.935	-2	2-13/O-2	-0.5
1948	StL-N	132	481	58	122	21	9	10	81	36	45	.254	.307	.397	84	-12	2			.986	-9	*1-128	-2.2
1949	StL-N	110	380	51	114	20	2	8	62	16	20	.300	.330	.426	97	-3	1			.984	-8	1-98	-1.1
1950	StL-N	13	26	0	6	1	0	0	6	3	1	.231	.310	.269	52	-2	0			.983	-1	/1-8	-0.2
1951	StL-N	80	300	20	79	12	0	3	41	9	13	.263	.287	.333	66	-15	1	2	-1	.991	-1	1-71	-2.0
1952	Phi-N	8	30	3	5	0	0	1	5	0	4	.167	.167	.267	19	-3	0	0	0	.976	0	/1-8	-0.3
1957	*Mil-N	30	79	5	21	2	1	2	8	3	7	.266	.293	.392	88	-2	0	0	0	.994	-0	1-20/O-1	-0.3
Total	8	412	1381	146	369	60	12	25	209	71	102	.267	.304	.382	81	-40	4	2		.987	-19	1-333/2-16,O-3	-6.5

■ BILL JONES Jones, William b: Syracuse, N.Y. Deb: 5/17/1882

YEAR	TM/L	G	AB	R	H	2B	3B	HR	RBI	BB	SO	AVG	OBP	SLG	PRO+	BR/A	SB	CS	SBR	FA	FR	G/POS	TPR
1882	Bal-a	4	15	1	1	0	0	0		0		.067	.067	.067	-59	-2				1.000	0	/O-2,C-2	-0.2
1884	Phi-U	4	14	2	2	0	0	0		1		.143	.200	.143	6	-2				.862	0	/C-4,O-1	-0.1
Total	2	8	29	3	3	0	0	0		1		.103	.133	.103	-25	-4				.857	1	/C-6,O-3	-0.3

■ BILL JONES Jones, William Dennis "Midget" b: 4/8/1887, Hartland, N.B., Can. d: 10/10/46, Boston, Mass. BL/TR, 5'6.5", 157 lbs. Deb: 6/20/11

YEAR	TM/L	G	AB	R	H	2B	3B	HR	RBI	BB	SO	AVG	OBP	SLG	PRO+	BR/A	SB	CS	SBR	FA	FR	G/POS	TPR
1911	Bos-N	24	51	6	11	2	1	0	3	15	7	.216	.394	.294	87	-0	1			.867	-1	O-18	-0.2
1912	Bos-N	3	2	0	1	0	0	0	2	0	1	.500	.500	.500	171	0	0			.000	0	H	0.0
Total	2	27	53	6	12	2	1	0	5	15	8	.226	.397	.302	89	-0	1			.867	-1	/O-18	-0.2

■ TEX JONES Jones, William Roderick b: 8/4/1885, Marion, Kan. d: 2/26/38, Wichita, Kan. BR/TR, 6', 192 lbs. Deb: 4/13/11

YEAR	TM/L	G	AB	R	H	2B	3B	HR	RBI	BB	SO	AVG	OBP	SLG	PRO+	BR/A	SB	CS	SBR	FA	FR	G/POS	TPR
1911	Chi-A	9	31	4	6	1	0	0	4	3		.194	.265	.226	39	-3	1			1.000	3	/1-9	0.0

■ TIM JONES Jones, William Timothy b: 12/1/62, Sumter, S.C. BL/TR, 5'10", 175 lbs. Deb: 7/26/88

YEAR	TM/L	G	AB	R	H	2B	3B	HR	RBI	BB	SO	AVG	OBP	SLG	PRO+	BR/A	SB	CS	SBR	FA	FR	G/POS	TPR
1988	StL-N	31	52	2	14	0	0	0	3	4	10	.269	.321	.269	70	-2	4	1	1	.955	5	/S-9,2-8,3-1	0.4
1989	StL-N	42	75	11	22	6	0	0	7	7	8	.293	.361	.373	107	1	1	0	0	1.000	-2	2-12,S-12/3-5,CO	0.0
1990	StL-N	67	128	9	28	7	1	1	12	12	20	.219	.291	.313	66	-6	3	4	-2	.944	2	S-29,2-19/3-6,P-1	-0.4
1991	StL-N	16	24	1	4	2	0	0	2	2	6	.167	.231	.250	35	-2	0	1	-1	1.000	-2	S-14/2-4	-0.5
1992	StL-N	67	145	9	29	4	0	0	3	11	29	.200	.256	.228	39	-11	5	2	0	.972	2	S-34,2-28/3-2,O-1	-0.8
1993	StL-N	29	61	13	16	6	0	0	1	9	8	.262	.366	.361	97	0	2	2	-1	.976	5	S-21/2-7	0.6
Total	6	252	485	45	113	25	1	1	28	45	81	.233	.302	.295	68	-20	15	10	-2	.964	10	S-119/2-78,3OPC	-0.7

■ WILLIE JONES Jones, Willie Edward "Puddin' Head" b: 8/16/25, Dillon, S.C. d: 10/18/83, Cincinnati, Ohio BR/TR, 6'1", 192 lbs. Deb: 9/10/47

YEAR	TM/L	G	AB	R	H	2B	3B	HR	RBI	BB	SO	AVG	OBP	SLG	PRO+	BR/A	SB	CS	SBR	FA	FR	G/POS	TPR
1947	Phi-N	18	62	5	14	0	1	0	10	7	0	.226	.304	.258	53	-4	2			.909	2	3-17	-0.2
1948	Phi-N	17	60	9	20	2	0	2	9	3	5	.333	.365	.467	126	2	0			.926	2	3-17	0.4
1949	Phi-N	149	532	71	130	35	1	19	77	65	66	.244	.328	.421	102	0	3			.948	-4	*3-145	-0.6
1950	*Phi-N★	157	610	100	163	28	6	25	88	61	40	.267	.337	.456	108	6	5			.954	-6	*3-157	-0.3
1951	Phi-N★	148	564	79	161	28	5	22	81	60	47	.285	.358	.470	123	17	6	2	1	.966	-9	*3-147	0.8
1952	Phi-N	147	541	60	135	12	3	18	72	53	36	.250	.323	.383	96	-3	5	3	-0	**.969**	4	*3-147	-0.3
1953	Phi-N	149	481	61	108	16	2	19	70	85	45	.225	.342	.385	90	-6	1	1	-0	**.975**	-3	*3-147	-1.2
1954	Phi-N	142	535	64	145	28	3	12	56	61	54	.271	.346	.402	94	-4	4	1	1	**.968**	-2	*3-141	-0.9
1955	Phi-N	146	516	65	133	20	3	16	81	77	51	.258	.357	.401	103	4	6	2	1	**.960**	-13	*3-146	-0.9
1956	Phi-N	149	520	88	144	20	4	17	78	92	49	.277	.387	.429	121	19	5	4	-1	**.973**	1	*3-149	2.1
1957	Phi-N	133	440	58	96	19	2	9	47	61	41	.218	.313	.332	76	-14	1	0	0	.966	-7	*3-126	-1.9
1958	Phi-N	118	398	52	108	15	1	14	60	49	45	.271	.354	.420	105	4	1	2	-1	**.967**	-13	*3-110/1-1	-1.0
1959	Phi-N	47	160	23	43	9	1	7	24	19	14	.269	.346	.469	113	3	0	0	0	.975	-3	3-46	0.0
	Cle-A	11	18	1	4	1	0	0	1	1	3	.222	.263	.278	51	-1	0	0	0	.929	2	/3-4	0.0
	Cin-N	72	233	33	58	12	1	7	31	28	26	.249	.332	.399	91	-3	0	2	-1	.966	-3	3-68	-0.7
1960	Cin-N	79	149	16	40	7	0	3	27	31	16	.268	.394	.376	110	4	1	0	0	.962	-3	3-46/2-1	0.0
1961	Cin-N	9	7	1	0	0	0	0	0	2	3	.000	.222	.000	-34	-1	0	0	0	.000	-0	/3-1	-0.2
Total	15	1691	5826	786	1502	252	33	190	812	755	541	.258	.345	.410	102	20	40	17		.963	-55	*3-1614/2-1,1-1	-4.9

■ BUBBER JONNARD Jonnard, Clarence James b: 11/23/1897, Nashville, Tenn. d: 8/23/77, New York, N.Y. BR/TR, 6'1", 185 lbs. Deb: 10/1/20 FC

YEAR	TM/L	G	AB	R	H	2B	3B	HR	RBI	BB	SO	AVG	OBP	SLG	PRO+	BR/A	SB	CS	SBR	FA	FR	G/POS	TPR
1920	Chi-A	2	5	0	0	0	0	0	0	0	1	.000	.000	.000	-99	-1	0	0	0	.857	0	/C-1	-0.1
1922	Pit-N	10	21	4	5	0	1	0	2	2	4	.238	.304	.333	64	-1	0	0	0	.974	2	C-10	0.1
1926	Phi-N	19	34	3	4	1	0	0	2	3	4	.118	.189	.147	-8	-5	0			.949	0	C-15	-0.4
1927	Phi-N	53	143	18	42	6	0	0	14	7	7	.294	.327	.336	77	-5	0			.967	-9	C-41	-1.1
1929	StL-N	18	31	1	3	0	0	0	2	0	6	.097	.097	.097	-51	-7	0			.957	1	C-18	-0.5
1935	Phi-N	1	1	0	0	0	0	0	0	0	1	.000	.000	.000	-91	-0	0			1.000	-0	/C-1	0.0
Total	6	103	235	26	54	7	1	0	20	12	23	.230	.267	.268	41	-20	0	0		.960	-6	/C-86	-2.0

■ EDDIE JOOST Joost, Edwin David b: 6/5/16, San Francisco, Cal BR/TR, 6', 175 lbs. Deb: 9/11/36 M

YEAR	TM/L	G	AB	R	H	2B	3B	HR	RBI	BB	SO	AVG	OBP	SLG	PRO+	BR/A	SB	CS	SBR	FA	FR	G/POS	TPR
1936	Cin-N	13	26	1	4	1	0	0	1	2	5	.154	.214	.192	11	-3	0			.947	-1	/S-7,2-5	-0.4
1937	Cin-N	6	12	0	1	0	0	0	0	0	0	.083	.083	.083	-57	-3	0			.875	0	/2-6	-0.2
1939	Cin-N	42	143	23	36	6	3	0	14	12	15	.252	.310	.336	73	-5	1			.957	-3	2-32/S-6	-0.6
1940	*Cin-N	88	278	24	60	7	2	1	24	32	40	.216	.301	.266	57	-15	4			.960	-1	S-78/2-7,3-4	-0.9
1941	Cin-N	152	537	67	136	25	4	4	40	69	59	.253	.340	.337	91	-5	9			.942	-6	*S-147/2-4,1-2,3-1	0.0
1942	Cin-N	142	562	65	126	30	3	6	41	62	57	.224	.307	.320	84	-11	9			.933	-10	*S-130,2-15	-1.4
1943	Bos-N	124	421	34	78	16	3	2	20	68	80	.185	.299	.252	61	-20	5			.945	13	3-67,2-60/S-1	-0.3
1945	Bos-N	35	141	16	35	7	1	0	9	13	7	.248	.312	.312	73	-5	0			.945	-7	2-19,3-16	-1.1
1947	Phi-A	151	540	76	111	22	3	13	64	114	110	.206	.348	.330	87	-6	6	6	-2	.956	-3	*S-151	-0.3
1948	Phi-A	135	509	99	127	22	2	16	55	119	87	.250	.393	.395	110	11	2	4	-2	.973	5	*S-135	2.1
1949	Phi-A★	144	525	128	138	25	3	23	81	149	80	.263	.429	.453	138	36	2	1	0	.969	8	*S-144	5.2
1950	Phi-A	131	476	79	111	12	3	18	58	103	68	.233	.373	.384	96	-1	5	1	1	.956	-7	*S-131	0.3
1951	Phi-A	140	553	107	160	28	5	19	78	106	70	.289	.409	.461	132	28	10	8	-2	.974	4	*S-140	3.9
1952	Phi-A☆	146	540	94	132	26	3	20	75	122	94	.244	.388	.415	116	16	5	8	-3	.962	-7	*S-146	1.7
1953	Phi-A	51	177	39	44	6	0	6	15	45	24	.249	.401	.384	109	4	3	2	-0	.958	-6	S-51	0.1
1954	Phi-A	19	47	7	17	3	0	1	9	10	10	.362	.474	.489	163	5	0	1	-1	.963	-3	/S-9,3-5,2-1,M	0.2
1955	Bos-A	55	119	15	23	2	0	5	17	17	21	.193	.299	.336	65	-6	0	0	0	.932	5	S-20,2-17/3-2	0.1
Total	17	1574	5606	874	1339	238	35	134	601	1043	827	.239	.361	.366	99	18	61	31		.958	-20	*S-1296,2-166/31	8.4

■ DUTCH JORDAN Jordan, Adolf Otto b: 1/5/1880, Pittsburgh, Pa. d: 12/23/72, W.Allegheny, Pa. BR/TR, 5'10", 185 lbs. Deb: 4/25/03

YEAR	TM/L	G	AB	R	H	2B	3B	HR	RBI	BB	SO	AVG	OBP	SLG	PRO+	BR/A	SB	CS	SBR	FA	FR	G/POS	TPR
1903	Bro-N	78	267	27	63	11	1	0	21	19		.236	.289	.285	66	-12	9			.928	-14	2-54,3-18/O-4,1-1	-2.3
1904	Bro-N	87	252	21	45	10	2	0	19	13		.179	.225	.234	43	-17	7			.958	-17	2-70,3-11/1-4	-3.5
Total	2	165	519	48	108	21	3	0	40	32		.208	.258	.260	55	-29	16			.945	-31	2-124/3-29,1-5,O-4	-5.8

■ BUCK JORDAN Jordan, Baxter Byerly b: 1/16/07, Cooleemee, N.C. d: 3/18/93, Salisbury, N.C. BL/TR, 6', 170 lbs. Deb: 9/15/27

YEAR	TM/L	G	AB	R	H	2B	3B	HR	RBI	BB	SO	AVG	OBP	SLG	PRO+	BR/A	SB	CS	SBR	FA	FR	G/POS	TPR
1927	NY-N	5	5	0	1	0	0	0	0	0	3	.200	.200	.200	7	-1	0			.000	0	H	-0.1
1929	NY-N	2	2	1	1	1	0	0	0	0	0	.500	.500	1.000	262	0	0			1.000	-0	/1-1	0.0
1931	Was-A	9	18	3	4	2	0	0	1	1	3	.222	.263	.333	56	-1	0	0	0	.978	-1	/1-7	-0.2
1932	Bos-N	49	212	27	68	12	3	2	29	4	5	.321	.333	.434	109	2	1			.991	-1	1-49	-0.3
1933	Bos-N	152	588	77	168	29	9	4	46	34	22	.286	.327	.386	112	7	4			.991	-3	*1-150	-1.1
1934	Bos-N	124	489	68	152	26	9	2	58	35	19	.311	.358	.413	114	9	3			.989	-3	*1-117	-0.4
1935	Bos-N	130	470	62	131	24	5	5	35	19	17	.279	.307	.383	91	-7	3			.983	1	1-95/3-8,O-2	-1.6
1936	Bos-N	138	555	81	179	27	5	3	66	45	22	.323	.375	.405	118	14	2			.993	1	*1-136	0.2
1937	Bos-N	8	8	1	2	0	0	0	0	0	0	.250	.250	.250	40	-1	0			.000	0	H	-0.1
	Cin-N	98	316	45	89	14	3	1	28	25	14	.282	.334	.354	92	-4	6			.989	-2	1-76	-1.4
	Yr	106	324	46	91	14	3	1	28	25	14	.281	.332	.352	91	-4	6			.989	-2	1-76	-1.5
1938	Cin-N	9	7	0	2	0	0	0	0	2	0	.286	.444	.286	107	0	0			.000	0	H	0.0
	Phi-N	87	310	31	93	18	1	0	18	17	4	.300	.336	.365	95	-2	1			.973	-4	3-58,1-17	-0.7
	Yr	96	317	31	95	18	1	0	18	19	4	.300	.339	.363	96	-2	1			.973	-4	3-58,1-17	-0.7
Total	10	811	2980	396	890	153	35	17	281	182	109	.299	.340	.391	106	18	20	0		.990	-12	1-648/3-66,O-2	-5.7

■ BRIAN JORDAN Jordan, Brian O'Neal b: 3/29/67, Baltimore, Md. BR/TR, 6'1", 205 lbs. Deb: 4/8/92

YEAR	TM/L	G	AB	R	H	2B	3B	HR	RBI	BB	SO	AVG	OBP	SLG	PRO+	BR/A	SB	CS	SBR	FA	FR	G/POS	TPR
1992	StL-N	55	193	17	40	9	4	5	22	10	48	.207	.250	.373	77	-7	7	2	1	.991	-1	O-53	-0.8
1993	StL-N	67	223	33	69	10	6	10	44	12	35	.309	.356	.543	139	11	6	6	-2	.973	-3	O-65	0.5
1994	StL-N	53	178	14	46	8	2	5	15	16	40	.258	.323	.410	91	-3	4	3	-1	.991	5	O-46/1-1	0.1
1995	StL-N	131	490	83	145	20	4	22	81	22	79	.296	.340	.488	116	9	24	9	2	.996	4	*O-126	1.1
1996	*StL-N	140	513	82	159	36	1	17	104	29	84	.310	.355	.483	120	14	22	5	4	.994	13	*O-136/1-1	2.6
1997	StL-N	47	145	17	34	5	0	0	10	10	21	.234	.311	.269	54	-9	6	1	1	1.000	1	O-44	-0.8
1998	StL-N	150	564	100	178	34	7	25	91	40	66	.316	.370	.534	132	26	17	5	2	.970	1	*O-141/3-1,D-3	2.7
Total	7	643	2306	346	671	122	24	84	367	139	373	.291	.342	.474	114	41	86	31	7	.987	20	O-611/D-3,1-2,3-1	5.4

■ SLATS JORDAN Jordan, Clarence Veasey b: 9/26/1879, Baltimore, Md. d: 12/7/53, Catonsville, Md. BL/TL, 6'1", 190 lbs. Deb: 9/28/01

YEAR	TM/L	G	AB	R	H	2B	3B	HR	RBI	BB	SO	AVG	OBP	SLG	PRO+	BR/A	SB	CS	SBR	FA	FR	G/POS	TPR
1901	Bal-A	1	3	0	0	0	0	0	0	0		.000	.000	.000	-96	-1	0			.867	-1	/1-1	-0.1
1902	Bal-A	1	4	0	0	0	0	0	0	0		.000	.000	.000	-96	-1	0			.000	-0	/O-1	-0.1
Total	2	2	7	0	0	0	0	0	0	0		.000	.000	.000	-96	-2	0			—	-1	/O-1,1-1	-0.2

■ JIMMY JORDAN Jordan, James William "Lord" b: 1/13/08, Tucapau, S.C. d: 12/4/57, Gastonia, N.C. BR/TR, 5'9", 157 lbs. Deb: 4/20/33

YEAR	TM/L	G	AB	R	H	2B	3B	HR	RBI	BB	SO	AVG	OBP	SLG	PRO+	BR/A	SB	CS	SBR	FA	FR	G/POS	TPR
1933	Bro-N	70	211	16	54	12	1	0	17	4	6	.256	.270	.322	71	-8	3			.969	12	S-51,2-11	0.7
1934	Bro-N	97	369	34	98	17	2	0	43	9	32	.266	.285	.322	66	-19	1			.956	-13	S-51,2-41/3-9	-2.6
1935	Bro-N	94	295	26	82	7	0	0	30	9	17	.278	.302	.302	64	-15	3			.983	27	2-46,S-28/3-5	1.6
1936	Bro-N	115	398	26	93	15	1	2	28	15	21	.234	.262	.291	48	-29	1			.970	-17	2-98/S-9,3-6	-3.9
Total	4	376	1273	102	327	51	4	2	118	37	76	.257	.279	.308	60	-71	8			.969	8	2-196,S-139/3-20	-4.2

■ KEVIN JORDAN Jordan, Kevin Wayne b: 10/9/69, San Francisco, Cal. BR/TR, 6'1", 185 lbs. Deb: 8/8/95

YEAR	TM/L	G	AB	R	H	2B	3B	HR	RBI	BB	SO	AVG	OBP	SLG	PRO+	BR/A	SB	CS	SBR	FA	FR	G/POS	TPR
1995	Phi-N	24	54	6	10	1	0	2	6	2	9	.185	.228	.315	41	-5	0	0	0	.984	6	/2-9,3-1	0.1
1996	Phi-N	43	131	15	37	10	0	3	12	5	20	.282	.314	.427	92	-2	2	1	0	1.000	-2	1-30/2-7,3-1	-0.6
1997	Phi-N	84	177	19	47	8	0	6	30	3	26	.266	.278	.412	78	-6	0	1	-1	.987	-5	1-25,3-12/2-6,D-1	-1.4
1998	Phi-N	112	250	23	69	13	0	2	27	8	30	.276	.304	.352	68	-12	0	0	0	1.000	0	1-24,2-22/3-6,D-8	-1.1
Total	4	263	612	63	163	32	0	13	75	18	85	.266	.292	.382	74	-24	2	2	-1	.996	-1	/1-79,2-44,3-20,D-9	-3.0

■ MIKE JORDAN Jordan, Michael Henry "Mitty" b: 2/7/1863, Lawrence, Mass. d: 9/25/40, Lawrence, Mass. 5'7.5", 155 lbs. Deb: 8/21/1890

YEAR	TM/L	G	AB	R	H	2B	3B	HR	RBI	BB	SO	AVG	OBP	SLG	PRO+	BR/A	SB	CS	SBR	FA	FR	G/POS	TPR
1890	Pit-N	37	125	8	12	1	0	0	6	15	19	.096	.210	.104	-9	-17	5			.947	2	O-37	-1.4

■ RICKY JORDAN Jordan, Paul Scott b: 5/26/65, Richmond, Cal. BR/TR, 6'3", 209 lbs. Deb: 7/17/88

YEAR	TM/L	G	AB	R	H	2B	3B	HR	RBI	BB	SO	AVG	OBP	SLG	PRO+	BR/A	SB	CS	SBR	FA	FR	G/POS	TPR
1988	Phi-N	69	273	41	84	15	1	11	43	7	39	.308	.325	.491	128	9	1	1	-0	.992	-5	1-69	-0.3
1989	Phi-N	144	523	63	149	22	3	12	75	23	62	.285	.321	.407	107	3	4	3	-1	.993	-11	*1-140	-2.1
1990	Phi-N	92	324	32	78	21	0	5	44	13	39	.241	.281	.352	73	-13	2	0	1	.995	-8	1-84	-2.7
1991	Phi-N	101	301	38	82	21	3	9	49	14	49	.272	.309	.452	113	4	0	2	-1	.987	-6	1-72	-0.8
1992	Phi-N	94	276	33	84	19	0	4	34	5	44	.304	.317	.417	106	1	3	0	1	.995	-6	1-54,O-11	-0.8
1993	*Phi-N	90	159	21	46	4	1	5	18	8	32	.289	.327	.421	100	-0	0	0	0	.990	-5	1-33	-0.8
1994	Phi-N	72	220	29	62	14	2	8	37	6	32	.282	.304	.473	96	-2	0	0	0	.993	-8	1-49	-1.4
1996	Sea-A	15	28	4	7	0	0	1	4	1	6	.250	.300	.357	65	-2	0	0	0	1.000	-1	/1-9,D-2	-0.3
Total	8	677	2104	261	592	116	10	55	304	77	303	.281	.311	.424	103	0	10	6	-1	.993	-49	1-510/O-11,D-2	-9.2

■ SCOTT JORDAN Jordan, Scott Allan b: 5/27/63, Waco, Tex. BR/TR, 6', 175 lbs. Deb: 9/2/88

YEAR	TM/L	G	AB	R	H	2B	3B	HR	RBI	BB	SO	AVG	OBP	SLG	PRO+	BR/A	SB	CS	SBR	FA	FR	G/POS	TPR
1988	Cle-A	7	9	0	1	0	0	0	1	0	3	.111	.111	.111	-37	-2	0	0	0	1.000	-1	/O-6	-0.3

■ TOM JORDAN Jordan, Thomas Jefferson b: 9/5/19, Lawton, Okla. BR/TR, 6'1.5", 195 lbs. Deb: 9/4/44

YEAR	TM/L	G	AB	R	H	2B	3B	HR	RBI	BB	SO	AVG	OBP	SLG	PRO+	BR/A	SB	CS	SBR	FA	FR	G/POS	TPR
1944	Chi-A	14	45	2	12	1	1	0	3	1	0	.267	.283	.333	77	-2	0	0	0	.947	-1	C-14	-0.2
1946	Chi-A	10	15	1	4	2	1	0	0	0	1	.267	.267	.533	124	0	0	0	0	1.000	1	/C-2	0.1
	Cle-A	14	35	2	7	1	0	1	3	3	1	.200	.263	.314	65	-2	1	1	-0	.974	-6	C-13	-0.8
	Yr	24	50	3	11	3	1	1	3	3	2	.220	.264	.380	83	-2	1	1	-0	.980	-5	C-15	-0.7
1948	StL-A	1	1	0	0	0	0	0	0	0	0	.000	.000	.000	-97	-0	0	0	-0	.000	0	H	0.0
Total	3	39	96	5	23	4	2	1	6	4	2	.240	.270	.354	78	-3	1	1	-0	.963	-6	/C-29	-0.9

■ TIM JORDAN Jordan, Timothy Joseph b: 2/14/1879, New York, N.Y. d: 9/13/49, Bronx, N.Y. BL/TL, 6'1", 170 lbs. Deb: 8/10/01

YEAR	TM/L	G	AB	R	H	2B	3B	HR	RBI	BB	SO	AVG	OBP	SLG	PRO+	BR/A	SB	CS	SBR	FA	FR	G/POS	TPR
1901	Was-A	6	20	2	4	1	0	0	2	3		.200	.304	.250	56	-1	0			.941	-1	/1-6	-0.2
1903	NY-A	2	8	2	1	0	0	0	0	0		.125	.125	.125	-23	-1	0			.889	-1	/1-2	-0.2
1906	Bro-N	129	450	67	118	20	8	**12**	78	59		.262	.352	.422	153	27	16			.978	-9	*1-126	1.5
1907	Bro-N	147	485	43	133	15	8	4	53	74		.274	.371	.363	141	25	10			.980	-6	*1-143	1.8

YEAR	TM/L	G	AB	R	H	2B	3B	HR	RBI	BB	SO	AVG	OBP	SLG	PRO+	BR/A	SB	CS	SBR	FA	FR	G/POS	TPR
1908	Bro-N	148	515	58	127	18	5	**12**	60	59		.247	.328	.371	128	16	9			.982	-15	*1-146	-0.2
1909	Bro-N	103	330	47	90	20	3	3	36	59		.273	.386	.379	142	19	13			.983	-9	1-95	1.0
1910	Bro-N	5	5	1	1	0	0	1	3	0	2	.200	.200	.800	195	0	0			.000	0	H	0.0
Total	7	540	1813	220	474	74	24	32	232	254	2	.261	.355	.382	139	86	48			.980	-41	1-518	3.7

■ ART JORGENS

Jorgens, Arndt Ludwig b: 5/18/05, Modum, Norway d: 3/1/80, Evanston, Ill. BR/TR, 5'9", 160 lbs. Deb: 4/26/29 F

YEAR	TM/L	G	AB	R	H	2B	3B	HR	RBI	BB	SO	AVG	OBP	SLG	PRO+	BR/A	SB	CS	SBR	FA	FR	G/POS	TPR
1929	NY-A	18	34	6	11	3	0	0	4	6	7	.324	.425	.412	125	2	0	2	-1	.979	-0	C-15	0.1
1930	NY-A	16	30	7	11	3	0	0	1	2	4	.367	.406	.467	126	1	0	0	0	.960	-0	C-16	0.2
1931	NY-A	46	100	12	27	1	2	0	14	9	3	.270	.330	.320	76	-3	0	1	-1	.962	-1	C-40	-0.3
1932	NY-A	56	151	13	33	7	1	2	19	14	11	.219	.285	.318	59	-10	0	0	0	.967	0	C-56	-0.6
1933	NY-A	21	50	9	11	3	0	2	13	12	3	.220	.371	.400	111	1	1	0	0	.982	2	C-19	0.4
1934	NY-A	58	183	14	38	6	1	0	20	23	24	.208	.296	.251	45	-15	2	0	1	.984	6	C-56	-0.5
1935	NY-A	36	84	6	20	2	0	0	8	12	10	.238	.333	.262	59	-5	0	0	0	1.000	6	C-33	0.2
1936	NY-A	31	66	5	18	3	1	0	5	2	3	.273	.294	.348	60	-4	0	0	0	.990	3	C-30	-0.1
1937	NY-A	13	23	3	3	1	0	0	3	2	5	.130	.200	.174	-5	-4	0	0	0	1.000	0	C-11	-0.3
1938	NY-A	9	17	3	4	2	0	0	2	3	3	.235	.350	.353	77	-1	0	0	0	.923	1	/C-8	0.0
1939	NY-A	3	0	1	0	0	0	0	0	0	0	—	—	—	—	0	0	0	0	1.000	0	/C-2	0.0
Total	11	307	738	79	176	31	5	4	89	85	73	.238	.317	.310	66	-37	3	3	-1	.978	17	C-286	-0.9

■ PINKY JORGENSEN

Jorgensen, Carl b: 11/21/14, Laton, Cal. BR/TR, 6'1", 195 lbs. Deb: 9/14/37

YEAR	TM/L	G	AB	R	H	2B	3B	HR	RBI	BB	SO	AVG	OBP	SLG	PRO+	BR/A	SB	CS	SBR	FA	FR	G/POS	TPR
1937	Cin-N	6	14	1	4	0	0	0	1	1	2	.286	.333	.286	73	-0	0			.875	0	/O-4	-0.1

■ SPIDER JORGENSEN

Jorgensen, John Donald b: 11/3/19, Folsom, Cal. BL/TR, 5'9", 155 lbs. Deb: 4/15/47

YEAR	TM/L	G	AB	R	H	2B	3B	HR	RBI	BB	SO	AVG	OBP	SLG	PRO+	BR/A	SB	CS	SBR	FA	FR	G/POS	TPR
1947	*Bro-N	129	441	57	121	29	8	5	67	58	45	.274	.360	.410	100	1	4			.949	-5	*3-128	-0.3
1948	Bro-N	31	90	15	27	6	2	1	13	16	13	.300	.411	.444	127	4	1			.887	-6	3-24	-0.3
1949	*Bro-N	53	134	15	36	5	1	1	14	23	13	.269	.376	.343	90	-1	0			.946	-5	3-36	-0.6
1950	Bro-N	2	2	0	0	0	0	0	1	1	0	.000	.333	.000	-4	-0	0			1.000	-0	/3-1	0.0
	NY-N	24	37	5	5	0	0	0	4	5	2	.135	.238	.135	1	-5	0			.913	1	/3-5	-0.4
	Yr	26	39	5	5	0	0	0	5	6	2	.128	.244	.128	1	-6	0			.917	1	/3-6	-0.4
1951	NY-N	28	51	5	12	0	0	2	8	3	2	.235	.291	.353	72	-2	0	0	0	1.000	-2	O-11/3-1	-0.5
Total	5	267	755	97	201	40	11	9	107	106	75	.266	.359	.384	95	-4	5	0		.940	-17	3-195/O-11	-2.1

■ MIKE JORGENSEN

Jorgensen, Michael b: 8/16/48, Passaic, N.J. BL/TL, 6', 195 lbs. Deb: 9/10/68 M

YEAR	TM/L	G	AB	R	H	2B	3B	HR	RBI	BB	SO	AVG	OBP	SLG	PRO+	BR/A	SB	CS	SBR	FA	FR	G/POS	TPR
1968	NY-N	8	14	0	2	1	0	0	0	0	4	.143	.143	.214	6	-2	0	0	0	1.000	-0	/1-4	-0.2
1970	NY-N	76	87	15	17	3	1	3	4	10	23	.195	.278	.356	69	-4	2	2	-1	.992	3	1-50,O-10	-0.3
1971	NY-N	45	118	16	26	1	1	5	11	11	24	.220	.303	.373	92	-1	1	2	-1	.951	-2	O-31/1-1	-0.6
1972	Mon-N	113	372	48	86	12	3	13	47	53	75	.231	.333	.384	102	1	12	13	-4	.995	0	1-76,O-28	-1.1
1973	Mon-N	138	413	49	95	16	2	9	47	64	49	.230	.338	.344	86	-6	16	7	1	**.995**	4	*1-123,O-11	-1.1
1974	Mon-N	131	287	45	89	16	1	11	59	70	39	.310	.448	.488	153	24	3	5	-2	.998	7	1-91,O-29	2.5
1975	Mon-N	144	445	58	116	18	0	18	67	79	75	.261	.380	.422	117	13	3	3	-1	.994	3	*1-133/O-6	0.7
1976	Mon-N	125	343	36	87	13	0	6	23	52	48	.254	.352	.344	94	-1	7	1	2	.989	0	1-81,O-41	-0.5
1977	Mon-N	19	20	3	4	1	0	0	0	3	4	.200	.304	.250	52	-1	0	0	0	1.000	1	/1-5	0.0
	Oak-A	66	203	18	50	4	1	8	32	25	44	.246	.335	.394	99	0	3	2	-0	.989	1	1-48,O-20/D-2	-0.3
1978	Tex-A	96	97	20	19	3	0	1	9	18	10	.196	.322	.258	65	-4	3	1	0	.994	6	1-78/O-9,D-1	0.1
1979	Tex-A	90	157	21	35	7	0	6	16	14	29	.223	.295	.382	82	-4	0	2	-1	.988	2	1-60,O-20/D-2	-0.6
1980	NY-N	119	321	43	82	11	0	7	43	46	55	.255	.349	.355	100	1	0	3	-2	.995	-1	1-72,O-31	-0.7
1981	NY-N	86	122	8	25	5	2	3	15	12	24	.205	.276	.352	79	-4	4	0	1	.991	1	1-40,O-19	-0.4
1982	NY-N	120	114	16	29	6	0	2	14	21	24	.254	.370	.360	106	2	2	0	1	.991	-3	1-56,O-16	-0.1
1983	NY-N	38	24	5	6	3	0	1	3	2	4	.250	.333	.500	129	1	0	1	-1	1.000	1	1-19	0.1
	Atl-N	57	48	5	12	1	0	1	8	8	8	.250	.357	.333	86	-1	0	0	0	1.000	-0	1-19/O-6	-0.1
	Yr	95	72	10	18	4	0	2	11	10	12	.250	.349	.389	100	0	0	1	-1	1.000	1	1-38/O-6	0.0
1984	Atl-N	31	26	4	7	1	0	0	5	3	6	.269	.345	.308	79	-1	0	1	-1	1.000	-1	/1-8,O-4	-0.3
	StL-N	59	98	5	24	4	2	1	12	10	17	.245	.315	.357	91	-1	0	0	0	.991	2	1-39	-0.1
	Yr	90	124	9	31	5	2	1	17	13	23	.250	.321	.347	87	-2	0	1	-1	.992	0	1-47/O-4	-0.4
1985	*StL-N	72	112	14	22	6	0	0	11	31	27	.196	.375	.250	79	-1	2	1	0	.994	-2	1-49/O-2	-0.6
Total	17	1633	3421	429	833	132	13	95	426	532	589	.243	.349	.373	100	10	58	44	-9	.994	22	*1-1052,O-283/D-5	-3.6

■ TERRY JORGENSEN

Jorgensen, Terry Allen b: 9/2/66, Kewaunee, Wis. BR/TR, 6'4", 208 lbs. Deb: 9/10/89

YEAR	TM/L	G	AB	R	H	2B	3B	HR	RBI	BB	SO	AVG	OBP	SLG	PRO+	BR/A	SB	CS	SBR	FA	FR	G/POS	TPR
1989	Min-A	10	23	1	4	1	0	0	2	4	5	.174	.296	.217	44	-2	0	0	0	.958	3	/3-9	0.2
1992	Min-A	22	58	5	18	1	0	0	5	3	11	.310	.355	.328	89	-1	1	2	-1	1.000	2	1-13/3-9,S-2	0.0
1993	Min-A	59	152	15	34	7	0	1	12	10	21	.224	.272	.289	51	-11	1	0	0	.982	8	3-45/1-9,S-6	-0.2
Total	3	91	233	21	56	9	0	1	19	17	37	.240	.295	.292	60	-13	2	2	-1	.975	14	/3-63,1-22,S-8	0.0

■ FELIX JOSE

Jose, Domingo Felix Andujar (b: Domingo Felix Andujar (Jose)) b: 5/2/65, Santo Domingo, D.R. BB/TR, 6'1", 190 lbs. Deb: 9/2/88

YEAR	TM/L	G	AB	R	H	2B	3B	HR	RBI	BB	SO	AVG	OBP	SLG	PRO+	BR/A	SB	CS	SBR	FA	FR	G/POS	TPR
1988	Oak-A	8	6	2	2	1	0	0	1	0	1	.333	.333	.500	135	0	1	0	0	1.000	-1	/O-6	0.0
1989	Oak-A	20	57	3	11	2	0	0	5	4	13	.193	.246	.228	36	-5	0	1	-1	.974	-0	O-19	-0.6
1990	Oak-A	101	341	42	90	12	0	8	39	16	65	.264	.307	.370	92	-4	8	2	1	.977	0	O-92/D-7	-0.5
	StL-N	25	85	12	23	4	1	3	13	8	16	.271	.333	.447	112	1	4	4	-1	1.000	-2	O-23	-0.2
1991	StL-N★	154	568	69	173	40	6	8	77	50	113	.305	.363	.438	123	18	20	12	-1	.990	4	*O-153	1.8
1992	StL-N	131	509	62	150	22	3	14	75	40	100	.295	.347	.432	123	15	28	12	1	.979	11	*O-127	2.6
1993	KC-A	149	499	64	126	24	3	6	43	36	95	.253	.304	.349	71	-21	31	13	2	.972	-10	*O-144/D-1	-3.2
1994	KC-A	99	366	56	111	28	1	11	55	35	75	.303	.364	.475	110	5	10	12	-4	.980	2	O-98	0.1
1995	KC-A	9	30	2	4	1	0	0	1	2	9	.133	.188	.167	-7	-5	0	0	0	1.000	2	/O-7	-0.3
Total	8	696	2461	312	690	134	14	50	309	191	487	.280	.334	.407	102	4	102	56	-3	.981	6	O-669/D-8	-0.3

■ RICK JOSEPH

Joseph, Ricardo Emelindo (Harrigan) b: 8/24/39, San Pedro De Macoris, D.R. d: 9/8/79, Santiago, D.R. BR/TR, 6'1", 195 lbs. Deb: 6/18/64

YEAR	TM/L	G	AB	R	H	2B	3B	HR	RBI	BB	SO	AVG	OBP	SLG	PRO+	BR/A	SB	CS	SBR	FA	FR	G/POS	TPR
1964	KC-A	17	54	3	12	2	0	0	1	3	11	.222	.263	.259	45	-4	0	1	-1	.981	-1	1-12/3-3	-0.7
1967	Phi-N	17	41	4	9	2	0	1	5	4	10	.220	.289	.341	79	-1	0	0	0	1.000	1	1-13	0.0
1968	Phi-N	66	155	20	34	5	0	3	12	16	35	.219	.297	.310	82	-3	0	1	-1	.992	1	1-30,3-14/O-1	-0.6
1969	Phi-N	99	264	35	72	15	0	6	37	22	57	.273	.331	.398	106	2	2	1	0	.956	7	3-58,1-17/2-1	0.8
1970	Phi-N	71	119	7	27	2	1	3	10	6	28	.227	.264	.336	61	-7	0	0	0	.917	-5	O-12,1-10/3-9	-1.3
Total	5	270	633	69	154	26	1	13	65	51	141	.243	.302	.349	85	-13	2	3	-1	.933	2	/3-84,1-82,O-13,2-1	-1.8

■ DUANE JOSEPHSON

Josephson, Duane Charles b: 6/3/42, New Hampton, Iowa d: 1/30/97, New Hampton, Iowa BR/TR, 6', 195 lbs. Deb: 9/15/65

YEAR	TM/L	G	AB	R	H	2B	3B	HR	RBI	BB	SO	AVG	OBP	SLG	PRO+	BR/A	SB	CS	SBR	FA	FR	G/POS	TPR
1965	Chi-A	4	9	2	1	0	0	0	0	2	4	.111	.273	.111	14	-1	0	0	0	1.000	1	/C-4	0.0
1966	Chi-A	11	38	3	9	1	0	0	3	3	3	.237	.293	.263	65	-2	0	0	0	.974	3	C-11	0.2
1967	Chi-A	62	189	11	45	5	1	1	9	6	24	.238	.262	.291	65	-9	0	3	-2	1.000	-6	C-59	-1.4
1968	Chi-A★	128	434	35	107	16	6	6	45	18	52	.247	.286	.353	92	-5	2	4	-2	.990	12	*C-122	1.5
1969	Chi-A	52	162	19	39	6	2	1	20	13	17	.241	.301	.321	71	-6	0	0	0	.984	-1	C-47	-0.5
1970	Chi-A	96	285	28	90	12	1	4	41	24	28	.316	.375	.407	111	5	0	1	-1	.985	-11	C-84	-0.3
1971	Bos-A	91	306	38	75	14	1	10	39	22	35	.245	.296	.395	88	-6	2	0	1	.989	-4	C-87	-0.7
1972	Bos-A	26	82	11	22	4	1	1	7	4	11	.268	.310	.378	99	-0	0	2	-1	.980	-1	1-16/C-6	-0.4
Total	8	470	1505	147	388	58	12	23	164	92	174	.258	.305	.358	89	-24	4	10	-5	.989	-7	C-420/1-16	-1.6

■ VON JOSHUA

Joshua, Von Everett b: 5/1/48, Oakland, Cal. BL/TL, 5'10", 170 lbs. Deb: 9/2/69 C

YEAR	TM/L	G	AB	R	H	2B	3B	HR	RBI	BB	SO	AVG	OBP	SLG	PRO+	BR/A	SB	CS	SBR	FA	FR	G/POS	TPR
1969	LA-N	14	8	2	2	0	0	0	0	0	2	.250	.250	.250	43	-1	1	0	0	.800	-2	/O-8	-0.3
1970	LA-N	72	109	23	29	1	3	1	8	6	24	.266	.304	.358	80	-3	2	2	-1	.941	-8	O-41	-1.3
1971	LA-N	11	7	2	0	0	0	0	0	0	1	.000	.000	.000	-99	-2	0	0	0	1.000	-1	/O-5	-0.3
1973	LA-N	75	159	19	40	4	1	2	17	8	29	.252	.292	.327	74	-6	7	2	1	.984	-5	O-46	-1.2
1974	*LA-N	81	124	11	29	5	1	1	16	7	17	.234	.280	.315	69	-5	3	2	-0	.943	-9	O-35	-1.6
1975	SF-N	129	507	75	161	25	10	7	43	32	75	.318	.359	.448	118	11	20	10	0	**.993**	6	*O-117	1.3

YEAR	TM/L	G	AB	R	H	2B	3B	HR	RBI	BB	SO	AVG	OBP	SLG	PRO+	BR/A	SB	CS	SBR	FA	FR	G/POS	TPR
1976	SF-N	42	156	13	41	5	2	0	2	4	20	.263	.281	.321	68	-7	1	3	-2	.948	-3	O-35	-1.3
	Mil-A	107	423	44	113	13	5	5	28	18	58	.267	.297	.357	93	-5	8	10	-4	.982	6	*O-105/D-1	-0.8
1977	Mil-A	144	536	58	140	25	7	9	49	21	74	.261	.289	.384	82	-15	12	9	-2	.970	-6	*O-140	-2.8
1979	LA-N	94	142	22	40	7	1	3	14	7	23	.282	.315	.408	97	-1	1	1	-0	.967	-9	O-46	-1.1
1980	SD-N	53	63	8	15	2	1	2	7	5	15	.238	.294	.397	97	-1	0	1	-1	1.000	-2	O-12/1-2	-0.3
Total	10	822	2234	277	610	87	31	30	184	108	338	.273	.307	.380	91	-34	55	40	-8	.975	-31	O-590/1-2,D-1	-9.7
■ **TED JOURDAN**	Jourdan, Theodore Charles b: 9/5/1895, New Orleans, La. d: 9/23/61, New Orleans, La. BL/TL, 6', 175 lbs. Deb: 9/18/16																						
1916	Chi-A	3	2	0	0	0	0	0	0	1	1	.000	.333	.000	1	-0	2			.000	0	H	0.0
1917	Chi-A	17	34	2	5	0	1	0	2	1	3	.147	.171	.206	15	-4	0			.973	-0	1-14	-0.5
1918	Chi-A	7	10	1	1	0	0	0	1	0	0	.100	.100	.100	-39	-2	0			1.000	-0	/1-2	-0.2
1920	Chi-A	48	150	16	36	5	2	0	8	17	17	.240	.337	.300	70	-6	3	2	-0	.982	-4	1-40	-1.1
Total	4	75	196	19	42	5	3	0	11	19	21	.214	.300	.270	56	-11	5	2		.981	-4	/1-56	-1.8
■ **POP JOY**	Joy, Aloysius C. b: 6/11/1860, Washington, D.C. d: 6/28/37, Washington, D.C. Deb: 6/3/1884																						
1884	Was-U	36	130	12	28	0	0	0		2		.215	.227	.215	36	-14				.966	0	1-36	-1.6
■ **JOYCE**	Joyce Deb: 8/14/1886																						
1886	Was-N	1	0	0	0	0	0	0	0	0	0	—	—	—	—	0	0			.000	-0	/O-1	0.0
■ **BILL JOYCE**	Joyce, William Michael "Scrappy Bill" b: 9/21/1865, St.Louis, Mo. d: 5/8/41, St.Louis, Mo. BL/TR, 5'11", 185 lbs. Deb: 4/19/1890 M																						
1890	Bro-P	133	489	121	123	18	18	1	78	**123**	77	.252	.413	.368	103	6	43			.811	-11	*3-133	0.0
1891	Bos-a	65	243	76	75	9	15	3	51	63	27	.309	.460	.506	179	29	36			.849	-1	3-64/1-1	2.6
1892	Bro-N	97	372	89	91	15	12	6	45	82	55	.245	.392	.398	144	25	23			.862	-19	3-94/O-3	0.8
1894	Was-N	99	355	103	126	25	14	17	89	87	33	.355	.496	.648	**180**	51	21			.866	-3	*3-99	3.7
1895	Was-N	126	474	110	148	25	13	17	95	**96**	54	.312	.442	.527	151	40	29			.844	-9	*3-126	2.7
1896	Was-N	81	310	85	97	16	10	8	51	67	20	.313	.454	.506	153	28	32			.888	-7	3-48,2-33	2.0
	NY-N	49	165	36	61	9	2	5	43	34	14	.370	.500	.539	179	22	13			.883	0	3-49,M	2.0
	Yr	130	475	121	158	25	12	**13**	94	101	34	.333	.470	.518	162	50	45			.885	-7	3-97,2-33	4.0
1897	NY-N	109	388	109	118	15	13	3	64	78		.304	.441	.433	135	26	33			.852	-1	*3-106/1-2,M	2.3
1898	NY-N	145	508	91	131	20	9	10	91	88		.258	.386	.392	127	22	34			.966	8	*1-130,3-14/2-2,M	2.8
Total	8	904	3304	820	970	152	106	70	607	718	280	.294	.435	.467	144	249	264			.851	-41	3-733,1-133/2-35,O	18.9
■ **WALLY JOYNER**	Joyner, Wallace Keith b: 6/16/62, Atlanta, Ga. BL/TL, 6'2", 203 lbs. Deb: 4/8/86																						
1986	*Cal-A★	154	593	82	172	27	3	22	100	57	58	.290	.354	.457	120	16	5	2	0	.989	9	*1-152	1.4
1987	Cal-A	149	564	100	161	33	1	34	117	72	64	.285	.371	.528	140	32	8	2	1	.993	-7	*1-149	1.5
1988	Cal-A	158	597	81	176	31	2	13	85	55	51	.295	.359	.419	120	17	8	2	1	.995	12	*1-156	1.7
1989	Cal-A	159	593	78	167	30	2	16	79	46	58	.282	.340	.420	115	11	3	2	-0	**.997**	-4	*1-159	-0.6
1990	Cal-A	83	310	35	83	15	0	8	41	41	34	.268	.355	.394	111	5	2	1	0	.995	2	1-83	0.1
1991	Cal-A	143	551	79	166	34	3	21	96	52	66	.301	.363	.488	133	24	2	0	1	.994	1	*1-141	1.6
1992	KC-A	149	572	66	154	36	2	9	66	55	50	.269	.338	.386	100	-0	11	5	0	.993	14	*1-145/D-4	0.4
1993	KC-A	141	497	83	145	36	3	15	65	66	67	.292	.378	.467	119	14	5	9	-4	.994	20	*1-140	1.8
1994	KC-A	97	363	52	113	20	3	8	57	47	43	.311	.390	.449	111	7	3	2	-0	.991	3	1-86,D-11	0.1
1995	KC-A	131	465	69	144	28	0	12	83	69	65	.310	.401	.447	119	15	3	2	-0	**.998**	12	*1-126/D-2	1.5
1996	*SD-N	121	433	59	120	29	1	8	65	69	71	.277	.380	.404	114	11	5	3	-0	**.997**	4	*1-119	0.3
1997	SD-N	135	455	59	149	29	2	13	83	51	51	.327	.398	.486	140	27	3	5	-2	**.996**	1	*1-131	1.3
1998	*SD-N	131	439	58	131	30	1	12	80	51	44	.298	.373	.453	125	16	1	2	-1	.993	-1	*1-127	0.4
Total	13	1751	6432	901	1881	378	23	191	1017	731	722	.292	.368	.447	121	195	59	37	-5	.994	65	*1-1714/D-17	11.5
■ **FRANK JUDE**	Jude, Frank b: 1884, Libby, Minn. d: 5/4/61, Brownsville, Tex. BR/TR, 5'7", 150 lbs. Deb: 7/9/06																						
1906	Cin-N	80	308	31	64	6	4	1	31	16		.208	.261	.263	61	-14	7			.965	-3	O-80	-2.4
■ **JOE JUDGE**	Judge, Joseph Ignatius b: 5/25/1894, Brooklyn, N.Y. d: 3/11/63, Washington, D.C. BL/TL, 5'8.5", 155 lbs. Deb: 9/20/15 C																						
1915	Was-A	12	41	7	17	2	0	0	9	4	6	.415	.500	.463	185	5	2	3	-1	.990	-1	1-10/O-2	0.3
1916	Was-A	103	336	42	74	10	8	0	28	54	44	.220	.333	.298	91	-2	18			.986	4	*1-103	-0.3
1917	Was-A	102	393	62	112	15	15	2	30	50	40	.285	.369	.415	141	19	17			.988	-1	*1-100	1.6
1918	Was-A	130	502	56	131	23	7	1	46	49	32	.261	.332	.341	105	2	20			.985	2	*1-130	-0.1
1919	Was-A	135	521	83	150	33	12	2	31	81	35	.288	.386	.409	124	19	23			.988	-4	*1-133	1.1
1920	Was-A	126	493	103	164	19	15	5	51	65	34	.333	.416	.462	136	28	12	12	-4	.992	-8	*1-124	1.3
1921	Was-A	153	622	87	187	26	11	7	72	68	35	.301	.372	.412	105	5	21	6	3	.996	-3	*1-152	0.1
1922	Was-A	148	591	84	174	32	15	10	81	50	20	.294	.355	.450	114	11	5	15	-8	.996	3	*1-147	0.0
1923	Was-A	113	405	56	127	24	6	2	63	58	20	.314	.406	.417	123	16	11	7	-1	**.993**	8	*1-112	1.6
1924	*Was-A	140	516	71	167	38	9	3	79	53	21	.324	.393	.450	121	16	13	8	-1	.994	-2	*1-140	0.4
1925	*Was-A	112	376	65	118	31	5	8	66	55	21	.314	.406	.487	128	17	7	12	-5	**.993**	3	*1-109	0.9
1926	Was-A	134	453	70	132	25	11	7	92	53	25	.291	.367	.442	113	8	7	5	-1	.994	10	*1-128	0.9
1927	Was-A	137	522	68	161	29	11	2	71	45	22	.308	.366	.418	104	3	10	5	0	**.996**	-6	*1-136	-1.1
1928	Was-A	153	542	78	166	31	10	3	93	80	19	.306	.396	.417	115	14	16	4	2	.996	1	*1-149	0.4
1929	Was-A	143	543	83	171	35	8	6	71	73	33	.315	.397	.442	115	14	12	5	1	**.996**	3	*1-142	0.3
1930	Was-A	126	442	83	144	29	11	10	80	60	29	.326	.410	.509	131	22	13	6	0	**.998**	2	*1-117	1.2
1931	Was-A	35	74	11	21	3	0	0	9	8	8	.284	.354	.324	79	-2	0	0	0	.994	1	1-15	-0.2
1932	Was-A	82	291	45	75	16	3	3	29	37	19	.258	.343	.364	84	-6	3	3	-1	.997	1	1-78	-1.1
1933	Bro-N	42	112	7	24	2	1	0	9	7	10	.214	.261	.250	48	-7	1			.989	0	1-28	-1.1
	Bos-A	35	108	20	32	8	1	0	22	13	4	.296	.372	.389	103	1	2	1	0	1.000	-0	1-29	-0.2
1934	Bos-A	10	15	3	5	2	0	0	2	2	1	.333	.412	.467	118	0	0	0	0	1.000	0	/1-2	0.0
Total	20	2171	7898	1184	2352	433	159	71	1034	965	478	.298	.378	.420	115	182	213	92		.993	13	*1-2084/O-2	6.0
■ **WALLY JUDNICH**	Judnich, Walter Franklin b: 1/24/17, San Francisco, Cal d: 7/12/71, Glendale, Cal. BL/TL, 6'1", 205 lbs. Deb: 4/16/40																						
1940	StL-A	137	519	97	157	27	7	24	89	54	71	.303	.368	.520	125	18	8	5	-1	**.989**	-1	*O-133	0.9
1941	StL-A	146	546	90	155	40	6	14	83	80	45	.284	.377	.456	116	13	5	5	-2	.980	3	*O-140	0.5
1942	StL-A	132	457	78	143	22	6	17	82	74	41	.313	.413	.499	153	34	3	2	-0	**.991**	-2	*O-122	2.5
1946	StL-A	142	511	60	134	23	4	15	72	60	54	.262	.340	.411	104	2	0	4	-2	**.995**	11	*O-137	0.5
1947	StL-A	144	500	58	129	24	3	18	64	60	62	.258	.338	.426	109	5	2	5	-2	.989	-6	*1-129,O-15	-0.9
1948	*Cle-A	79	218	36	56	13	3	2	29	56	23	.257	.411	.372	112	7	2	3	-1	.970	-8	O-49,1-20	-0.5
1949	Pit-N	10	35	5	8	1	0	0	1	1	2	.229	.250	.257	35	-3	0			1.000	1	/O-8	-0.2
Total	7	790	2786	424	782	150	29	90	420	385	298	.281	.369	.452	119	75	20	24		.988	-2	O-604,1-149	2.8
■ **LYLE JUDY**	Judy, Lyle Leroy "Punch" b: 11/15/13, Lawrenceville, Ill d: 1/15/91, Ormond Beach, Fla. BR/TR, 5'10", 150 lbs. Deb: 9/17/35																						
1935	StL-N	8	11	2	0	0	0	0	0	2	2	.000	.154	.000	-53	-2	2			1.000	1	/2-5	-0.2
■ **RED JUELICH**	Juelich, John Samuel b: 9/20/16, St.Louis, Mo. d: 12/25/70, St.Louis, Mo. BR/TR, 5'11.5", 170 lbs. Deb: 5/30/39																						
1939	Pit-N	17	46	5	11	0	2	0	4	2	4	.239	.271	.326	61	-3	0			.935	-5	2-10/3-2	-0.8
■ **GEORGE JUMONVILLE**	Jumonville, George Benedict b: 5/16/17, Mobile, Ala. d: 12/12/96, Mobile, Ala. BR/TR, 6', 175 lbs. Deb: 9/13/40																						
1940	Phi-N	11	34	0	3	0	0	0	0	1	6	.088	.139	.088	-38	-6	0			.952	-4	S-10/3-1	-1.0
1941	Phi-N	6	7	1	3	0	0	1	2	0	0	.429	.429	.857	266	1	0			1.000	1	/2-1,S-1	0.2
Total	2	17	41	1	6	0	0	1	2	1	6	.146	.186	.220	12	-5	0			.953	-4	/S-11,2-1,3-1	-0.8
■ **ED JURAK**	Jurak, Edward James b: 10/24/57, Los Angeles, Cal. BR/TR, 6'2", 185 lbs. Deb: 6/30/82																						
1982	Bos-A	12	21	3	7	0	0	0	7	2	4	.333	.391	.333	96	-0	0	0	0	.923	2	3-11/O-1	0.1
1983	Bos-A	75	159	19	44	8	4	0	18	18	25	.277	.354	.377	95	-1	1	2	-1	.943	9	S-38,1-19,3-12,/2D	0.8
1984	Bos-A	47	66	6	16	3	1	1	7	12	12	.242	.359	.364	96	-0	0	2	-1	1.000	5	1-19,2-14/3-9,S-2	0.3
1985	Bos-A	26	13	4	3	0	0	0	0	1	3	.231	.286	.231	42	-1	0	0	0	.833	4	/3-7,S-3,1-1,O-1,D	0.2

YEAR	TM/L	G	AB	R	H	2B	3B	HR	RBI	BB	SO	AVG	OBP	SLG	PRO+	BR/A	SB	CS	SBR	FA	FR	G/POS	TPR
1988	Oak-A	3	1	1	0	0	0	0	0	0	0	.000	.000	.000	-99	-0	0	0	0	.000	-0	/3-1,D-1	0.0
1989	SF-N	30	42	2	10	0	0	0	1	5	5	.238	.319	.238	63	-2	0	0	0	.875	-2	/S-6,3-5,2-4,O-2,1	-0.4
Total	6	193	302	35	80	11	5	1	33	38	49	.265	.349	.344	88	-4	1	4	-2	.941	17	/S-49,3-45,12DO	1.0

■ **BILLY JURGES** Jurges, William Frederick b: 5/9/08, Bronx, N.Y. d: 3/3/97, Clearwater, Fla. BR/TR, 5′11″, 175 lbs. Deb: 5/4/31 MC

YEAR	TM/L	G	AB	R	H	2B	3B	HR	RBI	BB	SO	AVG	OBP	SLG	PRO+	BR/A	SB	CS	SBR	FA	FR	G/POS	TPR
1931	Chi-N	88	293	34	59	15	5	0	23	25	41	.201	.264	.287	47	-22	2			.963	11	3-54,2-33/S-3	-0.6
1932	*Chi-N	115	396	40	100	24	4	2	52	19	26	.253	.288	.348	71	-16	1			**.964**	**32**	*S-108/3-5	2.4
1933	Chi-N	143	487	49	131	17	6	5	50	26	39	.269	.313	.359	92	-6	3			.958	20	*S-143	2.6
1934	Chi-N	100	358	43	88	15	2	8	33	19	34	.246	.289	.366	76	-13	1			.966	14	S-98	0.7
1935	*Chi-N	146	519	69	125	33	1	1	59	42	39	.241	.304	.314	66	-24	3			**.964**	**30**	*S-146	1.3
1936	Chi-N	118	429	51	120	25	1	1	42	23	25	.280	.321	.350	79	-13	4			.960	17	*S-116	1.1
1937	Chi-N☆	129	450	53	134	18	10	1	65	42	41	.298	.365	.389	101	2	2			**.975**	-7	*S-128	0.3
1938	*Chi-N	137	465	53	114	18	3	1	47	58	53	.245	.335	.303	75	-14	3			.953	-0	*S-136	-0.4
1939	NY-N☆	138	543	84	155	21	11	6	63	47	34	.285	.349	.398	99	-0	3			**.965**	15	*S-137	2.7
1940	NY-N†	63	214	23	54	3	3	2	36	25	14	.252	.347	.322	85	-3	2			.967	-1	S-63	0.1
1941	NY-N	134	471	50	138	25	2	5	61	47	36	.293	.361	.386	108	6	0			.957	7	*S-134	2.3
1942	NY-N	127	464	45	119	7	1	2	30	43	42	.256	.324	.289	79	-11	1			.978	7	*S-124	0.4
1943	NY-N	136	481	46	110	8	2	4	29	53	38	.229	.310	.279	70	-17	2			.955	1	S-99,3-28	-1.0
1944	NY-N	85	246	28	52	2	1	1	23	23	20	.211	.279	.240	47	-17	4			.961	-1	3-61,S-10/2-1	-1.7
1945	NY-N	61	176	22	57	3	1	3	24	24	11	.324	.405	.403	123	6	2			.937	2	3-44/S-8	1.0
1946	Chi-N	82	221	26	49	9	2	0	17	43	28	.222	.351	.281	82	-3	3			.976	-3	S-73/3-7,2-2	-0.3
1947	Chi-N	14	40	5	8	2	0	1	2	9	9	.200	.347	.325	83	-1	0			.925	-4	S-14	-0.4
Total	17	1816	6253	721	1613	245	55	43	656	568	530	.258	.325	.335	82	-147	36			.964	140	*S-1540,3-199/2-36	10.5

■ **JOE JUST** Just, Joseph Erwin (b: Joseph Erwin Juszczak) b: 1/8/16, Milwaukee, Wis. BR/TR, 5′11″, 185 lbs. Deb: 5/13/44

YEAR	TM/L	G	AB	R	H	2B	3B	HR	RBI	BB	SO	AVG	OBP	SLG	PRO+	BR/A	SB	CS	SBR	FA	FR	G/POS	TPR
1944	Cin-N	11	11	0	2	0	0	0	0	0	2	.182	.250	.182	24	-1	0			.923	0	C-10	-0.1
1945	Cin-N	14	34	2	5	0	0	0	2	4	7	.147	.237	.147	8	-4	0			.947	-2	C-14	-0.5
Total	2	25	45	2	7	0	0	0	2	4	9	.156	.240	.156	12	-5	0			.941	-1	/C-24	-0.6

■ **DAVID JUSTICE** Justice, David Christopher b: 4/14/66, Cincinnati, Ohio BL/TL, 6′3″, 200 lbs. Deb: 5/24/89

YEAR	TM/L	G	AB	R	H	2B	3B	HR	RBI	BB	SO	AVG	OBP	SLG	PRO+	BR/A	SB	CS	SBR	FA	FR	G/POS	TPR
1989	Atl-N	16	51	7	12	3	0	1	3	3	9	.235	.291	.353	81	-1	2	1	0	1.000	-1	O-16	-0.3
1990	Atl-N	127	439	76	124	23	2	28	78	64	92	.282	.374	.535	139	23	11	6	-0	.981	-2	1-69,O-61	1.5
1991	*Atl-N	109	396	67	109	25	1	21	87	65	81	.275	.381	.503	138	21	8	8	-2	.968	5	*O-106	2.2
1992	*Atl-N	144	484	78	124	19	5	21	72	79	85	.256	.363	.446	121	14	2	4	-2	.976	14	*O-140	2.5
1993	*Atl-N★	157	585	90	158	15	4	40	120	78	90	.270	.359	.515	129	24	3	5	-2	.985	9	*O-157	2.7
1994	Atl-N★	104	352	61	110	16	2	19	59	69	45	.313	.428	.531	145	26	2	4	-2	.947	2	*O-102	2.3
1995	*Atl-N	120	411	73	104	17	2	24	78	73	68	.253	.368	.479	118	11	4	2	0	.984	6	*O-120	1.4
1996	Atl-N	40	140	23	45	9	0	6	25	21	22	.321	.414	.514	135	8	1	1	-0	1.000	5	O-40	1.1
1997	*Cle-A†	139	495	84	163	31	1	33	101	80	79	.329	.423	.596	156	42	3	5	-2	.984	-5	O-78,D-61	2.8
1998	*Cle-A	146	540	94	151	39	2	21	88	76	98	.280	.369	.476	114	11	9	3	1	1.000	-1	*D-123,O-21	0.4
Total	10	1102	3893	653	1100	197	19	214	711	608	669	.283	.381	.508	131	180	45	39	-10	.976	32	O-841,D-184/1-69	16.6

■ **SKIP JUTZE** Jutze, Alfred Henry b: 5/28/46, Bayside, N.Y. BR/TR, 5′11″, 195 lbs. Deb: 9/1/72

YEAR	TM/L	G	AB	R	H	2B	3B	HR	RBI	BB	SO	AVG	OBP	SLG	PRO+	BR/A	SB	CS	SBR	FA	FR	G/POS	TPR
1972	StL-N	21	71	1	17	2	0	0	5	1	16	.239	.250	.268	48	-5	0	1	-1	.964	0	C-17	-0.5
1973	Hou-N	90	278	18	62	6	0	0	18	19	37	.223	.275	.245	45	-20	0	1	-1	.984	-6	C-86	-2.5
1974	Hou-N	8	13	0	3	0	0	0	1	1	1	.231	.286	.231	48	-1	0	0	0	1.000	-0	/C-7	-0.1
1975	Hou-N	51	93	9	21	2	0	0	6	2	4	.226	.242	.247	39	-8	1	0	0	.988	3	C-47	-0.3
1976	Hou-N	42	92	7	14	2	3	0	6	4	16	.152	.188	.239	22	-10	0	0	0	.986	2	C-42	-0.8
1977	Sea-A	42	109	10	24	2	0	3	15	7	12	.220	.267	.321	60	-6	0	4	-2	.984	-2	C-40	-1.0
Total	6	254	656	45	141	14	3	3	51	34	86	.215	.255	.259	44	-50	1	6	-3	.983	-3	C-239	-5.2

■ **HERB JUUL** Juul, Herbert Victor b: 2/2/1886, Chicago, Ill. d: 11/14/28, Chicago, Ill. BL/TL, 5′11″, 150 lbs. Deb: 7/11/11

YEAR	TM/L	G	AB	R	H	2B	3B	HR	RBI	BB	SO	AVG	OBP	SLG	PRO+	BR/A	SB	CS	SBR	FA	FR	G/POS	TPR
1911	Cin-N	2	2	0	0	0	0	0	0	0	0	.000	.000	.000	-99	-1	0			.000	-0	/P-1	0.0

■ **JIM KAAT** Kaat, James Lee b: 11/7/38, Zeeland, Mich. BL/TL, 6′4″, 217 lbs. Deb: 8/2/59 C

YEAR	TM/L	G	AB	R	H	2B	3B	HR	RBI	BB	SO	AVG	OBP	SLG	PRO+	BR/A	SB	CS	SBR	FA	FR	G/POS	TPR
1959	Was-A	3	1	0	0	0	0	0	0	0	1	.000	.000	.000	-99	-0	0	0	0	1.000	0	/P-3	0.0
1960	Was-A	13	14	0	2	0	0	0	0	0	6	.143	.143	.143	-23	-2	0	0	0	1.000	0	P-13	0.0
1961	Min-A	47	63	10	15	3	1	0	1	4	13	.238	.294	.317	60	-4	0	0	0	.968	3	P-36	0.0
1962	Min-A☆	48	100	9	18	3	1	1	10	8	40	.180	.241	.260	33	-9	0	0	0	.967	6	P-39	0.0
1963	Min-A	36	61	2	8	1	0	1	8	2	19	.131	.185	.197	7	-8	0	0	0	.984	4	P-31	0.0
1964	Min-A	46	83	11	14	1	0	3	11	11	31	.169	.266	.289	54	-5	0	0	0	.928	3	P-36	0.0
1965	*Min-A	56	93	6	23	4	0	1	9	3	29	.247	.271	.323	65	-4	2	0	1	.929	3	P-45	0.0
1966	Min-A★	47	118	12	23	2	1	2	13	5	41	.195	.228	.280	42	-9	0	0	0	.956	0	P-41	0.0
1967	Min-A	45	99	7	17	3	1	1	4	7	26	.172	.226	.253	38	-8	0	0	0	.952	1	P-42	0.0
1968	Min-A	36	77	7	12	3	0	0	5	2	18	.156	.177	.195	12	-8	0	0	0	.976	-0	P-30	0.0
1969	Min-A	43	87	8	18	8	0	2	10	4	20	.207	.250	.368	69	-4	0	0	0	.826	-3	P-40	0.0
1970	*Min-A	56	76	17	15	1	0	1	8	6	20	.197	.265	.250	42	-6	0	0	0	.935	2	P-45	0.0
1971	Min-A	54	93	6	15	3	0	0	5	2	16	.161	.179	.194	5	-12	2	0	1	.982	-0	P-39	0.0
1972	Min-A	24	45	3	13	3	0	2	4	1	16	.289	.304	.489	127	1	0	1	-1	.923	-0	P-15	0.0
1973	Min-A	31	0	1	0	0	0	0	0	0	0	—	—	—	—	0	0	0	0	.969	-1	P-29	0.0
	Chi-A	7	0	0	0	0	0	0	0	0	0	—	—	—	—	0	0	0	0	1.000	-0	/P-7	0.0
	Yr	38	0	1	0	0	0	0	0	0	0	—	—	—	—	0	0	0	0	.973	-2	P-36	0.0
1974	Chi-A	42	1	0	0	0	0	0	0	0	0	.000	.000	.000	-98	-0	0	0	0	.959	-2	P-42	0.0
1975	Chi-A★	43	0	0	0	0	0	0	0	0	0	—	—	—	—	0	0	0	0	.982	-2	P-43	0.0
1976	*Phi-N	42	79	4	14	3	1	1	8	2	24	.177	.198	.278	33	-7	0	0	0	.949	-3	P-38	0.0
1977	Phi-N	36	53	4	10	3	0	0	2	2	12	.189	.218	.245	23	-6	0	0	0	.897	-2	P-35	0.0
1978	Phi-N	26	48	4	7	1	0	0	4	0	15	.146	.163	.167	-8	-7	0	0	0	1.000	-2	P-26	0.0
1979	Phi-N	3	1	0	0	0	0	0	0	0	1	.000	.500	.000	47	0	0	0	0	1.000	-0	/P-3	0.0
	NY-A	40	0	0	0	0	0	0	0	0	0	—	—	—	—	0	0	0	0	.909	-1	P-40	0.0
1980	NY-A	4	0	0	0	0	0	0	0	0	0	—	—	—	—	0	0	0	0	.800	1	/P-4	0.0
	StL-N	49	35	4	5	1	0	1	2	2	13	.143	.189	.257	23	-4	1	0	0	.952	-2	P-49	0.0
1981	StL-N	41	8	2	3	1	0	0	2	1	0	.375	.444	.500	163	1	0	0	0	.895	1	P-41	0.0
1982	*StL-N	62	12	0	0	0	0	0	0	1	4	.000	.077	.000	-76	-3	0	0	0	.917	1	P-62	0.0
1983	StL-N	24	4	0	0	0	0	0	0	0	2	.000	.000	.000	-99	-1	0	0	0	.889	0	P-24	0.0
Total	25	1004	1251	117	232	44	5	16	106	63	367	.185	.229	.267	38	-104	5	1	1	.947	6	P-898	0.0

■ **JACK KADING** Kading, John Frederick b: 11/17/1884, Waukesha, Wis. d: 6/2/64, Chicago, Ill. BR/TR, 6′3″, 190 lbs. Deb: 9/12/10

YEAR	TM/L	G	AB	R	H	2B	3B	HR	RBI	BB	SO	AVG	OBP	SLG	PRO+	BR/A	SB	CS	SBR	FA	FR	G/POS	TPR
1910	Pit-N	8	23	5	7	2	1	0	4	4	5	.304	.407	.478	149	1	0			1.000	1	/1-8	0.3
1914	Chi-F	3	3	0	0	0	0	0	0	0	0	.000	.000	.000	-99	-1	0			.000	0	H	-0.1
Total	2	11	26	5	7	2	1	0	4	4	5	.269	.367	.423	123	1	0			1.000	1	/1-8	0.2

■ **JAKE KAFORA** Kafora, Frank Jacob "Tomatoes" b: 10/16/1888, Chicago, Ill. d: 3/23/28, Chicago, Ill. BR/TR, 6′, 180 lbs. Deb: 10/5/13

YEAR	TM/L	G	AB	R	H	2B	3B	HR	RBI	BB	SO	AVG	OBP	SLG	PRO+	BR/A	SB	CS	SBR	FA	FR	G/POS	TPR
1913	Pit-N	1	1	1	0	0	0	0	0	0	1	.000	.500	.000	52	0	0			1.000	-1	/C-1	-0.1
1914	Pit-N	21	23	2	3	0	0	0	0	0	6	.130	.200	.130	-1	-3	0			1.000	-1	C-17	-0.4
Total	2	22	24	3	3	0	0	0	0	0	7	.125	.222	.125	4	-3	0			1.000	-2	/C-18	-0.5

■ **IKE KAHDOT** Kahdot, Isaac Leonard "Chief" b: 10/22/01, Georgetown, Okla. BR/TR, 5′5.5″, 145 lbs. Deb: 9/5/22

YEAR	TM/L	G	AB	R	H	2B	3B	HR	RBI	BB	SO	AVG	OBP	SLG	PRO+	BR/A	SB	CS	SBR	FA	FR	G/POS	TPR
1922	Cle-A	4	2	0	0	0	0	0	0	0	1	.000	.000	.000	-99	-1	0	0	0	1.000	1	/3-2	0.0

■ **NICK KAHL** Kahl, Nicholas Alexander b: 4/10/1879, Coulterville, Ill. d: 7/13/59, Sparta, Ill. BR/TR, 5′9″, 185 lbs. Deb: 5/2/05

YEAR	TM/L	G	AB	R	H	2B	3B	HR	RBI	BB	SO	AVG	OBP	SLG	PRO+	BR/A	SB	CS	SBR	FA	FR	G/POS	TPR
1905	Cle-A	40	135	16	29	4	1	0	21	4		.215	.248	.259	60	-6	1			.940	-2	2-32/S-1,O-1	-0.9

YEAR	TM/L	G	AB	R	H	2B	3B	HR	RBI	BB	SO	AVG	OBP	SLG	PRO+	BR/A	SB	CS	SBR	FA	FR	G/POS	TPR
■ **BOB KAHLE**	Kahle, Robert Wayne b: 11/23/15, New Castle, Ind. d: 12/16/88, Inglewood, Cal. BR/TR, 6′, 170 lbs. Deb: 4/21/38																						
1938	Bos-N	8	3	2	1	0	0	0	0	0	0	.333	.333	.333	93	-0	0			.000	0	H	0.0
■ **OWEN KAHN**	Kahn, Owen Earle "Jack" b: 6/5/05, Richmond, Va. d: 1/17/81, Richmond, Va. BR/TR, 5′11″, 160 lbs. Deb: 5/24/30																						
1930	Bos-N	1	0	1	0	0	0	0	0	0	0	—	—	—	—	0	0			.000	0	R	0.0
■ **MIKE KAHOE**	Kahoe, Michael Joseph b: 9/3/1873, Yellow Springs, O d: 5/14/49, Akron, Ohio BR/TR, 6′, 185 lbs. Deb: 9/22/1895																						
1895	Cin-N	3	4	0	0	0	0	0	0	0	0	.000	.000	.000	-96	-1	0			1.000	-1	/C-3	-0.1
1899	Cin-N	14	42	2	7	1	1	0	4	0		.167	.167	.238	10	-5	1			.957	4	C-13	-0.1
1900	Cin-N	52	175	18	33	3	3	1	9	4		.189	.215	.257	31	-17	3			.963	5	C-51/S-1	-0.7
1901	Cin-N	4	13	0	4	0	0	0	0	1		.308	.357	.308	100	0	0			1.000	-2	/C-4	-0.2
	Chi-N	67	237	21	53	12	2	1	21	8		.224	.249	.304	62	-12	5			.974	9	C-63/1-6	0.3
	Yr	71	250	21	57	12	2	1	21	9		.228	.255	.304	64	-12	5			.974	7	C-67/1-6	0.1
1902	Chi-N	7	18	0	4	1	0	0	2	0		.222	.222	.278	56	-1	0			.875	-1	/C-4,3-2,S-1	-0.1
	StL-A	55	197	21	48	9	2	2	28	6		.244	.270	.340	69	-9	4			.967	-0	C-53	-0.3
1903	StL-A	77	244	26	46	7	5	0	23	11		.189	.227	.258	46	-16	1			.971	-3	C-71/O-2	-1.2
1904	StL-A	72	236	9	51	6	1	0	12	8		.216	.242	.250	59	-11	4			.968	1	C-69	-0.3
1905	Phi-N	16	51	2	13	2	0	0	4	1		.255	.269	.294	70	-2	1			.975	0	C-15	-0.1
1907	Chi-N	5	10	0	4	0	0	0	1	0		.400	.400	.400	142	0	0			1.000	-1	/C-3,1-1	-0.1
	Was-A	17	47	3	9	1	0	0	1	0		.191	.191	.213	31	-4	0			.976	0	C-15	-0.2
1908	Was-A	17	27	1	5	1	0	0	0	0		.185	.185	.222	35	-2	0			.983	4	C-11	0.3
1909	Was-A	4	8	0	1	0	0	0	0	0		.125	.125	.125	-22	-1	2			.867	-0	/C-3	-0.1
Total	11	410	1309	103	278	43	14	4	105	39	0	.212	.237	.276	52	-81	21			.968	15	C-378/1-7,O-2,3S	-2.9
■ **AL KAISER**	Kaiser, Alfred Edward "Deerfoot" b: 8/3/1886, Cincinnati, Ohio d: 4/11/69, Cincinnati, Ohio BR/TR, 5′9″, 165 lbs. Deb: 4/18/11																						
1911	Chi-N	26	84	16	21	0	5	0	7	7	12	.250	.308	.369	89	-2	6			.905	-3	O-22	-0.6
	Bos-N	66	197	20	40	5	2	2	15	10	26	.203	.249	.279	44	-15	4			.922	-6	O-58	-2.4
	Yr	92	281	36	61	5	7	2	22	17	38	.217	.267	.306	57	-17	10			.918	-9	O-80	-3.0
1912	Bos-N	4	13	0	0	0	0	0	0	0	3	.000	.000	.000	-98	-4	0			.900	0	/O-4	-0.4
1914	Ind-F	59	187	22	43	10	0	1	16	17	41	.230	.301	.299	58	-14	6			.918	-3	O-50/1-1	-2.0
Total	3	155	481	58	104	15	7	3	38	34	82	.216	.274	.295	53	-34	16			.917	-12	O-134/1-1	-5.4
■ **JOHN KALAHAN**	Kalahan, John Joseph b: 9/30/1878, Philadelphia, Pa. d: 6/20/52, Philadelphia, Pa. BR/TR, 6′, 165 lbs. Deb: 9/29/03																						
1903	Phi-A	1	5	0	0	0	0	0	0	0		.000	.000	.000	-96	-1	0			1.000	-1	/C-1	-0.2
■ **CHARLIE KALBFUS**	Kalbfus, Charles Henry "Skinny" b: 12/28/1864, Washington, D.C. d: 11/18/41, Washington, D.C. BR/TR, 5′11″, 145 lbs. Deb: 4/18/1884																						
1884	Was-U	1	5	1	1	0	0	0		0		.200	.200	.200	22	-1				.000	-0	/O-1	-0.1
■ **FRANK KALIN**	Kalin, Frank Bruno "Fats" (b: Frank Bruno Kalinkiewicz) b: 10/3/17, Steubenville, Ohio d: 1/12/75, Weirton, W.Va. BR/TR, 6′, 200 lbs. Deb: 9/25/40																						
1940	Pit-N	3	3	0	0	0	0	0	1	2	0	.000	.400	.000	19	-0	0			.667	-1	/O-2	-0.1
1943	Chi-A	4	4	0	0	0	0	0	0	0	0	.000	.000	.000	-99	-1	0	0	0	.000	0	H	-0.1
Total	2	7	7	0	0	0	0	0	1	2	0	.000	.222	.000	-34	-1	0	0		.667	-1	/O-2	-0.2
■ **AL KALINE**	Kaline, Albert William b: 12/19/34, Baltimore, Md. BR/TR, 6′2″, 180 lbs. Deb: 6/25/53 H																						
1953	Det-A	30	28	9	7	0	0	1	2	1	5	.250	.300	.357	78	-1	1	0	0	1.000	-7	O-20	-0.8
1954	Det-A	138	504	42	139	18	3	4	43	22	45	.276	.306	.347	80	-15	9	5	-0	.971	11	*O-135	-1.1
1955	Det-A★	152	588	121	**200**	24	8	27	102	82	57	**.340**	.425	.546	163	53	6	8	-3	.979	7	*O-152	5.0
1956	Det-A★	153	617	96	194	32	10	27	128	70	55	.314	.385	.530	139	33	7	1	2	.984	17	*O-153	4.2
1957	Det-A★	149	577	83	170	29	4	23	90	43	38	.295	.347	.478	120	14	11	9	-2	.985	7	*O-145	1.1
1958	Det-A★	146	543	84	170	34	7	16	85	54	47	.313	.377	.490	127	20	7	4	-0	.994	**23**	*O-145	3.6
1959	Det-A★	136	511	86	167	19	2	27	94	72	42	.327	.414	**.530**	149	36	10	4	1	.989	11	*O-136	4.0
1960	Det-A★	147	551	77	153	29	4	15	68	65	47	.278	.357	.426	108	7	19	4	3	.987	9	*O-142	1.2
1961	Det-A★	153	586	116	190	**41**	7	19	82	66	42	.324	.396	.515	138	32	14	1	4	.990	12	*O-147/3-1	3.8
1962	Det-A★	100	398	78	121	16	6	29	94	47	39	.304	.379	.593	152	28	4	0	1	.983	12	*O-100	3.4
1963	Det-A★	145	551	89	172	24	3	27	101	54	48	.312	.378	.514	142	31	6	4	-1	.992	-2	*O-140	2.1
1964	Det-A†	146	525	77	154	31	5	17	68	75	51	.293	.385	.469	134	26	4	1	1	.990	11	*O-136	3.2
1965	Det-A★	125	399	72	112	18	2	18	72	72	49	.281	.391	.471	142	24	6	0	2	.985	-4	*O-112/3-1	1.8
1966	Det-A★	142	479	85	138	29	1	29	88	81	66	.288	.396	.534	161	40	5	5	-2	**.993**	5	*O-136	3.9
1967	Det-A†	131	458	94	141	28	2	25	78	83	47	.308	.415	.541	176	46	8	2	1	.983	8	*O-130	5.2
1968	*Det-A	102	327	49	94	14	1	10	53	55	39	.287	.395	.428	145	20	6	4	-1	.978	-1	O-74,1-22	1.5
1969	Det-A	131	456	74	124	17	0	21	69	54	61	.272	.350	.447	117	10	1	2	-1	.966	1	*O-118/1-9	0.3
1970	Det-A	131	467	64	130	24	4	16	71	77	49	.278	.382	.450	127	19	2	2	-1	.988	1	O-91,1-52	1.2
1971	Det-A★	133	405	69	119	19	2	15	54	82	57	.294	.421	.462	144	28	4	6	-2	**1.000**	-6	*O-129/1-5	1.4
1972	*Det-A	106	278	46	87	11	2	10	32	28	33	.313	.380	.475	148	17	1	0	0	.991	-6	O-84,1-11	0.8
1973	Det-A	91	310	40	79	13	0	10	45	29	28	.255	.325	.394	95	-2	4	1	1	1.000	-5	O-63,1-36	-1.2
1974	Det-A★	147	558	71	146	28	2	13	64	65	75	.262	.340	.389	105	4	2	2	-1	.000	0	*D-146	0.0
Total	22	2834	10116	1622	3007	498	75	399	1583	1277	1020	.297	.379	.480	134	468	137	65	2	.986	103	*O-2488,D-146,1/3	44.6
■ **WILLIE KAMM**	Kamm, William Edward b: 2/2/1900, San Francisco, Cal. d: 12/21/88, Belmont, Cal. BR/TR, 5′10.5″, 170 lbs. Deb: 4/18/23																						
1923	Chi-A	149	544	57	159	39	9	6	87	62	82	.292	.366	.430	110	8	18	13	-2	.960	8	*3-149	2.5
1924	Chi-A	147	528	58	134	28	6	6	93	64	59	.254	.337	.364	83	-14	10	9	-2	**.971**	8	*3-146	0.3
1925	Chi-A	152	509	82	142	32	4	6	83	**90**	36	.279	.391	.393	105	7	11	13	-5	**.957**	-0	*3-152	1.2
1926	Chi-A	143	480	63	141	24	10	0	62	77	24	.294	.396	.385	108	9	12	4	1	**.978**	14	*3-142	3.1
1927	Chi-A	148	540	85	146	32	13	0	59	70	18	.270	.354	.378	92	-5	8	9	-3	**.972**	1	*3-146	-0.1
1928	Chi-A	155	552	70	170	30	12	1	84	73	22	.308	.391	.411	112	12	17	9	-0	**.977**	-3	*3-155	1.7
1929	Chi-A	147	523	72	140	33	6	3	63	75	23	.268	.363	.371	90	-6	12	5	1	**.978**	4	*3-145	0.4
1930	Chi-A	112	331	49	89	21	6	3	47	51	20	.269	.368	.396	97	-0	5	4	-1	.939	15	*3-106	1.7
1931	Chi-A	18	59	9	15	4	1	0	9	7	6	.254	.333	.356	86	-1	1	1	-0	.938	2	3-18	0.1
	Cle-A	114	410	68	121	31	4	0	66	64	13	.295	.392	.390	100	2	13	9	-2	.947	1	*3-114	0.8
	Yr	132	469	77	136	35	5	0	75	71	19	.290	.384	.386	99	1	14	10	-2	.945	3	*3-132	0.9
1932	Cle-A	148	524	76	150	34	9	3	83	75	36	.286	.379	.403	96	-2	6	3	0	.967	7	*3-148	1.4
1933	Cle-A	133	447	59	126	17	2	1	47	54	27	.282	.359	.336	81	-10	6	3	0	**.984**	1	*3-131	-0.2
1934	Cle-A	121	386	52	104	23	3	0	42	62	38	.269	.372	.345	84	-7	7	1	2	**.978**	11	*3-118	1.0
1935	Cle-A	6	18	2	6	0	0	0	1	0	1	.333	.333	.333	72	-1	0	1	-1	.875	-2	/3-4	-0.3
Total	13	1693	5851	802	1643	348	85	29	826	824	405	.281	.372	.384	97	-8	126	84	-13	.967	66	*3-1674	13.6
■ **ALEX KAMPOURIS**	Kampouris, Alexis William b: 11/13/12, Sacramento, Cal. d: 5/29/93, Sacramento, Cal. BR/TR, 5′8″, 155 lbs. Deb: 7/31/34																						
1934	Cin-N	19	66	6	13	1	0	0	3	3	18	.197	.254	.212	27	-7	2			.946	-1	2-16	-0.7
1935	Cin-N	148	499	46	123	26	5	7	62	32	84	.246	.295	.361	77	-17	8			.957	-1	*2-141/S-6	-0.7
1936	Cin-N	122	355	43	85	10	4	5	46	24	46	.239	.289	.332	72	-15	3			.969	28	*2-119/O-1	1.9
1937	Cin-N	146	458	62	114	21	4	17	71	60	65	.249	.342	.424	112	8	2			.961	3	*2-146	2.0
1938	Cin-N	21	74	13	19	1	0	2	7	10	13	.257	.353	.351	97	-0	0			.973	0	2-21	0.1
	NY-N	82	268	35	66	9	1	5	37	27	50	.246	.318	.343	81	-7	0			.972	13	2-79	1.1
	Yr	103	342	48	85	10	1	7	44	37	63	.249	.325	.345	84	-7	0			.972	14	*2-100	1.2
1939	NY-N	74	201	23	50	12	2	5	29	30	41	.249	.349	.403	101	1	0			.973	10	2-62,3-11	1.3
1941	Bro-N	16	51	8	16	4	2	2	9	11	8	.314	.444	.588	181	6	0			.987	0	2-15	0.7
1942	Bro-N	10	21	3	5	2	1	0	3	0	4	.238	.238	.429	92	-0	0			.970	2	/2-9	0.2
1943	Bro-N	19	44	9	10	4	1	0	4	17	6	.227	.452	.364	136	4	0			.946	-1	2-18	0.3
	Was-A	51	145	24	30	4	0	2	13	30	25	.207	.361	.276	91	0	7	1	2	.936	-3	3-33,2-10/O-1	-0.1
Total	9	708	2182	272	531	94	20	45	284	244	360	.243	.325	.367	91	-28	22	1		.964	50	2-636/3-44,S-6,O-2	6.1

YEAR	TM/L	G	AB	R	H	2B	3B	HR	RBI	BB	SO	AVG	OBP	SLG	PRO+	BR/A	SB	CS	SBR	FA	FR	G/POS	TPR

■ FRANK KANE   Kane, Francis Thomas "Sugar" (a.k.a. Frank Thomas Kiley In 1915) b: 3/9/1895, Whitman, Mass. d: 12/2/62, Brockton, Mass.   BL/TR, 5'11.5", 175 lbs.   Deb: 9/13/15

YEAR	TM/L	G	AB	R	H	2B	3B	HR	RBI	BB	SO	AVG	OBP	SLG	PRO+	BR/A	SB	CS	SBR	FA	FR	G/POS	TPR
1915	Bro-F	3	10	2	2	0	1	0	2	0	0	.200	.200	.400	67	-1	0			1.000	1	/O-2	0.0
1919	NY-A	1	1	0	0	0	0	0	0	0	0	.000	.000	.000	-99	-0	0			.000	0	H	0.0
Total	2	4	11	2	2	0	1	0	2	0	0	.182	.182	.364	52	-1	0			1.000	1	/O-2	0.0

■ JIM KANE   Kane, James Joseph "Shamus"   b: 11/27/1881, Scranton, Pa.   d: 10/2/47, Omaha, Neb.   BL/TL, 6'2", 225 lbs.   Deb: 4/21/08

1908	Pit-N	55	145	16	35	3	3	0	22	12		.241	.299	.303	93	-1	5			.966	-2	1-40	-0.4

■ JOHN KANE   Kane, John Francis   b: 9/24/1882, Chicago, Ill.   d: 1/28/34, St.Anthony, Idaho   BR/TR, 5'6", 138 lbs.   Deb: 4/11/07

YEAR	TM/L	G	AB	R	H	2B	3B	HR	RBI	BB	SO	AVG	OBP	SLG	PRO+	BR/A	SB	CS	SBR	FA	FR	G/POS	TPR
1907	Cin-N	79	262	40	65	9	4	3	19	22		.248	.325	.347	106	2	20			.959	-1	O-42,3-25/S-6,2-2	0.1
1908	Cin-N	130	455	61	97	11	7	3	23	43		.213	.299	.288	90	-4	30			**.981**	4	*O-127/2-1	-0.6
1909	Chi-N	20	45	6	4	1	0	0	5	2		.089	.146	.111	-20	-6	1			.917	3	/O-8,S-3,3-3,2-2	-0.4
1910	*Chi-N	32	62	11	15	0	0	1	12	9	10	.242	.338	.290	84	-1	2			1.000	-7	O-18/2-6,3-4,S-2	-0.8
Total	4	261	824	118	181	21	11	7	59	76	10	.220	.303	.297	89	-9	53			.975	-0	O-195/3-32,2-11,S	-1.7

■ JOHN KANE   Kane, John Francis   b: 2/19/1900, Chicago, Ill.   d: 7/25/56, Chicago, Ill.   BB/TR, 5'10.5", 162 lbs.   Deb: 9/3/25

1925	Chi-A	14	56	6	10	1	0	0	3	0	3	.179	.193	.196	-1	-9	0	0	0	.935	1	/S-8,2-6	-0.6

■ TOM KANE   Kane, Thomas Joseph "Sugar"   b: 12/15/06, Chicago, Ill.   d: 11/26/73, Chicago, Ill.   BR/TR, 5'10.5", 160 lbs.   Deb: 8/3/38

1938	Bos-N	2	2	0	0	0	0	0	2	0	.000	.500	.000	53	0	0			1.000	-1	/2-2	-0.1

■ JERRY KANE   Kane, William Jeremiah   b: 4/1869, Baltimore, Md.   d: 6/16/49, E.St.Louis, Ill.   BR/TR, 6', 175 lbs.   Deb: 5/2/1890

1890	StL-a	8	25	3	5	0	0	0	2	2		.200	.259	.200	31	-2	0			.907	-1	/1-5,C-4	-0.3

■ ROD KANEHL   Kanehl, Roderick Edwin "Hot Rod"   b: 4/1/34, Wichita, Kan.   BR/TR, 6'1", 180 lbs.   Deb: 4/15/62

YEAR	TM/L	G	AB	R	H	2B	3B	HR	RBI	BB	SO	AVG	OBP	SLG	PRO+	BR/A	SB	CS	SBR	FA	FR	G/POS	TPR
1962	NY-N	133	351	52	87	10	2	4	27	23	36	.248	.296	.322	65	-17	8	6	-1	.944	15	2-62,3-30,O-20,/1S	0.1
1963	NY-N	109	191	26	46	6	0	1	9	5	26	.241	.268	.288	59	-10	6	3	0	.974	-7	O-58,3-13,2-12,/1-3	-1.9
1964	NY-N	98	254	25	59	7	1	1	11	7	18	.232	.256	.280	52	-16	3	1	0	.988	19	2-34,O-25,3-19,/1-2	0.4
Total	3	340	796	103	192	23	3	6	47	35	80	.241	.277	.300	60	-44	17	10	-1	.950	27	2-108,O-103/31S	-1.4

■ GABE KAPLER   Kapler, Gabriel Stefan   b: 8/31/75, Hollywood, Cal.   BR/TR, 6'2", 190 lbs.   Deb: 9/20/98

1998	Det-A	7	25	3	5	0	1	0	0	1	4	.200	.231	.200	32	-3	2	0	l	1.000	-1	/O-6,D-1	-0.3

■ HEINIE KAPPEL   Kappel, Henry   b: 9/1863, Philadelphia, Pa.   d: 8/27/05, Philadelphia, Pa.   BR/TR, 5'8", 160 lbs.   Deb: 5/22/1887   F

1887	Cin-a	23	78	11	22	3	2	0	15	2		.282	.309	.372	87	-2	3			.667	-3	/3-9,O-7,2-6,S-1	-0.4
1888	Cin-a	36	143	18	37	4	4	1	15	2		.259	.274	.364	98	-1	20			.790	-12	S-25,2-10/3-1	-1.2
1889	Col-a	46	173	25	47	7	5	3	21	21	28	.272	.354	.422	127	6	10			.791	-2	S-23,3-23	0.5
Total	3	105	394	54	106	14	11	4	51	25	28	.269	.318	.391	109	3	33			.796	-17	/S-49,3-33,2-16,O-7	-1.1

■ JOE KAPPEL   Kappel, Joseph   b: 4/27/1857, Philadelphia, Pa.   d: 7/8/29, Philadelphia, Pa.   BR , 5'11", 175 lbs.   Deb: 5/26/1884   F

1884	Phi-N	4	15	1	1	0	0	0	0	2	.067	.067	.067	-61	-3				.727	-3	/C-4	-0.5
1890	Phi-a	56	208	29	50	8	1	1	22	20		.240	.310	.303	83	-5	12			.851	-5	O-23,S-18,3-11,/C2	-0.8
Total	2	60	223	30	51	8	1	1	22	20	2	.229	.295	.287	74	-7	12			.773	-8	/O-23,S-18,3-11,/C2	-1.3

■ RON KARKOVICE   Karkovice, Ronald Joseph   b: 8/8/63, Union, N.J.   BR/TR, 6'1", 215 lbs.   Deb: 8/17/86

YEAR	TM/L	G	AB	R	H	2B	3B	HR	RBI	BB	SO	AVG	OBP	SLG	PRO+	BR/A	SB	CS	SBR	FA	FR	G/POS	TPR
1986	Chi-A	37	97	13	24	7	0	4	13	9	37	.247	.318	.443	101	-0	1	0	0	.996	14	C-37	1.6
1987	Chi-A	39	85	7	6	0	0	2	7	7	40	.071	.160	.141	-19	-15	3	0	1	.982	10	C-37/D-1	-0.2
1988	Chi-A	46	115	10	20	4	0	3	9	7	30	.174	.228	.287	43	-9	4	2	0	.995	9	C-46	0.2
1989	Chi-A	71	182	21	48	9	2	3	24	10	56	.264	.309	.385	97	-1	0	0	0	.986	17	C-68/D-2	1.9
1990	Chi-A	68	183	30	45	10	0	6	20	16	52	.246	.310	.399	99	-1	2	0	1	.994	6	C-64/D-2	0.9
1991	Chi-A	75	167	25	41	13	0	5	22	15	42	.246	.311	.413	101	-0	0	0	0	.988	11	C-69/O-1	1.4
1992	Chi-A	123	342	39	81	12	1	13	50	30	89	.237	.304	.392	95	-3	10	4	1	.990	5	*C-119/O-1	0.8
1993	*Chi-A	128	403	60	92	17	1	20	54	29	126	.228	.290	.424	91	-7	2	2	-1	.994	13	*C-127	1.2
1994	Chi-A	77	207	33	44	9	1	11	29	36	68	.213	.329	.425	94	-2	0	3	-2	.993	-4	C-76	-0.3
1995	Chi-A	113	323	44	70	14	1	13	51	39	84	.217	.311	.387	84	-8	2	3	-1	.991	-7	*C-113	-0.9
1996	Chi-A	111	355	44	78	22	0	10	38	24	93	.220	.271	.366	62	-22	0	0	0	.993	11	*C-111	-0.4
1997	Chi-A	51	138	10	25	3	0	6	18	11	32	.181	.257	.333	55	-10	0	0	0	.996	-3	C-51	-1.0
Total	12	939	2597	336	574	120	6	96	335	233	749	.221	.292	.383	81	-77	24	14	-1	.992	82	C-918/D-5,O-2	5.2

■ BILL KARLON   Karlon, William John "Hank"   b: 1/21/09, Palmer, Mass.   d: 12/7/64, Ware, Mass.   BR/TR, 6'1", 190 lbs.   Deb: 4/28/30

1930	NY-A	2	5	0	0	0	0	0	0	0	1	.000	.000	.000	-99	-2	0	0	0	1.000	-0	/O-1	-0.2

■ MARTY KAROW   Karow, Martin Gregory (b: Martin Gregory Karowsky)   b: 7/18/04, Braddock, Pa.   d: 4/27/86, Bryan, Texas   BR/TR, 5'10.5", 170 lbs.   Deb: 6/21/27

1927	Bos-A	6	10	0	2	0	0	0	0	0	0	.200	.200	.300	29	-1	0	0	0	1.000	0	/S-3,3-2	-0.1

■ ERIC KARROS   Karros, Eric Peter   b: 11/4/67, Hackensack, N.J.   BR/TR, 6'4", 216 lbs.   Deb: 9/1/91

YEAR	TM/L	G	AB	R	H	2B	3B	HR	RBI	BB	SO	AVG	OBP	SLG	PRO+	BR/A	SB	CS	SBR	FA	FR	G/POS	TPR
1991	LA-N	14	14	0	1	1	0	0	1	1	6	.071	.133	.143	-23	-2	0	0	0	1.000	0	1-10	-0.3
1992	LA-N	149	545	63	140	30	1	20	88	37	103	.257	.307	.426	107	3	2	4	-2	.993	11	*1-143	0.3
1993	LA-N	158	619	74	153	27	2	23	80	34	82	.247	.289	.409	89	-12	0	1	-1	.992	15	*1-157	-1.0
1994	LA-N	111	406	51	108	21	1	14	46	29	53	.266	.318	.426	98	-3	2	0	1	.991	16	*1-109	0.4
1995	*LA-N	143	551	83	164	29	3	32	105	61	115	.298	.372	.535	149	37	4	4	-1	.995	4	*1-143	2.5
1996	*LA-N	154	608	84	158	29	1	34	111	53	121	.260	.320	.479	116	11	8	0	2	.990	3	*1-154	0.1
1997	LA-N	162	628	86	167	28	0	31	104	61	116	.266	.333	.459	113	9	15	7	0	.992	1	*1-162	-0.5
1998	LA-N	139	507	59	150	20	1	23	87	47	93	.296	.359	.475	123	16	7	2	1	.991	6	*1-136/D-2	1.2
Total	8	1030	3878	500	1041	185	9	177	622	323	689	.268	.327	.458	113	59	38	18	1	.992	57	*1-1014/D-2	2.7

■ JOHN KARST   Karst, John Gottlieb "King"   b: 10/15/1893, Philadelphia, Pa.   d: 5/21/76, Cape May Court House, N.J.   BL/TR, 5'11.5", 175 lbs.   Deb: 10/6/15

1915	Bro-N	1	0	0	0	0	0	0	0	0	0	—	—	—	—		0	0		1.000	0	/3-1	0.0

■ EDDIE KASKO   Kasko, Edward Michael   b: 6/27/32, Linden, N.J.   BR/TR, 6', 180 lbs.   Deb: 4/18/57   M

YEAR	TM/L	G	AB	R	H	2B	3B	HR	RBI	BB	SO	AVG	OBP	SLG	PRO+	BR/A	SB	CS	SBR	FA	FR	G/POS	TPR
1957	StL-N	134	479	59	131	16	5	1	35	33	53	.273	.320	.334	75	-16	6	1	1	.961	-7	*3-120,S-13/2-1	-2.0
1958	StL-N	104	259	20	57	8	1	2	22	21	25	.220	.279	.282	47	-19	1	2	-1	.961	6	S-77,2-12/3-1	-0.8
1959	Cin-N	118	329	39	93	14	1	2	31	14	38	.283	.312	.350	74	-12	2	2	-1	.976	12	S-84,3-31/2-2	0.6
1960	Cin-N	126	479	56	140	21	1	6	51	46	37	.292	.362	.378	101	2	9	9	-3	.966	0	3-86,2-33,S-15	0.3
1961	*Cin-N★	126	469	64	127	22	1	2	27	32	36	.271	.323	.335	74	-17	4	3	-1	.964	-18	*S-112,3-12/2-6	-2.6
1962	Cin-N	134	533	74	148	26	2	4	41	35	44	.278	.328	.356	81	-14	3	3	-1	.941	-8	*3-114,S-21	-2.0
1963	Cin-N	76	199	25	48	9	0	3	10	21	29	.241	.314	.332	83	-4	0	2	-1	.959	-1	3-48,S-15/2-1	-0.1
1964	Hou-N	133	448	45	109	16	1	2	22	37	52	.243	.302	.283	70	-17	4	6	-2	**.978**	10	*S-128/3-2	-0.1
1965	Hou-N	68	215	18	53	7	1	1	10	11	20	.247	.296	.302	74	-8	1	3	-2	.976	-10	S-59/3-2	-1.7
1966	Bos-A	58	136	11	29	7	0	1	12	15	19	.213	.291	.287	61	-7	1	0	0	.976	8	S-20,3-10/2-8	0.3
Total	10	1077	3546	411	935	146	13	22	261	265	353	.264	.318	.331	76	-112	31	31	-9	.971	-9	S-544,3-426/2-63	-8.5

■ RAY KATT   Katt, Raymond Frederick   b: 5/9/27, New Braunfels, Tex.   BR/TR, 6'2", 200 lbs.   Deb: 9/16/52   C

YEAR	TM/L	G	AB	R	H	2B	3B	HR	RBI	BB	SO	AVG	OBP	SLG	PRO+	BR/A	SB	CS	SBR	FA	FR	G/POS	TPR
1952	NY-N	9	27	4	6	0	0	0	1	1	5	.222	.250	.222	32	-2	0	0	0	1.000	1	/C-8	-0.1
1953	NY-N	8	29	2	5	1	0	0	1	1	3	.172	.200	.207	6	-4	0	0	0	.975	1	/C-8	-0.4
1954	NY-N	86	200	26	51	7	1	9	33	19	29	.255	.320	.435	94	-2	1	0	0	.973	-7	C-82	-0.6
1955	NY-N	124	326	27	70	7	2	7	28	22	38	.215	.269	.313	54	-22	0	0	0	.987	-8	*C-122	-2.6
1956	NY-N	37	101	10	23	4	0	7	14	6	16	.228	.278	.475	98	-4	0	1	-1	.973	6	C-37	0.0
	StL-N	47	158	11	41	4	0	6	20	6	24	.259	.291	.399	83	-4	0	1	-1	.984	-2	C-47	-0.5
	Yr	84	259	21	64	8	0	13	34	12	40	.247	.286	.429	89	-9	0	2	-2	.982	-1	C-84	-0.5
1957	NY-N	72	165	11	38	3	1	2	17	15	35	.230	.302	.297	62	-9	1	0	0	.981	-6	C-68	-1.3
1958	StL-N	19	41	1	7	1	0	1	4	4	6	.171	.244	.268	34	-4	0	0	0	.971	5	C-14	-0.3

YEAR	TM/L	G	AB	R	H	2B	3B	HR	RBI	BB	SO	AVG	OBP	SLG	PRO+	BR/A	SB	CS	SBR	FA	FR	G/POS	TPR
1959	StL-N	15	24	0	7	2	0	0	2	0	8	.292	.292	.375	71	-1	0	0	0	.976	-0	C-14	-0.1
Total	8	417	1071	92	248	29	4	32	120	74	164	.232	.285	.356	69	-49	2	2	-1	.981	-22	C-400	-5.9
■ BENNY KAUFF	Kauff, Benjamin Michael b: 1/5/1890, Pomeroy, Ohio d: 11/17/61, Columbus, Ohio BL/TL, 5'8", 157 lbs. Deb: 4/20/12																						
1912	NY-A	5	11	4	3	0	0	0	2	3		.273	.429	.273	96	0	1			1.000	-1	/O-4	-0.1
1914	Ind-F	154	571	**120**	**211**	**44**	13	8	95	72	55	**.370**	**.447**	.534	150	34	**75**			.953	16	*O-154	4.4
1915	Bro-F	136	483	92	165	23	11	12	83	85	50	**.342**	**.446**	**.509**	**170**	**42**	**55**			.959	15	*O-136	**5.3**
1916	NY-N	154	552	71	146	22	15	9	74	68	65	.264	.348	.408	139	26	40	26	-4	.962	2	*O-154	1.9
1917	*NY-N	153	559	89	172	22	4	5	68	59	54	.308	.379	.388	140	28	30			.976	-4	*O-153	1.7
1918	NY-N	67	270	41	85	19	4	2	39	16	30	.315	.355	.437	144	13	9			.952	-1	O-67	1.0
1919	NY-N	135	491	73	136	27	7	10	67	39	45	.277	.334	.422	128	15	21			.950	-3	*O-134	0.4
1920	NY-N	55	157	31	43	12	3	3	26	25	14	.274	.380	.446	138	8	3	7	-3	.960	-1	O-51	0.2
Total	8	859	3094	521	961	169	57	49	454	367	313	.311	.389	.450	146	167	234	33		.960	23	O-853	14.8
■ DICK KAUFFMAN	Kauffman, Howard Richard b: 6/22/1888, E.Lewisburg, Pa. d: 4/16/48, Mifflinburg, Pa. BB/TR, 6'3", 190 lbs. Deb: 9/17/14																						
1914	StL-A	7	15	1	4	1	0	0	2	0	3	.267	.267	.333	83	-0	0			.967	-1	/1-7	-0.2
1915	StL-A	37	124	9	32	8	2	0	14	5	27	.258	.298	.355	99	-1	0	3	-2	.984	-1	1-32/O-1	-0.5
Total	2	44	139	10	36	9	2	0	16	5	30	.259	.295	.353	97	-1	0	3		.982	-2	/1-39,O-1	-0.7
■ TONY KAUFMANN	Kaufmann, Anthony Charles b: 12/16/1900, Chicago, Ill. d: 6/4/82, Elgin, Ill. BR/TR, 5'11", 165 lbs. Deb: 9/23/21 C																						
1921	Chi-N	2	5	0	2	1	0	0	0	0	1	.400	.400	.600	161	0	0	0	0	1.000	-1	/P-2	0.0
1922	Chi-N	38	45	4	9	2	1	1	4	2	14	.200	.234	.356	49	-4	0	0	0	.933	-1	P-37	0.0
1923	Chi-N	33	74	10	16	2	0	2	10	7	17	.216	.284	.324	60	-4	0	0	0	.962	-1	P-33	0.0
1924	Chi-N	35	76	6	24	5	0	1	14	3	10	.316	.342	.421	102	0	0	0	0	.981	-1	P-34	0.0
1925	Chi-N	31	78	8	15	7	0	2	13	2	17	.192	.213	.359	42	-7	0	0	0	.981	-0	P-31	0.0
1926	Chi-N	30	60	9	15	2	0	1	7	2	10	.250	.274	.333	62	-3	1			**1.000**	-2	P-26	0.0
1927	Chi-N	9	16	2	5	0	0	1	6	4	4	.313	.450	.500	154	1	0			1.000	2	/P-9	0.0
	Phi-N	8	7	1	1	0	0	1	2	0	1	.143	.143	.571	83	-0	0			1.000	-1	/P-5,O-1	0.0
	StL-N	1	0	0	0	0	0	0	0	0	0	—	—	—	—	0	0			.000	0	/P-1	0.0
	Yr	18	23	3	6	0	0	2	8	4	5	.261	.370	.522	136	1	0			1.000	1	P-15/O-1	0.0
1928	StL-N	5	0	0	0	0	0	0	0	0	0	—	—	—	—	0	0			1.000	-0	/P-4	0.0
1929	NY-N	39	32	18	1	0	0	0	1	6	4	.031	.184	.031	-43	-7	3			.964	-4	O-16	-1.0
1930	StL-N	2	3	1	1	0	0	0	0	1	1	.333	.500	.333	103	0	0			1.000	-0	/P-2	0.0
1931	StL-N	20	18	1	2	0	0	0	0	1	3	.111	.158	.111	-26	-3	0			.929	-1	P-15/O-1	-0.1
1935	StL-N	7	0	2	0	0	0	0	0	0	0	—	—	—	—	0	0			1.000	0	/P-3	0.0
Total	12	260	414	62	91	19	1	9	57	28	82	.220	.269	.336	57	-27	4	0		.972	-9	P-202/O-18	-1.1
■ CHARLIE KAVANAGH	Kavanagh, Charles Hugh "Silk" b: 6/9/1893, Chicago, Ill. d: 9/6/73, Reedsburg, Wis. BR/TR, 5'9", 165 lbs. Deb: 6/11/14																						
1914	Chi-A	6	5	0	1	0	0	0	0	0	2	.200	.333	.200	62	-0	0			.000	0	H	0.0
■ LEO KAVANAGH	Kavanagh, Leo Daniel b: 8/9/1894, Chicago, Ill. d: 8/10/50, Chicago, Ill. BR/TR, 5'9", 180 lbs. Deb: 4/22/14																						
1914	Chi-F	5	11	0	3	0	0	0	1	1	0	.273	.333	.273	70	-1	0			1.000	-1	/S-5	-0.1
■ MARTY KAVANAGH	Kavanagh, Martin Joseph b: 6/13/1891, Harrison, N.J. d: 7/28/60, Eloise, Mich. BR/TR, 6', 187 lbs. Deb: 4/18/14																						
1914	Det-A	128	439	60	109	21	6	4	35	41	42	.248	.318	.351	98	-2	16	14	-4	.929	-7	*2-115/1-4	-1.5
1915	Det-A	113	332	55	98	14	13	4	49	42	44	.295	.378	.452	141	16	8	8	-2	.987	-15	1-44,2-42/S-2,O3	-0.2
1916	Det-A	58	78	6	11	4	0	0	5	9	15	.141	.239	.192	29	-7	0			1.000	0	O-11/2-2,3-1	-0.8
	Cle-A	19	44	4	11	2	1	1	10	2	5	.250	.283	.409	102	-0	0			.894	-0	/2-9,1-1,3-1	0.0
	Yr	77	122	10	22	6	1	1	15	11	20	.180	.254	.270	55	-7	0			1.000	-0	O-11,2-11/3-2,1-1	-0.8
1917	Cle-A	14	14	1	0	0	0	0	0	3	2	.000	.176	.000	-43	-2	0			1.000	0	/O-2	-0.2
1918	Cle-A	13	38	4	8	2	0	0	6	7	7	.211	.348	.263	77	-1	1			.967	-1	1-12	-0.3
	StL-N	12	44	6	8	1	0	1	8	3	1	.182	.234	.273	56	-2	1			1.000	-2	/O-8,2-4	-0.5
	Det-A	13	44	2	12	3	0	0	9	11	6	.273	.418	.341	135	3	0			.964	-1	1-12	0.1
Total	5	370	1033	138	257	47	20	10	122	118	122	.249	.330	.362	104	4	26	22		.926	-26	2-172/1-73,O-23,3S	-3.4
■ KAVANAUGH	Kavanaugh Deb: 9/11/1872																						
1872	Eck-n	5	23	3	6	1	0	0	2	0	1	.261	.261	.304	86	-0	0	0	0	.921	-1	/1-4,O-2	0.0
■ BILL KAY	Kay, Walter Brocton "King Bill" b: 2/14/1878, New Castle, Va. d: 12/3/45, Roanoke, Va. BL/TR, 6'2", 180 lbs. Deb: 8/12/07																						
1907	Was-A	25	60	8	20	1	1	0	7	0		.333	.333	.383	139	2	0			1.000	-0	O-12	0.2
■ EDDIE KAZAK	Kazak, Edward Terrance (b: Edward Terrance Tkaczuk) b: 7/18/20, Steubenville, O. BR/TR, 6', 175 lbs. Deb: 9/29/48																						
1948	StL-N	6	22	1	6	3	0	0	2	0	2	.273	.273	.409	78	-1	0			.900	1	/3-6	0.0
1949	StL-N★	92	326	43	99	15	3	6	42	29	17	.304	.362	.423	105	2	0			.926	-4	3-80/2-5	-0.2
1950	StL-N	93	207	21	53	2	2	5	23	18	19	.256	.319	.357	74	-8	0			.936	1	3-48	-0.7
1951	StL-N	11	33	2	6	2	0	0	4	5	5	.182	.289	.242	44	-3	0	0	0	.933	-1	3-10	-0.4
1952	StL-N	3	2	1	0	0	0	0	0	0	0	.000	.000	.000	-99	-1	0	0	0	1.000	0	/3-1	0.0
	Cin-N	13	15	1	1	0	1	0	0	0	2	.067	.067	.200	-29	-3	0	0	0	.667	-1	/3-3,1-1	-0.3
	Yr	16	17	2	1	0	1	0	0	0	2	.059	.059	.176	-37	-3	0	0	0	.750	-0	/3-4,1-1	-0.3
Total	5	218	605	69	165	22	6	11	71	52	45	.273	.332	.383	87	-12	0	0		.927	-3	3-148/2-5,1-1	-1.6
■ TED KAZANSKI	Kazanski, Theodore Stanley b: 1/25/34, Hamtramck, Mich. BR/TR, 6'1", 175 lbs. Deb: 6/25/53																						
1953	Phi-N	95	360	39	78	17	5	2	27	26	53	.217	.275	.308	52	-26	1	1	-0	.949	-19	S-95	-3.8
1954	Phi-N	39	104	7	14	2	0	1	8	4	14	.135	.167	.183	-9	-17	0	1	-1	.945	-7	S-38	-2.2
1955	Phi-N	9	12	1	1	0	0	1	1	1	1	.083	.154	.333	25	-1	0	0	0	1.000	1	/S-4,3-4	-0.1
1956	Phi-N	117	379	35	80	11	1	4	34	20	41	.211	.253	.277	43	-31	0	2	-1	.979	-10	*2-116/S-1	-3.5
1957	Phi-N	62	185	15	49	7	1	3	11	17	20	.265	.327	.362	88	-3	1	1	-0	.968	-3	3-36,2-22/S-3	-0.4
1958	Phi-N	95	289	21	66	12	2	3	35	22	34	.228	.292	.315	62	-16	2	3	-1	.988	-13	2-59,S-22,3-16	-2.6
Total	6	417	1329	118	288	49	9	14	116	90	163	.217	.270	.299	51	-94	4	8	-4	.981	-51	2-197,S-163/3-56	-12.6
■ BOB KEARNEY	Kearney, Robert Henry b: 10/3/56, San Antonio, Tex. BR/TR, 6', 190 lbs. Deb: 9/25/79																						
1979	SF-N	2	0	0	0	0	0	0	0	1	0	—	1.000	—	211	0	0	0	0	.000	0	/C-1	0.0
1981	Oak-A	1	0	0	0	0	0	0	0	0	0	—	—	—	—	0	0	0	0	.000	0	/C-1	0.0
1982	Oak-A	22	71	7	12	3	0	0	5	3	10	.169	.224	.211	21	-8	0	0	0	.970	5	C-22	-0.2
1983	Oak-A	108	298	33	76	11	0	8	32	21	50	.255	.313	.372	93	-3	1	4	-2	.982	5	*C-101/D-3	0.4
1984	Sea-A	133	431	39	97	24	1	7	43	18	72	.225	.259	.334	64	-22	7	5	-1	.988	5	*C-133	-1.2
1985	Sea-A	108	305	24	74	14	1	6	27	11	59	.243	.278	.354	71	-12	1	1	-0	**.995**	6	*C-108	-0.2
1986	Sea-A	81	204	23	49	10	0	6	25	12	35	.240	.282	.377	77	-7	0	2	-1	.989	14	C-79	1.0
1987	Sea-A	24	47	5	8	4	1	0	1	1	9	.170	.188	.298	25	-5	0	0	0	.981	6	C-24	0.2
Total	8	479	1356	131	316	66	3	27	133	67	235	.233	.275	.346	70	-57	9	12	-5	.987	41	C-469/D-3	-0.0
■ TEDDY KEARNS	Kearns, Edward Joseph b: 1/1/1900, Trenton, N.J. d: 12/21/49, Trenton, N.J. BR/TR, 5'11", 180 lbs. Deb: 10/1/20																						
1920	Phi-A	1	1	0	0	0	0	0	0	0	0	.000	.000	.000	-99	-0	0	0	0	.000	0	H	0.0
1924	Chi-N	4	16	0	4	0	1	0	1	1	1	.250	.294	.375	77	-1	0	0	0	1.000	-0	/1-4	-0.1
1925	Chi-N	3	2	0	1	0	0	0	0	0	0	.500	.500	.500	154	0	0	0	0	1.000	-0	/1-3	0.0
Total	3	8	19	0	5	0	1	0	1	1	1	.263	.300	.368	76	-1	0	0	0	1.000	-0	/1-7	-0.1
■ TOM KEARNS	Kearns, Thomas J. "Dasher" b: 11/9/1859, Rochester, N.Y. d: 12/7/38, Buffalo, N.Y. BR/TR, 5'7", 160 lbs. Deb: 8/26/1880																						
1880	Buf-N	2	7	0	0	0	0	0	0	0	0	.000	.000	.000	-98	-1				.667	-1	/C-2	-0.3
1882	Det-N	4	13	2	4	2	0	0	1	0	4	.308	.308	.462	143	1				.733	-3	/2-4	-0.2
1884	Det-N	21	79	9	16	0	1	0	7	2	10	.203	.222	.228	45	-5				.810	-10	2-21	-1.3
Total	3	27	99	11	20	2	1	0	8	2	14	.202	.218	.242	48	-6				.801	-14	/2-25,C-2	-1.8

YEAR	TM/L	G	AB	R	H	2B	3B	HR	RBI	BB	SO	AVG	OBP	SLG	PRO+	BR/A	SB	CS	SBR	FA	FR	G/POS	TPR
■ EDDIE KEARSE	Kearse, Edward Paul "Truck" b: 2/23/16, San Francisco, Cal d: 7/15/68, Eureka, Cal. BR/TR, 6'1", 195 lbs. Deb: 6/13/42																						
1942	NY-A	11	26	2	5	0	0	0	2	3	1	.192	.276	.192	34	-2	1	0	0	1.000	3	C-11	0.2
■ CHICK KEATING	Keating, Walter Francis b: 8/8/1891, Philadelphia, Pa. d: 7/13/59, Philadelphia, Pa. BR/TR, 5'9.5", 155 lbs. Deb: 9/26/13																						
1913	Chi-N	2	5	0	1	1	0	0	0	0	1	.200	.200	.400	69	-0	0			1.000	-1	/S-2	-0.1
1914	Chi-N	20	30	3	3	0	1	0	0	6	9	.100	.250	.167	25	-3	0			.951	0	S-14	-0.2
1915	Chi-N	4	8	1	0	0	0	0	0	0	3	.000	.000	.000	-99	-2	1			.750	-0	/S-2	-0.2
1926	Phi-N	4	2	0	0	0	0	0	0	0	0	.000	.000	.000	-95	-1	0			1.000	-0	/2-2,S-2,3-1	-0.1
Total	4	30	45	4	4	1	1	0	0	6	13	.089	.196	.156	4	-5	1			.903	-1	/S-20,2-2,3-1	-0.6
■ GREG KEATLEY	Keatley, Gregory Steven b: 9/12/53, Princeton, W.Va. BR/TR, 6'2", 200 lbs. Deb: 9/27/81																						
1981	KC-A	2	0	0	0	0	0	0	0	0	0	—	—	—	—	0	0	0	0	1.000	-0	/C-2	0.0
■ PAT KEEDY	Keedy, Charles Patrick b: 1/10/58, Birmingham, Ala. BR/TR, 6'4", 205 lbs. Deb: 9/10/85																						
1985	Cal-A	3	4	1	2	1	0	1	1	0	0	.500	.500	1.500	424	2	0	1	-1	.000	-0	/3-2,O-1	0.1
1987	Chi-A	17	41	6	7	1	0	2	2	2	14	.171	.209	.341	42	-4	1	0	0	.943	4	3-11/1-2,2-1,SOD	0.1
1989	Cle-A	9	14	3	3	2	0	0	1	2	5	.214	.313	.357	87	-0	0	0	0	1.000	-0	/O-3,3-2,1-1,S-1,D	0.0
Total	3	29	59	10	12	4	0	3	4	4	19	.203	.254	.424	77	-2	1	1	-0	.929	3	/3-15,O-5,1-3,DS2	0.2
■ WILLIE KEELER	Keeler, William Henry "Wee Willie" (b: William Henry O'Kelleher) b: 3/3/1872, Brooklyn, N.Y. d: 1/1/23, Brooklyn, N.Y. BL/TL, 5'4.5", 140 lbs. Deb: 9/30/1892 H																						
1892	NY-N	14	53	7	17	3	0	0	6	3	3	.321	.368	.377	128	2	5			.878	-3	3-14	-0.1
1893	NY-N	7	24	5	8	2	1	1	7	5	1	.333	.448	.625	183	3	3			.667	-5	/O-3,2-2,S-2	-0.2
	Bro-N	20	80	14	25	1	1	1	9	4	4	.313	.353	.387	101	0	2			.833	-1	3-12/O-8	-0.1
	Yr	27	104	19	33	3	2	2	16	9	5	.317	.377	.442	121	3	5			.833	-6	3-12,O-11/2-2,S-2	-0.3
1894	*Bal-N	129	590	165	219	27	22	5	94	40	6	.371	.427	.517	121	20	32			.938	3	*O-128/2-1	1.1
1895	*Bal-N	131	565	162	213	24	15	4	78	37	12	.377	.429	.494	134	28	47			.946	0	*O-131	1.4
1896	*Bal-N	126	544	153	210	22	13	4	82	37	9	.386	.432	.496	142	33	67			.969	6	*O-126	2.4
1897	*Bal-N	129	564	145	**239**	27	19	0	74	35		**.424**	.464	.539	164	52	64			.970	-2	*O-129	3.4
1898	Bal-N	129	561	126	**216**	7	2	1	44	31		**.385**	.420	.410	136	26	28			.961	0	*O-128/3-1	1.6
1899	Bro-N	141	570	**140**	216	12	13	1	61	37		.379	.425	.451	137	30	45			.979	-2	*O-141	1.5
1900	*Bro-N	136	563	106	**204**	13	12	4	68	30		.362	.402	.449	127	19	41			.940	5	*O-136/2-1	1.3
1901	Bro-N	136	595	123	202	18	12	2	43	21		.339	.369	.420	125	18	23			**.985**	-6	*O-125,3-10/2-3	0.3
1902	Bro-N	133	559	86	186	20	5	0	38	21		.333	.365	.386	131	19	19			**.978**	2	*O-133	1.3
1903	NY-A	132	512	95	160	14	7	0	32	32		.313	.368	.367	114	10	24			.935	-9	*O-128/3-4	-0.8
1904	NY-A	143	543	78	186	14	8	2	40	35		.343	.390	.409	146	28	21			.935	-3	*O-142	1.9
1905	NY-A	149	560	81	169	14	4	4	38	43		.302	.357	.363	115	9	19			.968	-3	*O-137,2-12/3-3	0.0
1906	NY-A	152	592	96	180	8	3	2	33	40		.304	.353	.338	106	4	23			.987	-2	*O-152	-0.6
1907	NY-A	107	423	50	99	5	2	0	17	15		.234	.265	.255	61	-19	7			.969	-3	*O-107	-2.9
1908	NY-A	91	323	38	85	3	1	1	14	31		.263	.337	.288	102	2	14			.936	-1	O-88	-0.3
1909	NY-A	99	360	44	95	7	5	1	32	24		.264	.327	.319	104	2	10			.968	-5	O-95	-0.8
1910	NY-N	19	10	5	3	0	0	0	0	3	1	.300	.462	.300	123	1	1			1.000	-1	/O-2	0.0
Total	19	2123	8591	1719	2932	241	145	33	810	524	36	.341	.388	.415	125	286	495			.960	-30	*O-2039/3-44,2-19,S	10.4
■ BOB KEELY	Keely, Robert William b: 8/22/09, St.Louis, Mo. BR/TR, 6', 175 lbs. Deb: 7/25/44 C																						
1944	StL-N	1	0	0	0	0	0	0	0	0	0	—	—	—	—	0	0			1.000	-0	/C-1	0.0
1945	StL-N	1	1	0	0	0	0	0	0	0	0	.000	.000	.000	-98	-0	0			1.000	-0	/C-1	0.0
Total	2	2	1	0	0	0	0	0	0	0	0	.000	.000	.000	-98	-0	0			1.000	-0	/C-2	0.0
■ BILL KEEN	Keen, William Brown "Buster" b: 8/16/1892, Oglethorpe, Ga. d: 7/16/47, South Point, Ohio BR/TR, 6', 181 lbs. Deb: 8/8/11																						
1911	Pit-N	6	7	0	0	0	0	0	0	1	4	.000	.125	.000	-61	-2	0			1.000	-0	/1-1	-0.2
■ JIM KEENAN	Keenan, James William b: 2/10/1858, New Haven, Conn. d: 9/21/26, Cincinnati, Ohio BR/TR, 5'10", 186 lbs. Deb: 5/17/1875																						
1875	NH-n	5	13	1	1	0	0	0	0	0	0	.077	.077	.077	-53	-2	0	0	0	.800	-3	/C-3,3-2,O-1	-0.5
1880	Buf-N	2	7	1	1	0	0	0	0	1	1	.143	.250	.143	36	-0				.947	3	/C-2	0.2
1882	Pit-a	25	96	10	21	7	0	1		1		.219	.227	.323	87	-1				.906	1	C-22/O-3,S-1	0.1
1884	Ind-a	68	249	36	73	14	4	3		16		.293	.343	.418	151	14				.923	-2	C-59/1-6,O-2,S-2,P	1.5
1885	Cin-a	36	132	16	35	2	2	1	15	8		.265	.307	.333	100	-0				.926	-1	C-33/1-4,P-1	0.1
1886	Cin-a	44	148	31	40	4	3	3	24	18		.270	.357	.399	132	6	0			.915	0	C-30/O-7,3-5,1-4,P	0.7
1887	Cin-a	47	174	19	44	4	1	0	17	11		.253	.301	.287	63	-9	7			.934	9	C-38,1-11	0.2
1888	Cin-a	85	313	38	73	9	8	1	40	22		.233	.294	.323	93	-3	9			.946	3	C-69,1-16	0.4
1889	Cin-a	87	300	52	86	10	11	6	60	48	35	.287	.395	.453	137	15	18			.962	1	C-66,1-21/3-1	1.8
1890	Cin-N	54	202	21	28	4	2	3	19	19	36	.139	.216	.223	28	-19	5			.950	4	C-50/1-2,O-1,3-1	-0.9
1891	Cin-N	75	252	30	51	7	5	4	33	33	39	.202	.302	.317	80	-6	2			.974	-4	1-41,C-34/3-1	-0.8
Total	10	523	1873	254	452	61	36	22	208	177	111	.241	.314	.348	99	-4	41	0		.935	14	C-403,1-105/O3PS	3.3
■ GEORGE KEERL	Keerl, George Henry b: 4/10/1847, Baltimore, Md. d: 9/9/23, Menominee, Mich. BR/TR, 5'7", 145 lbs. Deb: 5/5/1875																						
1875	Chi-n	6	23	2	3	0	0	0	3	0	2	.130	.130	.130	-9	-2	0	0	0	.815	-2	/2-6	-0.4
■ JIM KEESEY	Keesey, James Ward b: 10/27/02, Perryville, Md. d: 9/5/51, Boise, Idaho BR/TR, 6'0.5", 170 lbs. Deb: 9/6/25																						
1925	Phi-A	5	5	1	2	0	0	0	1	0	2	.400	.400	.400	97	-0	0	0	0	1.000	-0	/1-2	0.0
1930	Phi-A	11	12	2	3	1	0	0	2	1	2	.250	.308	.333	60	-1	0	0	0	.909	-0	/1-3	-0.1
Total	2	16	17	3	5	1	0	0	3	1	4	.294	.333	.353	71	-1	0	0	0	.923	-1	/1-5	-0.1
■ BILL KEISTER	Keister, William Hoffman "Wagon Tongue" b: 8/17/1874, Baltimore, Md. d: 8/19/24, Baltimore, Md. BL/TR, 5'5.5", 168 lbs. Deb: 5/20/1896																						
1896	Bal-N	15	58	8	14	3	0	0	5	3	5	.241	.302	.293	56	-4	4			.923	-5	/2-8,3-6	-0.7
1898	Bos-N	10	30	5	5	2	0	0	4	0		.167	.167	.233	14	-3	0			1.000	1	/S-4,2-4,O-1	-0.2
1899	Bal-N	136	523	96	172	22	16	3	73	16		.329	.368	.449	117	10	33			.895	-30	S-90,2-46/O-1	-1.0
1900	StL-N	126	497	78	149	26	10	1	72	25		.300	.347	.398	106	3	32			.927	-23	*2-116/S-7,3-3	-1.3
1901	Bal-A	115	442	78	145	20	**21**	2	93	18		.328	.365	.482	128	15	24			.851	-23	*S-112	0.1
1902	Was-A	119	483	82	145	33	9	9	90	14		.300	.329	.462	117	8	27			.912	-4	O-65,2-40,3-14,/S-2	0.2
1903	Phi-N	100	400	53	128	27	7	3	63	14		.320	.352	.445	131	14	11			.940	3	*O-100	1.1
Total	7	621	2433	400	758	133	63	18	400	90	5	.312	.349	.440	116	43	131			.870	-80	S-215,2-214,O/3	-1.8
■ MICKEY KELIHER	Keliher, Maurice Michael b: 1/11/1890, Washington, D.C. d: 9/7/30, Washington, D.C. BL/TL, 6', 175 lbs. Deb: 9/9/11																						
1911	Pit-N	3	7	0	0	0	0	0	0	0	5	.000	.000	.000	-96	-2	0			.875	-0	/1-3	-0.2
1912	Pit-N	2	0	1	0	0	0	0	0	0	0	—	—	—	—	0	0			.000	0	R	0.0
Total	2	5	7	1	0	0	0	0	0	0	5	.000	.000	.000	-96	-2	0			.875	-0	/1-3	-0.2
■ SKEETER KELL	Kell, Everett Lee b: 10/11/29, Swifton, Ark. BR/TR, 5'9", 160 lbs. Deb: 4/19/52 F																						
1952	Phi-A	75	213	24	47	8	3	0	17	14	18	.221	.275	.286	53	-14	5	1	1	.963	-5	2-68	-1.5
■ GEORGE KELL	Kell, George Clyde b: 8/23/22, Swifton, Ark. BR/TR, 5'9", 175 lbs. Deb: 9/28/43 FH																						
1943	Phi-A	1	5	1	1	0	1	0	1	0	0	.200	.200	.600	131	0	0	0	0	1.000	0	/3-1	0.0
1944	Phi-A	139	514	51	138	15	3	0	44	22	23	.268	.300	.309	75	-17	5	2	0	.958	-5	*3-139	-2.1
1945	Phi-A	147	567	50	154	30	3	4	56	27	15	.272	.306	.356	92	-8	2	0	1	**.964**	22	*3-147	2.0
1946	Phi-A	26	87	3	26	6	1	0	11	10	6	.299	.378	.391	116	2	0	0	0	.979	3	3-26	0.6
	Det-A	105	434	67	142	19	9	4	41	30	14	.327	.371	.440	119	10	3	2	-0	.984	5	*3-105/1-1	1.8
	Yr	131	521	70	168	25	10	4	52	40	20	.322	.372	.432	118	12	3	2	-0	**.983**	8	*3-131/1-1	2.4
1947	Det-A★	152	588	75	188	29	5	5	93	61	16	.320	.387	.412	118	16	9	11	-4	.962	18	*3-152	3.1
1948	Det-A☆	92	368	47	112	24	3	2	44	33	15	.304	.369	.402	102	1	2	2	-1	.969	-8	3-92	-0.8
1949	Det-A★	134	522	97	179	38	9	3	59	71	13	**.343**	.424	.467	136	28	7	5	-1	.975	1	*3-134	2.5

YEAR	TM/L	G	AB	R	H	2B	3B	HR	RBI	BB	SO	AVG	OBP	SLG	PRO+	BR/A	SB	CS	SBR	FA	FR	G/POS	TPR
1950	Det-A★	157	641	114	**218**	**56**	6	8	101	66	18	.340	.403	.484	122	21	3	3	-1	**.982**	-3	*3-157	1.4
1951	Det-A★	147	598	92	**191**	**36**	3	2	59	61	18	.319	.386	.400	112	12	10	3	1	**.960**	9	*3-147	2.0
1952	Det-A	39	152	11	45	8	0	1	17	15	13	.296	.359	.368	102	1	0	1	-1	.959	-2	3-39	-0.3
	Bos-A†	75	276	41	88	15	2	6	40	31	10	.319	.390	.453	124	9	0	1	-1	.959	-7	3-73	0.1
	Yr	114	428	52	133	23	2	7	57	46	23	.311	.379	.423	117	10	0	2	-1	.959	-9	*3-112	-0.2
1953	Bos-A★	134	460	68	141	41	2	12	73	52	22	.307	.383	.483	126	17	5	2	0	**.972**	-14	*3-124/O-7	0.0
1954	Bos-A	26	93	15	24	3	0	0	10	15	3	.258	.361	.290	72	-3	0	0	0	.920	-3	3-25	-0.7
	Chi-A†	71	233	25	66	10	0	5	48	18	12	.283	.335	.391	95	-2	1	1	-0	.996	-11	1-32,3-31/O-2	-1.7
	Yr	97	326	40	90	13	0	5	58	33	15	.276	.343	.362	88	-5	1	1	-0	.936	-14	3-56,1-32/O-2	-2.4
1955	Chi-A	128	429	44	134	24	1	8	81	51	36	.312	.393	.429	118	12	2	2	-1	**.976**	-19	*3-105,1-24/O-1	-0.9
1956	Chi-A	21	80	7	25	5	0	1	11	8	6	.313	.375	.412	106	1	0	0	0	1.000	-4	3-18/1-4	-0.3
	Bal-A★	102	345	45	90	17	2	8	37	25	31	.261	.316	.391	93	-5	0	1	-1	.974	-7	3-97/1-2,2-1	-1.1
	Yr	123	425	52	115	22	2	9	48	33	37	.271	.328	.395	96	-4	0	1	-1	**.978**	-11	*3-115/1-6,2-1	-1.4
1957	Bal-A★	99	310	28	92	9	0	9	44	25	16	.297	.353	.413	116	6	2	0	1	.979	-4	3-80,1-22	0.3
Total	15	1795	6702	881	2054	385	50	78	870	621	287	.306	.368	.414	111	100	51	36	-6	.969	-29	*3-1692/1-85,O-10,2	5.9

■ DUKE KELLEHER Kelleher, Albert Aloysius b: 9/30/1893, New York, N.Y. d: 9/28/47, Staten Island, N.Y. TR , Deb: 8/18/16

YEAR	TM/L	G	AB	R	H	2B	3B	HR	RBI	BB	SO	AVG	OBP	SLG	PRO+	BR/A	SB	CS	SBR	FA	FR	G/POS	TPR
1916	NY-N	1	0	0	0	0	0	0	0	0	0	—	—	—	—	0	0			.000	0	/C-1	0.0

■ FRANKIE KELLEHER Kelleher, Francis Eugene b: 8/22/16, San Francisco, Cal d: 4/13/79, Stockton, Cal. BR/TR, 6'1", 195 lbs. Deb: 7/18/42

YEAR	TM/L	G	AB	R	H	2B	3B	HR	RBI	BB	SO	AVG	OBP	SLG	PRO+	BR/A	SB	CS	SBR	FA	FR	G/POS	TPR
1942	Cin-N	38	110	13	20	3	1	3	12	16	20	.182	.286	.309	74	-4	0			.986	0	O-30	-0.5
1943	Cin-N	9	10	1	0	0	0	0	0	2	0	.000	.167	.000	-51	-2	0			1.000	-0	/O-1	-0.2
Total	2	47	120	14	20	3	1	3	12	18	20	.167	.275	.283	64	-6	0			.986	0	/O-31	-0.7

■ JOHN KELLEHER Kelleher, John Patrick b: 9/13/1893, Brookline, Mass. d: 8/21/60, Brighton, Mass. BR/TR, 5'11", 150 lbs. Deb: 7/31/12

YEAR	TM/L	G	AB	R	H	2B	3B	HR	RBI	BB	SO	AVG	OBP	SLG	PRO+	BR/A	SB	CS	SBR	FA	FR	G/POS	TPR
1912	StL-N	8	12	0	4	1	0	0	1	0	2	.333	.333	.417	107	0	0			1.000	1	/3-3	0.1
1916	Bro-N	2	3	0	0	0	0	0	0	0	0	.000	.000	.000	-97	-1	0			1.000	-1	/S-1,3-1	-0.2
1921	Chi-N	95	301	31	93	11	7	4	47	16	16	.309	.346	.432	104	2	2	5	-2	.947	3	3-37,2-27,1-11,S/O	0.6
1922	Chi-N	63	193	23	50	7	1	0	20	15	14	.259	.316	.306	60	-11	5	7	-3	.932	4	3-46/S-7,1-4	-0.6
1923	Chi-N	66	193	27	59	10	0	6	21	14	9	.306	.353	.451	110	2	2	4	-2	.975	-7	1-22,S-14,3-11,/2-6	-0.5
1924	Bos-N	1	1	0	0	0	0	0	0	0	1	.000	.000	.000	-99	-0	0	0	0	.000	0	H	0.0
Total	6	235	703	81	206	29	8	10	89	45	42	.293	.337	.400	92	-8	9	16		.924	-0	/3-98,1-37,2-33,SO	-0.6

■ MICK KELLEHER Kelleher, Michael Dennis b: 7/25/47, Seattle, Wash. BR/TR, 5'9", 176 lbs. Deb: 9/1/72 C

YEAR	TM/L	G	AB	R	H	2B	3B	HR	RBI	BB	SO	AVG	OBP	SLG	PRO+	BR/A	SB	CS	SBR	FA	FR	G/POS	TPR
1972	StL-N	23	63	5	10	2	1	0	1	6	15	.159	.232	.222	30	-6	0	0	0	.984	5	S-23	0.2
1973	StL-N	43	38	4	7	2	0	0	2	4	11	.184	.279	.237	44	-3	0	0	0	.955	9	S-42	0.8
1974	Hou-N	19	57	4	9	0	0	0	2	5	10	.158	.226	.158	9	-7	1	1	-0	.944	4	S-18	-0.1
1975	StL-N	7	4	0	0	0	0	0	0	0	1	.000	.000	.000	-97	-1	0	0	0	.909	2	/S-7	0.1
1976	Chi-N	124	337	28	77	12	1	0	22	15	32	.228	.266	.270	48	-23	0	4	-2	.980	12	*S-101,3-22/2-5	-0.3
1977	Chi-N	63	122	14	28	5	2	0	11	9	12	.230	.288	.303	53	-8	0	0	0	.976	18	2-40,S-14/3-1	1.3
1978	Chi-N	68	95	8	24	1	0	0	6	7	11	.253	.304	.263	53	-6	4	1	1	1.000	18	3-37,2-17,S-10	1.4
1979	Chi-N	73	142	14	36	4	1	0	10	7	9	.254	.298	.296	57	-8	2	0	1	.966	22	3-32,2-29,S-14	1.6
1980	Chi-N	105	96	12	14	1	1	0	4	9	17	.146	.219	.177	11	-11	1	3	-2	.974	25	2-57,3-31,S-17	1.5
1981	Det-A	61	77	10	17	4	0	0	6	7	10	.221	.286	.273	59	-4	0	0	0	.930	6	3-39,2-11/S-9	0.3
1982	Det-A	2	1	0	0	0	0	0	0	0	0	.000	.000	.000	-99	-0	0	0	0	1.000	-0	/2-1,3-1	-0.1
	Cal-A	34	49	9	8	1	0	0	1	5	5	.163	.255	.184	23	-5	1	1	-0	.965	7	S-28/3-6	0.3
	Yr	36	50	9	8	1	0	0	1	5	5	.160	.250	.180	20	-5	1	1	-0	.965	7	S-28/3-7,2-1	0.2
Total	11	622	1081	108	230	32	6	0	65	74	133	.213	.268	.253	43	-82	9	10	-3	.976	128	S-283,3-169,2-160	7.0

■ CHARLIE KELLER Keller, Charles Ernest "King Kong" b: 9/12/16, Middletown, Md. d: 5/23/90, Frederick, Md. BL/TR, 5'10", 190 lbs. Deb: 4/22/39 F

YEAR	TM/L	G	AB	R	H	2B	3B	HR	RBI	BB	SO	AVG	OBP	SLG	PRO+	BR/A	SB	CS	SBR	FA	FR	G/POS	TPR
1939	*NY-A	111	398	87	133	21	6	11	83	81	49	.334	.447	.500	144	30	6	3	0	.969	-3	*O-105	2.2
1940	NY-A★	138	500	102	143	18	15	21	93	**106**	65	.286	.411	.508	142	34	8	2	1	.967	2	*O-136	2.8
1941	*NY-A★	140	507	102	151	24	10	33	122	102	65	.298	.416	.580	163	47	6	4	-1	.980	4	*O-137	4.1
1942	*NY-A	152	544	106	159	24	9	26	108	114	61	.292	.417	.513	164	49	14	2	3	.985	-0	*O-152	4.4
1943	*NY-A†	141	512	97	139	15	11	31	86	**106**	60	.271	.396	.525	**167**	**45**	7	5	-1	.994	4	*O-141	4.3
1945	NY-A	44	163	26	49	7	4	10	34	31	21	.301	.412	.577	178	16	0	2	-1	1.000	4	O-44	1.7
1946	NY-A★	150	538	98	148	29	10	30	101	113	101	.275	.405	.533	158	44	1	4	-2	.979	-1	*O-149	3.5
1947	NY-A†	45	151	36	36	6	1	13	36	41	18	.238	.404	.550	165	14	0	0	0	.967	-2	O-43	1.0
1948	NY-A	83	247	41	66	15	2	6	44	41	25	.267	.372	.417	111	4	1	1	-0	.977	-5	O-66	-0.4
1949	NY-A	60	116	17	29	4	1	3	16	25	15	.250	.392	.379	104	2	2	0	1	.976	-6	O-31	-0.5
1950	Det-A	50	51	7	16	1	3	2	16	13	6	.314	.453	.569	155	5	0	0	0	1.000	-1	/O-6	0.3
1951	Det-A	54	62	6	16	2	0	3	21	11	12	.258	.370	.435	117	2	0	0	0	1.000	1	/O-8	0.2
1952	NY-A	2	1	0	0	0	0	0	0	0	1	.000	.000	.000	-99	-0	0	0	0	.000	-0	/O-1	-0.1
Total	13	1170	3790	725	1085	166	72	189	760	784	499	.286	.410	.518	152	293	45	23	-0	.980	-4	*O-1019	23.5

■ HAL KELLER Keller, Harold Kefauver b: 7/7/27, Middletown, Md. BL/TR, 6'1", 200 lbs. Deb: 9/13/49 F

YEAR	TM/L	G	AB	R	H	2B	3B	HR	RBI	BB	SO	AVG	OBP	SLG	PRO+	BR/A	SB	CS	SBR	FA	FR	G/POS	TPR
1949	Was-A	3	3	1	1	0	0	0	0	0	0	.333	.333	.333	78	-0	0	0	0	.000	0	H	0.0
1950	Was-A	11	28	1	6	3	0	1	5	2	2	.214	.267	.429	79	-1	0	0	0	1.000	-2	/C-8	-0.2
1952	Was-A	11	23	2	4	2	0	0	0	1	1	.174	.208	.261	31	-2	0	0	0	.967	-0	C-11	-0.2
Total	3	25	54	4	11	5	0	1	5	3	3	.204	.246	.352	60	-4	0	0	0	.982	-2	/C-19	-0.4

■ FRANK KELLERT Kellert, Frank William b: 7/6/24, Oklahoma City, Okla. d: 11/19/76, Oklahoma City, Okla. BR/TR, 6'2.5", 185 lbs. Deb: 4/18/53

YEAR	TM/L	G	AB	R	H	2B	3B	HR	RBI	BB	SO	AVG	OBP	SLG	PRO+	BR/A	SB	CS	SBR	FA	FR	G/POS	TPR
1953	StL-A	2	4	0	0	0	0	0	0	0	0	.000	.000	.000	-98	-1	0	0	0	1.000	-0	/1-1	-0.1
1954	Bal-A	10	34	3	7	2	0	0	1	5	4	.206	.308	.265	62	-2	0	0	0	1.000	-1	/1-9	-0.4
1955	*Bro-N	39	80	12	26	4	2	4	19	9	10	.325	.393	.575	149	6	0	1	-1	.983	-0	1-22	0.4
1956	Chi-N	71	129	10	24	3	1	4	17	12	22	.186	.255	.318	54	-9	0	0	0	.991	3	1-27	-0.8
Total	4	122	247	25	57	9	3	8	37	26	36	.231	.304	.389	85	-6	0	1	-1	.990	1	/1-59	-0.9

■ RED KELLETT Kellett, Donald Stafford b: 7/15/09, Brooklyn, N.Y. d: 11/3/70, Ft.Lauderdale, Fla. BR/TR, 6', 185 lbs. Deb: 7/2/34

YEAR	TM/L	G	AB	R	H	2B	3B	HR	RBI	BB	SO	AVG	OBP	SLG	PRO+	BR/A	SB	CS	SBR	FA	FR	G/POS	TPR
1934	Bos-A	9	9	0	0	0	0	0	0	1	5	.000	.100	.000	-68	-2	0	0	0	.778	1	/S-4,2-2,3-1	-0.1

■ JOE KELLEY Kelley, Joseph James b: 12/9/1871, Cambridge, Mass. d: 8/14/43, Baltimore, Md. BR/TR, 5'11", 190 lbs. Deb: 7/27/1891 MCH

YEAR	TM/L	G	AB	R	H	2B	3B	HR	RBI	BB	SO	AVG	OBP	SLG	PRO+	BR/A	SB	CS	SBR	FA	FR	G/POS	TPR
1891	Bos-N	12	45	7	11	1	1	0	3	2	7	.244	.277	.311	63	-2	0			.852	-1	O-12	-0.3
1892	Pit-N	56	205	26	49	7	7	0	28	17	21	.239	.297	.341	93	-2	8			.919	2	O-56	-0.3
	Bal-N	10	33	3	7	0	0	0	4	4	7	.212	.316	.212	59	-1	2			.824	-3	O-10	-0.4
	Yr	66	238	29	56	7	7	0	32	21	28	.235	.300	.324	88	-4	10			.908	-1	O-66	-0.7
1893	Bal-N	125	502	120	153	27	16	9	76	77	44	.305	.401	.476	131	22	33			.940	7	*O-125	1.9
1894	*Bal-N	129	507	165	199	48	20	6	111	107	36	.393	.502	.602	158	53	46			.951	2	*O-129	3.5
1895	*Bal-N	131	518	148	189	26	19	10	134	77	29	.365	.456	.546	154	43	54			.964	11	*O-131	3.5
1896	*Bal-N	131	519	148	189	31	19	8	100	91	19	.364	.469	.543	164	53	**87**			.958	4	*O-131	3.8
1897	*Bal-N	131	505	113	183	31	9	5	118	70		.362	.447	.489	147	37	44			.959	-2	*O-130/S-3,3-2	2.2
1898	Bal-N	124	464	71	149	18	15	2	110	56		.321	.398	.438	137	23	24			.969	1	*O-122/3-2	1.4
1899	Bro-N	143	538	108	175	21	14	6	93	70		.325	.410	.450	133	26	31			.977	8	*O-143	2.0
1900	*Bro-N	121	454	90	145	23	17	6	91	53		.319	.398	.485	135	21	26			.959	1	O-77,1-32,3-13	1.4
1901	Bro-N	120	492	77	151	22	12	4	65	40		.307	.363	.425	124	15	18			.975	7	*1-115/3-5	1.9
1902	Bal-A	60	222	50	69	17	7	1	34	34		.311	.405	.464	134	11	12			.973	-0	O-48/3-8,1-5	0.7
	Cin-N	40	156	24	50	9	2	1	12	15		.321	.380	.423	135	6	3			.971	3	O-20,2-10/3-9,SM	0.9
1903	Cin-N	105	383	85	121	22	4	3	45	51		.316	.402	.418	120	10	18			.947	-7	O-67,S-12,2/31M	0.1
1904	Cin-N	123	449	75	126	21	13	0	63	49		.281	.359	.385	119	10	15			.988	0	*1-117/O-6,2-1,M	0.8
1905	Cin-N	90	321	43	89	7	6	1	37	27		.277	.346	.346	96	-2	8			.974	-3	O-85/1-2,M	-0.9
1906	Cin-N	129	465	43	106	19	11	1	53	44		.228	.300	.323	90	-6	9			.966	-5	*O-122/1-3,S-1,3-1	-1.9

YEAR	TM/L	G	AB	R	H	2B	3B	HR	RBI	BB	SO	AVG	OBP	SLG	PRO+	BR/A	SB	CS	SBR	FA	FR	G/POS	TPR
1908	Bos-N	73	228	25	59	8	2	2	17	27		.259	.342	.338	119	6	5			.938	-4	O-51,1-11,M	-0.1
Total	17	1853	7006	1421	2220	358	194	65	1194	911	163	.317	.402	.451	132	321	443			.955	20	*O-1465,1-291/32S	20.2

■ MIKE KELLEY
Kelley, Michael Joseph   b: 12/2/1875, Templeton, Mass.   d: 6/6/55, Minneapolis, Minn.   BR/TR, 6′, 210 lbs.   Deb: 7/15/1899

| 1899 | Lou-N | 76 | 282 | 48 | 68 | 11 | 2 | 3 | 33 | 21 | | .241 | .307 | .326 | 74 | -10 | 10 | | | .974 | -0 | 1-76 | -0.9 |

■ FRANK KELLIHER
Kelliher, Francis Mortimer "Yucka"   b: 5/23/1899, Somerville, Mass.   d: 3/4/56, Somerville, Mass.   BL/TL, 5′9.5″, 175 lbs.   Deb: 9/19/19

| 1919 | Was-A | 1 | 1 | 0 | 0 | 0 | 0 | 0 | 0 | 0 | 0 | .000 | .000 | .000 | -99 | -0 | 0 | | | .000 | 0 | H | 0.0 |

■ NATE KELLOGG
Kellogg, Nathaniel Monroe   b: 9/28/1858, Rochester, Iowa   d: 15,   5′9″, 175 lbs.   Deb: 8/27/1885

| 1885 | Det-N | 5 | 17 | 4 | 2 | 1 | 0 | 0 | 0 | 1 | 5 | .118 | .167 | .176 | 11 | -2 | | | | .783 | -2 | /S-5 | -0.3 |

■ BILL KELLOGG
Kellogg, William Dearstyne   b: 5/25/1884, Albany, N.Y.   d: 12/12/71, Baltimore, Md.   BR/TR, 5′10″, 153 lbs.   Deb: 4/14/14

| 1914 | Cin-N | 71 | 126 | 14 | 22 | 0 | 1 | 0 | 7 | 14 | 28 | .175 | .262 | .190 | 34 | -10 | 7 | | | .988 | -1 | 1-38,2-11/O-2,3-1 | -1.2 |

■ RED KELLY
Kelly, Albert Michael   b: 11/15/1884, Union, Ill.   d: 2/4/61, Zephyrhills, Fla.   BR/TR, 5′11.5″, 165 lbs.   Deb: 6/18/10

| 1910 | Chi-A | 14 | 45 | 6 | 7 | 0 | 1 | 0 | 1 | 7 | | .156 | .296 | .200 | 58 | -2 | 0 | | | 1.000 | -1 | O-14 | -0.4 |

■ CHARLIE KELLY
Kelly, Charles H.   Deb: 6/14/1883

1883	Phi-N	2	7	1	1	0	1	0	0	0	3	.143	.143	.429	71	-0				.700	0	/3-2	0.0
1886	Phi-a	1	3	0	0	0	0	0	0	0		.000	.000	.000	-99	-1	0			.333	-1	/S-1	-0.2
Total	2	3	10	1	1	0	1	0	0	0	3	.100	.100	.300	19	-1				.700	0	/3-2,S-1	-0.2

■ PAT KELLY
Kelly, Dale Patrick   b: 8/27/55, Santa Maria, Cal.   BR/TR, 6′3″, 210 lbs.   Deb: 5/28/80

| 1980 | Tor-A | 3 | 7 | 0 | 2 | 0 | 0 | 0 | 0 | 0 | 4 | .286 | .286 | .286 | 55 | -0 | 0 | 0 | 0 | 1.000 | 1 | /C-3 | 0.1 |

■ GEORGE KELLY
Kelly, George Lange "Highpockets"   b: 9/10/1895, San Francisco, Cal.   d: 10/13/84, Burlingame, Cal.   BR/TR, 6′4″, 190 lbs.   Deb: 8/18/15   FCH

1915	NY-N	17	38	2	6	0	0	1	4	1	9	.158	.179	.237	27	-3	0	1	-1	.983	-0	/1-9,O-4	-0.5
1916	NY-N	49	76	4	12	2	1	0	3	6	24	.158	.220	.211	34	-6	1			.981	-3	1-13,O-12/3-1	-1.1
1917	NY-N	11	7	0	0	0	0	0	0	0	3	.000	.000	.000	-99	-2	0			1.000	-1	/O-4,P-1,1-1,2-1	-0.2
	Pit-N	8	23	2	2	0	1	0	0	1	9	.087	.125	.174	-9	-3	0			.971	-1	/1-8	-0.5
	Yr	19	30	2	2	0	1	0	0	1	12	.067	.097	.133	-30	-5	0			.972	-1	/1-9,O-4,P-1,2-1	-0.7
1919	NY-N	32	107	12	31	6	2	1	14	3	15	.290	.315	.411	119	2	1			.994	-3	1-32	-0.2
1920	NY-N	155	590	69	157	22	11	11	94	41	92	.266	.320	.397	106	0	4	16	-8	.994	6	*1-155	-0.4
1921	*NY-N	149	587	95	181	42	9	23	122	40	73	.308	.356	.528	131	23	4	12	-6	.990	12	*1-149	2.5
1922	*NY-N	151	592	96	194	33	8	17	107	30	65	.328	.364	.466	119	14	12	3	2	.993	10	*1-151	1.8
1923	*NY-N	145	560	82	172	23	5	16	103	47	64	.307	.362	.452	115	11	14	7	0	.993	-6	*1-145	-0.2
1924	*NY-N	144	571	91	185	37	9	21	136	38	52	.324	.371	.531	143	32	7	2	1	.993	-1	*1-125,O-14/2-5,3-1	2.3
1925	NY-N	147	586	87	181	29	3	20	99	35	54	.309	.350	.471	112	9	5	2	0	.981	16	*2-108,1-25,O-17	2.3
1926	NY-N	136	499	70	151	24	4	13	80	36	52	.303	.352	.445	115	9	4			**.993**	8	*1-114,2-18	1.1
1927	Cin-N	61	222	27	60	16	4	5	21	11	23	.270	.308	.446	103	-0	1			.992	-3	1-49,2-13/O-2	-0.6
1928	Cin-N	116	402	46	119	33	7	3	58	28	35	.296	.345	.435	104	2	2			.991	9	1-99,O-13	0.2
1929	Cin-N	147	577	73	169	45	9	5	103	33	61	.293	.332	.428	91	-10	7			.993	4	*1-147	-1.9
1930	Cin-N	51	188	18	54	10	1	5	35	7	20	.287	.313	.431	81	-6	1			.993	2	1-50	-0.9
	Chi-N	39	166	22	55	6	1	3	19	7	16	.331	.362	.434	91	-2	0			.998	4	1-39	-0.2
	Yr	90	354	40	109	16	2	8	54	14	36	.308	.336	.432	86	-9	1			.995	5	1-89	-1.1
1932	Bro-N	64	202	23	49	9	1	4	22	22	27	.243	.317	.356	82	-5	0			.984	-2	1-62/O-1	-1.1
Total	16	1622	5993	819	1778	337	76	148	1020	386	694	.297	.342	.452	110	68	65	43		.992	49	*1-1373,2-145/O3P	2.4

■ PAT KELLY
Kelly, Harold Patrick   b: 7/30/44, Philadelphia, Pa.   BL/TL, 6′1″, 185 lbs.   Deb: 9/6/67

1967	Min-A	8	1	1	0	0	0	0	0	0	1	.000	.000	.000	-93	-0	0	0		.000	0	H	0.0
1968	Min-A	12	35	2	4	2	0	1	2	3	10	.114	.205	.257	37	-3	0	2	-1	.955	0	O-10	-0.5
1969	KC-A	112	417	61	110	20	4	8	32	49	70	.264	.348	.388	105	3	40	13	4	.980	12	*O-107	1.4
1970	KC-A	136	452	56	106	16	1	6	38	76	105	.235	.347	.314	84	-8	34	16	1	.963	11	*O-118	-0.2
1971	Chi-A	67	213	32	62	6	3	3	22	36	29	.291	.396	.390	119	7	14	9	1	.991	1	O-61	0.4
1972	Chi-A	119	402	57	105	14	7	5	24	55	69	.261	.356	.368	113	8	32	9	4	.968	-2	*O-109	0.6
1973	Chi-A★	144	550	77	154	24	5	1	44	65	91	.280	.358	.347	96	-1	22	15	-2	.978	2	*O-141/D-1	-0.8
1974	Chi-A	122	424	60	119	16	3	4	21	46	58	.281	.354	.361	103	3	18	11	1	.976	-5	D-67,O-53	-0.7
1975	Chi-A	133	471	73	129	21	7	9	45	58	69	.274	.356	.406	113	9	18	10	-1	**.991**	-3	*O-115,D-14	0.1
1976	Chi-A	107	311	42	79	20	3	5	34	45	45	.254	.346	.386	116	5	15	7	0	.950	-4	D-63,O-26	0.2
1977	Bal-A	120	360	50	92	13	0	10	49	53	75	.256	.357	.375	106	5	25	7	3	.984	-14	*O-109/D-1	-1.0
1978	Bal-A	100	274	38	75	12	1	11	40	34	41	.274	.358	.445	133	12	10	8	-2	.969	-6	O-80/D-2	0.1
1979	*Bal-A	68	153	25	44	11	0	9	25	20	25	.288	.374	.536	147	10	4	5	-2	1.000	-3	O-24,D-18	0.4
1980	Bal-A	89	200	38	52	10	1	3	26	34	54	.260	.368	.365	102	2	16	2	4	1.000	-3	O-36,D-30	-0.1
1981	Cle-A	48	75	8	16	4	0	1	16	14	9	.213	.337	.307	88	-1	2	4	-2	1.000	-2	D-18/O-8	-0.6
Total	15	1385	4338	620	1147	189	35	76	418	588	768	.264	.356	.377	107	54	250	118	4	.978	-15	O-997,D-214	-0.5

■ JIM KELLY
Kelly, James Robert (Also Played Under Real Name Of Robert John Taggert In 1918)   b: 2/1/1884, Bloomfield, N.J.   d: 4/10/61, Kingsport, Tenn.   BL/TR, 5′10.5″, 180 lbs.   Deb: 4/26/14

1914	Pit-N	32	44	4	10	2	1	0	3	2	3	.227	.261	.318	75	-2	0			1.000	0	/O-7	-0.2
1915	Pit-F	148	524	68	154	12	17	4	50	35	46	.294	.340	.405	110	-2	38			.952	14	*O-148	0.5
1918	Bos-N	35	146	19	48	1	4	0	4	9	9	.329	.376	.390	140	7	4			.955	1	O-35	0.6
Total	3	215	714	91	212	15	22	4	57	46	58	.297	.343	.396	114	5	42			.954	15	O-190	0.9

■ TOM KELLY
Kelly, Jay Thomas   b: 8/15/50, Graceville, Minn.   BL/TL, 5′11″, 188 lbs.   Deb: 5/11/75   M

| 1975 | Min-A | 49 | 127 | 11 | 23 | 5 | 1 | 1 | 11 | 15 | 22 | .181 | .268 | .244 | 45 | -9 | 0 | 0 | 0 | .985 | 1 | 1-43/O-2 | -1.0 |

■ JOHN KELLY
Kelly, John B.   b: 3/13/1879, Clifton Heights, Pa.   d: 3/19/44, Baltimore, Md.   5′9″, 165 lbs.   Deb: 4/11/07

| 1907 | StL-N | 53 | 197 | 12 | 37 | 5 | 0 | 0 | 6 | 13 | | .188 | .245 | .213 | 45 | -12 | 7 | | | .968 | -1 | O-52 | -1.7 |

■ JOHN KELLY
Kelly, John Francis "Honest John" or "Father"   b: 3/3/1859, Paterson, N.J.   d: 4/13/08, Paterson, N.J.   BR/TR, 6′, 185 lbs.   Deb: 6/7/1879

1879	Cle-N	1	4	0	1	0	0	0	0	0	0	.250	.250	.250	66	-0				.571	-1	/C-1,1-1	-0.1
1882	Cle-N	30	104	6	14	2	0	0	5	1	24	.135	.143	.154	-5	-12				.800	-14	C-30	-2.3
1883	Bal-a	48	202	18	46	9	2	0		3		.228	.239	.292	68	-7				.803	-16	C-38,O-13	-2.0
	Phi-N	1	3	0	0	0	0	0	0	0	0	.000	.000	.000	-99	-1				1.000	1	/O-1	0.0
1884	Cin-U	38	142	23	40	5	1	1		0	6	.282	.311	.352	93	-5				.865	-3	C-37/O-2	-0.3
	Was-U	4	14	1	5	1	0	0		0		.357	.357	.429	142	0				.967	1	/C-3,O-1	0.1
	Yr	42	156	24	45	6	1	1		0	6	.288	.315	.359	97	-5				.874	-1	C-40/O-3	-0.2
Total	4	122	469	48	106	17	3	1	5	10	26	.226	.242	.281	63	-25				.831	-32	C-109/O-17,1-1	-4.6

■ KICK KELLY
Kelly, John O. "Diamond John"   b: 10/31/1856, New York, N.Y.   d: 3/27/26, Malba, N.Y.   6′0.5″, 185 lbs.   Deb: 5/1/1879   MU

1879	Syr-N	10	36	4	4	1	0	0		0		.111	.111	.139	-20	-4				.827	-1	/C-8,1-2	-0.5
	Tro-N	6	22	1	5	0	0	0	0	0	1	.227	.227	.227	54	-1				.789	-3	/C-3,O-2,3-1	-0.3
	Yr	16	58	5	9	1	0	0		0		.155	.155	.172	9	-5				.817	-4	C-11/1-2,O-2,3-1	-0.8

■ JOE KELLY
Kelly, Joseph Henry   b: 9/23/1886, Weir City, Kan.   d: 8/16/77, St.Joseph, Mo.   BR/TR, 5′10″, 175 lbs.   Deb: 4/14/14

1914	Pit-N	141	508	47	113	19	9	1	48	39	59	.222	.283	.301	77	-15	21			.946	4	*O-139	-2.0
1916	Chi-N	54	169	18	43	7	1	2	15	9	16	.254	.296	.343	87	-3	10			.953	-1	O-46	-0.7
1917	Bos-N	116	445	41	99	9	8	3	36	26	45	.222	.268	.299	78	-12	21			.946	-2	O-110	-0.8
1918	Bos-N	47	155	20	36	2	4	0	15	6	12	.232	.265	.297	74	-5	12			.933	-4	O-45	-0.9
1919	Bos-N	18	64	3	9	1	0	0	3	0	11	.141	.154	.156	-7	-8	2			.943	-4	O-16	-1.1
Total	5	376	1341	129	300	38	22	6	117	80	143	.224	.272	.298	75	-44	66			.945	16	O-362	-5.2

YEAR	TM/L	G	AB	R	H	2B	3B	HR	RBI	BB	SO	AVG	OBP	SLG	PRO+	BR/A	SB	CS	SBR	FA	FR	G/POS	TPR
■ JOE KELLY	Kelly, Joseph James b: 4/23/1900, New York, N.Y. d: 11/24/67, Lynbrook, N.Y. BL/TL, 6', 180 lbs. Deb: 4/13/26																						
1926	Chi-N	65	176	16	59	15	3	0	32	7	11	.335	.361	.455	117	4	0			.953	-5	O-39	-0.3
1928	Chi-N	32	52	3	11	1	0	1	7	1	3	.212	.255	.288	42	-4	0			.974	0	1-10	-0.5
Total	2	97	228	19	70	16	3	1	39	8	14	.307	.336	.417	100	-1	0			.953	-4	/O-39,1-10	-0.8
■ KING KELLY	Kelly, Michael Joseph b: 12/31/1857, Troy, N.Y. d: 11/8/1894, Boston, Mass. BR/TR, 5'10", 170 lbs. Deb: 5/1/1878 MH																						
1878	Cin-N	60	237	29	67	7	1	0	27	7	7	.283	.303	.321	116	5				.765	11	*O-47,C-17/3-2	1.3
1879	Cin-N	77	345	78	120	20	12	2	47	8	14	.348	.363	.493	**188**	32				.832	12	3-33,O-29,C-21,/2-1	**3.9**
1880	Chi-N	84	344	72	100	17	9	1	60	12	22	.291	.315	.401	133	11				.779	-3	*O-64,C-17,3/S2P	0.7
1881	Chi-N	82	353	84	114	**27**	3	2	55	16	14	.323	.352	.433	139	15				.841	-0	*O-72,C-11/3-8	1.3
1882	Chi-N	84	377	81	115	**37**	4	1	55	10	27	.305	.323	.432	134	13				.810	-1	S-42,O-38,C-12,/31	1.3
1883	Chi-N	98	428	92	109	28	10	3	61	16	35	.255	.282	.388	95	-4				.813	3	*O-82,C-38/2-3,3P	0.0
1884	Chi-N	108	452	**120**	160	28	5	13	95	46	24	.354	**.414**	.524	178	**39**				.794	-6	O-63,C-28,S3/1P2	3.1
1885	*Chi-N	107	438	**124**	126	24	7	9	75	46	24	.288	.355	.436	136	15				.867	3	O-69,C-37/2-6,31	1.8
1886	*Chi-N	118	451	**155**	175	32	11	4	79	83	33	**.388**	**.483**	.534	183	45	53			.811	3	O-56,C-53/1-9,32S	4.6
1887	Bos-N	116	484	120	156	34	11	8	63	55	40	.322	.393	.488	143	29	84			.856	-11	O-61,2-30,C/PS3M	1.7
1888	Bos-N	107	440	85	140	22	11	9	71	31	39	.318	.368	.480	166	32	56			.905	-3	C-76,O-34	3.4
1889	Bos-N	125	507	120	149	**41**	5	9	78	65	40	.294	.376	.448	122	14	68			.848	-9	*O-113,C-23	0.3
1890	Bos-P	89	340	83	111	18	6	4	66	52	22	.326	.419	.450	124	12	51			.915	-3	C-56,S-27/O-6,13PM	1.1
1891	Cin-a	82	283	56	84	15	7	1	53	51	28	.297	.408	.410	123	9	22			.904	14	C-66/3-8,O-7,21PS	2.3
	Bos-a	4	15	2	4	0	0	1	4	0	2	.267	.267	.467	111	-0	1			.950	-1	/C-4	0.0
	Yr	86	298	58	88	15	7	2	57	51	30	.295	.402	.413	123	9	23			.906	13	C-70/3-8,O-7,21PS	2.3
	Bos-N	16	52	7	12	1	0	0	5	6	10	.231	.322	.250	60	-3	6			.844	-5	C-11/O-6	-0.6
1892	*Bos-N	78	281	40	53	7	0	2	41	39	32	.189	.287	.235	54	-16	24			.912	0	C-72/O-2,3-2,1-2,P	-0.9
1893	NY-N	20	67	9	18	1	0	0	15	6	5	.269	.329	.284	63	-3	3			.895	-4	C-17/O-1	-0.5
Total	16	1455	5894	1357	1813	359	102	69	950	549	418	.308	.368	.438	136	243	368			.820	1	O-750,C-583/3S21P	24.8
■ MIKE KELLY	Kelly, Michael Raymond b: 6/2/70, Los Angeles, Cal. BR/TR, 6'4", 195 lbs. Deb: 4/5/94																						
1994	Atl-N	30	77	14	21	10	1	2	9	2	17	.273	.300	.506	103	-0	0	1	-1	.962	-5	O-25	-0.6
1995	Atl-N	97	137	26	26	6	1	3	17	11	49	.190	.260	.314	49	-10	7	3	0	.940	-16	O-83	-2.7
1996	Cin-N	19	49	5	9	4	0	1	7	9	11	.184	.333	.327	75	-2	4	0	1	.972	1	O-17	0.0
1997	Cin-N	73	140	27	41	13	2	6	19	10	30	.293	.340	.543	125	4	6	1	1	.978	-3	O-59/D-1	0.2
1998	TB-A	106	279	39	67	11	2	10	33	22	80	.240	.296	.401	76	-11	13	6	0	1.000	-8	O-93/D-6	-1.8
Total	5	325	682	111	164	44	6	22	85	54	187	.240	.301	.419	83	-18	30	11	2	.978	-31	O-277/D-7	-4.9
■ PAT KELLY	Kelly, Patrick Franklin b: 10/14/67, Philadelphia, Pa. BR/TR, 6', 182 lbs. Deb: 5/20/91																						
1991	NY-A	96	298	35	72	12	4	3	23	15	52	.242	.289	.339	73	-11	12	1	3	.926	7	3-80,2-19	-0.1
1992	NY-A	106	318	38	72	22	2	7	27	25	72	.226	.303	.374	89	-5	8	5	-1	.978	6	*2-101/D-1	0.3
1993	NY-A	127	406	49	111	24	1	7	51	24	68	.273	.322	.389	93	-5	14	11	-2	.978	9	*2-125	0.5
1994	NY-A	93	286	35	80	21	2	3	41	19	51	.280	.335	.399	92	-4	6	5	-1	.978	1	2-93	0.0
1995	*NY-A	89	270	32	64	12	1	4	29	23	65	.237	.309	.333	68	-13	8	3	1	.983	6	2-87/D-1	-0.1
1996	NY-A	13	21	4	3	0	0	0	2	2	9	.143	.217	.143	-6	-3	0	1	-1	.970	5	2-10/D-3	0.1
1997	NY-A	67	120	25	29	6	1	2	10	14	37	.242	.326	.358	79	-4	8	1	2	.981	14	2-48,D-16	1.2
1998	StL-N	53	153	18	33	5	0	4	14	13	48	.216	.286	.327	59	-9	5	1	1	.964	-1	2-41/O-3,S-2	-0.6
Total	8	644	1872	236	464	102	11	30	197	135	402	.248	.310	.362	80	-53	61	28	2	.978	48	2-524/3-80,D-21,OS	1.3
■ SPEED KELLY	Kelly, Robert Brown b: 8/19/1884, Bryan, Ohio d: 5/6/49, Goshen, Ind. BR/TR, 6'2", 185 lbs. Deb: 7/13/09																						
1909	Was-A	17	42	3	6	2	1	0	1	3		.143	.200	.238	40	-3	1			.852	-1	3-10/2-3,O-1	-0.5
■ ROBERTO KELLY	Kelly, Roberto Conrado (Gray) "Bobby" b: 10/1/64, Panama City, Pan. BR/TR, 6'2", 192 lbs. Deb: 7/29/87																						
1987	NY-A	23	52	12	14	3	0	1	7	5	15	.269	.333	.385	91	-1	9	3	1	.955	-0	O-17/D-2	0.0
1988	NY-A	38	77	9	19	4	1	1	7	3	15	.247	.275	.364	78	-2	5	2	0	.986	-2	O-30/D-3	-0.4
1989	NY-A	137	441	65	133	18	3	9	48	41	89	.302	.369	.417	123	14	35	12	3	.984	7	*O-137	2.1
1990	NY-A	162	641	85	183	32	4	15	61	33	148	.285	.324	.418	106	3	42	17	2	.988	8	*O-160/D-1	1.0
1991	NY-A	126	486	68	130	22	2	20	69	45	77	.267	.336	.444	114	8	32	9	4	.986	3	*O-125	1.3
1992	NY-A★	152	580	81	158	31	2	10	66	41	96	.272	.325	.384	99	-2	28	5	5	.983	10	*O-146	1.0
1993	Cin-N★	78	320	44	102	17	3	9	35	17	43	.319	.357	.475	120	9	21	5	3	.995	5	O-77	1.5
1994	Cin-N	47	179	29	54	8	0	3	21	11	35	.302	.352	.397	96	-1	9	8	-2	.992	3	O-47	-0.1
	Atl-N	63	255	44	73	15	3	6	24	24	36	.286	.348	.439	101	0	10	3	1	.985	-2	O-63	-0.1
	Yr	110	434	73	127	23	3	9	45	35	71	.293	.350	.422	99	-0	19	11	-1	.988	1	*O-110	-0.2
1995	Mon-N	24	95	11	26	4	0	1	9	7	14	.274	.337	.347	78	-3	4	3	-1	1.000	-1	O-24	-0.5
	*LA-N	112	409	47	114	19	2	6	48	15	65	.279	.311	.379	89	-8	15	7	0	.969	-4	*O-110	-1.4
	Yr	136	504	58	140	23	2	7	57	22	79	.278	.316	.373	87	-11	19	10	-0	.974	-5	*O-134	-1.9
1996	Min-A	98	322	41	104	17	4	6	47	23	53	.323	.381	.457	109	5	10	2	2	.990	-1	O-93/D-2	0.3
1997	Min-A	75	247	39	71	19	2	5	37	17	50	.287	.338	.441	100	-0	7	4	-0	1.000	-4	O-59,D-12	-0.6
	*Sea-A	30	121	19	36	7	0	7	22	5	17	.298	.331	.529	121	3	2	1	0	1.000	0	O-29/D-1	0.3
	Yr	105	368	58	107	26	2	12	59	22	67	.291	.336	.470	107	3	9	5	-0	1.000	-4	O-88,D-13	-0.3
1998	*Tex-A	75	257	48	83	7	3	16	46	8	46	.323	.351	.560	126	9	0	2	-1	.976	-4	O-71/D-2	0.2
Total	12	1240	4482	642	1300	223	29	115	547	295	799	.290	.340	.430	107	34	229	83	19	.985	19	*O-1188/D-23	4.6
■ VAN KELLY	Kelly, Van Howard b: 3/18/46, Charlotte, N.C. BL/TR, 5'11", 180 lbs. Deb: 6/13/69																						
1969	SD-N	73	209	16	51	7	1	3	15	12	24	.244	.285	.330	75	-8	0	1	-1	.971	-3	3-49,2-10	-1.2
1970	SD-N	38	89	9	15	3	0	1	9	15	21	.169	.288	.236	44	-7	0	1	-1	.971	1	3-27/2-1	-0.7
Total	2	111	298	25	66	10	1	4	24	27	45	.221	.286	.302	65	-14	0	2	-1	.971	-3	/3-76,2-11	-1.9
■ BILL KELLY	Kelly, William Henry "Big Bill" b: 12/28/1898, Syracuse, N.Y. d: 4/8/90, Syracuse, N.Y. BR/TR, 6', 190 lbs. Deb: 9/6/20																						
1920	Phi-A	9	13	0	3	1	0	0	0	0	2	.231	.231	.308	41	-1	0	0	0	1.000	0	/1-2	-0.1
1928	Phi-N	23	71	6	12	1	1	0	5	7	20	.169	.244	.211	19	-8	0			.991	1	1-23	-0.9
Total	2	32	84	6	15	2	1	0	5	7	22	.179	.242	.226	22	-10	0	0		.992	2	/1-25	-1.0
■ BILL KELLY	Kelly, William J. b: New York, N.Y. Deb: 5/4/1871																						
1871	Kek-n	18	67	16	15	1	1	0	7	6	1	.224	.288	.269	60	-3	0	0	0	.833	1	O-18	-0.1
■ BILLY KELLY	Kelly, William Joseph b: 5/1/1886, Baltimore, Md. d: 6/3/40, Detroit, Mich. BR/TR, 6'0.5", 183 lbs. Deb: 5/2/10																						
1910	StL-N	2	2	1	0	0	0	0	0	1	0	.000	.333	.000	-1	-0	0			.000	0	/C-1	0.0
1911	Pit-N	6	8	0	1	0	0	0	0	0	2	.125	.125	.125	-29	-1	0			1.000	1	/C-1	0.0
1912	Pit-N	48	132	20	42	3	2	1	11	2	16	.318	.328	.394	99	-1	8			.990	-9	C-39	-0.6
1913	Pit-N	48	82	11	22	2	2	0	9	2	12	.268	.302	.341	87	-2	1			.960	4	C-40	0.4
Total	4	104	224	32	65	5	4	1	20	5	30	.290	.312	.362	89	-4	9			.977	-5	/C-81	-0.2
■ BILLY KELSEY	Kelsey, George William b: 8/24/1881, Covington, Ohio d: 4/25/68, Springfield, Ohio BR/TR, 5'10", 150 lbs. Deb: 10/4/07																						
1907	Pit-N	2	5	1	2	0	0	0	0	0		.400	.400	.400	149	0	0			1.000	-1	/C-2	0.0
■ KEN KELTNER	Keltner, Kenneth Frederick "Butch" b: 10/31/16, Milwaukee, Wis. d: 12/12/91, New Berlin, Wis. BR/TR, 6', 190 lbs. Deb: 10/2/37																						
1937	Cle-A	1	1	0	0	0	0	0	0	0	0	.000	.000	.000	-99	-0	0	0	0	1.000	0	/3-1	0.0
1938	Cle-A	149	576	86	159	31	9	26	113	33	75	.276	.319	.497	103	-2	4	3	-1	.956	-10	*3-149	-0.9
1939	Cle-A	154	587	84	191	35	11	13	97	51	41	.325	.379	.489	125	20	6	6	-2	**.974**	6	*3-154	2.4
1940	Cle-A★	149	543	67	138	24	10	15	77	51	56	.254	.322	.418	93	-7	10	5	0	.953	-6	*3-148	-0.9
1941	Cle-A★	149	581	83	156	31	13	23	84	51	56	.269	.330	.485	119	12	2	2	-1	**.971**	23	*3-149	3.5
1942	Cle-A★	152	624	72	179	34	4	6	78	20	36	.287	.312	.383	101	-3	4	3	-1	**.945**	16	*3-151	1.4
1943	Cle-A★	110	427	47	111	31	3	4	39	36	20	.260	.317	.375	109	3	2	2	-1	.969	6	*3-107	1.0

YEAR	TM/L	G	AB	R	H	2B	3B	HR	RBI	BB	SO	AVG	OBP	SLG	PRO+	BR/A	SB	CS	SBR	FA	FR	G/POS	TPR
1944	Cle-A★	149	573	74	169	41	9	13	91	53	29	.295	.355	.466	139	26	4	3	-1	.968	15	*3-149	4.4
1946	Cle-A★	116	398	47	96	17	1	13	45	30	38	.241	.294	.387	95	-5	0	3	-2	.965	-2	*3-112	-0.7
1947	Cle-A	151	541	49	139	29	3	11	76	59	45	.257	.331	.383	101	-0	5	4	-1	.972	-9	*3-150	-1.0
1948	*Cle-A★	153	558	91	166	24	4	31	119	89	52	.297	.395	.522	146	36	2	1	0	.969	0	*3-153	3.3
1949	Cle-A	80	246	35	57	9	2	8	30	38	26	.232	.335	.382	91	-4	0	1	-1	.980	-1	3-69	-0.7
1950	Bos-A	13	28	2	9	2	0	0	2	3	6	.321	.387	.393	91	-0	0	0	0	.947	-2	/3-8,1-1	-0.2
Total	13	1526	5683	737	1570	308	69	163	852	514	480	.276	.338	.441	113	75	39	33	-8	.965	36	*3-1500/1-1	11.6

■ JOHN KELTY

Kelty, John James "Chief" b: 6/1866, Jersey City, N.J. 5'10", 175 lbs. Deb: 4/19/1890

YEAR	TM/L	G	AB	R	H	2B	3B	HR	RBI	BB	SO	AVG	OBP	SLG	PRO+	BR/A	SB	CS	SBR	FA	FR	G/POS	TPR
1890	Pit-N	59	207	24	49	10	2	1	27	22	42	.237	.322	.319	98	0	10			.898	-3	O-59	-0.4

■ BILL KEMMER

Kemmer, William Edward (b: William Edward Kemmerer) b: 11/15/1873, Pennsylvania d: 6/8/45, Washington, D.C. BR/TR, 6'2", Deb: 6/3/1895

YEAR	TM/L	G	AB	R	H	2B	3B	HR	RBI	BB	SO	AVG	OBP	SLG	PRO+	BR/A	SB	CS	SBR	FA	FR	G/POS	TPR
1895	Lou-N	11	38	5	7	0	0	1	3	2	4	.184	.225	.263	27	-4	0			.809	2	/3-9,1-2	-0.1

■ RUDY KEMMLER

Kemmler, Rudolph (b: Rudolph Kemler) b: 1860, Chicago, Ill. d: 6/20/09, Chicago, Ill. BR/TR, Deb: 7/26/1879

YEAR	TM/L	G	AB	R	H	2B	3B	HR	RBI	BB	SO	AVG	OBP	SLG	PRO+	BR/A	SB	CS	SBR	FA	FR	G/POS	TPR
1879	Pro-N	2	7	0	1	0	0	0	0	0	1	.143	.143	.143	-6	-1				.833	2	/C-2	0.1
1881	Cle-N	1	3	0	0	0	0	0	0	0	1	.000	.000	.000	-99	-1				1.000	1	/C-1	0.0
1882	Cin-a	3	11	0	1	1	0	0		0		.091	.091	.182	-10	-1				.909	-1	/C-3,O-1	-0.2
	Pit-a	24	99	7	25	4	0	0		1		.253	.260	.293	90	-1				.920	3	C-23/O-1	0.2
	Yr	27	110	7	26	5	0	0		1		.236	.243	.282	79	-2				.919	1	C-26/O-2	0.0
1883	Col-a	84	318	27	66	6	2	0		13		.208	.239	.239	59	-13				.872	-9	*C-82/O-2	-1.5
1884	Col-a	61	211	28	42	3	3	0		15		.199	.252	.242	67	-7				.906	-19	C-58/1-2,O-1	-2.0
1885	Pit-a	18	64	2	13	2	1	0	5	2		.203	.239	.266	60	-3				.870	-3	C-18	-0.3
1886	StL-a	35	123	13	17	2	0	0	6	8		.138	.197	.154	10	-13	0			.914	4	C-32/1-3	-0.5
1889	Col-a	8	26	2	3	0	0	0	0	3	3	.115	.207	.115	-8	-4	0			.930	1	/C-8	-0.2
Total	8	236	862	79	168	18	6	0	11	42	5	.195	.234	.230	52	-42	0			.894	-22	C-227/1-5,O-5	-4.4

■ STEVE KEMP

Kemp, Steven F. b: 8/7/54, San Angelo, Tex. BL/TL, 6', 195 lbs. Deb: 4/7/77

YEAR	TM/L	G	AB	R	H	2B	3B	HR	RBI	BB	SO	AVG	OBP	SLG	PRO+	BR/A	SB	CS	SBR	FA	FR	G/POS	TPR
1977	Det-A	151	552	75	142	29	4	18	88	71	93	.257	.347	.422	103	3	3	3	-1	.981	-3	*O-148	-0.7
1978	Det-A	159	582	75	161	18	4	15	79	97	87	.277	.381	.399	116	16	2	3	-1	.977	8	*O-157	1.6
1979	Det-A★	134	490	88	156	26	3	26	105	68	70	.318	.404	.543	148	34	5	6	-2	.976	6	*O-120,D-11	3.1
1980	Det-A	135	508	88	149	23	3	21	101	69	64	.293	.382	.474	130	22	5	1	1	.995	6	O-85,D-46	2.4
1981	Det-A	105	372	52	103	18	4	9	49	70	48	.277	.393	.419	129	17	9	3	1	.986	3	O-92,D-12	1.7
1982	Chi-A	160	580	91	166	23	1	19	98	89	83	.286	.384	.428	123	21	7	7	-2	.976	-7	*O-154/D-2	0.8
1983	NY-A	109	373	53	90	17	3	12	49	41	37	.241	.320	.399	100	-0	1	0	0	.987	1	*O-101/D-2	-0.2
1984	NY-A	94	313	37	91	12	1	7	41	40	54	.291	.373	.403	119	9	4	1	1	.972	-2	O-75,D-12	0.5
1985	Pit-N	92	236	19	59	13	2	2	21	25	54	.250	.322	.347	88	-4	1	0	0	1.000	-1	O-63	-0.6
1986	Pit-N	13	16	1	3	0	0	1	1	4	6	.188	.350	.375	98	0	1	0	0	1.000	0	/O-4	0.1
1988	Tex-A	16	36	2	8	0	0	0	2	2	9	.222	.263	.222	36	-3	1	0	0	1.000	-2	/O-5,1-1,D-7	-0.4
Total	11	1168	4058	581	1128	179	25	130	634	576	605	.278	.370	.431	119	115	39	24	-3	.982	10	*O-1004/D-92,1-1	8.3

■ FRED KENDALL

Kendall, Fred Lyn b: 1/31/49, Torrance, Cal. BR/TR, 6'1", 190 lbs. Deb: 9/8/69 FC

YEAR	TM/L	G	AB	R	H	2B	3B	HR	RBI	BB	SO	AVG	OBP	SLG	PRO+	BR/A	SB	CS	SBR	FA	FR	G/POS	TPR
1969	SD-N	10	26	2	4	0	0	0	0	2	5	.154	.214	.154	5	-3	0	0	0	1.000	-1	/C-9	-0.4
1970	SD-N	4	9	0	0	0	0	0	1	0	0	.000	.000	.000	-99	-3	0	0	0	1.000	-1	/C-2,1-1,O-1	-0.4
1971	SD-N	49	111	2	19	1	0	1	7	7	16	.171	.220	.207	23	-11	1	0	0	1.000	1	C-39/1-1,3-1	-1.0
1972	SD-N	91	273	18	59	3	4	6	18	11	42	.216	.249	.322	66	-14	0	0	0	.995	3	C-82/1-1	-0.9
1973	SD-N	145	507	39	143	22	3	10	59	30	35	.282	.323	.396	107	3	3	1	0	.984	-17	*C-138	-0.8
1974	SD-N	141	424	32	98	15	2	8	45	49	33	.231	.311	.333	84	-10	0	1	-1	.983	-23	*C-133	-3.0
1975	SD-N	103	286	16	57	12	1	0	24	26	28	.199	.266	.248	46	-21	0	1	-1	.977	-8	C-85	-2.7
1976	SD-N	146	456	30	112	17	0	2	39	36	42	.246	.305	.296	77	-14	1	1	-0	.994	-19	*C-146	-3.1
1977	Cle-A	103	317	18	79	13	1	3	39	16	27	.249	.287	.325	69	-14	0	1	-1	.991	-13	*C-102/D-1	-2.5
1978	Bos-A	20	41	3	8	1	0	0	4	1	2	.195	.214	.220	20	-4	0	0	0	1.000	3	1-13/C-5,D-1	-0.2
1979	SD-N	46	102	8	17	2	0	1	6	11	7	.167	.248	.216	29	-10	0	0	0	.977	5	C-40/1-2	-0.5
1980	SD-N	19	24	2	7	0	0	0	2	0	3	.292	.292	.292	67	-1	0	0	0	.938	0	C-14/1-1	-0.1
Total	12	877	2576	170	603	86	11	31	244	189	240	.234	.288	.312	72	-102	5	5	-2	.987	-71	C-795/1-19,D-2,3O	-15.6

■ JASON KENDALL

Kendall, Jason Daniel b: 6/26/74, San Diego, Cal. BR/TR, 6', 180 lbs. Deb: 4/1/96 F

YEAR	TM/L	G	AB	R	H	2B	3B	HR	RBI	BB	SO	AVG	OBP	SLG	PRO+	BR/A	SB	CS	SBR	FA	FR	G/POS	TPR
1996	Pit-N★	130	414	54	124	23	5	3	42	35	30	.300	.375	.401	102	3	5	2	0	.980	-0	*C-129	1.0
1997	Pit-N	144	486	71	143	36	4	8	49	49	53	.294	.394	.434	115	13	18	6	2	.990	13	*C-142	3.6
1998	Pit-N★	149	535	95	175	36	3	12	75	51	51	.327	.417	.473	128	25	26	5	5	.992	4	*C-144	4.4
Total	3	423	1435	220	442	95	12	23	166	135	134	.308	.397	.439	116	41	49	13	7	.987	17	C-415	9.0

■ AL KENDERS

Kenders, Albert Daniel George b: 4/4/37, Barrington, N.J. BR/TR, 6', 185 lbs. Deb: 8/14/61

YEAR	TM/L	G	AB	R	H	2B	3B	HR	RBI	BB	SO	AVG	OBP	SLG	PRO+	BR/A	SB	CS	SBR	FA	FR	G/POS	TPR
1961	Phi-N	10	23	0	4	1	0	0	1	1	0	.174	.208	.217	13	-3	0	0	0	1.000	-2	C-10	-0.4

■ EDDIE KENNA

Kenna, Edward Aloysius "Scrap Iron" b: 9/30/1897, San Francisco, Cal. d: 8/21/72, San Francisco, Cal BR/TR, 5'7.5", 150 lbs. Deb: 6/2/28

YEAR	TM/L	G	AB	R	H	2B	3B	HR	RBI	BB	SO	AVG	OBP	SLG	PRO+	BR/A	SB	CS	SBR	FA	FR	G/POS	TPR
1928	Was-A	41	118	14	35	4	2	1	20	14	8	.297	.376	.390	102	1	1	5	-3	.942	-3	C-33	-0.2

■ ED KENNEDY

Kennedy, Edward b: 4/1/1856, Carbondale, Pa. d: 5/20/05, New York, N.Y. 5'6", 150 lbs. Deb: 5/1/1883

YEAR	TM/L	G	AB	R	H	2B	3B	HR	RBI	BB	SO	AVG	OBP	SLG	PRO+	BR/A	SB	CS	SBR	FA	FR	G/POS	TPR
1883	NY-a	94	356	57	78	6	7	2		17		.219	.255	.292	72	-11				.884	-7	*O-94	-1.7
1884	*NY-a	103	378	49	72	6	2	1		16		.190	.225	.225	49	-20				.915	6	*O-100/S-1,2-1,C-1	-1.5
1885	NY-a	96	349	35	71	8	4	2	21	12		.203	.238	.266	64	-13				.841	2	*O-96	-1.3
1886	Bro-a	6	22	1	4	0	0	0	2	2		.182	.250	.182	36	-2	1			.909	-1	/O-6	-0.2
Total	4	299	1105	142	225	20	13	5	23	47		.204	.239	.259	61	-47	1			.878	0	O-296/C-1,2-1,S-1	-4.7

■ JIM KENNEDY

Kennedy, James Earl b: 11/1/46, Tulsa, Okla. BL/TR, 5'9", 160 lbs. Deb: 6/14/70 F

YEAR	TM/L	G	AB	R	H	2B	3B	HR	RBI	BB	SO	AVG	OBP	SLG	PRO+	BR/A	SB	CS	SBR	FA	FR	G/POS	TPR
1970	StL-N	12	24	1	3	0	0	0	0	0	0	.125	.125	.125	-32	-4	0	0	0	.909	1	/S-7,2-5	-0.3

■ JOHN KENNEDY

Kennedy, John Edward b: 5/29/41, Chicago, Ill. BR/TR, 6', 185 lbs. Deb: 9/5/62

YEAR	TM/L	G	AB	R	H	2B	3B	HR	RBI	BB	SO	AVG	OBP	SLG	PRO+	BR/A	SB	CS	SBR	FA	FR	G/POS	TPR
1962	Was-A	14	42	6	11	0	1	1	2	2	7	.262	.295	.381	81	-1	0	1	-1	.974	0	/S-9,3-2	-0.1
1963	Was-A	36	62	3	11	1	1	0	4	6	22	.177	.261	.226	38	-5	2	0	1	.954	6	3-26/S-2	0.2
1964	Was-A	148	482	55	111	16	4	7	35	29	119	.230	.281	.324	68	-21	3	3	-1	.941	9	*3-106,S-49/2-2	-1.2
1965	*LA-N	104	105	12	18	3	0	1	5	8	33	.171	.243	.229	36	-9	1	0	0	.971	11	3-95/S-5	0.2
1966	*LA-N	125	274	15	55	9	2	3	24	10	64	.201	.242	.281	49	-20	1	2	-1	.965	13	3-87,S-28,2-15	-0.6
1967	NY-A	78	179	22	35	4	0	1	17	17	35	.196	.269	.235	52	-10	2	1	0	.915	7	S-36,3-34/2-2	-0.1
1969	Sea-A	61	128	18	30	3	1	4	14	14	25	.234	.315	.367	92	-2	4	0	1	.916	-4	S-33,3-23	-0.2
1970	Mil-A	25	55	8	14	2	0	2	6	5	9	.255	.317	.400	96	-0	0	1	-1	.921	-1	2-16/3-5,S-4,1-1	-0.1
	Bos-A	43	129	15	33	7	1	4	17	6	14	.256	.294	.419	88	-2	0	0	0	.960	3	3-33/2-2	0.0
	Yr	68	184	23	47	9	1	6	23	11	23	.255	.301	.413	91	-3	0	1	-1	.962	1	3-38,2-18/S-4,1-1	-0.1
1971	Bos-A	74	272	41	75	12	5	5	22	14	42	.276	.321	.412	99	-1	1	1	-0	.974	-18	2-37,S-33/3-5	-1.3
1972	Bos-A	71	212	22	52	11	1	2	22	18	40	.245	.313	.335	88	-3	0	1	-1	.962	-6	2-32,S-27,3-11	-0.5
1973	Bos-A	67	155	17	28	9	1	1	16	12	45	.181	.249	.271	44	-12	0	0	0	.980	7	2-31,3-24/D-9	-0.3
1974	Bos-A	10	15	3	2	0	0	1	1	1	6	.133	.188	.333	44	-1	0	0	0	.778	-1	/2-6,3-4	-0.2
Total	12	856	2110	237	475	77	17	32	185	142	461	.225	.282	.323	70	-87	14	10	-2	.953	26	3-455,S-226,2/D1	-4.2

■ JOHN KENNEDY

Kennedy, John Irvin b: 10/12/26, Jacksonville, Fla. d: 4/27/98, Jacksonville, Fla. BR/TR, 5'10", 175 lbs. Deb: 4/22/57

YEAR	TM/L	G	AB	R	H	2B	3B	HR	RBI	BB	SO	AVG	OBP	SLG	PRO+	BR/A	SB	CS	SBR	FA	FR	G/POS	TPR
1957	Phi-N	5	2	1	0	0	0	0	0	0	1	.000	.000	.000	-99	-1	0	0	0	.500	0	/3-2	0.0

■ JUNIOR KENNEDY

Kennedy, Junior Raymond b: 8/9/50, Fort Gibson, Okla. BR/TR, 6', 185 lbs. Deb: 8/9/74 F

YEAR	TM/L	G	AB	R	H	2B	3B	HR	RBI	BB	SO	AVG	OBP	SLG	PRO+	BR/A	SB	CS	SBR	FA	FR	G/POS	TPR
1974	Cin-N	22	19	2	3	0	0	0	0	6	4	.158	.360	.158	49	-1	0	0	0	.909	-1	2-17/3-5	-0.2
1978	Cin-N	89	157	22	40	2	2	0	11	31	28	.255	.381	.293	91	-0	4	1	1	.979	13	2-71/3-4	1.7
1979	Cin-N	83	220	29	60	7	0	1	17	28	31	.273	.355	.318	85	-4	4	3	-1	.980	-1	2-59/S-5,3-4	-0.1

YEAR	TM/L	G	AB	R	H	2B	3B	HR	RBI	BB	SO	AVG	OBP	SLG	PRO+	BR/A	SB	CS	SBR	FA	FR	G/POS	TPR
1980	Cin-N	104	337	31	88	16	3	1	34	36	34	.261	.332	.335	87	-5	3	1	0	.988	2	*2-103	0.3
1981	Cin-N	27	44	5	11	1	0	0	5	1	5	.250	.267	.273	52	-3	0	0	0	.980	2	2-16/3-5	0.0
1982	Chi-N	105	242	22	53	3	1	2	25	21	34	.219	.281	.264	52	-15	1	4	-2	.978	13	2-71,S-28/3-7	0.0
1983	Chi-N	17	22	3	3	0	0	0	3	1	6	.136	.174	.136	-12	-3	0	0	0	1.000	2	/2-7,3-4,S-1	-0.1
Total	7	447	1041	114	258	29	6	4	95	124	142	.248	.328	.299	75	-31	12	9	-2	.982	30	2-344/S-34,3-29	1.6

■ DOC KENNEDY
Kennedy, Michael Joseph b: 8/11/1853, Brooklyn, N.Y. d: 5/23/20, Grove, N.Y. BR/TR, 5'9.5", 185 lbs. Deb: 5/1/1879

YEAR	TM/L	G	AB	R	H	2B	3B	HR	RBI	BB	SO	AVG	OBP	SLG	PRO+	BR/A	SB	CS	SBR	FA	FR	G/POS	TPR
1879	Cle-N	49	193	19	56	8	2	1	18	2	10	.290	.297	.368	119	4				.891	3	C-46/1-4	0.8
1880	Cle-N	66	250	26	50	10	1	0	18	5	12	.200	.216	.248	58	-10				.899	-1	*C-65/O-2	-1.0
1881	Cle-N	39	150	19	47	7	1	0	15	5	13	.313	.335	.373	129	5				.920	5	C-35/O-3,3-1	1.0
1882	Cle-N	1	3	0	1	0	0	0	0	1	0	.333	.500	.333	180	0				.857	3	/C-1	0.3
1883	Buf-N	5	19	3	6	0	0	0	2	2	2	.316	.381	.316	113	0				.583	-2	/O-4,1-1	-0.1
Total	5	160	615	67	160	25	4	1	53	15	37	.260	.278	.319	98	-1				.901	9	C-147/O-9,1-5,3-1	1.0

■ RAY KENNEDY
Kennedy, Raymond Lincoln b: 5/19/1895, Pittsburgh, Pa. d: 1/18/69, Casselberry, Fla. BR/TR, 5'9", 165 lbs. Deb: 9/8/16

YEAR	TM/L	G	AB	R	H	2B	3B	HR	RBI	BB	SO	AVG	OBP	SLG	PRO+	BR/A	SB	CS	SBR	FA	FR	G/POS	TPR
1916	StL-A	1	1	0	0	0	0	0	0	0	0	.000	.000	.000	-99	-0	0			.000	0	H	0.0

■ BOB KENNEDY
Kennedy, Robert Daniel b: 8/18/20, Chicago, Ill. BR/TR, 6'2", 193 lbs. Deb: 9/14/39 FMC

YEAR	TM/L	G	AB	R	H	2B	3B	HR	RBI	BB	SO	AVG	OBP	SLG	PRO+	BR/A	SB	CS	SBR	FA	FR	G/POS	TPR
1939	Chi-A	3	8	0	2	0	0	0	1	0	0	.250	.250	.250	27	-1	0	0	0	.750	-1	/3-2	-0.2
1940	Chi-A	154	606	74	153	23	3	3	52	42	58	.252	.301	.315	59	-36	3	7	-3	.938	-3	*3-154	-3.8
1941	Chi-A	76	257	16	53	9	3	1	29	17	23	.206	.255	.276	41	-22	5	3	-0	.934	3	3-71	-1.7
1942	Chi-A	113	412	37	95	18	5	0	38	22	41	.231	.270	.299	61	-22	11	7	-1	.956	4	3-96,O-16	-1.9
1946	Chi-A	113	411	43	106	13	5	5	34	24	42	.258	.300	.350	85	-10	6	8	-3	.965	4	O-75,3-29	-1.2
1947	Chi-A	115	428	47	112	19	3	6	48	18	38	.262	.291	.362	84	-11	3	4	-2	.968	-3	*O-106/3-1	-2.2
1948	Chi-A	30	113	4	28	8	1	0	14	4	17	.248	.274	.336	64	-6	0	2	-1	.970	-0	O-30	-0.9
	*Cle-A	66	73	10	22	3	2	0	5	4	6	.301	.338	.397	98	-1	0	0	0	1.000	-13	O-50/2-2,1-1	-1.4
	Yr	96	186	14	50	11	3	0	19	8	23	.269	.299	.360	77	-7	0	2	-1	.981	-13	O-80/2-2,1-1	-2.3
1949	Cle-A	121	424	49	117	23	5	9	57	37	40	.276	.334	.417	100	-2	5	5	-2	.990	3	O-98,3-21	-0.6
1950	Cle-A	146	540	79	157	27	5	9	54	53	31	.291	.355	.409	99	-2	3	4	-2	.987	1	*O-144	-0.8
1951	Cle-A	108	321	30	79	15	4	7	29	34	33	.246	.320	.383	95	-3	4	2	0	.968	-1	*O-106	-0.7
1952	Cle-A	22	40	6	12	3	1	0	12	9	5	.300	.429	.425	148	3	1	0	0	1.000	0	O-13/3-3	0.3
1953	Cle-A	100	161	22	38	5	0	3	22	19	11	.236	.320	.323	76	-5	0	2	-1	1.000	-21	O-89	-3.0
1954	Cle-A	1	0	0	0	0	0	0	0	0	0	—	—	—	—	0	0	0	0	.000	-0	/O-1	0.0
	Bal-A	106	323	37	81	13	2	6	45	28	43	.251	.311	.359	90	-6	2	1	0	.938	-6	3-71,O-21	-1.5
	Yr	107	323	37	81	13	2	6	45	28	43	.251	.311	.359	90	-6	2	1	0	.938	-7	3-71,O-22	-1.5
1955	Bal-A	26	70	10	10	1	0	0	5	10	10	.143	.250	.157	12	-9	0	1	-1	1.000	-1	O-14/1-6,3-1	-1.1
	Chi-A	83	214	28	65	10	2	9	43	16	16	.304	.352	.495	122	6	0	2	-1	.938	-13	3-55,O-20/1-3	-0.9
	Yr	109	284	38	75	11	2	9	48	26	26	.264	.326	.412	97	-2	0	3	-2	.938	-13	3-56,O-34/1-9	-2.0
1956	Chi-A	8	13	0	1	0	0	0	0	2	4	.077	.200	.077	-24	-2	0	0	0	1.000	-1	/3-6	-0.3
	Det-A	69	177	17	41	5	0	4	22	24	19	.232	.330	.328	74	-6	2	2	-1	.931	-3	O-29,3-27	-1.0
	Yr	77	190	17	42	5	0	4	22	26	23	.221	.321	.311	67	-9	2	2	-1	.909	-4	3-33,O-29	-1.3
1957	Chi-A	4	2	0	0	0	0	0	0	0	1	.000	.000	.000	-99	-1	0	0	0	.000	0	H	-0.1
	Bro-N	19	31	5	4	1	0	1	4	1	5	.129	.156	.258	8	-4	0	0	0	1.000	-4	/O-9,3-3	-0.9
Total	16	1483	4624	514	1176	196	41	63	514	364	443	.254	.310	.355	80	-142	45	50	-17	.978	-55	O-821,3-540/1-10,2	-23.9

■ SNAPPER KENNEDY
Kennedy, Sherman Montgomery b: 11/1/1878, Conneaut, Ohio d: 8/15/45, Pasadena, Tex. BB/TR, 5'10", 165 lbs. Deb: 5/1/02

YEAR	TM/L	G	AB	R	H	2B	3B	HR	RBI	BB	SO	AVG	OBP	SLG	PRO+	BR/A	SB	CS	SBR	FA	FR	G/POS	TPR
1902	Chi-N	1	5	0	0	0	0	0	0	0		.000	.000	.000	-99	-1	0			1.000	1	/O-1	-0.1

■ TERRY KENNEDY
Kennedy, Terrence Edward b: 6/4/56, Euclid, Ohio BL/TR, 6'3", 220 lbs. Deb: 9/4/78 F

YEAR	TM/L	G	AB	R	H	2B	3B	HR	RBI	BB	SO	AVG	OBP	SLG	PRO+	BR/A	SB	CS	SBR	FA	FR	G/POS	TPR
1978	StL-N	10	29	0	5	0	0	0	2	4	3	.172	.273	.172	27	-3	0	0	0	.980	0	C-10	-0.3
1979	StL-N	33	109	11	31	7	0	2	17	6	20	.284	.322	.404	96	-1	0	0	0	.993	-4	C-32	-0.4
1980	StL-N	84	248	28	63	12	3	4	34	28	34	.254	.330	.375	93	-2	0	0	0	.967	-3	C-41,O-28	-0.5
1981	SD-N★	101	382	32	115	24	1	2	41	22	53	.301	.342	.385	114	6	0	2	-1	.964	-8	*C-100	0.0
1982	SD-N	153	562	75	166	42	1	21	97	26	91	.295	.332	.486	133	21	1	0	0	.990	-18	*C-139,1-12	0.8
1983	SD-N☆	149	549	47	156	27	2	17	98	51	89	.284	.347	.434	119	13	1	3	-2	.986	-8	*C-143/1-4	1.0
1984	*SD-N	148	530	54	127	16	1	14	57	33	99	.240	.287	.353	79	-16	1	2	-1	.982	-14	*C-147	-2.6
1985	SD-N★	143	532	54	139	27	1	10	74	31	102	.261	.302	.372	89	-9	0	0	0	.986	0	*C-140/1-5	-0.2
1986	SD-N	141	432	46	114	22	1	12	57	37	74	.264	.325	.403	102	0	0	3	-2	.990	-0	*C-123	0.6
1987	Bal-A★	143	512	51	128	13	1	18	62	35	112	.250	.299	.385	82	-14	1	0	0	.993	-16	*C-142	-1.9
1988	Bal-A	85	265	20	60	10	0	3	16	15	53	.226	.270	.298	61	-14	0	0	0	.994	-8	C-79	-1.7
1989	*SF-N	125	355	19	85	15	0	5	34	35	56	.239	.308	.324	83	-8	1	3	-2	.986	-3	*C-121/1-2	-0.7
1990	SF-N	107	303	25	84	22	0	2	26	31	38	.277	.344	.370	100	0	1	2	-1	.991	-12	*C-103	-0.8
1991	SF-N	69	171	12	40	7	1	3	13	11	31	.234	.284	.339	77	-6	0	0	0	.978	-3	C-58/1-2	-0.7
Total	14	1491	4979	474	1313	244	12	113	628	365	855	.264	.316	.386	97	-31	6	15	-7	.985	-100	*C-1378/O-28,1-25	-7.4

■ ED KENNEDY
Kennedy, William Edward b: 4/5/1861, Bellevue, Ky. d: 12/22/12, Cheyenne, Wyoming BR/TR, 5'7", 160 lbs. Deb: 5/17/1884

YEAR	TM/L	G	AB	R	H	2B	3B	HR	RBI	BB	SO	AVG	OBP	SLG	PRO+	BR/A	SB	CS	SBR	FA	FR	G/POS	TPR
1884	Cin-U	13	48	6	10	1	1	0		1		.208	.224	.271	46	-5				.857	0	/3-8,S-4,O-1	-0.4

■ JERRY KENNEY
Kenney, Gerald T b: 6/30/45, St.Louis, Mo. BL/TR, 6'1", 170 lbs. Deb: 9/5/67

YEAR	TM/L	G	AB	R	H	2B	3B	HR	RBI	BB	SO	AVG	OBP	SLG	PRO+	BR/A	SB	CS	SBR	FA	FR	G/POS	TPR
1967	NY-A	20	58	4	18	2	0	1	5	10	8	.310	.412	.397	145	4	2	1	0	.952	-4	S-18	0.2
1969	NY-A	130	447	49	115	14	2	2	34	48	36	.257	.331	.311	83	-9	25	14	-1	.975	11	3-83,O-31,S-10	0.1
1970	NY-A	140	404	46	78	10	7	4	35	52	44	.193	.285	.282	60	-22	20	6	2	.960	15	*3-135/2-2	-0.6
1971	NY-A	120	325	50	85	10	3	0	20	56	38	.262	.372	.311	101	3	9	8	-2	.953	11	*3-109/S-5,1-1	1.2
1972	NY-A	50	119	16	25	2	0	0	7	16	13	.210	.304	.227	62	-5	3	0	1	.969	5	S-45/3-1	0.6
1973	Cle-A	5	16	0	4	0	1	0	2	2	0	.250	.333	.375	97	-0	0	0	0	1.000	-2	/2-5	-0.1
Total	6	465	1369	165	325	38	13	7	103	184	139	.237	.329	.299	82	-30	59	29	0	.962	36	3-328/S-78,O-31,21	1.4

■ JOHN KENNEY
Kenney, John Deb: 5/2/1872

YEAR	TM/L	G	AB	R	H	2B	3B	HR	RBI	BB	SO	AVG	OBP	SLG	PRO+	BR/A	SB	CS	SBR	FA	FR	G/POS	TPR
1872	Atl-n	5	19	0	0	0	0	0	1	0	1	.000	.000	.000	-85	-4	0	0	0	.692	-2	/2-3,O-3	-0.5

■ JEFF KENT
Kent, Jeffrey Franklin b: 3/7/68, Bellflower, Cal. BR/TR, 6'1", 185 lbs. Deb: 4/12/92

YEAR	TM/L	G	AB	R	H	2B	3B	HR	RBI	BB	SO	AVG	OBP	SLG	PRO+	BR/A	SB	CS	SBR	FA	FR	G/POS	TPR
1992	Tor-A	65	192	36	46	13	1	8	35	20	47	.240	.330	.443	110	2	2	1	0	.915	-3	3-49,2-17/1-3	-0.1
	NY-N	37	113	16	27	8	1	3	15	7	29	.239	.289	.407	97	-1	0	2	-1	.980	8	2-34/3-1,S-1	0.7
1993	NY-N	140	496	65	134	24	0	21	80	30	88	.270	.322	.446	104	2	4	4	-1	.969	-19	*2-127,3-12/S-2	-1.4
1994	NY-N	107	415	53	121	24	5	14	68	23	84	.292	.344	.475	112	6	1	4	-2	.976	0	*2-107	0.9
1995	NY-N	125	472	65	131	22	3	20	65	29	89	.278	.330	.464	110	5	3	3	-1	.984	-8	*2-122	0.4
1996	NY-N	89	335	45	97	20	1	9	39	21	56	.290	.333	.436	106	2	4	3	-1	.925	6	3-89	0.7
	*Cle-A	39	102	16	27	7	0	3	16	10	22	.265	.336	.422	90	-2	2	1	0	.992	3	1-20/2-9,3-6,D-5	0.0
1997	*SF-N	155	580	90	145	38	2	29	121	48	133	.250	.321	.472	107	4	11	3	2	.979	11	*2-148,1-13	2.3
1998	SF-N	137	526	94	156	37	3	31	128	48	110	.297	.365	.555	139	29	9	4	0	.972	11	*2-134/1-1	4.8
Total	7	894	3231	480	884	193	16	138	567	236	658	.274	.334	.471	112	47	36	25	-4	.976	9	2-698,3-157/1DS	8.3

■ DICK KENWORTHY
Kenworthy, Richard Lee b: 4/1/41, Red Oak, Iowa BR/TR, 5'9", 170 lbs. Deb: 9/8/62

YEAR	TM/L	G	AB	R	H	2B	3B	HR	RBI	BB	SO	AVG	OBP	SLG	PRO+	BR/A	SB	CS	SBR	FA	FR	G/POS	TPR
1962	Chi-A	3	4	0	0	0	0	0	0	0	3	.000	.000	.000	-99	-1	0	0	0	1.000	1	/2-2	0.0
1964	Chi-A	2	2	0	0	0	0	0	0	0	1	.000	.000	.000	-99	-1	0	0	0	.000	0	H	-0.1
1965	Chi-A	3	1	0	0	0	0	0	0	1	0	.000	.667	.000	113	0	0	0	0	.000	0	H	0.0
1966	Chi-A	9	25	1	5	0	0	0	0	0	0	.200	.200	.200	16	-3	0	0	0	.875	-3	/3-6	-0.6
1967	Chi-A	50	97	9	22	4	1	4	11	4	17	.227	.265	.412	101	-0	0	2	-1	.971	1	3-35	-0.1
1968	Chi-A	58	122	2	27	2	0	0	2	5	21	.221	.252	.238	49	-8	0	1	-1	.938	4	3-38	-0.4
Total	6	125	251	12	54	6	1	4	13	10	42	.215	.251	.295	63	-12	0	3	-2	.948	4	/3-79,2-2	-1.2

YEAR	TM/L	G	AB	R	H	2B	3B	HR	RBI	BB	SO	AVG	OBP	SLG	PRO+	BR/A	SB	CS	SBR	FA	FR	G/POS	TPR

■ BILL KENWORTHY   Kenworthy, William Jennings "Duke"   b: 7/4/1886, Cambridge, Ohio   d: 9/21/50, Eureka, Cal.   BR/TR, 5'7", 165 lbs.   Deb: 8/28/12

1912	Was-A	12	38	6	9	1	0	2	2			.237	.293	.263	59	-2	3			1.000	-0	O-12	-0.3
1914	KC-F	146	545	93	173	40	14	15	91	36	44	.317	.372	.525	148	25	37			.952	21	*2-145	4.5
1915	KC-F	122	396	59	118	30	7	3	52	28	32	.298	.355	.432	126	7	20			.936	-7	*2-108/O-7	0.0
1917	StL-A	5	10	1	1	0	0	0	1	1	1	.100	.182	.100	-14	-1	1			.889	1	/2-4	0.0
Total	4	285	989	159	301	71	21	18	146	67	77	.304	.360	.473	135	28	61			.945	14	2-257/O-19	4.2

■ JOE KEOUGH   Keough, Joseph William   b: 1/7/46, Pomona, Cal.   BL/TL, 6', 185 lbs.   Deb: 8/7/68   F

1968	Oak-A	34	98	7	21	2	1	2	18	8	11	.214	.274	.316	82	-2	1	0	0	.962	1	O-29/1-1	-0.3
1969	KC-A	70	166	17	31	2	0	0	13	13	13	.187	.254	.199	28	-16	5	2	0	1.000	-3	O-49/1-1	-2.2
1970	KC-A	57	183	28	59	6	2	4	21	23	18	.322	.398	.443	132	8	1	1	-0	.985	-2	O-34,1-18	0.7
1971	KC-A	110	351	34	87	14	2	3	30	35	26	.248	.318	.325	83	-8	0	6	-4	.982	-6	*O-100	-2.4
1972	KC-A	56	64	8	14	2	0	0	5	8	7	.219	.324	.250	73	-2	2	0	1	1.000	-3	O-16	-0.5
1973	Chi-A	5	1	1	0	0	0	0	0	0	0	.000	.000	.000	-97	-0	0	0	0	.000	0	H	0.0
Total	6	332	863	95	212	26	5	9	81	87	75	.246	.318	.319	82	-19	9	9	-3	.984	-9	O-228/1-20	-4.7

■ MARTY KEOUGH   Keough, Richard Martin   b: 4/14/35, Oakland, Cal.   BL/TL, 6', 180 lbs.   Deb: 4/21/56   F

1956	Bos-A	3	2	1	0	0	0	0	1	1	0	.000	.333	.000	-5	-0	0	0	0	.000	0	H	0.0
1957	Bos-A	9	17	1	1	0	0	0	0	4	3	.059	.238	.059	-14	-3	0	0	0	1.000	0	/O-7	-0.3
1958	Bos-A	68	118	21	26	3	3	1	9	7	29	.220	.264	.322	57	-7	1	1	-0	.974	-5	O-25/1-2	-1.4
1959	Bos-A	96	251	40	61	13	5	7	27	26	40	.243	.321	.418	97	-1	3	1	0	.993	-1	O-69/1-3	-0.6
1960	Bos-A	38	105	15	26	6	1	1	9	8	8	.248	.301	.352	73	-4	2	2	-1	1.000	1	O-29	-1.3
	Cle-A	65	149	19	37	5	0	3	11	9	23	.248	.296	.342	74	-6	2	3	-1	.986	-4	O-42	-1.3
	Yr	103	254	34	63	11	1	4	20	17	31	.248	.298	.346	74	-10	4	5	-2	.992	-3	O-71	-1.8
1961	Was-A	135	390	57	97	18	9	9	34	32	60	.249	.309	.410	92	-6	12	5	1	.978	2	*O-100,1-10	-0.9
1962	Cin-N	111	230	34	64	8	2	7	27	21	31	.278	.349	.422	102	1	3	1	0	.968	-5	O-71,1-29	-0.8
1963	Cin-N	95	172	21	39	8	2	6	21	25	37	.227	.338	.401	109	2	1	4	-2	.992	-3	1-46,O-28	-0.5
1964	Cin-N	109	276	29	71	9	1	9	28	22	58	.257	.314	.395	95	-2	1	2	-1	.991	-6	O-81/1-4	-1.2
1965	Cin-N	62	43	14	5	0	0	0	3	3	14	.116	.191	.116	-10	-6	0	0	0	.988	-1	1-32/O-4	-0.7
1966	Atl-N	17	17	1	1	0	0	0	1	1	6	.059	.111	.059	-50	-2	0	0	0	1.000	-2	/1-4,O-3	-0.6
	Chi-N	33	26	3	6	1	0	0	5	5	9	.231	.375	.269	82	-0	1	0	0	1.000	-2	/O-5	-0.2
	Yr	50	43	4	7	1	0	0	6	6	15	.163	.280	.186	32	-4	1	0	0	.667	-3	/O-8,1-4	-0.8
Total	11	841	1796	256	434	71	23	43	176	164	318	.242	.311	.379	86	-35	26	19	-4	.984	-25	O-464,1-130	-9.0

■ JOHN KERINS   Kerins, John Nelson   b: 7/15/1858, Indianapolis, Ind   d: 9/8/19, Louisville, Ky.   BR/TR, 5'10", 177 lbs.   Deb: 5/1/1884   MU

1884	Ind-a	94	364	58	78	10	3	6		6		.214	.229	.308	76	-10				.972	6	*1-87/C-5,O-5,3-1	-1.3
1885	Lou-a	112	456	65	111	9	16	3	51	20		.243	.281	.353	100	-1				.947	3	*1-96,C-19/O-3,3-1	-0.6
1886	Lou-a	120	487	113	131	19	9	4	50	66		.269	.360	.370	122	12	26			.933	39	C-65,1-47/O-7,S-1	4.6
1887	Lou-a	112	476	101	140	18	19	5	57	38		.294	.349	.443	118	9	49			.970	25	1-74,C-35/O-5	2.4
1888	Lou-a	83	319	38	75	11	4	2	41	25		.235	.297	.313	98	-0	16			.844	-2	O-47,C-33/1-4,32M	0.3
1889	Lou-a	2	9	2	3	1	0	0	3	0	1	.333	.333	.444	123	0	0			.500	-1	/O-2,C-1	-0.1
	Bal-a	16	53	7	15	2	0	0	12	2	4	.283	.321	.321	82	-1	2			.981	-2	/1-9,C-4,O-2,S-1	-0.3
	Yr	18	62	9	18	3	0	0	15	2	5	.290	.323	.339	87	-1	2			.981	-2	/1-9,C-5,O-4,S-1	-0.4
1890	StL-a	18	63	8	8	2	0	0	3	6		.127	.225	.159	12	-7	2			.968	1	1-17/C-1,M	-0.6
Total	7	557	2227	392	561	72	51	20	217	165	5	.252	.308	.357	102	2	95			.963	73	1-334,C-163/O3S2	4.4

■ ORIE KERLIN   Kerlin, Orie Milton "Cy"   b: 1/23/1891, Summerfield, La.   d: 10/29/74, Shreveport, La.   BL/TR, 5'7", 149 lbs.   Deb: 6/6/15

| 1915 | Pit-F | 3 | 1 | 0 | 0 | 0 | 0 | 0 | 0 | 0 | 0 | .000 | .000 | .000 | -99 | -0 | 0 | | | .000 | -0 | /C-3 | 0.0 |

■ BILL KERN   Kern, William George   b: 2/28/33, Coplay, Pa.   BR/TR, 6'2", 184 lbs.   Deb: 9/19/62

| 1962 | KC-A | 8 | 16 | 1 | 4 | 1 | 0 | 0 | 1 | 0 | 3 | .250 | .250 | .438 | 77 | -1 | 0 | 0 | 0 | 1.000 | 1 | /O-3 | 0.0 |

■ JOE KERNAN   Kernan, Joseph   b: Baltimore, Md.   Deb: 4/14/1873

| 1873 | Mar-n | 2 | 8 | 1 | 3 | 0 | 0 | 0 | 1 | 0 | 0 | .375 | .375 | .375 | 161 | 1 | 0 | 0 | 0 | .700 | 1 | /2-1,O-1 | 0.1 |

■ GEORGE KERNEK   Kernek, George Boyd   b: 1/12/40, Holdenville, Okla.   BL/TL, 6'3", 170 lbs.   Deb: 9/5/65

1965	StL-N	10	31	6	9	3	0	2	4	2	4	.290	.333	.452	109	0	0	0	0	.972	-0	/1-7	0.0
1966	StL-N	20	50	5	12	0	0	0	3	4	9	.240	.309	.280	65	-2	1	0	0	.984	-0	1-16	-0.3
Total	2	30	81	11	21	3	0	2	6	6	13	.259	.318	.346	82	-2	1	0	0	.980	-0	/1-23	-0.3

■ RUSS KERNS   Kerns, Russell Eldon   b: 11/10/20, Fremont, Ohio   BL/TR, 6', 188 lbs.   Deb: 8/18/45

| 1945 | Det-A | 1 | 1 | 0 | 0 | 0 | 0 | 0 | 0 | 0 | 0 | .000 | .000 | .000 | -94 | -0 | 0 | 0 | 0 | .000 | 0 | H | 0.0 |

■ JOHN KERR   Kerr, John Francis   b: 11/26/1898, San Francisco, Cal.   d: 10/19/93, Long Beach, Cal.   BR/TR, 5'8", 158 lbs.   Deb: 5/1/23

1923	Det-A	19	42	4	9	1	0	1	4	5		.214	.283	.238	39	-4	0	0	0	.877	4	S-15	0.1
1924	Det-A	17	11	3	3	0	0	1	0	1		.273	.273	.273	42	-1	0	0	0	.000	-0	/3-3,O-2	-0.1
1929	Chi-A	127	419	50	108	20	4	1	39	31	24	.258	.310	.332	66	-21	9	8	-2	.971	24	*2-122/S-1	0.6
1930	Chi-A	70	266	37	77	11	6	3	27	21	23	.289	.351	.410	95	-2	4	2	0	.980	8	2-52,S-20	0.3
1931	Chi-A	128	444	51	119	17	2	2	50	35	22	.268	.324	.329	77	-15	9	3	1	.968	8	*2-117/3-7,S-1	0.1
1932	Was-A	51	132	14	36	6	1	0	15	13	3	.273	.338	.333	75	-5	3	2	0	.954	-1	2-17,S-14/3-8	-0.3
1933	*Was-A	28	40	5	8	0	0	0	3	2		.200	.256	.200	22	-4	0	0	0	.966	3	2-16/3-1	-0.1
1934	Was-A	31	103	8	28	4	0	0	12	6	13	.272	.324	.311	67	-5	1	1	-0	.971	10	3-17,2-13	0.5
Total	8	471	1457	172	388	59	13	6	145	115	92	.266	.323	.337	73	-57	26	16	-2	.970	48	2-337/S-51,3-36,O-2	1.1

■ DOC KERR   Kerr, John Jonas   b: 1/17/1882, Dellroy, Ohio   d: 6/9/37, Baltimore, Md.   BB/TR, 5'10.5", 190 lbs.   Deb: 4/22/14

1914	Pit-F	42	71	3	17	4	2	1	7	10	13	.239	.333	.394	99	-1	0			.970	1	C-18	0.1
	Bal-F	14	34	4	9	1	1	0	1	1	6	.265	.286	.353	71	-2	1			.979	5	C-13/1-1	0.3
	Yr	56	105	7	26	5	3	1	8	11	19	.248	.319	.381	90	-3	1			.974	5	C-31/1-1	0.4
1915	Bal-F	3	6	1	2	0	0	0	1	0		.333	.429	.333	112	0	0			1.000	-1	/C-2,1-1	-0.1
Total	2	59	111	8	28	5	3	1	8	12	19	.252	.325	.378	91	-3	1			.975	4	/C-33,1-2	0.3

■ BUDDY KERR   Kerr, John Joseph   b: 11/6/22, Astoria, N.Y.   BR/TR, 6'2", 180 lbs.   Deb: 9/8/43

1943	NY-N	27	98	14	28	3	0	2	12	8	5	.286	.352	.378	110	1	1			.955	5	S-27	0.8
1944	NY-N	150	548	68	146	31	4	9	63	37	32	.266	.316	.387	97	-3	14			.954	17	*S-149	2.6
1945	NY-N	149	546	53	136	20	5	4	40	41	34	.249	.304	.319	72	-21	5			.964	28	*S-148	1.9
1946	NY-N	145	497	50	124	20	3	6	40	53	31	.249	.324	.338	87	-8	7			.982	6	*S-126,3-18	0.6
1947	NY-N	138	547	73	157	23	5	7	49	36	49	.287	.331	.386	89	-9	2			.977	12	*S-138	1.0
1948	NY-N★	144	496	41	119	16	4	0	46	56	36	.240	.317	.288	64	-23	9			.967	3	*S-143	-1.2
1949	NY-N	90	220	16	46	4	0	0	19	21	23	.209	.284	.227	39	-19	0			.959	6	S-89	-0.8
1950	Bos-N	155	507	45	115	24	6	2	46	50	50	.227	.296	.310	64	-27	0			.965	2	*S-155	-1.3
1951	Bos-N	69	172	18	32	4	1	1	18	22	20	.186	.282	.227	41	-14	0	0	0	.969	13	S-63/2-5	0.3
Total	9	1067	3631	378	903	145	25	31	333	324	280	.249	.312	.328	76	-123	38	0	0	.967	92	*S-1038/3-18,2-5	3.9

■ MEL KERR   Kerr, John Melville   b: 5/22/03, Souris, Man., Can.   d: 8/9/80, Vero Beach, Fla.   BL/TL, 5'11.5", 155 lbs.   Deb: 9/16/25   C

| 1925 | Chi-N | 1 | 0 | 1 | 0 | 0 | 0 | 0 | 0 | 0 | 0 | — | — | — | — | | 0 | 0 | 0 | .000 | 0 | R | 0.0 |

■ DAN KERWIN   Kerwin, Daniel Patrick (b: Daniel Patrick Kervin)   b: 7/9/1879, Philadelphia, Pa.   d: 7/13/60, Philadelphia, Pa.   BL/TL, 5'9", 164 lbs.   Deb: 9/27/03

| 1903 | Cin-N | 2 | 6 | 1 | 4 | 1 | 0 | 0 | 1 | 0 | 2 | .667 | .778 | .833 | 323 | 2 | | | | .500 | -1 | /O-2 | 0.1 |

■ DON KESSINGER   Kessinger, Donald Eulon   b: 7/17/42, Forrest City, Ark.   BB/TR, 6'1", 175 lbs.   Deb: 9/7/64   FM

| 1964 | Chi-N | 4 | 12 | 1 | 2 | 0 | 0 | 0 | 1 | 0 | 0 | .167 | .167 | .167 | -6 | -2 | 0 | 0 | 0 | 1.000 | -1 | /S-4 | -0.3 |
| 1965 | Chi-N | 106 | 309 | 19 | 62 | 4 | 3 | 0 | 14 | 20 | 44 | .201 | .254 | .233 | 37 | -25 | 1 | 2 | -1 | .948 | 21 | *S-105 | 0.1 |

YEAR	TM/L	G	AB	R	H	2B	3B	HR	RBI	BB	SO	AVG	OBP	SLG	PRO+	BR/A	SB	CS	SBR	FA	FR	G/POS	TPR
1966	Chi-N	150	533	50	146	8	2	1	43	26	46	.274	.308	.302	70	-21	13	7	-0	.951	-10	*S-148	-1.9
1967	Chi-N	145	580	61	134	10	7	0	42	33	80	.231	.277	.272	55	-33	6	13	-6	.973	-3	*S-143	-3.1
1968	Chi-N★	160	655	63	157	14	7	1	32	38	86	.240	.283	.287	67	-25	9	9	-3	.962	18	*S-159	0.8
1969	Chi-N★	158	664	109	181	38	6	4	53	61	70	.273	.335	.366	85	-13	11	8	-2	**.976**	25	*S-157	2.9
1970	Chi-N★	154	631	100	168	21	14	1	39	66	59	.266	.338	.349	75	-22	12	6	0	.972	9	*S-154	0.6
1971	Chi-N★	155	617	77	159	18	6	2	38	52	54	.258	.318	.316	70	-24	15	8	-0	.966	4	*S-154	0.0
1972	Chi-N★	149	577	77	158	20	6	1	39	67	44	.274	.351	.334	87	-8	8	7	-2	.965	8	*S-146	2.0
1973	Chi-N	160	577	52	151	22	3	0	43	57	44	.262	.328	.310	72	-20	6	6	-2	.964	17	*S-158	1.6
1974	Chi-N★	153	599	83	155	20	7	1	42	62	54	.259	.332	.321	80	-15	7	7	-2	.958	2	*S-150	0.5
1975	Chi-N	154	601	77	146	26	10	0	46	68	47	.243	.321	.319	75	-19	4	7	-3	.967	-2	*S-140,3-13	-1.0
1976	StL-N	145	502	55	120	22	6	1	40	61	51	.239	.323	.313	80	-12	3	0	1	.969	-4	*S-113,2-31/3-2	0.0
1977	StL-N	59	134	14	32	4	0	0	7	14	26	.239	.311	.269	58	-8	0	0	0	.978	2	S-26,2-24/3-4	-0.2
	Chi-A	39	119	12	28	3	2	0	11	13	7	.235	.311	.294	66	-5	2	1	0	.959	-4	S-21,2-13/3-9	-0.7
1978	Chi-A	131	431	35	110	18	1	1	31	36	34	.255	.313	.309	75	-14	2	4	-2	.974	-19	*S-123/2-9	-2.0
1979	Chi-A	56	110	14	22	6	0	1	7	10	12	.200	.267	.282	48	-8	1	0	0	.988	-1	S-54/1-1,2-1,M	-0.4
Total	16	2078	7651	899	1931	254	80	14	527	684	759	.252	.316	.312	72	-274	100	85	-21	.966	61	*S-1955/2-78,3-28,1	-1.1

■ **KEITH KESSINGER** Kessinger, Robert Keith b: 2/19/67, Forrest City, Ark. BB/TR, 6'2", 185 lbs. Deb: 9/15/93 F

YEAR	TM/L	G	AB	R	H	2B	3B	HR	RBI	BB	SO	AVG	OBP	SLG	PRO+	BR/A	SB	CS	SBR	FA	FR	G/POS	TPR
1993	Cin-N	11	27	4	7	1	0	1	3	4	4	.259	.355	.407	103	0	0	0	0	.935	-1	S-11	0.0

■ **HENRY KESSLER** Kessler, Henry "Lucky" b: 1847, Brooklyn, N.Y. d: 1/9/1900, Franklin, Pa. BR/TR, 5'10", 144 lbs. Deb: 8/4/1873

YEAR	TM/L	G	AB	R	H	2B	3B	HR	RBI	BB	SO	AVG	OBP	SLG	PRO+	BR/A	SB	CS	SBR	FA	FR	G/POS	TPR
1873	Atl-n	1	5	0	1	0	0	0	1	0	0	.200	.200	.200	21	-0	0	0	0	.882	0	/1-1	0.0
1874	Atl-n	14	56	8	17	1	0	0	4	0	2	.304	.304	.321	114	1	0	0	0	.737	-3	/C-9,2-4,O-4,3-1	-0.1
1875	Atl-n	25	105	17	26	2	0	0	7	1	2	.248	.255	.267	93	-0	0	2	-1	.794	-1	S-18/O-7,C-3,1-1,2	-0.2
1876	Cin-N	59	248	26	64	5	0	0	11	7	10	.258	.278	.278	100	2				.788	-8	S-46,O-16	-0.7
1877	Cin-N	6	20	0	2	0	0	0	0	2	1	.100	.182	.100	-10	-2				.500	-5	/C-5,1-1	-0.7
Total	3 n	40	166	25	44	3	0	0	12	1	4	.265	.269	.283	98	1	0	2	-1	.739	-4	/S-18,C-12,O213	-0.3
Total	2	65	268	26	66	5	0	0	11	9	11	.246	.271	.265	91	-1				.788	-14	/S-46,O-16,C-5,1-1	-1.4

■ **FRED KETCHUM** Ketchum, Frederick L. b: 7/27/1875, Elmira, N.Y. d: 3/12/08, Cortland, N.Y. BL/TR, 5'8", 157 lbs. Deb: 9/12/1899

YEAR	TM/L	G	AB	R	H	2B	3B	HR	RBI	BB	SO	AVG	OBP	SLG	PRO+	BR/A	SB	CS	SBR	FA	FR	G/POS	TPR
1899	Lou-N	15	61	13	18	1	0	0	5	0		.295	.306	.311	70	-3	2			1.000	-4	O-15	-0.7
1901	Phi-A	5	22	5	5	0	0	0	2	0		.227	.227	.227	25	-2	0			.875	-1	/O-5	-0.3
Total	2	20	83	18	23	1	0	0	7	0		.277	.286	.289	58	-5	2			.960	-5	/O-20	-1.0

■ **PHIL KETTER** Ketter, Philip (b: Philip Ketterer) b: 4/13/1884, St.Louis, Mo. d: 4/9/65, St.Louis, Mo. TR , Deb: 5/23/12

YEAR	TM/L	G	AB	R	H	2B	3B	HR	RBI	BB	SO	AVG	OBP	SLG	PRO+	BR/A	SB	CS	SBR	FA	FR	G/POS	TPR
1912	StL-A	2	6	1	2	0	0	0	0	0		.333	.333	.333	94	-0	0			1.000	-1	/C-2	-0.1

■ **SAM KHALIFA** Khalifa, Sam b: 12/5/63, Fontana, Cal. BR/TR, 5'11", 170 lbs. Deb: 6/25/85

YEAR	TM/L	G	AB	R	H	2B	3B	HR	RBI	BB	SO	AVG	OBP	SLG	PRO+	BR/A	SB	CS	SBR	FA	FR	G/POS	TPR
1985	Pit-N	95	320	30	76	14	3	2	31	34	56	.237	.311	.319	77	-9	5	2	0	.967	13	S-95	1.3
1986	Pit-N	64	151	8	28	6	0	0	4	19	28	.185	.276	.225	39	-12	0	2	-1	.961	14	S-60/2-6	0.5
1987	Pit-N	5	17	1	3	0	0	0	2	0	2	.176	.176	.176	-6	-3	0	0	0	.917	-5	/S-5	-0.7
Total	3	164	488	39	107	20	3	2	37	53	86	.219	.296	.285	62	-24	5	4	-1	.964	22	S-160/2-6	1.1

■ **HOD KIBBIE** Kibbie, Horace Kent b: 7/18/03, Ft.Worth, Tex. d: 10/19/75, Ft.Worth, Tex. BR/TR, 5'10", 150 lbs. Deb: 6/13/25

YEAR	TM/L	G	AB	R	H	2B	3B	HR	RBI	BB	SO	AVG	OBP	SLG	PRO+	BR/A	SB	CS	SBR	FA	FR	G/POS	TPR
1925	Bos-N	11	41	5	11	2	0	0	2	5	6	.268	.348	.317	78	-1	0	0	0	.904	-0	/2-8,S-3	-0.1

■ **JACK KIBBLE** Kibble, John Westly "Happy" b: 1/2/1892, Seatonville, Ill. d: 12/13/69, Roundup, Mont. BB/TR, 5'9.5", 154 lbs. Deb: 9/10/12

YEAR	TM/L	G	AB	R	H	2B	3B	HR	RBI	BB	SO	AVG	OBP	SLG	PRO+	BR/A	SB	CS	SBR	FA	FR	G/POS	TPR
1912	Cle-A	5	8	1	0	0	0	0	0	0		.000	.111	.000	-65	-2	0			1.000	4	/3-4,2-1	0.2

■ **STEVE KIEFER** Kiefer, Steven George b: 10/18/60, Chicago, Ill. BR/TR, 6'1", 180 lbs. Deb: 9/3/84 F

YEAR	TM/L	G	AB	R	H	2B	3B	HR	RBI	BB	SO	AVG	OBP	SLG	PRO+	BR/A	SB	CS	SBR	FA	FR	G/POS	TPR
1984	Oak-A	23	40	7	7	1	2	0	2	2	10	.175	.214	.300	43	-3	2	1	0	.904	1	S-17/3-2,D-3	-0.2
1985	Oak-A	40	66	8	13	1	1	1	10	1	18	.197	.209	.288	37	-6	0	0	0	.881	3	3-34/D-2	-0.3
1986	Mil-A	2	6	0	0	0	0	0	0	0	4	.000	.000	.000	-97	-2	0	0	0	1.000	3	/S-2	0.1
1987	Mil-A	28	99	17	20	4	0	5	17	7	28	.202	.262	.394	69	-5	0	0	0	.966	-3	3-26/2-4	-0.7
1988	Mil-A	7	10	2	3	1	0	1	1	2	3	.300	.462	.700	219	2	0	0	0	1.000	-1	/2-4,3-4	0.1
1989	NY-A	5	8	0	1	0	0	0	0	0	5	.125	.125	.125	-30	-1	0	0	0	1.000	-1	/3-5	-0.3
Total	6	105	229	34	44	7	3	7	30	12	68	.192	.239	.341	56	-15	2	1	0	.920	1	/3-71,S-19,2-8,D-5	-1.3

■ **BILL KIENZLE** Kienzle, William H. b: Philadelphia, Pa. BL/TL, Deb: 9/15/1882

YEAR	TM/L	G	AB	R	H	2B	3B	HR	RBI	BB	SO	AVG	OBP	SLG	PRO+	BR/A	SB	CS	SBR	FA	FR	G/POS	TPR
1882	Phi-a	9	33	8	11	3	2	0	9	5		.333	.421	.545	200	3				.842	-1	/O-9	0.2
1884	Phi-U	67	299	76	76	13	8	0		21		.254	.303	.351	106	-6				.772	-2	O-67	-0.9
Total	2	76	332	84	87	16	10	0	9	26		.262	.316	.370	116	-3				.781	-3	/O-76	-0.7

■ **BROOKS KIESCHNICK** Kieschnick, Michael Brooks b: 6/6/72, Robstown, Tex. BL/TR, 6'4", 225 lbs. Deb: 4/3/96

YEAR	TM/L	G	AB	R	H	2B	3B	HR	RBI	BB	SO	AVG	OBP	SLG	PRO+	BR/A	SB	CS	SBR	FA	FR	G/POS	TPR
1996	Chi-N	25	29	6	10	2	0	1	6	3	8	.345	.406	.517	138	2	0	0	0	.833	-3	/O-8	-0.1
1997	Chi-N	39	90	9	18	2	0	4	12	12	21	.200	.294	.356	67	-4	1	0	0	.952	-1	O-27	-0.6
Total	2	64	119	15	28	4	0	5	18	15	29	.235	.321	.395	84	-3	1	0	0	.938	-4	/O-35	-0.7

■ **PETE KILDUFF** Kilduff, Peter John b: 4/4/1893, Weir City, Kan. d: 2/14/30, Pittsburg, Kan. BR/TR, 5'7", 155 lbs. Deb: 4/18/17

YEAR	TM/L	G	AB	R	H	2B	3B	HR	RBI	BB	SO	AVG	OBP	SLG	PRO+	BR/A	SB	CS	SBR	FA	FR	G/POS	TPR
1917	NY-N	31	78	12	16	3	0	1	12	4	11	.205	.253	.282	66	-3	2			.954	-2	2-21/S-5,3-1	-0.5
	Chi-N	56	202	23	56	9	5	0	15	12	19	.277	.324	.371	105	1	11			.920	-14	S-51/2-5	-1.2
	Yr	87	280	35	72	12	5	1	27	16	30	.257	.304	.346	95	-2	13			.917	-16	S-56,2-26/3-1	-1.7
1918	Chi-N	30	93	7	19	2	2	0	13	7	7	.204	.267	.269	62	-4	1			.935	-3	2-30	-0.6
1919	Chi-N	31	88	5	24	4	2	0	8	10	5	.273	.360	.364	117	2	1			.974	-4	3-14/2-8,S-7	-0.1
	Bro-N	32	73	9	22	3	1	0	8	12	11	.301	.407	.370	132	4	5			.862	-4	3-26/2-1	0.1
	Yr	63	161	14	46	7	3	0	16	22	16	.286	.382	.366	124	6	6			.903	-8	3-40/2-9,S-7	0.0
1920	*Bro-N	141	478	62	130	26	8	0	58	58	43	.272	.351	.360	101	2	2	9	-5	.967	8	*2-134/3-5	1.0
1921	Bro-N	107	372	45	107	15	10	3	45	31	36	.288	.344	.406	94	-3	6	6	-2	.963	13	*2-105/3-1	1.1
Total	5	428	1384	163	374	62	28	4	159	134	132	.270	.338	.364	98	-2	28	15		.963	-7	2-304/S-63,3-47	-0.2

■ **JOHN KILEY** Kiley, John Frederick b: 7/1/1859, Dedham, Mass. d: 12/18/40, Norwood, Mass. BL/TL, 5'7", 147 lbs. Deb: 5/1/1884

YEAR	TM/L	G	AB	R	H	2B	3B	HR	RBI	BB	SO	AVG	OBP	SLG	PRO+	BR/A	SB	CS	SBR	FA	FR	G/POS	TPR
1884	Was-a	14	56	9	12	2	2	0		3		.214	.267	.321	103	0				.571	-4	O-14	-0.3
1891	Bos-N	1	2	0	0	0	0	0	0	1	1	.000	.500	.000	45	0	0			1.000	0	/P-1	0.0
Total	2	15	58	9	12	2	2	0	0	4	1	.207	.281	.310	102	0	0			.571	-4	/O-14,P-1	-0.3

■ **PAT KILHULLEN** Kilhullen, Joseph Isadore b: 8/10/1890, Carbondale, Pa. d: 11/2/22, Oakland, Cal. BR/TR, 5'9", 175 lbs. Deb: 6/10/14

YEAR	TM/L	G	AB	R	H	2B	3B	HR	RBI	BB	SO	AVG	OBP	SLG	PRO+	BR/A	SB	CS	SBR	FA	FR	G/POS	TPR
1914	Pit-N	1	1	0	0	0	0	0	0	0	0	.000	.000	.000	-99	-0	0			.000	0	/C-1	0.0

■ **HARMON KILLEBREW** Killebrew, Harmon Clayton "Killer" b: 6/29/36, Payette, Idaho BR/TR, 5'11", 213 lbs. Deb: 6/23/54 H

YEAR	TM/L	G	AB	R	H	2B	3B	HR	RBI	BB	SO	AVG	OBP	SLG	PRO+	BR/A	SB	CS	SBR	FA	FR	G/POS	TPR
1954	Was-A	9	13	1	4	1	0	0	3	2	3	.308	.400	.385	122	0	0	0	0	1.000	-2	/2-3	-0.2
1955	Was-A	38	80	12	16	1	0	4	7	9	31	.200	.281	.363	76	-3	0	0	0	.935	5	3-23/2-3	0.2
1956	Was-A	44	99	10	22	2	0	5	13	10	39	.222	.294	.394	80	-3	0	0	0	.951	-0	3-20/2-4	-0.3
1957	Was-A	9	31	4	9	2	0	2	5	2	8	.290	.333	.548	139	1	0	0	0	.947	-1	/3-7,2-1	0.1
1958	Was-A	13	31	2	6	0	0	0	2	0	12	.194	.219	.194	15	-4	0	0	0	1.000	0	/3-9	-0.4
1959	Was-A★	153	546	98	132	20	2	**42**	105	90	116	.242	.356	.516	137	28	3	2	-0	.938	-8	*3-150/O-4	2.0
1960	Was-A	124	442	84	122	19	1	31	80	71	106	.276	.377	.534	145	28	1	0	0	.987	-9	1-71,3-65	1.3
1961	Min-A★	150	541	94	156	20	7	46	122	107	109	.288	.409	.606	159	46	1	2	-1	.987	-10	*1-119,3-45/O-2	2.6
1962	Min-A	155	552	85	134	21	1	**48**	**126**	106	142	.243	.369	.545	137	29	1	2	-1	.967	-10	*O-151/1-4	0.9
1963	Min-A★	142	515	88	133	18	0	**45**	96	72	105	.258	.353	**.555**	147	32	0	0	0	.987	-3	*O-137	2.2
1964	Min-A★	158	577	95	156	11	1	**49**	111	93	135	.270	.379	.548	153	42	0	0	0	.971	-7	*O-157	2.9
1965	*Min-A★	113	401	78	108	16	1	25	75	72	69	.269	.386	.501	144	25	0	0	0	.988	-9	1-72,3-44/O-1	1.2
1966	Min-A★	162	569	89	160	27	1	39	110	**103**	98	.281	.393	.538	155	42	0	2	-1	.951	-17	*3-107,1-42,O-18	2.0

YEAR	TM/L	G	AB	R	H	2B	3B	HR	RBI	BB	SO	AVG	OBP	SLG	PRO+	BR/A	SB	CS	SBR	FA	FR	G/POS	TPR
1967	Min-A★	163	547	105	147	24	1	**44**	113	**131**	111	.269	.413	.558	170	52	1	0	0	.992	-8	*1-160/3-3	3.8
1968	Min-A★	100	295	40	62	7	2	17	40	70	70	.210	.365	.420	131	13	0	0	0	.994	3	1-77,3-11	1.3
1969	*Min-A★	162	555	106	153	20	2	**49**	**140**	**145**	84	.276	**.430**	.584	177	63	8	2	1	.929	-21	*3-105,1-80	3.9
1970	*Min-A★	157	527	96	143	20	1	41	113	128	84	.271	.416	.546	161	48	0	3	-2	.948	-29	*3-138,1-28	1.4
1971	Min-A★	147	500	61	127	19	1	28	**119**	**114**	96	.254	.393	.464	137	28	3	2	-0	.997	-15	1-90,3-64	0.4
1972	Min-A	139	433	53	100	13	2	26	74	94	91	.231	.369	.450	136	22	0	1	-1	.992	11	*1-130	2.5
1973	Min-A	69	248	29	60	9	1	5	32	41	59	.242	.352	.347	94	-1	0	0	0	.998	4	1-57/D-9	-0.1
1974	Min-A	122	333	28	74	7	0	13	54	45	61	.222	.315	.360	91	-4	0	0	0	.992	2	D-57,1-33	-0.6
1975	KC-A	106	312	25	62	13	0	14	44	54	70	.199	.319	.375	93	-3	1	2	-1	1.000	-1	D-92/1-6	-0.7
Total	22	2435	8147	1283	2086	290	24	573	1584	1559	1699	.256	.379	.509	142	482	19	18	-5	.992	-123	1-969,3-791,OD/2	26.4

■ RED KILLEFER

Killefer, Wade Hampton b: 4/13/1885, Bloomingdale, Mich d: 9/4/58, Los Angeles, Cal. BR/TR, 5'9", 175 lbs. Deb: 9/16/07 F

YEAR	TM/L	G	AB	R	H	2B	3B	HR	RBI	BB	SO	AVG	OBP	SLG	PRO+	BR/A	SB	CS	SBR	FA	FR	G/POS	TPR
1907	Det-A	1	4	0	0	0	0	0	0	0		.000	.000	.000	-97	-1	0			1.000	0	/O-1	-0.1
1908	Det-A	28	75	9	16	1	0	0	11	3		.213	.253	.227	54	-4	4			.956	-5	2-16/S-7,3-4	-1.1
1909	Det-A	23	61	6	17	2	2	1	4	3		.279	.343	.426	137	2	2			.912	-1	2-17/O-1	0.1
	Was-A	40	121	11	21	1	0	0	5	13		.174	.265	.182	43	-7	4			.957	-3	O-24/3-6,C-3,2-3,S	-1.2
	Yr	63	182	17	38	3	2	1	9	16		.209	.291	.264	76	-4	6			.957	-4	O-25,2-20/3-6,CS	-1.1
1910	Was-A	106	345	35	79	17	1	0	24	29		.229	.318	.284	93	-1	17			.940	-5	2-88,O-12	-0.9
1914	Cin-N	42	141	16	39	6	1	0	12	20	18	.277	.386	.333	111	3	11			.968	-4	O-37/2-5,3-1	-0.3
1915	Cin-N	155	555	75	151	25	11	1	41	38	33	.272	.340	.362	110	8	12	18	-7	.970	5	*O-150/1-2	-0.3
1916	Cin-N	70	234	29	57	9	1	1	18	21	8	.244	.327	.303	96	-0	7			.966	-2	O-68	-0.6
	NY-N	2	1	0	1	0	0	0	1	1	0	1.000	1.000	1.000	544	1	0			.000	0	H	0.1
	Yr	72	235	29	58	9	1	1	19	22	8	.247	.332	.306	99	1	7			.966	-2	O-68	-0.5
Total	7	467	1537	181	381	61	16	3	116	128	59	.248	.328	.314	98	0	57	18		.965	-16	O-293,2-129/3SC1	-4.3

■ BILL KILLEFER

Killefer, William Lavier "Reindeer Bill"
b: 10/10/1887, Bloomingdale, Mich d: 7/3/60, Elsmere, Del. BR/TR, 5'10.5", 200 lbs. Deb: 9/13/09 FMC

YEAR	TM/L	G	AB	R	H	2B	3B	HR	RBI	BB	SO	AVG	OBP	SLG	PRO+	BR/A	SB	CS	SBR	FA	FR	G/POS	TPR
1909	StL-A	11	29	0	4	0	0	0	1	0		.138	.138	.138	-14	-4	2			.905	2	C-11	-0.1
1910	StL-A	74	193	14	24	2	2	0	7	12		.124	.184	.155	7	-21	0			.938	12	C-73	-0.3
1911	Phi-N	6	16	3	3	0	0	0	2	0	2	.188	.188	.188	5	-2	0			.975	2	/C-6	0.0
1912	Phi-N	85	268	18	60	6	3	1	21	4	14	.224	.241	.280	40	-23	6			.973	17	C-85	0.2
1913	Phi-N	120	360	25	88	14	3	0	24	4	17	.244	.255	.300	56	-21	2			.988	13	*C-118/1-1	0.2
1914	Phi-N	98	299	27	70	10	1	0	27	8	17	.234	.261	.274	56	-17	3			.978	18	C-90	0.9
1915	*Phi-N	105	320	26	76	9	2	0	24	18	14	.237	.287	.278	70	-11	5	3	-0	.972	14	*C-104	1.1
1916	Phi-N	97	286	22	62	5	4	3	27	8	14	.217	.246	.294	63	-13	2			**.985**	-1	C-91	-0.8
1917	Phi-N	125	409	28	112	12	0	0	31	15	21	.274	.306	.303	84	-8	4			**.984**	10	*C-120/O-1	1.3
1918	*Chi-N	104	331	30	77	10	3	0	22	17	10	.233	.276	.281	68	-13	5			.982	9	*C-104	0.6
1919	Chi-N	103	315	17	90	10	2	0	22	15	8	.286	.322	.330	96	-2	5			**.987**	17	*C-100	2.6
1920	Chi-N	62	191	16	42	7	1	0	16	8	5	.220	.280	.267	56	-10	2	2	-1	.977	18	C-61	1.2
1921	Chi-N	45	133	11	43	1	0	0	16	4	4	.323	.357	.331	83	-3	3	3	-1	.964	-1	C-42,M	-0.3
Total	13	1035	3150	237	751	86	21	4	240	113	126	.238	.273	.283	63	-147	39	8		.976	131	*C-1005/O-1,1-1	6.6

■ GENE KIMBALL

Kimball, Eugene Boynton b: 8/31/1850, Rochester, N.Y. d: 8/2/1882, Rochester, N.Y. 5'10", 160 lbs. Deb: 5/4/1871

YEAR	TM/L	G	AB	R	H	2B	3B	HR	RBI	BB	SO	AVG	OBP	SLG	PRO+	BR/A	SB	CS	SBR	FA	FR	G/POS	TPR
1871	Cle-n	29	131	18	25	1	0	0	9	3	2	.191	.209	.198	19	-12	5	1	1	.743	-7	2-17/O-9,S-6,3-2	-1.3

■ DICK KIMBLE

Kimble, Richard Lewis b: 7/27/15, Buchtel, Ohio BL/TR, 5'9", 160 lbs. Deb: 8/20/45

YEAR	TM/L	G	AB	R	H	2B	3B	HR	RBI	BB	SO	AVG	OBP	SLG	PRO+	BR/A	SB	CS	SBR	FA	FR	G/POS	TPR
1945	Was-A	20	49	5	12	1	1	0	1	5	2	.245	.315	.306	88	-1	0	0	0	.950	-3	S-15	-0.3

■ BRUCE KIMM

Kimm, Bruce Edward b: 6/29/51, Cedar Rapids, Iowa BR/TR, 5'11", 175 lbs. Deb: 5/4/76 C

YEAR	TM/L	G	AB	R	H	2B	3B	HR	RBI	BB	SO	AVG	OBP	SLG	PRO+	BR/A	SB	CS	SBR	FA	FR	G/POS	TPR
1976	Det-A	63	152	13	40	8	0	1	6	15	20	.263	.329	.336	91	-1	4	3	-1	.970	4	C-61/D-2	0.4
1977	Det-A	14	25	2	2	1	0	0	1	0	4	.080	.115	.120	-34	-5	0	1	-1	.958	3	C-12/D-2	-0.2
1979	Chi-N	9	11	0	1	0	0	0	0	0	0	.091	.091	.091	-46	-2	0	1	-1	.969	2	/C-9	-0.1
1980	Chi-A	100	251	20	61	10	1	0	19	17	26	.243	.291	.291	60	-13	1	3	-2	.985	-1	C-98	-1.4
Total	4	186	439	35	104	19	1	1	26	32	50	.237	.290	.292	62	-22	5	8	-3	.977	8	C-180/D-4	-1.3

■ WALLY KIMMICK

Kimmick, Walter Lyons b: 5/30/1897, Turtle Creek, Pa. d: 7/24/89, Boswell, Pa. BR/TR, 5'11", 174 lbs. Deb: 9/13/19

YEAR	TM/L	G	AB	R	H	2B	3B	HR	RBI	BB	SO	AVG	OBP	SLG	PRO+	BR/A	SB	CS	SBR	FA	FR	G/POS	TPR
1919	StL-N	2	1	1	0	0	0	0	0	1	0	.000	.500	.000	61	0	1			1.000	0	/S-1	0.0
1921	Cin-N	3	6	0	1	0	0	0	1	0	1	.167	.167	.167	-12	-1	0	0	0	.667	-0	/3-2	-0.1
1922	Cin-N	39	89	11	22	2	1	0	12	3	12	.247	.272	.292	46	-7	0	0	0	.965	2	S-30/2-3,3-1	-0.3
1923	Cin-N	29	80	11	18	2	1	0	6	5	15	.225	.271	.275	45	-6	3	0	1	.972	8	2-17/3-4,S-1	0.3
1925	Phi-N	70	141	16	43	3	2	1	10	22	26	.305	.399	.376	91	-1	0	3	-2	.904	-3	S-28,3-21,2-13	-0.3
1926	Phi-N	20	28	0	6	2	1	0	2	3	7	.214	.290	.357	70	-1	0			1.000	-2	/1-5,S-4,3-4,2-1	-0.3
Total	6	163	345	39	90	9	5	1	31	34	61	.261	.327	.325	67	-17	4	3		.933	4	/S-64,2-34,3-32,1-5	-0.7

■ JERRY KINDALL

Kindall, Gerald Donald "Slim" b: 5/27/35, St.Paul, Minn. BR/TR, 6'2.5", 175 lbs. Deb: 7/1/56

YEAR	TM/L	G	AB	R	H	2B	3B	HR	RBI	BB	SO	AVG	OBP	SLG	PRO+	BR/A	SB	CS	SBR	FA	FR	G/POS	TPR
1956	Chi-N	32	55	7	9	1	1	0	0	6	17	.164	.246	.218	27	-6	1	0	0	.956	2	S-18	-0.2
1957	Chi-N	72	181	18	29	3	0	6	12	8	48	.160	.196	.276	25	-19	1	0	0	.920	-4	2-28,3-19/S-9	-2.1
1958	Chi-N	3	6	0	1	1	0	0	0	0	3	.167	.167	.333	29	-1	0	0	0	1.000	1	/2-3	0.1
1960	Chi-N	89	246	17	59	16	2	2	23	5	52	.240	.255	.346	63	-13	4	3	-1	.966	14	2-82/S-2	0.7
1961	Chi-N	96	310	37	75	22	3	9	44	18	89	.242	.288	.419	84	-8	2	2	-1	.950	7	2-50,S-47	0.6
1962	Cle-A	154	530	51	123	21	1	13	55	45	107	.232	.292	.349	74	-20	4	3	-1	.978	21	*2-154	1.6
1963	Cle-A	86	234	27	48	4	1	5	20	18	71	.205	.268	.295	58	-13	3	1	0	.958	3	S-46,2-37/1-4	-0.5
1964	Cle-A	23	25	5	9	1	0	2	2	2	7	.360	.407	.640	188	3	0	0	0	.989	3	1-23	0.6
	Min-A	62	128	8	19	2	0	1	6	7	44	.148	.199	.188	8	-16	0	0	0	.969	5	2-51/S-7,1-1	-0.9
	Yr	85	153	13	28	3	0	3	8	9	51	.183	.233	.261	37	-13	0	0	0	.969	8	2-51,1-24/S-7	-0.3
1965	Min-A	125	342	41	67	12	1	6	36	36	97	.196	.278	.289	59	-18	2	2	-1	.963	-1	*2-106,3-10/S-7	-1.2
Total	9	742	2057	211	439	83	9	44	198	145	535	.213	.268	.327	62	-111	17	11	-2	.967	50	2-511,S-136/3-29,1	-1.3

■ RALPH KINER

Kiner, Ralph McPherran b: 10/27/22, Santa Rita, N.Mex. BR/TR, 6'2", 195 lbs. Deb: 4/16/46 H

YEAR	TM/L	G	AB	R	H	2B	3B	HR	RBI	BB	SO	AVG	OBP	SLG	PRO+	BR/A	SB	CS	SBR	FA	FR	G/POS	TPR
1946	Pit-N	144	502	63	124	17	3	**23**	81	74	109	.247	.345	.430	116	10	3			.969	1	*O-140	0.5
1947	Pit-N	152	565	118	177	23	4	**51**	127	98	81	.313	.417	**.639**	**172**	**57**	1			.983	13	*O-152	**6.0**
1948	Pit-N★	156	555	104	147	19	5	**40**	123	112	61	.265	.391	.533	145	36	1			.975	7	*O-154	3.4
1949	Pit-N★	152	549	116	170	19	5	**54**	**127**	**117**	61	.310	.432	**.658**	**183**	**66**	6			.979	-1	*O-152	**5.6**
1950	Pit-N★	150	547	112	149	21	6	**47**	118	122	79	.272	.408	.590	154	44	2			.965	-3	*O-150	3.4
1951	Pit-N★	151	531	**124**	164	31	6	**42**	109	**137**	57	.309	**.452**	**.627**	182	67	2	1	0	.967	-5	O-94,1-58	5.4
1952	Pit-N☆	149	516	90	126	17	2	**37**	87	**110**	77	.244	.384	.500	140	30	3	0	1	.970	-6	*O-149	1.9
1953	Pit-N	41	148	27	40	6	1	7	29	25	21	.270	.383	.466	121	5	1	0	0	1.000	1	O-41	0.4
	Chi-N★	117	414	73	117	14	2	28	87	75	67	.283	.394	.529	135	22	1	1	-0	.964	-4	*O-116	1.3
	Yr	158	562	100	157	20	3	35	116	100	88	.279	.391	.512	131	27	2	1	0	.973	-3	*O-157	1.7
1954	Chi-N	147	557	88	159	36	5	22	73	76	90	.285	.373	.487	121	17	2	0	1	.971	-0	*O-147	1.1
1955	Cle-A	113	321	56	78	13	0	18	54	65	46	.243	.370	.452	116	8	0	0	0	.986	-5	O-87	-0.1
Total	10	1472	5205	971	1451	216	39	369	1015	1011	749	.279	.398	.548	148	363	22	2		.974	-2	*O-1382/1-58	28.9

■ CHICK KING

King, Charles Gilbert b: 11/10/30, Paris, Tenn. BR/TR, 6'2", 190 lbs. Deb: 8/27/54

YEAR	TM/L	G	AB	R	H	2B	3B	HR	RBI	BB	SO	AVG	OBP	SLG	PRO+	BR/A	SB	CS	SBR	FA	FR	G/POS	TPR
1954	Det-A	11	28	4	6	0	1	0	3	3	8	.214	.290	.286	59	-2	0	0	0	.958	1	/O-7	-0.1
1955	Det-A	7	21	3	5	0	0	0	0	1	2	.238	.273	.238	39	-2	0	0	0	.923	-0	/O-6	-0.2
1956	Det-A	7	9	0	2	0	0	0	0	1	4	.222	.300	.222	40	-1	0	0	0	.800	-1	/O-4	-0.2
1958	Chi-N	8	8	1	2	0	0	0	1	3	1	.250	.455	.250	95	0	0	0	0	1.000	-2	/O-7	-0.2
1959	Chi-N	7	3	3	0	0	0	0	0	0	1	.000	.000	.000	-99	-1	0	0	0	1.000	-0	/O-1	-0.1
	StL-N	5	7	0	3	0	0	0	1	0	2	.429	.429	.429	121	0	0	0	0	1.000	-0	/O-4	0.0

YEAR	TM/L	G	AB	R	H	2B	3B	HR	RBI	BB	SO	AVG	OBP	SLG	PRO+	BR/A	SB	CS	SBR	FA	FR	G/POS	TPR
	Yr	12	10	3	3	0	0	0	1	0	3	.300	.300	.300	59	-1	0	0	0	1.000	-0	/O-5	-0.1
Total	5	45	76	11	18	0	1	0	5	8	18	.237	.310	.263	56	-5	0	0	0	.947	-3	/O-29	-0.8
■ LEE KING King, Edward Lee b: 3/28/1894, Waltham, Mass. d: 9/7/38, Newton Center, Mass. BR/TR, 5′10″, 160 lbs. Deb: 6/24/16																							
1916	Phi-A	42	144	13	27	1	2	0	8	7	15	.188	.230	.222	38	-11	4			1.000	-10	O-22,S-11/3-5,2-2	-2.5
1919	Bos-N	2	1	0	0	0	0	0	0	0	0	.000	.000	.000	-99	-0	0			.000	0	H	0.0
Total	2	44	145	13	27	1	2	0	8	7	15	.186	.229	.221	37	-12	4			1.000	-10	/O-22,S-11,3-5,2-2	-2.5
■ HAL KING King, Harold b: 2/1/44, Oviedo, Fla. BL/TR, 6′1″, 200 lbs. Deb: 9/6/67																							
1967	Hou-N	15	44	2	11	1	2	0	6	2	9	.250	.283	.364	87	-1	0	0	0	1.000	-2	C-11	-0.3
1968	Hou-N	27	55	4	8	2	1	0	2	7	16	.145	.242	.218	40	-4	0	0	0	.968	-4	C-19	-0.8
1970	Atl-N	89	204	29	53	8	0	11	30	32	41	.260	.366	.461	113	4	1	0	0	.985	-11	C-62	-0.4
1971	Atl-N	86	198	14	41	9	0	5	19	29	43	.207	.320	.328	79	-5	0	0	0	.983	-2	C-60	-0.5
1972	Tex-A	50	122	12	22	5	0	4	12	25	35	.180	.333	.320	99	1	0	0	0	.970	-7	C-38	-0.6
1973	*Cin-N	35	43	5	8	0	0	4	10	6	10	.186	.286	.465	110	0	0	0	0	1.000	-1	/C-9	0.0
1974	Cin-N	20	17	1	3	1	0	0	3	3	4	.176	.300	.235	52	-1	0	0	0	1.000	0	/C-5	-0.1
Total	7	322	683	67	146	26	3	24	82	104	158	.214	.325	.366	93	-6	1	0	0	.982	-26	C-204	-2.7
■ JIM KING King, James Hubert b: 8/27/32, Elkins, Ark. BL/TR, 6′, 185 lbs. Deb: 4/17/55																							
1955	Chi-N	113	301	43	77	12	3	11	45	24	39	.256	.315	.425	95	-3	2	1	0	.990	5	O-93	-0.1
1956	Chi-N	118	317	32	79	13	2	15	54	30	40	.249	.316	.445	103	1	1	2	-1	.990	14	O-82	1.0
1957	StL-N	22	35	1	11	0	0	0	2	4	2	.314	.385	.314	89	-0	0	0	0	1.000	-2	/O-8	-0.3
1958	SF-N	34	56	8	12	2	1	2	8	10	8	.214	.343	.393	96	-0	0	1	-1	1.000	-2	O-15	-0.3
1961	Was-A	110	263	43	71	12	1	11	46	38	45	.270	.366	.449	118	7	4	0	1	.980	-6	O-91/C-1	-0.2
1962	Was-A	132	333	39	81	15	0	11	35	55	37	.243	.355	.387	101	2	4	2	0	.979	2	*O-101	-0.1
1963	Was-A	136	459	61	106	16	5	24	62	45	43	.231	.301	.444	106	2	3	0	1	.987	1	*O-123	-0.2
1964	Was-A	134	415	46	100	15	1	18	56	55	65	.241	.337	.412	108	5	3	1	0	.973	8	*O-121	0.8
1965	Was-A	120	258	46	55	10	2	14	49	44	50	.213	.339	.430	119	7	1	0	0	.993	-2	O-88	0.3
1966	Was-A	117	310	41	77	14	2	10	30	38	41	.248	.330	.403	111	4	4	0	1	.987	0	O-85	0.3
1967	Was-A	47	100	10	21	2	2	1	12	15	13	.210	.331	.300	91	-1	1	1	-0	.962	-3	O-31/C-1	-0.5
	Chi-A	23	50	2	6	1	0	0	2	4	16	.120	.185	.140	-3	-6	0	0	0	1.000	-2	O-12	-1.0
	Cle-A	19	21	2	3	0	0	0	0	1	2	.143	.182	.143	-3	-3	0	0	0	1.000	-0	/O-1	-0.3
	Yr	89	171	14	30	3	2	1	14	20	31	.175	.273	.234	53	-10	1	1	-0	.971	-5	O-44/C-1	-1.8
Total	11	1125	2918	374	699	112	19	117	401	363	401	.240	.328	.411	104	15	23	8	2	.984	13	O-851/C-2	-0.6
■ JEFF KING King, Jeffrey Wayne b: 12/26/64, Marion, Ind. BR/TR, 6′1″, 180 lbs. Deb: 6/2/89																							
1989	Pit-N	75	215	31	42	13	3	5	19	20	34	.195	.270	.353	80	-6	4	2	0	.995	-2	1-46,3-13/2-7,S-1	-1.2
1990	*Pit-N	127	371	46	91	17	1	14	53	21	50	.245	.288	.410	93	-5	3	3	-1	.938	16	*3-115/1-1	1.1
1991	Pit-N	33	109	16	26	1	1	4	18	14	15	.239	.331	.376	100	0	3	1	0	.975	1	3-33	0.1
1992	*Pit-N	130	480	56	111	21	2	14	65	27	56	.231	.275	.371	82	-13	4	6	-2	.953	-4	3-73,1-32,2-32,/SO	-2.2
1993	Pit-N	158	611	82	180	35	3	9	98	59	54	.295	.361	.406	105	5	8	6	-1	.964	21	*3-156/2-2,S-2	2.5
1994	Pit-N	94	339	36	89	23	0	5	42	30	38	.263	.322	.375	80	-10	3	2	-0	.955	11	3-91/2-1	0.1
1995	Pit-N	122	445	61	118	27	2	18	87	55	63	.265	.347	.456	108	5	7	4	-0	.942	-1	3-84,1-35/2-8,S-2	0.0
1996	Pit-N	155	591	91	160	36	4	30	111	70	95	.271	.350	.497	117	14	15	1	4	.997	-2	1-92,2-71,3-17	1.2
1997	KC-A	155	543	84	129	30	1	28	112	89	96	.238	.347	.451	104	3	16	5	2	**.996**	20	*1-150/D-2	1.0
1998	KC-A	131	486	83	128	17	1	24	93	42	73	.263	.325	.451	95	-5	10	2	2	.995	7	*1-112,D-16/3-4	-0.7
Total	10	1180	4190	586	1074	220	18	151	698	427	574	.256	.328	.426	99	-12	73	32	3	.953	66	3-586,1-468,2/DSO	1.9
■ LEE KING King, Lee b: 12/26/1892, Hundred, W.Va. d: 9/16/67, Shinnston, W.Va. BR/TR, 5′8″, 160 lbs. Deb: 9/20/16																							
1916	Pit-N	8	18	0	2	0	0	0	1	0	7	.111	.111	.111	-31	-3	0			.714	-1	/O-8	-0.5
1917	Pit-N	111	381	32	95	14	5	1	35	15	58	.249	.281	.320	82	-9	8			.968	9	*O-102	-0.6
1918	Pit-N	36	112	9	26	3	2	1	11	11	15	.232	.301	.321	87	-2	3			.909	-8	O-36	-1.3
1919	NY-N	21	20	5	2	1	0	0	1	1	6	.100	.143	.150	-12	-3	0			.667	-3	/O-7	-0.6
1920	NY-N	93	261	32	72	11	4	7	42	21	38	.276	.335	.429	120	6	3	7	-3	.951	-11	O-84	-1.4
1921	NY-N	39	94	17	21	4	2	0	7	13	6	.223	.324	.309	68	-4	0	2	-1	.921	-5	O-35/1-1	-1.2
	Phi-N	64	216	25	58	19	4	4	32	8	37	.269	.298	.449	88	-5	1	4	-2	.911	-2	O-57	-1.3
	Yr	103	310	42	79	23	6	4	39	21	43	.255	.306	.406	83	-8	1	6	-3	.914	-7	O-92/1-1	-2.5
1922	Phi-N	19	53	8	12	5	1	2	13	8	6	.226	.328	.472	95	-1	0	0	0	.946	-0	O-15	-0.2
	*NY-N	20	34	6	6	3	0	0	2	5	2	.176	.282	.265	41	-3	1	0	0	1.000	0	/1-5,O-5	-0.3
	Yr	39	87	14	18	8	1	2	15	13	8	.207	.310	.391	76	-3	1	0	0	.961	-0	O-20/1-5	-0.5
Total	7	411	1189	134	294	60	18	15	144	82	175	.247	.299	.366	87	-22	16	13		.940	-21	O-349/1-6	-7.4
■ LYNN KING King, Lynn Paul "Dig" b: 11/28/07, Villisca, Iowa d: 5/11/72, Atlantic, Iowa BL/TR, 5′9″, 165 lbs. Deb: 9/21/35																							
1935	StL-N	8	22	6	4	0	0	0	0	4	1	.182	.308	.182	34	-2	2			1.000	2	/O-6	0.0
1936	StL-N	78	100	12	19	2	1	0	10	9	14	.190	.257	.230	32	-9	2			.984	-4	O-34	-1.4
1939	StL-N	89	85	10	20	2	0	0	11	15	3	.235	.350	.259	62	-4	2			.982	-10	O-44	-1.4
Total	3	175	207	28	43	4	1	0	21	28	18	.208	.302	.237	45	-15	6			.986	-12	/O-84	-2.8
■ MART KING King, Marshal Ney b: 12/1849, Troy, N.Y. d: 10/19/11, Troy, N.Y. TR , 5′9.5″, 176 lbs. Deb: 5/8/1871																							
1871	Chi-n	20	101	23	21	1	0	2	16	8	1	.208	.266	.277	51	-8	5	0	2	.786	-3	O-11/C-9,S-3,3-1	-0.6
1872	Tro-n	3	11	0	0	0	0	0	1	0	1	.000	.000	.000	-99	-2	0	0	0	.857	-0	/O-3	-0.2
Total	2 n	23	112	23	21	1	0	2	17	8	2	.188	.242	.250	39	-10	5	0	2	.810	-3	/O-14,C-9,S-3,3-1	-0.8
■ SAM KING King, Samuel Warren b: 5/17/1852, Peabody, Mass. d: 8/11/22, Peabody, Mass. TL , 6′, Deb: 5/1/1884																							
1884	Was-a	12	45	3	8	2	0	0		1		.178	.213	.222	48	-2				.912	-1	1-12	-0.5
■ STEVE KING King, Stephen F. b: 1842, Troy, N.Y. d: 7/8/1895, Troy, N.Y. 5′9″, 175 lbs. Deb: 5/9/1871																							
1871	Tro-n	29	144	45	57	10	6	0	34	1	1	.396	.400	.549	167	12	3	3	-1	.833	3	*O-29	0.9
1872	Tro-n	25	128	33	39	8	0	0	21	1	2	.305	.310	.367	106	1	1	1	-0	.776	1	O-25	0.1
Total	2 n	54	272	78	96	18	6	0	55	2	3	.353	.358	.463	139	12	4	4	-1	.807	4	/O-54	1.0
■ WES KINGDON Kingdon, Westcott William b: 7/4/1900, Los Angeles, Cal. d: 4/19/75, Capistrano, Cal. BR/TR, 5′8″, 148 lbs. Deb: 6/12/32																							
1932	Was-A	18	34	10	11	3	1	0	3	5	2	.324	.410	.471	129	2	0	0	0	.929	-2	/3-8,S-4	0.1
■ MIKE KINGERY Kingery, Michael Scott b: 3/29/61, St.James, Minn. BL/TL, 6′, 180 lbs. Deb: 7/7/86																							
1986	KC-A	62	209	25	54	8	5	3	14	12	30	.258	.299	.388	83	-5	7	3	0	.973	-3	O-59	-1.0
1987	Sea-A	120	354	38	99	25	4	9	52	27	43	.280	.334	.449	100	-0	7	9	-3	.992	10	*O-114/D-4	0.3
1988	Sea-A	57	123	21	25	6	0	1	9	19	23	.203	.315	.276	64	-5	3	1	0	.989	-1	O-44,1-10	-0.7
1989	Sea-A	31	76	14	17	3	0	2	6	7	14	.224	.289	.342	75	-3	1	1	-0	1.000	3	O-23	-0.1
1990	SF-N	105	207	24	61	7	1	0	24	12	19	.295	.336	.338	89	-3	6	1	1	.978	-12	O-95	-1.5
1991	SF-N	91	110	13	20	2	2	0	8	15	21	.182	.280	.236	48	-7	1	0	0	.975	-7	O-38/1-6	-1.5
1992	Oak-A	12	28	3	3	0	0	0	1	1	3	.107	.138	.107	-32	-5	0	0	0	1.000	-2	O-10	-0.8
1994	Col-N	105	301	56	105	27	8	4	41	30	26	.349	.411	.532	123	10	5	7	-3	.979	-5	O-98/1-1	0.1
1995	*Col-N	119	350	66	94	18	4	8	37	45	40	.269	.352	.411	78	-13	13	5	1	.979	-11	*O-108/1-5	-2.6
1996	Pit-N	117	276	32	68	12	2	3	27	23	29	.246	.307	.337	68	-13	2	1	0	.985	-8	O-83	-2.2
Total	10	819	2034	292	546	108	26	30	219	191	248	.268	.333	.391	86	-45	45	28	-3	.984	-37	O-672/1-22,D-4	-10.0
■ DAVE KINGMAN Kingman, David Arthur b: 12/21/48, Pendleton, Ore. BR/TR, 6′6″, 210 lbs. Deb: 7/30/71																							
1971	*SF-N	41	115	17	32	10	2	6	24	9	35	.278	.336	.557	151	7	5	0	2	.981	-4	1-20,O-14	0.3
1972	SF-N	135	472	65	106	17	4	29	83	51	140	.225	.306	.462	114	7	16	6	1	.932	3	3-59,1-56,O-22	0.6
1973	SF-N	112	305	54	62	10	1	24	55	41	122	.203	.302	.479	109	2	8	5	-1	.910	3	3-60,1-46/P-2	0.3
1974	SF-N	121	350	41	78	18	2	18	55	37	125	.223	.303	.440	101	-1	8	8	-2	.983	2	1-91,3-21/O-2	-0.7

YEAR	TM/L	G	AB	R	H	2B	3B	HR	RBI	BB	SO	AVG	OBP	SLG	PRO+	BR/A	SB	CS	SBR	FA	FR	G/POS	TPR
1975	NY-N	134	502	65	116	22	1	36	88	34	153	.231	.285	.494	119	7	7	5	-1	.958	4	O-71,1-58,3-12	0.4
1976	NY-N★	123	474	70	113	14	1	37	86	28	135	.238	.288	.506	130	13	7	4	-0	.959	3	*O-111,1-16	1.2
1977	NY-N	58	211	22	44	7	0	9	28	13	66	.209	.264	.370	71	-10	3	2	-0	.974	-2	O-45,1-17	-1.5
	SD-N	56	168	16	40	9	0	11	39	12	48	.238	.297	.488	119	3	2	3	-1	.964	2	O-28,1-13/3-2	0.2
	Yr	114	379	38	84	16	0	20	67	25	114	.222	.279	.422	92	-7	5	5	-2	.970	-0	O-73,1-30/3-2	-1.3
	Cal-A	10	36	4	7	2	0	2	4	1	16	.194	.237	.417	77	-1	0	0	0	.974	-1	/1-8,O-2	-0.2
	NY-A	8	24	5	6	2	0	4	7	2	13	.250	.333	.833	208	3	0	1	-1	.000	0	/D-6	0.2
	Yr	18	60	9	13	4	0	6	11	3	29	.217	.277	.583	131	2	0	1	-1	.974	-1	/1-8,D-6,O-2	0.0
1978	Chi-N	119	395	65	105	17	4	28	79	39	111	.266	.341	.542	128	13	3	4	-2	.978	0	*O-100/1-6	0.8
1979	Chi-N†	145	532	97	153	19	5	**48**	115	45	131	.288	.348	**.613**	143	28	4	2	0	.954	5	*O-139	2.8
1980	Chi-N★	81	255	31	71	8	0	18	57	21	44	.278	.333	.522	126	8	2	2	-1	.941	1	O-61/1-2	0.6
1981	NY-N	100	353	40	78	11	3	22	59	55	105	.221	.328	.456	122	10	6	0	2	.974	-6	1-56,O-48	0.2
1982	NY-N	149	535	80	109	9	1	**37**	99	59	156	.204	.288	.432	99	-3	4	0	1	.986	-14	*1-143	-2.4
1983	NY-N	100	248	25	49	7	0	13	29	22	57	.198	.266	.383	79	-8	2	1	0	.994	-5	1-50/O-5	-1.7
1984	Oak-A	147	549	68	147	23	1	35	118	44	119	.268	.329	.505	136	24	2	1	0	1.000	-2	*D-139/1-9	1.8
1985	Oak-A	158	592	66	141	16	0	30	91	62	114	.238	.313	.417	105	3	3	2	-0	1.000	-1	*D-149/1-9	-0.2
1986	Oak-A	144	561	70	118	19	0	35	94	33	126	.210	.258	.431	90	-11	3	3	-1	.895	-1	*D-140/1-3	-1.6
Total	16	1941	6677	901	1575	240	25	442	1210	608	1816	.236	.305	.478	115	94	85	49	-4	.957	-11	O-648,1-603,D3/P	1.1

■ HARRY KINGMAN Kingman, Henry Lees b: 4/3/1892, Tientsin, China d: 12/27/82, Oakland, Cal. BL/TL, 6'1.5", 165 lbs. Deb: 7/1/14

1914	NY-A	4	3	0	0	0	0	0	0	1	2	.000	.250	.000	-24	-0	0			1.000	-0	/1-1	-0.1

■ GENE KINGSALE Kingsale, Eugene Humphrey b: 8/20/76, Solito, Aruba BB/TR, 6'3", 170 lbs. Deb: 9/3/96

1996	Bal-A	3	0	0	0	0	0	0	0	0	0	—	—	—	—	0	0	0	0	1.000	-1	/O-2	-0.1
1998	Bal-A	11	2	1	0	0	0	0	0	0	1	.000	.000	.000	-99	-1	0	0	0	1.000	-2	/O-4	-0.2
Total	2	14	2	1	0	0	0	0	0	0	1	.000	.000	.000	-99	-1	0	0	0	1.000	-2	/O-6	-0.3

■ MIKE KINKADE Kinkade, Michael A. b: 5/6/73, Livonia, Mich. BR/TR, 6'1", 210 lbs. Deb: 9/8/98

1998	NY-N	3	2	1	0	0	0	0	0	0	0	.000	.000	.000	-99	-1	0	0	0	.000	0	/3-1	-0.1

■ WALT KINLOCK Kinlock, Walter b: 1878, St.Joseph, Mo. Deb: 8/1/1895

1895	StL-N	1	3	0	1	0	0	0	0	0	2	.333	.333	.333	73	-0	0			1.000	1	/3-1	0.0

■ BOB KINSELLA Kinsella, Robert Francis "Red" b: 1/5/1899, Springfield, Ill. d: 12/30/51, Los Angeles, Cal. BL/TR, 5'9.5", 165 lbs. Deb: 9/20/19

1919	NY-N	3	9	1	2	0	0	0	0	0	3	.222	.222	.222	34	-1	1			.500	-2	/O-3	-0.3
1920	NY-N	1	3	0	1	0	0	0	1	0	2	.333	.333	.333	93	-0	0	0	0	.500	-1	/O-1	-0.1
Total	2	4	12	1	3	0	0	0	1	0	5	.250	.250	.250	49	-1	1	0		.500	-2	/O-4	-0.4

■ KINSLER Kinsler b: Staten Island, N.Y. Deb: 6/8/1893

1893	NY-N	1	3	1	0	0	0	0	0	1	1	.000	.250	.000	-31	-1	0			1.000	-0	/O-1	-0.1

■ TOM KINSLOW Kinslow, Thomas F. b: 1/12/1866, Washington, D.C. d: 2/22/01, Washington, D.C. BR/TR, 5'10", 160 lbs. Deb: 6/4/1886

1886	Was-N	3	8	1	2	0	0	0	1	0	1	.250	.250	.250	56	-0	0			1.000	-0	/C-3	0.0
1887	NY-a	2	6	0	0	0	0	0	0	0		.000	.000	.000	-99	-2	0			1.000	-0	/C-2	-0.1
1890	Bro-P	64	242	30	64	11	6	4	46	10	22	.264	.299	.409	83	-8	2			.909	11	C-64	0.7
1891	Bro-N	61	228	22	54	6	0	0	33	9	22	.237	.266	.263	55	-13	3			.922	-9	C-61	-1.5
1892	Bro-N	66	246	37	75	6	11	2	40	13	16	.305	.342	.443	142	11	4			.933	5	C-66	1.9
1893	Bro-N	78	312	38	76	8	4	4	45	11	13	.244	.272	.333	63	-18	4			.932	-2	C-76/O-2	-1.1
1894	Bro-N	62	223	39	68	5	6	2	41	20	11	.305	.362	.408	92	-3	4			.907	-9	C-61/1-1	-0.4
1895	Pit-N	19	62	10	14	2	0	0	5	2	2	.226	.250	.258	33	-6	1			.962	-2	C-18	-0.5
1896	Lou-N	8	25	4	7	0	1	0	7	1	5	.280	.308	.360	79	-1	0			.810	-2	/C-5,1-1	-0.2
1898	Was-N	3	9	0	1	0	0	0	0	0		.111	.111	.111	-36	-2	0			.800	-1	/C-3,1-1	-0.2
	StL-N	14	53	5	15	2	1	0	4	1		.283	.309	.358	89	-1	0			.925	1	C-14	0.1
	Yr	17	62	5	16	2	1	0	4	1		.258	.281	.323	72	-3	0			.909	0	C-17/1-1	-0.1
Total	10	380	1414	186	376	40	29	12	222	67	92	.266	.301	.361	81	-43	18			.923	-7	C-373/1-3,O-2	-1.3

■ WALT KINZIE Kinzie, Walter Harris b: 3/1858, Chicago, Ill. d: 11/5/09, Chicago, Ill. BR/TR, 5'10.5", 161 lbs. Deb: 7/17/1882

1882	Det-N	13	53	5	5	0	1	0	2	0	8	.094	.094	.132	-28	-7				.852	-4	S-13	-1.0
1884	Chi-N	19	82	4	13	3	0	2	8	0	13	.159	.159	.268	29	-7				.831	-3	S-17/3-2	-0.8
	StL-a	2	9	0	1	0	0	0		0		.111	.111	.111	-26	-1				.727	-3	/2-2	-0.4
Total	2	34	144	9	19	3	1	2	10	0	21	.132	.132	.208	6	-15				.840	-9	/S-30,2-2,3-2	-2.2

■ ED KIPPERT Kippert, Edward August "Kickapoo" b: 1/3/1880, Detroit, Mich. d: 6/3/60, Detroit, Mich. BR/TR, 5'10.5", 180 lbs. Deb: 4/14/14

1914	Cin-N	2	2	0	0	0	0	0	0	0	0	.000	.000	.000	-97	-0	0			1.000	-1	/O-2	-0.1

■ JIM KIRBY Kirby, James Herschel b: 5/5/23, Nashville, Tenn. BR/TR, 5'11", 175 lbs. Deb: 5/1/49

1949	Chi-N	3	2	0	1	0	0	0	0	0	0	.500	.500	.500	174	0	0			.000	0	H	0.0

■ LA RUE KIRBY Kirby, La Rue b: 12/30/1889, Eureka, Mich. d: 6/10/61, Lansing, Mich. BB/TR, 6', 185 lbs. Deb: 8/7/12

1912	NY-N	3	5	1	1	1	0	0	0	0	0	.200	.200	.400	60	-0	0			1.000	0	/P-3	0.0
1914	StL-F	52	195	21	48	6	3	2	18	14	30	.246	.303	.338	71	-11	5			.973	2	O-50	-1.2
1915	StL-F	61	178	15	38	7	2	0	16	17	31	.213	.282	.275	54	-13	3			.969	-3	O-52/P-1	-2.0
Total	3	116	378	37	87	14	5	2	34	31	61	.230	.292	.310	63	-25	8			.971	-1	O-102/P-4	-3.2

■ WAYNE KIRBY Kirby, Wayne Leonard b: 1/22/64, Williamsburg, Va. BL/TR, 5'10", 185 lbs. Deb: 9/12/91

1991	Cle-A	21	43	4	9	2	0	0	5	2	6	.209	.244	.256	38	-4	1	2	-1	1.000	-1	O-21	-0.6
1992	Cle-A	21	18	9	3	1	0	1	1	3	2	.167	.286	.389	89	-0	0	3	-2	1.000	-0	/O-2,D-4	-0.2
1993	Cle-A	131	458	71	123	19	5	6	60	37	58	.269	.327	.371	88	-8	17	5	2	.983	13	*O-123/D-5	0.4
1994	Cle-A	78	191	33	56	6	0	5	23	13	30	.293	.341	.403	91	-3	11	4	1	.959	-11	O-68/D-2	-1.3
1995	*Cle-A	101	188	29	39	10	2	1	14	13	32	.207	.262	.298	45	-16	10	3	1	.990	-10	O-68/D-7	-2.4
1996	Cle-A	27	16	3	4	1	0	0	1	2	2	.250	.333	.313	65	-1	0	1	-1	1.000	-6	O-18	-0.7
	*LA-N	65	188	23	51	10	1	1	11	17	17	.271	.335	.351	88	-3	4	2	0	.969	-3	O-53	-0.7
1997	LA-N	46	65	6	11	2	0	0	4	10	12	.169	.280	.200	31	-7	0	0	0	1.000	-2	O-26	-0.9
1998	NY-N	26	31	5	6	0	1	0	0	1	9	.194	.219	.258	23	-4	1	1	-0	1.000	-3	O-19	-0.7
Total	8	516	1198	183	302	51	9	14	119	98	168	.252	.312	.345	75	-44	44	21	1	.981	-24	O-398/D-18	-7.1

■ TOM KIRK Kirk, Thomas Daniel b: 9/27/27, Philadelphia, Pa. d: 8/1/74, Philadelphia, Pa. BL/TL, 5'10.5", 182 lbs. Deb: 6/24/47

1947	Phi-A	1	1	0	0	0	0	0	0	0	0	.000	.000	.000	-98	-0	0	0	0	.000	0	H	0.0

■ JAY KIRKE Kirke, Judson Fabian b: 6/16/1888, Fleischmanns, N.Y d: 8/31/68, New Orleans, La. BL/TR, 6', 195 lbs. Deb: 9/28/10

1910	Det-A	8	25	3	5	1	0	0	3	1		.200	.231	.240	44	-2	1			.917	-3	/2-7,O-1	-0.5
1911	Bos-N	20	89	9	32	5	5	0	12	2	6	.360	.380	.528	142	4	3			.929	-1	O-14/1-3,2-1,S-1,3	0.3
1912	Bos-N	103	359	53	115	11	4	4	62	9	46	.320	.339	.407	102	-1	7			.903	-2	O-72,3-14/S-2,1-1	-0.5
1913	Bos-N	18	38	3	9	2	0	0	3	1	6	.237	.293	.289	65	-2	0			.923	2	O-13	0.0
1914	Cle-A	67	242	18	66	10	2	1	25	7	30	.273	.296	.343	89	-4	5	10	-5	.974	0	O-42,1-18	-1.2
1915	Cle-A	87	339	35	105	19	2	2	40	14	21	.310	.346	.395	120	6	5	6	-2	.986	-1	1-87	0.1
1918	NY-N	17	56	1	14	1	0	0	3	1	3	.250	.263	.268	63	-3	0			.978	1	1-16	-0.3
Total	7	320	1148	122	346	49	13	7	148	35	112	.301	.328	.385	103	-0	21	16		.927	-4	O-142,1-125/32S	-2.1

■ WILLIE KIRKLAND Kirkland, Willie Charles b: 2/17/34, Siluria, Ala. BL/TR, 6'1", 206 lbs. Deb: 4/15/58

1958	SF-N	122	418	48	108	25	6	14	56	43	69	.258	.335	.447	107	4	3	2	-0	.961	-0	*O-115	-0.3
1959	SF-N	126	463	64	126	22	3	22	68	42	84	.272	.337	.475	116	9	5	3	-0	.969	1	*O-117	0.4
1960	SF-N	146	515	59	130	21	10	21	65	44	86	.252	.316	.454	115	8	12	7	-1	.978	4	*O-143	0.4

YEAR	TM/L	G	AB	R	H	2B	3B	HR	RBI	BB	SO	AVG	OBP	SLG	PRO+	BR/A	SB	CS	SBR	FA	FR	G/POS	TPR
1961	Cle-A	146	525	84	136	22	5	27	95	48	77	.259	.322	.474	113	7	7	0	2	.974	8	*O-138	1.0
1962	Cle-A	137	419	56	84	9	1	21	72	43	62	.200	.275	.377	76	-16	9	1	2	.972	0	*O-125	-2.0
1963	Cle-A	127	427	51	98	13	2	15	47	45	99	.230	.304	.375	90	-6	8	2	1	.984	7	*O-112	-0.4
1964	Bal-A	66	150	14	30	5	0	3	22	17	26	.200	.286	.293	62	-8	3	2	-0	.989	0	O-58	-1.0
	Was-A	32	102	8	22	6	0	5	13	6	30	.216	.259	.422	86	-2	0	0	0	.907	-3	O-27	-0.7
	Yr	98	252	22	52	11	0	8	35	23	56	.206	.275	.345	72	-10	3	2	-0	.964	-3	O-85	-1.7
1965	Was-A	123	312	38	72	9	1	14	54	19	65	.231	.275	.401	91	-5	3	2	-0	.987	-6	O-92	-1.6
1966	Was-A	124	163	21	31	2	1	6	17	16	50	.190	.263	.325	68	-7	2	0	1	.983	-12	O-68	-2.1
Total	9	1149	3494	443	837	134	29	148	509	323	648	.240	.307	.422	99	-15	52	19	4	.974	-2	O-995	-6.3

■ ED KIRKPATRICK

Kirkpatrick, Edgar Leon b: 10/8/44, Spokane, Wash. BL/TR, 5'11.5", 195 lbs. Deb: 9/13/62

YEAR	TM/L	G	AB	R	H	2B	3B	HR	RBI	BB	SO	AVG	OBP	SLG	PRO+	BR/A	SB	CS	SBR	FA	FR	G/POS	TPR
1962	LA-A	3	6	0	0	0	0	0	0	0	2	.000	.000	.000	-99	-2	0	0	0	1.000	1	/C-1	-0.1
1963	LA-A	34	77	4	15	5	0	2	7	6	19	.195	.262	.338	71	-3	1	0	0	.986	-0	C-14,O-10	-0.3
1964	LA-A	75	219	20	53	13	3	2	22	23	30	.242	.320	.356	97	-1	2	2	-1	.969	-2	O-63	-0.7
1965	Cal-A	19	73	8	19	5	0	3	8	3	9	.260	.289	.452	110	1	1	2	-1	.969	1	O-19	-0.1
1966	Cal-A	117	312	31	60	7	4	9	44	51	67	.192	.315	.327	87	-4	7	4	-0	.994	-6	*O-102/1-3	-1.6
1967	Cal-A	3	8	0	0	0	0	0	0	0	2	.000	.000	.000	-99	-2	0	0	0	1.000	-2	/C-2,O-1	-0.5
1968	Cal-A	89	161	23	37	4	0	1	15	25	32	.230	.337	.273	90	-1	1	3	-2	.982	-5	O-45/C-4,1-2	-1.1
1969	KC-A	120	315	40	81	11	4	14	49	43	42	.257	.352	.451	122	9	3	5	-2	.995	8	O-82/C-8,1-2,3-2,2	1.2
1970	KC-A	134	424	59	97	17	2	18	62	55	65	.229	.319	.406	98	-1	4	4	-1	.978	-8	C-89,O-19,1-16	-0.9
1971	KC-A	120	365	46	80	12	1	9	46	48	60	.219	.313	.332	83	-8	3	4	-2	.992	-1	O-61,C-59	-1.1
1972	KC-A	113	364	43	100	15	1	9	43	51	50	.275	.368	.396	128	14	3	5	-2	.991	-5	*C-108/1-1	1.3
1973	KC-A	126	429	61	113	24	3	6	45	46	48	.263	.336	.375	93	-4	3	7	-3	.990	-5	*O-108,C-14/D-8	-1.7
1974	*Pit-N	116	271	32	67	9	0	6	38	51	30	.247	.370	.347	105	4	1	2	-1	.993	-4	1-59,O-14/C-6	-0.5
1975	*Pit-N	89	144	15	34	5	0	5	16	18	22	.236	.321	.375	93	-1	1	0	0	1.000	-1	1-28,O-14	-0.3
1976	Pit-N	83	146	14	34	9	0	0	16	14	15	.233	.300	.295	69	-6	1	0	0	.990	-1	1-25/O-9,3-1	-0.8
1977	Pit-N	21	28	5	4	2	0	1	4	8	6	.143	.333	.321	75	-1	1	0	0	.972	-1	1-10/O-2,3-1	-0.2
	Tex-A	20	48	2	9	1	0	0	3	4	11	.188	.250	.208	26	-5	2	0	1	1.000	1	/O-6,1-3,C-1,D-5	-0.4
	Mil-A	29	77	8	21	4	0	0	6	10	8	.273	.364	.325	89	-1	0	1	-1	.973	-2	O-22/3-1,D-3	-0.4
	Yr	49	125	10	30	5	0	0	9	14	19	.240	.321	.280	65	-6	2	1	0	.980	-2	O-28/D-8,1-3,C-1,3	-0.8
Total	16	1311	3467	411	824	143	18	85	424	456	518	.238	.330	.363	97	-12	34	39	-13	.989	-32	O-577,C-306,1/D32	-8.2

■ ENOS KIRKPATRICK

Kirkpatrick, Enos Claire b: 12/8/1885, Pittsburgh, Pa. d: 4/14/64, Pittsburgh, Pa. BR/TR, 5'10", 175 lbs. Deb: 8/24/12

YEAR	TM/L	G	AB	R	H	2B	3B	HR	RBI	BB	SO	AVG	OBP	SLG	PRO+	BR/A	SB	CS	SBR	FA	FR	G/POS	TPR
1912	Bro-N	32	94	13	18	1	1	0	6	9	15	.191	.269	.223	37	-8	5			.968	6	3-29/S-3	-0.2
1913	Bro-N	48	89	13	22	4	1	1	5	3	18	.247	.287	.348	79	-3	5			.897	-1	S-10/1-8,2-6,3-4	-0.4
1914	Bal-F	55	174	22	44	7	2	2	16	18	30	.253	.330	.351	83	-7	10			.932	-5	3-36,S-11/O-3,1-1	-1.0
1915	Bal-F	68	171	22	41	8	2	0	19	24	15	.240	.337	.310	80	-6	12			.911	-3	3-28,2-21/1-5,S-5	-0.9
Total	4	203	528	70	125	20	6	3	46	54	78	.237	.315	.314	74	-24	32			.936	-2	/3-97,S-29,2-27,10	-2.5

■ JOE KIRRENE

Kirrene, Joseph John b: 10/4/31, San Francisco, Cal. BR/TR, 6'2", 195 lbs. Deb: 10/1/50

YEAR	TM/L	G	AB	R	H	2B	3B	HR	RBI	BB	SO	AVG	OBP	SLG	PRO+	BR/A	SB	CS	SBR	FA	FR	G/POS	TPR
1950	Chi-A	1	4	0	1	0	0	0	0	0	1	.250	.250	.250	29	-0	0	0	0	1.000	-1	/3-1	-0.1
1954	Chi-A	9	23	4	7	1	0	0	4	5	2	.304	.448	.348	116	1	1	0	0	.947	-2	/3-9	-0.1
Total	2	10	27	4	8	1	0	0	4	5	3	.296	.424	.333	105	1	1	0	0	.952	-3	/3-10	-0.2

■ ERNIE KISH

Kish, Ernest Alexander b: 2/6/18, Washington, D.C. d: 12/21/93, Kirtland, Ohio BL/TR, 5'9.5", 170 lbs. Deb: 7/29/45

YEAR	TM/L	G	AB	R	H	2B	3B	HR	RBI	BB	SO	AVG	OBP	SLG	PRO+	BR/A	SB	CS	SBR	FA	FR	G/POS	TPR
1945	Phi-A	43	110	10	27	5	1	0	10	9	9	.245	.320	.309	83	-2	0	3	-2	.932	-4	O-30	-1.0

■ BILL KISSINGER

Kissinger, William Francis "Shang" b: 8/15/1871, Dayton, Ky. d: 4/20/29, Cincinnati, Ohio BR/TR, 185 lbs. Deb: 5/30/1895

YEAR	TM/L	G	AB	R	H	2B	3B	HR	RBI	BB	SO	AVG	OBP	SLG	PRO+	BR/A	SB	CS	SBR	FA	FR	G/POS	TPR
1895	Bal-N	2	5	1	1	0	0	0	0	0	1	.200	.200	.200	3	-1	0			1.000	-0	/P-2	0.0
	StL-N	33	97	8	24	6	1	0	8	0	11	.247	.247	.330	49	-8	1			.975	-5	P-24/S-4,O-4,3-1	-0.6
	Yr	35	102	9	25	6	1	0	8	0	12	.245	.245	.324	46	-9	1			**.976**	-5	P-26/S-4,O-4,3-1	-0.6
1896	StL-N	23	73	8	22	4	0	0	12	0	4	.301	.301	.356	76	-3	0			.906	0	P-20/O-3,3-1	-0.2
1897	StL-N	14	39	7	13	3	2	0	6	3		.333	.381	.513	137	2	0			.786	-2	/O-7,P-7	-0.1
Total	3	72	214	24	60	13	3	0	26	3	16	.280	.290	.369	73	-9	1			.935	-6	/P-53,O-14,S-4,3-2	-0.9

■ CHRIS KITSOS

Kitsos, Christopher Anestos b: 2/11/28, New York, N.Y. BB/TR, 5'9", 165 lbs. Deb: 4/21/54

YEAR	TM/L	G	AB	R	H	2B	3B	HR	RBI	BB	SO	AVG	OBP	SLG	PRO+	BR/A	SB	CS	SBR	FA	FR	G/POS	TPR
1954	Chi-N	1	0	0	0	0	0	0	0	0	0	—	—	—	—	0	0	0	0	1.000	0	/S-1	0.0

■ RON KITTLE

Kittle, Ronald Dale b: 1/5/58, Gary, Indiana BR/TR, 6'4", 220 lbs. Deb: 9/2/82

YEAR	TM/L	G	AB	R	H	2B	3B	HR	RBI	BB	SO	AVG	OBP	SLG	PRO+	BR/A	SB	CS	SBR	FA	FR	G/POS	TPR
1982	Chi-A	20	29	3	7	2	0	1	7	3	12	.241	.313	.414	97	-0	0	0	0	1.000	-2	/O-5,D-3	-0.2
1983	*Chi-A★	145	520	75	132	19	3	35	100	39	150	.254	.316	.504	117	10	8	3	1	.964	-9	*O-139/D-2	-0.3
1984	Chi-A	139	466	67	100	15	0	32	74	49	137	.215	.298	.453	100	-2	3	6	-3	.972	3	*O-124/D-7	-0.5
1985	Chi-A	116	379	51	87	12	0	26	58	31	92	.230	.296	.467	101	1	1	4	-2	.989	-3	O-57,D-57	-0.8
1986	Chi-A	86	296	34	63	11	0	17	48	28	87	.213	.287	.422	87	-6	2	1	0	1.000	2	D-62,O-20	-0.6
	NY-A	30	80	8	19	2	0	4	12	7	23	.237	.299	.412	92	-1	2	0	1	1.000	0	D-24/O-1	-0.1
	Yr	116	376	42	82	13	0	21	60	35	110	.218	.290	.420	89	-7	4	1	1	1.000	2	D-86,O-21	-0.7
1987	NY-A	59	159	21	44	5	0	12	28	10	36	.277	.324	.535	123	5	0	1	-1	1.000	1	D-49/O-2	0.3
1988	Cle-A	75	225	31	58	8	0	18	43	16	65	.258	.329	.533	134	9	0	0	0	.000	0	D-63	0.8
1989	Chi-A	51	169	26	51	10	0	11	37	22	42	.302	.385	.556	166	15	0	1	-1	.982	-3	1-27,D-17/O-5	0.8
1990	Chi-A	83	277	29	68	14	0	16	43	24	77	.245	.313	.469	118	6	0	0	0	.987	-4	D-54,1-25	-0.2
	Bal-A	22	61	4	10	2	0	2	3	2	14	.164	.203	.295	39	-5	0	0	0	1.000	-1	D-13/1-5	-0.7
	Yr	105	338	33	78	16	0	18	46	26	91	.231	.293	.438	104	0	0	0	0	.989	-5	D-67,1-30	-0.9
1991	Chi-A	17	47	7	9	0	0	2	7	5	9	.191	.296	.319	72	-2	0	0	0	.982	-1	1-15	-0.4
Total	10	843	2708	356	648	100	3	176	460	236	744	.239	.309	.473	110	28	16	16	-5	.974	-17	O-353,D-351/1-72	-1.9

■ MALACHI KITTRIDGE

Kittridge, Malachi Jeddidah "Jeddidah" b: 10/12/1869, Clinton, Mass. d: 6/23/28, Gary, Ind. BR/TR, 5'7", 170 lbs. Deb: 4/19/1890 M

YEAR	TM/L	G	AB	R	H	2B	3B	HR	RBI	BB	SO	AVG	OBP	SLG	PRO+	BR/A	SB	CS	SBR	FA	FR	G/POS	TPR
1890	Chi-N	96	333	46	67	8	3	3	35	39	53	.201	.287	.270	60	-17	7			.944	2	*C-96	-0.6
1891	Chi-N	79	296	26	62	8	5	2	27	17	28	.209	.252	.291	58	-17	4			.940	-0	C-79	-0.9
1892	Chi-N	69	229	19	41	5	0	0	10	11	27	.179	.217	.201	26	-21	2			.946	15	C-69	-0.1
1893	Chi-N	70	255	32	59	9	5	2	30	17	15	.231	.279	.329	62	-15	3			.939	6	C-70	-0.3
1894	Chi-N	51	168	36	53	8	2	0	23	26	20	.315	.407	.387	88	-3	2			.925	2	C-51	0.3
1895	Chi-N	60	212	30	48	6	3	3	29	16	9	.226	.284	.325	54	-16	6			.976	-2	C-59	-1.0
1896	Chi-N	65	215	17	48	4	1	1	19	14	14	.223	.274	.265	41	-19	6			.962	1	C-64/P-1	-0.9
1897	Chi-N	79	262	25	53	5	5	1	30	22		.202	.264	.271	40	-24	9			.952	3	C-79	-1.0
1898	Lou-N	86	287	27	70	8	5	1	31	15		.244	.281	.317	73	-11	9			.944	-11	C-86	-1.3
1899	Lou-N	45	129	11	26	2	1	0	12	26		.202	.340	.233	58	-6	3			.974	7	C-43	0.4
	Was-N	44	133	14	20	3	0	0	11	10		.150	.215	.173	7	-17	2			.949	4	C-43	-0.9
	Yr	89	262	25	46	5	1	0	23	36		.176	.280	.202	33	-23	5			.961	11	C-86	-0.5
1901	Bos-N	114	381	24	96	14	0	2	40	32		.252	.312	.304	72	-14	2			**.984**	12	*C-113	1.0
1902	Bos-N	80	255	18	60	7	0	2	30	24		.235	.304	.286	81	-5	4			.981	6	C-72	0.9
1903	Bos-N	32	99	10	21	2	0	0	6	11		.212	.291	.232	52	-6	1			.981	5	C-30	0.2
	Was-A	60	192	8	41	4	1	0	16	10		.214	.252	.245	49	-12	1			.978	-3	C-60	-0.9
1904	Was-A	81	265	11	64	7	0	0	24	8		.242	.266	.268	70	-9	2			.982	1	C-79,M	0.0
1905	Was-A	77	238	16	39	8	0	0	14	15		.164	.213	.197	32	-18	1			.978	4	C-76	-0.7
1906	Was-A	22	68	5	13	0	0	0	3	1		.191	.203	.191	25	-6	0			.946	-2	C-22	-0.7
	Cle-A	5	10	0	1	0	0	0	0	0		.100	.100	.100	-38	-2	0			.938	-1	/C-5	-0.2
	Yr	27	78	5	14	0	0	0	3	1		.179	.190	.179	16	-8	0			.945	-3	C-27	-0.9
Total	16	1215	4027	375	882	108	31	17	390	314	166	.219	.277	.274	56	-236	64			.961	47	*C-1196/P-1	-6.7

■ DANNY KLASSEN

Klassen, Daniel Victor b: 9/22/75, Leamington, Ont., Can. BR/TR, 6', 175 lbs. Deb: 7/4/98

YEAR	TM/L	G	AB	R	H	2B	3B	HR	RBI	BB	SO	AVG	OBP	SLG	PRO+	BR/A	SB	CS	SBR	FA	FR	G/POS	TPR
1998	Ari-N	29	108	12	21	2	1	3	8	9	33	.194	.263	.315	49	-8	1	1	-0	.964	-5	2-29	-1.1

■ **BOBBY KLAUS** Klaus, Robert Francis b: 12/27/37, Spring Grove, Ill. BR/TR, 5'10", 170 lbs. Deb: 4/21/64 F

YEAR	TM/L	G	AB	R	H	2B	3B	HR	RBI	BB	SO	AVG	OBP	SLG	PRO+	BR/A	SB	CS	SBR	FA	FR	G/POS	TPR
1964	Cin-N	40	93	10	17	5	1	2	6	4	13	.183	.216	.323	48	-7	1	0	0	.972	4	2-18,3-11/S-3	-0.2
	NY-N	56	209	25	51	8	3	2	11	25	30	.244	.325	.340	90	-2	3	4	-2	.986	-4	2-25,3-28/S-5	-0.6
	Yr	96	302	35	68	13	4	4	17	29	43	.225	.293	.334	76	-9	4	4	-1	.981	0	2-43,3-39/S-8	-0.8
1965	NY-N	119	288	30	55	12	0	2	12	45	49	.191	.302	.253	61	-14	1	6	-3	.968	15	2-72,S-28,3-25	0.3
Total	2	215	590	65	123	25	4	6	29	74	92	.208	.298	.295	69	-23	5	10	-5	.973	16	2-115/3-64,S-36	-0.5

■ **BILLY KLAUS** Klaus, William Joseph b: 12/9/28, Fox Lake, Ill. BL/TR, 5'10", 165 lbs. Deb: 4/16/52 F

YEAR	TM/L	G	AB	R	H	2B	3B	HR	RBI	BB	SO	AVG	OBP	SLG	PRO+	BR/A	SB	CS	SBR	FA	FR	G/POS	TPR
1952	Bos-N	7	4	3	0	0	0	0	0	1	1	.000	.200	.000	-42	-1	0	0	0	.500	-1	/S-4	-0.2
1953	Mil-N	2	2	1	0	0	0	0	0	0	0	.000	.000	.000	-99	-1	0	0	0	.000	0	H	-0.1
1955	Bos-A	135	541	83	153	26	2	7	60	60	44	.283	.354	.377	89	-8	6	0	2	.955	-7	*S-126/3-8	-0.3
1956	Bos-A	135	520	91	141	29	5	7	59	90	43	.271	.380	.387	92	-5	1	0	0	.945	-4	*3-106,S-26	-0.5
1957	Bos-A	127	477	76	120	18	4	10	42	55	53	.252	.329	.369	85	-9	2	0	1	.961	11	*S-118	1.5
1958	Bos-A	61	88	5	14	4	0	1	7	5	16	.159	.204	.239	20	-10	0	0	0	.883	-6	S-27	-1.6
1959	Bal-A	104	321	33	80	11	0	3	25	51	38	.249	.352	.312	86	-4	2	4	-2	.970	-12	S-59,3-49/2-1	-1.4
1960	Bal-A	46	43	8	9	2	0	1	6	9	9	.209	.346	.326	84	-1	0	0	0	.960	8	2-30,S-12/3-2	0.8
1961	Was-A	91	251	26	57	8	2	7	30	30	34	.227	.314	.359	81	-7	2	2	-1	.961	-5	3-51,S-18/2-1,O-1	-1.0
1962	Phi-N	102	248	30	51	8	2	4	20	29	43	.206	.291	.302	61	-13	1	1	-0	.983	-6	3-53,S-30,2-11	-1.7
1963	Phi-N	11	18	1	1	0	0	0	0	1	4	.056	.105	.056	-53	-4	0	0	0	1.000	-2	/S-5,3-3	-0.6
Total	11	821	2513	357	626	106	15	40	250	331	285	.249	.337	.351	82	-62	14	7	0	.955	-24	S-425,3-272/2-43,O	-5.1

■ **OLLIE KLEE** Klee, Ollie Chester "Babe" b: 5/20/1900, Piqua, Ohio d: 2/9/77, Toledo, Ohio BL/TL, 5'9.5", 160 lbs. Deb: 8/10/25

YEAR	TM/L	G	AB	R	H	2B	3B	HR	RBI	BB	SO	AVG	OBP	SLG	PRO+	BR/A	SB	CS	SBR	FA	FR	G/POS	TPR
1925	Cin-N	3	1	0	0	0	0	0	0	0	1	.000	.000	.000	-99	-0	0	0	0	.000	-1	/O-1	-0.1

■ **CHUCK KLEIN** Klein, Charles Herbert b: 10/7/04, Indianapolis, Ind. d: 3/28/58, Indianapolis, Ind. BL/TR, 6', 185 lbs. Deb: 7/30/28 CH

YEAR	TM/L	G	AB	R	H	2B	3B	HR	RBI	BB	SO	AVG	OBP	SLG	PRO+	BR/A	SB	CS	SBR	FA	FR	G/POS	TPR
1928	Phi-N	64	253	41	91	14	4	11	34	14	22	.360	.396	.577	146	16	0			.978	1	O-63	1.2
1929	Phi-N	149	616	126	219	45	6	**43**	145	54	61	.356	.407	.657	149	44	5			.966	-2	*O-149	2.9
1930	Phi-N	156	648	**158**	250	**59**	8	40	170	54	50	.386	.436	.687	155	55	4			.960	23	*O-156	**5.8**
1931	Phi-N	148	594	**121**	200	34	10	**31**	**121**	59	49	.337	.398	**.584**	149	39	7			.971	-5	*O-148	2.4
1932	Phi-N	154	650	**152**	**226**	50	15	**38**	137	60	49	.348	.404	**.646**	158	51	**20**			.960	9	*O-154	4.9
1933	Phi-N★	152	606	101	**223**	**44**	7	**28**	**120**	56	36	**.368**	**.422**	**.602**	168	**52**	15			.986	9	*O-152	**5.5**
1934	Chi-N★	115	435	78	131	27	2	20	80	47	38	.301	.372	.510	136	22	3			.962	-3	*O-110	1.4
1935	*Chi-N	119	434	71	127	14	4	21	73	41	42	.293	.355	.488	123	14	4			.958	-1	*O-111	0.8
1936	Chi-N	29	109	19	32	5	0	5	18	16	14	.294	.384	.477	128	4	0			.917	1	O-29	0.4
	Phi-N	117	492	83	152	30	7	20	86	33	45	.309	.352	.520	120	12	6			.930	-4	*O-117	0.2
	Yr	146	601	102	184	35	7	25	104	49	59	.306	.358	.512	122	16	6			.927	-4	*O-146	0.6
1937	Phi-N	115	406	74	132	20	2	15	57	39	21	.325	.386	.495	127	15	3			.949	-4	*O-102	0.7
1938	Phi-N	129	458	53	113	22	2	8	61	38	30	.247	.304	.356	83	-11	7			.960	-3	*O-119	-1.8
1939	Phi-N	25	47	8	9	2	1	1	9	10	4	.191	.333	.340	84	-1	1			1.000	-0	O-11/1-1	-0.1
	Pit-N	85	270	37	81	16	4	11	47	26	17	.300	.361	.511	134	12	1			.951	-2	O-66	0.8
	Yr	110	317	45	90	18	5	12	56	36	21	.284	.357	.486	127	11	2			.958	-2	O-77/1-1	0.7
1940	Phi-N	116	354	39	77	16	2	7	37	44	30	.218	.304	.333	79	-10	2			.984	-3	O-96	-1.8
1941	Phi-N	50	73	6	9	0	0	1	3	10	6	.123	.229	.164	12	-8	0			.958	-1	O-14	-1.0
1942	Phi-N	14	14	0	1	0	0	0	0	0	2	.071	.071	.071	-61	-3	0			.000	0	H	-0.3
1943	Phi-N	12	20	0	2	0	0	0	3	0	3	.100	.100	.100	-44	-4	1			.000	-1	/O-2	-0.5
1944	Phi-N	4	7	1	1	0	0	0	0	0	2	.143	.143	.143	-20	-1	0			1.000	1	/O-1	-0.1
Total	17	1753	6486	1168	2076	398	74	300	1201	601	521	.320	.379	.543	135	298	79			.962	16	*O-1600/1-1	21.4

■ **LOU KLEIN** Klein, Louis Frank b: 10/22/18, New Orleans, La. d: 6/20/76, Metairie, La. BR/TR, 5'11", 170 lbs. Deb: 4/21/43 MC

YEAR	TM/L	G	AB	R	H	2B	3B	HR	RBI	BB	SO	AVG	OBP	SLG	PRO+	BR/A	SB	CS	SBR	FA	FR	G/POS	TPR
1943	*StL-N	154	627	91	180	28	14	7	62	50	70	.287	.342	.410	112	8	9			.973	-19	*2-126,S-51	-0.1
1945	StL-N	19	57	12	13	4	1	1	6	14	9	.228	.389	.386	113	2	0			.929	-0	/S-7,O-7,3-4,2-2	0.2
1946	StL-N	23	93	12	18	3	0	1	4	9	7	.194	.265	.258	47	-7	1			.975	-3	2-23	-0.9
1949	StL-N	58	114	25	25	6	0	2	12	22	20	.219	.355	.325	80	-3	0			.890	-4	S-21/2-9,3-7	-0.5
1951	Cle-A	2	2	0	0	0	0	0	0	0	1	.000	.000	.000	-99	-1	0	0	0	.000	0	H	-0.1
	Phi-A	49	144	22	33	7	0	5	17	10	12	.229	.279	.382	76	-6	0	0	0	.975	-4	2-42	-0.8
	Yr	51	146	22	33	7	0	5	17	10	13	.226	.276	.377	74	-6	0	0	0	.975	-4	2-42	-0.9
Total	5	305	1037	162	269	48	15	16	101	105	119	.259	.330	.381	97	-6	10	0		.975	-30	2-202/S-79,3-11,O-7	-2.2

■ **RED KLEINOW** Kleinow, John Peter b: 7/20/1879, Milwaukee, Wis. d: 10/9/29, New York, N.Y. BR/TR, 5'10", 165 lbs. Deb: 5/3/04

YEAR	TM/L	G	AB	R	H	2B	3B	HR	RBI	BB	SO	AVG	OBP	SLG	PRO+	BR/A	SB	CS	SBR	FA	FR	G/POS	TPR
1904	NY-A	68	209	12	43	8	4	0	16	15		.206	.259	.282	68	-8	4			.966	-6	C-62/3-2,O-1	-0.8
1905	NY-A	88	253	23	56	6	3	1	24	20		.221	.284	.281	71	-8	7			.978	-7	C-83/1-3	-0.9
1906	NY-A	96	268	30	59	9	3	0	31	24		.220	.287	.276	69	-9	8			.974	-1	C-95/1-1	-0.2
1907	NY-A	90	269	30	71	6	4	0	26	24		.264	.327	.316	97	-1	5			.970	-6	C-86/1-1	0.2
1908	NY-A	96	279	16	47	3	2	1	13	22		.168	.237	.204	43	-17	5			.973	-4	C-89/2-2	-1.6
1909	NY-A	78	206	24	47	11	4	0	15	25		.228	.315	.320	100	0	7			.966	-3	C-77	0.4
1910	NY-A	6	12	2	5	0	0	0	2	1		.417	.462	.417	166	1	2			1.000	0	/C-5	0.1
	Bos-A	50	147	9	22	1	0	1	8	20		.150	.251	.177	34	-11	3			.968	4	C-49	-0.2
	Yr	56	159	11	27	1	0	1	10	21		.170	.267	.195	44	-10	5			.970	4	C-54	-0.1
1911	Bos-A	8	14	0	3	0	0	0	0	2		.214	.313	.214	48	-1	1			1.000	0	/C-8	0.0
	Phi-N	4	8	0	1	1	0	0	0	0	1	.125	.125	.250	4	-1	0			1.000	-0	/C-4	-0.1
Total	8	584	1665	146	354	45	20	3	135	153	1	.213	.282	.269	71	-54	42			.972	-23	C-558/1-5,2-2,3O	-3.1

■ **RYAN KLESKO** Klesko, Ryan Anthony b: 6/12/71, Westminster, Cal. BL/TL, 6'3", 220 lbs. Deb: 9/12/92

YEAR	TM/L	G	AB	R	H	2B	3B	HR	RBI	BB	SO	AVG	OBP	SLG	PRO+	BR/A	SB	CS	SBR	FA	FR	G/POS	TPR
1992	Atl-N	13	14	0	0	0	0	0	1	0	5	.000	.067	.000	-75	-3	0	0	0	1.000	-1	/1-5	-0.4
1993	Atl-N	22	17	3	6	1	0	2	5	3	4	.353	.450	.765	216	3	0	0	0	1.000	-1	/1-3,O-2	0.2
1994	Atl-N	92	245	42	68	13	3	17	47	26	48	.278	.349	.563	130	10	1	0	0	.921	-11	O-74/1-6	-0.2
1995	*Atl-N	107	329	48	102	25	2	23	70	47	72	.310	.399	.608	156	27	5	4	-1	.942	-10	*O-102/1-4	1.3
1996	*Atl-N	153	528	90	149	21	4	34	93	68	129	.282	.366	.530	126	19	6	3	0	.975	-5	*O-144/1-2	1.1
1997	*Atl-N	143	467	67	122	23	6	24	84	48	130	.261	.335	.490	111	6	4	4	-1	.969	-9	*O-130,1-22	-0.7
1998	*Atl-N	129	427	69	117	29	1	18	70	56	66	.274	.362	.473	112	8	5	3	-0	.994	-1	*O-120/1-7	0.5
Total	7	659	2027	319	564	112	16	118	370	248	454	.278	.361	.524	124	69	21	14	-2	.966	-37	O-572/1-49	1.8

■ **JAY KLEVEN** Kleven, Jay Allen b: 12/2/49, Oakland, Cal. BR/TR, 6'2", 190 lbs. Deb: 6/20/76

YEAR	TM/L	G	AB	R	H	2B	3B	HR	RBI	BB	SO	AVG	OBP	SLG	PRO+	BR/A	SB	CS	SBR	FA	FR	G/POS	TPR
1976	NY-N	2	5	0	1	0	0	0	2	0	1	.200	.200	.200	15	-1	0	0	0	1.000	0	/C-2	0.0

■ **LOU KLIMCHOCK** Klimchock, Louis Stephen b: 10/15/39, Hostetter, Pa. BL/TR, 5'11", 180 lbs. Deb: 9/27/58

YEAR	TM/L	G	AB	R	H	2B	3B	HR	RBI	BB	SO	AVG	OBP	SLG	PRO+	BR/A	SB	CS	SBR	FA	FR	G/POS	TPR
1958	KC-A	2	10	2	2	0	0	1	1	0	1	.200	.200	.500	84	-0	0	0	0	1.000	-1	/2-2	-0.1
1959	KC-A	17	66	10	18	1	0	4	13	1	6	.273	.284	.470	101	-0	0	0	0	.949	-4	2-16	-0.3
1960	KC-A	10	10	0	3	0	0	0	0	0	0	.300	.300	.300	62	-1	0	0	0	.000	0	/2-1	-0.1
1961	KC-A	57	121	8	26	4	1	1	16	5	13	.215	.246	.289	42	-10	0	0	0	.976	-5	1-11/O-7,3-6,2-1	-1.7
1962	Mil-N	8	8	0	0	0	0	0	0	0	2	.000	.000	.000	-99	-2	0	0	0	.000	0	H	-0.2
1963	Was-A	9	14	1	2	0	0	0	2	0	1	.143	.143	.143	-20	-2	0	0	0	1.000	1	/2-3	-0.1
	Mil-N	24	46	6	9	1	0	0	1	0	12	.196	.196	.217	19	-5	0	1	-1	.988	0	1-12	-0.6
1964	Mil-N	10	21	3	7	2	0	0	2	1	2	.333	.364	.429	121	1	0	0	0	1.000	-3	/3-4,2-2	-0.2
1965	Mil-N	34	39	3	3	0	0	0	3	2	8	.077	.122	.077	-42	-7	0	0	0	.923	1	/1-4	-0.7
1966	NY-N	5	5	0	0	0	0	0	0	0	3	.000	.000	.000	-99	-1	0	0	0	.000	0	H	-0.1
1968	Cle-A	11	15	0	2	0	0	0	3	1	0	.133	.188	.133	-2	-2	0	0	0	.500	-3	/3-4,1-1,2-1	-0.5
1969	Cle-A	90	258	26	74	13	2	6	26	18	14	.287	.333	.422	107	2	0	0	0	.934	-16	3-56,2-21/C-1	-1.3
1970	Cle-A	41	56	5	9	0	0	1	2	3	9	.161	.217	.214	18	-6	0	0	0	1.000	-1	/1-5,2-5	-0.7
Total	12	318	669	64	155	21	3	13	69	31	71	.232	.267	.330	63	-35	0	1	-1	.906	-30	/3-70,2-52,1-33,OC	-6.6

YEAR	TM/L	G	AB	R	H	2B	3B	HR	RBI	BB	SO	AVG	OBP	SLG	PRO+	BR/A	SB	CS	SBR	FA	FR	G/POS	TPR
■ **BOBBY KLINE**	Kline, John Robert b: 1/27/29, St.Petersburg, Fla BR/TR, 6', 179 lbs. Deb: 4/11/55																						
1955	Was-A	77	140	12	31	5	0	0	9	11	27	.221	.288	.257	50	-10	0	0	0	.943	13	S-69/2-4,3-3,P-1	0.7
■ **JOHNNY KLING**	Kling, John "Noisy" b: 2/25/1875, Kansas City, Mo. d: 1/31/47, Kansas City, Mo. BR/TR, 5'9.5", 160 lbs. Deb: 9/11/00 FM																						
1900	Chi-N	15	51	8	15	3	1	0	7	2		.294	.321	.392	100	-0	0			.901	-2	C-15	-0.1
1901	Chi-N	74	256	26	70	6	3	0	21	9		.273	.301	.320	83	-6	8			.952	-10	C-69/1-1,O-1	-0.9
1902	Chi-N	114	431	49	123	19	3	0	57	29		.285	.330	.343	111	5	24			.974	6	*C-112/S-1	2.4
1903	Chi-N	132	491	67	146	29	13	3	68	22		.297	.330	.428	119	9	23			.969	2	*C-132	2.3
1904	Chi-N	123	452	41	110	18	0	2	46	16		.243	.271	.296	75	-14	7			.974	-12	*C-104,O-10/1-6	-1.5
1905	Chi-N	111	380	26	83	8	6	1	52	28		.218	.272	.279	62	-18	13			.966	0	*C-106/O-4,1-1	-0.7
1906	*Chi-N	107	343	45	107	15	8	2	46	23		.312	.357	.420	134	12	14			**.982**	5	C-96/O-3	2.9
1907	*Chi-N	104	334	44	95	15	8	1	43	27		.284	.342	.386	120	7	9			**.987**	6	C-98/1-2	2.5
1908	*Chi-N	126	424	51	117	23	5	4	59	21		.276	.315	.382	117	7	16			.979	2	*C-117/O-6,1-2	2.2
1910	*Chi-N	91	297	31	80	17	2	2	32	37	27	.269	.354	.360	109	4	3			.979	-5	C-86	0.8
1911	Chi-N	27	80	8	14	3	2	1	5	8	14	.175	.250	.300	54	-5	1			.969	5	C-25	0.2
	Bos-N	75	241	32	54	8	1	2	24	30	29	.224	.310	.290	63	-12	0			.951	-5	C-71/3-1	-1.0
	Yr	102	321	40	68	11	3	3	29	38	43	.212	.295	.293	61	-17	1			.956	-0	C-96/3-1	-0.8
1912	Bos-N	81	252	26	80	10	3	2	30	15	30	.317	.356	.405	106	2	3			.958	5	C-74,M	1.3
1913	Cin-N	80	209	20	57	7	6	0	23	14	14	.273	.318	.364	95	-2	2			.975	7	C-63	1.1
Total	13	1260	4241	474	1151	181	61	20	513	281	114	.271	.318	.357	100	-11	123			.971	3	*C-1168/O-24,13S	11.5
■ **RUDY KLING**	Kling, Rudolph A. b: 3/23/1870, St.Louis, Mo. d: 3/14/37, St.Louis, Mo. BR/TR, 5'10", 178 lbs. Deb: 9/21/02																						
1902	StL-N	4	10	1	2	0	0	0	0	4		.200	.429	.200	99	0	1			.842	-2	/S-4	-0.1
■ **JOE KLINGER**	Klinger, Joseph John b: 8/2/02, Canonsburg, Pa. d: 7/31/60, Little Rock, Ark. BR/TR, 6', 190 lbs. Deb: 9/13/27																						
1927	NY-N	3	5	0	2	0	0	0	0	0	2	.400	.400	.400	115	0	0			1.000	0	/O-1	0.0
1930	Chi-A	4	8	0	3	0	0	0	1	0	0	.375	.375	.375	94	-0	0	0	0	1.000	-1	/C-2,1-2	-0.1
Total	2	7	13	0	5	0	0	0	1	0	2	.385	.385	.385	102	0	0	0		1.000	-1	/1-2,C-2,O-1	-0.1
■ **NAP KLOZA**	Kloza, John Clarence b: 9/7/03, Poland d: 6/11/62, Milwaukee, Wis. BR/TR, 5'11", 180 lbs. Deb: 8/16/31																						
1931	StL-A	3	7	1	1	0	0	0	0	1	4	.143	.250	.143	5	-1	0	0	0	1.000	-0	/O-3	-0.1
1932	StL-A	19	13	4	2	0	1	0	2	4	4	.154	.353	.308	69	-1	0	0	0	1.000	-1	/O-3	-0.2
Total	2	22	20	5	3	0	1	0	2	5	8	.150	.320	.250	48	-1	0	0	0	1.000	-2	/O-6	-0.3
■ **JOE KLUGMANN**	Klugmann, Joe b: 3/26/1895, St.Louis, Mo. d: 7/18/51, Moberly, Mo. BR/TR, 5'11", 175 lbs. Deb: 9/23/21																						
1921	Chi-N	6	21	3	6	0	0	0	2	1	2	.286	.348	.286	69	-1	0	1	-1	.969	0	/2-5	-0.1
1922	Chi-N	2	2	0	0	0	0	0	0	0	0	.000	.000	.000	-98	-1	0	0	0	1.000	1	/2-2	0.0
1924	Bro-N	31	79	7	13	2	1	0	3	2	9	.165	.185	.215	7	-10	0	0	0	.929	-1	2-28/S-1	-1.2
1925	Cle-A	38	85	12	28	9	2	0	12	8	4	.329	.387	.482	119	2	3	1	0	.959	-3	2-29/1-4,3-2	0.0
Total	4	77	187	22	47	11	3	0	17	11	15	.251	.296	.342	67	-10	3	2	-0	.947	-3	/2-64,1-4,3-2,S-1	-1.3
■ **ELMER KLUMPP**	Klumpp, Elmer Edward b: 8/26/06, St.Louis, Mo. d: 10/18/96, Menomonee Falls, Wis. BR/TR, 6', 184 lbs. Deb: 4/17/34																						
1934	Was-A	12	15	2	2	0	0	0	0	0	1	.133	.188	.133	-17	-3	0	0	0	.889	-1	C-11	-0.3
1937	Bro-N	5	11	0	1	0	0	0	2	1	4	.091	.167	.091	-28	-2	0			1.000	1	/C-3	-0.1
Total	2	17	26	2	3	0	0	0	2	1	5	.115	.179	.115	-21	-5	0	0		.943	-0	/C-14	-0.4
■ **BILLY KLUSMAN**	Klusman, William F. b: 3/24/1865, Cincinnati, Ohio d: 6/24/07, Cincinnati, Ohio BR/TR, 5'10.5", 185 lbs. Deb: 6/21/1888																						
1888	Bos-N	28	107	9	18	4	0	2	11	5	13	.168	.205	.262	47	-6	3			.914	-9	2-28	-1.4
1890	StL-a	15	65	9	18	4	1	1	11	1		.277	.288	.415	94	-1	1			.896	-3	2-15	-0.3
Total	2	43	172	18	36	8	1	3	22	6	13	.209	.236	.320	67	-8	4			.908	-12	/2-43	-1.7
■ **TED KLUSZEWSKI**	Kluszewski, Theodore Bernard "Big Klu" b: 9/10/24, Argo, Ill. d: 3/29/88, Cincinnati, Ohio BL/TL, 6'2", 225 lbs. Deb: 4/18/47 C																						
1947	Cin-N	9	10	1	1	0	0	0	2	1	2	.100	.182	.100	-23	-2	0			1.000	-0	/1-2	-0.2
1948	Cin-N	113	379	49	104	23	4	12	57	18	32	.274	.307	.451	107	1	1			.990	1	1-98	0.2
1949	Cin-N	136	531	63	164	26	2	8	68	19	24	.309	.333	.411	97	-3	3			.989	-7	*1-134	-1.1
1950	Cin-N	134	538	76	165	37	0	25	111	33	28	.307	.348	.515	123	16	3			.987	-11	*1-131	0.1
1951	Cin-N	154	607	74	157	35	2	13	77	35	33	.259	.301	.387	83	-16	6	2	1	**.997**	-6	*1-154	-2.9
1952	Cin-N	135	497	62	159	24	11	16	86	47	28	.320	.383	.509	146	30	3	3	-1	**.993**	-10	*1-133	1.5
1953	Cin-N★	149	570	97	180	25	0	40	108	55	34	.316	.380	.570	142	34	2	0	1	**.995**	-18	*1-147	1.1
1954	Cin-N★	149	573	104	187	28	3	**49**	**141**	78	35	.326	.410	.642	165	53	0	2	-1	**.996**	-4	*1-149	4.0
1955	Cin-N★	153	612	116	**192**	25	0	47	113	66	40	.314	.384	.585	144	38	1	1	-0	**.995**	-9	*1-153	1.9
1956	Cin-N★	138	517	91	156	14	1	35	102	49	31	.302	.366	.536	130	21	1	0	0	.990	-5	*1-131	0.8
1957	Cin-N	69	127	12	34	7	0	6	21	5	5	.268	.301	.465	95	-1	0	0	0	.989	0	1-23	-0.3
1958	Pit-N	100	301	29	88	13	4	4	37	26	16	.292	.351	.402	101	1	0	0	0	.994	-5	1-72	-0.9
1959	Pit-N	60	122	11	32	10	1	2	17	5	14	.262	.291	.410	85	-3	0	0	0	1.000	-1	1-20	-0.5
	*Chi-A	31	101	11	30	2	1	2	10	9	10	.297	.355	.396	107	1	0	1	-1	1.000	-2	1-29	-0.4
1960	Chi-A	81	181	20	53	9	0	5	39	22	10	.293	.369	.425	116	4	0	1	-1	.997	-2	1-39	-0.1
1961	LA-A	107	263	32	64	12	0	15	39	24	23	.243	.307	.460	91	-4	0	0	0	.989	-5	1-66	-1.4
Total	15	1718	5929	848	1766	290	29	279	1028	492	365	.298	.354	.498	122	169	20	10		.993	-82	*1-1481	1.8
■ **MICKEY KLUTTS**	Klutts, Gene Ellis b: 9/20/54, Montebello, Cal. BR/TR, 5'11", 189 lbs. Deb: 7/7/76																						
1976	NY-A	2	3	0	0	0	0	0	0	0	1	.000	.000	.000	-99	-1	0	0	0	.875	0	/S-2	0.0
1977	NY-A	5	15	3	4	1	0	1	4	2	1	.267	.389	.533	150	1	0	1	-1	1.000	2	/3-4,S-1	0.3
1978	NY-A	1	2	1	2	1	0	0	0	0	0	1.000	1.000	1.500	608	2	0	0	0	.750	0	/3-1	0.2
1979	Oak-A	24	73	3	14	2	1	1	4	7	20	.192	.262	.288	51	-5	0	1	-1	.882	-2	S-10/2-8,3-6,D-2	-0.7
1980	Oak-A	75	197	20	53	14	0	4	21	13	41	.269	.314	.401	102	-0	1	4	-2	.947	-6	3-62/S-8,2-7,D-1	-0.9
1981	*Oak-A	15	46	9	17	0	0	5	11	2	9	.370	.396	.696	220	7	0	0	0	.957	-5	3-14	0.2
1982	Oak-A	55	157	10	28	8	0	0	14	9	18	.178	.223	.229	26	-16	0	0	0	.946	-3	3-49	-2.0
1983	Tor-A	22	43	3	11	0	0	3	5	1	11	.256	.289	.465	98	-0	0	1	-1	1.000	-3	3-17/D-2	-0.4
Total	8	199	536	49	129	26	1	14	59	34	101	.241	.290	.371	84	-13	1	7	-4	.948	-16	3-153/S-21,2-15,D-5	-3.3
■ **CLYDE KLUTTZ**	Kluttz, Clyde Franklin b: 12/12/17, Rockwell, N.C. d: 5/12/79, Salisbury, N.C. BR/TR, 6', 198 lbs. Deb: 4/20/42																						
1942	Bos-N	72	210	21	56	10	1	1	31	7	13	.267	.294	.338	86	-4	0			.979	0	C-57	0.0
1943	Bos-N	66	207	13	51	7	0	0	20	15	9	.246	.297	.280	68	-8	0			.973	2	C-55	-0.2
1944	Bos-N	81	229	20	64	12	2	2	19	13	14	.279	.318	.376	91	-3	0			.980	4	C-58	0.4
1945	Bos-N	25	81	9	24	4	1	0	10	2	6	.296	.313	.370	89	-1	0			.987	-0	C-19	-0.1
	NY-N	73	222	25	62	14	0	4	21	15	10	.279	.331	.396	100	-1	1			.978	-6	C-57	-0.3
	Yr	98	303	34	86	18	1	4	31	17	16	.284	.326	.389	97	-2	1			.981	-6	C-76	-0.4
1946	NY-N	5	8	0	3	0	0	0	1	0	1	.375	.375	.375	112	0	0			.857	-1	/C-2	0.0
	StL-N	52	136	8	36	7	0	0	14	10	10	.265	.315	.316	76	-4	0			.980	2	C-49	0.0
	Yr	57	144	8	39	7	0	0	15	10	11	.271	.318	.319	78	-4	0			.976	1	C-51	0.0
1947	Pit-N	73	232	26	70	9	2	6	42	17	18	.302	.355	.435	106	2	1			.987	3	C-69	0.9
1948	Pit-N	94	271	26	60	12	2	4	20	20	19	.221	.275	.325	61	-15	3			.978	0	C-91	-1.0
1951	StL-A	4	4	2	2	1	0	0	1	1	0	.500	.600	.750	256	1	0	0	0	1.000	1	/C-1	0.2
	Was-A	53	159	15	49	9	0	1	22	20	8	.308	.389	.384	111	3	0	0	0	.968	-7	C-46	-0.2
	Yr	57	163	17	51	10	0	1	23	21	8	.313	.395	.393	115	4	0	0	0	.968	-6	C-47	0.0
1952	Was-A	58	144	7	33	5	0	1	11	12	11	.229	.293	.285	63	-7	0	0	0	.979	-1	C-52	-0.6
Total	9	656	1903	172	510	90	8	19	212	132	119	.268	.318	.354	86	-39	5	0		.978	-3	C-556	-0.9
■ **JOE KMAK**	Kmak, Joseph Robert b: 5/3/63, Napa, Cal. BR/TR, 6', 185 lbs. Deb: 4/6/93																						
1993	Mil-A	51	110	9	24	5	0	0	7	14	13	.218	.317	.264	59	-6	6	2	1	1.000	2	C-50	-0.2

YEAR	TM/L	G	AB	R	H	2B	3B	HR	RBI	BB	SO	AVG	OBP	SLG	PRO+	BR/A	SB	CS	SBR	FA	FR	G/POS	TPR
1995	Chi-N	19	53	7	13	3	0	1	6	6	12	.245	.333	.358	84	-1	0	0	0	1.000	-1	C-18/3-1	-0.1
Total	2	70	163	16	37	8	0	1	13	20	25	.227	.323	.294	67	-7	6	2	1	1.000	0	/C-68,3-1	-0.3

■ OTTO KNABE

Knabe, Franz Otto "Dutch" b: 6/12/1884, Carrick, Pa. d: 5/17/61, Philadelphia, Pa. BR/TR, 5'8", 175 lbs. Deb: 10/3/05 M

YEAR	TM/L	G	AB	R	H	2B	3B	HR	RBI	BB	SO	AVG	OBP	SLG	PRO+	BR/A	SB	CS	SBR	FA	FR	G/POS	TPR
1905	Pit-N	3	10	0	3	1	0	0	2	3		.300	.462	.400	154	1	0			.786	0	/3-3	0.1
1907	Phi-N	129	444	67	113	16	9	1	34	52		.255	.339	.338	114	8	18			.960	1	*2-121/O-5	0.9
1908	Phi-N	151	555	63	121	26	8	0	27	49		.218	.290	.294	84	-10	27			.969	11	*2-151	0.0
1909	Phi-N	113	402	40	94	13	3	0	34	35		.234	.308	.281	82	-8	9			.938	8	*2-110/O-1	-0.3
1910	Phi-N	137	510	73	133	18	6	1	44	47	42	.261	.327	.325	87	-8	15			.954	14	*2-136	0.3
1911	Phi-N	142	528	99	125	15	6	1	42	94	35	.237	.352	.294	80	-10	23			.950	4	*2-142	-1.0
1912	Phi-N	126	426	56	120	11	4	0	46	55	20	.282	.366	.326	85	-7	16			.952	1	*2-123	-0.9
1913	Phi-N	148	571	70	150	25	7	2	53	45	26	.263	.320	.342	85	-11	14			.959	12	*2-148	-0.2
1914	Bal-F	147	469	45	106	26	2	2	42	53	28	.226	.307	.303	65	-30	10			.956	1	*2-144,M	-3.1
1915	Bal-F	103	320	38	81	16	2	1	25	37	16	.253	.334	.325	83	-11	7			.975	7	2-94/O-1,M	-0.3
1916	Pit-N	28	89	4	17	3	1	0	9	6	6	.191	.258	.247	55	-5	1			.962	-0	2-28	-0.5
	Chi-N	51	145	17	40	8	0	0	7	9	18	.276	.327	.331	92	-1	3			.939	6	2-42/S-1,3-1,O-1	0.6
	Yr	79	234	21	57	11	1	0	16	15	24	.244	.300	.299	79	-6	4			.948	5	2-70/S-1,3-1,O-1	0.1
Total	11	1278	4469	572	1103	178	48	8	365	485	191	.247	.325	.313	84	-92	143			.957	64	*2-1239/O-8,3-4,S-1	-4.4

■ COTTON KNAUPP

Knaupp, Henry Antone b: 8/13/1889, San Antonio, Tex. d: 7/6/67, New Orleans, La. BR/TR, 5'9", 165 lbs. Deb: 8/30/10

YEAR	TM/L	G	AB	R	H	2B	3B	HR	RBI	BB	SO	AVG	OBP	SLG	PRO+	BR/A	SB	CS	SBR	FA	FR	G/POS	TPR
1910	Cle-A	18	59	3	14	3	1	0	11	8		.237	.338	.322	105	1	1			.884	-8	S-18	-0.8
1911	Cle-A	13	39	2	4	1	0	0	0	0		.103	.103	.128	-35	-7	3			.964	2	S-13	-0.5
Total	2	31	98	5	18	4	1	0	11	8		.184	.252	.245	48	-6	4			.913	-6	/S-31	-1.3

■ ALAN KNICELY

Knicely, Alan Lee b: 5/19/55, Harrisonburg, Va. BR/TR, 6'0.5", 194 lbs. Deb: 8/12/79

YEAR	TM/L	G	AB	R	H	2B	3B	HR	RBI	BB	SO	AVG	OBP	SLG	PRO+	BR/A	SB	CS	SBR	FA	FR	G/POS	TPR
1979	Hou-N	7	6	0	0	0	0	0	0	2	3	.000	.250	.000	-27	-1	0	0	0	1.000	-2	/C-3,3-1	-0.3
1980	Hou-N	1	1	0	0	0	0	0	0	0	1	.000	.000	.000	-99	-0	0	0	0	.000	0	/H	0.0
1981	Hou-N	3	7	2	4	0	0	2	2	0	1	.571	.571	1.429	477	3	0	0	0	1.000	0	/C-2,O-1	0.3
1982	Hou-N	59	133	10	25	2	0	2	12	14	30	.188	.270	.248	50	-9	0	1	-1	.977	-9	C-23,O-16/3-1	-1.9
1983	Cin-N	59	98	11	22	3	0	2	10	16	28	.224	.333	.316	78	-2	0	2	-1	1.000	-2	C-31/O-8,1-2	-0.5
1984	Cin-N	10	29	0	4	0	0	0	5	3	6	.138	.219	.138	2	-4	0	0	0	.984	0	/1-8,C-1	-0.4
1985	Cin-N	48	158	17	40	9	0	5	26	16	34	.253	.326	.405	98	-0	0	0	0	.968	-14	C-46	-1.3
	Phi-N	7	7	0	0	0	0	0	0	0	4	.000	.000	.000	-97	-2	0	0	0	1.000	-0	/1-1	-0.2
	Yr	55	165	17	40	9	0	5	26	16	38	.242	.313	.388	91	-2	0	0	0	.968	-14	C-46/1-1	-1.5
1986	StL-N	34	82	8	16	3	0	1	6	17	21	.195	.333	.268	68	-3	1	1	-0	.995	-1	1-29/C-2	-0.6
Total	8	228	521	48	111	17	0	12	61	68	128	.213	.306	.315	73	-19	1	4	-2	.979	-26	C-108/1-40,O-25,3-2	-4.9

■ AUSTIN KNICKERBOCKER

Knickerbocker, Austin Jay b: 10/15/18, Bangall, N.Y. d: 2/18/97, Clinton Corners, N.Y. BR/TR, 5'11", 185 lbs. Deb: 4/19/47

YEAR	TM/L	G	AB	R	H	2B	3B	HR	RBI	BB	SO	AVG	OBP	SLG	PRO+	BR/A	SB	CS	SBR	FA	FR	G/POS	TPR
1947	Phi-A	21	48	8	12	3	2	0	2	3	4	.250	.294	.396	89	-1	0	1	-1	.943	0	O-14	-0.2

■ BILL KNICKERBOCKER

Knickerbocker, William Hart b: 12/29/11, Los Angeles, Cal. d: 9/8/63, Sebastopol, Cal. BR/TR, 5'11", 170 lbs. Deb: 4/12/33

YEAR	TM/L	G	AB	R	H	2B	3B	HR	RBI	BB	SO	AVG	OBP	SLG	PRO+	BR/A	SB	CS	SBR	FA	FR	G/POS	TPR
1933	Cle-A	80	279	20	63	16	3	2	32	11	30	.226	.255	.326	51	-21	1	4	-2	.939	2	S-80	-1.5
1934	Cle-A	146	593	82	188	32	5	4	67	25	40	.317	.347	.408	93	-8	6	6	-2	.962	-7	*S-146	-0.7
1935	Cle-A	132	540	77	161	34	5	0	55	27	31	.298	.332	.380	82	-15	2	12	-7	.956	9	*S-128	-0.5
1936	Cle-A	155	618	81	182	35	3	8	73	56	30	.294	.354	.400	85	-15	5	14	-7	.952	-1	*S-155	-1.1
1937	StL-A	121	491	53	128	29	5	4	61	30	32	.261	.303	.365	67	-26	3	2	-0	.958	-13	*S-115/2-6	-2.9
1938	NY-A	46	128	15	32	8	3	0	21	11	10	.250	.309	.383	73	-6	0	0	0	.982	-2	2-34/S-3	-0.5
1939	NY-A	6	13	2	2	1	0	0	1	0	0	.154	.154	.231	-3	-2	0	0	0	1.000	2	/2-2,S-2	0.0
1940	NY-A	45	124	17	30	8	1	1	10	14	8	.242	.333	.347	80	-4	1	1	-0	.985	-3	S-19,3-17	-0.4
1941	Chi-A	89	343	51	84	23	2	7	29	41	27	.245	.329	.385	89	-6	6	5	-1	.970	-17	2-88	-1.7
1942	Phi-A	87	289	25	73	12	0	1	19	29	30	.253	.323	.304	77	-8	1	2	-1	.964	-12	2-81/S-1	-1.7
Total	10	907	3418	423	943	198	27	28	368	244	238	.276	.326	.374	79	-109	25	46	-20	.955	-42	S-649,2-211/3-17	-11.0

■ LON KNIGHT

Knight, Alonzo P. b: 6/16/1853, Philadelphia, Pa. d: 4/23/32, Philadelphia, Pa. BR/TR, 5'11.5", 165 lbs. Deb: 9/4/1875 MU

YEAR	TM/L	G	AB	R	H	2B	3B	HR	RBI	BB	SO	AVG	OBP	SLG	PRO+	BR/A	SB	CS	SBR	FA	FR	G/POS	TPR
1875	Ath-n	13	47	5	6	2	0	0	2	0	2	.128	.128	.170	2	-5	2	0	1	.875	-0	P-13/S-1	-0.1
1876	Phi-N	55	240	32	60	9	3	0	24	2	2	.250	.256	.313	89	-3				.804	-7	P-34,1-13/O-9,2-6	-0.6
1880	Wor-N	49	201	31	48	11	3	0	21	5	8	.239	.257	.323	88	-3				.863	5	O-49	0.0
1881	Det-N	83	340	67	92	16	3	1	52	23	21	.271	.317	.344	104	1				.890	1	*O-82/2-1,1-1	0.1
1882	Det-N	86	347	39	72	12	6	0	24	16	21	.207	.242	.277	66	-13				.867	1	*O-84/1-2	-1.1
1883	Phi-a	97	429	98	108	23	9	1	53	21		.252	.287	.354	97	-3				.858	0	*O-93/3-3,2-2,M	-0.3
1884	Phi-a	108	484	94	131	18	12	1		10		.271	.287	.364	104	0				.911	11	*O-108/P-2,1-1,M	0.8
1885	Phi-a	29	119	17	25	1	1	0	14	9		.210	.271	.235	58	-6				.921	4	O-29/P-1	-0.2
	Pro-N	25	81	8	13	1	0	0	8	11	17	.160	.261	.173	44	-4				.957	1	O-25/P-1	-0.4
Total	7	532	2241	386	549	91	37	3	196	97	69	.245	.277	.323	90	-30				.887	17	O-479/P-38,1-17,23	-1.7

■ RAY KNIGHT

Knight, Charles Ray b: 12/28/52, Albany, Ga. BR/TR, 6'2", 190 lbs. Deb: 9/10/74 MC

YEAR	TM/L	G	AB	R	H	2B	3B	HR	RBI	BB	SO	AVG	OBP	SLG	PRO+	BR/A	SB	CS	SBR	FA	FR	G/POS	TPR
1974	Cin-N	14	11	1	2	1	0	0	2	1	2	.182	.250	.273	47	-1	0	0	0	1.000	1	3-14	0.0
1977	Cin-N	80	92	8	24	5	1	1	13	9	16	.261	.327	.370	85	-2	1	1	-0	.941	4	3-37,2-17/O-5,S-3	0.3
1978	Cin-N	83	65	7	13	3	0	1	4	3	13	.200	.235	.292	47	-5	0	0	0	.868	5	3-60/2-4,O-3,1-1,S	0.0
1979	*Cin-N	150	551	64	175	37	4	10	79	38	57	.318	.365	.454	121	16	4	4	-1	.962	-15	*3-149	-0.2
1980	Cin-N★	162	618	71	163	39	7	14	78	36	62	.264	.309	.417	101	-1	1	2	-1	.969	-15	*3-162	-2.1
1981	Cin-N	106	386	43	100	23	1	6	34	33	51	.259	.324	.370	95	-3	2	4	-2	.957	-13	*3-105	-2.2
1982	Hou-N★	158	609	72	179	36	6	6	70	48	58	.294	.350	.402	119	14	2	5	-2	.990	-2	1-96,3-67	0.3
1983	Hou-N	145	507	43	154	36	4	9	70	42	62	.304	.362	.444	130	19	0	3	-2	.993	-11	*1-143	-0.1
1984	Hou-N	88	278	15	62	10	0	2	29	14	30	.223	.263	.281	57	-17	0	3	-2	.946	-2	3-54,1-24	-2.4
	NY-N	27	93	13	26	4	0	1	6	7	13	.280	.337	.355	96	-0	0	0	0	.962	-4	3-27/1-3	-0.5
	Yr	115	371	28	88	14	0	3	35	21	43	.237	.282	.299	67	-17	0	3	-2	.951	-6	3-81,1-27	-2.9
1985	NY-N	90	271	22	59	12	0	6	36	13	32	.218	.256	.328	64	-14	1	1	-0	.958	-11	3-73/2-2,1-1	-2.7
1986	*NY-N	137	486	51	145	24	2	11	76	40	63	.298	.357	.424	118	11	2	1	0	.948	-11	*3-132/1-1	-0.2
1987	Bal-A	150	563	46	144	24	0	14	65	39	90	.256	.311	.373	82	-15	0	0	0	.956	10	*3-130,D-14/1-6	-0.7
1988	Det-A	105	299	34	65	12	2	3	33	20	30	.217	.273	.301	63	-15	1	1	-0	.991	-3	1-64,D-25,3-11,/O-2	-2.4
Total	13	1495	4829	490	1311	266	27	84	595	343	579	.271	.325	.390	99	-11	14	25	-11	.957	-67	*3-1021,1-339/D2OS	-12.9

■ JOHN KNIGHT

Knight, John Wesley "Schoolboy" b: 10/6/1885, Philadelphia, Pa. d: 12/19/65, Walnut Creek, Cal. BR/TR, 6'2.5", 180 lbs. Deb: 4/14/05

YEAR	TM/L	G	AB	R	H	2B	3B	HR	RBI	BB	SO	AVG	OBP	SLG	PRO+	BR/A	SB	CS	SBR	FA	FR	G/POS	TPR
1905	Phi-A	88	325	28	66	12	1	3	29	9		.203	.227	.274	58	-16	4			.895	-28	S-79/3-4	-4.8
1906	Phi-A	74	253	29	49	7	2	3	20	19		.194	.250	.273	62	-11	6			.922	0	3-67/2-7	-1.0
1907	Phi-A	40	139	6	29	7	1	0	12	10		.209	.272	.273	72	-4	1			.862	-0	3-40	-0.4
	Bos-A	98	360	31	78	9	3	2	29	19		.217	.256	.275	70	-13	8			.924	7	3-92/2-4	-0.3
	Yr	138	499	37	107	16	4	2	41	29		.214	.260	.275	71	-17	9			.906	7	*3-132/2-4	-0.7
1909	NY-A	116	360	46	85	8	5	0	40	37		.236	.311	.286	88	-4	15			.901	1	S-76,1-19,2-17,/3-3	-0.3
1910	NY-A	117	414	58	129	25	4	3	45	34		.312	.372	.413	138	17	23			.929	-1	S-79,1-23/2-7,3O	2.2
1911	NY-A	132	470	69	126	16	7	3	62	42		.268	.342	.351	88	-8	18			.907	3	S-82,1-27,2-21,/3-1	0.0
1912	Was-A	32	93	10	15	2	1	0	9	16		.161	.284	.204	40	-7	4			.926	-5	2-27/1-5	-1.2
1913	NY-A	70	250	24	59	10	0	0	24	25	27	.236	.310	.276	72	-9	7			.980	8	1-50,2-21	-0.2
Total	8	767	2664	301	636	96	24	14	270	211	27	.239	.300	.309	84	-55	86			.909	-15	S-316,3-211,12/O	-6.0

■ JOE KNIGHT

Knight, Joseph William "Quiet Joe"
b: 9/28/1859, Port Stanley, Ont., Canada d: 10/16/38, Lynhurst, Ont., Canada BL/TL, 5'11", 185 lbs. Deb: 5/16/1884

YEAR	TM/L	G	AB	R	H	2B	3B	HR	RBI	BB	SO	AVG	OBP	SLG	PRO+	BR/A	SB	CS	SBR	FA	FR	G/POS	TPR
1884	Phi-N	6	24	2	6	3	0	0	2	0	2	.250	.250	.375	98	-0				.789	-0	/P-6	0.0
1890	Cin-N	127	481	67	150	26	8	4	67	38	31	.312	.367	.424	131	18	17			.925	-6	*O-127	0.6
Total	2	133	505	69	156	29	8	4	69	38	33	.309	.362	.422	130	18	17			.925	-6	O-127/P-6	0.6

■ PETE KNISELY
Knisely, Peter Cole b: 8/11/1887, Waynesburg, Pa. d: 7/1/48, Brownsville, Pa. BR/TR, 5'9", 185 lbs. Deb: 9/4/12

YEAR	TM/L	G	AB	R	H	2B	3B	HR	RBI	BB	SO	AVG	OBP	SLG	PRO+	BR/A	SB	CS	SBR	FA	FR	G/POS	TPR
1912	Cin-N	21	67	10	22	7	3	0	7	4	5	.328	.375	.522	148	4	3			.939	-2	O-13/2-3,S-1	0.1
1913	Chi-N	2	2	0	0	0	0	0	0	0	1	.000	.000	.000	-99	-1	0			.000	0	H	-0.1
1914	Chi-N	37	69	5	9	0	1	0	5	5	6	.130	.200	.159	7	-8	0			.975	2	O-17	-0.7
1915	Chi-N	64	134	12	33	9	0	0	17	15	18	.246	.331	.313	95	-0	1	2	-1	.940	-7	O-33/2-9	-1.1
Total	4	124	272	27	64	16	4	0	29	24	30	.235	.307	.324	86	-5	4	2		.951	-7	/O-63,2-12,S-1	-1.8

■ CHUCK KNOBLAUCH
Knoblauch, Edward Charles b: 7/7/68, Houston, Tex. BR/TR, 5'9", 181 lbs. Deb: 4/9/91

YEAR	TM/L	G	AB	R	H	2B	3B	HR	RBI	BB	SO	AVG	OBP	SLG	PRO+	BR/A	SB	CS	SBR	FA	FR	G/POS	TPR
1991	*Min-A	151	565	78	159	24	6	1	50	59	40	.281	.354	.350	91	-5	25	5	5	.975	-1	*2-148/S-2	0.2
1992	Min-A★	155	600	104	178	19	6	2	56	88	60	.297	.391	.358	108	10	34	13	2	.992	-16	*2-154/S-1,D-1	0.0
1993	Min-A	153	602	82	167	27	4	2	41	65	44	.277	.357	.346	89	-7	29	11	2	.988	-5	*2-148/S-6,O-1	-0.5
1994	Min-A★	109	445	85	139	**45**	3	5	51	41	56	.312	.383	.461	116	12	35	6	7	.994	-23	*2-109/S-1	0.0
1995	Min-A	136	538	107	179	34	8	11	63	78	95	.333	.427	.487	137	33	46	18	3	.985	-8	*2-136/S-2	3.3
1996	Min-A★	153	578	140	197	35	**14**	13	72	98	74	.341	.452	.517	142	43	45	14	5	**.988**	-27	*2-151/D-2	2.8
1997	Min-A★	156	611	117	178	26	10	9	58	84	84	.291	.392	.411	108	11	62	10	**13**	.985	-16	*2-154/S-1,D-1	1.6
1998	*NY-A	150	603	117	160	25	4	17	64	76	70	.265	.364	.405	102	4	31	12	2	.981	-11	*2-149/D-1	0.4
Total	8	1163	4542	830	1357	235	55	60	455	589	523	.299	.390	.414	112	101	307	89	39	.986	-108	*2-1149/S-13,D-5,O	7.8

■ MIKE KNODE
Knode, Kenneth Thomson b: 11/8/1895, Westminster, Md. d: 12/20/80, South Bend, Ind. BR/TR, 5'10", 160 lbs. Deb: 6/28/20 F

YEAR	TM/L	G	AB	R	H	2B	3B	HR	RBI	BB	SO	AVG	OBP	SLG	PRO+	BR/A	SB	CS	SBR	FA	FR	G/POS	TPR
1920	StL-N	42	65	11	15	1	1	0	12	5	6	.231	.306	.277	71	-2	0	1	-1	.824	-0	/O-9,2-4,S-2,3-2	-0.4

■ RAY KNODE
Knode, Robert Troxell "Bob" b: 1/28/01, Westminster, Md. d: 4/13/82, Battle Creek, Mich BL/TL, 5'10", 160 lbs. Deb: 6/30/23 F

YEAR	TM/L	G	AB	R	H	2B	3B	HR	RBI	BB	SO	AVG	OBP	SLG	PRO+	BR/A	SB	CS	SBR	FA	FR	G/POS	TPR
1923	Cle-A	22	38	7	11	0	0	2	4	2	4	.289	.325	.447	102	-0	1	0	0	.992	0	1-21	0.0
1924	Cle-A	11	37	6	9	1	0	0	4	3	0	.243	.300	.270	47	-3	2	1	0	.992	1	1-10	-0.2
1925	Cle-A	45	108	13	27	5	0	0	11	10	4	.250	.314	.296	55	-7	3	3	-1	.990	1	1-34	-0.9
1926	Cle-A	31	24	6	8	1	1	0	4	3	4	.333	.407	.458	124	1	0	0	0	.984	1	1-11	0.1
Total	4	109	207	32	55	7	1	2	23	18	12	.266	.324	.338	70	-9	6	4	-1	.990	2	/1-76	-1.0

■ PUNCH KNOLL
Knoll, Charles Elmer b: 10/7/1881, Evansville, Ind. d: 2/8/60, Evansville, Ind. BR/TR, 5'7.5", 170 lbs. Deb: 4/27/05

YEAR	TM/L	G	AB	R	H	2B	3B	HR	RBI	BB	SO	AVG	OBP	SLG	PRO+	BR/A	SB	CS	SBR	FA	FR	G/POS	TPR
1905	Was-A	79	244	24	52	10	5	0	29	9		.213	.247	.295	75	-8	3			.927	-1	O-63/C-5,1-2	-1.3

■ BOBBY KNOOP
Knoop, Robert Frank b: 10/18/38, Sioux City, Iowa BR/TR, 6'1", 170 lbs. Deb: 4/13/64 MC

YEAR	TM/L	G	AB	R	H	2B	3B	HR	RBI	BB	SO	AVG	OBP	SLG	PRO+	BR/A	SB	CS	SBR	FA	FR	G/POS	TPR
1964	LA-A	162	486	42	105	8	1	7	38	46	109	.216	.291	.280	66	-23	3	2	-0	.978	**37**	*2-161	2.8
1965	Cal-A	142	465	47	125	24	4	7	43	31	101	.269	.315	.383	99	-1	3	4	-2	.971	13	*2-142	2.5
1966	Cal-A★	161	590	54	137	18	**11**	17	72	43	144	.232	.285	.386	94	-6	1	5	-3	**.981**	17	*2-161	2.0
1967	Cal-A	159	511	51	125	18	5	9	38	44	136	.245	.306	.352	98	-2	2	2	-1	.986	1	*2-159	1.0
1968	Cal-A	152	494	48	123	20	4	3	39	35	128	.249	.303	.324	93	-5	3	2	-0	.981	16	*2-151	2.2
1969	Cal-A	27	71	5	14	1	0	1	6	13	16	.197	.321	.254	66	-3	1	3	-2	.977	2	2-27	-0.1
	Chi-A	104	345	34	79	14	1	6	41	35	68	.229	.304	.328	73	-12	2	0	1	.985	23	*2-104	2.0
	Yr	131	416	39	93	15	1	7	47	48	84	.224	.307	.315	72	-15	3	3	-1	.984	25	*2-131	1.9
1970	Chi-A	130	402	34	92	13	2	5	36	34	79	.229	.292	.308	63	-20	0	1	-1	.984	**35**	*2-126	2.5
1971	KC-A	72	161	14	33	8	1	1	11	15	36	.205	.273	.286	59	-9	1	0	0	.968	-1	2-52/3-1	-0.6
1972	KC-A	44	97	8	23	5	0	0	7	9	16	.237	.302	.289	77	-3	0	0	0	.972	8	2-33/3-4	0.7
Total	9	1153	3622	337	856	129	29	56	331	305	833	.236	.298	.334	83	-84	16	17	-5	.980	150	*2-1116/3-5	15.0

■ RANDY KNORR
Knorr, Randy Duane b: 11/12/68, San Gabriel, Cal. BR/TR, 6'2", 215 lbs. Deb: 9/5/91

YEAR	TM/L	G	AB	R	H	2B	3B	HR	RBI	BB	SO	AVG	OBP	SLG	PRO+	BR/A	SB	CS	SBR	FA	FR	G/POS	TPR
1991	Tor-A	3	1	0	0	0	0	0	0	1	1	.000	.500	.000	49	0	0	0	0	1.000	1	/C-3	0.1
1992	Tor-A	8	19	1	5	0	0	1	2	1	5	.263	.300	.421	96	-0	0	0	0	1.000	1	/C-8	0.1
1993	*Tor-A	39	101	11	25	3	2	4	20	9	29	.248	.309	.436	97	-1	0	0	0	1.000	-1	C-39	0.0
1994	Tor-A	40	124	20	30	2	0	7	19	10	35	.242	.304	.427	86	-3	0	0	0	.993	-0	C-40	-0.1
1995	Tor-A	45	132	18	28	8	0	3	16	11	28	.212	.273	.341	59	-8	0	0	0	.971	-2	C-45	-0.7
1996	Hou-N	37	87	7	17	5	0	1	7	5	18	.195	.247	.287	44	-7	0	1	-1	1.000	8	C-33	0.1
1997	Hou-N	4	8	1	3	0	0	1	1	0	2	.375	.375	.750	193	1	0	0	0	1.000	1	/C-3,1-2	0.2
1998	Fla-N	15	49	4	10	4	1	2	11	1	10	.204	.220	.449	70	-2	0	0	0	.989	-2	C-15	-0.3
Total	8	191	521	62	118	22	3	19	76	38	128	.226	.282	.390	75	-21	0	1	-1	.990	6	C-186/1-2	-0.6

■ GEORGE KNOTHE
Knothe, George Bertram b: 1/12/1898, Bayonne, N.J. d: 7/3/81, Dover, N.J. BR/TR, 5'10", 165 lbs. Deb: 4/25/32 F

YEAR	TM/L	G	AB	R	H	2B	3B	HR	RBI	BB	SO	AVG	OBP	SLG	PRO+	BR/A	SB	CS	SBR	FA	FR	G/POS	TPR
1932	Phi-N	6	12	2	1	1	0	0	0	0	0	.083	.083	.167	-31	-2	0			.923	-1	/2-5	-0.3

■ FRITZ KNOTHE
Knothe, Wilfred Edgar b: 5/1/03, Passaic, N.J. d: 3/27/63, Passaic, N.J. BR/TR, 5'10.5", 180 lbs. Deb: 4/12/32 F

YEAR	TM/L	G	AB	R	H	2B	3B	HR	RBI	BB	SO	AVG	OBP	SLG	PRO+	BR/A	SB	CS	SBR	FA	FR	G/POS	TPR
1932	Bos-N	89	344	45	82	19	1	1	36	39	37	.238	.318	.308	72	-13	5			.947	-3	3-87	-1.0
1933	Bos-N	44	158	15	36	5	2	1	6	13	25	.228	.291	.304	76	-5	1			.978	-7	3-33/S-9	-1.0
	Phi-N	41	113	10	17	2	0	0	11	6	19	.150	.193	.168	3	-14	2			.949	15	3-32/2-4	0.3
	Yr	85	271	25	53	7	2	1	17	19	44	.196	.251	.247	42	-20	3			.961	8	3-65/S-9,2-4	-0.7
Total	2	174	615	70	135	26	3	2	53	58	81	.220	.289	.281	59	-32	8			.953	5	3-152/S-9,2-4	-1.7

■ JOE KNOTTS
Knotts, Joseph Steven b: 3/3/1884, Greensboro, Pa. d: 9/15/50, Philadelphia, Pa. BR/TR, Deb: 9/18/07

YEAR	TM/L	G	AB	R	H	2B	3B	HR	RBI	BB	SO	AVG	OBP	SLG	PRO+	BR/A	SB	CS	SBR	FA	FR	G/POS	TPR
1907	Bos-N	3	8	0	0	0	0	0	0	1		.000	.111	.000	-65	-2	0			1.000	-0	/C-3	-0.2

■ ED KNOUFF
Knouff, Edward "Fred" b: 6/1868, Philadelphia, Pa. d: 9/14/1900, Philadelphia, Pa. BR/TR, 210 lbs. Deb: 7/1/1885

YEAR	TM/L	G	AB	R	H	2B	3B	HR	RBI	BB	SO	AVG	OBP	SLG	PRO+	BR/A	SB	CS	SBR	FA	FR	G/POS	TPR
1885	Phi-a	14	48	5	9	0	0	0	2	2		.188	.220	.188	28	-4				.867	1	P-14/O-1	0.0
1886	Bal-a	1	3	0	0	0	0	0	0	0		.000	.250	.000	-20	-0	0			1.000	1	/P-1	0.0
1887	Bal-a	9	31	4	9	0	0	0	3	1		.290	.313	.290	73	-1	1			.889	-1	/P-9,O-3	-0.1
	StL-a	15	56	4	10	1	2	0	6	1		.179	.207	.268	29	-6	1			.800	-2	/O-9,P-6	-0.4
	Yr	24	87	8	19	1	2	0	9	2		.218	.244	.276	43	-7	2			.897	-3	P-15,O-12	-0.5
1888	StL-a	9	31	1	3	0	0	0	1	3		.097	.200	.097	-3	-4	1			.842	-2	/P-9	0.0
	Cle-a	2	6	0	1	1	0	0	0	1		.167	.286	.333	101	0	0			1.000	1	/P-2,2-1	0.0
	Yr	11	37	1	4	1	0	0	1	4		.108	.214	.135	12	-4	1			.880	-1	P-11/2-1	0.0
1889	Phi-a	3	12	2	3	1	0	0	2	1	1	.250	.308	.333	84	-0	1			1.000	-1	/P-3	0.0
Total	5	53	187	16	35	3	2	0	14	9	1	.187	.236	.225	35	-15	4			.891	-3	/P-44,O-13,2-1	-0.5

■ JAKE KNOWDELL
Knowdell, Jacob Augustus b: 7/27/1840, Brooklyn, N.Y. 5'7.5", 148 lbs. Deb: 6/20/1874

YEAR	TM/L	G	AB	R	H	2B	3B	HR	RBI	BB	SO	AVG	OBP	SLG	PRO+	BR/A	SB	CS	SBR	FA	FR	G/POS	TPR
1874	Atl-n	24	86	8	12	1	1	0	3	1	3	.140	.149	.174	4	-8	1	0	0	.824	-4	C-21/O-4	-0.9
1875	Atl-n	43	163	17	32	2	0	0	9	1	3	.196	.201	.209	49	-7	0	1	-1	.781	-8	C-33,S-11/O-4,2-1	-1.3
1878	Mil-N	4	14	2	3	1	0	0	2	0	3	.214	.214	.286	59	-1				.875	-2	/C-2,O-1,S-1	-0.3
Total	2 n	67	249	25	44	3	1	0	12	2	6	.177	.183	.197	32	-15	1	1	-0	.796	-12	/C-54,S-11,O-8,2-1	-2.2

■ JIMMY KNOWLES
Knowles, James "Darby" b: 9/1856, Toronto, Ont., Can. d: 2/11/12, Jersey City, N.J. 5'9", 160 lbs. Deb: 5/2/1884

YEAR	TM/L	G	AB	R	H	2B	3B	HR	RBI	BB	SO	AVG	OBP	SLG	PRO+	BR/A	SB	CS	SBR	FA	FR	G/POS	TPR
1884	Pit-a	46	182	19	42	5	7	0		5		.231	.259	.335	91	-2				.961	-0	1-46	-0.7
	Bro-a	41	153	19	36	5	1	1		3		.235	.255	.301	80	-3				.953	1	1-30,3-11	-0.6
	Yr	87	335	38	78	10	8	1		8		.233	.257	.319	86	-5				.958	1	1-76,3-11	-1.3
1886	Was-N	115	443	43	94	16	11	3	35	15	73	.212	.238	.318	72	-15	20			.899	**28**	2-62,3-53	1.5
1887	NY-a	16	60	12	15	1	1	0	6	1		.250	.262	.300	59	-3	6			.934	-3	2-16/3-1	-0.5
1890	Roc-a	123	491	83	138	12	8	5	84	59		.281	.359	.369	124	16	55			.881	7	*3-123	2.4
1892	NY-N	16	59	9	9	1	0	0	7	6	8	.153	.231	.169	22	-5	2			.792	-5	3-15/S-1	-0.9
Total	5	357	1388	185	334	40	28	9	132	89	81	.241	.288	.329	91	-13	83			.861	28	3-203/2-78,1-76,S-1	1.2

■ ANDY KNOX
Knox, Andrew Jackson "Dasher" b: 1/6/1864, Philadelphia, Pa. d: 9/14/40, Philadelphia, Pa. BR/TR, Deb: 9/19/1890

YEAR	TM/L	G	AB	R	H	2B	3B	HR	RBI	BB	SO	AVG	OBP	SLG	PRO+	BR/A	SB	CS	SBR	FA	FR	G/POS	TPR
1890	Phi-a	21	75	6	19	3	0	0	8	9		.253	.333	.293	87	-1	5			.963	-2	1-21	-0.3

■ CLIFF KNOX
Knox, Clifford Hiram "Bud" b: 1/7/02, Coalville, Iowa d: 9/24/65, Oskaloosa, Iowa BB/TR, 5'11.5", 178 lbs. Deb: 7/1/24

YEAR	TM/L	G	AB	R	H	2B	3B	HR	RBI	BB	SO	AVG	OBP	SLG	PRO+	BR/A	SB	CS	SBR	FA	FR	G/POS	TPR
1924	Pit-N	6	18	1	4	0	0	0	2	2	0	.222	.300	.222	41	-1	0	0	0	.917	2	/C-6	0.1

YEAR	TM/L	G	AB	R	H	2B	3B	HR	RBI	BB	SO	AVG	OBP	SLG	PRO+	BR/A	SB	CS	SBR	FA	FR	G/POS	TPR
■ **JOHN KNOX**	Knox, John Clinton b: 7/26/48, Newark, N.J. BL/TR, 6', 170 lbs. Deb: 8/1/72																						
1972	*Det-A	14	13	1	1	1	0	0	0	1	2	.077	.143	.154	-11	-2	0	0	0	1.000	4	/2-4	0.2
1973	Det-A	12	32	1	9	1	0	0	3	3	3	.281	.343	.313	80	-1	1	1	-0	1.000	-3	/2-9	-0.3
1974	Det-A	55	88	11	27	1	1	0	6	6	13	.307	.351	.341	96	-0	5	4	-1	.956	8	2-33/3-1,D-2	0.7
1975	Det-A	43	86	8	23	1	0	0	2	10	9	.267	.344	.279	74	-2	1	2	-1	.980	-1	2-23/3-3,D-3	-0.4
Total	4	124	219	21	60	4	1	0	11	20	27	.274	.335	.301	79	-5	7	7	-2	.973	8	/2-69,D-5,3-4	0.2
■ **NICK KOBACK**	Koback, Nicholas Nicholie b: 7/19/35, Hartford, Conn. BR/TR, 6', 187 lbs. Deb: 7/29/53																						
1953	Pit-N	7	16	1	2	0	1	0	0	1	4	.125	.176	.250	10	-2	0	0	0	1.000	-3	/C-6	-0.5
1954	Pit-N	4	10	0	0	0	0	0	0	0	8	.000	.000	.000	-99	-3	0	0	0	1.000	0	/C-4	-0.3
1955	Pit-N	5	7	0	2	0	0	0	0	0	1	.286	.286	.286	53	-0	0	0	0	1.000	0	/C-2	0.0
Total	3	16	33	1	4	0	1	0	0	1	13	.121	.147	.182	-15	-6	0	0	0	1.000	-3	/C-12	-0.8
■ **BARNEY KOCH**	Koch, Barnett b: 3/23/23, Campbell, Neb. d: 6/6/87, Tacoma, Wash. BR/TR, 5'8", 140 lbs. Deb: 7/23/44																						
1944	Bro-N	33	96	11	21	2	0	0	1	3	9	.219	.242	.240	37	-8	0			.956	-6	2-29/S-1	-1.3
■ **BRAD KOCHER**	Kocher, Bradley Wilson b: 1/16/1888, White Haven, Pa. d: 1/13/65, White Haven, Pa. BR/TR, 5'11", 188 lbs. Deb: 4/24/12																						
1912	Det-A	29	63	5	13	3	1	0	9	2		.206	.231	.286	49	-4	0			.904	-3	C-24	-0.6
1915	NY-N	4	11	3	5	0	1	0	2	0	1	.455	.455	.636	243	2	0			1.000	-1	/C-3	0.1
1916	NY-N	34	65	1	7	2	0	0	1	2	10	.108	.134	.138	-17	-9	0			.978	-7	C-30	-1.7
Total	3	67	139	9	25	5	2	0	12	4	11	.180	.203	.245	34	-12	0			.943	-11	/C-57	-2.2
■ **PETE KOEGEL**	Koegel, Peter John b: 7/31/47, Mineola, N.Y. BR/TR, 6'6.5", 230 lbs. Deb: 9/1/70																						
1970	Mil-A	7	8	2	2	0	0	1	1	1	3	.250	.333	.625	157	1	0	0	0	1.000	-0	/O-1	0.0
1971	Mil-A	2	3	0	0	0	0	0	0	2	2	.000	.400	.000	22	-0	0	0	0	1.000	-0	/1-1	0.0
	Phi-N	12	26	1	6	1	0	0	3	2	7	.231	.286	.269	58	-1	0	0	0	1.000	-1	/C-7,O-1	-0.2
1972	Phi-N	41	49	3	7	2	0	0	1	6	16	.143	.236	.184	20	-5	0	0	0	1.000	-2	/1-8,C-5,3-4,O-2	-0.8
Total	3	62	86	6	15	3	0	1	5	11	28	.174	.268	.244	45	-6	0	0	0	.971	-3	/C-12,1-9,3-4,O-4	-1.0
■ **BEN KOEHLER**	Koehler, Benard James b: 1/26/1877, Schoerndorn, Germany d: 5/21/61, South Bend, Ind. BR/TR, 5'10.5", 175 lbs. Deb: 4/23/05																						
1905	StL-A	142	536	55	127	14	6	2	47	32		.237	.285	.297	89	-7	22			.969	6	*O-124,1-12/2-6	-0.8
1906	StL-A	66	186	27	41	1	1	0	15	24		.220	.322	.237	79	-3	9			.957	-4	O-52/2-7,S-1,3-1	-1.0
Total	2	208	722	82	168	15	7	2	62	56		.233	.295	.281	87	-10	31			.966	2	O-176/2-13,1-12,3S	-1.8
■ **PIP KOEHLER**	Koehler, Horace Levering b: 1/16/02, Gilbert, Pa. d: 12/8/86, Tacoma, Wash. BR/TR, 5'10", 165 lbs. Deb: 4/22/25																						
1925	NY-N	12	2	1	0	0	0	0	0	0	1	.000	.000	.000	-99	-1	0	0	0	1.000	-1	/O-3	-0.1
■ **BRIAN KOELLING**	Koelling, Brian Wayne b: 6/11/69, Cincinnati, Ohio BR/TR, 6'1", 185 lbs. Deb: 8/21/93																						
1993	Cin-N	7	15	2	1	0	0	0	0	0	2	.067	.125	.067	-47	-3	0	0	0	.941	1	/2-3,S-2	-0.2
■ **LEN KOENECKE**	Koenecke, Leonard George b: 1/18/04, Baraboo, Wis. d: 9/17/35, Toronto, Ont., Can BL/TR, 5'11", 180 lbs. Deb: 4/12/32																						
1932	NY-N	42	137	33	35	5	0	4	14	11	13	.255	.320	.380	89	-2	3			.924	-5	O-35	-0.9
1934	Bro-N	123	460	79	147	31	7	14	73	70	38	.320	.411	.509	152	36	8			**.994**	2	*O-121	3.1
1935	Bro-N	100	325	43	92	13	2	4	27	43	45	.283	.369	.372	102	2	0			.966	-4	O-91	-0.5
Total	3	265	922	155	274	49	9	22	114	124	96	.297	.383	.441	125	36	11			.976	-7	O-247	1.7
■ **MARK KOENIG**	Koenig, Mark Anthony b: 7/19/04, San Francisco, Cal. d: 4/22/93, Willows, Cal. BB/TR, 6', 180 lbs. Deb: 9/8/25																						
1925	NY-A	28	110	14	23	6	1	0	4	5	4	.209	.243	.282	34	-12	0	1	-1	.944	-3	S-28	-1.1
1926	*NY-A	147	617	93	167	26	8	5	62	43	37	.271	.319	.363	79	-21	4	3	-1	.931	-0	*S-141	-0.6
1927	*NY-A	123	526	99	150	20	11	3	62	25	21	.285	.320	.382	84	-14	3	2	-0	.936	14	*S-122	1.2
1928	*NY-A	132	533	89	170	19	10	4	63	32	19	.319	.360	.415	106	4	3	5	-2	.923	-20	*S-125	-0.3
1929	NY-A	116	373	44	109	27	5	3	41	23	17	.292	.335	.416	99	-2	1	1	-0	.911	-13	S-61,3-37/2-1	-0.7
1930	NY-A	21	74	9	17	5	0	0	9	6	5	.230	.296	.297	53	-5	0	0	0	.905	2	S-19	-0.1
	Det-A	76	267	37	64	9	2	1	16	20	15	.240	.295	.300	50	-20	2	0	1	.922	-14	S-70/P-2,3-2,O-1	-2.4
	Yr	97	341	46	81	14	2	1	25	26	20	.238	.295	.299	51	-25	2	0	1	.918	-13	S-89/P-2,3-2,O-1	-2.5
1931	Det-A	106	364	33	92	24	4	1	39	14	12	.253	.282	.349	63	-20	8	2	1	.955	-23	2-55,S-35/P-3	-3.4
1932	*Chi-N	33	102	15	36	5	1	3	11	3	5	.353	.377	.510	137	5	0			.932	10	S-31	1.7
1933	Chi-N	80	218	32	62	12	1	3	25	15	9	.284	.330	.390	105	1	5			.922	5	3-37,S-26/2-2	1.0
1934	Cin-N	151	633	60	172	26	6	1	67	15	24	.272	.289	.336	68	-29	5			.930	6	3-64,S-58,2-26,/1-4	-1.6
1935	NY-N	107	396	40	112	12	0	3	37	13	18	.283	.306	.336	74	-15	0			.968	-11	2-64,S-21,3-15	-1.9
1936	*NY-N	42	58	7	16	4	0	1	7	8	4	.276	.373	.397	109	1	0			.905	-1	S-10/2-8,3-3	0.0
Total	12	1162	4271	572	1190	195	49	28	443	222	190	.279	.316	.367	81	-126	31	14		.927	-50	S-747,3-158,2/P10	-8.2
■ **HENRY KOHLER**	Kohler, Henry C. b: 5/5/1852, Baltimore, Md. d: 8/27/34, Baltimore, Md. Deb: 7/12/1871																						
1871	Kek-n	3	12	0	2	1	0	0	1	0	0	.167	.167	.250	17	-1	0	0	0	.000	-0	/C-2,1-2,3-1	-0.1
1873	Mar-n	6	25	2	3	0	0	0	1	0	1	.120	.120	.120	-37	-4	0	0	0	.686	-4	/3-6,C-1,1-1,O-1	-0.6
1874	Bal-n	2	4	0	0	0	0	0	0	0	0	.000	.000	.000	-99	-1	0	0	0	.714	-1	/1-1	-0.1
Total	3 n	11	41	2	5	1	0	0	2	0	1	.122	.122	.146	-24	-6	0	0	0	.700	-5	/3-7,1-4,C-3,O-1	-0.8
■ **DICK KOKOS**	Kokos, Richard Jerome (b: Richard Jerome Kokoszka) b: 2/28/28, Chicago, Ill. d: 4/9/86, Chicago, Ill. BL/TL, 5'8.5", 170 lbs. Deb: 7/8/48																						
1948	StL-A	71	258	40	77	15	3	4	40	28	32	.298	.374	.426	110	3	4	3	-1	.964	-1	O-71	-0.1
1949	StL-A	143	501	80	131	28	1	23	77	66	91	.261	.351	.459	109	4	3	5	-2	.981	8	*O-138	0.3
1950	StL-A	143	490	77	128	27	5	18	67	88	73	.261	.375	.447	106	4	8	8	-2	.970	9	*O-127	0.5
1953	StL-A	107	299	41	72	12	0	13	38	56	53	.241	.361	.411	106	3	0	5	-3	.963	-1	O-83	-0.4
1954	Bal-A	11	10	1	2	0	0	1	1	4	3	.200	.429	.500	166	1	0	0	0	1.000	0	/O-1	-0.1
Total	5	475	1558	239	410	82	9	59	223	242	252	.263	.365	.441	108	16	15	21	-8	.971	16	O-420	0.4
■ **GARY KOLB**	Kolb, Gary Alan b: 3/13/40, Rock Falls, Ill. BL/TR, 6', 195 lbs. Deb: 9/7/60																						
1960	StL-N	9	3	1	0	0	0	0	0	0	0	.000	.000	.000	-92	-1	0	0	0	1.000	-0	/O-2	-0.1
1962	StL-N	6	14	1	5	0	0	0	0	1	3	.357	.400	.357	96	-0	0	0	0	1.000	-1	/O-6	-0.1
1963	StL-N	75	96	23	26	1	5	3	10	22	26	.271	.407	.479	141	6	2	1	0	.981	-11	O-58/C-1,3-1	-0.7
1964	Mil-N	36	64	7	12	1	0	0	2	6	10	.188	.257	.203	31	-6	3	2	-0	1.000	-6	O-14/3-7,2-6,C-2	-1.3
1965	Mil-N	24	27	3	7	0	0	0	1	1	6	.259	.286	.259	54	-2	0	0	0	1.000	-3	O-13	-0.5
	NY-N	40	90	8	15	2	0	1	7	3	28	.167	.194	.222	17	-10	3	0	1	.976	-1	O-29/1-1,3-1	-1.2
	Yr	64	117	11	22	2	0	1	8	4	34	.188	.215	.231	26	-11	3	0	1	.981	-4	O-42/1-1,3-1	-1.7
1968	Pit-N	74	119	16	26	4	1	2	6	11	17	.218	.285	.319	82	-3	2	1	0	.900	-2	O-25,C-10/3-4,2-1	-0.6
1969	Pit-N	29	37	4	3	1	0	0	3	2	14	.081	.128	.108	-34	-7	0	0	0	1.000	0	/C-7	-0.7
Total	7	293	450	63	94	9	6	6	29	46	104	.209	.282	.296	65	-21	10	4	1	.965	-23	O-147/C-20,3-13,21	-5.2
■ **DON KOLLOWAY**	Kolloway, Donald Martin "Butch" or "Cab" b: 8/4/18, Posen, Ill. d: 6/30/94, Blue Island, Ill. BR/TR, 6'3", 200 lbs. Deb: 9/16/40																						
1940	Chi-A	10	40	5	9	1	0	0	3	0	3	.225	.225	.250	23	-5	1	0	0	.922	-2	2-10	-0.5
1941	Chi-A	71	280	33	76	8	3	3	24	6	12	.271	.292	.354	71	-13	11	4	1	.955	-7	2-62/1-4	-1.5
1942	Chi-A	147	601	72	164	**40**	4	3	60	30	39	.273	.311	.368	92	-8	16	14	-4	.966	-9	*2-116,1-33	-1.6
1943	Chi-A	85	348	29	75	14	4	1	33	9	30	.216	.235	.287	53	-22	11	7	-1	.968	-1	2-85	-2.1
1946	Chi-A	123	482	45	135	23	4	3	53	9	29	.280	.293	.363	86	-12	14	6	1	.972	3	2-90,3-31	-0.1
1947	Chi-A	124	485	49	135	25	4	2	35	17	34	.278	.303	.359	87	-11	11	4	1	.962	5	2-99,1-11/3-8	0.1
1948	Chi-A	119	417	60	114	14	4	6	38	18	18	.273	.303	.369	81	-13	2	4	-2	.966	11	2-83,3-18	0.0
1949	Chi-A	4	4	0	0	0	0	0	0	0	1	.000	.000	.000	-99	-1	0	0	0	.000	0	/3-2	-0.1
	Det-A	126	483	71	142	19	3	2	47	49	25	.294	.361	.358	91	-6	7	7	-2	.956	-21	2-62,1-57/3-7	-2.6
	Yr	130	487	71	142	19	3	2	47	49	26	.292	.359	.355	89	-7	7	7	-2	.956	-21	2-62,1-57/3-9	-2.7
1950	Det-A	125	467	55	135	20	4	6	62	29	28	.289	.331	.388	81	-15	1	3	-2	.989	3	*1-118/2-1	-1.5
1951	Det-A	78	212	28	54	7	0	1	17	15	12	.255	.307	.302	65	-10	2	3	-1	.992	6	1-59	-0.8

YEAR	TM/L	G	AB	R	H	2B	3B	HR	RBI	BB	SO	AVG	OBP	SLG	PRO+	BR/A	SB	CS	SBR	FA	FR	G/POS	TPR
1952	Det-A	65	173	19	42	9	0	2	21	7	19	.243	.280	.329	69	-8	0	2	-1	.979	-1	1-32/2-8	-1.1
1953	Phi-A	2	1	0	0	0	0	0	0	0	1	.000	.000	.000	-96	-0	0	0	0	.000	0	/3-1	0.0
Total	12	1079	3993	466	1081	180	30	29	393	189	251	.271	.305	.353	80	-124	76	54	-10	.964	-13	2-616,1-314/3-67	-11.8
■ KARL KOLSETH	Kolseth, Karl Dickey "Koley" b: 12/25/1892, Cambridge, Mass. d: 5/3/56, Cumberland, Md. BL/TR, 6', 182 lbs. Deb: 9/30/15																						
1915	Bal-F	6	23	1	6	1	1	0	1	1	0	.261	.292	.391	89	-1	0			.915	-2	/1-6	-0.3
■ FRED KOMMERS	Kommers, Frederick Raymond "Bugs" b: 3/31/1886, Chicago, Ill. d: 6/14/43, Chicago, Ill. BL/TR, 6', 175 lbs. Deb: 6/25/13																						
1913	Pit-N	40	155	14	36	5	4	0	22	10	29	.232	.279	.316	73	-6	1			.979	-2	O-40	-1.0
1914	StL-F	76	244	33	75	9	8	3	41	24	36	.307	.376	.447	117	3	7			.908	-2	O-67	-0.2
	Bal-F	16	42	5	9	1	0	1	1	7	7	.214	.340	.310	75	-2	0			.938	-2	O-12	-0.5
	Yr	92	286	38	84	10	8	4	42	31	43	.294	.371	.427	111	1	7			.911	-4	O-79	-0.7
Total	2	132	441	52	120	15	12	4	64	41	72	.272	.340	.388	99	-5	8			.938	-6	O-119	-1.7
■ BRAD KOMMINSK	Komminsk, Brad Lynn b: 4/4/61, Lima, Ohio BR/TR, 6'2", 205 lbs. Deb: 8/14/83																						
1983	Atl-N	19	36	2	8	2	0	0	4	5	7	.222	.317	.278	62	-2	0	0	0	.944	-1	O-13	-0.3
1984	Atl-N	90	301	37	61	10	0	8	36	29	77	.203	.277	.316	62	-15	18	8	1	.993	-2	O-80	-2.1
1985	Atl-N	106	300	52	68	12	3	4	21	38	71	.227	.316	.327	75	-9	10	8	-2	.959	-4	O-92	-1.9
1986	Atl-N	5	5	1	2	0	0	0	1	0	1	.400	.400	.400	115	0	0	1	-1	1.000	-0	/3-2,O-2	-0.1
1987	Mil-A	7	15	0	1	0	0	0	0	1	7	.067	.125	.067	-46	-3	1	0	0	1.000	0	/O-5,D-1	-0.3
1989	Cle-A	71	198	27	47	8	2	8	33	24	55	.237	.323	.419	106	1	8	2	1	.995	3	O-68	0.4
1990	SF-N	8	5	2	1	0	0	0	0	1	2	.200	.333	.200	52	-0	0	0	0	1.000	-3	/O-7	-0.3
	Bal-A	46	101	18	24	4	0	3	8	14	29	.238	.342	.366	101	0	1	1	-0	1.000	-5	O-40/D-2	-0.5
1991	Oak-A	24	25	1	3	1	0	0	2	2	9	.120	.185	.160	-4	-4	1	0	0	1.000	-6	O-22	-0.9
Total	8	376	986	140	215	37	5	23	105	114	258	.218	.303	.336	75	-31	39	20	-0	.984	-17	O-329/D-3,3-2	-6.0
■ PAUL KONERKO	Konerko, Paul Henry b: 3/5/76, Providence, R.I. BR/TR, 6'3", 205 lbs. Deb: 9/8/97																						
1997	LA-N	6	7	0	1	0	0	0	0	1	2	.143	.250	.143	7	-1	0	0	0	1.000	-1	/1-1,3-1	-0.1
1998	LA-N	49	144	14	31	1	0	4	16	10	30	.215	.276	.306	55	-10	0	1	-1	.995	-1	1-23,3-11,O-11	-1.3
	Cin-N	26	73	7	16	3	0	3	13	6	10	.219	.287	.384	71	-3	0	0	0	1.000	1	/3-9,1-7,O-7,D-3	-0.3
	Yr	75	217	21	47	4	0	7	29	16	40	.217	.280	.332	60	-13	0	1	-1	.996	-0	1-30,3-20,O-18,/D-3	-1.6
Total	2	81	224	21	48	4	0	7	29	17	42	.214	.279	.326	59	-14	0	1	-1	.996	-1	/1-31,3-21,O-18,D-3	-1.7
■ ED KONETCHY	Konetchy, Edward Joseph "Big Ed" b: 9/3/1885, LaCrosse, Wis. d: 5/27/47, Ft.Worth, Tex. BR/TR, 6'2.5", 195 lbs. Deb: 6/29/07																						
1907	StL-N	91	331	34	83	11	9	2	30	26		.251	.317	.356	115	5	13			.975	4	1-91	0.8
1908	StL-N	154	545	46	135	19	12	5	50	38		.248	.309	.354	117	9	16			.986	11	*1-154	2.0
1909	StL-N	152	576	88	165	23	14	4	80	65		.286	.366	.396	145	31	25			.985	5	*1-152	3.7
1910	StL-N	144	520	87	157	23	16	3	78	78	59	.302	.397	.425	145	32	18			**.991**	8	*1-144/P-1	**4.1**
1911	StL-N	158	571	90	165	**38**	13	6	88	81	63	.289	.384	.433	132	25	27			**.991**	-6	*1-158	1.9
1912	StL-N	143	538	81	169	26	13	8	82	62	66	.314	.389	.455	134	25	25			.991	6	*1-142/O-1	2.8
1913	StL-N	140	504	75	139	18	17	8	68	53	41	.276	.353	.427	124	15	27			**.995**	7	*1-140/P-1	2.2
1914	Pit-N	154	563	56	140	23	9	4	51	32	48	.249	.291	.343	92	-8	20			**.995**	5	*1-154	-0.7
1915	Pit-F	152	576	79	181	31	18	10	93	41	52	.314	.363	.483	138	18	27			**.994**	-0	*1-152	1.5
1916	Bos-N	158	566	76	147	29	13	3	70	43	46	.260	.320	.373	117	11	13			.990	9	*1-158	1.5
1917	Bos-N	130	474	56	129	19	13	2	54	36	40	.272	.330	.380	125	13	16			**.994**	2	*1-129	1.1
1918	Bos-N	119	437	33	103	15	5	2	56	32	35	.236	.291	.307	86	-8	5			**.992**	-2	*1-112/O-6,P-1	-1.6
1919	Bro-N	132	486	46	145	24	9	1	47	29	39	.298	.342	.391	117	10	14			**.994**	7	*1-132	1.3
1920	*Bro-N	131	497	62	153	22	12	5	63	33	18	.308	.352	.431	120	12	3	2	-0	.990	1	*1-130	1.0
1921	Bro-N	55	197	25	53	6	5	3	23	19	21	.269	.336	.396	90	-3	3	3	-1	.987	-1	1-54	-0.6
	Phi-N	72	268	38	86	17	4	8	59	21	17	.321	.379	.504	122	8	3	0	1	.986	6	1-71	1.3
	Yr	127	465	63	139	23	9	11	82	40	38	.299	.361	.458	109	6	6	3	0	.986	4	*1-125	0.7
Total	15	2085	7649	972	2150	344	182	74	992	689	545	.281	.346	.403	122	196	255	5		.990	59	*1-2073/O-7,P-3	22.3
■ MIKE KONNICK	Konnick, Michael Aloysius b: 1/13/1889, Glen Lyon, Pa. d: 7/9/71, Wilkes-Barre, Pa. BR/TR, 5'9", 180 lbs. Deb: 10/3/09																						
1909	Cin-N	2	5	0	2	1	0	0	1	0		.400	.400	.600	211	1	0			1.000	-1	/C-2	0.0
1910	Cin-N	1	3	0	0	0	0	0	0	1	0	.000	.250	.000	-27	-0	0			1.000	-1	/S-1	-0.1
Total	2	3	8	0	2	1	0	0	1	1	0	.250	.333	.375	117	0	0			1.000	-1	/C-2,S-1	-0.1
■ BRUCE KONOPKA	Konopka, Bruno Bruce b: 9/16/19, Hammond, Ind. d: 9/27/96, Denver, Colo. BL/TL, 6'2", 190 lbs. Deb: 6/7/42																						
1942	Phi-A	5	10	2	3	0	0	0	1	1	0	.300	.364	.300	88	-0	0	0	0	1.000	-0	/1-3	0.0
1943	Phi-A	2	2	0	0	0	0	0	0	0	1	.000	.000	.000	-99	-0	0	0	0	.000	0	H	-0.1
1946	Phi-A	38	93	7	22	4	1	0	9	4	8	.237	.268	.301	59	-5	0	0	0	.994	1	1-20/O-1	-0.6
Total	3	45	105	9	25	4	1	0	10	5	9	.238	.273	.295	59	-6	0	0	0	.995	1	/1-23,O-1	-0.7
■ HARRY KOONS	Koons, Henry M. b: 1863, Philadelphia, Pa. BR/TR, 5'8", 174 lbs. Deb: 4/17/1884																						
1884	Alt-U	21	78	8	18	2	1	0		2		.231	.250	.282	60	-6				.866	5	3-21/C-1	-0.1
	CP-U	1	3	0	0	0	0	0		0		.000	.000	.000	-99	-1				.000	0	/3-1	-0.1
	Yr	22	81	8	18	2	1	0		2		.222	.241	.272	54	-7				.866	5	3-22/C-1	-0.2
■ GEORGE KOPACZ	Kopacz, George Felix "Sonny" b: 2/26/41, Chicago, Ill. BL/TL, 6'1", 195 lbs. Deb: 9/18/66																						
1966	Atl-N	6	9	1	0	0	0	0	0	1	5	.000	.100	.000	-68	-2	0	0	0	.909	-1	/1-2	-0.3
1970	Pit-N	10	16	1	3	0	0	0	0	0	5	.188	.188	.188	1	-2	0	0	0	1.000	-1	/1-3	-0.3
Total	2	16	25	2	3	0	0	0	0	1	10	.120	.154	.120	-25	-4	0	0	0	.964	-1	/1-5	-0.6
■ WALLY KOPF	Kopf, Walter Henry b: 7/10/1899, Stonington, Conn. d: 4/30/79, Hamilton Co., Ohio BB/TR, 5'11", 168 lbs. Deb: 10/1/21 F																						
1921	NY-N	2	3	0	1	0	0	0	0	1	1	.333	.500	.333	125	0	0	0	0	1.000	2	/3-2	0.2
■ LARRY KOPF	Kopf, William Lorenz (a.k.a. Fred Brady In 1913) b: 11/3/1890, Bristol, Conn. d: 10/15/86, Anderson Twp., O. BB/TR, 5'9", 160 lbs. Deb: 9/2/13 F																						
1913	Cle-A	6	10	2	3	1	0	0	1	0	0	.300	.300	.400	102	-0	0			.923	2	/2-4,3-1	0.2
1914	Phi-A	37	69	8	13	2	2	0	12	8	14	.188	.300	.275	76	-2	6			.899	1	S-13/3-8,2-5	0.3
1915	Phi-A	118	386	39	87	10	2	1	33	41	45	.225	.314	.269	77	-10	5	9	-4	.920	-8	S-74,3-42/2-2	-1.6
1916	Cin-N	11	40	2	11	2	0	0	5	1	8	.275	.293	.325	92	-1	1			.942	-2	S-11	-0.3
1917	Cin-N	148	573	81	146	19	8	2	26	28	48	.255	.297	.326	95	-5	17			.916	-11	*S-145	-1.0
1919	*Cin-N	135	503	51	136	18	5	0	58	28	27	.270	.313	.326	95	-4	18			.943	-34	*S-135	-3.4
1920	Cin-N	126	458	56	112	15	6	0	59	35	24	.245	.305	.303	76	-13	14	13	-4	.929	-33	*S-123/2-2,3-2,O-1	-4.3
1921	Cin-N	107	367	36	80	8	3	1	25	43	20	.218	.310	.264	56	-22	3	14	-8	.947	-15	S-93/2-4,3-3,O-1	-3.6
1922	Bos-N	126	466	59	124	6	3	1	37	45	22	.266	.332	.298	67	-22	8	9	-3	.944	-14	2-78,S-33,3-13	-3.1
1923	Bos-N	39	138	15	38	3	1	0	10	13	6	.275	.338	.312	75	-5	0	3	-2	.905	-8	S-37/2-4	-1.0
Total	10	853	3010	349	750	84	30	5	266	242	214	.249	.312	.302	78	-82	72	48		.928	-122	S-664/2-99,3-69,O-2	-17.8
■ MERLIN KOPP	Kopp, Merlin Henry "Manny" b: 1/2/1892, Toledo, Ohio d: 5/6/60, Sacramento, Cal. BB/TR, 5'8", 158 lbs. Deb: 8/2/15																						
1915	Was-A	16	32	2	8	0	0	0	0	5	7	.250	.351	.250	79	-1	1			.933	-1	/O-9	-0.2
1918	Phi-A	96	363	60	85	7	7	0	18	42	55	.234	.320	.292	84	-6	22			.972	12	O-96	0.0
1919	Phi-A	75	235	34	53	2	4	1	12	42	43	.226	.348	.281	77	-6	16			.924	-2	O-65	-1.3
Total	3	187	630	96	146	9	11	1	30	89	105	.232	.332	.286	81	-12	39			.953	8	O-170	-1.5
■ JOE KOPPE	Koppe, Joseph (b: Joseph Kopchia) b: 10/19/30, Detroit, Mich. BR/TR, 5'10", 165 lbs. Deb: 8/9/58																						
1958	Mil-N	16	9	3	4	0	0	0	0	1	1	.444	.500	.444	167	1	0	0	0	.833	5	/S-3	0.6
1959	Phi-N	126	422	68	110	18	7	7	28	41	80	.261	.329	.386	88	-7	7	7	-2	.954	5	*S-113,2-11	0.6
1960	Phi-N	58	170	13	29	6	1	1	13	23	47	.171	.273	.235	41	-14	3	2	-0	.956	-12	S-55/3-2	-2.3
1961	Phi-N	6	3	1	0	0	0	0	0	0	0	.000	.000	.000	-99	-1	0	0	0	.800	0	/S-5	-0.1
	LA-A	91	338	46	85	12	2	5	40	45	77	.251	.341	.343	75	-12	3	3	-1	.947	-6	S-88/2-3,3-1	-1.0

YEAR	TM/L	G	AB	R	H	2B	3B	HR	RBI	BB	SO	AVG	OBP	SLG	PRO+	BR/A	SB	CS	SBR	FA	FR	G/POS	TPR
1962	LA-A	128	375	47	85	16	0	4	40	73	84	.227	.356	.301	81	-7	2	1	0	.957	4	*S-118/2-5,3-4	0.8
1963	LA-A	76	143	11	30	4	1	1	12	9	30	.210	.261	.273	53	-9	0	0	0	.962	8	S-19,3-18,2-14,/O-3	0.0
1964	LA-A	54	113	10	29	4	1	0	6	14	16	.257	.339	.310	91	-1	0	0	0	.945	15	S-31,2-13/3-3	1.6
1965	Cal-A	23	33	3	7	1	0	1	2	3	10	.212	.278	.333	75	-1	1	0	0	.979	9	2-10/S-4,3-4	0.9
Total	8	578	1606	202	379	61	12	19	141	209	345	.236	.327	.324	76	-50	16	13	-3	.952	29	S-436/2-56,3-32,O-3	1.1

■ GEORGE KOPSHAW Kopshaw, George Karl b: 7/5/1895, Passaic, N.J. d: 12/26/34, Lynchburg, Va. BR/TR, 5'11.5", 176 lbs. Deb: 8/4/23

YEAR	TM/L	G	AB	R	H	2B	3B	HR	RBI	BB	SO	AVG	OBP	SLG	PRO+	BR/A	SB	CS	SBR	FA	FR	G/POS	TPR
1923	StL-N	2	5	1	1	1	0	0	0	0	1	.200	.200	.400	56	-0	0	0	0	1.000	-1	/C-1	-0.1

■ STEVE KORCHECK Korcheck, Stephen Joseph "Hoss" b: 8/11/32, McClellandtown, Pa. BR/TR, 6'1", 205 lbs. Deb: 9/6/54

YEAR	TM/L	G	AB	R	H	2B	3B	HR	RBI	BB	SO	AVG	OBP	SLG	PRO+	BR/A	SB	CS	SBR	FA	FR	G/POS	TPR
1954	Was-A	2	7	0	1	0	0	0	0	0	2	.143	.143	.143	-23	-1	0	0	0	.857	-1	/C-2	-0.2
1955	Was-A	13	36	3	10	2	0	0	2	0	5	.278	.297	.333	73	-1	0	0	0	1.000	1	C-12	0.0
1958	Was-A	21	51	6	4	2	1	0	1	1	16	.078	.096	.157	-32	-9	0	0	0	.975	0	C-20	-0.9
1959	Was-A	22	51	3	8	2	0	0	4	5	13	.157	.232	.196	19	-6	0	0	0	.974	6	C-22	0.1
Total	4	58	145	12	23	6	1	0	7	6	36	.159	.197	.214	13	-18	0	0	0	.976	7	/C-56	-1.0

■ ART KORES Kores, Arthur Emil "Dutch" b: 7/22/1886, Milwaukee, Wis. d: 3/26/74, Milwaukee, Wis. BR/TR, 5'9", 167 lbs. Deb: 7/24/15

YEAR	TM/L	G	AB	R	H	2B	3B	HR	RBI	BB	SO	AVG	OBP	SLG	PRO+	BR/A	SB	CS	SBR	FA	FR	G/POS	TPR
1915	StL-F	60	201	18	47	9	2	1	22	21	13	.234	.306	.313	71	-11	6			.960	19	3-60	1.2

■ ANDY KOSCO Kosco, Andrew John b: 10/5/41, Youngstown, Ohio BR/TR, 6'3", 207 lbs. Deb: 8/13/65

YEAR	TM/L	G	AB	R	H	2B	3B	HR	RBI	BB	SO	AVG	OBP	SLG	PRO+	BR/A	SB	CS	SBR	FA	FR	G/POS	TPR
1965	Min-A	23	55	3	13	4	0	1	6	1	15	.236	.250	.364	69	-2	0	0	0	1.000	0	O-14/1-2	-0.3
1966	Min-A	57	158	11	35	5	0	2	13	7	31	.222	.255	.291	53	-10	0	1	-1	.986	-1	O-40/1-5	-1.4
1967	Min-A	9	28	4	4	1	0	0	4	2	4	.143	.200	.179	12	-3	0	0	0	.923	-0	/O-7	-0.4
1968	NY-A	131	466	47	112	19	1	15	59	16	71	.240	.270	.382	99	-3	2	2	-1	.960	3	O-95,1-28	-0.9
1969	LA-N	120	424	51	105	13	2	19	74	21	66	.248	.285	.422	103	-1	0	1	-1	.981	-6	*O-109/1-3	-1.5
1970	LA-N	74	224	21	51	12	0	8	27	1	40	.228	.231	.388	66	-12	1	1	-0	.981	-2	O-58/1-1	-1.7
1971	Mil-A	98	264	27	60	6	2	10	39	24	57	.227	.292	.379	90	-4	1	3	-2	.988	-3	O-45,1-29,3-12	-1.3
1972	Cal-A	49	142	15	34	4	2	6	13	5	23	.239	.270	.423	110	1	1	0	0	.985	0	O-36	0.0
	Bos-A	17	47	5	10	2	1	3	6	2	9	.213	.260	.489	113	0	0	0	0	1.000	0	O-12	0.0
	Yr	66	189	20	44	6	3	9	19	7	32	.233	.268	.439	111	1	1	0	0	.988	1	O-48	0.0
1973	*Cin-N	47	118	17	33	7	0	9	21	13	26	.280	.351	.568	159	9	0	0	0	1.000	-5	O-36/1-1	0.2
1974	Cin-N	33	37	3	7	2	0	0	5	7	8	.189	.318	.243	59	-2	0	0	0	.846	-2	/3-8,O-1	-0.4
Total	10	658	1963	204	464	75	8	73	267	99	350	.236	.275	.394	92	-28	5	8	-3	.979	-16	O-453/1-69,3-20	-7.7

■ CLEM KOSHOREK Koshorek, Clement John "Scooter" b: 6/20/25, Royal Oak, Mich. d: 9/8/91, Royal Oak, Mich. BR/TR, 5'4.5", 165 lbs. Deb: 4/15/52

YEAR	TM/L	G	AB	R	H	2B	3B	HR	RBI	BB	SO	AVG	OBP	SLG	PRO+	BR/A	SB	CS	SBR	FA	FR	G/POS	TPR
1952	Pit-N	98	322	27	84	17	0	0	15	26	39	.261	.320	.314	74	-11	4	7	-3	.949	1	S-33,2-27,3-26	-1.0
1953	Pit-N	1	1	0	0	0	0	0	0	0	1	.000	.000	.000	-99	-0	0	0	0	.000	0	H	0.0
Total	2	99	323	27	84	17	0	0	15	26	40	.260	.319	.313	74	-11	4	7	-3	.949	1	/S-33,2-27,3-26	-1.0

■ COREY KOSKIE Koskie, Cordel Leonard b: 6/28/73, Anola, Man., Can. BL/TR, 6'3", 215 lbs. Deb: 9/9/98

YEAR	TM/L	G	AB	R	H	2B	3B	HR	RBI	BB	SO	AVG	OBP	SLG	PRO+	BR/A	SB	CS	SBR	FA	FR	G/POS	TPR
1998	Min-A	11	29	2	4	0	0	1	2	2	10	.138	.194	.241	12	-4	0	0	0	.941	-1	3-10	-0.5

■ KEVIN KOSLOFSKI Koslofski, Kevin Craig b: 9/24/66, Decatur, Ill. BL/TR, 5'8", 165 lbs. Deb: 6/28/92

YEAR	TM/L	G	AB	R	H	2B	3B	HR	RBI	BB	SO	AVG	OBP	SLG	PRO+	BR/A	SB	CS	SBR	FA	FR	G/POS	TPR
1992	KC-A	55	133	20	33	0	2	3	13	12	23	.248	.315	.346	83	-3	2	1	0	.991	-1	O-52	-0.5
1993	KC-A	15	26	4	7	0	0	1	2	4	5	.269	.387	.385	102	0	0	1	-1	1.000	-0	O-13/D-1	-0.1
1994	KC-A	2	4	2	1	0	0	0	0	2	1	.250	.500	.250	97	0	0	0	0	.750	0	/O-2	0.0
1996	Mil-A	25	42	5	9	3	2	0	6	4	12	.214	.298	.381	67	-2	0	0	0	.972	-4	O-22/D-1	-0.6
Total	4	97	205	31	50	3	4	4	21	22	41	.244	.326	.356	83	-5	2	2	-1	.983	-5	/O-89,D-2	-1.2

■ MIKE KOSMAN Kosman, Michael Thomas b: 12/10/17, Hamtramck, Mich. BR/TR, 5'9", 160 lbs. Deb: 4/20/44

YEAR	TM/L	G	AB	R	H	2B	3B	HR	RBI	BB	SO	AVG	OBP	SLG	PRO+	BR/A	SB	CS	SBR	FA	FR	G/POS	TPR
1944	Cin-N	1	0	0	0	0	0	0	0	0	0	—	—	—	—	0	0			.000	0	R	0.0

■ FRED KOSTER Koster, Frederick Charles "Fritz" b: 12/21/05, Louisville, Ky. d: 4/24/79, St.Matthews, Ky. BL/TL, 5'10.5", 165 lbs. Deb: 4/27/31

YEAR	TM/L	G	AB	R	H	2B	3B	HR	RBI	BB	SO	AVG	OBP	SLG	PRO+	BR/A	SB	CS	SBR	FA	FR	G/POS	TPR
1931	Phi-N	76	151	21	34	2	2	0	8	14	21	.225	.291	.265	47	-11	4			.923	-4	O-41	-1.7

■ FRANK KOSTRO Kostro, Frank Jerry b: 8/4/37, Windber, Pa. BR/TR, 6'2", 190 lbs. Deb: 9/2/62

YEAR	TM/L	G	AB	R	H	2B	3B	HR	RBI	BB	SO	AVG	OBP	SLG	PRO+	BR/A	SB	CS	SBR	FA	FR	G/POS	TPR
1962	Det-A	16	41	5	11	3	0	0	3	1	6	.268	.286	.341	66	-2	0	0	0	.967	1	3-11	-0.1
1963	Det-A	31	52	4	12	1	0	0	0	9	13	.231	.344	.250	67	-2	0	0	0	.929	-1	/3-6,1-3,O-3	-0.3
	LA-A	43	99	6	22	2	1	2	10	6	17	.222	.267	.323	68	-4	0	0	0	.960	-2	3-19/1-5,O-3	-0.7
	Yr	74	151	10	34	3	1	2	10	15	30	.225	.295	.298	68	-6	0	0	0	.953	-3	3-25/1-8,O-6	-1.0
1964	Min-A	59	103	10	28	5	0	3	12	4	21	.272	.306	.408	96	-1	0	0	0	.912	-3	3-12/2-7,O-2,1-1	-0.4
1965	Min-A	20	31	2	5	2	0	0	1	4	5	.161	.257	.226	37	-3	0	0	0	.923	-1	/2-7,3-6,O-2	-0.3
1967	Min-A	32	31	4	10	0	0	0	2	3	2	.323	.382	.323	102	0	0	0	0	1.000	-1	/O-3,3-1	-0.1
1968	Min-A	63	108	9	26	4	1	0	9	6	20	.241	.281	.296	71	-4	0	0	0	1.000	-1	O-24/1-5	-0.7
1969	Min-A	2	2	0	0	0	0	0	0	0	1	.000	.000	.000	-98	-1	0	0	0	.000	0	H	-0.1
Total	7	266	467	40	114	17	2	5	37	33	85	.244	.295	.321	74	-16	0	0	0	.926	-8	/3-55,O-37,2-14,1	-2.7

■ MARK KOTSAY Kotsay, Mark Steven b: 12/2/75, Whittier, Cal. BL/TL, 6', 180 lbs. Deb: 7/11/97

YEAR	TM/L	G	AB	R	H	2B	3B	HR	RBI	BB	SO	AVG	OBP	SLG	PRO+	BR/A	SB	CS	SBR	FA	FR	G/POS	TPR
1997	Fla-N	14	52	5	10	1	1	0	4	4	7	.192	.250	.250	33	-5	3	0	1	1.000	2	O-14	-0.2
1998	Fla-N	154	578	72	161	25	7	11	68	34	61	.279	.320	.403	90	-10	10	5	0	.984	22	*O-145/1-3	1.1
Total	2	168	630	77	171	26	8	11	72	38	68	.271	.314	.390	85	-15	13	5	1	.985	24	O-159/1-3	0.9

■ BRIAN KOWITZ Kowitz, Brian Mark b: 8/7/69, Baltimore, Md. BL/TL, 5'10", 180 lbs. Deb: 6/4/95

YEAR	TM/L	G	AB	R	H	2B	3B	HR	RBI	BB	SO	AVG	OBP	SLG	PRO+	BR/A	SB	CS	SBR	FA	FR	G/POS	TPR
1995	Atl-N	10	24	3	4	1	0	0	3	2	5	.167	.259	.208	24	-3	0	1	-1	1.000	-2	/O-8	-0.5

■ ERNIE KOY Koy, Ernest Anyz "Chief" b: 9/17/09, Sealy, Tex. BR/TR, 6', 200 lbs. Deb: 4/19/38

YEAR	TM/L	G	AB	R	H	2B	3B	HR	RBI	BB	SO	AVG	OBP	SLG	PRO+	BR/A	SB	CS	SBR	FA	FR	G/POS	TPR
1938	Bro-N	142	521	78	156	29	13	11	76	38	76	.299	.352	.468	121	14	15			.984	-1	*O-135/3-1	0.8
1939	Bro-N	125	425	57	118	37	5	8	67	39	64	.278	.338	.445	105	2	11			.962	-0	*O-114	-0.2
1940	Bro-N	24	48	9	11	2	1	1	8	3	3	.229	.275	.375	73	-2	1			1.000	-4	O-19	-0.6
	StL-N	93	348	44	108	19	5	8	52	28	59	.310	.368	.463	121	10	12			.970	-3	O-91	0.3
	Yr	117	396	53	119	21	6	9	60	31	62	.301	.357	.452	115	8	13			.973	-6	*O-110	-0.3
1941	StL-N	13	40	5	8	1	0	2	4	1	8	.200	.220	.375	61	-2	0			1.000	-2	O-12	-0.5
	Cin-N	67	204	24	51	11	2	2	27	14	22	.250	.301	.353	84	-5	1			.990	-1	O-49	-1.0
	Yr	80	244	29	59	12	2	4	31	15	30	.242	.288	.357	80	-7	1			.991	-3	O-61	-1.5
1942	Cin-N	3	2	0	0	0	0	0	0	0	2	.000	.000	.000	-99	-0	0			.000	0	H	-0.1
	Phi-N	91	258	21	63	9	3	4	26	14	50	.244	.283	.349	89	-5	0			.981	-9	O-78	-1.8
	Yr	94	260	21	63	9	3	4	26	14	52	.242	.281	.346	87	-5	0			.981	-9	O-78	-1.9
Total	5	558	1846	238	515	108	29	36	260	137	284	.279	.332	.427	107	11	40			.977	-20	O-498/3-1	-3.1

■ AL KOZAR Kozar, Albert Kenneth b: 7/5/21, McKees Rocks, Pa. BR/TR, 5'9.5", 173 lbs. Deb: 4/19/48

YEAR	TM/L	G	AB	R	H	2B	3B	HR	RBI	BB	SO	AVG	OBP	SLG	PRO+	BR/A	SB	CS	SBR	FA	FR	G/POS	TPR
1948	Was-A	150	577	61	144	25	8	1	58	66	52	.250	.327	.326	76	-20	4	2	0	.967	-21	*2-149	-3.1
1949	Was-A	105	350	46	94	15	2	4	31	25	23	.269	.321	.357	81	-11	2	1	0	.977	-7	*2-102	-1.4
1950	Was-A	20	55	7	11	1	0	0	3	5	8	.200	.267	.218	27	-6	0	0	0	.962	-0	2-15	-0.6
	Chi-A	10	10	4	3	0	0	1	2	0	3	.300	.300	.600	129	0	0	0	0	1.000	3	/2-4,3-1	0.3
	Yr	30	65	11	14	1	0	1	5	5	11	.215	.271	.277	42	-6	0	0	0	.968	2	2-19/3-1	-0.3
Total	3	285	992	118	252	41	10	6	94	96	86	.254	.321	.334	76	-37	6	3	0	.971	-26	2-270/3-1	-4.8

■ JOE KRACHER Kracher, Joseph Peter "Jug" b: 11/4/15, Philadelphia, Pa. d: 12/24/81, San Angelo, Tex. BR/TR, 5'11", 185 lbs. Deb: 9/17/39

YEAR	TM/L	G	AB	R	H	2B	3B	HR	RBI	BB	SO	AVG	OBP	SLG	PRO+	BR/A	SB	CS	SBR	FA	FR	G/POS	TPR
1939	Phi-N	5	5	1	1	0	0	0	0	2	1	.200	.429	.200	76	0	0			1.000	-1	/C-2	-0.1

■ CLARENCE KRAFT Kraft, Clarence Otto "Big Boy" b: 6/9/1887, Evansville, Ind. d: 3/26/58, Fort Worth, Tex. BR/TR, 6', 190 lbs. Deb: 5/1/14

YEAR	TM/L	G	AB	R	H	2B	3B	HR	RBI	BB	SO	AVG	OBP	SLG	PRO+	BR/A	SB	CS	SBR	FA	FR	G/POS	TPR
1914	Bos-N	3	3	0	1	0	0	0	0	0	1	.333	.333	.333	99	-0	0			1.000	0	/1-1	0.0

■ ED KRANEPOOL
Kranepool, Edward Emil b: 11/8/44, New York, N.Y. BL/TL, 6'3", 215 lbs. Deb: 9/22/62

YEAR	TM/L	G	AB	R	H	2B	3B	HR	RBI	BB	SO	AVG	OBP	SLG	PRO+	BR/A	SB	CS	SBR	FA	FR	G/POS	TPR
1962	NY-N	3	6	0	1	1	0	0	0	0	1	.167	.167	.333	30	-1	0	0	0	1.000	1	/1-3	0.0
1963	NY-N	86	273	22	57	12	2	2	14	18	50	.209	.258	.289	56	-15	4	2	0	.954	-2	O-55,1-20	-2.3
1964	NY-N	119	420	47	108	19	4	10	45	32	50	.257	.313	.393	100	-1	0	1	-1	.991	3	*1-104/O-6	-0.4
1965	NY-N☆	153	525	44	133	24	4	10	53	39	71	.253	.307	.371	94	-5	1	4	-2	.992	-2	*1-147	-1.8
1966	NY-N	146	464	51	118	15	2	16	57	41	66	.254	.319	.399	100	-0	1	1	-0	.992	5	*1-132,O-11	-0.4
1967	NY-N	141	469	37	126	17	1	10	54	37	51	.269	.323	.373	100	0	0	4	-2	.992	4	*1-139	-0.7
1968	NY-N	127	373	29	86	13	1	3	20	19	39	.231	.272	.295	70	-14	0	3	-2	.994	5	*1-113/O-2	-2.2
1969	*NY-N	112	353	36	84	9	2	11	49	37	32	.238	.310	.368	88	-6	3	2	-0	.993	3	*1-106/O-2	-1.2
1970	NY-N	43	47	2	8	0	0	0	3	5	2	.170	.250	.170	15	-6	0	0	0	1.000	0	/1-8	-0.6
1971	NY-N	122	421	61	118	20	4	14	58	38	33	.280	.341	.447	123	12	0	4	-2	**.998**	-3	*1-108,O-11	-0.3
1972	NY-N	122	327	28	88	15	1	8	34	34	35	.269	.340	.394	111	5	1	0	0	.996	-1	*1-108/O-1	-0.4
1973	*NY-N	100	284	28	68	12	2	1	35	30	28	.239	.312	.306	73	-10	1	0	0	.998	-0	1-51,O-32	-1.5
1974	NY-N	94	217	20	65	11	1	4	24	18	14	.300	.353	.415	116	4	1	0	0	.977	-6	O-33,1-24	-0.4
1975	NY-N	106	325	42	105	16	0	4	43	27	21	.323	.375	.409	123	10	1	1	-0	.997	-0	1-82/O-4	0.4
1976	NY-N	123	415	47	121	17	1	10	49	35	38	.292	.347	.410	121	10	1	0	0	.996	-6	1-86,O-31	-0.2
1977	NY-N	108	281	28	79	17	0	10	40	23	20	.281	.336	.448	113	4	1	4	-2	.984	-1	O-42,1-41	-0.2
1978	NY-N	66	81	7	17	2	0	3	19	8	12	.210	.289	.346	79	-2	0	0	0	1.000	-2	O-12/1-3	-0.5
1979	NY-N	82	155	7	36	5	0	2	17	13	18	.232	.296	.303	66	-7	0	1	-1	1.000	0	1-29/O-8	-1.0
Total	18	1853	5436	536	1418	225	25	118	614	454	581	.261	.319	.377	97	-21	15	27	-12	.994	-2	*1-1304,O-250	-13.7

■ CHARLIE KRAUSE
Krause, Charles b: 10/2/1873, Detroit, Mich. d: 3/30/48, Eloise, Mich. TR , Deb: 7/27/01

YEAR	TM/L	G	AB	R	H	2B	3B	HR	RBI	BB	SO	AVG	OBP	SLG	PRO+	BR/A	SB	CS	SBR	FA	FR	G/POS	TPR
1901	Cin-N	1	4	0	1	0	0	0	0	0		.250	.250	.250	48	-0	0			.000	0	/2-1	0.0

■ DANNY KRAVITZ
Kravitz, Daniel "Dusty" or "Beak" b: 12/21/30, Lopez, Pa. BL/TR, 5'11", 195 lbs. Deb: 4/17/56

YEAR	TM/L	G	AB	R	H	2B	3B	HR	RBI	BB	SO	AVG	OBP	SLG	PRO+	BR/A	SB	CS	SBR	FA	FR	G/POS	TPR
1956	Pit-N	32	68	6	18	2	2	2	10	5	9	.265	.315	.441	103	0	1	1	-0	.944	0	C-26/3-2	0.1
1957	Pit-N	19	41	2	6	1	0	0	4	2	10	.146	.186	.171	-3	-6	0	0	0	1.000	0	C-15	-0.5
1958	Pit-N	45	100	9	24	3	2	1	5	11	10	.240	.315	.340	76	-3	0	0	0	.967	-6	C-37	-0.8
1959	Pit-N	52	162	18	41	9	1	3	21	5	14	.253	.275	.377	72	-7	0	1	-1	.986	-1	C-45	-0.6
1960	Pit-N	8	6	0	0	0	0	0	0	1	2	.000	.143	.000	-57	-1	0	0	0	1.000	-0	/C-1	-0.1
	KC-A	59	175	17	41	7	2	4	14	11	19	.234	.280	.366	73	-7	0	0	0	.971	-4	C-47	-0.8
Total	5	215	552	52	130	22	7	10	54	35	64	.236	.281	.355	70	-25	1	2	-1	.973	-10	C-171/3-2	-2.7

■ FRANK KREEGER
Kreeger, Frank Deb: 7/28/1884

YEAR	TM/L	G	AB	R	H	2B	3B	HR	RBI	BB	SO	AVG	OBP	SLG	PRO+	BR/A	SB	CS	SBR	FA	FR	G/POS	TPR
1884	KC-U	1	3	0	0	0	0	0		0		.000	.000	.000	-99	-1				.000	-1	/O-1,P-1	-0.1

■ MIKE KREEVICH
Kreevich, Michael Andreas b: 6/10/08, Mt.Olive, Ill. d: 4/25/94, Pana, Ill. BR/TR, 5'7.5", 168 lbs. Deb: 9/7/31

YEAR	TM/L	G	AB	R	H	2B	3B	HR	RBI	BB	SO	AVG	OBP	SLG	PRO+	BR/A	SB	CS	SBR	FA	FR	G/POS	TPR
1931	Chi-N	5	12	0	2	0	0	0	0	0	6	.167	.167	.167	-10	-2	1			1.000	-0	/O-4	-0.2
1935	Chi-A	6	23	3	10	2	0	0	2	1	0	.435	.458	.522	149	2	1	1	-0	1.000	-2	/3-6	-0.1
1936	Chi-A	137	550	99	169	32	11	5	69	61	46	.307	.378	.433	96	-3	10	5	0	.964	-2	*O-133	-0.9
1937	Chi-A	144	583	94	176	29	**16**	12	73	43	45	.302	.350	.468	104	2	10	1	2	**.988**	7	*O-138	0.6
1938	Chi-A★	129	489	73	145	26	12	6	73	55	23	.297	.371	.436	99	-1	13	5	1	.975	4	*O-127	0.0
1939	Chi-A	145	541	85	175	30	8	5	77	59	40	.323	.390	.436	108	8	23	10	1	.975	16	*O-139/3-4	1.8
1940	Chi-A	144	582	86	154	27	10	8	55	34	49	.265	.305	.387	77	-21	15	7	0	.982	12	*O-144	-1.6
1941	Chi-A	121	436	44	101	16	8	0	37	35	26	.232	.289	.305	58	-27	17	5	2	**.994**	0	*O-113	-3.1
1942	Phi-A	116	444	57	113	19	1	1	30	47	31	.255	.326	.309	79	-11	7	9	-3	.981	4	*O-107	-1.7
1943	StL-A	60	161	24	41	6	0	0	10	26	13	.255	.358	.292	89	-1	4	1	1	.993	5	O-51	0.2
1944	*StL-A	105	402	55	121	15	6	5	44	27	24	.301	.348	.405	108	4	3	3	-1	.986	-1	*O-100	-0.3
1945	StL-A	84	295	34	70	11	1	2	21	37	27	.237	.322	.302	78	-8	4	1	1	.991	4	O-81	-0.8
	Was-A	45	158	22	44	8	2	1	23	21	9	.278	.363	.373	124	5	7	5	-1	.971	-2	O-40	0.0
	Yr	129	453	56	114	19	3	3	44	58	36	.252	.337	.327	92	-3	11	6	-0	.985	2	*O-121	-0.8
Total	12	1241	4676	676	1321	221	75	45	514	446	339	.283	.346	.391	92	-54	115	53		.982	46	*O-1177/3-10	-6.1

■ CHARLIE KREHMEYER
Krehmeyer, Charles L. b: 7/5/1863, St.Louis, Mo. d: 2/10/26, St.Louis, Mo. BL/TL, 5'11", 179 lbs. Deb: 7/8/1884

YEAR	TM/L	G	AB	R	H	2B	3B	HR	RBI	BB	SO	AVG	OBP	SLG	PRO+	BR/A	SB	CS	SBR	FA	FR	G/POS	TPR
1884	StL-a	21	70	3	16	0	1	0	5	2		.229	.250	.257	64	-3				.619	-5	O-15/C-7,1-1	-0.7
1885	Lou-a	7	31	4	7	1	1	0	5	1		.226	.250	.323	80	-1				.909	-1	/C-4,O-2,1-1	-0.2
	StL-N	1	3	0	0	0	0	0	0	0	2	.000	.000	.000	-99	-1				.429	-2	/C-1	-0.2
Total	2	29	104	7	23	1	2	0	10	3	2	.221	.243	.269	64	-4				.571	-7	/O-17,C-12,1-2	-1.1

■ MICKEY KREITNER
Kreitner, Albert Joseph b: 10/10/22, Nashville, Tenn. BR/TR, 6'3", 190 lbs. Deb: 9/28/43

YEAR	TM/L	G	AB	R	H	2B	3B	HR	RBI	BB	SO	AVG	OBP	SLG	PRO+	BR/A	SB	CS	SBR	FA	FR	G/POS	TPR
1943	Chi-N	3	8	0	3	0	0	0	2	1	2	.375	.444	.375	140	0	0			1.000	-1	/C-3	0.0
1944	Chi-N	39	85	3	13	2	0	0	1	8	16	.153	.234	.176	17	-9	0			.992	-1	C-39	-0.9
Total	2	42	93	3	16	2	0	0	3	9	18	.172	.252	.194	27	-9	0			.992	-1	/C-42	-0.9

■ RALPH KREITZ
Kreitz, Ralph Wesley "Red" b: 11/13/1885, Plum Creek, Neb. d: 7/20/41, Portland, Ore. BR/TR, 5'9.5", 175 lbs. Deb: 8/1/11

YEAR	TM/L	G	AB	R	H	2B	3B	HR	RBI	BB	SO	AVG	OBP	SLG	PRO+	BR/A	SB	CS	SBR	FA	FR	G/POS	TPR
1911	Chi-A	7	17	0	4	1	0	0	0	2		.235	.316	.294	73	-1	0			1.000	-3	/C-7	-0.3

■ JIMMY KREMERS
Kremers, James Edward b: 10/8/65, Little Rock, Ark. BL/TR, 6'3", 205 lbs. Deb: 6/5/90

YEAR	TM/L	G	AB	R	H	2B	3B	HR	RBI	BB	SO	AVG	OBP	SLG	PRO+	BR/A	SB	CS	SBR	FA	FR	G/POS	TPR
1990	Atl-N	29	73	7	8	1	1	1	2	6	27	.110	.177	.192	1	-10	0	0	0	.992	-3	C-27	-1.3

■ WAYNE KRENCHICKI
Krenchicki, Wayne Richard b: 9/17/54, Trenton, N.J. BL/TR, 6'1", 180 lbs. Deb: 6/15/79

YEAR	TM/L	G	AB	R	H	2B	3B	HR	RBI	BB	SO	AVG	OBP	SLG	PRO+	BR/A	SB	CS	SBR	FA	FR	G/POS	TPR
1979	Bal-A	16	21	1	4	1	0	0	0	0	0	.190	.190	.238	15	-2	0	0	0	.875	1	/3-7,2-6	-0.1
1980	Bal-A	9	14	1	2	0	0	0	0	1	3	.143	.200	.143	-4	-2	0	0	0	1.000	0	/S-6,2-1,D-1	-0.2
1981	Bal-A	33	56	7	12	4	0	0	6	4	9	.214	.267	.286	59	-3	0	0	0	.964	4	S-16/2-7,3-6,D-1	0.3
1982	Cin-N	94	187	19	53	6	1	2	21	13	23	.283	.330	.358	91	-2	5	3	-0	.955	7	3-70/2-9	0.4
1983	Cin-N	51	77	6	21	2	0	0	11	8	4	.273	.349	.299	78	-2	0	0	0	.980	1	3-39/2-1	-0.1
	Det-A	59	133	18	37	7	0	1	16	11	27	.278	.338	.353	93	-1	0	0	0	.934	-8	3-48/2-6,S-6,1-3	-0.9
1984	Cin-N	97	181	18	54	9	2	6	22	19	23	.298	.365	.470	127	6	0	1	-1	.967	3	3-62/1-3,2-3	0.9
1985	Cin-N	90	173	16	47	9	0	4	25	28	20	.272	.373	.393	109	3	0	0	0	.967	4	3-52/2-3	0.7
1986	Mon-N	101	221	21	53	6	2	2	23	22	32	.240	.309	.312	72	-8	2	4	-2	.991	1	1-41,3-24/2-1,O-1	-1.2
Total	8	550	1063	107	283	44	5	15	124	106	141	.266	.334	.359	92	-11	7	8	-3	.955	14	3-308/1-47,2SDO	-0.2

■ CHUCK KRESS
Kress, Charles Steven b: 12/9/21, Philadelphia, Pa. BL/TL, 6', 190 lbs. Deb: 4/16/47

YEAR	TM/L	G	AB	R	H	2B	3B	HR	RBI	BB	SO	AVG	OBP	SLG	PRO+	BR/A	SB	CS	SBR	FA	FR	G/POS	TPR
1947	Cin-N	11	27	4	4	0	0	0	0	6	4	.148	.303	.148	23	-3	0			.983	1	/1-8	-0.2
1949	Cin-N	27	29	3	6	3	0	0	3	3	5	.207	.281	.310	58	-2	0			.974	0	1-16	-0.2
	Chi-A	97	353	45	98	17	6	1	44	39	44	.278	.349	.368	93	-4	6	7	-2	.994	-0	1-95	-0.7
1950	Chi-A	3	8	0	0	0	0	0	0	0	2	.000	.000	.000	-99	-2	0	0	0	1.000	-0	/1-2	-0.2
1954	Det-A	24	37	4	7	0	1	0	3	1	4	.189	.211	.243	24	-4	0	1	-1	.971	-0	/1-7,O-1	-0.5
	Bro-N	13	12	1	1	0	0	0	2	0	0	.083	.083	.083	-55	-3	0	0	0	.500	-0	/1-1	-0.3
Total	4	175	466	57	116	20	7	1	52	49	59	.249	.320	.328	74	-18	6	8		.990	0	1-129/O-1	-2.1

■ RED KRESS
Kress, Ralph b: 1/2/07, Columbia, Cal. d: 11/29/62, Los Angeles, Cal. BR/TR, 5'11.5", 165 lbs. Deb: 9/24/27 C

YEAR	TM/L	G	AB	R	H	2B	3B	HR	RBI	BB	SO	AVG	OBP	SLG	PRO+	BR/A	SB	CS	SBR	FA	FR	G/POS	TPR
1927	StL-A	7	23	3	7	2	1	1	3	3	3	.304	.385	.609	150	2	0	0	0	.974	1	/S-7	0.3
1928	StL-A	150	560	78	153	26	10	3	81	48	70	.273	.332	.371	82	-15	5	4	-1	.929	-17	*S-150	-1.4
1929	StL-A	147	557	82	170	38	4	9	107	52	54	.305	.366	.436	102	1	5	8	-3	**.946**	-2	*S-146	1.3
1930	StL-A	154	614	94	192	43	8	16	112	50	56	.313	.366	.487	110	9	3	12	-6	.938	-12	*S-123,3-31	0.6
1931	StL-A	150	605	87	188	46	8	16	114	46	48	.311	.360	.493	118	14	3	16	-9	.936	-11	3-84,O-40,S-38,1-10	-0.2
1932	StL-A	14	52	2	9	0	1	2	9	4	6	.173	.232	.327	41	-5	1	1	-0	.909	2	3-14	-0.2
	Chi-A	135	515	83	147	42	4	9	57	47	36	.285	.346	.435	108	5	6	3	0	.956	11	O-64,S-53,3-19,/1-1	1.6
	Yr	149	567	85	156	42	5	11	66	51	42	.275	.336	.425	101	-1	7	4	-0	.956	13	O-64,S-53,3-33,/1-1	1.4
1933	Chi-A	129	467	47	116	20	5	10	78	37	40	.248	.304	.377	83	-13	4	4	-1	.978	-4	*1-111/O-8	-2.8

YEAR	TM/L	G	AB	R	H	2B	3B	HR	RBI	BB	SO	AVG	OBP	SLG	PRO+	BR/A	SB	CS	SBR	FA	FR	G/POS	TPR
1934	Chi-A	8	14	3	4	0	0	0	1	3	3	.286	.412	.286	80	-0	0	0	0	1.000	-4	/2-3	-0.4
	Was-A	56	171	18	39	4	3	4	24	17	19	.228	.298	.357	71	-8	3	0	1	.993	-2	1-30,O-10/2-6,S3	-1.1
	Yr	64	185	21	43	4	3	4	25	20	22	.232	.307	.351	72	-8	3	0	1	.993	-6	1-30,O-10/2-9,S3	-1.5
1935	Was-A	84	252	32	75	13	4	2	42	25	16	.298	.361	.405	101	0	3	3	-1	.964	17	S-53/1-5,P-3,O-2,2	1.7
1936	Was-A	109	391	51	111	20	6	8	51	39	25	.284	.349	.427	96	-4	6	0	2	.927	9	S-64,2-33/1-5	1.2
1938	StL-A	150	566	74	171	33	3	7	79	69	47	.302	.378	.408	97	-1	5	4	-1	**.965**	-15	*S-150	-0.5
1939	StL-A	13	43	5	12	1	0	0	8	6	2	.279	.367	.302	72	-2	1	0	0	.933	-3	S-13	-0.3
	Det-A	51	157	19	38	7	0	1	22	17	16	.242	.316	.306	55	-10	2	1	0	.959	2	S-25,2-16/3-4	-0.5
	Yr	64	200	24	50	8	0	1	30	23	18	.250	.327	.305	59	-12	3	1	0	.951	-1	S-38,2-16/3-4	-0.8
1940	Det-A	33	99	13	22	3	1	1	11	10	12	.222	.294	.303	50	-7	0	0	0	.924	9	3-17,S-12	0.2
1946	NY-N	1	1	0	0	0	0	0	0	1	0	.000	.500	.000	48	0	0	0	0	1.000	1	/P-1	0.0
Total	14	1391	5087	691	1454	298	58	89	799	474	453	.286	.347	.420	96	-35	47	56		.944	-16	S-835,3-170,1O/2P	-0.5

■ CHAD KREUTER

Kreuter, Chadden Michael b: 8/26/64, Greenbrae, Cal. BB/TR, 6'2", 195 lbs. Deb: 9/14/88

YEAR	TM/L	G	AB	R	H	2B	3B	HR	RBI	BB	SO	AVG	OBP	SLG	PRO+	BR/A	SB	CS	SBR	FA	FR	G/POS	TPR
1988	Tex-A	16	51	3	14	2	1	1	5	7	13	.275	.362	.412	113	1	0	0	0	.990	2	C-16	0.4
1989	Tex-A	87	158	16	24	3	0	5	9	27	40	.152	.276	.266	52	-10	0	1	-1	.992	12	C-85	0.4
1990	Tex-A	22	22	2	1	1	0	0	2	8	9	.045	.300	.091	14	-2	0	0	0	.977	-1	C-20/D-1	-0.3
1991	Tex-A	3	4	0	0	0	0	0	0	0	1	.000	.000	.000	-99	-1	0	0	0	1.000	0	/C-1	-0.1
1992	Det-A	67	190	22	48	9	0	2	16	20	38	.253	.324	.332	83	-4	0	1	-1	.983	5	C-62/D-1	0.3
1993	Det-A	119	374	59	107	23	3	15	51	49	92	.286	.373	.484	129	16	2	1	0	.988	3	*C-112/1-1,D-2	2.3
1994	Det-A	65	170	17	38	8	0	1	19	28	36	.224	.333	.288	62	-9	0	1	-1	.987	-2	C-64/1-1,O-1	-0.8
1995	Sea-A	26	75	12	17	5	0	1	8	5	22	.227	.293	.333	62	-4	0	0	0	.976	0	C-23	-0.2
1996	Chi-A	46	114	14	25	8	0	3	18	13	29	.219	.310	.368	74	-5	0	0	0	.990	-5	C-38/1-2	-0.7
1997	Chi-A	19	37	6	8	2	1	1	3	8	9	.216	.356	.405	102	0	0	1	-1	.984	-2	C-13/1-2	-0.2
	Ana-A	70	218	19	51	7	1	4	18	21	57	.234	.301	.330	65	-11	0	2	-1	.994	8	C-67/D-2	-0.1
	Yr	89	255	25	59	9	2	5	21	29	66	.231	.310	.341	70	-11	0	3	-2	.992	5	C-80/1-2,D-2	-0.3
1998	Chi-A	93	245	26	62	9	1	2	33	32	45	.253	.346	.322	77	-7	1	0	0	.985	-10	C-91	-1.1
	Ana-A	3	7	1	1	1	0	0	0	1	4	.143	.250	.286	39	-1	0	0	0	.882	-0	/C-3	-0.1
	Yr	96	252	27	63	10	1	2	33	33	49	.250	.344	.321	76	-8	1	0	0	.981	-10	C-94	-1.2
Total	11	636	1665	197	396	78	7	35	182	219	395	.238	.330	.356	83	-37	3	7	-3	.987	8	C-595/1-6,D-6,O-1	-0.2

■ PAUL KRICHELL

Krichell, Paul Bernard b: 12/19/1882, New York, N.Y. d: 6/4/57, Bronx, N.Y. BR/TR, 5'7", 150 lbs. Deb: 5/12/11

YEAR	TM/L	G	AB	R	H	2B	3B	HR	RBI	BB	SO	AVG	OBP	SLG	PRO+	BR/A	SB	CS	SBR	FA	FR	G/POS	TPR
1911	StL-A	28	82	6	19	3	0	0	8	4		.232	.276	.268	54	-5	2			.943	-2	C-25	-0.4
1912	StL-A	59	161	19	35	6	0	0	8	19		.217	.304	.255	62	-7	2			.959	-1	C-59	-0.3
Total	2	87	243	25	54	9	0	0	16	23		.222	.295	.259	60	-12	4			.955	-3	/C-84	-0.7

■ BILL KRIEG

Krieg, William Frederick b: 1/29/1859, Petersburg, Ill. d: 3/25/30, Chillicothe, Ill. BR/TR, 5'8", 180 lbs. Deb: 4/20/1884

YEAR	TM/L	G	AB	R	H	2B	3B	HR	RBI	BB	SO	AVG	OBP	SLG	PRO+	BR/A	SB	CS	SBR	FA	FR	G/POS	TPR
1884	CP-U	71	279	35	69	15	4	0		11		.247	.276	.330	83	-14				.932	15	C-53,O-20/S-1,1-1	0.4
1885	Chi-N	1	3	0	0	0	0	0	0	0	2	.000	.000	.000	-88	-1				.800	2	/O-1	0.1
	Bro-a	17	60	7	9	4	0	1	5	2		.150	.177	.267	39	-4				.910	-4	C-12/1-5	-0.7
1886	Was-N	27	98	11	25	6	3	1	15	3	12	.255	.277	.408	113	1	2			.975	-1	1-27	-0.3
1887	Was-N	25	95	9	24	4	1	2	17	7	5	.253	.311	.379	95	-1	2			.973	-3	1-16/O-9	-0.4
Total	4	141	535	62	127	29	8	4	37	23	19	.237	.270	.344	85	-18	4			.929	9	/C-65,1-49,O-30,S-1	-0.9

■ JOHN KRONER

Kroner, John Harold b: 11/13/08, St.Louis, Mo. d: 8/26/68, St.Louis, Mo. BR/TR, 6', 185 lbs. Deb: 9/29/35

YEAR	TM/L	G	AB	R	H	2B	3B	HR	RBI	BB	SO	AVG	OBP	SLG	PRO+	BR/A	SB	CS	SBR	FA	FR	G/POS	TPR
1935	Bos-A	2	4	1	1	0	0	0	0	1	1	.250	.400	.250	67	-0	0	0	0	1.000	-1	/3-2	-0.1
1936	Bos-A	84	298	40	87	17	8	4	62	26	24	.292	.349	.443	89	-6	2	3	-1	.964	-2	2-38,3-28,S-18,/O-1	-0.4
1937	Cle-A	86	283	29	67	14	1	2	26	22	25	.237	.292	.314	52	-21	1	1	-0	.969	-3	2-64,3-11	-1.9
1938	Cle-A	51	117	13	29	16	0	1	17	19	6	.248	.353	.410	92	-1	0	1	-1	.974	12	2-31/1-7,3-3,S-1	1.0
Total	4	223	702	83	184	47	9	7	105	68	56	.262	.327	.385	75	-29	3	5	-2	.968	6	2-133/3-44,S-19,1O	-1.4

■ MIKE KRSNICH

Krsnich, Michael b: 9/24/31, W.Allis, Wis. BR/TR, 6'1", 190 lbs. Deb: 4/23/60 F

YEAR	TM/L	G	AB	R	H	2B	3B	HR	RBI	BB	SO	AVG	OBP	SLG	PRO+	BR/A	SB	CS	SBR	FA	FR	G/POS	TPR
1960	Mil-N	4	9	0	3	1	0	0	2	0	0	.333	.333	.444	120	0	0	0	0	1.000	-0	/O-3	0.0
1962	Mil-N	11	12	0	1	1	0	0	2	0	4	.083	.083	.167	-36	-2	0	0	0	1.000	-0	/O-3,1-1,3-1	-0.3
Total	2	15	21	0	4	2	0	0	4	0	4	.190	.190	.286	28	-2	0	0	0	1.000	-0	/O-6,3-1,1-1	-0.3

■ ROCKY KRSNICH

Krsnich, Rocco Peter b: 8/5/27, W.Allis, Wis. BR/TR, 6'1", 174 lbs. Deb: 9/13/49 F

YEAR	TM/L	G	AB	R	H	2B	3B	HR	RBI	BB	SO	AVG	OBP	SLG	PRO+	BR/A	SB	CS	SBR	FA	FR	G/POS	TPR
1949	Chi-A	16	55	7	12	3	1	1	9	6	4	.218	.295	.364	76	-2	0	1	-1	.935	4	3-16	0.0
1952	Chi-A	40	91	11	21	7	2	1	15	12	9	.231	.327	.385	97	-0	0	0	0	.959	11	3-37	1.0
1953	Chi-A	64	129	9	26	8	0	1	14	12	11	.202	.270	.287	49	-9	0	2	-1	.929	9	3-57	-0.2
Total	3	120	275	27	59	18	3	3	38	30	24	.215	.294	.335	70	-12	0	3	-2	.942	23	3-110	0.8

■ OTTO KRUEGER

Krueger, Arthur William "Oom Paul" b: 9/17/1876, Chicago, Ill. d: 2/20/61, St.Louis, Mo. BR/TR, 5'7", 165 lbs. Deb: 9/16/1899

YEAR	TM/L	G	AB	R	H	2B	3B	HR	RBI	BB	SO	AVG	OBP	SLG	PRO+	BR/A	SB	CS	SBR	FA	FR	G/POS	TPR
1899	Cle-N	13	44	4	10	1	0	0	2	8		.227	.358	.250	73	-1	1			.763	-2	/3-9,S-2,2-2	-0.3
1900	StL-N	12	35	8	14	3	2	1	3	10		.400	.543	.686	240	8	0			.852	-6	2-12	0.2
1901	StL-N	142	520	77	143	16	12	2	79	50		.275	.353	.363	114	11	19			.881	-9	*3-142	0.3
1902	StL-N	128	467	55	124	7	8	0	46	29		.266	.313	.315	97	-2	14			.897	0	*S-107,3-18	0.6
1903	Pit-N	80	256	42	63	6	8	1	28	21		.246	.323	.344	87	-4	5			.884	-5	S-29,O-28,3-13,/2-3	-0.9
1904	Pit-N	86	268	34	52	6	2	1	26	29		.194	.282	.243	61	-12	8			.905	-5	O-33,S-32,3-10	-1.9
1905	Phi-N	46	114	10	21	1	1	0	12	13		.184	.273	.211	47	-7	1			.930	-9	S-23/O-6,3-1	-1.7
Total	7	507	1704	230	427	40	33	5	196	160		.251	.326	.322	94	-7	48			.902	-36	S-193,3-193/O-67,2	-3.7

■ ERNIE KRUEGER

Krueger, Ernest George b: 12/27/1890, Chicago, Ill. d: 4/22/76, Waukegan, Ill. BR/TR, 5'10.5", 185 lbs. Deb: 8/4/13

YEAR	TM/L	G	AB	R	H	2B	3B	HR	RBI	BB	SO	AVG	OBP	SLG	PRO+	BR/A	SB	CS	SBR	FA	FR	G/POS	TPR
1913	Cle-A	5	6	0	0	0	0	0	0	0	2	.000	.000	.000	-97	-1	0			1.000	-0	/C-4	-0.2
1915	NY-A	10	29	3	5	1	0	0	0	0	5	.172	.200	.207	22	-3	0	1	-1	.905	-4	/C-8	-0.7
1917	NY-N	8	10	0	0	0	0	0	0	0	4	.000	.000	.000	-99	-2	0			.857	-2	/C-5	-0.5
	Bro-N	31	81	10	22	2	2	1	6	5	7	.272	.330	.383	115	1	1			.979	1	C-23	0.5
	Yr	39	91	10	22	2	2	1	6	5	11	.242	.296	.341	94	-1	1			.973	-1	C-28	0.0
1918	Bro-N	30	87	4	25	4	2	0	7	4	9	.287	.319	.379	113	1	2			.986	6	C-23	0.9
1919	Bro-N	80	226	24	56	7	4	5	36	19	25	.248	.312	.381	105	1	4			.963	5	C-66	1.4
1920	*Bro-N	52	146	21	42	4	2	1	17	16	13	.288	.358	.363	104	1	2	0	1	.959	-4	C-46	0.1
1921	Bro-N	65	163	18	43	11	4	3	20	14	12	.264	.322	.436	95	-1	2	2	-1	.969	-2	C-52	-0.1
1925	Cin-N	37	88	7	27	4	0	1	7	6	8	.307	.351	.386	90	-1	1	2	-1	.946	-4	C-30	-0.4
Total	8	318	836	87	220	33	14	11	93	64	85	.263	.319	.376	97	-4	12	5		.964	-3	C-257	1.0

■ CHRIS KRUG

Krug, Everett Ben b: 12/25/39, Los Angeles, Cal. BR/TR, 6'4", 200 lbs. Deb: 5/30/65 C

YEAR	TM/L	G	AB	R	H	2B	3B	HR	RBI	BB	SO	AVG	OBP	SLG	PRO+	BR/A	SB	CS	SBR	FA	FR	G/POS	TPR
1965	Chi-N	60	169	16	34	5	0	5	24	13	52	.201	.262	.320	61	-9	0	1	-1	.980	1	C-58	-0.6
1966	Chi-N	11	28	1	6	1	0	0	1	1	8	.214	.241	.250	36	-2	0	0	0	1.000	3	C-10	0.1
1969	SD-N	8	17	0	1	0	0	0	0	1	6	.059	.111	.059	-53	-3	0	0	0	.938	-1	/C-7	-0.4
Total	3	79	214	17	41	6	0	5	25	15	66	.192	.248	.290	50	-15	0	1	-1	.980	3	/C-75	-0.9

■ GENE KRUG

Krug, Gary Eugene b: 2/12/55, Garden City, Kan. BL/TL, 6'4", 225 lbs. Deb: 4/29/81

YEAR	TM/L	G	AB	R	H	2B	3B	HR	RBI	BB	SO	AVG	OBP	SLG	PRO+	BR/A	SB	CS	SBR	FA	FR	G/POS	TPR
1981	Chi-N	7	5	0	2	0	0	0	0	1	1	.400	.500	.400	151	0	0	0	0	.000	0	/H	0.0

■ HENRY KRUG

Krug, Henry Charles b: 12/4/1876, San Francisco, Cal. d: 1/14/08, San Francisco, Cal BR/TR, Deb: 7/26/02

YEAR	TM/L	G	AB	R	H	2B	3B	HR	RBI	BB	SO	AVG	OBP	SLG	PRO+	BR/A	SB	CS	SBR	FA	FR	G/POS	TPR
1902	Phi-N	53	198	20	45	3	3	0	14	7		.227	.261	.273	65	-9	2			.947	-7	O-28,2-13/S-9,3-6	-1.7

■ MARTY KRUG

Krug, Martin John b: 9/10/1888, Koblenz, Germany d: 6/27/66, Glendale, Cal. BR/TR, 5'9", 165 lbs. Deb: 5/29/12

YEAR	TM/L	G	AB	R	H	2B	3B	HR	RBI	BB	SO	AVG	OBP	SLG	PRO+	BR/A	SB	CS	SBR	FA	FR	G/POS	TPR
1912	Bos-A	24	39	6	12	2	1	0	7	5		.308	.386	.410	122	1	2			.895	-2	/S-13,2-4	0.0
1922	Chi-N	127	450	67	124	23	4	4	60	43	43	.276	.343	.371	82	-11	7	9	-3	.937	-6	*3-104,2-23/S-1	-1.1
Total	2	151	489	73	136	25	5	4	67	48	43	.278	.346	.374	85	-10	9	9		.910	-8	3-104/2-27,S-14	-1.1

YEAR	TM/L	G	AB	R	H	2B	3B	HR	RBI	BB	SO	AVG	OBP	SLG	PRO+	BR/A	SB	CS	SBR	FA	FR	G/POS	TPR
■ **ART KRUGER** Kruger, Arthur T. b: 3/16/1881, San Antonio, Tex. d: 11/28/49, Hondo, Cal. BR/TR, 6′, 185 lbs. Deb: 4/11/07																							
1907	Cin-N	100	317	25	74	10	9	0	28	18		.233	.285	.322	87	-6	10			.972	0	O-96	-1.0
1910	Cle-A	47	168	14	26	4	2	0	10	15		.155	.237	.202	37	-12	10			.947	2	O-47	-1.4
	Bos-N	1	1	0	0	0	0	0	0	0	0	.000	.000	.000	-96	-0	0			.000	0	H	0.0
	Cle-A	15	55	5	12	2	1	0	4	5		.218	.295	.291	82	-1	2			.974	2	O-15	0.0
1914	KC-F	122	441	45	114	24	7	4	47	23	59	.259	.297	.372	85	-18	11			.963	-7	*O-120	-3.2
1915	KC-F	80	240	24	57	9	2	2	26	12	29	.237	.277	.317	70	-14	5			.984	0	O-66	-1.9
Total	4	365	1222	113	283	49	21	6	115	73	88	.232	.281	.321	76	-52	38			.968	-2	O-344	-7.5
■ **JOHN KRUK** Kruk, John Martin b: 2/9/61, Charleston, W.Va. BL/TL, 5′10″, 204 lbs. Deb: 4/7/86																							
1986	SD-N	122	278	33	86	16	2	4	38	45	58	.309	.406	.424	132	14	2	4	-2	.981	-5	O-74/1-9	0.5
1987	SD-N	138	447	72	140	14	2	20	91	73	93	.313	.410	.488	142	29	18	10	-1	.996	3	*1-101,O-29	2.3
1988	SD-N	120	378	54	91	17	1	9	44	80	68	.241	.373	.362	114	10	5	3	-0	.995	-2	1-63,O-55	0.2
1989	SD-N	31	76	7	14	0	0	3	6	17	14	.184	.333	.303	83	-1	0	0	0	.962	1	O-27	0.0
	Phi-N	81	281	46	93	13	6	5	38	27	39	.331	.390	.473	146	17	3	0	1	.983	-4	O-72/1-7	1.2
	Yr	112	357	53	107	13	6	8	44	44	53	.300	.377	.437	132	15	3	0	1	.977	-3	O-99/1-7	1.2
1990	Phi-N	142	443	52	129	25	8	7	67	69	70	.291	.387	.431	125	17	10	5	0	.986	-5	O-87,1-61	0.7
1991	Phi-N☆	152	538	84	158	27	6	21	92	67	100	.294	.373	.483	141	29	7	0	2	.997	-1	*1-102,O-52	2.4
1992	Phi-N★	144	507	86	164	30	4	10	70	92	88	.323	.428	.458	151	39	3	5	-2	.993	-12	*1-121,O-35	1.8
1993	*Phi-N★	150	535	100	169	33	5	14	85	111	87	.316	.433	.475	145	40	6	2	1	.993	-11	*1-144	1.7
1994	Phi-N	75	255	35	77	17	0	5	38	42	51	.302	.401	.427	113	7	4	1	1	.995	-1	1-69	0.0
1995	Chi-A	45	159	13	49	7	0	2	23	26	33	.308	.405	.390	113	4	0	1	-1	.909	-1	D-42/1-1	0.0
Total	10	1200	3897	582	1170	199	34	100	592	649	701	.300	.400	.446	134	205	58	31	-1	.995	-37	1-678,O-431/D-42	10.8
■ **DICK KRYHOSKI** Kryhoski, Richard David b: 3/24/25, Leonia, N.J. BL/TL, 6′2″, 200 lbs. Deb: 4/19/49																							
1949	NY-A	54	177	18	52	10	3	1	27	9	17	.294	.335	.401	94	-2	2	4	-2	.983	-1	1-51	-0.5
1950	Det-A	53	169	20	37	10	0	4	19	8	11	.219	.258	.349	53	-13	0	1	-1	.991	-0	1-47	-1.4
1951	Det-A	119	421	58	121	19	4	12	57	28	29	.287	.335	.437	107	2	1	2	-1	.991	3	*1-112	-0.1
1952	StL-A	111	342	38	83	13	1	11	42	23	42	.243	.296	.383	86	-8	2	0	1	.989	-5	1-86	-1.6
1953	StL-A	104	338	35	94	18	4	16	50	26	33	.278	.333	.497	119	7	0	5	-3	.992	5	1-88	0.6
1954	Bal-A	100	300	32	78	13	2	1	34	19	24	.260	.308	.327	80	-9	0	0	0	.992	3	1-69	-1.0
1955	KC-A	28	47	2	10	2	0	0	2	6	7	.213	.302	.255	50	-3	0	1	-1	.988	0	1-14	-0.4
Total	7	569	1794	203	475	85	14	45	231	119	163	.265	.315	.403	93	-26	5	13	-6	.990	5	1-467	-4.4
■ **TONY KUBEK** Kubek, Anthony Christopher b: 10/12/36, Milwaukee, Wis. BL/TR, 6′3″, 191 lbs. Deb: 4/20/57																							
1957	*NY-A	127	431	56	128	21	3	3	39	24	48	.297	.338	.381	98	-2	6	6	-2	.938	1	O-50,S-41,3-38,/2-1	-0.2
1958	*NY-A☆	138	559	66	148	21	1	2	48	25	57	.265	.297	.317	72	-22	5	4	-1	.961	20	*S-134/O-3,1-1,2-1	0.9
1959	NY-A★	132	512	67	143	25	7	6	51	24	46	.279	.314	.391	95	-5	3	3	-1	.968	-1	S-67,O-53,3-17,/2-1	-0.3
1960	*NY-A	147	568	77	155	25	3	14	62	31	42	.273	.314	.401	98	-4	3	0	1	.968	-4	*S-136,O-29	0.3
1961	*NY-A★	153	617	84	170	38	6	8	46	27	60	.276	.307	.395	91	-10	1	3	-2	.959	13	*S-145	1.3
1962	*NY-A	45	169	28	53	6	1	4	17	12	17	.314	.359	.432	115	3	2	1	0	.954	5	S-35/O-6	1.2
1963	*NY-A	135	557	72	143	21	3	7	44	28	68	.257	.295	.343	79	-16	4	2	0	.980	10	*S-132/O-1	0.3
1964	NY-A	106	415	46	95	16	3	8	31	26	55	.229	.276	.340	69	-18	4	1	1	.978	4	S-99	-0.6
1965	NY-A	109	339	26	74	5	3	5	35	20	48	.218	.262	.295	58	-19	1	3	-2	.964	-10	S-93/O-3,1-1	-2.6
Total	9	1092	4167	522	1109	178	30	57	373	217	441	.266	.305	.364	85	-92	29	23	-5	.967	39	S-882,O-145/321	0.3
■ **TED KUBIAK** Kubiak, Theodore Rodger b: 5/12/42, New Brunswick, N.J. BB/TR, 6′, 175 lbs. Deb: 4/14/67																							
1967	KC-A	53	102	6	16	2	1	0	5	12	20	.157	.246	.196	33	-8	0	0	0	.984	-3	S-20,2-10/3-5	-1.1
1968	Oak-A	48	120	10	30	5	2	0	8	8	18	.250	.308	.325	96	-1	1	1	-0	.929	-3	2-24,S-12	-0.2
1969	Oak-A	92	305	38	76	9	1	2	27	25	35	.249	.308	.305	75	-10	2	0	1	.976	-0	S-42,2-33	-0.3
1970	Mil-A	158	540	63	136	9	6	4	41	72	51	.252	.340	.313	81	-12	4	9	-4	.989	-17	2-91,S-73	-1.9
1971	Mil-A	89	260	26	59	6	5	3	17	41	31	.227	.332	.323	87	-3	0	5	-3	.971	-3	2-48,S-39	-0.1
	StL-N	32	72	8	18	3	2	1	10	11	12	.250	.349	.389	105	1	1	0	0	.959	-4	S-17,2-14	-0.1
1972	Tex-A	46	116	5	26	3	0	0	7	12	12	.224	.302	.250	69	-4	0	1	-1	.990	-3	2-25,S-15/3-1	-0.6
	*Oak-A	51	94	14	17	4	1	0	8	9	11	.181	.252	.245	51	-6	0	0	0	.988	2	2-49/3-1	-0.2
	Yr	97	210	19	43	7	1	0	15	21	23	.205	.280	.248	61	-10	0	1	-1	.989	-1	2-74,S-15/3-2	-0.8
1973	*Oak-A	106	182	15	40	6	1	3	17	12	19	.220	.268	.313	67	-9	1	1	-0	.973	6	2-83,S-26/3-2	0.1
1974	Oak-A	99	220	22	46	3	0	0	18	18	15	.209	.269	.223	46	-15	1	1	-0	.995	-9	2-71,S-19,3-14,/D-2	-2.2
1975	Oak-A	20	28	2	7	1	0	0	4	2	2	.250	.300	.286	68	-1	0	0	0	1.000	2	/S-7,3-7,2-6	0.2
	SD-N	87	196	13	44	5	0	0	14	24	18	.224	.309	.250	60	-10	3	1	0	.954	1	3-64,2-11/1-1	-0.9
1976	SD-N	96	212	16	50	5	2	0	26	25	28	.236	.316	.278	76	-6	0	3	-2	.971	-9	3-27,2-25/S-6,1-1	-1.7
Total	10	977	2447	238	565	61	21	13	202	271	272	.231	.309	.289	73	-85	13	22	-9	.981	-39	2-490,S-276,3/1D	-9.0
■ **JACK KUBISZYN** Kubiszyn, John Henry b: 12/19/36, Buffalo, N.Y. BR/TR, 5′11″, 170 lbs. Deb: 4/23/61																							
1961	Cle-A	25	42	4	9	0	0	0	0	2	5	.214	.250	.214	26	-4	0	0	0	1.000	3	/3-8,S-7,2-2	-0.1
1962	Cle-A	25	59	3	10	2	0	1	2	5	7	.169	.234	.254	32	-6	0	0	0	.964	2	S-18/3-1	-0.2
Total	2	50	101	7	19	2	0	1	2	7	12	.188	.241	.238	30	-10	0	0	0	.969	5	/S-25,3-9,2-2	-0.3
■ **GIL KUBSKI** Kubski, Gilbert Thomas b: 10/12/54, Longview, Tex. BL/TR, 6′3″, 185 lbs. Deb: 9/2/80																							
1980	Cal-A	22	63	11	16	3	0	0	6	6	10	.254	.319	.302	73	-2	1	1	-0	1.000	1	O-20	-0.3
■ **STEVE KUCZEK** Kuczek, Stanislaw Leo b: 12/28/24, Amsterdam, N.Y. BR/TR, 6′, 160 lbs. Deb: 9/29/49																							
1949	Bos-N	1	1	0	1	1	0	0	0	0	0	1.000	1.000	2.000	723	1	0			.000	0	H	0.1
■ **BILL KUEHNE** Kuehne, William J. (b: William J. Knelme) b: 10/24/1858, Leipzig, Germany d: 10/27/21, Sulphur Springs, O BR/TR, 185 lbs. Deb: 5/1/1883																							
1883	Col-a	95	374	38	85	8	14	1		2		.227	.231	.332	86	-5				.833	-5	*3-69,2-18/S-7,O-3	-0.9
1884	Col-a	110	415	48	98	13	16	5		9		.236	.254	.381	113	6				.881	11	*3-110	1.6
1885	Pit-a	104	411	54	93	9	19	0	43	15		.226	.257	.341	89	-6				.865	-1	*3-97/S-7	-0.5
1886	Pit-a	117	481	73	98	16	17	1	48	19		.204	.237	.314	72	-17	26			.899	-1	O-54,3-47,1-18	-1.8
1887	Pit-N	102	402	68	120	18	15	1	41	14	39	.299	.324	.425	113	6	17			.883	-13	*S-91/3-4,1-4,O-3	-0.5
1888	Pit-N	138	524	60	123	22	11	3	62	9	68	.235	.250	.336	93	-5	34			.910	0	3-75,S-63	-0.2
1889	Pit-N	97	390	43	96	20	5	5	57	9	36	.246	.263	.362	82	-12	15			.885	-1	3-75,O-13/2-5,S1	-0.9
1890	Pit-P	126	528	66	126	21	12	5	73	28	37	.239	.277	.352	74	-22	21			.850	6	*3-126	-0.9
1891	Col-a	68	261	32	56	9	0	2	22	10	22	.215	.244	.272	50	-18	21			.885	-2	3-68	-1.5
	Lou-a	41	159	28	44	3	1	1	18	8	13	.277	.315	.327	85	-4	10			.904	3	3-41	0.1
	Yr	109	420	60	100	12	1	3	40	18	35	.238	.271	.293	64	-21	31			.893	0	*3-109	-1.4
1892	Lou-N	76	287	22	48	4	5	0	36	13	36	.167	.203	.216	29	-25	6			.874	-3	3-76	-2.4
	StL-N	6	24	1	4	1	0	0	0	0	3	.167	.200	.208	25	-2	1			.895	0	/3-5,S-1	-0.2
	Cin-N	6	24	3	5	1	0	1	4	1	5	.208	.240	.375	87	-1	0			.941	2	/3-4,2-2	0.1
	StL-N	1	4	0	0	0	0	0	0	0	1	.000	.000	.000	-99	-1	0			1.000	1	/3-1	0.0
	Yr	89	339	26	57	6	5	1	40	14	45	.168	.203	.224	32	-29	7			.880	-0	3-86/2-2,S-1	-2.5
Total	10	1087	4284	536	996	145	115	25	404	137	260	.232	.258	.338	82	-105	151			.876	-4	3-798,S-171/O21	-8.0
■ **HARVEY KUENN** Kuenn, Harvey Edward b: 12/4/30, W.Allis, Wis. d: 2/28/88, Peoria, Ariz. BR/TR, 6′2″, 190 lbs. Deb: 9/6/52 MC																							
1952	Det-A	19	80	2	26	2	2	0	8	2	1	.325	.349	.400	107	1	2	1	0	.962	2	S-19	0.4
1953	Det-A★	155	679	94	**209**	33	7	2	48	50	31	.308	.356	.386	101	1	6	5	-1	.973	-21	*S-155	-0.9
1954	Det-A☆	155	656	81	**201**	28	6	5	48	29	13	.306	.337	.390	100	-1	9	9	-3	.966	3	*S-155	1.2
1955	Det-A★	145	620	101	190	**38**	5	8	62	40	27	.306	.349	.423	109	6	8	3	1	.956	-28	*S-141	-0.9
1956	Det-A★	146	591	96	**196**	32	7	12	88	55	34	.332	.391	.470	126	22	9	5	-0	**.968**	-20	*S-141/O-1	1.4
1957	Det-A★	151	624	74	173	30	6	9	44	47	28	.277	.328	.388	92	-7	5	8	-3	.955	-49	*S-136,3-17/1-1	-4.8
1958	Det-A☆	139	561	73	179	**39**	3	8	54	51	34	.319	.376	.442	116	13	5	10	-5	.984	15	*O-138	1.6

YEAR	TM/L	G	AB	R	H	2B	3B	HR	RBI	BB	SO	AVG	OBP	SLG	PRO+	BR/A	SB	CS	SBR	FA	FR	G/POS	TPR
1959	Det-A★	139	561	99	**198**	**42**	7	9	71	48	37	**.353**	.405	.501	140	31	7	2	1	.988	1	*O-137	2.5
1960	Cle-A★	126	474	65	146	24	0	9	54	55	25	.308	.381	.416	119	14	3	0	1	.966	1	*O-119/3-5	1.0
1961	SF-N	131	471	60	125	22	4	5	46	47	34	.265	.333	.361	87	-8	5	4	-1	.988	-7	O-93,3-32/S-1	-2.1
1962	*SF-N	130	487	73	148	23	5	10	68	49	37	.304	.369	.433	116	12	3	6	-3	.970	-9	*O-105,3-30	-0.5
1963	SF-N	120	417	61	121	13	2	6	31	44	38	.290	.361	.374	113	8	2	1	0	.975	-30	O-64,3-53	-2.7
1964	SF-N	111	351	42	92	16	2	4	22	35	32	.262	.331	.353	91	-4	0	1	-1	.952	-13	O-88,1-11/3-2	-2.3
1965	SF-N	23	59	4	14	0	0	0	6	10	3	.237	.357	.237	69	-2	3	1	0	1.000	-1	O-14/1-7	-0.4
	Chi-N	54	120	11	26	5	0	0	6	22	13	.217	.338	.258	69	-4	1	0	0	.975	-3	O-35/1-1	-0.8
	Yr	77	179	15	40	5	0	0	12	32	16	.223	.344	.251	69	-6	4	1	1	.981	-4	O-49/1-8	-1.2
1966	Chi-N	3	3	0	1	0	0	0	0	0	1	.333	.333	.333	85	-0	0	0	0	.000	-0	/O-1	0.0
	Phi-N	86	159	15	47	9	0	0	15	10	16	.296	.337	.352	92	-2	0	0	0	1.000	-6	O-31,1-13/3-1	-1.0
	Yr	89	162	15	48	9	0	0	15	10	17	.296	.337	.352	92	-2	0	0	0	1.000	-7	O-32,1-13/3-1	-1.0
Total	15	1833	6913	951	2092	356	56	87	671	594	404	.303	.359	.408	108	80	68	56	-13	.978	-163	O-826,S-748,3/1	-8.3

■ **JOE KUHEL** Kuhel, Joseph Anthony b: 6/25/06, Cleveland, Ohio d: 2/26/84, Kansas City, Kan. BL/TL, 6', 180 lbs. Deb: 7/31/30 M

YEAR	TM/L	G	AB	R	H	2B	3B	HR	RBI	BB	SO	AVG	OBP	SLG	PRO+	BR/A	SB	CS	SBR	FA	FR	G/POS	TPR
1930	Was-A	18	63	9	18	3	3	0	17	5	6	.286	.348	.429	95	-1	1	0	0	.981	-1	1-16	-0.2
1931	Was-A	139	524	70	141	34	8	8	85	47	45	.269	.335	.410	94	-5	7	5	-1	.991	-7	*1-139	-2.4
1932	Was-A	101	347	52	101	21	5	4	52	32	19	.291	.353	.415	99	-0	5	2	0	.994	-2	1-85	-0.8
1933	*Was-A	153	602	89	194	34	10	11	107	59	48	.322	.385	.467	126	22	17	8	0	**.996**	-7	*1-153	0.1
1934	Was-A	63	263	49	76	12	3	3	25	30	14	.289	.364	.392	99	-0	2	7	-4	.994	-4	1-63	-1.3
1935	Was-A	151	633	99	165	25	9	2	74	78	44	.261	.345	.338	80	-17	5	4	-1	.991	0	*1-151	-3.3
1936	Was-A	149	588	107	189	42	8	16	118	64	30	.321	.392	.502	126	23	15	7	0	.993	-2	*1-149	0.6
1937	Was-A	136	547	73	155	24	11	6	61	63	39	.283	.357	.400	95	-4	6	3	0	.993	3	*1-136	-1.6
1938	Chi-A	117	412	67	110	27	4	8	51	72	35	.267	.376	.410	95	-2	9	7	-2	.988	-7	*1-111	-2.2
1939	Chi-A	139	546	107	164	24	9	15	56	64	51	.300	.376	.460	110	8	18	5	2	.992	-4	*1-136	-0.7
1940	Chi-A	155	603	111	169	28	8	27	94	87	59	.280	.374	.488	120	18	12	5	1	.988	-5	*1-155	-0.1
1941	Chi-A	153	600	99	150	39	5	12	63	70	55	.250	.331	.392	92	-8	20	5	3	.994	-1	*1-151	-1.6
1942	Chi-A	115	413	60	103	14	4	4	52	60	22	.249	.347	.332	94	-2	22	9	1	.991	-4	*1-112	-1.2
1943	Chi-A	153	531	55	113	21	1	5	46	76	45	.213	.319	.284	77	-13	14	8	-1	.995	1	*1-153	-2.4
1944	Was-A	139	518	90	144	26	7	4	51	68	40	.278	.364	.378	117	13	11	6	-0	.987	-2	*1-138	0.4
1945	Was-A	142	533	73	152	29	13	2	75	79	31	.285	.378	.400	137	27	10	5	0	.989	-6	*1-141	1.2
1946	Was-A	14	20	2	3	0	0	0	2	5	2	.150	.320	.150	36	-1	0	0	0	1.000	0	/1-5	-0.2
	Chi-A	64	238	24	65	9	3	4	20	21	24	.273	.335	.387	105	1	4	4	-1	.994	-2	1-63	-0.6
	Yr	78	258	26	68	9	3	4	22	26	26	.264	.333	.368	100	-0	4	4	-1	.994	-2	1-68	-0.8
1947	Chi-A	3	3	0	0	0	0	0	0	0	3	.000	.000	.000	-99	-1	0	0	0	.000	0	H	-0.1
Total	18	2104	7984	1236	2212	412	111	131	1049	980	612	.277	.359	.406	104	56	178	90	-1	.992	-48	*1-2057	-16.4

■ **KENNY KUHN** Kuhn, Kenneth Harold b: 3/20/37, Louisville, Ky. BL/TR, 5'10.5", 175 lbs. Deb: 7/7/55

YEAR	TM/L	G	AB	R	H	2B	3B	HR	RBI	BB	SO	AVG	OBP	SLG	PRO+	BR/A	SB	CS	SBR	FA	FR	G/POS	TPR
1955	Cle-A	4	6	0	2	0	0	0	0	1	0	.333	.429	.333	103	0	1	0	0	1.000	-2	/S-4	-0.1
1956	Cle-A	27	22	7	6	1	0	0	2	0	4	.273	.273	.318	54	-1	0	1	-1	1.000	2	S-17/2-5	0.0
1957	Cle-A	40	53	5	9	0	0	0	5	4	9	.170	.228	.170	10	-6	0	0	0	.974	-3	2-14/3-2,S-1	-0.9
Total	3	71	81	12	17	1	0	0	7	5	13	.210	.256	.222	30	-8	1	1	-0	.963	-3	/S-22,2-19,3-2	-1.0

■ **WALT KUHN** Kuhn, Walter Charles "Red" b: 2/2/1884, Fresno, Cal. d: 6/14/35, Fresno, Cal. BR/TR, 5'7", 162 lbs. Deb: 4/18/12

YEAR	TM/L	G	AB	R	H	2B	3B	HR	RBI	BB	SO	AVG	OBP	SLG	PRO+	BR/A	SB	CS	SBR	FA	FR	G/POS	TPR
1912	Chi-A	76	178	16	36	7	0	0	10	20		.202	.286	.242	53	-10	5			.966	9	C-75/2-1	0.4
1913	Chi-A	26	50	5	8	1	0	0	5	13	8	.160	.333	.180	52	-2	1			.980	-2	C-24	-0.3
1914	Chi-A	17	40	4	11	1	0	0	0	8	11	.275	.396	.300	111	1	2	3	-1	.987	-1	C-16	0.0
Total	3	119	268	25	55	9	0	0	15	41	19	.205	.313	.239	62	-12	8	3		.971	6	C-115/2-1	0.1

■ **CHARLIE KUHNS** Kuhns, Charles B. b: 10/27/1877, Freeport, Pa. d: 7/15/22, Pittsburgh, Pa. 5'9", 160 lbs. Deb: 6/4/1897

YEAR	TM/L	G	AB	R	H	2B	3B	HR	RBI	BB	SO	AVG	OBP	SLG	PRO+	BR/A	SB	CS	SBR	FA	FR	G/POS	TPR
1897	Pit-N	1	3	0	0	0	0	0	0	1		.000	.250	.000	-32	-1	0			.667	0	/3-1	0.0
1899	Bos-N	7	18	2	5	0	0	0	3	2		.278	.350	.278	67	-1	0			.813	-1	/S-3,3-3	-0.1
Total	2	8	21	2	5	0	0	0	3	3		.238	.333	.238	53	-1	0			.733	-1	/3-4,S-3	-0.1

■ **DUANE KUIPER** Kuiper, Duane Eugene b: 6/19/50, Racine, Wis. BL/TR, 6', 175 lbs. Deb: 9/9/74

YEAR	TM/L	G	AB	R	H	2B	3B	HR	RBI	BB	SO	AVG	OBP	SLG	PRO+	BR/A	SB	CS	SBR	FA	FR	G/POS	TPR
1974	Cle-A	10	22	7	11	2	0	0	4	2	2	.500	.542	.591	228	4	1	1	-0	1.000	1	/2-8	0.5
1975	Cle-A	90	346	42	101	11	1	0	25	30	26	.292	.362	.329	97	-0	19	18	-5	.972	-14	2-87/D-1	-1.5
1976	Cle-A	135	506	47	133	13	6	0	37	30	42	.263	.305	.312	82	-12	10	17	-7	**.987**	20	*2-128/1-5,D-2	0.9
1977	Cle-A	148	610	62	169	15	8	1	50	37	55	.277	.326	.333	83	-14	11	11	-3	.985	2	*2-148	-0.5
1978	Cle-A	149	547	52	155	18	6	0	43	19	35	.283	.312	.338	84	-12	4	9	-4	.979	-19	*2-149	-2.5
1979	Cle-A	140	479	46	122	9	5	0	39	37	27	.255	.313	.294	65	-23	4	9	-4	**.988**	-4	*2-140	-2.1
1980	Cle-A	42	149	10	42	5	0	0	9	13	8	.282	.340	.315	80	-4	0	1	-1	.995	-8	2-42	-0.9
1981	Cle-A	72	206	15	53	6	0	0	14	8	13	.257	.285	.286	66	-9	1	1	-0	.983	-5	2-72	-1.1
1982	SF-N	107	218	26	61	9	1	0	17	32	24	.280	.377	.330	100	1	2	2	-1	.978	-7	2-51	-0.4
1983	SF-N	72	176	14	44	2	2	0	14	27	13	.250	.356	.284	82	-3	0	1	-1	.988	-9	2-64	-1.0
1984	SF-N	83	115	8	23	1	0	0	11	12	10	.200	.276	.209	39	-9	0	1	-1	.969	6	2-31/1-1	-0.3
1985	SF-N	9	5	0	3	0	0	0	0	1	0	.600	.667	.600	270	1	0	0	0	.000	0	/H	0.1
Total	12	1057	3379	329	917	91	29	1	263	248	255	.271	.326	.316	81	-79	52	71	-27	.983	-36	2-920/1-6,D-3	-8.8

■ **JEFF KUNKEL** Kunkel, Jeffrey William b: 3/25/62, W.Palm Beach, Fla. BR/TR, 6'2", 180 lbs. Deb: 7/23/84 F

YEAR	TM/L	G	AB	R	H	2B	3B	HR	RBI	BB	SO	AVG	OBP	SLG	PRO+	BR/A	SB	CS	SBR	FA	FR	G/POS	TPR
1984	Tex-A	50	142	13	29	2	3	3	7	2	35	.204	.221	.324	47	-10	4	3	-1	.922	-1	S-48/D-1	-0.9
1985	Tex-A	2	4	1	1	0	0	0	0	0	3	.250	.250	.250	37	-0	0	0	0	1.000	1	/S-2	0.1
1986	Tex-A	8	13	3	3	0	0	1	2	0	2	.231	.231	.462	81	-0	0	0	0	.769	-0	/S-5,D-1	-0.1
1987	Tex-A	15	32	1	7	0	0	1	2	0	10	.219	.242	.313	46	-3	0	1	-1	.955	2	2-10/3-0,O-3,1SD	-0.1
1988	Tex-A	55	154	14	35	8	3	2	15	4	35	.227	.252	.357	67	-7	0	1	-1	.949	6	2-28,S-19,3/OPD	0.0
1989	Tex-A	108	293	39	79	21	2	8	29	20	75	.270	.323	.437	110	3	3	2	-0	.936	2	S-59,O-30/2-8,3PD	0.8
1990	Tex-A	99	200	17	34	11	1	3	17	11	66	.170	.221	.280	39	-17	2	1	0	.958	9	S-67,3-15,2-13,/OD	-0.4
1992	Chi-N	20	29	0	4	2	0	0	1	0	8	.138	.138	.207	-3	-4	0	0	0	1.000	4	/S-6,2-3,O-3	0.0
Total	8	357	867	88	192	44	9	18	73	37	234	.221	.260	.355	69	-38	9	8	-2	.940	22	S-207/2-62,O3DP1	-0.6

■ **RUSTY KUNTZ** Kuntz, Russell Jay b: 2/4/55, Orange, Cal. BR/TR, 6'3", 190 lbs. Deb: 9/1/79 C

YEAR	TM/L	G	AB	R	H	2B	3B	HR	RBI	BB	SO	AVG	OBP	SLG	PRO+	BR/A	SB	CS	SBR	FA	FR	G/POS	TPR
1979	Chi-A	5	11	0	1	0	0	0	0	2	6	.091	.231	.091	-9	-2	0	0	0	1.000	1	/O-5	-0.1
1980	Chi-A	36	62	5	14	4	0	0	3	5	13	.226	.284	.290	58	-4	1	0	0	.979	-5	O-34	-0.9
1981	Chi-A	67	55	15	14	2	0	0	4	6	8	.255	.339	.291	85	-1	1	0	0	1.000	-13	O-51/D-5	-1.5
1982	Chi-A	21	26	4	5	1	0	0	3	2	8	.192	.250	.231	33	-2	0	0	0	1.000	-7	O-20/D-1	-1.0
1983	Chi-A	28	42	6	11	1	0	0	1	6	13	.262	.354	.286	76	-1	1	0	0	.976	-6	O-27/D-1	-0.7
	Min-A	31	100	13	19	3	0	3	5	12	28	.190	.277	.310	59	-6	0	0	0	.986	0	O-30	-0.7
	Yr	59	142	19	30	4	0	3	6	18	41	.211	.300	.303	64	-7	1	0	0	.982	-6	O-57/D-1	-1.4
1984	*Det-A	84	140	32	40	12	0	2	22	25	28	.286	.398	.414	126	6	2	2	-1	.987	-16	O-67,D-10	-1.2
1985	Det-A	5	5	0	0	0	0	0	0	2	2	.000	.286	.000	-13	-1	0	1	-1	.000	-0	/1-1,D-3	-0.2
Total	7	277	441	75	104	23	0	5	38	60	106	.236	.330	.322	81	-10	5	3	-0	.988	-46	O-235/D-19,1-1	-6.3

■ **WHITEY KUROWSKI** Kurowski, George John b: 4/19/18, Reading, Pa. BR/TR, 5'11", 193 lbs. Deb: 9/23/41

YEAR	TM/L	G	AB	R	H	2B	3B	HR	RBI	BB	SO	AVG	OBP	SLG	PRO+	BR/A	SB	CS	SBR	FA	FR	G/POS	TPR
1941	StL-N	5	9	1	3	2	0	0	2	0	2	.333	.400	.556	157	1	0			1.000	-1	/3-4	0.0
1942	*StL-N	115	366	51	93	17	3	9	42	33	60	.254	.326	.391	102	0	7			.944	9	*3-104/S-1,O-1	1.1
1943	*StL-N☆	139	522	69	150	24	8	13	70	31	54	.287	.330	.439	116	8	3			.952	1	*3-137/S-2	1.2
1944	*StL-N★	149	555	95	150	25	7	20	87	58	40	.270	.341	.449	119	13	2			**.965**	4	*3-146/2-9,S-1	1.8
1945	StL-N†	133	511	84	165	27	3	21	102	45	45	.323	.383	.511	144	28	1			.964	2	*3-131/S-6	3.3
1946	*StL-N★	142	519	76	156	32	5	14	89	72	47	.301	.391	.462	136	25	2			**.966**	0	*3-138	2.9
1947	StL-N★	146	513	108	159	27	6	27	104	87	56	.310	.420	.544	148	37	4			.954	-14	*3-141	2.3
1948	StL-N	77	220	34	47	8	0	2	33	42	28	.214	.352	.277	68	-8	0			.939	-11	3-65	-2.0

YEAR	TM/L	G	AB	R	H	2B	3B	HR	RBI	BB	SO	AVG	OBP	SLG	PRO+	BR/A	SB	CS	SBR	FA	FR	G/POS	TPR
1949	StL-N	10	14	0	2	0	0	0	0	1	0	.143	.200	.143	-6	-2	0			1.000	-0	/3-2	-0.3
Total	9	916	3229	518	925	162	32	106	529	369	332	.286	.366	.455	124	102	19			.957	-10	3-868/S-10,2-9,O-1	10.3

■ CRAIG KUSICK Kusick, Craig Robert b: 9/30/48, Milwaukee, Wis. BR/TR, 6′3″, 232 lbs. Deb: 9/8/73

1973	Min-A	15	48	4	12	2	0	0	4	7	9	.250	.357	.292	81	-1	0	0	0	.989	-1	1-11/O-2,D-2	-0.3
1974	Min-A	76	201	36	48	7	1	8	26	35	36	.239	.354	.403	114	4	0	0	0	.996	4	1-75	0.4
1975	Min-A	57	156	14	37	8	0	6	27	21	23	.237	.346	.404	110	2	0	0	0	.990	1	1-51	0.1
1976	Min-A	109	266	33	69	13	0	11	36	35	44	.259	.348	.432	125	8	5	1	1	.977	3	D-79,1-23	1.0
1977	Min-A	115	268	34	68	12	0	12	45	49	60	.254	.375	.433	121	9	3	1	0	.972	-2	D-85,1-23	0.5
1978	Min-A	77	191	23	33	3	2	4	20	37	38	.173	.310	.272	64	-8	3	2	-0	.987	2	D-35,1-27/O-9	-1.0
1979	Min-A	24	54	8	13	4	0	3	6	3	11	.241	.281	.481	97	-0	0	0	0	1.000	-0	D-12/1-8	-0.1
	Tor-A	24	54	3	11	1	0	2	7	7	7	.204	.306	.333	72	-2	0	0	0	.978	1	1-20/P-1,D-1	-0.2
	Yr	48	108	11	24	5	0	5	13	10	18	.222	.294	.407	85	-3	0	0	0	.983	1	1-28,D-13/P-1	-0.3
Total	7	497	1238	155	291	50	3	46	171	194	228	.235	.345	.392	106	13	11	4	1	.988	8	1-238,D-214/O-11,P	0.4

■ ART KUSNYER Kusnyer, Arthur William b: 12/19/45, Akron, Ohio BR/TR, 6′2″, 198 lbs. Deb: 9/21/70 C

1970	Chi-A	4	10	0	1	0	0	0	0	0	4	.100	.100	.100	-43	-2	0	0	0	.941	1	/C-3	-0.1
1971	Cal-A	6	13	0	2	0	0	0	0	0	3	.154	.154	.154	-14	-2	0	0	0	.958	1	/C-6	-0.1
1972	Cal-A	64	179	13	37	2	1	2	13	16	33	.207	.276	.263	64	-8	0	0	0	.975	-3	C-63	-0.9
1973	Cal-A	41	64	5	8	2	0	0	3	2	12	.125	.152	.156	-14	-10	0	1	-1	.979	1	C-41	-0.9
1976	Mil-A	15	34	2	4	1	0	0	3	1	5	.118	.167	.147	-8	-5	1	0	0	.938	-1	C-14	-0.5
1978	KC-A	9	13	1	3	1	0	1	2	2	4	.231	.333	.538	138	1	0	0	0	.946	3	/C-9	0.4
Total	6	139	313	21	55	6	1	3	21	21	61	.176	.232	.230	37	-26	1	1	-0	.970	2	C-136	-2.1

■ JUL KUSTUS Kustus, Joseph J. "Joe" or "Kul" b: 9/5/1882, Detroit, Mich. d: 4/27/16, Eloise, Mich. BR/TR, 5′10″, Deb: 4/17/09

1909	Bro-N	53	173	12	25	5	0	1	11	11		.145	.204	.191	23	-16	9			.951	0	O-50	-2.0

■ RANDY KUTCHER Kutcher, Randy Scott b: 4/20/60, Anchorage, Alaska BR/TR, 5′11″, 175 lbs. Deb: 6/19/86

1986	SF-N	71	186	28	44	9	1	7	16	11	41	.237	.279	.409	92	-3	6	5	-1	.990	-1	O-51,S-13/3-4,2-3	-0.6
1987	SF-N	14	16	7	3	1	1	0	1	1	5	.188	.235	.375	61	-1	1	0	0	1.000	1	/O-6,2-2,3-2,S-1	0.0
1988	Bos-A	19	12	2	2	1	0	0	0	0	2	.167	.167	.250	14	-1	0	1	-1	1.000	0	/O-7,3-2,D-7	-0.2
1989	Bos-A	77	160	28	36	10	3	2	18	11	46	.225	.275	.363	74	-6	3	0	1	.982	-3	O-57/3-6,C-1,D-6	-0.9
1990	*Bos-A	63	74	18	17	4	1	1	5	13	18	.230	.345	.351	91	-1	3	3	-1	1.000	-0	O-34,3-11/2-5,D-5	-0.2
Total	5	244	448	83	102	25	6	10	40	36	112	.228	.285	.377	82	-12	13	9	-2	.989	-3	O-155/3-25,DS2C	-1.9

■ JOE KUTINA Kutina, Joseph Peter b: 1/16/1885, Chicago, Ill. d: 4/13/45, Chicago, Ill. BR/TR, 6′2″, 205 lbs. Deb: 9/6/11

1911	StL-A	26	101	12	26	6	2	3	15	2		.257	.279	.446	105	-0	2			.981	-1	1-26	-0.1
1912	StL-A	69	205	18	42	9	3	1	18	13		.205	.262	.293	61	-11	0			.985	-3	1-51/O-1	-1.5
Total	2	95	306	30	68	15	5	4	33	15		.222	.268	.343	76	-11	2			.984	-4	/1-77,O-1	-1.6

■ AL KVASNAK Kvasnak, Alexander b: 1/11/21, Sagamore, Pa. BR/TR, 6′1″, 170 lbs. Deb: 4/15/42

1942	Was-A	5	11	3	2	0	0	0	0	2	1	.182	.308	.182	40	-1	0	0	0	1.000	-0	/O-3	-0.1

■ ANDY KYLE Kyle, Andrew Ewing b: 10/29/1889, Toronto, Ont., Can. d: 9/6/71, Toronto, Ont., Can. BL/TL, 5′8″, 160 lbs. Deb: 9/7/12

1912	Cin-N	9	21	3	7	1	0	0	4	4	2	.333	.440	.381	129	1	0			1.000	0	/O-7	0.1

■ CHET LAABS Laabs, Chester Peter b: 4/30/12, Milwaukee, Wis. d: 1/26/83, Warren, Mich. BR/TR, 5′8″, 175 lbs. Deb: 5/5/37

1937	Det-A	72	242	31	58	13	5	8	37	24	66	.240	.308	.434	83	-8	6	2	1	.971	-7	O-62	-1.5
1938	Det-A	64	211	26	50	7	3	7	37	15	52	.237	.288	.398	66	-12	3	2	-0	.971	-1	O-53	-1.4
1939	Det-A	5	16	1	5	1	1	0	2	2	0	.313	.389	.500	117	0	0	0	0	.933	1	/O-5	0.1
	StL-A	95	317	52	95	20	5	10	62	33	62	.300	.368	.489	115	6	4	1	1	.972	-0	O-79	0.3
	Yr	100	333	53	100	21	6	10	64	35	62	.300	.369	.489	115	7	4	1	1	.969	1	O-84	0.4
1940	StL-A	105	218	32	59	11	5	10	40	34	59	.271	.372	.505	122	7	3	3	-1	.969	-7	O-63	-0.3
1941	StL-A	118	392	64	109	23	6	15	59	51	59	.278	.361	.482	117	9	5	2	0	.982	-2	*O-100	0.2
1942	StL-A	144	520	90	143	21	7	27	99	88	88	.275	.380	.498	144	30	0	3	-2	.970	-4	*O-139	1.7
1943	StL-A★	151	580	83	145	27	7	17	85	73	105	.250	.338	.409	115	11	5	7	-3	.976	2	*O-150	0.2
1944	*StL-A	66	201	28	47	10	2	5	23	29	33	.234	.330	.378	96	-1	3	1	0	1.000	-2	O-55	-0.5
1945	StL-A	35	109	15	26	4	3	1	8	16	17	.239	.352	.358	101	1	0	0	0	.986	-4	O-35	-0.5
1946	StL-A	80	264	40	69	13	0	16	52	20	50	.261	.316	.492	117	5	3	1	0	.987	1	O-72	0.3
1947	Phi-A	15	32	5	7	1	0	1	5	4	4	.219	.306	.344	79	-1	0	0	0	1.000	1	/O-7	-0.1
Total	11	950	3102	467	813	151	44	117	509	389	595	.262	.346	.452	113	47	32	22	-4	.977	-21	O-820	-1.5

■ COCO LABOY Laboy, Jose Alberto b: 7/3/39, Ponce, P.R. BR/TR, 5′10″, 170 lbs. Deb: 4/8/69

1969	Mon-N	157	562	53	145	29	1	18	83	40	96	.258	.312	.409	100	-1	0	2	-1	.944	4	*3-156	0.1
1970	Mon-N	137	432	37	86	26	1	5	53	31	81	.199	.256	.299	48	-33	0	2	-1	.946	-4	*3-132/2-3	-3.9
1971	Mon-N	76	151	10	38	4	0	1	14	11	19	.252	.302	.298	70	-6	0	1	-1	.937	1	3-65/2-2	-0.6
1972	Mon-N	28	69	6	18	2	0	3	14	10	16	.261	.354	.420	117	2	0	0	0	.980	-2	3-24/2-3,S-2	0.0
1973	Mon-N	22	33	2	4	1	0	1	2	5	8	.121	.237	.242	32	-3	0	0	0	.889	1	3-20/2-1	-0.2
Total	5	420	1247	108	291	62	2	28	166	97	220	.233	.292	.354	77	-41	0	5	-3	.944	-0	3-397/2-9,S-2	-4.6

■ CANDY LaCHANCE LaChance, George Joseph b: 2/15/1870, Putnam, Conn. d: 8/18/32, Waterville, Conn. BB/TR, 6′1″, 183 lbs. Deb: 8/15/1893

1893	Bro-N	11	35	1	6	1	0	0	6	2	12	.171	.237	.200	17	-4	0			.654	-6	/C-6,O-5	-0.8
1894	Bro-N	68	257	48	83	13	8	5	52	16	32	.323	.365	.494	114	5	20			.979	-8	1-56,C-10/O-3	-0.2
1895	Bro-N	127	536	99	167	22	8	8	108	29	48	.312	.356	.427	110	7	37			.983	-6	*1-125/O-3	0.3
1896	Bro-N	89	348	60	99	10	13	7	58	23	32	.284	.331	.448	111	3	17			.986	-3	*1-89	0.1
1897	Bro-N	126	520	86	160	28	16	4	90	15		.308	.333	.446	111	5	26			.978	-4	*1-126	0.1
1898	Bro-N	136	526	62	130	23	7	5	65	31		.247	.299	.346	85	-12	23			.988	-20	1-74,S-48,O-13	-2.9
1899	Bal-N	125	472	65	145	23	10	1	75	21		.307	.350	.405	101	-1	31			.984	-7	*1-125	-0.6
1901	Cle-A	133	548	81	166	22	9	1	75	7		.303	.314	.381	96	-5	11			.979	-3	*1-133	-0.8
1902	Bos-A	138	541	60	151	13	4	6	56	18		.279	.309	.351	80	-15	8			.983	-11	*1-138	-2.8
1903	*Bos-A	141	522	60	134	22	6	1	53	28		.257	.303	.328	85	-10	12			.984	-11	*1-141	-2.4
1904	Bos-A	157	573	55	130	19	5	1	47	23		.227	.265	.283	69	-20	7			**.992**	-14	*1-157	-4.2
1905	Bos-A	12	41	1	6	1	0	0	5	6		.146	.255	.171	36	-3	0			.988	-0	1-12	-0.4
Total	12	1263	4919	678	1377	197	86	39	690	219	124	.280	.318	.379	93	-49	192			.984	-93	*1-1176/S-48,O-24,C	-14.6

■ RENE LACHEMANN Lachemann, Rene George b: 5/4/45, Los Angeles, Cal. BR/TR, 6′, 198 lbs. Deb: 5/4/65 FMC

1965	KC-A	92	216	20	49	7	1	9	29	12	57	.227	.268	.394	87	-5	0	0	0	.980	2	C-75	0.1
1966	KC-A	7	5	0	1	1	0	0	0	0	1	.200	.200	.400	70	-0	0	0	0	1.000	1	/C-6	0.1
1968	Oak-A	19	60	3	9	1	0	0	4	1	11	.150	.177	.167	5	-7	0	0	0	.967	-6	C-16	-1.5
Total	3	118	281	23	59	9	1	9	33	13	69	.210	.247	.345	70	-12	0	0	0	.978	-3	/C-97	-1.3

■ PETE LaCOCK LaCock, Ralph Pierre b: 1/17/52, Burbank, Cal. BL/TL, 6′3″, 210 lbs. Deb: 9/6/72

1972	Chi-N	5	6	3	3	0	0	0	4	0	1	.500	.500	.500	167	1	1	0	0	1.000	-1	/O-3	0.0
1973	Chi-N	11	16	1	4	1	0	0	3	1	2	.250	.294	.313	63	-1	0	0	0	1.000	-0	/O-5	-0.1
1974	Chi-N	35	110	9	20	4	1	1	8	12	16	.182	.268	.264	47	-8	0	0	0	.974	1	O-22,1-11	-0.9
1975	Chi-N	106	249	30	57	8	1	6	30	37	27	.229	.329	.341	82	-5	0	2	-1	.988	1	1-53,O-26	-1.0
1976	Chi-N	106	244	34	54	9	2	8	28	42	37	.221	.338	.373	93	-2	1	4	-2	.975	-4	1-54,O-19	-1.3
1977	*KC-A	88	218	25	66	12	1	3	29	15	25	.303	.350	.408	105	2	2	1	0	.990	1	1-29,D-26,O-12	0.1
1978	*KC-A	118	322	44	95	21	2	5	48	21	27	.295	.338	.419	109	3	1	0	0	.993	-6	*1-106	-0.7
1979	KC-A	132	408	54	113	25	4	3	56	37	26	.277	.339	.380	92	-4	2	1	0	**.997**	1	*1-108,D-16	-1.0
1980	*KC-A	114	156	14	32	6	0	1	18	17	10	.205	.287	.263	51	-10	1	0	0	.997	-3	1-86,O-29	-1.5
Total	9	715	1729	214	444	86	11	27	224	182	171	.257	.329	.366	89	-25	8	8	-2	.991	-9	1-447,O-116/D-42	-6.4

■ LEE LACY Lacy, Leondaus b: 4/10/48, Longview, Tex. BR/TR, 6'1", 175 lbs. Deb: 6/30/72

YEAR	TM/L	G	AB	R	H	2B	3B	HR	RBI	BB	SO	AVG	OBP	SLG	PRO+	BR/A	SB	CS	SBR	FA	FR	G/POS	TPR
1972	LA-N	60	243	34	63	7	3	0	12	19	37	.259	.313	.313	80	-6	5	3	-0	.973	-8	2-58	-1.2
1973	LA-N	57	135	14	28	2	0	0	8	15	34	.207	.287	.222	45	-10	2	3	-1	.965	-1	2-41	-1.0
1974	*LA-N	48	78	13	22	6	0	0	8	2	14	.282	.300	.359	87	-2	2	0	1	.968	2	2-34/3-1	0.2
1975	LA-N	101	306	44	96	11	5	7	40	22	29	.314	.360	.451	129	11	5	9	-4	.935	-4	2-43,O-43/S-1	0.2
1976	Atl-N	50	180	25	49	4	2	3	20	6	12	.272	.299	.367	83	-4	2	2	-1	.969	-10	2-44/O-5,3-1	-1.4
	LA-N	53	158	17	42	7	1	0	14	16	13	.266	.333	.323	88	-2	1	2	-1	.979	1	O-37/3-3,2-2	-0.4
	Yr	103	338	42	91	11	3	3	34	22	25	.269	.316	.346	86	-6	3	4	-2	.970	-10	2-46,O-42/3-4	-1.8
1977	*LA-N	75	169	28	45	7	0	6	21	10	21	.266	.307	.414	92	-2	4	0	1	1.000	-13	O-32,2-22,3-12	-1.3
1978	*LA-N	103	245	29	64	16	4	13	40	27	30	.261	.337	.518	136	11	7	4	-0	.971	-5	O-44,2-24/3-9,S-1	0.5
1979	*Pit-N	84	182	17	45	9	3	5	15	22	36	.247	.332	.412	97	-1	6	1	1	.973	-2	O-41/2-5	-0.3
1980	Pit-N	109	278	45	93	20	4	7	33	28	33	.335	.399	.511	150	19	18	9	0	.984	5	O-88/3-3	2.2
1981	Pit-N	78	213	31	57	11	4	2	10	11	29	.268	.307	.385	92	-3	24	3	5	.977	3	O-63/3-1	0.5
1982	Pit-N	121	359	66	112	16	3	5	31	32	57	.312	.370	.415	116	8	40	15	3	.965	-8	*O-113/3-2	0.0
1983	Pit-N	108	288	40	87	12	3	4	13	22	36	.302	.352	.406	107	3	31	13	2	1.000	-8	O-98	-0.6
1984	Pit-N	138	474	66	152	26	3	12	70	32	61	.321	.364	.464	131	18	21	11	-0	**.996**	4	*O-127/2-2	2.0
1985	Bal-A	121	492	69	144	22	4	9	48	39	95	.293	.347	.409	109	6	10	3	1	.984	4	*O-115/D-5	0.7
1986	Bal-A	130	491	77	141	18	0	11	47	37	71	.287	.337	.391	99	-1	4	6	-2	.992	6	*O-120/D-3	-0.1
1987	Bal-A	87	258	35	63	13	3	7	28	32	49	.244	.328	.399	94	-2	3	2	-0	.973	2	O-80/D-4	-0.3
Total	16	1523	4549	650	1303	207	42	91	458	372	657	.286	.342	.410	108	43	185	86	4	.983	-31	*O-1006,2-275/3DS	-0.3

■ GUY LACY Lacy, Osceola Guy b: 6/12/1897, Cleveland, Tenn. d: 11/19/53, Cleveland, Tenn. BR/TR, 5'11.5", 170 lbs. Deb: 5/7/26

YEAR	TM/L	G	AB	R	H	2B	3B	HR	RBI	BB	SO	AVG	OBP	SLG	PRO+	BR/A	SB	CS	SBR	FA	FR	G/POS	TPR
1926	Cle-A	13	24	2	4	0	0	1	2	2	2	.167	.259	.292	43	-2	0	0	0	.976	1	2-11/3-2	-0.1

■ HI LADD Ladd, Arthur Clifford b: 2/9/1870, Willimantic, Conn. d: 5/7/48, Cranston, R.I. BL/TR, 6'4", 180 lbs. Deb: 7/12/1898

YEAR	TM/L	G	AB	R	H	2B	3B	HR	RBI	BB	SO	AVG	OBP	SLG	PRO+	BR/A	SB	CS	SBR	FA	FR	G/POS	TPR
1898	Pit-N	1	1	0	0	0	0	0	0	0		.000	.000	.000	-99	-0	0			.000	0	H	0.0
	Bos-N	1	4	1	1	0	0	0	0	0		.250	.250	.250	41	-0	0			1.000	-0	/O-1	0.0
	Yr	2	5	1	1	0	0	0	0	0		.200	.200	.200	14	-1	0			1.000	-0	/O-1	0.0

■ STEVE LADEW Ladew, Stephen b: St.Louis, Mo. Deb: 9/27/1889

YEAR	TM/L	G	AB	R	H	2B	3B	HR	RBI	BB	SO	AVG	OBP	SLG	PRO+	BR/A	SB	CS	SBR	FA	FR	G/POS	TPR
1889	KC-a	2	4	0	0	0	0	0	0	0	3	.000	.000	.000	-95	-1	0			1.000	-0	/O-1,P-1	-0.1

■ JOE LAFATA Lafata, Joseph Joseph b: 8/3/21, Detroit, Mich. BL/TL, 6', 163 lbs. Deb: 4/17/47

YEAR	TM/L	G	AB	R	H	2B	3B	HR	RBI	BB	SO	AVG	OBP	SLG	PRO+	BR/A	SB	CS	SBR	FA	FR	G/POS	TPR
1947	NY-N	62	95	13	21	1	0	2	18	15	18	.221	.333	.295	68	-4	1			.974	-1	O-19/1-2	-0.6
1948	NY-N	1	1	0	0	0	0	0	0	0	1	.000	.000	.000	-99	-0	0			.000	0	H	0.0
1949	NY-N	64	140	18	33	2	2	3	16	9	23	.236	.282	.343	67	-7	1			.984	-4	1-47	-1.1
Total	3	127	236	31	54	3	2	5	34	24	42	.229	.303	.322	67	-11	2			.985	-5	/1-49,O-19	-1.7

■ FLIP LAFFERTY Lafferty, Frank Bernard b: 5/4/1854, Scranton, Pa. d: 2/8/10, Wilmington, Del. TR , Deb: 9/15/1876

YEAR	TM/L	G	AB	R	H	2B	3B	HR	RBI	BB	SO	AVG	OBP	SLG	PRO+	BR/A	SB	CS	SBR	FA	FR	G/POS	TPR
1876	Phi-N	1	3	0	0	0	0	0	0	0	0	.000	.000	.000	-99	-1				.750	0	/P-1	0.0
1877	Lou-N	4	17	2	1	1	0	0	0	0	4	.059	.059	.118	-39	-3				.750	-1	/O-4	-0.4
Total	2	5	20	2	1	1	0	0	0	0	4	.050	.050	.100	-46	-3				.750	-1	/O-4,P-1	-0.4

■ TY LaFOREST LaForest, Byron Joseph b: 4/18/17, Edmundston, N.B., Canada d: 5/5/47, Arlington, Mass. BR/TR, 5'9", 165 lbs. Deb: 8/4/45

YEAR	TM/L	G	AB	R	H	2B	3B	HR	RBI	BB	SO	AVG	OBP	SLG	PRO+	BR/A	SB	CS	SBR	FA	FR	G/POS	TPR
1945	Bos-A	52	204	25	51	7	4	2	16	10	35	.250	.285	.353	83	-5	4	4	-1	.966	1	3-45/O-5	-0.5

■ ROGER LaFRANCOIS LaFrancois, Roger Victor b: 8/2/54, Norwich, Conn. BL/TR, 6'2", 215 lbs. Deb: 5/27/82

YEAR	TM/L	G	AB	R	H	2B	3B	HR	RBI	BB	SO	AVG	OBP	SLG	PRO+	BR/A	SB	CS	SBR	FA	FR	G/POS	TPR
1982	Bos-A	8	10	1	4	1	0	0	1	0	0	.400	.400	.500	137	0	0	0	0	1.000	-0	/C-8	0.0

■ MIKE LAGA Laga, Michael Russell b: 6/14/60, Ridgewood, N.J. BL/TL, 6'2", 210 lbs. Deb: 9/1/82

YEAR	TM/L	G	AB	R	H	2B	3B	HR	RBI	BB	SO	AVG	OBP	SLG	PRO+	BR/A	SB	CS	SBR	FA	FR	G/POS	TPR
1982	Det-A	27	88	6	23	9	0	3	11	4	23	.261	.293	.466	104	0	1	0	0	.994	-2	1-19/D-8	-0.3
1983	Det-A	12	21	2	4	0	0	0	2	1	9	.190	.227	.190	17	-2	0	0	0	1.000	0	/1-5,D-6	-0.2
1984	Det-A	9	11	1	6	0	0	0	1	1	2	.545	.583	.545	216	2	0	0	0	1.000	0	/1-4,D-4	0.2
1985	Det-A	9	36	3	6	1	0	2	6	0	9	.167	.167	.361	40	-3	0	0	0	.974	1	/1-4,D-5	-0.3
1986	Det-A	15	45	6	9	1	0	3	8	5	13	.200	.280	.422	88	-1	0	0	0	1.000	-0	1-12/D-2	-0.2
	StL-N	18	46	7	10	4	0	3	8	5	18	.217	.308	.500	120	1	0	0	0	1.000	2	1-16	0.2
1987	StL-N	17	29	4	4	1	0	1	4	2	7	.138	.194	.276	22	-3	0	0	0	.973	1	1-12	-0.3
1988	StL-N	41	100	5	13	0	0	1	4	2	21	.130	.147	.160	-12	-14	0	0	0	1.000	1	1-37	-1.7
1989	SF-N	17	20	1	4	1	0	1	7	1	6	.200	.238	.400	82	-1	0	0	0	1.000	-0	/1-4	-0.1
1990	SF-N	23	27	4	5	1	0	2	4	1	7	.185	.241	.444	88	-1	0	0	0	1.000	1	1-10	0.0
Total	9	188	423	39	84	18	0	16	55	22	115	.199	.242	.355	63	-22	1	0	0	.996	2	1-123/D-25	-2.7

■ JOE LAHOUD Lahoud, Joseph Michael b: 4/14/47, Danbury, Conn. BL/TL, 6', 202 lbs. Deb: 4/10/68

YEAR	TM/L	G	AB	R	H	2B	3B	HR	RBI	BB	SO	AVG	OBP	SLG	PRO+	BR/A	SB	CS	SBR	FA	FR	G/POS	TPR
1968	Bos-A	29	78	5	15	1	0	1	6	16	16	.192	.330	.244	71	-2	0	2	-1	.926	-3	O-25	-0.9
1969	Bos-A	101	218	32	41	5	0	9	21	40	43	.188	.317	.335	78	-6	2	1	0	.979	-7	O-66/1-1	-1.7
1970	Bos-A	17	49	6	12	1	0	2	5	7	6	.245	.339	.388	93	-0	0	0	0	.963	2	O-13	0.1
1971	Bos-A	107	256	39	55	9	3	14	32	40	45	.215	.330	.438	108	3	2	2	-1	.993	3	O-69	0.2
1972	Mil-A	111	316	35	75	9	3	12	34	45	54	.237	.332	.399	119	8	3	4	-2	.974	-2	O-97	0.0
1973	Mil-A	96	225	29	46	9	0	5	26	27	36	.204	.304	.311	75	-7	5	5	-2	1.000	2	D-41,O-40	-0.9
1974	Cal-A	127	325	46	88	16	3	13	44	47	57	.271	.368	.458	145	19	4	5	-2	.976	-6	*O-106,D-10	0.8
1975	Cal-A	76	192	21	41	6	2	6	33	48	33	.214	.373	.359	116	6	2	1	0	1.000	-3	D-35,O-29	0.2
1976	Cal-A	42	96	8	17	4	0	0	4	18	16	.177	.319	.219	63	-4	0	0	0	.962	-2	O-26/D-3	-0.7
	Tex-A	38	89	10	20	3	1	1	5	10	16	.225	.303	.315	79	-2	1	0	0	1.000	-2	D-22/O-5	-0.4
	Yr	80	185	18	37	7	1	1	9	28	32	.200	.312	.265	72	-6	1	0	0	.964	-4	O-31,D-25	-1.1
1977	*KC-A	34	65	8	17	5	0	2	8	11	16	.262	.368	.431	116	2	1	0	0	.952	-1	O-15/D-4	0.1
1978	KC-A	13	16	0	2	0	0	0	0	0	1	.125	.125	.125	-29	-3	0	0	0	.000	-0	/O-1,D-1	-0.3
Total	11	791	1925	239	429	68	12	65	218	309	339	.223	.335	.372	103	14	20	20	-6	.979	-19	O-492,D-116/1-1	-3.5

■ DICK LAJESKIE Lajeskie, Richard Edward b: 1/8/26, Passaic, N.J. d: 8/15/76, Ramsey, N.J. BR/TR, 5'11", 175 lbs. Deb: 9/10/46

YEAR	TM/L	G	AB	R	H	2B	3B	HR	RBI	BB	SO	AVG	OBP	SLG	PRO+	BR/A	SB	CS	SBR	FA	FR	G/POS	TPR
1946	NY-N	6	10	3	2	0	0	0	0	3	2	.200	.429	.200	81	0	0			.964	5	/2-4	0.5

■ NAP LAJOIE Lajoie, Napoleon "Larry" b: 9/5/1874, Woonsocket, R.I. d: 2/7/59, Daytona Beach, Fla. BR/TR, 6'1", 195 lbs. Deb: 8/12/1896 MH

YEAR	TM/L	G	AB	R	H	2B	3B	HR	RBI	BB	SO	AVG	OBP	SLG	PRO+	BR/A	SB	CS	SBR	FA	FR	G/POS	TPR
1896	Phi-N	39	175	36	57	12	7	4	42	1	11	.326	.330	.543	129	5	7			.995	-3	1-39	0.2
1897	Phi-N	127	545	107	197	40	23	9	127	15		.361	.392	**.569**	156	39	20			.984	-6	*1-108,O-19/3-2	2.8
1898	Phi-N	147	608	113	197	**43**	11	6	**127**	21		.324	.354	.461	139	26	25			.949	-1	*2-146/1-1	3.2
1899	Phi-N	77	312	70	118	19	9	6	70	12		.378	.419	.554	172	29	13			.954	23	2-67/O-5	4.9
1900	Phi-N	102	451	95	152	33	12	7	92	10		.337	.362	.510	140	21	22			**.954**	30	*2-102/3-1	**5.0**
1901	Phi-A	131	544	**145**	**232**	**48**	14	**14**	**125**	24		**.426**	**.463**	**.643**	**196**	**67**	27			**.960**	**29**	*2-119,S-12	**8.9**
1902	Phi-A	1	4	0	1	0	0	0	1	0		.250	.250	.250	37	-0	1			1.000	-0	/2-1	-0.1
	Cle-A	86	348	81	132	35	5	7	64	19		.379	.421	.569	180	36	19			.974	30	2-86	6.3
	Yr	87	352	81	133	35	5	7	65	19		.378	.419	.565	178	36	20			.974	29	2-87	**6.2**
1903	Cle-A	125	485	90	167	41	11	7	93	24		**.344**	.379	**.518**	**170**	**39**	21			.955	**40**	*2-122/1-1,3-1	**8.4**
1904	Cle-A	140	553	92	**208**	**49**	15	5	**102**	27		**.376**	**.413**	**.546**	**204**	**63**	29			.962	-1	2-95,S-44/1-2	**7.1**
1905	Cle-A	65	249	29	82	12	2	2	41	17		.329	.377	.418	150	14	11			.991	9	2-59/1-5,M	2.5
1906	Cle-A	152	602	88	**214**	**48**	9	0	91	30		.355	.392	.465	170	46	20			**.973**	31	*2-130,3-15/S-7,M	**8.4**
1907	Cle-A	137	509	53	152	30	6	2	63	30		.299	.345	.393	134	18	24			**.969**	**46**	*2-128/1-9,M	**6.7**
1908	Cle-A	157	581	77	168	32	6	2	74	47		.289	.352	.375	136	23	15			**.964**	**49**	*2-156/1-1,M	**7.8**
1909	Cle-A	128	469	56	152	33	7	1	47	35		.324	.378	.431	149	26	13			.959	19	*2-120/1-8,M	4.6
1910	Cle-A	159	591	94	**227**	**51**	7	4	76	60		.384	.445	.514	198	**66**	26			.966	15	*2-149,1-10	**8.5**
1911	Cle-A	90	315	36	115	20	1	2	60	26		.365	.420	.454	142	18	13			.990	-7	1-41,2-37	1.0
1912	Cle-A	117	448	66	165	34	4	0	90	28		.368	.414	.462	146	26	18			.959	5	2-97,1-20	2.7

YEAR	TM/L	G	AB	R	H	2B	3B	HR	RBI	BB	SO	AVG	OBP	SLG	PRO+	BR/A	SB	CS	SBR	FA	FR	G/POS	TPR
1913	Cle-A	137	465	66	156	25	2	1	68	33	17	.335	.398	.404	131	19	17			**.970**	9	*2-126	2.8
1914	Cle-A	121	419	37	108	14	3	0	50	32	15	.258	.313	.305	83	-9	14	15	-5	.959	6	2-80,1-31	-1.0
1915	Phi-A	129	490	40	137	24	5	1	61	11	16	.280	.301	.355	100	-3	10	6	-1	.962	14	*2-110,S-10/1-5,3-2	1.2
1916	Phi-A	113	426	33	105	14	4	2	35	14	26	.246	.272	.312	79	-13	15			.973	30	*2-105/1-5,O-2	2.2
Total	21	2480	9589	1504	3242	657	163	82	1599	516	85	.338	.380	.466	150	558	380	21		.963	367	*2-2035,1-286/SO3	94.1
■ EDDIE LAKE	Lake, Edward Erving "Sparky" b: 3/18/16, Antioch, Cal. d: 6/7/95, Castro Valley, Cal. BR/TR, 5'7", 160 lbs. Deb: 9/26/39																						
1939	StL-N	2	4	0	1	0	0	0	0	1	0	.250	.400	.250	74	-0	0			.857	-1	/S-2	-0.1
1940	StL-N	32	66	12	14	3	0	2	7	12	17	.212	.342	.348	86	-1	1			.957	-7	2-17/S-6	-0.7
1941	StL-N	45	76	9	8	2	0	0	0	15	22	.105	.253	.132	10	-9	3			.903	6	S-15,3-15/2-5	-0.2
1943	Bos-A	75	216	26	43	10	0	3	16	47	35	.199	.345	.287	84	-2	3	6	-3	.961	3	S-63	0.3
1944	Bos-A	57	126	21	26	5	0	0	8	23	22	.206	.329	.246	66	-5	5	2	0	.927	-5	S-41/P-6,2-3,3-1	-0.7
1945	Bos-A	133	473	81	132	27	1	11	51	106	37	.279	**.412**	.410	136	27	9	7	-2	.948	19	*S-130/2-1	5.7
1946	Det-A	155	587	105	149	24	1	8	31	103	69	.254	.369	.339	93	-2	15	9	-1	.947	-21	*S-155	-1.6
1947	Det-A	158	602	96	127	19	6	12	46	120	54	.211	.343	.322	83	-11	11	10	-3	.943	-29	*S-158	-3.6
1948	Det-A	64	198	51	52	6	0	2	18	57	20	.263	.427	.323	99	3	3	3	-1	.972	-3	2-45,3-17	0.2
1949	Det-A	94	240	38	47	9	1	1	15	61	33	.196	.359	.254	63	-10	2	8	-4	.959	-10	S-38,2-19,3-18	-2.1
1950	Det-A	20	7	3	0	0	0	0	1	1	3	.000	.125	.000	-64	-2	0	0	0	.000	0	/S-1,3-1	-0.2
Total	11	835	2595	442	599	105	9	39	193	546	312	.231	.366	.323	91	-11	52	45		.947	-48	S-609/2-90,3-52,P-6	-3.0
■ FRED LAKE	Lake, Frederick Lovett b: 10/16/1866, Nova Scotia, Can. d: 11/24/31, Boston, Mass. BR/TR, 5'10", 170 lbs. Deb: 5/7/1891 M																						
1891	Bos-N	5	7	1	1	0	0	0	0	2	4	.143	.333	.143	36	-1	0			1.000	-0	/C-4,O-1	-0.1
1894	Lou-N	16	42	8	12	2	0	1	10	11	6	.286	.474	.405	122	3	2			.864	-3	/2-6,S-5,C-5	0.0
1897	*Bos-N	19	62	2	15	4	0	0	5	1		.242	.254	.306	45	-5	2			.970	-1	C-18	-0.4
1898	Pit-N	5	13	1	1	0	0	0	1	2		.077	.200	.077	-20	-2	0			1.000	-0	/1-3	-0.2
1910	Bos-N	3	1	0	0	0	0	0	0	1	0	.000	.500	.000	46	0	0			.000	0	HM	0.0
Total	5	48	125	12	29	6	0	1	16	17	10	.232	.342	.304	68	-5	4			.930	-5	/C-27,2-6,S-5,1O	-0.7
■ STEVE LAKE	Lake, Steven Michael b: 3/14/57, Inglewood, Cal. BR/TR, 6'1", 190 lbs. Deb: 4/9/83																						
1983	Chi-N	38	85	9	22	4	1	1	7	2	6	.259	.284	.365	75	-3	0	0	0	1.000	4	C-32	0.2
1984	*Chi-N	25	54	4	12	4	0	2	7	0	7	.222	.236	.407	71	-2	0	0	0	.955	0	C-24	-0.1
1985	Chi-N	58	119	5	18	2	0	1	11	3	21	.151	.179	.193	4	-15	1	0	0	.995	6	C-55	-0.8
1986	Chi-N	10	19	4	8	1	0	0	4	1	2	.421	.450	.474	144	1	0	0	0	1.000	-0	C-10	0.1
	StL-N	26	49	4	12	1	0	2	10	2	5	.245	.275	.388	81	-1	0	0	0	.976	1	C-26	0.0
	Yr	36	68	8	20	2	0	2	14	3	7	.294	.324	.412	100	-0	0	0	0	.983	1	C-36	0.1
1987	*StL-N	74	179	19	45	7	2	2	19	10	18	.251	.291	.346	67	-9	0	0	0	.996	-2	C-59	-0.7
1988	StL-N	36	54	5	15	3	0	1	4	3	15	.278	.339	.389	107	1	0	0	0	.983	-1	C-19	0.1
1989	Phi-N	58	155	9	39	5	1	2	14	12	20	.252	.305	.335	83	-3	0	0	0	.990	3	C-55	0.2
1990	Phi-N	29	80	4	20	2	0	0	6	3	12	.250	.286	.275	55	-5	0	0	0	.993	4	C-28	0.0
1991	Phi-N	58	158	12	36	4	1	1	11	2	26	.228	.237	.285	47	-11	0	0	0	.993	2	C-58	-0.7
1992	Phi-N	20	53	3	13	2	0	1	2	1	8	.245	.259	.340	69	-2	0	0	0	.975	0	C-17	-0.2
1993	Chi-N	44	120	11	27	6	0	5	13	4	19	.225	.250	.400	72	-5	0	0	0	.985	1	C-41	-0.3
Total	11	476	1125	89	267	41	5	18	108	43	159	.237	.269	.331	64	-56	1	0	0	.989	18	C-424	-2.2
■ AL LAKEMAN	Lakeman, Albert Wesley "Moose" b: 12/31/18, Cincinnati, Ohio d: 5/25/76, Spartanburg, S.C. BR/TR, 6'2", 195 lbs. Deb: 4/19/42 C																						
1942	Cin-N	20	38	0	6	1	0	0	2	3	10	.158	.238	.184	24	-4	0			.970	3	C-17	0.0
1943	Cin-N	22	55	5	14	2	1	0	6	3	11	.255	.293	.327	80	-2	0			1.000	-2	C-21	-0.2
1944	Cin-N	1	1	0	0	0	0	0	0	0	1	.000	.000	.000	-99	-0	0			.000	0	H	0.0
1945	Cin-N	76	258	22	66	9	4	8	31	17	45	.256	.304	.415	101	-1	0			.963	-11	C-74	-0.7
1946	Cin-N	23	30	0	4	0	0	0	4	2	7	.133	.188	.133	-9	-4	0			1.000	-0	/C-6	-0.5
1947	Cin-N	2	2	0	0	0	0	0	0	0	1	.000	.000	.000	-99	-1	0			.000	0	H	-0.1
	Phi-N	55	182	11	29	3	0	6	19	5	39	.159	.186	.275	22	-21	0			.995	-5	1-29,C-23	-2.6
	Yr	57	184	11	29	3	0	6	19	5	40	.158	.184	.272	20	-22	0			.995	-5	1-29,C-23	-2.7
1948	Phi-N	32	68	2	11	2	0	1	4	5	22	.162	.219	.235	23	-7	0			1.000	-2	C-22/P-1	-0.8
1949	Bos-N	3	6	0	1	0	0	0	0	1	0	.167	.286	.167	26	-1	0			1.000	1	/1-2	0.0
1954	Det-A	5	6	0	0	0	0	0	0	0	1	.000	.000	.000	-99	-2	0	0	0	1.000	1	/C-4	-0.1
Total	9	239	646	40	131	17	5	15	66	36	137	.203	.248	.314	55	-42	0	0		.974	-16	C-167/1-31,P-1	-5.0
■ TIM LAKER	Laker, Timothy John b: 11/27/69, Encino, Cal. BR/TR, 6'3", 195 lbs. Deb: 8/18/92																						
1992	Mon-N	28	46	8	10	3	0	0	4	2	14	.217	.250	.283	51	-3	1	1	-0	.991	5	C-28	0.3
1993	Mon-N	43	86	3	17	2	1	0	7	2	16	.198	.225	.244	24	-9	2	0	1	.987	2	C-43	-0.5
1995	Mon-N	64	141	17	33	8	1	3	20	14	38	.234	.308	.369	75	-5	0	1	-1	.977	3	C-61	0.0
1997	Bal-A	7	14	0	0	0	0	0	1	2	9	.000	.125	.000	-66	-3	0	0	0	.966	-2	/C-7	-0.5
1998	TB-A	3	5	1	1	0	0	0	0	1	1	.200	.333	.200	42	-0	0	1	-1	1.000	-0	/C-2,D-1	-0.1
	Pit-N	14	24	2	9	1	0	1	2	1	3	.375	.400	.542	139	1	0	0	0	1.000	-1	/1-4,C-1	0.0
Total	5	159	316	31	70	14	2	4	34	22	81	.222	.276	.316	56	-20	3	3	-1	.982	7	C-142/1-4,D-1	-0.8
■ DAN LALLY	Lally, Daniel J. b: 8/12/1867, Jersey City, N.J. d: 4/14/36, Milwaukee, Wis. BR/TR, 5'11.5", 210 lbs. Deb: 8/19/1891																						
1891	Pit-N	41	143	24	32	6	2	1	17	16	20	.224	.319	.315	87	-2	0			.839	-7	O-41	-0.9
1897	StL-N	87	355	56	99	15	5	2	42	9		.279	.310	.366	80	-12	12			.897	2	O-84/1-3	-1.3
Total	2	128	498	80	131	21	7	3	59	25	20	.263	.313	.351	82	-14	12			.886	-4	O-125/1-3	-2.2
■ RAY LAMANNO	Lamanno, Raymond Simond b: 11/17/19, Oakland, Cal. d: 2/9/94, Berkeley, Cal. BR/TR, 6', 185 lbs. Deb: 9/11/41																						
1941	Cin-N	1	0	0	0	0	0	0	0	0	0	—	1.000	—	197	0	0			1.000	-0	/C-1	0.0
1942	Cin-N	111	371	40	98	12	2	12	43	31	54	.264	.324	.404	113	5	0			.978	-11	*C-104	0.2
1946	Cin-N★	85	239	18	58	12	0	1	30	11	26	.243	.285	.305	70	-10	0			.974	2	C-61	-0.5
1947	Cin-N	118	413	33	106	21	3	5	50	28	39	.257	.307	.358	77	-15	0			.986	9	*C-109	0.1
1948	Cin-N	127	385	31	93	12	0	0	27	48	32	.242	.329	.273	67	-16	2			.978	-11	*C-125	-2.0
Total	5	442	1408	122	355	57	5	18	150	118	151	.252	.314	.338	82	-36	2			.980	-11	C-400	-2.2
■ BILL LAMAR	Lamar, William Harmong "Good Time Bill" b: 3/21/1897, Rockville, Md. d: 5/24/70, Rockport, Mass. BL/TR, 6'1", 185 lbs. Deb: 9/19/17																						
1917	NY-A	11	41	2	10	0	0	0	3	0	2	.244	.244	.244	48	-3	1			1.000	0	O-11	-0.3
1918	NY-A	28	110	12	25	3	0	0	2	6	2	.227	.267	.255	56	-6	2			.884	-2	O-27	-1.1
1919	NY-A	11	16	1	3	1	0	0	0	2	1	.188	.278	.250	48	-1	1			1.000	-1	/O-3,1-1	-0.2
	Bos-A	48	148	18	43	5	1	0	14	5	9	.291	.314	.338	88	-3	3			.922	-2	O-36	-0.8
	Yr	59	164	19	46	6	1	0	14	7	10	.280	.310	.329	83	-4	4			.926	-3	O-39/1-1	-1.0
1920	*Bro-N	24	44	5	12	4	0	0	4	0	1	.273	.273	.364	79	-1	0	0	0	1.000	-3	O-12	-0.5
1921	Bro-N	3	3	2	1	0	0	0	0	0	0	.333	.333	.333	74	-0	0	0	0	.000	-1	/O-1	-0.1
1924	Phi-A	87	367	68	121	22	5	7	48	18	21	.330	.361	.474	113	5	8	8	-2	.971	4	O-87	0.1
1925	Phi-A	138	568	85	202	39	8	3	77	21	17	.356	.379	.468	107	4	2	6	-3	.953	4	*O-131	-0.3
1926	Phi-A	116	419	62	119	17	6	5	50	18	15	.284	.315	.389	78	-15	4	5	-2	.954	-3	*O-107	-2.6
1927	Phi-A	84	324	48	97	23	3	4	47	16	10	.299	.334	.426	91	-5	4	8	-4	.952	-3	O-79	-1.6
Total	9	550	2040	303	633	114	23	19	245	86	78	.310	.339	.417	94	-24	25	27		.952	-7	O-494/1-1	-7.4
■ LYMAN LAMB	Lamb, Laymon Raymond b: 3/17/1895, Lincoln, Neb. d: 10/5/55, Fayetteville, Ark. BR/TR, 5'7", 150 lbs. Deb: 9/14/20																						
1920	StL-A	9	24	4	9	2	0	0	4	0	7	.375	.375	.458	116	0	2	0	1	1.000	-2	/O-7	-0.1
1921	StL-A	45	134	18	34	9	2	1	17	4	12	.254	.281	.373	62	-8	0	0	0	.942	-9	3-25/2-7,O-6	-1.5
Total	2	54	158	22	43	11	2	1	21	4	19	.272	.294	.386	70	-8	2	0	1	1.000	-11	/3-25,O-13,2-7	-1.6
■ PETE LAMER	Lamer, Pierre b: 12/1873, New York, N.Y. d: 10/24/31, Brooklyn, N.Y. TR , 5'10", 170 lbs. Deb: 9/10/02																						
1902	Chi-N	2	9	2	2	0	0	0	0	0		.222	.222	.222	38	-1	0			.857	-0	/C-2	-0.1

YEAR	TM/L	G	AB	R	H	2B	3B	HR	RBI	BB	SO	AVG	OBP	SLG	PRO+	BR/A	SB	CS	SBR	FA	FR	G/POS	TPR
1907	Cin-N	1	2	0	0	0	0	0	0	0	0	.000	.000	.000	-96	-0	0			1.000	-0	/C-1	-0.1
Total	2	3	11	2	2	0	0	0	0	0		.182	.182	.182	13	-1	0			.867	-1	/C-3	-0.2
■ **GENE LAMONT** Lamont, Gene William b: 12/25/46, Rockford, Ill. BL/TR, 6'1", 195 lbs. Deb: 9/2/70 MC																							
1970	Det-A	15	44	3	13	3	1	1	4	2	9	.295	.340	.477	122	1	0	0	0	1.000	1	C-15	0.3
1971	Det-A	7	15	2	1	0	0	0	1	0	5	.067	.067	.067	-60	-3	0	0	0	.952	2	/C-7	-0.1
1972	Det-A	1	0	0	0	0	0	0	0	0	0	—	—	—	—	0	0	0	0	1.000	-0	/C-1	0.0
1974	Det-A	60	92	9	20	4	0	3	8	7	19	.217	.273	.359	78	-3	0	0	0	.974	8	C-60	0.7
1975	Det-A	4	8	1	3	1	0	0	1	0	2	.375	.375	.500	139	0	1	0	0	.944	1	/C-4	0.2
Total	5	87	159	15	37	8	1	4	14	9	35	.233	.278	.371	80	-4	1	0	0	.977	12	/C-87	1.1
■ **BOBBY LaMOTTE** LaMotte, Robert Eugene b: 2/15/1898, Savannah, Ga. d: 11/2/70, Chatham, Ga. BR/TR, 5'11", 160 lbs. Deb: 9/1/20																							
1920	Was-A	4	3	0	0	0	0	0	0	1	1	.000	.250	.000	-31	-1	0	0	0	.750	0	/S-1,3-1	0.0
1921	Was-A	16	41	5	8	0	0	0	2	5	0	.195	.283	.195	25	-5	0	0	0	.940	2	S-12	-0.2
1922	Was-A	68	214	22	54	10	2	1	23	15	21	.252	.307	.332	70	-10	6	1	1	.954	8	3-62/S-6	0.4
1925	StL-A	97	356	61	97	20	4	2	51	34	22	.272	.338	.368	75	-14	5	5	-2	.926	2	S-93/3-3	-0.3
1926	StL-A	36	79	11	16	4	3	0	9	11	6	.203	.300	.329	61	-5	0	0	0	.919	-2	S-30/3-1	-0.4
Total	5	221	693	99	175	34	9	3	85	66	50	.253	.320	.341	69	-33	11	6	-0	.927	10	S-142/3-67	-0.5
■ **KEITH LAMPARD** Lampard, Christopher Keith b: 12/20/45, Warrington, England BL/TR, 6'2", 197 lbs. Deb: 9/15/69																							
1969	Hou-N	9	12	2	3	0	0	1	2	0	3	.250	.250	.500	108	0	0	0	0	1.000	1	/O-1	0.1
1970	Hou-N	53	72	8	17	8	1	0	5	5	24	.236	.295	.375	82	-2	0	0	0	1.000	-1	O-16/1-2	-0.3
Total	2	62	84	10	20	8	1	1	7	5	27	.238	.289	.393	85	-2	0	0	0	1.000	1	/O-17,1-2	-0.2
■ **TOM LAMPKIN** Lampkin, Thomas Michael b: 3/4/64, Cincinnati, Ohio BL/TR, 5'11", 185 lbs. Deb: 9/10/88																							
1988	Cle-A	4	4	0	0	0	0	0	0	1	0	.000	.200	.000	-38	-1	0	0	0	1.000	-1	/C-3	-0.2
1990	SD-N	26	63	4	14	0	1	1	4	4	9	.222	.269	.302	56	-4	0	1	-1	.971	1	C-20	-0.3
1991	SD-N	38	58	4	11	3	1	0	3	3	9	.190	.230	.276	40	-5	0	0	0	1.000	0	C-11	-0.4
1992	SD-N	9	17	3	4	0	0	0	0	6	1	.235	.458	.235	100	1	2	0	1	1.000	-2	/C-7,O-1	0.0
1993	Mil-A	73	162	22	32	8	0	4	25	20	26	.198	.286	.321	64	-8	7	3	0	.978	-3	C-60/O-3,D-1	-0.9
1995	SF-N	65	76	8	21	2	0	1	9	9	8	.276	.360	.342	89	-1	2	0	1	1.000	-2	C-17/O-6	-0.1
1996	SF-N	66	177	26	41	8	0	6	29	20	22	.232	.327	.379	89	-3	1	5	-3	.992	7	C-53	0.4
1997	StL-N	108	229	28	56	8	1	7	22	28	30	.245	.337	.380	88	-4	2	1	0	.989	-6	C-86	-0.6
1998	StL-N	93	216	25	50	12	1	6	28	24	32	.231	.328	.380	84	-5	3	2	-0	.986	-3	C-62/O-5,1-2	-0.4
Total	9	482	1002	120	229	41	4	25	120	115	137	.229	.319	.352	79	-29	17	12	-2	.987	-8	C-319/O-15,1-2,D-1	-2.5
■ **RICK LANCELLOTTI** Lancellotti, Richard Anthony b: 7/5/56, Providence, R.I. BL/TL, 6'3", 195 lbs. Deb: 8/27/82																							
1982	SD-N	17	39	2	7	2	0	0	4	2	8	.179	.220	.231	28	-4	0	0	0	1.000	-2	/1-7,O-3	-0.6
1986	SF-N	15	18	2	4	0	0	2	6	0	7	.222	.222	.556	113	0	0	0	0	1.000	1	/1-1,O-1	0.1
1990	Bos-A	4	8	0	0	0	0	0	1	0	3	.000	.000	.000	-96	-2	0	0	0	1.000	0	/1-2	-0.2
Total	3	36	65	4	11	2	0	2	11	2	18	.169	.194	.292	35	-6	0	0	0	1.000	-0	/1-10,O-4	-0.7
■ **GROVER LAND** Land, Grover Cleveland b: 9/22/1884, Frankfort, Ky. d: 7/22/58, Phoenix, Ariz. BR/TR, 6', 190 lbs. Deb: 9/2/08 C																							
1908	Cle-A	8	16	1	3	0	0	0	2	0		.188	.188	.188	22	-1	0			.955	-1	/C-8	-0.3
1909	Cle-A	1	4	0	2	0	0	0	1	0		.500	.500	.500	207	0	0			1.000	0	/C-1	0.1
1910	Cle-A	34	111	4	23	0	0	0	7	2		.207	.228	.207	36	-8	1			.982	5	C-33	-0.1
1911	Cle-A	35	107	5	15	1	2	0	10	3		.140	.164	.187	-2	-15	2			.961	1	C-34/1-1	-1.1
1913	Cle-A	17	47	3	11	1	0	0	9	4	1	.234	.321	.255	67	-2	1			.924	1	C-17	0.0
1914	Bro-F	102	335	24	92	6	2	0	29	12	23	.275	.306	.304	67	-20	7			.970	0	C-97	-1.3
1915	Bro-F	96	290	25	75	13	2	0	22	6	20	.259	.279	.317	68	-17	3			.960	-6	C-81	-1.9
Total	7	293	910	62	221	21	6	0	80	27	44	.243	.271	.279	55	-64	14			.964	-2	C-271/1-1	-4.6
■ **DOC LAND** Land, William Gilbert (b: Doc Burrell Land) b: 5/14/03, Binnsville, Miss. d: 4/14/86, Livingston, Ala. BL/TL, 5'11", 165 lbs. Deb: 10/6/29																							
1929	Was-A	1	3	0	0	0	0	0	0	1	0	.000	.250	.000	-30	-1	0	0	0	1.000	-0	/O-1	-0.1
■ **KEN LANDENBERGER** Landenberger, Kenneth Henry "Red" b: 7/29/28, Lyndhurst, Ohio d: 7/28/60, Cleveland, Ohio BL/TL, 6'3", 200 lbs. Deb: 9/20/52																							
1952	Chi-A	2	5	0	1	0	0	0	0	0	2	.200	.200	.200	11	-1	0	0	0	1.000	0	/1-1	0.0
■ **RAFAEL LANDESTOY** Landestoy, Rafael Silvialdo (Santana) b: 5/28/53, Bani, D.R. BB/TR, 5'10", 165 lbs. Deb: 8/27/77 C																							
1977	*LA-N	15	18	6	5	0	0	0	0	3	2	.278	.381	.278	80	-0	2	0	1	1.000	3	/2-8,S-3	0.3
1978	Hou-N	59	218	18	58	5	1	0	9	8	23	.266	.292	.298	70	-9	7	4	-0	.980	-13	S-50/O-3,2-2	-1.8
1979	Hou-N	129	282	33	76	9	6	0	30	29	24	.270	.340	.344	92	-3	13	4	2	.971	-2	*2-114/S-3	0.2
1980	*Hou-N	149	393	42	97	13	8	1	27	31	37	.247	.307	.328	84	-9	23	12	-0	.991	-6	2-94,S-65/3-3	-0.7
1981	Hou-N	35	74	6	11	1	1	0	4	16	9	.149	.300	.189	43	-5	4	1	1	.966	-4	2-31	-0.8
	Cin-N	12	11	2	2	0	0	0	1	1	0	.182	.250	.182	24	-1	1	0	0	1.000	-0	/2-3	-0.1
	Yr	47	85	8	13	1	1	0	5	17	9	.153	.294	.188	40	-6	5	1	1	.967	-5	2-34	-0.9
1982	Cin-N	73	111	11	21	3	0	1	9	8	14	.189	.250	.243	38	-9	2	0	1	1.000	4	3-21,2-16/O-3,S-2	-0.5
1983	Cin-N	7	5	0	0	0	0	0	0	0	0	.000	.000	.000	-97	-1	0	0	0	1.000	-1	/1-2,3-1,O-1	-0.2
	*LA-N	64	64	6	11	1	1	1	1	3	8	.172	.209	.266	31	-6	0	2	-1	1.000	2	2-14,3-10,O-10,/S-1	-0.5
	Yr	71	69	6	11	1	1	1	1	3	8	.159	.194	.246	21	-7	0	2	-1	1.000	1	2-14,3-11,O-11,/1S	-0.7
1984	LA-N	53	54	10	10	0	0	1	2	1	6	.185	.200	.241	24	-6	2	1	0	.886	1	2-14,3-11/O-5	-0.4
Total	8	596	1230	134	291	32	17	4	83	100	123	.237	.297	.300	70	-50	54	24	2	.976	-17	2-296,S-124/3O1	-4.5
■ **JIM LANDIS** Landis, James Henry b: 3/9/34, Fresno, Cal. BR/TR, 6'1", 180 lbs. Deb: 4/16/57																							
1957	Chi-A	96	274	38	58	11	3	2	16	45	61	.212	.329	.296	72	-10	14	4	2	.985	4	O-90	-0.9
1958	Chi-A	142	523	72	145	23	7	15	64	52	80	.277	.352	.434	117	12	19	7	2	.986	6	*O-142	1.2
1959	*Chi-A	149	515	78	140	26	7	5	60	78	68	.272	.376	.379	109	10	20	9	1	.993	16	*O-148	1.8
1960	Chi-A	148	494	89	125	25	6	10	49	80	84	.253	.367	.389	106	6	23	6	3	.985	13	*O-147	1.5
1961	Chi-A	140	534	87	151	18	8	22	85	65	71	.283	.365	.470	123	18	19	5	3	.988	19	*O-139	3.1
1962	Chi-A★	149	534	82	122	21	6	15	61	80	105	.228	.339	.375	92	-5	19	7	2	.995	10	*O-144	-0.2
1963	Chi-A	133	396	56	89	6	6	13	45	47	75	.225	.316	.369	93	-3	8	6	-1	**.993**	1	*O-124	-1.0
1964	Chi-A	106	298	30	62	8	4	1	18	36	64	.208	.306	.272	64	-14	5	0	2	.995	-4	*O-101	-2.1
1965	KC-A	118	364	46	87	15	1	3	36	57	84	.239	.347	.310	90	-3	8	3	1	.985	6	*O-108	-0.2
1966	Cle-A	85	158	23	35	5	1	3	14	20	25	.222	.317	.323	84	-3	2	1	0	1.000	-11	O-61	-1.7
1967	Det-A	25	48	4	10	0	0	2	4	7	12	.208	.309	.333	87	-1	0	2	-1	.952	0	O-12	-0.2
	Bos-A	5	7	1	1	0	0	1	1	1	3	.143	.250	.571	126	0	0	0	0	1.000	-1	/O-5	-0.1
	Yr	30	55	5	11	0	0	3	5	8	15	.200	.302	.364	92	-0	0	2	-1	.960	-1	O-17	-0.3
	Hou-N	50	143	19	36	11	1	1	14	20	35	.252	.348	.364	107	2	2	1	0	1.000	-1	O-44	-0.1
Total	11	1346	4288	625	1061	169	50	93	467	588	767	.247	.346	.375	100	10	139	51	11	.989	58	*O-1265	1.1
■ **KEN LANDREAUX** Landreaux, Kenneth Francis b: 12/22/54, Los Angeles, Cal. BL/TR, 5'10", 165 lbs. Deb: 9/11/77																							
1977	Cal-A	23	76	6	19	5	1	0	5	5	15	.250	.296	.342	76	-3	1	1	-0	.970	5	O-22	0.1
1978	Cal-A	93	260	37	58	7	5	5	23	20	20	.223	.284	.346	79	-8	7	3	0	.986	-7	O-83/D-1	-1.8
1979	Min-A	151	564	81	172	27	5	15	83	37	57	.305	.352	.450	110	8	10	3	1	.981	-8	*O-147	-0.6
1980	Min-A★	129	484	56	136	23	11	7	62	39	42	.281	.337	.417	98	-2	8	6	-1	.976	-9	*O-120/D-6	-1.7
1981	*LA-N	99	390	48	98	16	4	7	41	25	42	.251	.298	.367	91	-6	18	4	3	**1.000**	-4	O-95	-1.1
1982	LA-N	129	461	71	131	23	7	7	50	39	54	.284	.345	.410	113	8	31	10	3	.986	2	*O-117	1.1
1983	*LA-N	141	481	63	135	25	3	17	66	34	52	.281	.331	.451	115	8	30	11	2	.990	-2	*O-137	0.5
1984	LA-N	134	438	39	110	11	5	11	47	29	35	.251	.299	.374	89	-7	10	9	-2	.986	-16	*O-129	-3.1
1985	*LA-N	147	482	70	129	26	2	12	50	33	37	.268	.316	.405	103	1	15	5	2	.975	-7	*O-140	-1.0
1986	LA-N	103	283	34	74	13	2	4	29	22	39	.261	.317	.364	94	-3	10	5	0	.955	-5	O-85	-1.1

YEAR	TM/L	G	AB	R	H	2B	3B	HR	RBI	BB	SO	AVG	OBP	SLG	PRO+	BR/A	SB	CS	SBR	FA	FR	G/POS	TPR
1987	LA-N	115	182	17	37	4	0	6	23	16	28	.203	.271	.324	58	-11	5	3	-0	.951	-6	O-63	-1.9
Total	11	1264	4101	522	1099	180	45	91	479	299	421	.268	.321	.400	99	-15	145	60	8	.981	-57	*O-1138/D-7	-10.6

■ HOBIE LANDRITH

Landrith, Hobert Neal b: 3/16/30, Decatur, Ill. BL/TR, 5'10", 170 lbs. Deb: 7/30/50 C

YEAR	TM/L	G	AB	R	H	2B	3B	HR	RBI	BB	SO	AVG	OBP	SLG	PRO+	BR/A	SB	CS	SBR	FA	FR	G/POS	TPR
1950	Cin-N	4	14	1	3	0	0	0	1	2	1	.214	.313	.214	41	-1	0			1.000	-1	/C-4	-0.2
1951	Cin-N	4	13	3	5	1	0	0	0	1	1	.385	.429	.462	137	1	0	0	0	1.000	1	/C-4	0.2
1952	Cin-N	15	50	1	13	4	0	0	4	0	4	.260	.260	.340	65	-2	0	1	-1	1.000	0	C-14	-0.2
1953	Cin-N	52	154	15	37	3	1	3	16	12	8	.240	.299	.331	64	-8	2	0	1	.985	0	C-47	-0.5
1954	Cin-N	48	81	12	16	0	0	5	14	18	9	.198	.343	.383	86	-1	1	0	0	.986	4	C-42	0.4
1955	Cin-N	43	87	9	22	3	0	4	7	10	14	.253	.330	.425	93	-1	0	1	-1	1.000	4	C-27	0.3
1956	Chi-N	111	312	22	69	10	3	4	32	39	38	.221	.310	.311	69	-13	0	2	-1	.975	-3	C-99	-1.3
1957	StL-N	75	214	18	52	6	0	3	26	25	27	.243	.322	.313	70	-8	0	2	-1	.987	5	C-67	-0.2
1958	StL-N	70	144	9	31	4	0	3	13	26	21	.215	.335	.306	68	-6	0	1	-1	.992	2	C-45	-0.2
1959	SF-N	109	283	30	71	14	0	3	29	43	23	.251	.350	.332	85	-5	0	4	-2	.992	7	*C-109	0.5
1960	SF-N	71	190	18	46	10	0	1	20	23	11	.242	.324	.311	79	-5	1	1	-0	.966	-5	C-70	-0.7
1961	SF-N	43	71	11	17	4	0	2	10	12	7	.239	.349	.380	97	-0	0	0	0	.985	2	C-30	0.2
1962	NY-N	23	45	6	13	3	0	1	7	8	3	.289	.396	.422	118	1	0	0	0	.968	-1	C-21	0.1
	Bal-A	60	167	18	37	4	1	4	17	19	9	.222	.305	.329	75	-6	0	0	0	.982	5	C-60	0.1
1963	Bal-A	2	1	0	0	0	0	0	0	0	0	.000	.000	.000	-99	-0	0	0	0	1.000	-0	/C-1	0.0
	Was-A	42	103	6	18	3	0	1	7	15	12	.175	.280	.233	46	-7	0	0	0	.978	2	C-37	-0.5
	Yr	44	104	6	18	3	0	1	7	15	12	.173	.277	.231	44	-7	0	0	0	.978	2	C-38	-0.5
Total	14	772	1929	179	450	69	5	34	203	253	188	.233	.323	.327	76	-63	5	12		.983	22	C-677	-2.0

■ CED LANDRUM

Landrum, Cedric Bernard b: 9/3/63, Butler, Ala. BL/TR, 5'7", 167 lbs. Deb: 5/28/91

YEAR	TM/L	G	AB	R	H	2B	3B	HR	RBI	BB	SO	AVG	OBP	SLG	PRO+	BR/A	SB	CS	SBR	FA	FR	G/POS	TPR
1991	Chi-N	56	86	28	20	2	1	0	6	10	18	.233	.313	.279	65	-4	27	5	5	.968	-9	O-44	-0.9
1993	NY-N	22	19	2	5	1	0	0	1	0	5	.263	.263	.316	55	-1	0	0	0	.000	-1	/O-3	-0.2
Total	2	78	105	30	25	3	1	0	7	10	23	.238	.304	.286	63	-5	27	5	5	.968	-11	/O-47	-1.1

■ DON LANDRUM

Landrum, Donald Leroy b: 2/16/36, Santa Rosa, Cal. BL/TR, 6', 180 lbs. Deb: 9/28/57

YEAR	TM/L	G	AB	R	H	2B	3B	HR	RBI	BB	SO	AVG	OBP	SLG	PRO+	BR/A	SB	CS	SBR	FA	FR	G/POS	TPR
1957	Phi-N	2	7	1	1	1	0	0	0	2	1	.143	.333	.286	71	-0	0	0	0	1.000	1	/O-2	0.0
1960	StL-N	13	49	7	12	0	1	2	3	4	6	.245	.315	.408	88	-1	3	0	1	1.000	-0	O-13	-0.1
1961	StL-N	28	66	5	11	2	0	1	3	5	14	.167	.225	.242	22	-7	1	0	0	1.000	-3	O-25/2-1	-1.1
1962	StL-N	32	35	11	11	0	0	0	3	4	2	.314	.385	.314	82	-1	2	0	1	1.000	-6	O-26	-0.7
	Chi-N	83	238	29	67	5	2	1	15	30	31	.282	.369	.332	87	-3	9	2	2	.969	-1	O-59	-0.6
	Yr	115	273	40	78	5	2	1	18	34	33	.286	.371	.330	85	-4	11	2	2	.973	-7	O-85	-1.3
1963	Chi-N	84	227	27	55	4	1	1	10	13	42	.242	.295	.282	64	-10	6	3	0	.972	-4	O-57	-1.9
1964	Chi-N	11	11	2	0	0	0	0	0	1	2	.000	.083	.000	-71	-2	0	0	0	1.000	1	/O-1	-0.2
1965	Chi-N	131	425	60	96	20	4	6	34	36	84	.226	.301	.334	77	-13	14	8	-1	.988	1	*O-115	-1.8
1966	SF-N	72	102	9	19	4	0	1	7	9	18	.186	.259	.255	42	-8	1	1	-0	.968	-5	O-54	-1.5
Total	8	456	1160	151	272	36	8	12	75	104	200	.234	.308	.310	69	-45	36	14	2	.982	-16	O-352/2-1	-7.9

■ JESSE LANDRUM

Landrum, Jesse Glenn b: 7/31/12, Crockett, Tex. d: 6/27/83, Beaumont, Tex. BR/TR, 5'11.5", 175 lbs. Deb: 4/26/38

YEAR	TM/L	G	AB	R	H	2B	3B	HR	RBI	BB	SO	AVG	OBP	SLG	PRO+	BR/A	SB	CS	SBR	FA	FR	G/POS	TPR
1938	Chi-A	4	6	0	0	0	0	0	1	0	2	.000	.000	.000	-98	-2	0	0	0	1.000	-1	/2-3	-0.2

■ TITO LANDRUM

Landrum, Terry Lee b: 10/25/54, Joplin, Mo. BR/TR, 5'11", 175 lbs. Deb: 7/23/80

YEAR	TM/L	G	AB	R	H	2B	3B	HR	RBI	BB	SO	AVG	OBP	SLG	PRO+	BR/A	SB	CS	SBR	FA	FR	G/POS	TPR
1980	StL-N	35	77	6	19	2	2	0	7	6	17	.247	.310	.325	75	-3	3	2	-0	.976	-5	O-29	-0.9
1981	StL-N	81	119	13	31	5	4	0	10	6	14	.261	.302	.370	87	-2	4	2	0	1.000	-13	O-67	-1.8
1982	StL-N	79	72	12	20	3	0	2	14	8	18	.278	.358	.403	111	1	0	1	-1	1.000	5	O-56	0.5
1983	StL-N	6	5	0	1	0	1	0	0	1	2	.200	.333	.600	154	0	1	0	0	1.000	-2	/O-5	-0.1
	*Bal-A	26	42	8	13	2	0	1	4	1	11	.310	.326	.429	108	0	0	2	-1	1.000	-6	O-26	-0.7
1984	StL-N	105	173	21	47	9	1	3	26	10	27	.272	.311	.387	98	-1	3	4	-2	.979	-21	O-88	-2.7
1985	*StL-N	85	161	21	45	8	2	4	21	19	30	.280	.356	.429	119	4	1	4	-2	1.000	-11	O-73	-1.0
1986	StL-N	96	205	24	43	7	1	2	17	20	41	.210	.283	.283	57	-12	3	1	0	.993	-4	O-78	-1.8
1987	StL-N	30	50	5	10	1	0	0	6	7	14	.200	.298	.220	39	-4	1	1	-0	1.000	-2	O-23/1-1	-0.7
	LA-N	51	67	8	16	3	0	1	4	3	16	.239	.282	.328	63	-4	1	1	-0	.971	-5	O-31	-0.9
	Yr	81	117	13	26	4	0	1	10	10	30	.222	.289	.282	53	-8	2	2	-1	.987	-7	O-54/1-1	-1.6
1988	Bal-A	13	24	2	3	0	1	0	2	4	6	.125	.250	.208	31	-2	0	0	0	1.000	-3	O-12/D-1	-0.5
Total	9	607	995	120	248	40	12	13	111	85	196	.249	.312	.353	84	-22	17	18	-6	.992	-65	O-488/D-1,1-1	-10.6

■ CHAPPY LANE

Lane, George M. b: Pittsburgh, Pa. BR, 165 lbs. Deb: 5/16/1882

YEAR	TM/L	G	AB	R	H	2B	3B	HR	RBI	BB	SO	AVG	OBP	SLG	PRO+	BR/A	SB	CS	SBR	FA	FR	G/POS	TPR
1882	Pit-a	57	214	26	38	8	2	3		5		.178	.196	.276	60	-8				.974	5	1-43,O-13/C-2	-0.7
1884	Tol-a	57	215	26	49	9	5	1		2		.228	.242	.330	82	-5				.948	4	1-46/O-9,3-2,C-1	-0.6
Total	2	114	429	52	87	17	7	4		7		.203	.219	.303	72	-13				.961	9	/1-89,O-22,C-3,3-2	-1.3

■ HUNTER LANE

Lane, James Hunter "Dodo" b: 7/20/1900, Pulaski, Tenn. d: 9/12/94, Memphis, Tenn. BR/TR, 5'11", 165 lbs. Deb: 5/13/24

YEAR	TM/L	G	AB	R	H	2B	3B	HR	RBI	BB	SO	AVG	OBP	SLG	PRO+	BR/A	SB	CS	SBR	FA	FR	G/POS	TPR
1924	Bos-N	7	15	0	1	0	0	0	0	1	1	.067	.125	.067	-49	-3	0	0	0	.909	-1	/3-4,2-1	-0.4

■ MARVIN LANE

Lane, Marvin b: 1/18/50, Sandersville, Ga. BR/TR, 5'11", 180 lbs. Deb: 9/4/71

YEAR	TM/L	G	AB	R	H	2B	3B	HR	RBI	BB	SO	AVG	OBP	SLG	PRO+	BR/A	SB	CS	SBR	FA	FR	G/POS	TPR
1971	Det-A	8	14	0	2	0	0	0	1	1	3	.143	.200	.143	-1	-2	0	0	0	1.000	-1	/O-6	-0.3
1972	Det-A	8	6	2	0	0	0	0	0	0	2	.000	.000	.000	-97	-1	0	0	0	1.000	-1	/O-3	-0.2
1973	Det-A	6	8	2	2	0	0	1	2	2	2	.250	.400	.625	173	1	0	0	0	1.000	-1	/O-4	0.0
1974	Det-A	50	103	16	24	4	1	2	9	19	24	.233	.352	.350	99	0	2	0	1	.986	-3	O-46/D-1	-0.3
1976	Det-A	18	48	3	9	1	0	0	5	6	11	.188	.278	.208	42	-3	0	0	0	.960	-2	O-15	-0.6
Total	5	90	179	23	37	5	1	3	17	28	42	.207	.314	.296	74	-5	2	0	1	.983	-8	/O-74,D-1	-1.4

■ DICK LANE

Lane, Richard Harrison b: 6/28/27, Highland Park, Mich. BR/TR, 5'11", 178 lbs. Deb: 6/20/49

YEAR	TM/L	G	AB	R	H	2B	3B	HR	RBI	BB	SO	AVG	OBP	SLG	PRO+	BR/A	SB	CS	SBR	FA	FR	G/POS	TPR
1949	Chi-A	12	42	4	5	0	0	0	4	5	3	.119	.213	.119	-11	-7	0	1	-1	1.000	1	O-11	-0.7

■ DON LANG

Lang, Donald Charles b: 3/15/15, Selma, Cal. BR/TR, 6', 175 lbs. Deb: 7/4/38

YEAR	TM/L	G	AB	R	H	2B	3B	HR	RBI	BB	SO	AVG	OBP	SLG	PRO+	BR/A	SB	CS	SBR	FA	FR	G/POS	TPR
1938	Cin-N	21	50	5	13	3	1	1	11	2	7	.260	.288	.420	95	-1	0			.976	2	3-15/2-1,S-1	0.1
1948	StL-N	117	323	30	87	14	1	4	31	47	38	.269	.364	.356	90	-3	2			.964	9	3-95/2-2	0.5
Total	2	138	373	35	100	17	2	5	42	49	45	.268	.355	.365	91	-4	2			.966	10	3-110/2-3,S-1	0.6

■ BILL LANGE

Lange, William Alexander "Little Eva" b: 6/6/1871, San Francisco, Cal d: 7/23/50, San Francisco, Cal. BR/TR, 6'1.5", 190 lbs. Deb: 4/27/1893

YEAR	TM/L	G	AB	R	H	2B	3B	HR	RBI	BB	SO	AVG	OBP	SLG	PRO+	BR/A	SB	CS	SBR	FA	FR	G/POS	TPR
1893	Chi-N	117	469	92	132	8	7	8	88	52	20	.281	.358	.380	98	-2	47			.888	2	2-57,O-40/3-8,SC	0.1
1894	Chi-N	111	442	84	145	16	9	6	90	56	18	.328	.405	.446	100	-1	65			.910	4	*O-109/S-2,3-1	-0.3
1895	Chi-N	123	478	120	186	27	16	10	98	55	24	.389	.456	.575	155	38	67			.924	10	*O-123	3.1
1896	Chi-N	122	469	114	153	21	16	4	92	65	24	.326	.414	.465	126	19	84			.932	10	*O-121/C-1	1.6
1897	Chi-N	118	479	119	163	24	14	5	83	48		.340	.406	.480	128	19	**73**			.946	2	*O-118	1.1
1898	Chi-N	113	442	79	141	16	11	5	69	36		.319	.377	.439	134	18	22			.970	10	*O-111/1-2	1.9
1899	Chi-N	107	416	81	135	21	7	1	58	38		.325	.382	.416	122	13	41			.976	12	O-94,1-14	1.6
Total	7	811	3195	689	1055	133	80	39	578	350	86	.330	.401	.459	124	105	399			.942	50	O-716/2-57,1S3C	9.1

■ SAM LANGFORD

Langford, Elton b: 5/21/1899, Briggs, Tex. d: 7/31/93, Plainview, Tex. BL/TR, 6', 180 lbs. Deb: 4/13/26

YEAR	TM/L	G	AB	R	H	2B	3B	HR	RBI	BB	SO	AVG	OBP	SLG	PRO+	BR/A	SB	CS	SBR	FA	FR	G/POS	TPR
1926	Bos-A	1	1	1	0	0	0	0	0	0	0	.000	.000	.000	-99	-0	0	0	0	.000	0	H	0.0
1927	Cle-A	20	67	10	18	5	0	1	7	5	7	.269	.347	.388	90	-1	0	1	-1	1.000	-2	O-20	-0.5
1928	Cle-A	110	427	50	118	17	8	4	50	21	35	.276	.312	.382	81	-13	3	7	-3	.972	-8	*O-107	-3.1
Total	3	131	495	61	136	22	8	5	57	26	42	.275	.316	.382	81	-14	3	8	-4	.976	-11	O-127	-3.6

■ BOB LANGSFORD

Langsford, Robert William (b: Robert Hugo Lankswert) b: 8/5/1865, Louisville, Ky. d: 1/10/07, Louisville, Ky. BR/TR, Deb: 6/18/1899

YEAR	TM/L	G	AB	R	H	2B	3B	HR	RBI	BB	SO	AVG	OBP	SLG	PRO+	BR/A	SB	CS	SBR	FA	FR	G/POS	TPR
1899	Lou-N	1	4	0	0	0	0	0	0	0		.000	.000	.000	-99	-1	0			1.000	-0	/S-1	-0.1

YEAR	TM/L	G	AB	R	H	2B	3B	HR	RBI	BB	SO	AVG	OBP	SLG	PRO+	BR/A	SB	CS	SBR	FA	FR	G/POS	TPR
■ HAL LANIER Lanier, Harold Clifton b: 7/4/42, Denton, N.C. BR/TR, 6'2", 180 lbs. Deb: 6/18/64 FMC																							
1964	SF-N	98	383	40	105	16	3	2	28	5	44	.274	.284	.347	75	-13	2	1	0	.979	10	2-98/S-3	0.6
1965	SF-N	159	522	41	118	15	9	0	39	21	67	.226	.256	.289	52	-33	2	1	0	.976	-5	*2-158/S-1	-2.7
1966	SF-N	149	459	37	106	14	2	3	37	16	49	.231	.257	.290	50	-31	1	0	0	.991	28	*2-112,S-41	0.8
1967	SF-N	151	525	37	112	16	3	0	42	16	61	.213	.239	.255	42	-39	2	2	-1	.974	29	*S-137,2-34	0.2
1968	SF-N	151	486	37	100	14	1	0	27	12	57	.206	.225	.239	39	-36	2	2	-1	**.979**	14	*S-150	-0.8
1969	SF-N	150	495	37	113	9	1	0	35	25	68	.228	.265	.251	46	-36	0	1	-1	.969	**29**	*S-150	0.8
1970	SF-N	134	438	33	101	13	1	2	41	21	41	.231	.266	.279	47	-33	1	2	-1	.967	13	*S-130/2-4,1-2	-0.7
1971	*SF-N	109	206	21	48	8	0	1	13	15	26	.233	.285	.286	63	-10	0	0	0	.957	5	3-83,2-13/S-8,1-3	-0.4
1972	NY-A	60	103	5	22	3	0	0	6	2	13	.214	.236	.243	44	-7	1	2	-1	.973	9	3-47/S-9,2-3	0.1
1973	NY-A	35	86	9	18	3	0	0	5	3	10	.209	.244	.244	39	-7	0	0	0	.960	1	S-26/2-8,3-1	-0.4
Total	10	1196	3703	297	843	111	20	8	273	136	436	.228	.256	.275	50	-245	11	11	-3	.971	132	S-655,2-430,3/1	-2.5
■ RIMP LANIER Lanier, Lorenzo b: 10/19/48, Tuskegee, Ala. BL/TR, 5'8", 150 lbs. Deb: 9/11/71																							
1971	Pit-N	6	4	0	0	0	0	0	0	0	1	.000	.200	.000	-39	-1	0	0	0	.000	0	H	-0.1
■ RAY LANKFORD Lankford, Raymond Lewis b: 6/5/67, Los Angeles, Cal. BL/TL, 5'11", 198 lbs. Deb: 8/21/90																							
1990	StL-N	39	126	12	36	10	1	3	12	13	27	.286	.353	.452	119	3	8	2	1	.989	2	O-35	0.6
1991	StL-N	151	566	83	142	23	**15**	9	69	41	114	.251	.303	.392	93	-6	44	20	1	.984	11	*O-149	0.3
1992	StL-N	153	598	87	175	40	6	20	86	72	147	.293	.373	.480	144	35	42	24	-2	.996	10	*O-153	4.3
1993	StL-N	127	407	64	97	17	3	7	45	81	111	.238	.369	.346	95	0	14	14	-4	.978	3	*O-121	-0.4
1994	StL-N	109	416	89	111	25	5	19	57	58	113	.267	.362	.488	121	13	11	10	-3	.978	3	*O-104	1.0
1995	StL-N	132	483	81	134	35	2	25	82	63	110	.277	.363	.513	128	19	24	8	2	.990	7	*O-129	2.5
1996	*StL-N	149	545	100	150	36	8	21	86	79	133	.275	.370	.486	125	20	35	7	6	**.997**	15	*O-144	3.6
1997	StL-N★	133	465	94	137	36	3	31	98	95	125	.295	.414	.585	160	43	21	11	-0	.971	6	*O-131	4.3
1998	StL-N	154	533	94	156	37	1	31	105	86	151	.293	.394	.540	141	33	26	5	5	.986	4	*O-145/D-1	4.0
Total	9	1147	4139	704	1138	259	44	166	640	588	1031	.275	.368	.479	127	160	225	101	7	.986	61	*O-1111/D-1	20.2
■ RED LANNING Lanning, Lester Alfred b: 5/13/1895, Harvard, Ill. d: 6/13/62, Bristol, Conn. BL/TL, 5'9", 165 lbs. Deb: 6/20/16																							
1916	Phi-A	19	33	5	6	2	0	0	1	10	9	.182	.372	.242	89	0	0			.909	-4	/O-9,P-6	-0.4
■ CARNEY LANSFORD Lansford, Carney Ray b: 2/7/57, San Jose, Cal. BR/TR, 6'2", 195 lbs. Deb: 4/8/78 F																							
1978	Cal-A	121	453	63	133	23	2	8	52	31	67	.294	.344	.406	115	8	20	9	1	.942	-26	*3-117/S-2,D-1	-1.9
1979	*Cal-A	157	654	114	188	30	5	19	79	39	115	.287	.330	.436	108	6	20	8	1	**.983**	-24	*3-157	-1.8
1980	Cal-A	151	602	87	157	27	3	15	80	50	93	.261	.317	.390	95	-5	14	5	1	.955	-24	*3-150	-3.0
1981	Bos-A	102	399	61	134	23	3	4	52	34	28	**.336**	.391	.439	131	16	15	10	-2	.951	-0	3-86,D-16	1.3
1982	Bos-A	128	482	65	145	28	4	11	63	46	48	.301	.364	.444	114	9	9	4	0	.968	-13	*3-114,D-13	-0.6
1983	Oak-A	80	299	43	92	16	2	10	45	22	33	.308	.361	.475	136	14	3	8	-4	.957	-5	3-78/S-1	0.4
1984	Oak-A	151	597	70	179	31	5	14	74	40	62	.300	.347	.439	124	18	9	3	1	.957	-8	*3-151	0.9
1985	Oak-A	98	401	51	111	18	2	13	46	18	27	.277	.314	.429	109	4	2	3	-1	.976	-32	3-97	-3.1
1986	Oak-A	151	591	80	168	16	4	19	72	39	51	.284	.334	.421	112	9	16	7	1	.982	-18	*3-100,1-60/2-1,D-3	-1.5
1987	Oak-A	151	554	89	160	27	4	19	76	60	44	.289	.368	.455	125	20	27	8	3	**.980**	-3	*3-142,1-17/D-4	1.7
1988	*Oak-A★	150	556	80	155	20	2	7	57	35	35	.279	.329	.360	96	-3	29	8	4	**.979**	-12	*3-143/1-9,2-1,D-1	-1.2
1989	*Oak-A	148	551	81	185	28	2	2	52	51	25	.336	.401	.405	132	26	37	15	2	.957	-26	*3-136,1-15/D-3	0.2
1990	*Oak-A	134	507	58	136	15	1	3	50	45	50	.268	.335	.320	88	-7	16	14	-4	**.970**	-21	*3-126/1-5,D-5	-3.2
1991	Oak-A	5	16	0	1	0	0	0	1	0	2	.063	.063	.063	-69	-4	0	0	0	1.000	-1	/3-4,D-1	-0.5
1992	*Oak-A	135	496	65	130	30	1	7	75	43	39	.262	.330	.369	101	0	7	2	1	.965	-23	*3-119,1-18/S-1,D-2	-2.3
Total	15	1862	7158	1007	2074	332	40	151	874	553	719	.290	.346	.411	112	112	224	104	5	.966	-235	*3-1720,1-124/DS2	-14.6
■ JODY LANSFORD Lansford, Joseph Dale b: 1/15/61, San Jose, Cal. BR/TR, 6'5", 225 lbs. Deb: 7/31/82 F																							
1982	SD-N	13	22	6	4	0	0	0	3	6	4	.182	.357	.182	58	-1	0	1	-1	.986	-1	/1-9	-0.3
1983	SD-N	12	8	1	2	0	0	1	2	0	3	.250	.250	.625	140	0	0	0	0	1.000	0	/1-8	0.0
Total	2	25	30	7	6	0	0	1	5	6	7	.200	.333	.300	82	-1	0	1	-1	.988	-1	/1-17	-0.3
■ MIKE LANSING Lansing, Michael Thomas b: 4/3/68, Rawlins, Wyo. BR/TR, 6', 180 lbs. Deb: 4/7/93																							
1993	Mon-N	141	491	64	141	29	1	3	45	46	56	.287	.354	.369	90	-6	23	5	4	.942	6	3-81,S-51,2-25	0.8
1994	Mon-N	106	394	44	105	21	2	5	35	30	37	.266	.329	.368	81	-11	12	8	-1	.983	1	2-82,3-27,S-12	-0.7
1995	Mon-N	127	467	47	119	30	2	10	62	28	65	.255	.301	.392	78	-15	27	4	6	.991	7	*2-127/S-2	0.4
1996	Mon-N	159	641	99	183	40	2	11	53	44	85	.285	.341	.406	94	-6	23	8	2	.985	-10	*2-159/S-2	-0.3
1997	Mon-N	144	572	86	161	45	2	20	70	45	92	.281	.339	.472	110	7	11	5	0	.987	-6	*2-144	1.0
1998	Col-N	153	584	73	161	39	2	12	66	39	88	.276	.326	.411	75	-22	10	3	1	.987	5	*2-153/3-1	-0.5
Total	6	830	3149	413	870	204	11	61	331	232	423	.276	.333	.406	88	-53	106	33	12	.986	3	2-690,3-109/S-67	0.7
■ PETE LAPAN Lapan, Peter Nelson b: 6/25/1891, Easthampton, Mass d: 1/5/53, Norwalk, Cal. BR/TR, 5'7", 165 lbs. Deb: 9/16/22																							
1922	Was-A	11	34	7	11	1	0	1	6	3	4	.324	.378	.441	119	1	1	0	0	.958	-0	C-11	0.2
1923	Was-A	2	2	0	0	0	0	0	0	0	0	.000	.000	.000	-99	-1	0	0	0	.000	0	H	-0.1
Total	2	13	36	7	11	1	0	1	6	3	4	.306	.359	.417	107	0	1	0	0	.958	-0	/C-11	0.1
■ RALPH LaPOINTE LaPointe, Ralph Robert b: 1/8/22, Winooski, Vt. d: 9/13/67, Burlington, Vt. BR/TR, 5'11", 185 lbs. Deb: 4/15/47																							
1947	Phi-N	56	211	33	65	7	0	1	15	17	15	.308	.362	.355	95	-1	8			.956	-10	S-54	-0.8
1948	StL-N	87	222	27	50	3	0	0	15	18	19	.225	.283	.239	40	-18	1			.965	8	2-44,S-25/3-1	-0.7
Total	2	143	433	60	115	10	0	1	30	35	34	.266	.322	.296	66	-19	9			.955	-2	/S-79,2-44,3-1	-1.5
■ FRANK LaPORTE LaPorte, Frank Breyfogle "Pot" b: 2/6/1880, Uhrichsville, Ohio d: 9/25/39, Newcomerstown, O. BR/TR, 5'8", 175 lbs. Deb: 9/29/05																							
1905	NY-A	11	40	4	16	1	0	1	12	1		.400	.415	.500	170	3	1			.918	-3	2-11	0.0
1906	NY-A	123	454	60	120	23	9	2	54	22		.264	.300	.368	99	-2	10			.904	-6	*3-114/2-5,O-1	-0.5
1907	NY-A	130	470	56	127	20	11	0	48	27		.270	.317	.360	107	3	10			.896	-11	3-64,O-63/1-1	-0.9
1908	Bos-A	62	156	14	37	1	3	0	15	12		.237	.296	.282	86	-2	3			.950	10	2-27,3-12/O-5	0.8
	NY-A	39	145	7	38	3	4	1	15	8		.262	.301	.359	113	2	3			.934	-3	2-26,O-11	-0.3
	Yr	101	301	21	75	4	7	1	30	20		.249	.298	.319	98	-1	6			.942	6	2-53,O-16,3-12	0.5
1909	NY-A	89	309	35	92	19	3	0	31	18		.298	.340	.379	126	8	5			.938	-15	2-83	-1.0
1910	NY-A	124	432	43	114	14	6	2	67	33		.264	.321	.338	100	-0	16			.959	-11	2-79,O-23,3-15	-1.5
1911	StL-A	136	507	71	159	37	12	2	82	34		.314	.361	.446	130	18	4			.950	-6	*2-133/3-3	0.9
1912	StL-A	80	266	32	83	11	4	1	38	20		.312	.367	.395	122	7	7			.944	-3	2-39,O-32	0.2
	Was-A	40	136	13	42	9	1	0	17	12		.309	.365	.390	115	3	3			.939	3	2-37	0.4
	Yr	120	402	45	125	20	5	1	55	32		.311	.366	.393	120	10	10			.941	0	2-76,O-32	0.6
1913	Was-A	79	242	25	61	5	4	0	18	17	16	.252	.309	.306	78	-7	10			.952	3	3-46,2-13,O-12	-0.5
1914	Ind-F	133	505	86	157	27	12	4	**107**	36	36	.311	.361	.436	105	-4	15			.956	6	*2-132	0.1
1915	New-F	148	550	55	139	28	10	2	56	48	33	.253	.314	.351	92	-16	14			.960	5	*2-146	-1.0
Total	11	1194	4212	501	1185	198	79	15	560	288	85	.281	.331	.377	107	12	101			.952	-31	2-731,3-254,O/1	-3.3
■ JACK LAPP Lapp, John Walker b: 9/10/1884, Frazer, Pa. d: 2/6/20, Philadelphia, Pa. BL/TR, 5'8", 160 lbs. Deb: 9/11/08																							
1908	Phi-A	13	35	4	5	0	1	0	1	5		.143	.268	.200	49	-2	0			.947	-3	C-13	-0.4
1909	Phi-A	21	56	8	19	3	1	0	10	3		.339	.373	.429	150	3	1			.938	1	C-19	0.6
1910	*Phi-A	71	192	18	45	4	3	0	17	20		.234	.310	.286	88	-2	0			.980	6	C-63	1.1
1911	*Phi-A	68	167	35	59	10	3	1	26	24		.353	.435	.467	154	13	4			.972	-6	C-57/1-4	1.2
1912	Phi-A	91	281	26	82	15	6	1	35	19		.292	.337	.399	114	4	3			.958	-14	C-83	-0.2
1913	*Phi-A	82	238	23	54	4	4	1	20	37	26	.227	.336	.290	85	-3	3			.968	-14	C-78/1-1	-1.1
1914	*Phi-A	69	199	22	46	7	2	0	19	31	14	.231	.338	.286	91	-1	1	4	-2	.977	-7	C-67	-0.5
1915	Phi-A	112	312	26	85	16	5	2	31	30	29	.272	.340	.375	118	6	5	2	0	.967	-4	C-89,1-12	0.9

YEAR	TM/L	G	AB	R	H	2B	3B	HR	RBI	BB	SO	AVG	OBP	SLG	PRO+	BR/A	SB	CS	SBR	FA	FR	G/POS	TPR
1916	Chi-A	40	101	6	21	0	1	0	7	8	10	.208	.266	.228	48	-6	1			.989	-0	C-34	-0.5
Total	9	567	1581	168	416	59	26	5	166	177	79	.263	.340	.343	105	12	16	6		.969	-39	C-503/1-17	1.1
■ NORM LARKER	Larker, Norman Howard John b: 12/27/30, Beaver Meadows, Pa. BL/TL, 6', 200 lbs. Deb: 4/15/58																						
1958	LA-N	99	253	32	70	16	5	4	29	29	21	.277	.358	.427	103	2	1	1	-0	.985	-2	O-43,1-35	-0.4
1959	*LA-N	108	311	37	90	14	1	8	49	26	25	.289	.348	.418	96	-2	0	1	-1	.990	4	1-55,O-30	-0.3
1960	LA-N★	133	440	56	142	26	3	5	78	36	24	.323	.375	.430	112	8	1	0	0	.993	4	*1-119/O-2	0.3
1961	LA-N	97	282	29	76	16	1	5	38	24	22	.270	.329	.387	82	-7	0	0	0	.995	2	1-86/O-1	-1.2
1962	Hou-N	147	506	58	133	19	5	9	63	70	47	.263	.360	.374	105	5	1	1	-0	.991	6	*1-135/O-6	0.2
1963	Mil-N	64	147	15	26	6	0	1	14	24	24	.177	.301	.238	58	-7	0	2	-1	.992	4	1-42	-0.6
	SF-N	19	14	0	1	0	0	0	0	2	2	.071	.188	.071	-22	-2	0	0	0	.929	-0	1-11	-0.3
	Yr	83	161	15	27	6	0	1	14	26	26	.168	.291	.224	51	-9	0	2	-1	.987	4	1-53	-0.9
Total	6	667	1953	227	538	97	15	32	271	211	165	.275	.351	.390	97	-3	3	5	-2	.991	17	1-483/O-82	-2.3
■ BARRY LARKIN	Larkin, Barry Louis b: 4/28/64, Cincinnati, Ohio BR/TR, 6', 190 lbs. Deb: 8/13/86 F																						
1986	Cin-N	41	159	27	45	4	3	3	19	9	21	.283	.321	.403	94	-1	8	0	2	.976	-0	S-36/2-3	0.4
1987	Cin-N	125	439	64	107	16	2	12	43	36	52	.244	.308	.371	76	-16	21	6	3	.965	-0	*S-119	-0.3
1988	Cin-N★	151	588	91	174	32	5	12	56	41	24	.296	.350	.429	118	13	40	7	8	.960	10	*S-148	4.5
1989	Cin-N☆	97	325	47	111	14	4	4	36	20	23	.342	.383	.446	132	13	10	5	0	.976	16	S-82	3.8
1990	*Cin-N★	158	614	85	185	25	6	7	67	49	49	.301	.360	.396	103	4	30	5	6	.977	20	*S-156	4.3
1991	Cin-N★	123	464	88	140	27	4	20	69	55	64	.302	.379	.506	141	26	24	6	4	.976	18	*S-119	5.8
1992	Cin-N	140	533	76	162	32	6	12	78	63	58	.304	.382	.454	132	24	15	4	2	.983	8	*S-140	4.7
1993	Cin-N★	100	384	57	121	20	3	8	51	51	33	.315	.397	.445	125	15	14	1	4	.965	-6	S-99	2.1
1994	Cin-N†	110	427	78	119	23	5	9	52	64	58	.279	.373	.419	107	6	26	2	7	**.980**	2	*S-110	2.4
1995	*Cin-N★	131	496	98	158	29	6	15	66	61	49	.319	.396	.492	133	25	51	5	**12**	.980	-10	*S-130	3.7
1996	Cin-N★	152	517	117	154	32	4	33	89	96	52	.298	.415	.567	155	44	36	10	5	.975	1	*S-151	6.0
1997	Cin-N†	73	224	34	71	17	3	4	20	47	24	.317	.442	.473	138	15	14	3	2	.980	-7	S-63/D-2	1.6
1998	Cin-N	145	538	93	166	34	10	17	72	79	69	.309	.399	.504	130	26	26	3	6	.979	-20	*S-145	2.6
Total	13	1546	5708	955	1713	305	61	156	718	671	576	.300	.378	.457	123	193	315	57	60	.974	33	*S-1498/2-3,D-2	41.6
■ ED LARKIN	Larkin, Edward Francis b: 7/1/1885, Wyalusing, Pa. d: 3/28/34, Wyalusing, Pa. BR/TR, 5'8", Deb: 10/2/09																						
1909	Phi-A	2	6	0	1	0	0	0	1	1		.167	.286	.167	42	-0	0			.769	-2	/C-2	-0.2
■ GENE LARKIN	Larkin, Eugene Thomas b: 10/24/62, Flushing, N.Y. BB/TR, 6'3", 205 lbs. Deb: 5/21/87																						
1987	*Min-A	85	233	23	62	11	2	4	28	25	31	.266	.342	.382	89	-3	1	4	-2	.989	-2	D-40,1-26	-1.0
1988	Min-A	149	505	56	135	30	2	8	70	68	55	.267	.371	.382	108	8	3	2	-0	.994	-5	D-86,1-60	-0.4
1989	Min-A	136	446	61	119	25	1	6	46	54	57	.267	.358	.368	98	0	5	2	0	.992	-7	1-67,D-41,O-32	-1.3
1990	Min-A	119	401	46	108	26	4	5	42	42	55	.269	.346	.392	99	0	5	3	-0	1.000	-2	O-47,D-43,1-28	-0.7
1991	*Min-A	98	255	34	73	14	1	2	19	30	21	.286	.364	.373	99	1	2	3	-1	.968	-10	O-47,1-39/2-1,3D	-1.4
1992	Min-A	115	337	38	83	18	1	6	42	28	43	.246	.312	.359	85	-7	7	2	1	.992	-6	1-55,O-43/D-4	-1.7
1993	Min-A	56	144	17	38	7	1	1	19	21	16	.264	.365	.347	92	-1	0	1	-1	1.000	-8	O-28,1-18/3-2,D-3	-1.1
Total	7	758	2321	275	618	131	12	32	266	268	278	.266	.352	.374	97	-2	23	17	-3	.992	-40	1-293,D-221,O/32	-7.6
■ TERRY LARKIN	Larkin, Frank S. d: 9/16/1894, Brooklyn, N.Y. BR/TR, Deb: 5/20/1876																						
1876	NY-N	1	4	0	0	0	0	0	0	0	0	.000	.000	.000	-99	-1				.500	-0	/P-1	0.0
1877	Har-N	58	228	28	52	6	5	1	18	5	23	.228	.245	.311	83	-4				.885	-1	*P-56/3-2,2-1	0.0
1878	Chi-N	58	226	33	65	9	4	0	32	**17**	17	.288	.337	.363	122	5				.858	-4	*P-56/O-1,3-1	0.1
1879	Chi-N	60	228	26	50	12	2	0	18	8	24	.219	.246	.289	71	-7				.918	-7	*P-58/O-3	-0.1
1880	Tro-N	6	20	1	3	1	0	0	1	3	4	.150	.261	.200	56	-1				1.000	-0	/P-5,O-2,S-1	-0.1
1884	Was-U	17	70	11	17	0	0	0		4		.243	.284	.243	63	-5				.726	-4	3-17	-0.8
	Ric-a	40	139	17	28	1	4	0		9		.201	.265	.266	75	-3				.907	0	2-40	-0.2
Total	6	240	915	116	215	29	15	1	69	46	68	.235	.274	.303	86	-16				.884	-16	P-176/2-41,3-20,OS	-1.1
■ HENRY LARKIN	Larkin, Henry E. "Ted" b: 1/12/1860, Reading, Pa. d: 1/31/42, Reading, Pa. BR/TR, 5'10", 175 lbs. Deb: 5/1/1884 M																						
1884	Phi-a	85	326	59	90	21	9	3	37	15		.276	.324	.423	133	11				.856	-7	*O-85/2-2	0.2
1885	Phi-a	108	453	114	149	**37**	14	8	88	26		.329	.372	.525	171	34				.882	12	*O-108	3.8
1886	Phi-a	139	565	133	180	**36**	16	2	74	59		.319	**.390**	.450	161	40	32			.866	5	*O-139	3.6
1887	Phi-a	126	497	105	154	22	12	3	88	48		.310	.380	.421	123	16	37			.895	3	O-93,1-23,2-10	1.2
1888	Phi-a	135	546	92	147	28	12	7	101	33		.269	.326	.403	134	20	20			.967	-8	*1-122,2-14	0.1
1889	Phi-a	133	516	105	164	23	12	3	74	83	41	.318	.428	.426	145	36	11			.973	-4	*1-131/3-1,2-1	1.9
1890	Cle-P	125	506	93	167	32	15	5	112	65	18	.330	.419	.482	153	41	5			.978	-8	*1-125/O-1,M	2.1
1891	Phi-a	133	526	94	147	27	14	10	93	66	56	.279	.376	.441	130	19	2			.974	-5	*1-111,O-23	0.6
1892	Was-N	119	464	76	130	13	7	8	96	39	21	.280	.346	.390	126	14	21			.969	1	*1-117/O-2	0.9
1893	Was-N	81	319	54	101	20	3	4	73	50	5	.317	.422	.436	132	17	1			.963	-9	1-81	0.5
Total	10	1184	4718	925	1429	259	114	53	836	484	141	.303	.380	.440	141	247	129			.971	-21	1-710,O-451/2-27,3	14.9
■ STEPHEN LARKIN	Larkin, Stephen Karari b: 7/24/73, Cincinnati, Ohio BL/TL, 6', 190 lbs. Deb: 9/27/98 F																						
1998	Cin-N	1	3	0	1	0	0	0	0	0	1	.333	.333	.333	73	-0	0	0	0	1.000	-0	/1-1	0.0
■ BOB LARMORE	Larmore, Robert McKahan "Red" b: 12/6/1896, Anderson, Ind. d: 1/15/64, St.Louis, Mo. BR/TR, 5'10.5", 185 lbs. Deb: 5/14/18																						
1918	StL-N	4	7	0	2	0	0	0	1	0	2	.286	.286	.286	77	-0	0			.778	-1	/S-2	-0.1
■ SAM LaROQUE	LaRoque, Samuel H. J. b: 2/26/1864, St.Mathias, Que., Canada TR, 5'11", 190 lbs. Deb: 7/30/1888																						
1888	Det-N	2	9	1	4	0	0	0	2	1	1	.444	.500	.444	203	1	0			.789	0	/2-2	0.1
1890	Pit-N	111	434	59	105	20	4	1	40	35	29	.242	.316	.313	95	-2	27			.925	-10	2-78,S-31/1-2,O-1	-0.5
1891	Pit-N	1	4	0	0	0	0	0	0	0	1	.000	.000	.000	-99	-1	0			.714	0	/3-1	-0.1
	Lou-a	10	35	6	11	2	1	1	8	5	8	.314	.429	.514	172	3	1			.875	-3	2-10/1-1	0.0
Total	3	124	482	66	120	22	5	2	50	41	39	.249	.326	.328	101	1	28			.916	-13	/2-90,S-31,1-3,3O	-0.5
■ VIC LaROSE	LaRose, Victor Raymond b: 12/23/44, Los Angeles, Cal. BR/TR, 5'11", 180 lbs. Deb: 9/13/68																						
1968	Chi-N	4	2	0	0	0	0	0	0	0	1	.000	.333	.000	6	-0	0	0	0	1.000	1	/2-2,S-2	0.1
■ HARRY LaROSS	LaRoss, Harry Raymond "Spike" b: 1/2/1888, Easton, Pa. d: 3/22/54, Chicago, Ill. BR/TR, 5'11.5", 170 lbs. Deb: 6/24/14																						
1914	Cin-N	22	48	7	11	1	0	0	5	2	10	.229	.260	.250	50	-3	4			.739	-6	O-20	-1.0
■ SWEDE LARSEN	Larsen, Erling Adeli b: 11/15/13, Jersey City, N.J. BR/TR, 5'11", 170 lbs. Deb: 6/17/36																						
1936	Bos-N	3	1	0	0	0	0	0	0	0	0	.000	.000	.000	-99	-0	0			1.000	-0	/2-2	-0.1
■ TONY LaRUSSA	LaRussa, Anthony b: 10/4/44, Tampa, Fla. BR/TR, 6'1", 190 lbs. Deb: 5/10/63 MC																						
1963	KC-A	34	44	4	11	1	1	0	1	7	12	.250	.353	.318	85	-1	0	0	0	.957	2	S-14/2-3	0.2
1968	Oak-A	5	3	0	1	0	0	0	0	0	0	.333	.333	.333	108	0	0	0	0	.000	0	H	0.0
1969	Oak-A	8	8	0	0	0	0	0	0	0	1	.000	.000	.000	-99	-2	0	0	0	.000	0	H	-0.2
1970	Oak-A	52	106	6	21	4	1	0	6	15	19	.198	.303	.255	57	-6	0	0	0	.969	-1	2-44	-0.4
1971	Oak-A	23	8	3	0	0	0	0	0	0	4	.000	.000	.000	-99	-2	0	0	0	.833	4	/2-7,S-4,3-2	0.2
	Atl-N	9	7	1	2	0	0	0	0	1	1	.286	.375	.286	84	-0	0	0	0	.933	0	/2-9	0.1
1973	Chi-N	1	0	1	0	0	0	0	0	0	0	—	—	—	—	0	0	0	0	.000	0	R	0.0
Total	6	132	176	15	35	5	2	0	7	23	37	.199	.295	.250	54	-11	0	0	0	.963	6	/2-63,S-18,3-2	-0.1
■ AL LARY	Lary, Alfred Allen b: 9/26/28, Northport, Ala. BR/TR, 6'3", 185 lbs. Deb: 9/6/54 F																						
1954	Chi-N	2	2	0	1	0	0	0	0	0	0	.500	.500	.500	160	0	0	0	0	1.000	0	/P-1	0.0
1955	Chi-N	4	0	1	0	0	0	0	0	0	0	—	—	—	—	0	0	0	0	.000	0	R	0.0

YEAR	TM/L	G	AB	R	H	2B	3B	HR	RBI	BB	SO	AVG	OBP	SLG	PRO+	BR/A	SB	CS	SBR	FA	FR	G/POS	TPR
1962	Chi-N	23	6	1	1	0	0	0	0	2	1	.167	.375	.167	49	-0	0	0	0	.857	-0	P-15	0.0
Total	3	29	8	2	2	0	0	0	0	2	2	.250	.400	.250	75	-0	0	0	0	.889	-0	/P-16	0.0

■ LYN LARY Lary, Lynford Hobart "Broadway" b: 1/28/06, Armona, Cal. d: 1/9/73, Downey, Cal. BR/TR, 6', 165 lbs. Deb: 5/11/29

YEAR	TM/L	G	AB	R	H	2B	3B	HR	RBI	BB	SO	AVG	OBP	SLG	PRO+	BR/A	SB	CS	SBR	FA	FR	G/POS	TPR
1929	NY-A	80	236	48	73	9	2	5	26	24	15	.309	.380	.428	115	6	4	1	1	.943	5	3-55,S-14/2-2	1.4
1930	NY-A	117	464	93	134	20	8	3	52	45	40	.289	.357	.386	92	-5	14	2	**3**	.940	-8	*S-113	0.3
1931	NY-A	155	610	100	171	35	9	10	107	88	54	.280	.376	.416	115	15	13	10	-2	.946	9	*S-155	3.4
1932	NY-A	91	280	56	65	14	4	3	39	52	28	.232	.358	.343	87	-4	9	3	1	.941	2	S-80/1-5,2-2,3-2,O	0.5
1933	NY-A	52	127	25	28	3	3	0	13	28	17	.220	.361	.291	79	-3	2	1	0	.938	2	3-28,S-16/1-3,O-1	0.1
1934	NY-A	1	0	0	0	0	0	0	0	1	0	—	1.000	—	189	0	0	0	0	.800	-0	/1-1	0.0
	Bos-A	129	419	58	101	20	4	2	54	66	51	.241	.344	.322	68	-19	12	5	1	**.965**	-5	*S-129	-1.5
	Yr	130	419	58	101	20	4	2	54	67	51	.241	.346	.322	68	-19	12	5	1	.965	-5	*S-129/1-1	-1.5
1935	Was-A	39	103	8	20	4	0	0	7	12	10	.194	.278	.233	35	-10	3	0	1	.953	-4	S-30	-1.1
	StL-A	93	371	78	107	25	7	2	35	64	43	.288	.396	.410	104	4	25	4	5	.962	13	S-93	2.5
	Yr	132	474	86	127	29	7	2	42	76	53	.268	.371	.371	90	-5	28	4	**6**	.960	9	*S-123	1.4
1936	StL-A	155	619	112	179	30	6	2	52	117	54	.289	.404	.367	89	-6	**37**	9	**6**	.956	-4	*S-155	0.6
1937	Cle-A	156	644	110	187	46	7	8	77	88	64	.290	.378	.421	100	2	18	8	1	.963	6	*S-156	1.7
1938	Cle-A	141	568	94	152	36	4	3	51	88	65	.268	.366	.361	84	-12	23	6	3	.964	-0	*S-141	0.2
1939	Cle-A	3	2	0	0	0	0	0	0	0	1	.000	.000	.000	-99	-1	0	0	0	.000	-1	/S-2	-0.1
	Bro-N	29	31	7	5	1	1	0	1	12	6	.161	.409	.258	80	-0	1			.947	1	S-12/3-7	0.2
	StL-N	34	75	11	14	3	0	0	9	16	15	.187	.330	.227	49	-5	1			.961	-6	S-30/3-3	-0.8
	Yr	63	106	18	19	4	1	0	10	28	21	.179	.356	.236	59	-5	2			.958	-4	S-42,3-10	-0.6
1940	StL-A	27	54	5	3	1	1	0	3	4	7	.056	.136	.111	-35	-11	0	0	0	.952	1	S-12/2-1	-0.9
Total	12	1302	4603	805	1239	247	56	38	526	705	470	.269	.369	.372	90	-47	162	49		.956	11	*S-1138/3-95,12O	6.5

■ DON LASSETTER Lassetter, Donald O'Neal b: 3/27/33, Newnan, Ga. BR/TR, 6'3", 200 lbs. Deb: 9/21/57

YEAR	TM/L	G	AB	R	H	2B	3B	HR	RBI	BB	SO	AVG	OBP	SLG	PRO+	BR/A	SB	CS	SBR	FA	FR	G/POS	TPR
1957	StL-N	4	13	2	2	0	1	0	0	1	3	.154	.214	.308	37	-1	0	0	0	1.000	1	/O-3	-0.1

■ CHRIS LATHAM Latham, Christopher Joseph b: 5/26/73, Coeur D'Alene, Idaho BB/TR, 6', 195 lbs. Deb: 4/12/97

YEAR	TM/L	G	AB	R	H	2B	3B	HR	RBI	BB	SO	AVG	OBP	SLG	PRO+	BR/A	SB	CS	SBR	FA	FR	G/POS	TPR
1997	Min-A	15	22	4	4	1	0	0	1	0	8	.182	.182	.227	6	-3	0	0	0	.917	-3	O-10	-0.6
1998	Min-A	34	94	14	15	1	0	1	5	13	36	.160	.262	.202	23	-11	4	2	0	.972	-1	O-32	-1.2
Total	2	49	116	18	19	2	0	1	6	13	44	.164	.248	.207	20	-14	4	2	0	.964	-4	/O-42	-1.8

■ JUICE LATHAM Latham, George Warren "Jumbo" b: 9/6/1852, Utica, N.Y. d: 5/26/14, Utica, N.Y. BR/TR, 5'8", 164 lbs. Deb: 4/19/1875 M

YEAR	TM/L	G	AB	R	H	2B	3B	HR	RBI	BB	SO	AVG	OBP	SLG	PRO+	BR/A	SB	CS	SBR	FA	FR	G/POS	TPR
1875	Bos-n	16	78	23	21	4	0	0	13	0	2	.269	.269	.321	100	-0	0	0	0	.927	0	1-16	0.0
	NH-n	20	76	6	15	1	0	0	5	0	4	.197	.197	.211	48	-3	6	0	2	.954	3	1-14/S-4,3-3,M	0.1
	Yr	36	154	29	36	5	0	0	18	0	6	.234	.234	.266	78	-3	6	0	2	.941	3	1-30/S-4,3-3	0.1
1877	Lou-N	59	278	42	81	10	6	0	22	5	6	.291	.304	.371	94	-5				.950	2	*1-59	-0.3
1882	Phi-a	74	323	47	92	10	2	0	38	10		.285	.306	.328	102	-1				**.972**	-0	*1-74,M	-0.9
1883	Lou-a	88	368	60	92	7	6	0		12		.250	.274	.302	92	-2				.956	-3	*1-67,2-14/S-9	-1.0
1884	Lou-a	77	308	31	52	3	3	0	23	8		.169	.197	.198	31	-22				.961	3	*1-76/3-1	-2.7
Total	4	298	1277	180	317	30	17	0	83	35	6	.248	.270	.298	82	-30				.960	1	1-276/2-14,S-9,3-1	-4.9

■ ARLIE LATHAM Latham, Walter Arlington "The Freshest Man On Earth"
b: 3/15/1860, W.Lebanon, N.H. d: 11/29/52, Garden City, N.Y. BR/TR, 5'8", 150 lbs. Deb: 7/5/1880 MUC

YEAR	TM/L	G	AB	R	H	2B	3B	HR	RBI	BB	SO	AVG	OBP	SLG	PRO+	BR/A	SB	CS	SBR	FA	FR	G/POS	TPR
1880	Buf-N	22	79	9	10	3	1	0	3	1	8	.127	.138	.190	10	-7				.887	-2	S-12,O-10/C-1	-0.8
1883	StL-a	98	406	86	96	12	7	0		18		.236	.269	.300	79	-11				.866	22	*3-98/C-1	0.9
1884	StL-a	110	474	115	130	17	12	1		18		.274	.309	.367	116	7				.864	**40**	*3-110/C-1	4.2
1885	*StL-a	110	485	84	100	15	3	1	35	18		.206	.242	.256	55	-26				.875	1	*3-109/C-2	-2.1
1886	*StL-a	134	578	**152**	174	23	8	1	47	55		.301	.368	.374	127	17	60			.827	0	*3-133/2-1	1.8
1887	*StL-a	136	627	163	198	35	10	2	83	45		.316	.366	.413	106	0	129			.877	2	*3-132/2-5,C-2	0.4
1888	*StL-a	133	570	119	151	19	5	2	31	43		.265	.325	.326	98	-4	**109**			.882	3	*3-133/S-1	0.1
1889	StL-a	118	512	110	126	13	3	4	49	42	30	.246	.317	.307	69	-24	69			.883	9	*3-116/2-3	-0.9
1890	Chi-P	52	214	47	49	7	2	1	20	22	22	.229	.310	.294	59	-13	32			.880	3	3-52	-0.6
	Cin-N	41	164	35	41	6	2	0	15	23	18	.250	.346	.311	92	-1	20			.853	5	3-41/O-1	0.5
1891	Cin-N	135	533	119	145	20	10	7	53	74	35	.272	.372	.386	120	15	87			.879	20	*3-135/C-1	3.7
1892	Cin-N	152	622	111	148	20	4	0	44	60	54	.238	.310	.283	81	-13	66			.883	-5	*3-142/2-9,O-1	-1.2
1893	Cin-N	127	531	101	150	18	6	2	49	62	20	.282	.368	.350	89	-7	57			.892	-11	*3-127	-1.3
1894	Cin-N	129	524	129	164	23	6	4	60	60	24	.313	.393	.403	89	-9	59			.860	-10	*3-127/2-2	-1.5
1895	Cin-N	112	460	93	143	14	6	2	69	42	25	.311	.375	.380	91	-6	48			.861	-16	*3-108/1-3,2-1	-1.6
1896	StL-N	8	35	3	7	0	0	0	5	4	3	.200	.282	.200	29	-3	2			.744	-1	/3-8,M	-0.4
1899	Was-N	6	6	1	1	0	0	0	0	1		.167	.286	.167	26	-1	0			1.000	-0	/O-1,2-1	-0.1
1909	NY-N	4	2	1	0	0	0	0	0	0		.000	.000	.000	-99	-0	1			1.000	1	/2-2	0.0
Total	17	1627	6822	1478	1833	245	85	27	563	588	239	.269	.334	.341	91	-84	739			.870	60	*3-1571/2-24,OSC1	1.1

■ CHICK LATHERS Lathers, Charles Ten Eyck b: 10/22/1888, Detroit, Mich. d: 7/26/71, Petoskey, Mich. BL/TR, 6', 180 lbs. Deb: 5/1/10

YEAR	TM/L	G	AB	R	H	2B	3B	HR	RBI	BB	SO	AVG	OBP	SLG	PRO+	BR/A	SB	CS	SBR	FA	FR	G/POS	TPR
1910	Det-A	41	82	4	19	2	0	0	3	8		.232	.300	.256	70	-3	0			.926	5	3-14/2-7,S-4	0.2
1911	Det-A	29	45	5	10	1	0	0	4	5		.222	.314	.244	54	-3	0			.867	-3	/2-9,3-8,S-4,1-3	-0.5
Total	2	70	127	9	29	3	0	0	7	13		.228	.305	.252	64	-5	0			.933	2	/3-22,2-16,S-8,1-3	-0.3

■ TACKS LATIMER Latimer, Clifford Wesley b: 11/30/1877, Loveland, Ohio d: 4/24/36, Loveland, Ohio BR/TR, 6', 160 lbs. Deb: 10/1/1898

YEAR	TM/L	G	AB	R	H	2B	3B	HR	RBI	BB	SO	AVG	OBP	SLG	PRO+	BR/A	SB	CS	SBR	FA	FR	G/POS	TPR
1898	NY-N	5	17	1	5	1	0	0	1	0		.294	.294	.353	88	-0	0			.889	-1	/C-4,O-2	-0.1
1899	Lou-N	9	29	3	8	1	0	0	4	2		.276	.323	.310	74	-1	1			.980	3	/C-8,1-1	0.2
1900	Pit-N	4	12	1	4	1	0	0	2	0		.333	.333	.417	106	0	0			.947	0	/C-4	0.0
1901	Bal-A	1	4	0	1	0	0	0	0	0		.250	.250	.250	37	-0	0			1.000	-0	/C-1	-0.1
1902	Bro-N	8	24	0	1	0	0	0	0	0		.042	.042	.042	-74	-5	0			.947	-0	/C-8	-0.5
Total	5	27	86	5	19	3	0	0	7	2		.221	.239	.256	41	-7	1			.949	2	/C-25,O-2,1-1	-0.5

■ CHARLIE LAU Lau, Charles Richard b: 4/12/33, Romulus, Mich. d: 3/18/84, Key Colony Beach, Fla. BL/TR, 6', 190 lbs. Deb: 9/12/56 C

YEAR	TM/L	G	AB	R	H	2B	3B	HR	RBI	BB	SO	AVG	OBP	SLG	PRO+	BR/A	SB	CS	SBR	FA	FR	G/POS	TPR
1956	Det-A	3	9	1	2	0	0	0	0	0	1	.222	.222	.222	18	-1	0	0	0	1.000	1	/C-3	0.0
1958	Det-A	30	68	8	10	1	2	0	6	12	15	.147	.293	.221	41	-5	0	0	0	.985	1	C-27	-0.4
1959	Det-A	2	6	0	1	0	0	0	0	0	2	.167	.167	.167	-8	-1	0	0	0	1.000	1	/C-2	0.0
1960	Mil-N	21	53	4	10	2	0	0	2	6	10	.189	.271	.226	41	-4	0	0	0	1.000	5	C-16	0.1
1961	Mil-N	28	82	3	17	5	0	0	5	14	11	.207	.330	.268	65	-4	1	1	-0	.968	-3	C-25	-0.6
	Bal-A	17	47	3	8	0	0	1	4	1	3	.170	.188	.234	12	-6	0	0	0	.990	5	C-17	-0.1
1962	Bal-A	81	197	21	58	11	2	6	37	7	11	.294	.322	.462	115	3	1	0	0	.996	-5	C-56	0.0
1963	Bal-A	29	48	4	9	2	0	0	6	1	5	.188	.204	.229	22	-5	0	0	0	.964	1	/C-8	-0.4
	KC-A	62	187	15	55	11	0	3	26	14	17	.294	.343	.401	102	1	1	0	0	.982	-10	C-50	-0.8
	Yr	91	235	19	64	13	0	3	32	15	22	.272	.316	.366	88	-4	1	0	0	.979	-9	C-58	-1.2
1964	KC-A	43	118	11	32	7	1	2	9	10	18	.271	.328	.398	98	-0	0	0	0	.990	-6	C-35	-0.5
	Bal-A	62	158	16	41	15	1	1	14	17	27	.259	.335	.386	100	0	0	0	0	.992	-3	C-47	-0.1
	Yr	105	276	27	73	22	2	3	23	27	45	.264	.332	.391	99	-0	0	0	0	.991	-9	C-82	-0.6
1965	Bal-A	68	132	15	39	5	2	2	18	17	18	.295	.376	.409	120	4	0	0	0	.989	-6	C-35	0.0
1966	Bal-A	18	12	1	6	2	1	0	5	4	1	.500	.625	.833	320	4	0	0	0	.000	0	H	0.4
1967	Bal-A	11	8	0	1	1	0	0	3	2	2	.125	.300	.250	65	-0	0	0	0	.000	0	H	0.0
	Atl-N	52	45	3	9	1	0	1	5	4	9	.200	.265	.289	59	-2	0	0	0	.000	0	H	-0.3
Total	11	527	1170	105	298	63	9	16	140	109	150	.255	.321	.365	89	-17	3	1	0	.988	-21	C-321	-2.7

■ BILLY LAUDER Lauder, William b: 2/23/1874, New York, N.Y. d: 5/20/33, Norwalk, Conn. BR/TR, 5'10", 160 lbs. Deb: 6/25/1898 C

YEAR	TM/L	G	AB	R	H	2B	3B	HR	RBI	BB	SO	AVG	OBP	SLG	PRO+	BR/A	SB	CS	SBR	FA	FR	G/POS	TPR
1898	Phi-N	97	361	42	95	14	7	2	67	19		.263	.300	.357	92	-5	6			.866	-17	3-97	-2.0
1899	Phi-N	151	583	74	156	17	6	3	90	34		.268	.310	.333	79	-18	15			.893	-14	*3-151	-2.7

YEAR	TM/L	G	AB	R	H	2B	3B	HR	RBI	BB	SO	AVG	OBP	SLG	PRO+	BR/A	SB	CS	SBR	FA	FR	G/POS	TPR
1901	Phi-A	2	8	1	1	0	0	0	0	0		.125	.125	.125	-29	-1	0			.833	1	/3-2	-0.1
1902	NY-N	125	482	41	113	20	1	0	43	10		.234	.250	.280	64	-22	19			.907	3	*3-121/O-4	-1.9
1903	NY-N	108	395	52	111	13	0	0	53	14		.281	.307	.314	74	-14	19			.908	-7	*3-108	-1.8
Total	5	483	1829	210	476	64	14	5	253	77		.260	.291	.319	76	-60	59			.894	-33	3-479/O-4	-8.5
■ **TIM LAUDNER**	Laudner, Timothy Jon b: 6/7/58, Mason City, Iowa BR/TR, 6'3", 212 lbs. Deb: 8/28/81																						
1981	Min-A	14	43	4	7	2	0	2	5	3	17	.163	.234	.349	62	-2	0	0	0	1.000	-1	C-12/D-2	-0.3
1982	Min-A	93	306	37	78	19	1	7	33	34	74	.255	.329	.392	95	-2	0	2	-1	.976	-15	C-93	-1.4
1983	Min-A	62	168	20	31	9	0	6	18	15	49	.185	.251	.345	60	-10	0	0	0	.986	6	C-57/D-4	-0.2
1984	Min-A	87	262	31	54	16	1	10	35	18	78	.206	.260	.389	73	-10	0	0	0	.978	9	C-81/D-2	0.2
1985	Min-A	72	164	16	39	5	0	7	19	12	45	.238	.294	.396	82	-4	0	1	-1	.969	-4	C-68/1-1	-0.7
1986	Min-A	76	193	21	47	10	0	10	29	24	56	.244	.336	.451	109	2	1	0	0	.984	-15	C-68	-0.8
1987	*Min-A	113	288	30	55	7	1	16	43	23	80	.191	.253	.389	65	-16	1	0	0	.987	-8	*C-101/1-7,D-2	-1.7
1988	Min-A★	117	375	38	94	18	1	13	54	36	89	.251	.318	.408	99	-1	0	0	0	.992	0	*C-109/1-3,D-4	0.7
1989	Min-A	100	239	24	53	11	1	6	27	25	65	.222	.295	.351	76	-8	1	0	0	.991	0	C-68,D-19,1-11	-0.5
Total	9	734	2038	221	458	97	5	77	263	190	553	.225	.293	.391	83	-50	3	3	-1	.984	-27	C-657/D-33,1-22	-4.7
■ **CHUCK LAUER**	Lauer, John Charles b: 1865, Pittsburgh, Pa. TR , Deb: 7/17/1884																						
1884	Pit-a	13	44	5	5	0	0	0		0		.114	.114	.114	-25	-6				.938	-1	O-10/P-3,1-1	-0.5
1889	Pit-N	4	16	2	3	0	0	0	1	0	5	.188	.188	.188	5	-2	0			.815	1	/C-3,O-1	-0.1
1890	Chi-N	2	8	1	2	1	0	0	2	0	0	.250	.250	.375	78	-0	0			.833	0	/C-2	0.0
Total	3	19	68	8	10	1	0	0	3	0	5	.147	.147	.162	-5	-8	0			.944	-0	/O-11,C-5,P-3,1-1	-0.6
■ **BEN LAUGHLIN**	Laughlin, Benjamin Deb: 4/28/1873																						
1873	Res-n	12	50	3	12	0	0	0	6	0	0	.240	.240	.240	47	-3	0	0	0	.725	-1	2-12	-0.3
■ **BILL LAUTERBORN**	Lauterborn, William Bernard b: 6/9/1879, Hornell, N.Y. d: 4/19/65, Andover, N.Y. BR/TR, 5'6", 140 lbs. Deb: 9/20/04																						
1904	Bos-N	20	69	7	19	2	0	0	2	1		.275	.286	.304	85	-1	1			.943	-3	2-20	-0.4
1905	Bos-N	67	200	11	37	1	1	0	9	12		.185	.238	.200	32	-17	1			.843	-7	3-29,2-23/S-3,O-2	-2.4
Total	2	87	269	18	56	3	1	0	11	13		.208	.250	.227	45	-18	2			.929	-10	/2-43,3-29,S-3,O-2	-2.8
■ **COOKIE LAVAGETTO**	Lavagetto, Harry Arthur b: 12/1/12, Oakland, Cal. d: 8/10/90, Orinda, Cal. BR/TR, 6', 170 lbs. Deb: 4/17/34 MC																						
1934	Pit-N	87	304	41	67	16	3	3	46	32	39	.220	.295	.322	64	-16	6			.961	-14	2-83	-2.4
1935	Pit-N	78	231	27	67	9	4	0	19	18	15	.290	.341	.364	87	-4	1			.951	-11	2-42,3-15	-1.2
1936	Pit-N	60	197	21	48	15	2	2	26	15	13	.244	.300	.371	78	-6	0			.951	-1	2-37,3-13/S-1	-0.5
1937	Bro-N	149	503	64	142	26	6	8	70	74	41	.282	.375	.406	110	9	13			.949	-7	*2-100,3-45	1.0
1938	Bro-N☆	137	487	68	133	34	6	6	79	68	31	.273	.364	.405	109	7	15			.929	-11	*3-132/2-4	-0.2
1939	Bro-N☆	153	587	93	176	28	5	10	87	78	30	.300	.387	.416	112	12	14			.948	-5	*3-149	0.9
1940	Bro-N★	118	448	56	115	21	3	4	43	70	32	.257	.361	.344	90	-4	4			.932	-14	*3-116	-1.5
1941	*Bro-N★	132	441	75	122	24	7	1	78	80	21	.277	.388	.370	109	9	7			.938	-20	*3-120	-0.9
1946	Bro-N	88	242	36	57	9	1	3	27	38	17	.236	.339	.318	86	-3	3			.927	-5	3-67	-0.8
1947	*Bro-N	41	69	6	18	1	0	3	11	12	5	.261	.370	.406	102	0	0			.961	3	3-18/1-3	0.3
Total	10	1043	3509	487	945	183	37	40	486	485	244	.269	.360	.377	98	4	63			.936	-85	3-675,2-266/1-3,S-1	-5.3
■ **MIKE LaVALLIERE**	LaValliere, Michael Eugene b: 8/18/60, Charlotte, N.C. BL/TR, 5'9", 190 lbs. Deb: 9/9/84																						
1984	Phi-N	6	7	0	0	0	0	0	0	2	2	.000	.222	.000	-32	-1	0	0	0	1.000	2	/C-6	0.1
1985	StL-N	12	34	2	5	1	0	0	6	7	3	.147	.293	.176	34	-3	0	0	0	1.000	-2	C-12	-0.4
1986	StL-N	110	303	18	71	10	2	3	30	36	37	.234	.318	.310	74	-10	0	1	-1	.988	2	*C-108	-0.3
1987	Pit-N	121	340	33	102	19	0	1	36	43	32	.300	.380	.365	98	1	0	0	0	.992	8	*C-112	1.5
1988	Pit-N	120	352	24	92	18	0	2	47	50	34	.261	.356	.330	99	2	3	2	-0	.987	-0	*C-114	1.0
1989	Pit-N	68	190	15	60	10	0	2	23	29	24	.316	.406	.400	136	10	0	2	-1	.991	-7	C-65	0.6
1990	*Pit-N	96	279	27	72	15	0	3	31	44	20	.258	.363	.344	99	1	0	3	-2	.990	2	C-95	0.7
1991	*Pit-N	108	336	25	97	11	2	3	41	33	27	.289	.356	.360	103	2	2	1	0	**.998**	2	*C-105	1.1
1992	*Pit-N	95	293	22	75	13	1	2	29	44	21	.256	.355	.328	95	-0	0	3	-2	.994	-1	C-92/3-1	0.2
1993	Pit-N	1	5	0	1	0	0	0	0	0	0	.200	.200	.200	7	-1	0	0	0	1.000	1	/C-1	0.0
	*Chi-A	37	97	6	25	2	0	0	8	4	14	.258	.287	.278	54	-6	0	1	-1	1.000	4	C-37	-0.1
1994	Chi-A	59	139	6	39	4	0	1	24	20	15	.281	.375	.331	86	-2	0	2	-1	.991	4	C-57	0.4
1995	Chi-A	46	98	7	24	6	0	1	19	9	15	.245	.308	.337	71	-4	0	0	0	.996	6	C-46	0.3
Total	12	879	2473	185	663	109	5	18	294	321	244	.268	.354	.338	94	-11	5	15	-8	.992	21	C-850/3-1	5.1
■ **DOC LAVAN**	Lavan, John Leonard (b: John Leonard Laven) b: 10/28/1890, Grand Rapids, Mich d: 5/29/52, Detroit, Mich. BR/TR, 5'8.5", 151 lbs. Deb: 6/22/13																						
1913	StL-A	46	149	8	21	2	1	0	4	10	46	.141	.210	.168	11	-17	3			.899	-5	S-46	-1.9
	Phi-A	5	14	1	1	0	1	0	1	0	0	.071	.071	.214	-17	-2	0			1.000	0	/S-5	-0.2
	Yr	51	163	9	22	2	2	0	5	10	46	.135	.199	.172	9	-19	3			.906	-5	S-51	-2.1
1914	StL-A	75	239	21	63	7	4	1	21	17	39	.264	.318	.339	101	-0	6	12	-5	.916	-12	S-74	-1.3
1915	StL-A	157	514	44	112	17	7	1	48	42	83	.218	.281	.284	72	-19	13	19	-8	.913	5	*S-157	-1.0
1916	StL-A	110	343	32	81	13	1	0	19	32	38	.236	.305	.280	80	-9	7			.950	**34**	*S-106	3.4
1917	StL-A	118	355	19	85	8	5	0	30	19	34	.239	.284	.290	78	-10	5			.923	12	*S-110/2-7	0.7
1918	Was-A	117	464	44	129	17	2	0	45	14	21	.278	.302	.323	90	-8	12			.917	-10	*S-117/O-1	-1.4
1919	StL-N	100	356	25	86	12	2	1	25	11	30	.242	.264	.295	72	-13	4			.929	9	S-99	0.2
1920	StL-N	142	516	52	149	21	10	1	63	19	38	.289	.318	.374	102	-0	11	14	-5	.942	16	*S-138	2.4
1921	StL-N	150	560	58	145	23	11	2	82	23	30	.259	.291	.350	70	-25	7	7	-2	.950	**19**	*S-150	0.6
1922	StL-N	89	264	24	60	8	1	0	27	13	10	.227	.271	.265	41	-23	3	1	0	.937	15	S-82/3-5	-0.1
1923	StL-N	50	111	10	22	6	0	1	12	9	7	.198	.264	.279	44	-9	0	3	-2	.924	1	S-40/3-4,1-3,2-1	-0.7
1924	StL-N	4	6	0	0	0	0	0	0	0	0	.000	.000	.000	-99	-2	0	0	0	1.000	2	/2-2,S-2	0.0
Total	12	1163	3891	338	954	134	45	7	377	209	376	.245	.288	.308	75	-136	71	56		.930	86	*S-1126/2-10,310	0.7
■ **ART LaVIGNE**	LaVigne, Arthur David b: 1/26/1885, Worcester, Mass. d: 7/18/50, Worcester, Mass. BR/TR, 5'10", 162 lbs. Deb: 4/24/14																						
1914	Buf-F	51	90	10	14	2	0	0	4	7	25	.156	.216	.178	8	-13	0			.967	6	C-34/1-3	-0.5
■ **JOHNNY LAVIN**	Lavin, John b: Troy, N.Y. 5'11", 175 lbs. Deb: 9/10/1884																						
1884	StL-a	16	52	9	11	2	0	0		3		.212	.268	.250	68	-2				.750	-3	O-16	-0.5
■ **RUDY LAW**	Law, Rudy Karl b: 10/7/56, Waco, Tex. BL/TL, 6'1", 165 lbs. Deb: 9/12/78																						
1978	LA-N	11	12	2	3	0	0	0	1	1	2	.250	.308	.250	58	-1	3	1	0	1.000	-2	/O-6	-0.3
1980	LA-N	128	388	55	101	5	4	1	23	23	27	.260	.307	.302	72	-14	40	13	4	.988	-1	*O-106	-1.6
1982	Chi-A	121	336	55	107	15	8	3	32	23	41	.318	.362	.438	118	8	36	10	5	.973	-5	O-94/D-3	0.6
1983	*Chi-A	141	501	95	142	20	7	3	34	42	36	.283	.341	.369	92	-5	77	12	16	**.994**	-4	*O-132/D-3	0.4
1984	Chi-A	136	487	68	122	14	7	6	37	39	42	.251	.310	.345	77	-15	29	17	-2	.985	-2	*O-130	-2.3
1985	Chi-A	125	390	62	101	21	6	4	36	27	40	.259	.312	.374	84	-9	29	6	5	.987	-5	*O-120/D-3	-1.2
1986	KC-A	87	307	42	80	26	5	1	36	29	22	.261	.328	.388	92	-3	14	6	1	.987	-8	O-77/D-2	-1.3
Total	7	749	2421	379	656	101	37	18	199	184	210	.271	.326	.366	88	-38	228	65	29	.986	-27	O-665/D-11	-5.7
■ **VANCE LAW**	Law, Vance Aaron b: 10/1/56, Boise, Idaho BR/TR, 6'2", 190 lbs. Deb: 6/1/80 F																						
1980	Pit-N	25	74	11	17	2	2	0	3	3	7	.230	.260	.311	58	-4	2	0	1	.964	-3	2-11/S-8,3-1	-0.6
1981	Pit-N	30	67	1	9	0	1	0	3	2	15	.134	.159	.164	-8	-9	1	1	-0	1.000	5	2-19/S-7,3-2	-0.4
1982	Chi-A	114	359	40	101	20	1	5	54	26	46	.281	.332	.384	96	-2	4	2	0	.953	-3	S-85,3-39,2-10,/O-1	0.1
1983	*Chi-A	145	408	55	99	21	5	4	42	51	56	.243	.328	.348	83	-9	3	1	0	.966	5	*3-139/2-3,S-2,OD	-0.5
1984	Chi-A	151	481	60	121	18	2	17	59	41	75	.252	.312	.403	92	-6	4	1	1	.955	-12	*3-137,2-22/O-5,S-4	-1.9
1985	Mon-N	147	519	75	138	30	6	10	52	86	96	.266	.372	.405	124	19	6	5	-1	.985	-1	*2-126,1-20,3-11,/O	2.2
1986	Mon-N	112	360	37	81	17	2	5	44	37	66	.225	.299	.325	73	-13	3	5	-2	.993	17	2-94,1-20,3-13,/PO	0.5
1987	Mon-N	133	436	52	119	27	1	12	56	51	62	.273	.349	.422	100	0	8	5	-1	.980	-9	*2-106,3-22,1-17,/P	-0.6

YEAR	TM/L	G	AB	R	H	2B	3B	HR	RBI	BB	SO	AVG	OBP	SLG	PRO+	BR/A	SB	CS	SBR	FA	FR	G/POS	TPR
1988	Chi-N★	151	556	73	163	29	2	11	78	55	79	.293	.360	.412	116	12	1	4	-2	.953	-12	*3-150/O-1	-0.3
1989	*Chi-N	130	408	38	96	22	3	7	42	38	73	.235	.300	.355	81	-10	2	2	-1	.949	-18	*3-119/O-1	-3.1
1991	Oak-A	74	134	11	28	7	1	0	9	18	27	.209	.303	.276	65	-6	0	0	0	.951	-6	3-67/S-3,O-3,1-1,P	-1.2
Total	11	1212	3802	453	972	193	26	71	442	408	602	.256	.329	.376	94	-28	34	26	-5	.956	-37	3-700,2-391,S/1OPD	-5.8
■ GARLAND LAWING	Lawing, Garland Frederick "Knobby" b: 8/29/19, Gastonia, N.C. d: 9/27/96, Murrells Inlet, S.C. BR/TR, 6'1", 180 lbs. Deb: 5/29/46																						
1946	Cin-N	2	3	0	0	0	0	0	0	0	2	.000	.000	.000	-99	-1	0			.000	-1	/O-1	-0.1
	NY-N	8	12	2	2	0	0	0	0	0	3	.167	.167	.167	-5	-2	0			1.000	-1	/O-4	-0.3
	Yr	10	15	2	2	0	0	0	0	0	5	.133	.133	.133	-24	-2	0			1.000	-1	/O-5	-0.4
■ TOM LAWLESS	Lawless, Thomas James b: 12/19/56, Erie, Pa. BR/TR, 5'11", 170 lbs. Deb: 7/15/82																						
1982	Cin-N	49	165	19	35	6	0	0	4	9	30	.212	.253	.248	40	-13	16	5	2	.978	7	2-47	-0.2
1984	Cin-N	43	80	10	20	2	0	1	2	8	12	.250	.318	.313	74	-3	6	3	0	1.000	-3	2-23/3-6	-0.5
	Mon-N	11	17	1	3	1	0	0	0	0	4	.176	.176	.235	15	-2	1	0	0	1.000	0	/2-9	-0.1
	Yr	54	97	11	23	3	0	1	2	8	16	.237	.295	.299	66	-4	7	3	0	1.000	-3	2-32/3-6	-0.6
1985	*StL-N	47	58	8	12	3	1	0	8	5	4	.207	.270	.293	58	-3	2	1	0	.971	9	3-13,2-11	0.6
1986	StL-N	46	39	5	11	1	0	0	3	2	8	.282	.317	.308	74	-1	8	1	2	.875	3	3-12/2-7,O-1	0.3
1987	*StL-N	19	25	5	2	1	0	0	0	3	5	.080	.179	.120	-19	-4	2	0	1	1.000	-1	/2-7,3-3,O-1	-0.5
1988	StL-N	54	65	9	10	2	1	1	3	7	9	.154	.236	.262	42	-5	6	0	2	1.000	2	3-24/O-6,2-5,1-1	-0.2
1989	Tor-A	59	70	20	16	1	0	0	3	7	12	.229	.299	.243	55	-4	12	1	3	1.000	1	O-16,3-12,D-12,/2C	0.0
1990	Tor-A	15	12	1	1	0	0	0	1	0	1	.083	.083	.083	-52	-2	0	2	-1	.800	2	/3-4,O-2,2-1,D-5	-0.1
Total	8	343	531	78	110	17	2	2	24	41	85	.207	.264	.258	46	-38	53	13	8	.988	20	2-117/3-74,ODC1	-0.7
■ MIKE LAWLOR	Lawlor, Michael H. b: 3/11/1854, Troy, N.Y. d: 8/3/18, Troy, N.Y. TR, 6', 180 lbs. Deb: 5/27/1880																						
1880	Tro-N	4	9	1	1	0	0	0	0	1	1	.111	.200	.111	8	-1				.867	1	/C-4	0.0
1884	Was-U	2	7	0	0	0	0	0		0		.000	.000	.000	-99	-2				1.000	1	/C-2	-0.1
Total	2	6	16	1	1	0	0	0	0	1	1	.063	.118	.063	-39	-3				.920	2	/C-6	-0.1
■ JIM LAWRENCE	Lawrence, James Ross b: 2/12/39, Hamilton, Ont., Can. BL/TR, 6'1", 185 lbs. Deb: 5/30/63																						
1963	Cle-A	2	0	0	0	0	0	0	0	0	0	—	—	—	—	0	0	0	0	.750	0	/C-2	0.0
■ BILL LAWRENCE	Lawrence, William Henry b: 3/11/06, San Mateo, Cal. d: 6/15/97, Redwood City, Cal. BR/TR, 6'4", 194 lbs. Deb: 4/13/32																						
1932	Det-A	25	46	10	10	1	0	0	3	5	5	.217	.294	.239	38	-4	0	2	-1	1.000	2	O-15	-0.4
■ OTIS LAWRY	Lawry, Otis Carroll "Rabbit" b: 11/1/1893, Fairfield, Me. d: 10/23/65, China, Maine BL/TR, 5'8", 133 lbs. Deb: 6/28/16																						
1916	Phi-A	41	123	10	25	0	0	0	4	9	21	.203	.263	.203	42	-9	4			.905	-10	2-29/O-5	-2.0
1917	Phi-A	30	55	7	9	1	0	0	1	2	9	.164	.193	.182	15	-6	1			.921	-3	2-17/O-1	-0.9
Total	2	71	178	17	34	1	0	0	5	11	30	.191	.242	.197	34	-14	5			.911	-13	/2-46,O-6	-2.9
■ MARCUS LAWTON	Lawton, Marcus Dwayne b: 8/18/65, Gulfport, Miss. BB/TR, 6'1", 160 lbs. Deb: 8/11/89 F																						
1989	NY-A	10	14	1	3	0	0	0	0	0	3	.214	.214	.214	21	-1	1	0	0	.818	-2	/O-8,D-1	-0.3
■ MATT LAWTON	Lawton, Matthew b: 11/3/71, Gulfport, Miss. BL/TR, 5'9", 180 lbs. Deb: 9/5/95 F																						
1995	Min-A	21	60	11	19	4	1	1	12	7	11	.317	.414	.467	128	3	1	1	-0	.972	-2	O-19/D-1	0.0
1996	Min-A	79	252	34	65	7	1	6	42	28	28	.258	.342	.365	78	-8	4	4	-1	.985	8	O-75/D-1	-0.3
1997	Min-A	142	460	74	114	29	3	14	60	76	81	.248	.366	.415	102	3	7	4	-0	.976	-1	*O-138	-0.1
1998	Min-A	152	557	91	155	36	6	21	77	86	64	.278	.389	.478	124	22	16	8	0	.990	18	*O-151	3.4
Total	4	394	1329	210	353	76	11	42	191	197	184	.266	.374	.434	107	20	28	17	-2	.984	23	O-383/D-2	3.0
■ GENE LAYDEN	Layden, Eugene Francis b: 3/14/1894, Pittsburgh, Pa. d: 12/12/84, Pittsburgh, Pa. BL/TL, 5'10", 160 lbs. Deb: 7/29/15																						
1915	NY-A	3	7	2	2	0	0	0	0	0	1	.286	.286	.286	71	-0	0	1	-1	.750	-1	/O-2	-0.2
■ PETE LAYDON	Laydon, Peter John b: 12/30/19, Dallas, Tex. d: 7/18/82, Edna, Tex. BR/TR, 5'11", 185 lbs. Deb: 4/28/48																						
1948	StL-A	41	104	11	26	2	1	0	4	6	10	.250	.297	.288	55	-7	4	2	0	.973	-1	O-30	-0.9
■ HERMAN LAYNE	Layne, Herman b: 2/13/01, New Haven, W.Va. d: 8/27/73, Gallipolis, Ohio BR/TR, 5'11", 165 lbs. Deb: 4/16/27																						
1927	Pit-N	11	6	3	0	0	0	0	0	1	0	.000	.143	.000	-55	-1	0			.000	-1	/O-2	-0.3
■ HILLIS LAYNE	Layne, Ivoria Hillis "Tony" b: 2/23/18, Whitwell, Tenn. BL/TR, 6', 170 lbs. Deb: 9/16/41																						
1941	Was-A	13	50	8	14	2	0	0	6	4	5	.280	.333	.320	77	-2	1	1	-0	.953	0	3-13	-0.1
1944	Was-A	33	87	6	17	2	0	0	8	6	10	.195	.263	.218	40	-7	2	0	1	.949	1	3-18/2-3	-0.5
1945	Was-A	61	147	23	44	5	4	1	14	10	7	.299	.352	.408	132	5	0	1	-1	.956	-5	3-33	0.1
Total	3	107	284	37	75	9	4	1	28	20	22	.264	.321	.335	92	-3	3	2	-0	.953	-3	/3-64,2-3	-0.5
■ LES LAYTON	Layton, Lester Lee b: 11/18/21, Nardin, Okla. BR/TR, 6', 165 lbs. Deb: 4/24/48																						
1948	NY-N	63	91	14	21	4	4	2	12	6	21	.231	.286	.429	90	-2	1			.951	-1	O-20	-0.3
■ JOHNNY LAZOR	Lazor, John Paul b: 9/9/12, Taylor, Wash. BL/TR, 5'9.5", 180 lbs. Deb: 4/22/43																						
1943	Bos-A	83	208	21	47	10	2	0	13	21	25	.226	.297	.293	72	-7	5	6	-2	.979	-3	O-63	-1.6
1944	Bos-A	16	24	0	2	1	0	0	0	1	0	.083	.120	.125	-30	-4	0	0	0	1.000	0	/O-6,C-1	-0.4
1945	Bos-A	101	335	35	104	19	2	5	45	18	17	.310	.346	.424	120	7	3	2	-0	.961	-8	O-81	-0.6
1946	Bos-A	23	29	1	4	0	0	1	4	2	11	.138	.194	.241	20	-3	0	0	0	1.000	-2	/O-7	-0.6
Total	4	223	596	57	157	30	4	6	62	42	53	.263	.312	.357	92	-7	8	8	-2	.971	-13	O-157/C-1	-3.2
■ TONY LAZZERI	Lazzeri, Anthony Michael "Poosh 'Em Up Tony" b: 12/6/03, San Francisco, Cal. d: 8/6/46, San Francisco, Cal. BR/TR, 5'11.5", 170 lbs. Deb: 4/13/26 CH																						
1926	*NY-A	155	589	79	162	28	14	18	114	54	96	.275	.338	.462	109	4	16	7	1	.961	-20	*2-149/S-5,3-1	-1.0
1927	*NY-A	153	570	92	176	29	8	18	102	69	82	.309	.383	.482	127	22	22	14	-2	.971	5	*2-113,S-38/3-9	3.1
1928	*NY-A	116	404	62	134	30	11	10	82	43	50	.332	.397	.535	148	27	15	5	2	.956	-11	*2-110	2.0
1929	NY-A	147	545	101	193	37	11	18	106	68	45	.354	.429	.561	164	52	9	10	-3	.969	-4	*2-147	4.8
1930	NY-A	143	571	109	173	34	15	9	121	60	62	.303	.372	.462	115	13	4	4	-1	.971	6	2-77,3-60/S-8,1O	2.3
1931	NY-A	135	484	67	129	27	7	8	83	79	80	.267	.371	.401	109	8	18	9	0	.958	-3	2-90,3-39	1.1
1932	*NY-A	142	510	79	153	28	16	15	113	82	64	.300	.399	.506	140	31	11	11	-3	.978	6	*2-134/3-5	3.8
1933	NY-A☆	139	523	94	154	22	12	18	104	73	62	.294	.383	.486	137	28	15	7	0	.968	-14	*2-138	2.1
1934	NY-A	123	438	59	117	24	6	14	67	71	64	.267	.369	.445	117	11	11	1	3	.976	-13	2-92,3-30	0.7
1935	NY-A	130	477	72	130	18	6	13	83	63	75	.273	.361	.417	107	5	11	5	0	.970	-21	*2-118/S-9	-0.6
1936	*NY-A	150	537	82	154	29	6	14	109	97	65	.287	.397	.441	110	11	8	5	-1	.968	-32	*2-148/S-2	-0.9
1937	*NY-A	126	446	56	109	21	3	14	70	71	76	.244	.348	.399	87	-9	7	1	2	.966	-8	*2-125	-0.6
1938	*Chi-N	54	120	21	32	5	0	5	23	22	30	.267	.380	.433	120	4	0			.946	-8	S-25/3-7,2-4,O-1	-0.2
1939	Bro-N	14	39	6	11	2	0	3	6	10	7	.282	.451	.564	165	4	1			.914	0	2-11/3-2	0.5
	NY-N	13	44	7	13	0	0	1	8	7	6	.295	.392	.364	103	1	0			.889	-2	3-13	-0.2
	Yr	27	83	13	24	2	0	4	14	17	13	.289	.422	.458	133	5	1			.897	-2	3-15,2-11	0.3
Total	14	1740	6297	986	1840	334	115	178	1191	869	864	.292	.380	.467	122	213	148	79		.967	-119	*2-1456,3-166/SO1	16.9
■ FREDDY LEACH	Leach, Frederick b: 11/23/1897, Springfield, Mo. d: 12/10/81, Hagerman, Idaho BL/TR, 5'11", 183 lbs. Deb: 5/24/23																						
1923	Phi-N	52	104	5	27	4	0	1	16	3	14	.260	.280	.327	54	-7	1	2	-1	.950	-6	O-26	-1.5
1924	Phi-N	8	28	6	13	2	1	2	7	2	1	.464	.500	.821	221	5	0	0	0	1.000	-1	/O-7	0.3
1925	Phi-N	65	292	47	91	15	4	5	28	5	21	.312	.323	.442	86	-7	1	2	-1	.952	-2	O-65	-1.4
1926	Phi-N	129	492	73	162	29	7	11	71	16	33	.329	.352	.484	117	10	6			.979	1	*O-123	0.2
1927	Phi-N	140	536	69	164	30	4	12	83	21	32	.306	.342	.444	108	4	2			.981	14	*O-140	0.9
1928	Phi-N	145	588	83	179	36	11	13	96	30	30	.304	.342	.469	107	4	4			.978	11	*O-120,1-25	0.4
1929	NY-N	113	411	74	119	22	6	8	47	17	14	.290	.324	.431	85	-11	10			.974	-12	O-95	-2.7
1930	NY-N	126	544	90	178	19	13	13	71	22	25	.327	.361	.482	104	2	3			.978	-3	*O-124	-0.8

YEAR	TM/L	G	AB	R	H	2B	3B	HR	RBI	BB	SO	AVG	OBP	SLG	PRO+	BR/A	SB	CS	SBR	FA	FR	G/POS	TPR
1931	NY-N	129	515	75	159	30	5	6	61	29	9	.309	.348	.421	109	5	4			.976	-4	*O-125	-0.7
1932	Bos-N	84	223	21	55	9	2	1	29	18	10	.247	.306	.318	71	-9	1			.977	-2	O-50	-1.4
Total	10	991	3733	543	1147	196	53	72	509	163	189	.307	.341	.446	101	-4	32	4		.975	-5	O-875/1-25	-6.7
■ RICK LEACH	Leach, Richard Max b: 5/4/57, Ann Arbor, Mich. BL/TL, 6′, 195 lbs. Deb: 4/30/81																						
1981	Det-A	54	83	9	16	3	1	1	11	16	15	.193	.323	.289	75	-2	0	1	-1	1.000	-1	1-32,O-15/D-2	-0.6
1982	Det-A	82	218	23	52	7	2	3	12	21	29	.239	.305	.330	74	-8	4	0	1	.995	-1	1-56,O-14/D-4	-1.0
1983	Det-A	99	242	22	60	17	0	3	26	19	21	.248	.305	.355	83	-6	2	2	-1	.994	3	1-73,O-13/D-3	-0.7
1984	Tor-A	65	88	11	23	6	2	0	7	8	14	.261	.323	.375	89	-1	0	0	0	1.000	-1	O-23,1-15/P-1,D-6	-0.3
1985	Tor-A	16	35	2	7	0	1	0	1	3	9	.200	.263	.257	42	-3	0	0	0	.987	-0	1-10/O-4	-0.3
1986	Tor-A	110	246	35	76	14	1	5	39	13	24	.309	.344	.435	108	2	0	0	0	.978	-8	D-42,O-39/1-7	-0.7
1987	Tor-A	98	195	26	55	13	1	3	25	25	25	.282	.372	.405	104	2	0	1	-1	.981	-6	O-43,D-30/1-5	-0.6
1988	Tor-A	87	199	21	55	13	1	0	23	18	27	.276	.336	.352	93	-2	0	1	-1	1.000	-4	O-49,D-25/1-4	-0.9
1989	Tex-A	110	239	32	65	14	1	1	23	32	33	.272	.360	.351	100	1	2	1	0	.951	-4	D-44,O-41/1-4	-0.5
1990	SF-N	78	174	24	51	13	0	2	16	21	20	.293	.372	.402	117	5	0	2	-1	.989	-3	O-52/1-7	-0.1
Total	10	799	1719	205	460	100	10	18	183	176	217	.268	.338	.369	94	-11	8	8	-2	.983	-26	O-293,1-213,D/P	-5.7
■ TOMMY LEACH	Leach, Thomas William b: 11/4/1877, French Creek, N.Y. d: 9/29/69, Haines City, Fla. BR/TR, 5′6.5″, 150 lbs. Deb: 9/28/1898																						
1898	Lou-N	3	10	0	1	0	0	0	0	0		.100	.100	.100	-43	-2	0			.727	-0	/3-3,2-1	-0.2
1899	Lou-N	106	406	75	117	10	6	5	57	37		.288	.349	.379	100	-0	19			.908	1	3-80,S-25/2-2	0.3
1900	*Pit-N	51	160	20	34	1	2	1	16	21		.213	.304	.262	57	-9	8			.864	1	3-31/S-8,2-7,O-4	-0.7
1901	Pit-N	98	374	64	114	12	13	2	44	20		.305	.347	.422	119	8	16			.903	9	3-92/S-4	1.7
1902	Pit-N	135	514	97	143	14	**22**	**6**	85	45		.278	.341	.426	132	18	25			.926	13	*3-134	3.3
1903	*Pit-N	127	507	97	151	16	17	7	87	40		.298	.352	.438	121	12	22			.879	7	*3-127	1.9
1904	Pit-N	146	579	92	149	15	12	2	56	45		.257	.316	.335	98	-1	23			.907	**36**	*3-146	4.1
1905	Pit-N	131	499	71	128	10	14	2	53	37		.257	.309	.345	92	-6	17			.988	11	O-71,3-58/2-2,S-2	0.5
1906	Pit-N	133	476	66	136	10	7	1	39	33		.286	.333	.342	106	3	21			.929	2	3-65,O-60/S-1	0.4
1907	Pit-N	149	547	102	166	19	12	4	43	40		.303	.352	.404	135	20	43			.980	11	*O-111,3-33/S-6,2-1	3.1
1908	Pit-N	152	583	93	151	24	16	5	41	54		.259	.324	.381	125	15	24			.937	-4	*3-150/O-2	1.9
1909	*Pit-N	151	587	**126**	153	29	8	6	43	66		.261	.337	.368	110	6	27			.969	3	*O-138,3-13	0.5
1910	Pit-N	135	529	83	143	24	5	4	52	38	62	.270	.319	.357	92	-7	18			.966	9	*O-131/S-2,2-1	-0.5
1911	Pit-N	108	386	60	92	12	6	3	43	46	50	.238	.323	.324	78	-11	19			.987	2	O-89,S-13/3-1	-1.3
1912	Pit-N	28	97	24	29	4	2	0	19	12	9	.299	.376	.381	109	1	6			.986	4	O-24	0.4
	Chi-N	82	265	50	64	10	3	2	32	55	20	.242	.378	.325	93	0	14			.975	5	O-73/3-4	0.2
	Yr	110	362	74	93	14	5	2	51	67	29	.257	.377	.340	98	2	20			.978	9	O-97/3-4	0.6
1913	Chi-N	131	456	**99**	131	23	10	6	32	77	44	.287	.391	.421	132	21	21			**.990**	3	*O-121/3-2	1.9
1914	Chi-N	153	577	80	152	24	9	7	46	79	50	.263	.353	.373	116	13	16			.968	9	*O-136,3-16	1.7
1915	Cin-N	107	335	42	75	7	5	0	17	56	38	.224	.338	.275	85	-4	20	14	-2	.959	-4	O-96	-1.6
1918	Pit-N	30	72	14	14	2	3	0	5	19	5	.194	.363	.306	101	1	2			.952	-2	O-23/S-3	-0.2
Total	19	2156	7959	1355	2143	266	172	63	810	820	278	.269	.340	.370	108	79	361	14		.975	114	*O-1079,3-955/S2	17.4
■ DAN LEAHY	Leahy, Daniel C. b: 8/8/1870, Knoxville, Tenn. d: 12/30/03, Knoxville, Tenn. 5′9″, 155 lbs. Deb: 9/2/1896																						
1896	Phi-N	2	6	0	2	1	0	0	1	1	2	.333	.429	.500	146	0	0			.857	1	/S-2	0.1
■ TOM LEAHY	Leahy, Thomas Joseph b: 6/2/1869, New Haven, Conn. d: 6/11/51, New Haven, Conn. TR , 168 lbs. Deb: 5/18/1897																						
1897	Pit-N	24	92	10	24	3	3	0	12	7		.261	.320	.359	82	-3	3			.935	-3	O-13/C-6,3-6	-0.5
	Was-N	19	52	12	20	2	1	0	7	9		.385	.529	.462	164	6	6			.727	-4	O-10/3-5,2-3,C-1	0.2
	Yr	43	144	22	44	5	4	0	19	16		.306	.405	.396	114	4	9			.881	-7	O-23,3-11/C-7,2-3	-0.3
1898	Was-N	15	55	10	10	2	0	0	5	8		.182	.297	.218	48	-3	6			.913	0	3-12/2-3	-0.3
1901	Mil-A	33	99	18	24	6	2	0	10	11		.242	.348	.343	97	0	3			.941	-5	C-28/O-2,2-1	-0.2
	Phi-A	5	15	1	5	1	0	0	1	1		.333	.375	.400	110	0	0			1.000	-1	/O-2,C-1,S-1	0.0
	Yr	38	114	19	29	7	2	0	11	12		.254	.351	.351	99	0	3			.944	-6	C-29/O-4,2-1,S-1	-0.2
1905	StL-N	35	97	3	22	1	3	0	7	8		.227	.286	.299	77	-3	0			.946	-9	C-29	-0.9
Total	4	131	410	54	105	15	9	0	42	44		.256	.348	.337	93	-2	18			.942	-21	/C-65,O-27,3-23,2S	-1.7
■ FRED LEAR	Lear, Frederick Francis "King" b: 4/7/1894, New York, N.Y. d: 10/13/55, E.Orange, N.J. BR/TR, 6′0.5″, 180 lbs. Deb: 6/7/15																						
1915	Phi-A	2	2	0	0	0	0	0	0	0	2	.000	.000	.000	-99	-0	0			.600	-0	/3-2	-0.1
1918	Chi-N	2	1	0	0	0	0	0	0	1	0	.000	.500	.000	56	0	0			.000	0	H	0.0
1919	Chi-N	40	76	8	17	3	1	1	11	8	11	.224	.306	.329	90	-1	2			.990	-2	/1-9,2-9,S-3	-0.3
1920	NY-N	31	87	12	22	0	1	1	7	8	15	.253	.323	.310	83	-2	0	2	-1	.951	-3	3-24/2-1	-0.5
Total	4	75	166	20	39	3	2	2	18	17	28	.235	.314	.313	84	-3	2	2		.924	-5	/3-26,2-10,1-9,S-3	-0.9
■ BILL LEARD	Leard, William Wallace "Wild Bill" b: 10/14/1885, Oneida, N.Y. d: 1/15/70, San Francisco, Cal BR/TR, 5′10″, 155 lbs. Deb: 7/21/17																						
1917	Bro-N	3	3	0	0	0	0	0	0	0	1	.000	.000	.000	-97	-1	0			.000	0	/2-1	-0.1
■ JACK LEARY	Leary, John J. b: 1858, New Haven, Conn. TL , 5′11″, 186 lbs. Deb: 8/21/1880																						
1880	Bos-N	1	3	1	0	0	0	0	0	1	0	.000	.250	.000	-7	-0				1.000	1	/O-1,P-1	0.0
1881	Det-N	3	11	2	3	1	1	0	4	1	1	.273	.333	.545	165	1				.833	0	/O-2,P-2	0.1
1882	Pit-a	60	257	32	75	7	3	1		5		.292	.305	.354	128	7				.759	-14	3-33,O-27/P-3,12	-0.6
	Bal-a	4	18	3	4	1	0	0		0		.222	.222	.278	73	-0				.900	-0	/P-3,O-1	0.0
	Yr	64	275	35	79	8	3	1		5		.287	.300	.349	124	7				.759	-14	3-33,O-28/P-6,12	-0.6
1883	Lou-a	40	165	16	31	1	3	3		2		.188	.198	.285	58	-7				.816	-1	S-40	-0.7
	Bal-a	3	11	1	2	0	2	0		0		.182	.182	.545	122	0				.727	-1	/2-3	-0.1
	Yr	43	176	17	33	1	5	3		2		.188	.197	.301	62	-7				.816	-2	S-40/2-3	-0.8
1884	Alt-U	8	33	1	3	0	0	0		1		.091	.118	.091	-35	-6				.692	-2	/O-6,P-3,3-1	-0.6
	CP-U	10	40	0	7	1	0	0		0		.175	.175	.200	13	-5				.840	1	/2-4,3-3,O-3,P-2	-0.3
	Yr	18	73	1	10	1	0	0		1		.137	.149	.151	-9	-12				.625	-1	/O-9,P-5,3-4,2-4	-0.9
Total	5	129	538	56	125	11	9	4	4	10	1	.232	.246	.309	84	-11				.725	-17	/S-40,O-40,3P21	-2.2
■ JOHN LEARY	Leary, John Louis "Jack" b: 5/2/1891, Waltham, Mass. d: 8/18/61, Waltham, Mass. BR/TR, 5′11.5″, 180 lbs. Deb: 4/14/14																						
1914	StL-A	144	533	35	141	28	7	0	45	10	71	.265	.282	.343	91	-9	9	15	-6	.987	-4	*1-130,C-15	-2.4
1915	StL-A	75	227	19	55	10	0	0	15	5	36	.242	.268	.286	69	-10	2	4	-2	.985	-2	1-53,C-11	-1.6
Total	2	219	760	54	196	38	7	0	60	15	107	.258	.278	.326	85	-19	11	19	-8	.987	-7	1-183/C-26	-4.0
■ HAL LEATHERS	Leathers, Harold Langford "Chuck" b: 12/2/1898, Selma, Cal. d: 4/12/77, Modesto, Cal. BL/TR, 5′8″, 152 lbs. Deb: 9/13/20																						
1920	Chi-N	9	23	3	7	1	0	1	1	1	1	.304	.333	.478	129	1	1	0	0	.825	-1	/S-6,2-3	0.1
■ EMIL LEBER	Leber, Emil Bohmiel b: 5/15/1881, Cleveland, Ohio d: 11/6/24, Cleveland, Ohio BR/TR, 5′11″, 170 lbs. Deb: 9/2/05																						
1905	Cle-A	2	6	1	0	0	0	0	0	1		.000	.143	.000	-53	-1	0			1.000	-0	/3-2	-0.1
■ BEVO LeBOURVEAU	LeBourveau, De Witt Wiley b: 8/24/1894, Dana, Cal. d: 12/10/47, Nevada City, Cal. BL/TR, 5′11″, 175 lbs. Deb: 9/9/19																						
1919	Phi-N	17	63	4	17	0	0	0	0	10	8	.270	.370	.270	88	-0	2			1.000	2	O-15	0.1
1920	Phi-N	84	261	29	67	7	2	3	12	11	36	.257	.295	.333	76	-8	9	6	-1	.949	3	O-72	-1.2
1921	Phi-N	93	281	42	83	12	5	6	35	29	51	.295	.361	.438	102	1	4	5	-2	.911	-8	O-76	-1.4
1922	Phi-N	74	167	24	45	8	3	2	20	24	29	.269	.368	.389	87	-3	0	3	-2	.920	-3	O-42	-1.0
1929	Phi-A	12	16	1	5	0	1	0	2	5	1	.313	.476	.438	132	1	0	1	-1	1.000	0	/O-3	0.0
Total	5	280	788	100	217	27	11	11	69	79	125	.275	.345	.379	91	-9	15	15		.935	-7	O-208	-3.5
■ RICKY LEDEE	Ledee, Ricardo Alberto b: 11/22/73, Ponce, P.R. BL/TL, 6′2″, 190 lbs. Deb: 6/14/98																						
1998	*NY-A	42	79	13	19	5	2	1	12	7	29	.241	.302	.392	81	-2	3	1	0	.981	-5	O-42	-0.7

YEAR	TM/L	G	AB	R	H	2B	3B	HR	RBI	BB	SO	AVG	OBP	SLG	PRO+	BR/A	SB	CS	SBR	FA	FR	G/POS	TPR

■ AARON LEDESMA Ledesma, Aaron David b: 6/3/71, Union City, Cal. BR/TR, 6'2", 200 lbs. Deb: 7/2/95

1995	NY-N	21	33	4	8	0	0	0	3	6	7	.242	.359	.242	64	-1	0	0	0	.875	-2	3-10/1-2,S-2	-0.3
1997	Bal-A	43	88	24	31	5	1	2	11	13	9	.352	.441	.500	149	7	1	0	0	.973	-1	2-22,3-11/1-5,S-4	0.7
1998	TB-A	95	299	30	97	16	3	0	29	9	51	.324	.346	.398	89	-5	9	7	-2	.970	6	S-58,2-19/3-7,1D	0.5
Total	3	159	420	58	136	21	4	2	43	28	67	.324	.369	.407	100	1	10	7	-1	.970	3	/S-64,2-41,31D	0.9

■ MIKE LEDWITH Ledwith, Michael b: Brooklyn, N.Y. d: 1/2/29, Bronx, N.Y. Deb: 8/19/1874

| 1874 | Atl-n | 1 | 4 | 1 | 1 | 0 | 0 | 0 | 1 | 0 | 0 | .250 | .250 | .250 | 69 | -0 | 0 | 0 | 0 | .600 | -1 | /C-1 | -0.1 |

■ CLIFF LEE Lee, Clifford Walker b: 8/4/1896, Lexington, Neb. d: 8/25/80, Denver, Colo. BR/TR, 6'1", 175 lbs. Deb: 5/15/19

1919	Pit-N	42	112	5	22	2	4	0	2	6	8	.196	.237	.286	55	-6	2			.962	-11	C-28/O-6	-1.7
1920	Pit-N	37	76	9	18	2	2	0	8	4	14	.237	.275	.316	67	-3	0	1	-1	.974	0	C-19/O-2	-0.3
1921	Phi-N	88	286	31	88	14	4	3	29	13	34	.308	.338	.427	94	-3	5	2	0	.987	-7	1-48,O-27/C-2	-1.2
1922	Phi-N	122	422	65	136	29	6	17	77	32	43	.322	.371	.540	121	11	2	3	-1	.967	-5	O-89,1-18/3-1	-0.1
1923	Phi-N	107	355	54	114	20	4	11	47	20	39	.321	.357	.493	110	3	3	3	-1	.959	-11	O-83,1-16	-1.3
1924	Phi-N	21	56	4	14	3	2	1	7	2	5	.250	.276	.429	77	-2	0	1	-1	1.000	-1	O-13/1-4	-0.4
	Cin-N	6	6	1	2	1	0	0	2	0	2	.333	.333	.500	122	0	0	0	0	.000	-0	/O-1	0.0
	Yr	27	62	5	16	4	2	1	9	2	7	.258	.281	.435	82	-2	0	1	-1	1.000	-1	O-14/1-4	-0.4
1925	Cle-A	77	230	43	74	15	6	4	42	21	33	.322	.378	.491	118	6	2	1	0	.951	-3	O-70	-0.1
1926	Cle-A	21	40	4	7	1	0	1	2	6	2	.175	.283	.275	45	-3	0	0	0	1.000	0	/O-9,C-3	-0.4
Total	8	521	1583	216	475	87	28	38	216	104	186	.300	.344	.462	103	2	14	11		.960	-36	O-300/1-86,C-52,3-1	-5.5

■ DEREK LEE Lee, Derek Gerald b: 7/28/66, Chicago, Ill. BL/TR, 6'1", 200 lbs. Deb: 6/27/93

| 1993 | Min-A | 15 | 33 | 3 | 5 | 1 | 0 | 0 | 4 | 1 | 4 | .152 | .176 | .182 | -4 | -5 | 0 | 0 | 0 | 1.000 | -2 | O-13 | -0.7 |

■ DERREK LEE Lee, Derrek Leon b: 9/6/75, Sacramento, Cal. BR/TR, 6'5", 205 lbs. Deb: 4/28/97

1997	SD-N	22	54	9	14	1	0	4	9	4	24	.259	.365	.370	101	0	0	0	0	1.000	1	1-21	0.0
1998	Fla-N	141	454	62	106	29	1	17	74	47	120	.233	.319	.414	92	-6	5	2	0	.993	10	*1-132	-0.6
Total	2	163	508	71	120	32	1	18	78	56	144	.236	.324	.409	93	-6	5	2	0	.993	11	1-153	-0.6

■ DUD LEE Lee, Ernest Dudley (a.k.a. Ernest Dudley In 1920-21) b: 8/22/1899, Denver, Colo. d: 1/7/71, Denver, Colo. BL/TR, 5'9", 150 lbs. Deb: 10/3/20

1920	StL-A	1	2	2	2	0	0	0	1	0	0	1.000	1.000	1.000	418	-1	0	0		.333	-1	/S-1	0.0
1921	StL-A	72	180	18	30	4	2	0	11	14	34	.167	.235	.211	14	-24	1	1	-0	.922	5	S-31,2-30/3-3	-1.5
1924	Bos-A	94	288	36	73	9	4	0	29	40	17	.253	.350	.313	72	-11	8	4	0	.937	-8	S-90	-0.9
1925	Bos-A	84	255	22	57	7	3	0	19	34	19	.224	.315	.275	51	-19	2	3	-1	.924	17	S-84	0.4
1926	Bos-A	2	7	2	1	0	0	0	0	0	0	.143	.250	.143	6	-1	0	0	0	1.000	-1	/S-2	-0.2
Total	5	253	732	80	163	20	9	0	60	88	70	.223	.311	.275	50	-54	12	8	-1	.928	12	S-208/2-30,3-3	-2.2

■ HAL LEE Lee, Harold Burnham "Sheriff" b: 2/15/05, Ludlow, Miss. d: 9/4/89, Pascagoula, Miss. BR/TR, 5'11", 180 lbs. Deb: 4/19/30

1930	Bro-N	22	37	5	6	0	0	1	4	4	5	.162	.244	.243	19	-5	0			1.000	-1	O-12	-0.6
1931	Phi-N	44	131	13	29	10	0	2	12	10	18	.221	.282	.344	62	-7	0			.967	-1	O-38	-1.1
1932	Phi-N	149	595	76	180	42	10	18	85	36	45	.303	.343	.497	110	7	6			.965	11	*O-148	0.8
1933	Phi-N	46	167	25	48	12	2	0	12	18	13	.287	.360	.383	100	0	1			.981	1	O-45	-0.1
	Bos-N	88	312	32	69	15	9	1	28	18	26	.221	.266	.337	77	-10	1			.977	2	O-87	-1.4
	Yr	134	479	57	117	27	11	1	40	36	39	.244	.300	.353	87	-9	2			.978	3	*O-132	-1.5
1934	Bos-N	139	521	70	152	23	6	8	79	47	43	.292	.353	.405	111	8	3			.985	5	*O-128/2-4	0.7
1935	Bos-N	112	422	49	128	18	6	0	39	18	25	.303	.333	.374	98	-2	0			.962	6	*O-110	-0.1
1936	Bos-N	152	565	46	143	24	7	3	64	52	50	.253	.318	.336	82	-15	4			.973	-6	*O-150	-2.6
Total	7	752	2750	316	755	144	40	33	323	203	225	.275	.326	.392	95	-25	15			.973	16	O-718/2-4	-4.4

■ LEONIDAS LEE Lee, Leonidas Pyrrhus (b: Leonidas Pyrrhus Funkhouser) b: 12/13/1860, St.Louis, Mo. d: 6/11/12, Hendersonville, N.C. Deb: 7/17/1877

| 1877 | StL-N | 4 | 18 | 0 | 5 | 1 | 0 | 0 | 1 | 0 | 0 | .278 | .278 | .333 | 97 | -0 | | | | .667 | -2 | /O-4,S-1 | -0.2 |

■ LERON LEE Lee, Leron b: 3/4/48, Bakersfield, Cal. BL/TR, 6', 196 lbs. Deb: 9/5/69

1969	StL-N	7	23	3	5	0	0	0	3	8	1	.217	.308	.261	60	-1	0	0	0	1.000	-0	/O-7	-0.2
1970	StL-N	121	264	28	60	13	1	6	23	24	66	.227	.294	.352	71	-11	5	1	1	.969	-5	O-77	-1.8
1971	StL-N	25	28	3	5	1	0	1	2	4	12	.179	.281	.321	68	-1	0	1	-1	.800	-3	O-8	-0.5
	SD-N	79	256	29	70	20	2	4	21	18	45	.273	.321	.414	115	4	4	5	-2	.920	-4	O-68	-0.5
	Yr	104	284	32	75	21	2	5	23	22	57	.264	.317	.405	108	2	4	6	-3	.914	-6	O-76	-1.0
1972	SD-N	101	370	50	111	23	7	12	47	29	58	.300	.356	.497	151	23	2	5	0	.975	4	O-96	2.1
1973	SD-N	118	333	36	79	7	2	3	30	33	61	.237	.308	.297	74	-12	4	0	1	.970	2	O-84	-1.2
1974	Cle-A	79	232	18	54	13	0	5	25	16	42	.233	.279	.353	82	-6	3	2	-0	.958	4	O-62/D-2	-0.6
1975	Cle-A	13	23	3	3	1	0	0	2	3	5	.130	.231	.174	16	-3	1	0	0	1.000	-1	/O-5,D-3	-0.3
	LA-N	48	43	2	11	0	0	0	2	3	9	.256	.304	.349	85	-1	0	0	0	1.000	-1	/O-4	-0.3
1976	LA-N	23	45	1	6	0	1	0	2	2	9	.133	.170	.178	-1	-6	0	0	0	1.000	-2	O-10	-0.9
Total	8	614	1617	173	404	83	13	31	152	133	315	.250	.309	.375	95	-15	19	14	-3	.962	-5	O-421/D-5	-4.2

■ MANUEL LEE Lee, Manuel Lora "Manny" (b: Manuel Lora (Lee)) b: 6/17/65, San Pedro De Macoris, D.R. BB/TR, 5'9", 161 lbs. Deb: 4/10/85

1985	*Tor-A	64	40	9	8	0	0	0	2	9	9	.200	.238	.200	21	-4	1	4	-2	.971	19	2-38/S-8,3-5,D-8	1.2
1986	Tor-A	35	78	8	16	0	1	1	7	4	10	.205	.244	.269	39	-7	0	1	-1	.990	4	2-29/S-5/3-2	-0.3
1987	Tor-A	56	121	14	31	2	3	1	11	6	13	.256	.291	.347	67	-6	2	0	1	.966	12	2-27,S-26/D-1	0.8
1988	Tor-A	116	381	38	111	16	3	2	38	26	64	.291	.337	.365	96	-2	3	3	-1	.988	10	2-98,S-23/3-8,D-2	1.2
1989	*Tor-A	99	300	27	78	9	2	3	34	20	60	.260	.306	.333	82	-7	4	2	0	.985	-2	2-40,S-28,3-17,D/O	-0.6
1990	Tor-A	117	391	45	95	12	4	6	41	26	90	.243	.290	.340	74	-14	3	1	0	**.993**	-10	*2-112/S-9	-2.1
1991	*Tor-A	138	445	41	104	18	3	0	29	24	107	.234	.276	.288	54	-28	7	2	1	.967	-28	*S-138	-4.5
1992	*Tor-A	128	396	49	104	10	1	3	39	50	73	.263	.345	.316	83	-8	6	2	1	.987	-18	*S-128	-1.6
1993	Tex-A	73	205	31	45	3	1	1	12	22	39	.220	.301	.259	54	-13	2	4	-2	.968	4	S-72/D-1	-0.5
1994	Tex-A	95	335	41	93	18	2	2	38	21	66	.278	.320	.361	76	-12	3	1	0	.967	4	S-85,2-13	0.1
1995	StL-N	1	1	1	1	0	0	0	0	0	0	1.000	1.000	1.000	431	0	0	0	0	.800	1	/2-1	0.1
Total	11	922	2693	304	686	88	20	19	249	201	531	.255	.307	.323	73	-100	31	20	-3	.972	-4	S-522,2-358/3DO	-6.3

■ TERRY LEE Lee, Terry James b: 3/13/62, San Francisco, Cal. BR/TR, 6'5", 215 lbs. Deb: 9/3/90

1990	Cin-N	12	19	1	4	1	0	0	3	2	2	.211	.286	.263	50	-1	0	0	0	1.000	0	/1-6	-0.1
1991	Cin-N	3	6	0	0	0	0	0	0	1	2	.000	.000	.000	-96	-2	0	0	0	1.000	2	/1-2	0.0
Total	2	15	25	1	4	1	0	0	3	3	4	.160	.222	.200	17	-3	0	0	0	1.000	2	/1-8	-0.1

■ TRAVIS LEE Lee, Travis Reynolds b: 5/26/75, San Diego, Cal. BL/TL, 6'0", 205 lbs. Deb: 3/31/98

| 1998 | Ari-N | 146 | 562 | 71 | 151 | 20 | 2 | 22 | 72 | 67 | 123 | .269 | .347 | .429 | 99 | -0 | 8 | 1 | 2 | .998 | -4 | *1-146 | 1.5 |

■ BILLY LEE Lee, William Joseph b: 1/9/1892, Bayonne, N.J. d: 1/6/84, West Hazleton, Pa. BR/TR, 5'9", 165 lbs. Deb: 4/15/15

1915	StL-A	18	59	2	11	1	0	0	4	6	5	.186	.262	.203	41	-4	1	1	0	1.000	2	O-15/3-1	-0.3
1916	StL-A	7	11	1	2	0	0	0	0	1	1	.182	.250	.182	31	-1	0			1.000	0	/O-4	-0.2
Total	2	25	70	3	13	1	0	0	4	7	6	.186	.260	.200	39	-5	1	1		1.000	2	/O-19,3-1	-0.5

■ WATTY LEE Lee, Wyatt Arnold b: 8/12/1879, Lynch Station, Va. d: 3/6/36, Washington, D.C. BL/TL, 5'10.5", 171 lbs. Deb: 4/30/01

1901	Was-A	43	129	15	33	6	3	0	12	7		.256	.304	.349	82	-3	0			.948	0	P-36/O-7	-0.2
1902	Was-A	109	391	61	100	21	5	4	45	33		.256	.319	.366	89	-6	8			.916	0	O-96,P-13	-1.1
1903	Was-A	75	231	17	48	8	4	0	13	18		.208	.265	.277	62	-11	5			.930	7	O-47,P-22	-0.6
1904	Pit-N	8	12	1	4	0	1	0	0	0		.333	.333	.500	152	1	0			.889	0	/P-5	0.0
Total	4	235	763	94	185	35	13	4	70	58		.242	.300	.338	80	-20	13			.917	8	O-150/P-76	-1.9

YEAR	TM/L	G	AB	R	H	2B	3B	HR	RBI	BB	SO	AVG	OBP	SLG	PRO+	BR/A	SB	CS	SBR	FA	FR	G/POS	TPR
■ **GENE LEEK**	Leek, Eugene Harold b: 7/15/36, San Diego, Cal. BR/TR, 6', 185 lbs. Deb: 4/22/59																						
1959	Cle-A	13	36	7	8	3	0	1	5	2	7	.222	.263	.389	80	-1	0	0	0	.955	-2	3-13/S-1	-0.3
1961	LA-A	57	199	16	45	9	1	5	20	7	54	.226	.260	.357	57	-13	0	1	-1	.958	18	3-49/S-7,O-1	0.6
1962	LA-A	7	14	0	2	0	0	0	0	0	6	.143	.143	.143	-24	-2	0	0	0	1.000	0	/3-4	-0.2
Total	3	77	249	23	55	12	1	6	25	9	67	.221	.254	.349	55	-16	0	1	-1	.959	16	/3-66,S-8,O-1	0.1
■ **DAVE LEEPER**	Leeper, David Dale b: 10/30/59, Santa Ana, Cal. BL/TL, 5'11", 170 lbs. Deb: 9/10/84																						
1984	KC-A	4	6	1	0	0	0	0	0	0	1	.000	.000	.000	-99	-2	0	0	0	1.000	-0	/O-2,D-1	-0.2
1985	KC-A	15	34	1	3	0	0	0	4	1	3	.088	.114	.088	-43	-7	0	0	0	.929	-1	/O-8	-0.8
Total	2	19	40	2	3	0	0	0	4	1	4	.075	.098	.075	-52	-8	0	0	0	.944	-1	/O-10,D-1	-1.0
■ **GEORGE LEES**	Lees, George Edward b: 2/2/1895, Bethlehem, Pa. d: 1/2/80, Harrisburg, Pa. BR/TR, 5'9", 150 lbs. Deb: 5/7/21																						
1921	Chi-A	20	42	3	9	2	0	0	4	0	3	.214	.214	.262	21	-5	0	1	-1	.951	-2	C-16	-0.7
■ **JIM LEFEBVRE**	Lefebvre, James Kenneth b: 1/7/42, Inglewood, Cal. BB/TR, 6', 185 lbs. Deb: 4/12/65 MC																						
1965	*LA-N	157	544	57	136	21	4	12	69	71	92	.250	.339	.369	106	5	3	5	-2	.970	-12	*2-156	0.5
1966	*LA-N★	152	544	69	149	23	3	24	74	48	72	.274	.336	.460	129	19	1	1	-0	.980	-11	*2-119,3-40	1.7
1967	LA-N	136	494	51	129	18	5	8	50	44	64	.261	.325	.366	106	3	1	5	-3	.955	6	3-92,2-34/1-5	0.8
1968	LA-N	84	286	23	69	12	1	5	31	26	55	.241	.307	.343	102	0	0	0	0	.978	-10	2-62,3-16/O-5,1-3	-0.8
1969	LA-N	95	275	29	65	15	2	4	44	48	37	.236	.352	.349	104	3	2	1	0	.985	1	3-44,2-37/1-6	0.7
1970	LA-N	109	314	33	79	15	1	4	44	29	42	.252	.317	.344	81	-9	1	1	-0	.988	-4	2-70,3-21/1-1	-0.8
1971	LA-N	119	388	40	95	14	2	12	68	39	55	.245	.317	.384	104	1	0	2	-1	.988	-17	*2-102/3-7	-0.9
1972	LA-N	70	169	11	34	8	0	5	24	17	30	.201	.274	.337	75	-6	0	0	0	.987	-1	2-33,3-11	-0.6
Total	8	922	3014	313	756	126	18	74	404	322	447	.251	.326	.378	105	18	8	15	-7	.979	-48	2-613,3-231/1-15,O	0.6
■ **JOE LEFEBVRE**	Lefebvre, Joseph Henry b: 2/22/56, Concord, N.H. BL/TR, 5'10", 175 lbs. Deb: 5/22/80																						
1980	*NY-A	74	150	26	34	1	1	8	21	27	30	.227	.345	.407	107	2	0	0	0	.975	-14	O-71	-1.4
1981	SD-N	86	246	31	63	13	4	8	31	35	33	.256	.353	.439	133	11	6	4	-1	.994	4	O-84	1.3
1982	SD-N	102	239	25	57	9	0	4	21	18	50	.238	.295	.326	78	-8	0	0	0	.972	-17	3-39,O-36/C-3	-2.8
1983	SD-N	18	20	1	5	0	0	0	1	2	3	.250	.318	.250	61	-1	0	0	0	1.000	-2	/O-6,3-4,C-2	-0.3
	*Phi-N	101	258	34	80	20	8	8	38	31	46	.310	.390	.543	158	20	5	3	-0	.990	-9	O-74/3-9,C-3	0.9
	Yr	119	278	35	85	20	8	8	39	33	49	.306	.385	.522	151	19	5	3	-0	.990	-11	O-80,3-13/C-5	0.6
1984	Phi-N	52	160	22	40	9	0	3	18	23	37	.250	.351	.363	99	1	0	2	-1	.966	0	O-47/3-1	-0.2
1986	Phi-N	14	18	0	2	0	0	0	0	3	5	.111	.238	.111	-1	-2	0	0	0	1.000	-0	/O-3	-0.3
Total	6	447	1091	139	281	52	13	31	130	139	204	.258	.346	.414	115	22	11	9	-2	.986	-37	O-321/3-53,C-8	-2.8
■ **BILL LEFEBVRE**	Lefebvre, Wilfred Henry "Lefty" b: 11/11/15, Natick, R.I. BL/TL, 5'11.5", 180 lbs. Deb: 6/10/38																						
1938	Bos-A	1	1	1	1	0	0	1	1	0	0	1.000	1.000	4.000	1048	1	0	0	0	.000	-0	/P-1	0.0
1939	Bos-A	7	10	3	3	0	0	0	1	2	2	.300	.417	.300	83	-0	0	0	0	1.000	-1	/P-5	0.0
1943	Was-A	7	14	0	4	3	0	0	1	1	0	.286	.333	.500	148	1	0	0	0	1.000	-0	/P-6	0.0
1944	Was-A	60	62	4	16	2	2	0	8	12	9	.258	.378	.355	115	2	0	0	0	.933	-0	P-24/1-2	0.0
Total	4	75	87	8	24	5	2	1	11	15	11	.276	.382	.414	129	4	0	0	0	.960	-1	/P-36,1-2	0.0
■ **AL LEFEVRE**	Lefevre, Alfredo Modesto b: 9/16/1898, New York, N.Y. d: 1/21/82, Glen Cove, N.Y. BR/TR, 5'10.5", 160 lbs. Deb: 6/28/20																						
1920	NY-N	17	27	5	4	0	1	0	0	0	13	.148	.148	.222	5	-3	0	0	0	1.000	3	/S-9,2-6,3-1	0.0
■ **WADE LEFLER**	Lefler, Wade Hampton b: 6/5/1896, Cooleemee, N.C. d: 3/6/81, Hickory, N.C. BL/TR, 5'11", 162 lbs. Deb: 4/16/24																						
1924	Bos-N	1	1	0	0	0	0	0	0	0	1	.000	.000	.000	-99	-0	0	0	0	.000	0	H	0.0
	Was-A	5	8	0	5	3	0	0	4	0	0	.625	.625	1.000	325	2	0	0	0	1.000	-0	/O-1	0.2
Total	1	6	9	0	5	3	0	0	4	0	1	.556	.556	.889	279	2	0	0	0	1.000	-0	/O-1	0.2
■ **RON LeFLORE**	LeFlore, Ronald b: 6/16/48, Detroit, Mich. BR/TR, 6', 200 lbs. Deb: 8/1/74																						
1974	Det-A	59	254	37	66	8	1	2	13	13	58	.260	.304	.323	78	-7	23	9	2	.935	3	O-59	-0.6
1975	Det-A	136	550	66	142	13	6	8	37	33	139	.258	.303	.347	80	-15	28	20	-4	.973	6	*O-134	-1.9
1976	Det-A★	135	544	93	172	23	8	4	39	51	111	.316	.377	.410	125	18	58	20	5	.973	16	*O-132/D-1	3.5
1977	Det-A	154	652	100	212	30	10	16	57	37	121	.325	.365	.475	121	18	39	19	0	.972	2	*O-152	1.3
1978	Det-A	155	666	**126**	198	30	3	12	62	65	104	.297	.363	.405	113	12	**68**	16	11	.976	9	*O-155	2.6
1979	Det-A	148	600	110	180	22	10	9	57	52	95	.300	.356	.415	104	4	78	14	15	.990	4	*O-113,D-34	1.6
1980	Mon-N	139	521	95	134	21	11	4	39	62	99	.257	.337	.363	95	-2	**97**	19	**18**	.957	6	*O-130	1.6
1981	Chi-A	82	337	46	83	10	4	0	24	28	70	.246	.306	.300	77	-10	36	11	4	.960	-1	O-82	-0.9
1982	Chi-A	91	334	58	96	15	4	4	25	22	91	.287	.331	.392	98	-1	28	14	0	.939	-4	O-83/D-2	-0.7
Total	9	1099	4458	731	1283	172	57	59	353	363	888	.288	.344	.392	103	16	455	142	51	.968	41	*O-1040/D-37	6.5
■ **LOU LEGETT**	Legett, Louis Alfred "Doc" b: 6/1/01, New Orleans, La. d: 3/6/88, New Orleans, La. BR/TR, 5'10", 166 lbs. Deb: 5/8/29																						
1929	Bos-N	39	81	7	13	2	0	0	6	3	18	.160	.190	.185	-7	-14	2			.914	-1	C-28	-1.2
1933	Bos-A	8	5	1	1	1	0	0	1	0	0	.200	.200	.400	56	-0	0	0	0	1.000	1	/C-2	0.0
1934	Bos-A	19	38	4	11	0	0	0	1	2	4	.289	.325	.289	56	-2	0	0	0	.977	-0	C-17	-0.2
1935	Bos-A	2	0	1	0	0	0	0	0	0	0	—	—	—	—	0	0	0	0	.000	0	R	0.0
Total	4	68	124	13	25	3	0	0	8	5	22	.202	.233	.226	16	-16	2	0		.938	-1	/C-47	-1.4
■ **GREG LEGG**	Legg, Gregory Lynn b: 4/21/60, San Jose, Cal. BR/TR, 6'1", 185 lbs. Deb: 4/18/86																						
1986	Phi-N	11	20	2	9	1	0	0	1	0	3	.450	.450	.500	156	1	0	0	0	.941	2	/2-4,S-1	0.4
1987	Phi-N	3	2	1	0	0	0	0	0	0	0	.000	.000	.000	-97	-1	0	0	0	1.000	-0	/2-1,S-1,3-1	-0.1
Total	2	14	22	3	9	1	0	0	1	0	3	.409	.409	.455	132	1	0	0	0	.952	2	/2-5,S-2,3-1	0.3
■ **MIKE LEHANE**	Lehane, Michael Patrick b: 4/15/1865, New York, N.Y. BR , 6'1.5", 180 lbs. Deb: 4/26/1884																						
1884	Was-U	3	12	1	4	2	0	0		0		.333	.333	.500	154	0				.688	-1	/S-3,O-1,3-1	0.0
1890	Col-a	140	512	54	108	19	5	0	56	43		.211	.276	.268	65	-23	13			**.982**	10	*1-140	-1.8
1891	Col-a	137	511	59	110	12	7	1	52	34	77	.215	.268	.272	58	-29	16			**.981**	7	*1-137	-2.5
Total	3	280	1035	114	222	33	12	1	108	77	77	.214	.273	.272	62	-51	29			.982	16	1-277/S-3,3-1,O-1	-4.3
■ **PAUL LEHNER**	Lehner, Paul Eugene "Peanuts" or "Gulliver" b: 7/1/20, Dolomite, Ala. d: 12/27/67, Birmingham, Ala. BL/TL, 5'9", 165 lbs. Deb: 9/10/46																						
1946	StL-A	16	45	6	10	1	2	0	5	1	5	.222	.239	.333	56	-3	0	0	0	.941	-3	O-12	-0.7
1947	StL-A	135	483	59	120	25	9	7	48	28	29	.248	.294	.381	85	-12	5	5	-2	.980	-6	*O-127	-2.7
1948	StL-A	103	333	23	92	15	4	2	46	30	19	.276	.336	.363	84	-8	0	2	-1	.974	-6	O-89/1-2	-2.0
1949	StL-A	104	297	25	68	13	0	3	37	16	20	.229	.271	.303	50	-23	0	2	-1	.987	2	O-56,1-18	-2.5
1950	Phi-A	114	427	48	132	17	5	9	52	32	33	.309	.357	.436	104	1	1	1	-0	.981	6	*O-101	0.3
1951	Phi-A	9	28	1	4	1	0	0	1	1	1	.143	.172	.179	-5	-4	0	0	0	1.000	1	/O-6	-0.3
	Chi-A	23	72	9	15	3	1	0	3	10	4	.208	.305	.278	60	-4	0	0	0	.980	-4	O-20	-0.8
	StL-A	21	67	2	9	5	0	1	2	6	5	.134	.205	.254	23	-8	0	1	-1	1.000	-1	O-18	-1.0
	Cle-A	12	13	2	3	0	0	0	1	1	2	.231	.286	.231	43	-1	0	0	0	1.000	-0	/O-1	-0.1
	Yr	65	180	14	31	9	1	1	7	18	12	.172	.247	.250	35	-17	0	1	-1	.991	-4	O-45	-2.2
1952	Bos-A	3	3	0	2	0	0	0	2	2	0	.667	.800	.667	288	1	0	0	0	1.000	-0	/O-2	0.1
Total	7	540	1768	175	455	80	21	22	197	127	118	.257	.309	.364	78	-60	6	11	-5	.981	-11	O-432/1-20	-9.7
■ **CLARENCE LEHR**	Lehr, Clarence Emanuel "King" b: 5/16/1886, Escanaba, Mich. d: 1/31/48, Highland Park, Mich. BR/TR, 5'11", 165 lbs. Deb: 5/18/11																						
1911	Phi-N	23	27	2	4	0	0	0	2	0	7	.148	.148	.148	-17	-4	0			1.000	-1	/O-5,2-4,S-4	-0.5
■ **HANK LEIBER**	Leiber, Henry Edward b: 1/17/11, Phoenix, Ariz. d: 11/8/93, Tucson, Ariz. BR/TR, 6'1.5", 205 lbs. Deb: 4/16/33																						
1933	NY-N	6	10	1	2	0	0	0	0	0	2	.200	.200	.200	15	-1	0			1.000	1	/O-1	0.0
1934	NY-N	63	187	17	45	5	3	2	25	4	13	.241	.257	.332	58	-12	1			.971	-6	O-51	-1.9
1935	NY-N	154	613	110	203	37	4	22	107	48	29	.331	.389	.512	143	36	0			.965	-15	*O-154	1.5

YEAR	TM/L	G	AB	R	H	2B	3B	HR	RBI	BB	SO	AVG	OBP	SLG	PRO+	BR/A	SB	CS	SBR	FA	FR	G/POS	TPR
1936	*NY-N	101	337	44	94	19	7	9	67	37	41	.279	.352	.457	118	8	1			.961	-7	O-86/1-1	-0.3
1937	*NY-N	51	184	24	54	7	3	4	32	15	27	.293	.347	.429	108	2	1			.988	-7	O-46	-0.6
1938	NY-N★	98	360	50	97	18	4	12	65	31	45	.269	.327	.442	109	3	0			.974	-9	O-89	-0.8
1939	Chi-N	112	365	65	113	16	1	24	88	59	42	.310	.411	.556	155	29	1			.977	4	O-98	2.9
1940	Chi-N†	117	440	68	133	24	2	17	86	45	68	.302	.371	.482	136	21	1			.985	-6	*O-103,1-12	0.9
1941	Chi-N†	53	162	20	35	5	0	7	25	16	25	.216	.291	.377	90	-3	0			.964	-4	O-29,1-15	-1.0
1942	NY-N	58	147	11	32	6	0	4	23	19	27	.218	.315	.340	91	-1	0			.990	-0	O-41/P-1	-0.4
Total	10	813	2805	410	808	137	24	101	518	274	319	.288	.356	.462	122	83	5			.973	-49	O-698/1-28,P-1	0.3

■ NEMO LEIBOLD Leibold, Harry Loran b: 2/17/1892, Butler, Ind. d: 2/4/77, Detroit, Mich. BL/TR, 5′6.5″, 157 lbs. Deb: 4/12/13

YEAR	TM/L	G	AB	R	H	2B	3B	HR	RBI	BB	SO	AVG	OBP	SLG	PRO+	BR/A	SB	CS	SBR	FA	FR	G/POS	TPR
1913	Cle-A	93	286	37	74	11	6	0	12	21	43	.259	.309	.339	87	-5	16			.945	-0	O-74	-1.0
1914	Cle-A	115	402	46	106	13	3	0	32	54	56	.264	.354	.311	96	-0	12	14	-5	.931	9	*O-107	-0.1
1915	Cle-A	57	207	28	53	5	4	0	4	24	16	.256	.339	.319	95	-1	5	3	-0	.969	9	O-52	0.6
	Chi-A	36	74	10	17	1	0	0	11	15	11	.230	.360	.243	78	-1	1	3	-2	1.000	5	O-22	0.1
	Yr	93	281	38	70	6	4	0	15	39	27	.249	.345	.299	91	-2	6	6	-2	.978	14	O-74	0.7
1916	Chi-A	45	82	5	20	1	2	0	13	7	7	.244	.303	.305	82	-2	7			1.000	-5	O-24	-0.8
1917	*Chi-A	125	428	59	101	12	6	0	29	74	34	.236	.350	.292	94	-0	27			.961	-1	*O-122	-0.8
1918	Chi-A	116	440	57	110	14	7	0	31	63	32	.250	.344	.314	97	0	13			.979	8	*O-114	0.2
1919	*Chi-A	122	434	81	131	18	2	0	26	72	30	.302	.404	.353	113	11	17			.928	7	*O-122	1.0
1920	Chi-A	108	413	61	91	16	3	1	28	55	30	.220	.316	.281	59	-23	7	15	-7	.977	6	*O-105	-3.2
1921	Bos-A	123	467	88	143	26	6	0	31	41	27	.306	.363	.388	94	-4	13	7	-0	.949	4	*O-117	-0.8
1922	Bos-A	81	271	42	70	8	1	1	18	41	14	.258	.360	.306	76	-8	1	6	-3	.966	6	O-71	-1.0
1923	Bos-A	12	18	1	2	0	0	0	0	1	2	.111	.158	.111	-28	-3	0	1	-1	.909	-3	O-10	-0.7
	Was-A	95	315	68	96	13	4	1	22	53	16	.305	.408	.381	114	9	7	6	-2	.980	1	O-84	0.3
	Yr	107	333	69	98	13	4	1	22	54	18	.294	.396	.366	106	5	7	7	-2	.977	-2	O-94	-0.4
1924	*Was-A	84	246	41	72	6	4	0	20	42	10	.293	.398	.350	97	1	7	5	-1	.994	-3	O-70	-0.6
1925	*Was-A	56	84	14	23	1	1	0	7	8	7	.274	.337	.310	66	-4	1	0	0	.972	-6	O-26/3-1	-1.0
Total	13	1268	4167	638	1109	145	49	3	284	571	335	.266	.357	.327	91	-30	134	60		.961	37	*O-1120/3-1	-7.8

■ ELMER LEIFER Leifer, Elmer Edwin b: 5/23/1893, Clarington, Ohio d: 9/26/48, Everett, Wash. BL/TR, 5′9.5″, 170 lbs. Deb: 9/7/21

YEAR	TM/L	G	AB	R	H	2B	3B	HR	RBI	BB	SO	AVG	OBP	SLG	PRO+	BR/A	SB	CS	SBR	FA	FR	G/POS	TPR
1921	Chi-A	9	10	0	3	0	0	0	1	0	4	.300	.300	.300	54	-1	0	0	0	1.000	-1	/3-1,O-1	-0.1

■ JOHN LEIGHTON Leighton, John Atkinson b: 10/4/1861, Peabody, Mass. d: 10/31/56, Lynn, Mass. 5′11″, 170 lbs. Deb: 7/12/1890

YEAR	TM/L	G	AB	R	H	2B	3B	HR	RBI	BB	SO	AVG	OBP	SLG	PRO+	BR/A	SB	CS	SBR	FA	FR	G/POS	TPR
1890	Syr-a	7	27	6	8	2	0	0	0	3		.296	.367	.370	131	1	2			.938	-0	/O-7	0.0

■ BILL LEINHAUSER Leinhauser, William Charles b: 11/4/1893, Philadelphia, Pa. d: 4/14/78, Elkins Park, Pa. BR/TR, 5′10″, 150 lbs. Deb: 5/18/12

YEAR	TM/L	G	AB	R	H	2B	3B	HR	RBI	BB	SO	AVG	OBP	SLG	PRO+	BR/A	SB	CS	SBR	FA	FR	G/POS	TPR
1912	Det-A	1	4	0	0	0	0	0	0	0		.000	.000	.000	-99	-1	0			1.000	0	/O-1	-0.1

■ ED LEIP Leip, Edgar Ellsworth b: 11/29/10, Trenton, N.J. d: 11/24/83, Zephyrhills, Fla. BR/TR, 5′9″, 160 lbs. Deb: 9/16/39

YEAR	TM/L	G	AB	R	H	2B	3B	HR	RBI	BB	SO	AVG	OBP	SLG	PRO+	BR/A	SB	CS	SBR	FA	FR	G/POS	TPR
1939	Was-A	9	32	4	11	1	0	0	2	2	4	.344	.382	.375	102	0	0	1	-1	.951	-1	/2-8	-0.1
1940	Pit-N	3	5	2	1	0	0	0	0	0	0	.200	.200	.200	11	-1	0			1.000	-0	/2-2	-0.1
1941	Pit-N	15	25	1	5	0	2	0	3	1	2	.200	.231	.360	65	-1	1			.889	2	/2-7,3-1	0.1
1942	Pit-N	3	0	0	0	0	0	0	0	0	0	—	—	—	—	0	0			.000	0	R	0.0
Total	4	30	62	7	17	1	2	0	5	3	6	.274	.308	.355	80	-2	1	1		.931	0	/2-17,3-1	-0.1

■ SCOTT LEIUS Leius, Scott Thomas b: 9/24/65, Yonkers, N.Y. BR/TR, 6′3″, 195 lbs. Deb: 9/3/90

YEAR	TM/L	G	AB	R	H	2B	3B	HR	RBI	BB	SO	AVG	OBP	SLG	PRO+	BR/A	SB	CS	SBR	FA	FR	G/POS	TPR
1990	Min-A	14	25	4	6	1	0	1	4	2	2	.240	.296	.400	87	-0	0	0	0	1.000	3	S-12/3-1	0.3
1991	*Min-A	109	199	35	57	7	2	5	20	30	35	.286	.380	.417	115	5	5	5	-2	.953	-2	3-79,S-19/O-2	0.3
1992	Min-A	129	409	50	102	18	2	2	35	34	61	.249	.309	.318	73	-14	6	5	-1	.955	4	*3-125,S-10	-1.1
1993	Min-A	10	18	4	3	0	0	0	2	2	4	.167	.250	.167	14	-2	0	0	0	.947	4	/S-9	0.2
1994	Min-A	97	350	57	86	16	1	14	49	37	58	.246	.320	.417	88	-7	2	4	-2	.969	-1	3-95/S-2	-0.9
1995	Min-A	117	372	51	92	16	5	4	45	49	54	.247	.338	.349	79	-11	2	1	0	.945	-4	*3-112/S-7,D-3	-1.4
1996	Cle-A	27	43	3	6	4	0	1	3	2	8	.140	.178	.302	18	-6	0	0	0	1.000	1	/3-8,1-7,2-6,D-1	-0.5
1998	KC-A	17	46	2	8	0	0	0	4	1	6	.174	.191	.174	-4	-7	0	0	0	.867	-0	3-15/S-2,D-1	-0.7
Total	8	520	1462	206	360	62	10	27	162	157	228	.246	.321	.358	80	-42	15	15	-5	.953	5	3-435/S-61,1-7,2DO	-3.8

■ FRANK LEJA Leja, Frank John b: 2/7/36, Holyoke, Mass. d: 5/3/91, Boston, Mass. BL/TL, 6′4″, 205 lbs. Deb: 5/1/54

YEAR	TM/L	G	AB	R	H	2B	3B	HR	RBI	BB	SO	AVG	OBP	SLG	PRO+	BR/A	SB	CS	SBR	FA	FR	G/POS	TPR
1954	NY-A	12	5	2	1	0	0	0	0	0	1	.200	.200	.200	10	-1	0	0	0	1.000	0	/1-6	-0.1
1955	NY-A	7	2	1	0	0	0	0	0	0	1	.000	.000	.000	-99	-1	0	0	0	1.000	0	/1-2	-0.1
1962	LA-A	7	16	0	0	0	0	0	0	1	6	.000	.059	.000	-85	-4	0	0	0	.953	-0	/1-4	-0.5
Total	3	26	23	3	1	0	0	0	0	1	8	.043	.083	.043	-67	-5	0	0	0	.958	-0	/1-12	-0.7

■ LARRY LeJEUNE LeJeune, Sheldon Aldenbert b: 7/22/1885, Chicago, Ill. d: 4/21/52, Eloise, Mich. BR/TR, 6′, 185 lbs. Deb: 5/10/11

YEAR	TM/L	G	AB	R	H	2B	3B	HR	RBI	BB	SO	AVG	OBP	SLG	PRO+	BR/A	SB	CS	SBR	FA	FR	G/POS	TPR
1911	Bro-N	6	19	2	3	0	0	0	2	2	8	.158	.238	.158	12	-2	2			.818	-2	/O-6	-0.5
1915	Pit-N	18	65	4	11	0	1	0	2	2	7	.169	.206	.200	23	-6	4	3	-1	.940	2	O-18	-0.6
Total	2	24	84	6	14	0	1	0	4	4	15	.167	.213	.190	21	-8	6	3		.918	1	/O-24	-1.1

■ DON LeJOHN LeJohn, Donald Everett b: 5/13/34, Daisytown, Pa. BR/TR, 5′10″, 175 lbs. Deb: 6/30/65

YEAR	TM/L	G	AB	R	H	2B	3B	HR	RBI	BB	SO	AVG	OBP	SLG	PRO+	BR/A	SB	CS	SBR	FA	FR	G/POS	TPR
1965	*LA-N	34	78	2	20	2	0	0	7	5	13	.256	.301	.282	70	-3	0	1	-1	.959	1	3-26	-0.4

■ JACK LELIVELT Lelivelt, John Frank b: 11/14/1885, Chicago, Ill. d: 1/20/41, Seattle, Wash. BL/TL, 5′11.5″, 175 lbs. Deb: 6/24/09 F

YEAR	TM/L	G	AB	R	H	2B	3B	HR	RBI	BB	SO	AVG	OBP	SLG	PRO+	BR/A	SB	CS	SBR	FA	FR	G/POS	TPR
1909	Was-A	91	318	25	93	8	6	0	24	19		.292	.334	.355	124	8	8			.970	8	O-91	1.4
1910	Was-A	110	347	40	92	10	3	0	33	40		.265	.343	.311	110	5	20			.964	4	O-86/1-7	0.6
1911	Was-A	72	225	29	72	12	4	0	22	22		.320	.386	.409	124	8	7			.939	4	O-49/1-7	0.8
1912	NY-A	36	149	12	54	6	7	2	23	4		.362	.383	.537	153	9	7			.963	-1	O-36	0.6
1913	NY-A	18	28	2	6	0	1	0	4	2	2	.214	.267	.286	61	-1	1			1.000	1	/O-5	-0.1
	Cle-A	23	23	0	9	2	0	0	7	0	3	.391	.391	.478	150	1	1			.000	-1	/O-1	0.1
	Yr	41	51	2	15	2	1	0	11	2	5	.294	.321	.373	101	-0	2			1.000	1	/O-6	0.0
1914	Cle-A	34	64	6	21	5	1	0	13	2	10	.328	.348	.438	131	2	2	3	-1	.933	-3	O-13/1-1	-0.3
Total	6	384	1154	114	347	43	22	2	126	89	15	.301	.353	.381	124	31	46	3		.962	13	O-281/1-15	3.1

■ JOHNNIE LeMASTER LeMaster, Johnnie Lee b: 6/19/54, Portsmouth, Ohio BR/TR, 6′2″, 167 lbs. Deb: 9/2/75

YEAR	TM/L	G	AB	R	H	2B	3B	HR	RBI	BB	SO	AVG	OBP	SLG	PRO+	BR/A	SB	CS	SBR	FA	FR	G/POS	TPR
1975	SF-N	22	74	4	14	4	0	2	9	4	15	.189	.241	.324	53	-5	2	1	0	.967	-1	S-22	-0.4
1976	SF-N	33	100	9	21	3	2	0	9	2	21	.210	.225	.280	42	-8	2	0	1	.937	11	S-31	0.7
1977	SF-N	68	134	13	20	5	1	0	8	13	27	.149	.224	.201	15	-16	2	1	0	.934	7	S-54/3-2	-0.5
1978	SF-N	101	272	23	64	18	3	1	14	21	45	.235	.293	.335	78	-9	6	6	-2	.966	2	S-96/2-2	0.2
1979	SF-N	108	343	42	87	11	2	3	29	23	55	.254	.304	.324	77	-12	9	5	-0	.959	0	*S-106	-0.1
1980	SF-N	135	405	33	87	16	6	3	31	25	57	.215	.260	.306	59	-23	0	1	-1	.957	-14	*S-134	-2.5
1981	SF-N	104	324	27	82	9	1	0	28	24	46	.253	.307	.287	70	-12	3	7	-3	.964	-8	*S-103	-1.5
1982	SF-N	130	436	34	94	14	1	2	30	31	78	.216	.268	.266	50	-29	13	4	2	.963	-8	*S-130	-2.5
1983	SF-N	141	534	81	128	16	1	6	30	60	96	.240	.319	.307	77	-16	39	19	0	.964	-22	*S-139	-2.6
1984	SF-N	132	451	46	98	13	2	4	32	31	97	.217	.268	.282	56	-27	17	5	2	.964	4	*S-129	-0.9
1985	SF-N	12	16	1	0	0	0	0	0	1	5	.000	.059	.000	-86	-4	0	0	0	.955	-1	S-10	-0.5
	Cle-A	11	20	0	3	0	0	0	2	0	6	.150	.150	.150	-18	-3	0	1	-1	.949	3	S-10	0.0
	Pit-N	22	58	4	9	0	0	1	6	5	12	.155	.222	.207	21	-6	1	0	0	.983	13	S-21	0.9
1987	Oak-A	20	24	3	2	0	0	0	1	1	4	.083	.120	.083	-48	-5	0	1	-1	1.000	5	/3-8,S-7,2-5,D-1	0.0
Total	12	1039	3191	320	709	109	19	22	229	241	564	.222	.278	.289	60	-174	94	51	-2	.961	-9	S-992/3-10,2-7,D-1	-9.7

■ STEVE LEMBO Lembo, Stephen Neal b: 11/13/26, Brooklyn, N.Y. d: 12/4/89, Flushing, N.Y. BR/TR, 6′1″, 185 lbs. Deb: 9/16/50

YEAR	TM/L	G	AB	R	H	2B	3B	HR	RBI	BB	SO	AVG	OBP	SLG	PRO+	BR/A	SB	CS	SBR	FA	FR	G/POS	TPR
1950	Bro-N	5	6	0	1	0	0	0	0	1	0	.167	.286	.167	22	-1	0			1.000	2	/C-5	0.2
1952	Bro-N	2	5	0	1	0	0	0	1	0	1	.200	.200	.200	11	-1	0	0	0	1.000	0	/C-2	0.0
Total	2	7	11	0	2	0	0	0	1	1	1	.182	.250	.182	18	-1	0	0		1.000	3	/C-7	0.2

YEAR	TM/L	G	AB	R	H	2B	3B	HR	RBI	BB	SO	AVG	OBP	SLG	PRO+	BR/A	SB	CS	SBR	FA	FR	G/POS	TPR
■ MARK LEMKE	Lemke, Mark Alan b: 8/13/65, Utica, N.Y. BB/TR, 5'9", 167 lbs. Deb: 9/17/88																						
1988	Atl-N	16	58	8	13	4	0	0	2	4	5	.224	.274	.293	60	-3	0	2	-1	.970	4	2-16	0.1
1989	Atl-N	14	55	4	10	2	1	2	10	5	7	.182	.250	.364	72	-2	0	1	-1	1.000	-2	2-14	-0.4
1990	Atl-N	102	239	22	54	13	0	0	21	21	22	.226	.288	.280	54	-15	0	1	-1	.989	23	3-45,2-44/S-1	0.9
1991	*Atl-N	136	269	36	63	11	2	2	23	29	27	.234	.309	.312	71	-10	1	2	-1	.978	13	*2-110,3-15	0.4
1992	*Atl-N	155	427	38	97	7	4	6	26	50	39	.227	.308	.304	70	-16	0	3	-2	.984	-10	*2-145,3-13	-2.7
1993	*Atl-N	151	493	52	124	19	2	7	49	65	50	.252	.339	.341	82	-11	1	2	-1	.982	6	*2-150	-0.2
1994	Atl-N	104	350	40	103	15	0	3	31	38	37	.294	.363	.363	88	-5	0	3	-2	.994	7	*2-103	0.5
1995	*Atl-N	116	399	42	101	16	5	5	38	44	40	.253	.327	.356	78	-12	2	2	-1	.990	-11	*2-115	-1.7
1996	*Atl-N	135	498	64	127	17	0	5	37	53	48	.255	.327	.319	68	-22	5	2	0	.977	7	*2-133	-0.7
1997	Atl-N	109	351	33	86	17	1	2	26	33	51	.245	.310	.316	63	-18	2	0	1	.980	8	*2-104	-0.3
1998	Bos-A	31	91	10	17	4	0	0	7	6	15	.187	.237	.231	22	-10	0	1	-1	1.000	-6	2-31	-1.5
Total	11	1069	3230	349	795	125	15	32	270	348	341	.246	.319	.324	71	-126	11	19	-8	.984	40	2-965/3-73,S-1	-5.6
■ CHET LEMON	Lemon, Chester Earl b: 2/12/55, Jackson, Miss. BR/TR, 6', 195 lbs. Deb: 9/9/75																						
1975	Chi-A	9	35	2	9	2	0	0	1	2	6	.257	.297	.314	72	-1	1	0	0	.923	-4	/3-6,O-1,D-2	-0.5
1976	Chi-A	132	451	46	111	15	5	4	38	28	65	.246	.300	.328	83	-10	13	7	-0	.992	11	*O-131	-0.4
1977	Chi-A	150	553	99	151	38	4	19	67	52	88	.273	.347	.459	118	13	8	7	-2	.978	**35**	*O-149	4.0
1978	Chi-A★	105	357	51	107	24	6	13	55	39	46	.300	.381	.510	147	22	5	9	-4	.983	14	O-95,D-10	2.8
1979	Chi-A★	148	556	79	177	**44**	2	17	86	56	68	.318	.394	.496	138	31	7	11	-5	.977	9	*O-147/D-1	2.8
1980	Chi-A	147	514	76	150	32	6	11	51	71	56	.292	.390	.442	128	22	6	6	-2	.981	2	*O-139/2-1,D-6	1.6
1981	Chi-A	94	328	50	99	23	6	9	50	33	48	.302	.388	.491	155	24	5	8	-3	.984	2	O-93	2.0
1982	Det-A	125	436	75	116	20	1	19	52	56	69	.266	.369	.447	122	15	1	4	-2	.984	1	*O-121/D-1	1.0
1983	Det-A	145	491	78	125	21	5	24	69	54	70	.255	.352	.464	126	18	0	7	-4	.988	11	*O-145	2.0
1984	*Det-A★	141	509	77	146	34	6	20	76	51	83	.287	.360	.495	135	24	5	5	-2	.995	16	*O-140/D-1	3.3
1985	Det-A	145	517	69	137	28	4	18	68	45	93	.265	.336	.439	111	7	0	2	-1	.990	11	*O-144	1.2
1986	Det-A	126	403	45	101	21	3	12	53	39	53	.251	.329	.407	99	-0	2	1	0	.985	3	*O-124	-0.1
1987	*Det-A	146	470	75	130	30	3	20	75	70	82	.277	.380	.481	132	23	0	0	0	.992	3	*O-145	2.0
1988	Det-A	144	512	67	135	29	4	17	64	59	65	.264	.348	.436	123	16	1	2	-1	.974	4	*O-144	1.5
1989	Det-A	127	414	45	98	19	2	7	47	46	71	.237	.325	.343	90	-4	1	5	-3	.985	-6	*O-111,D-13	-1.7
1990	Det-A	104	322	39	83	16	4	5	32	48	61	.258	.361	.379	106	4	3	2	-0	.973	6	O-96/D-6	0.8
Total	16	1988	6868	973	1875	396	61	215	884	749	1024	.273	.357	.442	121	203	58	76	-28	.984	116	*O-1925/D-40,3-6,2	22.3
■ JIM LEMON	Lemon, James Robert b: 3/23/28, Covington, Va. BR/TR, 6'4", 200 lbs. Deb: 8/20/50 MC																						
1950	Cle-A	12	34	4	6	1	0	1	1	3	12	.176	.243	.294	38	-3	0	0	0	.824	-2	O-10	-0.5
1953	Cle-A	16	46	5	8	1	0	1	5	3	15	.174	.224	.261	32	-5	0	0	0	.913	-1	O-11/1-2	-0.6
1954	Was-A	37	128	12	30	2	3	2	13	9	34	.234	.285	.344	76	-5	0	0	0	.951	-3	O-33	-1.0
1955	Was-A	10	25	3	5	2	0	1	3	3	4	.200	.286	.400	88	-1	0	0	0	.923	-0	/O-6	-0.1
1956	Was-A	146	538	77	146	21	**11**	27	96	65	138	.271	.352	.502	123	16	2	4	-2	.963	8	*O-141	1.4
1957	Was-A	137	518	58	147	23	6	17	64	49	94	.284	.349	.450	118	12	1	7	-4	.971	-3	*O-131/1-3	-0.3
1958	Was-A	142	501	65	123	15	9	26	75	50	120	.246	.315	.467	114	8	2	4	-2	.978	0	*O-137	-0.1
1959	Was-A	147	531	73	148	18	3	33	100	46	99	.279	.337	.510	130	20	5	2	0	.969	3	*O-142	1.6
1960	Was-A★	148	528	81	142	10	1	38	100	67	114	.269	.359	.508	133	23	2	0	1	.960	-1	*O-145	1.6
1961	Min-A	129	423	57	109	26	1	14	52	44	98	.258	.333	.423	95	-3	1	1	-0	.940	-6	*O-120	-1.6
1962	Min-A	12	17	1	3	0	0	1	5	3	4	.176	.300	.353	72	-1	0	0	0	1.000	-1	/O-3	-0.2
1963	Min-A	7	17	0	2	0	0	0	1	1	5	.118	.167	.118	-18	-3	0	0	0	.800	-1	/O-4	-0.4
	Phi-N	31	59	6	16	2	0	2	6	8	18	.271	.358	.407	121	2	0	0	0	.963	-2	O-18	0.0
	Chi-A	36	80	4	16	0	1	1	8	12	32	.200	.304	.262	62	-4	0	0	0	.979	-3	1-25	-0.8
Total	12	1010	3445	446	901	121	35	164	529	363	787	.262	.335	.460	114	57	13	18	-7	.961	-12	O-901/1-30	-1.0
■ BOB LEMON	Lemon, Robert Granville b: 9/22/20, San Bernardino, Cal. BL/TR, 6', 185 lbs. Deb: 9/9/41 MCH																						
1941	Cle-A	5	4	0	1	0	0	0	0	0	1	.250	.250	.250	34	-0	0	0	0	1.000	0	/3-1	0.0
1942	Cle-A	5	5	0	0	0	0	0	0	0	3	.000	.000	.000	-99	-1	0	0	0	.500	0	/3-1	-0.1
1946	Cle-A	55	89	9	16	3	0	1	4	7	18	.180	.240	.247	39	-8	0	1	-1	.976	6	P-32,O-12	-0.3
1947	Cle-A	47	56	11	18	4	3	2	5	6	9	.321	.387	.607	179	5	0	0	0	.983	4	P-37/O-2	-0.1
1948	*Cle-A☆	52	119	20	34	9	0	5	21	8	23	.286	.331	.487	119	2	0	0	0	.965	8	P-43	0.0
1949	Cle-A☆	46	108	17	29	6	2	7	19	10	20	.269	.331	.556	135	4	0	0	0	.963	6	P-37	0.0
1950	Cle-A★	72	136	21	37	9	1	6	26	13	25	.272	.340	.485	113	2	0	0	0	.957	5	P-44	0.0
1951	Cle-A★	56	102	11	21	4	1	3	13	9	22	.206	.270	.353	72	-5	0	0	0	.976	4	P-42	0.0
1952	Cle-A★	54	124	14	28	5	0	2	9	4	21	.226	.250	.315	60	-7	0	0	0	.982	7	P-42	0.0
1953	Cle-A☆	51	112	12	26	9	1	2	17	7	20	.232	.277	.384	79	-4	2	0	1	.972	8	P-41	0.0
1954	*Cle-A★	40	98	11	21	4	1	2	10	6	24	.214	.260	.337	61	-6	0	0	0	.963	4	P-36	0.0
1955	Cle-A	49	78	11	19	0	0	1	9	13	16	.244	.352	.282	69	-3	0	0	0	.983	2	P-35	0.0
1956	Cle-A	43	93	8	18	0	0	5	12	9	21	.194	.272	.355	63	-5	0	0	0	.934	4	P-39	0.0
1957	Cle-A	25	46	2	3	1	0	1	1	0	14	.065	.065	.152	-43	-9	0	0	0	1.000	3	P-21	0.0
1958	Cle-A	15	13	1	3	0	0	0	1	1	4	.231	.286	.231	45	-1	0	0	0	1.000	1	P-11	0.0
Total	15	615	1183	148	274	54	9	37	147	93	241	.232	.289	.386	82	-36	2	1	0	.969	62	P-460/O-14,3-2	-0.5
■ DON LENHARDT	Lenhardt, Donald Eugene "Footsie" b: 10/4/22, Alton, Ill. BR/TR, 6'3", 190 lbs. Deb: 4/18/50 C																						
1950	StL-A	139	480	75	131	22	6	22	81	90	94	.273	.390	.481	118	13	3	2	-0	.988	-12	1-86,O-39,3-10	-0.2
1951	StL-A	31	103	9	27	3	0	5	18	6	13	.262	.303	.437	95	-1	1	0	0	.982	-2	O-27/1-1	-0.4
	Chi-A	64	199	23	53	9	1	10	45	24	25	.266	.351	.472	124	6	1	1	-0	.983	-2	O-53/1-2	0.2
	Yr	95	302	32	80	12	1	15	63	30	38	.265	.335	.460	114	5	2	1	0	.983	-4	O-80/1-3	-0.2
1952	Bos-A	30	105	18	31	4	0	7	24	15	18	.295	.383	.533	142	6	0	1	-1	.981	-2	O-27	0.2
	Det-A	45	144	18	27	2	1	3	13	28	18	.188	.320	.278	67	-6	0	1	-1	.989	3	O-43	-0.5
	StL-A	18	48	5	13	4	1	1	5	4	8	.271	.327	.458	114	1	0	0	0	1.000	0	O-11/1-2	0.0
	Yr	93	297	41	71	10	2	11	42	47	44	.239	.343	.397	102	1	0	2	-1	.988	2	O-81/1-2	-0.3
1953	StL-A	97	303	37	96	15	0	10	35	41	41	.317	.400	.465	131	14	1	2	-1	.969	2	O-77/3-6	1.2
1954	Bal-A	13	33	2	5	1	0	0	1	3	9	.152	.222	.182	12	-4	0	0	0	1.000	-1	/O-7,1-2	-0.5
	Bos-A	44	66	5	18	4	0	3	17	3	9	.273	.314	.470	101	-0	0	0	0	1.000	-3	O-13/3-1	-0.4
	Yr	57	99	7	23	5	0	3	18	6	18	.232	.283	.374	74	-4	0	0	0	1.000	-4	O-20/1-2,3-1	-0.9
Total	5	481	1481	192	401	64	9	61	239	214	235	.271	.365	.450	114	28	6	7	-2	.980	-15	O-297/1-93,3-17	-0.4
■ PATRICK LENNON	Lennon, Patrick Orlando b: 4/27/68, Whiteville, N.C. BR/TR, 6'2", 200 lbs. Deb: 9/15/91																						
1991	Sea-A	9	8	2	1	1	0	0	1	3	1	.125	.364	.250	73	-0	0	0	0	1.000	0	/O-1,D-5	0.0
1992	Sea-A	1	2	0	0	0	0	0	0	0	0	.000	.000	.000	-99	-1	0	0	0	1.000	-0	/1-1	-0.1
1996	KC-A	14	30	5	7	3	0	0	1	7	10	.233	.378	.333	82	-1	0	0	0	.947	-1	O-11/D-1	-0.2
1997	Oak-A	56	116	14	34	6	1	1	14	15	35	.293	.374	.388	101	1	0	1	-1	.948	-5	O-36,D-17	-0.6
1998	Tor-A	2	4	1	2	2	0	0	0	0	1	.500	.500	1.000	277	1	0	0	0	1.000	-0	/O-2	0.1
Total	5	82	160	22	44	12	1	1	16	25	47	.275	.373	.381	98	0	0	1	-1	.951	-6	/O-50,D-23,1-1	-0.8
■ BOB LENNON	Lennon, Robert Albert "Arch" b: 9/15/28, Brooklyn, N.Y. BL/TL, 6', 200 lbs. Deb: 9/9/54																						
1954	NY-N	3	3	0	0	0	0	0	0	0	0	.000	.000	.000	-99	-1	0	0	0	.000	0	H	-0.1
1956	NY-N	26	55	3	10	1	0	0	1	4	17	.182	.237	.200	19	-6	0	0	0	.885	-4	O-21	-1.2
1957	Chi-N	9	21	2	3	1	0	1	3	1	9	.143	.182	.333	35	-2	0	0	0	1.000	-1	/O-4	-0.4
Total	3	38	79	5	13	2	0	1	4	5	26	.165	.214	.228	19	-9	0	0	0	.900	-6	/O-25	-1.7
■ BILL LENNON	Lennon, William F. b: 1848, Brooklyn, N.Y. 5'7", 145 lbs. Deb: 5/4/1871 MU																						
1871	Kek-n	12	48	5	11	3	0	0	5	1	0	.229	.245	.292	52	-3	1	0	0	.887	-2	C-12/S-2,O-1,M	-0.3
1872	Nat-n	11	54	11	12	1	0	0	6	0	0	.222	.222	.241	36	-5	0	0	0	.765	-5	C-11/1-1	-0.7

YEAR	TM/L	G	AB	R	H	2B	3B	HR	RBI	BB	SO	AVG	OBP	SLG	PRO+	BR/A	SB	CS	SBR	FA	FR	G/POS	TPR
1873	Mar-n	5	19	2	4	0	0	0	2	0	0	.211	.211	.211	33	-1	0	0	0	.942	-2	/1-4,C-1,3-1	-0.2
Total	3 n	28	121	18	27	4	0	0	13	1	0	.223	.230	.256	42	-9	1	0	0	.817	-9	/C-24,1-5,S-2,30	-1.2

■ ED LENNOX
Lennox, James Edgar "Eggie" b: 11/3/1885, Camden, N.J. d: 10/26/39, Camden, N.J. BR/TR, 5'10", 174 lbs. Deb: 8/8/06

YEAR	TM/L	G	AB	R	H	2B	3B	HR	RBI	BB	SO	AVG	OBP	SLG	PRO+	BR/A	SB	CS	SBR	FA	FR	G/POS	TPR
1906	Phi-A	6	17	1	1	1	0	0	0	1		.059	.111	.118	-28	-2	0			.909	5	/3-6	0.3
1909	Bro-N	126	435	33	114	18	9	2	44	47		.262	.337	.359	120	10	11			**.959**	-4	*3-121	1.2
1910	Bro-N	110	367	19	95	19	4	3	32	36	39	.259	.333	.357	104	2	7			.950	-16	*3-100	-1.2
1912	Chi-N	27	81	13	19	4	1	1	16	12	10	.235	.347	.346	90	-1	1			.934	-5	3-24	-0.6
1914	Pit-F	124	430	71	134	25	10	11	84	71	38	.312	.414	.493	148	24	19			.954	-15	*3-123	1.3
1915	Pit-F	55	53	1	16	3	1	1	9	7	12	.302	.383	.453	136	2	0			1.000	2	/3-3	0.5
Total	6	448	1383	138	379	70	25	18	185	174	99	.274	.361	.400	122	34	38			.953	-32	3-377	1.5

■ JIM LENTINE
Lentine, James Matthew b: 7/16/54, Los Angeles, Cal. BR/TR, 6', 175 lbs. Deb: 9/3/78

YEAR	TM/L	G	AB	R	H	2B	3B	HR	RBI	BB	SO	AVG	OBP	SLG	PRO+	BR/A	SB	CS	SBR	FA	FR	G/POS	TPR
1978	StL-N	8	11	1	2	0	0	0	1	0	0	.182	.250	.182	23	-1	1	0	0	1.000	-0	/O-3	-0.1
1979	StL-N	11	23	2	9	1	0	0	1	3	6	.391	.462	.435	145	2	0	1	-1	1.000	-0	/O-8	0.1
1980	StL-N	9	10	1	1	0	0	0	1	0	2	.100	.100	.100	-43	-2	0	0	0	1.000	-2	/O-6	-0.4
	Det-A	67	161	19	42	8	1	1	17	28	30	.261	.377	.342	96	0	2	1	0	.963	-3	O-55/D-9	-0.4
Total	3	95	205	23	54	9	1	1	20	31	38	.263	.368	.332	92	-1	3	2	-0	.969	-5	/O-72,D-9	-0.8

■ EDDIE LEON
Leon, Eduardo Antonio b: 8/11/46, Tucson, Ariz. BR/TR, 6', 175 lbs. Deb: 9/9/68

YEAR	TM/L	G	AB	R	H	2B	3B	HR	RBI	BB	SO	AVG	OBP	SLG	PRO+	BR/A	SB	CS	SBR	FA	FR	G/POS	TPR
1968	Cle-A	6	1	0	0	0	0	0	0	0	1	.000	.000	.000	-99	-0	0	0	0	1.000	3	/S-6	0.3
1969	Cle-A	64	213	20	51	6	0	3	19	19	37	.239	.302	.310	69	-9	2	2	-1	.952	9	S-64	0.6
1970	Cle-A	152	549	58	136	20	4	10	56	47	89	.248	.309	.353	78	-16	1	2	-1	.982	8	*2-141,S-23/3-1	0.5
1971	Cle-A	131	429	35	112	12	2	4	35	34	69	.261	.317	.326	76	-13	3	5	-2	.983	0	*2-107,S-24	-0.4
1972	Cle-A	89	225	14	45	2	1	4	16	20	47	.200	.268	.271	59	-11	0	2	-1	.993	-1	2-36,S-35	-0.8
1973	Chi-A	127	399	37	91	10	3	3	30	34	103	.228	.294	.291	63	-19	1	5	-3	.972	-2	*S-122/2-3	-0.9
1974	Chi-A	31	46	1	5	1	0	0	3	2	12	.109	.146	.130	-20	-7	0	0	0	.962	8	S-21/2-7,3-2,D-1	0.3
1975	NY-A	1	0	0	0	0	0	0	0	0	0	—	—	—	—	0	0	0	0	.000	0	/S-1	0.0
Total	8	601	1862	165	440	51	10	24	159	156	358	.236	.298	.313	69	-76	7	16	-8	.963	25	S-296,2-294/3-3,D-1	-0.4

■ LEONARD
Leonard Deb: 9/12/1892

YEAR	TM/L	G	AB	R	H	2B	3B	HR	RBI	BB	SO	AVG	OBP	SLG	PRO+	BR/A	SB	CS	SBR	FA	FR	G/POS	TPR
1892	StL-N	1	0	0	0	0	0	0	0	1	0	—	1.000	—	219	0	1			.000	-0	/O-1	0.0

■ ANDY LEONARD
Leonard, Andrew Jackson b: 6/1/1846, County Cavan, Ireland d: 8/21/03, Boston, Mass. BR/TR, 5'7", 168 lbs. Deb: 5/5/1871

YEAR	TM/L	G	AB	R	H	2B	3B	HR	RBI	BB	SO	AVG	OBP	SLG	PRO+	BR/A	SB	CS	SBR	FA	FR	G/POS	TPR
1871	Oly-n	31	148	33	43	8	3	0	30	3	1	.291	.305	.385	102	1	14	3	2	.863	-2	2-19,O-11/S-1	0.0
1872	Bos-n	46	240	57	84	7	1	2	43	0	2	.350	.350	.412	127	6	8	5	-1	.828	-4	*O-38/3-6,2-4,S-1	0.1
1873	Bos-n	58	302	81	95	12	7	0	61	4	0	.315	.324	.401	105	-1	5	6	-2	.714	-1	*O-45,2-12/1-2,S-1	-0.2
1874	Bos-n	71	339	68	106	18	4	0	50	2	2	.313	.317	.389	118	5	11	3	2	.807	1	*O-51,2-11,S-11	0.6
1875	Bos-n	80	396	87	127	14	6	1	74	2	6	.321	.324	.394	143	15	14	8	-1	.806	-0	*O-73/S-3,3-3,2-2	1.2
1876	Bos-N	64	303	53	85	10	2	0	27	4	6	.281	.290	.327	103	1				.925	-1	O-35,2-30	0.0
1877	Bos-N	58	272	46	78	5	0	0	27	5	5	.287	.300	.305	88	-4				.875	-4	O-37,S-21	-0.8
1878	Bos-N	60	262	41	68	8	5	0	16	3	19	.260	.268	.328	88	-4				.777	-7	*O-60	-1.3
1880	Cin-N	33	133	15	28	3	0	1	17	8	11	.211	.255	.256	75	-3				.833	-12	S-23,3-10	-1.3
Total	5 n	286	1425	326	455	59	21	3	258	11	11	.319	.325	.396	121	26	52	25	1	.778	-7	O-218/2-48,S-17,31	1.7
Total	4	215	970	155	259	26	7	1	87	20	41	.267	.282	.311	91	-11				.856	-23	O-132/S-44,2-30,3	-3.4

■ JEFFREY LEONARD
Leonard, Jeffrey b: 9/22/55, Philadelphia, Pa. BR/TR, 6'2", 200 lbs. Deb: 9/2/77

YEAR	TM/L	G	AB	R	H	2B	3B	HR	RBI	BB	SO	AVG	OBP	SLG	PRO+	BR/A	SB	CS	SBR	FA	FR	G/POS	TPR
1977	LA-N	11	10	1	3	0	1	0	2	1	4	.300	.364	.500	130	0	0	0	0	1.000	-2	O-10	-0.2
1978	Hou-N	8	26	2	10	2	0	0	4	1	2	.385	.407	.462	154	2	0	1	-1	1.000	1	/O-8	0.2
1979	Hou-N	134	411	47	119	15	5	0	47	46	68	.290	.364	.350	102	2	23	10	1	.959	-7	*O-123	-0.8
1980	*Hou-N	88	216	29	46	7	5	3	20	19	46	.213	.277	.333	75	-8	4	1	1	.979	-2	O-56,1-11	-1.3
1981	Hou-N	7	18	1	3	1	1	0	3	0	4	.167	.167	.333	41	-2	1	0	0	1.000	-0	/1-2,O-2	-0.2
	SF-N	37	127	20	39	11	3	4	26	12	21	.307	.371	.535	158	9	4	2	0	1.000	2	O-28/1-5	1.1
	Yr	44	145	21	42	12	4	4	29	12	25	.290	.348	.510	145	8	5	2	0	1.000	2	O-30/1-7	0.9
1982	SF-N	80	278	32	72	16	1	9	49	19	65	.259	.311	.421	103	0	18	5	2	.958	-5	O-74/1-1	-0.4
1983	SF-N	139	516	74	144	17	7	21	87	35	116	.279	.326	.461	120	11	26	7	4	.975	8	*O-136	1.9
1984	SF-N	136	514	76	155	27	2	21	86	47	123	.302	.360	.484	140	26	17	7	1	.970	6	*O-131	3.0
1985	SF-N	133	507	49	122	20	3	17	62	21	107	.241	.272	.393	88	-11	11	6	-0	.977	3	*O-126	-1.3
1986	SF-N	89	341	48	95	11	3	6	42	20	62	.279	.324	.381	99	-1	16	3	3	.970	3	O-87	0.2
1987	*SF-N★	131	503	70	141	29	4	19	63	21	68	.280	.312	.467	108	3	16	7	1	.966	-4	*O-127	-0.4
1988	SF-N	44	160	12	41	8	1	2	20	9	24	.256	.296	.356	90	-2	7	5	-1	.987	-3	O-43	-0.8
	Mil-A	94	374	45	88	19	0	8	44	16	68	.235	.272	.350	72	-14	10	4	1	.985	3	O-91/D-2	-1.4
1989	Sea-A★	150	566	69	144	20	1	24	93	38	125	.254	.307	.420	100	-2	6	1	1	.982	2	*D-123,O-26	-0.3
1990	Sea-A	134	478	39	120	20	0	10	75	37	97	.251	.309	.356	84	-10	4	2	0	.983	-8	O-79,D-48	-2.2
Total	14	1415	5045	614	1342	223	37	144	723	342	1000	.266	.316	.411	103	3	163	61	12	.974	-3	*O-1147,D-173/1-19	-2.9

■ JOE LEONARD
Leonard, Joseph Howard b: 11/15/1894, W.Chicago, Ill. d: 5/1/20, Washington, D.C. BL/TR, 5'7.5", 156 lbs. Deb: 5/7/14

YEAR	TM/L	G	AB	R	H	2B	3B	HR	RBI	BB	SO	AVG	OBP	SLG	PRO+	BR/A	SB	CS	SBR	FA	FR	G/POS	TPR
1914	Pit-N	53	126	17	25	2	2	0	4	12	21	.198	.268	.246	56	-7	4			.909	-8	3-38/S-1	-1.5
1916	Cle-A	3	2	1	0	0	0	0	0	0	1	.000	.000	.000	-94	-0	0			1.000	0	/2-1	0.0
	Was-A	42	168	20	46	7	0	0	14	22	23	.274	.358	.315	103	1	4			.952	-8	3-42	-0.5
	Yr	45	170	21	46	7	0	0	14	22	24	.271	.354	.312	101	1	4			.952	-7	3-42/2-1	-0.5
1917	Was-A	99	297	30	57	6	7	0	23	45	40	.192	.302	.259	72	-9	6			.925	-2	3-68,1-19/S-1,O-1	-1.2
1919	Was-A	71	198	26	51	8	3	2	20	20	28	.258	.329	.359	94	-2	3			.944	-9	2-28,3-25/1-4,O-1	-1.0
1920	Was-A	1	0	0	0	0	0	0	0	0	0	—	—	—	—	0	0	0	0	.000	0	R	0.0
Total	5	269	791	94	179	23	12	2	61	99	113	.226	.315	.293	82	-16	17	0		.937	-27	3-173/2-29,1-23,OS	-4.2

■ MARK LEONARD
Leonard, Mark David b: 8/14/64, Mountain View, Cal. BL/TR, 6', 195 lbs. Deb: 7/21/90

YEAR	TM/L	G	AB	R	H	2B	3B	HR	RBI	BB	SO	AVG	OBP	SLG	PRO+	BR/A	SB	CS	SBR	FA	FR	G/POS	TPR
1990	SF-N	11	17	3	3	1	0	1	2	3	8	.176	.300	.412	97	-0	0	0	0	1.000	-1	/O-7	-0.1
1991	SF-N	64	129	14	31	7	1	2	14	12	25	.240	.310	.357	90	-2	0	1	-1	1.000	-6	O-34	-0.9
1992	SF-N	55	128	13	30	7	0	4	16	16	31	.234	.333	.383	108	2	0	1	-1	.984	0	O-37	0.1
1993	Bal-A	10	15	1	1	1	0	0	3	3	7	.067	.222	.133	-2	-2	0	0	0	.833	-1	/O-4,D-3	-0.3
1994	SF-N	14	11	2	4	1	1	0	2	3	2	.364	.500	.636	203	2	0	0	0	1.000	-1	/O-2	0.1
1995	SF-N	14	21	4	4	1	0	1	4	5	2	.190	.346	.381	94	-0	0	0	0	1.000	-1	/O-6	-0.1
Total	6	168	321	37	73	18	2	8	41	42	75	.227	.324	.371	97	-1	0	2	-1	.985	-9	/O-90,D-3	-1.2

■ JOHN LEOVICH
Leovich, John Joseph b: 5/5/18, Portland, Ore. BR/TR, 6'0.5", 200 lbs. Deb: 5/1/41

YEAR	TM/L	G	AB	R	H	2B	3B	HR	RBI	BB	SO	AVG	OBP	SLG	PRO+	BR/A	SB	CS	SBR	FA	FR	G/POS	TPR
1941	Phi-A	1	2	0	1	1	0	0	0	0	0	.500	.500	1.000	296	1	0	0	0	.000	-0	/C-1	0.0

■ TED LEPCIO
Lepcio, Thaddeus Stanley b: 7/28/30, Utica, N.Y. BR/TR, 5'10", 177 lbs. Deb: 4/15/52

YEAR	TM/L	G	AB	R	H	2B	3B	HR	RBI	BB	SO	AVG	OBP	SLG	PRO+	BR/A	SB	CS	SBR	FA	FR	G/POS	TPR
1952	Bos-A	84	274	34	72	17	2	5	26	24	41	.263	.329	.394	93	-3	3	3	-1	.972	8	2-57,3-25/S-1	0.6
1953	Bos-A	66	161	17	38	4	2	4	11	17	24	.236	.313	.360	77	-5	0	0	0	.981	17	2-34,S-20,3-11	1.4
1954	Bos-A	116	398	42	102	19	4	8	45	42	62	.256	.332	.384	86	-8	3	4	-2	.971	16	2-80,3-24,S-14	1.2
1955	Bos-A	51	134	19	31	9	0	6	15	12	36	.231	.313	.433	91	-2	1	1	-0	.943	6	3-45	0.3
1956	Bos-A	83	284	34	74	10	0	15	51	30	77	.261	.338	.454	96	-3	1	3	-2	.966	7	2-57,3-22	0.8
1957	Bos-A	79	232	24	56	10	2	9	37	29	61	.241	.328	.418	97	-1	0	0	0	.976	9	2-68	1.3
1958	Bos-A	50	136	10	27	3	0	6	14	12	47	.199	.268	.353	65	-7	0	1	-1	.980	-3	2-40	-0.8
1959	Bos-A	3	3	1	1	1	0	0	1	0	2	.333	.333	.667	160	0	0	0	0	1.000	0	/2-1	0.0
	Det-A	76	215	25	60	8	0	7	24	17	49	.279	.332	.414	98	-1	2	0	1	.951	-6	S-35,2-24,3-11	-0.2
	Yr	79	218	26	61	9	0	7	25	17	51	.280	.332	.417	99	-1	2	0	1	.951	-6	S-35,2-25,3-11	-0.2
1960	Phi-N	69	141	16	32	7	0	2	8	17	41	.227	.319	.319	75	-4	0	3	-2	.942	-5	3-50,S-14/2-5	-1.1
1961	Chi-A	5	2	0	0	0	0	0	0	1	0	.000	.333	.000	-2	-0	0	0	0	.000	-0	/3-1	0.0
	Min-A	47	112	11	19	3	1	7	19	8	31	.170	.231	.402	62	-7	1	0	0	.919	2	3-35,2-22/S-6	-0.3

YEAR	TM/L	G	AB	R	H	2B	3B	HR	RBI	BB	SO	AVG	OBP	SLG	PRO+	BR/A	SB	CS	SBR	FA	FR	G/POS	TPR
	Yr	52	114	11	19	3	1	7	19	9	31	.167	.234	.395	62	-7	1	0	0	.895	2	3-36,2-22/S-6	-0.3
Total	10	729	2092	233	512	91	11	69	251	209	471	.245	.319	.398	87	-41	11	15	-6	.972	51	2-388,3-224/S-90	3.2
■ **PETE LePINE**	LePine, Louis Joseph b: 9/5/1876, Montreal, Que., Can d: 12/3/49, Woonsocket, R.I. BL/TL, 5'10", 142 lbs. Deb: 7/21/02																						
1902	Det-A	30	96	8	20	3	2	1	19	8		.208	.276	.313	62	-5	1			1.000	-2	O-19/1-8	-0.7
■ **DON LEPPERT**	Leppert, Don Eugene "Tiger" b: 11/20/30, Memphis, Tenn. BL/TR, 5'8", 175 lbs. Deb: 4/11/55																						
1955	Bal-A	40	70	6	8	0	1	0	2	9	10	.114	.215	.143	-2	-10	1	1	-0	.937	-7	2-35	-1.7
■ **DON LEPPERT**	Leppert, Donald George b: 10/19/31, Indianapolis, Ind. BR/TR, 6'2", 220 lbs. Deb: 6/18/61 C																						
1961	Pit-N	22	60	6	16	2	1	3	5	1	11	.267	.279	.483	97	-1	0	0	0	.968	1	C-21	0.1
1962	Pit-N	45	139	14	37	6	1	3	18	12	21	.266	.329	.388	92	-2	0	1	-1	.989	4	C-44	0.3
1963	Was-A☆	73	211	20	50	11	0	6	24	20	29	.237	.306	.374	90	-3	0	0	0	.984	-8	C-60	-0.9
1964	Was-A	50	122	6	19	3	0	3	12	11	32	.156	.226	.254	33	-11	0	0	0	.990	1	C-43	-0.9
Total	4	190	532	46	122	22	2	15	59	44	93	.229	.291	.363	78	-16	0	1	-1	.985	-2	C-168	-1.4
■ **DUTCH LERCHEN**	Lerchen, Bertram Roe b: 4/4/1889, Detroit, Mich. d: 1/7/62, Detroit, Mich. BR/TR, 5'8", 160 lbs. Deb: 8/14/10 F																						
1910	Bos-A	6	15	1	0	0	0	0	0	1		.000	.063	.000	-78	-3	0			.929	-3	/S-6	-0.8
■ **GEORGE LERCHEN**	Lerchen, George Edward b: 12/1/22, Detroit, Mich. BB/TR, 5'11", 175 lbs. Deb: 4/15/52 F																						
1952	Det-A	14	32	1	5	1	0	1	3	7	10	.156	.308	.281	64	-1	1	0	0	1.000	-0	/O-7	-0.2
1953	Cin-N	22	17	2	5	1	0	0	2	5	6	.294	.455	.353	113	1	0	0	0	1.000	-0	/O-1	0.0
Total	2	36	49	3	10	2	0	1	5	12	16	.204	.361	.306	82	-1	1	0	0	1.000	-1	/O-8	-0.2
■ **WALT LERIAN**	Lerian, Walter Irvin "Peck" b: 2/10/03, Baltimore, Md. d: 10/22/29, Baltimore, Md. BR/TR, 5'11", 170 lbs. Deb: 4/16/28																						
1928	Phi-N	96	239	28	65	16	2	2	25	41	29	.272	.385	.381	97	1	1			.977	-3	C-74	0.4
1929	Phi-N	105	273	28	61	13	2	6	25	53	37	.223	.354	.352	71	-12	0			**.986**	1	*C-103	-0.3
Total	2	201	512	56	126	29	4	8	50	94	66	.246	.368	.365	83	-11	1			.982	-1	C-177	0.1
■ **BRIAN LESHER**	Lesher, Brian Herbert b: 3/5/71, Wilrijk, Belgium BR/TL, 6'5", 205 lbs. Deb: 8/25/96																						
1996	Oak-A	26	82	11	19	3	0	5	16	5	17	.232	.284	.451	84	-3	0	0	0	.977	-3	O-25/1-1	-0.5
1997	Oak-A	46	131	17	30	4	1	4	16	9	30	.229	.279	.366	68	-7	4	1	1	.958	2	O-32/1-3,D-3	-0.5
1998	Oak-A	7	7	0	1	1	0	0	1	0	3	.143	.143	.286	8	-1	0	0	0	1.000	1	/O-4,1-1	0.0
Total	3	79	220	28	50	8	1	9	33	14	50	.227	.277	.395	72	-10	4	1	1	.967	-0	/O-61,1-5,D-3	-1.0
■ **ROY LESLIE**	Leslie, Roy Reid b: 8/23/1894, Bailey, Tex. d: 4/9/72, Sherman, Tex. BR/TR, 6'1", 175 lbs. Deb: 9/6/17																						
1917	Chi-N	7	19	1	4	0	0	0	1	1	5	.211	.250	.211	39	-1	1			.969	-0	/1-6	-0.2
1919	StL-N	12	24	2	5	1	0	0	4	4	3	.208	.321	.250	78	-0	0			.957	-0	/1-9	-0.1
1922	Phi-N	141	513	44	139	23	2	6	50	37	49	.271	.320	.359	68	-25	3	7	-3	.990	-4	*1-139	-3.6
Total	3	160	556	47	148	24	2	6	55	42	57	.266	.318	.349	68	-27	4	7		.988	-4	1-154	-3.9
■ **SAM LESLIE**	Leslie, Samuel Andrew "Sambo" b: 7/26/05, Moss Point, Miss. d: 1/21/79, Pascagoula, Miss. BL/TL, 6', 192 lbs. Deb: 10/6/29																						
1929	NY-N	1	1	0	0	0	0	0	1	0	0	.000	.000	.000	-99	-0	0			1.000	-0	/O-1	-0.1
1930	NY-N	2	2	0	1	0	0	0	0	0	1	.500	.500	.500	146	0	0			.000	0	H	0.0
1931	NY-N	53	53	11	16	4	0	3	5	1	2	.302	.315	.547	131	2	3			1.000	0	/1-6	0.2
1932	NY-N	77	75	5	22	4	0	1	15	2	5	.293	.329	.387	94	-1	0			1.000	-0	/1-2	-0.1
1933	NY-N	40	137	21	44	12	3	3	27	12	9	.321	.380	.518	157	10	0			.990	-0	1-35	0.7
	Bro-N	96	364	41	104	11	4	5	46	23	14	.286	.340	.379	110	5	1			.982	-6	1-95	-1.2
	Yr	136	501	62	148	23	7	8	73	35	23	.295	.351	.417	123	15	1			.984	-6	*1-130	-0.5
1934	Bro-N	146	546	75	181	29	6	9	102	69	34	.332	.409	.456	138	32	5			.993	5	*1-138	2.4
1935	Bro-N	142	520	72	160	30	7	5	93	55	19	.308	.379	.421	117	14	4			.989	-0	*1-138	0.0
1936	*NY-N	117	417	49	123	19	5	6	54	23	16	.295	.335	.408	100	-1	0			.991	0	1-99	-1.0
1937	*NY-N	72	191	25	59	7	2	3	30	20	12	.309	.380	.414	114	4	1			.990	3	1-44	0.2
1938	NY-N	76	154	12	39	7	1	1	16	11	6	.253	.307	.331	75	-5	0			.988	-3	1-32	-1.1
Total	10	822	2460	311	749	123	28	36	389	216	118	.304	.366	.421	117	60	14			.989	-2	1-589/O-1	0.0
■ **CHARLIE LETCHAS**	Letchas, Charlie b: 10/3/15, Thomasville, Ga. d: 3/14/95, Tampa, Fla. BR/TR, 5'10", 150 lbs. Deb: 9/16/39																						
1939	Phi-N	12	44	2	10	2	0	1	3	1	2	.227	.244	.341	57	-3	0			.933	-1	2-12	-0.3
1941	Was-A	2	8	0	1	0	0	0	1	1	1	.125	.222	.125	-6	-1	0	0	0	.800	-1	/2-2	-0.2
1944	Phi-N	116	396	29	94	8	0	0	33	32	27	.237	.298	.258	59	-21	0			.968	6	2-47,3-32,S-29	-1.0
1946	Phi-N	6	13	1	3	0	0	0	0	1	1	.231	.286	.231	49	-1	0			1.000	1	/2-4	0.0
Total	4	136	461	32	108	10	0	1	37	35	31	.234	.291	.262	58	-26	0	0		.959	5	/2-65,3-32,S-29	-1.5
■ **TOM LETCHER**	Letcher, Frederick Thomas b: 1/1868, Bryan, Ohio BL , Deb: 9/27/1891																						
1891	Mil-a	6	21	3	4	1	0	0	2	0	1	.190	.190	.238	19	-2	1			.857	0	/O-6	-0.2
■ **LEUTZ**	Leutz Deb: 5/7/1872																						
1872	Eck-n	4	12	2	1	0	0	0	0	0	0	.083	.083	.083	-57	-2	0	0	0	.733	-3	/C-4	-0.4
■ **JESSE LEVAN**	Levan, Jesse Roy b: 7/15/26, Reading, Pa. BL/TR, 6', 172 lbs. Deb: 9/27/47																						
1947	Phi-N	2	9	3	4	0	0	0	1	0	0	.444	.444	.444	142	1	0			1.000	-1	/O-2	0.0
1954	Was-A	7	10	1	3	0	0	0	0	0	0	.300	.300	.300	68	-0	0	0	0	.000	-0	/3-4,1-1	-0.1
1955	Was-A	16	16	1	3	0	0	1	4	0	2	.188	.188	.375	51	-1	0	0	0	.000	0	H	-0.1
Total	3	25	35	5	10	0	0	1	5	0	2	.286	.286	.371	80	-1	0	0		—	-1	/3-4,O-2,1-1	-0.2
■ **JIM LEVEY**	Levey, James Julius b: 9/13/06, Pittsburgh, Pa. d: 3/14/70, Dallas, Tex. BB/TR, 5'10.5", 154 lbs. Deb: 9/17/30																						
1930	StL-A	8	37	7	9	2	0	0	3	3	2	.243	.300	.297	50	-3	0	0	0	.958	2	/S-8	0.0
1931	StL-A	139	498	53	104	19	2	5	38	35	83	.209	.264	.285	43	-42	13	8	-1	.920	-10	*S-139	-3.8
1932	StL-A	152	568	59	159	30	8	4	63	21	48	.280	.310	.382	74	-23	6	4	-1	.939	-18	*S-152	-2.7
1933	StL-A	141	529	43	103	10	4	2	36	26	68	.195	.237	.240	25	-57	4	6	-2	.945	-6	*S-138	-5.4
Total	4	440	1632	162	375	61	14	11	140	85	201	.230	.272	.305	48	-125	23	18	-4	.936	-33	S-437	-11.9
■ **CHARLIE LEVIS**	Levis, Charles H. b: 6/21/1860, St.Louis, Mo. d: 10/16/26, St.Louis, Mo. BR , Deb: 4/17/1884																						
1884	Bal-U	87	373	59	85	11	4	5		3		.228	.234	.319	60	-30				.955	-0	*1-87	-3.6
	Was-U	1	3	0	0	0	0	0		0		.000	.000	.000	-99	-1				1.000	0	/1-1	-0.1
	Yr	88	376	59	85	11	4	5		3		.226	.232	.316	59	-31				.955	-0	1-88	-3.7
	Ind-a	3	10	0	2	0	0	0		0		.200	.200	.200	32	-1				1.000	0	/1-3	-0.1
1885	Bal-a	1	4	2	1	0	0	0	0	0		.250	.400	.250	110	0				.889	-0	/1-1	0.0
Total	2	92	390	61	88	11	4	5	0	3		.226	.234	.313	59	-32				.956	-0	/1-92	-3.8
■ **JESSE LEVIS**	Levis, Jesse b: 4/14/68, Philadelphia, Pa. BL/TR, 5'9", 180 lbs. Deb: 4/24/92																						
1992	Cle-A	28	43	2	12	4	0	1	3	0	5	.279	.279	.442	101	-0	0	0	0	.985	1	C-21/D-1	0.1
1993	Cle-A	31	63	7	11	2	0	0	4	2	10	.175	.200	.206	9	-8	0	0	0	.991	1	C-29	-0.6
1994	Cle-A	1	1	0	1	0	0	0	0	0	0	1.000	1.000	1.000	417	0	0	0	0	.000	0	/H	0.0
1995	Cle-A	12	18	1	6	2	0	0	3	1	0	.333	.368	.444	109	0	0	0	0	1.000	0	C-12	0.1
1996	Mil-A	104	233	27	55	6	1	1	21	38	15	.236	.348	.283	60	-13	0	0	0	**.998**	4	C-90/D-6	-0.5
1997	Mil-A	99	200	19	57	7	0	1	19	24	17	.285	.364	.335	83	-4	1	0	0	.994	-10	C-78/D-8	-1.0
1998	Mil-N	22	37	4	13	0	0	0	4	7	6	.351	.478	.351	119	2	1	0	0	1.000	1	C-14	0.4
Total	7	297	595	60	155	21	1	3	54	72	53	.261	.345	.314	71	-23	2	0	1	.995	-3	C-244/D-15	-1.5
■ **ED LEVY**	Levy, Edward Clarence (b: Edward Clarence Whitner) b: 10/28/16, Birmingham, Ala. BR/TR, 6'5.5", 190 lbs. Deb: 4/16/40																						
1940	Phi-N	1	1	0	0	0	0	0	0	0	0	.000	.000	.000	-99	-0	0			.000	0	H	0.0
1942	NY-A	13	41	5	5	0	0	0	3	4	5	.122	.200	.122	-9	-6	1	0	0	.992	2	1-13	-0.5

YEAR	TM/L	G	AB	R	H	2B	3B	HR	RBI	BB	SO	AVG	OBP	SLG	PRO+	BR/A	SB	CS	SBR	FA	FR	G/POS	TPR
1944	NY-A	40	153	12	37	11	2	4	29	6	19	.242	.270	.418	92	-3	1	1	-0	.962	-1	O-36	-0.6
Total	3	54	195	17	42	11	2	4	32	10	24	.215	.254	.354	70	-9	2	1		.962	0	/O-36,1-13	-1.1

■ LEWIS Lewis b: Brooklyn, N.Y. Deb: 7/12/1890

YEAR	TM/L	G	AB	R	H	2B	3B	HR	RBI	BB	SO	AVG	OBP	SLG	PRO+	BR/A	SB	CS	SBR	FA	FR	G/POS	TPR
1890	Buf-P	1	5	1	1	0	0	0	0	0	0	.200	.200	.200	8	-1	0			.000	0	/O-1,P-1	-0.1

■ ALLAN LEWIS Lewis, Allan Sydney "The Panamanian Express" b: 12/12/41, Colon, Panama BB/TR, 6', 170 lbs. Deb: 4/11/67

YEAR	TM/L	G	AB	R	H	2B	3B	HR	RBI	BB	SO	AVG	OBP	SLG	PRO+	BR/A	SB	CS	SBR	FA	FR	G/POS	TPR
1967	KC-A	34	6	7	1	0	0	0	0	0	3	.167	.167	.167	-1	-1	14	5	1	.000	0	H	0.0
1968	Oak-A	26	4	9	1	0	0	0	0	1	0	.250	.400	.250	105	0	8	4	0	.000	-0	/O-1	0.0
1969	Oak-A	12	1	2	0	0	0	0	0	0	0	.000	.000	.000	-99	-0	0	0	0	.000	0	H	0.0
1970	Oak-A	25	8	8	2	0	0	1	1	0	0	.250	.250	.625	139	0	7	1	2	1.000	-0	/O-2	0.2
1972	*Oak-A	24	10	5	2	1	0	0	2	0	1	.200	.200	.300	50	-1	8	3	1	.900	-1	/O-6	-0.1
1973	*Oak-A	35	0	16	0	0	0	0	0	0	0	—	—	—	—	0	7	4	-0	1.000	-0	/O-1,D-6	-0.1
Total	6	156	29	47	6	1	0	1	3	1	4	.207	.233	.345	69	-1	44	17	3	.923	-2	/O-10,D-6	0.0

■ DARREN LEWIS Lewis, Darren Joel b: 8/28/67, Berkeley, Cal. BR/TR, 6', 189 lbs. Deb: 8/21/90

YEAR	TM/L	G	AB	R	H	2B	3B	HR	RBI	BB	SO	AVG	OBP	SLG	PRO+	BR/A	SB	CS	SBR	FA	FR	G/POS	TPR
1990	Oak-A	25	35	4	8	0	0	0	1	7	4	.229	.372	.229	75	-1	2	0	1	1.000	-5	O-23/D-2	-0.5
1991	SF-N	72	222	41	55	5	3	1	15	36	30	.248	.358	.311	93	-1	13	7	-0	1.000	3	O-68	0.1
1992	SF-N	100	320	38	74	8	1	1	18	29	46	.231	.297	.272	66	-14	28	8	4	1.000	0	O-94	-1.3
1993	SF-N	136	522	84	132	17	7	2	48	30	40	.253	.302	.324	70	-22	46	15	5	**1.000**	8	*O-131	-1.2
1994	SF-N	114	451	70	116	15	**9**	4	29	53	50	.257	.341	.357	86	-8	30	13	1	**.993**	3	*O-113	-0.7
1995	SF-N	74	309	47	78	10	3	1	16	17	37	.252	.304	.314	65	-15	21	7	2	.995	8	O-73	-0.8
	*Cin-N	58	163	19	40	3	0	0	8	17	20	.245	.324	.264	58	-9	11	11	-3	.992	1	O-57	-1.3
	Yr	132	472	66	118	13	3	1	24	34	57	.250	.311	.297	63	-25	32	18	-1	.994	8	*O-130	-2.1
1996	Chi-A	141	337	55	77	12	2	4	53	45	40	.228	.325	.312	65	-17	21	5	3	.990	-11	*O-138	-2.5
1997	Chi-A	81	77	15	18	1	0	0	5	11	14	.234	.330	.247	56	-5	11	4	1	1.000	-12	O-64/D-6	-1.6
	LA-N	26	77	7	23	3	1	1	10	6	17	.299	.349	.403	104	0	3	2	-0	.980	1	O-25	0.1
1998	*Bos-A	155	585	95	157	25	3	8	63	70	94	.268	.354	.362	87	-9	29	12	2	.992	3	*O-152/D-1	-0.8
Total	9	982	3098	475	778	99	29	22	266	321	392	.251	.328	.323	76	-102	215	84	14	.995	-1	O-938/D-9	-10.5

■ FRED LEWIS Lewis, Frederick Miller b: 10/13/1858, Buffalo, N.Y. d: 6/5/45, Utica, N.Y. BB/TR, 5'10.5", 194 lbs. Deb: 7/2/1881

YEAR	TM/L	G	AB	R	H	2B	3B	HR	RBI	BB	SO	AVG	OBP	SLG	PRO+	BR/A	SB	CS	SBR	FA	FR	G/POS	TPR
1881	Bos-N	27	114	17	25	6	0	0	9	7	5	.219	.264	.272	72	-3				.837	-2	O-27	-0.6
1883	Phi-N	38	160	21	40	7	0	0	18	4	13	.250	.268	.294	78	-4				.814	1	O-38	-0.3
	StL-a	49	209	37	63	8	4	1	33	1		.301	.305	.392	116	3				.848	-0	O-49	0.2
1884	StL-a	73	300	59	97	25	3	0		16		.323	.366	.427	152	17				.853	3	O-73	1.6
	StL-U	8	30	6	9	1	0	0		3		.300	.364	.333	109	-0				.909	-2	/O-8	-0.2
1885	StL-N	45	181	12	53	9	0	1	27	9	10	.293	.326	.359	130	6				.957	7	O-45	1.1
1886	Cin-a	77	324	72	103	14	6	2	32	20		.318	.365	.417	140	14	8			.884	-2	O-76/3-1	0.9
Total	5	317	1318	224	390	70	13	4	119	60	28	.296	.330	.378	124	32	8			.866	4	O-316/3-1	2.7

■ DUFFY LEWIS Lewis, George Edward b: 4/18/1888, San Francisco, Cal d: 6/17/79, Salem, N.H. BL/TL, 5'10.5", 165 lbs. Deb: 4/16/10 C

YEAR	TM/L	G	AB	R	H	2B	3B	HR	RBI	BB	SO	AVG	OBP	SLG	PRO+	BR/A	SB	CS	SBR	FA	FR	G/POS	TPR
1910	Bos-A	151	541	64	153	29	7	8	68	32		.283	.328	.407	127	14	10			.944	10	*O-149	1.9
1911	Bos-A	130	469	64	144	32	4	7	86	25		.307	.355	.437	122	12	11			.939	5	*O-125	1.0
1912	*Bos-A	154	581	85	165	36	9	6	109	52		.284	.346	.408	110	5	9			.947	7	*O-154	0.4
1913	Bos-A	149	551	54	164	31	12	0	90	30	55	.298	.336	.397	112	6	12			.960	11	*O-142/P-1,3-1	1.1
1914	Bos-A	146	510	53	142	37	9	2	79	57	41	.278	.357	.398	127	16	22	31	-12	.952	-2	*O-142	-0.4
1915	*Bos-A	152	557	69	162	31	7	2	76	45	63	.291	.348	.382	122	14	14	7	0	.952	-7	*O-152	-0.1
1916	*Bos-A	152	563	56	151	29	5	1	56	33	56	.268	.313	.343	97	-4	16			.970	-1	*O-151	-1.4
1917	Bos-A	150	553	55	167	29	9	1	65	29	54	.302	.342	.392	125	14	8			.972	4	*O-150	1.1
1919	NY-A	141	559	67	152	23	4	7	89	17	42	.272	.293	.365	84	-14	8			.985	-6	*O-141	-3.2
1920	NY-A	107	365	34	99	8	1	4	61	24	32	.271	.320	.332	70	-16	2	8	-4	.961	-2	O-99	-2.9
1921	Was-A	27	102	11	19	4	1	0	14	8	10	.186	.252	.245	29	-11	1	1	-0	.980	-2	O-27	-1.5
Total	11	1459	5351	612	1518	289	68	38	793	352	353	.284	.333	.384	108	36	113	47		.959	16	*O-1432/3-1,P-1	-4.0

■ JACK LEWIS Lewis, John David b: 2/14/1884, Pittsburgh, Pa. d: 2/25/56, Steubenville, Ohio BR/TR, 5'8", 158 lbs. Deb: 9/16/11

YEAR	TM/L	G	AB	R	H	2B	3B	HR	RBI	BB	SO	AVG	OBP	SLG	PRO+	BR/A	SB	CS	SBR	FA	FR	G/POS	TPR
1911	Bos-A	18	59	7	16	0	0	0	6	7		.271	.368	.271	80	-1	2			.931	-2	2-18	-0.3
1914	Pit-F	117	394	32	92	14	5	1	48	17	46	.234	.276	.302	58	-30	9			.949	9	*2-115/S-1	-2.3
1915	Pit-F	82	231	24	61	6	5	0	26	8	31	.264	.292	.333	76	-11	7			.962	-2	2-45,S-11/O-6,13	-1.4
Total	3	217	684	63	169	20	10	1	80	32	77	.247	.290	.310	66	-42	18			.951	5	2-178/S-12,O-6,13	-4.0

■ BUDDY LEWIS Lewis, John Kelly b: 8/10/16, Gastonia, N.C. BL/TR, 6'1", 175 lbs. Deb: 9/16/35

YEAR	TM/L	G	AB	R	H	2B	3B	HR	RBI	BB	SO	AVG	OBP	SLG	PRO+	BR/A	SB	CS	SBR	FA	FR	G/POS	TPR
1935	Was-A	8	28	0	3	0	0	0	2	0	5	.107	.107	.107	-46	-6	0	0	0	.941	-0	/3-6	-0.6
1936	Was-A	143	601	100	175	21	13	6	67	47	46	.291	.347	.399	89	-12	6	6	-2	.933	5	*3-139	-0.3
1937	Was-A	156	668	107	210	32	6	10	79	52	44	.314	.367	.425	104	3	11	5	0	.938	-19	*3-156	-1.0
1938	Was-A★	151	656	122	194	35	9	12	91	58	35	.296	.354	.431	103	1	17	9	-0	.912	-0	*3-151	0.2
1939	Was-A	140	536	87	171	23	**16**	10	75	72	27	.319	.402	.478	134	28	10	9	-2	.933	14	*3-134	3.7
1940	Was-A	148	600	101	190	38	10	6	63	74	36	.317	.393	.443	124	23	15	10	-2	.960	-1	*O-112,3-36	1.5
1941	Was-A	149	569	97	169	29	11	9	72	82	30	.297	.386	.434	122	19	10	7	-1	.972	3	O-96,3-49	1.6
1945	Was-A	69	258	42	86	14	7	2	37	37	15	.333	.423	.465	172	25	1	2	-1	.981	4	O-69	2.5
1946	Was-A	150	582	82	170	28	13	7	45	59	26	.292	.359	.421	125	18	5	3	-0	.970	4	*O-145	1.6
1947	Was-A★	140	506	67	132	15	4	6	48	51	27	.261	.330	.342	89	-7	6	6	-2	.968	1	*O-130	-1.6
1949	Was-A	95	257	25	63	14	4	3	28	41	12	.245	.355	.366	93	-2	2	2	-1	.979	-0	O-67	-0.6
Total	11	1349	5261	830	1563	249	93	71	607	573	303	.297	.368	.420	112	90	83	59	-11	.927	11	3-671,O-619	7.0

■ JOHNNY LEWIS Lewis, Johnny Joe b: 8/10/39, Greenville, Ala. BL/TR, 6'1", 189 lbs. Deb: 4/14/64 C

YEAR	TM/L	G	AB	R	H	2B	3B	HR	RBI	BB	SO	AVG	OBP	SLG	PRO+	BR/A	SB	CS	SBR	FA	FR	G/POS	TPR
1964	StL-N	40	94	10	22	2	2	2	7	13	23	.234	.327	.362	86	-2	2	2	-1	.966	-1	O-36	-0.4
1965	NY-N	148	477	64	117	15	3	15	45	59	117	.245	.332	.384	105	3	4	7	-3	.975	1	*O-142	-0.5
1966	NY-N	65	166	21	32	6	1	5	20	21	43	.193	.283	.331	72	-6	2	0	1	.988	-3	O-49	-1.1
1967	NY-N	13	34	2	4	1	0	0	2	2	11	.118	.167	.147	-10	-5	0	0	0	1.000	-0	O-10	-0.6
Total	4	266	771	97	175	24	6	22	74	95	194	.227	.314	.359	90	-9	8	9	-3	.977	-3	O-237	-2.6

■ MARK LEWIS Lewis, Mark David b: 11/30/69, Hamilton, Ohio BR/TR, 6'1", 190 lbs. Deb: 4/26/91

YEAR	TM/L	G	AB	R	H	2B	3B	HR	RBI	BB	SO	AVG	OBP	SLG	PRO+	BR/A	SB	CS	SBR	FA	FR	G/POS	TPR
1991	Cle-A	84	314	29	83	15	1	0	30	15	45	.264	.298	.318	70	-13	2	2	-1	.966	-14	2-50,S-36	-2.4
1992	Cle-A	122	413	44	109	21	0	5	30	25	69	.264	.311	.351	87	-8	4	5	-2	.954	-9	*S-121/3-1	-1.1
1993	Cle-A	14	52	6	13	2	0	1	5	0	7	.250	.250	.346	59	-3	3	0	1	.964	-3	S-13	-0.4
1994	Cle-A	20	73	6	15	5	0	1	8	2	13	.205	.227	.315	38	-7	1	0	0	.902	-7	S-13/3-6,2-1	-1.2
1995	*Cin-N	81	171	25	58	13	1	3	30	21	33	.339	.411	.480	135	9	0	3	-2	.968	2	3-72/2-2,S-2	0.9
1996	Det-A	145	545	69	147	30	3	11	55	42	109	.270	.328	.396	82	-15	6	1	1	.987	-7	*2-144/D-1	-1.1
1997	*SF-N	118	341	50	91	14	6	10	42	23	62	.267	.321	.431	97	-3	3	2	-0	.945	-12	3-69,2-29/D-1	-1.3
1998	Phi-N	142	518	52	129	21	2	9	54	48	111	.249	.316	.349	71	-21	3	3	-1	.978	16	*2-140	0.4
Total	8	726	2427	281	645	121	13	40	254	176	449	.266	.319	.376	83	-61	22	16	-3	.978	-36	2-366,S-185,3/D	-6.2

■ PHIL LEWIS Lewis, Philip b: 10/8/1884, Pittsburgh, Pa. d: 8/8/59, Port Wentworth, Ga. BR/TR, 6', 195 lbs. Deb: 4/14/05

YEAR	TM/L	G	AB	R	H	2B	3B	HR	RBI	BB	SO	AVG	OBP	SLG	PRO+	BR/A	SB	CS	SBR	FA	FR	G/POS	TPR
1905	Bro-N	118	433	32	110	9	2	3	33	16		.254	.282	.305	81	-11	16			.904	-6	*S-118	-1.6
1906	Bro-N	136	452	40	110	8	4	0	37	43		.243	.309	.279	90	-5	14			.922	-22	*S-135	-2.6
1907	Bro-N	136	475	52	118	11	1	0	30	23		.248	.286	.276	83	-11	16			.938	-20	*S-136	-3.2
1908	Bro-N	118	415	22	91	5	6	1	30	13		.219	.243	.267	66	-17	9			.943	-7	*S-116	-2.6
Total	4	508	1775	146	429	33	13	4	130	95		.242	.281	.282	80	-44	55			.926	-55	S-505	-10.0

■ BILL LEWIS Lewis, William Henry "Buddy" b: 10/15/04, Ripley, Tenn. d: 10/24/77, Memphis, Tenn. BR/TR, 5'9", 165 lbs. Deb: 6/3/33

YEAR	TM/L	G	AB	R	H	2B	3B	HR	RBI	BB	SO	AVG	OBP	SLG	PRO+	BR/A	SB	CS	SBR	FA	FR	G/POS	TPR
1933	StL-N	15	35	8	14	1	0	1	8	2	3	.400	.432	.514	161	3	0			1.000	1	/C-8	0.4
1935	Bos-N	6	4	1	0	0	0	0	0	1	1	.000	.200	.000	-45	-1	0			.000	0	/C-1	-0.1

YEAR	TM/L	G	AB	R	H	2B	3B	HR	RBI	BB	SO	AVG	OBP	SLG	PRO+	BR/A	SB	CS	SBR	FA	FR	G/POS	TPR
1936	Bos-N	29	62	11	19	2	0	0	3	12	7	.306	.419	.339	113	2	0			.967	-4	C-21	-0.1
Total	3	50	101	20	33	3	0	1	11	15	11	.327	.414	.386	124	4	0			.981	-3	/C-30	0.2
■ **JIM LEYRITZ**	Leyritz, James Joseph b: 12/27/63, Lakewood, Ohio BR/TR, 6', 195 lbs. Deb: 6/8/90																						
1990	NY-A	92	303	28	78	13	1	5	25	27	51	.257	.332	.356	92	-3	2	3	-1	.929	-19	3-69,O-14,C-11	-2.3
1991	NY-A	32	77	8	14	3	0	0	4	13	15	.182	.300	.221	46	-5	0	1	-1	.909	-8	3-18/C-5,1-3,D-1	-1.4
1992	NY-A	63	144	17	37	6	0	7	26	14	22	.257	.348	.444	121	4	0	1	-1	.990	3	D-31,C-18/1-2,3O2	0.6
1993	NY-A	95	259	43	80	14	0	14	53	37	59	.309	.411	.525	155	21	0	0	0	.993	-6	1-29,O-28,D-21,C-12	1.2
1994	NY-A	75	249	47	66	12	0	17	58	35	61	.265	.369	.518	130	11	0	0	0	1.000	-3	C-37,D-25,1-10	0.8
1995	*NY-A	77	264	37	71	12	0	7	37	37	73	.269	.375	.394	102	2	1	1	-0	.993	-3	C-46,1-18,D-15	0.0
1996	*NY-A	88	265	23	70	10	0	7	40	30	68	.264	.359	.381	87	-4	2	0	1	.995	-3	C-55,3-13,D/1O2	-0.5
1997	Ana-A	84	294	47	81	7	0	11	50	37	56	.276	.362	.412	102	1	1	1	-0	1.000	-1	C-58,1-15,D-13	0.2
	Tex-A	37	85	11	24	4	0	0	14	23	22	.282	.450	.329	102	2	1	0	0	.984	-1	C-11/1-9,D-9	0.1
	Yr	121	379	58	105	11	0	11	64	60	78	.277	.384	.393	102	3	2	1	0	.998	-2	C-69,1-24,D-22	0.3
1998	Bos-A	52	129	17	37	6	0	8	24	21	34	.287	.395	.519	135	7	0	0	0	1.000	1	D-39/C-1,1-1	0.5
	*SD-N	62	143	17	38	10	0	4	18	21	40	.266	.386	.420	121	5	0	0	0	.987	-3	C-24,1-20/3-1,O-1	0.2
Total	9	757	2212	295	596	97	1	80	349	295	501	.269	.370	.423	110	42	7	7	-2	.995	-44	C-278,D-166,13/O2	-0.6
■ **CARLOS LEZCANO**	Lezcano, Carlos Manuel (Rubio) b: 9/30/55, Arecibo, P.R. BR/TR, 6'2", 185 lbs. Deb: 4/10/80																						
1980	Chi-N	42	88	15	18	4	1	3	12	11	29	.205	.300	.375	81	-2	1	2	-1	.948	-4	O-39	-0.8
1981	Chi-N	7	14	1	1	0	0	0	2	0	4	.071	.071	.071	-57	-3	0	0	0	1.000	-1	/O-5	-0.4
Total	2	49	102	16	19	4	1	3	14	11	33	.186	.272	.333	64	-5	1	2	-1	.952	-4	/O-44	-1.2
■ **SIXTO LEZCANO**	Lezcano, Sixto Joaquin (Curras) b: 11/28/53, Arecibo, P.R. BR/TR, 5'11", 175 lbs. Deb: 9/10/74																						
1974	Mil-A	15	54	5	13	2	0	2	9	4	9	.241	.293	.389	95	-0	1	1	-0	.972	2	O-15	0.1
1975	Mil-A	134	429	55	106	19	3	11	43	46	93	.247	.326	.382	99	-1	5	5	-2	.977	-3	*O-129/D-2	-1.0
1976	Mil-A	145	513	53	146	19	5	7	56	51	112	.285	.352	.382	117	11	14	10	-2	.973	8	*O-142/D-3	1.3
1977	Mil-A	109	400	50	109	21	4	21	49	52	78	.273	.359	.503	132	18	6	5	-1	.988	13	*O-108	2.4
1978	Mil-A	132	442	62	129	21	4	15	61	64	83	.292	.383	.459	135	22	3	3	-1	.979	10	*O-127/D-3	2.6
1979	Mil-A	138	473	84	152	29	3	28	101	77	74	.321	.420	.573	165	45	4	3	-1	.986	4	*O-135/D-1	4.0
1980	Mil-A	112	411	51	94	19	3	18	55	39	75	.229	.300	.421	98	-2	1	1	-0	.983	6	*O-108/D-4	-0.1
1981	StL-N	72	214	26	57	8	2	5	28	40	40	.266	.382	.393	117	6	0	1	-1	.973	-4	O-65	0.0
1982	SD-N	138	470	73	136	26	6	16	84	78	69	.289	.393	.472	149	33	2	1	0	.990	16	*O-134	4.6
1983	SD-N	97	317	41	74	11	2	8	49	47	66	.233	.334	.356	95	-2	0	0	0	.968	5	O-91	0.1
	*Phi-N	18	39	8	11	1	0	0	7	5	9	.282	.364	.308	89	-0	1	0	0	1.000	-1	O-15	-0.1
	Yr	115	356	49	85	12	2	8	56	52	75	.239	.337	.351	94	-2	1	0	0	.971	5	*O-106	0.0
1984	Phi-N	109	256	36	71	6	2	14	40	38	43	.277	.371	.480	135	12	0	1	-1	.981	-1	O-87	0.9
1985	Pit-N	72	116	16	24	2	0	3	9	35	17	.207	.395	.302	98	2	0	0	0	.967	-2	O-40	-0.1
Total	12	1291	4134	560	1122	184	34	148	591	576	768	.271	.363	.440	125	143	37	31	-8	.980	52	*O-1196/D-13	14.7
■ **STEVE LIBBY**	Libby, Stephen Augustus b: 12/8/1853, Scarborough, Me. d: 3/31/35, Milford, Conn. 6'1.5", 168 lbs. Deb: 5/10/1879																						
1879	Buf-N	1	2	0	0	0	0	0	0	0	1	.000	.000	.000	-98	-0				1.000	0	/1-1	0.0
■ **AL LIBKE**	Libke, Albert Walter b: 9/12/18, Tacoma, Wash. BL/TR, 6'4", 215 lbs. Deb: 4/19/45																						
1945	Cin-N	130	449	41	127	23	5	4	53	34	62	.283	.336	.383	102	0	6			.963	2	*O-108/P-4,1-2	-0.4
1946	Cin-N	124	431	32	109	22	1	5	42	43	50	.253	.322	.343	92	-5	0			.972	-5	*O-115/P-1	-1.6
Total	2	254	880	73	236	45	6	9	95	77	112	.268	.329	.364	97	-5	6			.967	-3	O-223/P-5,1-2	-2.0
■ **FRANKIE LIBRAN**	Libran, Francisco (Rosas) b: 5/6/48, Mayaguez, P.R. BR/TR, 6', 168 lbs. Deb: 9/3/69																						
1969	SD-N	10	10	1	1	1	0	0	1	1	2	.100	.182	.200	7	-1	0	0	0	1.000	1	/S-9	0.0
■ **JOHN LICKERT**	Lickert, John Wilbur b: 4/4/60, Pittsburgh, Pa. BR/TR, 5'11", 175 lbs. Deb: 9/19/81																						
1981	Bos-A	1	0	0	0	0	0	0	0	0	0	—	—	—	—	0	0	0	0	1.000	-0	/C-1	0.0
■ **DAVE LIDDELL**	Liddell, David Alexander (b: b: 6/15/66, Los Angeles, Cal. BR/TR, 6', 190 lbs. Deb: 6/3/90																						
1990	NY-N	1	1	1	1	0	0	0	0	0	0	1.000	1.000	1.000	453	0	0	0	0	1.000	-0	/C-1	0.0
■ **MIKE LIEBERTHAL**	Lieberthal, Michael Scott b: 1/18/72, Glendale, Cal. BR/TR, 6', 170 lbs. Deb: 6/30/94																						
1994	Phi-N	24	79	6	21	3	1	1	5	3	5	.266	.301	.367	71	-3	0	0	0	.969	-3	C-22	-0.5
1995	Phi-N	16	47	1	12	2	0	0	4	5	5	.255	.327	.298	66	-2	0	0	0	.991	3	C-14	0.1
1996	Phi-N	50	166	21	42	8	0	7	23	10	30	.253	.303	.428	89	-3	0	0	0	.990	0	C-43	0.0
1997	Phi-N	134	455	59	112	27	1	20	77	44	76	.246	.318	.442	97	-4	3	4	-2	.988	-11	*C-129/D-1	-0.8
1998	Phi-N	86	313	39	80	15	3	8	45	17	44	.256	.309	.399	80	-9	2	1	0	.988	-1	C-83	-0.4
Total	5	310	1060	126	267	55	5	36	154	79	160	.252	.312	.415	87	-21	5	5	-2	.987	-12	C-291/D-1	-1.6
■ **FRED LIESE**	Liese, Frederick Richard b: 10/7/1885, Wisconsin d: 6/30/67, Los Angeles, Cal. BL/TL, 5'8", 150 lbs. Deb: 4/14/10																						
1910	Bos-N	5	4	0	0	0	0	0	0	1	2	.000	.200	.000	-39	-1	0			.000	0	H	-0.1
■ **GENE LILLARD**	Lillard, Robert Eugene b: 11/12/13, Santa Barbara, Cal d: 4/12/91, Goleta, Cal. BR/TR, 5'10.5", 178 lbs. Deb: 5/8/36 F																						
1936	Chi-N	19	34	6	7	1	0	0	2	3	8	.206	.270	.235	36	-3	0			.947	-1	/S-4,3-3	-0.3
1939	Chi-N	23	10	3	1	0	0	0	0	6	3	.100	.438	.100	51	-0	0			1.000	0	P-20	0.0
1940	StL-N	2	0	0	0	0	0	0	0	0	0	—	—	—	—	0	0			1.000	0	/P-2	0.0
Total	3	44	44	9	8	1	0	0	2	9	11	.182	.321	.205	43	-3	0			1.000	-1	/P-22,S-4,3-3	-0.3
■ **BILL LILLARD**	Lillard, William Beverly b: 1/10/18, Goleta, Cal. BR/TR, 5'10", 170 lbs. Deb: 9/11/39 F																						
1939	Phi-A	7	19	4	6	1	0	0	1	3	1	.316	.409	.368	102	0	0	0	0	.974	2	/S-7	0.3
1940	Phi-A	73	206	26	49	8	2	1	21	28	28	.238	.332	.311	69	-9	0	1	-1	.921	-18	S-69/2-1	-2.1
Total	2	80	225	30	55	9	2	1	22	31	29	.244	.339	.316	72	-9	0	1	-1	.927	-16	/S-76,2-1	-1.8
■ **JIM LILLIE**	Lillie, James J. "Grasshopper" (b: James J. Lilly) b: 7/27/1861, New Haven, Conn. d: 11/9/1890, Kansas City, Mo. Deb: 5/17/1883																						
1883	Buf-N	50	201	25	47	7	3	1	29	1	31	.234	.238	.313	64	-9				.835	-7	O-47/P-3,C-2,S32	-1.4
1884	Buf-N	114	471	68	105	12	5	3	53	5	71	.223	.231	.289	60	-22				.852	16	*O-114/P-2	-0.7
1885	Buf-N	112	430	49	107	13	3	2	30	6	39	.249	.259	.307	80	-11				.862	0	*O-112/S-3,1-1	-1.3
1886	KC-N	114	416	37	73	9	0	0	22	11	80	.175	.197	.197	19	-41	13			.884	11	*O-114/P-1	-3.0
Total	4	390	1518	179	332	41	11	6	134	23	221	.219	.230	.272	54	-82	13			.863	21	O-387/P-6,S-4,C123	-6.4
■ **BOB LILLIS**	Lillis, Robert Perry b: 6/2/30, Altadena, Cal. BR/TR, 5'11", 160 lbs. Deb: 8/30/58 MC																						
1958	LA-N	20	69	10	27	3	1	1	5	4	2	.391	.432	.507	143	4	1	2	-1	.964	-3	S-19	0.2
1959	LA-N	30	48	7	11	2	0	0	2	3	4	.229	.275	.271	43	-4	0	0	0	.919	8	S-20	0.5
1960	LA-N	48	60	6	16	4	0	0	6	2	6	.267	.290	.333	66	-3	2	0	1	.982	15	S-23,3-14/2-1	1.3
1961	LA-N	19	9	0	1	0	0	0	1	1	1	.111	.200	.111	-13	-1	0	0	0	1.000	1	3-12/2-1,S-1	0.0
	StL-N	86	230	24	50	4	0	0	21	7	13	.217	.247	.235	26	-24	3	3	-1	.928	2	S-56,2-24	-1.8
	Yr	105	239	24	51	4	0	0	22	8	14	.213	.245	.230	25	-25	3	3	-1	.924	3	S-57,2-25,3-12	-1.8
1962	Hou-N	129	457	38	114	12	4	1	30	28	23	.249	.293	.300	64	-24	7	3	0	.972	9	S-99,2-33/3-9	-0.4
1963	Hou-N	147	469	31	93	13	1	1	19	15	35	.198	.230	.237	37	-39	3	4	-2	.957	-5	*S-124,2-19/3-6	-4.0
1964	Hou-N	109	332	31	89	11	2	0	17	11	10	.268	.292	.313	75	-12	4	9	-4	.995	1	2-52,S-43,3-12	-1.0
1965	Hou-N	124	408	34	90	12	1	0	20	20	10	.221	.267	.255	51	-27	2	2	-1	.968	-12	*S-104/3-9,2-6	-3.5
1966	Hou-N	68	164	14	38	6	0	0	11	7	4	.232	.263	.268	52	-11	1	1	-0	.951	-9	2-35,S-18/3-6	-1.8
1967	Hou-N	37	82	3	20	1	0	0	5	1	8	.244	.253	.256	48	-6	0	1	-1	.947	3	S-23/2-3,3-2	-0.2
Total	10	817	2328	198	549	68	9	3	137	99	116	.236	.271	.277	54	-145	23	25	-8	.959	8	S-530,2-174/3-70	-10.7
■ **LOU LIMMER**	Limmer, Louis b: 3/10/25, New York, N.Y. BL/TL, 6'2", 190 lbs. Deb: 4/22/51																						
1951	Phi-A	94	214	25	34	9	1	5	30	28	40	.159	.256	.280	44	-17	1	0	0	.988	2	1-58	-1.7

YEAR	TM/L	G	AB	R	H	2B	3B	HR	RBI	BB	SO	AVG	OBP	SLG	PRO+	BR/A	SB	CS	SBR	FA	FR	G/POS	TPR
1954	Phi-A	115	316	41	73	10	3	14	32	35	37	.231	.308	.415	96	-3	2	3	-1	.988	2	1-79	-0.6
Total	2	209	530	66	107	19	4	19	62	63	77	.202	.287	.360	75	-20	3	3	-1	.988	4	1-137	-2.3

■ RUFINO LINARES Linares, Rufino (b: Rufino De La Cruz (Linares)) b: 2/28/51, San Pedro De Macoris, D.R. d: 5/16/98, San Pedro De Macoris, D.R. BR/TR, 6', 170 lbs. Deb: 4/10/81

YEAR	TM/L	G	AB	R	H	2B	3B	HR	RBI	BB	SO	AVG	OBP	SLG	PRO+	BR/A	SB	CS	SBR	FA	FR	G/POS	TPR
1981	Atl-N	78	253	27	67	9	2	5	25	9	28	.265	.290	.375	85	-6	8	4	0	.963	3	O-60	-0.5
1982	Atl-N	77	191	28	57	7	1	2	17	7	29	.298	.327	.377	92	-2	5	2	0	1.000	0	O-53	-0.3
1984	Atl-N	34	58	4	12	3	0	1	10	6	12	.207	.281	.310	62	-3	0	0	0	.958	1	O-13	-0.3
1985	Cal-A	18	43	7	11	2	0	3	11	2	5	.256	.289	.512	114	1	2	0	1	1.000	-1	D-14/O-2	0.0
Total	4	207	545	66	147	21	3	11	63	24	74	.270	.302	.380	88	-10	15	6	1	.977	4	O-128/D-14	-1.1

■ CARL LIND Lind, Henry Carl "Hooks" b: 9/19/03, New Orleans, La. d: 8/4/46, New York, N.Y. BR/TR, 6', 160 lbs. Deb: 9/14/27

YEAR	TM/L	G	AB	R	H	2B	3B	HR	RBI	BB	SO	AVG	OBP	SLG	PRO+	BR/A	SB	CS	SBR	FA	FR	G/POS	TPR
1927	Cle-A	12	37	2	5	0	0	0	1	5	7	.135	.256	.135	4	-5	1	0	0	.969	2	2-11/S-1	-0.3
1928	Cle-A	154	650	102	191	42	4	1	54	36	48	.294	.331	.375	84	-15	8	5	-1	.960	4	*2-154	-0.7
1929	Cle-A	66	225	19	54	8	1	0	13	13	17	.240	.282	.284	44	-19	0	2	-1	.957	16	2-64/3-1	-0.1
1930	Cle-A	24	69	8	17	3	0	0	6	3	7	.246	.278	.290	43	-6	0	1	-1	.940	11	S-22/2-2	0.5
Total	4	256	981	131	267	53	5	1	74	57	79	.272	.313	.339	69	-45	9	8	-2	.960	33	2-231/S-23,3-1	-0.6

■ JACK LIND Lind, Jackson Hugh b: 6/8/46, Denver, Col. BB/TR, 6', 170 lbs. Deb: 9/10/74 C

YEAR	TM/L	G	AB	R	H	2B	3B	HR	RBI	BB	SO	AVG	OBP	SLG	PRO+	BR/A	SB	CS	SBR	FA	FR	G/POS	TPR
1974	Mil-A	9	17	4	4	2	0	0	1	3	2	.235	.350	.353	103	0	0	0	0	1.000	-0	/S-5,2-4	0.1
1975	Mil-A	17	20	1	1	0	0	0	0	2	12	.050	.136	.050	-45	-4	1	0	0	.919	5	/S-9,3-6,1-1	0.2
Total	2	26	37	5	5	2	0	0	1	5	14	.135	.238	.189	23	-4	1	0	0	.943	5	/S-14,3-6,2-4,1-1	0.3

■ JOSE LIND Lind, Jose (Salgado) "Chico" b: 5/1/64, Toa Baja, P.R. BR/TR, 5'11", 175 lbs. Deb: 8/28/87

YEAR	TM/L	G	AB	R	H	2B	3B	HR	RBI	BB	SO	AVG	OBP	SLG	PRO+	BR/A	SB	CS	SBR	FA	FR	G/POS	TPR
1987	Pit-N	35	143	21	46	8	4	0	11	8	12	.322	.358	.434	108	1	2	1	0	.995	6	2-35	0.9
1988	Pit-N	154	611	82	160	24	4	2	49	42	75	.262	.309	.324	83	-13	15	4	2	.987	3	*2-153	-0.2
1989	Pit-N	153	578	52	134	21	3	2	48	39	64	.232	.283	.289	66	-26	15	1	4	.976	-14	*2-151	-3.3
1990	*Pit-N	152	514	46	134	28	5	1	48	35	52	.261	.309	.340	82	-13	8	0	2	.991	17	*2-152	0.9
1991	*Pit-N	150	502	53	133	16	6	3	54	30	56	.265	.309	.339	83	-11	7	4	-0	.989	23	*2-149	1.5
1992	*Pit-N	135	468	38	110	14	1	0	39	26	29	.235	.277	.269	56	-27	3	1	0	**.992**	12	*2-134	-1.3
1993	KC-A	136	431	33	107	13	2	0	37	13	36	.248	.274	.288	48	-31	3	2	-0	**.994**	-4	*2-136	-3.1
1994	KC-A	85	290	34	78	16	2	1	31	16	34	.269	.307	.348	66	-15	9	5	-0	.988	2	2-84/D-1	-0.9
1995	KC-A	29	97	4	26	3	0	0	6	3	8	.268	.290	.299	53	-7	0	1	-1	.992	-2	2-29	-0.7
	Cal-A	15	43	5	7	2	0	0	1	3	4	.163	.217	.209	12	-6	0	0	0	1.000	4	2-15	-0.1
	Yr	44	140	9	33	5	0	0	7	6	12	.236	.267	.271	40	-12	0	1	-1	.995	1	2-44	-0.8
Total	9	1044	3677	368	935	145	27	9	324	215	370	.254	.297	.316	70	-148	62	19	7	.988	46	*2-1038/D-1	-6.3

■ EM LINDBECK Lindbeck, Emerit Desmond b: 8/27/35, Kewanee, Ill. BL/TR, 6', 185 lbs. Deb: 4/22/60

YEAR	TM/L	G	AB	R	H	2B	3B	HR	RBI	BB	SO	AVG	OBP	SLG	PRO+	BR/A	SB	CS	SBR	FA	FR	G/POS	TPR
1960	Det-A	2	1	0	0	0	0	0	0	1	0	.000	.500	.000	46	0	0	0	0	.000	0	H	0.0

■ JOHNNY LINDELL Lindell, John Harlan b: 8/30/16, Greeley, Colo. d: 8/27/85, Newport Beach, Cal. BR/TR, 6'4.5", 217 lbs. Deb: 4/18/41

YEAR	TM/L	G	AB	R	H	2B	3B	HR	RBI	BB	SO	AVG	OBP	SLG	PRO+	BR/A	SB	CS	SBR	FA	FR	G/POS	TPR
1941	NY-A	1	1	0	0	0	0	0	0	0	0	.000	.000	.000	-99	-0	0	0	0	.000	0	H	0.0
1942	NY-A	27	24	1	6	1	0	0	4	0	5	.250	.250	.292	53	-2	0	0	0	.923	-0	P-23	0.0
1943	*NY-A☆	122	441	53	108	17	**12**	4	51	51	55	.245	.329	.365	102	1	2	5	-2	.966	-2	*O-122	-1.0
1944	NY-A	149	594	91	178	33	**16**	18	103	44	56	.300	.351	.500	137	25	5	4	-1	.986	9	*O-149	2.7
1945	NY-A	41	159	26	45	6	3	1	20	17	10	.283	.363	.377	110	2	2	1	0	.982	0	O-41	0.0
1946	NY-A	102	332	41	86	10	5	10	40	32	47	.259	.328	.410	104	1	4	1	1	.982	-0	O-74,1-14	-0.3
1947	*NY-A	127	476	66	131	18	7	11	67	32	70	.275	.322	.412	104	0	1	2	-1	.978	7	*O-118	0.1
1948	NY-A	88	309	58	98	17	2	13	55	35	50	.317	.387	.511	139	16	0	0	0	.994	2	O-79	1.3
1949	*NY-A	78	211	33	51	10	0	6	27	35	27	.242	.350	.374	92	-3	3	0	1	.983	-6	O-65	-1.0
1950	NY-A	7	21	2	4	0	0	0	2	4	2	.190	.320	.190	34	-2	0	0	0	.857	-2	/O-6	-0.4
	StL-N	36	113	16	21	5	2	5	16	15	24	.186	.287	.398	74	-5	0			.984	-2	O-33	-0.8
1953	Pit-N	58	91	11	26	6	1	4	15	16	15	.286	.404	.505	136	5	0	0	0	.962	2	P-27/1-2	0.0
	Phi-N	11	18	3	7	1	0	0	2	6	2	.389	.542	.444	162	2	0	0	0	1.000	-1	/P-5,O-2	0.0
	Yr	69	109	14	33	7	1	4	17	22	17	.303	.429	.495	141	8	0	0	0	.964	1	P-32/1-2,O-2	0.0
1954	Phi-N	7	5	0	1	0	0	0	2	2	3	.200	.429	.200	70	-0	0	0	0	.000	0	H	0.0
Total	12	854	2795	401	762	124	48	72	404	289	366	.273	.344	.429	113	43	17	13		.980	7	O-689/P-55,1-16	0.6

■ JIM LINDEMAN Lindeman, James William b: 1/10/62, Evanston, Ill. BR/TR, 6'1", 200 lbs. Deb: 9/3/86

YEAR	TM/L	G	AB	R	H	2B	3B	HR	RBI	BB	SO	AVG	OBP	SLG	PRO+	BR/A	SB	CS	SBR	FA	FR	G/POS	TPR
1986	StL-N	19	55	7	14	1	0	1	6	2	10	.255	.281	.327	68	-3	1	1	-0	.992	-1	1-17/3-1,O-1	-0.5
1987	*StL-N	75	207	20	43	13	0	8	28	11	56	.208	.258	.386	67	-11	3	1	0	.976	-1	O-49,1-20	-1.3
1988	StL-N	17	43	3	9	1	0	2	7	2	9	.209	.244	.372	74	-2	0	0	0	.941	-2	O-12/1-3	-0.4
1989	StL-N	73	45	8	5	1	0	0	2	3	18	.111	.167	.133	-13	-7	0	0	0	.989	0	1-42/O-5	-0.7
1990	Det-A	12	32	5	7	1	0	2	8	2	13	.219	.265	.438	92	-1	0	0	0	1.000	-1	D-10/1-1,O-1	-0.2
1991	Phi-N	65	95	13	32	5	0	0	12	13	14	.337	.417	.389	129	4	0	1	-1	1.000	-5	O-30/1-1	-0.2
1992	Phi-N	29	39	6	10	1	0	1	6	3	11	.256	.310	.359	89	-1	0	0	0	1.000	-3	/O-9	-0.4
1993	Hou-N	9	23	2	8	3	0	0	0	0	7	.348	.348	.478	123	1	0	0	0	1.000	1	/1-9	0.1
1994	NY-N	52	137	18	37	8	1	7	20	6	35	.270	.306	.496	106	0	0	0	0	.948	-3	O-33/1-4	-0.3
Total	9	351	676	82	165	34	1	21	89	42	173	.244	.292	.391	83	-17	4	3	-1	.970	-14	O-140/1-97,D-10,3-1	-3.9

■ BOB LINDEMANN Lindemann, John Frederick Mann b: 6/5/1881, Philadelphia, Pa. d: 12/19/51, Williamsport, Pa. BB/TR, 6', 175 lbs. Deb: 8/28/01

YEAR	TM/L	G	AB	R	H	2B	3B	HR	RBI	BB	SO	AVG	OBP	SLG	PRO+	BR/A	SB	CS	SBR	FA	FR	G/POS	TPR
1901	Phi-A	3	9	0	1	0	0	0	0	0		.111	.111	.111	-37	-2	0			.600	-0	/O-3	-0.2

■ WALT LINDEN Linden, Walter Charles b: 3/27/24, Chicago, Ill. BR/TR, 6'1", 190 lbs. Deb: 4/30/50

YEAR	TM/L	G	AB	R	H	2B	3B	HR	RBI	BB	SO	AVG	OBP	SLG	PRO+	BR/A	SB	CS	SBR	FA	FR	G/POS	TPR
1950	Bos-N	3	5	0	2	1	0	0	0	1	0	.400	.500	.600	201	1	0			1.000	-1	/C-3	0.0

■ CHRIS LINDSAY Lindsay, Christian Haller "Pinky" or "The Crab" b: 7/24/1878, Beaver County, Pa. d: 1/25/41, Cleveland, Ohio BR/TR, 6', 190 lbs. Deb: 7/6/05

YEAR	TM/L	G	AB	R	H	2B	3B	HR	RBI	BB	SO	AVG	OBP	SLG	PRO+	BR/A	SB	CS	SBR	FA	FR	G/POS	TPR
1905	Det-A	88	329	38	88	14	1	0	31	18		.267	.315	.316	100	-0	10			.978	-0	1-88	-0.4
1906	Det-A	141	499	59	112	16	2	0	33	45		.224	.293	.265	73	-15	18			.977	-8	*1-122,2-17/3-1	-2.9
Total	2	229	828	97	200	30	3	0	64	63		.242	.301	.285	83	-15	28			.978	-8	1-210/2-17,3-1	-3.3

■ BILL LINDSAY Lindsay, William Gibbons b: 2/24/1881, Madison, N.C. d: 7/14/63, Greensboro, N.C. BL/TR, 5'10.5", 165 lbs. Deb: 6/21/11

YEAR	TM/L	G	AB	R	H	2B	3B	HR	RBI	BB	SO	AVG	OBP	SLG	PRO+	BR/A	SB	CS	SBR	FA	FR	G/POS	TPR
1911	Cle-A	19	66	6	16	2	0	0	5	1		.242	.265	.273	49	-5	2			.883	2	3-15/2-1	-0.2

■ DOUG LINDSEY Lindsey, Michael Douglas b: 9/22/67, Austin, Tex. BR/TR, 6'2", 200 lbs. Deb: 10/6/91

YEAR	TM/L	G	AB	R	H	2B	3B	HR	RBI	BB	SO	AVG	OBP	SLG	PRO+	BR/A	SB	CS	SBR	FA	FR	G/POS	TPR
1991	Phi-N	1	3	0	0	0	0	0	0	0	3	.000	.000	.000	-99	-1	0	0	0	1.000	0	/C-1	-0.1
1993	Phi-N	2	2	0	1	0	0	0	0	0	1	.500	.500	.500	171	0	0	0	0	1.000	-0	/C-2	0.0
	Chi-A	2	1	0	0	0	0	0	0	0	0	.000	.000	.000	-99	-0	0	0	0	1.000	0	/C-2	0.0
Total	2	5	6	0	1	0	0	0	0	0	4	.167	.167	.167	-8	-1	0	0	0	1.000	1	/C-5	-0.1

■ BILL LINDSEY Lindsey, William Donald b: 4/12/60, Staten Island, N.Y. BR/TR, 6'3", 195 lbs. Deb: 7/18/87

YEAR	TM/L	G	AB	R	H	2B	3B	HR	RBI	BB	SO	AVG	OBP	SLG	PRO+	BR/A	SB	CS	SBR	FA	FR	G/POS	TPR
1987	Chi-A	9	16	2	3	0	0	0	1	0	3	.188	.188	.188	-0	-2	0	0	0	1.000	2	/C-9	0.0

■ CHUCK LINDSTROM Lindstrom, Charles William b: 9/7/36, Chicago, Ill. BR/TR, 5'11", 175 lbs. Deb: 9/28/58 F

YEAR	TM/L	G	AB	R	H	2B	3B	HR	RBI	BB	SO	AVG	OBP	SLG	PRO+	BR/A	SB	CS	SBR	FA	FR	G/POS	TPR
1958	Chi-A	1	1	1	1	0	1	0	1	1	0	1.000	1.000	3.000	975	1	0	0	0	1.000	-0	/C-1	0.1

■ FREDDIE LINDSTROM Lindstrom, Frederick Charles (b: Frederick Anthony Lindstrom) b: 11/21/05, Chicago, Ill. d: 10/4/81, Chicago, Ill. BR/TR, 5'11", 170 lbs. Deb: 4/15/24 FH

YEAR	TM/L	G	AB	R	H	2B	3B	HR	RBI	BB	SO	AVG	OBP	SLG	PRO+	BR/A	SB	CS	SBR	FA	FR	G/POS	TPR
1924	*NY-N	52	79	19	20	3	1	0	4	6	10	.253	.314	.316	71	-3	3	1	0	.911	7	2-23,3-11	0.5
1925	NY-N	104	356	43	102	15	12	4	33	22	20	.287	.332	.430	97	-3	5	9	-4	.957	-1	3-96/2-1,S-1	-0.2
1926	NY-N	140	543	90	164	19	9	9	76	39	21	.302	.351	.420	108	5	11			.962	-3	*3-138/O-1	1.1
1927	NY-N	138	562	107	172	36	8	7	58	40	40	.306	.354	.436	111	8	10			.968	1	3-87,O-51	1.0

YEAR	TM/L	G	AB	R	H	2B	3B	HR	RBI	BB	SO	AVG	OBP	SLG	PRO+	BR/A	SB	CS	SBR	FA	FR	G/POS	TPR
1928	NY-N	153	646	99	**231**	39	9	14	107	25	21	.358	.383	.511	131	27	15			**.958**	15	*3-153	4.8
1929	NY-N	130	549	99	175	23	6	15	91	30	28	.319	.354	.464	101	-0	10			.966	7	*3-128	1.1
1930	NY-N	148	609	127	231	39	7	22	106	48	33	.379	.425	.575	142	41	15			.953	6	*3-148	4.8
1931	NY-N	78	303	38	91	12	6	5	36	26	12	.300	.356	.429	113	5	5			.975	-7	O-73/2-4	-0.6
1932	NY-N	144	595	83	161	26	5	15	92	27	28	.271	.303	.407	91	-9	6			.982	0	*O-128,3-15	-1.6
1933	Pit-N	138	538	70	167	39	10	5	55	33	22	.310	.350	.448	127	18	1			.988	11	*O-130	2.3
1934	Pit-N	97	383	59	111	24	4	4	49	23	21	.290	.333	.405	94	-3	1			.990	1	O-92	-0.6
1935	*Chi-N	90	342	49	94	22	4	3	62	10	13	.275	.297	.389	82	-9	1			.979	-2	O-50,3-33	-1.1
1936	Bro-N	26	106	12	28	4	0	0	10	5	7	.264	.297	.302	61	-6	1			.982	1	O-26	-0.5
Total	13	1438	5611	895	1747	301	81	103	779	334	276	.311	.351	.449	110	71	84	10		.959	37	3-809,O-551/2-28,S	11.0

■ **CARL LINHART** Linhart, Carl James b: 12/14/29, Zborov, Czech. BL/TR, 5'11", 184 lbs. Deb: 8/2/52

YEAR	TM/L	G	AB	R	H	2B	3B	HR	RBI	BB	SO	AVG	OBP	SLG	PRO+	BR/A	SB	CS	SBR	FA	FR	G/POS	TPR
1952	Det-A	3	2	0	0	0	0	0	0	0	0	.000	.000	.000	-99	-1	0	0	0	.000	0	H	-0.1

■ **BOB LINTON** Linton, Claud Clarence b: 4/18/03, Emerson, Ark. d: 4/3/80, Destin, Fla. BL/TR, 6', 185 lbs. Deb: 4/26/29

YEAR	TM/L	G	AB	R	H	2B	3B	HR	RBI	BB	SO	AVG	OBP	SLG	PRO+	BR/A	SB	CS	SBR	FA	FR	G/POS	TPR
1929	Pit-N	17	18	0	2	0	0	0	1	1	2	.111	.158	.111	-31	-4	0			1.000	0	/C-8	-0.3

■ **LARRY LINTZ** Lintz, Larry b: 10/10/49, Martinez, Cal. BB/TR, 5'9", 150 lbs. Deb: 7/14/73

YEAR	TM/L	G	AB	R	H	2B	3B	HR	RBI	BB	SO	AVG	OBP	SLG	PRO+	BR/A	SB	CS	SBR	FA	FR	G/POS	TPR
1973	Mon-N	52	116	20	29	1	0	0	3	17	18	.250	.351	.259	69	-4	12	4	1	.945	2	2-34,S-15	0.2
1974	Mon-N	113	319	60	76	10	1	0	20	44	50	.238	.334	.276	68	-12	50	7	11	.961	-13	2-67,S-31/3-1	-0.8
1975	Mon-N	46	132	18	26	0	0	0	3	23	18	.197	.316	.197	43	-9	17	9	-0	.970	-6	2-39/S-2	-1.4
	StL-N	27	18	6	5	1	0	0	1	3	2	.278	.381	.333	96	0	4	0	1	.889	9	/2-6,S-6	1.0
	Yr	73	150	24	31	1	0	0	4	26	20	.207	.324	.213	49	-9	21	9	1	.963	3	2-45/S-8	-0.4
1976	Oak-A	68	1	21	0	0	0	0	0	2	0	.000	.667	.000	111	0	31	11	3	1.000	-0	D-19/2-5,O-3	0.3
1977	Oak-A	41	30	11	4	1	0	0	0	8	13	.133	.333	.167	42	-2	13	5	1	1.000	11	2-28/S-2,3-1,D-5	1.0
1978	Cle-A	3	0	1	0	0	0	0	0	0	0	—	—	—	—	0	1	2	-1	.000	0	R	-0.1
Total	6	350	616	137	140	13	1	0	27	97	101	.227	.336	.252	63	-27	128	38	16	.962	3	2-179/S-56,D-24,O3	0.2

■ **PHIL LINZ** Linz, Philip Francis b: 6/4/39, Baltimore, Md. BR/TR, 6'1", 180 lbs. Deb: 4/13/62

YEAR	TM/L	G	AB	R	H	2B	3B	HR	RBI	BB	SO	AVG	OBP	SLG	PRO+	BR/A	SB	CS	SBR	FA	FR	G/POS	TPR
1962	NY-A	71	129	28	37	8	0	1	14	6	17	.287	.319	.372	88	-2	6	2	1	.937	-3	S-21/3-8,2-5,O-2	-0.3
1963	*NY-A	72	186	22	50	9	0	2	12	15	18	.269	.330	.349	91	-2	1	6	-3	.963	1	S-22,3-13,O-12,/2-6	-0.3
1964	*NY-A	112	368	63	92	21	3	5	25	43	61	.250	.332	.364	92	-3	3	4	-2	.952	11	S-55,3-41/2-5,O-3	1.0
1965	NY-A	99	285	37	59	12	1	2	16	30	33	.207	.283	.277	60	-15	2	1	0	.954	11	S-71/3-4,O-4,2-1	0.1
1966	Phi-N	40	70	4	14	3	0	0	6	2	14	.200	.222	.243	29	-7	0	0	0	.971	1	3-14/S-6,2-3	-0.6
1967	Phi-N	23	18	4	4	2	0	1	5	2	1	.222	.300	.500	124	0	0	0	0	.833	-1	/S-7,3-1	-0.1
	NY-N	24	58	8	12	2	0	0	1	4	10	.207	.270	.241	48	-4	0	0	0	.964	-2	2-11/S-8,3-1,O-1	-0.6
	Yr	47	76	12	16	4	0	1	6	6	11	.211	.277	.303	66	-3	0	0	0	.963	-4	S-15,2-11/3-2,O-1	-0.7
1968	NY-N	78	258	19	54	7	0	0	17	10	41	.209	.244	.236	45	-17	1	0	0	.968	-12	2-71	-2.9
Total	7	519	1372	185	322	64	4	11	96	112	195	.235	.296	.311	72	-49	13	13	-4	.952	6	S-190,2-102/3-82,O	-3.7

■ **JOHNNY LIPON** Lipon, John Joseph "Skids" b: 11/10/22, Martins Ferry, O. d: 8/17/98, Houston, Tex. BR/TR, 6', 175 lbs. Deb: 8/16/42 MC

YEAR	TM/L	G	AB	R	H	2B	3B	HR	RBI	BB	SO	AVG	OBP	SLG	PRO+	BR/A	SB	CS	SBR	FA	FR	G/POS	TPR
1942	Det-A	34	131	5	25	2	0	0	9	7	7	.191	.232	.206	22	-14	1	3	-2	.945	7	S-34	-0.6
1946	Det-A	14	20	4	6	0	0	0	1	5	3	.300	.440	.300	103	0	0	0	0	.933	3	/S-8,3-1	0.4
1948	Det-A	121	458	65	133	18	8	5	52	68	22	.290	.384	.397	105	5	4	4	-1	.970	-12	*S-117/2-1,3-1	-0.1
1949	Det-A	127	439	57	110	14	6	3	59	75	24	.251	.362	.330	84	-8	2	4	-2	.965	4	*S-120	0.2
1950	Det-A	147	601	104	176	27	6	2	63	81	26	.293	.378	.368	89	-8	9	6	-1	.958	9	*S-147	1.1
1951	Det-A	129	487	56	129	15	1	0	38	49	27	.265	.335	.300	72	-18	7	6	-2	.949	-13	*S-125	-2.3
1952	Det-A	39	136	17	30	4	2	0	12	16	6	.221	.303	.279	62	-7	3	1	0	.978	-3	S-39	-0.6
	Bos-A	79	234	25	48	8	1	0	18	32	20	.205	.301	.248	50	-15	1	1	-0	.982	14	S-69/3-7	0.4
	Yr	118	370	42	78	12	3	0	30	48	26	.211	.301	.259	54	-22	4	2	0	**.981**	12	*S-108/3-7	-0.2
1953	Bos-A	60	145	18	31	7	0	0	13	14	16	.214	.283	.262	46	-11	1	0	0	.951	4	S-58	-0.4
	StL-A	7	9	0	2	0	0	0	1	0	1	.222	.222	.222	20	-1	0	0	0	1.000	-1	/3-6,2-1	-0.2
	Yr	67	154	18	33	7	0	0	14	14	17	.214	.280	.260	44	-12	1	0	0	.951	3	S-58/3-6,2-1	-0.6
1954	Cin-N	1	1	0	0	0	0	0	0	0	0	.000	.000	.000	-97	-0	0	0	0	.000	0	H	0.0
Total	9	758	2661	351	690	95	24	10	266	347	152	.259	.346	.324	77	-77	28	25	-7	.961	13	S-717/3-15,2-2	-2.1

■ **NIG LIPSCOMB** Lipscomb, Gerard b: 2/24/11, Rutherfordton, N.C d: 2/27/78, Huntersville, N.C. BR/TR, 6', 175 lbs. Deb: 4/23/37

YEAR	TM/L	G	AB	R	H	2B	3B	HR	RBI	BB	SO	AVG	OBP	SLG	PRO+	BR/A	SB	CS	SBR	FA	FR	G/POS	TPR
1937	StL-A	36	96	11	31	9	1	0	8	11	10	.323	.398	.438	110	2	0	0	0	.963	2	2-27/P-3,3-1	0.6

■ **BOB LIPSKI** Lipski, Robert Peter b: 7/7/38, Scranton, Pa. BL/TR, 6'1", 180 lbs. Deb: 4/28/63

YEAR	TM/L	G	AB	R	H	2B	3B	HR	RBI	BB	SO	AVG	OBP	SLG	PRO+	BR/A	SB	CS	SBR	FA	FR	G/POS	TPR
1963	Cle-A	2	1	0	0	0	0	0	0	0	1	.000	.000	.000	-99	-0	0	0	0	1.000	0	/C-2	0.0

■ **NELSON LIRIANO** Liriano, Nelson Arturo (Bonilla) b: 6/3/64, Puerto Plata, D.R. BB/TR, 5'10", 172 lbs. Deb: 8/25/87

YEAR	TM/L	G	AB	R	H	2B	3B	HR	RBI	BB	SO	AVG	OBP	SLG	PRO+	BR/A	SB	CS	SBR	FA	FR	G/POS	TPR
1987	Tor-A	37	158	29	38	6	2	2	10	16	22	.241	.310	.342	71	-6	13	2	3	.995	3	2-37	0.1
1988	Tor-A	99	276	36	73	6	2	3	23	11	40	.264	.298	.333	76	-9	12	5	1	.961	-13	2-80,D-11/3-1	-1.9
1989	*Tor-A	132	418	51	110	26	3	5	53	43	51	.263	.335	.376	102	1	16	7	1	.980	-18	*2-122/D-5	-1.2
1990	Tor-A	50	170	16	36	7	2	1	15	16	20	.212	.283	.294	61	-9	3	5	-2	.983	-12	2-49	-2.3
	Min-A	53	185	30	47	5	7	0	13	22	24	.254	.333	.357	87	-3	5	2	0	.968	-15	2-50/S-1,D-2	-1.8
	Yr	103	355	46	83	12	9	1	28	38	44	.234	.310	.327	75	-12	8	7	-2	.975	-28	2-99/D-2,S-1	-4.1
1991	KC-A	10	22	5	9	0	0	0	1	0	2	.409	.409	.409	127	1	0	1	-1	1.000	1	2-10	0.1
1993	Col-N	48	151	28	46	6	3	2	15	18	22	.305	.379	.424	98	-0	6	4	-1	.975	-13	S-35,2-16/3-1	-1.1
1994	Col-N	87	255	39	65	17	5	3	31	42	44	.255	.360	.396	83	-6	0	2	-1	.973	-5	2-79/S-3,3-2	-0.9
1995	Pit-N	107	259	29	74	12	1	5	38	24	34	.286	.351	.398	95	-1	2	2	-1	.981	-18	2-67/3-5,S-1	-1.7
1996	Pit-N	112	217	23	58	14	2	3	30	14	22	.267	.312	.392	82	-6	2	0	1	.984	-6	2-36/3-9,S-5	-1.0
1997	LA-N	76	88	10	20	6	0	1	11	6	12	.227	.277	.330	63	-5	0	0	0	.949	-4	2-17/1-2,3-1,S-1	-0.8
1998	Col-N	12	17	0	0	0	0	0	0	0	7	.000	.000	.000	-84	-5	0	0	0	1.000	-1	/2-3,S-1	-0.5
Total	11	823	2216	296	576	105	27	25	240	212	300	.260	.326	.366	84	-49	59	30	-0	.976	-103	2-566/S-47,3-19,D1	-13.0

■ **JOE LIS** Lis, Joseph Anthony b: 8/15/46, Somerville, N.J. BR/TR, 6', 195 lbs. Deb: 9/5/70

YEAR	TM/L	G	AB	R	H	2B	3B	HR	RBI	BB	SO	AVG	OBP	SLG	PRO+	BR/A	SB	CS	SBR	FA	FR	G/POS	TPR
1970	Phi-N	13	37	1	7	2	0	1	4	5	11	.189	.286	.324	65	-2	0	0	0	.947	0	/O-9	-0.2
1971	Phi-N	59	123	16	26	6	0	6	10	16	43	.211	.312	.407	102	0	0	1	-1	.978	-3	O-35	-0.5
1972	Phi-N	62	140	13	34	6	0	6	18	30	34	.243	.380	.414	122	5	0	1	-1	.996	1	1-30,O-14	0.3
1973	Min-A	103	253	37	62	11	1	9	25	28	66	.245	.327	.403	101	0	0	1	-1	.987	2	1-96/D-1	-0.4
1974	Min-A	24	41	5	8	0	0	0	3	5	12	.195	.298	.195	43	-3	0	0	0	.992	0	1-18	-0.4
	Cle-A	57	109	15	22	3	0	6	16	14	30	.202	.293	.394	97	-1	1	0	0	1.000	-0	1-31/3-9,O-1,D-9	-0.2
	Yr	81	150	20	30	3	0	6	19	19	42	.200	.294	.340	82	-4	1	0	0	.997	-0	1-49/3-9,D-9,O-1	-0.6
1975	Cle-A	9	13	4	4	2	0	2	8	3	3	.308	.471	.923	286	3	0	0	0	1.000	-0	/1-8,D-1	0.3
1976	Cle-A	20	51	4	16	1	0	2	7	8	8	.314	.407	.451	153	4	0	0	0	1.000	-0	1-17/D-1	0.3
1977	Sea-A	9	13	1	3	0	0	0	1	1	2	.231	.286	.231	43	-1	0	0	0	1.000	-1	/1-4,C-1	-0.2
Total	8	356	780	96	182	31	1	32	92	110	209	.233	.334	.399	105	6	1	3	-2	.992	-1	1-204/O-59,D-12,3C	-1.0

■ **RICK LISI** Lisi, Riccardo Patrick Emilio b: 3/17/56, Halifax, N.S., Can. BR/TR, 6', 175 lbs. Deb: 5/9/81

YEAR	TM/L	G	AB	R	H	2B	3B	HR	RBI	BB	SO	AVG	OBP	SLG	PRO+	BR/A	SB	CS	SBR	FA	FR	G/POS	TPR
1981	Tex-A	9	16	6	5	0	0	0	1	4	0	.313	.450	.313	130	1	0	1	-1	1.000	-2	/O-8	-0.2

■ **PAT LISTACH** Listach, Patrick Alan b: 9/12/67, Natchitoches, La. BB/TR, 5'9", 170 lbs. Deb: 4/8/92

YEAR	TM/L	G	AB	R	H	2B	3B	HR	RBI	BB	SO	AVG	OBP	SLG	PRO+	BR/A	SB	CS	SBR	FA	FR	G/POS	TPR
1992	Mil-A	149	579	93	168	19	6	1	47	55	124	.290	.353	.349	99	1	54	18	5	.966	-7	*S-148/2-1,O-1	1.0
1993	Mil-A	98	356	50	87	15	1	3	30	37	70	.244	.321	.317	73	-13	18	9	0	.975	-16	S-95/O-6	-2.1
1994	Mil-A	16	54	8	16	3	0	0	2	3	8	.296	.333	.352	74	-2	2	1	0	.958	-0	S-16	-0.1
1995	Mil-A	101	334	35	73	8	2	0	25	25	61	.219	.277	.254	37	-31	13	3	2	1.000	-1	2-59,S-36,O-11,/3-2	-2.2
1996	Mil-A	87	317	51	76	16	2	1	33	36	51	.240	.319	.312	58	-20	25	5	5	.982	-0	O-68,2-12/S-7	-1.5
1997	Hou-N	52	132	13	24	2	2	0	6	11	24	.182	.250	.227	27	-14	4	2	0	.951	-8	S-31/O-6	-2.0
Total	6	503	1772	250	444	63	13	5	143	167	338	.251	.318	.309	68	-79	116	38	12	.967	-33	S-333/O-92,2-72,3-2	-6.9

YEAR	TM/L	G	AB	R	H	2B	3B	HR	RBI	BB	SO	AVG	OBP	SLG	PRO+	BR/A	SB	CS	SBR	FA	FR	G/POS	TPR

■ **PETE LISTER**   Lister, Morris Elmer   b: 7/21/1881, Savanna, Ill.   d: 3/27/47, St.Petersburg, Fla   BR/TR,   Deb: 9/14/07

| 1907 | Cle-A | 22 | 65 | 5 | 18 | 2 | 0 | 0 | 4 | 3 | | .277 | .319 | .308 | 99 | -0 | 2 | | | .974 | -1 | 1-22 | -0.2 |

■ **SCOTT LITTLE**   Little, Dennis Scott   b: 1/19/63, E.St.Louis, Ill.   BR/TR, 6', 198 lbs.   Deb: 7/27/89

| 1989 | Pit-N | 3 | 4 | 0 | 1 | 0 | 0 | 0 | 0 | 0 | 1 | .250 | .250 | .250 | 45 | -0 | 0 | 0 | 0 | 1.000 | 1 | /O-1 | 0.1 |

■ **HARRY LITTLE**   Little, Harry A.   b: St.Louis, Mo.   TR,   Deb: 7/16/1877

1877	StL-N	3	12	2	2	0	0	0	0	1	6	.167	.231	.167	29	-1				1.000	-0	/O-3	-0.1
	Lou-N	1	3	0	0	0	0	0	0	0	1	.000	.250	.000	-13	-0				.857	0	/2-1	0.0
	Yr	4	15	2	2	0	0	0	0	2	7	.133	.235	.133	19	-1				1.000	-0	/O-3,2-1	-0.1

■ **MARK LITTLE**   Little, Mark Travis   b: 7/11/72, Edwardsville, Ill.   BR/TR, 6', 195 lbs.   Deb: 9/12/98

| 1998 | StL-N | 7 | 12 | 0 | 1 | 0 | 0 | 0 | 0 | 2 | 5 | .083 | .214 | .083 | -18 | -2 | 1 | 0 | 0 | 1.000 | -0 | /O-7 | -0.2 |

■ **BRYAN LITTLE**   Little, Richard Bryan "Twig"   b: 10/8/59, Houston, Tex.   BB/TR, 5'10", 160 lbs.   Deb: 7/29/82   C

1982	Mon-N	29	42	6	9	0	0	0	3	4	6	.214	.283	.214	40	-3	2	1	0	1.000	-2	2-16,S-10	-0.5
1983	Mon-N	106	350	48	91	15	3	1	36	50	22	.260	.356	.329	91	-2	4	5	-2	.968	-32	S-66,2-51	-3.0
1984	Mon-N	85	266	31	65	11	1	0	9	34	19	.244	.332	.293	81	-6	2	3	-1	.982	-22	2-77/S-2	-2.8
1985	Chi-A	73	188	35	47	9	1	2	27	26	21	.250	.350	.340	87	-3	0	1	-1	.989	-6	2-68/3-2,S-1	-0.7
1986	Chi-A	20	35	3	6	1	0	0	2	4	4	.171	.256	.200	25	-4	0	0	0	1.000	0	2-12/S-7,3-1	-0.3
	NY-A	14	41	3	8	1	0	0	0	2	7	.195	.233	.220	24	-4	0	0	0	.975	5	2-14	0.1
	Yr	34	76	6	14	2	0	0	2	6	11	.184	.244	.211	25	-8	0	0	0	.983	6	2-26/S-7,3-1	-0.2
Total	5	327	922	126	226	37	5	3	77	120	79	.245	.336	.306	80	-22	8	10	-4	.987	-56	2-238/S-86,3-3	-7.2

■ **JACK LITTLE**   Little, William Arthur   b: 3/12/1891, Mart, Tex.   d: 7/27/61, Dallas, Tex.   BR/TR, 5'11", 175 lbs.   Deb: 7/2/12

| 1912 | NY-A | 3 | 12 | 1 | 3 | 0 | 0 | 0 | 0 | 0 | 1 | .250 | .357 | .250 | 70 | -0 | 2 | | | 1.000 | 0 | /O-3 | 0.0 |

■ **DENNIS LITTLEJOHN**   Littlejohn, Dennis Gerald   b: 10/4/54, Santa Monica, Cal.   BR/TR, 6'2", 200 lbs.   Deb: 7/9/78

1978	SF-N	2	0	0	0	0	0	0	0	0	0	—	—	—		-0	0	0	0	.000	0	/C-2	0.0
1979	SF-N	63	193	15	38	6	1	1	13	21	46	.197	.276	.254	49	-14	0	0	0	.986	5	C-63	-0.6
1980	SF-N	13	29	2	7	1	0	0	2	7	7	.241	.389	.276	91	0	0	0	0	.983	2	C-10	0.2
Total	3	78	222	17	45	7	1	1	15	28	53	.203	.292	.257	55	-14	0	0	0	.985	7	/C-75	-0.4

■ **LARRY LITTLETON**   Littleton, Larry Marvin   b: 4/3/54, Charlotte, N.C.   BR/TR, 6'1", 185 lbs.   Deb: 4/12/81

| 1981 | Cle-A | 26 | 23 | 2 | 0 | 0 | 0 | 0 | 1 | 3 | 6 | .000 | .115 | .000 | -65 | -5 | 0 | 0 | 0 | 1.000 | -10 | O-24 | -1.6 |

■ **GREG LITTON**   Litton, Jon Gregory   b: 7/13/64, New Orleans, La.   BR/TR, 6', 190 lbs.   Deb: 5/2/89

1989	*SF-N	71	143	12	36	5	3	4	17	7	29	.252	.291	.413	102	-0	0	2	-1	.953	-5	3-34,2-15/S-9,OC	-0.6
1990	SF-N	93	204	17	50	9	1	4	24	11	45	.245	.287	.314	68	-9	1	0	0	.985	-11	O-56,2-18/S-7,3-5	-2.1
1991	SF-N	59	127	13	23	7	1	1	15	11	25	.181	.252	.276	50	-9	0	2	-1	.989	-2	1-15,2-15,3/SOCP	-1.2
1992	SF-N	68	140	9	32	5	0	4	15	11	33	.229	.285	.350	84	-3	0	1	-1	.992	-3	2-31,3-10/1-8,SO	-0.7
1993	Sea-A	72	174	25	52	17	0	3	25	18	30	.299	.368	.448	116	4	0	1	-1	1.000	0	O-22,3-17,1D/3S	0.3
1994	Bos-A	11	21	2	2	0	0	0	1	0	5	.095	.095	.095	-48	-5	0	0	0	1.000	2	/2-4,1-3,3-2,D-1	-0.3
Total	6	374	809	78	195	43	5	13	97	58	167	.241	.295	.355	81	-22	1	6	-3	.997	-18	2-100/O-91,31SDCP	-4.6

■ **JACK LITTRELL**   Littrell, Jack Napier   b: 1/22/29, Louisville, Ky.   BR/TR, 6', 179 lbs.   Deb: 4/19/52

1952	Phi-A	4	2	0	0	0	0	0	0	1	2	.000	.333	.000	-2	-0	0	0	0	1.000	0	/S-2,3-1	0.0
1954	Phi-A	9	30	7	9	2	0	1	3	6	3	.300	.417	.467	141	2	1	0	0	.976	-1	/S-9	0.2
1955	KC-A	37	70	5	14	0	0	1	4	4	12	.200	.243	.229	27	-7	0	0	0	.947	5	S-22/1-6,2-4	-0.6
1957	Chi-N	61	153	8	29	4	2	1	9	9	43	.190	.235	.261	34	-14	0	0	0	.944	1	S-47/2-6,3-5	-0.9
Total	4	111	255	22	52	6	3	2	17	20	60	.204	.262	.275	45	-20	1	0	0	.949	0	/S-80,2-10,1-6,3-6	-1.3

■ **DANNY LITWHILER**   Litwhiler, Daniel Webster   b: 8/31/16, Ringtown, Pa.   BR/TR, 5'10.5", 198 lbs.   Deb: 4/25/40   C

1940	Phi-N	36	142	10	49	2	5	5	17	3	13	.345	.363	.493	139	7	1			.986	1	O-34	0.6
1941	Phi-N	151	590	72	180	29	6	18	66	39	43	.305	.350	.466	134	23	1			.964	17	*O-150	3.2
1942	Phi-N★	151	591	59	160	25	9	9	56	27	42	.271	.310	.389	109	4	2			1.000	-2	*O-151	-0.6
1943	Phi-N	36	139	23	36	6	0	5	17	11	14	.259	.313	.410	113	1	1			.989	5	O-34	0.5
	*StL-N	80	258	40	72	14	3	7	31	19	31	.279	.333	.438	117	5	1			1.000	1	O-70	0.3
	Yr	116	397	63	108	20	3	12	48	30	45	.272	.326	.428	115	6	2			.996	6	*O-104	0.8
1944	*StL-N	140	492	53	130	25	5	15	82	37	56	.264	.328	.427	109	5	2			.974	-1	*O-136	-0.2
1946	StL-N	6	5	0	0	0	0	0	0	1	1	.000	.167	.000	-49	-1	0			.000	0	H	-0.1
	Bos-N	79	247	29	72	12	2	6	38	19	23	.291	.347	.453	125	7	1			.985	-3	O-65/3-2	0.1
	Yr	85	252	29	72	12	2	6	38	20	24	.286	.343	.444	121	6	1			.985	-3	O-65/3-2	0.0
1947	Bos-N	91	226	38	59	5	2	7	31	25	43	.261	.337	.394	96	-2	1			.976	-6	O-66	-1.0
1948	Bos-N	13	33	0	9	2	0	0	6	4	2	.273	.385	.333	97	0	0			1.000	2	/O-8	0.1
	Cin-N	106	338	51	93	19	2	14	44	48	41	.275	.365	.467	128	13	1			.988	2	O-83,3-15	1.1
	Yr	119	371	51	102	21	2	14	50	52	43	.275	.367	.456	125	13	1			.990	4	O-91,3-15	1.2
1949	Cin-N	102	292	35	85	18	1	11	44	44	42	.291	.384	.473	127	12	0			.987	-5	O-82/3-3	0.3
1950	Cin-N	54	112	15	29	4	0	6	12	20	21	.259	.371	.455	116	3	0			.958	-3	O-29	-0.1
1951	Cin-N	12	29	3	8	1	0	2	2	5	2	.276	.323	.517	120	1	0			.933	-2	/O-7	0.0
Total	11	1057	3494	428	982	162	32	107	451	299	377	.281	.342	.438	119	78	11	0		.982	9	O-915/3-20	4.2

■ **PADDY LIVINGSTON**   Livingston, Patrick Joseph   b: 1/14/1880, Cleveland, Ohio   d: 9/19/77, Cleveland, Ohio   BR/TR, 5'8", 197 lbs.   Deb: 9/2/01   C

1901	Cle-A	1	2	0	0	0	0	0	0	0		.000	.333	.000	-2	-0	0			1.000	1	/C-1	-0.1
1906	Cin-N	50	139	8	22	1	4	0	8	12		.158	.259	.223	48	-8	0			.960	3	C-47	-0.1
1909	Phi-A	64	175	15	41	6	4	0	15	15		.234	.323	.314	99	-0	4			.969	9	C-64	1.7
1910	Phi-A	37	120	11	25	4	3	0	9	6		.208	.264	.292	75	-4	2			.968	4	C-37	0.4
1911	Phi-A	27	71	9	17	4	0	0	8	7		.239	.316	.296	72	-3	1			.977	5	C-26	0.4
1912	Cle-A	20	47	5	11	2	1	0	3	1		.234	.280	.319	69	-2	0			.976	0	C-14	-0.1
1917	StL-N	7	20	0	4	0	0	0	2	0	1	.200	.200	.200	23	-2	0			1.000	1	/C-6	-0.1
Total	7	206	574	48	120	17	12	0	45	41	1	.209	.287	.280	73	-18	7			.969	21	C-195	2.1

■ **MICKEY LIVINGSTON**   Livingston, Thompson Orville   b: 11/15/14, Newberry, S.C.   d: 4/3/83, Newberry, S.C.   BR/TR, 6'1.5", 185 lbs.   Deb: 9/17/38

1938	Was-A	2	4	0	3	2	0	0	1	0	1	.750	.750	1.250	421	2	0	0	0	.667	-1	/C-2	0.1
1941	Phi-N	95	207	16	42	6	1	0	18	20	38	.203	.276	.242	49	-14	2			.974	-1	C-71/1-1	-1.0
1942	Phi-N	89	239	20	49	6	1	2	22	25	20	.205	.283	.264	64	-11	0			.987	-6	C-78/1-6	-1.2
1943	Phi-N	84	265	25	66	9	2	3	18	19	18	.249	.304	.332	87	-5	1			.988	-2	C-84/1-2	-0.1
	Chi-N	36	111	11	29	5	4	1	16	12	8	.261	.333	.432	122	3	1			1.000	4	C-31/1-4	0.4
	Yr	120	376	36	95	14	6	4	34	31	26	.253	.313	.362	98	-2	2			.991	-3	*C-115/1-6	0.3
1945	*Chi-N	71	224	19	57	4	2	2	23	19	16	.254	.324	.317	80	-6	2			.990	-1	C-68/1-1	-0.2
1946	Chi-N	66	176	14	45	10	4	0	20	20	19	.256	.338	.369	103	1	0			.981	2	C-56	0.5
1947	Chi-N	19	33	2	7	2	0	0	3	1	5	.212	.235	.273	36	-3	0			1.000	-0	/C-7	-0.3
	NY-N	5	6	0	1	0	0	0	0	1	0	.167	.286	.167	23	-1	0			.800	1	/C-1	0.0
	Yr	24	39	2	8	2	0	0	3	2	5	.205	.244	.256	34	-4	0			.970	-1	/C-8	-0.3
1948	NY-N	45	99	9	21	4	1	2	12	21	11	.212	.350	.333	85	-1	1			.980	-1	C-42	0.0
1949	NY-N	19	57	6	17	2	0	4	12	2	8	.298	.333	.544	132	-1	0			.985	-1	C-19	-0.2
	Bos-N	28	64	6	15	2	1	0	6	3	5	.234	.290	.297	61	-4	0			.977	1	C-22	-0.2
	Yr	47	121	12	32	4	1	4	18	5	13	.264	.310	.413	95	-1	0			.980	1	C-41	0.0
1951	Bro-N	2	5	0	2	0	0	0	0	0	0	.400	.500	.400	142	0	0			1.000	-0	/C-2	0.0
Total	10	561	1490	128	354	56	9	19	153	144	141	.238	.310	.326	82	-37	7	0		.984	-11	C-483/1-14	-1.8

YEAR	TM/L	G	AB	R	H	2B	3B	HR	RBI	BB	SO	AVG	OBP	SLG	PRO+	BR/A	SB	CS	SBR	FA	FR	G/POS	TPR
■ **SCOTT LIVINGSTONE**	Livingstone, Scott Louis b: 7/15/65, Dallas, Tex. BL/TR, 6', 198 lbs. Deb: 7/19/91																						
1991	Det-A	44	127	19	37	5	0	2	11	10	25	.291	.343	.378	98	-0	2	1	0	.980	1	3-43	0.0
1992	Det-A	117	354	43	100	21	0	4	46	21	36	.282	.323	.376	95	-3	1	3	-2	.962	-6	*3-112	-1.1
1993	Det-A	98	304	39	89	10	2	2	39	19	32	.293	.334	.359	87	-6	1	3	-2	.955	-3	3-62,D-32	-1.1
1994	Det-A	15	23	0	5	1	0	0	1	1	4	.217	.250	.261	32	-2	0	0	0	1.000	0	/1-5,3-1,D-5	-0.2
	SD-N	57	180	11	49	12	1	2	10	6	22	.272	.296	.383	78	-6	2	2	-1	.942	-1	3-50	-0.7
1995	SD-N	99	196	26	66	15	0	5	32	15	22	.337	.384	.490	133	9	2	1	0	.991	-2	1-43,3-13/2-4	0.4
1996	*SD-N	102	172	20	51	4	1	2	20	9	22	.297	.331	.366	89	-3	0	1	-1	.993	0	1-22,3-16	-0.5
1997	SD-N	23	26	1	4	1	0	0	3	2	1	.154	.214	.192	8	-4	0	0	0	.750	2	/3-3,1-2,2-1	-0.2
	StL-N	42	41	3	7	1	0	0	3	1	10	.171	.190	.195	1	-6	1	0	0	1.000	-0	/3-2,O-1,D-1	-0.6
	Yr	65	67	4	11	2	0	0	6	3	11	.164	.200	.194	4	-9	1	0	0	.778	1	/3-5,1-2,2-1,O-1,D	-0.8
1998	Mon-N	76	110	1	23	6	0	0	12	5	15	.209	.243	.264	33	-11	1	1	-0	.938	-1	3-17/1-3,D-5	-1.2
Total	8	673	1533	163	431	76	4	17	177	89	189	.281	.321	.369	86	-32	10	12	-4	.958	-9	3-319/1-75,D-43,2O	-5.2
■ **ABEL LIZOTTE**	Lizotte, Abel b: 4/13/1870, Lewiston, Me. d: 12/4/26, Wilkes-Barre, Pa. 5'8", 174 lbs. Deb: 9/17/1896																						
1896	Pit-N	7	29	3	3	0	0	0	3	2	2	.103	.161	.103	-31	-5	1			.952	1	/1-7	-0.4
■ **WINSTON LLENAS**	Llenas, Winston Enriquillo (Davila) b: 9/23/43, Santiago, D.R. BR/TR, 5'10", 165 lbs. Deb: 8/15/68 C																						
1968	Cal-A	16	39	5	5	1	0	0	1	2	5	.128	.190	.154	6	-4	0	0	0	.800	-3	/3-9	-0.9
1969	Cal-A	34	47	4	8	2	0	0	0	2	10	.170	.204	.213	18	-5	0	0	0	.929	-2	/3-9	-0.8
1972	Cal-A	44	64	3	17	3	0	0	7	3	8	.266	.299	.313	87	-1	0	0	0	.950	-1	3-10/2-2,O-2	-0.3
1973	Cal-A	78	130	16	35	1	0	1	25	10	16	.269	.326	.300	84	-3	0	0	0	1.000	-4	2-20,3-11/O-4,D-4	-0.6
1974	Cal-A	72	138	16	36	6	0	2	17	11	19	.261	.315	.348	96	-1	0	0	0	1.000	-8	O-32,2-15,D-10,/3-2	-1.0
1975	Cal-A	56	113	6	21	4	0	0	11	10	11	.186	.252	.221	37	-9	0	1	-1	1.000	4	2-12,O-10/1-6,3D	-0.6
Total	6	300	531	50	122	17	0	3	61	38	69	.230	.284	.279	66	-24	0	1	-1	1.000	-13	/2-49,O-48,3-44,D1	-4.2
■ **MIKE LOAN**	Loan, William Joseph b: 9/27/1894, Philadelphia, Pa. d: 11/21/66, Springfield, Pa. BR/TR, 5'11", 185 lbs. Deb: 9/18/12																						
1912	Phi-N	1	2	1	1	0	0	0	0	0	0	.500	.500	.500	163	0	0			1.000	-1	/C-1	0.0
■ **BOB LOANE**	Loane, Robert Kenneth b: 8/6/14, Berkeley, Cal. BR/TR, 6', 190 lbs. Deb: 7/29/39																						
1939	Was-A	3	9	2	0	0	0	0	1	4	4	.000	.308	.000	-16	-1	0	0	0	.909	2	/O-3	0.0
1940	Bos-N	13	22	4	5	3	0	0	1	2	5	.227	.292	.364	84	-1	2			1.000	0	O-10	0.0
Total	2	16	31	6	5	3	0	0	2	6	9	.161	.297	.258	54	-2	2	0		.969	2	/O-13	0.0
■ **FRANK LOBERT**	Lobert, Frank John b: 11/26/1883, Williamsport, Pa. d: 5/29/32, Pittsburgh, Pa. BR/TR, 6', 180 lbs. Deb: 6/6/14 F																						
1914	Bal-F	11	30	3	6	0	1	0	2	0	0	.200	.200	.267	26	-4	0			.870	-2	/3-7,2-1	-0.5
■ **HANS LOBERT**	Lobert, John Bernard "Honus" b: 10/18/1881, Wilmington, Del. d: 9/14/68, Philadelphia, Pa. BR/TR, 5'9", 170 lbs. Deb: 9/21/03 FMC																						
1903	Pit-N	5	13	1	1	1	0	0	0	1		.077	.143	.154	-15	-2	1			.778	-1	/3-3,2-1,S-1	-0.3
1905	Chi-N	14	46	7	9	2	0	0	1	3		.196	.260	.239	47	-3	4			.918	0	3-13/O-1	-0.3
1906	Cin-N	79	268	39	83	5	5	0	19	19		.310	.366	.366	123	7	20			.959	-11	3-35,S-31,2-10,/O-1	-0.2
1907	Cin-N	148	537	61	132	9	12	1	41	37		.246	.299	.313	88	-8	30			.941	-18	*S-142/3-5	-2.5
1908	Cin-N	155	570	71	167	17	18	4	63	46		.293	.348	.407	145	27	47			.921	-26	3-99,S-35,O-21	0.6
1909	Cin-N	122	425	50	90	13	5	4	52	48		.212	.304	.294	86	-6	30			.921	-14	*3-122	-1.7
1910	Cin-N	93	314	43	97	6	6	3	40	30	9	.309	.369	.395	128	11	41			.932	-2	3-90	1.2
1911	Phi-N	147	541	94	154	20	9	9	72	66	31	.285	.368	.405	115	11	40			.954	-17	*3-147	-0.4
1912	Phi-N	65	257	37	84	12	5	2	33	19	13	.327	.373	.436	113	4	13			.976	-13	3-64	-0.9
1913	Phi-N	150	573	98	172	28	11	7	55	42	34	.300	.353	.424	117	11	41			**.974**	-15	*3-145/S-3,2-1	-0.2
1914	Phi-N	135	505	83	139	24	5	1	52	49	32	.275	.343	.349	99	-0	31			**.943**	-26	*3-133/S-2	-2.3
1915	NY-N	106	386	46	97	18	4	0	38	25	24	.251	.304	.319	94	-3	14	15	-5	.950	-5	*3-103	-1.1
1916	NY-N	48	76	6	17	3	2	0	11	5	8	.224	.272	.316	84	-2	2			.961	2	3-20	0.1
1917	NY-N	50	52	4	10	1	0	1	5	5	5	.192	.276	.269	70	-2	2			.906	2	3-21	0.0
Total	14	1317	4563	640	1252	159	82	32	482	395	156	.274	.337	.366	109	46	316	15		.944	-142	3-1000,S-214/O-23,2	-8.0
■ **HARRY LOCHHEAD**	Lochhead, Robert Henry b: 3/29/1876, Stockton, Cal. d: 8/22/09, Stockton, Cal. BR/TR, 5'11", 172 lbs. Deb: 4/16/1899																						
1899	Cle-N	148	541	52	129	7	1	1	43	21		.238	.280	.261	52	-35	23			.909	2	*S-146/2-1,P-1	-2.0
1901	Det-A	1	4	2	2	0	0	0	0	0		.500	.600	.500	198	1	0			.857	-0	/S-1	0.0
	Phi-A	9	34	3	3	0	0	0	2	3		.088	.162	.088	-28	-6	0			.757	-8	/S-9	-1.3
	Yr	10	38	5	5	0	0	0	2	3		.132	.214	.132	-3	-5	0			.773	-9	S-10	-1.3
Total	2	158	579	57	134	7	1	1	45	24		.231	.275	.252	48	-40	23			.903	-7	S-156/P-1,2-1	-3.3
■ **DON LOCK**	Lock, Don Wilson b: 7/27/36, Wichita, Kan. BR/TR, 6'2", 202 lbs. Deb: 7/17/62																						
1962	Was-A	71	225	30	57	6	2	12	37	30	63	.253	.341	.458	114	4	4	5	-2	.973	3	O-67	0.1
1963	Was-A	149	531	71	134	20	1	27	82	70	151	.252	.342	.446	119	14	7	3	0	.980	15	*O-146	2.2
1964	Was-A	152	512	73	127	17	4	28	80	79	137	.248	.350	.461	124	17	4	2	0	.987	13	*O-149	2.4
1965	Was-A	143	418	52	90	15	1	16	39	57	115	.215	.317	.371	96	-2	1	3	-2	.969	2	*O-136	-0.7
1966	Was-A	138	386	52	90	13	1	16	48	57	126	.233	.335	.396	110	6	2	6	-3	.977	7	*O-129	0.5
1967	Phi-N	112	313	46	79	13	1	14	51	43	98	.252	.352	.435	123	10	9	5	-0	.973	-2	O-97	0.4
1968	Phi-N	99	248	27	52	7	2	8	34	26	64	.210	.285	.351	90	-3	3	4	-2	.955	-5	O-78	-1.5
1969	Phi-N	4	4	0	0	0	0	0	0	0	1	.000	.000	.000	-99	-1	0	0	0	.000	-0	/O-1	-0.1
	Bos-A	53	58	8	13	1	0	1	2	11	21	.224	.348	.293	77	-1	0	1	-1	1.000	-6	O-28/1-4	-0.9
Total	8	921	2695	359	642	92	12	122	373	373	776	.238	.334	.417	111	43	30	29	-8	.976	27	O-831/1-4	2.4
■ **MARSHALL LOCKE**	Locke, Marshall Pinkney Wilder b: 3/12/1857, Ashland, Ohio d: 3/6/40, Ashland, Ohio Deb: 7/5/1884																						
1884	Ind-a	7	29	5	7	0	1	0	5	0		.241	.241	.310	81	-1				.800	-1	/O-7	-0.2
■ **KEITH LOCKHART**	Lockhart, Keith Virgil b: 11/10/64, Whittier, Cal. BL/TR, 5'10", 170 lbs. Deb: 4/5/94																						
1994	SD-N	27	43	4	9	0	0	2	6	4	10	.209	.292	.349	68	-2	1	0	0	1.000	-1	3-13/2-5,S-1,O-1	-0.3
1995	KC-A	94	274	41	88	19	3	6	33	14	21	.321	.363	.478	115	6	8	1	2	.974	-8	2-61,3-17,D-14	0.2
1996	KC-A	138	433	49	118	33	3	7	55	30	40	.273	.323	.411	84	-11	11	6	-0	.975	2	2-84,3-55/D-1	-0.5
1997	*Atl-N	96	147	25	41	5	3	6	32	14	17	.279	.346	.476	111	2	0	0	0	.983	-6	2-20,3-11/D-4	-0.3
1998	*Atl-N	109	366	50	94	21	0	9	37	29	37	.257	.313	.388	79	-11	2	2	-1	.984	-4	2-98/3-1,D-2	-1.0
Total	5	464	1263	169	350	78	9	30	163	91	125	.277	.330	.424	92	-17	22	9	1	.978	-17	2-268/3-97,D-21,OS	-1.9
■ **GENE LOCKLEAR**	Locklear, Gene b: 7/19/49, Lumberton, N.C. BL/TR, 5'10", 165 lbs. Deb: 4/5/73																						
1973	Cin-N	29	26	6	5	0	0	0	0	2	5	.192	.276	.192	34	-2	0	0	0	1.000	-1	/O-5	-0.4
	SD-N	67	154	20	37	6	1	3	25	21	22	.240	.331	.351	97	-1	9	4	0	.952	2	O-37	0.0
	Yr	96	180	26	42	6	1	3	25	23	27	.233	.324	.328	87	-3	9	4	0	.954	1	O-42	-0.4
1974	SD-N	39	74	7	20	3	2	1	3	4	12	.270	.308	.405	103	-0	0	1	-1	1.000	1	O-12	-0.1
1975	SD-N	100	237	31	76	11	1	5	27	22	26	.321	.381	.439	135	11	4	2	0	.970	-1	O-51	0.9
1976	SD-N	43	67	9	15	3	0	0	8	4	15	.224	.268	.269	57	-4	0	0	0	.952	-1	O-11	-0.5
	NY-A	13	32	2	7	1	0	0	1	2	7	.219	.265	.250	52	-2	0	0	0	1.000	-1	/O-3,D-6	-0.3
1977	NY-A	1	5	1	3	0	0	0	2	0	0	.600	.600	.600	231	1	0	0	0	.667	-0	/O-1	0.1
Total	5	292	595	76	163	24	4	9	66	55	87	.274	.337	.373	105	3	13	7	-0	.962	-0	O-120/D-6	-0.3
■ **STU LOCKLIN**	Locklin, Stuart Carlton b: 7/22/28, Appleton, Wis. BL/TL, 6'1.5", 190 lbs. Deb: 6/23/55																						
1955	Cle-A	16	18	4	3	1	0	0	0	3	4	.167	.286	.222	37	-2	0	0	0	1.000	-3	/O-7	-0.4
1956	Cle-A	9	6	0	1	0	0	0	0	0	1	.167	.167	.167	-12	-1	0	0	0	1.000	-0	/O-1	-0.1
Total	2	25	24	4	4	1	0	0	0	3	5	.167	.259	.208	26	-3	0	0	0	1.000	-3	/O-8	-0.5
■ **WHITEY LOCKMAN**	Lockman, Carroll Walter b: 7/25/26, Lowell, N.C. BL/TR, 6'1", 175 lbs. Deb: 7/5/45 MC																						
1945	NY-N	32	129	16	44	9	0	3	18	13	10	.341	.410	.481	145	8	1			.961	-4	O-32	0.2

YEAR	TM/L	G	AB	R	H	2B	3B	HR	RBI	BB	SO	AVG	OBP	SLG	PRO+	BR/A	SB	CS	SBR	FA	FR	G/POS	TPR
1947	NY-N	2	2	0	1	0	0	0	1	0	0	.500	.500	.500	165	0	0			.000	0	H	0.0
1948	NY-N	146	584	117	167	24	10	18	59	68	63	.286	.361	.454	119	15	8			.987	7	*O-144	1.4
1949	NY-N	151	617	97	186	32	7	11	65	62	31	.301	.368	.429	113	12	12			.973	4	*O-151	0.9
1950	NY-N	129	532	72	157	28	5	6	52	42	29	.295	.349	.400	96	-3	1			.978	9	*O-128	0.1
1951	*NY-N	153	614	85	173	27	7	12	73	50	32	.282	.339	.407	99	-1	4	5	-2	.986	4	*1-119,O-34	-0.6
1952	NY-N★	154	606	99	176	17	4	13	58	67	52	.290	.363	.396	110	9	2	4	-2	.992	2	*1-154	0.4
1953	NY-N	150	607	85	179	22	4	9	61	52	36	.295	.351	.389	91	-7	3	4	-2	.989	7	*1-120,O-30	-0.8
1954	*NY-N	148	570	73	143	17	3	16	60	59	31	.251	.321	.375	80	-17	2	2	-1	.987	-8	*1-145/O-2	-3.2
1955	NY-N	147	576	76	157	19	0	15	49	39	34	.273	.322	.384	86	-12	3	3	-1	.983	-4	O-81,1-68	-2.4
1956	NY-N	48	169	13	46	7	1	1	10	16	17	.272	.335	.343	83	-4	0	2	-1	.960	-1	O-39/1-7	-0.8
	StL-N	70	193	14	48	0	2	0	10	18	8	.249	.313	.269	59	-11	2	2	-1	.955	-8	O-57/1-2	-2.3
	Yr	118	362	27	94	7	3	1	20	34	25	.260	.323	.304	70	-14	2	4	-2	.957	-8	O-96/1-9	-3.1
1957	NY-N	133	456	51	113	9	4	7	30	39	19	.248	.310	.331	73	-17	5	5	-2	.991	-6	*1-102,O-27	-3.3
1958	SF-N	92	122	15	29	5	0	2	7	13	8	.238	.311	.328	71	-5	0	0	0	1.000	-11	O-25,2-15/1-7	-1.6
1959	Bal-A	38	69	7	15	1	1	0	2	8	4	.217	.299	.261	56	-4	0	0	0	.992	-4	1-22/2-5,O-1	-0.8
	Cin-N	52	84	10	22	5	1	0	7	4	6	.262	.295	.345	68	-4	0	0	0	.971	0	1-20/2-6,3-1,O-1	-0.4
1960	Cin-N	21	10	6	2	0	0	1	1	2	3	.200	.385	.500	138	1	0	0	0	1.000	0	/1-5	0.1
Total	15	1666	5940	836	1658	222	49	114	563	552	383	.279	.342	.391	95	-40	43	27		.989	-9	1-771,O-752/2-26,3	-13.1

■ SKIP LOCKWOOD

Lockwood, Claude Edward b: 8/17/46, Boston, Mass. BR/TR, 6', 190 lbs. Deb: 4/23/65

YEAR	TM/L	G	AB	R	H	2B	3B	HR	RBI	BB	SO	AVG	OBP	SLG	PRO+	BR/A	SB	CS	SBR	FA	FR	G/POS	TPR
1965	KC-A	42	33	4	4	0	0	0	0	7	11	.121	.293	.121	23	-3	0	0	0	1.000	2	/3-7	-0.1
1969	Sea-A	6	7	0	0	0	0	0	0	0	2	.000	.000	.000	-99	-2	0	0	0	1.000	0	/P-6	0.0
1970	Mil-A	27	53	2	12	1	0	1	2	1	11	.226	.241	.302	48	-4	0	0	0	.970	-1	P-27	0.0
1971	Mil-A	36	62	2	5	1	0	1	4	5	20	.081	.149	.145	-17	-10	0	0	0	**1.000**	-3	P-33	0.0
1972	Mil-A	31	53	3	7	0	0	0	0	3	12	.132	.193	.132	-2	-7	0	1	-1	.958	-3	P-29	0.0
1973	Mil-A	37	0	0	0	0	0	0	0	0	0	—	—	—	—	0	0	0	0	.944	0	P-37	0.0
1974	Cal-A	37	0	0	0	0	0	0	0	0	0	—	—	—	—	0	0	0	0	1.000	-0	P-37	0.0
1975	NY-N	24	6	0	1	0	0	0	1	0	0	.167	.167	.167	-8	-1	0	0	0	.800	-1	P-24	0.0
1976	NY-N	56	18	2	6	1	0	0	2	2	3	.333	.400	.389	132	1	0	1	-1	.867	-0	P-56	0.0
1977	NY-N	63	15	1	3	0	0	0	1	0	1	.200	.200	.200	8	-2	0	0	0	.875	-2	P-63	0.0
1978	NY-N	57	11	1	2	1	0	1	1	0	5	.182	.182	.545	100	-0	0	0	0	.900	-2	P-57	0.0
1979	NY-N	28	2	0	0	0	0	0	0	0	1	.000	.000	.000	-99	-1	0	0	0	.800	-1	P-27	0.0
1980	Bos-A	24	0	0	0	0	0	0	0	0	0	—	—	—	—	0	0	0	0	1.000	-1	P-24	0.0
Total	13	468	260	15	40	4	0	3	11	18	66	.154	.214	.204	19	-28	0	2	-1	.947	-11	P-420/3-7	-0.1

■ MILO LOCKWOOD

Lockwood, Milo Hathaway b: 4/7/1858, Solon, Ohio d: 10/9/1897, Economy, Pa. 5'10", 160 lbs. Deb: 4/17/1884

YEAR	TM/L	G	AB	R	H	2B	3B	HR	RBI	BB	SO	AVG	OBP	SLG	PRO+	BR/A	SB	CS	SBR	FA	FR	G/POS	TPR
1884	Was-U	20	67	9	14	1	0	0		8		.209	.293	.224	61	-5				.773	2	O-11,P-11/3-3	-0.2

■ DARIO LODIGIANI

Lodigiani, Dario Antonio b: 6/6/16, San Francisco, Cal BR/TR, 5'8", 150 lbs. Deb: 4/18/38 C

YEAR	TM/L	G	AB	R	H	2B	3B	HR	RBI	BB	SO	AVG	OBP	SLG	PRO+	BR/A	SB	CS	SBR	FA	FR	G/POS	TPR
1938	Phi-A	93	325	36	91	15	1	6	44	34	25	.280	.361	.388	90	-5	3	0	1	.953	-6	2-80,3-13	-0.5
1939	Phi-A	121	393	46	102	22	4	6	44	42	18	.260	.337	.382	85	-9	2	0	1	.944	2	3-89,2-28	-0.4
1940	Phi-A	1	1	0	0	0	0	0	0	0	0	.000	.000	.000	-99	-0	0	0	0	.000	0	H	-0.0
1941	Chi-A	87	322	39	77	19	2	4	40	31	19	.239	.316	.348	76	-11	0	4	-2	.962	6	3-86	-0.5
1942	Chi-A	59	168	9	47	7	0	0	15	18	10	.280	.353	.321	92	-1	3	4	-2	.944	6	3-43/2-7	0.4
1946	Chi-A	44	155	12	38	8	0	0	13	16	14	.245	.324	.297	77	-4	4	0	1	.935	-5	3-44	-0.8
Total	6	405	1364	142	355	71	7	16	156	141	86	.260	.338	.358	84	-31	12	8	-1	.947	3	3-275,2-115	-1.8

■ PAUL LoDUCA

LoDuca, Paul Anthony b: 4/12/72, Brooklyn, N.Y. BR/TR, 5'10", 193 lbs. Deb: 6/21/98

YEAR	TM/L	G	AB	R	H	2B	3B	HR	RBI	BB	SO	AVG	OBP	SLG	PRO+	BR/A	SB	CS	SBR	FA	FR	G/POS	TPR
1998	LA-N	6	14	2	4	1	0	0	1	0	1	.286	.286	.357	71	-1	0	0	0	1.000	-1	/C-4	-0.1

■ GEORGE LOEPP

Loepp, George Herbert b: 9/11/01, Detroit, Mich. d: 9/4/67, Los Angeles, Cal. BR/TR, 5'11", 170 lbs. Deb: 8/29/28

YEAR	TM/L	G	AB	R	H	2B	3B	HR	RBI	BB	SO	AVG	OBP	SLG	PRO+	BR/A	SB	CS	SBR	FA	FR	G/POS	TPR
1928	Bos-A	15	51	6	9	3	1	0	3	5	12	.176	.250	.275	38	-5	0	0	0	.949	-0	O-14	-0.6
1930	Was-A	50	134	23	37	7	1	0	14	20	9	.276	.382	.343	85	-2	0	4	-2	.958	-5	O-48	-1.1
Total	2	65	185	29	46	10	2	0	17	25	21	.249	.347	.324	73	-7	0	4	-2	.956	-6	/O-62	-1.7

■ KENNY LOFTON

Lofton, Kenneth b: 5/31/67, E.Chicago, Ind. BL/TL, 6', 180 lbs. Deb: 9/14/91

YEAR	TM/L	G	AB	R	H	2B	3B	HR	RBI	BB	SO	AVG	OBP	SLG	PRO+	BR/A	SB	CS	SBR	FA	FR	G/POS	TPR
1991	Hou-N	20	74	9	15	1	0	0	0	5	19	.203	.253	.216	35	-6	2	1	0	.977	0	O-20	-0.7
1992	Cle-A	148	576	96	164	15	8	5	42	68	54	.285	.362	.365	106	6	**66**	12	**13**	.982	17	*O-143	3.3
1993	Cle-A	148	569	116	185	28	8	1	42	81	83	.325	.410	.408	121	21	**70**	14	**13**	.979	13	*O-146	4.1
1994	Cle-A★	112	459	105	**160**	32	9	12	57	52	56	.349	.417	.536	143	30	**60**	12	**11**	.993	8	*O-112	4.2
1995	*Cle-A★	118	481	93	149	22	**13**	7	53	40	49	.310	.364	.453	110	7	**54**	15	7	.970	1	*O-114/D-2	1.1
1996	*Cle-A★	154	662	132	210	35	4	14	67	61	82	.317	.375	.446	107	8	**75**	17	**12**	.975	10	*O-152	2.3
1997	*Atl-N†	122	493	90	164	20	6	5	48	64	83	.333	.411	.428	118	16	27	20	-4	.983	11	*O-122	2.0
1998	*Cle-A★	154	600	101	169	31	6	12	64	87	80	.282	.374	.413	101	3	54	10	10	.978	5	*O-154	1.4
Total	8	976	3914	742	1216	184	54	56	373	458	506	.311	.384	.428	113	85	408	101	62	.980	64	O-963/D-2	17.7

■ DICK LOFTUS

Loftus, Richard Joseph b: 3/7/01, Concord, Mass. d: 1/21/72, Concord, Mass. BL/TR, 6', 155 lbs. Deb: 4/20/24

YEAR	TM/L	G	AB	R	H	2B	3B	HR	RBI	BB	SO	AVG	OBP	SLG	PRO+	BR/A	SB	CS	SBR	FA	FR	G/POS	TPR
1924	Bro-N	46	81	18	22	6	0	0	8	7	2	.272	.330	.346	84	-2	1	0	0	1.000	-3	O-29/1-1	-0.6
1925	Bro-N	51	131	16	31	6	0	0	13	5	5	.237	.275	.282	44	-11	2	0	1	.977	1	O-38	-1.1
Total	2	97	212	34	53	12	0	0	21	12	7	.250	.296	.307	59	-13	3	0	1	.985	-3	/O-67,1-1	-1.7

■ TOM LOFTUS

Loftus, Thomas Joseph b: 11/15/1856, St.Louis, Mo. d: 4/16/10, Dubuque, Iowa BR , 168 lbs. Deb: 8/17/1877 M

YEAR	TM/L	G	AB	R	H	2B	3B	HR	RBI	BB	SO	AVG	OBP	SLG	PRO+	BR/A	SB	CS	SBR	FA	FR	G/POS	TPR
1877	StL-N	3	11	2	2	0	0	0	0	0	1	.182	.182	.182	16	-1				.778	2	/O-3	0.0
1883	StL-a	6	22	1	4	0	0	0		2		.182	.250	.182	39	-1				.882	0	/O-6	-0.1
Total	2	9	33	3	6	0	0	0	0	2	1	.182	.229	.182	32	-2				.846	2	/O-9	-0.1

■ JOHNNY LOGAN

Logan, John "Yatcha" b: 3/23/27, Endicott, N.Y. BR/TR, 5'11", 175 lbs. Deb: 4/17/51

YEAR	TM/L	G	AB	R	H	2B	3B	HR	RBI	BB	SO	AVG	OBP	SLG	PRO+	BR/A	SB	CS	SBR	FA	FR	G/POS	TPR
1951	Bos-N	62	169	14	37	7	1	0	16	18	13	.219	.298	.272	59	-10	0	0	0	.958	4	S-58	-0.2
1952	Bos-N	117	456	56	129	21	3	4	42	31	33	.283	.334	.368	98	-2	1	2	-1	**.972**	18	*S-117	2.4
1953	Mil-N	150	611	100	167	27	8	11	73	41	33	.273	.326	.398	93	-7	2	2	-1	**.975**	21	*S-150	2.3
1954	Mil-N	154	560	66	154	17	7	8	66	51	51	.275	.342	.373	92	-7	2	0	1	**.969**	14	*S-154	2.1
1955	Mil-N★	154	595	95	177	**37**	5	13	83	58	58	.297	.364	.442	118	16	3	3	-1	.963	8	*S-154	3.5
1956	Mil-N	148	545	69	153	27	5	15	46	46	49	.281	.342	.431	113	9	3	0	1	.968	3	*S-148	2.6
1957	*Mil-N☆	129	494	59	135	19	7	10	49	31	49	.273	.321	.401	100	-2	5	0	2	.960	24	*S-129	3.6
1958	*Mil-N★	145	530	54	120	20	0	11	53	40	57	.226	.287	.326	68	-26	1	2	-1	.959	10	*S-144	-0.4
1959	Mil-N☆	138	470	59	137	17	0	13	50	57	45	.291	.372	.411	118	13	1	3	-2	.975	-3	*S-138	2.0
1960	Mil-N	136	482	52	118	14	4	7	42	43	40	.245	.309	.334	82	-12	1	1	-0	.956	2	*S-136	0.0
1961	Mil-N	18	19	0	2	1	0	0	1	1	3	.105	.150	.158	-19	-3	0	0	0	1.000	-0	/S-2	-0.4
	Pit-N	27	52	5	12	4	0	0	5	4	8	.231	.286	.308	57	-3	0	0	0	1.000	0	/3-7,S-6	-0.2
	Yr	45	71	5	14	5	0	0	6	5	11	.197	.250	.268	38	-6	0	0	0	.964	0	/S-8,3-7	-0.6
1962	Pit-N	44	80	7	24	3	0	1	12	7	6	.300	.356	.375	96	-0	0	0	0	.980	2	3-19	0.2
1963	Pit-N	81	181	15	42	2	1	0	9	23	27	.232	.325	.254	69	-6	0	0	0	.920	2	S-44/3-4	-0.2
Total	13	1503	5244	651	1407	216	41	93	547	451	472	.268	.331	.378	95	-41	19	13	-2	.965	105	*S-1380/3-30	17.3

■ PETE LOHMAN

Lohman, George F. b: 10/21/1864, Washington Co., Minn. d: 11/21/28, Los Angeles, Cal. Deb: 5/11/1891

YEAR	TM/L	G	AB	R	H	2B	3B	HR	RBI	BB	SO	AVG	OBP	SLG	PRO+	BR/A	SB	CS	SBR	FA	FR	G/POS	TPR
1891	Was-a	32	109	18	21	1	4	1	11	16	17	.193	.302	.303	76	-3	1			.914	-3	C-21/O-8,3-4,S-1,2	-0.4

■ HOWARD LOHR

Lohr, Howard Sylvester b: 6/3/1892, Philadelphia, Pa. d: 6/9/77, Philadelphia, Pa. BR/TR, 6', 165 lbs. Deb: 6/17/14

YEAR	TM/L	G	AB	R	H	2B	3B	HR	RBI	BB	SO	AVG	OBP	SLG	PRO+	BR/A	SB	CS	SBR	FA	FR	G/POS	TPR
1914	Cin-N	18	47	6	10	1	1	0	7	0	8	.213	.213	.277	44	-3	2			.926	-3	O-17	-0.8
1916	Cle-A	3	7	0	1	0	0	0	1	0	1	.143	.143	.143	-13	-1	1			1.000	-1	/O-3	-0.2
Total	2	21	54	6	11	1	1	0	8	0	9	.204	.204	.259	36	-4	3			.933	-4	/O-20	-1.0

YEAR	TM/L	G	AB	R	H	2B	3B	HR	RBI	BB	SO	AVG	OBP	SLG	PRO+	BR/A	SB	CS	SBR	FA	FR	G/POS	TPR
■ JACK LOHRKE	Lohrke, Jack Wayne "Lucky" b: 2/25/24, Los Angeles, Cal. BR/TR, 6', 180 lbs. Deb: 4/18/47																						
1947	NY-N	112	329	44	79	12	4	11	35	46	29	.240	.337	.401	95	-3	3			.939	-2	*3-111	-0.4
1948	NY-N	97	280	35	70	15	1	5	31	30	30	.250	.323	.364	85	-6	3			.898	-2	3-50,2-36	-0.6
1949	NY-N	55	180	32	48	11	4	5	22	16	12	.267	.333	.456	110	2	3			.969	4	2-23,3-19,S-15	0.7
1950	NY-N	30	43	4	8	0	0	0	4	4	8	.186	.255	.186	18	-5	0			.958	0	3-16/2-1	-0.5
1951	*NY-N	23	40	3	8	0	0	1	3	10	2	.200	.360	.275	73	-1	0	0	0	.943	-1	3-17/S-1	-0.2
1952	Phi-N	25	29	4	6	0	0	0	1	4	3	.207	.303	.207	44	-2	0	0	0	1.000	1	/S-5,3-3,2-1	-0.1
1953	Phi-N	12	13	3	2	0	0	0	0	1	2	.154	.214	.154	-2	-2	0	0	0	.750	1	/2-2,S-2,3-1	-0.1
Total	7	354	914	125	221	38	9	22	96	111	86	.242	.327	.375	87	-17	9	0		.928	2	3-217/2-63,S-23	-1.2
■ ALBERTO LOIS	Lois, Alberto (b: Alberto Louis (Pie)) b: 5/6/56, Hato Mayor, D.R. BR/TR, 5'9", 175 lbs. Deb: 9/8/78																						
1978	Pit-N	3	4	0	1	0	1	0	0	0	1	.250	.250	.750	163	0	0	0	0	1.000	-0	/O-2	0.0
1979	Pit-N	11	0	6	0	0	0	0	0	0	0	—	—	—	—	0	1	1	-0	.000	0	/R	-0.1
Total	2	14	4	6	1	0	1	0	0	0	1	.250	.250	.750	163	0	1	1	-0	1.000	-0	/O-2	-0.1
■ RON LOLICH	Lolich, Ronald John b: 9/19/46, Portland, Ore. BR/TR, 6'1", 185 lbs. Deb: 7/18/71																						
1971	Chi-A	2	8	0	1	1	0	0	0	0	2	.125	.125	.250	4	-1	0	0	0	1.000	-1	/O-2	-0.2
1972	Cle-A	24	80	4	15	1	0	2	8	4	20	.188	.226	.275	47	-5	0	0	0	1.000	-1	O-22	-0.8
1973	Cle-A	61	140	16	32	7	0	2	15	7	27	.229	.265	.321	63	-7	0	2	-1	.909	-4	O-32,D-12	-1.4
Total	3	87	228	20	48	9	0	4	23	11	49	.211	.247	.303	56	-13	0	2	-1	.953	-5	/O-56,D-12	-2.4
■ SHERM LOLLAR	Lollar, John Sherman b: 8/23/24, Durham, Ark. d: 9/24/77, Springfield, Mo. BR/TR, 6'1", 185 lbs. Deb: 4/20/46 C																						
1946	Cle-A	28	62	7	15	6	0	1	9	5	9	.242	.299	.387	97	-1	0	1	-1	.990	-3	C-24	-0.4
1947	*NY-A	11	32	4	7	0	1	1	6	1	5	.219	.242	.375	71	-1	0	1	-1	1.000	1	/C-9	-0.1
1948	NY-A	22	38	0	8	0	0	0	4	1	6	.211	.231	.211	18	-4	0	0	0	.976	1	C-10	-0.3
1949	StL-A	109	284	28	74	9	1	8	49	32	22	.261	.340	.384	88	-6	0	1	-1	.988	-3	C-93	-0.5
1950	StL-A☆	126	396	55	111	22	3	13	65	64	25	.280	.391	.449	110	7	2	0	1	.981	-5	*C-109	0.7
1951	StL-A	98	310	44	78	21	0	8	44	43	26	.252	.350	.397	99	-0	1	0	0	**.995**	-2	C-85/3-1	0.2
1952	Chi-A	132	375	35	90	15	0	13	50	54	34	.240	.354	.384	104	3	1	0	0	.989	-2	*C-120	0.7
1953	Chi-A	113	334	46	96	19	0	8	54	47	29	.287	.388	.416	114	8	1	0	0	**.994**	-2	*C-107/1-1	1.1
1954	Chi-A☆	107	316	31	77	13	0	7	34	37	28	.244	.336	.351	85	-6	0	1	-1	.993	-3	C-93	-0.5
1955	Chi-A☆	138	426	67	111	13	1	16	61	68	34	.261	.375	.408	108	6	2	2	-1	.995	10	*C-136	2.0
1956	Chi-A★	136	450	55	132	28	2	11	75	53	34	.293	.387	.438	116	12	2	0	1	**.993**	4	*C-132	2.0
1957	Chi-A	101	351	33	90	11	2	11	70	35	24	.256	.346	.393	101	1	2	0	1	.998	-2	C-96	0.4
1958	Chi-A☆	127	421	53	115	16	0	20	84	57	37	.273	.370	.454	128	17	2	1	0	.987	2	*C-116	2.6
1959	*Chi-A★	140	505	63	134	22	3	22	84	55	49	.265	.348	.451	119	13	4	3	-1	.993	10	*C-122,1-24	2.8
1960	Chi-A★	129	421	43	106	23	0	7	46	42	39	.252	.331	.356	87	-7	2	0	1	**.995**	-2	*C-123	-0.2
1961	Chi-A	116	337	38	95	10	1	7	41	37	22	.282	.363	.380	100	1	0	0	0	**.998**	-10	*C-107	-0.3
1962	Chi-A	84	220	17	59	12	0	2	26	32	23	.268	.369	.350	95	-0	1	0	0	.991	-8	C-66	-0.6
1963	Chi-A	35	73	4	17	4	0	0	6	8	7	.233	.317	.288	72	-2	0	0	0	.981	-2	C-23/1-2	-0.4
Total	18	1752	5351	623	1415	244	14	155	808	671	453	.264	.359	.402	104	40	20	10	0	.992	-16	*C-1571/1-27,3-1	9.2
■ DOUG LOMAN	Loman, Douglas Edward b: 5/9/58, Bakersfield, Cal. BL/TL, 5'11", 185 lbs. Deb: 9/3/84																						
1984	Mil-A	23	76	13	21	4	0	2	12	15	7	.276	.402	.408	130	4	0	2	-1	.967	3	O-23	0.5
1985	Mil-A	24	66	10	14	3	2	0	7	1	12	.212	.224	.318	47	-5	0	0	0	1.000	1	O-20	-0.4
Total	2	47	142	23	35	7	2	2	19	16	19	.246	.327	.366	93	-1	0	2	-1	.981	4	/O-43	0.1
■ GEORGE LOMBARD	Lombard, George Paul b: 9/14/75, Atlanta, Ga. BL/TR, 6', 208 lbs. Deb: 9/4/98																						
1998	Atl-N	6	6	2	2	0	0	1	1	0	1	.333	.333	.833	185	1	1	0	0	1.000	-0	/O-2	0.1
■ ERNIE LOMBARDI	Lombardi, Ernesto Natali "Schnozz" or "Bocci" b: 4/6/08, Oakland, Cal. d: 9/26/77, Santa Cruz, Cal. BR/TR, 6'3", 230 lbs. Deb: 4/15/31 H																						
1931	Bro-N	73	182	20	54	7	1	4	23	12	12	.297	.340	.412	102	0	1			.984	3	C-50	0.6
1932	Cin-N	118	413	43	125	22	9	11	68	41	19	.303	.371	.479	131	18	0			.963	-11	*C-110	1.3
1933	Cin-N	107	350	30	99	21	1	4	47	16	17	.283	.322	.383	102	0	2			.972	-16	C-95	-1.0
1934	Cin-N	132	417	42	127	19	4	9	62	16	22	.305	.335	.434	107	3	0			.989	-3	*C-111	0.5
1935	Cin-N	120	332	36	114	23	3	12	64	16	6	.343	.379	.539	148	21	0			.983	-6	C-82	1.9
1936	Cin-N☆	121	387	42	129	23	2	12	68	19	16	.333	.375	.496	142	21	1			.962	-13	*C-105	1.2
1937	Cin-N☆	120	368	41	123	22	1	9	59	14	17	.334	.362	.473	132	14	1			.973	-18	C-90	0.2
1938	Cin-N★	129	489	60	167	30	1	19	95	40	14	**.342**	.391	.524	154	34	0			.985	-3	*C-123	3.8
1939	*Cin-N★	130	450	43	129	26	2	20	85	35	19	.287	.342	.487	120	11	0			.984	4	*C-120	2.1
1940	*Cin-N★	109	376	50	120	22	0	14	74	31	14	.319	.382	.489	137	19	0			.989	-4	*C-101	2.2
1941	Cin-N	117	398	33	105	12	1	10	60	36	14	.264	.325	.374	96	-2	1			.983	-1	*C-116	0.6
1942	Bos-N★	105	309	32	102	14	0	11	46	37	12	**.330**	.403	.482	162	24	1			.980	-16	C-85	1.5
1943	NY-N★	104	295	19	90	7	0	10	51	16	11	.305	.347	.431	123	8	1			.971	-14	C-73	-0.1
1944	NY-N	117	373	37	95	13	0	10	58	33	25	.255	.317	.370	93	-4	0			.968	-15	*C-100	-1.3
1945	NY-N†	115	368	46	113	7	1	19	70	43	11	.307	.387	.486	140	20	0			.983	2	C-96	2.7
1946	NY-N	88	238	19	69	4	1	12	39	18	24	.290	.347	.466	129	8	0			.978	1	C-63	1.3
1947	NY-N	48	110	8	31	5	0	4	21	7	9	.282	.325	.436	100	-0	0			.980	-3	C-24	-0.2
Total	17	1853	5855	601	1792	277	27	190	990	430	262	.306	.358	.460	126	195	8			.979	-113	*C-1544	17.3
■ PHIL LOMBARDI	Lombardi, Phillip Arden b: 2/20/63, Abilene, Tex. BR/TR, 6'2", 200 lbs. Deb: 4/26/86																						
1986	NY-A	20	36	6	10	3	0	2	6	4	7	.278	.366	.528	141	2	0	0	0	.867	-1	/O-8,C-3	0.1
1987	NY-A	5	8	0	1	0	0	0	0	0	2	.125	.125	.125	-34	-2	0	0	0	1.000	-0	/C-3	-0.2
1989	NY-N	18	48	4	11	1	0	1	3	5	8	.229	.302	.313	80	-1	0	0	0	.980	-1	C-16/1-1	-0.2
Total	3	43	92	10	22	4	0	3	9	9	17	.239	.314	.380	95	-1	0	0	0	.975	-2	/C-22,O-8,1-1	-0.3
■ STEVE LOMBARDOZZI	Lombardozzi, Stephen Paul b: 4/26/60, Malden, Mass. BR/TR, 6', 175 lbs. Deb: 7/12/85																						
1985	Min-A	28	54	10	20	4	1	0	6	6	6	.370	.433	.481	142	3	3	2	-0	.982	11	2-26	1.4
1986	Min-A	156	453	53	103	20	5	8	33	52	76	.227	.308	.347	76	-15	3	1	0	**.991**	-3	*2-155	-1.2
1987	*Min-A	136	432	51	103	19	3	8	38	33	66	.238	.299	.352	69	-19	5	1	1	.977	-1	*2-133	-1.2
1988	Min-A	103	287	34	60	15	2	3	27	35	48	.209	.299	.307	68	-12	2	5	-2	.986	-7	2-90,S-12/3-5	-1.8
1989	Hou-N	21	37	5	8	3	1	1	3	4	9	.216	.293	.432	109	0	0	0	0	.922	0	2-18/3-1	0.1
1990	Hou-N	2	1	0	0	0	0	0	0	1	1	.000	.500	.000	52	0	0	0	0	.000	0	/H	0.0
Total	6	446	1264	153	294	61	12	20	107	131	206	.233	.308	.347	76	-42	13	9	-2	.983	1	2-422/S-12,3-6	-2.7
■ WALTER LONERGAN	Lonergan, Walter E. b: 9/22/1885, Boston, Mass. d: 1/23/58, Lexington, Mass. BR/TR, 5'7", 156 lbs. Deb: 8/17/11																						
1911	Bos-A	10	26	2	7	0	0	0	1	1		.269	.296	.269	59	-1	1			.935	-1	/2-7,S-1,3-1	-0.2
■ LONG	Long Deb: 8/29/1888																						
1888	Lou-a	1	2	0	0	0	0	0	0	1		.000	.333	.000	11	-0	0			.000	-0	/O-1	0.0
■ DAN LONG	Long, Daniel W. b: 8/27/1867, Boston, Mass. d: 4/30/29, Sausalito, Cal. Deb: 8/27/1890																						
1890	Bal-a	21	77	19	12	0	0	0	2	14		.156	.301	.156	33	-6	16			.939	-1	O-21	-0.6
■ HERMAN LONG	Long, Herman C. "Germany" or "Flying Dutchman" b: 4/13/1866, Chicago, Ill. d: 9/17/09, Denver, Colo. BL/TR, 5'8.5", 160 lbs. Deb: 4/17/1889																						
1889	KC-a	136	574	137	158	32	6	3	60	64	63	.275	.358	.368	101	-0	89			.874	32	*S-128/2-8,O-1	3.3
1890	Bos-N	101	431	95	108	15	3	8	52	40	34	.251	.320	.355	90	-8	49			.898	11	*S-101	0.8
1891	Bos-N	139	577	129	163	21	12	9	76	80	51	.282	.377	.407	115	9	60			.902	15	*S-139	2.8
1892	*Bos-N	151	646	115	181	33	6	6	78	44	36	.280	.334	.378	105	1	57			.889	14	*S-141,O-12/3-1	1.9
1893	Bos-N	128	552	**149**	159	22	6	6	58	73	32	.288	.376	.382	94	-6	38			.883	16	*S-123/2-5	1.4
1894	Bos-N	104	475	136	154	28	11	12	79	35	17	.324	.375	.505	103	-2	24			.885	3	*S-98/O-5,2-3	0.5
1895	Bos-N	124	535	109	169	23	10	9	75	31	12	.316	.357	.447	99	-5	35			.891	-7	*S-122/2-2	-0.5

YEAR	TM/L	G	AB	R	H	2B	3B	HR	RBI	BB	SO	AVG	OBP	SLG	PRO+	BR/A	SB	CS	SBR	FA	FR	G/POS	TPR
1896	Bos-N	120	502	106	173	26	8	6	101	26	16	.345	.383	.464	116	9	38			.897	10	*S-120	1.9
1897	*Bos-N	107	450	89	145	32	7	3	69	23		.322	.358	.444	105	0	22			.905	-3	*S-107/O-1	0.0
1898	Bos-N	144	589	99	156	21	10	6	99	39		.265	.311	.365	89	-11	20			.923	1	*S-142/2-2	-0.3
1899	Bos-N	145	578	91	153	30	8	6	100	45		.265	.321	.375	83	-17	20			.929	-10	*S-143/1-2	-1.4
1900	Bos-N	125	486	80	127	19	4	**12**	66	44		.261	.325	.391	86	-12	26			.937	-6	*S-125	-0.8
1901	Bos-N	138	518	54	112	14	6	3	68	25		.216	.254	.284	51	-34	20			**.946**	-3	*S-138	-2.5
1902	Bos-N	120	439	40	101	11	0	2	44	31		.230	.282	.269	69	-16	24			**.946**	23	*S-107,2-13	1.5
1903	NY-A	22	80	6	15	3	0	0	8	2		.188	.207	.225	28	-7	3			.889	-5	S-22	-1.1
	Det-A	69	239	21	53	12	0	0	23	10		.222	.256	.272	60	-12	11			.879	0	S-38,2-31	-0.9
	Yr	91	319	27	68	15	0	0	31	12		.213	.244	.260	52	-19	14			.883	-4	S-60,2-31	-2.0
1904	Phi-N	1	4	0	1	0	0	0	0	0		.250	.250	.250	56	-0	0			.889	1	/2-1	0.1
Total	16	1874	7675	1456	2128	342	97	91	1056	612	261	.277	.335	.383	93	-109	536			.906	94	*S-1794/2-65,O13	6.7

■ **JIMMIE LONG** Long, James Albert b: 6/29/1898, Ft.Dodge, Iowa d: 9/14/70, Ft.Dodge, Iowa BR/TR, 5'11", 160 lbs. Deb: 9/12/22

YEAR	TM/L	G	AB	R	H	2B	3B	HR	RBI	BB	SO	AVG	OBP	SLG	PRO+	BR/A	SB	CS	SBR	FA	FR	G/POS	TPR
1922	Chi-A	3	3	0	0	0	0	0	0	1	0	.000	.250	.000	-30	-1	0	0	0	1.000	-1	/C-2	-0.1

■ **JIM LONG** Long, James M. b: 11/15/1862, Louisville, Ky. d: 12/12/32, Louisville, Ky. Deb: 8/9/1891

YEAR	TM/L	G	AB	R	H	2B	3B	HR	RBI	BB	SO	AVG	OBP	SLG	PRO+	BR/A	SB	CS	SBR	FA	FR	G/POS	TPR
1891	Lou-a	6	25	5	6	0	0	0	4	3	6	.240	.367	.240	75	-0	1			.857	1	/O-6	0.0
1893	Bal-N	55	226	31	48	8	1	2	25	16	27	.212	.276	.283	48	-18	23			.893	-1	O-55	-1.8
Total	2	61	251	36	54	8	1	2	29	19	33	.215	.286	.279	51	-18	24			.890	-0	/O-61	-1.8

■ **JEOFF LONG** Long, Jeoffrey Keith b: 10/9/41, Covington, Ky. BR/TR, 6'1", 200 lbs. Deb: 7/31/63

YEAR	TM/L	G	AB	R	H	2B	3B	HR	RBI	BB	SO	AVG	OBP	SLG	PRO+	BR/A	SB	CS	SBR	FA	FR	G/POS	TPR
1963	StL-N	5	5	0	1	0	0	0	0	0	1	.200	.200	.200	14	-1	0	0	0	.000	0	H	-0.1
1964	StL-N	28	43	5	10	1	0	1	4	6	18	.233	.340	.326	81	-1	0	0	0	.833	-2	/O-4,1-3	-0.3
	Chi-A	23	35	0	5	0	0	0	5	4	15	.143	.231	.143	7	-4	0	0	0	1.000	-1	/1-5,O-5	-0.5
Total	2	56	83	5	16	1	0	1	9	10	34	.193	.287	.241	48	-6	0	0	0	.750	-2	/O-9,1-8	-0.9

■ **DALE LONG** Long, Richard Dale b: 2/6/26, Springfield, Mo. d: 1/27/91, Palm Coast, Fla. BL/TL, 6'4", 210 lbs. Deb: 4/21/51 C

YEAR	TM/L	G	AB	R	H	2B	3B	HR	RBI	BB	SO	AVG	OBP	SLG	PRO+	BR/A	SB	CS	SBR	FA	FR	G/POS	TPR
1951	Pit-N	10	12	1	2	0	0	1	1	0	3	.167	.167	.417	50	-1	0	0	0	1.000	-0	/1-1	-0.1
	StL-A	34	105	11	25	5	1	2	11	10	22	.238	.310	.362	79	-3	0	0	0	.988	-1	1-28/O-1	-0.5
1955	Pit-N	131	419	59	122	19	**13**	16	79	48	72	.291	.365	.513	132	19	0	1	-1	.988	6	*1-119	1.7
1956	Pit-N★	148	517	64	136	20	7	27	91	54	85	.263	.333	.485	119	13	1	0	0	.982	-3	*1-138	0.1
1957	Pit-N	7	22	0	4	1	0	0	5	4	10	.182	.308	.227	48	-2	0	0	0	1.000	0	/1-7	-0.2
	Chi-N	123	397	55	121	19	0	21	62	52	63	.305	.387	.511	141	23	1	1	-0	.995	-1	*1-104	1.6
	Yr	130	419	55	125	20	0	21	67	56	73	.298	.382	.496	136	22	1	1	-0	.995	-1	*1-111	1.4
1958	Chi-N	142	480	68	130	26	4	20	75	66	64	.271	.361	.467	119	13	2	0	1	.992	-2	*1-137/C-2	0.4
1959	Chi-N	110	296	34	70	10	3	14	37	31	53	.236	.309	.432	96	-3	0	0	0	.985	-2	1-85	-0.9
1960	SF-N	37	54	4	9	0	0	3	6	7	7	.167	.262	.333	66	-3	0	0	0	1.000	0	1-10	-0.3
	*NY-A	26	41	6	15	3	1	3	10	5	6	.366	.435	.707	216	6	0	0	0	.988	-1	1-11	0.5
1961	Was-A	123	377	52	94	20	4	17	49	39	41	.249	.321	.459	107	3	0	0	0	.983	-5	1-95	-1.0
1962	Was-A	67	191	17	46	8	0	4	24	18	22	.241	.310	.346	77	-6	5	1	1	.996	-0	1-51	-0.9
	*NY-A	41	94	12	28	4	0	4	17	18	9	.298	.411	.468	140	6	1	0	0	.992	1	1-31	0.6
	Yr	108	285	29	74	12	0	8	41	36	31	.260	.345	.386	98	-0	6	1	1	.995	1	1-82	-0.3
1963	NY-A	14	15	1	3	0	0	0	0	1	3	.200	.250	.200	28	-1	0	0	0	.917	-1	/1-2	-0.2
Total	10	1013	3020	384	805	135	33	132	467	353	460	.267	.345	.464	116	65	10	3	1	.988	-7	1-819/C-2,O-1	0.8

■ **RYAN LONG** Long, Ryan Marcus b: 2/3/73, Houston, Tex. BR/TR, 6'2", 215 lbs. Deb: 7/16/97

YEAR	TM/L	G	AB	R	H	2B	3B	HR	RBI	BB	SO	AVG	OBP	SLG	PRO+	BR/A	SB	CS	SBR	FA	FR	G/POS	TPR
1997	KC-A	6	9	2	2	0	0	0	2	0	3	.222	.300	.222	38	-1	0	0	0	1.000	-1	/O-5,D-1	-0.1

■ **TOM LONG** Long, Thomas Augustus b: 6/1/1890, Mitchum, Ala. d: 6/15/72, Mobile, Ala. BR/TR, 5'10.5", 165 lbs. Deb: 9/11/11

YEAR	TM/L	G	AB	R	H	2B	3B	HR	RBI	BB	SO	AVG	OBP	SLG	PRO+	BR/A	SB	CS	SBR	FA	FR	G/POS	TPR
1911	Was-A	14	48	1	11	3	0	0	5	1		.229	.245	.292	50	-3	4			.875	-2	O-13	-0.6
1912	Was-A	1	1	0	0	0	0	0	0	0		.000	.000	.000	-99	-0	0			.000	0	H	0.0
1915	StL-N	140	507	61	149	21	**25**	2	61	31	50	.294	.339	.446	137	20	19	15	-3	.927	-4	*O-136	0.7
1916	StL-N	119	403	37	118	11	10	1	33	10	43	.293	.312	.377	112	4	21	14	-2	.945	-8	*O-106	-1.3
1917	StL-N	144	530	49	123	12	14	3	41	37	44	.232	.285	.325	89	-8	21			.919	-19	*O-137	-4.0
Total	5	418	1489	148	401	47	49	6	140	79	137	.269	.309	.379	110	13	65	29		.928	-33	O-392	-5.2

■ **TONY LONGMIRE** Longmire, Anthony Eugene b: 8/12/68, Vallejo, Cal. BL/TR, 6'1", 197 lbs. Deb: 9/3/93

YEAR	TM/L	G	AB	R	H	2B	3B	HR	RBI	BB	SO	AVG	OBP	SLG	PRO+	BR/A	SB	CS	SBR	FA	FR	G/POS	TPR
1993	*Phi-N	11	13	1	3	0	0	0	1	0	1	.231	.231	.231	24	-1	0	0	0	1.000	0	/O-2	-0.1
1994	Phi-N	69	139	10	33	11	0	0	17	10	27	.237	.293	.317	58	-9	2	1	0	.941	-2	O-32	-1.1
1995	Phi-N	59	104	21	37	7	0	3	19	11	19	.356	.422	.510	143	7	1	1	-0	1.000	0	O-23	0.6
Total	3	139	256	32	73	18	0	3	37	21	47	.285	.344	.391	91	-3	3	2	-0	.967	-2	/O-57	-0.6

■ **JOE LONNETT** Lonnett, Joseph Paul b: 2/7/27, Beaver Falls, Pa. BR/TR, 5'10", 180 lbs. Deb: 4/22/56 C

YEAR	TM/L	G	AB	R	H	2B	3B	HR	RBI	BB	SO	AVG	OBP	SLG	PRO+	BR/A	SB	CS	SBR	FA	FR	G/POS	TPR
1956	Phi-N	16	22	2	4	0	0	0	0	2	7	.182	.250	.182	19	-2	0	0	0	1.000	0	/C-7	-0.2
1957	Phi-N	67	160	12	27	5	0	5	15	22	39	.169	.273	.294	54	-10	0	0	0	.997	5	C-65	-0.3
1958	Phi-N	17	50	0	7	2	0	0	2	2	11	.140	.173	.180	-6	-8	0	0	0	.988	2	C-15	-0.5
1959	Phi-N	43	93	8	16	1	0	1	10	14	17	.172	.287	.215	36	-8	0	1	-1	.983	-6	C-43	-1.3
Total	4	143	325	22	54	8	0	6	27	40	74	.166	.262	.246	37	-29	0	1	-1	.992	1	C-130	-2.3

■ **BRUCE LOOK** Look, Bruce Michael b: 6/9/43, Lansing, Mich. BL/TR, 5'11", 183 lbs. Deb: 4/17/68 F

YEAR	TM/L	G	AB	R	H	2B	3B	HR	RBI	BB	SO	AVG	OBP	SLG	PRO+	BR/A	SB	CS	SBR	FA	FR	G/POS	TPR
1968	Min-A	59	118	7	29	4	0	0	9	20	24	.246	.355	.280	90	-1	0	1	-1	.996	2	C-41	0.3

■ **DEAN LOOK** Look, Dean Zachary b: 7/23/37, Lansing, Mich. BR/TR, 5'11", 185 lbs. Deb: 9/22/61 F

YEAR	TM/L	G	AB	R	H	2B	3B	HR	RBI	BB	SO	AVG	OBP	SLG	PRO+	BR/A	SB	CS	SBR	FA	FR	G/POS	TPR
1961	Chi-A	3	6	0	0	0	0	0	0	0	1	.000	.000	.000	-99	-2	0	0	0	1.000	-0	/O-1	-0.2

■ **STAN LOPATA** Lopata, Stanley Edward "Stash" b: 9/12/25, Delray, Mich. BR/TR, 6'2", 210 lbs. Deb: 9/19/48

YEAR	TM/L	G	AB	R	H	2B	3B	HR	RBI	BB	SO	AVG	OBP	SLG	PRO+	BR/A	SB	CS	SBR	FA	FR	G/POS	TPR
1948	Phi-N	6	15	2	2	1	0	0	2	0	4	.133	.133	.200	-11	-2	0			1.000	0	/C-4	-0.2
1949	Phi-N	83	240	31	65	9	2	8	27	21	44	.271	.330	.425	104	1	1			.973	-3	C-58	0.1
1950	*Phi-N	58	129	10	27	2	2	1	11	22	25	.209	.325	.279	61	-7	1			.974	1	C-51	-0.4
1951	Phi-N	3	5	0	0	0	0	0	0	0	0	.000	.000	.000	-99	-1	0	0	0	1.000	0	/C-1	-0.1
1952	Phi-N	57	179	25	49	9	1	4	27	36	33	.274	.395	.402	123	7	1	1	-0	.987	6	C-55	1.6
1953	Phi-N	81	234	34	56	12	3	8	31	28	39	.239	.321	.419	91	-3	3	1	0	.987	4	C-80	0.5
1954	Phi-N	86	259	42	75	14	5	14	42	33	37	.290	.372	.544	136	13	1	3	-2	.989	9	C-75/1-1	2.3
1955	Phi-N★	99	303	49	82	9	3	22	58	58	62	.271	.391	.538	146	21	4	1	1	.995	4	C-66,1-24	2.6
1956	Phi-N☆	146	535	96	143	33	7	32	95	75	93	.267	.358	.535	138	28	5	2	0	.982	-18	*C-102,1-39	1.3
1957	Phi-N	116	388	50	92	18	2	18	67	56	81	.237	.335	.433	108	4	2	2	-1	.988	-9	*C-108	-0.1
1958	Phi-N	86	258	36	64	9	0	9	33	60	63	.248	.394	.388	109	6	0	1	-1	.987	-9	C-80	0.1
1959	Mil-N	25	48	0	5	0	0	0	4	3	13	.104	.157	.104	-31	-9	0	0	0	1.000	-3	C-11/1-2	1.2
1960	Mil-N	7	8	0	1	0	0	0	0	1	3	.125	.222	.125	-2	-1	0	0	0	.944	1	/C-4	0.0
Total	13	853	2601	375	661	116	25	116	397	393	497	.254	.354	.452	115	56	18	11		.986	-15	C-695/1-66	6.5

■ **DAVEY LOPES** Lopes, David Earl b: 5/3/45, E.Providence, R.I. BR/TR, 5'9", 170 lbs. Deb: 9/22/72 C

YEAR	TM/L	G	AB	R	H	2B	3B	HR	RBI	BB	SO	AVG	OBP	SLG	PRO+	BR/A	SB	CS	SBR	FA	FR	G/POS	TPR
1972	LA-N	11	42	6	9	4	0	0	1	7	6	.214	.327	.310	84	-1	4	0	1	.964	-2	2-11	-0.1
1973	LA-N	142	535	77	147	13	5	6	37	62	77	.275	.355	.351	101	2	36	16	1	.984	-13	*2-135/O-5,S-2,3-1	-0.2
1974	*LA-N	145	530	95	141	26	3	10	35	66	71	.266	.352	.383	110	8	59	18	7	.965	-22	*2-143	0.0
1975	LA-N	155	618	108	162	24	6	8	41	91	93	.262	.359	.359	104	6	**77**	12	**16**	.979	-23	*2-137,O-24,S-14	0.6
1976	LA-N	117	427	72	103	17	7	4	20	56	49	.241	.335	.342	94	-2	**63**	10	**13**	.964	-20	*2-100,O-19	-0.4
1977	*LA-N	134	502	85	142	19	5	11	53	73	69	.283	.376	.406	110	10	47	12	7	.979	8	*2-130	3.4
1978	*LA-N★	151	587	93	163	25	4	17	58	71	70	.278	.356	.421	117	13	45	4	**11**	.974	3	*2-147/O-2	4.0
1979	LA-N★	153	582	109	154	20	6	28	73	97	88	.265	.373	.464	129	25	44	4	**11**	.981	-34	*2-152	1.2
1980	LA-N★	141	553	79	139	15	3	10	49	58	71	.251	.324	.344	88	-8	23	7	3	.980	-16	*2-140	-1.3

YEAR	TM/L	G	AB	R	H	2B	3B	HR	RBI	BB	SO	AVG	OBP	SLG	PRO+	BR/A	SB	CS	SBR	FA	FR	G/POS	TPR
1981	*LA-N★	58	214	35	44	2	0	5	17	22	35	.206	.289	.285	66	-10	20	2	5	.993	-4	2-55	-0.5
1982	Oak-A	128	450	58	109	19	3	11	42	40	51	.242	.305	.371	89	-8	28	12	1	.977	-19	*2-125/O-6	-1.9
1983	Oak-A	147	494	64	137	13	4	17	67	51	61	.277	.347	.423	118	12	22	4	4	.983	-38	*2-123,D-12/O-7,3-5	-1.7
1984	Oak-A	72	230	32	59	11	1	9	36	31	36	.257	.347	.430	122	7	12	0	4	.965	-8	O-42,2-17/3-5,D-9	0.2
	*Chi-N	16	17	5	4	1	0	0	0	6	5	.235	.435	.294	99	0	3	0	1	1.000	-2	/O-9,2-2	-0.1
1985	Chi-N	99	275	52	78	11	0	11	44	46	37	.284	.386	.444	118	8	47	4	12	.991	-12	O-79/3-4,2-1	0.6
1986	Chi-N	59	157	38	47	8	2	6	22	31	16	.299	.421	.490	140	10	17	6	2	.902	-4	3-32,O-22	0.6
	*Hou-N	37	98	11	23	2	1	1	13	12	9	.235	.318	.306	75	-3	8	2	1	1.000	5	O-19/3-5	0.2
	Yr	96	255	49	70	10	3	7	35	43	25	.275	.383	.420	117	7	25	8	3	1.000	1	O-41,3-37	0.8
1987	Hou-N	47	43	4	10	2	0	1	6	13	8	.233	.411	.349	108	1	2	1	0	.857	-1	/O-5	0.0
Total	16	1812	6354	1023	1671	232	50	155	614	833	852	.263	.351	.388	107	69	557	114	99	.977	-201	*2-1418,O-239/3DS	4.6

■ AL LOPEZ

Lopez, Alfonso Ramon b: 8/20/08, Tampa, Fla. BR/TR, 5'11", 165 lbs. Deb: 9/27/28 MH

YEAR	TM/L	G	AB	R	H	2B	3B	HR	RBI	BB	SO	AVG	OBP	SLG	PRO+	BR/A	SB	CS	SBR	FA	FR	G/POS	TPR
1928	Bro-N	3	12	0	0	0	0	0	0	0	0	.000	.000	.000	-99	-4	0			1.000	-2	/C-3	-0.5
1930	Bro-N	128	421	60	130	20	4	6	57	33	35	.309	.362	.418	89	-7	3			.983	5	*C-126	0.7
1931	Bro-N	111	360	38	97	13	4	0	40	28	33	.269	.324	.328	76	-12	1			.977	-8	*C-105	-1.2
1932	Bro-N	126	404	44	111	18	6	1	43	34	35	.275	.331	.356	87	-7	3			.976	-2	*C-125	-0.2
1933	Bro-N	126	372	39	112	11	4	3	41	21	39	.301	.338	.376	108	4	10			.991	18	*C-124/2-1	3.0
1934	Bro-N★	140	439	58	120	23	2	7	54	49	44	.273	.349	.383	101	1	2			.982	-7	*C-137/2-2,3-2	0.1
1935	Bro-N	128	379	50	95	12	4	3	39	35	36	.251	.316	.327	75	-13	2			.980	6	*C-126	-0.1
1936	Bos-N	128	426	46	103	12	5	7	50	41	41	.242	.311	.343	81	-12	1			.975	10	*C-127/1-1	0.4
1937	Bos-N	105	334	31	68	11	1	3	38	35	57	.204	.281	.269	55	-21	3			.984	8	*C-102	-0.7
1938	Bos-N	71	236	19	63	6	1	1	14	11	24	.267	.305	.314	78	-8	5			.989	3	C-71	-0.1
1939	Bos-N	131	412	32	104	22	1	8	49	40	45	.252	.319	.369	91	-6	1			.986	3	*C-129	0.3
1940	Bos-N	36	119	20	35	3	1	2	17	6	8	.294	.328	.387	102	-0	1			.987	2	C-36	0.4
	Pit-N	59	174	15	45	6	2	1	24	13	13	.259	.310	.333	78	-5	5			.992	4	C-59	0.2
	Yr	95	293	35	80	9	3	3	41	19	21	.273	.317	.355	87	-5	6			**.990**	6	C-95	0.6
1941	Pit-N★	114	317	33	84	9	1	5	43	31	23	.265	.330	.347	91	-3	0			.980	-0	*C-114	0.5
1942	Pit-N	103	289	17	74	8	2	1	26	34	17	.256	.338	.308	88	-3	0			**.995**	6	C-99	0.9
1943	Pit-N	118	372	40	98	9	4	1	39	44	25	.263	.341	.317	88	-5	2			**.991**	8	*C-116/3-1	1.2
1944	Pit-N	115	331	27	76	12	1	1	34	34	24	.230	.303	.281	62	-16	4			**.984**	4	*C-115	-0.6
1945	Pit-N	91	243	22	53	8	0	0	18	35	12	.218	.317	.251	57	-13	1			.992	8	C-91	-0.1
1946	Pit-N	56	150	13	46	2	0	1	12	23	14	.307	.399	.340	108	3	1			.985	1	C-56	0.7
1947	Cle-A	61	126	9	33	1	0	0	14	9	13	.262	.311	.270	64	-6	1	1	-0	1.000	0	C-57	-0.4
Total	19	1950	5916	613	1547	206	43	51	652	556	538	.261	.326	.337	83	-133	46	1		.985	66	*C-1918/3-3,2-3,1-1	4.5

■ ART LOPEZ

Lopez, Arturo (Rodriguez) b: 6/8/37, Mayaguez, P.R. BL/TL, 5'9", 170 lbs. Deb: 4/12/65

YEAR	TM/L	G	AB	R	H	2B	3B	HR	RBI	BB	SO	AVG	OBP	SLG	PRO+	BR/A	SB	CS	SBR	FA	FR	G/POS	TPR
1965	NY-A	38	49	5	7	0	0	0	0	1	6	.143	.160	.143	-13	-7	0	0	0	.958	-2	O-16	-1.0

■ CARLOS LOPEZ

Lopez, Carlos Antonio (Morales) b: 9/27/50, Mazatlan, Mexico BR/TR, 6', 190 lbs. Deb: 9/17/76

YEAR	TM/L	G	AB	R	H	2B	3B	HR	RBI	BB	SO	AVG	OBP	SLG	PRO+	BR/A	SB	CS	SBR	FA	FR	G/POS	TPR
1976	Cal-A	9	10	1	0	0	0	0	0	2	3	.000	.167	.000	-52	-2	2	0	1	1.000	-1	/O-4,D-1	-0.3
1977	Sea-A	99	297	39	84	18	1	8	34	14	61	.283	.322	.431	104	1	16	4	2	.972	3	O-90/D-2	0.3
1978	Bal-A	129	193	21	46	6	0	4	20	9	34	.238	.276	.332	75	-7	5	7	-3	.988	-25	*O-114/D-1	-3.8
Total	3	237	500	61	130	24	1	12	54	25	98	.260	.301	.384	90	-8	23	11	0	.979	-23	O-208/D-4	-3.8

■ HECTOR LOPEZ

Lopez, Hector Headley (Swainson) b: 7/9/29, Colon, Panama BR/TR, 5'11", 182 lbs. Deb: 5/12/55

YEAR	TM/L	G	AB	R	H	2B	3B	HR	RBI	BB	SO	AVG	OBP	SLG	PRO+	BR/A	SB	CS	SBR	FA	FR	G/POS	TPR
1955	KC-A	128	483	50	140	15	2	15	68	33	58	.290	.339	.422	103	0	1	4	-2	.936	15	3-93,2-36	1.6
1956	KC-A	151	561	91	153	27	3	18	69	63	73	.273	.349	.428	104	2	4	5	-2	.940	1	*3-121,O-20/2-8,S-4	0.3
1957	KC-A	121	391	51	115	19	4	11	35	41	66	.294	.361	.448	118	9	1	6	-3	.937	4	*3-111/2-4,O-3	1.3
1958	KC-A	151	564	84	147	28	4	17	73	49	61	.261	.322	.415	99	-1	2	2	-1	.974	6	2-96,3-55/S-1,O-1	1.2
1959	KC-A	35	135	22	38	10	3	6	24	8	23	.281	.326	.533	129	5	1	0	0	.933	-12	2-33	-0.4
	NY-A	112	406	60	115	16	2	16	69	28	54	.283	.339	.451	119	9	3	1	0	.926	-5	3-76,O-35	0.3
	Yr	147	541	82	153	26	5	22	93	36	77	.283	.336	.471	122	14	4	1	1	.926	-17	3-76,O-35,2-33	-0.1
1960	*NY-A	131	408	66	116	14	6	9	42	46	64	.284	.362	.414	116	9	1	1	-0	.976	-0	*O-106/2-5,3-1	0.4
1961	*NY-A	93	243	27	54	7	2	3	22	24	38	.222	.295	.305	64	-13	1	0	0	.977	1	O-72	-1.5
1962	*NY-A	106	335	45	92	19	1	6	48	33	53	.275	.340	.391	99	-0	0	1	-1	.984	3	O-84/2-1,3-1	-0.2
1963	*NY-A	130	433	54	108	13	4	14	52	35	71	.249	.306	.395	95	-3	1	2	-1	.957	-3	*O-124/2-1	-1.4
1964	*NY-A	127	285	34	74	9	3	10	34	24	54	.260	.319	.418	101	0	1	1	-0	.971	-13	*O-103/3-1	-1.7
1965	NY-A	111	283	25	74	12	2	7	39	26	61	.261	.326	.392	104	1	0	0	0	.942	-8	O-75/1-2	-1.0
1966	NY-A	54	117	14	25	4	1	4	16	8	20	.214	.270	.368	84	-3	0	0	0	.936	-2	O-29	-0.7
Total	12	1450	4644	623	1251	193	37	136	591	418	696	.269	.333	.415	104	17	16	23	-9	.967	-13	O-652,3-459,2/S1	-1.8

■ JAVY LOPEZ

Lopez, Javier (Torres) b: 11/5/70, Ponce, P.R. BR/TR, 6'3", 185 lbs. Deb: 9/18/92

YEAR	TM/L	G	AB	R	H	2B	3B	HR	RBI	BB	SO	AVG	OBP	SLG	PRO+	BR/A	SB	CS	SBR	FA	FR	G/POS	TPR
1992	*Atl-N	9	16	3	6	2	0	0	2	0	1	.375	.375	.500	137	1	0	0	0	1.000	1	/C-9	0.2
1993	Atl-N	8	16	1	6	1	1	1	2	0	2	.375	.412	.750	201	2	0	0	0	.975	2	/C-7	0.4
1994	Atl-N	80	277	27	68	9	0	13	35	17	61	.245	.301	.419	83	-7	0	2	-1	.995	2	C-75	-0.2
1995	*Atl-N	100	333	37	105	11	4	14	51	14	57	.315	.347	.498	116	7	0	1	-1	.988	2	C-93	1.3
1996	*Atl-N	138	489	56	138	19	1	23	69	28	84	.282	.325	.466	100	-1	1	6	-3	.994	19	*C-135	2.1
1997	*Atl-N★	123	414	52	122	28	1	23	68	40	82	.295	.364	.534	129	17	1	1	-0	.993	-3	*C-117	2.0
1998	*Atl-N★	133	489	73	139	21	1	34	106	30	85	.284	.333	.540	119	12	5	3	-0	**.995**	11	*C-128/D-1	3.2
Total	7	591	2034	249	584	91	8	108	333	129	372	.287	.336	.499	112	30	7	13	-6	.993	34	C-564/D-1	9.0

■ LUIS LOPEZ

Lopez, Luis Antonio b: 9/1/64, Brooklyn, N.Y. BR/TR, 6'1", 190 lbs. Deb: 9/14/90

YEAR	TM/L	G	AB	R	H	2B	3B	HR	RBI	BB	SO	AVG	OBP	SLG	PRO+	BR/A	SB	CS	SBR	FA	FR	G/POS	TPR
1990	LA-N	6	6	0	0	0	0	0	0	0	2	.000	.000	.000	-99	-2	0	0	0	1.000	-0	/1-1	-0.2
1991	Cle-A	35	82	7	18	4	1	0	7	4	7	.220	.264	.293	54	-5	0	0	0	1.000	-2	C-12,1-10/3-1,OD	-0.8
Total	2	41	88	7	18	4	1	0	7	4	9	.205	.247	.273	43	-7	0	0	0	.977	-2	/C-12,1-11,D-6,O3	-1.0

■ LUIS LOPEZ

Lopez, Luis Manuel (Santos) b: 9/4/70, Cidra, P.R. BB/TR, 5'11", 175 lbs. Deb: 9/7/93

YEAR	TM/L	G	AB	R	H	2B	3B	HR	RBI	BB	SO	AVG	OBP	SLG	PRO+	BR/A	SB	CS	SBR	FA	FR	G/POS	TPR
1993	SD-N	17	43	1	5	1	0	0	1	0	8	.116	.116	.140	-31	-8	0	0	0	.983	3	2-15	-0.5
1994	SD-N	77	235	29	65	16	1	2	20	15	39	.277	.328	.379	86	-5	3	2	-0	.941	2	S-43,2-29/3-5	0.1
1996	*SD-N	63	139	10	25	3	0	2	11	9	35	.180	.235	.245	28	-15	0	0	0	.981	-3	S-35,2-22/3-2	-1.4
1997	NY-N	78	178	19	48	12	1	1	19	12	42	.270	.330	.365	85	-4	2	4	-2	.966	7	S-45,2-20/3-4	0.4
1998	NY-N	117	266	37	67	13	2	2	22	20	60	.252	.314	.338	70	-12	2	2	-1	.975	-16	2-50,S-39,3-11,/O-9	-2.3
Total	5	352	861	96	210	45	4	7	73	56	184	.244	.299	.330	66	-43	7	8	-3	.955	-7	S-162,2-136/3-22,O	-3.7

■ MENDY LOPEZ

Lopez, Mendy (Aude) b: 10/15/74, Pimentel, D.R. BR/TR, 6'2", 190 lbs. Deb: 6/3/98

YEAR	TM/L	G	AB	R	H	2B	3B	HR	RBI	BB	SO	AVG	OBP	SLG	PRO+	BR/A	SB	CS	SBR	FA	FR	G/POS	TPR
1998	KC-A	74	206	18	50	10	2	1	15	12	40	.243	.288	.325	57	-13	5	2	0	.956	18	S-72/3-2	1.0

■ BRIS LORD

Lord, Bristol Robotham "The Human Eyeball" b: 9/21/1883, Upland, Pa. d: 11/13/64, Annapolis, Md. BR/TR, 5'9", 185 lbs. Deb: 4/21/05

YEAR	TM/L	G	AB	R	H	2B	3B	HR	RBI	BB	SO	AVG	OBP	SLG	PRO+	BR/A	SB	CS	SBR	FA	FR	G/POS	TPR
1905	*Phi-A	66	238	38	57	14	0	0	13	14		.239	.285	.298	83	-5	3			.963	1	O-61	-0.8
1906	Phi-A	118	434	50	101	13	7	1	44	27		.233	.281	.302	80	-10	12			.941	-2	*O-115	-2.0
1907	Phi-A	57	170	12	31	3	0	1	11	14		.182	.249	.218	48	-10	2			.951	-1	O-53/P-1	-1.4
1909	Cle-A	69	249	26	67	7	3	1	25	8		.269	.295	.333	94	-2	10			.992	6	O-67	0.1
1910	Cle-A	58	210	23	46	8	7	0	17	12		.219	.268	.324	84	-5	4			.958	4	O-56	-0.4
	*Phi-A	70	279	53	78	13	11	1	20	23		.280	.337	.416	137	11	6			.980	4	O-70	1.2
	Yr	128	489	76	124	21	18	1	37	35		.254	.307	.376	114	6	10			.972	8	*O-126	0.8
1911	*Phi-A	134	574	92	178	37	11	3	55	35		.310	.355	.429	120	14	15			.963	8	*O-132	1.4
1912	Phi-A	97	378	63	90	12	9	0	25	34		.238	.309	.317	82	-9	15			.942	-0	O-97	-1.4
1913	Bos-N	73	235	22	59	12	1	6	26	8	22	.251	.276	.387	86	-5	7			.914	-10	O-62	-1.9
Total	8	742	2767	379	707	119	49	13	236	175	22	.256	.304	.348	95	-22	74			.957	8	O-713/P-1	-5.2

YEAR	TM/L	G	AB	R	H	2B	3B	HR	RBI	BB	SO	AVG	OBP	SLG	PRO+	BR/A	SB	CS	SBR	FA	FR	G/POS	TPR
■ **HARRY LORD**	Lord, Harry Donald b: 3/8/1882, Porter, Me. d: 8/9/48, Westbrook, Maine BL/TR, 5'10.5", 165 lbs. Deb: 9/25/07 M																						
1907	Bos-A	10	38	4	6	1	0	0	3	1		.158	.179	.184	16	-4	1			.919	0	3-10	-0.3
1908	Bos-A	145	560	61	145	15	6	2	37	22		.259	.297	.318	97	-3	23			.902	-10	*3-144	-0.8
1909	Bos-A	136	534	86	166	12	7	0	31	20		.311	.345	.360	120	11	36			.929	-7	*3-134	0.9
1910	Bos-A	77	288	25	72	5	5	1	32	14		.250	.294	.313	88	-5	17			.927	-5	3-70/S-1	-0.9
	Chi-A	44	165	26	49	6	3	0	10	14		.297	.352	.370	131	6	17			.952	-11	3-44	-0.4
	Yr	121	453	51	121	11	8	1	42	28		.267	.315	.333	103	1	34			.935	-16	*3-114/S-1	-1.3
1911	Chi-A	141	561	103	180	18	18	3	61	32		.321	.364	.433	126	18	43			.941	-17	*3-138	0.3
1912	Chi-A	151	570	81	152	19	12	5	54	52		.267	.333	.368	104	2	28			.895	-27	*3-106,O-45	-2.6
1913	Chi-A	150	547	62	144	18	12	1	42	45	39	.263	.327	.346	98	-2	24			.924	-31	*3-150	-3.4
1914	Chi-A	21	69	8	13	1	1	1	3	5	3	.188	.243	.275	57	-4	2	2	-1	.933	-6	3-19/O-1	-1.1
1915	Buf-F	97	359	50	97	12	6	1	21	21	15	.270	.311	.345	83	-14	15			.946	-14	3-92/O-1,M	-2.6
Total	9	972	3691	506	1024	107	70	14	294	226	57	.277	.326	.356	104	6	206	2		.924	-127	3-907/O-47,S-1	-10.9
■ **CARLTON LORD**	Lord, William Carlton b: 1/7/1900, Philadelphia, Pa. d: 8/15/47, Chester, Pa. BR/TR, 5'11", 170 lbs. Deb: 7/12/23																						
1923	Phi-N	17	47	3	11	2	0	0	2	2	3	.234	.265	.277	39	-4	0	1	-1	.833	-1	3-14	-0.4
■ **MARK LORETTA**	Loretta, Mark David b: 8/14/71, Santa Monica, Cal. BR/TR, 6', 175 lbs. Deb: 9/4/95																						
1995	Mil-A	19	50	13	13	3	0	1	3	4	7	.260	.327	.380	79	-2	1	1	-0	.979	-1	S-13/2-4,D-1	-0.2
1996	Mil-A	73	154	20	43	3	0	1	13	14	15	.279	.339	.318	65	-8	2	1	0	.989	7	2-28,3-23,S-21	0.1
1997	Mil-A	132	418	56	120	17	5	5	47	47	60	.287	.362	.388	95	-2	5	5	-2	.980	10	2-63,S-44,1-19,3/D	1.0
1998	Mil-N	140	434	55	137	29	0	6	54	42	47	.316	.385	.424	109	7	9	6	-1	.992	5	1-70,S-56,3-22,2/O	1.2
Total	4	364	1056	144	313	52	5	13	117	107	129	.296	.367	.392	95	-4	17	13	-3	.976	20	S-134,2-108/13DO	2.1
■ **SCOTT LOUCKS**	Loucks, Scott Gregory b: 11/11/56, Anchorage, Alaska BR/TR, 6', 178 lbs. Deb: 9/1/80																						
1980	Hou-N	8	3	4	1	0	0	0	0	0	2	.333	.333	.333	94	-0	0	0	0	1.000	-2	/O-4	-0.2
1981	Hou-N	10	7	2	4	0	0	0	0	1	3	.571	.625	.571	254	2	1	0	0	1.000	-2	/O-5	0.0
1982	Hou-N	44	49	6	11	2	0	0	3	3	17	.224	.269	.265	54	-3	4	1	1	.978	-7	O-37	-1.0
1983	Hou-N	7	14	2	3	0	0	0	0	1	4	.214	.267	.214	37	-1	2	2	-1	1.000	0	/O-6	-0.2
1985	Pit-N	4	7	1	2	2	0	0	1	2	2	.286	.444	.571	184	1	0	0	0	1.000	-1	/O-4	0.0
Total	5	73	80	15	21	4	0	0	4	7	28	.262	.322	.313	83	-2	7	3	0	.985	-10	/O-56	-1.4
■ **BALDY LOUDEN**	Louden, William P. b: 8/27/1885, Piedmont, W.Va. d: 12/8/35, Piedmont, W.Va. BR/TR, 5'11", 175 lbs. Deb: 9/13/07																						
1907	NY-A	4	9	4	1	0	0	0	0	2		.111	.273	.111	21	-1	1			.750	1	/3-3	0.0
1912	Det-A	122	403	57	97	12	4	1	36	58		.241	.352	.298	89	-3	28			.951	23	2-87,3-26/S-5	1.8
1913	Det-A	76	191	28	46	4	5	0	23	24	22	.241	.344	.314	94	-1	6			.906	0	2-30,3-26/S-6,O-5	0.0
1914	Buf-F	126	431	73	135	11	4	6	63	52	41	.313	.391	.399	113	3	35			.931	-18	*S-115	-0.5
1915	Buf-F	141	469	67	132	18	5	4	48	64	45	.281	.372	.367	106	-1	30			.978	14	2-88,S-27,3-19	1.8
1916	Cin-N	134	439	38	96	16	4	1	32	54	54	.219	.313	.280	85	-6	12			**.968**	17	*2-108,S-23	1.8
Total	6	603	1942	267	507	61	22	12	202	254	162	.261	.355	.334	98	-7	112			.961	37	2-313,S-176/3-74,O	4.9
■ **CHARLIE LOUDENSLAGER**	Loudenslager, Charles Edward b: 5/21/1881, Baltimore, Md. d: 10/31/33, Baltimore, Md. TR , 5'9", 186 lbs. Deb: 4/15/04																						
1904	Bro-N	1	2	0	0	0	0	0	0	0		.000	.000	.000	-99	-0	0			1.000	-1	/2-1	-0.1
■ **BILL LOUGHLIN**	Loughlin, William H. b: Baltimore, Md. Deb: 5/9/1883																						
1883	Bal-a	1	5	0	2	0	0	0		0		.400	.400	.400	154	0				.000	-0	/O-1	0.0
■ **LOUGHRAN**	Loughran b: New York, N.Y. Deb: 6/6/1884																						
1884	NY-N	9	29	4	3	1	1	0	3	7	11	.103	.278	.207	54	-1				.857	-3	/C-9,O-1	-0.3
■ **TOM LOVELACE**	Lovelace, Thomas Rivers b: 10/19/1897, Wolfe City, Tex. d: 7/12/79, Dallas, Tex. BR/TR, 5'11", 170 lbs. Deb: 9/23/22																						
1922	Pit-N	1	1	0	0	0	0	0	0	0	0	.000	.000	.000	-99	-0	0	0	0	.000	0	H	0.0
■ **LEN LOVETT**	Lovett, Leonard Walker b: 7/17/1852, Lancaster Co., Pa d: 11/18/22, Newark, Del. BR/TR, Deb: 8/4/1873																						
1873	Res-n	1	5	1	2	0	0	0	1	0	0	.400	.400	.400	150	0	0	0	0	.500	-0	/P-1	0.0
1875	Cen-n	6	21	2	5	1	0	0	2	1	5	.238	.273	.286	103	0	0	0	0	.700	-1	/O-6	0.0
Total	2 n	7	26	3	7	1	0	0	3	1	5	.269	.296	.308	113	1	0	0	0	.700	-1	/O-6,P-1	0.0
■ **MEM LOVETT**	Lovett, Merritt Marwood b: 6/15/12, Chicago, Ill. d: 9/19/95, Downers Grove, Ill. BR/TR, 5'9.5", 165 lbs. Deb: 9/4/33																						
1933	Chi-A	1	1	0	0	0	0	0	0	0	0	.000	.000	.000	-99	-0	0	0	0	.000	0	H	0.0
■ **JAY LOVIGLIO**	Loviglio, John Paul b: 5/30/56, Freeport, N.Y. BR/TR, 5'9", 160 lbs. Deb: 9/2/80																						
1980	Phi-N	16	5	7	0	0	0	0	0	1	0	.000	.167	.000	-47	-1	1	2	-1	1.000	1	/2-1	-0.1
1981	Chi-A	14	15	5	4	0	0	0	2	1	1	.267	.313	.267	70	-1	2	2	-1	.786	3	/3-4,2-3,D-2	0.2
1982	Chi-A	15	31	5	6	0	0	0	2	1	4	.194	.219	.194	14	-4	2	1	0	.964	4	2-13/D-2	0.1
1983	Chi-N	1	1	0	0	0	0	0	0	0	1	.000	.000	.000	-95	-0	0	0	0	.000	0	/H	0.0
Total	4	46	52	17	10	0	0	0	4	3	6	.192	.236	.192	21	-5	5	5	-2	.971	9	/2-17,D-4,3-4	0.2
■ **JOE LOVITTO**	Lovitto, Joseph b: 1/6/51, San Pedro, Cal. BB/TR, 6', 185 lbs. Deb: 4/15/72																						
1972	Tex-A	117	330	23	74	9	1	1	19	37	54	.224	.306	.267	75	-10	13	11	-3	.976	4	*O-103	-1.5
1973	Tex-A	26	44	3	6	1	0	0	0	5	7	.136	.224	.159	10	-5	1	0	0	.898	1	3-20/O-3	-0.4
1974	Tex-A	113	283	27	63	9	3	2	26	25	36	.223	.286	.297	69	-11	6	8	-3	.972	-12	*O-107/1-5	-3.2
1975	Tex-A	50	106	17	22	3	0	1	8	13	16	.208	.294	.264	59	-5	2	2	-1	.985	-6	O-38/1-2,C-1,D-2	-1.4
Total	4	306	763	70	165	22	4	4	53	80	113	.216	.292	.271	67	-31	22	21	-6	.975	-14	O-251/3-20,1-7,DC	-6.5
■ **TOREY LOVULLO**	Lovullo, Salvatore Anthony b: 7/25/65, Santa Monica, Cal. BB/TR, 6', 180 lbs. Deb: 9/10/88																						
1988	Det-A	12	21	2	8	1	1	1	2	1	2	.381	.409	.667	204	3	0	0	0	1.000	-0	/2-9,3-3	0.3
1989	Det-A	29	87	8	10	2	0	1	4	14	20	.115	.238	.172	18	-9	0	0	0	1.000	-3	1-18,3-11	-1.4
1991	NY-A	22	51	0	9	2	0	0	2	5	7	.176	.250	.216	30	-5	0	0	0	.940	0	3-22	-0.5
1993	Cal-A	116	367	42	92	20	0	6	30	36	49	.251	.319	.354	78	-11	7	6	-2	.981	-24	2-91,3-14/S-9,O1D	-3.3
1994	Sea-A	36	72	9	16	5	0	2	7	9	13	.222	.309	.375	74	-3	1	0	0	1.000	3	2-20/3-5,D-2	0.1
1996	Oak-A	65	82	15	18	4	0	3	9	11	17	.220	.326	.378	79	-3	1	2	-1	1.000	2	1-42,3-11/2-2,SOD	-0.3
1998	Cle-A	6	19	1	4	1	0	0	1	1	2	.211	.250	.263	33	-2	0	0	0	.947	-1	/2-5,3-1	-0.3
Total	7	286	699	77	157	35	1	13	55	77	110	.225	.304	.333	70	-30	9	8	-2	.983	-24	2-127/3-67,1SDO	-5.4
■ **FLETCHER LOW**	Low, Fletcher b: 4/7/1893, Essex, Mass. d: 6/6/73, Hanover, N.H. BR/TR, 5'10.5", 175 lbs. Deb: 10/7/15																						
1915	Bos-N	1	4	1	1	0	1	0	1	0	0	.250	.250	.750	207	0	0			1.000	-0	/3-1	0.0
■ **CHARLIE LOWE**	Lowe, Charles b: Baltimore, Md. Deb: 9/28/1872																						
1872	Atl-n	7	31	1	5	0	0	0	3	0	2	.161	.161	.161	-0	-4	0	0	0	.820	-1	/2-7	-0.4
■ **DICK LOWE**	Lowe, Richard Alvern b: 1/28/1854, Evansville, Wis. d: 6/28/22, Janesville, Wis. Deb: 6/26/1884																						
1884	Det-N	1	3	0	1	0	0	0	0	0	1	.333	.333	.333	117	0				.125	-3	/C-1	-0.2
■ **BOBBY LOWE**	Lowe, Robert Lincoln "Link" b: 7/10/1868, Pittsburgh, Pa. d: 12/8/51, Detroit, Mich. BR/TR, 5'10", 150 lbs. Deb: 4/19/1890 M																						
1890	Bos-N	52	207	35	58	13	2	2	21	26	32	.280	.366	.391	112	3	15			.951	-9	S-24,O-15,3-12	-0.4
1891	Bos-N	125	497	92	129	19	5	6	74	53	54	.260	.342	.354	92	-7	43			.927	-6	*O-107,2-17/S-2,3P	-1.5
1892	*Bos-N	124	475	79	115	16	7	3	57	37	47	.242	.308	.324	84	-11	36			.928	13	O-90,3-14,S-13,2-10	0.0
1893	Bos-N	126	526	130	157	19	5	14	89	55	29	.298	.369	.433	105	0	22			.936	1	*2-121/S-5	0.4
1894	Bos-N	133	613	158	212	34	11	17	115	50	25	.346	.401	.520	112	8	23			.927	-6	*2-130/S-2,3-1	0.6
1895	Bos-N	99	412	101	122	12	7	7	62	40	16	.296	.370	.410	94	-5	24			.954	15	*2-99	1.2
1896	Bos-N	73	306	59	98	11	4	2	48	20	12	.320	.370	.402	98	-2	15			.965	25	2-73	2.3
1897	*Bos-N	123	499	87	154	24	8	5	106	32		.309	.355	.419	98	-4	16			.952	-4	*2-123	-0.1

YEAR	TM/L	G	AB	R	H	2B	3B	HR	RBI	BB	SO	AVG	OBP	SLG	PRO+	BR/A	SB	CS	SBR	FA	FR	G/POS	TPR
1898	Bos-N	147	559	65	152	11	7	4	94	29		.272	.311	.338	82	-15	12			.958	16	*2-145/S-2	1.0
1899	Bos-N	152	559	81	152	5	9	4	88	35		.272	.316	.335	72	-24	17			.954	3	*2-148/S-4	-1.1
1900	Bos-N	127	474	65	132	11	5	3	71	26		.278	.323	.342	74	-18	15			.951	-7	*2-127	-1.8
1901	Bos-N	129	491	47	125	11	1	3	47	17		.255	.284	.299	63	-24	22			.912	-5	*3-111,2-18	-2.7
1902	Chi-N	119	472	41	116	13	3	0	31	11		.246	.270	.286	74	-16	16			.957	26	*2-117/3-2	1.5
1903	Chi-N	32	105	14	28	5	3	0	15	4		.267	.319	.371	99	-0	5			.948	4	2-22/1-6,3-1	0.4
1904	Pit-N	1	1	0	0	0	0	0	0	0		.000	.000	.000	-97	-0	0			.000	0	H	0.0
	Det-A	140	506	47	105	14	6	0	40	17		.208	.236	.259	58	-25	15			.964	-0	*2-140,M	-2.4
1905	Det-A	58	181	17	35	7	2	0	9	13		.193	.255	.254	61	-8	3			.980	-3	O-24,3-22/2-6,S1	-1.2
1906	Det-A	41	145	11	30	3	0	1	12	4		.207	.233	.248	49	-9	3			.915	8	S-19,2-17/3-5	0.0
1907	Det-A	17	37	2	9	2	0	0	5	4		.243	.317	.297	93	-0	0			.870	-4	3-10/O-4,S-2	-0.5
Total	18	1818	7065	1131	1929	230	85	71	984	473	215	.273	.325	.360	86	-158	302			.951	68	*2-1313,O-240,3/S1P	-4.3

■ MIKE LOWELL Lowell, Michael Averett b: 2/24/74, San Juan, P.R. BR/TR, 6′4″, 195 lbs. Deb: 9/13/98

YEAR	TM/L	G	AB	R	H	2B	3B	HR	RBI	BB	SO	AVG	OBP	SLG	PRO+	BR/A	SB	CS	SBR	FA	FR	G/POS	TPR
1998	NY-A	8	15	1	4	0	0	0	0	0	1	.267	.267	.267	40	-1	0	0	0	1.000	-0	/3-7	-0.2

■ JOHN LOWENSTEIN Lowenstein, John Lee b: 1/27/47, Wolf Point, Mont. BL/TR, 6′, 175 lbs. Deb: 9/2/70

YEAR	TM/L	G	AB	R	H	2B	3B	HR	RBI	BB	SO	AVG	OBP	SLG	PRO+	BR/A	SB	CS	SBR	FA	FR	G/POS	TPR
1970	Cle-A	17	43	5	11	3	1	1	6	1	9	.256	.273	.442	89	-1	1	0	0	1.000	4	2-10/3-2,O-2,S-1	0.4
1971	Cle-A	58	140	15	26	5	0	4	9	16	28	.186	.269	.307	58	-8	1	5	-3	.986	-6	2-29,O-18/S-3	-1.6
1972	Cle-A	68	151	16	32	8	1	6	21	20	43	.212	.304	.397	104	1	2	4	-2	1.000	-2	O-58/1-2	-0.6
1973	Cle-A	98	305	42	89	16	1	6	40	23	41	.292	.341	.410	109	3	5	3	-0	.931	-10	O-51,2-25/3-8,1D	-0.7
1974	Cle-A	140	508	65	123	14	2	8	48	53	85	.242	.316	.325	85	-9	36	17	1	.986	-1	*O-100,3-28,1-12,/2	-1.5
1975	Cle-A	91	265	37	64	5	1	12	33	28	28	.242	.314	.404	102	0	15	10	-2	.983	-5	O-36,D-31/3-8,2-2	-0.9
1976	Cle-A	93	229	33	47	8	2	2	14	25	35	.205	.283	.284	67	-9	11	8	-2	.972	-5	O-61,D-11/1-9	-2.0
1977	Cle-A	81	149	24	36	6	1	4	12	21	29	.242	.335	.376	97	-0	1	8	-5	1.000	-3	O-39,D-19/1-1	-1.0
1978	Tex-A	77	176	28	39	8	3	5	21	37	29	.222	.363	.386	110	4	16	3	3	.926	-9	3-25,D-21,O-16	-0.4
1979	*Bal-A	97	197	33	50	8	2	11	34	30	37	.254	.355	.482	128	8	16	4	2	.992	-8	O-72/1-1,3-1,D-3	0.0
1980	Bal-A	104	196	38	61	8	0	4	27	32	29	.311	.408	.413	127	9	7	3	0	.992	-11	O-91/D-3	-0.4
1981	Bal-A	83	189	19	47	7	0	6	20	22	32	.249	.330	.381	105	1	7	6	-2	.990	-12	O-73/D-4	-1.5
1982	Bal-A	122	322	69	103	15	2	24	66	54	59	.320	.419	.602	177	35	7	6	-2	**1.000**	-7	*O-111	2.4
1983	*Bal-A	122	310	52	87	13	2	15	60	49	55	.281	.381	.481	138	17	2	1	0	.982	-11	*O-107/2-1,D-1	0.3
1984	Bal-A	105	270	34	64	13	0	8	28	33	54	.237	.322	.374	94	-2	1	0	0	.971	-8	O-67,D-22/1-2	-1.2
1985	Bal-A	12	26	0	2	0	0	0	2	2	3	.077	.143	.077	-39	-5	0	0	0	1.000	-0	/O-4,D-6	-0.5
Total	16	1368	3476	510	881	137	18	116	441	446	596	.253	.340	.403	108	43	128	78	-8	.984	-96	O-906,D-125/321S	-9.2

■ TERRELL LOWERY Lowery, Quenton Terrell b: 10/25/70, Oakland, Cal. BR/TR, 6′3″, 180 lbs. Deb: 9/13/97

YEAR	TM/L	G	AB	R	H	2B	3B	HR	RBI	BB	SO	AVG	OBP	SLG	PRO+	BR/A	SB	CS	SBR	FA	FR	G/POS	TPR
1997	Chi-N	9	14	2	4	0	0	0	0	3	3	.286	.412	.286	85	-0	1	0	0	1.000	1	/O-6	0.1
1998	Chi-N	24	15	2	3	1	0	0	1	3	7	.200	.333	.267	57	-1	0	0	0	.929	-7	O-22	-0.8
Total	2	33	29	4	7	1	0	0	1	6	10	.241	.371	.276	70	-1	1	0	0	.957	-7	/O-28	-0.7

■ PEANUTS LOWREY Lowrey, Harry Lee b: 8/27/18, Culver City, Cal. d: 7/2/86, Inglewood, Cal. BR/TR, 5′8.5″, 170 lbs. Deb: 4/14/42 C

YEAR	TM/L	G	AB	R	H	2B	3B	HR	RBI	BB	SO	AVG	OBP	SLG	PRO+	BR/A	SB	CS	SBR	FA	FR	G/POS	TPR
1942	Chi-N	27	58	4	11	0	0	1	4	4	4	.190	.242	.241	43	-4	0			.978	-1	O-19	-0.6
1943	Chi-N	130	480	59	140	25	12	1	63	35	24	.292	.340	.400	115	8	13			.982	14	*O-113,S-16/2-3	1.7
1945	*Chi-N	143	523	72	148	22	7	7	89	48	27	.283	.343	.392	106	4	11			.987	4	*O-138/S-2	0.0
1946	Chi-N★	144	540	75	139	24	5	4	54	56	22	.257	.328	.343	92	-6	10			.979	8	*O-126,3-20	-0.3
1947	Chi-N	115	448	56	126	17	5	5	37	38	26	.281	.339	.375	93	-5	2			.945	9	3-91,O-25/2-6	0.4
1948	Chi-N	129	435	47	128	12	3	2	54	34	31	.294	.347	.349	93	-4	2			.983	-1	*O-103/3-9,2-2,S-1	-1.1
1949	Chi-N	38	111	18	30	5	0	2	10	9	8	.270	.325	.369	88	-2	3			.966	-4	O-31/3-1	-0.8
	Cin-N	89	309	48	85	16	2	2	25	37	11	.275	.354	.359	91	-3	1			.995	8	O-78	0.1
	Yr	127	420	66	115	21	2	4	35	46	19	.274	.347	.362	90	-5	4			.989	4	*O-109/3-1	-0.7
1950	Cin-N	91	264	34	60	14	0	1	11	36	7	.227	.320	.292	62	-14	0			.987	1	O-72/2-1	-1.5
	StL-N	17	56	10	15	0	0	1	4	6	1	.268	.349	.321	74	-2	0			1.000	1	/2-6,3-5,O-4	-0.1
	Yr	108	320	44	75	14	0	2	15	42	8	.234	.325	.297	64	-16	0			.982	2	O-76/2-7,3-5	-1.6
1951	StL-N	114	370	52	112	19	5	5	40	35	12	.303	.366	.422	111	6	0	1	-1	.983	-1	O-85,3-11/2-3	0.1
1952	StL-N	132	374	48	107	18	2	1	48	34	13	.286	.352	.353	96	-1	3	2	-0	.978	-9	*O-106/3-6	-1.5
1953	StL-N	104	182	26	49	9	2	5	27	15	21	.269	.325	.423	93	-2	1	0	0	1.000	-10	O-38,2-10/3-1	-1.2
1954	StL-N	74	61	6	7	1	2	0	5	9	9	.115	.229	.197	12	-8	0	0	0	1.000	-5	O-12	-1.3
1955	Phi-N	54	106	9	20	4	0	0	8	7	10	.189	.239	.226	25	-11	2	0	1	.973	-6	O-28/2-2,1-1	-1.7
Total	13	1401	4317	564	1177	186	45	37	479	403	226	.273	.336	.362	92	-45	48	3		.983	9	O-978,3-144/2S1	-7.8

■ DWIGHT LOWRY Lowry, Dwight (b: Dwight Lowery) b: 10/23/57, Lumberton, N.C. d: 7/10/97, Jamestown, N.Y. BL/TR, 6′3″, 210 lbs. Deb: 4/3/84

YEAR	TM/L	G	AB	R	H	2B	3B	HR	RBI	BB	SO	AVG	OBP	SLG	PRO+	BR/A	SB	CS	SBR	FA	FR	G/POS	TPR
1984	Det-A	32	45	8	11	2	0	2	7	3	11	.244	.292	.422	95	-0	0	0	0	1.000	5	C-31	0.5
1986	Det-A	56	150	21	46	4	0	3	18	17	19	.307	.392	.393	115	4	0	0	0	.992	-1	C-55/1-1,O-1	0.6
1987	Det-A	13	25	0	5	2	0	0	1	0	6	.200	.200	.280	27	-3	0	0	0	1.000	1	C-12/1-1	-0.2
1988	Min-A	7	7	0	0	0	0	0	0	0	2	.000	.000	.000	-97	-2	0	0	0	1.000	2	/C-5	0.0
Total	4	108	227	29	62	8	0	5	26	20	38	.273	.343	.374	96	-1	0	0	0	.995	7	C-103/1-2,O-1	0.9

■ JOHN LOWRY Lowry, John D. b: Baltimore, Md. Deb: 6/12/1875

YEAR	TM/L	G	AB	R	H	2B	3B	HR	RBI	BB	SO	AVG	OBP	SLG	PRO+	BR/A	SB	CS	SBR	FA	FR	G/POS	TPR
1875	Was-n	6	22	2	3	0	0	0	0	1	0	.136	.174	.136	10	-2	0	1	-1	.727	-1	/O-6	-0.3

■ WILLIE LOZADO Lozado, William b: 5/12/59, New York, N.Y. BR/TR, 6′, 166 lbs. Deb: 7/16/84

YEAR	TM/L	G	AB	R	H	2B	3B	HR	RBI	BB	SO	AVG	OBP	SLG	PRO+	BR/A	SB	CS	SBR	FA	FR	G/POS	TPR
1984	Mil-A	43	107	15	29	8	2	1	20	12	23	.271	.345	.411	113	2	0	3	-2	.925	-1	3-36/S-6,2-1,D-1	-0.1

■ STEVE LUBRATICH Lubratich, Steven George b: 5/1/55, Oakland, Cal. BR/TR, 6′, 170 lbs. Deb: 9/27/81

YEAR	TM/L	G	AB	R	H	2B	3B	HR	RBI	BB	SO	AVG	OBP	SLG	PRO+	BR/A	SB	CS	SBR	FA	FR	G/POS	TPR
1981	Cal-A	7	21	2	3	1	0	0	1	0	2	.143	.143	.190	-5	-3	1	0	0	1.000	2	/3-6	-0.1
1983	Cal-A	57	156	12	34	9	0	0	7	4	17	.218	.237	.276	41	-13	0	1	-1	.949	16	S-23,3-22,2-14	0.5
Total	2	64	177	14	37	10	0	0	8	4	19	.209	.227	.266	36	-15	1	1	-0	.988	18	/3-28,S-23,2-14	0.4

■ HAL LUBY Luby, Hugh Max b: 6/13/13, Blackfoot, Idaho d: 5/4/86, Eugene, Ore. BR/TR, 5′10″, 185 lbs. Deb: 9/10/36

YEAR	TM/L	G	AB	R	H	2B	3B	HR	RBI	BB	SO	AVG	OBP	SLG	PRO+	BR/A	SB	CS	SBR	FA	FR	G/POS	TPR
1936	Phi-A	9	38	3	7	1	0	0	3	0	7	.184	.205	.211	3	-6	2	0	1	.880	-4	/2-9	-0.8
1944	NY-N	111	323	30	82	10	2	2	35	52	15	.254	.364	.316	93	-1	2			.943	16	3-65,2-45/1-1	1.9
Total	2	120	361	33	89	11	2	2	38	52	22	.247	.349	.305	83	-7	4	0		.954	12	/3-65,2-54,1-1	1.1

■ JOHNNY LUCADELLO Lucadello, John b: 2/22/19, Thurber, Tex. BB/TR, 5′11″, 160 lbs. Deb: 9/24/38

YEAR	TM/L	G	AB	R	H	2B	3B	HR	RBI	BB	SO	AVG	OBP	SLG	PRO+	BR/A	SB	CS	SBR	FA	FR	G/POS	TPR
1938	StL-A	7	20	1	3	1	0	0	0	0	0	.150	.150	.200	-13	-4	0	0	0	.909	-1	/3-6	-0.5
1939	StL-A	9	30	0	7	2	0	0	4	2	4	.233	.281	.300	48	-2	0	0	0	.912	-4	/2-7	-0.6
1940	StL-A	17	63	15	20	4	2	2	10	6	4	.317	.394	.540	137	3	1	0	0	.968	0	2-16	0.5
1941	StL-A	107	351	58	98	22	4	2	31	48	23	.279	.366	.382	95	-2	5	2	0	.962	-16	2-70,S-12/3-6,O-1	-1.1
1946	StL-A	87	210	21	52	7	1	1	15	36	20	.248	.358	.305	82	-4	0	1	-1	.942	-7	3-37,2-19	-1.0
1947	NY-A	12	12	0	1	0	0	0	0	1	5	.083	.154	.083	-33	-2	0	0	0	1.000	-2	/2-5	-0.4
Total	6	239	686	95	181	36	7	5	60	93	56	.264	.353	.359	88	-10	6	3	0	.965	-29	2-117/3-49,S-12,O-1	-3.1

■ RED LUCAS Lucas, Charles Frederick "The Nashville Narcissus" b: 4/28/02, Columbia, Tenn. d: 7/9/86, Nashville, Tenn. BL/TR, 5′9.5″, 170 lbs. Deb: 4/19/23

YEAR	TM/L	G	AB	R	H	2B	3B	HR	RBI	BB	SO	AVG	OBP	SLG	PRO+	BR/A	SB	CS	SBR	FA	FR	G/POS	TPR
1923	NY-N	3	2	0	0	0	0	0	0	0	1	.000	.000	.000	-99	-1	0	0	0	1.000	1	/P-3	0.0
1924	Bos-N	33	33	5	11	1	0	0	5	1	4	.333	.353	.364	96	-0	0	0	0	1.000	1	P-27/3-2	0.0
1925	Bos-N	6	20	1	3	0	0	0	2	2	4	.150	.227	.150	-2	-3	0	0	0	.968	0	/2-6	-0.3
1926	Cin-N	66	76	15	23	4	4	0	14	10	13	.303	.384	.461	130	3	0			1.000	-1	P-39/2-1	0.0
1927	Cin-N	80	150	14	47	5	2	0	28	12	10	.313	.368	.373	102	1	0			.983	-6	P-37/2-5,S-3,O-1	-0.4
1928	Cin-N	39	73	8	23	2	1	0	7	4	6	.315	.351	.370	90	-1	0			**1.000**	-0	P-27	0.0
1929	Cin-N	76	140	15	41	6	0	0	13	13	15	.293	.353	.336	75	-5	1			.949	0	P-32	0.0
1930	Cin-N	80	113	18	38	4	1	2	19	17	4	.336	.423	.442	115	4	0			**1.000**	-3	P-33	0.0
1931	Cin-N	97	153	15	43	4	0	0	17	12	9	.281	.333	.307	78	-4	0			.984	1	P-29	0.0

YEAR	TM/L	G	AB	R	H	2B	3B	HR	RBI	BB	SO	AVG	OBP	SLG	PRO+	BR/A	SB	CS	SBR	FA	FR	G/POS	TPR
1932	Cin-N	76	150	13	43	11	2	0	19	10	9	.287	.335	.387	97	-1	0			.973	-0	P-31	0.0
1933	Cin-N	75	122	14	35	6	1	1	15	12	6	.287	.356	.377	111	2	0			**1.000**	0	P-29	0.0
1934	Pit-N	68	105	11	23	5	1	0	8	6	16	.219	.261	.286	45	-8	1			.939	-3	P-29	0.0
1935	Pit-N	47	66	6	21	6	0	0	10	7	11	.318	.392	.409	112	1	0			.968	-1	P-20	0.0
1936	Pit-N	69	108	11	26	4	1	0	14	8	17	.241	.293	.296	58	-6	0			.976	-1	P-27	0.0
1937	Pit-N	59	82	8	22	3	0	0	17	7	6	.268	.326	.305	72	-3	0			1.000	-2	P-20	0.0
1938	Pit-N	33	46	1	5	0	0	0	2	3	2	.109	.163	.109	-24	-8	0			1.000	-1	P-13	0.0
Total	16	907	1439	155	404	61	13	3	190	124	133	.281	.340	.347	84	-29	2	0		.981	-14	P-396/2-12,S-3,3O	-0.7

■ FRED LUCAS

Lucas, Frederick Warrington "Fritz" b: 1/19/03, Vineland, N.J. d: 3/11/87, Cambridge, Md. BR/TR, 5'10", 165 lbs. Deb: 7/15/35

YEAR	TM/L	G	AB	R	H	2B	3B	HR	RBI	BB	SO	AVG	OBP	SLG	PRO+	BR/A	SB	CS	SBR	FA	FR	G/POS	TPR
1935	Phi-N	20	34	1	9	0	0	0	2	3	6	.265	.324	.265	55	-2	0			.944	-2	O-10	-0.4

■ JOHNNY LUCAS

Lucas, John Charles "Buster" b: 2/10/03, Glen Carbon, Ill. d: 10/31/70, Maryville, Ill. BR/TL, 5'10", 186 lbs. Deb: 4/15/31

YEAR	TM/L	G	AB	R	H	2B	3B	HR	RBI	BB	SO	AVG	OBP	SLG	PRO+	BR/A	SB	CS	SBR	FA	FR	G/POS	TPR
1931	Bos-A	3	2	0	0	0	0	0	0	0	1	.000	.000	.000	-99	-1	0	0	0	.000	-1	/O-2	-0.2
1932	Bos-A	1	1	0	0	0	0	0	0	0	0	.000	.000	.000	-99	-0	0	0	0	.000	0	H	0.0
Total	2	4	3	0	0	0	0	0	0	0	1	.000	.000	.000	-99	-1	0	0	0	—	-1	/O-2	-0.2

■ FRANK LUCE

Luce, Frank Edward b: 12/6/1896, Spencer, Ohio d: 2/3/42, Milwaukee, Wis. BL/TR, 5'11", 180 lbs. Deb: 9/17/23

YEAR	TM/L	G	AB	R	H	2B	3B	HR	RBI	BB	SO	AVG	OBP	SLG	PRO+	BR/A	SB	CS	SBR	FA	FR	G/POS	TPR
1923	Pit-N	9	12	2	6	0	0	0	3	2	2	.500	.571	.500	181	2	2	1	0	1.000	-2	/O-5	0.0

■ JOE LUCEY

Lucey, Joseph Earl "Scootch" b: 3/27/1897, Holyoke, Mass. d: 7/30/80, Holyoke, Mass. BR/TR, 6', 168 lbs. Deb: 7/6/20

YEAR	TM/L	G	AB	R	H	2B	3B	HR	RBI	BB	SO	AVG	OBP	SLG	PRO+	BR/A	SB	CS	SBR	FA	FR	G/POS	TPR
1920	NY-A	3	3	0	0	0	0	0	0	0	0	.000	.000	.000	-97	-1	0	0	0	1.000	0	/2-1,S-1	0.0
1925	Bos-A	10	15	0	2	0	0	0	0	0	4	.133	.133	.133	-32	-3	0	0	0	.889	-1	/P-7,S-3	-0.3
Total	2	13	18	0	2	0	0	0	0	0	4	.111	.111	.111	-43	-4	0	0	0	.778	-0	/P-7,S-4,2-1	-0.3

■ FRED LUDERUS

Luderus, Frederick William b: 9/12/1885, Milwaukee, Wis. d: 1/5/61, Three Lakes, Wis. BL/TR, 5'11.5", 185 lbs. Deb: 9/23/09

YEAR	TM/L	G	AB	R	H	2B	3B	HR	RBI	BB	SO	AVG	OBP	SLG	PRO+	BR/A	SB	CS	SBR	FA	FR	G/POS	TPR
1909	Chi-N	11	37	8	11	1	1	1	9	3		.297	.366	.459	152	2	0			.950	-2	1-11	0.1
1910	Chi-N	24	54	5	11	1	1	0	3	4	3	.204	.259	.259	52	-3	0			.975	-0	1-17	-0.4
	Phi-N	21	68	10	20	5	2	0	14	9	5	.294	.385	.426	132	3	2			.985	1	1-19	0.4
	Yr	45	122	15	31	6	3	0	17	13	8	.254	.331	.352	98	-0	2			.981	0	1-36	0.0
1911	Phi-N	146	551	69	166	24	11	16	99	40	76	.301	.353	.472	128	18	6			.985	-2	*1-146	1.6
1912	Phi-N	148	572	77	147	31	5	10	69	44	65	.257	.318	.381	85	-14	8			.990	10	*1-146	-0.6
1913	Phi-N	155	588	67	154	32	7	18	86	34	51	.262	.304	.432	105	0	5			.984	1	*1-155	0.0
1914	Phi-N	121	443	55	110	16	5	12	55	33	31	.248	.308	.388	100	-2	2			.975	1	*1-121	-0.3
1915	*Phi-N	141	499	55	157	36	7	7	62	42	36	.315	.376	.457	150	29	9	7	-2	.993	10	*1-141	3.7
1916	Phi-N	146	508	52	143	26	3	5	53	41	32	.281	.341	.374	115	9	8			.982	-2	*1-146	0.3
1917	Phi-N	154	522	57	136	24	4	5	72	65	35	.261	.349	.351	110	8	5			.991	5	*1-154	0.8
1918	Phi-N	125	468	54	135	23	2	5	67	42	33	.288	.351	.378	115	8	4			.988	7	*1-125	1.1
1919	Phi-N	138	509	60	149	30	6	5	49	54	48	.293	.365	.405	123	15	6			.985	10	*1-138	2.2
1920	Phi-N	16	32	1	5	2	0	0	4	3	6	.156	.229	.219	28	-3	0	1	-1	.983	0	/1-7	-0.4
Total	12	1346	4851	570	1344	251	54	84	642	414	421	.277	.340	.403	113	72	55	8		.986	39	*1-1326	8.5

■ BILL LUDWIG

Ludwig, William Lawrence b: 5/27/1882, Louisville, Ky. d: 9/5/47, Louisville, Ky. BR/TR, Deb: 4/16/08

YEAR	TM/L	G	AB	R	H	2B	3B	HR	RBI	BB	SO	AVG	OBP	SLG	PRO+	BR/A	SB	CS	SBR	FA	FR	G/POS	TPR
1908	StL-N	66	187	15	34	2	2	0	8	16		.182	.246	.214	50	-10	3			.952	-3	C-62	-1.0

■ ROY LUEBBE

Luebbe, Roy John b: 9/17/1900, Parkersburg, Iowa d: 8/21/85, Papillion, Neb. BB/TR, 6', 175 lbs. Deb: 8/22/25

YEAR	TM/L	G	AB	R	H	2B	3B	HR	RBI	BB	SO	AVG	OBP	SLG	PRO+	BR/A	SB	CS	SBR	FA	FR	G/POS	TPR
1925	NY-A	8	15	1	0	0	0	0	3	2	6	.000	.118	.000	-69	-4	0	0	0	1.000	1	/C-8	-0.2

■ HENRY LUFF

Luff, Henry T. b: 9/14/1856, Philadelphia, Pa. d: 10/11/16, Philadelphia, Pa. 5'11", 175 lbs. Deb: 4/21/1875

YEAR	TM/L	G	AB	R	H	2B	3B	HR	RBI	BB	SO	AVG	OBP	SLG	PRO+	BR/A	SB	CS	SBR	FA	FR	G/POS	TPR
1875	NH-n	38	166	15	45	10	3	2	18	0	5	.271	.271	.404	150	9	3	3	-1	.689	-4	3-30,P-10/O-4,S-1	0.2
1882	Det-N	3	11	1	3	2	0	0	1	0	0	.273	.273	.455	129	0				.667	-1	/2-3,O-1	-0.1
	Cin-a	28	120	16	28	2	2	0	6	2		.233	.246	.283	74	-4				.922	-2	1-27/O-1	-0.8
1883	Lou-a	6	23	1	4	0	0	0	2	0		.174	.174	.174	13	-2				.868	-1	/1-4,O-2	-0.3
1884	Phi-U	26	111	9	30	4	2	0		4		.270	.296	.342	100	-3				.733	-3	O-12/1-6,3-5,2-3	-0.6
	KC-U	5	19	0	1	0	0	0		1		.053	.100	.053	-60	-4				.444	-4	/3-4,O-4	-0.8
	Yr	31	130	9	31	4	2	0		5		.238	.267	.300	78	-7				.706	-7	O-16/3-9,1-6,2-3	-1.4
Total	3	68	284	27	66	8	4	0	9	7	0	.232	.251	.289	73	-13				.911	-12	/1-37,O-20,3-9,2-6	-2.6

■ ROB LUKACHYK

Lukachyk, Robert James b: 7/24/68, Jersey City, N.J. BL/TR, 6', 185 lbs. Deb: 7/5/96

YEAR	TM/L	G	AB	R	H	2B	3B	HR	RBI	BB	SO	AVG	OBP	SLG	PRO+	BR/A	SB	CS	SBR	FA	FR	G/POS	TPR
1996	Mon-N	2	2	0	0	0	0	0	0	0	1	.000	.000	.000	-98	-1	0	0	0	.000	0	/H	-0.1

■ MATT LUKE

Luke, Matthew Clifford b: 2/26/71, Long Beach, Cal. BL/TL, 6'5", 220 lbs. Deb: 4/3/96

YEAR	TM/L	G	AB	R	H	2B	3B	HR	RBI	BB	SO	AVG	OBP	SLG	PRO+	BR/A	SB	CS	SBR	FA	FR	G/POS	TPR
1996	NY-A	1	0	1	0	0	0	0	0	0	0	—	—	—	—	0	0	0	0	.000	0	/R	0.0
1998	LA-N	33	77	10	22	7	0	3	11	3	18	.286	.313	.494	113	1	0	0	0	.958	3	O-15,1-12	0.3
	Cle-A	2	2	0	0	0	0	0	0	0	0	.000	.000	.000	-97	-1	0	0	0	.000	0	/H	-0.1
	LA-N	69	160	24	34	5	1	9	23	14	42	.213	.280	.425	86	-4	2	1	0	1.000	3	O-48/1-6	-0.2
Total	2	105	239	35	56	12	1	12	34	17	60	.234	.288	.444	93	-4	2	1	0	.958	5	/O-63,1-18	0.0

■ EDDIE LUKON

Lukon, Edward Paul "Mongoose" b: 8/5/20, Burgettstown, Pa. d: 11/7/96, Canonsburg, Pa. BL/TL, 5'10", 168 lbs. Deb: 8/6/41

YEAR	TM/L	G	AB	R	H	2B	3B	HR	RBI	BB	SO	AVG	OBP	SLG	PRO+	BR/A	SB	CS	SBR	FA	FR	G/POS	TPR
1941	Cin-N	23	86	6	23	3	0	0	3	6	6	.267	.315	.302	74	-3	1			.980	2	O-22	-0.2
1945	Cin-N	2	8	1	1	0	0	0	0	0	1	.125	.125	.125	-31	-1	0			1.000	0	/O-2	-0.2
1946	Cin-N	102	312	31	78	8	8	12	34	26	29	.250	.310	.442	116	4	3			.985	2	O-83	0.3
1947	Cin-N	86	200	26	41	6	1	11	33	28	36	.205	.306	.410	89	-4	0			1.000	-2	O-55	-0.8
Total	4	213	606	64	143	17	9	23	70	60	72	.236	.307	.408	99	-4	4			.989	3	O-162	-0.9

■ MIKE LUM

Lum, Michael Ken-Wai b: 10/27/45, Honolulu, Hawaii BL/TL, 6', 180 lbs. Deb: 9/12/67 C

YEAR	TM/L	G	AB	R	H	2B	3B	HR	RBI	BB	SO	AVG	OBP	SLG	PRO+	BR/A	SB	CS	SBR	FA	FR	G/POS	TPR
1967	Atl-N	9	26	1	6	0	0	0	1	1	4	.231	.259	.231	42	-2	0	1	-1	.944	1	/O-6	-0.2
1968	Atl-N	122	232	22	52	7	3	3	21	14	35	.224	.280	.319	79	-6	3	5	-2	.976	-9	O-95	-2.4
1969	*Atl-N	121	168	20	45	8	0	1	22	16	18	.268	.332	.333	86	-3	0	0	0	.992	-8	O-89	-1.3
1970	Atl-N	123	291	25	74	17	2	7	28	17	43	.254	.307	.399	83	-8	3	2	-0	.988	-3	O-98	-1.5
1971	Atl-N	145	454	56	122	14	1	13	55	47	43	.269	.344	.390	101	1	0	3	-2	.990	9	*O-125/1-1	0.3
1972	Atl-N	123	369	40	84	14	2	9	38	50	52	.228	.325	.350	84	-7	1	4	-2	.976	4	*O-109/1-2	-1.0
1973	Atl-N	138	513	74	151	26	6	16	82	41	89	.294	.354	.462	116	10	2	5	-2	.991	-3	1-84,O-64	-0.4
1974	Atl-N	106	361	50	84	11	2	11	50	45	49	.233	.321	.366	88	-6	0	2	-1	.994	-5	1-60,O-50	-1.9
1975	Atl-N	124	364	32	83	8	2	8	36	39	38	.228	.303	.327	72	-14	2	4	-2	.992	-1	1-60,O-38	-2.3
1976	*Cin-N	84	136	15	31	5	1	3	20	22	24	.228	.340	.346	93	-1	0	1	-1	1.000	-6	O-38	-1.0
1977	Cin-N	81	125	14	20	1	0	5	16	9	33	.160	.222	.288	35	-12	2	0	1	1.000	-3	O-24/1-8	-1.5
1978	Cin-N	86	146	15	39	7	1	6	23	22	18	.267	.363	.452	126	5	0	0	0	.907	-1	O-43/1-7	0.3
1979	Atl-N	111	217	27	54	6	0	6	27	18	34	.249	.306	.359	75	-7	0	2	-1	.998	2	1-51/O-3	-0.9
1980	Atl-N	93	83	7	17	3	0	0	5	18	19	.205	.347	.241	65	-3	0	0	0	1.000	-3	O-19,1-10	-0.7
1981	Atl-N	10	11	1	1	0	0	0	0	2	2	.091	.231	.091	-6	-1	0	0	0	1.000	0	/O-1	-0.1
	Chi-N	41	58	5	14	1	0	2	7	5	5	.241	.313	.362	87	-1	0	0	0	.923	-4	O-14/1-1	-0.6
	Yr	51	69	6	15	1	0	2	7	7	7	.217	.299	.319	72	-2	0	0	0	.938	-4	O-15/1-1	-0.7
Total	15	1517	3554	404	877	128	20	90	431	366	506	.247	.322	.370	89	-54	13	29	-14	.986	-29	O-816,1-284	-15.2

■ HARRY LUMLEY

Lumley, Harry G "Judge" b: 9/29/1880, Forest City, Pa. d: 5/22/38, Binghamton, N.Y. BL/TL, 5'10", 183 lbs. Deb: 4/14/04 M

YEAR	TM/L	G	AB	R	H	2B	3B	HR	RBI	BB	SO	AVG	OBP	SLG	PRO+	BR/A	SB	CS	SBR	FA	FR	G/POS	TPR
1904	Bro-N	150	577	79	161	23	**18**	**9**	78	41		.279	.331	.428	137	23	30			.955	4	*O-150	1.9
1905	Bro-N	130	505	50	148	19	10	7	47	36		.293	.340	.412	134	19	22			.912	-1	*O-129	1.2
1906	Bro-N	133	484	72	157	23	12	9	61	48		.324	.386	**.477**	**184**	**45**	35			.949	1	*O-131	4.3
1907	Bro-N	127	454	47	121	23	11	9	66	31		.267	.316	.425	144	19	18			.959	-4	*O-118	1.2
1908	Bro-N	127	440	36	95	13	12	4	39	29		.216	.266	.327	93	-5	4			.955	-5	*O-116	-1.8
1909	Bro-N	55	172	13	43	8	3	0	14	16		.250	.314	.331	104	1	1			.948	2	O-52,M	0.0

YEAR	TM/L	G	AB	R	H	2B	3B	HR	RBI	BB	SO	AVG	OBP	SLG	PRO+	BR/A	SB	CS	SBR	FA	FR	G/POS	TPR
1910	Bro-N	8	21	3	3	0	0	0	0	3	6	.143	.280	.143	25	-2	0			.833	-1	/O-4	-0.3
Total	7	730	2653	300	728	109	66	38	305	204	6	.274	.328	.408	135	99	110			.946	-5	O-700	6.5
■ **JERRY LUMPE**	Lumpe, Jerry Dean b: 6/2/33, Lincoln, Mo. BL/TR, 6'2", 185 lbs. Deb: 4/17/56 C																						
1956	NY-A	20	62	12	16	3	0	0	4	5	11	.258	.313	.306	66	-3	1	1	-0	.916	3	S-17/3-1	0.1
1957	*NY-A	40	103	15	35	6	2	0	11	9	13	.340	.393	.437	128	4	2	2	-1	.956	-2	3-30/S-6	0.2
1958	*NY-A	81	232	34	59	8	4	3	32	23	21	.254	.324	.362	92	-3	1	2	-1	.943	4	3-65/S-5	0.1
1959	NY-A	18	45	2	10	0	0	0	2	6	7	.222	.314	.222	52	-3	0	0	0	1.000	2	3-12/S-4,2-1	0.0
	KC-A	108	403	47	98	11	5	3	28	41	32	.243	.313	.318	72	-15	2	1	0	.986	-10	2-61,S-56/3-4	-1.6
	Yr	126	448	49	108	11	5	3	30	47	39	.241	.313	.308	70	-17	2	1	0	.987	-8	2-62,S-60,3-16	-1.6
1960	KC-A	146	574	69	156	19	3	8	53	48	49	.272	.328	.357	85	-12	1	1	-0	.982	-7	*2-134,S-15	-0.5
1961	KC-A	148	569	81	167	29	9	3	54	48	39	.293	.351	.392	96	-3	1	0	0	.979	16	*2-147	2.9
1962	KC-A	156	641	89	193	34	10	10	83	44	38	.301	.346	.432	103	2	0	2	-1	.986	-4	*2-156/S-2	1.4
1963	KC-A	157	595	75	161	26	7	5	59	58	44	.271	.335	.363	91	-6	3	2	-0	.988	2	*2-155	1.1
1964	Det-A☆	158	624	75	160	21	6	6	46	50	61	.256	.314	.338	80	-16	2	1	0	.983	-21	*2-158	-2.6
1965	Det-A	145	502	72	129	15	3	4	39	56	34	.257	.335	.323	87	-7	7	0	2	.985	-18	*2-139	-1.2
1966	Det-A	113	385	30	89	14	3	1	26	24	44	.231	.276	.291	62	-19	0	3	-2	.991	-6	2-95	-2.2
1967	Det-A	81	177	19	41	4	0	4	17	16	18	.232	.295	.322	80	-4	0	0	0	.963	-3	2-54/3-6	-0.5
Total	12	1371	4912	620	1314	190	52	47	454	428	411	.268	.327	.356	87	-84	20	15	-3	.984	-44	*2-1100,3-118,S-105	-2.8
■ **DON LUND**	Lund, Donald Andrew b: 5/18/23, Detroit, Mich. BR/TR, 6', 200 lbs. Deb: 7/3/45 C																						
1945	Bro-N	4	3	0	0	0	0	0	0	1	1	.000	.250	.000	-27	-0	0			.000	0	H	0.0
1947	Bro-N	11	20	5	6	2	0	2	5	3	7	.300	.391	.700	178	2	0			1.000	-0	/O-5	0.2
1948	Bro-N	27	69	9	13	4	0	1	5	5	16	.188	.243	.290	42	-6	1			.977	-2	O-25	-0.8
	StL-A	63	161	21	40	7	4	3	25	10	17	.248	.305	.398	84	-5	0	0	0	1.000	-4	O-45	-1.1
1949	Det-A	2	2	0	0	0	0	0	0	0	1	.000	.000	.000	-99	-1	0	0	0	.000	0	H	-0.1
1952	Det-A	8	23	1	7	0	0	0	1	3	3	.304	.385	.304	93	-0	0	1	-1	1.000	0	/O-7	-0.1
1953	Det-A	131	421	51	108	21	4	9	47	39	65	.257	.323	.390	93	-5	3	3	-1	.980	1	*O-123	-0.9
1954	Det-A	35	54	4	7	2	0	0	3	4	3	.130	.190	.167	-2	-8	1	0	0	.971	-8	O-31	-1.6
Total	7	281	753	91	181	36	8	15	86	65	113	.240	.305	.369	81	-22	5	4		.983	-12	O-236	-4.4
■ **GORDY LUND**	Lund, Gordon Thomas b: 2/23/41, Iron Mountain, Mich BR/TR, 5'11", 170 lbs. Deb: 8/1/67																						
1967	Cle-A	3	8	1	2	1	0	0	0	0	2	.250	.250	.375	82	-0	0	0	0	.667	-2	/S-2	-0.2
1969	Sea-A	20	38	4	10	0	0	0	1	5	7	.263	.349	.263	75	-1	1	1	-0	.927	-1	S-17/2-1,3-1	-0.1
Total	2	23	46	5	12	1	0	0	1	5	9	.261	.333	.283	76	-1	1	1	-0	.902	-2	/S-19,3-1,2-1	-0.3
■ **TOM LUNDSTEDT**	Lundstedt, Thomas Robert b: 4/10/49, Davenport, Iowa BB/TR, 6'4", 195 lbs. Deb: 8/31/73																						
1973	Chi-N	4	5	0	0	0	0	0	0	0	1	.000	.000	.000	-93	-1	0	0	0	1.000	1	/C-4	-0.1
1974	Chi-N	22	32	1	3	0	0	0	0	5	7	.094	.216	.094	-11	-5	0	0	0	.987	2	C-22	-0.3
1975	Min-A	18	28	2	3	0	0	0	1	4	5	.107	.219	.107	-5	-4	0	0	0	1.000	1	C-14/D-2	-0.2
Total	3	44	65	3	6	0	0	0	1	9	13	.092	.203	.092	-15	-10	0	0	0	.993	4	/C-40,D-2	-0.6
■ **HARRY LUNTE**	Lunte, Harry August b: 9/15/1892, St.Louis, Mo. d: 7/27/65, St.Louis, Mo. BR/TR, 5'11.5", 165 lbs. Deb: 5/19/19																						
1919	Cle-A	26	77	2	15	2	0	0	2	1	7	.195	.215	.221	21	-8	0			.935	-2	S-24	-1.0
1920	*Cle-A	23	71	6	14	0	0	0	7	5	6	.197	.250	.197	19	-8	0	1	-1	.979	3	S-21/2-2	-0.4
Total	2	49	148	8	29	2	0	0	9	6	13	.196	.232	.209	20	-16	0	1		.955	1	/S-45,2-2	-1.4
■ **TONY LUPIEN**	Lupien, Ulysses John b: 4/23/17, Chelmsford, Mass. BL/TL, 5'10.5", 185 lbs. Deb: 9/12/40																						
1940	Bos-A	10	19	5	9	3	2	0	4	1	1	.474	.500	.842	232	4	0	0	0	1.000	-0	/1-8	0.3
1942	Bos-A	128	463	63	130	25	7	3	70	50	20	.281	.351	.384	103	2	10	12	-4	.992	-7	*1-121	-1.7
1943	Bos-A	154	608	65	155	21	9	4	47	54	23	.255	.317	.339	90	-8	16	9	-1	.993	4	*1-153	-1.5
1944	Phi-N	153	597	82	169	23	9	5	52	56	29	.283	.347	.377	107	6	18			.992	1	*1-151	-0.1
1945	Phi-N	15	54	1	17	1	0	0	3	6	0	.315	.383	.333	103	1	2			1.000	3	1-15	0.2
1948	Chi-A	154	617	69	152	19	3	6	54	74	38	.246	.327	.316	74	-23	11	7	-1	.993	-4	*1-154	-2.8
Total	6	614	2358	285	632	92	30	18	230	241	111	.268	.337	.355	94	-19	57	28		.993	-4	1-602	-5.6
■ **AL LUPLOW**	Luplow, Alvin David b: 3/13/39, Saginaw, Mich. BL/TR, 5'11", 180 lbs. Deb: 9/16/61																						
1961	Cle-A	5	18	0	1	0	0	0	0	2	6	.056	.150	.056	-44	-4	0	0	0	1.000	2	/O-5	-0.3
1962	Cle-A	97	318	54	88	15	3	14	45	36	44	.277	.361	.475	127	12	1	0	0	.960	-3	O-86	0.5
1963	Cle-A	100	295	34	69	6	2	7	27	33	62	.234	.317	.339	85	-6	4	4	-1	.994	3	O-85	-0.8
1964	Cle-A	19	18	1	2	0	0	0	1	1	8	.111	.158	.111	-24	-3	0	0	0	1.000	-1	/O-5	-0.4
1965	Cle-A	53	45	3	6	2	0	1	4	3	14	.133	.188	.244	22	-5	0	1	-1	1.000	-2	/O-6	-0.7
1966	NY-N	111	334	31	84	9	1	7	31	38	46	.251	.332	.347	91	-3	2	6	-3	.987	-12	*O-101	-2.4
1967	NY-N	41	112	11	23	1	0	3	9	8	19	.205	.264	.295	61	-6	0	0	0	.966	-4	O-33	-1.2
	Pit-N	55	103	13	19	1	0	1	8	6	14	.184	.236	.223	32	-9	1	0	0	.961	3	O-25	-0.8
	Yr	96	215	24	42	2	0	4	17	14	33	.195	.251	.260	47	-15	1	0	0	.963	-1	O-58	-2.0
Total	7	481	1243	147	292	34	6	33	125	127	213	.235	.312	.352	85	-23	8	11	-4	.977	-14	O-346	-6.1
■ **SCOTT LUSADER**	Lusader, Scott Edward b: 9/30/64, Chicago, Ill. BL/TL, 5'10", 165 lbs. Deb: 9/1/87																						
1987	Det-A	23	47	8	15	3	1	1	8	5	7	.319	.385	.489	135	2	1	0	0	.967	-5	O-22/D-1	-0.2
1988	Det-A	16	16	3	1	0	0	1	3	1	4	.063	.118	.250	-0	-2	0	0	0	1.000	-1	/O-4,D-6	-0.4
1989	Det-A	40	103	15	26	4	0	1	8	9	21	.252	.313	.320	81	-3	3	0	1	.933	-6	O-33/D-1	-0.8
1990	Det-A	45	87	13	21	2	0	2	16	12	8	.241	.333	.333	86	-1	0	0	0	.982	-7	O-42/D-2	-0.9
1991	NY-A	11	7	2	1	0	0	0	1	1	3	.143	.250	.143	12	-1	0	1	-1	1.000	-1	/O-4,D-1	-0.3
Total	5	135	260	41	64	9	1	5	36	28	43	.246	.319	.346	86	-5	4	1	1	.961	-20	O-105/D-11	-2.6
■ **ERNIE LUSH**	Lush, Ernest Benjamin b: 10/31/1884, Bridgeport, Conn. d: 2/26/37, Detroit, Mich. BR/TL, Deb: 7/20/10 F																						
1910	StL-N	1	4	0	0	0	0	0	0	1	1	.000	.200	.000	-42	-1	0			1.000	-0	/O-1	-0.1
■ **JOHNNY LUSH**	Lush, John Charles b: 10/8/1885, Williamsport, Pa. d: 11/18/46, Beverly Hills, Cal BL/TL, 5'9.5", 165 lbs. Deb: 4/22/04																						
1904	Phi-N	106	369	39	102	22	3	2	42	27		.276	.336	.369	122	9	12			.950	-10	1-62,O-33/P-7	-0.5
1905	Phi-N	6	16	3	5	0	0	0	1	1		.313	.389	.313	114	0	0			.667	-1	/O-3,P-2	-0.1
1906	Phi-N	76	212	28	56	7	1	0	15	14		.264	.310	.307	92	-2	6			.907	5	P-37,O-22/1-2	0.0
1907	Phi-N	17	40	5	8	1	1	0	5	1		.200	.220	.275	56	-2	1			1.000	0	/P-8,O-4	-0.2
	StL-N	27	82	6	23	2	3	0	5	5		.280	.322	.378	123	2	4			.917	-3	P-20/O-7	-0.3
	Yr	44	122	11	31	3	4	0	10	6		.254	.289	.344	101	-0	5			.941	-3	P-28,O-11	-0.5
1908	StL-N	45	89	7	15	2	0	0	2	7		.169	.229	.191	36	-6	1			.926	0	P-38	0.0
1909	StL-N	45	92	11	22	5	0	0	14	6		.239	.293	.293	87	-2	2			.945	-1	P-34/O-3	-0.1
1910	StL-N	47	93	8	21	1	3	0	10	8	11	.226	.287	.301	74	-3	2			.928	-2	P-36	0.0
Total	7	369	993	107	252	40	11	2	94	69	11	.254	.307	.322	98	-4	28			.926	-12	P-182/O-72,1-64	-1.2
■ **BILLY LUSH**	Lush, William Lucas b: 11/10/1873, Bridgeport, Conn. d: 8/28/51, Hawthorne, N.Y. BB/TR, 5'7", 165 lbs. Deb: 9/3/1895 F																						
1895	Was-N	5	18	2	6	0	0	0	2	2	1	.333	.400	.333	92	-0	0			.692	-1	/O-5	-0.1
1896	Was-N	97	352	74	87	9	11	4	45	66	49	.247	.369	.369	95	-1	28			.885	-2	*O-91/2-3	-0.9
1897	Was-N	3	12	1	0	0	0	0	0	2		.000	.143	.000	-61	-3	0			1.000	1	/O-3	-0.2
1901	Bos-N	7	27	2	5	1	1	0	3	3		.185	.267	.296	58	-2	0			.960	3	/O-7	0.0
1902	Bos-N	120	413	68	92	8	1	2	19	76		.223	.346	.262	87	-2	30			.952	11	*O-116/3-1	0.1
1903	Det-A	119	423	71	116	18	14	1	33	70		.274	.379	.390	135	21	14			.968	12	*O-101,3-12/2-3,S-3	2.8
1904	Cle-A	138	477	76	123	13	8	1	50	72		.258	.359	.325	118	13	12			.959	3	*O-138	0.9
Total	7	489	1722	294	429	49	35	8	152	291	50	.249	.360	.332	107	27	84			.943	25	O-461/3-13,2-6,S-3	2.6

YEAR	TM/L	G	AB	R	H	2B	3B	HR	RBI	BB	SO	AVG	OBP	SLG	PRO+	BR/A	SB	CS	SBR	FA	FR	G/POS	TPR
■ CHARLIE LUSKEY Luskey, Charles Melton b: 4/6/1876, Washington, D.C. d: 12/20/62, Bethesda, Md. BR/TR, 5'7", 165 lbs. Deb: 9/12/01																							
1901	Was-A	11	41	8	8	3	1	0	3	2		.195	.233	.317	52	-3	0			.818	-1	/O-8,C-3	-0.4
■ LUKE LUTENBERG Lutenberg, Charles William b: 10/4/1864, Quincy, Ill. d: 12/24/38, Quincy, Ill. BR/TR, 6'2", 225 lbs. Deb: 7/7/1894																							
1894	Lou-N	69	250	42	48	10	4	0	23	23	21	.192	.284	.264	35	-27	4			.977	1	1-67/2-2	-1.9
■ LYLE LUTTRELL Luttrell, Lyle Kenneth b: 2/22/30, Bloomington, Ill. d: 7/11/84, Chattanooga, Tenn BR/TR, 6', 180 lbs. Deb: 5/15/56																							
1956	Was-A	38	122	17	23	5	3	2	9	8	19	.189	.256	.328	53	-9	5	1	1	.939	-7	S-37	-1.1
1957	Was-A	19	45	4	9	4	0	0	5	3	8	.200	.250	.289	47	-3	0	0	0	.927	-5	S-17	-0.8
Total	2	57	167	21	32	9	3	2	14	11	27	.192	.254	.317	52	-12	5	1	1	.936	-12	/S-54	-1.9
■ RED LUTZ Lutz, Louis William b: 12/17/1898, Cincinnati, Ohio d: 2/22/84, Cincinnati, Ohio BR/TR, 5'10", 170 lbs. Deb: 5/31/22																							
1922	Cin-N	1	1	0	1	1	0	0	0	0	0	1.000	1.000	2.000	669	1	0	0	0	.000	0	/C-1	0.1
■ JOE LUTZ Lutz, Rollin Joseph b: 2/18/25, Keokuk, Iowa BL/TL, 6', 195 lbs. Deb: 4/17/51 C																							
1951	StL-A	14	36	7	6	0	1	0	2	6	9	.167	.286	.222	38	-3	0	0	0	1.000	-1	1-11	-0.5
■ RUBE LUTZKE Lutzke, Walter John b: 11/17/1897, Milwaukee, Wis. d: 3/6/38, Granville, Wis. BR/TR, 5'11", 175 lbs. Deb: 4/18/23																							
1923	Cle-A	143	511	71	131	20	6	3	65	59	57	.256	.338	.337	78	-16	9	6	-1	.939	17	*3-141/S-2	1.3
1924	Cle-A	106	341	37	83	18	3	0	42	38	46	.243	.328	.314	65	-17	4	0	1	.947	19	*3-103/2-3	1.0
1925	Cle-A	81	238	31	52	9	0	1	16	26	29	.218	.295	.269	44	-20	2	4	-2	.936	-0	3-69,2-10	-1.7
1926	Cle-A	142	475	42	124	28	6	0	59	34	35	.261	.313	.345	71	-21	6	3	0	.960	-1	*3-142	-1.2
1927	Cle-A	100	311	35	78	12	3	0	41	22	29	.251	.307	.309	60	-19	2	1	0	.938	6	3-98	-0.8
Total	5	572	1876	216	468	87	18	4	223	179	196	.249	.319	.321	66	-93	23	14	-2	.945	42	3-553/2-13,S-2	-1.4
■ GREG LUZINSKI Luzinski, Gregory Michael b: 11/22/50, Chicago, Ill. BR/TR, 6'1", 225 lbs. Deb: 9/9/70 C																							
1970	Phi-N	8	12	0	2	0	0	0	0	3	5	.167	.333	.167	39	-1	0	1	-1	1.000	1	/1-3	-0.1
1971	Phi-N	28	100	13	30	8	0	3	15	12	32	.300	.386	.470	141	6	2	0	1	.996	6	1-28	1.1
1972	Phi-N	150	563	66	158	33	5	18	68	42	114	.281	.334	.453	119	12	0	4	-2	.960	1	*O-145/1-2	0.4
1973	Phi-N	161	610	76	174	26	4	29	97	51	135	.285	.347	.484	125	19	3	3	-1	**.993**	-2	*O-159	0.9
1974	Phi-N	85	302	29	82	14	1	7	48	29	76	.272	.335	.394	99	-0	3	0	1	.981	7	O-82	0.3
1975	Phi-N★	161	596	85	179	35	3	34	**120**	89	151	.300	.398	.540	152	43	3	6	-3	.966	-7	*O-159	2.8
1976	*Phi-N★	149	533	74	162	28	1	21	95	50	107	.304	.375	.478	137	26	1	2	-1	.964	-8	*O-144	1.2
1977	*Phi-N★	149	554	99	171	35	3	39	130	80	140	.309	.399	.594	155	43	3	2	-0	.964	-5	*O-148	3.2
1978	*Phi-N★	155	540	85	143	32	2	35	101	100	135	.265	.390	.526	152	40	8	7	-2	.984	-7	*O-154	2.6
1979	Phi-N	137	452	47	114	23	1	18	81	56	103	.252	.347	.427	107	5	3	3	-1	.946	-15	*O-125	-1.7
1980	*Phi-N	106	368	44	84	19	1	19	56	60	100	.228	.346	.440	112	6	3	0	1	.993	-12	*O-105	-0.9
1981	Chi-A	104	378	55	100	15	1	21	62	58	80	.265	.367	.476	144	22	0	0	0	.000	0	*D-103	1.9
1982	Chi-A	159	583	87	170	37	1	18	102	89	120	.292	.391	.451	130	27	1	1	-0	.000	0	*D-156	2.1
1983	*Chi-A	144	502	73	128	26	1	32	95	70	117	.255	.358	.502	129	20	2	1	0	1.000	0	*D-139/1-2	1.5
1984	Chi-A	125	412	47	98	13	0	13	58	56	80	.238	.333	.364	89	-5	5	1	1	.000	0	*D-114	-0.7
Total	15	1821	6505	880	1795	344	24	307	1128	845	1495	.276	.366	.478	129	262	37	31	-8	.972	-40	*O-1221,D-512/1-35	14.6
■ MITCH LYDEN Lyden, Mitchell Scott b: 12/14/64, Portland, Ore. BR/TR, 6'3", 225 lbs. Deb: 6/16/93																							
1993	Fla-N	6	10	2	3	0	0	1	1	0	3	.300	.300	.600	127	0	0	0	0	1.000	-1	/C-2	-0.1
■ SCOTT LYDY Lydy, Donald Scott b: 10/26/68, Mesa, Ariz. BR/TR, 6'5", 195 lbs. Deb: 5/18/93																							
1993	Oak-A	41	102	11	23	5	0	2	7	8	39	.225	.288	.333	71	-4	2	0	1	.958	-2	O-38/D-2	-0.6
■ JERRY LYNCH Lynch, Gerald Thomas b: 7/17/30, Bay City, Mich. BL/TR, 6'1", 189 lbs. Deb: 4/15/54																							
1954	Pit-N	98	284	27	68	4	5	8	36	20	43	.239	.292	.373	73	-12	2	2	-1	.965	-4	O-83	-2.0
1955	Pit-N	88	282	43	80	18	6	5	28	22	33	.284	.336	.443	106	2	2	2	-1	.950	-2	O-71/C-2	-0.4
1956	Pit-N	19	19	1	3	0	1	0	0	1	4	.158	.200	.263	24	-2	0	0	0	1.000	0	/O-1	-0.2
1957	Cin-N	67	124	11	32	4	1	4	13	6	18	.258	.292	.403	79	-4	0	0	0	1.000	-2	O-24/C-2	-0.7
1958	Cin-N	122	420	58	131	20	5	16	68	18	54	.312	.340	.498	112	6	1	4	-2	.970	-7	*O-101	-0.8
1959	Cin-N	117	379	49	102	16	3	17	58	29	50	.269	.323	.462	103	1	2	0	1	.979	2	O-98	-0.2
1960	Cin-N	102	159	23	46	8	2	6	27	16	25	.289	.358	.478	124	5	0	0	0	.913	-4	O-32	0.0
1961	*Cin-N	96	181	33	57	13	2	13	50	27	25	.315	.407	.624	166	17	2	2	-1	.948	-4	O-44	1.0
1962	Cin-N	114	288	41	81	15	4	12	57	24	38	.281	.339	.486	115	5	3	3	-1	.970	-0	O-73	0.0
1963	Cin-N	22	32	5	8	3	0	2	9	1	5	.250	.294	.531	129	1	0	0	0	1.000	-1	/O-7	-0.1
	Pit-N	88	237	26	63	6	3	10	36	22	28	.266	.331	.443	120	6	0	1	-1	.960	-6	O-64	-0.4
	Yr	110	269	31	71	9	3	12	45	23	33	.264	.327	.454	121	7	0	1	-1	.962	-7	O-71	-0.5
1964	Pit-N	114	297	35	81	14	2	16	66	26	57	.273	.333	.495	130	11	0	1	-1	.983	-13	O-78	-0.6
1965	Pit-N	73	121	7	34	1	0	5	16	8	26	.281	.331	.413	108	1	0	2	-1	.903	-3	O-26	-0.5
1966	Pit-N	64	56	5	12	1	0	1	6	4	10	.214	.267	.286	54	-3	0	0	0	1.000	-0	/O-4	-0.4
Total	13	1184	2879	364	798	123	34	115	470	224	416	.277	.331	.463	110	34	12	17	-7	.964	-46	O-706/C-4	-5.3
■ HENRY LYNCH Lynch, Henry W. b: 4/8/1866, Worcester, Mass. d: 11/23/25, Worcester, Mass. BB, 5'7", 143 lbs. Deb: 9/21/1893																							
1893	Chi-N	4	14	0	3	2	0	0	2	1	1	.214	.267	.357	66	-1	0			.833	-1	/O-4	-0.2
■ DANNY LYNCH Lynch, Matt Dan "Dummy" b: 2/7/26, Dallas, Tex. d: 6/30/78, Plano, Tex. BR/TR, 5'11", 174 lbs. Deb: 9/14/48																							
1948	Chi-N	7	7	3	2	0	0	1	1	1	1	.286	.375	.714	197	1	0			1.000	0	/2-1	0.1
■ MIKE LYNCH Lynch, Michael Joseph b: 9/10/1875, St.Paul, Minn. d: 4/1/47, Jennings Lodge, Ore TR, 5'10", 155 lbs. Deb: 4/24/02																							
1902	Chi-N	7	28	4	4	0	0	0	0	2		.143	.200	.143	6	-3	0			.929	-1	/O-7	-0.5
■ TOM LYNCH Lynch, Thomas James b: 4/3/1860, Bennington, Vt. d: 3/28/55, Cohoes, N.Y. BL/TR, 5'10.5", 170 lbs. Deb: 8/18/1884 U																							
1884	Wil-U	16	58	6	16	3	1	0		5		.276	.333	.362	108	-1				.846	-3	/C-8,O-8,1-1	-0.3
	Phi-N	13	48	7	15	4	2	0	3	4	5	.313	.365	.479	171	4				.860	-2	/C-7,O-7	0.3
1885	Phi-N	13	53	7	10	3	0	0	1	10	3	.189	.317	.245	86	-0				.838	3	O-13	0.2
Total	2	42	159	20	41	10	3	0	4	19	8	.258	.337	.358	119	3				.887	-2	/O-28,C-15,1-1	0.2
■ WALT LYNCH Lynch, Walter Edward "Jabber" b: 4/15/1897, Buffalo, N.Y. d: 12/21/76, Daytona Beach, Fla TR, 6', 176 lbs. Deb: 7/8/22																							
1922	Bos-A	3	2	1	1	0	0	0	0	0	0	.500	.500	.500	163	0	0	0	0	1.000	0	/C-3	0.0
■ BYRD LYNN Lynn, Byrd "Birdie" b: 3/13/1889, Unionville, Ill. d: 2/5/40, Napa, Cal. BR/TR, 5'11", 165 lbs. Deb: 4/16/16																							
1916	Chi-A	31	40	4	9	1	0	0	3	4	7	.225	.311	.250	68	-1	2			.952	8	C-13	0.8
1917	*Chi-A	35	72	7	16	2	0	0	5	7	11	.222	.300	.250	67	-3	1			.959	-2	C-29	-0.3
1918	Chi-A	5	8	0	2	0	0	0	0	2	1	.250	.400	.250	95	0	0			1.000	-1	/C-4	-0.1
1919	*Chi-A	29	66	4	15	4	0	0	4	4	9	.227	.271	.288	57	-4	0			.982	1	C-28	-0.2
1920	Chi-A	16	25	0	8	2	1	0	3	1	3	.320	.346	.480	117	0	0	0	0	1.000	-1	C-14	0.0
Total	5	116	211	15	50	9	1	0	15	18	31	.237	.303	.289	72	-7	3	0		.969	5	/C-88	0.2
■ FRED LYNN Lynn, Fredric Michael b: 2/3/52, Chicago, Ill. BL/TL, 6'1", 190 lbs. Deb: 9/5/74																							
1974	Bos-A	15	43	5	18	2	2	2	10	6	6	.419	.500	.698	226	7	0	0	0	1.000	-0	O-12/D-1	0.6
1975	*Bos-A★	145	528	**103**	175	**47**	7	21	105	62	90	.331	.405	**.566**	158	40	10	5	0	.983	13	*O-144	4.7
1976	Bos-A★	132	507	76	159	32	8	10	65	48	67	.314	.374	.467	130	18	14	9	-1	.984	14	*O-128/D-5	2.6
1977	Bos-A★	129	497	81	129	29	5	18	76	51	63	.260	.332	.447	98	-2	2	3	-1	.994	8	*O-125/D-1	-0.1
1978	Bos-A★	150	541	75	161	33	3	22	82	75	50	.298	.384	.492	131	22	3	6	-3	.984	8	*O-149	2.1
1979	Bos-A★	147	531	116	177	42	1	39	122	82	79	**.333**	.426	**.637**	**173**	**55**	2	2	-1	.987	7	*O-143/D-1	5.2
1980	Bos-A★	110	415	67	125	32	3	12	61	58	39	.301	.387	.480	129	18	12	0	4	.994	9	*O-110	2.5
1981	Cal-A★	76	256	28	56	8	1	5	31	38	42	.219	.327	.316	86	-4	1	2	-1	.978	1	O-69	-0.6
1982	*Cal-A★	138	472	89	141	38	1	21	86	58	72	.299	.379	.517	143	28	7	8	-3	.991	-3	*O-133	1.9

YEAR	TM/L	G	AB	R	H	2B	3B	HR	RBI	BB	SO	AVG	OBP	SLG	PRO+	BR/A	SB	CS	SBR	FA	FR	G/POS	TPR
1983	Cal-A★	117	437	56	119	20	3	22	74	55	83	.272	.356	.483	130	18	2	2	-1	.993	-2	*O-113/D-2	1.2
1984	Cal-A	142	517	84	140	28	4	23	79	77	97	.271	.367	.474	132	23	2	2	-1	.982	-10	*O-140	0.9
1985	Bal-A	124	448	59	118	12	1	23	68	53	100	.263	.343	.449	118	11	7	3	0	.994	2	*O-123	0.9
1986	Bal-A	112	397	67	114	13	1	23	67	53	59	.287	.374	.499	137	21	2	2	-1	.984	-4	*O-107/D-1	1.3
1987	Bal-A	111	396	49	100	24	0	23	60	39	72	.253	.321	.487	113	6	3	7	-3	.991	-3	*O-101/D-8	-0.3
1988	Bal-A	87	301	37	76	13	1	18	37	28	66	.252	.316	.482	123	8	2	2	-1	.991	0	O-83/D-2	0.6
	Det-A	27	90	9	20	1	0	7	19	5	16	.222	.271	.467	106	0	0	0	0	1.000	0	O-22/D-3	0.0
	Yr	114	391	46	96	14	1	25	56	33	82	.246	.306	.478	120	8	2	2	-1	.992	1	*O-105/D-5	0.6
1989	Det-A	117	353	44	85	11	1	11	46	47	71	.241	.332	.371	100	1	1	1	-0	.992	-1	O-68,D-46	-0.3
1990	SD-N	90	196	18	47	3	1	6	23	22	44	.240	.320	.357	85	-4	2	0	1	1.000	-4	O-55	-0.9
Total	17	1969	6925	1063	1960	388	43	306	1111	857	1116	.283	.364	.484	129	266	72	54	-11	.988	35	*O-1825/D-70	22.3

■ JERRY LYNN

Lynn, Jerome Edward b: 4/14/16, Scranton, Pa. d: 9/25/72, Scranton, Pa. BR/TR, 5'10", 164 lbs. Deb: 9/19/37

YEAR	TM/L	G	AB	R	H	2B	3B	HR	RBI	BB	SO	AVG	OBP	SLG	PRO+	BR/A	SB	CS	SBR	FA	FR	G/POS	TPR
1937	Was-A	1	3	0	2	1	0	0	0	0	0	.667	.667	1.000	329	1	0	0	0	1.000	1	/2-1	0.2

■ RUSS LYON

Lyon, Russell Mayo b: 6/26/13, Ball Ground, Ga. d: 12/24/75, Charleston, S.C. BR/TR, 6'1", 230 lbs. Deb: 4/21/44

YEAR	TM/L	G	AB	R	H	2B	3B	HR	RBI	BB	SO	AVG	OBP	SLG	PRO+	BR/A	SB	CS	SBR	FA	FR	G/POS	TPR
1944	Cle-A	7	11	1	2	0	0	0	0	1	1	.182	.250	.182	25	-1	0	0	0	.909	0	/C-3	-0.1

■ BARRY LYONS

Lyons, Barry Stephen b: 6/3/60, Biloxi, Miss. BR/TR, 6'1", 202 lbs. Deb: 4/19/86

YEAR	TM/L	G	AB	R	H	2B	3B	HR	RBI	BB	SO	AVG	OBP	SLG	PRO+	BR/A	SB	CS	SBR	FA	FR	G/POS	TPR
1986	NY-N	6	9	1	0	0	0	0	2	1	2	.000	.100	.000	-72	-2	0	0	0	.941	0	/C-3	-0.2
1987	NY-N	53	130	15	33	4	1	4	24	8	24	.254	.307	.392	88	-3	0	0	0	.984	0	C-49	0.0
1988	NY-N	50	91	5	21	7	1	0	11	3	12	.231	.255	.330	70	-4	0	0	0	.979	-2	C-32/1-1	-0.5
1989	NY-N	79	235	15	58	13	0	3	27	11	28	.247	.286	.340	82	-6	0	1	-1	.980	1	C-76	-0.2
1990	NY-N	24	80	8	19	0	0	2	7	2	9	.237	.265	.313	58	-5	0	0	0	.980	3	C-23	0.0
	LA-N	3	5	1	1	0	0	1	2	0	1	.200	.200	.800	166	0	0	0	0	1.000	-1	/C-2	0.0
	Yr	27	85	9	20	0	0	3	9	2	10	.235	.261	.341	65	-4	0	0	0	.980	3	C-25	0.0
1991	LA-N	9	9	0	0	0	0	0	0	0	2	.000	.000	.000	-99	-2	0	0	0	1.000	1	/C-6	-0.1
	Cal-A	2	5	0	1	0	0	0	0	0	0	.200	.200	.200	11	-1	0	0	0	1.000	0	/1-2	-0.1
1995	Chi-A	27	64	8	17	2	0	5	16	4	14	.266	.309	.531	119	1	0	0	0	.987	3	C-16/1-4,D-6	0.4
Total	7	253	628	53	150	26	2	15	89	29	92	.239	.278	.358	78	-20	0	1	-1	.981	6	C-207/1-7,D-6	-0.7

■ DENNY LYONS

Lyons, Dennis Patrick Aloysius b: 3/12/1866, Cincinnati, Ohio d: 1/2/29, W.Covington, Ky. BR/TR, 5'10", 185 lbs. Deb: 9/18/1885

YEAR	TM/L	G	AB	R	H	2B	3B	HR	RBI	BB	SO	AVG	OBP	SLG	PRO+	BR/A	SB	CS	SBR	FA	FR	G/POS	TPR
1885	Pro-N	4	16	3	2	1	0	0	1	0	3	.125	.125	.188	-0	-2				.824	-0	/3-4	-0.2
1886	Phi-a	32	123	22	26	3	1	0	11	8		.211	.281	.252	67	-5	7			.807	-7	3-32	-0.9
1887	Phi-a	137	570	128	209	43	14	6	102	47		.367	.421	.523	162	47	73			.866	-6	*3-137	3.5
1888	Phi-a	111	456	93	135	22	5	6	83	41		.296	.363	.406	147	25	39			.878	-13	*3-111	1.2
1889	Phi-a	131	510	135	168	36	4	9	82	79	44	.329	.426	.469	157	41	10			.860	9	*3-130/1-1	4.5
1890	Phi-a	88	339	79	120	29	5	7	73	57		.354	**.461**	**.531**	**197**	44	21			.909	9	3-88	4.8
1891	StL-a	120	451	124	142	24	3	11	84	88	58	.315	.445	.455	137	22	9			.871	-6	*3-120	1.8
1892	NY-N	108	389	71	100	16	7	8	51	59	37	.257	.359	.396	130	15	11			.871	-6	*3-108	1.3
1893	Pit-N	131	490	103	150	19	16	3	105	97	29	.306	.430	.429	131	27	19			.918	5	*3-131	2.8
1894	Pit-N	71	254	51	82	14	4	4	50	42	12	.323	.427	.457	114	8	14			.898	7	3-71	1.1
1895	StL-N	33	129	24	38	6	0	2	25	14	5	.295	.377	.388	99	0	3			.894	-5	3-33	-0.3
1896	Pit-N	118	436	77	134	25	6	4	71	67	25	.307	.406	.420	123	17	13			.893	-15	*3-116	0.4
1897	Pit-N	37	131	22	27	6	4	2	17	22		.206	.346	.359	89	-1	5			.989	-1	1-35/3-2	-0.2
Total	13	1121	4294	932	1333	244	69	62	755	621	213	.310	.407	.443	139	237	224			.882	-27	*3-1083/1-36	19.8

■ ED LYONS

Lyons, Edward Hoyte "Mouse" b: 5/12/23, Winston-Salem, N.C BR/TR, 5'9", 165 lbs. Deb: 9/15/47 C

YEAR	TM/L	G	AB	R	H	2B	3B	HR	RBI	BB	SO	AVG	OBP	SLG	PRO+	BR/A	SB	CS	SBR	FA	FR	G/POS	TPR
1947	Was-A	7	26	2	4	0	0	0	0	2	2	.154	.214	.154	3	-3	0	0	0	1.000	4	/2-7	0.1

■ HARRY LYONS

Lyons, Harry P. b: 3/25/1866, Chester, Pa. d: 6/30/12, Mauricetown, N.J. BR/TR, 5'10.5", 157 lbs. Deb: 8/29/1887

YEAR	TM/L	G	AB	R	H	2B	3B	HR	RBI	BB	SO	AVG	OBP	SLG	PRO+	BR/A	SB	CS	SBR	FA	FR	G/POS	TPR
1887	Phi-N	1	4	0	0	0	0	0	0	1	0	.000	.200	.000	-38	-1	0			.500	-0	/O-1	-0.1
	*StL-a	2	8	2	1	0	0	0	1	0		.125	.125	.125	-27	-1	2			1.000	1	/2-1,O-1	-0.1
1888	*StL-a	123	499	66	97	10	5	4	63	20		.194	.230	.259	51	-30	36			.891	6	*O-122/3-2,S-1,2-1	-2.6
1889	NY-N	5	20	1	2	0	1	0	2	2	0	.100	.182	.200	7	-3	0			1.000	-1	/O-5	-0.3
1890	Roc-a	133	584	83	152	11	11	3	58	27		.260	.294	.332	91	-9	47			.920	11	*O-132/3-2,C-1,P-1	-0.2
1892	NY-N	96	411	67	98	5	2	0	53	33	29	.238	.297	.260	70	-14	25			.910	3	O-96	-1.5
1893	NY-N	47	187	27	51	5	2	0	21	14	6	.273	.323	.321	71	-8	10			.917	2	O-47	-0.6
Total	6	407	1713	246	401	31	21	7	198	97	35	.234	.277	.289	69	-66	120			.908	21	O-404/3-4,2-2,PCS	-5.4

■ PAT LYONS

Lyons, Patrick Jerry b: 3/1860, Canada d: 1/20/14, Springfield, Ohio TR , Deb: 7/21/1890

YEAR	TM/L	G	AB	R	H	2B	3B	HR	RBI	BB	SO	AVG	OBP	SLG	PRO+	BR/A	SB	CS	SBR	FA	FR	G/POS	TPR
1890	Cle-N	11	38	2	2	1	0	0	1	4	4	.053	.143	.079	-36	-7	0			.839	-5	2-11	-1.0

■ STEVE LYONS

Lyons, Stephen John b: 6/3/60, Tacoma, Wash. BL/TR, 6'3", 195 lbs. Deb: 4/15/85

YEAR	TM/L	G	AB	R	H	2B	3B	HR	RBI	BB	SO	AVG	OBP	SLG	PRO+	BR/A	SB	CS	SBR	FA	FR	G/POS	TPR
1985	Bos-A	133	371	52	98	14	3	5	30	32	64	.264	.324	.358	83	-8	12	9	-2	.973	-8	*O-114/3-1,S-1,D-5	-2.1
1986	Bos-A	59	124	20	31	7	2	1	14	12	23	.250	.316	.363	84	-3	2	3	-1	.972	-5	O-55	-1.0
	Chi-A	42	123	10	25	2	1	0	6	7	24	.203	.252	.236	33	-11	2	3	-1	.987	1	O-35/3-3,1-1,D-1	-1.2
	Yr	101	247	30	56	9	3	1	20	19	47	.227	.285	.300	58	-14	4	6	-2	.978	-4	O-90/3-3,1-1,D-1	-2.2
1987	Chi-A	76	193	26	54	11	1	1	19	12	37	.280	.322	.363	79	-6	3	1	0	.971	11	3-51,O-15/2-1,D-6	0.4
1988	Chi-A	146	472	59	127	28	3	5	45	32	59	.269	.317	.373	93	-5	1	2	-1	.927	10	*3-128,O-14/2-4,C1	0.3
1989	Chi-A	140	443	51	117	21	3	2	50	35	68	.264	.319	.339	88	-7	9	6	-1	.982	-8	2-70,1-40,3O/SCD	-1.7
1990	Chi-A	94	146	22	28	6	1	1	11	10	41	.192	.248	.267	45	-11	1	0	0	.991	-1	1-61,2-15/O-7,3SDP	-1.4
1991	Bos-A	87	212	15	51	10	1	4	17	11	35	.241	.278	.354	70	-9	10	3	1	1.000	0	O-45,2-16,3/1SDP	-0.8
1992	Atl-N	11	14	0	1	0	1	0	1	0	4	.071	.071	.214	-21	-2	0	0	0	1.000	-2	/O-6,2-2	-0.4
	Mon-N	16	13	2	3	0	0	0	1	1	3	.231	.286	.231	48	-1	1	2	-1	1.000	-2	/O-8,1-1	-0.4
	Yr	27	27	2	4	0	1	0	2	1	7	.148	.179	.222	13	-3	1	2	-1	1.000	-3	O-14/2-2,1-1	-0.8
	Bos-A	21	28	3	7	0	1	0	2	2	1	.250	.300	.321	69	-1	0	1	-1	1.000	-0	/1-8,O-5,2-1,D-2	-0.2
1993	Bos-A	28	23	4	3	1	0	0	0	2	5	.130	.200	.174	1	-3	1	2	-1	1.000	-2	O-10/2-9,C-1,13D	-0.5
Total	9	853	2162	264	545	100	17	19	196	156	364	.252	.304	.340	77	-67	42	32	-7	.979	-4	O-334,3-229,21/DSCP	-9.0

■ TERRY LYONS

Lyons, Terence Hilbert b: 12/14/08, New Holland, Ohio d: 9/9/59, Dayton, Ohio BR/TR, 6'0.5", 165 lbs. Deb: 4/19/29

YEAR	TM/L	G	AB	R	H	2B	3B	HR	RBI	BB	SO	AVG	OBP	SLG	PRO+	BR/A	SB	CS	SBR	FA	FR	G/POS	TPR
1929	Phi-N	1	0	0	0	0	0	0	0	0	0	—	—	—	—	0	0	0	0	.000	0	/1-1	0.0

■ TED LYONS

Lyons, Theodore Amar b: 12/28/1900, Lake Charles, La. d: 7/25/86, Sulphur, La. BB/TR, 5'11", 200 lbs. Deb: 7/2/23 MCH

YEAR	TM/L	G	AB	R	H	2B	3B	HR	RBI	BB	SO	AVG	OBP	SLG	PRO+	BR/A	SB	CS	SBR	FA	FR	G/POS	TPR
1923	Chi-A	9	5	0	1	0	0	0	1	1	3	.200	.333	.200	43	-0	0	0	0	1.000	1	/P-9	0.0
1924	Chi-A	41	77	10	17	0	1	0	6	5	13	.221	.277	.247	37	-7	0	0	0	.902	-3	P-41	0.0
1925	Chi-A	43	97	6	18	3	0	0	7	3	13	.186	.218	.216	11	-13	0	0	0	.957	2	P-43	0.0
1926	Chi-A	41	104	7	22	1	1	0	3	1	10	.212	.219	.240	20	-12	0	0	0	.955	4	P-39	0.0
1927	Chi-A	41	110	16	28	6	2	1	9	6	17	.255	.293	.373	74	-5	0	0	0	.979	0	P-39	0.0
1928	Chi-A	49	91	10	23	2	0	0	8	1	9	.253	.261	.275	41	-8	0	0	0	.920	2	P-39	0.0
1929	Chi-A	40	91	7	20	4	0	0	11	9	13	.220	.290	.264	44	-8	0	0	0	.946	2	P-37/O-1	0.0
1930	Chi-A	57	122	20	38	6	3	1	15	2	18	.311	.323	.434	93	-2	0	0	0	.938	3	P-42	0.0
1931	Chi-A	42	33	6	5	0	0	0	3	2	1	.152	.200	.152	-7	-5	0	0	0	.957	-1	P-22	0.0
1932	Chi-A	49	73	11	19	2	1	1	10	4	10	.260	.308	.356	76	-3	0	0	0	.964	-1	P-33	0.0
1933	Chi-A	51	91	11	26	2	1	1	11	4	6	.286	.316	.363	83	-2	0	1	-1	.983	0	P-36	0.0
1934	Chi-A	50	97	9	20	4	0	1	16	3	19	.206	.245	.278	34	-10	0	0	0	.939	2	P-30	0.0
1935	Chi-A	29	82	5	18	4	0	0	6	3	4	.220	.256	.268	35	-8	0	0	0	**1.000**	-1	P-23	0.0
1936	Chi-A	26	70	2	11	0	0	0	5	5	12	.157	.213	.157	-7	-12	0	0	0	**1.000**	1	P-26	0.0
1937	Chi-A	23	57	6	12	0	0	0	3	9	14	.211	.318	.211	36	-5	0	0	0	**1.000**	0	P-22	0.0
1938	Chi-A	24	72	9	14	2	0	0	4	2	9	.194	.216	.222	10	-10	0	0	0	.982	2	P-23	0.0
1939	Chi-A☆	21	61	5	18	3	0	0	8	5	7	.295	.348	.344	76	-2	0	0	0	.912	-1	P-21	0.0
1940	Chi-A	22	75	4	18	4	0	0	7	2	7	.240	.260	.293	43	-6	0	0	0	.923	-2	P-22	0.0

YEAR	TM/L	G	AB	R	H	2B	3B	HR	RBI	BB	SO	AVG	OBP	SLG	PRO+	BR/A	SB	CS	SBR	FA	FR	G/POS	TPR
1941	Chi-A	22	74	8	20	2	0	0	6	2	6	.270	.289	.297	56	-5	0	0	0	.981	1	P-22	0.0
1942	Chi-A	20	67	10	16	4	0	0	10	3	7	.239	.282	.299	65	-3	0	0	0	.980	1	P-20	0.0
1946	Chi-A	5	14	0	0	0	0	0	0	1	3	.000	.067	.000	-83	-3	0	0	0	1.000	0	/P-5,M	0.0
Total	21	705	1563	162	364	49	9	5	149	73	201	.233	.270	.285	44	-130	0	1	-1	.958	11	P-594/O-1	0.0

■ BILL LYONS Lyons, William Allen b: 4/26/58, Alton, Ill. BR/TR, 6'1", 175 lbs. Deb: 7/20/83

YEAR	TM/L	G	AB	R	H	2B	3B	HR	RBI	BB	SO	AVG	OBP	SLG	PRO+	BR/A	SB	CS	SBR	FA	FR	G/POS	TPR
1983	StL-N	42	60	3	10	1	1	0	3	1	11	.167	.180	.217	10	-7	3	2	-0	.985	2	2-23/3-8,S-2	-0.5
1984	StL-N	46	73	13	16	3	0	0	3	9	13	.219	.305	.260	62	-3	3	1	0	.991	14	2-25,S-11/3-3	1.2
Total	2	88	133	16	26	4	1	0	6	10	24	.195	.252	.241	39	-11	6	3	0	.989	16	/2-48,S-13,3-11	0.7

■ DAD LYTLE Lytle, Edward Benson "Pop" b: 3/10/1862, Racine, Wis. d: 12/21/50, Long Beach, Cal. BR/TR, 5'11", 160 lbs. Deb: 8/11/1890

YEAR	TM/L	G	AB	R	H	2B	3B	HR	RBI	BB	SO	AVG	OBP	SLG	PRO+	BR/A	SB	CS	SBR	FA	FR	G/POS	TPR
1890	Chi-N	1	4	1	0	0	0	0	0	0	1	.000	.000	.000	-96	-1	0			1.000	1	/O-1	0.0
	Pit-N	15	55	2	8	1	0	0	0	8	9	.145	.254	.164	25	-5	0			.837	-6	/2-8,O-7	-1.0
	Yr	16	59	3	8	1	0	0	0	8	10	.136	.239	.153	16	-6	0			.824	-5	/O-8,2-8	-1.0

■ JIM LYTTLE Lyttle, James Lawrence b: 5/20/46, Hamilton, Ohio BL/TR, 6', 186 lbs. Deb: 5/17/69

YEAR	TM/L	G	AB	R	H	2B	3B	HR	RBI	BB	SO	AVG	OBP	SLG	PRO+	BR/A	SB	CS	SBR	FA	FR	G/POS	TPR
1969	NY-A	28	83	7	15	4	0	0	4	4	19	.181	.218	.229	26	-8	1	2	-1	.983	1	O-28	-1.0
1970	NY-A	87	126	20	39	7	1	3	14	10	26	.310	.360	.452	129	5	3	6	-3	.989	-9	O-70	-0.9
1971	NY-A	49	86	7	17	5	0	1	7	8	18	.198	.274	.291	64	-4	0	2	-1	1.000	-3	O-29	-1.0
1972	Chi-A	44	82	8	19	5	2	0	5	1	28	.232	.241	.341	70	-3	0	1	-1	1.000	-2	O-21	-0.7
1973	Mon-N	49	116	12	30	5	0	4	19	9	14	.259	.312	.422	98	-1	0	2	-1	.974	2	O-36	-0.1
1974	Mon-N	25	9	1	3	0	0	0	2	1	3	.333	.400	.333	101	0	0	0	0	1.000	-6	O-18	-0.6
1975	Mon-N	44	55	7	15	4	0	0	6	13	6	.273	.412	.345	107	1	0	1	-1	1.000	-3	O-16	-0.3
1976	Mon-N	42	85	6	23	4	1	1	8	7	13	.271	.326	.376	95	-1	0	0	0	.977	-3	O-29	-0.4
	LA-N	23	68	3	15	3	0	0	5	8	12	.221	.303	.265	63	-3	0	1	-1	1.000	4	O-18	0.0
	Yr	65	153	9	38	7	1	1	13	15	25	.248	.315	.327	81	-4	0	1	-1	.990	2	O-47	-0.4
Total	8	391	710	71	176	37	5	9	70	61	139	.248	.308	.352	86	-14	4	15	-8	.988	-18	O-265	-5.0

■ KEVIN MAAS Maas, Kevin Christian b: 1/20/65, Castro Valley, Cal. BL/TL, 6'3", 209 lbs. Deb: 6/29/90

YEAR	TM/L	G	AB	R	H	2B	3B	HR	RBI	BB	SO	AVG	OBP	SLG	PRO+	BR/A	SB	CS	SBR	FA	FR	G/POS	TPR
1990	NY-A	79	254	42	64	9	0	21	41	43	76	.252	.367	.535	149	17	1	2	-1	.983	-3	1-57,D-18	0.8
1991	NY-A	148	500	69	110	14	1	23	63	83	128	.220	.336	.390	100	1	5	1	1	.983	-1	*D-109,1-36	-0.6
1992	NY-A	98	286	35	71	12	0	11	35	25	63	.248	.309	.406	99	-1	3	1	0	.986	-3	D-62,1-22	-0.7
1993	NY-A	59	151	20	31	4	0	9	25	24	32	.205	.318	.411	97	-1	1	1	-0	.984	-1	D-31,1-17	-0.4
1995	Min-A	22	57	5	11	4	0	1	5	7	11	.193	.281	.316	55	-4	0	0	0	.936	-2	D-12/1-8	-0.7
Total	5	406	1248	171	287	43	1	65	169	182	310	.230	.332	.422	107	12	10	5	0	.982	-10	D-232,1-140	-1.6

■ JOHN MABRY Mabry, John Steven b: 10/17/70, Wilmington, Del. BL/TR, 6'4", 195 lbs. Deb: 4/23/94

YEAR	TM/L	G	AB	R	H	2B	3B	HR	RBI	BB	SO	AVG	OBP	SLG	PRO+	BR/A	SB	CS	SBR	FA	FR	G/POS	TPR
1994	StL-N	6	23	2	7	3	0	0	3	2	4	.304	.360	.435	108	0	0	0	0	1.000	1	/O-6	0.1
1995	StL-N	129	388	35	119	21	1	5	41	24	45	.307	.350	.405	99	-1	0	3	-2	.994	2	1-73,O-39	-0.7
1996	*StL-N	151	543	63	161	30	2	13	74	37	84	.297	.345	.431	104	3	3	2	-0	.994	-11	*1-146,O-14	-2.2
1997	StL-N	116	388	40	110	19	0	5	36	39	77	.284	.353	.371	91	-4	0	1	-1	1.000	-6	O-78,1-49/3-1	-1.6
1998	StL-N	142	377	41	94	22	0	9	46	30	76	.249	.306	.379	77	-13	0	2	-1	.971	-10	O-80,3-38,1-16	-2.5
Total	5	544	1719	181	491	95	3	32	200	132	286	.286	.340	.400	94	-15	3	8	-4	.995	-24	1-284,O-217/3-39	-6.9

■ HARVEY MacDONALD Mac Donald, Harvey Forsyth b: 5/18/1898, New York, N.Y. d: 10/4/65, Manoa, Pa. BL/TL, 5'11", 170 lbs. Deb: 6/12/28

YEAR	TM/L	G	AB	R	H	2B	3B	HR	RBI	BB	SO	AVG	OBP	SLG	PRO+	BR/A	SB	CS	SBR	FA	FR	G/POS	TPR
1928	Phi-N	13	16	0	4	0	0	0	2	2	3	.250	.333	.250	53	-1	0			1.000	-0	/O-2	-0.1

■ MACEY Macey b: Columbus, Ohio Deb: 10/2/1890

YEAR	TM/L	G	AB	R	H	2B	3B	HR	RBI	BB	SO	AVG	OBP	SLG	PRO+	BR/A	SB	CS	SBR	FA	FR	G/POS	TPR
1890	Phi-a	1	1	0	0	0	0	0	0	0		.000	.000	.000	-99	-0	0			1.000	-1	/C-1	-0.1

■ MIKE MACFARLANE Macfarlane, Michael Andrew b: 4/12/64, Stockton, Cal. BR/TR, 6'1", 205 lbs. Deb: 7/23/87

YEAR	TM/L	G	AB	R	H	2B	3B	HR	RBI	BB	SO	AVG	OBP	SLG	PRO+	BR/A	SB	CS	SBR	FA	FR	G/POS	TPR
1987	KC-A	8	19	0	4	1	0	0	3	2	2	.211	.286	.263	46	-1	0	0	0	1.000	-1	/C-8	-0.2
1988	KC-A	70	211	25	56	15	0	4	26	21	37	.265	.335	.393	102	1	0	0	0	.994	-15	C-68	-0.9
1989	KC-A	69	157	13	35	6	0	2	19	7	27	.223	.265	.299	59	-9	0	0	0	.996	2	C-59/D-4	-0.4
1990	KC-A	124	400	37	102	24	4	6	58	25	69	.255	.310	.380	94	-4	1	0	0	.991	-19	*C-112/D-5	-1.7
1991	KC-A	84	267	34	74	18	2	13	41	17	52	.277	.334	.506	128	9	1	0	0	.993	-12	C-69/D-4	0.2
1992	KC-A	129	402	51	94	28	3	17	48	30	89	.234	.311	.445	107	2	1	5	-3	.993	-1	*C-104,D-13	0.4
1993	KC-A	117	388	55	106	27	0	20	67	40	83	.273	.365	.497	122	12	2	5	-2	.985	4	*C-114	1.9
1994	KC-A	92	314	53	80	17	3	14	47	35	71	.255	.362	.462	106	3	1	0	0	.993	4	C-81/D-8	1.1
1995	*Bos-A	115	364	45	82	18	1	15	51	38	78	.225	.322	.404	85	-9	2	1	0	.993	-4	*C-111/D-3	-0.5
1996	KC-A	112	379	58	104	24	2	19	54	31	57	.274	.341	.499	109	4	3	3	-1	.993	-11	C-99/D-9	-0.2
1997	KC-A	82	257	34	61	14	2	8	35	24	47	.237	.317	.401	84	-6	0	2	-1	.991	-14	C-81	-1.5
1998	KC-A	3	11	1	1	0	0	0	0	0	2	.091	.091	.091	-50	-2	0	0	0	1.000	-0	/C-3	-0.2
	Oak-A	78	207	28	52	12	0	7	34	12	34	.251	.305	.411	86	-5	1	0	0	.989	-2	C-70	-0.3
	Yr	81	218	29	53	12	0	7	34	12	36	.243	.295	.394	79	-7	1	0	0	.990	-3	C-73	-0.5
Total	12	1083	3376	434	851	204	17	125	483	282	648	.252	.327	.434	100	-5	12	16	-6	.992	-70	C-979/D-46	-2.3

■ ED MacGAMWELL Mac Gamwell, Edward M. b: 1/10/1879, Buffalo, N.Y. d: 5/26/24, Albany, N.Y. BL/TL, Deb: 4/14/05

YEAR	TM/L	G	AB	R	H	2B	3B	HR	RBI	BB	SO	AVG	OBP	SLG	PRO+	BR/A	SB	CS	SBR	FA	FR	G/POS	TPR
1905	Bro-N	4	16	0	4	0	0	0	0	1		.250	.294	.250	68	-1	0			.951	-1	/1-4	-0.1

■ KEN MACHA Macha, Kenneth Edward b: 9/29/50, Monroeville, Pa. BR/TR, 6'2", 217 lbs. Deb: 9/14/74 FC

YEAR	TM/L	G	AB	R	H	2B	3B	HR	RBI	BB	SO	AVG	OBP	SLG	PRO+	BR/A	SB	CS	SBR	FA	FR	G/POS	TPR
1974	Pit-N	5	5	1	3	1	0	0	1	0	0	.600	.600	.800	300	1	0	0	0	1.000	-0	/C-1	0.1
1977	Pit-N	35	95	2	26	4	0	0	11	6	17	.274	.317	.316	68	-4	1	1	-0	.964	-5	3-17,1-11/O-4	-1.0
1978	Pit-N	29	52	5	11	1	1	0	5	12	10	.212	.359	.269	75	-1	2	0	1	.970	-3	3-21	-0.4
1979	Mon-N	25	36	8	10	3	1	0	4	2	9	.278	.333	.417	104	0	0	0	0	1.000	1	3-13/1-2,O-2,C-1	0.1
1980	Mon-N	49	107	10	31	5	1	1	8	11	17	.290	.361	.383	108	1	0	2	-1	.910	-5	3-33/1-2,C-1,O-1	-0.6
1981	Tor-A	37	85	4	17	2	0	0	6	8	15	.200	.269	.224	41	-6	1	1	-0	.892	-1	3-19,1-16/C-1,D-2	-0.9
Total	6	180	380	30	98	16	3	1	35	39	68	.258	.330	.324	80	-9	4	4	-1	.938	-13	3-103/1-31,O-7,CD	-2.7

■ MIKE MACHA Macha, Michael William b: 2/17/54, Victoria, Tex. BR/TR, 5'11", 180 lbs. Deb: 4/20/79 F

YEAR	TM/L	G	AB	R	H	2B	3B	HR	RBI	BB	SO	AVG	OBP	SLG	PRO+	BR/A	SB	CS	SBR	FA	FR	G/POS	TPR
1979	Atl-N	6	13	2	2	0	0	0	1	1	5	.154	.214	.154	2	-2	0	0	0	.769	0	/3-3	-0.1
1980	Tor-A	5	8	0	0	0	0	0	0	0	1	.000	.000	.000	-96	-2	0	0	0	.778	1	/3-2,C-1	-0.2
Total	2	11	21	2	2	0	0	0	1	1	6	.095	.136	.095	-33	-4	0	0	0	.773	1	/3-5,C-1	-0.3

■ ROBERT MACHADO Machado, Robert Alexis b: 6/3/73, Caracas, Venez. BR/TR, 6'1", 205 lbs. Deb: 7/24/96

YEAR	TM/L	G	AB	R	H	2B	3B	HR	RBI	BB	SO	AVG	OBP	SLG	PRO+	BR/A	SB	CS	SBR	FA	FR	G/POS	TPR
1996	Chi-A	4	6	1	4	1	0	0	2	0	0	.667	.667	.833	290	2	0	0	0	1.000	-1	/C-4	0.1
1997	Chi-A	10	15	1	3	0	1	0	2	1	6	.200	.250	.333	53	-1	0	0	0	1.000	2	C-10	0.1
1998	Chi-A	34	111	14	23	6	0	3	15	7	22	.207	.254	.342	55	-8	0	0	0	.981	-2	C-34	-0.8
Total	3	48	132	16	30	7	1	3	19	8	28	.227	.271	.364	65	-7	0	0	0	.984	-2	/C-48	-0.6

■ DAVE MACHEMER Machemer, David Ritchie b: 5/24/51, St.Joseph, Mo. BR/TR, 5'11.5", 180 lbs. Deb: 6/21/78

YEAR	TM/L	G	AB	R	H	2B	3B	HR	RBI	BB	SO	AVG	OBP	SLG	PRO+	BR/A	SB	CS	SBR	FA	FR	G/POS	TPR
1978	Cal-A	10	22	6	6	1	0	1	2	2	1	.273	.333	.455	124	1	0	1	-1	1.000	-2	/2-5,3-3,S-1	-0.2
1979	Det-A	19	26	8	5	1	0	0	2	3	2	.192	.276	.231	37	-2	0	3	-2	.972	5	2-11/O-1,D-1	0.1
Total	2	29	48	14	11	2	0	1	4	5	3	.229	.302	.333	74	-2	0	4	-2	.978	2	/2-16,3-3,D-1,OS	-0.1

■ CONNIE MACK Mack, Cornelius Alexander "The Tall Tactician" (b: Cornelius Alexander McGillicuddy)
b: 12/22/1862, E.Brookfield, Mass d: 2/8/56, Philadelphia, Pa. BR/TR, 6'1", 150 lbs. Deb: 9/11/1886 FMH

YEAR	TM/L	G	AB	R	H	2B	3B	HR	RBI	BB	SO	AVG	OBP	SLG	PRO+	BR/A	SB	CS	SBR	FA	FR	G/POS	TPR
1886	Was-N	10	36	4	13	2	1	0	5	0	2	.361	.361	.472	161	2	0			.957	9	C-10	1.1
1887	Was-N	82	314	35	63	6	1	0	20	8	17	.201	.228	.226	28	-30	26			.906	3	C-76/O-5,2-2	-1.7
1888	Was-N	85	300	49	56	5	6	3	29	17	18	.187	.249	.273	70	-9	31			.916	5	C-79/O-4,S-1,1-1	0.3
1889	Was-N	98	386	51	113	16	1	0	42	15	12	.293	.333	.339	94	-3	26			.891	5	C-45,O-34,1-22	0.3
1890	Buf-P	123	503	95	134	15	12	0	53	47	13	.266	.353	.344	94	-1	16			.925	-11	*C-112/O-9,1-5	-0.2
1891	Pit-N	75	280	43	60	10	0	0	29	19	11	.214	.286	.250	58	-14	4			.926	9	C-72/1-3	0.0

YEAR	TM/L	G	AB	R	H	2B	3B	HR	RBI	BB	SO	AVG	OBP	SLG	PRO+	BR/A	SB	CS	SBR	FA	FR	G/POS	TPR
1892	Pit-N	97	346	39	84	9	4	1	31	21	22	.243	.298	.301	81	-8	11			**.951**	24	C-92/O-3,1-1	2.0
1893	Pit-N	37	133	22	38	3	1	0	15	10	9	.286	.358	.323	83	-3	4			.941	6	C-37	0.5
1894	Pit-N	69	228	32	57	7	1	1	21	20	14	.250	.321	.303	52	-18	8			.947	5	C-69,M	-0.5
1895	Pit-N	14	49	12	15	2	0	0	4	7	1	.306	.404	.347	100	1	1			.962	-2	C-12/1-1,M	0.0
1896	Pit-N	33	120	9	26	4	1	0	16	5	8	.217	.248	.267	37	-11	0			.974	1	1-28/C-5,M	-0.8
Total	11	723	2695	391	659	79	28	5	265	169	127	.245	.305	.300	72	-95	127			.927	53	C-609/1-61,O-55,2S	1.0

■ DENNY MACK

Mack, Dennis Joseph (b: Dennis Joseph McGee) b: 1851, Easton, Pa. d: 4/10/1888, Wilkes-Barre, Pa. BR/TR, 5′7″, 164 lbs. Deb: 5/6/1871 MU

YEAR	TM/L	G	AB	R	H	2B	3B	HR	RBI	BB	SO	AVG	OBP	SLG	PRO+	BR/A	SB	CS	SBR	FA	FR	G/POS	TPR
1871	Rok-n	25	122	34	30	7	1	0	17	8	7	.246	.292	.320	79	-2	12	0	4	.936	0	*1-24/P-3,S-1,O-1	0.2
1872	Ath-n	47	205	68	59	9	1	0	34	**23**	9	.288	.360	.341	116	5	9	5	-0	.948	-3	1-26,S-21	0.2
1873	Phi-n	48	205	55	60	5	0	0	20	15	9	.293	.341	.317	93	-2	6	2	1	.936	2	*1-42/O-4,S-3,2-1	0.2
1874	Phi-n	56	246	48	51	8	4	0	22	2	3	.207	.214	.272	53	-13	4	0	1	.900	-4	*1-56	-1.2
1876	StL-N	48	180	32	39	5	0	1	7	11	5	.217	.262	.261	79	-3				.886	-8	S-41/2-5,O-2	-1.0
1880	Buf-N	17	59	5	12	0	0	0	3	5	7	.203	.266	.203	60	-2				.940	-2	S-16/2-1	-0.3
1882	Lou-a	72	264	41	48	3	1	0		16		.182	.229	.201	49	-13				.898	-3	S-49,2-24/O-5,M	-1.2
1883	Pit-a	60	224	26	44	5	3	0		13		.196	.241	.246	60	-9				.844	4	S-38,1-25/2-1	-0.6
Total	4 n	176	778	205	200	29	6	0	93	48	28	.257	.300	.310	85	-12	31	7	5	.926	-4	1-148/S-25,O-5,P2	-0.6
Total	4	197	727	104	143	13	4	1	10	45	12	.197	.244	.230	60	-27				.886	-8	S-144/2-31,1-25,O-7	-3.1

■ EARLE MACK

Mack, Earle Thaddeus (b: Earle Thaddeus McGillicuddy)
b: 2/1/1890, Spencer, Mass. d: 2/4/67, Upper Darby Township, Pa. BL/TR, 5′8″, 140 lbs. Deb: 10/5/10 FMC

YEAR	TM/L	G	AB	R	H	2B	3B	HR	RBI	BB	SO	AVG	OBP	SLG	PRO+	BR/A	SB	CS	SBR	FA	FR	G/POS	TPR
1910	Phi-A	1	4	0	2	0	1	0	0	0		.500	.500	1.000	372	1	0			1.000	-1	/C-1	0.1
1911	Phi-A	2	4	0	0	0	0	0	0	0		.000	.000	.000	-99	-1	0			.000	0	/3-2	-0.1
1914	Phi-A	2	8	0	0	0	0	0	1	0	0	.000	.000	.000	-99	-2	1			1.000	0	/1-2	-0.2
Total	3	5	16	0	2	0	1	0	1	0	0	.125	.125	.250	11	-2	1			1.000	-1	/1-2,3-2,C-1	-0.2

■ JOE MACK

Mack, Joe John (b: Joseph John Maciarz) b: 1/4/12, Chicago, Ill. BB/TL, 5′11.5″, 185 lbs. Deb: 4/17/45

YEAR	TM/L	G	AB	R	H	2B	3B	HR	RBI	BB	SO	AVG	OBP	SLG	PRO+	BR/A	SB	CS	SBR	FA	FR	G/POS	TPR
1945	Bos-N	66	260	30	60	13	1	3	44	34	39	.231	.320	.323	79	-7	1			.991	0	1-65	-1.1

■ REDDY MACK

Mack, Joseph (b: Joseph McNamara) b: 5/2/1866, Ireland d: 12/30/16, Newport, Ky. 5′8″, 182 lbs. Deb: 9/16/1885

YEAR	TM/L	G	AB	R	H	2B	3B	HR	RBI	BB	SO	AVG	OBP	SLG	PRO+	BR/A	SB	CS	SBR	FA	FR	G/POS	TPR
1885	Lou-a	11	41	7	10	1	0	0	5	2		.244	.295	.268	79	-1				.885	0	2-11	0.0
1886	Lou-a	137	483	82	118	23	11	1	56	68		.244	.342	.344	109	5	13			.900	6	*2-137	1.5
1887	Lou-a	128	478	117	147	23	8	1	69	83		.308	.415	.395	124	19	22			.912	5	*2-128	2.3
1888	Lou-a	112	446	77	97	13	5	3	34	52		.217	.320	.289	98	2	18			.907	4	*2-112	0.9
1889	Bal-a	136	519	84	125	24	7	1	87	60	69	.241	.329	.320	84	-11	23			.897	-11	*2-135/O-1	-1.2
1890	Bal-a	26	95	14	27	3	5	0	11	10		.284	.370	.421	127	3	7			.932	1	2-26	0.4
Total	6	550	2062	381	524	87	36	6	262	275	69	.254	.352	.340	104	18	83			.905	5	2-549/O-1	3.9

■ QUINN MACK

Mack, Quinn David b: 9/11/65, Los Angeles, Cal. BL/TL, 5′10″, 185 lbs. Deb: 6/16/94 F

YEAR	TM/L	G	AB	R	H	2B	3B	HR	RBI	BB	SO	AVG	OBP	SLG	PRO+	BR/A	SB	CS	SBR	FA	FR	G/POS	TPR
1994	Sea-A	5	21	1	5	3	0	0	2	1	3	.238	.273	.381	65	-1	2	0	1	1.000	-0	/O-4,D-1	-0.1

■ RAY MACK

Mack, Raymond James (b: Raymond James Mlckovsky) b: 8/31/16, Cleveland, Ohio d: 5/7/69, Bucyrus, Ohio BR/TR, 6′, 200 lbs. Deb: 9/9/38

YEAR	TM/L	G	AB	R	H	2B	3B	HR	RBI	BB	SO	AVG	OBP	SLG	PRO+	BR/A	SB	CS	SBR	FA	FR	G/POS	TPR
1938	Cle-A	2	6	2	2	0	1	0	2	0	1	.333	.333	.667	147	0	0	0	0	1.000	2	/2-2	0.2
1939	Cle-A	36	112	12	17	4	1	1	6	12	19	.152	.240	.232	22	-14	0	2	-1	.976	2	2-34/3-1	-1.0
1940	Cle-A★	146	530	60	150	21	5	12	69	51	77	.283	.346	.409	98	-2	4	2	0	.965	-9	*2-146	-0.1
1941	Cle-A	145	500	54	114	22	4	9	44	54	69	.228	.303	.342	74	-20	8	4	0	.970	-5	*2-145	-1.4
1942	Cle-A	143	481	43	108	14	6	2	45	41	51	.225	.288	.291	67	-22	9	3	1	.969	-4	*2-143	-1.7
1943	Cle-A	153	545	56	120	25	2	7	62	47	61	.220	.285	.312	79	-16	8	3	1	.967	-2	*2-153	-1.0
1944	Cle-A	83	284	24	66	15	3	0	29	28	45	.232	.301	.306	77	-9	4	1	1	.951	10	2-83	0.7
1946	Cle-A	61	171	13	35	6	2	1	9	23	27	.205	.299	.281	67	-8	2	2	-1	.970	1	2-61	-0.4
1947	NY-A	1	0	0	0	0	0	0	0	0	0	—	—	—	—	0	0	0	0	.000	0	R	0.0
	Chi-N	21	78	9	17	6	0	2	12	5	15	.218	.274	.372	73	-3	0			.965	7	2-21	0.5
Total	9	791	2707	273	629	113	24	34	278	261	365	.232	.301	.330	76	-93	35	17		.966	3	2-788/3-1	-4.2

■ SHANE MACK

Mack, Shane Lee b: 12/7/63, Los Angeles, Cal. BR/TR, 6′, 190 lbs. Deb: 5/25/87 F

YEAR	TM/L	G	AB	R	H	2B	3B	HR	RBI	BB	SO	AVG	OBP	SLG	PRO+	BR/A	SB	CS	SBR	FA	FR	G/POS	TPR
1987	SD-N	105	238	28	57	11	3	4	25	18	47	.239	.301	.361	77	-8	4	6	-2	.982	-8	O-91	-2.0
1988	SD-N	56	119	13	29	3	0	0	12	14	21	.244	.338	.269	78	-3	5	1	1	.983	-3	O-55	-0.6
1990	Min-A	125	313	50	102	10	4	8	44	29	69	.326	.392	.460	129	13	13	4	2	.988	1	*O-109/D-4	1.3
1991	*Min-A	143	442	79	137	27	8	18	74	34	79	.310	.367	.529	139	22	13	9	-2	.977	-9	*O-140/D-1	0.9
1992	Min-A	156	600	101	189	31	6	16	75	64	106	.315	.395	.467	136	30	26	14	-1	.988	1	*O-155	2.8
1993	Min-A	128	503	66	139	30	4	10	61	41	76	.276	.336	.412	99	-1	15	5	2	.986	14	*O-128	1.1
1994	Min-A	81	303	55	101	21	2	15	61	32	51	.333	.408	.564	147	22	4	1	1	.990	1	O-75/D-4	1.9
1997	Bos-A	60	130	13	41	7	0	3	17	9	24	.315	.373	.438	109	2	2	1	0	1.000	-7	O-45/D-5	-0.6
1998	Oak-A	3	2	1	0	0	0	0	0	0	0	.000	.000	.000	-99	-1	0	0	0	.000	0	/H	-0.1
	KC-A	66	207	30	58	15	1	6	29	15	36	.280	.346	.449	100	0	8	2	1	.982	-2	O-32,D-21	-0.2
	Yr	69	209	31	58	15	1	6	29	15	36	.278	.343	.445	99	-0	8	2	1	.982	-2	O-32,D-21	-0.3
Total	9	923	2857	436	853	155	28	80	398	256	509	.299	.367	.456	119	76	90	43	1	.985	-12	O-830/D-35	4.5

■ PETE MACKANIN

Mackanin, Peter b: 8/1/51, Chicago, Ill. BR/TR, 6′2″, 190 lbs. Deb: 7/3/73 C

YEAR	TM/L	G	AB	R	H	2B	3B	HR	RBI	BB	SO	AVG	OBP	SLG	PRO+	BR/A	SB	CS	SBR	FA	FR	G/POS	TPR
1973	Tex-A	44	90	3	9	2	0	0	2	4	26	.100	.147	.122	-24	-15	0	0	0	.947	2	S-33,3-10	-1.1
1974	Tex-A	2	6	0	1	0	1	0	0	0	2	.167	.167	.500	88	-0	0	0	0	1.000	2	/S-2	0.2
1975	Mon-N	130	448	59	101	19	6	12	44	31	99	.225	.279	.375	77	-16	11	5	0	.966	18	*2-127/S-1,3-1	1.0
1976	Mon-N	114	380	36	85	15	2	8	33	15	66	.224	.257	.337	65	-19	6	2	1	.965	-2	*2-100/3-8,S-3,O-1	-1.5
1977	Mon-N	55	85	9	19	2	2	1	6	4	17	.224	.258	.329	58	-5	3	1	0	1.000	3	/2-9,S-8,3-5,O-4	-0.1
1978	Phi-N	5	8	0	2	0	0	0	1	0	4	.250	.250	.250	40	-1	0	0	0	1.000	0	/1-1,3-1	-0.1
1979	Phi-N	13	9	2	1	0	0	1	2	1	2	.111	.200	.444	69	-0	0	0	0	1.000	3	/2-2,S-2,3-2	0.2
1980	Min-A	108	319	31	85	18	0	4	35	14	34	.266	.297	.361	74	-12	6	2	1	.968	16	2-71,S-30/1-4,3D	1.0
1981	Min-A	77	225	21	52	7	1	4	18	7	40	.231	.258	.324	63	-11	1	2	-1	.980	-5	2-31,S-28,1-10,/3D	-1.4
Total	9	548	1570	161	355	63	12	30	141	76	290	.226	.265	.339	65	-79	27	12	1	.968	36	2-340,S-107/31DO	-1.8

■ ERIC MacKENZIE

Mac Kenzie, Eric Hugh b: 8/29/32, Glendon, Alberta, Can. BL/TR, 6′, 185 lbs. Deb: 4/23/55

YEAR	TM/L	G	AB	R	H	2B	3B	HR	RBI	BB	SO	AVG	OBP	SLG	PRO+	BR/A	SB	CS	SBR	FA	FR	G/POS	TPR
1955	KC-A	1	1	0	0	0	0	0	0	0	0	.000	.000	.000	-99	-0	0	0	0	.000	0	/C-1	0.0

■ GORDON MacKENZIE

Mac Kenzie, Henry Gordon b: 7/9/37, St.Petersburg, Fla BR/TR, 5′11″, 175 lbs. Deb: 8/13/61 C

YEAR	TM/L	G	AB	R	H	2B	3B	HR	RBI	BB	SO	AVG	OBP	SLG	PRO+	BR/A	SB	CS	SBR	FA	FR	G/POS	TPR
1961	KC-A	11	24	1	3	0	0	0	1	1	6	.125	.160	.125	-22	-4	0	0	0	1.000	-0	/C-7	-0.4

■ FELIX MACKIEWICZ

Mackiewicz, Felix Thaddeus b: 11/20/17, Chicago, Ill. d: 12/20/93, Olivette, Mo. BR/TR, 6′2″, 195 lbs. Deb: 9/7/41

YEAR	TM/L	G	AB	R	H	2B	3B	HR	RBI	BB	SO	AVG	OBP	SLG	PRO+	BR/A	SB	CS	SBR	FA	FR	G/POS	TPR
1941	Phi-A	5	14	3	4	0	1	0	0	1	0	.286	.333	.429	103	0	0	0	0	1.000	-1	/O-3	-0.1
1942	Phi-A	6	14	3	3	2	0	0	2	0	4	.214	.214	.357	59	-1	0	0	0	1.000	0	/O-3	-0.1
1943	Phi-A	9	16	1	1	0	0	0	0	2	8	.063	.167	.063	-32	-3	0	0	0	1.000	0	/O-3	-0.3
1945	Cle-A	120	359	42	98	14	7	2	37	44	41	.273	.356	.368	115	7	5	5	-2	.987	5	*O-112	0.6
1946	Cle-A	78	258	35	67	15	4	0	16	16	32	.260	.305	.349	88	-5	5	1	1	.983	-2	O-72	-1.0
1947	Cle-A	2	5	0	0	0	0	0	0	0	2	.000	.000	.000	-99	-1	0	0	0	1.000	-0	/O-2	-0.2
	Was-A	3	6	1	1	1	0	0	0	0	1	.167	.167	.333	38	-1	0	0	0	1.000	-1	/O-3	-0.2
	Yr	5	11	1	1	1	0	0	0	0	3	.091	.091	.182	-26	-2	0	0	0	1.000	-1	/O-5	-0.4
Total	6	223	672	85	174	32	12	2	55	63	88	.259	.325	.351	97	-3	10	6	-1	.986	2	O-198	-1.3

■ STEVE MACKO

Macko, Steven Joseph b: 9/6/54, Burlington, Iowa d: 11/15/81, Arlington, Tex. BL/TR, 5′10″, 160 lbs. Deb: 8/18/79

YEAR	TM/L	G	AB	R	H	2B	3B	HR	RBI	BB	SO	AVG	OBP	SLG	PRO+	BR/A	SB	CS	SBR	FA	FR	G/POS	TPR
1979	Chi-N	19	40	2	9	1	0	0	3	4	8	.225	.295	.250	46	-3	0	0	0	1.000	4	2-10/3-4	0.2
1980	Chi-N	6	20	2	6	2	0	0	2	0	3	.300	.300	.400	87	-0	0	0	0	1.000	1	/S-3,3-2,2-1	0.1
Total	2	25	60	4	15	3	0	0	5	4	11	.250	.297	.300	59	-3	0	0	0	1.000	6	/2-11,3-6,S-3	0.3

YEAR	TM/L	G	AB	R	H	2B	3B	HR	RBI	BB	SO	AVG	OBP	SLG	PRO+	BR/A	SB	CS	SBR	FA	FR	G/POS	TPR
■ **LONNIE MACLIN**	Maclin, Lonnie Lee b: 2/17/67, Clayton, Mo. BL/TL, 5'11", 185 lbs. Deb: 9/7/93																						
1993	StL-N	12	13	2	1	0	0	0	1	0	5	.077	.077	.077	-60	-3	1	0	0	1.000	-2	/O-5	-0.4
■ **MAX MACON**	Macon, Max Cullen b: 10/14/15, Pensacola, Fla. d: 8/5/89, Jupiter, Fla. BL/TL, 6'3", 175 lbs. Deb: 4/21/38																						
1938	StL-N	46	36	5	11	0	0	0	3	2	4	.306	.342	.306	75	-1	0			.946	0	P-38/O-1	0.0
1940	Bro-N	2	1	0	1	0	0	0	0	0	0	1.000	1.000	1.000	427	0	0			.000	-0	/P-2	0.0
1942	Bro-N	26	43	4	12	2	1	0	1	2	4	.279	.311	.372	98	-0	1			.960	-0	P-14	0.0
1943	Bro-N	45	55	7	9	0	0	0	6	0	1	.164	.164	.164	-5	-7	1			1.000	0	P-25/1-3	-0.2
1944	Bos-N	106	366	38	100	15	3	3	36	12	23	.273	.296	.355	79	-11	7			.977	-2	1-72,O-22/P-1	-1.8
1947	Bos-N	1	1	0	0	0	0	0	0	0	0	.000	.000	.000	-99	-0	0			1.000	0	/P-1	0.0
Total	6	226	502	54	133	17	4	3	46	16	32	.265	.288	.333	72	-19	9			.965	-2	/P-81,1-75,O-23	-2.0
■ **WADDY MacPHEE**	Mac Phee, Walter Scott b: 12/23/1899, Brooklyn, N.Y. d: 1/20/80, Charlotte, N.C. BR/TR, 5'8", 140 lbs. Deb: 9/27/22																						
1922	NY-N	2	7	2	2	0	1	0	0	1	0	.286	.375	.571	140	0	0	0	0	.889	1	/3-2	0.1
■ **JIMMY MACULLAR**	Macullar, James F. "Little Mac" b: 1/16/1855, Boston, Mass. d: 4/8/24, Baltimore, Md. BR/TL, 5'6", 155 lbs. Deb: 5/5/1879 MU																						
1879	Syr-N	64	246	24	52	9	0	0	13	3	27	.211	.221	.248	61	-9				.864	1	S-37,O-26/2-4,3M	-0.7
1882	Cin-a	79	299	44	70	6	6	0	22	14		.234	.268	.294	85	-5				.922	-0	*O-79	-0.5
1883	Cin-a	14	48	4	8	2	0	0	4	4		.167	.231	.208	40	-3				.900	-4	O-14/S-1	-0.6
1884	Bal-a	107	360	73	73	16	6	4		36		.203	.290	.314	93	-2				.866	1	*S-107	0.0
1885	Bal-a	100	320	52	61	7	6	3	26	49		.191	.306	.278	87	-3				.877	0	*S-98/O-2,P-1	-0.1
1886	Bal-a	85	268	49	55	7	1	0	26	49		.205	.332	.239	82	-2	23			.852	-10	S-82/O-2,2-1,P-1	-1.0
Total	6	449	1541	246	319	47	19	7	91	155	27	.207	.285	.276	83	-25	23			.865	-11	S-325,O-123/2-5,P3	-2.9
■ **GENE MADDEN**	Madden, Eugene b: 6/5/1890, Elm Grove, W.Va. d: 4/6/49, Utica, N.Y. BL/TR, 5'10", 155 lbs. Deb: 4/20/16																						
1916	Pit-N	1	1	0	0	0	0	0	0	0	0	.000	.000	.000	-99	-0	0			.000	0	H	0.0
■ **FRANK MADDEN**	Madden, Francis A. "Red" b: 10/17/1892, Pittsburgh, Pa. d: 4/30/52, Pittsburgh, Pa. Deb: 7/4/14																						
1914	Pit-F	2	2	0	1	0	0	0	1	0	0	.500	.500	.500	174	0	0			.000	0	/C-1	0.0
■ **BUNNY MADDEN**	Madden, Thomas Francis b: 9/14/1882, Boston, Mass. d: 1/20/54, Cambridge, Mass. BR/TR, 5'10", 190 lbs. Deb: 6/3/09																						
1909	Bos-A	10	17	0	4	0	0	0	1	0		.235	.235	.235	48	-1	0			.941	1	/C-7	0.1
1910	Bos-A	14	35	4	13	3	0	0	4	3		.371	.436	.457	175	3	0			.938	-3	C-12	0.1
1911	Bos-A	4	15	2	3	0	0	0	2	2		.200	.294	.200	39	-1	0			1.000	-2	/C-4	-0.3
	Phi-N	28	76	4	21	1	1	0	4	0	13	.276	.276	.316	65	-4	0			.924	3	C-22	0.1
Total	3	56	143	10	41	4	1	0	11	5	13	.287	.315	.329	87	-3	0			.935	-1	/C-45	-0.0
■ **TOMMY MADDEN**	Madden, Thomas Joseph b: 7/31/1883, Philadelphia, Pa. d: 7/26/30, Philadelphia, Pa. BL/TL, 5'11", 160 lbs. Deb: 9/10/06																						
1906	Bos-N	4	15	1	4	0	0	0	0	1		.267	.313	.267	83	-0	0			1.000	-0	/O-4	-0.1
1910	NY-A	1	1	0	0	0	0	0	0	0		.000	.000	.000	-95	-0	0			.000	-0	H	-0.1
Total	2	5	16	1	4	0	0	0	0	1		.250	.294	.250	71	-1	0			1.000	-1	/O-4	-0.2
■ **CLARENCE MADDERN**	Maddern, Clarence James b: 9/26/21, Bisbee, Ariz. d: 8/9/86, Tucson, Ariz. BR/TR, 6'1", 185 lbs. Deb: 9/19/46																						
1946	Chi-N	3	3	0	0	0	0	0	0	0	0	.000	.250	.000	-27	-0	0			1.000	-0	/O-2	-0.1
1948	Chi-N	80	214	16	54	12	1	4	27	10	25	.252	.301	.374	85	-5	0			.981	-2	O-55	-1.0
1949	Chi-N	10	9	1	3	0	0	1	2	2	0	.333	.455	.667	202	1	0			1.000	0	/1-1	0.2
1951	Cle-A	11	12	0	2	0	0	0	0	0	1	.167	.167	.167	-10	-2	0	0	0	.667	-0	/O-1	-0.2
Total	4	104	238	17	59	12	1	5	29	12	26	.248	.301	.370	84	-6	0	0		.973	-2	/O-58,1-1	-1.1
■ **ELLIOTT MADDOX**	Maddox, Elliott b: 12/21/47, East Orange, N.J. BR/TR, 5'11", 181 lbs. Deb: 4/7/70																						
1970	Det-A	109	258	30	64	13	4	3	24	30	42	.248	.333	.364	92	-3	2	3	-1	.919	0	3-40,O-37,S-19,/2-1	-0.5
1971	Was-A	128	258	38	56	8	2	1	18	51	42	.217	.346	.275	83	-4	10	4	1	.990	-3	*O-103,3-12	-1.0
1972	Tex-A	98	294	40	74	7	2	0	10	49	53	.252	.362	.289	100	2	20	10	0	.990	4	O-94	0.2
1973	Tex-A	100	172	24	41	1	0	1	17	29	28	.238	.358	.262	80	-3	5	4	-1	.981	-7	O-89/3-7,D-1	-1.4
1974	NY-A	137	466	75	141	26	2	3	45	69	48	.303	.397	.386	128	20	6	5	-1	.986	9	*O-135/2-2,3-1	2.3
1975	NY-A	55	218	36	67	10	3	1	23	21	24	.307	.386	.394	123	8	9	3	1	1.000	8	O-55/2-1	1.4
1976	*NY-A	18	46	4	10	2	0	0	3	4	3	.217	.280	.261	60	-2	0	1	-1	1.000	-1	O-13/D-2	-0.4
1977	Bal-A	49	107	14	28	7	0	2	9	13	9	.262	.363	.383	110	2	2	2	-1	.990	-4	O-45/3-1	-0.4
1978	NY-N	119	389	43	100	18	2	2	39	71	38	.257	.374	.329	102	4	2	11	-6	.988	-3	O-79,3-43/1-1	-0.9
1979	NY-N	86	224	21	60	13	0	1	12	20	27	.268	.336	.339	88	-3	3	2	-0	.985	-1	O-65,3-11	-0.7
1980	NY-N	130	411	35	101	16	1	4	34	52	44	.246	.339	.319	87	-6	1	9	-5	.956	-3	*3-115/O-4,1-2	-1.6
Total	11	1029	2843	360	742	121	16	18	234	409	358	.261	.361	.334	100	16	60	54	-14	.989	-1	O-719,3-230/S21D	-3.0
■ **GARRY MADDOX**	Maddox, Garry Lee b: 9/1/49, Cincinnati, Ohio BR/TR, 6'3", 184 lbs. Deb: 4/25/72																						
1972	SF-N	125	458	62	122	26	7	12	58	14	97	.266	.294	.432	103	-1	13	6	0	.979	4	*O-121	-0.2
1973	SF-N	144	587	81	187	30	10	11	76	24	73	.319	.352	.460	118	13	24	10	1	.969	8	*O-140	1.6
1974	SF-N	135	538	74	153	31	3	8	50	29	64	.284	.325	.398	97	-4	21	9	1	.986	7	*O-131	-0.2
1975	SF-N	17	52	4	7	1	0	1	4	6	3	.135	.237	.212	24	-5	1	1	-0	1.000	3	O-13	-0.3
	Phi-N	99	374	50	109	25	8	4	46	36	54	.291	.361	.433	115	8	24	3	5	.983	18	O-97	2.7
	Yr	116	426	54	116	26	8	5	50	42	57	.272	.346	.406	104	2	25	4	5	.985	21	*O-110	2.4
1976	*Phi-N	146	531	75	175	37	6	6	68	42	59	.330	.383	.456	133	23	29	12	2	.989	24	*O-144	4.5
1977	*Phi-N	139	571	85	167	27	10	14	74	24	58	.292	.326	.448	101	-1	22	6	3	.977	14	*O-138	1.1
1978	*Phi-N	155	598	62	172	34	3	11	68	39	89	.288	.333	.410	106	3	33	7	6	.983	21	*O-154	2.4
1979	Phi-N	148	548	70	154	28	6	13	61	17	71	.281	.308	.425	95	-6	26	13	0	.996	**27**	*O-140	1.6
1980	*Phi-N	143	549	59	142	31	3	11	73	18	52	.259	.282	.386	80	-16	25	5	5	.976	14	*O-143	-0.3
1981	*Phi-N	94	323	37	85	7	1	5	40	17	42	.263	.302	.337	78	-10	9	4	0	.977	9	O-94	-0.3
1982	Phi-N	119	412	39	117	27	2	8	61	12	32	.284	.304	.417	98	-3	7	5	-1	**.992**	7	*O-111	0.1
1983	*Phi-N	97	324	27	89	14	2	4	32	17	31	.275	.313	.367	89	-5	7	6	-2	.977	-0	O-95	-1.0
1984	Phi-N	77	241	29	68	11	0	5	19	13	29	.282	.319	.390	97	-1	3	2	-0	1.000	0	O-69	-0.4
1985	Phi-N	105	218	22	52	8	1	4	23	13	26	.239	.284	.339	72	-8	4	2	0	.980	-12	O-94	-2.4
1986	Phi-N	6	7	1	3	0	0	0	1	2	1	.429	.556	.429	169	1	0	1	-1	1.000	-1	/O-3	-0.1
Total	15	1749	6331	777	1802	337	62	117	754	323	781	.285	.323	.413	100	-11	248	92	19	.983	142	*O-1687	8.8
■ **JERRY MADDOX**	Maddox, Jerry Glenn b: 7/28/53, Whittier, Cal. BR/TR, 6'2", 200 lbs. Deb: 6/3/78																						
1978	Atl-N	7	14	1	3	0	0	0	1	1	2	.214	.267	.214	32	-1	0	0	0	.909	-0	/3-5	-0.2
■ **ART MADISON**	Madison, Arthur b: 1/14/1871, Clarksburg, Mass. d: 1/27/33, N.Adams, Mass. BR/TR, 5'9", 165 lbs. Deb: 9/9/1895																						
1895	Phi-N	11	34	6	12	3	0	0	8	1	1	.353	.371	.441	109	0	4			.955	-1	/S-6,2-3,3-2	0.0
1899	Pit-N	42	118	20	32	2	4	0	19	11		.271	.338	.356	91	-1	1			.953	-5	2-19,S-15/3-2	-0.4
Total	2	53	152	26	44	5	4	0	27	12	1	.289	.345	.375	95	-1	5			.926	-6	/2-22,S-21,3-4	-0.4
■ **SCOTTI MADISON**	Madison, Charles Scott b: 9/12/59, Pensacola, Fla. BB/TR, 5'11", 195 lbs. Deb: 7/6/85																						
1985	Det-A	6	11	0	0	0	0	0	1	2	0	.000	.154	.000	-54	-2	0	0	0	1.000	-0	/C-1,D-3	-0.2
1986	Det-A	2	7	0	0	0	0	0	1	0	3	.000	.000	.000	-99	-2	0	0	0	.667	-1	/3-1,D-1	-0.3
1987	KC-A	7	15	4	4	3	0	0	0	1	5	.267	.313	.467	100	-0	0	0	0	1.000	-1	/1-4,C-3	-0.1
1988	KC-A	16	35	4	6	2	0	0	2	4	5	.171	.256	.229	37	-3	1	0	0	1.000	-2	/C-4,O-3,1-2,D-4	-0.4
1989	Cin-N	40	98	13	17	7	0	1	7	8	9	.173	.243	.276	46	-7	0	1	-1	1.000	2	3-26	-0.5
Total	5	71	166	21	27	12	0	1	11	15	22	.163	.236	.253	37	-14	1	1	-0	.985	-1	/3-27,D-8,C-8,10	-1.5
■ **ED MADJESKI**	Madjeski, Edward William (b: Edward William Majewski) b: 7/20/08, Far Rockaway, N.Y d: 11/11/94, Montgomery, Ohio BR/TR, 5'11", 178 lbs. Deb: 5/2/32																						
1932	Phi-A	17	35	4	8	0	0	0	3	3	6	.229	.289	.229	35	-3	0	0	0	1.000	2	/C-8	-0.1

YEAR	TM/L	G	AB	R	H	2B	3B	HR	RBI	BB	SO	AVG	OBP	SLG	PRO+	BR/A	SB	CS	SBR	FA	FR	G/POS	TPR
1933	Phi-A	51	142	17	40	4	0	0	17	4	21	.282	.301	.310	62	-8	0	0	0	.958	-4	C-41	-0.9
1934	Phi-A	8	8	1	3	1	0	0	2	0	1	.375	.375	.500	129	0	0	0	0	.000	-1	/C-1	0.0
	Chi-A	85	281	36	62	14	2	5	32	14	31	.221	.260	.338	52	-21	2	0	1	.973	2	C-79	-1.4
	Yr	93	289	37	65	15	2	5	34	14	32	.225	.263	.343	54	-21	2	0	1	.971	2	C-80	-1.4
1937	NY-N	5	15	0	3	0	0	0	2	0	2	.200	.200	.200	9	-2	0			1.000	-2	/C-5	-0.4
Total	4	166	481	58	116	19	2	5	56	21	61	.241	.274	.320	53	-34	2	0		.970	-2	C-134	-2.8

■ BILL MADLOCK

Madlock, Bill b: 1/2/51, Memphis, Tenn. BR/TR, 5'11", 185 lbs. Deb: 9/7/73

YEAR	TM/L	G	AB	R	H	2B	3B	HR	RBI	BB	SO	AVG	OBP	SLG	PRO+	BR/A	SB	CS	SBR	FA	FR	G/POS	TPR
1973	Tex-A	21	77	16	27	5	3	1	5	7	9	.351	.412	.532	171	7	3	2	-0	.918	-6	3-21	0.1
1974	Chi-N	128	453	65	142	21	5	9	54	42	39	.313	.378	.442	124	14	11	7	-1	.946	-12	*3-121	0.1
1975	Chi-N★	130	514	77	182	29	7	7	64	42	34	**.354**	.406	.479	139	27	9	7	-2	.943	-11	*3-128	1.5
1976	Chi-N	142	514	68	174	36	1	15	84	56	27	**.339**	.415	.500	146	32	15	11	-2	.961	-20	*3-136	0.9
1977	SF-N	140	533	70	161	28	1	12	46	43	33	.302	.361	.426	111	8	13	10	-2	.949	-17	*3-126/2-6	-1.2
1978	SF-N	122	447	76	138	26	3	15	44	48	39	.309	.380	.481	145	26	16	5	2	.974	-24	*2-114/1-3	1.3
1979	SF-N	69	249	37	65	9	2	7	41	18	19	.261	.311	.398	99	-2	11	3	2	.976	-14	2-63/1-5	-1.0
	*Pit-N	85	311	48	102	17	3	7	44	34	22	.328	.396	.469	129	13	21	8	2	.969	-6	3-85	0.8
	Yr	154	560	85	167	26	5	14	85	52	41	.298	.359	.438	117	13	32	11	3	.969	-20	3-85,2-63/1-5	-0.2
1980	Pit-N	137	494	62	137	22	4	10	53	45	33	.277	.343	.399	105	3	16	10	-1	.955	-17	*3-127,1-12	-1.8
1981	Pit-N★	82	279	35	95	23	1	6	45	34	17	**.341**	.418	.495	153	20	18	6	2	.956	-4	3-78	1.8
1982	Pit-N	154	568	92	181	33	3	19	95	48	39	.319	.376	.488	136	27	18	6	2	.952	-6	*3-146/1-3	1.9
1983	Pit-N★	130	473	68	153	21	0	12	68	49	24	**.323**	.389	.444	127	18	3	4	-2	.958	-14	*3-126	0.2
1984	Pit-N	103	403	38	102	16	0	4	44	26	29	.253	.300	.323	75	-14	3	1	0	.942	-8	3-98/1-1	-2.4
1985	Pit-N	110	399	49	100	23	1	10	41	39	42	.251	.325	.388	100	-0	3	3	-1	.940	-16	3-98,1-12	-2.0
	*LA-N	34	114	20	41	4	0	2	15	10	11	.360	.425	.447	149	8	7	1	2	.948	3	3-32	1.2
	Yr	144	513	69	141	27	1	12	56	49	53	.275	.347	.402	110	7	10	4	1	.943	-13	*3-130,1-12	-0.8
1986	LA-N	111	379	38	106	17	0	10	60	30	43	.280	.341	.404	112	6	3	3	-1	.910	-8	*3-101/1-2	-0.6
1987	LA-N	21	61	5	11	1	0	3	7	6	5	.180	.265	.344	61	-4	0	0	0	.912	-4	3-16/1-1	-0.8
	*Det-A	87	326	56	91	17	0	14	50	28	45	.279	.354	.460	119	9	4	3	-1	.989	-2	D-64,1-22/3-1	0.3
Total	15	1806	6594	920	2008	348	34	163	860	605	510	.305	.369	.442	123	200	174	90	-2	.948	-185	*3-1440,2-183/D1	0.3

■ SAL MADRID

Madrid, Salvador b: 6/9/20, ElPaso, Tex. d: 2/24/77, Ft.Wayne, Ind. BR/TR, 5'9", 165 lbs. Deb: 9/17/47

YEAR	TM/L	G	AB	R	H	2B	3B	HR	RBI	BB	SO	AVG	OBP	SLG	PRO+	BR/A	SB	CS	SBR	FA	FR	G/POS	TPR
1947	Chi-N	8	24	0	3	1	0	0	1	1	6	.125	.160	.167	-14	-4	0			.956	4	/S-8	0.0

■ DAVE MAGADAN

Magadan, David Joseph b: 9/30/62, Tampa, Fla. BL/TR, 6'3", 200 lbs. Deb: 9/7/86

YEAR	TM/L	G	AB	R	H	2B	3B	HR	RBI	BB	SO	AVG	OBP	SLG	PRO+	BR/A	SB	CS	SBR	FA	FR	G/POS	TPR
1986	NY-N	10	18	3	8	0	0	0	3	3	1	.444	.524	.444	175	2	0	0	0	1.000	1	/1-9	0.3
1987	NY-N	85	192	21	61	13	1	3	24	22	22	.318	.388	.443	126	8	0	0	0	.981	3	3-50,1-13	0.9
1988	*NY-N	112	314	39	87	15	0	1	35	60	39	.277	.396	.334	117	11	0	1	-1	.988	-1	1-71,3-48	0.4
1989	NY-N	127	374	47	107	22	3	4	41	49	37	.286	.370	.393	124	13	1	0	0	.991	3	1-87,3-28	1.0
1990	NY-N	144	451	74	148	28	6	6	72	74	55	.328	**.425**	.457	143	30	2	1	0	**.998**	3	*1-113,3-19	2.5
1991	NY-N	124	418	58	108	23	0	4	51	83	50	.258	.384	.342	106	8	1	1	-0	.996	2	*1-122	0.1
1992	NY-N	99	321	33	91	9	1	3	28	56	44	.283	.390	.346	111	8	1	0	0	.941	-13	3-93/1-2	-0.5
1993	Fla-N	66	227	22	65	12	0	4	29	44	30	.286	.404	.392	108	5	0	1	-1	.961	2	3-63/1-2	0.5
	Sea-A	71	228	27	59	11	0	1	21	36	33	.259	.360	.320	83	-4	2	0	1	.991	-1	1-41,3-27/D-2	-0.7
1994	Fla-N	74	211	30	58	7	0	1	17	39	25	.275	.390	.322	86	-2	0	0	0	.958	-5	3-48,1-16	-0.8
1995	Hou-N	127	348	44	109	24	0	2	51	71	56	.313	.430	.399	129	19	2	1	0	.922	-7	*3-100,1-11	1.1
1996	Chi-N	78	169	23	43	10	0	3	17	29	23	.254	.364	.367	91	-1	0	2	-1	.963	-7	3-51,1-10	-1.0
1997	Oak-A	128	271	38	82	10	1	4	30	50	40	.303	.415	.391	114	8	1	0	0	.940	0	3-49,1-30,D-25	0.6
1998	Oak-A	35	109	12	35	8	0	1	13	13	12	.321	.393	.422	116	3	0	1	-1	.918	2	3-30/1-7	0.4
Total	13	1280	3651	471	1061	192	12	37	432	629	467	.291	.396	.380	115	106	10	8	-2	.950	-19	3-606,1-534/D-27	4.8

■ EVER MAGALLANES

Magallanes, Everado (Espinoza) b: 11/6/65, Chihuahua, Mexico BL/TR, 5'10", 165 lbs. Deb: 5/17/91

YEAR	TM/L	G	AB	R	H	2B	3B	HR	RBI	BB	SO	AVG	OBP	SLG	PRO+	BR/A	SB	CS	SBR	FA	FR	G/POS	TPR
1991	Cle-A	3	2	0	0	0	0	0	0	1	1	.000	.333	.000	1	-0	0	0	0	1.000	-1	/S-2	-0.1

■ LEE MAGEE

Magee, Leo Christopher (b: Leopold Christopher Hoernschemeyer)
b: 6/4/1889, Cincinnati, Ohio d: 3/14/66, Columbus, Ohio BB/TR, 5'11", 165 lbs. Deb: 7/4/11 M

YEAR	TM/L	G	AB	R	H	2B	3B	HR	RBI	BB	SO	AVG	OBP	SLG	PRO+	BR/A	SB	CS	SBR	FA	FR	G/POS	TPR
1911	StL-N	26	69	9	18	1	1	0	8	8	8	.261	.338	.304	82	-1	4			.975	-2	2-18/S-3	-0.4
1912	StL-N	128	458	60	133	13	8	0	40	39	29	.290	.347	.354	94	-3	16			.956	7	O-85,2-23/1-6,S-1	-0.1
1913	StL-N	137	531	54	142	13	7	2	31	34	30	.267	.314	.330	85	-11	23			.982	13	*O-108,2-22/1-6,S-2	-0.3
1914	StL-N	142	529	59	150	23	4	2	40	42	24	.284	.337	.353	107	4	36			.970	5	*O-102,1-39/2-6	0.4
1915	Bro-F	121	452	87	146	19	10	4	49	22	19	.323	.356	.436	123	6	34			.937	-1	*2-115/1-2,M	0.7
1916	NY-A	131	510	57	131	18	4	3	45	50	31	.257	.324	.325	93	-4	29	25	-6	.975	5	*O-128/2-2	-1.4
1917	NY-A	51	173	17	38	4	1	0	8	13	18	.220	.278	.254	62	-8	3			.938	-8	O-50	-2.1
	StL-A	36	112	11	19	1	0	0	4	6	6	.170	.212	.179	20	-11	3			.971	6	3-20/2-6,1-5,O-1	-0.5
	Yr	87	285	28	57	5	1	0	12	19	24	.200	.252	.225	46	-18	6			.938	-2	O-51,3-20/2-6,1-5	-2.6
1918	Cin-N	119	459	61	133	22	13	0	28	28	19	.290	.331	.394	123	11	19			.956	9	*2-114/3-3	3.0
1919	Bro-N	45	181	16	43	7	2	0	7	5	8	.238	.262	.298	67	-8	5			.938	-1	2-36/3-9	-0.7
	Chi-N	79	267	36	78	12	4	1	17	18	16	.292	.339	.378	115	5	14			.978	-6	O-45,S-13,3-10,/2-7	-0.4
	Yr	124	448	52	121	19	6	1	24	23	24	.270	.309	.346	95	-3	19			.978	-7	O-45,2-43,3-19,S-13	-1.1
Total	9	1015	3741	467	1031	133	54	12	277	265	208	.276	.325	.350	98	-20	186	25		.969	27	O-519,2-349/13S	-1.8

■ SHERRY MAGEE

Magee, Sherwood Robert b: 8/6/1884, Clarendon, Pa. d: 3/13/29, Philadelphia, Pa. BR/TR, 5'11", 179 lbs. Deb: 6/29/04 U

YEAR	TM/L	G	AB	R	H	2B	3B	HR	RBI	BB	SO	AVG	OBP	SLG	PRO+	BR/A	SB	CS	SBR	FA	FR	G/POS	TPR
1904	Phi-N	95	364	51	101	15	12	3	57	14		.277	.308	.409	125	9	11			.921	5	O-94/1-1	0.8
1905	Phi-N	155	603	100	180	24	17	5	98	44		.299	.354	.420	135	25	48			.963	10	*O-155	2.8
1906	Phi-N	154	563	77	159	36	8	6	67	52		.282	.348	.407	135	22	55			.982	11	*O-154	2.8
1907	Phi-N	140	503	75	165	28	12	4	**85**	53		.328	.396	.455	169	40	46			.978	7	*O-139	4.6
1908	Phi-N	143	508	79	144	30	16	2	57	49		.283	.359	.417	143	25	40			.970	2	*O-142	2.3
1909	Phi-N	143	522	60	141	33	14	2	66	43		.270	.339	.398	128	16	38			.970	-6	*O-143	0.4
1910	Phi-N	154	519	**110**	172	39	17	6	**123**	94	36	**.331**	**.445**	**.507**	**172**	**51**	49			.974	-13	*O-154	3.2
1911	Phi-N	121	445	79	128	32	5	15	94	49	33	.288	.366	.483	135	19	22			**.981**	3	*O-120	1.6
1912	Phi-N	132	464	79	142	25	9	6	66	55	54	.306	.388	.438	118	12	30			.963	-11	*O-124/1-6	-0.6
1913	Phi-N	138	470	92	144	36	6	11	70	38	36	.306	.369	.479	136	21	23			.968	-10	*O-123/1-4	0.5
1914	Phi-N	146	544	96	**171**	**39**	11	15	**103**	55	42	.314	.380	**.509**	154	34	25			.940	9	O-67,S-39,1-32,/2-8	4.5
1915	Bos-N	156	571	72	160	34	12	2	87	54	39	.280	.350	.392	130	21	15	12	-3	.981	15	*O-135,1-21	2.9
1916	Bos-N	122	419	44	101	17	5	3	54	44	52	.241	.322	.327	104	3	10			.978	-5	*O-120/1-2,S-1	-1.0
1917	Bos-N	72	246	24	63	8	4	1	29	13	23	.256	.302	.333	100	-0	7			.954	2	O-65/1-2	-0.3
	Cin-N	45	137	17	44	8	4	0	23	16	7	.321	.400	.438	164	11	4			.989	4	O-41/1-2	1.4
	Yr	117	383	41	107	16	8	1	52	29	30	.279	.338	.371	124	10	11			.967	6	*O-106/1-4	1.1
1918	Cin-N	115	400	46	119	15	13	2	**76**	37	18	.298	.370	.415	142	20	14			.981	-2	1-66,O-38/2-6	1.5
1919	*Cin-N	56	163	11	35	6	1	0	21	26	19	.215	.337	.264	84	-2	4			.990	-3	O-47/2-1,3-1	-0.9
Total	16	2087	7441	1112	2169	425	166	83	1176	736	359	.291	.364	.427	137	324	441	12		.970	16	*O-1861,1-136/S23	26.5

■ WENDELL MAGEE

Magee, Wendell Errol b: 8/3/72, Hattiesburg, Miss. BR/TR, 6', 225 lbs. Deb: 8/16/96

YEAR	TM/L	G	AB	R	H	2B	3B	HR	RBI	BB	SO	AVG	OBP	SLG	PRO+	BR/A	SB	CS	SBR	FA	FR	G/POS	TPR
1996	Phi-N	38	142	9	29	7	0	2	14	9	33	.204	.252	.296	43	-12	0	0	0	.978	3	O-37	-1.0
1997	Phi-N	38	115	7	23	4	0	1	9	9	20	.200	.258	.261	36	-11	1	4	-2	.960	5	O-38	-0.8
1998	Phi-N	20	75	9	22	6	1	1	11	7	11	.293	.354	.440	103	0	0	0	0	.941	0	O-19	0.1
Total	3	96	332	25	74	17	1	4	34	25	64	.223	.277	.316	55	-22	1	4	-2	.965	8	/O-94	-1.7

■ HARL MAGGERT

Maggert, Harl Vestin b: 2/13/1883, Cromwell, Ind. d: 1/7/63, Fresno, Cal. BL/TR, 5'8", 155 lbs. Deb: 9/4/07 F

YEAR	TM/L	G	AB	R	H	2B	3B	HR	RBI	BB	SO	AVG	OBP	SLG	PRO+	BR/A	SB	CS	SBR	FA	FR	G/POS	TPR
1907	Pit-N	3	6	1	0	0	0	0	0	2		.000	.250	.000	-21	-1	1			1.000	0	/O-2	-0.1
1912	Phi-A	74	242	39	62	8	6	1	13	36		.256	.357	.351	107	3	10			.939	-6	O-61	-0.6
Total	2	77	248	40	62	8	6	1	13	38		.250	.354	.343	104	2	11			.942	-6	/O-63	-0.7

YEAR	TM/L	G	AB	R	H	2B	3B	HR	RBI	BB	SO	AVG	OBP	SLG	PRO+	BR/A	SB	CS	SBR	FA	FR	G/POS	TPR

■ HARL MAGGERT   Maggert, Harl Warren   b: 5/4/14, Los Angeles, Cal.   d: 7/10/86, Citrus Heights, Cal.   BR/TR, 6′, 190 lbs.   Deb: 4/19/38   F

| 1938 | Bos-N | 66 | 89 | 12 | 25 | 3 | 0 | 3 | 19 | 10 | 20 | .281 | .354 | .416 | 123 | 3 | 0 | | | .944 | -0 | O-10/3-8 | 0.2 |

■ STUBBY MAGNER   Magner, Edmund Burke   b: 2/20/1888, Kalamazoo, Mich.   d: 9/6/56, Chillicothe, Ohio   BR/TR, 5′3″, 135 lbs.   Deb: 7/12/11

| 1911 | NY-A | 13 | 33 | 3 | 7 | 0 | 0 | 0 | 4 | 4 | | .212 | .297 | .212 | 40 | -3 | 1 | | | .970 | -0 | /S-6,2-5 | -0.3 |

■ JOHN MAGNER   Magner, John T.   b: 1855, St.Louis, Mo.   Deb: 7/14/1879   U

| 1879 | Cin-N | 1 | 4 | 0 | 0 | 0 | 0 | 0 | | 0 | | .000 | .000 | .000 | -99 | -1 | | | | .500 | -0 | /O-1 | -0.1 |

■ GEORGE MAGOON   Magoon, George Henry "Maggie" or "Topsy"   b: 3/27/1875, St.Albans, Maine   d: 12/6/43, Rochester, N.H.   BR/TR, 5′10″, 160 lbs.   Deb: 6/29/1898

1898	Bro-N	93	343	35	77	7	0	1	39	30		.224	.293	.254	57	-19	7			.925	13	S-93	-0.1
1899	Bal-N	62	207	26	53	8	3	0	31	26		.256	.353	.324	82	-5	7			.923	5	S-62	0.5
	Chi-N	59	189	24	43	5	1	0	21	24		.228	.333	.265	67	-7	5			.896	6	S-59	0.3
	Yr	121	396	50	96	13	4	0	52	50		.242	.344	.295	75	-12	12			.909	12	*S-121	0.8
1901	Cin-N	127	460	47	116	16	7	1	53	52		.252	.331	.324	97	-1	15			.919	-20	*S-112,2-15	-1.1
1902	Cin-N	45	162	29	44	9	2	0	23	13		.272	.344	.352	105	1	7			.930	4	2-41/S-3	0.7
1903	Cin-N	42	139	6	30	6	0	0	9	19		.216	.314	.259	58	-8	2			.971	5	2-32/3-9	-0.2
	Chi-A	94	334	32	76	11	3	0	25	30		.228	.303	.278	79	-8	4			.936	-21	2-94	-2.6
Total	5	522	1834	199	439	62	16	2	201	194		.239	.321	.294	78	-45	47			.916	-8	S-329,2-182/3-9	-2.5

■ TOM MAGRANN   Magrann, Thomas Joseph   b: 12/9/63, Hollywood, Fla.   BR/TR, 6′3″, 177 lbs.   Deb: 9/7/89

| 1989 | Cle-A | 9 | 10 | 0 | 0 | 0 | 0 | 0 | 0 | 0 | 4 | .000 | .000 | .000 | -98 | -3 | 0 | 0 | 0 | 1.000 | 3 | /C-9 | 0.1 |

■ FREDDIE MAGUIRE   Maguire, Frederick Edward   b: 5/10/1899, Roxbury, Mass.   d: 11/3/61, Boston, Mass.   BR/TR, 5′11″, 155 lbs.   Deb: 9/22/22

1922	NY-N	5	12	4	4	0	0	0	1	0	1	.333	.333	.333	72	-0	1	0	0	.944	2	/2-3	0.1
1923	*NY-N	41	30	11	6	1	0	0	2	2	4	.200	.250	.233	29	-3	1	0	0	.881	12	2-16/3-1	0.9
1928	Chi-N	140	574	67	160	24	7	1	41	25	38	.279	.312	.350	74	-22	6			.976	51	*2-138	3.1
1929	Bos-N	138	496	54	125	26	8	0	41	19	40	.252	.284	.337	55	-36	8			.971	8	*2-138/S-1	-2.0
1930	Bos-N	146	516	54	138	21	5	0	52	20	22	.267	.297	.328	53	-40	4			.969	-4	*2-146	-3.2
1931	Bos-N	148	492	36	112	18	2	0	26	16	26	.228	.259	.272	45	-39	3			**.976**	9	*2-148	-2.1
Total	6	618	2120	226	545	90	22	1	163	82	131	.257	.289	.322	57	-140	23	0		.971	77	2-589/S-1,3-1	-3.2

■ JACK MAGUIRE   Maguire, Jack   b: 2/5/25, St.Louis, Mo.   BR/TR, 5′11″, 165 lbs.   Deb: 4/18/50

1950	NY-N	29	40	3	7	2	0	0	3	3	13	.175	.233	.225	21	-5	0			1.000	1	/O-9,1-2	-0.3
1951	NY-N	16	20	6	8	1	1	1	4	2	2	.400	.455	.700	204	3	0	0	0	1.000	-0	/O-8	0.2
	Pit-N	8	5	1	0	0	0	0	0	1	0	.000	.167	.000	-50	-1	0	0	0	1.000	1	/2-1,3-1	0.0
	Yr	24	25	7	8	1	1	1	4	3	2	.320	.393	.560	151	2	0	0	0	1.000	0	/O-8,2-1,3-1	0.2
	StL-A	41	127	15	31	2	1	1	14	12	21	.244	.309	.299	63	-6	1	0	0	.969	-0	O-26/3-5,2-2	-0.7
Total	2	94	192	25	46	5	2	2	21	18	36	.240	.305	.318	66	-9	1			.979	2	/O-43,3-6,2-3,1-2	-0.8

■ JIM MAHADY   Mahady, James Bernard   b: 4/22/01, Cortland, N.Y.   d: 8/9/36, Cortland, N.Y.   BR/TR, 5′11″, 170 lbs.   Deb: 10/2/21

| 1921 | NY-N | 1 | 0 | 0 | 0 | 0 | 0 | 0 | 0 | 0 | 0 | — | — | — | | | 0 | 0 | 0 | 1.000 | 0 | /2-1 | 0.0 |

■ ART MAHAN   Mahan, Arthur Leo   b: 6/8/13, Somerville, Mass.   BL/TL, 5′11″, 178 lbs.   Deb: 4/30/40

| 1940 | Phi-N | 146 | 544 | 55 | 133 | 24 | 5 | 2 | 39 | 40 | 37 | .244 | .297 | .318 | 73 | -21 | 4 | | | .992 | 4 | *1-145/P-1 | -3.1 |

■ FRANK MAHAR   Mahar, Frank Edward   b: 12/4/1878, Natick, Mass.   d: 12/5/61, Somerville, Mass.   TR, 5′10.5″,   Deb: 8/29/02

| 1902 | Phi-N | 1 | 1 | 0 | 0 | 0 | 0 | 0 | 0 | 0 | | .000 | .000 | .000 | -99 | -0 | | | | .000 | 0 | H | 0.0 |

■ BILLY MAHARG   Maharg, William Joseph   b: 3/19/1881, Philadelphia, Pa.   d: 11/20/53, Philadelphia, Pa.   BR/TR, 5′4.5″, 155 lbs.   Deb: 5/18/12

1912	Det-A	1	1	0	0	0	0	0	0	0	0	.000	.000	.000	-99	-0				1.000	1	/3-1	-0.0
1916	Phi-N	1	1	0	0	0	0	0	0	0	0	.000	.000	.000	-97	-0				.000	-0	/O-1	-0.1
Total	2	2	2	0	0	0	0	0	0	0	0	.000	.000	.000	-99	-0				—	0	/O-1,3-1	-0.1

■ RON MAHAY   Mahay, Ronald Matthew   b: 6/28/71, Crestwood, Ill.   BL/TL, 6′2″, 185 lbs.   Deb: 5/21/95

1995	Bos-A	5	20	3	4	2	0	1	3	1	6	.200	.273	.450	81	-1	0	0	0	1.000	-1	/O-5	-0.1
1997	Bos-A	28	0	0	0	0	0	0	0	0	0	—	—	—		-0	0	0	0	1.000	-0	P-28	0.0
1998	Bos-A	29	0	0	0	0	0	0	0	0	1	.000	1.000	.000	191	-0	0	0	0	1.000	-1	P-29	0.1
Total	3	62	20	3	4	2	0	1	3	2	6	.200	.304	.450	90	-0	0	0	0	.857	-1	/P-57,O-5	0.0

■ TOM MAHER   Maher, Thomas Francis   b: 7/6/1870, Philadelphia, Pa.   d: 8/25/29, Philadelphia, Pa.   Deb: 4/24/02

| 1902 | Phi-N | 1 | 0 | 0 | 0 | 0 | 0 | 0 | 0 | 0 | 0 | — | — | — | | | 0 | | | .000 | 0 | R | — |

■ GREG MAHLBERG   Mahlberg, Gregory John   b: 8/8/52, Milwaukee, Wis.   BR/TR, 5′10″, 180 lbs.   Deb: 9/24/78

1978	Tex-A	1	1	0	0	0	0	0	0	0	0	.000	.000	.000	-99	-0	0	0	0	1.000	0	/C-1	0.0
1979	Tex-A	7	17	2	2	0	0	1	1	2	4	.118	.211	.294	35	-2	0	0	0	1.000	-2	/C-7	-0.3
Total	2	8	18	2	2	0	0	1	1	2	4	.111	.200	.278	28	-2	0	0	0	1.000	-2	/C-8	-0.3

■ DAN MAHONEY   Mahoney, Daniel J.   b: 3/20/1864, Springfield, Mass.   d: 2/1/04, Springfield, Mass.   BR/TR, 5′9.5″, 165 lbs.   Deb: 8/20/1892

1892	Cin-N	5	21	1	4	0	1	0	1	1	4	.190	.227	.286	56	-1	0			.943	2	/C-5	0.1
1895	Was-N	6	12	2	2	0	0	0	1	0	0	.167	.167	.167	-14	-2	0			1.000	-1	/C-2,1-1	-0.2
Total	2	11	33	3	6	0	1	0	2	1	4	.182	.206	.242	28	-3	0			.949	1	/C-7,1-1	-0.1

■ DANNY MAHONEY   Mahoney, Daniel Joseph   b: 9/6/1888, Haverhill, Mass.   d: 9/28/60, Utica, N.Y.   BR/TR, 5′6.5″, 145 lbs.   Deb: 5/15/11

| 1911 | Cin-N | 1 | 0 | 0 | 0 | 0 | 0 | 0 | 0 | 0 | 0 | — | — | — | | | 0 | | | .000 | 0 | R | — |

■ MIKE MAHONEY   Mahoney, George W. "Big Mike"   b: 12/5/1873, Boston, Mass.   d: 1/3/40, Boston, Mass.   BR, 6′4″, 220 lbs.   Deb: 5/18/1897

1897	Bos-N	2	2	1	1	0	0	0	1	0		.500	.500	.500	155	0	0			1.000	0	/C-1,P-1	0.0
1898	StL-N	2	7	0	0	0	0	0	0	0		.000	.000	.000	-98	-2	0			.920	0	/1-2	-0.2
Total	2	4	9	1	1	0	0	0	1	0		.111	.111	.111	-36	-2	0			.920	-0	/1-2,P-1,C-1	-0.2

■ JIM MAHONEY   Mahoney, James Thomas "Moe"   b: 5/26/34, Englewood, N.J.   BR/TR, 6′, 175 lbs.   Deb: 7/28/59   C

1959	Bos-A	31	23	10	3	0	0	1	4	3	7	.130	.148	.261	33	-2	0	0	0	.940	10	S-30	0.9
1961	Was-A	43	108	10	26	0	1	0	6	5	23	.241	.274	.259	44	-8	1	2	-1	.968	12	S-31/2-2	0.4
1962	Cle-A	41	74	12	18	4	0	3	5	3	14	.243	.273	.419	86	-2	0	0	0	.964	8	S-23/2-8,3-1	0.8
1965	Hou-N	5	5	0	1	0	0	0	0	0	3	.200	.200	.200	14	-1	0	0	0	1.000	0	/S-5	0.0
Total	4	120	210	32	48	4	1	4	15	11	47	.229	.267	.314	57	-13	1	2	-1	.962	31	/S-89,2-10,3-1	2.1

■ BOB MAIER   Maier, Robert Phillip   b: 9/5/15, Dunellen, N.J.   d: 8/4/93, S.Plainfield, N.J.   BR/TR, 5′8″, 180 lbs.   Deb: 4/17/45

| 1945 | *Det-A | 132 | 486 | 58 | 128 | 25 | 7 | 1 | 34 | 38 | 32 | .263 | .317 | .350 | 88 | -8 | 7 | 11 | -5 | .936 | -13 | *3-124/O-5 | -2.4 |

■ EMIL MAILHO   Mailho, Emil Pierre "Lefty"   b: 12/16/09, Berkeley, Cal.   BL/TL, 5′10″, 165 lbs.   Deb: 4/14/36

| 1936 | Phi-A | 21 | 18 | 5 | 1 | 0 | 0 | 0 | 0 | 6 | 5 | .056 | .261 | .056 | -18 | -3 | 0 | 0 | 0 | 1.000 | -0 | /O-1 | -0.3 |

■ CHARLIE MAISEL   Maisel, Charles Louis   b: 4/21/1894, Catonsville, Md.   d: 8/25/53, Baltimore, Md.   BR/TR, 6′,   Deb: 10/2/15

| 1915 | Bal-F | 1 | 4 | 0 | 0 | 0 | 0 | 0 | 0 | 0 | 0 | .000 | .000 | .000 | -97 | -1 | 0 | | | 1.000 | 0 | /C-1 | -0.1 |

■ FRITZ MAISEL   Maisel, Frederick Charles "Flash"   b: 12/23/1889, Catonsville, Md.   d: 4/22/67, Baltimore, Md.   BR/TR, 5′7.5″, 170 lbs.   Deb: 8/11/13   F

1913	NY-A	51	187	33	48	4	3	0	12	34	20	.257	.371	.310	99	1	25			.950	-5	3-51	0.5
1914	NY-A	150	548	78	131	23	9	2	47	76	69	.239	.334	.325	98	0	**74**	17	**12**	.928	-18	*3-148	-0.1
1915	NY-A	135	530	77	149	16	6	4	46	48	35	.281	.342	.357	109	5	51	12	**8**	.940	-9	*3-134	1.0
1916	NY-A	53	158	18	36	5	0	0	7	20	18	.228	.318	.259	72	-5	4			.980	-5	O-26,3-11/2-4	-1.2
1917	NY-A	113	404	46	80	4	4	0	20	36	18	.198	.267	.218	51	-23	29			.967	-1	*2-100/3-7	-2.2

YEAR	TM/L	G	AB	R	H	2B	3B	HR	RBI	BB	SO	AVG	OBP	SLG	PRO+	BR/A	SB	CS	SBR	FA	FR	G/POS	TPR
1918	StL-A	90	284	43	66	4	2	0	16	46	17	.232	.341	.261	84	-3	11			.949	-4	3-79/O-1	-0.6
Total	6	592	2111	295	510	56	24	6	148	260	177	.242	.327	.299	88	-25	194	29		.938	-43	3-430,2-104/O-27	-3.4
■ **GEORGE MAISEL**	Maisel, George John b: 3/12/1892, Catonsville, Md. d: 11/20/68, Baltimore, Md. BR/TR, 5'10.5", 180 lbs. Deb: 5/1/13 F																						
1913	StL-A	11	18	2	3	2	0	0	1	1	7	.167	.211	.278	44	-1	0			.833	-2	/O-5	-0.4
1916	Det-A	8	5	2	0	0	0	0	0	0	2	.000	.000	.000	-97	-1	0			.857	2	/3-3	0.1
1921	Chi-N	111	393	54	122	7	2	0	43	11	13	.310	.334	.338	78	-12	17	7	1	.978	0	*O-108	-1.8
1922	Chi-N	38	84	9	16	1	1	0	6	8	2	.190	.261	.226	26	-9	1	3	-2	1.000	-2	O-26	-1.4
Total	4	168	500	67	141	10	3	0	50	20	24	.282	.314	.314	66	-23	18	10		.979	-2	O-139/3-3	-3.5
■ **HANK MAJESKI**	Majeski, Henry "Heeney" b: 12/13/16, Staten Island, N.Y d: 8/9/91, Staten Island, N.Y. BR/TR, 5'9", 180 lbs. Deb: 5/17/39																						
1939	Bos-N	106	367	35	100	16	1	7	54	18	30	.272	.310	.379	91	-6	2			.945	12	3-99	0.7
1940	Bos-N	3	3	0	0	0	0	0	0	0	0	.000	.000	.000	-99	-1	0			.000	0	H	-0.1
1941	Bos-N	19	55	5	8	5	0	0	3	1	13	.145	.161	.236	11	-7	0			.911	1	3-11	-0.6
1946	NY-A	8	12	1	1	0	0	0	0	0	3	.083	.083	.250	-9	-2	0	0	0	.750	-1	/3-2	-0.3
	Phi-A	78	264	25	66	14	3	1	25	26	13	.250	.320	.337	84	-6	3	2	-0	.967	8	3-72	0.3
	Yr	86	276	26	67	14	4	1	25	26	16	.243	.310	.333	80	-7	3	2	-0	.964	7	3-74	0.0
1947	Phi-A	141	479	54	134	26	5	8	72	53	31	.280	.358	.405	110	6	1	0	0	**.988**	7	*3-134/S-4,2-1	1.5
1948	Phi-A	148	590	88	183	41	4	12	120	48	43	.310	.368	.454	118	13	2	1	0	**.975**	1	*3-142/S-8	1.3
1949	Phi-A	114	448	62	124	26	5	9	67	29	23	.277	.326	.417	99	-3	0	1	-1	.957	-4	*3-113	-1.0
1950	Chi-A	122	414	47	128	18	2	6	46	42	34	.309	.377	.406	103	2	1	4	-2	.970	10	*3-112	0.8
1951	Chi-A	12	35	4	9	4	0	0	6	1	0	.257	.278	.371	76	-1	0	0	0	.950	-0	/3-9	-0.2
	Phi-A	89	323	41	92	19	4	5	42	35	24	.285	.358	.415	106	3	1	2	-1	.974	14	3-88	1.4
	Yr	101	358	45	101	23	4	5	48	36	24	.282	.351	.411	104	1	1	2	-1	.972	14	3-97	1.2
1952	Phi-A	34	117	14	30	2	2	2	20	19	10	.256	.365	.359	96	-0	0	1	-1	.976	4	3-34	0.3
	Cle-A	36	54	7	16	2	0	0	9	7	7	.296	.377	.333	106	1	0	0	0	.913	-0	3-11/2-3	0.0
	Yr	70	171	21	46	4	2	2	29	26	17	.269	.369	.351	101	1	0	1	-1	.966	4	3-45/2-3	0.3
1953	Cle-A	50	50	6	15	1	0	2	12	3	8	.300	.352	.440	116	1	0	0	0	1.000	-2	2-10/3-7,O-1	-0.1
1954	*Cle-A	57	121	10	34	4	0	3	17	7	14	.281	.320	.388	92	-2	0	0	0	.990	4	2-25,3-10	0.4
1955	Cle-A	36	48	3	9	2	0	2	6	8	3	.188	.328	.354	80	-1	0	0	0	1.000	-2	/3-9,2-4	-0.3
	Bal-A	16	41	2	7	1	0	0	2	2	4	.171	.209	.195	10	-5	0	0	0	1.000	-3	/3-8,2-5	-0.9
	Yr	52	89	5	16	3	0	2	8	10	7	.180	.277	.281	50	-6	0	0	0	1.000	-5	3-17/2-9	-1.2
Total	13	1069	3421	404	956	181	27	57	501	299	260	.279	.342	.398	100	-9	10	11		.968	49	3-861/2-48,S-12,O-1	3.2
■ **MIKE MAKSUDIAN**	Maksudian, Michael Bryant b: 5/28/66, Belleville, Ill. BL/TR, 5'11", 220 lbs. Deb: 9/2/92																						
1992	Tor-A	3	3	0	0	0	0	0	0	0	0	.000	.000	.000	-96	-1	0	0	0	.000	0	/1-1	-0.1
1993	Min-A	5	12	2	2	1	0	0	2	4	2	.167	.375	.250	71	-0	0	0	0	1.000	1	/1-4,3-1	0.0
1994	Chi-N	26	26	6	7	2	0	0	4	10	4	.269	.472	.346	120	2	0	1	-1	1.000	-0	/1-3,C-2,3-2	0.0
Total	3	34	41	8	9	3	0	0	6	14	6	.220	.418	.293	92	1	0	1	-1	1.000	1	/1-8,3-3,C-2	-0.1
■ **JOSE MALAVE**	Malave, Jose Francisco b: 5/31/71, Cumana, Venez. BR/TR, 6'2", 212 lbs. Deb: 5/23/96																						
1996	Bos-A	41	102	12	24	3	0	4	17	2	25	.235	.257	.382	58	-7	0	0	0	.978	-6	O-38	-1.2
1997	Bos-A	4	4	0	0	0	0	0	0	0	2	.000	.000	.000	-98	-1	0	0	0	1.000	-1	/O-4	-0.2
Total	2	45	106	12	24	3	0	4	17	2	27	.226	.248	.368	52	-8	0	0	0	.979	-7	/O-42	-1.4
■ **CHARLIE MALAY**	Malay, Charles Francis b: 6/13/1879, Brooklyn, N.Y. d: 9/18/49, Brooklyn, N.Y. BB/TR, 5'11.5", 175 lbs. Deb: 4/24/05 F																						
1905	Bro-N	102	349	33	88	7	2	1	31	22		.252	.300	.292	83	-7	13			.932	-9	2-75,O-25/S-1	-1.8
■ **JOE MALAY**	Malay, Joseph Charles b: 10/25/05, Brooklyn, N.Y. d: 3/19/89, Bridgeport, Conn. BL/TL, 6', 175 lbs. Deb: 9/7/33 F																						
1933	NY-N	8	24	0	3	0	0	0	2	0	0	.125	.125	.125	-29	-4	0			1.000	2	/1-8	-0.3
1935	NY-N	1	1	0	1	0	0	0	0	0	0	1.000	1.000	1.000	447	0	0			.000	0	H	0.0
Total	2	9	25	0	4	0	0	0	2	0	0	.160	.160	.160	-9	-3	0			1.000	2	/1-8	-0.3
■ **CANDY MALDONADO**	Maldonado, Candido (Guadarrama) b: 9/5/60, Humacao, P.R. BR/TR, 6', 190 lbs. Deb: 9/7/81																						
1981	LA-N	11	12	0	1	0	0	0	0	0	5	.083	.083	.083	-55	-2	0	0	0	1.000	-2	/O-9	-0.5
1982	LA-N	6	4	0	0	0	0	0	0	1	2	.000	.200	.000	-41	-1	0	0	0	1.000	-1	/O-3	-0.1
1983	*LA-N	42	62	5	12	1	1	1	6	5	14	.194	.254	.290	51	-4	0	0	0	1.000	-8	O-33	-1.3
1984	LA-N	116	254	25	68	14	0	5	28	19	29	.268	.321	.382	98	-1	0	3	-2	.955	-16	*O-102/3-4	-2.2
1985	*LA-N	121	213	20	48	7	1	5	19	19	40	.225	.289	.338	77	-7	1	1	-0	.984	-22	*O-113	-3.3
1986	SF-N	133	405	49	102	31	3	18	85	20	77	.252	.292	.477	114	5	4	4	-1	.983	-4	*O-101/3-1	-0.3
1987	*SF-N	118	442	69	129	28	4	20	85	34	78	.292	.351	.509	131	18	8	8	-2	.973	-6	*O-116	0.6
1988	SF-N	142	499	53	127	23	1	12	68	37	89	.255	.315	.377	102	1	6	5	-1	.962	-3	*O-139	-0.8
1989	*SF-N	129	345	39	75	23	0	9	41	37	69	.217	.299	.362	91	-5	4	1	1	.974	-6	*O-116	-1.3
1990	Cle-A	155	590	76	161	32	2	22	95	49	134	.273	.334	.446	117	12	3	5	-2	.993	7	*O-134,D-20	1.3
1991	Mil-A	34	111	11	23	6	0	5	20	13	23	.207	.290	.396	90	-2	1	0	0	.976	-2	O-24	-0.4
	*Tor-A	52	177	26	49	9	0	7	28	23	53	.277	.379	.446	123	6	3	0	1	.990	0	O-52/D-9	0.6
	Yr	86	288	37	72	15	0	12	48	36	76	.250	.345	.427	111	5	4	0	1	.986	-2	O-76/D-9	0.2
1992	*Tor-A	137	489	64	133	25	4	20	66	59	112	.272	.359	.462	123	15	2	2	-1	.978	5	*O-132/D-4	1.7
1993	Chi-N	70	140	8	26	5	0	3	15	13	40	.186	.260	.286	47	-11	0	0	0	.914	-5	O-41	-1.7
	Cle-A	28	81	11	20	2	0	5	20	11	18	.247	.337	.457	112	1	0	1	-1	.976	-3	O-26/D-2	-0.3
1994	Cle-A	42	92	14	18	5	1	5	12	19	31	.196	.333	.435	96	-1	1	1	-0	1.000	-1	D-25/O-5	-0.3
1995	Tor-A	61	160	22	43	13	0	7	25	25	45	.269	.374	.481	121	5	1	1	-0	.988	-8	O-58/D-1	-0.4
	Tex-A	13	30	6	7	3	0	2	5	7	5	.233	.378	.533	131	1	0	1	-1	1.000	-0	O-11	0.0
	Yr	74	190	28	50	16	0	9	30	32	50	.263	.375	.489	123	7	1	2	-1	.990	-8	O-69/D-1	-0.4
Total	15	1410	4106	498	1042	227	17	146	618	391	864	.254	.325	.424	107	31	34	33	-10	.977	-74	*O-1215/D-61,3-5	-8.7
■ **JIM MALER**	Maler, James Michael b: 8/16/58, New York, N.Y. BR/TR, 6'4", 230 lbs. Deb: 9/3/81																						
1981	Sea-A	12	23	1	8	1	0	0	2	2	1	.348	.423	.391	131	1	1	0	0	1.000	-0	/1-5,D-2	0.1
1982	Sea-A	64	221	18	50	8	3	4	26	12	35	.226	.275	.344	67	-10	0	0	0	.991	3	1-57/D-5	-1.0
1983	Sea-A	26	66	5	12	1	0	1	3	5	11	.182	.260	.242	38	-6	0	3	-2	1.000	0	1-19/D-5	-0.8
Total	3	102	310	24	70	10	3	5	31	19	47	.226	.284	.326	65	-15	1	3	-2	.994	3	/1-81,D-12	-1.7
■ **TONY MALINOSKY**	Malinosky, Anthony Francis b: 10/5/09, Collinsville, Ill. BR/TR, 5'10.5", 165 lbs. Deb: 4/26/37																						
1937	Bro-N	35	79	7	18	2	0	0	3	9	11	.228	.307	.253	53	-5	0			.833	-9	3-13,S-11	-1.4
■ **BOBBY MALKMUS**	Malkmus, Robert Edward b: 7/4/31, Newark, N.J. BR/TR, 5'9", 180 lbs. Deb: 6/1/57																						
1957	Mil-N	13	22	6	2	0	1	0	0	3	3	.091	.200	.182	4	-3	0	0	0	.972	4	/2-7	0.1
1958	Was-A	41	70	5	13	2	1	0	3	4	15	.186	.230	.243	31	-7	0	0	0	.964	8	2-26/3-2,S-1	0.2
1959	Was-A	6	0	0	0	0	0	0	0	0	0	—	—	—	—	0	0	0	0	.000	0	R	0.0
1960	Phi-N	79	133	16	28	4	1	1	12	11	28	.211	.271	.278	51	-9	2	2	-1	1.000	7	S-29,2-23,3-12	-0.1
1961	Phi-N	121	342	39	79	8	2	7	31	20	43	.231	.277	.327	61	-20	1	3	-2	.988	16	2-58,S-34,3-25	0.3
1962	Phi-N	8	5	3	1	1	0	0	0	0	1	.200	.200	.400	58	-0	0	0	0	1.000	2	/S-1	0.2
Total	6	268	572	69	123	15	5	8	46	38	90	.215	.266	.301	53	-39	3	5	-2	.982	36	2-114/S-65,3-39	0.7
■ **JERRY MALLETT**	Mallett, Gerald Gordon b: 9/18/35, Bonne Terre, Mo. BR/TR, 6'5", 208 lbs. Deb: 9/19/59																						
1959	Bos-A	4	15	1	4	0	0	0	1	1	3	.267	.313	.267	58	-1	0	0	0	1.000	3	/O-4	0.2
■ **LES MALLON**	Mallon, Leslie Clyde b: 11/21/05, Sweetwater, Tex. d: 4/17/91, Granbury, Tex. BR/TR, 5'8", 160 lbs. Deb: 4/14/31																						
1931	Phi-N	122	375	41	116	19	2	1	45	29	40	.309	.359	.379	91	-4	0			.956	6	2-97/1-5,S-3,3-3	0.8
1932	Phi-N	103	347	44	90	16	0	5	31	28	28	.259	.318	.349	71	-14	1			.955	-31	2-88/3-5	-4.1
1934	Bos-N	42	166	23	49	6	1	0	18	15	12	.295	.354	.343	95	-1	0			.967	-4	2-42	-0.3

YEAR	TM/L	G	AB	R	H	2B	3B	HR	RBI	BB	SO	AVG	OBP	SLG	PRO+	BR/A	SB	CS	SBR	FA	FR	G/POS	TPR
1935	Bos-N	116	412	48	113	24	2	2	25	28	37	.274	.322	.357	89	-7	3			.975	-14	2-73,3-36/O-1	-1.3
Total	4	383	1300	156	368	65	5	8	119	100	117	.263	.336	.359	85	-26	4			.962	-43	2-300/3-44,1-5,SO	-4.9

■ BEN MALLONEE
Mallonee, Howard Bennett "Lefty" b: 3/31/1894, Baltimore, Md. d: 2/19/78, Baltimore, Md. BL/TL, 5'6", 150 lbs. Deb: 9/14/21

YEAR	TM/L	G	AB	R	H	2B	3B	HR	RBI	BB	SO	AVG	OBP	SLG	PRO+	BR/A	SB	CS	SBR	FA	FR	G/POS	TPR
1921	Phi-A	7	25	2	6	1	0	0	4	1	2	.240	.269	.280	40	-2	1	0	0	1.000	0	/O-6	-0.2

■ JULE MALLONEE
Mallonee, Julius Norris b: 4/4/1900, Charlotte, N.C. d: 12/26/34, Charlotte, N.C. BL/TR, 6'2", 180 lbs. Deb: 8/4/25

YEAR	TM/L	G	AB	R	H	2B	3B	HR	RBI	BB	SO	AVG	OBP	SLG	PRO+	BR/A	SB	CS	SBR	FA	FR	G/POS	TPR
1925	Chi-A	2	3	1	0	0	0	0	0	1	0	.000	.250	.000	-34	-1	0	0	0	1.000	-0	/O-1	-0.1

■ JIM MALLORY
Mallory, James Baugh "Sunny Jim" b: 9/1/18, Lawrenceville, Va. BR/TR, 6'1", 170 lbs. Deb: 9/8/40

YEAR	TM/L	G	AB	R	H	2B	3B	HR	RBI	BB	SO	AVG	OBP	SLG	PRO+	BR/A	SB	CS	SBR	FA	FR	G/POS	TPR
1940	Was-A	4	12	2	2	0	0	0	0	1	1	.167	.231	.167	5	-2	0	0	0	1.000	1	/O-3	-0.1
1945	StL-N	13	43	3	10	2	0	0	5	0	2	.233	.233	.279	41	-4	0			.923	-2	O-11	-0.6
	NY-N	37	94	10	28	1	0	0	9	6	7	.298	.340	.309	80	-2	1			.979	-0	O-21	-0.4
	Yr	50	137	13	38	3	0	0	14	6	9	.277	.308	.299	68	-6	1			.959	-2	O-32	-1.0
Total	2	54	149	15	40	3	0	0	14	7	10	.268	.301	.289	63	-8	1	0		.964	-1	/O-35	-1.1

■ SHELDON MALLORY
Mallory, Sheldon b: 7/16/53, Argo, Ill. BL/TL, 6'2", 175 lbs. Deb: 4/10/77

YEAR	TM/L	G	AB	R	H	2B	3B	HR	RBI	BB	SO	AVG	OBP	SLG	PRO+	BR/A	SB	CS	SBR	FA	FR	G/POS	TPR
1977	Oak-A	64	126	19	27	4	1	0	5	11	18	.214	.293	.262	53	-8	12	5	1	.977	-3	O-45/1-4,D-7	-1.2

■ MARTY MALLOY
Malloy, Marty Thomas b: 4/6/72, Gainesville, Fla. BL/TR, 5'10", 160 lbs. Deb: 9/6/98

YEAR	TM/L	G	AB	R	H	2B	3B	HR	RBI	BB	SO	AVG	OBP	SLG	PRO+	BR/A	SB	CS	SBR	FA	FR	G/POS	TPR
1998	*Atl-N	11	28	3	5	1	0	1	1	2	2	.179	.233	.321	41	-3	0	0	0	1.000	2	2-10	0.0

■ HARRY MALMBERG
Malmberg, Harry William "Swede" b: 7/31/26, Fairfield, Ala. d: 10/29/76, San Francisco, Cal BR/TR, 6'1", 170 lbs. Deb: 4/12/55 C

YEAR	TM/L	G	AB	R	H	2B	3B	HR	RBI	BB	SO	AVG	OBP	SLG	PRO+	BR/A	SB	CS	SBR	FA	FR	G/POS	TPR
1955	Det-A	67	208	25	45	5	2	0	19	29	19	.216	.312	.260	56	-12	0	1	-1	.985	6	2-65	-0.2

■ EDDIE MALONE
Malone, Edward Russell b: 6/16/20, Chicago, Ill. BR/TR, 5'10", 175 lbs. Deb: 7/17/49

YEAR	TM/L	G	AB	R	H	2B	3B	HR	RBI	BB	SO	AVG	OBP	SLG	PRO+	BR/A	SB	CS	SBR	FA	FR	G/POS	TPR
1949	Chi-A	55	170	17	46	7	2	1	16	29	19	.271	.377	.353	97	-0	2	1	0	.990	-3	C-51	0.0
1950	Chi-A	31	71	2	16	2	0	0	10	10	8	.225	.321	.254	50	-5	0	0	0	1.000	2	C-21	-0.2
Total	2	86	241	19	62	9	2	1	26	39	27	.257	.361	.324	83	-5	2	1	0	.993	-2	/C-72	-0.2

■ FERGY MALONE
Malone, Ferguson G. b: 1842, Ireland d: 1/1/05, Seattle, Wash. BR/TL, 5'8", 156 lbs. Deb: 6/3/1871 MU

YEAR	TM/L	G	AB	R	H	2B	3B	HR	RBI	BB	SO	AVG	OBP	SLG	PRO+	BR/A	SB	CS	SBR	FA	FR	G/POS	TPR
1871	Ath-n	27	134	33	46	7	1	1	33	9	4	.343	.385	.433	136	7	9	3	1	.856	9	*C-27	1.0
1872	Ath-n	41	213	46	60	5	3	0	39	4	5	.282	.295	.333	92	-2	3	0	1	**.884**	4	C-24,1-17	0.3
1873	Phi-n	53	259	59	75	11	2	0	43	14	7	.290	.326	.347	97	-2	2	1	0	.898	5	*C-53/S-1,M	0.2
1874	Chi-n	47	223	33	56	5	0	0	28	4	0	.251	.264	.274	72	-7	2	1	0	.820	4	*C-47,M	-0.1
1875	Phi-n	29	123	15	28	2	1	0	10	1	2	.228	.234	.260	69	-4	1	0	0	.919	-3	1-22/C-6,O-2	-0.6
1876	Phi-N	22	96	14	22	2	0	0	6	0	1	.229	.229	.250	60	-4				.777	-2	C-20/O-3,S-1	-0.5
1884	Phi-U	1	4	0	1	0	0	0		0		.250	.250	.250	56	-0				.818	-1	/C-1,M	-0.1
Total	5 n	197	952	186	265	30	7	1	153	32	18	.278	.302	.328	93	-7	17	5	2	.856	19	C-157/1-39,O-2,S-1	0.8
Total	2	23	100	14	23	2	0	0	6	0	1	.230	.230	.250	60	-4				.780	-3	/C-21,O-3,S-1	-0.6

■ LEW MALONE
Malone, Lewis Aloysius b: 3/13/1897, Baltimore, Md. d: 2/17/72, Brooklyn, N.Y. BR/TR, 5'11", 175 lbs. Deb: 5/31/15

YEAR	TM/L	G	AB	R	H	2B	3B	HR	RBI	BB	SO	AVG	OBP	SLG	PRO+	BR/A	SB	CS	SBR	FA	FR	G/POS	TPR
1915	Phi-A	76	201	17	41	4	4	1	17	21	40	.204	.283	.279	70	-8	7	1	2	.919	-4	2-43,3-12/O-4,S-2	-1.0
1916	Phi-A	5	4	1	0	0	0	0	0	1	2	.000	.200	.000	-42	-1	0			1.000	-0	/S-1	-0.1
1917	Bro-N	1	0	1	0	0	0	0	0	0	0	—	—	—	—	0	0			.000	0	R	0.0
1919	Bro-N	51	162	9	33	7	3	0	11	6	18	.204	.232	.284	54	-9	1			.934	-6	3-47/2-2,S-2	-1.6
Total	4	133	367	28	74	11	7	1	28	28	60	.202	.260	.278	62	-18	8	1		.910	-11	/3-59,2-45,S-5,O-4	-2.7

■ JOHN MALONEY
Maloney, John Deb: 9/15/1876

YEAR	TM/L	G	AB	R	H	2B	3B	HR	RBI	BB	SO	AVG	OBP	SLG	PRO+	BR/A	SB	CS	SBR	FA	FR	G/POS	TPR
1876	NY-N	2	7	1	2	0	1	0	2	0	1	.286	.286	.571	206	1				.800	-0	/O-2	0.0
1877	Har-N	1	4	0	1	0	0	0	0	0	0	.250	.250	.250	65	-0				.250	-1	/O-1	-0.1
Total	2	3	11	1	3	0	1	0	2	0	1	.273	.273	.455	152	1				.556	-1	/O-3	-0.1

■ PAT MALONEY
Maloney, Patrick William b: 1/19/1888, Grosvenor Dale, Conn. d: 6/27/79, Pawtucket, R.I. BR/TR, 6', 150 lbs. Deb: 6/19/12

YEAR	TM/L	G	AB	R	H	2B	3B	HR	RBI	BB	SO	AVG	OBP	SLG	PRO+	BR/A	SB	CS	SBR	FA	FR	G/POS	TPR
1912	NY-A	25	79	9	17	1	0	0	4	6		.215	.279	.228	43	-6	3			.926	2	O-20	-0.4

■ BILLY MALONEY
Maloney, William Alphonse b: 6/5/1878, Lewiston, Me. d: 9/2/60, Breckenridge, Tex. BL/TR, 5'10", 177 lbs. Deb: 5/2/01

YEAR	TM/L	G	AB	R	H	2B	3B	HR	RBI	BB	SO	AVG	OBP	SLG	PRO+	BR/A	SB	CS	SBR	FA	FR	G/POS	TPR
1901	Mil-A	86	290	42	85	3	4	0	22	7		.293	.328	.331	87	-5	11			.952	9	C-72/O-8	0.9
1902	StL-A	30	112	8	23	3	0	0	11	6		.205	.258	.232	37	-9	0			.906	-4	O-23/C-7	-1.4
	Cin-N	27	89	13	22	4	0	1	7	2		.247	.272	.326	77	-3	8			.848	-3	O-18/C-7	-0.6
1905	Chi-N	145	558	78	145	17	14	2	56	43		.260	.325	.351	98	-2	**59**			.954	3	*O-145	-0.6
1906	Bro-N	151	566	71	125	15	7	0	32	49		.221	.286	.272	80	-13	38			.966	11	*O-151	-1.1
1907	Bro-N	144	502	51	115	7	10	0	32	31		.229	.287	.283	86	-9	25			.967	5	*O-144	-1.1
1908	Bro-N	113	359	31	70	5	7	3	17	24		.195	.255	.273	71	-12	14			.947	4	*O-107/C-4	-1.4
Total	6	696	2476	294	585	54	42	6	177	162		.236	.294	.299	83	-53	155			.954	25	O-596/C-90	-5.3

■ FRANK MALZONE
Malzone, Frank James b: 2/28/30, Bronx, N.Y. BR/TR, 5'10", 180 lbs. Deb: 9/17/55

YEAR	TM/L	G	AB	R	H	2B	3B	HR	RBI	BB	SO	AVG	OBP	SLG	PRO+	BR/A	SB	CS	SBR	FA	FR	G/POS	TPR
1955	Bos-A	6	20	2	7	1	0	0	1	1	3	.350	.381	.400	101	0	0	0	0	1.000	2	/3-4	0.2
1956	Bos-A	27	103	15	17	3	1	2	11	9	8	.165	.232	.272	29	-11	1	0	0	.931	1	3-26	-0.9
1957	Bos-A★	153	634	82	185	31	5	15	103	31	41	.292	.326	.427	98	-3	2	1	0	**.954**	14	*3-153	1.5
1958	Bos-A★	155	627	76	185	30	2	15	87	33	53	.295	.334	.421	100	-1	1	3	-2	.950	17	*3-155	1.6
1959	Bos-A★	154	604	90	169	34	2	19	92	42	58	.280	.328	.437	103	-1	6	0	2	.953	8	*3-154	0.9
1960	Bos-A★	152	595	60	161	30	2	14	79	36	42	.271	.317	.398	89	-10	2	3	-1	.948	8	*3-151	-0.5
1961	Bos-A	151	590	74	157	21	4	14	87	44	49	.266	.318	.386	85	-13	1	3	-2	.950	-5	*3-149	-1.8
1962	Bos-A	156	619	74	175	20	3	21	95	35	43	.283	.321	.426	96	-5	0	1	-1	.967	5	*3-156	0.1
1963	Bos-A★	151	580	66	169	25	2	15	71	31	45	.291	.331	.419	105	3	0	2	-1	.964	4	*3-148	0.6
1964	Bos-A☆	148	537	62	142	19	0	13	56	37	43	.264	.314	.372	86	-10	0	0	0	.959	-0	*3-143	-1.3
1965	Bos-A	106	364	40	87	20	0	3	34	28	38	.239	.295	.319	70	-14	1	1	-0	.969	-3	3-96	-2.1
1966	Cal-A	82	155	6	32	5	0	2	12	10	11	.206	.255	.277	54	-9	0	0	0	.925	-1	3-35	-1.2
Total	12	1441	5428	647	1486	239	21	133	728	337	434	.274	.318	.399	91	-71	14	14	-4	.955	47	*3-1370	-2.7

■ GUS MANCUSO
Mancuso, August Rodney "Blackie" b: 12/5/05, Galveston, Tex. d: 10/26/84, Houston, Tex. BR/TR, 5'10", 185 lbs. Deb: 4/30/28 FC

YEAR	TM/L	G	AB	R	H	2B	3B	HR	RBI	BB	SO	AVG	OBP	SLG	PRO+	BR/A	SB	CS	SBR	FA	FR	G/POS	TPR
1928	StL-N	11	38	2	7	0	1	0	3	0	5	.184	.184	.237	9	-5	0			.984	4	C-11	0.0
1930	*StL-N	76	227	39	83	17	2	7	59	18	16	.366	.415	.551	127	10	1			.969	1	C-61	1.4
1931	*StL-N	67	187	13	49	16	1	1	23	18	13	.262	.327	.374	85	-4	2			.972	6	C-56	0.6
1932	StL-N	103	310	25	88	23	1	5	43	30	15	.284	.347	.413	100	1	0			.977	8	C-82	1.3
1933	*NY-N	144	481	39	127	17	2	6	56	48	21	.264	.331	.345	95	-2	0			.972	2	*C-142	0.8
1934	NY-N	122	383	32	94	14	0	7	46	27	19	.245	.295	.337	70	-16	0			.977	6	*C-122	-0.4
1935	NY-N★	128	447	33	133	18	2	5	56	30	16	.298	.342	.380	95	-3	1			.972	-5	*C-126	-0.1
1936	*NY-N	139	519	55	156	21	3	9	63	39	28	.301	.351	.405	104	3	0			.977	5	*C-138	1.4
1937	*NY-N★	86	287	30	80	17	1	4	39	17	20	.279	.319	.387	90	-4	1			.982	16	C-81	1.5
1938	NY-N	52	158	19	55	8	0	2	15	17	13	.348	.411	.437	132	8	0			.977	4	C-44	1.4
1939	Chi-N	80	251	17	58	10	0	2	17	24	19	.231	.298	.295	59	-14	0			.981	5	C-76	-0.6
1940	Bro-N	60	144	16	33	8	0	0	16	13	7	.229	.293	.285	56	-8	0			.982	7	C-56	0.1
1941	StL-N	106	328	25	75	13	1	2	37	37	19	.229	.309	.293	66	-14	0			.989	11	*C-105	0.4
1942	StL-N	5	13	0	1	0	0	0	1	0	0	.077	.077	.077	-51	-2	0			.917	-1	/C-3	-0.4
	NY-N	39	109	4	21	1	1	0	8	14	7	.193	.285	.220	48	-7	1			.982	3	C-38	-0.2
	Yr	44	122	4	22	1	1	0	9	14	7	.180	.265	.205	38	-9	1			.977	1	C-41	-0.6
1943	NY-N	94	252	11	50	5	0	2	20	28	16	.198	.284	.242	52	-15	0			.974	-0	C-77	-1.1
1944	NY-N	78	195	15	49	4	1	1	25	30	20	.251	.351	.297	84	-3	0			.976	5	C-72	0.5
1945	Phi-N	70	176	11	35	5	0	0	16	28	10	.199	.309	.227	52	-11	2			.988	1	C-70	-0.7
Total	17	1460	4505	386	1194	197	16	53	543	418	264	.265	.328	.351	85	-89	8			.977	75	*C-1360	5.9

YEAR	TM/L	G	AB	R	H	2B	3B	HR	RBI	BB	SO	AVG	OBP	SLG	PRO+	BR/A	SB	CS	SBR	FA	FR	G/POS	TPR

■ FRANK MANCUSO
Mancuso, Frank Octavius b: 5/23/18, Houston, Tex. BR/TR, 6', 195 lbs. Deb: 4/18/44 F

1944	*StL-A	88	244	19	50	11	0	1	24	20	32	.205	.271	.262	50	-16	1	0	0	.953	-6	C-87	-1.8
1945	StL-A	119	365	39	98	13	3	1	38	46	44	.268	.354	.329	94	-2	0	2	-1	.989	-6	*C-115	-0.2
1946	StL-A	87	262	22	63	8	3	3	23	30	31	.240	.323	.328	78	-7	1	0	0	.973	-18	C-85	-2.1
1947	Was-A	43	131	5	30	5	1	0	13	5	11	.229	.257	.282	51	-9	0	0	0	.958	-4	C-35	-1.1
Total	4	337	1002	85	241	37	7	5	98	101	118	.241	.314	.306	74	-34	2	2	-1	.972	-34	C-322	-5.2

■ CARL MANDA
Manda, Carl Alan b: 11/16/1888, Little River, Kan. d: 3/9/83, Artesia, N.Mex. BR/TR, 5'10", 170 lbs. Deb: 9/11/14

| 1914 | Chi-A | 9 | 15 | 2 | 4 | 0 | 0 | 0 | 1 | 3 | 3 | .267 | .389 | .267 | 99 | 0 | 1 | | | .971 | 4 | /2-7 | 0.5 |

■ JIM MANGAN
Mangan, James Daniel b: 9/24/29, San Francisco, Cal. BR/TR, 5'10", 190 lbs. Deb: 4/16/52

1952	Pit-N	11	13	1	2	0	0	0	2	1	3	.154	.214	.154	4	-2	0	0	0	.833	-1	/C-4	-0.2
1954	Pit-N	14	26	2	5	0	0	0	2	4	9	.192	.300	.192	32	-2	0	0	0	1.000	0	/C-7	-0.2
1956	NY-N	20	20	2	2	0	0	0	1	4	6	.100	.250	.100	-1	-3	0	0	0	1.000	0	C-15	-0.2
Total	3	45	59	5	9	0	0	0	5	9	18	.153	.265	.153	15	-7	0	0	0	.985	-0	/C-26	-0.6

■ ANGEL MANGUAL
Mangual, Angel Luis (Guilbe) b: 3/19/47, Juana Diaz, P.R. BR/TR, 5'10", 180 lbs. Deb: 9/15/69 F

1969	Pit-N	6	4	1	1	0	0	0	1	0	0	.250	.250	.500	108	0	0	0	0	.000	-1	/O-3	-0.1
1971	*Oak-A	94	287	32	82	8	1	4	30	17	27	.286	.326	.362	97	-2	1	4	-2	.988	-2	O-81	-1.0
1972	Oak-A	91	272	19	67	13	2	5	32	14	48	.246	.286	.364	97	-2	0	1	-1	.971	3	O-74	-0.3
1973	*Oak-A	74	192	20	43	4	1	3	13	8	34	.224	.259	.302	61	-11	1	1	-0	.947	-5	O-50,D-14/1-2,2-1	-1.9
1974	*Oak-A	115	365	37	85	14	4	9	43	17	59	.233	.267	.367	87	-8	3	0	1	.961	-7	O-74,D-37/3-1	-1.9
1975	Oak-A	62	109	13	24	3	0	1	6	3	18	.220	.241	.275	47	-8	0	1	-1	.978	-9	O-39,D-15	-1.9
1976	Oak-A	8	12	0	2	1	0	0	1	0	1	.167	.167	.250	22	-1	0	1	-1	1.000	-2	/O-7	-0.4
Total	7	450	1241	122	304	44	8	22	125	59	187	.245	.280	.346	83	-32	5	8	-3	.969	-23	O-328/D-66,1-2,32	-7.5

■ PEPE MANGUAL
Mangual, Jose Manuel (Guilbe) b: 5/23/52, Ponce, P.R. BR/TR, 5'10", 165 lbs. Deb: 9/6/72 F

1972	Mon-N	8	11	2	3	0	0	0	1	5		.273	.333	.273	73	-0	0	1	-1	1.000	-1	/O-3	-0.2
1973	Mon-N	33	62	9	11	2	1	3	7	6	18	.177	.250	.387	71	-3	2	4	-2	.966	-3	O-22	-0.9
1974	Mon-N	23	61	10	19	3	0	0	4	5	15	.311	.364	.361	98	-0	5	0	2	1.000	-6	O-22	-0.6
1975	Mon-N	140	514	84	126	16	2	9	45	74	115	.245	.345	.337	86	-8	33	11	3	.972	-4	*O-138	-1.5
1976	Mon-N	66	215	34	56	9	1	3	16	50	49	.260	.404	.353	112	6	17	7	1	.968	1	O-62	0.4
	NY-N	41	102	15	19	5	2	1	9	10	32	.186	.259	.304	63	-5	7	3	0	.985	-2	O-38	-0.9
	Yr	107	317	49	75	14	3	4	25	60	81	.237	.364	.338	99	2	24	10	1	.973	-3	*O-100	-0.5
1977	NY-N	8	7	1	1	0	0	0	2	1	4	.143	.250	.143	9	-1	0	0	0	.833	-1	/O-4	-0.2
Total	6	319	972	155	235	35	6	16	83	147	238	.242	.345	.340	89	-11	64	26	4	.972	-18	O-289	-3.9

■ GEORGE MANGUS
Mangus, George Graham b: 5/22/1890, Red Creek, N.Y. d: 8/10/33, Rutland, Mass. BL/TR, 5'11.5", 165 lbs. Deb: 8/20/12

| 1912 | Phi-N | 10 | 25 | 2 | 5 | 3 | 0 | 0 | 3 | 1 | 6 | .200 | .231 | .320 | 47 | -2 | 0 | | | .750 | -1 | /O-5 | -0.4 |

■ CLYDE MANION
Manion, Clyde Jennings "Pete" b: 10/30/1896, Jefferson City, Mo d: 9/4/67, Detroit, Mich. BR/TR, 5'11", 175 lbs. Deb: 5/5/20

1920	Det-A	32	80	4	22	4	1	0	8	4	7	.275	.318	.350	79	-3	0	0	0	.940	-2	C-30	-0.3
1921	Det-A	12	10	0	2	0	0	0	2	2	2	.200	.385	.200	53	-1	0	0	0	1.000	1	/C-3	-0.1
1922	Det-A	42	69	9	19	4	1	0	12	4	6	.275	.315	.362	79	-2	0	1	-1	.932	-2	C-22/1-1	-0.4
1923	Det-A	23	22	0	3	0	0	0	2	2	2	.136	.208	.136	-8	-3	0	0	0	.857	-0	/C-3,1-1	-0.4
1924	Det-A	14	13	1	3	0	0	0	2	1	1	.231	.286	.231	35	-1	0	0	0	.750	-1	/C-3,1-1	-0.2
1926	Det-A	75	176	15	35	4	0	0	14	24	16	.199	.295	.222	36	-16	1	1	-0	.972	-0	C-74	-1.3
1927	Det-A	1	0	0	0	0	0	0	0	1	0	—	1.000	—	174	0	0	0	0	.000	0	H	0.0
1928	StL-A	76	243	25	55	5	1	2	31	15	18	.226	.274	.280	44	-20	3	0	1	.980	12	C-71	-0.1
1929	StL-A	35	111	16	27	2	0	0	11	15	3	.243	.333	.261	53	-7	1	0	0	.976	5	C-34	0.1
1930	StL-A	57	148	12	32	1	0	1	11	24	17	.216	.326	.243	45	-12	0	1	-1	.985	11	C-56	0.3
1932	Cin-N	49	135	7	28	4	0	0	12	14	16	.207	.282	.237	43	-11	0			.970	4	C-47	-0.4
1933	Cin-N	36	84	3	14	1	0	0	3	8	7	.167	.239	.179	21	-8	0			.981	4	C-34	-0.3
1934	Cin-N	25	54	4	10	0	0	0	3	4	8	.185	.241	.185	16	-6	0			1.000	3	C-24	-0.3
Total	13	477	1145	96	250	25	3	3	112	118	102	.218	.293	.253	45	-90	5	3		.973	33	C-401/1-3	-3.3

■ PHIL MANKOWSKI
Mankowski, Philip Anthony b: 1/9/53, Buffalo, N.Y. BL/TR, 6', 180 lbs. Deb: 8/30/76

1976	Det-A	24	85	9	23	2	1	1	4	4	9	.271	.303	.353	88	-1	0	0	0	.971	-1	3-23	0.1
1977	Det-A	94	286	21	79	7	3	3	27	16	41	.276	.319	.353	79	-8	1	2	-1	.964	13	3-85/2-1	0.3
1978	Det-A	88	222	28	61	8	0	4	20	22	28	.275	.346	.365	97	-0	2	3	-1	.972	-1	3-80/D-1	-0.3
1979	Det-A	42	99	11	22	4	0	0	8	10	16	.222	.294	.263	50	-7	0	0	0	.963	-0	3-36/D-1	-0.7
1980	NY-N	8	12	1	2	1	0	0	1	2	4	.167	.286	.250	52	-1	0	0	0	.571	-1	/3-3	-0.2
1982	NY-N	13	35	2	8	1	0	0	4	1	6	.229	.250	.257	42	-3	0	1	-1	.957	-1	3-13	-0.2
Total	6	269	739	72	195	23	4	8	64	55	103	.264	.318	.338	79	-20	3	6	-3	.962	13	3-240/D-2,2,1	-1.2

■ CHARLIE MANLOVE
Manlove, Charles Henry Weeks "Chick" b: 10/8/1862, Philadelphia, Pa. d: 2/12/52, Altoona, Pa. BR/TR, 5'9", 165 lbs. Deb: 5/31/1884

1884	Alt-U	2	7	1	3	0	0	0				.429	.429	.429	158	0				1.000	-1	/C-1,O-1	-0.1
	NY-N	3	10	0	0	0	0	0	0	0	4	.000	.000	.000	-98	-2				.833	-1	/C-3,O-1	-0.3
Total	1	5	17	1	3	0	0	0	0	0	4	.176	.176	.176	9	-2				.880	-2	/C-4,O-2	-0.4

■ GARTH MANN
Mann, Ben Garth "Red" b: 11/16/15, Brandon, Tex. d: 9/11/80, Italy, Tex. BR/TR, 6', 155 lbs. Deb: 5/14/44

| 1944 | Chi-N | 1 | 0 | 1 | 0 | 0 | 0 | 0 | | | | — | — | — | | | 0 | 0 | | .000 | 0 | R | 0.0 |

■ FRED MANN
Mann, Fred J. b: 4/1/1858, Sutton, Vt. d: 4/6/16, Springfield, Mass. BL, 5'10.5", 178 lbs. Deb: 5/1/1882

1882	Wor-N	19	77	12	18	5	0	2		2	15	.234	.253	.299	74	-2				.703	-6	3-18/1-1	-0.8
	Phi-a	29	121	13	28	7	4	0		4		.231	.256	.355	93	-2				.798	-10	3-29	-1.1
1883	Col-a	96	394	61	98	18	13	1			18	.249	.282	.368	117	8				.854	-3	*O-82/1-9,3-6,S-1	0.3
1884	Col-a	99	366	70	101	12	18	7			25	.276	.341	.464	174	31				.857	-8	*O-97/2-2	2.1
1885	Pit-a	99	391	60	99	17	6	0	41	31		.253	.318	.327	106	4				.908	-8	*O-97/3-3	-0.6
1886	Pit-a	116	440	85	110	16	14	2	60	45		.250	.335	.364	119	11	26			.878	-3	*O-116	0.4
1887	Cle-a	64	259	45	80	15	7	2	41	23		.309	.385	.444	135	13	25			.879	1	O-64	1.0
	Phi-a	55	229	42	63	14	6	0	32	15		.275	.336	.389	102	0	16			.916	-4	O-55	-0.4
	Yr	119	488	87	143	29	13	2	73	38		.293	.362	.418	119	13	41			.896	-3	*O-119	0.6
Total	6	577	2277	388	597	104	68	12	181	163	15	.262	.323	.383	122	63	67			.881	-39	O-511/3-56,1-10,2S	0.9

■ JOHNNY MANN
Mann, John Leo b: 2/4/1898, Fontanet, Ind. d: 3/31/77, Terre Haute, Ind. BR/TR, 5'11", 160 lbs. Deb: 4/18/28

| 1928 | Chi-A | 6 | 6 | 0 | 2 | 0 | 0 | 0 | 1 | 1 | 0 | .333 | .429 | .333 | 104 | 0 | 0 | 0 | 0 | 1.000 | 0 | /3-2 | 0.0 |

■ KELLY MANN
Mann, Kelly John b: 8/17/67, Santa Monica, Cal. BR/TR, 6'3", 215 lbs. Deb: 9/4/89

1989	Atl-N	7	24	1	5	2	0	0	1	0	6	.208	.240	.292	50	-2	0	0	0	1.000	2	/C-7	0.1
1990	Atl-N	11	28	2	4	1	0	1	2	0	6	.143	.143	.286	14	-3	0	0	0	1.000	-1	/C-10	-0.4
Total	2	18	52	3	9	3	0	1	3	0	12	.173	.189	.288	30	-5	0	0	0	1.000	1	/C-17	-0.3

■ LES MANN
Mann, Leslie "Major" b: 11/18/1893, Lincoln, Neb. d: 1/14/62, Pasadena, Cal. BR/TR, 5'9", 172 lbs. Deb: 4/30/13

1913	Bos-N	120	407	54	103	24	7	3	51	18	73	.253	.291	.369	86	-9	7			.960	-2	*O-120	-1.7
1914	*Bos-N	126	389	44	96	16	11	4	40	24	50	.247	.293	.375	99	-2	9			.952	13	*O-123	0.6
1915	Chi-F	135	470	74	144	12	19	4	58	36	40	.306	.357	.438	131	10	18			.969	5	*O-130/S-1	1.0
1916	Chi-N	127	415	46	113	19	9	2	29	19	31	.272	.307	.361	95	-3	11	7	-1	.972	-8	*O-115	-1.9
1917	Chi-N	117	444	63	121	19	10	1	44	27	46	.273	.316	.367	101	1	14			.953	0	*O-116	-0.7
1918	*Chi-N	129	489	69	141	27	7	2	55	38	45	.288	.342	.384	118	10	21			.961	-3	*O-129	0.9
1919	Chi-N	80	299	31	68	8	3	1	22	11	29	.227	.257	.318	72	-11	12			.982	2	O-78	-1.7
	Bos-N	40	145	15	41	4	3	1	20	9	14	.283	.329	.441	136	6	7			.929	3	O-40	0.6

YEAR	TM/L	G	AB	R	H	2B	3B	HR	RBI	BB	SO	AVG	OBP	SLG	PRO+	BR/A	SB	CS	SBR	FA	FR	G/POS	TPR
	Yr	120	444	46	109	14	12	4	42	20	43	.245	.281	.358	92	-6	19			.962	4	*O-118	-1.1
1920	Bos-N	115	424	48	117	7	8	3	32	38	42	.276	.341	.351	104	3	7	7	-2	.980	3	*O-110	-0.5
1921	StL-N	97	256	57	84	12	7	7	30	23	28	.328	.390	.512	140	14	5	5	-2	.969	0	O-79	0.8
1922	StL-N	84	147	42	51	14	2	2	20	16	12	.347	.415	.497	141	9	0	1	-1	.978	-11	O-57	-0.5
1923	StL-N	38	89	20	33	5	2	5	11	9	5	.371	.434	.640	184	11	0	0	0	.979	-3	O-26	0.6
	Cin-N	8	1	1	0	0	0	0	0	0	0	.000	.000	.000	-99	-0	0	0	0	.000	0	H	0.0
	Yr	46	90	21	33	5	2	5	11	9	5	.367	.430	.633	181	10	0	0	0	.979	-3	O-26	0.6
1924	Bos-N	32	102	13	28	7	4	0	10	8	10	.275	.333	.422	105	1	1	0	0	1.000	2	O-28	0.1
1925	Bos-N	60	184	27	63	11	4	2	20	5	11	.342	.373	.478	127	7	6	1	1	.992	-2	O-57	0.3
1926	Bos-N	50	129	23	39	8	2	1	20	9	9	.302	.348	.419	116	2	5			.966	-6	O-46	-0.6
1927	Bos-N	29	66	8	17	3	1	0	6	8	3	.258	.338	.333	87	-1	2			.955	-2	O-24	-0.4
	NY-N	29	67	13	22	4	1	2	10	8	7	.328	.400	.507	142	4	2			1.000	-4	O-22	-0.1
	Yr	58	133	21	39	7	2	2	16	16	10	.293	.369	.421	116	3	4			.973	-6	O-46	-0.5
1928	NY-N	82	193	29	51	7	1	2	25	18	9	.264	.330	.342	76	-7	2			.952	-19	O-68	-2.8
Total	16	1498	4716	677	1332	203	106	44	503	324	464	.282	.332	.398	109	43	129	21		.966	-32	*O-1368/S-1	-6.9

■ JIM MANNING
Manning, James H. b: 1/31/1862, Fall River, Mass. d: 10/22/29, Edinburg, Tex. BB/TR, 5'7", 157 lbs. Deb: 5/16/1884 M

YEAR	TM/L	G	AB	R	H	2B	3B	HR	RBI	BB	SO	AVG	OBP	SLG	PRO+	BR/A	SB	CS	SBR	FA	FR	G/POS	TPR
1884	Bos-N	89	345	52	83	8	6	2	35	19	47	.241	.280	.316	88	-5				.878	1	O-73/S-9,2-9,3-3	-0.4
1885	Bos-N	84	306	34	63	8	9	2	27	19	36	.206	.252	.310	84	-5				.898	9	*O-83/S-1	0.2
	Det-N	20	78	15	21	4	0	1	9	4	10	.269	.305	.359	114	1				.802	-7	S-20	-0.5
	Yr	104	384	49	84	12	9	3	36	23	46	.219	.263	.320	90	-4				.898	3	O-83,S-21	-0.3
1886	Det-N	26	97	14	18	2	3	0	7	6	10	.186	.233	.268	51	-6	7			.947	-1	O-26/S-1	-0.7
1887	Det-N	13	52	5	10	1	0	0	3	5	4	.192	.276	.212	36	-4	3			.867	-4	O-10/S-3	-0.8
1889	KC-a	132	506	68	103	16	7	3	68	54	61	.204	.297	.281	61	-27	58			.927	-10	O-69,2-63/S-1,3-1	-3.0
Total	5	364	1384	188	298	39	25	8	149	107	168	.215	.278	.297	73	-46	68			.903	-11	O-261/2-72,S-35,3-4	-5.2

■ JACK MANNING
Manning, John E. b: 12/20/1853, Braintree, Mass. d: 8/15/29, Boston, Mass. BR/TR, 5'8.5", 158 lbs. Deb: 4/23/1873 M

YEAR	TM/L	G	AB	R	H	2B	3B	HR	RBI	BB	SO	AVG	OBP	SLG	PRO+	BR/A	SB	CS	SBR	FA	FR	G/POS	TPR
1873	Bos-n	32	159	29	43	6	1	0	22	1	11	.270	.275	.321	71	-7	1	0	0	.940	1	1-29/O-5	-0.3
1874	Bal-n	42	174	32	61	8	2	0	18	2	2	.351	.358	.420	149	9	0	0	0	.839	-2	P-22,2-22/S-4,13	0.1
	Har-n	1	5	1	1	0	0	0	0	0	0	.200	.200	.200	27	-0	0	0	0	.167	-2	/3-1	-0.2
	Yr	43	179	33	62	8	2	0	18	2	2	.346	.354	.413	146	9	0	0	0	.793	-4	P-22,2-22/S-4,31	-0.1
1875	Bos-n	77	348	71	94	11	3	1	46	2	9	.270	.274	.328	104	1	5	5	-2	.802	-1	*O-65,P-27/1-3,3-1	-0.1
1876	Bos-N	70	288	52	76	13	0	2	25	7	5	.264	.281	.330	101	0				.777	-5	*O-56,P-34/S-1,2-1	-0.5
1877	Cin-N	57	252	47	80	16	7	0	36	5	6	.317	.331	.437	157	16				.742	-13	S-26,1-17,OP/2M	0.2
1878	Bos-N	60	248	41	63	10	1	0	23	10	16	.254	.283	.302	86	-4				.753	-13	*O-59/P-3	-1.9
1880	Cin-N	48	190	20	41	6	3	2	17	7	15	.216	.244	.311	87	-2				.798	-3	O-47/1-1	-0.6
1881	Buf-N	1	1	0	0	0	0	0	0	0	0	.000	.000	.000	-99	-0				1.000	0	/O-1	0.0
1883	Phi-N	98	420	60	112	31	5	0	37	20	37	.267	.300	.364	110	6				.853	10	*O-98	1.3
1884	Phi-N	104	424	71	115	29	4	5	52	40	67	.271	.334	.394	134	18				.847	-1	*O-104	1.3
1885	Phi-N	107	445	61	114	24	4	3	40	37	27	.256	.313	.348	116	9				.896	-6	*O-107	0.0
1886	Bal-a	137	556	78	124	18	7	1	45	50		.223	.291	.286	83	-10	24			.887	-10	*O-137	-2.0
Total	3 n	152	686	133	199	25	6	1	86	5	22	.290	.295	.348	106	3	6	5	-1	.785	-4	/O-70,P-49,12S3	-0.5
Total	9	682	2824	430	725	147	31	13	275	176	173	.257	.301	.345	108	33	24			.844	-40	O-621/P-47,S-27,12	-2.2

■ RICK MANNING
Manning, Richard Eugene b: 9/2/54, Niagara Falls, N.Y. BL/TR, 6'1", 180 lbs. Deb: 5/23/75

YEAR	TM/L	G	AB	R	H	2B	3B	HR	RBI	BB	SO	AVG	OBP	SLG	PRO+	BR/A	SB	CS	SBR	FA	FR	G/POS	TPR
1975	Cle-A	120	480	69	137	16	5	3	35	44	62	.285	.348	.358	100	1	19	11	-1	.974	13	*O-118/D-1	0.8
1976	Cle-A	138	552	73	161	24	7	6	43	41	75	.292	.341	.393	116	10	16	10	-1	.987	8	*O-136	1.2
1977	Cle-A	68	252	33	57	7	3	5	18	21	35	.226	.286	.337	71	-10	9	5	-0	.990	5	O-68	-0.8
1978	Cle-A	148	566	65	149	27	3	3	50	38	62	.263	.311	.337	83	-13	12	12	-4	.995	5	*O-144	-1.8
1979	Cle-A	144	560	67	145	12	2	3	51	55	48	.259	.326	.304	71	-21	30	8	4	.986	15	*O-141/D-1	-0.8
1980	Cle-A	140	471	55	110	17	4	3	52	63	66	.234	.326	.306	74	-15	12	6	0	.990	8	*O-139	-1.3
1981	Cle-A	103	360	47	88	15	3	4	33	40	57	.244	.320	.336	90	-4	25	3	6	.987	13	*O-103	1.2
1982	Cle-A	152	562	71	152	18	2	8	44	54	60	.270	.334	.352	89	-7	12	8	-1	.978	6	*O-152	-0.7
1983	Cle-A	50	194	20	54	6	0	1	10	12	22	.278	.320	.325	75	-6	7	3	0	.987	3	O-50	-0.4
	Mil-A	108	375	40	86	14	4	3	33	26	40	.229	.281	.312	68	-17	11	2	2	.991	6	*O-108	-1.2
	Yr	158	569	60	140	20	4	4	43	38	62	.246	.294	.316	71	-23	18	5	2	.990	9	*O-158	-1.6
1984	Mil-A	119	341	53	85	10	5	7	31	34	32	.249	.319	.370	94	-3	5	7	-3	.987	-14	*O-114/D-1	-2.2
1985	Mil-A	79	216	19	47	9	1	2	18	14	19	.218	.265	.296	54	-14	1	0	0	.976	-6	O-74/D-2	-2.1
1986	Mil-A	89	205	31	52	7	3	8	27	17	20	.254	.314	.434	98	-1	5	3	-0	.988	-5	O-83/D-5	-0.8
1987	Mil-A	97	114	21	26	7	1	0	13	12	18	.228	.302	.307	60	-6	4	0	1	.958	-19	O-78/D-2	-2.4
Total	13	1555	5248	664	1349	189	43	56	458	471	616	.257	.319	.341	84	-108	168	78	4	.985	40	*O-1508/D-12	-11.3

■ TIM MANNING
Manning, Timothy Edward b: 12/3/1853, Henley-On-Thames, England d: 6/11/34, Oak Park, Ill. BR/TR, 5'10", 170 lbs. Deb: 5/1/1882

YEAR	TM/L	G	AB	R	H	2B	3B	HR	RBI	BB	SO	AVG	OBP	SLG	PRO+	BR/A	SB	CS	SBR	FA	FR	G/POS	TPR
1882	Pro-N	21	76	7	8	0	0	0	8	5	13	.105	.160	.105	-13	-9				.787	-10	S-17/C-4	-1.8
1883	Bal-a	35	121	23	26	5	0	0		14		.215	.296	.256	77	-3				.913	3	2-35	0.1
1884	Bal-a	91	341	49	70	14	5	2		26		.205	.275	.293	82	-6				.907	-2	*2-91	-0.6
1885	Bal-a	43	157	17	32	8	1	0	16	10		.204	.265	.268	70	-5				.919	3	2-41/3-3	-0.1
	Pro-N	10	35	3	2	1	0	0	0	1	11	.057	.083	.086	-47	-5				.854	-3	S-10	-0.8
Total	4	200	730	99	138	28	6	2	24	56	24	.189	.256	.252	63	-29				.911	-9	2-167/S-27,C-4,3-3	-3.2

■ DON MANNO
Manno, Donald D. b: 5/4/15, Williamsport, Pa. d: 3/11/95, Williamsport, Pa. BR/TR, 6'1", 190 lbs. Deb: 9/22/40

YEAR	TM/L	G	AB	R	H	2B	3B	HR	RBI	BB	SO	AVG	OBP	SLG	PRO+	BR/A	SB	CS	SBR	FA	FR	G/POS	TPR
1940	Bos-N	3	7	1	2	0	0	1	4	0	2	.286	.286	.714	177	1	0			1.000	0	/O-2	0.1
1941	Bos-N	22	30	2	5	1	0	0	4	3	7	.167	.242	.200	27	-3	0			1.000	-1	/O-5,3-3,1-1	-0.5
Total	2	25	37	3	7	1	0	1	8	3	9	.189	.250	.297	56	-2	0			1.000	-1	/O-7,3-3,1-1	-0.4

■ FRED MANRIQUE
Manrique, Fred Eloy (Reyes) b: 11/5/61, Edo Bolivar, Venez. BR/TR, 6'1", 175 lbs. Deb: 8/23/81

YEAR	TM/L	G	AB	R	H	2B	3B	HR	RBI	BB	SO	AVG	OBP	SLG	PRO+	BR/A	SB	CS	SBR	FA	FR	G/POS	TPR
1981	Tor-A	14	28	1	4	0	0	0	1	0	12	.143	.172	.143	-8	-4	0	1	-1	.949	3	S-11/3-2,D-1	-0.1
1984	Tor-A	10	9	0	3	0	0	0	1	0	1	.333	.333	.333	82	-0	0	0	0	.938	3	/2-9,D-1	0.2
1985	Mon-N	9	13	5	4	1	1	1	1	1	3	.308	.357	.769	219	2	0	0	0	1.000	2	/2-2,S-2,3-1	0.4
1986	StL-N	13	17	2	3	0	0	1	1	1	1	.176	.222	.353	57	-1	1	0	0	1.000	-2	/3-4,2-1	-0.2
1987	Chi-A	115	298	30	77	13	3	4	29	19	69	.258	.305	.362	74	-11	5	3	-0	.984	19	2-92,S-23/D-5	1.1
1988	Chi-A	140	345	43	81	10	6	5	37	21	54	.235	.285	.342	75	-12	6	5	-1	.985	12	*2-129,S-12/D-1	0.4
1989	Chi-A	65	187	23	56	13	1	2	30	8	30	.299	.335	.412	112	3	0	4	-2	.961	-5	2-57/S-2,3-1	-0.3
	Tex-A	54	191	23	55	12	0	2	22	9	33	.288	.320	.382	96	-1	4	1	1	.963	-11	S-37,2-17/3-6,D-1	-0.9
	Yr	119	378	46	111	25	1	4	52	17	63	.294	.327	.397	104	1	4	5	-2	.952	-16	2-74,S-39/3-7,D-1	-1.2
1990	Min-A	69	228	22	54	10	0	5	29	4	35	.237	.256	.346	63	-12	2	0	1	.974	-10	2 67/D-1	-2.0
1991	Oak-A	9	21	2	3	0	0	0	0	2	1	.143	.217	.143	2	-3	0	0	0	.955	-0	/S-7,2-2	-0.3
Total	9	498	1337	151	340	59	11	20	151	65	239	.254	.293	.360	79	-40	18	14	-3	.976	11	2-376/S-94,3-14,D	-1.7

■ JOHN MANSELL
Mansell, John b: 1861, Auburn, N.Y. d: 2/20/25, Romulus, N.Y. BL , 5'10", 168 lbs. Deb: 5/9/1882 F

YEAR	TM/L	G	AB	R	H	2B	3B	HR	RBI	BB	SO	AVG	OBP	SLG	PRO+	BR/A	SB	CS	SBR	FA	FR	G/POS	TPR
1882	Phi-a	31	126	17	30	3	1	0	17	4		.238	.262	.278	73	-4				.791	-4	O-31	-0.7

■ MIKE MANSELL
Mansell, Michael R. b: 1/15/1858, Auburn, N.Y. d: 12/4/02, Auburn, N.Y. BL , 5'11", 175 lbs. Deb: 5/1/1879 F

YEAR	TM/L	G	AB	R	H	2B	3B	HR	RBI	BB	SO	AVG	OBP	SLG	PRO+	BR/A	SB	CS	SBR	FA	FR	G/POS	TPR
1879	Syr-N	67	242	24	52	4	2	1	13	5	45	.215	.231	.260	69	-7				.881	15	*O-67	0.5
1880	Cin-N	53	187	22	36	6	2	2	12	4	37	.193	.209	.278	64	-7				.865	12	O-53	0.4
1882	Pit-a	79	347	59	96	**18**	**16**	2		7		.277	.291	.438	150	17				.829	3	*O-79	1.8
1883	Pit-a	96	412	90	106	12	13	3		25		.257	.300	.371	120	10				.883	4	*O-96	1.1
1884	Pit-a	27	100	15	14	0	3	1		7		.140	.204	.230	41	-6				.796	-1	O-27	-0.8
	Phi-a	20	70	6	14	1	1	0		5		.200	.253	.243	59	-3				.762	-1	O-20	-0.4
	Ric-a	29	113	21	34	2	5	0		8		.301	.363	.407	153	7				.763	-5	O-29	0.1

YEAR	TM/L	G	AB	R	H	2B	3B	HR	RBI	BB	SO	AVG	OBP	SLG	PRO+	BR/A	SB	CS	SBR	FA	FR	G/POS	TPR
	Yr	76	283	42	62	3	9	1		20		.219	.280	.304	89	-3				.775	-7	O-76	-1.1
Total	5	371	1471	237	352	43	42	9	25	61	82	.239	.271	.344	106	11				.854	27	O-371	2.7

■ TOM MANSELL

Mansell, Thomas E. "Brick" b: 1/1/1855, Auburn, N.Y. d: 10/6/34, Auburn, N.Y. BL/TR, 5′8″, 160 lbs. Deb: 5/1/1879 F

YEAR	TM/L	G	AB	R	H	2B	3B	HR	RBI	BB	SO	AVG	OBP	SLG	PRO+	BR/A	SB	CS	SBR	FA	FR	G/POS	TPR
1879	Tro-N	40	177	29	43	6	0	0	11	3	9	.243	.256	.277	81	-3				.742	-6	O-40	-1.1
	Syr-N	1	4	0	1	0	0	0	0	0	0	.250	.250	.250	74	-0				1.000	-0	/O-1	0.0
	Yr	41	181	29	44	6	0	0	11	3	9	.243	.255	.276	81	-3				.747	-6	O-41	-1.1
1883	Det-N	34	131	22	29	4	1	0	10	8	13	.221	.266	.267	66	-5				.758	-2	O-34/P-1	-0.6
	StL-a	28	112	23	45	8	1	0	24	7		.402	.437	.491	188	10				.786	-6	O-28	0.4
1884	Cin-a	65	266	49	66	4	6	0	23	15		.248	.301	.308	94	-2				.752	-11	O-65	-1.3
	Col-a	23	77	9	15	1	3	0	6	6		.195	.262	.286	85	-1				.667	-4	O-23	-0.5
	Yr	88	343	58	81	5	9	0	29	21		.236	.292	.303	93	-2				.739	-15	O-88	-1.8
Total	3	191	767	132	199	23	11	0	74	39	22	.259	.300	.318	100	-0				.751	-28	O-191/P-1	-3.1

■ FELIX MANTILLA

Mantilla, Felix (Lamela) b: 7/29/34, Isabela, P.R. BR/TR, 6′, 160 lbs. Deb: 6/21/56

YEAR	TM/L	G	AB	R	H	2B	3B	HR	RBI	BB	SO	AVG	OBP	SLG	PRO+	BR/A	SB	CS	SBR	FA	FR	G/POS	TPR
1956	Mil-N	35	53	9	15	1	1	0	3	1	8	.283	.309	.340	79	-2	0	1	-1	1.000	9	S-15/3-3	0.8
1957	*Mil-N	71	182	28	43	9	1	4	21	14	34	.236	.298	.363	82	-5	2	0	1	.931	6	S-35,2-13/3-7,O-1	0.5
1958	*Mil-N	85	226	37	50	5	1	7	19	20	20	.221	.285	.345	72	-10	2	0	1	.987	-6	O-43,2-21/S-5,3-2	-1.6
1959	Mil-N	103	251	26	54	5	0	3	19	16	31	.215	.268	.271	48	-19	6	1	1	.970	4	2-60,S-23/3-9,O-7	-0.9
1960	Mil-N	63	148	21	38	7	0	3	11	7	16	.257	.295	.365	86	-3	3	1	0	.956	-12	2-26,S-25/O-8	-1.3
1961	Mil-N	45	93	13	20	3	0	1	5	10	16	.215	.298	.280	58	-6	1	1	-0	.933	-4	S-19,2-10,O-10,/3-6	-0.9
1962	NY-N	141	466	54	128	17	4	11	59	37	51	.275	.335	.399	94	-4	3	1	0	.948	-7	3-95,S-25,2-14	-0.7
1963	Bos-A	66	178	27	56	8	0	6	15	20	14	.315	.384	.461	131	8	2	1	0	.965	-5	S-27,O-11/2-5	0.5
1964	Bos-A	133	425	69	123	20	1	30	64	41	46	.289	.357	.553	142	23	0	1	-1	.984	-6	O-48,2-45/3-7,S-6	2.0
1965	Bos-A★	150	534	60	147	17	2	18	92	79	84	.275	.377	.416	118	15	7	3	0	.976	-22	*2-123,O-27/1-2	0.3
1966	Hou-N	77	151	16	33	5	0	6	22	11	32	.219	.280	.371	85	-4	1	0	0	.990	-2	1-14,3-14/2-9,O-1	-0.6
Total	11	969	2707	360	707	97	10	89	330	256	352	.261	.331	.403	100	-6	27	10	2	.977	-44	2-326,S-180,O3/1	-1.9

■ MICKEY MANTLE

Mantle, Mickey Charles "The Commerce Comet" b: 10/20/31, Spavinaw, Okla. d: 8/13/95, Dallas, Tex. BB/TR, 5′11″, 198 lbs. Deb: 4/17/51 CH

YEAR	TM/L	G	AB	R	H	2B	3B	HR	RBI	BB	SO	AVG	OBP	SLG	PRO+	BR/A	SB	CS	SBR	FA	FR	G/POS	TPR
1951	*NY-A	96	341	61	91	11	5	13	65	43	74	.267	.349	.443	117	7	8	7	-2	.959	-6	O-86	-0.3
1952	*NY-A☆	142	549	94	171	37	7	23	87	75	111	.311	.394	.530	166	**47**	4	1	1	.968	3	*O-141/3-1	4.6
1953	*NY-A★	127	461	105	136	24	3	21	92	79	90	.295	.398	.497	145	30	8	4	0	.982	1	*O-121/S-1	2.7
1954	NY-A★	146	543	**129**	163	17	12	27	102	102	107	.300	.411	.525	160	47	5	2	0	.975	-1	*O-144/S-4,2-1	4.1
1955	*NY-A★	147	517	121	158	25	**11**	**37**	99	**113**	97	.306	**.433**	**.611**	**181**	**61**	8	1	2	.995	8	*O-145/S-2	**6.3**
1956	*NY-A★	150	533	**132**	188	22	5	**52**	**130**	112	99	**.353**	.467	**.705**	**213**	**89**	10	1	2	.990	8	*O-144	**8.7**
1957	*NY-A★	144	474	**121**	173	28	6	34	94	**146**	75	.365	.515	.665	223	**91**	16	3	3	.979	0	*O-139	**8.6**
1958	*NY-A★	150	519	**127**	158	21	1	**42**	97	**129**	120	.304	.445	.592	**189**	**69**	18	3	4	.977	-0	*O-150	**6.5**
1959	NY-A★	144	541	104	154	23	4	31	75	93	126	.285	.392	.514	**152**	40	21	3	5	**.995**	8	*O-143	**4.5**
1960	*NY-A★	153	527	**119**	145	17	6	**40**	94	111	125	.275	.402	.558	**166**	**51**	14	3	2	.991	-1	*O-150	**4.4**
1961	*NY-A★	153	514	**132**	163	16	6	54	128	**126**	112	.317	.452	**.687**	**210**	**84**	12	1	3	.983	4	*O-150	**8.0**
1962	*NY-A★	123	377	96	121	15	1	30	89	**122**	78	.321	**.488**	**.605**	**198**	**61**	9	0	3	.978	-6	*O-117	**5.0**
1963	*NY-A†	65	172	40	54	8	0	15	35	40	32	.314	.443	.622	197	24	2	1	0	.990	-2	O-52	2.0
1964	*NY-A★	143	465	92	141	25	2	35	111	99	102	.303	**.426**	.591	**177**	**51**	6	3	0	.978	-13	*O-132	3.3
1965	NY-A†	122	361	44	92	12	1	19	46	73	76	.255	.380	.452	136	19	4	1	1	.966	-4	*O-108	1.2
1966	NY-A	108	333	40	96	12	1	23	56	57	76	.288	.392	.538	171	31	1	1	-0	1.000	-7	O-97	2.1
1967	NY-A★	144	440	63	108	17	0	22	55	107	113	.245	.394	.434	150	32	1	1	-0	.993	0	*1-131	2.7
1968	NY-A★	144	435	57	103	14	1	18	54	106	97	.237	.387	.398	143	28	6	2	1	.988	-3	*1-131	1.7
Total	18	2401	8102	1677	2415	344	72	536	1509	1733	1710	.298	.423	.557	173	863	153	38	23	.982	-9	*O-2019,1-262/S23	76.1

■ JEFF MANTO

Manto, Jeffrey Paul b: 8/23/64, Bristol, Pa. BR/TR, 6′3″, 210 lbs. Deb: 6/7/90

YEAR	TM/L	G	AB	R	H	2B	3B	HR	RBI	BB	SO	AVG	OBP	SLG	PRO+	BR/A	SB	CS	SBR	FA	FR	G/POS	TPR
1990	Cle-A	30	76	12	17	5	1	2	14	21	18	.224	.392	.395	121	3	0	1	-1	.990	1	1-25/3-5	0.2
1991	Cle-A	47	128	15	27	7	0	2	13	14	22	.211	.308	.313	72	-5	2	0	1	.929	1	3-32,1-14/C-5,O-1	-0.3
1993	Phi-N	8	18	0	1	0	0	0	0	0	3	.056	.105	.056	-56	-4	0	0	0	1.000	-0	/3-6,S-1	-0.4
1995	Bal-A	89	254	31	65	9	0	17	38	24	69	.256	.325	.492	107	2	0	3	-2	.959	-2	3-69,D-13/1-4	-0.3
1996	Bos-A	10	30	5	8	3	1	2	4	3	6	.267	.353	.633	140	2	0	0	0	.963	4	/2-4,S-4	0.5
	Sea-A	21	54	7	10	3	0	1	4	9	12	.185	.302	.296	52	-4	0	1	-1	.971	0	3-16/O-1,D-2	-0.4
	Bos-A	12	18	3	2	0	0	0	2	5	6	.111	.304	.111	11	-2	0	0	0	.960	4	3-10/1-1	0.1
	Yr	43	102	15	20	6	1	3	10	17	24	.196	.317	.363	70	-5	0	1	-1	.967	8	3-26/2-4,S-4,DO1	0.2
1997	Cle-A	16	30	3	8	3	0	2	7	1	10	.267	.290	.567	113	0	0	0	0	1.000	-1	/3-7,1-6,O-1	-0.1
1998	Cle-A	7	14	3	1	0	0	0	1	1	5	.071	.133	.071	-43	-3	0	0	0	1.000	-1	/1-4,3-2,2-1	-0.4
	Det-A	16	30	6	8	2	0	1	3	3	11	.267	.353	.433	102	0	1	0	0	.977	-2	1-10/O-1,D-6	-0.1
	Cle-A	8	23	5	7	1	0	2	5	1	5	.304	.333	.609	133	1	0	1	-1	1.000	0	/3-6,1-3	0.0
	Yr	31	67	14	16	3	0	3	9	5	21	.239	.301	.418	83	-2	1	1	-0	.979	-2	1-17/3-8,D-6,2-1,O	-0.5
Total	7	264	675	90	154	33	2	29	91	82	167	.228	.320	.412	91	-10	3	6	-3	.957	5	3-153/1-67,D2SCO	-1.2

■ CHUCK MANUEL

Manuel, Charles Fuqua b: 1/4/44, Northfork, W.Va. BL/TR, 6′4″, 200 lbs. Deb: 4/8/69 C

YEAR	TM/L	G	AB	R	H	2B	3B	HR	RBI	BB	SO	AVG	OBP	SLG	PRO+	BR/A	SB	CS	SBR	FA	FR	G/POS	TPR
1969	*Min-A	83	164	14	34	6	0	2	24	28	33	.207	.323	.280	69	-6	1	0	0	.967	-6	O-46	-1.4
1970	*Min-A	59	64	4	12	0	0	1	7	6	17	.188	.268	.234	39	-5	0	0	0	1.000	-3	O-11	-0.8
1971	Min-A	18	16	1	2	1	0	0	1	1	8	.125	.176	.188	3	-2	0	0	0	.000	-0	/O-1	-0.3
1972	Min-A	63	122	6	25	5	0	1	8	4	16	.205	.236	.270	48	-8	0	0	0	.977	-1	O-28	-1.1
1974	LA-N	4	3	0	1	0	0	0	1	1	0	.333	.500	.333	142	0	0	0	0	.000	0	H	0.0
1975	LA-N	15	15	0	2	0	0	0	2	0	3	.133	.133	.133	-27	-3	0	0	0	.000	0	H	-0.3
Total	6	242	384	25	76	12	0	4	43	40	77	.198	.277	.260	52	-24	1	0	0	.973	-9	/O-86	-3.9

■ JERRY MANUEL

Manuel, Jerry b: 12/23/53, Hahira, Ga. BB/TR, 6′, 165 lbs. Deb: 9/18/75 MC

YEAR	TM/L	G	AB	R	H	2B	3B	HR	RBI	BB	SO	AVG	OBP	SLG	PRO+	BR/A	SB	CS	SBR	FA	FR	G/POS	TPR
1975	Det-A	6	18	0	1	0	0	0	0	0	4	.056	.056	.056	-66	-4	0	0	0	.944	3	/2-6	-0.1
1976	Det-A	54	43	4	6	1	0	0	2	3	9	.140	.213	.163	11	-5	1	0	0	.921	10	2-47/S-4,D-1	0.7
1980	Mon-N	7	6	0	0	0	0	0	0	0	2	.000	.000	.000	-99	-2	0	0	0	.941	3	/S-7	0.1
1981	*Mon-N	27	55	10	11	5	0	3	10	6	11	.200	.279	.455	104	-0	0	0	0	.987	-0	2-23/S-2	0.0
1982	SD-N	2	5	0	1	0	1	0	1	1	0	.200	.333	.600	165	0	0	0	0	1.000	-1	/2-1,S-1,3-1	-0.1
Total	5	96	127	14	19	6	1	3	13	10	26	.150	.217	.283	42	-10	1	0	0	.949	14	/2-77,S-14,3-1,D-1	0.6

■ FRANK MANUSH

Manush, Frank Benjamin b: 9/18/1883, Tuscumbia, Ala. d: 1/5/65, Laguna Beach, Cal. BR/TR, 5′10.5″, 175 lbs. Deb: 8/31/08 F

YEAR	TM/L	G	AB	R	H	2B	3B	HR	RBI	BB	SO	AVG	OBP	SLG	PRO+	BR/A	SB	CS	SBR	FA	FR	G/POS	TPR
1908	Phi-A	23	77	6	12	2	1	0	0	2		.156	.188	.208	27	-6	2			.933	-5	3-20/2-2	-1.2

■ HEINIE MANUSH

Manush, Henry Emmett b: 7/20/01, Tuscumbia, Ala. d: 5/12/71, Sarasota, Fla. BL/TL, 6′1″, 200 lbs. Deb: 4/20/23 FCH

YEAR	TM/L	G	AB	R	H	2B	3B	HR	RBI	BB	SO	AVG	OBP	SLG	PRO+	BR/A	SB	CS	SBR	FA	FR	G/POS	TPR
1923	Det-A	109	308	59	103	20	5	4	54	20	21	.334	.406	.471	133	15	3	5	-2	.953	-5	O-79	0.3
1924	Det-A	120	422	83	122	24	8	9	68	27	30	.289	.355	.448	108	3	14	5	1	.979	-6	*O-106/1-1	-0.8
1925	Det-A	99	278	46	84	14	3	5	47	24	21	.302	.362	.428	101	0	8	3	1	.982	-5	O-73	-0.8
1926	Det-A	136	498	95	188	35	8	14	86	31	28	**.378**	.421	.564	153	37	11	5	0	.967	-4	*O-120	2.4
1927	Det-A	151	593	102	177	31	18	6	90	47	29	.298	.354	.442	104	2	12	8	-1	.971	-3	*O-149	-1.1
1928	StL-A	154	638	104	**241**	**47**	20	13	108	39	14	.378	.414	.575	153	46	17	5	2	.992	2	*O-154	3.8
1929	StL-A	142	574	85	204	**45**	10	6	81	43	24	.355	.401	.500	126	22	9	8	-2	.987	-2	*O-141	0.7
1930	StL-A	49	198	26	65	16	4	2	29	5	7	.328	.345	.480	103	0	3	1	0	.990	2	O-48	-0.1
	Was-A	88	356	74	129	33	8	7	65	26	17	.362	.406	.559	141	22	4	3	-1	.988	-2	O-86	1.2
	Yr	137	554	100	194	49	12	9	94	31	24	.350	.385	.531	128	22	7	4	-0	.989	1	*O-134	1.1
1931	Was-A	146	616	110	189	41	11	6	70	36	27	.307	.351	.438	106	4	3	3	-1	.977	-11	*O-143	-1.6
1932	Was-A	149	625	121	214	41	14	14	116	36	29	.342	.383	.520	133	29	7	2	1	.988	-0	*O-146	1.8
1933	*Was-A	153	658	115	**221**	32	**17**	5	95	36	18	.336	.372	.459	120	18	6	4	-1	.982	-2	*O-150	0.7
1934	Was-A★	137	556	88	194	42	11	11	89	36	23	.349	.392	.523	140	30	7	3	0	.980	-0	*O-131	2.3
1935	Was-A	119	479	68	131	26	9	4	56	35	17	.273	.328	.390	88	-10	2	0	1	.985	3	*O-111	-1.0

YEAR	TM/L	G	AB	R	H	2B	3B	HR	RBI	BB	SO	AVG	OBP	SLG	PRO+	BR/A	SB	CS	SBR	FA	FR	G/POS	TPR
1936	Bos-A	82	313	43	91	15	5	0	45	17	11	.291	.329	.371	69	-16	1	3	-2	.966	-8	O-72	-2.5
1937	Bro-N	132	466	57	155	25	7	4	73	40	24	.333	.389	.442	123	16	6			.970	-12	*O-123	0.0
1938	Bro-N	17	51	9	12	3	1	0	6	5	4	.235	.304	.333	73	-2	1			1.000	1	O-12	-0.1
	Pit-N	15	13	2	4	1	1	0	4	2	0	.308	.400	.538	155	1	0			.000	0	H	0.1
	Yr	32	64	11	16	4	2	0	10	7	4	.250	.324	.375	90	-1	1			1.000	1	O-12	0.0
1939	Pit-N	10	12	0	0	0	0	0	1	1	1	.000	.077	.000	-79	-3	0			1.000	-0	/O-1	-0.3
Total	17	2008	7654	1287	2524	491	160	110	1183	506	345	.330	.377	.479	121	214	114	58		.979	-50	*O-1845/1-1	5.0

■ **KIRT MANWARING** Manwaring, Kirt Dean b: 7/15/65, Elmira, N.Y. BR/TR, 5'11", 190 lbs. Deb: 9/15/87

YEAR	TM/L	G	AB	R	H	2B	3B	HR	RBI	BB	SO	AVG	OBP	SLG	PRO+	BR/A	SB	CS	SBR	FA	FR	G/POS	TPR
1987	SF-N	6	7	0	1	0	0	0	0	0	1	.143	.250	.143	8	-1	0	0	0	.909	-1	/C-6	-0.2
1988	SF-N	40	116	12	29	7	0	1	15	2	21	.250	.281	.336	80	-3	0	1	-1	.979	-2	C-40	-0.4
1989	*SF-N	85	200	14	42	4	2	0	18	11	28	.210	.265	.250	49	-13	2	1	0	.982	-0	C-81	-1.1
1990	SF-N	8	13	0	2	0	1	0	1	0	3	.154	.154	.308	25	-1	0	0	0	1.000	2	/C-8	0.1
1991	SF-N	67	178	16	40	9	0	0	19	9	22	.225	.274	.275	57	-10	1	1	-0	.988	1	C-67	-0.6
1992	SF-N	109	349	24	85	10	5	4	26	29	42	.244	.311	.335	88	-6	2	1	0	.994	1	*C-108	0.0
1993	SF-N	130	432	48	119	15	1	5	49	41	76	.275	.347	.350	90	-5	1	3	-2	**.998**	-0	*C-130	0.0
1994	SF-N	97	316	30	79	17	1	1	29	25	50	.250	.311	.320	68	-15	1	1	-0	.993	5	C-97	-0.5
1995	SF-N	118	379	21	95	15	2	4	36	27	72	.251	.317	.332	74	-14	1	0	0	.990	-13	*C-118	-1.9
1996	SF-N	49	145	9	34	6	0	1	14	16	24	.234	.323	.297	67	-6	0	1	-1	.993	1	C-49	-0.4
	Hou-N	37	82	5	18	3	0	0	4	3	16	.220	.264	.256	41	-7	0	0	0	.995	5	C-37	-0.1
	Yr	86	227	14	52	9	0	1	18	19	40	.229	.303	.282	59	-13	0	1	-1	.994	6	C-86	-0.5
1997	Col-N	104	337	22	76	6	4	1	27	30	78	.226	.293	.276	41	-30	1	5	-3	.994	-11	*C-100	-3.8
1998	Col-N	110	291	30	72	12	3	2	26	38	49	.247	.340	.330	63	-16	1	5	-3	.988	4	*C-108	-0.8
Total	12	960	2845	231	692	104	19	19	264	231	482	.243	.310	.313	67	-128	10	19	-8	.991	-9	C-949	-9.7

■ **CLIFF MAPES** Mapes, Clifford Franklin b: 3/13/22, Sutherland, Neb. d: 12/5/96, Pryor, Okla. BL/TR, 6'3", 205 lbs. Deb: 4/20/48

YEAR	TM/L	G	AB	R	H	2B	3B	HR	RBI	BB	SO	AVG	OBP	SLG	PRO+	BR/A	SB	CS	SBR	FA	FR	G/POS	TPR
1948	NY-A	53	88	19	22	11	1	1	12	6	13	.250	.298	.432	94	-2	1	1	-0	.958	1	O-21	-0.1
1949	*NY-A	111	304	56	75	13	3	7	38	58	50	.247	.369	.378	98	0	6	0	**2**	.976	3	*O-108	0.0
1950	*NY-A	108	356	60	88	14	6	12	61	47	61	.247	.338	.421	96	-3	1	6	-3	.950	-7	*O-102	-1.7
1951	NY-A	45	51	6	11	3	1	2	8	4	14	.216	.273	.431	92	-1	0	0	0	1.000	-9	O-34	-1.0
	StL-A	56	201	32	55	7	2	7	30	26	33	.274	.360	.433	110	3	0	1	-1	.983	-1	O-53	-0.1
	Yr	101	252	38	66	10	3	9	38	30	47	.262	.343	.433	109	2	0	1	-1	.986	-10	O-87	-1.1
1952	Det-A	86	193	26	38	7	0	9	23	27	42	.197	.295	.373	84	-5	0	1	-1	.967	-10	O-63	-1.8
Total	5	459	1193	199	289	55	13	38	172	168	213	.242	.338	.406	97	-8	8	9	-3	.969	-23	O-381	-4.7

■ **HOWARD MAPLE** Maple, Howard Albert "Mape" b: 7/20/03, Adrian, Mo. d: 11/9/70, Portland, Ore. BL/TR, 5'7", 175 lbs. Deb: 5/19/32

YEAR	TM/L	G	AB	R	H	2B	3B	HR	RBI	BB	SO	AVG	OBP	SLG	PRO+	BR/A	SB	CS	SBR	FA	FR	G/POS	TPR
1932	Was-A	44	41	6	10	0	1	0	7	7	7	.244	.367	.293	74	-1	0	0	0	1.000	-3	C-41	-0.3

■ **GEORGE MAPPES** Mappes, George Richard "Dick" b: 12/25/1865, St.Louis, Mo. d: 2/20/34, St.Louis, Mo. Deb: 9/23/1885

YEAR	TM/L	G	AB	R	H	2B	3B	HR	RBI	BB	SO	AVG	OBP	SLG	PRO+	BR/A	SB	CS	SBR	FA	FR	G/POS	TPR
1885	Bal-a	6	19	2	4	0	1	0	0	1		.211	.250	.316	79	-0				.875	-2	/2-6	-0.2
1886	StL-N	6	14	1	2	0	0	0	0	1	5	.143	.200	.143	6	-2	0			1.000	-1	/C-3,3-2,2-1	-0.2
Total	2	12	33	3	6	0	1	0	0	2	5	.182	.229	.242	48	-2	0			.848	-3	/2-7,C-3,3-2	-0.4

■ **RABBIT MARANVILLE** Maranville, Walter James Vincent b: 11/11/1891, Springfield, Mass. d: 1/5/54, New York, N.Y. BR/TR, 5'5", 155 lbs. Deb: 9/10/12 MH

YEAR	TM/L	G	AB	R	H	2B	3B	HR	RBI	BB	SO	AVG	OBP	SLG	PRO+	BR/A	SB	CS	SBR	FA	FR	G/POS	TPR
1912	Bos-N	26	86	8	18	2	0	0	8	9	14	.209	.292	.233	44	-6	1			.929	5	S-26	0.1
1913	Bos-N	143	571	68	141	13	8	2	48	68	62	.247	.330	.308	81	-12	25			.949	15	*S-143	1.7
1914	*Bos-N	156	586	74	144	23	6	4	78	45	56	.246	.306	.326	88	-9	28			.938	**52**	*S-156	**5.9**
1915	Bos-N	149	509	51	124	23	6	2	43	45	65	.244	.308	.324	96	-3	18	12	-2	.941	21	*S-149	3.0
1916	Bos-N	155	604	79	142	16	13	4	38	50	69	.235	.296	.325	94	-5	32	15	1	**.947**	22	*S-155	2.9
1917	Bos-N	142	561	69	146	19	13	3	43	40	47	.260	.312	.357	111	6	27			.947	14	*S-142	3.0
1918	Bos-N	11	38	3	12	0	1	0	3	4	0	.316	.381	.368	134	2	0			.932	2	S-11	0.4
1919	Bos-N	131	480	44	128	18	10	5	43	36	23	.267	.319	.377	113	7	12			.941	**29**	*S-131	**4.7**
1920	Bos-N	134	493	48	131	19	15	1	43	28	24	.266	.305	.371	98	-3	14	11	-2	.948	14	*S-133	2.1
1921	Pit-N	153	612	90	180	25	12	1	70	47	38	.294	.347	.379	90	-8	25	12	0	.962	-11	*S-153	-0.4
1922	Pit-N	155	672	115	198	26	15	0	63	61	43	.295	.355	.378	88	-11	24	13	-1	.961	7	*S-138,2-18	1.0
1923	Pit-N	141	581	78	161	19	9	1	41	42	34	.277	.327	.346	76	-20	14	11	-2	**.965**	12	*S-141	0.4
1924	Pit-N	152	594	62	158	33	20	2	71	35	53	.266	.307	.399	86	-13	18	14	-3	**.973**	5	*2-152	-1.0
1925	Chi-N	75	266	37	62	10	3	0	23	29	20	.233	.308	.293	54	-18	6	5	-1	.955	4	S-74,M	-0.7
1926	Bro-N	78	234	32	55	8	5	0	24	26	24	.235	.312	.312	69	-10	7			.948	10	S-60,2-18	0.6
1927	StL-N	9	29	0	7	1	0	0	0	2	2	.241	.290	.276	51	-2	0			.962	3	/S-9	0.2
1928	*StL-N	112	366	40	88	14	10	1	34	36	27	.240	.310	.342	69	-17	3			.969	-5	*S-112/2-2	-0.9
1929	Bos-N	146	560	87	159	26	10	0	55	47	33	.284	.344	.366	79	-18	13			.961	20	*S-145/2-1	1.8
1930	Bos-N	142	558	85	157	26	8	2	43	48	23	.281	.344	.367	75	-22	9			**.965**	-13	*S-138/3-4	-1.7
1931	Bos-N	145	562	69	146	22	5	0	33	56	34	.260	.329	.317	77	-17	9			.949	-24	*S-137,2-11	-2.7
1932	Bos-N	149	571	67	134	20	4	0	37	46	28	.235	.295	.284	59	-32	4			**.975**		*2-149	-1.9
1933	Bos-N	143	478	46	104	15	4	0	38	36	34	.218	.274	.266	59	-25	2			.971	-27	*2-142	-4.7
1935	Bos-N	23	67	3	10	2	0	0	5	3	3	.149	.186	.179	-2	-10	0			.963	-5	2-20	-1.3
Total	23	2670	10078	1255	2605	380	177	28	884	839	756	.258	.318	.340	82	-246	291	93		.952	155	*S-2153,2-513/3-4	12.5

■ **JOHNNY MARCUM** Marcum, John Alfred "Footsie" b: 9/9/09, Campbellsburg, Ky. d: 9/10/84, Louisville, Ky. BL/TR, 5'11", 197 lbs. Deb: 9/7/33

YEAR	TM/L	G	AB	R	H	2B	3B	HR	RBI	BB	SO	AVG	OBP	SLG	PRO+	BR/A	SB	CS	SBR	FA	FR	G/POS	TPR
1933	Phi-A	5	12	2	2	0	0	0	0	2	1	.167	.286	.167	22	-1	0	0	0	1.000	0	/P-5	0.0
1934	Phi-A	58	112	10	30	4	0	1	13	3	5	.268	.287	.330	61	-7	0	1	-1	.949	-0	P-37	0.0
1935	Phi-A	64	119	13	37	2	1	2	17	9	5	.311	.359	.395	96	-1	0	0	0	.896	-3	P-39	0.0
1936	Bos-A	48	88	6	18	3	0	2	7	3	5	.205	.231	.307	30	-10	0	0	0	.950	0	P-31	0.0
1937	Bos-A	51	86	12	23	8	0	0	13	7	4	.267	.323	.360	69	-4	0	0	0	.981	1	P-37	0.0
1938	Bos-A	19	37	3	5	0	0	0	3	6	9	.135	.256	.135	1	-6	0	0	0	1.000	-1	P-15	0.0
1939	StL-A	16	22	3	10	1	0	0	5	1	2	.455	.478	.500	147	2	0	0	0	1.000	-0	P-12	0.0
	Chi-A	38	57	7	16	0	0	0	12	5	1	.281	.339	.281	58	-3	0	0	0	.941	-1	P-19	0.0
	Yr	54	79	10	26	1	0	0	17	6	3	.329	.376	.342	83	-2	0	0	0	.962	-1	P-31	0.0
Total	7	299	533	56	141	18	1	5	70	36	32	.265	.311	.330	62	-30	0	1	-1	.953	-4	P-195	0.0

■ **RED MARION** Marion, John Wyeth b: 3/14/14, Richburg, S.C. d: 3/13/75, San Jose, Cal. BR/TR, 6'2", 175 lbs. Deb: 9/16/35 F

YEAR	TM/L	G	AB	R	H	2B	3B	HR	RBI	BB	SO	AVG	OBP	SLG	PRO+	BR/A	SB	CS	SBR	FA	FR	G/POS	TPR
1935	Was-A	4	11	1	2	1	0	1	1	0	2	.182	.182	.545	85	-0	0	0	0	.833	-0	/O-3	-0.1
1943	Was-A	14	17	2	3	0	0	0	1	3	1	.176	.300	.176	42	-1	0	0	0	1.000	-1	/O-4	-0.2
Total	2	18	28	3	5	1	0	1	2	3	3	.179	.258	.321	63	-2	0	0	0	.923	-1	/O-7	-0.3

■ **MARTY MARION** Marion, Martin Whiteford "Slats" or "The Octopus" b: 12/1/17, Richburg, S.C. BR/TR, 6'2", 170 lbs. Deb: 4/16/40 FMC

YEAR	TM/L	G	AB	R	H	2B	3B	HR	RBI	BB	SO	AVG	OBP	SLG	PRO+	BR/A	SB	CS	SBR	FA	FR	G/POS	TPR
1940	StL-N	125	435	44	121	18	1	3	46	21	34	.278	.311	.345	76	-14	9			.949	-6	*S-125	-1.1
1941	StL-N	155	547	50	138	22	3	3	58	42	48	.252	.308	.320	72	-20	8			.954	7	*S-155	-0.2
1942	*StL-N	147	485	66	134	**38**	5	0	54	48	50	.276	.343	.375	102	1	8			.960	7	*S-147	1.9
1943	*StL-N★	129	418	38	117	15	3	1	52	32	37	.280	.334	.337	90	-5	1			.970	25	*S-128	3.1
1944	*StL-N★	144	506	50	135	26	2	6	63	43	50	.267	.324	.362	91	-6	1			**.972**	5	*S-144	1.0
1945	StL-N†	123	430	63	119	27	5	1	59	39	39	.277	.340	.370	95	-3	2			.967	-2	*S-122	0.5
1946	*StL-N★	146	498	51	116	29	4	3	46	59	53	.233	.318	.325	79	-13	1			.973	**19**	*S-145	1.5
1947	StL-N★	149	540	57	147	19	6	4	74	49	58	.272	.334	.352	79	-16	3			**.981**	**20**	*S-141	1.1
1948	StL-N†	144	567	70	143	26	4	4	43	37	54	.252	.298	.333	67	-27	1			**.974**	9	*S-142	-0.9
1949	StL-N☆	134	515	61	140	31	2	5	70	37	42	.272	.323	.369	81	-14	0			.976	17	*S-134	1.2
1950	StL-N★	106	372	36	92	10	2	4	40	44	55	.247	.327	.317	67	-17	1			.978	-1	*S-101	-1.0
1952	StL-A	67	186	16	46	11	0	2	19	19	17	.247	.320	.339	81	-5	0	2	-1	.980	-7	S-63,M	-0.9
1953	StL-A	3	7	0	0	0	0	0	0	0	0	.000	.000	.000	-98	-2	0	0	0	1.000	-1	/3-2,M	-0.4
Total	13	1572	5506	602	1448	272	37	36	624	470	537	.263	.323	.345	81	-140	35	2		.969	92	*S-1547/3-2	5.8

■ ROGER MARIS Maris, Roger Eugene (b: Roger Eugene Maras) b: 9/10/34, Hibbing, Minn. d: 12/14/85, Houston, Tex. BL/TR, 6', 204 lbs. Deb: 4/16/57

YEAR	TM/L	G	AB	R	H	2B	3B	HR	RBI	BB	SO	AVG	OBP	SLG	PRO+	BR/A	SB	CS	SBR	FA	FR	G/POS	TPR
1957	Cle-A	116	358	61	84	9	5	14	51	60	79	.235	.346	.405	106	3	8	4	0	.975	5	*O-112	0.3
1958	Cle-A	51	182	26	41	5	1	9	27	17	33	.225	.291	.412	94	-2	4	2	0	.967	5	*O-47	0.0
	KC-A	99	401	61	99	14	3	19	53	28	52	.247	.299	.439	99	-2	0	0	0	.975	-4	O-99	-1.2
	Yr	150	583	87	140	19	4	28	80	45	85	.240	.297	.431	97	-4	4	2	0	.972	1	*O-146	-1.2
1959	KC-A★	122	433	69	118	21	7	16	72	58	53	.273	.362	.464	123	14	2	1	0	.975	6	*O-117	1.5
1960	*NY-A★	136	499	98	141	18	7	39	**112**	70	65	.283	.374	**.581**	164	42	2	2	-1	.985	3	*O-131	3.8
1961	*NY-A★	161	590	**132**	159	16	4	**61**	**142**	94	67	.269	.376	.620	170	57	0	0	0	.968	-11	*O-160	3.5
1962	*NY-A★	157	590	92	151	34	1	33	100	87	78	.256	.357	.485	128	23	1	0	0	.991	-4	*O-154	1.0
1963	*NY-A	90	312	53	84	14	1	23	53	35	40	.269	.347	.542	146	18	1	0	0	.988	2	O-86	1.7
1964	*NY-A	141	513	86	144	12	2	26	71	62	78	.281	.365	.464	127	19	3	0	1	.996	-0	*O-137	1.4
1965	NY-A	46	155	22	37	7	0	8	27	29	29	.239	.359	.439	126	6	0	0	0	.971	-2	O-43	0.2
1966	NY-A	119	348	37	81	9	2	13	43	36	60	.233	.310	.382	101	0	0	0	0	.993	-7	O-95	-1.1
1967	*StL-N	125	410	64	107	18	7	9	55	52	61	.261	.350	.405	117	10	0	0	0	.991	2	*O-118	0.6
1968	*StL-N	100	310	25	79	18	2	5	45	24	38	.255	.310	.374	106	2	0	0	0	.983	3	O-84	0.0
Total	12	1463	5101	826	1325	195	42	275	851	652	733	.260	.348	.476	128	191	21	9	1	.982	-3	*O-1383	11.7

■ GENE MARKLAND Markland, Cleneth Eugene "Mousey" b: 12/26/19, Detroit, Mich. BR/TR, 5'10", 160 lbs. Deb: 4/25/50

YEAR	TM/L	G	AB	R	H	2B	3B	HR	RBI	BB	SO	AVG	OBP	SLG	PRO+	BR/A	SB	CS	SBR	FA	FR	G/POS	TPR
1950	Phi-A	5	8	2	1	0	0	0	0	3	0	.125	.364	.125	30	-1	0	0	0	1.000	0	/2-5	-0.1

■ HARRY MARNIE Marnie, Harry Sylvester b: 7/6/18, Philadelphia, Pa. BR/TR, 6'1", 178 lbs. Deb: 9/15/40

YEAR	TM/L	G	AB	R	H	2B	3B	HR	RBI	BB	SO	AVG	OBP	SLG	PRO+	BR/A	SB	CS	SBR	FA	FR	G/POS	TPR
1940	Phi-N	11	34	4	6	0	0	0	4	4	2	.176	.263	.176	24	-3	0			.984	6	2-11	0.3
1941	Phi-N	61	158	12	38	3	3	0	11	13	25	.241	.298	.297	71	-6	0			.990	5	2-39,S-16/3-3	0.2
1942	Phi-N	24	30	3	5	0	0	0	0	1	2	.167	.194	.167	6	-4	1			.971	8	2-11/S-7,3-1	0.5
Total	3	96	222	19	49	3	3	0	15	18	29	.221	.279	.261	55	-13	1			.987	19	/2-61,S-23,3-4	1.0

■ FRED MAROLEWSKI Marolewski, Fred Daniel "Fritz" b: 10/6/28, Chicago, Ill. BR/TR, 6'2.5", 205 lbs. Deb: 9/19/53

YEAR	TM/L	G	AB	R	H	2B	3B	HR	RBI	BB	SO	AVG	OBP	SLG	PRO+	BR/A	SB	CS	SBR	FA	FR	G/POS	TPR
1953	StL-N	1	0	0	0	0	0	0	0	0	0	—	—	—	—	0	0	0	0	.000	0	/1-1	0.0

■ OLLIE MARQUARDT Marquardt, Albert Ludwig b: 9/22/02, Toledo, Ohio d: 2/7/68, Port Clinton, Ohio BR/TR, 5'9", 156 lbs. Deb: 4/14/31

YEAR	TM/L	G	AB	R	H	2B	3B	HR	RBI	BB	SO	AVG	OBP	SLG	PRO+	BR/A	SB	CS	SBR	FA	FR	G/POS	TPR
1931	Bos-A	17	39	4	7	1	0	0	2	3	4	.179	.238	.205	18	-5	0	1	-1	.946	-3	2-13/S-1,3-1	-0.7

■ GONZALO MARQUEZ Marquez, Gonzalo Enrique (Moya) b: 3/31/46, Carupano, Venez. d: 12/20/84, Valencia, Venez. BL/TL, 5'11", 180 lbs. Deb: 8/11/72

YEAR	TM/L	G	AB	R	H	2B	3B	HR	RBI	BB	SO	AVG	OBP	SLG	PRO+	BR/A	SB	CS	SBR	FA	FR	G/POS	TPR
1972	*Oak-A	23	21	2	8	0	0	0	4	3	4	.381	.480	.381	167	2	1	1	-0	.929	-0	/1-2	0.2
1973	Oak-A	23	25	1	6	1	0	0	2	0	4	.240	.240	.280	49	-2	0	0	0	.000	-1	/2-2,1-1,O-1,D-1	-0.3
	Chi-N	19	58	5	13	2	0	1	4	3	4	.224	.274	.310	57	-3	0	0	0	.994	2	1-18	-0.2
1974	Chi-N	11	11	1	0	0	0	0	0	1	2	.000	.083	.000	-72	-3	0	0	0	1.000	-0	/1-1	-0.3
Total	3	76	115	9	27	3	0	1	10	7	14	.235	.290	.287	62	-6	1	1	-0	.989	1	/1-22,2-2,D-1,O-1	-0.6

■ LUIS MARQUEZ Marquez, Luis Angel (Sanchez) "Canena" b: 10/28/25, Aguadilla, P.R. d: 3/1/88, Aguadilla, P.R. BR/TR, 5'10.5", 174 lbs. Deb: 4/18/51

YEAR	TM/L	G	AB	R	H	2B	3B	HR	RBI	BB	SO	AVG	OBP	SLG	PRO+	BR/A	SB	CS	SBR	FA	FR	G/POS	TPR
1951	Bos-N	68	122	19	24	5	1	0	11	10	20	.197	.274	.254	46	-9	4	4	-1	1.000	-2	O-43	-1.4
1954	Chi-N	17	12	2	1	0	0	0	0	2	4	.083	.214	.083	-19	-2	3	0	1	1.000	-4	O-14	-0.6
	Pit-N	14	9	3	1	0	0	0	0	4	0	.111	.385	.111	37	-1	0	0	0	1.000	-1	/O-4	-0.2
	Yr	31	21	5	2	0	0	0	0	6	4	.095	.296	.095	7	-3	3	0	1	1.000	-5	O-18	-0.8
Total	2	99	143	24	26	5	1	0	11	16	24	.182	.278	.231	40	-12	7	4	-0	1.000	-7	/O-61	-2.2

■ BOB MARQUIS Marquis, Robert Rudolph b: 12/23/24, Oklahoma City, Okla. BL/TL, 6'1", 170 lbs. Deb: 4/17/53

YEAR	TM/L	G	AB	R	H	2B	3B	HR	RBI	BB	SO	AVG	OBP	SLG	PRO+	BR/A	SB	CS	SBR	FA	FR	G/POS	TPR
1953	Cin-N	40	44	9	12	1	1	2	3	4	11	.273	.333	.477	107	0	0	0	0	.905	-2	O-10	-0.2

■ ROGER MARQUIS Marquis, Roger Julian "Noonie" b: 4/5/37, Holyoke, Mass. BL/TL, 6', 190 lbs. Deb: 9/25/55

YEAR	TM/L	G	AB	R	H	2B	3B	HR	RBI	BB	SO	AVG	OBP	SLG	PRO+	BR/A	SB	CS	SBR	FA	FR	G/POS	TPR
1955	Bal-A	1	1	0	0	0	0	0	0	0	0	.000	.000	.000	-99	-0	0	0	0	.000	-0	/O-1	-0.1

■ LEFTY MARR Marr, Charles W. b: 9/19/1862, Cincinnati, Ohio d: 1/11/12, New Britain, Conn. BL/TL, Deb: 10/3/1886

YEAR	TM/L	G	AB	R	H	2B	3B	HR	RBI	BB	SO	AVG	OBP	SLG	PRO+	BR/A	SB	CS	SBR	FA	FR	G/POS	TPR
1886	Cin-a	8	29	2	8	1	1	0	2	1		.276	.323	.379	116	0	1			.696	-1	/O-8	-0.1
1889	Col-a	139	546	110	167	26	**15**	1	75	87	32	.306	.407	.414	141	34	29			.856	12	3-66,O-47,S-26,/1C	4.1
1890	Cin-N	130	527	91	157	17	12	1	73	46	29	.298	.361	.381	117	11	44			.930	-11	O-64,3-63/S-3	0.0
1891	Cin-N	72	286	32	74	9	7	0	32	25	15	.259	.323	.339	92	-3	16			.835	-10	O-72	-1.4
	Cin-a	14	57	9	11	1	0	0	4	7	4	.193	.281	.211	38	-5	2			.923	-1	O-14	-0.5
Total	4	363	1445	244	417	54	35	2	186	166	80	.289	.368	.379	118	38	92			.853	-10	O-205,3-129/S1C	2.1

■ ELI MARRERO Marrero, Elieser b: 11/17/73, Havana, Cuba BR/TR, 6'1", 180 lbs. Deb: 9/3/97

YEAR	TM/L	G	AB	R	H	2B	3B	HR	RBI	BB	SO	AVG	OBP	SLG	PRO+	BR/A	SB	CS	SBR	FA	FR	G/POS	TPR
1997	StL-N	17	45	4	11	2	0	2	7	2	13	.244	.277	.422	81	-1	4	0	1	.969	1	C-17	0.1
1998	StL-N	83	254	28	62	18	1	4	20	28	42	.244	.319	.370	79	-8	6	2	1	.991	-2	C-73/1-2	-0.4
Total	2	100	299	32	73	20	1	6	27	30	55	.244	.313	.378	79	-9	10	2	2	.987	-2	/C-90,1-2	-0.3

■ ORESTE MARRERO Marrero, Oreste Vilato (Vazquez) b: 10/31/69, Bayamon, P.R. BL/TL, 6', 195 lbs. Deb: 8/12/93

YEAR	TM/L	G	AB	R	H	2B	3B	HR	RBI	BB	SO	AVG	OBP	SLG	PRO+	BR/A	SB	CS	SBR	FA	FR	G/POS	TPR
1993	Mon-N	32	81	10	17	5	1	1	4	14	16	.210	.326	.333	74	-3	1	3	-2	.991	-0	1-32	-0.7
1996	LA-N	10	8	2	3	1	0	0	1	1	3	.375	.444	.500	161	1	0	0	0	1.000	-0	/1-1	0.1
Total	2	42	89	12	20	6	1	1	5	15	19	.225	.337	.348	81	-2	1	3	-2	.991	-1	/1-33	-0.6

■ WILLIAM MARRIOTT Marriott, William Earl b: 4/18/1893, Pratt, Kan. d: 8/11/69, Berkeley, Cal. BL/TR, 6', 170 lbs. Deb: 9/6/17

YEAR	TM/L	G	AB	R	H	2B	3B	HR	RBI	BB	SO	AVG	OBP	SLG	PRO+	BR/A	SB	CS	SBR	FA	FR	G/POS	TPR
1917	Chi-N	3	6	0	0	0	0	0	0	0	1	.000	.000	.000	-93	-1	0			.667	-0	/O-1	-0.2
1920	Chi-N	14	43	7	12	4	2	0	5	6	5	.279	.367	.465	135	2	1	1	-0	.892	-4	2-14	-0.2
1921	Chi-N	30	38	3	12	1	1	0	7	4	1	.316	.381	.395	105	0	0	1	-1	.826	-1	/2-6,S-1,3-1,O-1	-0.1
1925	Bos-N	103	370	37	99	9	1	1	40	28	26	.268	.322	.305	67	-18	3	8	-4	.928	3	3-89/O-1	-1.2
1926	Bro-N	109	360	39	96	13	9	3	42	17	20	.267	.303	.378	84	-9	12			.927	-8	*3-104	-1.1
1927	Bro-N	6	9	0	1	0	1	0	1	2	2	.111	.273	.333	61	-1	0			.889	1	/3-2	0.0
Total	6	265	826	86	220	27	14	4	95	57	55	.266	.317	.347	78	-27	16	10		.925	-9	3-196/2-20,O-3,S-1	-2.8

■ ARMANDO MARSANS Marsans, Armando b: 10/3/1887, Matanzas, Cuba d: 9/3/60, Havana, Cuba BR/TR, 5'10", 157 lbs. Deb: 7/4/11

YEAR	TM/L	G	AB	R	H	2B	3B	HR	RBI	BB	SO	AVG	OBP	SLG	PRO+	BR/A	SB	CS	SBR	FA	FR	G/POS	TPR
1911	Cin-N	58	138	17	36	2	2	0	11	15	11	.261	.346	.304	86	-2	11			.968	-5	O-34/1-1,3-1	-0.9
1912	Cin-N	110	416	59	132	19	7	1	38	20	17	.317	.353	.404	110	5	35			.975	-3	O-98/1-6	-0.3
1913	Cin-N	118	435	49	129	7	6	0	38	17	25	.297	.327	.340	91	-5	37			.963	-5	O-94,1-22/3-2,S-1	-1.5
1914	Cin-N	36	124	16	37	3	0	0	22	14	6	.298	.374	.323	105	1	13			.916	1	O-36	0.0
	StL-F	9	40	5	14	0	2	0	2	3	0	.350	.395	.450	123	1	4			.927	0	/2-7,S-2	0.1
1915	StL-F	36	124	16	22	3	0	0	6	14	5	.177	.261	.202	29	-13	5			.975	3	O-35	-1.3
1916	StL-A	151	528	51	134	12	1	1	60	57	41	.254	.333	.286	91	-5	46	26	-2	.977	5	*O-150	-1.0
1917	StL-A	75	257	31	59	12	0	0	20	20	6	.230	.285	.276	74	-8	11			.963	-4	O-67/3-5,2-1	-1.8
	NY-A	25	88	10	20	4	0	0	15	8	3	.227	.292	.273	72	-3	6			.974	3	O-25	-0.1
	Yr	100	345	41	79	16	0	0	35	28	9	.229	.287	.275	73	-11	17			.967	-1	O-92/3-5,2-1	-1.9
1918	NY-A	37	123	13	29	5	1	0	9	5	3	.236	.266	.293	67	-5	3			.943	-6	O-36	-1.5
Total	8	655	2273	267	612	67	19	2	221	173	117	.269	.325	.318	88	-35	171	26		.967	-11	O-575/1-29,2-8,3S	-8.3

■ FRED MARSH Marsh, Fred Francis b: 1/5/24, Valley Falls, Kan. BR/TR, 5'10", 180 lbs. Deb: 4/19/49

YEAR	TM/L	G	AB	R	H	2B	3B	HR	RBI	BB	SO	AVG	OBP	SLG	PRO+	BR/A	SB	CS	SBR	FA	FR	G/POS	TPR
1949	Cle-A	1	0	0	0	0	0	0	0	0	0	—	—	—	—	0	0	0	0	.000	0	R	0.0
1951	StL-A	130	445	44	108	21	4	4	43	36	56	.243	.299	.335	69	-20	4	4	-1	.928	3	*3-117/S-3,2-2	-1.9
1952	StL-A	11	24	3	5	1	0	0	1	5	4	.208	.345	.250	65	-1	0	1	-1	.963	2	/2-9,S-3	0.1
	Was-A	9	24	1	1	0	0	0	0	1	1	.042	.080	.042	-68	-5	0	0	0	1.000	-2	/2-5,O-2	-0.8
	StL-A	76	223	25	64	8	1	2	26	22	29	.287	.351	.359	95	-1	3	2	-0	.945	-15	S-57,3-21	-1.4
	Yr	96	271	29	70	9	1	2	28	28	37	.258	.328	.321	79	-7	3	3	-1	.945	-15	S-60,3-21,2-14,/O-2	-2.1
1953	Chi-A	67	95	22	19	1	0	2	2	13	26	.200	.303	.274	55	-6	0	3	-2	.940	7	3-32,S-17/1-5,2-2	-0.1
1954	Chi-A	62	98	21	30	5	2	0	4	9	16	.306	.364	.398	105	1	4	2	0	.975	18	3-36/S-3,1-2,O-1	1.9

YEAR	TM/L	G	AB	R	H	2B	3B	HR	RBI	BB	SO	AVG	OBP	SLG	PRO+	BR/A	SB	CS	SBR	FA	FR	G/POS	TPR
1955	Bal-A	89	303	30	66	7	1	2	19	35	33	.218	.301	.267	58	-18	1	2	-1	.983	-15	2-76,3-18,S-16	-2.9
1956	Bal-A	20	24	2	3	0	0	0	0	4	3	.125	.250	.125	2	-3	1	0	0	.929	0	/S-8,3-8,2-5	-0.2
Total	7	465	1236	148	296	43	8	10	96	125	171	.239	.310	.311	69	-54	13	14	-5	.928	-2	3-232,S-107/210	-5.3

■ **TOM MARSH** Marsh, Thomas Owen b: 12/27/65, Toledo, Ohio BR/TR, 6'2", 180 lbs. Deb: 6/5/92

YEAR	TM/L	G	AB	R	H	2B	3B	HR	RBI	BB	SO	AVG	OBP	SLG	PRO+	BR/A	SB	CS	SBR	FA	FR	G/POS	TPR
1992	Phi-N	42	125	7	25	3	2	2	16	2	23	.200	.219	.304	47	-9	0	1	-1	.971	-1	O-35	-1.2
1994	Phi-N	8	18	3	5	1	1	0	3	1	1	.278	.316	.444	93	-0	0	0	0	.889	-1	/O-7	-0.2
1995	Phi-N	43	109	13	32	3	1	3	15	4	25	.294	.319	.422	93	-1	0	1	-1	.939	-0	O-29	-0.3
Total	3	93	252	23	62	7	4	5	34	7	49	.246	.269	.365	71	-11	0	2	-1	.952	-3	/O-71	-1.7

■ **CHARLIE MARSHALL** Marshall, Charles Anthony (b: Charles Anthony Marczlewicz) b: 8/28/19, Wilmington, Del. BR/TR, 5'10.5", 178 lbs. Deb: 6/14/41

YEAR	TM/L	G	AB	R	H	2B	3B	HR	RBI	BB	SO	AVG	OBP	SLG	PRO+	BR/A	SB	CS	SBR	FA	FR	G/POS	TPR
1941	StL-N	1	0	0	0	0	0	0	0	0	0	—	—	—	—	0	0			1.000	-0	/C-1	0.0

■ **DAVE MARSHALL** Marshall, David Lewis b: 1/14/43, Artesia, Cal. BL/TR, 6'1", 190 lbs. Deb: 9/7/67

YEAR	TM/L	G	AB	R	H	2B	3B	HR	RBI	BB	SO	AVG	OBP	SLG	PRO+	BR/A	SB	CS	SBR	FA	FR	G/POS	TPR
1967	SF-N	1	0	0	0	0	0	0	0	0	0	—	—	—		0	0	0	0	.000	0	R	0.0
1968	SF-N	76	174	17	46	5	1	1	16	20	37	.264	.344	.322	101	1	2	1	0	.924	-6	O-50	-0.8
1969	SF-N	110	267	32	62	7	1	2	33	40	68	.232	.343	.288	80	-6	1	8	-5	.956	-10	O-87	-2.5
1970	NY-N	92	189	21	46	10	1	6	29	17	43	.243	.306	.402	88	-4	4	1	1	.973	-1	O-43	-0.6
1971	NY-N	100	214	28	51	9	1	3	21	26	54	.238	.326	.332	88	-3	3	1	0	.989	-4	O-64	-0.9
1972	NY-N	72	156	21	39	5	0	4	11	22	28	.250	.346	.359	103	1	3	3	-1	.972	-3	O-42	-0.5
1973	SD-N	39	49	4	14	5	0	0	4	8	9	.286	.397	.388	128	2	0	1	-1	1.000	-1	/O-8	0.1
Total	7	490	1049	123	258	41	4	16	114	133	239	.246	.336	.338	92	-8	13	15	-5	.966	-24	O-294	-5.2

■ **DOC MARSHALL** Marshall, Edward Herbert "Eddie" b: 6/4/06, New Albany, Miss. BR/TR, 5'11", 150 lbs. Deb: 9/28/29

YEAR	TM/L	G	AB	R	H	2B	3B	HR	RBI	BB	SO	AVG	OBP	SLG	PRO+	BR/A	SB	CS	SBR	FA	FR	G/POS	TPR
1929	NY-N	5	15	6	6	2	0	0	2	1	0	.400	.438	.533	140	1	0			1.000	-2	/2-5	-0.1
1930	NY-N	78	223	33	69	5	3	0	21	13	9	.309	.350	.359	73	-9	0			.947	-3	S-45,2-17/3-5	-0.6
1931	NY-N	68	194	15	39	6	2	0	10	8	8	.201	.233	.253	31	-19	1			.956	4	2-47,S-11/3-3	-1.2
1932	NY-N	68	226	18	56	8	1	0	28	6	11	.248	.270	.292	52	-15	1			.922	-3	S-63	-1.2
Total	4	219	658	72	170	21	6	0	61	28	28	.258	.291	.309	56	-42	2			.931	-4	S-119/2-69,3-8	-3.1

■ **JOE MARSHALL** Marshall, Joseph Hanley "Home Run Joe" b: 2/19/1876, Audubon, Minn. d: 9/11/31, Santa Monica, Cal BR/TR, 5'8", 170 lbs. Deb: 9/7/03

YEAR	TM/L	G	AB	R	H	2B	3B	HR	RBI	BB	SO	AVG	OBP	SLG	PRO+	BR/A	SB	CS	SBR	FA	FR	G/POS	TPR
1903	Pit-N	10	23	2	6	1	2	0	2	0		.261	.261	.478	106	-0	0			1.000	-4	/S-3,O-3,2-1	-0.4
1906	StL-N	33	95	2	15	1	2	0	7	6		.158	.216	.211	34	-7	0			.903	-1	O-23/1-4	-1.1
Total	2	43	118	4	21	2	4	0	9	6		.178	.224	.263	50	-7	0			.903	-5	/O-26,1-4,S-3,2-1	-1.5

■ **KEITH MARSHALL** Marshall, Keith Alan b: 7/2/51, San Francisco, Cal. BR/TR, 6'2", 175 lbs. Deb: 4/7/73

YEAR	TM/L	G	AB	R	H	2B	3B	HR	RBI	BB	SO	AVG	OBP	SLG	PRO+	BR/A	SB	CS	SBR	FA	FR	G/POS	TPR
1973	KC-A	8	9	0	2	1	0	0	3	1	4	.222	.300	.333	73	-0	0	0	0	1.000	-3	/O-8	-0.3

■ **MIKE MARSHALL** Marshall, Michael Allen b: 1/12/60, Libertyville, Ill. BR/TR, 6'5", 220 lbs. Deb: 9/7/81

YEAR	TM/L	G	AB	R	H	2B	3B	HR	RBI	BB	SO	AVG	OBP	SLG	PRO+	BR/A	SB	CS	SBR	FA	FR	G/POS	TPR
1981	*LA-N	14	25	2	5	3	0	0	1	1	4	.200	.259	.320	66	-1	0	0	0	1.000	-1	/1-3,3-3,O-2	-0.2
1982	LA-N	49	95	10	23	3	0	5	9	13	23	.242	.339	.432	117	2	2	0	1	1.000	-4	O-19,1-13	-0.2
1983	*LA-N	140	465	47	132	17	1	17	65	43	127	.284	.351	.434	117	10	7	3	0	.976	-7	*O-109,1-33	-0.1
1984	LA-N☆	134	495	68	127	27	0	21	65	40	93	.257	.316	.438	111	6	4	3	-1	.981	4	*O-118,1-15	0.5
1985	*LA-N	135	518	72	152	27	2	28	95	37	137	.293	.344	.515	141	26	3	10	-5	.991	-0	*O-125/1-7	1.7
1986	LA-N	103	330	47	77	11	0	19	53	27	90	.233	.299	.439	109	2	4	4	-1	.963	-2	O-97	-0.4
1987	LA-N	104	402	45	118	19	0	16	72	18	79	.294	.330	.460	109	4	0	5	-3	.987	-6	*O-102	-0.8
1988	*LA-N	144	542	63	150	27	2	20	82	24	93	.277	.316	.445	120	11	4	1	1	.966	-1	O-90,1-53	0.4
1989	LA-N	105	377	41	98	21	1	11	42	33	78	.260	.328	.408	111	5	2	5	-2	.978	-2	*O-102	-0.2
1990	NY-N	53	163	24	39	8	1	6	27	7	40	.239	.283	.411	89	-3	0	2	-1	.993	-1	1-42/O-1	-0.8
	*Bos-A	30	112	10	32	6	1	4	12	4	26	.286	.316	.464	111	1	0	0	0	1.000	1	D-14/1-8,O-8	0.1
1991	Bos-A	22	62	4	18	4	0	1	7	0	19	.290	.290	.403	86	-1	0	0	0	.979	-3	/1-5,O-4,D-7	-0.4
	Cal-A	2	7	0	0	0	0	0	0	0	1	.000	.000	.000	-99	-2	0	0	0	1.000	0	/1-1,D-1	-0.2
	Yr	24	69	4	18	4	0	1	7	0	20	.261	.261	.362	67	-3	0	0	0	.984	-2	/D-8,1-6,O-4	-0.6
Total	11	1035	3593	433	971	173	8	148	530	247	810	.270	.324	.446	115	60	26	33	-12	.978	-21	O-777,1-180/D-22,3	-0.6

■ **MAX MARSHALL** Marshall, Milo May b: 9/18/13, Shenandoah, Iowa d: 9/16/93, Salem, Ore. BL/TR, 6'1", 180 lbs. Deb: 5/10/42

YEAR	TM/L	G	AB	R	H	2B	3B	HR	RBI	BB	SO	AVG	OBP	SLG	PRO+	BR/A	SB	CS	SBR	FA	FR	G/POS	TPR
1942	Cin-N	131	530	49	135	17	6	7	43	34	38	.255	.301	.349	90	-8	4			.976	-10	*O-129	-2.7
1943	Cin-N	132	508	55	120	11	8	4	39	34	52	.236	.287	.313	74	-18	8			.981	-5	*O-129	-3.2
1944	Cin-N	66	229	36	56	13	2	4	23	21	10	.245	.308	.371	94	-2	3			.965	2	O-59	-0.4
Total	3	329	1267	140	311	41	16	15	105	89	100	.245	.297	.339	84	-28	15			.975	-14	O-317	-6.3

■ **JIM MARSHALL** Marshall, Rufus James b: 5/25/31, Danville, Ill. BL/TL, 6'1", 190 lbs. Deb: 4/15/58 MC

YEAR	TM/L	G	AB	R	H	2B	3B	HR	RBI	BB	SO	AVG	OBP	SLG	PRO+	BR/A	SB	CS	SBR	FA	FR	G/POS	TPR
1958	Bal-A	85	191	17	41	4	3	5	19	18	30	.215	.282	.346	76	-7	3	2	-0	1.000	-5	1-52/O-8	-1.5
	Chi-N	26	81	12	22	2	0	5	11	12	13	.272	.372	.481	126	3	1	0	0	.992	-4	1-15,O-11	-0.1
1959	Chi-N	108	294	39	74	10	1	11	40	33	39	.252	.327	.405	95	-2	0	1	-1	.997	1	1-72/O-8	-0.7
1960	SF-N	75	118	19	28	2	2	2	13	17	24	.237	.333	.339	90	-1	0	1	-1	.968	-3	1-28/O-6	-0.7
1961	SF-N	44	36	5	8	0	0	1	7	3	8	.222	.282	.306	58	-2	0	0	0	1.000	-0	/1-4,O-2	-0.2
1962	NY-N	17	32	6	11	1	0	3	4	3	6	.344	.400	.656	175	3	0	0	0	1.000	-0	/1-5,O-1	0.3
	Pit-N	55	100	13	22	5	1	2	12	15	19	.220	.322	.350	80	-3	1	0	0	1.000	1	1-26	-0.3
	Yr	72	132	19	33	6	1	5	16	18	25	.250	.340	.424	103	1	1	0	0	1.000	1	1-31/O-1	0.0
Total	5	410	852	111	206	24	7	29	106	101	139	.242	.323	.388	93	-9	5	4	-1	.994	-10	1-202/O-36	-3.2

■ **WILLARD MARSHALL** Marshall, Willard Warren b: 2/8/21, Richmond, Va. BL/TR, 6'1", 205 lbs. Deb: 4/14/42

YEAR	TM/L	G	AB	R	H	2B	3B	HR	RBI	BB	SO	AVG	OBP	SLG	PRO+	BR/A	SB	CS	SBR	FA	FR	G/POS	TPR
1942	NY-N★	116	401	41	103	9	2	11	59	26	20	.257	.307	.372	98	-2	1			.975	-0	*O-107	-0.9
1946	NY-N	131	510	63	144	18	3	13	48	33	29	.282	.327	.406	107	3	3			.978	2	*O-125	-0.2
1947	NY-N★	155	587	102	171	19	6	36	107	67	30	.291	.366	.528	134	26	3			.972	12	*O-155	2.9
1948	NY-N	143	537	72	146	21	8	14	86	64	34	.272	.350	.419	107	5	2			.983	4	*O-142	0.1
1949	NY-N★	141	499	81	153	19	3	12	70	78	20	.307	.401	.429	123	19	4			.974	6	*O-138	1.8
1950	Bos-N	105	298	38	70	10	2	5	40	36	5	.235	.319	.332	77	-10	1			.958	1	O-85	-1.2
1951	Bos-N	136	469	65	132	24	7	11	62	48	18	.281	.351	.433	118	11	0	3	-2	**1.000**	-8	*O-136	-0.3
1952	Bos-N	21	66	5	15	4	1	2	11	4	4	.227	.271	.409	89	-1	0	0	0	.938	1	O-16	-0.1
	Cin-N	107	397	52	106	23	1	8	46	37	21	.267	.333	.390	100	-0	0	1	-1	.985	2	*O-105	-0.3
	Yr	128	463	57	121	27	2	10	57	41	25	.261	.324	.393	99	-1	0	1	-1	.979	3	*O-121	-0.4
1953	Cin-N	122	357	51	95	14	6	17	62	41	28	.266	.342	.482	111	5	0	0	0	.995	6	O-95	0.8
1954	Chi-A	47	71	7	18	2	0	1	7	11	9	.254	.354	.324	84	-1	0	0	0	.960	-7	O-29	-0.9
1955	Chi-A	22	41	6	7	0	0	0	6	13	1	.171	.370	.171	48	-2	0	0	0	.957	-1	O-12	-0.4
Total	11	1246	4233	583	1160	103	39	130	604	458	219	.274	.347	.423	109	51	14	4		.979	20	*O-1145	1.3

■ **BILL MARSHALL** Marshall, William Henry b: 2/14/11, Dorchester, Mass. d: 5/5/77, Sacramento, Cal. BR/TR, 5'8.5", 156 lbs. Deb: 6/20/31

YEAR	TM/L	G	AB	R	H	2B	3B	HR	RBI	BB	SO	AVG	OBP	SLG	PRO+	BR/A	SB	CS	SBR	FA	FR	G/POS	TPR
1931	Bos-A	1	0	1	0	0	0	0	0	0	0	—	—	—	—	0	0	0	0	.000	0	R	0.0
1934	Cin-N	6	8	0	1	0	0	0	0	0	2	.125	.125	.125	-34	-1	0			.875	1	/2-2	-0.1
Total	2	7	8	1	1	0	0	0	0	0	2	.125	.125	.125	-34	-1	0	0		.875	1	/2-2	-0.1

■ **DOC MARSHALL** Marshall, William Riddle b: 9/22/1875, Butler, Pa. d: 12/11/59, Clinton, Ill. BR/TR, 6', 185 lbs. Deb: 4/15/04

YEAR	TM/L	G	AB	R	H	2B	3B	HR	RBI	BB	SO	AVG	OBP	SLG	PRO+	BR/A	SB	CS	SBR	FA	FR	G/POS	TPR
1904	Phi-N	8	20	1	2	0	0	0	1	0		.100	.100	.100	-40	-3	0			.944	2	/C-7	-0.1
	NY-N	1	0	0	0	0	0	0	0	0		—	—	—	—	0	0			.000	0	/C-1	0.0
	Bos-N	13	43	3	9	0	1	0	2	2		.209	.244	.256	56	-2	2			.955	1	C-10/O-1	0.0
	NY-N	10	17	3	6	1	0	0	2	1		.353	.389	.412	141	1	0			.955	2	/C-2,O-2,2-1	0.3
	Yr	32	80	7	17	1	1	0	5	3		.213	.241	.250	52	-5	2			.952	5	C-20/O-3,2-1	0.2
1906	NY-N	38	102	8	17	3	2	0	7	7		.167	.234	.235	45	-7	7			1.000	-2	O-16,C-13/1-2	-0.9
	StL-N	39	123	6	34	4	1	0	10	6		.276	.315	.325	104	0	1			.961	9	C-38	1.4
	Yr	77	225	14	51	7	3	0	17	13		.227	.278	.284	76	-7	8			.969	7	C-51,O-16/1-2	0.5

YEAR	TM/L	G	AB	R	H	2B	3B	HR	RBI	BB	SO	AVG	OBP	SLG	PRO+	BR/A	SB	CS	SBR	FA	FR	G/POS	TPR
1907	StL-N	84	268	19	54	8	2	2	18	12		.201	.246	.269	64	-12	2			.952	5	C-83	0.1
1908	StL-N	6	14	0	1	0	0	0	1	0		.071	.071	.071	-57	-2	0			1.000	2	/C-6	0.0
	Chi-N	12	20	4	6	0	1	0	3	0		.300	.300	.400	118	0	0			1.000	5	/C-4,O-3	0.6
	Yr	18	34	4	7	0	1	0	4	0		.206	.206	.265	49	-2	0			1.000	7	C-10/O-3	0.6
1909	Bro-N	50	149	7	30	7	1	0	10	6		.201	.232	.262	55	-8	3			.968	-5	C-49/O-1	-1.1
Total	5	261	756	51	159	23	8	2	54	34		.210	.251	.270	64	-34	15			.961	19	C-213/O-23,1-2,2-1	0.3

■ **DOC MARTEL** Martel, Leon Alphonse "Marty" b: 1/29/1883, Weymouth, Mass. d: 10/11/47, Washington, D.C. BR/TR, 6', 185 lbs. Deb: 7/6/09

YEAR	TM/L	G	AB	R	H	2B	3B	HR	RBI	BB	SO	AVG	OBP	SLG	PRO+	BR/A	SB	CS	SBR	FA	FR	G/POS	TPR
1909	Phi-N	24	41	1	11	3	1	0	7	4		.268	.333	.390	123	1	0			.974	4	C-12	0.7
1910	Bos-N	10	31	0	4	0	0	0	1	2	3	.129	.182	.129	-9	-4	0			.980	-0	1-10	-0.5
Total	2	34	72	1	15	3	1	0	8	6	3	.208	.269	.278	64	-3	0			.974	4	/C-12,1-10	0.2

■ **AL MARTIN** Martin, Albert (a.k.a. Albert May In 1872) Deb: 5/7/1872

YEAR	TM/L	G	AB	R	H	2B	3B	HR	RBI	BB	SO	AVG	OBP	SLG	PRO+	BR/A	SB	CS	SBR	FA	FR	G/POS	TPR
1872	Eck-n	4	18	2	5	0	0	0	2	0	0	.278	.278	.278	84	-0	0	0	0	.636	-3	/2-4	-0.3
1874	Atl-n	7	29	1	4	0	0	0	1	0	1	.138	.138	.138	-13	-3	0	0	0	.646	-2	/2-6,O-1	-0.4
1875	Atl-n	6	26	1	3	0	0	0	1	0	0	.115	.115	.115	-22	-3	0	0	0	.909	-1	/O-6	-0.3
Total	3 n	17	73	4	12	0	0	0	4	0	1	.164	.164	.164	9	-6	0	0	0	.643	-6	/2-10,O-7	-1.0

■ **AL MARTIN** Martin, Albert Lee b: 11/24/67, West Covina, Cal. BL/TL, 6'2", 210 lbs. Deb: 7/28/92

YEAR	TM/L	G	AB	R	H	2B	3B	HR	RBI	BB	SO	AVG	OBP	SLG	PRO+	BR/A	SB	CS	SBR	FA	FR	G/POS	TPR
1992	Pit-N	12	12	1	2	0	1	0	2	0	5	.167	.167	.333	39	-1	0	0	0	1.000	-2	/O-7	-0.3
1993	Pit-N	143	480	85	135	26	8	18	64	42	122	.281	.340	.481	117	11	16	9	-1	.975	-10	*O-136	-0.3
1994	Pit-N	82	276	48	79	12	4	9	33	34	56	.286	.369	.457	112	5	15	6	1	.979	2	O-77	0.7
1995	Pit-N	124	439	70	124	25	3	13	41	44	92	.282	.351	.442	105	3	20	11	-1	.977	-3	*O-121	-0.4
1996	Pit-N	155	630	101	189	40	1	18	72	54	116	.300	.357	.452	109	8	38	12	4	.965	-14	*O-152	-0.6
1997	Pit-N	113	423	64	123	24	7	13	59	45	83	.291	.363	.473	115	9	23	7	3	.957	-8	*O-110	0.1
1998	Pit-N	125	440	57	105	15	2	12	47	32	91	.239	.298	.364	69	-20	20	3	4	.985	6	*O-114/D-2	-1.1
Total	7	754	2700	426	757	142	26	83	318	251	565	.280	.345	.444	104	15	132	48	11	.974	-29	O-717/D-2	-1.9

■ **BILLY MARTIN** Martin, Alfred Manuel b: 5/16/28, Berkeley, Cal. d: 12/25/89, Johnson City, N.Y. BR/TR, 5'11.5", 165 lbs. Deb: 4/18/50 MC

YEAR	TM/L	G	AB	R	H	2B	3B	HR	RBI	BB	SO	AVG	OBP	SLG	PRO+	BR/A	SB	CS	SBR	FA	FR	G/POS	TPR
1950	NY-A	34	36	10	9	1	0	1	8	3	3	.250	.308	.361	73	-2	0	0	0	.976	-1	2-22/3-1	-0.2
1951	*NY-A	51	58	10	15	1	2	0	2	4	9	.259	.328	.345	85	-1	0	1	-1	.988	16	2-23/S-6,3-2,O-1	1.4
1952	*NY-A	109	363	32	97	13	3	3	33	22	31	.267	.323	.344	91	-5	3	6	-3	.984	18	*2-107	1.6
1953	*NY-A	149	587	72	151	24	6	15	75	43	56	.257	.314	.395	94	-7	6	7	-2	.985	-1	*2-146,S-18	-0.3
1955	*NY-A	20	70	8	21	2	0	1	9	7	9	.300	.364	.371	100	0	1	2	-1	.977	1	2-17/S-3	0.2
1956	*NY-A★	121	458	76	121	24	5	9	49	30	56	.264	.314	.397	90	-9	7	3	0	.980	-14	*2-105,3-16	-1.4
1957	NY-A	43	145	12	35	5	2	1	12	3	14	.241	.262	.324	60	-8	2	1	0	.947	-3	2-26,3-13	-1.0
	KC-A	73	265	33	68	9	3	9	27	12	20	.257	.296	.415	91	-4	7	1	2	.987	-20	2-52,3-20/S-2	-1.9
	Yr	116	410	45	103	14	5	10	39	15	34	.251	.284	.383	80	-12	9	2	2	.973	-23	2-78,3-33/S-2	-2.9
1958	Det-A	131	498	56	127	19	1	7	42	16	62	.255	.282	.339	65	-24	5	3	-0	.958	-18	S-88,3-41	-3.5
1959	Cle-A	73	242	37	63	7	0	9	24	8	18	.260	.292	.401	92	-4	0	2	-1	.997	-11	2-67/3-4	-1.1
1960	Cin-N	103	317	34	78	17	1	3	16	27	34	.246	.305	.334	74	-11	0	1	-1	.975	-13	2-97	-1.7
1961	Mil-N	6	6	1	0	0	0	0	0	0	1	.000	.000	.000	-99	-2	0	0	0	.000	0	H	-0.2
	Min-A	108	374	44	92	15	5	6	36	13	42	.246	.277	.361	65	-19	3	2	-0	.963	-15	*2-105/S-1	-2.4
Total	11	1021	3419	425	877	137	28	64	333	188	355	.257	.301	.369	81	-96	34	29	-7	.980	-61	2-767,S-118/3-97,O	-10.5

■ **PHONNEY MARTIN** Martin, Alphonse Case b: 8/4/1845, New York, N.Y. d: 5/24/33, Hollis, N.Y. 5'7", 148 lbs. Deb: 4/26/1872

YEAR	TM/L	G	AB	R	H	2B	3B	HR	RBI	BB	SO	AVG	OBP	SLG	PRO+	BR/A	SB	CS	SBR	FA	FR	G/POS	TPR
1872	Tro-n	25	117	27	36	2	1	0	14	0	1	.308	.308	.342	98	-0	0	0	0	.780	-2	O-25/P-8	-0.1
	Eck-n	18	78	13	12	0	0	0	9	1	2	.154	.165	.154	-2	-8	3	1	0	.806	2	P-10/O-9,M	-0.2
	Yr	43	195	40	48	2	1	0	23	1	3	.246	.250	.267	62	-7	3	1	0	.776	-0	O-34,P-18	-0.3
1873	Mut-n	31	140	12	31	1	0	0	14	0	4	.221	.221	.229	34	-11	0	1	-1	.680	-7	O-30/P-6	-1.1
Total	2 n	74	335	52	79	3	1	0	37	1	7	.236	.238	.251	50	-19	3	2	-0	.747	-7	/O-64,P-24	-1.4

■ **BABE MARTIN** Martin, Boris Michael (b: Boris Michael Martinovich)
b: 3/28/20, Seattle, Wash. d: 10/30/97, Columbia, S.C. BR/TR, 5'11.5", 194 lbs. Deb: 9/25/44

YEAR	TM/L	G	AB	R	H	2B	3B	HR	RBI	BB	SO	AVG	OBP	SLG	PRO+	BR/A	SB	CS	SBR	FA	FR	G/POS	TPR
1944	StL-A	2	4	0	3	1	0	0	1	0	0	.750	.750	1.000	376	1	0	0	0	1.000	-0	/O-1	0.1
1945	StL-A	54	185	13	37	5	2	2	16	11	24	.200	.245	.281	50	-12	0	1	-1	.992	6	O-48/1-6	-1.0
1946	StL-A	3	9	0	2	0	0	0	1	1	2	.222	.300	.222	45	-1	0	0	0	1.000	1	/C-2	0.0
1948	Bos-A	4	4	0	2	0	0	0	0	0	1	.500	.500	.500	158	0	0	0	0	.000	0	/C-1	0.0
1949	Bos-A	2	2	0	0	0	0	0	0	0	0	.000	.000	.000	-93	-1	0	0	0	.000	0	/C-1	-0.1
1953	StL-A	4	2	0	0	0	0	0	0	1	0	.000	.333	.000	-4	-0	0	0	0	.000	0	/C-1	0.0
Total	6	69	206	13	44	6	2	2	18	13	27	.214	.260	.291	56	-12	0	1	-1	.992	6	/O-49,1-6,C-5	-1.0

■ **FRANK MARTIN** Martin, Frank b: 2/28/1879, Chicago, Ill. d: 9/30/24, Chicago, Ill. Deb: 6/30/1897

YEAR	TM/L	G	AB	R	H	2B	3B	HR	RBI	BB	SO	AVG	OBP	SLG	PRO+	BR/A	SB	CS	SBR	FA	FR	G/POS	TPR
1897	Lou-N	2	8	1	2	0	0	0	0	0		.250	.250	.250	33	-1	0			.813	0	/2-2	0.0
1898	Chi-N	1	4	0	0	0	0	0	0	0		.000	.000	.000	-99	-1	0			1.000	0	/2-1	-0.1
1899	NY-N	17	54	5	14	2	0	0	1	2		.259	.298	.296	66	-3	0			.824	2	3-17	0.0
Total	3	20	66	6	16	2	0	0	1	2		.242	.275	.273	52	-4	0			.870	3	/3-17,2-3	-0.1

■ **HERSH MARTIN** Martin, Hershel Ray b: 9/19/09, Birmingham, Ala. d: 11/17/80, Cuba, Mo. BB/TR, 6'2", 190 lbs. Deb: 4/23/37

YEAR	TM/L	G	AB	R	H	2B	3B	HR	RBI	BB	SO	AVG	OBP	SLG	PRO+	BR/A	SB	CS	SBR	FA	FR	G/POS	TPR
1937	Phi-N	141	579	102	164	35	7	8	49	69	66	.283	.362	.409	101	1	11			.978	5	*O-139	0.1
1938	Phi-N☆	120	466	58	139	36	6	3	39	34	48	.298	.347	.421	113	8	8			.965	1	*O-116	0.5
1939	Phi-N	111	393	59	111	28	5	1	22	42	27	.282	.355	.387	102	2	4			.976	11	O-95	0.9
1940	Phi-N	33	83	10	21	6	1	0	5	9	9	.253	.326	.349	90	-1	0			.979	-0	O-23	-0.2
1944	NY-A	85	328	49	99	12	4	9	47	34	26	.302	.371	.445	128	12	5	2	0	.964	3	O-80	1.1
1945	NY-A	117	408	53	109	18	6	7	53	65	31	.267	.368	.392	115	9	4	1	1	.984	3	*O-102	0.8
Total	6	607	2257	331	643	135	29	28	215	253	207	.285	.359	.408	109	31	33	3		.974	22	O-555	3.2

■ **JERRY MARTIN** Martin, Jerry Lindsey b: 5/11/49, Columbia, S.C. BR/TR, 6'1", 195 lbs. Deb: 9/7/74 F

YEAR	TM/L	G	AB	R	H	2B	3B	HR	RBI	BB	SO	AVG	OBP	SLG	PRO+	BR/A	SB	CS	SBR	FA	FR	G/POS	TPR
1974	Phi-N	13	14	2	3	1	0	0	1	1	5	.214	.267	.286	52	-1	0	0	0	1.000	-3	O-11	-0.5
1975	Phi-N	57	113	15	24	7	1	2	11	11	16	.212	.288	.345	72	-4	2	2	-1	.979	-3	O-49	-1.0
1976	*Phi-N	130	121	30	30	7	0	2	15	7	28	.248	.289	.355	80	-3	3	2	-0	.975	-30	*O-110/1-1	-3.7
1977	*Phi-N	116	215	34	56	16	3	6	28	18	42	.260	.329	.447	101	0	6	4	-1	.984	-19	*O-106/1-1	-2.2
1978	*Phi-N	128	266	40	72	13	4	9	36	28	65	.271	.342	.451	119	6	9	5	-0	.987	-15	*O-112	-1.3
1979	Chi-N	150	534	74	145	34	3	19	73	38	85	.272	.323	.453	100	-1	2	4	-2	.981	-2	*O-144	-1.1
1980	Chi-N	141	494	57	112	22	2	23	73	38	107	.227	.285	.419	88	-10	8	3	1	.978	-12	*O-129	-2.8
1981	SF-N	72	241	23	58	5	3	4	25	21	52	.241	.309	.336	85	-5	6	2	1	.993	-4	O-64	-1.1
1982	KC-A	147	519	52	138	22	1	15	65	38	138	.266	.318	.399	95	-4	1	1	-0	.980	4	*O-142/D-3	-0.4
1983	KC-A	13	44	4	14	2	0	2	13	1	7	.318	.333	.500	125	1	1	0	0	.957	-2	O-13	0.0
1984	NY-N	51	91	6	14	1	0	3	5	6	29	.154	.206	.264	32	-9	0	0	0	1.000	-1	O-30/1-3	-1.1
Total	11	1018	2652	337	666	130	17	85	345	207	574	.251	.309	.409	93	-29	38	23	-2	.982	-87	O-910/1-5,D-3	-15.2

■ **JACK MARTIN** Martin, John Christopher b: 4/19/1887, Plainfield, N.J. d: 7/4/80, Plainfield, N.J. BR/TR, 5'9", 159 lbs. Deb: 4/25/12

YEAR	TM/L	G	AB	R	H	2B	3B	HR	RBI	BB	SO	AVG	OBP	SLG	PRO+	BR/A	SB	CS	SBR	FA	FR	G/POS	TPR
1912	NY-A	71	231	30	52	6	1	0	17	37		.225	.347	.260	70	-7	14			.898	3	S-65/3-4,2-1	0.1
1914	Bos-N	33	85	10	18	2	0	0	5	6	7	.212	.264	.235	49	-5	0			.949	0	3-26/1-1,2-1	-0.5
	Phi-N	83	292	26	74	5	3	0	21	27	29	.253	.319	.291	77	-8	6			.930	-3	S-83	-0.4
	Yr	116	377	36	92	7	3	0	26	33	36	.244	.307	.279	71	-13	6			.930	-3	S-83,3-26/1-1,2-1	-0.9
Total	2	187	608	66	144	13	4	0	43	70	36	.237	.323	.271	71	-21	20			.915	-0	S-148/3-30,2-2,1-1	-0.8

■ **PEPPER MARTIN** Martin, John Leonard Roosevelt "The Wild Horse Of The Osage"
b: 2/29/04, Temple, Okla. d: 3/5/65, McAlester, Okla. BR/TR, 5'8", 170 lbs. Deb: 4/16/28 C

YEAR	TM/L	G	AB	R	H	2B	3B	HR	RBI	BB	SO	AVG	OBP	SLG	PRO+	BR/A	SB	CS	SBR	FA	FR	G/POS	TPR
1928	*StL-N	39	13	11	4	0	0	0	0	1	2	.308	.400	.308	86	-0	2			1.000	-2	/O-4	-0.2
1930	StL-N	6	1	5	0	0	0	0	0	0	0	.000	.000	.000	-97	-0	0			.000	0	H	0.0

YEAR	TM/L	G	AB	R	H	2B	3B	HR	RBI	BB	SO	AVG	OBP	SLG	PRO+	BR/A	SB	CS	SBR	FA	FR	G/POS	TPR
1931	*StL-N	123	413	68	124	32	8	7	75	30	40	.300	.351	.467	114	7	16			.967	0	*O-110	0.1
1932	StL-N	85	323	47	77	19	6	4	34	30	31	.238	.305	.372	79	-10	9			.976	-1	O-69,3-15	-1.4
1933	StL-N★	145	599	**122**	189	36	12	8	57	67	46	.316	.387	.456	133	27	**26**			.943	-3	*3-145	3.5
1934	*StL-N★	110	454	74	131	25	11	5	49	32	41	.289	.337	.425	96	-3	**23**			.936	-5	*3-107/P-1	-0.3
1935	StL-N★	135	539	121	161	41	6	9	54	33	58	.299	.341	.447	106	4	20			.904	-14	*3-114,O-16	-0.7
1936	StL-N	143	572	121	177	36	11	11	76	58	66	.309	.373	.469	126	20	**23**			.976	-10	*O-127,3-15/P-1	0.5
1937	StL-N☆	98	339	60	103	27	8	5	38	33	50	.304	.366	.475	124	11	9			.973	11	O-82/3-5	1.9
1938	StL-N	91	269	34	79	18	2	2	38	18	34	.294	.340	.398	97	-1	4			.986	-3	O-62/3-4	-0.6
1939	StL-N	88	281	48	86	17	7	3	37	30	35	.306	.375	.448	113	6	6			.975	-4	O-51,3-22	0.0
1940	StL-N	86	228	28	72	15	4	3	39	22	24	.316	.378	.456	122	7	6			.974	-3	O-63/3-2	0.2
1944	StL-N	40	86	15	24	4	0	2	4	15	11	.279	.386	.395	118	3	2			.980	-4	O-29	-0.2
Total	13	1189	4117	754	1227	270	75	59	501	369	438	.298	.358	.443	112	70	146			.973	-36	O-613,3-429/P-2	2.8

■ J. C. MARTIN

Martin, Joseph Clifton b: 12/13/36, Axton, Va. BL/TR, 6'2", 200 lbs. Deb: 9/10/59 C

YEAR	TM/L	G	AB	R	H	2B	3B	HR	RBI	BB	SO	AVG	OBP	SLG	PRO+	BR/A	SB	CS	SBR	FA	FR	G/POS	TPR
1959	Chi-A	3	4	0	1	0	0	0	1	0	1	.250	.250	.250	38	-0	0	0	0	.667	-0	/3-2	0.0
1960	Chi-A	7	20	0	2	1	0	0	2	0	6	.100	.100	.150	-34	-4	0	0	0	1.000	-0	/3-5,1-1	-0.4
1961	Chi-A	110	274	26	63	8	3	5	32	21	31	.230	.290	.336	68	-13	1	2	-1	.988	9	1-60,3-36	-0.7
1962	Chi-A	18	26	0	2	0	0	0	2	0	3	.077	.077	.077	-59	-6	0	0	0	1.000	-1	/C-6,1-1,3-1	-0.6
1963	Chi-A	105	259	25	53	11	1	5	28	26	35	.205	.280	.313	67	-11	0	0	0	.983	14	C-98/1-3,3-1	0.6
1964	Chi-A	122	294	23	58	10	1	4	22	16	30	.197	.244	.279	46	-22	0	0	0	.986	8	*C-120	-1.0
1965	Chi-A	119	230	21	60	12	0	2	21	24	29	.261	.336	.339	98	-0	2	1	0	.982	1	*C-112/1-4,3-2	0.4
1966	Chi-A	67	157	13	40	5	3	2	20	14	24	.255	.320	.363	103	0	0	0	0	.982	-1	C-63	0.3
1967	Chi-A	101	252	22	59	12	1	4	22	30	41	.234	.318	.337	97	-1	4	4	-1	.987	3	C-96/1-1	0.6
1968	NY-N	78	244	20	55	9	2	3	31	21	31	.225	.300	.316	84	-4	0	0	0	.994	-3	C-53,1-14	-0.6
1969	*NY-N	66	177	12	37	5	1	4	21	12	32	.209	.259	.316	59	-10	0	0	0	.996	-6	C-48/1-2	-1.5
1970	Chi-N	40	77	11	12	1	0	1	4	20	11	.156	.337	.208	44	-6	0	0	0	.983	2	C-36/1-3	-0.3
1971	Chi-N	47	125	13	33	5	0	2	17	12	16	.264	.338	.352	84	-3	1	1	-0	.996	2	C-43/O-1	0.1
1972	Chi-N	25	50	3	12	3	0	0	7	5	9	.240	.309	.300	67	-2	1	0	0	.970	-3	C-17	-0.5
Total	14	908	2189	189	487	82	12	32	230	201	299	.222	.293	.315	72	-81	9	8	-2	.987	26	C-692/1-89,3-47,O-1	-3.6

■ MIKE MARTIN

Martin, Joseph Michael b: 12/3/58, Portland, Ore. BL/TR, 6'2", 193 lbs. Deb: 8/15/86

YEAR	TM/L	G	AB	R	H	2B	3B	HR	RBI	BB	SO	AVG	OBP	SLG	PRO+	BR/A	SB	CS	SBR	FA	FR	G/POS	TPR
1986	Chi-N	8	13	1	1	1	0	0	0	2	4	.077	.200	.154	-1	-2	0	0	0	1.000	0	/C-8	-0.2

■ JOE MARTIN

Martin, Joseph Samuel "Silent Joe" b: 1/1/1876, Hollidaysburg, Pa. d: 5/25/64, Altoona, Pa. BL/TR, 5'9.5", 155 lbs. Deb: 4/28/03

YEAR	TM/L	G	AB	R	H	2B	3B	HR	RBI	BB	SO	AVG	OBP	SLG	PRO+	BR/A	SB	CS	SBR	FA	FR	G/POS	TPR
1903	Was-A	35	119	11	27	4	5	0	7	5		.227	.258	.345	78	-3	2			.892	-5	2-15,3-13/O-7	-0.8
	StL-A	44	173	18	37	6	4	0	7	6		.214	.249	.295	64	-8	0			.983	-3	O-38/2-6,3-1	-1.4
	Yr	79	292	29	64	10	9	0	14	11		.219	.252	.315	70	-11	2			.959	-8	O-45,2-21,3-14	-2.2

■ NORBERTO MARTIN

Martin, Norberto Edonal (McDonald) b: 12/10/66, San Pedro De Macoris, D.R. BR/TR, 5'10", 164 lbs. Deb: 9/20/93

YEAR	TM/L	G	AB	R	H	2B	3B	HR	RBI	BB	SO	AVG	OBP	SLG	PRO+	BR/A	SB	CS	SBR	FA	FR	G/POS	TPR
1993	Chi-A	8	14	3	5	0	0	0	2	1	1	.357	.400	.357	108	0	0	0	0	.957	3	/2-5,D-1	0.3
1994	Chi-A	45	131	19	36	7	1	1	16	9	16	.275	.321	.366	78	-4	4	2	0	.982	-6	2-28/S-6,3-5,O-2,D	-0.8
1995	Chi-A	72	160	17	43	7	4	2	17	3	25	.269	.287	.400	80	-5	5	0	2	.950	-3	2-17,O-12,D-10,/3S	-0.5
1996	Chi-A	70	140	30	49	7	0	1	14	6	17	.350	.377	.421	107	1	10	2	2	.943	10	S-24,D-22,2-10,/3-3	1.2
1997	Chi-A	71	213	24	64	7	1	2	27	6	31	.300	.320	.371	83	-6	1	4	-2	.960	-12	S-28,3-17/2-9,D-6	-1.6
1998	Ana-A	79	195	20	42	2	0	1	13	6	29	.215	.239	.241	25	-21	3	1	0	.982	10	2-54,D-10/3-5,OS	-0.9
Total	6	345	853	113	239	30	6	7	89	31	119	.280	.306	.354	72	-35	23	9	2	.976	2	2-123/S-67,D-50,3O	-2.3

■ STU MARTIN

Martin, Stuart McGuire b: 11/17/13, Rich Square, N.C. d: 1/11/97, Severn, N.C. BL/TR, 6', 155 lbs. Deb: 4/14/36

YEAR	TM/L	G	AB	R	H	2B	3B	HR	RBI	BB	SO	AVG	OBP	SLG	PRO+	BR/A	SB	CS	SBR	FA	FR	G/POS	TPR
1936	StL-N☆	92	332	63	99	21	4	6	41	29	27	.298	.356	.440	114	6	17			.949	-13	2-83/S-3	-0.1
1937	StL-N	90	223	34	58	6	1	1	17	32	18	.260	.353	.309	80	-5	3			.946	-6	2-48/1-9,S-1	-0.9
1938	StL-N	114	417	54	116	26	2	1	27	30	28	.278	.328	.357	84	-9	4			.967	10	2-99	-1.3
1939	StL-N	120	425	60	114	26	7	3	30	33	40	.268	.325	.384	85	-9	4			**.977**	-3	*2-107/1-1	-0.7
1940	StL-N	112	369	45	88	12	6	4	32	33	35	.238	.301	.336	71	-14	4			.972	-25	3-73,2-33	-3.8
1941	Pit-N	88	233	37	71	13	2	0	19	10	17	.305	.341	.378	103	1	2			.972	-4	2-53/3-2,1-1	0.0
1942	Pit-N	42	120	16	27	4	2	1	12	8	10	.225	.273	.317	71	-5	1			.979	-11	2-30/1-1,S-1	-1.5
1943	Chi-N	64	118	13	26	4	0	0	5	15	10	.220	.308	.254	64	-5	1			.980	1	2-22/3-8,1-2	-0.3
Total	8	722	2237	322	599	112	24	16	183	190	185	.268	.327	.361	86	-41	36			.966	-71	2-475/3-83,1-14,S-5	-8.6

■ GENE MARTIN

Martin, Thomas Eugene b: 1/12/47, Americus, Ga. BL/TR, 6'0.5", 190 lbs. Deb: 7/28/68

YEAR	TM/L	G	AB	R	H	2B	3B	HR	RBI	BB	SO	AVG	OBP	SLG	PRO+	BR/A	SB	CS	SBR	FA	FR	G/POS	TPR
1968	Was-A	9	11	1	4	1	0	1	1	0	1	.364	.364	.727	232	2	0	0	0	.000	-1	/O-2	0.1

■ JOE MARTIN

Martin, William Joseph "Smokey Joe" b: 8/28/11, Seymour, Mo. d: 9/28/60, Buffalo, N.Y. BR/TR, 5'11.5", 181 lbs. Deb: 4/27/36

YEAR	TM/L	G	AB	R	H	2B	3B	HR	RBI	BB	SO	AVG	OBP	SLG	PRO+	BR/A	SB	CS	SBR	FA	FR	G/POS	TPR
1936	NY-N	7	15	0	4	1	0	0	2	0	4	.267	.313	.333	75	-1	0			1.000	1	/3-7	0.0
1938	Chi-A	1	0	0	0	0	0	0	0	0	0	—	—	—	—	0	0	0	0	.000	0	R	0.0
Total	2	8	15	0	4	1	0	0	2	0	4	.267	.313	.333	75	-1	0	0		1.000	1	/3-7	0.0

■ BILLY MARTIN

Martin, William Lloyd b: 2/13/1894, Washington, D.C. d: 9/14/49, Arlington, Va. BR/TR, 5'8.5", 170 lbs. Deb: 10/6/14

YEAR	TM/L	G	AB	R	H	2B	3B	HR	RBI	BB	SO	AVG	OBP	SLG	PRO+	BR/A	SB	CS	SBR	FA	FR	G/POS	TPR
1914	Bos-N	1	3	0	0	0	0	0	0	0	0	.000	.000	.000	-99	-1	0			.500	-1	/S-1	-0.2

■ SANDY MARTINEZ

Martinez, Angel Sandy (Martinez) b: 10/3/72, Villa Mella, D.R. BL/TR, 6'2", 200 lbs. Deb: 6/24/95

YEAR	TM/L	G	AB	R	H	2B	3B	HR	RBI	BB	SO	AVG	OBP	SLG	PRO+	BR/A	SB	CS	SBR	FA	FR	G/POS	TPR
1995	Tor-A	62	191	12	46	12	0	2	25	7	45	.241	.271	.335	57	-12	0	0	0	.986	-3	C-61	-1.1
1996	Tor-A	76	229	17	52	9	3	3	18	16	58	.227	.289	.332	57	-15	0	0	0	.993	6	C-75	-0.5
1997	Tor-A	3	2	1	0	0	0	0	0	1	1	.000	.333	.000	-3	-0	0	0	0	.933	2	/C-3	0.1
1998	*Chi-N	45	87	7	23	9	1	0	7	13	21	.264	.366	.391	94	-0	1	0	0	.985	0	C-33	0.2
Total	4	186	509	37	121	30	4	5	50	37	125	.238	.297	.342	63	-28	1	0	0	.988	5	C-172	-1.3

■ CARLOS MARTINEZ

Martinez, Carlos Alberto Escobar (b: Carlos Alberto Escobar (Martinez))
b: 8/11/64, LaGuaira, Venez. BR/TR, 6'5", 175 lbs. Deb: 9/2/88

YEAR	TM/L	G	AB	R	H	2B	3B	HR	RBI	BB	SO	AVG	OBP	SLG	PRO+	BR/A	SB	CS	SBR	FA	FR	G/POS	TPR
1988	Chi-A	17	55	5	9	1	0	0	0	0	12	.164	.164	.182	-3	-7	1	0	0	.909	3	3-15/D-2	-0.5
1989	Chi-A	109	350	44	105	22	0	5	32	21	57	.300	.341	.406	112	5	4	1	1	.912	-6	3-68,1-34,O-10,/D-1	-0.2
1990	Chi-A	92	272	18	61	6	5	4	24	10	40	.224	.252	.327	62	-15	0	4	-2	.988	-5	1-82/O-1,D-3	-2.9
1991	Cle-A	72	257	22	73	14	0	5	30	10	43	.284	.316	.397	95	-2	3	2	-0	.968	-4	D-41,1-31	-1.0
1992	Cle-A	69	228	23	60	9	1	5	35	7	21	.263	.288	.377	87	-5	1	2	-1	.996	-5	1-37,3-28/D-4	-1.3
1993	Cle-A	80	262	26	64	10	0	5	31	20	29	.244	.298	.340	71	-11	1	1	-0	.934	-9	3-35,1-22,D-19	-2.2
1995	Cal-A	26	61	7	11	1	0	1	9	6	7	.180	.265	.246	34	-6	0	0	0	.968	2	3-16/1-4,D-2	-0.4
Total	7	465	1485	145	383	63	6	25	161	74	209	.258	.295	.359	81	-41	10	10	-3	.986	-25	1-210,3-162/D-72,O	-8.5

■ CARMELO MARTINEZ

Martinez, Carmelo (Salgado) b: 7/28/60, Dorado, P.R. BR/TR, 6'2", 220 lbs. Deb: 8/22/83

YEAR	TM/L	G	AB	R	H	2B	3B	HR	RBI	BB	SO	AVG	OBP	SLG	PRO+	BR/A	SB	CS	SBR	FA	FR	G/POS	TPR
1983	Chi-N	29	89	8	23	3	0	6	16	4	19	.258	.290	.494	108	0	0	0	0	.992	-0	1-26/3-1,O-1	-0.1
1984	*SD-N	149	488	64	122	28	2	13	66	68	82	.250	.346	.395	108	6	1	3	-2	.976	21	*O-142/1-2	2.2
1985	SD-N	150	514	64	130	28	1	21	72	87	82	.253	.364	.434	124	18	0	4	-2	.978	13	*O-150/1-3	2.5
1986	SD-N	113	244	28	58	10	0	9	25	35	46	.238	.336	.389	101	1	1	1	-0	.978	-0	O-60,1-26/3-1	-0.2
1987	SD-N	139	447	59	122	21	2	15	70	70	82	.273	.375	.430	117	12	5	5	-2	.968	-3	O-78,1-65	0.1
1988	SD-N	121	365	48	86	12	0	18	65	35	57	.236	.303	.416	106	2	1	1	-0	.993	10	O-64,1-41	0.7
1989	SD-N	111	267	23	59	12	2	6	39	32	54	.221	.304	.348	86	-5	0	0	0	.982	1	O-65,1-32	-0.7
1990	Phi-N	71	198	23	48	8	0	8	31	29	37	.242	.339	.404	104	1	2	1	0	.994	-2	1-43,O-20	-0.4
	*Pit-N	12	19	3	4	1	0	2	4	1	5	.211	.250	.579	126	0	0	0	0	1.000	0	/1-5,O-2	0.1
	Yr	83	217	26	52	9	0	10	35	30	42	.240	.332	.419	106	2	2	1	0	.995	-2	1-48,O-22	-0.3
1991	Pit-N	11	16	1	4	0	0	0	0	1	2	.250	.294	.250	55	-1	0	0	0	.945	-1	/1-8	-0.2
	KC-A	44	121	17	25	6	0	4	17	27	25	.207	.351	.355	96	0	0	1	-1	.991	4	1-43/D-1	0.1
	Cin-N	53	138	12	32	5	0	6	19	15	37	.232	.307	.399	93	-1	0	0	0	.985	0	1-25,O-16	-0.3
Total	9	1003	2906	350	713	134	7	108	424	404	528	.245	.340	.408	108	35	10	16	-7	.980	41	O-598,1-319/3-2,D-1	3.8

YEAR	TM/L	G	AB	R	H	2B	3B	HR	RBI	BB	SO	AVG	OBP	SLG	PRO+	BR/A	SB	CS	SBR	FA	FR	G/POS	TPR
■ TINO MARTINEZ	Martinez, Constantino b: 12/7/67, Tampa, Fla. BL/TR, 6'2", 210 lbs. Deb: 8/20/90																						
1990	Sea-A	24	68	4	15	4	0	0	5	9	9	.221	.312	.279	66	-3	0	0	0	1.000	0	1-23	-0.4
1991	Sea-A	36	112	11	23	2	0	4	9	11	24	.205	.276	.330	67	-5	0	0	0	.993	2	1-29/D-5	-0.5
1992	Sea-A	136	460	53	118	19	2	16	66	42	77	.257	.321	.411	103	1	2	1	0	.995	1	1-78,D-47	-0.5
1993	Sea-A	109	408	48	108	25	1	17	60	45	56	.265	.345	.456	112	6	0	3	-2	.997	-3	*1-103/D-6	-0.7
1994	Sea-A	97	329	42	86	21	0	20	61	29	52	.261	.323	.508	108	2	1	2	-1	.997	-2	1-82/D-8	-0.7
1995	*Sea-A★	141	519	92	152	35	3	31	111	62	91	.293	.373	.551	135	26	0	0	0	.993	4	*1-139/D-1	1.6
1996	*NY-A	155	595	82	174	28	0	25	117	68	85	.292	.367	.466	109	8	2	1	0	**.996**	-4	*1-151/D-3	-0.9
1997	*NY-A★	158	594	96	176	31	2	44	141	75	75	.296	.378	.577	146	39	3	1	0	.994	5	*1-150/D-9	2.7
1998	*NY-A	142	531	92	149	33	1	28	123	61	83	.281	.361	.505	125	19	2	1	0	.992	-2	*1-142	0.3
Total	9	998	3616	520	1001	198	9	185	693	402	552	.277	.353	.490	119	94	10	9	-2	.995	1	1-897/D-79	0.9
■ DAVE MARTINEZ	Martinez, David b: 9/26/64, New York, N.Y. BL/TL, 5'10", 175 lbs. Deb: 6/15/86																						
1986	Chi-N	53	108	13	15	1	1	1	7	6	22	.139	.191	.194	6	-14	4	2	0	.988	-4	O-46	-1.9
1987	Chi-N	142	459	70	134	18	8	8	36	57	96	.292	.373	.418	105	5	16	8	0	.980	1	*O-139	0.2
1988	Chi-N	75	256	27	65	10	1	4	34	21	46	.254	.315	.348	86	-4	7	3	0	.970	-1	O-72	-0.7
	Mon-N	63	191	24	49	3	5	2	12	17	48	.257	.317	.356	89	-3	16	6	1	.992	-5	O-60	-0.8
	Yr	138	447	51	114	13	6	6	46	38	94	.255	.316	.351	87	-7	23	9	2	.979	-5	*O-132	-1.5
1989	Mon-N	126	361	41	99	16	7	3	27	27	57	.274	.325	.382	100	-0	23	4	5	.967	-18	*O-118	-1.8
1990	Mon-N	118	391	60	109	13	5	11	39	24	48	.279	.322	.422	107	2	13	11	-3	.989	-3	*O-108/P-1	-0.5
1991	Mon-N	124	396	47	117	18	5	7	42	20	54	.295	.334	.419	112	5	16	7	1	.982	-1	*O-112	0.4
1992	Cin-N	135	393	47	100	20	5	3	31	42	54	.254	.326	.354	90	-5	12	8	-1	.991	-4	*O-111,1-21	-1.4
1993	SF-N	91	241	28	58	12	1	5	27	27	39	.241	.317	.361	84	-6	6	3	0	.993	-5	O-73	-1.2
1994	SF-N	97	235	23	58	9	3	4	27	21	22	.247	.314	.362	79	-7	3	4	-2	1.000	-5	O-58,1-25	-1.6
1995	Chi-A	119	303	49	93	16	4	5	37	32	41	.307	.375	.436	115	7	8	2	1	.976	-10	O-59,1-47/P-1,D-5	-0.6
1996	Chi-A	146	440	85	140	20	8	10	53	52	52	.318	.394	.468	123	16	15	7	0	.988	-17	*O-121,1-23	-0.3
1997	Chi-A	145	504	78	144	16	6	12	55	55	69	.286	.359	.413	105	5	12	6	0	.996	-4	*O-105,1-52/D-1	-0.5
1998	TB-A	90	309	31	79	11	0	3	20	35	52	.256	.335	.320	69	-13	8	7	-2	.994	3	O-86/1-1,D-1	-1.3
Total	13	1524	4587	623	1260	183	59	78	447	436	700	.275	.340	.391	97	-11	159	78	1	.986	-70	*O-1268,1-169/D-7,P	-12.0
■ DOMINGO MARTINEZ	Martinez, Domingo Emilio (La Fontaine) b: 8/4/67, Santo Domingo, D.R. BR/TR, 6'2", 215 lbs. Deb: 9/11/92																						
1992	Tor-A	7	8	2	5	0	0	1	3	0	1	.625	.625	1.000	333	2	0	0	0	1.000	-1	/1-7	0.2
1993	Tor-A	8	14	2	4	0	0	1	3	1	7	.286	.333	.500	120	0	0	0	0	1.000	1	/1-7,3-1	0.1
Total	2	15	22	4	9	0	0	2	6	1	8	.409	.435	.682	196	3	0	0	0	1.000	0	/1-14,3-1	0.3
■ EDGAR MARTINEZ	Martinez, Edgar b: 1/2/63, New York, N.Y. BR/TR, 5'11", 175 lbs. Deb: 9/12/87																						
1987	Sea-A	13	43	6	16	5	2	0	5	2	5	.372	.413	.581	152	3	0	0	0	1.000	1	3-12/D-1	0.4
1988	Sea-A	14	32	0	9	4	0	0	5	4	7	.281	.361	.406	110	0	0	0	0	.929	-4	3-13	-0.4
1989	Sea-A	65	171	20	41	5	0	2	20	17	26	.240	.319	.304	74	-5	2	1	0	.949	-6	3-61	-1.2
1990	Sea-A	144	487	71	147	27	2	11	49	74	62	.302	.399	.433	131	23	1	4	-2	.928	-1	*3-143/D-2	2.1
1991	Sea-A	150	544	98	167	35	1	14	52	84	72	.307	.407	.452	137	31	0	3	-2	.962	3	*3-144/D-2	3.2
1992	Sea-A★	135	528	100	181	**46**	3	18	73	54	61	**.343**	.408	.544	164	44	14	4	2	.943	1	*3-103,D-28/1-2	4.6
1993	Sea-A	42	135	20	32	7	0	4	13	28	19	.237	.368	.378	100	1	0	0	0	.889	-4	D-24,3-16	-0.4
1994	Sea-A	89	326	47	93	23	1	13	51	53	42	.285	.390	.482	121	11	6	2	1	.950	6	3-64,D-23	1.5
1995	*Sea-A★	145	511	**121**	182	**52**	0	29	113	116	87	**.356**	**.482**	.628	**184**	**70**	4	3	-1	.800	-1	*D-138/3-4,1-3	5.4
1996	Sea-A★	139	499	121	163	52	2	26	103	123	84	.327	.467	.595	166	57	3	3	-1	.967	-1	*D-134/1-4,3-2	4.2
1997	*Sea-A★	155	542	104	179	35	1	28	108	119	86	.330	.460	.554	164	59	2	4	-2	.986	-1	*D-144/1-7,3-1	4.4
1998	Sea-A	154	556	86	179	46	1	29	102	106	96	.322	**.433**	.565	157	50	1	1	-0	1.000	2	*D-147/1-4	4.0
Total	12	1245	4374	794	1389	337	13	174	694	780	647	.318	.427	.520	150	345	33	25	-5	.946	-6	D-643,3-563/1-20	27.8
■ FELIX MARTINEZ	Martinez, Felix (Mata) b: 5/18/74, Nagua, D.R. BB/TR, 6', 168 lbs. Deb: 9/3/97																						
1997	KC-A	16	31	3	7	1	1	0	3	6	8	.226	.351	.323	76	-1	0	0	0	.975	2	S-12/D-2	0.2
1998	KC-A	34	85	7	11	1	1	0	5	5	21	.129	.187	.165	-7	-13	3	1	0	.956	2	S-32/2-2	-0.9
Total	2	50	116	10	18	2	2	0	8	11	29	.155	.234	.207	16	-14	3	1	0	.960	4	/S-44,2-2,D-2	-0.7
■ TONY MARTINEZ	Martinez, Gabriel Antonio (Diaz) b: 3/18/40, Perico, Cuba d: 8/24/91, Miami, Fla. BR/TR, 5'10", 165 lbs. Deb: 4/9/63																						
1963	Cle-A	43	141	10	22	4	0	0	8	5	18	.156	.185	.184	4	-18	1	1	-0	.961	-6	S-41	-2.4
1964	Cle-A	9	14	1	3	1	0	0	2	0	2	.214	.214	.286	38	-1	0	1	-1	1.000	4	/2-4,S-1	0.2
1965	Cle-A	4	3	0	0	0	0	0	0	0	0	.000	.000	.000	-99	-1	0	0	0	.000	0	H	-0.1
1966	Cle-A	17	17	2	5	0	0	0	0	1	6	.294	.333	.294	82	-0	1	1	-0	.833	1	/S-5,2-4	0.1
Total	4	73	175	13	30	5	0	0	10	6	26	.171	.199	.200	13	-20	2	3	-1	.958	-1	/S-47,2-8	-2.2
■ GREG MARTINEZ	Martinez, Gregory Alfred b: 1/27/72, Las Vegas, Nev. BB/TR, 5'10", 168 lbs. Deb: 3/31/98																						
1998	Mil-N	13	3	2	0	0	0	0	0	1	2	.000	.250	.000	-27	-1	2	0	1	.000	-2	/O-6	-0.2
■ BUCK MARTINEZ	Martinez, John Albert b: 11/7/48, Redding, Cal. BR/TR, 5'10", 190 lbs. Deb: 6/18/69																						
1969	KC-A	72	205	14	47	6	1	4	23	8	25	.229	.258	.327	62	-11	0	0	0	.972	-1	C-55/O-1	-1.0
1970	KC-A	6	9	1	1	0	0	0	0	2	1	.111	.273	.111	10	-1	0	0	0	.958	2	/C-5	0.1
1971	KC-A	22	46	3	7	2	0	0	1	5	9	.152	.235	.196	23	-5	0	1	-1	.968	2	C-21	-0.3
1973	KC-A	14	32	2	8	1	0	1	6	4	5	.250	.333	.375	92	-0	0	0	0	.966	-1	C-14	-0.1
1974	KC-A	43	107	10	23	3	1	1	8	14	19	.215	.317	.290	71	-4	0	1	-1	.977	1	C-38	-0.2
1975	KC-A	80	226	15	51	9	2	3	23	21	28	.226	.294	.323	72	-8	1	0	0	.980	-0	C-79	-0.5
1976	*KC-A	95	267	24	61	13	3	5	34	16	45	.228	.272	.356	82	-7	0	0	0	.991	5	C-94	0.1
1977	KC-A	29	80	3	18	4	0	1	9	3	12	.225	.253	.313	53	-5	0	1	-1	.993	3	C-28	-0.3
1978	Mil-A	89	256	26	56	10	1	1	20	14	42	.219	.259	.277	51	-17	1	1	-0	.978	-3	C-89	-1.9
1979	Mil-A	69	196	17	53	8	0	4	26	8	25	.270	.299	.372	80	-6	0	1	-1	.967	-2	C-68/P-1	-0.6
1980	Mil-A	76	219	16	49	9	0	3	17	12	33	.224	.267	.306	58	-13	1	0	0	.985	11	C-76	0.1
1981	Tor-A	45	128	13	29	8	1	4	21	11	16	.227	.293	.398	92	-2	1	0	0	.991	2	C-45	0.2
1982	Tor-A	96	260	26	63	17	0	10	37	24	34	.242	.306	.423	90	-4	1	1	-0	.988	6	C-93	0.4
1983	Tor-A	88	221	27	56	14	0	10	33	29	39	.253	.340	.452	109	3	0	1	-1	.989	-3	C-85	0.2
1984	Tor-A	102	232	24	51	13	1	5	37	29	49	.220	.312	.349	80	-6	0	3	-2	.995	-4	C-98/D-1	-0.9
1985	Tor-A	42	99	11	16	3	0	4	14	10	12	.162	.245	.313	50	-7	0	0	0	.988	4	C-42	-0.2
1986	Tor-A	81	160	13	29	8	0	2	12	20	25	.181	.272	.269	47	-12	0	0	0	.994	-1	C-78/D-1	-1.0
Total	17	1049	2743	245	618	128	10	58	321	230	419	.225	.287	.343	73	-105	5	10	-5	.984	19	*C-1008/D-2,P-1,O-1	-5.9
■ JOSE MARTINEZ	Martinez, Jose (Azcuiz) b: 7/26/42, Cardenas, Cuba BR/TR, 5'10", 190 lbs. Deb: 6/18/69 C																						
1969	Pit-N	77	168	20	45	6	0	1	16	9	32	.268	.309	.321	78	-5	1	3	-2	.975	10	2-42,S-20/3-5,O-2	0.7
1970	Pit-N	19	20	1	1	0	0	0	0	1	5	.050	.095	.050	-61	-5	0	0	0	1.000	3	/3-7,2-4,S-1	-0.1
Total	2	96	188	21	46	6	0	1	16	10	37	.245	.286	.293	63	-9	1	3	-2	.966	13	/2-46,S-21,3-12,O-2	0.6
■ MANNY MARTINEZ	Martinez, Manuel (De Jesus) b: 10/3/70, San Pedro De Macoris, D.R. BR/TR, 6'2", 169 lbs. Deb: 6/14/96																						
1996	Sea-A	9	17	3	4	2	1	0	3	3	5	.235	.350	.471	105	0	2	0	1	1.000	0	/O-8	0.1
	Phi-N	13	36	2	8	0	2	0	0	1	11	.222	.263	.333	55	-2	2	1	0	.955	0	O-11	-0.3
1998	Pit-N	73	180	21	45	11	2	6	24	9	44	.250	.293	.433	84	-5	0	3	-2	.989	-8	O-62	-1.5
Total	2	95	233	26	57	13	5	6	27	13	60	.245	.293	.421	81	-7	4	4	-1	.984	-8	/O-81	-1.7
■ MARTY MARTINEZ	Martinez, Orlando (Oliva) b: 8/23/41, Havana, Cuba BB/TR, 6'1", 175 lbs. Deb: 5/2/62 MC																						
1962	Min-A	37	18	13	3	0	1	0	3	3	4	.167	.286	.278	51	-1	0	0	0	.920	8	S-11/3-1	0.7
1967	Atl-N	44	73	14	21	2	1	0	5	11	11	.288	.388	.342	112	2	0	1	-1	.920	4	S-25/2-9,C-3,3-2,1	0.8
1968	Atl-N	113	356	34	82	5	3	0	12	29	28	.230	.292	.261	67	-14	6	6	-2	.955	-5	S-54,3-37,2-16,C-14	-1.6
1969	Hou-N	78	198	14	61	5	4	0	15	10	21	.308	.341	.374	102	0	0	0	0	1.000	-9	O-21,S-17,3/CP2	-0.8

YEAR	TM/L	G	AB	R	H	2B	3B	HR	RBI	BB	SO	AVG	OBP	SLG	PRO+	BR/A	SB	CS	SBR	FA	FR	G/POS	TPR
1970	Hou-N	75	150	12	33	3	0	0	12	9	22	.220	.264	.240	38	-13	0	0	0	.990	-6	S-29,3-10/C-6,2-4	-1.6
1971	Hou-N	32	62	4	16	3	1	0	4	3	6	.258	.292	.339	80	-2	1	0	0	.968	1	/2-9,S-7,1-4,3-3	0.0
1972	StL-N	9	7	0	3	0	0	0	2	0	1	.429	.429	.429	146	0	0	0	0	1.000	0	/S-3,2-2,3-1	0.1
	Oak-A	22	40	3	5	0	0	0	1	3	6	.125	.186	.125	-7	-5	0	0	0	.944	3	2-17/S-6,3-1	-0.1
	Tex-A	26	41	3	6	1	1	0	3	2	8	.146	.186	.220	21	-4	0	1	-1	.944	-2	/S-5,3-4,2-1	-0.7
	Yr	48	81	6	11	1	1	0	4	5	14	.136	.186	.173	8	-9	0	1	-1	.946	2	2-18,S-11/3-5	-0.8
Total	7	436	945	97	230	19	11	0	57	70	107	.243	.298	.287	70	-37	7	8	-3	.950	-5	S-157/3-74,2CO1P	-3.2
■ **PABLO MARTINEZ** Martinez, Pablo Made (Valera) b: 6/29/69, Sabana Grande, D.R. BB/TR, 5'10", 155 lbs. Deb: 7/20/96																							
1996	Atl-N	4	2	1	1	0	0	0	0	0	0	.500	.500	.500	156	0	0	1	-1	1.000	1	/S-1	0.0
■ **RAMON MARTINEZ** Martinez, Ramon E. b: 10/10/72, Philadelphia, Pa. BR/TR, 6'1", 170 lbs. Deb: 6/20/98																							
1998	SF-N	19	19	4	6	1	0	0	0	4	2	.316	.435	.368	116	1	0	0	0	1.000	5	2-14	0.6
■ **CHITO MARTINEZ** Martinez, Reyenaldo Ignacio b: 12/19/65, Belize City, British Honduras (Belize) BL/TL, 5'10", 180 lbs. Deb: 7/5/91																							
1991	Bal-A	67	216	32	58	12	1	13	33	11	51	.269	.304	.514	127	6	1	1	-0	.982	2	O-54/1-1,D-4	0.7
1992	Bal-A	83	198	26	53	10	1	5	25	31	47	.268	.372	.404	114	5	0	1	-1	.973	1	O-52/D-4	0.5
1993	Bal-A	8	15	0	0	0	0	0	0	4	4	.000	.211	.000	-37	-3	0	0	0	1.000	-2	/O-5,D-2	-0.5
Total	3	158	429	58	111	22	2	18	58	46	102	.259	.333	.445	115	8	1	2	-1	.978	2	O-111/D-10,1-1	0.7
■ **HECTOR MARTINEZ** Martinez, Rodolfo Hector (Santos) b: 5/11/39, Las Villas, Cuba BR/TR, 5'10", 160 lbs. Deb: 9/30/62																							
1962	KC-A	1	1	0	0	0	0	0	0	0	1	.000	.000	.000	-96	-0	0	0	0	.000	0	H	0.0
1963	KC-A	6	14	2	4	0	0	1	3	1	3	.286	.375	.500	135	1	0	1	-1	1.000	0	/O-3	0.0
Total	2	7	15	2	4	0	0	1	3	1	4	.267	.353	.467	120	0	0	1	-1	1.000	0	/O-3	0.0
■ **TED MARTINEZ** Martinez, Teodoro Noel (Encarnacion) b: 12/10/47, Barahona, D.R. BR/TR, 6', 165 lbs. Deb: 7/18/70																							
1970	NY-N	4	16	0	1	0	0	0	0	0	3	.063	.063	.063	-66	-4	0	0	0	1.000	1	/2-4,S-1	-0.3
1971	NY-N	38	125	16	36	5	2	1	10	4	22	.288	.326	.384	102	0	6	0	2	.976	-7	S-23,2-13/3-3,O-1	-0.2
1972	NY-N	103	330	22	74	5	5	1	19	12	49	.224	.254	.279	52	-21	7	4	-0	.994	1	2-47,S-42,O-15,/3-2	-1.5
1973	*NY-N	92	263	34	67	11	0	1	14	13	38	.255	.295	.308	68	-11	3	5	-2	.941	-4	S-44,O-21,3-14,/2-5	-1.4
1974	NY-N	116	334	32	73	15	7	2	43	14	40	.219	.250	.323	61	-19	3	2	-0	.952	14	S-75,3-12,2-11,O-10	0.2
1975	StL-N	16	21	1	4	2	0	0	2	0	2	.190	.190	.286	30	-2	0	0	0	1.000	-1	/O-7,2-2,S-1,3-1	-0.4
	*Oak-A	86	87	7	15	0	0	0	3	2	9	.172	.200	.172	6	-11	1	1	-0	.955	4	S-45,2-31,3-14	-0.5
1977	LA-N	67	137	21	41	6	1	1	10	2	20	.299	.309	.380	84	-3	3	4	-2	.992	14	2-27,S-13,3-12	1.1
1978	LA-N	54	55	13	14	1	0	1	5	4	14	.255	.317	.327	80	-1	3	2	-0	.912	10	S-17,3-16,2-10	1.0
1979	LA-N	81	112	19	30	5	1	0	2	4	16	.268	.293	.330	71	-5	3	2	-0	.769	-0	3-23,S-21,2-18	-0.4
Total	9	657	1480	165	355	50	16	7	108	55	213	.240	.271	.309	62	-77	29	20	-3	.956	31	S-282,2-168/3-97,O	-2.4
■ **JOE MARTY** Marty, Joseph Anton b: 9/1/13, Sacramento, Cal. d: 10/4/84, Sacramento, Cal. BR/TR, 6', 182 lbs. Deb: 4/22/37																							
1937	Chi-N	88	290	41	84	17	2	5	44	28	30	.290	.356	.414	104	2	3			.976	-2	O-84	-0.3
1938	*Chi-N	76	235	32	57	8	3	7	35	18	26	.243	.305	.391	88	-4	0			.987	-4	O-68	-1.0
1939	Chi-N	23	76	6	10	1	0	2	10	4	13	.132	.175	.224	6	-10	2			.933	-2	O-21	-1.3
	Phi-N	91	299	32	76	12	6	9	44	24	27	.254	.310	.425	98	-2	1			.974	3	O-79/P-1	-0.2
	Yr	114	375	38	86	13	6	11	54	28	40	.229	.283	.384	79	-13	3			.968	1	*O-100/P-1	-1.5
1940	Phi-N	123	455	52	123	21	8	13	50	17	50	.270	.298	.437	105	0	2			.974	2	*O-118	-0.3
1941	Phi-N	137	477	60	128	19	3	8	39	51	41	.268	.344	.371	105	4	6			.964	-6	*O-132	-1.1
Total	5	538	1832	223	478	78	22	44	222	142	187	.261	.318	.400	97	-11	14			.972	-9	O-502/P-1	-4.2
■ **BOB MARTYN** Martyn, Robert Gordon b: 8/15/30, Weiser, Idaho BL/TR, 6', 176 lbs. Deb: 6/18/57																							
1957	KC-A	58	131	10	35	2	4	1	12	11	20	.267	.324	.366	87	-2	1	3	-2	.976	-3	O-49	-1.0
1958	KC-A	95	226	25	59	10	7	2	23	26	36	.261	.337	.394	99	-0	1	4	-2	.967	-5	O-63	-1.0
1959	KC-A	1	1	0	0	0	0	0	0	0	0	.000	.000	.000	-98	-0	0	0	0	.000	0	R	0.0
Total	3	154	358	35	94	12	11	3	35	37	56	.263	.332	.383	94	-3	2	7	-4	.970	-8	O-112	-2.0
■ **GARY MARTZ** Martz, Gary Arthur b: 1/10/51, Spokane, Wash. BR/TR, 6'4", 210 lbs. Deb: 7/8/75																							
1975	KC-A	1	1	0	0	0	0	0	0	0	0	.000	.000	.000	-97	-0	0	0	0	1.000	-0	/O-1	-0.1
■ **JOHN MARZANO** Marzano, John Robert b: 2/14/63, Philadelphia, Pa. BR/TR, 5'11", 197 lbs. Deb: 7/31/87																							
1987	Bos-A	52	168	20	41	11	0	5	24	7	41	.244	.287	.399	77	-6	0	1	-1	.986	1	C-52	-0.2
1988	Bos-A	10	29	3	4	1	0	0	1	1	3	.138	.167	.172	-5	-4	0	0	0	1.000	5	C-10	0.2
1989	Bos-A	7	18	5	8	3	0	1	3	0	2	.444	.444	.778	224	3	0	0	0	1.000	-0	/C-7	0.3
1990	Bos-A	32	83	8	20	4	0	0	6	5	10	.241	.284	.289	58	-5	0	1	-1	1.000	4	C-32	0.1
1991	Bos-A	49	114	10	30	8	0	0	9	1	16	.263	.276	.333	64	-6	0	0	0	.985	-2	C-48	-0.6
1992	Bos-A	19	50	4	4	2	1	0	1	2	12	.080	.132	.160	-17	-8	0	0	0	.968	0	C-18/D-1	-0.7
1995	Tex-A	2	6	1	2	0	0	0	0	0	0	.333	.333	.333	72	-0	0	0	0	1.000	-0	/C-2	0.0
1996	Sea-A	41	106	8	26	6	0	0	6	7	15	.245	.316	.302	57	-7	0	0	0	.986	-0	C-39	-0.5
1997	Sea-A	39	87	7	25	3	0	1	10	7	15	.287	.340	.356	83	-2	0	0	0	.976	4	C-37/D-1	0.3
1998	Sea-A	50	133	13	31	7	1	4	12	9	24	.233	.325	.391	85	-3	0	0	0	.997	8	C-48/D-1	0.8
Total	10	301	794	79	191	45	2	11	72	39	138	.241	.291	.344	67	-37	0	2	-1	.988	20	C-293/D-3	-0.3
■ **CLYDE MASHORE** Mashore, Clyde Wayne b: 5/29/45, Concord, Cal. BR/TR, 5'11", 184 lbs. Deb: 7/11/69																							
1969	Cin-N	2	1	1	0	0	0	0	0	0	0	.000	.000	.000	-95	-0	0	0	0	.000	0	H	0.0
1970	Mon-N	13	25	2	4	0	0	1	3	4	11	.160	.276	.280	49	-2	0	0	0	1.000	-2	O-10	-0.4
1971	Mon-N	66	114	20	22	5	0	1	7	10	22	.193	.258	.263	48	-8	1	0	0	.967	-11	O-47/3-1	-2.2
1972	Mon-N	93	176	23	40	7	1	3	23	14	41	.227	.284	.330	73	-6	6	1	1	.988	-13	O-74	-2.2
1973	Mon-N	67	103	12	21	3	0	3	14	15	28	.204	.305	.320	71	-4	4	3	-1	.958	-3	O-44/2-1	-0.9
Total	5	241	419	58	87	15	1	8	47	43	102	.208	.281	.305	64	-20	11	4	1	.974	-28	O-175/2-1,3-1	-5.7
■ **DAMON MASHORE** Mashore, Damon Wayne b: 10/31/69, Ponce, P.R. BR/TR, 5'11", 195 lbs. Deb: 6/5/96																							
1996	Oak-A	50	105	20	28	7	1	3	12	16	31	.267	.369	.438	105	1	4	0	1	.985	-11	O-48	-0.9
1997	Oak-A	92	279	55	69	10	2	3	18	50	82	.247	.371	.330	86	-3	5	4	-1	.991	-0	O-89	-0.6
1998	Ana-A	43	98	13	23	6	0	2	11	9	22	.235	.318	.357	75	-4	1	0	0	1.000	-4	O-35/D-7	-0.7
Total	3	185	482	88	120	23	3	8	41	75	135	.249	.360	.359	88	-6	10	4	1	.991	-15	O-172/D-7	-2.2
■ **PHIL MASI** Masi, Philip Samuel b: 1/6/16, Chicago, Ill. d: 3/29/90, Mt.Prospect, Ill. BR/TR, 5'10", 180 lbs. Deb: 4/23/39																							
1939	Bos-N	46	114	14	29	7	2	1	14	9	15	.254	.315	.377	92	-2	0			.960	-3	C-42	-0.3
1940	Bos-N	63	138	11	27	4	1	1	14	14	14	.196	.270	.261	50	-10	0			.966	-1	C-52	-0.7
1941	Bos-N	87	180	17	40	8	2	3	18	16	13	.222	.286	.339	79	-6	4			.978	-7	C-83	-0.8
1942	Bos-N	57	87	14	19	3	1	0	9	12	4	.218	.313	.276	74	-3	2			.961	2	C-39/O-4	0.1
1943	Bos-N	80	238	27	65	9	1	2	28	27	20	.273	.347	.345	102	1	7			.991	-6	C-73	0.0
1944	Bos-N	89	251	33	69	13	5	3	23	31	20	.275	.355	.402	108	3	4			.977	-0	C-63,1-12/3-2	0.6
1945	Bos-N†	114	371	55	101	25	4	7	46	42	32	.272	.348	.418	112	5	9			.980	1	C-95/1-7	1.1
1946	Bos-N★	133	397	52	106	17	5	3	62	55	41	.267	.358	.358	102	2	5			.981	-5	*C-124	0.4
1947	Bos-N★	126	411	54	125	22	4	9	50	47	27	.304	.377	.443	120	12	7			**.989**	-6	*C-123	1.4
1948	*Bos-N★	113	376	43	95	19	0	5	44	35	26	.253	.318	.343	80	-10	2			.988	1	*C-109	-0.2
1949	Bos-N	37	105	13	22	2	0	0	6	14	10	.210	.303	.229	47	-8	1			.993	-2	C-37	-0.7
	Pit-N	48	135	16	37	6	1	2	13	17	16	.274	.355	.378	94	-1	1			.994	-2	C-44/1-2	0.0
	Yr	85	240	29	59	8	1	2	19	31	26	.246	.332	.313	74	-8	2			**.994**	-3	C-81/1-2	-0.7
1950	Chi-A	122	377	38	105	17	2	7	55	49	36	.279	.366	.390	96	-2	2	1	0	**.996**	-1	*C-114	0.2
1951	Chi-A	84	225	24	61	11	2	4	28	32	27	.271	.367	.391	107	3	1	0	0	.979	-0	C-78	0.6
1952	Chi-A	30	63	9	16	1	1	0	7	10	10	.254	.356	.302	84	-1	0	0	0	.956	0	C-25	0.0
Total	14	1229	3468	420	917	164	31	47	417	410	311	.264	.344	.370	97	-14	45	1		.983	-27	*C-1101/1-21,O-4,3	1.7

YEAR	TM/L	G	AB	R	H	2B	3B	HR	RBI	BB	SO	AVG	OBP	SLG	PRO+	BR/A	SB	CS	SBR	FA	FR	G/POS	TPR
■ HARRY MASKREY Maskrey, Harry H. b: 12/21/1861, Mercer, Pa. d: 8/17/30, Mercer, Pa. Deb: 9/21/1882 F																							
1882	Lou-a	1	4	0	0	0	0	0		0		.000	.000	.000	-99	-1				.000	-1	/O-1	-0.1
■ LEECH MASKREY Maskrey, Samuel Leech b: 2/11/1854, Mercer, Pa. d: 4/1/22, Mercer, Pa. BR/TR, 5'8", 150 lbs. Deb: 5/2/1882 F																							
1882	Lou-a	76	288	30	65	14	2	0		9		.226	.249	.288	85	-4				.902	-0	*O-76/2-1	-0.4
1883	Lou-a	96	361	50	73	13	8	1		10		.202	.224	.291	70	-11				.914	9	*O-96/S-1	-0.2
1884	Lou-a	105	412	48	103	13	4	0	36	17		.250	.281	.301	94	-2				.896	2	*O-103/3-3,S-1	-0.2
1885	Lou-a	109	423	54	97	8	11	1	46	19		.229	.269	.307	82	-9				.899	-3	*O-108/3-3	-1.3
1886	Lou-a	5	19	1	3	1	0	0	2	1		.158	.200	.211	27	-2	0			.800	-1	/O-5	-0.3
	Cin-a	27	98	7	19	3	1	0	10	5		.194	.240	.245	51	-6	4			.926	1	O-26/3-2	-0.5
	Yr	32	117	8	22	4	1	0	12	6		.188	.234	.239	47	-7	4			.915	-0	O-31/3-2	-0.8
Total	5	418	1601	190	360	52	26	2	94	61		.225	.256	.294	80	-33	4			.904	7	O-414/3-8,S-2,2-1	-2.9
■ CHARLIE MASON Mason, Charles E. b: 6/25/1853, New Orleans, La. d: 10/21/36, Philadelphia, Pa. BR/TR, 175 lbs. Deb: 4/26/1875 M																							
1875	Cen-n	12	47	5	11	0	0	0	3	0	1	.234	.234	.234	69	-1	0	0	0	.719	0	O-10/1-2,C-1	-0.1
	Was-n	8	33	2	3	0	0	0	1	0	3	.091	.091	.091	-38	-4	0	0	0	.909	2	/O-8,P-1	-0.2
	Yr	20	80	7	14	0	0	0	4	0	4	.175	.175	.175	23	-6	0	0	0	.796	2	O-18/1-2,C-1,P-1	-0.3
1883	Phi-a	1	2	0	1	0	0	0	1	0		.500	.500	.500	207	0				.000	-0	/O-1	0.0
■ DON MASON Mason, Donald Stetson b: 12/20/44, Boston, Mass. BL/TR, 5'11", 160 lbs. Deb: 4/14/66																							
1966	SF-N	42	25	8	3	0	0	1	1	0	2	.120	.120	.240	-3	-3	0	1	-1	.905	5	/2-9	0.1
1967	SF-N	4	3	0	0	0	0	0	0	0	0	.000	.000	.000	-99	-1	0	0	0	1.000	1	/2-2	0.0
1968	SF-N	10	19	3	3	0	0	0	1	1	4	.158	.200	.158	9	-2	1	1	-0	1.000	-1	/2-5,S-4,3-2	-0.4
1969	SF-N	104	250	43	57	4	2	0	13	36	29	.228	.325	.260	67	-10	1	5	-3	.956	10	2-51,3-21/S-7	0.1
1970	SF-N	46	36	4	5	0	0	0	1	5	7	.139	.244	.139	5	-5	0	0	0	.950	2	2-14	-0.3
1971	SD-N	113	344	43	73	12	1	2	11	27	35	.212	.270	.270	57	-20	6	4	-1	.965	-12	2-90/3-3	-2.7
1972	SD-N	9	11	1	2	0	0	0	0	1	1	.182	.250	.182	26	-1	0	0	0	.692	-0	/2-3	-0.1
1973	SD-N	8	8	0	0	0	0	0	0	0	2	.000	.000	.000	-99	-2	0	0	0	.750	1	/2-1	-0.2
Total	8	336	696	102	143	16	3	3	27	70	80	.205	.278	.250	52	-44	8	11	-4	.955	5	2-175/3-26,S-11	-3.5
■ JIM MASON Mason, James Percy b: 8/14/50, Mobile, Ala. BL/TR, 6'2", 190 lbs. Deb: 9/26/71																							
1971	Was-A	3	9	0	3	0	0	0	0	1	3	.333	.400	.333	116	0	0	0	0	.955	2	/S-3	0.3
1972	Tex-A	46	147	10	29	3	0	0	10	9	39	.197	.248	.218	41	-11	0	0	0	.948	-6	S-32,3-10	-1.4
1973	Tex-A	92	238	23	49	7	2	3	19	23	48	.206	.276	.290	62	-12	0	1	-1	.947	9	S-74,2-19/3-1	0.4
1974	NY-A	152	440	41	110	18	6	5	37	35	87	.250	.305	.352	90	-6	1	2	-1	.964	-4	*S-152	0.8
1975	NY-A	94	223	17	34	3	2	2	16	22	49	.152	.229	.211	25	-22	0	2	-1	.955	-10	S-93/2-1	-2.6
1976	*NY-A	93	217	17	39	7	1	1	14	9	37	.180	.212	.235	31	-19	0	0	0	.966	7	S-93	-0.4
1977	Tor-A	22	79	10	13	3	0	0	2	7	10	.165	.233	.203	20	-9	1	1	-0	.971	-5	S-22	-1.2
	Tex-A	36	55	9	12	3	0	1	7	6	10	.218	.295	.327	69	-2	0	0	0	.976	7	S-32/3-1,D-1	0.6
	Yr	58	134	19	25	6	0	1	9	13	20	.187	.259	.254	40	-11	1	1	-0	.973	3	S-54/3-1,D-1	-0.6
1978	Tex-A	55	105	10	20	4	0	0	3	5	17	.190	.227	.229	28	-10	0	0	0	.938	1	S-42,3-11/2-1,D-1	-0.7
1979	Mon-N	40	71	3	13	5	1	0	6	7	16	.183	.256	.282	47	-5	0	2	-1	.966	0	S-33/3-6	-0.4
Total	9	633	1584	140	322	53	12	12	114	124	316	.203	.262	.275	54	-96	2	8	-4	.959	2	S-576/3-29,2-21,D-2	-4.6
■ GORDON MASSA Massa, Gordon Richard "Moose" or "Duke" b: 9/2/35, Cincinnati, Ohio BL/TR, 6'3", 210 lbs. Deb: 9/24/57																							
1957	Chi-N	6	15	2	7	1	0	0	3	4	3	.467	.579	.533	205	3	0	0	0	1.000	-3	/C-6	0.0
1958	Chi-N	2	2	0	0	0	0	0	0	0	2	.000	.000	.000	-99	-1	0	0	0	.000	0	H	-0.1
Total	2	8	17	2	7	1	0	0	3	4	5	.412	.524	.471	172	2	0	0	0	1.000	-3	/C-6	-0.1
■ ROY MASSEY Massey, Roy Hardee "Red" b: 10/9/1890, Sevierville, Tenn. d: 6/23/54, Atlanta, Ga. BL/TR, 5'11", 170 lbs. Deb: 4/16/18																							
1918	Bos-N	66	203	20	59	6	2	0	18	23	20	.291	.363	.340	120	5	1			.954	-3	O-45/3-2,1-1,S-1	0.0
■ BILL MASSEY Massey, William Harry "Big Bill" b: 1/1871, Philadelphia, Pa. d: 10/9/40, Manila, Philippines BR/TR, 5'11", 168 lbs. Deb: 9/18/1894																							
1894	Cin-N	13	53	7	15	3	0	0	5	3	2	.283	.321	.340	57	-4	0			.991	-1	1-10/2-2,3-1	-0.4
■ MIKE MASSEY Massey, William Herbert b: 9/28/1893, Galveston, Tex. d: 10/17/71, Shreveport, La. BB/TR, 6', 195 lbs. Deb: 4/12/17																							
1917	Bos-N	31	91	12	18	0	0	0	2	15	15	.198	.318	.198	63	-3	2			.900	-8	2-25	-1.1
■ DAN MASTELLER Masteller, Dan Patrick b: 3/17/68, Toledo, Ohio BL/TL, 6', 185 lbs. Deb: 6/23/95																							
1995	Min-A	71	198	21	47	12	0	3	21	18	19	.237	.304	.343	68	-9	1	2	-1	.994	-4	1-48,O-22/D-8	-1.8
■ VICTOR MATA Mata, Victor Jose (Abreu) b: 6/17/61, Santiago, D.R. BR/TR, 6'1", 165 lbs. Deb: 7/22/84																							
1984	NY-A	30	70	8	23	5	0	1	6	0	12	.329	.338	.443	119	1	1	1	-0	.942	-6	O-28	-0.5
1985	NY-A	6	7	1	1	0	0	0	0	0	0	.143	.143	.143	-22	-1	0	0	0	1.000	-2	/O-3	-0.3
Total	2	36	77	9	24	5	0	1	6	0	12	.312	.321	.416	106	0	1	1	-0	.943	-7	/O-31	-0.8
■ TOM MATCHICK Matchick, John Thomas b: 9/7/43, Hazleton, Pa. BL/TR, 6', 175 lbs. Deb: 9/2/67																							
1967	Det-A	8	6	1	1	0	0	0	0	0	2	.167	.167	.167	-1	-1	0	0	0	1.000	0	/S-1	-0.1
1968	*Det-A	80	227	18	46	6	2	3	14	10	46	.203	.249	.286	60	-11	0	2	-1	.950	-14	S-59,2-13/1-6	-2.4
1969	Det-A	94	298	25	72	11	2	0	32	15	51	.242	.278	.292	57	-17	3	0	1	.972	-7	2-47,3-27/S-6,1-2	-2.0
1970	Bos-A	10	14	2	1	0	0	0	0	2	2	.071	.188	.071	-24	-2	0	1	-1	1.000	-1	/3-2,2-1,S-1	-0.4
	KC-A	55	158	11	31	3	2	0	11	5	23	.196	.226	.241	29	-15	0	0	0	.985	13	S-43,2-10/3-1	0.2
	Yr	65	172	13	32	3	2	0	11	7	25	.186	.222	.227	24	-18	0	1	-1	.985	12	S-44,2-11/3-3	-0.2
1971	Mil-A	42	114	6	25	1	0	1	7	7	23	.219	.264	.254	48	-8	3	2	-0	.979	1	3-41/2-1	-0.8
1972	Bal-A	3	9	0	2	0	0	0	0	0	1	.222	.222	.222	32	-1	0	1	-1	.857	-1	/3-3	-0.2
Total	6	292	826	63	178	21	6	4	64	39	148	.215	.255	.270	49	-55	6	6	-2	.967	-8	S-110/3-74,2-72,1-8	-5.7
■ MIKE MATHENY Matheny, Michael Scott b: 9/22/70, Columbus, Ohio BR/TR, 6'3", 205 lbs. Deb: 4/7/94																							
1994	Mil-A	28	53	3	12	3	0	1	2	3	13	.226	.293	.340	60	-3	0	1	-1	.989	3	C-27	0.0
1995	Mil-A	80	166	13	41	9	1	0	21	12	28	.247	.306	.313	58	-10	2	1	0	.986	5	C-80	-0.2
1996	Mil-A	106	313	31	64	15	2	8	46	14	80	.204	.245	.342	45	-27	3	2	-0	.985	-2	*C-104/D-1	-2.2
1997	Mil-A	123	320	29	78	16	1	4	32	17	68	.244	.297	.338	64	-17	0	1	-1	.993	18	*C-121/1-2	0.7
1998	Mil-N	108	320	24	76	13	0	6	27	11	63	.237	.278	.334	58	-20	1	0	0	.987	-7	*C-107	-2.0
Total	5	445	1172	100	271	56	4	19	128	57	252	.231	.279	.334	56	-78	6	5	-1	.989	17	C-439/1-2,D-1	-3.7
■ JOE MATHES Mathes, Joseph John b: 7/28/1891, Milwaukee, Wis. d: 12/21/78, St.Louis, Mo. BB/TR, 6'0.5", 180 lbs. Deb: 9/19/12																							
1912	Phi-A	4	14	0	2	0	0	0	0	0		.143	.200	.143	-2	-2	0			.889	-1	/3-4	-0.3
1914	StL-F	26	85	10	25	3	0	0	6	9	11	.294	.362	.329	85	-3	1			.938	-4	2-23	-0.7
1916	Bos-N	2	0	0	0	0	0	0	0	0	0	—	—	—	—	0	0			.000	-1	/2-2	-0.1
Total	3	32	99	10	27	3	0	0	6	9	11	.273	.339	.303	74	-4	1			.921	-6	/2-25,3-4	-1.1
■ EDDIE MATHEWS Mathews, Edwin Lee b: 10/13/31, Texarkana, Tex. BL/TR, 6'1", 200 lbs. Deb: 4/15/52 MCH																							
1952	Bos-N	145	528	80	128	23	5	25	58	59	115	.242	.320	.447	114	8	6	4	-1	.957	-10	*3-142	-0.5
1953	Mil-N★	157	579	110	175	31	8	**47**	135	99	83	.302	.406	.627	**175**	**64**	1	3	-2	.939	3	*3-157	5.8
1954	Mil-N	138	476	96	138	21	4	40	103	113	61	.290	.428	.603	**177**	57	10	3	1	.966	-2	*3-127,O-10	5.2
1955	Mil-N★	141	499	108	144	23	5	41	101	**109**	98	.289	.417	.601	175	56	3	4	-2	.952	-4	*3-137	4.9
1956	Mil-N☆	151	552	103	150	21	2	37	95	91	86	.272	.376	.518	146	36	6	0	2	.944	-12	*3-150	2.8
1957	*Mil-N★	148	572	109	167	28	9	32	94	90	79	.292	.388	.540	157	47	3	1	0	.964	-2	*3-147	4.8
1958	*Mil-N☆	149	546	97	137	18	1	31	77	85	85	.251	.354	.458	123	18	5	0	2	.955	5	*3-149	2.6
1959	Mil-N★	148	594	118	182	16	8	**46**	114	80	71	.306	.391	.593	172	59	2	1	0	.961	3	*3-148	6.2
1960	Mil-N★	153	548	108	152	19	7	39	124	111	113	.277	.401	.551	**170**	**55**	7	3	0	.950	-13	*3-153	4.2
1961	Mil-N★	152	572	103	175	23	6	32	91	**93**	95	.306	.405	.535	156	48	12	7	-1	.961	-6	*3-151	4.2

YEAR	TM/L	G	AB	R	H	2B	3B	HR	RBI	BB	SO	AVG	OBP	SLG	PRO+	BR/A	SB	CS	SBR	FA	FR	G/POS	TPR
1962	Mil-N★	152	536	106	142	25	6	29	90	**101**	90	.265	.383	.496	138	30	4	2	0	.964	2	*3-140/1-7	3.3
1963	Mil-N	158	547	82	144	27	4	23	84	**124**	119	.263	**.400**	.453	147	39	3	4	-2	**.968**	15	*3-121,O-42	5.3
1964	Mil-N	141	502	83	117	19	1	23	74	85	100	.233	.345	.412	112	9	2	2	-1	.962	2	*3-128/1-7	0.9
1965	Mil-N	156	546	77	137	23	0	32	95	73	110	.251	.342	.469	125	18	1	0	0	.956	9	*3-153	2.6
1966	Atl-N	134	452	72	113	21	4	16	53	63	82	.250	.342	.420	109	6	1	1	-0	.946	-2	*3-127	0.1
1967	Hou-N	101	328	39	78	13	2	10	38	48	65	.238	.337	.381	109	4	2	4	-2	.987	-4	1-79,3-24	-0.7
	Det-A	36	108	14	25	3	0	6	19	15	23	.231	.336	.426	121	3	0	0	0	.933	-2	3-21,1-13	0.0
1968	*Det-A	31	52	4	11	0	0	3	8	5	12	.212	.281	.385	97	-0	0	0	0	.974	-1	/1-6,3-6	-0.1
Total	17	2391	8537	1509	2315	354	72	512	1453	1444	1487	.271	.378	.509	145	559	68	39	-3	.956	-20	*3-2181,1-112/O-52	51.6

■ NELSON MATHEWS

Mathews, Nelson Elmer b: 7/21/41, Columbia, Ill. BR/TR, 6′4″, 195 lbs. Deb: 9/9/60 F

YEAR	TM/L	G	AB	R	H	2B	3B	HR	RBI	BB	SO	AVG	OBP	SLG	PRO+	BR/A	SB	CS	SBR	FA	FR	G/POS	TPR
1960	Chi-N	3	8	1	2	0	0	0	0	0	2	.250	.250	.250	38	-1	0	0	0	1.000	0	/O-2	-0.1
1961	Chi-N	3	9	0	1	0	0	0	0	0	2	.111	.111	.111	-40	-2	0	0	0	1.000	0	/O-2	-0.2
1962	Chi-N	15	49	5	15	2	0	2	13	5	4	.306	.393	.469	126	2	3	3	-1	.962	-2	O-14	-0.2
1963	Chi-N	61	155	12	24	3	2	4	10	16	48	.155	.234	.277	44	-11	3	4	-2	.979	-2	O-46	-1.9
1964	KC-A	157	573	58	137	27	5	14	60	43	143	.239	.293	.377	82	-14	2	3	-1	.968	9	*O-154	-1.4
1965	KC-A	67	184	17	39	7	7	2	15	24	49	.212	.303	.359	89	-3	0	2	-1	.981	-2	O-57	-0.9
Total	6	306	978	93	218	39	14	22	98	88	248	.223	.289	.359	78	-29	8	12	-5	.972	4	O-275	-4.7

■ BOBBY MATHEWS

Mathews, Robert T. b: 11/21/1851, Baltimore, Md. d: 4/17/1898, Baltimore, Md. BR/TR, 5′5.5″, 140 lbs. Deb: 5/4/1871 U

YEAR	TM/L	G	AB	R	H	2B	3B	HR	RBI	BB	SO	AVG	OBP	SLG	PRO+	BR/A	SB	CS	SBR	FA	FR	G/POS	TPR
1871	Kek-n	19	89	15	24	3	1	0	10	2	0	.270	.286	.326	74	-3	2	1	0	.840	-0	P-19	0.0
1872	Bal-n	50	223	36	50	1	0	0	21	3	2	.224	.235	.229	41	-16	1	1	-0	.780	-6	*P-49/O-8,3-3	-0.3
1873	Mut-n	52	223	40	43	3	3	0	13	10	3	.193	.227	.233	37	-16	1	1	-0	.759	-3	*P-52/O-5	-0.1
1874	Mut-n	65	298	46	72	6	1	0	30	3	4	.242	.249	.268	64	-12	2	0	1	.774	-2	*P-65/3-1,O-1	-0.1
1875	Mut-n	70	264	23	48	6	2	0	15	2	5	.182	.188	.220	39	-16	1	2	-1	.838	-6	*P-70/O-1	0.0
1876	NY-N	56	218	19	40	4	1	0	9	3	2	.183	.195	.211	40	-12				.810	-3	*P-56/O-1	0.0
1877	Cin-N	15	59	5	10	0	0	0	0	1	2	.169	.183	.169	13	-5				.862	-3	P-15/O-1,S-1	-0.2
1879	Pro-N	43	173	25	35	2	0	1	10	7	12	.202	.233	.231	55	-8				.956	-5	P-27,O-21/3-5	-0.9
1881	Pro-N	16	57	6	11	1	0	0	4	5	6	.193	.258	.211	50	-3				.810	-3	P-14/O-5	-0.2
	Bos-N	19	71	2	12	2	0	0	4	0	5	.169	.169	.197	15	-7				.818	-4	O-18/P-5	-0.9
	Yr	35	128	8	23	3	0	0	8	5	11	.180	.211	.203	32	-10				.811	-7	O-23,P-19	-1.1
1882	Bos-N	45	169	17	38	6	0	0	13	8	18	.225	.260	.260	67	-6				.867	-10	P-34,O-13/S-1	-0.6
1883	Phi-a	45	167	15	31	2	0	0	11	5		.186	.209	.198	29	-13				.874	-2	P-44/O-3	-0.1
1884	Phi-a	49	184	26	34	5	1	0		7		.185	.215	.223	40	-12				.775	-1	P-49/O-1	0.1
1885	Phi-a	48	179	22	30	3	0	0	12	10		.168	.212	.184	24	-16				.881	-0	P-48/O-1	0.0
1886	Phi-a	24	88	16	21	3	0	0	10	3		.239	.264	.273	67	-3	1			.843	-0	P-24/O-1	-0.1
1887	Phi-a	7	25	5	5	0	0	0	0	4		.200	.310	.200	44	-2	0			.889	0	/P-7	0.0
Total	5 n	256	1097	160	237	19	7	0	89	20	14	.216	.230	.246	49	-64	7	5	-1	.797	-18	P-255/O-15,3-4	-0.5
Total	10	367	1390	158	267	28	2	1	73	53	45	.192	.222	.217	42	-87	1			.845	-30	P-323/O-65,3-5,S-2	-2.9

■ JIMMY MATHISON

Mathison, James Michael Ignatius b: 11/11/1878, Baltimore, Md. d: 7/4/11, Baltimore, Md. TR , Deb: 8/29/02

YEAR	TM/L	G	AB	R	H	2B	3B	HR	RBI	BB	SO	AVG	OBP	SLG	PRO+	BR/A	SB	CS	SBR	FA	FR	G/POS	TPR
1902	Bal-A	29	91	12	24	2	1	0	7	9		.264	.368	.308	85	-1	2			.889	-3	3-28/S-1	-0.3

■ JOHN MATIAS

Matias, John Roy b: 8/15/44, Honolulu, Hawaii BL/TL, 5′11″, 170 lbs. Deb: 4/7/70

YEAR	TM/L	G	AB	R	H	2B	3B	HR	RBI	BB	SO	AVG	OBP	SLG	PRO+	BR/A	SB	CS	SBR	FA	FR	G/POS	TPR
1970	Chi-A	58	117	7	22	2	0	2	6	3	22	.188	.215	.256	28	-11	1	0	0	.941	-4	O-22,1-18	-1.8

■ FRANCISCO MATOS

Matos, Francisco Aguirre (Mancebo) b: 7/23/69, Santo Domingo, D.R. BR/TR, 6′1″, 160 lbs. Deb: 7/17/94

YEAR	TM/L	G	AB	R	H	2B	3B	HR	RBI	BB	SO	AVG	OBP	SLG	PRO+	BR/A	SB	CS	SBR	FA	FR	G/POS	TPR
1994	Oak-A	14	28	1	7	1	0	0	2	1	2	.250	.276	.286	49	-2	1	0	0	.925	1	2-12/D-2	-0.1

■ C. V. MATTESON

Matteson, Clifford Virgil b: 11/1861, Ohio d: 12/18/31, Seville, Ohio Deb: 6/13/1884

YEAR	TM/L	G	AB	R	H	2B	3B	HR	RBI	BB	SO	AVG	OBP	SLG	PRO+	BR/A	SB	CS	SBR	FA	FR	G/POS	TPR
1884	StL-U	1	4	0	0	0	0	0		0		.000	.000	.000	-97	-1				.000	-1	/O-1,P-1	-0.1

■ GARY MATTHEWS

Matthews, Gary Nathaniel b: 7/5/50, San Fernando, Cal. BR/TR, 6′3″, 190 lbs. Deb: 9/6/72 C

YEAR	TM/L	G	AB	R	H	2B	3B	HR	RBI	BB	SO	AVG	OBP	SLG	PRO+	BR/A	SB	CS	SBR	FA	FR	G/POS	TPR
1972	SF-N	20	62	11	18	1	1	4	14	7	13	.290	.362	.532	149	4	0	1	-1	.971	-1	O-19	0.2
1973	SF-N	148	540	74	162	22	10	12	58	58	83	.300	.369	.444	119	15	17	5	2	.983	6	*O-145	1.7
1974	SF-N	154	561	87	161	27	6	16	82	70	69	.287	.369	.442	120	16	11	9	-2	.970	5	*O-151	1.2
1975	SF-N	116	425	67	119	22	3	12	58	65	53	.280	.378	.431	119	12	13	4	2	.967	8	*O-113	1.8
1976	SF-N	156	587	79	164	28	4	20	84	75	94	.279	.362	.443	124	19	12	5	1	.975	-3	*O-156	1.1
1977	Atl-N	148	555	89	157	25	5	17	64	67	90	.283	.362	.438	101	1	22	8	2	.965	8	*O-145	0.6
1978	Atl-N	129	474	75	135	20	5	18	62	61	92	.285	.369	.462	118	11	8	7	-2	.969	2	*O-127	0.6
1979	Atl-N★	156	631	97	192	34	5	27	90	60	75	.304	.365	.502	125	21	18	6	2	.974	1	*O-156	1.7
1980	Atl-N	155	571	79	159	17	3	19	75	42	93	.278	.328	.419	104	2	11	3	2	.960	-3	*O-143	-0.6
1981	*Phi-N	101	359	62	108	21	3	9	67	59	42	.301	.404	.451	136	19	15	2	3	.963	1	*O-100	2.2
1982	Phi-N	162	616	89	173	31	1	19	83	66	87	.281	.352	.427	114	12	21	4	4	.966	3	*O-162	1.5
1983	*Phi-N	132	446	66	115	18	2	10	50	69	81	.258	.357	.374	104	4	13	9	-2	.974	-1	*O-122	-0.3
1984	*Chi-N	147	491	101	143	21	2	14	82	**103**	97	.291	**.417**	.428	126	22	17	8	0	.955	-4	*O-145	1.4
1985	Chi-N	97	298	45	70	12	0	13	40	59	64	.235	.365	.406	104	3	2	0	1	.977	-2	O-85	-0.1
1986	Chi-N	123	370	49	96	16	1	21	46	60	59	.259	.363	.478	121	11	3	2	-0	.940	-8	*O-105	-0.1
1987	Chi-N	44	42	3	11	3	0	0	8	4	11	.262	.326	.333	72	-2	0	0	0	1.000	-0	/O-2	-0.2
	Sea-A	45	119	10	28	1	0	3	15	15	22	.235	.321	.319	67	-5	0	1	-1	.000	0	D-39	-0.7
Total	16	2033	7147	1083	2011	319	51	234	978	940	1125	.281	.367	.439	116	164	183	74	11	.968	12	*O-1876/D-39	12.0

■ BOB MATTHEWS

Matthews, Robert b: Camden, N.J. Deb: 9/25/1891

YEAR	TM/L	G	AB	R	H	2B	3B	HR	RBI	BB	SO	AVG	OBP	SLG	PRO+	BR/A	SB	CS	SBR	FA	FR	G/POS	TPR
1891	Phi-a	1	3	1	1	0	0	0	0	0	1	.333	.600	.333	163	1	0			.000	-0	/O-1	0.0

■ WID MATTHEWS

Matthews, Wid Curry "Matty" b: 10/20/1896, Raleigh, Ill d: 10/5/65, Hollywood, Cal. BL/TL, 5′8.5″, 155 lbs. Deb: 4/18/23

YEAR	TM/L	G	AB	R	H	2B	3B	HR	RBI	BB	SO	AVG	OBP	SLG	PRO+	BR/A	SB	CS	SBR	FA	FR	G/POS	TPR
1923	Phi-A	129	485	52	133	11	6	1	25	50	27	.274	.343	.328	76	-16	16	16	-5	.947	-8	*O-127	-3.7
1924	Was-A	53	169	25	51	10	4	0	13	11	4	.302	.355	.408	100	-0	3	8	-4	.985	5	O-44	-0.2
1925	Was-A	10	9	2	4	0	0	0	1	0	1	.444	.444	.444	129	0	0	0	0	1.000	-0	/O-1	0.0
Total	3	192	663	79	188	21	10	1	39	61	32	.284	.348	.350	83	-16	19	24	-9	.957	-4	O-172	-3.9

■ STEVE MATTHIAS

Matthias, Stephen J. b: 1860, Mitchellville, Md. BR/TR, 5′8″, 160 lbs. Deb: 4/20/1884

YEAR	TM/L	G	AB	R	H	2B	3B	HR	RBI	BB	SO	AVG	OBP	SLG	PRO+	BR/A	SB	CS	SBR	FA	FR	G/POS	TPR
1884	CP-U	37	142	24	39	7	1	0		5		.275	.299	.338	93	-5				.840	2	S-36/O-2	-0.2

■ BOBBY MATTICK

Mattick, Robert James b: 12/5/15, Sioux City, Iowa BR/TR, 5′11″, 178 lbs. Deb: 5/5/38 FM

YEAR	TM/L	G	AB	R	H	2B	3B	HR	RBI	BB	SO	AVG	OBP	SLG	PRO+	BR/A	SB	CS	SBR	FA	FR	G/POS	TPR
1938	Chi-N	1	1	0	1	0	0	0	1	0	0	1.000	1.000	1.000	439	0	0			.000	0	/S-1	0.0
1939	Chi-N	51	178	16	51	12	1	0	23	6	19	.287	.314	.365	80	-5	1			.927	7	S-48	0.6
1940	Chi-N	128	441	30	96	15	0	0	33	19	33	.218	.250	.252	39	-36	5			.946	10	*S-126/3-1	-1.6
1941	Cin-N	20	60	8	11	3	0	0	7	8	7	.183	.279	.233	45	-4	1			.982	-2	S-12/3-5,2-1	-0.5
1942	Cin-N	6	10	0	2	1	0	0	0	0	1	.200	.200	.300	45	-1	0			1.000	1	/S-3	0.1
Total	5	206	690	54	161	31	1	0	64	33	60	.233	.269	.281	52	-46	7			.943	17	S-190/3-6,2-1	-1.4

■ WALLY MATTICK

Mattick, Walter Joseph "Chink" b: 3/12/1887, St.Louis, Mo. d: 11/5/68, Los Altos, Cal. BR/TR, 5′10″, 180 lbs. Deb: 4/11/12 F

YEAR	TM/L	G	AB	R	H	2B	3B	HR	RBI	BB	SO	AVG	OBP	SLG	PRO+	BR/A	SB	CS	SBR	FA	FR	G/POS	TPR
1912	Chi-A	90	285	45	74	7	9	1	35	27		.260	.334	.358	101	0	15			.982	-3	O-79	-0.7
1913	Chi-A	71	207	15	39	8	1	0	11	18	16	.188	.253	.237	44	-15	3			.977	2	O-64	-1.7
1918	StL-N	8	14	0	2	0	0	0	1	2	3	.143	.333	.143	49	-1	0			1.000	0	/O-3	0.0
Total	3	169	506	60	115	15	10	1	47	47	19	.227	.302	.302	77	-15	18			.980	-1	O-146	-2.4

■ MIKE MATTIMORE

Mattimore, Michael Joseph b: 1859, Renovo, Pa. d: 4/28/31, Butte, Mont. BL/TL, 5′8.5″, 160 lbs. Deb: 5/3/1887

YEAR	TM/L	G	AB	R	H	2B	3B	HR	RBI	BB	SO	AVG	OBP	SLG	PRO+	BR/A	SB	CS	SBR	FA	FR	G/POS	TPR
1887	NY-N	8	32	5	8	1	0	0	4	0	6	.250	.250	.281	50	-2	1			.889	-1	/P-7,O-2	0.0
1888	Phi-a	41	142	22	38	6	5	0	12	12		.268	.333	.380	129	5	16			.915	5	P-26,O-16	0.2
1889	Phi-a	23	73	10	17	1	2	1	8	9	7	.233	.333	.342	94	-0	6			.944	-3	O-12/1-7,P-5	-0.3

YEAR	TM/L	G	AB	R	H	2B	3B	HR	RBI	BB	SO	AVG	OBP	SLG	PRO+	BR/A	SB	CS	SBR	FA	FR	G/POS	TPR
	KC-a	19	75	6	12	1	1	0	5	3	16	.160	.192	.200	11	-9	0			.844	-2	O-19/P-1	-0.9
	Yr	42	148	16	29	2	3	1	13	12	23	.196	.265	.270	52	-10	6			.873	-5	O-31/1-7,P-6	-1.2
1890	Bro-a	33	129	14	17	1	1	0	7	16		.132	.238	.155	17	-13	11			.887	-6	P-19,O-14	-0.9
Total	4	124	451	57	92	10	9	1	36	40	29	.204	.278	.273	64	-20	34			.853	-7	/O-63,P-58,1-7	-1.9

■ DON MATTINGLY
Mattingly, Donald Arthur b: 4/20/61, Evansville, Ind. BL/TL, 6', 175 lbs. Deb: 9/8/82

YEAR	TM/L	G	AB	R	H	2B	3B	HR	RBI	BB	SO	AVG	OBP	SLG	PRO+	BR/A	SB	CS	SBR	FA	FR	G/POS	TPR
1982	NY-A	7	12	0	2	0	0	0	1	0	1	.167	.167	.167	-8	-2	0	0	0	1.000	1	/O-6,1-1	-0.1
1983	NY-A	91	279	34	79	15	4	4	32	21	31	.283	.336	.409	108	3	0	0	0	.974	-10	O-48,1-42/2-1	-1.1
1984	NY-A★	153	603	91	**207**	**44**	2	23	110	41	33	**.343**	.386	.537	**159**	46	1	1	-0	**.996**	13	*1-133,O-19	4.9
1985	NY-A★	159	652	107	211	**48**	3	35	**145**	56	41	.324	.379	.567	159	51	2	2	-1	**.995**	-11	*1-159	2.8
1986	NY-A★	162	677	117	**238**	**53**	2	31	113	53	35	.352	.399	**.573**	**163**	**57**	0	0	0	**.996**	-7	*1-160/3-3,D-1	3.7
1987	NY-A★	141	569	93	186	38	2	30	115	51	38	.327	.383	.559	147	38	1	4	-2	**.996**	-4	*1-140/D-1	2.0
1988	NY-A★	144	599	94	186	37	0	18	88	41	29	.311	.358	.462	129	22	1	0	0	.993	-4	*1-143/O-1,D-1	0.6
1989	NY-A★	158	631	79	191	37	2	23	113	51	30	.303	.356	.477	134	27	3	0	1	.995	-5	*1-145,D-17/O-1	1.1
1990	NY-A	102	394	40	101	16	0	5	42	28	20	.256	.311	.335	80	-10	1	0	0	.997	6	1-89,D-13/O-1	-1.2
1991	NY-A	152	587	64	169	35	0	9	68	46	42	.288	.344	.394	103	3	2	0	1	.996	-4	*1-127,D-22	-1.0
1992	NY-A	157	640	89	184	40	0	14	86	39	43	.287	.329	.416	108	5	3	0	1	**.997**	7	*1-143,D-15	0.3
1993	NY-A	134	530	78	154	27	2	17	86	61	42	.291	.366	.445	121	16	0	0	0	**.998**	-2	*1-130/D-5	0.3
1994	NY-A	97	372	62	113	20	1	6	51	60	24	.304	.400	.411	114	10	0	0	0	**.998**	3	1-97	0.4
1995	*NY-A	128	458	59	132	32	2	7	49	40	35	.288	.347	.413	98	-2	0	2	-1	.994	-1	*1-125/D-1	-1.4
Total	14	1785	7003	1007	2153	442	20	222	1099	588	444	.307	.363	.471	128	264	14	9	-1	.996	-19	*1-1634/D-76,O32	11.3

■ RALPH MATTIS
Mattis, Ralph "Matty" b: 8/24/1890, Roxborough, Pa. d: 9/13/60, Williamsport, Pa. BR/TR, 5'11", 172 lbs. Deb: 4/22/14

YEAR	TM/L	G	AB	R	H	2B	3B	HR	RBI	BB	SO	AVG	OBP	SLG	PRO+	BR/A	SB	CS	SBR	FA	FR	G/POS	TPR
1914	Pit-F	36	85	14	21	4	1	0	8	9	11	.247	.326	.318	77	-4	2			.938	2	O-24	-0.4

■ CLOY MATTOX
Mattox, Cloy Mitchell "Monk" b: 11/24/02, Leesville, Va. d: 8/3/85, Danville, Va. BL/TR, 5'8", 168 lbs. Deb: 9/1/29 F

YEAR	TM/L	G	AB	R	H	2B	3B	HR	RBI	BB	SO	AVG	OBP	SLG	PRO+	BR/A	SB	CS	SBR	FA	FR	G/POS	TPR
1929	Phi-A	3	6	0	1	0	0	0	0	1	1	.167	.286	.167	19	-1	0	0	0	.875	-0	/C-3	-0.1

■ JIM MATTOX
Mattox, James Powell b: 12/17/1896, Leesville, Va. d: 10/12/73, Myrtle Beach, S.C. BL/TR, 5'9.5", 168 lbs. Deb: 4/30/22 F

YEAR	TM/L	G	AB	R	H	2B	3B	HR	RBI	BB	SO	AVG	OBP	SLG	PRO+	BR/A	SB	CS	SBR	FA	FR	G/POS	TPR
1922	Pit-N	29	51	11	15	1	1	0	3	1	3	.294	.308	.353	69	-2	0	0	0	.984	1	C-21	-0.1
1923	Pit-N	22	32	4	6	1	1	0	1	0	5	.188	.235	.281	35	-3	0	0	0	.960	1	/C-8	-0.2
Total	2	51	83	15	21	2	2	0	4	1	8	.253	.279	.325	56	-5	0	0	0	.978	2	/C-29	-0.3

■ LEN MATUSZEK
Matuszek, Leonard James b: 9/27/54, Toledo, Ohio BL/TR, 6'2", 195 lbs. Deb: 9/3/81

YEAR	TM/L	G	AB	R	H	2B	3B	HR	RBI	BB	SO	AVG	OBP	SLG	PRO+	BR/A	SB	CS	SBR	FA	FR	G/POS	TPR
1981	Phi-N	13	11	1	3	1	0	0	1	3	1	.273	.429	.364	121	1	0	1	-1	1.000	2	/1-1,3-1	0.1
1982	Phi-N	25	39	1	3	1	0	0	3	1	10	.077	.122	.103	-36	-7	0	1	-1	.750	-2	/3-8,1-3	-1.1
1983	Phi-N	28	80	12	22	6	1	4	16	4	14	.275	.310	.525	129	2	0	1	-1	1.000	1	1-21	0.0
1984	Phi-N	101	262	40	65	17	1	12	43	39	54	.248	.354	.458	125	9	4	3	-1	.990	4	1-81/O-1	0.8
1985	Tor-A	62	151	23	32	6	2	2	15	11	24	.212	.265	.318	57	-9	2	1	0	1.000	0	D-54/1-5	-1.0
	*LA-N	43	63	10	14	2	1	3	13	8	14	.222	.319	.429	111	1	0	1	-1	1.000	-1	O-17,1-10/3-1	-0.2
1986	LA-N	91	199	26	52	7	0	9	28	21	47	.261	.335	.432	118	4	2	2	-1	1.000	-4	O-37,1-31	-0.3
1987	LA-N	16	15	0	1	0	0	0	0	1	4	.067	.125	.067	-49	-3	0	0	0	1.000	0	/1-3	-0.3
Total	7	379	820	113	192	40	5	30	119	88	168	.234	.314	.405	99	-2	8	10	-4	.990	-2	1-155/O-55,D-54,3	-2.0

■ GENE MAUCH
Mauch, Gene William "Skip" b: 11/18/25, Salina, Kan. BR/TR, 5'10", 165 lbs. Deb: 4/18/44 M

YEAR	TM/L	G	AB	R	H	2B	3B	HR	RBI	BB	SO	AVG	OBP	SLG	PRO+	BR/A	SB	CS	SBR	FA	FR	G/POS	TPR
1944	Bro-N	5	15	2	2	1	0	0	2	2	3	.133	.235	.200	24	-2	0			1.000	-2	/S-5	-0.3
1947	Pit-N	16	30	8	9	0	0	0	1	7	6	.300	.432	.300	95	0	0			.963	-2	/2-6,S-4	-0.1
1948	Bro-N	12	13	1	2	0	0	0	0	1	4	.154	.214	.154	1	-2	0			.950	1	/2-7,S-1	0.0
	Chi-N	53	138	18	28	3	2	1	7	26	10	.203	.329	.275	68	-5	1			.925	-6	2-26,S-19	-0.9
	Yr	65	151	19	30	3	2	1	7	27	14	.199	.320	.265	62	-7	1			.929	-5	2-33,S-20	-0.9
1949	Chi-N	72	150	15	37	6	2	1	7	21	15	.247	.339	.333	83	-3	3			.971	12	2-25,S-19/3-7	1.0
1950	Bos-N	48	121	17	28	5	0	1	15	14	9	.231	.316	.298	67	-6	1			.968	-1	2-28/3-7,S-5	-0.5
1951	Bos-N	19	20	5	2	0	0	0	1	7	4	.100	.333	.100	24	-2	0	0	0	1.000	-0	S-10/3-3,2-2	-0.2
1952	StL-N	7	3	0	0	0	0	0	0	1	2	.000	.250	.000	-25	-0	0	0	0	.500	0	/S-2	-0.1
1956	Bos-A	7	25	4	8	0	0	0	1	3	3	.320	.393	.320	80	-1	0	0	0	.935	-2	/2-6	-0.2
1957	Bos-A	65	222	23	60	10	3	2	28	22	26	.270	.339	.369	88	-3	1	0	0	.962	-10	2-58	-0.8
Total	9	304	737	93	176	25	7	5	62	104	82	.239	.335	.312	75	-23	6	0		.958	-10	2-158/S-65,3-17	-2.1

■ AL MAUL
Maul, Albert Joseph "Smiling Al" b: 10/9/1865, Philadelphia, Pa. d: 5/3/58, Philadelphia, Pa. BR/TR, 6', 175 lbs. Deb: 6/20/1884

YEAR	TM/L	G	AB	R	H	2B	3B	HR	RBI	BB	SO	AVG	OBP	SLG	PRO+	BR/A	SB	CS	SBR	FA	FR	G/POS	TPR
1884	Phi-U	1	4	0	0	0	0	0		0		.000	.000	.000	-99	-1				1.000	-0	/P-1	0.0
1887	Phi-N	16	56	15	17	2	2	1	4	15	10	.304	.451	.464	146	4	5			.897	2	/O-8,P-7,1-2	0.3
1888	Pit-N	74	259	21	54	9	4	0	31	21	45	.208	.276	.274	82	-4	9			.975	-1	1-38,O-34/P-3	-0.9
1889	Pit-N	68	257	37	71	6	6	4	44	29	41	.276	.356	.393	121	8	18			.946	11	O-64/P-6	1.3
1890	Pit-P	45	162	31	42	6	2	0	21	22	12	.259	.348	.321	86	-2	5			.904	4	P-30,O-15/S-1	-0.1
1891	Pit-N	47	149	15	28	2	4	0	14	20	28	.188	.284	.255	59	-7	4			.877	-2	O-40/P-8	-0.9
1893	Was-N	44	134	10	34	8	4	0	12	33	14	.254	.405	.373	110	4	1			.889	1	P-37/O-7	0.1
1894	Was-N	41	124	23	30	3	3	2	20	14	11	.242	.352	.363	75	-5	1			.877	2	P-28,O-12	-0.1
1895	Was-N	22	72	9	18	5	2	0	16	6	7	.250	.308	.375	76	-3	0			.933	1	P-16/O-4	-0.1
1896	Was-N	8	28	6	8	1	1	0	5	3	2	.286	.355	.393	97	-0	0			.923	-1	/P-8	0.0
1897	Was-N	1	1	0	0	0	0	0	0	0		.000	.000	.000	-99	-0	0			1.000	0	/P-1	0.0
	Bal-N	2	3	0	1	0	0	0	0	0		.333	.333	.333	76	-0	0			1.000	-0	/P-2	0.0
	Yr	3	4	0	1	0	0	0	0	0		.250	.250	.250	32	-0	0			1.000	-0	/P-3	0.0
1898	Bal-N	29	93	21	19	3	2	0	10	16		.204	.333	.280	75	-3	1			.978	-5	P-28/O-1	0.0
1899	Bro-N	4	11	2	3	0	0	0	0	1		.273	.333	.273	66	-0	0			.900	0	/P-4	0.0
1900	Phi-N	5	15	2	3	0	0	0	1	2		.200	.294	.200	38	-1	0			.917	0	/P-5	0.0
1901	NY-N	3	8	1	3	0	0	0	1	0		.375	.375	.375	122	0	0			1.000	0	/P-3	0.0
Total	15	410	1376	193	331	45	30	7	179	182	170	.241	.336	.332	91	-12	44			.910	13	P-187,O-185/1-40,S	-0.4

■ MARK MAULDIN
Mauldin, Marshall Reese b: 11/5/14, Atlanta, Ga. d: 9/2/90, Union City, Ga. BR/TR, 5'11", 170 lbs. Deb: 9/10/34

YEAR	TM/L	G	AB	R	H	2B	3B	HR	RBI	BB	SO	AVG	OBP	SLG	PRO+	BR/A	SB	CS	SBR	FA	FR	G/POS	TPR
1934	Chi-A	10	38	3	10	2	0	1	3	0	3	.263	.263	.395	66	-2	0	0	0	.906	-0	3-10	-0.2

■ ROB MAURER
Maurer, Robert John b: 1/7/67, Evansville, Ind. BL/TL, 6'3", 210 lbs. Deb: 9/8/91

YEAR	TM/L	G	AB	R	H	2B	3B	HR	RBI	BB	SO	AVG	OBP	SLG	PRO+	BR/A	SB	CS	SBR	FA	FR	G/POS	TPR
1991	Tex-A	13	16	0	1	1	0	0	2	2	6	.063	.211	.125	-5	-2	0	0	0	1.000	1	/1-4,D-2	-0.1
1992	Tex-A	8	9	1	2	0	0	0	1	1	2	.222	.300	.222	50	-1	0	0	0	1.000	0	/1-3,D-1	0.0
Total	2	21	25	1	3	1	0	0	3	3	8	.120	.241	.160	14	-3	0	0	0	1.000	1	/1-7,D-3	-0.1

■ CARMEN MAURO
Mauro, Carmen Louis b: 11/10/26, St.Paul, Minn. BL/TR, 6', 167 lbs. Deb: 10/1/48

YEAR	TM/L	G	AB	R	H	2B	3B	HR	RBI	BB	SO	AVG	OBP	SLG	PRO+	BR/A	SB	CS	SBR	FA	FR	G/POS	TPR
1948	Chi-N	3	5	2	1	0	0	1	1	2	0	.200	.429	.800	235	1	0			1.000	1	/O-2	0.1
1950	Chi-N	62	185	19	42	4	3	1	10	13	31	.227	.285	.297	54	-12	3			.946	-3	O-49	-1.8
1951	Chi-N	13	29	3	5	1	0	0	3	2	6	.172	.250	.207	24	-3	0	0	0	.900	1	/O-6	-0.3
1953	Bro-N	8	9	1	0	0	0	0	0	0	4	.000	.000	.000	-98	-3	0	0	0	1.000	-0	/O-1	-0.3
	Was-A	17	23	1	4	0	1	0	2	1	3	.174	.208	.261	27	-2	0	0	0	1.000	-0	/O-6	-0.3
	Phi-A	64	165	14	44	4	4	0	17	19	21	.267	.342	.339	81	-4	3	4	-2	.969	-1	O-49/3-1	-0.8
	Yr	81	188	15	48	4	5	0	19	20	24	.255	.327	.330	76	-6	3	4	-2	.971	-1	O-55/3-1	-1.1
Total	4	167	416	40	96	9	8	2	33	37	65	.231	.298	.305	61	-23	6	4		.958	-4	O-113/3-1	-3.4

■ BOB MAVIS
Mavis, Robert Henry b: 4/8/18, Milwaukee, Wis. BL/TR, 5'7", 160 lbs. Deb: 9/17/49

YEAR	TM/L	G	AB	R	H	2B	3B	HR	RBI	BB	SO	AVG	OBP	SLG	PRO+	BR/A	SB	CS	SBR	FA	FR	G/POS	TPR
1949	Det-A	1	0	0	0	0	0	0	0	0	0	—	—	—	—	0	0	0	0	.000	0	R	0.0

■ DAL MAXVILL
Maxvill, Charles Dallan b: 2/18/39, Granite City, Ill. BR/TR, 5'11", 160 lbs. Deb: 6/10/62 C

YEAR	TM/L	G	AB	R	H	2B	3B	HR	RBI	BB	SO	AVG	OBP	SLG	PRO+	BR/A	SB	CS	SBR	FA	FR	G/POS	TPR
1962	StL-N	79	189	20	42	3	1	1	18	17	39	.222	.290	.265	46	-14	1	2	-1	.962	-2	S-76/3-1	-1.2
1963	StL-N	53	51	12	12	2	0	0	3	6	11	.235	.316	.275	66	-2	0	0	0	.974	7	S-24/2-9,3-3	0.6

YEAR	TM/L	G	AB	R	H	2B	3B	HR	RBI	BB	SO	AVG	OBP	SLG	PRO+	BR/A	SB	CS	SBR	FA	FR	G/POS	TPR
1964	*StL-N	37	26	4	6	0	0	0	4	0	7	.231	.231	.231	28	-2	1	0	0	.972	6	2-15,S-13/3-1,O-1	0.4
1965	StL-N	68	89	10	12	2	2	0	10	7	15	.135	.206	.202	14	-10	0	0	0	.993	13	2-49,S-12	0.5
1966	StL-N	134	394	25	96	14	3	0	24	37	61	.244	.312	.294	69	-15	3	0	1	.967	24	*S-128/2-5,O-1	2.1
1967	*StL-N	152	476	37	108	14	4	1	41	48	66	.227	.299	.279	67	-19	0	2	-1	.974	3	*S-148/2-7	-0.4
1968	*StL-N	151	459	51	116	8	5	1	24	52	71	.253	.330	.298	91	-3	0	2	-1	.969	-9	*S-151	0.2
1969	StL-N	132	372	27	65	10	2	2	32	44	52	.175	.264	.228	39	-30	1	1	-0	.969	21	*S-131	0.4
1970	StL-N	152	399	35	80	5	2	0	28	51	56	.201	.291	.223	39	-33	0	0	0	**.982**	**38**	*S-136,2-22	1.9
1971	StL-N	142	356	31	80	10	1	0	24	43	45	.225	.310	.258	60	-17	1	2	-1	.979	**29**	*S-140	2.6
1972	StL-N	105	276	22	61	6	1	1	23	31	47	.221	.300	.261	61	-13	0	1	-1	.980	9	S-95,2-11	0.7
	*Oak-A	27	36	2	9	1	0	0	1	1	11	.250	.270	.278	67	-2	0	1	-1	.983	4	2-24/S-4	0.3
1973	Oak-A	29	19	0	4	0	0	0	1	1	3	.211	.250	.211	33	-2	0	0	0	.966	4	S-18,2-11/3-1	0.2
	Pit-N	74	217	19	41	4	3	0	17	22	40	.189	.264	.235	40	-17	0	0	0	.971	4	S-74	-0.5
1974	Pit-N	8	22	3	4	0	0	0	0	2	4	.182	.250	.182	23	-2	0	0	0	.946	1	/S-8	-0.1
	*Oak-A	60	52	3	10	0	0	0	2	8	10	.192	.300	.192	47	-3	0	0	0	1.000	9	2-30,S-29/3-1	0.8
1975	Oak-A	20	10	1	2	0	0	0	0	0	0	.200	.200	.200	14	-1	0	0	0	.955	2	S-20/2-2	0.2
Total	14	1423	3443	302	748	79	24	6	252	370	538	.217	.295	.259	57	-188	7	11	-5	.973	160	*S-1207,2-185/3-7,O	8.7

■ CHARLIE MAXWELL

Maxwell, Charles Richard "Smokey" b: 4/8/27, Lawton, Mich. BL/TL, 5'11", 185 lbs. Deb: 9/20/50

YEAR	TM/L	G	AB	R	H	2B	3B	HR	RBI	BB	SO	AVG	OBP	SLG	PRO+	BR/A	SB	CS	SBR	FA	FR	G/POS	TPR
1950	Bos-A	3	8	1	0	0	0	0	0	1	3	.000	.111	.000	-63	-2	0	0	0	1.000	1	/O-2	-0.1
1951	Bos-A	49	80	8	15	1	0	3	12	9	18	.188	.270	.313	52	-6	0	1	-1	.926	-1	O-13	-0.8
1952	Bos-A	8	15	0	1	1	0	0	0	3	11	.067	.222	.133	0	-2	0	0	0	.966	2	/1-3,O-3	-0.1
1954	Bos-A	74	104	9	26	4	1	0	5	12	21	.250	.328	.308	67	-4	3	0	1	1.000	-7	O-27	-1.2
1955	Bal-A	4	4	0	0	0	0	0	0	0	1	.000	.000	.000	-99	-1	0	0	0	.000	0	H	-0.1
	Det-A	55	109	19	29	7	1	7	18	8	20	.266	.328	.541	134	4	0	0	0	.967	2	O-26/1-2	0.5
	Yr	59	113	19	29	7	1	7	18	8	21	.257	.317	.522	126	3	0	0	0	.967	2	O-26/1-2	0.4
1956	Det-A☆	141	500	96	163	14	3	28	87	79	74	.326	.420	.534	150	37	1	1	-0	.987	13	*O-136	4.2
1957	Det-A★	138	492	75	136	23	3	24	82	76	84	.276	.379	.482	130	21	3	2	-0	**.997**	14	*O-137	2.8
1958	Det-A	131	397	56	108	14	4	13	65	64	54	.272	.373	.426	111	7	6	1	1	.986	-1	*O-114,1-14	0.1
1959	Det-A	145	518	81	130	12	2	31	95	81	91	.251	.359	.461	117	13	0	2	-1	.986	10	*O-136	1.5
1960	Det-A	134	482	70	114	16	5	24	81	58	75	.237	.326	.440	102	1	5	0	2	**.996**	8	*O-120	0.4
1961	Det-A	79	131	11	30	4	2	5	18	20	24	.229	.336	.405	94	-1	0	0	0	.965	2	O-25	-0.1
1962	Det-A	30	67	5	13	2	0	1	9	8	10	.194	.280	.269	47	-5	0	0	0	.966	-1	O-15/1-1	-0.6
	Chi-A	69	206	30	61	8	3	9	43	34	32	.296	.396	.495	139	12	0	0	0	.990	-1	O-56/1-6	0.8
	Yr	99	273	35	74	10	3	10	52	42	42	.271	.368	.440	115	7	0	0	0	.985	-1	O-71/1-7	0.2
1963	Chi-A	71	130	17	30	4	2	3	17	31	27	.231	.379	.362	111	3	0	0	0	1.000	-4	O-24,1-17	-0.2
1964	Chi-A	2	2	0	0	0	0	0	0	0	0	.000	.000	.000	-99	-1	0	0	0	.000	0	H	-0.1
Total	14	1133	3245	478	856	110	26	148	532	484	545	.264	.363	.451	116	77	18	7	1	.988	37	O-834/1-43	7.0

■ JASON MAXWELL

Maxwell, Jason Ramond b: 3/21/72, Lewisburg, Tenn. BR/TR, 6', 185 lbs. Deb: 9/1/98

YEAR	TM/L	G	AB	R	H	2B	3B	HR	RBI	BB	SO	AVG	OBP	SLG	PRO+	BR/A	SB	CS	SBR	FA	FR	G/POS	TPR
1998	Chi-N	7	3	2	1	0	0	1	2	0	2	.333	.333	1.333	295	1	0	0	0	1.000	0	/2-1	0.1

■ CARLOS MAY

May, Carlos b: 5/17/48, Birmingham, Ala. BL/TR, 6', 215 lbs. Deb: 9/6/68 F

YEAR	TM/L	G	AB	R	H	2B	3B	HR	RBI	BB	SO	AVG	OBP	SLG	PRO+	BR/A	SB	CS	SBR	FA	FR	G/POS	TPR
1968	Chi-A	17	67	4	12	1	0	0	1	3	15	.179	.214	.194	24	-6	0	0	0	.960	-2	O-17	-1.0
1969	Chi-A★	100	367	62	103	18	2	18	62	58	66	.281	.387	.488	137	19	1	4	-2	.982	-1	*O-100	1.0
1970	Chi-A	150	555	83	158	28	4	12	68	79	96	.285	.377	.414	114	12	12	5	1	.991	1	*O-141/1-7	0.6
1971	Chi-A	141	500	64	147	21	7	7	70	62	61	.294	.379	.406	119	14	16	7	1	.986	-5	*1-130/O-9	-0.3
1972	Chi-A☆	148	523	83	161	26	3	12	68	79	70	.308	.408	.438	149	35	23	14	-2	.983	-1	*O-145/1-5	2.9
1973	Chi-A	149	553	62	148	20	0	20	96	53	73	.268	.337	.412	106	4	8	6	-1	.992	1	D-75,O-70/1-2	-0.1
1974	Chi-A	149	551	66	137	19	2	8	58	46	76	.249	.308	.334	82	-12	8	9	-3	.988	6	*O-129,D-13	-1.6
1975	Chi-A	128	454	55	123	19	2	8	53	67	46	.271	.375	.374	111	9	12	7	-1	.989	1	1-63,O-46,D-19	0.3
1976	Chi-A	20	63	7	11	2	0	0	3	9	5	.175	.278	.206	43	-4	4	0	1	1.000	-1	D-10/O-9	-0.5
	*NY-A	87	288	38	80	11	2	3	40	34	32	.278	.364	.361	114	6	1	1	-0	.950	0	D-71/O-7,1-1	0.4
	Yr	107	351	45	91	13	2	3	43	43	37	.259	.348	.333	101	2	5	1	1	.970	-1	D-81,O-16/1-1	-0.1
1977	NY-A	65	181	21	41	7	1	2	16	17	24	.227	.296	.309	66	-8	0	0	0	1.000	-1	D-53/O-4	-1.1
	Cal-A	11	18	0	6	0	0	0	1	5	1	.333	.478	.333	131	1	0	0	0	1.000	0	/1-3,D-1	0.1
	Yr	76	199	21	47	7	1	2	17	22	25	.236	.315	.312	73	-7	0	0	0	1.000	-1	D-54/O-4,1-3	-1.0
Total	10	1165	4120	545	1127	172	23	90	536	512	565	.274	.360	.392	111	70	85	53	-6	.984	-1	O-677,D-242,1-211	0.7

■ DAVE MAY

May, David La France b: 12/23/43, New Castle, Del. BL/TR, 5'10.5", 186 lbs. Deb: 7/28/67 F

YEAR	TM/L	G	AB	R	H	2B	3B	HR	RBI	BB	SO	AVG	OBP	SLG	PRO+	BR/A	SB	CS	SBR	FA	FR	G/POS	TPR
1967	Bal-A	36	85	12	20	1	1	1	7	6	13	.235	.286	.306	75	-3	0	0	0	.969	-0	O-19	-0.4
1968	Bal-A	84	152	15	29	6	3	0	7	19	27	.191	.285	.270	69	-5	3	3	-1	.984	-11	O-61	-2.2
1969	*Bal-A	78	120	8	29	6	0	3	10	9	23	.242	.305	.367	86	-2	2	1	0	.940	-4	O-40	-0.8
1970	Bal-A	25	31	6	6	0	1	1	6	4	4	.194	.286	.355	75	-1	0	0	0	1.000	-2	/O-9	-0.4
	Mil-A	100	342	36	82	8	1	7	31	44	56	.240	.330	.330	82	-8	8	6	-1	.989	8	O-99	-0.6
	Yr	125	373	42	88	8	2	8	37	48	60	.236	.326	.332	81	-9	8	6	-1	.989	6	*O-108	-1.0
1971	Mil-A	144	501	74	139	20	3	16	65	50	59	.277	.347	.425	119	12	15	9	-1	.975	10	*O-142	1.6
1972	Mil-A	143	500	49	119	20	2	9	45	47	56	.238	.307	.340	94	-4	11	13	-5	.985	15	*O-138	0.0
1973	Mil-A★	156	624	96	189	23	4	25	93	44	78	.303	.354	.473	134	26	6	7	-2	.979	3	*O-152/D-2	2.0
1974	Mil-A	135	477	56	108	15	1	10	42	28	73	.226	.274	.325	72	-18	4	3	-1	.989	-3	*O-121/D-8	-2.8
1975	Atl-N	82	203	28	56	8	0	12	40	25	27	.276	.361	.493	130	8	1	1	-0	.964	-1	O-53	0.5
1976	Atl-N	105	214	27	46	5	3	3	23	26	31	.215	.303	.308	69	-8	5	1	1	.972	-0	O-60	-1.0
1977	Tex-A	120	340	46	82	14	1	7	42	32	43	.241	.314	.350	80	-9	4	3	-1	.969	-4	*O-111/D-5	-1.8
1978	Mil-A	39	77	9	15	4	0	2	11	9	10	.195	.295	.325	74	-3	0	0	0	.944	0	O-16/D-8	-0.3
	Pit-N	5	4	0	0	0	0	0	0	1	1	.000	.200	.000	-38	-1	1	0	0	.000	0	H	-0.1
Total	12	1252	3670	462	920	130	20	96	422	344	501	.251	.320	.375	97	-16	60	47	-10	.978	10	*O-1021/D-23	-6.3

■ DERRICK MAY

May, Derrick Brant b: 7/14/68, Rochester, N.Y. BL/TR, 6'4", 225 lbs. Deb: 9/6/90 F

YEAR	TM/L	G	AB	R	H	2B	3B	HR	RBI	BB	SO	AVG	OBP	SLG	PRO+	BR/A	SB	CS	SBR	FA	FR	G/POS	TPR
1990	Chi-N	17	61	8	15	3	0	1	11	2	7	.246	.270	.344	63	-3	1	0	0	.972	0	O-17	-0.3
1991	Chi-N	15	22	4	5	2	0	1	3	2	1	.227	.292	.455	102	-0	0	0	0	1.000	0	/O-7	0.0
1992	Chi-N	124	351	33	96	11	0	8	45	14	40	.274	.307	.373	89	-5	5	3	-0	.969	-11	*O-108	-1.9
1993	Chi-N	128	465	62	137	25	2	10	77	31	41	.295	.340	.422	104	2	10	3	1	.970	1	*O-122	0.2
1994	Chi-N	100	345	43	98	19	2	8	51	30	34	.284	.341	.420	99	-1	3	2	-0	.994	2	O-92	-0.1
1995	Mil-A	32	113	15	28	3	1	1	9	5	18	.248	.286	.319	54	-8	0	1	-1	.971	-0	O-32	-0.9
	Hou-N	78	206	29	62	15	1	8	41	19	24	.301	.363	.500	134	9	5	0	2	.974	-5	O-55/1-1	0.5
1996	Hou-N	109	259	24	65	12	3	5	33	30	33	.251	.333	.378	95	-2	2	2	-1	.970	4	O-71	0.0
1997	Phi-N	83	149	8	34	5	1	1	13	8	26	.228	.260	.295	47	-12	4	1	1	.961	-3	O-56	-1.5
1998	Mon-N	85	180	13	43	8	0	5	15	11	24	.239	.283	.367	69	-9	0	0	0	.984	-2	O-49/D-2	-1.1
Total	9	771	2151	239	583	103	10	48	298	152	248	.271	.322	.395	91	-28	30	12	2	.974	-13	O-609/D-2,1-1	-5.1

■ JERRY MAY

May, Jerry Lee b: 12/14/43, Staunton, Va. d: 6/30/96, Swoope, Va. BR/TR, 6'2.5", 195 lbs. Deb: 9/19/64

YEAR	TM/L	G	AB	R	H	2B	3B	HR	RBI	BB	SO	AVG	OBP	SLG	PRO+	BR/A	SB	CS	SBR	FA	FR	G/POS	TPR
1964	Pit-N	11	31	1	8	0	0	0	3	3	9	.258	.324	.258	66	-1	0	0	0	.988	4	C-11	0.3
1965	Pit-N	4	2	0	1	0	0	0	1	0	0	.500	.500	.500	182	0	0	0	0	1.000	-0	/C-4	0.0
1966	Pit-N	42	52	6	13	4	0	1	2	2	15	.250	.291	.385	86	-1	0	1	-1	.984	8	C-41	0.7
1967	Pit-N	110	325	23	88	13	2	3	22	36	55	.271	.349	.351	100	1	0	0	0	.993	-0	*C-110	0.7
1968	Pit-N	137	416	26	91	15	2	1	33	41	80	.219	.293	.272	72	-14	0	0	0	.988	4	*C-135	-0.1
1969	Pit-N	62	190	21	44	8	0	7	23	9	53	.232	.274	.384	84	-5	1	1	-0	.994	-5	C-52	-0.8
1970	Pit-N	51	139	13	29	4	2	1	16	21	25	.209	.317	.288	65	-7	0	0	0	.994	13	C-45	0.8
1971	KC-A	71	218	16	55	13	2	1	24	27	37	.252	.335	.344	93	-1	0	0	0	.997	0	C-71	0.1
1972	KC-A	53	116	10	22	5	1	1	4	14	13	.190	.277	.276	65	-5	0	0	0	.979	-1	C-41	-0.5
1973	KC-A	11	30	4	4	1	1	0	2	3	5	.133	.235	.233	30	-3	0	0	0	.940	-2	C-11	-0.4

YEAR	TM/L	G	AB	R	H	2B	3B	HR	RBI	BB	SO	AVG	OBP	SLG	PRO+	BR/A	SB	CS	SBR	FA	FR	G/POS	TPR
	NY-N	4	8	0	2	0	0	0	0	1	1	.250	.333	.250	65	-0	0	0	0	1.000	-1	/C-4	-0.1
Total	10	556	1527	120	357	63	10	15	130	157	293	.234	.310	.318	81	-35	1	2	-1	.990	21	C-525	0.7

■ LEE MAY

May, Lee Andrew b: 3/23/43, Birmingham, Ala. BR/TR, 6'3", 205 lbs. Deb: 9/1/65 FC

YEAR	TM/L	G	AB	R	H	2B	3B	HR	RBI	BB	SO	AVG	OBP	SLG	PRO+	BR/A	SB	CS	SBR	FA	FR	G/POS	TPR
1965	Cin-N	5	4	1	0	0	0	0	0	0	1	.000	.000	.000	-94	-1	0	0	0	.000	0	H	-0.1
1966	Cin-N	25	75	14	25	5	1	2	10	0	14	.333	.333	.507	119	2	0	1	-1	.972	-1	1-16	-0.1
1967	Cin-N	127	438	54	116	29	2	12	57	19	80	.265	.310	.422	97	-3	4	8	-4	.994	2	1-81,O-48	-1.2
1968	Cin-N	146	559	78	162	32	1	22	80	34	100	.290	.337	.469	132	20	4	7	-3	.996	0	*1-122,O-33	0.8
1969	Cin-N★	158	607	85	169	32	3	38	110	45	142	.278	.334	.529	132	23	5	4	-1	.993	-1	*1-156/O-7	0.9
1970	*Cin-N	153	605	78	153	34	2	34	94	38	125	.253	.299	.484	106	1	1	1	-0	.993	0	*1-153	-1.2
1971	Cin-N★	147	553	85	154	17	3	39	98	42	135	.278	.334	.532	145	29	3	0	1	.994	-7	*1-143	1.1
1972	Hou-N★	148	592	87	168	31	2	29	98	52	145	.284	.344	.490	137	27	3	1	0	.996	-3	*1-146	1.2
1973	Hou-N	148	545	65	147	24	3	28	105	34	122	.270	.315	.479	117	10	1	1	-0	.993	-3	*1-144	-0.5
1974	Hou-N	152	556	59	149	26	0	24	85	17	97	.268	.298	.444	110	3	1	0	0	.994	1	*1-145	-0.5
1975	Bal-A	146	580	67	152	28	3	20	99	36	91	.262	.311	.424	113	7	1	2	-1	.993	3	*1-144/D-2	0.0
1976	Bal-A	148	530	61	137	17	4	25	**109**	41	104	.258	.315	.447	130	17	4	1	1	.996	0	1-94,D-52	1.0
1977	Bal-A	150	585	75	148	16	2	27	99	38	119	.253	.299	.426	101	-2	2	2	-1	.995	-7	*1-110,D-39	-1.7
1978	Bal-A	148	556	56	137	16	1	25	80	31	110	.246	.287	.414	101	-2	5	2	0	.973	-0	*D-140/1-4	-0.7
1979	*Bal-A	124	456	59	116	15	0	19	69	28	100	.254	.299	.412	93	-6	3	4	-2	.913	-1	*D-117/1-2	-1.2
1980	Bal-A	78	222	20	54	10	2	7	31	15	53	.243	.291	.401	88	-4	2	0	1	1.000	-0	D-58/1-7	-0.6
1981	*KC-A	26	55	3	16	3	0	0	8	3	14	.291	.328	.345	95	-0	0	1	-1	1.000	-1	/1-8,D-4	-0.2
1982	KC-A	42	91	12	28	5	2	3	12	14	18	.308	.400	.505	147	6	0	0	0	.989	-2	1-32/D-2	0.3
Total	18	2071	7609	959	2031	340	31	354	1244	487	1570	.267	.315	.459	116	126	39	35	-9	.994	-19	*1-1507,D-414/O-88	-2.7

■ PINKY MAY

May, Merrill Glend b: 1/18/11, Laconia, Ind. BR/TR, 5'11.5", 165 lbs. Deb: 4/21/39 F

YEAR	TM/L	G	AB	R	H	2B	3B	HR	RBI	BB	SO	AVG	OBP	SLG	PRO+	BR/A	SB	CS	SBR	FA	FR	G/POS	TPR
1939	Phi-N	135	464	49	133	27	3	2	62	41	20	.287	.346	.371	95	-3	4			**.956**	8	*3-132	0.7
1940	Phi-N★	136	501	59	147	24	2	1	48	58	33	.293	.371	.355	105	6	2			.954	13	*3-135/S-1	2.1
1941	Phi-N	142	490	46	131	17	4	0	39	55	30	.267	.344	.318	91	-5	2			**.972**	**25**	*3-140	2.4
1942	Phi-N	115	345	25	82	15	0	0	18	51	17	.238	.338	.281	86	-4	3			.963	17	*3-107	1.5
1943	Phi-N	137	415	31	117	19	2	1	48	56	21	.282	.369	.345	111	8	2			**.963**	11	*3-132	2.2
Total	5	665	2215	210	610	102	11	4	215	261	121	.275	.354	.337	98	2	13			.962	74	3-646/S-1	8.9

■ MILT MAY

May, Milton Scott b: 8/1/50, Gary, Ind. BL/TR, 6', 190 lbs. Deb: 9/8/70 FC

YEAR	TM/L	G	AB	R	H	2B	3B	HR	RBI	BB	SO	AVG	OBP	SLG	PRO+	BR/A	SB	CS	SBR	FA	FR	G/POS	TPR
1970	Pit-N	5	4	1	2	1	0	0	2	0	0	.500	.600	.750	265	1	0	0	0	.000	0	H	0.1
1971	*Pit-N	49	126	15	35	1	0	6	25	9	16	.278	.326	.429	113	2	0	0	0	1.000	3	C-31	0.6
1972	*Pit-N	57	139	12	39	10	0	0	14	10	13	.281	.329	.353	96	-1	0	0	0	.985	5	C-33	0.5
1973	Pit-N	101	283	29	76	8	1	7	31	34	26	.269	.351	.378	105	2	0	1	-1	.973	-6	C-79	-0.1
1974	Hou-N	127	405	47	117	17	4	7	54	39	33	.289	.353	.402	116	8	0	1	-1	**.993**	2	*C-116	1.5
1975	Hou-N	111	386	29	93	15	1	4	52	26	41	.241	.289	.316	73	-15	1	2	-1	.986	1	*C-102	-1.1
1976	Det-A	6	25	2	7	1	0	0	1	0	1	.280	.280	.320	73	-1	0	0	0	1.000	1	/C-6	0.0
1977	Det-A	115	397	32	99	9	3	12	46	26	31	.249	.296	.378	78	-13	0	0	0	.986	7	*C-111	-0.3
1978	Det-A	105	352	24	88	9	0	10	37	27	26	.250	.307	.361	85	-7	0	0	0	.979	1	C-94	-0.4
1979	Det-A	6	11	1	3	2	0	0	3	1	1	.273	.333	.455	107	0	0	0	0	1.000	1	/C-5	0.1
	Chi-A	65	202	23	51	13	0	7	28	14	27	.252	.307	.421	94	-2	0	0	0	.981	1	C-65	0.1
	Yr	71	213	24	54	15	0	7	31	15	28	.254	.309	.423	95	-2	0	0	0	.982	2	C-70	0.2
1980	SF-N	111	358	27	93	16	2	6	50	25	40	.260	.310	.366	90	-5	0	1	-1	.986	-4	*C-103	-0.7
1981	SF-N	97	316	20	98	17	0	2	33	34	29	.310	.377	.383	118	8	1	4	-2	.989	-1	C-93	0.9
1982	SF-N	114	395	29	104	19	0	9	39	28	38	.263	.312	.380	93	-4	0	1	-1	.987	-1	*C-110	-0.2
1983	SF-N	66	186	18	46	6	0	6	20	21	23	.247	.324	.376	96	-1	2	2	-1	.981	-2	C-56	-0.1
	Pit-N	7	12	0	3	0	0	0	0	1	1	.250	.308	.250	55	-1	0	0	0	1.000	2	/C-4	0.1
	Yr	73	198	18	49	6	0	6	20	22	24	.247	.323	.369	94	-2	2	2	-1	.983	0	C-60	0.0
1984	Pit-N	50	96	4	17	3	0	1	8	10	15	.177	.255	.240	40	-8	0	1	-1	.993	5	C-26	-0.3
Total	15	1192	3693	313	971	147	11	77	443	305	361	.263	.321	.371	93	-37	4	13	-7	.986	14	*C-1034	0.7

■ JOHN MAYBERRY

Mayberry, John Claiborn b: 2/18/49, Detroit, Mich. BL/TL, 6'3", 220 lbs. Deb: 9/10/68 C

YEAR	TM/L	G	AB	R	H	2B	3B	HR	RBI	BB	SO	AVG	OBP	SLG	PRO+	BR/A	SB	CS	SBR	FA	FR	G/POS	TPR
1968	Hou-N	4	9	0	0	0	0	0	0	0	2	.000	.100	.000	-69	-2	0	0	0	1.000	-0	/1-2	-0.3
1969	Hou-N	5	4	0	0	0	0	0	0	1	1	.000	.200	.000	-41	-1	0	0	0	.000	0	H	-0.1
1970	Hou-N	50	148	23	32	3	2	5	14	21	33	.216	.322	.365	87	-3	1	1	-0	.995	3	1-45	-0.3
1971	Hou-N	46	137	16	25	0	1	7	14	13	32	.182	.263	.350	74	-5	0	0	0	.997	-3	1-37	-1.2
1972	KC-A	149	503	65	150	24	3	25	100	78	74	.298	.396	.507	168	43	0	2	-1	**.995**	-0	*1-146	3.3
1973	KC-A★	152	510	87	142	20	2	26	100	**122**	79	.278	**.420**	.478	141	33	3	0	1	.994	-5	*1-149/D-1	1.7
1974	KC-A★	126	427	63	100	13	1	22	69	77	72	.234	.359	.424	118	11	4	2	0	.990	-2	*1-106,D-16	0.2
1975	KC-A	156	554	95	161	38	1	34	106	**119**	73	.291	.419	.547	**167**	**53**	5	3	-0	.988	3	*1-131,D-27	4.6
1976	*KC-A	161	594	76	138	22	2	13	95	82	73	.232	.327	.342	95	-2	3	2	-0	.996	3	*1-160/D-2	-1.7
1977	*KC-A	153	543	73	125	22	1	23	82	83	86	.230	.340	.401	100	1	1	3	-2	**.995**	-6	*1-145/D-8	-1.5
1978	Tor-A	152	515	51	129	15	2	22	70	60	57	.250	.333	.416	107	5	1	2	-1	.993	-14	*1-139/D-7	-1.9
1979	Tor-A	137	464	61	127	22	1	21	74	69	60	.274	.374	.461	122	16	1	1	-0	.995	-8	*1-135	-0.1
1980	Tor-A	149	501	62	124	19	2	30	82	77	80	.248	.351	.473	118	13	0	0	0	.994	-4	*1-136/D-8	0.0
1981	Tor-A	94	290	34	72	6	1	17	43	44	45	.248	.363	.452	125	10	1	1	-0	.993	-6	1-80,D-10	-0.1
1982	Tor-A	17	33	7	9	0	0	2	3	7	5	.273	.415	.455	127	1	0	0	0	1.000	-1	D-13/1-4	0.0
	NY-A	69	215	20	45	7	0	8	27	28	38	.209	.315	.353	84	-4	0	0	0	.996	-4	1-63/D-4	-1.1
	Yr	86	248	27	54	7	0	10	30	35	43	.218	.329	.367	90	-3	0	0	0	.996	-4	1-67,D-17	-1.1
Total	15	1620	5447	733	1379	211	19	255	879	881	810	.253	.363	.439	122	170	20	17	-4	.994	-49	*1-1478/D-96	1.5

■ LEE MAYE

Maye, Arthur Lee b: 12/11/34, Tuscaloosa, Ala. BL/TR, 6'2", 190 lbs. Deb: 7/17/59

YEAR	TM/L	G	AB	R	H	2B	3B	HR	RBI	BB	SO	AVG	OBP	SLG	PRO+	BR/A	SB	CS	SBR	FA	FR	G/POS	TPR
1959	Mil-N	51	140	17	42	5	1	4	16	7	26	.300	.338	.436	114	2	2	2	-1	.976	1	O-44	0.0
1960	Mil-N	41	83	14	25	6	0	0	2	7	21	.301	.363	.373	110	1	5	0	2	.968	-1	O-19	0.1
1961	Mil-N	110	373	68	101	11	5	14	41	36	50	.271	.340	.440	112	6	10	1	2	.972	-2	O-96	0.0
1962	Mil-N	99	349	40	85	10	0	10	41	25	58	.244	.296	.358	77	-12	9	3	1	.977	1	O-94	-1.6
1963	Mil-N	124	442	67	120	22	7	11	34	36	52	.271	.331	.428	118	10	14	2	3	.983	-8	*O-111	-0.2
1964	Mil-N	153	588	96	179	**44**	5	10	74	34	54	.304	.347	.447	121	16	5	10	-5	.961	-1	*O-135/3-5	0.3
1965	Mil-N	15	53	8	16	2	0	2	7	2	6	.302	.339	.453	120	1	0	0	0	.962	1	O-13	0.2
	Hou-N	108	415	38	104	17	7	3	36	20	37	.251	.287	.347	83	-11	1	5	-3	.953	3	*O-103	-1.6
	Yr	123	468	46	120	19	7	5	43	22	43	.256	.293	.359	88	-9	1	5	-3	.954	4	*O-116	-1.4
1966	Hou-N	115	358	38	103	12	4	9	36	20	26	.288	.325	.419	113	5	4	3	-1	.949	-1	O-97	-0.1
1967	Cle-A	115	297	43	77	20	4	9	27	26	47	.259	.321	.444	123	8	3	3	-1	.981	-10	O-77/2-1	-0.7
1968	Cle-A	109	299	20	84	13	2	4	26	15	24	.281	.317	.378	112	3	0	0	0	.984	1	O-80/1-1	0.0
1969	Cle-A	43	108	9	27	5	0	1	15	8	15	.250	.308	.324	74	-4	1	0	0	.982	1	O-28	-0.4
	Was-A	71	238	41	69	9	3	9	26	20	25	.290	.345	.466	132	9	1	3	-2	.944	-6	O-65	-0.2
	Yr	114	346	50	96	14	3	10	41	28	40	.277	.333	.422	112	5	2	3	-1	.957	-5	O-93	-0.6
1970	Was-A	96	255	28	67	12	1	7	30	21	32	.263	.321	.400	103	0	4	2	0	1.000	-8	O-68/3-1	-1.1
	Chi-A	6	6	0	1	0	0	0	1	0	1	.167	.167	.167	-8	-1	0	0	0	.000	0	H	-0.1
	Yr	102	261	28	68	12	1	7	31	21	33	.261	.318	.395	100	-1	4	2	0	1.000	-8	O-68/3-1	-1.2
1971	Chi-A	32	44	6	9	2	0	1	7	5	7	.205	.286	.318	69	-2	0	0	0	1.000	-1	O-10	-0.3
Total	13	1288	4048	533	1109	190	39	94	419	282	481	.274	.324	.410	108	32	59	34	-3	.970	-31	*O-1040/3-6,1-1,2-1	-5.7

■ ED MAYER

Mayer, Edward H. b: 8/16/1866, Marshall, Ill. d: 5/18/13, Chicago, Ill. 5'8.5", 155 lbs. Deb: 4/19/1890

YEAR	TM/L	G	AB	R	H	2B	3B	HR	RBI	BB	SO	AVG	OBP	SLG	PRO+	BR/A	SB	CS	SBR	FA	FR	G/POS	TPR
1890	Phi-N	117	484	49	117	25	5	1	70	22	36	.242	.286	.320	75	-17	20			.878	-4	*3-114/O-4	-1.5
1891	Phi-N	68	268	24	50	2	4	0	31	14	29	.187	.238	.224	34	-23	7			.895	-6	3-31,O-29/S-7,2-1	-2.5
Total	2	185	752	73	167	27	9	1	101	36	65	.222	.269	.286	60	-40	27			.882	-10	3-145/O-33,S-7,2-1	-4.0

YEAR	TM/L	G	AB	R	H	2B	3B	HR	RBI	BB	SO	AVG	OBP	SLG	PRO+	BR/A	SB	CS	SBR	FA	FR	G/POS	TPR
■ **SAM MAYER**	Mayer, Samuel Frankel (b: Samuel Frankel Erskine) b: 2/28/1893, Atlanta, Ga. d: 7/1/62, Atlanta, Ga. BR/TL, 5'10", 164 lbs. Deb: 9/14/15 F																						
1915	Was-A	11	29	5	7	0	0	1	4	4	2	.241	.333	.345	101	0	1	2	-1	1.000	0	/O-9,P-1,1-1	-0.1
■ **WALLY MAYER**	Mayer, Walter A. b: 7/8/1890, Cincinnati, Ohio d: 11/18/51, Minnetonka, Minn. BR/TR, 5'11", 168 lbs. Deb: 9/28/11																						
1911	Chi-A	1	3	0	0	0	0	0	0	0	2	.000	.400	.000	16	-0	0			.900	-1	/C-1	-0.1
1912	Chi-A	9	9	1	0	0	0	0	0	1		.000	.100	.000	-73	-2	0			1.000	-0	/C-6	-0.2
1914	Chi-A	40	85	7	14	3	1	0	5	14	23	.165	.290	.224	55	-4	1	1	-0	.968	5	C-33/3-1	0.3
1915	Chi-A	22	54	3	12	3	1	0	5	5	8	.222	.288	.315	78	-2	0	2	-1	.990	-1	C-20	-0.3
1917	Bos-A	4	12	2	2	0	0	0	0	5	2	.167	.412	.167	78	0	0			.964	2	/C-4	0.2
1918	Bos-A	26	49	7	11	4	0	0	5	7	7	.224	.321	.306	91	-0	0			.964	-1	C-23	0.0
1919	StL-A	30	62	2	14	4	1	0	5	8	11	.226	.314	.323	77	-2	0			.959	6	C-25	0.5
Total	7	132	274	22	53	14	3	0	20	42	51	.193	.303	.266	68	-10	1	3		.969	10	C-112/3-1	0.4
■ **PADDY MAYES**	Mayes, Adair Bushyhead b: 3/17/1885, Locust Grove, Okla. d: 5/28/62, Fayetteville, Ark. BL/TR, 5'11", 160 lbs. Deb: 6/11/11																						
1911	Phi-N	5	5	1	0	0	0	0	0	1	2	.000	.286	.000	-17	-1	0			1.000	-0	/O-2	-0.1
■ **BUSTER MAYNARD**	Maynard, James Walter b: 3/25/13, Henderson, N.C. d: 9/7/77, Durham, N.C. BR/TR, 5'11", 170 lbs. Deb: 9/17/40																						
1940	NY-N	7	29	6	8	2	2	1	2	2	6	.276	.323	.586	145	2	0			.929	-1	/O-7	0.0
1942	NY-N	89	190	17	47	4	1	4	32	19	19	.247	.319	.342	93	-2	3			.982	-0	O-58,3-10/2-1	-0.4
1943	NY-N	121	393	43	81	8	2	9	32	24	27	.206	.252	.305	60	-21	3			.965	-6	O-74,3-22	-3.4
1946	NY-N	7	4	2	0	0	0	0	0	1	1	.000	.200	.000	-41	-1	0			.750	-1	/O-3	-0.2
Total	4	224	616	68	136	14	5	14	66	46	53	.221	.276	.328	74	-22	6			.967	-8	O-142/3-32,2-1	-4.0
■ **CHICK MAYNARD**	Maynard, Le Roy Evans b: 11/2/1896, Turners Falls, Mass. d: 1/31/57, Bangor, Maine BL/TR, 5'9", 150 lbs. Deb: 6/27/22																						
1922	Bos-A	12	24	1	3	0	0	0	0	3	2	.125	.222	.125	-8	-4	0	1	-1	.872	-2	S-12	-0.6
■ **BRENT MAYNE**	Mayne, Brent Danem b: 4/19/68, Loma Linda, Cal. BL/TR, 6'1", 190 lbs. Deb: 9/18/90																						
1990	KC-A	5	13	2	3	0	0	0	1	3	3	.231	.375	.231	74	-0	0	1	-1	.970	1	/C-5	0.0
1991	KC-A	85	231	22	58	8	0	3	31	23	42	.251	.319	.325	78	-7	2	4	-2	.987	4	C-80/D-1	0.0
1992	KC-A	82	213	16	48	10	0	0	18	11	26	.225	.263	.272	49	-15	0	4	-2	.990	2	C-62/3-8,D-1	-1.2
1993	KC-A	71	205	22	52	9	1	2	22	18	31	.254	.317	.337	72	-8	3	2	-0	.995	6	C-68/D-1	0.1
1994	KC-A	46	144	19	37	5	1	2	20	14	27	.257	.323	.347	70	-6	1	0	0	.996	6	C-42/D-3	0.2
1995	KC-A	110	307	23	77	18	1	1	27	25	41	.251	.313	.326	66	-15	0	1	-1	.995	11	*C-103	0.2
1996	NY-N	70	99	9	26	6	0	1	6	12	22	.263	.342	.354	88	-2	0	1	-1	1.000	-4	C-21	-0.5
1997	Oak-A	85	256	29	74	12	0	6	22	18	33	.289	.345	.406	97	-1	1	0	0	.996	-10	C-83	-0.5
1998	SF-N	94	275	26	75	15	0	3	32	37	47	.273	.361	.360	91	-2	2	1	0	.991	-7	C-88	-0.4
Total	9	648	1743	168	450	83	3	18	179	161	272	.258	.324	.340	76	-56	9	14	-6	.993	10	C-552/3-8,D-6	-2.1
■ **EDDIE MAYO**	Mayo, Edward Joseph "Hotshot" (b: Edward Joseph Mayoski) b: 4/15/10, Holyoke, Mass. BL/TR, 5'11", 178 lbs. Deb: 5/22/36 C																						
1936	*NY-N	46	141	11	28	4	1	1	8	11	12	.199	.257	.262	40	-12	0			.981	5	3-40	-0.6
1937	Bos-N	65	172	19	39	6	1	1	18	15	20	.227	.293	.291	65	-9	1			.956	-4	3-50	-1.1
1938	Bos-N	8	14	2	3	0	0	1	4	1	0	.214	.267	.429	98	-0	0			.923	2	/3-6,S-2	0.1
1943	Phi-A	128	471	49	103	10	1	0	28	34	32	.219	.278	.244	54	-27	2	0	1	**.976**	-3	*3-123	-3.0
1944	Det-A	154	607	76	151	18	3	5	63	57	23	.249	.317	.313	76	-18	9	13	-5	.978	**29**	*2-143,S-11	1.6
1945	*Det-A†	134	501	71	143	24	3	10	54	47	29	.285	.347	.405	111	6	7	7	-2	**.980**	18	*2-124	3.1
1946	Det-A	51	202	21	51	9	2	0	22	14	12	.252	.301	.317	68	-9	6	2	1	.965	-11	2-49	-1.6
1947	Det-A	142	535	66	149	28	4	6	48	48	28	.279	.338	.379	96	-3	3	7	-3	.983	-23	*2-142	-2.1
1948	Det-A	106	370	35	92	20	1	2	42	30	19	.249	.310	.324	67	-18	1	9	-5	.975	-10	2-86,3-10	-2.7
Total	9	834	3013	350	759	119	16	26	287	257	175	.252	.313	.328	78	-89	29	38		.978	3	2-544,3-229/S-13	-6.3
■ **JACKIE MAYO**	Mayo, John Lewis b: 7/26/25, Litchfield, Ill. BL/TR, 6'1", 190 lbs. Deb: 9/19/48																						
1948	Phi-N	12	35	7	8	2	1	0	3	7	7	.229	.386	.343	101	0	1			1.000	1	O-11	0.1
1949	Phi-N	45	39	3	5	0	0	0	2	4	5	.128	.209	.128	-8	-6	0			.889	-7	O-25	-1.3
1950	*Phi-N	18	36	1	8	3	0	0	3	2	5	.222	.263	.306	50	-3	0			.958	-3	O-15	-0.5
1951	Phi-N	9	7	1	1	0	0	0	0	0	0	.143	.143	.143	-23	-1	0	0	0	1.000	-2	/O-5	-0.3
1952	Phi-N	50	119	13	29	5	0	1	4	12	17	.244	.313	.311	74	-4	1	3	-2	1.000	4	O-27/1-6	-0.3
1953	Phi-N	5	4	0	0	0	0	0	0	0	1	.000	.000	.000	-99	-1	0	0	0	.000	-0	/O-1	-0.2
Total	6	139	240	25	51	10	1	1	12	25	35	.213	.292	.275	56	-15	2	3		.972	-7	/O-84,1-6	-2.5
■ **WILLIE MAYS**	Mays, Willie Howard "Say Hey" b: 5/6/31, Westfield, Ala. BR/TR, 5'11", 180 lbs. Deb: 5/25/51 CH																						
1951	*NY-N	121	464	59	127	22	5	20	68	57	60	.274	.356	.472	120	12	7	4	-0	.976	11	*O-121	1.9
1952	NY-N	34	127	17	30	2	4	4	23	16	17	.236	.326	.409	102	0	4	1	1	.991	8	O-34	0.7
1954	*NY-N★	151	565	119	195	33	**13**	41	110	66	57	**.345**	.415	**.667**	176	**61**	8	5	-1	.985	16	*O-151	**6.7**
1955	NY-N★	152	580	123	185	18	**13**	**51**	127	79	60	.319	.404	**.659**	**176**	**62**	24	4	**5**	.982	**20**	*O-152	**7.7**
1956	NY-N★	152	578	101	171	27	8	36	84	68	65	.296	.371	.557	146	37	**40**	10	**6**	.979	12	*O-152	**4.7**
1957	NY-N★	152	585	112	195	26	**20**	35	97	76	62	.333	.411	**.626**	**174**	**61**	**38**	19	0	.980	11	*O-150	**6.3**
1958	SF-N★	152	600	**121**	208	33	11	29	96	78	56	.347	.423	.583	**167**	**58**	**31**	6	**6**	.980	17	*O-151	**7.2**
1959	SF-N★	151	575	125	180	43	5	34	104	65	58	.313	.385	.583	157	45	**27**	4	**6**	.984	7	*O-147	5.0
1960	SF-N★	153	595	107	**190**	29	12	29	103	61	70	.319	.386	.555	164	51	25	10	2	.981	14	*O-152	**5.9**
1961	SF-N★	154	572	**129**	176	32	3	40	123	81	77	.308	.395	.584	162	50	18	9	0	.980	10	*O-153	5.0
1962	*SF-N★	162	621	130	189	36	5	**49**	141	78	85	.304	.385	.615	167	56	18	2	4	.991	14	*O-161	**6.4**
1963	SF-N★	157	596	115	187	32	7	38	103	66	83	.314	.384	.582	176	57	8	3	1	.981	13	*O-157/S-1	**6.6**
1964	SF-N★	157	578	121	171	21	9	**47**	111	82	72	.296	.384	**.607**	**171**	**54**	19	5	3	.984	14	*O-155/1-1,S-1,3-1	6.5
1965	SF-N★	157	558	118	177	21	3	**52**	112	76	71	.317	**.399**	**.645**	**184**	**61**	9	4	0	.983	16	*O-151	**7.3**
1966	SF-N★	152	552	99	159	29	4	37	103	70	81	.288	.370	.556	149	36	5	1	1	.982	12	*O-150	4.3
1967	SF-N★	141	486	83	128	22	2	22	70	51	92	.263	.336	.453	125	15	6	0	2	.976	-2	*O-134	1.0
1968	SF-N★	148	498	84	144	20	5	23	79	67	81	.289	.376	.488	158	36	12	6	0	.978	0	*O-142/1-1	3.3
1969	SF-N★	117	403	64	114	17	3	13	58	49	71	.283	.365	.437	126	14	6	2	1	.976	-7	*O-108/1-1	0.2
1970	SF-N★	139	478	94	139	15	2	28	83	79	90	.291	.395	.506	141	29	5	0	2	.975	2	*O-129/1-5	2.6
1971	*SF-N★	136	417	82	113	24	5	18	61	**112**	123	.271	**.429**	.482	160	39	23	3	5	.970	-2	O-84,1-48	3.6
1972	SF-N	19	49	8	9	2	0	0	3	17	5	.184	.394	.224	79	-0	3	0	1	1.000	-1	O-14	-0.1
	NY-N★	69	195	27	52	9	1	8	19	43	43	.267	.402	.446	144	13	1	5	-3	.974	0	O-49,1-11	0.8
	Yr	88	244	35	61	11	1	8	22	60	48	.250	.400	.402	131	13	4	5	-2	.979	-1	O-63,1-11	0.7
1973	*NY-N★	66	209	24	44	10	0	6	25	27	47	.211	.304	.344	81	-6	1	0	0	.991	-5	O-45,1-17	-1.4
Total	22	2992	10881	2062	3283	523	140	660	1903	1464	1526	.302	.387	.557	157	844	338	103	40	.981	180	*O-2842/1-84,S-2,3	92.2
■ **BILL MAZEROSKI**	Mazeroski, William Stanley "Maz" b: 9/5/36, Wheeling, W.Va. BR/TR, 5'11.5", 183 lbs. Deb: 7/7/56 C																						
1956	Pit-N	81	255	30	62	8	1	3	14	18	24	.243	.293	.318	66	-12	0	0	0	.981	11	2-81	0.5
1957	Pit-N	148	526	59	149	27	7	8	54	27	49	.283	.319	.407	96	-4	3	3	-1	.978	4	*2-144	1.1
1958	Pit-N★	152	567	69	156	24	6	19	68	25	71	.275	.309	.439	98	-4	1	1	-0	.980	19	*2-152	2.5
1959	Pit-N★	135	493	50	119	15	6	7	59	29	54	.241	.285	.339	66	-25	1	3	-2	.981	-9	*2-133	-2.5
1960	*Pit-N★	151	538	58	147	21	5	11	64	40	50	.273	.325	.392	95	-4	4	0	1	**.989**	**25**	*2-151	3.8
1961	Pit-N	152	558	71	148	21	2	13	59	26	55	.265	.302	.380	79	-17	2	1	0	.975	**31**	*2-152	2.9
1962	Pit-N★	159	572	55	155	24	9	14	81	37	47	.271	.318	.418	95	-5	0	3	-2	.985	**41**	*2-159	5.0
1963	Pit-N†	142	534	43	131	22	3	8	52	32	46	.245	.288	.343	80	-14	2	0	1	.984	**57**	*2-138	6.0
1964	Pit-N☆	162	601	66	161	22	8	10	64	29	52	.268	.302	.381	91	-8	1	1	-0	.975	**34**	*2-162	4.1
1965	Pit-N	130	494	52	134	17	1	6	54	18	34	.271	.300	.346	81	-13	2	1	0	**.988**	26	*2-127	2.5
1966	Pit-N	162	621	56	163	22	7	16	82	31	62	.262	.299	.398	91	-8	4	3	-1	**.992**	**41**	*2-162	4.5
1967	Pit-N★	163	639	62	167	25	3	9	77	30	55	.261	.294	.352	84	-14	1	2	-1	.981	17	*2-163	1.4
1968	Pit-N	143	506	36	127	18	2	3	42	38	38	.251	.306	.312	87	-8	3	4	-2	.981	**26**	*2-142	2.8
1969	Pit-N	67	227	13	52	7	1	3	25	22	16	.229	.303	.308	73	-8	1	1	-0	.988	14	2-65	1.1

YEAR	TM/L	G	AB	R	H	2B	3B	HR	RBI	BB	SO	AVG	OBP	SLG	PRO+	BR/A	SB	CS	SBR	FA	FR	G/POS	TPR
1970	*Pit-N	112	367	29	84	14	0	7	39	27	40	.229	.285	.324	64	-19	2	0	1	.987	24	*2-102	1.3
1971	*Pit-N	70	193	17	49	3	1	1	16	15	8	.254	.308	.295	72	-7	0	0	0	.986	-1	2-46/3-7	-0.5
1972	*Pit-N	34	64	3	12	4	0	0	3	3	5	.188	.224	.250	35	-6	0	0	0	.986	3	2-15/3-3	-0.2
Total	17	2163	7755	769	2016	294	62	138	853	447	706	.260	.302	.367	84	-176	27	23	-6	.983	362	*2-2094/3-10	36.3
■ **MEL MAZZERA**	Mazzera, Melvin Leonard "Mike" b: 1/31/14, Stockton, Cal. d: 12/19/97, Stockton, Cal. BL/TL, 5'11", 180 lbs. Deb: 9/9/35																						
1935	StL-A	12	30	4	7	2	0	1	2	4	9	.233	.324	.400	82	-1	0	0	0	.950	-1	O-10	-0.2
1937	StL-A	7	7	1	2	2	0	0	0	0	2	.286	.286	.571	110	0	0	0	0	.000	0	H	0.0
1938	StL-A	86	204	33	57	8	2	6	29	12	25	.279	.329	.426	88	-5	1	1	-0	.976	-1	O-47	-0.7
1939	StL-A	33	110	21	33	5	2	3	22	10	20	.300	.364	.464	108	1	0	0	0	.983	0	O-25	0.0
1940	Phi-N	69	156	16	37	5	4	0	13	19	15	.237	.320	.321	80	-4	1			.985	-4	O-42,1-11	-1.0
Total	5	207	507	75	136	22	8	10	66	45	71	.268	.333	.402	90	-8	2	1		.978	-6	O-124/1-11	-1.9
■ **LEE MAZZILLI**	Mazzilli, Lee Louis b: 3/25/55, New York, N.Y. BB/TR, 6'1", 185 lbs. Deb: 9/7/76																						
1976	NY-N	24	77	9	15	2	0	2	7	14	10	.195	.326	.299	83	-1	5	4	-1	.983	2	O-23	-0.1
1977	NY-N	159	537	66	134	24	3	6	46	72	72	.250	.342	.339	87	-8	22	15	-2	.992	11	*O-156	-0.5
1978	NY-N	148	542	78	148	28	5	16	61	69	82	.273	.356	.432	124	17	20	13	-2	.987	14	*O-144	2.4
1979	NY-N★	158	597	78	181	34	4	15	79	93	74	.303	.397	.449	135	32	34	12	3	.989	8	*O-143,1-15	3.7
1980	NY-N	152	578	82	162	31	4	16	76	82	92	.280	.373	.431	127	23	41	15	3	.983	1	1-92,O-66	2.0
1981	NY-N	95	324	36	74	14	5	6	34	46	53	.228	.328	.358	96	-1	17	7	1	.970	-0	O-89	-0.4
1982	Tex-A	58	195	23	47	8	0	4	17	28	26	.241	.339	.344	93	-1	11	6	-0	.945	-3	O-26,D-24	-0.6
	NY-A	37	128	20	34	2	0	6	17	15	15	.266	.347	.422	112	2	2	3	-1	.995	-3	1-23/O-2,D-9	-0.3
	Yr	95	323	43	81	10	0	10	34	43	41	.251	.342	.375	100	1	13	9	-2	.949	-6	D-33,O-28,1-23	-0.9
1983	Pit-N	109	246	37	59	9	0	5	24	49	43	.240	.370	.337	95	0	15	5	2	.985	0	O-57/1-7	0.0
1984	Pit-N	111	266	37	63	11	1	4	21	40	42	.237	.339	.331	89	-3	8	1	2	.989	-7	O-74/1-5	-1.1
1985	Pit-N	92	117	20	33	8	0	1	9	29	17	.282	.425	.376	127	6	4	1	1	.986	-1	1-19/O-5	0.5
1986	Pit-N	61	93	18	21	2	1	1	8	26	25	.226	.395	.301	93	0	3	3	-1	1.000	-3	O-18/1-7	-0.4
	*NY-N	39	58	10	16	3	0	2	7	12	11	.276	.417	.431	138	4	1	1	-0	1.000	-1	O-10/1-8	0.2
	Yr	100	151	28	37	5	1	3	15	38	36	.245	.403	.351	109	4	4	4	-1	1.000	-4	O-28,1-15	-0.2
1987	NY-N	88	124	26	38	8	1	3	24	21	14	.306	.407	.460	136	7	5	3	-0	1.000	-6	O-25,1-13	0.0
1988	*NY-N	68	116	9	17	2	0	0	12	12	16	.147	.233	.164	16	-12	4	1	1	1.000	-4	O-18,1-16	-1.9
1989	NY-N	48	60	10	11	2	0	2	7	17	19	.183	.364	.317	101	1	3	0	1	.889	-4	O-10/1-8	-0.3
	*Tor-A	28	66	12	15	3	0	4	11	17	16	.227	.400	.455	143	5	2	0	1	.944	-1	D-19/1-2,O-2	0.4
Total	14	1475	4124	571	1068	191	24	93	460	642	627	.259	.361	.385	109	70	197	90	5	.986	4	O-868,1-215/D-52	3.6
■ **JIMMY McALEER**	McAleer, James Robert "Loafer" b: 7/10/1864, Youngstown, Ohio d: 4/29/31, Youngstown, Ohio BR/TR, 6', 175 lbs. Deb: 4/24/1889 M																						
1889	Cle-N	110	447	66	105	6	6	0	35	30	49	.235	.289	.275	59	-24	37			.955	9	*O-110	-1.5
1890	Cle-P	86	341	58	91	8	7	1	42	37	33	.267	.340	.340	89	-4	21			.940	11	O-86	0.3
1891	Cle-N	136	565	97	135	16	11	1	61	49	47	.239	.305	.312	77	-18	51			.924	5	*O-136	-1.5
1892	*Cle-N	149	571	92	136	26	7	4	70	63	54	.238	.318	.329	92	-6	40			.948	12	*O-149	-0.1
1893	Cle-N	91	350	63	83	5	1	2	41	35	21	.237	.314	.274	54	-24	32			.928	4	*O-91	-2.0
1894	Cle-N	64	253	36	73	15	1	2	40	13	17	.289	.331	.379	68	-14	14			.953	3	O-64	-1.2
1895	*Cle-N	131	528	84	143	17	2	0	68	38	37	.271	.327	.311	61	-31	32			.934	3	*O-131	-3.2
1896	*Cle-N	116	455	70	131	16	4	1	54	47	32	.288	.361	.347	82	-11	24			.958	7	*O-116	-1.2
1897	Cle-N	24	91	6	20	2	0	0	10	7		.220	.283	.242	37	-8	4			.947	-1	O-24	-0.9
1898	Cle-N	106	366	47	87	3	0	0	48	46		.238	.331	.246	67	-13	7			.965	3	*O-104/2-2	-1.7
1901	Cle-A	3	7	0	1	0	0	0	0	0		.143	.143	.143	-22	-1	0			1.000	-1	/O-2,P-1,3-1,M	-0.2
1902	StL-A	2	3	0	2	0	0	0	0	0		.667	.667	.667	274	1	0			.000	-1	/O-2,M	0.0
1907	StL-A	2	0	0	0	0	0	0	0	0		—	—	—	—	0	0			.000	0	RM	0.0
Total	13	1020	3977	619	1007	114	39	11	469	365	290	.253	.322	.310	72	-154	262			.944	54	*O-1015/2-2,3-1,P-1	-13.2
■ **JACK McALEESE**	McAleese, John James b: 1877, Sharon, Pa. d: 11/15/50, New York, N.Y. BR/TR, 5'8", Deb: 8/10/01																						
1901	Chi-A	1	1	0	0	0	0	0	0	0		.000	.000	.000	-99	-0	0			1.000	0	/P-1	0.0
1909	StL-A	85	267	33	57	7	0	0	12	32		.213	.318	.240	82	-3	18			.910	-3	O-79/3-2	-1.1
Total	2	86	268	33	57	7	0	0	12	32		.213	.317	.239	82	-4	18			.910	-3	/O-79,3-2,P-1	-1.1
■ **BILL McALLESTER**	McAllester, William Lusk b: 12/29/1889, Chattanooga, Tenn. d: 3/3/70, Chattanooga, Tenn. BR/TR, 6', 175 lbs. Deb: 5/2/13																						
1913	StL-A	49	85	3	13	4	0	0	6	11	12	.153	.250	.200	33	-7	2			.908	-4	C-39	-0.9
■ **SPORT McALLISTER**	McAllister, Lewis William b: 7/23/1874, Austin, Miss. d: 7/17/62, Wyandotte, Mich. BB/TR, 5'11", 180 lbs. Deb: 8/7/1896																						
1896	Cle-N	8	27	2	6	2	0	0	1	0	2	.222	.250	.296	41	-2	1			.500	-6	/O-4,C-2,P-1	-0.8
1897	Cle-N	43	137	23	30	5	1	0	11	12		.219	.287	.270	45	-11	3			.894	-6	O-28/S-4,P-4,1C2	-1.6
1898	Cle-N	17	57	8	13	3	1	0	9	5		.228	.290	.316	75	-2	0			.941	1	/P-9,O-8	0.0
1899	Cle-N	113	418	29	99	6	8	1	31	19		.237	.273	.297	61	-23	5			.943	-15	O-79,C-17/3-7,1SP2	-3.8
1901	Det-A	90	306	45	92	9	4	3	57	15		.301	.344	.386	97	-2	17			.898	-19	C-35,1-28,O-11,3/S	-1.6
1902	Det-A	21	67	8	14	1	0	1	8	2		.209	.243	.269	41	-5	0			1.000	-0	/1-5,S-5,2-3,C3O	-0.5
	Bal-A	3	11	0	1	0	0	0	1	1		.091	.167	.091	-26	-2	0			.923	-0	/2-2,1-1	-0.2
	Det-A	45	162	11	34	4	2	0	24	3		.210	.229	.259	34	-14	1			.991	-1	1-21,O-11/C-7,3S	-1.5
	Yr	69	240	19	49	5	2	1	33	6		.204	.230	.254	33	-22	1			.992	-1	1-27,O-12/C-9,S32D	-2.2
1903	Det-A	78	265	31	69	8	2	0	22	10		.260	.297	.306	84	-5	5			.888	-7	S-46,C-18/O-5,31	-0.9
Total	7	418	1450	157	358	38	18	5	164	67	2	.247	.287	.308	67	-68	32			.914	-55	O-147/C-83,1S3P2	-10.9
■ **JIM McANANY**	McAnany, James b: 9/4/36, Los Angeles, Cal. BR/TR, 5'10", 196 lbs. Deb: 9/19/58																						
1958	Chi-A	5	13	0	0	0	0	0	0	0	5	.000	.000	.000	-99	-4	0	0	0	1.000	1	/O-3	-0.3
1959	*Chi-A	67	210	22	58	9	3	0	27	19	26	.276	.339	.348	90	-3	2	1	0	.966	-1	O-67	-0.6
1960	Chi-A	3	2	0	0	0	0	0	0	0	2	.000	.000	.000	-99	-1	0	0	0	.000	0	H	-0.1
1961	Chi-N	11	10	1	3	1	0	0	0	1	3	.300	.364	.400	101	0	0	0	0	.000	-0	/O-1	0.0
1962	Chi-N	7	6	0	0	0	0	0	0	1	2	.000	.143	.000	-56	-1	0	0	0	.000	0	H	-0.1
Total	5	93	241	23	61	10	3	0	27	21	38	.253	.316	.320	75	-8	2	1	0	.968	-1	/O-71	-1.1
■ **BUB McATEE**	McAtee, Michael James "Butch" b: 3/1845, Troy, N.Y. d: 10/18/1876, Troy, N.Y. TR, 5'9", 160 lbs. Deb: 5/8/1871																						
1871	Chi-n	26	135	34	37	8	2	0	10	5	2	.274	.300	.363	81	-5	5	3	-0	.943	1	*1-26	-0.2
1872	Tro-n	25	129	30	28	3	1	0	15	1	2	.217	.223	.256	46	-8	0	2	-1	.948	1	1-25	-0.5
Total	2 n	51	264	64	65	11	3	0	25	6	4	.246	.263	.311	65	-13	5	5	-2	.945	2	/1-51	-0.7
■ **IKE McAULEY**	McAuley, James Earl b: 8/19/1891, Wichita, Kan. d: 4/6/28, Des Moines, Iowa BR/TR, 5'9.5", 150 lbs. Deb: 9/10/14																						
1914	Pit-N	15	24	3	3	0	0	0	0	0	8	.125	.125	.125	-27	-4	0			.900	1	/S-5,3-3,2-2	-0.3
1915	Pit-N	5	15	0	2	1	0	0	0	0	6	.133	.133	.200	0	-2	0			.917	-3	/S-5	-0.5
1916	Pit-N	4	8	1	2	0	0	0	1	0	1	.250	.250	.250	53	-0	0			.938	1	/S-4	0.0
1917	StL-N	3	7	0	2	0	0	0	1	0	1	.286	.286	.286	78	-0	0			.833	-2	/S-3	-0.3
1925	Chi-N	37	125	10	35	7	2	0	11	11	12	.280	.343	.368	80	-4	1	0	0	.949	-8	S-37	-0.7
Total	5	64	179	14	44	8	2	0	13	11	28	.246	.293	.313	62	-10	1	0		.940	-12	/S-54,3-3,2-2	-1.8
■ **GENE McAULIFFE**	McAuliffe, Eugene Leo b: 2/28/1872, Randolph, Mass. d: 4/29/53, Randolph, Mass. BR/TR, 6'1", 180 lbs. Deb: 8/17/04																						
1904	Bos-N	1	2	0	1	0	0	0	0	0		.500	.500	.500	217	0	0			.667	-1	/C-1	0.0
■ **DICK McAULIFFE**	McAuliffe, Richard John b: 11/29/39, Hartford, Conn. BL/TR, 5'11", 176 lbs. Deb: 9/17/60																						
1960	Det-A	8	27	2	7	0	1	0	1	2	6	.259	.310	.333	72	-1	0	0	0	.884	1	/S-7	0.1
1961	Det-A	80	285	36	73	12	4	6	33	24	39	.256	.323	.389	87	-6	2	3	-1	.933	-29	S-55,3-22	-3.1
1962	Det-A	139	471	50	124	20	5	12	63	64	76	.263	.351	.403	99	0	4	2	0	.965	-21	2-70,3-49,S-16	-1.2
1963	Det-A	150	568	77	149	18	6	13	61	64	75	.262	.337	.384	98	-1	11	5	0	.963	-24	*S-133,2-15	-1.4
1964	Det-A	162	557	85	134	18	7	24	66	77	96	.241	.336	.427	109	7	8	5	-1	.958	-8	*S-160	1.1

YEAR	TM/L	G	AB	R	H	2B	3B	HR	RBI	BB	SO	AVG	OBP	SLG	PRO+	BR/A	SB	CS	SBR	FA	FR	G/POS	TPR
1965	Det-A★	113	404	61	105	13	6	15	54	49	62	.260	.343	.433	118	10	6	9	-4	.956	-15	*S-112	-0.2
1966	Det-A★	124	430	83	118	16	8	23	56	66	80	.274	.375	.509	148	28	5	7	-3	.964	-11	*S-105,3-15	2.5
1967	Det-A★	153	557	92	133	16	7	22	65	105	118	.239	.366	.411	126	21	6	5	-1	.965	-14	*2-145,S-43	1.9
1968	*Det-A	151	570	**95**	142	24	10	16	56	82	99	.249	.346	.411	125	18	8	7	-2	.986	-20	*2-148/S-5	0.7
1969	Det-A	74	271	49	71	10	5	11	33	47	41	.262	.371	.458	125	10	2	5	-2	.976	-0	2-72	1.4
1970	Det-A	146	530	73	124	21	1	12	50	101	62	.234	.360	.345	95	-0	5	6	-2	.975	-6	*2-127,S-15,3-12	0.4
1971	Det-A	128	477	67	99	16	6	18	57	53	67	.208	.293	.379	86	-10	4	1	1	.987	7	*2-123/S-7	0.9
1972	*Det-A	122	408	47	98	16	3	8	30	59	59	.240	.339	.353	103	3	0	0	0	.975	-7	*2-116/S-3,3-1	0.2
1973	Det-A	106	343	39	94	18	1	12	47	49	52	.274	.366	.437	118	9	0	4	-2	.986	5	*2-102/S-2,D-1	1.7
1974	Bos-A	100	272	32	57	13	1	5	24	39	40	.210	.311	.320	76	-8	2	0	1	.971	-8	2-53,3-40/S-3,D-3	-1.4
1975	Bos-A	7	15	0	2	0	0	0	1	1	2	.133	.188	.133	-7	-2	0	0	0	.769	-2	/3-7	-0.4
Total	16	1763	6185	888	1530	231	71	197	697	882	974	.247	.344	.403	108	78	63	59	-17	.977	-150	2-971,S-666,3/D	3.2

■ GEORGE McAVOY

McAvoy, George Robert b: 3/12/1884, E.Liverpool, Ohio Deb: 7/17/14

YEAR	TM/L	G	AB	R	H	2B	3B	HR	RBI	BB	SO	AVG	OBP	SLG	PRO+	BR/A	SB	CS	SBR	FA	FR	G/POS	TPR
1914	Phi-N	1	1	0	0	0	0	0	0	0	0	.000	.000	.000	-94	-0	0			.000	0	H	0.0

■ WICKEY McAVOY

McAvoy, James Eugene b: 10/22/1894, Rochester, N.Y. d: 7/6/73, Rochester, N.Y. BR/TR, 5'11", 172 lbs. Deb: 9/29/13

YEAR	TM/L	G	AB	R	H	2B	3B	HR	RBI	BB	SO	AVG	OBP	SLG	PRO+	BR/A	SB	CS	SBR	FA	FR	G/POS	TPR
1913	Phi-A	4	9	0	1	0	0	0	0	0	4	.111	.200	.111	-9	-1	0			1.000	1	/C-4	0.0
1914	Phi-A	8	16	1	2	0	1	0	0	0	4	.125	.125	.250	13	-2	0			.971	1	/C-8	-0.1
1915	Phi-A	68	184	12	35	7	2	0	6	11	32	.190	.236	.250	47	-13	0	2	-1	.931	5	C-64	-0.6
1917	Phi-A	10	24	1	6	1	0	1	4	0	3	.250	.250	.417	105	-0	0			.955	3	/C-8	0.4
1918	Phi-A	83	271	14	66	5	3	0	32	13	23	.244	.283	.284	70	-10	5			.960	5	C-74/P-1,1-1,O-1	0.1
1919	Phi-A	62	170	10	24	5	2	0	11	14	21	.141	.207	.194	13	-20	1			.973	-3	C-57	-1.9
Total	6	235	674	38	134	18	8	1	53	38	87	.199	.245	.254	47	-46	6	2		.954	13	C-215/O-1,1-1,P-1	-2.1

■ ALGIE McBRIDE

McBride, Algernon Griggs b: 5/23/1869, Washington, D.C. d: 1/10/56, Georgetown, Ohio BL/TL, 5'9", 152 lbs. Deb: 5/12/1896

YEAR	TM/L	G	AB	R	H	2B	3B	HR	RBI	BB	SO	AVG	OBP	SLG	PRO+	BR/A	SB	CS	SBR	FA	FR	G/POS	TPR
1896	Chi-N	9	29	2	7	1	1	1	7	7	3	.241	.389	.448	116	1	0			.917	0	/O-9	0.0
1898	Cin-N	120	486	94	147	14	12	2	43	51		.302	.383	.393	114	9	16			.959	7	*O-120	0.8
1899	Cin-N	64	251	57	87	12	5	1	23	30		.347	.431	.446	138	15	5			.950	-2	O-64	0.7
1900	Cin-N	112	436	59	120	15	8	4	59	25		.275	.320	.374	94	-5	12			.915	-9	*O-110	-2.0
1901	Cin-N	30	123	19	29	7	0	2	18	7		.236	.282	.341	86	-3	0			.968	-2	O-28	-0.7
	NY-N	68	264	27	74	11	0	2	29	12		.280	.317	.345	95	-2	3			.948	-4	O-65	-1.0
	Yr	98	387	46	103	18	0	4	47	19		.266	.306	.344	92	-4	3			.956	-6	O-93	-1.7
Total	5	403	1589	258	464	60	26	12	179	132	3	.292	.356	.385	108	15	36			.946	-10	O-396	-2.2

■ BAKE McBRIDE

McBride, Arnold Ray b: 2/3/49, Fulton, Mo. BL/TR, 6'2", 190 lbs. Deb: 7/26/73

YEAR	TM/L	G	AB	R	H	2B	3B	HR	RBI	BB	SO	AVG	OBP	SLG	PRO+	BR/A	SB	CS	SBR	FA	FR	G/POS	TPR
1973	StL-N	40	63	8	19	3	0	0	5	4	10	.302	.362	.349	98	0	0	1	-1	.976	1	O-17	-0.1
1974	StL-N	150	559	81	173	19	5	6	56	43	57	.309	.372	.394	115	12	30	11	2	.990	14	*O-144	2.3
1975	StL-N	116	413	70	124	10	9	5	36	34	52	.300	.355	.404	107	4	26	8	3	.990	7	*O-107	1.0
1976	StL-N☆	72	272	40	91	13	4	3	24	18	28	.335	.389	.445	135	12	10	5	0	.981	9	O-66	2.0
1977	StL-N	43	122	21	32	5	1	4	20	7	19	.262	.302	.418	93	-2	9	3	1	1.000	-5	O-33	-0.7
	*Phi-N	85	280	55	95	20	5	11	41	25	25	.339	.399	.564	149	19	27	4	6	.986	1	O-73	2.2
	Yr	128	402	76	127	25	6	15	61	32	44	.316	.371	.520	133	18	36	7	7	.990	-4	*O-106	1.5
1978	*Phi-N	122	472	68	127	20	4	10	49	28	68	.269	.317	.392	96	-3	28	3	7	**.996**	5	*O-119	0.3
1979	Phi-N	151	582	82	163	16	12	12	60	41	77	.280	.332	.411	98	-2	25	14	-1	.989	15	*O-147	0.6
1980	*Phi-N	137	554	68	171	33	10	9	87	26	58	.309	.345	.453	115	10	13	10	-2	.990	6	*O-133	0.9
1981	*Phi-N	58	221	26	60	17	1	2	21	11	25	.271	.306	.385	91	-3	5	0	2	.987	-4	O-56	-0.8
1982	Cle-A	27	85	8	31	3	3	0	13	2	12	.365	.379	.471	132	4	2	2	-1	1.000	-2	O-22	0.0
1983	Cle-A	70	230	21	67	8	1	1	18	9	26	.291	.321	.348	81	-6	8	2	1	.977	0	O-46,D-15	-0.7
Total	11	1071	3853	548	1153	167	55	63	430	248	457	.299	.348	.420	109	45	183	63	17	.989	46	O-963/D-15	7.0

■ GEORGE McBRIDE

McBride, George Florian b: 11/20/1880, Milwaukee, Wis. d: 7/2/73, Milwaukee, Wis. BR/TR, 5'11", 170 lbs. Deb: 9/12/01 MC

YEAR	TM/L	G	AB	R	H	2B	3B	HR	RBI	BB	SO	AVG	OBP	SLG	PRO+	BR/A	SB	CS	SBR	FA	FR	G/POS	TPR
1901	Mil-A	3	12	0	2	0	0	0	0	1		.167	.231	.167	12	-1	0			1.000	-1	/S-3	-0.2
1905	Pit-N	27	87	9	19	4	0	0	7	6		.218	.277	.264	60	-4	2			.902	-4	3-17/S-8	-0.8
	StL-N	81	281	22	61	1	2	2	34	14		.217	.264	.256	57	-15	10			.938	-2	S-80/1-1	-1.6
	Yr	108	368	31	80	5	2	2	41	20		.217	.267	.258	58	-19	12			.935	-6	S-88,3-17/1-1	-2.4
1906	StL-N	90	313	24	53	8	2	0	13	17		.169	.215	.208	33	-25	5			.944	9	S-90	-1.5
1908	Was-A	155	518	47	120	10	6	0	34	41		.232	.292	.274	92	-4	12			.948	32	*S-155	3.4
1909	Was-A	156	504	38	118	16	0	0	34	36		.234	.294	.266	81	-10	17			**.935**	11	*S-156	0.4
1910	Was-A	154	514	54	118	19	4	1	55	61		.230	.321	.288	95	-1	11			.939	27	*S-154	3.5
1911	Was-A	154	557	58	131	11	4	0	59	52		.235	.312	.269	64	-26	15			.941	24	*S-154	0.8
1912	Was-A	152	521	56	118	13	7	1	52	38		.226	.288	.284	63	-25	17			**.941**	**31**	*S-152	1.9
1913	Was-A	150	499	52	107	18	7	1	52	43	46	.214	.286	.285	66	-22	12			**.960**	11	*S-150	0.4
1914	Was-A	156	503	49	102	12	4	0	24	43	70	.203	.274	.243	53	-28	12	14	-5	**.958**	12	*S-156	-1.0
1915	Was-A	146	476	54	97	8	6	1	30	29	60	.204	.251	.252	50	-31	10	5	0	**.968**	9	*S-146	-1.1
1916	Was-A	139	466	36	106	15	4	1	36	23	58	.227	.271	.283	67	-20	8			.957	13	*S-139	0.0
1917	Was-A	50	141	6	27	3	0	0	9	10	17	.191	.265	.213	46	-9	1			.943	-1	S-41/3-6,2-2	-0.9
1918	Was-A	18	53	2	7	0	0	0	1	0	11	.132	.132	.132	-21	-8	1			.986	2	S-14/2-2	-0.6
1919	Was-A	15	40	3	8	1	1	0	4	3	6	.200	.256	.275	49	-3	0			.932	1	S-15	-0.2
1920	Was-A	13	41	6	9	1	0	0	3	2	3	.220	.256	.244	34	-4	0	0	0	.966	-3	S-13	-0.6
Total	16	1659	5526	516	1203	140	47	7	447	419	271	.218	.281	.264	65	-236	133	19		.948	169	*S-1626/3-23,2-4,1	1.9

■ JOHN McBRIDE

McBride, John F. Deb: 10/12/1890

YEAR	TM/L	G	AB	R	H	2B	3B	HR	RBI	BB	SO	AVG	OBP	SLG	PRO+	BR/A	SB	CS	SBR	FA	FR	G/POS	TPR
1890	Phi-a	1	2	0	0	0	0	0	0	0		.000	.000	.000	-99	-1	0			1.000	1	/O-1	0.0

■ TOM McBRIDE

McBride, Thomas Raymond b: 11/2/14, Bonham, Tex. BR/TR, 6', 190 lbs. Deb: 4/23/43

YEAR	TM/L	G	AB	R	H	2B	3B	HR	RBI	BB	SO	AVG	OBP	SLG	PRO+	BR/A	SB	CS	SBR	FA	FR	G/POS	TPR
1943	Bos-A	26	96	11	23	3	1	0	7	7	3	.240	.291	.292	70	-4	2	0	1	.984	0	O-24	-0.5
1944	Bos-A	71	216	29	53	7	3	0	24	8	13	.245	.276	.306	67	-10	4	0	1	.992	-1	O-57/1-5	-1.2
1945	Bos-A	100	344	38	105	11	7	1	47	26	17	.305	.354	.387	112	5	2	2	-1	.984	-0	O-81,1-11	-0.1
1946	*Bos-A	61	153	21	46	5	2	0	19	9	6	.301	.340	.359	90	-2	0	1	-1	1.000	-7	O-43	-1.2
1947	Bos-A	2	5	0	1	0	0	0	0	0	0	.200	.200	.200	11	-1	0	0	0	1.000	1	/O-1	0.0
	Was-A	56	166	19	45	4	2	0	15	15	9	.271	.331	.319	84	-4	3	1	0	.972	-4	O-51/3-1	-1.0
	Yr	58	171	19	46	4	2	0	15	15	9	.269	.328	.316	81	-4	3	1	0	.973	-3	O-52/3-1	-1.0
1948	Was-A	92	206	22	53	9	1	1	29	28	15	.257	.346	.325	81	-5	2	2	-1	.983	2	O-55	-0.6
Total	6	408	1186	140	326	39	16	2	141	93	63	.275	.328	.340	88	-20	13	6	0	.985	-9	O-312/1-16,3-1	-4.6

■ SWAT McCABE

McCabe, James Arthur b: 11/20/1881, Towanda, Pa. d: 12/9/44, Bristol, Conn. BL/TR, 5'10", Deb: 9/23/09

YEAR	TM/L	G	AB	R	H	2B	3B	HR	RBI	BB	SO	AVG	OBP	SLG	PRO+	BR/A	SB	CS	SBR	FA	FR	G/POS	TPR
1909	Cin-N	3	11	2	6	1	0	0	0	0		.545	.545	.636	269	2	1			.625	-1	/O-3	0.1
1910	Cin-N	13	35	3	9	1	0	0	5	1	2	.257	.297	.286	73	-1	0			1.000	1	/O-9	-0.1
Total	2	16	46	5	15	2	0	0	5	1	2	.326	.354	.370	118	1	1			.875	-1	/O-12	0.0

■ JOE McCABE

McCabe, Joseph Robert b: 8/27/38, Indianapolis, Ind. BR/TR, 6', 190 lbs. Deb: 4/18/64

YEAR	TM/L	G	AB	R	H	2B	3B	HR	RBI	BB	SO	AVG	OBP	SLG	PRO+	BR/A	SB	CS	SBR	FA	FR	G/POS	TPR
1964	Min-A	14	19	1	3	0	0	0	2	0	8	.158	.158	.158	-12	-3	0	0	0	1.000	0	C-12	-0.2
1965	Was-A	14	27	1	5	0	0	1	5	4	13	.185	.290	.296	68	-1	1	0	0	.972	-3	C-11	-0.3
Total	2	28	46	2	8	0	0	1	7	4	21	.174	.240	.239	36	-4	1	0	0	.986	-2	/C-23	-0.5

■ BILL McCABE

McCabe, William Francis b: 10/28/1892, Chicago, Ill. d: 9/2/66, Chicago, Ill. BB/TR, 5'9.5", 180 lbs. Deb: 4/16/18

YEAR	TM/L	G	AB	R	H	2B	3B	HR	RBI	BB	SO	AVG	OBP	SLG	PRO+	BR/A	SB	CS	SBR	FA	FR	G/POS	TPR
1918	*Chi-N	29	45	9	8	0	1	0	5	4	7	.178	.245	.222	42	-3	2			.939	5	2-13/O-4	0.3
1919	Chi-N	33	84	8	13	3	1	0	5	9	15	.155	.253	.214	41	-6	3			.950	-1	O-20/S-4,3-1	-0.9
1920	Chi-N	3	2	1	1	0	0	0	0	0	0	.500	.500	.500	184	0	0	0	0	.000	0	H	0.0
	*Bro-N	41	68	10	10	0	0	0	3	2	6	.147	.171	.147	-8	-9	1	2	-1	.882	4	S-13/O-6,2-4,3-3	-0.7

YEAR	TM/L	G	AB	R	H	2B	3B	HR	RBI	BB	SO	AVG	OBP	SLG	PRO+	BR/A	SB	CS	SBR	FA	FR	G/POS	TPR
	Yr	44	70	11	11	0	0	0	3	2	6	.157	.181	.157	-2	-9	1	2	-1	.882	4	S-13/O-6,2-4,3-3	-0.7
Total	3	106	199	28	32	3	2	0	13	15	28	.161	.227	.196	26	-18	6	2		.943	8	/O-30,S-17,2-17,3-4	-1.3
■ HARRY McCAFFERY	McCaffery, Harry Charles b: 11/25/1858, St.Louis, Mo. d: 4/19/28, St.Louis, Mo. BR/TR, 5′10.5″, 185 lbs. Deb: 6/15/1882 U																						
1882	Lou-a	1	4	1	1	0	0	0		0		.250	.250	.250	73	-0				1.000	-1	/2-1	-0.1
	StL-a	38	153	23	42	8	6	0		3		.275	.288	.405	127	4				.891	4	O-23/2-8,3-7,1-1	0.7
	Yr	39	157	24	43	8	6	0		3		.274	.287	.401	125	4				.891	3	O-23/2-9,3-7,1-1	0.6
1883	StL-a	5	18	0	1	0	0	0	1	1		.056	.105	.056	-44	-3				.889	1	/O-5	-0.2
1885	Cin-a	1	5	0	0	0	0	0	0	0		.000	.000	.000	-98	-1				.000	-0	/P-1	0.0
Total	3	45	180	24	44	8	6	0	1	4		.244	.261	.356	101	-0				.891	4	/O-28,2-9,3-7,P1	0.4
■ SPARROW McCAFFREY	McCaffrey, Charles P. b: 1868, Philadelphia, Pa. d: 4/29/1894, Philadelphia, Pa. 120 lbs. Deb: 8/13/1889																						
1889	Col-a	2	1	1	1	0	0	0	0	1	0	1.000	1.000	1.000	495	1	0			.000	0	/C-2	0.1
■ BRIAN McCALL	McCall, Brian Allen "Bam" b: 1/25/43, Kentfield, Cal. BL/TL, 5′10″, 170 lbs. Deb: 9/18/62																						
1962	Chi-A	4	8	2	3	0	0	2	3	0	2	.375	.375	1.125	287	2	0	0	0	1.000	0	/O-1	0.2
1963	Chi-A	3	7	1	0	0	0	0	0	1	2	.000	.125	.000	-62	-2	0	0	0	1.000	-0	/O-2	-0.2
Total	2	7	15	3	3	0	0	2	3	1	4	.200	.250	.600	126	0	0	0	0	1.000	0	/O-3	0.0
■ JACK McCANDLESS	McCandless, Scott Cook b: 5/5/1891, Pittsburgh, Pa. d: 8/17/61, Pittsburgh, Pa. BL/TR, 6′, 170 lbs. Deb: 9/10/14																						
1914	Bal-F	11	31	5	8	0	1	0	1	3	0	.258	.343	.323	79	-1	0			1.000	-0	/O-8	-0.2
1915	Bal-F	117	406	47	87	6	7	5	34	41	99	.214	.296	.300	66	-24	9			.945	3	*O-105	-2.9
Total	2	128	437	52	95	6	8	5	35	44	99	.217	.299	.302	67	-26	9			.948	3	O-113	-3.1
■ EMMETT McCANN	McCann, Robert Emmett b: 3/4/02, Philadelphia, Pa. d: 4/15/37, Philadelphia, Pa. BR/TR, 5′11″, 150 lbs. Deb: 4/19/20																						
1920	Phi-A	13	34	4	9	1	1	0	3	3	1	.265	.342	.353	84	-1	0	1	-1	.907	-0	S-11	-0.1
1921	Phi-A	52	157	15	35	5	0	0	15	4	6	.223	.242	.255	27	-17	2	1	0	.949	-0	S-32/3-9,2-2,1-1	-1.4
1926	Bos-A	6	3	0	0	0	0	0	0	1	1	.000	.250	.000	-32	-1	0	0	0	1.000	-0	/S-1,3-1	-0.1
Total	3	71	194	19	44	6	1	0	18	8	8	.227	.261	.268	36	-19	2	2	-1	.939	-1	/S-44,3-10,2-2,1-1	-1.6
■ ROGER McCARDELL	McCardell, Roger Morton b: 8/29/32, Gorsuch Mills, Md. d: 11/13/96, Perry Point, Md. BR/TR, 6′, 200 lbs. Deb: 5/8/59																						
1959	SF-N	4	4	0	0	0	0	0	0	0	0	.000	.000	.000	-99	-1	0	0	0	1.000	0	/C-3	-0.1
■ BILL McCARREN	McCarren, William Joseph b: 11/4/1895, Fortenia, Pa. d: 9/11/83, Denver, Colo. BR/TR, 5′11.5″, 170 lbs. Deb: 5/4/23																						
1923	Bro-N	69	216	28	53	10	1	3	27	22	39	.245	.326	.343	79	-6	0	1	-1	.927	-2	3-66/O-1	-0.3
■ ALEX McCARTHY	McCarthy, Alexander George b: 5/12/1888, Chicago, Ill. d: 3/12/78, Salisbury, Md. BR/TR, 5′9″, 150 lbs. Deb: 10/7/10																						
1910	Pit-N	3	12	1	1	0	1	0	0	0	2	.083	.083	.250	-3	-2	0			.875	0	/S-3	-0.2
1911	Pit-N	50	150	18	36	5	1	2	31	14	24	.240	.305	.327	74	-6	4			.981	-1	S-33,2-11/3-1,O-1	-0.4
1912	Pit-N	111	401	53	111	12	4	1	41	30	26	.277	.332	.334	84	-9	8			.962	3	*2-105/3-4	-0.8
1913	Pit-N	31	74	7	15	5	0	0	10	7	7	.203	.298	.270	66	-3	1			.902	-2	S-12,3-12/2-6	-0.5
1914	Pit-N	57	173	14	26	0	1	1	14	6	17	.150	.192	.179	11	-19	2			.975	11	3-36,2-10/S-6	-0.8
1915	Pit-N	21	49	3	10	0	1	0	3	5	10	.204	.291	.245	64	-2	1	2	-1	.950	1	/2-9,S-5,3-4,1-1	-0.2
	Chi-N	23	72	4	19	3	0	1	6	5	7	.264	.329	.347	105	0	2	3	-1	.972	11	2-12,3-12/S-1	1.2
	Yr	44	121	7	29	3	1	1	9	10	17	.240	.313	.306	88	-1	3	5	-2	.964	12	2-21,3-16/S-6,1-1	1.0
1916	Chi-N	37	107	10	26	2	3	0	6	11	7	.243	.341	.318	93	-0	1			.931	-2	2-34/S-3	-0.2
	Pit-N	50	146	11	29	3	0	0	3	15	10	.199	.282	.219	54	-7	3			.955	-5	S-39/2-7,3-5	-1.2
	Yr	87	253	21	55	5	3	0	9	26	17	.217	.308	.261	72	-7	4			.951	-7	S-42,2-41/3-5	-1.4
1917	Pit-N	49	151	15	33	4	0	0	8	11	13	.219	.276	.245	58	-7	1			.964	7	3-26,2-13/S-9	0.1
Total	8	432	1335	136	306	34	11	5	122	104	123	.229	.295	.282	67	-55	23	5		.957	23	2-207,S-111,3/10	-3.0
■ JERRY McCARTHY	McCarthy, Jerome Francis b: 5/23/23, Brooklyn, N.Y. d: 10/3/65, Oceanside, N.Y. BL/TL, 6′1″, 205 lbs. Deb: 6/19/48																						
1948	StL-A	2	3	0	1	0	0	0	0	0	0	.333	.333	.333	76	-0	0	0	0	.600	-1	/1-2	-0.1
■ JACK McCARTHY	McCarthy, John Arthur b: 3/26/1869, Gilbertville, Mass d: 9/11/31, Chicago, Ill. BL/TL, 5′9″, 155 lbs. Deb: 8/3/1893																						
1893	Cin-N	49	195	28	55	8	3	0	22	22	7	.282	.355	.354	86	-4	6			.887	-1	O-47/1-2	-0.6
1894	Cin-N	40	167	29	45	9	1	0	21	17	6	.269	.348	.335	63	-10	3			.895	2	O-25,1-15	-0.8
1898	Pit-N	137	537	75	155	13	12	4	78	34		.289	.336	.380	107	4	7			.935	4	*O-137	-0.3
1899	Pit-N	138	560	108	171	22	17	3	67	39		.305	.355	.421	113	8	28			.961	-5	*O-138	-0.7
1900	Chi-N	124	503	68	148	16	7	0	48	24		.294	.329	.354	92	-6	22			.944	-1	*O-123	-1.5
1901	Cle-A	86	343	60	110	14	7	0	32	30		.321	.382	.402	123	12	9			.949	-1	O-86	0.4
1902	Cle-A	95	359	45	102	31	5	0	41	24		.284	.329	.398	105	2	12			.944	-5	O-95	-0.9
1903	Cle-A	108	415	47	110	20	8	0	43	19		.265	.299	.352	96	-2	15			.964	-3	*O-108	-1.3
	Chi-N	24	101	11	28	5	0	0	14	4		.277	.305	.327	82	-3	8			.947	-3	O-24	-0.7
1904	Chi-N	115	432	36	114	14	2	0	51	23		.264	.307	.306	89	-6	14			.961	-5	*O-115	-1.8
1905	Chi-N	59	170	16	47	4	3	0	14	10		.276	.320	.335	92	-2	8			.986	2	O-37/1-6	-0.2
1906	Bro-N	91	322	23	98	13	1	0	35	20		.304	.347	.351	128	9	9			.924	2	O-86	0.8
1907	Bro-N	25	91	4	20	2	0	0	8	2		.220	.237	.242	54	-5	4			1.000	-4	O-25	-1.2
Total	12	1091	4195	550	1203	171	66	7	474	268	13	.287	.333	.364	100	-3	145			.946	-17	*O-1046/1-23	-8.8
■ JOHNNY McCARTHY	McCarthy, John Joseph b: 1/7/10, Chicago, Ill. d: 9/13/73, Mundelein, Ill. BL/TL, 6′1.5″, 185 lbs. Deb: 9/2/34																						
1934	Bro-N	17	39	7	7	2	0	1	5	2	2	.179	.220	.308	42	-3	0			.961	1	1-13	-0.3
1935	Bro-N	22	48	9	12	1	1	0	4	2	9	.250	.280	.313	60	-3	1			.982	-3	1-19	-0.7
1936	NY-N	4	16	1	7	0	0	1	2	0	1	.438	.438	.625	185	2	1			.981	1	/1-4	0.3
1937	*NY-N	114	420	53	117	19	3	10	65	24	37	.279	.322	.410	96	-3	2			.987	2	*1-110	-1.3
1938	NY-N	134	470	55	128	13	4	8	59	39	28	.272	.329	.368	91	-6	3			.993	-3	*1-125	-2.4
1939	NY-N	50	80	12	21	6	1	1	11	3	8	.262	.298	.400	85	-2	0			1.000	-4	1-12/O-4,P-1	-0.7
1940	NY-N	51	67	6	16	4	0	0	5	2	8	.239	.261	.299	53	-4	0			1.000	1	/1-6	-0.4
1941	NY-N	14	40	1	13	3	0	0	12	3	0	.325	.372	.400	115	1	0			.987	0	/1-8,O-1	0.1
1943	Bos-N	78	313	32	95	24	6	2	33	10	19	.304	.327	.438	122	7	1			.996	1	1-78	0.3
1946	Bos-N	2	7	0	1	0	0	0	1	2	0	.143	.333	.143	37	-0	0			1.000	-1	/1-2	-0.1
1948	NY-N	56	57	6	15	0	1	2	12	3	2	.263	.300	.404	88	-1	0			.966	-0	/1-6	-0.2
Total	11	542	1557	182	432	72	16	25	209	90	114	.277	.319	.392	95	-14	8			.990	-5	1-383/O-5,P-1	-5.4
■ JOE McCARTHY	McCarthy, Joseph N. b: 12/25/1881, Syracuse, N.Y. d: 1/12/37, Syracuse, N.Y. BR/TR, Deb: 9/27/05																						
1905	NY-A	1	2	0	0	0	0	0	0	0		.000	.000	.000	-90	-0	0			1.000	0	/C-1	0.0
1906	StL-N	15	37	3	9	2	0	0	2	2		.243	.282	.297	84	-1	0			.984	-0	C-15	0.0
Total	2	16	39	3	9	2	0	0	2	2		.231	.268	.282	74	-1	0			.985	-0	/C-16	0.0
■ TOMMY McCARTHY	McCarthy, Thomas Francis Michael b: 7/24/1863, Boston, Mass. d: 8/5/22, Boston, Mass. BR/TR, 5′7″, 170 lbs. Deb: 7/10/1884 MH																						
1884	Bos-U	53	209	37	45	2	2	0		6		.215	.237	.244	47	-19				.794	-2	O-48/P-7	-1.9
1885	Bos-N	40	148	16	27	2	0	0	11	5	25	.182	.209	.196	33	-11				.865	3	O-40	-0.8
1886	Phi-N	8	27	6	5	2	1	0	3	2	3	.185	.241	.333	73	-1	1			.818	-1	/O-8,P-1	-0.2
1887	Phi-N	18	70	7	13	4	0	0	6	2	5	.186	.219	.243	27	-7	15			.818	-9	/O-8,2-5,S-3,3-2	-1.4
1888	*StL-a	131	511	107	140	20	3	1	68	38		.274	.328	.331	100	-2	93			.932	30	*O-131/P-2	2.2
1889	StL-a	140	604	136	176	24	7	2	63	46	26	.291	.348	.364	91	-12	57			.893	14	*O-140/2-2,P-1	-0.1
1890	StL-a	133	548	137	192	28	9	6	69	66		.350	.430	.467	144	27	**83**			.893	7	*O-102,3-32/2-1,M	2.8
1891	StL-a	136	578	127	179	21	6	8	95	50	19	.310	.375	.408	108	1	37			.895	-1	*O-113,2-14,S/3P	-0.2
1892	*Bos-N	152	603	119	146	19	5	4	63	93	29	.242	.347	.310	91	-6	53			.883	2	*O-152	-1.0
1893	Bos-N	116	462	107	160	28	6	5	111	64	10	.346	.429	.465	128	18	46			.902	3	*O-108/2-7,S-3	1.3
1894	Bos-N	127	539	118	188	21	8	13	126	59	17	.349	.419	.490	110	7	43			.904	11	*O-127/S-2,2-1,P-1	0.7
1895	Bos-N	117	452	90	131	13	2	2	73	72	12	.290	.391	.341	83	-10	18			.885	-10	*O-109/2-9	-2.3

YEAR	TM/L	G	AB	R	H	2B	3B	HR	RBI	BB	SO	AVG	OBP	SLG	PRO+	BR/A	SB	CS	SBR	FA	FR	G/POS	TPR
1896	Bro-N	104	377	62	94	8	4	3	47	34	17	.249	.316	.316	71	-15	22			.920	-2	*O-103	-2.2
Total	13	1275	5128	1069	1496	192	53	44	735	537	163	.292	.364	.376	99	-31	468			.897	45	*O-1189/2-39,3SP	-3.1

■ **BILL McCARTHY** McCarthy, William John b: 2/14/1886, Boston, Mass. d: 2/4/28, Washington, D.C. TR , Deb: 6/5/05

YEAR	TM/L	G	AB	R	H	2B	3B	HR	RBI	BB	SO	AVG	OBP	SLG	PRO+	BR/A	SB	CS	SBR	FA	FR	G/POS	TPR
1905	Bos-N	1	3	0	0	0	0	0	0	0		.000	.000	.000	-99	-1	0			.667	-0	/C-1	-0.1
1907	Cin-N	3	8	1	1	0	0	0	0	0		.125	.125	.125	-21	-1	0			1.000	-1	/C-3	-0.2
Total	2	4	11	1	1	0	0	0	0	0		.091	.091	.091	-43	-2	0			.842	-1	/C-4	-0.3

■ **FRANK McCARTON** McCarton, Francis b: 10/6/1854, Middletown, Conn. d: 6/17/07, New York, N.Y. Deb: 4/26/1872

YEAR	TM/L	G	AB	R	H	2B	3B	HR	RBI	BB	SO	AVG	OBP	SLG	PRO+	BR/A	SB	CS	SBR	FA	FR	G/POS	TPR
1872	Man-n	19	85	17	28	4	1	0	10	1	3	.329	.337	.400	134	4	0	0	0	.791	-2	O-19	0.2

■ **DAVID McCARTY** McCarty, David Andrew b: 11/23/69, Houston, Tex. BR/TL, 6'5", 215 lbs. Deb: 5/17/93

YEAR	TM/L	G	AB	R	H	2B	3B	HR	RBI	BB	SO	AVG	OBP	SLG	PRO+	BR/A	SB	CS	SBR	FA	FR	G/POS	TPR
1993	Min-A	98	350	36	75	15	2	2	21	19	80	.214	.257	.286	45	-27	2	6	-3	.959	5	O-67,1-36/D-2	-2.9
1994	Min-A	44	131	21	34	8	2	1	12	7	32	.260	.322	.374	79	-4	2	1	0	.981	1	1-32,O-14	-0.6
1995	Min-A	25	55	10	12	3	1	0	4	4	18	.218	.283	.309	54	-4	0	1	-1	.993	-2	1-18/O-5	-0.7
	SF-N	12	20	1	5	1	0	0	2	2	4	.250	.318	.300	66	-1	1	0	0	.833	-1	/O-4,1-2	-0.2
1996	SF-N	91	175	16	38	3	0	6	24	18	43	.217	.297	.337	70	-8	2	1	0	.990	-4	1-51,O-20	-1.5
1998	Sea-A	8	18	1	5	0	0	1	2	5	4	.278	.435	.444	130	1	1	0	0	1.000	-1	/O-5,1-2	0.0
Total	5	278	749	85	169	30	5	10	65	55	181	.226	.287	.319	61	-43	8	9	-3	.989	-3	1-141,O-115/D-2	-5.9

■ **LEW McCARTY** McCarty, George Lewis b: 11/17/1888, Milton, Pa. d: 6/9/30, Reading, Pa. BR/TR, 5'11.5", 192 lbs. Deb: 8/30/13

YEAR	TM/L	G	AB	R	H	2B	3B	HR	RBI	BB	SO	AVG	OBP	SLG	PRO+	BR/A	SB	CS	SBR	FA	FR	G/POS	TPR
1913	Bro-N	9	26	1	6	0	0	0	2	2	2	.231	.286	.231	47	-2	0			1.000	0	/C-9	-0.1
1914	Bro-N	90	284	20	72	14	2	1	30	14	22	.254	.293	.327	83	-7	1			.970	1	C-84	0.1
1915	Bro-N	84	276	19	66	9	4	0	19	7	23	.239	.261	.301	68	-11	7	4	-0	.969	-8	C-81	-1.5
1916	Bro-N	55	150	17	47	6	1	0	13	14	16	.313	.383	.367	127	5	4			.985	-4	C-27,1-17	0.4
	NY-N	25	68	6	27	3	4	0	9	7	9	.397	.453	.559	222	10	0			.993	0	C-24	1.3
	Yr	80	218	23	74	9	5	0	22	21	25	.339	.405	.427	155	15	4			.989	-3	C-51,1-17	1.7
1917	*NY-N	56	162	15	40	3	2	2	19	14	6	.247	.311	.327	99	-0	1			.979	-3	C-54	0.1
1918	NY-N	86	257	16	69	7	3	0	24	17	13	.268	.321	.319	97	-1	3			.975	-7	C-75	-0.2
1919	NY-N	85	210	17	59	5	4	2	21	18	15	.281	.341	.371	115	4	2			.970	-8	C-59	0.1
1920	NY-N	36	38	2	5	0	0	0	0	4	2	.132	.214	.132	1	-5	2	0	1	1.000	2	/C-5	-0.2
	StL-N	5	7	0	2	0	0	0	0	5	0	.286	.583	.286	160	1	0	0	0	1.000	-1	/C-3	0.1
	Yr	41	45	2	7	0	0	0	0	9	2	.156	.296	.156	33	-3	2	0	1	1.000	1	/C-8	-0.1
1921	StL-N	1	1	0	0	0	0	0	0	0	1	.000	.000	.000	-99	-0	0	0	0	.000	0	H	0.0
Total	9	532	1479	113	393	47	20	5	137	102	109	.266	.318	.335	97	-5	20	4		.975	-28	C-421/1-17	0.1

■ **TIM McCARVER** McCarver, James Timothy b: 10/16/41, Memphis, Tenn. BL/TR, 6'1", 195 lbs. Deb: 9/10/59

YEAR	TM/L	G	AB	R	H	2B	3B	HR	RBI	BB	SO	AVG	OBP	SLG	PRO+	BR/A	SB	CS	SBR	FA	FR	G/POS	TPR
1959	StL-N	8	24	3	4	1	0	0	0	2	1	.167	.231	.208	17	-3	0	0	0	.971	-2	/C-6	-0.5
1960	StL-N	10	10	3	2	0	0	0	0	0	2	.200	.200	.200	9	-1	0	0	0	1.000	-0	/C-5	-0.1
1961	StL-N	22	67	5	16	2	1	1	6	0	5	.239	.239	.343	47	-5	0	0	0	.969	-2	C-20	-0.6
1963	StL-N	127	405	39	117	12	7	4	51	27	43	.289	.336	.383	97	-1	5	2	0	.994	-0	*C-126	0.3
1964	*StL-N	143	465	53	134	19	3	9	52	40	44	.288	.346	.400	101	1	2	0	1	.987	-9	*C-137	-0.2
1965	StL-N	113	409	48	113	17	2	11	48	31	26	.276	.329	.408	97	-2	5	1	1	**.995**	-4	*C-111	0.1
1966	StL-N★	150	543	50	149	19	**13**	12	68	36	38	.274	.322	.424	105	3	9	6	-1	.992	-4	*C-148	0.8
1967	*StL-N★	138	471	68	139	26	3	14	69	54	32	.295	.374	.452	137	23	8	8	-2	**.997**	4	*C-130	3.4
1968	*StL-N	128	434	35	110	15	6	5	48	26	31	.253	.297	.350	95	-3	4	3	-1	.986	3	*C-109	0.8
1969	StL-N	138	515	46	134	27	3	7	51	49	26	.260	.327	.365	93	-5	4	9	-4	.986	9	*C-136	0.8
1970	Phi-N	44	164	16	47	11	1	4	14	14	10	.287	.346	.439	112	2	2	2	-1	.991	0	C-44	0.4
1971	Phi-N	134	474	51	132	20	5	8	46	43	26	.278	.340	.392	107	4	5	3	-0	.985	-8	*C-125	0.1
1972	Phi-N	45	152	14	36	8	0	2	14	17	15	.237	.322	.329	83	-3	1	2	-1	.989	-3	C-40	-0.6
	Mon-N	77	239	19	60	5	1	5	20	19	14	.251	.309	.343	84	-5	4	4	-1	.990	1	C-45,O-14/3-6	-0.5
	Yr	122	391	33	96	13	1	7	34	36	29	.246	.314	.338	83	-8	5	6	-2	.990	-3	C-85,O-14/3-6	-1.1
1973	StL-N	130	331	30	88	16	4	3	49	38	31	.266	.345	.366	97	-1	2	0	1	.986	-6	1-77,C-11	-1.2
1974	StL-N	74	106	13	23	0	1	0	11	22	6	.217	.366	.236	72	-3	0	1	-1	.969	-1	C-21/1-6	-0.4
	Bos-A	11	28	3	7	1	0	0	1	4	1	.250	.344	.286	77	-1	1	0	0	1.000	1	/C-8,D-2	0.1
1975	Bos-A	12	21	1	8	2	1	0	3	1	3	.381	.409	.571	161	2	0	0	0	.957	-0	/C-7,1-1	0.2
	Phi-N	47	59	6	15	2	0	1	7	14	7	.254	.397	.339	102	1	0	0	0	.984	1	C-10/1-1	0.2
1976	*Phi-N	90	155	26	43	11	2	3	29	35	14	.277	.414	.432	136	9	2	1	0	1.000	5	C-41/1-2	1.6
1977	*Phi-N	93	169	28	54	13	2	6	30	28	11	.320	.422	.527	146	12	3	5	-2	.988	2	C-42/1-3	1.2
1978	*Phi-N	90	146	18	36	9	1	1	14	28	24	.247	.375	.342	101	1	2	2	-1	.995	2	C-34,1-11	0.3
1979	Phi-N	79	137	13	33	5	1	1	12	19	12	.241	.338	.314	76	-4	2	0	1	.989	3	C-31/O-1	0.0
1980	Phi-N	6	5	2	1	1	0	0	2	1	0	.200	.333	.400	98	-0	0	0	0	1.000	-0	/1-2	0.0
Total	21	1909	5529	590	1501	242	57	97	645	548	422	.271	.340	.388	102	23	61	49	-11	.990	-9	*C-1387,1-103/O3D	6.2

■ **AL McCAULEY** McCauley, Allen A. b: 3/4/1863, Indianapolis, Ind. d: 8/24/17, Wayne Twnshp., Ind BL/TL, 6', 180 lbs. Deb: 6/21/1884

YEAR	TM/L	G	AB	R	H	2B	3B	HR	RBI	BB	SO	AVG	OBP	SLG	PRO+	BR/A	SB	CS	SBR	FA	FR	G/POS	TPR
1884	Ind-a	17	53	7	10	0	1	0	5	12		.189	.358	.226	97	1				1.000	0	P-10/1-5,O-3	-0.2
1890	Phi-N	112	418	63	102	25	7	1	42	57	38	.244	.346	.344	99	0	8			.973	-6	*1-116	-1.1
1891	Was-a	59	206	36	58	5	8	1	31	30	13	.282	.378	.398	128	8	9			.969	-2	1-59	0.3
Total	3	188	677	106	170	30	16	2	78	99	51	.251	.357	.352	107	9	17			.971	-7	1-180/P-10,O-3	-1.0

■ **JIM McCAULEY** McCauley, James Adelbert b: 3/24/1863, Stanley, N.Y. d: 9/14/30, Canandaigua, N.Y. BL/TR, 6', 180 lbs. Deb: 9/17/1884

YEAR	TM/L	G	AB	R	H	2B	3B	HR	RBI	BB	SO	AVG	OBP	SLG	PRO+	BR/A	SB	CS	SBR	FA	FR	G/POS	TPR
1884	StL-a	1	2	0	0	0	0	0		0		.000	.000	.000	-97	-0				.818	1	/C-1	0.1
1885	Buf-N	24	84	4	15	2	1	0	7	11	12	.179	.274	.226	61	-3				.936	-1	C-21/O-4	-0.2
	Chi-N	3	6	1	1	0	0	0	0	2	3	.167	.375	.167	70	-0				.800	-3	/C-2,O-2	-0.3
	Yr	27	90	5	16	2	1	0	7	13	15	.178	.282	.222	62	-3				.927	-3	C-23/O-6	-0.5
1886	Bro-a	11	30	5	7	1	0	0	3	11		.233	.439	.267	122	2	2			.846	-1	C-11	0.2
Total	3	39	122	10	23	3	1	0	10	24	15	.189	.322	.230	76	-2	2			.893	-3	/C-35,O-6	-0.2

■ **PAT McCAULEY** McCauley, Patrick M. b: 6/10/1870, Ware, Mass. d: 1/23/17, Newark, N.J. TR , 5'10.5", 156 lbs. Deb: 9/5/1893

YEAR	TM/L	G	AB	R	H	2B	3B	HR	RBI	BB	SO	AVG	OBP	SLG	PRO+	BR/A	SB	CS	SBR	FA	FR	G/POS	TPR
1893	StL-N	5	16	0	1	0	0	0	0	0	1	.063	.063	.063	-67	-4	0			.808	1	/C-5	-0.2
1896	Was-N	26	84	14	21	3	0	3	11	7	8	.250	.315	.393	86	-2	3			.917	0	C-24/O-1	0.0
1903	NY-A	6	19	0	1	0	0	0	1	0		.053	.053	.053	-64	-4	0			.920	-2	/C-6	-0.6
Total	3	37	119	14	23	3	0	3	12	7	9	.193	.244	.294	44	-10	3			.900	-2	/C-35,O-1	-0.8

■ **BILL McCAULEY** McCauley, William H. b: 12/20/1869, Washington, D.C. d: 1/27/26, Washington, D.C. Deb: 8/31/1895

YEAR	TM/L	G	AB	R	H	2B	3B	HR	RBI	BB	SO	AVG	OBP	SLG	PRO+	BR/A	SB	CS	SBR	FA	FR	G/POS	TPR
1895	Was-N	1	2	0	0	0	0	0	0	0	0	.000	.000	.000	-99	-1	0			.714	0	/S-1	0.0

■ **HARRY McCHESNEY** McChesney, Harry Vincent "Pud" b: 6/1/1880, Pittsburgh, Pa. d: 8/11/60, Pittsburgh, Pa. BR/TR, 5'0", 165 lbs. Deb: 9/17/04

YEAR	TM/L	G	AB	R	H	2B	3B	HR	RBI	BB	SO	AVG	OBP	SLG	PRO+	BR/A	SB	CS	SBR	FA	FR	G/POS	TPR
1904	Chi-N	22	88	9	23	6	2	0	11	4		.261	.293	.375	106	0	2			.967	-2	O-22	-0.3

■ **SCOTT McCLAIN** McClain, Scott Michael b: 5/19/72, Simi Valley, Cal. BR/TR, 6'3", 209 lbs. Deb: 5/14/98

YEAR	TM/L	G	AB	R	H	2B	3B	HR	RBI	BB	SO	AVG	OBP	SLG	PRO+	BR/A	SB	CS	SBR	FA	FR	G/POS	TPR
1998	TB-A	9	20	2	2	0	0	0	0	2	6	.100	.217	.100	-13	-3	0	0	0	.966	0	/1-5,3-3	-0.3

■ **PETE McCLANAHAN** McClanahan, Robert Hugh b: 10/24/06, Coldspring, Tex. d: 10/28/87, Mont Belvieu, Tex. BR/TR, 5'9", 170 lbs. Deb: 4/24/31

YEAR	TM/L	G	AB	R	H	2B	3B	HR	RBI	BB	SO	AVG	OBP	SLG	PRO+	BR/A	SB	CS	SBR	FA	FR	G/POS	TPR
1931	Pit-N	7	4	2	2	0	0	0	0	2	0	.500	.667	.500	220	1	0			.000	0	H	0.1

■ **HARVEY McCLELLAN** McClellan, Harvey McDowell "Little Mac" b: 12/22/1894, Cynthiana, Ky. d: 11/6/25, Cynthiana, Ky. BR/TR, 5'9.5", 143 lbs. Deb: 5/31/19

YEAR	TM/L	G	AB	R	H	2B	3B	HR	RBI	BB	SO	AVG	OBP	SLG	PRO+	BR/A	SB	CS	SBR	FA	FR	G/POS	TPR
1919	Chi-A	7	12	2	4	0	0	0	1	1	1	.333	.385	.333	102	0	0			1.000	1	/3-3,S-2	0.1
1920	Chi-A	10	18	4	6	1	1	0	5	4	1	.333	.455	.500	153	2	2	0	1	.917	-3	/S-4,3-2	-0.1
1921	Chi-A	63	196	20	35	4	1	1	14	14	18	.179	.237	.224	18	-24	2	3	-1	.968	18	2-21,S-15,O-15,/3-5	-0.6
1922	Chi-A	91	301	28	68	17	3	2	28	16	32	.226	.272	.322	55	-21	3	2	-0	.971	-5	3-71/S-8,2-2,O-1	-1.9
1923	Chi-A	141	550	67	129	29	3	1	41	27	44	.235	.270	.304	52	-40	14	11	-2	.958	-18	*S-139/2-2	-4.6

YEAR	TM/L	G	AB	R	H	2B	3B	HR	RBI	BB	SO	AVG	OBP	SLG	PRO+	BR/A	SB	CS	SBR	FA	FR	G/POS	TPR
1924	Chi-A	32	85	9	15	3	0	0	9	6	7	.176	.239	.212	17	-11	2	0	1	.938	3	S-21/2-7,3-1,O-1	-0.5
Total	6	344	1162	130	257	54	8	4	98	68	103	.221	.267	.292	46	-94	23	16		.952	-4	S-189/3-82,2-32,O	-7.6

■ BILL McCLELLAN
McClellan, William Henry b: 3/22/1856, Chicago, Ill. d: 7/3/29, Chicago, Ill. BL/TL, 5'5.5", 156 lbs. Deb: 5/20/1878

YEAR	TM/L	G	AB	R	H	2B	3B	HR	RBI	BB	SO	AVG	OBP	SLG	PRO+	BR/A	SB	CS	SBR	FA	FR	G/POS	TPR
1878	Chi-N	48	205	26	46	6	1	0	29	2	13	.224	.232	.263	59	-9				.866	-9	*2-42/S-5,O-1	-1.4
1881	Pro-N	68	259	30	43	3	1	0	16	15	21	.166	.212	.185	26	-21				.855	-8	S-50,O-17/2-1	-2.5
1883	Phi-N	80	326	42	75	21	4	1	33	19	18	.230	.272	.328	89	-3				.849	5	*S-78/O-2,3-1	0.3
1884	Phi-N	111	450	71	116	13	2	3	33	28	43	.258	.301	.316	99	1				.852	-12	*S-111/O-1	-0.9
1885	Bro-a	112	464	85	124	22	7	0	46	28		.267	.317	.345	108	5				.837	-5	3-57,2-55	0.3
1886	Bro-a	141	595	131	152	33	9	1	68	56		.255	.322	.346	108	5	43			.907	-7	*2-141	0.4
1887	Bro-a	136	548	109	144	24	6	1	53	80		.263	.363	.334	94	-2	70			.879	-23	*2-136	-1.7
1888	Bro-a	74	278	33	57	7	3	0	21	40		.205	.307	.252	80	-4	13			.905	-7	2-56,O-18	-0.9
	Cle-a	22	72	6	16	0	0	0	5	6		.222	.282	.222	64	-3	6			.875	-4	O-15/2-5,S-2	-0.6
	Yr	96	350	39	73	7	3	0	26	46		.209	.302	.246	77	-7	19			.897	-11	2-61,O-33/S-2	-1.5
Total	8	792	3197	533	773	129	33	6	304	274	95	.242	.305	.308	90	-31	132			.893	-68	2-436,S-246/3-58,O	-7.0

■ LLOYD McCLENDON
McClendon, Lloyd Glenn b: 1/11/59, Gary, Ind. BR/TR, 5'11", 195 lbs. Deb: 4/6/87 C

YEAR	TM/L	G	AB	R	H	2B	3B	HR	RBI	BB	SO	AVG	OBP	SLG	PRO+	BR/A	SB	CS	SBR	FA	FR	G/POS	TPR
1987	Cin-N	45	72	8	15	5	0	2	13	4	15	.208	.250	.361	57	-5	1	0	0	.981	-2	C-12/1-5,3-1,O-1	-0.6
1988	Cin-N	72	137	9	30	4	0	3	14	15	22	.219	.305	.314	75	-4	4	0	0	1.000	-3	C-23,O-17,1-12,/3-2	-0.6
1989	*Chi-N	92	259	47	74	12	1	12	40	37	31	.286	.377	.479	133	12	6	4	-1	.962	-7	O-45,1-28/3-6,C-5	0.1
1990	Chi-N	49	107	5	17	3	0	1	10	14	21	.159	.256	.215	29	-10	1	0	0	.980	1	O-23/C-8,1-8	-1.0
	Pit-N	4	3	1	1	0	0	1	2	0	1	.333	.333	1.333	349	1	0	0	0	.000	-0	/O-1	0.1
	Yr	53	110	6	18	3	0	2	12	14	22	.164	.258	.245	37	-9	1	0	0	.980	1	O-24/C-8,1-8	-0.9
1991	*Pit-N	85	163	24	47	7	0	7	24	18	23	.288	.366	.460	133	7	2	1	0	.966	-7	O-32,1-22/C-2	-0.2
1992	*Pit-N	84	190	26	48	8	1	3	20	28	24	.253	.355	.353	102	1	1	3	-2	.964	-7	O-60,1-18	-0.9
1993	Pit-N	88	181	21	40	11	1	2	19	23	17	.221	.309	.326	70	-7	0	3	-2	.967	-9	O-61/1-6	-2.0
1994	Pit-N	51	92	9	22	4	0	4	12	4	11	.239	.278	.413	76	-4	0	1	-1	.967	-2	O-20/1-2	-0.6
Total	8	570	1204	150	294	54	3	35	154	143	165	.244	.328	.381	94	-9	15	12	-3	.966	-36	O-260,1-101/C-50,3	-5.7

■ JEFF McCLESKEY
McCleskey, Jefferson Lamar b: 11/6/1891, Americus, Ga. d: 5/11/71, Americus, Ga. BL/TR, 5'11", 160 lbs. Deb: 9/8/13

YEAR	TM/L	G	AB	R	H	2B	3B	HR	RBI	BB	SO	AVG	OBP	SLG	PRO+	BR/A	SB	CS	SBR	FA	FR	G/POS	TPR
1913	Bos-N	2	3	0	0	0	0	0	0	1	0	.000	.250	.000	-25	-0	0			.750	-0	/3-2	-0.1

■ McCLOSKEY
McCloskey b: Brooklyn, N.Y. Deb: 5/25/1875

YEAR	TM/L	G	AB	R	H	2B	3B	HR	RBI	BB	SO	AVG	OBP	SLG	PRO+	BR/A	SB	CS	SBR	FA	FR	G/POS	TPR
1875	Was-n	11	40	1	7	0	0	0	4	1	2	.175	.195	.175	31	-3	0	1	-1	.673	-7	C-11	-0.9

■ BILL McCLOSKEY
McCloskey, William George b: 5/1854, Pennsylvania 5'8", 155 lbs. Deb: 8/18/1884

YEAR	TM/L	G	AB	R	H	2B	3B	HR	RBI	BB	SO	AVG	OBP	SLG	PRO+	BR/A	SB	CS	SBR	FA	FR	G/POS	TPR
1884	Wil-U	9	30	0	3	0	0	0		0		.100	.100	.100	-38	-6				.588	1	/O-5,C-5	-0.4

■ HAL McCLURE
McClure, Harold Murray "Mac" b: 8/8/1859, Lewisburg, Pa. d: 3/1/19, Lewisburg, Pa. BR/TR, 6', 165 lbs. Deb: 5/10/1882

YEAR	TM/L	G	AB	R	H	2B	3B	HR	RBI	BB	SO	AVG	OBP	SLG	PRO+	BR/A	SB	CS	SBR	FA	FR	G/POS	TPR
1882	Bos-N	2	6	1	2	0	0	0	0	0	1	.333	.333	.333	115	0				.750	-0	/O-2	0.0

■ LARRY McCLURE
McClure, Lawrence Ledwith b: 10/3/1885, Wayne, W.Va. d: 8/31/49, Huntington, W.Va. BR/TR, 5'6.5", 130 lbs. Deb: 7/26/10

YEAR	TM/L	G	AB	R	H	2B	3B	HR	RBI	BB	SO	AVG	OBP	SLG	PRO+	BR/A	SB	CS	SBR	FA	FR	G/POS	TPR
1910	NY-A	1	1	0	0	0	0	0	0	0		.000	.000	.000	-95	-0	0			.000	0	/O-1	0.0

■ AMBY McCONNELL
McConnell, Ambrose Moses b: 4/29/1883, N.Pownal, Vt. d: 5/20/42, Utica, N.Y. BL/TR, 5'7", 150 lbs. Deb: 4/17/08

YEAR	TM/L	G	AB	R	H	2B	3B	HR	RBI	BB	SO	AVG	OBP	SLG	PRO+	BR/A	SB	CS	SBR	FA	FR	G/POS	TPR
1908	Bos-A	140	502	77	140	10	6	2	43	38		.279	.343	.335	117	10	31			.939	-19	*2-126/S-3	-1.2
1909	Bos-A	121	453	61	108	7	8	0	36	34		.238	.300	.289	84	-8	26			.954	15	*2-121	0.5
1910	Bos-A	11	35	6	6	0	0	0	1	5		.171	.310	.171	50	-2	4			.959	-1	2-10	-0.3
	Chi-A	33	120	13	33	2	3	0	5	7		.275	.320	.342	112	1	4			.952	-1	2-32	0.0
	Yr	44	155	19	39	2	3	0	6	12		.252	.318	.303	97	-0	8			.954	-2	2-42	-0.3
1911	Chi-A	104	396	45	111	11	5	1	34	23		.280	.331	.341	90	-5	7			**.973**	-7	*2-103	-1.4
Total	4	409	1506	202	398	30	22	3	119	107		.264	.324	.319	98	-3	72			.954	-13	2-392/S-3	-2.4

■ GEORGE McCONNELL
McConnell, George Neely "Slats" b: 9/16/1877, Shelbyville, Tenn d: 5/10/64, Chattanooga, Tenn. BR/TR, 6'3", 190 lbs. Deb: 4/13/09

YEAR	TM/L	G	AB	R	H	2B	3B	HR	RBI	BB	SO	AVG	OBP	SLG	PRO+	BR/A	SB	CS	SBR	FA	FR	G/POS	TPR
1909	NY-A	13	43	4	9	0	1	0	5	1		.209	.227	.256	52	-2	1			.964	2	1-11/P-2	-0.2
1912	NY-A	42	91	11	27	4	2	0	8	4		.297	.333	.385	99	-0	0			.913	5	P-23/1-2	0.0
1913	NY-A	39	67	4	12	2	0	0	2	0	11	.179	.179	.209	13	-7	0			.965	5	P-35/1-1	0.0
1914	Chi-N	1	2	0	0	0	0	0	0	0	1	.000	.000	.000	-99	-0	0			1.000	0	/P-1	0.0
1915	Chi-F	53	125	14	31	6	2	1	18	0	16	.248	.254	.352	74	-7	2			.974	3	P-44	0.0
1916	Chi-N	28	57	2	9	0	0	0	0	2	4	.158	.200	.158	10	-6	0			.952	2	P-28	0.0
Total	6	176	385	35	88	12	5	1	33	7	32	.229	.248	.294	57	-24	3			.953	16	P-133/1-14	-0.2

■ SAM McCONNELL
McConnell, Samuel Faulkner b: 6/8/1895, Philadelphia, Pa. d: 6/27/81, Phoenixville, Pa. BL/TR, 5'6.5", 150 lbs. Deb: 4/19/15

YEAR	TM/L	G	AB	R	H	2B	3B	HR	RBI	BB	SO	AVG	OBP	SLG	PRO+	BR/A	SB	CS	SBR	FA	FR	G/POS	TPR
1915	Phi-A	6	11	1	2	1	0	0	0	1	3	.182	.250	.273	58	-1	0			.842	2	/3-5	0.1

■ DON McCORMACK
McCormack, Donald Ross b: 9/18/55, Omak, Wash. BR/TR, 6'3", 205 lbs. Deb: 9/30/80

YEAR	TM/L	G	AB	R	H	2B	3B	HR	RBI	BB	SO	AVG	OBP	SLG	PRO+	BR/A	SB	CS	SBR	FA	FR	G/POS	TPR
1980	Phi-N	2	1	0	1	0	0	0	0	0	0	1.000	1.000	1.000	436	0	0	0	0	1.000	1	/C-2	0.1
1981	Phi-N	3	4	0	1	0	0	0	0	0	1	.250	.250	.250	40	-0	0	0	0	1.000	0	/C-3	0.0
Total	2	5	5	0	2	0	0	0	0	0	1	.400	.400	.400	121	0	0	0	0	1.000	1	/C-5	0.1

■ FRANK McCORMICK
McCormick, Frank Andrew "Buck" b: 6/9/11, New York, N.Y. d: 11/21/82, Manhasset, N.Y. BR/TR, 6'4", 205 lbs. Deb: 9/11/34 C

YEAR	TM/L	G	AB	R	H	2B	3B	HR	RBI	BB	SO	AVG	OBP	SLG	PRO+	BR/A	SB	CS	SBR	FA	FR	G/POS	TPR
1934	Cin-N	12	16	1	5	2	1	0	5	0	1	.313	.313	.563	132	1	0			.941	-1	/1-2	0.0
1937	Cin-N	24	83	5	27	5	0	0	9	2	4	.325	.341	.386	102	0	1			1.000	1	1-20/2-4,O-1	-0.2
1938	Cin-N★	151	640	89	**209**	40	4	5	106	18	17	.327	.348	.425	115	11	1			.995	-3	*1-151	-1.0
1939	*Cin-N★	156	630	99	**209**	41	4	18	**128**	40	16	.332	.374	.495	131	26	1			**.996**	2	*1-156	1.0
1940	*Cin-N★	155	618	93	**191**	**44**	3	19	127	52	26	.309	.367	.482	131	25	2			**.995**	1	*1-155	1.1
1941	Cin-N★	154	603	77	162	31	5	17	97	40	13	.269	.318	.421	107	3	2			**.995**	1	*1-154	-0.8
1942	Cin-N★	145	564	58	156	24	0	13	89	45	18	.277	.332	.388	111	6	1			.993	6	*1-144	0.3
1943	Cin-N†	126	472	56	143	28	0	8	56	29	15	.303	.345	.413	120	10	2			.995	3	*1-120	0.8
1944	Cin-N☆	153	581	85	177	37	3	20	102	57	17	.305	.371	.482	144	32	7			.992	12	*1-153	3.7
1945	Cin-N†	152	580	68	160	33	0	10	81	56	22	.276	.345	.384	105	4	6			.994	5	*1-151	-0.1
1946	Phi-N★	135	504	46	143	20	2	11	66	36	21	.284	.333	.397	110	4	2			**.999**	4	*1-134	0.1
1947	Phi-N	15	40	7	9	2	0	1	8	3	2	.225	.279	.350	69	-2	0			.989	-1	1-12	-0.3
	Bos-N	81	212	24	75	18	2	2	43	11	8	.354	.386	.486	133	9	2			.996	-1	1-46	0.7
	Yr	96	252	31	84	20	2	3	51	14	10	.333	.368	.464	123	7	2			.995	-2	1-58	0.4
1948	*Bos-N	75	180	14	45	9	2	4	34	10	9	.250	.289	.389	84	-5	0			.987	3	1-50	-0.3
Total	13	1534	5723	722	1711	334	26	128	951	399	189	.299	.348	.434	118	125	27			.995	31	*1-1448/2-4,O-1	5.0

■ MOOSE McCORMICK
McCormick, Harry Elwood b: 2/28/1881, Philadelphia, Pa. d: 7/9/62, Lewisburg, Pa. BL/TL, 5'11", 180 lbs. Deb: 4/14/04

YEAR	TM/L	G	AB	R	H	2B	3B	HR	RBI	BB	SO	AVG	OBP	SLG	PRO+	BR/A	SB	CS	SBR	FA	FR	G/POS	TPR
1904	NY-N	59	203	28	54	9	5	1	26	13		.266	.323	.374	110	2	13			.916	-5	O-55	-0.6
	Pit-N	66	238	25	69	10	6	2	23	13		.290	.332	.408	124	6	6			.940	-6	O-66	-0.4
	Yr	125	441	53	123	19	11	3	49	26		.279	.328	.392	118	8	19			.928	-11	*O-121	-1.0
1908	Phi-N	11	22	0	2	0	0	0	2	2		.091	.167	.091	-17	-3	0			1.000	-0	/O-5	-0.4
	NY-N	73	252	31	76	16	3	0	32	4		.302	.315	.389	119	4	6			.901	-11	O-65	-1.1
	Yr	84	274	31	78	16	3	0	34	6		.285	.302	.365	108	1	6			.910	-11	O-70	-1.5
1909	NY-N	110	413	68	120	21	8	3	27	49		.291	.373	.402	138	19	4			.924	-14	*O-110	0.1
1912	*NY-N	42	39	4	13	4	1	0	8	6	9	.333	.422	.487	144	2	1			.667	-13	/O-6,1-1	0.0
1913	*NY-N	57	80	9	22	2	3	0	15	5	13	.275	.318	.375	97	-1	0			.909	-2	O-15	-0.3
Total	5	418	1247	165	356	62	26	6	133	92	22	.285	.340	.391	122	30	30			.920	-40	O-322/1-1	-2.7

■ JIM McCORMICK
McCormick, James Ambrose b: 11/2/1868, Spencer, Mass. d: 2/1/48, Saco, Maine BR/TR, 6'1", 160 lbs. Deb: 9/10/1892

YEAR	TM/L	G	AB	R	H	2B	3B	HR	RBI	BB	SO	AVG	OBP	SLG	PRO+	BR/A	SB	CS	SBR	FA	FR	G/POS	TPR
1892	StL-N	3	11	0	0	0	0	0	0	1	5	.000	.083	.000	-78	-2	0			1.000	-0	/2-2,3-1	-0.2

YEAR	TM/L	G	AB	R	H	2B	3B	HR	RBI	BB	SO	AVG	OBP	SLG	PRO+	BR/A	SB	CS	SBR	FA	FR	G/POS	TPR
■ JERRY McCORMICK	McCormick, John b: Philadelphia, Pa. d: 9/19/05, Philadelphia, Pa. Deb: 5/1/1883																						
1883	Bal-a	93	389	40	102	16	6	0		2		.262	.266	.334	89	-6				.799	0	*3-93	-0.5
1884	Phi-U	67	295	41	84	12	2	0		4		.285	.294	.339	99	-9				.811	14	3-54/2-5,O-5,S-3,P	0.4
	Was-U	42	157	23	34	8	2	0		1		.217	.222	.293	57	-13				.792	-6	3-38/S-4	-1.7
	Yr	109	452	64	118	20	4	0		5		.261	.269	.323	84	-22				**.806**	8	3-92/S-7,2-5,O-5,P	-1.3
Total	2	202	841	104	220	36	10	0		7		.262	.268	.328	86	-28				.802	8	3-185/S-7,O-5,2P	-1.8
■ MIKE McCORMICK	McCormick, Michael J. "Kid" or "Dude" b: 5/1883, Scotland d: 11/18/53, Jersey City, N.J. BR/TR, 5′3″, 155 lbs. Deb: 4/14/04																						
1904	Bro-N	105	347	28	64	5	4	0	27	43		.184	.278	.222	56	-16	22			**.914**	-3	*3-104/2-1	-1.7
■ MIKE McCORMICK	McCormick, Myron Winthrop b: 5/6/17, Angels Camp, Cal. d: 4/14/76, Ventura, Cal. BR/TR, 6′, 200 lbs. Deb: 4/16/40																						
1940	*Cin-N	110	417	48	125	20	0	1	30	13	36	.300	.326	.355	87	-8	8			.986	8	*O-107	-0.6
1941	Cin-N	110	369	52	106	17	3	4	31	30	24	.287	.341	.382	103	1	4			.976	7	*O-101	0.3
1942	Cin-N	40	135	18	32	2	3	1	11	13	7	.237	.304	.319	82	-3	0			.990	1	O-38	-0.4
1943	Cin-N	4	15	0	2	0	0	0	0	2	0	.133	.235	.133	8	-2	0			.909	-0	/O-4	-0.3
1946	Cin-N	23	74	10	16	2	0	0	5	8	4	.216	.293	.243	55	-4	0			1.000	1	O-21	-0.5
	Bos-N	59	164	23	43	6	2	1	16	11	7	.262	.309	.341	83	-4	0			.973	-2	O-48	-0.8
	Yr	82	238	33	59	8	2	1	21	19	11	.248	.304	.311	75	-8	0			.982	-1	O-69	-1.3
1947	Bos-N	92	284	42	81	13	7	3	36	20	21	.285	.332	.412	99	-1	1			.981	-12	O-79	-1.6
1948	*Bos-N	115	343	45	104	22	7	1	39	32	34	.303	.363	.417	112	6	1			.975	-11	*O-100	-1.0
1949	*Bro-N	55	139	17	29	5	1	2	14	14	12	.209	.281	.302	54	-9	1			1.000	-6	O-49	-1.7
1950	NY-N	4	4	0	0	0	0	0	0	0	2	.000	.000	.000	-99	-1	0			.000	0	H	-0.1
	Chi-A	55	138	16	32	4	3	0	10	16	6	.232	.312	.304	60	-8	0	1	-1	.982	-1	O-44	-1.1
1951	Was-A	81	243	31	70	9	3	1	23	29	20	.288	.364	.362	98	0	1	2	-1	.966	1	O-62	-0.2
Total	10	748	2325	302	640	100	29	14	215	188	173	.275	.330	.361	90	-33	16	3		.980	-14	O-653	-8.0
■ BARRY McCORMICK	McCormick, William J. b: 12/25/1874, Maysville, Ky. d: 1/28/56, Cincinnati, Ohio TR , 5′9″, Deb: 9/25/1895 U																						
1895	Lou-N	3	12	2	3	0	1	0	0	0	0	.250	.250	.417	75	-1	1			1.000	-2	/S-2,2-1	-0.2
1896	Chi-N	45	168	22	37	3	1	1	23	14	30	.220	.280	.268	43	-14	9			.835	-5	3-35/S-6,2-3,O-1	-1.6
1897	Chi-N	101	419	87	112	8	10	2	55	33		.267	.324	.348	75	-16	44			.851	-3	3-56,S-46/2-1	-1.4
1898	Chi-N	137	530	76	131	15	9	2	78	47		.247	.314	.321	82	-12	15			.888	4	*3-136/S-1,2-1	-0.7
1899	Chi-N	102	376	48	97	15	2	2	52	25		.258	.311	.324	76	-12	14			.941	5	2-99/S-3	-0.1
1900	Chi-N	110	379	35	83	13	5	3	48	38		.219	.292	.303	67	-17	8			.907	-9	S-84,3-21/2-5	-1.7
1901	Chi-N	115	427	45	100	15	6	1	32	31		.234	.288	.304	75	-14	12			.911	0	*S-112/3-3	-0.5
1902	StL-A	139	504	55	124	14	4	3	51	37		.246	.304	.308	71	-19	10			.905	-11	*3-132/S-7,O-1	-2.8
1903	StL-A	61	207	13	45	6	1	1	16	18		.217	.283	.271	69	-7	5			.969	-4	2-28,3-28/S-4	-1.0
	Was-A	63	219	14	47	10	2	0	23	10		.215	.255	.279	59	-11	3			.960	8	2-63	0.0
	Yr	124	426	27	92	16	3	1	39	28		.216	.269	.275	64	-18	8			.962	4	2-91,3-28/S-4	-1.0
1904	Was-A	113	404	36	88	11	1	0	39	27		.218	.274	.250	67	-14	9			.938	-1	*2-113	-1.4
Total	10	989	3645	433	867	110	42	15	417	280	30	.238	.297	.303	71	-139	130			.885	-17	3-411,2-314,S/O	-11.4
■ BARNEY McCOSKY	McCosky, William Barney b: 4/11/17, Coal Run, Pa. d: 9/6/96, Venice, Fla. BL/TR, 6′1″, 184 lbs. Deb: 4/18/39																						
1939	Det-A	147	611	120	190	33	14	4	58	70	45	.311	.384	.430	100	1	20	4	4	.986	9	*O-145	0.8
1940	*Det-A	143	589	123	**200**	39	**19**	4	57	67	41	.340	.408	.491	120	18	13	9	-2	.983	-1	*O-141	0.8
1941	Det-A	127	494	80	160	25	8	3	55	61	33	.324	.401	.425	108	7	8	3	1	.985	5	*O-122	0.5
1942	Det-A	154	600	75	176	28	11	7	50	68	37	.293	.365	.412	109	7	11	5	0	.981	3	*O-154	0.3
1946	Det-A	25	91	11	18	5	0	1	11	17	9	.198	.324	.286	67	-4	0	0	0	.966	-1	O-24	-0.6
	Phi-A	92	308	33	109	17	4	1	34	43	13	.354	.433	.445	146	21	2	2	-1	.981	-4	O-85	1.3
	Yr	117	399	44	127	22	4	2	45	60	22	.318	.407	.409	127	17	2	2	-1	.978	-4	*O-109	0.7
1947	Phi-A	137	546	77	179	22	7	1	52	57	29	.328	.395	.399	119	16	1	4	-2	.983	4	*O-136	1.1
1948	Phi-A	135	515	95	168	21	5	0	46	68	22	.326	.405	.386	111	11	1	3	-2	.990	-3	*O-134	-0.1
1950	Phi-A	66	179	19	43	10	1	0	11	22	12	.240	.323	.307	63	-10	0	0	0	.987	-5	O-42	-1.6
1951	Phi-A	12	27	4	8	2	0	1	1	3	4	.296	.367	.481	125	1	0	0	0	1.000	-1	/O-7	0.0
	Cin-N	25	50	2	16	2	1	1	11	4	2	.320	.370	.460	120	1	0	0	0	1.000	-3	O-11	-0.2
	Cle-A	31	61	8	13	3	0	0	2	8	5	.213	.304	.262	57	-4	1	0	0	1.000	-1	O-16	-0.5
1952	Cle-A	54	80	14	17	4	1	1	6	8	5	.213	.284	.325	74	-3	1	1	-0	.944	-5	O-19	-1.0
1953	Cle-A	22	21	3	4	3	0	0	3	1	4	.190	.227	.333	51	-2	0	0	0	.000	0	H	-0.2
Total	11	1170	4172	664	1301	214	71	24	397	497	261	.312	.386	.414	109	62	58	31	-1	.984	-1	*O-1036	0.6
■ WILLIE McCOVEY	McCovey, Willie Lee "Stretch" b: 1/10/38, Mobile, Ala. BL/TL, 6′4″, 210 lbs. Deb: 7/30/59 H																						
1959	SF-N	52	192	32	68	9	5	13	38	22	35	.354	.431	.656	189	24	2	0	1	.989	-2	1-51	2.0
1960	SF-N	101	260	37	62	15	3	13	51	45	53	.238	.351	.469	130	11	1	1	-0	.985	-3	1-71	0.2
1961	SF-N	106	328	59	89	12	3	18	50	37	60	.271	.354	.491	126	12	1	2	-1	.985	-2	1-84	0.3
1962	*SF-N	91	229	41	67	6	1	20	54	29	35	.293	.372	.590	156	17	3	3	-1	.976	-2	O-57,1-17	1.1
1963	SF-N★	152	564	103	158	19	5	**44**	102	50	119	.280	.350	.566	161	42	1	1	-0	.942	3	*O-135,1-23	3.9
1964	SF-N	130	364	55	80	14	1	18	54	61	73	.220	.340	.412	108	5	2	1	0	.935	-6	O-83,1-26	-0.6
1965	SF-N	160	540	93	149	17	4	39	92	88	118	.276	.383	.539	152	39	0	4	-2	.991	-3	*1-156	2.7
1966	SF-N★	150	502	85	148	26	6	36	96	76	100	.295	.394	.586	163	44	2	1	0	.984	-3	*1-145	3.3
1967	SF-N	135	456	73	126	17	4	31	91	71	110	.276	.381	.535	162	37	3	3	-1	.989	1	*1-127	3.1
1968	SF-N★	148	523	81	153	16	4	**36**	**105**	72	71	.293	.383	**.545**	**176**	**49**	4	2	0	.985	3	*1-146	4.6
1969	SF-N★	149	491	101	157	26	2	**45**	**126**	121	66	.320	**.458**	**.656**	**212**	**79**	0	0	0	.992	-6	*1-148	**6.3**
1970	SF-N★	152	495	98	143	39	2	39	126	**137**	75	.289	.446	**.612**	**183**	**64**	0	0	0	.989	13	*1-146	**6.2**
1971	*SF-N★	105	329	45	91	13	0	18	70	64	57	.277	.401	.480	151	24	0	2	-1	.983	-2	1-95	1.4
1972	SF-N	81	263	30	56	8	0	14	35	38	45	.213	.317	.403	102	1	0	0	0	.986	-5	1-74	-1.2
1973	SF-N	130	383	52	102	14	3	29	75	105	78	.266	.425	.546	161	35	1	0	0	.988	1	*1-117	2.8
1974	SD-N	128	344	53	87	19	1	22	63	96	76	.253	.417	.506	164	34	1	0	0	.987	-6	*1-104	2.2
1975	SD-N	122	413	43	104	17	0	23	68	57	80	.252	.347	.460	130	16	1	0	0	.986	-1	*1-115	0.9
1976	SD-N	71	202	20	41	9	0	7	36	21	39	.203	.281	.351	86	-5	0	0	0	.991	5	1-51	-0.4
	Oak-A	11	24	0	5	0	0	0	0	3	4	.208	.296	.208	52	-1	0	0	0	.000	0	/D-9	-0.2
1977	SF-N	141	478	54	134	21	0	28	86	67	106	.280	.369	.500	131	21	3	0	1	.989	-7	*1-136	0.7
1978	SF-N	108	351	32	80	19	2	12	64	36	57	.228	.300	.396	97	-3	1	0	0	.987	-4	1-97	-1.2
1979	SF-N	117	353	34	88	9	0	15	57	36	70	.249	.321	.402	103	0	0	2	-1	.987	-1	1-89	-0.7
1980	SF-N	48	113	8	23	8	0	1	16	13	23	.204	.291	.301	67	-5	0	0	0	.992	-2	1-27	-0.9
Total	22	2588	8197	1229	2211	353	46	521	1555	1345	1550	.270	.377	.515	148	540	26	22	-5	.987	-30	*1-2045,O-275/D-9	36.5
■ ART McCOY	McCoy, Arthur Gray b: 7/1864, Danville, Pa. d: 3/22/04, Danville, Pa. 168 lbs. Deb: 7/8/1889																						
1889	Was-N	2	6	0	0	0	0	0	0	2	1	.000	.250	.000	29	-1	0			.889	-2	/2-2	-0.2
■ BENNY McCOY	McCoy, Benjamin Jenison b: 11/9/15, Jenison, Mich. BL/TR, 5′9″, 170 lbs. Deb: 9/14/38																						
1938	Det-A	7	15	2	3	1	0	0	0	1	2	.200	.250	.267	28	-2	0	0	0	.963	2	/2-6,3-1	0.1
1939	Det-A	55	192	38	58	13	6	1	33	29	26	.302	.394	.448	107	2	3	1	0	.958	-2	2-34,S-16	0.4
1940	Phi-A	134	490	56	126	26	5	7	62	65	44	.257	.345	.373	88	-8	2	2	-1	.951	-16	*2-130/3-1	-1.5
1941	Phi-A	141	517	86	140	12	7	8	61	95	50	.271	.384	.368	102	5	3	3	-1	.963	-13	*2-135	0.1
Total	4	337	1214	182	327	52	18	16	156	190	122	.269	.369	.381	97	-2	8	6	-1	.957	-28	2-305/S-16,3-2	-0.9
■ QUINTON McCRACKEN	McCracken, Quinton Antoine b: 3/16/70, Wilmington, N.C. BB/TR, 5′8″, 170 lbs. Deb: 9/17/95																						
1995	Col-N	3	1	0	0	0	0	0	0	0	1	.000	.000	.000	-78	-0	0	0	0	.000	-0	/O-1	-0.1
1996	Col-N	124	283	50	82	13	6	3	40	32	62	.290	.364	.410	84	-8	17	6	2	.957	-15	O-93	-2.2
1997	Col-N	147	325	69	95	11	1	3	36	42	62	.292	.375	.360	76	-11	28	11	2	.980	-16	*O-132	-2.7
1998	TB-A	155	614	77	179	38	7	7	59	41	107	.292	.339	.410	90	-9	19	10	-0	.992	9	*O-153	-0.4
Total	4	429	1223	196	356	62	14	13	135	115	232	.291	.354	.397	84	-29	64	27	3	.982	-22	O-379	-5.4

YEAR	TM/L	G	AB	R	H	2B	3B	HR	RBI	BB	SO	AVG	OBP	SLG	PRO+	BR/A	SB	CS	SBR	FA	FR	G/POS	TPR
■ TOM McCRAW	McCraw, Tommy Lee b: 11/21/40, Malvern, Ark. BL/TL, 6', 183 lbs. Deb: 6/4/63 C																						
1963	Chi-A	102	280	38	71	11	3	6	33	21	46	.254	.313	.379	94	-2	15	4	2	.993	-1	1-97	-0.5
1964	Chi-A	125	368	47	96	11	5	6	36	32	65	.261	.327	.367	95	-2	15	7	0	.992	-7	1-84,O-36	-1.4
1965	Chi-A	133	273	38	65	12	1	5	21	25	48	.238	.309	.344	91	-4	12	7	-1	.993	-8	1-72,O-64	-1.6
1966	Chi-A	151	389	49	89	16	4	5	48	29	40	.229	.291	.329	83	-9	20	11	-1	.990	-2	*1-121,O-41	-1.9
1967	Chi-A	125	453	55	107	18	3	11	45	33	55	.236	.290	.362	95	-4	24	10	1	.991	11	*1-123/O-6	0.1
1968	Chi-A	136	477	51	112	16	12	9	44	36	58	.235	.295	.375	101	-0	20	5	3	.986	2	*1-135	-0.5
1969	Chi-A	93	240	21	62	12	2	2	25	21	24	.258	.326	.350	85	-5	1	3	-2	.989	-10	1-44,O-41	-2.1
1970	Chi-A	129	332	39	73	11	2	6	31	21	50	.220	.275	.319	61	-18	12	3	2	.987	-3	1-59,O-49	-2.6
1971	Was-A	122	207	33	44	6	4	7	25	19	38	.213	.294	.382	96	-2	3	3	-1	.958	-9	O-60,1-30	-1.6
1972	Cle-A	129	391	43	101	13	5	7	33	41	47	.258	.335	.371	106	4	12	10	-2	1.000	-1	O-84,1-38	-0.7
1973	Cal-A	99	264	25	70	7	0	3	24	30	42	.265	.345	.326	97	-0	3	2	-0	1.000	2	O-34,1-25/D-8	-0.2
1974	Cal-A	56	119	21	34	8	0	3	17	12	13	.286	.351	.429	131	5	2	1	0	1.000	2	1-29,O-12/D-3	0.5
	Cle-A	45	112	17	34	8	0	3	17	5	11	.304	.339	.455	128	4	0	1	-1	.990	2	1-38/O-1	0.3
	Yr	101	231	38	68	16	0	6	34	17	24	.294	.345	.442	130	8	2	2	-1	.994	4	1-67,O-13/D-3	0.8
1975	Cle-A	23	51	7	14	1	1	2	5	7	7	.275	.362	.451	129	2	4	1	1	1.000	-2	1-16/O-3	0.0
Total	13	1468	3956	484	972	150	42	75	404	332	544	.246	.311	.362	94	-33	143	68	2	.991	-22	1-911,O-431/D-11	-12.2
■ RODNEY McCRAY	McCray, Rodney Duncan b: 9/13/63, Detroit, Mich. BR/TR, 5'10", 175 lbs. Deb: 4/30/90																						
1990	Chi-A	32	6	8	0	0	0	0	0	1	4	.000	.143	.000	-58	-1	6	0	2	1.000	-5	O-13/D-7	-0.4
1991	Chi-A	17	7	2	2	0	0	0	0	0	2	.286	.286	.286	60	-0	1	1	-0	1.000	-2	/O-8,D-6	-0.2
1992	NY-N	18	1	3	1	0	0	0	1	0	0	1.000	1.000	1.000	475	0	2	0	1	1.000	-4	O-13	-0.3
Total	3	67	14	13	3	0	0	0	1	1	6	.214	.267	.214	36	-1	9	1	2	1.000	-10	/O-34,D-13	-0.9
■ FRANK McCREA	McCrea, Francis William b: 9/6/1896, Jersey City, N.J. d: 2/25/81, Dover, N.J. BR/TR, 5'9", 155 lbs. Deb: 9/26/25																						
1925	Cle-A	1	5	1	1	0	0	0	0	0	0	.200	.200	.200	2	-1	0	0	0	1.000	-1	/C-1	-0.1
■ WALT McCREDIE	McCredie, Walter Henry b: 11/29/1876, Manchester, Iowa d: 7/29/34, Portland, Ore. BL/TR, 6'2", 195 lbs. Deb: 4/20/03																						
1903	Bro-N	56	213	40	69	5	0	0	20	24		.324	.397	.347	116	6	10			.925	-4	O-56	-0.2
■ TOM McCREERY	McCreery, Thomas Livingston b: 10/19/1874, Beaver, Pa. d: 7/3/41, Beaver, Pa. BB/TR, 5'11", 180 lbs. Deb: 6/8/1895																						
1895	Lou-N	31	108	18	35	3	1	0	10	8	15	.324	.376	.370	99	0	3			.875	-6	O-18/P-8,S-4,3-1,1	-0.7
1896	Lou-N	115	441	87	155	23	**21**	7	65	42	58	.351	.409	.546	157	35	26			.916	1	*O-111/2-1,P-1	2.2
1897	Lou-N	89	338	55	96	5	6	4	40	38		.284	.356	.370	95	-2	13			.856	-5	*O-89	-1.2
	NY-N	49	177	36	53	8	5	1	27	22		.299	.380	.418	114	4	15			.900	-2	O-45/2-3	-0.1
	Yr	138	515	91	149	13	11	5	67	60		.289	.365	.386	101	2	28			.869	-7	*O-134/2-3	-1.3
1898	NY-N	35	121	15	24	4	3	1	17	19		.198	.307	.306	78	-3	3			.820	-5	O-35	-1.0
	Pit-N	53	190	33	59	5	7	2	20	26		.311	.394	.442	142	11	3			.934	-1	O-51	0.6
	Yr	88	311	48	83	9	10	3	37	45		.267	.360	.389	117	8	6			.901	-6	O-86	-0.4
1899	Pit-N	118	455	76	147	21	9	2	64	47		.323	.390	.422	123	15	11			.911	-7	O-97/S-9,2-7	0.1
1900	Pit-N	43	132	20	29	4	3	1	13	16		.220	.304	.318	71	-5	2			.887	2	O-35/P-1	-0.5
1901	Bro-N	91	335	47	97	11	14	3	53	32		.290	.355	.433	124	10	13			.947	4	O-82/1-4,S-2	0.8
1902	Bro-N	112	430	49	105	8	4	4	57	29		.244	.295	.309	86	-8	16			.979	-1	*1-108/O-4	-1.1
1903	Bro-N	40	141	13	37	5	2	0	10	20		.262	.354	.326	97	0	5			.892	-2	O-38	-0.4
	Bos-N	23	83	15	18	2	1	1	10	9		.217	.293	.301	72	-3	6			.900	0	O-23	-0.4
	Yr	63	224	28	55	7	3	1	20	29		.246	.332	.317	88	-3	11			.896	-2	O-61	-0.8
Total	9	799	2951	464	855	99	76	26	386	308	73	.290	.359	.401	113	54	116			.905	-22	O-628,1-113/S2P3	-1.7
■ FRANK McCUE	McCue, Frank Aloysius b: 10/4/1898, Chicago, Ill. d: 7/5/53, Chicago, Ill. BB/TR, 5'9", 150 lbs. Deb: 9/15/22																						
1922	Phi-A	2	5	0	0	0	0	0	0	0	0	.000	.000	.000	-97	-1	0	0	0	.000	0	/3-2	-0.1
■ CLYDE McCULLOUGH	McCullough, Clyde Edward b: 3/4/17, Nashville, Tenn. d: 9/18/82, San Francisco, Cal. BR/TR, 5'11.5", 180 lbs. Deb: 4/28/40 C																						
1940	Chi-N	9	26	4	4	1	0	0	1	5	5	.154	.290	.192	36	-2	0			1.000	3	/C-7	0.1
1941	Chi-N	125	418	41	95	9	2	9	53	34	67	.227	.289	.323	75	-15	5			.982	-8	*C-119	-1.3
1942	Chi-N	109	337	39	95	22	1	5	31	25	47	.282	.331	.398	117	6	7			.980	-1	C-97	1.4
1943	Chi-N	87	266	20	63	5	2	2	23	24	33	.237	.302	.293	73	-9	6			.977	-16	C-81	-2.1
1946	Chi-N	95	307	38	88	18	5	4	34	22	39	.287	.338	.417	116	5	2			.991	-2	C-89	0.8
1947	Chi-N	86	234	25	59	12	4	3	30	20	20	.252	.314	.376	86	-5	1			.984	7	C-64	0.5
1948	Chi-N☆	69	172	10	36	4	2	1	7	15	25	.209	.273	.273	50	-12	0			.973	5	C-51	-0.5
1949	Pit-N	91	241	30	57	9	3	4	21	24	30	.237	.316	.349	76	-8	1			.985	8	C-90	0.4
1950	Pit-N	103	279	28	71	16	4	6	34	31	35	.254	.340	.405	92	-3	3			.985	-8	*C-100	-0.7
1951	Pit-N	92	259	26	77	9	2	8	39	27	31	.297	.366	.440	113	5	2	0	1	.988	10	C-87	1.8
1952	Pit-N	66	172	10	40	5	1	1	15	10	18	.233	.283	.291	58	-10	0	1	-1	.981	7	C-61/1-1	-0.1
1953	Chi-N☆	77	229	21	59	3	2	6	23	15	23	.258	.303	.367	72	-10	0	0	0	.987	-3	C-73	-1.0
1954	Chi-N	31	81	9	21	7	0	3	17	5	5	.259	.310	.457	96	-1	0	0	0	.981	-2	C-26/3-3	-0.1
1955	Chi-N	44	81	7	16	0	0	0	10	8	15	.198	.278	.198	29	-8	0	0	0	.989	7	C-37	0.0
1956	Chi-N	14	19	0	4	1	0	0	1	0	5	.211	.211	.263	27	-2	0	0	0	1.000	1	/C-7	-0.1
Total	15	1098	3121	308	785	121	28	52	339	265	398	.252	.314	.358	85	-69	27	1		.984	7	C-989/3-3,1-1	-0.9
■ HARRY McCURDY	McCurdy, Harry Henry "Hank" b: 9/15/1899, Stevens Point, Wis. d: 7/21/72, Houston, Tex. BL/TR, 5'11", 187 lbs. Deb: 7/4/22																						
1922	StL-N	13	27	3	8	2	2	0	5	1	1	.296	.321	.519	119	1	0	0	0	.967	-1	/C-9,1-2	0.0
1923	StL-N	67	185	17	49	11	2	0	15	11	11	.265	.306	.346	73	-7	3	1	0	.969	-7	C-58	-1.1
1926	Chi-A	44	86	16	28	7	2	1	11	6	10	.326	.370	.488	127	3	0	1	-1	.974	-4	C-25/1-8	0.0
1927	Chi-A	86	262	34	75	19	3	1	27	32	24	.286	.366	.393	99	0	6	4	-1	.972	-3	C-82	0.2
1928	Chi-A	49	103	12	27	10	0	2	13	8	15	.262	.315	.417	92	-2	1	3	-2	.964	-4	C-34	-0.4
1930	Phi-N	80	148	23	49	6	2	1	25	15	12	.331	.393	.419	90	-2	0			.966	-5	C-41	-0.4
1931	Phi-N	66	150	21	43	9	0	1	25	23	16	.287	.382	.367	95	-0	2			.968	-1	C-45	0.1
1932	Phi-N	62	136	13	32	6	1	1	14	17	13	.235	.325	.316	65	-6	0			.974	-1	C-42	-0.5
1933	Phi-N	73	54	9	15	1	0	2	12	16	6	.278	.451	.407	130	3	0			.000	0	/C-2	0.3
1934	Cin-N	3	6	0	0	0	0	0	1	0	0	.000	.000	.000	-99	-2	0			1.000	1	/1-1	-0.1
Total	10	543	1157	148	326	71	12	9	148	129	108	.282	.355	.387	92	-13	12	9		.970	-24	C-338/1-11	-1.9
■ TERRY McDANIEL	McDaniel, Terrence Keith b: 12/6/66, Kansas City, Mo. BR/TR, 5'9", 205 lbs. Deb: 8/31/91																						
1991	NY-N	23	29	3	6	1	0	0	2	1	11	.207	.233	.241	34	-3	2	0	1	1.000	-3	O-14	-0.5
■ RAY McDAVID	McDavid, Ray Darnell b: 7/20/71, San Diego, Cal. BL/TR, 6'3", 190 lbs. Deb: 7/15/94																						
1994	SD-N	9	28	2	7	1	0	0	2	1	8	.250	.276	.286	48	-2	1	0	0	1.000	-0	/O-7	-0.2
1995	SD-N	11	17	2	3	0	0	0	0	2	6	.176	.263	.176	19	-2	1	1	-0	1.000	-2	/O-7	-0.4
Total	2	20	45	4	10	1	0	0	2	3	14	.222	.271	.244	37	-4	2	1	0	1.000	-2	/O-14	-0.6
■ RED McDERMOTT	McDermott, Frank A. b: 11/12/1889, Philadelphia, Pa. d: 9/11/64, Philadelphia, Pa. BR/TR, 5'6", 150 lbs. Deb: 8/6/12																						
1912	Det-A	5	15	2	4	1	0	0	0	0		.267	.313	.333	87	-0	1			1.000	-0	/O-5	-0.1
■ JOE McDERMOTT	McDermott, Joseph Deb: 5/4/1871																						
1871	Kek-n	2	8	3	2	0	0	0	1	1	1	.250	.333	.250	70	-0	1	0	0	.500	-0	/O-2	0.0
1872	Eck-n	7	32	3	9	3	0	0	3	1	2	.281	.303	.375	126	1	0	0	0	.643	-1	/P-7	0.0
Total	2 n	9	40	6	11	3	0	0	4	2	3	.275	.310	.350	112	1	1	0	0	.643	-1	/P-7,O-2	0.0
■ MICKEY McDERMOTT	McDermott, Maurice Joseph "Maury" b: 8/29/28, Poughkeepsie, N.Y. BL/TL, 6'2", 170 lbs. Deb: 4/24/48 C																						
1948	Bos-A	7	8	2	3	1	0	0	0	0	0	.375	.375	.500	125	0	0	0	0	1.000	1	/P-7	0.0
1949	Bos-A	12	33	3	7	3	0	0	6	3	6	.212	.278	.303	50	-2	0	0	0	.941	-0	P-12	0.0
1950	Bos-A	39	44	11	16	5	0	0	12	9	3	.364	.472	.477	131	2	0	0	0	.938	1	P-38	0.0

YEAR	TM/L	G	AB	R	H	2B	3B	HR	RBI	BB	SO	AVG	OBP	SLG	PRO+	BR/A	SB	CS	SBR	FA	FR	G/POS	TPR
1951	Bos-A	43	66	8	18	1	1	1	6	3	14	.273	.314	.364	76	-2	0	1	-1	.950	1	P-34	0.0
1952	Bos-A	36	62	10	14	1	1	1	7	4	11	.226	.273	.323	60	-3	0	0	0	.944	-0	P-30	0.0
1953	Bos-A	45	93	9	28	8	0	1	13	2	13	.301	.316	.419	92	-1	0	1	-1	.957	1	P-32	0.0
1954	Was-A	54	95	7	19	3	0	0	4	7	12	.200	.255	.232	36	-9	0	0	0	.955	1	P-30	0.0
1955	Was-A	70	95	10	25	4	0	1	10	6	16	.263	.314	.337	79	-3	1	0	0	.943	0	P-31	0.0
1956	*NY-A	46	52	4	11	0	0	1	4	8	13	.212	.317	.269	58	-3	0	0	0	1.000	-0	P-23	0.0
1957	KC-A	58	49	6	12	1	0	4	7	9	16	.245	.362	.510	133	2	0	0	0	.960	1	P-29/1-2	0.0
1958	Det-A	4	3	0	1	0	0	0	1	0	2	.333	.333	.333	78	-0	0	0	0	.000	-0	/P-2	0.0
1961	StL-N	22	14	1	1	1	0	0	3	0	4	.071	.071	.143	-41	-3	0	0	0	1.000	-0	P-19	0.0
	KC-A	7	5	0	1	1	0	0	1	1	2	.200	.333	.400	93	-0	0	0	0	.500	-0	/P-4	0.0
Total	12	443	619	71	156	29	2	9	74	52	112	.252	.312	.349	76	-22	1	2	-1	.951	4	P-291/1-2	0.0

■ **TERRY McDERMOTT** McDermott, Terrence Michael b: 3/20/51, Rockville Cen., N.Y BR/TR, 6'3", 205 lbs. Deb: 9/12/72

YEAR	TM/L	G	AB	R	H	2B	3B	HR	RBI	BB	SO	AVG	OBP	SLG	PRO+	BR/A	SB	CS	SBR	FA	FR	G/POS	TPR
1972	LA-N	9	23	2	3	0	0	0	0	2	8	.130	.200	.130	-5	-3	0	0	0	1.000	-1	/1-7	-0.5

■ **SANDY McDERMOTT** McDermott, Thomas Nathaniel b: 3/15/1856, Zanesville, Ohio d: 11/23/22, Mansfield, Ohio Deb: 6/18/1885

YEAR	TM/L	G	AB	R	H	2B	3B	HR	RBI	BB	SO	AVG	OBP	SLG	PRO+	BR/A	SB	CS	SBR	FA	FR	G/POS	TPR
1885	Bal-a	1	0	0	0	0	0	0	0	0		—	—	—	—	0				.000	0	/2-1	0.0

■ **McDONALD** McDonald Deb: 5/18/1872

YEAR	TM/L	G	AB	R	H	2B	3B	HR	RBI	BB	SO	AVG	OBP	SLG	PRO+	BR/A	SB	CS	SBR	FA	FR	G/POS	TPR
1872	Eck-n	1	4	0	0	0	0	0	0	0	0	.000	.000	.000	-99	-1	0	0	0	.333	-1	/S-1	-0.2

■ **TEX McDONALD** McDonald, Charles E. (b: Charles C. Crabtree) b: 1/31/1891, Farmersville, Tex. d: 3/31/43, Houston, Tex. BL/TR, 5'10", 160 lbs. Deb: 4/11/12

YEAR	TM/L	G	AB	R	H	2B	3B	HR	RBI	BB	SO	AVG	OBP	SLG	PRO+	BR/A	SB	CS	SBR	FA	FR	G/POS	TPR
1912	Cin-N	61	140	16	36	3	4	1	15	13	24	.257	.329	.357	90	-2	5			.915	-9	S-42	-0.7
1913	Cin-N	11	10	1	3	0	0	0	2	0	1	.300	.300	.300	72	-0	0			.000	0	/S-1	0.0
	Bos-N	62	145	24	52	4	4	0	18	15	17	.359	.422	.441	144	9	4			.869	-1	3-31/2-6,O-1	0.8
	Yr	73	155	25	55	4	4	0	20	15	18	.355	.415	.432	140	8	4			.869	-1	3-31/2-6,S-1,O-1	0.8
1914	Pit-F	67	223	27	71	16	7	3	29	13	23	.318	.361	.493	132	6	9			.925	-3	O-29,2-27/S-5	0.2
	Buf-F	69	250	32	74	13	6	3	32	20	26	.296	.353	.432	111	-0	11			.953	-3	O-61,2-10	-0.6
	Yr	136	473	59	145	29	13	6	61	33	49	.307	.357	.461	121	5	20			.943	-6	O-90,2-37/S-5	-0.4
1915	Buf-F	87	251	31	68	9	6	6	39	27	34	.271	.346	.426	114	1	5			.924	-7	O-65	-1.0
Total	4	357	1019	131	304	45	27	13	135	88	125	.298	.359	.434	118	12	34			.936	-22	O-156/S-48,2-43,3	-1.3

■ **JACK McDONALD** McDonald, Daniel b: 1847, Brooklyn, N.Y. d: 11/23/1880, Brooklyn, N.Y. 5'11", 154 lbs. Deb: 5/2/1872

YEAR	TM/L	G	AB	R	H	2B	3B	HR	RBI	BB	SO	AVG	OBP	SLG	PRO+	BR/A	SB	CS	SBR	FA	FR	G/POS	TPR
1872	Atl-n	15	62	9	16	3	1	0	4	0	1	.258	.258	.339	70	-3	0	0	0	.720	-2	O-15	-0.3

■ **DAVE McDONALD** McDonald, David Bruce b: 5/20/43, New Albany, Ind. BL/TR, 6'3", 215 lbs. Deb: 9/15/69

YEAR	TM/L	G	AB	R	H	2B	3B	HR	RBI	BB	SO	AVG	OBP	SLG	PRO+	BR/A	SB	CS	SBR	FA	FR	G/POS	TPR
1969	NY-A	9	23	0	5	1	0	0	2	2	5	.217	.280	.261	54	-1	0	1	-1	.960	-1	/1-7	-0.3
1971	Mon-N	24	39	3	4	2	0	1	4	4	14	.103	.186	.231	17	-4	0	0	0	.983	-1	/1-8,O-1	-0.6
Total	2	33	62	3	9	3	0	1	6	6	19	.145	.221	.242	31	-6	0	1	-1	.972	-1	/1-15,O-1	-0.9

■ **ED McDONALD** McDonald, Edward C. b: 10/28/1886, Albany, N.Y. d: 3/11/46, Albany, N.Y. BR/TR, 6', 180 lbs. Deb: 8/5/11

YEAR	TM/L	G	AB	R	H	2B	3B	HR	RBI	BB	SO	AVG	OBP	SLG	PRO+	BR/A	SB	CS	SBR	FA	FR	G/POS	TPR
1911	Bos-N	54	175	28	36	7	3	1	21	40	39	.206	.359	.297	78	-4	11			.955	-6	3-53/S-1	-0.9
1912	Bos-N	121	459	70	119	23	6	2	34	70	91	.259	.363	.349	94	-2	22			.940	-2	*3-118	-0.3
1913	Chi-N	1	0	0	0	0	0	0	0	0	0	—	—	—	—	0	0			.000	0	R	0.0
Total	3	176	634	98	155	30	9	3	55	110	130	.244	.362	.334	89	-6	33			.945	-7	3-171/S-1	-1.2

■ **JIM McDONALD** McDonald, James b: Philadelphia, Pa. BR/TR, 6', 180 lbs. Deb: 6/2/02

YEAR	TM/L	G	AB	R	H	2B	3B	HR	RBI	BB	SO	AVG	OBP	SLG	PRO+	BR/A	SB	CS	SBR	FA	FR	G/POS	TPR
1902	NY-N	2	9	0	3	0	0	0	1	0		.333	.333	.333	107	0	0			1.000	-0	/O-2	-0.1

■ **JIM McDONALD** McDonald, James A. b: 8/6/1860, San Francisco, Cal. d: 9/14/14, San Francisco, Cal. Deb: 6/20/1884

YEAR	TM/L	G	AB	R	H	2B	3B	HR	RBI	BB	SO	AVG	OBP	SLG	PRO+	BR/A	SB	CS	SBR	FA	FR	G/POS	TPR
1884	Was-U	2	6	0	1	0	0	0		0		.167	.167	.167	1	-1				.700	-1	/C-1,O-1	-0.2
	Pit-a	38	145	11	23	3	0	0		2		.159	.170	.179	14	-13				.795	-6	3-22,O-15/2-1	-1.9
1885	Buf-N	5	14	0	0	0	0	0	0	0	4	.000	.000	.000	-97	-3				.875	2	/S-4,O-1	-0.1
Total	2	45	165	11	24	3	0	0	0	2	4	.145	.156	.164	4	-17				.848	-6	/3-22,O-17,S-4,2C	-2.2

■ **JASON McDONALD** McDonald, Jason Adam b: 3/20/72, Modesto, Cal. BB/TR, 5'8", 175 lbs. Deb: 6/5/97

YEAR	TM/L	G	AB	R	H	2B	3B	HR	RBI	BB	SO	AVG	OBP	SLG	PRO+	BR/A	SB	CS	SBR	FA	FR	G/POS	TPR
1997	Oak-A	78	236	47	62	11	4	4	14	36	49	.263	.363	.394	99	1	13	8	-1	.961	-10	O-74	-1.1
1998	Oak-A	70	175	25	44	9	0	1	16	27	33	.251	.361	.320	82	-4	10	4	1	.956	-3	O-60	-0.7
Total	2	148	411	72	106	20	4	5	30	63	82	.258	.362	.363	92	-3	23	12	-0	.958	-13	O-134	-1.8

■ **JOE McDONALD** McDonald, Malcolm Joseph b: 4/9/1888, Texas d: 5/30/63, Baytown, Tex. BR/TR, 5'11", 175 lbs. Deb: 9/6/10

YEAR	TM/L	G	AB	R	H	2B	3B	HR	RBI	BB	SO	AVG	OBP	SLG	PRO+	BR/A	SB	CS	SBR	FA	FR	G/POS	TPR
1910	StL-A	10	32	4	5	0	0	0	1	1		.156	.182	.156	6	-3	0			.821	-3	3-10	-0.7

■ **JIM McDONNELL** McDonnell, James William "Mack" b: 8/15/22, Gagetown, Mich. d: 4/24/93, Detroit, Mich. BL/TR, 5'11", 165 lbs. Deb: 9/23/43

YEAR	TM/L	G	AB	R	H	2B	3B	HR	RBI	BB	SO	AVG	OBP	SLG	PRO+	BR/A	SB	CS	SBR	FA	FR	G/POS	TPR
1943	Cle-A	2	1	1	0	0	0	0	0	2	1	.000	.667	.000	108	0	0	0	0	1.000	-0	/C-1	0.0
1944	Cle-A	20	43	5	10	0	0	0	4	4	3	.233	.298	.233	55	-2	0	0	0	.900	-2	C-13	-0.4
1945	Cle-A	28	51	3	10	2	0	0	8	2	4	.196	.226	.235	36	-4	0	0	0	.980	8	C-23	0.5
Total	3	50	95	9	20	2	0	0	12	8	8	.211	.272	.232	48	-6	0	0	0	.953	6	/C-37	0.1

■ **ED McDONOUGH** McDonough, Edward Sebastian b: 9/11/1886, Elgin, Ill. d: 9/2/26, Elgin, Ill. BR/TR, 6', 160 lbs. Deb: 8/3/09

YEAR	TM/L	G	AB	R	H	2B	3B	HR	RBI	BB	SO	AVG	OBP	SLG	PRO+	BR/A	SB	CS	SBR	FA	FR	G/POS	TPR
1909	Phi-N	1	1	0	0	0	0	0	0	0		.000	.000	.000	-99	-0	0			1.000	0	/C-1	0.0
1910	Phi-N	5	9	1	1	0	0	0	0	0	1	.111	.111	.111	-34	-2	0			1.000	-1	/C-4	-0.2
Total	2	6	10	1	1	0	0	0	0	0	1	.100	.100	.100	-40	-2	0			1.000	-1	/C-5	-0.2

■ **GIL McDOUGALD** McDougald, Gilbert James b: 5/19/28, San Francisco, Cal BR/TR, 6'1", 180 lbs. Deb: 4/20/51

YEAR	TM/L	G	AB	R	H	2B	3B	HR	RBI	BB	SO	AVG	OBP	SLG	PRO+	BR/A	SB	CS	SBR	FA	FR	G/POS	TPR
1951	*NY-A	131	402	72	123	23	4	14	63	56	54	.306	.396	.488	143	25	14	5	1	.949	-16	3-82,2-55	1.2
1952	*NY-A★	152	555	65	146	16	5	11	78	57	73	.263	.336	.369	102	1	6	5	-1	.968	12	*3-117,2-38	1.2
1953	*NY-A	141	541	82	154	27	7	10	83	60	65	.285	.361	.416	113	10	3	4	-2	.953	6	*3-136,2-26	1.2
1954	NY-A	126	394	66	102	22	2	12	48	62	64	.259	.367	.416	118	11	3	4	-2	.989	1	2-92,3-35	1.6
1955	*NY-A	141	533	79	152	10	8	13	53	65	77	.285	.365	.407	109	7	6	4	-1	**.985**	19	*2-126,3-17	3.5
1956	*NY-A☆	120	438	79	136	13	3	13	56	68	59	.311	.407	.443	128	20	3	8	-4	.970	3	S-92,2-31/3-5	2.8
1957	*NY-A★	141	539	87	156	25	**9**	13	62	59	71	.289	.364	.442	121	16	2	5	-2	.976	15	*S-121,2-21/3-7	4.2
1958	*NY-A★	138	503	69	126	19	1	14	65	59	75	.250	.333	.376	98	-1	6	2	1	.977	-3	*2-115,S-19	0.6
1959	NY-A★	127	434	44	109	16	8	4	34	35	40	.251	.311	.353	85	-9	0	3	-2	.989	8	2-53,S-52,3-25	0.5
1960	*NY-A	119	337	54	87	16	4	8	34	38	45	.258	.339	.401	105	2	2	4	-2	.945	-3	3-84,2-42	0.0
Total	10	1336	4676	697	1291	187	51	112	576	559	623	.276	.358	.410	112	81	45	44	-13	.984	42	2-599,3-508,S-284	16.8

■ **ODDIBE McDOWELL** McDowell, Oddibe b: 8/25/62, Hollywood, Fla. BL/TL, 5'9", 165 lbs. Deb: 5/19/85

YEAR	TM/L	G	AB	R	H	2B	3B	HR	RBI	BB	SO	AVG	OBP	SLG	PRO+	BR/A	SB	CS	SBR	FA	FR	G/POS	TPR
1985	Tex-A	111	406	63	97	14	5	18	42	36	85	.239	.306	.431	98	-2	25	7	3	.993	10	*O-103/D-4	0.8
1986	Tex-A	154	572	105	152	24	7	18	49	65	112	.266	.342	.427	105	4	33	15	1	.991	3	*O-148/D-1	0.3
1987	Tex-A	128	407	65	98	26	4	14	52	51	99	.241	.325	.428	97	-2	24	2	6	.989	-2	*O-125	-0.1
1988	Tex-A	120	437	55	108	19	5	6	37	41	89	.247	.315	.355	85	-9	33	10	4	.989	-3	*O-113/D-3	-1.2
1989	Cle-A	69	239	33	53	5	2	3	22	25	36	.222	.298	.297	67	-10	12	5	1	.992	2	O-64/D-2	-1.0
	Atl-N	76	280	56	85	18	4	7	24	27	37	.304	.365	.471	134	12	15	10	-2	.978	5	O-68	1.4
1990	Atl-N	113	305	47	74	14	0	7	25	21	53	.243	.296	.357	74	-11	13	2	3	.971	-6	O-72	-1.6
1994	Tex-A	59	183	34	48	5	1	1	15	28	39	.262	.360	.317	77	-5	14	2	3	.983	-4	O-53/D-2	-0.7
Total	7	830	2829	458	715	125	28	74	266	294	550	.253	.325	.395	94	-23	169	53	19	.987	5	O-746/D-12	-2.1

■ **PRYOR McELVEEN** McElveen, Pryor Mynatt "Humpty" b: 11/5/1881, Atlanta, Ga. d: 10/27/51, Pleasant Hill, Tenn. BR/TR, 5'10", 168 lbs. Deb: 4/26/09

YEAR	TM/L	G	AB	R	H	2B	3B	HR	RBI	BB	SO	AVG	OBP	SLG	PRO+	BR/A	SB	CS	SBR	FA	FR	G/POS	TPR
1909	Bro-N	81	258	22	51	8	1	3	25	14		.198	.242	.271	61	-13	6			.938	-5	3-37,O-13,S-10,/12	-1.8
1910	Bro-N	74	213	19	48	8	3	1	26	22	47	.225	.307	.305	81	-5	6			.943	-5	3-54/S-6,2-3,C-1	-0.9
1911	Bro-N	16	31	1	6	0	0	0	5	0	3	.194	.194	.194	9	-4	0			.929	-1	/2-5,S-1	-0.5
Total	3	171	502	42	105	16	4	4	56	36	50	.209	.268	.281	67	-22	12			.941	-11	/3-91,S-17,2O1C	-3.2

YEAR	TM/L	G	AB	R	H	2B	3B	HR	RBI	BB	SO	AVG	OBP	SLG	PRO+	BR/A	SB	CS	SBR	FA	FR	G/POS	TPR
■ LEE McELWEE	McElwee, Leland Stanford b: 5/23/1894, LaMesa, Cal. d: 2/8/57, Union, Maine BR/TR, 5'10.5", 160 lbs. Deb: 7/3/16																						
1916	Phi-A	54	155	9	41	3	0	0	10	8	17	.265	.301	.284	79	-4	0			.883	-2	3-30/O-9,2-3,1-1,S	-0.6
■ FRANK McELYEA	McElyea, Frank b: 8/4/18, Hawthorne Twsp., Ill. d: 4/19/87, Evansville, Ind. BR/TR, 6'6", 221 lbs. Deb: 9/10/42																						
1942	Bos-N	7	4	2	0	0	0	0	0	0	0	.000	.000	.000	-99	-1	0			1.000	-0	/O-1	-0.1
■ JOE McEWING	McEwing, Joseph Earl b: 10/19/72, Bristol, Pa. BR/TR, 5'10", 170 lbs. Deb: 9/2/98																						
1998	StL-N	10	20	5	4	1	0	0	1	1	3	.200	.273	.250	38	-2	0	1	-1	1.000	-0	/2-6,O-3	-0.3
■ GUY McFADDEN	McFadden, Guy G. b: 9/3/1872, Topeka, Kan. d: 3/10/11, Topeka, Kan. Deb: 8/24/1895																						
1895	StL-N	4	14	1	3	0	0	0	2	0	2	.214	.214	.214	11	-2	0			.968	-1	/1-4	-0.2
■ LEON McFADDEN	McFadden, Leon b: 4/26/44, Little Rock, Ark. BR/TR, 6'2", 195 lbs. Deb: 9/6/68																						
1968	Hou-N	16	47	2	13	1	0	0	1	6	10	.277	.358	.298	101	0	1	0	0	.968	-1	S-16	0.2
1969	Hou-N	44	74	3	13	2	0	0	3	4	9	.176	.218	.203	19	-8	1	2	-1	.944	-3	O-17/S-8	-1.2
1970	Hou-N	2	0	0	0	0	0	0	0	0	0	—	—	—	—	0	0	0	0	.000	0	R	0.0
Total	3	62	121	5	26	3	0	0	4	10	19	.215	.275	.240	50	-8	2	2	-1	.966	-4	/S-24,O-17	-1.0
■ ALEX McFARLAN	McFarlan, Alexander Shepherd b: 11/11/1866, Kentucky d: 3/2/39, Pewee Valley, Ky. Deb: 6/19/1892 F																						
1892	Lou-N	14	42	2	7	0	0	0	1	8	11	.167	.300	.167	46	-2	1			.773	-3	O-12/2-2	-0.5
■ CHRIS McFARLAND	McFarland, Christopher b: 8/17/1861, Fall River, Mass. d: 5/24/18, New Bedford, Mass. 5'9", 170 lbs. Deb: 4/19/1884																						
1884	Bal-U	3	14	2	3	1	0	0		0		.214	.214	.286	46	-1				.571	-1	/O-3,P-1	-0.2
■ ED McFARLAND	McFarland, Edward William b: 8/3/1874, Cleveland, Ohio d: 11/28/59, Cleveland, Ohio BR/TR, 5'10", 180 lbs. Deb: 7/7/1893																						
1893	Cle-N	8	22	5	9	2	1	0	6	1	2	.409	.458	.591	168	2	0			1.000	-4	/O-5,3-2,C-1	-0.1
1896	StL-N	83	290	48	70	13	4	3	36	15	17	.241	.281	.345	67	-15	7			.961	8	C-80/O-2	0.2
1897	StL-N	31	107	14	35	5	2	1	17	8		.327	.374	.439	116	2	2			.965	2	C-23/1-3,O-3,2-1	0.6
	Phi-N	38	130	18	29	3	5	1	16	14		.223	.308	.346	74	-5	2			.951	-2	C-37	-0.2
	Yr	69	237	32	64	8	7	2	33	22		.270	.337	.388	93	-3	4			.957	0	C-60/1-3,O-3,2-1	0.4
1898	Phi-N	121	429	65	121	21	5	3	71	44		.282	.352	.375	113	8	4			.960	-1	*C-121	1.7
1899	Phi-N	96	324	59	108	22	9	2	57	36		.333	.403	.475	146	21	9			.968	13	C-94	3.7
1900	Phi-N	94	344	50	105	14	8	0	38	29		.305	.364	.392	110	5	9			**.963**	-3	C-93/3-1	0.9
1901	Phi-N	74	295	33	84	14	2	1	32	18		.285	.326	.356	96	-2	11			.970	2	C-74	0.8
1902	Chi-A	75	246	29	56	9	2	1	25	19		.228	.291	.293	65	-11	8			.967	2	C-69/1-1	-0.2
1903	Chi-A	61	201	15	42	7	2	1	19	14		.209	.264	.279	66	-8	3			.968	-0	C-56/1-1	-0.3
1904	Chi-A	50	160	22	44	11	3	0	20	17		.275	.348	.381	136	7	2			.975	-11	C-49	0.1
1905	Chi-A	80	250	24	70	13	4	0	31	23		.280	.345	.364	130	9	5			.973	6	C-70	2.4
1906	*Chi-A	12	23	0	4	1	0	0	3	3		.174	.269	.217	54	-1	0			.973	-1	/C-7	-0.1
1907	Chi-A	52	138	11	39	9	1	0	8	12		.283	.340	.362	128	4	3			.972	-2	C-43	0.7
1908	Bos-A	19	48	5	10	2	1	0	4	1		.208	.224	.292	66	-2	0			.978	4	C-13	0.3
Total	14	894	3007	398	826	146	49	13	383	254	19	.275	.335	.369	104	13	65			.967	14	C-830/O-10,1-5,32	10.5
■ HERM McFARLAND	McFarland, Hermas Walter b: 3/11/1870, Des Moines, Iowa d: 9/21/35, Richmond, Va. BL/TR, 5'6", 150 lbs. Deb: 4/21/1896																						
1896	Lou-N	30	110	11	21	4	1	1	12	9	14	.191	.252	.273	40	-10	4			.833	-3	O-28/C-1	-1.3
1898	Cin-N	19	64	10	18	1	3	0	11	7		.281	.361	.391	108	1	3			.968	-2	O-17	-0.3
1901	Chi-A	132	473	83	130	21	9	4	59	75		.275	.384	.383	116	14	33			.946	5	*O-132	0.8
1902	Chi-A	7	27	5	5	0	0	0	4	2		.185	.241	.185	20	-3	1			1.000	-0	/O-7	-0.4
	Bal-A	61	242	54	78	19	6	3	36	36		.322	.418	.488	144	16	10			.965	6	O-61	1.7
	Yr	68	269	59	83	19	6	3	40	38		.309	.402	.457	133	13	11			.967	6	O-68	1.3
1903	NY-A	103	362	41	88	16	9	5	45	46		.243	.333	.378	106	3	13			.939	-3	*O-103	-0.6
Total	5	352	1278	204	340	61	28	13	167	175	14	.266	.362	.388	110	21	64			.941	2	O-348/C-1	-0.1
■ HOWIE McFARLAND	McFarland, Howard Alexander b: 3/7/10, ElReno, Okla. d: 4/7/93, Wichita, Kan. BR/TR, 6', 175 lbs. Deb: 7/16/45																						
1945	Was-A	6	11	0	1	0	0	0	2	0	3	.091	.091	.091	-52	-2	0	0	0	1.000	-0	/O-3	-0.3
■ ORLANDO McFARLANE	McFarlane, Orlando Dejesus (Quesada) b: 6/28/38, Oriente, Cuba BR/TR, 6', 180 lbs. Deb: 4/23/62																						
1962	Pit-N	8	23	0	2	0	0	0	1	1	4	.087	.125	.087	-42	-5	0	0	0	1.000	2	/C-8	-0.2
1964	Pit-N	37	78	5	19	5	0	0	1	4	27	.244	.280	.308	66	-4	0	0	0	.983	-6	C-35/O-1	-0.9
1966	Det-A	49	138	16	35	7	0	5	13	9	46	.254	.304	.413	102	0	0	0	0	.991	-2	C-33	0.0
1967	Cal-A	12	22	0	5	0	0	0	3	1	7	.227	.261	.227	47	-1	0	0	0	.935	-1	/C-6	-0.2
1968	Cal-A	18	31	1	9	0	0	0	2	5	9	.290	.389	.290	112	1	0	0	0	.977	-0	/C-9	0.1
Total	5	124	292	22	70	12	0	5	20	20	93	.240	.291	.332	78	-9	0	0	0	.985	-8	/C-91,O-1	-1.2
■ PATSY McGAFFIGAN	McGaffigan, Mark Andrew b: 9/12/1888, Carlyle, Ill. d: 12/22/40, Carlyle, Ill. BR/TR, 5'8", 140 lbs. Deb: 4/16/17																						
1917	Phi-N	19	60	5	10	1	0	0	6	0	7	.167	.167	.183	7	-7	1			.920	-1	S-17/O-1	-0.7
1918	Phi-N	54	192	17	39	3	2	1	8	16	23	.203	.268	.255	56	-10	3			.948	-12	2-53/S-1	-2.1
Total	2	73	252	22	49	4	2	1	14	16	30	.194	.245	.238	45	-16	4			.923	-12	/2-53,S-18,O-1	-2.8
■ EDDIE McGAH	McGah, Edward Joseph b: 9/30/21, Oakland, Cal. BR/TR, 6', 183 lbs. Deb: 4/26/46																						
1946	Bos-A	15	37	2	8	1	1	0	1	7	7	.216	.341	.297	75	-1	0	0	0	.981	-2	C-14	-0.3
1947	Bos-A	9	14	1	0	0	0	0	2	3	0	.000	.176	.000	-45	-3	0	0	0	.964	2	/C-7	-0.1
Total	2	24	51	3	8	1	1	0	3	10	7	.157	.295	.216	41	-4	0	0	0	.975	-0	/C-21	-0.4
■ AMBROSE McGANN	McGann, Ambrose b: 1875, Baltimore, Md. 170 lbs. Deb: 5/2/1895																						
1895	Lou-N	20	73	9	21	5	2	0	9	8	6	.288	.358	.411	105	1	6			.852	-2	/S-8,3-6,O-5	-0.1
■ DAN McGANN	McGann, Dennis Lawrence "Cap" b: 7/15/1871, Shelbyville, Ky. d: 12/13/10, Louisville, Ky. BB/TR, 6', 190 lbs. Deb: 8/8/1896																						
1896	Bos-N	43	171	25	55	6	7	2	30	12	10	.322	.383	.474	118	4	2			.905	-17	2-43	-0.9
1898	Bal-N	145	535	99	161	18	8	5	106	53		.301	.404	.393	126	22	33			.983	2	*1-145	2.1
1899	Bro-N	63	214	49	52	11	4	2	32	21		.243	.362	.360	96	-0	16			.985	2	1-61	0.1
	Was-N	76	280	65	96	9	8	5	58	14		.343	.410	.486	147	18	11			.990	2	1-76	1.8
	Yr	139	494	114	148	20	12	7	90	35		.300	.389	.431	124	18	27			**.988**	4	*1-137	1.9
1900	StL-N	121	444	79	132	10	9	4	58	32		.297	.376	.387	112	8	26			**.990**	-1	*1-121/2-1	0.6
1901	StL-N	103	423	73	115	15	9	6	56	16		.272	.333	.392	116	8	17			.984	-3	*1-103	0.4
1902	Bal-A	68	250	40	79	10	8	0	42	19		.316	.378	.420	116	6	17			.987	3	1-68	0.7
	NY-N	61	227	25	68	5	7	0	21	12		.300	.356	.383	129	8	12			.981	2	1-61	0.9
1903	NY-N	129	482	75	130	21	6	3	50	32		.270	.331	.357	92	-5	36			**.988**	-0	*1-129	-0.7
1904	NY-N	141	517	81	148	22	6	6	71	36		.286	.354	.387	123	14	42			**.991**	3	*1-141	1.5
1905	*NY-N	136	491	88	147	23	14	5	75	55		.299	.391	.434	143	27	22			**.991**	5	*1-136	2.9
1906	NY-N	134	451	62	107	14	8	0	37	60		.237	.344	.304	100	2	30			**.995**	3	*1-133	0.2
1907	NY-N	81	262	29	78	9	1	2	36	29		.298	.383	.363	129	10	9			.994	5	1-81	1.5
1908	Bos-N	135	475	52	114	8	5	2	55	38		.240	.321	.291	97	0	9			.988	5	*1-121/2-9	0.3
Total	12	1436	5222	842	1482	181	100	42	727	429	10	.284	.364	.381	117	122	282			.989	10	*1-1376/2-53	11.4
■ CHIPPY McGARR	McGarr, James B. b: 5/10/1863, Worcester, Mass. d: 6/6/04, Worcester, Mass. BR/TR, 5'7", 168 lbs. Deb: 7/11/1884 U																						
1884	CP-U	19	70	10	11	2	0	0		0		.157	.157	.186	4	-10				.905	-6	2-13/O-6	-1.5
1886	Phi-a	71	267	41	71	9	3	2	31	9		.266	.295	.345	99	-1	17			.850	1	S-71	0.0
1887	Phi-a	137	536	93	158	23	6	1	63	23		.295	.326	.366	93	-6	84			.875	-1	*S-137	-0.5
1888	StL-a	34	132	17	31	1	0	0	13	6		.235	.268	.242	58	-7	25			.895	-3	2-33/S-1	-0.7
1889	KC-a	25	108	22	31	3	0	0	16	6	11	.287	.330	.315	79	-3	12			.857	-2	3-11/O-6,2-5,S-3	-0.4
	Bal-a	3	7	1	1	0	0	0	0	1	1	.143	.250	.143	13	-1	0			.583	-2	/S-3	-0.2

YEAR	TM/L	G	AB	R	H	2B	3B	HR	RBI	BB	SO	AVG	OBP	SLG	PRO+	BR/A	SB	CS	SBR	FA	FR	G/POS	TPR
	Yr	28	115	23	32	3	0	0	16	7	12	.278	.325	.304	76	-4	12			.857	-4	3-11/O-6,S-6,2-5	-0.6
1890	Bos-N	121	487	68	115	12	7	1	51	34	38	.236	.291	.296	66	-23	39			**.933**	-2	*3-115/S-5,O-1	-1.8
1893	Cle-N	63	249	38	77	12	0	0	28	20	15	.309	.363	.357	87	-5	24			.886	0	3-63	-0.3
1894	Cle-N	128	523	94	144	24	6	2	74	28	29	.275	.316	.356	59	-36	31			.902	-7	*3-128	-3.3
1895	*Cle-N	112	419	85	111	14	2	2	59	34	33	.265	.322	.322	63	-24	19			.870	-5	*3-108/2-4	-2.3
1896	*Cle-N	113	455	68	122	16	4	1	53	22	30	.268	.302	.327	62	-26	16			.924	-7	*3-113/C-1	-2.6
Total	10	826	3253	537	872	116	28	9	388	183	157	.268	.310	.329	71	-144	267			.903	-33	3-538,S-220/2OC	-13.6

■ JIM McGARR

McGarr, James Vincent "Reds" b: 11/9/1888, Philadelphia, Pa. d: 7/21/81, Miami, Fla. BR/TR, 5'9.5", 170 lbs. Deb: 5/18/12

YEAR	TM/L	G	AB	R	H	2B	3B	HR	RBI	BB	SO	AVG	OBP	SLG	PRO+	BR/A	SB	CS	SBR	FA	FR	G/POS	TPR
1912	Det-A	1	4	0	0	0	0	0	0	0	0	.000	.000	.000	-99	-1	0			.800	-0	/2-1	-0.2

■ DAN McGARVEY

McGarvey, Daniel Francis b: 12/2/1887, Philadelphia, Pa. d: 3/7/47, Philadelphia, Pa. Deb: 5/18/12

YEAR	TM/L	G	AB	R	H	2B	3B	HR	RBI	BB	SO	AVG	OBP	SLG	PRO+	BR/A	SB	CS	SBR	FA	FR	G/POS	TPR
1912	Det-A	1	3	0	0	0	0	0	0	1		.000	.400	.000	18	-0	0			.667	0	/O-1	0.0

■ JACK McGEACHY

McGeachy, John Charles b: 5/23/1864, Clinton, Mass. d: 4/5/30, Cambridge, Mass. BR/TR, 5'8", 165 lbs. Deb: 6/17/1886

YEAR	TM/L	G	AB	R	H	2B	3B	HR	RBI	BB	SO	AVG	OBP	SLG	PRO+	BR/A	SB	CS	SBR	FA	FR	G/POS	TPR
1886	Det-N	6	27	3	9	0	1	0	4	0	3	.333	.333	.407	121	1	2			.875	-1	/O-6	0.0
	StL-N	59	226	31	46	12	3	2	24	1	37	.204	.207	.310	59	-11	8			.880	2	O-55/2-2,3-2	-1.0
	Yr	65	253	34	55	12	4	2	28	1	40	.217	.220	.320	66	-10	10			.880	1	O-61/2-2,3-2	-1.0
1887	Ind-N	99	405	49	109	17	3	1	56	5	16	.269	.280	.333	72	-15	27			.894	7	*O-98/3-1,P-1	-0.9
1888	Ind-N	118	452	45	99	15	2	0	30	5	21	.219	.231	.261	56	-23	49			.932	5	*O-117/S-1,P-1	-2.1
1889	Ind-N	131	532	83	142	32	1	2	63	9	39	.267	.282	.342	73	-22	37			.918	9	*O-131/P-3	-1.4
1890	Bro-P	104	443	84	108	24	4	1	65	19	12	.244	.278	.323	57	-30	21			.906	-1	*O-104	-2.8
1891	Phi-a	50	201	24	46	4	3	2	13	6	12	.229	.255	.308	59	-12	9			.920	2	O-50	-1.0
	Bos-a	41	178	26	45	2	1	1	21	12	8	.253	.304	.292	72	-7	11			.910	-4	O-41	-1.1
	Yr	91	379	50	91	6	4	3	34	18	20	.240	.278	.301	65	-19	20			.916	-2	O-91	-2.1
Total	6	608	2464	345	604	106	18	9	276	57	148	.245	.265	.314	65	-120	164			.909	18	O-602/P-5,3-3,2S	-10.3

■ MIKE McGEARY

McGeary, Michael Henry b: 1851, Philadelphia, Pa. BR/TR, 5'7", 138 lbs. Deb: 5/9/1871 M

YEAR	TM/L	G	AB	R	H	2B	3B	HR	RBI	BB	SO	AVG	OBP	SLG	PRO+	BR/A	SB	CS	SBR	FA	FR	G/POS	TPR
1871	Tro-n	29	148	42	39	4	0	0	12	6	0	.264	.292	.291	67	-6	**20**	4	4	**.897**	-2	*C-26/S-3	-0.3
1872	Ath-n	47	225	68	81	9	2	0	35	2	1	.360	.366	.418	140	10	13	8	-1	.867	7	C-23,S-23/O-1	1.1
1873	Ath-n	52	275	63	83	8	1	0	31	1	1	.302	.304	.338	84	-7	3	6	-3	.805	-5	*S-44,C-13/3-1	-1.1
1874	Ath-n	54	271	61	87	10	2	0	22	1	2	.321	.324	.373	113	2	10	2	2	.837	7	C-28,S-26/O-4	0.8
1875	Phi-n	68	310	71	90	6	2	0	37	1	1	.290	.293	.323	109	2	19	4	3	.743	4	3-27,2-23,S-18,/OM	0.7
1876	StL-N	61	276	48	72	3	0	0	30	2	1	.261	.266	.272	84	-4				.889	5	*2-56/C-5,O-1,3-1	0.1
1877	StL-N	57	258	35	65	3	2	0	20	2	6	.252	.258	.279	73	-7				.883	7	2-39,3-19	0.1
1879	Pro-N	85	374	62	103	7	2	0	35	5	13	.275	.285	.305	96	-2				.884	1	*2-73,3-12	0.5
1880	Pro-N	18	59	5	8	0	0	0	1	0	6	.136	.136	.136	-8	-6				.887	3	3-17/2-2,S-1,M	-0.3
	Cle-N	31	111	14	28	2	1	0	6	4	3	.252	.278	.288	94	-1				.887	-4	3-29/O-2	-0.4
	Yr	49	170	19	36	2	1	0	7	4	9	.212	.230	.235	60	-7				.887	-1	3-46/2-2,O-2,S-1	-0.7
1881	Cle-N	11	41	1	9	0	0	0	5	0	6	.220	.220	.220	41	-3				.724	-7	3-11,M	-0.9
1882	Det-N	34	133	14	19	4	1	0	2	2	20	.143	.156	.188	10	-13				.928	8	S-33/2-3	-0.3
Total	5 n	250	1229	305	380	37	7	0	137	11	5	.309	.315	.351	104	0	65	24	5	.808	12	S-114/C-90,3-28,2O	1.2
Total	6	297	1252	179	304	19	6	0	99	15	55	.243	.252	.268	72	-35				.885	13	2-173/3-89,S-34,CO	-1.2

■ DAN McGEE

McGee, Daniel Aloysius b: 9/29/11, New York, N.Y. d: 12/4/91, Lakehurst, N.J. BR/TR, 5'8.5", 152 lbs. Deb: 7/14/34

YEAR	TM/L	G	AB	R	H	2B	3B	HR	RBI	BB	SO	AVG	OBP	SLG	PRO+	BR/A	SB	CS	SBR	FA	FR	G/POS	TPR
1934	Bos-N	7	22	2	3	0	0	0	1	3	6	.136	.240	.136	4	-3	0			.951	3	/S-7	0.0

■ FRANK McGEE

McGee, Francis De Sales b: 4/28/1899, Columbus, Ohio d: 1/30/34, Columbus, Ohio BR/TR, 5'11.5", 175 lbs. Deb: 9/19/25

YEAR	TM/L	G	AB	R	H	2B	3B	HR	RBI	BB	SO	AVG	OBP	SLG	PRO+	BR/A	SB	CS	SBR	FA	FR	G/POS	TPR
1925	Was-A	2	3	0	0	0	0	0	0	0	1	.000	.000	.000	-99	-1	0	0	0	1.000	0	/1-2	-0.1

■ PAT McGEE

McGee, Patrick b: Philadelphia, Pa. d: 6/21/1889, New York, N.Y. Deb: 9/24/1874

YEAR	TM/L	G	AB	R	H	2B	3B	HR	RBI	BB	SO	AVG	OBP	SLG	PRO+	BR/A	SB	CS	SBR	FA	FR	G/POS	TPR
1874	Atl-n	16	65	4	11	1	0	0	6	0	3	.169	.169	.185	15	-5	0	0	0	.795	-1	O-15/S-2,2-1	-0.5
1875	Mut-n	25	95	4	17	2	0	0	9	0	10	.179	.179	.200	30	-7	0	0	0	.848	-2	O-25	-0.7
	Atl-n	18	65	3	10	3	1	0	5	1	4	.154	.167	.231	42	-3	0	0	0	.912	6	O-13/2-6,3-1	0.3
	Yr	43	160	7	27	5	1	0	14	1	14	.169	.174	.213	34	-10	0	0	0	.875	4	O-38/2-6,3-1	-0.4
Total	2 n	59	225	11	38	6	1	0	20	1	17	.169	.173	.204	29	-15	0	0	0	.849	3	/O-53,2-7,S-2,3-1	-0.9

■ WILLIE McGEE

McGee, Willie Dean b: 11/2/58, San Francisco, Cal. BB/TR, 6'1", 175 lbs. Deb: 5/10/82

YEAR	TM/L	G	AB	R	H	2B	3B	HR	RBI	BB	SO	AVG	OBP	SLG	PRO+	BR/A	SB	CS	SBR	FA	FR	G/POS	TPR
1982	*StL-N	123	422	43	125	12	8	4	56	12	58	.296	.319	.391	97	-3	24	12	0	.958	-9	*O-117	-1.6
1983	StL-N★	147	601	75	172	22	8	5	75	26	98	.286	.316	.374	90	-9	39	8	7	.987	8	*O-145	0.2
1984	StL-N	145	571	82	166	19	11	6	50	29	80	.291	.326	.394	104	2	43	10	7	.985	11	*O-141	1.6
1985	*StL-N★	152	612	114	**216**	26	**18**	10	82	34	86	**.353**	.387	.503	148	38	56	16	7	.978	13	*O-149	5.4
1986	StL-N	124	497	65	127	22	7	7	48	37	82	.256	.308	.370	87	-10	19	16	-4	**.991**	15	*O-121	-0.2
1987	*StL-N★	153	620	76	177	37	11	11	105	24	90	.285	.314	.434	94	-7	16	4	2	.981	8	*O-152/S-1	-0.1
1988	StL-N★	137	562	73	164	24	6	3	50	32	84	.292	.331	.372	100	0	41	6	9	.975	10	*O-135	1.6
1989	StL-N	58	199	23	47	10	2	3	17	10	34	.236	.276	.352	76	-7	8	6	-1	.976	2	O-47	-0.8
1990	StL-N	125	501	76	168	32	5	3	62	38	86	**.335**	.383	.437	125	17	28	9	3	.957	16	*O-124	3.4
	*Oak-A	29	113	23	31	3	2	0	15	10	18	.274	.333	.336	91	-1	3	0	1	.986	1	O-28/D-1	0.0
1991	SF-N	131	497	67	155	30	3	4	43	34	74	.312	.358	.408	119	12	17	9	-0	.978	-2	*O-128	0.7
1992	SF-N	138	474	56	141	20	2	1	36	29	88	.297	.339	.354	102	1	13	4	2	.976	3	*O-119	0.4
1993	SF-N	130	475	53	143	28	1	4	46	38	67	.301	.354	.389	102	2	10	9	-2	.979	0	*O-126	-0.3
1994	SF-N	45	156	19	44	3	0	5	23	15	24	.282	.345	.397	97	-1	3	0	1	.988	0	O-42	0.0
1995	*Bos-A	67	200	32	57	11	3	2	15	9	41	.285	.316	.400	82	-6	5	2	0	.973	-7	O-64	-1.3
1996	*StL-N	123	309	52	95	15	2	5	41	18	60	.307	.350	.417	102	1	5	2	0	.962	-4	O-83/1-6	-0.5
1997	StL-N	122	300	29	90	19	4	3	38	22	59	.300	.348	.420	101	0	8	2	1	.981	-9	O-81/D-3	-0.9
1998	StL-N	120	269	27	68	10	1	3	34	14	49	.253	.290	.331	61	-15	7	2	-1	.938	-13	O-88/1-1,D-3	-2.8
Total	17	2069	7378	985	2186	343	94	79	836	431	1178	.296	.336	.400	102	15	345	117	33	.976	43	*O-1890/1-7,D-7,S-1	4.8

■ DAN McGEEHAN

McGeehan, Daniel De Sales b: 6/7/1885, Jeddo, Pa. d: 7/12/55, Hazleton, Pa. BR/TR, 5'6", 135 lbs. Deb: 4/22/11 F

YEAR	TM/L	G	AB	R	H	2B	3B	HR	RBI	BB	SO	AVG	OBP	SLG	PRO+	BR/A	SB	CS	SBR	FA	FR	G/POS	TPR
1911	StL-N	3	9	0	2	0	0	0	1	0	1	.222	.222	.222	25	-1	0			.818	-1	/2-3	-0.2

■ ED McGHEE

McGhee, Warren Edward b: 9/29/24, Perry, Ark. d: 2/13/86, Memphis, Tenn. BR/TR, 5'11", 170 lbs. Deb: 9/20/50

YEAR	TM/L	G	AB	R	H	2B	3B	HR	RBI	BB	SO	AVG	OBP	SLG	PRO+	BR/A	SB	CS	SBR	FA	FR	G/POS	TPR
1950	Chi-A	3	6	0	1	0	1	0	0	0	1	.167	.167	.500	67	-0	0	0	0	1.000	-0	/O-1	-0.1
1953	Phi-A	104	358	36	94	11	4	1	29	32	43	.263	.328	.324	74	-13	4	3	-1	.982	7	O-99	-1.0
1954	Phi-A	21	53	5	11	2	0	2	9	4	8	.208	.263	.358	69	-3	0	1	-1	.933	1	O-13	-0.3
	Chi-A	42	75	12	17	1	0	0	5	12	8	.227	.333	.240	57	-4	5	0	2	.982	-3	O-34	-0.7
	Yr	63	128	17	28	3	0	2	14	16	16	.219	.306	.289	62	-7	5	1	1	.960	-3	O-47	-1.0
1955	Chi-A	26	13	6	1	0	0	0	0	6	1	.077	.368	.077	24	-1	2	1	0	.923	-6	O-17	-0.7
Total	4	196	505	59	124	14	5	3	43	54	61	.246	.322	.311	70	-21	11	5	0	.975	-2	O-164	-2.8

■ BILL McGHEE

McGhee, William Mac "Fibber" b: 9/5/05, Shawmut, Ala. d: 3/10/84, Decatur, Ga. BL/TL, 5'10.5", 185 lbs. Deb: 7/5/44

YEAR	TM/L	G	AB	R	H	2B	3B	HR	RBI	BB	SO	AVG	OBP	SLG	PRO+	BR/A	SB	CS	SBR	FA	FR	G/POS	TPR
1944	Phi-A	77	287	27	83	12	0	1	19	21	20	.289	.338	.341	96	-2	2	1	0	.989	-0	1-75	-0.6
1945	Phi-A	93	250	24	63	6	1	0	19	24	16	.252	.320	.284	76	-7	3	2	-0	.989	-5	O-48/1-8	-1.6
Total	2	170	537	51	146	18	1	1	38	45	36	.272	.329	.315	87	-9	5	3	-0	.990	-5	/1-83,O-48	-2.2

■ BILL McGILVRAY

McGilvray, William Alexander "Big Bill" b: 4/29/1883, Portland, Ore. d: 5/23/52, Denver, Colo. BL/TL, 6', 160 lbs. Deb: 4/17/08

YEAR	TM/L	G	AB	R	H	2B	3B	HR	RBI	BB	SO	AVG	OBP	SLG	PRO+	BR/A	SB	CS	SBR	FA	FR	G/POS	TPR
1908	Cin-N	2	2	0	0	0	0	0	0	0		.000	.000	.000	-99	-0	0			.000	0	H	-0.1

■ TIM McGINLEY

McGinley, Timothy S. b: Philadelphia, Pa. d: 11/2/1899, Oakland, Cal. 5'9.5", 155 lbs. Deb: 4/30/1875

YEAR	TM/L	G	AB	R	H	2B	3B	HR	RBI	BB	SO	AVG	OBP	SLG	PRO+	BR/A	SB	CS	SBR	FA	FR	G/POS	TPR
1875	Cen-n	13	52	5	12	0	1	0	5	0	4	.231	.231	.269	80	-1	0	0	0	.646	-7	C-12/O-2	-0.6
	NH-n	32	131	13	36	3	1	0	10	0	7	.275	.275	.313	119	3	1	1	-0	.807	-5	C-32,3-2	-0.1
	Yr	45	183	18	48	3	2	0	15	0	11	.262	.262	.301	107	2	1	1	-0	.762	-11	C-44/O-2,3-2	-0.7

YEAR	TM/L	G	AB	R	H	2B	3B	HR	RBI	BB	SO	AVG	OBP	SLG	PRO+	BR/A	SB	CS	SBR	FA	FR	G/POS	TPR
1876	Bos-N	9	40	5	6	0	0	0	2	0	1	.150	.150	.150	0	-4				.600	-3	/O-6,C-3	-0.7
■ FRANK McGINN	McGinn, Frank J. b: 1869, Cincinnati, Ohio d: 11/19/1897, Cincinnati, Ohio Deb: 6/9/1890																						
1890	Pit-N	1	4	0	0	0	0	0	0	0	2	.000	.000	.000	-99	-1	0			1.000	-0	/O-1	-0.1
■ RUSS McGINNIS	McGinnis, Russell Brent b: 6/18/63, Coffeyville, Kan. BR/TR, 6'3", 225 lbs. Deb: 6/3/92																						
1992	Tex-A	14	33	2	8	4	0	0	4	3	7	.242	.306	.364	90	-0	0	0	0	1.000	-3	C-10/1-2,3-2	-0.4
1995	KC-A	3	5	1	0	0	0	0	0	1	1	.000	.167	.000	-51	-1	0	0	0	1.000	-1	/1-1,3-1,O-1	-0.2
Total	2	17	38	3	8	4	0	0	4	4	8	.211	.286	.316	69	-2	0	0	0	1.000	-4	/C-10,3-3,1-3,O-1	-0.6
■ JOHN McGLONE	McGlone, John T. b: 1864, Brooklyn, N.Y. d: 11/24/27, Brooklyn, N.Y. 5'10", 165 lbs. Deb: 10/7/1886																						
1886	Was-N	4	15	2	1	0	0	0	1	0	3	.067	.067	.067	-63	-3	0			.846	-1	/3-4	-0.4
1887	Cle-a	21	79	14	20	2	1	0	10	7		.253	.337	.304	82	-1	15			.854	1	3-21	0.0
1888	Cle-a	55	203	22	37	1	3	1	22	16		.182	.249	.232	56	-9	26			.787	-6	3-48/O-7	-1.4
Total	3	80	297	38	58	3	4	1	33	23	3	.195	.265	.242	58	-14	41			.810	-7	/3-73,O-7	-1.8
■ ART McGOVERN	McGovern, Arthur John b: 2/27/1882, St.John, N.B., Can. d: 11/14/15, Thornton, R.I. BR/TR, 5'10", 160 lbs. Deb: 4/21/05																						
1905	Bos-A	15	44	1	5	1	0	0	1	4		.114	.204	.136	9	-4	0			.951	-4	C-15	-0.8
■ BEAUTY McGOWAN	McGowan, Frank Bernard b: 11/8/01, Branford, Conn. d: 5/6/82, Hamden, Conn. BL/TR, 5'11", 190 lbs. Deb: 4/12/22																						
1922	Phi-A	99	300	36	69	10	5	1	20	40	46	.230	.323	.307	63	-16	6	5	-1	.965	9	O-82	-1.4
1923	Phi-A	95	287	41	73	9	1	1	19	36	25	.254	.340	.303	69	-12	4	3	-1	.971	-0	O-79	-1.7
1928	StL-A	47	168	35	61	13	4	2	18	16	15	.363	.425	.524	143	11	2	1	0	.962	-1	O-47	0.6
1929	StL-A	125	441	62	112	26	6	2	51	61	34	.254	.346	.354	78	-14	5	2	0	.975	7	*O-117	-1.4
1937	Bos-N	9	12	0	1	0	0	0	0	1	2	.083	.154	.083	-37	-2	0			1.000	-1	/O-2	-0.3
Total	5	375	1208	174	316	58	16	6	108	154	122	.262	.347	.351	80	-33	17	11		.970	13	O-327	-4.2
■ JOHN McGRAW	McGraw, John Joseph "Mugsy" or "Little Napoleon" b: 4/7/1873, Truxton, N.Y. d: 2/25/34, New Rochelle, N.Y. BL/TR, 5'7", 155 lbs. Deb: 8/26/1891 MH																						
1891	Bal-a	33	115	17	31	3	5	0	14	12	17	.270	.359	.383	111	2	4			.811	-15	S-21/O-9,2-3	-1.0
1892	Bal-N	79	286	41	77	13	2	1	26	32	21	.269	.355	.339	107	3	15			.897	1	O-34,2-34/S-8,3-3	0.4
1893	Bal-N	127	480	123	154	9	10	5	64	101	11	.321	.454	.412	129	27	38			.894	-23	*S-117,O-11	0.7
1894	*Bal-N	124	512	156	174	18	14	1	92	91	12	.340	.451	.436	110	13	78			.892	-2	*3-118/2-6	0.9
1895	*Bal-N	96	388	110	143	13	6	2	48	60	9	.369	.459	.448	131	21	61			.878	9	*3-95/2-1	2.6
1896	*Bal-N	23	77	20	25	2	2	0	14	11	4	.325	.422	.403	116	2	13			.833	-2	3-18/1-1	0.1
1897	*Bal-N	106	391	90	127	15	3	0	48	99		.325	**.471**	.379	126	24	44			.886	-13	*3-105	1.1
1898	Bal-N	143	515	**143**	176	8	10	0	53	**112**		.342	.475	.396	148	43	43			.900	-12	*3-137/O-3	3.0
1899	Bal-N	117	399	**140**	156	13	3	1	33	**124**		.391	**.547**	.446	165	50	73			.945	2	*3-117,M	4.8
1900	StL-N	99	334	84	115	10	4	2	33	85		.344	**.505**	.416	157	37	29			.909	-9	*3-99	2.5
1901	Bal-A	73	232	71	81	14	9	0	28	61		.349	.508	.487	169	28	24			.890	-20	3-69,M	0.8
1902	Bal-A	20	63	14	18	3	2	1	3	17		.286	.451	.444	143	5	5			.864	-8	3-19,M	-0.3
	NY-N	35	107	13	25	0	0	0	5	26		.234	.401	.234	97	2	7			.926	-3	S-34,M	0.2
1903	NY-N	12	11	2	3	0	0	0	1	1		.273	.467	.273	108	0	1			.000	-2	/2-2,O-2,S-1,3-1,M	-0.2
1904	NY-N	5	12	0	4	0	0	0	0	3		.333	.467	.333	142	1	0			.947	3	/2-2,S-2,M	0.4
1905	NY-N	3	0	0	0	0	0	0	0	0		—	—	—	—	0	1			.000	-0	/O-1,M	0.0
1906	NY-N	4	2	0	0	0	0	0	0	1		.000	.333	.000	4	-0	0			.000	0	/3-1,M	0.0
Total	16	1099	3924	1024	1309	121	70	13	462	836	74	.334	.466	.410	135	258	436			.898	-92	3-782,S-183/O21	16.0
■ FRED McGRIFF	McGriff, Frederick Stanley b: 10/31/63, Tampa, Fla. BL/TL, 6'3", 215 lbs. Deb: 5/17/86																						
1986	Tor-A	3	5	1	1	0	0	0	0	0	2	.200	.200	.200	9	-1	0	0	0	1.000	-0	/1-1,D-2	-0.1
1987	Tor-A	107	295	58	73	16	0	20	43	60	104	.247	.376	.505	128	13	3	2	-0	.983	-1	D-90,1-14	0.7
1988	Tor-A	154	536	100	151	35	4	34	82	79	149	.282	.378	.552	156	40	6	1	1	**.997**	-5	*1-153	2.3
1989	*Tor-A	161	551	98	148	27	3	**36**	92	119	132	.269	.402	.525	**162**	**49**	7	4	-0	.989	-1	*1-159/D-2	3.5
1990	Tor-A	153	557	91	167	21	1	35	88	94	108	.300	.403	.530	156	43	5	3	-0	.996	9	*1-147/D-6	4.1
1991	SD-N	153	528	84	147	19	1	31	106	105	135	.278	.400	.494	146	35	4	1	1	.990	-11	*1-153	1.5
1992	SD-N★	152	531	79	152	30	4	**35**	104	96	108	.286	.396	.556	164	46	8	6	-1	.991	-1	*1-151	3.5
1993	SD-N	83	302	52	83	11	1	18	46	42	55	.275	.365	.497	126	11	4	3	-1	.983	-6	1-83	-0.2
	*Atl-N	68	255	59	79	18	1	19	55	34	51	.310	.393	.612	163	22	1	0	0	.992	-1	1-66	1.6
	Yr	151	557	111	162	29	2	37	101	76	106	.291	.378	.549	143	33	5	3	-0	.987	-7	*1-149	1.4
1994	Atl-N★	113	424	81	135	25	1	34	94	50	76	.318	.392	.623	156	34	7	3	0	.994	-5	*1-112	1.9
1995	*Atl-N★	144	528	85	148	27	1	27	93	65	99	.280	.365	.489	119	14	3	6	-3	.996	0	*1-144	-0.1
1996	*Atl-N★	159	617	81	182	37	1	28	107	68	116	.295	.367	.494	118	16	7	3	0	.992	5	*1-158	0.6
1997	*Atl-N	152	564	77	156	25	1	22	97	68	112	.277	.358	.441	106	6	5	0	2	.990	-4	*1-149	-1.1
1998	TB-A	151	564	73	160	33	0	19	81	79	118	.284	.374	.443	107	7	7	2	1	.995	-4	*1-135,D-14	-1.0
Total	13	1753	6257	1019	1782	324	19	358	1088	959	1365	.285	.382	.514	137	337	67	34	-0	.992	-24	*1-1625,D-114	17.2
■ TERRY McGRIFF	McGriff, Terence Roy b: 9/23/63, Fort Pierce, Fla. BR/TR, 6'2", 195 lbs. Deb: 7/11/87																						
1987	Cin-N	34	89	6	20	3	0	2	11	8	17	.225	.289	.326	60	-5	0	0	0	.983	4	C-33	0.0
1988	Cin-N	35	96	9	19	3	0	1	4	12	31	.198	.287	.260	56	-5	1	0	0	.990	3	C-32	0.0
1989	Cin-N	6	11	1	3	0	0	0	2	2	3	.273	.385	.273	88	-0	0	0	0	.929	1	/C-6	0.1
1990	Cin-N	2	4	0	0	0	0	0	0	0	1	.000	.000	.000	-96	-1	0	0	0	1.000	1	/C-1	0.0
	Hou-N	4	5	0	0	0	0	0	0	0	0	.000	.000	.000	-99	-1	0	0	0	.900	0	/C-4	-0.1
	Yr	6	9	0	0	0	0	0	0	0	1	.000	.000	.000	-99	-2	0	0	0	.938	1	/C-5	-0.1
1993	Fla-N	3	7	0	0	0	0	0	0	1	2	.000	.125	.000	-60	-2	0	0	0	1.000	-0	/C-3	-0.2
1994	StL-N	42	114	10	25	6	0	0	13	13	11	.219	.310	.272	55	-7	0	0	0	.991	3	C-39	-0.2
Total	6	126	326	26	67	12	0	3	30	36	65	.206	.288	.270	51	-22	1	0	0	.985	11	C-118	-0.4
■ MARK McGRILLIS	McGrillis, Mark A. b: 10/22/1872, Philadelphia, Pa. d: 5/16/35, Philadelphia, Pa. Deb: 9/17/1892																						
1892	StL-N	1	3	0	0	0	0	0	0	0	1	.000	.000	.000	-99	-1	0			1.000	-0	/3-1	-0.1
■ JOE McGUCKIN	McGuckin, Joseph W. b: 3/13/1862, Paterson, N.J. d: 12/31/03, Yonkers, N.Y. 5'8.5", 160 lbs. Deb: 8/27/1890																						
1890	Bal-a	11	37	2	4	0	0	0	2	6		.108	.250	.108	6	-4	3			.962	3	O-11	-0.1
■ JOHN McGUINNESS	McGuinness, John James b: 1857, Ireland d: 12/19/16, Binghamton, N.Y. 5'10.5", 150 lbs. Deb: 5/6/1876																						
1876	NY-N	1	4	0	0	0	0	0	0	0	0	.000	.000	.000	-99	-1				.500	-2	/2-1,C-1	-0.2
1879	Syr-N	12	51	7	15	1	1	0	4	0	6	.294	.294	.353	126	1				.928	-1	1-12	0.1
1884	Phi-U	53	220	25	52	8	1	0		5		.236	.253	.282	67	-15				.959	-0	1-48/2-5,S-1	-1.9
Total	3	66	275	32	67	9	2	0	4	5	6	.244	.257	.291	75	-15				.954	-2	/1-60,2-6,S-1,C-1	-2.0
■ RYAN McGUIRE	McGuire, Ryan Byron b: 11/23/71, Bellflower, Cal. BL/TL, 6'2", 210 lbs. Deb: 6/5/97																						
1997	Mon-N	84	199	22	51	15	2	3	17	19	34	.256	.321	.397	87	-4	1	4	-2	.960	1	O-44,1-30/D-3	-0.7
1998	Mon-N	130	210	17	39	9	0	1	10	32	55	.186	.293	.243	43	-17	0	0	0	.980	-8	1-78,O-46	-2.8
Total	2	214	409	39	90	24	2	4	27	51	89	.220	.307	.318	65	-21	1	4	-2	.987	-7	1-108/O-90,D-3	-3.5
■ JIM McGUIRE	McGuire, James A. b: 2/4/1875, Dunkirk, N.Y. d: 1/26/17, Buffalo, N.Y. TR , Deb: 9/10/01																						
1901	Cle-A	18	69	4	16	2	0	0	3	0		.232	.232	.261	38	-6	0			.913	1	S-18	-0.3
■ DEACON McGUIRE	McGuire, James Thomas b: 11/18/1863, Youngstown, Ohio d: 10/31/36, Duck Lake, Mich. BR/TR, 6'1", 185 lbs. Deb: 6/21/1884 MC																						
1884	Tol-a	45	151	12	28	7	0	1		5		.185	.217	.252	50	-8				.906	-8	C-41/O-4,S-3	-1.2
1885	Det-N	34	121	11	23	4	2	0	9	5	23	.190	.222	.256	54	-6				.920	14	C-31/O-3	1.0
1886	Phi-N	50	167	25	33	7	1	2	18	19	25	.198	.280	.287	72	-5	2			.899	-6	C-49/O-1	-0.5
1887	Phi-N	41	150	22	46	6	6	2	23	11	8	.307	.362	.467	122	4	3			.884	-1	C-41	0.6
1888	Phi-N	12	51	7	17	4	2	0	11	4	9	.333	.382	.490	168	4	0			.800	-5	C-10/3-2	-0.1

YEAR	TM/L	G	AB	R	H	2B	3B	HR	RBI	BB	SO	AVG	OBP	SLG	PRO+	BR/A	SB	CS	SBR	FA	FR	G/POS	TPR
	Det-N	3	13	0	0	0	0	0	0	0	4	.000	.000	.000	-99	-3	0			.810	-2	/C-3	-0.5
	Yr	15	64	7	17	4	2	0	11	4	13	.266	.309	.391	117	1	0			.802	-7	C-13/3-2	-0.6
	Cle-a	26	94	15	24	1	3	1	13	7		.255	.333	.362	126	3	2			.891	-1	C-17/1-6,O-3	0.3
1890	Roc-a	87	331	46	99	16	4	4	53	21		.299	.356	.408	135	14	8			.938	8	C-71,1-15/O-3,P-1	2.4
1891	Was-a	114	413	55	125	22	10	3	66	43	34	.303	.382	.426	137	20	10			.911	-12	*C-98,O-18/3-3,1-1	1.5
1892	Was-N	97	315	46	73	14	4	4	43	61	48	.232	.360	.340	115	8	7			.936	-1	C-89/1-8,O-1	1.2
1893	Was-N	63	237	29	61	14	3	1	26	26	12	.257	.338	.354	86	-5	3			.889	-5	C-50,1-12	-0.5
1894	Was-N	104	425	67	130	18	6	6	78	33	19	.306	.366	.419	92	-6	11			.918	-1	*C-104	0.2
1895	Was-N	132	533	89	179	30	8	10	97	40	18	.336	.388	.478	124	18	16			.936	11	*C-132/S-1	3.3
1896	Was-N	108	389	60	125	25	3	2	70	30	14	.321	.379	.416	110	5	12			.936	-1	*C-98/1-1	1.3
1897	Was-N	93	327	51	112	17	7	4	53	21		.343	.386	.474	127	12	9			.947	8	C-73/1-6	2.3
1898	Was-N	131	489	59	131	18	3	1	57	24		.268	.310	.323	82	-12	10			.967	4	C-93,1-37,M	0.0
1899	Was-N	59	199	25	54	3	1	1	12	16		.271	.335	.312	79	-5	3			.973	-4	C-56/1-1	-0.5
	Bro-N	46	157	22	50	12	4	0	23	12		.318	.385	.446	125	5	4			.971	2	C-46	1.0
	Yr	105	356	47	104	15	5	1	35	28		.292	.357	.371	99	0	7			.972	-2	*C-102/1-1	0.5
1900	*Bro-N	71	241	20	69	15	2	0	34	19		.286	.348	.365	91	-3	2			.952	-6	C-69	-0.3
1901	Bro-N	85	301	28	89	16	4	0	40	18		.296	.342	.375	105	2	4			.960	-4	C-81/1-3	0.6
1902	Det-A	73	229	27	52	14	1	2	23	24		.227	.300	.323	71	-9	0			.952	-5	C-70	-0.6
1903	Det-A	72	248	15	62	12	1	0	21	19		.250	.306	.306	87	-4	3			.960	-6	C-69/1-1	-0.2
1904	NY-A	101	322	17	67	12	2	0	20	27		.208	.276	.258	66	-12	2			.970	13	C-97/1-1	1.3
1905	NY-A	72	228	9	50	7	2	0	33	18		.219	.291	.268	69	-8	3			.975	-6	C-71	-0.7
1906	NY-A	51	144	11	43	5	0	0	14	12		.299	.365	.333	108	2	3			.966	-1	C-49/1-1	0.5
1907	NY-A	1	1	0	0	0	0	0	0	0		.000	.000	.000	-93	-0	0			1.000	1	/C-1	0.0
	Bos-A	6	4	1	3	0	0	1	1	0		.750	.750	1.500	620	2	0			.000	0	HM	0.2
	Yr	7	5	1	3	0	0	1	1	0		.600	.600	1.200	470	2	0			1.000	1	/C-1	0.2
1908	Bos-A	1	1	0	0	0	0	0	0	0		.000	.000	.000	-97	-0	0			.000	0	HM	0.0
	Cle-A	1	4	0	1	1	0	0	2	0		.250	.250	.500	142	0	0			1.000	-0	/1-1	0.0
	Yr	2	5	0	1	1	0	0	2	0		.200	.200	.400	93	-0	0			1.000	-0	/1-1	0.0
1910	Cle-A	1	3	0	1	0	0	0	0	0		.333	.500	.333	159	0	0			1.000	-1	/C-1,M	-0.1
1912	Det-A	1	2	1	1	0	0	0	0	0		.500	.500	.500	192	0	0			.714	-0	/C-1	0.1
Total	26	1781	6290	770	1748	300	79	45	840	515	214	.278	.341	.372	101	14	117			.938	-16	*C-1611/1-94,O3SP	12.6

■ MICKEY McGUIRE

McGuire, M C Adolphus b: 1/18/41, Dayton, Ohio BR/TR, 5'10", 170 lbs. Deb: 9/7/62

YEAR	TM/L	G	AB	R	H	2B	3B	HR	RBI	BB	SO	AVG	OBP	SLG	PRO+	BR/A	SB	CS	SBR	FA	FR	G/POS	TPR
1962	Bal-A	6	4	0	0	0	0	0	0	0	0	.000	.000	.000	-99	-1	0	0	0	1.000	-0	/S-5	-0.1
1967	Bal-A	10	17	2	4	0	0	0	2	0	2	.235	.235	.235	40	-1	0	0	0	1.000	-2	/2-4	-0.4
Total	2	16	21	2	4	0	0	0	2	0	2	.190	.190	.190	11	-2	0	0	0	1.000	-3	/S-5,2-4	-0.5

■ BILL McGUIRE

McGuire, William Patrick b: 2/14/64, Omaha, Neb. BR/TR, 6'3", 205 lbs. Deb: 8/2/88

YEAR	TM/L	G	AB	R	H	2B	3B	HR	RBI	BB	SO	AVG	OBP	SLG	PRO+	BR/A	SB	CS	SBR	FA	FR	G/POS	TPR
1988	Sea-A	9	16	1	3	0	0	0	2	3	2	.188	.316	.188	43	-1	0	0	0	1.000	-0	/C-9	-0.1
1989	Sea-A	14	28	2	5	0	0	1	4	2	6	.179	.233	.286	44	-2	0	0	0	1.000	4	C-14	0.3
Total	2	23	44	3	8	0	0	1	6	5	8	.182	.265	.250	44	-3	0	0	0	1.000	4	/C-23	0.2

■ BILL McGUNNIGLE

McGunnigle, William Henry "Gunner" b: 1/1/1855, Boston, Mass. d: 3/9/1899, Brockton, Mass. BR/TR, 5'9", 155 lbs. Deb: 5/2/1879 M

YEAR	TM/L	G	AB	R	H	2B	3B	HR	RBI	BB	SO	AVG	OBP	SLG	PRO+	BR/A	SB	CS	SBR	FA	FR	G/POS	TPR
1879	Buf-N	47	171	22	30	0	1	0	5	5	24	.175	.199	.187	27	-13				.918	1	O-34,P-14	-1.0
1880	Buf-N	7	22	0	4	0	0	0	1	0	4	.182	.182	.182	23	-2				1.000	-2	/P-5,O-3	-0.2
	Wor-N	1	4	0	0	0	0	0	0	0	2	.000	.000	.000	-92	-1				1.000	-1	/O-1	-0.2
	Yr	8	26	0	4	0	0	0	1	0	6	.154	.154	.154	5	-3				1.000	-2	/P-5,O-4	-0.4
1882	Cle-N	1	5	2	1	0	0	0	0	0	1	.200	.200	.200	30	-0				.000	-1	/O-1	-0.1
Total	3	56	202	24	35	0	1	0	6	5	31	.173	.193	.183	25	-16				.900	-1	/O-39,P-19	-1.5

■ MARK McGWIRE

McGwire, Mark David b: 10/1/63, Pomona, Cal. BR/TR, 6'5", 225 lbs. Deb: 8/22/86

YEAR	TM/L	G	AB	R	H	2B	3B	HR	RBI	BB	SO	AVG	OBP	SLG	PRO+	BR/A	SB	CS	SBR	FA	FR	G/POS	TPR
1986	Oak-A	18	53	10	10	1	0	3	9	4	18	.189	.259	.377	76	-2	0	1	-1	.833	-3	3-16	-0.6
1987	Oak-A★	151	557	97	161	28	4	**49**	118	71	131	.289	.374	**.618**	168	53	1	1	-0	.992	-7	*1-145/3-8,O-3	3.3
1988	*Oak-A★	155	550	87	143	22	1	32	99	76	117	.260	.354	.478	135	26	0	0	0	.993	-8	*1-154/O-1	0.6
1989	*Oak-A★	143	490	74	113	17	0	33	95	83	94	.231	.345	.467	132	21	1	0	-0	.995	7	*1-141/D-2	1.6
1990	*Oak-A★	156	523	87	123	16	0	39	108	**110**	116	.235	.375	.489	146	35	2	1	0	.997	-5	*1-154/D-2	1.8
1991	Oak-A†	154	483	62	97	22	0	22	75	93	116	.201	.333	.383	103	4	2	1	0	.997	2	*1-152	-0.4
1992	*Oak-A★	139	467	87	125	22	0	42	104	90	105	.268	.391	**.585**	**180**	50	0	1	-1	.995	-10	*1-139	3.1
1993	Oak-A	27	84	16	28	6	0	9	24	21	19	.333	.472	.726	231	16	0	1	-1	1.000	-1	1-25	1.2
1994	Oak-A	47	135	26	34	3	0	9	25	37	40	.252	.413	.474	140	10	0	0	0	.988	-2	1-40/D-5	0.4
1995	Oak-A†	104	317	75	87	13	0	39	90	88	77	.274	.447	.685	200	51	1	1	-0	.986	-1	1-91,D-10	3.8
1996	Oak-A★	130	423	104	132	21	0	**52**	113	116	112	.312	**.468**	**.730**	**201**	70	0	0	0	.990	-5	*1-109,D-18	4.8
1997	Oak-A★	105	366	48	104	24	0	34	81	58	98	.284	.388	.628	162	33	1	0	0	.994	-1	*1-101	2.1
	StL-N	51	174	38	44	3	0	24	42	43	61	.253	.414	.684	183	22	2	0	1	.998	-1	1-50	1.6
1998	StL-N★	155	509	130	152	21	0	**70**	147	**162**	155	.299	**.473**	**.752**	**213**	**93**	1	0	0	.992	-7	*1-151	7.2
Total	13	1535	5131	941	1353	219	5	457	1130	1052	1259	.264	.395	.576	164	482	11	8	-2	.993	-41	*1-1452/D-37,3-24,O	30.5

■ JIM McHALE

McHale, James Bernard "J.B." b: 12/17/1875, Miners Mills, Pa. d: 6/17/59, Los Angeles, Cal. BR/TR, 5'11", 165 lbs. Deb: 4/14/08

YEAR	TM/L	G	AB	R	H	2B	3B	HR	RBI	BB	SO	AVG	OBP	SLG	PRO+	BR/A	SB	CS	SBR	FA	FR	G/POS	TPR
1908	Bos-A	21	67	9	15	2	2	0	7	4		.224	.278	.313	90	-1	4			.970	-2	O-19	-0.4

■ JOHN McHALE

McHale, John Joseph b: 9/21/21, Detroit, Mich. BL/TR, 6', 200 lbs. Deb: 5/28/43

YEAR	TM/L	G	AB	R	H	2B	3B	HR	RBI	BB	SO	AVG	OBP	SLG	PRO+	BR/A	SB	CS	SBR	FA	FR	G/POS	TPR
1943	Det-A	4	3	0	0	0	0	0	0	1	1	.000	.250	.000	-23	-0	0	0	0	.000	0	H	0.0
1944	Det-A	3	1	0	0	0	0	0	0	0	0	.000	.000	.000	-95	-0	0	0	0	.000	0	H	0.0
1945	*Det-A	19	14	0	2	0	0	0	1	1	4	.143	.250	.143	14	-1	0	0	0	1.000	0	/1-3	-0.1
1947	Det-A	39	95	10	20	1	0	3	11	7	24	.211	.265	.316	59	-6	1	1	-0	.995	-1	1-25	-0.8
1948	Det-A	1	1	0	0	0	0	0	0	0	0	.000	.000	.000	-97	-0	0	0	0	.000	0	H	0.0
Total	5	64	114	10	22	1	0	3	12	9	29	.193	.258	.281	49	-8	1	1	-0	.995	-1	/1-28	-0.9

■ BOB McHALE

McHale, Robert Emmet "Rabbit" b: 2/25/1872, Michigan Bluff, Cal. d: 6/9/52, Sacramento, Cal. Deb: 5/9/1898

YEAR	TM/L	G	AB	R	H	2B	3B	HR	RBI	BB	SO	AVG	OBP	SLG	PRO+	BR/A	SB	CS	SBR	FA	FR	G/POS	TPR
1898	Was-N	11	33	5	6	2	0	0	7	1		.182	.270	.242	47	-2	1			.900	-1	/O-9,S-1,1-1	-0.4

■ AUSTIN McHENRY

McHenry, Austin Bush "Mac" b: 9/22/1895, Wrightsville, O. d: 11/27/22, Jefferson Twsp., Ohio BR/TR, 5'11", 152 lbs. Deb: 6/22/18

YEAR	TM/L	G	AB	R	H	2B	3B	HR	RBI	BB	SO	AVG	OBP	SLG	PRO+	BR/A	SB	CS	SBR	FA	FR	G/POS	TPR
1918	StL-N	80	272	32	71	12	6	1	29	21	24	.261	.319	.360	111	3	8			.952	2	O-80	0.0
1919	StL-N	110	371	41	106	19	11	1	47	19	57	.286	.322	.404	125	10	7			.985	1	*O-103	0.4
1920	StL-N	137	504	66	142	19	11	10	65	25	73	.282	.316	.423	115	7	8	11	-4	.952	2	*O-133	-0.4
1921	StL-N	152	574	92	201	37	8	17	102	38	48	.350	.393	.531	145	36	10	20	-9	.965	7	*O-152	2.3
1922	StL-N	64	238	31	72	18	3	5	43	14	27	.303	.344	.466	112	3	2	2	-1	.935	7	O-61	0.5
Total	5	543	1959	262	592	105	39	34	286	117	229	.302	.343	.448	126	59	35	33		.960	18	O-529	2.8

■ VANCE McHENRY

McHenry, Vance Loren b: 7/10/56, Chico, Cal. BR/TR, 5'9", 165 lbs. Deb: 8/13/81

YEAR	TM/L	G	AB	R	H	2B	3B	HR	RBI	BB	SO	AVG	OBP	SLG	PRO+	BR/A	SB	CS	SBR	FA	FR	G/POS	TPR
1981	Sea-A	15	18	3	4	0	0	0	2	1	1	.222	.263	.222	39	-1	0	0	0	.893	0	S-13/D-1	-0.1
1982	Sea-A	3	1	0	0	0	0	0	0	0	0	.000	.000	.000	-97	-0	0	0	0	.500	-0	/S-1,D-1	-0.1
Total	2	18	19	3	4	0	0	0	2	1	1	.211	.250	.211	32	-2	0	0	0	.867	-0	/S-14,D-2	-0.2

■ IRISH McILVEEN

McIlveen, Henry Cooke b: 7/27/1880, Belfast, Ireland d: 10/18/60, Lorain, Ohio BL/TL, 5'11.5", 180 lbs. Deb: 7/10/06

YEAR	TM/L	G	AB	R	H	2B	3B	HR	RBI	BB	SO	AVG	OBP	SLG	PRO+	BR/A	SB	CS	SBR	FA	FR	G/POS	TPR
1906	Pit-N	5	5	1	2	0	0	0	0	0		.400	.400	.400	143	0	0			1.000	0	/P-2	0.0
1908	NY-A	44	169	17	36	3	3	0	8	14		.213	.277	.266	76	-4	6			.949	0	O-44	-0.7
1909	NY-A	4	3	0	0	0	0	0	0	1		.000	.250	.000	-20	-0	0			.000	0	H	0.0
Total	3	53	177	18	38	3	3	0	8	15		.215	.280	.266	76	-4	6			.949	0	/O-44,P-2	-0.7

■ STUFFY McINNIS

McInnis, John Phalen "Jack" b: 9/19/1890, Gloucester, Mass. d: 2/16/60, Ipswich, Mass. BR/TR, 5'9.5", 162 lbs. Deb: 4/12/09 M

YEAR	TM/L	G	AB	R	H	2B	3B	HR	RBI	BB	SO	AVG	OBP	SLG	PRO+	BR/A	SB	CS	SBR	FA	FR	G/POS	TPR
1909	Phi-A	19	46	4	11	0	0	1	4	2		.239	.286	.304	85	-1	0			.886	4	S-14	0.4

YEAR	TM/L	G	AB	R	H	2B	3B	HR	RBI	BB	SO	AVG	OBP	SLG	PRO+	BR/A	SB	CS	SBR	FA	FR	G/POS	TPR
1910	Phi-A	38	73	10	22	2	4	0	12	7		.301	.363	.438	152	4	3			.927	-5	S-17/2-5,3-4,O-1	0.0
1911	*Phi-A	126	468	76	150	20	10	3	77	25		.321	.361	.425	121	12	23			.982	-15	1-97,S-24	-0.1
1912	Phi-A	153	568	83	186	25	13	3	101	49		.327	.384	.433	138	28	27			.984	3	*1-153	2.8
1913	*Phi-A	148	543	79	176	30	4	4	90	45	31	.324	.382	.416	137	24	16			**.992**	-2	*1-148	2.3
1914	*Phi-A	149	576	74	181	12	8	1	95	19	27	.314	.341	.368	118	10	25	19	-4	**.995**	0	*1-149	0.2
1915	Phi-A	119	456	44	143	14	4	0	49	14	17	.314	.337	.362	113	5	8	8	-2	.989	5	*1-119	0.5
1916	Phi-A	140	512	42	151	25	3	1	60	25	19	.295	.331	.361	114	6	7			.992	7	*1-140	0.8
1917	Phi-A	150	567	50	172	19	4	0	44	33	19	.303	.342	.351	113	7	18			.993	2	*1-150	0.4
1918	*Bos-A	117	423	40	115	11	5	0	56	19	10	.272	.306	.322	91	-6	10			**.992**	4	1-94,3-23	-0.6
1919	Bos-A	120	440	32	134	12	5	1	58	23	11	.305	.341	.361	103	1	8			.995	3	*1-118	-0.1
1920	Bos-A	148	559	50	166	21	3	2	71	18	19	.297	.321	.356	83	-15	6	11	-5	**.996**	-1	*1-148	-2.4
1921	Bos-A	152	584	72	179	31	10	0	76	21	9	.307	.335	.394	88	-12	2	4	-2	**.999**	4	*1-152	-1.3
1922	Cle-A	142	537	58	164	28	7	1	78	15	5	.305	.325	.389	85	-13	1	5	-3	**.997**	-5	*1-140	-2.6
1923	Bos-N	154	607	70	191	23	9	2	95	26	12	.315	.343	.392	97	-3	7	8	-3	.991	4	*1-154	-1.0
1924	Bos-N	146	581	57	169	23	7	1	59	15	6	.291	.311	.360	83	-15	9	3	1	.994	7	*1-146	-1.7
1925	*Pit-N	59	155	19	57	10	4	0	24	17	1	.368	.437	.484	126	7	1	1	-0	.993	1	1-46	0.5
1926	Pit-N	47	127	12	38	6	1	0	13	7	3	.299	.336	.362	83	-3	1			.988	-1	1-40	-0.6
1927	Phi-N	1	0	0	0	0	0	0	0	0	0	—	—	—	—	0	0			1.000	-0	/1-1,M	0.0
Total	19	2128	7822	872	2405	312	101	20	1062	380	189	.307	.343	.381	106	35	172	59		.993	17	*1-1995/S-55,32O	-2.5

■ **TIM McINTOSH** McIntosh, Timothy Allen b: 3/21/65, Minneapolis, Minn. BR/TR, 5'11", 195 lbs. Deb: 9/3/90

YEAR	TM/L	G	AB	R	H	2B	3B	HR	RBI	BB	SO	AVG	OBP	SLG	PRO+	BR/A	SB	CS	SBR	FA	FR	G/POS	TPR
1990	Mil-A	5	5	1	1	0	0	1	1	0	2	.200	.200	.800	168	0	0	0	0	.875	-0	/C-4	0.0
1991	Mil-A	7	11	2	4	1	0	1	1	0	4	.364	.364	.727	199	1	0	0	0	.000	-2	/O-4,1-1,D-2	0.0
1992	Mil-A	35	77	7	14	3	0	0	6	3	9	.182	.232	.221	28	-7	1	3	-2	.983	1	C-14,O-10/1-7,D-3	-0.8
1993	Mil-A	1	0	0	0	0	0	0	0	0	0	—	—	—	—	0	0	0	0	.000	0	/C-1	0.0
	Mon-N	20	21	2	2	1	0	0	2	0	7	.095	.095	.143	-36	-4	0	0	0	1.000	-3	/O-7,C-5	-0.7
1996	NY-A	3	3	0	0	0	0	0	0	0	0	.000	.000	.000	-99	-1	0	0	0	.000	-0	/C-1,1-1,3-1	-0.1
Total	5	71	117	12	21	5	0	2	10	3	22	.179	.213	.274	34	-11	1	3	-2	.973	-4	/C-25,O-21,1-9,D3	-1.6

■ **MATTY McINTYRE** McIntyre, Matthew W. b: 6/12/1880, Stonington, Conn. d: 4/2/20, Detroit, Mich. BL/TL, 5'11", 175 lbs. Deb: 7/3/01

YEAR	TM/L	G	AB	R	H	2B	3B	HR	RBI	BB	SO	AVG	OBP	SLG	PRO+	BR/A	SB	CS	SBR	FA	FR	G/POS	TPR
1901	Phi-A	82	308	38	85	12	4	0	46	30		.276	.346	.341	87	-5	11			.921	-3	O-82	-1.2
1904	Det-A	152	578	74	146	11	10	2	46	44		.253	.310	.317	101	1	11			.959	12	*O-152	0.5
1905	Det-A	131	495	59	130	21	5	0	30	48		.263	.330	.325	107	5	9			.968	17	*O-131	1.7
1906	Det-A	133	493	63	128	19	11	0	39	56		.260	.338	.343	110	7	29			.982	12	*O-133	1.4
1907	Det-A	20	81	6	23	1	1	0	9	7		.284	.341	.321	107	1	3			1.000	3	O-20	0.3
1908	*Det-A	151	569	**105**	168	24	13	0	28	83		.295	.392	.383	146	32	20			**.977**	16	*O-151	4.7
1909	*Det-A	125	476	65	116	18	9	1	34	54		.244	.325	.326	101	1	13			.975	-0	*O-122	-0.4
1910	Det-A	83	305	40	72	15	5	0	25	39		.236	.323	.318	94	-2	4			.946	4	O-77	-0.2
1911	Chi-A	146	569	102	184	19	11	1	52	64		.323	.397	.401	127	22	17			.948	-2	*O-146	1.2
1912	Chi-A	49	84	10	14	0	0	0	10	14		.167	.300	.167	36	-6	3			1.000	-1	O-25	-0.8
Total	10	1072	3958	562	1066	140	69	4	319	439		.269	.346	.343	110	57	120			.964	56	*O-1039	7.2

■ **OTTO McIVOR** McIvor, Edward Otto b: 7/26/1884, Greenville, Tex. d: 5/4/54, Dallas, Tex. BB/TL, 5'11.5", 175 lbs. Deb: 4/18/11

YEAR	TM/L	G	AB	R	H	2B	3B	HR	RBI	BB	SO	AVG	OBP	SLG	PRO+	BR/A	SB	CS	SBR	FA	FR	G/POS	TPR
1911	StL-N	30	62	11	14	2	1	1	9	9	14	.226	.333	.339	91	-1	0			.926	-3	O-17	-0.5

■ **DAVE McKAY** McKay, David Lawrence b: 3/14/50, Vancouver, B.C., Can BB/TR, 6'1", 195 lbs. Deb: 8/22/75 C

YEAR	TM/L	G	AB	R	H	2B	3B	HR	RBI	BB	SO	AVG	OBP	SLG	PRO+	BR/A	SB	CS	SBR	FA	FR	G/POS	TPR
1975	Min-A	33	125	8	32	4	1	2	16	6	14	.256	.295	.352	81	-3	1	1	-0	.923	2	3-33	-0.2
1976	Min-A	45	138	8	28	2	0	0	8	9	27	.203	.272	.217	43	-9	1	2	-1	.911	-1	3-41/S-2,D-1	-1.3
1977	Tor-A	95	274	18	54	4	3	3	22	7	51	.197	.223	.266	32	-26	2	1	0	.968	7	2-40,3-32,S-20,/D-2	-1.6
1978	Tor-A	145	504	59	120	20	8	7	45	20	91	.238	.269	.351	71	-20	4	4	-1	.984	-7	*2-140/S-3,3-2,D-1	-1.8
1979	Tor-A	47	156	19	34	9	0	0	12	7	19	.218	.256	.276	43	-12	1	1	-0	.974	6	2-46/3-2	-0.3
1980	Oak-A	123	295	29	72	16	1	1	29	10	57	.244	.283	.315	68	-13	1	1	-0	.977	-6	2-62,3-54,S-10	-1.6
1981	*Oak-A	79	224	25	59	11	1	4	21	16	43	.263	.318	.375	104	1	4	1	1	.926	-4	3-43,2-38/S-7	-0.1
1982	Oak-A	78	212	25	42	4	1	4	17	11	35	.198	.238	.283	44	-17	6	1	1	.968	-3	2-59,3-16/S-3	-1.7
Total	8	645	1928	191	441	70	15	21	170	86	337	.229	.268	.313	62	-100	20	12	-1	.976	-6	2-385,3-223/S-45,D	-8.6

■ **ED McKEAN** McKean, Edwin John "Mack" b: 6/6/1864, Grafton, Ohio d: 8/16/19, Cleveland, Ohio BR/TR, 5'9", 160 lbs. Deb: 4/16/1887

YEAR	TM/L	G	AB	R	H	2B	3B	HR	RBI	BB	SO	AVG	OBP	SLG	PRO+	BR/A	SB	CS	SBR	FA	FR	G/POS	TPR
1887	Cle-a	132	539	97	154	16	13	2	54	60		.286	.358	.375	108	7	76			.847	-8	*S-123/2-8,O-4	0.1
1888	Cle-a	131	548	94	164	21	15	6	68	28		.299	.340	.425	149	28	52			.909	3	S-78,O-48/2-9,3-1	3.0
1889	Cle-N	123	500	88	159	22	8	5	75	42	25	.318	.375	.424	126	17	35			.907	6	*S-122/2-1	2.6
1890	Cle-N	136	530	95	157	15	14	7	61	87	25	.296	.401	.417	141	31	23			.903	-18	*S-134/2-3	1.9
1891	Cle-N	141	603	115	170	13	12	6	69	64	19	.282	.352	.373	107	4	14			.887	-12	*S-141	0.1
1892	*Cle-N	129	531	76	139	14	10	0	93	49	28	.262	.325	.326	93	-5	19			.862	-45	*S-129	-4.1
1893	Cle-N	125	545	103	169	29	24	4	133	50	14	.310	.372	.473	117	9	16			.902	-4	*S-125	1.0
1894	Cle-N	130	554	116	198	30	15	8	128	49	12	.357	.412	.509	116	13	33			.905	-21	*S-130	0.0
1895	*Cle-N	131	565	131	193	32	17	8	119	45	25	.342	.397	.501	123	17	12			.909	-19	*S-131	0.3
1896	*Cle-N	133	571	100	193	29	12	7	112	45	9	.338	.388	.468	118	13	13			.915	-33	*S-133	-1.3
1897	Cle-N	125	523	83	143	21	14	2	78	40		.273	.330	.379	82	-15	15			.920	-30	*S-125	-3.6
1898	Cle-N	151	604	89	172	23	1	9	94	56		.285	.346	.371	107	5	11			.932	-36	*S-151	-2.2
1899	StL-N	67	277	40	72	7	3	3	40	20		.260	.310	.339	76	-10	4			.886	-17	S-42,1-15,2-10	-2.1
Total	13	1654	6890	1227	2083	272	158	67	1124	635	157	.302	.364	.417	114	116	323			.900	-233	*S-1564/O-52,213	-4.3

■ **BILL McKECHNIE** McKechnie, William Boyd "Deacon" b: 8/7/1886, Wilkinsburg, Pa. d: 10/29/65, Bradenton, Fla. BB/TR, 5'10", 160 lbs. Deb: 9/8/07 MCH

YEAR	TM/L	G	AB	R	H	2B	3B	HR	RBI	BB	SO	AVG	OBP	SLG	PRO+	BR/A	SB	CS	SBR	FA	FR	G/POS	TPR
1907	Pit-N	3	8	0	1	0	0	0	0	0		.125	.125	.125	-21	-1	0			1.000	-1	/3-2,2-1	-0.2
1910	Pit-N	71	212	23	46	1	2	0	12	11	23	.217	.256	.241	42	-16	4			.971	8	2-36,S-14/3-8,1-4	-0.8
1911	Pit-N	104	321	40	73	8	7	2	37	28	18	.227	.293	.315	68	-15	9			.975	-0	1-57,2-17,S-12,/3-6	-1.5
1912	Pit-N	24	73	8	18	0	1	0	4	4	5	.247	.286	.274	54	-5	2			.978	2	3-13/S-4,2-3,1-2	-0.3
1913	Bos-N	1	4	1	0	0	0	0	0	0	1	.000	.200	.000	-39	-1	0			1.000	0	/O-1	-0.1
	NY-A	45	112	7	15	0	0	0	8	8	17	.134	.198	.134	-2	-14	2			.950	5	2-28/S-7,3-2	-1.0
1914	Ind-F	149	570	107	173	24	6	2	38	53	36	.304	.368	.377	93	-12	47			.939	23	*3-149	1.6
1915	New-F	127	451	49	113	22	5	1	43	41	31	.251	.316	.328	86	-16	28			.956	2	*3-117/O-1,M	-1.0
1916	NY-N	71	260	22	64	9	1	0	17	7	20	.246	.269	.288	75	-8	7			.940	-3	3-71	-1.1
	Cin-N	37	130	4	36	3	0	0	10	3	12	.277	.293	.300	84	-3	4			.960	-4	3-35	-0.7
	Yr	108	390	26	100	12	1	0	27	10	32	.256	.277	.292	78	-11	11			.947	-8	*3-106	-1.8
1917	Cin-N	48	134	11	34	3	1	0	15	7	7	.254	.296	.291	84	-3	5			.943	-7	2-26,S-13/3-4	-0.9
1918	Pit-N	126	435	34	111	13	9	2	43	24	22	.255	.297	.340	91	-5	12			.966	-1	*3-126	-0.4
1920	Pit-N	40	133	13	29	3	1	1	13	4	7	.218	.241	.278	47	-9	7	4	-0	.943	-1	3-20,S-10/2-6,1-1	-1.0
Total	11	846	2843	319	713	86	33	8	240	190	199	.251	.301	.313	76	-108	127	4		.952	22	3-553,2-117/1SO	-7.4

■ **FRANK McKEE** McKee, Frank b: Philadelphia, Pa. Deb: 6/11/1884

YEAR	TM/L	G	AB	R	H	2B	3B	HR	RBI	BB	SO	AVG	OBP	SLG	PRO+	BR/A	SB	CS	SBR	FA	FR	G/POS	TPR
1884	Was-U	4	17	2	3	0	0	0		1		.176	.222	.176	23	-2				.200	-2	/O-3,3-2,C-1	-0.3

■ **RED McKEE** McKee, Raymond Ellis b: 7/20/1890, Shawnee, Ohio d: 8/5/72, Saginaw, Mich. BL/TR, 5'11", 180 lbs. Deb: 4/19/13

YEAR	TM/L	G	AB	R	H	2B	3B	HR	RBI	BB	SO	AVG	OBP	SLG	PRO+	BR/A	SB	CS	SBR	FA	FR	G/POS	TPR
1913	Det-A	68	187	18	53	3	4	1	20	21	21	.283	.359	.358	112	3	7			.950	-5	C-62	0.4
1914	Det-A	34	64	7	12	1	1	0	8	14	16	.188	.342	.234	71	-2	1	2	-1	.964	-6	C-27	-0.7
1915	Det-A	55	106	10	29	5	0	1	17	13	16	.274	.353	.349	105	1	1			.954	-6	C-35	-0.3
1916	Det-A	32	76	3	16	1	2	0	4	6	11	.211	.268	.276	61	-4	0			.955	-5	C-26	-0.7
Total	4	189	433	38	110	10	7	2	49	54	64	.254	.339	.323	95	-1	9	2		.954	-22	C-150	-1.3

■ **WALT McKEEL** McKeel, Walt Thomas b: 1/17/72, Wilson, N.C. BR/TR, 6'2", 200 lbs. Deb: 9/14/96

YEAR	TM/L	G	AB	R	H	2B	3B	HR	RBI	BB	SO	AVG	OBP	SLG	PRO+	BR/A	SB	CS	SBR	FA	FR	G/POS	TPR
1996	Bos-A	1	0	0	0	0	0	0	0	0	0	—	—	—	—	0	0	0	0	.000	0	/C-1	0.0

YEAR	TM/L	G	AB	R	H	2B	3B	HR	RBI	BB	SO	AVG	OBP	SLG	PRO+	BR/A	SB	CS	SBR	FA	FR	G/POS	TPR
1997	Bos-A	5	3	0	0	0	0	0	0	0	1	.000	.000	.000	-98	-1	0	0	0	1.000	0	/C-4,1-1	-0.1
Total	2	6	3	0	0	0	0	0	0	0	1	.000	.000	.000	-98	-1	0	0	0	1.000	0	/C-5,1-1	-0.1
■ **JIM McKEEVER**	McKeever, James b: 4/19/1861, St.John, N.B., Can. d: 8/19/1897, Boston, Mass. 5'10", 170 lbs. Deb: 4/17/1884																						
1884	Bos-U	16	66	13	9	0	0	0	0			.136	.136	.136	-17	-11				.869	-6	C-12/O-4	-1.4
■ **JOHN McKELVEY**	McKelvey, John Wellington b: 8/27/1847, Rochester, N.Y. d: 5/31/44, Rochester, N.Y. BR/TR, 5'7.5", 175 lbs. Deb: 4/21/1875																						
1875	NH-n	43	188	26	43	3	1	0	10	5	8	.229	.249	.255	86	-1	3	1	0	.656	-8	O-39/3-5	-0.7
■ **RUSS McKELVY**	McKelvy, Russell Errett b: 9/8/1854, Swissvale, Pa. d: 10/19/15, Omaha, Neb. BR/TR, Deb: 5/1/1878																						
1878	Ind-N	63	253	33	57	4	3	2	36	5	38	.225	.240	.289	84	-4				.846	6	*O-62/P-4	-0.1
1882	Pit-a	1	4	0	0	0	0	0		0		.000	.000	.000	-99	-1				.000	-0	/O-1	-0.1
Total	2	64	257	33	57	4	3	2	36	5	38	.222	.237	.284	81	-4				.846	5	/O-63,P-4	-0.2
■ **ED McKENNA**	McKenna, Edward J. b: St.Louis, Mo. Deb: 7/29/1874																						
1874	Phi-n	1	4	0	0	0	0	0	0	0	1	.000	.000	.000	-97	-1	0	0	0	1.000	0	/1-1	-0.1
1877	StL-N	1	5	0	1	0	0	0	0	0	1	.200	.200	.200	28	-0				1.000	-0	/O-1	-0.1
1884	Was-U	32	117	19	22	1	0	0		4		.188	.215	.197	26	-14				.876	-14	C-23,O-10/3-7	-2.3
Total	2	33	122	19	23	1	0	0	0	4	1	.189	.214	.197	26	-14				.556	-14	/C-23,O-11,3-7	-2.4
■ **DAVE McKEOUGH**	McKeough, David J. b: 12/1/1863, Utica, N.Y. d: 7/11/01, Utica, N.Y. 5'7", 158 lbs. Deb: 4/22/1890																						
1890	Roc-a	62	218	38	49	5	0	0	20	29		.225	.316	.248	72	-6	14			.929	-4	C-47,S-13/2-2,3-1	-0.5
1891	Phi-a	15	54	4	14	1	1	0	3	8	6	.259	.355	.315	89	-1	0			.854	-4	C-14/S-1	-0.3
Total	2	77	272	42	63	6	1	0	23	37	6	.232	.324	.261	75	-7	14			.912	-9	/C-61,S-14,2-2,3-1	-0.8
■ **RICH McKINNEY**	McKinney, Charles Richard b: 11/22/46, Piqua, Ohio BR/TR, 5'11", 185 lbs. Deb: 6/26/70																						
1970	Chi-A	43	119	12	20	5	0	4	17	11	25	.168	.244	.311	50	-8	3	2	-0	.931	2	3-23,S-11	-0.6
1971	Chi-A	114	369	35	100	11	2	8	46	35	37	.271	.337	.377	99	-0	0	0	0	.968	-9	2-67,O-25/3-5	-0.6
1972	NY-A	37	121	10	26	2	0	1	7	7	13	.215	.258	.256	55	-7	1	0	0	.917	-3	3-33	-1.1
1973	Oak-A	48	65	9	16	3	0	1	7	7	4	.246	.319	.338	90	-1	0	0	0	.900	-1	3-17/2-7,O-3,D-6	-0.1
1974	Oak-A	5	7	0	1	0	0	0	0	0	0	.143	.143	.143	-19	-1	0	0	0	1.000	-2	/2-3	-0.4
1975	Oak-A	8	7	0	1	0	0	0	2	1	2	.143	.250	.143	14	-1	0	0	0	1.000	-0	/1-1,D-2	-0.1
1977	Oak-A	86	198	13	35	7	0	6	21	16	43	.177	.238	.303	47	-15	0	1	-1	.978	-4	1-32,D-18/3-7,O2	-2.2
Total	7	341	886	79	199	28	2	20	100	77	124	.225	.289	.328	73	-33	4	3	-1	.911	-17	/3-85,2-80,1ODS	-5.1
■ **BOB McKINNEY**	McKinney, Robert Francis b: 10/4/1875, McSherrystown, Pa. d: 8/19/46, Hanover, Pa. BR/TR, 5'7", 165 lbs. Deb: 7/23/01																						
1901	Phi-A	2	2	0	0	0	0	0	0	0		.000	.000	.000	-96	-1	0			.000	-1	/2-1,3-1	-0.2
■ **ALEX McKINNON**	McKinnon, Alexander J. b: 8/14/1856, Boston, Mass. d: 7/24/1887, Charlestown, Mass BR, 5'11.5", 170 lbs. Deb: 5/1/1884 M																						
1884	NY-N	116	470	66	128	21	13	3	73	8	62	.272	.285	.391	108	3				.955	-2	*1-116	-1.2
1885	StL-N	100	411	42	121	21	6	1	44	8	31	.294	.308	.382	130	13				**.978**	-2	*1-100,M	-0.1
1886	StL-N	122	491	75	148	24	7	8	72	21	23	.301	.330	.428	138	21	10			.963	-6	*1-119/O-3	0.1
1887	Pit-N	48	200	26	68	16	4	1	30	8	9	.340	.365	.475	140	10	6			.977	3	1-48	0.7
Total	4	386	1572	209	465	82	30	13	219	45	125	.296	.315	.411	127	47	16			.967	-7	1-383/O-3	-0.5
■ **JIM McKNIGHT**	McKnight, James Arthur b: 6/1/36, Bee Branch, Ark. d: 2/24/94, Van Buren County, Ark. BR/TR, 6'1", 185 lbs. Deb: 9/22/60 F																						
1960	Chi-N	3	6	0	2	0	0	0	1	0	1	.333	.333	.333	84	-0	0	0	0	.667	-2	/2-1,O-1	-0.2
1962	Chi-N	60	85	6	19	0	1	0	5	2	13	.224	.241	.247	30	-8	0	0	0	.955	3	/3-9,O-5,2-2	-0.6
Total	2	63	91	6	21	0	1	0	6	2	14	.231	.247	.253	34	-8	0	0	0	.875	1	/3-9,O-6,2-3	-0.8
■ **JEFF McKNIGHT**	McKnight, Jefferson Alan b: 2/18/63, Conway, Ark. BB/TR, 6', 188 lbs. Deb: 6/6/89 F																						
1989	NY-N	6	12	2	3	0	0	0	0	2	1	.250	.357	.250	80	-0	0	0	0	1.000	-3	/2-4,1-1,3-1,S-1	-0.3
1990	Bal-A	29	75	11	15	2	0	1	4	5	17	.200	.259	.267	49	-5	0	0	0	1.000	-3	1-15/O-8,2-5,S-1,D	-0.9
1991	Bal-A	16	41	2	7	1	0	0	2	2	7	.171	.209	.195	13	-5	1	0	0	1.000	-0	/O-7,1-2,D-4	-0.5
1992	NY-N	31	85	10	23	3	1	2	13	2	8	.271	.287	.400	94	-1	0	1	-1	.980	-3	2-14/1-9,3-3,S-3,O	-0.5
1993	NY-N	105	164	19	42	3	1	2	13	13	31	.256	.315	.323	72	-6	0	0	0	.943	-7	S-29,2-15,1-10,/3C	-1.2
1994	NY-N	31	27	1	4	1	0	0	2	4	12	.148	.258	.185	18	-3	0	0	0	1.000	-0	/1-2	-0.3
Total	6	218	404	45	94	10	2	5	34	28	76	.233	.286	.304	63	-21	1	1	-0	.996	-16	/1-39,2-38,SO3DC	-3.7
■ **ED McLANE**	McLane, Edward Cameron b: 8/20/1881, Weston, Mass. d: 8/21/75, Baltimore, Md. 5'10", 179 lbs. Deb: 10/6/07																						
1907	Bro-N	1	2	0	0	0	0	0	0	0		.000	.333	.000	5	-0	0			.333	-1	/O-1	-0.1
■ **ART McLARNEY**	McLarney, Arthur James b: 12/20/08, Ft.Worden, Wash. d: 12/20/84, Seattle, Wash. BB/TR, 6', 168 lbs. Deb: 8/23/32																						
1932	NY-N	9	23	2	3	1	0	0	3	1	3	.130	.167	.174	-8	-4	0			1.000	-1	/S-7	-0.4
■ **POLLY McLARRY**	McLarry, Howard Zell b: 3/25/1891, Leonard, Tex. d: 11/4/71, Bonham, Tex. BL/TR, 6', 185 lbs. Deb: 9/2/12																						
1912	Chi-A	2	2	0	0	0	0	0	0	0		.000	.000	.000	-99	-1	0			.000	0	H	-0.1
1915	Chi-N	68	127	16	25	3	0	1	12	14	20	.197	.277	.244	58	-6	2	2	-1	.957	3	2-21,1-18	-0.4
Total	2	70	129	16	25	3	0	1	12	14	20	.194	.273	.240	56	-7	2	2		.957	3	/2-21,1-18	-0.5
■ **BARNEY McLAUGHLIN**	McLaughlin, Bernard b: 1857, Ireland d: 2/13/21, Lowell, Mass. BR/TR, Deb: 8/2/1884 F																						
1884	KC-U	42	162	15	37	7	3	0		9		.228	.269	.309	86	-8				.762	-4	O-24,2-12/P-7,S-2	-1.0
1887	Phi-N	50	205	26	45	8	3	1	26	11	27	.220	.263	.302	53	-13	2			.879	-11	2-50	-2.0
1890	Syr-a	86	329	43	87	8	1	2	40	47		.264	.360	.313	110	7	13			.902	-12	S-86	0.0
Total	3	178	696	84	169	23	7	3	66	67	27	.243	.312	.309	86	-14	15			.900	-27	/S-88,2-62,O-24,P-7	-3.0
■ **FRANK McLAUGHLIN**	McLaughlin, Francis Edward b: 6/19/1856, Lowell, Mass. d: 4/5/17, Lowell, Mass. BR/TR, 5'9", 160 lbs. Deb: 8/9/1882 F																						
1882	Wor-N	15	55	7	12	0	2	1	4	0	11	.218	.218	.345	76	-2				.760	-3	S-14/O-1	-0.4
1883	Pit-a	29	114	15	25	2	0	1		6		.219	.258	.263	72	-3				.802	-1	S-25/O-4,2-2,P-2	-0.3
1884	Cin-U	16	67	10	16	4	1	2		2		.239	.261	.418	95	-3				.740	-7	S-16	-0.8
	CP-U	15	67	11	16	4	1	0		1		.239	.250	.328	74	-4				.888	6	2-14/S-1,O-1	0.2
	KC-U	32	123	17	28	11	0	1		9		.228	.280	.341	101	-4				.847	-9	2-10,O-10/3-9,SP	-1.1
	Yr	63	257	38	60	19	2	3		12		.233	.268	.358	92	-10				.873	-10	2-24,S-22,O-11,/3P	-1.7
Total	3	107	426	60	97	21	4	5	4	18	11	.228	.259	.331	85	-15				.769	-15	/S-61,2-26,O-16,3P	-2.4
■ **JAMES McLAUGHLIN**	McLaughlin, James b: San Francisco, Cal. Deb: 5/3/1884																						
1884	Was-U	10	37	3	7	3	0	0		0		.189	.189	.270	39	-4				.696	-3	/S-9,3-1	-0.6
■ **KID McLAUGHLIN**	McLaughlin, James Anson "Sunshine" b: 4/12/1888, Randolph, N.Y. d: 11/13/34, Allegany, N.Y. BL/TR, 5'8.5", 158 lbs. Deb: 6/30/14																						
1914	Cin-N	3	2	1	0	0	0	0	0	0	0	.000	.000	.000	-97	-0	0			1.000	-1	/O-2	-0.1
■ **JIM McLAUGHLIN**	McLaughlin, James Robert b: 1/3/02, St.Louis, Mo. d: 12/18/68, Mount Vernon, Ill. BR/TR, 5'8.5", 168 lbs. Deb: 4/18/32																						
1932	StL-A	1	1	0	0	0	0	0	1	0	0	.000	.000	.000	-95	-0	0	0	0	.000	0	/3-1	0.0
■ **TOM McLAUGHLIN**	McLaughlin, Thomas b: 3/28/1860, Louisville, Ky. d: 7/21/21, Louisville, Ky. TR, Deb: 7/17/1883																						
1883	Lou-a	42	146	16	28	1	2	0		5		.192	.219	.226	47	-8				.844	4	S-19,O-17/1-5,32	-0.4
1884	Lou-a	98	335	41	67	11	6	0	21	22		.200	.262	.269	77	-7				.892	19	*S-94/3-4,2-1	1.1
1885	Lou-a	112	411	49	87	13	9	2	41	15		.212	.245	.302	72	-13				.883	1	*2-93,S-19	-0.8
1886	NY-a	74	250	27	34	3	1	0	16	26		.136	.220	.156	19	-22	13			.886	7	S-63,2-10/O-1	-1.2
1891	Was-a	14	41	9	11	0	1	0	3	7	6	.268	.400	.317	111	1	3			.871	-0	S-14	0.2
Total	5	340	1183	142	227	28	19	2	81	75	6	.192	.247	.253	61	-49	16			.886	30	S-209,2-106/O31	-1.1
■ **RALPH McLAURIN**	McLaurin, Ralph Edgar b: 5/23/1885, Kissimmee, Fla. d: 2/11/43, McColl, S.C. Deb: 9/5/08																						
1908	StL-N	8	22	2	5	0	0	0	0	0		.227	.227	.227	47	-1	0			.875	-0	/O-6	-0.2

YEAR	TM/L	G	AB	R	H	2B	3B	HR	RBI	BB	SO	AVG	OBP	SLG	PRO+	BR/A	SB	CS	SBR	FA	FR	G/POS	TPR
■ **LARRY McLEAN**	McLean, John Bannerman b: 7/18/1881, Fredericton, N.B., Canada d: 3/24/21, Boston, Mass. BR/TR, 6'5", 228 lbs. Deb: 4/26/01																						
1901	Bos-A	9	19	4	4	1	0	0	2	0		.211	.211	.263	31	-2	1			1.000	0	/1-5	-0.1
1903	Chi-N	1	4	0	0	0	0	0	1	1		.000	.200	.000	-42	-1	0			.889	-0	/C-1	-0.1
1904	StL-N	27	84	5	14	2	1	0	4	4		.167	.205	.214	31	-7	1			.954	-2	C-24	-0.7
1906	Cin-N	12	35	3	7	2	0	0	2	4		.200	.282	.257	65	-1	0			.954	-1	C-12	-0.2
1907	Cin-N	113	374	35	108	9	9	0	54	13		.289	.313	.361	107	1	4			.975	-3	C-89,1-13	0.7
1908	Cin-N	99	309	24	67	9	4	1	28	15		.217	.258	.282	74	-10	2			.963	-6	C-69,1-19	-1.1
1909	Cin-N	95	324	26	83	12	2	2	36	21		.256	.307	.324	97	-2	1			.978	-6	C-95	0.1
1910	Cin-N	127	423	27	126	14	7	2	71	26	23	.298	.340	.378	114	6	4			.983	-4	*C-119	1.4
1911	Cin-N	107	328	24	94	7	2	0	34	20	18	.287	.330	.320	85	-7	1			.968	8	C-98	1.0
1912	Cin-N	102	333	17	81	15	1	1	27	18	15	.243	.284	.303	63	-18	1			.973	-2	C-98	-1.0
1913	StL-N	48	152	7	41	9	0	0	12	6	9	.270	.297	.329	80	-4	0			.981	-8	C-42	-0.9
	*NY-N	30	75	3	24	4	0	0	9	4	4	.320	.354	.373	107	1	1			.953	-4	C-28	-0.1
	Yr	78	227	10	65	13	0	0	21	10	13	.286	.316	.344	89	-4	1			.970	-12	C-70	-1.0
1914	NY-N	79	154	8	40	6	0	0	14	4	9	.260	.283	.299	76	-5	4			.973	-4	C-74	-0.5
1915	NY-N	13	33	0	5	0	0	0	4	0	1	.152	.152	.152	-9	-4	0			.985	2	C-12	-0.2
Total	13	862	2647	183	694	90	26	6	298	136	79	.262	.301	.323	86	-53	20			.973	-29	C-761/1-37	-1.7
■ **MARK McLEMORE**	McLemore, Mark Tremell b: 10/4/64, San Diego, Cal. BB/TR, 5'11", 195 lbs. Deb: 9/13/86																						
1986	Cal-A	5	4	0	0	0	0	0	0	1	2	.000	.200	.000	-40	-1	0	1	-1	1.000	4	/2-2	0.2
1987	Cal-A	138	433	61	102	13	3	3	41	48	72	.236	.312	.300	66	-20	25	8	3	.974	-5	*2-132/S-6,D-3	-1.6
1988	Cal-A	77	233	38	56	11	2	2	16	25	28	.240	.314	.330	83	-5	13	7	-0	.979	7	2-63/3-5,D-1	0.4
1989	Cal-A	32	103	12	25	3	1	0	14	7	19	.243	.297	.291	68	-4	6	1	1	.966	3	2-27/D-1	0.0
1990	Cal-A	20	48	4	7	2	0	0	2	4	9	.146	.212	.188	13	-6	1	0	0	1.000	-1	/2-8,S-8,D-1	-0.6
	Cle-A	8	12	2	2	0	0	0	0	0	6	.167	.167	.167	-7	-2	0	0	0	1.000	3	/3-4,2-3,D-1	0.1
	Yr	28	60	6	9	2	0	0	2	4	15	.150	.203	.183	9	-7	1	0	0	1.000	2	2-11/S-8,3-4,D-2	-0.5
1991	Hou-N	21	61	6	9	1	0	0	2	6	13	.148	.224	.164	11	-7	0	1	-1	.975	1	2-19	-0.7
1992	Bal-A	101	228	40	56	7	2	0	27	21	26	.246	.309	.294	68	-9	11	5	0	.978	9	2-70,D-17	0.0
1993	Bal-A	148	581	81	165	27	5	4	72	64	92	.284	.356	.368	91	-6	21	15	-3	.987	12	*O-124,2-25/3-4,D-1	0.1
1994	Bal-A	104	343	44	88	11	1	3	29	51	50	.257	.354	.321	72	-13	20	5	3	.981	-3	2-96/O-7,D-1	-0.8
1995	Tex-A	129	467	73	122	20	5	5	41	59	71	.261	.348	.358	82	-11	21	11	-0	.986	-1	O-73,2-66/D-2	-1.0
1996	*Tex-A	147	517	84	150	23	4	5	46	87	69	.290	.392	.379	92	-4	27	10	2	.985	20	*2-147/O-1	2.5
1997	Tex-A	89	349	47	91	17	2	1	25	40	54	.261	.340	.330	72	-13	7	5	-1	.980	-6	2-89/O-1	-1.5
1998	*Tex-A	126	461	79	114	15	1	5	53	89	64	.247	.371	.317	78	-12	12	4	1	.975	-7	*2-122/D-2	-0.9
Total	13	1145	3840	571	987	150	26	28	368	502	575	.257	.344	.332	78	-113	164	73	5	.980	34	2-869,O-206/DS3	-3.8
■ **RALPH McLEOD**	McLeod, Ralph Alton b: 10/19/16, N.Quincy, Mass. BL/TL, 6', 170 lbs. Deb: 9/14/38																						
1938	Bos-N	6	7	1	2	1	0	0	0	0	2	.286	.286	.429	105	-0	0			1.000	-0	/O-1	0.0
■ **JIM McLEOD**	McLeod, Soule James b: 9/12/08, Jones, La. d: 8/3/81, Little Rock, Ark. BR/TR, 6', 187 lbs. Deb: 5/22/30																						
1930	Was-A	18	34	3	9	1	0	0	1	1	5	.265	.306	.294	53	-2	1	1	-0	1.000	-1	3-10/S-7	-0.2
1932	Was-A	7	0	1	0	0	0	0	0	1	0	—	1.000	—	183	0	0	0	0	1.000	0	/S-1	0.1
1933	Phi-N	67	232	20	45	6	1	0	15	12	25	.194	.237	.228	30	-21	1			.914	-6	3-67/S-1	-2.5
Total	3	92	266	24	54	7	1	0	16	14	30	.203	.248	.237	33	-23	2	1		.922	-6	/3-77,S-9	-2.6
■ **JACK McMAHON**	McMahon, John Henry b: 10/15/1869, Waterbury, Conn. d: 12/30/1894, Bridgeport, Conn. BR/TL, 5'10", 165 lbs. Deb: 8/8/1892																						
1892	NY-N	40	147	21	33	5	7	1	24	10	9	.224	.278	.374	99	-1	3			.973	-2	1-36/C-5	-0.4
1893	NY-N	11	30	5	10	2	1	0	4	2	0	.333	.375	.467	123	1	0			.891	-1	C-11	0.0
Total	2	51	177	26	43	7	8	1	28	12	9	.243	.295	.390	103	-0	3			.900	-3	/1-36,C-16	-0.4
■ **FRANK McMANUS**	McManus, Francis E. b: 9/21/1875, Lawrence, Mass. d: 9/1/23, Syracuse, N.Y. TR , 5'7", 150 lbs. Deb: 9/14/1899																						
1899	Was-N	7	21	3	8	1	0	0	2	2		.381	.435	.429	139	1	3			.931	0	/C-7	0.2
1903	Bro-N	2	7	0	0	0	0	0	0	0		.000	.000	.000	-99	-2	0			.929	1	/C-2	-0.1
1904	Det-A	1	0	0	0	0	0	0	0	0		—	—	—	—	0	0			.000	0	/C-1	0.0
	NY-A	4	7	0	0	0	0	0	0	0		.000	.000	.000	-96	-2	0			.900	-1	/C-4	-0.3
	Yr	5	7	0	0	0	0	0	0	0		.000	.000	.000	-97	-2	0			.900	-1	/C-5	-0.3
Total	3	14	35	3	8	1	0	0	2	2		.229	.270	.257	50	-2	3			.925	-0	/C-14	-0.2
■ **JIM McMANUS**	McManus, James Michael b: 7/20/36, Brookline, Mass. BL/TL, 6'4", 215 lbs. Deb: 9/21/60																						
1960	KC-A	5	13	3	4	0	0	1	2	1	2	.308	.357	.538	138	1	0	0	0	1.000	-0	/1-3	0.0
■ **MARTY McMANUS**	McManus, Martin Joseph b: 3/14/1900, Chicago, Ill. d: 2/18/66, St.Louis, Mo. BR/TR, 5'10.5", 160 lbs. Deb: 9/26/20 M																						
1920	StL-A	1	3	0	1	0	1	0	1	0	0	.333	.333	1.000	237	0	0	0	0	.667	-0	/3-1	0.0
1921	StL-A	121	412	49	107	19	8	3	64	27	30	.260	.308	.367	68	-21	5	3	-0	.952	-11	2-96,3-13/1-9,S-2	-2.7
1922	StL-A	154	606	88	189	34	11	11	109	38	41	.312	.358	.459	108	6	9	6	-1	.964	3	*2-153/1-1	1.1
1923	StL-A	154	582	86	180	35	10	15	94	49	50	.309	.367	.481	116	11	14	10	-2	.960	-1	*2-133,1-20	0.8
1924	StL-A	123	442	71	147	23	5	5	80	55	40	.333	.409	.441	112	9	13	9	-2	.972	7	*2-119	1.5
1925	StL-A	154	587	108	169	**44**	8	13	90	73	69	.288	.371	.457	104	2	5	11	-5	.967	4	*2-154/O-1	0.3
1926	StL-A	149	549	102	156	30	10	9	68	55	62	.284	.350	.424	97	-4	5	7	-3	.958	15	3-84,2-61/1-4	1.5
1927	Det-A	108	369	60	99	19	7	9	69	34	38	.268	.332	.431	95	-4	8	7	-2	.960	-2	S-39,2-35,3-22,/1-6	-0.1
1928	Det-A	139	500	78	144	37	5	8	73	51	32	.288	.355	.430	104	2	11	13	-5	.955	0	3-92,1-45/S-2	0.0
1929	Det-A	154	599	99	168	32	8	18	90	60	52	.280	.347	.451	103	2	16	11	-2	.972	8	*3-150/S-8	1.4
1930	Det-A	132	484	74	155	40	4	9	89	59	28	.320	.396	.475	118	14	**23**	8	2	**.966**	6	*3-130/S-3,1-1	2.6
1931	Det-A	107	362	39	98	17	3	3	53	49	22	.271	.361	.359	87	-6	7	3	0	.950	13	3-79,2-21/1-1	1.2
	Bos-A	17	62	8	18	4	0	1	9	8	1	.290	.371	.403	110	1	1	1	-0	1.000	8	3-11/2-7	0.9
	Yr	124	424	47	116	21	3	4	62	57	23	.274	.362	.366	90	-5	8	4	0	.956	21	3-90,2-28/1-1	2.1
1932	Bos-A	93	302	39	71	19	4	5	24	36	30	.235	.317	.374	80	-9	1	2	-1	.969	6	2-49,3-30/S-2,1M	0.0
1933	Bos-A	106	366	51	104	30	4	3	36	49	21	.284	.369	.413	108	5	3	0	1	.957	-5	3-76,2-26/1-4,M	0.6
1934	Bos-N	119	435	56	120	18	0	8	47	32	42	.276	.330	.372	95	-4	5			.964	-5	2-73,3-37	-0.3
Total	15	1831	6660	1008	1926	401	88	120	996	675	558	.289	.357	.430	101	5	126	91		.965	44	2-927,3-725/1SO	8.8
■ **JIMMY McMATH**	McMath, Jimmy Lee b: 8/10/49, Tuscaloosa, Ala. BL/TL, 6'1.5", 195 lbs. Deb: 9/7/68																						
1968	Chi-N	6	14	0	2	0	0	0	2	0	6	.143	.143	.143	-13	-2	0	0	0	1.000	0	/O-3	-0.2
■ **GEORGE McMILLAN**	McMillan, George A. "Reddy" b: Evansville, Ind. 5'8", 175 lbs. Deb: 8/11/1890																						
1890	NY-N	10	35	4	5	0	0	0	1	7	4	.143	.286	.143	26	-3	1			.800	-1	O-10	-0.4
■ **NORM McMILLAN**	McMillan, Norman Alexis "Bub" b: 10/5/1895, Latta, S.C. d: 9/28/69, Marion, S.C. BR/TR, 6', 175 lbs. Deb: 4/12/22																						
1922	*NY-A	33	78	7	20	1	2	0	11	6	10	.256	.310	.321	63	-4	4	1	1	.921	-8	O-26/3-5	-1.2
1923	Bos-A	131	459	37	116	24	5	0	42	28	44	.253	.299	.327	64	-25	13	5	1	.942	13	3-67,2-34,S-28	-0.2
1924	StL-A	76	201	25	56	12	2	0	27	12	17	.279	.332	.358	73	-8	6	4	-1	.966	-3	2-37,3-19/S-7,1-2	-1.0
1928	Chi-N	49	123	11	27	2	2	1	12	13	19	.220	.299	.293	56	-8	0			.977	-1	2-19,3-18	-0.7
1929	*Chi-N	124	495	77	134	35	5	5	55	36	43	.271	.324	.392	76	-19	13			.944	6	*3-120	-0.8
Total	5	413	1356	157	353	74	16	6	147	95	133	.260	.313	.352	69	-64	36	10		.944	7	3-229/2-90,S-35,O1	-3.9
■ **ROY McMILLAN**	McMillan, Roy David b: 7/17/29, Bonham, Tex. d: 11/2/97, Bonham, Tex. BR/TR, 5'11", 170 lbs. Deb: 4/17/51 MC																						
1951	Cin-N	85	199	21	42	4	0	1	8	17	26	.211	.273	.246	40	-17	0	0	0	.963	5	S-54,3-12/2-1	-0.9
1952	Cin-N	154	540	60	132	32	2	7	57	45	81	.244	.306	.350	82	-14	4	5	-2	.971	11	*S-154	0.7
1953	Cin-N	155	557	51	130	15	4	5	43	43	52	.233	.290	.302	54	-37	2	4	-2	.972	14	*S-155	-1.4
1954	Cin-N	154	588	86	147	21	2	4	42	47	54	.250	.311	.313	61	-33	4	2	0	.959	6	*S-154	-1.4
1955	Cin-N	151	470	50	126	21	2	1	37	66	33	.268	.366	.328	81	-10	4	4	-1	.969	17	*S-150	1.8

YEAR	TM/L	G	AB	R	H	2B	3B	HR	RBI	BB	SO	AVG	OBP	SLG	PRO+	BR/A	SB	CS	SBR	FA	FR	G/POS	TPR
1956	Cin-N★	150	479	51	126	16	7	3	62	76	54	.263	.370	.344	88	-5	4	3	-1	**.975**	**30**	*S-150	3.7
1957	Cin-N★	151	448	50	122	25	5	1	55	66	44	.272	.373	.357	91	-3	5	1	1	**.977**	-8	*S-151	0.4
1958	Cin-N	145	393	48	90	18	3	1	25	47	33	.229	.313	.298	60	-22	5	2	0	**.980**	4	*S-145	-0.6
1959	Cin-N	79	246	38	65	14	2	9	24	27	27	.264	.347	.447	106	2	0	2	-1	.974	-7	S-73	0.0
1960	Cin-N	124	399	42	94	12	2	10	42	35	40	.236	.304	.351	77	-12	2	0	1	.964	-13	*S-116,2-10	-1.7
1961	Mil-N	154	505	42	111	16	0	7	48	61	86	.220	.309	.293	65	-25	2	4	-2	**.975**	-0	*S-154	-1.4
1962	Mil-N	137	468	66	115	13	0	12	41	60	53	.246	.338	.350	87	-7	2	2	-1	.972	1	*S-135	0.5
1963	Mil-N	100	320	35	80	10	1	4	29	17	25	.250	.292	.325	78	-9	1	5	-3	.979	7	S-94	0.2
1964	Mil-N	8	13	1	4	0	0	0	2	0	2	.308	.308	.308	73	-0	1	0	0	.933	-1	/S-8	-0.1
	NY-N	113	379	30	80	8	2	1	25	14	16	.211	.247	.251	42	-29	3	1	0	.976	-1	*S-111	-2.3
	Yr	121	392	31	84	8	2	1	27	14	18	.214	.249	.253	43	-30	4	1	1	.975	-2	*S-119	-2.4
1965	NY-N	157	528	44	128	19	2	1	42	24	60	.242	.281	.292	64	-26	1	0	0	.964	-4	*S-153	-2.0
1966	NY-N	76	220	24	47	9	1	1	12	20	25	.214	.285	.277	59	-12	1	1	-0	.975	6	S-71	-0.1
Total	16	2093	6752	739	1639	253	35	68	594	665	711	.243	.316	.321	72	-259	41	36	-9	.972	66	*S-2028/3-12,2-11	-4.6

■ TOM McMILLAN
McMillan, Thomas Erwin b: 9/13/51, Richmond, Va. BR/TR, 5'9", 165 lbs. Deb: 9/17/77

YEAR	TM/L	G	AB	R	H	2B	3B	HR	RBI	BB	SO	AVG	OBP	SLG	PRO+	BR/A	SB	CS	SBR	FA	FR	G/POS	TPR
1977	Sea-A	2	5	0	0	0	0	0	0	0	0	.000	.000	.000	-99	-1	0	0	0	1.000	-0	/S-2	-0.2

■ TOMMY McMILLAN
McMillan, Thomas Law "Rebel" b: 4/18/1888, Pittston, Pa. d: 7/15/66, Orlando, Fla. BR/TR, 5'5", 130 lbs. Deb: 8/19/08

YEAR	TM/L	G	AB	R	H	2B	3B	HR	RBI	BB	SO	AVG	OBP	SLG	PRO+	BR/A	SB	CS	SBR	FA	FR	G/POS	TPR
1908	Bro-N	43	147	9	35	3	0	0	3	9		.238	.296	.259	80	-3	5			.873	-5	S-29,O-14	-0.9
1909	Bro-N	108	373	18	79	15	1	0	24	20		.212	.254	.257	61	-18	11			.914	-10	*S-105/2-2,3-1	-3.0
1910	Bro-N	23	74	2	13	1	0	0	2	6	10	.176	.237	.189	26	-7	4			.898	-1	S-23	-0.8
	Cin-N	82	248	20	46	0	3	0	13	31	23	.185	.281	.210	46	-16	7			.927	10	S-82	-0.4
	Yr	105	322	22	59	1	3	0	15	37	33	.183	.271	.205	41	-23	11			.921	8	*S-105	-1.2
1912	NY-A	41	149	24	34	2	0	0	12	15		.228	.303	.242	53	-9	18			.948	-8	S-41	-1.3
Total	4	297	991	73	207	21	4	0	54	81	33	.209	.273	.238	56	-53	45			.917	-15	S-280/O-14,2-2,3-1	-6.4

■ BILLY McMILLON
McMillon, William Edward b: 11/17/71, Otero, N.Mex. BL/TL, 5'11", 172 lbs. Deb: 7/26/96

YEAR	TM/L	G	AB	R	H	2B	3B	HR	RBI	BB	SO	AVG	OBP	SLG	PRO+	BR/A	SB	CS	SBR	FA	FR	G/POS	TPR
1996	Fla-N	28	51	4	11	0	0	0	4	5	14	.216	.286	.216	36	-5	0	0	0	1.000	-2	O-15	-0.6
1997	Fla-N	13	18	0	2	1	0	0	1	0	7	.111	.111	.167	-30	-3	0	0	0	1.000	0	/O-2	-0.3
	Phi-N	24	72	10	21	4	1	2	13	6	17	.292	.346	.458	109	1	2	1	0	.957	3	O-21	0.3
	Yr	37	90	10	23	5	1	2	14	6	24	.256	.302	.400	83	-2	2	1	0	.957	3	O-23	0.0
Total	2	65	141	14	34	5	1	2	18	11	38	.241	.296	.333	66	-7	2	1	0	.970	1	/O-38	-0.6

■ HUGH McMULLEN
McMullen, Hugh Raphael b: 12/16/01, LaCygne, Kan. d: 5/23/86, Whittier, Cal. BB/TR, 6'1", 180 lbs. Deb: 9/19/25

YEAR	TM/L	G	AB	R	H	2B	3B	HR	RBI	BB	SO	AVG	OBP	SLG	PRO+	BR/A	SB	CS	SBR	FA	FR	G/POS	TPR
1925	NY-N	5	15	1	2	1	0	0	0	0	3	.133	.133	.200	-17	-3	0	0	0	1.000	-2	/C-5	-0.4
1926	NY-N	57	91	5	17	2	0	0	6	2	18	.187	.204	.209	11	-11	1			.942	-0	C-56	-0.9
1928	Was-A	1	1	0	0	0	0	0	0	0	1	.000	.000	.000	-99	-0	0	0	0	.000	0	H	0.0
1929	Cin-N	1	1	0	0	0	0	0	0	0	0	.000	.000	.000	-99	-0	0			1.000	0	/C-1	0.0
Total	4	64	108	6	19	3	0	0	6	2	22	.176	.191	.204	5	-15	1	0		.947	-2	/C-62	-1.3

■ KEN McMULLEN
McMullen, Kenneth Lee b: 6/1/42, Oxnard, Cal. BR/TR, 6'3", 195 lbs. Deb: 9/17/62

YEAR	TM/L	G	AB	R	H	2B	3B	HR	RBI	BB	SO	AVG	OBP	SLG	PRO+	BR/A	SB	CS	SBR	FA	FR	G/POS	TPR
1962	LA-N	6	11	0	3	0	0	0	0	0	3	.273	.273	.273	50	-1	0	0	0	1.000	-0	/O-2	-0.1
1963	LA-N	79	233	16	55	9	0	5	28	20	46	.236	.299	.339	89	-4	1	2	-1	.933	6	3-71/2-1,O-1	0.2
1964	LA-N	24	67	3	14	0	0	1	2	3	7	.209	.243	.254	43	-5	0	1	-1	.991	-3	1-13/3-4,O-3	-1.0
1965	Was-A	150	555	75	146	18	6	18	54	47	90	.263	.325	.414	110	7	2	0	1	.954	6	*3-142/O-8,1-1	1.0
1966	Was-A	147	524	48	122	19	4	13	54	44	89	.233	.292	.359	87	-9	3	1	0	.951	-1	*3-141/1-8,O-1	-1.4
1967	Was-A	146	563	73	138	22	2	16	67	46	84	.245	.303	.377	104	1	5	3	-0	.965	12	*3-145	1.3
1968	Was-A	151	557	66	138	11	2	20	62	63	66	.248	.327	.382	118	12	1	3	-2	.962	5	*3-145,S-11	1.9
1969	Was-A	158	562	83	153	25	2	19	87	70	103	.272	.354	.425	123	17	4	5	-2	.976	19	*3-154	3.6
1970	Was-A	15	59	5	12	2	0	0	3	5	10	.203	.266	.237	42	-5	0	0	0	.971	6	3-15	0.1
	Cal-A	124	422	50	98	9	3	14	61	59	81	.232	.331	.367	96	-2	1	0	0	.959	9	*3-122	0.6
	Yr	139	481	55	110	11	3	14	64	64	91	.229	.323	.351	89	-7	1	0	0	.960	15	*3-137	0.7
1971	Cal-A	160	593	63	148	19	2	21	68	53	74	.250	.314	.395	107	3	1	1	-0	.966	-1	*3-158	0.1
1972	Cal-A	137	472	36	127	18	1	9	34	48	59	.269	.337	.369	116	9	1	2	-1	.970	2	*3-137	1.0
1973	LA-N	42	85	6	21	5	0	5	18	6	13	.247	.297	.482	118	1	0	0	0	.922	5	3-24	0.6
1974	*LA-N	44	60	5	15	1	0	3	12	2	12	.250	.274	.417	95	-1	0	0	0	1.000	-1	/3-7,2-3	-0.1
1975	LA-N	39	46	4	11	1	1	2	14	7	12	.239	.340	.435	119	1	0	0	0	1.000	1	3-11/1-3	0.2
1976	Oak-A	98	186	20	41	6	2	5	23	22	33	.220	.306	.355	97	-1	1	1	-0	.952	-1	3-35,1-26,D-23,/O2	-0.5
1977	Mil-A	63	136	15	31	7	1	5	19	15	33	.228	.305	.404	91	-2	0	0	0	.978	2	D-29,1-11/3-7	-0.2
Total	16	1583	5131	568	1273	172	26	156	606	510	815	.248	.318	.383	105	23	20	19	-5	.961	66	*3-1318/1-62,DOS2	7.3

■ FRED McMULLIN
McMullin, Frederick William b: 10/13/1891, Scammon, Kan. d: 11/21/52, Los Angeles, Cal. BR/TR, 5'11", 170 lbs. Deb: 8/27/14

YEAR	TM/L	G	AB	R	H	2B	3B	HR	RBI	BB	SO	AVG	OBP	SLG	PRO+	BR/A	SB	CS	SBR	FA	FR	G/POS	TPR
1914	Det-A	1	1	0	0	0	0	0	0	0	1	.000	.000	.000	-97	-0	0			.667	0	/S-1	0.0
1916	Chi-A	68	187	8	48	3	0	0	10	19	30	.257	.332	.273	81	-4	9			.950	-4	3-63/S-2,2-1	-0.6
1917	*Chi-A	59	194	35	46	2	1	0	12	27	17	.237	.339	.258	81	-3	9			.932	-13	3-52/S-2	-1.7
1918	Chi-A	70	235	32	65	7	0	1	16	25	26	.277	.356	.319	103	2	7			.941	-2	3-69/2-1	0.2
1919	*Chi-A	60	170	31	50	8	4	0	19	11	18	.294	.355	.388	108	2	4			.931	-0	3-46/2-5	0.3
1920	Chi-A	46	127	14	25	1	4	0	13	9	13	.197	.255	.268	39	-11	1	1	-0	.962	-5	3-29/2-3,S-1	-1.5
Total	6	304	914	120	234	21	9	1	70	91	105	.256	.333	.302	85	-15	30	1		.942	-24	3-259/2-10,S-6	-3.3

■ JOHN McMULLIN
McMullin, John F. "Lefty" b: 1848, Philadelphia, Pa. d: 4/11/1881, Philadelphia, Pa. BR/TL, 5'9", 160 lbs. Deb: 5/9/1871

YEAR	TM/L	G	AB	R	H	2B	3B	HR	RBI	BB	SO	AVG	OBP	SLG	PRO+	BR/A	SB	CS	SBR	FA	FR	G/POS	TPR
1871	Tro-n	29	136	38	38	0	5	0	32	8	6	.279	.319	.353	92	-1	11	1	3	.871	0	*P-29/S-1	0.0
1872	Mut-n	54	237	48	61	6	1	0	25	11	6	.257	.290	.291	85	-2	8	2	1	.871	6	*O-53/P-3	0.5
1873	Ath-n	52	227	54	62	7	1	0	29	8	4	.273	.298	.313	76	-8	9	1	2	.828	-4	*O-51/P-1	-0.6
1874	Ath-n	55	260	61	90	10	2	2	32	8	13	.346	.366	.423	140	10	4	3	-1	.771	-4	*O-55	0.4
1875	Phi-n	54	222	33	57	9	4	2	19	5	12	.257	.273	.360	114	3	6	10	-4	.835	-1	*O-54/P-4	-0.1
Total	5 n	244	1082	234	308	32	13	4	137	40	41	.285	.310	.349	103	0	38	17	1	.829	-3	O-213/P-37,S-1	0.2

■ CARL McNABB
McNabb, Carl Mac "Skinny" b: 1/25/17, Stevenson, Ala. BR/TR, 5'9", 155 lbs. Deb: 4/20/45

YEAR	TM/L	G	AB	R	H	2B	3B	HR	RBI	BB	SO	AVG	OBP	SLG	PRO+	BR/A	SB	CS	SBR	FA	FR	G/POS	TPR
1945	Det-A	1	1	0	0	0	0	0	0	0	1	.000	.000	.000	-94	-0	0	0	0	.000	0	H	0.0

■ ERIC McNAIR
McNair, Donald Eric "Boob" b: 4/12/09, Meridian, Miss. d: 3/11/49, Meridian, Miss. BR/TR, 5'8.5", 160 lbs. Deb: 9/20/29

YEAR	TM/L	G	AB	R	H	2B	3B	HR	RBI	BB	SO	AVG	OBP	SLG	PRO+	BR/A	SB	CS	SBR	FA	FR	G/POS	TPR
1929	Phi-A	4	8	2	4	1	0	0	3	0	0	.500	.500	.625	181	1	1	0	0	1.000	-0	/S-4	0.1
1930	*Phi-A	78	237	27	63	12	2	0	34	9	19	.266	.296	.333	57	-16	5	2	0	.915	-7	S-31,3-29/2-5,O-1	-1.7
1931	*Phi-A	79	280	41	76	10	1	5	33	11	19	.271	.306	.368	72	-12	1	4	-2	.915	-6	3-47,2-16,S 13	-1.4
1932	Phi-A	135	554	87	158	**47**	3	18	95	28	29	.285	.323	.478	101	-2	8	4	0	.953	-7	*S-133	0.2
1933	Phi-A	89	310	57	81	15	4	7	48	15	32	.261	.302	.403	84	-8	2	1	0	.966	-2	S-46,2-27	-0.5
1934	Phi-A	151	599	80	168	20	4	17	82	35	42	.280	.321	.412	91	-10	7	8	-3	.951	4	*S-151	0.0
1935	Phi-A	137	526	55	142	22	2	4	57	35	33	.270	.319	.342	72	-22	3	7	-3	.955	-21	*S-121,3-11/1-2	-3.8
1936	Bos-A	128	494	68	141	36	2	4	74	27	34	.285	.329	.391	73	-22	3	3	-1	.966	-12	S-84,2-35,3-11	-2.4
1937	Bos-A	126	455	60	133	29	4	12	76	30	33	.292	.340	.453	94	-5	10	7	-1	.969	-6	*2-106/S-9,3-4,1-1	-0.4
1938	Bos-A	46	96	9	15	1	1	0	7	3	6	.156	.182	.188	-7	-16	0	1	-1	.870	3	S-15,2-14/3-3	-1.2
1939	Chi-A	129	479	62	155	18	5	7	82	38	41	.324	.375	.426	102	1	17	9	-0	.937	4	*3-103,2-19/S-9	0.7
1940	Chi-A	66	251	26	57	13	1	7	31	12	26	.227	.265	.371	62	-15	1	7	-4	.958	-17	2-65/3-1	-3.1
1941	Det-A	23	59	5	11	1	0	0	3	4	4	.186	.250	.203	19	-7	0	0	0	.970	-2	3-11/S-3	-0.9
1942	Det-A	26	68	5	11	2	0	1	4	3	5	.162	.197	.235	20	-7	0	1	-1	.881	-8	S-21	-1.5
	Phi-A	34	103	8	25	2	0	0	4	11	5	.243	.316	.262	64	-5	1	0	0	.952	-6	S-29/2-1	-0.9
	Yr	60	171	13	36	4	0	1	8	14	10	.211	.270	.251	46	-12	1	1	-0	.927	-13	S-50/2-1	-2.4
Total	14	1251	4519	592	1240	229	29	82	633	261	328	.274	.318	.392	80	-146	59	54	-15	.949	-83	S-669,2-288,3/10	-16.8

YEAR	TM/L	G	AB	R	H	2B	3B	HR	RBI	BB	SO	AVG	OBP	SLG	PRO+	BR/A	SB	CS	SBR	FA	FR	G/POS	TPR
■ **MIKE McNALLY** McNally, Michael Joseph "Minooka Mike" b: 9/9/1892, Minooka, Pa. d: 5/29/65, Bethlehem, Pa. BR/TR, 5'11", 150 lbs. Deb: 4/21/15																							
1915	Bos-A	23	53	7	8	0	1	0	0	3	7	.151	.196	.189	16	-6	0	2	-1	.891	1	3-18/2-5	-0.6
1916	*Bos-A	87	135	28	23	0	0	0	9	10	19	.170	.228	.170	20	-13	9			.964	7	2-35,3-14/S-7,O-1	-0.6
1917	Bos-A	42	50	9	15	1	0	0	2	6	3	.300	.375	.320	113	1	3			.935	6	3-14/S-9,2-6	0.8
1919	Bos-A	33	42	10	11	4	0	0	6	1	2	.262	.279	.357	83	-1	4			.950	9	S-11,3-11/2-3	0.9
1920	Bos-A	93	312	42	80	5	1	0	23	31	24	.256	.326	.279	64	-15	13	10	-2	.930	-9	2-76/S-8,1-6	-2.3
1921	*NY-A	71	215	36	56	4	2	1	24	14	15	.260	.306	.312	57	-14	5	6	-2	.974	18	3-49,2-16	0.5
1922	*NY-A	52	143	20	36	2	2	0	18	16	14	.252	.331	.294	63	-7	3	0	1	.983	-0	3-34/2-9,S-4,1-1	-0.4
1923	NY-A	30	38	5	8	0	0	0	1	3	4	.211	.268	.211	27	-4	2	0	1	1.000	0	S-13/3-7,2-5	-0.3
1924	NY-A	49	69	11	17	0	0	0	2	7	5	.246	.316	.246	46	-5	1	1	-0	.985	10	2-25,3-13/S-6	0.4
1925	Was-A	12	21	1	3	0	0	0	0	1	4	.143	.182	.143	-17	-4	0	0	0	1.000	1	/3-7,S-2,2-1	-0.3
Total	10	492	1078	169	257	16	6	1	85	92	97	.238	.299	.267	54	-69	40	19		.946	41	2-181,3-167/S10	-1.9
■ **GEORGE McNAMARA** McNamara, George Francis b: 1/11/01, Chicago, Ill. d: 6/12/90, Hinsdale, Ill. BL/TR, 6', 175 lbs. Deb: 9/28/22																							
1922	Was-A	3	11	3	3	0	0	0	1	1	2	.273	.333	.273	63	-1	0	0	0	1.000	-1	/O-3	-0.1
■ **JIM McNAMARA** McNamara, James Patrick b: 6/10/65, Nashua, N.H. BL/TR, 6'4", 210 lbs. Deb: 4/9/92																							
1992	SF-N	30	74	6	16	1	0	1	9	6	25	.216	.275	.270	58	-4	0	0	0	.993	-0	C-30	-0.3
1993	SF-N	4	7	0	1	0	0	0	1	0	1	.143	.143	.143	-24	-1	0	0	0	1.000	-0	/C-4	-0.1
Total	2	34	81	6	17	1	0	1	10	6	26	.210	.264	.259	51	-5	0	0	0	.993	-0	/C-34	-0.4
■ **DINNY McNAMARA** McNamara, John Raymond b: 9/16/05, Lexington, Mass. d: 12/20/63, Arlington, Mass. BL/TR, 5'9", 165 lbs. Deb: 7/2/27																							
1927	Bos-N	11	9	3	0	0	0	0	0	0	3	.000	.000	.000	-99	-3	0			1.000	0	/O-3	-0.2
1928	Bos-N	9	4	2	1	0	0	0	0	0	1	.250	.250	.250	33	-0	0			1.000	-0	/O-3	-0.1
Total	2	20	13	5	1	0	0	0	0	0	4	.077	.077	.077	-63	-3	0			1.000	0	/O-6	-0.3
■ **BOB McNAMARA** McNamara, Robert Maxey b: 9/19/16, Denver, Colo. BR/TR, 5'10", 170 lbs. Deb: 5/27/39																							
1939	Phi-A	9	9	0	2	1	0	0	3	1	1	.222	.300	.333	63	-1	0	0	0	1.000	0	/3-5,S-2,1-1,2-1	0.0
■ **TOM McNAMARA** McNamara, Thomas Henry b: 11/5/1895, Roxbury, Mass. d: 5/5/74, Danvers, Mass. BR/TR, 6'2", 200 lbs. Deb: 6/25/22																							
1922	Pit-N	1	1	0	0	0	0	0	0	0	0	.000	.000	.000	-99	-0	0	0	0	.000	0	H	0.0
■ **RUSTY McNEALY** McNealy, Robert Lee b: 8/12/58, Sacramento, Cal. BL/TL, 5'8", 160 lbs. Deb: 9/4/83																							
1983	Oak-A	15	4	5	0	0	0	0	0	0	0	.000	.000	.000	-99	-1	0	1	-1	1.000	-2	/O-5,D-7	-0.4
■ **EARL McNEELY** McNeely, George Earl b: 5/12/1898, Sacramento, Cal. d: 7/16/71, Sacramento, Cal. BR/TR, 5'9", 155 lbs. Deb: 8/9/24 C																							
1924	*Was-A	43	179	31	59	5	6	0	15	5	21	.330	.355	.425	104	0	3	1	0	.973	-2	O-42	-0.4
1925	*Was-A	122	385	76	110	14	2	3	37	48	54	.286	.378	.356	89	-5	15	16	-5	.975	-2	*O-112/1-1	-1.7
1926	Was-A	124	442	84	134	20	12	0	48	44	28	.303	.373	.403	105	4	18	6	2	.969	0	*O-118	-0.2
1927	Was-A	73	185	40	51	10	4	0	16	11	13	.276	.320	.373	80	-6	11	4	1	.977	-7	O-47/1-4	-1.4
1928	StL-A	127	496	66	117	27	7	0	44	37	39	.236	.299	.319	61	-29	8	6	-1	.984	7	*O-120	-3.0
1929	StL-A	69	230	27	56	8	1	1	18	7	13	.243	.272	.300	45	-19	2	1	0	.980	-7	O-62	-2.8
1930	StL-A	76	235	33	64	19	1	0	20	22	14	.272	.340	.362	75	-9	8	3	1	.939	-7	O-38,1-27	-1.8
1931	StL-A	49	102	12	23	4	0	0	15	9	5	.225	.288	.265	45	-8	4	4	-1	.969	-5	O-37/1-1	-1.5
Total	8	683	2254	369	614	107	33	4	213	183	187	.272	.335	.354	78	-71	69	41	-4	.974	-21	O-576/1-33	-12.8
■ **JEFF McNEELY** McNeely, Jeffrey Lavern b: 10/18/69, Monroe, N.C. BR/TR, 6'2", 190 lbs. Deb: 9/5/93																							
1993	Bos-A	21	37	10	11	1	1	0	1	7	9	.297	.409	.378	106	1	6	0	2	.917	-3	O-13/D-3	0.0
■ **NORM McNEIL** McNeil, Norman Francis b: 10/22/1892, Chicago, Ill. d: 4/11/42, Buffalo, N.Y. BR/TR, 5'11", 180 lbs. Deb: 6/21/19																							
1919	Bos-A	5	9	0	3	0	0	0	1	1	0	.333	.400	.333	113	0	0			.818	-2	/C-5	-0.1
■ **JERRY McNERTNEY** McNertney, Gerald Edward b: 8/7/36, Boone, Iowa BR/TR, 6'1", 195 lbs. Deb: 4/16/64 C																							
1964	Chi-A	73	186	16	40	5	0	3	23	19	24	.215	.298	.290	66	-8	0	0	0	.987	8	C-69	0.2
1966	Chi-A	44	59	3	13	0	0	0	1	7	6	.220	.303	.220	57	-3	1	1	-0	.969	5	C-37	0.3
1967	Chi-A	56	123	8	28	6	0	3	13	6	14	.228	.275	.350	87	-2	0	0	0	.996	13	C-52	1.4
1968	Chi-A	74	169	18	37	4	1	3	18	18	29	.219	.302	.308	84	-3	0	0	0	.985	14	C-64/1-1	1.6
1969	Sea-A	128	410	39	99	18	1	8	55	29	63	.241	.292	.349	80	-12	1	0	0	.988	2	*C-122	-0.4
1970	Mil-A	111	296	27	72	11	1	6	22	22	33	.243	.304	.348	79	-9	1	4	-2	.984	-9	C-94,1-13	-1.7
1971	StL-N	56	128	15	37	4	2	4	22	12	14	.289	.350	.445	119	3	0	0	0	.985	-3	C-36	0.2
1972	StL-N	39	48	3	10	3	1	0	9	6	16	.208	.296	.313	74	-2	0	0	0	.982	2	C-10	0.0
1973	Pit-N	9	4	0	1	0	0	0	0	0	0	.250	.250	.250	40	-0	0	0	0	1.000	1	/C-9	0.1
Total	9	590	1423	129	337	51	6	27	163	119	199	.237	.301	.338	81	-36	3	5	-2	.987	33	C-493/1-14	1.7
■ **PAT McNULTY** McNulty, Patrick Howard b: 2/27/1899, Cleveland, Ohio d: 5/4/63, Hollywood, Cal. BL/TR, 5'11", 160 lbs. Deb: 9/5/22																							
1922	Cle-A	22	59	10	16	2	1	0	5	9	5	.271	.368	.339	85	-1	4	1	1	.956	-3	O-22	-0.5
1924	Cle-A	101	291	46	78	13	5	0	26	33	22	.268	.347	.347	78	-9	10	7	-1	.961	-4	O-75	-1.8
1925	Cle-A	118	373	70	117	18	2	6	43	47	23	.314	.392	.421	105	4	7	7	-2	.965	-2	*O-111	-0.5
1926	Cle-A	48	56	3	14	2	1	0	6	5	9	.250	.311	.321	65	-3	0	1	-1	.909	-2	/O-9	-0.5
1927	Cle-A	19	41	3	13	1	0	0	4	4	3	.317	.378	.341	87	-1	1	2	-1	.906	-1	O-12	-0.2
Total	5	308	820	132	238	36	9	6	84	98	62	.290	.368	.378	91	-10	22	18	-4	.957	-11	O-229	-3.5
■ **BILL McNULTY** McNulty, William Francis b: 8/29/46, Sacramento, Cal. BR/TR, 6'4", 205 lbs. Deb: 7/9/69																							
1969	Oak-A	5	17	0	0	0	0	0	0	0	10	.000	.000	.000	-99	-5	0	0	0	1.000	1	/O-5	-0.4
1972	Oak-A	4	10	0	1	0	0	0	0	2	1	.100	.250	.100	7	-1	0	0	0	.800	-2	/3-3	-0.3
Total	2	9	27	0	1	0	0	0	0	2	11	.037	.103	.037	-61	-6	0	0	0	1.000	-0	/O-5,3-3	-0.7
■ **BID McPHEE** McPhee, John Alexander b: 11/1/1859, Massena, N.Y. d: 1/3/43, San Diego, Cal. BR/TR, 5'8", 152 lbs. Deb: 5/2/1882 M																							
1882	Cin-a	78	311	43	71	8	7	1	31	11		.228	.255	.309	84	-6				**.920**	-1	*2-78	-0.5
1883	Cin-a	96	367	61	90	10	10	2	42	18		.245	.281	.343	95	-3				**.928**	3	*2-96	0.1
1884	Cin-a	112	450	107	125	8	7	5	64	27		.278	.327	.360	118	8				.924	16	*2-112	2.4
1885	Cin-a	110	431	78	114	12	4	0	46	19		.265	.306	.311	94	-3				**.936**	6	*2-110	0.6
1886	Cin-a	140	560	139	150	23	12	**8**	70	59		.268	.343	.395	127	16	40			**.939**	31	*2-140	4.6
1887	Cin-a	129	540	137	156	20	**19**	2	87	55		.289	.360	.407	111	8	95			.924	26	*2-129	3.0
1888	Cin-a	111	458	88	110	12	10	4	51	43		.240	.312	.336	102	0	54			**.940**	31	*2-111	3.3
1889	Cin-a	135	540	109	145	25	7	5	57	60	29	.269	.346	.369	100	-0	63			**.946**	**41**	*2-135/3-1	4.0
1890	Cin-N	132	528	125	135	16	22	3	39	82	26	.256	.362	.386	119	14	55			.942	30	*2-132	4.5
1891	Cin-N	138	562	107	144	14	16	6	38	74	35	.256	.345	.370	107	6	33			**.954**	23	*2-138	3.1
1892	Cin-N	144	573	111	157	19	12	4	60	84	48	.274	.373	.370	127	22	44			.948	25	*2-144	4.5
1893	Cin-N	127	491	101	138	17	11	3	68	94	20	.281	.401	.379	105	7	25			.954	**34**	*2-127	3.5
1894	Cin-N	126	474	107	144	21	9	5	88	90	23	.304	.420	.418	99	2	33			.945	31	*2-126	2.9
1895	Cin-N	115	432	107	129	24	12	1	75	73	30	.299	.409	.417	109	8	30			.955	15	*2-115	2.3
1896	Cin-N	117	433	81	132	18	7	1	87	51	18	.305	.391	.386	99	-0	48			**.978**	6	*2-117	1.0
1897	Cin-N	81	282	45	85	13	7	1	39	35		.301	.386	.408	103	1	9			.966	12	2-81	1.5
1898	Cin-N	133	486	72	121	26	9	1	60	66		.249	.341	.346	91	-6	21			.956	-12	*2-130/O-3	-0.9
1899	Cin-N	111	373	60	104	17	7	1	65	40		.279	.360	.370	98	-0	18			.955	-4	*2-105/O-1	0.2
Total	18	2135	8291	1678	2250	303	188	53	1067	981	229	.271	.355	.372	106	72	568			.944	313	*2-2126/O-4,3-1	40.1
■ **MART McQUAID** McQuaid, Mortimer Martin b: 6/28/1861, Chicago, Ill. d: 3/5/28, Chicago, Ill. Deb: 8/15/1891																							
1891	StL-a	4	11	1	4	2	0	0	1	0	1	.364	.364	.545	139	0	1			1.000	-1	/2-3,O-1	0.0
1898	Was-N	1	4	0	0	0	0	0	0	0		.000	.000	.000	-99	-1	0			.333	-1	/O-1	-0.2
Total	2	5	15	1	4	2	0	0	1	0	1	.267	.267	.400	81	-1	1			.333	-1	/2-3,O-2	-0.2

YEAR	TM/L	G	AB	R	H	2B	3B	HR	RBI	BB	SO	AVG	OBP	SLG	PRO+	BR/A	SB	CS	SBR	FA	FR	G/POS	TPR
■ JERRY McQUAIG	McQuaig, Gerald Joseph b: 1/31/12, Douglas, Ga. BR/TR, 5′11″, 183 lbs. Deb: 8/25/34																						
1934	Phi-A	7	16	2	1	0	0	0	1	2	4	.063	.167	.063	-40	-3	0	0	0	.889	-1	/O-6	-0.5
■ MOX McQUERY	McQuery, William Thomas b: 6/28/1861, Garrard Co., Ky. d: 6/12/1900, Cincinnati, Ohio 6′4″, Deb: 8/20/1884																						
1884	Cin-U	35	132	31	37	5	0	2		8		.280	.321	.364	99	-4				.978	1	1-35	-0.6
1885	Det-N	70	278	34	76	15	4	3	30	8	29	.273	.294	.388	119	5				.976	5	1-69/O-1	0.2
1886	KC-N	122	449	62	111	27	4	4	38	36	44	.247	.303	.352	93	-5	4			.969	1	*1-122	-1.7
1890	Syr-a	122	461	64	142	17	6	2	55	53		.308	.383	.384	141	25	26			.972	-1	*1-122	1.5
1891	Was-a	68	261	40	63	9	4	2	37	18	19	.241	.305	.330	85	-5	3			.977	1	1-68	-0.7
Total	5	417	1581	231	429	73	18	13	160	123	92	.271	.327	.365	110	16	33			.973	7	1-416/O-1	-1.3
■ GLENN McQUILLEN	McQuillen, Glenn Richard "Red" b: 4/19/15, Strasburg, Va. d: 6/8/89, Gardenville, Md. BR/TR, 6′, 198 lbs. Deb: 6/16/38																						
1938	StL-A	43	116	14	33	4	0	0	13	4	12	.284	.308	.319	57	-8	0	1	-1	.971	-0	O-30	-0.8
1941	StL-A	7	21	4	7	2	1	0	3	1	2	.333	.364	.524	128	1	0	1	-1	.933	-0	/O-6	0.0
1942	StL-A	100	339	40	96	15	12	3	47	10	17	.283	.306	.425	103	-1	1	1	-0	.969	-5	O-77	-1.1
1946	StL-A	59	166	24	40	3	3	1	12	19	18	.241	.319	.313	73	-6	0	2	-1	.977	-2	O-48	-1.1
1947	StL-A	1	1	0	0	0	0	0	0	0	0	.000	.000	.000	-98	-0	0	0	0	.000	0	H	0.0
Total	5	210	643	82	176	24	16	4	75	34	49	.274	.311	.379	87	-14	1	5	-3	.970	-7	O-161	-3.0
■ GEORGE McQUINN	McQuinn, George Hartley b: 5/29/10, Arlington, Va. d: 12/24/78, Alexandria, Va. BL/TL, 5′11″, 165 lbs. Deb: 4/14/36																						
1936	Cin-N	38	134	5	27	3	4	0	13	10	22	.201	.262	.284	50	-10	0			.992	1	1-38	-1.3
1938	StL-A	148	602	100	195	42	7	12	82	58	49	.324	.384	.477	115	13	4	5	-2	.992	-0	*1-148	-0.6
1939	StL-A☆	154	617	101	195	37	13	20	94	65	42	.316	.383	.515	125	22	6	5	-1	.993	10	*1-154	1.3
1940	StL-A☆	151	594	78	166	39	10	16	84	57	58	.279	.343	.460	104	2	3	3	-1	**.992**	10	*1-150	-0.3
1941	StL-A	130	495	93	147	28	4	18	80	74	30	.297	.388	.479	124	18	5	4	-1	**.995**	8	*1-125	1.5
1942	StL-A☆	145	554	86	145	32	5	12	78	60	77	.262	.335	.403	105	3	1	1	-0	.991	1	*1-144	-0.5
1943	StL-A	125	449	53	109	19	2	12	74	56	65	.243	.327	.374	103	1	4	3	-1	.992	2	*1-122	-0.4
1944	*StL-A★	146	516	83	129	26	3	11	72	85	74	.250	.357	.376	103	4	4	3	-1	**.994**	-5	*1-146	-1.0
1945	StL-A†	139	483	69	134	31	3	7	61	65	51	.277	.364	.398	115	10	1	1	-0	.991	4	*1-136	0.5
1946	Phi-A	136	484	47	109	23	6	3	35	64	62	.225	.317	.316	78	-14	4	2	0	.988	3	*1-134	-1.9
1947	*NY-A★	144	517	84	157	24	3	13	80	78	66	.304	.395	.437	132	24	0	2	-1	.994	-2	*1-142	1.7
1948	NY-A★	94	302	33	75	11	4	11	41	40	38	.248	.336	.421	102	-0	0	2	-1	.993	-1	1-90	-0.3
Total	12	1550	5747	832	1588	315	64	135	794	712	634	.276	.357	.424	109	73	32	31		.992	31	*1-1529	-1.3
■ BRIAN McRAE	McRae, Brian Wesley b: 8/27/67, Bradenton, Fla. BB/TR, 6′, 185 lbs. Deb: 8/7/90 F																						
1990	KC-A	46	168	21	48	8	3	2	23	9	29	.286	.322	.405	104	0	4	3	-1	1.000	4	O-45	0.2
1991	KC-A	152	629	86	164	28	9	8	64	24	99	.261	.290	.372	81	-17	20	11	-1	.993	8	*O-150	-1.4
1992	KC-A	149	533	63	119	23	5	4	52	42	88	.223	.287	.308	65	-25	18	5	2	.993	10	*O-148	-1.6
1993	KC-A	153	627	78	177	28	9	12	69	37	105	.282	.326	.413	92	-8	23	14	-2	.983	5	*O-153	-0.8
1994	KC-A	114	436	71	119	22	6	4	40	54	67	.273	.361	.378	87	-7	28	8	4	.988	-6	*O-110/D-4	-1.1
1995	Chi-N	137	580	92	167	38	7	12	48	47	92	.288	.349	.440	108	6	27	8	3	.991	10	*O-137	1.5
1996	Chi-N	157	624	111	172	32	5	17	66	73	84	.276	.362	.425	104	5	37	9	6	.986	1	*O-155	0.8
1997	Chi-N	108	417	63	100	27	5	6	28	52	62	.240	.330	.372	81	-11	14	6	1	.996	7	*O-107	-0.6
	NY-N	45	145	23	36	5	2	5	15	13	22	.248	.319	.414	93	-2	3	4	-2	.957	-5	O-41	-0.9
	Yr	153	562	86	136	32	7	11	43	65	84	.242	.327	.383	84	-13	17	10	-1	.987	2	*O-148	-1.5
1998	NY-N	159	552	79	146	36	5	21	79	80	90	.264	.363	.462	113	11	20	11	-1	.987	-2	*O-154	0.7
Total	9	1220	4711	687	1248	247	56	91	484	431	738	.265	.333	.399	93	-47	194	79	11	.989	30	*O-1200/D-4	-3.2
■ HAL McRAE	McRae, Harold Abraham b: 7/10/45, Avon Park, Fla. BR/TR, 5′11″, 180 lbs. Deb: 7/11/68 FMC																						
1968	Cin-N	17	51	1	10	1	0	0	2	4	14	.196	.255	.216	40	-4	1	1	-0	.926	-4	2-16	-0.8
1970	*Cin-N	70	165	18	41	6	1	8	23	15	23	.248	.315	.442	100	-1	0	2	-1	.981	-5	O-46/3-6,2-1	-0.9
1971	Cin-N	99	337	39	89	24	2	9	34	11	35	.264	.291	.427	103	-0	3	2	-0	.966	-1	O-91	-0.6
1972	*Cin-N	61	97	9	27	4	0	5	26	2	10	.278	.307	.474	126	3	0	0	0	.867	-6	O-12,3-11	-0.4
1973	KC-A	106	338	36	79	18	3	9	50	34	38	.234	.315	.385	89	-5	2	2	-1	.963	-4	O-64,D-37/3-2	-1.3
1974	KC-A	148	539	71	167	36	4	15	88	54	68	.310	.378	.475	136	25	11	8	-2	.950	2	D-90,O-56/3-1	2.2
1975	KC-A★	126	480	58	147	38	6	5	71	47	47	.306	.373	.442	126	17	11	8	-2	.986	-1	*O-114,D-12/3-1	0.9
1976	*KC-A★	149	527	75	175	34	5	8	73	64	43	.332	**.412**	.461	154	**38**	22	12	-1	.970	-0	*D-117,O-31	3.4
1977	*KC-A	162	641	104	191	**54**	11	21	92	59	43	.298	.369	.515	137	32	18	14	-3	.958	4	*D-115,O-47	2.7
1978	*KC-A	156	623	90	170	39	5	16	72	51	62	.273	.334	.429	110	7	17	8	0	1.000	0	*D-153/O-3	0.3
1979	KC-A	101	393	55	113	32	4	10	74	38	46	.288	.356	.466	117	9	5	4	-1	.000	0	*D-100	0.5
1980	*KC-A	124	489	73	145	39	5	14	83	29	56	.297	.346	.483	123	14	10	2	2	1.000	-1	*D-110/O-9	1.2
1981	*KC-A	101	389	38	106	23	2	7	36	34	33	.272	.334	.396	111	5	3	4	-2	.909	0	D-97/O-4	0.0
1982	KC-A★	159	613	91	189	**46**	8	27	**133**	55	61	.308	.370	.542	146	38	4	4	-1	.500	-0	*D-158/O-1	3.0
1983	KC-A	157	589	84	183	41	6	12	82	50	68	.311	.374	.462	128	23	2	3	-1	.000	0	*D-156	1.6
1984	*KC-A	106	317	30	96	13	4	3	42	34	47	.303	.372	.397	112	6	0	3	-2	.000	0	D-94	0.2
1985	*KC-A	112	320	41	83	19	0	14	70	44	45	.259	.351	.450	117	8	0	1	-1	.000	0	*D-106	0.5
1986	KC-A	112	278	22	70	14	0	7	37	18	39	.252	.300	.378	81	-8	0	0	0	.000	0	D-75	-0.9
1987	KC-A	18	32	5	10	3	0	1	9	5	1	.313	.405	.500	135	2	0	0	0	.000	0	/D-7	0.1
Total	19	2084	7218	940	2091	484	66	191	1097	648	779	.290	.355	.454	122	210	109	78	-14	.966	-16	*D-1427,O-478/32	11.7
■ McREMER	McRemer Deb: 6/20/1884																						
1884	Was-U	1	3	0	0	0	0	0		0		.000	.000	.000	-99	-1				1.000	0	/O-1	-0.1
■ KEVIN McREYNOLDS	McReynolds, Walter Kevin b: 10/16/59, Little Rock, Ark. BR/TR, 6′1″, 210 lbs. Deb: 6/2/83																						
1983	SD-N	39	140	15	31	3	1	4	14	12	29	.221	.283	.343	75	-5	2	1	0	.989	0	O-38	-0.7
1984	*SD-N	147	525	68	146	26	6	20	75	34	69	.278	.322	.465	119	11	3	6	-3	.991	18	*O-143	2.3
1985	SD-N	152	564	61	132	24	4	15	75	43	81	.234	.292	.371	85	-12	4	0	1	.993	23	*O-150	0.7
1986	SD-N	158	560	89	161	31	6	26	96	66	83	.287	.364	.504	140	29	8	6	-1	.977	-14	*O-154	1.0
1987	NY-N	151	590	86	163	32	5	29	95	39	70	.276	.322	.495	119	13	14	1	4	.987	9	*O-150	2.0
1988	*NY-N	147	552	82	159	30	2	27	99	38	56	.288	.338	.496	144	28	21	0	6	.985	10	*O-147	4.3
1989	NY-N	148	545	74	148	25	3	22	85	46	74	.272	.329	.450	127	17	15	7	0	.969	15	*O-145	3.0
1990	NY-N	147	521	75	140	23	1	24	82	71	61	.269	.358	.455	122	16	9	2	2	.988	5	*O-144	2.0
1991	NY-N	143	522	65	135	32	1	16	74	49	46	.259	.325	.416	108	4	6	6	-2	.993	2	*O-141	0.1
1992	KC-A	109	373	45	92	25	0	13	49	67	48	.247	.361	.418	115	9	7	1	2	.986	-3	*O-106/D-1	0.5
1993	KC-A	110	351	44	86	22	4	11	42	37	56	.245	.319	.425	92	-5	2	2	-1	.990	0	*O-104/D-1	-0.7
1994	NY-N	51	180	23	46	11	2	4	21	20	34	.256	.330	.406	91	-2	2	0	1	1.000	2	O-47	0.0
Total	12	1502	5423	727	1439	284	35	211	807	522	707	.265	.331	.447	116	103	93	32	9	.987	68	*O-1469/D-2	14.5
■ PETE McSHANNIC	McShannic, Peter Robert b: 3/20/1864, Pittsburgh, Pa. d: 11/30/46, Toledo, Ohio BB/TR, 5′7″, 190 lbs. Deb: 9/15/1888																						
1888	Pit-N	26	98	5	19	1	0	0	5	1	9	.194	.218	.204	38	-7	3			.907	-0	3-26	-0.6
■ TRICK McSORLEY	McSorley, John Bernard b: 12/6/1852, St.Louis, Mo. d: 2/9/36, St.Louis, Mo. BR/TR, 5′4″, 142 lbs. Deb: 5/6/1875																						
1875	RS-n	15	52	4	11	0	0	0	2	0	3	.212	.212	.212	53	-2	3	0	1	.745	1	/3-9,O-7	0.0
1884	Tol-a	21	68	12	17	1	0	0		3		.250	.282	.265	77	-2				.974	1	1-16/O-5,3-1,P-1	-0.2
1885	StL-N	2	6	2	3	1	0	0	1	2	1	.500	.625	.667	340	2				.400	-2	/3-2	0.0
1886	StL-a	5	20	1	3	3	0	0	0	0		.150	.150	.300	38	-2	0			.765	-3	/S-5	-0.4
Total	3	28	94	15	23	5	0	0	1	5	1	.245	.283	.298	85	-1	0	0		.400	-4	/1-16,S-5,O-5,3P	-0.6
■ PAUL McSWEENEY	McSweeney, Paul A. b: 4/3/1867, St.Louis, Mo. d: 8/12/51, St.Louis, Mo. Deb: 9/20/1891																						
1891	StL-a	3	12	2	3	1	0	0	2	0	0	.250	.308	.333	73	-1	1			.643	-2	/2-3,3-1	-0.2

YEAR	TM/L	G	AB	R	H	2B	3B	HR	RBI	BB	SO	AVG	OBP	SLG	PRO+	BR/A	SB	CS	SBR	FA	FR	G/POS	TPR
■ **JIM McTAMANY** McTamany, James Edward b: 7/1/1863, Philadelphia, Pa. d: 4/16/16, Lenni, Pa. BR/TR, 5'8", 190 lbs. Deb: 8/15/1885																							
1885	Bro-a	35	131	21	36	7	2	1	13	9		.275	.321	.382	121	3				.896	-5	O-35	-0.3
1886	Bro-a	111	418	86	106	23	10	2	56	54		.254	.353	.371	126	14	18			.893	14	*O-111	2.2
1887	Bro-a	134	520	123	134	22	10	1	68	76		.258	.365	.344	97	1	66			.918	8	*O-134	0.5
1888	KC-a	130	516	94	127	12	10	4	41	67		.246	.345	.331	110	7	55			.913	6	*O-130	0.8
1889	Col-a	139	529	113	146	21	7	4	52	116	66	.276	.407	.365	127	27	40			.902	-5	*O-139	1.5
1890	Col-a	125	466	**140**	120	27	7	1	48	**112**		.258	.405	.352	132	27	43			.940	2	*O-125	2.2
1891	Col-a	81	304	59	76	17	9	3	35	58	48	.250	.374	.395	127	13	20			.929	-3	O-81	0.6
	Phi-a	58	218	57	49	6	3	3	21	43	44	.225	.365	.321	94	-1	13			.901	0	O-58	-0.2
	Yr	139	522	116	125	23	12	6	56	101	92	.239	.370	.364	112	12	33			.917	-2	*O-139	0.4
Total	7	813	3102	693	794	135	58	19	334	535	158	.256	.373	.355	117	91	255			.913	16	O-813	7.3
■ **BILL McTIGUE** McTigue, William Patrick "Rebel" b: 1/3/1891, Nashville, Tenn. d: 5/8/20, Nashville, Tenn. BL/TL, 6'1.5", 175 lbs. Deb: 5/2/11																							
1911	Bos-N	14	12	1	1	1	0	0	0	0	5	.083	.083	.167	-28	-2	0			.875	-1	P-14	0.0
1912	Bos-N	10	13	2	1	0	0	0	1	1	5	.077	.143	.077	-38	-2	0			1.000	1	P-10	0.0
1913	Bos-N	1	0	0	0	0	0	0	0	0	0	—	—	—	—	0	0			.000	0	R	0.0
1916	Det-A	3	1	0	0	0	0	0	0	0	0	.000	.000	.000	-97	-0	0			1.000	0	/P-3	0.0
Total	4	28	26	3	2	1	0	0	1	1	10	.077	.111	.115	-36	-5	0			.957	0	/P-27	0.0
■ **CAL McVEY** McVey, Calvin Alexander b: 8/30/1850, Montrose, Iowa d: 8/20/26, San Francisco, Cal BR/TR, 5'9", 170 lbs. Deb: 5/5/1871 M																							
1871	Bos-n	29	153	43	**66**	9	5	0	43	1	2	.431	.435	.556	177	14	6	0	2	.873	1	*C-29/O-5,3-1	1.1
1872	Bos-n	46	237	56	76	10	2	0	41	1	1	.321	.324	.380	110	1	6	1	1	.869	4	*C-40,O-11/3-1	0.4
1873	Bal-n	38	192	49	73	4	5	2	34	3	2	.380	.390	.484	159	13	1	0	0	.907	-1	C-25/O-6,S-5,213M	0.9
1874	Bos-n	70	343	**91**	**123**	21	6	3	**71**	1	3	.359	.360	.481	158	20	5	0	2	.710	-2	*O-57,C-23	1.6
1875	Bos-n	82	389	89	138	**36**	9	3	**87**	1	5	.355	.356	**.517**	193	33	7	0	2	.949	6	*1-55,O-23,C-16,/P	3.5
1876	Chi-N	63	308	62	107	15	0	1	53	2	4	.347	.352	.406	136	9				.959	4	*1-55,P-11/C-6,O3	0.9
1877	Chi-N	60	266	58	98	9	7	0	36	8	11	.368	.387	.455	147	12				.859	-13	*C-40,3-17,P/21	0.0
1878	Cin-N	61	271	43	83	10	4	2	28	5	10	.306	.319	.395	147	14				.814	-10	*3-61/C-3,M	0.6
1879	Cin-N	81	354	64	105	18	6	0	55	8	13	.297	.312	.381	134	13				.946	-7	*1-72/O-7,P-3,3CM	0.3
Total	5 n	265	1314	328	476	80	27	8	276	7	13	.362	.366	.482	161	82	25	1	7	.876	8	C-133,O-102/1S23P	7.5
Total	4	265	1199	227	393	52	17	3	172	23	38	.328	.340	.407	140	48				.951	-26	1-128/3-80,CPO2	1.8
■ **GEORGE McVEY** McVey, George W. b: 9/16/1865, Port Jervis, N.Y. d: 5/3/1896, Quincy, Ill. BR/TR, 6'1", 185 lbs. Deb: 9/19/1885																							
1885	Bro-a	6	21	2	3	0	0	0	1	2		.143	.217	.143	15	-2				.967	-0	/1-3,C-3	-0.2
■ **BILL McWILLIAMS** McWilliams, William Henry b: 11/28/10, Dubuque, Iowa d: 1/21/97, Garland, Tex. BR/TR, 6', 185 lbs. Deb: 7/8/31																							
1931	Bos-A	2	2	0	0	0	0	0	0	0	1	.000	.000	.000	-99	-1	0	0	0	.000	0	H	-0.1
■ **BOB MEACHAM** Meacham, Robert Andrew b: 8/25/60, Los Angeles, Cal. BB/TR, 6'1", 180 lbs. Deb: 6/30/83																							
1983	NY-A	22	51	5	12	2	0	0	4	4	10	.235	.304	.275	63	-2	8	0	2	.929	9	S-18/3-4	1.0
1984	NY-A	99	360	62	91	13	4	2	25	32	70	.253	.319	.328	83	-8	9	5	-0	.955	-12	S-96/2-2	-1.1
1985	NY-A	156	481	70	105	16	2	1	47	54	102	.218	.304	.266	59	-26	25	7	3	.963	-17	*S-155	-2.4
1986	NY-A	56	161	19	36	7	1	0	10	17	39	.224	.309	.280	62	-8	3	6	-3	.948	-5	S-56	-1.0
1987	NY-A	77	203	28	55	11	1	5	21	19	33	.271	.351	.409	102	1	6	5	-1	.961	-1	S-56,2-25/D-1	0.3
1988	NY-A	47	115	18	25	9	0	0	7	14	22	.217	.313	.296	72	-4	7	1	2	.959	-7	S-24,2-21/3-5	-0.8
Total	6	457	1371	202	324	58	8	8	114	140	276	.236	.316	.308	73	-47	58	24	3	.957	-32	S-405/2-48,3-9,D-1	-4.0
■ **CHARLIE MEAD** Mead, Charles Richard b: 4/9/21, Vermilion, Alberta, Canada BL/TR, 6'1.5", 185 lbs. Deb: 8/28/43																							
1943	NY-N	37	146	9	40	6	1	1	13	10	15	.274	.321	.349	93	-2	3			.976	1	O-37	-0.3
1944	NY-N	39	78	5	14	1	0	1	8	5	7	.179	.229	.231	30	-7	0			.981	2	O-23	-0.7
1945	NY-N	11	37	4	10	1	0	1	6	5	2	.270	.357	.378	103	0	0			.962	1	O-11	0.1
Total	3	87	261	18	64	8	1	3	27	20	24	.245	.299	.318	75	-9	3			.975	4	/O-71	-0.9
■ **LOUIE MEADOWS** Meadows, Michael Ray b: 4/29/61, Maysville, N.C. BL/TL, 5'11", 190 lbs. Deb: 7/3/86																							
1986	Hou-N	6	6	1	2	0	0	0	0	0	0	.333	.333	.333	87	-0	1	0	0	.000	-0	/O-1	0.0
1988	Hou-N	35	42	5	8	0	1	2	3	6	8	.190	.292	.381	95	-0	4	2	0	1.000	0	O-10	0.0
1989	Hou-N	31	51	5	9	0	0	3	10	1	14	.176	.192	.353	55	-3	1	2	-1	1.000	-4	O-14/1-1	-0.9
1990	Hou-N	15	14	3	2	0	0	0	0	2	4	.143	.250	.143	11	-2	0	0	0	1.000	-2	/O-9	-0.4
	Phi-N	15	14	1	1	0	0	0	0	1	2	.071	.133	.071	-42	-3	0	0	0	1.000	-2	/O-4	-0.5
	Yr	30	28	4	3	0	0	0	0	3	6	.107	.194	.107	-15	-4	0	0	0	1.000	-4	O-13	-0.9
Total	4	102	127	15	22	0	1	5	13	10	28	.173	.234	.307	54	-8	6	4	-1	1.000	-9	/O-38,1-1	-1.8
■ **PAT MEANEY** Meaney, Patrick J. b: 7/1871, Philadelphia, Pa. d: 10/20/22, Philadelphia, Pa. BR/TR, Deb: 5/18/12																							
1912	Det-A	1	2	0	0	0	0	0	0	1		.000	.500	.000	48	0	0			.833	-0	/S-1	0.0
■ **CHARLIE MEARA** Meara, Charles Edward "Goggy" b: 4/13/1891, New York, N.Y. d: 2/8/62, Bronx, N.Y. BL/TR, 5'10", 160 lbs. Deb: 6/1/14																							
1914	NY-A	4	7	2	2	0	0	0	1	2	2	.286	.444	.286	120	0	0	1	-1	1.000	-1	/O-3	-0.1
■ **PAT MEARES** Meares, Patrick James b: 9/6/68, Salina, Kan. BR/TR, 6', 188 lbs. Deb: 5/5/93																							
1993	Min-A	111	346	33	87	14	3	0	33	7	52	.251	.268	.309	55	-22	4	5	-2	.961	-1	*S-111	-1.7
1994	Min-A	80	229	29	61	12	1	2	24	14	50	.266	.314	.354	72	-10	5	1	1	.963	2	S-79	-0.1
1995	Min-A	116	390	57	105	19	4	12	49	15	68	.269	.315	.431	91	-6	10	4	1	.965	-9	*S-114/O-3	-0.4
1996	Min-A	152	517	66	138	26	7	8	67	17	90	.267	.302	.391	72	-23	9	4	0	.965	-30	*S-150/O-1	-3.7
1997	Min-A	134	439	63	121	23	3	10	60	18	86	.276	.328	.410	90	-7	7	7	-2	.969	13	*S-134	1.5
1998	Min-A	149	543	56	141	26	3	9	70	24	86	.260	.298	.368	72	-23	7	4	-0	.966	-16	*S-149	-2.4
Total	6	742	2464	304	653	120	21	41	303	95	432	.265	.305	.381	76	-90	42	25	-2	.965	-40	S-737/O-4	-6.8
■ **RAY MEDEIROS** Medeiros, Ray Antone "Pep" b: 5/9/26, Oakland, Cal. BR/TR, 5'10", 163 lbs. Deb: 4/25/45																							
1945	Cin-N	1	0	0	0	0	0	0	0	0	0	—	—	—	—	0	0			.000	0	R	0.0
■ **LUIS MEDINA** Medina, Luis Main b: 3/26/63, Santa Monica, Cal. BR/TL, 6'4", 200 lbs. Deb: 9/2/88																							
1988	Cle-A	16	51	10	13	0	0	6	8	2	18	.255	.309	.608	146	3	0	0	0	1.000	-0	1-16	0.1
1989	Cle-A	30	83	8	17	1	0	4	8	6	35	.205	.258	.361	72	-3	0	1	-1	.500	-1	D-25/O-3,1-1	-0.6
1991	Cle-A	5	16	0	1	0	0	0	0	1	7	.063	.118	.063	-48	-3	0	0	0	.000	0	/D-5	-0.4
Total	3	51	150	18	31	1	0	10	16	9	60	.207	.261	.413	85	-4	0	1	-1	1.000	-2	/D-30,1-17,O-3	-0.9
■ **JOE MEDWICK** Medwick, Joseph Michael "Ducky" or "Muscles" b: 11/24/11, Carteret, N.J. d: 3/21/75, St.Petersburg, Fla BR/TR, 5'10", 187 lbs. Deb: 9/2/32 H																							
1932	StL-N	26	106	13	37	12	1	2	12	2	10	.349	.367	.538	136	5	3			.970	0	O-26	0.4
1933	StL-N	148	595	92	182	40	10	18	98	26	56	.306	.337	.497	129	20	5			.980	8	*O-147	2.1
1934	*StL-N★	149	620	110	198	40	**18**	18	106	21	83	.319	.343	.529	122	16	3			.960	4	*O-149	1.4
1935	StL-N★	154	634	132	224	46	13	23	126	30	59	.353	.386	.576	149	41	4			.965	3	*O-154	3.6
1936	StL-N★	155	636	115	**223**	**64**	13	18	**138**	34	33	.351	.387	.577	157	47	3			.985	14	*O-155	5.3
1937	StL-N★	156	633	**111**	**237**	**56**	10	**31**	**154**	41	50	**.374**	.414	**.641**	**179**	**66**	4			**.988**	4	*O-156	**6.2**
1938	StL-N★	146	590	100	190	**47**	8	21	**122**	42	41	.322	.369	.536	138	29	0			.974	8	*O-144	3.2
1939	StL-N★	150	606	98	201	48	8	14	117	45	44	.332	.380	.507	128	23	6			.976	5	*O-149	2.2
1940	StL-N	37	158	21	48	12	0	3	20	6	8	.304	.329	.437	104	0	0			.988	-0	O-37	-0.2
	Bro-N★	106	423	62	127	18	12	14	66	26	28	.300	.345	.499	123	11	2			.980	5	*O-103	1.2
	Yr	143	581	83	175	30	12	17	86	32	36	.301	.341	.482	118	12	2			.982	5	*O-140	1.0
1941	*Bro-N★	133	538	100	171	33	10	18	88	38	35	.318	.364	.517	140	26	2			.983	1	*O-131	2.0
1942	Bro-N★	142	553	69	166	37	4	4	96	32	25	.300	.338	.403	115	9	2			.990	-3	*O-140	-0.1
1943	Bro-N	48	173	13	47	10	0	0	25	10	8	.272	.315	.329	86	-3	1			.971	-5	O-42	-1.1
	NY-N	78	324	41	91	20	3	5	45	9	14	.281	.300	.407	103	-1	0			.988	5	O-74/1-3	0.0

YEAR	TM/L	G	AB	R	H	2B	3B	HR	RBI	BB	SO	AVG	OBP	SLG	PRO+	BR/A	SB	CS	SBR	FA	FR	G/POS	TPR
	Yr	126	497	54	138	30	3	5	70	19	22	.278	.306	.380	97	-4	1			.983	-0	*O-116/1-3	-1.1
1944	NY-N★	128	490	64	165	24	3	7	85	38	24	.337	.386	.441	133	21	2			.993	8	*O-122	2.3
1945	NY-N	26	92	14	28	4	0	3	11	2	2	.304	.319	.446	110	1	2			.979	-1	O-23	-0.1
	Bos-N	66	218	17	62	13	0	0	26	12	12	.284	.325	.344	85	-4	3			1.000	1	O-38,1-15	-0.7
	Yr	92	310	31	90	17	0	3	37	14	14	.290	.323	.374	93	-4	5			.992	-0	O-61,1-15	-0.8
1946	Bro-N	41	77	7	24	4	0	2	18	6	5	.312	.369	.442	128	3	0			1.000	-3	O-18/1-1	-0.1
1947	StL-N	75	150	19	46	12	0	4	28	16	12	.307	.373	.467	117	4	0			1.000	-5	O-43	-0.3
1948	StL-N	20	19	0	4	0	0	0	2	1	2	.211	.250	.211	24	-2	0			.000	-0	/O-1	-0.2
Total	17	1984	7635	1198	2471	540	113	205	1383	437	551	.324	.362	.505	133	310	42			.980	49	*O-1852/1-19	27.1
■ **TOMMY MEE**	Mee, Thomas William "Judge" b: 3/18/1890, Chicago, Ill. d: 5/16/81, Chicago, Ill. BR/TR, 5'8", 165 lbs. Deb: 6/14/10																						
1910	StL-A	8	19	1	3	2	0	0	1	0		.158	.158	.263	34	-2	0			.828	-1	/S-6,2-1,3-1	-0.3
■ **DAD MEEK**	Meek, Frank J. b: 3/14/1867, St.Louis, Mo. d: 12/22/22, St.Louis, Mo. Deb: 5/10/1889																						
1889	StL-a	2	2	2	1	0	0	0	1	0	0	.500	.500	.500	164	0	1			.667	0	/C-2	0.0
1890	StL-a	4	16	3	5	0	0	0	1	0		.313	.313	.313	74	-1	1			.913	3	/C-4	0.2
Total	2	6	18	5	6	0	0	0	2	0	0	.333	.333	.333	84	-1	2			.898	3	/C-6	0.2
■ **SAMMY MEEKS**	Meeks, Samuel Mack b: 4/23/23, Anderson, S.C. BR/TR, 5'9", 160 lbs. Deb: 4/29/48																						
1948	Was-A	24	33	4	4	1	0	0	2	1	12	.121	.147	.152	-21	-6	0	0	0	.939	-0	S-10/2-1	-0.6
1949	Cin-N	16	36	10	11	2	0	2	6	2	6	.306	.342	.528	128	1	1			1.000	6	/2-8,S-3	0.7
1950	Cin-N	39	95	7	27	5	0	1	8	6	14	.284	.327	.368	82	-2	1			.951	-4	S-29/3-2	-0.5
1951	Cin-N	23	35	4	8	0	0	0	2	0	4	.229	.229	.229	23	-4	1	0	0	.929	-1	/3-4,S-1	-0.5
Total	4	102	199	25	50	8	0	3	18	9	36	.251	.284	.337	64	-11	3	0		.953	0	/S-43,2-9,3-6	-0.9
■ **DUTCH MEIER**	Meier, Arthur Ernst b: 3/30/1879, St.Louis, Mo. d: 3/23/48, Chicago, Ill. BR/TR, 5'10", 175 lbs. Deb: 5/12/06																						
1906	Pit-N	82	273	32	70	11	4	0	16	13		.256	.298	.326	90	-4	4			.975	-12	O-52,S-17	-1.9
■ **DAVE MEIER**	Meier, David Keith b: 8/8/59, Helena, Mont. BR/TR, 6', 185 lbs. Deb: 4/3/84																						
1984	Min-A	59	147	18	35	8	1	0	13	6	9	.238	.273	.306	57	-9	0	1	-1	.978	-4	O-50/3-1,D-4	-1.4
1985	Min-A	71	104	15	27	6	0	1	8	18	12	.260	.374	.346	93	-0	0	6	-4	.987	-9	O-63/D-3	-1.4
1987	Tex-A	13	21	4	6	1	0	0	0	0	4	.286	.286	.333	63	-1	0	0	0	.917	-1	/O-8	-0.2
1988	Chi-N	2	5	0	2	0	0	0	1	0	1	.400	.400	.400	125	0	0	0	0	1.000	-1	/3-1	-0.1
Total	4	145	277	37	70	15	1	1	22	24	26	.253	.317	.325	73	-10	0	7	-4	.978	-15	O-121/D-7,3-2	-3.1
■ **WALT MEINERT**	Meinert, Walter Henry b: 12/11/1890, New York, N.Y. d: 11/9/58, Decatur, Ill. BL/TL, 5'7.5", 150 lbs. Deb: 9/6/13																						
1913	StL-A	4	8	1	3	0	0	0	0	1	3	.375	.444	.375	144	1	1			1.000	-0	/O-2	0.0
■ **FRANK MEINKE**	Meinke, Frank Louis b: 10/18/1863, Chicago, Ill. d: 11/8/31, Chicago, Ill. BR , 5'10.5", 172 lbs. Deb: 5/1/1884 F																						
1884	Det-N	92	341	28	56	5	7	6	24	6	89	.164	.179	.273	42	-22				.839	-3	S-51,P-35/O-4,32	-1.3
1885	Det-N	1	3	0	0	0	0	0	0	0	1	.000	.000	.000	-99	-1				1.000	-0	/O-1,P-1	0.0
Total	2	93	344	28	56	5	7	6	24	6	90	.163	.177	.270	41	-22				1.000	-3	/S-51,P-36,O-5,23	-1.3
■ **BOB MEINKE**	Meinke, Robert Bernard b: 6/25/1887, Chicago, Ill. d: 12/29/52, Chicago, Ill. BR/TR, 5'10", 135 lbs. Deb: 8/22/10 F																						
1910	Cin-N	2	1	0	0	0	0	0	0	1	0	.000	.500	.000	51	0	0			1.000	1	/S-2	0.1
■ **GEORGE MEISTER**	Meister, George B. b: 6/5/1864, Dorzbach, Germany d: 8/24/08, Pittsburgh, Pa. Deb: 8/15/1884																						
1884	Tol-a	34	119	9	23	6	0	0	3			.193	.244	.244	58	-5				.817	-9	3-34	-1.4
■ **JOHN MEISTER**	Meister, John F. b: 5/10/1863, Allentown, Pa. d: 1/17/23, Philadelphia, Pa. 5'8", 175 lbs. Deb: 8/24/1886																						
1886	NY-a	45	186	35	44	7	3	2	21	4		.237	.253	.339	89	-3	1			.906	-8	2-45	-0.8
1887	NY-a	39	157	24	35	6	2	1	21	16		.223	.303	.306	73	-5	9			.930	-9	O-22,2-14/3-3,S-1	-1.2
Total	2	84	343	59	79	13	5	3	42	20		.230	.277	.324	81	-8	10			.905	-17	/2-59,O-22,3-3,S-1	-2.0
■ **KARL MEISTER**	Meister, Karl Daniel "Dutch" b: 5/15/1891, Marietta, Ohio d: 8/15/67, Marietta, Ohio BR/TR, 6', 178 lbs. Deb: 8/10/13																						
1913	Cin-N	4	7	1	2	1	0	0	2	0	4	.286	.286	.429	103	-0	0			.667	-2	/O-4	-0.2
■ **MOXIE MEIXELL**	Meixell, Merton Merrill b: 10/18/1887, Lake Crystal, Minn d: 8/17/82, Los Angeles, Cal. BL/TR, 5'10", 168 lbs. Deb: 7/7/12																						
1912	Cle-A	3	2	0	1	0	0	0	0	0		.500	.500	.500	181	0	0			.000	0	/O-1	0.0
■ **MIGUEL MEJIA**	Mejia, Miguel b: 3/25/75, San Pedro De Macoris, D.R. BR/TR, 6'1", 155 lbs. Deb: 4/4/96																						
1996	*StL-N	45	23	10	2	0	0	0	0	0	10	.087	.087	.087	-54	-5	6	3	0	.933	-6	O-21	-1.1
■ **ROBERTO MEJIA**	Mejia, Roberto Antonio (Diaz) b: 4/14/72, Hato Mayor, D.R. BR/TR, 5'11", 160 lbs. Deb: 7/15/93																						
1993	Col-N	65	229	31	53	14	5	5	20	13	63	.231	.276	.402	68	-11	4	1	1	.963	7	2-65	-0.2
1994	Col-N	38	116	11	28	8	1	4	14	15	33	.241	.328	.431	82	-3	3	1	0	.959	-3	2-34	-0.4
1995	Col-N	23	52	5	8	1	0	1	4	0	17	.154	.170	.231	3	-7	0	1	-1	.971	1	2-16	-0.7
1997	StL-N	7	14	0	1	1	0	0	2	0	5	.071	.071	.143	-46	-3	0	0	0	.900	-2	/2-3,O-1	-0.5
Total	4	133	411	47	90	24	6	10	40	28	118	.219	.272	.380	60	-25	7	3	0	.961	3	2-118/O-1	-1.8
■ **ROMAN MEJIAS**	Mejias, Roman (Gomez) b: 8/9/30, Abreus, Las Villas, Cuba BR/TR, 6', 175 lbs. Deb: 4/13/55																						
1955	Pit-N	71	167	14	36	8	1	3	21	9	13	.216	.256	.329	55	-11	1	3	-2	.926	-0	O-44	-1.5
1957	Pit-N	58	142	12	39	7	4	2	15	6	13	.275	.309	.423	97	-1	2	2	-1	1.000	-2	O-42	-0.5
1958	Pit-N	76	157	17	42	3	2	5	19	2	27	.268	.281	.408	82	-5	2	0	1	.973	-1	O-57	-0.7
1959	Pit-N	96	276	28	65	6	1	7	28	21	48	.236	.301	.341	71	-11	1	2	-1	.970	-0	O-85	-1.6
1960	Pit-N	3	1	1	0	0	0	0	0	0	1	.000	.000	.000	-99	-0	0	0	0	.000	0	H	0.0
1961	Pit-N	4	1	1	0	0	0	0	0	0	1	.000	.000	.000	-99	-0	0	0	0	1.000	-1	/O-2	-0.1
1962	Hou-N	146	566	82	162	12	3	24	76	30	83	.286	.329	.445	114	9	12	4	1	.946	-4	*O-142	-0.3
1963	Bos-A	111	357	43	81	18	0	11	39	14	36	.227	.262	.370	72	-14	4	1	1	.973	2	O-86	-1.6
1964	Bos-A	62	101	14	24	3	1	2	4	7	16	.238	.294	.347	74	-4	0	0	0	.962	-3	O-37	-0.8
Total	9	627	1768	212	449	57	12	54	202	89	238	.254	.296	.391	86	-38	22	12	-1	.963	-8	O-495	-7.1
■ **SAM MEJIAS**	Mejias, Samuel Elias b: 5/9/52, Santiago, D.R. BR/TR, 6', 170 lbs. Deb: 9/6/76 C																						
1976	StL-N	18	21	1	3	1	0	0	0	2	2	.143	.217	.190	16	-2	2	0	1	1.000	-3	O-17	-0.5
1977	Mon-N	74	101	14	23	4	1	3	8	2	17	.228	.243	.376	65	-5	1	0	0	.966	-12	O-56	-1.9
1978	Mon-N	67	56	9	13	1	0	0	6	2	5	.232	.259	.250	43	-4	0	0	0	.949	-14	O-52/P-1	-2.0
1979	Chi-N	31	11	4	2	0	0	0	0	2	5	.182	.308	.182	34	-1	0	0	0	.875	-8	O-23	-0.9
	Cin-N	7	2	1	1	0	0	0	0	0	0	.500	.500	.500	173	0	0	0	0	1.000	-2	/O-5	-0.2
	Yr	38	13	5	3	0	0	0	0	2	5	.231	.333	.231	53	-1	0	0	0	.889	-10	O-28	-1.1
1980	Cin-N	71	108	16	30	5	1	1	10	6	13	.278	.322	.370	93	-1	4	2	0	.989	-13	O-67	-1.7
1981	Cin-N	66	49	6	14	2	0	0	7	2	9	.286	.314	.327	80	-1	1	0	0	.972	-16	O-58	-1.9
Total	6	334	348	51	86	13	2	4	31	16	51	.247	.282	.330	69	-15	8	2	1	.973	-68	O-278/P-1	-9.1
■ **DUTCH MELE**	Mele, Albert Ernest b: 1/11/15, New York, N.Y. d: 2/12/75, Hollywood, Fla. BL/TL, 6'0.5", 195 lbs. Deb: 9/14/37																						
1937	Cin-N	6	14	1	2	1	0	0	1	1	1	.143	.200	.214	13	-2	0			1.000	-2	/O-5	-0.4
■ **SAM MELE**	Mele, Sabath Anthony b: 1/21/23, Astoria, N.Y. BR/TR, 6'1", 187 lbs. Deb: 4/15/47 MC																						
1947	Bos-A	123	453	71	137	14	8	12	73	37	35	.302	.356	.448	114	8	0	3	-2	.992	-3	*O-116/1-1	-0.3
1948	Bos-A	66	180	25	42	12	1	2	25	13	21	.233	.292	.344	66	-9	1	1	-0	.971	-4	O-55	-1.6
1949	Bos-A	18	46	1	9	1	1	0	7	7	14	.196	.302	.261	46	-4	2	0	1	.955	-0	O-11	-0.4
	Was-A	78	264	21	64	12	2	3	25	17	34	.242	.288	.337	67	-14	2	1	0	.966	-8	O-63,1-11	-2.5
	Yr	96	310	22	73	13	3	3	32	24	48	.235	.290	.326	63	-18	4	1	1	.964	-9	O-74,1-11	-2.9
1950	Was-A	126	435	57	119	21	6	12	86	51	40	.274	.351	.432	105	2	2	0	1	.990	-5	O-99,1-16	-0.7

YEAR	TM/L	G	AB	R	H	2B	3B	HR	RBI	BB	SO	AVG	OBP	SLG	PRO+	BR/A	SB	CS	SBR	FA	FR	G/POS	TPR
1951	Was-A	143	558	58	153	**36**	7	5	94	32	31	.274	.315	.391	92	-9	2	3	-1	.993	3	*O-124,1-15	-1.2
1952	Was-A	9	28	2	12	3	0	2	10	1	2	.429	.448	.750	237	5	0	0	0	.917	-1	/O-7	0.3
	Chi-A	123	423	46	105	18	2	14	59	48	40	.248	.328	.400	101	-0	1	2	-1	1.000	-6	*O-112/1-3	-1.2
	Yr	132	451	48	117	21	2	16	69	49	42	.259	.335	.421	109	4	1	2	-1	.994	-7	*O-119/1-3	-0.9
1953	Chi-A	140	481	64	132	26	8	12	82	58	47	.274	.353	.437	109	5	3	1	0	.996	-8	*O-138/1-2	-0.7
1954	Bal-A	72	230	17	55	9	4	5	32	18	26	.239	.294	.378	90	-5	1	0	0	.962	-4	O-62	-1.1
	Bos-A	42	132	22	42	6	0	7	23	12	12	.318	.384	.523	132	5	0	1	-1	.994	-4	1-22,O-13	-0.1
	Yr	114	362	39	97	15	4	12	55	30	38	.268	.327	.431	107	2	1	1	-0	.961	-8	O-75,1-22	-1.2
1955	Bos-A	14	31	1	4	2	0	0	1	0	7	.129	.129	.194	-13	-5	1	0	0	1.000	2	/O-7	-0.3
	Cin-N	35	62	4	13	1	0	2	7	5	13	.210	.279	.323	56	-4	0	1	-1	.960	-1	O-13/1-1	-0.6
1956	Cle-A	57	114	17	29	7	0	4	20	12	20	.254	.325	.421	94	-1	1	1	-1	.969	-0	O-20/1-8	-0.3
Total	10	1046	3437	406	916	168	39	80	544	311	342	.267	.329	.408	97	-26	15	14	-4	.985	-39	O-840/1-79	-10.7

■ FRANCISCO MELENDEZ Melendez, Francisco Javier (Villegas) b: 1/25/64, Rio Piedras, P.R. BL/TL, 6', 190 lbs. Deb: 8/26/84

YEAR	TM/L	G	AB	R	H	2B	3B	HR	RBI	BB	SO	AVG	OBP	SLG	PRO+	BR/A	SB	CS	SBR	FA	FR	G/POS	TPR
1984	Phi-N	21	23	0	3	0	0	0	2	1	5	.130	.167	.130	-15	-3	0	0	0	1.000	1	1-10	-0.3
1986	Phi-N	9	8	0	2	0	0	0	0	0	2	.250	.250	.250	37	-1	0	0	0	1.000	-0	/1-2	-0.1
1987	SF-N	12	16	2	5	0	0	1	1	0	3	.313	.313	.500	117	0	0	0	0	1.000	-1	/1-5	0.0
1988	SF-N	23	26	1	5	0	0	0	3	3	2	.192	.276	.192	38	-2	0	0	0	1.000	-1	/1-6,O-1	-0.4
1989	Bal-A	9	11	1	3	0	0	0	3	1	2	.273	.333	.273	75	-0	0	0	0	1.000	0	/1-5	0.0
Total	5	74	84	4	18	0	0	1	9	5	14	.214	.258	.250	43	-6	0	0	0	1.000	-1	/1-28,O-1	-0.8

■ LUIS MELENDEZ Melendez, Luis Antonio (Santana) b: 8/11/49, Aibonito, P.R. BR/TR, 6', 165 lbs. Deb: 9/7/70

YEAR	TM/L	G	AB	R	H	2B	3B	HR	RBI	BB	SO	AVG	OBP	SLG	PRO+	BR/A	SB	CS	SBR	FA	FR	G/POS	TPR
1970	StL-N	21	70	11	21	1	0	0	8	2	12	.300	.319	.314	69	-3	3	0	1	1.000	1	O-18	-0.2
1971	StL-N	88	173	25	39	3	1	0	11	24	29	.225	.320	.254	62	-8	2	0	1	.959	-10	O-66	-2.0
1972	StL-N	118	332	32	79	11	3	5	28	25	34	.238	.293	.334	79	-10	5	4	-1	.959	-6	*O-105	-2.3
1973	StL-N	121	341	35	91	18	1	2	35	27	50	.267	.321	.343	84	-7	2	7	-4	.990	2	O-95	-1.3
1974	StL-N	83	124	15	27	4	3	0	8	11	9	.218	.287	.298	64	-6	2	2	-1	.977	-8	O-46/S-1	-1.6
1975	StL-N	110	291	33	77	8	5	2	27	16	25	.265	.303	.347	77	-9	3	2	-0	.983	-6	O-89	-1.9
1976	StL-N	20	24	0	3	0	0	0	0	0	3	.125	.125	.125	-29	-4	0	0	0	1.000	-1	/O-8	-0.5
	SD-N	72	119	15	29	5	0	0	5	3	12	.244	.262	.286	60	-7	1	1	-0	.988	-12	O-60	-2.2
	Yr	92	143	15	32	5	0	0	5	3	15	.224	.240	.259	44	-11	1	1	-0	.990	-13	O-68	-2.7
1977	SD-N	8	3	1	0	0	0	0	0	1	1	.000	.250	.000	-29	-1	0	0	0	1.000	-1	/O-2	-0.1
Total	8	641	1477	167	366	50	13	9	122	109	175	.248	.300	.318	73	-54	18	16	-4	.977	-40	O-489/S-1	-12.1

■ SKI MELILLO Melillo, Oscar Donald "Spinach" b: 8/4/1899, Chicago, Ill. d: 11/14/63, Chicago, Ill. BR/TR, 5'8", 150 lbs. Deb: 4/18/26 C

YEAR	TM/L	G	AB	R	H	2B	3B	HR	RBI	BB	SO	AVG	OBP	SLG	PRO+	BR/A	SB	CS	SBR	FA	FR	G/POS	TPR
1926	StL-A	99	385	54	98	18	5	1	30	32	31	.255	.315	.335	66	-19	6	7	-2	.965	8	2-88,3-11	-1.0
1927	StL-A	107	356	45	80	18	2	0	26	25	28	.225	.276	.287	45	-30	3	6	-3	.935	-2	*2-101	-3.0
1928	StL-A	51	132	9	25	2	0	0	9	9	11	.189	.241	.205	18	-16	2	1	0	.961	4	2-28,3-19	-1.1
1929	StL-A	141	494	57	146	17	10	5	67	29	30	.296	.337	.401	86	-11	11	6	-0	.973	23	*2-141	1.6
1930	StL-A	149	574	62	147	30	10	5	59	23	44	.256	.287	.369	63	-34	15	9	-1	.979	**27**	*2-148	0.0
1931	StL-A	151	617	88	189	34	11	2	75	37	29	.306	.346	.407	94	-6	7	11	-5	.968	**33**	*2-151	2.9
1932	StL-A	154	612	71	148	19	11	3	66	36	42	.242	.286	.324	54	-42	6	6	-2	.981	11	*2-153	-2.4
1933	StL-A	132	496	50	145	23	6	3	79	29	18	.292	.333	.381	83	-12	12	10	-2	**.991**	23	*2-130	1.5
1934	StL-A	144	552	54	133	19	3	2	55	28	27	.241	.279	.297	45	-46	4	6	-2	**.981**	18	*2-141	-2.0
1935	StL-A	19	62	8	13	3	0	0	5	8	4	.210	.300	.258	43	-5	0	0	0	.970	0	2-18	-0.3
	Bos-A	106	400	45	104	13	2	1	39	38	22	.260	.327	.310	61	-22	3	2	-0	.973	18	*2-105	0.3
	Yr	125	462	53	117	16	2	1	44	46	26	.253	.324	.303	59	-27	3	2	-0	.973	19	*2-123	0.0
1936	Bos-A	98	327	39	74	12	4	0	32	28	16	.226	.287	.287	40	-31	0	0	0	.980	-8	2-93	-2.9
1937	Bos-A	26	56	8	14	2	0	0	6	5	4	.250	.311	.286	50	-4	0	1	-1	.939	-3	2-19/S-2,3-2	-0.7
Total	12	1377	5063	590	1316	210	64	22	548	327	306	.260	.306	.340	64	-279	69	65	-18	.973	151	*2-1316/3-32,S-2	-7.1

■ JOE MELLANA Mellana, Joseph Peter b: 3/11/05, Oakland, Cal. d: 11/1/69, Larkspur, Cal. BR/TR, 5'10", 180 lbs. Deb: 9/21/27

YEAR	TM/L	G	AB	R	H	2B	3B	HR	RBI	BB	SO	AVG	OBP	SLG	PRO+	BR/A	SB	CS	SBR	FA	FR	G/POS	TPR
1927	Phi-A	4	7	1	2	0	0	0	2	0	1	.286	.286	.286	46	-1	0	0	0	.889	2	/3-2	0.1

■ BILL MELLOR Mellor, William Harpin b: 6/6/1874, Camden, N.J. d: 11/5/40, Bridgeton, R.I. BR/TR, 6', 190 lbs. Deb: 7/28/02

YEAR	TM/L	G	AB	R	H	2B	3B	HR	RBI	BB	SO	AVG	OBP	SLG	PRO+	BR/A	SB	CS	SBR	FA	FR	G/POS	TPR
1902	Bal-A	10	36	4	13	3	0	0	5	3		.361	.410	.444	131	2	1			.978	-1	1-10	0.0

■ PAUL MELOAN Meloan, Paul B. "Molly" b: 8/23/1888, Paynesville, Mo. d: 2/11/50, Taft, Cal. BR/TL, 5'10.5", 175 lbs. Deb: 8/2/10

YEAR	TM/L	G	AB	R	H	2B	3B	HR	RBI	BB	SO	AVG	OBP	SLG	PRO+	BR/A	SB	CS	SBR	FA	FR	G/POS	TPR
1910	Chi-A	65	222	23	54	6	6	0	23	17		.243	.314	.324	104	1	4			.948	3	O-65	0.2
1911	Chi-A	1	3	0	1	0	0	0	1	0		.333	.333	.333	89	-0	0			.000	-1	/O-1	-0.1
	StL-A	64	206	30	54	11	2	3	14	15		.262	.318	.379	98	-1	7			.904	-6	O-54	-1.0
	Yr	65	209	30	55	11	2	3	15	15		.263	.318	.378	98	-1	7			.893	-6	O-55	-1.1
Total	2	130	431	53	109	17	8	3	38	32		.253	.316	.350	101	-0	11			.923	-3	O-120	-0.9

■ DAVE MELTON Melton, David Olin b: 10/3/28, Pampa, Tex. BR/TR, 6', 185 lbs. Deb: 4/17/56

YEAR	TM/L	G	AB	R	H	2B	3B	HR	RBI	BB	SO	AVG	OBP	SLG	PRO+	BR/A	SB	CS	SBR	FA	FR	G/POS	TPR
1956	KC-A	3	3	0	1	0	0	0	0	0	0	.333	.333	.333	76	-0	0	0	0	1.000	-1	/O-3	-0.1
1958	KC-A	9	6	0	0	0	0	0	0	0	5	.000	.000	.000	-98	-2	0	0	0	1.000	-0	/O-2	-0.2
Total	2	12	9	0	1	0	0	0	0	0	5	.111	.111	.111	-39	-2	0	0	0	1.000	-1	/O-5	-0.3

■ BILL MELTON Melton, William Edwin b: 7/7/45, Gulfport, Miss. BR/TR, 6'2", 200 lbs. Deb: 5/4/68

YEAR	TM/L	G	AB	R	H	2B	3B	HR	RBI	BB	SO	AVG	OBP	SLG	PRO+	BR/A	SB	CS	SBR	FA	FR	G/POS	TPR
1968	Chi-A	34	109	5	29	8	0	2	16	10	32	.266	.328	.394	117	2	1	1	-0	.968	3	3-33	0.6
1969	Chi-A	157	556	67	142	26	2	23	87	56	106	.255	.329	.433	106	4	1	2	-1	.952	7	*3-148,O-11	1.0
1970	Chi-A	141	514	74	135	15	1	33	96	56	107	.263	.345	.488	123	15	2	4	-2	1.000	9	O-71,3-70	1.8
1971	Chi-A☆	150	543	72	146	18	2	**33**	86	61	87	.269	.354	.492	133	23	3	3	-1	.968	27	*3-148	5.1
1972	Chi-A	57	208	22	51	5	0	7	30	23	31	.245	.320	.370	103	1	1	1	-0	.935	3	3-56	0.3
1973	Chi-A	152	560	83	155	29	1	20	87	75	66	.277	.364	.439	121	16	4	4	-1	.953	14	*3-151/D-1	2.9
1974	Chi-A	136	495	63	120	17	0	21	63	59	60	.242	.329	.404	107	5	3	2	-0	.939	-3	*3-123,D-11	0.0
1975	Chi-A	149	512	62	123	16	0	15	70	78	106	.240	.349	.359	99	2	5	4	-1	.945	1	*3-138,D-11	0.1
1976	Cal-A	118	341	31	71	17	3	6	42	44	53	.208	.302	.328	90	-4	2	0	1	.992	-3	D-51,1-30,3-21	-1.1
1977	Cle-A	50	133	17	32	11	0	0	14	17	21	.241	.336	.323	83	-3	1	3	-2	1.000	1	1-15,D-14,3-13	-0.5
Total	10	1144	3971	496	1004	162	9	160	591	479	669	.253	.340	.419	112	61	23	24	-8	.949	57	3-901/D-88,O-82,1	10.2

■ MITCH MELUSKEY Meluskey, Mitchell Wade b: 9/18/73, Yakima, Wash. BB/TR, 6', 185 lbs. Deb: 8/30/98

YEAR	TM/L	G	AB	R	H	2B	3B	HR	RBI	BB	SO	AVG	OBP	SLG	PRO+	BR/A	SB	CS	SBR	FA	FR	G/POS	TPR
1998	Hou-N	8	8	1	2	1	0	0	0	1	4	.250	.333	.375	85	-0	0	0	0	1.000	0	/C-3	0.0

■ BOB MELVIN Melvin, Robert Paul b: 10/28/61, Palo Alto, Cal. BR/TR, 6'4", 205 lbs. Deb: 5/25/85

YEAR	TM/L	G	AB	R	H	2B	3B	HR	RBI	BB	SO	AVG	OBP	SLG	PRO+	BR/A	SB	CS	SBR	FA	FR	G/POS	TPR
1985	Det-A	41	82	10	18	4	1	0	4	3	21	.220	.247	.293	47	-6	0	0	0	.989	8	C-41	0.3
1986	SF-N	89	268	24	60	14	2	5	25	15	69	.224	.265	.347	71	-12	3	2	-0	.988	7	C-84/3-1	0.0
1987	*SF-N	84	246	31	49	8	0	11	31	17	44	.199	.251	.366	64	-14	0	4	-2	.998	4	C-78/1-1	-0.8
1988	SF-N	92	273	23	64	13	1	8	27	13	46	.234	.269	.377	87	-6	0	2	-1	.984	-8	C-89/1-1	-0.9
1989	Bal-A	85	278	22	67	10	1	1	32	15	53	.241	.280	.295	64	-13	1	4	-2	.991	-9	C-75/D-9	-2.1
1990	Bal-A	93	301	30	73	14	1	5	37	11	53	.243	.269	.346	73	-12	0	1	-1	.997	1	C-76,D-10/1-1	-0.8
1991	Bal-A	79	228	11	57	10	0	1	23	11	46	.250	.285	.307	66	-11	0	0	0	.998	6	C-72/D-4	-0.1
1992	KC-A	32	70	5	22	5	0	0	6	5	13	.314	.360	.386	106	1	0	0	0	1.000	-0	C-21/1-3	0.1
1993	Bos-A	77	176	13	39	7	0	3	23	7	44	.222	.255	.313	49	-13	0	0	0	.994	-8	C-76/1-1	-1.7
1994	NY-A	9	14	2	4	0	0	1	3	0	3	.286	.286	.500	101	-0	0	0	0	1.000	-1	/C-4,1-4,D-1	-0.1
	Chi-A	11	19	3	3	0	0	0	1	1	4	.158	.200	.158	-6	-3	0	0	0	1.000	2	C-11	-0.1
	Yr	20	33	5	7	0	0	1	4	1	7	.212	.235	.303	39	-3	0	0	0	1.000	1	C-15/1-4,D-1	-0.2
Total	10	692	1955	174	456	85	6	35	212	98	396	.233	.270	.337	69	-89	4	13	-7	.993	2	C-627/D-24,1-11,3-1	-6.2

■ CARLOS MENDOZA Mendoza, Carlos Ramon b: 11/4/74, Bolivar, Venez. BL/TL, 5'11", 160 lbs. Deb: 9/3/97

YEAR	TM/L	G	AB	R	H	2B	3B	HR	RBI	BB	SO	AVG	OBP	SLG	PRO+	BR/A	SB	CS	SBR	FA	FR	G/POS	TPR
1997	NY-N	15	12	6	3	0	0	0	1	4	2	.250	.500	.250	108	1	0	0	0	1.000	-1	/O-3	0.0

YEAR	TM/L	G	AB	R	H	2B	3B	HR	RBI	BB	SO	AVG	OBP	SLG	PRO+	BR/A	SB	CS	SBR	FA	FR	G/POS	TPR
■ MINNIE MENDOZA Mendoza, Cristobal Rigoberto (Carreras) b: 11/16/33, Ceiba Del Agua, Cuba BR/TR, 6', 180 lbs. Deb: 4/9/70 C																							
1970	Min-A	16	16	2	3	0	0	0	2	0	1	.188	.188	.188	4	-2	0	0	0	1.000	0	/3-5,2-4	-0.2
■ MARIO MENDOZA Mendoza, Mario (Aizpuru) b: 12/26/50, Chihuahua, Mex. BR/TR, 5'11", 187 lbs. Deb: 4/26/74																							
1974	*Pit-N	91	163	10	36	1	2	0	15	8	35	.221	.262	.252	46	-12	1	1	-0	.964	5	S-87	-0.1
1975	Pit-N	56	50	8	9	1	0	0	2	3	17	.180	.226	.200	19	-5	0	0	0	.952	8	S-53/3-1	0.4
1976	Pit-N	50	92	6	17	5	0	0	12	4	15	.185	.219	.239	30	-9	0	1	-1	.967	12	S-45/3-2,2-1	0.6
1977	Pit-N	70	81	5	16	3	0	0	4	3	10	.198	.226	.235	23	-9	0	0	0	.928	12	S-45,3-19/P-1	0.5
1978	Pit-N	57	55	5	12	1	0	1	3	2	9	.218	.283	.291	58	-3	3	1	0	.980	9	2-21,3-18,S-14	0.8
1979	Sea-A	148	373	26	74	10	3	1	29	9	62	.198	.219	.249	26	-39	3	0	1	.968	28	*S-148	0.2
1980	Sea-A	114	277	27	68	6	3	2	14	16	42	.245	.287	.310	63	-14	3	4	-2	.959	12	*S-114	0.6
1981	Tex-A	88	229	18	53	6	1	0	22	7	25	.231	.257	.266	54	-14	2	1	0	.970	3	S-88	-0.3
1982	Tex-A	12	17	1	2	0	0	0	0	0	4	.118	.118	.118	-37	-3	0	0	0	.882	2	S-12	-0.1
Total	9	686	1337	106	287	33	9	4	101	52	219	.215	.247	.262	41	-108	12	8	-1	.961	91	S-606/3-40,2-22,P-1	2.6
■ MIKE MENDOZA Mendoza, Michael Joseph b: 11/26/55, Inglewood, Cal. BR/TR, 6'5", 215 lbs. Deb: 9/7/79																							
1979	Hou-N	2	0	0	0	0	0	0	0	0	0	—	—	—	—	0	0	0	0	.000	0	/P-1	0.0
■ JOCK MENEFEE Menefee, John b: 1/15/1868, Rowlesburg, W.Va. d: 3/11/53, Belle Vernon, Pa. BR/TR, 6', 165 lbs. Deb: 8/17/1892																							
1892	Pit-N	2	3	0	0	0	0	0	0	0	0	.000	.000	.000	-99	-1	0			1.000	0	/O-1,P-1	-0.1
1893	Lou-N	22	73	10	20	2	1	0	12	13	5	.274	.391	.329	100	1	2			.913	3	P-15/O-7	0.1
1894	Lou-N	29	79	7	13	1	0	0	4	8	7	.165	.250	.177	5	-12	2			.940	2	P-28/2-1	0.0
	Pit-N	13	47	6	12	1	2	0	7	3	3	.255	.300	.362	60	-3	2			.909	2	P-13	0.0
	Yr	42	126	13	25	2	2	0	11	11	10	.198	.268	.246	26	-15	4			.928	5	P-41/2-1	0.0
1895	Pit-N	2	0	0	0	0	0	0	0	0	0	—	—	—	—	0	0			.667	0	/P-2	0.0
1898	NY-N	1	5	0	0	0	0	0	0	0		.000	.000	.000	-99	-1	0			.750	0	/P-1	0.0
1900	Chi-N	17	46	5	5	0	0	0	4	2		.109	.180	.109	-20	-7	0			.889	-2	P-16	0.0
1901	Chi-N	48	152	19	39	5	3	0	13	8		.257	.327	.329	94	-1	4			.913	-2	O-24,P-21/1-2,2-1	-0.3
1902	Chi-N	65	216	24	50	4	1	0	15	15		.231	.303	.259	76	-5	4			.952	-4	O-23,P-22,1-18,/32	-0.8
1903	Chi-N	22	64	3	13	3	0	0	2	3		.203	.239	.250	40	-5	0			.896	3	P-20/1-2	-0.1
Total	9	221	685	74	152	16	7	0	57	52	15	.222	.295	.266	60	-35	14			.918	3	P-139/O-55,1-22,23	-1.2
■ DENIS MENKE Menke, Denis John b: 7/21/40, Algona, Iowa BR/TR, 6', 190 lbs. Deb: 4/14/62 C																							
1962	Mil-N	50	146	12	28	3	1	2	16	16	38	.192	.280	.267	49	-10	0	1	-1	.980	5	2-20,3-15/S-9,10	-0.4
1963	Mil-N	146	518	58	121	16	4	11	50	37	106	.234	.292	.344	83	-11	6	7	-2	.976	12	S-82,3-51,2-22,/1O	0.6
1964	Mil-N	151	505	79	143	29	5	20	65	68	77	.283	.373	.479	137	26	4	2	0	.964	2	*S-141,2-15/3-6	4.0
1965	Mil-N	71	181	16	44	13	1	4	18	18	28	.243	.315	.392	97	-1	1	3	-2	.967	-7	S-54/1-8,3-4	-0.7
1966	Atl-N	138	454	55	114	20	4	15	60	71	87	.251	.360	.412	112	9	0	7	-4	.955	-22	*S-106,3-39/1-7	-0.9
1967	Atl-N	129	418	37	95	14	3	7	39	65	62	.227	.335	.325	91	-3	5	7	-3	.965	-23	*S-124/3-3	-1.8
1968	Hou-N	150	542	56	135	23	6	6	56	64	81	.249	.335	.347	107	6	5	8	-3	.982	-17	*2-119,S-35/1-5,3-4	-0.5
1969	Hou-N★	154	553	72	149	25	5	10	90	87	87	.269	.373	.387	115	14	2	7	-4	.956	-9	*S-131,2-23/1-9,3-1	1.7
1970	Hou-N★	154	562	82	171	26	6	13	92	82	80	.304	.398	.441	130	26	6	5	-1	.954	-16	*S-133,2-21/1-5,3O	2.6
1971	Hou-N	146	475	57	117	26	3	1	43	59	68	.246	.332	.320	88	-6	4	5	-2	.997	-3	*1-101,3-32,S-17,/2	-1.9
1972	*Cin-N	140	447	41	104	19	2	9	50	58	76	.233	.327	.345	97	-1	0	1	-1	.955	1	*3-130,1-11	-0.3
1973	*Cin-N	139	241	38	46	10	0	3	26	69	53	.191	.375	.270	86	-1	1	1	-0	.966	16	*3-123/S-7,2-5,1-1	1.6
1974	Hou-N	30	29	2	3	1	0	0	1	4	10	.103	.212	.138	-1	-4	0	0	0	1.000	3	1-12/3-7,2-3,S-2	-0.1
Total	13	1598	5071	605	1270	225	40	101	606	698	853	.250	.346	.370	104	44	34	54	-22	.961	-58	S-841,3-420,21/O	3.9
■ MIKE MENOSKY Menosky, Michael William "Leaping Mike" b: 10/16/1894, Glen Campbell, Pa. d: 4/11/83, Detroit, Mich. BL/TR, 5'10", 163 lbs. Deb: 4/18/14																							
1914	Pit-F	68	140	26	37	4	1	2	9	16	30	.264	.352	.350	92	-3	5			.942	-3	O-41	-0.8
1915	Pit-F	17	21	3	2	0	0	0	1	2	0	.095	.208	.095	-13	-3	2			.917	-2	/O-9	-0.6
1916	Was-A	11	37	5	6	1	1	0	3	1	10	.162	.184	.243	29	-3	1			.952	1	/O-9	-0.3
1917	Was-A	114	322	46	83	12	10	1	34	45	55	.258	.359	.366	123	10	22			.982	8	O-94	1.4
1919	Was-A	116	342	62	98	15	3	6	39	44	46	.287	.379	.401	120	10	13			.979	0	*O-103	0.4
1920	Bos-A	141	532	80	158	24	9	3	64	65	52	.297	.383	.393	111	10	23	19	-5	.961	-3	*O-141	-0.7
1921	Bos-A	133	477	77	143	18	5	3	45	60	45	.300	.388	.377	99	2	12	6	0	.970	-4	*O-133	-1.1
1922	Bos-A	126	406	61	115	16	5	3	32	40	33	.283	.355	.369	90	-5	9	5	-0	.977	6	*O-103	-0.7
1923	Bos-A	84	188	22	43	8	4	0	25	22	19	.229	.310	.314	64	-10	3	6	-3	.920	3	O-49	-1.2
Total	9	810	2465	382	685	98	38	18	252	295	290	.278	.364	.370	100	7	90	36		.967	7	O-682	-3.6
■ ED MENSOR Mensor, Edward "The Midget" b: 11/7/1886, Woodville, Ore. d: 4/20/70, Salem, Ore. BB/TR, 5'6", 145 lbs. Deb: 7/15/12																							
1912	Pit-N	39	99	19	26	3	2	0	1	23	12	.263	.402	.333	104	2	10			.955	-2	O-32	-0.2
1913	Pit-N	44	56	9	10	1	0	0	1	8	13	.179	.292	.196	43	-4	2			.971	-1	O-18/2-1,S-1	-0.5
1914	Pit-N	44	89	15	18	2	1	1	6	22	13	.202	.372	.281	99	1	2			.969	2	O-25	0.2
Total	3	127	244	43	54	6	3	1	8	53	38	.221	.367	.283	89	-1	14			.964	-1	/O-75,S-1,2-1	-0.5
■ TED MENZE Menze, Theodore Charles b: 11/4/1897, St.Louis, Mo. d: 12/23/69, St.Louis, Mo. BR/TR, 5'9", 172 lbs. Deb: 4/23/18																							
1918	StL-N	1	3	0	0	0	0	0	0	0	2	.000	.000	.000	-99	-1	0			1.000	-0	/O-1	-0.1
■ RUDY MEOLI Meoli, Rudolph Bartholomew b: 5/1/51, Troy, N.Y. BL/TR, 5'9", 165 lbs. Deb: 9/9/71																							
1971	Cal-A	7	3	0	0	0	0	0	0	0	1	.000	.000	.000	-99	-1	0	0	0	.000	0	H	-0.1
1973	Cal-A	120	305	36	68	12	1	2	23	31	38	.223	.295	.289	70	-12	2	4	-2	.933	-2	S-95,3-13/2-8	-0.5
1974	Cal-A	36	90	9	22	2	0	0	3	8	10	.244	.306	.267	70	-3	2	4	-2	.946	2	3-20/S-8,1-1,2-1	-0.3
1975	Cal-A	70	126	12	27	2	1	0	6	15	20	.214	.298	.246	59	-6	3	0	1	.976	0	S-28,3-15,2-11,/D-3	-0.3
1978	Chi-N	47	29	10	3	0	1	0	2	6	4	.103	.257	.172	20	-3	1	0	0	.900	6	/2-6,3-5	0.4
1979	Phi-N	30	73	2	13	4	1	0	6	9	15	.178	.268	.260	43	-6	2	0	1	.984	3	S-16,2-15/3-1	0.0
Total	6	310	626	69	133	20	4	2	40	69	88	.212	.291	.267	61	-31	10	8	-2	.944	10	S-147/3-54,2-41,D1	-0.8
■ ORLANDO MERCADO Mercado, Orlando (Rodriguez) b: 11/7/61, Arecibo, P.R. BR/TR, 6', 195 lbs. Deb: 9/13/82																							
1982	Sea-A	9	17	1	2	0	0	1	6	0	5	.118	.118	.294	8	-2	0	0	0	1.000	1	/C-8,D-1	-0.1
1983	Sea-A	66	178	10	35	11	2	1	16	14	27	.197	.259	.298	51	-12	2	2	-1	.995	4	C-65	-0.6
1984	Sea-A	30	78	5	17	3	1	0	5	4	12	.218	.265	.282	52	-5	1	0	0	.992	-6	C-29	-1.0
1986	Tex-A	46	102	7	24	1	1	1	7	6	13	.235	.284	.294	56	-6	0	1	-1	.996	16	C-45	1.1
1987	Det-A	10	22	2	3	0	0	0	1	2	0	.136	.208	.136	-6	-3	0	0	0	.980	3	C-10	0.0
	LA-N	7	5	1	3	1	0	0	1	1	1	.600	.667	.800	294	2	0	0	0	1.000	0	/C-7	0.2
1988	Oak-A	16	24	3	3	0	0	1	1	3	8	.125	.222	.250	33	-2	0	0	0	.959	1	C-16	-0.1
1989	Min-A	19	38	1	4	0	0	0	1	4	4	.105	.190	.105	-14	-6	1	0	0	1.000	4	C-19	-0.1
1990	NY-N	42	90	10	19	1	0	3	7	8	11	.211	.290	.322	68	-4	0	0	0	.991	2	C-40	-0.1
	Mon-N	8	8	0	2	0	0	0	0	0	1	.250	.250	.250	39	-1	0	0	0	1.000	3	/C-8	0.2
	Yr	50	98	10	21	1	0	3	7	8	12	.214	.287	.316	66	-5	0	0	0	.992	4	C-48	0.1
Total	8	253	562	40	112	17	4	7	45	42	82	.199	.261	.281	48	-40	4	3	-1	.993	27	C-247/D-1	-0.5
■ ORLANDO MERCED Merced, Orlando Luis (Villanueva) b: 11/2/66, Hato Rey, P.R. BB/TR, 5'11", 170 lbs. Deb: 6/27/90																							
1990	Pit-N	25	24	3	5	1	0	0	0	1	9	.208	.240	.250	36	-2	0	0	0	.000	-0	/C-1,O-1	-0.3
1991	*Pit-N	120	411	83	113	17	2	10	50	64	81	.275	.374	.399	119	12	8	4	0	.988	-8	*1-105/O-7	-0.2
1992	*Pit-N	134	405	50	100	28	5	6	60	52	63	.247	.336	.385	105	3	5	4	-1	.995	0	*1-114,O-17	-0.5
1993	Pit-N	137	447	68	140	26	4	8	70	77	64	.313	.415	.443	130	23	3	3	-1	.965	3	*O-109,1-42	2.0
1994	Pit-N	108	386	48	105	21	3	9	51	42	58	.272	.345	.412	95	-2	4	1	1	.981	-9	O-68,1-55	-1.6
1995	Pit-N	132	487	75	146	29	4	15	83	52	74	.300	.369	.468	117	12	7	2	1	.976	1	*O-107,1-35	0.9
1996	Pit-N	120	453	69	130	24	1	17	80	51	74	.287	.359	.457	110	7	8	4	0	.988	15	*O-115/1-1	1.9
1997	Tor-A	98	368	45	98	23	2	9	40	47	62	.266	.354	.413	99	0	7	3	0	.985	8	O-96/1-1,D-1	0.6

YEAR	TM/L	G	AB	R	H	2B	3B	HR	RBI	BB	SO	AVG	OBP	SLG	PRO+	BR/A	SB	CS	SBR	FA	FR	G/POS	TPR
1998	Min-A	63	204	22	59	12	0	5	33	17	29	.289	.347	.422	98	-0	1	4	-2	.982	-1	1-38,O-13/D-8	-0.6
	Bos-A	9	9	0	0	0	0	0	2	2	3	.000	.182	.000	-47	-2	0	0	0	1.000	0	/O-1,D-1	-0.2
	Yr	72	213	22	59	12	0	5	35	19	32	.277	.339	.404	92	-2	1	4	-2	.982	-1	1-38,O-14/D-9	-0.8
	Chi-N	12	10	2	3	0	0	1	5	1	2	.300	.364	.600	140	1	0	0	0	1.000	-1	/O-4	0.0
Total	9	958	3204	465	899	181	21	80	474	406	519	.281	.363	.425	110	51	43	25	-2	.980	10	O-538,1-391/D-10,C	2.0

■ HENRY MERCEDES Mercedes, Henry Felipe (Perez) b: 7/23/69, Santo Domingo, D.R. BR/TR, 6'1", 210 lbs. Deb: 4/22/92

YEAR	TM/L	G	AB	R	H	2B	3B	HR	RBI	BB	SO	AVG	OBP	SLG	PRO+	BR/A	SB	CS	SBR	FA	FR	G/POS	TPR
1992	Oak-A	9	5	1	4	0	1	0	1	0	1	.800	.800	1.200	479	2	0	0	0	.875	-0	/C-9	0.2
1993	Oak-A	20	47	5	10	2	0	0	3	2	15	.213	.260	.255	42	-4	1	1	-0	.987	-0	C-18/D-1	-0.4
1995	KC-A	23	43	7	11	2	0	0	9	8	13	.256	.385	.302	81	-1	0	0	0	.986	-3	C-22	-0.2
1996	KC-A	4	4	1	1	0	0	0	0	0	1	.250	.250	.250	27	-0	0	0	0	1.000	-1	/C-4	-0.1
1997	Tex-A	23	47	4	10	4	0	0	4	6	25	.213	.302	.298	54	-3	0	0	0	.988	0	C-23	-0.2
Total	5	79	146	18	36	8	1	0	17	16	55	.247	.329	.315	71	-6	1	1	-0	.983	-4	/C-76,D-1	-0.7

■ LUIS MERCEDES Mercedes, Luis Roberto (Santana) b: 2/15/68, San Pedro De Macoris, D.R. BR/TR, 6', 180 lbs. Deb: 9/8/91

YEAR	TM/L	G	AB	R	H	2B	3B	HR	RBI	BB	SO	AVG	OBP	SLG	PRO+	BR/A	SB	CS	SBR	FA	FR	G/POS	TPR
1991	Bal-A	19	54	10	11	2	0	0	2	4	9	.204	.259	.241	41	-4	0	0	0	1.000	-2	O-15/D-1	-0.7
1992	Bal-A	23	50	7	7	2	0	0	4	8	9	.140	.271	.180	28	-5	0	1	-1	.956	2	O-16/D-7	-0.3
1993	Bal-A	10	24	1	7	2	0	0	0	5	4	.292	.414	.375	109	1	1	1	-0	1.000	-0	/O-8,D-2	0.0
	SF-N	18	25	1	4	0	1	0	3	1	3	.160	.250	.240	33	-2	0	1	-1	1.000	-1	/O-5	-0.4
Total	3	70	153	19	29	6	1	0	9	18	25	.190	.287	.242	47	-11	1	3	-2	.976	-2	/O-44,D-10	-1.4

■ WIN MERCER Mercer, George Barclay b: 6/20/1874, Chester, W.Va. d: 1/12/03, San Francisco, Cal BR/TR, 5'7", 140 lbs. Deb: 4/21/1894

YEAR	TM/L	G	AB	R	H	2B	3B	HR	RBI	BB	SO	AVG	OBP	SLG	PRO+	BR/A	SB	CS	SBR	FA	FR	G/POS	TPR
1894	Was-N	53	165	29	48	5	2	2	29	9	20	.291	.328	.382	73	-8	9			.944	2	P-50/O-4	-0.1
1895	Was-N	63	196	26	50	9	1	1	26	12	32	.255	.308	.327	65	-11	7			.874	-8	P-43/S-7,O-5,3-3,2	-0.8
1896	Was-N	49	156	23	38	1	1	1	14	9	18	.244	.302	.282	54	-10	9			.856	1	P-46/O-1	0.0
1897	Was-N	50	139	23	44	2	5	0	19	6		.317	.354	.403	100	-0	7			.858	-1	P-47	0.0
1898	Was-N	80	249	38	80	3	5	2	25	18		.321	.369	.398	120	6	14			.863	-9	P-33,S-23,O-19,/32	-0.4
1899	Was-N	108	375	73	112	6	7	1	35	32		.299	.360	.360	99	0	16			.846	-14	3-62,P-23,O-16,/S1	-1.6
1900	NY-N	76	248	32	73	4	0	0	27	26		.294	.366	.310	92	-1	15			.931	-2	P-33,3-19,O-14,/S2	-0.4
1901	Was-A	51	140	26	42	7	2	0	16	23		.300	.402	.379	119	5	10			.944	-2	P-24,O-16/1-7,S3	-0.1
1902	Det-A	35	100	8	18	2	0	0	6	6		.180	.226	.200	19	-11	1			.935	4	P-35	0.0
Total	9	565	1768	278	505	39	23	7	197	141	70	.286	.344	.346	87	-30	88			.903	-29	P-334/3-90,OS12	-3.4

■ JOHN MERCER Mercer, John Locke b: 6/22/1892, Taylortown, La. d: 12/22/82, Shreveport, La. BL/TL, 5'10.5", 155 lbs. Deb: 6/25/12

YEAR	TM/L	G	AB	R	H	2B	3B	HR	RBI	BB	SO	AVG	OBP	SLG	PRO+	BR/A	SB	CS	SBR	FA	FR	G/POS	TPR
1912	StL-N	1	1	0	0	0	0	0	0	0	0	.000	.000	.000	-99	-0	0			.500	-0	/1-1	-0.1

■ ANDY MERCHANT Merchant, James Anderson b: 8/30/50, Mobile, Ala. BL/TR, 5'11", 185 lbs. Deb: 9/28/75

YEAR	TM/L	G	AB	R	H	2B	3B	HR	RBI	BB	SO	AVG	OBP	SLG	PRO+	BR/A	SB	CS	SBR	FA	FR	G/POS	TPR
1975	Bos-A	1	4	1	2	0	0	0	0	1	0	.500	.600	.500	197	1	0	0	0	1.000	-1	/C-1	0.0
1976	Bos-A	2	2	0	0	0	0	0	0	0	2	.000	.000	.000	-89	-0	0	0	0	1.000	-0	/C-1	-0.1
Total	2	3	6	1	2	0	0	0	0	1	2	.333	.429	.333	109	0	0	0	0	1.000	-1	/C-2	-0.1

■ ART MEREWETHER Merewether, Arthur Francis "Merry" b: 7/7/02, E.Providence, R.I. d: 2/2/97, Bayside, N.Y. BR/TR, 5'9.5", 155 lbs. Deb: 7/10/22

YEAR	TM/L	G	AB	R	H	2B	3B	HR	RBI	BB	SO	AVG	OBP	SLG	PRO+	BR/A	SB	CS	SBR	FA	FR	G/POS	TPR
1922	Pit-N	1	1	0	0	0	0	0	0	0	0	.000	.000	.000	-99	-0	0	0	0	.000	0	H	0.0

■ FRED MERKLE Merkle, Frederick Charles b: 12/20/1888, Watertown, Wis. d: 3/2/56, Daytona Beach, Fla. BR/TR, 6'1", 190 lbs. Deb: 9/21/07 C

YEAR	TM/L	G	AB	R	H	2B	3B	HR	RBI	BB	SO	AVG	OBP	SLG	PRO+	BR/A	SB	CS	SBR	FA	FR	G/POS	TPR
1907	NY-N	15	47	0	12	1	0	0	5	1		.255	.271	.277	69	-2	0			.949	-1	1-15	-0.4
1908	NY-N	38	41	6	11	2	1	1	7	4		.268	.333	.439	140	2	0			1.000	-2	1-11/O-5,2-1,3-1	-0.1
1909	NY-N	79	236	15	45	9	1	0	20	16		.191	.245	.237	49	-14	8			.976	-3	1-70/2-1	-2.0
1910	NY-N	144	506	75	148	35	14	4	70	44	59	.292	.353	.441	131	18	23			.981	1	*1-144	1.9
1911	*NY-N	149	541	80	153	24	10	12	84	43	60	.283	.342	.431	112	7	49			.985	15	*1-148	2.1
1912	*NY-N	129	479	82	148	22	6	11	84	42	70	.309	.374	.449	121	13	37			.980	-1	*1-129	1.0
1913	*NY-N	153	563	78	147	30	13	2	69	41	60	.261	.315	.371	95	-5	35			.986	-4	*1-153	-1.1
1914	NY-N	146	512	71	132	25	7	7	63	52	80	.258	.327	.375	112	7	23			.990	3	*1-146	0.7
1915	NY-N	140	505	52	151	25	3	4	62	36	39	.299	.348	.384	129	16	20	15	-3	.989	-1	*1-110,O-30	0.9
1916	NY-N	112	401	45	95	19	3	7	44	33	46	.237	.308	.352	108	3	17			.984	0	*1-112	-0.1
	*Bro-N	23	69	6	16	1	0	0	2	7	4	.232	.312	.246	70	-2	2			.992	-1	1-15/O-4	-0.4
	Yr	135	470	51	111	20	3	7	46	40	50	.236	.308	.336	102	1	19			.985	-1	*1-127/O-4	-0.5
1917	Bro-N	2	8	1	1	1	0	0	0	0	1	.125	.125	.250	13	-1	0			1.000	0	/1-2	-0.1
	Chi-N	146	549	65	146	30	9	3	57	42	60	.266	.323	.370	104	2	13			.983	-3	*1-140/O-6	-0.7
	Yr	148	557	66	147	31	9	3	57	42	61	.264	.320	.368	103	1	13			.983	-3	*1-142/O-6	-0.8
1918	*Chi-N	129	482	55	143	25	5	3	65	35	36	.297	.349	.388	122	12	21			.990	1	*1-129	0.9
1919	Chi-N	133	498	52	133	20	6	3	62	33	35	.267	.315	.349	99	-1	20			.985	-10	*1-132/2-1	-1.7
1920	Chi-N	92	330	33	94	20	4	3	38	24	32	.285	.335	.397	108	3	3	5	-2	.985	-0	1-85/O-1	-0.1
1925	NY-A	7	13	4	5	1	0	0	1	1	1	.385	.429	.462	128	1	1	0	0	1.000	-0	/1-5	0.0
1926	NY-A	1	2	0	0	0	0	0	0	0	0	.000	.000	.000	-99	-1	0	0	0	1.000	-0	/1-1	-0.1
Total	16	1638	5782	720	1580	290	82	60	733	454	583	.273	.331	.383	109	58	272	20		.985	-5	*1-1547/O-46,2-3,3	0.7

■ LOU MERLONI Merloni, Louis William b: 4/6/71, Framingham, Mass. BR/TR, 5'10", 188 lbs. Deb: 5/10/98

YEAR	TM/L	G	AB	R	H	2B	3B	HR	RBI	BB	SO	AVG	OBP	SLG	PRO+	BR/A	SB	CS	SBR	FA	FR	G/POS	TPR
1998	Bos-A	39	96	10	27	6	0	1	15	7	20	.281	.343	.375	87	-2	1	0	0	.974	-3	2-32/3-5,S-1	-0.3

■ ED MERRILL Merrill, Edward Mason b: 5/1860, Maysville, Ky. d: 8/18/24, Chicago, Ill. 5'11", 176 lbs. Deb: 5/5/1882

YEAR	TM/L	G	AB	R	H	2B	3B	HR	RBI	BB	SO	AVG	OBP	SLG	PRO+	BR/A	SB	CS	SBR	FA	FR	G/POS	TPR
1882	Lou-a	1	0	0	0	0	0	0		0		—	—	—	—	0				.000	-0	/O-1	0.0
	Wor-N	2	8	0	1	0	0	0	4	0	1	.125	.125	.125	-19	-1				.714	-1	/3-2	-0.1
1884	Ind-a	55	196	14	35	3	1	0		6		.179	.207	.204	35	-13				.900	-4	2-55	-1.5
Total	2	58	204	14	36	3	1	0	4	6	1	.176	.204	.201	33	-14				.900	-5	/2-55,3-2,O-1	-1.6

■ LLOYD MERRIMAN Merriman, Lloyd Archer "Citation" b: 8/2/24, Clovis, Cal. BL/TL, 6', 195 lbs. Deb: 4/24/49

YEAR	TM/L	G	AB	R	H	2B	3B	HR	RBI	BB	SO	AVG	OBP	SLG	PRO+	BR/A	SB	CS	SBR	FA	FR	G/POS	TPR
1949	Cin-N	103	287	35	66	12	5	4	26	21	36	.230	.285	.348	68	-14	2			.969	-1	O-86	-1.7
1950	Cin-N	92	298	44	77	15	3	2	31	30	23	.258	.330	.349	79	-9	6			.989	-4	O-84	-1.6
1951	Cin-N	114	359	34	87	23	2	5	36	31	34	.242	.303	.359	76	-12	8	4	0	.997	9	*O-102	-0.7
1954	Cin-N	73	112	12	30	8	1	0	16	23	10	.268	.406	.357	98	1	3	0	1	.981	-1	O-25	0.0
1955	Chi-A	1	1	0	0	0	0	0	0	0	0	.000	.000	.000	-97	-0	0	0	0	.000	0	H	0.0
	Chi-N	72	145	15	31	6	1	1	8	21	21	.214	.313	.290	62	-8	1	0	0	.977	-6	O-47	-1.5
Total	5	455	1202	140	291	64	12	12	117	126	124	.242	.317	.345	75	-42	20	4		.985	-2	O-344	-5.5

■ GEORGE MERRITT Merritt, George Washington b: 4/14/1880, Paterson, N.J. d: 2/21/38, Memphis, Tenn. TR , 6', 160 lbs. Deb: 9/6/01

YEAR	TM/L	G	AB	R	H	2B	3B	HR	RBI	BB	SO	AVG	OBP	SLG	PRO+	BR/A	SB	CS	SBR	FA	FR	G/POS	TPR
1901	Pit-N	4	11	2	3	0	1	0	0	0		.273	.385	.455	139	1	0			1.000	-0	/P-3	0.0
1902	Pit-N	2	9	2	3	1	0	0	2	0		.333	.333	.444	135	0	0			1.000	1	/O-2	0.1
1903	Pit-N	9	27	4	4	0	1	0	3	2		.148	.233	.222	29	-3	1			.889	-2	/O-7,P-1	-0.4
Total	3	15	47	8	10	1	2	0	5	2		.213	.288	.319	74	-2	1			.929	-1	/O-9,P-4	-0.3

■ HERM MERRITT Merritt, Herman G. b: 11/12/1900, Independence, Kan. d: 5/26/27, Kansas City, Mo. BR/TR, Deb: 8/24/21

YEAR	TM/L	G	AB	R	H	2B	3B	HR	RBI	BB	SO	AVG	OBP	SLG	PRO+	BR/A	SB	CS	SBR	FA	FR	G/POS	TPR
1921	Det-A	20	46	3	17	1	2	0	6	1	5	.370	.396	.478	123	2	1	0	0	.882	-6	S-17	-0.3

■ JOHN MERRITT Merritt, John Howard b: 10/12/1894, Tupelo, Miss. d: 11/3/55, Tupelo, Miss. BR/TL, 5'11", 170 lbs. Deb: 9/27/13

YEAR	TM/L	G	AB	R	H	2B	3B	HR	RBI	BB	SO	AVG	OBP	SLG	PRO+	BR/A	SB	CS	SBR	FA	FR	G/POS	TPR
1913	NY-N	1	0	0	0	0	0	0	0	0	0	—	—	—	—	0	0			.000	-0	/O-1	0.0

■ BILL MERRITT Merritt, William Henry b: 7/30/1870, Lowell, Mass. d: 11/17/37, Lowell, Mass. BR/TR, 5'7", 160 lbs. Deb: 8/8/1891

YEAR	TM/L	G	AB	R	H	2B	3B	HR	RBI	BB	SO	AVG	OBP	SLG	PRO+	BR/A	SB	CS	SBR	FA	FR	G/POS	TPR
1891	Chi-N	11	42	4	9	1	0	0	4	2	2	.214	.250	.238	42	-3	0			.955	-3	C-11/1-1	-0.5
1892	Lou-N	46	168	22	33	4	2	1	13	11	15	.196	.246	.262	58	-9	3			.940	-3	C-46	-0.8
1893	Bos-N	39	141	30	49	6	3	3	26	13	13	.348	.403	.496	128	5	3			.945	-4	C-37/O-2	0.3
1894	Bos-N	10	26	3	6	1	0	0	6	8	0	.231	.412	.269	62	-1	0			.881	1	/C-8,O-1	0.0

YEAR	TM/L	G	AB	R	H	2B	3B	HR	RBI	BB	SO	AVG	OBP	SLG	PRO+	BR/A	SB	CS	SBR	FA	FR	G/POS	TPR
	Pit-N	36	109	18	30	1	2	1	18	15	7	.275	.363	.349	73	-4	2			.952	-1	C-28/1-4,O-2	-0.2
	Cin-N	29	113	17	37	6	1	1	21	9	3	.327	.387	.425	92	-2	4			.953	-3	C-24/3-3,1-1,O-1	-0.2
	Yr	75	248	38	73	8	3	2	45	32	10	.294	.379	.375	81	-7	6			.941	-3	C-60/1-5,O-4,3-3	-0.4
1895	Cin-N	22	79	9	14	2	0	0	12	6	5	.177	.235	.203	13	-10	2			.955	-1	C-20/2-1	-0.8
	Pit-N	67	239	32	68	5	1	0	27	18	16	.285	.340	.314	73	-9	2			.935	-2	C-63/1-2	-0.4
	Yr	89	318	41	82	7	1	0	39	24	21	.258	.314	.286	57	-20	4			.939	-3	C-83/1-2,2-1	-1.2
1896	Pit-N	77	282	26	82	8	2	1	42	18	10	.291	.336	.344	83	-7	3			.941	2	C-62/3-5,2-3,1-3,S	0.2
1897	Pit-N	62	209	21	55	6	1	1	26	9		.263	.297	.316	64	-11	2			.946	-4	C-53/1-7	-0.8
1899	Bos-N	1	2	0	0	0	0	0	0	0	0	.000	.333	.000	-5	-0	0			1.000	0	/C-1	0.0
Total	8	400	1410	182	383	40	12	8	195	109	71	.272	.327	.334	75	-52	21			.942	-19	C-353/1-18,3-8,O2S	-3.2
■ **JACK MERSON**	Merson, John Warren b: 1/17/22, Elk Ridge, Md. BR/TR, 5'11", 175 lbs. Deb: 9/14/51																						
1951	Pit-N	13	50	6	18	2	2	1	14	1	7	.360	.373	.540	138	2	0	0	0	.987	2	2-13	0.5
1952	Pit-N	111	398	41	98	20	2	5	38	22	38	.246	.287	.344	72	-15	1	1	-0	.978	-6	2-81,3-27	-1.9
1953	Bos-A	1	4	0	0	0	0	0	0	0	0	.000	.000	.000	-95	-1	0	0	0	.875	0	/2-1	-0.1
Total	3	125	452	47	116	22	4	6	52	23	45	.257	.294	.363	78	-14	1	1	-0	.978	-3	/2-95,3-27	-1.5
■ **SAM MERTES**	Mertes, Samuel Blair "Sandow" b: 8/6/1872, San Francisco, Cal. d: 3/11/45, San Francisco, Cal BR/TR, 6', 225 lbs. Deb: 6/30/1896																						
1896	Phi-N	37	143	20	34	4	4	0	14	8	10	.238	.288	.322	61	-8	19			.907	-1	O-35/S-1,2-1	-1.0
1898	Chi-N	83	269	45	80	4	8	1	47	34		.297	.388	.383	121	9	27			.880	2	O-60,S-14/2-4,1-2	0.7
1899	Chi-N	117	426	83	127	13	16	9	81	33		.298	.349	.467	126	13	45			.923	-1	*O-108/1-3,S-1	0.4
1900	Chi-N	127	481	72	142	25	4	7	60	42		.295	.356	.407	114	9	38			.923	-5	O-88,1-33/S-7	-0.2
1901	Chi-A	137	545	94	151	16	17	5	98	52		.277	.347	.396	108	7	46			.940	-6	*2-132/O-5	0.5
1902	Chi-A	129	497	60	140	23	7	1	79	37		.282	.334	.362	97	-2	46			.922	6	*O-120/S-5,CP123	-0.3
1903	NY-N	138	517	100	145	**32**	14	7	**104**	61		.280	.360	.437	122	14	45			**.973**	8	*O-137/C-1,1-1	1.3
1904	NY-N	148	532	83	147	28	11	4	78	54		.276	.346	.393	123	14	47			.956	-1	*O-147/S-1	0.5
1905	*NY-N	150	551	81	154	27	17	5	108	56		.279	.351	.417	126	17	52			.960	-11	*O-150	-0.1
1906	NY-N	71	253	37	60	9	6	1	33	29		.237	.323	.332	102	1	21			.970	1	O-71	-0.1
	StL-N	53	191	20	47	7	4	0	19	16		.246	.304	.325	100	-0	10			.890	-6	O-53	-1.0
	Yr	124	444	57	107	16	10	1	52	45		.241	.315	.329	101	1	31			.938	-5	*O-124	-1.1
Total	10	1190	4405	695	1227	188	108	40	721	422	10	.279	.346	.398	113	73	396			.938	-14	O-974,2-138/1SC3P	0.7
■ **LENNIE MERULLO**	Merullo, Leonard Richard b: 5/5/17, Boston, Mass. BR/TR, 5'11", 168 lbs. Deb: 9/12/41 F																						
1941	Chi-N	7	17	3	6	1	0	0	1	2	0	.353	.421	.412	140	1	1			.968	2	/S-7	0.3
1942	Chi-N	143	515	53	132	23	3	2	37	35	45	.256	.310	.324	89	-8	14			.946	-1	*S-143	0.0
1943	Chi-N	129	453	37	115	18	3	1	25	26	42	.254	.297	.313	78	-14	7			.940	-12	*S-125	-1.8
1944	Chi-N	66	193	20	41	8	1	1	16	16	18	.212	.276	.280	57	-11	3			.937	2	S-56/1-1	-0.5
1945	*Chi-N	121	394	40	94	18	0	2	37	31	30	.239	.297	.299	68	-17	7			.948	-4	*S-118	-1.3
1946	Chi-N	65	126	14	19	8	0	0	7	11	13	.151	.219	.214	24	-13	2			.946	18	S-44	0.7
1947	Chi-N	108	373	24	90	16	1	0	29	15	26	.241	.274	.290	52	-26	4			.949	7	*S-108	-1.4
Total	7	639	2071	191	497	92	8	6	152	136	174	.240	.291	.301	69	-88	38			.945	11	S-601/1-1	-4.0
■ **MATT MERULLO**	Merullo, Matthew Bates b: 8/4/65, Winchester, Mass. BL/TR, 6'2", 200 lbs. Deb: 4/12/89 F																						
1989	Chi-A	31	81	5	18	1	0	1	8	6	14	.222	.276	.272	56	-5	0	1	-1	.973	-4	C-27/D-1	-0.8
1991	Chi-A	80	140	8	32	1	0	5	21	9	18	.229	.275	.343	72	-6	0	0	0	.989	-1	C-27,1-16/D-6	-0.6
1992	Chi-A	24	50	3	9	1	1	0	3	1	8	.180	.212	.240	27	-5	0	0	0	.971	-1	C-16/D-1	-0.5
1993	Chi-A	8	20	1	1	0	0	0	0	0	1	.050	.050	.050	-75	-5	0	0	0	.000	0	/D-6	-0.5
1994	Cle-A	4	10	1	1	0	0	0	0	2	1	.100	.250	.100	-5	-2	0	0	0	.957	-0	/C-4	-0.2
1995	Min-A	76	195	19	55	14	1	1	27	14	27	.282	.340	.379	87	-4	0	1	-1	.987	-9	C-46,D-13/1-2	-1.1
Total	6	223	496	37	116	17	2	7	59	32	69	.234	.286	.319	64	-25	0	2	-1	.981	-14	C-120/D-27,1-18	-3.7
■ **STEVE MESNER**	Mesner, Stephan Mathias b: 1/13/18, Los Angeles, Cal. d: 4/6/81, San Diego, Cal. BR/TR, 5'9", 178 lbs. Deb: 9/23/38																						
1938	Chi-N	2	4	2	1	0	0	0	0	1	1	.250	.400	.250	80	-0	0			.667	-1	/S-1	-0.1
1939	Chi-N	17	43	7	12	4	0	0	6	3	4	.279	.340	.372	90	-1	0			.927	1	S-12/2-1,3-1	0.2
1941	StL-N	24	69	8	10	1	0	0	10	5	6	.145	.203	.159	3	-9	0			.958	5	3-22	-0.3
1943	Cin-N	137	504	53	137	26	1	0	52	26	20	.272	.309	.327	85	-11	6			.944	1	*3-130	-0.9
1944	Cin-N	121	414	31	100	17	4	1	47	34	20	.242	.301	.309	75	-14	1			.951	-7	*3-120	-2.1
1945	Cin-N	150	540	52	137	19	1	1	52	52	18	.254	.322	.298	74	-18	4			.971	12	*3-148/2-3	-0.2
Total	6	451	1574	153	397	67	6	2	167	121	69	.252	.308	.306	75	-52	11			.956	10	3-421/S-13,2-4	-3.4
■ **BOBBY MESSENGER**	Messenger, Charles Walter b: 3/19/1884, Bangor, Me. d: 7/10/51, Bath, Maine BB/TR, 5'10.5", 165 lbs. Deb: 8/30/09																						
1909	Chi-A	31	112	18	19	1	1	0	0	13		.170	.268	.196	49	-6	7			.950	-2	O-31	-1.0
1910	Chi-A	9	26	7	6	0	1	0	4	4		.231	.375	.308	119	1	3			.846	-0	/O-8	0.0
1911	Chi-A	13	17	4	2	0	1	0	0	3		.118	.250	.235	37	-1	0			.875	-1	/O-4	-0.2
1914	StL-A	1	2	0	0	0	0	0	0	0	0	.000	.000	.000	-99	-0	0			.000	-0	/O-1	-0.1
Total	4	54	157	29	27	1	3	0	4	20	0	.172	.282	.217	57	-7	10			.918	-3	/O-44	-1.3
■ **TOM MESSITT**	Messitt, Thomas John b: 7/27/1874, Frankfort, Pa. d: 9/22/34, Chicago, Ill. 5'9", 177 lbs. Deb: 9/14/1899																						
1899	Lou-N	3	11	0	1	0	0	0	0	0		.091	.091	.091	-50	-2	0			1.000	1	/C-3	-0.1
■ **AL METCALF**	Metcalf, Alfred Tristram b: 12/31/1852, Brooklyn, N.Y. d: 9/2/14, Brooklyn, N.Y. Deb: 5/27/1875																						
1875	Mut-n	8	32	2	7	0	0	0	1	0	3	.219	.219	.219	50	-2	2	0	1	.667	-2	/3-5,O-2,S-1	-0.2
■ **MIKE METCALFE**	Metcalfe, Michael Henry b: 1/2/73, Quantico, Va. BR/TR, 5'10", 175 lbs. Deb: 9/18/98																						
1998	LA-N	4	1	0	0	0	0	0	0	0	1	.000	.000	.000	-99	-0	2	0	1	.000	0	/2-1	0.0
■ **SCAT METHA**	Metha, Frank Joseph b: 12/13/13, Los Angeles, Cal. d: 3/2/75, Fountain Valley, Cal. BR/TR, 5'11", 165 lbs. Deb: 4/22/40																						
1940	Det-A	26	37	6	9	0	1	0	3	2	8	.243	.282	.297	46	-3	0	1	-1	.960	4	2-10/3-6	0.0
■ **BUD METHENY**	Metheny, Arthur Beauregard b: 6/1/15, St.Louis, Mo. BL/TL, 5'11", 190 lbs. Deb: 4/27/43																						
1943	*NY-A	103	360	51	94	18	2	9	36	39	34	.261	.333	.397	113	5	2	3	-1	.963	-12	O-91	-1.4
1944	NY-A	137	518	72	124	16	1	14	67	56	57	.239	.316	.355	89	-8	5	5	-2	.956	-8	*O-132	-2.6
1945	NY-A	133	509	64	126	18	2	8	53	54	31	.248	.325	.338	88	-7	5	2	0	.984	-6	*O-128	-2.2
1946	NY-A	3	3	0	0	0	0	0	0	0	0	.000	.000	.000	-99	-1	0	0	0	.000	0	H	-0.1
Total	4	376	1390	187	344	52	5	31	156	149	122	.247	.323	.359	94	-11	12	10	-2	.968	-26	O-351	-6.3
■ **CATFISH METKOVICH**	Metkovich, George Michael b: 10/8/20, Angels Camp, Cal. d: 5/17/95, Costa Mesa, Cal. BL/TL, 6'1", 185 lbs. Deb: 7/16/43																						
1943	Bos-A	78	321	34	79	14	4	5	27	19	38	.246	.294	.361	90	-5	1	3	-2	.955	-3	O-76/1-2	-1.5
1944	Bos-A	134	549	94	152	28	8	9	59	31	57	.277	.319	.406	108	3	13	4	2	.962	5	O-82,1-50	0.3
1945	Bos-A	138	539	65	140	26	3	5	62	51	70	.260	.331	.347	94	-4	19	6	2	.985	-4	1-97,O-42	-1.6
1946	*Bos-A	86	281	42	69	15	2	4	25	36	39	.246	.333	.356	88	-4	8	3	1	.948	-11	O-81	-1.9
1947	Cle-A	126	473	68	120	22	7	5	40	32	51	.254	.302	.362	86	-11	5	3	-0	.989	1	*O-119/1-1	-1.7
1949	Chi-A	93	338	50	80	9	4	5	45	41	24	.237	.321	.331	75	-13	5	4	-1	.968	-7	O-87	-2.5
1951	Pit-N	120	423	51	124	21	3	3	40	28	23	.293	.338	.378	90	-6	3	2	-0	.994	1	O-69,1-37	-0.9
1952	Pit-N	125	373	41	101	18	3	7	41	32	29	.271	.335	.391	98	-1	5	2	0	.988	-7	1-72,O-33	-1.1
1953	Pit-N	26	41	5	6	0	1	1	7	6	3	.146	.255	.268	37	-4	0	0	0	1.000	-1	/1-5,O-4	-0.5
	Chi-N	61	124	19	29	9	0	2	12	16	10	.234	.326	.355	76	-4	2	1	0	1.000	-5	O-38/1-7	-1.0
	Yr	87	165	24	35	9	1	3	19	22	13	.212	.309	.333	66	-8	2	1	0	1.000	-6	O-42,1-12	-1.5
1954	Mil-N	68	123	7	34	5	1	1	15	15	15	.276	.360	.358	94	-1	0	0	0	1.000	1	1-18,O-13	-0.1
Total	10	1055	3585	476	934	167	36	47	373	307	359	.261	.323	.367	91	-49	61	28	2	.976	-28	O-644,1-289	-12.5

YEAR	TM/L	G	AB	R	H	2B	3B	HR	RBI	BB	SO	AVG	OBP	SLG	PRO+	BR/A	SB	CS	SBR	FA	FR	G/POS	TPR
■ CHARLIE METRO	Metro, Charles (b: Charles Moreskonich) b: 4/28/19, Nanty Glo, Pa. BR/TR, 5′11.5″, 178 lbs. Deb: 5/4/43 MC																						
1943	Det-A	44	40	12	8	0	0	0	2	3	6	.200	.256	.200	32	-3	1	1	-0	.966	-2	O-14	-0.6
1944	Det-A	38	78	8	15	0	1	0	5	3	10	.192	.222	.218	25	-8	1	0	0	1.000	-2	O-20	-1.0
	Phi-A	24	40	4	4	0	0	0	1	7	6	.100	.234	.100	-3	-5	0	0	0	1.000	-1	O-11/3-5,2-2	-0.7
	Yr	62	118	12	19	0	1	0	6	10	16	.161	.227	.178	16	-13	1	0	0	1.000	-2	O-31/3-5,2-2	-1.7
1945	Phi-A	65	200	18	42	10	1	3	15	23	33	.210	.291	.315	76	-6	1	1	-0	.972	-5	O-57	-1.5
Total	3	171	358	42	69	10	2	3	23	36	55	.193	.266	.257	51	-22	3	2	-0	.980	-9	O-102/3-5,2-2	-3.8
■ LENNY METZ	Metz, Leonard Raymond b: 7/6/1899, Louisville, Colo. d: 2/24/53, Denver, Colo. BR/TR, 5′10.5″, 170 lbs. Deb: 9/11/23																						
1923	Phi-N	12	37	4	8	0	0	0	3	4	3	.216	.310	.216	37	-3	0	0	0	.969	1	/2-6,S-6	-0.2
1924	Phi-N	7	7	1	2	0	0	0	1	1	0	.286	.375	.286	71	-0	0	0	0	.846	0	/S-6	0.0
1925	Phi-N	11	14	1	0	0	0	0	0	0	2	.000	.000	.000	-92	-4	0	0	0	1.000	2	/S-9,2-2	-0.2
Total	3	30	58	6	10	0	0	0	4	5	5	.172	.250	.172	11	-8	0	0	0	.951	3	/S-21,2-8	-0.4
■ ROGER METZGER	Metzger, Roger Henry b: 10/10/47, Fredericksburg, Tex BB/TR, 6′, 165 lbs. Deb: 6/16/70																						
1970	Chi-N	1	2	0	0	0	0	0	0	0	0	.000	.000	.000	-89	-1	0	0	0	.833	1	/S-1	0.1
1971	Hou-N	150	562	64	132	14	**11**	0	26	44	50	.235	.295	.299	70	-22	15	6	1	.977	-5	*S-148	-0.7
1972	Hou-N	153	641	84	142	12	3	2	38	60	71	.222	.289	.259	58	-34	23	9	2	.971	5	*S-153	-0.7
1973	Hou-N	154	580	67	145	11	**14**	1	35	39	70	.250	.301	.322	73	-21	10	4	1	**.982**	-19	*S-149	-2.1
1974	Hou-N	143	572	66	145	18	10	0	30	37	73	.253	.299	.320	76	-19	9	7	-2	.976	-11	*S-143	-1.3
1975	Hou-N	127	450	54	102	7	9	2	26	41	39	.227	.291	.296	68	-20	4	5	-2	.977	11	*S-126	0.2
1976	Hou-N	152	481	37	101	13	8	0	29	52	63	.210	.287	.270	65	-23	1	1	-0	**.986**	-3	*S-150/2-2	-0.9
1977	Hou-N	97	269	24	50	9	6	0	16	32	24	.186	.272	.264	49	-20	2	0	1	.973	-4	S-96/2-1	-1.4
1978	Hou-N	45	123	11	27	4	1	0	6	12	9	.220	.289	.268	61	-6	0	0	0	.964	-4	S-42/2-1	-0.6
	SF-N	75	235	17	61	6	1	0	17	12	17	.260	.296	.294	68	-10	8	1	2	.974	-12	S-74	-1.3
	Yr	120	358	28	88	10	2	0	23	24	26	.246	.293	.285	66	-17	8	1	2	.970	-16	*S-116/2-1	-1.9
1979	SF-N	94	259	24	65	7	8	0	31	23	31	.251	.312	.340	83	-6	11	3	2	.956	2	S-78,2-10/3-1	0.6
1980	SF-N	28	27	5	2	0	0	0	0	3	2	.074	.167	.074	-31	-5	0	0	0	.971	3	S-13/2-1	-0.2
Total	11	1219	4201	453	972	101	71	5	254	355	449	.231	.293	.293	67	-188	83	36	3	.976	-36	*S-1173/2-15,3-1	-8.3
■ WILLIAM METZIG	Metzig, William Andrew b: 12/4/18, Ft.Dodge, Iowa BR/TR, 6′1″, 180 lbs. Deb: 9/19/44																						
1944	Chi-A	5	16	1	2	0	0	0	1	1	4	.125	.176	.125	-13	-2	0	0	0	1.000	2	/2-5	0.0
■ ALEX METZLER	Metzler, Alexander b: 1/4/03, Fresno, Cal. d: 11/30/73, Fresno, Cal. BL/TR, 5′9″, 167 lbs. Deb: 9/16/25																						
1925	Chi-N	9	38	2	7	2	0	0	2	3	7	.184	.244	.237	23	-4	0	0	0	1.000	2	/O-9	-0.3
1926	Phi-A	20	67	8	16	3	0	0	12	7	5	.239	.311	.284	53	-5	1	0	0	1.000	2	O-17	-0.4
1927	Chi-A	134	543	87	173	29	11	3	61	61	39	.319	.396	.429	117	15	15	11	-2	.965	16	*O-134	1.9
1928	Chi-A	139	464	71	141	18	14	3	55	77	30	.304	.410	.422	121	17	16	8	0	.968	-4	*O-134	0.5
1929	Chi-A	146	568	80	156	23	13	2	49	80	45	.275	.367	.371	92	-5	9	5	-0	.960	1	*O-142	-1.3
1930	Chi-A	56	79	12	14	4	0	0	5	11	6	.177	.278	.228	31	-8	0	2	-1	.969	-5	O-27	-1.4
	StL-A	56	209	30	54	6	3	1	23	21	12	.258	.326	.330	65	-11	5	1	1	.951	-5	O-56	-1.8
	Yr	112	288	42	68	10	3	1	28	32	18	.236	.313	.302	57	-19	5	3	-0	.955	-10	O-83	-3.2
Total	6	560	1968	290	561	85	41	9	207	260	144	.285	.374	.384	97	-0	46	27	-2	.965	6	O-519	-2.8
■ HENSLEY MEULENS	Meulens, Hensley Filemon Acasio "Bam-Bam" b: 6/23/67, Willemstad, Curacao BR/TR, 6′3″, 212 lbs. Deb: 8/23/89																						
1989	NY-A	8	28	2	5	0	0	0	1	2	8	.179	.233	.179	18	-3	0	1	-1	.875	2	/3-8	-0.1
1990	NY-A	23	83	12	20	7	0	3	10	9	25	.241	.337	.434	113	1	1	0	0	.963	3	O-23	0.4
1991	NY-A	96	288	37	64	8	1	6	29	18	97	.222	.277	.319	64	-14	3	0	1	.967	2	O-73,D-13/1-7	-1.4
1992	NY-A	2	5	1	3	0	0	1	1	1	0	.600	.667	1.200	416	2	0	0	0	1.000	0	/3-2	0.2
1993	NY-A	30	53	8	9	1	1	2	5	8	19	.170	.279	.340	67	-3	0	1	-1	1.000	-4	O-24/1-3,3-1	-0.8
1997	Mon-N	16	24	6	7	1	0	2	6	4	10	.292	.393	.583	152	2	0	1	-1	1.000	-2	/O-8,1-3	-0.1
1998	Ari-N	7	15	1	1	0	0	1	1	0	6	.067	.067	.267	-19	-3	0	0	0	1.000	-1	/O-4	-0.4
Total	7	182	496	67	109	17	2	15	53	42	165	.220	.290	.353	76	-17	4	3	-1	.972	-0	O-132/1-13,D-13,3	-2.2
■ IRISH MEUSEL	Meusel, Emil Frederick b: 6/9/1893, Oakland, Cal. d: 3/1/63, Long Beach, Cal. BR/TR, 5′11.5″, 178 lbs. Deb: 10/1/14 FC																						
1914	Was-A	1	2	0	0	0	0	0	0	0	0	.000	.000	.000	-96	-0	0			1.000	-0	/O-1	-0.1
1918	Phi-N	124	473	48	132	25	6	4	62	30	21	.279	.323	.383	108	3	18			.972	8	*O-120/2-4	0.6
1919	Phi-N	135	521	65	159	26	7	5	59	15	13	.305	.327	.411	113	7	24			.968	-2	*O-128	-0.4
1920	Phi-N	138	518	75	160	27	8	14	69	32	27	.309	.349	.473	129	17	17	11	-2	.929	-5	*O-129/1-3	0.2
1921	Phi-N	84	343	59	121	21	7	12	51	18	17	.353	.385	.560	136	17	8	4	0	.929	2	O-84	1.2
	*NY-N	62	243	37	80	12	6	2	36	15	12	.329	.373	.453	117	6	5	9	-4	.971	-1	O-62	-0.3
	Yr	146	586	96	201	33	13	14	87	33	29	.343	.380	.515	129	23	13	13	-4	.947	1	*O-146	0.9
1922	*NY-N	154	617	100	204	28	17	16	132	35	33	.331	.369	.509	123	19	12	10	-2	.980	-8	*O-154	-0.3
1923	*NY-N	146	595	102	177	22	14	19	**125**	38	16	.297	.341	.477	115	10	8	8	-2	.949	-8	*O-145	-0.9
1924	*NY-N	139	549	75	170	26	9	6	102	33	18	.310	.351	.423	109	7	11	7	-1	.967	-7	*O-138	-1.0
1925	NY-N	135	516	82	169	35	8	21	111	26	19	.328	.363	.548	135	24	5	4	-1	.959	0	*O-126	1.4
1926	NY-N	129	449	51	131	25	10	6	65	16	18	.292	.322	.432	103	-0	5			.958	-5	*O-112	-1.3
1927	Bro-N	42	74	7	18	3	1	1	7	11	5	.243	.341	.351	85	-1	0			1.000	-0	O-17	-0.3
Total	11	1289	4900	701	1521	250	93	106	819	269	199	.310	.348	.464	118	107	113	53		.959	-25	*O-1216/2-4,1-3	-1.2
■ BOB MEUSEL	Meusel, Robert William "Long Bob" b: 7/19/1896, San Jose, Cal. d: 11/28/77, Downey, Cal. BR/TR, 6′3″, 190 lbs. Deb: 4/14/20 F																						
1920	NY-A	119	460	75	151	40	7	11	83	20	72	.328	.359	.517	126	14	4	4	-1	.947	-10	O-64,3-45/1-2	0.0
1921	*NY-A	149	598	104	190	40	16	24	135	34	88	.318	.356	.559	128	20	17	6	2	.934	5	*O-147	1.5
1922	*NY-A	121	473	61	151	26	11	16	84	40	58	.319	.376	.522	129	18	13	8	-1	.950	-0	*O-121	0.9
1923	*NY-A	132	460	59	144	29	10	9	91	31	52	.313	.359	.478	117	9	13	15	-5	.953	-7	*O-121	-1.0
1924	NY-A	143	579	93	188	40	11	12	120	32	43	.325	.365	.494	120	14	26	14	-1	.951	-7	*O-143/3-2	-0.3
1925	NY-A	156	624	101	181	34	12	**33**	**138**	54	55	.290	.348	.542	125	18	13	14	-5	.985	-9	*O-131,3-27	-0.2
1926	*NY-A	108	413	73	130	22	3	12	81	37	32	.315	.373	.470	120	11	16	17	-5	.960	-6	*O-107	-0.7
1927	*NY-A	135	516	75	174	47	9	8	103	45	58	.337	.393	.510	137	27	24	10	1	.950	-4	*O-131	1.5
1928	*NY-A	131	518	77	154	45	5	11	113	39	56	.297	.349	.467	116	10	6	9	-4	.975	4	*O-131	0.2
1929	NY-A	100	391	46	102	15	3	10	57	17	42	.261	.292	.391	79	-14	1	5	-3	.968	3	O-96	-1.9
1930	Cin-N	113	443	62	128	30	8	10	62	26	63	.289	.330	.460	93	-7	9			.962	-4	*O-112	-1.7
Total	11	1407	5475	826	1693	368	95	156	1067	375	619	.309	.356	.497	119	121	142	102		.958	-35	*O-1304/3-74,1-2	-1.7
■ BENNY MEYER	Meyer, Bernhard "Earache" b: 1/1/1888, Hematite, Mo. d: 2/6/74, Festus, Mo. BR/TR, 5′9″, 170 lbs. Deb: 4/9/13 C																						
1913	Bro-N	38	87	12	17	0	1	1	10	10	14	.195	.278	.253	51	-5	8			.943	-2	O-26/C-1	-0.9
1914	Bal-F	143	500	76	152	18	10	5	40	71	53	.304	.395	.410	116	6	23			.916	-11	*O-132/S-4	-1.0
1915	Bal-F	35	120	20	29	2	0	0	5	37	13	.242	.424	.258	91	-0	6			.931	-3	O-34	-0.6
	Buf-F	93	333	37	77	8	6	1	29	40	37	.231	.316	.300	72	-17	9			.947	-6	O-88	-3.0
	Yr	128	453	57	106	10	6	1	34	77	50	.234	.348	.289	78	-17	15			.943	-10	*O-122	-3.6
1925	Phi-N	1	1	1	1	1	0	0	0	0	0	1.000	1.000	2.000	594	1	0	0	0	.000	0	/2-1	0.1
Total	4	310	1041	146	276	29	17	7	84	158	117	.265	.365	.346	95	-15	46	0		.931	-22	O-280/S-4,2-1,C-1	-5.4
■ DAN MEYER	Meyer, Daniel Thomas b: 8/3/52, Hamilton, Ohio BL/TR, 5′11″, 180 lbs. Deb: 9/14/74																						
1974	Det-A	13	50	5	10	1	1	3	7	1	1	.200	.231	.440	86	-1	1	0	0	.967	1	O-12	-0.1
1975	Det-A	122	470	56	111	17	3	8	47	26	25	.236	.279	.336	70	-19	8	3	1	.950	-0	O-74,1-46	-2.6
1976	Det-A	105	294	37	74	8	4	2	16	17	22	.252	.293	.327	78	-8	10	0	3	.988	-4	O-47,1-19/D-1	-1.3
1977	Sea-A	159	582	75	159	24	4	22	90	43	51	.273	.324	.442	107	5	11	8	-2	.992	1	*1-159	-0.6
1978	Sea-A	123	444	38	101	18	1	8	56	24	39	.227	.267	.327	66	-21	7	3	0	.989	-2	*1-121/O-2,D-1	-3.0
1979	Sea-A	144	525	72	146	21	7	20	74	29	35	.278	.321	.459	106	3	11	7	-1	.936	-14	*3-101,O-31,1-15	-1.4
1980	Sea-A	146	531	56	146	25	6	11	71	31	42	.275	.316	.407	96	-4	8	4	0	.961	-10	*O-123/3-5,1-4,D-7	-1.9

YEAR	TM/L	G	AB	R	H	2B	3B	HR	RBI	BB	SO	AVG	OBP	SLG	PRO+	BR/A	SB	CS	SBR	FA	FR	G/POS	TPR
1981	Sea-A	83	252	26	66	10	1	3	22	10	16	.262	.293	.345	80	-7	4	3	-1	.961	-2	3-49,O-14/1-3,D-3	-1.1
1982	Oak-A	120	383	28	92	17	3	8	59	18	33	.240	.274	.363	77	-13	1	1	-0	.990	-3	1-58,D-38,O-11	-2.2
1983	Oak-A	69	169	15	32	9	0	1	13	19	11	.189	.271	.260	50	-11	0	0	0	.987	-6	1-41,D-12,O-11,/3-1	-2.0
1984	Oak-A	20	22	1	7	3	1	0	4	0	2	.318	.318	.545	143	1	0	0	0	.944	0	/1-3,D-1	0.1
1985	Oak-A	14	12	2	0	0	0	0	0	1	0	.000	.077	.000	-83	-3	0	0	0	.000	-0	/3-1,O-1,D-1	-0.4
Total	12	1118	3734	411	944	153	31	86	459	219	277	.253	.296	.379	86	-80	61	29	1	.991	-38	1-469,O-326,3/D	-16.5

■ GEORGE MEYER Meyer, George Francis b: 8/3/09, Chicago, Ill. d: 1/3/92, Hoffman Estates, Ill. BR/TR, 5'9", 160 lbs. Deb: 9/3/38

YEAR	TM/L	G	AB	R	H	2B	3B	HR	RBI	BB	SO	AVG	OBP	SLG	PRO+	BR/A	SB	CS	SBR	FA	FR	G/POS	TPR
1938	Chi-A	24	81	10	24	2	2	0	9	11	17	.296	.387	.370	89	-1	3	1	0	.967	6	2-24	0.6

■ DUTCH MEYER Meyer, Lambert Dalton b: 10/6/15, Waco, Tex. BR/TR, 5'10.5", 181 lbs. Deb: 6/23/37

YEAR	TM/L	G	AB	R	H	2B	3B	HR	RBI	BB	SO	AVG	OBP	SLG	PRO+	BR/A	SB	CS	SBR	FA	FR	G/POS	TPR
1937	Chi-N	1	0	0	0	0	0	0	0	0	0	—	—	—	—	0	0			.000	0	R	0.0
1940	Det-A	23	58	12	15	3	0	0	6	4	10	.259	.317	.310	58	-4	2	0	1	.960	0	2-21	-0.2
1941	Det-A	46	153	12	29	9	1	1	14	8	13	.190	.230	.281	31	-16	1	1	-0	.972	6	2-40	-0.7
1942	Det-A	14	52	5	17	3	0	2	9	4	4	.327	.386	.500	137	2	0	1	-1	.989	6	2-14	0.9
1945	Cle-A	130	524	71	153	29	8	7	48	40	32	.292	.342	.418	125	15	2	4	-2	.978	-32	*2-130	-1.2
1946	Cle-A	72	207	13	48	5	3	0	16	26	16	.232	.321	.285	75	-7	0	1	-1	.977	-13	2-64	-1.8
Total	6	286	994	113	262	49	12	10	93	82	75	.264	.322	.367	94	-9	5	7		.977	-32	2-269	-3.0

■ LEO MEYER Meyer, Leo b: 3/29/1888, Iowa d: 9/2/68, Smyrna, Del. TR , Deb: 9/27/09

YEAR	TM/L	G	AB	R	H	2B	3B	HR	RBI	BB	SO	AVG	OBP	SLG	PRO+	BR/A	SB	CS	SBR	FA	FR	G/POS	TPR
1909	Bro-N	7	23	1	3	0	0	0	0	2		.130	.200	.130	3	-3	0			.882	2	/S-7	-0.1

■ SCOTT MEYER Meyer, Scott William b: 8/19/57, Evergreen Park, Ill BR/TR, 6'1", 195 lbs. Deb: 9/10/78

YEAR	TM/L	G	AB	R	H	2B	3B	HR	RBI	BB	SO	AVG	OBP	SLG	PRO+	BR/A	SB	CS	SBR	FA	FR	G/POS	TPR
1978	Oak-A	8	9	1	1	1	0	0	0	0	4	.111	.111	.222	-9	-1	0	0	0	1.000	-1	/C-7	-0.2

■ JOEY MEYER Meyer, Tanner Joe b: 5/10/62, Honolulu, Hawaii BR/TR, 6'3", 260 lbs. Deb: 4/4/88

YEAR	TM/L	G	AB	R	H	2B	3B	HR	RBI	BB	SO	AVG	OBP	SLG	PRO+	BR/A	SB	CS	SBR	FA	FR	G/POS	TPR
1988	Mil-A	103	327	22	86	18	0	11	45	23	88	.263	.313	.419	102	0	0	1	-1	.986	-0	D-66,1-33	-0.4
1989	Mil-A	53	147	13	33	6	0	7	29	12	36	.224	.283	.408	93	-2	1	0	0	.982	-1	D-31,1-18	-0.4
Total	2	156	474	35	119	24	0	18	74	35	124	.251	.304	.416	100	-2	1	1	-0	.984	-1	/D-97,1-51	-0.8

■ BILLY MEYER Meyer, William Adam b: 1/14/1892, Knoxville, Tenn. d: 3/31/57, Knoxville, Tenn. BR/TR, 5'9.5", 170 lbs. Deb: 9/6/13 M

YEAR	TM/L	G	AB	R	H	2B	3B	HR	RBI	BB	SO	AVG	OBP	SLG	PRO+	BR/A	SB	CS	SBR	FA	FR	G/POS	TPR
1913	Chi-A	1	1	0	1	0	0	0	0	0	0	1.000	1.000	1.000	490	0	0			.857	1	/C-1	0.1
1916	Phi-A	50	138	6	32	2	2	1	12	8	11	.232	.274	.297	75	-5	3			.961	7	C-48	0.6
1917	Phi-A	62	162	9	38	5	1	0	9	7	14	.235	.271	.278	68	-7	0			.962	9	C-55	0.7
Total	3	113	301	15	71	7	3	1	21	15	25	.236	.274	.289	73	-11	3			.960	18	C-104	1.4

■ LEVI MEYERLE Meyerle, Levi Samuel "Long Levi" b: 7/1845, Philadelphia, Pa. d: 11/4/21, Philadelphia, Pa. BR/TR, 6'1", 177 lbs. Deb: 5/20/1871

YEAR	TM/L	G	AB	R	H	2B	3B	HR	RBI	BB	SO	AVG	OBP	SLG	PRO+	BR/A	SB	CS	SBR	FA	FR	G/POS	TPR
1871	Ath-n	26	130	45	64	9	3	**4**	40	2	1	**.492**	**.500**	**.700**	**243**	**23**	4	0	1	.646	-8	*3-26/P-1	0.9
1872	Ath-n	27	146	31	48	10	5	1	31	0	1	.329	.329	.486	147	7	0	0	0	.773	5	O-26/3-1	0.9
1873	Phi-n	48	238	53	83	14	4	3	58	2	0	.349	.354	.479	140	10	5	0	2	.743	-6	*3-48/S-1	0.3
1874	Chi-n	53	254	65	100	19	1	1	45	3	4	**.394**	**.401**	.488	**182**	**22**	3	1	0	.833	-15	2-31,3-14/S-5,O-5	0.4
1875	Phi-n	68	301	55	95	14	8	1	54	0	2	.316	.316	.425	149	13	7	2	1	.859	-10	2-36,3-20,1-16	0.3
1876	Phi-N	55	256	46	87	12	8	0	34	3	2	.340	.347	.449	165	17				.791	-3	*3-49/O-3,2-3,P-2	1.3
1877	Cin-N	27	107	11	35	7	2	0	15	0	4	.327	.327	.430	154	6				.822	1	S-18,2-12/O-1	0.7
1884	Phi-U	3	11	0	1	1	0	0		0		.091	.091	.182	-21	-2				.789	-1	/1-2,O-1	-0.3
Total	5 n	222	1069	249	390	66	21	10	228	7	8	.365	.369	.494	166	76	19	3	4	.704	-35	3-109/2-67,O1SP	2.8
Total	3	85	374	57	123	20	10	0	49	3	6	.329	.334	.436	156	21				.891	-4	/3-49,S-18,2O1P	1.7

■ HENRY MEYERS Meyers, Henry L. b: 1860, Philadelphia, Pa. d: 6/28/1898, Harrisburg, Pa. Deb: 8/30/1890

YEAR	TM/L	G	AB	R	H	2B	3B	HR	RBI	BB	SO	AVG	OBP	SLG	PRO+	BR/A	SB	CS	SBR	FA	FR	G/POS	TPR
1890	Phi-a	5	19	2	3	0	0	0	1	1		.158	.238	.158	17	-2	2			.684	-3	/3-5	-0.4

■ CHIEF MEYERS Meyers, John Tortes b: 7/29/1880, Riverside, Cal. d: 7/25/71, San Bernardino, Cal. BR/TR, 5'11", 194 lbs. Deb: 4/16/09

YEAR	TM/L	G	AB	R	H	2B	3B	HR	RBI	BB	SO	AVG	OBP	SLG	PRO+	BR/A	SB	CS	SBR	FA	FR	G/POS	TPR
1909	NY-N	90	220	15	61	10	5	1	30	22		.277	.359	.382	128	7	3			.963	2	C-64	1.6
1910	NY-N	127	365	25	104	18	0	1	62	40	18	.285	.362	.342	106	4	5			.969	5	*C-117	2.0
1911	*NY-N	133	391	48	130	18	9	1	61	25	33	.332	.392	.432	126	14	7			.979	-3	*C-128	2.2
1912	*NY-N	126	371	60	133	16	5	6	54	47	20	.358	.441	.477	147	26	8			.973	-10	*C-122	2.7
1913	*NY-N	120	378	37	118	18	5	3	47	37	22	.312	.387	.410	127	14	7			.967	1	*C-116	2.6
1914	NY-N	134	381	33	109	13	5	1	55	34	25	.286	.357	.354	116	8	4			.970	-12	*C-126	0.6
1915	NY-N	110	289	24	67	10	5	1	26	26	18	.232	.311	.311	94	-2	4	4	-1	**.986**	-4	C-96	0.0
1916	*Bro-N	80	239	21	59	10	3	0	21	26	15	.247	.336	.314	97	0	2			.984	7	C-74	1.5
1917	Bro-N	47	132	8	28	3	0	0	3	13	7	.212	.283	.235	58	-6	4			.974	-6	C-44	-1.0
	Bos-N	25	68	5	17	4	4	0	4	4	4	.250	.311	.426	133	2	0			1.000	7	C-24	1.2
	Yr	72	200	13	45	7	4	0	7	17	11	.225	.292	.300	82	-4	4			.984	1	C-68	0.2
Total	9	992	2834	276	826	120	41	14	363	274	162	.291	.367	.378	117	67	44	4		.974	-14	C-911	13.4

■ LOU MEYERS Meyers, Lewis Henry "Crazy Horse" b: 12/9/1859, Cincinnati, Ohio d: 11/30/20, Cincinnati, Ohio BR/TR, 5'11", 165 lbs. Deb: 5/10/1884

YEAR	TM/L	G	AB	R	H	2B	3B	HR	RBI	BB	SO	AVG	OBP	SLG	PRO+	BR/A	SB	CS	SBR	FA	FR	G/POS	TPR
1884	Cin-U	2	3	1	0	0	0	0		1		.000	.250	.000	-17	-1				.667	-2	/C-2,O-1	-0.2

■ MICKEY MICELOTTA Micelotta, Robert Peter b: 10/20/28, Corona, N.Y. BR/TR, 5'11", 185 lbs. Deb: 4/20/54

YEAR	TM/L	G	AB	R	H	2B	3B	HR	RBI	BB	SO	AVG	OBP	SLG	PRO+	BR/A	SB	CS	SBR	FA	FR	G/POS	TPR
1954	Phi-N	13	3	2	0	0	0	0	0	1	1	.000	.250	.000	-28	-1	0	0	0	1.000	0	/S-1	0.0
1955	Phi-N	4	4	0	0	0	0	0	0	0	0	.000	.000	.000	-99	-1	0	0	0	1.000	0	/S-2	-0.1
Total	2	17	7	2	0	0	0	0	0	1	1	.000	.125	.000	-64	-2	0	0	0	1.000	1	/S-3	-0.1

■ GENE MICHAEL Michael, Eugene Richard "Stick" b: 6/2/38, Kent, Ohio BB/TR, 6'2", 183 lbs. Deb: 7/15/66 MC

YEAR	TM/L	G	AB	R	H	2B	3B	HR	RBI	BB	SO	AVG	OBP	SLG	PRO+	BR/A	SB	CS	SBR	FA	FR	G/POS	TPR
1966	Pit-N	30	33	9	5	2	1	0	2	0	7	.152	.152	.273	15	-4	0	0	0	.903	5	/S-8,2-2,3-1	0.2
1967	LA-N	98	223	20	45	3	1	0	7	11	30	.202	.246	.224	39	-18	1	3	-2	.950	5	S-83	-1.0
1968	NY-A	61	116	8	23	3	0	1	8	2	23	.198	.218	.250	43	-8	3	2	-0	.939	-1	S-43/P-1	-0.7
1969	NY-A	119	412	41	112	24	4	2	31	43	56	.272	.342	.364	101	1	7	4	-0	.968	-1	*S-118	1.3
1970	NY-A	134	435	42	93	10	1	2	38	50	93	.214	.295	.255	56	-26	3	1	0	.957	2	*S-123/3-4,2-3	-0.9
1971	NY-A	139	456	36	102	15	0	3	35	48	64	.224	.302	.276	69	-18	3	3	-1	.973	17	*S-136	1.6
1972	NY-A	126	391	29	91	7	4	1	32	32	45	.233	.292	.279	73	-13	4	2	0	.969	24	*S-121	3.0
1973	NY-A	129	418	30	94	11	1	3	47	26	51	.225	.270	.278	56	-24	1	3	-2	.965	5	*S-129	-0.5
1974	NY-A	81	177	19	46	9	0	0	13	14	24	.260	.314	.311	82	-4	0	0	0	.970	5	2-45,S-39/3-2	0.5
1975	Det-A	56	145	15	31	2	0	3	13	8	28	.214	.255	.290	51	-9	0	0	0	.938	-4	S-44/2-7,3-4	-1.0
Total	10	973	2806	249	642	86	12	15	226	234	421	.229	.290	.284	66	-124	22	18	-4	.962	55	S-844/2-57,3-11,P-1	2.5

■ CASS MICHAELS Michaels, Casimir Eugene (Played In 1943 Under Real Name Of Casimir Eugene Kwietniewski)
b: 3/4/26, Detroit, Mich. d: 11/12/82, Grosse Pointe, Mich. BR/TR, 5'11", 175 lbs. Deb: 8/19/43

YEAR	TM/L	G	AB	R	H	2B	3B	HR	RBI	BB	SO	AVG	OBP	SLG	PRO+	BR/A	SB	CS	SBR	FA	FR	G/POS	TPR
1943	Chi-A	2	7	0	0	0	0	0	0	0	0	.000	.000	.000	-99	-2	0	0	0	1.000	-1	/3-2	-0.4
1944	Chi-A	27	68	4	12	4	1	0	5	2	5	.176	.200	.265	33	-6	0	0	0	.930	6	S-21/3-3	0.1
1945	Chi-A	129	445	47	109	8	5	2	54	37	28	.245	.307	.299	78	-12	8	7	-2	.936	10	*S-126/2-1	0.6
1946	Chi-A	91	291	37	75	8	0	1	22	29	36	.258	.333	.296	80	-7	9	3	1	.957	3	2-66,3-13/S-6	0.1
1947	Chi-A	110	355	31	97	15	4	3	34	39	28	.273	.350	.363	102	1	10	5	0	.982	11	2-60,3-44/S-2	1.7
1948	Chi-A	145	484	47	120	12	6	5	56	69	42	.248	.344	.329	82	-11	8	2	1	.957	13	S-85,2-55/O-1	1.0
1949	Chi-A★	154	561	73	173	27	9	6	83	101	50	.308	.417	.421	126	25	5	7	-3	.976	12	*2-154	3.9
1950	Chi-A	36	138	21	43	6	3	4	19	13	8	.312	.375	.486	122	4	0	0	0	.964	-6	2-35	-0.1
	Was-A★	106	388	48	97	8	4	4	47	55	39	.250	.345	.322	75	-14	2	3	-1	.975	8	*2-104	-0.3
	Yr	142	526	69	140	14	7	8	66	68	47	.266	.352	.365	88	-9	2	3	-1	.972	2	*2-139	-0.4
1951	Was-A	138	485	59	125	20	4	4	45	61	41	.258	.342	.340	86	-8	1	1	-0	.964	-23	*2-128	-2.6
1952	Was-A	22	86	10	20	4	1	1	7	7	15	.233	.290	.337	77	-3	0	0	0	.977	1	2-22	-0.1
	StL-A	55	166	21	44	8	2	3	25	23	16	.265	.354	.392	104	1	1	0	0	.916	-0	3-42/2-8	0.1
	Phi-A	55	200	22	50	4	5	1	18	23	11	.250	.330	.335	80	-5	3	0	1	.993	-13	2-55	-1.5

YEAR	TM/L	G	AB	R	H	2B	3B	HR	RBI	BB	SO	AVG	OBP	SLG	PRO+	BR/A	SB	CS	SBR	FA	FR	G/POS	TPR
	Yr	132	452	53	114	16	8	5	50	53	42	.252	.332	.356	89	-7	4	0	1	.989	-13	2-85,3-42	-1.5
1953	Phi-A	117	411	53	103	10	0	12	42	51	56	.251	.335	.363	85	-8	7	0	**2**	.970	-11	*2-110	-1.1
1954	Chi-A	101	282	35	74	13	2	7	44	56	31	.262	.392	.397	113	7	10	4	1	.958	-4	3-91/2-2	0.2
Total	12	1288	4367	508	1142	147	46	53	501	566	406	.262	.349	.353	92	-39	64	32	0	.973	3	2-800,S-240,3/O	1.6

■ RALPH MICHAELS Michaels, Ralph Joseph b: 5/3/02, Etna, Pa. d: 8/5/88, Monroeville, Pa. BR/TR, 5′10.5″, 178 lbs. Deb: 4/16/24

YEAR	TM/L	G	AB	R	H	2B	3B	HR	RBI	BB	SO	AVG	OBP	SLG	PRO+	BR/A	SB	CS	SBR	FA	FR	G/POS	TPR
1924	Chi-N	8	11	0	4	0	0	0	2	0	1	.364	.364	.364	95	-0	0	0	0	.929	1	/S-4	0.1
1925	Chi-N	22	50	10	14	1	0	0	6	6	9	.280	.357	.300	69	-2	1	0	0	.975	3	3-15/1-1,2-1,S-1	0.2
1926	Chi-N	2	0	1	0	0	0	0	0	0	0	—	—	—	—	0	0	2	0	.000	0	H	0.0
Total	3	32	61	11	18	1	0	0	8	6	10	.295	.358	.311	73	-2	1	0		.933	3	/3-15,S-5,2-1,1-1	0.3

■ ED MICKELSON Mickelson, Edward Allen b: 9/9/26, Ottawa, Ill. BR/TR, 6′3″, 205 lbs. Deb: 9/18/50

YEAR	TM/L	G	AB	R	H	2B	3B	HR	RBI	BB	SO	AVG	OBP	SLG	PRO+	BR/A	SB	CS	SBR	FA	FR	G/POS	TPR
1950	StL-N	5	10	1	1	0	0	0	0	2	3	.100	.250	.100	-4	-1	0			1.000	1	/1-4	-0.1
1953	StL-A	7	15	1	2	1	0	0	2	2	6	.133	.235	.200	18	-2	0	0	0	1.000	0	/1-3	-0.2
1957	Chi-N	6	12	0	0	0	0	0	1	0	4	.000	.000	.000	-99	-3	0	0	0	1.000	1	/1-2	-0.3
Total	3	18	37	2	3	1	0	0	3	4	13	.081	.171	.108	-23	-7	0	0		1.000	2	/1-9	-0.6

■ EZRA MIDKIFF Midkiff, Ezra Millington "Salt Rock" b: 11/13/1882, Salt Rock, W.Va. d: 3/20/57, Huntington, W.Va. BL/TR, 5′10″, 180 lbs. Deb: 10/5/09

YEAR	TM/L	G	AB	R	H	2B	3B	HR	RBI	BB	SO	AVG	OBP	SLG	PRO+	BR/A	SB	CS	SBR	FA	FR	G/POS	TPR
1909	Cin-N	1	2	0	0	0	0	0	0	0		.000	.000	.000	-99	-0	0			.000	-1	/3-1	-0.1
1912	NY-A	21	86	9	21	1	0	0	9	7		.244	.301	.256	56	-5	4			.901	2	3-21	-0.3
1913	NY-A	83	284	22	56	9	1	0	14	12	33	.197	.232	.236	37	-23	9			.957	18	3-76/S-4,2-2	-0.5
Total	3	105	372	31	77	10	1	0	23	19	33	.207	.247	.239	41	-28	13			.942	18	/3-98,S-4,2-2	-0.9

■ DOUG MIENTKIEWICZ Mientkiewicz, Douglas Andrew b: 6/19/74, Toledo, Ohio BL/TR, 6′2″, 195 lbs. Deb: 9/18/98

YEAR	TM/L	G	AB	R	H	2B	3B	HR	RBI	BB	SO	AVG	OBP	SLG	PRO+	BR/A	SB	CS	SBR	FA	FR	G/POS	TPR
1998	Min-A	8	25	1	5	1	0	0	2	4	3	.200	.310	.240	46	-2	1	1	-0	1.000	-1	/1-8	-0.3

■ ED MIERKOWICZ Mierkowicz, Edward Frank "Butch" or "Mouse" b: 3/6/24, Wyandotte, Mich. BR/TR, 6′4″, 205 lbs. Deb: 8/31/45

YEAR	TM/L	G	AB	R	H	2B	3B	HR	RBI	BB	SO	AVG	OBP	SLG	PRO+	BR/A	SB	CS	SBR	FA	FR	G/POS	TPR
1945	*Det-A	10	15	0	2	2	0	0	2	1	3	.133	.188	.267	29	-1	0	0	0	1.000	-1	/O-6	-0.3
1947	Det-A	21	42	6	8	1	0	1	1	1	12	.190	.209	.286	36	-4	1	0	0	.947	-1	O-10	-0.5
1948	Det-A	3	5	0	1	0	0	0	1	2	2	.200	.429	.200	69	-0	0	0	0	1.000	0	/O-1	0.0
1950	StL-N	1	1	0	0	0	0	0	0	0	1	.000	.000	.000	-95	-0	0	0	0	.000	0	H	0.0
Total	4	35	63	6	11	3	0	1	4	4	18	.175	.224	.270	36	-6	1	0		.968	-2	/O-17	-0.8

■ MATT MIESKE Mieske, Matthew Todd b: 2/13/68, Midland, Mich. BR/TR, 6′, 192 lbs. Deb: 5/3/93

YEAR	TM/L	G	AB	R	H	2B	3B	HR	RBI	BB	SO	AVG	OBP	SLG	PRO+	BR/A	SB	CS	SBR	FA	FR	G/POS	TPR
1993	Mil-A	23	58	9	14	0	0	3	7	4	14	.241	.290	.397	84	-2	0	2	-1	.936	-2	O-22	-0.5
1994	Mil-A	84	259	39	67	13	1	10	38	21	62	.259	.322	.432	88	-5	3	5	-2	.976	-3	O-80/D-1	-1.1
1995	Mil-A	117	267	42	67	13	1	12	48	27	45	.251	.329	.442	93	-3	2	4	-2	.979	-3	*O-108/D-2	-0.9
1996	Mil-A	127	374	46	104	24	3	14	64	26	76	.278	.328	.471	95	-4	1	5	-3	.996	1	*O-122	-0.7
1997	Mil-A	84	253	39	63	15	3	5	21	19	50	.249	.301	.391	78	-8	1	0	0	.962	-4	O-74/D-5	-1.2
1998	Chi-N	77	97	16	29	7	0	1	12	11	17	.299	.376	.402	99	0	0	0	0	.974	-14	O-62	-1.4
Total	6	512	1308	191	344	72	8	45	190	108	264	.263	.324	.433	90	-22	7	16	-8	.978	-24	O-468/D-8	-5.8

■ LARRY MIGGINS Miggins, Lawrence Edward "Irish" b: 8/20/25, Bronx, N.Y. BR/TR, 6′4″, 198 lbs. Deb: 10/3/48

YEAR	TM/L	G	AB	R	H	2B	3B	HR	RBI	BB	SO	AVG	OBP	SLG	PRO+	BR/A	SB	CS	SBR	FA	FR	G/POS	TPR
1948	StL-N	1	1	1	0	0	0	0	0	0	0	.000	.000	.000	-95	-0	0			.000	0	H	0.0
1952	StL-N	42	96	7	22	5	1	2	10	3	19	.229	.253	.365	69	-4	0	1	-1	.967	-4	O-25/1-1	-1.1
Total	2	43	97	8	22	5	1	2	10	3	19	.227	.250	.361	67	-5	0	1		.967	-4	/O-25,1-1	-1.1

■ JOHN MIHALIC Mihalic, John Michael b: 11/13/11, Cleveland, Ohio d: 4/24/87, Ft.Oglethorpe, Ga. BR/TR, 5′11″, 172 lbs. Deb: 9/18/35

YEAR	TM/L	G	AB	R	H	2B	3B	HR	RBI	BB	SO	AVG	OBP	SLG	PRO+	BR/A	SB	CS	SBR	FA	FR	G/POS	TPR
1935	Was-A	6	22	4	5	3	0	0	6	2	3	.227	.292	.364	71	-1	1	0	0	.966	-1	/S-6	-0.1
1936	Was-A	25	88	15	21	2	1	0	8	14	14	.239	.343	.284	60	-5	2	1	0	.972	1	2-25	-0.2
1937	Was-A	38	107	13	27	5	2	0	8	17	9	.252	.355	.336	79	-3	2	1	0	.981	4	2-28/S-3	0.3
Total	3	69	217	32	53	10	3	0	22	33	26	.244	.344	.318	70	-9	5	2	0	.977	4	/2-53,S-9	0.0

■ EDDIE MIKSIS Miksis, Edward Thomas b: 9/11/26, Burlington, N.J. BR/TR, 6′0.5″, 185 lbs. Deb: 6/17/44

YEAR	TM/L	G	AB	R	H	2B	3B	HR	RBI	BB	SO	AVG	OBP	SLG	PRO+	BR/A	SB	CS	SBR	FA	FR	G/POS	TPR
1944	Bro-N	26	91	12	20	2	0	0	11	6	11	.220	.268	.242	45	-7	4			.896	-4	3-15,S-10	-1.0
1946	Bro-N	23	48	3	7	0	0	0	5	3	3	.146	.212	.146	2	-6	0			.970	0	3-13/2-1	-0.6
1947	*Bro-N	45	86	18	23	1	0	4	10	9	8	.267	.337	.419	96	-1	0			1.000	3	2-13,O-11/3-5,S-2	0.3
1948	Bro-N	86	221	28	47	7	1	2	16	19	27	.213	.278	.281	50	-15	5			.967	4	2-54,3-22/S-5	-1.0
1949	*Bro-N	50	113	17	25	5	0	1	6	7	8	.221	.267	.292	48	-8	3			.978	6	3-29/S-4,2-3,1-1	-0.3
1950	Bro-N	51	76	13	19	2	1	2	10	5	10	.250	.296	.382	75	-3	3			.964	5	2-15,S-15/3-7	0.3
1951	Bro-N	19	10	6	2	1	0	0	0	1	2	.200	.333	.300	70	-0	0	0	0	1.000	2	/3-6,2-1	0.2
	Chi-N	102	421	48	112	13	3	4	35	33	36	.266	.319	.340	76	-14	11	5	0	.969	3	*2-102	-0.6
	Yr	121	431	54	114	14	3	4	35	34	38	.265	.320	.339	76	-14	11	5	0	.969	5	*2-103/3-6	-0.4
1952	Chi-N	93	383	44	89	20	1	2	19	20	32	.232	.272	.305	59	-21	4	4	-1	.950	-13	2-54,S-40	-3.1
1953	Chi-N	142	577	61	145	17	6	8	39	33	59	.251	.293	.343	64	-31	13	4	2	.954	-13	2-92,S-53	-3.3
1954	Chi-N	38	99	9	20	3	0	2	3	3	9	.202	.225	.293	33	-10	1	0	0	.961	4	2-21/3-2,O-1	-0.4
1955	Chi-N	131	481	52	113	14	2	9	41	32	55	.235	.283	.328	62	-27	3	6	-3	**.989**	5	*O-111,3-18	-3.0
1956	Chi-N	114	356	54	85	10	3	9	27	32	40	.239	.303	.360	79	-11	4	2	0	.975	-3	3-48,O-33,2-19,/S-2	-1.4
1957	StL-N	49	38	3	8	0	0	1	2	7	7	.211	.333	.289	68	-2	0	0	0	1.000	-11	O-31	-1.3
	Bal-A	1	1	0	0	0	0	0	0	0	0	.000	.000	.000	-99	-0	0	0	0	.000	0	H	0.0
1958	Bal-A	3	2	0	0	0	0	0	0	0	1	.000	.000	.000	-99	-1	0	0	0	.000	0	/S-1	-0.1
	Cin-N	69	50	15	7	0	0	0	4	5	5	.140	.218	.140	-2	-7	1	1	-0	1.000	-4	O-32,3-14/2-7,S1	-1.2
Total	14	1042	3053	383	722	95	17	44	228	215	313	.236	.288	.322	62	-164	52	22		.962	-17	2-382,O-219,3S/1	-16.5

■ HORACE MILAN Milan, Horace Robert b: 4/7/1894, Linden, Tenn. d: 6/29/55, Texarkana, Ark. BR/TR, 5′9″, 175 lbs. Deb: 8/29/15 F

YEAR	TM/L	G	AB	R	H	2B	3B	HR	RBI	BB	SO	AVG	OBP	SLG	PRO+	BR/A	SB	CS	SBR	FA	FR	G/POS	TPR
1915	Was-A	11	27	6	11	1	1	0	7	8	7	.407	.543	.519	214	5	2			1.000	-3	O-10	0.2
1917	Was-A	31	73	8	21	3	1	0	9	4	9	.288	.342	.356	114	1	4			.932	-4	O-23	-0.4
Total	2	42	100	14	32	4	2	0	16	12	16	.320	.404	.400	144	6	6			.944	-6	/O-33	-0.2

■ CLYDE MILAN Milan, Jesse Clyde "Deerfoot" b: 3/25/1887, Linden, Tenn. d: 3/3/53, Orlando, Fla. BL/TR, 5′9″, 168 lbs. Deb: 8/19/07 FMC

YEAR	TM/L	G	AB	R	H	2B	3B	HR	RBI	BB	SO	AVG	OBP	SLG	PRO+	BR/A	SB	CS	SBR	FA	FR	G/POS	TPR
1907	Was-A	48	183	22	51	3	3	0	9	8		.279	.323	.328	117	3	8			.929	4	O-47	0.6
1908	Was-A	130	485	55	116	10	12	1	32	38		.239	.304	.315	110	5	29			.959	9	*O-122	1.1
1909	Was-A	130	400	36	80	12	4	1	15	31		.200	.268	.257	69	-14	10			.972	5	*O-120	-1.6
1910	Was-A	142	531	89	148	17	6	0	16	71		.279	.379	.333	129	22	44			.946	11	*O-142	2.9
1911	Was-A	154	616	109	194	24	8	3	35	74		.315	.395	.394	123	21	58			.957	11	*O-154	2.3
1912	Was-A	154	601	105	184	19	11	1	79	63		.306	.377	.379	116	13	**88**			.935	8	*O-154	1.3
1913	Was-A	154	579	92	174	18	9	3	54	58	25	.301	.367	.378	116	12	**75**			.932	-7	*O-154	-0.3
1914	Was-A	115	437	63	129	19	11	1	39	32	26	.295	.346	.396	118	8	38	21	-1	.949	-4	*O-113	-0.2
1915	Was-A	153	573	83	165	13	7	2	66	53	32	.288	.353	.346	107	5	40	19	1	.946	-0	*O-151	-0.2
1916	Was-A	150	565	58	154	14	3	1	45	56	31	.273	.343	.313	98	-0	34	21	-2	.961	17	*O-149	0.7
1917	Was-A	155	579	60	170	15	4	0	48	58	26	.294	.364	.333	114	11	20			.962	-5	*O-153	-0.2
1918	Was-A	128	503	56	146	18	5	0	56	36	14	.290	.344	.346	110	5	26			.972	2	*O-124	0.1
1919	Was-A	88	321	43	92	12	6	0	37	40	16	.287	.371	.361	107	4	11			.953	-3	O-86	-0.5
1920	Was-A	126	506	70	163	22	5	3	41	28	12	.322	.364	.403	106	4	10	12	-4	.971	8	*O-123	-0.2
1921	Was-A	113	406	55	117	19	11	1	40	37	13	.288	.351	.397	95	-4	4	5	-2	.931	2	O-99	-1.0
1922	Was-A	42	74	8	17	5	0	0	5	2	2	.230	.250	.297	44	-6	0	0	0	1.000	1	O-12,M	-0.6
Total	16	1982	7359	1004	2100	240	105	17	617	685	197	.285	.353	.353	109	92	495	78		.953	58	*O-1903	4.2

■ LARRY MILBOURNE Milbourne, Lawrence William b: 2/14/51, Port Norris, N.J. BB/TR, 6′, 165 lbs. Deb: 4/6/74

YEAR	TM/L	G	AB	R	H	2B	3B	HR	RBI	BB	SO	AVG	OBP	SLG	PRO+	BR/A	SB	CS	SBR	FA	FR	G/POS	TPR
1974	Hou-N	112	136	31	38	2	1	0	9	10	14	.279	.329	.309	83	-3	6	2	1	.974	17	2-87/S-8,O-4	1.7
1975	Hou-N	73	151	17	32	1	2	1	9	6	14	.212	.247	.265	45	-12	1	2	-1	.968	10	2-43,S-22	0.0
1976	Hou-N	59	145	22	36	4	0	0	7	14	10	.248	.319	.276	77	-4	6	1	1	.965	-1	2-32	-0.2

YEAR	TM/L	G	AB	R	H	2B	3B	HR	RBI	BB	SO	AVG	OBP	SLG	PRO+	BR/A	SB	CS	SBR	FA	FR	G/POS	TPR
1977	Sea-A	86	242	24	53	10	0	2	21	6	20	.219	.244	.285	44	-19	3	1	0	.982	4	2-41,S-40/3-1,D-1	-0.9
1978	Sea-A	93	234	31	53	6	2	2	20	9	6	.226	.255	.295	55	-14	5	7	-3	.989	16	3-32,S-23,2-15,D-10	0.1
1979	Sea-A	123	356	40	99	13	4	2	26	19	20	.278	.315	.354	79	-11	5	3	-0	.981	-17	S-65,2-49,3-11	-2.0
1980	Sea-A	106	258	31	68	6	6	0	26	19	13	.264	.317	.333	78	-8	7	6	-2	.976	0	2-38,S-34/3-6,D-8	-0.4
1981	*NY-A	61	163	24	51	7	2	1	12	9	14	.313	.353	.399	118	4	2	0	1	.955	-7	S-39,2-14/3-3,D-3	0.2
1982	NY-A	14	27	2	4	1	0	0	0	1	4	.148	.179	.185	0	-4	0	1	-1	.917	1	/S-9,2-3,3-3	-0.3
	Min-A	29	98	9	23	1	1	0	1	7	8	.235	.286	.265	51	-6	1	1	-0	.981	-10	2-26	-1.6
	Cle-A	82	291	29	80	11	4	2	25	12	20	.275	.308	.361	83	-7	2	5	-2	.981	-6	2-63,S-21/3-9,D-1	-1.1
	Yr	125	416	40	107	13	5	2	26	20	32	.257	.295	.327	70	-17	3	7	-3	.979	-15	2-92,S-30,3-12,/D-1	-3.0
1983	Phi-N	41	66	3	16	0	1	0	4	4	7	.242	.286	.273	56	-4	2	1	0	.963	1	2-27/S-8,3-3	-0.3
	NY-A	31	70	5	14	4	0	0	2	5	10	.200	.263	.257	46	-5	1	1	-0	1.000	3	2-19/S-6,3-4	-0.1
1984	Sea-A	79	211	22	56	5	1	1	22	12	16	.265	.305	.313	72	-8	0	2	-1	.900	-9	3-40,2-14/S-5,D-6	-1.8
Total	11	989	2448	290	623	71	24	11	184	133	176	.254	.295	.317	70	-101	41	33	-8	.974	1	2-471,S-280,3/DO	-6.7
■ **DON MILES**	Miles, Donald Ray b: 3/13/36, Indianapolis, Ind. BL/TR, 6′1″, 210 lbs. Deb: 9/9/58																						
1958	LA-N	8	22	2	4	0	0	0	0	0	6	.182	.217	.182	7	-3	0	0	0	1.000	2	/O-5	-0.2
■ **DEE MILES**	Miles, Wilson Daniel b: 2/15/09, Kellerman, Ala. d: 11/2/76, Birmingham, Ala. BL/TR, 6′, 175 lbs. Deb: 7/7/35																						
1935	Was-A	60	215	28	57	5	2	0	29	7	13	.265	.291	.307	57	-14	6	4	-1	.970	2	O-45	-1.3
1936	Was-A	25	59	8	14	1	2	0	7	1	5	.237	.250	.322	43	-6	0	1	-1	.958	0	O-10	-0.6
1939	Phi-A	106	320	49	96	17	6	1	37	15	17	.300	.331	.400	88	-7	3	4	-2	.968	-7	O-77	-1.6
1940	Phi-A	88	236	26	71	9	6	1	23	8	18	.301	.327	.403	90	-4	1	1	-0	.945	-1	O-50	-0.8
1941	Phi-A	80	170	14	53	7	1	0	15	4	8	.312	.331	.365	86	-4	0	1	-1	1.000	0	O-35	-0.6
1942	Phi-A	99	346	41	94	12	5	0	22	12	10	.272	.300	.335	79	-11	5	3	-0	.984	-3	O-81	-1.9
1943	Bos-A	45	121	9	26	2	2	0	10	3	3	.215	.234	.264	45	-9	0	2	-1	.968	-1	O-25	-1.3
Total	7	503	1467	175	411	53	24	2	143	50	74	.280	.306	.353	76	-53	15	16	-5	.971	-10	O-323	-8.1
■ **MIKE MILEY**	Miley, Michael Wilfred b: 3/30/53, Yazoo City, Miss. d: 1/6/77, Baton Rouge, La. BB/TR, 6′1″, 185 lbs. Deb: 7/6/75																						
1975	Cal-A	70	224	17	39	3	2	4	26	16	54	.174	.232	.259	42	-18	0	1	-1	.939	-9	S-70	-2.1
1976	Cal-A	14	38	4	7	2	0	0	4	4	8	.184	.262	.237	50	-2	1	0	0	.981	-2	S-14	-0.2
Total	2	84	262	21	46	5	2	4	30	20	62	.176	.237	.256	43	-20	1	1	-0	.945	-11	/S-84	-2.3
■ **FELIX MILLAN**	Millan, Felix Bernardo (Martinez) b: 8/21/43, Yabucoa, P.R. BR/TR, 5′11″, 172 lbs. Deb: 6/2/66																						
1966	Atl-N	37	91	20	25	6	0	0	5	2	6	.275	.290	.341	74	-3	3	1	0	.973	-2	2-25/S-1,3-1	-0.4
1967	Atl-N	41	136	13	32	3	3	2	6	4	10	.235	.268	.346	75	-5	0	3	-2	.972	3	2-41	-0.1
1968	Atl-N	149	570	49	165	22	2	1	33	22	26	.289	.323	.340	99	-1	6	6	-2	.980	3	*2-145	1.0
1969	*Atl-N★	162	652	98	174	23	5	6	57	34	35	.267	.311	.345	83	-15	14	3	2	**.980**	-16	*2-162	-1.6
1970	Atl-N†	142	590	100	183	25	5	2	37	35	23	.310	.354	.380	91	-7	16	5	2	.979	-19	*2-142	-1.2
1971	Atl-N★	143	577	65	167	20	8	2	45	37	22	.289	.335	.362	92	-6	11	7	-1	.982	6	*2-141	1.2
1972	Atl-N	125	498	46	128	19	3	1	38	23	28	.257	.294	.313	66	-22	6	4	-1	.987	-16	*2-120	-3.5
1973	*NY-N	153	638	82	185	23	4	3	37	35	22	.290	.333	.353	91	-7	2	2	-1	.989	-4	*2-153	-0.3
1974	NY-N	136	518	50	139	15	2	1	33	31	14	.268	.320	.311	78	-15	5	1	1	.979	-20	*2-134	-2.9
1975	NY-N	162	676	81	191	37	2	1	56	36	28	.283	.330	.348	92	-8	1	6	-3	.972	-25	*2-162	-2.8
1976	NY-N	139	531	55	150	25	2	1	35	41	19	.282	.342	.343	101	1	2	4	-2	.977	-24	*2-136	-1.8
1977	NY-N	91	314	40	78	11	2	2	21	18	9	.248	.296	.315	67	-15	1	1	-0	.977	-16	2-89	-2.6
Total	12	1480	5791	699	1617	229	38	22	403	318	242	.279	.324	.343	87	-103	67	43	-6	.980	-129	*2-1450/3-1,S-1	-15.0
■ **KEVIN MILLAR**	Millar, Kevin Charles b: 9/24/71, Los Angeles, Cal. BR/TR, 6′1″, 195 lbs. Deb: 4/11/98																						
1998	Fla-N	2	2	1	1	0	0	0	0	1	0	.500	.667	.500	219	1	0	0	0	.833	1	/3-2	0.1
■ **FRANK MILLARD**	Millard, Frank E. b: 7/4/1865, E.St.Louis, Ill. d: 7/4/1892, Galveston, Tex. Deb: 5/4/1890																						
1890	StL-a	1	1	0	0	0	0	0	0	1		.000	.500	.000	42	0	0			.625	1	/2-1	0.0
■ **DUSTY MILLER**	Miller, Charles Bradley b: 9/10/1868, Oil City, Pa. d: 9/3/45, Memphis, Tenn. BL/TR, 5′11.5″, 170 lbs. Deb: 9/23/1889																						
1889	Bal-a	11	40	4	6	1	1	0	6	2	11	.150	.209	.225	23	-4	3			.636	-7	/S-8,O-3	-1.0
1890	StL-a	26	96	17	21	5	3	1	10	8		.219	.279	.365	78	-4	4			.872	3	O-24/S-3	-0.2
1895	Cin-N	132	529	103	177	31	16	10	112	33	34	.335	.378	.510	123	14	43			.937	11	*O-132	1.2
1896	Cin-N	125	504	91	162	38	12	4	93	33	30	.321	.368	.468	112	6	76			.902	-2	*O-125	-0.5
1897	Cin-N	119	440	83	139	27	1	4	70	48		.316	.393	.409	105	3	29			.929	2	*O-119	-0.3
1898	Cin-N	152	586	99	175	24	12	3	90	38		.299	.351	.396	106	3	32			.929	8	*O-152	0.0
1899	Cin-N	80	323	44	81	12	5	0	37	9		.251	.278	.319	62	-18	18			.927	7	O-80	-1.5
	StL-N	10	39	3	8	1	0	0	3	3		.205	.279	.231	40	-3	1			.875	-1	O-10	-0.4
	Yr	90	362	47	89	13	5	0	40	12		.246	.278	.309	60	-21	19			.921	6	O-90	-1.9
Total	7	655	2557	444	769	139	50	22	421	174	75	.301	.352	.420	102	-3	206			.923	21	O-645/S-11	-2.7
■ **BRUCE MILLER**	Miller, Charles Bruce b: 3/4/47, Fort Wayne, Ind. BR/TR, 6′1″, 185 lbs. Deb: 8/4/73																						
1973	SF-N	12	21	1	3	0	0	0	2	2	3	.143	.217	.143	2	-3	0	0	0	.900	1	/3-4,2-3,S-1	-0.2
1974	SF-N	73	198	19	55	7	1	0	16	11	15	.278	.319	.323	76	-6	1	1	-0	.938	13	3-41,S-13/2-9	0.8
1975	SF-N	99	309	22	74	6	3	1	31	15	26	.239	.277	.288	55	-19	0	1	-1	.949	10	3-68,2-21/S-6	-0.9
1976	SF-N	12	25	1	4	1	0	0	2	2	5	.160	.222	.200	20	-3	0	0	0	.920	-1	/2-8,3-2	-0.4
Total	4	196	553	43	136	14	4	1	51	30	49	.246	.287	.291	59	-30	1	2	-1	.944	22	3-115/2-41,S-20	-0.7
■ **CHARLIE MILLER**	Miller, Charles Elmer b: 1/4/1892, Warrensburg, Mo. d: 4/23/72, Warrensburg, Mo. TR , Deb: 9/18/12																						
1912	StL-A	1	2	0	0	0	0	0	0	0		.000	.000	.000	-99	-1	0			1.000	-0	/S-1	-0.1
■ **CHARLIE MILLER**	Miller, Charles Hess b: 12/30/1877, Conestoga, Pa. d: 1/13/51, Millersville, Pa. BR/TR, 6′, 190 lbs. Deb: 10/2/15																						
1915	Bal-F	1	1	0	0	0	0	0	0	0	0	.000	.000	.000	-97	-0	0			.000	0	H	0.0
■ **CHUCK MILLER**	Miller, Charles Marion b: 9/18/1889, Woodville, Ohio d: 6/16/61, Houston, Tex. BL/TL, 5′8.5″, 155 lbs. Deb: 9/19/13																						
1913	StL-N	4	12	0	2	0	0	0	1	0	2	.167	.167	.167	-5	-2	0			1.000	-1	/O-3	-0.3
1914	StL-N	36	36	4	7	1	0	0	2	3	9	.194	.256	.222	43	-2	2			1.000	-3	O-14	-0.6
Total	2	40	48	4	9	1	0	0	3	3	11	.188	.235	.208	31	-4	2			1.000	-4	/O-17	-0.9
■ **DUSTY MILLER**	Miller, Dakin Evans b: 9/3/1876, Malvern, Iowa d: 4/19/50, Stockton, Cal. BL/TR, 5′10″, 175 lbs. Deb: 4/17/02																						
1902	Chi-N	51	187	17	46	4	1	0	13	7		.246	.299	.278	80	-4	10			.955	1	O-51	-0.7
■ **DAMIAN MILLER**	Miller, Damian Donald b: 10/13/69, LaCrosse, Wis. BR/TR, 6′3″, 202 lbs. Deb: 8/10/97																						
1997	Min-A	25	66	5	18	1	0	2	13	2	12	.273	.294	.379	73	-3	0	0	0	1.000	-1	C-20/D-3	-0.3
1998	Ari-N	57	168	17	48	14	2	3	14	11	43	.286	.337	.446	100	-0	1	0	0	.986	2	C-46/O-2,1-1,D-2	0.6
Total	2	82	234	22	66	15	2	5	27	13	55	.282	.325	.427	93	-3	1	0	0	.989	1	/C-66,D-5,O-2,1-1	0.3
■ **DARRELL MILLER**	Miller, Darrell Keith b: 2/26/58, Washington, D.C. BR/TR, 6′2″, 200 lbs. Deb: 8/14/84																						
1984	Cal-A	17	41	5	7	0	0	0	1	4	9	.171	.244	.171	17	-5	0	0	0	.990	-1	1-16/O-1	-0.6
1985	Cal-A	51	48	8	18	2	1	2	7	1	10	.375	.400	.583	166	4	0	1	-1	.952	-11	O-45/C-1,3-1,D-4	-0.7
1986	Cal-A	33	57	6	13	2	1	0	4	4	8	.228	.279	.298	58	-3	0	0	0	1.000	-10	O-23,C-10/D-2	-1.3
1987	Cal-A	53	108	14	26	5	0	4	16	9	13	.241	.311	.398	89	-2	1	0	0	.984	-6	C-33,O-18/3-1,D-1	-0.6
1988	Cal-A	70	140	21	31	4	1	2	7	9	29	.221	.292	.307	70	-6	2	1	0	.987	3	C-53/O-8,D-1	0.0
Total	5	224	394	54	95	13	3	8	35	27	69	.241	.303	.350	80	-11	3	2	-0	.987	-25	/C-97,O-95,1-16,D3	-3.2
■ **BING MILLER**	Miller, Edmund John b: 8/30/1894, Vinton, Iowa d: 5/7/66, Philadelphia, Pa. BR/TR, 6′, 185 lbs. Deb: 4/16/21 FC																						
1921	Was-A	114	420	57	121	28	8	9	71	25	50	.288	.334	.457	105	1	3	4	-2	.945	2	*O-109	-0.6
1922	Phi-A	143	535	90	179	29	12	21	90	24	42	.335	.371	.551	134	24	10	10	-3	.977	5	*O-139	1.5
1923	Phi-A	123	458	68	137	25	4	12	64	27	34	.299	.344	.450	106	2	9	3	1	.978	-1	*O-119	-0.5

YEAR	TM/L	G	AB	R	H	2B	3B	HR	RBI	BB	SO	AVG	OBP	SLG	PRO+	BR/A	SB	CS	SBR	FA	FR	G/POS	TPR
1924	Phi-A	113	398	62	136	22	4	6	62	12	24	.342	.376	.462	114	7	11	5	0	.973	-2	O-94/1-7	-0.1
1925	Phi-A	124	474	78	151	29	10	10	81	19	14	.319	.355	.485	105	1	11	6	-0	.975	-10	*O-115,1-12	-1.6
1926	Phi-A	38	110	13	32	6	2	2	13	11	6	.291	.355	.436	100	-0	4	1	1	1.000	-5	O-34/1-1	-0.6
	StL-A	94	353	60	117	27	5	4	50	22	12	.331	.382	.470	116	8	7	9	-3	.939	4	O-94	0.2
	Yr	132	463	73	149	33	7	6	63	33	18	.322	.376	.462	112	7	11	10	-3	.950	-1	*O-128/1-1	-0.4
1927	StL-A	143	492	83	160	32	7	5	75	30	26	.325	.375	.449	109	6	8	7	-2	.970	4	*O-126	0.1
1928	Phi-A	139	510	76	168	34	7	8	85	27	24	.329	.372	.471	117	12	10	6	-1	.968	0	*O-133	0.3
1929	*Phi-A	147	556	84	184	32	16	8	93	40	25	.331	.380	.489	118	14	24	9	2	.970	6	*O-145	1.1
1930	*Phi-A	154	585	89	177	38	7	9	100	47	22	.303	.357	.438	96	-4	13	13	-4	.976	5	*O-154	-1.2
1931	*Phi-A	137	534	75	150	43	5	8	77	36	16	.281	.338	.425	94	-6	5	3	-0	.987	6	*O-137	-0.9
1932	Phi-A	95	305	40	90	17	4	7	58	20	11	.295	.343	.446	99	-1	7	3	0	.979	1	O-84	-0.4
1933	Phi-A	67	120	22	33	7	1	2	17	12	7	.275	.346	.400	96	-1	4	2	0	1.000	-6	O-30/1-6	-0.8
1934	Phi-A	81	177	22	43	10	2	1	22	16	14	.243	.309	.339	70	-8	1	0	0	1.000	-3	O-46	-1.2
1935	Bos-A	78	138	18	42	8	1	3	26	10	8	.304	.356	.442	99	-1	0	1	-1	.962	-2	O-29	-0.4
1936	Bos-A	30	47	9	14	2	1	1	6	5	5	.298	.377	.447	97	-0	0	0	0	1.000	-3	O-13	-0.3
Total	16	1820	6212	946	1934	389	96	116	990	383	340	.311	.359	.461	108	52	127	82	-11	.971	2	*O-1601/1-26	-5.4

■ EDDIE MILLER
Miller, Edward Lee b: 6/29/57, San Pablo, Cal. BB/TR, 5'9", 175 lbs. Deb: 9/5/77

YEAR	TM/L	G	AB	R	H	2B	3B	HR	RBI	BB	SO	AVG	OBP	SLG	PRO+	BR/A	SB	CS	SBR	FA	FR	G/POS	TPR
1977	Tex-A	17	6	7	2	0	0	0	1	1	1	.333	.429	.333	110	0	3	1	0	1.000	-0	/O-2,D-3	0.0
1978	Atl-N	6	21	5	3	1	0	0	2	2	4	.143	.250	.190	22	-2	3	0	1	1.000	-1	/O-5	-0.2
1979	Atl-N	27	113	12	35	1	0	0	5	5	24	.310	.350	.319	78	-3	15	2	3	.988	3	O-27	0.2
1980	Atl-N	11	19	3	3	0	0	0	0	0	5	.158	.158	.158	-11	-3	1	2	-1	1.000	-3	/O-9	-0.8
1981	Atl-N	50	134	29	31	3	1	0	7	7	29	.231	.285	.269	56	-8	23	5	4	.985	-1	O-36	-0.7
1982	Det-A	14	25	3	1	0	0	0	0	4	4	.040	.250	.040	-14	-4	0	3	-2	1.000	-0	/O-8,D-1	-0.6
1984	SD-N	13	14	4	4	0	1	1	2	0	4	.286	.286	.643	155	1	4	0	1	1.000	-1	/O-8	0.1
Total	7	138	332	63	79	5	2	1	17	19	71	.238	.297	.274	57	-18	49	13	7	.989	-4	/O-95,D-4	-2.0

■ EDDIE MILLER
Miller, Edward Robert "Eppie" b: 11/26/16, Pittsburgh, Pa. d: 7/31/97, Lake Worth, Fla. BR/TR, 5'9", 180 lbs. Deb: 9/9/36

YEAR	TM/L	G	AB	R	H	2B	3B	HR	RBI	BB	SO	AVG	OBP	SLG	PRO+	BR/A	SB	CS	SBR	FA	FR	G/POS	TPR
1936	Cin-N	5	10	0	1	0	0	0	0	1	1	.100	.182	.100	-24	-2	0			.938	-0	/S-4,2-1	-0.2
1937	Cin-N	36	60	3	9	3	1	0	5	3	8	.150	.190	.233	15	-7	0			.926	7	S-30/3-4	0.1
1939	Bos-N	77	296	32	79	12	2	4	31	16	21	.267	.315	.361	88	-6	4			.970	12	S-77	1.3
1940	Bos-N★	151	569	78	157	33	3	14	79	41	43	.276	.330	.418	111	7	8			**.970**	15	*S-151	3.5
1941	Bos-N★	154	585	54	140	27	3	6	68	35	72	.239	.288	.326	76	-20	8			**.966**	12	*S-154	0.4
1942	Bos-N★	142	534	47	130	28	2	6	47	22	42	.243	.279	.337	81	-15	11			**.983**	4	*S-142	-0.2
1943	Cin-N★	154	576	49	129	26	4	2	71	33	43	.224	.271	.293	64	-28	8			**.979**	**27**	*S-154	1.1
1944	Cin-N†	155	536	48	112	21	5	4	55	41	41	.209	.269	.289	59	-30	9			.971	12	*S-155	-0.5
1945	Cin-N	115	421	46	100	27	2	13	49	18	38	.238	.275	.404	89	-9	4			**.975**	5	*S-115	0.5
1946	Cin-N†	91	299	30	58	10	0	6	36	25	34	.194	.258	.288	57	-18	5			.970	24	S-88	1.1
1947	Cin-N†	151	545	69	146	**38**	4	19	87	49	40	.268	.333	.457	109	5	5			.972	-5	*S-151	0.7
1948	Phi-N	130	468	45	115	20	1	14	61	19	40	.246	.281	.382	79	-15	1			.966	-14	*S-122	-2.2
1949	Phi-N	85	266	21	55	10	1	6	29	29	21	.207	.294	.320	66	-13	1			.986	-10	2-82/S-1	-2.0
1950	StL-N	64	172	17	39	8	0	3	22	19	21	.227	.307	.326	64	-9	0			.980	14	S-51/2-1	0.8
Total	14	1510	5337	539	1270	263	28	97	640	351	465	.238	.290	.352	80	-160	64			.972	102	*S-1395/2-84,3-4	4.4

■ ED MILLER
Miller, Edwin J. "Big Ed" b: 11/24/1888, Annville, Pa. d: 4/17/80, S.Lebanon Twsp, Pa BR/TR, 6', 180 lbs. Deb: 6/29/12

YEAR	TM/L	G	AB	R	H	2B	3B	HR	RBI	BB	SO	AVG	OBP	SLG	PRO+	BR/A	SB	CS	SBR	FA	FR	G/POS	TPR
1912	StL-A	13	46	4	9	1	0	0	5	2		.196	.245	.217	34	-4	1			.951	-4	/1-8,S-5	-0.8
1914	StL-A	41	58	8	8	0	1	0	4	4	13	.138	.219	.172	18	-6	1	3	-2	.981	-2	/1-8,2-5,O-5,3-2	-1.0
1918	Cle-A	32	96	9	22	4	3	0	3	12	10	.229	.321	.333	89	-1	2			.977	1	1-22/O-4	-0.2
Total	3	86	200	21	39	5	4	0	12	18	23	.195	.275	.260	58	-11	4	3		.972	-5	/1-38,O-9,2-5,S3	-2.0

■ ELMER MILLER
Miller, Elmer b: 7/28/1890, Sandusky, Ohio d: 11/28/44, Beloit, Wis. BR/TR, 6', 175 lbs. Deb: 4/26/12

YEAR	TM/L	G	AB	R	H	2B	3B	HR	RBI	BB	SO	AVG	OBP	SLG	PRO+	BR/A	SB	CS	SBR	FA	FR	G/POS	TPR
1912	StL-N	12	37	5	7	1	0	0	3	4	9	.189	.268	.216	34	-3	1			1.000	0	O-11	-0.4
1915	NY-A	26	83	4	12	1	0	0	3	4	14	.145	.193	.157	5	-10	0			.955	-4	O-26	-1.7
1916	NY-A	43	152	12	34	3	2	1	18	11	18	.224	.280	.289	70	-6	8			.969	5	O-42	-0.4
1917	NY-A	114	379	43	95	11	3	3	35	40	44	.251	.336	.319	99	1	11			.961	-6	*O-112	-1.2
1918	NY-A	67	202	18	49	9	2	1	22	19	17	.243	.317	.322	91	-2	2			.947	4	O-62	-0.2
1921	*NY-A	56	242	41	72	9	8	4	36	19	16	.298	.356	.450	102	0	2	2	-1	.947	3	O-56	-0.1
1922	NY-A	51	172	31	46	7	2	3	18	11	12	.267	.311	.384	79	-6	2	3	-1	.982	-2	O-51	-1.2
	Bos-A	44	147	16	28	2	3	4	16	5	10	.190	.222	.327	42	-13	3	1	0	.957	-0	O-35	-1.6
	Yr	95	319	47	74	9	5	7	34	16	22	.232	.271	.357	62	-19	5	4	-1	.970	-2	O-86	-2.8
Total	7	413	1414	170	343	43	20	16	151	113	140	.243	.307	.335	80	-40	29	6		.960	-0	O-395	-6.8

■ ELMER MILLER
Miller, Elmer Joseph "Lefty" b: 4/17/03, Detroit, Mich. d: 1/8/87, Corona, Cal. BL/TL, 5'11", 189 lbs. Deb: 6/21/29

YEAR	TM/L	G	AB	R	H	2B	3B	HR	RBI	BB	SO	AVG	OBP	SLG	PRO+	BR/A	SB	CS	SBR	FA	FR	G/POS	TPR
1929	Phi-N	31	38	3	9	1	0	1	4	1	5	.237	.256	.342	44	-3	0			.750	2	/P-8,O-4	-0.1

■ KOHLY MILLER
Miller, Frank A. b: 1/1874, Cumru Township, Pa. d: 3/29/51, Reading, Pa. Deb: 9/16/1892

YEAR	TM/L	G	AB	R	H	2B	3B	HR	RBI	BB	SO	AVG	OBP	SLG	PRO+	BR/A	SB	CS	SBR	FA	FR	G/POS	TPR
1892	Was-N	1	3	0	0	0	0	0	0	0	1	.000	.000	.000	-99	-1	0			.400	-1	/S-1	-0.2
	StL-N	1	4	0	0	0	0	0	0	0	0	.000	.000	.000	-99	-1	0			.500	-1	/3-1	-0.2
	Yr	2	7	0	0	0	0	0	0	0	1	.000	.000	.000	-99	-2	0			.400	-2	/S-1,3-1	-0.4
1897	Phi-N	3	11	2	2	0	0	0	1	2		.182	.308	.182	32	-1	0			.857	-2	/2-3	-0.3
Total	2	5	18	2	2	0	0	0	1	2	1	.111	.200	.111	-13	-3	0			.857	-5	/2-3,3-1,S-1	-0.7

■ GEORGE MILLER
Miller, George C. b: 2/19/1853, Newport, Ky. d: 7/24/29, Norwood, Ohio BR/TR, 5'5", 160 lbs. Deb: 9/6/1877

YEAR	TM/L	G	AB	R	H	2B	3B	HR	RBI	BB	SO	AVG	OBP	SLG	PRO+	BR/A	SB	CS	SBR	FA	FR	G/POS	TPR
1877	Cin-N	11	37	4	6	1	0	0	3	5	2	.162	.262	.189	50	-2				.918	0	C-11	-0.1
1884	Cin-a	6	20	6	5	1	1	0	3	1		.250	.318	.400	127	1				.975	2	/C-6	0.3
Total	2	17	57	10	11	2	1	0	6	6	2	.193	.281	.263	79	-1				.938	2	/C-17	0.2

■ DOGGIE MILLER
Miller, George Frederick "Foghorn" or "Calliope"
b: 8/15/1864, Brooklyn, N.Y. d: 4/6/09, Brooklyn, N.Y. BR/TR, 5'6", 145 lbs. Deb: 5/1/1884 M

YEAR	TM/L	G	AB	R	H	2B	3B	HR	RBI	BB	SO	AVG	OBP	SLG	PRO+	BR/A	SB	CS	SBR	FA	FR	G/POS	TPR
1884	Pit-a	89	347	46	78	10	2	0		13		.225	.257	.265	69	-12				.798	-5	O-49,C-36/3-3,2-1	-1.3
1885	Pit-a	42	166	19	27	3	1	0	13	4		.163	.182	.193	19	-15				.893	-5	C-33/O-6,S-2,3-2	-1.5
1886	Pit-a	83	317	70	80	15	1	2	36	43		.252	.343	.325	110	5	35			.918	-22	C-61,O-23/2-1	-0.9
1887	Pit-N	87	342	58	83	17	4	1	34	35	13	.243	.317	.325	83	-6	33			.928	-22	C-73,O-14/3-1	-1.9
1888	Pit-N	103	404	50	112	17	5	0	36	18	16	.277	.319	.344	121	10	27			.908	-15	C-68,O-32/3-4	0.0
1889	Pit-N	104	422	77	113	25	3	6	56	31	11	.268	.321	.384	107	3	16			.889	-5	C-76,O-27/3-3	0.4
1890	Pit-N	138	549	85	150	24	3	4	66	68	11	.273	.357	.350	120	17	32			.850	1	3-88,O-25,S-13,C/2	2.0
1891	Pit-N	135	548	80	156	19	6	4	57	59	26	.285	.357	.363	113	10	35			.938	-16	C-41,S-37,3-34,O/1	0.1
1892	Pit-N	149	623	103	158	15	12	2	59	69	14	.254	.335	.326	100	1	28			.906	-11	O-76,C-63,S-19,/3-2	-0.7
1893	Pit-N	41	154	23	28	6	1	0	17	17	8	.182	.284	.234	39	-13	3			.916	-0	C-40	-0.8
1894	StL-N	127	481	93	163	9	11	8	86	58	9	.339	.414	.453	109	9	17			.832	-14	3-52,C-41,21/OSM	0.0
1895	StL-N	121	490	81	143	15	4	5	74	25	12	.292	.334	.369	82	-13	18			.829	-23	3-46,C-46,O-21,/S1	-2.7
1896	Lou-N	98	324	54	89	17	4	1	33	27	9	.275	.334	.361	87	-6	16			.922	-16	C-48,2-25/O-8,31S	-1.4
Total	13	1317	5167	839	1380	192	57	33	567	467	129	.267	.333	.345	97	-12	260			.918	-153	C-636,O-309,3/S21	-8.7

■ HUGHIE MILLER
Miller, Hugh Stanley "Cotton" b: 12/28/1887, St.Louis, Mo. d: 12/24/45, Jefferson Barracks, Mo. BR/TR, 6'1.5", 175 lbs. Deb: 6/18/11

YEAR	TM/L	G	AB	R	H	2B	3B	HR	RBI	BB	SO	AVG	OBP	SLG	PRO+	BR/A	SB	CS	SBR	FA	FR	G/POS	TPR
1911	Phi-N	1	0	0	0	0	0	0	0	0	0	—	—	—	—	0	0			.000	0	R	0.0
1914	StL-F	132	490	51	109	20	5	0	46	27	57	.222	.264	.284	47	-44	4			.990	0	*1-130	-5.0
1915	StL-F	7	6	0	3	1	0	0	3	0	0	.500	.500	.667	216	1	0			1.000	-0	/1-6	0.1
Total	3	140	496	51	112	21	5	0	49	27	57	.226	.267	.288	49	-43	4			.990	-0	1-136	-4.9

■ JAKE MILLER
Miller, Jacob George (b: Jacob George Munzing) b: 12/1/1895, Baltimore, Md. d: 8/24/74, Towson, Md. BR/TR, 5'10", 170 lbs. Deb: 7/16/22

YEAR	TM/L	G	AB	R	H	2B	3B	HR	RBI	BB	SO	AVG	OBP	SLG	PRO+	BR/A	SB	CS	SBR	FA	FR	G/POS	TPR
1922	Pit-N	3	11	0	1	0	0	0	0	2	0	.091	.231	.091	-14	-2	1	0	0	.889	0	/O-3	-0.2

YEAR	TM/L	G	AB	R	H	2B	3B	HR	RBI	BB	SO	AVG	OBP	SLG	PRO+	BR/A	SB	CS	SBR	FA	FR	G/POS	TPR
■ **HACK MILLER**	Miller, James Eldridge b: 2/13/13, Celeste, Tex. d: 11/21/66, Dallas, Tex. BR/TR, 5'11.5", 215 lbs. Deb: 4/18/44																						
1944	Det-A	5	5	1	1	0	0	1	3	1	1	.200	.333	.800	207	1	0	0	0	1.000	0	/C-5	0.1
1945	Det-A	2	4	0	3	0	0	0	1	0	0	.750	.750	.750	315	1	0	0	0	1.000	-0	/C-2	0.1
Total	2	7	9	1	4	0	0	1	4	1	1	.444	.500	.778	250	2	0	0	0	1.000	-0	/C-7	0.2
■ **JIM MILLER**	Miller, James McCurdy "Rabbit" b: 10/2/1880, Pittsburgh, Pa. d: 2/7/37, Pittsburgh, Pa. BR/TR, 5'8", 165 lbs. Deb: 9/9/01																						
1901	NY-N	18	58	3	8	0	0	0	3	6		.138	.219	.138	5	-7	1			.936	-2	2-18	-0.8
■ **JOHN MILLER**	Miller, John Allen b: 3/14/44, Alhambra, Cal. BR/TR, 5'11", 195 lbs. Deb: 9/11/66																						
1966	NY-A	6	23	1	2	0	0	1	2	0	9	.087	.087	.217	-16	-3	0	0	0	1.000	-1	/1-3,O-3	-0.5
1969	LA-N	26	38	3	8	1	0	1	1	2	9	.211	.250	.316	62	-2	0	0	0	1.000	-2	/O-6,1-5,3-2,2-1	-0.5
Total	2	32	61	4	10	1	0	2	3	2	18	.164	.190	.279	33	-6	0	0	0	1.000	-3	/O-9,1-8,3-2,2-1	-1.0
■ **DOTS MILLER**	Miller, John Barney b: 9/9/1886, Kearny, N.J. d: 9/5/23, Saranac Lake, N.Y. BR/TR, 5'11.5", 170 lbs. Deb: 4/16/09																						
1909	*Pit-N	151	560	71	156	31	13	3	87	39		.279	.329	.396	115	8	14			**.953**	-11	*2-150	-0.7
1910	Pit-N	120	444	45	101	13	10	1	48	33	41	.227	.284	.309	69	-19	11			.946	-19	*2-119/1-1,S-1	-4.2
1911	Pit-N	137	470	82	126	17	8	6	78	51	48	.268	.348	.377	99	-1	17			.943	-6	*2-129	-1.0
1912	Pit-N	148	567	74	156	33	12	4	87	37	45	.275	.324	.397	98	-4	18			.985	1	*1-147	-0.5
1913	Pit-N	154	580	75	158	24	20	7	90	37	52	.272	.317	.419	114	8	20			.985	-4	*1-150/S-3	0.2
1914	StL-N	155	573	67	166	27	10	4	88	34	52	.290	.339	.393	119	12	16			.993	0	1-91,S-60/2-5	1.6
1915	StL-N	150	553	73	146	17	10	2	72	43	48	.264	.324	.342	101	1	27	19	-3	.991	4	1-94,2-55/3-9,S-3	0.0
1916	StL-N	143	505	47	120	22	7	1	46	40	49	.238	.300	.315	89	-6	18			.993	2	1-93,2-38,S-21,/3-1	-0.6
1917	StL-N	148	544	61	135	15	9	2	45	33	52	.248	.295	.320	91	-6	14			.960	19	2-92,1-46,S-11	1.7
1919	StL-N	101	346	38	80	10	4	1	24	13	23	.231	.265	.292	72	-13	6			.981	2	1-68,2-28	-1.4
1920	Phi-N	98	343	41	87	12	2	1	27	16	17	.254	.289	.309	68	-14	13	6	0	.948	-9	2-59,3-17,S-12,/1O	-2.1
1921	Phi-N	84	320	37	95	11	3	0	23	15	27	.297	.330	.350	74	-11	3	5	-2	.940	1	3-41,1-38/2-6	-1.1
Total	12	1589	5805	711	1526	232	108	32	715	391	454	.263	.314	.357	95	-46	177	30		.988	-20	1-737,2-681,S/3O	-8.1
■ **JOE MILLER**	Miller, Joseph A. b: 2/17/1861, Baltimore, Md. d: 4/23/28, Wheeling, W.Va. BR, 5'9.5", 165 lbs. Deb: 5/1/1884																						
1884	Tol-a	105	423	46	101	12	8	1		26		.239	.284	.312	91	-4				.864	1	*S-105	-0.2
1885	Lou-a	98	339	44	62	9	5	0	24	28		.183	.249	.239	55	-17				.891	3	*S-79,3-11/2-8	-1.1
Total	2	203	762	90	163	21	13	1	24	54		.214	.269	.280	75	-21				.876	4	S-184/3-11,2-8	-1.3
■ **JOE MILLER**	Miller, Joseph Wick b: 7/24/1850, Germany d: 8/30/1891, White Bear Lake, Minn. 5'10.5", 169 lbs. Deb: 6/26/1872 M																						
1872	Nat-n	1	4	0	1	0	0	0	0	0	0	.250	.250	.250	46	-0	0	0	0	.923	-0	/1-1	0.0
1875	Wes-n	13	50	4	6	1	0	0	0	0	3	.120	.120	.140	-9	-5	0	0	0	.870	4	2-13	-0.2
	Chi-n	15	54	1	8	0	0	0	1	0	7	.148	.148	.148	3	-5	0	0	0	.788	-3	2-14/O-1	-0.7
	Yr	28	104	5	14	1	0	0	1	0	10	.135	.135	.144	-3	-10	0	0	0	.832	1	2-27/O-1	-0.9
Total	2 n	29	108	5	15	1	0	0	1	0	10	.139	.139	.148	-1	-11	0	0	0	.870	1	/2-27,O-1,1-1	-0.9
■ **KEITH MILLER**	Miller, Keith Alan b: 6/12/63, Midland, Mich. BR/TR, 5'11", 185 lbs. Deb: 6/16/87																						
1987	NY-N	25	51	14	19	2	2	0	1	2	6	.373	.407	.490	144	3	8	1	2	.967	2	2-16	0.7
1988	NY-N	40	70	9	15	1	1	1	5	6	10	.214	.276	.300	69	-3	0	5	-3	.946	-7	2-16/S-8,3-6,O-1	-1.4
1989	NY-N	57	143	15	33	7	0	1	7	5	27	.231	.262	.301	63	-7	6	0	2	.967	-4	2-23,O-14/S-8,3-2	-0.9
1990	NY-N	88	233	42	60	8	0	1	12	23	46	.258	.329	.305	76	-7	16	3	3	.980	5	O-61,2-11/S-4	0.0
1991	NY-N	98	275	41	77	22	1	4	23	23	44	.280	.347	.411	113	5	14	4	2	.972	0	2-60,O-28/3-2,S-2	0.8
1992	KC-A	106	416	57	118	24	4	4	38	31	46	.284	.354	.389	105	3	16	6	1	.971	-20	2-93,O-16/D-1	-1.4
1993	KC-A	37	108	9	18	3	0	0	3	8	19	.167	.231	.194	15	-13	3	1	0	.889	-6	3-21/O-4,2-3,D-6	-1.8
1994	KC-A	5	15	1	2	0	0	0	0	0	3	.133	.133	.133	-30	-3	0	0	0	1.000	1	/O-4,3-2	-0.2
1995	KC-A	9	15	2	5	0	0	1	3	2	4	.333	.412	.533	142	1	0	0	0	1.000	-0	/O-4,D-4	0.1
Total	9	465	1326	190	347	67	8	12	92	100	205	.262	.325	.351	88	-21	63	20	7	.969	-28	2-222,O-132/3SD	-4.1
■ **ED MILLER**	Miller, L. Edward b: Tecumseh, Mich. Deb: 7/18/1884																						
1884	Tol-a	8	24	2	6	0	0	0	1	1		.250	.280	.250	72	-1				.615	-1	/O-8	-0.1
■ **HACK MILLER**	Miller, Lawrence H. b: 1/1/1894, New York, N.Y. d: 9/17/71, Oakland, Cal. BR/TR, 5'9", 195 lbs. Deb: 9/22/16																						
1916	Bro-N	3	3	0	1	0	1	0	1	1	1	.333	.500	1.000	345	1	0			1.000	-1	/O-3	0.0
1918	*Bos-A	12	29	2	8	2	0	0	4	0	4	.276	.276	.345	89	-1	0			1.000	-3	O-10	-0.4
1922	Chi-N	122	466	61	164	28	5	12	78	26	39	.352	.389	.511	128	18	3	3	-1	.959	-3	*O-116	0.6
1923	Chi-N	135	485	74	146	24	2	20	88	27	39	.301	.343	.482	116	9	6	5	-1	.978	6	*O-129	0.4
1924	Chi-N	53	131	17	44	8	1	4	25	8	11	.336	.379	.504	133	6	1	0	0	.948	-4	O-32	0.0
1925	Chi-N	24	86	10	24	3	2	2	9	2	9	.279	.303	.430	84	-2	0	1	-1	.878	-3	O-21	-0.7
Total	6	349	1200	164	387	65	11	38	205	64	103	.322	.361	.490	120	31	10	9		.962	-8	O-311	-0.1
■ **LEMMIE MILLER**	Miller, Lemmie Earl b: 6/2/60, Dallas, Tex. BR/TR, 6'1", 190 lbs. Deb: 5/22/84																						
1984	LA-N	8	12	1	2	0	0	0	0	1	2	.167	.231	.167	13	-1	0	0	0	1.000	-1	/O-5	-0.3
■ **OTTO MILLER**	Miller, Lowell Otto "Moonie" b: 6/1/1889, Minden, Neb. d: 3/29/62, Brooklyn, N.Y. BR/TR, 6', 196 lbs. Deb: 7/16/10 C																						
1910	Bro-N	31	66	5	11	3	0	0	2	2	19	.167	.203	.212	22	-7	1			.987	9	C-28	0.4
1911	Bro-N	25	62	7	13	2	2	0	8	0	4	.210	.210	.306	46	-5	2			.927	-3	C-22	-0.6
1912	Bro-N	98	316	35	88	18	1	1	31	18	50	.278	.325	.351	88	-6	11			.975	13	C-94	1.6
1913	Bro-N	104	320	26	87	11	7	0	26	10	31	.272	.294	.350	81	-9	7			.971	14	*C-103/1-1	1.4
1914	Bro-N	54	169	17	39	6	1	0	9	7	20	.231	.261	.278	59	-9	0			.964	0	C-50/1-1	-0.5
1915	Bro-N	84	254	20	57	4	6	0	25	6	28	.224	.245	.287	60	-13	3			.981	8	C-83	0.2
1916	*Bro-N	73	216	16	55	9	2	1	17	7	29	.255	.281	.329	85	-4	6			.968	4	C-69	0.5
1917	Bro-N	92	274	19	63	5	4	1	17	14	29	.230	.272	.288	70	-10	5			.979	1	C-91	-0.2
1918	Bro-N	75	228	8	44	6	1	0	8	9	20	.193	.230	.228	40	-16	1			.972	4	C-62/1-1	-0.8
1919	Bro-N	51	164	18	37	5	0	0	5	7	14	.226	.257	.256	53	-9	2			.966	2	C-51	-0.3
1920	*Bro-N	90	301	16	87	9	2	0	33	9	18	.289	.312	.332	82	-7	0	5	-3	**.986**	-2	C-89	-0.6
1921	Bro-N	91	286	22	67	8	6	1	27	9	26	.234	.260	.315	50	-21	2	1	0	.972	9	C-91	-0.7
1922	Bro-N	59	180	20	47	11	1	1	23	6	13	.261	.285	.350	63	-10	0	0	0	.968	3	C-57	-0.4
Total	13	927	2836	229	695	97	33	5	231	104	301	.245	.275	.308	67	-125	40	6		.973	62	C-890/1-3	0.0
■ **KEITH MILLER**	Miller, Neal Keith b: 3/7/63, Dallas, Tex. BB/TR, 5'11", 175 lbs. Deb: 4/23/88																						
1988	Phi-N	47	48	4	8	3	0	0	6	5	13	.167	.245	.229	36	-4	0	0	0	1.000	-3	/O-4,3-3,S-1	-0.8
1989	Phi-N	8	10	0	3	1	0	0	0	0	3	.300	.300	.400	98	-0	0	0	0	1.000	-1	/O-2	-0.1
Total	2	55	58	4	11	4	0	0	6	5	16	.190	.254	.259	47	-4	0	0	0	1.000	-4	/O-6,3-3,S-1	-0.9
■ **NORM MILLER**	Miller, Norman Calvin b: 2/5/46, Los Angeles, Cal. BL/TR, 5'11", 195 lbs. Deb: 9/11/65																						
1965	Hou-N	11	15	2	3	0	1	0	1	1	7	.200	.250	.333	67	-1	0	0	0	1.000	-0	/O-2	-0.1
1966	Hou-N	11	34	1	5	0	0	1	3	2	8	.147	.194	.235	20	-4	0	0	0	1.000	0	/O-8,3-2	-0.4
1967	Hou-N	64	190	15	39	9	3	1	14	19	42	.205	.278	.300	68	-8	2	0	1	.967	1	O-53	-1.0
1968	Hou-N	79	257	35	61	18	2	6	28	22	48	.237	.310	.393	112	3	6	5	-1	.971	-3	O-74	-0.5
1969	Hou-N	119	409	58	108	21	4	4	50	47	77	.264	.350	.364	102	2	4	4	-1	.984	-1	*O-114	-0.7
1970	Hou-N	90	226	29	54	9	0	4	29	41	33	.239	.358	.332	90	-2	3	1	0	.947	-5	O-72/C-1	-0.9
1971	Hou-N	45	74	5	19	5	0	2	10	5	13	.257	.313	.405	105	0	0	0	0	1.000	-5	O-20/C-1	-0.5
1972	Hou-N	67	107	18	26	4	0	4	13	13	23	.243	.331	.393	107	1	1	0	0	1.000	-4	O-29	-0.4
1973	Hou-N	3	3	0	0	0	0	0	0	0	2	.000	.000	.000	-99	-1	0	0	0	.000	-0	/O-1	-0.1
	Atl-N	9	8	2	3	1	0	1	6	3	3	.375	.545	.875	267	2	0	0	0	.667	-0	/O-1	0.2
	Yr	12	11	2	3	1	0	1	6	3	5	.273	.429	.636	181	1	0	0	0	.667	-1	/O-2	0.1
1974	Atl-N	42	41	1	7	1	0	1	5	7	9	.171	.292	.268	55	-2	0	0	0	1.000	-1	/O-4	-0.3
Total	10	540	1364	166	325	68	10	24	159	160	265	.238	.325	.356	95	-9	16	10	-1	.972	-18	O-378/C-2,3-2	-4.7

YEAR	TM/L	G	AB	R	H	2B	3B	HR	RBI	BB	SO	AVG	OBP	SLG	PRO+	BR/A	SB	CS	SBR	FA	FR	G/POS	TPR
■ **ORLANDO MILLER**	Miller, Orlando (Salmon) b: 1/13/69, Changuinola, Pan. BR/TR, 6′1″, 180 lbs. Deb: 7/8/94																						
1994	Hou-N	16	40	3	13	0	1	2	9	2	12	.325	.386	.525	142	2	1	0	0	1.000	-1	S-11/2-3	0.2
1995	Hou-N	92	324	36	85	20	1	5	36	22	71	.262	.319	.377	89	-6	3	4	-2	.964	5	S-89	0.5
1996	Hou-N	139	468	43	120	26	2	15	58	14	116	.256	.293	.417	92	-8	3	7	-3	.958	-12	*S-117,3-29	-1.4
1997	Det-A	50	111	13	26	7	1	2	10	5	24	.234	.292	.369	72	-5	1	0	0	.979	-0	S-31,D-11/3-4,1-3	-0.3
Total	4	297	943	95	244	53	5	24	113	43	223	.259	.306	.402	90	-17	8	11	-4	.964	-9	S-248/3-33,D-11,12	-1.0
■ **OTTO MILLER**	Miller, Otis Louis b: 2/2/01, Belleville, Ill. d: 7/26/59, Belleville, Ill. BR/TR, 5′10.5″, 168 lbs. Deb: 4/17/27																						
1927	StL-A	51	76	8	17	5	0	0	8	8	5	.224	.306	.289	53	-5	0	1	-1	.938	-4	S-35,3-11	-0.8
1930	Bos-A	112	370	49	106	22	5	0	40	26	21	.286	.333	.373	82	-10	2	4	-2	.948	-6	3-83,2-15	-1.1
1931	Bos-A	107	389	38	106	12	1	0	43	15	20	.272	.301	.308	64	-21	1	1	-0	.953	-1	3-75,2-25	-1.5
1932	Bos-A	2	2	0	0	0	0	0	0	0	0	.000	.000	.000	-99	-1	0	0	0	.000	0	H	-0.1
Total	4	272	837	95	229	39	6	0	91	49	46	.274	.315	.335	71	-36	3	6	-3	.949	-11	3-169/2-40,S-35	-3.5
■ **RALPH MILLER**	Miller, Ralph Joseph b: 2/29/1896, Ft.Wayne, Ind. d: 3/18/39, Ft.Wayne, Ind. BR/TR, 6′, 190 lbs. Deb: 4/14/20																						
1920	Phi-N	97	338	28	74	14	1	0	28	11	32	.219	.246	.266	45	-24	3	4	-2	.940	0	3-91/1-3,S-2,O-1	-2.3
1921	Phi-N	57	204	19	62	10	0	3	26	6	10	.304	.327	.397	84	-5	3	5	-2	.910	0	S-46,3-10	-0.2
1924	*Was-A	9	15	1	2	0	0	0	0	1	1	.133	.188	.133	-17	-3	0	0	0	.941	0	/2-3	-0.2
Total	3	163	557	48	138	24	1	3	54	18	43	.248	.274	.311	59	-31	6	9	-4	.927	1	3-101/S-48,2-3,1O	-2.7
■ **RAY MILLER**	Miller, Raymond Peter b: 2/12/1888, Pittsburgh, Pa. d: 4/7/27, Pittsburgh, Pa. BL/TL, 5′10″, 168 lbs. Deb: 4/14/17																						
1917	Cle-A	19	21	1	4	1	0	0	2	8	3	.190	.414	.238	92	0	0			1.000	1	/1-4	0.2
	Pit-N	6	27	1	4	1	0	0	0	2	3	.148	.207	.185	20	-3	0			1.000	0	/1-6	-0.3
Total	1	25	48	2	8	2	0	0	2	10	6	.167	.310	.208	56	-2	0			1.000	2	/1-10	-0.1
■ **RICK MILLER**	Miller, Richard Alan b: 4/19/48, Grand Rapids, Mich. BL/TL, 6′, 185 lbs. Deb: 9/4/71																						
1971	Bos-A	15	33	9	11	5	0	1	7	8	8	.333	.463	.576	180	4	0	2	-1	.969	1	O-14	0.3
1972	Bos-A	89	98	13	21	4	1	3	15	11	27	.214	.294	.367	91	-1	0	2	-1	.967	-11	O-75	-1.7
1973	Bos-A	143	441	65	115	17	7	6	43	51	59	.261	.341	.372	95	-2	12	7	-1	.978	-4	*O-137	-1.3
1974	Bos-A	114	280	41	73	8	1	5	22	37	47	.261	.347	.350	94	-1	13	2	3	.989	2	*O-105	0.0
1975	*Bos-A	77	108	21	21	2	1	0	15	21	20	.194	.326	.231	55	-6	3	2	-0	.981	-8	O-65	-1.6
1976	Bos-A	105	269	40	76	15	3	0	27	34	47	.283	.363	.361	100	1	11	10	-3	.991	5	O-82/D-4	0.0
1977	Bos-A	86	189	34	48	9	3	0	24	22	30	.254	.341	.333	76	-6	11	5	0	.992	-7	O-79/D-1	-1.5
1978	Cal-A	132	475	66	125	25	4	1	37	54	70	.263	.343	.339	96	-1	3	13	-7	.989	15	*O-129	0.2
1979	*Cal-A	120	427	60	125	15	5	2	28	50	69	.293	.368	.365	102	3	5	4	-1	.989	10	*O-117/D-2	0.7
1980	Cal-A	129	412	52	113	14	3	2	38	48	71	.274	.351	.337	92	-3	7	3	0	.984	5	*O-118	-0.2
1981	Bos-A	97	316	38	92	17	2	2	33	28	36	.291	.351	.377	103	2	3	5	-2	.987	-3	O-95	-0.7
1982	Bos-A	135	409	50	104	13	2	4	38	40	41	.254	.324	.325	75	-14	5	6	-2	.983	-6	*O-127	-2.5
1983	Bos-A	104	262	41	75	10	2	2	21	28	30	.286	.357	.363	92	-2	3	3	-1	.993	0	O-66/1-2,D-2	-0.5
1984	Bos-A	95	123	17	32	5	1	0	12	17	22	.260	.350	.317	82	-2	1	1	-0	.974	-7	O-31/1-8	-1.1
1985	Bos-A	41	45	5	15	2	0	0	9	5	6	.333	.400	.378	110	1	1	0	0	1.000	-2	/O-8,D-4	-0.1
Total	15	1482	3887	552	1046	161	35	28	369	454	583	.269	.348	.350	92	-29	78	65	-16	.986	-10	*O-1248/D-13,1-10	-10.0
■ **ROD MILLER**	Miller, Rodney Carter b: 1/16/40, Portland, Ore. BL/TR, 5′10″, 160 lbs. Deb: 9/28/57																						
1957	Bro-N	1	1	0	0	0	0	0	0	0	1	.000	.000	.000	-91	-0	0	0	0	.000	0	H	0.0
■ **DOC MILLER**	Miller, Roy Oscar b: 2/4/1883, Chatham, Ontario, Canada d: 7/31/38, Jersey City, N.J. BL/TL, 5′10.5″, 170 lbs. Deb: 5/4/10																						
1910	Chi-N	1	1	0	0	0	0	0	0	0	0	.000	.000	.000	-99	-0	0			.000	0	H	0.0
	Bos-N	130	482	48	138	27	4	3	55	33	52	.286	.333	.378	103	0	17			.951	-12	*O-130	-1.9
	Yr	131	483	48	138	27	4	3	55	33	52	.286	.333	.377	102	-0	17			.951	-12	*O-130	-1.9
1911	Bos-N	146	577	69	**192**	36	3	7	91	43	43	.333	.379	.442	120	13	32			.961	2	*O-146	0.8
1912	Bos-N	51	201	26	47	8	1	2	24	14	17	.234	.287	.313	63	-11	6			.948	3	O-50	-1.1
	Phi-N	67	177	24	51	12	5	0	21	9	13	.288	.323	.412	94	-2	3			.986	2	O-40	-0.2
	Yr	118	378	50	98	20	6	2	45	23	30	.259	.303	.360	78	-13	9			.964	5	O-90	-1.3
1913	Phi-N	69	87	9	30	6	0	0	11	6	6	.345	.400	.414	127	3	2			.800	-4	O-12	-0.1
1914	Cin-N	93	192	8	49	7	2	0	33	16	18	.255	.313	.313	83	-4	4			.976	-4	O-47	-1.1
Total	5	557	1717	184	507	96	15	12	235	121	149	.295	.343	.390	102	-0	64			.958	-13	O-425	-3.6
■ **RUDY MILLER**	Miller, Rudel Charles b: 7/12/1900, Kalamazoo, Mich. d: 1/22/94, Kalamazoo, Mich. BR/TR, 6′1″, 180 lbs. Deb: 9/19/29																						
1929	Phi-A	2	4	1	1	0	0	0	1	3	0	.250	.571	.250	115	0	0	0	0	.750	-0	/3-2	0.0
■ **TOM MILLER**	Miller, Thomas P. "Reddy" b: Philadelphia, Pa. d: 5/29/1876, Philadelphia, Pa. Deb: 10/24/1874																						
1874	Ath-n	4	16	1	8	0	0	0	5	0	0	.500	.500	.500	204	2	0	0	0	.793	0	/C-4,O-1	0.1
1875	StL-n	56	214	18	35	2	0	0	12	1	8	.164	.167	.173	20	-15	2	0	1	.827	-3	*C-53/3-2	-1.4
Total	2 n	60	230	19	43	2	0	0	17	1	8	.187	.190	.196	37	-14	2	0	1	.824	-3	/C-57,3-2,O-1	-1.3
■ **TOM MILLER**	Miller, Thomas Royall b: 7/5/1897, Powhatan Court House, Va. d: 8/13/80, Richmond, Va. BL/TR, 5′11″, 180 lbs. Deb: 7/29/18																						
1918	Bos-N	2	2	0	0	0	0	0	0	0	0	.000	.000	.000	-99	-0	1			.000	0	H	-0.1
1919	Bos-N	7	6	2	2	0	0	0	0	0	1	.333	.333	.333	105	0	0			.000	0	H	0.0
Total	2	9	8	2	2	0	0	0	0	0	1	.250	.250	.250	53	-0	1				0	-0,-0	-0.1
■ **WARD MILLER**	Miller, Ward Taylor "Windy" or "Grump" b: 7/5/1884, Mt.Carroll, Ill. d: 9/4/58, Dixon, Ill. BL/TR, 5′11″, 177 lbs. Deb: 4/14/09																						
1909	Pit-N	15	56	2	8	0	1	0	4	4		.143	.213	.179	20	-5	2			.967	-1	O-14	-0.8
	Cin-N	43	113	17	35	3	1	0	4	6		.310	.345	.354	118	2	9			.981	-7	O-26	-0.6
	Yr	58	169	19	43	3	2	0	8	10		.254	.300	.296	84	-3	11			.976	-8	O-40	-1.4
1910	Cin-N	81	126	21	30	6	0	0	10	22	13	.238	.356	.286	92	-0	10			.944	2	O-26	0.0
1912	Chi-N	86	241	45	74	11	4	0	22	26	18	.307	.377	.386	109	4	11			.943	-8	O-64	-0.8
1913	Chi-N	80	203	23	48	5	7	1	16	34	33	.236	.349	.345	98	1	13			.980	3	O-63	0.2
1914	StL-F	121	402	49	118	17	7	4	50	59	36	.294	.397	.400	112	3	18			.953	10	*O-111	0.8
1915	StL-F	154	536	80	164	19	9	1	63	79	39	.306	.400	.381	114	7	33			.963	3	*O-154	0.2
1916	StL-A	146	485	72	129	17	5	1	50	72	76	.266	.371	.328	116	13	25	21	-5	.943	-5	*O-136	-0.6
1917	StL-A	43	82	13	17	1	1	1	2	16	15	.207	.350	.280	96	0	7			.966	-4	O-25	-0.5
Total	8	769	2244	322	623	79	35	8	221	318	230	.278	.375	.355	108	24	128	21		.957	-8	O-619	-2.1
■ **WARREN MILLER**	Miller, Warren Lemuel "Gitz" b: 7/14/1885, Philadelphia, Pa. d: 8/12/56, Philadelphia, Pa. BL/TL, 5′10″, 160 lbs. Deb: 7/29/09																						
1909	Was-A	26	51	5	11	0	0	0	1	4		.216	.273	.216	57	-2	0			1.000	-1	O-15	-0.5
1911	Was-A	21	34	3	5	0	0	0	0	0		.147	.147	.147	-18	-5	0			.778	-2	/O-9	-0.7
Total	2	47	85	8	16	0	0	0	1	4		.188	.225	.188	25	-8	0			.931	-3	/O-24	-1.2
■ **BILL MILLER**	Miller, William Alexander b: 5/23/1879, Bad Schwalbach, Germany d: 9/8/57, Ashtabula, Ohio BL/TL, 6′2″, 170 lbs. Deb: 8/23/02																						
1902	Pit-N	1	5	0	1	0	0	0	2	0		.200	.200	.200	23	-0	0			.000	-0	/O-1	-0.1
■ **JOE MILLETTE**	Millette, Joseph Anthony b: 8/12/66, Walnut Creek, Cal. BR/TR, 6′1″, 180 lbs. Deb: 7/16/92																						
1992	Phi-N	33	78	5	16	0	0	0	2	5	10	.205	.271	.205	37	-6	1	0	0	.974	10	S-26/3-3,2-1	0.6
1993	Phi-N	10	10	3	2	0	0	0	2	1	2	.200	.273	.200	29	-1	0	0	0	1.000	3	/S-7,3-3	0.3
Total	2	43	88	8	18	0	0	0	4	6	12	.205	.271	.205	36	-7	1	0	0	.978	13	/S-33,3-6,2-1	0.9
■ **RALPH MILLIARD**	Milliard, Ralph Gregory b: 12/30/73, Willemstad, Curacao BR/TR, 5′11″, 170 lbs. Deb: 5/12/96																						
1996	Fla-N	24	62	7	10	2	0	0	1	14	16	.161	.316	.194	40	-5	2	0	1	.955	5	2-24	0.2
1997	Fla-N	8	30	2	6	0	0	0	2	3	3	.200	.314	.200	40	-2	1	1	-0	1.000	4	/2-8	0.1
1998	NY-N	10	1	3	0	0	0	0	0	0	1	.000	.000	.000	-99	-0	0	0	0	.833	1	/2-5,S-1	0.1
Total	3	42	93	12	16	2	0	0	3	17	20	.172	.313	.194	38	-8	3	1	0	.963	10	/2-37,S-1	0.4

WALLY MILLIES
Millies, Walter Louis b: 10/18/06, Chicago, Ill. d: 2/28/95, Oak Lawn, Ill. BR/TR, 5'10.5", 170 lbs. Deb: 9/23/34

YEAR	TM/L	G	AB	R	H	2B	3B	HR	RBI	BB	SO	AVG	OBP	SLG	PRO+	BR/A	SB	CS	SBR	FA	FR	G/POS	TPR
1934	Bro-N	2	7	0	0	0	0	0	0	0	0	.000	.000	.000	-99	-2	0			1.000	1	/C-2	-0.1
1936	Was-A	74	215	26	67	10	2	0	25	11	8	.312	.345	.377	83	-6	1	0	0	.968	1	C-72	-0.2
1937	Was-A	59	179	21	40	7	1	0	28	9	15	.223	.261	.274	36	-18	1	0	0	.971	2	C-56	-1.2
1939	Phi-N	84	205	12	48	3	0	0	12	9	5	.234	.270	.249	41	-17	0			.964	-7	C-84	-2.1
1940	Phi-N	26	43	1	3	0	0	0	0	4	4	.070	.149	.070	-39	-8	0			.958	2	C-24	-0.5
1941	Phi-N	1	2	0	0	0	0	0	0	0	0	.000	.000	.000	-99	-1	0			.800	0	/C-1	0.0
Total	6	246	651	60	158	20	3	0	65	33	32	.243	.280	.283	47	-51	2	0		.966	-2	C-239	-4.1

JOCKO MILLIGAN
Milligan, John b: 8/8/1861, Philadelphia, Pa. d: 8/29/23, Philadelphia, Pa. BR/TR, 6', 192 lbs. Deb: 5/1/1884

YEAR	TM/L	G	AB	R	H	2B	3B	HR	RBI	BB	SO	AVG	OBP	SLG	PRO+	BR/A	SB	CS	SBR	FA	FR	G/POS	TPR
1884	Phi-a	66	268	39	77	20	3	3		8		.287	.308	.418	126	6				**.939**	13	C-65/O-1	2.3
1885	Phi-a	67	265	35	71	15	4	2	39	7		.268	.289	.377	103	-0				.935	11	C-61/1-6,O-2	1.4
1886	Phi-a	75	301	52	76	17	3	5	45	21		.252	.301	.379	111	3	18			.919	5	C-40,1-29/O-5,3-2	0.7
1887	Phi-a	95	377	54	114	27	4	2	50	21		.302	.344	.411	110	4	8			.966	3	1-50,C-47/O-1	0.5
1888	*StL-a	63	219	19	55	6	2	5	37	17		.251	.311	.365	105	-0	3			.941	8	C-58/1-5	1.1
1889	StL-a	72	273	53	100	30	2	12	76	16	19	.366	.408	.623	170	21	2			.933	14	C-66/1-9	3.3
1890	Phi-P	62	234	38	69	9	3	3	57	19	19	.295	.363	.397	101	-0	2			.893	4	C-59/1-3	0.7
1891	Phi-a	118	455	75	138	**35**	12	11	106	56	51	.303	.397	.505	153	30	2			.939	0	C-87,1-32	3.1
1892	Was-N	88	323	40	89	20	9	4	43	26	24	.276	.335	.430	135	12	2			.947	5	C-59,1-28	1.9
1893	Bal-N	24	102	19	25	5	2	1	19	5	7	.245	.294	.363	73	-5	2			.981	1	1-22/C-1	-0.3
	NY-N	42	147	16	34	5	6	1	25	14	14	.231	.302	.367	77	-6	2			.934	14	C-42	0.9
	Yr	66	249	35	59	10	8	2	44	19	21	.237	.299	.365	76	-10	4			.932	15	C-43,1-22	0.6
Total	10	772	2964	440	848	189	50	49	497	210	134	.286	.341	.433	122	65	41			.930	78	C-585,1-184/O-9,3-2	15.6

RANDY MILLIGAN
Milligan, Randy Andre b: 11/27/61, San Diego, Cal. BR/TR, 6'1", 228 lbs. Deb: 9/12/87

YEAR	TM/L	G	AB	R	H	2B	3B	HR	RBI	BB	SO	AVG	OBP	SLG	PRO+	BR/A	SB	CS	SBR	FA	FR	G/POS	TPR
1987	NY-N	3	1	0	0	0	0	0	0	1	1	.000	.500	.000	49	0	0	0	0	.000	0	/H	0.0
1988	Pit-N	40	82	10	18	5	0	3	8	20	24	.220	.379	.390	123	3	1	2	-1	.987	-1	1-25/O-2	0.0
1989	Bal-A	124	365	56	98	23	5	12	45	74	75	.268	.396	.458	144	24	9	5	-0	.995	2	*1-117/D-1	1.7
1990	Bal-A	109	362	64	96	20	1	20	60	88	68	.265	.412	.492	157	31	6	3	0	.990	5	1-98/D-9	2.9
1991	Bal-A	141	483	57	127	17	2	16	70	84	108	.263	.374	.406	121	16	0	5	-3	.990	3	*1-106,D-25/O-9	0.8
1992	Bal-A	137	462	71	111	21	1	11	53	106	81	.240	.386	.361	108	10	0	1	-1	.994	-6	*1-129/D-6	-0.6
1993	Cin-N	83	234	30	64	11	1	6	29	46	49	.274	.395	.406	115	7	0	2	-1	.994	5	1-61/O-9	0.6
	Cle-A	19	47	7	20	7	0	0	7	14	4	.426	.557	.574	206	8	0	0	0	1.000	-1	1-18/D-1	0.6
1994	Mon-N	47	82	10	19	2	0	2	12	14	21	.232	.344	.329	76	-3	0	0	0	.978	2	1-33	-0.2
Total	8	703	2118	305	553	106	10	70	284	447	431	.261	.393	.420	127	97	16	18	-6	.992	9	1-587/D-42,O-20	5.8

JACK MILLS
Mills, Abbott Paige b: 10/23/1889, S.Williamstown, Mass. d: 6/3/73, Washington, D.C. BL/TR, 6', 165 lbs. Deb: 7/1/11

YEAR	TM/L	G	AB	R	H	2B	3B	HR	RBI	BB	SO	AVG	OBP	SLG	PRO+	BR/A	SB	CS	SBR	FA	FR	G/POS	TPR
1911	Cle-A	13	17	5	5	0	0	0	1	1		.294	.368	.294	85	-0	1			1.000	2	/3-7	0.1

CHARLIE MILLS
Mills, Charles b: 9/1844, Brooklyn, N.Y. d: 4/10/1874, Brooklyn, N.Y. 6', Deb: 5/18/1871 U

YEAR	TM/L	G	AB	R	H	2B	3B	HR	RBI	BB	SO	AVG	OBP	SLG	PRO+	BR/A	SB	CS	SBR	FA	FR	G/POS	TPR
1871	Mut-n	32	146	27	36	4	3	0	22	1	0	.247	.252	.315	68	-5	2	0	1	.866	-2	*C-29/O-4,3-1	-0.4
1872	Mut-n	6	31	6	4	0	0	0	2	0	0	.129	.129	.129	-22	-4	0	0	0	.667	-1	/O-4,C-3	-0.4
Total	2 n	38	177	33	40	4	3	0	24	1	0	.226	.230	.282	53	-9	2	0	1	.854	-3	/C-32,O-8,3-1	-0.8

BUSTER MILLS
Mills, Colonel Buster "Bus" b: 9/16/08, Ranger, Tex. d: 12/1/91, Arlington, Tex. BR/TR, 5'11.5", 195 lbs. Deb: 4/18/34 MC

YEAR	TM/L	G	AB	R	H	2B	3B	HR	RBI	BB	SO	AVG	OBP	SLG	PRO+	BR/A	SB	CS	SBR	FA	FR	G/POS	TPR
1934	StL-N	29	72	7	17	4	1	1	8	4	11	.236	.295	.361	70	-3	0			1.000	-0	O-18	-0.4
1935	Bro-N	17	56	12	12	2	1	1	7	5	11	.214	.323	.339	80	-1	0			.971	-2	O-17	-0.4
1937	Bos-A	123	505	85	149	25	8	7	58	46	41	.295	.361	.418	92	-6	11	8	-2	.946	-5	*O-120	-1.5
1938	StL-A	123	466	66	133	24	4	3	46	43	46	.285	.350	.373	81	-13	7	8	-3	.964	3	*O-113	-1.5
1940	NY-A	34	63	10	25	3	3	1	15	7	5	.397	.457	.587	176	7	0	0	0	1.000	-2	O-14	0.4
1942	Cle-A	80	195	19	54	4	2	1	26	23	18	.277	.353	.333	99	0	5	4	-1	.973	2	O-53	-0.1
1946	Cle-A	9	22	1	6	0	0	0	3	3	5	.273	.360	.273	84	-0	0	1	-1	1.000	-0	/O-6	-0.2
Total	7	415	1379	200	396	62	19	14	163	131	137	.287	.355	.390	91	-17	23	21		.964	-5	O-341	-3.7

EVERETT MILLS
Mills, Everett b: 1/20/1845, Newark, N.J. d: 6/22/08, Newark, N.J. 6'1", 174 lbs. Deb: 5/5/1871 M

YEAR	TM/L	G	AB	R	H	2B	3B	HR	RBI	BB	SO	AVG	OBP	SLG	PRO+	BR/A	SB	CS	SBR	FA	FR	G/POS	TPR
1871	Oly-n	32	157	38	43	6	4	1	24	3	1	.274	.287	.382	95	-0	2	3	-1	.967	3	*1-32	0.2
1872	Bal-n	55	266	55	79	14	2	0	34	3	2	.297	.305	.365	100	-1	0	2	-1	.931	2	*1-55,M	0.1
1873	Bal-n	54	263	64	87	19	**9**	0	57	2	1	.331	.336	.471	138	12	1	0	0	**.949**	2	*1-53/O-1	1.1
1874	Har-n	53	244	39	69	6	1	0	19	4	2	.283	.294	.316	91	-3	1	1	-0	.920	-2	*1-53	-0.4
1875	Har-n	80	342	59	89	8	4	1	48	0	3	.260	.260	.316	94	-3	6	4	-1	.945	2	*1-80	-0.2
1876	Har-N	63	254	28	66	8	1	0	23	1	3	.260	.263	.299	80	-6				.939	-2	*1-63	-0.9
Total	5 n	274	1272	255	367	53	20	2	182	12	9	.289	.295	.366	104	4	10	10	-3	.941	6	1-273/O-1	0.8

FRANK MILLS
Mills, Frank Le Moyne b: 5/13/1895, Knoxville, Ohio d: 8/31/83, Youngstown, Ohio BL/TR, 6', 180 lbs. Deb: 9/22/14

YEAR	TM/L	G	AB	R	H	2B	3B	HR	RBI	BB	SO	AVG	OBP	SLG	PRO+	BR/A	SB	CS	SBR	FA	FR	G/POS	TPR
1914	Cle-A	4	8	0	1	0	0	0	0	1	2	.125	.222	.125	4	-1	0			.900	-1	/C-2	-0.2

BRAD MILLS
Mills, James Bradley b: 1/19/57, Exeter, Cal. BL/TR, 6', 195 lbs. Deb: 6/8/80 C

YEAR	TM/L	G	AB	R	H	2B	3B	HR	RBI	BB	SO	AVG	OBP	SLG	PRO+	BR/A	SB	CS	SBR	FA	FR	G/POS	TPR
1980	Mon-N	21	60	1	18	1	0	0	8	5	6	.300	.354	.317	88	-1	0	1	-1	.977	-1	3-18	-0.3
1981	*Mon-N	17	21	3	5	1	0	0	1	2	1	.238	.304	.286	67	-1	0	0	0	1.000	0	/3-7,2-2	-0.1
1982	Mon-N	54	67	6	15	3	0	1	2	5	11	.224	.278	.313	64	-3	0	0	0	.867	-3	3-13	-0.7
1983	Mon-N	14	20	1	5	0	0	0	1	2	3	.250	.318	.250	60	-1	0	0	0	1.000	-1	/3-3,1-1	-0.2
Total	4	106	168	11	43	5	0	1	12	14	21	.256	.313	.304	73	-6	0	1	-1	.959	-5	/3-41,2-2,1-1	-1.3

RUPERT MILLS
Mills, Rupert Frank b: 10/12/1892, Newark, N.J. d: 7/20/29, Lake Hopatcong, N.J. BR/TR, 6'2", 185 lbs. Deb: 6/23/15

YEAR	TM/L	G	AB	R	H	2B	3B	HR	RBI	BB	SO	AVG	OBP	SLG	PRO+	BR/A	SB	CS	SBR	FA	FR	G/POS	TPR
1915	New-F	41	134	12	27	5	1	0	16	6	21	.201	.241	.254	42	-13	6			.976	0	1-37	-1.5

BILL MILLS
Mills, William Henry b: 11/2/20, Boston, Mass. BR/TR, 5'10", 175 lbs. Deb: 5/19/44

YEAR	TM/L	G	AB	R	H	2B	3B	HR	RBI	BB	SO	AVG	OBP	SLG	PRO+	BR/A	SB	CS	SBR	FA	FR	G/POS	TPR
1944	Phi-A	5	4	0	1	0	0	0	0	1	1	.250	.400	.250	89	0	0	0	0	.000	0	/C-1	0.0

PETE MILNE
Milne, William James b: 4/10/25, Mobile, Ala. BL/TR, 6'1", 180 lbs. Deb: 9/15/48

YEAR	TM/L	G	AB	R	H	2B	3B	HR	RBI	BB	SO	AVG	OBP	SLG	PRO+	BR/A	SB	CS	SBR	FA	FR	G/POS	TPR
1948	NY-N	12	27	0	6	0	1	0	2	1	6	.222	.250	.296	47	-2	0			.867	-2	/O-9	-0.5
1949	NY-N	31	29	5	7	1	0	1	6	3	6	.241	.313	.379	85	-1	0			1.000	-0	/O-1	-0.1
1950	NY-N	4	4	1	1	0	1	0	1	0	1	.250	.250	.750	151	0	0			.000	0	H	0.0
Total	3	47	60	6	14	1	2	1	9	4	13	.233	.281	.367	73	-2	0			.882	-2	/O-10	-0.6

BRIAN MILNER
Milner, Brian Tate b: 11/17/59, Fort Worth, Tex. BR/TR, 6'2", 200 lbs. Deb: 6/23/78

YEAR	TM/L	G	AB	R	H	2B	3B	HR	RBI	BB	SO	AVG	OBP	SLG	PRO+	BR/A	SB	CS	SBR	FA	FR	G/POS	TPR
1978	Tor-A	2	9	3	4	0	1	0	2	0	1	.444	.444	.667	204	1	0	0	0	.800	-3	/C-2	-0.1

EDDIE MILNER
Milner, Eddie James b: 5/21/55, Columbus, Ohio BL/TL, 5'11", 173 lbs. Deb: 9/2/80

YEAR	TM/L	G	AB	R	H	2B	3B	HR	RBI	BB	SO	AVG	OBP	SLG	PRO+	BR/A	SB	CS	SBR	FA	FR	G/POS	TPR
1980	Cin-N	6	3	1	0	0	0	0	0	0	0	.000	.000	.000	-99	-1	0	0	0	.000	0	/H	-0.1
1981	Cin-N	8	5	0	1	1	0	0	1	1	1	.200	.333	.400	106	0	0	0	0	1.000	-1	/O-4	-0.1
1982	Cin-N	113	407	61	109	23	5	4	31	41	40	.268	.336	.378	98	-1	18	12	-2	.987	-3	*O-107	-0.8
1983	Cin-N	146	502	77	131	23	6	9	33	68	60	.261	.350	.384	100	1	41	12	5	.990	20	*O-139	2.2
1984	Cin-N	117	336	44	78	8	4	7	29	51	50	.232	.337	.342	87	-5	21	13	-2	.983	10	*O-108	0.1
1985	Cin-N	145	453	82	115	19	7	3	33	61	31	.254	.344	.347	89	-5	35	13	3	.983	15	*O-135	0.9
1986	Cin-N	145	424	70	110	22	6	15	47	36	56	.259	.317	.446	104	1	18	11	-1	.990	5	*O-127	0.3
1987	*SF-N	101	214	38	54	14	0	4	19	24	33	.252	.328	.374	90	-3	10	9	-2	.993	-9	O-84	-1.7
1988	Cin-N	23	51	3	9	1	0	0	2	4	9	.176	.236	.196	24	-5	2	2	-1	.968	-0	O-15	-0.7
Total	9	804	2395	376	607	111	28	42	195	286	280	.253	.335	.376	94	-17	145	72	0	.987	38	O-719	0.1

JOHN MILNER
Milner, John David "The Hammer" b: 12/28/49, Atlanta, Ga. BL/TL, 6', 185 lbs. Deb: 9/15/71

YEAR	TM/L	G	AB	R	H	2B	3B	HR	RBI	BB	SO	AVG	OBP	SLG	PRO+	BR/A	SB	CS	SBR	FA	FR	G/POS	TPR
1971	NY-N	9	18	1	3	1	0	0	1	0	3	.167	.167	.222	9	-2	0	0	0	1.000	1	/O-3	-0.1

YEAR	TM/L	G	AB	R	H	2B	3B	HR	RBI	BB	SO	AVG	OBP	SLG	PRO+	BR/A	SB	CS	SBR	FA	FR	G/POS	TPR
1972	NY-N	117	362	52	86	12	2	17	38	51	74	.238	.340	.423	118	9	2	1	0	.965	3	O-91,1-10	0.8
1973	*NY-N	129	451	69	108	12	3	23	72	62	84	.239	.333	.432	112	7	1	1	-0	.989	-7	1-95,O-29	-0.9
1974	NY-N	137	507	70	128	19	0	20	63	66	77	.252	.339	.408	110	6	10	2	2	.994	-1	*1-133	-0.2
1975	NY-N	91	220	24	42	11	0	7	29	33	22	.191	.302	.336	81	-6	1	1	-0	.985	6	O-31,1-29	-0.3
1976	NY-N	127	443	56	120	25	4	15	78	65	53	.271	.364	.447	137	22	0	7	-4	.985	4	*O-112,1-12	1.7
1977	NY-N	131	388	43	99	20	3	12	57	61	55	.255	.356	.415	111	7	6	2	1	.994	-1	1-87,O-22	0.1
1978	Pit-N	108	295	39	80	17	0	6	38	34	25	.271	.347	.390	101	1	5	0	2	1.000	-2	O-69,1-28	-0.3
1979	*Pit-N	128	326	52	90	9	4	16	60	53	37	.276	.379	.475	126	12	3	5	-2	.958	-2	O-64,1-48	0.4
1980	Pit-N	114	238	31	58	6	0	8	34	52	29	.244	.379	.370	108	5	2	2	-1	.991	-5	1-70,O-11	-0.5
1981	Pit-N	34	59	6	14	1	0	2	9	5	3	.237	.297	.356	82	-1	0	0	0	.980	-2	/1-8,O-8	-0.5
	*Mon-N	31	76	6	18	5	0	3	9	12	6	.237	.341	.421	114	1	0	1	-1	.978	1	1-21	0.1
	Yr	65	135	12	32	6	0	5	18	17	9	.237	.322	.393	100	-0	0	1	-1	.979	-2	1-29/O-8	-0.4
1982	Mon-N	26	28	1	3	0	0	0	2	4	2	.107	.219	.107	-6	-4	0	0	0	1.000	0	/1-5	-0.4
	Pit-N	33	25	5	6	2	0	2	8	6	3	.240	.406	.560	163	2	1	0	0	1.000	-0	/1-1	0.3
	Yr	59	53	6	9	2	0	2	10	10	5	.170	.313	.321	76	-2	1	0	0	1.000	0	/1-6	-0.1
Total	12	1215	3436	455	855	140	16	131	498	504	473	.249	.347	.413	112	59	31	22	-4	.991	-4	1-547,O-440	0.2

■ MIKE MILOSEVICH Milosevich, Michael "Mollie" b: 1/13/15, Zeigler, Ill. d: 2/3/66, E.Chicago, Ind. BR/TR, 5'10.5", 172 lbs. Deb: 4/30/44

YEAR	TM/L	G	AB	R	H	2B	3B	HR	RBI	BB	SO	AVG	OBP	SLG	PRO+	BR/A	SB	CS	SBR	FA	FR	G/POS	TPR
1944	NY-A	94	312	27	77	11	4	0	32	30	37	.247	.313	.308	75	-10	1	2	-1	.954	7	S-91	0.3
1945	NY-A	30	69	5	15	2	0	0	7	6	6	.217	.289	.246	54	-4	0	0	0	.957	1	S-22/2-1	-0.2
Total	2	124	381	32	92	13	4	0	39	36	43	.241	.309	.297	71	-14	1	2	-1	.954	8	S-113/2-1	0.1

■ DON MINCHER Mincher, Donald Ray b: 6/24/38, Huntsville, Ala. BL/TR, 6'3", 213 lbs. Deb: 4/18/60

YEAR	TM/L	G	AB	R	H	2B	3B	HR	RBI	BB	SO	AVG	OBP	SLG	PRO+	BR/A	SB	CS	SBR	FA	FR	G/POS	TPR
1960	Was-A	27	79	10	19	4	1	2	5	11	11	.241	.333	.392	96	-0	0	1	-1	.977	-4	1-20	-0.7
1961	Min-A	35	101	18	19	5	1	5	11	22	11	.188	.333	.406	91	-1	0	1	-1	.969	-2	1-29	-0.6
1962	Min-A	86	121	20	29	1	1	9	29	34	24	.240	.406	.488	134	7	0	0	0	.978	-1	1-25	0.4
1963	Min-A	82	225	41	58	8	0	17	42	30	51	.258	.353	.520	138	11	0	0	0	.983	-5	1-60	0.4
1964	Min-A	120	287	45	68	12	4	23	56	27	51	.237	.303	.547	130	10	0	0	0	.992	-0	1-76	0.7
1965	*Min-A	128	346	43	87	17	3	22	65	49	73	.251	.348	.509	134	15	1	3	-2	.992	-5	1-99/O-1	0.4
1966	Min-A	139	431	53	108	30	0	14	62	58	68	.251	.342	.418	110	6	3	2	-0	.992	3	*1-130	0.1
1967	Cal-A★	147	487	81	133	23	3	25	76	69	69	.273	.368	.487	157	35	0	3	-2	.994	-2	*1-142/O-1	2.4
1968	Cal-A	120	399	35	94	12	1	13	48	43	65	.236	.316	.368	111	5	0	2	-1	.991	-3	*1-113	-0.9
1969	Sea-A★	140	427	53	105	14	0	25	78	78	69	.246	.369	.454	131	19	10	11	-4	.995	8	*1-122	1.4
1970	Oak-A	140	463	62	114	18	0	27	74	56	71	.246	.331	.460	120	11	5	4	-1	.990	2	*1-137	0.1
1971	Oak-A	28	92	9	22	6	1	2	8	20	14	.239	.375	.391	120	3	1	1	-0	.996	3	1-27	0.3
	Was-A	100	323	35	94	15	1	10	45	53	52	.291	.394	.437	143	20	2	1	0	.990	3	1-88	1.6
	Yr	128	415	44	116	21	2	12	53	73	66	.280	.390	.427	138	23	3	2	-0	.991	6	*1-115	1.9
1972	Tex-A	61	191	23	45	10	0	6	39	46	23	.236	.389	.382	136	11	2	1	0	.994	6	1-59	1.4
	*Oak-A	47	54	2	8	1	0	0	5	10	16	.148	.281	.167	37	-4	0	2	-1	.988	-1	1-11	-0.7
	Yr	108	245	25	53	11	0	6	44	56	39	.216	.366	.335	115	7	2	3	-1	.993	5	1-70	0.7
Total	13	1400	4026	530	1003	176	16	200	643	606	668	.249	.351	.450	127	149	24	32	-12	.990	2	*1-1138/O-2	6.3

■ ED MINCHER Mincher, Edward John b: 1851, Baltimore, Md. Deb: 5/4/1871

YEAR	TM/L	G	AB	R	H	2B	3B	HR	RBI	BB	SO	AVG	OBP	SLG	PRO+	BR/A	SB	CS	SBR	FA	FR	G/POS	TPR
1871	Kek-n	9	36	4	8	0	0	0	5	0	0	.222	.222	.222	28	-3	1	0	0	.852	-0	/O-9	-0.2
1872	Nat-n	11	53	5	6	0	0	0	4	0	1	.113	.113	.113	-26	-9	0	0	0	.837	2	O-11	-0.4
Total	2 n	20	89	9	14	0	0	0	9	0	1	.157	.157	.157	-5	-12	1	0	0	.842	2	/O-20	-0.6

■ DAN MINNEHAN Minnehan, Daniel Joseph b: 11/28/1865, Troy, N.Y. d: 8/8/29, Troy, N.Y. BR/TR, 5'10", 145 lbs. Deb: 9/20/1895

YEAR	TM/L	G	AB	R	H	2B	3B	HR	RBI	BB	SO	AVG	OBP	SLG	PRO+	BR/A	SB	CS	SBR	FA	FR	G/POS	TPR
1895	Lou-N	8	34	6	13	0	0	0	6	1	1	.382	.400	.382	109	1	0			.920	-0	/3-7,O-2	0.0

■ RYAN MINOR Minor, Ryan Dale b: 1/5/74, Canton, Ohio BR/TR, 6'7", 225 lbs. Deb: 9/13/98

YEAR	TM/L	G	AB	R	H	2B	3B	HR	RBI	BB	SO	AVG	OBP	SLG	PRO+	BR/A	SB	CS	SBR	FA	FR	G/POS	TPR
1998	Bal-A	9	14	3	6	1	0	0	1	0	3	.429	.429	.500	143	1	0	0	0	.833	0	/3-6,1-3,D-1	0.1

■ MINNIE MINOSO Minoso, Saturnino Orestes Armas (Arrieta) b: 11/29/22, Havana, Cuba BR/TR, 5'10", 175 lbs. Deb: 4/19/49 C

YEAR	TM/L	G	AB	R	H	2B	3B	HR	RBI	BB	SO	AVG	OBP	SLG	PRO+	BR/A	SB	CS	SBR	FA	FR	G/POS	TPR
1949	Cle-A	9	16	2	3	0	0	1	1	2	2	.188	.350	.375	94	-0	0	1	-1	1.000	-1	/O-7	-0.2
1951	Cle-A	8	14	3	6	2	0	0	2	1	1	.429	.529	.571	209	2	0	0	0	.952	-0	/1-7	0.2
	Chi-A★	138	516	109	167	32	14	10	74	71	41	.324	.419	.498	150	38	31	10	3	.961	-12	O-82,3-68/S-1	2.6
	Yr	146	530	112	173	34	**14**	10	76	72	42	.326	.422	.500	152	41	**31**	10	3	.961	-12	O-82,3-68/1-7,S-1	2.8
1952	Chi-A★	147	569	96	160	24	9	13	61	71	46	.281	.375	.424	121	17	**22**	16	-3	.979	4	*O-143/3-9,S-1	1.2
1953	Chi-A★	151	556	104	174	24	8	15	104	74	43	.313	.410	.466	132	27	**25**	16	-2	.967	6	*O-147,3-10	2.5
1954	Chi-A★	153	568	119	182	29	**18**	19	116	77	46	.320	.416	**.535**	154	43	18	11	-1	.978	13	*O-146/3-9	5.0
1955	Chi-A	139	517	79	149	26	7	10	70	76	43	.288	.390	.424	115	13	19	8	1	.971	12	*O-138/3-2	2.0
1956	Chi-A	151	545	106	172	29	**11**	21	88	86	40	.316	.430	.525	149	42	12	6	0	.974	3	*O-148/3-8,1-1	3.6
1957	Chi-A★	153	568	96	176	**36**	5	12	103	79	54	.310	.413	.454	136	32	18	15	-4	.984	6	*O-152/3-1	2.6
1958	Cle-A	149	556	94	168	25	2	24	80	59	53	.302	.384	.484	141	32	14	14	-4	.975	13	*O-147/3-1	3.3
1959	Cle-A★	148	570	92	172	32	0	21	92	54	46	.302	.379	.468	136	29	8	10	-4	.985	16	*O-148	3.4
1960	Chi-A★	154	591	89	**184**	32	4	20	105	52	63	.311	.380	.481	132	27	17	13	-3	.980	5	*O-154	2.0
1961	Chi-A	152	540	91	151	28	3	14	82	67	46	.280	.376	.420	114	13	9	4	0	.956	3	*O-147	0.8
1962	StL-N	39	97	14	19	5	0	1	10	7	17	.196	.271	.278	44	-8	4	0	1	.972	-1	O-27	-0.9
1963	Was-A	109	315	38	72	12	2	4	30	33	38	.229	.317	.317	79	-8	8	6	-1	.955	-5	O-74/3-8	-1.9
1964	Chi-A	30	31	4	7	0	0	1	5	5	3	.226	.351	.323	91	-0	0	0	0	1.000	0	/O-5	0.0
1976	Chi-A	3	8	0	1	0	0	0	0	0	2	.125	.125	.125	-27	-1	0	0	0	.000	0	/D-3	-0.1
1980	Chi-A	2	2	0	0	0	0	0	0	0	0	.000	.000	.000	-99	-1	0	0	0	.000	0	/H	-0.1
Total	17	1835	6579	1136	1963	336	83	186	1023	814	584	.298	.391	.459	130	297	205	130	-16	.974	62	*O-1665,3-116/1DS	26.0

■ DOUG MIRABELLI Mirabelli, Douglas Anthony b: 10/18/70, Kingman, Ariz. BR/TR, 6'1", 205 lbs. Deb: 8/27/96

YEAR	TM/L	G	AB	R	H	2B	3B	HR	RBI	BB	SO	AVG	OBP	SLG	PRO+	BR/A	SB	CS	SBR	FA	FR	G/POS	TPR
1996	SF-N	9	18	2	4	1	0	0	1	3	4	.222	.333	.278	66	-1	0	0	0	1.000	-1	/C-8	-0.1
1997	SF-N	6	7	0	1	0	0	0	0	1	3	.143	.250	.143	6	-1	0	0	0	1.000	0	/C-6	-0.1
1998	SF-N	10	17	2	4	2	0	1	4	2	6	.235	.316	.529	118	0	0	0	0	.974	1	C-10	0.2
Total	3	25	42	4	9	3	0	1	5	6	13	.214	.313	.357	77	-1	0	0	0	.988	-0	/C-24	0.0

■ WILLY MIRANDA Miranda, Guillermo (Perez) b: 5/24/26, Velasco, Cuba d: 9/7/96, Baltimore, Md. BB/TR, 5'9.5", 150 lbs. Deb: 5/6/51

YEAR	TM/L	G	AB	R	H	2B	3B	HR	RBI	BB	SO	AVG	OBP	SLG	PRO+	BR/A	SB	CS	SBR	FA	FR	G/POS	TPR
1951	Was-A	7	9	2	4	0	0	0	0	0	0	.444	.444	.444	143	1	0	0	0	.818	-0	/S-2,1-1	0.0
1952	Chi-A	12	8	1	2	1	0	0	0	3	0	.250	.455	.375	131	1	0	0	0	1.000	4	/S-4,3-4,2-1	0.5
	StL-A	7	11	2	1	0	1	0	1	3	1	.091	.286	.273	54	-1	0	0	0	.900	-1	/S-7	-0.1
	Chi-A	58	142	13	31	3	1	0	7	10	14	.218	.275	.254	47	-10	1	0	0	.975	11	S-50/2-1,3-1	0.4
	Yr	77	161	16	34	4	2	0	8	16	15	.211	.287	.261	52	-10	1	0	0	.970	14	S-61/3-5,2-2	0.8
1953	StL-A	17	6	2	1	0	0	0	0	1	1	.167	.286	.167	24	-1	1	1	-0	.933	3	/S-8,3-6	0.3
	NY-A	48	58	12	13	0	0	1	5	5	10	.224	.286	.276	54	-4	1	1	-0	.984	17	S-45	1.4
	Yr	65	64	14	14	0	0	1	5	6	11	.219	.286	.266	51	-4	2	2	-1	.979	20	S-53/3-6	1.7
1954	NY-A	92	116	12	29	4	2	1	12	10	10	.250	.310	.345	82	-3	0	3	-2	.948	16	S-88/2-4,3-1	1.5
1955	Bal-A	153	487	42	124	12	6	1	38	42	58	.255	.315	.310	74	-19	4	3	-1	.958	19	*S-153/2-1	1.2
1956	Bal-A	148	461	38	100	16	4	2	34	46	73	.217	.288	.282	55	-31	3	6	-3	.962	2	*S-147	-2.0
1957	Bal-A	115	314	29	61	3	0	0	20	24	42	.194	.251	.204	28	-31	2	1	0	.966	-3	*S-115	-2.6
1958	Bal-A	102	214	15	43	6	0	1	8	14	25	.201	.250	.243	38	-18	1	1	-0	.962	-2	*S-102	-1.4
1959	Bal-A	65	88	8	14	5	0	0	7	7	16	.159	.221	.216	21	-10	0	0	0	.974	22	S-47,3-11/2-5	1.4
Total	9	824	1914	176	423	50	14	6	132	165	250	.221	.284	.271	54	-126	13	16	-6	.962	88	S-768/3-23,2-12,1-1	0.6

■ JOHN MISSE Misse, John Beverly b: 5/30/1885, Highland, Kan. d: 3/18/70, St.Joseph, Mo. BR/TR, 5'8", 150 lbs. Deb: 5/26/14

YEAR	TM/L	G	AB	R	H	2B	3B	HR	RBI	BB	SO	AVG	OBP	SLG	PRO+	BR/A	SB	CS	SBR	FA	FR	G/POS	TPR
1914	StL-F	99	306	28	60	8	1	0	22	36	52	.196	.281	.229	38	-31	3			.948	14	2-50,S-48/3-2	-1.4

■ CLARENCE MITCHELL

Mitchell, Clarence Elmer b: 2/22/1891, Franklin, Neb. d: 11/6/63, Grand Island, Neb. BL/TL, 5'11.5", 190 lbs. Deb: 6/2/11 C

YEAR	TM/L	G	AB	R	H	2B	3B	HR	RBI	BB	SO	AVG	OBP	SLG	PRO+	BR/A	SB	CS	SBR	FA	FR	G/POS	TPR
1911	Det-A	5	4	2	2	0	0	0	0	1		.500	.600	.500	198	1	0			1.000	-1	/P-5	0.0
1916	Cin-N	56	117	11	28	2	1	0	11	4	6	.239	.264	.274	67	-5	1			.985	-2	P-29/1-9,O-3	-0.5
1917	Cin-N	47	90	13	25	3	0	0	5	5	5	.278	.316	.311	97	-0	0			.982	-0	P-32/1-6,O-5	-0.1
1918	Bro-N	10	24	2	6	1	1	0	2	0	3	.250	.250	.375	90	-0	0			.750	-2	/O-6,1-2,P-1	-0.4
1919	Bro-N	34	49	7	18	1	0	1	2	4	4	.367	.415	.449	156	3	0			.976	1	P-23	0.0
1920	*Bro-N	55	107	9	25	2	2	0	11	8	9	.234	.287	.290	64	-5	1	0	0	1.000	1	P-19,1-11/O-4	-0.4
1921	Bro-N	46	91	11	24	5	0	0	12	5	7	.264	.316	.319	66	-4	3	1	0	.945	3	P-37/1-4	0.0
1922	Bro-N	56	155	21	45	6	3	3	28	19	6	.290	.371	.426	106	2	0	0	0	.992	3	1-42/P-5	0.2
1923	Phi-N	53	78	10	21	3	2	1	9	4	11	.269	.305	.397	75	-3	0	0	0	.880	-3	P-29	0.0
1924	Phi-N	69	102	7	26	3	0	0	13	2	7	.255	.276	.284	45	-8	1	0	0	**1.000**	3	P-30	0.0
1925	Phi-N	52	92	7	18	2	0	0	13	5	9	.196	.237	.217	16	-12	2	0	1	**1.000**	4	P-32/1-2	0.0
1926	Phi-N	39	78	8	19	4	0	0	6	5	5	.244	.289	.295	55	-5	0			.986	4	P-28/1-4	0.0
1927	Phi-N	18	42	5	10	2	0	1	6	2	1	.238	.273	.357	67	-2	0			.963	1	P-13	0.0
1928	Phi-N	5	4	0	1	0	0	0	0	0	0	.250	.250	.250	30	-0	0			1.000	0	/P-3	0.0
	*StL-N	19	56	0	7	1	0	0	1	0	3	.125	.125	.143	-30	-11	0			.982	2	P-19	0.0
	Yr	24	60	0	8	1	0	0	1	0	3	.133	.133	.150	-26	-11	0			.983	3	P-22	0.0
1929	StL-N	26	66	9	18	3	1	0	9	4	6	.273	.314	.348	63	-4	1			.974	-1	P-25	0.0
1930	StL-N	1	2	0	1	0	0	0	0	0	0	.500	.500	.500	138	0	0			.000	-0	/P-1	0.0
	NY-N	24	47	9	12	1	0	0	1	1	5	.255	.271	.277	33	-5	0			1.000	2	P-24	0.0
	Yr	25	49	9	13	1	0	0	1	1	5	.265	.280	.286	38	-5	0			1.000	2	P-25	0.0
1931	NY-N	27	73	5	16	2	0	1	4	2	4	.219	.240	.288	42	-6	0			.885	-2	P-27	0.0
1932	NY-N	8	10	2	2	0	0	0	0	1	1	.200	.273	.200	30	-1	0			.833	-1	/P-8	0.0
Total	18	650	1287	138	324	41	10	7	133	72	92	.252	.293	.315	64	-65	9	1		.972	14	P-390/1-80,O-18	-1.2

■ FRED MITCHELL

Mitchell, Frederick Francis (b: Frederick Francis Yapp) b: 6/5/1878, Cambridge, Mass. d: 10/13/70, Newton, Mass. BR/TR, 5'9.5", 185 lbs. Deb: 4/27/01 MC

YEAR	TM/L	G	AB	R	H	2B	3B	HR	RBI	BB	SO	AVG	OBP	SLG	PRO+	BR/A	SB	CS	SBR	FA	FR	G/POS	TPR
1901	Bos-A	20	44	5	7	0	2	0	4	2		.159	.196	.250	23	-5	0			.875	-0	P-17/2-2,S-1	-0.1
1902	Bos-A	1	1	0	0	0	0	0	0	0		.000	.000	.000	-97	-0	0			.667	0	/P-1	0.0
	Phi-A	19	48	7	9	1	1	0	3	1		.188	.204	.250	24	-5	1			.942	2	P-18/O-1	-0.1
	Yr	20	49	7	9	1	1	0	3	1		.184	.200	.245	22	-5	1			.927	2	P-19/O-1	-0.1
1903	Phi-N	29	95	11	19	4	0	0	10	0		.200	.200	.242	27	-9	0			.857	-3	P-28	0.0
1904	Phi-N	25	82	9	17	3	1	0	3	5		.207	.253	.268	63	-4	1			.981	3	P-13/1-9,3-2,O-1	-0.2
	Bro-N	8	24	3	7	1	1	0	6	1		.292	.346	.417	139	1	0			.906	1	/P-8	0.0
	Yr	33	106	12	24	4	2	0	9	6		.226	.274	.302	80	-3	1			.952	4	P-21/1-9,3-2,O-1	-0.2
1905	Bro-N	27	79	4	15	0	0	0	8	4		.190	.238	.190	30	-7	0			.881	-2	P-12/1-7,3-4,S-1,O	-0.7
1910	NY-A	68	196	16	45	7	2	0	18	9		.230	.274	.286	71	-7	6			.968	-15	C-62	-1.8
1913	Bos-N	4	3	0	1	0	0	0	0	0	2	.333	.333	.333	89	-0	0			.000	0	H	0.0
Total	7	201	572	55	120	16	7	0	52	22	2	.210	.245	.262	52	-35	8			.904	-14	/P-97,C-62,13OS2	-2.9

■ JOHNNY MITCHELL

Mitchell, John Franklin b: 8/9/1894, Detroit, Mich. d: 11/4/65, Birmingham, Mich. BB/TR, 5'8", 155 lbs. Deb: 5/21/21

YEAR	TM/L	G	AB	R	H	2B	3B	HR	RBI	BB	SO	AVG	OBP	SLG	PRO+	BR/A	SB	CS	SBR	FA	FR	G/POS	TPR
1921	NY-A	13	42	4	11	1	0	0	2	4	4	.262	.326	.286	56	-3	1	0	0	.958	-6	/S-7,2-5	-0.7
1922	NY-A	4	4	1	0	0	0	0	0	0	1	.000	.000	.000	-98	-1	0	1	-1	1.000	-1	/S-4	-0.2
	Bos-A	59	203	20	51	4	1	1	8	16	17	.251	.318	.296	61	-11	1	2	-1	.962	-5	S-58	-1.1
	Yr	63	207	21	51	4	1	1	8	16	18	.246	.313	.290	58	-12	1	2	-1	.963	-6	S-62	-1.3
1923	Bos-A	92	347	40	78	15	4	0	19	34	18	.225	.296	.291	55	-23	7	11	-5	.961	-0	S-87/2-5	-1.9
1924	Bro-N	64	243	42	64	10	0	1	16	37	22	.263	.361	.317	86	-3	3	1	0	.951	-1	S-64	0.4
1925	Bro-N	97	336	45	84	8	3	0	18	28	19	.250	.308	.292	55	-22	2	0	1	.947	-4	S-90	-1.5
Total	5	329	1175	152	288	38	8	2	63	119	81	.245	.317	.296	62	-63	14	14	-4	.955	-16	S-310/2-10	-5.0

■ KEITH MITCHELL

Mitchell, Keith Alexander b: 8/6/69, San Diego, Cal. BR/TR, 5'10", 180 lbs. Deb: 7/23/91

YEAR	TM/L	G	AB	R	H	2B	3B	HR	RBI	BB	SO	AVG	OBP	SLG	PRO+	BR/A	SB	CS	SBR	FA	FR	G/POS	TPR
1991	*Atl-N	48	66	11	21	0	0	2	5	8	12	.318	.392	.409	118	2	3	1	0	.970	-7	O-34	-0.5
1994	Sea-A	46	128	21	29	2	0	5	15	18	22	.227	.327	.359	75	-5	0	0	0	.980	-7	O-38/D-6	-1.1
1996	Cin-N	11	15	2	4	1	0	1	3	1	3	.267	.313	.533	117	0	0	0	0	.875	-1	O-5	0.0
1998	Bos-A	23	33	4	9	2	0	0	6	7	5	.273	.400	.333	94	0	1	0	0	1.000	-3	D-12,O-10	-0.3
Total	4	128	242	38	63	5	0	8	29	34	42	.260	.354	.380	92	-2	4	1	1	.969	-17	/O-87,D-18	-1.9

■ KEVIN MITCHELL

Mitchell, Kevin Darnell b: 1/13/62, San Diego, Cal. BR/TR, 5'11", 210 lbs. Deb: 9/4/84

YEAR	TM/L	G	AB	R	H	2B	3B	HR	RBI	BB	SO	AVG	OBP	SLG	PRO+	BR/A	SB	CS	SBR	FA	FR	G/POS	TPR
1984	NY-N	7	14	0	3	0	0	0	1	0	3	.214	.214	.214	21	-1	0	1	-1	.833	-1	/3-5	-0.3
1986	*NY-N	108	328	51	91	22	2	12	43	33	61	.277	.345	.466	125	10	3	3	-1	.983	-11	O-68,S-24/3-7,1-2	-0.1
1987	SD-N	62	196	19	48	7	1	7	26	20	38	.245	.315	.398	91	-3	0	0	0	.945	4	3-51/O-3	0.0
	*SF-N	69	268	49	82	13	1	15	44	28	50	.306	.376	.530	144	16	9	6	-1	.962	-5	3-68/O-3,S-1	0.9
	Yr	131	464	68	130	20	2	22	70	48	88	.280	.350	.474	121	13	9	6	-1	.954	-2	*3-119/O-6,S-1	0.9
1988	SF-N	148	505	60	127	25	7	19	80	48	85	.251	.323	.442	123	13	5	5	-2	.943	-5	*3-102,O-40	0.5
1989	*SF-N★	154	543	100	158	34	6	**47**	**125**	87	115	.291	.392	**.635**	**194**	**66**	3	4	-2	.978	7	*O-147/3-2	**7.0**
1990	SF-N★	140	524	90	152	24	2	35	93	58	87	.290	.363	.544	151	35	4	7	-3	.971	7	*O-138	3.6
1991	SF-N	113	371	52	95	13	1	27	69	43	57	.256	.341	.515	142	20	2	3	-1	.970	3	*O-100/1-1	2.0
1992	Sea-A	99	360	48	103	24	0	9	67	35	46	.286	.354	.428	117	8	0	2	-1	1.000	-0	O-69,D-26	0.5
1993	Cin-N	93	323	56	110	21	3	19	64	25	48	.341	.390	.601	160	26	1	0	0	.957	1	O-87	2.6
1994	Cin-N	95	310	57	101	18	1	30	77	59	62	.326	.438	.681	188	41	2	0	1	.972	4	O-89/1-1	4.2
1996	Bos-A	27	92	9	28	4	0	2	13	11	14	.304	.385	.413	100	0	0	0	0	.935	-3	O-21/D-4	-0.3
	Cin-N	37	114	18	37	11	0	6	26	26	16	.325	.450	.579	168	12	0	0	0	.978	-2	O-31/1-3	0.9
1997	Cle-A	20	59	7	9	1	0	4	11	9	11	.153	.275	.373	65	-3	1	0	0	.000	-1	D-16/O-1	-0.4
1998	Oak-A	51	127	14	29	7	1	2	21	9	26	.228	.279	.346	63	-7	0	0	0	1.000	-2	D-23,O-10/1-2	-1.0
Total	13	1223	4134	630	1173	224	25	234	760	491	719	.284	.363	.520	143	234	30	31	-10	.971	-5	O-807,3-235/DS1	20.1

■ DALE MITCHELL

Mitchell, Loren Dale b: 8/23/21, Colony, Okla. d: 1/5/87, Tulsa, Okla. BL/TL, 6'1", 195 lbs. Deb: 9/15/46

YEAR	TM/L	G	AB	R	H	2B	3B	HR	RBI	BB	SO	AVG	OBP	SLG	PRO+	BR/A	SB	CS	SBR	FA	FR	G/POS	TPR
1946	Cle-A	11	44	7	19	3	0	0	5	1	2	.432	.444	.500	175	4	1	0	0	1.000	-0	O-11	0.4
1947	Cle-A	123	493	69	156	16	10	1	34	23	14	.316	.347	.396	109	4	2	5	-2	.977	-9	*O-115	-1.4
1948	*Cle-A	141	608	82	204	30	8	4	56	45	17	.336	.383	.431	119	16	13	18	-7	**.991**	4	*O-140	0.4
1949	Cle-A★	149	640	81	**203**	16	**23**	3	56	43	11	.317	.360	.428	110	7	10	3	1	**.994**	3	*O-149	0.3
1950	Cle-A	130	506	81	156	27	5	3	49	67	21	.308	.390	.399	106	6	3	7	-3	.972	-11	*O-127	-1.3
1951	Cle-A	134	510	83	148	21	7	11	62	53	16	.290	.358	.424	117	11	7	7	-2	.992	-6	*O-124	-0.1
1952	Cle-A★	134	511	61	165	26	3	5	58	52	9	.323	.387	.415	132	22	6	6	-2	.992	-5	*O-128	1.0
1953	Cle-A	134	500	76	150	26	4	13	60	42	20	.300	.354	.446	118	11	3	1	0	.970	-6	*O-125	0.1
1954	*Cle-A	53	60	6	17	1	0	1	6	9	1	.283	.377	.350	98	0	0	0	0	.889	-1	/O-6,1-1	-0.1
1955	Cle-A	61	58	4	15	2	1	0	10	4	3	.259	.306	.328	68	-3	0	0	0	1.000	-1	/1-8,O-3	-0.4
1956	Cle-A	38	30	2	4	0	0	0	6	7	2	.133	.297	.133	17	-3	0	0	0	.000	-0	/O-1	-0.4
	*Bro-N	19	24	3	7	1	0	0	1	0	3	.292	.292	.333	63	-1	0	0	0	1.000	-0	/O-2	-0.2
Total	11	1127	3984	555	1244	169	61	41	403	346	119	.312	.368	.416	114	74	45	47	-15	.985	-32	O-931/1-9	-1.7

■ MIKE MITCHELL

Mitchell, Michael Francis b: 12/12/1879, Springfield, Ohio d: 7/16/61, Phoenix, Ariz. BR/TR, 6'1", 185 lbs. Deb: 4/11/07

YEAR	TM/L	G	AB	R	H	2B	3B	HR	RBI	BB	SO	AVG	OBP	SLG	PRO+	BR/A	SB	CS	SBR	FA	FR	G/POS	TPR
1907	Cin-N	148	558	64	163	17	12	3	47	37		.292	.339	.382	121	12	17			.962	22	*O-146/1-2	3.2
1908	Cin-N	119	406	41	90	9	6	1	37	46		.222	.304	.281	89	-4	18			.959	1	*O-118/1-1	-0.9
1909	Cin-N	145	523	83	162	17	**17**	4	86	57		.310	.378	.430	152	31	37			.962	6	*O-145/1-1	3.4
1910	Cin-N	156	583	79	167	16	**18**	5	88	59	56	.286	.356	.401	126	18	35			.958	-3	*O-149/1-7	0.8
1911	Cin-N	142	529	74	154	22	22	2	84	44	34	.291	.348	.427	121	12	35			.971	11	*O-140	1.6
1912	Cin-N	147	552	60	156	14	13	4	78	41	43	.283	.333	.377	97	-4	23			.947	-0	*O-144	-1.1
1913	Chi-N	82	279	37	73	11	6	4	35	32	33	.262	.340	.387	107	3	15			.941	4	O-82	0.3
	Pit-N	54	199	25	54	8	2	1	16	14	15	.271	.319	.347	94	-2	8			.946	7	O-54	0.3
	Yr	136	478	62	127	19	8	5	51	46	48	.266	.331	.370	102	1	23			.943	11	*O-136	0.6

YEAR	TM/L	G	AB	R	H	2B	3B	HR	RBI	BB	SO	AVG	OBP	SLG	PRO+	BR/A	SB	CS	SBR	FA	FR	G/POS	TPR
1914	Pit-N	76	273	31	64	11	5	2	23	16	16	.234	.279	.333	86	-6	5			.984	9	O-76	0.0
	Was-A	55	193	20	55	5	3	1	20	22	19	.285	.361	.358	112	3	9	7	-2	.957	4	O-53	0.3
Total	8	1124	4095	514	1138	130	104	27	514	368	216	.278	.340	.380	114	64	202	7		.959	61	*O-1107/1-11	7.9

■ BOBBY MITCHELL
Mitchell, Robert McKasha b: 2/6/1856, Cincinnati, Ohio d: 5/1/33, Springfield, Ohio BL/TL, 5'5", 135 lbs. Deb: 9/6/1877

YEAR	TM/L	G	AB	R	H	2B	3B	HR	RBI	BB	SO	AVG	OBP	SLG	PRO+	BR/A	SB	CS	SBR	FA	FR	G/POS	TPR
1877	Cin-N	13	49	5	10	3	0	0	5	1	2	.204	.220	.265	59	-2				.920	-1	P-12/O-2	-0.1
1878	Cin-N	13	49	4	12	0	0	0	8	1	4	.245	.260	.245	74	-1				.944	0	/P-9,S-2,O-1	0.0
1879	Cle-N	30	109	11	16	2	2	0	6	0	14	.147	.147	.202	14	-10				.714	-6	P-23/O-9	-0.5
1882	StL-a	1	4	0	0	0	0	0		0		.000	.000	.000	-96	-1				.000	-1	/O-1,P-1	-0.1
Total	4	57	211	20	38	5	2	0	19	2	20	.180	.188	.223	35	-14				.811	-7	/P-45,O-13,S-2	-0.7

■ BOBBY MITCHELL
Mitchell, Robert Van b: 4/7/55, Salt Lake City, Utah BL/TL, 5'10", 170 lbs. Deb: 9/1/80

YEAR	TM/L	G	AB	R	H	2B	3B	HR	RBI	BB	SO	AVG	OBP	SLG	PRO+	BR/A	SB	CS	SBR	FA	FR	G/POS	TPR
1980	LA-N	9	3	1	1	0	0	0	0	1	0	.333	.500	.333	139	0	0	0	0	1.000	-3	/O-8	-0.3
1981	LA-N	10	8	0	1	0	0	0	0	1	4	.125	.222	.125	1	-1	0	0	0	1.000	-3	/O-7	-0.4
1982	Min-A	124	454	48	113	11	6	2	28	54	53	.249	.331	.313	76	-13	8	9	-3	.997	14	*O-121	-0.6
1983	Min-A	59	152	26	35	4	2	1	15	28	21	.230	.354	.303	80	-3	1	1	-0	.990	-3	O-44	-0.8
Total	4	202	617	75	150	15	8	3	43	84	78	.243	.337	.308	76	-17	9	10	-3	.996	5	O-180	-2.1

■ BOBBY MITCHELL
Mitchell, Robert Vance b: 10/22/43, Norristown, Pa. BR/TR, 6'4", 190 lbs. Deb: 7/5/70

YEAR	TM/L	G	AB	R	H	2B	3B	HR	RBI	BB	SO	AVG	OBP	SLG	PRO+	BR/A	SB	CS	SBR	FA	FR	G/POS	TPR
1970	NY-A	10	22	1	5	2	0	0	4	2	3	.227	.320	.318	81	-1	0	2	-1	1.000	1	/O-7	-0.1
1971	Mil-A	35	55	7	10	1	1	2	6	6	18	.182	.262	.345	72	-2	0	2	-1	.974	1	O-19	-0.4
1973	Mil-A	47	130	12	29	6	0	5	20	5	32	.223	.252	.385	79	-4	4	1	1	.960	-4	O-20,D-19	-0.9
1974	Mil-A	88	173	27	42	6	2	5	20	18	46	.243	.318	.387	103	0	7	6	-2	.969	-5	D-53,O-26	-0.8
1975	Mil-A	93	229	39	57	14	3	9	41	25	69	.249	.323	.454	117	4	3	4	-2	.992	-4	O-72,D-11	-0.3
Total	5	273	609	86	143	29	6	21	91	56	168	.235	.301	.406	100	-2	14	15	-5	.984	-11	O-144/D-83	-2.5

■ RALPH MITTERLING
Mitterling, Ralph "Sarge" b: 4/19/1890, Freeburg, Pa. d: 1/22/56, Pittsburgh, Pa. BR/TR, 5'10", 165 lbs. Deb: 7/7/16

YEAR	TM/L	G	AB	R	H	2B	3B	HR	RBI	BB	SO	AVG	OBP	SLG	PRO+	BR/A	SB	CS	SBR	FA	FR	G/POS	TPR
1916	Phi-A	13	39	1	6	0	0	0	2	3	6	.154	.214	.154	11	-4	0			.944	-2	O-12	-0.8

■ GEORGE MITTERWALD
Mitterwald, George Eugene b: 6/7/45, Berkeley, Cal. BR/TR, 6'2", 206 lbs. Deb: 9/15/66 C

YEAR	TM/L	G	AB	R	H	2B	3B	HR	RBI	BB	SO	AVG	OBP	SLG	PRO+	BR/A	SB	CS	SBR	FA	FR	G/POS	TPR
1966	Min-A	3	5	1	1	0	0	0	0	0	0	.200	.200	.200	14	-1	0	0	0	1.000	1	/C-3	0.0
1968	Min-A	11	34	1	7	1	0	0	1	3	8	.206	.270	.235	52	-2	0	0	0	.961	0	C-10	-0.1
1969	*Min-A	69	187	18	48	8	0	5	13	17	47	.257	.329	.380	96	-1	0	1	-1	.987	11	C-63/O-1	1.2
1970	*Min-A	117	369	36	82	12	2	15	46	34	84	.222	.291	.388	84	-9	3	5	-2	.996	24	*C-117	2.0
1971	Min-A	125	388	38	97	13	1	13	44	39	104	.250	.319	.389	97	-2	3	3	-1	.986	-10	*C-120	-0.9
1972	Min-A	64	163	12	30	4	1	1	8	9	37	.184	.227	.239	37	-13	0	1	-1	.984	6	C-61	-0.6
1973	Min-A	125	432	50	112	15	0	16	64	39	111	.259	.328	.405	101	0	3	1	0	.992	-1	*C-122/D-3	0.5
1974	Chi-N	78	215	17	54	7	0	7	28	18	42	.251	.315	.381	90	-3	1	3	-2	.974	-4	C-68	-0.6
1975	Chi-N	84	200	19	44	4	3	5	26	19	42	.220	.288	.345	72	-8	0	0	0	.976	-1	C-59,1-10	-0.8
1976	Chi-N	101	303	19	65	7	0	5	28	16	63	.215	.254	.287	49	-20	1	2	-1	.981	0	C-64,1-25	-2.2
1977	Chi-N	110	349	40	83	22	0	9	43	28	69	.238	.296	.378	72	-15	3	1	0	.989	12	*C-109/1-1	0.1
Total	11	887	2645	251	623	93	7	76	301	222	607	.236	.298	.362	80	-73	14	17	-6	.987	40	C-796/1-36,D-3,O-1	-1.4

■ JOHNNY MIZE
Mize, John Robert "The Big Cat" b: 1/7/13, Demorest, Ga. d: 6/2/93, Demorest, Ga. BL/TR, 6'2", 215 lbs. Deb: 4/16/36 CH

YEAR	TM/L	G	AB	R	H	2B	3B	HR	RBI	BB	SO	AVG	OBP	SLG	PRO+	BR/A	SB	CS	SBR	FA	FR	G/POS	TPR
1936	StL-N	126	414	76	136	30	8	19	93	50	32	.329	.402	.577	162	35	1			.994	1	1-97/O-8	2.5
1937	StL-N★	145	560	103	204	40	7	25	113	56	57	.364	.427	.595	171	55	2			.988	-13	*1-144	2.5
1938	StL-N	149	531	85	179	34	**16**	27	102	74	47	.337	.422	**.614**	172	52	0			.989	-2	*1-140	3.4
1939	StL-N★	153	564	104	197	44	14	**28**	108	92	49	**.349**	.444	**.626**	**174**	**60**	0			.987	-4	*1-152	3.9
1940	StL-N★	155	579	111	182	31	13	**43**	**137**	82	49	.314	.404	**.636**	**173**	**56**	7			.990	-7	*1-153	3.4
1941	StL-N★	126	473	67	150	**39**	8	16	100	70	45	.317	.406	.535	153	34	4			.994	3	*1-122	2.8
1942	NY-N★	142	541	97	165	25	7	26	**110**	60	39	.305	.380	**.521**	161	40	3			**.995**	-3	*1-138	3.0
1946	NY-N★	101	377	70	127	18	3	22	70	62	26	.337	.437	.576	185	43	3			.989	5	*1-101	4.4
1947	NY-N★	154	586	**137**	177	26	2	**51**	**138**	74	42	.302	.384	.614	160	48	2			**.996**	9	*1-154	4.9
1948	NY-N★	152	560	110	162	26	4	**40**	125	94	37	.289	.395	.564	156	44	4			.991	4	*1-152	4.6
1949	NY-N★	106	388	59	102	15	0	18	62	50	19	.263	.351	.441	111	6	1			.994	2	*1-101	0.7
	*NY-A	13	23	4	6	1	0	1	2	4	2	.261	.393	.435	119	1	0	0	0	.980	-0	/1-6	0.0
1950	*NY-A	90	274	43	76	12	0	25	72	29	24	.277	.351	.595	143	14	0	1	-1	.996	-3	1-72	0.8
1951	*NY-A	113	332	37	86	14	1	10	49	36	24	.259	.339	.398	102	1	1	0	0	.994	-4	1-93	-0.7
1952	*NY-A	78	137	9	36	9	0	4	29	11	15	.263	.327	.416	112	2	0	0	0	.987	1	1-27	0.1
1953	*NY-A★	81	104	6	26	3	0	4	27	12	17	.250	.339	.394	101	0	0	0	0	1.000	-0	1-15	-0.1
Total	15	1884	6443	1118	2011	367	83	359	1337	856	524	.312	.397	.562	157	490	28	1		.992	-14	*1-1667/O-8	36.2

■ JOHN MIZEROCK
Mizerock, John Joseph b: 12/8/60, Punxsutawney, Pa. BL/TR, 5'11", 190 lbs. Deb: 4/12/83

YEAR	TM/L	G	AB	R	H	2B	3B	HR	RBI	BB	SO	AVG	OBP	SLG	PRO+	BR/A	SB	CS	SBR	FA	FR	G/POS	TPR
1983	Hou-N	33	85	8	13	4	1	1	10	12	15	.153	.265	.259	49	-6	0	0	0	.967	1	C-33	-0.4
1985	Hou-N	15	38	6	9	4	0	0	6	2	8	.237	.293	.342	79	-1	0	0	0	.966	3	C-15	0.3
1986	Hou-N	44	81	9	15	1	1	1	6	24	16	.185	.377	.259	81	-1	0	0	0	.987	4	C-42	0.5
1989	Atl-N	11	27	1	6	0	0	0	2	0	3	.222	.222	.222	27	-3	0	0	0	1.000	1	C-11	-0.2
Total	4	103	231	24	43	9	2	2	24	38	42	.186	.309	.268	64	-10	0	0	0	.979	8	C-101	0.2

■ BILL MIZEUR
Mizeur, William Francis "Bad Bill" b: 6/22/1897, Nokomis, Ill. d: 8/27/76, Decatur, Ill. BL/TR, 6', 180 lbs. Deb: 9/30/23

YEAR	TM/L	G	AB	R	H	2B	3B	HR	RBI	BB	SO	AVG	OBP	SLG	PRO+	BR/A	SB	CS	SBR	FA	FR	G/POS	TPR
1923	StL-A	1	1	0	0	0	0	0	0	0	0	.000	.000	.000	-95	-0	0	0	0	.000	0	H	0.0
1924	StL-A	1	1	0	0	0	0	0	0	0	0	.000	.000	.000	-94	-0	0	0	0	.000	0	H	0.0
Total	2	2	2	0	0	0	0	0	0	0	0	.000	.000	.000	-94	-1	0	0	0		0	-0,-0	0.0

■ DAVE MOATES
Moates, David Allan b: 1/30/48, Great Lakes, Ill. BL/TL, 5'9", 163 lbs. Deb: 9/21/74

YEAR	TM/L	G	AB	R	H	2B	3B	HR	RBI	BB	SO	AVG	OBP	SLG	PRO+	BR/A	SB	CS	SBR	FA	FR	G/POS	TPR
1974	Tex-A	1	0	0	0	0	0	0	0	0	0	—	—	—		0	0	0	0	.000	0	R	0.0
1975	Tex-A	54	175	21	48	9	0	3	14	13	15	.274	.324	.377	99	-1	9	2	2	.984	1	O-51/D-1	0.0
1976	Tex-A	85	137	21	33	7	1	0	13	11	18	.241	.297	.307	75	-4	6	3	0	.991	-10	O-66/D-7	-1.7
Total	3	140	312	42	81	16	1	3	27	24	33	.260	.313	.346	88	-5	15	5	2	.987	-9	O-117/D-8	-1.7

■ DANNY MOELLER
Moeller, Daniel Edward b: 3/23/1885, DeWitt, Iowa d: 4/14/51, Florence, Ala. BB/TR, 5'11", 165 lbs. Deb: 9/24/07

YEAR	TM/L	G	AB	R	H	2B	3B	HR	RBI	BB	SO	AVG	OBP	SLG	PRO+	BR/A	SB	CS	SBR	FA	FR	G/POS	TPR
1907	Pit-N	11	42	4	12	1	1	0	3	4		.286	.348	.357	119	1	2			.800	-2	O-11	-0.2
1908	Pit-N	36	109	14	21	3	1	0	9	9		.193	.254	.239	57	-5	4			.950	-5	O-27	-1.3
1912	Was-A	132	519	90	143	26	10	6	46	52		.276	.346	.399	112	7	30			.944	10	*O-132	1.0
1913	Was-A	153	589	88	139	15	10	5	42	72	103	.236	.322	.321	86	-9	62			.926	6	*O-153	-1.1
1914	Was-A	151	571	83	143	19	10	1	45	71	89	.250	.341	.324	96	-1	26	25	-7	.930	-1	*O-150	-1.8
1915	Was-A	118	438	65	99	11	10	2	23	59	63	.226	.319	.311	87	-7	32	10	4	.952	-3	*O-116	-1.2
1916	Was-A	78	240	30	59	8	1	1	23	30	35	.246	.335	.300	92	-2	13			.963	2	O-63	-0.4
	Cle-A	25	30	5	2	0	0	0	1	5	6	.067	.200	.067	-19	-4	2			1.000	-2	/O-8,2-1	-0.7
	Yr	103	270	35	61	8	1	1	24	35	41	.226	.319	.274	78	-6	15			.966	-1	O-71/2-1	-1.1
Total	7	704	2538	379	618	83	43	15	192	302	296	.243	.328	.328	93	-20	171	35		.938	5	O-660/2-1	-5.7

■ JOE MOFFETT
Moffett, Joseph W. b: 6/1859, Wheeling, W.Va. 6', 179 lbs. Deb: 5/6/1884 F

YEAR	TM/L	G	AB	R	H	2B	3B	HR	RBI	BB	SO	AVG	OBP	SLG	PRO+	BR/A	SB	CS	SBR	FA	FR	G/POS	TPR
1884	Tol-a	56	204	17	41	5	3	0		2		.201	.209	.255	49	-12				.957	-5	1-38,3-11/2-4,O-3	-2.0

■ SAM MOFFETT
Moffett, Samuel R. b: 3/14/1857, Wheeling, W.Va. d: 5/5/07, Butte, Mont. BR/TR, 6', 175 lbs. Deb: 5/15/1884 F

YEAR	TM/L	G	AB	R	H	2B	3B	HR	RBI	BB	SO	AVG	OBP	SLG	PRO+	BR/A	SB	CS	SBR	FA	FR	G/POS	TPR
1884	Cle-N	67	256	26	47	12	2	0	15	8	56	.184	.208	.246	41	-17				.827	6	O-42,P-24/1-2,32	-0.8
1887	Ind-N	11	41	6	5	1	0	0	1	1	6	.122	.143	.146	-20	-7	2			.857	-3	/P-6,O-5	-0.4
1888	Ind-N	10	35	6	4	0	0	0	0	5	4	.114	.225	.114	11	-3	0			.750	-3	/P-7,O-3	-0.2
Total	3	88	332	38	56	13	2	0	16	14	66	.169	.202	.220	30	-27	2			.821	1	/O-50,P-37,1-2,23	-1.4

YEAR	TM/L	G	AB	R	H	2B	3B	HR	RBI	BB	SO	AVG	OBP	SLG	PRO+	BR/A	SB	CS	SBR	FA	FR	G/POS	TPR
■ **JOHN MOHARDT**	Mohardt, John Henry b: 1/21/1898, Pittsburgh, Pa. d: 11/24/61, LaJolla, Cal. BR/TR, 5'10", 165 lbs. Deb: 4/15/22																						
1922	Det-A	5	1	2	1	0	0	0	0	1	0	1.000	1.000	1.000	436	1	0	1	-1	1.000	-1	/O-3	-0.1
■ **KID MOHLER**	Mohler, Ernest Follette b: 12/13/1874, Oneida, Ill. d: 11/4/61, San Francisco, Cal. BR/TL, 5'4.5", 145 lbs. Deb: 9/29/1894																						
1894	Was-N	3	9	0	1	0	0	0	0	2	4	.111	.273	.111	-5	-2	0			.952	2	/2-3	0.0
■ **JOHNNY MOKAN**	Mokan, John Leo b: 9/23/1895, Buffalo, N.Y. d: 2/10/85, Buffalo, N.Y. BR/TR, 5'7", 165 lbs. Deb: 4/15/21																						
1921	Pit-N	19	52	7	14	3	2	0	9	5	3	.269	.333	.404	92	-1	0	0	0	.946	0	O-15	-0.1
1922	Pit-N	31	89	9	23	3	1	0	8	9	3	.258	.327	.315	65	-4	0	1	-1	.903	-4	O-23	-1.0
	Phi-N	47	151	20	38	7	1	3	27	16	25	.252	.327	.371	73	-6	1	0	0	.905	-6	O-37/3-2	-1.4
	Yr	78	240	29	61	10	2	3	35	25	28	.254	.327	.350	70	-11	1	1	-0	.905	-10	O-60/3-2	-2.4
1923	Phi-N	113	400	76	125	23	3	10	48	53	31	.313	.401	.460	113	8	6	11	-5	.969	7	*O-105/3-1	0.4
1924	Phi-N	96	366	50	95	15	1	7	44	30	27	.260	.321	.363	74	-14	7	5	-1	.986	-0	O-94	-2.1
1925	Phi-N	75	209	30	69	11	2	6	42	27	9	.330	.417	.488	120	7	3	5	-2	.984	-12	O-68	-1.0
1926	Phi-N	127	456	68	138	23	5	6	62	41	31	.303	.365	.414	104	3	4			.967	-8	*O-123	-1.3
1927	Phi-N	74	213	22	61	13	2	0	33	25	21	.286	.361	.366	94	-1	5			.962	-9	O-63	-1.4
Total	7	582	1936	282	563	98	17	32	273	206	150	.291	.364	.409	97	-8	26	22		.966	-32	O-528/3-3	-7.9
■ **FENTON MOLE**	Mole, Fenton Le Roy "Muscles" b: 6/14/25, San Leandro, Cal. BL/TL, 6'1.5", 200 lbs. Deb: 9/1/49																						
1949	NY-A	10	27	2	5	2	1	0	2	3	5	.185	.267	.333	58	-2	0	0	0	1.000	1	/1-8	-0.1
■ **BEN MOLINA**	Molina, Benjamin Jose b: 7/20/74, Rio Piedras, P.R. BR/TR, 5'11", 200 lbs. Deb: 9/21/98																						
1998	Ana-A	2	1	0	0	0	0	0	0	0	0	.000	.000	.000	-99	-0	0	0	0	1.000	-0	/C-2	0.0
■ **IZZY MOLINA**	Molina, Islay b: 6/3/71, New York, N.Y. BR/TR, 6', 200 lbs. Deb: 8/15/96																						
1996	Oak-A	14	25	0	5	2	0	0	1	1	3	.200	.231	.280	29	-3	0	0	0	1.000	0	C-12/D-1	-0.2
1997	Oak-A	48	111	6	22	3	1	3	7	3	17	.198	.219	.324	40	-10	0	0	0	.992	5	C-48	-0.3
1998	Oak-A	6	2	1	1	0	0	0	0	0	0	.500	.500	.500	166	0	0	0	0	1.000	2	/C-5	0.2
Total	3	68	138	7	28	5	1	3	8	4	20	.203	.225	.319	40	-13	0	0	0	.993	7	/C-65,D-1	-0.3
■ **BOB MOLINARO**	Molinaro, Robert Joseph b: 5/21/50, Newark, N.J. BL/TR, 6', 190 lbs. Deb: 9/18/75																						
1975	Det-A	6	19	2	5	0	1	0	1	1	0	.263	.300	.368	84	-0	0	0	0	1.000	-0	/O-6	-0.1
1977	Det-A	4	4	0	1	1	0	0	0	0	2	.250	.250	.500	94	-0	0	0	0	.000	0	H	0.0
	Chi-A	1	2	0	1	0	0	0	0	0	1	.500	.500	.500	174	0	1	0	0	1.000	-0	/O-1	0.0
	Yr	5	6	0	2	1	0	0	0	0	3	.333	.333	.500	119	0	1	0	0	1.000	-0	/O-1	0.0
1978	Chi-A	105	286	39	75	5	5	6	27	19	12	.262	.315	.378	93	-3	22	6	3	1.000	-7	O-62,D-32	-1.0
1979	Bal-A	8	6	0	0	0	0	0	0	1	3	.000	.143	.000	-60	-1	1	0	0	1.000	-1	/O-5	-0.2
1980	Chi-A	119	344	48	100	16	4	5	36	26	29	.291	.353	.404	107	4	18	7	1	.957	-2	O-49,D-47	-0.1
1981	Chi-A	47	42	7	11	1	1	1	9	8	1	.262	.392	.405	133	2	1	0	0	1.000	-0	/O-2,D-4	0.2
1982	Chi-N	65	66	6	13	1	0	1	12	6	5	.197	.264	.258	45	-5	1	1	-0	1.000	-1	/O-4	-0.7
	Phi-N	19	14	0	4	0	0	0	2	3	1	.286	.412	.286	96	0	1	0	0	.000	0	H	0.0
	Yr	84	80	6	17	1	0	1	14	9	6	.213	.292	.262	55	-5	2	1	0	1.000	-1	/O-4	-0.7
1983	Phi-N	19	18	1	2	1	0	1	3	0	2	.111	.111	.333	19	-2	0	0	0	.000	0	H	-0.3
	Det-A	8	2	3	0	0	0	0	0	1	1	.000	.333	.000	1	-0	1	1	-0	.000	0	/D-1	-0.1
Total	8	401	803	106	212	25	11	14	90	65	57	.264	.328	.375	95	-6	46	15	5	.980	-12	O-129/D-84	-2.3
■ **PAUL MOLITOR**	Molitor, Paul Leo b: 8/22/56, St.Paul, Minn. BR/TR, 6', 185 lbs. Deb: 4/7/78																						
1978	Mil-A	125	521	73	142	26	4	6	45	19	54	.273	.303	.372	89	-9	30	12	2	.976	-5	2-91,S-31/3-1,D-2	-0.1
1979	Mil-A	140	584	88	188	27	16	9	62	48	48	.322	.375	.469	126	21	33	13	2	.979	1	*2-122,S-10/D-8	3.3
1980	Mil-A†	111	450	81	137	29	2	9	37	48	48	.304	.375	.438	126	17	34	7	6	.971	-2	2-91,S-12/3-1,D-7	2.8
1981	*Mil-A	64	251	45	67	11	0	2	19	25	29	.267	.341	.335	100	1	10	6	-1	.976	2	O-46,D-16	-0.1
1982	*Mil-A	160	666	**136**	201	26	8	19	71	69	93	.302	.368	.450	132	29	41	9	7	.942	-1	*3-150/S-4,D-6	3.1
1983	Mil-A	152	608	95	164	28	6	15	47	59	74	.270	.336	.410	113	10	41	8	8	.966	2	*3-146/D-2	1.7
1984	Mil-A	13	46	3	10	1	0	0	6	2	8	.217	.250	.239	38	-4	1	0	0	.933	4	/3-7,D-4	0.0
1985	Mil-A★	140	576	93	171	28	3	10	48	54	80	.297	.358	.408	110	8	21	7	2	.953	-2	*3-135/D-4	0.6
1986	Mil-A	105	437	62	123	24	6	9	55	40	81	.281	.342	.426	104	2	20	5	3	.944	2	3-91,D-10/O-4	0.5
1987	Mil-A	118	465	**114**	164	**41**	5	16	75	69	67	.353	.438	.566	159	42	45	10	8	.947	-10	D-58,3-41,2-19	3.5
1988	Mil-A★	154	609	115	190	34	6	13	60	71	54	.312	.386	.452	132	28	41	10	6	.941	-8	*3-105,D-49/2-1	2.4
1989	Mil-A	155	615	84	194	35	4	11	56	64	67	.315	.384	.439	133	28	27	11	2	.950	4	*3-112,D-28,2-16	3.4
1990	Mil-A	103	418	64	119	27	6	12	45	37	51	.285	.344	.464	125	13	18	3	4	.988	-1	2-60,1-37/3-2,D-4	1.4
1991	Mil-A★	158	665	**133**	**216**	32	**13**	17	75	77	62	.325	.400	.489	148	45	19	8	1	.986	-1	*D-112,1-46	3.6
1992	Mil-A★	158	609	89	195	36	7	12	89	73	66	.320	.396	.461	142	36	31	6	6	.996	-4	*D-108,1-48	3.1
1993	*Tor-A★	160	636	121	**211**	37	5	22	111	77	71	.332	.406	.509	144	40	22	4	4	.985	-1	*D-137,1-23	3.5
1994	Tor-A★	115	454	86	155	30	4	14	75	55	48	.341	.414	.518	138	27	20	0	6	1.000	0	*D-110/1-5	2.4
1995	Tor-A	130	525	63	142	31	2	15	60	61	57	.270	.352	.423	101	1	12	0	4	.000	0	*D-129	-0.3
1996	Min-A	161	660	99	**225**	41	8	9	113	56	72	.341	.395	.468	115	17	18	6	2	.993	0	*D-143,1-17	0.8
1997	Min-A	135	538	63	164	32	4	10	89	45	73	.305	.358	.435	104	4	11	4	1	.991	-1	*D-122,1-12	-0.4
1998	Min-A	126	502	75	141	29	5	4	69	45	41	.281	.341	.382	88	-8	9	2	2	1.000	0	*D-115/1-9	-1.3
Total	21	2683	10835	1782	3319	605	114	234	1307	1094	1244	.306	.372	.448	122	346	504	131	73	.950	-21	*D-1174,3-791,21/SO	33.9
■ **FRED MOLLENKAMP**	Mollenkamp, Frederick Henry b: 3/15/1890, Cincinnati, Ohio d: 11/1/48, Cincinnati, Ohio Deb: 8/29/14																						
1914	Phi-N	3	8	0	1	0	0	0	0	2	0	.125	.300	.125	26	-1	0			1.000	2	/1-3	0.1
■ **FRITZ MOLLWITZ**	Mollwitz, Frederick August b: 6/16/1890, Coburg, Germany d: 10/3/67, Bradenton, Fla. BR/TR, 6'2", 170 lbs. Deb: 9/26/13																						
1913	Chi-N	2	7	1	3	0	0	0	0	0	0	.429	.429	.429	145	0	0			1.000	-0	/1-2	0.0
1914	Chi-N	13	20	0	3	0	0	0	1	0	3	.150	.150	.150	-11	-3	1			.962	-1	/1-4,O-1	-0.4
	Cin-N	32	111	12	18	2	0	0	5	3	9	.162	.198	.180	12	-12	2			.991	1	1-32	-1.3
	Yr	45	131	12	21	2	0	0	6	3	12	.160	.191	.176	9	-15	3			.989	0	1-36/O-1	-1.7
1915	Cin-N	153	525	36	136	21	3	1	51	15	49	.259	.281	.316	79	-14	19	11	-1	**.996**	0	*1-153	-2.2
1916	Cin-N	65	183	12	41	4	4	0	16	5	12	.224	.245	.290	65	-8	6			.981	-1	1-54	-1.2
	Chi-N	33	71	1	19	2	0	0	11	7	6	.268	.333	.296	85	-1	4			.976	-1	1-19/O-6	-0.3
	Yr	98	254	13	60	6	4	0	27	12	18	.236	.271	.291	71	-9	10			.980	-2	1-73/O-6	-1.5
1917	Pit-N	36	140	15	36	4	1	0	12	8	8	.257	.297	.300	81	-3	4			.994	-1	1-36/2-1	-0.6
1918	Pit-N	119	432	43	116	12	7	0	45	23	24	.269	.305	.329	90	-6	23			.990	-0	*1-119	-1.2
1919	Pit-N	56	168	11	29	2	4	0	12	15	18	.173	.249	.232	43	-11	9			.994	-3	1-53/O-1	-1.8
	StL-N	25	83	7	19	3	0	0	5	7	3	.229	.289	.265	71	-3	2			.994	1	1-25	-0.3
	Yr	81	251	18	48	5	4	0	17	22	21	.191	.262	.243	52	-14	11			.994	-3	1-78/O-1	-2.1
Total	7	534	1740	138	420	50	19	1	158	83	132	.241	.278	.294	72	-60	70	11		.991	-6	1-497/O-8,2-1	-9.3
■ **BLAS MONACO**	Monaco, Blas b: 11/16/15, San Antonio, Tex. BB/TR, 5'11", 170 lbs. Deb: 8/18/37																						
1937	Cle-A	5	7	0	2	0	1	0	2	0	2	.286	.375	.571	134	0	0	0	0	1.000	0	/2-3	0.1
1946	Cle-A	12	6	2	0	0	0	0	0	1	1	.000	.143	.000	-62	-1	0	0	0	.000	0	H	-0.1
Total	2	17	13	2	2	0	1	0	2	1	3	.154	.267	.308	53	-1	0	0	0	1.000	0	/2-3	0.0
■ **SHANE MONAHAN**	Monahan, Shane Hartland b: 8/12/74, Syosset, N.Y. BL/TR, 6', 195 lbs. Deb: 7/09/98																						
1998	Sea-A	62	211	17	51	8	1	4	28	8	53	.242	.269	.346	59	-13	1	2	-1	.992	1	O-62	-1.4
■ **FREDDIE MONCEWICZ**	Moncewicz, Frederick Alfred b: 9/1/03, Brockton, Mass. d: 4/23/69, Brockton, Mass. BR/TR, 5'8.5", 175 lbs. Deb: 6/19/28																						
1928	Bos-A	3	1	0	0	0	0	0	0	0	1	.000	.000	.000	-99	-0	0	0	0	1.000	0	/S-2	0.0
■ **ALEX MONCHAK**	Monchak, Alex b: 12/22/19, Bayonne, N.J. BR/TR, 6', 180 lbs. Deb: 6/22/40 C																						
1940	Phi-N	19	14	1	2	0	0	0	0	0	6	.143	.143	.143	-22	-2	1			.833	0	/S-9,2-1	-0.2

YEAR	TM/L	G	AB	R	H	2B	3B	HR	RBI	BB	SO	AVG	OBP	SLG	PRO+	BR/A	SB	CS	SBR	FA	FR	G/POS	TPR
■ **RICK MONDAY**	Monday, Robert James b: 11/20/45, Batesville, Ark. BL/TL, 6'3", 200 lbs. Deb: 9/3/66																						
1966	KC-A	17	41	4	4	1	1	0	2	6	16	.098	.213	.171	12	-5	1	1	-0	.964	-1	O-15	-0.7
1967	KC-A	124	406	52	102	14	6	14	58	42	107	.251	.324	.419	122	10	3	6	-3	.972	15	*O-113	1.9
1968	Oak-A★	148	482	56	132	24	7	8	49	72	143	.274	.373	.402	142	26	14	6	1	.978	-0	*O-144	2.2
1969	Oak-A	122	399	57	108	17	4	12	54	72	100	.271	.389	.424	133	20	12	3	2	.964	-2	*O-119	1.5
1970	Oak-A	112	376	63	109	19	7	10	37	58	99	.290	.388	.457	137	20	17	11	-2	.981	1	*O-109	1.5
1971	*Oak-A	116	355	53	87	9	3	18	56	49	93	.245	.337	.439	121	9	6	9	-4	.984	-0	*O-111	0.1
1972	Chi-N	138	434	68	108	22	5	11	42	78	102	.249	.365	.399	105	5	12	9	-2	**.996**	-6	*O-134	-0.9
1973	Chi-N	149	554	93	148	24	5	26	56	92	124	.267	.372	.469	123	18	5	12	-6	.973	1	*O-148	0.7
1974	Chi-N	142	538	84	158	19	7	20	58	70	94	.294	.377	.467	130	22	7	9	-3	.984	2	*O-139	1.5
1975	Chi-N	136	491	89	131	29	4	17	60	83	95	.267	.374	.446	121	15	8	3	1	.973	1	*O-131	1.2
1976	Chi-N	137	534	107	145	20	5	32	77	60	125	.272	.347	.507	129	18	5	9	-4	.993	7	*O-103,1-32	1.6
1977	*LA-N	118	392	47	90	13	1	15	48	60	109	.230	.332	.383	91	-4	1	4	-2	.991	-11	*O-115/1-3	-2.2
1978	*LA-N★	119	342	54	87	14	1	19	57	49	100	.254	.349	.468	127	12	2	4	-2	.995	-11	*O-103/1-1	-0.5
1979	LA-N	12	33	2	10	0	0	0	2	5	6	.303	.395	.303	94	0	0	0	0	.964	-0	O-10	0.0
1980	LA-N	96	194	35	52	7	1	10	25	28	49	.268	.363	.469	133	9	2	2	-1	.969	-7	O-50	-0.1
1981	*LA-N	66	130	24	41	1	2	11	25	24	42	.315	.426	.608	198	17	1	2	-1	.962	-6	O-41	1.0
1982	LA-N	104	210	37	54	6	4	11	42	39	51	.257	.376	.481	142	12	2	1	0	.943	-7	O-57/1-4	0.4
1983	*LA-N	99	178	21	44	7	1	6	20	29	42	.247	.353	.399	108	3	0	0	0	.969	-4	O-44/1-4	-0.3
1984	LA-N	31	47	4	9	2	0	1	7	8	16	.191	.309	.298	72	-2	0	0	0	.987	-1	1-10/O-2	-0.4
Total	19	1986	6136	950	1619	248	64	241	775	924	1513	.264	.362	.443	124	207	98	91	-25	.979	-29	*O-1688/1-54	8.5
■ **RAUL MONDESI**	Mondesi, Raul Ramon (Avelino) b: 3/12/71, San Cristobal, D.R. BR/TR, 5'11", 202 lbs. Deb: 7/19/93																						
1993	LA-N	42	86	13	25	3	1	4	10	4	16	.291	.322	.488	120	2	4	1	1	.951	-5	O-40	-0.2
1994	LA-N	112	434	63	133	27	8	16	56	16	78	.306	.334	.516	126	13	11	8	-2	.965	2	*O-112	1.1
1995	*LA-N★	139	536	91	153	23	6	26	88	33	96	.285	.332	.496	126	16	27	4	6	.980	14	*O-138	3.2
1996	*LA-N	157	634	98	188	40	7	24	88	32	122	.297	.335	.495	125	19	14	7	0	.967	16	*O-157	3.0
1997	LA-N	159	616	95	191	42	5	30	87	44	105	.310	.362	.541	143	35	32	15	1	.989	17	*O-159	4.8
1998	LA-N	148	580	85	162	26	5	30	90	30	112	.279	.318	.497	115	10	16	10	-1	.980	0	*O-148	0.7
Total	6	757	2886	445	852	161	32	130	419	159	529	.295	.336	.508	127	96	104	45	4	.976	45	O-754	12.6
■ **DON MONEY**	Money, Donald Wayne "Brooks" b: 6/7/47, Washington, D.C. BR/TR, 6'1", 190 lbs. Deb: 4/10/68																						
1968	Phi-N	4	13	1	3	2	0	0	2	2	4	.231	.333	.385	115	0	0	1	-1	1.000	-1	/S-4	-0.1
1969	Phi-N	127	450	41	103	22	2	6	42	43	83	.229	.298	.327	77	-14	1	3	-2	.969	17	*S-126	1.6
1970	Phi-N	120	447	66	132	25	4	14	66	43	68	.295	.366	.463	124	15	4	7	-3	.961	11	*3-119/S-2	2.2
1971	Phi-N	121	439	40	98	22	8	7	38	31	80	.223	.279	.358	79	-13	4	1	1	.953	5	3-68,O-40,2-20	-0.8
1972	Phi-N	152	536	54	119	16	2	15	52	41	92	.222	.280	.343	74	-19	5	7	-3	**.978**	20	*3-151/S-2	-0.3
1973	Mil-A	145	556	75	158	28	2	11	61	53	53	.284	.350	.401	113	10	22	5	4	**.971**	-23	*3-124,S-21	-0.8
1974	Mil-A☆	159	629	85	178	32	3	15	65	62	80	.283	.349	.415	120	16	19	6	2	**.989**	-10	*3-157/2-1,D-1	0.8
1975	Mil-A	109	405	58	112	16	1	15	43	31	51	.277	.333	.432	114	7	7	9	-3	.951	-21	3-99/S-7	-1.8
1976	Mil-A★	117	439	51	117	18	4	12	62	47	50	.267	.337	.408	120	11	6	5	-1	.958	-4	*3-103,D-10/S-1	0.4
1977	Mil-A†	152	570	86	159	28	3	25	83	57	70	.279	.352	.470	122	17	8	5	-1	.981	-3	*2-116,O-23,3-15,/D	2.0
1978	Mil-A★	137	518	88	152	30	2	14	54	48	70	.293	.361	.440	124	16	3	0	1	.994	-2	1-61,2-36,3-25,D/S	1.4
1979	Mil-A	92	350	52	83	20	1	6	38	40	47	.237	.319	.351	81	-9	1	0	0	1.000	-2	D-33,3-26,1-19,2-16	-1.2
1980	Mil-A	86	289	39	74	17	1	17	46	40	36	.256	.348	.498	133	13	0	0	0	.940	0	3-55,1-14,D-14,/2-2	1.1
1981	*Mil-A	60	185	17	40	7	0	2	14	19	27	.216	.293	.286	71	-7	0	0	0	.977	-5	3-56/1-1,D-2	-1.3
1982	*Mil-A	96	275	40	78	14	3	16	55	32	38	.284	.360	.531	150	18	0	2	-1	.923	5	D-66,3-16,1-11,/2-1	1.8
1983	Mil-A	43	114	5	17	5	0	1	8	11	17	.149	.224	.219	24	-12	0	0	0	.980	4	D-28,3-11/1-2	-0.9
Total	16	1720	6215	798	1623	302	36	176	729	600	866	.261	.330	.406	106	49	80	51	-7	.968	-7	*3-1025,2-192,DS1/O	4.1
■ **FRANK MONROE**	Monroe, Frank W. b: Hamilton, Ohio Deb: 7/18/1884																						
1884	Ind-a	2	8	1	0	0	0	0	0			.000	.000	.000	-99	-2				1.000	-1	/O-1,C-1	-0.3
■ **JOHN MONROE**	Monroe, John Allen b: 8/24/1898, Farmersville, Tex. d: 6/19/56, Conroe, Tex. BL/TR, 5'10", 160 lbs. Deb: 4/16/21																						
1921	NY-N	19	21	4	3	0	0	1	3	3	6	.143	.280	.286	50	-2	0	0	0	.846	2	/2-8,S-1	0.0
	Phi-N	41	133	13	38	4	2	1	8	11	9	.286	.345	.368	82	-3	2	2	-1	.938	5	2-28/3-9	0.3
	Yr	60	154	17	41	4	2	2	11	14	15	.266	.335	.357	79	-4	2	2	-1	.920	7	2-36/3-9,S-1	0.3
■ **ED MONTAGUE**	Montague, Edward Francis b: 7/24/05, San Francisco, Cal. d: 6/17/88, Daly City, Cal. BR/TR, 5'10", 165 lbs. Deb: 5/14/28																						
1928	Cle-A	32	51	12	12	0	1	0	3	6	7	.235	.339	.275	62	-3	0	0	0	.914	5	S-15/3-9	0.4
1930	Cle-A	58	179	37	47	5	2	1	16	37	38	.263	.392	.330	82	-3	1	5	-3	.917	-15	S-46,3-13	-1.4
1931	Cle-A	64	193	27	55	8	3	1	26	21	22	.285	.358	.373	87	-3	3	4	-2	.924	16	S-64	1.5
1932	Cle-A	66	192	29	47	5	1	0	24	21	24	.245	.326	.281	55	-12	3	3	-1	.891	-13	S-57,3-11	-2.1
Total	4	220	615	105	161	18	7	2	69	85	91	.262	.357	.324	74	-21	7	12	-5	.912	-7	S-182/3-33	-1.6
■ **WILLIE MONTANEZ**	Montanez, Guillermo (Naranjo) b: 4/1/48, Catano, P.R. BL/TL, 6'1", 193 lbs. Deb: 4/12/66																						
1966	Cal-A	8	2	2	0	0	0	0	0	0	2	.000	.000	.000	-99	-1	1	0	0	1.000	0	/1-2	0.0
1970	Phi-N	18	25	3	6	0	0	0	3	1	4	.240	.269	.240	39	-2	0	0	0	1.000	-1	O-10/1-5	-0.3
1971	Phi-N	158	599	78	153	27	6	30	99	67	105	.255	.333	.471	126	19	4	7	-3	.972	5	*O-158/1-9	1.3
1972	Phi-N	147	531	60	131	**39**	3	13	64	58	108	.247	.322	.405	103	2	1	3	-2	.985	14	*O-130,1-14	0.8
1973	Phi-N	146	552	69	145	16	5	11	65	46	80	.263	.326	.370	90	-7	2	6	-3	.994	-6	1-99,O-51	-2.7
1974	Phi-N	143	527	55	160	33	1	7	79	32	57	.304	.347	.410	107	4	3	6	-3	.992	-1	*1-137/O-1	-1.0
1975	Phi-N	21	84	9	24	8	0	2	16	4	12	.286	.318	.452	108	0	1	0	0	.990	2	1-21	0.1
	SF-N	135	518	52	158	26	2	8	85	45	50	.305	.365	.409	110	7	5	3	-0	.994	-1	*1-134	-0.3
	Yr	156	602	61	182	34	2	10	101	49	62	.302	.359	.415	110	8	6	3	0	.993	0	*1-155	-0.2
1976	SF-N	60	230	22	71	15	2	2	20	15	15	.309	.354	.417	115	4	2	1	0	.989	4	1-58	0.4
	Atl-N	103	420	52	135	14	0	9	64	21	32	.321	.354	.419	112	6	0	4	-2	.986	-6	*1-103	-1.0
	Yr	163	650	74	206	29	2	11	84	36	47	.317	.354	.418	113	10	2	5	-2	.987	-1	*1-161	-0.6
1977	Atl-N★	136	544	70	156	31	1	20	68	35	60	.287	.330	.458	97	-3	1	1	-0	.992	-4	*1-134	-1.6
1978	NY-N	159	609	66	156	32	0	17	96	60	92	.256	.324	.392	103	1	9	4	0	.995	3	*1-158	-0.6
1979	NY-N	109	410	36	96	19	0	5	47	25	48	.234	.280	.317	65	-21	0	1	-1	.989	3	*1-108	-2.6
	Tex-A	38	144	19	46	6	0	8	24	8	14	.319	.359	.528	137	7	0	1	-1	.995	1	1-19,D-17	0.6
1980	SD-N	128	481	39	132	12	4	6	63	36	52	.274	.329	.353	96	-3	3	4	-2	.994	1	*1-124	-1.1
	Mon-N	14	19	1	4	0	0	0	1	3	3	.211	.318	.211	50	-1	0	1	-1	1.000	0	/1-4	-0.2
	Yr	142	500	40	136	12	4	6	64	39	55	.272	.328	.348	94	-4	3	5	-2	.994	1	*1-128	-1.3
1981	Mon-N	26	62	6	11	0	1	0	5	4	9	.177	.227	.210	24	-6	0	0	0	.992	1	1-16	-0.6
	Pit-N	29	38	2	10	0	0	1	1	1	2	.263	.282	.342	74	-1	0	0	0	1.000	-1	1-11	-0.3
	Yr	55	100	8	21	0	1	1	6	5	11	.210	.248	.260	43	-7	0	0	0	.995	0	1-27	-0.9
1982	Pit-N	36	32	4	9	1	0	0	1	3	3	.281	.343	.313	82	-1	0	0	0	1.000	0	/1-2,O-2	-0.1
	Phi-N	18	16	0	1	0	0	0	1	1	3	.063	.118	.063	-47	-3	0	0	0	1.000	1	/1-6	-0.3
	Yr	54	48	4	10	1	0	0	2	4	6	.208	.269	.229	40	-4	0	0	0	1.000	1	/1-8,O-2	-0.4
Total	14	1632	5843	645	1604	279	25	139	802	465	751	.275	.331	.402	101	1	32	42	-16	.992	15	*1-1164,O-352/D-17	-9.5
■ **RENE MONTEAGUDO**	Monteagudo, Rene (Miranda) b: 3/12/16, Havana, Cuba d: 9/14/73, Hialeah, Fla. BL/TL, 5'7", 165 lbs. Deb: 9/6/38 F																						
1938	Was-A	5	6	0	3	0	0	0	1	0	0	.500	.500	.500	162	1	0	0	0	1.000	-1	/P-5	0.0
1940	Was-A	27	33	4	6	1	1	0	1	1	4	.182	.206	.273	24	-4	0	0	0	.941	-1	P-27	0.0
1944	Was-A	10	38	2	11	2	0	0	4	0	1	.289	.289	.342	84	-1	0	0	0	.929	-1	/O-9	-0.3
1945	Phi-N	114	193	26	58	6	0	0	15	28	7	.301	.389	.332	104	3	2			.918	-1	O-35,P-14	0.0
Total	4	156	270	32	78	9	1	0	21	29	12	.289	.358	.330	94	-2	2	0		.889	-4	/P-46,O-44	-0.3

YEAR	TM/L	G	AB	R	H	2B	3B	HR	RBI	BB	SO	AVG	OBP	SLG	PRO+	BR/A	SB	CS	SBR	FA	FR	G/POS	TPR
■ **FELIPE MONTEMAYOR**	Montemayor, Felipe Angel "Monty" b: 2/7/30, Monterrey, Mexico BL/TL, 6'2", 185 lbs. Deb: 4/14/53																						
1953	Pit-N	28	55	5	6	4	0	0	2	4	13	.109	.210	.182	3	-8	0	0	0	1.000	1	O-12	-0.7
1955	Pit-N	36	95	10	20	1	3	2	8	18	24	.211	.342	.347	85	-2	1	0	0	.957	-5	O-28	-0.8
Total	2	64	150	15	26	5	3	2	10	22	37	.173	.295	.287	55	-10	1	0	0	.974	-5	/O-40	-1.5
■ **AL MONTGOMERY**	Montgomery, Alvin Atlas b: 7/3/20, Loving, N.Mex. d: 4/26/42, Waverly, Va. BR/TR, 5'10.5", 185 lbs. Deb: 6/20/41																						
1941	Bos-N	42	52	4	10	1	0	0	4	9	8	.192	.323	.212	55	-3	0			.976	-6	C-30	-0.8
■ **RAY MONTGOMERY**	Montgomery, Raymond James b: 8/8/69, Bronxville, N.Y. BR/TR, 6'3", 195 lbs. Deb: 7/3/96																						
1996	Hou-N	12	14	4	3	1	0	1	4	1	5	.214	.267	.500	105	-0	0	0	0	1.000	-2	/O-6	-0.2
1997	Hou-N	29	68	8	16	4	1	0	4	5	18	.235	.288	.324	62	-4	0	0	0	1.000	-0	O-18	-0.5
1998	Hou-N	6	5	2	2	0	0	0	0	0	0	.400	.400	.400	111	0	0	0	0	1.000	-1	/O-2	0.0
Total	3	47	87	14	21	5	1	1	8	6	23	.241	.290	.356	71	-4	0	0	0	1.000	-3	/O-26	-0.7
■ **BOB MONTGOMERY**	Montgomery, Robert Edward b: 4/16/44, Nashville, Tenn. BR/TR, 6'1", 203 lbs. Deb: 9/6/70																						
1970	Bos-A	22	78	8	14	2	0	1	4	6	20	.179	.247	.244	33	-7	0	0	0	.981	0	C-22	-0.6
1971	Bos-A	67	205	19	49	11	2	2	24	16	43	.239	.304	.341	77	-6	1	0	0	.989	-3	C-66	-0.7
1972	Bos-A	24	77	7	22	1	0	2	7	3	17	.286	.313	.377	99	-0	0	0	0	.985	-2	C-22	-0.2
1973	Bos-A	34	128	18	41	6	2	7	25	7	36	.320	.356	.563	146	7	0	0	0	.974	1	C-33	0.9
1974	Bos-A	88	254	26	64	10	0	4	38	13	50	.252	.291	.339	75	-8	3	0	1	.977	-6	C-79/D-5	-1.1
1975	*Bos-A	62	195	16	44	10	1	2	26	4	37	.226	.245	.318	53	-12	1	1	-0	.987	-5	C-53/1-6,D-3	-1.6
1976	Bos-A	31	93	10	23	3	1	3	13	5	20	.247	.286	.398	88	-2	0	1	-1	.983	-1	C-30/D-1	-0.2
1977	Bos-A	17	40	6	12	2	0	2	7	4	9	.300	.378	.500	123	1	0	0	0	.982	-0	C-15	0.1
1978	Bos-A	10	29	2	7	1	1	0	5	2	12	.241	.290	.345	70	-1	0	0	0	.976	0	C-10	-0.1
1979	Bos-A	32	86	13	30	4	1	0	7	4	24	.349	.378	.419	109	1	1	0	0	.984	-4	C-31	-0.2
Total	10	387	1185	125	306	50	8	23	156	64	268	.258	.300	.372	83	-28	6	2	1	.983	-19	C-361/D-9,1-6	-3.7
■ **CHARLIE MONTOYO**	Montoyo, Jose Carlos (Diaz) b: 10/17/65, Florida, P.R. BR/TR, 5'10", 170 lbs. Deb: 9/7/93																						
1993	Mon-N	4	5	1	2	1	0	0	3	0	0	.400	.400	.600	157	0	0	0	0	.000	0	/2-3	0.0
■ **AL MONTREUIL**	Montreuil, Allan Arthur b: 8/23/43, New Orleans, La. BR/TR, 5'5", 158 lbs. Deb: 9/1/72																						
1972	Chi-N	5	11	0	1	0	0	0	0	1	4	.091	.167	.091	-23	-2	0	0	0	1.000	0	/2-5	-0.2
■ **DAN MONZON**	Monzon, Daniel Francisco b: 5/17/46, Bronx, N.Y. d: 1/21/96, Santo Domingo, D.R. BR/TR, 5'10", 182 lbs. Deb: 4/25/72																						
1972	Min-A	55	55	13	15	1	0	0	5	8	12	.273	.365	.291	92	-0	1	0	0	.977	9	2-13/3-5,S-3,O-1	1.1
1973	Min-A	39	76	10	17	1	1	0	4	11	9	.224	.330	.263	66	-3	1	0	0	.968	9	2-17,3-14/O-1	0.7
Total	2	94	131	23	32	2	1	0	9	19	21	.244	.344	.275	77	-3	2	0	1	.971	18	/2-30,3-19,S-3,O-2	1.8
■ **JOE MOOCK**	Moock, Joseph Geoffrey b: 3/12/44, Plaquemine, La. BL/TR, 6'1", 180 lbs. Deb: 9/1/67																						
1967	NY-N	13	40	2	9	2	0	0	5	0	7	.225	.225	.275	43	-3	0	0	0	.917	2	3-12	-0.2
■ **GEORGE MOOLIC**	Moolic, George Henry "Prunes" b: 3/12/1865, Lawrence, Mass. d: 2/19/15, Methuen, Mass. BR/TR, 5'7", 145 lbs. Deb: 5/1/1886																						
1886	Chi-N	16	56	9	8	3	0	0	2	2	17	.143	.172	.196	10	-6	0			.945	3	C-15/O-2	-0.2
■ **WALLY MOON**	Moon, Wallace Wade b: 4/3/30, Bay, Ark. BL/TR, 6', 175 lbs. Deb: 4/13/54 C																						
1954	StL-N	151	635	106	193	29	9	12	76	71	73	.304	.375	.435	109	10	18	10	-1	.978	2	*O-148	0.4
1955	StL-N	152	593	86	175	24	8	19	76	47	65	.295	.350	.459	113	10	11	11	-3	.975	-9	*O-100,1-51	-1.0
1956	StL-N	149	540	86	161	22	11	16	68	80	50	.298	.390	.469	129	24	12	9	-2	.988	0	O-97,1-52	1.5
1957	StL-N★	142	516	86	152	28	5	24	73	62	57	.295	.371	.508	131	22	5	6	-2	.966	-9	*O-133	0.4
1958	StL-N	108	290	36	69	10	3	7	38	47	30	.238	.344	.366	85	-5	2	3	-1	.984	-8	O-82	-1.9
1959	*LA-N★	145	543	93	164	26	**11**	19	74	81	64	.302	.396	.495	126	22	15	6	1	.983	-4	*O-143/1-1	1.2
1960	LA-N	138	469	74	140	21	6	13	69	67	53	.299	.387	.452	121	15	6	10	-4	.986	4	*O-127	0.9
1961	LA-N	134	463	79	152	25	3	17	88	89	79	.328	**.438**	.505	137	28	7	5	-1	.970	-9	*O-133	1.1
1962	LA-N	95	244	36	59	9	1	4	31	30	33	.242	.327	.336	84	-5	5	2	0	.981	-2	O-36,1-32	-1.1
1963	LA-N	122	343	41	90	13	2	8	48	45	43	.262	.350	.382	119	9	5	5	-2	.962	-13	O-96	-1.1
1964	LA-N	68	118	8	26	2	1	2	9	12	22	.220	.292	.305	74	-4	1	1	-0	1.000	-3	O-23	-0.7
1965	*LA-N	53	89	6	18	3	0	1	11	13	22	.202	.304	.270	67	-4	2	0	1	1.000	-2	O-23	-0.7
Total	12	1457	4843	737	1399	212	60	142	661	644	591	.289	.374	.445	117	123	89	68	-14	.978	-50	*O-1141,1-136	-1.0
■ **AL MOORE**	Moore, Albert James b: 8/4/02, Brooklyn, N.Y. d: 11/29/74, AtSea N.Y.To P.R BR/TR, 5'10", 174 lbs. Deb: 9/27/25																						
1925	NY-N	2	8	0	1	0	0	0	0	1	2	.125	.222	.125	-9	-1	0	1	-1	1.000	-0	/O-2	-0.2
1926	NY-N	28	81	12	18	4	0	0	10	5	7	.222	.267	.272	46	-6	2			.966	3	O-20	-0.5
Total	2	30	89	12	19	4	0	0	10	6	9	.213	.263	.258	41	-7	2	1		.968	3	/O-22	-0.7
■ **JUNIOR MOORE**	Moore, Alvin Earl b: 1/25/53, Waskom, Tex. BR/TR, 5'11", 185 lbs. Deb: 8/2/76																						
1976	Atl-N	20	26	1	7	1	0	0	2	4	4	.269	.387	.308	93	0	0	0	0	.929	1	/3-6,2-1,O-1	0.1
1977	Atl-N	112	361	41	94	9	3	5	34	33	29	.260	.324	.343	71	-15	4	5	-2	.942	-4	*3-104/2-1	-2.2
1978	Chi-A	24	65	8	19	0	1	0	4	6	7	.292	.352	.323	90	-1	1	1	-0	.857	-0	D-12/3-6,O-5	-0.2
1979	Chi-A	88	201	24	53	6	2	1	23	12	20	.264	.305	.328	71	-8	0	2	-1	.966	-9	O-61,D-10/2-2	-2.0
1980	Chi-A	45	121	9	31	4	1	1	10	7	11	.256	.297	.331	72	-5	0	2	-1	.929	-2	3-34/O-3,1-1,D-2	-0.9
Total	5	289	774	83	204	20	7	7	73	62	71	.264	.320	.335	73	-28	5	10	-5	.936	-14	3-150/O-70,D-24,21	-5.2
■ **ANSE MOORE**	Moore, Ansel Winn b: 9/22/17, Delhi, La. d: 10/29/93, Pearl, Miss. BL/TR, 6'1", 190 lbs. Deb: 4/17/46																						
1946	Det-A	51	134	16	28	4	0	1	8	12	9	.209	.279	.261	48	-9	1	1	-0	.971	1	O-32	-1.1
■ **ARCHIE MOORE**	Moore, Archie Francis b: 8/30/41, Upper Darby, Pa. BL/TL, 6'2", 190 lbs. Deb: 4/20/64																						
1964	NY-A	31	23	4	4	2	0	0	1	2	9	.174	.240	.261	39	-2	0	0	0	1.000	-2	/O-8,1-7	-0.4
1965	NY-A	9	17	1	7	2	0	1	4	4	4	.412	.524	.706	248	4	0	0	0	.889	-0	/O-5	0.3
Total	2	40	40	5	11	4	0	1	5	6	13	.275	.370	.450	128	2	0	0	0	.929	-2	/O-13,1-7	-0.1
■ **CHARLEY MOORE**	Moore, Charles Wesley b: 12/1/1884, Jackson Co., Ind. d: 7/29/70, Portland, Ore. BR/TR, 5'10", 160 lbs. Deb: 4/16/12																						
1912	Chi-N	5	9	2	2	0	1	0	2	0	1	.222	.222	.444	80	-0	0			.800	1	/S-2,2-1,3-1	0.0
■ **CHARLIE MOORE**	Moore, Charles William b: 6/21/53, Birmingham, Ala. BR/TR, 5'11", 180 lbs. Deb: 9/8/73																						
1973	Mil-A	8	27	0	5	0	1	0	3	2	4	.185	.241	.259	42	-2	0	0	0	.981	3	/C-8	0.1
1974	Mil-A	72	204	17	50	10	4	0	19	21	34	.245	.316	.333	87	-3	3	4	-2	.985	3	C-61/D-6	0.0
1975	Mil-A	73	241	26	70	20	1	1	29	17	31	.290	.337	.394	106	1	1	5	-3	.960	-6	C-47,O-22/D-1	-0.6
1976	Mil A	87	241	33	46	7	4	3	16	43	45	.191	.316	.290	80	-5	1	2	-1	.969	-3	C-49,O-28/3-1,D-2	-0.9
1977	Mil-A	138	375	42	93	15	6	5	45	31	39	.248	.307	.360	81	-10	1	7	-4	.980	-7	*C-137	-1.7
1978	Mil-A	96	268	30	72	7	1	5	31	12	24	.269	.300	.358	84	-6	4	2	0	.983	-2	C-95	-0.6
1979	Mil-A	111	337	45	101	16	2	5	38	29	32	.300	.357	.404	105	3	8	5	-1	.979	9	*C-106	1.4
1980	Mil-A	111	320	42	93	13	2	2	30	24	28	.291	.340	.363	96	-2	10	5	0	.989	-15	*C-105	-1.3
1981	*Mil-A	48	156	16	47	8	3	1	9	12	13	.301	.351	.410	125	5	1	4	-2	.970	-0	C-34/O-8,D-6	0.3
1982	*Mil-A	133	456	53	116	22	4	6	45	29	49	.254	.300	.360	86	-10	2	10	-5	.988	5	*O-115,C-20/2-1	-1.2
1983	Mil-A	151	529	65	150	27	6	2	49	55	42	.284	.355	.369	108	7	11	4	1	.978	0	*O-150/C-7,D-1	0.3
1984	Mil-A	70	188	13	44	7	1	2	17	10	26	.234	.276	.314	66	-9	0	4	-2	.984	-3	O-61/C-7	-1.6
1985	Mil-A	105	349	35	81	13	4	0	31	27	53	.232	.289	.292	60	-19	4	0	1	.977	5	*C-102/O-3	-0.8
1986	Mil-A	80	235	24	61	12	3	3	39	21	38	.260	.320	.374	86	-5	5	5	-2	.992	13	C-72/O-4,2-1,D-2	1.0
1987	Tor-A	51	107	15	23	10	1	1	7	13	12	.215	.306	.355	73	-4	0	0	0	.984	6	C-44/O-5	0.4
Total	15	1334	4033	456	1052	187	43	36	408	346	470	.261	.321	.355	89	-59	51	57	-19	.980	9	C-894,O-396/D23	-5.2
■ **DEE MOORE**	Moore, D C b: 4/6/14, Hedley, Tex. d: 7/2/97, Williston, N.Dak. BR/TR, 5'11", 190 lbs. Deb: 9/12/36																						
1936	Cin-N	6	10	4	4	2	1	0	1	0	3	.400	.400	.800	230	2	0			1.000	-0	/P-2,C-1	0.0

YEAR	TM/L	G	AB	R	H	2B	3B	HR	RBI	BB	SO	AVG	OBP	SLG	PRO+	BR/A	SB	CS	SBR	FA	FR	G/POS	TPR
1937	Cin-N	7	13	2	1	0	0	0	0	1	2	.077	.200	.077	-23	-2	0			.931	2	/C-6	0.0
1943	Bro-N	37	79	8	20	3	0	0	12	11	8	.253	.344	.291	84	-1	1			.982	-6	C-15/3-9	-0.7
	Phi-N	37	113	13	27	4	1	1	8	15	8	.239	.328	.319	91	-1	0			.960	-0	C-21/O-6,3-5,1-1	0.0
	Yr	74	192	21	47	7	1	1	20	26	16	.245	.335	.307	88	-2	1			.968	-7	C-36,3-14/O-6,1-1	-0.7
1946	Phi-N	11	13	2	1	0	0	0	1	7	3	.077	.400	.077	41	-0	0			1.000	0	/C-6,1-2	0.0
Total	4	98	228	29	53	9	2	1	22	34	24	.232	.335	.303	85	-3	1			.962	-5	/C-49,3-14,O-6,1P	-0.7

■ GENE MOORE

Moore, Eugene Jr. "Rowdy" b: 8/26/09, Lancaster, Tex. d: 3/12/78, Jackson, Miss. BL/TL, 5'11", 175 lbs. Deb: 9/19/31 F

YEAR	TM/L	G	AB	R	H	2B	3B	HR	RBI	BB	SO	AVG	OBP	SLG	PRO+	BR/A	SB	CS	SBR	FA	FR	G/POS	TPR
1931	Cin-N	4	14	2	2	1	0	0	1	0	0	.143	.143	.214	-6	-2	0			1.000	0	/O-3	-0.2
1933	StL-N	11	38	6	15	3	2	0	8	4	10	.395	.452	.579	183	4	1			.967	0	O-10	0.4
1934	StL-N	9	18	2	5	1	0	0	1	2	2	.278	.350	.333	79	-0	0			.923	1	/O-3	0.0
1935	StL-N	3	3	0	0	0	0	0	0	0	1	.000	.000	.000	-96	-1	0			.000	0	H	-0.1
1936	Bos-N	151	637	91	185	38	12	13	67	40	80	.290	.335	.449	117	12	6			.977	15	*O-151	2.0
1937	Bos-N☆	148	561	88	159	29	10	16	70	61	73	.283	.358	.456	132	23	11			.978	14	*O-148	3.1
1938	Bos-N	54	180	27	49	8	3	3	19	16	20	.272	.338	.400	114	3	1			.981	1	O-47	0.2
1939	Bro-N	107	306	45	69	13	6	3	39	40	50	.225	.315	.337	73	-12	4			.961	-6	O-86/1-1	-2.1
1940	Bro-N	10	26	3	7	2	0	0	2	1	3	.269	.296	.346	72	-1	0			1.000	-1	/O-6	-0.2
	Bos-N	103	363	46	106	24	1	5	39	25	32	.292	.338	.405	110	4	2			.986	6	O-94	0.6
	Yr	113	389	49	113	26	1	5	41	26	35	.290	.335	.401	107	3	2			.986	5	*O-100	0.4
1941	Bos-N	129	397	42	108	17	8	5	43	45	37	.272	.349	.393	114	7	5			.968	4	*O-110	0.5
1942	Was-A	1	2	0	0	0	0	0	0	0	1	.000	.000	.000	-99	-1	0	0	0	.000	-1	/O-1	-0.1
1943	Was-A	92	254	41	68	14	3	2	39	19	29	.268	.321	.370	106	1	0	2	-1	.985	0	O-57/1-1	-0.3
1944	*StL-A	110	390	56	93	13	6	6	58	24	37	.238	.284	.349	76	-13	0	5	-3	.968	2	O-98/1-1	-2.1
1945	StL-A	110	354	48	92	16	2	5	50	40	26	.260	.337	.359	97	-1	1	3	-2	.970	-3	*O-100	-1.2
Total	14	1042	3543	497	958	179	53	58	436	317	401	.270	.333	.400	105	24	31	10		.975	32	O-914/1-3	0.5

■ FERDIE MOORE

Moore, Ferdinand Depage b: 2/21/1896, Camden, N.J. d: 5/6/47, Atlantic City, N.J. Deb: 10/2/14

YEAR	TM/L	G	AB	R	H	2B	3B	HR	RBI	BB	SO	AVG	OBP	SLG	PRO+	BR/A	SB	CS	SBR	FA	FR	G/POS	TPR
1914	Phi-A	2	4	1	2	0	0	0	1	0	2	.500	.500	.500	209	0	0			.895	-1	/1-2	0.0

■ GARY MOORE

Moore, Gary Douglas b: 2/24/45, Tulsa, Okla. BR/TL, 5'10", 175 lbs. Deb: 5/3/70

YEAR	TM/L	G	AB	R	H	2B	3B	HR	RBI	BB	SO	AVG	OBP	SLG	PRO+	BR/A	SB	CS	SBR	FA	FR	G/POS	TPR
1970	LA-N	7	16	2	3	0	2	0	0	0	1	.188	.188	.438	65	-1	1	0	0	1.000	-1	/O-5,1-1	-0.2

■ EDDIE MOORE

Moore, Graham Edward b: 1/18/1899, Barlow, Ky. d: 2/10/76, Ft.Myers, Fla. BR/TR, 5'7", 165 lbs. Deb: 9/25/23

YEAR	TM/L	G	AB	R	H	2B	3B	HR	RBI	BB	SO	AVG	OBP	SLG	PRO+	BR/A	SB	CS	SBR	FA	FR	G/POS	TPR
1923	Pit-N	6	26	6	7	1	0	0	1	2	3	.269	.321	.308	65	-1	1	0	0	.923	-5	/S-6	-0.5
1924	Pit-N	72	209	47	75	8	4	2	13	27	12	.359	.437	.464	139	13	6	7	-2	.988	4	O-35,3-13/2-4	1.3
1925	*Pit-N	142	547	106	163	29	8	6	77	73	26	.298	.383	.413	97	-1	19	7	2	.952	-6	*2-122,O-15/3-3	-0.4
1926	Pit-N	43	132	19	30	8	1	0	19	12	6	.227	.292	.303	57	-8	3			.911	-11	2-24/3-9,S-1	-1.8
	Bos-N	54	184	17	49	3	2	0	15	16	12	.266	.325	.304	77	-6	6			.973	-3	2-39,S-14/3-1	-0.7
	Yr	97	316	36	79	11	3	0	34	28	18	.250	.311	.304	68	-14	9			.950	-14	2-63,S-15,3-10	-2.5
1927	Bos-N	112	411	53	124	14	4	1	32	39	17	.302	.364	.363	103	2	5			.947	-2	3-52,2-39,O-16,/S-1	0.3
1928	Bos-N	68	215	27	51	9	0	2	18	19	12	.237	.299	.307	62	-12	7			.958	6	O-54/2-1	-1.0
1929	Bro-N	111	402	48	119	18	6	0	48	44	16	.296	.370	.371	86	-8	3			.955	-18	2-74,S-36/O-2,3-1	-1.6
1930	Bro-N	76	196	24	55	13	1	1	20	21	7	.281	.356	.372	77	-7	1			.991	3	2-23,O-23,S-17,/3-1	-0.2
1932	NY-N	37	87	9	23	3	0	1	6	9	6	.264	.340	.333	84	-2	1			.930	3	S-21/3-6,2-5	0.3
1934	Cle-A	27	65	4	10	2	0	0	8	10	4	.154	.267	.185	18	-8	0	0	0	.932	1	2-18/3-3,S-2	-0.6
Total	10	748	2474	360	706	108	26	13	257	272	121	.285	.359	.366	89	-37	52	14		.956	-29	2-349,O-145/S-98,3	-4.9

■ HARRY MOORE

Moore, Henry S. Deb: 4/17/1884

YEAR	TM/L	G	AB	R	H	2B	3B	HR	RBI	BB	SO	AVG	OBP	SLG	PRO+	BR/A	SB	CS	SBR	FA	FR	G/POS	TPR
1884	Was-U	111	461	77	155	23	5	1		19		.336	.363	.414	139	10				.820	-9	*O-105/S-8	-0.1

■ JACKIE MOORE

Moore, Jackie Spencer b: 2/19/39, Jay, Fla. BR/TR, 6', 180 lbs. Deb: 4/18/65 MC

YEAR	TM/L	G	AB	R	H	2B	3B	HR	RBI	BB	SO	AVG	OBP	SLG	PRO+	BR/A	SB	CS	SBR	FA	FR	G/POS	TPR
1965	Det-A	21	53	2	5	0	0	0	2	6	12	.094	.186	.094	-17	-8	0	0	0	.985	4	C-20	-0.4

■ JIMMY MOORE

Moore, James William b: 4/24/03, Paris, Tenn. d: 3/7/86, Memphis, Tenn. BR/TR, 6'0.5", 187 lbs. Deb: 8/31/30

YEAR	TM/L	G	AB	R	H	2B	3B	HR	RBI	BB	SO	AVG	OBP	SLG	PRO+	BR/A	SB	CS	SBR	FA	FR	G/POS	TPR
1930	Chi-A	16	39	4	8	2	0	0	2	6	3	.205	.326	.256	52	-3	0	0	0	.900	0	O-11	-0.3
	*Phi-A	15	50	10	19	3	0	2	12	2	4	.380	.404	.560	136	3	1	1	-0	.958	-0	O-13	0.1
	Yr	31	89	14	27	5	0	2	14	8	7	.303	.367	.427	100	0	1	1	-0	.932	-0	O-24	-0.2
1931	*Phi-A	49	143	18	32	5	1	2	21	11	13	.224	.284	.315	54	-10	0	1	-1	.973	0	O-36	-1.2
Total	2	80	232	32	59	10	1	4	35	19	20	.254	.316	.358	71	-10	1	2	-1	.958	0	/O-60	-1.4

■ JERRIE MOORE

Moore, Jeremiah S. b: Detroit, Mich. d: 9/26/1890, Wayne, Mich. BL, 5'11", 170 lbs. Deb: 4/17/1884

YEAR	TM/L	G	AB	R	H	2B	3B	HR	RBI	BB	SO	AVG	OBP	SLG	PRO+	BR/A	SB	CS	SBR	FA	FR	G/POS	TPR
1884	Alt-U	20	80	10	25	3	1	1		0		.313	.313	.412	116	-1				.800	-8	C-12/O-9	-0.7
	Cle-N	9	30	1	6	0	0	0	10	0	5	.200	.200	.200	25	-3				.887	-1	/C-9	-0.3
1885	Det-N	6	23	2	4	1	0	0	0	1	3	.174	.208	.217	38	-2				.800	-3	/C-6	-0.4
Total	2	35	133	13	35	4	1	1	10	1	8	.263	.269	.331	83	-5				.830	-12	/C-27,O-9	-1.4

■ JOHNNY MOORE

Moore, John Francis b: 3/23/02, Waterville, Conn. d: 4/4/91, Bradenton, Fla. BL/TR, 5'10.5", 175 lbs. Deb: 9/15/28

YEAR	TM/L	G	AB	R	H	2B	3B	HR	RBI	BB	SO	AVG	OBP	SLG	PRO+	BR/A	SB	CS	SBR	FA	FR	G/POS	TPR
1928	Chi-N	4	4	0	0	0	0	0	0	0	0	.000	.000	.000	-99	-1	0			.000	0	H	-0.1
1929	Chi-N	37	63	13	18	1	0	2	8	4	6	.286	.338	.397	81	-2	0			.971	-0	O-15	-0.3
1931	Chi-N	39	104	19	25	3	1	2	16	7	5	.240	.288	.346	69	-5	1			.964	1	O-22	-0.5
1932	*Chi-N	119	443	59	135	24	5	13	64	22	38	.305	.342	.470	117	9	4			.983	1	*O-109	0.3
1933	Cin-N	135	514	60	135	19	5	1	44	29	16	.263	.306	.325	81	-12	4			.974	5	*O-132	-1.6
1934	Cin-N	16	42	5	8	1	1	0	5	3	2	.190	.244	.262	36	-4	0			1.000	-0	O-10	-0.4
	Phi-N	116	458	68	157	34	6	11	93	40	18	.343	.397	.515	125	16	7			.981	7	*O-115	1.7
	Yr	132	500	73	165	35	7	11	98	43	20	.330	.384	.494	120	13	7			.983	6	*O-125	1.3
1935	Phi-N	153	600	84	194	33	3	19	93	45	50	.323	.375	.483	117	14	4			.973	-10	*O-150	-0.1
1936	Phi-N	124	472	85	155	24	3	16	68	26	22	.328	.365	.494	117	10	1			.948	-8	*O-112	-0.2
1937	Phi-N	96	307	46	98	16	2	9	59	18	18	.319	.357	.472	114	5	2			.943	-3	O-72	0.0
1945	Chi-N	7	6	0	1	0	0	0	2	1	1	.167	.286	.167	28	-1	0			.000	0	H	-0.1
Total	10	846	3013	439	926	155	26	73	452	195	176	.307	.352	.449	109	30	23			.970	-7	O-737	-1.3

■ JO-JO MOORE

Moore, Joseph Gregg "The Gause Ghost" b: 12/25/08, Gause, Tex. BL/TR, 5'11", 155 lbs. Deb: 9/17/30

YEAR	TM/L	G	AB	R	H	2B	3B	HR	RBI	BB	SO	AVG	OBP	SLG	PRO+	BR/A	SB	CS	SBR	FA	FR	G/POS	TPR
1930	NY-N	3	5	1	1	0	0	0	0	0	1	.200	.200	.200	-3	-1	0			1.000	-0	/O-1	-0.1
1931	NY-N	4	8	0	2	1	0	0	3	0	1	.250	.250	.375	68	-0	1			1.000	0	/O-1	-0.1
1932	NY-N	86	361	53	110	15	2	2	27	20	18	.305	.341	.374	94	-3	4			.982	-4	O-86	-1.2
1933	*NY-N	132	524	56	153	16	5	0	42	21	27	.292	.323	.342	91	-6	4			.966	3	*O-132	-1.0
1934	NY-N†	139	580	106	192	37	4	15	61	31	23	.331	.370	.486	130	24	5			.954	-10	*O-131	0.8
1935	NY-N★	155	681	108	201	28	9	15	71	53	24	.295	.353	.429	111	10	5			.972	2	*O-155	0.6
1936	*NY-N☆	152	649	110	205	29	9	7	63	37	27	.316	.358	.421	110	9	2			.981	8	*O-149	1.0
1937	*NY-N★	142	580	89	180	37	10	6	57	46	37	.310	.364	.440	116	13	7			.975	-7	*O-140	0.1
1938	NY-N☆	125	506	76	153	23	6	11	56	22	27	.302	.335	.437	110	5	2			.978	-5	*O-114	-0.3
1939	NY-N	138	562	80	151	23	2	10	47	45	17	.269	.324	.370	85	-12	5			.986	3	*O-136	-1.4
1940	NY-N★	138	543	83	150	33	4	6	46	43	30	.276	.337	.385	98	-1	7			.982	-1	*O-133	-1.0
1941	NY-N	121	428	47	117	16	2	7	40	30	15	.273	.322	.369	93	-5	4			.972	-4	*O-116	-1.6
Total	12	1335	5427	809	1615	258	53	79	513	348	247	.298	.344	.408	105	33	46			.975	-14	*O-1294	-4.2

■ KELVIN MOORE

Moore, Kelvin Orlando b: 9/26/57, Leroy, Ala. BR/TL, 6'1", 195 lbs. Deb: 8/28/81

YEAR	TM/L	G	AB	R	H	2B	3B	HR	RBI	BB	SO	AVG	OBP	SLG	PRO+	BR/A	SB	CS	SBR	FA	FR	G/POS	TPR
1981	*Oak-A	14	47	5	12	0	1	1	3	5	15	.255	.327	.362	103	0	1	0	0	1.000	-1	1-13	-0.1
1982	Oak-A	21	67	6	15	1	1	2	6	3	23	.224	.257	.358	70	-3	0	1	-1	.971	-2	1-20	-0.6
1983	Oak-A	41	124	12	26	4	0	5	16	10	39	.210	.274	.363	78	-4	2	4	-2	.994	-3	1-40	-1.1
Total	3	76	238	23	53	5	2	8	25	18	77	.223	.280	.361	81	-7	3	5	-2	.989	-5	/1-73	-1.8

YEAR	TM/L	G	AB	R	H	2B	3B	HR	RBI	BB	SO	AVG	OBP	SLG	PRO+	BR/A	SB	CS	SBR	FA	FR	G/POS	TPR
■ **KERWIN MOORE**	Moore, Kerwin Lamar b: 10/29/70, Detroit, Mich. BB/TR, 6'1", 190 lbs. Deb: 8/30/96																						
1996	Oak-A	22	16	4	1	1	0	0	0	2	6	.063	.167	.125	-25	-3	1	0	0	1.000	-5	O-18/D-2	-0.8
■ **MOLLY MOORE**	Moore, Maurice d: 2/24/1881, New York, N.Y. Deb: 6/30/1875																						
1875	Atl-n	21	86	5	19	4	0	0	5	0	4	.221	.221	.267	79	-1	0	1	-1	.747	-5	S-14/1-8,O-2,C23	-0.6
■ **RANDY MOORE**	Moore, Randolph Edward b: 6/21/06, Naples, Tex. d: 6/12/92, Mt.Pleasant, Tex. BL/TR, 6', 185 lbs. Deb: 4/12/27																						
1927	Chi-A	6	15	0	0	0	0	0	0	0	2	.000	.000	.000	-99	-4	0	0	0	1.000	1	/O-4	-0.4
1928	Chi-A	24	61	6	13	4	1	0	5	3	5	.213	.250	.311	47	-5	0	1	-1	.946	0	O-16	-0.6
1930	Bos-N	83	191	24	55	9	0	2	34	10	13	.288	.323	.366	69	-10	3			.986	-2	O-34,3-13	-1.2
1931	Bos-N	83	192	19	50	8	1	3	34	13	3	.260	.311	.359	83	-5	1			.952	0	O-29,3-22/2-1	-0.5
1932	Bos-N	107	351	41	103	21	2	3	43	15	11	.293	.322	.390	94	-3	1			.987	-7	O-41,3-31,1-22,/C-1	-1.3
1933	Bos-N	135	497	64	150	23	7	8	70	40	16	.302	.356	.425	133	20	3			.979	-0	*O-122,1-10	1.3
1934	Bos-N	123	422	55	120	21	2	7	64	40	16	.284	.346	.393	105	3	2			.965	-2	O-72,1-37	-0.4
1935	Bos-N	125	407	42	112	20	4	4	42	26	16	.275	.319	.373	93	-5	1			.950	0	O-78,1-21	-1.0
1936	Bro-N	42	88	4	21	3	0	0	14	8	1	.239	.302	.273	55	-5	0			.964	-4	O-21	-1.0
1937	Bro-N	13	22	3	3	1	0	0	2	3	2	.136	.240	.182	16	-3	0			.889	0	C-10	-0.2
	StL-N	8	7	0	0	0	0	0	0	0	0	.000	.000	.000	-98	-2	0			.000	-0	/O-1	-0.2
	Yr	21	29	3	3	1	0	0	2	3	2	.103	.188	.138	-10	-4	0			.889	-0	C-10/O-1	-0.4
Total	10	749	2253	258	627	110	17	27	308	158	85	.278	.326	.378	95	-19	11	1		.969	-15	O-418/1-90,3-66,C2	-5.5
■ **BOBBY MOORE**	Moore, Robert Vincent b: 10/27/65, Cincinnati, Ohio BR/TR, 5'9", 165 lbs. Deb: 9/5/91																						
1991	KC-A	18	14	3	5	1	0	0	0	1	2	.357	.400	.429	129	1	3	2	-0	1.000	-4	O-13	-0.4
■ **TERRY MOORE**	Moore, Terry Bluford b: 5/27/12, Vernon, Ala. d: 3/29/95, Collinsville, Ill. BR/TR, 5'11", 195 lbs. Deb: 4/16/35 MC																						
1935	StL-N	119	456	63	131	34	3	6	53	15	40	.287	.314	.414	90	-7	13			.984	14	*O-117	0.3
1936	StL-N	143	590	85	156	39	4	5	47	37	52	.264	.309	.369	82	-16	9			.977	22	*O-133	0.1
1937	StL-N	115	461	76	123	17	3	5	43	32	41	.267	.317	.349	79	-13	13			.988	14	*O-106	-0.3
1938	StL-N	94	312	49	85	21	3	4	21	46	19	.272	.366	.397	104	3	9			.987	9	O-75/3-6	0.9
1939	StL-N★	130	417	65	123	25	2	17	77	43	38	.295	.362	.487	119	10	6			**.994**	11	*O-121/P-1	1.7
1940	StL-N★	136	537	92	163	33	4	17	64	42	44	.304	.356	.475	121	14	18			.987	17	*O-133	2.4
1941	StL-N★	122	493	86	145	26	4	6	68	52	31	.294	.364	.400	108	5	3			.984	7	*O-121	0.5
1942	*StL-N★	130	489	80	141	26	3	6	49	56	26	.288	.364	.391	112	8	10			.986	-3	*O-126/3-1	-0.1
1946	*StL-N	91	278	32	73	14	1	3	28	18	26	.263	.312	.353	85	-6	0			.982	1	O-66	-0.8
1947	StL-N	127	460	61	130	17	1	7	45	38	39	.283	.339	.370	84	-10	1			.983	1	*O-120	-1.5
1948	StL-N	91	207	30	48	11	0	4	18	27	12	.232	.321	.343	75	-7	0			.993	-10	O-71	-2.0
Total	11	1298	4700	719	1318	263	28	80	513	406	368	.280	.340	.399	98	-18	82			.985	83	*O-1189/3-7,P-1	1.2
■ **SCRAPPY MOORE**	Moore, William Allen b: 12/16/1892, St.Louis, Mo. d: 10/13/64, Little Rock, Ark. BR/TR, 5'8", 153 lbs. Deb: 6/21/17																						
1917	StL-A	4	8	1	1	0	0	0	0	1	0	.125	.222	.125	6	-1	0			.750	0	/3-2	-0.1
■ **BILL MOORE**	Moore, William Henry "Willie" b: 12/12/03, Kansas City, Mo. d: 5/24/72, Kansas City, Mo. BL/TR, 5'11", 170 lbs. Deb: 9/7/26																						
1926	Bos-A	5	18	2	3	0	0	0	0	0	2	.167	.167	.167	-13	-3	0	0	0	1.000	0	/C-5	-0.2
1927	Bos-A	44	69	7	15	2	0	0	4	13	8	.217	.341	.246	56	-4	0	0	0	.938	2	C-42	0.0
Total	2	49	87	9	18	2	0	0	4	13	10	.207	.310	.230	43	-7	0	0	0	.946	2	/C-47	-0.2
■ **BILL MOORE**	Moore, William Ross b: 10/10/60, Los Angeles, Cal. BR/TL, 6'1", 185 lbs. Deb: 7/19/86																						
1986	Mon-N	6	12	0	2	0	0	0	0	0	4	.167	.167	.167	-8	-2	0	0	0	1.000	-1	/1-3,O-1	-0.3
■ **ANDRES MORA**	Mora, Andres (Ibarra) b: 5/25/55, Rio Bravo, Mex. BR/TR, 6', 180 lbs. Deb: 4/13/76																						
1976	Bal-A	73	220	18	48	11	0	6	25	13	49	.218	.262	.350	83	-6	1	0	0	.951	-2	D-34,O-31	-1.0
1977	Bal-A	77	233	32	57	8	2	13	44	5	53	.245	.264	.464	100	-2	0	0	0	1.000	-9	O-57/3-1,D-5	-1.3
1978	Bal-A	76	229	21	49	8	0	8	14	13	47	.214	.259	.354	75	-9	0	1	-1	.978	1	O-69/D-1	-1.1
1980	Cle-A	9	18	0	2	0	0	0	0	0	0	.111	.111	.111	-39	-3	0	0	0	1.000	0	/O-3	-0.4
Total	4	235	700	71	156	27	2	27	83	31	149	.223	.258	.383	83	-19	1	1	-0	.978	-10	O-160/D-40,3-1	-3.8
■ **JOSE MORALES**	Morales, Jose Manuel (Hernandez) b: 12/30/44, Frederiksted, V.I. BR/TR, 6', 195 lbs. Deb: 8/13/73 C																						
1973	Oak-A	6	14	0	4	1	0	0	1	1	5	.286	.333	.357	100	-0	0	1	-1	.000	0	/D-3	-0.1
	Mon-N	5	5	0	2	0	0	0	0	0	0	.400	.400	.400	118	0	0	0	0	.000	0	H	0.0
1974	Mon-N	25	26	3	7	4	0	1	5	1	7	.269	.296	.538	123	1	0	0	0	.800	-1	/C-2	0.0
1975	Mon-N	93	163	18	49	6	1	2	24	14	21	.301	.356	.387	102	0	0	2	-1	.983	4	1-27/O-6,C-5	0.2
1976	Mon-N	104	158	12	50	11	0	4	37	3	20	.316	.337	.462	120	3	0	0	0	.977	1	1-21,C-12	0.4
1977	Mon-N	65	74	3	15	4	1	1	9	5	12	.203	.253	.324	55	-5	0	0	0	1.000	-2	/C-8,1-8	-0.7
1978	Min-A	101	242	22	76	13	1	2	38	20	35	.314	.369	.401	114	5	0	1	-1	.000	0	D-77/C-1,1-1,O-1	0.2
1979	Min-A	92	191	21	51	5	1	2	27	14	27	.267	.324	.335	75	-6	0	0	0	1.000	-0	D-77/1-1	-0.9
1980	Min-A	97	241	36	73	17	2	8	36	22	19	.303	.364	.490	123	7	0	0	0	1.000	-1	D-86/C-2,1-2	0.4
1981	Bal-A	38	86	6	21	3	0	2	14	3	13	.244	.270	.349	77	-3	0	0	0	1.000	-0	D-22/1-3	-0.4
1982	Bal-A	3	3	0	0	0	0	0	0	0	2	.000	.000	.000	-99	-1	0	0	0	.000	0	/H	-0.1
	LA-N	35	30	1	9	1	0	1	8	4	8	.300	.382	.433	131	1	0	0	0	.000	0	H	0.0
1983	*LA-N	47	53	4	15	3	0	3	8	1	11	.283	.296	.509	120	1	0	0	0	.951	-0	/1-4	0.1
1984	LA-N	22	19	0	3	0	0	0	0	1	2	.158	.200	.158	2	-2	0	0	0	.000	0	H	-0.3
Total	12	733	1305	126	375	68	6	26	207	89	182	.287	.336	.408	102	1	0	4	-2	.981	2	D-265/1-67,C-30,O-7	-1.2
■ **JERRY MORALES**	Morales, Julio Ruben (Torres) b: 2/18/49, Yabucao, P.R. BR/TR, 5'10", 175 lbs. Deb: 9/5/69																						
1969	SD-N	19	41	5	8	2	0	1	6	5	7	.195	.283	.317	71	-2	0	2	-1	1.000	-1	O-19	-0.4
1970	SD-N	28	58	6	9	0	1	1	4	3	11	.155	.197	.241	17	-7	0	0	0	.926	-5	O-26	-1.3
1971	SD-N	12	17	1	2	0	0	0	1	2	2	.118	.211	.118	-5	-2	0	0	0	1.000	-1	/O-7	-0.4
1972	SD-N	115	347	38	83	15	7	4	18	35	54	.239	.309	.357	96	-3	4	6	-2	.987	4	O-96/3-4	-0.6
1973	SD-N	122	388	47	109	23	2	9	34	27	55	.281	.328	.420	115	6	6	5	-1	.991	1	*O-100	0.1
1974	Chi-N	151	534	70	146	21	7	15	82	46	63	.273	.333	.423	106	3	2	12	-7	.975	-7	*O-143	-1.6
1975	Chi-N	153	578	62	156	21	0	12	91	50	65	.270	.333	.369	91	-7	3	7	-3	.979	0	*O-151	-1.7
1976	Chi-N	140	537	66	147	17	0	16	67	41	49	.274	.325	.395	95	-4	3	8	-4	.983	3	*O-136	-1.1
1977	Chi-N★	136	490	56	142	34	5	11	69	43	75	.290	.350	.447	101	0	0	3	-2	.985	-7	*O-128	-1.4
1978	StL-N	130	457	44	109	19	8	4	46	33	44	.239	.291	.341	77	-15	4	4	-1	.977	-0	*O-126	-2.3
1979	Det-A	129	440	50	93	23	1	14	56	30	56	.211	.265	.364	65	-23	10	4	1	.986	-9	*O-119/D-7	-3.5
1980	NY-N	94	193	19	49	7	1	3	30	13	31	.254	.304	.347	84	-4	2	3	-1	.973	-7	O-63	-1.5
1981	Chi-N	84	245	27	70	6	2	1	25	22	29	.286	.347	.339	91	-2	1	1	-0	.986	-6	O-72	-1.1
1982	Chi-N	65	116	14	33	2	2	4	30	9	7	.284	.336	.440	112	2	1	2	-1	1.000	-5	O-41	-0.5
1983	Chi-N	63	87	11	17	9	0	0	11	7	19	.195	.255	.299	51	-6	0	0	0	1.000	-6	O-29	-1.3
Total	15	1441	4528	516	1173	199	36	95	570	366	567	.259	.316	.382	91	-64	37	57	-23	.983	-44	*O-1256/D-7,3-4	-18.6
■ **RICH MORALES**	Morales, Richard Angelo b: 9/20/43, San Francisco, Cal. BR/TR, 5'11", 170 lbs. Deb: 8/8/67 C																						
1967	Chi-A	8	10	0	0	0	0	0	0	0	2	.000	.000	.000	-99	-2	0	0	0	.944	2	/S-7	-0.1
1968	Chi-A	10	29	2	5	0	0	0	0	2	5	.172	.226	.172	22	-3	0	0	0	.966	2	/S-7,2-5	0.0
1969	Chi-A	55	121	12	26	0	1	0	6	7	18	.215	.269	.231	39	-10	1	0	0	.976	10	2-38,S-13/3-1	0.4
1970	Chi-A	62	112	6	18	2	0	1	2	9	16	.161	.230	.205	20	-12	1	0	0	.967	6	S-24,3-20,2-12	-0.4
1971	Chi-A	84	185	19	45	8	0	2	14	22	26	.243	.336	.319	84	-3	2	3	-1	.976	-1	S-57,3-18/2-3,O-1	0.0
1972	Chi-A	110	287	24	59	7	1	2	20	19	49	.206	.262	.258	54	-16	2	3	-1	.968	-1	S-86,2-16,3-14	-0.9
1973	Chi-A	7	4	1	0	0	0	0	1	1	1	.000	.200	.000	-38	-1	0	0	0	1.000	1	/3-5,2-2	0.0
	SD-N	90	244	9	40	6	1	0	16	27	36	.164	.247	.197	27	-24	0	1	-1	.988	22	2-79,S-10	0.2

YEAR	TM/L	G	AB	R	H	2B	3B	HR	RBI	BB	SO	AVG	OBP	SLG	PRO+	BR/A	SB	CS	SBR	FA	FR	G/POS	TPR
1974	SD-N	54	61	8	12	3	0	1	5	8	6	.197	.290	.295	67	-3	1	0	0	.933	7	S-29,2-18/3-6,1-1	0.6
Total	8	480	1053	81	205	26	3	6	64	95	159	.195	.268	.242	46	-74	7	7	-2	.970	47	S-233,2-173/31O	-0.2

■ **CHARLIE MORAN** Moran, Charles Barthell "Uncle Charlie" b: 2/22/1878, Nashville, Tenn. d: 6/14/49, Horse Cave, Ky. BR/TR, 5'8", 180 lbs. Deb: 9/9/03 U

YEAR	TM/L	G	AB	R	H	2B	3B	HR	RBI	BB	SO	AVG	OBP	SLG	PRO+	BR/A	SB	CS	SBR	FA	FR	G/POS	TPR
1903	StL-N	4	14	2	6	0	0	0	1	0		.429	.429	.429	149	1	1			1.000	-1	/P-3,S-1	0.0
1908	StL-N	21	63	2	11	1	2	0	2	0		.175	.175	.254	38	-5	0			.903	-3	C-16	-0.7
Total	2	25	77	4	17	1	2	0	3	0		.221	.221	.286	61	-4	1			.903	-4	/C-16,P-3,S-1	-0.7

■ **CHARLES MORAN** Moran, Charles Vincent b: 3/26/1879, Washington, D.C. d: 4/11/34, Washington, D.C. TR , Deb: 4/29/03

YEAR	TM/L	G	AB	R	H	2B	3B	HR	RBI	BB	SO	AVG	OBP	SLG	PRO+	BR/A	SB	CS	SBR	FA	FR	G/POS	TPR
1903	Was-A	98	373	41	84	14	5	1	24	33		.225	.297	.298	77	-10	8			**.943**	5	S-96/2-2	-0.1
1904	Was-A	62	243	27	54	10	0	0	7	23		.222	.289	.263	77	-6	7			.919	-13	S-61/3-1	-2.0
	StL-A	82	272	15	47	3	1	0	14	25		.173	.242	.191	40	-18	2			.937	-3	3-81/O-1	-2.0
	Yr	144	515	42	101	13	1	0	21	48		.196	.265	.225	58	-23	9			.938	-16	3-82,S-61/O-1	-4.0
1905	StL-A	27	82	6	16	1	0	0	5	10		.195	.290	.207	62	-3	3			.954	-4	2-20/3-5	-0.7
Total	3	269	970	89	201	28	6	1	50	91		.207	.279	.252	66	-36	20			.935	-15	S-157/3-87,2-22,O-1	-4.8

■ **HERBIE MORAN** Moran, John Herbert b: 2/16/1884, Costello, Pa. d: 9/21/54, Clarkson, N.Y. BL/TR, 5'5", 150 lbs. Deb: 4/16/08

YEAR	TM/L	G	AB	R	H	2B	3B	HR	RBI	BB	SO	AVG	OBP	SLG	PRO+	BR/A	SB	CS	SBR	FA	FR	G/POS	TPR
1908	Phi-A	19	59	4	9	0	0	0	4	6		.153	.242	.153	27	-4	1			.952	1	O-19	-0.5
	Bos-N	8	29	3	8	0	0	0	2	2		.276	.364	.276	106	0	1			1.000	2	/O-8	0.3
1909	Bos-N	8	31	8	7	1	0	0	0	5		.226	.333	.258	80	-1	0			1.000	-1	/O-8	-0.1
1910	Bos-N	20	67	11	8	0	0	0	3	13	14	.119	.280	.119	17	-7	6			.958	4	O-20	-0.4
1912	Bro-N	130	508	77	140	18	10	1	40	69	38	.276	.368	.356	102	4	28			.961	8	*O-129	0.5
1913	Bro-N	132	515	71	137	15	5	0	26	45	29	.266	.333	.315	83	-10	21			.950	2	*O-129	-1.4
1914	Cin-N	107	395	43	93	10	5	1	35	41	29	.235	.312	.294	78	-10	26			.954	-5	*O-107	-2.2
	*Bos-N	41	154	24	41	3	1	0	4	17	11	.266	.347	.299	93	-1	4			.940	-8	O-41	-1.1
	Yr	148	549	67	134	13	6	1	39	58	40	.244	.322	.295	82	-11	30			.950	-13	*O-148	-3.3
1915	Bos-N	130	419	59	84	13	5	0	21	66	41	.200	.320	.255	79	-8	16	10	-1	.964	-6	*O-123	-2.3
Total	7	595	2177	300	527	60	26	2	135	264	162	.242	.332	.296	83	-35	103	10		.957	-2	O-584	-7.2

■ **PAT MORAN** Moran, Patrick Joseph b: 2/7/1876, Fitchburg, Mass. d: 3/7/24, Orlando, Fla. BR/TR, 5'10", 180 lbs. Deb: 5/15/01 M

YEAR	TM/L	G	AB	R	H	2B	3B	HR	RBI	BB	SO	AVG	OBP	SLG	PRO+	BR/A	SB	CS	SBR	FA	FR	G/POS	TPR
1901	Bos-N	52	180	12	38	5	1	2	18	3		.211	.228	.283	44	-13	3			.973	-5	C-28,1-13/3-4,SO2	-1.6
1902	Bos-N	80	251	22	60	5	5	1	24	17		.239	.303	.311	88	-3	6			**.982**	1	C-71/1-3,O-1	0.5
1903	Bos-N	109	389	40	102	25	5	7	54	29		.262	.331	.406	114	6	8			.967	19	*C-107/1-1	3.5
1904	Bos-N	113	398	26	90	11	3	4	34	18		.226	.267	.299	77	-11	10			.957	4	C-72,3-39/1-2	0.1
1905	Bos-N	85	267	22	64	11	5	2	22	8		.240	.270	.341	83	-7	3			**.986**	13	C-78	1.4
1906	*Chi-N	70	226	22	57	13	1	0	35	7		.252	.281	.319	82	-6	6			.979	3	C-61	0.4
1907	*Chi-N	65	198	8	45	5	1	1	19	10		.227	.271	.278	68	-8	5			.973	0	C-59	-0.2
1908	Chi-N	50	150	12	39	5	1	0	12	13		.260	.323	.307	97	-0	6			.968	1	C-45	0.5
1909	Chi-N	77	246	18	54	11	1	1	23	16		.220	.278	.285	73	-8	2			.984	1	C-74	0.0
1910	Phi-N	68	199	13	47	7	1	0	11	17	16	.236	.306	.281	69	-8	6			.989	0	C-56	-0.2
1911	Phi-N	34	103	2	19	3	0	0	8	3	13	.184	.208	.214	18	-11	0			.984	-1	C-32	-1.0
1912	Phi-N	13	26	1	3	1	0	0	1	1	7	.115	.148	.154	-16	-4	0			.955	-2	C-13	-0.5
1913	Phi-N	1	1	0	0	0	0	0	0	0	0	.000	.000	.000	-96	-0	0			.000	0	H	0.0
1914	Phi-N	1	0	0	0	0	0	0	1	0	0	—	—	—	—	0	0			.000	0	/C-1	0.0
Total	14	818	2634	198	618	102	24	18	262	142	36	.235	.283	.312	78	-74	55			.976	34	C-697/3-43,1OS2	2.9

■ **AL MORAN** Moran, Richard Alan b: 12/5/38, Detroit, Mich. BR/TR, 6'1.5", 190 lbs. Deb: 4/9/63

YEAR	TM/L	G	AB	R	H	2B	3B	HR	RBI	BB	SO	AVG	OBP	SLG	PRO+	BR/A	SB	CS	SBR	FA	FR	G/POS	TPR
1963	NY-N	119	331	26	64	5	2	1	23	36	60	.193	.274	.230	46	-22	3	7	-3	.951	6	*S-116/3-1	-1.3
1964	NY-N	16	22	2	5	0	0	0	4	2	2	.227	.292	.227	50	-1	0	0	0	.957	4	S-15/3-1	0.3
Total	2	135	353	28	69	5	2	1	27	38	62	.195	.276	.229	46	-23	3	7	-3	.951	10	S-131/3-2	-1.0

■ **ROY MORAN** Moran, Roy Ellis "Deedle" b: 9/17/1884, Vincennes, Ind. d: 7/18/66, Atlanta, Ga. BR/TR, 5'8", 155 lbs. Deb: 9/3/12

YEAR	TM/L	G	AB	R	H	2B	3B	HR	RBI	BB	SO	AVG	OBP	SLG	PRO+	BR/A	SB	CS	SBR	FA	FR	G/POS	TPR
1912	Was-A	7	13	1	2	0	0	0	0	8		.154	.476	.154	82	1	3			.889	-0	/O-6	0.0

■ **BILL MORAN** Moran, William L. b: 10/10/1869, Joliet, Ill. d: 4/8/16, Joliet, Ill. 175 lbs. Deb: 5/7/1892

YEAR	TM/L	G	AB	R	H	2B	3B	HR	RBI	BB	SO	AVG	OBP	SLG	PRO+	BR/A	SB	CS	SBR	FA	FR	G/POS	TPR
1892	StL-N	24	81	2	11	1	0	0	5	2	12	.136	.157	.148	-8	-11	0			.891	-4	C-22/O-2	-1.3
1895	Chi-N	15	55	8	9	2	1	1	9	3	2	.164	.220	.291	29	-6	2			.827	-2	C-15	-0.5
Total	2	39	136	10	20	3	1	1	14	5	14	.147	.183	.206	10	-17	2			.866	-6	/C-37,O-2	-1.8

■ **BILLY MORAN** Moran, William Nelson b: 11/27/33, Montgomery, Ala. BR/TR, 5'11", 185 lbs. Deb: 4/15/58

YEAR	TM/L	G	AB	R	H	2B	3B	HR	RBI	BB	SO	AVG	OBP	SLG	PRO+	BR/A	SB	CS	SBR	FA	FR	G/POS	TPR
1958	Cle-A	115	257	26	58	11	0	1	18	13	23	.226	.263	.280	51	-17	3	2	-0	.960	13	2-74,S-38	0.0
1959	Cle-A	11	17	1	5	0	0	0	2	0	1	.294	.294	.294	64	-1	0	0	0	1.000	-1	/2-6,S-5	-0.1
1961	LA-A	54	173	17	45	7	1	2	22	17	16	.260	.330	.347	73	-7	0	0	0	.966	-5	2-51/S-2	-0.6
1962	LA-A★	160	659	90	186	25	3	17	74	39	80	.282	.326	.407	99	-2	5	1	1	.986	19	*2-160	3.4
1963	LA-A	153	597	67	164	29	5	7	65	31	57	.275	.314	.375	98	-3	1	1	-0	.973	15	*2-151	2.7
1964	LA-A	50	198	26	53	10	1	0	11	13	20	.268	.316	.328	88	-4	1	3	-2	.929	-7	3-47/2-3,S-1	-1.3
	Cle-A	69	151	14	31	6	0	1	10	18	16	.205	.294	.265	57	-8	0	1	-1	.972	3	3-42,2-15/1-2	-0.6
	Yr	119	349	40	84	16	1	1	21	31	36	.241	.306	.301	73	-12	1	4	-2	.947	-4	3-89,2-18/1-2,S-1	-1.9
1965	Cle-A	22	24	1	3	0	0	0	0	2	5	.125	.222	.125	1	-3	0	0	0	1.000	1	/2-7,S-1	-0.2
Total	7	634	2076	242	545	88	10	28	202	133	218	.263	.310	.355	85	-45	10	8	-2	.976	39	2-467/3-89,S-47,1-2	3.3

■ **MICKEY MORANDINI** Morandini, Michael Robert b: 4/22/66, Kittanning, Pa. BL/TR, 5'11", 171 lbs. Deb: 9/1/90

YEAR	TM/L	G	AB	R	H	2B	3B	HR	RBI	BB	SO	AVG	OBP	SLG	PRO+	BR/A	SB	CS	SBR	FA	FR	G/POS	TPR
1990	Phi-N	25	79	9	19	4	0	1	3	6	19	.241	.294	.329	71	-3	3	0	1	.990	1	2-25	-0.1
1991	Phi-N	98	325	38	81	11	4	1	20	29	45	.249	.315	.317	79	-9	13	2	3	.986	8	2-97	0.4
1992	Phi-N	127	422	47	112	8	8	3	30	25	64	.265	.306	.344	84	-9	8	3	1	.991	11	*2-124/S-3	0.6
1993	*Phi-N	120	425	57	105	19	9	3	33	34	73	.247	.310	.355	79	-13	13	2	3	.990	-1	*2-111	-0.8
1994	Phi-N	87	274	40	80	16	5	2	26	34	33	.292	.378	.409	103	2	10	5	0	.985	4	2-79	0.9
1995	Phi-N★	127	494	65	140	34	7	6	49	42	80	.283	.350	.417	101	1	9	6	-1	.989	-1	*2-122	0.6
1996	Phi-N	140	539	64	135	24	6	3	32	49	87	.250	.323	.334	73	-20	26	5	5	.982	-9	*2-137	-1.5
1997	Phi-N	150	553	83	163	40	2	1	39	62	91	.295	.374	.380	98	1	16	13	-3	.990	-15	*2-146/S-1	-0.8
1998	*Chi-N	154	582	93	172	20	4	8	53	72	84	.296	.382	.385	97	1	13	1	3	**.993**	-17	*2-152	-0.2
Total	9	1028	3693	496	1007	176	45	28	285	353	576	.273	.344	.367	89	-50	111	37	11	.988	-18	2-993/S-4	-0.9

■ **MIKE MORDECAI** Mordecai, Michael Howard b: 12/13/67, Birmingham, Ala. BB/TR, 5'11", 175 lbs. Deb: 5/8/94

YEAR	TM/L	G	AB	R	H	2B	3B	HR	RBI	BB	SO	AVG	OBP	SLG	PRO+	BR/A	SB	CS	SBR	FA	FR	G/POS	TPR
1994	Atl-N	4	4	1	1	0	0	1	3	1	0	.250	.400	1.000	244	1	0	0	0	1.000	-0	/S-4	0.1
1995	*Atl-N	69	75	10	21	6	0	3	11	9	16	.280	.357	.480	115	2	0	0	0	1.000	-2	2-21/1-9,3-6,S-6,O	0.0
1996	*Atl-N	66	108	12	26	5	0	2	8	9	24	.241	.299	.343	65	-5	1	0	0	.985	-1	2-20,3-10/S-6,1-1	-0.5
1997	Atl-N	61	81	8	14	2	1	0	3	6	16	.173	.230	.222	19	-10	0	1	-1	1.000	-2	3-19/2-4,S-4,1OD	-1.2
1998	Mon-N	73	119	12	24	4	2	3	10	9	20	.202	.258	.345	57	-8	1	0	0	.953	-2	S-30,2-21,3-11,/1-1	-0.7
Total	5	273	387	43	86	17	3	9	35	34	76	.222	.285	.351	65	-21	2	1	0	.987	-7	/2-66,S-50,31OD	-2.3

■ **RAY MOREHART** Morehart, Raymond Anderson b: 12/2/1899, Terrell, Tex. d: 1/13/89, Dallas, Tex. BL/TR, 5'9", 157 lbs. Deb: 8/9/24

YEAR	TM/L	G	AB	R	H	2B	3B	HR	RBI	BB	SO	AVG	OBP	SLG	PRO+	BR/A	SB	CS	SBR	FA	FR	G/POS	TPR
1924	Chi-A	31	100	10	20	4	2	0	8	17	7	.200	.316	.280	56	-6	3	1	0	.873	-12	S-27/2-2	-1.4
1926	Chi-A	73	192	27	61	10	3	0	21	11	15	.318	.358	.401	101	0	3	11	-6	.950	-5	2-48	-0.9
1927	NY-A	73	195	45	50	7	2	1	20	29	18	.256	.353	.328	80	-5	4	4	-1	.945	4	2-53	-0.1
Total	3	177	487	82	131	21	7	1	49	57	40	.269	.347	.347	83	-11	10	16	-7	.946	-13	2-103/S-27	-2.4

■ **DANNY MOREJON** Morejon, Daniel (Torres) b: 7/21/30, Havana, Cuba BR/TR, 6'1", 175 lbs. Deb: 7/11/58

YEAR	TM/L	G	AB	R	H	2B	3B	HR	RBI	BB	SO	AVG	OBP	SLG	PRO+	BR/A	SB	CS	SBR	FA	FR	G/POS	TPR
1958	Cin-N	12	26	4	5	0	0	0	1	9	2	.192	.400	.192	60	-1	1	0	0	1.000	-2	O-11	-0.4

■ **KEITH MORELAND** Moreland, Bobby Keith b: 5/2/54, Dallas, Tex. BR/TR, 6', 200 lbs. Deb: 10/1/78

YEAR	TM/L	G	AB	R	H	2B	3B	HR	RBI	BB	SO	AVG	OBP	SLG	PRO+	BR/A	SB	CS	SBR	FA	FR	G/POS	TPR
1978	Phi-N	1	2	0	0	0	0	0	0	0	0	.000	.000	.000	-99	-1	0	0	0	1.000	0	/C-1	0.0

YEAR	TM/L	G	AB	R	H	2B	3B	HR	RBI	BB	SO	AVG	OBP	SLG	PRO+	BR/A	SB	CS	SBR	FA	FR	G/POS	TPR
1979	Phi-N	14	48	3	18	3	2	0	8	3	5	.375	.412	.521	148	3	0	0	0	1.000	-0	C-13	0.3
1980	*Phi-N	62	159	13	50	8	0	4	29	8	14	.314	.347	.440	112	2	3	1	0	.967	-1	C-39/3-4,O-2	0.3
1981	*Phi-N	61	196	16	50	7	0	6	37	15	13	.255	.311	.383	92	-2	1	2	-1	.982	-7	C-50/3-7,1-2,O-2	-1.0
1982	Chi-N	138	476	50	124	17	2	15	68	46	71	.261	.330	.399	100	0	0	6	-4	.989	-21	O-86,C-44/3-2	-2.7
1983	Chi-N	154	533	76	161	30	3	16	70	68	73	.302	.384	.460	127	20	0	3	-2	.976	-6	*O-151/C-3	0.9
1984	*Chi-N	140	495	59	138	17	3	16	80	34	71	.279	.329	.422	101	-0	1	4	-2	.976	-7	*O-103,1-29/3-8,C-3	-1.5
1985	Chi-N	161	587	74	180	30	3	14	106	68	58	.307	.380	.440	116	13	12	3	2	.976	-9	*O-148,1-12,3-11,/C	0.1
1986	Chi-N	156	586	72	159	30	0	12	79	53	48	.271	.332	.384	90	-8	3	6	-3	.980	-9	*O-121,3-24,C-13,1	-2.5
1987	Chi-N	153	563	63	150	29	1	27	88	39	66	.266	.314	.465	99	-2	3	3	-1	.934	4	*3-150/1-1	-0.1
1988	SD-N	143	511	40	131	23	0	5	64	40	51	.256	.310	.331	86	-9	2	3	-1	.994	-3	1-73,O-64/3-2	-2.3
1989	Det-A	90	318	34	95	16	0	5	35	27	33	.299	.357	.396	115	6	3	2	-0	1.000	-6	D-51,1-31,3-12,/C-1	-0.4
	Bal-A	33	107	11	23	4	0	1	10	4	12	.215	.243	.280	49	-7	0	0	0	.000	0	D-29	-0.8
	Yr	123	425	45	118	20	0	6	45	31	45	.278	.330	.367	99	-1	3	2	-0	1.000	-6	D-80,1-31,3-12,/C-1	-1.2
Total	12	1306	4581	511	1279	214	14	121	674	405	515	.279	.339	.411	103	15	28	33	-11	.979	-65	O-677,3-220,C1/D	-9.7

■ HARRY MORELOCK
Morelock, A. Harry b: 11/1869, Philadelphia, Pa. Deb: 8/21/1891

YEAR	TM/L	G	AB	R	H	2B	3B	HR	RBI	BB	SO	AVG	OBP	SLG	PRO+	BR/A	SB	CS	SBR	FA	FR	G/POS	TPR
1891	Phi-N	4	14	1	1	0	0	0	0	3	3	.071	.235	.071	-9	-2	0			.824	-4	/S-4	-0.5
1892	Phi-N	1	3	0	0	0	0	0	0	1	0	.000	.250	.000	-23	-0	0			.600	-1	/3-1	-0.1
Total	2	5	17	1	1	0	0	0	0	4	3	.059	.238	.059	-11	-2	0			.824	-4	/S-4,3-1	-0.6

■ JOSE MORENO
Moreno, Jose De Los Santos (b: Jose De Los Santos Mauricio (Moreno)) b: 11/1/57, Santo Domingo, D.R. BB/TR, 6', 175 lbs. Deb: 5/24/80

YEAR	TM/L	G	AB	R	H	2B	3B	HR	RBI	BB	SO	AVG	OBP	SLG	PRO+	BR/A	SB	CS	SBR	FA	FR	G/POS	TPR
1980	NY-N	37	46	6	9	2	1	2	9	3	12	.196	.245	.413	83	-1	1	0	0	.917	0	/2-4,3-4	-0.1
1981	SD-N	34	48	5	11	2	0	0	6	1	8	.229	.245	.271	50	-3	4	1	1	1.000	-0	/O-9,2-1	-0.3
1982	Cal-A	11	3	3	0	0	0	0	0	2	0	.000	.400	.000	21	-0	0	2	-1	1.000	1	/2-2,D-1	0.0
Total	3	82	97	14	20	4	1	2	15	6	20	.206	.252	.330	66	-5	5	3	-0	.947	1	/O-9,2-7,3-4,D-1	-0.4

■ OMAR MORENO
Moreno, Omar Renan (Quintero) b: 10/24/52, Puerto Armuelles, Panama BL/TL, 6'2", 180 lbs. Deb: 9/6/75

YEAR	TM/L	G	AB	R	H	2B	3B	HR	RBI	BB	SO	AVG	OBP	SLG	PRO+	BR/A	SB	CS	SBR	FA	FR	G/POS	TPR
1975	Pit-N	6	6	1	1	0	0	0	0	1	1	.167	.286	.167	28	-1	1	0	0	.000	-1	/O-1	-0.1
1976	Pit-N	48	122	24	33	4	1	2	12	16	24	.270	.360	.369	106	1	15	5	2	.960	-1	O-42	0.1
1977	Pit-N	150	492	69	118	19	9	7	34	38	102	.240	.296	.358	72	-20	53	16	6	.977	8	*O-147	-1.0
1978	Pit-N	155	515	95	121	15	7	2	33	81	104	.235	.342	.303	78	-12	**71**	22	8	.984	17	*O-152	0.6
1979	*Pit-N	162	695	110	196	21	12	8	69	51	104	.282	.334	.381	90	-9	**77**	21	11	.975	23	*O-162	1.8
1980	Pit-N	162	676	87	168	20	**13**	2	36	57	101	.249	.309	.325	76	-21	96	33	9	.990	27	*O-162	0.9
1981	Pit-N	103	434	62	120	18	8	1	35	26	76	.276	.322	.362	91	-5	39	14	3	.997	10	*O-103	0.4
1982	Pit-N	158	645	82	158	18	9	3	44	44	121	.245	.294	.315	68	-27	60	26	2	.983	13	*O-157	-1.7
1983	Hou-N	97	405	48	98	12	11	0	25	22	72	.242	.283	.326	73	-16	30	13	1	.977	9	O-97	-1.0
	NY-A	48	152	17	38	9	1	1	17	8	31	.250	.287	.342	75	-5	7	3	0	.992	-0	O-48	-0.6
1984	NY-A	117	355	37	92	12	6	4	38	18	48	.259	.297	.361	84	-8	20	11	-1	.985	3	*O-108/D-1	-0.9
1985	NY-A	34	66	12	13	4	1	1	4	1	16	.197	.209	.333	47	-5	1	1	-0	1.000	0	O-26/D-1	-0.6
	KC-A	24	70	9	17	1	3	2	12	3	8	.243	.284	.429	91	-1	0	1	-1	1.000	-3	O-21	-0.6
	Yr	58	136	21	30	5	4	3	16	4	24	.221	.248	.382	70	-6	1	2	-1	1.000	-3	O-47/D-1	-1.2
1986	Atl-N	118	359	46	84	18	6	4	27	21	77	.234	.276	.351	68	-16	17	16	-5	.970	-3	O-97	-2.7
Total	12	1382	4992	699	1257	171	87	37	386	387	885	.252	.308	.343	79	-146	487	182	37	.982	103	*O-1323/D-2	-5.4

■ CHET MORGAN
Morgan, Chester Collins "Chick" b: 6/6/10, Cleveland, Miss. d: 9/20/91, Pasadena, Tex. BL/TR, 5'9", 160 lbs. Deb: 4/19/35

YEAR	TM/L	G	AB	R	H	2B	3B	HR	RBI	BB	SO	AVG	OBP	SLG	PRO+	BR/A	SB	CS	SBR	FA	FR	G/POS	TPR
1935	Det-A	14	23	2	4	1	0	0	1	5	0	.174	.321	.217	43	-2	0	0	0	.909	-0	/O-4	-0.2
1938	Det-A	74	306	50	87	6	1	0	27	20	12	.284	.330	.310	58	-19	5	6	-2	.980	0	O-74	-2.2
Total	2	88	329	52	91	7	1	0	28	25	12	.277	.330	.304	57	-21	5	6	-2	.977	0	/O-78	-2.4

■ ED MORGAN
Morgan, Edward Carre b: 5/22/04, Cairo, Ill. d: 4/9/80, New Orleans, La. BR/TR, 6'0.5", 180 lbs. Deb: 4/11/28

YEAR	TM/L	G	AB	R	H	2B	3B	HR	RBI	BB	SO	AVG	OBP	SLG	PRO+	BR/A	SB	CS	SBR	FA	FR	G/POS	TPR
1928	Cle-A	76	265	42	83	24	6	4	54	21	17	.313	.366	.494	123	8	5	5	-2	.968	1	1-36,O-21,3-14	0.4
1929	Cle-A	93	318	60	101	19	10	3	37	37	24	.318	.392	.469	116	8	4	3	-1	.908	-11	O-80	-0.8
1930	Cle-A	150	584	122	204	47	11	26	136	62	66	.349	.413	.601	148	41	8	4	0	.987	-3	*1-129,O-19	2.2
1931	Cle-A	131	462	87	162	33	4	11	86	83	46	.351	.451	.511	144	33	4	5	-2	.984	2	*1-117/3-3	2.1
1932	Cle-A	144	532	96	156	32	7	4	68	94	44	.293	.402	.402	102	5	7	6	-2	.985	-8	*1-142/3-1	-1.5
1933	Cle-A	39	121	10	32	3	3	1	13	7	9	.264	.305	.364	73	-5	1	1	-0	.997	2	1-32/O-1	-0.6
1934	Bos-A	138	528	95	141	28	4	3	79	81	46	.267	.367	.352	80	-14	7	1	2	.988	-7	*1-137	-3.0
Total	7	771	2810	512	879	186	45	52	473	385	252	.313	.398	.467	117	76	36	25	-4	.986	-23	1-593,O-121/3-18	-1.2

■ EDDIE MORGAN
Morgan, Edwin Willis "Pepper" b: 11/19/14, Brady Lake, Ohio d: 6/27/82, Lakewood, Ohio BL/TL, 5'10", 160 lbs. Deb: 4/14/36

YEAR	TM/L	G	AB	R	H	2B	3B	HR	RBI	BB	SO	AVG	OBP	SLG	PRO+	BR/A	SB	CS	SBR	FA	FR	G/POS	TPR
1936	StL-N	8	18	4	5	0	0	1	3	2	4	.278	.350	.444	113	0	0			.889	-0	/O-4	0.0
1937	Bro-N	31	48	4	9	3	0	0	5	9	7	.188	.316	.250	55	-3	0			.984	-3	/1-7,O-7	-0.6
Total	2	39	66	8	14	3	0	1	8	11	11	.212	.325	.303	70	-2	0			.842	-3	/O-11,1-7	-0.6

■ BILL MORGAN
Morgan, Henry William b: 10/1857, Washington, D.C. Deb: 5/4/1875

YEAR	TM/L	G	AB	R	H	2B	3B	HR	RBI	BB	SO	AVG	OBP	SLG	PRO+	BR/A	SB	CS	SBR	FA	FR	G/POS	TPR
1875	RS-n	19	69	11	18	4	0	0	1	5	4	.261	.311	.319	132	3	2	1	0	.824	-5	O-10/P-7,3-7	-0.2
1878	Mil-N	14	56	2	11	0	0	0	5	3	9	.196	.237	.196	41	-4				.769	-6	O-13/3-3,2-1	-0.9
1882	Pit-a	17	66	10	17	2	1	0		4		.258	.300	.318	114	1				.688	-8	O-11/C-7	-0.6
1884	Ric-a	6	20	0	2	0	0	0		1		.100	.143	.100	-20	-3				.850	-2	/C-3,O-2,2-1	-0.4
	Bal-U	2	9	1	2	0	0	0		1		.222	.300	.222	55	-1				.909	0	/C-1,2-1,O-1	-0.1
Total	3	39	151	13	32	2	1	0	5	9	9	.212	.256	.238	64	-6				.743	-16	/O-27,C-11,2-3,3-3	-2.0

■ RED MORGAN
Morgan, James Edward b: 10/6/1883, Neola, Iowa d: 3/25/81, New York, N.Y. TR , Deb: 6/20/06

YEAR	TM/L	G	AB	R	H	2B	3B	HR	RBI	BB	SO	AVG	OBP	SLG	PRO+	BR/A	SB	CS	SBR	FA	FR	G/POS	TPR
1906	Bos-A	88	307	20	66	6	3	1	21	16		.215	.270	.264	67	-11	7			.866	-13	3-88	-2.4

■ JOE MORGAN
Morgan, Joe Leonard b: 9/19/43, Bonham, Tex. BL/TR, 5'7", 160 lbs. Deb: 9/21/63 H

YEAR	TM/L	G	AB	R	H	2B	3B	HR	RBI	BB	SO	AVG	OBP	SLG	PRO+	BR/A	SB	CS	SBR	FA	FR	G/POS	TPR
1963	Hou-N	8	25	5	6	0	1	0	3	5	5	.240	.367	.320	106	0	1	0	0	.909	-3	/2-7	-0.1
1964	Hou-N	10	37	4	7	0	0	0	0	6	7	.189	.302	.189	44	-3	0	1	-1	.949	-0	2-10	-0.3
1965	Hou-N	157	601	100	163	22	12	14	40	**97**	77	.271	.375	.418	132	28	20	9	1	.969	-2	*2-157	4.3
1966	Hou-N†	122	425	60	121	14	8	5	42	89	43	.285	.412	.391	134	25	11	8	-2	.965	-16	*2-117	1.6
1967	Hou-N	133	494	73	136	27	11	6	42	81	51	.275	.380	.411	131	22	29	5	**6**	.979	-5	*2-130/O-1	3.4
1968	Hou-N	10	20	6	5	0	1	0	0	7	4	.250	.444	.350	144	2	3	0	1	.882	-4	/2-5,O-1	-0.1
1969	Hou-N	147	535	94	126	18	5	15	43	110	74	.236	.367	.372	110	11	49	14	6	.972	-4	*2-132,O-14	2.5
1970	Hou-N★	144	548	102	147	28	9	8	52	102	55	.268	.384	.396	114	15	42	13	5	.979	11	*2-142	4.1
1971	Hou-N	160	583	87	149	27	**11**	13	56	88	52	.256	.354	.407	118	15	40	8	7	.986	-3	*2-157	3.5
1972	*Cin-N★	149	552	**122**	161	23	4	16	73	**115**	44	.292	**.419**	.435	152	44	58	17	7	**.990**	-7	*2-149	5.5
1973	*Cin-N★	157	576	116	167	35	2	26	82	111	61	.290	.408	.493	157	48	67	15	**11**	.990	-8	*2-154	6.1
1974	Cin-N★	149	512	107	150	31	3	22	67	120	69	.293	**.430**	.494	160	47	58	12	10	.982	-13	*2-142	5.2
1975	*Cin-N★	146	498	107	163	27	6	17	94	**132**	52	.327	**.471**	.508	**169**	**55**	67	10	14	**.986**	-7	*2-142	**7.1**
1976	*Cin-N★	141	472	113	151	30	5	27	111	114	41	.320	**.453**	**.576**	**186**	**58**	60	9	13	.981	-23	*2-133	5.8
1977	Cin-N★	153	521	113	150	21	6	22	78	117	58	.288	.420	.478	138	33	49	10	9	**.993**	-18	*2-151	3.5
1978	Cin-N★	132	441	68	104	27	0	13	75	79	40	.236	.354	.385	107	6	19	5	3	.980	-31	*2-124	-1.4
1979	*Cin-N★	127	436	70	109	26	1	9	32	93	45	.250	.383	.376	107	8	28	6	5	.980	-13	*2-121	0.8
1980	*Hou-N★	141	461	66	112	17	5	11	49	**93**	47	.243	.370	.373	117	14	24	6	4	.988	-12	*2-130	1.4
1981	SF-N	90	308	47	74	16	1	8	31	66	37	.240	.374	.377	116	9	14	5	1	.991	-11	2-87	0.5
1982	SF-N	134	463	68	134	19	4	14	61	85	60	.289	.402	.438	135	25	24	4	5	.989	-6	*2-120/3-3	3.1
1983	*Phi-N	123	404	72	93	20	1	16	59	89	54	.230	.374	.403	117	12	18	2	4	.971	-2	*2-117	2.1
1984	Oak-A	116	365	50	89	21	0	6	43	66	39	.244	.361	.351	105	5	8	3	1	.977	-31	*2-100/D-5	-2.3
Total	22	2649	9277	1650	2517	449	96	268	1133	1865	1015	.271	.395	.427	133	478	689	162	110	.981	-206	*2-2527/O-16,D-5,3	56.3

■ JOE MORGAN
Morgan, Joseph Michael b: 11/19/30, Walpole, Mass. BL/TR, 5'10", 170 lbs. Deb: 4/14/59 MC

YEAR	TM/L	G	AB	R	H	2B	3B	HR	RBI	BB	SO	AVG	OBP	SLG	PRO+	BR/A	SB	CS	SBR	FA	FR	G/POS	TPR
1959	Mil-N	13	23	2	5	1	0	0	1	2	4	.217	.280	.261	49	-2	0	0	0	.913	-2	/2-7	-0.4

YEAR	TM/L	G	AB	R	H	2B	3B	HR	RBI	BB	SO	AVG	OBP	SLG	PRO+	BR/A	SB	CS	SBR	FA	FR	G/POS	TPR
	KC-A	20	21	2	4	0	1	0	3	3	7	.190	.292	.286	58	-1	0	0	0	1.000	-1	/3-2	-0.2
1960	Phi-N	26	83	5	11	2	2	0	2	6	11	.133	.191	.205	8	-11	0	0	0	.971	1	3-24	-1.0
	Cle-A	22	47	6	14	2	0	2	4	6	4	.298	.377	.468	131	2	0	0	0	.889	-2	3-12/O-2	0.0
1961	Cle-A	4	10	0	2	0	0	0	0	1	3	.200	.273	.200	29	-1	0	0	0	1.000	0	/O-2	-0.1
1964	StL-N	3	3	0	0	0	0	0	0	0	2	.000	.000	.000	-92	-1	0	0	0	.000	0	H	-0.1
Total	4	88	187	15	36	5	3	2	10	18	31	.193	.263	.283	49	-13	0	0	0	.944	-3	/3-38,2-7,O-4	-1.8

■ KEVIN MORGAN Morgan, Kevin Lee b: 3/3/70, Lafayette, La. BR/TR, 6′1″, 170 lbs. Deb: 6/15/97

YEAR	TM/L	G	AB	R	H	2B	3B	HR	RBI	BB	SO	AVG	OBP	SLG	PRO+	BR/A	SB	CS	SBR	FA	FR	G/POS	TPR
1997	NY-N	1	1	0	0	0	0	0	0	0	0	.000	.000	.000	-99	-0	0	0	0	1.000	0	/3-1	0.0

■ RAY MORGAN Morgan, Raymond Caryll b: 6/14/1889, Baltimore, Md. d: 2/15/40, Baltimore, Md. BR/TR, 5′8.5″, 155 lbs. Deb: 8/7/11

YEAR	TM/L	G	AB	R	H	2B	3B	HR	RBI	BB	SO	AVG	OBP	SLG	PRO+	BR/A	SB	CS	SBR	FA	FR	G/POS	TPR
1911	Was-A	25	89	11	19	2	0	0	5	4		.213	.247	.236	36	-8	2			.900	-3	3-25	-1.1
1912	Was-A	81	273	40	65	10	7	1	30	29		.238	.318	.337	87	-5	11			.939	-7	2-76/S-4,3-1	-1.3
1913	Was-A	138	481	58	131	19	8	0	57	68	63	.272	.369	.345	107	7	19			.950	-6	*2-134/S-4	-0.1
1914	Was-A	147	491	50	126	22	8	1	49	62	34	.257	.352	.340	104	4	24	17	-3	.948	-9	*2-146	-1.1
1915	Was-A	62	193	21	45	5	4	0	21	30	15	.233	.342	.301	91	-1	6	5	-1	.965	-4	2-57/S-2,3-2	-0.6
1916	Was-A	99	315	41	84	12	4	1	29	59	29	.267	.398	.340	123	13	14			.957	-17	2-82/S-9,1-3,3-1	-0.1
1917	Was-A	101	338	32	90	9	1	1	33	40	29	.266	.346	.308	101	1	7			.961	-8	2-95/3-3	-0.2
1918	Was-A	88	300	25	70	11	1	0	30	28	14	.233	.311	.277	79	-7	4			.959	-5	2-80/O-2	-0.8
Total	8	741	2480	278	630	90	33	4	254	320	184	.254	.348	.322	98	4	87	22		.953	-58	2-670/3-32,S-19,1O	-5.3

■ BOBBY MORGAN Morgan, Robert Morris b: 6/29/26, Oklahoma City, Okla. BR/TR, 5′9″, 175 lbs. Deb: 4/18/50

YEAR	TM/L	G	AB	R	H	2B	3B	HR	RBI	BB	SO	AVG	OBP	SLG	PRO+	BR/A	SB	CS	SBR	FA	FR	G/POS	TPR
1950	Bro-N	67	199	38	45	10	3	7	21	32	43	.226	.342	.412	95	-1	0			.969	6	3-52,S-10	0.5
1952	*Bro-N	67	191	36	45	8	0	7	16	46	35	.236	.392	.387	115	6	2	2	-1	.968	3	3-60/2-5,S-4	0.8
1953	*Bro-N	69	196	35	51	6	2	7	33	33	47	.260	.370	.418	103	1	2	2	-1	.920	-2	3-36,S-21	0.0
1954	Phi-N	135	455	58	119	25	2	14	50	70	68	.262	.360	.418	102	2	3	1	0	.954	-22	*S-129/3-8,2-5	-0.9
1955	Phi-N	136	483	61	112	20	2	10	49	73	72	.232	.333	.344	81	-12	6	4	-1	.980	-13	2-88,S-41/3-6,1-1	-1.6
1956	Phi-N	8	25	1	5	0	0	0	1	6	4	.200	.355	.200	56	-1	0	0	0	.857	1	/3-5,2-3	0.0
	StL-N	61	113	14	22	7	0	3	20	15	24	.195	.289	.336	67	-5	0	2	-1	.980	1	2-13,3-11/S-6	-0.5
	Yr	69	138	15	27	7	0	3	21	21	28	.196	.302	.312	65	-7	0	2	-1	.877	1	3-16,2-16/S-6	-0.5
1957	Phi-N	2	0	0	0	0	0	0	0	0	0	—	—	—	—	0	0	0	0	1.000	0	/2-1	0.0
	Chi-N	125	425	43	88	20	2	5	27	52	87	.207	.295	.299	61	-23	5	0	2	.976	8	*2-116,3-12	-0.5
	Yr	127	425	43	88	20	2	5	27	52	87	.207	.295	.299	61	-23	5	0	2	.976	8	*2-117,3-12	-0.5
1958	Chi-N	1	1	0	0	0	0	0	0	0	1	.000	.000	.000	-99	-0	0	0	0	.000	0	H	0.0
Total	8	671	2088	286	487	96	11	53	217	327	381	.233	.339	.366	88	-33	18	11		.978	-18	2-231,S-211,3/1	-2.2

■ VERN MORGAN Morgan, Vernon Thomas b: 8/8/28, Emporia, Va. d: 11/8/75, Minneapolis, Minn. BL/TR, 6′1″, 190 lbs. Deb: 8/10/54 C

YEAR	TM/L	G	AB	R	H	2B	3B	HR	RBI	BB	SO	AVG	OBP	SLG	PRO+	BR/A	SB	CS	SBR	FA	FR	G/POS	TPR
1954	Chi-N	24	64	3	15	2	0	0	2	1	10	.234	.246	.266	33	-6	0	0	0	.895	-4	3-15	-1.1
1955	Chi-N	7	7	1	1	0	0	0	1	3	4	.143	.400	.143	52	-0	0	0	0	.667	-1	/3-2	-0.1
Total	2	31	71	4	16	2	0	0	3	4	14	.225	.267	.254	36	-7	0	0	0	.864	-5	/3-17	-1.2

■ BILL MORGAN Morgan, William Deb: 8/6/1883

YEAR	TM/L	G	AB	R	H	2B	3B	HR	RBI	BB	SO	AVG	OBP	SLG	PRO+	BR/A	SB	CS	SBR	FA	FR	G/POS	TPR
1883	Pit-a	32	114	12	18	2	1	0		7		.158	.207	.193	31	-8				.825	-2	S-21/O-6,C-5,2-2	-0.8
1884	Was-a	45	162	8	28	1	1	0		8		.173	.216	.191	39	-10				.781	-5	O-31,C-12/2-2,S-2	-1.3
Total	2	77	276	20	46	3	2	0		15		.167	.212	.192	35	-18				.771	-6	/O-37,S-23,C-17,2-4	-2.1

■ MOE MORHARDT Morhardt, Meredith Goodwin b: 1/16/37, Manchester, Conn. BL/TL, 6′1″, 185 lbs. Deb: 9/7/61

YEAR	TM/L	G	AB	R	H	2B	3B	HR	RBI	BB	SO	AVG	OBP	SLG	PRO+	BR/A	SB	CS	SBR	FA	FR	G/POS	TPR
1961	Chi-N	7	18	3	5	0	0	0	1	3	5	.278	.381	.278	78	-0	0	0	0	.962	-1	/1-7	-0.2
1962	Chi-N	18	16	1	2	0	0	0	2	2	8	.125	.222	.125	-4	-2	0	0	0	.000	0	H	-0.2
Total	2	25	34	4	7	0	0	0	3	5	13	.206	.308	.206	39	-3	0	0	0	.962	-1	/1-7	-0.4

■ GENE MORIARITY Moriarity, Eugene John b: 1/5/1865, Holyoke, Mass. BL/TL, 5′8″, 130 lbs. Deb: 6/18/1884

YEAR	TM/L	G	AB	R	H	2B	3B	HR	RBI	BB	SO	AVG	OBP	SLG	PRO+	BR/A	SB	CS	SBR	FA	FR	G/POS	TPR
1884	Bos-N	4	16	1	1	0	0	0	0	0	8	.063	.063	.063	-61	-3				.714	-1	/O-4	-0.3
	Ind-a	10	37	4	8	0	2	0	4	0		.216	.216	.324	76	-1				.769	-1	/O-7,P-2,3-1	-0.2
1885	Det-N	11	39	1	1	1	0	0	0	0	10	.026	.026	.051	-75	-7				.905	2	/O-6,3-4,S-1,P-1	-0.5
1892	StL-N	47	177	20	31	4	1	3	19	4	37	.175	.207	.260	43	-13	7			.820	2	O-47	-1.2
Total	3	72	269	26	41	5	3	3	23	4	55	.152	.174	.227	24	-24	7			.822	2	/O-64,3-5,P-3,S-1	-2.2

■ ED MORIARTY Moriarty, Edward Jerome b: 10/12/12, Holyoke, Mass. d: 9/29/91, Holyoke, Mass. BR/TR, 5′10.5″, 180 lbs. Deb: 6/21/35

YEAR	TM/L	G	AB	R	H	2B	3B	HR	RBI	BB	SO	AVG	OBP	SLG	PRO+	BR/A	SB	CS	SBR	FA	FR	G/POS	TPR
1935	Bos-N	8	34	4	11	2	1	1	1	0	6	.324	.324	.529	136	1	0			.923	-4	/2-8	-0.2
1936	Bos-N	6	6	1	1	0	0	0	0	0	1	.167	.167	.167	-11	-1	0			.000	0	H	-0.1
Total	2	14	40	5	12	2	1	1	1	0	7	.300	.300	.475	114	0	0			.923	-4	/2-8	-0.3

■ GEORGE MORIARTY Moriarty, George Joseph b: 6/7/1884, Chicago, Ill. d: 4/8/64, Miami, Fla. BR/TR, 6′, 185 lbs. Deb: 9/27/03 FMU

YEAR	TM/L	G	AB	R	H	2B	3B	HR	RBI	BB	SO	AVG	OBP	SLG	PRO+	BR/A	SB	CS	SBR	FA	FR	G/POS	TPR
1903	Chi-N	1	5	1	0	0	0	0	0	0		.000	.000	.000	-99	-1	0			1.000	-0	/3-1	-0.2
1904	Chi-N	4	13	0	0	0	0	0	0	1		.000	.071	.000	-77	-3	0			.778	-0	/3-2,O-2	-0.3
1906	NY-A	65	197	22	46	7	7	0	23	17		.234	.298	.340	90	-3	8			.912	1	3-39,O-15/1-5,2-1	-0.1
1907	NY-A	126	437	51	121	16	5	0	43	25		.277	.320	.336	101	0	28			.899	-10	3-91,1-22/O-9,2S	-0.9
1908	NY-A	101	348	25	82	12	1	0	27	11		.236	.269	.276	76	-9	22			.976	8	1-52,3-28,O-10,/2-4	-0.2
1909	*Det-A	133	473	43	129	20	4	1	39	24		.273	.309	.338	100	-1	34			**.939**	2	*3-106,1-24	0.5
1910	Det-A	136	490	53	123	24	3	2	60	33		.251	.308	.324	92	-5	33			.927	-1	*3-134	-0.3
1911	Det-A	130	478	51	116	20	4	1	60	27		.243	.287	.308	63	-25	28			.929	-4	*3-129/1-1	-2.7
1912	Det-A	105	375	38	93	23	1	0	54	26		.248	.316	.315	83	-8	27			.987	-8	1-71,3-33	-1.7
1913	Det-A	105	347	29	83	5	2	0	30	24	25	.239	.302	.265	67	-14	33			.938	-3	3-94/O-7	-1.7
1914	Det-A	132	465	56	118	19	5	1	40	39	27	.254	.318	.323	90	-6	34	15	1	.956	17	*3-126/1-3	1.8
1915	Det-A	31	38	2	8	1	0	0	0	5	7	.211	.318	.237	63	-2	1	1	-0	.875	-0	3-12/1-1,2-1,O-1	-0.2
1916	Chi-A	7	5	1	1	0	0	0	0	2	0	.200	.429	.200	88	0	0			1.000	1	/1-1,3-1	0.1
Total	13	1076	3671	372	920	147	32	5	376	234	59	.251	.303	.312	84	-77	248	16		.931	3	3-796,1-180/O2S	-5.9

■ BILL MORIARTY Moriarty, William Joseph b: 8/1883, Chicago, Ill. d: 12/25/16, Elgin, Ill. BR/TR, 6′2″, 180 lbs. Deb: 4/29/09 F

YEAR	TM/L	G	AB	R	H	2B	3B	HR	RBI	BB	SO	AVG	OBP	SLG	PRO+	BR/A	SB	CS	SBR	FA	FR	G/POS	TPR
1909	Cin-N	6	20	1	4	1	0	0	1	0		.200	.200	.250	40	-1	2			.944	0	/S-6	-0.1

■ BILL MORLEY Morley, William M. (b: William Morley Jennings) b: 1/23/1890, Holland, Mich. d: 5/14/85, Lubbock, Tex. BR/TR, 5′11″, 170 lbs. Deb: 9/8/13

YEAR	TM/L	G	AB	R	H	2B	3B	HR	RBI	BB	SO	AVG	OBP	SLG	PRO+	BR/A	SB	CS	SBR	FA	FR	G/POS	TPR
1913	Was-A	2	3	0	0	0	0	0	0	0	0	.000	.000	.000	-98	-1	0			.000	0	/2-1	-0.1

■ RUSS MORMAN Morman, Russell Lee b: 4/28/62, Independence, Mo. BR/TR, 6′4″, 220 lbs. Deb: 8/3/86

YEAR	TM/L	G	AB	R	H	2B	3B	HR	RBI	BB	SO	AVG	OBP	SLG	PRO+	BR/A	SB	CS	SBR	FA	FR	G/POS	TPR
1986	Chi-A	49	159	18	40	5	0	4	17	16	36	.252	.328	.358	84	-3	1	0	0	.989	-3	1-47	-0.9
1988	Chi-A	40	75	8	18	2	0	0	3	3	17	.240	.269	.267	51	-5	0	0	0	.981	-3	1-22,O-10/D-3	-0.9
1989	Chi-A	37	58	5	13	2	0	0	8	6	16	.224	.297	.259	59	-3	1	0	0	.988	1	1-35/D-1	-0.3
1990	KC-A	12	37	5	10	4	2	1	3	3	3	.270	.325	.568	147	2	0	0	0	1.000	-0	/O-8,1-3,D-1	0.1
1991	KC-A	12	23	1	6	0	0	0	1	1	5	.261	.292	.261	54	-1	0	0	0	1.000	0	/1-8,O-2,D-1	-0.2
1994	Fla-N	13	33	2	7	0	1	1	2	2	9	.212	.278	.364	64	-2	0	0	0	.987	2	/1-8	-0.1
1995	Fla-N	34	72	9	20	2	1	3	7	3	12	.278	.316	.458	101	-0	0	0	0	.955	-2	O-18/1-3	-0.3
1996	Fla-N	6	6	0	1	1	0	0	0	1	2	.167	.286	.333	65	-0	0	0	0	1.000	-0	/1-2	-0.1
1997	Fla-N	4	7	3	2	1	0	1	2	0	2	.286	.286	.857	194	1	1	0	0	1.000	0	/O-2,1-1	0.1
Total	9	207	470	51	117	17	4	10	43	35	102	.249	.306	.366	82	-12	3	0	1	.989	-7	1-129/O-40,D-6	-2.6

■ JEFF MORONKO Moronko, Jeffrey Robert b: 8/17/59, Houston, Tex. BR/TR, 6′2″, 190 lbs. Deb: 9/1/84

YEAR	TM/L	G	AB	R	H	2B	3B	HR	RBI	BB	SO	AVG	OBP	SLG	PRO+	BR/A	SB	CS	SBR	FA	FR	G/POS	TPR
1984	Cle-A	7	19	1	3	1	0	0	3	3	5	.158	.273	.211	35	-2	0	0	0	.895	-0	/3-6,D-1	-0.2
1987	NY-A	7	11	0	1	0	0	0	0	0	2	.091	.167	.091	-29	-2	0	0	0	1.000	-0	/3-3,S-2,O-2	-0.2
Total	2	14	30	1	4	1	0	0	3	3	7	.133	.235	.167	12	-4	0	0	0	.926	-0	/3-9,O-2,S-2,D-1	-0.4

YEAR	TM/L	G	AB	R	H	2B	3B	HR	RBI	BB	SO	AVG	OBP	SLG	PRO+	BR/A	SB	CS	SBR	FA	FR	G/POS	TPR
■ JOHN MORRILL	Morrill, John Francis "Honest John" b: 2/19/1855, Boston, Mass. d: 4/2/32, Brookline, Mass. BR/TR, 5'10.5", 155 lbs. Deb: 4/24/1876 M																						
1876	Bos-N	66	278	38	73	5	2	0	26	3	5	.263	.270	.295	87	-4				.857	7	2-37,C-23/O-5,1-3	0.3
1877	Bos-N	61	242	47	73	5	1	0	28	6	15	.302	.319	.331	101	0				.864	-9	3-30,1-18,O-11,/2-3	-0.8
1878	Bos-N	60	233	26	56	5	1	0	23	5	16	.240	.256	.270	68	-9				.957	2	*1-59/O-1,3-1	-0.8
1879	Bos-N	84	348	56	98	18	5	0	49	14	32	.282	.309	.362	118	6				.878	3	3-51,1-33	0.8
1880	Bos-N	86	342	51	81	16	8	2	44	11	37	.237	.261	.348	108	3				.966	0	1-46,3-40/P-3	0.0
1881	Bos-N	81	311	47	90	19	3	1	39	12	30	.289	.316	.379	123	8				.969	9	*1-74/2-4,P-3,3-2	1.0
1882	Bos-N	83	349	73	101	19	11	2	54	18	29	.289	.324	.424	137	14				.964	-3	*1-76/S-3,2-2,03PM	0.3
1883	Bos-N	97	404	83	129	33	16	6	68	15	68	.319	.344	.525	155	25				**.974**	-1	*1-81/O-7,3-6,S2PM	1.4
1884	Bos-N	111	438	80	114	19	7	3	61	30	87	.260	.308	.356	109	5				.971	3	*1-91,2-17/P-7,3OM	-0.2
1885	Bos-N	111	394	74	89	20	7	4	44	64	78	.226	.334	.343	124	14				.969	2	*1-92,2-17/3-2,M	0.5
1886	Bos-N	117	430	86	106	25	6	7	69	56	81	.247	.333	.381	121	13	9			.895	-3	S-55,1-42,2-20,/PM	0.6
1887	Bos-N	127	504	79	141	32	6	12	81	37	86	.280	.330	.438	112	7	19			.984	4	*1-127,M	-0.2
1888	Bos-N	135	486	60	96	18	7	4	39	55	68	.198	.282	.288	81	-9	21			.979	9	*1-133/2-2,M	-1.3
1889	Was-N	44	146	20	27	5	0	2	16	30	23	.185	.328	.260	70	-5	12			.980	-1	1-40/3-3,2-1,P-1,M	-0.7
1890	Bos-P	2	7	1	1	0	0	0	2	2	1	.143	.333	.143	28	-1	0			.750	-1	/S-1,1-1	-0.1
Total	15	1265	4912	821	1275	239	80	43	643	358	656	.260	.310	.367	111	68	61			.971	22	1-916,3-138,2/SOCP	0.8
■ DOYT MORRIS	Morris, Doyt Theodore b: 7/15/16, Stanley, N.C. d: 7/4/84, Gastonia, N.C. BR/TR, 6'4", 195 lbs. Deb: 6/6/37																						
1937	Phi-A	6	13	0	2	0	0	0	0	0	3	.154	.154	.154	-23	-2	0	0	0	1.000	-0	/O-3	-0.2
■ E. MORRIS	Morris, E. b: Trenton, N.J. Deb: 9/11/1884																						
1884	Bal-U	1	3	0	0	0	0	0		0		.000	.000	.000	-91	-1				.500	-1	/O-1,P-1	-0.1
■ JOHN MORRIS	Morris, John Daniel b: 2/23/61, N.Bellmore, N.Y. BL/TL, 6'1", 185 lbs. Deb: 8/5/86																						
1986	StL-N	39	100	8	24	0	1	1	14	7	15	.240	.290	.290	61	-5	6	2	1	.986	-1	O-31	-0.7
1987	*StL-N	101	157	22	41	6	4	3	23	11	22	.261	.314	.408	88	-3	5	2	0	.989	-15	O-74	-1.8
1988	StL-N	20	38	3	11	2	1	0	3	1	7	.289	.308	.395	99	-0	0	0	0	.857	-5	O-16	-0.6
1989	StL-N	96	117	8	28	4	1	2	14	4	22	.239	.264	.342	70	-5	1	0	0	1.000	-13	O-51	-1.9
1990	StL-N	18	18	0	2	0	0	0	0	3	6	.111	.238	.111	-1	-2	0	0	0	1.000	-2	/O-6	-0.4
1991	Phi-N	85	127	15	28	2	1	1	6	12	25	.220	.293	.276	61	-6	2	0	1	.974	-10	O-57	-1.8
1992	Cal-A	43	57	4	11	1	0	1	3	4	11	.193	.258	.263	46	-4	1	0	0	1.000	-3	O-14/D-6	-0.7
Total	7	402	614	60	145	15	8	8	63	42	108	.236	.288	.326	69	-26	15	4	2	.981	-49	O-249/D-6	-7.9
■ WALTER MORRIS	Morris, John Walter b: 1/31/1880, Rockwall, Tex. d: 8/2/61, Dallas, Tex. BR/TR, 5'11", Deb: 8/31/08																						
1908	StL-N	23	73	1	13	1	1	0	2	0		.178	.178	.219	28	-6	1			.938	4	S-23	-0.2
■ P. MORRIS	Morris, P. b: Rockford, Ill. Deb: 5/14/1884																						
1884	Was-U	1	3	0	0	0	0	0		0		.000	.000	.000	-99	-1				.750	0	/S-1	-0.1
■ HAL MORRIS	Morris, William Harold b: 4/9/65, Fort Rucker, Ala. BL/TL, 6'4", 215 lbs. Deb: 7/29/88																						
1988	NY-A	15	20	1	2	0	0	0	0	0	9	.100	.100	.100	-44	-4	0	0	0	1.000	-1	/O-4,D-1	-0.5
1989	NY-A	15	18	2	5	0	0	0	4	1	4	.278	.316	.278	69	-1	0	0	0	1.000	-2	/O-5,1-2,D-1	-0.2
1990	*Cin-N	107	309	50	105	22	3	7	36	21	32	.340	.384	.498	135	14	9	3	1	.995	-0	1-80/O-6	0.9
1991	Cin-N	136	478	72	152	33	1	14	59	46	61	.318	.379	.479	135	22	10	4	1	.992	4	*1-128/O-1	1.9
1992	Cin-N	115	395	41	107	21	3	6	53	45	53	.271	.348	.385	105	3	6	6	-2	**.999**	5	*1-109	-0.1
1993	Cin-N	101	379	48	120	18	0	7	49	34	51	.317	.376	.420	112	7	2	2	-1	.994	3	1-98	0.2
1994	Cin-N	112	436	60	146	30	4	10	78	34	62	.335	.389	.491	129	19	6	2	1	**.994**	1	*1-112	1.0
1995	*Cin-N	101	359	53	100	25	2	11	51	29	58	.279	.334	.451	105	2	1	1	-0	.994	5	1-99	-0.2
1996	Cin-N	142	528	82	165	32	4	16	80	50	76	.313	.377	.479	123	18	7	5	-1	.993	-2	*1-140	0.2
1997	Cin-N	96	333	42	92	20	1	1	33	23	43	.276	.329	.351	77	-11	3	1	0	.990	-4	1-89	-2.3
1998	KC-A	127	472	50	146	27	2	1	40	32	52	.309	.354	.381	88	-8	1	0	0	.990	-5	1-46,O-39,D-39	-1.9
Total	11	1067	3727	501	1140	228	20	73	483	315	501	.306	.363	.437	112	63	45	24	-1	.994	5	1-903/O-55,D-41	-1.0
■ JIM MORRISON	Morrison, James Forrest b: 9/23/52, Pensacola, Fla. BR/TR, 5'11", 182 lbs. Deb: 9/18/77																						
1977	Phi-N	5	7	3	3	0	0	0	1	1	1	.429	.500	.429	145	1	0	0	0	.875	1	/3-5	0.1
1978	*Phi-N	53	108	12	17	1	1	3	10	10	21	.157	.235	.269	40	-9	1	1	-0	.968	13	2-31/3-3,O-1	0.6
1979	Chi-A	67	240	38	66	14	0	14	35	15	48	.275	.328	.508	122	6	11	3	2	.982	1	2-48,3-29	1.1
1980	Chi-A	162	604	66	171	40	0	15	57	36	74	.283	.332	.424	106	4	9	6	-1	.969	-3	*2-161/S-1,D-1	1.1
1981	Chi-A	90	290	27	68	8	1	10	34	10	29	.234	.265	.372	84	-7	3	2	-0	.956	8	3-87/2-1,D-1	-0.2
1982	Chi-A	51	166	17	37	7	3	7	19	13	15	.223	.279	.428	91	-3	0	1	-1	.914	-14	3-50/D-1	-1.9
	Pit-N	44	86	10	24	4	1	4	15	5	14	.279	.319	.488	119	2	2	0	1	.964	2	3-26/O-2,2-1,S-1	0.4
1983	Pit-N	66	158	16	48	7	2	6	25	9	25	.304	.349	.487	126	5	2	6	-3	.973	3	2-28,3-26/S-7	0.6
1984	Pit-N	100	304	38	87	14	2	11	45	20	52	.286	.332	.454	119	7	0	1	-1	.938	0	3-61,2-26/S-2,1-1	0.7
1985	Pit-N	92	244	17	62	10	0	4	22	8	44	.254	.281	.344	75	-9	3	0	1	.961	1	3-59,2-15/O-1	-0.8
1986	Pit-N	154	537	58	147	35	4	23	88	47	88	.274	.337	.482	120	13	9	8	-2	.946	-13	*3-151/2-1,S-1	-0.5
1987	Pit-N	96	348	41	92	22	1	9	46	27	57	.264	.319	.411	91	-5	8	5	-1	.975	1	3-82,S-17/2-9	-0.4
	*Det-A	34	117	15	24	1	1	4	19	2	26	.205	.225	.333	47	-9	2	1	0	.962	3	3-16/2-3,S-3,O1D	-0.6
1988	Det-A	24	74	7	16	5	0	0	6	0	14	.216	.216	.284	40	-6	0	2	-1	1.000	-0	D-14/1-4,3-4,O-2,S	-0.8
	Atl-N	51	92	6	14	2	0	2	13	10	13	.152	.235	.239	35	-8	0	1	-1	.933	0	3-20/O-4,P-3	-0.9
Total	12	1089	3375	371	876	170	16	112	435	213	521	.260	.308	.419	98	-18	50	37	-7	.949	2	3-619,2-324/SDO1P	-1.5
■ JON MORRISON	Morrison, Jonathan W. b: 1859, London, Ontario, Canada 5'9.5", 167 lbs. Deb: 8/1/1884																						
1884	Ind-a	44	182	26	48	6	8	1		7		.264	.306	.401	132	6				.784	3	O-44	0.7
1887	NY-a	9	34	7	4	0	0	0	3	6		.118	.268	.118	10	-4	0			.600	-4	/O-9	-0.7
Total	2	53	216	33	52	6	8	1	3	13		.241	.299	.356	110	3	0			.756	-1	/O-53	0.0
■ TOM MORRISON	Morrison, Thomas J. b: 1875, St.Louis, Mo. 5'3", 145 lbs. Deb: 9/18/1895																						
1895	Lou-N	6	22	3	6	0	2	0	4	1	1	.273	.304	.455	100	-0	0			1.000	-3	/S-3,3-3	-0.2
1896	Lou-N	8	27	3	4	1	0	0	0	4	4	.148	.258	.185	19	-3	0			.864	-1	/3-5,O-2,S-1	-0.3
Total	2	14	49	6	10	1	2	0	4	5	5	.204	.278	.306	55	-3	0			.839	-3	/3-8,S-4,O-2	-0.5
■ JACK MORRISSEY	Morrissey, John Albert "King" b: 5/2/1876, Lansing, Mich. d: 10/30/36, Lansing, Mich. BB/TR, 5'10", 160 lbs. Deb: 9/18/02																						
1902	Cin-N	12	39	5	11	1	1	0	3	4		.282	.349	.359	108	0	0			.941	-2	2-11/O-1	-0.1
1903	Cin-N	29	89	14	22	1	0	0	9	14		.247	.350	.258	67	-4	3			.922	-10	2-17/O-8,S-2	-1.3
Total	2	41	128	19	33	2	1	0	12	18		.258	.349	.289	78	-3	3			.930	-12	/2-28,O-9,S-2	-1.4
■ JOHN MORRISSEY	Morrissey, John J. b: 12/30/1856, Janesville, Wis. d: 4/29/1884, Janesville, Wis. Deb: 5/2/1881 F																						
1881	Buf-N	12	47	3	10	2	0	0	3	0	3	.213	.213	.255	47	-3				.865	-2	3-12	-0.4
1882	Det-N	2	7	1	2	0	0	0	0	0	2	.286	.286	.286	84	-0				.714	-1	/3-2	-0.1
Total	2	14	54	4	12	2	0	0	3	0	5	.222	.222	.259	52	-3				.841	-3	/3-14	-0.5
■ JO-JO MORRISSEY	Morrissey, Joseph Anselm b: 1/16/04, Warren, R.I. d: 5/2/50, Worcester, Mass. BR/TR, 6'1.5", 178 lbs. Deb: 4/12/32																						
1932	Cin-N	89	269	15	65	10	1	0	13	14	15	.242	.282	.286	55	-17	2			.967	8	S-45,2-42,3-12,/O-1	-0.4
1933	Cin-N	148	534	43	123	20	0	0	26	20	22	.230	.261	.268	52	-33	5			.964	-9	2-88,S-63,3-15	-3.5
1936	Chi-A	17	38	3	7	1	0	0	6	2	3	.184	.225	.211	8	-6	0	0	0	.895	0	/3-9,S-4,2-1	-0.4
Total	3	254	841	61	195	31	1	0	45	36	40	.232	.266	.271	51	-56	7	0		.971	-0	2-131,S-112/3-36,O	-4.3
■ TOM MORRISSEY	Morrissey, Thomas J. b: 1861, Janesville, Wis. d: 9/23/41, Janesville, Wis. 5'11", 180 lbs. Deb: 9/27/1884 F																						
1884	Mil-U	12	47	3	8	2	0	0		0		.170	.170	.213	28	-8				.710	-1	3-12	-0.8

YEAR	TM/L	G	AB	R	H	2B	3B	HR	RBI	BB	SO	AVG	OBP	SLG	PRO+	BR/A	SB	CS	SBR	FA	FR	G/POS	TPR
■ **BUD MORSE**	Morse, Newell Obediah b: 9/4/04, Berkeley, Cal. d: 4/6/87, Sparks, Nev. BL/TR, 5′9″, 150 lbs. Deb: 9/14/29																						
1929	Phi-A	8	27	1	2	0	0	0	0	0	2	.074	.074	.074	-60	-6	0	0	0	.975	2	/2-8	-0.4
■ **HAP MORSE**	Morse, Peter Raymond "Pete" b: 12/6/1886, St.Paul, Minn. d: 6/19/74, St.Paul, Minn. BR/TR, 5′8″, 160 lbs. Deb: 4/18/11																						
1911	StL-N	4	8	0	0	0	0	0	0	1	2	.000	.111	.000	-70	-2	0			.750	-0	/S-2,O-1	-0.2
■ **CHARLIE MORTON**	Morton, Charles Hazen b: 10/12/1854, Kingsville, Ohio d: 12/9/21, Massillon, Ohio BR/TR, 150 lbs. Deb: 5/2/1882 MU																						
1882	Pit-a	25	103	12	29	0	3	0		5		.282	.315	.340	127	3				.816	1	O-25/3-3,S-1	0.4
	StL-a	9	32	2	2	0	1	0		2		.063	.118	.125	-17	-4				.708	-4	/2-7,O-3	-0.8
	Yr	34	135	14	31	0	4	0		7		.230	.268	.289	90	-1				.821	-3	O-28/2-7,3-3,S-1	-0.4
1884	Tol-a	32	111	11	18	6	2	0		7		.162	.212	.252	49	-6				.861	-1	3-16,O-15/P-3,2M	-0.5
1885	Det-N	22	79	9	14	1	2	0	3	5	10	.177	.226	.241	51	-4				.750	2	3-18/S-4,M	-0.2
Total	3	88	325	34	63	7	8	0	3	19	10	.194	.238	.265	66	-11				.841	-3	/O-43,3-37,2-8,SP	-1.1
■ **GUY MORTON**	Morton, Guy Jr. "Moose" b: 11/4/30, Tuscaloosa, Ala. BR/TR, 6′2″, 200 lbs. Deb: 9/17/54 F																						
1954	Bos-A	1	1	0	0	0	0	0	0	0	1	.000	.000	.000	-90	-0	0	0	0	.000	0	H	0.0
■ **BUBBA MORTON**	Morton, Wycliffe Nathaniel b: 12/13/31, Washington, D.C. BR/TR, 5′10.5″, 180 lbs. Deb: 4/19/61																						
1961	Det-A	77	108	26	31	5	1	2	19	9	25	.287	.347	.407	98	-0	3	1	0	.952	-4	O-30	-0.5
1962	Det-A	90	195	30	51	6	3	4	17	32	32	.262	.366	.385	99	0	1	1	-0	.991	-2	O-62/1-3	-0.4
1963	Det-A	6	11	2	1	0	0	0	2	2	1	.091	.231	.091	-5	-2	0	0	0	.875	-0	/O-3	-0.2
	Mil-N	15	28	1	5	0	0	0	4	2	3	.179	.258	.179	28	-2	0	0	0	1.000	-1	/O-9	-0.4
1966	Cal-A	15	50	4	11	1	0	0	4	2	6	.220	.250	.240	43	-4	1	1	-0	1.000	0	O-14	-0.5
1967	Cal-A	80	201	23	63	9	3	0	32	22	29	.313	.387	.388	135	9	0	3	-2	1.000	-6	O-61	-0.1
1968	Cal-A	81	163	13	44	6	0	1	18	14	18	.270	.343	.325	107	2	2	1	0	.985	-4	O-50/3-1	-0.5
1969	Cal-A	87	172	18	42	10	1	7	32	28	29	.244	.360	.436	128	7	0	0	0	1.000	-0	O-49/1-1	0.5
Total	7	451	928	117	248	37	8	14	128	111	143	.267	.352	.370	106	10	7	7	-2	.988	-17	O-278/1-4,3-1	-2.1
■ **WALT MORYN**	Moryn, Walter Joseph "Moose" b: 4/12/26, St.Paul, Minn. d: 7/21/96, Winfield, Ill. BL/TR, 6′2″, 205 lbs. Deb: 6/29/54																						
1954	Bro-N	48	91	16	25	4	2	2	14	7	11	.275	.333	.429	94	-1	0	0	0	.881	-0	O-20	-0.2
1955	Bro-N	11	19	3	5	1	0	1	3	5	4	.263	.417	.474	132	1	0	0	0	.833	-2	/O-7	-0.1
1956	Chi-N	147	529	69	151	27	3	23	67	50	67	.285	.351	.478	122	16	4	2	0	.983	10	*O-141	1.9
1957	Chi-N	149	568	76	164	33	0	19	88	50	90	.289	.349	.447	114	11	0	2	-1	.960	7	*O-147	0.9
1958	Chi-N☆	143	512	77	135	26	7	26	77	62	83	.264	.352	.494	123	16	1	2	-1	.978	5	*O-141	1.3
1959	Chi-N	117	381	41	89	14	1	14	48	44	66	.234	.318	.386	87	-7	0	0	0	.989	0	*O-104	-1.2
1960	Chi-N	38	109	12	32	4	0	2	11	13	19	.294	.369	.385	108	2	2	1	0	.964	0	O-30	0.1
	StL-N	75	200	24	49	4	3	11	35	17	38	.245	.304	.460	97	-1	0	0	0	.990	-3	O-62	-0.7
	Yr	113	309	36	81	8	3	13	46	30	57	.262	.327	.434	101	0	2	1	0	.981	-3	O-92	-0.6
1961	StL-N	17	32	0	4	2	0	0	2	1	5	.125	.152	.188	-10	-5	0	0	0	.889	-1	/O-7	-0.7
	Pit-N	40	65	6	13	1	0	3	9	2	10	.200	.235	.354	53	-5	0	0	0	.950	1	O-11	-0.4
	Yr	57	97	6	17	3	0	3	11	3	15	.175	.208	.299	31	-10	0	0	0	.931	-0	O-18	-1.1
Total	8	785	2506	324	667	116	16	101	354	251	393	.266	.338	.446	108	27	7	7	-2	.972	17	O-670	0.9
■ **ROSS MOSCHITTO**	Moschitto, Rosaire Allen b: 2/15/45, Fresno, Cal. BR/TR, 6′2″, 175 lbs. Deb: 4/15/65																						
1965	NY-A	96	27	12	5	0	0	1	3	0	12	.185	.185	.296	35	-2	0	0	0	.941	-26	O-89	-3.1
1967	NY-A	14	9	1	1	0	0	0	0	1	2	.111	.200	.111	-6	-1	0	0	0	1.000	-2	/O-8	-0.4
Total	2	110	36	13	6	0	0	1	3	1	14	.167	.189	.250	25	-4	0	0	0	.944	-28	/O-97	-3.5
■ **LLOYD MOSEBY**	Moseby, Lloyd Anthony b: 11/5/59, Portland, Ark. BL/TR, 6′3″, 200 lbs. Deb: 5/24/80																						
1980	Tor-A	114	389	44	89	24	1	9	46	25	85	.229	.282	.365	73	-15	4	6	-2	.982	6	*O-104/D-6	-1.6
1981	Tor-A	100	378	36	88	16	2	9	43	24	86	.233	.280	.357	78	-12	11	8	-2	.989	3	*O-100	-1.5
1982	Tor-A	147	487	51	115	20	9	9	52	33	106	.236	.295	.370	74	-18	11	7	-1	.992	-1	*O-145	-2.3
1983	Tor-A	151	539	104	170	31	7	18	81	51	85	.315	.380	.499	132	23	27	8	3	.983	10	*O-147	3.2
1984	Tor-A	158	592	97	166	28	**15**	18	92	78	122	.280	.372	.470	126	22	39	9	6	.990	17	*O-156	4.0
1985	*Tor-A	152	584	92	151	30	7	18	70	76	91	.259	.348	.426	108	7	37	15	2	.980	1	*O-152	0.5
1986	Tor-A★	152	589	89	149	24	5	21	86	64	122	.253	.332	.418	100	0	32	11	3	.984	3	*O-147/D-3	0.1
1987	Tor-A	155	592	106	167	27	4	26	96	70	124	.282	.360	.473	116	14	39	7	8	.980	-8	*O-153/D-2	0.8
1988	Tor-A	128	472	77	113	17	7	10	42	70	93	.239	.345	.369	99	1	31	8	5	.984	-6	*O-125/D-1	-0.4
1989	*Tor-A	135	502	72	111	25	3	11	43	56	101	.221	.307	.349	86	-9	24	7	3	.986	-3	*O-120,D-14	-1.4
1990	Det-A	122	431	64	107	16	5	14	51	48	77	.248	.331	.406	104	2	17	5	2	.983	8	*O-116/D-4	1.0
1991	Det-A	74	260	37	68	15	1	6	35	21	43	.262	.324	.396	97	-1	8	1	2	.955	-1	O-64/D-7	-0.2
Total	12	1588	5815	869	1494	273	66	169	737	616	1135	.257	.334	.414	102	15	280	92	29	.984	28	*O-1529/D-37	2.2
■ **ARNIE MOSER**	Moser, Arnold Robert b: 8/9/15, Houston, Tex. BR/TR, 5′11″, 165 lbs. Deb: 6/20/37																						
1937	Cin-N	5	5	0	0	0	0	0	0	0	2	.000	.000	.000	-99	-1	0			.000	0	H	-0.1
■ **JERRY MOSES**	Moses, Gerald Braheen b: 8/9/46, Yazoo City, Miss. BR/TR, 6′3″, 210 lbs. Deb: 5/9/65																						
1965	Bos-A	4	4	1	1	0	0	1	1	0	2	.250	.250	1.000	224	1	0	0	0	.000	0	H	0.1
1968	Bos-A	6	18	2	6	0	0	2	4	1	4	.333	.368	.667	196	2	0	1	-1	.963	-3	/C-6	-0.1
1969	Bos-A	53	135	13	41	9	1	4	17	5	23	.304	.333	.474	117	3	0	1	-1	.981	-5	C-36	-0.2
1970	Bos-A☆	92	315	26	83	18	1	6	35	21	45	.263	.314	.384	85	-7	1	1	-0	.990	2	C-88/O-1	0.0
1971	Cal-A	69	181	12	41	8	2	4	15	10	34	.227	.267	.359	82	-5	0	0	0	.977	5	C-63/O-1	0.1
1972	Cle-A	52	141	9	31	3	0	4	14	11	29	.220	.290	.326	81	-3	0	0	0	.982	1	C-39/1-3	-0.2
1973	NY-A	21	59	5	15	2	0	0	3	2	6	.254	.279	.288	62	-3	0	0	0	1.000	5	C-17/D-1	0.2
1974	Det-A	74	198	19	47	6	3	4	19	11	38	.237	.284	.359	81	-5	0	1	-1	.985	0	C-74	-0.3
1975	SD-N	13	19	1	3	2	0	0	1	2	3	.158	.238	.263	42	-2	0	0	0	.900	-1	/C-5	-0.2
	Chi-A	2	2	1	1	0	1	0	0	0	0	.500	.500	1.500	441	1	0	0	0	1.000	-0	/1-1,D-1	0.1
Total	9	386	1072	89	269	48	8	25	109	63	184	.251	.297	.381	89	-19	1	4	-2	.984	3	C-328/1-4,D-2,O-2	-0.5
■ **JOHN MOSES**	Moses, John William b: 8/9/57, Los Angeles, Cal. BB/TL, 5′10″, 170 lbs. Deb: 8/23/82																						
1982	Sea-A	22	44	7	14	5	1	1	3	4	5	.318	.375	.545	145	3	5	1	1	.947	-4	O-19	-0.1
1983	Sea-A	93	130	19	27	4	1	0	6	12	20	.208	.280	.254	46	-9	11	5	0	.979	-9	O-71,D-10	-1.9
1984	Sea-A	19	35	3	12	1	1	0	2	2	5	.343	.395	.429	129	1	1	0	0	1.000	-4	O-19/D-1	-0.3
1985	Sea-A	33	62	4	12	0	0	0	3	2	8	.194	.219	.194	14	-7	5	2	0	1.000	-7	O-29	-1.5
1986	Sea-A	103	399	56	102	16	3	3	34	34	65	.256	.314	.333	76	-13	25	18	-3	.987	2	O-93/1-7,D-4	-1.8
1987	Sea-A	116	390	58	96	16	4	3	38	29	49	.246	.303	.331	65	-20	23	15	-2	.987	-2	*O-100/1-16,D-5	-2.6
1988	Min-A	105	206	33	65	10	3	2	12	15	21	.316	.368	.422	117	5	11	6	-0	1.000	-14	O-82/D-2	-1.1
1989	Min-A	129	242	33	68	12	3	1	31	19	23	.281	.336	.368	92	-2	14	7	0	.988	-24	*O-108/1-2,P-1,D-3	-2.8
1990	Min-A	115	172	26	38	3	1	1	14	19	19	.221	.306	.267	58	-9	2	3	-1	1.000	-17	O-85,D-10/1-6,P-2	-3.0
1991	Det-A	13	21	5	1	1	0	0	1	2	7	.048	.130	.095	-36	-4	4	0	1	1.000	-2	O-12	-0.5
1992	Sea-A	21	22	3	3	1	0	0	1	5	4	.136	.296	.182	37	-2	0	0	0	1.000	-4	O-18/D-1	-0.6
Total	11	769	1723	247	438	69	17	11	145	143	226	.254	.315	.333	75	-58	101	57	-4	.990	-86	O-636/D-36,1-31,P-3	-16.2
■ **WALLY MOSES**	Moses, Wallace b: 10/8/10, Uvalda, Ga. d: 10/10/90, Vidalia, Ga. BL/TL, 5′10″, 160 lbs. Deb: 4/17/35 C																						
1935	Phi-A	85	345	60	112	21	3	5	35	25	18	.325	.375	.446	113	6	3	4	-2	.943	0	O-80	0.2
1936	Phi-A	146	585	98	202	35	11	7	66	62	32	.345	.410	.479	121	20	12	6	0	.974	3	*O-144	1.5
1937	Phi-A☆	154	649	113	208	48	13	25	86	54	38	.320	.374	.550	132	28	9	7	-2	.958	6	*O-154	2.5
1938	Phi-A	142	589	86	181	29	8	8	49	58	31	.307	.369	.424	101	1	15	5	2	.966	5	*O-139	0.2
1939	Phi-A	115	437	68	134	28	7	3	33	44	23	.307	.370	.423	105	3	7	4	-0	.965	-1	*O-103	-0.1
1940	Phi-A	142	537	91	166	41	9	9	50	75	44	.309	.396	.469	126	22	6	4	-1	.974	4	*O-133	1.8
1941	Phi-A	116	438	78	132	31	4	4	35	62	27	.301	.388	.418	116	12	3	3	-1	.975	9	*O-109	1.3

YEAR	TM/L	G	AB	R	H	2B	3B	HR	RBI	BB	SO	AVG	OBP	SLG	PRO+	BR/A	SB	CS	SBR	FA	FR	G/POS	TPR
1942	Chi-A	146	577	73	156	28	4	7	49	74	27	.270	.353	.369	106	5	16	10	-1	.980	7	*O-145	0.3
1943	Chi-A	150	599	82	147	22	**12**	3	48	55	47	.245	.310	.337	89	-9	56	14	8	.979	9	*O-148	0.0
1944	Chi-A	136	535	82	150	26	9	3	34	52	22	.280	.345	.379	108	6	21	7	2	.975	-2	*O-134	-0.1
1945	Chi-A†	140	569	79	168	**35**	15	2	50	69	33	.295	.373	.420	134	25	11	5	0	.977	9	*O-139	2.7
1946	Chi-A	56	168	20	46	9	1	4	16	17	20	.274	.344	.411	115	3	2	2	-1	1.000	-1	O-36	0.0
	*Bos-A	48	175	23	36	11	3	2	17	14	15	.206	.268	.337	65	-9	2	4	-2	.979	0	O-44	-1.3
	Yr	104	343	43	82	20	4	6	33	31	35	.239	.306	.373	88	-6	4	6	-2	.989	-0	O-80	-1.3
1947	Bos-A	90	255	32	70	18	2	2	27	27	16	.275	.344	.384	95	-2	3	0	1	.974	-3	O-58	-0.7
1948	Bos-A	78	189	26	49	12	1	2	29	21	19	.259	.340	.365	83	-5	5	0	2	.981	1	O-45	-0.4
1949	Phi-A	110	308	49	85	19	3	1	25	51	19	.276	.381	.367	102	2	1	3	-2	.983	-3	O-92	-0.6
1950	Phi-A	88	265	47	70	16	5	2	21	40	17	.264	.365	.385	94	-2	0	1	-1	.987	5	O-62	0.0
1951	Phi-A	70	136	17	26	6	0	0	9	21	9	.191	.304	.235	46	-10	2	2	-1	.984	2	O-27	-0.9
Total	17	2012	7356	1124	2138	435	110	89	679	821	457	.291	.364	.416	109	97	174	81	4	.973	51	*O-1792	6.4

■ DOC MOSKIMAN

Moskiman, William Bankhead b: 12/20/1879, Oakland, Cal. d: 1/11/53, San Leandro, Cal. BR/TR, 6′, 170 lbs. Deb: 8/23/10

YEAR	TM/L	G	AB	R	H	2B	3B	HR	RBI	BB	SO	AVG	OBP	SLG	PRO+	BR/A	SB	CS	SBR	FA	FR	G/POS	TPR
1910	Bos-A	5	9	1	1	0	0	0	1	2		.111	.273	.111	20	-1	0			1.000	0	/1-2,O-1	0.0

■ JIM MOSOLF

Mosolf, James Frederick b: 8/21/05, Puyallup, Wash. d: 12/28/79, Dallas, Ore. BL/TR, 5′10″, 186 lbs. Deb: 9/9/29

YEAR	TM/L	G	AB	R	H	2B	3B	HR	RBI	BB	SO	AVG	OBP	SLG	PRO+	BR/A	SB	CS	SBR	FA	FR	G/POS	TPR
1929	Pit-N	8	13	3	6	1	1	0	2	1	1	.462	.500	.692	188	2	0			1.000	0	/O-3	0.2
1930	Pit-N	40	51	16	17	2	1	0	9	8	7	.333	.424	.412	103	1	0			.765	-3	O-12/P-1	-0.3
1931	Pit-N	39	44	7	11	1	0	1	8	8	5	.250	.365	.341	92	-0	0			1.000	-1	/O-4	-0.1
1933	Chi-N	31	82	13	22	5	1	1	9	5	8	.268	.326	.390	104	0	0			.964	1	O-22	0.0
Total	4	118	190	39	56	9	3	2	28	22	21	.295	.374	.405	107	3	0			.929	-4	/O-41,P-1	-0.2

■ JULIO MOSQUERA

Mosquera, Julio Alberto (Cervantes) b: 1/29/72, Panama City, Panama BR/TR, 6′, 165 lbs. Deb: 8/17/96

YEAR	TM/L	G	AB	R	H	2B	3B	HR	RBI	BB	SO	AVG	OBP	SLG	PRO+	BR/A	SB	CS	SBR	FA	FR	G/POS	TPR
1996	Tor-A	8	22	2	5	2	0	0	2	0	3	.227	.261	.318	46	-2	0	1	-1	1.000	1	/C-8	-0.1
1997	Tor-A	3	8	0	2	1	0	0	0	0	2	.250	.250	.375	60	-0	0	0	0	1.000	-1	/C-3	-0.1
Total	2	11	30	2	7	3	0	0	2	0	5	.233	.258	.333	49	-2	0	1	-1	1.000	1	/C-11	-0.2

■ CHARLIE MOSS

Moss, Charles Crosby b: 3/20/11, Meridian, Miss. d: 10/9/91, Meridian, Miss. BR/TR, 5′10″, 160 lbs. Deb: 5/19/34

YEAR	TM/L	G	AB	R	H	2B	3B	HR	RBI	BB	SO	AVG	OBP	SLG	PRO+	BR/A	SB	CS	SBR	FA	FR	G/POS	TPR
1934	Phi-A	10	10	3	2	0	0	0	1	0	0	.200	.200	.200	4	-1	0	0	0	1.000	-1	/C-6	-0.2
1935	Phi-A	4	3	1	1	0	0	0	1	1	0	.333	.500	.333	120	0	0	0	0	.000	0	/C-1	0.0
1936	Phi-A	33	44	2	11	1	1	0	10	6	5	.250	.340	.318	65	-2	1	0	0	.929	-2	C-19	-0.3
Total	3	47	57	6	14	1	1	0	12	7	5	.246	.328	.298	58	-4	1	0	0	.935	-2	/C-26	-0.5

■ HOWIE MOSS

Moss, Howard Glenn b: 10/17/19, Gastonia, N.C. d: 5/7/89, Baltimore, Md. BR/TR, 5′11.5″, 185 lbs. Deb: 4/14/42

YEAR	TM/L	G	AB	R	H	2B	3B	HR	RBI	BB	SO	AVG	OBP	SLG	PRO+	BR/A	SB	CS	SBR	FA	FR	G/POS	TPR
1942	NY-N	7	14	0	0	0	0	0	0	0	4	.000	.000	.000	-99	-3	0			1.000	0	/O-3	-0.4
1946	Cin-N	7	26	1	5	0	0	0	1	0	4	.192	.222	.192	19	-3	0			1.000	0	/O-6	-0.3
	Cle-A	8	32	2	2	0	0	0	0	3	9	.063	.143	.063	-44	-6	0	1	-1	.857	0	/3-8	-0.7
Total	2	22	72	3	7	0	0	0	1	3	17	.097	.145	.097	-32	-12	0	1		1.000	0	/O-9,3-8	-1.4

■ LES MOSS

Moss, John Lester b: 5/14/25, Tulsa, Okla. BR/TR, 5′11″, 205 lbs. Deb: 9/10/46 MC

YEAR	TM/L	G	AB	R	H	2B	3B	HR	RBI	BB	SO	AVG	OBP	SLG	PRO+	BR/A	SB	CS	SBR	FA	FR	G/POS	TPR
1946	StL-A	12	35	4	13	3	0	0	5	3	5	.371	.436	.457	142	2	1	0	0	.968	1	C-12	0.4
1947	StL-A	96	274	17	43	5	2	6	27	35	48	.157	.255	.255	41	-22	0	0	0	.983	-5	C-96	-2.3
1948	StL-A	107	335	35	86	12	1	14	46	39	50	.257	.334	.424	98	-2	0	0	0	.988	-9	*C-103	-0.4
1949	StL-A	97	278	28	81	11	0	10	39	49	32	.291	.399	.439	117	8	0	1	-1	.970	-5	C-83	0.7
1950	StL-A	84	222	24	59	6	0	8	34	26	32	.266	.343	.401	87	-5	0	1	-1	.957	-1	C-60	-0.4
1951	StL-A	16	47	5	8	2	0	1	7	6	8	.170	.264	.277	45	-4	0	0	0	.967	-0	C-12	-0.3
	Bos-A	71	202	18	40	6	0	3	26	25	34	.198	.289	.272	48	-15	0	0	0	.984	-1	C-69	-1.3
	Yr	87	249	23	48	8	0	4	33	31	42	.193	.285	.273	47	-19	0	0	0	.981	-1	C-81	-1.6
1952	StL-A	52	118	11	29	3	0	3	12	15	13	.246	.331	.347	86	-2	0	1	-1	.957	-3	C-39	-0.5
1953	StL-A	78	239	21	66	14	1	2	28	18	31	.276	.329	.368	86	-5	0	1	-1	.978	-6	C-71	-0.8
1954	Bal-A	50	126	7	31	3	0	0	5	14	16	.246	.321	.270	68	-5	0	0	0	.972	-2	C-38	-0.6
1955	Bal-A	29	56	5	19	1	0	2	6	7	4	.339	.413	.464	146	4	0	1	-1	1.000	2	C-17	0.5
	Chi-A	32	59	5	15	2	0	2	7	6	10	.254	.333	.390	91	-1	0	0	0	.990	-0	C-32	0.0
	Yr	61	115	10	34	3	0	4	13	13	14	.296	.372	.426	116	3	0	1	-1	.994	2	C-49	0.5
1956	Chi-A	56	127	20	31	4	0	10	22	18	15	.244	.338	.512	120	3	0	0	0	.994	-6	C-49	-0.2
1957	Chi-A	42	115	10	31	3	0	2	12	20	18	.270	.378	.348	99	1	0	0	0	.980	-7	C-39	-0.5
1958	Chi-A	2	1	0	0	0	0	0	0	1	0	.000	.500	.000	51	0	0	0	0	.000	0	H	0.0
Total	13	824	2234	210	552	75	4	63	276	282	316	.247	.333	.369	86	-44	1	5	-3	.978	-42	C-720	-5.7

■ JOHNNY MOSTIL

Mostil, John Anthony "Bananas" b: 6/1/1896, Chicago, Ill. d: 12/10/70, Midlothian, Ill. BR/TR, 5′8.5″, 168 lbs. Deb: 6/20/18

YEAR	TM/L	G	AB	R	H	2B	3B	HR	RBI	BB	SO	AVG	OBP	SLG	PRO+	BR/A	SB	CS	SBR	FA	FR	G/POS	TPR
1918	Chi-A	10	33	4	9	2	2	0	4	1	6	.273	.294	.455	125	1	1			.923	-2	/2-9	-0.1
1921	Chi-A	100	326	43	98	21	7	3	42	28	35	.301	.379	.436	109	5	10	12	-4	.946	0	O-91/2-1	-0.5
1922	Chi-A	132	458	74	139	28	14	7	70	38	39	.303	.375	.472	120	13	14	10	-2	.966	5	*O-123	0.7
1923	Chi-A	153	546	91	159	37	15	3	64	62	51	.291	.376	.430	113	11	41	16	**3**	.974	22	*O-143/3-5,S-1	2.5
1924	Chi-A	118	385	75	125	22	5	4	49	45	41	.325	.401	.439	120	12	7	11	-5	.974	7	*O-102	0.8
1925	Chi-A	153	605	**135**	181	36	16	2	50	**90**	52	.299	.400	.421	115	16	**43**	20	1	**.985**	7	*O-153	1.3
1926	Chi-A	148	600	120	197	41	15	4	42	79	55	.328	.415	.467	134	32	**35**	14	**2**	.968	17	*O-147	4.0
1927	Chi-A	13	16	3	2	0	0	0	1	0	1	.125	.176	.125	-21	-3	1	0	0	.857	-2	/O-6	-0.4
1928	Chi-A	133	503	69	136	19	8	0	51	66	54	.270	.360	.340	86	-8	23	21	-6	.976	18	*O-131	-0.5
1929	Chi-A	12	35	4	8	3	0	0	3	6	2	.229	.341	.314	71	-1	1	1	-0	.963	-1	O-11	-0.3
Total	10	972	3507	618	1054	209	82	23	376	415	336	.301	.386	.427	113	78	176	105		.971	72	O-907/2-10,3-5,S-1	7.5

■ ANDY MOTA

Mota, Andres Alberto (Matos) b: 3/4/66, Santo Domingo, D.R. BR/TR, 5′10″, 180 lbs. Deb: 8/31/91 F

YEAR	TM/L	G	AB	R	H	2B	3B	HR	RBI	BB	SO	AVG	OBP	SLG	PRO+	BR/A	SB	CS	SBR	FA	FR	G/POS	TPR
1991	Hou-N	27	90	4	17	2	0	1	6	1	17	.189	.198	.244	25	-9	2	0	1	.970	-3	2-27	-1.2

■ JOSE MOTA

Mota, Jose Manuel (Matos) b: 3/16/65, Santo Domingo, D.R. BB/TR, 5′9″, 155 lbs. Deb: 5/25/91 F

YEAR	TM/L	G	AB	R	H	2B	3B	HR	RBI	BB	SO	AVG	OBP	SLG	PRO+	BR/A	SB	CS	SBR	FA	FR	G/POS	TPR
1991	SD-N	17	36	4	8	0	0	0	2	2	7	.222	.282	.222	42	-3	0	0	0	.962	0	2-13/S-3	-0.2
1995	KC-A	2	2	0	0	0	0	0	0	0	0	.000	.000	.000	-99	-1	0	0	0	1.000	0	/2-2	0.0
Total	2	19	38	4	8	0	0	0	2	2	7	.211	.268	.211	35	-3	0	0	0	.965	1	/2-15,S-3	-0.2

■ MANNY MOTA

Mota, Manuel Rafael (Geronimo) b: 2/18/38, Santo Domingo, D.R. BR/TR, 5′11″, 168 lbs. Deb: 4/16/62 FC

YEAR	TM/L	G	AB	R	H	2B	3B	HR	RBI	BB	SO	AVG	OBP	SLG	PRO+	BR/A	SB	CS	SBR	FA	FR	G/POS	TPR
1962	SF-N	47	74	9	13	1	0	0	9	7	8	.176	.256	.189	22	-8	3	2	-0	1.000	-2	O-27/3-7,2-3	-1.0
1963	Pit-N	59	126	20	34	2	3	0	7	7	18	.270	.313	.333	86	-2	0	2	-1	.953	-5	O-37/2-1	-1.1
1964	Pit-N	115	271	43	75	8	3	5	32	10	31	.277	.310	.384	94	-2	4	1	1	.961	-16	O-93/C-1,2-1	-2.2
1965	Pit N	121	294	47	82	7	6	4	29	22	32	.279	.333	.384	101	0	2	2	-1	.985	-14	O-95	-1.9
1966	Pit-N	116	322	54	107	16	7	5	46	25	28	.332	.387	.472	137	17	7	7	-2	.994	-11	O-96/3-4	-0.1
1967	Pit-N	120	349	53	112	14	8	4	56	14	46	.321	.351	.441	125	10	3	2	-0	.988	-6	O-99/3-2	0.0
1968	Pit-N	111	331	35	93	10	2	1	33	20	19	.281	.324	.332	99	-1	4	2	0	.981	-7	O-92/2-1,3-1	-1.4
1969	Mon-N	31	89	6	28	1	1	0	0	6	11	.315	.358	.348	98	-0	1	3	-2	.907	-2	O-22	-0.6
	LA-N	85	294	35	95	6	4	3	30	26	25	.323	.380	.401	128	11	5	4	-1	.969	0	O-80	0.6
	Yr	116	383	41	123	7	5	3	30	32	36	.321	.375	.389	120	11	6	7	-2	.954	-2	*O-102	0.0
1970	LA-N	124	417	63	127	12	6	3	37	47	37	.305	.379	.384	110	7	11	6	-0	.973	0	*O-111/3-1	0.2
1971	LA-N	91	269	24	84	13	5	0	34	20	20	.312	.362	.398	122	8	4	3	-1	.965	-9	O-80	-0.6
1972	LA-N	118	371	57	120	16	5	5	48	27	15	.323	.377	.434	133	16	4	4	-1	.993	-8	O-99	0.2
1973	LA-N★	89	293	33	92	11	2	0	23	25	12	.314	.370	.365	109	4	1	3	-2	1.000	-6	O-74	-0.7
1974	*LA-N	66	57	5	16	2	0	0	16	5	4	.281	.349	.316	91	-1	0	0	0	1.000	-1	/O-3	-0.2
1975	LA-N	52	49	3	13	1	0	0	10	5	1	.265	.357	.286	84	-1	0	0	0	1.000	-0	/O-5	-0.1
1976	LA-N	50	52	1	15	3	0	0	13	7	5	.288	.373	.346	107	1	0	0	0	1.000	1	/O-6	0.1
1977	*LA-N	49	38	5	15	1	0	1	4	10	0	.395	.521	.500	176	5	1	1	-0	1.000	-0	/O-1	0.5
1978	*LA-N	37	33	2	10	1	0	0	6	3	4	.303	.361	.333	95	-0	0	0	0	.000	0	H	-0.1

YEAR	TM/L	G	AB	R	H	2B	3B	HR	RBI	BB	SO	AVG	OBP	SLG	PRO+	BR/A	SB	CS	SBR	FA	FR	G/POS	TPR
1979	LA-N	47	42	1	15	0	0	0	3	3	4	.357	.400	.357	110	1	0	0	0	.000	-0	/O-1	0.0
1980	LA-N	7	7	0	3	0	0	0	2	0	0	.429	.429	.429	143	0	0	0	0	.000	0	/H	0.0
1982	LA-N	1	1	0	0	0	0	0	0	0	0	.000	.000	.000	-99	-0	0	0	0	.000	0	/H	0.0
Total	20	1536	3779	496	1149	125	52	31	438	289	320	.304	.358	.389	112	65	50	42	-10	.979	-87	*O-1021/3-15,2-6,C	-8.4

■ DARRYL MOTLEY
Motley, Darryl De Wayne b: 1/21/60, Muskogee, Okla. BR/TR, 5'9", 196 lbs. Deb: 8/10/81

YEAR	TM/L	G	AB	R	H	2B	3B	HR	RBI	BB	SO	AVG	OBP	SLG	PRO+	BR/A	SB	CS	SBR	FA	FR	G/POS	TPR
1981	KC-A	42	125	15	29	4	0	2	8	7	15	.232	.278	.312	70	-5	1	3	-2	.968	3	O-39	-0.5
1983	KC-A	19	68	9	16	1	2	3	11	2	8	.235	.268	.441	91	-1	2	1	0	.978	1	O-18/D-1	-0.1
1984	*KC-A	146	522	64	148	25	6	15	70	28	73	.284	.321	.441	108	4	10	12	-4	.984	-2	*O-138	-0.6
1985	*KC-A	123	383	45	85	20	1	17	49	18	57	.222	.261	.413	81	-12	6	4	-1	.967	-8	*O-114/D-7	-2.4
1986	KC-A	72	217	22	44	9	1	7	20	11	31	.203	.241	.350	57	-13	0	2	-1	.979	-8	O-66/D-2	-2.4
	Atl-N	5	10	1	2	1	0	0	0	1	1	.200	.273	.300	55	-1	0	0	0	1.000	-0	/O-3	-0.1
1987	Atl-N	6	8	0	0	0	0	0	1	0	1	.000	.000	.000	-95	-2	0	0	0	1.000	-0	/O-2	-0.3
Total	6	413	1333	156	324	60	10	44	159	67	186	.243	.282	.402	86	-30	19	22	-8	.976	-15	O-380/D-10	-6.4

■ BITSY MOTT
Mott, Elisha Matthew b: 6/12/18, Arcadia, Fla. BR/TR, 5'8", 155 lbs. Deb: 4/17/45

YEAR	TM/L	G	AB	R	H	2B	3B	HR	RBI	BB	SO	AVG	OBP	SLG	PRO+	BR/A	SB	CS	SBR	FA	FR	G/POS	TPR
1945	Phi-N	90	289	21	64	8	0	0	22	27	25	.221	.290	.249	52	-18	2			.944	13	S-63,2-27/3-7	0.0

■ CHAD MOTTOLA
Mottola, Charles Edward b: 10/15/71, Augusta, Ga. BR/TR, 6'3", 220 lbs. Deb: 4/22/96

YEAR	TM/L	G	AB	R	H	2B	3B	HR	RBI	BB	SO	AVG	OBP	SLG	PRO+	BR/A	SB	CS	SBR	FA	FR	G/POS	TPR
1996	Cin-N	35	79	10	17	3	0	3	6	6	16	.215	.271	.367	66	-4	2	2	-1	1.000	-2	O-31	-0.7

■ CURT MOTTON
Motton, Curtell Howard b: 9/24/40, Darnell, La. BR/TR, 5'7.5", 175 lbs. Deb: 7/5/67 C

YEAR	TM/L	G	AB	R	H	2B	3B	HR	RBI	BB	SO	AVG	OBP	SLG	PRO+	BR/A	SB	CS	SBR	FA	FR	G/POS	TPR
1967	Bal-A	27	65	5	13	2	0	2	9	5	14	.200	.278	.323	78	-2	0	1	-1	.973	1	O-18	-0.3
1968	Bal-A	83	217	27	43	7	0	8	25	31	43	.198	.301	.341	94	-1	1	3	-2	.989	2	O-54	-0.4
1969	*Bal-A	56	89	15	27	6	0	6	21	13	10	.303	.398	.573	167	8	3	1	0	1.000	-3	O-20	0.5
1970	Bal-A	52	84	16	19	3	1	3	19	18	20	.226	.369	.393	109	2	1	2	-1	1.000	-1	O-21	-0.1
1971	*Bal-A	38	53	13	10	1	0	4	8	10	12	.189	.317	.434	112	1	0	0	0	1.000	-2	O-16	-0.2
1972	Mil-A	6	6	1	1	0	0	1	2	1	2	.167	.286	.667	181	1	0	0	0	.000	-1	/O-3	-0.1
	Cal-A	42	39	6	6	1	0	0	1	5	12	.154	.250	.179	31	-3	0	0	0	1.000	-0	/O-9	-0.4
	Yr	48	45	7	7	1	0	1	3	6	14	.156	.255	.244	52	-3	0	0	0	1.000	-1	O-12	-0.5
1973	Bal-A	5	6	2	2	0	0	1	4	1	1	.333	.429	.833	250	1	0	0	0	.000	-0	/O-1,D-1	0.1
1974	*Bal-A	7	8	0	0	0	0	0	0	2	2	.000	.200	.000	-40	-1	0	0	0	1.000	-0	/O-2,D-1	-0.2
Total	8	316	567	85	121	20	1	25	89	86	116	.213	.322	.384	105	4	5	7	-3	.991	-5	O-144/D-2	-1.1

■ FRANK MOTZ
Motz, Frank H. b: 10/1/1868, Freeburg, Pa. d: 3/18/44, Akron, Ohio 6', 160 lbs. Deb: 8/27/1890

YEAR	TM/L	G	AB	R	H	2B	3B	HR	RBI	BB	SO	AVG	OBP	SLG	PRO+	BR/A	SB	CS	SBR	FA	FR	G/POS	TPR
1890	Phi-N	1	2	1	0	0	0	0	0	1	1	.000	.333	.000	-1	-0	1			1.000	0	/1-1	0.0
1893	Cin-N	43	156	16	40	7	1	2	25	19	10	.256	.352	.353	85	-3	3			.981	6	1-43	0.1
1894	Cin-N	18	69	8	14	4	0	0	12	9	1	.203	.304	.261	36	-7	2			.995	4	1-18	-0.3
Total	3	62	227	25	54	11	1	2	37	29	12	.238	.337	.322	68	-11	6			.985	10	/1-62	-0.2

■ ALLIE MOULTON
Moulton, Albert Theodore b: 1/16/1886, Medway, Mass. d: 7/10/68, Peabody, Mass. BR/TR, 5'6", 155 lbs. Deb: 9/25/11

YEAR	TM/L	G	AB	R	H	2B	3B	HR	RBI	BB	SO	AVG	OBP	SLG	PRO+	BR/A	SB	CS	SBR	FA	FR	G/POS	TPR
1911	StL-A	4	15	4	1	0	0	0	1	4		.067	.263	.067	-6	-2	0			.938	-1	/2-4	-0.3

■ FRANK MOUNTAIN
Mountain, Frank Henry b: 5/17/1860, Ft.Edward, N.Y. d: 11/19/39, Schenectady, N.Y. BR/TR, 5'11", 185 lbs. Deb: 7/19/1880

YEAR	TM/L	G	AB	R	H	2B	3B	HR	RBI	BB	SO	AVG	OBP	SLG	PRO+	BR/A	SB	CS	SBR	FA	FR	G/POS	TPR
1880	Tro-N	2	9	1	2	0	0	0	0	0	4	.222	.222	.222	49	-0				1.000	0	/P-2	0.0
1881	Det-N	7	25	0	4	1	1	0	4	2	8	.160	.222	.280	55	-1				.923	-1	/P-7	0.0
1882	Wor-N	5	16	1	1	0	0	0	1	0	5	.063	.063	.063	-58	-3				.889	-1	/P-5	0.0
	Phi-a	9	36	5	12	3	0	0		2		.333	.368	.417	147	2				.917	1	/P-8,O-1	0.0
	Wor-N	20	70	8	19	2	2	2	5	3	18	.271	.301	.443	132	2				.870	-3	P-13/O-6,1-2,S-1	-0.2
1883	Col-a	70	276	36	60	14	5	3		9		.217	.242	.337	92	-2				.848	2	P-59,O-12	0.0
1884	Col-a	58	210	26	50	7	3	4		9		.238	.283	.357	117	4				.919	2	P-42,O-17	0.0
1885	Pit-a	5	20	1	2	0	1	0	1	1		.100	.143	.200	8	-2				.846	0	/P-5	0.0
1886	Pit-a	18	55	6	8	1	1	0	2	13		.145	.319	.200	64	-2	3			.959	-0	1-16/P-2	-0.3
Total	7	194	717	84	158	28	13	9	13	39	35	.220	.265	.333	96	-2	3			.880	0	P-143/O-36,1-18,S-1	-0.5

■ JAMES MOUTON
Mouton, James Raleigh b: 12/19/68, Denver, Colo. BR/TR, 5'9", 175 lbs. Deb: 4/4/94

YEAR	TM/L	G	AB	R	H	2B	3B	HR	RBI	BB	SO	AVG	OBP	SLG	PRO+	BR/A	SB	CS	SBR	FA	FR	G/POS	TPR
1994	Hou-N	99	310	43	76	11	0	2	16	27	69	.245	.316	.300	65	-16	24	5	4	.982	-5	O-96	-1.8
1995	Hou-N	104	298	42	78	18	2	4	27	25	59	.262	.327	.376	91	-4	25	8	3	1.000	-7	O-94	-1.0
1996	Hou-N	122	300	40	79	15	1	3	34	38	55	.263	.346	.350	91	-3	21	9	1	.971	-4	*O-108	-0.8
1997	Hou-N	86	180	24	38	9	1	3	23	18	30	.211	.290	.322	62	-10	9	7	-2	1.000	-7	O-61	-1.9
1998	SD-N	55	63	8	12	2	1	0	7	7	11	.190	.271	.254	42	-6	4	3	-1	.969	-5	O-33/D-1	-1.1
Total	5	466	1151	157	283	55	5	12	107	115	224	.246	.320	.334	77	-39	83	32	6	.985	-28	O-392/D-1	-6.6

■ LYLE MOUTON
Mouton, Lyle Joseph b: 5/13/69, Lafayette, La. BR/TR, 6'4", 240 lbs. Deb: 6/7/95

YEAR	TM/L	G	AB	R	H	2B	3B	HR	RBI	BB	SO	AVG	OBP	SLG	PRO+	BR/A	SB	CS	SBR	FA	FR	G/POS	TPR
1995	Chi-A	58	179	23	54	16	0	5	27	19	46	.302	.375	.475	125	7	1	0	0	.990	-0	O-53/D-2	0.5
1996	Chi-A	87	214	25	63	8	1	7	39	22	50	.294	.366	.439	107	3	3	0	1	.970	-7	O-47,D-28	-0.6
1997	Chi-A	88	242	26	65	9	0	5	23	14	66	.269	.311	.368	80	-8	4	4	-1	.969	-4	O-67,D-11	-1.4
1998	Bal-A	18	39	5	12	2	0	2	7	4	8	.308	.372	.513	130	2	0	0	0	1.000	-3	O-16/D-2	-0.1
Total	4	251	674	79	194	35	1	19	96	59	170	.288	.350	.427	104	3	8	4	0	.978	-14	O-183/D-43	-1.6

■ RAY MOWE
Mowe, Raymond Benjamin b: 7/12/1889, Rochester, Ind. d: 8/14/68, Sarasota, Fla. BL/TR, 5'7.5", 160 lbs. Deb: 9/25/13

YEAR	TM/L	G	AB	R	H	2B	3B	HR	RBI	BB	SO	AVG	OBP	SLG	PRO+	BR/A	SB	CS	SBR	FA	FR	G/POS	TPR
1913	Bro-N	5	9	0	1	0	0	0	0	0	1	.111	.200	.111	-10	-1	0			.941	1	/S-2	0.0

■ MIKE MOWREY
Mowrey, Harry Harlan b: 4/20/1884, Browns Mill, Pa. d: 3/20/47, Chambersburg, Pa. BR/TR, 5'10", 180 lbs. Deb: 9/24/05

YEAR	TM/L	G	AB	R	H	2B	3B	HR	RBI	BB	SO	AVG	OBP	SLG	PRO+	BR/A	SB	CS	SBR	FA	FR	G/POS	TPR
1905	Cin-N	7	30	4	8	1	0	0	6	1		.267	.290	.300	69	-1	0			.759	-0	/3-7	-0.1
1906	Cin-N	21	53	3	17	3	0	0	6	5		.321	.379	.377	130	2	2			.930	4	3-15/2-1,S-1	0.6
1907	Cin-N	138	448	43	113	16	6	1	44	35		.252	.308	.321	93	-4	10			.929	-19	*3-127,S-11	-2.1
1908	Cin-N	77	227	17	50	9	1	0	23	12		.220	.266	.269	73	-7	5			.936	-7	3-56/S-3,O-3,2-1	-1.4
1909	Cin-N	38	115	10	22	5	0	0	5	20		.191	.311	.235	70	-3	2			.947	1	3-22,S-13	-0.2
	StL-N	12	29	3	7	1	0	0	4	4		.241	.333	.276	95	-0	1			.921	-1	/2-7,3-2	-0.1
	Yr	50	144	13	29	6	0	0	9	24		.201	.315	.243	75	-3	3			.948	-1	3-24,S-13/2-7	-0.3
1910	StL-N	143	489	69	138	24	6	2	70	67	38	.282	.375	.368	121	15	21			.927	12	*3-141	3.2
1911	StL-N	137	471	59	126	29	7	0	61	59	46	.268	.355	.359	103	3	15			.944	7	*3-134/S-1	1.1
1912	StL-N	114	408	59	104	13	8	2	50	46	29	.255	.335	.341	87	-7	19			.931	3	*3-108	-0.3
1913	StL-N	132	450	61	117	18	4	0	33	53	40	.260	.342	.318	90	-4	21			.953	16	*3-131	1.4
1914	Pit-N	79	284	24	72	7	5	1	25	22	20	.254	.316	.324	94	-2	8			.960	-2	3-78	-0.2
1915	Pit-F	151	521	56	146	26	6	1	49	66	39	.280	.367	.359	105	-2	40			**.959**	-19	*3-151	-1.6
1916	*Bro-N	144	495	57	121	22	6	0	60	50	60	.244	.320	.313	92	-3	16			**.965**	0	*3-144	0.2
1917	Bro-N	83	271	20	58	9	5	0	25	29	25	.214	.292	.284	75	-7	7			.952	-3	3-80/2-2	-1.0
Total	13	1276	4291	485	1099	183	54	7	461	469	297	.256	.334	.329	96	-21	167			.944	-10	*3-1196/S-29,2-11,O	-0.5

■ JOE MOWRY
Mowry, Joseph Aloysius b: 4/6/08, St.Louis, Mo. d: 2/9/94, St.Louis, Mo. BB/TR, 6', 198 lbs. Deb: 5/13/33

YEAR	TM/L	G	AB	R	H	2B	3B	HR	RBI	BB	SO	AVG	OBP	SLG	PRO+	BR/A	SB	CS	SBR	FA	FR	G/POS	TPR
1933	Bos-N	86	249	25	55	8	5	0	20	15	22	.221	.273	.293	67	-11	1			.994	1	O-64	-1.5
1934	Bos-N	25	79	9	17	3	0	1	4	3	13	.215	.244	.291	46	-6	0			.976	0	O-20/2-1	-0.7
1935	Bos-N	81	136	17	36	8	1	1	13	11	13	.265	.324	.360	91	-2	0			.970	-7	O-45	-1.0
Total	3	192	464	51	108	19	6	2	37	29	48	.233	.284	.313	71	-19	1			.985	-7	O-129/2-1	-3.2

■ MIKE MOYNAHAN
Moynahan, Michael b: 1856, Chicago, Ill. d: 4/9/1899, Chicago, Ill. BL/TR, Deb: 8/20/1880

YEAR	TM/L	G	AB	R	H	2B	3B	HR	RBI	BB	SO	AVG	OBP	SLG	PRO+	BR/A	SB	CS	SBR	FA	FR	G/POS	TPR
1880	Buf-N	27	100	12	33	5	1	0	14	6	9	.330	.368	.400	157	6				.862	-6	S-27	0.1
1881	Cle-N	33	135	12	31	5	1	0	8	3	14	.230	.246	.281	69	-5				.883	-2	O-32/3-1	-0.7
	Det-N	1	4	1	1	0	0	0	0	0	1	.250	.250	.250	55	-0				.857	1	/3-1	0.0
	Yr	34	139	13	32	5	1	0	8	3	15	.230	.246	.281	69	-5				.883	-2	O-32/3-2	-0.7

YEAR	TM/L	G	AB	R	H	2B	3B	HR	RBI	BB	SO	AVG	OBP	SLG	PRO+	BR/A	SB	CS	SBR	FA	FR	G/POS	TPR
1883	Phi-a	95	400	90	124	18	10	1	67	31		.310	.360	.412	137	15				.833	0	*S-95	1.5
1884	Phi-a	1	4	0	0	0	0	0		0		.000	.000	.000	-94	-1				.000	-0	/O-1	-0.1
	Cle-N	12	45	9	13	2	1	0	6	7	11	.289	.385	.378	136	2				.852	-0	/2-6,S-3,O-3	0.2
Total	4	169	688	124	202	30	13	1	95	47	35	.294	.339	.379	126	17				.837	-9	S-125/O-36,2-6,3-2	1.0

■ HEINIE MUELLER

Mueller, Clarence Francis b: 9/16/1899, Creve Coeur, Mo. d: 1/23/75, DeSoto, Mo. BL/TL, 5'8", 158 lbs. Deb: 9/25/20

YEAR	TM/L	G	AB	R	H	2B	3B	HR	RBI	BB	SO	AVG	OBP	SLG	PRO+	BR/A	SB	CS	SBR	FA	FR	G/POS	TPR
1920	StL-N	4	22	0	7	1	0	0	1	2	4	.318	.375	.364	117	1	1	0	0	1.000	0	/O-4	0.1
1921	StL-N	55	176	25	62	10	6	1	34	11	22	.352	.397	.494	137	9	2	4	-2	.976	-3	O-54	0.1
1922	StL-N	61	159	20	43	7	2	3	26	14	18	.270	.329	.396	91	-3	2	1	0	.947	-3	O-44	-0.8
1923	StL-N	78	265	39	91	16	9	5	41	18	16	.343	.392	.528	144	16	4	3	-1	.963	2	O-74	1.2
1924	StL-N	92	296	39	78	12	6	2	37	19	16	.264	.312	.365	82	-8	8	7	-2	.962	-2	O-53,1-27	-1.7
1925	StL-N	78	243	33	76	16	4	1	26	17	11	.313	.365	.424	99	-0	0	3	-2	.955	-3	O-72	-0.9
1926	StL-N	52	191	36	51	7	5	3	28	11	6	.267	.330	.403	93	-2	8			.950	-1	O-51	-0.6
	NY-N	85	305	36	76	6	2	4	29	21	17	.249	.300	.321	68	-14	7			.950	5	O-82	-1.5
	Yr	137	496	72	127	13	7	7	57	32	23	.256	.312	.353	78	-16	15			.950	4	*O-133	-2.1
1927	NY-N	84	190	33	55	6	1	3	19	25	12	.289	.384	.379	105	2	2			.944	-7	O-56/1-1	-0.7
1928	Bos-N	42	151	25	34	3	1	0	19	17	9	.225	.316	.258	54	-10	1			.985	6	O-41	-0.6
1929	Bos-N	46	93	10	19	2	1	0	11	12	12	.204	.302	.247	39	-9	2			1.000	-4	O-24	-1.3
1935	StL-A	16	27	0	5	1	0	0	1	1	4	.185	.214	.222	12	-4	0	0	0	.955	-1	/1-3,O-2	-0.4
Total	11	693	2118	296	597	87	37	22	272	168	147	.282	.342	.389	94	-20	37	18		.960	-11	O-557/1-31	-7.1

■ DON MUELLER

Mueller, Donald Frederick "Mandrake The Magician" b: 4/14/27, St.Louis, Mo. BL/TR, 6', 185 lbs. Deb: 8/2/48 F

YEAR	TM/L	G	AB	R	H	2B	3B	HR	RBI	BB	SO	AVG	OBP	SLG	PRO+	BR/A	SB	CS	SBR	FA	FR	G/POS	TPR
1948	NY-N	36	81	12	29	4	1	1	9	0	3	.358	.358	.469	121	2	0			.973	-1	O-22	0.0
1949	NY-N	51	56	5	13	4	0	0	1	5	6	.232	.295	.304	61	-3	0			1.000	-1	/O-6	-0.4
1950	NY-N	132	525	60	153	15	6	7	84	10	26	.291	.309	.383	80	-16	1			.986	-5	*O-125	-2.5
1951	NY-N	122	469	58	130	10	7	16	69	19	13	.277	.307	.431	95	-5	1	1	-0	.983	-2	*O-115	-1.1
1952	NY-N	126	456	61	128	14	7	12	49	34	24	.281	.333	.421	107	4	2	1	0	.987	-1	*O-120	-0.2
1953	NY-N	131	480	56	160	12	2	6	60	19	13	.333	.360	.404	97	-2	2	0	1	.972	-4	*O-122	-1.0
1954	*NY-N★	153	619	90	**212**	35	8	4	71	22	17	.342	.367	.444	110	8	2	3	-1	.979	-0	*O-153	0.0
1955	NY-N★	147	605	67	185	21	4	8	83	19	12	.306	.330	.393	91	-8	1	2	-1	.976	-11	*O-146	-2.7
1956	NY-N	138	453	38	122	12	1	5	41	15	7	.269	.293	.333	68	-20	0	1	-1	.989	-9	*O-117	-3.7
1957	NY-N	135	450	45	116	7	1	6	37	13	16	.258	.280	.318	60	-25	2	0	1	.989	-1	*O-115	-3.3
1958	Chi-A	70	166	7	42	5	0	0	16	11	9	.253	.299	.283	62	-8	0	0	0	.968	-5	O-43	-1.6
1959	Chi-A	4	4	0	2	0	0	0	0	0	0	.500	.500	.500	178	0	0	0	0	.000	0	H	0.0
Total	12	1245	4364	499	1292	139	37	65	520	167	146	.296	.324	.390	89	-74	11	8		.982	-38	*O-1084	-16.5

■ HEINIE MUELLER

Mueller, Emmett Jerome b: 7/20/12, St.Louis, Mo. d: 10/3/86, Orlando, Fla. BB/TR, 5'6", 167 lbs. Deb: 4/19/38

YEAR	TM/L	G	AB	R	H	2B	3B	HR	RBI	BB	SO	AVG	OBP	SLG	PRO+	BR/A	SB	CS	SBR	FA	FR	G/POS	TPR
1938	Phi-N	136	444	53	111	12	4	4	34	64	43	.250	.346	.322	87	-6	2			.967	-27	*2-111,3-21	-2.7
1939	Phi-N	115	341	46	95	19	4	9	43	33	34	.279	.342	.437	111	5	4			.964	-14	2-51,3-17,O-17,/S-1	-0.6
1940	Phi-N	97	263	24	65	13	2	3	28	37	23	.247	.344	.346	95	-1	2			.966	-9	2-34,O-31,3-13,/1-2	-0.9
1941	Phi-N	93	233	21	53	11	1	1	22	22	24	.227	.302	.296	72	-9	2			.980	-4	2-29,O-21,3-19	-1.2
Total	4	441	1281	144	324	55	11	17	127	156	124	.253	.337	.353	93	-11	10			.968	-54	2-225/3-70,O-69,1S	-5.4

■ RAY MUELLER

Mueller, Ray Coleman "Iron Man" b: 3/8/12, Pittsburg, Kan. d: 6/29/94, Lower Paxton Township, Pa. BR/TR, 5'9", 175 lbs. Deb: 5/11/35 C

YEAR	TM/L	G	AB	R	H	2B	3B	HR	RBI	BB	SO	AVG	OBP	SLG	PRO+	BR/A	SB	CS	SBR	FA	FR	G/POS	TPR
1935	Bos-N	42	97	10	22	5	0	3	11	3	11	.227	.250	.371	70	-5	0			.978	-2	C-40	-0.5
1936	Bos-N	24	71	5	14	4	0	0	5	5	17	.197	.250	.254	38	-6	0			.986	-4	C-23	-0.9
1937	Bos-N	64	187	21	47	9	2	2	26	18	36	.251	.317	.353	90	-3	1			.995	2	C-57	0.2
1938	Bos-N	83	274	23	65	8	6	4	35	16	28	.237	.282	.354	82	-8	3			.993	-2	C-75	-0.7
1939	Pit-N	86	180	14	42	8	1	2	18	14	22	.233	.289	.322	65	-9	0			.971	-3	C-81	-0.9
1940	Pit-N	4	3	1	1	0	0	0	1	2	0	.333	.600	.333	165	1	0			1.000	1	/C-4	0.1
1943	Cin-N	141	427	50	111	19	4	8	52	56	42	.260	.347	.379	111	7	1			.988	20	*C-140	3.8
1944	Cin-N★	155	555	54	159	24	4	10	73	53	47	.286	.353	.398	115	11	4			.983	-5	*C-155	1.6
1946	Cin-N	114	378	35	96	18	4	8	48	27	37	.254	.309	.386	100	-2	0			**.994**	10	*C-100	1.4
1947	Cin-N	71	192	17	48	11	0	6	33	16	25	.250	.311	.401	88	-4	1			.984	-1	C-55	-0.2
1948	Cin-N	14	34	2	7	1	0	0	2	4	3	.206	.289	.235	45	-3	0			.982	1	C-10	-0.1
1949	Cin-N	32	106	7	29	4	0	1	13	5	13	.274	.319	.340	76	-4	1			1.000	-3	C-31	-0.4
	NY-N	56	170	17	38	2	2	5	23	13	14	.224	.279	.347	67	-8	1			.982	1	C-56	-0.5
	Yr	88	276	24	67	6	2	6	36	18	27	.243	.294	.344	70	-12	2			.988	-2	C-87	-0.9
1950	NY-N	4	11	0	1	1	0	0	0	0	2	.091	.091	.182	-30	-2	0			1.000	2	/C-4	0.0
	Pit-N	67	156	17	42	7	0	6	24	11	14	.269	.321	.429	92	-2	2			.996	2	C-63	0.2
	Yr	71	167	17	43	8	0	6	24	11	16	.257	.307	.413	85	-4	2			.996	4	C-67	0.2
1951	Bos-N	28	70	8	11	2	0	1	9	7	11	.157	.234	.229	27	-7	0	0	0	1.000	3	C-23	-0.4
Total	14	985	2911	281	733	123	23	56	373	250	322	.252	.314	.368	91	-44	14	0		.988	21	C-917	2.7

■ WALTER MUELLER

Mueller, Walter John b: 12/6/1894, Central, Mo. d: 8/16/71, St.Louis, Mo. BR/TR, 5'8", 160 lbs. Deb: 5/7/22 F

YEAR	TM/L	G	AB	R	H	2B	3B	HR	RBI	BB	SO	AVG	OBP	SLG	PRO+	BR/A	SB	CS	SBR	FA	FR	G/POS	TPR
1922	Pit-N	32	122	21	33	5	1	2	18	5	7	.270	.305	.377	74	-5	1	0	0	.976	6	O-31	-0.1
1923	Pit-N	40	111	11	34	4	4	0	20	4	6	.306	.336	.414	95	-1	2	2	-1	.941	1	O-26	-0.2
1924	Pit-N	30	50	6	13	1	1	0	8	4	4	.260	.327	.320	73	-2	1	0	0	1.000	-1	O-15	-0.3
1926	Pit-N	19	62	8	15	0	1	0	3	0	2	.242	.242	.274	37	-5	0			.969	0	O-15	-0.6
Total	4	121	345	46	95	10	7	2	49	13	19	.275	.307	.362	74	-13	4	2		.966	7	/O-87	-1.2

■ BILL MUELLER

Mueller, William Lawrence "Hawk" b: 11/9/20, Bay City, Mich. BR/TR, 6'1.5", 180 lbs. Deb: 8/29/42

YEAR	TM/L	G	AB	R	H	2B	3B	HR	RBI	BB	SO	AVG	OBP	SLG	PRO+	BR/A	SB	CS	SBR	FA	FR	G/POS	TPR
1942	Chi-A	26	85	5	14	1	0	0	5	12	9	.165	.276	.176	29	-8	2	1	0	.978	7	O-26	-0.2
1945	Chi-A	13	9	3	0	0	0	0	0	2	1	.000	.182	.000	-47	-2	1	0	0	.778	-3	/O-7	-0.4
Total	2	39	94	8	14	1	0	0	5	14	10	.149	.266	.160	22	-9	3	1	0	.960	4	/O-33	-0.6

■ BILL MUELLER

Mueller, William Richard b: 3/17/71, Maryland Heights, Mo. BB/TR, 5'11", 175 lbs. Deb: 4/18/96

YEAR	TM/L	G	AB	R	H	2B	3B	HR	RBI	BB	SO	AVG	OBP	SLG	PRO+	BR/A	SB	CS	SBR	FA	FR	G/POS	TPR
1996	SF-N	55	200	31	66	15	1	0	19	24	26	.330	.404	.415	121	7	0	0	0	.966	-3	3-45/2-8	0.5
1997	*SF-N	128	390	51	114	26	3	7	44	48	71	.292	.374	.428	112	8	4	3	-1	.956	8	*3-122	1.6
1998	SF-N	145	534	93	157	27	0	9	59	79	83	.294	.386	.395	107	9	3	3	-1	.952	-0	*3-137,2-10	1.0
Total	3	328	1124	175	337	68	4	16	122	151	180	.300	.385	.410	111	23	7	6	-2	.955	5	3-304/2-18	3.1

■ MIKE MULDOON

Muldoon, Michael D. b: 1858, Ireland 5'8", 165 lbs. Deb: 5/1/1882

YEAR	TM/L	G	AB	R	H	2B	3B	HR	RBI	BB	SO	AVG	OBP	SLG	PRO+	BR/A	SB	CS	SBR	FA	FR	G/POS	TPR
1882	Cle-N	84	341	50	84	17	5	6	45	10	28	.246	.268	.378	108	3				.880	3	*3-61,O-23	0.7
1883	Cle-N	98	378	54	86	22	3	0	29	10	39	.228	.247	.302	67	-15				.825	-9	*3-98/O-2	-2.2
1884	Cle-N	110	422	46	101	16	6	2	38	18	67	.239	.270	.320	82	-9				.833	-7	*3-109/O-1,2-1	-1.4
1885	Bal-a	102	410	47	103	20	6	2	52	20		.251	.293	.344	102	1				.870	-3	*3-101/2-1	0.0
1886	Bal-a	101	381	57	76	13	8	0	23	34		.199	.269	.276	72	-12	12			.912	2	2-57,3-44	-0.5
Total	5	495	1932	254	450	88	28	10	187	92	134	.233	.270	.323	86	-31	12			.846	-14	3-413/2-59,O-26	-3.4

■ TONY MULLANE

Mullane, Anthony John "Count" or "The Apollo Of The Box"
b: 1/20/1859, Cork, Ireland d: 4/25/44, Chicago, Ill. BB/TR, 5'10.5", 165 lbs. Deb: 8/27/1881

YEAR	TM/L	G	AB	R	H	2B	3B	HR	RBI	BB	SO	AVG	OBP	SLG	PRO+	BR/A	SB	CS	SBR	FA	FR	G/POS	TPR
1881	Det-N	5	19	0	5	0	0	0	1	0	0	.263	.263	.263	63	-1				.882	0	/P-5	0.0
1882	Lou-a	77	303	46	78	13	1	0		13		.257	.288	.307	107	3				.959	10	*P-55,1-13,O-12,/2	-0.1
1883	StL-a	83	307	38	69	11	6	0	33	13		.225	.256	.300	74	-9				.851	2	P-53,O-30/2-3,1-2	-0.3
1884	Tol-a	95	352	49	97	19	3	3		33		.276	.339	.372	127	11				.885	7	P-67,O-19/1-7,3S2	0.0
1886	Cin-a	91	324	59	73	12	5	0	39	25		.225	.283	.293	78	-9	20			.899	-0	P-63,O-27/1-4,3S2	-0.6
1887	Cin-a	56	199	35	44	6	3	3	23	16		.221	.292	.327	71	-8	20			.944	-2	P-48/O-9	-0.2
1888	Cin-a	51	175	27	44	4	4	1	16	8		.251	.296	.337	97	-1	12			.888	-2	P-44/1-4,O-3,2-2	-0.2
1889	Cin-a	63	196	53	58	16	4	0	29	27	21	.296	.387	.418	125	7	24			.920	-1	P-33,3-18,O-12,/1-4	0.3
1890	Cin-N	81	286	41	79	9	8	0	34	39	30	.276	.375	.364	116	7	19			.941	-2	O-28,P-25,3-21,S/1	0.3

YEAR	TM/L	G	AB	R	H	2B	3B	HR	RBI	BB	SO	AVG	OBP	SLG	PRO+	BR/A	SB	CS	SBR	FA	FR	G/POS	TPR
1891	Cin-N	64	209	16	31	1	2	0	10	18	33	.148	.229	.172	17	-22	4			.958	-3	P-51,O-12/3-4	-0.6
1892	Cin-N	39	118	14	20	3	1	0	9	9	8	.169	.246	.212	39	-9	4			.926	5	P-37/1-2	0.0
1893	Cin-N	16	52	11	15	0	0	1	6	5	3	.288	.383	.346	92	-0	1			.939	0	P-15/3-1	0.0
	Bal-N	38	114	15	26	2	1	0	14	5	14	.228	.261	.263	39	-10	5			.943	2	P-34/O-2,1-1	-0.1
	Yr	54	166	26	41	2	1	1	20	10	17	.247	.302	.289	56	-11	6			.942	2	P-49/O-2,3-1,1-1	-0.1
1894	Bal-N	21	53	3	21	3	0	0	9	6	3	.396	.475	.453	120	2	2			.889	-1	P-21	0.0
	Cle-N	4	13	0	1	0	0	0	0	4	2	.077	.294	.077	-6	-2	1			.944	2	/P-4	0.0
	Yr	25	66	3	22	3	0	0	9	10	5	.333	.436	.379	94	-0	3			.911	1	P-25	0.0
Total	13	784	2720	407	661	99	38	8	223	221	114	.243	.307	.316	87	-42	112			.918	18	P-555,O-154/31S2	-1.5
■ **GREG MULLEAVY**	Mulleavy, Gregory Thomas "Moe" b: 9/25/05, Detroit, Mich. d: 2/1/80, Arcadia, Cal. BR/TR, 5'9", 167 lbs. Deb: 7/4/30 C																						
1930	Chi-A	77	289	27	76	14	5	0	28	20	23	.263	.311	.346	69	-14	5	2	0	.918	-5	S-73	-0.9
1932	Chi-A	1	3	0	0	0	0	0	0	0	0	.000	.000	.000	-99	-1	0	0	0	1.000	0	/2-1	-0.1
1933	Bos-A	1	0	1	0	0	0	0	0	0	0	—	—	—	—	0	0	0	0	.000	0	R	0.0
Total	3	79	292	28	76	14	5	0	28	20	23	.260	.308	.342	67	-15	5	2	0	.918	-5	/S-73,2-1	-1.0
■ **MULLEN**	Mullen Deb: 8/17/1872																						
1872	Cle-n	1	4	1	0	0	0	0	0	0	0	.000	.000	.000	-99	-1	0	0	0	.400	-0	/O-1	-0.1
■ **CHARLIE MULLEN**	Mullen, Charles George b: 3/15/1889, Seattle, Wash. d: 6/6/63, Seattle, Wash. BR/TR, 5'10.5", 155 lbs. Deb: 5/18/10																						
1910	Chi-A	41	123	15	24	2	1	0	13	4		.195	.220	.228	42	-8	4			.982	1	1-37/O-2	-0.9
1911	Chi-A	20	59	7	12	2	1	0	5	5		.203	.266	.271	51	-4	1			.969	0	1-20	-0.4
1914	NY-A	93	323	33	84	8	0	0	44	33	55	.260	.332	.285	86	-5	11	17	-7	.994	3	1-93	-1.2
1915	NY-A	40	90	11	24	1	0	0	7	10	12	.267	.340	.278	85	-1	5	2	0	.982	1	1-27	-0.1
1916	NY-A	59	146	11	39	9	1	0	18	9	13	.267	.310	.342	94	-2	7			.943	-4	2-20,1-17/O-6	-0.7
Total	5	253	741	77	183	22	3	0	87	61	80	.247	.306	.285	78	-20	28	19		.988	0	1-194/2-20,O-8	-3.3
■ **MOON MULLEN**	Mullen, Ford Parker b: 2/9/17, Olympia, Wash. BL/TR, 5'9", 165 lbs. Deb: 4/18/44																						
1944	Phi-N	118	464	51	124	9	4	0	31	28	32	.267	.315	.304	77	-14	4			.963	-7	*2-114/3-1	-1.5
■ **JOHN MULLEN**	Mullen, John b: Philadelphia, Pa. BL/TL, Deb: 9/9/1876																						
1876	Phi-N	1	3	0	0	0	0	0	0	0	0	.000	.000	.000	-99	-1				.714	0	/C-1	0.0
■ **BILLY MULLEN**	Mullen, William John b: 1/23/1896, St.Louis, Mo. d: 5/4/71, St.Louis, Mo. BR/TR, 5'8", 160 lbs. Deb: 10/2/20																						
1920	StL-A	2	4	0	0	0	0	0	0	0	0	.000	.000	.000	-97	-1	0	0	0	1.000	-1	/2-1	-0.2
1921	StL-A	4	4	0	0	0	0	0	0	2	1	.000	.333	.000	-8	-1	0	0	0	1.000	0	/3-2	0.0
1923	Bro-N	4	11	1	3	0	0	0	0	0	0	.273	.273	.273	46	-1	0	0	0	.875	-0	/3-4	-0.1
1926	Det-A	11	13	2	1	0	0	0	0	5	1	.077	.333	.077	11	-1	1	0	0	.875	-0	/3-9	-0.1
1928	StL-A	15	18	2	7	1	0	0	2	3	4	.389	.476	.444	139	1	0	0	0	.867	1	/3-6	0.2
Total	5	36	50	5	11	1	0	0	2	10	6	.220	.350	.240	56	-3	1	0	0	.884	-1	/3-21,2-1	-0.2
■ **FREDDIE MULLER**	Muller, Frederick William b: 12/21/07, Newark, Cal. d: 10/20/76, Davis, Cal. BR/TR, 5'10", 170 lbs. Deb: 7/8/33																						
1933	Bos-A	15	48	6	9	1	1	0	3	5	5	.188	.264	.250	37	-4	1	0	0	.923	-4	2-14	-0.7
1934	Bos-A	2	1	1	0	0	0	0	0	1	0	.000	.500	.000	36	-0	0	0	0	.800	-0	/2-1,3-1	0.0
Total	2	17	49	7	9	1	1	0	3	6	5	.184	.273	.245	38	-4	1	0	0	.914	-5	/2-15,3-1	-0.7
■ **EDDIE MULLIGAN**	Mulligan, Edward Joseph b: 8/27/1894, St.Louis, Mo. d: 3/15/82, San Rafael, Cal. BR/TR, 5'9", 152 lbs. Deb: 9/23/15																						
1915	Chi-N	11	22	5	8	1	0	0	2	5	1	.364	.481	.409	170	2	2	2	-1	.907	3	S-10/3-1	0.5
1916	Chi-N	58	189	13	29	3	4	0	9	8	30	.153	.200	.212	24	-17	1			.888	3	S-58	-1.2
1921	Chi-A	151	609	82	153	21	12	1	45	32	53	.251	.293	.330	59	-38	13	18	-7	.955	-13	*3-151/S-1	-4.6
1922	Chi-A	103	372	39	87	14	8	0	31	22	32	.234	.278	.315	55	-26	7	7	-2	.971	4	3-84/S-7	-1.6
1928	Pit-N	27	43	4	10	2	0	0	1	3	4	.233	.283	.279	45	-3	0			.929	0	/3-6,2-4	-0.3
Total	5	350	1235	143	287	41	24	1	88	70	120	.232	.278	.307	54	-82	23	27		.961	-3	3-242/S-76,2-4	-7.2
■ **JOHN MULLIGAN**	Mulligan, John Deb: 6/14/1884																						
1884	Was-U	1	4	2	1	0	0	0		0		.250	.250	.250	54	-0				1.000	1	/3-1	0.1
■ **SEAN MULLIGAN**	Mulligan, Sean Patrick b: 4/25/70, Lynwood, Cal. BR/TR, 6'2", 205 lbs. Deb: 9/1/96																						
1996	SD-N	2	1	0	0	0	0	0	0	0	0	.000	.000	.000	-99	-0	0	0	0	.000	0	/H	0.0
■ **GEORGE MULLIN**	Mullin, George Joseph "Wabash George" b: 7/4/1880, Toledo, Ohio d: 1/7/44, Wabash, Ind. BR/TR, 5'11", 188 lbs. Deb: 5/4/02																						
1902	Det-A	40	120	20	39	4	3	0	11	8		.325	.367	.408	113	2	1			.921	1	P-35/O-4	-0.1
1903	Det-A	46	126	11	35	9	1	1	12	2		.278	.295	.389	107	1	1			.936	5	P-41/O-1	0.0
1904	Det-A	53	155	14	45	10	2	0	8	10		.290	.337	.381	131	5	1			.936	7	P-45/O-2	-0.1
1905	Det-A	47	135	15	35	4	0	0	12	12		.259	.320	.289	93	-1	4			.962	7	P-44/O-1	0.0
1906	Det-A	50	142	13	32	6	4	0	6	4		.225	.247	.324	76	-4	2			.957	2	P-40/2-1,O-1	-0.1
1907	*Det-A	70	157	16	34	5	3	0	13	12		.217	.276	.287	77	-4	2			.961	4	P-46/1-1	0.0
1908	*Det-A	55	125	13	32	2	2	1	8	7		.256	.306	.328	102	0	2			.961	3	P-39	0.0
1909	*Det-A	53	126	13	27	7	0	0	17	13		.214	.288	.270	73	-4	2			.973	0	P-40/O-2	-0.1
1910	Det-A	50	129	15	33	6	2	1	11	8		.256	.299	.357	99	-1	1			.944	-0	P-38/O-2	-0.1
1911	Det-A	40	98	4	28	7	2	0	5	10		.286	.352	.398	104	0	1			.941	-2	P-30	0.0
1912	Det-A	38	90	13	25	5	1	0	12	17		.278	.393	.356	118	3	0			.929	0	P-30	0.0
1913	Det-A	12	20	1	7	0	0	0	1	4	1	.350	.458	.350	139	1	0			.952	1	/P-7	0.0
	Was-A	11	21	4	4	0	0	0	0	2	5	.190	.292	.190	41	-1	1			.958	1	P-11	0.0
	Yr	23	41	5	11	0	0	0	1	6	6	.268	.375	.268	89	-0	1			.956	1	P-18	0.0
1914	Ind-F	43	77	11	24	5	3	0	21	11	15	.312	.404	.455	121	1	0			.915	-4	P-36	0.0
1915	New-F	6	10	0	1	0	0	0	0	2	0	.100	.250	.100	0	-1	0			1.000	-1	/P-5	0.0
Total	14	614	1531	163	401	70	23	3	137	122	21	.262	.319	.344	99	-3	18			.947	24	P-487/O-13,1-1,2-1	-0.5
■ **HENRY MULLIN**	Mullin, Henry J. b: 4/1862, St.John, N.B., Canada d: 11/8/27, Beverly, Mass. BR , 5'9", 160 lbs. Deb: 6/4/1884																						
1884	Was-a	34	120	13	17	3	1	0		8		.142	.195	.183	27	-9				.869	-1	O-34/3-1	-0.9
	Bos-U	2	8	1	0	0	0	0		0		.000	.000	.000	-99	-2				1.000	3	/O-2	0.0
Total	1	36	128	14	17	3	1	0		8		.133	.184	.172	18	-11				.882	2	/O-36,3-1	-0.9
■ **JIM MULLIN**	Mullin, James Henry b: 10/16/1883, New York, N.Y. d: 1/24/25, Philadelphia, Pa. BR/TR, 5'10", 173 lbs. Deb: 6/1/04																						
1904	Phi-A	22	52	5	14	1	0	1	5	3		.269	.321	.346	106	0	2			.985	-5	/1-7,2-5,S-2,O-1	-0.6
	Was-A	27	102	10	19	2	2	0	4	4		.186	.224	.245	49	-6	3			.981	6	2-27	0.1
	Phi-A	19	58	4	10	0	0	0	4	2		.172	.238	.172	29	-4	2			.984	-1	1-19	-0.6
	Yr	68	212	19	43	3	2	1	13	9		.203	.252	.250	58	-10	7			.965	-0	2-32,1-26/S-2,O-1	-1.1
1905	Was-A	50	163	18	31	7	6	0	13	5		.190	.214	.307	67	-7	5			.928	-3	2-40/1-6	-1.1
Total	2	118	375	37	74	10	8	1	26	14		.197	.236	.275	62	-17	12			.946	-4	/2-72,1-32,S-2,O-1	-2.2
■ **PAT MULLIN**	Mullin, Patrick Joseph b: 11/1/17, Trotter, Pa. BL/TR, 6'2", 190 lbs. Deb: 9/18/40 C																						
1940	Det-A	4	4	0	0	0	0	0	0	0	0	.000	.000	.000	-91	-1	0	0	0	.000	-1	/O-1	-0.2
1941	Det-A	54	220	42	76	11	5	5	23	18	18	.345	.400	.509	126	8	5	1	1	.944	-4	O-51	0.1
1946	Det-A	93	276	34	68	13	4	3	35	25	36	.246	.311	.355	81	-7	3	5	-2	.949	-3	O-75	-1.6
1947	Det-A☆	116	398	62	102	28	6	15	62	63	66	.256	.359	.470	126	13	3	8	-4	.988	8	*O-106	1.2
1948	Det-A★	138	496	91	143	16	11	23	80	77	57	.288	.385	.504	132	22	1	2	-1	.972	0	*O-131	1.3
1949	Det-A	104	310	55	83	8	6	12	59	42	29	.268	.357	.448	112	4	1	2	-1	.989	-4	O-79	-0.4
1950	Det-A	69	142	16	31	5	0	6	23	20	23	.218	.315	.380	75	-6	1	4	-2	1.000	-1	O-32	-0.9
1951	Det-A	110	295	41	83	11	6	12	51	40	38	.281	.367	.481	128	11	2	2	-1	.939	-9	O-83	-0.2
1952	Det-A	97	255	29	64	13	5	7	35	31	30	.251	.332	.424	108	2	4	2	0	.979	2	O-65	0.2

YEAR	TM/L	G	AB	R	H	2B	3B	HR	RBI	BB	SO	AVG	OBP	SLG	PRO+	BR/A	SB	CS	SBR	FA	FR	G/POS	TPR
1953	Det-A	79	97	11	26	1	0	4	17	14	15	.268	.360	.402	107	1	0	1	-1	.944	-2	O-14	-0.2
Total	10	864	2493	381	676	106	43	87	385	330	312	.271	.358	.453	115	47	20	27	-10	.970	-14	O-637	-0.7

■ RANCE MULLINIKS
Mulliniks, Steven Rance b: 1/15/56, Tulare, Cal. BL/TR, 6', 170 lbs. Deb: 6/18/77

YEAR	TM/L	G	AB	R	H	2B	3B	HR	RBI	BB	SO	AVG	OBP	SLG	PRO+	BR/A	SB	CS	SBR	FA	FR	G/POS	TPR
1977	Cal-A	78	271	36	73	13	2	3	21	23	36	.269	.329	.365	93	-3	1	1	-0	.963	2	S-77	0.7
1978	Cal-A	50	119	6	22	3	1	1	6	8	23	.185	.242	.252	41	-9	2	0	1	.953	2	S-47/D-2	-0.3
1979	Cal-A	22	68	7	10	0	0	1	8	4	14	.147	.205	.191	8	-9	0	0	0	.957	-7	S-22	-1.4
1980	KC-A	36	54	8	14	3	0	0	6	7	10	.259	.344	.315	81	-1	0	0	0	.981	2	S-18,2-14	0.3
1981	KC-A	24	44	6	10	3	0	0	5	2	7	.227	.261	.295	61	-2	0	1	-1	.900	3	2-10/S-7,3-5	0.1
1982	Tor-A	112	311	32	76	25	0	4	35	37	49	.244	.327	.363	82	-8	3	2	-0	.938	-16	*3-102,S-16	-2.5
1983	Tor-A	129	364	54	100	34	3	10	49	57	43	.275	.374	.467	122	12	0	2	-1	.971	-18	*3-116,S-15/2-2	-0.8
1984	Tor-A	125	343	41	111	21	5	3	42	33	44	.324	.385	.440	123	11	2	3	-1	**.968**	-13	*3-119/S-3,2-1	-0.4
1985	*Tor-A	129	366	55	108	26	1	10	57	55	54	.295	.387	.454	126	15	2	0	1	**.971**	-16	*3-119	-0.3
1986	Tor-A	117	348	50	90	22	0	11	45	43	60	.259	.342	.417	103	2	1	1	-0	**.975**	-1	*3-110/2-1,D-5	-0.2
1987	Tor-A	124	332	37	103	28	1	11	44	34	55	.310	.374	.500	127	13	1	1	-0	.927	-6	3-96,D-22/S-1	0.4
1988	Tor-A	119	337	49	101	21	1	12	48	56	57	.300	.399	.475	143	21	1	0	0	1.000	-0	*D-108/3-7	1.9
1989	*Tor-A	103	273	25	65	11	2	3	29	34	40	.238	.322	.326	85	-5	0	0	0	.985	1	D-73,3-29	-0.5
1990	Tor-A	57	97	11	28	4	0	2	16	22	19	.289	.420	.392	126	5	2	1	0	.949	-0	3-22,D-10/1-3	0.4
1991	*Tor-A	97	240	27	60	12	1	2	24	44	44	.250	.366	.333	92	-1	0	0	0	1.000	0	D-81/3-5	-0.4
1992	Tor-A	3	2	1	1	0	0	0	0	1	0	.500	.667	.500	221	0	0	0	0	.000	0	/D-2	0.0
Total	16	1325	3569	445	972	226	17	73	435	460	555	.272	.357	.407	107	40	15	12	-3	.961	-68	3-730,D-303,S/21	-3.0

■ FRAN MULLINS
Mullins, Francis Joseph b: 5/14/57, Oakland, Cal. BR/TR, 6', 180 lbs. Deb: 9/1/80

YEAR	TM/L	G	AB	R	H	2B	3B	HR	RBI	BB	SO	AVG	OBP	SLG	PRO+	BR/A	SB	CS	SBR	FA	FR	G/POS	TPR
1980	Chi-A	21	62	9	12	4	0	0	3	9	8	.194	.296	.258	53	-4	0	1	-1	.981	-2	3-21	-0.7
1984	SF-N	57	110	8	24	8	0	2	10	9	29	.218	.277	.345	77	-4	3	1	0	.969	9	S-28,3-28/2-4	0.8
1986	Cle-A	28	40	3	7	4	0	0	5	2	11	.175	.214	.275	33	-4	0	0	0	.953	8	2-13,S-11/1-1,D-1	0.4
Total	3	106	212	20	43	16	0	2	18	20	48	.203	.272	.307	61	-11	3	2	-0	.968	15	/3-49,S-39,2-17,D1	0.5

■ JOE MULVEY
Mulvey, Joseph H. b: 10/27/1858, Providence, R.I. d: 8/21/28, Philadelphia, Pa. BR/TR, 5'11.5", 178 lbs. Deb: 5/31/1883

YEAR	TM/L	G	AB	R	H	2B	3B	HR	RBI	BB	SO	AVG	OBP	SLG	PRO+	BR/A	SB	CS	SBR	FA	FR	G/POS	TPR
1883	Pro-N	4	16	1	2	1	0	0	2	0	1	.125	.125	.188	-6	-2				.692	-3	/S-4	-0.4
	Phi-N	3	12	2	6	1	0	0	3	0	1	.500	.500	.583	250	2				.750	-1	/3-3	0.1
	Yr	7	28	3	8	2	0	0	5	0	2	.286	.286	.357	96	-0				.692	-3	/S-4,3-3	-0.3
1884	Phi-N	100	401	47	92	11	2	2	32	4	49	.229	.237	.282	66	-15				.834	11	*3-100	-0.3
1885	Phi-N	107	443	74	119	25	6	6	64	3	18	.269	.274	.393	116	6				.848	-7	*3-107	0.1
1886	Phi-N	107	430	71	115	16	10	2	53	15	31	.267	.292	.365	98	-2	27			.879	-19	*3-107/O-1	-1.6
1887	Phi-N	111	474	93	136	21	6	2	78	21	14	.287	.321	.369	86	-10	43			.865	-15	*3-111	-2.0
1888	Phi-N	100	398	37	86	12	3	0	39	9	33	.216	.235	.261	55	-20	18			.891	-14	*3-100	-3.2
1889	Phi-N	129	544	77	157	21	9	6	77	23	25	.289	.319	.393	91	-11	23			.893	1	*3-129	-0.4
1890	Phi-P	120	519	96	149	26	16	5	87	27	36	.287	.326	.428	98	-5	20			.857	-16	*3-120	-1.3
1891	Phi-a	113	453	62	115	9	13	5	66	17	32	.254	.287	.364	84	-13	11			.894	2	*3-113	-0.5
1892	Phi-N	25	98	9	14	1	1	0	4	6	9	.143	.200	.173	13	-10	2			.883	3	3-25	-0.6
1893	Was-N	55	226	21	53	9	4	0	19	7	8	.235	.264	.310	54	-16	2			.874	5	3-55	-0.8
1895	Bro-N	13	49	8	15	4	1	0	8	2	0	.306	.333	.429	104	0	1			.917	2	3-13	0.2
Total	12	987	4063	598	1059	157	71	28	532	134	257	.261	.287	.355	84	-97	147			.871	-48	3-983/S-4,O-1	-10.7

■ JERRY MUMPHREY
Mumphrey, Jerry Wayne b: 9/9/52, Tyler, Tex. BB/TR, 6'2", 185 lbs. Deb: 9/10/74

YEAR	TM/L	G	AB	R	H	2B	3B	HR	RBI	BB	SO	AVG	OBP	SLG	PRO+	BR/A	SB	CS	SBR	FA	FR	G/POS	TPR
1974	StL-N	5	2	2	0	0	0	0	0	0	0	.000	.000	.000	-99	-1	0	0	0	.000	-0	/O-1	-0.1
1975	StL-N	11	16	2	6	2	0	0	1	4	3	.375	.500	.500	172	2	0	0	0	1.000	1	/O-3	0.2
1976	StL-N	112	384	51	99	15	5	1	26	37	53	.258	.325	.331	86	-7	22	6	3	.993	6	O-94	-0.2
1977	StL-N	145	463	73	133	20	10	2	38	47	70	.287	.354	.387	100	1	22	15	-2	.971	-2	*O-133	-0.8
1978	StL-N	125	367	41	96	13	4	2	37	30	40	.262	.319	.335	84	-8	14	10	-2	.995	8	*O-116	-2.3
1979	StL-N	124	339	53	100	10	3	3	32	26	39	.295	.345	.369	94	-2	8	11	-4	.984	-13	*O-114	-2.4
1980	SD-N	160	564	61	168	24	3	4	59	49	90	.298	.354	.372	109	7	52	5	13	.974	8	*O-153	2.3
1981	*NY-A	80	319	44	98	11	5	6	32	24	27	.307	.356	.429	127	11	14	9	-1	.966	7	O-79	1.5
1982	NY-A	123	477	76	143	24	10	9	68	50	66	.300	.366	.449	124	16	11	3	2	.986	9	*O-123	2.3
1983	NY-A	83	267	41	70	11	4	7	36	28	33	.262	.332	.412	107	3	2	3	-1	.983	7	O-83	0.6
	Hou-N	44	143	17	48	10	2	1	17	22	23	.336	.428	.455	154	11	5	0	2	.990	0	O-43	1.2
1984	Hou-N★	151	524	66	152	20	3	9	83	56	79	.290	.359	.391	119	13	15	7	0	.988	0	*O-137	1.0
1985	Hou-N	130	444	52	123	25	2	8	61	37	57	.277	.333	.396	106	3	6	7	-2	.969	-0	*O-126	-0.3
1986	Chi-N	111	309	37	94	11	2	5	32	26	45	.304	.358	.401	101	1	2	3	-1	.982	-16	O-92	-1.9
1987	Chi-N	118	309	41	103	19	2	13	44	35	47	.333	.401	.534	140	18	1	1	-0	.992	-2	O-85	1.3
1988	Chi-N	63	66	3	9	2	0	0	9	7	16	.136	.219	.167	12	-7	0	0	0	1.000	-1	/O-4	-0.9
Total	15	1585	4993	660	1442	217	55	70	575	478	688	.289	.351	.396	109	61	174	80	4	.981	-3	*O-1386	1.5

■ JOHN MUNCE
Munce, John Lewis "Big John" b: 11/18/1857, Philadelphia, Pa. d: 3/15/17, Philadelphia, Pa. 5'8.5", 160 lbs. Deb: 8/19/1884

YEAR	TM/L	G	AB	R	H	2B	3B	HR	RBI	BB	SO	AVG	OBP	SLG	PRO+	BR/A	SB	CS	SBR	FA	FR	G/POS	TPR
1884	Wil-U	7	21	1	4	0	0	0		1		.190	.227	.190	27	-2				.667	-1	/O-7	-0.3

■ JAKE MUNCH
Munch, Jacob Ferdinand b: 11/16/1890, Morton, Pa. d: 6/8/66, Lansdowne, Pa. BL/TL, 6'2.5", 170 lbs. Deb: 5/27/18

YEAR	TM/L	G	AB	R	H	2B	3B	HR	RBI	BB	SO	AVG	OBP	SLG	PRO+	BR/A	SB	CS	SBR	FA	FR	G/POS	TPR
1918	Phi-A	22	30	3	8	0	1	0	0	0	5	.267	.267	.333	80	-1	0			.667	-2	/O-3,1-2	-0.3

■ GEORGE MUNDINGER
Mundinger, George b: 11/20/1854, New Orleans, La. d: 10/12/10, Covington, La. BR/TR, 6'2", 200 lbs. Deb: 5/9/1884

YEAR	TM/L	G	AB	R	H	2B	3B	HR	RBI	BB	SO	AVG	OBP	SLG	PRO+	BR/A	SB	CS	SBR	FA	FR	G/POS	TPR
1884	Ind-a	3	8	1	2	0	0	0	3	0		.250	.250	.250	65	-0				.750	-3	/C-3	-0.3

■ BILL MUNDY
Mundy, William Edward b: 6/28/1889, Salineville, Ohio d: 9/23/58, Kalamazoo, Mich. BL/TL, 5'10", 154 lbs. Deb: 8/17/13

YEAR	TM/L	G	AB	R	H	2B	3B	HR	RBI	BB	SO	AVG	OBP	SLG	PRO+	BR/A	SB	CS	SBR	FA	FR	G/POS	TPR
1913	Bos-A	16	47	4	12	0	0	0	4	4	12	.255	.314	.255	65	-2	0			.952	-2	1-14	-0.5

■ HORATIO MUNN
Munn, Horatio Brinsmade b: 7/26/1851, Newark, N.J. d: 2/17/10, Brooklyn, N.Y. Deb: 9/6/1875

YEAR	TM/L	G	AB	R	H	2B	3B	HR	RBI	BB	SO	AVG	OBP	SLG	PRO+	BR/A	SB	CS	SBR	FA	FR	G/POS	TPR
1875	Atl-n	1	4	0	0	0	0	0	0	0	0	.000	.000	.000	-99	-1	0	0	0	.833	-0	/2-1	-0.1

■ JOSE MUNOZ
Munoz, Jose Luis b: 11/11/67, Chicago, Ill. BB/TR, 5'11", 165 lbs. Deb: 4/7/96

YEAR	TM/L	G	AB	R	H	2B	3B	HR	RBI	BB	SO	AVG	OBP	SLG	PRO+	BR/A	SB	CS	SBR	FA	FR	G/POS	TPR
1996	Chi-A	17	27	7	7	0	0	0	1	4	1	.259	.355	.259	62	-1	0	0	0	.923	-2	/2-7,S-2,3-1,O-1,D	-0.3

■ NOE MUNOZ
Munoz, Noe b: 11/11/67, Escatepec, Mexico BR/TR, 6'2", 180 lbs. Deb: 4/30/95

YEAR	TM/L	G	AB	R	H	2B	3B	HR	RBI	BB	SO	AVG	OBP	SLG	PRO+	BR/A	SB	CS	SBR	FA	FR	G/POS	TPR
1995	LA-N	2	1	0	0	0	0	0	0	0	0	.000	.000	.000	-99	-0	0	0	0	1.000	1	/C-2	0.0

■ PEDRO MUNOZ
Munoz, Pedro Javier (Gonzalez) b: 9/19/68, Ponce, P.R. BR/TR, 5'10", 207 lbs. Deb: 9/1/90

YEAR	TM/L	G	AB	R	H	2B	3B	HR	RBI	BB	SO	AVG	OBP	SLG	PRO+	BR/A	SB	CS	SBR	FA	FR	G/POS	TPR
1990	Min-A	22	85	13	23	4	1	0	5	2	16	.271	.287	.341	70	-3	3	0	1	.972	-1	O-21/D-1	-0.5
1991	Min-A	51	138	15	39	7	1	7	26	9	31	.283	.331	.500	121	3	3	0	1	.989	0	O-44/D-2	0.4
1992	Min-A	127	418	44	113	16	3	12	71	17	90	.270	.300	.409	94	-5	4	5	-2	.987	-1	*O-122/D-3	-1.0
1993	Min-A	104	326	34	76	11	1	13	38	25	97	.233	.294	.393	82	-9	1	2	-1	.983	-6	*O-102	-1.7
1994	Min-A	75	244	35	72	15	2	11	36	19	67	.295	.351	.508	118	6	0	0	0	.965	-4	O-58,D-12	0.0
1995	Min-A	104	376	45	113	17	0	18	58	19	86	.301	.339	.489	112	5	0	3	-2	.926	-4	D-77,O-25/1-3	-0.6
1996	Oak-A	34	121	17	31	5	0	6	18	9	31	.256	.308	.446	89	-2	0	0	0	1.000	-3	D-18,O-14	-0.6
Total	7	517	1708	203	467	75	8	67	252	100	418	.273	.317	.444	100	-5	11	10	-3	.980	-19	O-386,D-113/1-3	-4.0

■ RED MUNSON
Munson, Clarence Hanford b: 7/31/1883, Cincinnati, Ohio d: 2/19/57, Mishawaka, Ind. TR, Deb: 8/28/05

YEAR	TM/L	G	AB	R	H	2B	3B	HR	RBI	BB	SO	AVG	OBP	SLG	PRO+	BR/A	SB	CS	SBR	FA	FR	G/POS	TPR
1905	Phi-N	9	26	1	3	1	0	0	2	0		.115	.115	.154	-21	-4	0			.857	-1	/C-8	-0.4

■ JOE MUNSON
Munson, Joseph Martin Napoleon (b: Joseph Martin Napoleon Carlson)
b: 11/6/1899, Renovo, Pa. d: 2/24/91, Drexel Hill, Pa. BL/TR, 5'9", 184 lbs. Deb: 9/18/25

YEAR	TM/L	G	AB	R	H	2B	3B	HR	RBI	BB	SO	AVG	OBP	SLG	PRO+	BR/A	SB	CS	SBR	FA	FR	G/POS	TPR
1925	Chi-N	9	35	5	13	3	1	0	3	3	1	.371	.436	.514	140	2	1	1	-0	1.000	-0	/O-9	0.1
1926	Chi-N	33	101	17	26	2	2	3	15	8	4	.257	.318	.406	93	-1	0			.898	-2	O-28	-0.5
Total	2	42	136	22	39	5	3	3	18	11	5	.287	.349	.434	105	1	1	1		.922	-2	/O-37	-0.4

■ THURMAN MUNSON
Munson, Thurman Lee b: 6/7/47, Akron, Ohio d: 8/2/79, Canton, Ohio BR/TR, 5′11″, 191 lbs. Deb: 8/8/69

YEAR	TM/L	G	AB	R	H	2B	3B	HR	RBI	BB	SO	AVG	OBP	SLG	PRO+	BR/A	SB	CS	SBR	FA	FR	G/POS	TPR
1969	NY-A	26	86	6	22	1	2	1	9	10	10	.256	.333	.349	94	-1	0	1	-1	.986	-1	C-25	-0.1
1970	NY-A	132	453	59	137	25	4	6	53	57	56	.302	.389	.415	128	19	5	7	-3	.989	6	*C-125	3.0
1971	NY-A★	125	451	71	113	15	4	10	42	52	65	.251	.337	.368	106	4	6	5	-1	**.998**	-1	*C-117/O-1	0.6
1972	NY-A	140	511	54	143	16	3	7	46	47	58	.280	.344	.364	115	9	6	7	-2	.977	-5	*C-132	0.9
1973	NY-A★	147	519	80	156	29	4	20	74	48	64	.301	.364	.487	143	28	4	6	-2	.984	6	*C-142/D-1	3.8
1974	NY-A★	144	517	64	135	19	2	13	60	44	66	.261	.320	.381	103	1	2	0	1	.974	2	*C-137/D-4	1.0
1975	NY-A★	157	597	83	190	24	3	12	102	45	52	.318	.372	.429	128	22	3	2	-0	.972	9	*C-130,D-22/1-2,O3	3.6
1976	*NY-A★	152	616	79	186	27	1	17	105	29	38	.302	.343	.432	127	19	14	11	-2	.981	-6	*C-121,D-21,O-11	1.4
1977	*NY-A★	149	595	85	183	28	5	18	100	39	55	.308	.352	.462	121	16	5	6	-2	.984	-5	*C-136,D-10	1.3
1978	*NY-A†	154	617	73	183	27	1	6	71	35	70	.297	.337	.373	102	1	2	3	-1	.986	-0	*C-125,D-14,O-13	0.2
1979	NY-A	97	382	42	110	18	3	3	39	32	37	.288	.343	.374	95	-2	1	2	-1	.978	-6	C-88/1-3,D-5	-0.5
Total	11	1423	5344	696	1558	229	32	113	701	438	571	.292	.350	.410	117	117	48	50	-16	.982	-1	*C-1278/D-77,O13	15.2

■ JOHN MUNYAN
Munyan, John B. b: 11/14/1860, Chester, Pa. d: 2/18/45, Endicott, N.Y. Deb: 7/12/1887

YEAR	TM/L	G	AB	R	H	2B	3B	HR	RBI	BB	SO	AVG	OBP	SLG	PRO+	BR/A	SB	CS	SBR	FA	FR	G/POS	TPR
1887	Cle-a	16	58	9	14	1	1	0	6	3		.241	.279	.293	61	-3	4			.762	-2	O-12/C-3,3-2	-0.4
1890	Col-a	2	7	1	1	0	0	0	0	0		.143	.250	.143	17	-1	0			.667	0	/O-2	-0.1
	StL-a	96	342	61	91	15	7	4	42	32		.266	.341	.386	100	-3	11			.939	-3	C-83/O-7,2-5,3-3,S	0.1
	Yr	98	349	62	92	15	7	4	42	32		.264	.339	.381	99	-4	11			.939	-3	C-83/O-9,2-5,3-3,S	0.0
1891	StL-a	62	182	44	42	4	3	0	20	43	39	.231	.389	.286	81	-4	13			.943	-6	C-45,O-12/S-5,3-3	-0.6
Total	3	176	589	115	148	20	11	4	68	78	39	.251	.351	.343	90	-11	28			.937	-10	C-131/O-33,3-8,S2	-1.0

■ BOBBY MURCER
Murcer, Bobby Ray b: 5/20/46, Oklahoma City, Okla BL/TR, 5′11″, 180 lbs. Deb: 9/8/65

YEAR	TM/L	G	AB	R	H	2B	3B	HR	RBI	BB	SO	AVG	OBP	SLG	PRO+	BR/A	SB	CS	SBR	FA	FR	G/POS	TPR
1965	NY-A	11	37	2	9	0	1	1	4	5	12	.243	.333	.378	102	0	0	0	0	.932	7	S-11	0.8
1966	NY-A	21	69	3	12	1	1	0	5	4	5	.174	.219	.217	27	-7	2	2	-1	.931	-4	S-18	-1.0
1969	NY-A	152	564	82	146	24	4	26	82	50	103	.259	.323	.454	120	12	7	5	-1	.964	-5	*O-118,3-31	-0.1
1970	NY-A	159	581	95	146	23	3	23	78	87	100	.251	.351	.420	118	14	15	10	-2	.992	10	*O-155	1.5
1971	NY-A★	146	529	94	175	25	6	25	94	91	60	.331	**.429**	.543	**185**	**61**	14	8	-1	.985	-1	*O-143	**5.5**
1972	NY-A★	153	585	**102**	171	30	7	33	96	63	67	.292	.363	.537	171	49	11	9	-2	.992	10	*O-151	**5.5**
1973	NY-A★	160	616	83	187	29	2	22	95	50	67	.304	.359	.464	135	27	6	7	-2	.985	2	*O-160	1.9
1974	NY-A★	156	606	69	166	25	4	10	88	57	59	.274	.338	.378	108	6	14	5	1	.978	0	*O-156	0.1
1975	SF-N★	147	526	80	157	29	4	11	91	91	45	.298	.404	.432	127	22	9	5	-0	.981	-8	*O-144	0.9
1976	SF-N	147	533	73	138	20	2	23	90	84	78	.259	.364	.433	122	17	12	7	-1	.961	-0	*O-146	1.0
1977	Chi-N	154	554	90	147	18	3	27	89	80	77	.265	.361	.455	106	5	16	7	1	.980	-4	*O-150/2-1,S-1	-0.5
1978	Chi-N	146	499	66	140	22	6	9	64	80	57	.281	.380	.403	106	6	14	5	1	.979	-17	*O-138	-1.6
1979	Chi-N	58	190	22	49	4	1	7	22	36	20	.258	.379	.400	103	2	2	3	-1	1.000	3	O-54	0.1
	NY-A	74	264	42	72	12	0	8	33	25	32	.273	.340	.409	103	1	1	1	-0	.983	-4	O-70	-0.6
1980	*NY-A	100	297	41	80	9	1	13	57	34	28	.269	.348	.438	116	7	2	0	1	.955	-9	O-59,D-33	-0.5
1981	*NY-A	50	117	14	31	6	0	6	24	12	15	.265	.333	.470	131	4	0	0	0	.000	0	D-33	0.3
1982	NY-A	65	141	12	32	6	0	7	30	12	15	.227	.292	.418	94	-2	2	1	0	.000	0	D-47	-0.3
1983	NY-A	9	22	2	4	2	0	1	1	1	1	.182	.217	.409	71	-1	0	0	0	.000	0	/D-5	-0.1
Total	17	1908	6730	972	1862	285	45	252	1043	862	841	.277	.361	.445	124	223	127	75	-7	.981	-19	*O-1644,D-118/3S2	12.9

■ SIMMY MURCH
Murch, Simeon Augustus b: 11/21/1880, Castine, Me. d: 6/6/39, Exeter, N.H. BR/TR, 6′4″, 220 lbs. Deb: 9/20/04

YEAR	TM/L	G	AB	R	H	2B	3B	HR	RBI	BB	SO	AVG	OBP	SLG	PRO+	BR/A	SB	CS	SBR	FA	FR	G/POS	TPR
1904	StL-N	13	51	3	7	1	0	0	1	1		.137	.154	.157	-4	-6	0			.905	-3	/2-6,3-6,S-1	-0.9
1905	StL-N	4	9	0	1	0	0	0	0	0		.111	.111	.111	-35	-1	0			.750	-3	/2-2,S-1	-0.5
1908	Bro-N	6	11	1	2	1	0	0	0	1		.182	.250	.273	70	-0	0			.964	-1	/1-2	-0.1
Total	3	23	71	4	10	2	0	0	1	2		.141	.164	.169	3	-8	0			.880	-6	/2-8,3-6,1-2,S-2	-1.5

■ WILBUR MURDOCH
Murdoch, Wilbur Edwin b: 3/14/1875, Avon, N.Y. d: 10/29/41, Los Angeles, Cal. Deb: 8/29/08

YEAR	TM/L	G	AB	R	H	2B	3B	HR	RBI	BB	SO	AVG	OBP	SLG	PRO+	BR/A	SB	CS	SBR	FA	FR	G/POS	TPR
1908	StL-N	27	62	5	16	3	0	0	5	3		.258	.292	.306	96	-0	4			.913	-5	O-16	-0.6

■ TIM MURNANE
Murnane, Timothy Hayes b: 6/4/1852, Naugatuck, Conn. d: 2/7/17, Boston, Mass. BL/TR, 5′9.5″, 172 lbs. Deb: 4/26/1872 M

YEAR	TM/L	G	AB	R	H	2B	3B	HR	RBI	BB	SO	AVG	OBP	SLG	PRO+	BR/A	SB	CS	SBR	FA	FR	G/POS	TPR
1872	Man-n	24	117	30	42	1	0	0	13	0	1	.359	.359	.368	131	5	1	0	0	.883	-5	1-24	0.1
1873	Ath-n	41	176	53	39	3	0	1	10	8	13	.222	.255	.256	49	-12	7	2	1	.797	-4	O-30,1-10/2-6	-1.0
1874	Ath-n	21	82	11	17	2	0	0	11	1	3	.207	.217	.232	40	-6	0	1	-1	.857	-5	O-14/2-6,1-3	-0.9
1875	Phi-n	69	313	71	85	5	0	1	30	7	7	.272	.287	.297	100	-1	**30**	9	4	.918	2	1-31,O-26,2-15	0.4
1876	Bos-N	69	308	60	87	4	3	2	34	8	12	.282	.301	.334	109	3				.927	-4	*1-65/O-3,2-1	-0.2
1877	Bos-N	35	140	23	39	7	1	1	15	6	7	.279	.308	.364	107	1				.815	-1	O-30/1-5	-0.1
1878	Pro-N	49	188	35	45	6	1	0	14	8	12	.239	.270	.282	82	-3				.940	1	*1-48/O-1	-0.4
1884	Bos-U	76	311	55	73	5	2	0		22		.235	.285	.264	68	-20				.950	-5	1-63,O-16,M	-2.9
Total	4 n	155	688	165	183	11	0	2	64	16	24	.266	.283	.291	82	-14	38	12	4	.830	-13	/O-70,1-68,2-27	-1.4
Total	4	229	947	173	244	22	7	3	63	44	31	.258	.291	.305	90	-20				.938	-8	1-181/O-50,2-1	-3.6

■ MURPHY
Murphy Deb: 8/16/1884

YEAR	TM/L	G	AB	R	H	2B	3B	HR	RBI	BB	SO	AVG	OBP	SLG	PRO+	BR/A	SB	CS	SBR	FA	FR	G/POS	TPR
1884	Bos-U	1	3	0	0	0	0	0		1		.000	.250	.000	-18	-1				.333	-3	/C-1,O-1	-0.3

■ CLARENCE MURPHY
Murphy, Clarence Deb: 6/17/1886

YEAR	TM/L	G	AB	R	H	2B	3B	HR	RBI	BB	SO	AVG	OBP	SLG	PRO+	BR/A	SB	CS	SBR	FA	FR	G/POS	TPR
1886	Lou-a	1	3	0	0	0	0	0	0	0		.000	.000	.000	-95	-1	0			1.000	0	/O-1	-0.1

■ CONNIE MURPHY
Murphy, Cornelius David "Stone Face" b: 11/1/1870, Northfield, Mass. d: 12/14/45, New Bedford, Mass. BL/TR, 5′8″, 155 lbs. Deb: 9/17/1893

YEAR	TM/L	G	AB	R	H	2B	3B	HR	RBI	BB	SO	AVG	OBP	SLG	PRO+	BR/A	SB	CS	SBR	FA	FR	G/POS	TPR
1893	Cin-N	6	17	3	3	1	0	0	2	1	2	.176	.222	.235	21	-2	0			.917	-2	/C-4	-0.3
1894	Cin-N	1	4	0	0	0	0	0	0	1	1	.000	.200	.000	-46	-1	0			.500	-1	/C-1	-0.2
Total	2	7	21	3	3	1	0	0	2	2	3	.143	.217	.190	6	-3	0			.857	-3	/C-5	-0.5

■ DALE MURPHY
Murphy, Dale Bryan b: 3/12/56, Portland, Ore. BR/TR, 6′5″, 215 lbs. Deb: 9/13/76

YEAR	TM/L	G	AB	R	H	2B	3B	HR	RBI	BB	SO	AVG	OBP	SLG	PRO+	BR/A	SB	CS	SBR	FA	FR	G/POS	TPR
1976	Atl-N	19	65	3	17	6	0	0	9	7	9	.262	.333	.354	89	-1	0	0	0	.974	-0	C-19	0.0
1977	Atl-N	18	76	5	24	8	1	2	14	0	8	.316	.316	.526	108	1	0	1	-1	.954	-2	C-18	-0.1
1978	Atl-N	151	530	66	120	14	3	23	79	42	145	.226	.287	.394	80	-16	11	7	-1	.984	4	*1-129,C-21	-2.2
1979	Atl-N	104	384	53	106	7	2	21	57	38	67	.276	.344	.469	111	5	6	1	1	.980	-9	1-76,C-27	-0.6
1980	Atl-N★	156	569	98	160	27	2	33	89	59	133	.281	.350	.510	133	23	9	6	-1	.985	11	*O-154/1-1	2.8
1981	Atl-N	104	369	43	91	12	1	13	50	44	72	.247	.327	.390	100	0	14	5	1	.981	4	*O-103/1-3	0.2
1982	*Atl-N★	162	598	113	168	23	2	36	**109**	93	134	.281	.380	.507	140	33	23	11	0	.979	-1	*O-162	2.9
1983	Atl-N★	162	589	131	178	24	4	36	**121**	90	110	.302	.396	**.540**	146	38	30	4	7	.985	5	*O-160	4.6
1984	Atl-N★	162	607	94	176	32	8	**36**	100	79	134	.290	.374	**.547**	145	36	19	7	2	.987	1	*O-160	3.4
1985	Atl-N★	162	616	**118**	185	32	2	**37**	111	**90**	141	.300	.390	.539	148	40	10	3	1	.980	-5	*O-161	3.3
1986	Atl-N★	160	614	89	163	29	7	29	83	75	141	.265	.347	.477	118	15	7	7	-2	.981	-4	*O-159	0.4
1987	Atl-N★	159	566	115	167	27	1	44	105	115	136	.295	.420	.580	154	47	16	6	1	.977	12	*O-159	5.4
1988	Atl-N	156	592	77	134	35	4	24	77	74	125	.226	.314	.421	104	3	3	5	-2	.992	18	*O-156	1.4
1989	Atl-N	154	574	60	131	16	0	20	84	65	142	.228	.309	.361	88	-8	3	2	-0	.985	4	*O-151	-0.9
1990	Atl-N	97	349	38	81	14	0	17	55	41	84	.232	.315	.418	94	-3	9	2	2	.981	4	O-97	0.0
	Phi-N	57	214	22	57	9	1	7	28	20	46	.266	.329	.416	104	1	0	1	-1	.992	3	O-55	0.2
	Yr	154	563	60	138	23	1	24	83	61	130	.245	.320	.417	98	-2	9	3	1	.985	7	*O-152	0.2
1991	Phi-N	153	544	66	137	33	1	18	81	48	93	.252	.313	.415	104	2	1	0	0	.983	4	*O-147	0.2
1992	Phi-N	18	62	5	10	1	0	2	7	1	13	.161	.175	.274	25	-6	0	0	0	.950	-3	O-16	-1.1
1993	Col-N	26	42	1	6	1	0	0	7	5	15	.143	.234	.167	8	-6	0	0	0	1.000	-1	O-13	-0.7
Total	18	2180	7960	1197	2111	350	39	398	1266	986	1748	.265	.348	.469	119	203	161	68	8	.983	45	*O-1853,1-209/C-85	19.2

■ DANNY MURPHY
Murphy, Daniel Francis b: 8/11/1876, Philadelphia, Pa. d: 11/22/55, Jersey City, N.J. BR/TR, 5′9″, 175 lbs. Deb: 9/17/00 C

YEAR	TM/L	G	AB	R	H	2B	3B	HR	RBI	BB	SO	AVG	OBP	SLG	PRO+	BR/A	SB	CS	SBR	FA	FR	G/POS	TPR
1900	NY-N	22	74	11	20	1	0	0	6	8		.270	.341	.284	77	-2	4			.888	-6	2-22	-0.6
1901	NY-N	5	20	0	4	0	0	0	0	1		.200	.238	.200	29	-2	0			.895	-3	/2-5	-0.4

YEAR	TM/L	G	AB	R	H	2B	3B	HR	RBI	BB	SO	AVG	OBP	SLG	PRO+	BR/A	SB	CS	SBR	FA	FR	G/POS	TPR
1902	Phi-A	76	291	48	91	11	8	1	48	13		.313	.351	.416	107	2	12			.963	-12	2-76	-0.6
1903	Phi-A	133	513	66	140	31	11	1	60	13		.273	.295	.382	97	-3	17			.949	-13	*2-133	-1.1
1904	Phi-A	150	557	78	160	30	17	7	77	22		.287	.320	.440	132	18	22			.941	13	*2-150	3.9
1905	*Phi-A	151	537	71	149	34	4	6	71	42		.277	.339	.389	129	17	23			.955	-8	*2-151	1.1
1906	Phi-A	119	448	48	135	28	6	2	60	21		.301	.341	.404	129	14	17			.955	-11	*2-119	0.4
1907	Phi-A	124	469	51	127	23	3	2	57	30		.271	.317	.345	109	4	11			.965	14	*2-122	1.8
1908	Phi-A	142	525	51	139	28	7	4	66	32		.265	.309	.368	112	5	16			.963	10	O-84,2-56/1-2	1.3
1909	Phi-A	149	541	61	152	28	14	5	69	35		.281	.332	.412	132	18	19			**.977**	-2	*O-149	1.2
1910	*Phi-A	151	560	70	168	28	18	4	64	31		.300	.338	.436	143	24	18			.974	-2	*O-151	1.7
1911	*Phi-A	141	508	104	167	27	11	6	66	50		.329	.398	.461	142	28	22			.961	6	*O-136/2-4	2.6
1912	Phi-A	36	130	27	42	6	2	2	20	16		.323	.401	.446	147	8	8			.891	-6	O-36	0.0
1913	Phi-A	40	59	3	19	5	1	0	6	4	8	.322	.365	.441	139	3	0			1.000	-2	/O-9	0.0
1914	Bro-F	52	161	16	49	9	0	4	32	17	16	.304	.374	.435	121	2	4			.986	1	O-46	0.1
1915	Bro-F	5	6	0	1	0	0	0	0	0	0	.167	.167	.167	-6	-1	0			1.000	-1	/2-1,O-1	-0.2
Total	16	1496	5399	705	1563	289	102	44	702	335	24	.289	.336	.405	124	137	193			.953	-22	2-839,O-612/1-2	11.2

■ **DANNY MURPHY** Murphy, Daniel Francis b: 8/23/42, Beverly, Mass. BL/TR, 5'11", 185 lbs. Deb: 6/18/60

YEAR	TM/L	G	AB	R	H	2B	3B	HR	RBI	BB	SO	AVG	OBP	SLG	PRO+	BR/A	SB	CS	SBR	FA	FR	G/POS	TPR
1960	Chi-N	31	75	7	9	2	0	1	6	4	13	.120	.175	.187	-1	-11	0	0	0	.976	-1	O-21	-1.3
1961	Chi-N	4	13	3	5	0	0	2	3	1	5	.385	.429	.846	225	2	0	0	0	1.000	0	/O-4	0.2
1962	Chi-N	14	35	5	7	3	1	0	3	2	9	.200	.243	.343	53	-2	0	0	0	1.000	-3	/O-5	-0.5
1969	Chi-A	17	1	0	0	0	0	0	0	2	0	.000	.667	.000	95	0	0	0	0	1.000	-0	P-17	0.0
1970	Chi-A	51	6	3	2	0	0	1	1	2	2	.333	.500	.833	252	1	0	0	0	.933	-1	P-51	0.0
Total	5	117	130	18	23	5	1	4	13	11	29	.177	.246	.323	53	-9	0	0	0	.947	-4	/P-68,O-30	-1.6

■ **DANNY MURPHY** Murphy, Daniel Joseph "Handsome Dan" b: 9/10/1864, Brooklyn, N.Y. d: 12/14/15, Brooklyn, N.Y. 156 lbs. Deb: 4/26/1892

YEAR	TM/L	G	AB	R	H	2B	3B	HR	RBI	BB	SO	AVG	OBP	SLG	PRO+	BR/A	SB	CS	SBR	FA	FR	G/POS	TPR
1892	NY-N	8	26	2	3	0	0	0	0	5	4	.115	.258	.115	14	-2	0			.900	-2	/C-8	-0.4

■ **DAVE MURPHY** Murphy, David Francis "Dirty Dave" b: 5/4/1876, Adams, Mass. d: 4/8/40, Adams, Mass. TR , Deb: 8/28/05

YEAR	TM/L	G	AB	R	H	2B	3B	HR	RBI	BB	SO	AVG	OBP	SLG	PRO+	BR/A	SB	CS	SBR	FA	FR	G/POS	TPR
1905	Bos-N	3	11	0	2	0	0	0	1	0		.182	.182	.182	9	-1	0			1.000	-2	/S-2,3-1	-0.4

■ **DWAYNE MURPHY** Murphy, Dwayne Keith b: 3/18/55, Merced, Cal. BL/TR, 6'1", 185 lbs. Deb: 4/8/78 C

YEAR	TM/L	G	AB	R	H	2B	3B	HR	RBI	BB	SO	AVG	OBP	SLG	PRO+	BR/A	SB	CS	SBR	FA	FR	G/POS	TPR
1978	Oak-A	60	52	15	10	2	0	0	5	7	14	.192	.288	.231	50	-3	0	1	-1	1.000	-10	O-45/D-5	-1.5
1979	Oak-A	121	388	57	99	10	4	11	40	84	80	.255	.389	.387	116	13	15	11	-2	.988	8	*O-118	1.3
1980	Oak-A	159	573	86	157	18	2	13	68	102	96	.274	.386	.380	119	19	26	15	-1	.990	24	*O-158	3.5
1981	*Oak-A	107	390	58	98	10	3	15	60	73	91	.251	.372	.408	131	18	10	4	1	.985	12	*O-106/D-1	2.8
1982	Oak-A	151	543	84	129	15	1	27	94	94	122	.238	.353	.418	116	14	26	8	3	.983	22	*O-147/S-1,D-1	3.4
1983	Oak-A	130	471	55	107	17	2	17	75	62	105	.227	.317	.380	97	-2	7	5	-1	.979	10	*O-124/D-7	0.3
1984	Oak-A	153	559	93	143	18	2	33	88	74	111	.256	.346	.472	133	24	4	5	-2	.988	21	*O-153	3.8
1985	Oak-A	152	523	77	122	21	3	20	59	84	123	.233	.343	.400	111	9	4	5	-2	.989	9	*O-150	1.1
1986	Oak-A	98	329	50	83	11	3	9	39	56	80	.252	.368	.386	114	8	3	1	0	.993	11	O-97/D-1	1.6
1987	Oak-A	82	219	39	51	7	0	8	35	58	61	.233	.394	.374	113	7	4	4	-1	.984	0	O-79/1-1,2-1	0.3
1988	Det-A	49	144	14	36	5	0	4	19	24	26	.250	.361	.368	109	2	1	1	-0	1.000	1	O-43/D-3	0.2
1989	Phi-N	98	156	20	34	5	0	9	27	29	44	.218	.341	.423	117	4	0	1	-1	.986	-6	O-52	-0.4
Total	12	1360	4347	648	1069	139	20	166	609	747	953	.246	.359	.402	116	113	100	61	-7	.987	102	*O-1272/D-18,2S	16.4

■ **ED MURPHY** Murphy, Edward Joseph b: 8/23/18, Joliet, Ill. d: 12/10/91, Joliet, Ill. BR/TR, 5'11", 190 lbs. Deb: 9/10/42

YEAR	TM/L	G	AB	R	H	2B	3B	HR	RBI	BB	SO	AVG	OBP	SLG	PRO+	BR/A	SB	CS	SBR	FA	FR	G/POS	TPR
1942	Phi-N	13	28	2	7	2	0	0	4	2	4	.250	.300	.321	86	-1	0			1.000	-0	/1-8	-0.1

■ **TONY MURPHY** Murphy, Francis J. b: 1863, Brooklyn, N.Y. 5'6", 145 lbs. Deb: 10/15/1884

YEAR	TM/L	G	AB	R	H	2B	3B	HR	RBI	BB	SO	AVG	OBP	SLG	PRO+	BR/A	SB	CS	SBR	FA	FR	G/POS	TPR
1884	NY-a	1	3	1	1	0	0	0		0		.333	.333	.333	121	0				1.000	-1	/C-1	-0.1

■ **FRANK MURPHY** Murphy, Francis Patrick b: 4/16/1875, N.Tarrytown, N.Y. d: 11/4/12, Central Islip, N.Y. Deb: 7/2/01

YEAR	TM/L	G	AB	R	H	2B	3B	HR	RBI	BB	SO	AVG	OBP	SLG	PRO+	BR/A	SB	CS	SBR	FA	FR	G/POS	TPR
1901	Bos-N	45	176	13	46	5	3	1	18	4		.261	.282	.341	73	-7	6			.939	4	O-45	-0.6
	NY-N	35	130	10	21	3	0	0	8	6		.162	.199	.185	12	-15	2			.847	-10	2-23,O-12	-2.5
	Yr	80	306	23	67	8	3	1	26	10		.219	.246	.275	49	-20	8			.940	-6	O-57,2-23	-3.1

■ **DUMMY MURPHY** Murphy, Herbert Courtland b: 12/18/1886, Olney, Ill. d: 8/10/62, Tallahassee, Fla. BR/TR, 5'10", 165 lbs. Deb: 4/14/14

YEAR	TM/L	G	AB	R	H	2B	3B	HR	RBI	BB	SO	AVG	OBP	SLG	PRO+	BR/A	SB	CS	SBR	FA	FR	G/POS	TPR
1914	Phi-N	9	26	1	4	1	0	0	3	0	4	.154	.185	.192	12	-3	0			.864	3	/S-9	0.1

■ **HOWARD MURPHY** Murphy, Howard b: 1/1/1882, Birmingham, Ala. d: 10/5/26, Fort Worth, Tex. BL/TR, 5'8.5", 150 lbs. Deb: 8/4/09

YEAR	TM/L	G	AB	R	H	2B	3B	HR	RBI	BB	SO	AVG	OBP	SLG	PRO+	BR/A	SB	CS	SBR	FA	FR	G/POS	TPR
1909	StL-N	25	60	3	12	0	0	0	3	4		.200	.250	.200	42	-4	1			.925	-2	O-19	-0.7

■ **EDDIE MURPHY** Murphy, John Edward b: 10/2/1891, Hancock, N.Y. d: 2/21/69, Dunmore, Pa. BL/TR, 5'9", 155 lbs. Deb: 8/26/12

YEAR	TM/L	G	AB	R	H	2B	3B	HR	RBI	BB	SO	AVG	OBP	SLG	PRO+	BR/A	SB	CS	SBR	FA	FR	G/POS	TPR
1912	Phi-A	33	142	24	45	4	1	0	6	11		.317	.370	.359	113	3	7			.947	0	O-33	0.1
1913	*Phi-A	137	508	105	150	14	7	1	30	70	44	.295	.391	.356	122	17	21			.942	-12	*O-135	-0.1
1914	*Phi-A	148	573	101	156	12	9	3	43	87	46	.272	.379	.340	121	19	36	32	-8	.941	-5	*O-148	-0.2
1915	Phi-A	68	260	37	60	3	4	0	17	29	15	.231	.315	.273	79	-6	13	3	2	.899	-5	O-58/3-6	-1.3
	Chi-A	70	273	51	86	11	5	0	26	39	12	.315	.410	.392	136	14	20	12	-1	.952	-1	O-70	0.9
	Yr	138	533	88	146	14	9	0	43	68	27	.274	.365	.334	109	8	33	15	1	.933	-6	*O-128/3-6	-0.4
1916	Chi-A	51	105	14	22	5	1	0	4	9	5	.210	.284	.276	68	-4	3			1.000	-3	O-24/3-1	-0.9
1917	Chi-A	53	51	9	16	2	1	0	16	5	1	.314	.386	.392	135	2	4			1.000	-4	/O-9	-0.2
1918	Chi-A	91	286	36	85	9	3	0	23	22	18	.297	.350	.350	110	3	6			.958	-10	O-63/2-8	-1.1
1919	*Chi-A	30	35	8	17	4	0	0	5	7	0	.486	.571	.600	228	7	0			.917	-0	/O-6	0.6
1920	Chi-A	58	118	22	40	2	1	0	19	12	4	.339	.405	.373	107	2	1	3	-2	.886	1	O-19/3-3	0.0
1921	Chi-A	6	5	1	1	0	0	0	0	0	0	.200	.200	.200	2	-1	0	0	0	.000	0	H	-0.1
1926	Pit-N	16	17	3	2	0	0	0	6	3	0	.118	.250	.118	2	-2	0			1.000	-0	/O-3	-0.3
Total	11	761	2373	411	680	66	32	4	195	294	145	.287	.374	.346	114	53	111	50		.942	-39	O-568/3-10,2-8	-2.6

■ **JOHN MURPHY** Murphy, John Patrick b: 1879, New Haven, Conn. d: 4/20/49, Andover, Mass. 5'7.5", 160 lbs. Deb: 9/10/02

YEAR	TM/L	G	AB	R	H	2B	3B	HR	RBI	BB	SO	AVG	OBP	SLG	PRO+	BR/A	SB	CS	SBR	FA	FR	G/POS	TPR
1902	StL-N	1	3	1	2	1	0	0	1	1		.667	.750	1.000	457	1	0			1.000	-1	/3-1	0.1
1903	Det-A	5	22	1	4	1	0	0	1	0		.182	.182	.227	23	-2	0			.852	-1	/S-5	-0.3
Total	2	6	25	2	6	2	0	0	2	1		.240	.269	.320	79	-1	0			.852	-2	/S-5,3-1	-0.2

■ **LARRY MURPHY** Murphy, Lawrence Patrick BL , Deb: 5/30/1891

YEAR	TM/L	G	AB	R	H	2B	3B	HR	RBI	BB	SO	AVG	OBP	SLG	PRO+	BR/A	SB	CS	SBR	FA	FR	G/POS	TPR
1891	Was-a	101	400	73	106	15	3	1	35	63	27	.265	.372	.325	104	6	29			.874	-5	*O-101	-0.3

■ **LEO MURPHY** Murphy, Leo Joseph "Red" b: 1/7/1889, Terre Haute, Ind. d: 8/12/60, Racine, Wis. BR/TR, 6'1", 179 lbs. Deb: 5/2/15

YEAR	TM/L	G	AB	R	H	2B	3B	HR	RBI	BB	SO	AVG	OBP	SLG	PRO+	BR/A	SB	CS	SBR	FA	FR	G/POS	TPR
1915	Pit-N	31	41	4	4	0	0	0	4	4	12	.098	.178	.098	-16	-6	0			.932	-3	C-20	-0.9

■ **MIKE MURPHY** Murphy, Michael Jerome b: 8/19/1888, Forestville, Pa. d: 10/26/52, Johnson City, N.Y. BR/TR, 5'9", 170 lbs. Deb: 5/17/12

YEAR	TM/L	G	AB	R	H	2B	3B	HR	RBI	BB	SO	AVG	OBP	SLG	PRO+	BR/A	SB	CS	SBR	FA	FR	G/POS	TPR
1912	StL-N	1	1	0	0	0	0	0	1	0	0	.000	.000	.000	-99	-0	0			.000	0	/C-1	0.0
1916	Phi-A	14	27	0	3	0	0	0	1	0	3	.111	.143	.111	-25	-4	0			.973	-3	C-12	-0.8
Total	2	15	28	0	3	0	0	0	2	1	3	.107	.138	.107	-28	-4	0			.973	-3	/C-13	-0.8

■ **MORGAN MURPHY** Murphy, Morgan Edward b: 2/14/1867, E.Providence, R.I. d: 10/3/38, Providence, R.I. BR/TR, 5'8", 160 lbs. Deb: 4/22/1890

YEAR	TM/L	G	AB	R	H	2B	3B	HR	RBI	BB	SO	AVG	OBP	SLG	PRO+	BR/A	SB	CS	SBR	FA	FR	G/POS	TPR
1890	Bos-P	68	246	38	56	10	2	2	32	24	31	.228	.301	.309	59	-15	16			.903	4	C-67/S-2,O-1,3-1	-0.5
1891	Bos-a	106	402	60	87	11	4	4	54	36	58	.216	.289	.294	68	-18	17			**.954**	11	*C-104/O-4	0.2
1892	Cin-N	74	234	29	46	8	2	2	24	25	57	.197	.277	.274	68	-9	4			.955	0	C-74	-0.4
1893	Cin-N	57	200	25	47	5	1	1	19	14	35	.235	.295	.285	53	-14	1			.932	-5	C-56/1-1	-1.2
1894	Cin-N	75	255	42	70	9	0	1	37	26	34	.275	.344	.322	59	-17	6			.901	-4	C-74/S-1,3-1	-1.2
1895	Cin-N	25	82	15	22	2	0	0	16	11	8	.268	.355	.293	65	-4	6			.907	-3	C-25	-0.4
1896	StL-N	49	175	12	45	5	2	0	11	8	14	.257	.290	.309	60	-10	1			.926	-2	C-48	-0.6
1897	StL-N	62	207	13	35	2	0	0	12	6		.169	.196	.179	-1	-30	1			.950	-3	C-53/1-8	-2.4

YEAR	TM/L	G	AB	R	H	2B	3B	HR	RBI	BB	SO	AVG	OBP	SLG	PRO+	BR/A	SB	CS	SBR	FA	FR	G/POS	TPR
1898	Pit-N	5	16	0	2	0	0	0	2	1		.125	.176	.125	-14	-2	0			.957	1	/C-5	-0.1
	Phi-N	25	86	6	17	3	0	0	11	6		.198	.258	.233	43	-6	0			.964	0	C-25	-0.4
	Yr	30	102	6	19	3	0	0	13	7		.186	.245	.216	34	-9	0			.963	1	C-30	-0.5
1900	Phi-N	11	36	2	10	0	1	0	3	0		.278	.278	.333	69	-2	0			.980	2	C-11	0.1
1901	Phi-A	9	28	5	6	1	0	0	6	0		.214	.214	.250	27	-3	1			.929	0	/C-8,1-1	-0.2
Total	11	566	1967	247	443	56	12	10	227	157	237	.225	.287	.281	54	-131	53			.936	2	C-550/1-10,O-5,S3	-7.1
■ PAT MURPHY	Murphy, Patrick J. b: 1/2/1857, Auburn, Mass. d: 5/16/27, Worcester, Mass. TR , 5'10", 160 lbs. Deb: 9/2/1887																						
1887	NY-N	17	56	4	12	2	0	0	4	2	4	.214	.241	.250	38	-5	1			.847	2	C-17	-0.1
1888	*NY-N	28	106	11	18	1	0	0	4	6	11	.170	.214	.179	27	-8	3			.913	3	C-28	-0.3
1889	NY-N	9	28	5	10	1	1	1	4	2	0	.357	.400	.571	170	2	0			.872	-2	/C-9	0.1
1890	NY-N	32	119	14	28	5	1	0	9	14	13	.235	.321	.294	79	-3	3			.905	-5	C-29/O-3,S-1	-0.5
Total	4	86	309	34	68	9	2	1	21	24	28	.220	.278	.272	64	-13	7			.895	-3	/C-83,O-3,S-1	-0.8
■ DICK MURPHY	Murphy, Richard Lee b: 10/25/31, Cincinnati, Ohio BL/TL, 5'11", 170 lbs. Deb: 6/13/54																						
1954	Cin-N	6	1	1	0	0	0	0	0	0	1	.000	.000	.000	-97	-0	0	0	0	.000	0	H	0.0
■ BUZZ MURPHY	Murphy, Robert R. b: 4/26/1895, Denver, Colo. d: 5/11/38, Denver, Colo. BL/TL, 5'8.5", 155 lbs. Deb: 7/14/18																						
1918	Bos-N	9	32	6	12	2	3	1	9	3	5	.375	.429	.719	259	6	0			1.000	-2	/O-9	0.4
1919	Was-A	79	252	19	66	7	4	0	28	19	32	.262	.326	.321	83	-5	5			.959	2	O-73	-0.9
Total	2	88	284	25	78	9	7	1	37	22	37	.275	.338	.366	101	0	5			.961	0	/O-82	-0.5
■ BILLY MURPHY	Murphy, William Eugene b: 5/7/44, Pineville, La. BR/TR, 6'1", 190 lbs. Deb: 4/15/66																						
1966	NY-N	84	135	15	31	4	1	3	13	7	34	.230	.273	.341	71	-5	1	2	-1	.955	-9	O-57	-1.8
■ WILLIE MURPHY	Murphy, William H. "Gentle Willie" b: 3/23/1864, Springfield, Mass. BL , 5'11", 198 lbs. Deb: 5/1/1884																						
1884	Cle-N	42	168	18	38	3	3	1	9	1	23	.226	.231	.298	63	-7				.720	-5	O-42	-1.2
	Was-a	5	21	3	10	0	0	0		1		.476	.542	.476	266	4				.700	-0	/O-4,2-1	0.3
Total	1	47	189	21	48	3	3	1	9	2	23	.254	.269	.317	83	-3				.718	-5	/O-46,2-1	-0.9
■ YALE MURPHY	Murphy, William Henry "Tot" or "Midget" b: 11/11/1869, Southville, Mass. d: 2/14/06, Southville, Mass. BL/TR, 5'3", 125 lbs. Deb: 4/19/1894																						
1894	*NY-N	74	280	64	76	6	2	0	28	51	23	.271	.384	.307	69	-12	28			.898	-11	S-49,O-20/3-3,21	-1.7
1895	NY-N	51	184	35	37	6	2	0	16	27	13	.201	.303	.255	46	-14	7			.944	-4	O-33/S-8,3-8,2-1	-1.7
1897	NY-N	5	8	1	0	0	0	0	1	2		.000	.200	.000	-46	-2	0			.800	-2	/S-3,2-2	-0.3
Total	3	130	472	100	113	12	4	0	45	80	36	.239	.350	.282	59	-28	35			.890	-17	/S-60,O-53,3-11,21	-3.7
■ TONY MURRAY	Murray, Anthony Joseph b: 4/30/04, Chicago, Ill. d: 3/19/74, Chicago, Ill. BR/TR, 5'10.5", 154 lbs. Deb: 10/6/23																						
1923	Chi-N	2	4	0	1	0	0	0	0	0	0	.250	.400	.250	75	-0	0	0	0	1.000	-2	/O-2	-0.2
■ EDDIE MURRAY	Murray, Eddie Clarence b: 2/24/56, Los Angeles, Cal. BB/TR, 6'2", 200 lbs. Deb: 4/7/77 FC																						
1977	Bal-A	160	611	81	173	29	2	27	88	48	104	.283	.336	.470	125	19	0	1	-1	.992	-4	*D-111,1-42/O-3	0.8
1978	Bal-A☆	161	610	85	174	32	3	27	95	70	97	.285	.360	.480	143	34	6	5	-1	.997	1	*1-157/3-3,D-1	2.4
1979	*Bal-A	159	606	90	179	30	2	25	99	72	78	.295	.372	.475	132	27	10	2	2	.994	-1	*1-157/D-2	1.7
1980	Bal-A	158	621	100	186	36	2	32	116	54	71	.300	.357	.519	138	31	7	2	1	.994	-9	*1-154/D-1	1.3
1981	Bal-A★	99	378	57	111	21	2	**22**	**78**	40	43	.294	.363	.534	156	26	2	3	-1	**.999**	10	1-99	3.0
1982	Bal-A★	151	550	87	174	30	1	32	110	70	82	.316	.395	.549	157	43	7	2	1	**.997**	1	*1-149/D-2	3.6
1983	*Bal-A★	156	582	115	178	30	3	33	111	86	90	.306	.398	.538	**158**	**47**	5	1	1	.993	4	*1-153/D-2	4.2
1984	Bal-A★	162	588	97	180	26	3	29	110	**107**	87	.306	**.415**	.509	157	**50**	10	2	2	.992	8	*1-159/D-3	4.9
1985	Bal-A★	156	583	111	173	37	1	31	124	84	68	.297	.387	.523	151	42	5	2	0	.987	13	*1-154/D-2	4.4
1986	Bal-A☆	137	495	61	151	25	1	17	84	78	49	.305	.400	.463	136	27	3	0	1	.989	-3	*1-119,D-16	1.6
1987	Bal-A	160	618	89	171	28	3	30	91	73	80	.277	.353	.477	121	18	1	2	-1	.993	12	*1-156/D-4	1.6
1988	Bal-A	161	603	75	171	27	2	28	84	75	78	.284	.363	.474	136	29	5	2	0	.989	10	*1-103,D-58	2.9
1989	LA-N	160	594	66	147	29	1	20	88	87	85	.247	.346	.401	115	13	7	2	1	**.996**	13	*1-159/3-2	1.5
1990	LA-N	155	558	96	184	22	3	26	95	82	64	.330	.417	.520	160	48	8	5	-1	.992	4	*1-150	4.1
1991	LA-N★	153	576	69	150	23	1	19	96	55	74	.260	.325	.403	106	4	10	3	1	.995	9	*1-149/3-1	0.4
1992	NY-N	156	551	64	144	37	2	16	93	66	74	.261	.340	.423	117	12	4	2	0	.991	-4	*1-154	-0.3
1993	NY-N	154	610	77	174	28	1	27	100	40	61	.285	.329	.467	112	8	2	2	-1	.988	-1	*1-154	-0.6
1994	Cle-A	108	433	57	110	21	1	17	76	31	53	.254	.304	.425	85	-11	8	4	0	.988	-2	D-82,1-26	-1.8
1995	*Cle-A	113	436	68	141	21	0	21	82	39	65	.323	.379	.516	128	18	5	1	1	.984	3	D-95,1-18	1.3
1996	Cle-A	88	336	33	88	9	1	12	45	34	45	.262	.330	.402	84	-8	3	0	1	1.000	0	D-87/1-1	-1.2
	*Bal-A	64	230	36	59	12	0	10	34	27	42	.257	.335	.439	94	-2	1	0	0	.000	0	D-62	-0.5
	Yr	152	566	69	147	21	1	22	79	61	87	.260	.332	.417	88	-11	4	0	1	1.000	0	*D-149/1-1	-1.7
1997	Ana-A	46	160	13	35	7	0	3	15	13	24	.219	.277	.319	55	-11	1	0	0	.000	0	D-45	-1.2
	LA-N	9	7	0	2	0	0	0	3	2	2	.286	.444	.286	104	0	0	0	0	.000	0	/H	0.0
Total	21	3026	11336	1627	3255	560	35	504	1917	1333	1516	.287	.363	.476	130	462	110	43	7	.993	63	*1-2413,D-573/3-6,O	34.1
■ ED MURRAY	Murray, Edward Francis b: 5/8/1895, Mystic, Conn. d: 11/8/70, Cheyenne, Wyoming BR/TR, 5'6", 145 lbs. Deb: 6/24/17																						
1917	StL-A	1	1	0	0	0	0	0	0	0	1	.000	.000	.000	-99	-0	0			.000	0	/S-1	0.0
■ GLENN MURRAY	Murray, Glenn Everett b: 11/23/70, Manning, S.C. BR/TR, 6'2", 225 lbs. Deb: 5/10/96																						
1996	Phi-N	38	97	8	19	3	0	2	6	7	36	.196	.250	.289	41	-8	1	1	-0	1.000	1	O-27	-0.8
■ JIM MURRAY	Murray, James Oscar b: 1/16/1878, Galveston, Tex. d: 4/25/45, Galveston, Tex. BR/TL, 5'10", 180 lbs. Deb: 9/2/02																						
1902	Chi-N	12	47	3	8	0	0	0	1	2		.170	.204	.170	16	-5	0			1.000	-1	O-12	-0.6
1911	StL-A	31	102	8	19	5	0	3	11	5		.186	.224	.324	54	-7	0			.935	-0	O-25	-0.8
1914	Bos-N	39	112	10	26	4	2	0	12	6	24	.232	.277	.304	73	-4	2			.941	-8	O-32	-1.4
Total	3	82	261	21	53	9	2	3	24	13	24	.203	.244	.287	56	-16	2			.949	-9	/O-69	-2.8
■ MIAH MURRAY	Murray, Jeremiah J. b: 1/1/1865, Boston, Mass. d: 1/11/22, Boston, Mass. BR/TR, 5'11.5", 170 lbs. Deb: 5/17/1884 U																						
1884	Pro-N	8	27	1	5	0	0	0	1	1	8	.185	.214	.185	27	-2				.836	-4	/C-7,O-1,1-1	-0.6
1885	Lou-a	12	43	4	8	0	0	0	3	2		.186	.239	.186	36	-3				.863	1	C-12/1-2	-0.1
1888	Was-N	12	42	1	4	1	0	0	3	1	7	.095	.116	.119	-26	-6	0			.912	-0	C-10/1-2	-0.5
1891	Was-a	2	8	0	0	0	0	0	0	0	1	.000	.000	.000	-99	-2	0			1.000	3	/C-2	0.1
Total	4	34	120	6	17	1	0	0	7	4	16	.142	.176	.150	3	-13	0			.884	-1	/C-31,1-5,O-1	-1.1
■ RED MURRAY	Murray, John Joseph b: 3/4/1884, Arnot, Pa. d: 12/4/58, Sayre, Pa. BR/TR, 5'10.5", 190 lbs. Deb: 6/16/06																						
1906	StL-N	46	144	18	37	9	7	1	16	9		.257	.305	.438	137	5	5			.962	-3	O-34/C-7	0.2
1907	StL-N	132	485	46	127	10	10	7	46	24		.262	.301	.367	113	5	23			.935	5	*O-131	0.5
1908	StL-N	154	593	64	167	19	15	7	62	37		.282	.332	.400	140	24	48			.914	-4	*O-154	1.6
1909	NY-N	149	570	74	150	15	12	**7**	91	45		.263	.319	.368	112	6	48			.947	3	*O-149	0.4
1910	NY-N	149	553	78	153	27	8	4	87	52	51	.277	.345	.376	110	7	57			.948	4	*O-148	0.4
1911	*NY-N	140	488	70	142	27	15	3	78	43	37	.291	.354	.426	114	8	48			.954	-11	*O-131	-0.9
1912	*NY-N	143	549	83	152	26	20	3	92	27	45	.277	.320	.413	97	-5	38			**.968**	2	*O-143	-1.0
1913	*NY-N	147	520	70	139	21	3	2	59	34	28	.267	.320	.331	85	-10	35			.965	10	*O-147	-0.7
1914	NY-N	86	139	19	31	6	3	0	23	9	7	.223	.270	.309	75	-5	11			1.000	-10	O-49	-1.7
1915	NY-N	45	127	12	28	1	2	3	11	7	15	.220	.261	.331	83	-3	2	3	-1	.959	-1	O-34	-0.7
	Chi-N	51	144	20	43	6	1	0	11	8	8	.299	.340	.354	110	2	6	5	-1	.966	1	O-40/2-1	0.0
	Yr	96	271	32	71	7	3	3	22	15	23	.262	.303	.343	98	-1	8	8	-2	.963	1	O-74/2-1	-0.7
1917	NY-N	22	22	1	1	1	0	0	3	4	3	.045	.192	.091	-12	-3	0			1.000	-3	O-11/C-1	-0.7
Total	11	1264	4334	555	1170	168	96	37	579	299	194	.270	.323	.379	108	30	321	8		.950	-6	*O-1171/C-8,2-1	-2.6

■ **LARRY MURRAY** Murray, Larry b: 4/1/53, Chicago, Ill. BB/TR, 5'11", 179 lbs. Deb: 9/7/74

YEAR	TM/L	G	AB	R	H	2B	3B	HR	RBI	BB	SO	AVG	OBP	SLG	PRO+	BR/A	SB	CS	SBR	FA	FR	G/POS	TPR
1974	NY-A	6	1	1	0	0	0	0	0	0	0	.000	.000	.000	-99	-0	0	1	-1	.000	-2	/O-3	-0.3
1975	NY-A	6	1	1	0	0	0	0	0	0	0	.000	.000	.000	-99	-0	0	0	0	1.000	-2	/O-4	-0.2
1976	NY-A	8	10	2	1	0	0	0	2	1	2	.100	.182	.100	-16	-1	2	0	1	1.000	-1	/O-7	-0.2
1977	Oak-A	90	162	19	29	5	2	1	9	17	36	.179	.257	.253	40	-13	12	3	2	.992	-13	O-78/S-1,D-3	-2.6
1978	Oak-A	11	12	1	1	0	0	0	0	3	2	.083	.267	.083	3	-1	0	0	0	1.000	-1	/O-6	-0.3
1979	Oak-A	105	226	25	42	11	2	2	20	28	34	.186	.276	.279	53	-15	6	6	-2	.963	-1	O-90/2-3	-2.0
Total	6	226	412	49	73	16	4	3	31	49	74	.177	.265	.257	44	-32	20	10	0	.975	-20	O-188/2-3,D-3,S-1	-5.6

■ **RAY MURRAY** Murray, Raymond Lee "Deacon" b: 10/12/17, Spring Hope, N.C. BR/TR, 6'3", 204 lbs. Deb: 4/25/48

YEAR	TM/L	G	AB	R	H	2B	3B	HR	RBI	BB	SO	AVG	OBP	SLG	PRO+	BR/A	SB	CS	SBR	FA	FR	G/POS	TPR
1948	Cle-A	4	4	0	0	0	0	0	0	0	3	.000	.000	.000	-99	-1	0	0	0	.000	0	H	-0.1
1950	Cle-A	55	139	16	38	8	2	1	13	12	13	.273	.331	.381	85	-4	1	0	0	.972	-5	C-45	-0.6
1951	Cle-A	1	1	0	1	0	0	0	1	0	0	1.000	1.000	1.000	468	1	0	0	0	1.000	1	/C-1	0.1
	Phi-A	40	122	10	26	6	0	0	13	14	8	.213	.294	.262	50	-8	0	0	0	.985	-3	C-39	-0.9
	Yr	41	123	10	27	6	0	0	14	14	8	.220	.299	.268	53	-8	0	0	0	.986	-2	C-40	-0.8
1952	Phi-A	44	136	14	28	5	0	1	10	9	13	.206	.255	.265	42	-11	0	0	0	.995	7	C-42	-0.1
1953	Phi-A	84	268	25	76	14	3	6	41	18	25	.284	.331	.425	99	-1	0	0	0	.989	4	C-78	0.6
1954	Bal-A	22	61	4	15	4	1	0	2	2	5	.246	.270	.344	73	-3	0	0	0	.989	1	C-21	-0.1
Total	6	250	731	69	184	37	6	8	80	55	67	.252	.305	.352	75	-27	1	0	0	.987	6	C-226	-1.1

■ **RICH MURRAY** Murray, Richard Dale b: 7/6/57, Los Angeles, Cal. BR/TR, 6'4", 195 lbs. Deb: 6/7/80 F

YEAR	TM/L	G	AB	R	H	2B	3B	HR	RBI	BB	SO	AVG	OBP	SLG	PRO+	BR/A	SB	CS	SBR	FA	FR	G/POS	TPR
1980	SF-N	53	194	19	42	8	2	4	24	11	48	.216	.259	.340	67	-9	2	1	0	.987	0	1-53	-1.3
1983	SF-N	4	10	0	2	0	0	0	1	0	3	.200	.200	.200	11	-1	0	0	0	1.000	-0	/1-3	-0.2
Total	2	57	204	19	44	8	2	4	25	11	51	.216	.256	.333	65	-10	2	1	0	.988	0	/1-56	-1.5

■ **BOBBY MURRAY** Murray, Robert Hayes b: 7/4/1894, St.Albans, Vt. d: 1/4/79, Nashua, N.H. BL/TR, 5'7", 155 lbs. Deb: 9/24/23

YEAR	TM/L	G	AB	R	H	2B	3B	HR	RBI	BB	SO	AVG	OBP	SLG	PRO+	BR/A	SB	CS	SBR	FA	FR	G/POS	TPR
1923	Was-A	10	37	2	7	1	0	0	2	1	4	.189	.211	.216	13	-5	1	0	0	1.000	2	3-10	-0.1

■ **TOM MURRAY** Murray, Thomas W. b: 1866, Savannah, Ga. Deb: 6/20/1894

YEAR	TM/L	G	AB	R	H	2B	3B	HR	RBI	BB	SO	AVG	OBP	SLG	PRO+	BR/A	SB	CS	SBR	FA	FR	G/POS	TPR
1894	Phi-N	1	2	0	0	0	0	0	0	0	2	.000	.000	.000	-99	-1	0			.833	0	/S-1	0.0

■ **BILL MURRAY** Murray, William Allenwood "Dasher" b: 9/6/1893, Vinalhaven, Me. d: 9/14/43, Boston, Mass. BB/TR, 5'11", 165 lbs. Deb: 6/27/17

YEAR	TM/L	G	AB	R	H	2B	3B	HR	RBI	BB	SO	AVG	OBP	SLG	PRO+	BR/A	SB	CS	SBR	FA	FR	G/POS	TPR
1917	Was-A	8	21	2	3	0	1	0	4	2	2	.143	.217	.238	39	-2	1			.889	-2	/2-6,S-1	-0.3

■ **IVAN MURRELL** Murrell, Ivan Augustus (Peters) b: 4/24/45, Almirante, Panama BR/TR, 6'2", 196 lbs. Deb: 9/28/63

YEAR	TM/L	G	AB	R	H	2B	3B	HR	RBI	BB	SO	AVG	OBP	SLG	PRO+	BR/A	SB	CS	SBR	FA	FR	G/POS	TPR
1963	Hou-N	2	5	1	1	0	0	0	0	0	2	.200	.200	.200	17	-1	0	0	0	1.000	-0	/O-2	-0.1
1964	Hou-N	10	14	1	2	1	0	0	1	0	6	.143	.143	.214	-1	-2	0	0	0	1.000	-1	/O-5	-0.3
1967	Hou-N	10	29	2	9	0	0	0	1	1	9	.310	.333	.310	88	-0	1	0	0	.846	-0	/O-6	-0.1
1968	Hou-N	32	59	3	6	1	1	0	3	1	17	.102	.117	.153	-20	-9	0	0	0	.931	2	O-15	-0.9
1969	SD-N	111	247	19	63	10	6	3	25	11	65	.255	.292	.381	91	-4	3	4	-2	.959	-3	O-72/1-2	-1.2
1970	SD-N	125	347	43	85	9	3	12	35	17	93	.245	.288	.392	84	-10	9	7	-2	.970	3	*O-101/1-1	-1.2
1971	SD-N	103	255	23	60	6	3	7	24	7	60	.235	.264	.365	82	-8	5	2	0	.978	0	O-72	-1.1
1972	SD-N	5	7	0	1	0	0	0	1	0	3	.143	.143	.143	-20	-1	0	0	0	1.000	0	/O-1	-0.1
1973	SD-N	93	210	23	48	13	1	9	21	2	52	.229	.236	.429	87	-6	2	0	1	.959	-1	O-37,1-24	-0.9
1974	Atl-N	73	133	11	33	1	1	2	12	5	35	.248	.275	.316	62	-7	0	0	0	.983	-1	O-32,1-13	-1.0
Total	10	564	1306	126	308	41	15	33	123	44	342	.236	.266	.366	77	-46	20	13	-2	.965	-2	O-343/1-40	-6.9

■ **DANNY MURTAUGH** Murtaugh, Daniel Edward b: 10/8/17, Chester, Pa. d: 12/2/76, Chester, Pa. BR/TR, 5'9", 165 lbs. Deb: 7/6/41 MC

YEAR	TM/L	G	AB	R	H	2B	3B	HR	RBI	BB	SO	AVG	OBP	SLG	PRO+	BR/A	SB	CS	SBR	FA	FR	G/POS	TPR
1941	Phi-N	85	347	34	76	8	1	0	11	26	31	.219	.275	.248	50	-23	**18**			.978	2	2-85/S-1	-1.5
1942	Phi-N	144	506	48	122	16	4	0	27	49	39	.241	.311	.289	80	-12	13			.939	6	S-60,3-53,2-32	0.0
1943	Phi-N	113	451	65	123	17	4	1	35	57	23	.273	.357	.335	104	4	4			.974	0	*2-113	1.2
1946	Phi-N	6	19	1	4	1	0	1	3	2	2	.211	.286	.421	102	-0	0			.958	-4	/2-6	-0.4
1947	Bos-N	3	8	0	1	0	0	0	0	1	2	.125	.222	.125	-6	-1	0			1.000	-0	/2-2,3-2	-0.1
1948	Pit-N	146	514	56	149	21	5	1	71	60	40	.290	.365	.356	94	-2	10			.979	1	*2-146	0.7
1949	Pit-N	75	236	16	48	7	2	2	24	29	17	.203	.291	.275	51	-16	2			.975	3	2-74	-1.0
1950	Pit-N	118	367	34	108	20	5	2	37	47	42	.294	.376	.392	99	1	2			.976	3	*2-108	0.8
1951	Pit-N	77	151	9	30	7	0	1	11	16	19	.199	.284	.265	47	-11	0	0	0	.970	-2	2-65/3-3	-1.2
Total	9	767	2599	263	661	97	21	8	219	287	215	.254	.331	.317	81	-61	49	0		.975	10	2-631/S-61,3-58	-1.5

■ **TONY MUSER** Muser, Anthony Joseph b: 8/1/47, Van Nuys, Cal. BL/TL, 6'2", 190 lbs. Deb: 9/14/69 C

YEAR	TM/L	G	AB	R	H	2B	3B	HR	RBI	BB	SO	AVG	OBP	SLG	PRO+	BR/A	SB	CS	SBR	FA	FR	G/POS	TPR
1969	Bos-A	2	9	0	1	0	0	0	1	1	1	.111	.200	.111	-10	-1	0	0	0	1.000	1	/1-2	-0.1
1971	Chi-A	11	16	2	5	0	1	0	0	1	1	.313	.353	.438	119	0	0	0	0	.963	0	/1-4	0.1
1972	Chi-A	44	61	6	17	2	2	1	9	2	6	.279	.302	.426	113	1	1	1	-0	.986	-0	1-29/O-1	-0.1
1973	Chi-A	109	309	38	88	14	3	4	30	33	36	.285	.354	.388	105	3	8	4	0	.992	-3	1-89,D-13/O-2	-0.6
1974	Chi-A	103	206	16	60	5	1	1	18	6	22	.291	.315	.340	86	-4	1	4	-2	.998	-4	1-80,D-13	-1.3
1975	Chi-A	43	111	11	27	3	0	0	6	7	8	.243	.288	.270	58	-6	2	1	0	.993	2	1-41	-0.6
	Bal-A	80	82	11	26	3	0	0	11	8	9	.317	.378	.354	115	2	0	0	0	.996	1	1-62	0.2
	Yr	123	193	22	53	6	0	0	17	15	17	.275	.327	.306	83	-4	2	1	0	.994	3	*1-103	-0.4
1976	Bal-A	136	326	25	74	7	1	1	30	21	34	.227	.274	.264	62	-16	1	1	-0	.991	1	*1-109,O-12,D-10	-2.2
1977	Bal-A	120	118	14	27	6	0	0	7	13	16	.229	.305	.280	65	-6	1	2	-1	.992	1	1-77,O-11/D-1	-0.6
1978	Mil-A	15	30	0	4	1	1	0	5	3	5	.133	.212	.233	25	-3	0	0	0	.988	-0	1-12	-0.4
Total	9	663	1268	123	329	41	9	7	117	95	138	.259	.312	.323	82	-30	14	13	-4	.992	-1	1-505/D-37,O-26	-5.6

■ **STAN MUSIAL** Musial, Stanley Frank "Stan The Man" b: 11/21/20, Donora, Pa. BL/TL, 6', 175 lbs. Deb: 9/17/41 H

YEAR	TM/L	G	AB	R	H	2B	3B	HR	RBI	BB	SO	AVG	OBP	SLG	PRO+	BR/A	SB	CS	SBR	FA	FR	G/POS	TPR
1941	StL-N	12	47	8	20	4	0	1	7	2	1	.426	.449	.574	175	4	1			1.000	0	O-11	0.4
1942	*StL-N	140	467	87	147	32	10	10	72	62	25	.315	.397	.490	148	28	6			.984	1	*O-135	2.5
1943	*StL-N★	157	617	108	**220**	**48**	**20**	13	81	72	18	**.357**	**.425**	**.562**	**176**	**60**	9			.982	11	*O-155	**6.4**
1944	*StL-N★	146	568	112	**197**	**51**	14	12	94	90	28	.347	**.440**	**.549**	**174**	**59**	7			.987	3	*O-146	**5.4**
1946	*StL-N★	156	624	**124**	**228**	**50**	**20**	16	103	73	31	**.365**	.434	**.587**	**180**	**65**	7			.989	-1	*1-114,O-42	**5.7**
1947	StL-N★	149	587	113	183	30	13	19	95	80	24	.312	.398	.504	132	28	4			.994	-7	*1-149	1.5
1948	StL-N★	155	611	**135**	**230**	**46**	**18**	39	**131**	79	34	**.376**	**.450**	**.702**	**196**	**81**	7			.981	-8	*O-155/1-2	**6.3**
1949	StL-N★	157	612	128	**207**	**41**	**13**	36	123	107	38	.338	**.438**	.624	174	65	3			**.991**	-19	*O-156/1-1	3.8
1950	StL-N★	146	555	105	192	41	7	28	109	87	36	**.346**	.437	**.596**	**161**	**51**	5			.964	-13	O-77,1-69	3.2
1951	StL-N★	152	578	**124**	205	30	**12**	32	108	98	40	**.355**	.449	.614	**182**	**69**	4	5	-2	.974	4	O-91,1-60	6.4
1952	StL-N★	154	578	**105**	**194**	**42**	6	21	91	96	29	**.336**	.432	**.538**	**167**	**56**	7	7	-2	.987	-7	*O-129,1-25/P-1	4.2
1953	StL-N★	157	593	127	200	**53**	9	30	113	**105**	32	.337	**.437**	.609	169	63	3	4	-2	.984	-9	*O-157	4.4
1954	StL-N★	153	591	**120**	195	**41**	9	35	126	103	39	.330	.433	.607	166	60	1	7	-4	**.990**	-2	*O-152,1-10	4.6
1955	StL-N★	154	562	97	179	30	5	33	108	80	39	.319	.411	.566	156	47	5	4	-1	.992	1	*1-110,O-51	3.8
1956	StL-N★	156	594	87	184	33	6	27	**109**	75	39	.310	.390	.522	142	36	2	0	1	.993	6	*1-103,O-53	3.3
1957	StL-N★	134	502	82	176	38	3	29	102	66	34	**.351**	**.428**	.612	172	52	1	1	-0	.992	2	*1-130	4.5
1958	StL-N★	135	472	64	159	35	2	17	62	72	26	.337	.426	.528	145	33	0	0	0	.989	8	*1-124	3.4
1959	StL-N★	115	341	37	87	13	2	14	44	60	25	.255	.367	.428	104	3	0	2	-1	.990	2	1-90/O-3	-0.1
1960	StL-N★	116	331	49	91	17	1	17	63	41	34	.275	.358	.486	118	8	1	1	-0	.990	-1	O-59,1-29	0.2
1961	StL-N★	123	372	46	107	22	4	15	70	52	35	.288	.376	.489	116	9	0	0	0	**.994**	0	*O-103	0.3
1962	StL-N★	135	433	57	143	18	1	19	82	64	46	.330	.420	.508	135	23	3	0	1	.977	-3	*O-119	1.4
1963	StL-N★	124	337	34	86	10	2	12	58	35	43	.255	.329	.404	100	0	2	0	1	.968	-7	O-96	-1.1
Total	22	3026	10972	1949	3630	725	177	475	1951	1599	696	.331	.418	.559	157	899	78	31		.984	-38	*O-1890,*1-1016/P-1	70.5

■ **DANNY MUSSER** Musser, William Daniel b: 9/5/05, Zion, Pa. BL/TR, 5'9.5", 160 lbs. Deb: 9/18/32

YEAR	TM/L	G	AB	R	H	2B	3B	HR	RBI	BB	SO	AVG	OBP	SLG	PRO+	BR/A	SB	CS	SBR	FA	FR	G/POS	TPR
1932	Was-A	1	2	0	1	0	0	0	0	0	0	.500	.500	.500	162	0	0	0	0	.000	0	/3-1	0.0

■ GEORGE MYATT

Myatt, George Edward "Mercury', "Stud" or "Foghor n" b: 6/14/14, Denver, Colo. BL/TR, 5'11", 167 lbs. Deb: 8/16/38 MC

YEAR	TM/L	G	AB	R	H	2B	3B	HR	RBI	BB	SO	AVG	OBP	SLG	PRO+	BR/A	SB	CS	SBR	FA	FR	G/POS	TPR
1938	NY-N	43	170	27	52	2	1	3	10	14	13	.306	.362	.382	104	1	10			.919	7	S-24,3-19	1.1
1939	NY-N	22	53	7	10	2	0	0	3	6	6	.189	.271	.226	35	-5	2			.907	1	3-14	-0.4
1943	Was-A	42	53	11	13	3	0	0	3	13	7	.245	.394	.302	109	1	3	0	1	.930	-1	2-11/S-2,3-2	0.2
1944	Was-A	140	538	86	153	19	6	0	40	54	44	.284	.357	.342	105	5	26	10	2	.957	-22	*2-121,S-15/O-3	-0.8
1945	Was-A	133	490	81	145	17	7	1	39	63	43	.296	.378	.365	127	18	30	11	2	.972	-19	2-94,O-32/3-6,S-1	0.6
1946	Was-A	15	34	7	8	1	0	0	4	2	3	.235	.297	.265	61	-2	1	1	-0	.900	-2	/3-7,2-2	-0.4
1947	Was-A	12	7	1	0	0	0	0	0	4	4	.000	.364	.000	6	-1	0	0	0	1.000	0	/2-1	-0.1
Total	7	407	1345	220	381	44	14	4	99	156	120	.283	.362	.346	108	19	72	22		.962	-35	2-229/3-48,S-42,O	0.2

■ GLENN MYATT

Myatt, Glenn Calvin b: 7/9/1897, Argenta, Ark. d: 8/9/69, Houston, Tex. BL/TR, 5'11", 165 lbs. Deb: 4/15/20

YEAR	TM/L	G	AB	R	H	2B	3B	HR	RBI	BB	SO	AVG	OBP	SLG	PRO+	BR/A	SB	CS	SBR	FA	FR	G/POS	TPR
1920	Phi-A	70	196	14	49	8	3	0	18	12	22	.250	.293	.321	62	-11	1	3	-2	.900	-5	O-37,C-22	-1.9
1921	Phi-A	44	69	6	14	2	0	0	5	6	7	.203	.267	.232	28	-7	1	0	0	.939	2	C-27	-0.4
1923	Cle-A	92	220	36	63	7	6	3	40	16	18	.286	.338	.414	97	-2	0	2	-1	.934	-8	C-69	-0.8
1924	Cle-A	105	342	55	117	22	7	8	73	33	12	.342	.402	.518	134	16	6	1	1	.978	-15	C-95	0.8
1925	Cle-A	106	358	51	97	15	9	11	54	29	24	.271	.329	.455	97	-4	3	1	0	.973	-18	C-98/O-1	-1.5
1926	Cle-A	56	117	14	29	5	2	0	13	13	13	.248	.323	.325	69	-5	1	0	0	1.000	-1	C-35	-0.4
1927	Cle-A	55	94	15	23	6	0	2	8	12	7	.245	.336	.372	83	-2	1	1	-0	.978	2	C-26	0.0
1928	Cle-A	58	125	9	36	7	2	1	15	13	13	.288	.355	.400	97	-0	0	2	-1	.967	-9	C-30	-0.8
1929	Cle-A	59	129	14	30	4	1	1	17	7	5	.233	.277	.302	47	-10	0	1	-1	.976	-1	C-41	-0.9
1930	Cle-A	86	265	30	78	23	2	2	37	18	17	.294	.342	.419	88	-5	2	3	-1	.977	-7	C-71	-0.6
1931	Cle-A	65	195	21	48	14	2	1	29	21	13	.246	.319	.354	73	-8	2	1	0	.991	-4	C-53	-0.8
1932	Cle-A	82	252	45	62	12	1	8	46	27	21	.246	.326	.397	81	-8	2	2	-1	.988	-8	C-65	-1.2
1933	Cle-A	40	77	10	18	4	0	0	7	15	8	.234	.372	.286	73	-2	0	1	-1	.965	-1	C-27	-0.2
1934	Cle-A	36	107	18	34	6	1	0	12	13	5	.318	.392	.393	101	1	1	0	0	.980	-1	C-34	0.2
1935	Cle-A	10	36	1	3	1	0	0	2	4	3	.083	.175	.111	-24	-7	0	0	0	1.000	-1	C-10	-0.7
	NY-N	13	18	2	4	0	1	1	6	0	3	.222	.222	.500	90	-0	0			1.000	-1	/C-4	-0.1
1936	Det-A	27	78	5	17	1	0	0	5	9	4	.218	.299	.231	32	-8	0	0	0	1.000	-2	C-27	-0.8
Total	16	1004	2678	346	722	137	37	38	387	248	195	.270	.334	.391	85	-63	20	18		.974	-78	C-734/O-38	-10.1

■ BUDDY MYER

Myer, Charles Solomon b: 3/16/04, Ellisville, Miss. d: 10/31/74, Baton Rouge, La. BL/TR, 5'10.5", 163 lbs. Deb: 9/26/25

YEAR	TM/L	G	AB	R	H	2B	3B	HR	RBI	BB	SO	AVG	OBP	SLG	PRO+	BR/A	SB	CS	SBR	FA	FR	G/POS	TPR
1925	*Was-A	4	8	1	2	0	0	0	0	0	1	.250	.250	.250	28	-1	0	0	0	1.000	-2	/S-4	-0.3
1926	Was-A	132	434	66	132	18	6	1	62	45	19	.304	.370	.380	98	-0	10	11	-4	.928	-18	*S-118/3-8	-1.0
1927	Was-A	15	51	7	11	1	0	0	7	8	3	.216	.322	.235	47	-4	3	1	0	.933	-3	S-15	-0.4
	Bos-A	133	469	59	135	22	11	2	47	48	15	.288	.359	.394	97	-2	9	5	-0	.940	7	*S-101,3-14,O-10,/2	1.4
	Yr	148	520	66	146	23	11	2	54	56	18	.281	.355	.379	92	-5	12	6	0	.939	4	*S-116,3-14,O-10,/2	1.0
1928	Bos-A	147	536	78	168	26	6	1	44	53	28	.313	.379	.390	104	5	**30**	16	-1	.967	4	*3-144	1.5
1929	Was-A	141	563	80	169	29	10	3	82	63	33	.300	.373	.403	99	0	18	7	1	.958	-15	2-88,3-53	-0.7
1930	Was-A	138	541	97	164	18	8	2	61	58	31	.303	.373	.377	90	-6	14	11	-2	.965	-19	*2-134/O-2	-1.8
1931	Was-A	139	591	114	173	33	11	4	56	58	42	.293	.360	.406	100	1	11	14	-5	**.984**	-17	*2-137	-1.1
1932	Was-A	143	577	120	161	38	16	5	52	69	33	.279	.360	.426	104	4	12	7	-1	.975	-18	*2-139	-0.7
1933	*Was-A	131	530	95	160	29	15	4	61	60	29	.302	.374	.436	115	12	6	8	-3	.978	-1	*2-129	1.4
1934	Was-A	139	524	103	160	33	8	3	57	102	32	.305	.419	.416	121	21	6	6	-2	.975	-13	*2-135	1.4
1935	Was-A☆	151	616	115	215	36	11	5	100	96	40	**.349**	.440	.468	139	41	7	6	-2	.979	8	*2-151	5.4
1936	Was-A	51	156	31	42	5	2	0	15	42	11	.269	.427	.327	94	1	7	2	1	.985	3	2-43	0.8
1937	Was-A☆	125	430	54	126	16	10	1	65	78	41	.293	.407	.384	105	7	2	6	-3	.966	-17	*2-119/O-1	-0.4
1938	Was-A	127	437	79	147	22	8	6	71	93	32	.336	.454	.465	140	33	9	5	-0	**.982**	2	*2-121	3.7
1939	Was-A	83	258	33	78	10	3	1	32	40	18	.302	.396	.376	106	4	4	1	1	.968	-1	2-65	0.7
1940	Was-A	71	210	28	61	14	4	0	29	34	10	.290	.389	.395	111	5	6	3	0	.967	4	2-54	1.1
1941	Was-A	53	107	14	27	3	1	0	9	18	10	.252	.360	.299	80	-2	2	0	1	.982	-8	2-24	-0.8
Total	17	1923	7038	1174	2131	353	130	38	850	965	428	.303	.389	.406	108	120	156	109	-19	.974	-103	*2-1340,S-238,3/O	10.2

■ GEORGE MYERS

Myers, George D. b: 11/13/1860, Buffalo, N.Y. d: 12/14/26, Buffalo, N.Y. BR/TR, 5'8", 170 lbs. Deb: 5/2/1884

YEAR	TM/L	G	AB	R	H	2B	3B	HR	RBI	BB	SO	AVG	OBP	SLG	PRO+	BR/A	SB	CS	SBR	FA	FR	G/POS	TPR
1884	Buf-N	78	325	34	59	9	2	2	32	13	33	.182	.213	.240	41	-22				.837	-10	C-49,O-34	-2.6
1885	Buf-N	89	326	40	67	7	2	0	19	23	40	.206	.258	.239	60	-14				.899	-6	C-69,O-23	-1.4
1886	StL-N	79	295	26	56	7	3	0	27	18	42	.190	.236	.234	46	-18	6			.928	-13	C-72/O-6,3-1	-2.1
1887	Ind-N	69	235	25	51	8	1	1	20	22	7	.217	.298	.272	62	-11	26			.929	-13	C-50,O-15/1-6,3-1	-1.7
1888	Ind-N	66	248	36	59	9	0	2	16	16	14	.238	.292	.298	87	-3	28			.929	-8	C-47,3-14,O-10,/1-1	-0.7
1889	Ind-N	43	149	22	29	3	0	0	12	17	13	.195	.294	.215	42	-11	12			.909	4	O-23,C-18/1-1	-0.5
Total	6	424	1578	183	321	43	8	5	126	109	149	.203	.260	.250	56	-80	72			.901	-46	C-305,O-111/3-16,1	-9.0

■ GREG MYERS

Myers, Gregory Richard b: 4/14/66, Riverside, Cal. BL/TR, 6'2", 205 lbs. Deb: 9/12/87

YEAR	TM/L	G	AB	R	H	2B	3B	HR	RBI	BB	SO	AVG	OBP	SLG	PRO+	BR/A	SB	CS	SBR	FA	FR	G/POS	TPR
1987	Tor-A	7	9	1	1	0	0	0	0	0	3	.111	.111	.111	-40	-2	0	0	0	1.000	2	/C-7	0.0
1989	Tor-A	17	44	0	5	2	0	0	1	2	9	.114	.152	.159	-12	-7	0	1	-1	1.000	2	C-11/D-6	-0.5
1990	Tor-A	87	250	33	59	7	1	5	22	22	33	.236	.298	.332	75	-9	0	1	-1	.993	-0	C-87	-0.5
1991	Tor-A	107	309	25	81	22	0	8	36	21	45	.262	.309	.411	94	-3	0	0	0	.979	-4	*C-104	-0.3
1992	Tor-A	22	61	4	14	6	0	1	13	5	5	.230	.288	.377	81	-2	0	0	0	.991	0	C-18/D-1	0.0
	Cal-A	8	17	0	4	1	0	0	0	0	6	.235	.235	.294	47	-1	0	0	0	1.000	2	/C-8	0.1
	Yr	30	78	4	18	7	0	1	13	5	11	.231	.277	.359	74	-3	0	0	0	.993	2	C-26/D-1	0.1
1993	Cal-A	108	290	27	74	10	0	7	40	17	47	.255	.301	.362	75	-11	3	3	-1	.986	-8	C-97/D-2	-1.5
1994	Cal-A	45	126	10	31	6	0	2	8	10	27	.246	.301	.341	64	-7	0	2	-1	.991	-2	C-41/D-1	-0.7
1995	Cal-A	85	273	35	71	12	2	9	38	17	49	.260	.306	.418	87	-6	0	1	-1	.989	-4	C-61,D-16	-0.7
1996	Min-A	97	329	37	94	22	3	6	47	19	52	.286	.325	.426	86	-7	0	0	0	.985	-12	C-90	-1.3
1997	Min-A	62	165	24	44	11	1	5	28	16	29	.267	.331	.436	97	-1	0	0	0	.986	-1	C-38,D-10	-0.1
	Atl-N	9	9	0	1	0	0	0	1	1	3	.111	.200	.111	-16	-2	0	0	0	1.000	2	/C-2	0.0
1998	*SD-N	69	171	19	42	10	0	4	20	17	36	.246	.314	.374	86	-4	0	1	-1	.987	-4	C-52	-0.5
Total	11	723	2053	215	521	109	7	47	254	147	344	.254	.305	.382	81	-61	3	9	-5	.987	-27	C-616/D-36	-6.0

■ HENRY MYERS

Myers, Henry C. b: 5/1858, Philadelphia, Pa. d: 4/18/1895, Philadelphia, Pa. BR/TR, 5'9", 159 lbs. Deb: 8/20/1881 M

YEAR	TM/L	G	AB	R	H	2B	3B	HR	RBI	BB	SO	AVG	OBP	SLG	PRO+	BR/A	SB	CS	SBR	FA	FR	G/POS	TPR
1881	Pro-N	1	4	0	0	0	0	0	0	0	2	.000	.000	.000	-99	-1				1.000	-0	/S-1	-0.1
1882	Bal-a	69	294	43	53	3	0	0		12		.180	.212	.190	40	-17				.822	-7	*S-68/P-6,M	-1.8
1884	Wil-U	6	24	3	3	0	0	0		0		.125	.125	.125	-23	-4				.875	4	/S-5,2-1	0.0
Total	3	76	322	46	56	3	0	0	0	12	2	.174	.204	.183	32	-22				.826	-3	/S-74,P-6,2-1	-1.9

■ HY MYERS

Myers, Henry Harrison b: 4/27/1889, E.Liverpool, Ohio d: 5/1/65, Minerva, Ohio BR/TR, 5'9.5", 175 lbs. Deb: 8/30/09

YEAR	TM/L	G	AB	R	H	2B	3B	HR	RBI	BB	SO	AVG	OBP	SLG	PRO+	BR/A	SB	CS	SBR	FA	FR	G/POS	TPR
1909	Bro-N	6	22	1	5	1	0	0	6	2		.227	.292	.273	78	-1	1			1.000	-1	/O-6	-0.2
1911	Bro-N	13	43	2	7	1	0	0	0	2	3	.163	.200	.186	9	-5	1			.889	-2	O-13	-0.8
1914	Bro-N	70	227	35	65	3	9	0	17	7	24	.286	.316	.379	104	0	2			.964	-6	O-60	-0.9
1915	Bro-N	153	605	69	150	21	7	2	46	17	51	.248	.275	.316	77	-18	19	22	-8	.964	7	*O-153	-3.0
1916	*Bro-N	113	412	54	108	12	14	3	36	21	35	.262	.308	.381	108	3	17			.969	1	*O-106	-0.2
1917	Bro-N	120	471	37	126	15	10	1	41	18	25	.268	.294	.348	94	-4	5			.982	-3	O-66,1-22,2-19,3-15	-1.2
1918	Bro-N	107	407	36	104	9	8	4	40	20	26	.256	.292	.346	95	-4	17			.975	13	*O-107	0.3
1919	Bro-N	133	512	62	157	23	**14**	5	**73**	23	34	.307	.339	**.436**	129	16	13			.979	9	*O-131	1.8
1920	*Bro-N	154	582	83	177	36	**22**	4	80	35	54	.304	.345	.462	126	18	9	13	-5	.978	4	*O-152/3-2	0.6
1921	Bro-N	144	549	51	158	14	4	4	68	22	51	.288	.318	.350	74	-20	8	6	-1	.968	6	*O-124,2-21/3-1	-2.4
1922	Bro-N	153	618	82	196	20	9	6	89	13	26	.317	.331	.408	90	-10	9	10	-3	.974	6	*O-152/2-1	-1.8
1923	StL-N	96	330	29	99	18	2	2	48	12	19	.300	.330	.385	90	-5	5	3	-0	.977	6	O-87	-0.4
1924	StL-N	43	124	12	26	5	1	1	15	3	10	.210	.228	.290	39	-11	1	2	-1	.945	-3	O-22,3-12/2-3	-1.6
1925	StL-N	1	1	0	0	0	0	0	0	0	0	.000	.000	.000	-98	-0	0	0	0	.000	0	H	0.0
	Cin-N	3	6	1	1	1	0	0	0	0	0	.167	.167	.333	25	-1	0	0	0	1.000	-1	/O-3	-0.1

YEAR	TM/L	G	AB	R	H	2B	3B	HR	RBI	BB	SO	AVG	OBP	SLG	PRO+	BR/A	SB	CS	SBR	FA	FR	G/POS	TPR
	StL-N	1	1	1	1	0	0	0	0	0	0	1.000	1.000	1.000	403	0	0	0	0	.000	0	H	0.0
	Yr	5	8	2	2	1	0	0	0	0	0	.250	.250	.375	58	-1	0	0	0	1.000	-1	/O-3	-0.1
Total	14	1310	4910	555	1380	179	100	32	559	195	358	.281	.312	.378	95	-42	107	56		.972	38	*O-1182/2-44,3-30,1	-9.9

■ BERT MYERS
Myers, James Albert b: 4/8/1874, Frederick, Md. d: 10/12/15, Washington, D.C. BR/TR, 5'10", Deb: 4/25/1896

YEAR	TM/L	G	AB	R	H	2B	3B	HR	RBI	BB	SO	AVG	OBP	SLG	PRO+	BR/A	SB	CS	SBR	FA	FR	G/POS	TPR
1896	StL-N	122	454	47	116	12	8	0	37	40	32	.256	.320	.317	71	-19	8			.867	-9	*3-121/S-1	-2.1
1898	Was-N	31	110	14	29	1	4	0	13	13		.264	.341	.345	97	-0	2			.835	-3	3-31	-0.3
1900	Phi-N	7	28	5	5	1	0	0	2	3		.179	.258	.214	31	-3	1			.909	2	/3-7	-0.1
Total	3	160	592	66	150	14	12	0	52	56	32	.253	.321	.318	74	-21	11			.863	-10	3-159/S-1	-2.5

■ AL MYERS
Myers, James Albert "Cod" b: 10/22/1863, Danville, Ill. d: 12/24/27, Marshall, Ill. BR/TR, 5'8.5", 165 lbs. Deb: 9/27/1884

YEAR	TM/L	G	AB	R	H	2B	3B	HR	RBI	BB	SO	AVG	OBP	SLG	PRO+	BR/A	SB	CS	SBR	FA	FR	G/POS	TPR
1884	Mil-U	12	46	6	15	6	0	0		0		.326	.326	.457	249	4				.848	2	2-12	0.6
1885	Phi-N	93	357	25	73	13	2	1	28	11	41	.204	.228	.261	59	-16				.884	-17	*2-93	-2.9
1886	KC-N	118	473	69	131	22	9	4	51	22	42	.277	.309	.387	104	0	3			.913	2	*2-118	0.6
1887	Was-N	105	362	45	84	9	5	2	36	40	26	.232	.312	.301	75	-11	18			.909	-5	2-78,S-27	-1.1
1888	Was-N	132	502	46	104	12	7	2	46	37	46	.207	.270	.271	77	-12	20			.918	-25	*2-132	-3.1
1889	Was-N	46	176	24	46	3	0	0	20	22	7	.261	.347	.278	81	-3	10			.942	3	2-46	0.2
	Phi-N	75	305	52	82	14	2	0	28	36	9	.269	.354	.328	84	-7	8			.853	-8	2-75	-0.9
	Yr	121	481	76	128	17	2	0	48	58	16	.266	.351	.310	83	-10	18			.886	-4	*2-121	-0.7
1890	Phi-N	117	487	95	135	29	7	2	81	57	46	.277	.365	.378	114	9	44			.948	14	*2-117	2.6
1891	Phi-N	135	514	67	118	27	2	2	69	69	46	.230	.331	.302	83	-10	8			.937	-10	*2-135	-1.2
Total	8	833	3222	429	788	135	34	13	359	294	263	.245	.314	.320	88	-45	111			.914	-42	2-806/S-27	-5.2

■ LYNN MYERS
Myers, Lynnwood Lincoln b: 2/23/14, Enola, Pa. BR/TR, 5'6.5", 145 lbs. Deb: 7/13/38 F

YEAR	TM/L	G	AB	R	H	2B	3B	HR	RBI	BB	SO	AVG	OBP	SLG	PRO+	BR/A	SB	CS	SBR	FA	FR	G/POS	TPR
1938	StL-N	70	227	18	55	10	2	1	19	9	25	.242	.271	.317	58	-13	9			.944	-1	S-69	-0.9
1939	StL-N	74	117	24	28	6	1	0	10	12	23	.239	.310	.308	63	-6	1			.897	5	S-36,3-13/2-5	0.1
Total	2	144	344	42	83	16	3	1	29	21	48	.241	.285	.314	60	-19	10			.930	4	S-105/3-13,2-5	-0.8

■ HAP MYERS
Myers, Ralph Edward b: 4/8/1888, San Francisco, Cal. d: 6/30/67, San Francisco, Cal. BR/TR, 6'3", 175 lbs. Deb: 4/16/10

YEAR	TM/L	G	AB	R	H	2B	3B	HR	RBI	BB	SO	AVG	OBP	SLG	PRO+	BR/A	SB	CS	SBR	FA	FR	G/POS	TPR
1910	Bos-A	3	6	0	2	0	0	0	0	0		.333	.333	.333	106	0	0			1.000	0	/O-2	0.0
1911	StL-A	11	37	4	11	1	0	0	1	1		.297	.316	.324	82	-1	0			.976	-2	1-11	-0.3
	Bos-A	13	38	3	14	2	0	0	0	4		.368	.429	.421	139	2	4			.947	-1	1-12	0.1
	Yr	24	75	7	25	3	0	0	1	5		.333	.375	.373	111	1	4			.963	-3	1-23	-0.2
1913	Bos-N	140	524	74	143	20	1	2	50	38	48	.273	.333	.326	87	-8	57			.987	5	*1-135	-0.5
1914	Bro-F	92	305	61	67	10	5	1	29	44	43	.220	.322	.295	69	-17	43			.989	1	1-88	-1.9
1915	Bro-F	118	341	61	98	9	1	1	36	32	39	.287	.352	.328	83	-7	28			.990	1	*1-107	-0.9
Total	5	377	1251	203	335	42	7	4	116	119	130	.268	.338	.322	85	-31	132			.987	4	1-353/O-2	-3.5

■ RICHIE MYERS
Myers, Richard b: 4/7/30, Sacramento, Cal. BR/TR, 5'6", 150 lbs. Deb: 4/21/56

YEAR	TM/L	G	AB	R	H	2B	3B	HR	RBI	BB	SO	AVG	OBP	SLG	PRO+	BR/A	SB	CS	SBR	FA	FR	G/POS	TPR
1956	Chi-N	4	1	1	0	0	0	0	0	0	0	.000	.000	.000	-99	-0	0	0	0	.000	0	H	0.0

■ ROD MYERS
Myers, Roderick Demond b: 1/14/73, Conroe, Tex. BL/TL, 6', 190 lbs. Deb: 6/21/96

YEAR	TM/L	G	AB	R	H	2B	3B	HR	RBI	BB	SO	AVG	OBP	SLG	PRO+	BR/A	SB	CS	SBR	FA	FR	G/POS	TPR
1996	KC-A	22	63	9	18	7	0	1	11	7	16	.286	.357	.444	101	0	3	2	-0	1.000	-3	O-19	-0.3
1997	KC-A	31	101	14	26	7	0	2	9	17	22	.257	.370	.386	95	-0	4	0	1	.982	-2	O-26	-0.1
Total	2	53	164	23	44	14	0	3	20	24	38	.268	.365	.409	98	-0	7	2	1	.989	-5	/O-45	-0.4

■ BILLY MYERS
Myers, William Harrison b: 8/14/10, Enola, Pa. d: 4/10/95, Carlisle, Pa. BR/TR, 5'8", 168 lbs. Deb: 4/16/35 F

YEAR	TM/L	G	AB	R	H	2B	3B	HR	RBI	BB	SO	AVG	OBP	SLG	PRO+	BR/A	SB	CS	SBR	FA	FR	G/POS	TPR
1935	Cin-N	117	445	60	119	15	10	5	36	29	81	.267	.315	.380	89	-8	10			.939	3	*S-112	0.1
1936	Cin-N	98	323	45	87	9	6	6	27	28	56	.269	.328	.390	99	-1	6			.938	8	S-98	1.2
1937	Cin-N	124	335	35	84	13	3	7	43	44	57	.251	.339	.370	97	-1	0			.948	4	*S-121/2-6	1.1
1938	Cin-N	134	442	57	112	18	6	12	47	41	80	.253	.317	.403	99	-1	2			.939	2	*S-123,2-11	1.1
1939	*Cin-N	151	509	79	143	18	6	9	56	71	90	.281	.369	.393	104	5	4			.951	6	*S-151	2.4
1940	*Cin-N	90	282	33	57	14	2	5	30	30	56	.202	.283	.319	65	-14	0			.961	-5	S-88	-1.1
1941	Chi-N	24	63	10	14	1	0	1	4	7	25	.222	.310	.286	71	-2	1			.939	4	S-19/2-1	0.3
Total	7	738	2399	319	616	88	33	45	243	250	445	.257	.328	.377	93	-22	23			.946	23	S-712/2-18	5.1

■ TIM NAEHRING
Naehring, Timothy James b: 2/1/67, Cincinnati, Ohio BR/TR, 6'2", 205 lbs. Deb: 7/15/90

YEAR	TM/L	G	AB	R	H	2B	3B	HR	RBI	BB	SO	AVG	OBP	SLG	PRO+	BR/A	SB	CS	SBR	FA	FR	G/POS	TPR
1990	Bos-A	24	85	10	23	6	0	2	12	8	15	.271	.333	.412	102	0	0	0	0	.918	-1	S-19/3-5,2-1	0.1
1991	Bos-A	20	55	1	6	1	0	0	3	6	15	.109	.197	.127	-8	-8	0	0	0	.956	-1	S-17/3-2,2-1	-0.8
1992	Bos-A	72	186	12	43	8	0	3	14	18	31	.231	.309	.323	72	-7	0	0	0	.992	16	S-30,2-23,3-10,/OD	1.1
1993	Bos-A	39	127	14	42	10	0	1	17	10	26	.331	.380	.433	111	2	1	0	0	.973	-4	2-15,D-10/3-9,S-4	-0.1
1994	Bos-A	80	297	41	82	18	1	7	42	30	56	.276	.350	.414	92	-3	1	3	-2	.981	-1	2-49,3-11/1-8,SD	-0.3
1995	*Bos-A	126	433	61	133	27	2	10	57	77	66	.307	.416	.448	121	17	0	2	-1	.954	7	*3-124/D-1	2.0
1996	Bos-A	116	430	77	124	16	0	17	65	49	63	.288	.366	.444	102	2	2	1	0	.963	1	*3-116/2-1	0.2
1997	Bos-A	70	259	38	74	18	1	9	40	38	40	.286	.379	.467	117	7	1	1	-0	.981	-7	3-68/D-1	0.0
Total	8	547	1872	254	527	104	4	49	250	236	312	.282	.367	.420	102	9	5	7	-3	.962	9	3-345/2-90,SD10	2.2

■ BILL NAGEL
Nagel, William Taylor b: 8/19/15, Memphis, Tenn. d: 10/8/81, Freehold, N.J. BR/TR, 6'1", 190 lbs. Deb: 4/20/39

YEAR	TM/L	G	AB	R	H	2B	3B	HR	RBI	BB	SO	AVG	OBP	SLG	PRO+	BR/A	SB	CS	SBR	FA	FR	G/POS	TPR
1939	Phi-A	105	341	39	86	19	4	12	39	25	86	.252	.307	.437	90	-7	2	1	0	.944	-15	2-56,3-43/P-1	-1.7
1941	Phi-N	17	56	2	8	1	1	0	6	3	14	.143	.186	.196	8	-7	0			.935	3	2-12/O-2,3-1	-0.3
1945	Chi-A	67	220	21	46	10	3	3	27	15	41	.209	.263	.323	71	-9	3	1	0	.984	-3	1-57/3-1	-1.7
Total	3	189	617	62	140	30	8	15	72	43	141	.227	.281	.374	77	-23	5	2		.942	-15	/2-68,1-57,3-45,OP	-3.7

■ LOU NAGELSEN
Nagelsen, Louis Marcellus (b: Louis Marcellus Nageleisen)
b: 6/29/1887, Piqua, Ohio d: 10/21/65, Fort Wayne, Ind. BR/TR, 6'2", 180 lbs. Deb: 9/10/12

YEAR	TM/L	G	AB	R	H	2B	3B	HR	RBI	BB	SO	AVG	OBP	SLG	PRO+	BR/A	SB	CS	SBR	FA	FR	G/POS	TPR
1912	Cle-A	2	3	0	0	0	0	0	0	0		.000	.000	.000	-97	-1	0			1.000	-1	/C-2	-0.2

■ RUSS NAGELSON
Nagelson, Russell Charles b: 9/19/44, Cincinnati, Ohio BL/TR, 6', 205 lbs. Deb: 9/11/68

YEAR	TM/L	G	AB	R	H	2B	3B	HR	RBI	BB	SO	AVG	OBP	SLG	PRO+	BR/A	SB	CS	SBR	FA	FR	G/POS	TPR
1968	Cle-A	5	3	0	1	0	0	0	0	2	2	.333	.600	.333	192	1	0	0	0	.000	0	H	0.1
1969	Cle-A	12	17	1	6	0	0	0	0	3	3	.353	.450	.353	123	1	0	0	0	1.000	-1	/O-3,1-1	0.0
1970	Cle-A	17	24	3	3	1	0	1	2	3	9	.125	.222	.292	39	-2	0	0	0	1.000	-0	/O-4	-0.3
	Det-A	28	32	5	6	0	0	0	2	5	6	.188	.297	.188	36	-3	0	0	0	1.000	-1	/O-4,1-1	-0.4
	Yr	45	56	8	9	1	0	1	4	8	15	.161	.266	.232	38	-5	0	0	0	1.000	-2	/O-8,1-1	-0.7
Total	3	62	76	9	16	1	0	1	4	13	20	.211	.326	.263	64	-3	0	0	0	1.000	-2	/O-11,1-2	-0.6

■ TOM NAGLE
Nagle, Thomas Edward b: 10/30/1865, Milwaukee, Wis. d: 3/9/46, Milwaukee, Wis. BR/TR, 5'10", 150 lbs. Deb: 4/22/1890

YEAR	TM/L	G	AB	R	H	2B	3B	HR	RBI	BB	SO	AVG	OBP	SLG	PRO+	BR/A	SB	CS	SBR	FA	FR	G/POS	TPR
1890	Chi-N	38	144	21	39	5	1	1	11	7	24	.271	.318	.340	88	-3	4			.939	-7	C-33/O-6	-0.6
1891	Chi-N	8	25	3	3	0	0	0	1	1	3	.120	.154	.120	-20	-4	0			.906	-3	/C-7,O-1	-0.6
Total	2	46	169	24	42	5	1	1	12	8	27	.249	.294	.308	73	-6	4			.935	-11	/C-40,O-7	-1.2

■ BILL NAHORODNY
Nahorodny, William Gerard b: 8/31/53, Hamtramck, Mich. BR/TR, 6'2", 200 lbs. Deb: 9/27/76

YEAR	TM/L	G	AB	R	H	2B	3B	HR	RBI	BB	SO	AVG	OBP	SLG	PRO+	BR/A	SB	CS	SBR	FA	FR	G/POS	TPR
1976	Phi-N	3	5	0	1	1	0	0	0	0	0	.200	.200	.400	65	-0	0	0	0	1.000	0	/C-2	0.0
1977	Chi-A	7	23	3	6	1	0	1	4	2	3	.261	.320	.435	104	0	0	0	0	1.000	-1	/C-7	-0.1
1978	Chi-A	107	347	29	82	11	2	8	35	23	52	.236	.288	.349	77	-11	1	0	0	.980	-3	*C-104/1-4,D-1	-1.2
1979	Chi-A	65	179	20	46	10	0	6	29	18	23	.257	.325	.413	98	-1	0	1	-1	.973	-0	C-60/D-3	0.0
1980	Atl-N	59	157	14	38	12	0	5	18	8	21	.242	.287	.414	91	-2	0	2	-1	.990	-7	C-54/1-1	-1.0
1981	Atl-N	14	13	0	3	1	0	0	2	1	3	.231	.286	.308	67	-1	0	0	0	1.000	0	/C-3,1-1	-0.1
1982	Cle-A	39	94	6	21	5	1	4	18	2	9	.223	.240	.426	79	-3	0	0	0	1.000	-3	C-35	-0.6
1983	Det-A	2	1	0	0	0	0	0	0	1	0	.000	.500	.000	53	0	0	0	0	.000	0	/H	0.0
1984	Sea-A	12	25	2	6	0	0	1	3	1	7	.240	.321	.360	89	-0	0	1	-1	.976	-3	C-10/1-1	-0.3
Total	9	308	844	74	203	41	3	25	109	56	118	.241	.292	.385	85	-18	1	4	-2	.983	-17	C-275/1-7,D-4	-3.3

YEAR	TM/L	G	AB	R	H	2B	3B	HR	RBI	BB	SO	AVG	OBP	SLG	PRO+	BR/A	SB	CS	SBR	FA	FR	G/POS	TPR
■ FRANK NALEWAY Naleway, Frank "Chick" b: 7/5/02, Chicago, Ill. d: 1/28/49, Chicago, Ill. BR/TR, 5'9.5", 165 lbs. Deb: 9/16/24																							
1924	Chi-A	1	2	0	0	0	0	0	0	1	0	.000	.333	.000	-10	-0	0	0	0	.750	-1	/S-1	-0.1
■ DOC NANCE Nance, William G. "Kid" (b: Willie G. Cooper) b: 8/2/1876, Ft.Worth, Tex. d: 5/28/58, Fort Worth, Tex. BR/TR, 5'7", 165 lbs. Deb: 8/19/1897																							
1897	Lou-N	35	120	25	29	5	3	3	17	20		.242	.355	.408	105	1	3			.986	4	O-35	0.2
1898	Lou-N	22	76	13	24	5	0	1	16	12		.316	.416	.421	142	5	2			.946	2	O-22	0.5
1901	Det-A	132	461	72	129	24	5	3	66	51		.280	.355	.373	98	-1	9			.932	1	*O-132	-0.9
Total	3	189	657	110	182	34	8	7	99	83		.277	.362	.385	104	5	14			.943	6	O-189	-0.2
■ AL NAPLES Naples, Aloysius Francis b: 8/29/27, St.George, N.Y. BR/TR, 5'9", 168 lbs. Deb: 6/25/49																							
1949	StL-A	2	7	0	1	1	0	0	0	0	1	.143	.143	.286	12	-1	0	0	0	.875	-1	/S-2	-0.2
■ DANNY NAPOLEON Napoleon, Daniel b: 1/11/42, Claysburg, Pa. BR/TR, 5'11", 190 lbs. Deb: 4/14/65																							
1965	NY-N	68	97	5	14	1	1	0	7	8	23	.144	.224	.175	15	-11	0	0	0	.941	1	O-15/3-7	-1.1
1966	NY-N	12	33	2	7	2	0	0	0	1	10	.212	.235	.273	42	-3	0	1	-1	.929	-0	O-10	-0.4
Total	2	80	130	7	21	3	1	0	7	9	33	.162	.227	.200	22	-14	0	1	-1	.938	1	/O-25,3-7	-1.5
■ HAL NARAGON Naragon, Harold Richard b: 10/1/28, Zanesville, Ohio BL/TR, 6', 175 lbs. Deb: 9/23/51 C																							
1951	Cle-A	3	8	0	2	0	0	0	0	1	0	.250	.400	.250	83	-0	0	0	0	.929	0	/C-2	0.0
1954	*Cle-A	46	101	10	24	2	2	0	12	9	12	.238	.300	.297	63	-5	0	0	0	1.000	-2	C-45	-0.5
1955	Cle-A	57	127	12	41	9	2	1	14	15	8	.323	.394	.449	122	4	1	0	0	.991	-4	C-52	0.2
1956	Cle-A	53	122	11	35	3	1	3	18	13	9	.287	.360	.402	99	-0	0	0	0	.988	-12	C-48	-1.0
1957	Cle-A	57	121	12	31	1	1	0	8	12	9	.256	.328	.281	69	-5	0	0	0	.990	-2	C-39	-0.6
1958	Cle-A	9	9	2	3	0	1	0	0	0	0	.333	.333	.556	144	0	0	0	0	.000	0	H	0.0
1959	Cle-A	14	36	6	10	4	1	0	5	3	2	.278	.350	.444	121	1	0	0	0	1.000	-1	C-10	0.0
	Was-A	71	195	12	47	3	2	0	11	8	9	.241	.275	.277	52	-13	0	1	-1	.993	-2	C-54	-1.2
	Yr	85	231	18	57	7	3	0	16	11	11	.247	.287	.303	63	-12	0	1	-1	.994	-3	C-64	-1.2
1960	Was-A	33	92	7	19	2	0	0	5	8	4	.207	.277	.228	39	-8	0	0	0	.978	-2	C-29	-0.9
1961	Min-A	57	139	10	42	2	1	2	11	4	8	.302	.326	.374	82	-4	0	0	0	.994	-5	C-36	-0.7
1962	Min-A	24	35	1	8	1	0	0	3	3	1	.229	.289	.257	47	-3	0	0	0	1.000	0	/C-9	-0.2
Total	10	424	985	83	262	27	11	6	87	76	62	.266	.323	.334	77	-31	1	1	-0	.991	-29	C-324	-4.9
■ BILL NARLESKI Narleski, William Edward "Cap" b: 6/9/1899, Perth Amboy, N.J. d: 7/22/64, Laurel Springs, N.J. BR/TR, 5'9", 160 lbs. Deb: 4/18/29 F																							
1929	Bos-A	96	260	30	72	16	1	0	25	21	22	.277	.333	.346	77	-9	4	4	-1	.957	-17	S-51,2-29/3-7	-1.9
1930	Bos-A	39	98	11	23	9	0	0	7	7	5	.235	.306	.327	63	-6	0	0	0	.915	-8	S-19,3-14/2-5	-1.1
Total	2	135	358	41	95	25	1	0	32	28	27	.265	.326	.341	73	-14	4	4	-1	.949	-25	/S-70,2-34,3-21	-3.0
■ JERRY NARRON Narron, Jerry Austin b: 1/15/56, Goldsboro, N.C. BL/TR, 6'3", 205 lbs. Deb: 4/13/79 C																							
1979	NY-A	61	123	17	21	3	1	4	18	9	26	.171	.227	.309	44	-10	0	0	0	.973	-4	C-56/D-1	-1.3
1980	Sea-A	48	107	7	21	3	0	4	18	13	18	.196	.283	.336	68	-5	0	0	0	.992	-10	C-39/D-1	-1.3
1981	Sea-A	76	203	13	45	5	0	3	17	16	35	.222	.285	.291	64	-9	0	0	0	.996	-14	C-65	-2.3
1983	Cal-A	10	22	1	3	0	0	1	4	1	3	.136	.174	.273	21	-2	0	0	0	.895	-1	/C-6,D-1	-0.3
1984	Cal-A	69	150	9	37	5	0	3	17	8	12	.247	.289	.340	74	-5	0	0	0	.994	-8	C-46/1-7	-1.2
1985	Cal-A	67	132	12	29	4	0	5	14	11	17	.220	.280	.364	75	-5	0	0	0	1.000	2	C-45/1-1,D-7	-0.1
1986	*Cal-A	57	95	5	21	3	1	1	8	9	14	.221	.295	.305	65	-5	0	0	0	.988	1	C-51/D-2	-0.1
1987	Sea-A	4	8	0	0	0	0	0	0	0	2	.000	.000	.000	-95	-2	0	0	0	1.000	-0	/C-3	-0.2
Total	8	392	840	64	177	23	2	21	96	67	127	.211	.272	.318	62	-44	0	0	0	.989	-33	C-311/D-12,1-8	-6.8
■ SAM NARRON Narron, Samuel b: 8/25/13, Middlesex, N.C. d: 12/31/96, Middlesex, N.C. BR/TR, 5'10", 180 lbs. Deb: 9/15/35 C																							
1935	StL-N	4	7	0	3	0	0	0	0	0	0	.429	.429	.429	126	0	0			1.000	-0	/C-1	0.0
1942	StL-N	10	10	0	4	0	0	0	1	0	0	.400	.400	.400	125	0	0			1.000	-0	/C-2	0.0
1943	*StL-N	10	11	0	1	0	0	0	0	1	2	.091	.167	.091	-24	-2	0			1.000	1	/C-3	-0.1
Total	3	24	28	0	8	0	0	0	1	1	2	.286	.310	.286	67	-1	0			1.000	1	/C-6	-0.1
■ COTTON NASH Nash, Charles Francis b: 7/24/42, Jersey City, N.J. BR/TR, 6'6", 220 lbs. Deb: 9/1/67																							
1967	Chi-A	3	3	1	0	0	0	0	0	1	0	.000	.250	.000	-21	-0	0	0	0	.833	-1	/1-3	-0.1
1969	Min-A	6	9	0	2	0	0	0	0	1	2	.222	.300	.222	47	-1	0	0	0	1.000	1	/1-6,O-1	0.0
1970	Min-A	4	4	1	1	0	0	0	2	1	1	.250	.400	.250	82	-0	0	1	-1	1.000	-0	/1-2	-0.1
Total	3	13	16	2	3	0	0	0	2	3	3	.188	.316	.188	45	-1	0	1	-1	.965	0	/1-11,O-1	-0.2
■ KEN NASH Nash, Kenneth Leland (Played One Game In 1912 under name of Costello) b: 7/14/1888, Weymouth, Mass. d: 2/16/77, Epsom, N.H. BB/TR, 5'8", 140 lbs. Deb: 7/4/12																							
1912	Cle-A	11	23	2	4	0	0	0	0	3		.174	.269	.174	27	-2	0			.826	-3	/S-8	-0.5
1914	StL-N	24	51	4	14	3	1	0	6	6	10	.275	.351	.373	116	1	0			.875	-6	3-10/2-6,S-3	-0.6
Total	2	35	74	6	18	3	1	0	6	9	10	.243	.325	.311	87	-1	0			.760	-10	/S-11,3-10,2-6	-1.1
■ BILLY NASH Nash, William Mitchell b: 6/24/1865, Richmond, Va. d: 11/15/29, E.Orange, N.J. BR/TR, 5'8.5", 167 lbs. Deb: 8/5/1884 MU																							
1884	Ric-a	45	166	31	33	8	8	1		12		.199	.281	.361	109	2				.828	8	3-45	0.9
1885	Bos-N	26	94	9	24	4	0	0	11	2	9	.255	.271	.298	87	-1				.864	-4	3-19/2-8	-0.4
1886	Bos-N	109	417	61	117	11	8	1	45	24	28	.281	.320	.353	108	4	16			.863	-5	*3-90,S-17/O-2	0.2
1887	Bos-N	121	475	100	140	24	12	6	94	60	30	.295	.376	.434	124	17	43			.884	9	*3-117/O-5	2.3
1888	Bos-N	135	526	71	149	18	15	4	75	50	46	.283	.350	.397	136	22	20			**.913**	26	*3-105,2-31	**4.9**
1889	Bos-N	128	481	84	132	20	2	3	76	79	44	.274	.379	.343	97	-0	26			.905	12	*3-128/P-1	1.4
1890	Bos-P	129	488	103	130	28	6	5	90	88	43	.266	.383	.379	97	-2	26			.866	18	*3-129/P-1	1.7
1891	Bos-N	140	537	92	148	24	9	5	95	74	50	.276	.369	.382	106	2	28			.900	-12	*3-140	-0.3
1892	*Bos-N	135	526	94	137	25	5	4	95	59	42	.260	.338	.350	99	-2	31			**.898**	24	*3-135/O-1	2.5
1893	Bos-N	128	485	115	141	27	6	10	123	85	29	.291	.399	.433	112	8	30			**.923**	3	*3-128	1.0
1894	Bos-N	132	512	132	148	23	6	8	87	91	23	.289	.399	.404	87	-11	20			**.933**	6	*3-132	-0.4
1895	Bos-N	132	508	97	147	23	6	10	108	74	19	.289	.383	.417	99	-2	18			.882	-8	*3-132	-0.7
1896	Phi-N	65	227	29	56	9	1	3	30	34	21	.247	.355	.335	83	-4	3			.911	7	3-65,M	0.3
1897	Phi-N	104	337	45	87	20	2	0	39	60		.258	.373	.329	89	-3	4			.919	-8	3-79,S-19/2-4	-0.7
1898	Phi-N	20	70	9	17	2	1	0	9	11		.243	.346	.300	89	-1	0			.958	-1	3-20	-0.1
Total	15	1549	5849	1072	1606	266	87	60	977	803	384	.275	.366	.381	103	29	265			.897	75	*3-1464/2-43,SOP	12.6
■ ROB NATAL Natal, Robert Marcel b: 11/13/65, Long Beach, Cal. BR/TR, 5'11", 190 lbs. Deb: 7/18/92																							
1992	Mon-N	5	6	0	0	0	0	0	0	1	1	.000	.143	.000	-57	-1	0	0	0	.909	-0	/C-4	-0.2
1993	Fla-N	41	117	3	25	4	1	1	6	6	22	.214	.276	.291	49	-8	1	0	0	1.000	3	C-38	-0.4
1994	Fla-N	10	29	2	8	2	0	0	2	5	5	.276	.382	.345	89	-0	1	0	0	.983	3	/C-8	0.3
1995	Fla-N	16	43	2	10	2	1	2	6	1	9	.233	.250	.465	83	-1	0	0	0	.988	-1	C-13	-0.1
1996	Fla-N	44	90	4	12	1	1	0	2	15	31	.133	.257	.167	15	-11	0	1	-1	.976	0	C-43	-1.0
1997	Fla-N	4	4	2	2	1	0	1	3	2	0	.500	.667	1.500	468	2	0	0	0	1.000	0	/C-4	0.3
Total	6	120	289	13	57	10	3	4	19	30	68	.197	.282	.294	52	-20	2	1	0	.986	5	C-110	-1.1
■ PETE NATON Naton, Peter Alphonsus b: 9/9/31, Flushing, N.Y. BR/TR, 6'1", 200 lbs. Deb: 6/16/53																							
1953	Pit-N	6	12	2	2	0	0	0	1	2	1	.167	.286	.167	22	-1	0	0	0	1.000	-1	/C-4	-0.2
■ SANDY NAVA Nava, Vincent P. (b: Irwin Sandy) b: 4/12/1850, San Francisco, Cal d: 6/15/06, Baltimore, Md. 5'6", 155 lbs. Deb: 5/5/1882																							
1882	Pro-N	28	97	15	20	2	0	0	7	1	13	.206	.214	.227	42	-6				.867	-7	C-27/O-1	-1.1
1883	Pro-N	29	100	18	24	4	2	0	16	3	17	.240	.262	.320	74	-3				.813	-4	C-27/O-2	-0.5
1884	Pro-N	34	116	10	11	0	0	0	6	11	35	.095	.173	.095	-13	-15				.887	1	C-27/S-6,2-1	-1.0
1885	Bal-a	8	27	2	5	1	0	0	4	1		.185	.214	.222	39	-2				.825	-5	/C-8	-0.6

YEAR	TM/L	G	AB	R	H	2B	3B	HR	RBI	BB	SO	AVG	OBP	SLG	PRO+	BR/A	SB	CS	SBR	FA	FR	G/POS	TPR
1886	Bal-a	2	5	0	1	0	0	0	0	0		.200	.200	.200	26	-0	1			.500	-1	/S-1,C-1	-0.1
Total	5	101	345	45	61	7	2	0	33	16	65	.177	.213	.209	33	-26	1			.857	-16	/C-90,S-7,O-3,2-1	-3.3
■ **TITO NAVARRO**	Navarro, Norberto (Rodriguez) b: 9/12/70, Rio Piedras, P.R. BB/TR, 5'10", 165 lbs. Deb: 9/6/93																						
1993	NY-N	12	17	1	1	0	0	0	1	0	4	.059	.059	.059	-69	-4	0	0	0	1.000	1	/S-2	-0.3
■ **EARL NAYLOR**	Naylor, Earl Eugene b: 5/19/19, Kansas City, Mo. d: 1/16/90, Winter Haven, Fla. BR/TR, 6', 190 lbs. Deb: 4/15/42																						
1942	Phi-N	76	168	9	33	4	1	0	14	11	18	.196	.246	.232	42	-12	1			.984	-5	O-34,P-20	-1.8
1943	Phi-N	33	120	12	21	2	0	3	14	12	16	.175	.256	.267	53	-7	1			.964	6	O-33	-0.3
1946	Bro-N	3	2	1	0	0	0	0	0	0	1	.000	.000	.000	-99	-1	0			.000	0	H	-0.1
Total	3	112	290	22	54	6	1	3	28	23	35	.186	.248	.245	46	-20	2			.971	1	/O-67,P-20	-2.2
■ **JACK NEAGLE**	Neagle, John Henry b: 1/2/1858, Syracuse, N.Y. d: 9/20/04, Syracuse, N.Y. BR/TR, 5'6", 155 lbs. Deb: 7/8/1879																						
1879	Cin-N	3	12	1	2	0	0	0	2	0	0	.167	.167	.167	11	-1				.000	-1	/O-2,P-2	-0.1
1883	Phi-N	18	73	6	12	1	0	0	4	1	9	.164	.176	.178	9	-8				.840	-2	O-12/P-8	-0.5
	Bal-a	9	35	3	10	4	0	0		2		.286	.324	.400	128	1				.769	-3	/P-6,O-5	-0.2
	Pit-a	27	101	14	19	0	1	0		5		.188	.226	.208	43	-6				.839	-3	P-16,O-15	-0.5
	Yr	36	136	17	29	4	1	0		7		.213	.252	.257	66	-5				.818	-6	P-22,O-20	-0.7
1884	Pit-a	43	148	13	22	6	0	0		6		.149	.187	.189	23	-12				.760	-5	P-38/O-6	-0.4
Total	3	100	369	37	65	11	1	0	6	14	9	.176	.208	.211	35	-26				.785	-14	/P-70,O-40	-1.7
■ **CHARLIE NEAL**	Neal, Charles Lenard b: 1/30/31, Longview, Tex. d: 11/18/96, Dallas, Tex. BR/TR, 5'10", 165 lbs. Deb: 4/17/56																						
1956	*Bro-N	62	136	22	39	5	1	2	14	14	19	.287	.353	.382	91	-1	2	2	-1	.972	2	2-51/S-1	0.2
1957	Bro-N	128	448	62	121	13	7	12	62	53	83	.270	.358	.411	96	-1	11	4	1	.949	-3	*S-100,3-23/2-3	0.7
1958	LA-N	140	473	87	120	9	6	22	65	61	91	.254	.345	.438	102	2	7	6	-2	.976	12	*2-132/S-9	2.2
1959	*LA-N★	151	616	103	177	30	**11**	19	83	43	86	.287	.338	.464	103	2	17	6	2	**.989**	20	*2-151/S-1	3.5
1960	LA-N★	139	477	60	122	23	2	8	40	48	75	.256	.325	.363	83	-11	5	5	-2	.977	-16	*2-136/S-3	-1.6
1961	LA-N	108	341	40	80	6	1	10	48	30	49	.235	.298	.346	65	-17	3	2	-0	.976	2	*2-104	-0.6
1962	NY-N	136	508	59	132	14	9	11	58	56	90	.260	.333	.388	91	-6	2	8	-4	.970	-8	2-85,S-39,3-12	-0.6
1963	NY-N	72	253	26	57	12	1	3	18	27	49	.225	.302	.316	77	-7	1	2	-1	.961	0	3-66/S-8	-0.8
	Cin-N	34	64	2	10	1	0	0	3	5	15	.156	.217	.172	13	-7	0	1	-1	.927	-2	3-19/2-1,S-1	-1.1
	Yr	106	317	28	67	13	1	3	21	32	64	.211	.286	.287	64	-14	1	3	-2	.955	-2	3-85/S-9,2-1	-1.9
Total	8	970	3316	461	858	113	38	87	391	337	557	.259	.331	.394	90	-47	48	36	-7	.978	7	2-663,S-162,3-120	1.9
■ **OFFA NEAL**	Neal, Theophilus Fountain b: 6/5/1876, Benton, Ill. d: 4/11/50, Mt.Vernon, Ill. BL/TR, 6', 185 lbs. Deb: 9/30/05																						
1905	NY-N	4	13	0	0	0	0	0	0	0		.000	.000	.000	-98	-3	0			1.000	-1	/3-3,2-1	-0.4
■ **GREASY NEALE**	Neale, Alfred Earle b: 11/5/1891, Parkersburg, W.Va. d: 11/2/73, Lake Worth, Fla. BL/TR, 6', 170 lbs. Deb: 4/12/16 C																						
1916	Cin-N	138	530	53	139	13	5	0	20	19	79	.262	.295	.306	87	-9	17			.973	11	*O-133	-0.6
1917	Cin-N	121	385	40	113	14	9	3	33	24	36	.294	.343	.400	133	14	25			.979	-5	*O-119	0.4
1918	Cin-N	107	371	57	100	11	11	1	32	24	38	.270	.324	.367	112	5	23			**.981**	10	*O-102	1.0
1919	*Cin-N	139	500	57	121	10	12	1	54	47	51	.242	.316	.316	93	-3	28			.959	2	*O-138	-1.2
1920	Cin-N	150	530	55	135	10	7	3	46	45	48	.255	.322	.317	85	-9	29	12	2	.987	14	*O-150	-0.4
1921	Phi-N	22	57	7	12	1	0	0	1	14	9	.211	.366	.228	56	-3	3	4	-2	.842	-5	O-16	-1.1
	Cin-N	63	241	39	58	10	5	0	12	22	16	.241	.307	.324	70	-10	9	6	-1	.964	1	O-60	-1.5
	Yr	85	298	46	70	11	5	0	13	36	25	.235	.319	.305	67	-13	12	10	-2	.950	-4	O-76	-2.6
1922	Cin-N	25	43	11	10	2	1	0	2	6	3	.233	.353	.326	77	-1	5	2	0	.864	-4	O-16	-0.5
1924	Cin-N	3	4	0	0	0	0	0	0	0	1	.000	.000	.000	-99	-1	0	0	0	1.000	-0	/O-2	-0.2
Total	8	768	2661	319	688	71	50	8	200	201	281	.259	.319	.332	94	-18	139	24		.972	24	O-736	-4.1
■ **JOE NEALE**	Neale, Joseph Hunt b: 5/7/1866, Wadsworth, Ohio d: 12/30/13, Akron, Ohio BR/TR, 5'8", 153 lbs. Deb: 6/21/1886																						
1886	Lou-a	2	5	0	0	0	0	0	0	0		.000	.000	.000	-95	-1	0			1.000	0	/O-2,P-1	-0.1
1887	Lou-a	5	19	3	1	0	0	0	1	3		.053	.182	.053	-32	-3	1			.833	0	/P-5	0.0
1890	StL-a	11	30	4	2	0	0	0	1	3		.067	.152	.067	-31	-5	0			1.000	-2	P-10/O-1	0.0
1891	StL-a	15	51	6	6	0	1	1	8	3	11	.118	.167	.216	8	-7	1			.933	2	P-15	0.0
Total	4	33	105	13	9	0	1	1	10	9	11	.086	.158	.133	-14	-16	2			.930	0	/P-31,O-3	-0.1
■ **JIM NEALON**	Nealon, James Joseph b: 12/15/1884, Sacramento, Cal. d: 4/2/10, San Francisco, Cal. BR/TR, 6'1.5", Deb: 4/12/06																						
1906	Pit-N	154	556	82	142	21	12	3	**83**	53		.255	.327	.353	107	4	15			.987	1	*1-154	0.1
1907	Pit-N	105	381	29	98	10	8	0	47	23		.257	.301	.325	95	-3	11			.978	0	*1-104	-0.7
Total	2	259	937	111	240	31	20	3	130	76		.256	.317	.342	102	1	26			.983	1	1-258	-0.6
■ **TOM NEEDHAM**	Needham, Thomas Joseph "Deerfoot" b: 5/17/1879, Steubenville, Ohio d: 12/13/26, Steubenville, Ohio BR/TR, 5'10", 180 lbs. Deb: 5/12/04																						
1904	Bos-N	84	269	18	70	12	3	4	19	11		.260	.292	.372	108	1	3			.945	4	C-77/O-1	1.4
1905	Bos-N	83	271	21	59	6	1	2	17	24		.218	.293	.269	70	-10	3			.949	-8	C-77/O-3,1-2	-1.1
1906	Bos-N	83	285	11	54	8	2	1	12	13		.189	.230	.242	49	-18	3			.962	-7	C-76/2-5,1-2,3-1,O	-2.0
1907	Bos-N	86	260	19	51	6	2	1	19	18		.196	.264	.246	60	-12	4			.967	-11	C-78/1-1	-1.8
1908	NY-N	54	91	8	19	3	0	0	11	12		.209	.339	.242	82	-1	0			.975	7	C-47	1.0
1909	Chi-N	13	28	3	4	0	0	0	0	0		.143	.143	.143	-11	-4	0			.980	1	/C-7	-0.2
1910	*Chi-N	31	76	9	14	3	1	0	10	10	10	.184	.287	.250	57	-4	1			.982	3	C-27/1-1	0.2
1911	Chi-N	27	62	4	12	2	0	0	5	9	14	.194	.315	.226	52	-4	2			.984	6	C-23	0.4
1912	Chi-N	33	90	12	16	5	0	0	10	7	13	.178	.260	.233	36	-8	3			.994	-1	C-32	-0.6
1913	Chi-N	20	42	5	10	4	1	0	11	4	8	.238	.304	.381	95	-0	0			.962	4	C-14/1-1	0.5
1914	Chi-N	9	17	3	2	1	0	0	3	1	4	.118	.167	.176	2	-2	1			.943	1	/C-7	0.0
Total	11	523	1491	113	311	50	10	8	117	109	49	.209	.274	.272	66	-60	20			.963	-1	C-465/1-7,2-5,03	-2.2
■ **TROY NEEL**	Neel, Troy Lee b: 9/14/65, Freeport, Tex. BL/TR, 6'4", 210 lbs. Deb: 5/30/92																						
1992	Oak-A	24	53	8	14	3	0	3	9	5	15	.264	.339	.491	137	2	0	1	-1	.846	-2	/O-9,1-2,D-9	0.0
1993	Oak-A	123	427	59	124	21	0	19	63	49	101	.290	.369	.473	132	19	3	5	-2	.981	-0	D-85,1-34	1.1
1994	Oak-A	83	278	43	74	13	0	15	48	38	61	.266	.358	.475	123	9	2	3	-1	.994	-0	1-45,D-35	0.2
Total	3	230	758	110	212	37	0	37	120	92	177	.280	.363	.475	129	31	5	9	-4	.986	-3	D-129/1-81,O-9	1.3
■ **CAL NEEMAN**	Neeman, Calvin Amandus b: 2/18/29, Valmeyer, Ill. BR/TR, 6'1", 192 lbs. Deb: 4/16/57																						
1957	Chi-N	122	415	37	107	17	1	10	39	22	87	.258	.300	.376	81	-11	0	0	0	.990	1	*C-118	-0.6
1958	Chi-N	76	201	30	52	7	0	12	29	21	41	.259	.338	.473	113	3	0	0	0	.992	1	C-71	0.8
1959	Chi-N	44	105	7	17	2	0	3	9	11	23	.162	.241	.267	36	-10	0	0	0	.994	-1	C-38	-1.0
1960	Chi-N	9	13	0	2	1	0	0	0	0	5	.154	.154	.231	4	-2	0	0	0	1.000	4	/C-9	0.2
	Phi-N	59	160	13	29	6	2	4	13	16	42	.181	.264	.319	59	-9	0	0	0	.979	5	C-52	-0.2
	Yr	68	173	13	31	7	2	4	13	16	47	.179	.257	.312	55	-11	0	0	0	.982	8	C-61	0.0
1961	Phi-N	19	31	0	7	1	0	0	2	4	8	.226	.314	.258	55	-2	1	0	0	.986	2	C-19	0.1
1962	Pit-N	24	50	5	9	1	1	1	5	3	10	.180	.226	.300	40	-4	0	0	0	.983	8	C-24	0.4
1963	Cle-A	9	9	0	0	0	0	0	0	1	5	.000	.100	.000	-70	-2	0	0	0	1.000	3	/C-9	0.1
	Was-A	14	18	1	1	0	0	0	0	1	0	.056	.105	.056	-54	-4	0	0	0	.970	2	C-12	-0.2
	Yr	23	27	1	1	0	0	0	0	2	5	.037	.103	.037	-59	-6	0	0	0	.985	5	C-21	-0.1
Total	7	376	1002	93	224	35	4	30	97	79	221	.224	.286	.356	72	-41	1	0	0	.988	24	C-352	-0.4
■ **DOUG NEFF**	Neff, Douglas Williams b: 10/8/1891, Harrisonburg, Va. d: 5/23/32, Cape Charles, Va. BR/TR, 5'9", 141 lbs. Deb: 6/26/14																						
1914	Was-A	3	2	0	0	0	0	0	0	0	0	.000	.000	.000	-96	-0	0			.889	2	/S-3	0.1
1915	Was-A	30	60	1	10	1	0	0	4	4	6	.167	.219	.183	20	-6	1	2	-1	.867	-4	3-12,2-10/S-7	-1.1
Total	2	33	62	1	10	1	0	0	4	4	6	.161	.212	.177	16	-6	1	2		.900	-2	/3-12,2-10,S-10	-1.0

YEAR	TM/L	G	AB	R	H	2B	3B	HR	RBI	BB	SO	AVG	OBP	SLG	PRO+	BR/A	SB	CS	SBR	FA	FR	G/POS	TPR
■ CY NEIGHBORS		Neighbors, Flemon Cecil b: 9/23/1880, Fayetteville, Mo. d: 5/20/64, Tacoma, Wash. BR, 5'10", 178 lbs. Deb: 4/29/08																					
1908	Pit-N	1	0	0	0	0	0	0	0	0		—	—	—	—	0	0			.000	-1	/O-1	-0.1
■ BOB NEIGHBORS		Neighbors, Robert Otis b: 11/9/17, Talihina, Okla. d: 8/8/52, North Korea (Mia) BR/TR, 5'11", 165 lbs. Deb: 9/16/39																					
1939	StL-A	7	11	3	2	0	0	1	1	0	1	.182	.182	.455	56	-1	0	0	0	.917	-0	/S-5	-0.1
■ MIKE NEILL		Neill, Michael Robert b: 4/27/70, Martinsville, Va. BL/TL, 6'2", 190 lbs. Deb: 7/27/98																					
1998	Oak-A	6	15	2	4	1	0	0	0	2	4	.267	.353	.333	82	-0	0	0	0	1.000	0	/O-6	0.0
■ TOMMY NEILL		Neill, Thomas White b: 11/7/19, Hartselle, Ala. d: 9/22/80, Houston, Tex. BL/TR, 6'2", 200 lbs. Deb: 9/10/46																					
1946	Bos-N	13	45	8	12	2	0	0	7	2	1	.267	.298	.311	72	-2	0			1.000	-1	O-13	-0.4
1947	Bos-N	7	10	1	2	0	1	0	0	1	2	.200	.333	.400	96	-0	0			1.000	-1	/O-2	-0.1
Total	2	20	55	9	14	2	1	0	7	3	3	.255	.305	.327	77	-2	0			1.000	-2	/O-15	-0.5
■ BERNIE NEIS		Neis, Bernard Edmund b: 9/26/1895, Bloomington, Ill. d: 11/29/72, Inverness, Fla. BB/TR, 5'7", 160 lbs. Deb: 4/14/20																					
1920	*Bro-N	95	249	38	63	11	2	2	22	26	35	.253	.329	.337	89	-3	9	9	-3	.957	-2	O-83	-1.3
1921	Bro-N	102	230	34	59	5	4	4	34	25	41	.257	.332	.365	81	-6	9	7	-2	.946	-6	O-77/2-1	-1.7
1922	Bro-N	61	70	15	16	4	1	1	9	13	8	.229	.349	.357	83	-2	3	2	-0	.897	-5	O-27	-0.7
1923	Bro-N	126	445	78	122	17	4	5	37	36	38	.274	.330	.364	85	-10	8	8	-2	.941	6	*O-111	-1.2
1924	Bro-N	80	211	43	64	8	3	4	26	27	17	.303	.385	.427	121	7	4	2	0	.937	-4	O-62	-0.1
1925	Bos-N	106	355	47	101	20	2	5	45	38	19	.285	.354	.394	100	-0	8	10	-4	.970	11	O-87	0.1
1926	Bos-N	30	93	16	20	5	2	0	8	8	10	.215	.277	.312	64	-5	4			.925	2	O-23	-0.5
1927	Cle-A	32	96	17	29	9	0	4	18	18	9	.302	.412	.521	140	6	0	1	-1	.978	5	O-29	0.8
	Chi-A	45	76	9	22	5	0	0	11	10	9	.289	.372	.355	92	-1	1	0	0	.927	-3	O-21	-0.4
	Yr	77	172	26	51	14	0	4	29	28	18	.297	.395	.448	120	6	1	1	-0	.962	2	O-50	0.4
Total	8	677	1825	297	496	84	18	25	210	201	186	.272	.346	.379	94	-13	46	39		.950	3	O-520/2-1	-5.0
■ ERNIE NEITZKE		Neitzke, Ernest Fredrich b: 11/13/1894, Toledo, Ohio d: 4/27/77, Sylvania, Ohio BR/TR, 5'10", 180 lbs. Deb: 6/2/21																					
1921	Bos-A	11	25	3	6	0	0	0	2	4	4	.240	.345	.240	53	-2	0	0	0	.875	-1	/O-8,P-2	-0.3
■ DAVE NELSON		Nelson, David Earl b: 6/20/44, Fort Sill, Okla. BR/TR, 5'10", 160 lbs. Deb: 4/11/68 C																					
1968	Cle-A	88	189	26	44	4	5	0	19	17	35	.233	.300	.307	85	-3	23	7	3	.987	-2	2-59,S-14	0.1
1969	Cle-A	52	123	11	25	0	0	0	6	9	26	.203	.263	.203	31	-11	4	3	-1	.966	4	2-33/O-2	-0.5
1970	Was-A	47	107	5	17	1	0	0	4	7	24	.159	.211	.168	6	-14	2	1	0	.986	1	2-33	-1.1
1971	Was-A	85	329	47	92	11	3	5	33	23	29	.280	.329	.377	105	1	17	8	0	.938	-13	3-84/2-1	-1.3
1972	Tex-A	145	499	68	113	16	3	2	28	67	81	.226	.324	.283	85	-7	51	17	5	.945	-12	*3-119,O-15	-1.8
1973	Tex-A★	142	576	71	165	24	4	7	48	34	78	.286	.326	.378	102	0	43	16	3	.984	-12	*2-140	0.0
1974	Tex-A	121	474	71	112	13	1	3	42	34	72	.236	.293	.287	69	-19	25	13	-0	.969	1	*2-120/D-1	-1.3
1975	Tex-A	28	80	9	17	1	0	2	10	8	10	.213	.292	.300	68	-3	6	0	2	.959	1	2-23/D-1	0.1
1976	*KC-A	78	153	24	36	4	2	1	17	14	26	.235	.299	.307	77	-4	15	5	2	.975	2	2-46,D-22/1-3	0.0
1977	KC-A	27	48	8	9	3	1	0	4	7	11	.188	.291	.292	59	-3	1	3	-2	.926	-2	2-11/D-7	-0.6
Total	10	813	2578	340	630	77	19	20	211	220	392	.244	.307	.312	81	-62	187	73	12	.976	-31	2-466,3-203/DOS1	-6.4
■ ROCKY NELSON		Nelson, Glenn Richard b: 11/18/24, Portsmouth, Ohio BL/TL, 5'11", 178 lbs. Deb: 4/27/49																					
1949	StL-N	82	244	28	54	8	4	4	32	11	12	.221	.258	.336	55	-16	1			1.000	-4	1-70	-2.0
1950	StL-N	76	235	27	58	10	4	1	20	26	9	.247	.324	.336	71	-10	4			.992	3	1-70	-0.8
1951	StL-N	9	18	3	4	1	0	0	1	1	0	.222	.263	.278	45	-1	0	0	0	1.000	-1	/1-4,O-1	-0.3
	Pit-N	71	195	29	52	7	4	1	14	10	7	.267	.302	.359	75	-7	1	1	-0	.990	1	1-32,O-12	-0.9
	Yr	80	213	32	56	8	4	1	15	11	7	.263	.299	.352	73	-8	1	1	-0	.991	-0	1-36,O-13	-1.2
	Chi-A	6	5	0	0	0	0	0	0	1	0	.000	.167	.000	-53	-1	0	0	0	.000	0	H	-0.1
1952	*Bro-N	37	39	6	10	1	0	0	3	7	4	.256	.370	.282	82	-1	0	0	0	1.000	-1	/1-5	-0.2
1954	Cle-A	4	4	0	0	0	0	0	0	0	1	.000	.000	.000	-98	-1	0	0	0	1.000	-0	/1-2	-0.1
1956	Bro-N	31	96	7	20	2	0	4	15	4	10	.208	.240	.354	53	-7	0	0	0	.991	2	1-25	-0.7
	StL-N	38	56	6	13	5	0	3	8	6	6	.232	.306	.482	108	0	0	0	0	1.000	1	1-14/O-8	0.0
	Yr	69	152	13	33	7	0	7	23	10	16	.217	.265	.401	73	-6	0	0	0	.993	2	1-39/O-8	-0.7
1959	Pit-N	98	175	31	51	11	0	6	32	23	19	.291	.383	.457	124	6	0	0	0	.994	-4	1-56/O-2	0.0
1960	*Pit-N	93	200	34	60	11	1	7	35	24	15	.300	.389	.470	133	10	1	2	-1	.996	1	1-73	0.6
1961	Pit-N	75	127	15	25	5	1	5	13	17	11	.197	.301	.370	77	-4	0	0	0	.996	-1	1-35	-0.7
Total	9	620	1394	186	347	61	14	31	173	130	94	.249	.318	.379	84	-31	7	3		.995	-3	1-386/O-23	-5.2
■ JAMIE NELSON		Nelson, James Victor b: 9/5/59, Clinton, Okla. BR/TR, 5'11", 180 lbs. Deb: 7/21/83																					
1983	Sea-A	40	96	9	21	3	0	1	5	13	12	.219	.312	.281	62	-5	4	2	0	.978	3	C-39	0.0
■ CANDY NELSON		Nelson, John W b: 3/14/1849, Brooklyn, N.Y. d: 9/4/10, Brooklyn, N.Y. BL/TR, 5'6", 145 lbs. Deb: 6/11/1872																					
1872	Tro-n	4	20	2	7	0	0	0	4	0	2	.350	.350	.350	114	0	0	0	0	1.000	-1	/O-3,S-1	0.0
	Eck-n	18	76	12	19	2	0	0	8	2	2	.250	.269	.276	80	-1	1	0	0	.818	1	/2-9,O-8,3-3	0.0
	Yr	22	96	14	26	2	0	0	12	2	4	.271	.286	.292	89	-0	1	0	0	.813	1	O-11/2-9,3-3,S-1	0.0
1873	Mut-n	36	168	28	55	4	1	0	22	1	2	.327	.331	.363	107	1	2	0	1	.869	-8	2-27/O-6,3-5,C-1,1	-0.6
1874	Mut-n	65	297	55	73	7	5	0	31	**9**	5	.246	.268	.303	80	-7	6	0	2	.824	-18	*2-51,S-14/O-1	-2.0
1875	Mut-n	70	276	28	55	7	1	0	23	9	0	.199	.225	.232	56	-12	4	2	0	.855	-0	2-49,3-23/S-2,O-1	-1.2
1878	Ind-N	19	84	12	11	1	0	0	5	5	11	.131	.180	.143	8	-8				.841	-6	S-19	-1.3
1879	Tro-N	28	106	17	28	7	1	0	10	8	4	.264	.316	.349	127	4				.834	4	S-24/O-4	0.8
1881	Wor-N	24	103	13	29	1	0	1	15	5	6	.282	.315	.320	95	-1				.898	2	S-24	0.3
1883	NY-a	97	417	75	127	19	6	0		31		.305	.353	.379	130	13				.875	-5	*S-97	0.9
1884	*NY-a	111	432	114	110	15	3	1		**74**		.255	.375	.310	129	19				.879	-17	*S-110/2-1	0.3
1885	NY-a	107	420	98	107	12	4	1	30	**61**		.255	.353	.310	120	15				.892	13	*S-107/3-1	2.6
1886	NY-a	109	413	89	93	7	2	0	23	64		.225	.332	.252	88	-2	14			.855	-8	S-73,O-36	-0.9
1887	NY-a	68	257	61	63	5	1	0	24	48		.245	.380	.272	87	0	29			.895	10	O-37,S-32/2-1	0.8
	NY-N	1	2	0	0	0	0	0	0	0	1	.000	.000	.000	-99	-1	0			.000	0	/3-1	0.0
1890	Bro-a	60	223	44	56	3	2	0	12	35		.251	.365	.283	94	1	12			.866	-8	S-57/O-4	-0.3
Total	4 n	193	837	125	209	20	7	0	88	21	11	.250	.268	.290	79	-18	13	2	3	.844	-25	2-136/3-31,OS1C	-3.8
Total	9	624	2457	523	624	70	19	3	119	331	22	.254	.349	.302	108	41	55			.875	-15	S-543/O-81,3-2,2-2	3.2
■ LYNN NELSON		Nelson, Lynn Bernard "Line Drive" b: 2/24/05, Sheldon, N.Dak. d: 2/15/55, Kansas City, Mo. BL/TR, 5'10.5", 170 lbs. Deb: 4/18/30																					
1930	Chi-N	37	18	0	4	1	1	0	2	0	1	.222	.222	.389	44	-2	0			.966	1	P-37	0.0
1933	Chi-N	29	21	5	5	1	1	0	1	1	3	.238	.273	.381	85	-0	0			1.000	1	P-24	0.0
1934	Chi-N	2	0	0	0	0	0	0	0	0	0	—	—	—	—	0	0			.000	-0	/P-2	0.0
1937	Phi-A	74	113	18	40	6	2	4	29	6	13	.354	.387	.549	135	6	1	0	0	1.000	-0	P-30/O-6	0.3
1938	Phi-A	67	112	12	31	0	0	0	15	7	12	.277	.319	.277	52	-8	0	0	0	.952	-0	P-32	0.0
1939	Phi-A	40	80	3	15	2	0	0	5	2	13	.188	.217	.213	10	-11	0	1	-1	.950	-1	P-35	0.0
1940	Det-A	19	23	4	8	0	0	1	3	0	6	.348	.348	.478	102	-0	0	0	0	1.000	0	/P-6	0.0
Total	7	268	367	42	103	10	4	5	55	16	48	.281	.313	.371	74	-16	1	1		.967	1	P-166/O-6	0.3
■ RAY NELSON		Nelson, Raymond "Kell" (b: Raymond Nelson Kellogg) b: 8/4/1875, Holyoke, Mass. d: 1/8/61, Mt.Vernon, N.Y. BR/TR, 5'9", 150 lbs. Deb: 5/6/01																					
1901	NY-N	39	130	12	26	2	0	0	7	10		.200	.262	.215	41	-9	3			.885	-3	2-39	-1.1
■ RICKY NELSON		Nelson, Ricky Lee b: 5/8/59, Eloy, Ariz. BL/TR, 6', 200 lbs. Deb: 5/17/83																					
1983	Sea-A	98	291	32	74	13	3	5	36	17	50	.254	.295	.371	79	-9	7	4	-0	.971	-8	O-91/D-1	-1.9
1984	Sea-A	9	15	2	3	0	0	1	2	2	4	.200	.294	.400	91	-0	0	0	0	1.000	-0	/O-2,D-3	-0.1
1985	Sea-A	6	2	2	0	0	0	0	0	0	1	.000	.000	.000	-99	-1	0	0	0	1.000	-1	/O-3	-0.2
1986	Sea-A	10	12	2	2	0	0	0	1	0	4	.167	.167	.167	-9	-2	1	0	0	.667	-0	/O-1,D-5	-0.2
Total	4	123	320	38	79	13	3	6	39	19	59	.247	.289	.363	75	-11	8	4	0	.965	-9	/O-97,D-9	-2.4

YEAR	TM/L	G	AB	R	H	2B	3B	HR	RBI	BB	SO	AVG	OBP	SLG	PRO+	BR/A	SB	CS	SBR	FA	FR	G/POS	TPR
■ ROB NELSON	Nelson, Robert Augustus b: 5/17/64, Pasadena, Cal. BL/TL, 6'4", 215 lbs. Deb: 9/9/86																						
1986	Oak-A	5	9	1	2	1	0	0	0	1	4	.222	.300	.333	78	-0	0	0	0	.800	0	/1-2,D-1	0.0
1987	Oak-A	7	24	1	4	1	0	0	0	0	12	.167	.167	.208	-2	-3	0	0	0	.968	3	/1-7	-0.1
	SD-N	10	11	0	1	0	0	0	1	1	8	.091	.167	.091	-31	-2	0	0	0	1.000	-0	/1-2	-0.2
1988	SD-N	7	21	4	4	0	0	1	3	2	9	.190	.261	.333	71	-1	0	0	0	.981	1	/1-5	-0.1
1989	SD-N	42	82	6	16	0	1	3	7	20	29	.195	.353	.329	96	0	1	3	-2	.991	3	1-31	0.1
1990	SD-N	5	5	0	0	0	0	0	0	0	4	.000	.000	.000	-99	-1	0	0	0	.000	0	/H	-0.2
Total	5	76	152	12	27	2	1	4	11	24	66	.178	.290	.283	62	-8	1	3	-2	.983	6	/1-47,D-1	-0.5
■ TEX NELSON	Nelson, Robert Sydney "Babe" b: 8/7/36, Dallas, Tex. BL/TL, 6'3", 220 lbs. Deb: 6/22/55																						
1955	Bal-A	25	31	4	6	0	0	0	1	7	13	.194	.342	.194	50	-2	0	0	0	.889	0	/O-6,1-2	-0.2
1956	Bal-A	39	68	5	14	2	0	0	5	7	22	.206	.280	.235	40	-6	0	0	0	.939	-3	O-24	-0.9
1957	Bal-A	15	23	2	5	0	2	0	5	1	5	.217	.280	.391	87	-1	0	0	0	1.000	-2	/O-8	-0.3
Total	3	79	122	11	25	2	2	0	11	15	40	.205	.297	.254	52	-8	0	0	0	.938	-5	/O-38,1-2	-1.4
■ TOMMY NELSON	Nelson, Tom Cousineau b: 5/1/17, Chicago, Ill. d: 9/24/73, San Diego, Cal. BR/TR, 5'11.5", 180 lbs. Deb: 4/17/45																						
1945	Bos-N	40	121	6	20	2	0	0	6	4	13	.165	.192	.182	4	-16	1			.910	-3	3-20,2-12	-1.8
■ DICK NEN	Nen, Richard Le Roy b: 9/24/39, South Gate, Cal. BL/TL, 6'2", 205 lbs. Deb: 9/18/63 F																						
1963	LA-N	7	8	2	1	0	0	1	1	3	3	.125	.364	.500	157	1	0	0	0	1.000	-1	/1-5	0.0
1965	Was-A	69	246	18	64	7	1	6	31	19	47	.260	.316	.370	96	-2	1	2	-1	.993	8	1-65	0.2
1966	Was-A	94	235	20	50	8	0	6	30	28	46	.213	.297	.323	79	-6	0	2	-1	.990	-2	1-76	-1.5
1967	Was-A	110	238	21	52	7	1	6	29	21	39	.218	.282	.332	84	-5	0	1	-1	.995	1	1-65/O-1	-0.9
1968	Chi-N	81	94	8	17	1	1	2	16	6	17	.181	.230	.277	48	-6	0	0	0	.987	-1	1-52	-0.9
1970	Was-A	6	5	1	1	0	0	0	0	0	0	.200	.200	.200	11	-1	0	0	0	1.000	0	/1-1	0.0
Total	6	367	826	70	185	23	3	21	107	77	152	.224	.291	.335	82	-19	1	5	-3	.992	7	1-264/O-1	-3.1
■ JACK NESS	Ness, John Charles b: 11/11/1884, Chicago, Ill. d: 12/4/57, DeLand, Fla. BR/TR, 6'2", 165 lbs. Deb: 5/9/11																						
1911	Det-A	12	39	6	6	0	0	0	2	2		.154	.195	.154	-2	-5	0			.977	1	1-12	-0.5
1916	Chi-A	75	258	32	69	7	5	1	34	9	32	.267	.310	.345	96	-2	4			.979	-5	1-69	-1.1
Total	2	87	297	38	75	7	5	1	36	11	32	.253	.295	.320	82	-8	4			.978	-4	/1-81	-1.6
■ GRAIG NETTLES	Nettles, Graig b: 8/20/44, San Diego, Cal. BL/TR, 6', 186 lbs. Deb: 9/6/67 FC																						
1967	Min-A	3	3	0	1	1	0	0	0	0	0	.333	.333	.667	175	0	0	0	0	.000	0	H	0.0
1968	Min-A	22	76	13	17	2	1	5	8	7	20	.224	.298	.474	125	2	0	0	0	.968	1	O-16/3-5,1-3	0.2
1969	*Min-A	96	225	27	50	9	2	7	26	32	47	.222	.322	.373	92	-2	1	2	-1	.987	-5	O-54,3-21	-1.1
1970	Cle-A	157	549	81	129	13	1	26	62	81	77	.235	.336	.404	99	-1	3	1	0	**.967**	28	*3-154/O-3	2.7
1971	Cle-A	158	598	78	156	18	1	28	86	82	56	.261	.353	.435	112	10	7	4	-0	.973	**42**	*3-158	5.3
1972	Cle-A	150	557	65	141	28	0	17	70	57	50	.253	.327	.395	110	7	2	3	-1	.956	5	*3-150	1.0
1973	NY-A	160	552	65	129	18	0	22	81	78	76	.234	.336	.386	107	6	0	0	0	.953	26	*3-157/D-2	3.1
1974	NY-A	155	566	74	139	21	1	22	75	59	75	.246	.320	.403	109	6	1	0	0	.961	16	*3-154/S-1	2.2
1975	NY-A★	157	581	71	155	24	4	21	91	51	88	.267	.328	.430	115	10	1	3	-2	.964	11	*3-157	1.9
1976	*NY-A	158	583	88	148	29	2	**32**	93	62	94	.254	.330	.475	135	24	11	6	-0	.965	17	*3-158/S-1	**4.1**
1977	*NY-A★	158	589	99	150	23	4	37	107	68	79	.255	.335	.496	124	18	2	5	-2	.974	-3	*3-156/D-1	1.1
1978	*NY-A★	159	587	81	162	23	2	27	93	59	69	.276	.348	.460	128	21	1	1	-0	.975	-6	*3-159/S-2	1.3
1979	NY-A★	145	521	71	132	15	1	20	73	59	53	.253	.329	.401	98	-2	1	2	-1	.966	9	*3-144	0.5
1980	*NY-A★	89	324	52	79	14	0	16	45	42	42	.244	.332	.435	110	4	0	0	0	.960	-3	3-88/S-1	0.0
1981	*NY-A	103	349	46	85	7	1	15	46	47	49	.244	.335	.398	112	6	0	2	-1	.972	8	3-97/D-4	1.2
1982	NY-A	122	405	47	94	11	2	18	55	51	49	.232	.319	.402	98	-1	1	5	-3	.934	8	*3-113/D-3	0.1
1983	NY-A	129	462	56	123	17	3	20	75	51	65	.266	.343	.446	120	12	0	1	-1	.956	1	*3-126/D-1	1.0
1984	*SD-N	124	395	56	90	11	1	20	65	58	55	.228	.334	.413	109	5	0	0	0	.936	-10	*3-119	-0.7
1985	SD-N★	137	440	66	115	23	1	15	61	72	59	.261	.365	.420	121	14	0	0	0	.959	-9	*3-130	0.4
1986	SD-N	126	354	36	77	9	0	16	55	41	62	.218	.302	.379	88	-6	0	1	-1	.941	-2	*3-114	-1.1
1987	Atl-N	112	177	16	37	8	1	5	33	22	25	.209	.296	.350	67	-8	1	0	0	.951	-0	3-40/1-6	-0.9
1988	Mon-N	80	93	5	16	4	0	1	14	9	19	.172	.245	.247	40	-7	0	0	0	.818	-2	3-12/1-5	-1.0
Total	22	2700	8986	1193	2225	328	28	390	1314	1088	1209	.248	.332	.421	110	117	32	36	-12	.961	132	*3-2412/O-73,1DS	21.3
■ JIM NETTLES	Nettles, James William b: 3/2/47, San Diego, Cal. BL/TL, 6', 186 lbs. Deb: 9/7/70 F																						
1970	Min-A	13	20	3	5	0	0	0	0	1	5	.250	.286	.250	48	-1	0	1	-1	1.000	-2	O-11	-0.5
1971	Min-A	70	168	17	42	5	1	6	24	19	24	.250	.326	.399	101	0	3	2	-0	.986	2	O-62	-0.1
1972	Min-A	102	235	28	48	5	2	4	15	32	52	.204	.302	.294	74	-7	4	3	-1	.982	-1	O-78/1-1	-1.3
1974	Det-A	43	141	20	32	5	1	6	17	15	26	.227	.306	.404	99	-0	3	4	-2	1.000	-1	O-41	-0.5
1979	KC-A	11	23	0	2	0	0	0	1	3	2	.087	.192	.087	-21	-4	0	0	0	1.000	0	/O-8,1-1	-0.4
1981	Oak-A	1	0	0	0	0	0	0	0	0	0	—	—	—	—	0	0	0	0	.000	-0	/O-1	0.0
Total	6	240	587	68	129	15	4	16	57	70	109	.220	.305	.341	83	-12	10	10	-3	.988	-3	O-201/1-2	-2.8
■ MORRIS NETTLES	Nettles, Morris b: 1/26/52, Los Angeles, Cal. BL/TL, 6'1", 170 lbs. Deb: 4/26/74																						
1974	Cal-A	56	175	27	48	4	0	0	8	16	38	.274	.335	.297	88	-2	20	11	-1	.990	-6	O-54	-1.2
1975	Cal-A	112	294	50	68	11	0	0	23	26	57	.231	.296	.269	65	-13	22	15	-2	.974	-2	O-90/D-9	-2.1
Total	2	168	469	77	116	15	0	0	31	42	95	.247	.311	.279	74	-16	42	26	-3	.980	-8	O-144/D-9	-3.3
■ MILO NETZEL	Netzel, Miles A. b: 5/12/1886, Eldred, Pa. d: 3/18/38, Oxnard, Cal. BL/TL, Deb: 9/16/09																						
1909	Cle-A	10	37	2	7	1	0	0	3	3		.189	.250	.216	46	-2	1			.800	-3	/3-6,O-2	-0.6
■ OTTO NEU	Neu, Otto Adam b: 9/24/1894, Springfield, Ohio d: 9/19/32, Kenton, Ohio BR/TR, 5'11", 170 lbs. Deb: 7/10/17																						
1917	StL-A	1	0	0	0	0	0	0	0	0	0	—	—	—	—	0	0			.000	0	/S-1	0.0
■ JOHNNY NEUN	Neun, John Henry b: 10/28/1900, Baltimore, Md. d: 3/28/90, Baltimore, Md. BB/TL, 5'10.5", 175 lbs. Deb: 4/14/25 MC																						
1925	Det-A	60	75	15	20	3	3	0	4	9	12	.267	.345	.387	87	-2	2	3	-1	.990	-1	1-13	-0.4
1926	Det-A	97	242	47	72	14	4	0	15	27	26	.298	.370	.388	97	-1	4	7	-3	.993	-3	1-49	-0.9
1927	Det-A	79	204	38	66	9	4	0	27	35	13	.324	.427	.407	116	7	22	7	2	.980	-3	1-53	0.3
1928	Det-A	36	108	15	23	3	1	0	5	7	10	.213	.261	.259	36	-10	2	2	-1	.975	-0	1-25	-1.2
1930	Bos-N	81	212	39	69	12	2	2	23	21	18	.325	.389	.429	101	1	9			.991	0	1-55	-0.4
1931	Bos-N	79	104	17	23	1	3	0	11	11	14	.221	.302	.288	62	-5	2			.994	-0	1-36	-0.7
Total	6	432	945	171	273	42	17	2	85	110	93	.289	.366	.376	91	-10	41	19		.987	-7	1-231	-3.3
■ ALEXANDER NEVIN	Nevin, Alexander Brown b: 10/3/1850, Allegheny City, Pa. d: 10/10/21, Pensacola, Fla. Deb: 6/17/1873																						
1873	Res-n	13	53	7	11	1	2	0	2	0	3	.208	.208	.302	54	-3	0	0	0	.579	-8	3-12/O-1	-0.8
■ PHIL NEVIN	Nevin, Phillip Joseph b: 1/19/71, Fullerton, Cal. BR/TR, 6'2", 180 lbs. Deb: 6/11/95																						
1995	Hou-N	18	60	4	7	1	0	0	1	7	13	.117	.221	.133	-4	-9	1	0	0	.933	1	3-16	-0.8
	Det-A	29	96	9	21	3	1	2	12	11	27	.219	.318	.333	70	-4	0	0	0	.963	-0	O-27/D-2	-0.5
1996	Det-A	38	120	15	35	5	0	8	19	8	39	.292	.341	.533	117	3	1	0	0	.943	5	3-24/O-9,C-4,D-1	0.7
1997	Det-A	93	251	32	59	16	1	9	35	25	68	.235	.307	.414	87	-5	0	1	-1	.986	-0	O-40,D-30,3-17,/1C	-0.8
1998	Ana-A	75	237	27	54	8	1	8	27	17	67	.228	.293	.371	71	-11	0	0	0	.989	-7	C-69/1-2,D-3	-1.3
Total	4	253	764	87	176	33	3	27	94	68	214	.230	.302	.387	78	-27	2	1	0	.972	-2	/O-76,C-74,3-57,D1	-2.7
■ DON NEWCOMBE	Newcombe, Donald "Newk" b: 6/14/26, Madison, N.J. BL/TR, 6'4", 225 lbs. Deb: 5/20/49																						
1949	*Bro-N★	39	96	8	22	4	0	0	10	5	16	.229	.267	.271	43	-8	0			**1.000**	1	P-38	0.0
1950	Bro-N★	40	97	8	24	3	1	1	8	10	19	.247	.318	.330	69	-4	0			.969	-0	P-40	0.0
1951	Bro-N★	40	103	11	23	3	1	0	8	8	9	.223	.286	.272	50	-7	0	0	0	.958	1	P-40	0.0
1954	Bro-N	31	47	6	15	1	0	0	4	4	6	.319	.373	.340	85	-1	0	0	0	.931	-1	P-29	0.0

YEAR	TM/L	G	AB	R	H	2B	3B	HR	RBI	BB	SO	AVG	OBP	SLG	PRO+	BR/A	SB	CS	SBR	FA	FR	G/POS	TPR
1955	*Bro-N★	57	117	18	42	9	1	7	23	6	18	.359	.395	.632	163	10	1	0	0	.907	-2	P-34	0.0
1956	*Bro-N	52	111	13	26	6	0	2	16	12	18	.234	.315	.342	71	-4	1	0	0	.985	0	P-38	0.0
1957	Bro-N	34	74	8	17	2	0	1	7	11	11	.230	.329	.297	64	-4	0	1	-1	.964	1	P-28	0.0
1958	LA-N	11	12	2	5	0	0	0	0	2	2	.417	.500	.417	141	1	0	0	0	1.000	0	P-11	0.0
	Cin-N	39	60	9	21	1	0	1	9	8	10	.350	.426	.417	118	2	0	0	0	1.000	-2	P-20	0.0
	Yr	50	72	11	26	1	0	1	9	10	12	.361	.439	.417	122	3	0	0	0	**1.000**	-2	P-31	0.0
1959	Cin-N	61	105	10	32	2	0	3	21	17	23	.305	.402	.410	113	3	0	0	0	.978	-1	P-30	0.0
1960	Cin-N	24	36	0	5	1	0	0	1	3	8	.139	.205	.167	3	-5	0	0	0	.895	-1	P-16	0.0
	Cle-A	24	20	1	6	1	0	0	1	1	7	.300	.333	.350	88	-0	0	0	0	.889	-1	P-20	0.0
Total	10	452	878	94	238	33	3	15	108	87	147	.271	.339	.367	85	-17	2	1		.963	-6	P-344	0.0

■ JOHN NEWELL

Newell, John A. b: 1/14/1868, Wilmington, Del. d: 1/28/19, Wilmington, Del. BR/TL, Deb: 7/22/1891

YEAR	TM/L	G	AB	R	H	2B	3B	HR	RBI	BB	SO	AVG	OBP	SLG	PRO+	BR/A	SB	CS	SBR	FA	FR	G/POS	TPR
1891	Pit-N	5	18	1	2	0	0	0	2	0	0	.111	.158	.111	-22	-3	0			.846	-2	/3-5	-0.4

■ T. E. NEWELL

Newell, T. E. b: St.Louis, Mo. Deb: 8/8/1877

YEAR	TM/L	G	AB	R	H	2B	3B	HR	RBI	BB	SO	AVG	OBP	SLG	PRO+	BR/A	SB	CS	SBR	FA	FR	G/POS	TPR
1877	StL-N	1	3	0	0	0	0	0	0	0	0	.000	.000	.000	-99	-1				.833	0	/S-1	0.0

■ MARC NEWFIELD

Newfield, Marc Alexander b: 10/19/72, Sacramento, Cal. BR/TR, 6′4″, 205 lbs. Deb: 7/6/93

YEAR	TM/L	G	AB	R	H	2B	3B	HR	RBI	BB	SO	AVG	OBP	SLG	PRO+	BR/A	SB	CS	SBR	FA	FR	G/POS	TPR
1993	Sea-A	22	66	5	15	3	0	1	7	2	8	.227	.261	.318	54	-4	0	1	-1	.000	-2	D-15/O-5	-0.7
1994	Sea-A	12	38	3	7	1	0	1	4	2	4	.184	.225	.289	31	-4	0	0	0	1.000	-1	/O-3,D-9	-0.5
1995	Sea-A	24	85	7	16	3	0	3	14	3	16	.188	.225	.329	42	-8	0	0	0	1.000	-0	O-24	-0.8
	SD-N	21	55	6	17	5	1	1	7	2	8	.309	.333	.491	118	1	0	0	0	1.000	-0	O-19	0.0
1996	SD-N	84	191	27	48	11	0	5	26	16	44	.251	.316	.387	89	-3	1	1	-0	.970	-7	O-51/1-2	-1.1
	Mil-A	49	179	21	55	15	0	7	31	11	26	.307	.361	.508	112	3	0	1	-1	.990	1	O-49	0.2
1997	Mil-A	50	157	14	36	8	0	1	18	14	27	.229	.301	.299	57	-10	0	0	0	.977	-3	O-28,D-18	-1.4
1998	Mil-N	93	186	15	44	7	0	3	25	19	29	.237	.311	.323	64	-10	0	1	-1	.962	-2	O-55/D-1	-1.2
Total	6	355	957	98	238	53	1	22	132	69	162	.249	.307	.375	76	-34	1	4	-2	.981	-14	O-234/D-43,1-2	-5.5

■ AL NEWMAN

Newman, Albert Dwayne b: 6/30/60, Kansas City, Mo. BB/TR, 5′9″, 183 lbs. Deb: 6/14/85

YEAR	TM/L	G	AB	R	H	2B	3B	HR	RBI	BB	SO	AVG	OBP	SLG	PRO+	BR/A	SB	CS	SBR	FA	FR	G/POS	TPR
1985	Mon-N	25	29	7	5	1	0	0	1	3	4	.172	.250	.207	31	-3	2	1	0	1.000	10	2-15/S-2	0.7
1986	Mon-N	95	185	23	37	3	0	1	8	21	20	.200	.282	.232	44	-14	11	11	-3	.967	9	2-59,S-22	-0.6
1987	*Min-A	110	307	44	68	15	5	0	29	34	27	.221	.299	.303	58	-18	15	11	-2	.982	-11	S-55,2-47,3-12,/OD	-2.5
1988	Min-A	105	260	35	58	7	0	0	19	29	34	.223	.301	.250	54	-15	12	3	2	.966	-4	3-60,S-28,2-23,/D-2	-1.6
1989	Min-A	141	446	62	113	18	2	0	38	59	46	.253	.343	.303	78	-11	25	12	0	.980	-22	2-84,3-37,S-31,/OD	-2.9
1990	Min-A	144	388	43	94	14	0	0	30	33	34	.242	.305	.278	60	-20	13	6	0	.993	-2	2-89,S-48,3-28,/O-3	-1.8
1991	*Min-A	118	246	25	47	5	0	0	19	23	21	.191	.263	.211	31	-22	4	5	-2	.987	-1	S-55,2-35,3/1OD	-2.2
1992	Tex-A	116	246	25	54	5	0	0	12	34	26	.220	.317	.240	60	-12	9	6	-1	.983	12	2-72,3-28,S-20,/OD	0.1
Total	8	854	2107	264	476	68	7	1	156	236	212	.226	.306	.266	58	-115	91	55	-6	.984	-10	2-424,S-261,3/DO1	-10.8

■ CHARLIE NEWMAN

Newman, Charles "Decker" b: 11/5/1868, Juda, Wis. d: 11/23/47, San Diego, Cal. BR/TR, Deb: 9/11/1892

YEAR	TM/L	G	AB	R	H	2B	3B	HR	RBI	BB	SO	AVG	OBP	SLG	PRO+	BR/A	SB	CS	SBR	FA	FR	G/POS	TPR
1892	NY-N	3	12	1	4	0	0	0	1	2	0	.333	.429	.333	133	1	3			.750	-0	/O-3	0.0
	Chi-N	16	61	4	10	0	0	0	2	1	6	.164	.177	.164	3	-7	2			.950	-3	O-16	-1.0
	Yr	19	73	5	14	0	0	0	3	3	6	.192	.224	.192	26	-7	5			.917	-3	O-19	-1.0

■ JEFF NEWMAN

Newman, Jeffrey Lynn b: 9/11/48, Fort Worth, Tex. BR/TR, 6′2″, 218 lbs. Deb: 6/30/76 MC

YEAR	TM/L	G	AB	R	H	2B	3B	HR	RBI	BB	SO	AVG	OBP	SLG	PRO+	BR/A	SB	CS	SBR	FA	FR	G/POS	TPR
1976	Oak-A	43	77	5	15	4	0	0	4	4	12	.195	.235	.247	43	-6	0	0	0	.981	6	C-43	0.1
1977	Oak-A	94	162	17	36	9	0	4	15	4	24	.222	.246	.352	61	-9	2	0	1	.970	10	C-94/P-1	0.3
1978	Oak-A	105	268	25	64	7	1	9	32	18	40	.239	.289	.373	90	-5	0	3	-2	.969	-5	C-61,1-36/D-2	-1.2
1979	Oak-A☆	143	516	53	119	17	2	22	71	27	88	.231	.270	.399	82	-15	2	1	0	.977	-1	C-81,1-46/3-7,D-7	-1.5
1980	Oak-A	127	438	37	102	19	1	15	56	25	81	.233	.276	.384	85	-11	3	4	-2	.982	-9	1-60,C-55/3-2,2D	-2.3
1981	*Oak-A	68	216	17	50	12	0	3	15	9	28	.231	.262	.329	73	-8	0	2	-1	.995	2	C-37,1-30	-0.8
1982	Oak-A	72	251	19	50	11	0	6	30	14	49	.199	.242	.315	54	-17	0	1	-1	.989	-1	C-67/1-3,3-1,D-1	-1.6
1983	Bos-A	59	132	11	25	4	0	3	7	10	31	.189	.257	.288	46	-10	0	1	-1	.990	2	C-51/D-6	-0.7
1984	Bos-A	24	63	5	14	2	0	1	3	5	16	.222	.279	.302	58	-4	0	0	0	.992	2	C-24	-0.1
Total	9	735	2123	189	475	85	4	63	233	116	369	.224	.266	.357	73	-84	7	12	-5	.981	7	C-513,1-175/D32P	-7.8

■ PATRICK NEWNAM

Newnam, Patrick Henry b: 12/10/1880, Hempstead, Tex. d: 6/20/38, San Antonio, Tex. BL/TR, 6′, 180 lbs. Deb: 5/29/10

YEAR	TM/L	G	AB	R	H	2B	3B	HR	RBI	BB	SO	AVG	OBP	SLG	PRO+	BR/A	SB	CS	SBR	FA	FR	G/POS	TPR
1910	StL-A	103	384	45	83	3	8	2	26	29		.216	.275	.281	79	-10	16			.972	-4	*1-103	-1.6
1911	StL-A	20	62	11	12	4	0	0	5	12		.194	.351	.258	74	-1	4			.986	1	1-20	-0.1
Total	2	123	446	56	95	7	8	2	31	41		.213	.287	.278	78	-11	20			.974	-3	1-123	-1.7

■ SKEETER NEWSOME

Newsome, Lamar Ashby b: 10/18/10, Phenix City, Ala. d: 8/31/89, Columbus, Ga. BR/TR, 5′9″, 170 lbs. Deb: 4/19/35

YEAR	TM/L	G	AB	R	H	2B	3B	HR	RBI	BB	SO	AVG	OBP	SLG	PRO+	BR/A	SB	CS	SBR	FA	FR	G/POS	TPR
1935	Phi-A	59	145	18	30	7	1	1	10	5	9	.207	.233	.290	35	-14	2	1	0	.956	8	S-24,2-13/3-4,O-1	-0.5
1936	Phi-A	127	471	41	106	15	2	0	46	25	27	.225	.266	.265	32	-51	13	4	2	.957	7	*S-123/2-2,3-1,O-1	-3.1
1937	Phi-A	122	438	53	111	22	1	1	30	37	22	.253	.312	.315	59	-27	11	5	0	.954	7	*S-122	-1.1
1938	Phi-A	17	48	7	13	4	0	0	7	1	4	.271	.286	.354	61	-3	1	1	-0	.971	1	S-15	-0.1
1939	Phi-A	99	248	22	55	9	1	0	17	19	12	.222	.277	.266	40	-22	5	7	-3	.950	1	S-93/2-2	-1.6
1941	Bos-A	93	227	28	51	6	0	2	17	22	11	.225	.296	.278	51	-16	10	4	1	.958	15	S-69,2-23	0.4
1942	Bos-A	29	95	7	26	6	0	0	9	9	5	.274	.337	.337	87	-2	2	1	0	.925	3	3-12,2-10/S-7	0.2
1943	Bos-A	114	449	48	119	21	2	1	22	21	21	.265	.301	.327	82	-11	5	6	-2	.962	14	S-98,3-15	0.9
1944	Bos-A	136	472	41	114	26	3	0	41	33	21	.242	.291	.309	72	-17	4	3	-1	.963	11	*S-126/2-8,3-1	0.3
1945	Bos-A	125	438	45	127	30	1	1	48	20	15	.290	.322	.370	98	-2	6	3	0	.963	22	2-82,S-33,3-11	2.9
1946	Phi-N	112	375	35	87	10	2	1	23	30	23	.232	.289	.277	63	-18	4			.955	-12	*S-107/2-3,3-2	-2.6
1947	Phi-N	95	310	36	71	8	2	2	22	24	24	.229	.284	.287	54	-21	4			.969	2	S-85/2-6,3-3	-1.5
Total	12	1128	3716	381	910	164	15	9	292	246	194	.245	.293	.304	62	-205	67	35		.959	78	S-902,2-149/3-49,O	-5.8

■ WARREN NEWSON

Newson, Warren Dale b: 7/3/64, Newnan, Ga. BL/TL, 5′7″, 202 lbs. Deb: 5/29/91

YEAR	TM/L	G	AB	R	H	2B	3B	HR	RBI	BB	SO	AVG	OBP	SLG	PRO+	BR/A	SB	CS	SBR	FA	FR	G/POS	TPR
1991	Chi-A	71	132	20	39	5	0	4	25	28	34	.295	.419	.424	137	8	2	2	-1	.962	-10	O-50/D-3	-0.3
1992	Chi-A	63	136	19	30	3	0	1	11	37	38	.221	.387	.265	87	-0	3	0	1	1.000	-4	O-50/D-4	-0.4
1993	*Chi-A	26	40	9	12	0	0	2	6	9	12	.300	.429	.450	139	3	0	0	0	1.000	-1	D-10/O-5	0.1
1994	Chi-A	63	102	16	26	5	0	2	7	14	23	.255	.345	.363	84	-2	1	0	0	.979	-4	O-34/D-3	-0.6
1995	Chi-A	51	85	19	20	0	2	3	9	23	27	.235	.404	.388	112	3	1	1	-0	.978	-1	O-24/D-7	0.1
	*Sea-A	33	72	15	21	2	0	2	6	16	18	.292	.420	.403	114	2	1	0	0	.971	-2	O-23	0.0
	Yr	84	157	34	41	2	2	5	15	39	45	.261	.411	.395	114	5	2	1	0	.975	-3	O-47/D-7	0.1
1996	*Tex-A	91	235	34	60	14	1	10	31	37	82	.255	.357	.451	97	-1	3	0	1	.992	2	O-66/D-9	0.0
1997	Tex-A	81	169	23	36	10	1	10	23	31	53	.213	.335	.462	100	-0	3	0	1	.949	-8	O-58/D-9	-0.8
1998	Tex-A	10	21	1	4	1	0	0	2	1	5	.190	.227	.238	20	-2	0	0	0	1.000	-1	/O-6,D-3	-0.4
Total	8	489	992	156	248	40	4	34	120	196	292	.250	.374	.401	103	10	14	3	2	.978	-29	O-316/D-48	-2.3

■ GUS NIARHOS

Niarhos, Constantine Gregory b: 12/6/20, Birmingham, Ala. BR/TR, 6′, 165 lbs. Deb: 6/9/46 C

YEAR	TM/L	G	AB	R	H	2B	3B	HR	RBI	BB	SO	AVG	OBP	SLG	PRO+	BR/A	SB	CS	SBR	FA	FR	G/POS	TPR
1946	NY-A	37	40	11	9	1	1	0	2	11	2	.225	.392	.300	94	0	1	0	0	.989	6	C-29	0.8
1948	NY-A	83	228	41	61	12	2	0	19	52	15	.268	.404	.338	99	3	1	3	-2	.990	11	C-82	1.6
1949	*NY-A	32	43	7	12	2	1	0	6	13	8	.279	.456	.372	120	2	0	0	0	1.000	4	C-30	0.7
1950	NY-A	1	0	0	0	0	0	0	0	0	0	—	—	—	—	0	0	0	0	.000	0	R	0.0
	Chi-A	41	105	17	34	4	0	0	16	14	6	.324	.408	.362	101	1	0	0	0	.978	8	C-36	1.0
	Yr	42	105	17	34	4	0	0	16	14	6	.324	.408	.362	101	1	0	0	0	.978	8	C-36	1.0
1951	Chi-A	66	168	27	43	6	0	1	10	47	9	.256	.419	.310	101	4	4	3	-1	.985	4	C-59	0.9
1952	Bos-A	29	58	4	6	0	0	0	4	12	9	.103	.268	.103	6	-7	0	0	0	.992	6	C-25	0.0
1953	Bos-A	16	35	6	7	1	1	0	2	4	4	.200	.300	.286	56	-2	0	1	-1	.985	4	C-16	0.1
1954	Phi-N	3	5	0	1	0	0	0	0	0	1	.200	.200	.200	5	-1	0	0	0	1.000	1	/C-3	0.0
1955	Phi-N	7	9	1	1	0	0	0	0	0	2	.111	.111	.111	-42	-2	0	0	0	1.000	1	/C-7	-0.1
Total	9	315	691	114	174	26	5	1	59	153	56	.252	.390	.308	89	-2	6	7	-2	.988	45	C-287	5.0

YEAR	TM/L	G	AB	R	H	2B	3B	HR	RBI	BB	SO	AVG	OBP	SLG	PRO+	BR/A	SB	CS	SBR	FA	FR	G/POS	TPR
■ SAM NICHOL	Nichol, Samuel Anderson b: 4/20/1869, County Antrim, Ireland d: 4/19/37, Steubenville, Ohio BR/TR, 5'10", 178 lbs. Deb: 10/5/1888																						
1888	Pit-N	8	22	3	1	0	0	0	0	2	2	.045	.125	.045	-47	-4	0			.952	0	/O-8	-0.3
1890	Col-a	14	56	7	9	0	0	0	4	2		.161	.190	.161	4	-7	3			.903	3	O-14	-0.4
Total	2	22	78	10	10	0	0	0	4	4	2	.128	.171	.128	-10	-10	3			.923	3	/O-22	-0.7
■ DON NICHOLAS	Nicholas, Donald Leigh b: 10/30/30, Phoenix, Ariz. BL/TR, 5'7", 150 lbs. Deb: 4/16/52																						
1952	Chi-A	3	2	0	0	0	0	0	0	0	0	.000	.000	.000	-99	-1	0	0	0	.000	0	H	-0.1
1954	Chi-A	7	0	3	0	0	0	0	0	1	0	—	1.000	—	185	0	0	1	-1	.000	0	H	0.0
Total	2	10	2	3	0	0	0	0	0	1	0	.000	.333	.000	-2	-0	0	1	-1		0	-0,-0	-0.1
■ SIMON NICHOLLS	Nicholls, Simon Burdette b: 7/18/1882, Germantown, Md. d: 3/12/11, Baltimore, Md. BL/TR, 5'11.5", 165 lbs. Deb: 9/18/03																						
1903	Det-A	2	8	0	3	0	0	0	0	0		.375	.375	.375	129	0	0			.600	-2	/S-2	-0.2
1906	Phi-A	12	44	1	8	1	0	0	1	3		.182	.234	.205	36	-3	0			.965	-2	S-12	-0.6
1907	Phi-A	124	460	75	139	12	2	0	23	24		.302	.338	.337	113	6	13			.930	-20	S-82,2-28,3-13	-1.3
1908	Phi-A	150	550	58	119	17	3	4	31	35		.216	.265	.280	72	-18	14			.913	-20	*S-120,2-23/3-7	-4.1
1909	Phi-A	21	71	10	15	2	1	0	3	3		.211	.243	.268	60	-3	0			.889	0	S-14/3-5,1-1	-0.3
1910	Cle-A	3	0	0	0	0	0	0	0	0		—	—	—	—	0	0			.000	-1	/S-3	-0.1
Total	6	312	1133	144	284	32	6	4	58	65		.251	.292	.300	86	-18	27			.917	-46	S-233/2-51,3-25,1-1	-6.6
■ AL NICHOLS	Nichols, Albert H. b: Brooklyn, N.Y. 5'11", 180 lbs. Deb: 4/24/1875																						
1875	Atl-n	32	131	4	20	2	0	0	9	0	6	.153	.153	.168	13	-10	0	0	0	.785	9	3-32	-0.1
1876	NY-N	57	212	20	38	4	0	0	9	2	3	.179	.187	.198	33	-14				.779	5	*3-57	-0.6
1877	Lou-N	6	19	1	4	0	1	0	0	0	2	.211	.211	.316	54	-1				.706	4	/2-3,S-1,3-1,1-1	0.3
Total	2	63	231	21	42	4	1	0	9	2	5	.182	.189	.208	35	-15				.785	9	/3-58,2-3,1-1,S-1	-0.3
■ ART NICHOLS	Nichols, Arthur Francis (b: Arthur Francis Meikle) b: 7/14/1871, Manchester, N.H. d: 8/9/45, Willimantic, Conn. BR/TR, 5'10", 175 lbs. Deb: 9/16/1898																						
1898	Chi-N	14	42	7	12	1	0	0	6	4		.286	.388	.310	101	0	6			.968	1	C-14	0.2
1899	Chi-N	17	47	5	12	2	0	1	11	0		.255	.286	.362	79	-2	3			.931	-1	C-15	-0.2
1900	Chi-N	8	25	1	5	0	0	0	0	3		.200	.286	.200	36	-2	1			.938	-1	/C-7	-0.2
1901	StL-N	93	308	50	75	11	3	1	33	10		.244	.290	.308	77	-9	14			.960	-4	C-47,O-40	-1.0
1902	StL-N	73	251	36	67	12	0	1	31	21		.267	.333	.327	108	3	18			.984	-7	1-56,C-11/O-4	-0.4
1903	StL-N	36	120	13	23	2	0	0	9	12		.192	.281	.208	42	-9	9			.972	-5	1-25/O-7,C-2	-1.4
Total	6	241	793	112	194	28	3	3	90	50		.245	.308	.299	81	-18	51			.952	-17	/C-96,1-81,O-51	-3.0
■ CARL NICHOLS	Nichols, Carl Edward b: 10/14/62, Los Angeles, Cal. BR/TR, 6', 208 lbs. Deb: 9/14/86																						
1986	Bal-A	5	5	0	0	0	0	0	0	1	4	.000	.167	.000	-51	-1	0	0	0	1.000	-0	/C-5	-0.1
1987	Bal-A	13	21	4	8	1	0	0	3	1	4	.381	.409	.429	126	1	0	0	0	1.000	1	C-13	0.2
1988	Bal-A	18	47	2	9	1	0	0	1	3	10	.191	.240	.213	29	-4	0	0	0	.987	6	C-13/O-3	0.2
1989	Hou-N	8	13	0	1	0	0	0	2	0	3	.077	.077	.077	-58	-3	0	0	0	1.000	-0	/C-6	-0.3
1990	Hou-N	32	49	7	10	3	0	0	11	8	11	.204	.328	.265	67	-2	0	0	0	.986	3	C-15/1-3,O-1	0.1
1991	Hou-N	20	51	3	10	3	0	0	1	5	17	.196	.268	.255	51	-3	0	0	0	.971	3	C-17	0.1
Total	6	96	186	16	38	8	0	0	18	18	49	.204	.278	.247	49	-13	0	0	0	.985	12	/C-69,O-4,1-3	0.2
■ ROY NICHOLS	Nichols, Roy b: 3/3/21, Little Rock, Ark. BR/TR, 5'11", 155 lbs. Deb: 5/6/44																						
1944	NY-N	11	9	3	2	1	0	0	0	2	2	.222	.364	.333	97	0	0			1.000	2	/2-1,3-1	0.2
■ REID NICHOLS	Nichols, Thomas Reid b: 8/5/58, Ocala, Fla. BR/TR, 5'11", 165 lbs. Deb: 9/16/80																						
1980	Bos-A	12	36	5	8	0	1	0	3	3	8	.222	.282	.278	51	-2	0	1	-1	.962	0	/O-9,D-1	-0.3
1981	Bos-A	39	48	13	9	0	1	0	3	2	6	.188	.220	.229	28	-4	0	1	-1	1.000	-4	O-27/3-1,D-7	-1.0
1982	Bos-A	92	245	35	74	16	1	7	33	14	28	.302	.342	.461	112	3	5	3	-0	.989	-2	O-82/D-4	0.0
1983	Bos-A	100	274	35	78	22	1	6	22	26	36	.285	.353	.438	108	3	7	5	-1	.994	2	O-72,D-18/S-1	0.2
1984	Bos-A	74	124	14	28	5	1	1	14	12	18	.226	.309	.306	68	-5	2	1	0	.988	-4	O-48/D-1	-1.0
1985	Bos-A	21	32	3	6	1	0	1	3	2	4	.188	.257	.313	53	-2	1	0	0	.933	-2	O-10/2-3,D-4	-0.4
	Chi-A	51	118	20	35	7	1	1	15	15	13	.297	.376	.398	108	2	5	5	-2	1.000	-12	O-48/D-1	-1.2
	Yr	72	150	23	41	8	1	2	18	17	17	.273	.351	.380	96	-0	6	5	-1	.988	-14	O-58/D-5,2-3	-1.6
1986	Chi-A	74	136	9	31	4	0	2	18	11	23	.228	.286	.301	58	-8	5	4	-1	.989	-4	O-53/2-2,D-3	-1.4
1987	Mon-N	77	147	22	39	8	2	4	20	14	13	.265	.333	.429	97	-1	2	1	0	.990	-4	O-59/3-3	-0.5
Total	8	540	1160	156	308	63	8	22	131	99	149	.266	.328	.391	91	-14	27	21	-5	.990	-29	O-408/D-39,2-5,3S	-5.6
■ DAVE NICHOLSON	Nicholson, David Lawrence b: 8/29/39, St.Louis, Mo. BR/TR, 6'2", 215 lbs. Deb: 5/24/60																						
1960	Bal-A	54	113	17	21	1	1	5	11	20	55	.186	.308	.345	77	-4	0	2	-1	.982	-5	O-44	-1.1
1962	Bal-A	97	173	25	30	4	1	9	15	27	76	.173	.289	.364	79	-6	3	4	-2	.983	-7	O-80	-1.7
1963	Chi-A	126	449	53	103	11	4	22	70	63	175	.229	.324	.419	108	5	2	1	0	.970	2	*O-123	0.1
1964	Chi-A	97	294	40	60	6	1	13	39	52	126	.204	.330	.364	95	-1	0	2	-1	.972	-2	O-92	-0.9
1965	Chi-A	54	85	11	13	2	1	2	12	9	40	.153	.234	.271	46	-6	0	0	0	1.000	-9	O-36	-1.7
1966	Hou-N	100	280	36	69	8	4	10	31	46	92	.246	.359	.411	122	9	1	1	-0	.968	2	O-90	0.7
1967	Atl-N	10	25	2	5	0	0	0	1	2	9	.200	.259	.200	34	-2	0	0	0	1.000	-0	/O-7	-0.3
Total	7	538	1419	184	301	32	12	61	179	219	573	.212	.320	.381	97	-4	6	10	-4	.974	-19	O-472	-4.9
■ FRED NICHOLSON	Nicholson, Fred "Shoemaker" b: 9/1/1894, Honey Grove, Tex. d: 1/23/72, Kilgore, Tex. BR/TR, 5'10.5", 173 lbs. Deb: 4/11/17																						
1917	Det-A	13	14	4	4	1	0	0	1	1	2	.286	.333	.357	111	0	0			1.000	-1	/O-3	-0.1
1919	Pit-N	30	66	8	18	2	2	1	6	6	11	.273	.333	.409	118	1	2			.939	-1	O-17/1-1	-0.1
1920	Pit-N	99	247	33	89	16	7	4	30	18	31	.360	.404	.530	162	19	9	6	-1	.957	2	O-58	1.7
1921	Bos-N	83	245	36	80	11	7	5	41	17	29	.327	.370	.490	133	11	5	4	-1	.983	-7	O-59/1-4,2-2	0.0
1922	Bos-N	78	222	31	56	4	5	2	29	23	24	.252	.336	.342	79	-7	5	7	-3	.915	-4	O-63	-1.7
Total	5	303	794	112	247	34	21	12	107	65	97	.311	.367	.452	124	25	21	17		.950	-11	O-200/1-5,2-2	-0.2
■ OVID NICHOLSON	Nicholson, Ovid Edward b: 12/30/1888, Salem, Ind. d: 3/24/68, Salem, Ind. BL/TR, 5'9.5", 155 lbs. Deb: 9/17/12																						
1912	Pit-N	6	11	2	5	0	0	0	3	1	2	.455	.500	.455	164	1	0			1.000	-1	/O-4	0.0
■ PARSON NICHOLSON	Nicholson, Thomas C. "Deacon" b: 4/14/1863, Blaine, Ohio d: 2/28/17, Bellaire, Ohio 5'6", 190 lbs. Deb: 9/14/1888																						
1888	Det-N	24	85	11	22	2	3	1	9	2	7	.259	.284	.388	113	1	6			.935	-2	2-24	0.0
1890	Tol-a	134	523	78	140	16	11	4	72	42		.268	.333	.363	102	-0	46			.929	-8	*2-134/C-1	0.0
1895	Was-N	10	38	7	7	2	1	0	5	7	4	.184	.311	.289	56	-2	6			.797	-2	S-10	-0.3
Total	3	168	646	96	169	20	15	5	86	51	11	.262	.325	.362	100	-2	58			.930	-12	2-158/S-10,C-1	-0.3
■ BILL NICHOLSON	Nicholson, William Beck "Swish" b: 12/11/14, Chestertown, Md. d: 3/8/96, Chestertown, Md. BL/TR, 6', 205 lbs. Deb: 6/13/36																						
1936	Phi-A	11	12	2	0	0	0	0	0	0	5	.000	.000	.000	-99	-4	0	0	0	1.000	-0	/O-1	-0.4
1939	Chi-N	58	220	37	65	12	5	5	38	20	29	.295	.354	.464	116	5	0			.955	1	O-58	0.4
1940	Chi-N★	135	491	78	146	27	7	25	98	50	67	.297	.366	.534	148	31	2			.950	-2	*O-123	2.2
1941	Chi-N★	147	532	74	135	26	1	26	98	82	91	.254	.357	.453	132	22	1			.971	6	*O-143	2.0
1942	Chi-N	152	588	83	173	22	11	21	78	76	80	.294	.382	.476	156	42	8			.986	11	*O-151	**4.8**
1943	Chi-N★	154	608	95	188	30	9	**29**	**128**	71	86	.309	.386	.531	166	50	4			.978	6	*O-154	4.9
1944	Chi-N★	156	582	**116**	167	35	8	**33**	**122**	93	71	.287	.391	.545	162	48	3			.979	2	*O-156	4.2
1945	*Chi-N†	151	559	82	136	28	4	13	88	92	73	.243	.356	.377	106	7	4			.990	1	*O-151	-0.1
1946	Chi-N	105	296	36	65	13	2	8	41	44	44	.220	.325	.358	95	-2	1			.973	2	O-80	-0.3
1947	Chi-N	148	487	69	119	28	1	26	75	87	83	.244	.364	.466	124	17	1			**.990**	-1	*O-140	0.9
1948	Chi-N	143	494	68	129	24	5	19	67	81	60	.261	.371	.445	125	18	2			.980	-3	*O-136	0.8
1949	Phi-N	98	299	42	70	8	3	11	40	45	53	.234	.344	.391	99	0	1			.995	3	O-91	-0.1
1950	Phi-N	41	58	3	13	2	1	3	10	8	16	.224	.318	.448	101	-0	0			.952	-2	O-15	-0.3
1951	Phi-N	85	170	23	41	9	2	8	30	25	24	.241	.342	.459	115	3	0	1	-1	.987	-3	O-41	-0.1

YEAR	TM/L	G	AB	R	H	2B	3B	HR	RBI	BB	SO	AVG	OBP	SLG	PRO+	BR/A	SB	CS	SBR	FA	FR	G/POS	TPR
1952	Phi-N	55	88	17	24	3	0	6	19	14	26	.273	.390	.511	150	6	0	0	0	1.000	-2	O-19	0.4
1953	Phi-N	38	62	12	13	5	1	2	16	12	20	.210	.338	.419	97	-0	0	0	0	1.000	-2	O-12	-0.3
Total	16	1677	5546	837	1484	272	60	235	948	800	828	.268	.365	.465	133	243	27	1		.979	17	*O-1471	19.0

■ GEORGE NICOL Nicol, George Edward b: 10/17/1870, Barry, Ill. d: 8/10/24, Milwaukee, Wis. TL, 5′7″, 155 lbs. Deb: 9/23/1890

YEAR	TM/L	G	AB	R	H	2B	3B	HR	RBI	BB	SO	AVG	OBP	SLG	PRO+	BR/A	SB	CS	SBR	FA	FR	G/POS	TPR
1890	StL-a	3	7	4	2	1	0	0	1	4		.286	.545	.429	164	1	0			1.000	-0	/P-3	0.0
1891	Chi-N	3	6	0	2	0	1	0	3	0	1	.333	.333	.667	189	1	0			.000	-1	/P-3	0.0
1894	Pit-N	8	20	8	9	1	0	0	3	0	1	.450	.450	.500	130	1	0			.800	-1	/P-8	0.0
	Lou-N	27	108	12	38	6	4	0	19	2	3	.352	.375	.481	113	2	4			.791	-5	O-26/P-1	-0.4
	Yr	35	128	20	47	7	4	0	22	2	4	.367	.386	.484	115	3	4			.791	-6	O-26/P-9	-0.4
Total	3	41	141	24	51	8	5	0	26	6	5	.362	.396	.489	121	4	4			.692	-7	/O-26,P-15	-0.4

■ HUGH NICOL Nicol, Hugh b: 1/1/1858, Campsie, Scotland d: 6/27/21, Lafayette, Ind. BR/TR, 5′4″, 145 lbs. Deb: 5/3/1881 M

YEAR	TM/L	G	AB	R	H	2B	3B	HR	RBI	BB	SO	AVG	OBP	SLG	PRO+	BR/A	SB	CS	SBR	FA	FR	G/POS	TPR
1881	Chi-N	26	108	13	22	2	0	0	7	4	12	.204	.232	.222	42	-7				.932	3	O-26/S-1	-0.4
1882	Chi-N	47	186	19	37	9	1	1	16	7	29	.199	.228	.274	58	-9				.887	10	O-47/S-8	0.1
1883	StL-a	94	368	73	105	13	3	0	39	18		.285	.319	.337	105	1				.916	12	*O-84,2-11	1.1
1884	StL-a	110	442	79	116	14	5	0		22		.262	.302	.317	99	-1				.873	23	*O-87,2-23/S-1,3-1	1.9
1885	*StL-a	112	425	59	88	11	1	0	45	34		.207	.271	.238	59	-20				.888	13	*O-111/3-1	-0.9
1886	StL-a	67	253	44	52	6	3	0	19	26		.206	.280	.253	64	-11	38			.942	-4	O-57/S-8,2-4	-1.4
1887	Cin-a	125	475	122	102	18	2	1	34	86		.215	.341	.267	69	-17	**138**			.918	-3	*O-125	-1.7
1888	Cin-a	135	548	112	131	10	2	1	35	67		.239	.330	.270	88	-6	103			.957	-3	*O-125,2-12/S-1	-1.1
1889	Cin-a	122	474	82	121	7	8	2	58	54	35	.255	.338	.316	84	-9	80			.918	1	*O-115/2-7,3-3	-0.9
1890	Cin-N	50	186	28	39	1	4	0	19	19	12	.210	.283	.258	58	-10	24			.921	-6	O-46/S-3,2-1	-1.5
Total	10	888	3465	631	813	91	29	5	272	337	88	.235	.307	.282	78	-88	383			.912	49	O-823/2-58,S-22,3-5	-4.8

■ STEVE NICOSIA Nicosia, Steven Richard b: 8/6/55, Paterson, N.J. BR/TR, 5′10″, 185 lbs. Deb: 7/8/78

YEAR	TM/L	G	AB	R	H	2B	3B	HR	RBI	BB	SO	AVG	OBP	SLG	PRO+	BR/A	SB	CS	SBR	FA	FR	G/POS	TPR
1978	Pit-N	3	5	0	0	0	0	0	0	1	0	.000	.167	.000	-48	-1	0	0	0	1.000	1	/C-1	0.0
1979	*Pit-N	70	191	22	55	16	0	4	13	23	17	.288	.364	.435	112	3	0	2	-1	.991	4	C-65	0.8
1980	Pit-N	60	176	16	38	8	0	1	22	19	16	.216	.296	.278	60	-9	0	1	-1	.984	-1	C-58	-0.9
1981	Pit-N	54	169	21	39	10	1	2	18	13	10	.231	.286	.337	74	-6	3	1	0	.982	1	C-52	-0.4
1982	Pit-N	39	100	6	28	3	0	1	7	11	13	.280	.351	.340	91	-1	0	1	-1	.990	3	C-35/O-3	0.3
1983	Pit-N	21	46	4	6	2	0	1	1	1	7	.130	.149	.239	6	-6	0	0	0	.988	-1	C-15	-0.7
	SF-N	15	33	4	11	0	0	0	6	3	2	.333	.389	.333	105	0	0	0	0	.984	2	/C-9	0.3
	Yr	36	79	8	17	2	0	1	7	4	9	.215	.253	.278	47	-6	0	0	0	.986	1	C-24	-0.4
1984	SF-N	48	132	9	40	11	2	2	19	8	14	.303	.343	.462	129	4	1	1	-0	.985	-5	C-41	0.0
1985	Mon-N	42	71	4	12	2	0	0	1	7	11	.169	.244	.197	26	-7	1	0	0	.988	-5	C-23/1-2	-1.2
	Tor-A	6	15	0	4	0	0	0	1	0	0	.267	.267	.267	46	-1	0	0	0	1.000	1	/C-6	0.0
Total	8	358	938	86	233	52	3	11	88	86	90	.248	.312	.345	82	-23	5	6	-2	.987	-1	C-305/O-3,1-2	-1.8

■ CHARLIE NIEBERGALL Niebergall, Charles Arthur "Nig" b: 5/23/1899, New York, N.Y. d: 8/29/82, Holiday, Fla. BR/TR, 5′10″, 160 lbs. Deb: 6/17/21

YEAR	TM/L	G	AB	R	H	2B	3B	HR	RBI	BB	SO	AVG	OBP	SLG	PRO+	BR/A	SB	CS	SBR	FA	FR	G/POS	TPR
1921	StL-N	5	6	1	1	0	0	0	0	0	0	.167	.167	.167	-12	-1	0	0	0	1.000	-1	/C-3	-0.1
1923	StL-N	9	28	2	3	1	0	0	1	2	2	.107	.167	.143	-18	-5	0	0	0	1.000	-0	/C-7	-0.5
1924	StL-N	40	58	6	17	6	0	0	7	3	9	.293	.339	.397	98	-0	0	0	0	.951	1	C-34	0.2
Total	3	54	92	9	21	7	0	0	8	5	11	.228	.276	.304	55	-6	0	0	0	.966	1	/C-44	-0.4

■ AL NIEHAUS Niehaus, Albert Bernard b: 6/1/1899, Cincinnati, Ohio d: 10/14/31, Cincinnati, Ohio BR/TR, 5′11″, 175 lbs. Deb: 4/22/25

YEAR	TM/L	G	AB	R	H	2B	3B	HR	RBI	BB	SO	AVG	OBP	SLG	PRO+	BR/A	SB	CS	SBR	FA	FR	G/POS	TPR
1925	Pit-N	17	64	7	14	8	0	0	7	1	5	.219	.242	.344	45	-6	0	0	0	.962	-1	1-15	-0.7
	Cin-N	51	147	16	44	10	2	0	14	13	10	.299	.360	.395	95	-1	1	4	-2	.988	2	1-45	-0.3
	Yr	68	211	23	58	18	2	0	21	14	15	.275	.326	.379	80	-7	1	4	-2	.981	1	1-60	-1.0

■ BERT NIEHOFF Niehoff, John Albert b: 5/13/1884, Louisville, Colo. d: 12/8/74, Inglewood, Cal. BR/TR, 5′10.5″, 170 lbs. Deb: 10/4/13 C

YEAR	TM/L	G	AB	R	H	2B	3B	HR	RBI	BB	SO	AVG	OBP	SLG	PRO+	BR/A	SB	CS	SBR	FA	FR	G/POS	TPR
1913	Cin-N	2	8	0	0	0	0	0	0	0	2	.000	.000	.000	-99	-2	0			.917	2	/3-2	0.0
1914	Cin-N	142	484	46	117	16	9	4	49	38	77	.242	.298	.337	86	-9	20			.924	7	*3-134/2-3	0.2
1915	*Phi-N	148	529	61	126	27	2	2	49	30	63	.238	.280	.308	77	-15	21	11	-0	.946	-7	*2-148	-2.3
1916	Phi-N	146	548	65	133	**42**	4	4	61	37	57	.243	.292	.356	95	-4	20	14	-2	.936	-2	*2-144/3-2	-0.4
1917	Phi-N	114	361	30	92	17	4	2	42	23	29	.255	.303	.341	93	-3	8			.945	18	2-96/1-7,3-6	2.2
1918	StL-N	22	84	5	15	2	0	0	5	3	10	.179	.207	.202	26	-7	2			.975	2	2-22	-0.5
	NY-N	7	23	3	6	0	0	0	1	0	4	.261	.261	.261	60	-1	0			.871	-2	/2-7	-0.4
	Yr	29	107	8	21	2	0	0	6	3	14	.196	.218	.215	33	-9	2			.954	-1	2-29	-0.9
Total	6	581	2037	210	489	104	19	12	207	131	242	.240	.288	.327	84	-42	71	25		.943	18	2-420,3-144/1-7	-1.2

■ MILT NIELSEN Nielsen, Milton Robert b: 2/8/25, Tyler, Minn. BL/TL, 5′11″, 190 lbs. Deb: 9/27/49

YEAR	TM/L	G	AB	R	H	2B	3B	HR	RBI	BB	SO	AVG	OBP	SLG	PRO+	BR/A	SB	CS	SBR	FA	FR	G/POS	TPR
1949	Cle-A	3	9	1	1	0	0	0	0	2	4	.111	.273	.111	4	-1	0	0	0	1.000	-0	/O-3	-0.2
1951	Cle-A	16	6	1	0	0	0	0	0	1	1	.000	.143	.000	-63	-1	0	0	0	.000	0	H	-0.1
Total	2	19	15	2	1	0	0	0	0	3	5	.067	.222	.067	-22	-3	0	0	0	1.000	-0	/O-3	-0.3

■ BUTCH NIEMAN Nieman, Elmer Le Roy b: 2/8/18, Herkimer, Kan. d: 11/2/93, Topeka, Kan. BL/TL, 6′2″, 195 lbs. Deb: 5/2/43

YEAR	TM/L	G	AB	R	H	2B	3B	HR	RBI	BB	SO	AVG	OBP	SLG	PRO+	BR/A	SB	CS	SBR	FA	FR	G/POS	TPR
1943	Bos-N	101	335	39	84	15	8	7	46	39	39	.251	.331	.406	114	5	4			.963	1	O-93	0.2
1944	Bos-N	134	468	65	124	16	6	16	65	47	47	.265	.332	.427	108	4	5			.975	-2	*O-126	-0.4
1945	Bos-N	97	247	43	61	15	0	14	56	43	33	.247	.361	.478	131	10	11			.932	0	O-57	0.7
Total	3	332	1050	147	269	46	14	37	167	129	119	.256	.339	.432	116	20	20			.961	-0	O-276	0.5

■ BOB NIEMAN Nieman, Robert Charles b: 1/26/27, Cincinnati, Ohio d: 3/10/85, Corona, Cal. BR/TR, 5′11″, 195 lbs. Deb: 9/14/51

YEAR	TM/L	G	AB	R	H	2B	3B	HR	RBI	BB	SO	AVG	OBP	SLG	PRO+	BR/A	SB	CS	SBR	FA	FR	G/POS	TPR
1951	StL-A	12	43	6	16	3	1	2	8	3	5	.372	.413	.628	174	4	0	0	0	.962	0	O-11	0.4
1952	StL-A	131	478	66	138	22	2	18	74	46	73	.289	.352	.456	120	12	0	4	-2	.976	1	*O-125	0.5
1953	Det-A	142	508	72	143	32	5	15	69	57	57	.281	.354	.453	118	12	0	3	-2	.979	3	*O-135	0.8
1954	Det-A	91	251	24	66	14	1	8	35	22	32	.263	.322	.422	105	1	0	2	-1	.984	-2	O-62	-0.5
1955	Chi-A	99	272	36	77	11	2	11	53	36	37	.283	.371	.460	119	7	1	0	0	.976	-7	O-78	-0.2
1956	Chi-A	14	40	3	12	1	0	2	4	4	4	.300	.364	.475	118	1	0	1	-1	1.000	1	O-10	0.0
	Bal-A	114	388	60	125	20	6	12	64	86	59	.322	.445	.497	161	38	1	5	-3	.980	7	*O-114	3.5
	Yr	128	428	63	137	21	6	14	68	90	63	.320	.438	.495	156	39	1	6	-3	.982	7	*O-124	3.5
1957	Bal-A	129	445	61	123	17	6	13	70	63	86	.276	.369	.429	125	16	4	4	-1	.980	5	*O-120	1.3
1958	Bal-A	105	366	56	119	20	2	16	60	44	57	.325	.398	.522	159	29	2	8	-4	.961	-7	*O-100	1.3
1959	Bal-A	118	360	49	105	18	2	21	60	42	55	.292	.369	.528	146	22	1	2	-1	.973	-0	O-97	1.6
1960	StL-N	81	188	19	54	13	5	4	31	24	31	.287	.374	.473	120	5	0	1	-1	.940	-8	O-55	-0.6
1961	StL-N	6	17	0	8	1	0	0	2	0	2	.471	.471	.529	150	1	0	0	0	1.000	-1	/O-4	0.0
	Cle-A	39	65	2	23	6	0	2	10	7	4	.354	.417	.538	157	5	1	0	0	.960	0	O-12	0.5
1962	Cle-A	2	1	0	0	0	0	0	1	0	1	.000	.000	.000	-99	-0	0	0	0	.000	0	H	0.0
	*SF-N	30	30	1	9	2	0	1	3	1	9	.300	.323	.467	111	0	0	0	0	1.000	-1	/O-3	0.0
Total	12	1113	3452	455	1018	180	32	125	544	435	512	.295	.375	.474	132	154	10	30	-15	.975	-8	O-926	8.6

■ AL NIEMIEC Niemiec, Alfred Joseph b: 5/18/11, Meriden, Conn. d: 10/29/95, Kirkland, Wash. BR/TR, 5′11″, 158 lbs. Deb: 9/19/34

YEAR	TM/L	G	AB	R	H	2B	3B	HR	RBI	BB	SO	AVG	OBP	SLG	PRO+	BR/A	SB	CS	SBR	FA	FR	G/POS	TPR
1934	Bos-A	9	32	2	7	0	0	0	3	3	4	.219	.286	.219	30	-3	0	0	0	1.000	4	/2-9	0.1
1936	Phi-A	69	203	22	40	3	2	1	20	26	16	.197	.291	.246	35	-21	2	2	-1	.972	10	2-52/S-5	-0.6
Total	2	78	235	24	47	3	2	1	23	29	20	.200	.291	.243	34	-24	2	2	-1	.976	15	/2-61,S-5	-0.5

■ TOM NIETO Nieto, Thomas Andrew b: 10/27/60, Downey, Cal. BR/TR, 6′1″, 205 lbs. Deb: 5/10/84

YEAR	TM/L	G	AB	R	H	2B	3B	HR	RBI	BB	SO	AVG	OBP	SLG	PRO+	BR/A	SB	CS	SBR	FA	FR	G/POS	TPR
1984	StL-N	33	86	7	24	4	0	3	12	5	18	.279	.319	.430	112	1	0	0	0	.994	4	C-32	0.6
1985	*StL-N	95	253	15	57	10	2	0	34	26	37	.225	.305	.281	65	-11	0	2	-1	.990	-4	C-95	-1.3
1986	Mon-N	30	65	5	13	3	1	1	7	6	21	.200	.278	.323	66	-3	0	1	-1	.978	-3	C-30	-0.5
1987	Min-A	41	105	7	21	7	1	1	12	8	24	.200	.276	.314	54	-7	0	0	0	.996	2	C-40/D-1	-0.3
1988	Min-A	24	60	1	4	0	0	0	0	1	17	.067	.097	.067	-52	-12	0	0	0	.991	3	C-24	-0.8

YEAR	TM/L	G	AB	R	H	2B	3B	HR	RBI	BB	SO	AVG	OBP	SLG	PRO+	BR/A	SB	CS	SBR	FA	FR	G/POS	TPR
1989	Phi-N	11	20	1	3	0	0	0	0	6	7	.150	.370	.150	54	-1	0	0	0	1.000	3	C-11	0.3
1990	Phi-N	17	30	1	5	0	0	0	4	3	11	.167	.265	.167	21	-3	0	0	0	.984	2	C-17	0.0
Total	7	251	619	37	127	24	4	5	69	55	135	.205	.281	.281	56	-36	0	3	-2	.991	7	C-249/D-1	-2.0

■ JOSE NIEVES

Nieves, Jose Miguel (Pinto) b: 6/16/75, Guacara, Venez. BR/TR, 6'1", 180 lbs. Deb: 8/7/98

YEAR	TM/L	G	AB	R	H	2B	3B	HR	RBI	BB	SO	AVG	OBP	SLG	PRO+	BR/A	SB	CS	SBR	FA	FR	G/POS	TPR
1998	Chi-N	2	1	0	0	0	0	0	0	0	0	.000	.000	.000	-97	-0	0	0	0	.000	-0	/S-1	-0.1

■ MELVIN NIEVES

Nieves, Melvin Ramos b: 12/28/71, San Juan, P.R. BB/TR, 6'2", 210 lbs. Deb: 9/1/92

YEAR	TM/L	G	AB	R	H	2B	3B	HR	RBI	BB	SO	AVG	OBP	SLG	PRO+	BR/A	SB	CS	SBR	FA	FR	G/POS	TPR
1992	Atl-N	12	19	0	4	1	0	0	1	2	7	.211	.286	.263	53	-1	0	0	0	.727	-1	/O-6	-0.3
1993	SD-N	19	47	4	9	0	0	2	3	3	21	.191	.255	.319	52	-3	0	0	0	.931	-1	O-15	-0.5
1994	SD-N	10	19	2	5	1	0	1	4	3	10	.263	.364	.474	120	1	0	0	0	1.000	1	/O-6	0.1
1995	SD-N	98	234	32	48	6	1	14	38	19	88	.205	.279	.419	84	-7	2	3	-1	.990	-6	O-79/1-2	-1.5
1996	Det-A	120	431	71	106	23	4	24	60	44	158	.246	.324	.485	101	-1	1	2	-1	.943	4	*O-105,D-11	-0.1
1997	Det-A	116	359	46	82	18	1	20	64	39	157	.228	.313	.451	97	-3	1	7	-4	.979	-2	O-99,D-10	-1.1
1998	Cin-N	83	119	8	30	4	0	2	17	26	42	.252	.386	.336	89	-1	0	0	0	1.000	-2	O-25/D-3	-0.3
Total	7	458	1228	163	284	53	6	63	187	136	483	.231	.316	.438	93	-15	4	12	-6	.962	-7	O-335/D-24,1-2	-3.7

■ TOM NILAND

Niland, Thomas James "Honest Tom" b: 4/14/1870, Brookfield, Mass. d: 4/30/50, Lynn, Mass. BR/TR, 5'11", 160 lbs. Deb: 4/19/1896

YEAR	TM/L	G	AB	R	H	2B	3B	HR	RBI	BB	SO	AVG	OBP	SLG	PRO+	BR/A	SB	CS	SBR	FA	FR	G/POS	TPR
1896	StL-N	18	68	3	12	0	1	0	3	5	4	.176	.243	.206	20	-8	0			.913	-4	O-13/S-5	-1.1

■ HARRY NILES

Niles, Herbert Clyde b: 9/10/1880, Buchanan, Mich. d: 4/18/53, Sturgis, Mich. BR/TR, 5'8", 175 lbs. Deb: 4/24/06

YEAR	TM/L	G	AB	R	H	2B	3B	HR	RBI	BB	SO	AVG	OBP	SLG	PRO+	BR/A	SB	CS	SBR	FA	FR	G/POS	TPR
1906	StL-A	142	541	71	124	14	4	2	31	46		.229	.297	.281	85	-9	30			.967	9	*O-108,3-34	-0.5
1907	StL-A	120	492	65	142	9	5	2	35	28		.289	.331	.339	114	7	19			.949	-5	*2-116/O-1	0.1
1908	NY-A	96	362	43	90	14	6	4	24	25		.249	.304	.354	112	4	18			.928	-24	2-85/O-7	-2.4
	Bos-A	17	32	4	8	0	0	1	3	6		.250	.385	.344	133	2	3			1.000	-1	/2-8,S-2	0.1
	Yr	113	394	47	98	14	6	5	27	31		.249	.312	.353	114	6	21			.934	-24	2-93/O-7,S-2	-2.3
1909	Bos-A	145	546	64	134	12	5	1	38	39		.245	.311	.291	88	-6	27			.952	-0	*O-117,3-13/S-9,2-5	-1.2
1910	Bos-A	18	57	6	12	3	0	1	3	4		.211	.262	.316	79	-2	1			.920	-0	O-15	-0.3
	Cle-A	70	240	25	51	6	4	1	18	15		.213	.267	.283	72	-8	9			.975	-4	O-50/S-7,3-5	-1.6
	Yr	88	297	31	63	9	4	2	21	19		.212	.266	.290	73	-10	10			.962	-4	O-65/S-7,3-5	-1.9
Total	5	608	2270	278	561	58	24	12	152	163		.247	.306	.310	95	-12	107			.960	-25	O-298,2-214/3-52,S	-5.8

■ BILL NILES

Niles, William E. b: 1/11/1867, Covington, Ky. d: 7/3/36, Springfield, Ohio 160 lbs. Deb: 5/13/1895

YEAR	TM/L	G	AB	R	H	2B	3B	HR	RBI	BB	SO	AVG	OBP	SLG	PRO+	BR/A	SB	CS	SBR	FA	FR	G/POS	TPR
1895	Pit-N	11	37	2	8	0	0	0	0	5	2	.216	.310	.216	39	-3	2			.930	1	3-10/2-1	-0.2

■ RABBIT NILL

Nill, George Charles b: 7/14/1881, Ft.Wayne, Ind. d: 5/24/62, Fort Wayne, Ind. BR/TR, 5'7", 160 lbs. Deb: 9/27/04

YEAR	TM/L	G	AB	R	H	2B	3B	HR	RBI	BB	SO	AVG	OBP	SLG	PRO+	BR/A	SB	CS	SBR	FA	FR	G/POS	TPR
1904	Was-A	15	48	4	8	0	1	0	3	5		.167	.273	.208	54	-2	0			.878	-4	2-15	-0.6
1905	Was-A	103	319	46	58	7	3	3	31	33		.182	.269	.251	68	-11	12			.897	-2	3-52,2-33/S-6	-1.2
1906	Was-A	89	315	37	74	8	2	0	15	47		.235	.340	.273	97	2	16			.882	5	S-31,2-25,3-15,O-15	0.8
1907	Was-A	66	215	21	47	7	3	0	25	15		.219	.282	.279	86	-3	6			.962	-2	2-39,O-18/3-1	-0.7
	Cle-A	12	43	5	12	1	0	0	2	3		.279	.326	.302	100	0	2			.815	-4	/3-7,S-4	-0.4
	Yr	78	258	26	59	8	3	0	27	18		.229	.289	.283	88	-3	8			.962	-5	2-39,O-18/3-8,S-4	-1.1
1908	Cle-A	11	23	3	5	0	0	0	1	0		.217	.217	.217	41	-2	0			.833	0	/S-6,O-3,2-1	-0.1
Total	5	296	963	116	204	23	9	3	77	103		.212	.297	.264	82	-17	36			.943	-6	2-113/3-75,S-47,O	-2.2

■ DAVE NILSSON

Nilsson, David Wayne b: 12/14/69, Brisbane, Queensland, Australia BL/TR, 6'3", 215 lbs. Deb: 5/18/92

YEAR	TM/L	G	AB	R	H	2B	3B	HR	RBI	BB	SO	AVG	OBP	SLG	PRO+	BR/A	SB	CS	SBR	FA	FR	G/POS	TPR
1992	Mil-A	51	164	15	38	8	0	4	25	17	18	.232	.304	.354	85	-3	2	2	-1	.992	0	C-46/1-3,D-2	-0.1
1993	Mil-A	100	296	35	76	10	2	7	40	37	36	.257	.339	.375	93	-2	3	6	-3	.981	-9	C-91/1-4,D-4	-0.9
1994	Mil-A	109	397	51	109	28	3	12	69	34	61	.275	.332	.451	95	-4	1	0	0	.994	-5	C-60,D-43/1-5	-0.7
1995	Mil-A	81	263	41	73	12	1	12	53	24	41	.278	.343	.468	103	0	2	0	1	.981	-2	O-58,D-14/1-7,C-2	-0.3
1996	Mil-A	123	453	81	150	33	2	17	84	57	68	.331	.409	.525	129	21	2	3	-1	.965	-2	O-61,D-40,1-24,/C-2	1.1
1997	Mil-A	156	554	71	154	33	0	20	81	65	88	.278	.356	.446	107	6	2	3	-1	.991	-7	1-74,D-59,O-22	-1.3
1998	Mil-N	102	309	39	83	14	1	12	56	33	48	.269	.341	.437	99	-0	2	2	-1	.984	-10	1-49,O-37/C-7	-1.4
Total	7	722	2436	333	683	138	9	84	408	267	360	.280	.353	.448	105	17	14	16	-5	.987	-35	C-208,O-178,1D	-3.6

■ AL NIXON

Nixon, Albert Richard "Humpty Dumpty" b: 4/11/1886, Atlantic City, N.J d: 11/9/60, Opelousas, La. BR/TL, 5'7.5", 164 lbs. Deb: 9/4/15

YEAR	TM/L	G	AB	R	H	2B	3B	HR	RBI	BB	SO	AVG	OBP	SLG	PRO+	BR/A	SB	CS	SBR	FA	FR	G/POS	TPR
1915	Bro-N	14	26	3	6	1	0	0	2	2	4	.231	.286	.269	67	-1	1	1	-0	1.000	-2	O-14	-0.4
1916	Bro-N	1	2	0	2	0	0	0	0	0	0	1.000	1.000	1.000	501	1	0			.000	-0	/O-1	0.1
1918	Bro-N	6	11	1	5	0	0	0	0	0	0	.455	.455	.455	178	1	0			1.000	-0	/O-4	0.1
1921	Bos-N	55	138	25	33	6	3	1	9	7	11	.239	.281	.348	69	-7	3	2	-0	.980	-2	O-43	-1.1
1922	Bos-N	86	318	35	84	14	4	2	22	9	19	.264	.284	.352	66	-17	6	6	-2	.975	1	O-79	-2.2
1923	Bos-N	88	321	53	88	12	4	0	19	24	14	.274	.334	.336	81	-9	2	3	-1	.987	9	O-80	-0.6
1926	Phi-N	93	311	38	91	18	2	4	41	13	20	.293	.323	.402	90	-5	5			.977	-2	O-88	-1.3
1927	Phi-N	54	154	18	48	7	0	0	18	5	5	.312	.333	.357	84	-4	1			.969	-1	O-44	-0.6
1928	Phi-N	25	64	7	15	2	0	0	7	6	4	.234	.300	.266	47	-5	1			1.000	-0	O-20	-0.6
Total	9	422	1345	180	372	60	13	7	118	66	77	.277	.314	.356	78	-45	19	12		.980	2	O-373	-6.6

■ TROT NIXON

Nixon, Christopher Trotman b: 4/11/74, Durham, N.C. BL/TL, 6'1", 195 lbs. Deb: 9/21/96

YEAR	TM/L	G	AB	R	H	2B	3B	HR	RBI	BB	SO	AVG	OBP	SLG	PRO+	BR/A	SB	CS	SBR	FA	FR	G/POS	TPR
1996	Bos-A	2	4	2	2	1	0	0	0	0	1	.500	.500	.750	206	1	1	0	0	1.000	-0	/O-2	0.1
1998	*Bos-A	13	27	3	7	1	0	0	0	1	3	.259	.286	.296	52	-2	0	0	0	1.000	0	/O-7,D-2	-0.2
Total	2	15	31	5	9	2	0	0	0	1	4	.290	.313	.355	72	-1	1	0	0	1.000	0	/O-9,D-2	-0.1

■ OTIS NIXON

Nixon, Otis Junior b: 1/9/59, Columbus Co., N.C. BB/TR, 6'2", 180 lbs. Deb: 9/9/83 F

YEAR	TM/L	G	AB	R	H	2B	3B	HR	RBI	BB	SO	AVG	OBP	SLG	PRO+	BR/A	SB	CS	SBR	FA	FR	G/POS	TPR
1983	NY-A	13	14	2	2	0	0	0	0	1	5	.143	.200	.143	-4	-2	2	0	1	.938	-1	/O-9	-0.2
1984	Cle-A	49	91	16	14	0	0	0	1	8	11	.154	.222	.154	6	-11	12	6	0	1.000	-2	O-46	-1.5
1985	Cle-A	104	162	34	38	4	0	3	9	8	27	.235	.271	.315	60	-9	20	11	-1	.971	-7	O-80,D-11	-1.8
1986	Cle-A	105	95	33	25	4	1	0	8	13	12	.263	.352	.326	88	-1	23	6	3	.969	-23	O-95/D-5	-2.2
1987	Cle-A	19	17	2	1	0	0	0	1	3	4	.059	.200	.059	-26	-3	2	3	-1	1.000	-4	O-17/D-2	-0.8
1988	Mon-N	90	271	47	66	8	2	0	15	28	42	.244	.314	.288	71	-9	46	13	6	.994	-2	O-82	-0.8
1989	Mon-N	126	258	41	56	7	2	0	21	33	36	.217	.306	.260	62	-12	37	12	4	.988	-15	O-98	-2.6
1990	Mon-N	119	231	46	58	6	2	1	20	28	33	.251	.332	.307	80	-6	50	13	7	.994	-9	O-88/S-1	-0.9
1991	Atl-N	124	401	81	119	10	1	0	26	47	40	.297	.373	.327	93	-2	72	21	9	.987	1	*O-115	0.6
1992	*Atl-N	120	456	79	134	14	2	2	22	39	54	.294	.349	.346	92	-4	41	18	2	.991	13	*O-111	0.9
1993	*Atl-N	134	461	77	124	12	3	1	24	61	63	.269	.354	.315	80	-11	47	13	6	.990	8	*O-116	0.1
1994	Bos-A	103	398	60	109	15	1	0	25	55	65	.274	.362	.317	74	-14	42	10	7	.989	2	*O-103	-0.7
1995	Tex-A	139	589	87	174	21	2	0	45	58	85	.295	.359	.338	81	-15	50	21	2	.989	5	*O-138	-1.0
1996	Tor-A	125	496	87	142	15	1	1	29	71	68	.286	.377	.327	80	-12	54	13	8	.994	12	*O-125	0.5
1997	Tor-A	103	401	54	105	12	1	1	26	52	54	.262	.347	.304	71	-15	47	10	8	.996	4	*O-102/D-1	-0.5
	LA-N	42	175	30	48	6	2	1	18	13	24	.274	.324	.349	83	-5	12	2	2	.990	3	O-42	0.0
1998	Min-A	110	448	71	133	6	6	1	20	44	56	.297	.362	.344	85	-8	37	7	7	.989	3	*O-108	-0.1
Total	16	1625	4964	847	1348	140	26	11	310	562	679	.272	.346	.317	78	-137	594	179	71	.990	-12	*O-1475/D-19,S-1	-11.0

■ DONELL NIXON

Nixon, Robert Donell b: 12/31/61, Evergreen, N.C. BR/TR, 6'1", 185 lbs. Deb: 4/7/87 F

YEAR	TM/L	G	AB	R	H	2B	3B	HR	RBI	BB	SO	AVG	OBP	SLG	PRO+	BR/A	SB	CS	SBR	FA	FR	G/POS	TPR
1987	Sea-A	46	132	17	33	4	0	3	12	13	28	.250	.327	.348	75	-5	21	7	2	1.000	0	O-32/D-6	-0.3
1988	SF-N	59	78	15	27	3	0	0	6	10	12	.346	.420	.385	138	4	11	8	-2	.983	-8	O-46	-0.7
1989	*SF-N	95	166	23	44	2	0	1	15	11	30	.265	.311	.295	76	-5	10	3	1	.967	-14	O-64	-2.0
1990	Bal-A	8	20	1	5	2	0	0	2	1	7	.250	.286	.350	79	-1	5	0	2	1.000	-1	/O-4,D-3	0.0
Total	4	208	396	56	109	11	0	4	35	35	77	.275	.337	.333	88	-6	47	18	3	.983	-23	O-146/D-9	-3.0

■ RUSS NIXON

Nixon, Russell Eugene b: 2/19/35, Cleves, Ohio BL/TR, 6'1", 200 lbs. Deb: 4/20/57 MC

YEAR	TM/L	G	AB	R	H	2B	3B	HR	RBI	BB	SO	AVG	OBP	SLG	PRO+	BR/A	SB	CS	SBR	FA	FR	G/POS	TPR
1957	Cle-A	62	185	15	52	7	1	2	18	12	12	.281	.325	.362	88	-3	0	1	-1	.984	-6	C-57	-0.8
1958	Cle-A	113	376	42	113	17	4	9	46	13	38	.301	.324	.439	111	4	0	3	-2	.991	-10	*C-101	-0.2

YEAR	TM/L	G	AB	R	H	2B	3B	HR	RBI	BB	SO	AVG	OBP	SLG	PRO+	BR/A	SB	CS	SBR	FA	FR	G/POS	TPR
1959	Cle-A	82	258	23	62	10	3	1	29	15	28	.240	.282	.314	66	-12	0	0	0	.985	-7	C-74	-1.6
1960	Cle-A	25	82	6	20	5	0	1	6	6	6	.244	.311	.341	79	-2	0	1	-1	.993	-0	C-25	-0.2
	Bos-A	80	272	24	81	17	3	5	33	13	23	.298	.330	.438	102	0	0	1	-1	.987	-17	C-74	-1.3
	Yr	105	354	30	101	22	3	6	39	19	29	.285	.325	.415	97	-2	0	2	-1	.989	-17	C-99	-1.5
1961	Bos-A	87	242	24	70	12	2	1	19	13	19	.289	.331	.368	84	-5	0	1	-1	.975	-3	C-66	-0.6
1962	Bos-A	65	151	11	42	7	2	1	19	8	14	.278	.314	.371	81	-4	0	0	0	1.000	-2	C-38	-0.5
1963	Bos-A	98	287	27	77	18	1	5	30	22	32	.268	.329	.390	98	-1	0	0	0	.992	-10	C-76	-0.8
1964	Bos-A	81	163	10	38	7	0	1	20	14	29	.233	.302	.294	64	-8	0	0	0	.990	-4	C-45	-1.0
1965	Bos-A	59	137	11	37	5	1	0	11	6	23	.270	.301	.321	72	-5	0	0	0	.981	-6	C-38	-1.0
1966	Min-A	51	96	5	25	2	1	0	7	7	13	.260	.317	.302	74	-3	0	0	0	.986	-4	C-32	-0.6
1967	Min-A	74	170	16	40	6	1	1	22	18	29	.235	.309	.300	74	-5	0	0	0	.994	-12	C-69	-1.5
1968	Bos-A	29	85	1	13	2	0	0	6	7	13	.153	.217	.176	19	-8	0	0	0	.994	-5	C-27	-1.3
Total	12	906	2504	215	670	115	19	27	266	154	279	.268	.313	.361	84	-53	0	7	-4	.988	-85	C-722	-11.4

■ RAY NOBLE Noble, Rafael Miguel (Magee) b: 3/15/19, Central Hatillo, Cuba d: 5/9/98, Brooklyn, N.Y. BR/TR, 5′11″, 210 lbs. Deb: 4/18/51

YEAR	TM/L	G	AB	R	H	2B	3B	HR	RBI	BB	SO	AVG	OBP	SLG	PRO+	BR/A	SB	CS	SBR	FA	FR	G/POS	TPR
1951	*NY-N	55	141	16	33	6	0	5	26	6	26	.234	.265	.383	72	-6	0	0	0	.974	-5	C-41	-0.9
1952	NY-N	6	5	0	0	0	0	0	0	0	1	.000	.000	.000	-99	-1	0	0	0	1.000	0	/C-5	-0.1
1953	NY-N	46	97	15	20	0	1	4	14	19	14	.206	.353	.351	83	-2	1	0	0	.982	-1	C-41	-0.1
Total	3	107	243	31	53	6	1	9	40	25	41	.218	.299	.362	74	-9	1	0	0	.979	-5	/C-87	-1.1

■ JUNIOR NOBOA Noboa, Milciades Arturo (Diaz) b: 11/10/64, Azua, D.R. BR/TR, 5′10″, 160 lbs. Deb: 8/22/84

YEAR	TM/L	G	AB	R	H	2B	3B	HR	RBI	BB	SO	AVG	OBP	SLG	PRO+	BR/A	SB	CS	SBR	FA	FR	G/POS	TPR
1984	Cle-A	23	11	3	4	0	0	0	0	0	2	.364	.364	.364	100	-0	1	0	0	1.000	4	2-19/D-1	0.4
1987	Cle-A	39	80	7	18	2	1	0	7	3	6	.225	.253	.275	40	-7	1	0	0	.983	4	2-21/S-8,3-5,D-1	-0.2
1988	Cal-A	21	16	4	1	0	0	0	0	0	1	.063	.063	.063	-67	-4	0	0	0	.967	9	/2-9,S-3,3-2	0.5
1989	Mon-N	21	44	3	10	0	0	0	1	1	3	.227	.244	.227	35	-4	0	0	0	1.000	7	2-13/S-4,3-1	0.4
1990	Mon-N	81	158	15	42	7	2	0	14	7	14	.266	.301	.335	78	-5	4	1	1	1.000	-17	2-31/O-9,3-8,S-7,P	-2.2
1991	Mon-N	67	95	5	23	3	0	1	2	1	8	.242	.250	.305	56	-6	2	3	-1	1.000	-3	/O-7,2-6,3-2,S-2,1	-1.0
1992	NY-N	46	47	7	7	0	0	0	3	3	8	.149	.216	.149	5	-6	0	0	0	.977	6	2-16/3-3,S-2	0.0
1994	Oak-A	17	40	3	13	1	1	0	6	2	5	.325	.357	.400	104	0	1	0	0	.943	1	2-14/S-1	0.2
	Pit-N	2	2	0	0	0	0	0	0	0	0	.000	.000	.000	-99	-1	0	0	0	1.000	0	/S-1	-0.1
Total	8	317	493	47	118	13	4	1	33	17	47	.239	.268	.288	54	-31	9	4	0	.981	10	2-129/S-28,3OD1P	-2.0

■ PAUL NOCE Noce, Paul David b: 12/16/59, San Francisco, Cal. BR/TR, 5′10″, 175 lbs. Deb: 6/1/87

YEAR	TM/L	G	AB	R	H	2B	3B	HR	RBI	BB	SO	AVG	OBP	SLG	PRO+	BR/A	SB	CS	SBR	FA	FR	G/POS	TPR
1987	Chi-N	70	180	17	41	9	2	3	14	6	49	.228	.261	.350	58	-11	5	3	-0	.983	19	2-36,S-35/3-2	1.0
1990	Cin-N	1	1	0	1	0	0	0	0	0	0	1.000	1.000	1.000	434	0	0	0	0	.000	0	/H	0.0
Total	2	71	181	17	42	9	2	3	14	6	49	.232	.265	.354	60	-11	5	3	-0	.983	19	/2-36,S-35,3-2	1.0

■ GEORGE NOFTSKER Noftsker, George Washington b: 8/24/1859, Shippensburg, Pa. d: 5/8/31, Shippensburg, Pa. BR/TR, 5′8″, 135 lbs. Deb: 4/17/1884

YEAR	TM/L	G	AB	R	H	2B	3B	HR	RBI	BB	SO	AVG	OBP	SLG	PRO+	BR/A	SB	CS	SBR	FA	FR	G/POS	TPR
1884	Alt-U	7	25	0	1	0	0	0		0		.040	.040	.040	-75	-6				.818	1	/O-5,C-3	-0.4

■ MATT NOKES Nokes, Matthew Dodge b: 10/31/63, San Diego, Cal. BL/TR, 6′1″, 185 lbs. Deb: 9/3/85

YEAR	TM/L	G	AB	R	H	2B	3B	HR	RBI	BB	SO	AVG	OBP	SLG	PRO+	BR/A	SB	CS	SBR	FA	FR	G/POS	TPR
1985	SF-N	19	53	3	11	2	0	2	5	1	9	.208	.236	.358	67	-3	0	0	0	.977	-1	C-14	-0.3
1986	Det-A	7	24	2	8	1	0	1	2	1	1	.333	.360	.500	132	1	0	0	0	1.000	2	/C-7	0.3
1987	*Det-A★	135	461	69	133	14	2	32	87	35	70	.289	.347	.536	135	22	2	1	0	.992	-9	*C-109,D-19/O-3,3-2	1.8
1988	Det-A	122	382	53	96	18	0	16	53	34	58	.251	.314	.424	109	4	0	1	-1	.989	-3	*C-110/D-4	0.8
1989	Det-A	87	268	15	67	10	0	9	39	17	37	.250	.300	.388	95	-3	1	0	0	.978	4	C-51,D-33	-0.7
1990	Det-A	44	111	12	30	5	1	3	8	4	14	.270	.308	.414	99	-0	0	0	0	.984	-3	D-24,C-19	-0.3
	NY-A	92	240	21	57	4	0	8	32	20	33	.237	.307	.354	84	-5	2	2	-1	.995	-7	C-46,D-30/O-2	-1.2
	Yr	136	351	33	87	9	1	11	40	24	47	.248	.307	.373	89	-6	2	2	-1	.993	-10	C-65,D-54/O-2	-1.5
1991	NY-A	135	456	52	122	20	0	24	77	25	49	.268	.313	.469	113	6	3	2	-0	.992	-14	*C-130/D-3	-0.1
1992	NY-A	121	384	42	86	9	1	22	59	37	62	.224	.297	.424	101	-1	0	1	-1	.993	-11	*C-111	-0.6
1993	NY-A	76	217	25	54	8	0	10	35	16	31	.249	.306	.424	97	-2	0	0	0	.992	-5	C-56,D-11	-0.4
1994	NY-A	28	79	11	23	3	0	7	19	5	16	.291	.333	.595	138	4	0	0	0	.975	0	C-17/1-4,D-5	0.4
1995	Bal-A	26	49	4	6	1	0	2	6	4	11	.122	.189	.265	16	-6	0	0	0	.989	3	C-16/D-2	-0.2
	Col-N	10	11	1	2	1	0	0	0	1	4	.182	.250	.273	29	-1	0	0	0	.909	-0	/C-3	-0.1
Total	11	902	2735	310	695	96	4	136	422	200	395	.254	.311	.441	106	15	8	7	-2	.990	-53	C-689,D-131/O-5,13	-0.6

■ JOE NOLAN Nolan, Joseph William b: 5/12/51, St.Louis, Mo. BL/TR, 6′, 190 lbs. Deb: 9/21/72

YEAR	TM/L	G	AB	R	H	2B	3B	HR	RBI	BB	SO	AVG	OBP	SLG	PRO+	BR/A	SB	CS	SBR	FA	FR	G/POS	TPR
1972	NY-N	4	10	0	0	0	0	0	0	1	3	.000	.091	.000	-74	-2	0	0	0	.938	-1	/C-3	-0.3
1975	Atl-N	4	4	0	1	0	0	0	0	1	0	.250	.400	.250	80	-0	0	0	0	1.000	-0	/C-1	0.0
1977	Atl-N	62	82	13	23	3	0	3	9	13	12	.280	.379	.427	103	1	1	0	0	1.000	-1	C-19	0.1
1978	Atl-N	95	213	22	49	7	3	4	22	34	28	.230	.339	.347	83	-4	3	2	-0	.979	-6	C-61	-1.0
1979	Atl-N	89	230	28	57	9	3	4	21	27	28	.248	.335	.365	85	-4	1	3	-2	.983	-7	C-74	-1.1
1980	Atl-N	17	22	2	6	1	0	0	2	2	4	.273	.333	.318	80	-1	0	0	0	1.000	1	/C-6	0.1
	Cin-N	53	154	14	48	7	0	3	24	13	8	.312	.365	.416	117	4	0	0	0	.982	1	C-51	0.7
	Yr	70	176	16	54	8	0	3	26	15	12	.307	.361	.403	112	3	0	0	0	.983	2	C-57	0.8
1981	Cin-N	81	236	25	73	18	1	1	26	24	19	.309	.375	.407	120	7	1	2	-1	**.995**	-11	C-81	-0.3
1982	Bal-A	77	219	24	51	7	1	6	35	16	35	.233	.285	.356	75	-8	1	1	-0	.978	-3	C-72	-0.9
1983	*Bal-A	73	184	25	51	11	1	5	24	16	31	.277	.342	.429	113	3	0	0	0	.980	-10	C-65	-0.5
1984	Bal-A	35	62	2	18	1	1	1	9	12	10	.290	.405	.387	123	3	0	0	0	.962	-1	D-11/C-6	0.2
1985	Bal-A	31	38	1	5	2	0	0	6	5	5	.132	.233	.184	16	-4	0	0	0	1.000	1	/C-5,D-4	-0.4
Total	11	621	1454	156	382	66	10	27	178	164	183	.263	.340	.378	95	-7	7	8	-3	.984	-37	C-444/D-15	-3.4

■ RED NONNENKAMP Nonnenkamp, Leo William b: 7/7/10, St.Louis, Mo. BL/TL, 5′11″, 165 lbs. Deb: 9/6/33

YEAR	TM/L	G	AB	R	H	2B	3B	HR	RBI	BB	SO	AVG	OBP	SLG	PRO+	BR/A	SB	CS	SBR	FA	FR	G/POS	TPR
1933	Pit-N	1	1	0	0	0	0	0	0	0	1	.000	.000	.000	-99	-0	0			.000	0	H	0.0
1938	Bos-A	87	180	37	51	4	1	0	18	21	13	.283	.358	.317	67	-8	6	1	1	.968	2	O-39/1-5	-0.6
1939	Bos-A	58	75	12	18	2	1	0	5	12	6	.240	.345	.293	62	-4	0	1	-1	.962	-3	O-15	-0.7
1940	Bos-A	9	7	0	0	0	0	0	1	0	4	.000	.125	.000	-62	-2	0	0	0	.000	0	H	-0.2
Total	4	155	263	49	69	6	2	0	24	33	24	.262	.347	.300	62	-14	6	2		.966	-1	/O-54,1-5	-1.5

■ PETE NOONAN Noonan, Peter John b: 11/24/1881, W.Stockbridge, Mass. d: 2/11/65, Great Barrington, Mass. BR/TR, 6′, 180 lbs. Deb: 6/20/04

YEAR	TM/L	G	AB	R	H	2B	3B	HR	RBI	BB	SO	AVG	OBP	SLG	PRO+	BR/A	SB	CS	SBR	FA	FR	G/POS	TPR
1904	Phi-A	39	114	13	23	3	1	2	13	1		.202	.209	.298	56	-6	1			.969	-4	C-22,1-10	-0.9
1906	Chi-N	5	3	0	1	0	0	0	0	0		.333	.333	.333	102	-0	0			1.000	0	/1-1	0.0
	StL-N	44	125	8	21	1	3	1	9	11		.168	.235	.248	53	-7	1			.957	3	C-23,1-16	-0.2
	Yr	49	128	8	22	1	3	1	9	11		.172	.237	.250	54	-7	1			.957	3	C-23,1-17	-0.2
1907	StL-N	74	237	19	53	7	3	1	16	9		.224	.252	.291	73	-9	3			.951	3	C-70	0.1
Total	3	162	479	40	98	11	7	4	38	21		.205	.238	.282	64	-22	5			.955	2	C-115/1-27	-1.0

■ TIM NORDBROOK Nordbrook, Timothy Charles b: 7/7/49, Baltimore, Md. BR/TR, 6′1″, 180 lbs. Deb: 9/13/74

YEAR	TM/L	G	AB	R	H	2B	3B	HR	RBI	BB	SO	AVG	OBP	SLG	PRO+	BR/A	SB	CS	SBR	FA	FR	G/POS	TPR
1974	Bal-A	6	15	4	4	0	0	0	1	2	2	.267	.353	.267	83	-0	1	0	0	1.000	1	/S-5,2-1	0.2
1975	Bal-A	40	34	6	4	1	0	0	0	7	7	.118	.268	.147	21	-3	0	0	0	.970	5	S-37/2-3	0.3
1976	Bal-A	27	22	4	5	0	0	0	0	3	5	.227	.320	.227	66	-1	0	0	0	1.000	3	2-14,S-12	0.3
	Cal-A	5	8	1	0	0	0	0	0	1	3	.000	.111	.000	-70	-2	1	0	0	.941	2	/S-4,2-1,D-1	0.1
	Yr	32	30	5	5	0	0	0	0	4	8	.167	.265	.167	30	-3	1	0	0	.978	5	S-16,2-15/D-1	0.4
1977	Chi-A	15	20	2	5	0	0	0	1	7	4	.250	.444	.250	95	0	1	0	0	.850	-2	S-11/3-1,D-2	0.0
	Tor-A	24	63	9	11	0	1	0	1	4	11	.175	.224	.206	18	-7	1	0	0	.989	1	S-24	-0.4
	Yr	39	83	11	16	0	1	0	2	11	15	.193	.287	.217	39	-7	2	0	1	.947	-1	S-35/D-2,3-1	-0.4
1978	Tor-A	7	0	1	0	0	0	0	0	0	0	—	1.000	—	200	0	0	0	0	1.000	2	/S-7	0.2
	Mil-A	2	5	0	0	0	0	0	0	1	1	.000	.167	.000	-49	-1	0	0	0	.909	0	/S-2	0.0
	Yr	9	5	1	0	0	0	0	0	1	1	.000	.286	.000	-13	-1	0	0	0	.941	2	/S-9	0.2

YEAR	TM/L	G	AB	R	H	2B	3B	HR	RBI	BB	SO	AVG	OBP	SLG	PRO+	BR/A	SB	CS	SBR	FA	FR	G/POS	TPR
1979	Mil-A	2	2	0	1	0	0	0	0	0	0	.500	.500	.500	171	0	0	0	0	1.000	-1	/S-2	0.0
Total	6	128	169	27	30	1	1	0	3	25	33	.178	.287	.195	38	-13	4	0	1	.961	12	S-104/2-19,D-3,3-1	0.7

■ WAYNE NORDHAGEN Nordhagen, Wayne Oren b: 7/4/48, Thief River Falls, Minn. BR/TR, 6'2", 205 lbs. Deb: 7/16/76

YEAR	TM/L	G	AB	R	H	2B	3B	HR	RBI	BB	SO	AVG	OBP	SLG	PRO+	BR/A	SB	CS	SBR	FA	FR	G/POS	TPR
1976	Chi-A	22	53	6	10	2	0	0	5	4	12	.189	.246	.226	39	-4	0	0	0	1.000	0	O-10/C-5,D-6	-0.4
1977	Chi-A	52	124	16	39	7	3	4	22	2	12	.315	.325	.516	125	4	1	0	0	.944	-10	O-46/C-3,D-2	-0.7
1978	Chi-A	68	206	28	62	16	0	5	35	5	18	.301	.318	.451	113	3	0	1	-1	.941	-8	O-36,D-16,C-12	-0.8
1979	Chi-A	78	193	20	54	15	0	7	25	13	22	.280	.325	.466	111	2	0	0	0	1.000	-0	D-47,O-12/C-5,P-2	0.0
1980	Chi-A	123	415	45	115	22	4	15	59	10	45	.277	.296	.458	104	0	0	1	-1	.969	-5	O-74,D-32	-0.9
1981	Chi-A	65	208	19	64	8	1	6	33	10	25	.308	.342	.442	127	7	0	1	-1	.947	-7	O-60	-0.2
1982	Tor-A	44	115	8	32	3	0	1	14	9	13	.278	.331	.330	75	-4	0	2	-1	1.000	-1	D-32,O-10	-0.7
	Pit-N	1	4	0	2	0	0	0	2	0	1	.500	.500	.500	175	0	0	0	0	1.000	0	/O-1	0.0
	Tor-A	28	70	4	18	3	0	0	6	1	9	.257	.268	.300	51	-5	0	0	0	.000	0	D-28	-0.6
1983	Chi-N	21	35	1	5	1	0	1	4	0	5	.143	.167	.257	15	-4	0	0	0	1.000	-1	/O-7	-0.6
Total	8	502	1423	147	401	77	8	39	205	54	162	.282	.309	.429	101	-1	1	5	-3	.962	-31	O-256,D-163/C-25,P	-4.9

■ LOU NORDYKE Nordyke, Louis Ellis b: 8/7/1876, Brighton, Iowa d: 9/27/45, Los Angeles, Cal. BL/TR, 6', 185 lbs. Deb: 4/18/06

YEAR	TM/L	G	AB	R	H	2B	3B	HR	RBI	BB	SO	AVG	OBP	SLG	PRO+	BR/A	SB	CS	SBR	FA	FR	G/POS	TPR
1906	StL-A	25	53	4	13	1	0	0	7	10		.245	.365	.264	102	1	3			.942	-3	1-12	-0.2

■ IRV NOREN Noren, Irving Arnold b: 11/29/24, Jamestown, N.Y. BL/TL, 6', 190 lbs. Deb: 4/18/50 C

YEAR	TM/L	G	AB	R	H	2B	3B	HR	RBI	BB	SO	AVG	OBP	SLG	PRO+	BR/A	SB	CS	SBR	FA	FR	G/POS	TPR
1950	Was-A	138	542	80	160	27	10	14	98	67	77	.295	.375	.459	118	14	5	2	0	.984	16	*O-121,1-17	2.3
1951	Was-A	129	509	82	142	33	5	8	86	51	35	.279	.345	.411	105	3	10	7	-1	.978	21	*O-126	1.8
1952	Was-A	12	49	4	12	3	1	0	2	6	3	.245	.327	.347	91	-1	1	0	0	1.000	3	O-12	0.2
	*NY-A	93	272	36	64	13	2	5	21	26	34	.235	.316	.353	91	-4	4	2	0	1.000	-7	O-60,1-19	-1.4
	Yr	105	321	40	76	16	3	5	23	32	37	.237	.318	.352	91	-4	5	2	0	1.000	-4	O-72,1-19	-1.2
1953	*NY-A	109	345	55	92	12	6	6	46	42	39	.267	.350	.388	103	1	3	3	-1	.991	-1	O-96	-0.4
1954	NY-A★	125	426	70	136	21	6	12	66	43	38	.319	.383	.481	140	23	4	6	-2	.980	-1	*O-116/1-1	1.5
1955	*NY-A	132	371	49	94	19	1	8	59	43	33	.253	.336	.375	92	-4	5	2	0	.980	-0	*O-126	-0.9
1956	NY-A	29	37	4	8	1	0	0	6	12	7	.216	.408	.243	78	-0	0	0	0	.875	-2	O-10/1-1	-0.3
1957	KC-A	81	160	8	34	8	0	2	16	11	19	.213	.267	.300	54	-10	0	0	0	.990	-2	1-25/O-6	-1.4
	StL-N	17	30	3	11	4	1	1	10	4	6	.367	.441	.667	189	4	0	1	-1	1.000	-2	/O-8	0.1
1958	StL-N	117	178	24	47	9	1	4	22	13	21	.264	.328	.393	87	-3	0	1	-1	.974	-17	O-77	-2.3
1959	StL-N	8	8	0	1	1	0	0	0	0	2	.125	.125	.250	-3	-1	0	0	0	.000	-1	/O-2,1-1	-0.2
	Chi-N	65	156	27	50	6	2	4	19	13	24	.321	.384	.462	125	6	2	0	1	1.000	3	O-40/1-1	0.8
	Yr	73	164	27	51	7	2	4	19	13	26	.311	.372	.451	118	4	2	0	1	1.000	2	O-42/1-2	0.6
1960	Chi-N	12	11	0	1	0	0	0	1	3	4	.091	.286	.091	9	-1	0	0	0	.833	-1	/1-1,O-1	-0.2
	LA-N	26	25	1	5	0	0	1	1	1	8	.200	.231	.320	46	-2	0	0	0	.000	0	H	-0.2
	Yr	38	36	1	6	0	0	1	2	4	12	.167	.250	.250	36	-3	0	0	0	1.000	-1	/1-1,O-1	-0.4
Total	11	1093	3119	443	857	157	35	65	453	335	350	.275	.349	.410	106	23	34	24	-4	.984	10	O-801/1-66	-0.6

■ DAN NORMAN Norman, Daniel Edmund b: 1/11/55, Los Angeles, Cal. BR/TR, 6'2", 195 lbs. Deb: 9/27/77

YEAR	TM/L	G	AB	R	H	2B	3B	HR	RBI	BB	SO	AVG	OBP	SLG	PRO+	BR/A	SB	CS	SBR	FA	FR	G/POS	TPR
1977	NY-N	7	16	2	4	1	0	0	0	4	2	.250	.400	.313	99	0	0	0	0	1.000	-1	/O-6	-0.1
1978	NY-N	19	64	7	17	0	1	4	10	2	14	.266	.288	.484	116	1	1	0	0	1.000	-1	O-18	0.0
1979	NY-N	44	110	9	27	3	1	3	11	10	26	.245	.314	.373	90	-2	2	0	1	.967	-0	O-33	-0.3
1980	NY-N	69	92	5	17	1	1	2	9	6	14	.185	.235	.283	45	-7	5	0	2	1.000	-3	O-19	-0.9
1982	Mon-N	53	66	6	14	3	0	2	7	7	20	.212	.288	.348	76	-2	0	1	-1	.969	-6	O-31	-0.9
Total	5	192	348	29	79	8	3	11	37	29	76	.227	.288	.362	81	-10	8	1	2	.981	-11	O-107	-2.2

■ BILL NORMAN Norman, Henry Willis Patrick b: 7/16/10, St.Louis, Mo. d: 4/21/62, Milwaukee, Wis. BR/TR, 6'2", 190 lbs. Deb: 8/8/31 MC

YEAR	TM/L	G	AB	R	H	2B	3B	HR	RBI	BB	SO	AVG	OBP	SLG	PRO+	BR/A	SB	CS	SBR	FA	FR	G/POS	TPR
1931	Chi-A	24	55	7	10	2	0	0	6	4	10	.182	.237	.218	22	-6	0	1	-1	.933	-1	O-17	-0.8
1932	Chi-A	13	48	6	11	3	1	0	2	2	3	.229	.260	.333	56	-3	0	0	0	.917	-2	O-13	-0.6
Total	2	37	103	13	21	5	1	0	8	6	13	.204	.248	.272	38	-10	0	1	-1	.928	-3	/O-30	-1.4

■ LES NORMAN Norman, Leslie Eugene b: 2/25/69, Warren, Mich. BR/TR, 6'1", 185 lbs. Deb: 5/29/95

YEAR	TM/L	G	AB	R	H	2B	3B	HR	RBI	BB	SO	AVG	OBP	SLG	PRO+	BR/A	SB	CS	SBR	FA	FR	G/POS	TPR
1995	KC-A	24	40	6	9	0	1	0	4	6	6	.225	.326	.275	58	-2	0	1	-1	.958	-2	O-17/D-5	-0.5
1996	KC-A	54	49	9	6	0	0	0	0	6	14	.122	.232	.122	-7	-8	1	1	-0	1.000	-7	O-38/D-7	-1.4
Total	2	78	89	15	15	0	1	0	4	12	20	.169	.275	.191	22	-10	1	2	-1	.986	-9	/O-55,D-12	-1.9

■ NELSON NORMAN Norman, Nelson Augusto b: 5/23/58, San Pedro De Macoris, D.R. BB/TR, 6'2", 160 lbs. Deb: 5/20/78

YEAR	TM/L	G	AB	R	H	2B	3B	HR	RBI	BB	SO	AVG	OBP	SLG	PRO+	BR/A	SB	CS	SBR	FA	FR	G/POS	TPR
1978	Tex-A	23	34	1	9	2	0	0	1	0	5	.265	.265	.324	64	-2	0	0	0	.984	10	S-18/3-6	0.9
1979	Tex-A	147	343	36	76	9	3	0	21	19	41	.222	.262	.265	43	-27	4	1	1	.952	-16	*S-142/2-1	-3.0
1980	Tex-A	17	32	4	7	0	0	0	1	1	1	.219	.242	.219	28	-3	0	1	-1	.943	7	S-17	0.4
1981	Tex-A	7	13	1	3	1	0	0	2	1	2	.231	.286	.308	75	-0	0	0	0	.963	3	/S-5	0.3
1982	Pit-N	3	3	0	0	0	0	0	0	0	0	.000	.000	.000	-97	-1	0	0	0	.000	-1	/2-2,S-1	-0.2
1987	Mon-N	1	4	0	0	0	0	0	0	0	1	.000	.000	.000	-97	-1	0	0	0	.667	-1	/S-1	-0.2
Total	6	198	429	42	95	12	3	0	25	21	50	.221	.258	.263	42	-34	4	2	0	.954	2	S-184/3-6,2-3	-1.8

■ JIM NORRIS Norris, James Francis b: 12/20/48, Brooklyn, N.Y. BL/TL, 5'10", 175 lbs. Deb: 4/7/77

YEAR	TM/L	G	AB	R	H	2B	3B	HR	RBI	BB	SO	AVG	OBP	SLG	PRO+	BR/A	SB	CS	SBR	FA	FR	G/POS	TPR
1977	Cle-A	133	440	59	119	23	6	2	37	64	57	.270	.363	.364	102	3	26	17	-2	.982	12	*O-124/1-3	0.8
1978	Cle-A	113	315	41	89	14	5	2	27	42	20	.283	.367	.378	111	6	12	7	-1	.988	0	O-78,D-15/1-6	0.2
1979	Cle-A	124	353	50	87	15	6	3	30	44	35	.246	.330	.348	83	-8	15	10	-2	.982	0	O-93,D-13	-1.3
1980	Tex-A	119	174	23	43	5	0	0	16	23	16	.247	.335	.276	72	-6	6	3	0	1.000	-18	O-82,1-10/D-1	-2.6
Total	4	489	1282	173	338	57	17	7	110	173	128	.264	.351	.351	95	-5	59	37	-5	.985	-5	O-377/D-29,1-19	-2.9

■ LEO NORRIS Norris, Leo John b: 5/17/08, Bay St.Louis, Miss d: 2/13/87, Zachary, La. BR/TR, 5'11", 165 lbs. Deb: 4/14/36

YEAR	TM/L	G	AB	R	H	2B	3B	HR	RBI	BB	SO	AVG	OBP	SLG	PRO+	BR/A	SB	CS	SBR	FA	FR	G/POS	TPR
1936	Phi-N	154	581	64	154	27	4	11	76	39	79	.265	.315	.382	79	-18	4			.936	-8	*S-121,2-38	-1.6
1937	Phi-N	116	381	45	98	24	3	9	36	21	53	.257	.296	.407	82	-11	3			.949	-12	2-74,3-24,S-20	-1.7
Total	2	270	962	109	252	51	7	20	112	60	132	.262	.307	.392	80	-29	7			.940	-21	S-141,2-112/3-24	-3.3

■ BILLY NORTH North, William Alex b: 5/15/48, Seattle, Wash. BB/TR, 5'11", 185 lbs. Deb: 9/3/71

YEAR	TM/L	G	AB	R	H	2B	3B	HR	RBI	BB	SO	AVG	OBP	SLG	PRO+	BR/A	SB	CS	SBR	FA	FR	G/POS	TPR
1971	Chi-N	8	16	3	6	0	0	0	0	4	6	.375	.524	.375	138	1	1	1	-0	1.000	-2	/O-6	-0.1
1972	Chi-N	66	127	22	23	2	3	0	4	13	33	.181	.262	.244	40	-10	6	0	2	.955	-8	O-48	-1.9
1973	Oak-A	146	554	98	158	10	5	5	34	78	89	.285	.376	.348	111	11	53	20	4	.980	24	*O-138/D-6	3.3
1974	*Oak-A	149	543	79	141	20	5	4	33	69	86	.260	.348	.337	105	5	**54**	26	1	.991	18	*O-138/D-8	1.9
1975	*Oak-A	140	524	74	143	17	5	1	43	81	80	.273	.374	.330	103	6	30	12	2	.975	20	*O-138/D-1	2.2
1976	Oak-A	154	590	91	163	20	5	2	31	73	95	.276	.358	.337	109	9	**75**	29	5	.978	6	*O-144/D-8	1.5
1977	Oak-A	56	184	32	48	3	3	1	9	32	25	.261	.376	.326	95	0	17	13	-3	.983	-4	O-52/D-1	-0.8
1978	Oak-A	24	52	5	11	4	0	0	5	9	13	.212	.349	.288	86	-1	3	2	-0	1.000	-2	O-17	-0.4
	*LA-N	110	304	54	71	10	0	0	10	65	48	.234	.372	.266	81	-4	27	8	3	.975	-2	*O-103	-0.7
1979	SF-N	142	460	87	119	15	4	5	30	96	84	.259	.388	.341	108	10	58	24	3	.987	3	*O-130	1.0
1980	SF-N	128	415	73	104	12	1	1	19	81	78	.251	.374	.292	90	-1	45	19	2	.982	10	*O-115	0.7
1981	SF-N	46	131	22	29	7	0	1	12	26	28	.221	.354	.298	88	-1	26	8	3	.966	-2	O-37	-0.2
Total	11	1169	3900	640	1016	120	31	20	230	627	665	.261	.366	.323	99	26	395	162	21	.981	61	*O-1066/D-24	6.5

■ HUB NORTHEN Northen, Hubbard Elwin b: 8/16/1885, Atlanta, Tex. d: 10/1/47, Shreveport, La. BL/TL, 5'8", 175 lbs. Deb: 9/10/10

YEAR	TM/L	G	AB	R	H	2B	3B	HR	RBI	BB	SO	AVG	OBP	SLG	PRO+	BR/A	SB	CS	SBR	FA	FR	G/POS	TPR
1910	StL-A	26	96	6	19	1	0	0	16	5		.198	.238	.208	42	-6	2			.926	-2	O-26	-1.1
1911	Cin-N	1	0	0	0	0	0	0	0	0	0	—	—	—		0	0			.000	0	H	0.0
	Bro-N	19	76	16	24	2	2	0	1	14	9	.316	.429	.395	137	5	4			.911	2	O-19	0.5
	Yr	20	76	16	24	2	2	0	1	14	9	.316	.429	.395	137	5	4			.911	2	O-19	0.5
1912	Bro-N	118	412	54	116	26	6	3	46	41	46	.282	.352	.396	109	5	8			.950	-7	*O-102	-0.8
Total	3	164	584	76	159	29	8	3	63	60	55	.272	.345	.365	103	3	14			.939	-7	O-147	-1.4

YEAR	TM/L	G	AB	R	H	2B	3B	HR	RBI	BB	SO	AVG	OBP	SLG	PRO+	BR/A	SB	CS	SBR	FA	FR	G/POS	TPR
■ RON NORTHEY	Northey, Ronald James b: 4/26/20, Mahanoy City, Pa. d: 4/16/71, Pittsburgh, Pa. BL/TR, 5'10", 195 lbs. Deb: 4/14/42 FC																						
1942	Phi-N	127	402	31	101	13	2	5	31	28	33	.251	.300	.331	89	-7	2			.952	1	*O-109	-1.2
1943	Phi-N	147	586	72	163	31	5	16	68	51	52	.278	.339	.430	127	17	2			.978	3	*O-145	1.4
1944	Phi-N	152	570	72	164	35	9	22	104	67	51	.288	.367	.496	146	33	1			.981	4	*O-151	3.0
1946	Phi-N	128	438	55	109	24	6	16	62	39	59	.249	.313	.441	116	6	1			.971	-6	*O-111	-0.6
1947	Phi-N	13	47	7	12	3	0	0	3	6	3	.255	.340	.319	79	-1	1			1.000	-1	O-13	-0.3
	StL-N	110	311	52	91	19	3	15	63	48	29	.293	.391	.518	133	15	0			.949	-12	O-94/3-2	0.0
	Yr	123	358	59	103	22	3	15	66	54	32	.288	.384	.492	127	14	1			.955	-13	*O-107/3-2	-0.3
1948	StL-N	96	246	40	79	10	1	13	64	38	25	.321	.420	.528	147	17	0			.989	-10	O-67	0.4
1949	StL-N	90	265	28	69	18	2	7	50	31	15	.260	.338	.423	98	-1	0			.980	-11	O-73	-1.5
1950	Cin-N	27	77	11	20	5	0	5	9	15	6	.260	.380	.519	134	4	0			.955	-5	O-24	-0.2
	Chi-N	53	114	11	32	9	0	4	20	10	9	.281	.339	.465	110	1	0			.976	-1	O-27	0.0
	Yr	80	191	22	52	14	0	9	29	25	15	.272	.356	.487	120	5	0			.969	-6	O-51	-0.2
1952	Chi-N	1	1	0	0	0	0	0	0	0	0	.000	.000	.000	-99	-0	0	0	0	.000	0	H	0.0
1955	Chi-A	14	14	1	5	2	0	1	4	3	3	.357	.471	.714	209	2	0	0	0	1.000	-1	/O-2	0.2
1956	Chi-A	53	48	4	17	2	0	3	23	8	1	.354	.446	.583	168	5	0	0	0	1.000	-1	/O-4	0.4
1957	Chi-A	40	27	0	5	1	0	0	7	11	5	.185	.421	.222	80	0	0	0	0	.000	0	H	0.0
	Phi-N	33	26	1	7	0	0	1	5	6	6	.269	.406	.385	118	1	0	0	0	.000	0	H	0.1
Total	12	1084	3172	385	874	172	28	108	513	361	297	.276	.352	.450	124	93	7	0		.972	-38	O-820/3-2	1.7
■ SCOTT NORTHEY	Northey, Scott Richard b: 10/15/46, Philadelphia, Pa. BR/TR, 6', 175 lbs. Deb: 9/2/69 F																						
1969	KC-A	20	61	11	16	2	2	1	7	7	19	.262	.338	.410	108	1	6	3	0	.973	-0	O-18	-0.1
■ JIM NORTHRUP	Northrup, James Thomas b: 11/24/39, Breckenridge, Mich. BL/TR, 6'3", 190 lbs. Deb: 9/30/64																						
1964	Det-A	5	12	1	1	1	0	0	0	0	3	.083	.083	.167	-32	-2	1	0	0	1.000	-1	/O-2	-0.3
1965	Det-A	80	219	20	45	12	3	2	16	12	50	.205	.253	.315	60	-12	1	1	-0	.976	-4	O-54	-1.9
1966	Det-A	123	419	53	111	24	6	16	58	33	52	.265	.325	.465	121	11	4	7	-3	.980	10	*O-113	1.3
1967	Det-A	144	495	63	134	18	6	10	61	43	83	.271	.333	.392	110	6	7	1	2	.972	-20	*O-143	-2.0
1968	*Det-A	154	580	76	153	29	7	21	90	50	87	.264	.326	.447	129	19	4	5	-2	.979	8	*O-151	1.9
1969	Det-A	148	543	79	160	31	5	25	66	52	83	.295	.360	.508	135	23	4	2	0	.985	4	*O-143	2.0
1970	Det-A	139	504	71	132	21	3	24	80	58	68	.262	.346	.458	119	13	3	6	-3	.993	3	*O-136	0.6
1971	Det-A	136	459	72	124	27	2	16	71	60	43	.270	.357	.442	121	13	7	4	-0	.981	-20	*O-108,1-32	-1.6
1972	*Det-A	134	426	40	111	15	2	8	42	38	47	.261	.324	.362	101	0	4	7	-3	.978	-16	*O-127/1-2	-2.8
1973	Det-A	119	404	55	124	14	7	12	44	38	41	.307	.368	.465	125	13	4	4	-1	.982	-9	*O-116	-0.2
1974	Det-A	97	376	41	89	12	1	11	42	36	46	.237	.303	.362	88	-6	0	0	0	.973	3	O-97	-0.8
	Mon-N	21	54	3	13	1	0	2	8	5	9	.241	.305	.370	84	-1	0	0	0	1.000	-2	O-13	-0.4
	Bal-A	8	7	2	4	0	0	1	3	2	1	.571	.667	1.000	386	3	0	0	0	1.000	-1	/O-6,D-1	0.2
1975	Bal-A	84	194	27	53	13	0	5	29	22	22	.273	.353	.418	125	6	0	1	-1	.979	-12	O-58/D-3	-0.8
Total	12	1392	4692	603	1254	218	42	153	610	449	635	.267	.335	.429	115	86	39	38	-11	.981	-57	*O-1267/1-34,D-4	-4.8
■ FRANK NORTON	Norton, Frank Prescott Deb: 5/5/1871																						
1871	Oly-n	1	1	0	0	0	0	0	0	0	1	.000	.000	.000	-99	-0	0	0	0	.000	-1	/3-1,O-1	-0.1
■ GREG NORTON	Norton, Gregory Blakemoor b: 7/6/72, San Leandro, Cal. BB/TR, 6'1", 190 lbs. Deb: 8/18/96																						
1996	Chi-A	11	23	4	5	0	0	2	3	4	6	.217	.333	.478	107	0	0	1	-1	.778	-2	/S-6,3-2,D-2	-0.2
1997	Chi-A	18	34	5	9	2	2	0	1	2	8	.265	.306	.441	96	-0	0	0	0	.864	0	3-11/D-2	0.0
1998	Chi-A	105	299	38	71	17	2	9	36	26	77	.237	.303	.398	82	-8	3	3	-1	.994	-7	1-79,3-11/2-1,D-2	-2.2
Total	3	134	356	47	85	19	4	11	40	32	91	.239	.305	.407	85	-9	3	4	-2	.904	-9	/1-79,3-24,D-6,S2	-2.4
■ WILLIE NORWOOD	Norwood, Willie b: 11/7/50, Greene County, Ala. BR/TR, 6', 185 lbs. Deb: 4/21/77																						
1977	Min-A	39	83	15	19	3	0	3	9	6	17	.229	.281	.373	78	-3	6	1	1	.952	-4	O-28/D-5	-0.6
1978	Min-A	125	428	56	109	22	3	8	46	28	64	.255	.305	.376	89	-7	25	10	2	.944	-2	*O-115/D-6	-1.3
1979	Min-A	96	270	32	67	13	3	6	30	20	51	.248	.300	.385	80	-8	9	5	-0	.974	-4	O-71,D-14	-1.5
1980	Min-A	34	73	6	12	2	0	1	8	3	13	.164	.197	.233	16	-8	1	1	-0	1.000	-1	O-17/D-9	-1.1
Total	4	294	854	109	207	40	6	18	93	57	145	.242	.292	.367	79	-26	41	17	2	.959	-12	O-231/D-34	-4.5
■ JOE NOSSEK	Nossek, Joseph Rudolph b: 11/8/40, Cleveland, Ohio BR/TR, 6', 178 lbs. Deb: 4/18/64 C																						
1964	Min-A	7	1	1	0	0	0	0	0	0	0	.000	.000	.000	-99	-0	0	0	0	.000	-1	/O-2	-0.1
1965	*Min-A	87	170	19	37	9	0	2	16	7	22	.218	.253	.306	55	-10	2	0	1	.970	-6	O-48/3-9	-1.8
1966	Min-A	4	0	0	0	0	0	0	0	0	0	—	—	—	—	0	0	0	0	.000	-1	/O-2	-0.1
	KC-A	87	230	13	60	10	3	1	27	8	21	.261	.286	.343	83	-6	4	2	0	.983	3	O-78/3-1	-0.6
	Yr	91	230	13	60	10	3	1	27	8	21	.261	.286	.343	82	-6	4	2	0	.983	2	O-80/3-1	-0.7
1967	KC-A	87	166	12	34	6	1	0	10	4	26	.205	.224	.253	42	-12	2	0	1	.982	-3	O-63	-1.9
1969	Oak-A	13	6	0	0	0	0	0	0	0	0	.000	.000	.000	-99	-2	0	0	0	1.000	-4	O-12	-0.6
	StL-N	9	5	2	1	0	0	0	0	0	3	.200	.200	.200	12	-1	0	0	0	1.000	0	/O-1	-0.1
1970	StL-N	1	1	0	0	0	0	0	0	0	0	.000	.000	.000	-98	-0	0	0	0	.000	0	H	0.0
Total	6	295	579	47	132	25	4	3	53	19	72	.228	.254	.301	60	-31	8	2	1	.980	-11	O-206/3-10	-5.2
■ LOU NOVIKOFF	Novikoff, Louis Alexander "The Mad Russian" b: 10/12/15, Glendale, Ariz. d: 9/30/70, South Gate, Cal. BR/TR, 5'10", 185 lbs. Deb: 4/15/41																						
1941	Chi-N	62	203	22	49	8	0	5	24	11	15	.241	.284	.355	82	-6	0			1.000	-4	O-54	-1.3
1942	Chi-N	128	483	48	145	25	5	7	64	24	28	.300	.337	.416	125	12	3			.964	-2	*O-120	0.4
1943	Chi-N	78	233	22	65	7	3	0	28	18	15	.279	.333	.335	95	-2	0			.980	-8	O-61	-1.4
1944	Chi-N	71	139	15	39	4	2	3	19	10	11	.281	.329	.403	106	1	1			.976	-5	O-29	-0.6
1946	Phi-N	17	23	0	7	1	0	0	3	1	2	.304	.333	.348	96	-0	0			1.000	0	/O-3	0.0
Total	5	356	1081	107	305	45	10	15	138	64	71	.282	.325	.384	107	6	4			.976	-19	O-267	-2.9
■ RUBE NOVOTNEY	Novotney, Ralph Joseph b: 8/5/24, Streator, Ill. d: 7/16/87, Redondo Beach, Cal. BR/TR, 6', 187 lbs. Deb: 4/29/49																						
1949	Chi-N	22	67	4	18	2	1	0	6	3	11	.269	.300	.328	70	-3	0			.958	0	C-20	-0.1
■ LES NUNAMAKER	Nunamaker, Leslie Grant b: 1/25/1889, Aurora, Neb. d: 11/14/38, Hastings, Neb. BR/TR, 6'2", 190 lbs. Deb: 4/28/11																						
1911	Bos-A	62	183	18	47	4	3	0	19	12		.257	.303	.311	72	-7	1			.972	6	C-59	0.4
1912	Bos-A	35	103	15	26	5	2	0	6	6		.252	.313	.340	82	-3	2			.971	-3	C-35	-0.3
1913	Bos-A	29	65	9	14	5	2	0	9	8	8	.215	.311	.354	92	-1	2			.977	3	C-27	0.5
1914	Bos-A	5	5	0	1	0	0	0	0	1	0	.200	.333	.200	61	-0	0			1.000	0	/C-3,1-1	0.0
	NY-A	87	257	19	68	10	3	2	29	22	34	.265	.327	.350	104	1	11	9	-2	.971	4	C-70/1-5	1.0
	Yr	92	262	19	69	10	3	2	29	23	34	.263	.328	.347	103	1	11	9	-2	.971	5	C-73/1-6	1.0
1915	NY-A	87	249	24	56	6	3	0	17	23	24	.225	.293	.273	70	-9	3	2	-0	.964	-4	C-77/1-2	-0.9
1916	NY-A	91	260	25	77	14	7	0	28	34	21	.296	.380	.404	133	11	4			.983	-6	C-79	1.1
1917	NY-A	104	310	22	81	9	2	0	33	21	25	.261	.310	.303	86	-5	5			.976	-4	C-91	-0.3
1918	StL-A	85	274	22	71	9	2	0	22	28	16	.259	.339	.307	98	-0	6			.979	0	C-81/1-1,O-1	0.7
1919	Cle-A	26	56	6	14	1	1	0	7	2	6	.250	.276	.304	59	-3	0			.927	-4	C-16	-0.7
1920	*Cle-A	34	54	10	18	3	3	0	14	4	5	.333	.379	.500	128	2	1	0	0	.963	1	C-17/1-6	0.4
1921	Cle-A	46	131	16	47	7	2	0	25	11	8	.359	.408	.443	115	3	1	1	-0	.970	4	C-46	0.8
1922	Cle-A	25	43	8	13	2	0	0	7	4	3	.302	.362	.349	85	-1	0	0	0	.936	-2	C-13	-0.3
Total	12	716	1990	194	533	75	30	2	216	176	150	.268	.332	.339	95	-12	36	12		.972	-5	C-614/1-15,O-1	2.4
■ ABRAHAM NUNEZ	Nunez, Abraham Orlando (Adames) b: 3/16/76, Santo Domingo, D.R. BB/TR, 5'11", 160 lbs. Deb: 8/27/97																						
1997	Pit-N	19	40	3	9	2	2	0	6	3	10	.225	.295	.375	73	-2	1	0	0	1.000	1	S-12/2-9	0.1
1998	Pit-N	24	52	6	10	2	0	1	2	12	14	.192	.344	.288	66	-2	4	2	0	.930	4	S-23	0.4
Total	2	43	92	9	19	4	2	1	8	15	24	.207	.324	.326	69	-4	5	2	0	.948	6	/S-35,2-9	0.5

YEAR	TM/L	G	AB	R	H	2B	3B	HR	RBI	BB	SO	AVG	OBP	SLG	PRO+	BR/A	SB	CS	SBR	FA	FR	G/POS	TPR
■ **JON NUNNALLY** Nunnally, Jonathan Keith b: 11/9/71, Pelham, N.C. BL/TR, 5'10", 190 lbs. Deb: 4/26/95																							
1995	KC-A	119	303	51	74	15	6	14	42	51	86	.244	.357	.472	112	5	6	4	-1	.971	-4	*O-107/D-4	-0.2
1996	KC-A	35	90	16	19	5	1	5	17	13	25	.211	.311	.456	91	-2	0	0	0	.968	-1	O-29/D-4	-0.3
1997	KC-A	13	29	8	7	0	1	1	4	5	7	.241	.353	.414	97	-0	0	0	0	1.000	-1	/O-9	-0.2
	Cin-N	65	201	38	64	12	3	13	35	26	51	.318	.402	.602	157	16	7	3	0	.984	-2	O-60	1.4
1998	Cin-N	74	174	29	36	9	0	7	20	34	38	.207	.340	.379	85	-3	3	4	-2	.956	-4	O-70	-1.0
Total	4	306	797	142	200	41	11	40	118	129	207	.251	.359	.481	114	17	16	11	-2	.971	-13	O-275/D-8	-0.3
■ **EMORY NUSZ** Nusz, Emory Moberly b: 4/2/1866, Frederick, Md. d: 8/3/1893, Point Of Rocks, Md. Deb: 4/26/1884																							
1884	Was-U	1	4	1	0	0	0	0		0		.000	.000	.000	-99	-1				.500	-0	/O-1	-0.1
■ **DIZZY NUTTER** Nutter, Everett Clarence b: 8/27/1893, Roseville, Ohio d: 7/25/58, Battle Creek, Mich. BL/TR, 5'9", 160 lbs. Deb: 9/7/19																							
1919	Bos-N	18	52	4	11	0	0	0	3	4	5	.212	.268	.212	47	-3	1			1.000	2	O-12	-0.3
■ **CHARLIE NYCE** Nyce, Charles Reiff (b: Charles Reiff Nice) b: 7/1/1870, Philadelphia, Pa. d: 5/9/08, Philadelphia, Pa. 5'8", 160 lbs. Deb: 5/28/1895																							
1895	Bos-N	9	35	7	8	5	0	2	9	4	2	.229	.325	.543	113	0	0			.889	-1	/S-9	0.0
■ **CHRIS NYMAN** Nyman, Christopher Curtis b: 6/6/55, Pomona, Cal. BR/TR, 6'4", 200 lbs. Deb: 7/28/82 F																							
1982	Chi-A	28	65	6	16	1	0	0	2	3	9	.246	.279	.262	50	-4	3	2	-0	.994	0	1-24/O-2	-0.6
1983	Chi-A	21	28	12	8	0	0	2	4	4	7	.286	.394	.500	139	2	2	2	-1	1.000	1	1-10,D-10	0.1
Total	2	49	93	18	24	1	0	2	6	7	16	.258	.317	.333	78	-3	5	4	-1	.996	1	/1-34,D-10,O-2	-0.5
■ **NYLS NYMAN** Nyman, Nyls Wallace Rex b: 3/7/54, Detroit, Mich. BL/TR, 6', 170 lbs. Deb: 9/6/74 F																							
1974	Chi-A	5	14	5	9	2	1	0	4	0	1	.643	.667	.929	347	4	1	0	0	1.000	1	/O-3	0.5
1975	Chi-A	106	327	36	74	6	3	2	28	11	34	.226	.256	.281	51	-21	10	4	1	.958	-4	O-94/D-4	-2.9
1976	Chi-A	8	15	2	2	1	0	0	1	0	3	.133	.133	.200	-3	-2	1	0	0	1.000	-1	/O-7	-0.3
1977	Chi-A	1	1	0	0	0	0	0	0	0	0	.000	.000	.000	-99	-0	0	0	0	.000	0	H	0.0
Total	4	120	357	43	85	9	4	2	33	11	38	.238	.267	.303	60	-19	12	4	1	.962	-4	O-104/D-4	-2.7
■ **REBEL OAKES** Oakes, Ennis Telfair b: 12/17/1883, Arizona, La. d: 3/1/48, Lisbon, La. BL/TR, 5'8", 170 lbs. Deb: 4/14/09 M																							
1909	Cin-N	120	415	55	112	10	5	3	31	40		.270	.341	.340	112	6	23			.979	-2	*O-113	0.0
1910	StL-N	131	468	50	118	14	6	0	43	38	38	.252	.315	.308	85	-9	18			.939	-7	*O-127	-2.3
1911	StL-N	154	551	69	145	13	6	2	59	41	35	.263	.320	.319	81	-14	25			.961	11	*O-151	-1.1
1912	StL-N	136	495	57	139	19	5	3	58	31	24	.281	.328	.358	90	-8	26			.947	-2	*O-136	-1.6
1913	StL-N	147	539	60	158	14	5	0	49	43	32	.293	.350	.338	98	-0	22			.968	-2	*O-145	-1.0
1914	Pit-F	145	571	82	178	18	10	7	75	35	22	.312	.359	.415	111	-0	28			.960	6	*O-145,M	-0.1
1915	Pit-F	153	580	55	161	24	5	0	82	37	19	.278	.323	.336	86	-19	21			.973	-3	*O-153,M	-3.3
Total	7	986	3619	428	1011	112	42	15	397	265	170	.279	.334	.346	95	-44	163			.961	1	O-970	-9.4
■ **PRINCE OANA** Oana, Henry Kauhane b: 1/22/08, Waipahu, Hawaii d: 6/19/76, Austin, Tex. BR/TR, 6'2", 193 lbs. Deb: 4/22/34																							
1934	Phi-N	6	21	3	5	1	0	0	3	0	1	.238	.238	.286	35	-2	0			1.000	1	/O-4	-0.1
1943	Det-A	20	26	5	10	2	1	1	7	1	2	.385	.407	.654	193	3	0	0	0	.750	-0	P-10	0.0
1945	Det-A	4	5	0	1	0	0	0	0	0	0	.200	.200	.200	15	-1	0	0	0	1.000	-0	/P-3	0.0
Total	3	30	52	8	16	3	1	1	10	1	3	.308	.321	.462	108	0	0	0		.778	0	/P-13,O-4	-0.1
■ **JOHNNY OATES** Oates, Johnny Lane b: 1/21/46, Sylva, N.C. BL/TR, 5'11", 188 lbs. Deb: 9/17/70 MC																							
1970	Bal-A	5	18	2	5	0	1	0	2	2	0	.278	.350	.389	102	0	0	0	0	.939	1	/C-4	0.1
1972	Bal-A	85	253	20	66	12	1	4	21	28	31	.261	.335	.364	105	2	5	7	-3	**.995**	-3	C-82	-0.1
1973	Atl-N	93	322	27	80	6	0	4	27	22	31	.248	.299	.304	63	-16	1	4	-2	.981	-6	C-86	-2.1
1974	Atl-N	100	291	22	65	10	0	1	21	23	24	.223	.280	.268	52	-19	2	3	-1	.992	12	C-91	-0.5
1975	Atl-N	8	18	0	4	1	0	0	0	1	4	.222	.263	.278	48	-1	0	0	0	1.000	-0	/C-6	-0.2
	Phi-N	90	269	28	77	14	0	1	25	33	29	.286	.364	.349	95	-1	1	0	0	.990	2	C-82	0.5
	Yr	98	287	28	81	15	0	1	25	34	33	.282	.358	.345	92	-2	1	0	0	.990	1	C-88	0.3
1976	*Phi-N	37	99	10	25	2	0	0	8	8	12	.253	.308	.273	64	-4	0	1	-1	.994	2	C-33	-0.3
1977	*LA-N	60	156	18	42	4	0	3	11	11	11	.269	.317	.353	80	-4	1	0	0	.987	5	C-56	0.2
1978	*LA-N	40	75	5	23	1	0	0	6	5	3	.307	.350	.320	89	-1	0	1	-1	.956	-2	C-24	-0.3
1979	LA-N	26	46	4	6	2	0	0	2	4	1	.130	.200	.174	36	-6	0	1	-1	.975	3	C-20	-0.4
1980	NY-A	39	64	6	12	3	0	1	3	2	3	.188	.224	.281	38	-6	1	2	-1	.991	3	C-39	-0.3
1981	NY-A	10	26	4	5	1	0	0	0	2	0	.192	.250	.231	40	-2	0	0	0	.963	1	C-10	-0.1
Total	11	593	1637	146	410	56	2	14	126	141	149	.250	.311	.313	73	-58	11	19	-8	.987	16	C-533	-3.5
■ **SHERMAN OBANDO** Obando, Sherman Omar (Gainor) b: 1/23/70, Bocas Del Toro, Pan. BR/TR, 6'4", 215 lbs. Deb: 4/10/93																							
1993	Bal-A	31	92	8	25	2	0	3	15	4	26	.272	.309	.391	83	-2	0	0	0	.929	-1	D-21/O-8	-0.4
1995	Bal-A	16	38	0	10	1	0	0	3	2	12	.263	.300	.289	53	-3	1	0	0	.923	-0	/O-7,D-7	-0.3
1996	Mon-N	89	178	30	44	9	0	8	22	22	48	.247	.333	.433	98	-1	2	0	1	.962	-1	O-47	-0.3
1997	Mon-N	41	47	3	6	1	0	2	9	6	14	.128	.241	.277	35	-5	0	0	0	1.000	-3	O-15/D-2	-0.8
Total	4	177	355	41	85	13	0	13	49	34	100	.239	.311	.386	81	-10	3	0	1	.957	-6	/O-77,D-30	-1.8
■ **HENRY OBERBECK** Oberbeck, Henry A. b: 5/17/1858, Missouri d: 8/26/21, St.Louis, Mo. Deb: 5/7/1883																							
1883	Pit-a	2	9	1	2	1	0	0		0		.222	.222	.333	80	-0				1.000	0	/1-2	0.0
	StL-a	4	14	0	0	0	0	0		0		.000	.000	.000	-95	-3				.833	1	/O-4	-0.2
	Yr	6	23	1	2	1	0	0		0		.087	.087	.130	-30	-3				.833	1	/O-4,1-2	-0.2
1884	Bal-U	33	125	19	23	4	0	0		3		.184	.203	.216	25	-15				.878	2	O-28/3-8,P-2	-1.2
	KC-U	27	90	7	17	3	0	0		7		.189	.247	.222	50	-8				.823	7	3-15/O-7,P-6,1-3	0.0
	Yr	60	215	26	40	7	0	0		10		.186	.222	.219	34	-23				.908	9	O-35,3-23/P-8,1-3	-1.2
Total	2	66	238	27	42	8	0	0		10		.176	.210	.210	28	-27				.901	9	/O-39,3-23,P-8,1-5	-1.4
■ **KEN OBERKFELL** Oberkfell, Kenneth Ray b: 5/4/56, Highland, Ill. BL/TR, 6', 210 lbs. Deb: 8/22/77																							
1977	StL-N	9	9	0	1	0	0	0	1	0	3	.111	.111	.111	-41	-2	0	0	0	1.000	-1	/2-6	-0.2
1978	StL-N	24	50	7	6	1	0	0	0	3	1	.120	.170	.140	-13	-8	0	0	0	.987	3	2-17/3-4	-0.4
1979	StL-N	135	369	53	111	19	5	1	35	57	35	.301	.400	.388	115	10	4	1	1	**.985**	-4	*2-117,3-17/S-2	1.4
1980	StL-N	116	422	58	128	27	6	3	46	51	23	.303	.380	.417	118	12	4	4	-1	.989	-8	*2-101,3-16	0.9
1981	StL-N	102	376	43	110	12	6	2	45	37	28	.293	.356	.372	104	3	13	5	1	.956	11	*3-102/S-1	1.3
1982	*StL-N	137	470	55	136	22	5	2	34	40	31	.289	.346	.370	99	0	11	9	-2	**.972**	11	*3-135/2-1	0.6
1983	StL-N	151	488	62	143	26	5	3	38	61	27	.293	.373	.385	110	9	12	6	0	**.960**	3	*3-127,2-32/S-1	1.2
1984	StL-N	50	152	17	47	11	1	0	11	16	10	.309	.379	.395	121	5	1	2	-1	.967	4	3-46/2-2,S-1	0.8
	Atl-N	50	172	21	40	8	1	1	10	15	17	.233	.294	.308	65	-8	1	3	-2	.964	-5	3-45/2-4	-1.6
	Yr	100	324	38	87	19	2	1	21	31	27	.269	.334	.349	90	-4	2	5	-2	.966	-1	3-91/2-6,S-1	-0.8
1985	Atl-N	134	412	30	112	19	4	3	35	51	38	.272	.360	.359	96	-0	1	2	-1	.963	-1	*3-117,2-16	-0.4
1986	Atl-N	151	503	62	136	24	3	5	48	83	40	.270	.376	.360	98	2	7	4	-0	.976	9	*3-130,2-41	1.0
1987	Atl-N	135	508	59	142	29	2	3	48	48	29	.280	.344	.362	83	-11	3	3	-1	.979	-4	*3-126,2-11	-1.8
1988	Atl-N	120	422	42	117	20	4	3	40	32	28	.277	.331	.365	95	-3	4	5	-2	.951	-7	*3-113/2-1	-1.3
	Pit-N	20	54	7	12	2	0	0	2	5	6	.222	.288	.259	59	-3	0	0	0	1.000	-4	2-11/S-3,3-2,1-1	-0.6
	Yr	140	476	49	129	22	4	3	42	37	34	.271	.326	.353	91	-5	4	5	-2	.952	-10	*3-115,2-12/S-3,1-1	-1.9
1989	Pit-N	14	40	2	5	1	0	0	2	2	2	.125	.167	.150	-9	-6	0	0	0	.988	-1	/1-9,2-3	-0.7
	*SF-N	83	116	17	37	5	1	2	15	8	8	.319	.373	.431	133	5	0	1	-1	.971	-4	3-38/1-7,2-7	0.0
	Yr	97	156	19	42	6	1	2	17	10	10	.269	.321	.359	97	-1	0	1	-1	.971	-5	3-38,1-16,2-10	-0.7
1990	Hou-N	77	150	10	31	6	1	1	12	15	17	.207	.283	.280	57	-9	1	1	-0	.935	-2	3-24,1-11,2-11	-1.2
1991	Hou-N	53	70	7	16	4	0	0	14	14	8	.229	.357	.286	88	-0	0	0	0	1.000	0	1-13/3-4	-0.1
1992	Cal-A	41	91	6	24	1	0	0	10	8	5	.264	.323	.275	69	-4	0	1	-1	.986	-7	2-21/1-2,D-5	-1.1
Total	16	1602	4874	558	1354	237	44	29	446	546	356	.278	.353	.362	97	-7	62	47	-10	.965	-5	*3-1046,2-402/1SD	-2.2

YEAR	TM/L	G	AB	R	H	2B	3B	HR	RBI	BB	SO	AVG	OBP	SLG	PRO+	BR/A	SB	CS	SBR	FA	FR	G/POS	TPR
■ MIKE O'BERRY	O'Berry, Preston Michael b: 4/20/54, Birmingham, Ala. BR/TR, 6'2", 195 lbs. Deb: 4/8/79																						
1979	Bos-A	43	59	8	10	1	0	1	4	5	16	.169	.246	.237	29	-6	0	0	0	.957	0	C-43	-0.5
1980	Chi-N	19	48	7	10	1	0	0	5	5	13	.208	.283	.229	41	-4	0	0	0	.982	4	C-19	0.1
1981	Cin-N	55	111	6	20	3	1	0	5	14	19	.180	.272	.252	49	-7	0	0	0	.983	3	C-55	-0.3
1982	Cin-N	21	45	5	10	2	0	0	3	10	13	.222	.364	.267	77	-1	0	0	0	.990	-1	C-21	-0.1
1983	Cal-A	26	60	7	10	1	0	1	5	3	11	.167	.206	.233	21	-7	0	0	0	1.000	-1	C-26	-0.6
1984	NY-A	13	32	3	8	2	0	0	5	2	2	.250	.294	.313	71	-1	0	0	0	1.000	1	C-12/3-1	0.0
1985	Mon-N	20	21	2	4	0	0	0	0	4	3	.190	.320	.190	49	-1	1	0	0	1.000	3	C-20	0.3
Total	7	197	376	38	72	10	1	3	27	43	77	.191	.276	.247	46	-27	1	0	0	.984	10	C-196/3-1	-1.1
■ JIM OBRADOVICH	Obradovich, James Thomas b: 9/13/49, Fort Campbell, Ky. BL/TL, 6'2", 200 lbs. Deb: 9/12/78																						
1978	Hou-N	10	17	3	3	0	1	0	2	1	3	.176	.222	.294	47	-1	0	0	0	1.000	-0	/1-3	-0.2
■ CHARLIE O'BRIEN	O'Brien, Charles Hugh b: 5/1/60, Tulsa, Okla. BR/TR, 6'2", 190 lbs. Deb: 6/2/85																						
1985	Oak-A	16	11	3	3	1	0	0	1	3	3	.273	.429	.364	129	1	0	0	0	.958	-0	C-16	0.1
1987	Mil-A	10	35	2	7	3	1	0	0	4	4	.200	.282	.343	63	-2	0	1	-1	1.000	6	C-10	0.4
1988	Mil-A	40	118	12	26	6	0	2	9	5	16	.220	.252	.322	59	-7	0	1	-1	.991	12	C-40	0.8
1989	Mil-A	62	188	22	44	10	0	6	35	21	11	.234	.339	.383	104	2	0	0	0	.986	7	C-62	1.1
1990	Mil-A	46	145	11	27	7	2	0	11	11	26	.186	.253	.262	45	-11	0	0	0	.992	5	C-46	-0.3
	NY-N	28	68	6	11	3	0	0	9	10	8	.162	.278	.206	36	-6	0	0	0	.986	9	C-28	0.5
1991	NY-N	69	168	16	31	6	0	2	14	17	25	.185	.275	.256	51	-11	0	2	-1	.991	19	C-67	1.0
1992	NY-N	68	156	15	33	12	0	2	13	16	18	.212	.289	.327	75	-5	0	1	-1	.979	5	C-64	0.2
1993	NY-N	67	188	15	48	11	0	4	23	14	14	.255	.314	.378	85	-4	1	1	-0	.986	11	C-65	1.0
1994	Atl-N	51	152	24	37	11	0	8	28	15	24	.243	.324	.474	102	0	0	0	0	.991	3	C-48	0.5
1995	*Atl-N	67	198	18	45	7	0	9	23	29	40	.227	.343	.399	92	-2	0	1	-1	.992	4	C-64	0.5
1996	Tor-A	109	324	33	77	17	0	13	44	29	68	.238	.332	.410	87	-7	0	1	-1	.995	3	*C-105	0.1
1997	Tor-A	69	225	22	49	15	1	4	27	22	45	.218	.318	.347	73	-9	0	2	-1	.995	19	C-69	1.3
1998	Chi-A	57	164	12	43	9	0	4	18	9	31	.262	.309	.390	82	-5	0	0	0	.988	1	C-57	0.0
	Ana-A	5	11	1	2	0	0	0	0	1	2	.182	.250	.182	15	-1	0	0	0	1.000	0	/C-5	-0.1
	Yr	62	175	13	45	9	0	4	18	10	33	.257	.305	.377	78	-6	0	0	0	.989	1	C-62	-0.1
Total	13	764	2151	212	483	118	4	54	255	206	335	.225	.309	.358	78	-66	1	10	-6	.990	103	C-746	7.1
■ EDDIE O'BRIEN	O'Brien, Edward Joseph b: 12/11/30, S.Amboy, N.J. BR/TR, 5'9", 165 lbs. Deb: 4/25/53 FC																						
1953	Pit-N	89	261	21	62	5	3	0	14	17	30	.238	.289	.280	50	-19	6	1	1	.935	-14	S-81	-2.6
1955	Pit-N	75	236	26	55	3	1	0	8	18	13	.233	.290	.254	47	-18	4	5	-2	.993	1	O-56/3-7,S-4	-2.1
1956	Pit-N	63	53	17	14	2	0	0	3	2	2	.264	.291	.302	61	-3	1	1	-0	.978	9	S-23/O-6,3-4,2-2,P	0.7
1957	Pit-N	3	4	0	0	0	0	0	0	0	0	.000	.000	.000	-99	-1	0	0	0	1.000	0	/P-3	0.0
1958	Pit-N	1	0	0	0	0	0	0	0	0	0	—	—	—	—	0	0	0	0	.000	-0	/P-1	0.0
Total	5	231	554	64	131	10	4	0	25	37	45	.236	.288	.269	48	-41	11	7	-1	.942	-4	S-108/O-62,3-11,P2	-4.0
■ DINK O'BRIEN	O'Brien, Frank Aloysius b: 9/13/1894, San Francisco, Cal. d: 11/4/71, Monterey Park, Cal. BR/TR, 5'8", 160 lbs. Deb: 4/26/23																						
1923	Phi-N	15	21	3	7	2	0	0	0	2	1	.333	.391	.429	104	0	0	0	0	.909	0	/C-9	0.1
■ GEORGE O'BRIEN	O'Brien, George Joseph b: 11/4/1889, Cleveland, Ohio d: 3/24/66, Columbus, Ohio BR/TR, 6', 185 lbs. Deb: 8/16/15																						
1915	StL-A	3	9	1	2	0	0	0	0	1	2	.222	.300	.222	59	-0	0			.933	-1	/C-3	-0.1
■ JERRY O'BRIEN	O'Brien, Jeremiah b: 2/2/1864, New York d: 7/4/11, Binghamton, N.Y. Deb: 7/30/1887																						
1887	Was-N	1	4	0	0	0	0	0	0	0	2	.000	.000	.000	-99	-1	0			.714	-0	/2-1	-0.1
■ JOHN O'BRIEN	O'Brien, John E. b: 10/22/1851, Columbus, Ohio d: 12/31/14, Fall River, Mass. TR , 5'11.5", 187 lbs. Deb: 4/19/1884																						
1884	Bal-U	18	77	7	19	1	1	0		2		.247	.266	.286	61	-6				.865	0	O-18	-0.5
■ JOHN O'BRIEN	O'Brien, John J. "Chewing Gum" b: 7/14/1870, St.John, N.B., Can d: 5/13/13, Lewiston, Maine BL/TR, 175 lbs. Deb: 4/22/1891																						
1891	Bro-N	43	167	22	41	4	2	0	26	12	17	.246	.308	.293	76	-5	4			.854	-22	2-43	-2.3
1893	Chi-N	4	14	3	5	0	1	0	1	2	2	.357	.471	.500	160	1	0			.900	-2	/2-4	0.0
1895	Lou-N	128	539	82	138	10	4	1	50	45	20	.256	.325	.295	65	-26	15			.938	3	*2-125/1-3	-1.4
1896	Lou-N	49	186	24	63	9	1	2	24	13	7	.339	.385	.430	119	5	4			.919	-1	2-49	0.6
	Was-N	73	270	38	72	6	3	4	33	27	12	.267	.344	.356	85	-6	4			.952	3	2-73	0.1
	Yr	122	456	62	135	15	4	6	57	40	19	.296	.361	.386	98	-1	8			.938	2	*2-122	0.7
1897	Was-N	86	320	37	78	12	2	3	45	19		.244	.309	.322	67	-16	6			.942	4	2-86	-0.6
1899	Bal-N	39	135	14	26	4	0	1	17	15		.193	.283	.244	43	-11	4			.966	7	2-39	-0.1
	Pit-N	79	279	26	63	2	4	1	33	21		.226	.285	.272	53	-18	8			.946	3	2-79	-1.0
	Yr	118	414	40	89	6	4	2	50	36		.215	.284	.263	50	-28	12			.953	10	*2-118	-1.1
Total	6	501	1910	246	486	47	17	12	229	154	58	.254	.322	.316	72	-75	45			.936	-6	2-498/1-3	-4.7
■ JACK O'BRIEN	O'Brien, John Joseph b: 2/5/1873, Watervliet, N.Y. d: 6/10/33, Watervliet, N.Y. BL/TR, 6'1", 165 lbs. Deb: 4/14/1899																						
1899	Was-N	127	468	68	132	11	5	6	51	31		.282	.331	.365	92	-6	17			.926	4	*O-121/3-4	-1.0
1901	Was-A	11	45	5	8	0	0	0	5	3		.178	.245	.178	19	-5	2			.929	-0	O-11	-0.5
	Cle-A	92	375	54	106	14	5	0	39	22		.283	.329	.347	91	-4	13			.941	-3	O-92/3-1	-1.3
	Yr	103	420	59	114	14	5	0	44	25		.271	.320	.329	83	-9	15			.939	-3	*O-103/3-1	-1.8
1903	*Bos-A	96	338	44	71	14	4	3	38	21		.210	.262	.302	65	-14	10			.958	-6	O-71,3-11/2-4,S-1	-2.6
Total	3	326	1226	171	317	39	14	9	133	77		.259	.308	.335	82	-29	42			.937	-5	O-295/3-16,2-4,S-1	-5.4
■ JACK O'BRIEN	O'Brien, John K. (b: John K. Bryne) b: 6/12/1860, Philadelphia, Pa. d: 11/20/10, Philadelphia, Pa. BR/TR, 5'10", 184 lbs. Deb: 5/2/1882																						
1882	Phi-a	62	241	44	73	13	3	3	37	13		.303	.339	.419	138	8				**.925**	11	C-45,O-18/3-1,1-1	1.9
1883	Phi-a	94	390	74	113	14	10	0	70	25		.290	.333	.377	119	7				.876	-1	C-58,O-25,3-19,/S-1	0.7
1884	Phi-a	36	138	25	39	6	1	1		9		.283	.340	.362	121	3				.930	-0	C-30/O-5,1-1	0.4
1885	Phi-a	62	225	35	60	9	1	2	30	20		.267	.340	.342	109	2				.903	-8	C-43/S-9,1-7,O-3,3	-0.3
1886	Phi-a	105	423	65	107	25	7	0	56	38		.253	.325	.345	109	4	23			.918	-15	C-36,3-27,1S/20	-0.7
1887	Bro-a	30	123	18	28	4	1	1	17	6		.228	.264	.301	56	-8	8			.839	-8	C-25/O-4,2-1	-1.0
1888	Bal-a	57	196	25	44	11	5	0	18	17		.224	.300	.332	105	1	14			.925	-15	C-37,O-13/1-7	-1.0
1890	Phi-a	109	433	80	113	24	14	4	80	52		.261	.356	.409	128	15	31			.976	4	*1-109/O-1,C-1	1.2
Total	8	555	2169	366	577	106	42	11	308	180		.266	.331	.369	115	34	76			.903	-31	C-275,1-149/O3S2	1.2
■ JOHNNY O'BRIEN	O'Brien, John Thomas b: 12/11/30, S.Amboy, N.J. BR/TR, 5'9", 170 lbs. Deb: 4/19/53 F																						
1953	Pit-N	89	279	28	69	13	2	2	22	21	36	.247	.309	.330	67	-13	1	1	-0	.982	-5	2-77/S-1	-1.4
1955	Pit-N	84	278	22	83	15	2	1	25	20	19	.299	.348	.378	94	-2	1	1	-0	.969	5	2-78	0.8
1956	Pit-N	73	104	13	18	1	0	0	3	5	7	.173	.211	.183	7	-13	0	0	0	.959	5	2-53/P-8,S-1	-0.5
1957	Pit-N	34	35	7	11	2	1	0	1	1	4	.314	.368	.429	117	1	0	0	0	.857	-2	P-16/S-8,2-2	-0.1
1958	Pit-N	3	1	1	0	0	0	0	0	0	1	.000	.000	.000	-99	-0	0	0	0	.000	0	H	0.0
	StL-N	12	2	3	0	0	0	0	0	1	0	.000	.333	.000	-2	-0	0	0	0	1.000	0	/S-5,P-1,2-1	0.0
	Yr	15	3	4	0	0	0	0	0	1	1	.000	.250	.000	-26	-1	0	0	0	1.000	0	/S-5,P-1,2-1	0.0
1959	Mil-N	44	116	16	23	4	0	1	8	11	15	.198	.273	.259	47	-9	0	0	0	.987	-3	2-37	-0.9
Total	6	339	815	90	204	35	5	4	59	59	82	.250	.307	.320	68	-38	2	2	-1	.974	0	2-248/P-25,S-15	-2.1
■ PETE O'BRIEN	O'Brien, Peter J. b: 6/17/1877, Binghamton, N.Y. d: 1/31/17, Jersey City, N.J. BL/TR, 5'7", 170 lbs. Deb: 9/21/01																						
1901	Cin-N	16	54	1	11	1	0	1	3	2		.204	.232	.278	51	-4	0			.889	-2	2-15	-0.5
1906	StL-A	151	524	44	122	9	4	2	57	42		.233	.293	.277	82	-10	25			.933	-41	*2-120,3-20,S-11	-5.5
1907	Cle-A	43	145	9	33	5	2	0	6	7		.228	.263	.290	76	-4	1			.949	-11	2-15,3-12,S-12	-1.7
	Was-A	39	134	6	25	3	1	0	12	12		.187	.259	.224	59	-6	4			.912	4	3-26,S-13/2-1	-0.1
	Yr	82	279	15	58	8	3	0	18	19		.208	.261	.258	68	-10	5			.911	-7	3-38,S-25,2-16	-1.8
Total	3	249	857	60	191	18	7	3	78	63		.223	.279	.271	76	-24	30			.930	-50	2-151/3-58,S-36	-7.8

YEAR	TM/L	G	AB	R	H	2B	3B	HR	RBI	BB	SO	AVG	OBP	SLG	PRO+	BR/A	SB	CS	SBR	FA	FR	G/POS	TPR
■ **PETE O'BRIEN**	O'Brien, Peter James b: 6/16/1867, Chicago, Ill. d: 6/30/37, York Township, Du Page County, Ill. BR/TR, 5'9.5", 165 lbs. Deb: 4/29/1890																						
1890	Chi-N	27	106	15	30	7	0	3	16	5	10	.283	.315	.434	113	1	4			.929	-2	2-27	0.1
■ **PETE O'BRIEN**	O'Brien, Peter Michael b: 2/9/58, Santa Monica, Cal. BL/TL, 6'1", 198 lbs. Deb: 9/3/82																						
1982	Tex-A	20	67	13	16	4	1	4	13	6	8	.239	.301	.507	124	2	1	0	0	1.000	-0	O-11/1-3,D-4	0.1
1983	Tex-A	154	524	53	124	24	5	8	53	58	62	.237	.314	.347	83	-11	5	4	-1	.993	13	*1-133,O-27/D-1	-0.7
1984	Tex-A	142	520	57	149	26	2	18	80	53	50	.287	.353	.448	116	11	3	5	-2	.992	1	*1-141/O-1	0.1
1985	Tex-A	159	573	69	153	34	3	22	92	69	53	.267	.347	.452	115	12	5	10	-5	.995	-6	*1-159	-0.8
1986	Tex-A	156	551	86	160	23	3	23	90	87	66	.290	.387	.468	128	24	4	4	-1	.992	2	*1-155	1.3
1987	Tex-A	159	569	84	163	26	1	23	88	59	61	.286	.354	.457	113	10	0	4	-2	.992	16	*1-158/O-2,D-1	1.2
1988	Tex-A	156	547	57	149	24	1	16	71	72	73	.272	.357	.408	111	9	1	4	-2	.995	13	*1-155/D-1	0.7
1989	Cle-A	155	554	75	144	24	1	12	55	83	48	.260	.358	.372	104	6	3	1	0	.994	3	*1-154/D-1	-0.4
1990	Sea-A	108	366	32	82	18	0	5	27	44	33	.224	.311	.314	74	-12	0	0	0	.995	4	1-97/O-6,D-6	-1.5
1991	Sea-A	152	560	58	139	29	3	17	88	44	61	.248	.304	.402	93	-6	0	1	-1	**.997**	1	*1-132,D-18,O-13	-1.5
1992	Sea-A	134	396	40	88	15	1	14	52	40	27	.222	.294	.371	85	-9	2	1	0	.996	2	1-81,D-36	-1.4
1993	Sea-A	72	210	30	54	7	0	7	27	26	21	.257	.339	.390	94	-2	0	0	0	.988	0	D-52/1-9,O-1	-0.4
Total	12	1567	5437	654	1421	254	21	169	736	641	563	.261	.340	.409	104	34	24	34	-13	.994	49	*1-1377,D-120/O-61	-3.3
■ **RAY O'BRIEN**	O'Brien, Raymond Joseph b: 10/31/1892, St.Louis, Mo. d: 3/31/42, St.Louis, Mo. BL/TL, 5'9", 175 lbs. Deb: 6/27/16																						
1916	Pit-N	16	57	5	12	3	2	0	3	1	14	.211	.224	.333	69	-2	0			.864	-1	O-14	-0.4
■ **SYD O'BRIEN**	O'Brien, Sydney Lloyd b: 12/18/44, Compton, Cal. BR/TR, 6'1", 185 lbs. Deb: 4/15/69																						
1969	Bos-A	100	263	47	64	10	5	9	29	15	37	.243	.287	.422	91	-4	2	3	-1	.939	-1	3-53,S-15,2-12	-0.5
1970	Chi-A	121	441	48	109	13	2	8	44	22	62	.247	.286	.340	69	-19	3	3	-1	.938	-6	3-68,2-43/S-5	-2.4
1971	Cal-A	90	251	25	50	8	1	5	21	15	33	.199	.247	.299	58	-15	0	2	-1	.961	-1	S-52/2-7,3-6,1-1,O	-1.2
1972	Cal-A	36	39	10	7	2	0	1	1	6	10	.179	.289	.308	82	-1	0	0	0	.889	1	/3-8,S-4,2-3,1-1	0.0
	Mil-A	31	58	5	12	2	0	1	5	2	13	.207	.233	.293	57	-3	0	1	-1	.852	-1	/3-9,2-7	-0.5
	Yr	67	97	15	19	4	0	2	6	8	23	.196	.257	.299	68	-4	0	1	-1	.861	0	3-17,2-10/S-4,1-1	-0.5
Total	4	378	1052	135	242	35	8	24	100	60	155	.230	.274	.347	72	-42	5	9	-4	.934	-8	3-144/S-76,2-72,1O	-4.6
■ **TOMMY O'BRIEN**	O'Brien, Thomas Edward "Obie" b: 12/19/18, Anniston, Ala. d: 11/5/78, Anniston, Ala. BR/TR, 5'11", 195 lbs. Deb: 4/24/43																						
1943	Pit-N	89	232	35	72	12	7	2	26	15	24	.310	.352	.448	126	7	0			.964	-6	O-48/3-9	-0.1
1944	Pit-N	85	156	27	39	6	2	3	20	21	12	.250	.343	.372	97	-0	1			.965	-9	O-48/3-1	-1.2
1945	Pit-N	58	161	23	54	6	5	0	18	9	13	.335	.374	.435	120	4	0			.961	-6	O-45	-0.4
1949	Bos-A	49	125	24	28	5	0	3	10	21	12	.224	.336	.336	73	-5	1	0	0	.984	-2	O-32	-0.8
1950	Bos-A	9	31	0	4	1	0	0	3	3	5	.129	.206	.161	-5	-5	0	0	0	1.000	-1	/O-9	-0.6
	Was-A	3	9	1	1	0	0	0	1	1	0	.111	.200	.111	-20	-2	0	0	0	1.000	1	/O-3	-0.1
	Yr	12	40	1	5	1	0	0	4	4	5	.125	.205	.150	-8	-7	0	0	0	1.000	-0	O-12	-0.7
Total	5	293	714	110	198	30	14	8	78	70	66	.277	.344	.392	100	-1	2	0		.970	-24	O-185/3-10	-3.2
■ **TOM O'BRIEN**	O'Brien, Thomas H. b: 6/22/1860, Salem, Mass. d: 4/21/21, Worcester, Mass. BR/TR, 6'1", 185 lbs. Deb: 6/14/1882																						
1882	Wor-N	22	89	9	18	1	1	0	7	1	10	.202	.211	.236	42	-6				.789	-2	O-20/2-2,3-1	-0.7
1883	Bal-a	33	138	16	37	6	4	0		5		.268	.294	.370	109	1				.825	-4	2-29/O-4	-0.2
1884	Bos-U	103	449	80	118	31	8	4		12		.263	.282	.394	105	-11				.853	1	*2-99/O-3,1-2,C-1	-0.7
1885	Bal-a	8	33	4	7	3	0	0	5	2		.212	.257	.303	78	-1				.932	1	/1-6,2-2	0.0
1887	NY-a	31	129	13	25	3	2	0	18	2		.194	.212	.248	29	-12	10			.963	-2	1-20/O-8,3-2,2-2,P	-1.3
1890	Roc-a	73	273	36	52	6	5	0	31	30		.190	.273	.249	58	-14	6			.971	-4	1-68/2-8	-1.9
Total	6	270	1111	158	257	50	20	4	61	52	10	.231	.267	.323	79	-43	16			.846	-10	2-142/1-96,O3PC	-4.8
■ **TOM O'BRIEN**	O'Brien, Thomas J. b: 2/20/1873, Verona, Pa. d: 2/4/01, Phoenix, Ariz. Deb: 5/10/1897																						
1897	*Bal-N	50	147	25	37	6	0	0	32	20		.252	.349	.293	70	-6	7			.968	0	1-25,O-24	-0.6
1898	Bal-N	18	60	9	13	0	0	0	14	10		.217	.338	.217	59	-3	0			.833	0	O-16	-0.3
	Pit-N	107	413	53	107	10	8	1	45	25		.259	.318	.329	87	-7	13			.924	-3	O-69,1-21/3-8,2S	-1.4
	Yr	125	473	62	120	10	8	1	59	35		.254	.321	.315	84	-10	13			.911	-3	O-85,1-21/3-8,2S	-1.7
1899	NY-N	150	573	100	170	21	10	6	77	44		.297	.351	.400	109	7	23			.933	-2	*O-127,3-21/S-2,21	-0.4
1900	*Pit-N	102	376	61	109	22	6	3	61	21		.290	.349	.404	107	3	12			.961	-11	1-65,O-25/2-4,S-2	-0.9
Total	4	427	1569	248	436	59	24	10	229	120		.278	.341	.365	97	-6	55			.928	-15	O-261,1-112/32S	-3.6
■ **DARBY O'BRIEN**	O'Brien, William D. b: 9/1/1863, Peoria, Ill. d: 6/15/1893, Peoria, Ill. BR/TR, 6'1", 186 lbs. Deb: 4/16/1887																						
1887	NY-a	127	522	97	157	30	13	5	73	40		.301	.355	.437	126	18	49			.913	6	*O-121,1-10/S-2,3P	1.7
1888	Bro-a	136	532	105	149	27	6	2	65	30		.280	.327	.365	122	12	55			.932	2	*O-136	0.9
1889	*Bro-a	136	567	146	170	30	11	5	80	61	76	.300	.384	.418	128	22	91			.906	-7	*O-136	1.0
1890	*Bro-N	85	350	78	110	28	6	2	63	32	43	.314	.378	.446	139	17	38			.960	4	O-85	1.5
1891	Bro-N	103	395	79	100	18	6	5	57	39	53	.253	.331	.367	104	2	31			.951	2	*O-103	0.0
1892	Bro-N	122	490	72	119	14	5	1	56	29	52	.243	.289	.298	81	-12	57			.956	4	*O-122	-1.3
Total	6	709	2856	577	805	147	47	20	394	231	224	.282	.344	.387	117	58	321			.934	11	O-703/1-10,S-2,P3	3.8
■ **BILLY O'BRIEN**	O'Brien, William Smith b: 3/14/1860, Albany, N.Y. d: 5/26/11, Kansas City, Mo. BR, 6', 185 lbs. Deb: 9/27/1884																						
1884	StP-U	8	30	1	7	3	0	0		0		.233	.233	.333	129	-2				.840	1	/3-8,P-2	0.0
	KC-U	4	17	2	4	0	0	0		0		.235	.235	.235	49	-2				.714	1	/3-3,1-1	-0.1
	Yr	12	47	3	11	3	0	0		0		.234	.234	.298	92	-3				.795	2	3-11/P-2,1-1	-0.1
1887	Was-N	113	453	71	126	16	12	**19**	73	21	17	.278	.317	.492	128	15	11			.974	-3	*1-104/O-4,3-4,2-2	0.1
1888	Was-N	133	528	42	119	15	2	9	66	9	70	.225	.238	.313	79	-13	10			.975	-4	*1-132/3-1	-3.0
1889	Was-N	2	8	1	0	0	0	0	0	1	1	.000	.111	.000	-72	-2	0			1.000	-0	/1-2	-0.2
1890	Bro-a	96	388	47	108	25	8	4	67	28		.278	.332	.415	124	10	5			.973	-2	*1-96	0.2
Total	5	356	1424	164	364	59	22	32	206	59	88	.256	.289	.395	108	7	26			.974	-8	1-335/3-16,O-4,2P	-3.0
■ **ALEX OCHOA**	Ochoa, Alex b: 3/29/72, Miami Lakes, Fla. BR/TR, 6', 185 lbs. Deb: 9/18/95																						
1995	NY-N	11	37	7	11	1	0	0	0	2	10	.297	.333	.324	77	-1	1	0	0	1.000	1	O-10	0.0
1996	NY-N	82	282	37	83	19	3	4	33	17	30	.294	.339	.426	105	1	4	3	-1	.966	3	O-76	0.2
1997	NY-N	113	238	31	58	14	1	3	22	18	32	.244	.302	.349	72	-10	3	4	-2	.982	-9	O-88/D-1	-2.1
1998	Min-A	94	249	35	64	14	2	2	25	10	35	.257	.288	.353	66	-13	6	3	0	.969	-4	O-74/D-3	-1.7
Total	4	300	806	110	216	48	6	9	80	47	107	.268	.312	.376	82	-22	14	10	-2	.973	-8	O-248/D-4	-3.6
■ **WHITEY OCK**	Ock, Harold David b: 3/17/12, Brooklyn, N.Y. d: 3/18/75, Mt.Kisco, N.Y. BR/TR, 5'11", 180 lbs. Deb: 9/29/35																						
1935	Bro-N	1	3	0	0	0	0	0	0	1	2	.000	.250	.000	-27	-1	0			1.000	-0	/C-1	-0.1
■ **DANNY O'CONNELL**	O'Connell, Daniel Francis b: 1/21/27, Paterson, N.J. d: 10/2/69, Clifton, N.J. BR/TR, 6', 180 lbs. Deb: 7/14/50 C																						
1950	Pit-N	79	315	39	92	16	1	8	32	24	33	.292	.342	.425	97	-2	7			.977	17	S-65,3-12	2.0
1953	Pit-N	149	588	88	173	26	8	7	55	57	42	.294	.361	.401	99	0	3	4	-2	.958	8	*3-104,2-47	0.6
1954	Mil-N	146	541	61	151	28	4	2	37	38	46	.279	.329	.357	84	-13	2	2	-1	.979	9	*2-103,3-35/1-8,S-1	0.1
1955	Mil-N	124	453	47	102	15	4	6	40	28	43	.225	.278	.316	60	-27	2	2	-1	.981	16	*2-114/3-7,S-1	-0.3
1956	Mil-N	139	498	71	119	17	9	2	42	76	42	.239	.344	.321	86	-8	3	3	-1	.985	-6	*2-138/3-4,S-1	-0.4
1957	Mil-N	48	183	29	43	9	1	1	8	19	20	.235	.314	.311	74	-7	1	0	0	.982	7	2-48	0.4
	NY-N	95	364	57	97	18	3	7	28	33	30	.266	.331	.390	93	-3	8	3	1	.980	6	2-68,3-30	0.9
	Yr	143	547	86	140	27	4	8	36	52	50	.256	.325	.364	87	-10	9	3	1	.981	12	*2-116,3-30	1.3
1958	SF-N	107	306	44	71	12	2	3	23	51	35	.232	.342	.314	77	-9	2	1	0	.986	3	*2-104/3-3	0.1
1959	SF-N	34	58	6	11	3	0	0	0	5	15	.190	.254	.241	34	-5	0	1	-1	.927	7	3-26/2-8	0.1
1961	Was-A	138	493	61	128	30	1	1	37	77	62	.260	.363	.331	88	-5	15	5	2	.939	1	3-73,2-61	0.5
1962	Was-A	84	236	24	62	7	2	2	18	23	28	.263	.328	.335	80	-6	5	1	1	.961	-1	3-41,2-22	-0.5
Total	10	1143	4035	527	1049	181	35	39	320	431	396	.260	.335	.351	84	-86	48	22		.980	67	2-713,3-335/S-68,1	3.5

YEAR	TM/L	G	AB	R	H	2B	3B	HR	RBI	BB	SO	AVG	OBP	SLG	PRO+	BR/A	SB	CS	SBR	FA	FR	G/POS	TPR
■ **JIMMY O'CONNELL**	O'Connell, James Joseph b: 2/11/01, Sacramento, Cal. d: 11/11/76, Bakersfield, Cal. BL/TR, 5'10.5", 175 lbs. Deb: 4/17/23																						
1923	*NY-N	87	252	42	63	9	2	6	39	34	32	.250	.351	.373	92	-2	7	3	0	.980	-8	O-64/1-8	-1.4
1924	NY-N	52	104	24	33	4	2	2	18	11	16	.317	.388	.452	128	4	2	1	0	.952	-7	O-29/2-1	-0.4
Total	2	139	356	66	96	13	4	8	57	45	48	.270	.361	.396	102	2	9	4	0	.974	-15	/O-93,1-8,2-1	-1.8
■ **JOHN O'CONNELL**	O'Connell, John Charles b: 6/13/04, Verona, Pa. d: 10/17/92, Canton, Ohio BR/TR, 6', 170 lbs. Deb: 8/16/28																						
1928	Pit-N	1	1	0	0	0	0	0	0	0	0	.000	.000	.000	-96	-0	0			1.000	1	/C-1	0.0
1929	Pit-N	2	7	1	1	1	0	0	0	1	1	.143	.250	.286	32	-1	0			1.000	-0	/C-2	-0.1
Total	2	3	8	1	1	1	0	0	0	1	1	.125	.222	.250	17	-1	0			1.000	0	/C-3	-0.1
■ **JOHN O'CONNELL**	O'Connell, John Joseph d: 5/14/08, Derry, N.H. 5'9.5", 170 lbs. Deb: 8/22/1891																						
1891	Bal-a	8	29	2	5	1	0	0	7	3	6	.172	.250	.207	31	-3	2			.938	-3	/S-3,2-3,O-2	-0.5
1902	Det-A	8	22	1	4	0	0	0	0	3		.182	.280	.182	29	-2	0			.919	1	/2-6,1-2	-0.1
Total	2	16	51	3	9	1	0	0	7	6	6	.176	.263	.196	30	-5	2			.885	-2	/2-9,S-3,1-2,O-2	-0.6
■ **PAT O'CONNELL**	O'Connell, Patrick b: 1862, Brooklyn, N.Y. d: 5/5/1892, Brooklyn, N.Y. Deb: 4/17/1890																						
1890	Bro-a	11	40	7	9	2	1	0	3	7		.225	.340	.325	100	0	3			.830	-1	3-10/1-1	0.0
■ **PAT O'CONNELL**	O'Connell, Patrick H. b: 6/10/1861, Bangor, Me. d: 1/24/43, Lewiston, Maine BR/TR, 5'10", 175 lbs. Deb: 7/22/1886																						
1886	Bal-a	42	166	20	30	3	2	0	8	11		.181	.236	.223	45	-10	10			.782	-4	O-41/1-1,P-1	-1.4
■ **DAN O'CONNOR**	O'Connor, Daniel Cornelius b: 8/1868, Guelph, Ont., Canada d: 3/3/42, Guelph, Ont., Canada BL/TR, 6'2", 185 lbs. Deb: 6/3/1890																						
1890	Lou-a	6	26	3	12	1	1	0	5	1		.462	.481	.577	217	4	5			1.000	-1	/1-6	0.2
■ **JOHNNY O'CONNOR**	O'Connor, John Charles "Bucky" b: 12/1/1891, Cahirciveen, Ire. d: 5/30/82, Bonner Springs, Kan. BR/TR, 5'9", Deb: 9/16/16																						
1916	Chi-N	1	0	0	0	0	0	0	0	0	0	—	—	—	—	0	0			.000	0	/C-1	0.0
■ **JACK O'CONNOR**	O'Connor, John Joseph "Rowdy Jack" or "Peach Pie" b: 6/2/1869, St.Louis, Mo. d: 11/14/37, St.Louis, Mo. BR/TR, 5'10", 170 lbs. Deb: 4/20/1887 M																						
1887	Cin-a	12	40	4	4	0	0	0	1	2		.100	.143	.100	-31	-7	3			.947	3	/O-7,C-5	-0.3
1888	Cin-a	36	137	14	28	3	1	1	17	6		.204	.243	.263	59	-7	12			.795	-0	O-34/C-2	-0.7
1889	Col-a	107	398	69	107	17	7	4	60	33	37	.269	.331	.377	107	3	26			**.955**	-1	C-84,O-19/2-4,1-3	0.8
1890	Col-a	121	457	89	148	14	10	2	66	38		.324	.377	.411	142	24	29			**.962**	10	*C-106/O-9,S-8,23	3.7
1891	Col-a	56	229	28	61	12	3	0	37	11	14	.266	.300	.345	90	-4	10			.878	3	O-40,C-21	-0.1
1892	*Cle-N	140	572	71	142	22	5	1	58	25	48	.248	.282	.309	76	-19	17			.935	9	*O-106,C-34	-1.1
1893	Cle-N	96	384	72	110	23	1	4	75	29	12	.286	.341	.383	87	-9	29			.949	-2	C-56,O-44	-0.7
1894	Cle-N	86	330	67	104	23	7	2	51	15	7	.315	.345	.445	86	-9	15			.942	7	C-45,O-33/1-7	-0.1
1895	Cle-N	89	340	51	99	14	10	0	58	30	22	.291	.354	.391	87	-8	11			.923	-6	C-47,1-41/3-1	-0.7
1896	*Cle-N	68	256	41	76	11	1	1	43	15	12	.297	.343	.359	81	-8	15			.966	-7	C-37,1-17,O-12	-0.9
1897	Cle-N	103	397	49	115	21	4	2	69	26		.290	.338	.378	84	-10	20			.941	-12	O-52,1-36,C-13	-2.1
1898	Cle-N	131	478	50	119	17	4	1	56	26		.249	.291	.308	72	-18	8			.983	3	1-69,C-48,O-15	-1.1
1899	StL-N	84	289	33	73	5	6	0	43	15		.253	.299	.311	66	-14	7			.943	2	C-57,1-26	-0.7
1900	StL-N	10	32	4	7	0	0	0	6	2		.219	.306	.219	46	-2	0			.957	-1	C-10	-0.2
	*Pit-N	43	147	15	35	4	1	0	19	3		.238	.263	.279	49	-10	5			.944	-9	C-40/1-2	-1.5
	Yr	53	179	19	42	4	1	0	25	5		.235	.271	.268	49	-13	5			.947	-10	C-50/1-2	-1.7
1901	Pit-N	61	202	16	39	7	3	0	22	10		.193	.238	.257	42	-15	2			.978	-1	C-59	-1.0
1902	Pit-N	49	170	13	50	1	2	1	28	3		.294	.306	.341	96	-1	2			.979	-3	C-42/1-6,O-1	0.0
1903	NY-A	64	212	13	43	4	1	0	12	8		.203	.235	.231	38	-16	4			.988	1	C-63/1-1	-0.9
1904	StL-A	14	47	4	10	1	0	0	2	2		.213	.245	.234	55	-2	0			.943	-4	C-14	-0.6
1906	StL-A	55	174	8	33	0	0	0	11	2		.190	.199	.190	23	-16	4			.990	10	C-51	-0.1
1907	StL-A	25	89	2	14	2	0	0	4	0		.157	.176	.180	13	-9	0			.991	-2	C-25	-1.0
1910	StL-A	1	0	0	0	0	0	0	0	0		—	—	—	—	0	0			1.000	-0	/C-1,M	0.0
Total	21	1451	5380	713	1417	201	66	19	738	301	152	.263	.307	.336	79	-157	219			.961	-2	C-860,O-372,1/S23	-9.3
■ **PADDY O'CONNOR**	O'Connor, Patrick Francis b: 8/4/1879, County Kerry, Ireland d: 8/17/50, Springfield, Mass. BR/TR, 5'8", 168 lbs. Deb: 4/17/08 C																						
1908	Pit-N	12	16	1	3	0	0	0	2	0		.188	.188	.188	20	-1	0			.889	-2	/C-4	-0.3
1909	*Pit-N	9	16	1	5	1	0	0	3	0		.313	.313	.375	104	-0	0			.700	-2	/C-3,3-1	-0.2
1910	Pit-N	6	4	0	1	0	0	0	0	1	1	.250	.400	.250	85	-0	0			1.000	-0	/C-1	0.0
1914	StL-N	10	9	0	0	0	0	0	0	2	2	.000	.250	.000	-24	-1	0			1.000	-0	/C-7	-0.2
1915	Pit-F	70	219	15	50	10	1	0	16	14	30	.228	.278	.283	58	-16	4			.987	4	C-66	-0.7
1918	NY-A	1	3	0	1	0	0	0	0	0	1	.333	.333	.333	99	-0	0			1.000	-0	/C-1	0.0
Total	6	108	267	17	60	11	1	0	21	17	34	.225	.276	.273	57	-18	4			.979	-0	/C-82,3-1	-1.4
■ **KEN O'DEA**	O'Dea, James Kenneth b: 3/16/13, Lima, N.Y. d: 12/17/85, Lima, N.Y. BL/TR, 6', 180 lbs. Deb: 4/21/35																						
1935	*Chi-N	76	202	30	52	13	2	6	38	26	18	.257	.345	.431	106	2	0			.964	-2	C-63	0.3
1936	Chi-N	80	189	36	58	10	3	2	38	38	18	.307	.423	.423	126	9	0			.979	-3	C-55	0.8
1937	Chi-N	83	219	31	66	7	5	4	32	24	26	.301	.370	.434	113	4	1			.985	-6	C-64	0.1
1938	*Chi-N	86	247	22	65	12	1	3	33	12	18	.263	.297	.356	77	-8	1			.970	4	C-71	-0.1
1939	NY-N	52	97	7	17	1	0	3	11	10	16	.175	.252	.278	42	-8	0			.947	-2	C-30	-0.9
1940	NY-N	48	96	9	23	4	1	0	12	16	15	.240	.348	.302	80	-2	0			.992	2	C-31	0.2
1941	NY-N	59	89	13	19	5	1	3	17	8	20	.213	.278	.393	86	-2	0			1.000	1	C-14	0.0
1942	*StL-N	58	192	22	45	7	1	5	32	17	23	.234	.297	.359	85	-4	0			.979	10	C-49	1.1
1943	*StL-N	71	203	15	57	11	2	3	25	19	25	.281	.345	.399	110	2	0			.989	6	C-56	1.2
1944	*StL-N	85	265	35	66	11	2	6	37	37	29	.249	.343	.374	100	0	1			.994	7	C-69	1.2
1945	StL-N†	100	307	36	78	18	2	4	43	50	31	.254	.359	.365	99	1	0			**.995**	3	C-91	0.9
1946	StL-N	22	57	2	7	2	0	1	3	8	8	.123	.231	.211	25	-6	0			.991	5	C-22	0.0
	Bos-N	12	32	4	7	0	0	0	2	8	4	.219	.375	.219	70	-1	0			1.000	-1	C-12	-0.1
	Yr	34	89	6	14	2	0	1	5	16	12	.157	.286	.213	41	-7	0			.994	4	C-34	-0.1
Total	12	832	2195	262	560	101	20	40	323	273	251	.255	.338	.374	95	-12	3			.983	26	C-627	4.7
■ **PAUL O'DEA**	O'Dea, Paul "Lefty" b: 7/3/20, Cleveland, Ohio d: 12/11/78, Cleveland, Ohio BL/TL, 6', 200 lbs. Deb: 4/19/44																						
1944	Cle-A	76	173	25	55	9	0	0	13	23	21	.318	.401	.370	126	7	2	2	-1	.949	-5	O-41/P-3,1-3	0.0
1945	Cle-A	87	221	21	52	2	2	1	21	20	26	.235	.299	.276	70	-8	3	0	1	.992	2	O-53/P-1	-0.9
Total	2	163	394	46	107	11	2	1	34	43	47	.272	.345	.317	95	-1	5	2	0	.975	-2	/O-94,P-4,1-3	-0.9
■ **HEINIE ODOM**	Odom, Herman Boyd b: 10/13/1900, Rusk, Tex. d: 8/31/70, Rusk, Tex. BB/TR, 6', 170 lbs. Deb: 4/22/25																						
1925	NY-A	1	1	0	1	0	0	0	0	0	0	1.000	1.000	1.000	416	0	0	0	0	1.000	0	/3-1	0.1
■ **BLUE MOON ODOM**	Odom, Johnny Lee b: 5/29/45, Macon, Ga. BR/TR, 6', 185 lbs. Deb: 9/5/64																						
1964	KC-A	5	5	1	0	0	0	0	0	1	4	.000	.167	.000	-47	-1	0	0	0	.800	0	/P-5	0.0
1965	KC-A	1	0	0	0	0	0	0	0	0	0	—	—	—	—	0	0	0	0	1.000	0	/P-1	0.0
1966	KC-A	17	31	1	3	0	0	0	2	3	16	.097	.176	.097	-20	-5	0	0	0	.970	2	P-14	0.0
1967	KC-A	33	28	4	8	1	0	0	0	1	14	.286	.310	.321	90	-0	0	1	-1	.897	0	P-29	0.0
1968	Oak-A★	42	78	14	17	2	0	1	2	6	29	.218	.282	.282	75	-2	0	0	0	.964	1	P-32	0.0
1969	Oak-A★	43	79	15	21	2	1	5	16	2	24	.266	.293	.506	125	2	0	0	0	.937	1	P-32	0.0
1970	Oak-A	37	54	8	13	2	0	3	7	3	18	.241	.281	.444	100	-0	1	0	0	.929	2	P-29	0.0
1971	Oak-A	37	50	8	8	0	1	1	1	2	24	.160	.192	.260	28	-5	0	0	0	.850	-1	P-25	0.0
1972	*Oak-A	59	66	16	8	1	0	2	2	1	29	.121	.134	.227	7	-8	4	2	0	.873	0	P-31	0.0
1973	*Oak-A	51	1	5	0	0	0	0	0	0	0	.000	.000	.000	-99	-0	1	2	-1	.875	-1	P-30	0.0
1974	*Oak-A	43	0	3	0	0	0	0	0	0	0	—	—	—	—	0	0	0	0	.821	1	P-34	0.0
1975	Oak-A	8	0	1	0	0	0	0	0	0	0	—	—	—	—	0	0	0	0	.750	0	/P-7	0.0
	Cle-A	3	0	0	0	0	0	0	0	0	0	—	—	—	—	0	0	0	0	1.000	-0	/P-3	0.0

YEAR	TM/L	G	AB	R	H	2B	3B	HR	RBI	BB	SO	AVG	OBP	SLG	PRO+	BR/A	SB	CS	SBR	FA	FR	G/POS	TPR
	Yr	11	0	1	0	0	0	0	0	0	0	—	—	—	—	0	0	0	0	.800	-0	P-10	0.0
	Atl-N	15	13	0	1	1	0	0	1	0	5	.077	.077	.154	-36	-2	0	0	0	.944	0	P-15	0.0
1976	Chi-A	8	0	0	0	0	0	0	0	0	0	—	—	—	—	0	0	0	0	.600	-1	/P-8	0.0
Total	13	402	405	76	79	9	2	12	31	19	163	.195	.235	.316	60	-22	6	5	-1	.904	5	P-295	0.0

■ HARRY O'DONNELL O'Donnell, Harry Herman "Butch" b: 4/2/1894, Philadelphia, Pa. d: 1/31/58, Philadelphia, Pa. BR/TR, 5'8", 175 lbs. Deb: 4/30/27

YEAR	TM/L	G	AB	R	H	2B	3B	HR	RBI	BB	SO	AVG	OBP	SLG	PRO+	BR/A	SB	CS	SBR	FA	FR	G/POS	TPR
1927	Phi-N	16	16	1	1	0	0	0	2	2	2	.063	.167	.063	-36	-3	0			1.000	1	C-12	-0.2

■ JOHN O'DONNELL O'Donnell, John b: Littlestown, Pa. Deb: 7/16/1884

YEAR	TM/L	G	AB	R	H	2B	3B	HR	RBI	BB	SO	AVG	OBP	SLG	PRO+	BR/A	SB	CS	SBR	FA	FR	G/POS	TPR
1884	Phi-U	1	4	0	1	0	0	0		0		.250	.250	.250	56	-0				.545	-2	/C-1	-0.2

■ LEFTY O'DOUL O'Doul, Francis Joseph b: 3/4/1897, San Francisco, Cal. d: 12/7/69, San Francisco, Cal. BL/TL, 6', 180 lbs. Deb: 4/29/19

YEAR	TM/L	G	AB	R	H	2B	3B	HR	RBI	BB	SO	AVG	OBP	SLG	PRO+	BR/A	SB	CS	SBR	FA	FR	G/POS	TPR
1919	NY-A	19	16	2	4	0	0	0	1	1	2	.250	.294	.250	53	-1	1			.500	-1	/P-3,O-1	-0.1
1920	NY-A	13	12	2	2	1	0	0	1	1	1	.167	.231	.250	26	-1	0	0	0	.000	-1	/P-2,O-1	-0.1
1922	NY-A	8	9	0	3	1	0	0	4	0	2	.333	.333	.444	99	-0	0	0	0	1.000	0	/P-6	0.0
1923	Bos-A	36	35	2	5	0	0	0	4	2	3	.143	.189	.143	-12	-6	0	0	0	.958	1	P-23/O-1	-0.1
1928	NY-N	114	354	67	113	19	4	8	46	30	8	.319	.372	.463	117	8	9			.962	-12	O-94	-0.9
1929	Phi-N	154	638	152	**254**	35	6	32	122	76	19	**.398**	**.465**	.622	157	58	2			.971	5	*O-154	4.7
1930	Phi-N	140	528	122	202	37	7	22	97	63	21	.383	.453	.604	142	38	3			.953	-5	*O-131	2.0
1931	Bro-N	134	512	85	172	32	11	7	75	48	16	.336	.396	.482	136	26	5			.954	-1	*O-132	1.6
1932	Bro-N	148	595	120	219	32	8	21	90	50	20	**.368**	.423	.555	164	54	11			.979	-5	*O-148	3.9
1933	Bro-N	43	159	14	40	5	1	5	21	15	6	.252	.320	.390	106	1	2			.947	-3	O-41	-0.4
	*NY-N★	78	229	31	70	9	1	9	35	29	17	.306	.388	.472	147	15	1			.974	-6	O-63	0.6
	Yr	121	388	45	110	14	2	14	56	44	23	.284	.361	.438	130	16	3			.962	-8	*O-104	0.2
1934	NY-N	83	177	27	56	4	3	9	46	18	7	.316	.383	.525	144	11	2			.968	-5	O-38	0.4
Total	11	970	3264	624	1140	175	41	113	542	333	122	.349	.413	.532	142	202	36	0		.964	-33	O-804/P-34	11.6

■ FRED ODWELL Odwell, Frederick William "Fritz" b: 9/25/1872, Downsville, N.Y. d: 8/19/48, Downsville, N.Y. BL/TR, 5'9.5", 160 lbs. Deb: 4/16/04

YEAR	TM/L	G	AB	R	H	2B	3B	HR	RBI	BB	SO	AVG	OBP	SLG	PRO+	BR/A	SB	CS	SBR	FA	FR	G/POS	TPR
1904	Cin-N	129	468	75	133	22	10	1	58	26		.284	.333	.380	110	4	30			.956	14	*O-126/2-1	1.2
1905	Cin-N	130	468	79	113	10	9	**9**	65	26		.241	.293	.359	85	-11	21			.967	4	*O-126	-1.4
1906	Cin-N	58	202	20	45	5	4	0	21	15		.223	.286	.287	76	-6	11			.963	3	O-57	-0.6
1907	Cin-N	94	274	24	74	5	7	0	24	22		.270	.336	.339	107	2	10			.975	5	O-84/2-1	0.5
Total	4	411	1412	198	365	42	30	10	168	89		.258	.313	.352	96	-10	72			.964	26	O-393/2-2	-0.3

■ CHUCK OERTEL Oertel, Charles Frank "Ducky" or "Snuffy" b: 3/12/31, Coffeyville, Kan. BL/TR, 5'8", 165 lbs. Deb: 9/1/58

YEAR	TM/L	G	AB	R	H	2B	3B	HR	RBI	BB	SO	AVG	OBP	SLG	PRO+	BR/A	SB	CS	SBR	FA	FR	G/POS	TPR
1958	Bal-A	14	12	4	2	0	0	1	1	1	1	.167	.231	.417	78	-0	0	0	0	1.000	-1	/O-2	-0.1

■ RON OESTER Oester, Ronald John b: 5/5/56, Cincinnati, Ohio BB/TR, 6'2", 190 lbs. Deb: 9/10/78 C

YEAR	TM/L	G	AB	R	H	2B	3B	HR	RBI	BB	SO	AVG	OBP	SLG	PRO+	BR/A	SB	CS	SBR	FA	FR	G/POS	TPR
1978	Cin-N	6	8	1	3	0	0	0	1	0	2	.375	.375	.375	110	0	0	0	0	1.000	1	/S-6	0.1
1979	Cin-N	6	3	0	0	0	0	0	0	0	1	.000	.000	.000	-99	-1	0	0	0	1.000	1	/S-2	0.0
1980	Cin-N	100	303	40	84	16	2	2	20	26	44	.277	.336	.363	95	-2	6	2	1	.980	-14	2-79,S-17/3-3	-1.0
1981	Cin-N	105	354	45	96	16	7	5	42	42	49	.271	.348	.398	110	5	2	5	-2	.980	5	*2-103/S-9	1.5
1982	Cin-N	151	549	63	143	19	4	9	47	35	82	.260	.305	.359	83	-13	5	6	-2	.972	4	*2-118,S-29,3-13	-0.4
1983	Cin-N	157	549	63	145	23	5	11	58	49	106	.264	.326	.384	93	-6	2	2	-1	.977	-25	*2-154	-2.5
1984	Cin-N	150	553	54	134	26	3	3	38	41	97	.242	.296	.316	69	-23	7	2	1	.980	-16	*2-147/S-1	-3.4
1985	Cin-N	152	526	59	155	26	3	1	34	51	65	.295	.357	.361	97	-1	5	0	2	.989	5	*2-149	1.1
1986	Cin-N	153	523	52	135	23	2	8	44	52	84	.258	.326	.356	84	-11	9	2	2	.978	18	*2-151	1.5
1987	Cin-N	69	237	28	60	9	6	2	23	22	51	.253	.317	.367	77	-8	2	3	-1	.974	6	2-69	0.0
1988	Cin-N	54	150	20	42	7	0	0	10	9	24	.280	.321	.327	83	-3	0	2	-1	.995	2	2-49/S-5	0.0
1989	Cin-N	109	305	23	75	15	0	1	14	32	47	.246	.318	.305	76	-9	1	0	0	.985	8	*2-102/S-2	0.2
1990	*Cin-N	64	154	10	46	10	1	0	13	10	29	.299	.341	.377	93	-1	1	2	-1	.982	-8	2-50/3-3	-1.0
Total	13	1276	4214	458	1118	190	33	42	344	369	681	.265	.325	.356	87	-71	40	26	-4	.980	-14	*2-1171/S-71,3-19	-3.9

■ BOB O'FARRELL O'Farrell, Robert Arthur b: 10/19/1896, Waukegan, Ill. d: 2/20/88, Waukegan, Ill. BR/TR, 5'9.5", 180 lbs. Deb: 9/5/15 M

YEAR	TM/L	G	AB	R	H	2B	3B	HR	RBI	BB	SO	AVG	OBP	SLG	PRO+	BR/A	SB	CS	SBR	FA	FR	G/POS	TPR
1915	Chi-N	2	3	0	1	0	0	0	0	0	0	.333	.333	.333	102	-0	0			.667	-1	/C-2	-0.1
1916	Chi-N	1	0	0	0	0	0	0	0	0	0	—	—	—	—	0	0			.000	0	/C-1	0.0
1917	Chi-N	3	8	1	3	2	0	0	1	1	0	.375	.444	.625	209	1	1			1.000	-1	/C-3	0.0
1918	*Chi-N	52	113	9	32	7	3	1	14	10	15	.283	.347	.425	132	4	0			.974	-6	C-45	0.1
1919	Chi-N	49	125	11	27	4	2	0	9	7	10	.216	.258	.280	61	-6	2			.965	-4	C-38	-0.7
1920	Chi-N	94	270	29	67	11	4	3	19	34	23	.248	.332	.352	95	-1	1	0	0	.956	-6	C-86	-0.1
1921	Chi-N	96	260	32	65	12	7	4	32	18	14	.250	.299	.396	82	-7	2	0	1	.967	-5	C-90	-0.7
1922	Chi-N	128	392	68	127	18	8	4	60	79	34	.324	.439	.441	125	19	5	3	-0	.977	16	*C-125	3.8
1923	Chi-N	131	452	73	144	25	4	12	84	67	38	.319	.408	.471	131	22	10	3	1	.976	1	*C-124	2.9
1924	Chi-N	71	183	25	44	6	2	3	28	30	13	.240	.347	.344	85	-3	2	0	1	.984	-2	C-57	-0.1
1925	Chi-N	17	22	2	4	0	1	0	3	2	5	.182	.250	.273	33	-2	0	0	0	1.000	-1	/C-3	-0.3
	StL-N	94	317	37	88	13	2	3	32	46	26	.278	.373	.360	86	-5	0	1	-1	.975	-5	C-92	-0.5
	Yr	111	339	39	92	13	3	3	35	48	31	.271	.365	.354	83	-7	0	1	-1	.975	-6	C-95	-0.8
1926	*StL-N	147	492	63	144	30	9	7	68	61	44	.293	.371	.433	111	8	1			.983	10	*C-146	2.7
1927	StL-N	61	178	19	47	10	1	0	18	23	22	.264	.348	.331	80	-4	3			.979	-0	C-53,M	-0.1
1928	StL-N	16	52	6	11	1	0	0	4	13	9	.212	.369	.231	59	-2	2			.985	0	C-14	-0.1
	NY-N	75	133	23	26	6	0	2	20	34	16	.195	.359	.286	70	-5	2			.988	-1	C-63	-0.2
	Yr	91	185	29	37	7	0	2	24	47	25	.200	.362	.270	67	-7	4			.987	-1	C-77	-0.3
1929	NY-N	91	248	35	76	14	3	4	42	28	30	.306	.384	.435	103	2	3			.979	-5	C-84	0.3
1930	NY-N	94	249	37	75	16	4	4	54	31	21	.301	.381	.446	101	1	1			.973	0	C-69	0.6
1931	NY-N	85	174	11	39	8	3	1	19	21	23	.224	.311	.322	72	-7	0			.980	1	C-80	-0.2
1932	NY-N	50	67	7	16	3	0	0	8	11	10	.239	.354	.284	76	-2	0			.969	2	C-41	0.1
1933	StL-N	55	163	16	39	4	2	2	20	15	25	.239	.303	.325	76	-5	0			.970	-5	C-50	-0.8
1934	Cin-N	44	123	10	30	8	3	1	9	11	19	.244	.306	.382	85	-3	0			.993	-0	C-42,M	-0.1
	Chi-N	22	67	3	15	3	0	0	5	3	11	.224	.257	.269	42	-6	0			1.000	2	C-22	-0.2
	Yr	66	190	13	45	11	3	1	14	14	30	.237	.289	.342	70	-8	0			.996	2	C-64	-0.3
1935	StL-N	14	10	0	0	0	0	0	0	2	0	.000	.167	.000	-49	-2	0			1.000	1	/C-8	-0.1
Total	21	1492	4101	517	1120	201	58	51	549	547	408	.273	.360	.388	97	-3	35	7		.976	-9	*C-1338	6.2

■ JOSE OFFERMAN Offerman, Jose Antonio (Dono) b: 11/8/68, San Pedro De Macoris, D.R. BB/TR, 6', 165 lbs. Deb: 8/19/90

YEAR	TM/L	G	AB	R	H	2B	3B	HR	RBI	BB	SO	AVG	OBP	SLG	PRO+	BR/A	SB	CS	SBR	FA	FR	G/POS	TPR
1990	LA-N	29	58	7	9	0	0	1	7	4	14	.155	.210	.207	15	-7	1	0	0	.946	-2	S-27	-0.7
1991	LA-N	52	113	10	22	2	0	0	3	25	32	.195	.345	.212	62	-4	3	2	-0	.945	2	S-50	0.0
1992	LA-N	149	534	67	139	20	8	1	30	57	98	.260	.332	.333	90	-6	23	16	-3	.935	-18	*S-149	-1.7
1993	LA-N	158	590	77	159	21	6	1	62	71	75	.269	.350	.331	88	-8	30	13	1	.950	-7	*S-158	-0.1
1994	LA-N	72	243	27	51	8	4	1	25	38	38	.210	.317	.288	63	-13	2	1	0	.967	-4	S-72	-1.0
1995	*LA-N★	119	429	69	123	14	6	4	33	69	67	.287	.389	.375	113	11	2	7	-4	.932	-10	*S-115	0.8
1996	KC-A	151	561	85	170	33	8	5	47	74	98	.303	.385	.417	103	5	24	10	1	.994	-1	1-96,2-38,S-36,/O-1	0.2
1997	KC-A	106	424	59	126	23	6	2	39	41	64	.297	.359	.394	94	-3	9	10	-3	.981	-20	*2-101/D-1	-1.9
1998	KC-A	158	607	102	191	28	**13**	7	66	89	96	.315	.407	.438	115	17	45	12	6	.974	1	*2-152/D-6	3.1
Total	9	994	3559	503	990	149	51	22	312	468	582	.278	.364	.367	96	-8	139	71	-1	.943	-58	S-607,2-291/1DO	-1.3

■ ROWLAND OFFICE Office, Rowland Johnie b: 10/25/52, Sacramento, Cal. BL/TL, 6', 170 lbs. Deb: 8/5/72

YEAR	TM/L	G	AB	R	H	2B	3B	HR	RBI	BB	SO	AVG	OBP	SLG	PRO+	BR/A	SB	CS	SBR	FA	FR	G/POS	TPR
1972	Atl-N	2	5	1	2	0	0	0	0	1	2	.400	.500	.400	145	0	0	0	0	1.000	0	/O-1	0.0
1974	Atl-N	131	248	20	61	16	1	3	31	16	30	.246	.292	.355	77	-8	5	3	-0	.994	-25	*O-119	-3.8
1975	Atl-N	126	355	30	103	14	1	3	30	23	41	.290	.339	.361	91	-4	2	2	-1	.967	-6	*O-107	-1.6
1976	Atl-N	99	359	51	101	17	1	4	34	37	49	.281	.352	.368	98	-0	2	8	-4	.986	-3	O-92	-1.2
1977	Atl-N	124	428	42	103	13	1	5	39	23	58	.241	.284	.311	53	-28	2	4	-2	.988	7	*O-104/1-1	-2.7

YEAR	TM/L	G	AB	R	H	2B	3B	HR	RBI	BB	SO	AVG	OBP	SLG	PRO+	BR/A	SB	CS	SBR	FA	FR	G/POS	TPR
1978	Atl-N	146	404	40	101	13	1	9	40	22	52	.250	.299	.354	73	-15	8	6	-1	.990	-3	*O-136	-2.5
1979	Atl-N	124	277	35	69	14	2	2	37	27	33	.249	.320	.336	74	-10	5	4	-1	.988	-13	O-97	-2.7
1980	Mon-N	116	292	36	78	13	4	6	30	36	39	.267	.348	.401	108	4	3	3	-1	.987	-11	O-97	-1.2
1981	Mon-N	26	40	4	7	0	0	0	0	4	6	.175	.250	.175	22	-4	0	0	0	.938	-3	O-15	-0.8
1982	Mon-N	3	3	0	1	1	0	0	0	0	1	.333	.333	.667	170	0	0	0	0	1.000	0	/O-1	0.0
1983	NY-A	2	2	0	0	0	0	0	1	0	0	.000	.000	.000	-99	-1	0	0	0	1.000	-1	/O-2	-0.1
Total	11	899	2413	259	626	101	11	32	242	189	311	.259	.317	.350	79	-66	27	30	-10	.985	-57	O-771/1-1	-16.6

■ JIM OGLESBY

Oglesby, James Dorn b: 8/10/05, Schofield, Mo. d: 9/1/55, Tulsa, Okla. BL/TL, 6', 190 lbs. Deb: 4/14/36

YEAR	TM/L	G	AB	R	H	2B	3B	HR	RBI	BB	SO	AVG	OBP	SLG	PRO+	BR/A	SB	CS	SBR	FA	FR	G/POS	TPR
1936	Phi-A	3	11	0	2	0	0	0	2	2	0	.182	.308	.182	24	-1	0	0	0	1.000	0	/1-3	-0.1

■ BEN OGLIVIE

Oglivie, Benjamin Ambrosio (Palmer) b: 2/11/49, Colon, Panama BL/TL, 6'2", 170 lbs. Deb: 9/4/71

YEAR	TM/L	G	AB	R	H	2B	3B	HR	RBI	BB	SO	AVG	OBP	SLG	PRO+	BR/A	SB	CS	SBR	FA	FR	G/POS	TPR
1971	Bos-A	14	38	2	10	3	0	0	4	0	5	.263	.263	.342	66	-2	0	0	0	.958	1	O-11	-0.1
1972	Bos-A	94	253	27	61	10	2	8	30	18	61	.241	.294	.391	97	-1	1	1	-0	.981	-1	O-65	-0.6
1973	Bos-A	58	147	16	32	9	1	2	9	9	32	.218	.272	.333	66	-7	1	1	-0	.983	0	O-32,D-13	-0.9
1974	Det-A	92	252	28	68	11	3	4	29	34	38	.270	.357	.385	109	4	12	3	2	.947	-5	O-63,1-10/D-4	-0.3
1975	Det-A	100	332	45	95	14	1	9	36	16	62	.286	.323	.416	103	0	11	8	-2	.975	6	O-86/1-5,D-2	0.1
1976	Det-A	115	305	36	87	12	3	15	47	11	44	.285	.317	.492	129	9	9	4	0	.986	1	O-64/1-9,D-1	0.8
1977	Det-A	132	450	63	118	24	2	21	61	40	80	.262	.327	.464	107	3	9	9	-3	.976	7	*O-118/D-2	0.3
1978	Mil-A	128	469	71	142	29	4	18	72	52	69	.303	.372	.497	142	26	11	7	-1	.980	1	O-89,D-27,1-11	2.1
1979	Mil-A	139	514	88	145	30	4	29	81	48	56	.282	.346	.525	131	21	12	5	1	.985	-0	*O-120,D-13/1-9	1.5
1980	Mil-A★	156	592	94	180	26	2	**41**	118	54	71	.304	.367	.563	156	43	11	9	-2	.978	21	*O-152/D-4	5.4
1981	*Mil-A	107	400	53	97	15	2	14	72	37	49	.243	.316	.395	109	4	2	2	-1	.982	-3	*O-101/D-6	-0.3
1982	*Mil-A★	159	602	92	147	22	1	34	102	70	81	.244	.327	.453	119	14	3	5	-2	.982	13	*O-159	2.0
1983	Mil-A★	125	411	49	115	19	3	13	66	60	64	.280	.377	.436	133	20	4	6	-2	.985	6	*O-113/D-8	2.0
1984	Mil-A	131	461	49	121	16	2	12	60	44	56	.262	.328	.384	100	0	0	6	-4	.970	-4	*O-125/D-1	-1.1
1985	Mil-A	101	341	40	99	17	2	10	61	37	51	.290	.363	.440	119	9	0	2	-1	.965	-3	O-91/D-4	0.2
1986	Mil-A	103	346	31	98	20	1	5	53	30	33	.283	.340	.390	95	-2	1	2	-1	.991	4	O-50,D-42	-0.2
Total	16	1754	5913	784	1615	277	33	235	901	560	852	.273	.340	.450	119	142	87	70	-16	.978	44	*O-1439,D-127/1-44	10.9

■ BRUCE OGRODOWSKI

Ogrodowski, Ambrose Francis "Brusie" b: 2/17/12, Hoytville, Pa. d: 3/5/56, San Francisco, Cal. BR/TR, 5'11", 175 lbs. Deb: 4/14/36

YEAR	TM/L	G	AB	R	H	2B	3B	HR	RBI	BB	SO	AVG	OBP	SLG	PRO+	BR/A	SB	CS	SBR	FA	FR	G/POS	TPR
1936	StL-N	94	237	28	54	15	1	1	20	10	20	.228	.259	.312	53	-16	0			.989	4	C-85	-0.8
1937	StL-N	90	279	37	65	10	3	3	31	11	17	.233	.267	.323	58	-17	2			.984	2	C-87	-1.0
Total	2	184	516	65	119	25	4	4	51	21	37	.231	.263	.318	56	-32	2			.986	6	C-172	-1.8

■ HAL O'HAGEN

O'Hagen, Harry P. b: 9/30/1873, Washington, D.C. d: 1/14/13, Newark, N.J. 6', 173 lbs. Deb: 9/24/1892

YEAR	TM/L	G	AB	R	H	2B	3B	HR	RBI	BB	SO	AVG	OBP	SLG	PRO+	BR/A	SB	CS	SBR	FA	FR	G/POS	TPR
1892	Was-N	1	4	1	1	0	0	0	0	0	2	.250	.250	.250	53	-0	0			1.000	1	/C-1	0.0
1902	Chi-N	31	108	10	21	1	3	0	10	11		.194	.269	.259	65	-4	8			.982	3	1-31	-0.2
	NY-N	4	11	0	1	0	0	0	0	0		.091	.091	.091	-44	-2	0			1.000	-1	/O-4	-0.3
	Cle-A	3	13	2	5	2	0	0	1	0		.385	.385	.538	160	1	2			1.000	1	/1-3	0.1
	NY-N	22	73	5	11	2	1	0	8	2		.151	.195	.205	24	-7	3			.973	-0	1-18/O-4	-0.8
	Yr	57	192	15	33	2	4	0	18	13		.172	.232	.224	45	-13	11			.979	2	1-49/O-8	-1.3
Total	2	61	209	18	39	5	4	0	19	13	2	.187	.241	.249	51	-12	13			.981	3	/1-52,O-8,C-1	-1.2

■ GREG O'HALLORAN

O'Halloran, Gregory Joseph b: 5/21/68, Toronto, Ont., Can. BL/TR, 6'2", 205 lbs. Deb: 5/16/94

YEAR	TM/L	G	AB	R	H	2B	3B	HR	RBI	BB	SO	AVG	OBP	SLG	PRO+	BR/A	SB	CS	SBR	FA	FR	G/POS	TPR
1994	Fla-N	12	11	1	2	0	0	0	1	0	1	.182	.182	.182	-5	-2	0	0	0	1.000	0	/C-1	-0.1

■ KID O'HARA

O'Hara, James Francis b: 12/19/1875, Wilkes-Barre, Pa. d: 12/1/54, Canton, Ohio BB/TR, 5'7.5", 152 lbs. Deb: 9/15/04

YEAR	TM/L	G	AB	R	H	2B	3B	HR	RBI	BB	SO	AVG	OBP	SLG	PRO+	BR/A	SB	CS	SBR	FA	FR	G/POS	TPR
1904	Bos-N	8	29	3	6	0	0	0	0	4		.207	.303	.207	60	-1	1			.923	0	/O-8	-0.2

■ TOM O'HARA

O'Hara, Thomas F. b: 7/13/1885, Waverly, N.Y. d: 6/8/54, Denver, Colo. Deb: 9/19/06

YEAR	TM/L	G	AB	R	H	2B	3B	HR	RBI	BB	SO	AVG	OBP	SLG	PRO+	BR/A	SB	CS	SBR	FA	FR	G/POS	TPR
1906	StL-N	14	53	8	16	1	0	0	0	3		.302	.339	.321	110	1	3			.889	-2	O-14	-0.2
1907	StL-N	48	173	11	41	2	1	0	5	12		.237	.286	.260	74	-5	1			.943	-1	O-47	-0.9
Total	2	62	226	19	57	3	1	0	5	15		.252	.299	.274	82	-5	4			.930	-3	/O-61	-1.1

■ BILL O'HARA

O'Hara, William Alexander b: 8/14/1883, Toronto, Ont., Can. d: 6/15/31, Jersey City, N.J. BL/TR, 5'10", Deb: 4/15/09

YEAR	TM/L	G	AB	R	H	2B	3B	HR	RBI	BB	SO	AVG	OBP	SLG	PRO+	BR/A	SB	CS	SBR	FA	FR	G/POS	TPR
1909	NY-N	115	360	48	85	9	3	1	30	41		.236	.318	.286	86	-5	31			.978	2	*O-111	-0.8
1910	StL-N	9	20	1	3	0	0	0	2	1	3	.150	.190	.150	-0	-3	0			1.000	-0	/O-4,P-1,1-1	-0.3
Total	2	124	380	49	88	9	3	1	32	42	3	.232	.311	.279	82	-7	31			.979	2	O-115/1-1,P-1	-1.1

■ LEN OKRIE

Okrie, Leonard Joseph b: 7/16/23, Detroit, Mich. BR/TR, 6', 185 lbs. Deb: 6/16/48 FC

YEAR	TM/L	G	AB	R	H	2B	3B	HR	RBI	BB	SO	AVG	OBP	SLG	PRO+	BR/A	SB	CS	SBR	FA	FR	G/POS	TPR
1948	Was-A	19	42	1	10	0	1	0	1	1	7	.238	.256	.286	45	-3	0	0	0	.981	2	C-17	-0.1
1950	Was-A	17	27	1	6	0	0	0	2	6	7	.222	.382	.222	61	-1	0	0	0	1.000	1	C-17	0.0
1951	Was-A	5	8	1	1	1	0	0	0	2	1	.125	.300	.250	51	-1	0	0	0	.850	1	/C-5	0.0
1952	Bos-A	1	1	0	0	0	0	0	0	0	1	.000	.000	.000	-93	-0	0	0	0	1.000	-0	/C-1	0.0
Total	4	42	78	3	17	1	1	0	3	9	16	.218	.307	.256	51	-5	0	0	0	.965	4	/C-40	-0.1

■ JIM OLANDER

Olander, James Bentley b: 2/21/63, Tucson, Ariz. BR/TR, 6'1", 185 lbs. Deb: 9/20/91

YEAR	TM/L	G	AB	R	H	2B	3B	HR	RBI	BB	SO	AVG	OBP	SLG	PRO+	BR/A	SB	CS	SBR	FA	FR	G/POS	TPR
1991	Mil-A	12	9	2	0	0	0	0	0	2	5	.000	.182	.000	-46	-2	0	0	0	1.000	-2	/O-9,D-2	-0.4

■ DAVE OLDFIELD

Oldfield, David b: 12/18/1864, Philadelphia, Pa. d: 8/28/39, Philadelphia, Pa. BB/TL, 5'7", 175 lbs. Deb: 6/28/1883

YEAR	TM/L	G	AB	R	H	2B	3B	HR	RBI	BB	SO	AVG	OBP	SLG	PRO+	BR/A	SB	CS	SBR	FA	FR	G/POS	TPR
1883	Bal-a	1	4	0	0	0	0	0		0		.000	.000	.000	-97	-1				.667	-1	/C-1	-0.2
1885	Bro-a	10	25	2	8	1	0	0	2	3		.320	.414	.360	145	2				.873	1	/C-9,O-2	0.3
1886	Bro-a	14	55	7	13	1	0	0	5	2		.236	.263	.255	62	-2	1			.833	-3	C-13/S-1,O-1	-0.3
	Was-N	21	71	2	10	2	0	0	2	5	15	.141	.197	.169	13	-7	0			.899	-3	C-12/O-9	-0.9
Total	3	46	155	11	31	4	0	0	9	10	15	.200	.253	.226	50	-9	1			.857	-7	/C-35,O-12,S-1	-1.1

■ JOHN OLDHAM

Oldham, John Hardin b: 11/6/32, Salinas, Cal. BR/TL, 6'3", 198 lbs. Deb: 9/2/56

YEAR	TM/L	G	AB	R	H	2B	3B	HR	RBI	BB	SO	AVG	OBP	SLG	PRO+	BR/A	SB	CS	SBR	FA	FR	G/POS	TPR
1956	Cin-N	1	0	0	0	0	0	0	0	0	0	—	—	—	—	0	0	0	0	.000	0	R	0.0

■ BOB OLDIS

Oldis, Robert Carl b: 1/5/28, Preston, Iowa BR/TR, 6'1", 185 lbs. Deb: 4/28/53 C

YEAR	TM/L	G	AB	R	H	2B	3B	HR	RBI	BB	SO	AVG	OBP	SLG	PRO+	BR/A	SB	CS	SBR	FA	FR	G/POS	TPR
1953	Was-A	7	16	0	4	0	0	0	3	1	2	.250	.294	.250	49	-1	0	0	0	1.000	2	/C-7	0.1
1954	Was-A	11	24	1	8	1	0	0	0	1	3	.333	.360	.375	107	0	0	0	0	.941	-1	/C-8,3-2	0.0
1955	Was-A	6	6	1	0	0	0	0	0	1	0	.000	.143	.000	-62	-1	0	0	0	1.000	0	/C-6	-0.1
1960	*Pit-N	22	20	1	4	1	0	0	1	1	2	.200	.238	.250	34	-2	0	0	0	1.000	3	C-22	0.1
1961	Pit-N	4	5	0	0	0	0	0	0	0	0	.000	.000	.000	-99	-1	0	0	0	1.000	3	/C-4	0.1
1962	Phi-N	38	80	9	21	1	0	1	10	13	10	.262	.366	.313	87	-1	0	1	-1	.987	1	C-30	0.0
1963	Phi-N	47	85	8	19	3	0	0	8	3	5	.224	.250	.259	47	-6	0	0	0	.979	5	C-43	0.0
Total	7	135	236	20	56	6	0	1	22	20	22	.237	.297	.275	60	-12	0	1	-1	.983	12	C-120/3-2	0.2

■ RUBE OLDRING

Oldring, Reuben Henry b: 5/30/1884, New York, N.Y. d: 9/9/61, Bridgeton, N.J. BR/TR, 5'10", 186 lbs. Deb: 10/2/05

YEAR	TM/L	G	AB	R	H	2B	3B	HR	RBI	BB	SO	AVG	OBP	SLG	PRO+	BR/A	SB	CS	SBR	FA	FR	G/POS	TPR
1905	NY-A	8	30	2	9	0	1	1	6	2		.300	.344	.467	140	1	4			.967	5	/S-8	0.7
1906	Phi-A	59	174	15	42	10	1	0	19	2		.241	.263	.310	77	-5	7			.897	2	3-49/S-3,2-2,1-1	-0.2
1907	Phi-A	117	441	48	126	27	8	1	40	7		.286	.305	.390	118	7	29			.974	-9	*O-117	-0.8
1908	Phi-A	116	434	38	96	14	2	1	39	18		.221	.267	.270	70	-15	13			.941	3	*O-116	-2.0
1909	Phi-A	90	326	39	75	13	8	1	28	20		.230	.287	.328	92	-4	17			.963	-1	O-89/1-1	-0.9
1910	Phi-A	134	546	79	168	27	14	4	57	23		.308	.340	.430	142	23	17			**.978**	-1	*O-134	1.7
1911	*Phi-A	121	495	84	147	11	14	3	59	21		.297	.332	.394	104	1	21			**.979**	-9	*O-119	-1.4
1912	Phi-A	99	395	61	119	14	5	1	24	10		.301	.324	.370	102	-1	17			.974	-3	O-98	-0.9
1913	*Phi-A	137	538	101	152	27	9	5	71	34	37	.283	.328	.394	113	6	40			.968	-7	*O-131/S-5	-0.6
1914	*Phi-A	119	466	68	129	21	7	3	49	18	35	.277	.308	.371	108	2	14	16	-5	.965	-6	*O-117	-1.7
1915	Phi-A	107	408	49	101	23	3	6	42	22	21	.248	.293	.363	100	-3	11	6	-0	.982	5	O-96/3-8	-0.3

YEAR	TM/L	G	AB	R	H	2B	3B	HR	RBI	BB	SO	AVG	OBP	SLG	PRO+	BR/A	SB	CS	SBR	FA	FR	G/POS	TPR
1916	Phi-A	40	146	10	36	8	3	0	14	9	9	.247	.290	.342	95	-2	1			.897	-2	O-40	-0.7
	NY-A	43	158	17	37	8	0	1	12	12	13	.234	.288	.304	76	-5	6			.957	-3	O-43	-1.2
	Yr	83	304	27	73	16	3	1	26	21	22	.240	.289	.322	85	-7	7			.926	-5	O-83	-1.9
1918	Phi-A	49	133	5	31	2	1	0	11	8	10	.233	.282	.263	64	-6	0			.949	-8	O-30/2-2,3-2	-1.8
Total	13	1239	4690	616	1268	205	76	27	471	206	125	.270	.307	.364	103	0	197	22		.966	-35	*O-1130/3-59,S21	-10.1

■ CHARLEY O'LEARY

O'Leary, Charles Timothy b: 10/15/1882, Chicago, Ill. d: 1/6/41, Chicago, Ill. BR/TR, 5'7", 165 lbs. Deb: 4/14/04 C

YEAR	TM/L	G	AB	R	H	2B	3B	HR	RBI	BB	SO	AVG	OBP	SLG	PRO+	BR/A	SB	CS	SBR	FA	FR	G/POS	TPR
1904	Det-A	135	456	39	97	10	3	1	16	21		.213	.254	.254	63	-19	9			.933	6	*S-135	-1.1
1905	Det-A	148	512	47	109	13	1	0	33	29		.213	.259	.242	59	-24	13			.933	-8	*S-148	-3.1
1906	Det-A	128	443	34	97	13	2	2	34	17		.219	.253	.271	62	-20	8			.926	-8	*S-127	-2.6
1907	*Det-A	139	465	61	112	19	1	0	34	32		.241	.298	.286	83	-8	11			.943	-5	*S-138	-1.1
1908	*Det-A	65	211	21	53	9	3	0	17	9		.251	.295	.322	96	-1	4			.920	-12	S-64/2-1	-1.4
1909	*Det-A	76	261	29	53	10	0	0	13	6		.203	.224	.241	45	-17	9			.922	-4	3-54,2-15/S-4,O-2	-2.2
1910	Det-A	65	211	23	51	7	1	0	9	9		.242	.276	.284	71	-8	7			.935	1	2-38,S-18/3-6	-0.7
1911	Det-A	74	256	29	68	8	2	0	25	21		.266	.336	.313	77	-7	10			.966	4	2-67/3-6	-0.5
1912	Det-A	3	10	1	2	0	0	0	1	0		.200	.200	.200	15	-1	0			1.000	2	/2-3	0.0
1913	StL-N	121	406	32	88	15	5	0	31	20	34	.217	.260	.278	55	-24	3			.951	-8	*S-103,2-15	-2.5
1934	StL-A	1	1	1	1	0	0	0	0	0	0	1.000	1.000	1.000	385	0	0	0	0	.000	0	H	0.0
Total	11	955	3232	317	731	104	18	3	213	164	34	.226	.270	.272	67	-129	74	0		.935	-32	S-737,2-139/3-66,O	-15.2

■ DAN O'LEARY

O'Leary, Daniel "Hustling Dan" b: 10/22/1856, Detroit, Mich. d: 6/24/22, Chicago, Ill. BL , 5'10", 165 lbs. Deb: 9/3/1879 M

YEAR	TM/L	G	AB	R	H	2B	3B	HR	RBI	BB	SO	AVG	OBP	SLG	PRO+	BR/A	SB	CS	SBR	FA	FR	G/POS	TPR
1879	Pro-N	2	7	1	3	0	0	0	2	0	0	.429	.429	.429	187	1				.000	-1	/O-2	0.0
1880	Bos-N	3	12	1	3	2	0	0	1	0	3	.250	.250	.417	126	0				1.000	-1	/O-3	-0.1
1881	Det-N	2	8	0	0	0	0	0	0	0	2	.000	.000	.000	-96	-2				.714	-1	/O-2	-0.2
1882	Wor-N	6	22	2	4	1	0	0	2	5	5	.182	.333	.227	82	-0				.800	-2	/O-6	-0.2
1884	Cin-U	32	132	14	34	0	2	1		5		.258	.285	.311	74	-8				.862	2	O-32,M	-0.6
Total	5	45	181	18	44	3	2	1	5	10	10	.243	.283	.298	75	-9				.843	-2	/O-45	-1.1

■ TROY O'LEARY

O'Leary, Troy Franklin b: 8/4/69, Compton, Cal. BL/TL, 6', 196 lbs. Deb: 5/9/93

YEAR	TM/L	G	AB	R	H	2B	3B	HR	RBI	BB	SO	AVG	OBP	SLG	PRO+	BR/A	SB	CS	SBR	FA	FR	G/POS	TPR
1993	Mil-A	19	41	3	12	3	0	0	3	5	9	.293	.370	.366	100	0	0	0	0	1.000	-1	O-19	-0.1
1994	Mil-A	27	66	9	18	1	1	2	7	5	12	.273	.333	.409	86	-1	1	1	-0	1.000	-1	O-21/D-1	-0.3
1995	Bos-A	112	399	60	123	31	6	10	49	29	64	.308	.357	.491	114	7	5	3	-0	.976	-5	*O-105/D-3	0.0
1996	Bos-A	149	497	68	129	28	5	15	81	47	80	.260	.328	.427	87	-10	3	2	-0	.971	-26	*O-146	-3.7
1997	Bos-A	146	499	65	154	32	4	15	80	39	70	.309	.361	.479	115	10	0	5	-3	.979	-1	*O-142/D-1	0.3
1998	*Bos-A	156	611	95	165	36	8	23	83	36	108	.270	.316	.468	100	-2	2	2	-1	.990	7	*O-155	0.1
Total	6	609	2113	300	601	131	24	65	303	161	343	.284	.339	.461	103	4	11	13	-5	.981	-27	O-588/D-5	-3.7

■ JOHN OLERUD

Olerud, John Garrett b: 8/5/68, Seattle, Wash. BL/TL, 6'5", 220 lbs. Deb: 9/3/89

YEAR	TM/L	G	AB	R	H	2B	3B	HR	RBI	BB	SO	AVG	OBP	SLG	PRO+	BR/A	SB	CS	SBR	FA	FR	G/POS	TPR
1989	Tor-A	6	8	2	3	0	0	0	0	0	1	.375	.375	.375	114	0	0	0	0	1.000	0	/1-5,D-1	0.0
1990	Tor-A	111	358	43	95	15	1	14	48	57	75	.265	.368	.430	120	11	0	2	-1	.986	-1	D-90,1-18	0.5
1991	*Tor-A	139	454	64	116	30	1	17	68	68	84	.256	.360	.438	115	10	0	2	-1	.996	-4	*1-135/D-1	-0.4
1992	*Tor-A	138	458	68	130	28	0	16	66	70	61	.284	.380	.450	126	17	1	0	0	.994	-2	*1-133/D-1	0.6
1993	*Tor-A★	158	551	109	200	**54**	2	24	107	114	65	**.363**	**.478**	.599	**186**	**74**	0	2	-1	.992	1	*1-137,D-20	**5.8**
1994	Tor-A	108	384	47	114	29	2	12	67	61	53	.297	.397	.477	124	15	1	2	-1	.993	2	*1-104/D-3	0.6
1995	Tor-A	135	492	72	143	32	0	8	54	84	54	.291	.398	.404	110	11	0	0	0	.997	-2	*1-133	-0.3
1996	Tor-A	125	398	59	109	25	0	18	61	60	37	.274	.382	.472	115	10	1	0	0	.998	-1	*1-101,D-15	0.0
1997	NY-N	154	524	90	154	34	1	22	102	85	67	.294	.405	.489	138	32	0	0	0	.995	5	*1-146	2.2
1998	NY-N	160	557	91	197	36	4	22	93	95	73	.354	.452	.550	159	54	2	2	-1	.996	3	*1-157	4.2
Total	10	1234	4184	645	1261	283	11	153	666	694	570	.301	.407	.484	135	234	5	10	-5	.995	2	*1-1069,D-131	13.2

■ FRANK OLIN

Olin, Franklin Walter b: 1/9/1860, Woodford, Vt. d: 5/21/51, St.Louis, Mo. BL , Deb: 7/4/1884

YEAR	TM/L	G	AB	R	H	2B	3B	HR	RBI	BB	SO	AVG	OBP	SLG	PRO+	BR/A	SB	CS	SBR	FA	FR	G/POS	TPR
1884	Was-a	21	83	12	32	4	1	0		7		.386	.433	.458	216	11				.775	-7	2-12,O-11	0.4
	Was-U	1	4	0	0	0	0	0		0		.000	.000	.000	-99	-1				.000	-0	/O-1	-0.1
	Tol-a	26	86	16	22	0	1	1		5		.256	.304	.314	99	-0				.875	0	O-26	0.0
1885	Det-N	1	4	1	2	0	0	0	0	0	0	.500	.500	.500	224	1				.667	-0	/3-1	0.0
Total	2	49	177	29	56	4	2	1	0	12	0	.316	.363	.379	148	10				.849	-7	/O-38,2-12,3-1	0.3

■ JOSE OLIVA

Oliva, Jose (Galvez) b: 3/3/71, San Pedro De Macoris, D.R. d: 12/22/97, San Cristobal, D.R. BR/TR, 6'3", 215 lbs. Deb: 7/1/94

YEAR	TM/L	G	AB	R	H	2B	3B	HR	RBI	BB	SO	AVG	OBP	SLG	PRO+	BR/A	SB	CS	SBR	FA	FR	G/POS	TPR
1994	Atl-N	19	59	9	17	5	0	6	11	7	10	.288	.364	.678	160	5	0	1	-1	.932	2	3-16	0.6
1995	Atl-N	48	109	7	17	4	0	5	12	7	22	.156	.207	.330	38	-10	0	0	0	.902	-1	3-25/1-1	-1.1
	StL-N	22	74	8	9	1	0	2	8	5	24	.122	.198	.216	9	-10	0	0	0	.977	-2	3-18/1-2	-1.3
	Yr	70	183	15	26	5	0	7	20	12	46	.142	.203	.284	26	-20	0	0	0	.933	-3	3-43/1-3	-2.4
Total	2	89	242	24	43	10	0	13	31	19	56	.178	.243	.380	60	-15	0	1	-1	.932	-2	/3-59,1-3	-1.8

■ TONY OLIVA

Oliva, Pedro (Lopez) b: 7/20/40, Pinar Del Rio, Cuba BL/TR, 6'2", 190 lbs. Deb: 9/9/62 C

YEAR	TM/L	G	AB	R	H	2B	3B	HR	RBI	BB	SO	AVG	OBP	SLG	PRO+	BR/A	SB	CS	SBR	FA	FR	G/POS	TPR
1962	Min-A	9	9	3	4	1	0	0	3	3	2	.444	.583	.556	201	2	0	0	0	1.000	-0	/O-2	0.1
1963	Min-A	7	7	0	3	0	0	0	1	0	2	.429	.429	.429	138	0	0	0	0	.000	0	H	0.0
1964	Min-A★	161	672	**109**	**217**	**43**	9	32	94	34	68	**.323**	.361	.557	150	42	12	6	0	.981	5	*O-159	4.1
1965	*Min-A★	149	576	107	**185**	40	5	16	98	55	64	**.321**	.384	.491	141	31	19	9	0	.964	7	*O-147	3.3
1966	Min-A★	159	622	99	**191**	32	7	25	87	42	72	.307	.356	.502	135	27	13	7	-0	.972	14	*O-159	3.5
1967	Min-A★	146	557	76	161	**34**	6	17	83	44	61	.289	.350	.463	128	19	11	3	2	.987	12	*O-146	2.7
1968	Min-A★	128	470	54	136	24	5	18	68	45	61	.289	.360	.477	145	25	10	9	-2	.983	8	*O-126	2.7
1969	*Min-A†	153	637	97	**197**	**39**	4	24	101	45	66	.309	.358	.496	134	26	10	13	-5	.982	13	*O-152	2.7
1970	*Min-A★	157	628	96	**204**	**36**	7	23	107	38	67	.325	.366	.514	138	30	5	4	-1	.968	21	*O-157	4.3
1971	Min-A†	126	487	73	164	30	3	22	81	25	44	**.337**	.372	**.546**	152	31	4	1	1	.969	-1	*O-121	2.6
1972	Min-A	10	28	1	9	1	0	0	1	2	5	.321	.367	.357	111	0	0	0	0	.857	-3	/O-9	-0.3
1973	Min-A	146	571	63	166	20	0	16	92	45	44	.291	.347	.410	108	6	2	1	0	.000	0	*D-142	0.2
1974	Min-A	127	459	43	131	16	2	13	57	27	31	.285	.328	.414	109	4	0	1	-1	.000	0	*D-112	0.1
1975	Min-A	131	455	46	123	10	0	13	58	41	45	.270	.348	.378	104	3	0	1	-1	.000	0	*D-120	-0.1
1976	Min-A	67	123	3	26	3	0	1	16	2	13	.211	.236	.260	44	-9	0	0	0	.000	0	D-32	-1.0
Total	15	1676	6301	870	1917	329	48	220	947	448	645	.304	.356	.476	130	238	86	55	-7	.975	76	*O-1178,D-406	24.9

■ ED OLIVARES

Olivares, Edward (Balzac) b: 11/5/38, Mayaguez, P.R. BR/TR, 5'11", 180 lbs. Deb: 9/16/60 F

YEAR	TM/L	G	AB	R	H	2B	3B	HR	RBI	BB	SO	AVG	OBP	SLG	PRO+	BR/A	SB	CS	SBR	FA	FR	G/POS	TPR
1960	StL-N	3	5	0	0	0	0	0	0	0	3	.000	.000	.000	-92	-1	0	0	0	.500	-0	/3-1	-0.2
1961	StL-N	21	30	2	5	0	0	0	1	0	4	.167	.167	.167	-10	-5	1	0	0	1.000	-2	O-10	-0.7
Total	2	24	35	2	5	0	0	0	1	0	7	.143	.143	.143	-21	-6	1	0	0	1.000	-3	/O-10,3-1	-0.9

■ AL OLIVER

Oliver, Albert b: 10/14/46, Portsmouth, Ohio BL/TL, 6', 195 lbs. Deb: 9/23/68

YEAR	TM/L	G	AB	R	H	2B	3B	HR	RBI	BB	SO	AVG	OBP	SLG	PRO+	BR/A	SB	CS	SBR	FA	FR	G/POS	TPR
1968	Pit-N	4	8	1	1	0	0	0	0	0	4	.125	.125	.125	-25	-1	0	0	0	1.000	0	/O-1	-0.1
1969	Pit-N	129	463	55	132	19	2	17	70	21	38	.285	.334	.445	119	10	8	5	-1	.991	-1	*1-106,O-21	-0.1
1970	*Pit-N	151	551	63	149	33	5	12	83	35	35	.270	.330	.414	100	-1	1	1	-0	.986	1	O-80,1-77	-1.0
1971	*Pit-N	143	529	69	149	31	7	14	64	27	72	.282	.323	.446	116	9	4	3	-1	.981	8	*O-116,1-25	1.0
1972	*Pit-N★	140	565	88	176	27	4	12	89	34	44	.312	.356	.437	127	19	2	4	-2	.985	1	*O-138/1-3	1.1
1973	Pit-N	158	654	90	191	38	7	20	99	22	52	.292	.320	.463	118	12	6	0	2	.964	-2	*O-109,1-50	0.3
1974	*Pit-N	147	617	96	198	38	12	11	85	33	58	.321	.360	.475	137	27	10	1	2	.986	7	O-98,1-49	3.0
1975	*Pit-N★	155	628	90	176	39	8	18	84	25	73	.280	.313	.454	112	6	4	2	0	.987	2	*O-153/1-4	0.1
1976	Pit-N★	121	443	62	143	22	5	12	61	26	29	.323	.367	.476	137	20	6	2	1	.984	7	*O-106/1-3	2.4
1977	Pit-N	154	568	75	175	29	6	19	82	40	38	.308	.358	.481	119	15	13	16	-6	.981	0	*O-148	0.3
1978	Tex-A	133	525	65	170	35	5	14	89	31	41	.324	.364	.490	138	24	8	9	-3	.987	6	*O-107,D-26	2.2
1979	Tex-A	136	492	69	159	28	4	12	76	34	34	.323	.372	.470	127	18	4	5	-2	.975	0	*O-119,D-10	1.1
1980	Tex-A★	163	656	96	209	43	3	19	117	39	47	.319	.361	.480	132	27	5	7	-3	.973	4	*O-157/1-1,D-4	2.2

YEAR	TM/L	G	AB	R	H	2B	3B	HR	RBI	BB	SO	AVG	OBP	SLG	PRO+	BR/A	SB	CS	SBR	FA	FR	G/POS	TPR
1981	Tex-A★	102	421	53	130	29	1	4	55	24	28	.309	.349	.411	125	12	3	0	1	1.000	-0	*D-101/1-1	1.0
1982	Mon-N★	160	617	90	**204**	**43**	2	22	**109**	61	59	**.331**	.394	.514	149	41	5	2	0	.986	-9	*1-159	2.5
1983	Mon-N★	157	614	70	184	**38**	3	8	84	44	44	.300	.348	.410	110	8	1	3	-2	.990	2	*1-153/O-1	0.0
1984	SF-N	91	339	27	101	19	2	0	34	20	27	.298	.339	.366	101	0	2	2	-1	.985	-1	1-82	-0.7
	Phi-N	28	93	9	29	7	0	0	14	7	9	.312	.360	.387	108	1	1	2	-1	.987	-3	1-19/O-5	-0.5
	Yr	119	432	36	130	26	2	0	48	27	36	.301	.343	.370	103	1	3	4	-2	.985	-4	*1-101/O-5	-1.2
1985	LA-N	35	79	1	20	5	0	0	8	5	11	.253	.298	.316	74	-3	1	0	0	.882	-2	O-17	-0.6
	*Tor-A	61	187	20	47	6	1	5	23	7	13	.251	.282	.374	76	-6	0	0	0	1.000	-0	D-59/1-1	-0.8
Total	18	2368	9049	1189	2743	529	77	219	1326	535	756	.303	.348	.451	122	238	84	64	-13	.980	19	*O-1376,1-733,D-200	13.4

■ DAVE OLIVER
Oliver, David Jacob b: 4/7/51, Stockton, Cal. BL/TR, 5′11″, 175 lbs. Deb: 9/25/77 C

YEAR	TM/L	G	AB	R	H	2B	3B	HR	RBI	BB	SO	AVG	OBP	SLG	PRO+	BR/A	SB	CS	SBR	FA	FR	G/POS	TPR
1977	Cle-A	7	22	2	7	0	1	0	3	4	0	.318	.444	.409	139	2	0	0	0	.949	1	/2-7	0.2

■ GENE OLIVER
Oliver, Eugene George b: 3/22/35, Moline, Ill. BR/TR, 6′2″, 225 lbs. Deb: 6/6/59

YEAR	TM/L	G	AB	R	H	2B	3B	HR	RBI	BB	SO	AVG	OBP	SLG	PRO+	BR/A	SB	CS	SBR	FA	FR	G/POS	TPR
1959	StL-N	68	172	14	42	9	0	6	28	7	41	.244	.274	.401	72	-7	3	2	-0	.955	-5	O-42/C-9,1-5	-1.5
1961	StL-N	22	52	8	14	2	0	4	9	6	10	.269	.367	.538	124	2	0	0	0	1.000	2	C-15/O-1	0.4
1962	StL-N	122	345	42	89	19	1	14	45	50	59	.258	.354	.441	102	1	5	2	0	.991	-4	C-98/O-8,1-3	0.0
1963	StL-N	39	102	10	23	4	0	6	18	13	19	.225	.313	.441	105	1	0	0	0	.981	1	C-35	0.3
	Mil-N	95	296	34	74	12	2	11	47	27	59	.250	.323	.416	112	5	4	4	-1	.985	-14	1-55,O-35/C-2	-1.5
	Yr	134	398	44	97	16	2	17	65	40	78	.244	.321	.422	110	5	4	4	-1	.985	-13	1-55,C-37,O-35	-1.2
1964	Mil-N	93	279	45	77	15	1	13	49	17	41	.276	.320	.477	120	7	3	7	-3	.982	-6	1-76/C-1	-0.6
1965	Mil-N	122	392	56	106	20	0	21	58	36	61	.270	.336	.482	127	13	5	4	-1	.976	1	C-64,1-52/O-1	1.5
1966	Atl-N	76	191	19	37	9	1	8	24	16	43	.194	.256	.377	72	-8	2	0	1	.990	11	C-48/1-5,O-2	0.7
1967	Atl-N	17	51	8	10	2	0	3	6	6	8	.196	.281	.412	97	-0	0	0	0	.968	2	C-14	0.3
	Phi-N	85	263	29	59	16	0	7	34	29	56	.224	.304	.365	90	-4	2	2	-1	.987	-12	C-79/1-2	-1.3
	Yr	102	314	37	69	18	0	10	40	35	64	.220	.300	.373	91	-4	2	2	-1	.984	-10	C-93/1-2	-1.0
1968	Bos-A	16	35	2	5	0	0	0	1	4	12	.143	.250	.143	20	-3	0	0	0	.984	-2	C-10/O-1	-0.5
	Chi-N	8	11	1	4	0	0	0	1	3	2	.364	.500	.364	152	1	0	0	0	1.000	0	/1-2,C-1,O-1	0.1
1969	Chi-N	23	27	0	6	3	0	0	0	1	9	.222	.276	.333	62	-1	0	0	0	1.000	2	/C-6	0.1
Total	10	786	2216	268	546	111	5	93	320	215	420	.246	.317	.427	103	5	24	21	-5	.985	-24	C-382,1-200/O-91	-2.0

■ JOE OLIVER
Oliver, Joseph Melton b: 7/24/65, Memphis, Tenn. BR/TR, 6′3″, 210 lbs. Deb: 7/15/89

YEAR	TM/L	G	AB	R	H	2B	3B	HR	RBI	BB	SO	AVG	OBP	SLG	PRO+	BR/A	SB	CS	SBR	FA	FR	G/POS	TPR
1989	Cin-N	49	151	13	41	8	0	3	23	6	28	.272	.304	.384	92	-2	0	0	0	.986	-1	C-47	0.0
1990	*Cin-N	121	364	34	84	23	0	8	52	37	75	.231	.305	.360	79	-11	1	1	-0	**.992**	2	*C-118	-0.2
1991	Cin-N	94	269	21	58	11	0	11	41	18	53	.216	.265	.379	76	-9	0	0	0	.980	-1	C-90	-0.6
1992	Cin-N	143	485	42	131	25	1	10	57	35	75	.270	.321	.388	97	-2	2	3	-1	.992	-1	*C-141/1-1	0.4
1993	Cin-N	139	482	40	115	28	0	14	75	27	91	.239	.280	.384	76	-18	0	0	0	.992	-9	*C-133,1-12/O-1	-2.0
1994	Cin-N	6	19	1	4	0	0	1	5	2	3	.211	.286	.368	70	-1	0	0	0	.980	2	/C-6	0.1
1995	Mil-A	97	337	43	92	20	0	12	51	27	66	.273	.332	.439	93	-4	2	4	-2	.982	-5	C-91/1-2,D-6	-0.5
1996	Cin-N	106	289	31	70	12	1	11	46	28	54	.242	.313	.405	87	-6	2	0	1	.992	10	C-97/1-3,O-3	0.9
1997	Cin-N	111	349	28	90	13	0	14	43	25	58	.258	.317	.415	89	-6	1	3	-2	.990	0	*C-106/1-4	-0.2
1998	Det-A	50	155	8	35	8	0	4	22	7	33	.226	.259	.355	57	-10	0	1	-1	.982	-3	C-48/1-2	-1.0
	Sea-A	29	85	12	19	3	0	2	10	10	15	.224	.305	.329	65	-4	1	0	0	.984	-4	C-29	-0.6
	Yr	79	240	20	54	11	0	6	32	17	48	.225	.276	.346	60	-14	1	1	-0	.983	-7	C-77/1-2	-1.6
Total	10	945	2985	273	739	151	2	90	425	222	551	.248	.303	.390	84	-73	9	12	-5	.989	-12	C-906/1-24,D-6,O-4	-3.7

■ NATE OLIVER
Oliver, Nathaniel "Peewee" b: 12/13/40, St.Petersburg, Fla. BR/TR, 5′10″, 160 lbs. Deb: 4/9/63

YEAR	TM/L	G	AB	R	H	2B	3B	HR	RBI	BB	SO	AVG	OBP	SLG	PRO+	BR/A	SB	CS	SBR	FA	FR	G/POS	TPR
1963	LA-N	65	163	23	39	2	3	1	9	13	25	.239	.299	.307	80	-4	3	4	-2	.961	5	2-57/S-2	0.4
1964	LA-N	99	321	28	78	9	0	0	21	31	57	.243	.310	.271	70	-12	7	4	-0	.967	-10	2-98/S-1	-1.6
1965	LA-N	8	1	3	1	0	0	0	0	0	0	1.000	1.000	1.000	498	1	1	0	0	1.000	1	/2-2	0.2
1966	*LA-N	80	119	17	23	2	0	0	3	13	17	.193	.278	.210	41	-9	3	3	-1	.977	11	2-68/S-2,3-1	0.4
1967	LA-N	77	232	18	55	6	2	0	7	13	50	.237	.283	.280	67	-10	3	2	-0	.973	-8	2-39,S-32/O-1	-1.5
1968	SF-N	36	73	3	13	2	0	0	1	1	13	.178	.189	.205	18	-7	0	1	-1	.950	1	2-14,S-13/3-1	-0.7
1969	NY-A	1	1	0	0	0	0	0	0	0	0	.000	.000	.000	-99	-0	0	0	0	.000	0	H	0.0
	Chi-N	44	44	15	7	3	0	1	4	1	10	.159	.196	.295	32	-4	0	1	-1	1.000	11	2-13	0.7
Total	7	410	954	107	216	24	5	2	45	72	172	.226	.284	.268	62	-47	17	15	-4	.969	10	2-291/S-50,3-2,O-1	-2.1

■ BOB OLIVER
Oliver, Robert Lee b: 2/8/43, Shreveport, La. BR/TR, 6′2″, 215 lbs. Deb: 9/10/65 F

YEAR	TM/L	G	AB	R	H	2B	3B	HR	RBI	BB	SO	AVG	OBP	SLG	PRO+	BR/A	SB	CS	SBR	FA	FR	G/POS	TPR
1965	Pit-N	3	2	1	0	0	0	0	0	0	0	.000	.000	.000	-99	-1	0	0	0	1.000	-0	/O-3	-0.1
1969	KC-A	118	394	43	100	8	4	13	43	21	74	.254	.295	.393	91	-6	5	5	-2	.977	5	O-98,1-12/3-8	-0.9
1970	KC-A	160	612	83	159	24	6	27	99	42	126	.260	.311	.451	108	4	3	3	-1	.993	-8	*1-115,3-46	-1.6
1971	KC-A	128	373	35	91	12	2	8	52	14	88	.244	.281	.351	79	-12	0	0	0	.988	-0	1-68,O-48/3-2	-2.0
1972	KC-A	16	63	7	17	2	1	1	6	2	12	.270	.292	.381	100	-0	1	0	0	.979	3	O-16	0.3
	Cal-A	134	509	47	137	20	4	19	70	27	97	.269	.310	.436	127	14	4	3	-1	.994	-6	*1-127/O-8	-0.4
	Yr	150	572	54	154	22	5	20	76	29	109	.269	.308	.430	124	13	5	3	-0	.994	-3	*1-127,O-24	-0.1
1973	Cal-A	151	544	51	144	24	1	18	89	33	100	.265	.313	.412	111	5	1	1	-0	.952	-1	3-49,O-47,1-32,D-12	-0.1
1974	Cal-A	110	359	22	89	9	1	8	55	16	51	.248	.282	.345	84	-8	2	1	0	.985	-12	1-57,3-46/O-4,D-1	-2.6
	Bal-A	9	20	1	3	2	0	0	4	0	5	.150	.150	.250	14	-2	1	1	-0	.974	1	/1-4,D-1	-0.2
	Yr	119	379	23	92	11	1	8	59	16	56	.243	.275	.340	81	-11	3	2	-0	.984	-11	1-61,3-46/O-4,D-2	-2.8
1975	NY-A	18	38	3	5	1	0	0	1	1	9	.132	.154	.158	-12	-6	0	0	0	1.000	-0	/1-8,3-1,D-3	-0.7
Total	8	847	2914	293	745	102	19	94	419	156	562	.256	.298	.400	100	-13	17	14	-3	.991	-19	1-423,O-224,3/D	-8.3

■ TOM OLIVER
Oliver, Thomas Noble "Rebel" b: 1/15/03, Montgomery, Ala. d: 2/26/88, Montgomery, Ala. BR/TR, 6′, 168 lbs. Deb: 4/14/30 C

YEAR	TM/L	G	AB	R	H	2B	3B	HR	RBI	BB	SO	AVG	OBP	SLG	PRO+	BR/A	SB	CS	SBR	FA	FR	G/POS	TPR
1930	Bos-A	154	646	86	189	34	2	0	46	42	25	.293	.339	.351	78	-21	6	6	-2	.982	15	*O-154	-1.7
1931	Bos-A	148	586	52	162	35	5	0	70	25	17	.276	.307	.353	77	-21	4	6	-2	**.993**	13	*O-148	-1.9
1932	Bos-A	122	455	39	120	23	3	0	37	25	12	.264	.305	.327	66	-23	1	6	-3	.983	8	*O-116	-2.4
1933	Bos-A	90	244	25	63	9	1	0	23	13	7	.258	.296	.303	60	-14	1	1	-0	.985	-1	O-86	-1.8
Total	4	514	1931	202	534	101	11	0	176	105	61	.277	.316	.340	73	-79	12	19	-8	.986	35	O-504	-7.8

■ LUIS OLMO
Olmo, Luis Francisco (Rodriguez) (b: Luis Francisco Rodriquez (Olmo)) b: 8/11/19, Arecibo, P.R. BR/TR, 5′11.5″, 190 lbs. Deb: 7/23/43

YEAR	TM/L	G	AB	R	H	2B	3B	HR	RBI	BB	SO	AVG	OBP	SLG	PRO+	BR/A	SB	CS	SBR	FA	FR	G/POS	TPR
1943	Bro-N	57	238	39	72	6	4	4	37	8	20	.303	.325	.412	112	2	3			.957	-2	O-57	-0.2
1944	Bro-N	136	520	65	134	20	5	9	85	17	37	.258	.284	.367	84	-13	10			.971	-8	O-64,2-42,3-31	-2.3
1945	Bro-N	141	556	62	174	27	**13**	10	110	36	33	.313	.356	.462	127	18	15			.971	-9	*O-106,3-31/2-1	0.4
1949	*Bro-N	38	105	15	32	4	1	1	14	5	11	.305	.336	.390	91	-1	2			.950	-4	O-34	-0.7
1950	Bos-N	69	154	23	35	7	1	5	22	18	23	.227	.308	.383	86	-4	3			.974	-9	O-55/3-1	-1.4
1951	Bos-N	21	56	4	11	1	1	0	4	4	4	.196	.250	.250	38	-5	0	1	-1	1.000	-3	O-16	-0.9
Total	6	462	1629	208	458	65	25	29	272	88	128	.281	.319	.405	102	-3	33	1		.968	-34	O-332/3-63,2-43	-5.1

■ BARNEY OLSEN
Olsen, Bernard Charles b: 9/11/19, Everett, Mass. d: 3/30/77, Everett, Mass. BR/TR, 5′11″, 179 lbs. Deb: 4/17/41

YEAR	TM/L	G	AB	R	H	2B	3B	HR	RBI	BB	SO	AVG	OBP	SLG	PRO+	BR/A	SB	CS	SBR	FA	FR	G/POS	TPR
1941	Chi-N	24	73	13	21	6	1	1	4	4	11	.288	.325	.438	118	1	0			.947	1	O-23	0.1

■ GREG OLSON
Olson, Gregory William b: 9/6/60, Marshall, Minn. BR/TR, 6′, 200 lbs. Deb: 6/27/89

YEAR	TM/L	G	AB	R	H	2B	3B	HR	RBI	BB	SO	AVG	OBP	SLG	PRO+	BR/A	SB	CS	SBR	FA	FR	G/POS	TPR
1989	Min-A	3	2	0	1	0	0	0	0	0	0	.500	.500	.500	171	0	0	0	0	1.000	0	/C-3	0.0
1990	Atl-N★	100	298	36	78	12	1	7	36	30	51	.262	.333	.379	90	-4	1	1	-0	.987	-7	C-97/3-1	-0.5
1991	*Atl-N	133	411	46	99	25	0	6	44	44	48	.241	.319	.345	82	-9	1	1	-0	.995	3	*C-127	0.0
1992	Atl-N	95	302	27	72	14	2	3	27	34	31	.238	.318	.328	78	-8	2	1	0	.998	7	C-94	0.5
1993	*Atl-N	83	262	23	59	10	0	4	24	29	27	.225	.305	.309	64	-13	1	0	0	.988	-2	C-81	-1.0
Total	5	414	1275	132	309	61	3	20	131	137	157	.242	.319	.342	79	-34	5	3	-0	.992	2	C-402/3-1	-1.0

■ IVY OLSON
Olson, Ivan Massie b: 10/14/1885, Kansas City, Mo. d: 9/1/65, Inglewood, Cal. BR/TR, 5′10.5″, 175 lbs. Deb: 4/12/11 C

YEAR	TM/L	G	AB	R	H	2B	3B	HR	RBI	BB	SO	AVG	OBP	SLG	PRO+	BR/A	SB	CS	SBR	FA	FR	G/POS	TPR
1911	Cle-A	140	545	89	142	20	8	1	50	34		.261	.311	.332	79	-17	20			.909	-16	*S-139/3-1	-2.3
1912	Cle-A	125	467	68	118	13	1	0	33	21		.253	.291	.285	63	-23	16			.917	6	S-56,3-36,2-21,/O-3	-1.3

YEAR	TM/L	G	AB	R	H	2B	3B	HR	RBI	BB	SO	AVG	OBP	SLG	PRO+	BR/A	SB	CS	SBR	FA	FR	G/POS	TPR
1913	Cle-A	104	370	47	92	13	3	0	32	22	28	.249	.296	.300	72	-13	7			.953	4	3-73,1-21/2-1	-1.0
1914	Cle-A	89	310	22	75	6	2	1	20	13	24	.242	.275	.284	65	-14	15	9	-1	.942	12	S-31,2-23,3-19,/O1	0.0
1915	Cin-N	63	207	18	48	5	4	0	14	12	13	.232	.274	.295	71	-7	10	6	-1	.938	13	2-39,3-15/1-7	0.6
	Bro-N	18	26	2	2	0	1	0	3	1	0	.077	.111	.154	-20	-4	0			.909	-1	/S-7,2-1,3-1,O-1	-0.5
	Yr	81	233	20	50	5	5	0	17	13	13	.215	.256	.279	61	-11	10	6	-1	.938	12	2-40,3-16/1-7,SO	0.1
1916	*Bro-N	108	351	29	89	13	4	1	38	21	27	.254	.298	.322	88	-5	14			.920	-12	*S-103/2-3,1-1	-1.4
1917	Bro-N	139	580	64	156	18	5	2	38	14	34	.269	.291	.328	87	-10	6			.941	-6	*S-133/3-6	-1.1
1918	Bro-N	126	506	63	121	16	4	1	17	27	18	.239	.286	.292	77	-14	21			.918	-25	*S-126	-3.9
1919	Bro-N	140	590	73	**164**	14	9	1	38	30	12	.278	.316	.337	94	-4	26			.947	-2	*S-140	0.3
1920	*Bro-N	143	637	71	162	13	11	1	46	20	19	.254	.278	.314	68	-27	4	7	-3	.935	-7	*S-125,2-21	-2.8
1921	Bro-N	151	652	88	174	22	10	3	35	28	26	.267	.301	.345	68	-30	4	9	-4	.943	5	*S-133,2-20	-1.6
1922	Bro-N	136	551	63	150	26	6	1	47	25	10	.272	.306	.347	69	-26	8	5	-1	.960	-6	2-85,S-51	-2.4
1923	Bro-N	82	292	33	76	11	1	1	35	14	10	.260	.296	.315	63	-16	5	0	2	.974	5	2-72/3-4,1-2,S-2	-0.8
1924	Bro-N	10	27	0	6	1	0	0	0	3	1	.222	.300	.259	53	-2	0	0	0	.941	-2	/S-8,2-2	-0.3
Total	14	1574	6111	730	1575	191	69	13	446	285	222	.258	.295	.318	74	-212	156	36		.932	-34	*S-1054,2-288,3/10	-18.5

■ KARL OLSON

Olson, Karl Arthur "Ole" b: 7/6/30, Kentfield, Cal. BR/TR, 6'3", 205 lbs. Deb: 6/30/51

YEAR	TM/L	G	AB	R	H	2B	3B	HR	RBI	BB	SO	AVG	OBP	SLG	PRO+	BR/A	SB	CS	SBR	FA	FR	G/POS	TPR
1951	Bos-A	5	10	0	1	0	0	0	0	0	3	.100	.100	.100	-42	-2	0	0	0	1.000	-1	/O-5	-0.3
1953	Bos-A	25	57	5	7	2	0	1	6	1	9	.123	.138	.211	-7	-9	0	0	0	.970	-4	O-24	-1.3
1954	Bos-A	101	227	25	59	12	2	1	20	12	23	.260	.297	.344	68	-10	2	1	0	.957	-8	O-78	-2.1
1955	Bos-A	26	48	7	12	1	2	0	1	1	10	.250	.265	.354	60	-3	0	0	0	1.000	-5	O-21	-0.8
1956	Was-A	106	313	34	77	10	2	4	22	28	41	.246	.310	.329	69	-14	1	1	-0	.990	-10	*O-101	-2.8
1957	Was-A	8	12	2	2	0	0	0	0	1	2	.167	.231	.167	10	-1	0	0	0	1.000	-1	/O-6	-0.3
	Det-A	8	14	1	2	0	0	0	1	0	6	.143	.143	.143	-21	-2	0	0	0	1.000	-1	/O-5	-0.4
	Yr	16	26	3	4	0	0	0	1	1	8	.154	.185	.154	-6	-4	0	0	0	1.000	-2	O-11	-0.7
Total	6	279	681	74	160	25	6	6	50	43	94	.235	.281	.316	57	-42	3	2	-0	.979	-28	O-240	-8.0

■ MARV OLSON

Olson, Marvin Clement "Sparky" b: 5/28/07, Gayville, S.Dak. d: 2/5/98, Tyndall, S.Dak. BR/TR, 5'7", 160 lbs. Deb: 9/13/31

YEAR	TM/L	G	AB	R	H	2B	3B	HR	RBI	BB	SO	AVG	OBP	SLG	PRO+	BR/A	SB	CS	SBR	FA	FR	G/POS	TPR
1931	Bos-A	15	53	8	10	1	0	0	5	9	3	.189	.306	.208	40	-4	0	0	0	.963	3	2-15	0.0
1932	Bos-A	115	403	58	100	14	6	0	25	61	26	.248	.347	.313	74	-14	1	5	-3	.955	-15	*2-106/3-1	-2.4
1933	Bos-A	3	1	1	0	0	0	0	0	0	1	.000	.000	.000	-99	-0	0	0	0	.000	0	/2-1	0.0
Total	3	133	457	67	110	15	6	0	30	70	30	.241	.342	.300	70	-18	1	5	-3	.956	-12	2-122/3-1	-2.4

■ TOM O'MALLEY

O'Malley, Thomas Patrick b: 12/25/60, Orange, N.J. BL/TR, 6', 190 lbs. Deb: 5/8/82

YEAR	TM/L	G	AB	R	H	2B	3B	HR	RBI	BB	SO	AVG	OBP	SLG	PRO+	BR/A	SB	CS	SBR	FA	FR	G/POS	TPR
1982	SF-N	92	291	26	80	12	4	2	27	33	39	.275	.351	.364	100	1	0	3	-2	.965	0	3-83/2-1,S-1	-0.3
1983	SF-N	135	410	40	106	16	1	5	45	52	47	.259	.348	.339	94	-2	2	4	-2	.940	1	*3-117	-0.5
1984	SF-N	13	25	2	3	0	0	0	0	2	2	.120	.185	.120	-13	-4	0	0	0	1.000	-0	/3-7	-0.5
	Chi-A	12	16	0	2	0	0	0	3	0	5	.125	.125	.125	-29	-3	0	0	0	1.000	-2	/3-6	-0.5
1985	Bal-A	8	14	1	1	0	0	1	2	0	2	.071	.071	.286	-8	-2	0	0	0	.833	-1	/3-3	-0.3
1986	Bal-A	56	181	19	46	9	0	1	18	17	21	.254	.318	.320	76	-6	0	1	-1	.938	-1	3-55	-0.9
1987	Tex-A	45	117	10	32	8	0	1	12	15	9	.274	.356	.368	92	-1	0	0	0	.962	-4	3-40/2-1	-0.6
1988	Mon-N	14	27	3	7	0	0	0	2	3	4	.259	.333	.259	69	-1	0	0	0	.905	1	/3-7	0.0
1989	NY-N	9	11	2	6	2	0	0	8	0	2	.545	.545	.727	274	2	0	0	0	1.000	-0	/3-3	0.2
1990	NY-N	82	121	14	27	7	0	3	14	11	20	.223	.288	.355	76	-4	0	0	0	.983	2	3-38/1-3	-0.2
Total	9	466	1213	117	310	54	5	13	131	133	151	.256	.332	.340	87	-19	2	8	-4	.951	-5	3-359/1-3,2-2,S-1	-3.6

■ OLLIE O'MARA

O'Mara, Oliver Edward b: 3/8/1891, St.Louis, Mo. d: 10/24/89, Reno, Nev. BR/TR, 5'9", 155 lbs. Deb: 9/8/12

YEAR	TM/L	G	AB	R	H	2B	3B	HR	RBI	BB	SO	AVG	OBP	SLG	PRO+	BR/A	SB	CS	SBR	FA	FR	G/POS	TPR
1912	Det-A	1	4	0	0	0	0	0	0	0		.000	.000	.000	-99	-1	0			.857	0	/S-1	-0.1
1914	Bro-N	67	247	41	65	10	2	1	7	16	26	.263	.316	.332	91	-3	14			.918	-12	S-63	-1.1
1915	Bro-N	149	577	77	141	26	3	0	31	51	40	.244	.308	.300	83	-11	11	12	-4	.906	-34	*S-149	-4.2
1916	*Bro-N	72	193	18	39	5	2	0	15	12	20	.202	.249	.249	52	-11	10			.898	-5	S-51	-1.5
1918	Bro-N	121	450	29	96	8	1	1	24	7	18	.213	.242	.242	48	-28	11			.951	-2	*3-121	-3.1
1919	Bro-N	2	7	1	0	0	0	0	0	0	0	.000	.000	.000	-98	-2	0			.875	-0	/3-2	-0.2
Total	6	412	1478	166	341	49	8	2	77	86	104	.231	.280	.279	69	-56	46	12		.907	-53	S-264,3-123	-10.2

■ TOM O'MEARA

O'Meara, Thomas Edward b: 12/12/1872, Chicago, Ill. d: 2/16/02, Fort Wayne, Ind. Deb: 9/29/1895

YEAR	TM/L	G	AB	R	H	2B	3B	HR	RBI	BB	SO	AVG	OBP	SLG	PRO+	BR/A	SB	CS	SBR	FA	FR	G/POS	TPR
1895	Cle-N	1	1	1	0	0	0	0	0	1	0	.000	.500	.000	34	-0	0			.500	-0	/C-1	0.0
1896	Cle-N	12	33	5	5	0	0	0	0	5	7	.152	.263	.152	10	-4	0			.914	-1	/C-9,1-1	-0.4
Total	2	13	34	6	5	0	0	0	0	6	7	.147	.275	.147	12	-4	0			.892	-1	/C-10,1-1	-0.4

■ O'NEAL

O'Neal Deb: 10/23/1874

YEAR	TM/L	G	AB	R	H	2B	3B	HR	RBI	BB	SO	AVG	OBP	SLG	PRO+	BR/A	SB	CS	SBR	FA	FR	G/POS	TPR
1874	Har-n	1	3	0	0	0	0	0	0	0	1	.000	.000	.000	-95	-1	0	0	0	.667	1	/O-1	0.0

■ DENNY O'NEIL

O'Neil, Dennis b: 11/22/1866, Holyoke, Mass. d: 11/15/22, Rushville, Ind. BL/TL, 6'2.5", 200 lbs. Deb: 6/18/1893

YEAR	TM/L	G	AB	R	H	2B	3B	HR	RBI	BB	SO	AVG	OBP	SLG	PRO+	BR/A	SB	CS	SBR	FA	FR	G/POS	TPR
1893	StL-N	7	25	3	3	0	0	0	2	4	0	.120	.241	.120	-3	-4	3			.986	-1	/1-7	-0.4

■ MICKEY O'NEIL

O'Neil, George Michael b: 4/12/1900, St.Louis, Mo. d: 4/8/64, St.Louis, Mo. BR/TR, 5'10", 185 lbs. Deb: 9/12/19 C

YEAR	TM/L	G	AB	R	H	2B	3B	HR	RBI	BB	SO	AVG	OBP	SLG	PRO+	BR/A	SB	CS	SBR	FA	FR	G/POS	TPR
1919	Bos-N	11	28	3	6	0	0	0	1	1	7	.214	.241	.214	39	-2	0			.981	3	C-11	0.2
1920	Bos-N	112	304	19	86	5	4	0	28	21	20	.283	.339	.326	96	-1	4	4	-1	.962	8	*C-105/2-1	1.3
1921	Bos-N	98	277	26	69	9	4	2	29	23	21	.249	.307	.332	73	-11	2	2	-1	.968	8	C-95	0.1
1922	Bos-N	83	251	18	56	5	2	0	26	14	11	.223	.267	.259	38	-23	1	0	0	.978	0	C-79	-1.8
1923	Bos-N	96	306	29	65	7	4	0	20	17	14	.212	.258	.261	39	-27	3	2	-0	.973	14	C-95	-0.9
1924	Bos-N	106	362	32	89	4	1	0	22	14	27	.246	.276	.262	47	-27	4	3	-1	.985	1	*C-106	-2.0
1925	Bos-N	70	222	29	57	6	5	2	30	21	16	.257	.327	.356	81	-6	1	2	-1	.972	-8	C-69	-1.1
1926	Bro-N	75	201	19	42	5	3	0	20	23	8	.209	.293	.264	52	-13	3			.965	-3	C-74	-1.2
1927	Was-A	5	6	0	0	0	0	0	0	0	1	.000	.000	.000	-99	-2	0	0	0	1.000	-0	/C-4	-0.2
	NY-N	16	38	2	5	0	0	0	3	5	2	.132	.233	.132	-0	-5	0			.969	3	C-16	-0.1
Total	9	672	1995	177	475	41	23	4	179	139	127	.238	.292	.288	58	-118	18	13		.972	26	C-654/2-1	-5.7

■ JOHN O'NEIL

O'Neil, John Francis b: 4/19/20, Shelbiana, Ky. BR/TR, 5'9", 155 lbs. Deb: 4/16/46

YEAR	TM/L	G	AB	R	H	2B	3B	HR	RBI	BB	SO	AVG	OBP	SLG	PRO+	BR/A	SB	CS	SBR	FA	FR	G/POS	TPR
1946	Phi-N	46	94	12	25	3	0	0	9	5	12	.266	.303	.298	73	-3	0			.940	4	S-32	0.2

■ FRED O'NEILL

O'Neill, Frederick James "Tip" b: 1865, London, Ontario, Canada d: 3/7/1892, London, Ont., Can. 5'7", 142 lbs. Deb: 5/3/1887

YEAR	TM/L	G	AB	R	H	2B	3B	HR	RBI	BB	SO	AVG	OBP	SLG	PRO+	BR/A	SB	CS	SBR	FA	FR	G/POS	TPR
1887	NY-a	6	26	4	8	1	1	0	3	1		.308	.357	.423	122	1	3			.800	-1	/O-6	-0.1

■ HARRY O'NEILL

O'Neill, Harry Mink b: 5/8/17, Philadelphia, Pa. d: 3/6/45, Iwo Jima, Marianas Islands BR/TR, 6'3", 205 lbs. Deb: 7/23/39

YEAR	TM/L	G	AB	R	H	2B	3B	HR	RBI	BB	SO	AVG	OBP	SLG	PRO+	BR/A	SB	CS	SBR	FA	FR	G/POS	TPR
1939	Phi-A	1	0	0	0	0	0	0	0	0	0	—	—	—	—	0	0	0	0	.000	0	/C-1	0.0

■ TIP O'NEILL

O'Neill, James Edward b: 5/25/1858, Woodstock, Ont., Canada d: 12/31/15, Montreal, Que., Can. BR/TR, 6'1.5", 167 lbs. Deb: 5/5/1883

YEAR	TM/L	G	AB	R	H	2B	3B	HR	RBI	BB	SO	AVG	OBP	SLG	PRO+	BR/A	SB	CS	SBR	FA	FR	G/POS	TPR
1883	NY-N	23	76	8	15	3	0	0	5	3	15	.197	.228	.237	42	-5				.917	-2	P-19/O-7	-0.2
1884	StL-a	78	297	49	82	13	11	3	54	12		.276	.309	.424	132	9				.811	-6	O-64,P-17/1-1	0.0
1885	*StL-a	52	206	44	72	7	4	3	38	13		.350	.399	.466	165	15				.881	-1	O-52	1.1
1886	*StL-a	138	579	106	190	28	14	3	**107**	47		.328	.385	.440	151	32	9			.927	8	*O-138	3.2
1887	*StL-a	124	517	**167**	**225**	**52**	**19**	**14**	**123**	50		**.435**	**.490**	**.691**	**205**	**68**	30			.895	-6	*O-124	**4.7**
1888	*StL-a	130	529	96	**177**	24	10	5	98	44		**.335**	.390	.446	151	27	26			.937	-1	*O-130	2.1
1889	StL-a	134	534	123	179	33	8	9	110	72	37	.335	.419	.478	137	23	28			.936	-2	*O-134	1.5
1890	Chi-P	137	577	112	174	20	16	3	75	65	36	.302	.377	.407	105	3	29			.926	-12	*O-137	-1.1
1891	StL-a	129	521	112	167	28	4	10	95	62	33	.321	.402	.447	124	12	25			.935	-13	*O-129	-0.4
1892	Cin-N	109	419	63	105	14	6	2	52	53	25	.251	.339	.327	103	3	14			.922	-3	*O-109	-0.5
Total	10	1054	4255	880	1386	222	92	52	757	421	146	.326	.392	.458	140	188	161			.917	-38	*O-1024/P-36,1-1	10.4

YEAR	TM/L	G	AB	R	H	2B	3B	HR	RBI	BB	SO	AVG	OBP	SLG	PRO+	BR/A	SB	CS	SBR	FA	FR	G/POS	TPR
■ **JIM O'NEILL**	O'Neill, James Leo b: 2/23/1893, Minooka, Pa. d: 9/5/76, Chambersburg, Pa. BR/TR, 5'10.5", 165 lbs. Deb: 4/15/20 F																						
1920	Was-A	86	294	27	85	17	7	1	40	13	30	.289	.324	.405	95	-3	7	3	0	.943	-5	S-80/2-2	-0.2
1923	Was-A	23	33	6	9	1	0	0	3	1	3	.273	.294	.303	60	-2	0	0	0	.946	3	/2-8,3-4,S-1,O-1	0.1
Total	2	109	327	33	94	18	7	1	43	14	33	.287	.321	.394	91	-5	7	3	0	.943	-3	/S-81,2-10,3-4,O-1	-0.1
■ **JOHN O'NEILL**	O'Neill, John J. b: New York, N.Y. TR , Deb: 9/6/1899																						
1899	NY-N	2	7	0	0	0	0	0	0	0		.000	.000	.000	-99	-2	0			.929	1	/C-2	-0.1
1902	NY-N	2	8	0	0	0	0	0	0	0		.000	.000	.000	-99	-2	0			.933	1	/C-2	-0.1
Total	2	4	15	0	0	0	0	0	0	0		.000	.000	.000	-99	-4	0			.931	2	/C-4	-0.2
■ **JACK O'NEILL**	O'Neill, John Joseph b: 1/10/1873, Maam, Ireland d: 6/29/35, Minooka, Pa. BR/TR, 5'10", 165 lbs. Deb: 4/21/02 F																						
1902	StL-N	63	192	13	27	1	1	0	12	13		.141	.214	.156	15	-19	2			.973	1	C-59	-1.3
1903	StL-N	75	246	23	58	9	1	0	27	13		.236	.288	.280	64	-11	11			.972	16	C-74	1.1
1904	Chi-N	51	168	8	36	5	0	1	19	6		.214	.258	.262	61	-8	1			.981	5	C-49	0.2
1905	Chi-N	53	172	16	34	4	2	0	12	8		.198	.277	.244	54	-10	6			.974	7	C-50	0.3
1906	Bos-N	61	167	14	30	5	1	0	4	12		.180	.243	.222	46	-10	0			.971	12	C-48/1-2,O-1	0.6
Total	5	303	945	74	185	24	5	1	74	52		.196	.258	.235	49	-58	20			.974	40	C-280/1-2,O-1	0.9
■ **MIKE O'NEILL**	O'Neill, Michael Joyce (a.k.a. Michael Joyce In 1901) b: 9/7/1877, Maam, Ireland d: 8/12/59, Scranton, Pa. BL/TL, 5'11", 185 lbs. Deb: 9/20/01 F																						
1901	StL-N	6	15	3	6	0	0	0	2	3		.400	.526	.400	179	2	0			.875	-1	/P-5	0.0
1902	StL-N	51	135	21	43	5	3	2	15	2		.319	.333	.444	145	6	0			.920	-0	P-36/O-3	0.0
1903	StL-N	41	110	12	25	2	2	0	6	8		.227	.303	.282	69	-4	3			.882	-1	P-19,O-13	-0.3
1904	StL-N	30	91	9	21	7	2	0	16	5		.231	.286	.352	101	-0	0			.910	1	P-25/O-3	0.0
1907	Cin-N	9	29	5	2	0	2	0	2	2		.069	.129	.207	5	-3	1			.864	-0	/O-9	-0.5
Total	5	137	380	50	97	14	9	2	41	20		.255	.306	.355	102	0	4			.907	-1	/P-85,O-28	-0.8
■ **PAUL O'NEILL**	O'Neill, Paul Andrew b: 2/25/63, Columbus, Ohio BL/TL, 6'4", 215 lbs. Deb: 9/3/85																						
1985	Cin-N	5	12	1	4	1	0	0	1	0	2	.333	.333	.417	103	0	0	0	0	1.000	1	/O-2	0.1
1986	Cin-N	3	2	0	0	0	0	0	0	1	1	.000	.333	.000	-0	-0	0	0	0	.000	0	/H	0.0
1987	Cin-N	84	160	24	41	14	1	7	28	18	29	.256	.331	.488	109	2	2	1	0	.949	-3	O-42/1-2,P-1	-0.3
1988	Cin-N	145	485	58	122	25	3	16	73	38	65	.252	.309	.414	102	0	8	6	-1	.984	1	*O-118,1-21	-0.6
1989	Cin-N	117	428	49	118	24	2	15	74	46	64	.276	.349	.446	122	12	20	5	3	.983	4	*O-115	1.7
1990	*Cin-N	145	503	59	136	28	0	16	78	53	103	.270	.342	.421	104	3	13	11	-3	.993	6	*O-141	0.4
1991	Cin-N★	152	532	71	136	36	0	28	91	73	107	.256	.347	.481	126	18	12	7	-1	.994	13	*O-150	2.8
1992	Cin-N	148	496	59	122	19	1	14	66	77	85	.246	.350	.373	102	3	6	3	0	**.997**	15	*O-143	1.7
1993	NY-A	141	498	71	155	34	1	20	75	44	69	.311	.369	.504	137	25	2	4	-2	.992	-11	*O-138/D-2	0.8
1994	NY-A★	103	368	68	132	25	1	21	83	72	56	**.359**	.464	.603	179	47	5	4	-1	.995	2	O-99/D-4	4.1
1995	*NY-A★	127	460	82	138	30	4	22	96	71	76	.300	.395	.526	138	27	1	2	-1	.987	-4	*O-121/D-4	1.7
1996	*NY-A	150	546	89	165	35	1	19	91	102	76	.302	.416	.474	124	24	0	1	-1	**1.000**	8	*O-146/1-1,D-3	2.6
1997	*NY-A★	149	553	89	179	42	0	21	117	75	92	.324	.404	.514	139	33	10	7	-1	.984	5	*O-146/1-2,D-2	3.1
1998	*NY-A★	152	602	95	191	40	2	24	116	57	103	.317	.378	.510	131	27	15	1	4	.987	6	*O-150/D-1	3.1
Total	14	1621	5645	815	1639	353	16	223	989	727	928	.290	.373	.477	126	220	94	52	-3	.990	41	*O-1511/1-26,D-16,P	21.2
■ **PEACHES O'NEILL**	O'Neill, Philip Bernard b: 8/30/1879, Anderson, Ind. d: 8/2/55, Anderson, Ind. BR/TR, 5'11", 165 lbs. Deb: 4/16/04																						
1904	Cin-N	8	15	0	4	0	0	0	1	1		.267	.313	.267	73	-0	0			.900	-3	/C-5,1-1	-0.4
■ **STEVE O'NEILL**	O'Neill, Stephen Francis b: 7/6/1891, Minooka, Pa. d: 1/26/62, Cleveland, Ohio BR/TR, 5'10", 165 lbs. Deb: 9/18/11 FMC																						
1911	Cle-A	9	27	1	4	1	0	0	1	4		.148	.281	.185	31	-2	2			.986	4	/C-9	0.2
1912	Cle-A	69	215	17	49	4	0	0	14	12		.228	.272	.247	47	-15	2			.961	9	C-68	0.1
1913	Cle-A	80	234	19	69	13	3	0	29	10	24	.295	.329	.376	103	0	5			.973	3	C-80	1.1
1914	Cle-A	87	269	28	68	12	2	0	20	15	35	.253	.292	.312	79	-8	1	3	-2	.956	0	C-82/1-1	-0.2
1915	Cle-A	121	386	32	91	14	2	2	34	26	41	.236	.293	.298	75	-13	2	3	-1	.968	5	*C-115	0.1
1916	Cle-A	130	378	30	89	23	0	0	29	24	33	.235	.288	.296	71	-14	2			.971	5	*C-128	0.0
1917	Cle-A	129	370	21	68	10	2	0	29	41	55	.184	.272	.222	47	-23	2			.980	1	*C-127	-1.3
1918	Cle-A	114	359	34	87	8	7	1	35	48	22	.242	.343	.312	89	-4	5			**.983**	1	*C-113	0.8
1919	Cle-A	125	398	46	115	35	7	2	47	48	21	.289	.373	.427	117	9	4			.977	-7	*C-123	1.3
1920	*Cle-A	149	489	63	157	39	5	3	55	69	39	.321	.408	.440	121	17	3	5	-2	.976	-5	*C-148	2.0
1921	Cle-A	106	335	39	108	22	1	1	50	57	22	.322	.424	.403	110	8	0	1	-1	.982	3	*C-105	1.6
1922	Cle-A	133	392	33	122	27	4	2	65	73	25	.311	.423	.416	118	15	2	2	-1	.974	-14	*C-130	0.6
1923	Cle-A	113	330	31	82	12	0	0	50	64	34	.248	.374	.285	75	-9	0	4	-2	.968	-12	*C-111	-1.7
1924	Bos-A	106	307	29	73	15	1	0	38	63	23	.238	.371	.293	73	-10	0	2	-1	.970	0	C-92	-0.5
1925	NY-A	35	91	7	26	5	0	1	13	10	3	.286	.363	.374	89	-1	0	0	0	.946	3	C-31	0.3
1927	StL-A	74	191	14	44	7	0	1	22	20	6	.230	.303	.283	51	-14	0	3	-2	.983	1	C-60	-1.0
1928	StL-A	10	24	4	7	1	0	0	6	8	0	.292	.485	.333	115	1	0	0	0	.958	-4	C-10	-0.2
Total	17	1590	4795	448	1259	248	34	13	537	592	383	.263	.349	.337	88	-61	30	23		.972	-6	*C-1532/1-1	3.2
■ **BILL O'NEILL**	O'Neill, William John b: 1/22/1880, St.John, N.B., Can. d: 7/20/20, Woodhaven, N.Y. BB/TR, 5'11", 175 lbs. Deb: 5/7/04																						
1904	Bos-A	17	51	7	10	1	0	0	5	2		.196	.226	.216	38	-4	0			.933	-2	/O-9,S-2	-0.7
	Was-A	95	365	33	89	10	1	1	16	22		.244	.294	.285	85	-6	22			.893	-12	O-93/2-3	-2.6
	Yr	112	416	40	99	11	1	1	21	24		.238	.286	.276	79	-10	22			.896	-14	*O-102/2-3,S-2	-3.3
1906	*Chi-A	94	330	37	82	4	1	1	21	22		.248	.301	.276	83	-6	19			.949	-6	O-93	-1.8
Total	2	206	746	77	181	15	2	2	42	46		.243	.293	.276	81	-15	41			.919	-20	O-195/2-3,S-2	-5.1
■ **RALPH ONIS**	Onis, Manuel Dominguez "Curly" b: 10/24/08, Tampa, Fla. d: 1/4/95, Tampa, Fla. BR/TR, 5'9", 180 lbs. Deb: 4/27/35																						
1935	Bro-N	1	1	0	1	0	0	0	0	0	0	1.000	1.000	1.000	449	0	0			.500	-0	/C-1	0.0
■ **EDDIE ONSLOW**	Onslow, Edward Joseph b: 2/17/1893, Meadville, Pa. d: 5/8/81, Dennison, Ohio BL/TL, 6', 170 lbs. Deb: 8/7/12 F																						
1912	Det-A	36	128	11	29	1	2	1	13	3		.227	.250	.289	56	-8	3			.972	-3	1-35	-1.2
1913	Det-A	17	55	7	14	1	0	0	8	5	9	.255	.328	.273	77	-1	1			.990	-1	1-17	-0.3
1918	Cle-A	2	6	0	1	0	0	0	0	0	1	.167	.167	.167	1	-1	0			.000	-1	/O-1	-0.2
1927	Was-A	9	18	1	4	1	0	0	1	1	0	.222	.263	.278	41	-2	0	0	0	1.000	0	/1-5	-0.2
Total	4	64	207	19	48	3	2	1	22	9	10	.232	.271	.280	59	-12	4	0		.979	-5	/1-57,O-1	-1.9
■ **JACK ONSLOW**	Onslow, John James b: 10/13/1888, Scottdale, Pa. d: 12/22/60, Concord, Mass. BR/TR, 5'11", 180 lbs. Deb: 5/2/12 FMC																						
1912	Det-A	36	69	7	11	1	0	0	4	10		.159	.284	.174	33	-6	1			.948	1	C-35/O-1	-0.2
1917	NY-N	9	8	1	2	1	0	0	0	0	1	.250	.333	.375	121	0	0			.929	-0	/C-9	0.0
Total	2	45	77	8	13	2	0	0	4	10	1	.169	.289	.195	41	-5	1			.947	0	/C-44,O-1	-0.2
■ **STEVE ONTIVEROS**	Ontiveros, Steven Robert b: 10/26/51, Bakersfield, Cal. BB/TR, 6', 185 lbs. Deb: 8/5/73																						
1973	SF-N	24	33	3	8	0	0	1	5	4	7	.242	.324	.333	79	-1	0	0	0	1.000	1	/1-5,O-1	0.0
1974	SF-N	120	343	45	91	15	1	4	33	57	41	.265	.375	.350	99	2	0	0	0	.929	-6	3-75,1-19/O-2	-0.6
1975	SF-N	108	325	21	94	16	0	3	31	55	44	.289	.395	.366	108	6	2	0	1	.923	-2	3-89/O-8,1-4	0.5
1976	SF-N	59	74	8	13	3	0	0	5	6	11	.176	.247	.216	31	-7	0	0	0	1.000	-5	/3-7,O-7,1-4	-1.3
1977	Chi-N	156	546	54	163	32	3	10	68	81	69	.299	.392	.423	107	7	3	3	-1	.955	-2	*3-155	0.3
1978	Chi-N	82	276	34	67	14	4	1	22	34	33	.243	.326	.333	75	-9	0	2	-1	.965	10	3-77/1-1	-0.1
1979	Chi-N	152	519	58	148	28	2	4	57	58	68	.285	.365	.370	92	-4	0	1	-1	.941	-4	*3-142/1-1	-1.1
1980	Chi-N	31	77	7	16	3	0	1	3	14	17	.208	.330	.286	68	-3	0	0	0	.929	-1	3-24	-0.4
Total	8	732	2193	230	600	111	10	24	224	309	290	.274	.367	.366	94	-8	5	6	-2	.944	-9	3-569/1-34,O-18	-2.7
■ **JOSE OQUENDO**	Oquendo, Jose Manuel (Contreras) b: 7/4/63, Rio Piedras, P.R. BB/TR, 5'10", 160 lbs. Deb: 5/2/83																						
1983	NY-N	120	328	29	70	7	0	1	17	19	60	.213	.261	.244	41	-26	8	9	-3	.960	6	*S-116	-1.4

YEAR	TM/L	G	AB	R	H	2B	3B	HR	RBI	BB	SO	AVG	OBP	SLG	PRO+	BR/A	SB	CS	SBR	FA	FR	G/POS	TPR
1984	NY-N	81	189	23	42	5	0	0	10	15	26	.222	.286	.249	52	-12	10	1	2	.972	2	S-67	-0.3
1986	StL-N	76	138	20	41	4	1	0	13	15	20	.297	.366	.341	97	-0	2	3	-1	.956	-6	S-29,2-21/3-1,O-1	-0.5
1987	*StL-N	116	248	43	71	9	0	1	24	54	29	.286	.414	.335	99	3	4	4	-1	1.000	3	O-46,2-32,S/31P	0.5
1988	StL-N	148	451	36	125	10	1	7	46	52	40	.277	.352	.350	101	2	4	6	-2	.997	8	2-69,3-47,S1O/PC	1.1
1989	StL-N	163	556	59	162	28	7	1	48	79	59	.291	.380	.372	112	12	3	5	-2	**.994**	20	*2-156/S-7,1-1	3.8
1990	StL-N	156	469	38	118	17	5	1	37	74	46	.252	.354	.316	85	-7	1	1	-0	**.996**	-1	*2-150/S-4	-0.5
1991	StL-N	127	366	37	88	11	4	1	26	67	48	.240	.359	.301	87	-3	1	2	-1	.988	15	*2-118,S-22/1-3,P-1	1.5
1992	StL-N	14	35	3	9	3	1	0	3	5	3	.257	.350	.400	115	1	0	0	0	1.000	0	/2-9,S-5	0.1
1993	StL-N	46	73	7	15	0	0	0	4	12	8	.205	.318	.205	44	-5	0	0	0	.988	14	S-22,2-16	1.0
1994	StL-N	55	129	13	34	2	2	0	9	21	16	.264	.367	.310	80	-3	1	1	-0	.945	-5	S-28,2-16	-0.6
1995	StL-N	88	220	31	46	8	3	2	17	35	21	.209	.318	.300	64	-11	1	1	-0	.981	6	2-62,S-24/3-2,O-1	-0.1
Total	12	1190	3202	339	821	104	24	14	254	448	376	.256	.349	.317	85	-49	35	33	-9	.992	63	2-649,S-364/O31PC	4.6
■ TOM ORAN	Oran, Thomas b: 1845, d: 9/22/1886, St.Louis, Mo. Deb: 5/4/1875																						
1875	RS-n	19	81	7	15	3	1	0	10	1	1	.185	.195	.247	58	-3	3	2	-0	.633	-4	O-19/S-1	-0.6
■ ERNIE ORAVETZ	Oravetz, Ernest Eugene b: 1/24/32, Johnstown, Pa. BB/TL, 5'4", 145 lbs. Deb: 4/11/55																						
1955	Was-A	100	263	24	71	5	1	0	25	26	19	.270	.338	.297	76	-8	1	2	-1	.967	-3	O-57	-1.5
1956	Was-A	88	137	20	34	3	2	0	11	27	20	.248	.372	.299	79	-3	1	0	0	.946	-2	O-31	-0.6
Total	2	188	400	44	105	8	3	0	36	53	39	.262	.350	.298	77	-11	2	2	-1	.961	-5	/O-88	-2.1
■ LUIS ORDAZ	Ordaz, Luis Javier b: 8/12/75, Maracaibo, Venez. BR/TR, 5'11", 170 lbs. Deb: 9/3/97																						
1997	StL-N	12	22	3	6	1	0	0	1	1	2	.273	.304	.318	64	-1	3	0	1	.964	1	S-11	0.1
1998	StL-N	57	153	9	31	5	0	0	8	12	18	.203	.261	.235	31	-16	2	0	1	.945	13	S-54/3-2,2-1	0.3
Total	2	69	175	12	37	6	0	0	9	13	20	.211	.266	.246	35	-17	5	0	2	.947	15	/S-65,3-2,2-1	0.4
■ TONY ORDENANA	Ordenana, Antonio (Rodriguez) "Mosquito" b: 10/30/18, Guanabacoa, Havana, Cuba d: 9/29/88, Miami, Fla. BR/TR, 5'9", 158 lbs. Deb: 10/3/43																						
1943	Pit-N	1	4	0	2	0	0	0	3	0	0	.500	.500	.500	183	0	0			1.000	1	/S-1	0.1
■ MAGGLIO ORDONEZ	Ordonez, Maggio (Delgado) b: 1/28/74, Caracas, Venez. BR/TR, 5'11", 170 lbs. Deb: 8/29/97																						
1997	Chi-A	21	69	12	22	6	0	4	11	2	8	.319	.338	.580	139	3	1	2	-1	1.000	2	O-19	0.4
1998	Chi-A	145	535	70	151	25	2	14	65	28	53	.282	.329	.415	94	-5	9	7	-2	.985	3	*O-145	-0.7
Total	2	166	604	82	173	31	2	18	76	30	61	.286	.330	.434	99	-2	10	9	-2	.987	4	O-164	-0.3
■ REY ORDONEZ	Ordonez, Reynaldo b: 1/11/71, Havana, Cuba BR/TR, 5'9", 160 lbs. Deb: 4/1/96																						
1996	NY-N	151	502	51	129	12	4	1	30	22	53	.257	.290	.303	59	-30	1	3	-2	.962	2	*S-150	-1.6
1997	NY-N	120	356	35	77	5	3	1	33	18	36	.216	.256	.256	36	-34	11	5	0	**.983**	16	*S-118	-0.8
1998	NY-N	153	505	46	124	20	2	1	42	23	60	.246	.280	.299	51	-36	3	6	-3	.975	11	*S-151	-1.3
Total	3	424	1363	132	330	37	9	3	105	63	149	.242	.277	.289	50	-100	15	14	-4	.972	29	S-419	-3.7
■ JOE ORENGO	Orengo, Joseph Charles b: 11/29/14, San Francisco, Cal d: 7/24/88, San Francisco, Cal. BR/TR, 6', 185 lbs. Deb: 4/18/39																						
1939	StL-N	7	3	0	0	0	0	0	0	0	1	.000	.000	.000	-94	-1	0			.667	-0	/S-7	-0.1
1940	StL-N	129	415	58	119	23	4	7	56	65	90	.287	.383	.412	113	9	9			.952	5	2-77,3-34,S-19	2.1
1941	NY-N	77	252	23	54	11	2	4	25	28	49	.214	.298	.321	73	-9	1			.958	18	3-59/S-9,2-6	1.2
1943	NY-N	83	266	28	58	8	2	6	29	36	46	.218	.311	.331	85	-5	1			.992	4	1-82	-0.5
	Bro-N	7	15	1	3	2	0	0	1	4	2	.200	.368	.333	103	0	0			1.000	-0	/3-6	0.0
	Yr	90	281	29	61	10	2	6	30	40	48	.217	.315	.331	86	-5	1			.992	4	1-82/3-6	-0.5
1944	Det-A	46	154	14	31	10	0	0	10	20	29	.201	.297	.266	58	-8	1	1	-0	.903	6	S-29,3-11/1-5,2-2	0.0
1945	Chi-A	17	15	5	1	0	0	0	1	3	2	.067	.222	.067	-15	-2	0	0	0	.923	1	/3-7,2-1	-0.1
Total	6	366	1120	129	266	54	8	17	122	156	219	.237	.332	.346	88	-16	12	1		.957	34	3-117/1-87,2-86,S	2.6
■ KEVIN ORIE	Orie, Kevin Leonard b: 9/1/72, West Chester, Pa. BR/TR, 6'4", 210 lbs. Deb: 4/1/97																						
1997	Chi-N	114	364	40	100	23	5	8	44	39	57	.275	.353	.431	102	1	2	2	-1	.971	11	*3-112/S-3	1.2
1998	Chi-N	64	204	24	37	14	0	2	21	18	35	.181	.258	.279	38	-19	1	1	-0	.966	-1	3-57	-1.9
	Fla-N	48	175	23	46	8	1	6	17	14	24	.263	.335	.423	99	-0	1	0	0	.939	6	3-48	0.7
	Yr	112	379	47	83	22	1	8	38	32	59	.219	.294	.346	65	-20	2	1	0	.952	6	*3-105	-1.2
Total	2	226	743	87	183	45	6	16	82	71	116	.246	.323	.388	83	-18	4	3	-1	.961	17	3-217/S-3	0.0
■ GEORGE ORME	Orme, George William b: 9/16/1891, Lebanon, Ind. d: 3/16/62, Indianapolis, Ind. BR/TR, 5'10", 160 lbs. Deb: 9/14/20																						
1920	Bos-A	4	6	4	2	0	0	0	1	3	0	.333	.556	.333	146	1	0	0	0	1.000	0	/O-3	0.1
■ JESS ORNDORFF	Orndorff, Jesse Walworth Thayer b: 1/15/1881, Chicago, Ill. d: 9/28/60, Cardiff-By-The- Sea, Cal. BB/TR, 6', 168 lbs. Deb: 4/18/07																						
1907	Bos-N	5	17	0	2	0	0	0	0	0		.118	.118	.118	-26	-2	0			.900	-2	/C-5	-0.5
■ FRANK O'ROURKE	O'Rourke, James Francis "Blackie" b: 11/28/1894, Hamilton, Ont., Can d: 5/14/86, Chatham, N.J. BR/TR, 5'10.5", 165 lbs. Deb: 6/12/12																						
1912	Bos-N	61	196	11	24	3	1	0	16	11	50	.122	.177	.148	-10	-30	1			.915	-7	S-59/3-1	-3.3
1917	Bro-N	64	198	18	47	7	1	0	15	14	25	.237	.294	.283	75	-6	11			.954	7	3-58	0.3
1918	Bro-N	4	12	0	2	0	0	0	2	1	3	.167	.231	.167	22	-1	0			.857	1	/2-2,O-1	0.0
1920	Was-A	14	54	8	16	1	0	0	5	2	5	.296	.321	.315	71	-2	2	1	0	.952	4	S-13/3-1	0.3
1921	Was-A	123	444	51	104	17	8	3	54	26	56	.234	.287	.329	60	-29	6	7	-2	.922	-7	*S-122	-2.5
1922	Bos-A	67	216	28	57	14	3	1	17	20	28	.264	.335	.370	84	-5	6	6	-2	.909	-12	S-49,3-20	-1.2
1924	Det-A	47	181	28	50	11	2	0	19	12	19	.276	.332	.359	79	-6	7	4	-0	.970	11	2-40/S-7	0.6
1925	Det-A	124	482	88	141	40	7	5	57	32	37	.293	.350	.436	100	-2	5	8	-3	**.971**	15	*2-118/3-6	1.1
1926	Det-A	111	363	43	88	16	1	1	41	35	33	.242	.321	.300	62	-20	8	6	-1	.936	10	3-60,2-41,S-10	-0.6
1927	StL-A	140	538	85	144	25	3	1	39	64	43	.268	.358	.331	77	-16	18	8	1	.955	11	*3-121,2-16/1-3	0.2
1928	StL-A	99	391	54	103	24	3	1	62	21	19	.263	.303	.348	68	-18	10	2	2	.954	-9	3-96/S-2	-2.0
1929	StL-A	154	585	81	147	23	9	2	62	41	28	.251	.306	.332	62	-34	14	7	0	.943	-18	*3-151/2-3,S-2	-4.3
1930	StL-A	115	400	52	107	15	4	1	41	35	30	.268	.326	.333	65	-21	11	9	-2	.950	10	3-84,S-23/1-3	-0.5
1931	StL-A	8	9	0	2	0	0	0	0	0	1	.222	.222	.222	17	-1	1	1	-0	1.000	1	/S-2,1-1	-0.1
Total	14	1131	4069	547	1032	196	42	15	430	314	377	.254	.315	.333	68	-189	100	59		.949	16	3-598,S-289,2/1O	-12.0
■ JIM O'ROURKE	O'Rourke, James Henry "Orator Jim" b: 9/1/1850, Bridgeport, Conn. d: 1/8/19, Bridgeport, Conn. BR/TR, 5'8", 185 lbs. Deb: 4/26/1872 FMUH																						
1872	Man-n	23	101	25	31	4	1	0	12	2	0	.307	.320	.366	117	3	1	0	0	.729	-2	S-16/C-8,3-2	0.0
1873	Bos-n	57	280	79	98	19	3	1	48	14	1	.350	.381	.450	135	10	4	2	0	.916	1	1-32,O-22/C-9	0.9
1874	Bos-n	70	331	82	104	15	8	**5**	61	4	5	.314	.322	.453	138	12	11	2	2	.943	1	*1-70	1.1
1875	Bos-n	75	358	97	106	13	7	**6**	72	9	6	.296	.313	.422	148	16	17	5	2	.800	-5	O-45,3-27/1-6,C-1	1.2
1876	Bos-N	70	312	61	102	17	3	2	43	15	17	.327	.358	.420	156	18				.856	-3	*O-68/1-2,C-1	1.3
1877	Bos-N	61	265	**68**	96	14	4	0	23	**20**	9	.362	**.407**	.445	162	19				.846	-0	*O-60/1-1	1.4
1878	Bos-N	60	255	44	71	17	7	1	29	5	21	.278	.292	.412	120	4				.860	4	*O-57/1-2,C-2	0.4
1879	Pro-N	81	362	69	126	19	9	1	46	13	10	.348	**.371**	.459	174	28				.785	-9	*O-56,1-20/C-5,3-3	1.5
1880	Bos-N	86	363	71	100	20	11	**6**	45	21	8	.275	.315	.441	158	22				.907	-3	O-37,1-19,S-17,3/C	1.8
1881	Buf-N	83	348	71	105	21	7	0	30	27	18	.302	.352	.402	139	16				.821	-20	*3-56,O-18/C-8,S1M	-0.2
1882	Buf-N	84	370	62	104	15	6	2	37	13	13	.281	.305	.370	114	5				.866	-0	*O-81/S-2,C-2,3M	0.4
1883	Buf-N	94	436	102	143	29	8	1	38	15	13	.328	.350	.438	135	17				.866	-12	O-61,C-33/3-8,SPM	0.6
1884	Buf-N	108	467	119	**162**	33	7	5	63	35	17	**.347**	.392	.480	167	35				.894	-9	*O-86,1-18,C/P3M	2.0
1885	NY-N	112	477	119	143	21	**16**	5	42	40	21	.300	.354	.442	158	31				.940	-16	*O-112/C-8	1.2
1886	NY-N	105	440	106	136	26	6	1	34	39	21	.309	.365	.402	132	17	14			.926	8	O-63,C-47/1-2	2.6
1887	NY-N	103	397	73	113	15	13	3	88	36	11	.285	.352	.411	116	10	46			.890	-9	C-40,3-38,O-28,/2-2	0.4
1888	*NY-N	107	409	50	112	16	6	4	50	24	30	.274	.319	.372	121	10	25			.960	-1	O-87,C-15/1-4,3-2	0.7
1889	*NY-N	128	502	89	161	36	7	3	81	40	34	.321	.372	.438	126	16	33			.893	-8	*O-128/C-1	0.4
1890	NY-P	111	478	112	172	37	5	9	115	33	20	.360	.410	.515	135	20	23			.930	5	*O-111	1.6
1891	NY-N	136	555	92	164	28	7	5	95	26	29	.295	.334	.398	118	10	19			.906	-1	*O-126,C-14	0.6

YEAR	TM/L	G	AB	R	H	2B	3B	HR	RBI	BB	SO	AVG	OBP	SLG	PRO+	BR/A	SB	CS	SBR	FA	FR	G/POS	TPR
1892	NY-N	115	448	62	136	28	5	0	56	30	30	.304	.354	.388	127	14	16			.913	-10	*O-111/C-4,1-1	-0.1
1893	Was-N	129	547	75	157	22	5	2	95	49	26	.287	.354	.356	92	-6	15			.927	5	O-87,1-33/C-9,M	-0.4
1904	NY-N	1	4	1	1	0	0	0	0	0		.250	.250	.250	52	-0	0			.800	-1	/C-1	-0.1
Total	4 n	225	1070	283	339	51	19	12	193	29	12	.317	.335	.434	138	40	33	9	5	.934	-5	1-108/O-67,3-29,CS	3.2
Total	19	1774	7435	1446	2304	414	132	50	1010	481	348	.310	.355	.421	133	286	191			.898	-80	*O-1377,C-209,31/SP2	16.1
■ CHARLIE O'ROURKE	O'Rourke, James Patrick b: 6/22/37, Walla Walla, Wash. BR/TR, 6'2", 195 lbs. Deb: 6/16/59																						
1959	StL-N	2	2	0	0	0	0	0	0	0	0	.000	.000	.000	-94	-1	0	0	0	.000	0	H	-0.1
■ QUEENIE O'ROURKE	O'Rourke, James Stephen b: 12/26/1883, Bridgeport, Conn. d: 12/22/55, Sparrows Point, Md BR/TR, 5'7", 150 lbs. Deb: 8/15/08 F																						
1908	NY-A	34	108	5	25	1	0	0	3	4		.231	.259	.241	62	-5	4			1.000	-6	O-14,S-11/2-4,3-3	-1.3
■ JOHN O'ROURKE	O'Rourke, John b: 8/23/1849, Bridgeport, Conn. d: 6/23/11, Boston, Mass. BL/TL, 6', 190 lbs. Deb: 5/1/1879 F																						
1879	Bos-N	72	317	69	108	17	11	6	**62**	8	32	.341	.357	**.521**	181	26				.882	2	*O-71	2.3
1880	Bos-N	81	313	30	86	22	8	3	36	18	32	.275	.314	.425	153	17				.871	5	*O-81	1.9
1883	NY-a	77	315	49	85	19	5	2		21		.270	.315	.381	118	6				.856	-3	*O-76/1-1	0.1
Total	3	230	945	148	279	58	24	11	98	47	64	.295	.329	.442	150	49				.871	4	O-228/1-1	4.3
■ JOE O'ROURKE	O'Rourke, Joseph Leo Jr. b: 10/28/04, Philadelphia, Pa. d: 6/27/90, Philadelphia, Pa. BL/TR, 5'7", 145 lbs. Deb: 4/19/29 F																						
1929	Phi-N	3	3	0	0	0	0	0	0	0	1	.000	.000	.000	-94	-1	0			.000	0	H	-0.1
■ PATSY O'ROURKE	O'Rourke, Joseph Leo Sr. b: 4/13/1881, Philadelphia, Pa. d: 4/18/56, Philadelphia, Pa. BR/TR, 5'7", 160 lbs. Deb: 4/16/08 F																						
1908	StL-N	53	164	8	32	4	2	0	16	14		.195	.263	.244	65	-6	2			.860	-7	S-53	-1.5
■ TOM O'ROURKE	O'Rourke, Thomas Joseph b: 10/1865, New York, N.Y. d: 7/19/29, New York, N.Y. TR , 5'9", 158 lbs. Deb: 5/11/1887																						
1887	Bos-N	22	78	12	12	3	0	0	10	7	6	.154	.233	.192	19	-8	4			.777	-5	C-21/O-1,3-1	-1.0
1888	Bos-N	20	74	3	13	0	0	0	4	1	9	.176	.187	.176	16	-7	2			.881	1	C-20/O-1	-0.4
1890	NY-N	2	7	1	0	0	0	0	0	1	0	.000	.125	.000	-63	-1	0			.864	1	/C-2	0.0
	Syr-a	41	153	16	33	8	0	0	12	12		.216	.277	.268	68	-6	2			.907	-12	C-40/1-1	-1.3
Total	3	85	312	32	58	11	0	0	26	21	15	.186	.242	.221	39	-23	8			.867	-15	/C-83,O-2,1-1,3-1	-2.7
■ TIM O'ROURKE	O'Rourke, Timothy Patrick "Voiceless Tim" b: 5/18/1864, Chicago, Ill. d: 4/20/38, Seattle, Wash. BL/TR, 5'10", 170 lbs. Deb: 5/27/1890																						
1890	Syr-a	87	332	48	94	13	6	1	46	36		.283	.360	.367	128	13	22			.866	-11	3-87	0.4
1891	Col-a	34	136	22	38	1	3	0	12	15	7	.279	.359	.331	104	1	9			.879	0	3-34	0.3
1892	Bal-N	63	239	40	74	8	4	0	35	24	19	.310	.373	.377	123	7	12			.869	-14	S-58/O-4,3-1	-0.4
1893	Bal-N	31	135	22	49	4	1	0	19	12	4	.363	.423	.407	119	4	5			.980	-4	O-25/3-5,S-1	-0.1
	Lou-N	92	352	80	99	8	4	0	53	77	15	.281	.421	.327	108	11	22			.865	-21	S-60,O-26/3-6	-0.6
	Yr	123	487	102	148	12	5	0	72	89	19	.304	.422	.349	112	16	27			.861	-25	S-61,O-51,3-11	-0.7
1894	Lou-N	55	220	46	61	3	3	0	27	23	9	.277	.351	.318	67	-11	9			.977	-1	1-30,O-18/S-3,32	-1.0
	StL-N	18	71	10	20	4	1	0	10	8	3	.282	.354	.366	74	-3	2			.861	-2	3-18	-0.4
	Was-N	7	25	4	5	2	1	0	2	2	1	.200	.259	.360	50	-2	0			.909	1	/2-4,S-3	-0.1
	Yr	80	316	60	86	9	5	0	39	33	13	.272	.345	.332	67	-16	11			.977	-2	1-30,3-21,O-18,/S2	-1.5
Total	5	387	1510	272	440	43	23	1	204	197	58	.291	.380	.352	105	20	81			.861	-51	3-154,S-125/O12	-1.9
■ DAVE ORR	Orr, David L. b: 9/29/1859, New York, N.Y. d: 6/2/15, Richmond Hill, N.Y. BR/TR, 5'11", 250 lbs. Deb: 5/17/1883 M																						
1883	NY-a	1	4	1	1	1	0	0		0		.250	.250	.500	130	0				1.000	0	/1-1	0.0
	NY-N	1	3	0	0	0	0	0	0	0	1	.000	.000	.000	-99	-1				1.000	0	/O-1	-0.1
	NY-a	12	46	5	15	3	3	2	11	0		.326	.326	.652	198	5				.938	-2	1-12	0.2
1884	*NY-a	110	458	82	**162**	32	13	9	112	5		**.354**	.362	.539	**195**	**45**				.960	-5	*1-110/O-3	2.4
1885	NY-a	107	444	76	152	29	**21**	6	77	8		.342	.358	**.543**	**197**	47				.966	-3	*1-107/P-3	2.7
1886	NY-a	136	571	93	**193**	25	**31**	7	91	17		.338	.363	**.527**	**186**	**52**	16			**.981**	-0	*1-136	3.1
1887	NY-a	84	345	63	127	25	10	2	66	22		.368	.408	.516	164	29	17			.969	-1	1-81/O-3,M	1.6
1888	Bro-a	99	394	57	120	20	5	1	59	7		.305	.330	.388	130	12	11			.979	4	*1-99	0.6
1889	Col-a	134	560	70	183	31	12	4	87	9	38	.327	.340	.446	129	18	12			.983	9	*1-134	1.5
1890	Bro-P	107	464	89	172	32	13	6	124	30	11	.371	.414	.534	144	25	10			.972	-5	*1-107	1.2
Total	8	791	3289	536	1125	198	108	37	627	98	50	.342	.366	.502	163	231	66			.973	-3	1-787/O-7,P-3	13.2
■ BILLY ORR	Orr, William John b: 4/22/1891, San Francisco, Cal d: 3/10/67, St.Helena, Cal. BR/TR, 5'11", 168 lbs. Deb: 5/3/13																						
1913	Phi-A	30	67	6	13	1	1	0	7	4	10	.194	.239	.239	41	-5	1			.967	-2	S-16/1-3,3-3,2-2	-0.6
1914	Phi-A	10	24	3	4	1	1	0	1	2	5	.167	.231	.292	59	-1	1	1	-0	.810	-4	/S-6,3-1	-0.6
Total	2	40	91	9	17	2	2	0	8	6	15	.187	.237	.253	46	-6	2	1		.927	-6	/S-22,3-4,1-3,2-2	-1.2
■ ERNIE ORSATTI	Orsatti, Ernest Ralph b: 9/8/02, Los Angeles, Cal. d: 9/4/68, Canoga Park, Cal. BL/TL, 5'7.5", 154 lbs. Deb: 9/4/27																						
1927	StL-N	27	92	15	29	7	3	0	12	11	12	.315	.388	.457	122	3	2			.922	-1	O-26	0.1
1928	*StL-N	27	69	10	21	6	0	3	15	10	11	.304	.400	.522	137	4	0			1.000	-2	O-17/1-5	0.1
1929	StL-N	113	346	64	115	21	7	3	39	33	43	.332	.394	.460	110	6	7			.974	4	O-77,1-10	0.4
1930	*StL-N	48	131	24	42	8	4	1	15	12	18	.321	.382	.466	100	0	1			.985	4	1-22,O-11	0.1
1931	*StL-N	70	158	27	46	16	6	0	19	14	16	.291	.349	.468	113	3	1			.988	-5	O-45/1-1	-0.5
1932	StL-N	101	375	44	126	27	6	2	44	18	29	.336	.368	.456	117	9	5			.976	-9	O-96/1-1	-0.6
1933	StL-N	120	436	55	130	21	6	0	38	33	33	.298	.348	.374	101	1	14			.986	2	*O-107/1-3	-0.4
1934	*StL-N	105	337	39	101	14	4	0	31	27	31	.300	.353	.365	87	-5	6			.986	-2	O-90	-1.1
1935	StL-N	90	221	28	53	9	3	1	24	18	25	.240	.297	.321	64	-11	10			.975	-5	O-60	-1.8
Total	9	701	2165	306	663	129	39	10	237	176	218	.306	.360	.416	102	8	46			.979	-14	O-529/1-42	-3.7
■ JOHN ORSINO	Orsino, John Joseph "Horse" b: 4/22/38, Teaneck, N.J. BR/TR, 6'3", 215 lbs. Deb: 7/14/61																						
1961	SF-N	25	83	5	23	3	2	4	12	3	13	.277	.310	.506	116	1	0	0	0	.959	-3	C-25	0.0
1962	*SF-N	18	48	4	13	2	0	0	4	5	11	.271	.340	.313	78	-1	0	0	0	.963	-2	C-16	-0.2
1963	Bal-A	116	379	53	103	18	1	19	56	38	53	.272	.352	.475	134	17	2	3	-1	.990	-7	*C-109/1-3	1.4
1964	Bal-A	81	248	21	55	10	0	8	23	23	55	.222	.293	.359	81	-7	0	0	0	.976	1	C-66/1-5	-0.4
1965	Bal-A	77	232	30	54	10	2	9	28	23	51	.233	.315	.409	102	1	1	0	0	.987	-8	C-62/1-5	-0.4
1966	Was-A	14	23	1	4	1	0	0	0	0	7	.174	.174	.217	12	-3	0	0	0	1.000	-0	/1-5,C-2	-0.3
1967	Was-A	1	1	0	0	0	0	0	0	0	1	.000	.000	.000	-99	-0	0	0	0	.000	0	H	0.0
Total	7	332	1014	114	252	44	5	40	123	92	191	.249	.321	.420	106	8	3	3	-1	.982	-18	C-280/1-18	0.1
■ JOE ORSULAK	Orsulak, Joseph Michael b: 5/31/62, Glen Ridge, N.J. BL/TL, 6'1", 196 lbs. Deb: 9/1/83																						
1983	Pit-N	7	11	0	2	0	0	0	1	0	2	.182	.182	.182	1	-1	0	1	-1	1.000	0	/O-4	-0.2
1984	Pit-N	32	67	12	17	1	2	0	3	1	7	.254	.275	.328	69	-3	3	1	0	1.000	-1	O-25	-0.5
1985	Pit-N	121	397	54	119	14	6	0	21	26	27	.300	.344	.365	100	-0	24	11	1	.976	-0	*O-115	-0.3
1986	Pit-N	138	401	60	100	19	6	2	19	28	38	.249	.300	.342	75	-14	24	11	1	.981	-5	*O-120	-2.2
1988	Bal-A	125	379	48	109	21	3	8	27	23	30	.288	.333	.422	113	6	9	8	-2	.979	-6	*O-117	-0.5
1989	Bal-A	123	390	59	111	22	5	7	55	41	35	.285	.356	.421	122	11	5	3	-0	.985	7	*O-109/D-5	1.5
1990	Bal-A	124	413	49	111	14	3	11	57	46	48	.269	.343	.397	110	6	6	8	-3	.989	11	*O-109/D-5	1.1
1991	Bal-A	143	486	57	135	22	1	5	43	28	45	.278	.322	.358	92	-6	6	2	1	.997	10	*O-132/D-2	0.2
1992	Bal-A	117	391	45	113	18	3	4	39	28	34	.289	.343	.381	100	0	5	4	-1	.983	4	*O-110/D-1	0.1
1993	NY-N	134	409	59	116	15	4	8	35	28	25	.284	.333	.399	96	-3	5	4	-1	.978	-6	*O-114/1-4	-1.2
1994	NY-N	96	292	39	76	3	0	8	42	16	21	.260	.305	.353	72	-12	4	2	0	.979	-8	O-90/1-6	-2.2
1995	NY-N	108	290	41	82	19	2	1	37	19	35	.283	.329	.372	87	-5	1	3	-2	.965	-8	O-86/1-1	-1.7
1996	Fla-N	120	217	23	48	6	1	2	19	16	38	.221	.275	.286	50	-16	1	1	-0	.956	-3	O-59/1-2	-2.0
1997	Mon-N	106	150	13	34	12	1	1	7	18	17	.227	.310	.340	70	-7	0	1	-1	1.000	-12	O-63,1-15/D-1	-2.0
Total	14	1494	4293	559	1173	186	37	57	405	318	402	.273	.327	.374	93	-44	93	60	-8	.982	-18	*O-1253/1-28,D-14	-9.9

■ **JORGE ORTA** Orta, Jorge (Nunez) b: 11/26/50, Mazatlan, Mexico BL/TR, 5'10", 175 lbs. Deb: 4/15/72

YEAR	TM/L	G	AB	R	H	2B	3B	HR	RBI	BB	SO	AVG	OBP	SLG	PRO+	BR/A	SB	CS	SBR	FA	FR	G/POS	TPR
1972	Chi-A	51	124	20	25	3	1	3	11	6	37	.202	.244	.315	64	-6	3	3	-1	.958	-0	S-18,2-14/3-9	-0.5
1973	Chi-A	128	425	46	113	9	10	6	40	37	87	.266	.326	.376	94	-3	8	8	-2	.969	-27	*2-122/S-1	-2.6
1974	Chi-A	139	525	73	166	31	2	10	67	40	88	.316	.368	.440	128	19	9	5	-0	.971	-13	*2-123,D-10/S-3	1.2
1975	Chi-A†	140	542	64	165	26	10	11	83	48	67	.304	.365	.450	128	19	16	9	-1	.978	-12	*2-135/D-2	1.4
1976	Chi-A	158	636	74	174	29	8	14	72	38	77	.274	.320	.410	112	8	24	8	2	.971	2	O-77,3-49,D-31	0.8
1977	Chi-A	144	564	71	159	27	8	11	84	46	49	.282	.338	.417	105	3	4	4	-1	.970	-47	*2-139	-3.5
1978	Chi-A	117	420	45	115	19	2	13	53	42	39	.274	.345	.421	114	8	1	2	-1	.984	-22	*2-114/D-2	-0.7
1979	Chi-A	113	325	49	85	18	3	11	46	44	33	.262	.351	.437	111	5	1	5	-3	.978	-11	D-62,2-41	-0.8
1980	Cle-A☆	129	481	78	140	18	3	10	64	71	44	.291	.384	.403	116	13	6	5	-1	.982	13	*O-120/D-7	2.0
1981	Cle-A	88	338	50	92	14	3	5	34	21	43	.272	.317	.376	100	-0	4	3	-1	.994	4	O-86	0.0
1982	LA-N	86	115	13	25	5	0	2	8	12	13	.217	.297	.313	73	-4	0	1	-1	.947	1	O-17	-0.4
1983	Tor-A	103	245	30	58	6	3	10	38	19	29	.237	.292	.408	85	-6	1	2	-1	1.000	-3	D-70,O-17	-1.2
1984	*KC-A	122	403	50	120	23	7	9	50	28	39	.298	.346	.457	119	10	0	1	-1	.980	-3	D-83,O-26/2-1	0.4
1985	*KC-A	110	300	32	80	21	1	4	45	22	28	.267	.321	.383	92	-4	2	1	0	.000	0	D-85	-0.5
1986	KC-A	106	336	35	93	14	2	9	46	23	34	.277	.323	.411	96	-2	0	3	-2	.000	0	D-87	-0.6
1987	KC-A	21	50	3	9	4	0	2	4	3	8	.180	.226	.380	55	-3	0	0	0	.000	0	D-12	-0.4
Total	16	1755	5829	733	1619	267	63	130	745	500	715	.278	.338	.412	108	56	79	60	-12	.974	-118	2-689,D-451,O/3S	-5.4

■ **FRANK ORTENZIO** Ortenzio, Frank Joseph b: 2/24/51, Fresno, Cal. BR/TR, 6'2", 215 lbs. Deb: 9/9/73

YEAR	TM/L	G	AB	R	H	2B	3B	HR	RBI	BB	SO	AVG	OBP	SLG	PRO+	BR/A	SB	CS	SBR	FA	FR	G/POS	TPR
1973	KC-A	9	25	1	7	2	0	1	6	2	6	.280	.333	.480	118	0	0	0	0	.983	1	/1-7,D-1	0.1

■ **AL ORTH** Orth, Albert Lewis "Smiling Al" or "The Curveless Wonder" b: 9/5/1872, Tipton, Ind. d: 10/8/48, Lynchburg, Va. BL/TR, 6', 200 lbs. Deb: 8/15/1895 U

YEAR	TM/L	G	AB	R	H	2B	3B	HR	RBI	BB	SO	AVG	OBP	SLG	PRO+	BR/A	SB	CS	SBR	FA	FR	G/POS	TPR
1895	Phi-N	11	45	8	16	4	0	1	13	1	6	.356	.370	.511	125	1	0			.842	-2	P-11	0.0
1896	Phi-N	25	82	12	21	3	3	1	13	3	11	.256	.282	.402	80	-3	2			.901	1	P-25	0.0
1897	Phi-N	53	152	26	50	7	4	1	17	3		.329	.342	.447	110	1	5			.929	0	P-36/O-6	0.0
1898	Phi-N	39	123	17	36	6	4	1	14	3		.293	.310	.431	117	2	1			.959	1	P-32/O-1	0.1
1899	Phi-N	22	62	5	13	3	1	1	5	1		.210	.222	.339	55	-4	2			.793	-4	P-21/O-1	0.0
1900	Phi-N	39	129	6	40	4	1	1	21	2		.310	.326	.380	95	-1	2			.943	1	P-33/O-3	0.0
1901	Phi-N	41	128	14	36	6	0	1	15	3		.281	.303	.352	88	-2	3			.945	1	P-35/O-4	-0.1
1902	Was-A	56	175	20	38	3	2	2	10	9		.217	.255	.291	51	-12	2			.923	-0	P-38,O-13/1-1,S-1	-0.4
1903	Was-A	55	162	19	49	9	7	0	11	4		.302	.323	.444	126	4	3			.920	-2	P-36/S-7,O-4,1-2	-0.1
1904	Was-A	31	102	7	22	3	1	0	11	1		.216	.238	.265	60	-5	2			.816	-2	O-18,P-10	-0.8
	NY-A	24	64	6	19	1	1	0	7	0		.297	.308	.344	101	-0	2			.968	1	P-20/O-2	0.0
	Yr	55	166	13	41	4	2	0	18	1		.247	.265	.295	76	-5	4			.969	-2	P-30,O-20	-0.8
1905	NY-A	55	131	13	24	3	1	1	8	4		.183	.213	.244	40	-9	2			.940	-0	P-40/1-1,O-1	-0.1
1906	NY-A	47	135	12	37	2	2	1	17	6		.274	.305	.341	93	-1	2			.934	0	P-45/O-1	0.1
1907	NY-A	44	105	11	34	6	0	1	13	4		.324	.355	.410	133	3	1			.920	2	P-36/O-1	0.0
1908	NY-A	38	69	4	20	1	2	0	4	2		.290	.310	.362	117	1	0			.980	-1	P-21	0.0
1909	NY-A	22	34	3	9	0	1	0	5	5		.265	.359	.324	115	1	1			1.000	-2	/2-6,P-1	-0.1
Total	15	602	1698	183	464	61	30	12	184	51	17	.273	.298	.366	91	-24	30			.932	-5	P-440/O-55,S-8,21	-1.4

■ **JUNIOR ORTIZ** Ortiz, Adalberto Colon b: 10/24/59, Humacao, P.R. BR/TR, 5'11", 176 lbs. Deb: 9/20/82

YEAR	TM/L	G	AB	R	H	2B	3B	HR	RBI	BB	SO	AVG	OBP	SLG	PRO+	BR/A	SB	CS	SBR	FA	FR	G/POS	TPR
1982	Pit-N	7	15	1	3	1	0	0	0	1	3	.200	.250	.267	43	-1	0	0	0	1.000	1	/C-7	0.0
1983	Pit-N	5	8	1	1	0	0	0	0	1	0	.125	.222	.125	-1	-1	0	0	0	1.000	0	/C-4	-0.1
	NY-N	68	185	10	47	5	0	0	12	3	34	.254	.270	.281	53	-12	1	0	0	.965	1	C-67	-0.9
	Yr	73	193	11	48	5	0	0	12	4	34	.249	.268	.275	51	-13	1	0	0	.967	1	C-71	-1.0
1984	NY-N	40	91	6	18	3	0	0	11	5	15	.198	.240	.231	33	-8	1	0	0	.980	-4	C-32	-1.1
1985	Pit-N	23	72	4	21	2	0	1	5	3	17	.292	.320	.361	91	-1	1	0	0	.985	1	C-23	0.1
1986	Pit-N	49	110	11	37	6	0	0	14	9	13	.336	.387	.391	112	2	0	1	-1	.983	-1	C-36	0.3
1987	Pit-N	75	192	16	52	8	1	1	22	15	23	.271	.324	.339	75	-7	0	2	-1	.975	-0	C-72	-0.4
1988	Pit-N	49	118	8	33	6	0	2	18	9	9	.280	.341	.381	109	1	1	4	-2	.983	-2	C-40	0.0
1989	Pit-N	91	230	16	50	6	1	1	22	20	20	.217	.286	.265	61	-12	2	2	-1	.995	-10	C-84	-2.0
1990	Min-A	71	170	18	57	7	1	0	18	12	16	.335	.386	.388	110	3	0	4	-2	1.000	2	C-68/D-3	0.5
1991	*Min-A	61	134	9	28	5	1	0	11	15	12	.209	.293	.261	52	-8	0	1	-1	.995	-0	C-60	-0.7
1992	Cle-A	86	244	20	61	7	0	0	24	12	23	.250	.296	.279	63	-12	1	3	-2	.989	-1	C-86	-1.1
1993	Cle-A	95	249	19	55	13	0	0	20	11	26	.221	.268	.273	46	-19	1	0	0	.990	11	C-95	-0.3
1994	Tex-A	29	76	3	21	2	0	0	9	5	11	.276	.329	.303	65	-4	0	1	-1	.992	-1	C-28	-0.4
Total	13	749	1894	142	484	71	4	5	186	121	222	.256	.306	.305	69	-78	8	18	-8	.986	-4	C-702/D-3	-6.1

■ **DAVID ORTIZ** Ortiz, David Americo (Arias) b: 11/18/75, Santo Domingo, D.R. BL/TL, 6'4", 230 lbs. Deb: 9/2/97

YEAR	TM/L	G	AB	R	H	2B	3B	HR	RBI	BB	SO	AVG	OBP	SLG	PRO+	BR/A	SB	CS	SBR	FA	FR	G/POS	TPR
1997	Min-A	15	49	10	16	3	0	1	6	2	19	.327	.353	.449	106	0	0	0	0	.989	1	1-11/D-1	0.0
1998	Min-A	86	278	47	77	20	0	9	46	39	72	.277	.376	.446	112	6	1	0	0	.989	0	1-71,D-10	-0.1
Total	2	101	327	57	93	23	0	10	52	41	91	.284	.373	.446	112	6	1	0	0	.989	1	/1-82,D-11	-0.1

■ **HECTOR ORTIZ** Ortiz, Hector (Montanez) b: 10/14/69, Rio Piedras, P.R. BR/TR, 6', 205 lbs. Deb: 9/14/98

YEAR	TM/L	G	AB	R	H	2B	3B	HR	RBI	BB	SO	AVG	OBP	SLG	PRO+	BR/A	SB	CS	SBR	FA	FR	G/POS	TPR
1998	KC-A	4	4	1	0	0	0	0	0	0	0	.000	.000	.000	-96	-1	0	0	0	1.000	-1	/C-3,1-1	-0.2

■ **JAVIER ORTIZ** Ortiz, Javier Victor b: 1/22/63, Boston, Mass. BR/TR, 6'4", 220 lbs. Deb: 6/15/90

YEAR	TM/L	G	AB	R	H	2B	3B	HR	RBI	BB	SO	AVG	OBP	SLG	PRO+	BR/A	SB	CS	SBR	FA	FR	G/POS	TPR
1990	Hou-N	30	77	7	21	5	1	1	10	12	11	.273	.371	.403	116	2	1	1	-0	.978	-3	O-25	-0.2
1991	Hou-N	47	83	7	23	4	1	1	5	14	14	.277	.381	.386	123	3	0	0	0	1.000	-3	O-24	0.0
Total	2	77	160	14	44	9	2	2	15	26	25	.275	.376	.394	120	5	1	1	-0	.987	-6	/O-49	-0.2

■ **JOSE ORTIZ** Ortiz, Jose Luis (Irizarry) b: 6/25/47, Ponce, P.R. BR/TR, 5'9.5", 155 lbs. Deb: 9/4/69

YEAR	TM/L	G	AB	R	H	2B	3B	HR	RBI	BB	SO	AVG	OBP	SLG	PRO+	BR/A	SB	CS	SBR	FA	FR	G/POS	TPR
1969	Chi-A	16	11	0	3	1	0	0	2	1	0	.273	.333	.364	90	-0	1	0	0	1.000	-2	/O-8	-0.3
1970	Chi-A	15	24	4	8	1	0	0	1	2	2	.333	.407	.375	113	1	0	0	0	1.000	1	/O-8	0.2
1971	Chi-N	36	88	10	26	7	1	0	3	4	10	.295	.347	.398	96	-0	2	2	-1	1.000	-2	O-30	-0.5
Total	3	67	123	14	37	9	1	0	6	7	12	.301	.358	.390	99	0	3	2	-0	1.000	-3	/O-46	-0.6

■ **LUIS ORTIZ** Ortiz, Luis Alberto (Galarza) b: 5/25/70, Santo Domingo, D.R. BR/TR, 6', 190 lbs. Deb: 8/31/93

YEAR	TM/L	G	AB	R	H	2B	3B	HR	RBI	BB	SO	AVG	OBP	SLG	PRO+	BR/A	SB	CS	SBR	FA	FR	G/POS	TPR
1993	Bos-A	9	12	0	3	0	0	0	1	0	2	.250	.250	.250	33	-1	0	0	0	1.000	1	/3-5,D-3	-0.1
1994	Bos-A	7	18	3	3	2	0	0	6	1	5	.167	.211	.278	23	-2	0	0	0	.000	0	/D-6	-0.2
1995	Tex-A	41	108	10	25	5	2	1	18	6	18	.231	.272	.343	57	-7	0	1	-1	.867	-5	3-35/D-3	-1.2
1996	Tex-A	3	7	1	2	0	1	1	1	0	1	.286	.286	1.000	196	1	0	0	0	.000	0	/D-1	0.1
Total	4	60	145	14	33	7	3	2	26	7	26	.228	.263	.359	58	-9	0	1	-1	.875	-4	/3-40,D-13	-1.4

■ **ROBERTO ORTIZ** Ortiz, Roberto Gonzalo (Nunez) b: 6/30/15, Camaguey, Cuba d: 9/15/71, Miami, Fla. BR/TR, 6'4", 200 lbs. Deb: 9/6/41 F

YEAR	TM/L	G	AB	R	H	2B	3B	HR	RBI	BB	SO	AVG	OBP	SLG	PRO+	BR/A	SB	CS	SBR	FA	FR	G/POS	TPR
1941	Was-A	22	79	10	26	1	2	1	17	3	10	.329	.354	.430	112	1	0	1	-1	.860	-2	O-21	-0.2
1942	Was-A	20	42	4	7	1	3	1	4	5	11	.167	.271	.405	89	-1	0	0	0	.941	-1	/O-9	-0.2
1943	Was-A	1	4	0	1	0	0	0	0	0	0	.250	.250	.250	48	-0	0	1	-1	1.000	0	/O-1	-0.1
1944	Was-A	85	316	36	80	11	4	5	35	19	47	.253	.312	.361	96	-2	4	1	1	.949	-3	O-80	-1.0
1949	Was-A	40	129	12	36	3	0	1	11	9	12	.279	.326	.326	74	-5	0	0	0	.946	-1	O-32	-0.8
1950	Was-A	39	75	4	17	2	1	0	8	7	12	.227	.301	.280	52	-5	0	0	0	1.000	-3	O-19	-0.8
	Phi-A	6	14	1	1	0	0	0	3	0	3	.071	.071	.071	-65	-3	0	0	0	1.000	-1	/O-3	-0.4
	Yr	45	89	5	18	2	1	0	11	7	15	.202	.268	.247	34	-9	0	0	0	1.000	-3	O-22	-1.2
Total	6	213	659	67	168	18	10	8	78	43	95	.255	.310	.349	84	-16	4	3	-1	.942	-10	O-165	-3.5

■ **JOHN ORTON** Orton, John Andrew b: 12/8/65, Santa Cruz, Cal. BR/TR, 6'1", 192 lbs. Deb: 8/20/89

YEAR	TM/L	G	AB	R	H	2B	3B	HR	RBI	BB	SO	AVG	OBP	SLG	PRO+	BR/A	SB	CS	SBR	FA	FR	G/POS	TPR
1989	Cal-A	16	39	4	7	1	0	0	4	2	17	.179	.220	.205	21	-4	0	0	0	.988	5	C-16	0.1
1990	Cal-A	31	84	8	16	5	0	1	6	5	31	.190	.244	.286	49	-6	0	1	-1	.987	1	C-31	-0.4
1991	Cal-A	29	69	7	14	4	0	0	3	10	17	.203	.313	.261	60	-3	0	1	-1	.994	9	C-28/D-1	0.6

YEAR	TM/L	G	AB	R	H	2B	3B	HR	RBI	BB	SO	AVG	OBP	SLG	PRO+	BR/A	SB	CS	SBR	FA	FR	G/POS	TPR
1992	Cal-A	43	114	11	25	3	0	2	12	7	32	.219	.276	.298	61	-6	1	1	-0	.981	8	C-43	0.4
1993	Cal-A	37	95	5	18	5	0	1	4	7	24	.189	.252	.274	40	-8	1	2	-1	.980	5	C-35/O-1	-0.2
Total	5	156	401	35	80	18	0	4	29	31	121	.200	.265	.274	49	-28	2	5	-2	.985	28	C-153/O-1,D-1	0.5

■ OSSIE ORWOLL   Orwoll, Oswald Christian b: 11/17/1900, Portland, Ore. d: 5/8/67, Decorah, Iowa BL/TL, 6', 174 lbs. Deb: 4/13/28

1928	Phi-A	64	170	28	52	13	2	0	22	16	24	.306	.366	.406	100	0	3	1	0	.983	-1	1-34,P-27	-0.3
1929	Phi-A	30	51	6	13	2	1	0	6	2	11	.255	.283	.333	56	-3	0	0	0	1.000	-2	P-12/O-9	-0.4
Total	2	94	221	34	65	15	3	0	28	18	35	.294	.347	.389	90	-3	3	1	0	.970	-3	/P-39,1-34,O-9	-0.7

■ FRED OSBORN   Osborn, Wilfred Pearl "Ossie" b: 11/28/1883, Nevada, Ohio d: 9/2/54, Upper Sandusky, O. BL/TR, 5'9", 178 lbs. Deb: 6/8/07

1907	Phi-N	56	163	22	45	2	3	0	9	3		.276	.298	.325	97	-1	4			1.000	-4	O-36/1-1	-0.7
1908	Phi-N	152	555	62	148	19	12	2	44	30		.267	.305	.355	107	3	16			.969	2	*O-152	-0.2
1909	Phi-N	58	189	14	35	4	1	0	19	12		.185	.238	.217	41	-13	6			.979	10	O-54	-0.6
Total	3	266	907	98	228	25	16	2	72	45		.251	.290	.321	91	-12	26			.975	8	O-242/1-1	-1.5

■ FRED OSBORNE   Osborne, Frederick W. b: Hampton, Iowa TL, Deb: 7/14/1890

| 1890 | Pit-N | 41 | 168 | 24 | 40 | 8 | 3 | 1 | 14 | 6 | 18 | .238 | .269 | .339 | 87 | -4 | 0 | | | .828 | 1 | O-35/P-8 | -0.3 |

■ BOBO OSBORNE   Osborne, Lawrence Sidney b: 10/12/35, Chattahoochee, Ga. b: 6'1", 205 lbs. Deb: 6/27/57 F

1957	Det-A	11	27	4	4	1	0	0	1	3	7	.148	.233	.185	15	-3	0	0	0	1.000	-1	/O-5,1-4	-0.4
1958	Det-A	2	2	0	0	0	0	0	0	0	0	.000	.000	.000	-93	-1	0	0	0	.000	0	H	-0.1
1959	Det-A	86	209	27	40	7	1	3	21	16	41	.191	.256	.278	44	-16	1	0	0	.983	-1	1-56/O-1	-2.1
1961	Det-A	71	93	8	20	7	0	2	13	20	15	.215	.354	.355	88	-1	1	0	0	.957	-2	/3-8,1-11	-0.4
1962	Det-A	64	74	12	17	1	0	0	7	16	25	.230	.374	.243	68	-3	0	0	0	.857	-2	3-13/1-7,C-1	-0.4
1963	Was-A	125	358	42	76	14	1	12	44	49	83	.212	.312	.358	87	-6	0	0	0	.988	-3	1-81,3-16	-1.3
Total	6	359	763	93	157	30	2	17	86	104	171	.206	.306	.317	71	-29	2	0	1	.987	-9	1-159/3-37,O-6,C-1	-4.7

■ KEITH OSIK   Osik, Keith Richard b: 10/22/68, Port Jefferson, N.Y. BR/TR, 6', 185 lbs. Deb: 4/5/96

1996	Pit-N	48	140	18	41	14	1	1	14	14	22	.293	.361	.429	105	1	1	0	0	.977	-3	C-41/3-2,O-2	0.1
1997	Pit-N	49	105	10	27	9	1	0	7	9	21	.257	.322	.362	77	-3	0	1	-1	.989	-3	C-32/2-4,1-1,3-1	-0.5
1998	Pit-N	39	98	8	21	4	0	0	7	13	16	.214	.319	.255	51	-7	1	2	-1	1.000	6	C-26/3-7	-0.4
Total	3	136	343	36	89	27	2	1	28	36	59	.259	.337	.359	81	-9	2	3	-1	.987	0	/C-99,3-10,2-4,O1	-0.4

■ HARRY OSTDIEK   Ostdiek, Henry Girard b: 4/12/1881, Ottumwa, Iowa d: 5/6/56, Minneapolis, Minn. BR/TR, 5'11", 185 lbs. Deb: 9/10/04

1904	Cle-A	7	18	1	3	0	1	0	3	3		.167	.318	.278	90	-1	0			.946	0	/C-7	0.0
1908	Bos-A	1	3	0	0	0	0	0	0	0		.000	.000	.000	-97	-1	0			.889	1	/C-1	0.0
Total	2	8	21	1	3	0	1	0	3	3		.143	.280	.238	65	-1	1			.935	0	/C-8	0.0

■ CHAMP OSTEEN   Osteen, James Champlin b: 2/24/1877, Hendersonville, N.C. d: 12/14/62, Greenville, S.C. BL/TR, 5'8", 150 lbs. Deb: 9/18/03

1903	Was-A	10	40	4	8	0	2	0	4	2		.200	.256	.300	65	-2	0			.938	1	S-10	0.0
1904	NY-A	28	107	15	21	1	4	2	9	1		.196	.218	.336	71	-4	0			.930	-2	3-17/S-8,1-4	-0.6
1908	StL-N	29	112	2	22	4	0	0	11	0		.196	.204	.232	41	-8	0			.847	-6	S-17,3-12	-1.6
1909	StL-N	16	45	6	9	1	0	0	7	7		.200	.308	.222	69	-1	1			.879	-6	S-16	-0.8
Total	4	83	304	27	60	6	6	2	31	10		.197	.233	.276	60	-15	1			.890	-13	/S-51,3-29,1-4	-3.0

■ RED OSTERGARD   Ostergard, Roy Lund b: 5/16/1896, Denmark, Wis. d: 1/13/77, Hemet, Cal. BR/TR, 5'10.5", 175 lbs. Deb: 6/14/21

| 1921 | Chi-A | 12 | 11 | 2 | 4 | 0 | 0 | 0 | 0 | 0 | 2 | .364 | .364 | .364 | 87 | -0 | 0 | 0 | 0 | .000 | 0 | H | 0.0 |

■ CHARLIE OSTERHOUT   Osterhout, Charles H. b: 1856, Syracuse, N.Y. d: 5/21/33, Syracuse, N.Y. TR, Deb: 6/23/1879

| 1879 | Syr-N | 2 | 8 | 0 | 0 | 0 | 0 | 0 | 0 | 0 | 0 | .000 | .000 | .000 | -99 | -2 | | | | 1.000 | -0 | /O-1,C-1 | -0.2 |

■ BRIAN OSTROSSER   Ostrosser, Brian Leonard b: 6/17/49, Hamilton, Ont., Can BL/TR, 6', 175 lbs. Deb: 8/5/73

| 1973 | NY-N | 4 | 5 | 0 | 0 | 0 | 0 | 0 | 0 | 0 | 0 | .000 | .000 | .000 | -99 | -1 | 0 | 0 | 0 | 1.000 | -0 | /S-4 | -0.2 |

■ JOHNNY OSTROWSKI   Ostrowski, John Thaddeus b: 10/17/17, Chicago, Ill. d: 11/13/92, Chicago, Ill. BR/TR, 5'10.5", 170 lbs. Deb: 9/24/43

1943	Chi-N	10	29	2	6	0	1	0	3	3	8	.207	.303	.276	69	-1	0			1.000	-2	/O-5,3-4	-0.4
1944	Chi-N	8	13	2	2	1	0	0	2	1	4	.154	.214	.231	25	-1	0			.500	-1	/O-2	-0.2
1945	Chi-N	7	10	4	3	2	0	0	1	0	0	.300	.300	.500	123	0	0			.750	-1	/3-4	-0.1
1946	Chi-N	64	160	20	34	4	2	3	12	20	31	.213	.300	.319	77	-5	1			.934	1	3-50/2-1	-0.3
1948	Bos-A	1	1	0	0	0	0	0	0	0	0	.000	.000	.000	-95	-0	0	0	0	.000	0	H	0.0
1949	Chi-A	49	158	19	42	9	4	5	31	15	41	.266	.333	.468	115	2	3	4	-1	.944	-4	O-41/3-8	-0.4
1950	Chi-A	21	45	9	10	1	1	2	2	9	8	.222	.364	.422	104	1	0	0	1	1.000	-1	O-14	-0.1
	Was-A	55	141	16	32	2	1	4	23	20	31	.227	.327	.340	75	-6	2	0	1	.947	-0	O-45	-0.6
	Chi-A	1	4	1	2	1	0	0	0	1		.500	.500	.750	223	1	0	0	0	1.000	-0	/O-1	0.0
	Yr	77	190	26	44	4	2	6	25	29	40	.232	.339	.368	85	-4	2	0	1	.958	-2	O-60	-0.7
Total	7	216	561	73	131	20	9	14	74	68	125	.234	.321	.376	89	-10	7	3		.950	-9	O-108/3-66,2-1	-2.1

■ WILLIS OTANEZ   Otanez, Willis Alexander b: 4/19/73, Las Vega Baja, D.R. BR/TR, 6'1", 200 lbs. Deb: 8/25/98

| 1998 | Bal-A | 3 | 5 | 0 | 1 | 0 | 0 | 0 | 0 | 0 | 2 | .200 | .200 | .200 | 5 | -1 | 0 | 0 | 0 | 1.000 | -1 | /O-2 | -0.1 |

■ REGGIE OTERO   Otero, Regino Jose (Gomez) b: 9/7/15, Havana, Cuba d: 10/21/88, Hialeah, Fla. BL/TR, 6', 165 lbs. Deb: 9/2/45 C

| 1945 | Chi-N | 14 | 23 | 1 | 9 | 0 | 0 | 0 | 5 | 2 | 2 | .391 | .440 | .391 | 135 | 1 | 0 | | | .967 | 0 | /1-8 | 0.1 |

■ RICKY OTERO   Otero, Ricardo (Figueroa) b: 4/15/72, Vega Baja, P.R. BB/TR, 5'7", 150 lbs. Deb: 4/26/95

1995	NY-N	35	51	5	7	2	0	0	1	3	10	.137	.185	.176	-4	-8	2	1	0	1.000	-2	O-23	-1.0
1996	Phi-N	104	411	54	112	11	7	2	32	34	33	.273	.331	.348	79	-12	16	10	-1	.985	13	*O-100	-0.3
1997	Phi-N	50	151	20	38	6	2	0	3	19	15	.252	.339	.318	73	-5	0	3	-2	1.000	6	O-42	-0.2
Total	3	189	613	79	157	19	9	2	36	56	55	.256	.321	.326	71	-25	18	14	-3	.990	16	O-165	-1.5

■ AMOS OTIS   Otis, Amos Joseph b: 4/26/47, Mobile, Ala. BR/TR, 5'11", 166 lbs. Deb: 9/6/67 C

1967	NY-N	19	59	6	13	2	0	1	5	3	13	.220	.292	.254	59	-3	0	4	-2	1.000	-2	O-16/3-1	-0.9
1969	NY-N	48	93	6	14	3	1	0	4	6	27	.151	.202	.204	14	-11	1	0	0	1.000	-2	O-35/3-3	-1.5
1970	KC-A★	159	620	91	176	36	9	11	58	68	67	.284	.356	.424	114	12	33	2	9	.990	14	*O-159	2.7
1971	KC-A★	147	555	80	167	26	4	15	79	40	74	.301	.356	.443	125	16	52	8	11	.990	20	*O-144	4.2
1972	KC-A†	143	540	75	158	28	2	11	54	50	59	.293	.356	.413	129	19	28	12	1	.992	10	*O-137	2.6
1973	KC-A★	148	583	89	175	21	4	26	93	63	47	.300	.369	.484	129	21	13	9	-2	.986	3	*O-135,D-14	1.6
1974	KC-A	146	552	87	157	31	9	12	73	58	67	.284	.355	.438	120	14	18	5	2	.986	10	*O-143/D-2	2.1
1975	KC-A	132	470	87	116	26	6	9	46	66	48	.247	.344	.385	103	3	39	11	5	.988	5	*O-130	0.5
1976	*KC-A★	153	592	93	165	40	2	18	86	55	100	.279	.345	.444	129	21	26	7	4	.992	-5	*O-152	1.4
1977	*KC-A	142	478	85	120	20	8	17	78	71	88	.251	.348	.433	110	8	23	7	3	.991	1	*O-140	0.6
1978	*KC-A	141	486	74	145	30	7	22	96	66	54	.298	.387	.525	150	33	32	8	5	.995	10	*O-136/D-1	4.2
1979	KC-A	151	577	100	170	28	2	18	90	68	92	.295	.372	.444	117	14	30	5	6	.992	5	*O-146/D-4	1.9
1980	*KC-A	107	394	56	99	16	3	10	53	39	70	.251	.320	.383	92	-4	16	1	4	.988	7	*O-105	0.2
1981	KC-A	99	372	49	100	22	3	9	57	31	59	.269	.328	.417	114	6	16	7	1	.993	11	O-97/D-1	1.4
1982	KC-A	125	475	73	136	25	3	11	88	37	65	.286	.340	.421	108	5	9	5	-0	.997	-1	*O-125	0.0
1983	KC-A	98	356	35	93	16	3	4	41	27	63	.261	.313	.357	84	-8	2	0	1	.996	3	O-96/D-1	-0.7
1984	Pit-N	40	97	6	16	4	0	0	10	7	15	.165	.221	.206	21	-10	0	0	0	.964	2	O-32	-1.0
Total	17	1998	7299	1092	2020	374	66	193	1007	757	1008	.277	.347	.425	114	136	341	93	47	.991	87	*O-1928/D-23,3-4	19.3

■ BILL OTIS   Otis, Paul Franklin b: 12/24/1889, Scituate, Mass. d: 12/15/90, Duluth, Minn. BL/TR, 5'10.5", 150 lbs. Deb: 7/4/12

| 1912 | NY-A | 4 | 17 | 1 | 1 | 0 | 0 | 0 | 0 | 2 | 3 | .059 | .200 | .059 | -24 | -3 | 0 | | | .917 | 1 | /O-4 | -0.2 |

YEAR	TM/L	G	AB	R	H	2B	3B	HR	RBI	BB	SO	AVG	OBP	SLG	PRO+	BR/A	SB	CS	SBR	FA	FR	G/POS	TPR
■ **MEL OTT**	Ott, Melvin Thomas "Master Melvin" b: 3/2/09, Gretna, La. d: 11/21/58, New Orleans, La. BL/TR, 5'9", 170 lbs. Deb: 4/27/26 MH																						
1926	NY-N	35	60	7	23	2	0	0	4	1	9	.383	.393	.417	120	2	1			.913	1	O-10	0.2
1927	NY-N	82	163	23	46	7	3	1	19	13	9	.282	.335	.380	91	-2	2			.982	-7	O-32	-1.1
1928	NY-N	124	435	69	140	26	4	18	77	52	36	.322	.397	.524	138	24	3			.970	-3	*O-115/2-5,3-1	1.4
1929	NY-N	150	545	138	179	37	2	42	151	**113**	38	.328	.449	.635	166	59	6			.973	9	*O-149/2-1	5.2
1930	NY-N	148	521	122	182	34	5	25	119	103	35	.349	**.458**	.578	152	48	9			.969	6	*O-146	3.8
1931	NY-N	138	497	104	145	23	8	29	115	**80**	44	.292	.392	.545	**153**	38	10			.981	8	*O-137	**3.6**
1932	NY-N	154	566	119	180	30	8	**38**	123	**100**	39	.318	**.424**	.601	**175**	**63**	6			.984	2	*O-154	**5.3**
1933	*NY-N	152	580	98	164	36	1	23	103	**75**	48	.283	.367	.467	139	30	1			.983	-14	*O-152	0.9
1934	NY-N★	153	582	119	190	29	10	**35**	**135**	85	43	.326	.415	.591	**170**	**58**	0			.974	-9	*O-153	4.1
1935	NY-N★	152	593	113	191	33	6	31	114	82	58	.322	.407	.555	159	50	7			**.990**	6	*O-137,3-15	4.9
1936	*NY-N★	150	534	120	175	28	6	**33**	135	111	41	.328	.448	**.588**	**179**	**63**	6			.985	-3	*O-148	5.2
1937	*NY-N★	151	545	99	160	28	2	**31**	95	**102**	69	.294	.408	.523	149	40	7			.939	0	3-60,O-91	3.7
1938	NY-N★	150	527	**116**	164	23	6	**36**	116	118	47	.311	**.442**	.583	**178**	**61**	2			.957	1	*3-113,O-37	6.1
1939	NY-N★	125	396	85	122	23	2	27	80	100	50	.308	**.449**	.581	173	45	2			.973	-5	O-96,3-20	3.6
1940	NY-N★	151	536	89	155	27	3	19	79	100	50	.289	.407	.457	137	31	6			.982	2	*O-111,3-42	2.8
1941	NY-N★	148	525	89	150	29	0	27	90	100	68	.286	.403	.495	149	37	5			.968	5	*O-145	3.3
1942	NY-N★	152	549	**118**	162	21	0	**30**	93	**109**	61	.295	.415	.497	**165**	**49**	6			.990	-1	*O-152,M	4.2
1943	NY-N★	125	380	65	89	12	2	18	47	95	48	.234	.391	.418	133	20	7			.975	1	*O-111/3-1,M	1.5
1944	NY-N★	120	399	91	115	16	4	26	82	90	47	.288	.423	.544	171	41	2			.986	-4	*O-103/3-4,M	3.2
1945	NY-N†	135	451	73	139	23	0	21	79	71	41	.308	.411	.499	150	32	1			.983	-4	*O-118,M	2.2
1946	NY-N	31	68	2	5	1	0	1	4	8	15	.074	.171	.132	-13	-10	0			1.000	-1	O-16,M	-1.3
1947	NY-N	4	4	0	0	0	0	0	0	0	0	.000	.000	.000	-99	-1	0			.000	0	HM	-0.1
Total	22	2730	9456	1859	2876	488	72	511	1860	1708	896	.304	.414	.533	155	776	89			.980	-10	*O-2313,3-256/2-6	62.7
■ **ED OTT**	Ott, Nathan Edward b: 7/11/51, Muncy, Pa. BL/TR, 5'10", 198 lbs. Deb: 6/10/74 C																						
1974	Pit-N	7	5	1	0	0	0	0	0	0	1	.000	.000	.000	-99	-1	0	0	0	1.000	-1	/O-2	-0.2
1975	Pit-N	5	5	0	1	0	0	0	0	0	0	.200	.200	.200	11	-1	0	0	0	1.000	-0	/C-2	-0.1
1976	Pit-N	27	39	2	12	2	0	0	5	3	5	.308	.357	.359	103	0	0	0	0	1.000	-1	/C-8	0.0
1977	Pit-N	104	311	40	82	14	3	7	38	32	41	.264	.336	.395	93	-3	7	7	-2	.982	-5	C-90	-0.8
1978	Pit-N	112	379	49	102	18	4	9	38	27	56	.269	.318	.409	97	-2	4	1	1	.975	-9	C-97/O-4	-0.8
1979	*Pit-N	117	403	49	110	20	2	7	51	26	62	.273	.317	.385	86	-8	0	1	-1	.994	-3	*C-116	-0.7
1980	Pit-N	120	392	35	102	14	0	8	41	33	47	.260	.318	.357	87	-7	1	6	-3	.983	-4	*C-117/O-3	-1.0
1981	Cal-A	75	258	20	56	8	1	2	22	17	42	.217	.268	.279	58	-14	2	1	0	.979	1	C-72	-1.1
Total	8	567	1792	196	465	76	10	33	195	138	254	.259	.314	.368	86	-36	14	16	-5	.983	-21	C-502/O-9	-4.7
■ **BILLY OTT**	Ott, William Joseph b: 11/23/40, New York, N.Y. BB/TR, 6'1", 180 lbs. Deb: 9/4/62																						
1962	Chi-N	12	28	3	4	0	0	1	2	2	10	.143	.200	.250	19	-3	0	0	0	1.000	-0	/O-7	-0.4
1964	Chi-N	20	39	4	7	3	0	0	1	3	10	.179	.238	.256	38	-3	0	1	-1	1.000	-2	O-10	-0.6
Total	2	32	67	7	11	3	0	1	3	5	20	.164	.222	.254	30	-6	0	1	-1	1.000	-2	/O-17	-1.0
■ **JOE OTTEN**	Otten, Joseph G. b: Murphysboro, Ill. TR, Deb: 7/5/1895																						
1895	StL-N	26	87	8	21	0	0	0	8	5	8	.241	.283	.241	36	-8	2			.947	-4	C-24/O-2	-0.8
■ **BILLY OTTERSON**	Otterson, William John b: 5/4/1862, Pittsburgh, Pa. d: 9/21/40, Pittsburgh, Pa. BR/TR, 5'7", 124 lbs. Deb: 9/4/1887																						
1887	Bro-a	30	100	16	20	4	1	2	15	8		.200	.259	.320	60	-6	8			.859	1	S-30	-0.4
■ **PHIL OUELLETTE**	Ouellette, Philip Roland b: 11/10/61, Salem, Ore. BB/TR, 6', 190 lbs. Deb: 9/10/86																						
1986	SF-N	10	23	1	4	0	0	0	0	3	3	.174	.269	.174	26	-2	0	0	0	1.000	0	/C-9	-0.2
■ **JOHNNY OULLIBER**	Oulliber, John Andrew b: 2/24/11, New Orleans, La. d: 12/26/80, New Orleans, La. BR/TR, 5'11", 165 lbs. Deb: 7/25/33																						
1933	Cle-A	22	75	9	20	1	0	0	3	4	5	.267	.313	.280	55	-5	0	0	0	1.000	-3	O-18	-0.9
■ **CHINK OUTEN**	Outen, William Austin b: 6/17/05, Mt.Holly, N.C. d: 9/11/61, Durham, N.C. BL/TR, 6', 200 lbs. Deb: 4/16/33																						
1933	Bro-N	93	153	20	38	10	0	4	17	20	15	.248	.335	.392	112	3	1			.982	-13	C-56	-0.9
■ **JIMMY OUTLAW**	Outlaw, James Paulus b: 1/20/13, Orme, Tenn. BR/TR, 5'8", 168 lbs. Deb: 4/20/37																						
1937	Cin-N	49	165	18	45	7	3	0	11	3	31	.273	.290	.352	77	-6	2			.914	4	3-41	-0.1
1938	Cin-N	4	0	1	0	0	0	0	0	0	0	—	—	—	—	0	0			.000	0	R	0.0
1939	Bos-N	65	133	15	35	2	0	0	5	10	14	.263	.315	.278	65	-6	1			.964	-3	O-39/3-2	-1.1
1943	Det-A	20	67	8	18	1	0	1	6	8	4	.269	.347	.328	91	-1	0	0	0	1.000	-0	O-16	-0.1
1944	Det-A	139	535	69	146	20	6	3	57	41	40	.273	.327	.350	88	-8	7	8	-3	.964	-3	*O-137	-2.2
1945	*Det-A	132	446	56	121	16	5	0	34	45	33	.271	.338	.330	88	-6	6	7	-2	.967	-4	*O-105,3-21	-1.8
1946	Det-A	92	299	36	78	14	2	2	31	29	24	.261	.328	.341	82	-7	5	4	-1	1.000	-8	O-43,3-38	-1.8
1947	Det-A	70	127	20	29	7	1	0	15	21	14	.228	.338	.299	76	-4	3	1	0	.983	-7	O-37/3-9	-1.2
1948	Det-A	74	198	33	56	12	0	0	25	31	15	.283	.383	.343	91	-1	0	1	-1	.920	1	3-47,O-13	-0.2
1949	Det-A	5	4	1	1	0	0	0	0	0	1	.250	.250	.250	32	-0	0	0	0	.000	0	H	0.0
Total	10	650	1974	257	529	79	17	6	184	188	176	.268	.333	.334	85	-39	24	21		.972	-19	O-390,3-158	-8.5
■ **MICKEY OWEN**	Owen, Arnold Malcolm b: 4/4/16, Nixa, Mo. BR/TR, 5'10", 190 lbs. Deb: 5/2/37 C																						
1937	StL-N	80	234	17	54	4	2	0	20	15	13	.231	.277	.265	47	-17	1			.974	-3	C-78	-1.6
1938	StL-N	122	397	45	106	25	2	4	36	32	14	.267	.325	.370	86	-8	2			.980	1	*C-116	-0.1
1939	StL-N	131	344	32	89	18	2	3	35	43	28	.259	.344	.349	82	-8	6			.982	4	*C-126	0.2
1940	StL-N	117	307	27	81	16	2	0	27	34	13	.264	.341	.329	81	-7	4			.980	3	*C-113	0.2
1941	*Bro-N★	128	386	32	89	15	2	1	44	34	14	.231	.296	.288	62	-19	1			.995	6	*C-128	-0.3
1942	Bro-N★	133	421	53	109	16	3	0	44	44	17	.259	.330	.311	87	-6	10			.987	5	*C-133	0.9
1943	Bro-N☆	106	365	31	95	11	2	0	54	25	15	.260	.309	.301	77	-11	4			.987	-6	*C-100/3-3,S-1	-1.0
1944	Bro-N☆	130	461	43	126	20	3	1	42	36	17	.273	.326	.336	88	-7	4			.979	-11	*C-125/2-1	-1.1
1945	Bro-N	24	84	5	24	9	0	0	11	10	2	.286	.368	.393	113	2	0			.963	-3	C-24	0.2
1949	Chi-N	62	198	15	54	9	3	2	18	12	13	.273	.318	.379	88	-4	1			.969	-1	C-59	-0.1
1950	Chi-N	86	259	22	63	11	0	2	21	13	16	.243	.282	.309	56	-17	2			.978	3	C-86	-1.0
1951	Chi-N	58	125	10	23	6	0	0	15	19	13	.184	.292	.232	42	-10	1	0	0	.969	8	C-57	0.0
1954	Bos-A	32	68	6	16	3	0	1	11	9	6	.235	.325	.324	70	-3	0	1	-1	.989	-2	C-30	-0.5
Total	13	1209	3649	338	929	163	21	14	378	326	181	.255	.318	.322	76	-114	36	1		.982	3	*C-1175/3-3,2-1,S-1	-4.4
■ **DAVE OWEN**	Owen, Dave b: 4/25/58, Cleburne, Tex. BB/TR, 6'2", 170 lbs. Deb: 9/6/83 F																						
1983	Chi-N	16	22	1	2	0	1	0	2	2	7	.091	.167	.182	-3	-3	1	0	0	1.000	4	S-14/3-3	0.1
1984	Chi-N	47	93	8	18	2	2	1	10	8	15	.194	.272	.290	53	-6	1	2	-1	.969	1	S-35/3 6,2 4	-0.4
1985	Chi-N	22	19	6	7	0	0	0	4	1	5	.368	.400	.368	105	0	1	1	-0	.917	2	/S-7,3-7,2-4	0.2
1988	KC-A	7	5	0	0	0	0	0	0	0	3	.000	.000	.000	-99	-1	0	0	0	.941	4	/S-7	0.3
Total	4	92	139	15	27	2	3	1	16	11	30	.194	.263	.273	47	-10	3	3	-1	.969	10	/S-63,3-16,2-8	0.2
■ **LARRY OWEN**	Owen, Lawrence Thomas b: 5/31/55, Cleveland, Ohio BR/TR, 5'11", 185 lbs. Deb: 8/14/81																						
1981	Atl-N	13	16	0	0	0	0	0	0	1	4	.000	.059	.000	-80	-4	0	0	0	.964	2	C-10	-0.2
1982	Atl-N	2	3	1	1	1	0	0	0	0	1	.333	.333	.667	167	0	0	0	0	1.000	-0	/C-2	0.0
1983	Atl-N	17	17	0	2	0	0	0	1	0	2	.118	.118	.118	-32	-3	0	1	-1	.970	1	C-16	-0.3
1985	Atl-N	26	71	7	17	3	0	2	12	8	17	.239	.316	.366	85	-1	0	0	0	.966	3	C-25	0.2
1987	KC-A	76	164	17	31	6	0	5	14	16	51	.189	.261	.317	51	-12	0	0	0	.983	19	C-75	1.0
1988	KC-A	37	81	5	17	1	0	1	3	9	23	.210	.304	.259	59	-4	0	0	0	.989	5	C-37	0.3
Total	6	171	352	30	68	11	0	8	30	34	98	.193	.268	.293	51	-24	0	1	-1	.980	29	C-165	1.0

YEAR	TM/L	G	AB	R	H	2B	3B	HR	RBI	BB	SO	AVG	OBP	SLG	PRO+	BR/A	SB	CS	SBR	FA	FR	G/POS	TPR
■ **MARV OWEN**	Owen, Marvin James "Freck" b: 3/22/06, Agnew, Cal. d: 6/22/91, Mountain View, Cal. BR/TR, 6'1", 175 lbs. Deb: 4/16/31																						
1931	Det-A	105	377	35	84	11	6	3	39	29	38	.223	.282	.308	53	-26	2	2	-1	.937	1	S-37,3-37,1-27,/2-4	-2.0
1933	Det-A	138	550	77	144	24	9	2	65	44	56	.262	.321	.349	76	-19	2	2	-1	.944	-11	*3-136	-2.1
1934	*Det-A	154	565	79	179	34	9	8	96	59	37	.317	.385	.451	115	13	3	3	-1	.956	-7	*3-154	1.0
1935	*Det-A	134	483	52	127	24	5	2	71	43	37	.263	.326	.346	76	-17	1	4	-2	.958	-10	*3-131	-2.3
1936	Det-A	154	583	72	172	20	4	9	105	53	41	.295	.361	.389	85	-13	9	6	-1	.952	-4	*3-153/1-2	-1.1
1937	Det-A	107	396	48	114	22	5	1	45	41	24	.288	.358	.376	83	-10	3	4	-2	**.970**	0	*3-106	-0.8
1938	Chi-A	141	577	84	162	23	6	6	55	45	31	.281	.337	.373	76	-22	6	4	-1	.948	0	*3-140	-1.8
1939	Chi-A	58	194	22	46	9	0	0	15	16	15	.237	.302	.284	49	-15	4	5	-2	.953	-2	3-55	-1.7
1940	Bos-A	20	57	4	12	0	0	0	6	8	4	.211	.308	.211	36	-5	0	0	0	.962	2	/3-9,1-8	-0.4
Total	9	1011	3782	473	1040	167	44	31	497	338	283	.275	.339	.367	80	-114	30	30	-9	.953	-30	3-921/1-37,S-37,2-4	-11.2
■ **SPIKE OWEN**	Owen, Spike Dee b: 4/19/61, Cleburne, Tex. BB/TR, 5'10", 170 lbs. Deb: 6/25/83 F																						
1983	Sea-A	80	306	36	60	11	3	2	21	24	44	.196	.259	.271	44	-23	10	6	-1	.970	-0	S-80	-1.6
1984	Sea-A	152	530	67	130	18	8	3	43	46	63	.245	.309	.326	77	-16	16	8	0	.977	16	*S-151	1.5
1985	Sea-A	118	352	41	91	10	6	6	37	34	27	.259	.324	.372	89	-5	11	5	0	.975	**30**	*S-117	3.5
1986	Sea-A	112	402	46	99	22	6	0	35	34	42	.246	.307	.331	73	-15	1	3	-2	.972	34	*S-112	2.7
	*Bos-A	42	126	21	23	2	1	1	10	17	9	.183	.285	.238	44	-10	3	1	0	.976	-2	S-42	-0.7
	Yr	154	528	67	122	24	7	1	45	51	51	.231	.301	.309	66	-24	4	4	-1	.973	**32**	*S-154	2.0
1987	Bos-A	132	437	50	113	17	7	2	48	53	43	.259	.340	.343	80	-12	11	8	-2	.975	-14	*S-130	-1.5
1988	*Bos-A	89	257	40	64	14	1	5	18	27	27	.249	.325	.370	90	-3	0	1	-1	.967	-1	S-76/D-7	0.1
1989	Mon-N	142	437	52	102	17	4	6	41	76	44	.233	.351	.332	95	-0	3	2	-0	**.979**	11	*S-142	2.2
1990	Mon-N	149	453	55	106	24	5	5	35	70	60	.234	.337	.342	91	-4	8	6	-1	**.989**	-12	*S-148	-0.8
1991	Mon-N	139	424	39	108	22	8	3	26	42	61	.255	.323	.366	95	-3	2	6	-3	.986	8	*S-133	1.1
1992	Mon-N	122	386	52	104	16	3	7	40	50	30	.269	.353	.381	109	5	9	4	0	.982	-10	*S-116	0.4
1993	NY-A	103	334	41	78	16	2	2	20	29	30	.234	.295	.311	65	-16	3	2	-0	.968	10	S-96/D-2	0.0
1994	Cal-A	82	268	30	83	17	2	3	37	49	17	.310	.418	.422	116	9	2	8	-4	.956	0	3-70/S-5,1-4,2-1,D	0.4
1995	Cal-A	82	218	17	50	9	3	1	28	18	22	.229	.288	.312	57	-14	3	2	-0	.945	-18	3-29,S-25,2-16	-2.9
Total	13	1544	4930	587	1211	215	59	46	439	569	519	.246	.326	.341	83	-107	82	62	-13	.977	51	*S-1373/3-99,2D1	4.4
■ **JAYHAWK OWENS**	Owens, Claude Jayhawk b: 2/10/69, Cincinnati, Ohio BR/TR, 6'1", 200 lbs. Deb: 6/6/93																						
1993	Col-N	33	86	12	18	5	0	3	6	6	30	.209	.277	.372	62	-5	1	0	0	.957	1	C-32	-0.2
1994	Col-N	6	12	4	3	0	1	0	1	3	3	.250	.400	.417	97	0	0	0	0	1.000	1	/C-6	0.1
1995	*Col-N	18	45	7	11	2	0	4	12	2	15	.244	.292	.556	91	-1	0	0	0	.988	2	C-16	0.2
1996	Col-N	73	180	31	43	9	1	4	17	27	56	.239	.341	.367	70	-9	4	1	1	.974	-3	C-68	-0.7
Total	4	130	323	54	75	16	2	11	36	38	104	.232	.321	.396	72	-15	5	1	1	.973	1	C-122	-0.6
■ **ERIC OWENS**	Owens, Eric Blake b: 2/3/71, Danville, Va. BR/TR, 6'1", 185 lbs. Deb: 6/6/95																						
1995	Cin-N	2	2	0	2	0	0	0	1	0	0	1.000	1.000	1.000	432	1	0	0	0	.000	0	/3-2	0.1
1996	Cin-N	88	205	26	41	6	0	0	9	23	38	.200	.284	.229	37	-18	16	2	4	.986	-5	O-52/2-6,3-5	-2.0
1997	Cin-N	27	57	8	15	0	0	0	3	4	11	.263	.311	.263	52	-4	3	2	-0	.938	-4	O-18/2-2	-0.9
1998	Mil-N	34	40	5	5	2	0	1	4	2	6	.125	.167	.250	6	-6	0	0	0	1.000	-4	O-16/2-4	-1.0
Total	4	151	304	39	63	8	0	1	17	29	55	.207	.278	.243	38	-27	19	4	3	.980	-14	/O-86,2-12,3-7	-3.8
■ **FRANK OWENS**	Owens, Frank Walter "Yip" b: 1/26/1886, Toronto, Ont., Can. d: 7/2/58, Minneapolis, Minn. BR/TR, 6', 170 lbs. Deb: 9/11/05																						
1905	Bos-A	1	2	0	0	0	0	0	0	0		.000	.000	.000	-99	-0	0			1.000	-0	/C-1	-0.1
1909	Chi-A	64	174	12	35	4	1	0	17	8		.201	.245	.236	54	-9	3			.959	-6	C-57	-1.2
1914	Bro-F	58	184	15	51	7	3	2	20	9	16	.277	.314	.380	89	-6	2			.967	-14	C-58	-1.7
1915	Bal-F	99	334	32	84	14	7	3	28	17	34	.251	.290	.362	80	-15	4			.976	2	C-99	-0.6
Total	4	222	694	59	170	25	11	5	65	34	50	.245	.284	.334	77	-30	9			.969	-19	C-215	-3.6
■ **JACK OWENS**	Owens, Furman Lee b: 5/6/08, Converse, S.C. d: 11/14/58, Greenville, S.C. BR/TR, 6'1", 186 lbs. Deb: 9/21/35																						
1935	Phi-A	2	8	0	2	0	0	0	1	0	1	.250	.250	.250	30	-1	0	0	0	.900	-0	/C-2	-0.1
■ **RED OWENS**	Owens, Thomas Llewellyn b: 11/1/1874, Pottsville, Pa. d: 8/20/52, Harrisburg, Pa. BR/TR, Deb: 7/28/1899																						
1899	Phi-N	8	21	0	1	0	0	0	1	2		.048	.130	.048	-52	-4	0			.914	-1	/2-8	-0.4
1905	Bro-N	43	168	14	36	6	2	1	20	6		.214	.241	.292	63	-8	1			.929	4	2-43	-0.4
Total	2	51	189	14	37	6	2	1	21	8		.196	.228	.265	49	-13	1			.927	3	/2-51	-0.8
■ **HENRY OXLEY**	Oxley, Henry Havelock b: 1/4/1858, Covehead, P.E.I., Canada d: 10/12/45, Somerville, Mass. 5'11", 163 lbs. Deb: 7/30/1884																						
1884	NY-N	2	4	0	0	0	0	0	0	1	2	.000	.200	.000	-31	-1				.900	1	/C-2	0.0
	NY-a	1	3	0	0	0	0	0		0		.000	.000	.000	-99	-1				.889	0	/C-1	0.0
Total	1	3	7	0	0	0	0	0	0	1	2	.000	.125	.000	-56	-1				.895	1	/C-3	0.0
■ **ANDY OYLER**	Oyler, Andrew Paul "Pepper" b: 5/5/1880, Newville, Pa. d: 10/24/70, E.Pennsboro Twsp., Pa. BR/TR, 5'6.5", 138 lbs. Deb: 5/8/02																						
1902	Bal-A	27	77	9	17	1	0	1	6	8		.221	.318	.273	62	-4	3			.947	-8	3-20/O-3,S-2,2-1	-1.1
■ **RAY OYLER**	Oyler, Raymond Francis b: 8/4/38, Indianapolis, Ind. d: 1/26/81, Seattle, Wash. BR/TR, 5'11", 165 lbs. Deb: 4/18/65																						
1965	Det-A	82	194	22	36	6	0	5	13	21	61	.186	.265	.294	58	-11	1	0	0	.955	6	S-57,2-11/1-1,3-1	-0.1
1966	Det-A	71	210	16	36	8	3	1	9	23	62	.171	.263	.252	48	-14	0	0	0	.965	15	S-69	0.6
1967	Det-A	148	367	33	76	14	2	1	29	37	91	.207	.283	.264	61	-17	0	2	-1	.964	15	*S-146	0.9
1968	*Det-A	111	215	13	29	6	1	1	12	20	59	.135	.215	.186	22	-20	0	2	-1	.977	9	*S-111	-0.5
1969	Sea-A	106	255	24	42	5	0	7	22	31	80	.165	.260	.267	48	-18	1	2	-1	.965	9	*S-106	-0.1
1970	Cal-A	24	24	2	2	0	0	0	1	3	6	.083	.185	.083	-24	-4	0	0	0	1.000	-1	S-13/3-2	-0.5
Total	6	542	1265	110	221	39	6	15	86	135	359	.175	.259	.251	48	-84	2	6	-3	.966	52	S-502/2-11,3-3,1-1	0.3
■ **CHARLIE PABOR**	Pabor, Charles Henry b: 9/24/1846, New York, N.Y. d: 4/23/13, New Haven, Conn. BL/TL, 5'8", 155 lbs. Deb: 5/4/1871 M																						
1871	Cle-n	29	142	24	42	2	4	0	18	1	3	.296	.301	.366	96	-0	1	0	0	.773	-5	*O-28/P-7,M	-0.3
1872	Cle-n	21	92	12	19	0	0	0	7	0	0	.207	.207	.207	29	-7	0	0	0	.863	-0	O-20/P-2	-0.4
1873	Atl-n	55	228	36	82	8	3	0	42	6	3	.360	.376	.421	153	16	2	0	1	.807	-4	*O-55	1.1
1874	Phi-n	17	77	11	17	0	1	0	1	0	0	.221	.221	.247	48	-4	0	1	-1	.553	-1	O-17	-0.5
1875	Atl-n	42	153	14	36	2	2	0	11	1	1	.235	.240	.275	90	-1	0	0	0	.803	1	O-42/P-1,M	0.1
	NH-n	6	23	4	8	0	2	0	2	0	1	.348	.348	.522	227	3	0	0	0	.818	-1	/O-6,M	0.2
	Yr	48	176	18	44	2	4	0	13	1	2	.250	.254	.307	108	2	0	0	0	.804	-0	O-48/P-1	0.3
Total	5 n	170	715	101	204	12	12	0	81	8	8	.285	.293	.336	102	7	3	1	0	.787	-11	O-168/P-10	0.2
■ **ED PABST**	Pabst, Edward D. A. b: 1868, St.Louis, Mo. d: 6/19/40, St.Louis, Mo. 5'11", 170 lbs. Deb: 9/26/1890																						
1890	Phi-a	8	25	7	10	2	0	0	3	5		.400	.500	.480	193	3	3			.963	4	/O-8	0.6
	StL-a	4	14	1	2	0	1	0	0	0		.143	.143	.286	23	-2	0			1.000	1	/O-4	0.0
	Yr	12	39	8	12	2	1	0	3	5		.308	.386	.410	131	1	3			.972	5	O-12	0.6
■ **JIM PACIOREK**	Paciorek, James Joseph b: 6/7/60, Detroit, Mich. BR/TR, 6'3", 203 lbs. Deb: 4/9/87 F																						
1987	Mil-A	48	101	16	23	5	0	2	10	12	20	.228	.310	.337	69	-4	1	0	0	.980	-4	1-21,3-15/O-5,D-2	-0.9
■ **JOHN PACIOREK**	Paciorek, John Francis b: 2/11/45, Detroit, Mich. BR/TR, 6'2", 200 lbs. Deb: 9/29/63 F																						
1963	Hou-N	1	3	4	3	0	0	0	3	2	0	1.000	1.000	1.000	509	2	0	0	0	1.000	0	/O-1	0.2
■ **TOM PACIOREK**	Paciorek, Thomas Marian b: 11/2/46, Detroit, Mich. BR/TR, 6'4", 215 lbs. Deb: 9/12/70 F																						
1970	LA-N	8	9	2	2	1	0	0	0	0	3	.222	.300	.333	73	-0	0	0	0	1.000	-1	/O-3	-0.1
1971	LA-N	2	2	0	1	0	0	0	1	0	0	.500	.500	.500	196	0	0	0	0	1.000	-0	/O-1	0.0
1972	LA-N	11	47	4	12	4	0	1	6	1	7	.255	.271	.404	92	-1	1	0	0	.979	1	/1-6,O-6	0.0
1973	LA-N	96	195	26	51	8	0	5	18	11	35	.262	.304	.379	92	-3	3	3	-1	.979	-15	O-77/1-4	-2.2

YEAR	TM/L	G	AB	R	H	2B	3B	HR	RBI	BB	SO	AVG	OBP	SLG	PRO+	BR/A	SB	CS	SBR	FA	FR	G/POS	TPR
1974	*LA-N	85	175	23	42	8	6	1	24	10	32	.240	.285	.371	86	-4	1	3	-2	.944	-16	O-77/1-1	-2.5
1975	LA-N	62	145	14	28	8	0	1	5	11	29	.193	.250	.269	46	-11	4	3	-1	.972	-9	O-54	-2.4
1976	Atl-N	111	324	39	94	10	4	4	36	19	57	.290	.335	.383	97	-1	2	3	-1	.983	-12	O-84,1-12/3-1	-2.0
1977	Atl-N	72	155	20	37	8	0	3	15	6	46	.239	.267	.348	57	-10	1	0	0	.984	-2	1-32/O-9,3-1	-1.3
1978	Atl-N	5	9	2	3	0	0	0	0	0	1	.333	.333	.333	78	-0	0	0	0	1.000	-0	/1-2	-0.1
	Sea-A	70	251	32	75	20	3	4	30	15	39	.299	.338	.450	121	6	2	2	-1	.980	-3	O-54,D-12/1-3	0.0
1979	Sea-A	103	310	38	89	23	4	6	42	28	62	.287	.356	.445	113	5	6	4	-1	1.000	-2	O-75,1-15	-0.1
1980	Sea-A	126	418	44	114	19	1	15	59	17	67	.273	.303	.431	98	-3	3	2	-0	1.000	-3	O-60,1-36,D-23	-1.0
1981	Sea-A★	104	405	50	132	28	2	14	66	35	50	.326	.385	.509	150	25	13	10	-2	.974	6	*O-103	2.7
1982	Chi-A	104	382	49	119	27	4	11	55	24	53	.312	.366	.490	133	17	3	3	-1	.993	-1	*1-102/O-6	0.9
1983	*Chi-A	115	420	65	129	32	3	9	63	25	58	.307	.350	.462	117	9	6	1	1	1.000	-10	1-67,O-55/D-2	-0.5
1984	Chi-A	111	363	35	93	21	2	4	29	25	69	.256	.311	.358	81	-9	6	0	2	.993	-13	1-67,O-41	-2.5
1985	Chi-A	46	122	14	30	2	0	0	9	8	22	.246	.298	.262	53	-8	2	0	1	.970	-2	O-23,D-12/1-6	-1.0
	NY-N	46	116	14	33	3	1	1	11	6	14	.284	.325	.353	92	-1	1	0	0	1.000	-5	O-29/1-8	-0.7
1986	Tex-A	88	213	17	61	7	0	4	22	3	41	.286	.306	.376	82	-5	1	3	-2	.967	-1	O-25,1-23,3-21,/SD	-1.0
1987	Tex-A	27	60	6	17	3	0	3	12	1	19	.283	.306	.483	105	0	0	1	-1	1.000	-0	1-12,O-12/D-3	-0.1
Total	18	1392	4121	494	1162	232	30	86	503	245	704	.282	.328	.415	102	6	55	38	-6	.979	-89	O-794,1-396/D3S	-13.9

■ FRANKIE PACK

Pack, Frank b: 4/10/28, Morristown, Tenn. BL/TR, 6', 190 lbs. Deb: 6/5/49

YEAR	TM/L	G	AB	R	H	2B	3B	HR	RBI	BB	SO	AVG	OBP	SLG	PRO+	BR/A	SB	CS	SBR	FA	FR	G/POS	TPR
1949	StL-A	1	1	0	0	0	0	0	0	0	1	.000	.000	.000	-96	-0	0	0	0	.000	0	H	0.0

■ DICK PADDEN

Padden, Richard Joseph "Brains" b: 9/17/1870, Martins Ferry, O. d: 10/31/22, Martins Ferry, O. BR/TR, 5'10", 165 lbs. Deb: 7/15/1896

YEAR	TM/L	G	AB	R	H	2B	3B	HR	RBI	BB	SO	AVG	OBP	SLG	PRO+	BR/A	SB	CS	SBR	FA	FR	G/POS	TPR
1896	Pit-N	61	219	33	53	4	8	2	24	14	9	.242	.294	.361	75	-9	8			.931	-12	2-61	-1.5
1897	Pit-N	134	517	84	146	16	10	2	58	38		.282	.350	.364	92	-5	18			.941	2	*2-134	0.3
1898	Pit-N	128	463	61	119	7	6	2	43	35		.257	.335	.311	87	-7	11			.947	-2	*2-128	0.0
1899	Was-N	134	451	66	125	20	7	2	61	24		.277	.337	.366	94	-4	27			.913	8	S-85,2-48	1.2
1901	StL-N	123	489	71	125	17	7	2	62	31		.256	.315	.331	92	-5	26			.950	1	*2-115/S-8	0.1
1902	StL-A	117	413	54	109	26	3	1	40	30		.264	.327	.349	89	-6	11			**.967**	18	*2-117	1.5
1903	StL-A	29	94	7	19	3	0	0	6	9		.202	.306	.234	65	-3	5			.955	6	2-29	0.4
1904	StL-A	132	453	42	108	19	4	0	36	40		.238	.325	.298	104	4	23			.959	-9	*2-132	-0.2
1905	StL-A	16	58	5	10	1	1	0	4	3		.172	.213	.224	41	-4	3			.950	0	2-16	-0.4
Total	9	874	3157	423	814	113	46	11	334	224	9	.258	.326	.333	90	-39	132			.950	11	2-780/S-93	1.4

■ TOM PADDEN

Padden, Thomas Francis b: 10/6/08, Manchester, N.H. d: 6/10/73, Manchester, N.H. BR/TR, 5'11.5", 170 lbs. Deb: 5/29/32

YEAR	TM/L	G	AB	R	H	2B	3B	HR	RBI	BB	SO	AVG	OBP	SLG	PRO+	BR/A	SB	CS	SBR	FA	FR	G/POS	TPR
1932	Pit-N	47	118	13	31	6	1	0	10	9	7	.263	.315	.331	75	-4	0			.985	-1	C-43	-0.3
1933	Pit-N	30	90	5	19	2	0	0	8	2	6	.211	.237	.233	35	-8	0			.984	6	C-27	0.0
1934	Pit-N	82	237	27	76	12	2	0	22	30	23	.321	.399	.388	109	5	3			.978	-5	C-76	0.3
1935	Pit-N	97	302	35	82	9	1	1	30	48	26	.272	.371	.318	84	-4	1			.966	14	C-94	1.4
1936	Pit-N	88	281	22	70	9	2	1	31	22	41	.249	.304	.306	63	-14	0			.976	2	C-87	-0.8
1937	Pit-N	35	98	14	28	2	0	0	8	13	11	.286	.369	.306	85	-1	1			.983	6	C-34	0.6
1943	Phi-N	17	41	5	12	0	0	0	1	2	6	.293	.341	.293	87	-1	0			1.000	4	C-16	0.4
	Was-A	3	3	1	0	0	0	0	0	1	1	.000	.250	.000	-25	-0	0	0	0	1.000	0	/C-2	0.0
Total	7	399	1170	122	318	40	6	2	110	127	121	.272	.345	.321	80	-28	5	0		.977	27	C-379	1.6

■ DEL PADDOCK

Paddock, Delmar Harold b: 6/8/1887, Volga, S.Dak. d: 2/6/52, Remer, Minn BL/TR, 5'9", 165 lbs. Deb: 4/14/12

YEAR	TM/L	G	AB	R	H	2B	3B	HR	RBI	BB	SO	AVG	OBP	SLG	PRO+	BR/A	SB	CS	SBR	FA	FR	G/POS	TPR
1912	Chi-A	1	1	0	0	0	0	0	0	0		.000	.000	.000	-99	-0	0			.000	0	H	0.0
	NY-A	46	156	26	45	5	3	1	14	23		.288	.393	.378	114	4	9			.894	-7	3-41/2-2,O-1	-0.3
	Yr	47	157	26	45	5	3	1	14	23		.287	.391	.376	113	3	9			.894	-7	3-41/2-2,O-1	-0.3

■ DON PADGETT

Padgett, Don Wilson b: 12/5/11, Caroleen, N.C. d: 12/9/80, High Point, N.C. BL/TR, 6', 190 lbs. Deb: 4/23/37

YEAR	TM/L	G	AB	R	H	2B	3B	HR	RBI	BB	SO	AVG	OBP	SLG	PRO+	BR/A	SB	CS	SBR	FA	FR	G/POS	TPR
1937	StL-N	123	446	62	140	22	6	10	74	30	43	.314	.357	.457	117	10	4			.955	3	*O-109	0.9
1938	StL-N	110	388	59	105	26	5	8	65	18	28	.271	.303	.425	93	-5	0			.962	5	O-71,1-16/C-6	-0.4
1939	StL-N	92	233	38	93	15	3	5	53	18	11	.399	.444	.554	157	19	1			.978	-3	C-61/1-6	1.8
1940	StL-N	93	240	24	58	15	1	6	41	26	14	.242	.321	.387	89	-4	1			.962	-8	C-72/1-2	-0.7
1941	StL-N	107	324	39	80	18	0	5	44	21	16	.247	.293	.349	75	-11	0			.959	-9	O-62,C-18/1-2	-2.4
1946	Bro-N	19	30	2	5	1	0	1	9	4	4	.167	.265	.300	59	-2	0			1.000	-1	C-10	-0.3
	Bos-N	44	98	6	25	3	0	2	21	5	7	.255	.291	.347	80	-3	0			.939	-6	C-26	-0.8
	Yr	63	128	8	30	4	0	3	30	9	11	.234	.285	.336	75	-5	0			.954	-7	C-36	-1.1
1947	Phi-N	75	158	14	50	8	1	0	24	16	5	.316	.383	.380	107	2	0			.962	-7	C-39	-0.3
1948	Phi-N	36	74	3	17	3	0	0	7	3	2	.230	.260	.270	44	-6	0			.957	-4	C-19	-0.9
Total	8	699	1991	247	573	111	16	37	338	141	130	.288	.336	.415	101	1	6			.962	-32	C-251,O-242/1-26	-3.1

■ ERNIE PADGETT

Padgett, Ernest Kitchen "Red" b: 3/1/1899, Philadelphia, Pa. d: 4/15/57, E.Orange, N.J. BR/TR, 5'8", 155 lbs. Deb: 10/3/23

YEAR	TM/L	G	AB	R	H	2B	3B	HR	RBI	BB	SO	AVG	OBP	SLG	PRO+	BR/A	SB	CS	SBR	FA	FR	G/POS	TPR
1923	Bos-N	4	11	3	2	0	0	0	0	2	0	.182	.308	.182	33	-1	0	0	0	.947	2	/S-2,2-1	0.1
1924	Bos-N	138	502	42	128	25	9	1	46	37	56	.255	.310	.347	79	-15	4	9	-4	.967	-11	*3-113,2-29	-2.2
1925	Bos-N	86	256	31	78	9	7	0	29	14	14	.305	.341	.395	96	-2	3	5	-2	.964	-20	2-47,S-18/3-7	-2.1
1926	Cle-A	36	62	7	13	0	1	0	6	8	3	.210	.300	.242	42	-5	1	0	0	.930	2	3-29/S-2	-0.2
1927	Cle-A	7	7	1	2	0	0	0	0	0	2	.286	.286	.286	48	-1	0	0	0	1.000	-0	/2-4	-0.1
Total	5	271	838	84	223	34	17	1	81	61	75	.266	.318	.351	80	-24	8	14	-6	.957	-27	3-149/2-81,S-22	-4.5

■ DENNIS PAEPKE

Paepke, Dennis Ray b: 4/17/45, Long Beach, Cal. BR/TR, 6', 202 lbs. Deb: 6/2/69

YEAR	TM/L	G	AB	R	H	2B	3B	HR	RBI	BB	SO	AVG	OBP	SLG	PRO+	BR/A	SB	CS	SBR	FA	FR	G/POS	TPR
1969	KC-A	12	27	2	3	1	0	0	0	2	3	.111	.172	.148	-10	-4	0	0	0	1.000	3	/C-8	-0.1
1971	KC-A	60	152	11	31	6	0	2	14	8	29	.204	.244	.283	49	-10	0	0	0	.994	-3	C-32,O-17	-1.5
1972	KC-A	2	6	0	0	0	0	0	0	1	2	.000	.143	.000	-55	-1	0	0	0	.842	1	/C-2	0.0
1974	KC-A	6	12	0	2	0	0	0	0	1	2	.167	.231	.167	15	-1	0	1	-1	1.000	-1	/C-4,O-1	-0.3
Total	4	80	197	13	36	7	0	2	14	12	36	.183	.230	.249	36	-17	0	1	-1	.984	-1	/C-46,O-18	-1.9

■ ANDY PAFKO

Pafko, Andrew "Handy Andy" or "Pruschka" b: 2/25/21, Boyceville, Wis. BR/TR, 6', 190 lbs. Deb: 9/24/43 C

YEAR	TM/L	G	AB	R	H	2B	3B	HR	RBI	BB	SO	AVG	OBP	SLG	PRO+	BR/A	SB	CS	SBR	FA	FR	G/POS	TPR
1943	Chi-N	13	58	7	22	3	0	0	10	2	5	.379	.400	.431	142	3	1			1.000	-2	O-13	0.0
1944	Chi-N	128	469	47	126	16	2	6	62	28	23	.269	.315	.350	87	-8	2			.983	15	*O-123	0.0
1945	*Chi-N†	144	534	64	159	24	12	12	110	45	36	.298	.361	.455	129	19	5			**.995**	3	*O-140	1.5
1946	Chi-N	65	234	18	66	6	4	3	39	27	15	.282	.366	.380	114	5	4			.978	11	O-64	1.3
1947	Chi-N★	129	513	68	155	25	7	13	66	31	39	.302	.346	.454	115	9	4			.985	7	*O-127	0.9
1948	Chi-N★	142	548	82	171	30	2	26	101	50	50	.312	.375	.516	145	32	3			.938	13	*3-139	4.3
1949	Chi-N★	144	519	79	146	29	2	18	69	63	33	.281	.369	.449	121	16	4			.987	-7	O-98,3-49	0.4
1950	Chi-N★	146	514	95	156	24	8	36	92	69	32	.304	.397	.591	158	43	4			.978	-1	*O-144	3.5
1951	Chi-N	49	178	26	47	5	3	12	35	17	10	.264	.342	.528	128	6	1	1	-0	.992	2	O-48	0.6
	Bro-N	84	277	42	69	11	0	18	58	35	27	.249	.350	.484	120	7	1	4	-2	.993	-2	O-76	0.1
	Yr	133	455	68	116	16	3	30	93	52	37	.255	.347	.501	123	14	2	5	-2	.993	0	*O-124	0.7
1952	*Bro-N	150	551	76	158	17	5	19	85	64	48	.287	.366	.439	121	16	4	3	-1	.988	-7	*O-139,3-13	0.3
1953	Mil-N	140	516	70	153	23	4	17	72	37	33	.297	.347	.455	114	9	2	1	0	.976	-4	*O-139	0.1
1954	Mil-N	138	510	61	146	22	4	14	69	37	36	.286	.339	.427	105	2	1	2	-1	.969	-4	*O-138	-0.8
1955	Mil-N	86	252	29	67	3	5	5	34	7	23	.266	.297	.377	81	-7	1	2	-1	.980	-8	O-58,3-12	-1.9
1956	Mil-N	45	93	15	24	5	0	2	9	10	13	.258	.330	.376	95	-1	0	0	0	.978	-5	O-37	-0.7
1957	*Mil-N	83	220	31	61	6	1	8	27	10	22	.277	.312	.423	102	-0	1	0	0	.982	-6	O-69	-0.9
1958	*Mil-N	95	164	17	39	7	1	3	23	15	17	.238	.309	.348	80	-5	0	0	0	1.000	-14	O-93	-2.2
1959	Mil-N	71	142	17	31	8	2	1	15	14	15	.218	.293	.324	70	-6	0	0	0	.978	-12	O-64	-2.0
Total	17	1852	6292	844	1796	264	62	213	976	561	477	.285	.351	.449	118	141	38	13		.984	-21	*O-1570,3-213	4.5

■ JOSE PAGAN

Pagan, Jose Antonio (Rodriguez) b: 5/5/35, Barceloneta, P.R. BR/TR, 5'9", 165 lbs. Deb: 8/4/59 C

YEAR	TM/L	G	AB	R	H	2B	3B	HR	RBI	BB	SO	AVG	OBP	SLG	PRO+	BR/A	SB	CS	SBR	FA	FR	G/POS	TPR
1959	SF-N	31	46	7	8	1	0	0	1	2	8	.174	.208	.196	9	-6	1	0	0	.900	3	3-18/S-5,2-3	-0.2

YEAR	TM/L	G	AB	R	H	2B	3B	HR	RBI	BB	SO	AVG	OBP	SLG	PRO+	BR/A	SB	CS	SBR	FA	FR	G/POS	TPR
1960	SF-N	18	49	8	14	2	2	0	2	1	6	.286	.300	.408	97	-0	2	2	-1	.917	-8	S-11/3-1	-0.9
1961	SF-N	134	434	38	110	15	2	5	46	31	45	.253	.306	.332	72	-18	8	5	-1	.964	-19	*S-132/O-4	-2.6
1962	*SF-N	164	580	73	150	25	6	7	57	47	77	.259	.315	.359	82	-15	13	9	-2	**.973**	-25	*S-164	-2.7
1963	SF-N	148	483	46	113	12	1	6	39	26	67	.234	.279	.300	67	-20	10	7	-1	.970	-18	*S-143/2-1,O-1	-3.2
1964	SF-N	134	367	33	82	10	1	1	28	35	66	.223	.293	.264	57	-20	5	4	-1	.958	-18	*S-132/O-8	-3.3
1965	SF-N	26	83	10	17	4	0	0	5	8	9	.205	.275	.253	48	-6	1	0	0	.941	-5	S-26	-1.0
	Pit-N	42	38	6	9	1	0	0	1	1	7	.237	.275	.263	52	-2	1	0	0	.923	8	3-15/S-7	0.6
	Yr	68	121	16	26	5	0	0	6	9	16	.215	.275	.256	50	-8	2	0	1	.923	3	S-33,3-15	-0.4
1966	Pit-N	109	368	44	97	15	6	4	54	13	38	.264	.296	.370	84	-8	0	2	-1	.949	3	3-83,S-18/2-3,O-3	-0.8
1967	Pit-N	81	211	17	61	6	2	1	19	10	28	.289	.330	.351	95	-1	1	1	-0	.938	10	3-25,O-23,S-16,/2C	0.9
1968	Pit-N	80	163	24	36	7	1	4	21	11	32	.221	.282	.350	90	-2	2	3	-1	.924	-5	3-30,O-19/S-8,21	-0.9
1969	Pit-N	108	274	29	78	11	4	9	42	17	46	.285	.329	.453	119	6	1	0	0	.954	-4	3-44,O-23/2-1	0.2
1970	*Pit-N	95	230	21	61	14	1	7	29	20	24	.265	.324	.426	101	-0	1	1	-0	.957	-3	3-53/O-4,1-1,2-1	-0.4
1971	*Pit-N	57	158	16	38	1	0	5	15	16	25	.241	.314	.342	86	-3	0	0	0	.980	-2	3-41/O-3,1-2	-0.6
1972	Pit-N	53	127	11	32	9	0	3	8	5	17	.252	.286	.394	93	-2	0	0	0	.899	-8	3-32/O-2	-1.1
1973	Phi-N	46	78	4	16	5	0	0	5	1	15	.205	.215	.269	33	-7	0	1	-1	.958	-1	3-16/1-5,O-2,2-1	-1.0
Total	15	1326	3689	387	922	138	26	52	372	244	510	.250	.300	.344	79	-105	46	35	-7	.963	-91	S-662,3-358/O21C	-17.0

■ MIKE PAGE

Page, Michael Randy b: 7/12/40, Woodruff, S.C. BL/TR, 6′2.5″, 210 lbs. Deb: 6/30/68

YEAR	TM/L	G	AB	R	H	2B	3B	HR	RBI	BB	SO	AVG	OBP	SLG	PRO+	BR/A	SB	CS	SBR	FA	FR	G/POS	TPR
1968	Atl-N	20	28	1	5	0	0	0	1	1	9	.179	.207	.179	16	-3	0	0	0	1.000	-1	/O-6	-0.5

■ MITCHELL PAGE

Page, Mitchell Otis b: 10/15/51, Los Angeles, Cal. BL/TR, 6′2″, 205 lbs. Deb: 4/9/77

YEAR	TM/L	G	AB	R	H	2B	3B	HR	RBI	BB	SO	AVG	OBP	SLG	PRO+	BR/A	SB	CS	SBR	FA	FR	G/POS	TPR
1977	Oak-A	145	501	85	154	28	8	21	75	78	95	.307	.407	.521	153	39	42	5	**10**	.954	7	*O-133/D-8	4.9
1978	Oak-A	147	516	62	147	25	7	17	70	53	95	.285	.356	.459	135	23	23	19	-5	.973	-1	*O-114,D-33	1.2
1979	Oak-A	133	478	51	118	11	2	9	42	52	93	.247	.325	.335	83	-11	17	16	-5	1.000	-0	*D-126/O-4	-2.0
1980	Oak-A	110	348	58	85	10	4	17	51	35	87	.244	.315	.443	113	5	14	7	0	.000	0	*D-101	0.2
1981	Oak-A	34	92	9	13	1	0	4	13	7	29	.141	.202	.283	40	-7	2	1	0	.000	0	D-29	-0.9
1982	Oak-A	31	78	14	20	5	0	4	7	7	24	.256	.333	.474	124	2	3	4	-2	.000	0	D-24	0.0
1983	Oak-A	57	79	16	19	3	0	0	1	10	22	.241	.341	.278	77	-2	3	3	-1	1.000	-2	D-34,O-10	-0.6
1984	Pit-N	16	12	2	4	1	0	0	0	3	4	.333	.467	.417	150	1	0	0	0	.000	0	H	0.1
Total	8	673	2104	297	560	84	21	72	259	245	449	.266	.348	.429	118	50	104	55	-2	.963	3	D-355,O-261	2.9

■ KARL PAGEL

Pagel, Karl Douglas b: 3/29/55, Madison, Wis. BL/TL, 6′2″, 190 lbs. Deb: 9/21/78

YEAR	TM/L	G	AB	R	H	2B	3B	HR	RBI	BB	SO	AVG	OBP	SLG	PRO+	BR/A	SB	CS	SBR	FA	FR	G/POS	TPR
1978	Chi-N	2	2	0	0	0	0	0	0	0	2	.000	.000	.000	-89	-0	0	0	0	.000	0	H	-0.1
1979	Chi-N	1	1	0	0	0	0	0	0	0	1	.000	.000	.000	-91	-0	0	0	0	.000	0	/H	0.0
1981	Cle-A	14	15	3	4	0	2	1	4	4	1	.267	.421	.733	230	3	0	0	0	1.000	2	/1-6,D-1	0.4
1982	Cle-A	23	18	3	3	0	0	0	2	7	11	.167	.400	.167	63	-0	0	0	0	.970	0	1-10/D-1	-0.1
1983	Cle-A	8	20	1	6	0	0	0	1	0	5	.300	.300	.300	63	-1	0	0	0	.000	-1	/O-1,D-5	-0.2
Total	5	48	56	7	13	0	2	1	7	11	20	.232	.358	.357	99	0	0	0	0	.985	1	/1-16,D-7,O-1	0.0

■ JIM PAGLIARONI

Pagliaroni, James Vincent "Pag" b: 12/8/37, Dearborn, Mich. BR/TR, 6′4″, 210 lbs. Deb: 8/13/55

YEAR	TM/L	G	AB	R	H	2B	3B	HR	RBI	BB	SO	AVG	OBP	SLG	PRO+	BR/A	SB	CS	SBR	FA	FR	G/POS	TPR
1955	Bos-A	1	0	0	0	0	0	0	1	0	0	—	—	—	—	-0	0	0	0	.000	0	/C-1	0.0
1960	Bos-A	28	62	7	19	5	2	2	9	13	11	.306	.434	.548	158	6	0	0	0	.990	-3	C-18	0.4
1961	Bos-A	120	376	50	91	17	0	16	58	55	74	.242	.345	.415	100	0	1	1	-0	.984	-4	*C-108	0.2
1962	Bos-A	90	260	39	67	14	0	11	37	36	55	.258	.359	.438	110	4	2	1	0	.987	-3	C-73	0.4
1963	Pit-N	92	252	27	58	5	0	11	26	36	57	.230	.331	.381	104	2	0	0	0	.988	4	C-85	1.0
1964	Pit-N	97	302	33	89	12	3	10	36	41	56	.295	.383	.454	135	15	1	0	0	.992	1	C-96	2.1
1965	Pit-N	134	403	42	108	15	0	17	65	41	84	.268	.340	.432	115	8	0	0	0	.994	-4	*C-131	1.1
1966	Pit-N	123	374	37	88	20	0	11	49	50	71	.235	.332	.377	96	-1	0	5	-3	**.997**	-14	*C-118	-1.1
1967	Pit-N	44	100	4	20	1	1	0	9	16	26	.200	.316	.230	59	-5	0	0	0	.984	-0	C-38	-0.3
1968	Oak-A	66	199	19	49	4	0	6	20	24	42	.246	.333	.357	115	4	0	0	0	.997	-9	C-63	-0.1
1969	Oak-A	14	27	1	4	1	0	1	2	5	2	.148	.303	.296	71	-1	0	0	0	.981	2	/C-7	0.1
	Sea-A	40	110	10	29	4	1	5	14	13	16	.264	.341	.455	123	3	0	0	0	.988	-6	C-29/1-2,O-1	-0.2
	Yr	54	137	11	33	5	1	6	16	18	18	.241	.333	.423	113	2	0	0	0	.987	-4	C-36/1-2,O-1	-0.1
Total	11	849	2465	269	622	98	7	90	326	330	494	.252	.346	.407	109	35	4	7	-3	.991	-36	C-767/1-2,O-1	3.6

■ MIKE PAGLIARULO

Pagliarulo, Michael Timothy b: 3/15/60, Medford, Mass. BL/TR, 6′2″, 195 lbs. Deb: 7/7/84

YEAR	TM/L	G	AB	R	H	2B	3B	HR	RBI	BB	SO	AVG	OBP	SLG	PRO+	BR/A	SB	CS	SBR	FA	FR	G/POS	TPR
1984	NY-A	67	201	24	48	15	3	7	34	15	46	.239	.292	.448	105	1	0	0	0	.955	6	3-67	0.6
1985	NY-A	138	380	55	91	16	2	19	62	45	86	.239	.326	.442	111	5	0	0	0	.951	-17	*3-134	-1.3
1986	NY-A	149	504	71	120	24	3	28	71	54	120	.238	.317	.464	111	6	4	1	1	.953	6	*3-143/S-2	1.0
1987	NY-A	150	522	76	122	26	3	32	87	53	111	.234	.307	.479	105	2	1	3	-2	.959	4	*3-147/1-1	0.3
1988	NY-A	125	444	46	96	20	1	15	67	37	104	.216	.280	.367	80	-13	1	0	0	.943	-0	*3-124	-1.4
1989	NY-A	74	223	19	44	10	0	4	16	19	43	.197	.266	.296	59	-12	1	1	-0	.936	-4	3-69/D-1	-1.7
	SD-N	50	148	12	29	7	0	3	14	18	39	.196	.287	.304	69	-6	2	0	1	.936	0	3-49	-0.5
1990	SD-N	128	398	29	101	23	2	7	38	39	66	.254	.325	.374	91	-5	1	3	-2	.955	2	*3-116	-0.4
1991	*Min-A	121	365	38	102	20	0	6	36	21	55	.279	.324	.384	91	-5	1	2	-1	.965	12	*3-118/2-1	0.7
1992	Min-A	42	105	10	21	4	0	0	9	1	17	.200	.215	.238	26	-10	1	0	0	.962	3	3-37/D-1	-0.8
1993	Min-A	83	253	31	74	16	4	3	23	18	34	.292	.351	.423	107	2	6	6	-2	.984	0	3-79	0.1
	Bal-A	33	117	24	38	9	0	6	21	8	15	.325	.373	.556	140	6	0	0	0	.937	-1	3-28/1-4	0.5
	Yr	116	370	55	112	25	4	9	44	26	49	.303	.358	.465	118	9	6	6	-2	.969	-1	*3-107/1-4	0.6
1995	Tex-A	86	241	27	56	16	0	4	27	15	49	.232	.280	.349	61	-14	0	0	0	.963	5	3-68,1-11	-1.0
Total	11	1246	3901	462	942	206	18	134	505	343	785	.241	.308	.407	93	-43	18	16	-4	.955	15	*3-1179/1-16,DS2	-3.9

■ TOM PAGNOZZI

Pagnozzi, Thomas Alan b: 7/30/62, Tucson, Ariz. BR/TR, 6′1″, 190 lbs. Deb: 4/12/87

YEAR	TM/L	G	AB	R	H	2B	3B	HR	RBI	BB	SO	AVG	OBP	SLG	PRO+	BR/A	SB	CS	SBR	FA	FR	G/POS	TPR
1987	*StL-N	27	48	8	9	1	0	2	9	4	13	.188	.250	.333	52	-3	1	0	0	1.000	-4	C-25/1-1	-0.6
1988	StL-N	81	195	17	55	9	0	0	15	11	32	.282	.320	.328	86	-4	0	0	0	.971	-2	C-28,1-28/3-5	-0.6
1989	StL-N	52	80	3	12	2	0	0	3	6	19	.150	.218	.175	13	-9	0	0	0	.982	-3	C-38/1-2,3-1	-1.2
1990	StL-N	69	220	20	61	15	0	2	23	14	37	.277	.323	.373	91	-3	1	1	-0	.989	10	C-63/1-2	1.0
1991	StL-N	140	459	38	121	24	5	2	57	36	63	.264	.323	.351	89	-7	9	13	-5	.991	-7	*C-139/1-3	-1.1
1992	StL-N★	139	485	33	121	26	3	7	44	28	64	.249	.292	.359	86	-10	2	5	-2	**.999**	-16	*C-138	-2.3
1993	StL-N	92	330	31	85	15	1	7	41	19	30	.258	.300	.373	80	-10	1	0	0	.991	-12	C-92	-1.7
1994	StL-N	70	243	21	66	12	1	7	40	21	39	.272	.330	.416	94	-2	0	0	0	.998	-7	C-70/1-1	-0.5
1995	StL-N	62	219	17	47	14	1	2	15	11	31	.215	.255	.315	50	-16	0	1	-1	.995	-2	C-61	-1.4
1996	*StL-N	119	407	48	110	23	0	13	55	24	78	.270	.314	.423	93	-5	4	1	1	.990	-0	*C-116/1-1	0.2
1997	StL-N	25	50	4	11	3	0	1	8	1	7	.220	.235	.340	49	-4	0	0	0	1.000	-5	C-13/1-2,3-1	-0.8
1998	StL-N	51	160	7	35	9	0	1	10	14	37	.219	.282	.294	50	-12	0	0	0	.982	-5	C-44	-1.3
Total	12	927	2896	247	733	153	11	44	320	189	450	.253	.301	.359	80	-85	18	21	-7	.992	-53	C-827/1-40,3-7	-10.3

■ REY PALACIOS

Palacios, Robert Rey b: 11/8/62, Brooklyn, N.Y. BR/TR, 5′10″, 190 lbs. Deb: 9/8/88

YEAR	TM/L	G	AB	R	H	2B	3B	HR	RBI	BB	SO	AVG	OBP	SLG	PRO+	BR/A	SB	CS	SBR	FA	FR	G/POS	TPR
1988	KC-A	5	11	2	1	0	0	0	0	0	4	.091	.091	.091	-48	-2	0	0	0	1.000	1	/C-3,3-1,D-1	-0.1
1989	KC-A	55	47	12	8	2	0	1	8	2	14	.170	.220	.277	39	-4	0	1	-1	.958	4	3-21,1-18,C-13,/OD	-0.1
1990	KC-A	41	56	8	13	3	0	2	9	5	24	.232	.295	.393	92	-1	2	2	-1	.992	4	C-27/1-7,3-3,O-1	0.4
Total	3	101	114	22	22	5	0	3	17	7	42	.193	.246	.316	57	-7	2	3	-1	.994	9	/C-43,1-25,3-25,DO	0.2

■ ERV PALICA

Palica, Ervin Martin (b: Ervin Martin Pavliecivich)
b: 2/9/28, Lomita, Cal. d: 5/29/82, Huntington Beach, Cal. BR/TR, 6′1.5″, 180 lbs. Deb: 4/21/45

YEAR	TM/L	G	AB	R	H	2B	3B	HR	RBI	BB	SO	AVG	OBP	SLG	PRO+	BR/A	SB	CS	SBR	FA	FR	G/POS	TPR
1945	Bro-N	2	0	0	0	0	0	0	0	0	0	—	—	—	—	0	0			.000	0	R	0.0
1947	Bro-N	3	0	0	0	0	0	0	0	0	0	—	—	—	—	0	0			.000	-0	/P-3	0.0
1948	Bro-N	45	39	6	5	1	1	0	3	4	12	.128	.209	.205	12	-5	0			1.000	-1	P-41	0.0
1949	*Bro-N	49	19	2	3	1	0	0	2	2	6	.158	.238	.211	20	-2	0			.875	-0	P-49	0.0
1950	Bro-N	48	68	4	15	4	0	1	8	0	8	.221	.221	.324	40	-6	2			.889	-4	P-43	0.0

YEAR	TM/L	G	AB	R	H	2B	3B	HR	RBI	BB	SO	AVG	OBP	SLG	PRO+	BR/A	SB	CS	SBR	FA	FR	G/POS	TPR
1951	Bro-N	20	13	1	2	0	0	0	0	2	5	.154	.267	.154	16	-1	0	0	0	1.000	1	P-19	0.0
1953	Bro-N	4	1	0	1	0	0	0	0	0	0	1.000	1.000	1.000	414	0	0	0	0	1.000	0	/P-4	0.0
1954	Bro-N	28	16	2	4	1	0	0	1	1	4	.250	.294	.313	56	-1	0	0	0	.875	-2	P-25	0.0
1955	Bal-A	33	55	3	13	1	0	0	3	4	18	.236	.288	.255	50	-4	0	0	0	.905	-1	P-33	0.0
1956	Bal-A	30	32	4	5	0	0	0	0	0	10	.156	.156	.156	-19	-6	0	0	0	.917	-0	P-29	0.0
Total	10	262	243	22	48	8	1	1	17	13	63	.198	.238	.251	31	-24	2	0		.921	-7	P-246	0.0

■ **ORLANDO PALMEIRO** Palmeiro, Orlando b: 1/19/69, Hoboken, N.J. BL/TR, 5'11", 155 lbs. Deb: 7/1/95

YEAR	TM/L	G	AB	R	H	2B	3B	HR	RBI	BB	SO	AVG	OBP	SLG	PRO+	BR/A	SB	CS	SBR	FA	FR	G/POS	TPR
1995	Cal-A	15	20	3	7	0	0	0	1	1	1	.350	.381	.350	93	-0	0	0	0	1.000	-2	/O-7,D-1	-0.2
1996	Cal-A	50	87	6	25	6	1	0	6	8	13	.287	.361	.379	87	-1	0	1	-1	1.000	-8	O-31/D-4	-0.9
1997	Ana-A	74	134	19	29	2	2	0	8	17	11	.216	.309	.261	51	-9	2	2	-1	.975	-9	O-52,D-11	-1.9
1998	Ana-A	75	165	28	53	7	2	0	21	20	11	.321	.395	.388	104	2	5	4	-1	1.000	-4	O-54/D-3	-0.4
Total	4	214	406	56	114	15	5	0	36	46	36	.281	.358	.342	82	-9	7	7	-2	.991	-22	O-144/D-19	-3.4

■ **RAFAEL PALMEIRO** Palmeiro, Rafael (Corrales) b: 9/24/64, Havana, Cuba BL/TL, 6', 188 lbs. Deb: 9/8/86

YEAR	TM/L	G	AB	R	H	2B	3B	HR	RBI	BB	SO	AVG	OBP	SLG	PRO+	BR/A	SB	CS	SBR	FA	FR	G/POS	TPR
1986	Chi-N	22	73	9	18	4	0	3	12	4	6	.247	.295	.425	89	-1	1	1	-0	.900	-0	O-20	-0.2
1987	Chi-N	84	221	32	61	15	1	14	30	20	26	.276	.339	.543	124	7	2	2	-1	1.000	-4	O-45,1-18	0.0
1988	Chi-N★	152	580	75	178	41	5	8	53	38	34	.307	.353	.436	120	14	12	2	2	.983	4	*O-147/1-5	1.7
1989	Tex-A	156	559	76	154	23	4	8	64	63	48	.275	.355	.374	104	4	4	3	-1	.991	10	*1-147/D-6	0.2
1990	Tex-A	154	598	72	**191**	35	6	14	89	40	59	.319	.365	.468	131	24	3	3	-1	.995	-1	*1-146/D-6	1.1
1991	Tex-A★	159	631	115	203	**49**	3	26	88	68	72	.322	.393	.532	156	48	4	3	-1	.992	-4	*1-157/D-2	3.3
1992	Tex-A	159	608	84	163	27	4	22	85	72	83	.268	.355	.434	124	20	2	3	-1	.995	14	*1-156/D-2	2.2
1993	Tex-A	160	597	**124**	176	40	2	37	105	73	85	.295	.376	.554	153	43	22	3	5	.997	16	*1-160	4.8
1994	Bal-A	111	436	82	139	32	0	23	76	54	63	.319	.396	.550	134	22	7	3	0	.996	-2	*1-111	0.9
1995	Bal-A	143	554	89	172	30	2	39	104	62	65	.310	.383	.583	145	35	3	1	0	.997	9	*1-142	2.9
1996	*Bal-A	162	626	110	181	40	2	39	142	95	96	.289	.385	.546	133	32	8	0	2	.995	5	*1-159/D-3	2.1
1997	*Bal-A	158	614	95	156	24	2	38	110	67	109	.254	.332	.485	113	10	5	2	0	.993	5	*1-155/D-3	0.0
1998	Bal-A★	162	619	98	183	36	1	43	121	79	91	.296	.382	.565	145	40	11	7	-1	.994	8	*1-159/D-3	2.9
Total	13	1782	6716	1061	1975	396	32	314	1079	735	837	.294	.368	.503	132	298	84	33	5	.994	59	*1-1515,O-212/D-25	21.9

■ **DEAN PALMER** Palmer, Dean William b: 12/27/68, Tallahassee, Fla. BR/TR, 6'2", 195 lbs. Deb: 9/1/89

YEAR	TM/L	G	AB	R	H	2B	3B	HR	RBI	BB	SO	AVG	OBP	SLG	PRO+	BR/A	SB	CS	SBR	FA	FR	G/POS	TPR
1989	Tex-A	16	19	0	2	2	0	0	1	0	12	.105	.105	.211	-13	-3	0	0	0	.667	-0	/3-6,S-1,O-1,D-6	-0.3
1991	Tex-A	81	268	38	50	9	2	15	37	32	98	.187	.281	.403	88	-5	0	2	-1	.944	-10	3-50,O-29/D-5	-1.7
1992	Tex-A	152	541	74	124	25	0	26	72	62	154	.229	.313	.420	107	4	10	4	1	.945	-10	*3-150	-0.6
1993	Tex-A	148	519	88	127	31	2	33	96	53	154	.245	.324	.503	123	15	11	10	-3	.922	-12	*3-148/S-1	0.0
1994	Tex-A	93	342	50	84	14	2	19	59	26	89	.246	.303	.465	94	-4	3	4	-2	.912	-2	3-91	-0.7
1995	Tex-A	36	119	30	40	6	0	9	24	21	21	.336	.451	.613	170	13	1	1	-0	.948	1	3-36	1.2
1996	*Tex-A	154	582	98	163	26	2	38	107	59	145	.280	.351	.527	112	9	2	0	1	.953	-24	*3-154/D-1	-1.4
1997	Tex-A	94	355	47	87	21	0	14	55	26	84	.245	.298	.423	81	-11	1	0	0	.959	-8	3-93	-1.8
	KC-A	49	187	23	52	10	1	9	31	15	50	.278	.338	.487	109	2	1	2	-1	.924	-7	3-48/D-1	-0.6
	Yr	143	542	70	139	31	1	23	86	41	134	.256	.312	.445	91	-9	2	2	-1	.948	-16	*3-141/D-1	-2.4
1998	KC-A★	152	572	84	159	27	2	34	119	48	134	.278	.340	.510	112	9	8	2	1	.921	-21	*3-129,D-22	-1.1
Total	9	975	3504	532	888	171	11	197	601	342	941	.253	.326	.477	108	28	37	25	-4	.935	-95	3-905/D-35,O-30,S-2	-7.0

■ **EDDIE PALMER** Palmer, Edwin Henry "Baldy" b: 6/1/1893, Petty, Tex. d: 1/9/83, Marlow, Okla. BR/TR, 5'9.5", 175 lbs. Deb: 9/6/17

YEAR	TM/L	G	AB	R	H	2B	3B	HR	RBI	BB	SO	AVG	OBP	SLG	PRO+	BR/A	SB	CS	SBR	FA	FR	G/POS	TPR
1917	Phi-A	16	52	7	11	1	0	0	5	7	7	.212	.305	.231	65	-2	1			.898	0	3-13/S-1	-0.2

■ **JOE PALMISANO** Palmisano, Joseph b: 11/19/02, West Point, Ga. d: 11/5/71, Albuquerque, N.Mex. BR/TR, 5'8", 160 lbs. Deb: 5/31/31

YEAR	TM/L	G	AB	R	H	2B	3B	HR	RBI	BB	SO	AVG	OBP	SLG	PRO+	BR/A	SB	CS	SBR	FA	FR	G/POS	TPR
1931	Phi-A	19	44	5	10	2	0	0	4	6	3	.227	.320	.273	54	-3	0	0	0	.960	-2	C-16/2-1	-0.3

■ **STAN PALYS** Palys, Stanley Francis b: 5/1/30, Blakely, Pa. BR/TR, 6'2", 190 lbs. Deb: 9/20/53

YEAR	TM/L	G	AB	R	H	2B	3B	HR	RBI	BB	SO	AVG	OBP	SLG	PRO+	BR/A	SB	CS	SBR	FA	FR	G/POS	TPR
1953	Phi-N	2	2	0	0	0	0	0	0	1	0	.000	.333	.000	-4	-0	0	0	0	.000	-0	/O-1	-0.1
1954	Phi-N	2	4	0	1	0	0	0	0	1	1	.250	.400	.250	74	-0	0	0	0	1.000	0	/O-1	0.0
1955	Phi-N	15	52	8	15	3	0	1	8	6	5	.288	.362	.404	105	0	1	0	0	1.000	-0	O-15	0.0
	Cin-N	79	222	29	51	14	0	7	30	12	35	.230	.272	.387	69	-11	1	1	-0	.992	2	O-55/1-1	-1.1
	Yr	94	274	37	66	17	0	8	38	18	40	.241	.290	.391	75	-10	2	1	0	.993	2	O-70/1-1	-1.1
1956	Cin-N	40	53	5	12	0	0	2	5	6	13	.226	.305	.340	69	-2	0	0	0	.929	-2	O-10	-0.5
Total	4	138	333	42	79	17	0	10	43	26	54	.237	.294	.378	74	-13	2	1	0	.988	-1	/O-82,1-1	-1.7

■ **JIM PANKOVITS** Pankovits, James Franklin b: 8/6/55, Pennington Gap, Va. BR/TR, 5'10", 195 lbs. Deb: 5/27/84

YEAR	TM/L	G	AB	R	H	2B	3B	HR	RBI	BB	SO	AVG	OBP	SLG	PRO+	BR/A	SB	CS	SBR	FA	FR	G/POS	TPR
1984	Hou-N	53	81	6	23	7	0	1	14	2	20	.284	.301	.407	105	0	2	1	0	.925	-5	2-15/S-4/O-3	-0.5
1985	Hou-N	75	172	24	42	3	0	4	14	17	29	.244	.316	.331	84	-4	1	0	0	.983	0	O-33,2-21/S-1,3-1	-0.4
1986	*Hou-N	70	113	12	32	6	1	1	7	11	25	.283	.347	.381	103	1	1	1	-0	.969	3	2-26/O-5,C-1	0.4
1987	Hou-N	50	61	7	14	2	0	1	8	6	13	.230	.299	.311	64	-3	2	0	1	1.000	5	/2-9,O-6,3-4	0.2
1988	Hou-N	68	140	13	31	7	1	2	12	8	28	.221	.273	.329	75	-5	2	1	0	.939	-2	2-31,3-11/1-2	-0.7
1990	Bos-A	2	0	0	0	0	0	0	0	0	0	—	—	—	—	0	0	0	0	.000	0	/2-2	0.0
Total	6	318	567	62	142	25	2	9	55	44	115	.250	.308	.349	86	-11	8	3	1	.961	1	2-104/O-47,3S1C	-1.0

■ **KEN PAPE** Pape, Kenneth Wayne b: 10/1/51, San Antonio, Tex. BR/TR, 5'11", 195 lbs. Deb: 5/17/76

YEAR	TM/L	G	AB	R	H	2B	3B	HR	RBI	BB	SO	AVG	OBP	SLG	PRO+	BR/A	SB	CS	SBR	FA	FR	G/POS	TPR
1976	Tex-A	21	23	7	5	1	0	1	4	3	2	.217	.357	.391	117	1	0	1	-1	.968	4	/S-6,3-4,2-1,D-3	0.5

■ **STAN PAPI** Papi, Stanley Gerard b: 2/4/51, Fresno, Cal. BR/TR, 6', 178 lbs. Deb: 4/11/74

YEAR	TM/L	G	AB	R	H	2B	3B	HR	RBI	BB	SO	AVG	OBP	SLG	PRO+	BR/A	SB	CS	SBR	FA	FR	G/POS	TPR
1974	StL-N	8	4	0	1	0	0	0	1	0	0	.250	.250	.250	40	-0	0	0	0	1.000	1	/S-7,2-1	0.0
1977	Mon-N	13	43	5	10	2	1	0	4	1	9	.233	.250	.326	55	-3	1	0	0	.952	-5	3-10/S-2,2-1	-0.7
1978	Mon-N	67	152	15	35	11	0	0	11	10	28	.230	.287	.303	65	-7	0	0	0	.976	-3	S-22,3-15/2-5	-0.8
1979	Bos-A	50	117	9	22	8	0	1	6	5	20	.188	.221	.282	33	-11	0	0	0	.982	13	2-26,S-21/D-1	0.4
1980	Bos-A	1	0	0	0	0	0	0	0	0	0	—	—	—	—	0	0	0	0	.000	0	/3-1	0.0
	Det-A	46	114	12	27	3	4	3	17	5	24	.237	.269	.412	82	-3	0	0	0	.973	-2	2-31,3-11/S-5,/1-1	-0.4
	Yr	47	114	12	27	3	4	3	17	5	24	.237	.269	.412	82	-3	0	0	0	.973	-2	2-31,3-12/S-5,1-1	-0.4
1981	Det-A	40	93	8	19	2	1	3	12	3	18	.204	.229	.344	61	-5	1	0	0	.941	-1	3-32/1-1,2-1,O-1,D	-0.7
Total	6	225	523	49	114	26	6	7	51	24	99	.218	.255	.331	60	-30	2	0	1	.931	3	/3-69,2-65,SD1O	-2.2

■ **ERIK PAPPAS** Pappas, Erik Daniel b: 4/25/66, Chicago, Ill. BR/TR, 6', 190 lbs. Deb: 4/19/91

YEAR	TM/L	G	AB	R	H	2B	3B	HR	RBI	BB	SO	AVG	OBP	SLG	PRO+	BR/A	SB	CS	SBR	FA	FR	G/POS	TPR
1991	Chi-N	7	17	1	3	0	0	0	2	1	5	.176	.222	.176	13	-2	0	0	0	1.000	1	/C-6	0.0
1993	StL-N	82	228	25	63	12	0	1	28	35	35	.276	.373	.342	95	-0	1	3	-2	.982	5	C-63,O-16/1-2	0.6
1994	StL-N	15	44	8	4	1	0	0	5	10	13	.091	.273	.114	6	-6	0	0	0	.955	-4	C-15	-1.0
Total	3	104	289	34	70	13	0	1	35	46	53	.242	.348	.298	76	-8	1	3	-2	.978	2	/C-84,O-16,1-2	-0.4

■ **CRAIG PAQUETTE** Paquette, Craig Harold b: 3/28/69, Long Beach, Cal. BR/TR, 6', 190 lbs. Deb: 6/1/93

YEAR	TM/L	G	AB	R	H	2B	3B	HR	RBI	BB	SO	AVG	OBP	SLG	PRO+	BR/A	SB	CS	SBR	FA	FR	G/POS	TPR
1993	Oak-A	105	393	35	86	20	4	12	46	14	108	.219	.246	.382	70	-19	4	2	0	.950	-9	*3-104/O-1,D-1	-2.7
1994	Oak-A	14	49	0	7	2	0	0	0	0	14	.143	.143	.184	-18	-9	1	0	0	1.000	1	3-14	-0.7
1995	Oak-A	105	283	42	64	13	1	13	49	12	88	.226	.260	.417	77	-11	5	2	0	.935	-12	3-75,O-20/S-8,1-3	-2.2
1996	KC-A	118	429	61	111	15	1	22	67	23	101	.259	.300	.452	87	-10	5	3	-0	.891	-11	3-51,O-47,1-19,S/D	-2.2
1997	KC-A	77	252	26	58	15	1	8	33	10	57	.230	.265	.393	67	-13	2	2	-1	.935	2	3-72/O-4	-1.1
1998	NY-N	7	19	3	5	2	0	0	0	0	6	.263	.263	.368	62	-1	1	0	0	1.000	-1	/3-4,1-2,O-1	-0.2
Total	6	426	1425	167	331	67	7	55	195	59	374	.232	.265	.405	73	-63	18	9	0	.938	-31	3-320/O-73,1-24,SD	-9.1

■ **AL PARDO** Pardo, Alberto Judas b: 9/8/62, Oviedo, Spain BB/TR, 6'2", 187 lbs. Deb: 7/3/85

YEAR	TM/L	G	AB	R	H	2B	3B	HR	RBI	BB	SO	AVG	OBP	SLG	PRO+	BR/A	SB	CS	SBR	FA	FR	G/POS	TPR
1985	Bal-A	34	75	3	10	1	0	0	1	3	15	.133	.167	.147	-14	-12	0	0	0	.979	3	C-29	-0.7
1986	Bal-A	16	51	3	7	1	0	1	3	0	14	.137	.137	.216	-6	-7	0	0	0	.987	-2	C-14/D-1	-0.9
1988	Phi-N	2	2	0	0	0	0	0	0	0	2	.000	.000	.000	-98	-0	0	0	0	1.000	-0	/C-2	-0.1

YEAR	TM/L	G	AB	R	H	2B	3B	HR	RBI	BB	SO	AVG	OBP	SLG	PRO+	BR/A	SB	CS	SBR	FA	FR	G/POS	TPR
1989	Phi-N	1	1	0	0	0	0	0	0	0	0	.000	.000	.000	-99	-0	0	0	0	1.000	0	/C-1	0.0
Total	4	53	129	6	17	2	0	1	4	3	31	.132	.152	.171	-12	-20	0	0	0	.982	1	/C-46,D-1	-1.7
■ **JOHNNY PAREDES**	Paredes, Johnny Alfonso (Isambert) b: 9/2/62, Maracaibo, Venez. BR/TR, 5'11", 165 lbs. Deb: 4/29/88																						
1988	Mon-N	35	91	6	17	2	0	1	10	9	17	.187	.282	.242	49	-6	5	2	0	.976	0	2-28/O-1	-0.5
1990	Det-A	6	8	2	1	0	0	0	0	1	0	.125	.222	.125	-0	-1	0	0	0	.917	1	/2-4	0.0
	Mon-N	3	6	0	2	1	0	0	1	1	0	.333	.429	.500	161	1	0	0	0	.889	1	/2-2	0.1
1991	Det-A	16	18	4	6	0	0	0	0	0	1	.333	.333	.333	84	-0	1	1	-0	.958	4	/2-7,3-1,S-1,D-2	0.3
Total	3	60	123	12	26	3	0	1	11	11	18	.211	.292	.260	56	-7	6	3	0	.965	6	/2-41,D-2,S-1,30	-0.1
■ **FREDDY PARENT**	Parent, Frederick Alfred b: 11/25/1875, Biddeford, Me. d: 11/2/72, Sanford, Maine BR/TR, 5'7", 154 lbs. Deb: 7/14/1899																						
1899	StL-N	2	8	0	1	0	0	0	1	0		.125	.125	.125	-31	-1	0			.889	-1	/2-2	-0.2
1901	Bos-A	138	517	87	158	23	9	4	59	41		.306	.367	.408	117	12	16			.918	-0	*S-138	2.1
1902	Bos-A	138	567	91	156	31	8	3	62	24		.275	.309	.374	86	-12	16			.932	4	*S-138	0.0
1903	*Bos-A	139	560	83	170	31	17	4	80	13		.304	.326	.441	122	13	24			.930	9	*S-139	2.8
1904	Bos-A	155	591	85	172	22	9	6	77	28		.291	.330	.389	120	12	20			.929	-8	*S-155	1.0
1905	Bos-A	153	602	55	141	16	5	0	33	47		.234	.296	.277	81	-12	25			.920	-11	*S-153	-2.1
1906	Bos-A	149	600	67	141	14	10	1	49	31		.235	.277	.297	80	-15	16			.933	-7	*S-143/2-6	-1.9
1907	Bos-A	114	409	51	113	19	5	1	26	22		.276	.321	.355	116	7	12			.978	-2	O-47,S-43/3-7,2-5	0.5
1908	Chi-A	119	391	28	81	7	5	0	35	50		.207	.300	.251	81	-6	9			.930	5	*S-118	0.1
1909	Chi-A	136	472	61	123	10	5	0	30	46		.261	.335	.303	106	5	32			.929	17	S-98,O-38/2-1	2.4
1910	Chi-A	81	258	23	46	6	1	1	16	29		.178	.266	.221	55	-13	14			.970	-3	O-62,2-11/S-4,3-1	-2.0
1911	Chi-A	3	9	2	4	1	0	0	3	2		.444	.545	.556	214	2	0			1.000	1	/2-3	0.2
Total	12	1327	4984	633	1306	180	74	20	471	333		.262	.315	.340	99	-8	184			.927	4	*S-1129,O-147/23	2.9
■ **MARK PARENT**	Parent, Mark Alan b: 9/16/61, Ashland, Ore. BR/TR, 6'5", 225 lbs. Deb: 9/20/86																						
1986	SD-N	8	14	1	2	0	0	0	0	1	3	.143	.200	.143	-4	-2	0	0	0	.889	-1	/C-3	-0.3
1987	SD-N	12	25	0	2	0	0	0	2	0	9	.080	.080	.080	-60	-6	0	0	0	1.000	0	C-10	-0.5
1988	SD-N	41	118	9	23	3	0	6	15	6	23	.195	.234	.373	73	-5	0	0	0	.986	5	C-36	0.3
1989	SD-N	52	141	12	27	4	0	7	21	8	34	.191	.235	.369	70	-6	1	0	0	1.000	6	C-41/1-1	0.2
1990	SD-N	65	189	13	42	11	0	3	16	16	29	.222	.283	.328	67	-9	1	0	0	.992	8	C-60	0.3
1991	Tex-A	3	1	0	0	0	0	0	0	0	1	.000	.000	.000	-99	-0	0	0	0	1.000	1	/C-3	0.0
1992	Bal-A	17	34	4	8	1	0	2	4	3	7	.235	.316	.441	107	0	0	0	0	.988	4	C-16	0.5
1993	Bal-A	22	54	7	14	2	0	4	12	3	14	.259	.298	.519	110	0	0	0	0	.989	-1	C-21/D-1	0.0
1994	Chi-N	44	99	8	26	4	0	3	16	13	24	.263	.354	.394	96	-0	0	1	-1	.976	4	C-37	0.4
1995	Pit-N	69	233	25	54	9	0	15	33	23	62	.232	.301	.464	96	-2	0	0	0	.990	-10	C-67	-0.7
	Chi-N	12	32	5	8	2	0	3	5	3	7	.250	.314	.594	135	1	0	0	0	1.000	2	C-10	0.4
	Yr	81	265	30	62	11	0	18	38	26	69	.234	.302	.479	101	-1	0	0	0	.992	-7	C-77	-0.3
1996	Det-A	38	104	13	25	6	0	7	17	3	27	.240	.262	.500	87	-3	0	0	0	.994	-4	C-33/1-1	-0.5
	*Bal-A	18	33	4	6	1	0	2	6	2	10	.182	.229	.394	54	-3	0	0	0	.987	2	C-18	0.0
	Yr	56	137	17	31	7	0	9	23	5	37	.226	.254	.474	79	-5	0	0	0	.992	-2	C-51/1-1	-0.5
1997	Phi-N	39	113	4	17	3	0	0	8	7	39	.150	.200	.177	-0	-17	0	1	-1	.996	-0	C-38	-1.6
1998	Phi-N	34	113	7	25	4	0	1	13	10	30	.221	.285	.283	47	-9	1	1	-0	.987	-3	C-34	-1.0
Total	13	474	1303	112	279	50	0	53	168	98	319	.214	.270	.375	71	-59	3	3	-1	.990	14	C-427/1-2,D-1	-2.5
■ **KELLY PARIS**	Paris, Kelly Jay b: 10/17/57, Encino, Cal. BR/TR, 6', 180 lbs. Deb: 9/1/82																						
1982	StL-N	12	29	1	3	0	0	0	1	0	7	.103	.103	.103	-42	-5	0	0	0	.867	2	/3-5,S-4	-0.3
1983	Cin-N	56	120	13	30	6	0	0	7	15	22	.250	.338	.300	75	-3	8	2	1	1.000	-2	3-16,2-10/S-7,1-3	-0.4
1985	Bal-A	5	9	0	0	0	0	0	0	0	1	.000	.000	.000	-99	-2	0	0	0	.857	-0	/2-2,D-2	-0.3
1986	Bal-A	5	10	0	2	0	0	0	0	0	3	.200	.200	.200	9	-1	0	1	-1	.857	1	/3-3,D-2	-0.1
1988	Chi-A	14	44	6	11	0	0	3	6	0	6	.250	.250	.455	93	-1	0	0	0	1.000	-0	/1-9,3-4,D-1	-0.1
Total	5	92	212	20	46	6	0	3	14	15	39	.217	.272	.288	54	-13	8	3	1	.944	1	/3-28,1-12,2-12,SD	-1.2
■ **TONY PARISSE**	Parisse, Louis Peter b: 6/25/11, Philadelphia, Pa. d: 6/2/56, Philadelphia, Pa. BR/TR, 5'10", 165 lbs. Deb: 9/22/43																						
1943	Phi-A	6	17	0	3	0	0	0	1	2	2	.176	.263	.176	30	-1	0	0	0	1.000	0	/C-5	-0.1
1944	Phi-A	4	4	0	0	0	0	0	0	0	1	.000	.000	.000	-99	-1	0	0	0	.500	-1	/C-2	-0.2
Total	2	10	21	0	3	0	0	0	1	2	3	.143	.217	.143	6	-2	0	0	0	.960	-0	/C-7	-0.3
■ **ACE PARKER**	Parker, Clarence McKay b: 5/17/12, Portsmouth, Va. BR/TR, 6', 180 lbs. Deb: 4/24/37																						
1937	Phi-A	38	94	8	11	0	1	2	13	4	17	.117	.153	.202	-11	-17	0	0	0	.905	-5	S-19/2-9,O-5	-1.9
1938	Phi-A	56	113	12	26	5	0	0	12	10	16	.230	.293	.274	44	-10	1	2	-1	.972	-5	S-26/2-9,3-9	-1.3
Total	2	94	207	20	37	5	1	2	25	14	33	.179	.231	.242	19	-26	1	2	-1	.934	-10	/S-45,2-18,3-9,O-5	-3.2
■ **PAT PARKER**	Parker, Clarence Perkins b: 5/22/1893, Somerville, Mass. d: 3/21/67, Claremont, N.H. BR/TR, 5'7", 160 lbs. Deb: 8/10/15																						
1915	StL-A	3	6	0	1	0	0	0	1	0	3	.167	.167	.167	-0	-1	0	1	-1	1.000	-0	/O-2	-0.2
■ **DAVE PARKER**	Parker, David Gene b: 6/9/51, Calhoun, Miss. BL/TR, 6'5", 230 lbs. Deb: 7/12/73 C																						
1973	Pit-N	54	139	17	40	9	1	4	14	2	27	.288	.308	.453	111	1	1	1	-0	.964	0	O-39	0.0
1974	*Pit-N	73	220	27	62	10	3	4	29	10	53	.282	.322	.409	107	1	3	3	-1	.964	1	O-49/1-6	-0.1
1975	*Pit-N	148	558	75	172	35	10	25	101	38	89	.308	.358	**.541**	148	33	8	6	-1	.972	11	*O-141	3.7
1976	Pit-N	138	537	82	168	28	10	13	90	30	80	.313	.351	.475	132	20	19	7	2	.956	7	*O-134	2.5
1977	Pit-N★	159	637	107	**215**	**44**	8	21	88	58	107	**.338**	.399	.531	143	39	17	19	-6	.965	33	*O-158/2-1	5.8
1978	Pit-N	148	581	102	194	32	12	30	117	57	92	**.334**	.395	**.585**	163	**48**	20	7	2	.960	8	*O-147	**5.3**
1979	*Pit-N★	158	622	109	193	45	7	25	94	67	101	.310	.385	.526	140	34	20	4	4	.960	9	*O-158	4.0
1980	Pit-N★	139	518	71	153	31	1	17	79	25	69	.295	.330	.458	116	9	10	7	-1	.965	4	*O-130	0.7
1981	Pit-N★	67	240	29	62	14	3	9	48	9	25	.258	.291	.454	106	0	6	2	1	.941	-2	O-60	-0.4
1982	Pit-N	73	244	41	66	19	3	6	29	22	45	.270	.333	.447	113	4	7	5	-1	.957	-1	O-63	0.0
1983	Pit-N	144	552	68	154	29	4	12	69	28	89	.279	.314	.411	97	-4	12	9	-2	.973	7	*O-142	-0.3
1984	Cin-N	156	607	73	173	28	0	16	94	41	89	.285	.331	.410	103	1	11	10	-3	.974	5	*O-151	-0.1
1985	Cin-N★	160	635	88	198	**42**	4	34	**125**	52	80	.312	.367	.551	146	37	5	13	-6	.972	13	*O-159	3.9
1986	Cin-N★	162	637	89	174	31	3	31	116	56	126	.273	.333	.477	116	12	1	6	-3	.970	-2	*O-159	0.1
1987	Cin-N	153	589	77	149	28	0	26	97	44	104	.253	.314	.433	91	-9	7	3	0	.967	8	*O-142/1-9	-0.5
1988	*Oak-A	101	377	43	97	18	1	12	55	32	70	.257	.315	.406	104	1	0	1	-1	.953	-0	D-61,O-34/1-1	-0.2
1989	*Oak-A	144	553	56	146	27	0	22	97	38	91	.264	.313	.432	112	6	0	0	0	1.000	0	*D-140/O-1	0.3
1990	Mil-A☆	157	610	71	176	30	3	21	92	41	102	.289	.337	.451	119	14	4	7	-3	.960	-1	*D-153/1-3	0.5
1991	Cal-A	119	466	45	108	22	2	11	56	29	91	.232	.281	.358	76	-16	3	2	-0	.000	0	*D-119	-2.2
	Tor-A	13	36	2	12	4	0	0	3	4	7	.333	.400	.444	128	1	0	1	-1	.000	0	D-11	0.0
	Yr	132	502	47	120	26	2	11	59	33	98	.239	.290	.365	80	-15	3	3	-1	.000	0	*D-130	-2.2
Total	19	2466	9358	1272	2712	526	75	339	1493	683	1537	.290	.342	.471	121	233	154	113	-22	.965	98	*O-1867,D-484/12	23.0
■ **DIXIE PARKER**	Parker, Douglas Woolley b: 4/24/1895, Forest Home, Ala. d: 5/15/72, Tuscaloosa, Ala. BL/TR, 5'11", 160 lbs. Deb: 7/28/23																						
1923	Phi-N	4	5	0	1	0	0	0	1	0	1	.200	.200	.200	5	-1	0	0	0	.500	-1	/C-2	-0.1
■ **SALTY PARKER**	Parker, Francis James b: 7/8/13, E.St.Louis, Ill. d: 7/27/92, Houston, Tex. BR/TR, 6', 173 lbs. Deb: 8/13/36 MC																						
1936	Det-A	11	25	6	7	2	0	0	4	2	3	.280	.333	.360	71	-1	0	2	-1	.906	3	/S-7,1-2	0.1
■ **WES PARKER**	Parker, Maurice Wesley b: 11/13/39, Evanston, Ill. BB/TL, 6'1", 180 lbs. Deb: 4/19/64																						
1964	LA-N	124	214	29	55	7	1	3	10	14	45	.257	.306	.341	88	-4	5	4	-1	.971	-10	O-69,1-31	-1.8
1965	*LA-N	154	542	80	129	24	7	8	51	75	95	.238	.336	.352	101	2	13	7	-0	**.997**	-1	*1-154/O-1	-0.8
1966	*LA-N	156	475	67	120	17	5	12	51	69	83	.253	.353	.385	114	11	7	3	0	.992	1	*1-140,O-14	0.3
1967	LA-N	139	413	56	102	16	5	5	31	65	83	.247	.359	.346	112	9	10	5	0	**.996**	5	*1-112,O-18	0.7
1968	LA-N	135	468	42	112	22	2	3	27	49	87	.239	.314	.314	96	-2	4	6	-2	**.999**	1	*1-114,O-28	-1.5

YEAR	TM/L	G	AB	R	H	2B	3B	HR	RBI	BB	SO	AVG	OBP	SLG	PRO+	BR/A	SB	CS	SBR	FA	FR	G/POS	TPR
1969	LA-N	132	471	76	131	23	4	13	68	56	46	.278	.357	.427	128	17	4	1	1	.995	0	*1-128/O-2	0.8
1970	LA-N	161	614	84	196	**47**	4	10	111	79	70	.319	.390	.458	134	31	8	2	1	**.996**	4	*1-161	2.2
1971	LA-N	157	533	69	146	24	1	6	62	63	63	.274	.352	.356	107	6	6	1	1	.996	3	*1-148,O-18	-0.3
1972	LA-N	130	427	45	119	14	3	4	59	62	43	.279	.371	.354	110	8	3	5	-2	**.997**	1	*1-120/O-5	-0.3
Total	9	1288	4157	548	1110	194	32	64	470	532	615	.267	.353	.375	112	78	60	34	-2	.996	4	*1-1108,O-155	-0.7

■ RICK PARKER Parker, Richard Alan b: 3/20/63, Kansas City, Mo. BR/TR, 6', 185 lbs. Deb: 5/4/90

YEAR	TM/L	G	AB	R	H	2B	3B	HR	RBI	BB	SO	AVG	OBP	SLG	PRO+	BR/A	SB	CS	SBR	FA	FR	G/POS	TPR
1990	SF-N	54	107	19	26	5	0	2	14	10	15	.243	.314	.346	84	-2	6	1	1	.978	-10	O-35/2-2,3-1,S-1	-1.2
1991	SF-N	13	14	0	1	0	0	0	1	1	5	.071	.133	.071	-42	-3	0	0	0	1.000	-1	/O-4	-0.4
1993	Hou-N	45	45	11	15	3	0	0	4	3	8	.333	.375	.400	112	1	1	2	-1	1.000	-5	O-16/2-1,S-1	-0.5
1994	NY-N	8	16	1	1	0	0	0	0	0	2	.063	.063	.063	-68	-4	0	0	0	1.000	0	/O-6	-0.4
1995	LA-N	27	29	3	8	0	0	0	4	2	4	.276	.323	.276	66	-1	1	1	-0	1.000	-2	O-21/3-2,S-2	-0.4
1996	LA-N	16	14	2	4	1	0	0	1	0	2	.286	.333	.357	89	-0	1	0	0	1.000	-1	/O-4	-0.1
Total	6	163	225	36	55	9	0	2	24	16	36	.244	.300	.311	69	-10	9	4	0	.990	-19	/O-86,S-4,3-3,2-3	-3.0

■ BILLY PARKER Parker, William David b: 1/14/47, Hayneville, Ala. BR/TR, 5'8", 168 lbs. Deb: 9/9/71

YEAR	TM/L	G	AB	R	H	2B	3B	HR	RBI	BB	SO	AVG	OBP	SLG	PRO+	BR/A	SB	CS	SBR	FA	FR	G/POS	TPR
1971	Cal-A	20	70	4	16	0	1	1	6	2	20	.229	.250	.300	59	-4	1	1	-0	.958	-1	2-20	-0.4
1972	Cal-A	36	80	11	17	2	0	2	8	9	17	.213	.292	.313	85	-2	0	2	-1	.951	-0	3-21/2-9,O-5,S-1	-0.4
1973	Cal-A	38	102	14	23	2	1	0	7	8	23	.225	.288	.265	61	-5	0	1	-1	.959	-3	2-32/S-3,D-1	-0.7
Total	3	94	252	29	56	4	2	3	21	19	60	.222	.279	.290	68	-11	1	4	-2	.963	-5	/2-61,3-21,O-5,SD	-1.5

■ FRANK PARKINSON Parkinson, Frank Joseph "Parky" b: 3/23/1895, Dickson City, Pa. d: 7/4/60, Trenton, N.J. BR/TR, 5'11", 175 lbs. Deb: 4/13/21

YEAR	TM/L	G	AB	R	H	2B	3B	HR	RBI	BB	SO	AVG	OBP	SLG	PRO+	BR/A	SB	CS	SBR	FA	FR	G/POS	TPR
1921	Phi-N	108	391	36	99	20	2	5	32	13	81	.253	.277	.353	61	-23	3	4	-2	.931	9	*S-105/3-1	-0.5
1922	Phi-N	141	545	86	150	18	6	15	70	55	93	.275	.344	.413	86	-12	3	4	-2	.963	**31**	*2-139	2.0
1923	Phi-N	67	219	21	53	12	0	3	28	13	31	.242	.288	.338	58	-14	0	4	-2	.950	3	2-37,S-15,3-11	-1.1
1924	Phi-N	62	156	14	33	7	0	1	19	14	28	.212	.281	.276	44	-12	3	1	0	.952	7	3-28,S-21,2-10	-0.2
Total	4	378	1311	157	335	57	8	24	149	95	233	.256	.308	.366	69	-61	9	13	-5	.962	50	2-186,S-141/3-40	0.2

■ ART PARKS Parks, Artie William b: 11/1/11, Paris, Ark. d: 12/6/89, Little Rock, Ark. BL/TR, 5'9", 170 lbs. Deb: 9/25/37

YEAR	TM/L	G	AB	R	H	2B	3B	HR	RBI	BB	SO	AVG	OBP	SLG	PRO+	BR/A	SB	CS	SBR	FA	FR	G/POS	TPR
1937	Bro-N	7	16	2	5	2	0	0	0	2	2	.313	.389	.438	122	1	0			1.000	0	/O-4	0.0
1939	Bro-N	71	239	27	65	13	2	1	19	28	14	.272	.348	.356	86	-4	2			.977	-4	O-65	-1.0
Total	2	78	255	29	70	15	2	1	19	30	16	.275	.351	.361	89	-3	2			.978	-4	/O-69	-1.0

■ DEREK PARKS Parks, Derek Gavin b: 9/29/68, Covina, Cal. BR/TR, 6', 205 lbs. Deb: 9/11/92

YEAR	TM/L	G	AB	R	H	2B	3B	HR	RBI	BB	SO	AVG	OBP	SLG	PRO+	BR/A	SB	CS	SBR	FA	FR	G/POS	TPR
1992	Min-A	7	6	1	2	0	0	0	0	1	1	.333	.500	.333	133	0	0	0	0	1.000	1	/C-7	0.2
1993	Min-A	7	20	3	4	0	0	0	1	1	2	.200	.238	.200	19	-2	0	0	0	.970	-0	/C-7	-0.2
1994	Min-A	31	89	6	17	6	0	1	9	4	20	.191	.242	.292	37	-9	0	1	-1	.993	-3	C-31	-1.0
Total	3	45	115	10	23	6	0	1	10	6	23	.200	.258	.278	40	-10	0	1	-1	.989	-2	/C-45	-1.0

■ BILL PARKS Parks, William Robert b: 6/4/1849, Easton, Pa. d: 10/10/11, Easton, Pa. BR/TR, 5'8", 150 lbs. Deb: 4/26/1875 M

YEAR	TM/L	G	AB	R	H	2B	3B	HR	RBI	BB	SO	AVG	OBP	SLG	PRO+	BR/A	SB	CS	SBR	FA	FR	G/POS	TPR
1875	Was-n	27	111	13	20	0	0	0	6	1	1	.180	.188	.180	29	-7	1	1	-0	.836	3	O-17,P-14,M	-0.1
	Phi-n	2	6	0	1	0	0	0	0	0	1	.167	.167	.167	16	-1	0	0	0	.500	-1	/P-2,O-2	0.0
	Yr	29	117	13	21	0	0	0	6	1	2	.179	.186	.179	29	-8	1	1	-0	.833	3	O-19,P-16	-0.1
1876	Bos-N	1	4	0	0	0	0	0	0	0	0	.000	.000	.000	-98	-1				.750	-0	/O-1	-0.1

■ SAM PARRILLA Parrilla, Samuel (Monge) b: 6/12/43, Santurce, P.R. d: 2/9/94, Brooklyn, N.Y. BR/TR, 5'11", 185 lbs. Deb: 4/11/70

YEAR	TM/L	G	AB	R	H	2B	3B	HR	RBI	BB	SO	AVG	OBP	SLG	PRO+	BR/A	SB	CS	SBR	FA	FR	G/POS	TPR
1970	Phi-N	11	16	0	2	1	0	0	0	1	4	.125	.176	.188	-3	-2	0	0	0	1.000	0	/O-3	-0.2

■ LANCE PARRISH Parrish, Lance Michael b: 6/15/56, Clairton, Pa. BR/TR, 6'3", 220 lbs. Deb: 9/5/77

YEAR	TM/L	G	AB	R	H	2B	3B	HR	RBI	BB	SO	AVG	OBP	SLG	PRO+	BR/A	SB	CS	SBR	FA	FR	G/POS	TPR
1977	Det-A	12	46	10	9	2	0	3	7	5	12	.196	.275	.435	85	-1	0	0	0	1.000	2	C-12	0.1
1978	Det-A	85	288	37	63	11	3	14	41	11	71	.219	.255	.424	85	-7	0	0	0	.987	5	C-79	-0.1
1979	Det-A	143	493	65	136	26	3	19	65	49	105	.276	.344	.456	110	6	6	7	-2	.989	5	*C-142	1.4
1980	Det-A★	144	553	79	158	34	6	24	82	31	109	.286	.327	.499	120	13	6	4	-1	.990	-5	*C-121,D-16/1-5,O-5	1.1
1981	Det-A	96	348	39	85	18	2	10	46	34	52	.244	.312	.394	98	-1	2	3	-1	.993	-2	C-90/D-5	-0.1
1982	Det-A★	133	486	75	138	19	2	32	87	40	99	.284	.340	.529	134	21	3	4	-2	.989	9	*C-132/O-1	3.3
1983	Det-A★	155	605	80	163	42	3	27	114	44	106	.269	.320	.483	120	15	1	3	-2	.995	0	*C-131,D-27	1.8
1984	*Det-A★	147	578	75	137	16	2	33	98	41	120	.237	.290	.443	100	-2	2	3	-1	.991	1	*C-127,D-22	0.4
1985	Det-A†	140	549	64	150	27	1	28	98	41	90	.273	.326	.479	118	12	2	6	-3	.993	-6	*C-120,D-22	0.9
1986	Det-A★	91	327	53	84	6	1	22	62	38	83	.257	.343	.483	122	10	0	0	0	.989	2	C-85/D-6	1.7
1987	Phi-N	130	466	42	114	21	0	17	67	47	104	.245	.315	.399	85	-10	0	1	-1	.989	-3	*C-127	-0.5
1988	Phi-N★	123	424	44	91	17	2	15	60	47	93	.215	.296	.370	88	-7	0	0	0	.988	-4	*C-117/1-1	-0.2
1989	Cal-A	124	433	48	103	12	1	17	50	42	104	.238	.308	.388	97	-3	1	1	-0	.993	-2	*C-122/D-2	0.2
1990	Cal-A★	133	470	54	126	14	0	24	70	46	107	.268	.340	.451	122	13	2	2	-1	.993	10	*C-131/1-4,D-1	3.1
1991	Cal-A	119	402	38	87	12	0	19	51	35	117	.216	.287	.388	85	-9	0	1	-1	.997	0	*C-111/1-3,D-5	-0.3
1992	Cal-A	24	83	7	19	2	0	4	11	5	22	.229	.273	.398	85	-2	0	0	0	.975	-5	C-22/D-2	-0.6
	Sea-A	69	192	19	45	11	1	8	21	19	48	.234	.307	.427	103	0	1	1	-0	.995	-4	C-34,1-16,D-14	-0.4
	Yr	93	275	26	64	13	1	12	32	24	70	.233	.297	.418	98	-2	1	1	-0	.987	-9	C-56,D-16,1-16	-1.0
1993	Cle-A	10	20	2	4	1	0	1	2	4	5	.200	.333	.400	97	-0	1	0	0	.950	4	C-10	0.4
1994	Pit-N	40	126	10	34	5	0	3	16	18	28	.270	.366	.381	94	-1	1	1	-0	.988	-2	C-38/1-1	-0.1
1995	Tor-A	70	178	15	36	9	0	4	22	15	52	.202	.268	.320	53	-13	0	0	0	1.000	9	C-67/D-1	0.0
Total	19	1988	7067	856	1782	305	27	324	1070	612	1527	.252	.315	.440	105	33	28	37	-14	.991	15	*C-1818,D-123/10	12.1

■ LARRY PARRISH Parrish, Larry Alton b: 11/10/53, Winter Haven, Fla. BR/TR, 6'3", 215 lbs. Deb: 9/6/74 MC

YEAR	TM/L	G	AB	R	H	2B	3B	HR	RBI	BB	SO	AVG	OBP	SLG	PRO+	BR/A	SB	CS	SBR	FA	FR	G/POS	TPR
1974	Mon-N	25	69	9	14	5	0	0	4	6	19	.203	.286	.275	54	-4	0	0	0	.986	8	3-24	0.3
1975	Mon-N	145	532	50	146	32	5	10	65	28	74	.274	.316	.410	96	-5	4	5	-2	.919	-3	*3-143/2-1,S-1	-1.0
1976	Mon-N	154	543	65	126	28	5	11	61	41	91	.232	.288	.363	81	-15	2	6	-3	.945	5	*3-153	-1.6
1977	Mon-N	123	402	50	99	19	2	11	46	37	71	.246	.316	.386	90	-6	2	4	-2	.936	-9	*3-115	-1.9
1978	Mon-N	144	520	68	144	39	4	15	70	32	103	.277	.321	.454	116	9	2	3	-1	.947	-5	*3-139	0.0
1979	Mon-N★	153	544	83	167	39	2	30	82	41	101	.307	.358	.551	146	32	5	1	1	.947	-9	*3-153	2.2
1980	Mon-N	126	452	55	115	27	3	15	72	36	80	.254	.315	.427	105	2	2	6	-3	.949	-8	*3-124	-1.1
1981	*Mon-N	97	349	41	85	19	3	8	44	28	73	.244	.300	.384	92	-5	0	0	0	.935	-17	3-95	-2.6
1982	Tex-A	128	440	59	116	15	0	17	62	30	84	.264	.316	.414	104	1	5	2	0	.962	-7	*O-124/3-3,D-2	-0.9
1983	Tex-A	145	555	76	151	26	4	26	88	46	91	.272	.331	.474	121	14	0	0	0	.962	-5	*O-132,D-13	0.5
1984	Tex-A	156	613	72	175	42	1	22	101	42	116	.285	.337	.465	116	12	2	4	-2	.982	4	O-81,D-63,3-12	1.0
1985	Tex-A	94	346	44	86	11	1	17	51	33	77	.249	.316	.434	101	0	0	2	-1	.991	-3	O-69,D-22/3-2	-0.6
1986	Tex-A	129	464	67	128	22	1	28	94	52	114	.276	.351	.509	127	17	3	1	0	.935	-5	D-98,3-30	0.9
1987	Tex-A★	152	557	79	149	22	1	32	100	49	154	.268	.330	.483	112	8	3	1	0	.918	-9	*D-122,3-28/O-1	-0.4
1988	Tex-A	68	248	22	47	9	1	7	26	20	79	.190	.256	.319	58	-14	0	0	0	.000	0	D-67	-1.6
	*Bos-A	52	158	10	41	5	0	7	26	8	32	.259	.299	.424	96	-1	0	1	-1	.988	3	1-36,D-14	-0.2
	Yr	120	406	32	88	14	1	14	52	28	111	.217	.272	.360	73	-15	0	1	-1	.988	3	D-81,1-36	-1.8
Total	15	1891	6792	850	1789	360	33	256	992	529	1359	.263	.321	.439	106	45	30	36	-13	.941	-62	*3-1021,O-407,D/1S2	-7.0

■ TOM PARROTT Parrott, Thomas William "Tacky Tom" b: 4/10/1868, Portland, Ore. d: 1/1/32, Dundee, Ore. BR/TR, 5'10.5", 170 lbs. Deb: 6/18/1893 F

YEAR	TM/L	G	AB	R	H	2B	3B	HR	RBI	BB	SO	AVG	OBP	SLG	PRO+	BR/A	SB	CS	SBR	FA	FR	G/POS	TPR
1893	Chi-N	7	27	4	7	1	0	0	3	1	2	.259	.286	.296	56	-2	0			.800	-1	/P-4,3-2,2-1	-0.1
	Cin-N	24	68	5	13	1	1	1	9	1	9	.191	.203	.279	27	-8	0			.915	1	P-22/O-1	-0.1
	Yr	31	95	9	20	2	1	1	12	2	11	.211	.227	.284	35	-9	0			.906	-0	P-26/3-2,2-1,O-1	-0.2
1894	Cin-N	68	229	51	74	12	6	4	40	17	10	.323	.372	.480	101	-1	4			.929	5	P-41,O-13,1/S32	0.1
1895	Cin-N	64	201	35	69	13	7	3	41	11	8	.343	.377	.522	125	6	10			.922	1	P-41,1-14/O-9	0.0
1896	StL-N	118	474	62	138	13	12	7	70	11	24	.291	.307	.414	93	-8	12			.951	13	*O-108/P-7,1-6	-0.2
Total	4	281	999	157	301	40	26	15	163	41	53	.301	.329	.438	96	-12	26			.940	19	O-131,P-115/132S	-0.3

YEAR	TM/L	G	AB	R	H	2B	3B	HR	RBI	BB	SO	AVG	OBP	SLG	PRO+	BR/A	SB	CS	SBR	FA	FR	G/POS	TPR
■ JIGGS PARROTT	Parrott, Walter Edward b: 7/14/1871, Portland, Ore. d: 4/16/1898, Phoenix, Ariz. 5'11", 160 lbs. Deb: 7/11/1892 F																						
1892	Chi-N	78	333	38	67	8	5	2	22	8	30	.201	.222	.273	49	-22	7			.891	-2	3-78	-2.0
1893	Chi-N	110	455	54	111	10	9	1	65	13	25	.244	.267	.312	54	-32	25			.904	9	*3-99/2-7,O-4	-1.7
1894	Chi-N	124	517	82	128	17	9	3	64	16	35	.248	.274	.333	43	-51	30			.931	-6	*2-123/3-1	-4.0
1895	Chi-N	3	4	0	1	0	0	0	0	0	0	.250	.250	.250	27	-0	0			.000	-2	/O-1,S-1,1-1	-0.2
Total	4	315	1309	174	307	35	23	6	151	37	90	.235	.258	.310	48	-105	62			.899	-1	3-178,2-130/O-5,1S	-7.9
■ CASEY PARSONS	Parsons, Casey Robert b: 4/14/54, Wenatchee, Wash. BL/TR, 6'1", 180 lbs. Deb: 5/31/81																						
1981	Sea-A	36	22	6	5	1	0	1	5	1	4	.227	.320	.409	105	0	0	0	0	1.000	-5	O-24/1-1	-0.5
1983	Chi-A	8	5	1	1	0	0	0	0	2	1	.200	.429	.200	77	-0	0	0	0	1.000	-1	/O-3,D-2	-0.1
1984	Chi-A	1	1	0	0	0	0	0	0	0	1	.000	.000	.000	-96	-0	0	0	0	.000	0	/H	0.0
1987	Cle-A	18	25	2	4	0	0	1	5	0	5	.160	.160	.280	13	-3	0	0	0	1.000	-1	/O-2,1-1,D-5	-0.4
Total	4	63	53	9	10	1	0	2	10	3	11	.189	.259	.321	57	-3	0	0	0	1.000	-6	/O-29,D-7,1-2	-1.0
■ DIXIE PARSONS	Parsons, Edward Dixon b: 5/12/16, Talladega, Ala. d: 10/31/91, Longview, Tex. BR/TR, 6'2", 180 lbs. Deb: 8/16/39																						
1939	Det-A	5	1	0	0	0	0	0	0	1	1	.000	.500	.000	36	-0	0	0	0	1.000	0	/C-4	0.0
1942	Det-A	63	188	8	37	4	0	2	11	13	22	.197	.249	.250	37	-16	1	0	0	.981	10	C-62	-0.2
1943	Det-A	40	106	2	15	3	0	0	4	6	16	.142	.188	.170	4	-13	0	0	0	.975	5	C-40	-0.6
Total	3	108	295	10	52	7	0	2	15	20	39	.176	.229	.220	26	-29	1	0	0	.979	15	C-106	-0.8
■ JOHN PARSONS	Parsons, John S. b: Napoleon, Ohio 5'6", 138 lbs. Deb: 10/15/1884																						
1884	Cin-a	1	3	0	0	0	0	0			0	.000	.000	.000	-95	-1				1.000	-1	/O-1	-0.1
■ ROY PARTEE	Partee, Roy Robert b: 9/7/17, Los Angeles, Cal. BR/TR, 5'10", 180 lbs. Deb: 4/23/43																						
1943	Bos-A	96	299	30	84	14	2	0	31	39	33	.281	.368	.341	106	4	0	0	0	.983	-6	C-91	0.4
1944	Bos-A	89	280	18	68	12	0	2	41	37	29	.243	.333	.307	85	-5	0	1	-1	.989	-6	C-85	-0.7
1946	*Bos-A	40	111	13	35	5	2	0	9	13	14	.315	.387	.396	113	2	0	0	0	.974	-6	C-38	-0.2
1947	Bos-A	60	169	14	39	2	0	0	16	18	23	.231	.305	.243	50	-11	0	0	0	.975	-1	C-54	-0.9
1948	StL-A	82	231	14	47	8	1	0	17	25	21	.203	.284	.247	41	-19	2	2	-1	.982	1	C-76	-1.5
Total	5	367	1090	89	273	41	5	2	114	132	120	.250	.334	.303	78	-29	2	3	-1	.982	-18	C-344	-2.9
■ STEVE PARTENHEIMER	Partenheimer, Harold Philip b: 8/30/1891, Greenfield, Mass. d: 6/16/71, Mansfield, Ohio BR/TR, 5'8.5", 145 lbs. Deb: 6/18/13 F																						
1913	Det-A	1	2	0	0	0	0	0	0	0	0	.000	.333	.000	-1	-0	0			.750	0	/3-1	0.0
■ JAY PARTRIDGE	Partridge, James Bugg b: 11/15/02, Mountville, Ga. d: 1/14/74, Nashville, Tenn. BL/TR, 5'11", 160 lbs. Deb: 4/12/27																						
1927	Bro-N	146	572	72	149	17	6	7	40	20	36	.260	.289	.348	70	-26	9			.938	-16	*2-140	-3.6
1928	Bro-N	37	73	18	18	0	1	0	12	13	6	.247	.368	.274	71	-2	2			.908	-5	2-18/3-2	-0.7
Total	2	183	645	90	167	17	7	7	52	33	42	.259	.299	.340	70	-28	11			.935	-20	2-158/3-2	-4.3
■ BEN PASCHAL	Paschal, Benjamin Edwin b: 10/13/1895, Enterprise, Ala. d: 11/10/74, Charlotte, N.C. BR/TR, 5'11", 185 lbs. Deb: 8/16/15																						
1915	Cle-A	9	9	0	1	0	0	0	0	0	3	.111	.111	.111	-33	-1	0			.000	0	H	-0.2
1920	Bos-A	9	28	5	10	0	0	0	5	5	2	.357	.455	.357	122	1	1	0	0	1.000	-0	/O-7	0.1
1924	NY-A	4	12	2	3	1	0	0	3	1	0	.250	.308	.333	65	-1	0	0	0	1.000	-0	/O-4	-0.1
1925	NY-A	89	247	49	89	16	5	12	56	22	29	.360	.417	.611	161	22	14	9	-1	.953	-4	O-66	1.2
1926	*NY-A	96	258	46	74	12	3	7	32	26	35	.287	.354	.438	107	2	7	6	-2	.935	-3	O-74	-0.7
1927	NY-A	50	82	16	26	9	2	2	16	4	10	.317	.349	.549	134	3	0	2	-1	.976	-5	O-27	-0.3
1928	*NY-A	65	79	12	25	6	1	1	15	8	11	.316	.379	.456	122	3	1	0	0	1.000	-6	O-25	-0.3
1929	NY-A	42	72	13	15	3	0	2	11	6	3	.208	.269	.333	58	-5	1	1	-0	.951	-1	O-20	-0.7
Total	8	364	787	143	243	47	11	24	138	72	93	.309	.369	.488	123	24	24	18		.953	-19	O-223	-1.0
■ JOHNNY PASEK	Pasek, John Paul b: 6/25/05, Niagara Falls, N.Y. d: 3/13/76, Niagara Falls, N.Y BR/TR, 5'10", 175 lbs. Deb: 7/28/33																						
1933	Det-A	28	61	6	15	4	0	0	4	7	7	.246	.324	.311	68	-3	2	0	1	.989	-1	C-28	-0.1
1934	Chi-A	4	9	1	3	0	0	0	0	1	1	.333	.400	.333	88	-0	0	0	0	1.000	0	/C-4	0.0
Total	2	32	70	7	18	4	0	0	4	8	8	.257	.333	.314	70	-3	2	0	1	.990	-1	/C-32	-0.1
■ DODE PASKERT	Paskert, George Henry b: 8/28/1881, Cleveland, Ohio d: 2/12/59, Cleveland, Ohio BR/TR, 5'11", 165 lbs. Deb: 9/21/07																						
1907	Cin-N	16	50	10	14	4	0	1	8	2		.280	.333	.420	130	2	2			.973	1	O-16	0.2
1908	Cin-N	118	395	40	96	14	4	1	36	27		.243	.298	.306	96	-2	25			.953	5	*O-116	-0.2
1909	Cin-N	104	322	49	81	7	4	0	33	34		.252	.327	.298	95	-1	23			.968	0	O-82/1-6	-0.5
1910	Cin-N	144	506	63	152	21	5	2	46	70	60	.300	.389	.374	128	20	51			.957	14	*O-139/1-2	2.9
1911	Phi-N	153	560	96	153	18	5	4	47	70	70	.273	.358	.345	96	-2	28			.979	8	*O-153	-0.2
1912	Phi-N	145	540	102	170	37	5	2	43	91	67	.315	.420	.413	120	19	36			.967	5	*O-141/2-2,3-1	1.6
1913	Phi-N	124	454	83	119	21	9	4	29	65	69	.262	.358	.374	105	4	12			.972	18	*O-120	1.7
1914	Phi-N	132	451	59	119	25	6	3	44	56	68	.264	.349	.366	106	4	23			.958	12	*O-128/S-4	1.1
1915	*Phi-N	109	328	51	80	17	4	3	39	35	38	.244	.319	.348	100	0	9	6	-1	.970	-2	O-92/1-5	-0.8
1916	Phi-N	149	555	82	155	30	7	8	46	54	76	.279	.346	.402	125	17	22	21	-6	.983	1	*O-146/S-1	0.5
1917	Phi-N	141	546	78	137	27	11	4	43	62	63	.251	.331	.363	108	6	19			**.984**	-2	*O-138	-0.4
1918	*Chi-N	127	461	69	132	24	3	3	59	53	49	.286	.362	.371	121	13	20			.980	-3	*O-121/3-6	0.3
1919	Chi-N	88	270	21	53	11	3	2	29	28	33	.196	.274	.281	67	-11	7			.969	-6	O-80	-2.4
1920	Chi-N	139	487	57	136	22	10	5	71	64	58	.279	.366	.396	117	12	16	14	-4	.956	1	*O-137	0.0
1921	Cin-N	27	92	8	16	1	1	0	4	4	8	.174	.208	.207	11	-12	0	2	-1	.984	1	O-24	-1.4
Total	15	1716	6017	868	1613	279	77	42	577	715	659	.268	.350	.361	108	70	293	43		.969	52	*O-1633/1-13,3S2	2.4
■ KEVIN PASLEY	Pasley, Kevin Patrick b: 7/22/53, Bronx, N.Y. BR/TR, 6', 185 lbs. Deb: 10/2/74																						
1974	LA-N	1	0	0	0	0	0	0	0	0	0	—	—	—	—	0	0	0	0	1.000	-0	/C-1	0.0
1976	LA-N	23	52	4	12	2	0	0	2	3	7	.231	.273	.269	55	-3	0	0	0	.971	5	C-23	0.2
1977	LA-N	2	3	0	1	0	0	0	0	0	0	.333	.333	.333	80	-0	0	0	0	1.000	1	/C-2	0.0
	Sea-A	4	13	1	5	0	0	0	2	1	2	.385	.429	.385	125	1	0	0	0	1.000	-2	/C-4	-0.1
1978	Sea-A	25	54	3	13	5	0	1	5	2	4	.241	.268	.389	83	-1	0	0	0	1.000	-0	C-25	-0.1
Total	4	55	122	8	31	7	0	1	9	6	13	.254	.289	.336	76	-4	0	0	0	.986	3	/C-55	0.0
■ DAN PASQUA	Pasqua, Daniel Anthony b: 10/17/61, Yonkers, N.Y. BL/TL, 6', 203 lbs. Deb: 5/30/85																						
1985	NY-A	60	148	17	31	3	1	9	25	16	38	.209	.291	.426	96	-1	0	0	0	1.000	1	O-37,D-14	-0.1
1986	NY-A	102	280	44	82	17	0	16	45	47	78	.293	.400	.525	151	21	2	0	1	.987	-2	O-81/1-5,D-3	1.7
1987	NY-A	113	318	42	74	7	1	17	42	40	99	.233	.320	.421	96	-2	0	2	-1	.985	-2	O-74,D-20,1-12	-0.8
1988	Chi-A	129	422	48	96	16	2	20	50	46	100	.227	.308	.417	101	0	1	0	0	**.996**	7	*O-112/1-7,D-2	0.4
1989	Chi-A	73	246	26	61	9	1	11	47	25	58	.248	.320	.427	111	3	1	2	-1	.993	2	O-66/D-5	0.2
1990	Chi-A	112	325	43	89	27	3	13	58	37	66	.274	.352	.495	137	16	1	1	-0	.962	0	D-57,O-43	1.3
1991	Chi-A	134	417	71	108	22	5	18	66	62	86	.259	.359	.465	129	17	0	2	-1	.991	-8	1-83,O-59/D-8	0.3
1992	Chi-A	93	265	26	56	16	1	6	33	36	57	.211	.308	.347	84	-5	0	1	-1	.963	-2	O-81/1-5,D-1	-1.0
1993	*Chi-A	78	176	22	36	10	1	5	20	26	51	.205	.307	.358	80	-5	2	2	-1	.984	-3	O-37,1-32/D-6	-1.0
1994	Chi-A	11	23	2	5	2	0	2	4	0	9	.217	.217	.565	95	-0	0	0	0	.867	-1	/O-5,1-3	-0.1
Total	10	905	2620	341	638	129	15	117	390	335	642	.244	.333	.438	112	42	7	10	-4	.984	-8	O-595,1-147,D-116	0.9
■ MIKE PASQUELLA	Pasquella, Michael John "Toney" (b: Michael John Pasquariello) b: 11/7/1898, Philadelphia, Pa. d: 4/5/65, Bridgeport, Conn. BR/TR, 5'11", 167 lbs. Deb: 7/9/19																						
1919	Phi-N	1	1	1	1	0	0	0	0	0	0	1.000	1.000	1.000	469	0	0			.000	0	/1-1	0.0
	StL-N	1	1	0	0	0	0	0	0	0	1	.000	.000	.000	-99	-0	0			.000	0	H	0.0
	Yr	2	2	1	1	0	0	0	0	0	1	.500	.500	.500	200	0	0			.000	0	/1-1	0.0
■ CLIFF PASTORNICKY	Pastornicky, Clifford Scott b: 11/18/58, Seattle, Wash. BR/TR, 5'10", 170 lbs. Deb: 6/14/83																						
1983	KC-A	10	32	4	4	0	0	2	5	0	3	.125	.125	.313	16	-4	0	0	0	.929	-0	3-10	-0.4

YEAR	TM/L	G	AB	R	H	2B	3B	HR	RBI	BB	SO	AVG	OBP	SLG	PRO+	BR/A	SB	CS	SBR	FA	FR	G/POS	TPR
■ **BOB PATE**	Pate, Robert Wayne b: 12/3/53, Los Angeles, Cal. BR/TR, 6'3.5", 200 lbs. Deb: 6/2/80																						
1980	Mon-N	23	39	3	10	2	0	0	5	3	6	.256	.310	.308	73	-1	0	1	-1	1.000	-4	O-18	-0.6
1981	Mon-N	8	6	0	2	0	0	0	0	1	0	.333	.429	.333	117	0	0	0	0	1.000	-2	/O-5	-0.2
Total	2	31	45	3	12	2	0	0	5	4	6	.267	.327	.311	79	-1	0	1	-1	1.000	-5	/O-23	-0.8
■ **FREDDIE PATEK**	Patek, Frederick Joseph "The Flea" b: 10/9/44, Seguin, Tex. BR/TR, 5'5", 148 lbs. Deb: 6/3/68																						
1968	Pit-N	61	208	31	53	4	2	2	18	12	37	.255	.302	.322	89	-3	18	7	1	.976	-1	S-52/O-5,3-1	0.2
1969	Pit-N	147	460	48	110	9	1	5	32	53	86	.239	.319	.296	75	-14	15	8	-0	.954	-2	*S-146	-0.2
1970	*Pit-N	84	237	42	58	10	5	1	19	29	46	.245	.327	.342	81	-6	8	2	1	.971	11	S-65	1.3
1971	KC-A	147	591	86	158	21	**11**	6	36	44	80	.267	.323	.371	97	-3	49	14	6	.968	10	*S-147	3.4
1972	KC-A†	136	518	59	110	25	4	0	32	47	64	.212	.282	.276	67	-21	33	7	6	.971	**30**	*S-136	3.8
1973	KC-A	135	501	82	117	19	5	5	45	54	63	.234	.312	.321	73	-18	36	14	2	.966	**35**	*S-135	3.8
1974	KC-A	149	537	72	121	18	6	3	38	77	69	.225	.326	.298	76	-15	33	15	1	.967	4	*S-149	1.0
1975	KC-A	136	483	58	110	14	5	5	45	42	65	.228	.292	.308	68	-20	32	7	5	.959	-7	*S-136/D-1	-0.7
1976	*KC-A★	144	432	58	104	19	3	1	43	50	63	.241	.322	.306	84	-8	51	15	6	.962	-6	*S-143/D-1	1.0
1977	*KC-A	154	497	72	130	26	6	5	60	41	84	.262	.324	.368	88	-8	**53**	13	8	.958	-19	*S-154	-0.2
1978	*KC-A★	138	440	54	109	23	1	2	46	42	56	.248	.315	.318	76	-13	38	11	5	.949	-25	*S-137	-1.7
1979	KC-A	106	306	30	77	17	0	1	37	16	42	.252	.295	.317	64	-15	11	12	-4	.955	-29	*S-104	-3.7
1980	Cal-A	86	273	41	72	10	5	5	34	15	26	.264	.304	.392	92	-4	7	6	-2	.953	-18	S-81	-1.5
1981	Cal-A	27	47	3	11	1	1	0	5	1	6	.234	.250	.298	57	-3	1	0	0	.983	2	2-16/3-7,S-3	0.0
Total	14	1650	5530	736	1340	216	55	41	490	523	787	.242	.311	.324	79	-151	385	131	37	.962	-15	*S-1588/2-16,3OD	6.5
■ **BOB PATRICK**	Patrick, Robert Lee b: 10/27/17, Ft.Smith, Ark. BR/TR, 6'2", 190 lbs. Deb: 9/20/41																						
1941	Det-A	5	7	2	2	0	0	0	0	0	1	.286	.286	.286	47	-1	0	0	0	.750	-1	/O-3	-0.2
1942	Det-A	4	8	1	2	1	0	1	3	1	0	.250	.333	.750	185	1	0	0	0	1.000	-0	/O-3	0.0
Total	2	9	15	3	4	1	0	1	3	1	1	.267	.313	.533	118	0	0	0	0	.889	-1	/O-6	-0.2
■ **HARRY PATTEE**	Pattee, Harry Ernest b: 1/17/1882, Charlestown, Mass. d: 7/17/71, Lynchburg, Va. BL/TR, 5'8", 149 lbs. Deb: 4/14/08																						
1908	Bro-N	80	264	19	57	5	2	0	9	25		.216	.286	.250	74	-7	24			.964	12	2-74	0.5
■ **DAN PATTERSON**	Patterson, Daniel Thomas b: 1846, New York, N.Y. TL , 5'9", 143 lbs. Deb: 5/18/1871																						
1871	Mut-n	32	151	31	31	2	0	0	13	1	0	.205	.211	.219	26	-13	2	1	0	.824	-2	*O-31/2-2	-0.9
1872	Eck-n	12	47	5	9	2	0	0	4	0	1	.191	.191	.234	36	-3	0	0	0	.882	2	O-11/1-1	0.0
1874	Mut-n	1	5	1	2	0	0	0	2	0	0	.400	.400	.400	153	0	0	0	0	1.000	-0	/1-1,O-1	0.0
1875	Atl-n	12	45	4	9	0	0	0	4	0	0	.200	.200	.200	45	-2	1	0	0	.636	-6	/2-7,O-7	-0.7
Total	4 n	57	248	41	51	4	0	0	23	1	1	.206	.209	.222	33	-17	3	1	0	.833	-7	/O-50,2-9,1-2	-1.6
■ **HAM PATTERSON**	Patterson, Hamilton b: 10/13/1877, Belleville, Ill. d: 11/25/45, E.St.Louis, Ill. BR/TR, 6'2", 185 lbs. Deb: 5/18/09 F																						
1909	StL-A	17	49	2	10	1	0	0	5	0		.204	.204	.224	38	-4	1			1.000	-1	/1-6,O-6	-0.6
	Chi-A	1	3	2	0	0	0	0	0	1		.000	.250	.000	-21	-0	0			1.000	1	/1-1	0.0
	Yr	18	52	4	10	1	0	0	5	1		.192	.208	.212	35	-4	1			1.000	-0	/1-7,O-6	-0.6
■ **HANK PATTERSON**	Patterson, Henry Joseph Colquit b: 7/17/07, San Francisco, Cal. d: 9/30/70, Panorama City, Cal. BR/TR, 5'11.5", 170 lbs. Deb: 9/5/32																						
1932	Bos-A	1	1	0	0	0	0	0	0	0	0	.000	.000	.000	-99	-0	0	0	0	.000	0	/C-1	0.0
■ **JOHN PATTERSON**	Patterson, John Allen b: 2/11/67, Key West, Fla. BB/TR, 5'9", 160 lbs. Deb: 4/6/92																						
1992	SF-N	32	103	10	19	1	1	0	4	5	24	.184	.229	.214	28	-10	5	1	1	.960	6	2-22/O-5	-0.3
1993	SF-N	16	16	1	3	0	0	1	2	0	5	.188	.188	.375	48	-1	0	1	-1	.000	0	H	-0.3
1994	SF-N	85	240	36	57	10	1	3	32	16	43	.237	.315	.325	70	-10	13	3	2	.979	-9	2-63	-1.5
1995	SF-N	95	205	27	42	5	3	1	14	14	41	.205	.294	.273	52	-14	4	2	0	.983	-6	2-53	-1.7
Total	4	228	564	74	121	16	5	5	52	35	113	.215	.289	.287	56	-35	22	7	2	.977	-9	2-138/O-5	-3.8
■ **CLAIRE PATTERSON**	Patterson, Lorenzo Claire b: 10/5/1887, Arkansas City, Kan. d: 3/28/13, Mojave, Cal. BL/TR, 6' ", 180 lbs. Deb: 9/5/09																						
1909	Cin-N	4	8	0	1	0	0	0	1	0		.125	.125	.125	-23	-1	0			1.000	-0	/O-2	-0.2
■ **MIKE PATTERSON**	Patterson, Michael Lee b: 1/26/58, Santa Monica, Cal. BL/TR, 5'10", 170 lbs. Deb: 4/15/81																						
1981	Oak-A	12	23	4	8	1	1	0	1	2	5	.348	.400	.478	160	2	0	1	-1	1.000	-1	/O-5,D-2	0.0
	NY-A	4	9	2	2	0	2	0	0	0	0	.222	.222	.667	150	0	0	0	0	1.000	-1	/O-4	0.0
	Yr	16	32	6	10	1	3	0	1	2	5	.313	.353	.531	158	2	0	1	-1	1.000	-1	/O-9,D-2	0.0
1982	NY-A	11	16	3	3	1	0	1	1	2	6	.188	.278	.438	94	-0	1	0	0	1.000	-3	/O-9,D-1	-0.3
Total	2	27	48	9	13	2	3	1	2	4	11	.271	.327	.500	135	2	1	1	-0	1.000	-5	/O-18,D-3	-0.3
■ **PAT PATTERSON**	Patterson, William Jennings Bryan b: 1/29/01, Belleville, Ill. d: 10/1/77, St.Louis, Mo. BR/TR, 6', 175 lbs. Deb: 4/14/21 F																						
1921	NY-N	23	35	5	14	0	0	1	5	2	5	.400	.432	.486	142	2	0	1	-1	.970	4	3-14/S-7	0.6
■ **GEORGE PATTISON**	Pattison, George Deb: 4/24/1884																						
1884	Phi-U	2	7	0	1	0	0	0		0		.143	.143	.143	-14	-1				.500	-0	/O-2	-0.1
■ **GENE PATTON**	Patton, Gene Tunney b: 7/8/26, Coatesville, Pa. BL/TR, 5'10", 165 lbs. Deb: 6/17/44																						
1944	Bos-N	1	0	0	0	0	0	0	0	0	0	—	—	—	—	0	0			.000	0	R	0.0
■ **BILL PATTON**	Patton, George William b: 10/12/12, Cornwall, Pa. d: 3/15/86, Philadelphia, Pa. BR/TR, 6'2", 180 lbs. Deb: 6/29/35																						
1935	Phi-A	9	10	1	3	1	0	0	2	2	3	.300	.417	.400	113	0	0	0	0	1.000	0	/C-3	0.1
■ **TOM PATTON**	Patton, Thomas Allen b: 9/5/35, Honey Brook, Pa. BR/TR, 5'9.5", 185 lbs. Deb: 4/30/57																						
1957	Bal-A	1	2	0	0	0	0	0	0	0	2	.000	.000	.000	-99	-1	0	0	0	1.000	1	/C-1	0.1
■ **LOU PAUL**	Paul, Louis BR/TR, Deb: 9/5/1876																						
1876	Phi-N	3	12	2	2	1	0	0	0	0	0	.167	.167	.250	37	-1				.643	-2	/C-3	-0.3
■ **CARLOS PAULA**	Paula, Carlos (Conill) b: 11/28/27, Havana, Cuba d: 4/25/83, Miami, Fla. BR/TR, 6'3", 195 lbs. Deb: 9/6/54																						
1954	Was-A	9	24	2	4	1	0	0	2	2	4	.167	.231	.208	22	-3	0	0	0	1.000	1	/O-6	-0.2
1955	Was-A	115	351	34	105	20	7	6	45	17	43	.299	.335	.447	115	5	2	3	-1	.941	-2	O-85	-0.2
1956	Was-A	33	82	8	15	2	1	3	13	8	15	.183	.256	.341	56	-6	0	2	-1	.974	-1	O-20	-0.9
Total	3	157	457	44	124	23	8	9	60	27	62	.271	.315	.416	99	-3	2	5	-2	.950	-2	O-111	-1.3
■ **GENE PAULETTE**	Paulette, Eugene Edward b: 5/26/1891, Centralia, Ill. d: 2/8/66, Little Rock, Ark. BR/TR, 6', 150 lbs. Deb: 6/16/11																						
1911	NY-N	10	12	1	2	0	0	0	1	0	1	.167	.167	.167	-6	-2	0			.938	-1	/1-7,S-1,3-1	-0.3
1916	StL-A	5	4	1	2	0	0	0	0	1	1	.500	.600	.500	242	1	0			.000	0	H	0.1
1917	StL-A	12	22	3	4	0	0	0	0	3	3	.182	.280	.182	43	-1	0			.982	0	/1-5,2-3,3-1	-0.1
	StL-N	95	332	32	88	21	7	0	34	16	16	.265	.303	.370	109	2	9			.993	-1	1-93	-0.3
1918	StL-N	125	461	33	126	15	3	0	52	27	16	.273	.316	.319	97	-2	11			.983	5	1-97,S-12/2-7,O3P	0.0
1919	StL-N	43	144	11	31	6	0	0	11	9	6	.215	.261	.257	60	-7	4			.990	2	1-35/S-3	-0.7
	Phi-N	67	243	20	63	8	3	1	31	19	10	.259	.316	.329	88	-3	10			.957	0	2-58,O-10/1-1	-0.1
	Yr	110	387	31	94	14	3	1	42	28	16	.243	.296	.302	78	-10	14			.957	2	2-58,1-36,O-10,/S-3	-0.8
1920	Phi-N	143	562	59	162	16	6	1	36	33	16	.288	.332	.343	90	-7	9	8	-2	.988	6	*1-139/S-2	-0.6
Total	6	500	1780	160	478	66	19	2	165	108	69	.269	.314	.330	92	-19	43	8		.988	11	1-377/2-68,SO3P	-2.0
■ **SI PAUXTIS**	Pauxtis, Simon Francis b: 7/20/1885, Pittston, Pa. d: 3/13/61, Philadelphia, Pa. BR/TR, 6' ", 175 lbs. Deb: 9/18/09																						
1909	Cin-N	4	8	2	1	0	0	0	0	0		.125	.222	.125	8	-1	0			1.000	-1	/C-4	-0.2
■ **DON PAVLETICH**	Pavletich, Donald Stephen b: 7/13/38, Milwaukee, Wis. BR/TR, 5'11", 209 lbs. Deb: 4/20/57																						
1957	Cin-N	1	1	0	0	0	0	0	0	0	0	.000	.000	.000	-93	-0	0	0	0	.000	0	H	0.0

YEAR	TM/L	G	AB	R	H	2B	3B	HR	RBI	BB	SO	AVG	OBP	SLG	PRO+	BR/A	SB	CS	SBR	FA	FR	G/POS	TPR
1959	Cin-N	1	0	1	0	0	0	0	0	0	0	—	—	—	—	0	0	0	0	.000	0	R	0.0
1962	Cin-N	34	63	7	14	3	0	1	7	8	18	.222	.310	.317	67	-3	0	0	0	1.000	1	1-25/C-2	-0.3
1963	Cin-N	71	183	18	38	11	0	5	18	17	12	.208	.275	.350	76	-6	0	0	0	.991	-3	1-57,C-13	-1.1
1964	Cin-N	34	91	12	22	4	0	5	11	10	17	.242	.317	.451	109	1	0	0	0	.983	-3	C-27/1-1	-0.1
1965	Cin-N	68	191	25	61	11	1	8	32	23	27	.319	.395	.513	144	11	1	1	-0	.986	-2	C-54/1-9	1.1
1966	Cin-N	83	235	29	69	13	2	12	38	18	37	.294	.346	.519	126	8	1	0	0	.975	-10	C-55,1-10	0.1
1967	Cin-N	74	231	25	55	14	3	6	34	21	38	.238	.313	.403	93	-2	2	1	0	.986	-5	C-66/1-6,3-1	-0.4
1968	Cin-N	46	98	11	28	3	1	2	11	8	23	.286	.352	.398	117	2	0	0	0	1.000	-0	1-22/C-5	0.1
1969	Chi-A	78	188	26	46	12	0	6	33	28	45	.245	.343	.404	103	1	0	0	0	.974	-6	C-51,1-13	-0.4
1970	Bos-A	32	65	4	9	1	1	0	6	10	15	.138	.253	.185	21	-7	1	0	0	1.000	1	1-16,C-10	-0.7
1971	Bos-A	14	27	5	7	1	0	1	3	5	5	.259	.375	.407	113	1	0	0	0	.973	-2	/C-8	-0.1
Total	12	536	1373	163	349	73	8	46	193	148	237	.254	.330	.420	103	6	5	2	0	.983	-31	C-291,1-159/3-1	-1.8

■ TED PAWELEK Pawelek, Theodore John "Porky" b: 8/15/19, Chicago Heights, Ill. d: 2/12/64, Chicago Heights, Ill. BL/TR, 5′10.5″, 202 lbs. Deb: 9/13/46

YEAR	TM/L	G	AB	R	H	2B	3B	HR	RBI	BB	SO	AVG	OBP	SLG	PRO+	BR/A	SB	CS	SBR	FA	FR	G/POS	TPR
1946	Chi-N	4	4	0	1	1	0	0	0	0	0	.250	.250	.500	112	0	0			.000	-0	/C-1	0.0

■ STAN PAWLOSKI Pawloski, Stanley Walter b: 9/6/31, Wanamie, Pa. BR/TR, 6′1″, 175 lbs. Deb: 9/24/55

YEAR	TM/L	G	AB	R	H	2B	3B	HR	RBI	BB	SO	AVG	OBP	SLG	PRO+	BR/A	SB	CS	SBR	FA	FR	G/POS	TPR
1955	Cle-A	2	8	0	1	0	0	0	0	0	2	.125	.125	.125	-31	-1	0	0	0	1.000	1	/2-2	0.0

■ FRED PAYNE Payne, Frederick Thomas b: 9/2/1880, Camden, N.Y. d: 1/16/54, Camden, N.Y. BR/TR, 5′10″, 162 lbs. Deb: 4/21/06

YEAR	TM/L	G	AB	R	H	2B	3B	HR	RBI	BB	SO	AVG	OBP	SLG	PRO+	BR/A	SB	CS	SBR	FA	FR	G/POS	TPR
1906	Det-A	72	222	23	60	5	5	0	20	13		.270	.316	.338	102	0	4			.966	-1	C-47,O-17	0.4
1907	*Det-A	53	169	17	28	2	2	0	14	7		.166	.221	.201	34	-13	4			.981	3	C-46/O-5	-0.7
1908	Det-A	20	45	3	3	0	0	0	2	3		.067	.176	.067	-20	-6	1			.954	-3	C-17/O-1	-0.9
1909	Chi-A	32	82	8	20	2	0	0	12	5		.244	.295	.268	82	-2	0			.987	-2	C-27/O-3	-0.1
1910	Chi-A	91	252	17	56	5	4	0	19	11		.222	.260	.274	70	-9	6			.974	-5	C-78/O-2	-0.7
1911	Chi-A	66	133	14	27	2	1	1	19	8		.203	.259	.256	45	-10	6			.963	-4	C-56	-1.0
Total	6	334	903	82	194	16	12	1	86	47		.215	.265	.262	64	-39	21			.972	-11	C-271/O-28	-3.0

■ GEORGE PAYNTER Paynter, George Washington (b: George Washington Paner) b: 7/6/1871, Cincinnati, Ohio d: 10/1/50, Cincinnati, Ohio BR/TR, 5′9″, 125 lbs. Deb: 8/12/1894

YEAR	TM/L	G	AB	R	H	2B	3B	HR	RBI	BB	SO	AVG	OBP	SLG	PRO+	BR/A	SB	CS	SBR	FA	FR	G/POS	TPR
1894	StL-N	1	4	0	0	0	0	0	0	1	0	.000	.200	.000	-48	-1	1			1.000	1	/O-1	0.0

■ JAY PAYTON Payton, Jason Lee b: 11/22/72, Zanesville, Ohio BR/TR, 5′10″, 185 lbs. Deb: 9/1/98

YEAR	TM/L	G	AB	R	H	2B	3B	HR	RBI	BB	SO	AVG	OBP	SLG	PRO+	BR/A	SB	CS	SBR	FA	FR	G/POS	TPR
1998	NY-N	15	22	2	7	1	0	0	0	1	4	.318	.348	.364	86	-0	0	0	0	1.000	-1	O-10	-0.1

■ JOHNNY PEACOCK Peacock, John Gaston b: 1/10/10, Fremont, N.C. d: 10/17/81, Wilson, N.C. BL/TR, 5′11″, 165 lbs. Deb: 9/23/37

YEAR	TM/L	G	AB	R	H	2B	3B	HR	RBI	BB	SO	AVG	OBP	SLG	PRO+	BR/A	SB	CS	SBR	FA	FR	G/POS	TPR
1937	Bos-A	9	32	3	10	2	1	0	6	1	0	.313	.333	.438	89	-1	0	0	0	.980	1	/C-9	0.1
1938	Bos-A	72	195	29	59	7	1	1	39	17	4	.303	.358	.364	78	-6	4	1	1	.984	-9	C-57/1-1,O-1	-1.1
1939	Bos-A	92	274	33	76	11	4	0	36	29	11	.277	.347	.347	75	-10	1	1	-0	.972	-8	C-84	-1.2
1940	Bos-A	63	131	20	37	4	1	0	13	23	10	.282	.390	.328	85	-2	1	1	-0	.994	-6	C-48	-0.6
1941	Bos-A	79	261	28	74	20	1	0	27	21	3	.284	.339	.368	85	-6	2	1	0	.988	-4	C-70	-0.3
1942	Bos-A	88	286	17	76	7	3	0	25	21	11	.266	.316	.311	74	-10	1	1	-0	.988	-6	C-82	-1.0
1943	Bos-A	48	114	7	23	3	1	0	7	10	9	.202	.266	.246	49	-7	1	1	-0	.972	-1	C-32	-0.7
1944	Bos-A	4	4	0	0	0	0	0	0	0	0	.000	.000	.000	-99	-1	0	0	0	1.000	0	/C-2	-0.1
	Phi-N	83	253	21	57	9	3	0	21	31	15	.225	.310	.285	70	-9	1			.990	1	C-73/2-1	-0.4
1945	Phi-N	33	74	6	15	6	0	0	6	6	0	.203	.262	.284	53	-5	1			.969	-5	C-23	-0.9
	Bro-N	48	110	11	28	5	1	0	14	24	10	.255	.388	.318	98	1	2			.975	1	C-38	0.3
	Yr	81	184	17	43	11	1	0	20	30	10	.234	.341	.304	82	-4	3			.973	-5	C-61	-0.6
Total	9	619	1734	175	455	74	16	1	194	183	73	.262	.333	.325	76	-56	14	6		.983	-37	C-518/2-1,O-1,1-1	-5.9

■ ELIAS PEAK Peak, Elias b: 5/23/1859, Philadelphia, Pa. d: 12/17/16, Philadelphia, Pa. Deb: 4/19/1884

YEAR	TM/L	G	AB	R	H	2B	3B	HR	RBI	BB	SO	AVG	OBP	SLG	PRO+	BR/A	SB	CS	SBR	FA	FR	G/POS	TPR
1884	Bos-U	1	3	2	2	0	0	0		1		.667	.750	.667	338	1				1.000	-0	/O-1	0.1
	Phi-U	54	215	35	42	6	4	0		7		.195	.221	.260	49	-20				.825	-6	2-47/O-5,S-2	-2.2
	Yr	55	218	37	44	6	4	0		8		.202	.230	.266	54	-19				.825	-6	2-47/O-6,S-2	-2.1

■ HARRY PEARCE Pearce, Harry James b: 7/12/1889, Philadelphia, Pa. d: 1/8/42, Philadelphia, Pa. BR/TR, 5′9″, 158 lbs. Deb: 10/2/17

YEAR	TM/L	G	AB	R	H	2B	3B	HR	RBI	BB	SO	AVG	OBP	SLG	PRO+	BR/A	SB	CS	SBR	FA	FR	G/POS	TPR
1917	Phi-N	7	16	2	4	3	0	0	2	0	4	.250	.294	.438	118	0	0			.967	5	/S-4	0.5
1918	Phi-N	60	164	16	40	3	2	0	18	9	31	.244	.295	.287	73	-5	5			.944	5	2-46/S-2,1-1,3-1	0.3
1919	Phi-N	68	244	24	44	3	3	0	9	8	27	.180	.209	.217	26	-22	6			.948	-1	2-43,S-23/3-2	-2.2
Total	3	135	424	42	88	9	5	0	29	17	62	.208	.247	.252	48	-27	11			.946	9	/2-89,S-29,3-3,1-1	-1.4

■ DICKEY PEARCE Pearce, Richard J. b: 2/29/1836, Brooklyn, N.Y. d: 10/12/08, Wareham, Mass. BR/TR, 5′3.5″, 161 lbs. Deb: 5/18/1871 MU

YEAR	TM/L	G	AB	R	H	2B	3B	HR	RBI	BB	SO	AVG	OBP	SLG	PRO+	BR/A	SB	CS	SBR	FA	FR	G/POS	TPR
1871	Mut-n	33	163	31	44	5	0	0	20	4	1	.270	.287	.301	76	-3	0	0	0	.793	-7	*S-33	-0.7
1872	Mut-n	44	206	32	40	1	1	1	23	4	1	.194	.210	.223	35	-14	1	1	-0	**.839**	-0	*S-42/O-2,M	-1.0
1873	Atl-n	55	262	42	72	5	0	1	26	8	2	.275	.296	.305	88	-1	2	0	1	.780	5	*S-55/1-1,2-1	0.2
1874	Atl-n	56	255	48	75	1	0	0	26	6	1	.294	.310	.298	109	4	1	0	0	**.845**	9	*S-56/3-2,2-1	0.9
1875	StL-n	70	311	51	77	6	3	0	29	7	7	.248	.264	.286	100	2	8	3	1	.830	13	*S-70/P-2,M	1.1
1876	StL-N	25	102	12	21	1	0	0	10	3	5	.206	.229	.216	51	-5				.902	5	S-23/O-1,2-1	0.0
1877	StL-N	8	29	1	5	0	0	0	4	1	4	.172	.200	.172	19	-3				.950	3	/S-8	0.0
Total	5 n	258	1197	204	308	18	4	2	124	29	12	.257	.275	.284	84	-12	12	4	1	.818	19	S-256/P-2,3-2,2O1	0.5
Total	2	33	131	13	26	1	0	0	14	4	9	.198	.222	.206	44	-7				.914	7	/S-31,2-1,O-1	0.0

■ DUCKY PEARCE Pearce, William C. b: 3/17/1885, Corning, Ohio d: 5/22/33, Brownstown, Ind. BR/TR, 6′1″, 185 lbs. Deb: 7/1/08

YEAR	TM/L	G	AB	R	H	2B	3B	HR	RBI	BB	SO	AVG	OBP	SLG	PRO+	BR/A	SB	CS	SBR	FA	FR	G/POS	TPR
1908	Cin-N	2	2	0	0	0	0	0	0	0		.000	.000	.000	-99	-0	0			1.000	1	/C-2	0.1
1909	Cin-N	2	2	0	0	0	0	0	0	0		.000	.000	.000	-99	-0	0			1.000	-0	/C-2	-0.1
Total	2	4	4	0	0	0	0	0	0	0		.000	.000	.000	-99	-1	0			1.000	1	/C-4	0.0

■ ALBIE PEARSON Pearson, Albert Gregory b: 9/12/34, Alhambra, Cal. BL/TL, 5′5″, 141 lbs. Deb: 4/14/58

YEAR	TM/L	G	AB	R	H	2B	3B	HR	RBI	BB	SO	AVG	OBP	SLG	PRO+	BR/A	SB	CS	SBR	FA	FR	G/POS	TPR
1958	Was-A	146	530	63	146	25	5	3	33	64	31	.275	.356	.358	99	1	7	8	-3	.980	6	*O-141	-0.4
1959	Was-A	25	80	9	15	1	0	0	2	14	3	.188	.309	.200	43	-6	1	1	-0	.974	-2	O-21	-1.0
	Bal-A	80	138	22	32	4	2	0	6	13	5	.232	.298	.290	64	-7	4	0	1	.987	-7	O-50	-1.4
	Yr	105	218	31	47	5	2	0	8	27	8	.216	.302	.257	56	-13	5	1	1	.983	-9	O-71	-2.4
1960	Bal-A	48	82	17	20	2	0	1	6	17	3	.244	.374	.305	87	-1	4	0	1	.975	-5	O-32	-0.6
1961	LA-A	144	427	92	123	21	3	7	41	96	40	.288	.422	.400	109	9	11	3	2	.956	-1	*O-113	0.3
1962	LA-A	160	614	**115**	160	29	6	5	42	95	36	.261	.361	.352	96	-1	15	6	1	.989	9	*O-160	-0.1
1963	LA-A★	154	578	92	176	26	5	6	47	92	37	.304	.403	.398	133	30	17	10	-1	.983	7	*O-148	2.9
1964	LA-A	107	265	34	59	5	1	2	16	35	22	.223	.316	.272	72	-9	6	4	-1	.978	-3	O-66	-1.7
1965	Cal-A	122	360	41	100	17	2	4	21	51	17	.278	.370	.369	114	8	12	1	3	.988	-4	*O-101	0.4
1966	Cal-A	2	3	0	0	0	0	0	0	0	1	.000	.000	.000	-99	-1	0	0	0	.000	-0	/O-1	-0.1
Total	9	988	3077	485	831	130	24	28	214	477	195	.270	.370	.355	102	24	77	33	3	.980	1	O-833	-1.7

■ CHARLIE PECHOUS Pechous, Charles Edward b: 10/5/1896, Chicago, Ill. d: 9/13/80, Kenosha, Wis. BR/TR, 6′, 170 lbs. Deb: 9/14/15

YEAR	TM/L	G	AB	R	H	2B	3B	HR	RBI	BB	SO	AVG	OBP	SLG	PRO+	BR/A	SB	CS	SBR	FA	FR	G/POS	TPR
1915	Chi-F	18	51	4	9	3	0	0	4	4	15	.176	.236	.235	35	-5	1			.938	-1	3-18	-0.6
1916	Chi-N	22	69	5	10	1	1	0	4	3	21	.145	.181	.188	12	-7	1			.940	8	3-22	0.2
1917	Chi-N	13	41	2	10	0	0	0	1	2	9	.244	.295	.244	61	-2	1			1.000	-2	/3-7,S-5	-0.4
Total	3	53	161	11	29	4	1	0	9	9	45	.180	.228	.217	32	-14	3			.947	6	/3-47,S-5	-0.8

■ HAL PECK Peck, Harold Arthur b: 4/20/17, Big Bend, Wis. d: 4/13/95, Milwaukee, Wis. BL/TL, 5′11″, 175 lbs. Deb: 5/13/43

YEAR	TM/L	G	AB	R	H	2B	3B	HR	RBI	BB	SO	AVG	OBP	SLG	PRO+	BR/A	SB	CS	SBR	FA	FR	G/POS	TPR
1943	Bro-N	1	1	0	0	0	0	0	0	0	0	.000	.000	.000	-99	-0	0			.000	0	H	0.0
1944	Phi-A	2	8	0	2	0	0	0	1	0	2	.250	.250	.250	44	-1	0	2	-1	1.000	-0	/O-2	-0.2
1945	Phi-A	112	449	51	124	22	9	5	39	37	28	.276	.331	.399	112	5	5	3	-0	.943	-9	*O-110	-1.1
1946	Phi-A	48	150	14	37	8	2	2	11	16	14	.247	.319	.367	92	-2	1	2	-1	.981	-3	O-35	-0.8

YEAR	TM/L	G	AB	R	H	2B	3B	HR	RBI	BB	SO	AVG	OBP	SLG	PRO+	BR/A	SB	CS	SBR	FA	FR	G/POS	TPR
1947	Cle-A	114	392	58	115	18	2	8	44	27	31	.293	.342	.411	112	5	3	3	-1	.983	-7	O-97	-0.8
1948	*Cle-A	45	63	12	18	3	0	0	8	4	8	.286	.328	.333	78	-2	1	0	0	1.000	-2	/O-9	-0.4
1949	Cle-A	33	29	1	9	1	0	0	9	3	3	.310	.375	.345	93	-0	0	0	0	1.000	-1	/O-2	-0.1
Total	7	355	1092	136	305	52	13	15	112	87	86	.279	.334	.392	106	5	10	10		.965	-21	O-255	-3.4
■ ROGER PECKINPAUGH Peckinpaugh, Roger Thorpe b: 2/5/1891, Wooster, Ohio d: 11/17/77, Cleveland, Ohio BR/TR, 5′10.5″, 165 lbs. Deb: 9/15/10 M																							
1910	Cle-A	15	45	1	9	0	0	0	6	1		.200	.234	.200	36	-3	3			.906	-6	S-14	-1.0
1912	Cle-A	70	236	18	50	4	1	1	22	16		.212	.262	.250	45	-17	11			.924	-2	S-68	-1.4
1913	Cle-A	1	0	1	0	0	0	0	0	0	0	—	—	—	—	0	0			.000	0	H	0.0
	NY-A	95	340	35	91	10	7	1	32	24	47	.268	.316	.347	94	-4	19			.931	-6	S-93	-0.1
	Yr	96	340	36	91	10	7	1	32	24	47	.268	.316	.347	94	-4	19			.931	-6	S-93	-0.1
1914	NY-A	157	570	55	127	14	6	3	51	51	73	.223	.288	.284	72	-20	38	17	1	.956	3	*S-157,M	-0.3
1915	NY-A	142	540	67	119	18	7	5	44	49	72	.220	.289	.307	79	-16	19	12	-2	.942	11	*S-142	0.5
1916	NY-A	145	552	65	141	22	8	4	58	62	50	.255	.332	.346	101	1	18			.946	1	*S-145	1.1
1917	NY-A	148	543	63	141	24	7	0	41	64	46	.260	.340	.330	103	3	17			.934	10	*S-148	2.2
1918	NY-A	122	446	59	103	15	3	0	43	43	41	.231	.303	.278	74	-14	12			.961	**25**	*S-122	1.8
1919	NY-A	122	453	89	138	20	2	7	33	59	37	.305	.390	.404	122	15	10			.943	28	*S-121	5.1
1920	NY-A	139	534	109	144	26	6	8	54	72	47	.270	.356	.386	93	-5	8	12	-5	.962	3	*S-137	0.6
1921	*NY-A	149	577	128	166	25	7	8	71	84	44	.288	.380	.397	96	-1	2	2	-1	.948	-5	*S-149	0.7
1922	Was-A	147	520	62	132	14	4	2	48	55	36	.254	.329	.308	70	-22	11	6	-0	.951	20	*S-147	1.3
1923	Was-A	154	568	73	150	18	4	2	62	64	30	.264	.340	.320	78	-17	10	8	-2	.948	**23**	*S-154	1.9
1924	*Was-A	155	523	72	142	20	5	2	73	72	45	.272	.360	.340	84	-11	9	6	-1	.963	9	*S-155	1.3
1925	*Was-A	126	422	67	124	16	4	4	64	49	23	.294	.367	.379	91	-5	13	4	2	.952	-16	*S-124/1-1	-0.5
1926	Was-A	57	147	19	35	4	1	1	14	28	12	.238	.360	.299	75	-4	3	0	1	.960	-1	S-46/1-1	0.0
1927	Chi-A	68	217	23	64	6	3	0	23	21	6	.295	.360	.350	87	-4	2	3	-1	.964	-1	S-60	0.0
Total	17	2012	7233	1006	1876	256	75	48	739	814	609	.259	.336	.335	87	-122	205	70		.949	97	*S-1982/1-2	13.2
■ BILL PECOTA Pecota, William Joseph b: 2/16/60, Redwood City, Cal. BR/TR, 6′2″, 190 lbs. Deb: 9/19/86																							
1986	KC-A	12	29	3	6	2	0	0	2	3	3	.207	.303	.276	58	-2	0	2	-1	.974	6	3-12/S-2,D-4	0.3
1987	KC-A	66	156	22	43	5	1	3	14	15	25	.276	.343	.378	89	-2	5	0	2	.977	7	S-36,3-17,2-15,/D-1	0.9
1988	KC-A	90	178	25	37	3	3	1	15	18	34	.208	.288	.275	58	-10	7	2	1	.976	11	S-41,3-21,1/OD2C	0.4
1989	KC-A	65	83	21	17	4	2	3	5	7	9	.205	.275	.410	91	-1	5	0	2	.988	4	S-29,O-15,2/31D	0.5
1990	KC-A	87	240	43	58	15	2	5	20	33	39	.242	.336	.383	102	1	8	5	-1	.986	6	2-50,S-21,3/O1D	0.9
1991	KC-A	125	398	53	114	23	2	6	45	41	45	.286	.356	.399	108	5	16	7	1	.983	-13	*3-102,2-34/S1DOP	-0.6
1992	NY-N	117	269	28	61	13	0	2	26	25	40	.227	.295	.297	69	-11	9	3	1	.926	10	3-48,S-39,2-38,/P1	0.2
1993	*Atl-N	72	62	17	20	2	1	0	5	2	5	.323	.344	.387	94	-1	1	1	-0	1.000	1	3-23/2-4,O-1	0.1
1994	Atl-N	64	112	11	24	5	0	2	16	16	16	.214	.313	.313	62	-6	1	0	0	.974	7	3-31/2-1,O-1	0.2
Total	9	698	1527	223	380	72	11	22	148	160	216	.249	.324	.354	87	-26	52	20	4	.968	39	3-272,S-177,2/O1DPC	2.9
■ LES PEDEN Peden, Leslie Earl "Gooch" b: 9/17/23, Azle, Tex. BR/TR, 6′1.5″, 212 lbs. Deb: 4/17/53 C																							
1953	Was-A	9	28	4	7	1	0	1	1	4	3	.250	.344	.393	101	0	0	0	0	1.000	-1	/C-8	0.0
■ STU PEDERSON Pederson, Stuart Russell b: 1/28/60, Palo Alto, Cal. BL/TL, 6′, 185 lbs. Deb: 9/8/85																							
1985	LA-N	8	4	1	0	0	0	0	1	0	2	.000	.000	.000	-99	-1	0	0	0	1.000	-1	/O-5	-0.3
■ JORGE PEDRE Pedre, Jorge Enrique b: 10/12/66, Culver City, Cal. BR/TR, 5′11″, 210 lbs. Deb: 9/7/91																							
1991	KC-A	10	19	2	5	1	1	0	3	3	5	.263	.364	.421	116	0	0	0	0	.971	-0	/C-9,1-1	0.1
1992	Chi-N	4	4	0	0	0	0	0	0	0	1	.000	.000	.000	-98	-1	0	0	0	1.000	-1	/C-4	-0.2
Total	2	14	23	2	5	1	1	0	3	3	6	.217	.308	.348	81	-1	0	0	0	.973	-1	/C-13,1-1	-0.1
■ AL PEDRIQUE Pedrique, Alfredo Jose (Garcia) b: 8/11/60, Aragua, Venez. BR/TR, 6′ ", 155 lbs. Deb: 4/14/87																							
1987	NY-N	5	6	1	0	0	0	0	0	1	2	.000	.143	.000	-61	-1	0	0	0	1.000	1	/S-4,2-1	0.0
	Pit-N	88	246	23	74	10	1	1	27	18	27	.301	.356	.362	90	-3	5	4	-1	.968	-12	S-76/3-3,2-2	-0.9
	Yr	93	252	24	74	10	1	1	27	19	29	.294	.350	.353	87	-4	5	4	-1	.969	-10	S-80/2-3,3-3	-0.9
1988	Pit-N	50	128	7	23	5	0	0	4	8	17	.180	.234	.219	31	-11	0	0	0	.974	2	S-46/3-5	-0.7
1989	Det-A	31	69	1	14	3	0	0	5	2	15	.203	.225	.246	34	-6	0	0	0	.960	8	3-12,S-12/2-8	0.2
Total	3	174	449	32	111	18	1	1	36	29	61	.247	.299	.298	64	-22	5	4	-1	.971	-1	S-138/3-20,2-11	-1.4
■ CHICK PEDROES Pedroes, Charles P. b: 10/27/1869, Chicago, Ill. d: 8/6/27, Chicago, Ill. Deb: 8/21/02																							
1902	Chi-N	2	6	0	0	0	0	0	0	0		.000	.000	.000	-99	-1	0			1.000	-0	/O-2	-0.2
■ HOMER PEEL Peel, Homer Hefner b: 10/10/02, Port Sullivan, Tex d: 4/8/97, Shreveport, La. BR/TR, 5′9.5″, 170 lbs. Deb: 9/13/27																							
1927	StL-N	2	2	0	0	0	0	0	0	0	1	.000	.000	.000	-97	-1	0			.000	-1	/O-1	-0.1
1929	Phi-N	53	156	16	42	12	1	0	19	12	7	.269	.329	.359	66	-8	1			.990	-2	O-39/1-1	-1.2
1930	StL-N	26	73	9	12	2	0	0	10	3	4	.164	.197	.192	-5	-12	0			.968	-4	O-21	-1.6
1933	*NY-N	84	148	16	38	1	1	1	12	14	10	.257	.325	.297	80	-3	0			.962	-12	O-45	-1.8
1934	NY-N	21	41	7	8	0	0	1	3	1	2	.195	.214	.268	29	-4	0			.929	-3	O-10	-0.7
Total	5	186	420	48	100	15	2	2	44	30	24	.238	.294	.298	53	-29	1			.974	-22	O-116/1-1	-5.4
■ JACK PEERSON Peerson, Jack Chiles b: 8/28/10, Brunswick, Ga. d: 10/23/66, Ft.Walton Beach, Fla. BR/TR, 5′11″, 175 lbs. Deb: 9/7/35																							
1935	Phi-A	10	19	3	6	1	0	0	1	1	1	.316	.350	.368	87	-0	0	0	0	.952	0	/S-4	0.0
1936	Phi-A	8	34	7	11	1	1	0	5	0	3	.324	.324	.412	82	-1	0	1	-1	.942	4	/S-7,2-1	0.2
Total	2	18	53	10	17	2	1	0	6	1	4	.321	.333	.396	84	-1	0	1	-1	.945	4	/S-11,2-1	0.2
■ CHARLIE PEETE Peete, Charles "Mule" b: 2/22/29, Franklin, Va. d: 11/27/56, Caracas, Venez. BL/TR, 5′9.5″, 190 lbs. Deb: 7/17/56																							
1956	StL-N	23	52	3	10	2	2	0	6	6	10	.192	.288	.308	60	-3	0	2	-1	1.000	-1	O-21	-0.7
■ MONTE PEFFER Peffer, Monte (b: Montague Pfeiffer) b: 10/8/1891, New York, N.Y. d: 9/27/41, New York, N.Y. BR/TR, 5′4.5″, 147 lbs. Deb: 9/29/13																							
1913	Phi-A	1	3	0	0	0	0	0	0	0	1	.000	.250	.000	-26	-0	0			.800	-0	/S-1	-0.1
■ JULIO PEGUERO Peguero, Julio Cesar b: 9/7/68, San Isidro, D.R. BB/TR, 6′, 160 lbs. Deb: 4/8/92																							
1992	Phi-N	14	9	3	2	0	0	0	0	3	3	.222	.417	.222	86	0	0	0	0	1.000	-5	O-14	-0.5
■ STEVE PEGUES Pegues, Steven Antone b: 5/21/68, Pontotoc, Miss. BR/TR, 6′2″, 190 lbs. Deb: 7/6/94																							
1994	Cin-N	11	10	1	3	0	0	0	0	1	3	.300	.364	.300	76	-0	0	0	0	.833	-1	/O-4	-0.1
	Pit-N	7	26	1	10	2	0	0	2	1	2	.385	.407	.462	124	1	1	0	0	1.000	-1	/O-7	0.0
	Yr	18	36	2	13	2	0	0	2	2	5	.361	.395	.417	112	1	1	0	0	.929	-2	O-11	-0.1
1995	Pit-N	82	171	17	42	8	0	6	16	4	36	.246	.267	.398	71	-8	1	2	-1	.954	-5	O-53	-1.4
Total	2	100	207	19	55	10	0	6	18	6	41	.266	.290	.401	78	-7	2	2	-1	.950	-7	/O-64	-1.5
■ HEINIE PEITZ Peitz, Henry Clement b: 11/28/1870, St.Louis, Mo. d: 10/23/43, Cincinnati, Ohio BR/TR, 5′11″, 165 lbs. Deb: 10/15/1892 FC																							
1892	StL-N	1	3	0	0	0	0	0	0	0	0	.000	.000	.000	-99	-1	0			1.000	-0	/C-1	-0.1
1893	StL-N	96	362	53	92	12	9	1	45	54	20	.254	.353	.345	86	-7	12			.948	9	C-74,S-11,O-10,/1-5	0.6
1894	StL-N	99	338	52	89	19	9	3	49	43	21	.263	.348	.399	80	-12	14			.897	4	3-47,C-39,1-14,/P-1	-0.3
1895	StL-N	90	334	44	95	14	12	2	65	29	20	.284	.345	.416	97	-2	9			.937	1	C-71,1-11,3-10	0.5
1896	Cin-N	68	211	33	63	12	5	2	34	30	15	.299	.386	.431	108	2	7			.968	1	C-67	0.9
1897	Cin-N	77	266	35	78	11	7	1	44	18		.293	.340	.398	89	-5	3			**.979**	7	C-71/P-2	0.8
1898	Cin-N	105	330	49	90	15	5	1	43	35		.273	.348	.358	96	-2	9			.945	-3	*C-101	0.5
1899	Cin-N	93	290	45	79	13	2	1	43	45		.272	.374	.341	95	-0	11			.977	-1	C-91/P-1	0.5
1900	Cin-N	91	294	34	75	14	1	2	34	20		.255	.318	.330	81	-8	5			.958	6	C-80/1-8	0.5
1901	Cin-N	82	269	24	82	13	5	1	24	23		.305	.364	.401	130	11	3			.982	2	C-49,2-21/3-6,1-2	1.8
1902	Cin-N	112	387	54	122	22	5	1	60	24		.315	.369	.406	127	12	7			.919	-2	2-48,C-47/1-6,3-6	1.7

YEAR	TM/L	G	AB	R	H	2B	3B	HR	RBI	BB	SO	AVG	OBP	SLG	PRO+	BR/A	SB	CS	SBR	FA	FR	G/POS	TPR
1903	Cin-N	105	358	45	93	15	3	0	42	37		.260	.331	.318	77	-11	7			.970	-2	C-78,1-11/3-9,2-4	-0.5
1904	Cin-N	84	272	32	66	13	2	1	30	14		.243	.282	.316	78	-8	1			.975	4	C-64,1-18/3-1	0.3
1905	Pit-N	88	278	18	62	10	0	0	27	24		.223	.289	.259	62	-13	2			.965	-11	C-87/2-1	-1.5
1906	Pit-N	40	125	13	30	8	0	0	20	13		.240	.321	.304	91	-1	1			.979	0	C-38	0.3
1913	StL-N	3	4	1	1	0	1	0	0	0	0	.250	.250	.750	182	0	0			.625	-2	/C-2,O-1	-0.1
Total	16	1234	4121	532	1117	191	66	16	560	409	76	.271	.342	.361	92	-46	91			.963	14	C-960/3-79,12OSP	5.9

■ JOE PEITZ Peitz, Joseph b: 11/8/1869, St.Louis, Mo. d: 12/4/19, St.Louis, Mo. Deb: 7/5/1894 F

YEAR	TM/L	G	AB	R	H	2B	3B	HR	RBI	BB	SO	AVG	OBP	SLG	PRO+	BR/A	SB	CS	SBR	FA	FR	G/POS	TPR
1894	StL-N	7	26	10	11	2	3	0	3	6	1	.423	.531	.731	202	5	2			.818	1	/O-7	0.3

■ EDDIE PELLAGRINI Pellagrini, Edward Charles b: 3/13/18, Boston, Mass. BR/TR, 5'9", 165 lbs. Deb: 4/22/46

YEAR	TM/L	G	AB	R	H	2B	3B	HR	RBI	BB	SO	AVG	OBP	SLG	PRO+	BR/A	SB	CS	SBR	FA	FR	G/POS	TPR
1946	Bos-A	22	71	7	15	3	1	2	4	3	18	.211	.253	.366	68	-3	1	0	0	.891	-0	3-14/S-9	-0.3
1947	Bos-A	74	231	29	47	8	1	4	19	23	35	.203	.281	.299	57	-14	2	2	-1	.926	-6	3-42,S-26	-2.0
1948	StL-A	105	290	31	69	8	3	2	27	34	40	.238	.320	.307	65	-14	1	2	-1	.964	**24**	S-98	1.3
1949	StL-A	79	235	26	56	8	1	2	15	14	24	.238	.284	.306	54	-16	2	1	0	.961	7	S-76	-0.4
1951	Phi-N	86	197	31	46	4	5	5	30	23	25	.234	.326	.381	91	-3	5	1	1	.990	-17	2-53/S-8,3-6	-1.6
1952	Cin-N	46	100	15	17	2	0	1	3	8	18	.170	.231	.220	26	-10	1	0	0	.983	10	2-22/1-8,S-1,3-1	0.1
1953	Pit-N	78	174	16	44	3	2	4	19	14	20	.253	.309	.362	75	-7	1	1	-0	.972	-4	2-31,3-12/S-3	-0.9
1954	Pit-N	73	125	12	27	6	0	0	16	9	21	.216	.290	.264	46	-10	0	0	0	.968	2	3-31/2-7,S-1	-0.8
Total	8	563	1423	167	321	42	13	20	133	128	201	.226	.295	.316	62	-76	13	7	-0	.956	15	S-222,2-113,3/1	-4.6

■ LOUIS PELOUZE Pelouze, Louis Henri b: 9/10/1863, Fort Monroe, Va. d: 1/9/39, New York, N.Y. BL/TL, 6', 175 lbs. Deb: 7/24/1886

YEAR	TM/L	G	AB	R	H	2B	3B	HR	RBI	BB	SO	AVG	OBP	SLG	PRO+	BR/A	SB	CS	SBR	FA	FR	G/POS	TPR
1886	StL-N	1	3	0	0	0	0	0	0	0	2	.000	.000	.000	-99	-1	0			1.000	0	/O-1	0.0

■ DAN PELTIER Peltier, Daniel Edward b: 6/30/68, Clifton Park, N.Y. BL/TL, 6'1", 200 lbs. Deb: 6/26/92

YEAR	TM/L	G	AB	R	H	2B	3B	HR	RBI	BB	SO	AVG	OBP	SLG	PRO+	BR/A	SB	CS	SBR	FA	FR	G/POS	TPR
1992	Tex-A	12	24	1	4	0	0	0	2	0	3	.167	.167	.167	-7	-3	0	0	0	.857	-3	O-10	-0.7
1993	Tex-A	65	160	23	43	7	1	1	17	20	27	.269	.354	.344	92	-1	0	4	-2	.950	-7	O-55/1-5	-1.1
1996	SF-N	31	59	3	15	2	0	0	9	7	9	.254	.333	.288	68	-2	0	0	0	1.000	-1	1-13/O-1	-0.5
Total	3	108	243	27	62	9	1	1	28	27	39	.255	.332	.313	77	-7	0	4	-2	.943	-11	/O-66,1-18	-2.3

■ JOHN PELTZ Peltz, John b: 4/23/1861, New Orleans, La. d: 2/27/06, New Orleans, La. BR/TR, Deb: 5/1/1884

YEAR	TM/L	G	AB	R	H	2B	3B	HR	RBI	BB	SO	AVG	OBP	SLG	PRO+	BR/A	SB	CS	SBR	FA	FR	G/POS	TPR
1884	Ind-a	106	393	40	86	13	17	3		7		.219	.236	.361	95	-3				.818	4	*O-106	-0.1
1888	Bal-a	1	4	1	1	0	0	0	0	0		.250	.250	.250	62	-0	1			.500	-0	/O-1	-0.1
1890	Bro-a	98	384	55	87	9	6	1	33	32		.227	.289	.289	73	-13	10			.904	3	*O-98	-1.2
	Syr-a	5	17	2	3	1	1	0	2	3		.176	.300	.353	103	0	0			.857	0	/O-5	0.0
	Tol-a	20	73	8	18	2	2	0	13	3		.247	.286	.329	79	-2	7			.886	-2	O-20	-0.4
	Yr	123	474	65	108	12	9	1	48	38		.228	.289	.297	75	-16	17			.900	1	*O-123	-1.6
Total	3	230	871	106	195	25	26	4	48	45		.224	.266	.326	84	-18	18			.865	5	O-230	-1.8

■ BROCK PEMBERTON Pemberton, Brock b: 11/5/53, Tulsa, Okla. BB/TL, 6'3", 190 lbs. Deb: 9/10/74

YEAR	TM/L	G	AB	R	H	2B	3B	HR	RBI	BB	SO	AVG	OBP	SLG	PRO+	BR/A	SB	CS	SBR	FA	FR	G/POS	TPR
1974	NY-N	11	22	0	4	0	0	0	1	0	3	.182	.182	.182	2	-3	0	1	-1	1.000	1	/1-4	-0.3
1975	NY-N	2	2	0	0	0	0	0	0	0	1	.000	.000	.000	-99	-1	0	0	0	.000	0	H	-0.1
Total	2	13	24	0	4	0	0	0	1	0	4	.167	.167	.167	-7	-3	0	1	-1	1.000	1	/1-4	-0.4

■ RUDY PEMBERTON Pemberton, Rudy Hector (Perez) b: 12/17/69, San Pedro De Macoris, D.R. BR/TR, 6'1", 185 lbs. Deb: 4/26/95

YEAR	TM/L	G	AB	R	H	2B	3B	HR	RBI	BB	SO	AVG	OBP	SLG	PRO+	BR/A	SB	CS	SBR	FA	FR	G/POS	TPR
1995	Det-A	12	30	3	9	3	1	0	3	1	5	.300	.344	.467	109	0	0	0	0	1.000	-0	/O-8,D-3	0.0
1996	Bos-A	13	41	11	21	8	0	1	10	2	4	.512	.556	.780	228	8	3	1	0	1.000	-3	O-13	0.4
1997	Bos-A	27	63	8	15	2	0	2	10	4	13	.238	.314	.365	75	-2	0	0	0	.949	-1	O-23	-0.4
Total	3	52	134	22	45	13	1	3	23	7	22	.336	.395	.515	131	6	3	1	0	.968	-5	/O-44,D-3	0.0

■ BERT PENA Pena, Adalberto (Rivera) b: 7/11/59, Santurce, P.R. BR/TR, 5'11", 165 lbs. Deb: 9/14/81

YEAR	TM/L	G	AB	R	H	2B	3B	HR	RBI	BB	SO	AVG	OBP	SLG	PRO+	BR/A	SB	CS	SBR	FA	FR	G/POS	TPR
1981	Hou-N	4	2	0	1	0	0	0	0	0	0	.500	.500	.500	194	0	0	0	0	1.000	0	/S-3	0.0
1983	Hou-N	4	8	0	1	0	0	0	0	2	2	.125	.300	.125	23	-1	0	0	0	1.000	-1	/S-4	-0.2
1984	Hou-N	24	39	3	8	1	0	1	4	3	8	.205	.262	.308	64	-2	0	0	0	.956	6	S-21	0.5
1985	Hou-N	20	29	7	8	2	0	0	4	1	6	.276	.300	.345	82	-1	0	0	0	1.000	-1	/3-7,S-6,2-2	-0.1
1986	Hou-N	15	29	3	6	1	0	0	2	5	5	.207	.324	.241	60	-1	1	0	0	.907	1	S-10/3-2,2-1	0.1
1987	Hou-N	21	46	5	7	0	0	0	0	2	7	.152	.204	.152	-4	-7	0	0	0	.982	-1	S-19/3-1	-0.7
Total	6	88	153	18	31	4	0	1	10	13	28	.203	.269	.248	45	-12	1	0	0	.953	3	/S-63,3-10,2-3	-0.4

■ ANGEL PENA Pena, Angel Maria b: 2/16/75, San Pedro De Macoris, D.R. BR/TR, 5'10", 225 lbs. Deb: 9/8/98

YEAR	TM/L	G	AB	R	H	2B	3B	HR	RBI	BB	SO	AVG	OBP	SLG	PRO+	BR/A	SB	CS	SBR	FA	FR	G/POS	TPR
1998	LA-N	6	13	1	3	0	0	0	0	0	6	.231	.231	.231	22	-2	0	0	0	1.000	1	/C-4	0.0

■ TONY PENA Pena, Antonio Francisco (Padilla) b: 6/4/57, Monte Cristi, D.R. BR/TR, 6', 181 lbs. Deb: 9/1/80 F

YEAR	TM/L	G	AB	R	H	2B	3B	HR	RBI	BB	SO	AVG	OBP	SLG	PRO+	BR/A	SB	CS	SBR	FA	FR	G/POS	TPR
1980	Pit-N	8	21	1	9	1	1	0	1	0	4	.429	.429	.571	174	2	0	1	-1	.952	2	/C-6	0.3
1981	Pit-N	66	210	16	63	9	1	2	17	8	23	.300	.329	.381	98	-1	1	2	-1	.985	2	C-64	0.2
1982	Pit-N★	138	497	53	147	28	4	11	63	17	57	.296	.324	.435	107	3	2	5	-2	.982	-7	*C-137	0.0
1983	Pit-N	151	542	51	163	22	3	15	70	31	73	.301	.339	.435	110	6	6	7	-2	.992	-0	*C-149	1.1
1984	Pit-N★	147	546	77	156	27	2	15	78	36	79	.286	.334	.425	112	8	12	8	-1	.991	13	*C-146	2.8
1985	Pit-N★	147	546	53	136	27	2	10	59	29	67	.249	.287	.361	81	-15	12	8	-1	.988	9	*C-146/1-1	0.0
1986	Pit-N★	144	510	56	147	26	2	10	52	53	69	.288	.356	.406	107	6	9	10	-3	.981	5	*C-139/1-4	1.7
1987	*StL-N	116	384	40	82	13	4	5	44	36	54	.214	.283	.307	55	-25	6	1	1	.988	-1	*C-112/1-4,O-2	-1.7
1988	StL-N	149	505	55	133	23	1	10	51	33	60	.263	.310	.372	94	-4	6	2	1	**.994**	6	*C-142/1-3	1.3
1989	StL-N★	141	424	36	110	17	2	4	37	35	33	.259	.319	.337	85	-8	5	3	-0	**.997**	11	*C-134/O-1	1.0
1990	*Bos-A	143	491	62	129	19	1	7	56	43	71	.263	.323	.348	84	-10	8	6	-1	.995	11	*C-142/1-1	0.8
1991	Bos-A	141	464	45	107	23	2	5	48	37	53	.231	.293	.321	66	-21	8	3	1	.995	9	*C-140	-0.4
1992	Bos-A	133	410	39	99	21	1	1	38	24	61	.241	.285	.305	61	-21	3	2	-0	.993	11	*C-132	-0.3
1993	Bos-A	126	304	20	55	11	0	4	19	25	46	.181	.248	.257	34	-29	1	3	-2	.995	22	*C-125/D-1	-0.3
1994	Cle-A	40	112	18	33	8	1	2	10	9	11	.295	.347	.438	100	-0	0	1	-1	.996	5	C-40	0.6
1995	*Cle-A	91	263	25	69	15	0	5	28	14	44	.262	.302	.376	74	-10	1	0	0	.987	10	C-91	0.5
1996	*Cle-A	67	174	14	34	4	0	1	27	15	25	.195	.259	.236	26	-20	0	1	-1	.992	7	C-67	-0.9
1997	Chi-A	31	67	4	11	1	0	0	8	8	13	.164	.253	.179	16	-8	0	0	0	1.000	3	C-30/3-1	-0.4
	*Hou-N	9	19	2	4	3	0	0	2	2	3	.211	.286	.368	72	-1	0	0	0	1.000	4	/C-8	0.3
Total	18	1988	6489	667	1687	298	27	107	708	455	846	.260	.311	.364	84	-149	80	63	-14	.991	121	*C-1950/1-13,O3D	6.6

■ GERONIMO PENA Pena, Geronimo (Martinez) b: 3/29/67, Distrito Nacional, D.R. BB/TR, 6'1", 195 lbs. Deb: 9/5/90

YEAR	TM/L	G	AB	R	H	2B	3B	HR	RBI	BB	SO	AVG	OBP	SLG	PRO+	BR/A	SB	CS	SBR	FA	FR	G/POS	TPR
1990	StL-N	18	45	5	11	2	0	0	2	4	14	.244	.320	.289	69	-2	1	1	-0	.982	-1	2-11	-0.3
1991	StL-N	104	185	38	45	8	3	5	17	18	45	.243	.327	.400	103	1	15	5	2	.976	-3	2-83/O-4	0.0
1992	StL-N	62	203	31	62	12	1	7	31	24	37	.305	.392	.478	150	14	13	8	-1	.984	8	2-57	2.3
1993	StL-N	74	254	34	65	19	2	5	30	25	71	.256	.332	.406	98	-1	13	5	1	.966	-1	2-64	0.2
1994	StL-N	83	213	33	54	13	1	11	34	24	54	.254	.346	.479	114	4	9	1	2	.990	5	2-59/3-1	1.4
1995	StL-N	32	101	20	27	6	1	1	8	16	30	.267	.373	.376	98	0	3	2	-0	.976	-2	2-25	-0.1
1996	Cle-A	5	9	1	1	0	0	1	2	1	4	.111	.200	.444	57	-1	0	0	0	.000	0	/3-3,2-1	-0.1
Total	7	378	1010	162	265	60	8	30	124	112	255	.262	.349	.427	111	16	54	22	3	.978	7	2-300/3-4,O-4	3.4

■ ROBERTO PENA Pena, Roberto Cesar "Baby" (b: Roberto Cesar Zapata (Pena))
b: 4/17/37, Santo Domingo, D.R. d: 7/23/82, Santiago, D.R. BR/TR, 5'8", 175 lbs. Deb: 4/12/65

YEAR	TM/L	G	AB	R	H	2B	3B	HR	RBI	BB	SO	AVG	OBP	SLG	PRO+	BR/A	SB	CS	SBR	FA	FR	G/POS	TPR
1965	Chi-N	51	170	17	37	5	1	2	12	16	19	.218	.293	.294	64	-8	1	2	-1	.930	-10	S-50	-1.6
1966	Chi-N	6	17	0	3	2	0	0	1	0	4	.176	.176	.294	28	-2	0	0	0	.957	0	/S-5	-0.1
1968	Phi-N	138	500	56	130	13	2	1	38	34	63	.260	.310	.300	84	-9	3	5	-2	.954	6	*S-133	1.0
1969	SD-N	139	472	44	118	16	3	4	30	21	63	.250	.286	.322	73	-18	0	3	-2	.977	-23	S-65,2-33,3-27,1-12	-3.7
1970	Oak-A	19	58	4	15	1	0	0	3	3	4	.259	.295	.276	61	-3	1	1	-0	.961	-1	S-12/3-5	-0.4
	Mil-A	121	416	36	99	19	1	3	42	25	45	.238	.284	.310	63	-21	3	5	-2	.981	-16	S-99,2-15/1-7	-2.8

YEAR	TM/L	G	AB	R	H	2B	3B	HR	RBI	BB	SO	AVG	OBP	SLG	PRO+	BR/A	SB	CS	SBR	FA	FR	G/POS	TPR
	Yr	140	474	40	114	20	1	3	45	28	49	.241	.286	.306	63	-24	4	6	-2	**.979**	-17	*S-111,2-15/1-7,3-5	-3.2
1971	Mil-A	113	274	17	65	9	3	3	28	15	37	.237	.279	.325	71	-11	2	1	0	.996	-5	1-50,3-37,S-23,/2-1	-1.8
Total	6	587	1907	174	467	65	10	13	154	114	235	.245	.291	.310	72	-72	10	17	-7	.962	-49	S-387/1-69,3-69,2	-9.4

■ ELMER PENCE

Pence, Elmer Clair b: 8/17/1900, Valley Springs, Cal. d: 9/17/68, San Francisco, Cal. BR/TR, 6', 185 lbs. Deb: 8/23/22

YEAR	TM/L	G	AB	R	H	2B	3B	HR	RBI	BB	SO	AVG	OBP	SLG	PRO+	BR/A	SB	CS	SBR	FA	FR	G/POS	TPR
1922	Chi-A	1	0	0	0	0	0	0	0	0	0	—	—	—	—	0	0	0	0	1.000	-0	/O-1	0.0

■ JIM PENDLETON

Pendleton, James Edward b: 1/7/24, St.Charles, Mo. d: 3/20/96, Houston, Tex. BR/TR, 6', 185 lbs. Deb: 4/17/53

YEAR	TM/L	G	AB	R	H	2B	3B	HR	RBI	BB	SO	AVG	OBP	SLG	PRO+	BR/A	SB	CS	SBR	FA	FR	G/POS	TPR
1953	Mil-N	120	251	48	75	12	4	7	27	7	36	.299	.323	.462	108	2	6	5	-1	.961	-13	*O-105/S-7	-1.4
1954	Mil-N	71	173	20	38	3	1	1	16	4	21	.220	.237	.266	33	-17	2	1	0	.950	-4	O-50	-2.3
1955	Mil-N	8	10	0	0	0	0	0	0	0	2	.000	.000	.000	-99	-3	0	0	0	1.000	-0	/S-1,3-1,O-1	-0.3
1956	Mil-N	14	11	0	0	0	0	0	0	1	3	.000	.083	.000	-80	-3	0	0	0	1.000	-0	/S-3,3-2,1-1,2-1	-0.3
1957	Pit-N	46	59	9	18	1	1	0	9	9	14	.305	.406	.356	110	1	0	0	0	.917	-3	/O-9,3-2,S-1	-0.2
1958	Pit-N	3	3	0	1	0	0	0	0	0	0	.333	.333	.333	79	-0	0	0	0	.000	0	H	0.0
1959	Cin-N	65	113	13	29	2	0	3	9	8	18	.257	.311	.354	75	-4	3	0	1	.971	0	O-24,3-16/S-3	-0.4
1962	Hou-N	117	321	30	79	12	2	8	36	14	57	.246	.282	.371	79	-11	0	0	0	.963	-6	O-90/1-8,3-3,S-2	-2.1
Total	8	444	941	120	240	30	8	19	97	43	151	.255	.292	.365	76	-35	11	6	-0	.959	-26	O-279/3-24,S-17,12	-7.0

■ TERRY PENDLETON

Pendleton, Terry Lee b: 7/16/60, Los Angeles, Cal. BB/TR, 5'9", 180 lbs. Deb: 7/18/84

YEAR	TM/L	G	AB	R	H	2B	3B	HR	RBI	BB	SO	AVG	OBP	SLG	PRO+	BR/A	SB	CS	SBR	FA	FR	G/POS	TPR
1984	StL-N	67	262	37	85	16	3	1	33	16	32	.324	.363	.420	123	7	20	5	3	.943	9	3-66	1.9
1985	*StL-N	149	559	56	134	16	3	5	69	37	75	.240	.287	.306	66	-25	17	12	-2	.965	23	*3-149	-0.7
1986	StL-N	159	578	56	138	26	5	1	59	34	59	.239	.282	.306	63	-30	24	6	4	.962	24	*3-156/O-1	-0.5
1987	*StL-N	159	583	82	167	29	4	12	96	70	74	.286	.365	.412	103	4	19	12	-2	.949	16	*3-158	1.6
1988	StL-N	110	391	44	99	20	2	6	53	21	51	.253	.295	.361	86	-7	3	3	-1	.963	11	*3-101	0.2
1989	StL-N	162	613	83	162	28	5	13	74	44	81	.264	.314	.390	97	-3	9	5	-0	**.971**	**30**	*3-161	2.9
1990	StL-N	121	447	46	103	20	2	6	58	30	58	.230	.280	.324	66	-21	7	5	-1	.947	7	*3-117	-1.5
1991	*Atl-N	153	586	94	**187**	34	8	22	86	43	70	**.319**	.367	.517	138	28	10	2	2	.950	**28**	*3-148	5.9
1992	*Atl-N★	160	640	98	**199**	39	1	21	105	37	67	.311	.349	.473	123	18	5	2	0	.960	13	*3-158	3.3
1993	*Atl-N	161	633	81	172	33	1	17	84	36	97	.272	.314	.408	91	-10	5	1	1	.959	12	*3-161	0.4
1994	Atl-N	77	309	25	78	18	3	7	30	12	57	.252	.280	.398	73	-13	2	0	1	.950	6	3-77	-0.6
1995	Fla-N	133	513	70	149	32	1	14	78	38	84	.290	.342	.439	104	2	1	2	-1	.952	0	*3-129	0.2
1996	Fla-N	111	406	30	102	20	1	7	58	26	75	.251	.301	.357	75	-15	0	2	-1	.961	7	*3-108	-0.9
	*Atl-N	42	162	21	33	6	0	4	17	15	36	.204	.271	.315	51	-12	2	1	0	.939	1	3-41	-1.0
	Yr	153	568	51	135	26	1	11	75	41	111	.238	.292	.345	68	-27	2	3	-1	.955	9	*3-149	-1.9
1997	Cin-N	50	113	11	28	9	0	1	17	12	14	.248	.320	.354	75	-4	2	1	0	.942	-6	3-32	-1.0
1998	KC-A	79	237	17	61	10	0	3	29	15	49	.257	.302	.338	63	-13	1	0	0	.957	-1	D-40,3-23	-1.5
Total	15	1893	7032	851	1897	356	39	140	946	486	979	.270	.318	.391	91	-94	127	59	3	.957	181	*3-1785/D-40,O-1	8.7

■ SHANNON PENN

Penn, Shannon Dion b: 9/11/69, Cincinnati, Ohio BB/TR, 5'10", 160 lbs. Deb: 4/28/95

YEAR	TM/L	G	AB	R	H	2B	3B	HR	RBI	BB	SO	AVG	OBP	SLG	PRO+	BR/A	SB	CS	SBR	FA	FR	G/POS	TPR
1995	Det-A	3	9	0	3	0	0	0	0	1	2	.333	.400	.333	94	-0	0	0	0	.864	2	/2-3	0.2
1996	Det-A	6	14	0	1	0	0	0	1	0	3	.071	.071	.071	-64	-3	0	0	0	.000	-0	/O-1,D-4	-0.4
Total	2	9	23	0	4	0	0	0	1	1	5	.174	.208	.174	-1	-3	0	0	0	.864	1	/D-4,2-3,O-1	-0.2

■ WILL PENNYFEATHER

Pennyfeather, William Nathaniel b: 5/25/68, Perth Amboy, N.J. BR/TR, 6'2", 195 lbs. Deb: 6/27/92

YEAR	TM/L	G	AB	R	H	2B	3B	HR	RBI	BB	SO	AVG	OBP	SLG	PRO+	BR/A	SB	CS	SBR	FA	FR	G/POS	TPR
1992	Pit-N	15	9	2	2	0	0	0	0	0	0	.222	.222	.222	26	-1	0	0	0	1.000	-4	O-10	-0.5
1993	Pit-N	21	34	4	7	1	0	0	2	0	6	.206	.206	.235	18	-4	0	1	-1	1.000	-5	O-17	-1.0
1994	Pit-N	4	3	0	0	0	0	0	0	0	0	.000	.000	.000	-99	-1	0	0	0	.000	-0	/O-1	-0.1
Total	3	40	46	6	9	1	0	0	2	0	6	.196	.196	.217	11	-6	0	1	-1	1.000	-9	/O-28	-1.6

■ JIMMY PEOPLES

Peoples, James Elsworth b: 10/8/1863, Big Beaver, Mich. d: 8/29/20, Detroit, Mich. TR , 5'8", 200 lbs. Deb: 5/29/1884 U

YEAR	TM/L	G	AB	R	H	2B	3B	HR	RBI	BB	SO	AVG	OBP	SLG	PRO+	BR/A	SB	CS	SBR	FA	FR	G/POS	TPR
1884	Cin-a	69	267	28	45	2	2	1	16	6		.169	.187	.202	26	-22				.829	0	S-47,C-14,O-10,/31	-1.9
1885	Cin-a	7	22	1	4	0	0	0	1	1		.182	.217	.182	27	-2				.826	-1	/C-5,P-2,O-1	-0.2
	Bro-a	41	151	21	30	4	1	1	15	5		.199	.229	.258	53	-8				.895	-2	C-37/S-2,1-1,3-1,O	-0.6
	Yr	48	173	22	34	4	1	1	16	6		.197	.228	.249	50	-10				.889	-4	C-42/P-2,O-2,S13	-0.8
1886	Bro-a	93	340	43	74	7	3	3	38	20		.218	.261	.282	70	-12	20			.879	19	C-76,S-14/O-8,3-1	1.2
1887	Bro-a	73	268	36	68	14	2	1	38	16		.254	.306	.332	77	-9	22			.853	-6	C-57/O-8,S-4,1-4,2	-0.8
1888	Bro-a	32	103	15	20	5	3	0	17	8		.194	.259	.301	79	-2	10			.904	10	C-25/S-5,O-2	0.9
1889	Col-a	29	100	13	23	6	2	1	16	6	8	.230	.274	.360	84	-3	3			.922	-4	C-22/O-5,2-2,S-1	-0.4
Total	6	344	1251	157	264	38	13	7	141	62	8	.211	.252	.279	62	-58	55			.886	15	C-236/S-73,O123P	-1.8

■ JOE PEPITONE

Pepitone, Joseph Anthony "Pepi" b: 10/9/40, Brooklyn, N.Y. BL/TL, 6'2", 200 lbs. Deb: 4/10/62 C

YEAR	TM/L	G	AB	R	H	2B	3B	HR	RBI	BB	SO	AVG	OBP	SLG	PRO+	BR/A	SB	CS	SBR	FA	FR	G/POS	TPR
1962	NY-A	63	138	14	33	3	2	7	17	3	21	.239	.255	.442	86	-4	1	1	-0	1.000	-9	O-32,1-16	-1.5
1963	*NY-A★	157	580	79	157	16	3	27	89	23	63	.271	.307	.448	109	5	3	5	-2	.995	4	*1-143,O-16	0.0
1964	*NY-A★	160	613	71	154	12	3	28	100	24	63	.251	.283	.418	90	-10	2	1	0	.988	-6	*1-155,O-30	-2.4
1965	NY-A★	143	531	51	131	18	3	18	62	43	59	.247	.306	.394	98	-2	4	2	0	**.997**	-3	*1-115,O-41	-1.4
1966	NY-A	152	585	85	149	21	4	31	83	29	58	.255	.292	.463	118	10	4	3	-1	**.995**	1	*1-119,O-55	0.1
1967	NY-A	133	501	45	126	18	3	13	64	34	62	.251	.303	.377	104	1	1	3	-2	.976	6	*O-123/1-6	-0.2
1968	NY-A	108	380	41	93	9	3	15	56	37	45	.245	.313	.403	119	8	8	2	1	.980	-6	O-92,1-12	-0.3
1969	NY-A	135	513	49	124	16	3	27	70	30	42	.242	.285	.442	105	-1	8	6	-1	**.995**	-6	*1-132	-1.9
1970	Hou-N	75	279	44	70	9	5	14	35	18	28	.251	.299	.470	107	1	5	2	0	.995	-1	1-50,O-28	-0.5
	Chi-N	56	213	38	57	9	2	12	44	15	15	.268	.316	.498	102	-1	0	2	-1	.992	2	O-56,1-13	-0.3
	Yr	131	492	82	127	18	7	26	79	33	43	.258	.306	.482	105	1	5	4	-1	.989	1	O-84,1-63	-0.8
1971	Chi-N	115	427	50	131	19	4	16	61	24	41	.307	.349	.482	117	8	1	2	-1	.990	-3	1-95,O-23	-0.6
1972	Chi-N	66	214	23	56	5	0	8	21	13	22	.262	.313	.397	91	-3	1	2	-1	.997	-0	1-66	-0.9
1973	Chi-N	31	112	16	30	3	0	3	18	8	6	.268	.322	.375	86	-2	3	1	0	.985	0	1-28	-0.4
	Atl-N	3	11	0	4	0	0	0	1	1	1	.364	.417	.364	110	0	0	0	0	.963	-1	/1-3	-0.1
	Yr	34	123	16	34	3	0	3	19	9	7	.276	.331	.374	88	-2	3	1	0	.983	-1	1-31	-0.5
Total	12	1397	5097	606	1315	158	35	219	721	302	526	.258	.303	.432	105	12	41	32	-7	.993	-21	1-953,O-496	-10.4

■ HENRY PEPLOSKI

Peploski, Henry Stephen "Pep" b: 9/15/05, Garlin, Poland d: 1/28/82, Dover, N.J. BL/TR, 5'9", 155 lbs. Deb: 9/19/29 F

YEAR	TM/L	G	AB	R	H	2B	3B	HR	RBI	BB	SO	AVG	OBP	SLG	PRO+	BR/A	SB	CS	SBR	FA	FR	G/POS	TPR
1929	Bos-N	6	10	1	2	0	0	0	1	1	3	.200	.273	.200	20	-1	0			1.000	-0	/3-2	-0.1

■ PEPPER PEPLOSKI

Peploski, Joseph Aloysius b: 9/12/1891, Brooklyn, N.Y. d: 7/13/72, New York, N.Y. BR/TR, 5'8", 155 lbs. Deb: 6/24/13 F

YEAR	TM/L	G	AB	R	H	2B	3B	HR	RBI	BB	SO	AVG	OBP	SLG	PRO+	BR/A	SB	CS	SBR	FA	FR	G/POS	TPR
1913	Det-A	2	4	1	2	0	0	0	0	0	0	.500	.500	.500	196	0	0			1.000	-1	/3-2	0.0

■ DON PEPPER

Pepper, Donald Hoyte b: 10/8/43, Saratoga Sprgs., N.Y BL/TR, 6'4.5", 215 lbs. Deb: 9/10/66

YEAR	TM/L	G	AB	R	H	2B	3B	HR	RBI	BB	SO	AVG	OBP	SLG	PRO+	BR/A	SB	CS	SBR	FA	FR	G/POS	TPR
1966	Det-A	4	3	0	0	0	0	0	0	0	1	.000	.000	.000	-98	-1	0	0	0	1.000	-0	/1-1	-0.1

■ RAY PEPPER

Pepper, Raymond Watson b: 8/5/05, Decatur, Ala. d: 3/24/96, Belle Mina, Ala. BR/TR, 6'2", 195 lbs. Deb: 4/15/32

YEAR	TM/L	G	AB	R	H	2B	3B	HR	RBI	BB	SO	AVG	OBP	SLG	PRO+	BR/A	SB	CS	SBR	FA	FR	G/POS	TPR
1932	StL-N	21	57	3	14	2	1	0	7	5	13	.246	.306	.316	66	-3	1			.971	-0	O-17	-0.4
1933	StL-N	3	9	2	2	0	0	1	2	0	1	.222	.222	.556	110	0	0			1.000	-0	/O-2	0.0
1934	StL-A	148	564	71	168	24	6	7	101	29	67	.298	.333	.399	81	-17	1	4	-2	.963	5	*O-136	-1.9
1935	StL-A	92	261	20	66	15	3	4	37	20	32	.253	.306	.379	73	-11	0	2	-1	.982	-3	O-57	-1.6
1936	StL-A	75	124	13	35	5	0	2	23	5	23	.282	.310	.371	66	-7	0	2	-1	.941	-2	O-18	-1.0
Total	5	339	1015	109	285	46	10	14	170	59	136	.281	.321	.387	77	-38	2	8		.967	-1	O-230	-4.9

■ JACK PERCONTE

Perconte, John Patrick b: 8/31/54, Joliet, Ill. BL/TR, 5'10", 160 lbs. Deb: 9/13/80

YEAR	TM/L	G	AB	R	H	2B	3B	HR	RBI	BB	SO	AVG	OBP	SLG	PRO+	BR/A	SB	CS	SBR	FA	FR	G/POS	TPR
1980	LA-N	14	17	2	4	0	0	0	2	2	1	.235	.316	.235	57	-1	3	0	1	1.000	3	/2-9	0.4
1981	LA-N	8	9	2	2	0	1	0	1	2	2	.222	.364	.444	133	0	1	1	-0	1.000	5	/2-2	0.5
1982	Cle-A	93	219	27	52	4	4	0	15	22	25	.237	.307	.292	66	-10	9	3	1	.976	8	2-82/D-2	0.2
1983	Cle-A	14	26	1	7	1	0	0	0	5	2	.269	.387	.308	91	-0	3	1	0	.950	8	2-13	0.8
1984	Sea-A	155	612	93	180	24	4	0	31	57	47	.294	.359	.346	97	-0	29	6	5	.981	0	*2-150	1.1

YEAR	TM/L	G	AB	R	H	2B	3B	HR	RBI	BB	SO	AVG	OBP	SLG	PRO+	BR/A	SB	CS	SBR	FA	FR	G/POS	TPR
1985	Sea-A	125	485	60	128	17	7	2	23	50	36	.264	.336	.340	85	-9	31	2	8	.986	0	*2-125	0.4
1986	Chi-A	24	73	6	16	1	0	0	4	11	10	.219	.321	.233	52	-4	2	0	1	.990	-7	2-24	-1.0
Total	7	433	1441	191	389	47	16	2	76	149	123	.270	.342	.329	86	-23	78	13	16	.982	18	2-405/D-2	2.4

■ TONY PEREZ

Perez, Atanasio (Rigal) b: 5/14/42, Ciego De Avila, Cuba BR/TR, 6'2", 205 lbs. Deb: 7/26/64 FMC

YEAR	TM/L	G	AB	R	H	2B	3B	HR	RBI	BB	SO	AVG	OBP	SLG	PRO+	BR/A	SB	CS	SBR	FA	FR	G/POS	TPR
1964	Cin-N	12	25	1	2	1	0	0	1	3	9	.080	.179	.120	-14	-4	0	0	0	.981	-1	/1-6	-0.6
1965	Cin-N	104	281	40	73	14	4	12	47	21	67	.260	.316	.466	110	3	0	2	-1	.989	-2	1-93	-0.5
1966	Cin-N	99	257	25	68	10	4	4	39	14	44	.265	.308	.381	83	-6	1	0	0	.989	-5	1-75	-1.6
1967	Cin-N★	156	600	78	174	28	7	26	102	33	102	.290	.331	.490	119	13	0	3	-2	.963	-22	*3-139,1-18/2-1	-1.5
1968	Cin-N★	160	625	93	176	25	7	18	92	51	92	.282	.342	.430	123	17	3	2	-0	.952	5	*3-160	2.6
1969	Cin-N★	160	629	103	185	31	2	37	122	63	131	.294	.360	.526	138	30	4	2	0	.937	1	*3-160	3.3
1970	*Cin-N★	158	587	107	186	28	6	40	129	83	134	.317	.405	.589	162	52	8	3	1	.923	-7	*3-153/1-8	4.3
1971	Cin-N	158	609	72	164	22	3	25	91	51	120	.269	.327	.438	117	12	4	1	1	.959	7	*3-148,1-44	1.8
1972	*Cin-N	136	515	64	146	33	7	21	90	55	121	.283	.353	.497	148	30	4	2	0	.993	-5	*1-136	1.4
1973	*Cin-N	151	564	73	177	33	3	27	101	74	117	.314	.396	.527	162	47	3	1	0	.991	-4	*1-151	3.3
1974	Cin-N★	158	596	81	158	28	2	28	101	61	112	.265	.335	.460	123	16	1	3	-2	**.996**	-6	*1-157	-0.1
1975	*Cin-N★	137	511	74	144	28	3	20	109	54	101	.282	.354	.466	124	15	1	2	-1	.993	-5	*1-132	0.1
1976	*Cin-N★	139	527	77	137	32	6	19	91	50	88	.260	.330	.452	117	10	10	5	0	.996	-4	*1-136	-0.2
1977	Mon-N	154	559	71	158	32	6	19	91	63	111	.283	.357	.463	122	17	4	3	-1	.992	9	*1-148	1.6
1978	Mon-N	148	544	63	158	38	3	14	78	38	104	.290	.339	.449	120	13	2	0	1	.991	-1	*1-145	0.4
1979	Mon-N	132	489	58	132	29	4	13	73	38	82	.270	.326	.425	104	2	2	1	0	.991	-6	*1-129	-1.3
1980	Bos-A	151	585	73	161	31	3	25	105	41	93	.275	.324	.467	108	5	1	0	0	.993	-1	*1-137,D-13	-0.4
1981	Bos-A	84	306	35	77	11	3	9	39	27	66	.252	.312	.395	97	-2	0	0	0	.993	0	1-56,D-23	-0.6
1982	Bos-A	69	196	18	51	14	2	6	31	19	48	.260	.326	.444	103	1	0	1	-1	.857	0	D-46/1-2	-0.2
1983	*Phi-N	91	253	18	61	11	2	6	43	28	57	.241	.319	.372	92	-3	1	0	0	.998	1	1-69	-0.5
1984	Cin-N	71	137	9	33	6	1	2	15	11	21	.241	.297	.343	76	-4	0	0	0	.990	-2	1-31	-0.8
1985	Cin-N	72	183	25	60	8	0	6	33	22	22	.328	.400	.470	136	9	0	2	-1	.995	-2	1-50	0.4
1986	Cin-N	77	200	14	51	12	1	2	29	25	25	.255	.338	.355	87	-3	0	0	0	.984	-3	1-55	-1.0
Total	23	2777	9778	1272	2732	505	79	379	1652	925	1867	.279	.344	.463	122	270	49	33	-5	.992	-54	*1-1778,3-760/D2	9.9

■ DANNY PEREZ

Perez, Daniel b: 2/26/71, ElPaso, Tex. BR/TR, 5'10", 188 lbs. Deb: 6/30/96

YEAR	TM/L	G	AB	R	H	2B	3B	HR	RBI	BB	SO	AVG	OBP	SLG	PRO+	BR/A	SB	CS	SBR	FA	FR	G/POS	TPR
1996	Mil-A	4	4	0	0	0	0	0	0	0	0	.000	.000	.000	-96	-1	0	0	0	1.000	-0	/O-3	-0.1

■ EDDIE PEREZ

Perez, Eduardo b: 5/4/68, Ciudad Ojeda, Venez. BR/TR, 6'1", 175 lbs. Deb: 9/10/95

YEAR	TM/L	G	AB	R	H	2B	3B	HR	RBI	BB	SO	AVG	OBP	SLG	PRO+	BR/A	SB	CS	SBR	FA	FR	G/POS	TPR
1995	Atl-N	7	13	1	4	1	0	1	4	0	2	.308	.308	.615	132	0	0	0	0	1.000	3	/C-5,1-1	0.3
1996	*Atl-N	68	156	19	40	9	1	4	17	8	19	.256	.297	.404	78	-5	0	0	0	.993	-0	C-54/1-7	-0.4
1997	*Atl-N	73	191	20	41	5	0	6	18	10	35	.215	.261	.335	54	-13	0	1	-1	.988	10	C-64/1-6	-0.1
1998	*Atl-N	61	149	18	50	12	0	6	32	15	28	.336	.404	.537	138	9	1	1	-0	.997	9	C-45/1-8,D-1	1.9
Total	4	209	509	58	135	27	1	17	71	33	84	.265	.316	.422	89	-9	1	2	-1	.992	21	C-168/1-22,D-1	1.7

■ EDUARDO PEREZ

Perez, Eduardo Atanasio b: 9/11/69, Cincinnati, Ohio BR/TR, 6'4", 215 lbs. Deb: 7/27/93 F

YEAR	TM/L	G	AB	R	H	2B	3B	HR	RBI	BB	SO	AVG	OBP	SLG	PRO+	BR/A	SB	CS	SBR	FA	FR	G/POS	TPR
1993	Cal-A	52	180	16	45	6	2	4	30	9	39	.250	.293	.372	75	-7	5	4	-1	.962	10	3-45/D-3	0.3
1994	Cal-A	38	129	10	27	7	0	5	16	12	29	.209	.277	.380	66	-7	3	0	1	.997	-3	1-38	-1.1
1995	Cal-A	29	71	9	12	4	1	1	7	12	9	.169	.306	.296	58	-4	0	2	-1	.883	1	3-23/D-1	-0.4
1996	Cin-N	18	36	8	8	0	0	3	5	5	9	.222	.317	.472	104	0	0	0	0	1.000	2	/1-8,3-3	0.1
1997	Cin-N	106	297	44	75	18	0	16	52	29	76	.253	.323	.475	104	1	5	1	1	.996	-5	1-67,O-12/3-8,D-1	-0.9
1998	Cin-N	84	172	20	41	4	0	4	30	21	45	.238	.328	.331	71	-7	0	1	-1	.985	7	1-51/3-1,O-1	-0.4
Total	6	327	885	107	208	39	3	33	140	88	207	.235	.310	.398	83	-24	13	8	-1	.994	12	1-164/3-80,O-13,D-5	-2.4

■ MARTY PEREZ

Perez, Martin Roman b: 2/28/47, Visalia, Cal. BR/TR, 5'11", 160 lbs. Deb: 9/9/69

YEAR	TM/L	G	AB	R	H	2B	3B	HR	RBI	BB	SO	AVG	OBP	SLG	PRO+	BR/A	SB	CS	SBR	FA	FR	G/POS	TPR
1969	Cal-A	13	13	3	3	0	0	0	0	2	1	.231	.333	.231	63	-1	0	0	0	1.000	6	/S-7,2-2,3-2	0.6
1970	Cal-A	3	3	0	0	0	0	0	1	0	0	.000	.000	.000	-99	-1	0	0	0	.833	1	/S-2	0.0
1971	Atl-N	130	410	28	93	15	3	4	32	25	44	.227	.273	.307	60	-22	1	2	-1	.955	-14	*S-126/2-1	-2.3
1972	Atl-N	141	479	33	109	13	1	1	28	30	55	.228	.277	.265	50	-31	0	3	-2	.957	-34	*S-141	-5.2
1973	Atl-N	141	501	66	125	15	5	8	57	49	66	.250	.319	.347	79	-14	2	3	-1	.962	-9	*S-139	-0.8
1974	Atl-N	127	447	51	116	20	5	2	34	35	51	.260	.315	.340	80	-12	2	0	1	.985	-9	*2-102,S-14/3-6	-1.5
1975	Atl-N	120	461	50	127	14	2	2	34	37	44	.275	.329	.328	80	-12	2	2	-1	.985	-8	*2-116/S-7	-1.5
1976	Atl-N	31	96	12	24	4	0	1	6	8	9	.250	.308	.323	74	-3	0	0	0	.976	-2	2-18,S-17/3-2	-0.3
	SF-N	93	332	37	86	13	1	2	26	30	28	.259	.320	.322	80	-8	3	4	-2	.979	7	2-89/S-5	0.3
	Yr	124	428	49	110	17	1	3	32	38	37	.257	.318	.322	79	-11	3	4	-2	.978	5	*2-107,S-22/3-2	0.0
1977	NY-A	1	4	0	2	0	0	0	0	0	1	.500	.500	.500	175	0	0	0	0	1.000	1	/3-1	0.1
	Oak-A	115	373	32	86	14	5	2	23	29	65	.231	.291	.311	65	-18	1	3	-2	.974	0	*2-105,3-12/S-4	-1.3
	Yr	116	377	32	88	14	5	2	23	29	66	.233	.293	.313	66	-17	1	3	-2	.974	1	*2-105,3-13/S-4	-1.2
1978	Oak-A	16	12	1	0	0	0	0	0	0	5	.000	.000	.000	-99	-3	0	0	0	1.000	2	3-11/S-3,2-1	-0.1
Total	10	931	3131	313	771	108	22	22	241	245	369	.246	.303	.316	70	-124	11	17	-7	.958	-59	S-465,2-434/3-34	-12.0

■ NEIFI PEREZ

Perez, Neifi Neftali (Diaz) b: 2/2/75, Villa Mella, D.R. BB/TR, 6', 175 lbs. Deb: 8/31/96

YEAR	TM/L	G	AB	R	H	2B	3B	HR	RBI	BB	SO	AVG	OBP	SLG	PRO+	BR/A	SB	CS	SBR	FA	FR	G/POS	TPR
1996	Col-N	17	45	4	7	2	0	0	3	0	8	.156	.156	.200	-6	-7	2	2	-1	.972	-0	S-14/2-4	-0.7
1997	Col-N	83	313	46	91	13	10	5	31	21	43	.291	.337	.444	83	-9	4	3	-1	.975	32	S-45,2-41/3-2	2.7
1998	Col-N	162	647	80	177	25	9	9	59	38	70	.274	.315	.382	67	-33	5	6	-2	.975	27	*S-162/C-1	0.8
Total	3	262	1005	130	275	40	19	14	93	59	121	.274	.315	.393	69	-49	11	11	-3	.975	58	S-221/2-45,3-2,C-1	2.8

■ ROBERT PEREZ

Perez, Robert Alexander (Jimenez) b: 6/4/69, Bolivar, Venez. BR/TR, 6'3", 205 lbs. Deb: 7/20/94

YEAR	TM/L	G	AB	R	H	2B	3B	HR	RBI	BB	SO	AVG	OBP	SLG	PRO+	BR/A	SB	CS	SBR	FA	FR	G/POS	TPR
1994	Tor-A	4	8	0	1	0	0	0	0	0	1	.125	.125	.125	-35	-2	0	0	0	1.000	-0	/O-4	-0.2
1995	Tor-A	17	48	2	9	2	0	1	3	0	5	.188	.188	.292	22	-6	0	0	0	1.000	-0	O-15	-0.6
1996	Tor-A	86	202	30	66	10	0	2	21	8	17	.327	.355	.406	92	-2	3	0	1	.983	-9	O-79/D-2	-1.1
1997	Tor-A	37	78	4	15	4	1	2	6	0	16	.192	.192	.346	36	-7	0	0	0	1.000	-3	O-25/D-7	-1.0
1998	Sea-A	17	35	3	6	1	0	2	6	0	5	.171	.171	.371	36	-3	0	0	0	1.000	-2	O-17	-0.5
	Mon-N	52	106	9	25	1	0	1	8	2	23	.236	.257	.274	39	-10	0	0	0	.852	-4	O-29	-1.4
Total	5	213	477	48	122	18	1	8	44	10	67	.256	.274	.348	59	-30	3	0	1	.975	-18	O-169/D-9	-4.8

■ TOMAS PEREZ

Perez, Tomas Orlando b: 12/29/73, Barquisimeto, Venez BB/TR, 5'11", 165 lbs. Deb: 5/3/95

YEAR	TM/L	G	AB	R	H	2B	3B	HR	RBI	BB	SO	AVG	OBP	SLG	PRO+	BR/A	SB	CS	SBR	FA	FR	G/POS	TPR
1995	Tor-A	41	98	12	24	3	1	1	8	7	18	.245	.295	.327	62	-6	0	1	-1	.954	1	S-31/2-7,3-1	-0.3
1996	Tor-A	91	295	24	74	13	4	1	19	25	29	.251	.312	.332	63	-16	1	2	-1	.970	12	2-75,3-11/S-5	-0.1
1997	Tor-A	40	123	9	24	3	2	0	9	11	28	.195	.267	.252	36	-11	1	1	-0	.993	9	S-32/2-8	0.0
1998	Tor-A	6	9	1	1	0	0	0	0	1	3	.111	.200	.111	-16	-2	0	0	0	1.000	-0	/S-4,2-1	-0.2
Total	4	178	525	46	123	19	7	2	36	44	78	.234	.296	.309	55	-35	2	4	-2	.971	21	/2-91,S-72,3-12	-0.6

■ TONY PEREZCHICA

Perezchica, Antonio Llamas (Gonzales) b: 4/20/66, Mexicali, Mex. BR/TR, 5'11", 165 lbs. Deb: 9/7/88

YEAR	TM/L	G	AB	R	H	2B	3B	HR	RBI	BB	SO	AVG	OBP	SLG	PRO+	BR/A	SB	CS	SBR	FA	FR	G/POS	TPR
1988	SF-N	7	8	1	1	0	0	0	1	2	1	.125	.300	.125	27	-1	0	0	0	1.000	-1	/2-6	-0.2
1990	SF-N	4	3	1	1	0	0	0	0	1	2	.333	.500	.333	139	0	0	0	0	1.000	-2	/2-2,S-2	-0.1
1991	SF-N	23	48	2	11	4	1	0	3	2	12	.229	.260	.354	73	-2	0	1	-1	.947	-3	S-13/2-6	-0.5
	Cle-A	17	22	4	8	2	0	0	0	3	5	.364	.440	.455	147	2	0	0	0	1.000	-1	/S-6,3-3,2-2,D-1	0.1
1992	Cle-A	18	20	2	2	1	0	0	1	2	6	.100	.182	.150	-6	-3	0	0	0	.875	-1	/3-9,2-4,S-4,D-1	-0.4
Total	4	69	101	10	23	7	1	0	5	10	26	.228	.297	.317	74	-4	0	1	-1	.944	-8	/S-25,2-20,3-12,D-2	-1.1

■ BRODERICK PERKINS

Perkins, Broderick Phillip b: 11/23/54, Pittsburg, Cal. BL/TL, 5'10", 180 lbs. Deb: 7/7/78

YEAR	TM/L	G	AB	R	H	2B	3B	HR	RBI	BB	SO	AVG	OBP	SLG	PRO+	BR/A	SB	CS	SBR	FA	FR	G/POS	TPR
1978	SD-N	62	217	14	52	14	1	2	33	5	29	.240	.257	.341	71	-10	4	0	1	.993	3	1-59	-0.9
1979	SD-N	57	87	8	23	0	0	0	8	8	12	.264	.326	.264	67	-4	0	0	0	.982	-1	1-28	-0.5
1980	SD-N	43	100	18	37	9	0	2	14	11	10	.370	.432	.520	175	10	2	1	0	.988	-4	1-20,O-10	0.5
1981	SD-N	92	254	27	71	18	3	2	40	14	16	.280	.317	.398	110	2	0	4	-2	.997	-3	1-80/O-3	-0.7
1982	SD-N	125	347	32	94	10	4	2	34	26	20	.271	.327	.340	92	-4	2	1	0	.994	-1	1-98,O-11	-1.0

YEAR	TM/L	G	AB	R	H	2B	3B	HR	RBI	BB	SO	AVG	OBP	SLG	PRO+	BR/A	SB	CS	SBR	FA	FR	G/POS	TPR
1983	Cle-A	79	184	23	50	10	0	0	24	9	19	.272	.306	.326	71	-7	1	5	-3	.991	0	1-19,O-17,D-16	-1.1
1984	Cle-A	58	66	5	13	1	0	0	4	7	10	.197	.284	.212	39	-5	0	0	0	1.000	-0	D-10/1-2	-0.6
Total	7	516	1255	127	340	62	8	8	157	80	116	.271	.317	.352	90	-18	9	11	-4	.993	-4	1-306/O-41,D-26	-4.3

■ **CY PERKINS** Perkins, Ralph Foster b: 2/27/1896, Gloucester, Mass. d: 10/2/63, Philadelphia, Pa. BR/TR, 5'10.5", 158 lbs. Deb: 9/25/15 MC

1915	Phi-A	7	20	2	4	1	0	0	0	3	3	.200	.304	.250	68	-1	0			.920	1	/C-6	0.0
1917	Phi-A	6	18	1	3	0	0	0	2	2	1	.167	.250	.167	28	-1	0			.978	4	/C-6	0.3
1918	Phi-A	68	218	9	41	4	1	1	14	8	15	.188	.217	.229	34	-18	1			.990	12	C-60	-0.1
1919	Phi-A	101	305	22	77	12	7	2	29	27	22	.252	.313	.357	87	-6	2			.971	7	C-87/S-8	1.0
1920	Phi-A	148	492	40	128	24	6	5	52	28	35	.260	.303	.364	75	-19	5	6	-2	.979	**23**	*C-146/2-1	1.1
1921	Phi-A	141	538	58	155	31	4	12	73	32	32	.288	.329	.428	91	-9	5	9	-4	.971	5	*C-141	0.0
1922	Phi-A	148	505	58	135	20	6	6	69	40	30	.267	.322	.366	77	-17	1	7	-4	.984	-4	*C-141	-1.7
1923	Phi-A	143	500	53	135	34	5	2	65	65	30	.270	.356	.370	90	-6	1	3	-2	.971	-7	*C-137	-0.8
1924	Phi-A	128	392	31	95	19	4	0	32	31	20	.242	.304	.311	58	-25	3	4	-2	.983	-0	*C-128	-1.8
1925	Phi-A	65	140	21	43	10	0	1	18	26	6	.307	.426	.400	104	2	0	0	0	.980	11	C-58/3-1	1.4
1926	Phi-A	63	148	14	43	6	0	0	19	18	7	.291	.371	.331	80	-4	0	2	-1	.984	9	C-55	0.6
1927	Phi-A	59	137	11	35	7	2	1	15	12	8	.255	.315	.358	70	-6	0	2	-1	.979	1	C-54/1-1	-0.4
1928	Phi-A	19	29	1	5	0	0	0	1	1	1	.172	.200	.172	-1	-4	0	1	-1	.982	4	C-19	-0.1
1929	Phi-A	38	76	4	16	4	0	0	9	5	4	.211	.259	.263	34	-8	0	0	0	.990	2	C-38	-0.4
1930	Phi-A	20	38	1	6	2	0	0	4	2	3	.158	.200	.211	4	-6	0	0	0	.964	0	C-19/1-1	-0.4
1931	NY-A	16	47	3	12	1	0	0	7	1	4	.255	.286	.277	51	-3	0	0	0	1.000	-5	C-16	-0.7
1934	Det-A	1	1	0	0	0	0	0	0	0	0	.000	.000	.000	-99	-0	0	0	0	.000	0	H	0.0
Total	17	1171	3604	329	933	175	35	30	409	301	221	.259	.319	.352	75	-131	18	34		.978	62	*C-1111/S-8,1-2,32	-2.0

■ **SAM PERLOZZO** Perlozzo, Samuel Benedict b: 3/4/51, Cumberland, Md. BR/TR, 5'9", 170 lbs. Deb: 9/13/77 C

1977	Min-A	10	24	6	7	0	2	0	0	2	3	.292	.346	.458	119	1	0	0	0	1.000	-3	2-10/3-1	-0.2
1979	SD-N	2	2	0	0	0	0	0	0	1	0	.000	.333	.000	-1	-0	0	0	0	.500	-1	/2-2	-0.2
Total	2	12	26	6	7	0	2	0	0	3	3	.269	.345	.423	110	0	0	0	0	.967	-5	/2-12,3-1	-0.4

■ **JOHN PERRIN** Perrin, John Stephenson b: 2/4/1898, Escanaba, Mich. d: 6/24/69, Detroit, Mich. BL/TR, 5'9", 160 lbs. Deb: 7/11/21

1921	Bos-A	4	13	3	3	0	0	0	1	0	3	.231	.231	.231	19	-2	0	0	0	1.000	-2	/O-4	-0.3

■ **NIG PERRINE** Perrine, John Grover b: 1/14/1885, Clinton, Wis. d: 8/13/48, Kansas City, Mo. BR/TR, 5'9", 160 lbs. Deb: 4/11/07

1907	Was-A	44	146	13	25	4	1	0	15	13		.171	.253	.212	53	-7	10			.946	-3	2-24,S-18/3-2	-1.2

■ **GEORGE PERRING** Perring, George Wilson b: 8/13/1884, Sharon, Wis. d: 8/20/60, Beloit, Wis. BR/TR, 6', 190 lbs. Deb: 4/25/08

1908	Cle-A	89	310	23	67	8	5	0	19	16		.216	.255	.274	72	-10	8			.928	-6	S-48,3-41	-1.6
1909	Cle-A	88	283	26	63	10	9	0	20	19		.223	.283	.322	87	-5	6			.932	6	3-67,S-11/2-4	0.5
1910	Cle-A	39	122	14	27	6	3	0	8	3		.221	.240	.320	74	-4	3			.931	2	3-33/1-4	-0.2
1914	KC-F	144	496	68	138	28	10	2	69	59	39	.278	.355	.387	106	-3	7			.934	9	*3-101,1-41/P-1,S-1	0.8
1915	KC-F	153	553	67	143	23	7	7	67	57	30	.259	.329	.363	99	-10	10			.958	15	*3-102,1-31,2-31,/S	0.9
Total	5	513	1764	198	438	75	34	9	183	154	69	.248	.311	.345	93	-32	34			.939	26	3-344/1-76,S-61,2P	0.4

■ **BOYD PERRY** Perry, Boyd Glenn b: 3/21/14, Snow Camp, N.C. d: 6/29/90, Burlington, N.C. BR/TR, 5'10", 158 lbs. Deb: 5/23/41

1941	Det-A	36	83	9	15	5	0	0	11	10	9	.181	.269	.241	32	-8	1	0	0	.974	-0	S-25,2-11	-0.6

■ **CLAY PERRY** Perry, Clayton Shields b: 12/18/1881, Clayton, Wis. d: 1/13/54, Rice Lake, Wis. BR/TR, 5'10.5", 175 lbs. Deb: 9/2/08

1908	Det-A	7	17	0	2	0	0	0	0	0		.118	.167	.118	-7	-2	0			.850	0	/3-7	-0.2

■ **GERALD PERRY** Perry, Gerald June b: 10/30/60, Savannah, Ga. BL/TR, 6', 190 lbs. Deb: 8/11/83

1983	Atl-N	27	39	5	14	2	0	1	6	5	4	.359	.432	.487	144	2	0	1	-1	.982	-2	/1-7,O-1	-0.1
1984	Atl-N	122	347	52	92	12	2	7	47	61	38	.265	.378	.372	104	4	15	12	-3	.988	-8	1-64,O-53	-1.2
1985	Atl-N	110	238	22	51	5	0	3	13	23	28	.214	.284	.273	53	-15	9	5	-0	.985	-0	1-55/O-1	-1.9
1986	Atl-N	29	70	6	19	2	0	2	11	8	4	.271	.346	.386	96	-0	0	1	-1	.889	-5	O-21/1-1	-0.7
1987	Atl-N	142	533	77	144	35	2	12	74	48	63	.270	.332	.411	91	-7	42	16	3	.990	-10	*1-136/O-7	-2.4
1988	Atl-N★	141	547	61	164	29	1	8	74	36	49	.300	.344	.400	108	5	29	14	0	.988	1	*1-141	-0.6
1989	Atl-N	72	266	24	67	11	0	4	21	32	28	.252	.339	.338	92	-2	10	6	-1	.987	1	1-72	-0.7
1990	KC-A	133	465	57	118	22	2	8	57	39	56	.254	.316	.361	90	-6	17	4	3	.986	2	D-68,1-51	-0.7
1991	StL-N	109	242	29	58	8	4	6	36	22	34	.240	.303	.380	90	-3	15	8	-0	.989	-4	1-61/O-5	-1.1
1992	StL-N	87	143	13	34	8	0	1	18	15	23	.238	.314	.315	81	-3	3	6	-3	.987	-4	1-29	-1.2
1993	StL-N	96	98	21	33	5	0	4	16	18	23	.337	.440	.510	157	9	1	1	-0	.976	-1	1-15/O-1	0.6
1994	StL-N	60	77	12	25	7	0	3	18	15	12	.325	.435	.532	153	7	1	1	-0	.990	-2	1-13	0.4
1995	StL-N	65	79	4	13	4	0	0	5	6	12	.165	.224	.215	16	-10	0	0	0	1.000	-1	1-11	-1.1
Total	13	1193	3144	383	832	150	11	59	396	328	374	.265	.336	.376	95	-20	142	75	-2	.988	-32	1-656/O-89,D-68	-10.7

■ **HERB PERRY** Perry, Herbert Edward b: 9/15/69, Live Oak, Fla. BR/TR, 6'2", 210 lbs. Deb: 5/3/94

1994	Cle-A	4	9	1	1	0	0	0	1	3	1	.111	.385	.111	36	-1	0	0	0	1.000	1	/1-2,3-2	0.0
1995	*Cle-A	52	162	23	51	13	1	3	23	13	28	.315	.380	.463	116	4	1	3	-2	1.000	0	1-45/3-1,D-6	-0.1
1996	Cle-A	7	12	1	1	1	0	0	0	1	2	.083	.154	.167	-19	-2	1	0	0	1.000	-0	/1-5,3-1	-0.2
Total	3	63	183	25	53	14	1	3	24	17	31	.290	.366	.426	104	1	2	3	-1	1.000	1	/1-52,D-6,3-4	-0.3

■ **BOB PERRY** Perry, Melvin Gray b: 9/14/34, New Bern, N.C. BR/TR, 6'2", 180 lbs. Deb: 5/17/63

1963	LA-A	61	166	16	42	9	0	3	14	9	31	.253	.303	.361	91	-2	1	1	-0	.946	-7	O-55	-1.3
1964	LA-A	70	221	19	61	8	1	3	16	14	52	.276	.319	.362	99	-1	1	1	-0	.975	-4	O-62	-0.9
Total	2	131	387	35	103	17	1	6	30	23	83	.266	.312	.362	95	-4	2	2	-1	.962	-11	O-117	-2.2

■ **HANK PERRY** Perry, William Henry "Socks" b: 7/28/1886, Howell, Mich. d: 7/18/56, Pontiac, Mich. BL/TR, 5'11", 190 lbs. Deb: 4/12/12

1912	Det-A	13	36	3	6	1	0	0	0	3		.167	.231	.194	23	-4	0			1.000	2	/O-7	-0.2

■ **JOHNNY PESKY** Pesky, John Michael (b: John Michael Paveskovich) b: 9/27/19, Portland, Ore. BL/TR, 5'9", 168 lbs. Deb: 4/14/42 MC

1942	Bos-A	147	620	105	**205**	29	9	2	51	42	36	.331	.375	.416	118	14	12	7	-1	.955	18	*S-147	4.1
1946	*Bos-A★	153	621	115	**208**	43	4	2	55	65	29	.335	.401	.427	124	22	9	8	-2	.969	12	*S-153	4.2
1947	Bos-A	155	638	106	**207**	27	8	0	39	72	22	.324	.393	.392	110	11	12	9	-2	.976	-11	*S-133,3-22	0.5
1948	Bos-A	143	565	124	159	26	6	3	55	99	32	.281	.394	.365	98	2	3	5	-2	.951	6	*3-141	0.4
1949	Bos-A	148	604	111	185	27	7	2	69	100	19	.306	.408	.384	103	6	8	4	0	.970	21	*3-148	2.4
1950	Bos-A	127	490	112	153	22	6	1	49	104	31	.312	.437	.388	103	7	2	1	0	.974	22	*3-116/S-8	2.5
1951	Bos-A	131	480	93	150	20	6	3	41	84	15	.313	.417	.398	110	10	2	2	-1	.961	9	*S-106,3-11/2-5	2.5
1952	Bos-A	25	67	10	10	2	0	0	2	15	5	.149	.313	.179	36	-5	0	3	-2	.917	-6	3-19/S-2	-1.4
	Det-A	69	177	26	45	4	0	1	9	41	11	.254	.394	.294	93	1	1	2	-1	.952	-6	S-41,2-22/3-3	-0.2
	Yr	94	244	36	55	6	0	1	11	56	16	.225	.372	.262	77	-5	1	5	-3	.953	-11	S-43,3-22,2-22	-1.6
1953	Det-A	103	308	43	90	22	1	2	24	27	10	.292	.353	.390	102	1	3	7	-3	.991	-14	2-73	-1.2
1954	Det-A	20	17	5	3	0	0	1	1	3	1	.176	.300	.353	80	-1	0	0	0	.000	0	H	-0.1
	Was-A	49	158	17	40	4	3	0	9	10	7	.253	.298	.316	72	-6	1	1	-0	.979	-8	2-37/S-1	-1.3
	Yr	69	175	22	43	4	3	1	10	13	8	.246	.298	.320	72	-7	1	1	-0	.979	-8	2-37/S-1	-1.4
Total	10	1270	4745	867	1455	226	50	17	404	662	218	.307	.394	.386	106	62	53	49	-14	.964	43	S-591,3-460,2-137	12.4

■ **ROBERTO PETAGINE** Petagine, Roberto Antonio (Guerra) b: 6/7/71, Nueva Esparta, Venez. BL/TL, 6'1", 170 lbs. Deb: 4/4/94

1994	Hou-N	8	7	0	0	0	0	0	0	1	3	.000	.125	.000	-67	-2	0	0	0	1.000	-0	/1-2	-0.2
1995	SD-N	89	124	15	29	8	0	3	17	26	41	.234	.367	.371	99	1	0	0	0	.996	1	1-51/O-2	-0.1
1996	NY-N	50	99	10	23	3	0	4	17	9	27	.232	.315	.384	87	-2	0	2	-1	.996	2	1-40	-0.3
1997	NY-N	12	15	2	1	1	0	0	2	3	6	.067	.222	.067	-21	-3	0	0	0	1.000	0	/1-6,O-1	-0.2

YEAR	TM/L	G	AB	R	H	2B	3B	HR	RBI	BB	SO	AVG	OBP	SLG	PRO+	BR/A	SB	CS	SBR	FA	FR	G/POS	TPR
1998	Cin-N	34	62	14	16	2	1	3	7	16	11	.258	.410	.468	125	3	1	0	0	1.000	-1	1-15,O-15	0.1
Total	5	193	307	41	69	13	1	10	43	55	88	.225	.348	.371	92	-3	1	2	-1	.997	3	1-114/O-18	-0.7
■ **BILL PETERMAN** Peterman, William David b: 3/20/21, Philadelphia, Pa. BR/TR, 6′2″, 185 lbs. Deb: 4/26/42																							
1942	Phi-N	1	1	0	1	0	0	0	0	0	0	1.000	1.000	1.000	512	0	0			.000	0	/C-1	0.1
■ **JOHN PETERS** Peters, John Paul b: 4/8/1850, Louisiana, Mo. d: 1/4/24, St.Louis, Mo. BR/TR, 5′7″, 180 lbs. Deb: 5/23/1874																							
1874	Chi-n	55	239	39	69	10	0	1	25	2	11	.289	.295	.343	103	1	2	2	-1	.799	3	S-36,2-19	0.1
1875	Chi-n	69	297	40	85	16	2	0	34	0	3	.286	.286	.354	120	5	12	6	0	.871	10	*S-65/2-6	1.1
1876	Chi-N	66	316	70	111	14	2	1	47	3	2	.351	.357	.418	141	11				**.932**	-1	*S-66/P-1	0.8
1877	Chi-N	60	265	45	84	10	3	0	41	1	7	.317	.320	.377	106	0				.883	19	*S-60	1.8
1878	Mil-N	55	246	33	76	6	1	0	22	5	8	.309	.323	.341	111	2				.853	5	2-34,S-22	0.9
1879	Chi-N	83	379	45	93	13	2	1	31	1	19	.245	.247	.298	74	-11				.837	-8	*S-83	-1.4
1880	Pro-N	86	359	30	82	5	0	0	24	5	15	.228	.239	.242	66	-12				**.900**	-1	*S-86	-0.7
1881	Buf-N	54	229	21	49	8	1	0	25	3	12	.214	.224	.258	52	-12				.869	7	S-53/O-1	-0.2
1882	Pit-a	78	333	46	96	10	1	0		4		.288	.297	.324	115	5				.883	6	*S-77/2-1	1.3
1883	Pit-a	8	28	3	3	0	0	0		0		.107	.107	.107	-32	-4				.818	3	/S-8	-0.1
1884	Pit-a	1	4	0	0	0	0	0		0		.000	.000	.000	-98	-1				.667	-1	/S-1	-0.2
Total	2 n	124	536	79	154	26	2	1	59	2	14	.287	.290	.349	112	6	14	8	-1	.846	14	S-101/2-25	1.2
Total	9	491	2159	293	594	66	10	2	190	22	63	.275	.282	.318	94	-23				.881	28	S-456/2-35,O-1,P-1	2.2
■ **JOHN PETERS** Peters, John William "Big Pete" or "Shotgun" b: 7/14/1893, Kansas City, Kan. d: 2/21/32, Kansas City, Mo. BR/TR, 6′, 192 lbs. Deb: 5/1/15																							
1915	Det-A	1	3	0	0	0	0	0	0	0	1	.000	.000	.000	-95	-1	0			1.000	1	/C-1	0.1
1918	Cle-A	1	1	0	0	0	0	0	0	1	1	.000	.500	.000	46	0	0			.500	-1	/C-1	-0.1
1921	Phi-N	55	155	7	45	4	0	3	23	6	13	.290	.329	.374	79	-5	1	0	0	.933	-13	C-44	-1.5
1922	Phi-N	55	143	15	35	9	1	4	24	9	18	.245	.308	.406	75	-6	0	1	-1	.953	-5	C-39	-0.9
Total	4	112	302	22	80	13	1	7	47	16	33	.265	.317	.384	76	-11	1	1		.934	-18	/C-85	-2.4
■ **RICK PETERS** Peters, Richard Devin b: 11/21/55, Lynwood, Cal. BB/TR, 5′9″, 170 lbs. Deb: 9/8/79																							
1979	Det-A	12	19	3	5	0	0	0	2	5	3	.263	.417	.263	85	-0	0	0	0	.000	-1	/3-3,2-2,O-1,D-3	-0.1
1980	Det-A	133	477	79	139	19	7	2	42	54	48	.291	.371	.373	102	3	13	7	-0	.977	0	*O-109,D-11	-0.2
1981	Det-A	63	207	26	53	7	3	0	15	29	28	.256	.353	.319	91	-1	1	6	-3	.991	3	O-38,D-19	-0.3
1983	Oak-A	55	178	20	51	7	0	0	20	12	21	.287	.335	.326	88	-3	4	9	-4	.986	5	O-47/D-8	-0.4
1986	Oak-A	44	38	7	7	1	0	0	1	7	7	.184	.311	.211	49	-2	2	2	-1	1.000	-5	O-27/2-1	-0.9
Total	5	307	919	135	255	34	10	2	80	107	107	.277	.358	.343	95	-3	20	24	-8	.983	1	O-222/D-41,2-3,3-3	-1.9
■ **RUSTY PETERS** Peters, Russell Dixon b: 12/14/14, Roanoke, Va. BR/TR, 5′11″, 170 lbs. Deb: 4/14/36																							
1936	Phi-A	45	119	12	26	3	2	3	16	4	28	.218	.244	.353	47	-11	1	1	-0	.898	1	S-25,3-10/O-2,2-1	-0.8
1937	Phi-A	116	339	39	88	17	6	3	43	41	59	.260	.339	.372	80	-10	4	4	-1	.966	-13	2-70,3-31,S-13	-1.8
1938	Phi-A	2	7	0	0	0	0	0	0	0	1	.000	.000	.000	-99	-2	0	0	0	.714	-2	/S-2	-0.4
1940	Cle-A	30	71	5	17	3	2	0	7	4	14	.239	.280	.338	61	-4	1	0	0	.922	-0	/2-9,S-6,3-6,1-1	-0.3
1941	Cle-A	29	63	6	13	2	0	0	2	7	10	.206	.286	.238	42	-5	0	1	-1	.891	2	S-11/3-9,2-3	-0.3
1942	Cle-A	34	58	6	13	5	1	0	2	2	14	.224	.250	.345	70	-3	0	0	0	.944	2	S-24/2-1,3-1	0.0
1943	Cle-A	79	215	22	47	6	2	1	19	18	29	.219	.282	.279	69	-9	1	1	-0	.913	-6	3-46,S-14/2-6,O-2	-1.5
1944	Cle-A	88	282	23	63	13	3	1	24	15	35	.223	.268	.301	65	-14	2	1	0	.976	-3	2-63,S-13/3-8	-1.4
1946	Cle-A	9	21	0	6	0	0	0	2	1	1	.286	.318	.286	74	-1	0	1	-1	1.000	0	/S-7	-0.1
1947	StL-A	39	47	10	16	4	0	0	2	6	8	.340	.415	.426	131	2	0	0	0	.955	7	2-13/S-2	1.0
Total	10	471	1222	123	289	53	16	8	117	98	199	.236	.295	.326	69	-57	9	9	-3	.966	-13	2-166,S-117,3/O1	-5.6
■ **BUDDY PETERSON** Peterson, Carl Francis b: 4/23/25, Portland, Ore. BR/TR, 5′9.5″, 170 lbs. Deb: 9/14/55																							
1955	Chi-A	6	21	7	6	1	0	0	2	3	1	.286	.400	.333	96	0	0	0	0	.962	-1	/S-6	0.0
1957	Bal-A	7	17	1	3	2	0	0	0	2	2	.176	.263	.294	55	-1	0	0	0	.963	-1	/S-7	-0.2
Total	2	13	38	8	9	3	0	0	2	5	3	.237	.341	.316	80	-1	0	0	0	.962	-2	/S-13	-0.2
■ **CAP PETERSON** Peterson, Charles Andrew b: 8/15/42, Tacoma, Wash. d: 5/16/80, Tacoma, Wash. BR/TR, 6′2″, 195 lbs. Deb: 9/12/62																							
1962	SF-N	4	6	1	1	0	0	0	1	4		.167	.286	.167	25	-1	0	0	0	1.000	-1	/S-2	-0.1
1963	SF-N	22	54	7	14	2	0	1	2	2	13	.259	.286	.352	83	-1	0	0	0	.917	-7	/2-8,3-5,O-3,S-1	-0.8
1964	SF-N	66	74	8	15	1	1	1	8	3	20	.203	.234	.284	44	-5	0	0	0	1.000	-3	O-10/1-2,2-1,3-1	-0.9
1965	SF-N	63	105	14	26	7	0	3	15	10	16	.248	.313	.400	97	-1	0	0	0	1.000	-4	O-27	-0.5
1966	SF-N	89	190	13	45	6	1	2	19	11	32	.237	.282	.311	63	-9	2	0	1	1.000	-3	O-51/1-2	-1.4
1967	Was-A	122	405	35	97	17	2	8	46	32	61	.240	.300	.351	95	-3	0	3	-2	.970	0	*O-101	-1.0
1968	Was-A	94	226	20	46	8	1	3	18	18	31	.204	.265	.288	70	-9	2	1	0	1.000	-1	O-53	-1.4
1969	Cle-A	76	110	8	25	3	0	1	14	24	18	.227	.370	.282	82	-1	0	0	0	.977	-2	O-30/3-4	-0.5
Total	8	536	1170	106	269	44	5	19	122	101	195	.230	.294	.325	80	-30	4	4	-1	.983	-18	O-275/3-10,2-9,1S	-6.6
■ **HARDY PETERSON** Peterson, Harding William b: 10/17/29, Perth Amboy, N.J. BR/TR, 6′, 205 lbs. Deb: 5/5/55																							
1955	Pit-N	32	81	7	20	6	0	1	10	7	7	.247	.315	.358	79	-2	0	0	0	.965	6	C-31	0.4
1957	Pit-N	30	73	10	22	2	1	2	11	9	10	.301	.378	.438	122	2	0	1	-1	.985	2	C-30	0.4
1958	Pit-N	2	6	0	2	0	0	0	0	1	0	.333	.429	.333	108	0	0	0	0	1.000	-0	/C-2	0.0
1959	Pit-N	2	1	0	0	0	0	0	0	0	0	.000	.000	.000	-99	-0	0	0	0	1.000	1	/C-2	0.0
Total	4	66	161	17	44	8	1	3	21	17	17	.273	.346	.391	99	-0	0	1	-1	.976	7	/C-65	0.8
■ **BOB PETERSON** Peterson, Robert A. b: 7/16/1884, Philadelphia, Pa. d: 11/27/62, Evesham Township, N.J. BR/TR, 6′1″, 160 lbs. Deb: 4/18/06																							
1906	Bos-A	39	118	10	24	1	1	1	9	11		.203	.277	.254	67	-4	1			.899	-7	C-30/2-3,1-2,O-1	-0.9
1907	Bos-A	4	13	1	1	0	0	0	0	0		.077	.077	.077	-51	-2	0			1.000	0	/C-4	-0.2
Total	2	43	131	11	25	1	1	1	9	11		.191	.259	.237	56	-6	1			.910	-7	/C-34,2-3,1-2,O-1	-1.1
■ **TED PETOSKEY** Petoskey, Frederick Lee b: 1/5/11, St.Charles, Mich. d: 11/30/96, Elgin, S.C. BR/TR, 5′11.5″, 183 lbs. Deb: 9/9/34																							
1934	Cin-N	6	7	0	0	0	0	0	1	0	5	.000	.000	.000	-99	-2	0			1.000	1	/O-2	-0.1
1935	Cin-N	4	5	0	2	0	0	0	0	0	1	.400	.400	.400	119	0	1			1.000	-1	/O-2	-0.1
Total	2	10	12	0	2	0	0	0	1	0	6	.167	.167	.167	-11	-2	1			1.000	0	/O-4	-0.2
■ **GENO PETRALLI** Petralli, Eugene James b: 9/25/59, Sacramento, Cal. BL/TR, 6′2″, 185 lbs. Deb: 9/4/82																							
1982	Tor-A	16	44	3	16	2	0	0	1	4	6	.364	.417	.409	117	1	0	0	0	.981	-2	C-12/3-3	-0.1
1983	Tor-A	6	4	0	0	0	0	0	0	1	1	.000	.200	.000	-37	-1	0	0	0	1.000	0	/C-5,D-1	0.0
1984	Tor-A	3	3	0	0	0	0	0	0	0	0	.000	.000	.000	-97	-1	0	0	0	1.000	0	/C-1,D-1	0.0
1985	Tex-A	42	100	7	27	2	0	0	11	8	12	.270	.330	.290	71	-4	1	0	0	.990	2	C-41	0.0
1986	Tex-A	69	137	17	35	9	3	2	18	5	14	.255	.282	.409	83	-4	3	0	1	.988	-8	C-41,3-15/2-2,D-2	-0.9
1987	Tex-A	101	202	28	61	11	2	7	31	27	29	.302	.390	.480	129	9	0	2	-1	.995	-0	C-63,3-17/1-5,2OD	1.0
1988	Tex-A	129	351	35	99	14	2	7	36	41	52	.282	.360	.393	108	5	0	1	-1	.981	-1	C-85,D-23/3-9,12	0.9
1989	Tex-A	70	184	18	56	7	0	4	23	17	24	.304	.369	.408	117	4	0	0	0	.989	-12	C-49,D-16	-0.6
1990	Tex-A	133	325	28	83	13	1	0	21	50	49	.255	.360	.302	87	-4	0	2	-1	.991	-4	*C-118/3-7,2-3	-0.2
1991	Tex-A	87	199	21	54	8	1	2	20	21	25	.271	.341	.352	94	-1	2	1	0	.972	-10	C-66/3-7,D-5	-0.8
1992	Tex-A	94	192	11	38	12	0	1	18	20	34	.198	.274	.276	56	-11	0	0	0	.990	3	C-54,D-14/3-4,2-2	-0.6
1993	Tex-A	59	133	16	32	5	0	1	13	22	17	.241	.348	.301	79	-3	2	0	1	.990	-7	C-39/2-1,3-1,D-2	-0.7
Total	12	809	1874	184	501	83	9	24	192	216	263	.267	.346	.360	95	-9	8	6	-1	.987	-37	C-574/D-66,3210	-2.0
■ **RICO PETROCELLI** Petrocelli, Americo Peter b: 6/27/43, Brooklyn, N.Y. BR/TR, 6′, 185 lbs. Deb: 9/21/63																							
1963	Bos-A	1	4	0	1	1	0	0	1	0	1	.250	.250	.500	101	-0	0	0	0	.833	-0	/S-1	0.0
1965	Bos-A	103	323	38	75	15	2	13	33	36	71	.232	.311	.412	98	-1	0	2	-1	.958	10	S-93	1.5
1966	Bos-A	139	522	58	124	20	1	18	59	41	99	.238	.297	.383	85	-11	1	1	-0	.954	1	*S-127/3-5	0.1
1967	*Bos-A★	142	491	53	127	24	2	17	66	49	93	.259	.332	.420	112	7	2	4	-2	.970	3	*S-141	2.3

YEAR	TM/L	G	AB	R	H	2B	3B	HR	RBI	BB	SO	AVG	OBP	SLG	PRO+	BR/A	SB	CS	SBR	FA	FR	G/POS	TPR
1968	Bos-A	123	406	41	95	17	2	12	46	31	73	.234	.295	.374	95	-3	0	1	-1	**.978**	11	*S-117/1-1	2.2
1969	Bos-A★	154	535	92	159	32	2	40	97	98	68	.297	.407	.589	167	48	3	5	-2	**.981**	5	*S-153/3-1	**6.9**
1970	Bos-A	157	583	82	152	31	3	29	103	67	82	.261	.339	.473	114	10	1	1	-0	.970	-10	*S-141,3-18	1.7
1971	Bos-A	158	553	82	139	24	4	28	89	91	108	.251	.359	.461	122	17	2	0	1	**.976**	-1	*3-156	1.7
1972	Bos-A	147	521	62	125	15	2	15	75	78	91	.240	.341	.363	104	4	0	1	-1	.970	-1	*3-146	0.1
1973	Bos-A	100	356	44	87	13	1	13	45	47	64	.244	.334	.396	99	-0	0	0	0	.980	5	3-99	0.4
1974	Bos-A	129	454	53	121	23	1	15	76	48	74	.267	.339	.421	110	5	1	0	0	.962	-19	*3-116/D-9	-1.4
1975	*Bos-A	115	402	31	96	15	1	7	59	41	66	.239	.314	.333	76	-12	0	2	-1	.960	-18	*3-113/D-1	-3.4
1976	Bos-A	85	240	17	51	7	1	3	24	34	36	.213	.310	.287	67	-9	0	5	-3	.967	-4	3-73/2-5,1-1,S-1,D	-1.8
Total	13	1553	5390	653	1352	237	22	210	773	661	926	.251	.336	.420	108	55	10	22	-10	.969	-18	S-774,3-727/D21	10.3

■ PAT PETTEE
Pettee, Patrick E. b: 1/10/1863, Natick, Mass. d: 10/9/34, Natick, Mass. BR/TR, 5'10", 170 lbs. Deb: 4/8/1891

YEAR	TM/L	G	AB	R	H	2B	3B	HR	RBI	BB	SO	AVG	OBP	SLG	PRO+	BR/A	SB	CS	SBR	FA	FR	G/POS	TPR
1891	Lou-a	2	5	1	0	0	0	0	0	3	1	.000	.375	.000	9	-0	1			.818	-1	/2-2	-0.1

■ NED PETTIGREW
Pettigrew, Jim Ned b: 8/25/1881, Honey Grove, Tex. d: 8/20/52, Duncan, Okla. BR/TR, 5'11", 175 lbs. Deb: 4/23/14

YEAR	TM/L	G	AB	R	H	2B	3B	HR	RBI	BB	SO	AVG	OBP	SLG	PRO+	BR/A	SB	CS	SBR	FA	FR	G/POS	TPR
1914	Buf-F	2	2	0	0	0	0	0	0	0	0	.000	.000	.000	-98	-1	0			.000	0	H	-0.1

■ JOE PETTINI
Pettini, Joseph Paul b: 1/26/55, Wheeling, W.Va. BR/TR, 5'9", 165 lbs. Deb: 7/10/80

YEAR	TM/L	G	AB	R	H	2B	3B	HR	RBI	BB	SO	AVG	OBP	SLG	PRO+	BR/A	SB	CS	SBR	FA	FR	G/POS	TPR
1980	SF-N	63	190	19	44	3	1	1	9	17	33	.232	.295	.274	61	-10	5	2	0	.955	-13	S-42,3-18/2-8	-1.9
1981	SF-N	35	29	3	2	1	0	0	2	4	5	.069	.182	.103	-18	-4	1	0	0	.920	4	2-12,S-12/3-9	0.0
1982	SF-N	29	39	5	8	1	0	0	2	3	4	.205	.262	.231	39	-3	0	1	-1	.934	-1	S-26/3-1	-0.3
1983	SF-N	61	86	11	16	0	1	0	7	9	11	.186	.263	.209	33	-8	4	1	1	.949	11	S-26,2-14,3-12	0.5
Total	4	188	344	38	70	5	2	1	20	33	53	.203	.273	.238	45	-25	10	4	1	.943	2	S-106/3-40,2-34	-1.7

■ GARY PETTIS
Pettis, Gary George b: 4/3/58, Oakland, Cal. BB/TR, 6'1", 165 lbs. Deb: 9/13/82

YEAR	TM/L	G	AB	R	H	2B	3B	HR	RBI	BB	SO	AVG	OBP	SLG	PRO+	BR/A	SB	CS	SBR	FA	FR	G/POS	TPR
1982	Cal-A	10	5	5	1	0	0	1	1	0	2	.200	.200	.800	159	0	0	0	0	1.000	-2	/O-8	-0.2
1983	Cal-A	22	85	19	25	2	3	3	6	7	15	.294	.348	.494	130	3	8	3	1	.982	2	O-21	0.5
1984	Cal-A	140	397	63	90	11	6	2	29	60	115	.227	.333	.300	77	-10	48	17	4	.983	1	*O-134	-0.9
1985	Cal-A	125	443	67	114	10	8	1	32	62	125	.257	.349	.323	86	-7	56	9	11	.990	17	*O-122	1.7
1986	*Cal-A	154	539	93	139	23	4	5	58	69	132	.258	.342	.343	88	-7	50	13	7	.985	21	*O-153/D-1	1.6
1987	Cal-A	133	394	49	82	13	2	1	17	52	124	.208	.302	.259	53	-26	24	5	4	.980	6	*O-131	-1.9
1988	Det-A	129	458	65	96	14	4	3	36	47	85	.210	.285	.277	60	-24	44	10	7	.987	10	*O-126/D-2	-1.0
1989	Det-A	119	444	77	114	8	6	1	18	84	106	.257	.375	.309	97	2	43	15	4	.988	5	*O-119	0.8
1990	Tex-A	136	423	66	101	16	8	3	31	57	118	.239	.335	.336	88	-6	38	15	2	.993	4	*O-128/D-2	-0.2
1991	Tex-A	137	282	37	61	7	5	0	19	54	91	.216	.342	.277	75	-8	29	13	1	.977	-11	*O-126/D-3	-1.9
1992	SD-N	30	30	0	6	1	0	0	0	2	11	.200	.250	.233	37	-2	1	0	0	.952	-3	O-14	-0.6
	Det-A	48	129	27	26	4	3	1	12	27	34	.202	.340	.302	81	-2	13	4	2	.993	5	O-46	0.3
Total	11	1183	3629	568	855	109	49	21	259	521	958	.236	.333	.310	80	-86	354	104	44	.986	54	*O-1128/D-8	-1.8

■ BOB PETTIT
Pettit, Robert Henry b: 7/19/1861, Williamstown, Mass. d: 11/1/10, Derby, Conn. BL/TR, 5'9", 160 lbs. Deb: 9/3/1887

YEAR	TM/L	G	AB	R	H	2B	3B	HR	RBI	BB	SO	AVG	OBP	SLG	PRO+	BR/A	SB	CS	SBR	FA	FR	G/POS	TPR
1887	Chi-N	32	138	29	36	3	3	2	12	8	15	.261	.301	.370	76	-6	16			.894	-1	O-32/C-1,P-1	-0.6
1888	Chi-N	43	169	23	43	1	4	4	23	7	9	.254	.288	.379	104	0	7			.931	-4	O-43	-0.5
1891	Mil-a	21	80	10	14	4	0	1	5	7	7	.175	.267	.262	43	-7	2			.932	-7	/2-9,O-7,3-6	-1.2
Total	3	96	387	62	93	8	7	7	40	22	31	.240	.288	.351	79	-13	25			.919	-11	/O-82,2-9,3-6,PC	-2.3

■ MARTY PEVEY
Pevey, Marty Ashley b: 12/25/62, Savannah, Ga. BL/TR, 6'1", 185 lbs. Deb: 5/16/89

YEAR	TM/L	G	AB	R	H	2B	3B	HR	RBI	BB	SO	AVG	OBP	SLG	PRO+	BR/A	SB	CS	SBR	FA	FR	G/POS	TPR
1989	Mon-N	13	41	2	9	1	1	0	3	0	8	.220	.220	.293	45	-3	0	0	0	.985	-2	C-11/O-1	-0.5

■ LARRY PEZOLD
Pezold, Lorenz Johannes b: 6/22/1893, New Orleans, La. d: 10/22/57, Baton Rouge, La. BR/TR, 5'9.5", 175 lbs. Deb: 7/27/14

YEAR	TM/L	G	AB	R	H	2B	3B	HR	RBI	BB	SO	AVG	OBP	SLG	PRO+	BR/A	SB	CS	SBR	FA	FR	G/POS	TPR
1914	Cle-A	23	71	4	16	0	1	0	5	9	6	.225	.313	.254	68	-3	2	3	-1	.827	-1	3-20/O-1	-0.5

■ FRED PFEFFER
Pfeffer, Nathaniel Frederick "Fritz" or "Dandelion"
b: 3/17/1860, Louisville, Ky. d: 4/10/32, Chicago, Ill. BR/TR, 5'10.5", 184 lbs. Deb: 5/1/1882 M

YEAR	TM/L	G	AB	R	H	2B	3B	HR	RBI	BB	SO	AVG	OBP	SLG	PRO+	BR/A	SB	CS	SBR	FA	FR	G/POS	TPR
1882	Tro-N	85	330	26	72	7	4	1	43	1	24	.218	.221	.273	60	-14				.857	11	*S-83/2-2	0.1
1883	Chi-N	96	371	41	87	22	7	1	45	8	50	.235	.251	.340	73	-13				.887	17	*2-79,S-18/3-1,1-1	0.5
1884	Chi-N	112	467	105	135	10	10	25	101	25	47	.289	.325	.514	147	22				.903	**46**	*2-112/P-1	**6.1**
1885	*Chi-N	112	469	90	113	12	7	5	73	26	47	.241	.281	.328	85	-11				.893	25	*2-109/P-5,O-1	1.7
1886	*Chi-N	118	474	88	125	17	8	7	95	36	46	.264	.316	.378	96	-6	30			.903	7	*2-118/1-1	0.6
1887	Chi-N	123	479	95	133	21	6	16	89	34	20	.278	.327	.447	100	-4	57			.917	25	*2-123/O-2	2.0
1888	Chi-N	135	517	90	129	22	10	8	57	32	38	.250	.297	.377	106	2	64			.931	**38**	*2-135	4.4
1889	Chi-N	134	531	85	121	15	7	7	77	53	51	.228	.302	.322	71	-22	45			.943	19	*2-134	0.4
1890	Chi-P	124	499	86	128	21	8	5	80	44	23	.257	.319	.361	78	-18	27			.916	24	*2-124	1.1
1891	Chi-N	137	498	93	123	12	9	7	77	79	60	.247	.353	.349	105	5	40			.921	25	*2-137	3.2
1892	Lou-N	124	470	78	121	14	9	2	76	67	36	.257	.353	.338	119	13	27			.933	12	*2-116,1-10/P-1,M	2.5
1893	Lou-N	125	508	85	129	29	12	3	75	51	18	.254	.322	.376	92	-7	32			.939	6	*2-125	0.2
1894	Lou-N	104	409	68	126	12	14	5	59	30	14	.308	.357	.443	99	-2	31			.937	12	*2-90,S-15/P-1	1.1
1895	Lou-N	11	45	8	13	1	0	0	5	5	3	.289	.360	.311	79	-1	2			.742	-3	/S-5,2-3,1-3	-0.3
1896	NY-N	4	14	1	2	0	0	0	4	1	1	.143	.250	.143	5	-2	0			.760	-1	/2-4	-0.3
	Chi-N	94	360	45	88	16	7	2	52	23	20	.244	.294	.344	65	-20	22			.947	9	*2-94	-0.4
	Yr	98	374	46	90	16	7	2	56	24	21	.241	.292	.337	63	-21	22			.939	8	2-98	-0.7
1897	Chi-N	32	114	10	26	0	1	0	11	12		.228	.318	.246	48	-8	5			.883	-6	2-32	-1.1
Total	16	1670	6555	1094	1671	231	119	94	1019	527	498	.255	.312	.369	92	-84	382			.920	266	*2-1537,S-121/1PO3	21.8

■ BOBBY PFEIL
Pfeil, Robert Raymond b: 11/13/43, Passaic, N.J. BR/TR, 6'1", 180 lbs. Deb: 6/26/69

YEAR	TM/L	G	AB	R	H	2B	3B	HR	RBI	BB	SO	AVG	OBP	SLG	PRO+	BR/A	SB	CS	SBR	FA	FR	G/POS	TPR
1969	NY-N	62	211	20	49	9	0	0	10	7	27	.232	.260	.275	49	-14	0	1	-1	.976	-4	3-49,2-11/O-2	-1.9
1971	Phi-N	44	70	5	19	3	0	2	9	6	9	.271	.329	.400	106	0	1	1	-0	1.000	-2	3-15/C-4,O-3,12S	-0.2
Total	2	106	281	25	68	12	0	2	19	13	36	.242	.278	.306	63	-14	1	2	-1	.980	-6	/3-64,2-12,O-5,CS1	-2.1

■ GEORGE PFISTER
Pfister, George Edward b: 9/4/18, Bound Brook, N.J. d: 8/14/97, St.Joseph, Mo. BR/TR, 6', 200 lbs. Deb: 9/27/41 C

YEAR	TM/L	G	AB	R	H	2B	3B	HR	RBI	BB	SO	AVG	OBP	SLG	PRO+	BR/A	SB	CS	SBR	FA	FR	G/POS	TPR
1941	Bro-N	1	2	0	0	0	0	0	0	0	0	.000	.000	.000	-96	-1	0			.000	0	/C-1	-0.1

■ MONTE PFYL
Pfyl, Meinhard Charles b: 5/11/1884, St.Louis, Mo. d: 10/18/45, San Francisco, Cal BL/TL, 6'3", 190 lbs. Deb: 7/30/07

YEAR	TM/L	G	AB	R	H	2B	3B	HR	RBI	BB	SO	AVG	OBP	SLG	PRO+	BR/A	SB	CS	SBR	FA	FR	G/POS	TPR
1907	NY-N	1	0	0	0	0	0	0	0	0		—	—	—	—	-0	0			.000	0	/1-1	0.0

■ ART PHELAN
Phelan, Arthur Thomas "Dugan" b: 8/14/1887, Niantic, Ill. d: 12/27/64, Ft.Worth, Tex. BR/TR, 5'8", 160 lbs. Deb: 6/25/10

YEAR	TM/L	G	AB	R	H	2B	3B	HR	RBI	BB	SO	AVG	OBP	SLG	PRO+	BR/A	SB	CS	SBR	FA	FR	G/POS	TPR
1910	Cin-N	23	42	7	9	0	0	0	4	7	6	.214	.327	.214	61	-2	5			1.000	-2	/3-8,2-5,O-3,S-1	-0.4
1912	Cin-N	130	461	56	112	9	11	3	54	46	37	.243	.314	.330	79	-14	25			.924	-2	*3-127/2-3	-1.4
1913	Chi-N	91	261	41	65	11	6	2	35	29	26	.249	.331	.360	97	-1	8			.931	-8	2-46,3-38/S-1	-0.9
1914	Chi-N	25	46	5	13	2	1	0	3	4	3	.283	.340	.370	111	1	0			.905	-0	/3-7,2-3,S-2	0.1
1915	Chi-N	133	448	41	98	16	7	3	35	55	42	.219	.307	.306	86	-7	12	9	-2	.939	-2	*3-110,2-24	-0.6
Total	5	402	1258	150	297	38	25	8	131	141	114	.236	.317	.325	86	-23	50	9		.931	-14	3-290/2-81,S-4,O-3	-3.2

■ DAN PHELAN
Phelan, Daniel T. b: 7/23/1864, Thomaston, Conn. d: 12/7/45, West Haven, Conn. Deb: 4/18/1890

YEAR	TM/L	G	AB	R	H	2B	3B	HR	RBI	BB	SO	AVG	OBP	SLG	PRO+	BR/A	SB	CS	SBR	FA	FR	G/POS	TPR
1890	Lou-a	8	32	4	8	1	1	0	4	0		.250	.250	.344	77	-1	1			.975	0	/1-8	-0.1

■ DICK PHELAN
Phelan, James Dickson b: 12/10/1854, Towanda, Pa. d: 2/13/31, San Antonio, Tex. BR , Deb: 4/17/1884

YEAR	TM/L	G	AB	R	H	2B	3B	HR	RBI	BB	SO	AVG	OBP	SLG	PRO+	BR/A	SB	CS	SBR	FA	FR	G/POS	TPR
1884	Bal-U	101	402	63	99	13	3	3		12		.246	.268	.316	69	-28				.872	-9	*2-100/3-5,O-1	-3.0
1885	Buf-N	4	16	2	2	0	0	1	3	0	3	.125	.125	.313	37	-1				.808	-1	/2-4	-0.2
	StL-N	2	4	1	1	1	0	0	1	0	2	.250	.250	.500	147	0				1.000	-1	/3-2	0.0
	Yr	6	20	3	3	1	0	1	4	0	5	.150	.150	.350	58	-1				.808	-2	/2-4,3-2	-0.2
Total	2	107	422	66	102	14	3	4	4	12	5	.242	.263	.318	69	-29				.869	-10	2-104/3-7,O-1	-3.2

■ NEALY PHELPS
Phelps, Cornelius Carman b: 11/19/1840, New York, N.Y. d: 2/12/1885, New York, N.Y. Deb: 7/1/1871

YEAR	TM/L	G	AB	R	H	2B	3B	HR	RBI	BB	SO	AVG	OBP	SLG	PRO+	BR/A	SB	CS	SBR	FA	FR	G/POS	TPR
1871	Kek-n	1	3	0	0	0	0	0	0	1	0	.000	.250	.000	-20	-0	0	0	0	.889	-0	/1-1	0.0
1873	Mut-n	1	6	0	0	0	0	0	0	0	0	.000	.000	.000	-99	-1	0	0	0	1.000	-0	/1-1,O-1	-0.1
1874	Mut-n	6	24	5	3	0	0	0	2	0	0	.125	.125	.125	-19	-3	0	0	0	.818	1	/O-6	-0.1
1875	Mut-n	2	6	1	2	1	0	0	0	0	1	.333	.333	.500	176	0	0	0	0	1.000	1	/O-2	0.1
1876	NY-N	1	3	0	0	0	0	0	0	0	1	.000	.000	.000	-99	-1				.667	-0	/O-1	-0.1
	Phi-N	1	4	0	0	0	0	0	0	0	0	.000	.000	.000	-99	-1				.571	-1	/C-1	-0.2
	Yr	2	7	0	0	0	0	0	0	0	1	.000	.000	.000	-99	-1				.667	-2	/O-1,C-1	-0.3
Total	4 n	10	39	6	5	1	0	0	2	1	1	.128	.150	.154	-3	-5	0	0	0	.857	2	/O-9,1-2	-0.1

■ ED PHELPS
Phelps, Edward Jaykill "Yaller" b: 3/3/1879, Albany, N.Y. d: 1/31/42, E.Greenbush, N.Y. BR/TR, 5'11", 185 lbs. Deb: 9/3/02

YEAR	TM/L	G	AB	R	H	2B	3B	HR	RBI	BB	SO	AVG	OBP	SLG	PRO+	BR/A	SB	CS	SBR	FA	FR	G/POS	TPR
1902	Pit-N	18	61	5	13	1	0	0	6	4		.213	.284	.230	56	-3	2			.968	-6	C-13/1-5	-0.8
1903	*Pit-N	81	273	32	77	7	3	2	31	17		.282	.338	.352	94	-2	2			.980	-8	C-76/1-3	-0.3
1904	Pit-N	94	302	29	73	5	3	0	28	15		.242	.289	.278	73	-9	2			.964	-11	C-91/1-1	-1.1
1905	Cin-N	44	156	18	36	5	3	0	18	12		.231	.306	.301	73	-5	4			.949	-6	C-44	-0.7
1906	Cin-N	12	40	3	11	0	2	1	5	3		.275	.326	.450	136	1	2			.987	-1	C-12	0.2
	Pit-N	43	118	9	28	3	1	0	12	9		.237	.302	.280	78	-3	1			.971	-3	C-40	-0.3
	Yr	55	158	12	39	3	3	1	17	12		.247	.308	.323	93	-2	3			.975	-4	C-52	-0.1
1907	Pit-N	43	113	11	24	1	0	0	12	9		.212	.282	.221	57	-5	1			.979	-3	C-35/1-1	-0.6
1908	Pit-N	34	64	3	15	2	2	0	11	2		.234	.269	.328	90	-1	0			.977	-0	C-20	0.0
1909	StL-N	104	306	43	76	13	1	0	22	39		.248	.350	.297	108	5	7			.954	-9	C-83	0.3
1910	StL-N	93	270	25	71	4	2	0	37	36	29	.263	.356	.293	93	-1	9			.976	-15	C-80	-0.9
1912	Bro-N	52	111	8	32	4	3	0	23	16	15	.288	.388	.378	114	3	1			.976	-4	C-32	0.1
1913	Bro-N	15	18	0	4	0	0	0	0	1	2	.222	.263	.222	38	-1	0			.875	-2	/C-4	-0.3
Total	11	633	1832	186	460	45	20	3	205	163	46	.251	.325	.302	88	-22	31			.968	-69	C-530/1-10	-4.4

■ BABE PHELPS
Phelps, Ernest Gordon "Blimp" b: 4/19/08, Odenton, Md. d: 12/10/92, Odenton, Md. BL/TR, 6'2", 225 lbs. Deb: 9/17/31

YEAR	TM/L	G	AB	R	H	2B	3B	HR	RBI	BB	SO	AVG	OBP	SLG	PRO+	BR/A	SB	CS	SBR	FA	FR	G/POS	TPR
1931	Was-A	3	3	0	1	0	0	0	0	0	0	.333	.333	.333	75	-0	0	0	0	.000	0	H	0.0
1933	Chi-N	3	7	0	2	0	0	0	2	0	1	.286	.286	.286	64	-0	0			1.000	1	/C-2	0.0
1934	Chi-N	44	70	7	20	5	2	2	12	1	8	.286	.296	.500	111	1	0			.981	-2	C-18	-0.1
1935	Bro-N	47	121	17	44	7	2	5	22	9	10	.364	.408	.579	165	11	0			.957	-2	C-34	1.0
1936	Bro-N	115	319	36	117	23	2	5	57	27	18	.367	.421	.498	145	21	1			.977	-16	C-98/O-1	0.9
1937	Bro-N	121	409	42	128	37	3	7	58	25	28	.313	.357	.469	121	11	2			.971	-7	*C-111	1.0
1938	Bro-N†	66	208	33	64	12	2	5	46	23	15	.308	.379	.457	126	8	2			.980	-4	C-55	0.6
1939	Bro-N★	98	323	33	92	21	2	6	42	24	24	.285	.336	.418	98	-1	0			.980	2	C-92	0.5
1940	Bro-N★	118	370	47	109	24	5	13	61	30	27	.295	.349	.492	122	10	2			.977	-9	C-99/1-1	0.8
1941	Bro-N	16	30	3	7	3	0	2	4	1	2	.233	.258	.533	114	0	0			.971	-1	C-11	0.0
1942	Pit-N	95	257	21	73	11	1	9	41	20	24	.284	.345	.440	126	8	2			.959	-3	C-72	1.1
Total	11	726	2117	239	657	143	19	54	345	160	157	.310	.362	.472	124	67	9	0		.974	-41	C-592/1-1,O-1	5.8

■ KEN PHELPS
Phelps, Kenneth Allen b: 8/6/54, Seattle, Wash. BL/TL, 6'1", 209 lbs. Deb: 9/20/80

YEAR	TM/L	G	AB	R	H	2B	3B	HR	RBI	BB	SO	AVG	OBP	SLG	PRO+	BR/A	SB	CS	SBR	FA	FR	G/POS	TPR
1980	KC-A	3	4	0	0	0	0	0	0	0	2	.000	.000	.000	-99	-1	0	0	0	1.000	-0	/1-2	-0.1
1981	KC-A	21	22	1	3	0	1	0	1	1	13	.136	.174	.227	15	-2	0	0	0	1.000	0	/1-2,D-4	-0.2
1982	Mon-N	10	8	0	2	0	0	0	0	0	3	.250	.333	.250	64	-0	0	0	0	.000	0	H	-0.1
1983	Sea-A	50	127	10	30	4	1	7	16	13	25	.236	.307	.449	101	-0	0	0	0	1.000	2	1-22,D-19	0.0
1984	Sea-A	101	290	52	70	9	0	24	51	61	73	.241	.382	.521	149	21	3	3	-1	.987	-1	D-84/1-9	1.6
1985	Sea-A	61	116	18	24	3	0	9	24	24	33	.207	.343	.466	118	3	2	0	1	1.000	-0	D-25/1-8	0.3
1986	Sea-A	125	344	69	85	16	4	24	64	88	96	.247	.409	.526	151	28	2	3	-1	.983	-4	1-55,D-52	1.8
1987	Sea-A	120	332	68	86	13	1	27	68	80	75	.259	.414	.548	145	24	1	1	-0	1.000	-0	*D-114/1-1	1.9
1988	Sea-A	72	190	37	54	8	0	14	32	51	35	.284	.438	.547	167	19	1	0	0	.952	0	D-68/1-3	1.8
	NY-A	45	107	17	24	5	0	10	22	19	26	.224	.341	.551	147	6	0	0	0	.000	-0	D-24/1-1	0.6
	Yr	117	297	54	78	13	0	24	54	70	61	.263	.405	.549	160	26	1	0	0	.952	-0	D-92/1-4	2.4
1989	NY-A	86	185	26	46	3	0	7	29	27	47	.249	.344	.378	105	2	0	0	0	.980	-1	D-55/1-8	-0.1
	*Oak-A	11	9	0	1	1	0	0	0	4	0	.111	.385	.222	78	-0	0	0	0	.000	-0	/1-1,D-1	0.0
	Yr	97	194	26	47	4	0	7	29	31	47	.242	.347	.371	104	2	0	0	0	.980	-1	D-56/1-9	-0.1
1990	Oak-A	32	59	6	11	2	0	1	6	12	10	.186	.324	.271	71	-2	0	0	0	.964	0	D-15/1-5	-0.2
	Cle-A	24	61	4	7	0	0	0	0	10	11	.115	.239	.115	2	-8	1	0	0	1.000	0	1-14/D-6	-0.9
	Yr	56	120	10	18	2	0	1	6	22	21	.150	.282	.192	36	-10	1	0	0	.992	0	D-21,1-19	-1.1
Total	11	761	1854	308	443	64	7	123	313	390	449	.239	.377	.480	132	89	10	7	-1	.987	-4	D-467,1-131	6.4

■ DAVE PHILLEY
Philley, David Earl b: 5/16/20, Paris, Tex. BB/TR, 6', 188 lbs. Deb: 9/6/41

YEAR	TM/L	G	AB	R	H	2B	3B	HR	RBI	BB	SO	AVG	OBP	SLG	PRO+	BR/A	SB	CS	SBR	FA	FR	G/POS	TPR
1941	Chi-A	7	9	4	2	1	0	0	0	3	3	.222	.417	.333	102	0	0	0	0	.000	-1	/O-2	-0.1
1946	Chi-A	17	68	10	24	2	3	0	17	4	4	.353	.389	.471	145	4	5	0	2	.983	5	O-17	1.0
1947	Chi-A	143	551	55	142	25	11	2	45	35	39	.258	.303	.354	85	-13	21	16	-3	.986	2	*O-133/3-4	-2.2
1948	Chi-A	137	488	51	140	28	3	5	42	50	33	.287	.353	.387	100	-0	8	10	-4	.978	15	*O-128	0.4
1949	Chi-A	146	598	84	171	20	8	0	44	54	51	.286	.347	.346	86	-12	13	4	2	.977	2	*O-145	-1.6
1950	Chi-A	156	619	69	150	21	5	14	80	52	57	.242	.302	.360	71	-30	6	3	0	.980	1	*O-154	-3.3
1951	Chi-A	7	25	0	6	2	0	0	2	2	3	.240	.296	.320	68	-1	0	0	0	.938	-0	/O-6	-0.2
	Phi-A	125	468	71	123	18	7	7	59	63	38	.263	.354	.376	95	-2	9	6	-1	.978	2	*O-120/3-2	-0.6
	Yr	132	493	71	129	20	7	7	61	65	41	.262	.351	.373	94	-3	9	6	-1	.976	2	*O-126/3-2	-0.8
1952	Phi-A	151	586	80	154	25	4	7	71	59	35	.263	.334	.355	86	-10	11	4	1	.991	13	*O-149/3-2	-0.3
1953	Phi-A	157	620	80	188	30	9	9	59	51	35	.303	.358	.424	106	5	13	5	1	.981	-4	*O-157/3-1	-0.4
1954	*Cle-A	133	452	48	102	13	3	12	60	57	48	.226	.312	.347	79	-13	2	4	-2	.984	-4	*O-129	-2.5
1955	Cle-A	43	104	15	31	4	2	2	9	12	10	.298	.371	.433	111	2	0	2	-1	1.000	-3	O-34	-0.3
	Bal-A	83	311	50	93	13	3	6	41	34	38	.299	.368	.418	119	8	1	2	-1	.970	-7	O-82/3-2	-0.3
	Yr	126	415	65	124	17	5	8	50	46	48	.299	.369	.422	116	9	1	4	-2	.976	-9	*O-116/3-2	-0.6
1956	Bal-A	32	117	13	24	4	2	1	17	18	13	.205	.311	.299	67	-6	3	1	0	.935	-4	O-31/3-5	-1.1
	Chi-A	86	279	44	74	14	2	4	47	28	27	.265	.334	.373	85	-6	1	3	-2	.978	-9	1-51,O-30	-2.0
	Yr	118	396	57	98	18	4	5	64	46	40	.247	.327	.351	80	-11	4	4	-1	.965	-13	O-61,1-51/3-5	-3.1
1957	Chi-A	22	71	9	23	4	0	0	9	4	10	.324	.360	.380	102	0	1	1	-0	.975	1	O-17/1-2	-0.1
	Det-A	65	173	15	49	8	1	2	16	7	16	.283	.311	.376	85	-4	3	1	0	.996	1	1-27,O-12/3-1	-0.5
	Yr	87	244	24	72	12	1	2	25	11	26	.295	.325	.377	90	-4	4	2	0	.965	2	O-29,1-29/3-1	-0.6
1958	Phi-N	91	207	30	64	11	4	3	31	15	20	.309	.359	.444	113	4	1	1	-0	1.000	-4	O-24,1-18	-0.2
1959	Phi-N	99	254	32	74	18	2	7	37	18	27	.291	.341	.461	109	3	0	0	0	1.000	1	O-34,1-24	0.1
1960	Phi-N	14	15	2	5	2	0	0	4	3	2	.333	.444	.467	149	1	0	0	0	.000	-2	/O-3,1-2	-0.1
	SF-N	39	61	5	10	0	0	1	7	6	14	.164	.239	.213	26	-6	0	0	0	.941	-1	O-10/3-3	-0.8
	Yr	53	76	7	15	2	0	1	11	9	16	.197	.282	.263	53	-5	0	0	0	.941	-3	O-13/3-3,1-2	-0.9
	Bal-A	14	34	6	9	2	1	1	5	4	5	.265	.342	.471	119	1	1	0	0	1.000	-0	/O-8,3-1	0.0
1961	Bal-A	99	144	13	36	9	2	1	23	10	20	.250	.299	.361	78	-5	2	0	1	1.000	-6	O-25/1-1	-1.1
1962	Bos-A	38	42	3	6	2	0	0	4	5	3	.143	.250	.190	20	-5	0	0	0	1.000	-0	/O-4	-0.5
Total	18	1904	6296	789	1700	276	72	84	729	594	551	.270	.335	.377	91	-86	101	63	-8	.981	-0	*O-1454,1-125/3-21	-16.7

■ ADOLFO PHILLIPS
Phillips, Adolfo Emilio (Lopez) b: 12/16/41, Bethania, Panama BR/TR, 6', 177 lbs. Deb: 9/2/64

YEAR	TM/L	G	AB	R	H	2B	3B	HR	RBI	BB	SO	AVG	OBP	SLG	PRO+	BR/A	SB	CS	SBR	FA	FR	G/POS	TPR
1964	Phi-N	13	13	4	3	0	0	0	0	3	3	.231	.375	.231	76	-0	0	0	0	1.000	-0	/O-4	-0.1
1965	Phi-N	41	87	14	20	4	0	3	5	5	34	.230	.272	.379	83	-2	3	3	-1	1.000	-4	O-32	-0.8
1966	Phi-N	2	3	1	0	0	0	0	0	0	0	.000	.000	.000	-99	-1	0	0	0	1.000	-0	/O-1	-0.1
	Chi-N	116	416	68	109	29	1	16	36	43	135	.262	.348	.452	119	11	32	15	1	.978	12	*O-111	1.9
	Yr	118	419	69	109	29	1	16	36	43	135	.260	.346	.449	118	10	32	15	1	.979	12	*O-112	1.8
1967	Chi-N	144	448	66	120	20	7	17	70	80	93	.268	.386	.458	134	23	24	10	1	.981	15	*O-141	3.4
1968	Chi-N	143	439	49	106	20	5	13	33	47	90	.241	.322	.399	108	5	9	7	-2	.979	6	*O-141	0.3

YEAR	TM/L	G	AB	R	H	2B	3B	HR	RBI	BB	SO	AVG	OBP	SLG	PRO+	BR/A	SB	CS	SBR	FA	FR	G/POS	TPR
1969	Chi-N	28	49	5	11	3	1	0	1	16	15	.224	.424	.327	100	1	1	3	-2	.956	-3	O-25	-0.4
	Mon-N	58	199	25	43	4	4	4	7	19	62	.216	.288	.337	74	-7	6	5	-1	.981	-1	O-53	-1.3
	Yr	86	248	30	54	7	5	4	8	35	77	.218	.319	.335	80	-6	7	8	-3	.973	-3	O-78	-1.7
1970	Mon-N	92	214	36	51	6	3	6	21	36	51	.238	.353	.379	96	-0	7	1	2	.985	-6	O-75	-0.8
1972	Cle-A	12	7	2	0	0	0	0	0	2	2	.000	.222	.000	-29	-1	0	0	0	1.000	-3	O-10	-0.4
Total	8	649	1875	270	463	86	21	59	173	251	485	.247	.344	.410	110	27	82	44	-2	.980	17	O-593	1.7

■ J. R. PHILLIPS
Phillips, Charles Gene b: 4/29/70, West Covina, Cal. BL/TL, 6'1", 185 lbs. Deb: 9/3/93

YEAR	TM/L	G	AB	R	H	2B	3B	HR	RBI	BB	SO	AVG	OBP	SLG	PRO+	BR/A	SB	CS	SBR	FA	FR	G/POS	TPR
1993	SF-N	11	16	1	5	1	1	1	4	0	5	.313	.313	.688	164	1	0	0	0	.971	0	/1-5	0.1
1994	SF-N	15	38	1	5	0	0	1	3	1	13	.132	.154	.211	-7	-6	1	0	0	.989	1	1-10	-0.5
1995	SF-N	92	231	27	45	9	0	9	28	19	69	.195	.256	.351	60	-14	1	1	-0	.993	-2	1-79/O-1	-2.2
1996	SF-N	15	25	3	5	0	0	2	5	1	13	.200	.231	.440	75	-1	0	0	0	.981	-1	1-10	-0.2
	Phi-N	35	79	9	12	5	0	5	10	10	38	.152	.256	.405	70	-4	0	0	0	.957	3	O-15,1-11	-0.2
	Yr	50	104	12	17	5	0	7	15	11	51	.163	.250	.413	71	-5	0	0	0	.992	3	1-21,O-15	-0.4
1997	Hou-N	13	15	2	2	0	0	1	4	0	7	.133	.133	.333	18	-2	0	0	0	1.000	-1	/1-3,O-3	-0.3
1998	Hou-N	36	58	4	11	0	0	2	9	7	22	.190	.277	.293	49	-4	0	0	0	.962	-2	1-12/O-6	-0.7
Total	6	217	462	47	85	15	1	21	63	38	167	.184	.248	.357	58	-30	2	1	0	.989	-1	1-130/O-25	-4.0

■ DAMON PHILLIPS
Phillips, Damon Roswell "Dee" b: 6/8/19, Corsicana, Tex. BR/TR, 6', 176 lbs. Deb: 7/19/42

YEAR	TM/L	G	AB	R	H	2B	3B	HR	RBI	BB	SO	AVG	OBP	SLG	PRO+	BR/A	SB	CS	SBR	FA	FR	G/POS	TPR
1942	Cin-N	28	84	4	17	2	0	0	6	7	5	.202	.264	.226	44	-6	0			.964	7	S-27	0.3
1944	Bos-N	140	489	35	126	30	1	1	53	28	34	.258	.301	.329	74	-17	1			.932	-4	3-90,S-60	-1.6
1946	Bos-N	2	2	0	1	0	0	0	0	0	0	.500	.500	.500	182	0	0			.000	0	H	0.0
Total	3	170	575	39	144	32	1	1	59	35	39	.250	.296	.315	70	-23	1			.956	3	/3-90,S-87	-1.3

■ EDDIE PHILLIPS
Phillips, Edward David b: 2/17/01, Worcester, Mass. d: 1/26/68, Buffalo, N.Y. BR/TR, 6', 178 lbs. Deb: 5/4/24

YEAR	TM/L	G	AB	R	H	2B	3B	HR	RBI	BB	SO	AVG	OBP	SLG	PRO+	BR/A	SB	CS	SBR	FA	FR	G/POS	TPR
1924	Bos-N	3	3	0	0	0	0	0	0	0	2	.000	.000	.000	-99	-1	0	0	0	1.000	0	/C-1	-0.1
1929	Det-A	68	221	24	52	13	1	2	21	20	16	.235	.302	.330	62	-13	0	1	-1	.967	-5	C-63	-1.2
1931	Pit-N	106	353	30	82	18	3	7	44	41	49	.232	.317	.360	82	-9	1			.986	-7	*C-103	-0.8
1932	NY-A	9	31	4	9	1	0	2	4	2	3	.290	.333	.516	123	1	1	0	0	1.000	1	/C-9	0.2
1934	Was-A	56	169	6	33	6	1	2	16	26	24	.195	.306	.278	54	-12	1	0	0	.984	-7	C-53	-1.5
1935	Cle-A	70	220	18	60	16	1	1	41	15	21	.273	.319	.368	76	-8	0	0	0	.980	-8	C-69	-1.3
Total	6	312	997	82	236	54	6	14	126	104	115	.237	.312	.345	72	-41	3	1		.980	-27	C-298	-4.7

■ EDDIE PHILLIPS
Phillips, Howard Edward b: 7/8/31, St.Louis, Mo. BB/TR, 6'1", 180 lbs. Deb: 9/10/53

YEAR	TM/L	G	AB	R	H	2B	3B	HR	RBI	BB	SO	AVG	OBP	SLG	PRO+	BR/A	SB	CS	SBR	FA	FR	G/POS	TPR
1953	StL-N	9	0	4	0	0	0	0	0	0	0	—	—	—	—	0	0	0	0	.000	0	R	0.0

■ JACK PHILLIPS
Phillips, Jack Dorn "Stretch" b: 9/6/21, Clarence, N.Y. BR/TR, 6'4", 193 lbs. Deb: 8/22/47

YEAR	TM/L	G	AB	R	H	2B	3B	HR	RBI	BB	SO	AVG	OBP	SLG	PRO+	BR/A	SB	CS	SBR	FA	FR	G/POS	TPR
1947	*NY-A	16	36	5	10	0	1	1	2	3	5	.278	.333	.417	109	0	0	0	0	.986	-2	1-10	-0.2
1948	NY-A	1	2	0	0	0	0	0	0	0	1	.000	.000	.000	-99	-1	0	0	0	.889	-0	/1-1	-0.1
1949	NY-A	45	91	16	28	4	1	1	10	12	9	.308	.388	.407	110	2	1	0	0	.977	-2	1-38	0.0
	Pit-N	18	56	6	13	3	1	0	3	4	6	.232	.283	.321	60	-3	1			1.000	-0	1-16/3-1	-0.3
1950	Pit-N	69	208	25	61	7	6	5	34	20	17	.293	.355	.457	108	2	1			.986	2	1-54/3-3,P-1	0.3
1951	Pit-N	70	156	12	37	7	3	0	12	15	17	.237	.304	.321	66	-7	1	2	-1	.991	-1	1-53/3-4	-1.1
1952	Pit-N	1	1	0	0	0	0	0	0	0	0	.000	.000	.000	-97	-0	0	0	0	1.000	-0	/1-1	0.0
1955	Det-A	55	117	15	37	8	2	1	20	10	12	.316	.370	.444	121	3	0	0	0	.992	-1	1-35/3-3	0.0
1956	Det-A	67	224	31	66	13	2	1	20	21	19	.295	.355	.384	95	-2	1	1	-0	.981	-1	1-56/2-1,O-1	-0.7
1957	Det-A	1	1	1	0	0	0	0	0	0	0	.000	.000	.000	-97	-0	0	0	0	.000	0	H	0.0
Total	9	343	892	111	252	42	16	9	101	85	86	.283	.345	.396	95	-6	5	3		.986	-6	1-264/3-11,O-1,2P	-2.1

■ BUBBA PHILLIPS
Phillips, John Melvin b: 2/24/28, West Point, Miss. d: 6/22/93, Hattiesburg, Miss. BR/TR, 5'9", 180 lbs. Deb: 4/30/55

YEAR	TM/L	G	AB	R	H	2B	3B	HR	RBI	BB	SO	AVG	OBP	SLG	PRO+	BR/A	SB	CS	SBR	FA	FR	G/POS	TPR
1955	Det-A	95	184	18	43	4	0	3	23	14	20	.234	.295	.304	63	-10	2	1	0	.992	-1	O-65/3-4	-1.3
1956	Chi-A	67	99	16	27	6	0	2	11	6	12	.273	.321	.394	87	-2	1	2	-1	1.000	-1	O-35/3-2	-0.5
1957	Chi-A	121	393	38	106	13	3	7	42	28	32	.270	.323	.372	89	-6	5	3	-0	.958	16	3-97,O-20	1.0
1958	Chi-A	84	260	26	71	10	0	5	30	15	14	.273	.315	.369	89	-4	3	0	1	.954	7	3-47,O-37	0.2
1959	*Chi-A	117	379	43	100	27	1	5	40	27	28	.264	.320	.380	92	-4	1	1	-0	.951	3	*3-100,O-23	-0.3
1960	Cle-A	113	304	34	63	14	1	4	33	14	37	.207	.252	.299	50	-22	1	0	0	.953	-8	3-85,O-25/S-1	-3.2
1961	Cle-A	143	546	64	144	23	1	18	72	29	61	.264	.307	.408	92	-8	1	0	0	.958	-18	*3-143	-2.5
1962	Cle-A	148	562	53	145	26	0	10	54	20	55	.258	.292	.358	76	-20	4	0	1	.977	-15	*3-145/O-3,2-1	-3.3
1963	Det-A	128	464	42	114	11	2	5	45	19	42	.246	.281	.310	63	-22	6	2	1	.961	1	*3-117/O-5	-2.2
1964	Det-A	46	87	14	22	1	0	3	6	10	13	.253	.330	.368	92	-1	1	2	-1	.983	2	3-22/O-1	0.0
Total	10	1062	3278	348	835	135	8	62	356	182	314	.255	.300	.358	79	-100	25	11	1	.960	-16	3-762,O-214/2-1,S-1	-12.1

■ JACK PHILLIPS
Phillips, John Stephen b: 5/24/19, St.Louis, Mo. d: 6/16/58, St.Louis, Mo. BR/TR, 6'1", 185 lbs. Deb: 7/13/45

YEAR	TM/L	G	AB	R	H	2B	3B	HR	RBI	BB	SO	AVG	OBP	SLG	PRO+	BR/A	SB	CS	SBR	FA	FR	G/POS	TPR
1945	NY-N	2	2	1	1	0	0	0	0	0	0	.500	.500	.500	176	0	0			1.000	-0	/P-1	0.0

■ TONY PHILLIPS
Phillips, Keith Anthony b: 4/25/59, Atlanta, Ga. BB/TR, 5'10", 175 lbs. Deb: 5/10/82

YEAR	TM/L	G	AB	R	H	2B	3B	HR	RBI	BB	SO	AVG	OBP	SLG	PRO+	BR/A	SB	CS	SBR	FA	FR	G/POS	TPR
1982	Oak-A	40	81	11	17	2	2	0	8	12	26	.210	.326	.284	73	-3	2	3	-1	.953	-5	S-39	-0.5
1983	Oak-A	148	412	54	102	12	3	4	35	48	70	.248	.329	.320	85	-8	16	5	2	.941	1	*S-101,2-63/3-4,D-1	0.5
1984	Oak-A	154	451	62	120	24	3	4	37	42	86	.266	.329	.359	97	-2	10	6	-1	.941	-11	S-91,2-90/O-1	-0.4
1985	Oak-A	42	161	23	45	12	2	4	17	13	34	.280	.333	.453	122	4	3	2	-0	.980	-0	3-31,2-24	0.4
1986	Oak-A	118	441	76	113	14	5	5	52	76	82	.256	.369	.345	103	5	15	10	-2	.976	1	2-88,3-30/O-4,SD	0.7
1987	Oak-A	111	379	48	91	20	0	10	46	57	76	.240	.339	.372	95	-2	7	6	-2	.974	-3	2-87,3-11/S-9,OD	-0.1
1988	*Oak-A	79	212	32	43	8	4	2	17	36	50	.203	.321	.307	80	-5	0	2	-1	.913	-20	3-32,O-31,2S/1D	-2.6
1989	*Oak-A	143	451	48	118	15	6	4	47	58	66	.262	.350	.348	101	2	3	8	-4	.985	-24	2-84,3-49,S-17,O/1	-2.3
1990	Det-A	152	573	97	144	23	5	8	55	99	85	.251	.365	.351	100	4	19	9	0	.931	6	*3-104,2-47,S/OD	1.3
1991	Det-A	146	564	87	160	28	4	17	72	79	95	.284	.375	.438	122	19	10	5	0	.992	6	O-56,3-46,2-36,DS	2.5
1992	Det-A	159	606	**114**	167	32	3	10	64	114	93	.276	.391	.388	118	20	12	10	-2	.968	4	O-69,2-57,D-34,3/S	2.0
1993	Det-A	151	566	113	177	27	0	7	57	**132**	102	.313	.446	.398	130	33	16	11	-2	.969	-1	*O-108,2-51/3-1,D-4	2.9
1994	Det-A	114	438	91	123	19	3	19	61	95	105	.281	.411	.468	126	20	13	5	1	.980	7	*O-104,2-12/D-6	2.4
1995	Cal-A	139	525	119	137	21	1	27	61	113	135	.261	.395	.459	122	21	13	10	-2	.924	4	3-88,O-48/D-2	2.0
1996	Chi-A	153	581	119	161	29	3	12	63	**125**	132	.277	.408	.399	111	16	13	8	-1	.981	16	*O-150/2-2,1-1	2.4
1997	Chi-A	36	129	23	40	6	0	2	9	29	29	.310	.440	.403	127	7	4	1	1	.972	2	O-28/3-9	0.9
	Ana-A	105	405	73	107	28	2	6	48	73	89	.264	.379	.388	101	3	9	9	-3	.968	-15	2-43,O-35,D-26,/3-1	-1.4
	Yr	141	534	96	147	34	2	8	57	102	118	.275	.394	.391	107	10	13	10	-2	.970	-13	O-63,2-43,D-26,3-10	-0.5
1998	Tor-A	13	48	9	17	5	0	1	7	9	6	.354	.475	.521	159	5	0	0	0	.960	-1	O-13	0.3
	NY-N	52	188	25	42	11	0	3	14	38	44	.223	.354	.330	80	-5	1	1	-0	.967	-1	O-51	-0.7
Total	17	2055	7211	1224	1924	336	46	145	770	1248	1405	.267	.378	.386	109	136	166	111	-17	.975	-34	O-724,2-711,3SD/1	10.3

■ MARR PHILLIPS
Phillips, Marr B. b: 6/16/1857, Pittsburgh, Pa. d: 4/1/28, Pittsburgh, Pa. BR, 5'6.5", 164 lbs. Deb: 5/1/1884

YEAR	TM/L	G	AB	R	H	2B	3B	HR	RBI	BB	SO	AVG	OBP	SLG	PRO+	BR/A	SB	CS	SBR	FA	FR	G/POS	TPR
1884	Ind-a	97	413	41	111	18	8	0		5		.269	.279	.351	107	3				.862	14	*S-97	1.6
1885	Det-N	33	139	13	29	5	0	0	17	0	13	.209	.209	.245	46	-8				.881	2	S-33	-0.5
	Pit-a	4	15	1	4	0	0	0	2	2		.267	.353	.267	99	0				.875	-1	/S-4	-0.1
1890	Roc-a	64	257	18	53	8	0	0	34	16		.206	.261	.237	51	-16	10			.918	6	S-64	-0.6
Total	3	198	824	73	197	31	8	0	53	23	13	.239	.263	.296	79	-21	10			.884	21	S-198	0.4

■ MIKE PHILLIPS
Phillips, Michael Dwaine b: 8/19/50, Beaumont, Tex. BL/TR, 6'1", 185 lbs. Deb: 4/15/73

YEAR	TM/L	G	AB	R	H	2B	3B	HR	RBI	BB	SO	AVG	OBP	SLG	PRO+	BR/A	SB	CS	SBR	FA	FR	G/POS	TPR
1973	SF-N	63	104	18	25	3	4	1	9	6	17	.240	.288	.375	79	-3	0	3	-2	.931	-0	3-28,S-20/2-7	-0.4
1974	SF-N	100	283	19	62	6	1	2	20	14	37	.219	.258	.269	45	-21	4	5	-2	.909	4	3-34,2-30,S-23	-1.6
1975	SF-N	10	31	3	6	0	0	0	1	6	4	.194	.324	.194	44	-2	1	0	0	.969	4	/2-6,3-6	0.2
	NY-N	116	383	31	98	10	7	1	28	25	47	.256	.303	.326	78	-12	3	0	1	.944	1	*S-115/2-1	0.1
	Yr	126	414	34	104	10	7	1	29	31	51	.251	.305	.316	76	-14	4	0	1	.944	4	*S-115/2-7,3-6	0.3
1976	NY-N	87	262	30	67	4	6	4	29	25	29	.256	.321	.363	99	-1	2	2	-1	.955	-9	S-53,2-19,3-10	-0.4

YEAR	TM/L	G	AB	R	H	2B	3B	HR	RBI	BB	SO	AVG	OBP	SLG	PRO+	BR/A	SB	CS	SBR	FA	FR	G/POS	TPR
1977	NY-N	38	86	5	18	2	1	1	3	2	15	.209	.244	.291	45	-7	0	1	-1	1.000	-5	S-24/3-9,2-4	-1.1
	StL-N	48	87	17	21	3	2	0	9	9	13	.241	.320	.322	74	-3	1	0	0	.971	5	2-31/S-5,3-5	0.4
	Yr	86	173	22	39	5	3	1	12	11	28	.225	.283	.306	60	-10	1	1	-0	.973	1	2-35,S-29,3-14	-0.7
1978	StL-N	76	164	14	44	8	1	1	28	13	25	.268	.330	.348	91	-2	0	0	0	.971	-1	2-55,S-10/3-1	0.1
1979	StL-N	44	97	10	22	3	1	1	6	10	9	.227	.306	.309	68	-4	0	0	0	.973	13	S-25,2-16/3-1	1.1
1980	StL-N	63	128	13	30	5	0	0	7	9	17	.234	.285	.273	55	-8	0	0	0	.971	13	S-37/2-9,3-8	0.9
1981	SD-N	14	29	1	6	0	1	0	0	0	3	.207	.207	.276	39	-2	1	0	0	.979	4	/2-9,S-1	0.2
	*Mon-N	34	55	5	12	2	0	0	4	5	15	.218	.283	.255	53	-3	0	1	-1	.974	0	S-26/2-6	-0.2
	Yr	48	84	6	18	2	1	0	4	5	18	.214	.258	.262	49	-6	1	1	-0	.974	4	S-27,2-15	0.0
1982	Mon-N	14	8	0	1	0	0	0	1	0	3	.125	.125	.125	-29	-1	0	0	0	1.000	3	2-10/S-2	0.1
1983	Mon-N	5	2	0	0	0	0	0	0	0	0	.000	.000	.000	-99	-1	0	0	0	.000	-1	/S-3,3-2	-0.2
Total	11	712	1719	166	412	46	24	11	145	124	234	.240	.294	.314	70	-70	12	12	-4	.956	29	S-344,2-203,3-104	-0.8

■ DICK PHILLIPS

Phillips, Richard Eugene b: 11/24/31, Racine, Wis. d: 3/29/98, Burnaby, B.C., Canada BL/TR, 6', 180 lbs. Deb: 4/15/62 C

YEAR	TM/L	G	AB	R	H	2B	3B	HR	RBI	BB	SO	AVG	OBP	SLG	PRO+	BR/A	SB	CS	SBR	FA	FR	G/POS	TPR
1962	SF-N	5	3	1	0	0	0	0	1	1	1	.000	.250	.000	-27	-1	0	0	0	1.000	-0	/1-1	-0.1
1963	Was-A	124	321	33	76	8	0	10	32	29	35	.237	.304	.355	84	-7	1	0	0	.994	4	1-68/2-5,3-4	-0.6
1964	Was-A	109	234	17	54	6	1	2	23	27	22	.231	.313	.291	70	-9	1	2	-1	.994	2	1-61/3-4	-1.1
1966	Was-A	25	37	3	6	0	0	0	4	2	5	.162	.225	.162	13	-4	0	0	0	1.000	-1	/1-5	-0.5
Total	4	263	595	54	136	14	1	12	60	59	63	.229	.302	.316	74	-20	2	2	-1	.995	5	1-135/3-8,2-5	-2.3

■ BILL PHILLIPS

Phillips, William B. b: 1857, St.John, N.B., Canada d: 10/7/1900, Chicago, Ill. BR/TR, 202 lbs. Deb: 5/1/1879

YEAR	TM/L	G	AB	R	H	2B	3B	HR	RBI	BB	SO	AVG	OBP	SLG	PRO+	BR/A	SB	CS	SBR	FA	FR	G/POS	TPR
1879	Cle-N	81	365	58	99	15	4	0	29	2	20	.271	.275	.334	101	0				.954	-5	*1-75,C-11/O-2	-0.6
1880	Cle-N	85	334	41	85	14	10	1	36	6	29	.254	.268	.365	115	5				.963	2	*1-85	-0.1
1881	Cle-N	85	357	51	97	18	10	1	44	5	19	.272	.282	.387	114	5				.966	-1	*1-85	-0.3
1882	Cle-N	78	335	40	87	17	7	4	47	7	18	.260	.275	.388	114	5				.971	3	*1-78/C-1	-0.1
1883	Cle-N	97	382	42	94	29	8	2	40	8	49	.246	.262	.380	93	-3				.967	-2	*1-97	-1.4
1884	Cle-N	111	464	58	128	25	12	3	46	18	80	.276	.303	.401	115	7				.959	-2	*1-111	-0.7
1885	Bro-a	99	391	65	118	16	11	3	63	27		.302	.364	.422	147	21				**.973**	0	*1-99	0.8
1886	Bro-a	141	585	68	160	26	15	0	72	33		.274	.313	.369	113	6	13			.978	-2	*1-141	-1.1
1887	Bro-a	132	533	82	142	34	11	2	101	45		.266	.330	.383	97	-3	16			**.982**	4	*1-132	-1.0
1888	KC-a	129	509	57	120	20	10	1	56	27		.236	.284	.320	88	-9	10			.980	3	*1-129	-1.7
Total	10	1038	4255	562	1130	214	98	17	534	178	215	.266	.299	.374	109	35	39			.971	1	*1-1032/C-12,O-2	-6.2

■ BILL PHYLE

Phyle, William Joseph b: 6/25/1875, Duluth, Minn. d: 8/6/53, Los Angeles, Cal. TR, Deb: 9/17/1898

YEAR	TM/L	G	AB	R	H	2B	3B	HR	RBI	BB	SO	AVG	OBP	SLG	PRO+	BR/A	SB	CS	SBR	FA	FR	G/POS	TPR
1898	Chi-N	4	9	1	1	0	0	0	0	2		.111	.273	.111	11	-1	0			.800	-1	/P-3	0.0
1899	Chi-N	10	34	2	6	0	0	0	1	0		.176	.176	.176	-3	-5	0			.935	1	P-10	0.0
1901	NY-N	25	66	8	12	2	0	0	3	2		.182	.206	.212	22	-7	0			.903	1	P-24/S-1	0.0
1906	StL-N	22	73	6	13	3	1	0	4	5		.178	.231	.247	51	-4	2			.935	2	3-21	-0.2
Total	4	61	182	17	32	5	1	0	8	9		.176	.215	.214	28	-17	2			.907	3	/P-37,3-21,S-1	-0.2

■ MIKE PIAZZA

Piazza, Michael Joseph b: 9/4/68, Norristown, Pa. BR/TR, 6'3", 197 lbs. Deb: 9/1/92

YEAR	TM/L	G	AB	R	H	2B	3B	HR	RBI	BB	SO	AVG	OBP	SLG	PRO+	BR/A	SB	CS	SBR	FA	FR	G/POS	TPR
1992	LA-N	21	69	5	16	3	0	1	7	4	12	.232	.284	.319	71	-3	0	0	0	.990	-2	C-16	-0.4
1993	LA-N★	149	547	81	174	24	2	35	112	46	86	.318	.374	.561	155	41	3	4	-2	.989	5	*C-146/1-1	5.1
1994	LA-N★	107	405	64	129	18	0	24	92	33	65	.319	.371	.541	143	24	1	3	-2	.985	-12	*C-104	1.7
1995	*LA-N★	112	434	82	150	17	0	32	93	39	80	.346	.401	.606	**177**	46	1	0	0	.990	-9	*C-112	4.4
1996	*LA-N★	148	547	87	184	16	0	36	105	81	93	.336	.423	.563	171	57	0	3	-2	.992	-5	*C-146	5.6
1997	LA-N★	152	556	104	201	32	1	40	124	69	77	.362	.435	.638	**191**	**73**	5	1	1	.986	-4	*C-139/D-7	7.6
1998	LA-N	37	149	20	42	5	0	9	30	11	27	.282	.331	.497	120	4	0	0	0	.993	3	C-37	1.0
	Fla-N	5	18	1	5	0	1	0	5	0	0	.278	.278	.389	73	-1	0	0	0	.968	0	/C-4	0.0
	NY-N★	109	394	67	137	33	0	23	76	47	53	.348	.421	.607	164	38	1	0	0	.989	1	C-99/D-4	4.5
	Yr	151	561	88	184	38	1	32	111	58	80	.328	.394	.570	150	41	1	0	0	.990	4	*C-140/D-4	5.5
Total	7	840	3119	511	1038	148	4	200	644	330	493	.333	.399	.575	163	279	11	11	-3	.989	-23	C-803/D-11,1-1	29.5

■ ROB PICCIOLO

Picciolo, Robert Michael b: 2/4/53, Santa Monica, Cal. BR/TR, 6'2", 185 lbs. Deb: 4/9/77 C

YEAR	TM/L	G	AB	R	H	2B	3B	HR	RBI	BB	SO	AVG	OBP	SLG	PRO+	BR/A	SB	CS	SBR	FA	FR	G/POS	TPR
1977	Oak-A	148	419	35	84	12	3	2	22	9	55	.200	.219	.258	30	-41	1	4	-2	.966	7	*S-148	-2.3
1978	Oak-A	78	93	16	21	1	0	2	7	2	13	.226	.242	.301	55	-6	1	1	-0	.958	12	S-41,2-19,3-13	0.9
1979	Oak-A	115	348	37	88	16	2	2	27	3	45	.253	.261	.328	61	-20	2	1	0	.964	-3	*S-105/2-6,3-4,O-1	-1.2
1980	Oak-A	95	271	32	65	9	2	5	18	2	63	.240	.245	.343	64	-15	1	1	-0	.977	-23	S-49,2-47/O-1	-3.1
1981	*Oak-A	82	179	23	48	5	3	4	13	5	22	.268	.292	.397	102	-0	0	1	-1	.981	-15	S-82	-1.0
1982	Oak-A	18	49	3	11	1	0	0	3	1	10	.224	.240	.245	35	-4	1	0	0	.979	3	S-18	0.1
	Mil-A	22	21	7	6	1	0	0	1	1	4	.286	.318	.333	84	-0	0	0	0	1.000	2	2-11/S-6,D-1	0.1
	Yr	40	70	10	17	2	0	0	4	2	14	.243	.264	.271	50	-5	1	0	0	.973	5	S-24,2-11/D-1	0.2
1983	Mil-A	14	27	2	6	3	0	0	1	0	4	.222	.222	.333	55	-2	0	0	0	1.000	2	/S-7,2-2,3-2,1-1,D	0.1
1984	Cal-A	87	119	18	24	6	0	1	9	0	21	.202	.202	.277	31	-11	0	1	-1	.974	13	S-66,3-13/2-9,O-1	0.4
1985	Oak-A	71	102	19	28	2	0	1	8	2	17	.275	.288	.324	73	-4	3	2	-0	.889	7	3-19,2-17,1-13,D/S	0.3
Total	9	730	1628	192	381	56	10	17	109	25	254	.234	.247	.312	55	-103	9	11	-4	.970	6	S-531,2-111/31DO	-5.7

■ NICK PICCIUTO

Picciuto, Nicholas Thomas b: 8/27/21, Newark, N.J. d: 1/10/97, Winchester, Va. BR/TR, 5'8.5", 165 lbs. Deb: 5/11/45

YEAR	TM/L	G	AB	R	H	2B	3B	HR	RBI	BB	SO	AVG	OBP	SLG	PRO+	BR/A	SB	CS	SBR	FA	FR	G/POS	TPR
1945	Phi-N	36	89	7	12	6	0	0	6	6	17	.135	.189	.202	9	-11	0			.839	-6	3-30/2-4	-1.6

■ VAL PICINICH

Picinich, Valentine John b: 9/8/1896, New York, N.Y. d: 12/5/42, Nobleboro, Maine BR/TR, 5'9", 165 lbs. Deb: 7/25/16 C

YEAR	TM/L	G	AB	R	H	2B	3B	HR	RBI	BB	SO	AVG	OBP	SLG	PRO+	BR/A	SB	CS	SBR	FA	FR	G/POS	TPR
1916	Phi-A	40	118	8	23	3	1	0	5	6	33	.195	.234	.237	44	-9	1			.967	-0	C-37	-0.7
1917	Phi-A	2	6	0	2	0	0	0	0	1	2	.333	.429	.333	135	0	0			.786	-1	/C-2	-0.1
1918	Was-A	47	148	13	34	3	3	0	12	9	25	.230	.274	.291	72	-6	0			.960	-2	C-46	-0.4
1919	Was-A	80	212	18	58	12	3	3	22	17	43	.274	.330	.401	106	1	6			.978	15	C-69	2.1
1920	Was-A	48	133	14	27	6	2	3	14	9	33	.203	.259	.346	61	-8	0	0	0	.978	9	C-45	0.4
1921	Was-A	45	141	10	39	9	0	0	12	16	21	.277	.354	.340	82	-3	0	3	-2	.966	3	C-45	0.0
1922	Was-A	76	210	16	48	12	2	0	19	23	33	.229	.311	.305	64	-11	1	0	0	.976	7	C-76	0.0
1923	Bos-A	87	268	33	74	21	1	2	31	46	32	.276	.386	.384	103	3	3	5	-2	.957	-2	C-81	0.3
1924	Bos-A	69	161	25	44	6	3	1	24	29	19	.273	.394	.366	97	0	5	1	1	.951	-4	C-52	0.0
1925	Bos-A	90	251	31	64	21	0	1	25	33	21	.255	.344	.351	77	-9	2	0	1	.968	-8	C-74/1-2	-1.1
1926	Cin-N	89	240	33	63	16	1	2	31	29	22	.262	.342	.363	92	-2	4			.967	-0	C-86	0.2
1927	Cin-N	65	173	16	44	8	3	0	12	24	15	.254	.345	.335	85	-3	3			.980	5	C-61	0.6
1928	Cin-N	96	324	29	98	15	1	7	35	20	25	.302	.343	.420	100	-1	1			.983	-3	C-93	0.4
1929	Bro-N	93	273	28	71	16	6	4	31	34	24	.260	.342	.407	86	-6	3			.979	-4	C-85	-0.2
1930	Bro-N	23	46	4	10	3	0	0	3	5	6	.217	.294	.283	41	-4	1			.944	-2	C-22	-0.4
1931	Bro-N	24	45	5	12	4	0	1	4	4	9	.267	.327	.422	100	-0	1			.967	1	C-15	0.1
1932	Bro-N	41	70	8	18	6	0	1	11	4	8	.257	.297	.386	84	-2	0			.985	-2	C-24	-0.3
1933	Bro-N	6	6	1	1	1	0	0	0	0	1	.167	.167	.333	42	-0	0			.889	0	/C-6	0.0
	Pit-N	16	52	6	13	4	0	1	7	5	10	.250	.316	.385	99	-0	0			.982	-3	C-16	-0.2
	Yr	22	58	7	14	5	0	1	7	5	11	.241	.302	.379	95	-0	0			.969	-3	C-22	-0.2
Total	18	1037	2877	298	743	166	26	26	298	314	382	.258	.334	.361	86	-60	31	9		.970	11	C-935/1-2	0.7

■ CHARLIE PICK

Pick, Charles Thomas b: 4/10/1888, Brookneal, Va. d: 6/26/54, Lynchburg, Va. BL/TR, 5'10", 160 lbs. Deb: 9/20/14

YEAR	TM/L	G	AB	R	H	2B	3B	HR	RBI	BB	SO	AVG	OBP	SLG	PRO+	BR/A	SB	CS	SBR	FA	FR	G/POS	TPR
1914	Was-A	10	23	0	9	0	0	0	1	4	4	.391	.481	.391	157	2	1	2	-1	.833	-0	/O-7	0.0
1915	Was-A	3	2	0	0	0	0	0	0	0	0	.000	.000	.000	-98	-0	0			.000	0	H	-0.1
1916	Phi-A	121	398	29	96	10	3	0	20	40	24	.241	.315	.281	83	-8	25	16	-2	.899	4	*3-108/O-8	-0.3
1918	*Chi-N	29	89	13	29	4	1	0	12	14	4	.326	.417	.393	144	5	7			.964	-0	2-20/3-8	0.7
1919	Chi-N	75	269	27	65	8	6	0	18	14	12	.242	.292	.316	82	-6	17			.946	12	2-71/3-3	1.0
	Bos-N	34	114	12	29	1	1	1	7	7	5	.254	.325	.307	94	-0	4			.924	-2	2-21/3-5,O-3,1-2	-0.2
	Yr	109	383	39	94	9	7	1	25	21	17	.245	.302	.313	86	-6	21			.942	10	2-92/3-8,O-3,1-2	0.8

YEAR	TM/L	G	AB	R	H	2B	3B	HR	RBI	BB	SO	AVG	OBP	SLG	PRO+	BR/A	SB	CS	SBR	FA	FR	G/POS	TPR
1920	Bos-N	95	383	34	105	16	6	2	28	23	11	.274	.320	.363	100	-0	10	16	-7	.952	0	2-94	-0.4
Total	6	367	1278	115	333	39	17	3	86	102	60	.261	.323	.325	95	-8	64	34		.949	14	2-206,3-124/O-18,1	0.7

■ EDDIE PICK Pick, Edgar Everett b: 5/7/1899, Attleboro, Mass. d: 5/13/67, Santa Monica, Cal. BB/TR, 6', 185 lbs. Deb: 9/13/23

YEAR	TM/L	G	AB	R	H	2B	3B	HR	RBI	BB	SO	AVG	OBP	SLG	PRO+	BR/A	SB	CS	SBR	FA	FR	G/POS	TPR
1923	Cin-N	9	8	2	3	0	0	0	2	3	3	.375	.545	.375	150	1	0	0	0	1.000	-1	/O-4	-0.1
1924	Cin-N	3	2	0	0	0	0	0	0	0	1	.000	.000	.000	-99	-1	0	0	0	1.000	-0	/O-1	-0.1
1927	Chi-N	54	181	23	31	5	2	2	15	20	26	.171	.254	.254	36	-16	0			.910	-6	3-49/2-1,O-1	-2.0
Total	3	66	191	25	34	5	2	2	17	23	30	.178	.266	.257	40	-16	0	0		1.000	-8	/3-49,O-6,2-1	-2.2

■ CALVIN PICKERING Pickering, Calvin E. b: 9/29/76, St.Thomas, V.I. BL/TL, 6'5", 283 lbs. Deb: 9/12/98

YEAR	TM/L	G	AB	R	H	2B	3B	HR	RBI	BB	SO	AVG	OBP	SLG	PRO+	BR/A	SB	CS	SBR	FA	FR	G/POS	TPR
1998	Bal-A	9	21	4	5	0	0	2	3	3	4	.238	.333	.524	121	1	1	0	0	.969	-1	/1-5,D-3	0.0

■ OLLIE PICKERING Pickering, Oliver Daniel b: 4/9/1870, Olney, Ill. d: 1/20/52, Vincennes, Ind. BL/TR, 5'10", 175 lbs. Deb: 8/9/1896

YEAR	TM/L	G	AB	R	H	2B	3B	HR	RBI	BB	SO	AVG	OBP	SLG	PRO+	BR/A	SB	CS	SBR	FA	FR	G/POS	TPR
1896	Lou-N	45	165	28	50	6	4	1	22	12	11	.303	.350	.406	103	0	13			.901	3	O-45	0.0
1897	Lou-N	63	246	34	62	5	2	1	20	25		.252	.326	.301	68	-11	20			.937	5	O-62	-0.9
	Cle-N	46	182	33	64	5	2	1	22	11		.352	.392	.418	108	2	18			.950	-0	O-46/2-1	-0.1
	Yr	109	428	67	126	10	4	2	42	36		.294	.353	.350	86	-8	38			.943	4	*O-108/2-1	-1.0
1901	Cle-A	137	547	102	169	25	6	0	40	58		.309	.383	.377	116	15	36			.949	15	*O-137	1.7
1902	Cle-A	69	293	46	75	5	2	3	26	19		.256	.306	.317	76	-9	22			.979	-2	O-64/1-2	-1.6
1903	Phi-A	137	512	93	144	18	6	1	36	53		.281	.353	.346	105	5	40			.970	4	*O-135	0.0
1904	Phi-A	124	455	56	103	10	3	0	30	45		.226	.299	.262	74	-12	17			.939	-0	*O-121	-2.2
1907	StL-A	151	576	63	159	15	10	0	60	35		.276	.321	.337	110	6	15			.949	-11	*O-151	-1.2
1908	Was-A	113	373	45	84	7	4	2	30	28		.225	.285	.282	92	-4	13			.940	-8	O-98	-1.7
Total	8	885	3349	500	910	96	39	9	286	286	11	.272	.334	.332	97	-8	194			.949	5	O-859/1-2,2-1	-6.0

■ URBANE PICKERING Pickering, Urbane Henry "Pick" b: 6/3/1899, Hoxie, Kan. d: 5/13/70, Modesto, Cal. BR/TR, 5'10", 180 lbs. Deb: 4/18/31

YEAR	TM/L	G	AB	R	H	2B	3B	HR	RBI	BB	SO	AVG	OBP	SLG	PRO+	BR/A	SB	CS	SBR	FA	FR	G/POS	TPR
1931	Bos-A	103	341	48	86	13	4	9	52	33	53	.252	.318	.393	91	-5	3	4	-2	.967	-2	3-74,2-16	-0.3
1932	Bos-A	132	457	47	119	28	5	2	40	39	71	.260	.320	.357	77	-16	3	4	-2	.941	-7	*3-126/C-1	-1.5
Total	2	235	798	95	205	41	9	11	92	72	124	.257	.319	.372	83	-21	6	8	-3	.951	-9	3-200/2-16,C-1	-1.8

■ DAVE PICKETT Pickett, David T. b: 5/26/1874, Brookline, Mass. d: 4/22/50, Easton, Mass. 5'7.5", 170 lbs. Deb: 7/21/1898

YEAR	TM/L	G	AB	R	H	2B	3B	HR	RBI	BB	SO	AVG	OBP	SLG	PRO+	BR/A	SB	CS	SBR	FA	FR	G/POS	TPR
1898	Bos-N	14	43	3	12	1	0	0	3	6		.279	.380	.302	91	-0	2			.955	-2	O-14	-0.3

■ JOHN PICKETT Pickett, John Thomas b: 2/20/1866, Chicago, Ill. d: 7/4/22, Chicago, Ill. BR/TR, Deb: 6/6/1889

YEAR	TM/L	G	AB	R	H	2B	3B	HR	RBI	BB	SO	AVG	OBP	SLG	PRO+	BR/A	SB	CS	SBR	FA	FR	G/POS	TPR
1889	KC-a	53	201	20	45	7	0	0	12	11	21	.224	.271	.259	48	-14	7			.900	-16	O-28,3-14,2-11	-2.6
1890	Phi-P	100	407	82	114	7	9	4	64	40	17	.280	.347	.371	90	-7	12			.893	-22	*2-100	-1.8
1892	Bal-N	36	141	13	30	2	3	1	12	7	10	.213	.260	.291	65	-6	2			.915	-5	2-36	-1.0
Total	3	189	749	115	189	16	12	5	88	58	48	.252	.311	.326	75	-27	21			.900	-42	2-147/O-28,3-14	-5.4

■ TY PICKUP Pickup, Clarence William b: 10/29/1897, Philadelphia, Pa. d: 8/2/74, Philadelphia, Pa. BR/TR, 6', 180 lbs. Deb: 4/30/18

YEAR	TM/L	G	AB	R	H	2B	3B	HR	RBI	BB	SO	AVG	OBP	SLG	PRO+	BR/A	SB	CS	SBR	FA	FR	G/POS	TPR
1918	Phi-N	1	1	0	1	0	0	0	0	0	0	1.000	1.000	1.000	478	0	0			1.000	-0	/O-1	0.0

■ GRACIE PIERCE Pierce, Grayson S. b: New York, N.Y. d: 8/28/1894, New York, N.Y. BR/TR, Deb: 5/2/1882 U

YEAR	TM/L	G	AB	R	H	2B	3B	HR	RBI	BB	SO	AVG	OBP	SLG	PRO+	BR/A	SB	CS	SBR	FA	FR	G/POS	TPR
1882	Lou-a	9	33	3	10	1	0	0		1		.303	.324	.333	129	1				.864	1	/2-9	0.2
	Bal-a	41	151	8	30	2	1	0		3		.199	.214	.225	52	-7				.796	-10	2-38/O-3,S-1	-1.5
	Yr	50	184	11	40	3	1	0		4		.217	.234	.245	66	-6				.808	-9	2-47/O-3,S-1	-1.3
1883	Col-a	11	41	5	7	0	0	0		0		.171	.171	.171	11	-4				.744	-1	/2-6,O-5	-0.4
	NY-N	18	62	3	5	0	1	0	2	1	9	.081	.095	.113	-37	-10				.850	-2	O-18/2-1	-1.1
1884	NY-a	5	20	2	5	1	0	0		0		.250	.250	.300	81	-0				1.000	-5	/O-3,2-3	-0.5
Total	3	84	307	21	57	4	2	0	2	5	9	.186	.199	.212	36	-20				.795	-17	/2-57,O-29,S-1	-3.3

■ JACK PIERCE Pierce, Lavern Jack b: 6/2/48, Laurel, Miss. BL/TR, 6', 210 lbs. Deb: 4/27/73

YEAR	TM/L	G	AB	R	H	2B	3B	HR	RBI	BB	SO	AVG	OBP	SLG	PRO+	BR/A	SB	CS	SBR	FA	FR	G/POS	TPR
1973	Atl-N	11	20	0	1	0	0	0	0	1	8	.050	.095	.050	-55	-4	0	0	0	1.000	1	/1-6	-0.4
1974	Atl-N	6	9	1	1	0	0	0	0	1	1	.111	.200	.111	-11	-1	0	0	0	.958	0	/1-2	-0.1
1975	Det-A	53	170	19	40	6	1	8	22	20	40	.235	.323	.424	105	1	0	0	0	.971	-4	1-49	-0.7
Total	3	70	199	20	42	6	1	8	22	22	48	.211	.296	.372	83	-5	0	0	0	.973	-3	/1-57	-1.2

■ MAURY PIERCE Pierce, Maurice b: Baltimore, Md. Deb: 4/23/1884

YEAR	TM/L	G	AB	R	H	2B	3B	HR	RBI	BB	SO	AVG	OBP	SLG	PRO+	BR/A	SB	CS	SBR	FA	FR	G/POS	TPR
1884	Was-U	2	7	0	1	0	0	0		0		.143	.143	.143	-14	-1				.778	0	/3-2	-0.1

■ ANDY PIERCY Piercy, Andrew J. b: 8/1856, San Jose, Cal. d: 12/27/32, San Jose, Cal. TR, Deb: 5/12/1881

YEAR	TM/L	G	AB	R	H	2B	3B	HR	RBI	BB	SO	AVG	OBP	SLG	PRO+	BR/A	SB	CS	SBR	FA	FR	G/POS	TPR
1881	Chi-N	2	8	1	2	0	0	0	0	0	1	.250	.250	.250	55	-0				.750	-1	/3-1,2-1	-0.2

■ JIM PIERSALL Piersall, James Anthony b: 11/14/29, Waterbury, Conn. BR/TR, 6', 175 lbs. Deb: 9/7/50 C

YEAR	TM/L	G	AB	R	H	2B	3B	HR	RBI	BB	SO	AVG	OBP	SLG	PRO+	BR/A	SB	CS	SBR	FA	FR	G/POS	TPR
1950	Bos-A	6	7	4	2	0	0	0	0	4	0	.286	.545	.286	107	0	0	0	0	1.000	1	/O-2	0.1
1952	Bos-A	56	161	28	43	8	0	1	16	28	26	.267	.379	.335	93	-1	3	3	-1	.928	-6	S-30,O-22/3-1	-0.7
1953	Bos-A	151	585	76	159	21	9	3	52	41	52	.272	.329	.354	80	-16	11	10	-3	.987	16	*O-151	-0.9
1954	Bos-A★	133	474	77	135	24	2	8	38	36	42	.285	.339	.395	90	-7	5	1	1	.985	0	*O-126	-1.1
1955	Bos-A	149	515	68	146	25	5	13	62	67	52	.283	.368	.427	104	3	6	1	1	.993	13	*O-147	1.1
1956	Bos-A★	155	601	91	176	**40**	6	14	87	58	48	.293	.356	.449	99	-2	7	7	-2	**.991**	**18**	*O-155	0.5
1957	Bos-A	151	609	103	159	27	5	19	63	62	54	.261	.333	.415	98	-2	14	6	1	.990	13	*O-151	0.2
1958	Bos-A	130	417	55	99	13	5	8	48	42	43	.237	.307	.350	75	-14	12	2	2	.985	9	*O-125	-0.9
1959	Cle-A	100	317	42	78	13	2	4	30	25	31	.246	.305	.338	79	-9	6	3	0	.982	0	*O-91/3-1	-1.3
1960	Cle-A	138	486	70	137	12	4	18	66	24	38	.282	.316	.434	104	0	18	5	2	.992	10	*O-134	0.7
1961	Cle-A	121	484	81	156	26	7	6	40	43	46	.322	.380	.442	122	15	8	2	1	**.991**	16	*O-120	2.5
1962	Was-A	135	471	38	115	20	4	4	31	39	53	.244	.302	.329	70	-20	12	7	-1	**.997**	7	*O-132	-2.1
1963	Was-A	29	94	9	23	1	0	1	5	6	11	.245	.290	.287	63	-5	4	0	1	1.000	1	O-25	-0.4
	NY-N	40	124	13	24	4	1	1	10	10	14	.194	.254	.266	49	-8	1	2	-1	1.000	-2	O-38	-1.4
	LA-A	20	52	4	16	1	0	0	4	5	5	.308	.368	.327	103	0	0	1	-1	1.000	-2	O-18	-0.4
1964	LA-A	87	255	28	80	11	0	2	13	16	32	.314	.354	.380	116	5	5	3	-0	1.000	-6	O-72	-0.5
1965	Cal-A	53	112	10	30	5	2	2	12	5	15	.268	.305	.402	101	-0	2	2	-1	.984	-4	O-41	-0.6
1966	Cal-A	75	123	14	26	5	0	0	14	13	19	.211	.287	.252	58	-6	1	2	-1	.973	-10	O-63	-2.1
1967	Cal-A	5	3	0	0	0	0	0	0	0	2	.000	.000	.000	-99	-1	0	0	0	1.000	-0	/O-1	-0.1
Total	17	1734	5890	811	1604	256	52	104	591	524	583	.272	.334	.386	92	-66	115	57	0	.990	73	*O-1614/S-30,3-2	-7.4

■ DAVE PIERSON Pierson, David P. b: 8/20/1855, Newark, N.J. d: 11/11/22, Trenton, N.J. BR/TR, 5'7", 142 lbs. Deb: 4/25/1876 F

YEAR	TM/L	G	AB	R	H	2B	3B	HR	RBI	BB	SO	AVG	OBP	SLG	PRO+	BR/A	SB	CS	SBR	FA	FR	G/POS	TPR
1876	Cin-N	57	233	33	55	4	1	0	13	1	9	.236	.239	.262	78	-4				.760	-2	C-31,O-30/S-1,3P	-0.5

■ DICK PIERSON Pierson, Edmund Dana b: 10/24/1857, Wilkes-Barre, Pa. d: 7/20/22, Newark, N.J. TR, Deb: 6/23/1885 F

YEAR	TM/L	G	AB	R	H	2B	3B	HR	RBI	BB	SO	AVG	OBP	SLG	PRO+	BR/A	SB	CS	SBR	FA	FR	G/POS	TPR
1885	NY-a	3	9	1	1	0	0	0	0	2		.111	.273	.111	27	-1				.682	-2	/2-3	-0.2

■ A.J. PIERZYNSKI Pierzynski, Anthony John b: 12/30/76, Bridgehampton, N.Y. BL/TR, 6'3", 218 lbs. Deb: 9/9/98

YEAR	TM/L	G	AB	R	H	2B	3B	HR	RBI	BB	SO	AVG	OBP	SLG	PRO+	BR/A	SB	CS	SBR	FA	FR	G/POS	TPR
1998	Min-A	7	10	1	3	0	0	0	1	1	2	.300	.417	.300	91	-0	0	0	0	1.000	3	/C-6	0.3

■ TONY PIET Piet, Anthony Francis (b: Anthony Francis Pietruszka) b: 12/7/06, Berwick, Pa. d: 12/1/81, Hinsdale, Ill. BR/TR, 6', 175 lbs. Deb: 8/15/31

YEAR	TM/L	G	AB	R	H	2B	3B	HR	RBI	BB	SO	AVG	OBP	SLG	PRO+	BR/A	SB	CS	SBR	FA	FR	G/POS	TPR
1931	Pit-N	44	167	22	50	12	4	0	24	13	24	.299	.354	.419	108	2	10			.987	-4	2-44/S-1	0.0
1932	Pit-N	154	574	66	162	25	8	7	85	46	56	.282	.343	.390	98	-1	19			.970	-28	*2-154	-2.0
1933	Pit-N	107	362	45	117	21	5	1	42	19	28	.323	.367	.417	124	11	12			.955	-5	2-97	1.2
1934	Cin-N	106	421	58	109	20	5	1	38	23	44	.259	.307	.337	74	-15	6			.934	-10	3-51,2-49	-2.0
1935	Cin-N	6	5	2	1	1	0	0	2	0	0	.200	.200	.400	59	-0	0			1.000	-0	/O-1	-0.1
	Chi-A	77	292	47	87	17	5	3	27	33	27	.298	.375	.421	103	2	2	1	0	.975	4	2-59,3-17	1.0
1936	Chi-A	109	352	69	96	15	2	7	42	66	48	.273	.400	.386	92	-2	15	5	2	.966	6	2-68,3-32	0.9
1937	Chi-A	100	332	34	78	15	1	4	38	32	36	.235	.314	.322	61	-20	14	6	1	.939	2	3-86,2-13	-1.4

YEAR	TM/L	G	AB	R	H	2B	3B	HR	RBI	BB	SO	AVG	OBP	SLG	PRO+	BR/A	SB	CS	SBR	FA	FR	G/POS	TPR
1938	Det-A	41	80	9	17	6	0	0	14	15	11	.213	.351	.287	58	-5	2	4	-2	.919	0	3-18/2-1	-0.6
Total	8	744	2585	352	717	132	30	23	312	247	274	.277	.350	.378	91	-29	80	16		.967	-37	2-485,3-204/O-1,S-1	-3.0
■ SANDY PIEZ Piez, Charles William b: 10/13/1892, New York, N.Y. d: 12/29/30, Atlantic City, N.J BR/TR, 5'10", 170 lbs. Deb: 4/17/14																							
1914	NY-N	37	8	9	3	0	1	0	3	0	1	.375	.375	.625	202	1	4			1.000	-1	/O-5	0.0
■ JOE PIGNATANO Pignatano, Joseph Benjamin b: 8/4/29, Brooklyn, N.Y. BR/TR, 5'10", 180 lbs. Deb: 4/28/57 C																							
1957	Bro-N	8	14	0	3	1	0	0	1	0	5	.214	.214	.286	30	-1	0	0	0	1.000	3	/C-6	0.2
1958	LA-N	63	142	18	31	4	0	9	17	16	26	.218	.306	.437	91	-2	4	1	1	1.000	10	C-57	1.0
1959	*LA-N	52	139	17	33	4	1	1	11	21	15	.237	.346	.302	69	-5	1	0	0	.997	7	C-49	0.4
1960	LA-N	58	90	11	21	4	0	2	9	15	17	.233	.343	.344	83	-2	1	1	-0	.984	15	C-40	1.5
1961	KC-A	92	243	31	59	10	3	4	22	36	42	.243	.350	.358	88	-3	2	2	-1	.979	1	C-83/3-2	0.1
1962	SF-N	7	5	2	1	0	0	0	0	4	0	.200	.556	.200	114	1	0	0	0	1.000	-1	/C-7	0.0
	NY-N	27	56	2	13	2	0	0	2	2	11	.232	.259	.268	41	-5	0	0	0	.991	4	C-25	0.0
	Yr	34	61	4	14	2	0	0	2	6	11	.230	.299	.262	51	-4	0	0	0	.992	4	C-32	0.0
Total	6	307	689	81	161	25	4	16	62	94	116	.234	.332	.351	80	-18	8	4	0	.990	39	C-267/3-2	3.2
■ JAY PIKE Pike, Jacob Emanuel b: Brooklyn, N.Y. BL/TL, Deb: 8/27/1877 F																							
1877	Har-N	1	4	0	1	0	0	0	0	0	0	.250	.250	.250	65	-0				.000	-1	/O-1	-0.1
■ JESS PIKE Pike, Jess Willard b: 7/31/15, Dustin, Okla. d: 3/28/84, San Diego, Cal. BL/TR, 6'3", 175 lbs. Deb: 4/18/46																							
1946	NY-N	16	41	4	7	1	1	1	6	6	9	.171	.277	.317	68	-2	0			.929	-2	O-10	-0.5
■ LIP PIKE Pike, Lipman Emanuel b: 5/25/1845, New York, N.Y. d: 10/10/1893, Brooklyn, N.Y. BL/TL, 5'8", 158 lbs. Deb: 5/9/1871 FM																							
1871	Tro-n	28	130	43	49	10	7	**4**	39	5	7	.377	.400	.654	194	15	3	2	-0	.850	1	O-18/2-7,1-4,M	1.0
1872	Bal-n	56	288	67	84	15	5	**6**	**60**	3	6	.292	.299	.441	119	5	8	1	2	.875	-13	O-25,2-24/3-9	-0.6
1873	Bal-n	56	286	71	90	14	8	**4**	50	7	4	.315	.331	.462	134	11	8	1	2	.704	-3	*O-56/2-2	0.9
1874	Har-n	52	234	58	83	**22**	5	1	50	5	1	.355	.368	**.504**	168	16	4	1	1	.856	14	O-27,S-20/2-7,3M	2.3
1875	StL-n	70	312	61	108	22	12	0	44	3	8	.346	.352	.494	**210**	**34**	25	10	2	.885	-2	*O-64,2-10/3-2,S-1	2.9
1876	StL-N	63	282	55	91	19	10	1	50	8	9	.323	.341	.472	178	23				.896	-4	*O-62/2-2	1.6
1877	Cin-N	58	262	45	78	12	4	**4**	23	9	7	.298	.321	.420	148	15				.802	-3	O-38,2-22/S-2,M	1.0
1878	Cin-N	31	145	28	47	5	1	0	11	4	9	.324	.342	.372	149	8				.824	-4	O-31	0.2
	Pro-N	5	22	4	5	0	1	0	4	1	1	.227	.261	.318	90	-0				.788	-3	/2-5	-0.3
	Yr	36	167	32	52	5	2	0	15	5	10	.311	.331	.365	140	7				.824	-7	O-31/2-5	-0.1
1881	Wor-N	5	18	1	2	0	0	0	0	4	3	.111	.273	.111	24	-1				.647	-1	/O-5	-0.2
1887	NY-a	1	4	0	0	0	0	0	0	0		.000	.000	.000	-99	-1	0			1.000	-0	/O-1	-0.1
Total	5 n	262	1250	300	414	83	37	15	243	23	26	.331	.343	.493	160	81	48	15	5	.835	-3	O-190/2-50,S-21,31	6.5
Total	5	163	733	133	223	36	16	5	88	26	29	.304	.328	.417	152	43	0			.833	-15	O-137/2-29,S-2	2.2
■ AL PILARCIK Pilarcik, Alfred James b: 7/3/30, Whiting, Ind. BL/TL, 5'10", 180 lbs. Deb: 7/13/56																							
1956	KC-A	69	239	28	60	10	1	4	22	30	32	.251	.335	.351	81	-6	9	2	2	.976	3	O-67	-0.5
1957	Bal-A	142	407	52	113	16	3	9	49	53	28	.278	.366	.398	116	10	14	7	0	.996	0	*O-126	0.4
1958	Bal-A	141	379	40	92	21	0	1	24	42	37	.243	.322	.306	78	-11	7	3	0	.986	-14	*O-119	-3.1
1959	Bal-A	130	273	37	77	12	1	3	16	30	25	.282	.355	.366	101	1	9	3	1	.978	-16	*O-106	-1.7
1960	Bal-A	104	194	30	48	5	1	4	17	15	16	.247	.315	.345	79	-6	0	2	-1	1.000	-11	O-75	-2.0
1961	KC-A	35	60	9	12	1	1	0	9	6	7	.200	.273	.250	40	-5	1	0	0	1.000	-1	O-21	-0.7
	Chi-A	47	62	9	11	1	0	1	6	9	5	.177	.282	.242	42	-5	1	1	-0	.944	-0	O-17	-0.6
	Yr	82	122	18	23	2	1	1	15	15	12	.189	.277	.246	41	-10	2	1	0	.971	-1	O-38	-1.3
Total	6	668	1614	205	413	66	7	22	143	185	150	.256	.336	.346	89	-22	41	18	2	.986	-39	O-531	-8.2
■ ANDY PILNEY Pilney, Antone James b: 1/19/13, Frontenac, Kan. d: 9/15/96, Kenner, La. BR/TR, 5'11", 174 lbs. Deb: 6/12/36																							
1936	Bos-N	3	2	0	0	0	0	0	0	0	1	.000	.000	.000	-99	-1	0			.000	0	H	-0.1
■ BABE PINELLI Pinelli, Ralph Arthur (b: Rinaldo Angelo Paolinelli) b: 10/18/1895, San Francisco, Cal d: 10/22/84, Daly City, Cal. BR/TR, 5'9", 165 lbs. Deb: 8/3/18 U																							
1918	Chi-A	24	78	7	18	1	1	1	7	7	8	.231	.302	.308	83	-2	3			.847	-7	3-24	-0.9
1920	Det-A	102	284	33	65	9	3	0	21	25	16	.229	.296	.282	55	-18	6	8	-3	.954	20	3-74,S-18/2-1	0.3
1922	Cin-N	156	547	77	167	19	7	1	72	48	37	.305	.368	.371	93	-4	17	22	-8	.945	21	*3-156	1.9
1923	Cin-N	117	423	44	117	14	5	0	51	27	29	.277	.320	.333	74	-16	10	14	-5	.938	9	*3-116	-0.2
1924	Cin-N	144	510	61	156	16	7	0	70	32	32	.306	.353	.365	94	-4	23	17	-3	.956	**27**	*3-143	3.0
1925	Cin-N	130	492	68	139	33	6	2	49	22	28	.283	.316	.386	80	-15	8	19	-9	.945	21	*3-109,S-17	0.6
1926	Cin-N	71	207	26	46	7	4	0	24	15	5	.222	.284	.295	58	-12	2			.978	1	3-40,S-27/2-3	-0.7
1927	Cin-N	30	76	11	15	2	0	1	4	6	7	.197	.265	.263	43	-6	2			.968	-1	3-15/S-9,2-5	-0.6
Total	8	774	2617	327	723	101	33	5	298	182	162	.276	.328	.346	79	-77	71	80		.947	90	3-677/S-71,2-9	3.4
■ LOU PINIELLA Piniella, Louis Victor b: 8/28/43, Tampa, Fla. BR/TR, 6'2", 198 lbs. Deb: 9/4/64 MC																							
1964	Bal-A	4	1	0	0	0	0	0	0	0	0	.000	.000	.000	-99	-0	0	0	0	.000	0	H	0.0
1968	Cle-A	6	5	1	0	0	0	0	1	0	0	.000	.000	.000	-99	-1	0	0	0	1.000	-0	/O-2	-0.2
1969	KC-A	135	493	43	139	21	6	11	68	33	56	.282	.331	.416	107	3	2	4	-2	.977	15	*O-129	1.0
1970	KC-A	144	542	54	163	24	5	11	88	35	42	.301	.345	.424	111	7	3	6	-3	.984	4	*O-139/1-1	0.2
1971	KC-A	126	448	43	125	21	5	3	51	21	43	.279	.314	.368	94	-5	5	3	-0	.986	1	*O-115	-1.1
1972	KC-A★	151	574	65	179	**33**	4	11	72	34	59	.312	.359	.441	138	25	7	2	1	.976	3	*O-150	2.5
1973	KC-A	144	513	53	128	28	1	9	69	30	65	.250	.294	.361	77	-16	5	7	-3	.986	-5	*O-128/D-9	-3.1
1974	NY-A	140	518	71	158	26	0	9	70	32	58	.305	.348	.407	119	12	1	8	-5	.989	11	*O-130/1-1,D-6	1.4
1975	NY-A	74	199	7	39	4	1	0	22	16	22	.196	.266	.226	41	-15	0	0	0	.986	-3	O-46,D-12	-2.0
1976	*NY-A	100	327	36	92	16	6	3	38	18	34	.281	.323	.394	110	3	0	1	-1	.982	2	O-49,D-38	0.1
1977	*NY-A	103	339	47	112	19	3	12	45	20	31	.330	.369	.510	138	17	2	2	-1	.975	-4	O-51,D-43/1-1	0.9
1978	*NY-A	130	472	67	148	34	5	6	69	34	36	.314	.362	.445	129	17	3	1	0	.969	2	*O-103,D-23	1.5
1979	NY-A	130	461	49	137	22	2	11	69	17	31	.297	.325	.425	103	1	3	2	-0	.982	3	*O-112,D-16	-0.1
1980	*NY-A	116	321	39	92	18	0	2	27	29	20	.287	.346	.361	96	-1	0	2	-1	.971	-7	*O-104/D-7	-1.3
1981	*NY-A	60	159	16	44	9	0	5	18	13	9	.277	.331	.428	119	4	0	1	-1	.986	1	O-36,D-19	0.2
1982	NY-A	102	261	33	80	17	1	6	37	18	18	.307	.354	.448	120	7	0	1	-1	1.000	-1	D-55,O-40	0.2
1983	NY-A	53	148	19	43	9	1	2	16	11	12	.291	.344	.405	109	2	1	1	-0	.959	-2	O-43/D-1	-0.1
1984	NY-A	29	86	8	26	4	1	1	6	7	5	.302	.355	.407	115	2	0	0	0	1.000	1	O-24/D-2	0.2
Total	18	1747	5867	651	1705	305	41	102	766	368	541	.291	.336	.409	109	61	32	41	-15	.981	21	*O-1401,D-231/1-3	0.3
■ ED PINKHAM Pinkham, Edward b: 1849, Brooklyn, N.Y. TL, 5'7", 142 lbs. Deb: 5/8/1871																							
1871	Chi-n	24	95	27	25	5	5	1	17	**18**	3	.263	.381	.453	125	2	5	2	0	.754	9	3-18/O-8,P-3	0.7
■ GEORGE PINKNEY Pinkney, George Burton b: 1/11/1862, Orange Prairie, Ill. d: 11/10/26, Peoria, Ill. BR/TR, 5'7", 160 lbs. Deb: 8/16/1884																							
1884	Cle-N	36	144	18	45	9	0	0	16	10	7	.313	.357	.375	126	4				.848	-8	2-25,S-11	-0.3
1885	Bro-a	110	447	77	124	16	5	0	42	27		.277	.328	.336	109	5				.904	-11	2-57,3-51/S-3	-0.2
1886	Bro-a	141	597	119	156	22	7	0	37	**70**		.261	.339	.322	106	6	32			.858	-16	*3-141/P-1	-0.6
1887	Bro-a	138	580	133	156	26	6	3	69	61		.267	.343	.348	92	-6	59			**.890**	13	*3-136/S-2	0.8
1888	Bro-a	143	575	**134**	156	18	8	4	52	66		.271	.358	.351	128	21	51			.898	-26	*3-143	-0.2
1889	*Bro-a	138	545	103	134	25	7	4	82	59	43	.246	.327	.339	90	-7	47			**.897**	-8	*3-138	-0.9
1890	*Bro-N	126	485	115	150	20	9	7	83	80	19	.309	.411	.431	145	30	47			.933	-15	*3-126	1.8
1891	Bro-N	135	501	80	137	19	6	2	71	67	32	.273	.367	.347	109	8	44			.904	-20	*3-130/S-5	-0.5
1892	StL-N	78	290	31	50	3	2	0	25	36	26	.172	.268	.197	43	-19	4			.888	-8	3-78	-2.2
1893	Lou-N	118	446	64	105	12	6	1	62	50	8	.235	.323	.296	71	-17	12			.923	-2	*3-118	-1.4
Total	10	1163	4610	874	1212	170	56	21	539	526	135	.263	.345	.338	103	26	296			.897	-99	*3-1061/2-82,S-21,P	-3.7

YEAR	TM/L	G	AB	R	H	2B	3B	HR	RBI	BB	SO	AVG	OBP	SLG	PRO+	BR/A	SB	CS	SBR	FA	FR	G/POS	TPR
■ **VADA PINSON**	Pinson, Vada Edward b: 8/11/38, Memphis, Tenn. d: 10/21/95, Oakland, Cal. BL/TL, 5'11", 181 lbs. Deb: 4/15/58 C																						
1958	Cin-N	27	96	20	26	7	0	1	8	11	18	.271	.352	.375	88	-1	2	1	0	1.000	2	O-27	-0.1
1959	Cin-N★	154	648	**131**	205	**47**	9	20	84	55	98	.316	.371	.509	128	25	21	6	3	.984	20	*O-154	3.9
1960	Cin-N★	154	652	107	187	**37**	12	20	61	47	96	.287	.339	.472	117	14	32	12	2	.981	9	*O-154	1.9
1961	*Cin-N	154	607	101	**208**	34	8	16	87	39	63	.343	.383	.504	131	27	23	10	1	.976	19	*O-153	3.7
1962	Cin-N	155	619	107	181	31	7	23	100	45	68	.292	.344	.477	114	11	26	8	3	.989	7	*O-152	1.2
1963	Cin-N	162	652	96	**204**	37	**14**	22	106	36	80	.313	.350	.514	141	32	27	8	3	.979	9	*O-162	3.8
1964	Cin-N	156	625	99	166	23	11	23	84	42	99	.266	.317	.448	109	6	8	2	1	.972	4	*O-156	0.4
1965	Cin-N	159	669	97	204	34	10	22	94	43	81	.305	.353	.484	125	21	21	8	2	**.992**	15	*O-159	3.1
1966	Cin-N	156	618	70	178	35	6	16	76	33	83	.288	.329	.442	103	2	18	10	-1	.964	5	*O-154	-0.1
1967	Cin-N	158	650	90	187	28	**13**	18	66	26	86	.288	.318	.454	106	4	26	8	3	.986	5	*O-157	0.4
1968	Cin-N	130	499	60	135	29	6	5	48	32	59	.271	.315	.383	102	1	17	11	-2	.978	-1	*O-123	-0.9
1969	StL-N	132	495	58	126	22	6	10	70	35	63	.255	.308	.384	92	-6	4	4	-1	**.996**	1	*O-124	-1.4
1970	Cle-A	148	574	74	164	28	6	24	82	28	69	.286	.322	.481	113	8	7	6	-2	.982	5	*O-141/1-7	0.4
1971	Cle-A	146	566	60	149	23	4	11	35	21	58	.263	.297	.376	82	-14	25	6	4	.978	4	*O-141/1-3	-1.5
1972	Cal-A	136	484	56	133	24	2	7	49	30	54	.275	.324	.376	114	7	17	6	2	.991	-5	*O-134/1-1	-0.3
1973	Cal-A	124	466	56	121	14	6	8	57	20	55	.260	.290	.367	91	-8	5	5	-2	.965	-4	*O-120	-1.9
1974	KC-A	115	406	46	112	18	2	6	41	21	45	.276	.315	.374	92	-5	21	5	3	.980	-5	*O-110/1-1,D-2	-1.2
1975	KC-A	103	319	38	71	14	5	4	22	10	21	.223	.251	.335	63	-17	5	6	-2	.993	-3	O-82/1-4,D-5	-2.6
Total	18	2469	9645	1366	2757	485	127	256	1170	574	1196	.286	.330	.442	110	106	305	122	18	.981	87	*O-2403/1-16,D-7	8.8
■ **WALLY PIPP**	Pipp, Walter Clement b: 2/17/1893, Chicago, Ill. d: 1/11/65, Grand Rapids, Mich BL/TL, 6'1", 180 lbs. Deb: 6/29/13																						
1913	Det-A	12	31	3	5	0	3	0	5	2	6	.161	.235	.355	73	-1	0			.977	-1	1-10	-0.2
1915	NY-A	136	479	59	118	20	13	4	60	66	81	.246	.339	.367	112	7	18	7	1	**.992**	3	*1-134	0.8
1916	NY-A	151	545	70	143	20	14	**12**	93	54	82	.262	.331	.417	122	12	16			.992	6	*1-148	1.3
1917	NY-A	155	587	82	143	29	12	**9**	70	60	66	.244	.320	.380	112	7	11			.990	4	*1-155	0.7
1918	NY-A	91	349	48	106	15	9	2	44	22	34	.304	.345	.415	127	9	11			.988	0	1-91	0.7
1919	NY-A	138	523	74	144	23	10	7	50	39	42	.275	.330	.398	103	1	9			.991	1	*1-138	-0.3
1920	NY-A	153	610	109	171	30	14	11	76	48	54	.280	.339	.430	99	-3	4	10	-5	.991	0	*1-153	-1.1
1921	*NY-A	153	588	96	174	35	9	8	97	45	28	.296	.347	.427	94	-6	17	10	-1	.991	-4	*1-153	-1.4
1922	*NY-A	152	577	96	190	32	10	9	90	56	32	.329	.392	.466	120	18	7	12	-5	.993	-5	*1-152	0.1
1923	*NY-A	144	569	79	173	19	8	6	108	36	28	.304	.352	.397	95	-5	6	13	-6	.992	-4	*1-144	-2.1
1924	NY-A	153	589	88	174	30	**19**	9	114	51	36	.295	.352	.457	108	4	12	5	1	**.994**	2	*1-153	-0.3
1925	NY-A	62	178	19	41	6	3	3	24	13	12	.230	.286	.348	61	-11	3	3	-1	.991	4	1-47	-1.0
1926	Cin-N	155	574	72	167	22	15	6	99	49	26	.291	.352	.413	108	6	8			.992	2	*1-155	-0.1
1927	Cin-N	122	443	49	115	19	6	2	41	32	13	.260	.309	.343	77	-15	2			**.996**	0	*1-114	-2.2
1928	Cin-N	95	272	30	77	11	3	2	26	23	13	.283	.341	.368	87	-5	1			.989	1	1-72	-1.0
Total	15	1872	6914	974	1941	311	148	90	997	596	551	.281	.341	.408	104	18	125	60		.992	9	*1-1819	-6.1
■ **JIM PIRIE**	Pirie, James Moir b: 3/31/1853, Ontario, Canada d: 6/2/34, Dundas, Ont., Can. 5'8", 169 lbs. Deb: 9/25/1883																						
1883	Phi-N	5	19	1	3	0	0	0	0	0	2	.158	.158	.158	-4	-2				.577	-4	/S-5	-0.6
■ **GREG PIRKL**	Pirkl, Gregory Daniel b: 8/7/70, Long Beach, Cal. BR/TR, 6'5", 225 lbs. Deb: 8/13/93																						
1993	Sea-A	7	23	1	4	0	0	1	4	0	4	.174	.174	.304	25	-2	0	0	0	1.000	1	/1-5,D-2	-0.2
1994	Sea-A	19	53	7	14	3	0	6	11	1	12	.264	.291	.660	133	2	0	0	0	.983	-1	D-10/1-7	0.0
1995	Sea-A	10	17	2	4	0	0	0	0	1	7	.235	.278	.235	35	-2	0	0	0	1.000	1	/1-6,D-1	-0.1
1996	Sea-A	7	21	2	4	1	0	1	1	0	3	.190	.190	.381	40	-2	0	0	0	1.000	0	/1-2,D-3	-0.2
	Bos-A	2	2	0	0	0	0	0	0	0	1	.000	.000	.000	-98	-1	0	0	0	.000	0	/H	-0.1
	Yr	9	23	2	4	1	0	1	1	0	4	.174	.174	.348	27	-3	0	0	0	1.000	0	/D-3,1-2	-0.3
Total	4	45	116	12	26	4	0	8	16	2	27	.224	.244	.466	77	-5	0	0	0	.994	0	/1-20,D-16	-0.6
■ **JIM PISONI**	Pisoni, James Pete b: 8/14/29, St.Louis, Mo. BR/TR, 5'10", 169 lbs. Deb: 9/25/53																						
1953	StL-A	3	12	1	1	0	0	1	1	0	5	.083	.083	.333	8	-2	0	0	0	1.000	-0	/O-3	-0.2
1956	KC-A	10	30	4	8	0	0	2	5	2	8	.267	.313	.467	103	-0	0	0	0	.966	4	/O-9	0.4
1957	KC-A	44	97	14	23	2	2	3	12	10	17	.237	.321	.392	92	-1	0	0	0	.989	-3	O-44	-0.6
1959	Mil-N	9	24	4	4	1	0	0	0	2	6	.167	.231	.208	20	-3	0	0	0	.941	-1	/O-9	-0.4
	NY-A	17	17	2	3	0	1	0	1	1	9	.176	.222	.294	42	-1	0	0	0	1.000	-3	O-15	-0.4
1960	NY-A	20	9	1	1	0	0	0	1	1	2	.111	.200	.111	-14	-1	0	0	0	.938	-5	O-18	-0.7
Total	5	103	189	26	40	3	3	6	20	16	47	.212	.280	.354	71	-8	0	0	0	.978	-7	/O-98	-1.9
■ **ALEX PITKO**	Pitko, Alexander "Spunk" b: 11/22/14, Burlington, N.J. BR/TR, 5'10", 180 lbs. Deb: 9/11/38																						
1938	Phi-N	7	19	2	6	1	0	0	2	3	3	.316	.409	.368	118	1	1			.889	-2	/O-7	-0.1
1939	Was-A	4	8	0	1	0	0	0	1	1	3	.125	.222	.125	-10	-1	0	0	0	1.000	-1	/O-3	-0.2
Total	2	11	27	2	7	1	0	0	3	4	6	.259	.355	.296	80	-1	1	0		.917	-3	/O-10	-0.3
■ **JAKE PITLER**	Pitler, Jacob Albert b: 4/22/1894, New York, N.Y. d: 2/3/68, Binghamton, N.Y. BR/TR, 5'8", 150 lbs. Deb: 5/30/17 C																						
1917	Pit-N	109	382	39	89	8	5	0	23	30	24	.233	.297	.280	75	-11	6			**.966**	-12	*2-106/O-3	-1.9
1918	Pit-N	2	1	1	0	0	0	0	0	1	0	.000	.500	.000	55	0	2			.667	0	/2-1	0.1
Total	2	111	383	40	89	8	5	0	23	31	24	.232	.298	.279	75	-10	8			.962	-11	2-107/O-3	-1.8
■ **CHRIS PITTARO**	Pittaro, Christopher Francis b: 9/16/61, Trenton, N.J. BB/TR, 5'11", 170 lbs. Deb: 4/8/85																						
1985	Det-A	28	62	10	15	3	1	0	7	5	13	.242	.299	.323	71	-2	1	1	-0	.881	-1	3-22/2-4,D-1	-0.3
1986	Min-A	11	21	0	2	0	0	0	0	0	8	.095	.095	.095	-47	-4	0	0	0	.969	2	/2-8,S-4	-0.2
1987	Min-A	14	12	6	4	0	0	0	0	1	0	.333	.385	.333	90	-0	1	0	0	1.000	2	/2-8,D-2	-0.2
Total	3	53	95	16	21	3	1	0	7	6	21	.221	.267	.274	48	-7	2	1	0	.968	4	/3-22,2-20,S-4,D-3	-0.3
■ **PINKY PITTINGER**	Pittinger, Clarke Alonzo b: 2/24/1899, Hudson, Mich. d: 11/4/77, Ft.Lauderdale, Fla. BR/TR, 5'10", 160 lbs. Deb: 4/15/21																						
1921	Bos-A	40	91	6	18	1	0	0	5	4	13	.198	.232	.209	13	-12	3	2	-0	.985	3	O-27/3-3,S-2,2-1	-1.0
1922	Bos-A	66	186	16	48	3	0	0	7	9	10	.258	.299	.274	51	-13	2	5	-2	.920	5	3-33,S-29	-0.6
1923	Bos-A	60	177	15	38	5	0	0	15	5	10	.215	.236	.243	26	-19	3	1	0	.959	-11	2-42,S-10/3-3	-2.8
1925	Chi-N	59	173	21	54	7	2	0	15	12	7	.312	.364	.376	88	-3	5	4	-1	.940	4	S-24,3-24	0.4
1927	Cin-N	31	84	17	23	5	0	1	10	2	5	.274	.291	.369	78	-3	4			.963	3	2-20/S-9,3-2	0.1
1928	Cin-N	40	38	12	9	0	1	0	4	0	1	.237	.237	.289	37	-4	2			.892	8	S-12/2-4,3-4	0.5
1929	Cin-N	77	210	31	62	11	0	0	27	5	4	.295	.318	.348	68	-11	8			.956	2	S-50/3-8,2-4	-0.2
Total	7	373	959	118	252	32	3	1	83	37	50	.263	.294	.306	55	-64	27	12		.938	13	S-136/3-77,2-71,O	-3.6
■ **JOE PITTMAN**	Pittman, Joseph Wayne b: 1/1/54, Houston, Tex. BR/TR, 6'1", 180 lbs. Deb: 4/25/81																						
1981	*Hou-N	52	135	11	38	4	2	0	7	11	16	.281	.336	.341	97	-1	4	4	-1	.980	-9	2-35/3-4	-1.0
1982	Hou-N	15	10	0	2	1	0	0	0	0	2	.200	.200	.300	41	-1	0	0	0	1.000	0	/3-3,O-1	-0.1
	SD-N	55	118	16	30	2	0	0	7	9	13	.254	.307	.271	66	-5	8	3	1	.964	-3	2-30,S-13	-0.6
	Yr	70	128	16	32	3	0	0	7	9	15	.250	.299	.273	65	-6	8	3	1	.964	-2	2-30,S-13/3-3,O-1	-0.7
1984	SF-N	17	22	2	5	0	0	0	2	0	6	.227	.227	.227	29	-2	1	1	-0	.900	-2	/S-6,2-5,3-2	-0.5
Total	3	139	285	29	75	7	2	0	16	20	37	.263	.311	.302	77	-9	13	8	-1	.974	-14	/2-70,S-19,3-9,O-1	-2.2
■ **GAYLEN PITTS**	Pitts, Gaylen Richard b: 6/6/46, Wichita, Kan. BR/TR, 6'1", 175 lbs. Deb: 5/12/74 C																						
1974	Oak-A	18	41	4	10	3	0	0	3	5	4	.244	.326	.317	92	-0	0	0	0	.909	0	3-11/2-6,1-1	0.0
1975	Oak-A	10	3	1	1	1	0	0	1	0	0	.333	.333	.667	181	0	0	0	0	.800	2	/3-6,S-2,2-1	0.2
Total	2	28	44	5	11	4	0	0	4	5	4	.250	.327	.341	98	-0	0	0	0	.895	2	/3-17,2-7,S-2,1-1	0.2
■ **HERMAN PITZ**	Pitz, Herman b: 7/18/1865, Brooklyn, N.Y. d: 9/3/24, Far Rockaway, N.Y. 5'6", 140 lbs. Deb: 4/18/1890																						
1890	Bro-a	61	189	26	26	0	0	0	6	45		.138	.312	.138	34	-13	25			.885	-7	C-34,3-16/O-9,S2	-1.4

YEAR	TM/L	G	AB	R	H	2B	3B	HR	RBI	BB	SO	AVG	OBP	SLG	PRO+	BR/A	SB	CS	SBR	FA	FR	G/POS	TPR
	Syr-a	29	95	17	21	0	0	0	3	13		.221	.321	.221	67	-3	14			.929	-5	C-27/S-1,O-1	-0.5
	Yr	90	284	43	47	0	0	0	9	58		.165	.315	.165	44	-16	39			.906	-12	C-61,3-16,O-10,/S2	-1.9
■ **PHIL PLANTIER** Plantier, Phillip Alan b: 1/27/69, Manchester, N.H. BL/TR, 5'11", 195 lbs. Deb: 8/21/90																							
1990	Bos-A	14	15	1	2	1	0	0	3	4	6	.133	.350	.200	55	-1	0	0	0	.000	-0	/O-1,D-4	-0.1
1991	Bos-A	53	148	27	49	7	1	11	35	23	38	.331	.424	.615	175	15	1	0	0	.976	-0	O-40/D-5	1.4
1992	Bos-A	108	349	46	86	19	0	7	30	44	83	.246	.334	.361	89	-5	2	3	-1	.975	2	O-76,D-23	-0.6
1993	SD-N	138	462	67	111	20	1	34	100	61	124	.240	.338	.509	121	13	4	5	-2	.990	14	*O-134	2.2
1994	SD-N	96	341	44	75	21	0	18	41	36	91	.220	.304	.440	93	-5	3	1	0	.988	6	O-91	0.0
1995	Hou-N	22	68	12	17	2	0	4	15	11	19	.250	.363	.456	123	2	0	0	0	.962	-3	O-20	-0.1
	SD-N	54	148	21	38	4	0	5	19	17	29	.257	.333	.385	92	-2	1	1	-0	.958	4	O-39	0.1
	Yr	76	216	33	55	6	0	9	34	28	48	.255	.343	.407	101	1	1	1	-0	.959	2	O-59	0.0
1996	Oak-A	73	231	29	49	8	1	7	31	28	56	.212	.305	.346	66	-12	2	2	-1	.973	4	O-68/D-1	-0.9
1997	SD-N	10	8	0	1	0	0	0	0	2	3	.125	.300	.125	18	-1	0	0	0	1.000	-1	/O-3	-0.1
	StL-N	42	113	13	29	8	0	5	18	11	27	.257	.339	.460	108	1	0	3	-2	.981	-1	O-32	-0.2
	Yr	52	121	13	30	8	0	5	18	13	30	.248	.336	.438	103	0	0	3	-2	.982	-2	O-35	-0.3
Total	8	610	1883	260	457	90	3	91	292	237	476	.243	.335	.439	103	6	13	15	-5	.980	25	O-504/D-33	1.7
■ **DON PLARSKI** Plarski, Donald Joseph b: 11/9/29, Chicago, Ill. d: 12/29/81, St.Louis, Mo. BR/TR, 5'6", 160 lbs. Deb: 7/20/55																							
1955	KC-A	8	11	0	1	0	0	0	0	0	2	.091	.091	.091	-50	-2	1	0	0	1.000	-2	/O-6	-0.4
■ **ELMO PLASKETT** Plaskett, Elmo Alexander b: 6/27/38, Frederiksted, V.I. d: 11/2/98, Christianstad, V.I. BR/TR, 5'10", 195 lbs. Deb: 9/8/62																							
1962	Pit-N	7	14	2	4	0	0	1	3	1	3	.286	.333	.500	120	0	0	0	0	1.000	-1	/C-4	-0.1
1963	Pit-N	10	21	1	3	0	0	0	2	0	5	.143	.143	.143	-17	-3	0	0	0	1.000	-2	/C-5,3-1	-0.5
Total	2	17	35	3	7	0	0	1	5	1	8	.200	.222	.286	41	-3	0	0	0	1.000	-3	/C-9,3-1	-0.6
■ **WHITEY PLATT** Platt, Mizell George b: 8/21/20, W.Palm Beach, Fla. d: 7/27/70, W.Palm Beach, Fla BR/TR, 6'2", 195 lbs. Deb: 9/16/42																							
1942	Chi-N	4	16	1	1	0	0	0	2	0	3	.063	.063	.063	-66	-3	0			1.000	0	/O-4	-0.4
1943	Chi-N	20	41	2	7	3	0	0	2	1	7	.171	.190	.244	25	-4	0			.952	-3	O-14	-0.9
1946	Chi-A	84	247	28	62	8	5	3	32	17	34	.251	.307	.360	89	-4	1	7	-4	.971	-3	O-61	-1.5
1948	StL-A	123	454	57	123	22	10	7	82	39	51	.271	.331	.410	94	-6	1	4	-2	.948	-6	*O-114	-2.0
1949	StL-A	102	244	29	63	8	2	3	29	24	27	.258	.325	.344	74	-10	0	1	-1	.986	0	O-59/1-2	-1.2
Total	5	333	1002	117	256	41	17	13	147	81	122	.255	.314	.369	83	-27	2	12		.964	-12	O-252/1-2	-6.0
■ **AL PLATTE** Platte, Alfred Frederick Joseph b: 4/13/1890, Grand Rapids, Mich d: 8/29/76, Grand Rapids, Mich BL/TL, 5'7", 160 lbs. Deb: 9/1/13																							
1913	Det-A	9	18	1	2	1	0	0	0	1	1	.111	.158	.167	-5	-2	0			.800	-1	/O-5	-0.4
■ **RANCE PLESS** Pless, Rance b: 12/6/25, Greeneville, Tenn. BR/TR, 6', 145 lbs. Deb: 4/21/56																							
1956	KC-A	48	85	4	23	3	1	0	9	10	13	.271	.354	.329	81	-2	0	1	-1	1.000	2	1-15/3-5	-0.1
■ **HERB PLEWS** Plews, Herbert Eugene b: 6/14/28, Helena, Mont. BL/TR, 5'11", 160 lbs. Deb: 4/18/56																							
1956	Was-A	91	256	24	69	10	7	1	25	26	40	.270	.339	.375	88	-4	1	2	-1	.947	-3	2-66/S-5,3-2	-0.4
1957	Was-A	104	329	51	89	19	4	1	26	28	39	.271	.331	.362	90	-4	0	3	-2	.979	-15	2-79,3-11/S-4	-1.5
1958	Was-A	111	380	46	98	12	6	2	29	17	45	.258	.291	.337	74	-14	2	3	-1	.976	-21	2-64,3-36	-3.3
1959	Was-A	27	40	4	9	0	0	0	2	3	5	.225	.279	.225	40	-3	0	1	-1	.971	1	/2-6	-0.2
	Bos-A	13	12	0	1	1	0	0	0	0	4	.083	.083	.167	-32	-2	0	0	0	.833	1	/2-2	-0.1
	Yr	40	52	4	10	1	0	0	2	3	9	.192	.236	.212	24	-5	0	1	-1	.951	2	/2-8	-0.3
Total	4	346	1017	125	266	42	17	4	82	74	133	.262	.314	.348	80	-28	3	9	-5	.967	-36	2-217/3-49,S-9	-5.5
■ **WALTER PLOCK** Plock, Walter S. b: 7/2/1869, Philadelphia, Pa. d: 4/28/1900, Richmond, Va. 6'3", 180 lbs. Deb: 8/21/1891																							
1891	Phi-N	2	5	2	2	0	0	0	0	0	1	.400	.500	.400	159	0	0			.000	-1	/O-2	-0.1
■ **BILL PLUMMER** Plummer, William Francis b: 3/21/47, Oakland, Cal. BR/TR, 6'1", 200 lbs. Deb: 4/19/68 MC																							
1968	Chi-N	2	2	0	0	0	0	0	0	0	1	.000	.000	.000	-94	-0	0	0	0	1.000	0	/C-1	0.0
1970	Cin-N	4	8	0	1	0	0	0	0	0	2	.125	.222	.125	-4	-1	0	0	0	.857	-2	/C-4	-0.3
1971	Cin-N	10	19	0	0	0	0	0	0	0	4	.000	.000	.000	-99	-5	0	0	0	1.000	0	/C-4,3-2	-0.5
1972	Cin-N	38	102	8	19	4	0	2	9	4	20	.186	.217	.284	44	-8	0	0	0	.994	0	C-36/1-1,3-1	-0.7
1973	Cin-N	50	119	8	18	3	0	2	11	18	26	.151	.268	.227	41	-9	1	0	0	.994	-1	C-42/3-5	-0.9
1974	Cin-N	50	120	7	27	7	0	2	10	6	21	.225	.262	.333	67	-6	1	0	0	.974	5	C-49/3-1	0.1
1975	Cin-N	65	159	17	29	7	0	1	19	24	28	.182	.297	.245	51	-10	1	0	0	.990	-3	C-63	-1.1
1976	Cin-N	56	153	16	38	6	1	4	19	14	36	.248	.311	.379	93	-2	0	2	-1	.977	6	C-54	0.5
1977	Cin-N	51	117	10	16	5	0	1	7	17	34	.137	.246	.205	22	-13	1	1	-0	.986	-1	C-50	-1.3
1978	Sea-A	41	93	6	20	5	0	2	7	12	19	.215	.305	.333	80	-2	0	0	0	.978	-5	C-40	-0.7
Total	10	367	892	72	168	37	1	14	82	95	191	.188	.269	.279	53	-57	4	3	-1	.984	0	C-343/3-9,1-1	-4.9
■ **BIFF POCOROBA** Pocoroba, Biff b: 7/25/53, Burbank, Cal. BB/TR, 5'10", 180 lbs. Deb: 4/25/75																							
1975	Atl-N	67	188	15	48	7	1	1	22	20	11	.255	.327	.319	77	-5	0	0	0	.970	-4	C-62	-0.8
1976	Atl-N	54	174	16	42	7	0	0	14	19	12	.241	.316	.282	66	-7	1	0	0	.978	4	C-54	-0.1
1977	Atl-N	113	321	46	93	24	1	8	44	57	27	.290	.398	.445	113	7	3	4	-2	.989	2	*C-100	1.1
1978	Atl-N★	92	289	21	70	8	0	6	34	29	14	.242	.316	.332	73	-10	0	3	-2	.990	1	C-79	-1.0
1979	Atl-N	28	38	6	12	4	0	0	4	7	0	.316	.422	.421	122	1	1	1	-0	.933	0	/C-7	0.2
1980	Atl-N	70	83	7	22	4	0	2	8	11	11	.265	.351	.386	102	0	1	0	0	.934	-1	C-10	0.1
1981	Atl-N	57	122	4	22	4	0	0	8	12	15	.180	.265	.213	36	-10	0	0	0	.938	-5	3-21/C-9	-1.6
1982	*Atl-N	56	120	5	33	7	0	2	22	13	12	.275	.351	.383	101	0	0	0	0	.988	-4	C-36/3-2	-0.3
1983	Atl-N	55	120	11	32	6	0	2	16	12	7	.267	.333	.367	87	-2	0	0	0	.983	-3	C-34	-0.3
1984	Atl-N	4	2	1	0	0	0	0	0	2	0	.000	.500	.000	48	0	0	0	0	.000	0	/H	0.0
Total	10	596	1457	132	374	71	2	21	172	182	109	.257	.342	.351	86	-25	6	8	-3	.982	-9	C-391/3-23	-2.7
■ **MIKE POEPPING** Poepping, Michael Harold b: 8/7/50, Little Falls, Minn. BR/TR, 6'6", 230 lbs. Deb: 9/6/75																							
1975	Min-A	14	37	0	5	1	0	0	1	5	7	.135	.238	.162	15	-4	0	0	0	.950	-2	O-13	-0.7
■ **JIMMY POFAHL** Pofahl, James Willard b: 6/18/17, Faribault, Minn. d: 9/14/84, Owatonna, Minn. BR/TR, 5'11", 185 lbs. Deb: 4/16/40																							
1940	Was-A	119	406	34	95	23	5	2	36	37	55	.234	.298	.330	67	-21	2	0	1	.952	-5	*S-112/2-4	-1.5
1941	Was-A	22	75	9	14	3	2	0	6	10	11	.187	.282	.280	52	-5	1	0	0	.934	-4	S-21	-0.7
1942	Was-A	84	283	22	59	7	2	0	28	29	30	.208	.282	.247	50	-18	4	3	-1	.956	1	S-49,2-15,3-14	-1.5
Total	3	225	764	65	168	33	9	2	70	76	96	.220	.290	.295	59	-44	7	3	0	.951	-8	S-182/2-19,3-14	-3.7
■ **JOHN POFF** Poff, John William b: 10/23/52, Chillicothe, Ohio BL/TL, 6'2", 190 lbs. Deb: 9/8/79																							
1979	Phi-N	12	19	2	2	1	0	0	1	1	4	.105	.150	.158	-15	-3	0	0	0	.875	-0	/O-4,1-1	-0.4
1980	Mil-A	19	68	7	17	1	2	1	7	3	7	.250	.282	.368	79	-2	0	0	0	1.000	-1	/O-7,1-3,D-7	-0.3
Total	2	31	87	9	19	2	2	1	8	4	11	.218	.253	.322	57	-5	0	0	0	.957	-1	/O-11,D-7,1-4	-0.7
■ **AARON POINTER** Pointer, Aaron Elton "Hawk" b: 4/19/42, Little Rock, Ark. BR/TR, 6'2", 185 lbs. Deb: 9/22/63																							
1963	Hou-N	2	5	0	1	0	0	0	0	0	1	.200	.200	.200	17	-1	0	0	0	1.000	-0	/O-1	-0.1
1966	Hou-N	11	26	5	9	1	0	1	5	5	6	.346	.469	.500	182	3	1	1	-0	1.000	2	O-11	0.4
1967	Hou-N	27	70	6	11	4	0	1	10	13	26	.157	.298	.257	62	-3	1	0	0	.951	1	O-22	-0.3
Total	3	40	101	11	21	5	0	2	15	18	33	.208	.339	.317	91	-0	2	1	0	.966	3	/O-34	0.0
■ **PLACIDO POLANCO** Polanco, Placido Enrique b: 10/10/75, Santo Domingo, D.R. BR/TR, 5'10", 168 lbs. Deb: 7/3/98																							
1998	StL-N	45	114	10	29	3	2	1	11	5	9	.254	.292	.342	64	-6	2	0	1	.952	11	S-28,2-14	0.8
■ **HUGH POLAND** Poland, Hugh Reid b: 1/19/13, Tompkinsville, Ky. d: 3/30/84, Guthrie, Ky. BL/TR, 5'11.5", 185 lbs. Deb: 4/22/43																							
1943	NY-N	4	12	1	1	0	1	0	2	1	0	.083	.154	.250	16	-1	0			.889	-2	/C-4	-0.3

YEAR	TM/L	G	AB	R	H	2B	3B	HR	RBI	BB	SO	AVG	OBP	SLG	PRO+	BR/A	SB	CS	SBR	FA	FR	G/POS	TPR
	Bos-N	44	141	5	27	7	0	0	13	4	11	.191	.214	.241	32	-13	0			.973	-2	C-38	-1.3
	Yr	48	153	6	28	7	1	0	15	5	11	.183	.209	.242	30	-14	0			.969	-4	C-42	-1.6
1944	Bos-N	8	23	1	3	1	0	0	2	0	1	.130	.130	.174	-14	-3	0			.939	1	/C-6	-0.2
1946	Bos-N	4	6	0	1	1	0	0	0	0	0	.167	.167	.333	40	-1	0			1.000	0	/C-2	0.0
1947	Phi-N	4	8	0	0	0	0	0	0	0	0	.000	.000	.000	-99	-2	0			1.000	1	/C-2	-0.2
	Cin-N	16	18	1	6	1	0	0	2	1	4	.333	.368	.389	102	0	0			.667	-1	/C-3	-0.1
	Yr	20	26	1	6	1	0	0	2	1	4	.231	.259	.269	41	-2	0			.867	-1	/C-5	-0.3
1948	Cin-N	3	3	0	1	0	0	0	0	0	0	.333	.333	.333	84	-0	0			.000	0	H	0.0
Total	5	83	211	8	39	10	1	0	19	6	16	.185	.207	.242	28	-20	0			.958	-4	/C-55	-2.1
■ **KEVIN POLCOVICH**	Polcovich, Kevin Michael b: 6/28/70, Auburn, N.Y. BR/TR, 5'9", 170 lbs. Deb: 5/17/97																						
1997	Pit-N	84	245	37	67	16	1	4	21	21	45	.273	.353	.396	94	-2	2	2	-1	.969	20	S-80/2-2,3-1	2.3
1998	Pit-N	81	212	18	40	12	0	0	14	15	33	.189	.259	.245	31	-21	4	3	-1	.916	14	S-54,2-15/3-8	-0.2
Total	2	165	457	55	107	28	1	4	35	36	78	.234	.310	.326	65	-23	6	5	-1	.948	35	S-134/2-17,3-9	2.1
■ **MARK POLHEMUS**	Polhemus, Mark S. "Humpty Dumpty" b: 10/4/1862, Brooklyn, N.Y. d: 11/12/23, Lynn, Mass. 5'6.5", 185 lbs. Deb: 7/13/1887																						
1887	Ind-N	20	75	6	18	1	0	0	8	2	9	.240	.260	.253	45	-5	4			.744	0	O-20	-0.5
■ **GUS POLIDOR**	Polidor, Gustavo Adolfo (Gonzalez) b: 10/26/61, Caracas, Venezuela d: 4/28/95, Caracas, Venezuela BR/TR, 6', 170 lbs. Deb: 9/7/85																						
1985	Cal-A	2	1	1	1	0	0	0	0	0	0	1.000	1.000	1.000	452	0	0	0	0	1.000	0	/S-1,O-1	0.0
1986	Cal-A	6	19	1	5	1	0	0	1	1	0	.263	.300	.316	69	-1	0	0	0	1.000	0	/2-4,S-1,3-1	-0.1
1987	Cal-A	63	137	12	36	3	0	2	15	2	15	.263	.279	.328	62	-8	0	0	0	.983	-6	S-46,3-11/2-3	-1.0
1988	Cal-A	54	81	4	12	3	0	0	4	3	11	.148	.179	.185	2	-11	0	0	0	.984	0	S-25,3-22/2-3,D-1	-1.0
1989	Mil-A	79	175	15	34	7	0	0	14	6	18	.194	.230	.234	31	-16	3	0	1	.923	3	3-30,2-29,S-21,/D-2	-1.1
1990	Mil-A	18	15	0	1	0	0	0	1	0	1	.067	.067	.067	-63	-3	0	0	0	1.000	2	3-14/2-2,S-2	-0.2
1993	Fla-N	7	6	0	1	1	0	0	0	0	2	.167	.167	.333	28	-1	0	0	0	.000	-0	/2-1,3-1	-0.1
Total	7	229	434	33	90	15	0	2	35	12	47	.207	.234	.256	35	-38	3	0	1	.970	-1	/S-96,3-79,2-42,DO	-3.5
■ **NICK POLLY**	Polly, Nicholas (b: Nicholas Joseph Polachanin) b: 4/18/17, Chicago, Ill. d: 1/17/93, Chicago, Ill. BR/TR, 5'11", 190 lbs. Deb: 9/11/37																						
1937	Bro-N	10	18	2	4	0	0	0	2	0	1	.222	.222	.222	21	-2	0			.850	2	/3-7	0.0
1945	Bos-A	4	7	0	1	0	0	0	1	0	0	.143	.143	.143	-17	-1	0	0	0	1.000	-0	/3-2	-0.1
Total	2	14	25	2	5	0	0	0	3	0	1	.200	.200	.200	11	-3	0	0		.870	2	/3-9	-0.1
■ **LUIS POLONIA**	Polonia, Luis Andrew (Almonte) b: 10/12/64, Santiago, D.R. BL/TL, 5'8", 152 lbs. Deb: 4/24/87																						
1987	Oak-A	125	435	78	125	16	10	4	49	32	64	.287	.336	.398	100	-0	29	7	5	.979	-1	*O-104,D-18	-0.1
1988	*Oak-A	84	288	51	84	11	4	2	27	21	40	.292	.340	.378	104	2	24	9	2	.988	1	O-76/D-2	0.2
1989	Oak-A	59	206	31	59	6	4	1	17	9	15	.286	.316	.369	96	-2	13	4	2	.985	5	O-55	0.3
	NY-A	66	227	39	71	11	2	2	29	16	29	.313	.363	.405	118	5	9	4	0	.982	4	O-53/D-9	0.8
	Yr	125	433	70	130	17	6	3	46	25	44	.300	.341	.388	108	4	22	8	2	.984	8	*O-108/D-9	1.1
1990	NY-A	11	22	2	7	0	0	0	3	0	1	.318	.318	.318	78	-1	1	0	0	.000	0	/D-4	0.0
	Cal-A	109	381	50	128	7	9	2	32	25	42	.336	.378	.417	125	13	20	14	-2	.980	-5	O-85,D-11	0.3
	Yr	120	403	52	135	7	9	2	35	25	43	.335	.375	.412	122	12	21	14	-2	.980	-5	O-85,D-15	0.3
1991	Cal-A	150	604	92	179	28	8	2	50	52	74	.296	.353	.379	103	3	48	23	1	.981	1	*O-143/D-4	0.1
1992	Cal-A	149	577	83	165	17	4	0	35	45	64	.286	.339	.329	87	-9	51	21	3	.980	2	O-99,D-47	-0.8
1993	Cal-A	152	576	75	156	17	6	1	32	48	53	.271	.329	.326	74	-20	55	24	2	.983	8	*O-141/D-4	-1.2
1994	NY-A	95	350	62	109	21	6	1	36	37	36	.311	.384	.414	110	6	20	12	-1	.976	2	O-84/D-2	0.5
1995	NY-A	67	238	37	62	9	3	2	15	25	29	.261	.331	.349	78	-7	10	4	1	1.000	5	O-64/D-1	-0.3
	*Atl-N	28	53	6	14	7	0	0	2	3	9	.264	.304	.396	80	-2	3	0	1	1.000	-4	O-15	-0.5
1996	Bal-A	58	175	25	42	4	1	2	14	10	20	.240	.285	.309	50	-13	8	6	-1	.983	-2	O-34,D-18	-1.7
	*Atl-N	22	31	3	13	0	0	0	2	1	3	.419	.438	.419	121	1	1	1	-0	.800	-2	/O-7	-0.1
Total	10	1175	4163	634	1214	154	57	19	343	324	479	.292	.345	.370	95	-23	292	129	10	.982	14	O-960,D-120	-2.5
■ **CARLOS PONCE**	Ponce, Carlos Antonio (Diaz) b: 2/7/59, Rio Piedras, P.R. BR/TR, 5'10", 170 lbs. Deb: 8/14/85																						
1985	Mil-A	21	62	4	10	2	0	1	5	1	9	.161	.175	.242	13	-7	0	0	0	1.000	-0	1-10/O-6,D-3	-0.9
■ **RALPH POND**	Pond, Ralph Benjamin b: 5/4/1888, Eau Claire, Wis. d: 9/8/47, Cleveland, Ohio Deb: 6/8/10																						
1910	Bos-A	1	4	0	1	0	0	0	0	0		.250	.250	.250	55	-0	1			.000	-1	/O-1	-0.1
■ **HARLIN POOL**	Pool, Harold G "Samson" b: 3/12/08, Lakeport, Cal. d: 2/15/63, Rodeo, Cal. BL/TR, 5'10", 195 lbs. Deb: 5/30/34																						
1934	Cin-N	99	358	38	117	22	5	2	50	17	18	.327	.369	.433	117	8	3			.953	0	O-94	0.4
1935	Cin-N	28	68	8	12	6	2	0	11	2	2	.176	.200	.324	39	-6	0			.962	-3	O-18	-1.0
Total	2	127	426	46	129	28	7	2	61	19	20	.303	.343	.415	105	2	3			.954	-3	O-112	-0.6
■ **ED POOLE**	Poole, Edward I. b: 9/7/1874, Canton, Ohio d: 3/11/19, Malvern, Ohio BR/TR, 5'10", 175 lbs. Deb: 10/6/00																						
1900	Pit-N	2	4	1	2	0	1	1	3	0		.500	.500	1.750	504	2	0			.500	-0	/O-1,P-1	0.0
1901	Pit-N	26	78	6	16	4	0	1	4	4		.205	.244	.295	54	-5	1			.933	-2	P-12,O-12/2-1,3-1	-0.5
1902	Pit-N	1	4	0	1	0	0	0	0	0		.250	.250	.250	52	-0	0			.667	-0	/P-1	0.0
	Cin-N	17	61	7	7	2	0	0	1	0		.115	.115	.148	-18	-8	0			1.000	-1	P-16/O-1	-0.1
	Yr	18	65	7	8	2	0	0	1	0		.123	.123	.154	-13	-9	0			**.976**	-1	P-17/O-1	-0.1
1903	Cin-N	25	70	7	17	1	0	0	7	2		.243	.264	.257	44	-5	0			.929	2	P-25	0.0
1904	Bro-N	25	62	3	8	1	0	0	0	0		.129	.129	.145	-16	-8	0			.973	3	P-25	0.0
Total	5	96	279	24	51	8	1	2	15	6		.183	.200	.240	29	-25	1			.954	3	/P-80,O-14,3-1,2-1	-0.6
■ **JIM POOLE**	Poole, James Robert "Easy" b: 5/12/1895, Taylorsville, N.C. d: 1/2/75, Hickory, N.C. BL/TR, 6', 175 lbs. Deb: 4/14/25																						
1925	Phi-A	133	480	65	143	29	8	5	67	27	37	.298	.338	.423	86	-12	5	4	-1	.982	-7	*1-123	-2.5
1926	Phi-A	112	361	49	106	23	5	8	63	23	25	.294	.339	.452	99	-2	4	3	-1	.992	0	*1-101/O-1	-0.8
1927	Phi-A	38	99	4	22	2	0	0	10	9	6	.222	.287	.242	36	-9	0	0	0	.993	0	1-31	-1.0
Total	3	283	940	118	271	54	13	13	140	59	68	.288	.333	.415	86	-23	9	7	-2	.987	-7	1-255/O-1	-4.3
■ **RAY POOLE**	Poole, Raymond Herman b: 1/16/20, Salisbury, N.C. BL/TR, 6', 180 lbs. Deb: 9/9/41																						
1941	Phi-A	2	2	0	0	0	0	0	0	0	1	.000	.000	.000	-99	-1	0	0	0	.000	0	H	-0.1
1947	Phi-A	13	13	1	3	0	0	0	1	1	4	.231	.286	.231	44	-1	0	0	0	.000	0	H	-0.1
Total	2	15	15	1	3	0	0	0	1	1	5	.200	.250	.200	25	-2	0	0	0		0	-0,-0	-0.2
■ **TOM POORMAN**	Poorman, Thomas Iverson b: 10/14/1857, Lock Haven, Pa. d: 2/18/05, Lock Haven, Pa. BL/TR, 5'7", 135 lbs. Deb: 5/5/1880																						
1880	Buf-N	19	70	5	11	1	0	0	1	0	13	.157	.157	.171	11	-6				.879	-2	P-11,O-10	-0.6
	Chi-N	7	25	3	5	1	2	0	0	0	2	.200	.200	.400	92	-0				.778	-2	/O-7,P-2	-0.1
	Yr	26	95	8	16	2	2	0	1	0	15	.168	.168	.232	33	-6				.750	-4	O-17,P-13	-0.7
1884	Tol-a	94	382	56	89	8	7	0		10		.233	.254	.291	75	-11				.845	4	*O-93/P-1	-0.8
1885	Bos-N	56	227	44	54	5	3	3	25	7	32	.238	.261	.326	92	-2				.867	-2	O-56	-0.6
1886	Bos-N	88	371	72	97	16	6	3	41	19	52	.261	.297	.361	103	1	31			.902	6	*O-88	0.4
1887	Phi-a	135	585	140	155	18	**19**	4	61	35		.265	.317	.381	94	-6	88			.911	3	*O-135/2-2,P-1	-0.5
1888	Phi-a	97	383	76	87	16	6	2	44	31		.227	.294	.316	96	-1	46			.898	-10	*O-97	-1.3
Total	6	496	2043	396	498	65	43	12	172	102	99	.244	.285	.335	90	-26	165			.885	-4	O-486/P-15,2-2	-3.5
■ **DAVE POPE**	Pope, David b: 6/17/21, Talladega, Ala. BL/TR, 5'10.5", 170 lbs. Deb: 7/1/52																						
1952	Cle-A	12	34	9	10	1	1	1	4	1	7	.294	.314	.471	124	1	0	0	0	1.000	-1	O-10	-0.1
1954	*Cle-A	60	102	21	30	2	1	4	13	10	22	.294	.357	.451	118	2	2	1	0	1.000	-4	O-29	-0.2
1955	Cle-A	35	104	17	31	5	0	6	22	12	31	.298	.376	.519	134	5	0	0	0	.954	-3	O-31	0.1
	Bal-A	86	222	21	55	8	4	1	30	16	34	.248	.304	.333	77	-8	5	2	0	1.000	-8	O-73	-1.9
	Yr	121	326	38	86	13	4	7	52	28	65	.264	.328	.393	97	-2	5	2	0	.986	-11	*O-104	-1.8
1956	Bal-A	12	19	1	3	0	0	0	1	0	7	.158	.200	.158	-5	-3	0	0	0	1.000	-1	/O-4	-0.4

YEAR	TM/L	G	AB	R	H	2B	3B	HR	RBI	BB	SO	AVG	OBP	SLG	PRO+	BR/A	SB	CS	SBR	FA	FR	G/POS	TPR
	Cle-A	25	70	6	17	3	1	0	3	1	12	.243	.254	.314	48	-5	0	0	0	1.000	-1	O-18	-0.7
	Yr	37	89	7	20	3	1	0	4	1	19	.225	.242	.281	38	-8	0	0	0	1.000	-2	O-22	-1.1
Total	4	230	551	75	146	19	7	12	73	40	113	.265	.319	.390	92	-9	7	3	0	.990	-18	O-165	-3.2

■ PAUL POPOVICH

Popovich, Paul Edward b: 8/18/40, Flemington, W.Va. BB/TR, 6', 175 lbs. Deb: 4/19/64

YEAR	TM/L	G	AB	R	H	2B	3B	HR	RBI	BB	SO	AVG	OBP	SLG	PRO+	BR/A	SB	CS	SBR	FA	FR	G/POS	TPR
1964	Chi-N	1	1	0	1	0	0	0	0	0	0	1.000	1.000	1.000	447	0	0	0	0	.000	0	H	0.0
1966	Chi-N	2	6	0	0	0	0	0	0	0	2	.000	.000	.000	-99	-2	0	0	0	.889	-1	/2-2	-0.3
1967	Chi-N	49	159	18	34	4	0	0	2	9	12	.214	.265	.239	43	-11	0	1	-1	.967	-4	S-31,2-17/3-2	-1.3
1968	LA-N	134	418	35	97	8	1	2	25	29	37	.232	.283	.270	72	-15	1	3	-2	.983	3	2-89,S-45/3-7	-0.5
1969	LA-N	28	50	5	10	0	0	0	4	1	4	.200	.216	.200	18	-5	0	0	0	.985	0	2-23/S-3	-0.4
	Chi-N	60	154	26	48	6	0	1	14	18	14	.312	.387	.370	100	1	0	1	-1	.974	-6	2-25/S-7,3-6,O-1	-0.4
	Yr	88	204	31	58	6	0	1	18	19	18	.284	.348	.328	85	-4	0	1	-1	.978	-6	2-48,S-10/3-6,O-1	-0.8
1970	Chi-N	78	186	22	47	5	1	4	20	18	18	.253	.325	.355	73	-7	0	1	-1	.990	-6	2-22,S-17,3-16	-1.0
1971	Chi-N	89	226	24	49	7	1	4	28	14	17	.217	.262	.310	54	-14	0	1	-1	.985	4	2-40,3-16/S-1	-0.9
1972	Chi-N	58	129	8	25	3	2	1	11	12	8	.194	.262	.271	47	-9	0	1	-1	.981	19	2-36/S-8,3-1	1.2
1973	Chi-N	99	280	24	66	6	3	2	24	18	27	.236	.284	.300	58	-16	3	2	-0	.981	26	2-84/S-9,3-1	1.5
1974	*Pit-N	59	83	9	18	2	1	0	5	5	10	.217	.261	.265	49	-6	0	0	0	.962	-1	2-12,S-10	-0.6
1975	Pit-N	25	40	5	8	1	0	0	1	3	2	.200	.273	.225	40	-3	0	0	0	1.000	-3	/2-8,S-8	-0.6
Total	11	682	1732	176	403	42	9	14	134	127	151	.233	.288	.292	62	-87	4	10	-5	.982	31	2-358,S-139/3-49,O	-3.3

■ GEORGE POPPLEIN

Popplein, George J. b: 8/1840, Baltimore, Md. d: 3/31/01, Baltimore, Md. Deb: 7/11/1873

YEAR	TM/L	G	AB	R	H	2B	3B	HR	RBI	BB	SO	AVG	OBP	SLG	PRO+	BR/A	SB	CS	SBR	FA	FR	G/POS	TPR
1873	Mar-n	1	4	0	0	0	0	0	0	0	0	.000	.000	.000	-99	-1	0	0	0	.500	-1	/S-1,O-1	-0.2

■ TOM POQUETTE

Poquette, Thomas Arthur b: 10/30/51, Eau Claire, Wis. BL/TR, 5'10", 175 lbs. Deb: 9/1/73 C

YEAR	TM/L	G	AB	R	H	2B	3B	HR	RBI	BB	SO	AVG	OBP	SLG	PRO+	BR/A	SB	CS	SBR	FA	FR	G/POS	TPR
1973	KC-A	21	28	4	6	1	0	0	3	1	4	.214	.267	.250	43	-2	1	1	-0	.870	-4	O-20	-0.7
1976	*KC-A	104	344	43	104	18	10	2	34	29	31	.302	.363	.430	131	13	6	5	-1	.979	-8	O-98/D-2	0.1
1977	*KC-A	106	342	43	100	23	6	2	33	19	21	.292	.339	.412	103	1	1	4	-2	1.000	-2	O-96	-0.6
1978	*KC-A	80	204	16	44	9	2	4	30	14	9	.216	.266	.338	67	-9	2	0	1	.955	4	O-63/D-1	-0.7
1979	KC-A	21	26	1	5	0	0	0	3	1	4	.192	.222	.192	13	-3	0	0	0	1.000	-2	O-10	-0.5
	Bos-A	63	154	14	51	9	0	2	23	8	7	.331	.376	.429	110	2	2	2	-1	.949	-7	O-43/D-4	-0.6
	Yr	84	180	15	56	9	0	2	26	9	11	.311	.354	.394	97	-1	2	2	-1	.954	-9	O-53/D-4	-1.1
1981	Bos-A	3	2	0	0	0	0	0	0	0	0	.000	.000	.000	-94	-0	0	0	0	.000	-1	/O-2	-0.2
	Tex-A	30	64	2	10	1	0	0	7	5	1	.156	.229	.172	18	-7	0	1	-1	.963	-3	O-18	-1.2
	Yr	33	66	2	10	1	0	0	7	5	1	.152	.222	.167	14	-7	0	1	-1	.963	-4	O-20	-1.4
1982	KC-A	24	62	4	9	1	0	0	3	4	5	.145	.209	.161	3	-8	1	0	0	.957	-1	O-23	-0.9
Total	7	452	1226	127	329	62	18	10	136	81	82	.268	.321	.373	92	-13	13	13	-4	.971	-24	O-373/D-7	-5.3

■ DAN PORTER

Porter, Daniel Edward b: 10/17/31, Decatur, Ill. BL/TL, 6', 164 lbs. Deb: 8/16/51

YEAR	TM/L	G	AB	R	H	2B	3B	HR	RBI	BB	SO	AVG	OBP	SLG	PRO+	BR/A	SB	CS	SBR	FA	FR	G/POS	TPR
1951	Was-A	13	19	2	4	0	0	0	0	2	4	.211	.286	.211	36	-2	0	0	0	1.000	-0	/O-3	-0.2

■ DARRELL PORTER

Porter, Darrell Ray b: 1/17/52, Joplin, Mo. BL/TR, 6', 193 lbs. Deb: 9/2/71

YEAR	TM/L	G	AB	R	H	2B	3B	HR	RBI	BB	SO	AVG	OBP	SLG	PRO+	BR/A	SB	CS	SBR	FA	FR	G/POS	TPR
1971	Mil-A	22	70	4	15	2	0	2	9	9	20	.214	.304	.329	80	-2	2	2	-1	.977	2	C-22	0.1
1972	Mil-A	18	56	2	7	1	0	1	2	5	21	.125	.210	.196	22	-5	0	0	0	.976	5	C-18	0.0
1973	Mil-A	117	350	50	89	19	2	16	67	57	85	.254	.365	.457	133	16	5	2	0	.977	-4	C-90,D-19	1.7
1974	Mil-A☆	131	432	59	104	15	4	12	56	50	88	.241	.326	.377	103	2	8	7	-2	.978	-3	*C-117/D-9	0.2
1975	Mil-A	130	409	66	95	12	5	18	60	89	77	.232	.376	.418	123	16	2	5	-2	.979	-2	*C-124/D-2	1.7
1976	Mil-A	119	389	43	81	14	1	5	32	51	61	.208	.302	.288	75	-12	2	0	1	.975	-5	*C-111/D-2	-1.4
1977	*KC-A	130	425	61	117	21	3	16	60	53	70	.275	.357	.452	118	11	1	0	0	.982	1	*C-125/D-1	1.5
1978	*KC-A★	150	520	77	138	27	6	18	78	75	75	.265	.360	.444	122	16	0	5	-3	.988	-6	*C-145/D-4	1.1
1979	KC-A★	157	533	101	155	23	10	20	112	**121**	65	.291	**.429**	.484	143	38	3	4	-2	.982	-2	*C-141,D-15	3.8
1980	*KC-A★	118	418	51	104	14	2	7	51	69	50	.249	.358	.342	92	-2	1	1	-0	.978	2	C-81,D-34	0.1
1981	StL-N	61	174	22	39	10	2	6	31	39	32	.224	.369	.408	117	5	1	2	-1	.979	-3	C-52	0.4
1982	*StL-N	120	373	46	86	18	5	12	48	66	66	.231	.349	.402	109	6	1	1	-0	.983	-5	*C-111	0.4
1983	StL-N	145	443	57	116	24	3	15	66	68	94	.262	.365	.431	120	13	1	3	-2	.989	-7	*C-133	1.0
1984	StL-N	127	422	56	98	16	3	11	68	60	79	.232	.335	.363	98	0	5	3	-0	.984	-12	*C-122	-0.6
1985	*StL-N	84	240	30	53	12	2	10	36	41	48	.221	.337	.412	109	3	6	1	1	.990	-2	C-82	0.7
1986	Tex-A	68	155	21	41	6	0	12	29	22	51	.265	.360	.535	136	8	1	1	-0	.994	2	C-25,D-19	1.1
1987	Tex-A	85	130	19	31	3	0	7	21	30	43	.238	.389	.423	115	4	0	0	0	1.000	-0	D-35/C-7,1-5	0.3
Total	17	1782	5539	765	1369	237	48	188	826	905	1025	.247	.357	.409	113	116	39	37	-11	.982	-38	*C-1506,D-140/1-5	12.1

■ IRV PORTER

Porter, Irving Marble b: 5/17/1888, Lynn, Mass. d: 2/20/71, Lynn, Mass. BB/TR, 5'9", 155 lbs. Deb: 8/20/14

YEAR	TM/L	G	AB	R	H	2B	3B	HR	RBI	BB	SO	AVG	OBP	SLG	PRO+	BR/A	SB	CS	SBR	FA	FR	G/POS	TPR
1914	Chi-A	1	4	1	1	0	0	0	0	0	1	.250	.250	.250	51	-0	0			1.000	-0	/O-1	-0.1

■ JAY PORTER

Porter, J W "J W" b: 1/17/33, Shawnee, Okla. BR/TR, 6'2", 180 lbs. Deb: 7/30/52

YEAR	TM/L	G	AB	R	H	2B	3B	HR	RBI	BB	SO	AVG	OBP	SLG	PRO+	BR/A	SB	CS	SBR	FA	FR	G/POS	TPR
1952	StL-A	33	104	12	26	4	1	0	7	10	10	.250	.316	.308	72	-4	4	0	1	.973	-1	O-29/3-2	-0.5
1955	Det-A	24	55	6	13	2	0	0	3	8	15	.236	.333	.273	66	-2	0	0	0	1.000	-3	/1-6,C-4,O-4	-0.6
1956	Det-A	14	21	0	2	0	0	0	3	0	8	.095	.095	.095	-49	-4	0	0	0	1.000	-1	/C-2,O-2	-0.5
1957	Det-A	58	140	14	35	8	0	2	18	14	20	.250	.323	.350	82	-3	0	0	0	.953	-3	O-27,C-12/1-3	-0.8
1958	Cle-A	40	85	13	17	1	0	4	19	9	23	.200	.284	.353	76	-3	0	0	0	1.000	-3	C-20/1-4,3-1	-0.5
1959	Was-A	37	106	8	24	4	0	1	10	11	16	.226	.305	.292	65	-5	0	0	0	.993	-1	C-34/1-2	-0.5
	StL-N	23	33	5	7	3	0	1	2	1	4	.212	.257	.394	66	-2	0	0	0	1.000	0	C-19/1-1	-0.1
Total	6	229	544	58	124	22	1	8	62	53	96	.228	.301	.316	68	-24	4	0	1	.990	-12	/C-91,O-62,1-16,3-3	-3.5

■ MATTHEW PORTER

Porter, Matthew Sheldon b: Kansas City, Mo. Deb: 6/27/1884 M

YEAR	TM/L	G	AB	R	H	2B	3B	HR	RBI	BB	SO	AVG	OBP	SLG	PRO+	BR/A	SB	CS	SBR	FA	FR	G/POS	TPR
1884	KC-U	3	12	1	1	1	0	0		0		.083	.083	.167	-30	-2				.750	1	/O-3,M	-0.1

■ DICK PORTER

Porter, Richard Twilley "Wiggles" or "Twitches"
b: 12/30/01, Princess Anne, Md. d: 9/24/74, Philadelphia, Pa. BL/TR, 5'10", 170 lbs. Deb: 4/16/29

YEAR	TM/L	G	AB	R	H	2B	3B	HR	RBI	BB	SO	AVG	OBP	SLG	PRO+	BR/A	SB	CS	SBR	FA	FR	G/POS	TPR
1929	Cle-A	71	192	26	63	16	5	1	24	17	14	.328	.386	.479	117	5	3	5	-2	.941	-5	O-28,2-20	-0.3
1930	Cle-A	119	480	100	168	43	8	4	57	55	31	.350	.420	.498	127	21	3	3	-1	.962	-4	*O-118	0.7
1931	Cle-A	114	414	82	129	24	3	1	38	56	36	.312	.395	.391	102	3	6	9	-4	.970	-6	*O-109/2-1	-1.3
1932	Cle-A	146	621	106	191	42	8	4	60	64	43	.308	.373	.420	99	-1	2	4	-2	.982	-11	*O-145	-2.1
1933	Cle-A	132	499	73	133	19	6	0	41	51	42	.267	.335	.329	73	-19	4	4	-1	**.996**	-1	*O-124	-2.6
1934	Cle-A	13	44	9	10	2	1	1	6	4	5	.227	.292	.386	73	-2	0	0	0	1.000	-1	O-10	-0.4
	Bos-A	80	265	30	80	13	6	0	56	21	15	.302	.355	.396	87	-5	5	2	0	.940	-6	O-65	-1.2
	Yr	93	309	39	90	15	7	1	62	25	20	.291	.346	.395	85	-7	5	2	0	.947	-7	O-75	-1.6
Total	6	675	2515	426	774	159	37	11	282	268	186	.308	.376	.414	99	2	23	27	-9	.973	-35	O-599/2-21	-7.2

■ BOB PORTER

Porter, Robert Lee b: 7/22/59, Yuma, Ariz. BL/TL, 5'10", 180 lbs. Deb: 5/13/81

YEAR	TM/L	G	AB	R	H	2B	3B	HR	RBI	BB	SO	AVG	OBP	SLG	PRO+	BR/A	SB	CS	SBR	FA	FR	G/POS	TPR
1981	Atl-N	17	14	2	4	1	0	0	4	2	1	.286	.375	.357	106	0	0	0	0	.000	0	/H	0.0
1982	Atl-N	24	27	1	3	0	0	0	0	1	9	.111	.143	.111	-27	-5	0	0	0	1.000	-1	/O-4,1-1	-0.6
Total	2	41	41	3	7	1	0	0	4	3	10	.171	.227	.195	19	-4	0	0	0	1.000	-1	/O-4,1-1	-0.6

■ JORGE POSADA

Posada, Jorge Rafael (Villeta) b: 8/17/71, Santurce, P.R. BB/TR, 6'2", 190 lbs. Deb: 9/4/95

YEAR	TM/L	G	AB	R	H	2B	3B	HR	RBI	BB	SO	AVG	OBP	SLG	PRO+	BR/A	SB	CS	SBR	FA	FR	G/POS	TPR
1995	*NY-A	1	0	0	0	0	0	0	0	0	0	—	—	—	—	0	0	0	0	1.000	-0	/C-1	0.0
1996	NY-A	8	14	1	1	0	0	0	0	1	6	.071	.133	.071	-46	-3	0	0	0	1.000	2	/C-4,D-3	-0.1
1997	*NY-A	60	188	29	47	12	0	6	25	30	33	.250	.362	.410	102	1	1	2	-1	.992	-7	C-60	-0.3
1998	*NY-A	111	358	56	96	23	0	17	63	47	92	.268	.353	.475	115	8	0	1	-1	.994	-4	C-99/1-1,D-6	0.9
Total	4	180	560	86	144	35	0	23	88	78	131	.257	.351	.443	107	6	1	3	-2	.993	-10	C-164/D-9,1-1	0.5

■ LEO POSADA

Posada, Leopoldo Jesus (Hernandez) b: 4/15/36, Havana, Cuba BR/TR, 5'11", 175 lbs. Deb: 9/21/60

YEAR	TM/L	G	AB	R	H	2B	3B	HR	RBI	BB	SO	AVG	OBP	SLG	PRO+	BR/A	SB	CS	SBR	FA	FR	G/POS	TPR
1960	KC-A	10	36	8	13	0	2	1	2	3	7	.361	.410	.556	158	3	1	0	0	1.000	-2	/O-9	0.1

YEAR	TM/L	G	AB	R	H	2B	3B	HR	RBI	BB	SO	AVG	OBP	SLG	PRO+	BR/A	SB	CS	SBR	FA	FR	G/POS	TPR
1961	KC-A	116	344	37	87	10	4	7	53	36	84	.253	.331	.366	85	-7	0	0	0	.973	-3	*O-102	-1.5
1962	KC-A	29	46	6	9	1	1	0	3	7	14	.196	.302	.261	51	-3	0	0	0	1.000	-0	O-11	-0.4
Total	3	155	426	51	109	11	7	8	58	46	105	.256	.334	.371	87	-8	1	0	0	.976	-5	O-122	-1.8
■ **SCOTT POSE**	Pose, Scott Vernon b: 2/11/67, Davenport, Iowa BL/TR, 5'11", 165 lbs. Deb: 4/5/93																						
1993	Fla-N	15	41	0	8	2	0	0	3	2	4	.195	.233	.244	26	-4	0	2	-1	1.000	-3	O-10	-0.9
1997	*NY-A	54	87	19	19	2	1	0	5	9	11	.218	.292	.264	47	-7	3	1	0	1.000	-9	O-45/D-5	-1.5
Total	2	69	128	19	27	4	1	0	8	11	15	.211	.273	.258	40	-11	3	3	-1	1.000	-12	/O-55,D-5	-2.4
■ **LEW POST**	Post, Lewis G. b: 4/12/1875, Woodland, Mich. d: 8/21/44, Chicago, Ill. Deb: 9/21/02																						
1902	Det-A	3	12	2	1	0	0	0	2	0		.083	.083	.083	-53	-2	0			.800	-1	/O-3	-0.3
■ **SAM POST**	Post, Samuel Gilbert b: 11/17/1896, Richmond, Va. d: 3/31/71, Portsmouth, Va. BL/TL, 6'1.5", 170 lbs. Deb: 4/22/22																						
1922	Bro-N	9	25	3	7	0	0	0	4	1	4	.280	.308	.280	53	-2	1	0	0	.982	-1	/1-8	-0.3
■ **WALLY POST**	Post, Walter Charles b: 7/9/29, St.Wendelin, Ohio d: 1/6/82, St.Henry, Ohio BR/TR, 6'1", 203 lbs. Deb: 9/18/49																						
1949	Cin-N	6	8	1	2	0	0	0	1	0	3	.250	.250	.250	34	-1	0			.750	-1	/O-3	-0.2
1951	Cin-N	15	41	6	9	3	0	1	7	3	4	.220	.273	.366	69	-2	0	0	0	.963	1	/O-9	-0.2
1952	Cin-N	19	58	5	9	1	0	2	7	4	20	.155	.222	.276	37	-5	0	0	0	1.000	2	O-16	-0.4
1953	Cin-N	11	33	3	8	1	0	1	4	4	6	.242	.324	.364	78	-1	1	0	0	.960	1	O-11	-0.1
1954	Cin-N	130	451	46	115	21	3	18	83	26	70	.255	.300	.435	86	-11	2	2	-1	.957	5	*O-116	-1.1
1955	Cin-N	154	601	116	186	33	3	40	109	60	102	.309	.374	.574	139	32	7	4	-0	.978	2	*O-154	2.6
1956	Cin-N	143	539	94	134	25	3	36	83	37	124	.249	.302	.506	105	2	6	0	2	.969	12	*O-136	0.9
1957	Cin-N	134	467	68	114	26	2	20	74	33	84	.244	.294	.437	87	-10	2	2	-1	.985	10	*O-124	-0.7
1958	Phi-N	110	379	51	107	21	3	12	62	32	74	.282	.343	.449	109	4	0	2	-1	.952	8	O-91	0.6
1959	Phi-N	132	468	62	119	17	6	22	94	36	101	.254	.312	.457	100	-1	0	0	0	.992	9	*O-120	0.1
1960	Phi-N	34	84	11	24	6	1	2	12	9	24	.286	.355	.452	119	2	0	0	0	1.000	1	O-22	0.2
	Cin-N	77	249	36	70	14	0	17	38	28	51	.281	.354	.542	139	13	0	2	-1	.985	4	O-67	1.3
	Yr	111	333	47	94	20	1	19	50	37	75	.282	.354	.520	134	15	0	2	-1	.989	5	O-89	1.5
1961	*Cin-N	99	282	44	83	16	3	20	57	22	61	.294	.348	.585	140	15	0	1	-1	.959	1	O-81	1.1
1962	Cin-N	109	285	43	75	10	3	17	62	32	67	.263	.342	.498	118	7	1	0	0	.935	-4	O-90	-0.1
1963	Cin-N	5	7	1	0	0	0	0	0	0	1	.000	.125	.000	-59	-1	0	0	0	1.000	0	/O-1	-0.1
	Min-A	21	47	6	9	0	1	2	6	2	17	.191	.224	.362	60	-3	0	0	0	1.000	-2	O-12	-0.5
1964	Cle-A	5	8	1	0	0	0	0	0	3	4	.000	.273	.000	-16	-1	0	0	0	.667	-1	/O-2	-0.2
Total	15	1204	4007	594	1064	194	28	210	699	331	813	.266	.325	.485	109	39	19	13		.970	46	*O-1055	3.2
■ **MIKE POTTER**	Potter, Michael Gary b: 5/16/51, Montebello, Cal. BR/TR, 6'1", 195 lbs. Deb: 9/6/76																						
1976	StL-N	9	16	0	0	0	0	0	0	1	6	.000	.059	.000	-82	-4	0	0	0	1.000	0	/O-4	-0.4
1977	StL-N	5	7	0	0	0	0	0	0	0	2	.000	.000	.000	-99	-2	0	0	0	.000	-0	/O-1	-0.2
Total	2	14	23	0	0	0	0	0	0	1	8	.000	.042	.000	-87	-6	0	0	0	1.000	-0	/O-5	-0.6
■ **JOHN POTTS**	Potts, John Frederick "Fred" b: 2/6/1887, Tipp City, Ohio d: 9/5/62, Cleveland, Ohio BL/TR, 5'7", 165 lbs. Deb: 4/18/14																						
1914	KC-F	41	102	14	27	4	0	1	9	25	13	.265	.414	.333	110	1	7			.933	-4	O-31	-0.4
■ **DAN POTTS**	Potts, Vivian b: 1/1869, Bristol, Pa. Deb: 10/3/1892																						
1892	Was-N	1	4	0	1	0	0	0	0	0	1	.250	.250	.250	53	-0	0			1.000	1	/C-1	0.0
■ **KEN POULSEN**	Poulsen, Ken Sterling b: 8/4/47, Van Nuys, Cal. BL/TR, 6'1", 190 lbs. Deb: 7/3/67																						
1967	Bos-A	5	5	0	1	1	0	0	0	0	2	.200	.200	.400	68	-0	0	0	0	.667	-1	/3-2,S-1	-0.1
■ **ALONZO POWELL**	Powell, Alonzo Sidney b: 12/12/64, San Francisco, Cal. BR/TR, 6'2", 190 lbs. Deb: 4/6/87																						
1987	Mon-N	14	41	3	8	3	0	0	4	5	17	.195	.283	.268	46	-3	0	0	0	1.000	-1	O-11	-0.5
1991	Sea-A	57	111	16	24	6	1	3	12	11	24	.216	.293	.369	82	-3	0	2	-1	.960	-9	O-40/1-7,D-7	-1.4
Total	2	71	152	19	32	9	1	3	16	16	41	.211	.290	.342	71	-6	0	2	-1	.968	-10	/O-51,D-7,1-7	-1.9
■ **JAKE POWELL**	Powell, Alvin Jacob b: 7/15/08, Silver Spring, Md d: 11/4/48, Washington, D.C. BR/TR, 5'11.5", 180 lbs. Deb: 8/3/30																						
1930	Was-A	3	4	1	0	0	0	0	0	0	1	.000	.000	.000	-99	-1	0	0	0	1.000	-0	/O-2	-0.1
1934	Was-A	9	35	6	10	2	0	0	1	4	2	.286	.359	.343	85	-1	1	1	-0	.955	1	/O-9	0.0
1935	Was-A	139	551	88	172	26	10	6	98	37	37	.312	.360	.428	107	4	15	7	0	.976	0	*O-136/2-2	0.0
1936	Was-A	53	210	40	62	11	5	1	30	18	21	.295	.357	.410	94	-2	10	4	1	.951	-7	O-53	-1.0
	*NY-A	87	328	62	99	13	3	7	48	33	30	.302	.366	.424	98	-1	16	7	1	.976	1	O-84	-0.3
	Yr	140	538	102	161	24	8	8	78	51	51	.299	.362	.418	96	-4	26	11	1	.967	-7	*O-137	-1.3
1937	*NY-A	97	365	54	96	22	3	3	45	25	36	.263	.314	.364	70	-17	7	5	-1	.981	1	O-94	-1.9
1938	*NY-A	45	164	27	42	12	1	2	20	15	20	.256	.326	.378	76	-6	3	1	0	.978	-3	O-43	-0.9
1939	NY-A	31	86	12	21	4	1	1	9	3	8	.244	.270	.349	58	-6	1	2	-1	.983	0	O-23	-0.7
1940	NY-A	12	27	3	5	0	0	0	2	1	4	.185	.214	.185	5	-4	0	0	0	1.000	0	/O-7	-0.4
1943	Was-A	37	132	14	35	10	2	0	20	5	13	.265	.297	.371	99	-1	3	5	-2	.978	2	O-33	-0.3
1944	Was-A	96	367	29	88	9	1	1	37	16	26	.240	.272	.278	60	-20	7	2	1	.980	0	O-90/3-1	-2.5
1945	Was-A	31	98	4	19	2	0	0	3	8	8	.194	.255	.214	40	-8	1	1	-0	.950	-1	O-27	-1.2
	Phi-N	48	173	13	40	5	0	1	14	8	13	.231	.265	.277	52	-11	1			.986	-4	O-44	-1.8
Total	11	688	2540	353	689	116	26	22	327	173	219	.271	.320	.363	81	-75	65	35		.975	-9	O-645/2-2,3-1	-11.1
■ **ABNER POWELL**	Powell, Charles Abner "Ab" b: 12/15/1860, Shenandoah, Pa. d: 8/7/53, New Orleans, La. BL/TR, 5'7", 160 lbs. Deb: 8/4/1884																						
1884	Was-U	48	191	36	54	10	5	0		3		.283	.294	.387	108	-4				.875	-2	O-30,P-18/3-2,S2	-0.6
1886	Bal-a	11	39	4	7	2	1	0	7	1		.179	.200	.282	52	-2	4			.917	1	/P-7,O-4	-0.2
	Cin-a	19	74	13	17	1	1	0	8	4		.230	.269	.270	67	-3	0			.760	0	O-13/S-6,P-4	-0.2
	Yr	30	113	17	24	3	2	0	15	5		.212	.246	.274	62	-5	4			.735	1	O-17,P-11/S-6	-0.4
Total	2	78	304	53	78	13	7	0	15	8		.257	.276	.345	91	-9	4			.817	-1	/O-47,P-29,S-7,32	-1.0
■ **HOSKEN POWELL**	Powell, Hosken b: 5/14/55, Selma, Ala. BL/TL, 6'1", 185 lbs. Deb: 4/5/78																						
1978	Min-A	121	381	55	94	20	2	3	31	45	31	.247	.326	.333	84	-7	11	5	0	.983	-1	*O-117	-1.3
1979	Min-A	104	338	49	99	17	3	2	36	33	25	.293	.361	.379	96	-1	5	1	1	.977	-2	O-93/D-5	-0.6
1980	Min-A	137	485	58	127	17	5	6	35	32	46	.262	.312	.355	76	-16	14	3	2	.968	7	*O-129	-1.1
1981	Min-A	80	264	30	63	11	3	2	25	17	31	.239	.287	.326	71	-10	7	4	-0	.970	2	O-64/D-8	-1.1
1982	Tor-A	112	265	43	73	13	4	3	26	12	23	.275	.307	.389	82	-7	4	4	-1	.974	-9	O-75,D-19	-2.0
1983	Tor-A	40	83	6	14	0	0	1	7	5	8	.169	.216	.205	16	-10	2	0	1	.981	-4	O-33/1-1,D-1	-1.3
Total	6	594	1816	241	470	78	17	17	160	144	164	.259	.316	.349	79	-50	43	17	3	.975	8	O-511/D-33,1-1	-7.4
■ **JIM POWELL**	Powell, James Edwin b: 8/30/1859, Richmond, Va. d: 11/20/29, Butte, Mont. 5'10", 170 lbs. Deb: 8/5/1884																						
1884	Ric-a	41	151	23	37	8	4	0		7		.245	.296	.351	112	2				.943	1	1-41	-0.2
■ **BOOG POWELL**	Powell, John Wesley b: 8/17/41, Lakeland, Fla. BL/TR, 6'4", 240 lbs. Deb: 9/26/61																						
1961	Bal-A	4	13	0	1	0	0	0	1	0	2	.077	.077	.077	-61	-3	0	0	0	1.000	-1	/O-3	-0.4
1962	Bal-A	124	400	44	97	13	2	15	53	38	79	.243	.311	.398	95	-4	1	1	-0	.969	-7	*O-112/1-1	-1.8
1963	Bal-A	140	491	67	130	22	2	25	82	49	87	.265	.331	.470	126	16	1	2	-1	.969	-8	*O-121,1-23	0.1
1964	Bal-A	134	424	74	123	17	0	39	99	76	91	.290	.400	**.606**	176	44	0	0	0	.974	4	*O-124/1-5	**4.4**
1965	Bal-A	144	472	54	117	20	2	17	72	71	93	.248	.351	.407	112	9	1	1	-0	.992	3	1-78,O-71	0.6
1966	*Bal-A	140	491	78	141	18	0	34	109	67	125	.287	.374	.532	159	38	0	4	-2	.989	-7	*1-136	2.1
1967	Bal-A	125	415	53	97	14	1	13	55	55	94	.234	.326	.366	105	3	1	3	-2	.986	-4	*1-114	-1.0
1968	Bal-A★	154	550	60	137	21	1	22	85	73	97	.249	.340	.411	127	18	7	1	2	.990	-5	*1-149	0.4
1969	*Bal-A★	152	533	83	162	25	0	37	121	72	76	.304	.388	.559	161	42	1	1	-0	.995	-2	*1-144	3.0
1970	*Bal-A★	154	526	82	156	28	0	35	114	104	80	.297	.417	.549	163	48	1	1	-0	.992	-2	*1-145	3.3

YEAR	TM/L	G	AB	R	H	2B	3B	HR	RBI	BB	SO	AVG	OBP	SLG	PRO+	BR/A	SB	CS	SBR	FA	FR	G/POS	TPR
1971	*Bal-A†	128	418	59	107	19	0	22	92	82	64	.256	.383	.459	139	24	1	0	0	.995	-3	*1-124	1.1
1972	Bal-A	140	465	53	117	20	1	21	81	65	92	.252	.348	.434	129	17	4	0	1	.988	-3	*1-133	0.5
1973	*Bal-A	114	370	52	98	13	1	11	54	85	64	.265	.402	.395	126	17	0	2	-1	.989	2	*1-111	0.9
1974	*Bal-A	110	344	37	91	13	1	12	45	52	58	.265	.361	.413	126	13	0	1	-1	.996	1	*1-102/D-1	0.7
1975	Cle-A	134	435	64	129	18	0	27	86	59	72	.297	.382	.524	154	31	1	3	-2	**.997**	-2	*1-121/D-5	2.0
1976	Cle-A	95	293	29	63	9	0	9	33	41	43	.215	.311	.338	91	-3	1	1	-0	.987	1	1-89	-0.9
1977	LA-N	50	41	0	10	0	0	0	5	12	9	.244	.415	.244	82	-0	0	0	0	.938	-1	/1-4	-0.1
Total	17	2042	6681	889	1776	270	11	339	1187	1001	1226	.266	.364	.462	134	310	20	21	-7	.991	-33	*1-1479,O-431/D-6	14.9

■ **DANTE POWELL** Powell, Le Jon Dante b: 8/25/73, Long Beach, Cal. BR/TR, 6'2", 185 lbs. Deb: 4/15/97

1997	*SF-N	27	39	8	12	1	0	1	3	4	11	.308	.372	.410	107	0	1	1	-0	1.000	-4	O-22	-0.4
1998	SF-N	8	4	2	2	0	0	1	1	3	0	.500	.714	1.250	410	2	0	0	0	1.000	-3	/O-8	-0.1
Total	2	35	43	10	14	1	0	2	4	7	11	.326	.420	.488	140	3	1	1	-0	1.000	-7	/O-30	-0.5

■ **MARTIN POWELL** Powell, Martin J. b: 3/25/1856, Fitchburg, Mass. d: 2/5/1888, Fitchburg, Mass. BL/TL, 6', 170 lbs. Deb: 6/18/1881

1881	Det-N	55	219	47	74	9	4	1	38	15	9	.338	.380	.429	148	12				.947	-3	1-55/C-1	0.4
1882	Det-N	80	338	44	81	13	0	0	29	19	27	.240	.280	.278	80	-7				.940	-5	*1-80	-1.9
1883	Det-N	101	421	76	115	17	5	1	48	28	23	.273	.318	.344	106	5				.950	-3	*1-101	-0.7
1884	Cin-U	43	185	46	59	4	2	1		13		.319	.364	.378	116	-1				.940	-2	1-43	-0.8
1885	Phi-a	19	75	5	12	0	3	0	5	1		.160	.192	.240	34	-6				.973	-0	1-19	-0.8
Total	5	298	1238	218	341	43	14	3	120	76	59	.275	.318	.340	104	2				.947	-13	1-298/C-1	-3.8

■ **PAUL POWELL** Powell, Paul Ray b: 3/19/48, San Angelo, Tex. BR/TR, 5'11", 185 lbs. Deb: 4/7/71

1971	Min-A	20	31	7	5	0	0	1	2	3	12	.161	.235	.258	38	-3	0	0	0	1.000	-2	O-15	-0.6
1973	LA-N	2	1	0	0	0	0	0	0	0	1	.000	.000	.000	-99	-0	0	0	0	.000	-0	/O-1	-0.1
1975	LA-N	8	10	2	2	1	0	0	0	1	2	.200	.273	.300	61	-1	0	0	0	.955	1	/C-7,O-1	0.0
Total	3	30	42	9	7	1	0	1	2	4	15	.167	.239	.262	41	-3	0	0	0	1.000	-2	/O-17,C-7	-0.7

■ **RAY POWELL** Powell, Raymond Reath "Rabbit" b: 11/20/1888, Siloam Springs, Ark. d: 10/16/62, Chillicothe, Mo. BL/TR, 5'9", 160 lbs. Deb: 4/16/13

1913	Det-A	2	0	0	0	0	0	0	0	0	0	—	—	—	—	0	0			.000	0	/O-1	0.0
1917	Bos-N	88	357	42	97	10	4	4	30	24	54	.272	.318	.356	113	5	12			.976	9	O-88	0.9
1918	Bos-N	53	188	31	40	7	5	0	20	29	30	.213	.321	.303	95	-0	2			.949	-0	O-53	-0.4
1919	Bos-N	123	470	51	111	12	12	2	33	41	79	.236	.303	.326	93	-4	16			.951	1	*O-122	-1.3
1920	Bos-N	147	609	69	137	12	12	6	29	44	83	.225	.282	.314	74	-21	10	18	-8	.956	5	*O-147	-3.8
1921	Bos-N	149	624	114	191	25	**18**	12	74	58	85	.306	.369	.462	125	22	6	17	-8	.954	3	*O-149	0.5
1922	Bos-N	142	550	82	163	22	11	6	37	59	66	.296	.369	.409	105	5	3	12	-6	.980	12	*O-136	0.0
1923	Bos-N	97	338	57	102	20	4	4	38	45	36	.302	.385	.420	117	10	1	6	-3	.941	-4	O-84	-0.3
1924	Bos-N	74	188	21	49	9	1	1	15	21	28	.261	.338	.335	85	-4	1	3	-2	.947	4	O-46	-0.4
Total	9	875	3324	467	890	117	67	35	276	321	461	.268	.336	.375	102	11	51	56		.959	29	O-826	-4.8

■ **LEROY POWELL** Powell, Robert Leroy b: 10/17/33, Flint, Mich. BR/TR, 6'1", 190 lbs. Deb: 9/16/55

1955	Chi-A	1	0	0	0	0	0	0	0	0	0	—	—	—	—	0	0	0	0	.000	0	R	0.0
1957	Chi-A	1	0	1	0	0	0	0	0	0	0	—	—	—	—	0	0	0	0	.000	0	R	0.0
Total	2	2	0	1	0	0	0	0	0	0	0	—	—	—	—	0	0	0	0		0	-0,-0	0.0

■ **TOM POWER** Power, Thomas E. b: San Francisco, Cal. d: 2/25/1898, San Francisco, Cal 5'11", 164 lbs. Deb: 8/27/1890

1890	Bal-a	38	125	11	26	3	1	0	6	13		.208	.293	.248	57	-7	6			.960	-4	1-26,2-12	-1.0

■ **VIC POWER** Power, Victor Pellot (b: Victor Felipe Pellot (Pove)) b: 11/1/27, Arecibo, P.R. BR/TR, 5'11", 195 lbs. Deb: 4/13/54

1954	Phi-A	127	462	36	118	17	5	8	38	19	19	.255	.288	.366	78	-16	2	1	0	.985	10	*O-101,1-21/S-1,3-1	-1.1
1955	KC-A★	147	596	91	190	34	10	19	76	35	27	.319	.357	.505	128	20	0	2	-1	.993	14	*1-144	2.4
1956	KC-A★	127	530	77	164	21	5	14	63	24	16	.309	.341	.447	106	3	2	2	-1	.993	8	1-76,2-47/O-7	0.8
1957	KC-A	129	467	48	121	15	1	14	42	19	21	.259	.292	.385	82	-13	3	2	-0	**.998**	12	*1-113/O-6,2-4	-0.8
1958	KC-A	52	205	35	62	13	4	4	27	7	3	.302	.325	.463	112	3	1	1	-0	.992	6	1-50/2-1	0.5
	Cle-A	93	385	63	122	24	6	12	53	13	11	.317	.341	.504	133	15	2	1	0	.977	6	3-42,1-41,2-27,/SO	2.1
	Yr	145	590	98	184	37	**10**	16	80	20	14	.312	.336	.490	125	17	3	2	-0	.992	11	1-91,3-42,2-28,/SO	2.6
1959	Cle-A★	147	595	102	172	31	6	10	60	40	22	.289	.336	.412	108	5	9	13	-5	**.995**	10	*1-121,2-21/3-7	0.4
1960	Cle-A★	147	580	69	167	26	3	10	84	24	20	.288	.316	.395	94	-7	9	5	-0	**.996**	21	*1-147/S-5,3-4	0.3
1961	Cle-A	147	563	64	151	34	4	5	63	38	16	.268	.316	.369	85	-13	4	3	-1	.994	18	*1-141/2-7	-0.7
1962	Min-A	144	611	80	177	28	2	16	63	22	35	.290	.318	.421	93	-7	7	1	2	.993	9	*1-142/2-2	-0.6
1963	Min-A	138	541	65	146	28	2	10	52	22	24	.270	.298	.384	88	-9	3	1	0	.992	-1	*1-124,2-18/3-5	-1.4
1964	Min-A	19	45	6	10	2	0	0	1	1	3	.222	.239	.267	40	-4	0	0	0	.990	1	1-12/2-1	-0.3
	LA-A	68	221	17	55	6	0	3	13	8	14	.249	.278	.317	72	-9	1	1	-0	1.000	2	1-48,3-28/2-5	-0.9
	Yr	87	266	23	65	8	0	3	14	9	17	.244	.272	.308	66	-13	1	1	-0	.998	4	1-60,3-28/2-6	-1.2
	Phi-N	18	48	1	10	4	0	0	3	2	3	.208	.240	.292	50	-3	0	0	0	.993	1	1-17	-0.3
1965	Cal-A	124	197	11	51	7	1	1	20	5	13	.259	.281	.320	72	-8	2	2	-1	.996	6	*1-107/2-6,3-2	-0.5
Total	12	1627	6046	765	1716	290	49	126	658	279	247	.284	.317	.411	97	-43	45	35	-7	.994	123	*1-1304,2-139,O/3S	-0.1

■ **MIKE POWERS** Powers, Ellis Foree b: 3/2/06, Toddspoint, Ky. d: 12/2/83, Louisville, Ky. BL/TL, 6'1", 185 lbs. Deb: 8/19/32

1932	Cle-A	14	33	4	6	4	0	0	5	2	2	.182	.229	.303	34	-3	0	0	0	.917	-2	/O-8	-0.5
1933	Cle-A	24	47	6	13	2	1	0	2	6	6	.277	.358	.362	87	-1	2	1	0	.952	-2	O-11	-0.3
Total	2	38	80	10	19	6	1	0	7	8	8	.237	.307	.338	65	-4	2	1	0	.939	-3	/O-19	-0.8

■ **JOHN POWERS** Powers, John Calvin b: 7/8/29, Birmingham, Ala. BL/TR, 6', 190 lbs. Deb: 9/24/55

1955	Pit-N	2	4	0	1	0	0	0	0	0	0	.250	.250	.250	34	-0	0	0	0	1.000	-0	/O-2	0.0
1956	Pit-N	11	21	0	1	0	0	0	0	1	4	.048	.091	.048	-63	-5	0	0	0	1.000	-0	/O-5	-0.5
1957	Pit-N	20	35	7	10	3	0	2	8	5	9	.286	.419	.543	161	3	0	0	0	1.000	0	/O-9	0.3
1958	Pit-N	57	82	6	15	1	0	2	2	8	19	.183	.256	.268	40	-7	0	0	0	1.000	0	O-14	-0.8
1959	Cin-N	43	43	8	11	2	1	2	4	3	13	.256	.319	.488	108	0	0	0	0	1.000	-1	/O-5	-0.1
1960	Bal-A	10	18	3	2	0	0	0	0	3	1	.111	.238	.111	-2	-3	0	0	0	.833	-1	/O-4	-0.4
	Cle-A	8	12	2	2	1	1	0	0	2	2	.167	.286	.417	90	-0	0	0	0	1.000	-1	/O-5	-0.1
	Yr	18	30	5	4	1	1	0	0	5	3	.133	.257	.233	34	-3	0	0	0	.929	-1	/O-9	-0.5
Total	6	151	215	26	42	7	2	6	14	22	48	.195	.282	.330	64	-11	0	0	0	.986	-2	/O-44	-1.6

■ **LES POWERS** Powers, Leslie Edwin b: 11/5/09, Seattle, Wash. d: 11/13/78, Santa Monica, Cal. BL/TL, 6', 175 lbs. Deb: 9/17/38

1938	NY-N	2	3	0	0	0	0	0	0	0	1	.000	.000	.000	-99	-1	0			.000	0	H	-0.1
1939	Phi-N	19	52	7	18	1	1	0	2	4	6	.346	.393	.404	118	1	0			.983	-2	1-13	-0.2
Total	2	21	55	7	18	1	1	0	2	4	7	.327	.373	.382	106	1	0			.983	-2	/1-13	-0.3

■ **DOC POWERS** Powers, Michael Riley b: 9/22/1870, Pittsfield, Mass. d: 4/26/09, Philadelphia, Pa. BR/TR, Deb: 6/12/1898

1898	Lou-N	34	99	13	27	4	3	1	19	5		.273	.308	.404	105	0	1			.962	-3	C-22/1-6,O-1	-0.1
1899	Lou-N	49	169	15	35	8	2	0	22	6		.207	.239	.278	42	-14	1			.942	-8	C-38/1-7	-1.7
	Was-N	14	38	3	10	2	0	0	3	1		.263	.282	.316	65	-2	0			.942	-0	C-12/1-1	-0.1
	Yr	63	207	18	45	10	2	0	25	7		.217	.247	.285	46	-16	1			.942	-8	C-50/1-8	-1.8
1901	Phi-A	116	431	53	108	26	5	1	47	18		.251	.292	.341	72	-17	10			.952	-5	*C-111/1-3	-1.0
1902	Phi-A	71	246	35	65	7	1	2	39	14		.264	.312	.325	74	-9	3			.950	5	C-68/1-3	0.3
1903	Phi-A	75	247	19	56	11	1	0	23	5		.227	.242	.279	54	-14	1			.982	-2	C-66/1-7	-1.0
1904	Phi-A	57	184	11	35	3	0	0	11	6		.190	.220	.207	33	-14	3			.965	-5	C-56/O-1	-1.4
1905	*Phi-A	21	60	6	10	0	0	0	5	0		.167	.180	.167	10	-6	2			.928	3	C-21	-0.1
	NY-A	11	33	3	6	1	0	0	2	1		.182	.206	.212	29	-3	0			.975	-0	/1-7,C-4	-0.3
	*Phi-A	19	61	2	8	0	0	0	5	3		.131	.172	.131	-3	-7	2			.991	-5	C-19	-1.2
	Yr	51	154	11	24	1	0	0	12	4		.156	.182	.162	9	-16	4			.957	-2	C-44/1-7	-1.6

YEAR	TM/L	G	AB	R	H	2B	3B	HR	RBI	BB	SO	AVG	OBP	SLG	PRO+	BR/A	SB	CS	SBR	FA	FR	G/POS	TPR
1906	Phi-A	58	185	5	29	1	0	0	7	1		.157	.170	.162	4	-20	2			.974	9	C-57/1-1	-0.6
1907	Phi-A	59	159	9	29	3	0	0	9	7		.182	.217	.201	33	-12	1			.983	14	C-59	0.7
1908	Phi-A	62	172	8	31	6	1	0	7	5		.180	.217	.227	41	-11	1			.967	7	C-60/1-2	0.1
1909	Phi-A	1	4	1	1	0	0	0	0	0		.250	.250	.250	57	-0	0			1.000	0	/C-1	0.0
Total	11	647	2088	183	450	72	13	4	199	72		.216	.248	.268	51	-129	27			.965	12	C-594/1-37,O-2	-6.4

■ PHIL POWERS Powers, Phillip B. "Grandmother" b: 7/26/1854, New York, N.Y. d: 12/22/14, New York, N.Y. BR/TR, 5'7", 166 lbs. Deb: 8/31/1878 U

YEAR	TM/L	G	AB	R	H	2B	3B	HR	RBI	BB	SO	AVG	OBP	SLG	PRO+	BR/A	SB	CS	SBR	FA	FR	G/POS	TPR
1878	Chi-N	8	31	2	5	1	1	0	2	1	5	.161	.188	.258	42	-2				.930	5	/C-8	0.3
1880	Bos-N	37	126	11	18	5	0	0	10	5	15	.143	.176	.183	22	-10				.851	-5	C-37/O-2	-1.4
1881	Cle-N	5	15	1	1	0	0	0	0	1	2	.067	.125	.067	-40	-2				.955	-1	/C-4,3-1	-0.3
1882	Cin-a	16	60	4	13	1	1	0	5	3		.217	.254	.267	72	-2				.921	3	C-10/1-5,O-1	0.1
1883	Cin-a	30	114	16	28	1	4	0	8	3		.246	.265	.325	84	-2				.893	-2	C-17,O-13	-0.3
1884	Cin-a	34	130	10	18	1	0	0	8	5		.138	.170	.146	4	-14				.891	5	C-31/O-2,1-2	-0.6
1885	Cin-a	15	60	6	16	2	0	0	7	0		.267	.267	.300	77	-2				.833	-3	C-15	-0.3
	Bal-a	9	34	6	4	1	0	0	2	1		.118	.143	.147	-8	-4				.844	-4	/C-8,O-1	-0.7
	Yr	24	94	12	20	3	0	0	9	1		.213	.221	.245	47	-6				.837	-7	C-23/O-1	-1.0
Total	7	154	570	56	103	12	6	0	42	19	22	.181	.207	.223	40	-37				.877	-2	C-130/O-19,1-7,3-1	-3.2

■ CARL POWIS Powis, Carl Edgar "Jug" b: 1/11/28, Philadelphia, Pa. BR/TR, 6', 185 lbs. Deb: 4/15/57

YEAR	TM/L	G	AB	R	H	2B	3B	HR	RBI	BB	SO	AVG	OBP	SLG	PRO+	BR/A	SB	CS	SBR	FA	FR	G/POS	TPR
1957	Bal-A	15	41	4	8	3	1	0	2	7	9	.195	.327	.317	82	-1	2	0	1	.909	-1	O-13	-0.2

■ ARQUIMEDEZ POZO Pozo, Arquimedez (Ortiz) b: 8/24/73, Santo Domingo, D.R. BR/TR, 5'10", 160 lbs. Deb: 9/12/95

YEAR	TM/L	G	AB	R	H	2B	3B	HR	RBI	BB	SO	AVG	OBP	SLG	PRO+	BR/A	SB	CS	SBR	FA	FR	G/POS	TPR
1995	Sea-A	1	1	0	0	0	0	0	0	0	0	.000	.000	.000	-99	-0	0	0	0	1.000	0	/2-1	0.0
1996	Bos-A	21	58	4	10	3	1	1	11	2	10	.172	.213	.310	30	-6	1	0	0	.930	3	2-10,3-10	-0.3
1997	Bos-A	4	15	0	4	1	0	0	3	0	5	.267	.267	.333	54	-1	0	0	0	.947	3	/3-4	0.2
Total	3	26	74	4	14	4	1	1	14	2	15	.189	.221	.311	33	-8	1	0	0	.952	6	/3-14,2-11	-0.1

■ JOHNNY PRAMESA Pramesa, John Steven b: 8/28/25, Barton, Ohio d: 9/9/96, Los Angeles, Cal. BR/TR, 6'2", 210 lbs. Deb: 4/24/49

YEAR	TM/L	G	AB	R	H	2B	3B	HR	RBI	BB	SO	AVG	OBP	SLG	PRO+	BR/A	SB	CS	SBR	FA	FR	G/POS	TPR
1949	Cin-N	17	25	2	6	1	0	1	2	3	5	.240	.321	.400	91	-0	0			.966	-1	C-13	-0.1
1950	Cin-N	74	228	14	70	10	1	5	30	19	15	.307	.363	.425	106	2	0			.981	0	C-73	0.5
1951	Cin-N	72	227	12	52	5	2	6	22	5	17	.229	.246	.348	57	-14	0	0	0	.968	-7	C-63	-1.9
1952	Chi-N	22	46	1	13	1	0	1	5	4	4	.283	.340	.370	96	-0	0	0	0	.958	2	C-17	0.2
Total	4	185	526	29	141	17	3	13	59	31	41	.268	.310	.386	84	-13	0	0		.973	-6	C-166	-1.3

■ DEL PRATT Pratt, Derrill Burnham b: 1/10/1888, Walhalla, S.C. d: 9/30/77, Texas City, Tex. BR/TR, 5'11", 175 lbs. Deb: 4/11/12

YEAR	TM/L	G	AB	R	H	2B	3B	HR	RBI	BB	SO	AVG	OBP	SLG	PRO+	BR/A	SB	CS	SBR	FA	FR	G/POS	TPR
1912	StL-A	152	570	76	172	26	15	5	69	36		.302	.348	.426	125	16	24			.943	14	*2-122,S-21/O-8,3-1	2.8
1913	StL-A	155	592	60	175	31	13	2	87	40	57	.296	.341	.402	121	13	37			.951	5	*2-146/1-9	1.6
1914	StL-A	158	584	85	165	34	13	5	65	50	45	.283	.341	.411	131	19	37	28	-6	.944	-2	*2-152/O-5,S-1	1.2
1915	StL-A	159	602	61	175	31	11	3	78	26	43	.291	.323	.394	119	10	32	23	-4	.965	12	*2-158	2.0
1916	StL-A	158	596	64	159	35	12	5	**103**	54	56	.267	.331	.391	123	14	26	17	-2	.966	22	*2-158	4.2
1917	StL-A	123	450	40	111	22	8	1	53	33	36	.247	.301	.338	98	-2	18			.959	15	*2-119/1-2	2.0
1918	NY-A	126	477	65	131	19	7	2	55	35	26	.275	.327	.356	104	1	12			.969	12	*2-126	2.3
1919	NY-A	140	527	69	154	27	7	4	56	36	24	.292	.342	.393	105	3	22			.969	**28**	*2-140	3.8
1920	NY-A	154	574	84	180	37	8	4	97	50	24	.314	.372	.427	107	6	12	10	-2	.971	12	*2-154	2.0
1921	Bos-A	135	521	80	169	36	10	5	102	44	10	.324	.378	.461	116	12	8	10	-4	.961	-1	*2-134	1.0
1922	Bos-A	154	607	73	183	44	7	6	86	53	20	.301	.361	.427	106	5	7	10	-4	.966	-13	*2-154	-0.8
1923	Det-A	101	297	43	92	18	3	0	40	25	9	.310	.375	.391	104	2	6	1	1	.947	-10	2-60,1-17,3-12	-0.6
1924	Det-A	121	429	56	130	32	3	1	77	31	10	.303	.353	.399	95	-4	6	9	-4	.948	-2	2-65,1-51/3-4,O-1	-1.1
Total	13	1836	6826	856	1996	392	117	43	968	513	360	.292	.345	.403	112	94	247	108		.960	91	*2-1688/1-79,S3O	20.4

■ FRANK PRATT Pratt, Francis Bruce "Truckhorse" b: 8/24/1897, Blocton, Ala. d: 3/8/74, Centreville, Ala. BL/TR, 5'9.5", 155 lbs. Deb: 5/13/21

YEAR	TM/L	G	AB	R	H	2B	3B	HR	RBI	BB	SO	AVG	OBP	SLG	PRO+	BR/A	SB	CS	SBR	FA	FR	G/POS	TPR
1921	Chi-A	1	1	0	0	0	0	0	0	0	0	.000	.000	.000	-99	-0	0	0	0	.000	0	H	0.0

■ LARRY PRATT Pratt, Lester John b: 10/8/1886, Gibson City, Ill. d: 1/8/69, Peoria, Ill. BR/TR, 6' ", 183 lbs. Deb: 9/19/14

YEAR	TM/L	G	AB	R	H	2B	3B	HR	RBI	BB	SO	AVG	OBP	SLG	PRO+	BR/A	SB	CS	SBR	FA	FR	G/POS	TPR
1914	Bos-A	5	4	0	0	0	0	0	0	0	4	.000	.000	.000	-99	-1	0			.923	2	/C-5	0.1
1915	Bro-F	20	49	5	9	1	0	1	2	2	18	.184	.216	.265	35	-5	2			.949	-1	C-17	-0.5
	New-F	5	4	2	2	2	0	0	0	3	1	.500	.714	1.000	403	2	2			1.000	-1	/C-3	0.2
	Yr	25	53	7	11	3	0	1	2	5	19	.208	.276	.321	69	-3	4			.953	-1	C-20	-0.3
Total	2	30	57	7	11	3	0	1	2	5	23	.193	.258	.298	58	-4	4			.949	0	/C-25	-0.2

■ TOM PRATT Pratt, Thomas J. b: 1/26/1844, Chelsea, Mass. d: 9/28/08, Philadelphia, Pa. TL , 5'7.5", 150 lbs. Deb: 10/18/1871 U

YEAR	TM/L	G	AB	R	H	2B	3B	HR	RBI	BB	SO	AVG	OBP	SLG	PRO+	BR/A	SB	CS	SBR	FA	FR	G/POS	TPR
1871	Ath-n	1	6	2	2	0	0	0	1	0	0	.333	.333	.333	93	-0	0	0	0	.786	-1	/1-1	0.0

■ TODD PRATT Pratt, Todd Alan b: 2/9/67, Bellevue, Neb. BR/TR, 6'3", 225 lbs. Deb: 7/29/92

YEAR	TM/L	G	AB	R	H	2B	3B	HR	RBI	BB	SO	AVG	OBP	SLG	PRO+	BR/A	SB	CS	SBR	FA	FR	G/POS	TPR
1992	Phi-N	16	46	6	13	1	0	2	10	4	12	.283	.340	.435	118	1	0	0	0	.972	-1	C-11	0.1
1993	*Phi-N	33	87	8	25	6	0	5	13	5	19	.287	.333	.529	128	3	0	0	0	.989	5	C-26	0.9
1994	Phi-N	28	102	10	20	6	1	2	9	12	29	.196	.281	.333	58	-6	0	1	-1	1.000	-1	C-28	-0.6
1995	Chi-N	25	60	3	8	2	0	0	4	6	21	.133	.212	.167	2	-9	0	0	0	.981	7	C-25	0.0
1997	NY-N	39	106	12	30	6	0	2	19	13	32	.283	.372	.396	105	1	0	1	-1	.990	5	C-36/D-1	0.7
1998	NY-N	41	69	9	19	9	1	2	18	2	20	.275	.296	.522	107	0	0	0	0	.973	-2	C-16/1-3	-0.1
Total	6	182	470	48	115	30	2	13	73	42	133	.245	.311	.400	87	-9	0	2	-1	.987	13	C-142/1-3,D-1	1.0

■ MEL PREIBISCH Preibisch, Melvin Adolphus "Primo" b: 11/23/14, Sealy, Tex. d: 4/12/80, Sealy, Tex. BR/TR, 5'11", 185 lbs. Deb: 9/17/40

YEAR	TM/L	G	AB	R	H	2B	3B	HR	RBI	BB	SO	AVG	OBP	SLG	PRO+	BR/A	SB	CS	SBR	FA	FR	G/POS	TPR
1940	Bos-N	11	40	3	9	2	0	0	5	2	4	.225	.262	.275	51	-3	0			1.000	1	O-11	-0.3
1941	Bos-N	5	4	0	0	0	0	0	0	1	2	.000	.200	.000	-42	-1	0			1.000	-1	/O-2	-0.2
Total	2	16	44	3	9	2	0	0	5	3	6	.205	.255	.250	42	-3	0			1.000	-0	/O-13	-0.5

■ BOBBY PRESCOTT Prescott, George Bertrand b: 3/27/31, Colon, Panama BR/TR, 5'11", 180 lbs. Deb: 6/17/61

YEAR	TM/L	G	AB	R	H	2B	3B	HR	RBI	BB	SO	AVG	OBP	SLG	PRO+	BR/A	SB	CS	SBR	FA	FR	G/POS	TPR
1961	KC-A	10	12	0	1	0	0	0	0	2	5	.083	.214	.083	-17	-2	0	0	0	.000	-1	/O-2	-0.3

■ JIM PRESLEY Presley, James Arthur b: 10/23/61, Pensacola, Fla. BR/TR, 6'1", 200 lbs. Deb: 6/24/84 C

YEAR	TM/L	G	AB	R	H	2B	3B	HR	RBI	BB	SO	AVG	OBP	SLG	PRO+	BR/A	SB	CS	SBR	FA	FR	G/POS	TPR
1984	Sea-A	70	251	27	57	12	1	10	36	6	63	.227	.248	.402	78	-9	1	1	-0	.958	-3	3-69/D-1	-1.3
1985	Sea-A	155	570	71	157	33	1	28	84	44	100	.275	.328	.484	118	13	2	2	-1	.961	7	*3-154	1.7
1986	Sea-A☆	155	616	83	163	33	4	27	107	32	172	.265	.305	.463	105	2	0	4	-2	.965	6	*3-155	0.2
1987	Sea-A	152	575	78	142	23	6	24	88	38	157	.247	.298	.433	86	-13	2	0	1	.953	11	*3-148/S-4,D-1	-0.3
1988	Sea-A	150	544	50	125	26	0	14	62	36	114	.230	.283	.355	74	-20	3	5	-2	.940	-13	*3-146/D-4	-3.6
1989	Sea-A	117	390	42	92	20	1	12	41	21	107	.236	.277	.385	82	-11	0	0	0	.924	-4	3-90,1-30/D-1	-1.6
1990	Atl-N	140	541	59	131	34	1	19	72	29	130	.242	.284	.414	85	-13	1	1	-0	.930	-3	*3-133,1-17	-1.7
1991	SD-N	20	59	3	8	0	0	1	5	4	16	.136	.203	.186	10	-7	0	1	-1	.923	-3	3-16	-1.2
Total	8	959	3546	413	875	181	14	135	495	210	859	.247	.292	.420	90	-57	9	14	-6	.949	-2	3-911/1-47,D-7,S-4	-7.8

■ WALT PRESTON Preston, Walter B. b: 1870, Richmond, Va. BL/TR, 6', 175 lbs. Deb: 4/18/1895

YEAR	TM/L	G	AB	R	H	2B	3B	HR	RBI	BB	SO	AVG	OBP	SLG	PRO+	BR/A	SB	CS	SBR	FA	FR	G/POS	TPR
1895	Lou-N	50	197	42	55	6	4	1	24	17	17	.279	.366	.365	95	-1	11			.893	-7	O-26,3-25	-0.7

■ JIM PRICE Price, Jimmie William b: 10/13/41, Harrisburg, Pa. BR/TR, 6', 195 lbs. Deb: 4/11/67

YEAR	TM/L	G	AB	R	H	2B	3B	HR	RBI	BB	SO	AVG	OBP	SLG	PRO+	BR/A	SB	CS	SBR	FA	FR	G/POS	TPR
1967	Det-A	44	92	9	24	4	0	0	8	4	10	.261	.292	.304	74	-3	0	0	0	.974	0	C-24	-0.2
1968	*Det-A	64	132	12	23	4	0	3	13	13	14	.174	.253	.273	58	-7	0	0	0	.996	2	C-42	-0.3
1969	Det-A	72	192	21	45	8	0	9	28	18	20	.234	.300	.417	95	-2	0	0	0	.989	4	C-51	0.4
1970	Det-A	52	132	12	24	4	0	5	15	21	23	.182	.294	.326	70	-5	0	0	0	.979	-1	C-38	-0.5
1971	Det-A	29	54	4	13	2	0	1	7	6	3	.241	.328	.333	84	-1	0	0	0	.981	1	C-25	0.1
Total	5	261	602	58	129	22	0	18	71	62	70	.214	.290	.341	78	-18	0	0	0	.985	5	C-180	-0.5

YEAR	TM/L	G	AB	R	H	2B	3B	HR	RBI	BB	SO	AVG	OBP	SLG	PRO+	BR/A	SB	CS	SBR	FA	FR	G/POS	TPR

■ **JACKIE PRICE**   Price, John Thomas Reid "Johnny"   b: 11/13/12, Winborn, Miss.   d: 10/2/67, San Francisco, Cal.   BL/TR, 5'10.5", 150 lbs.   Deb: 8/18/46

| 1946 | Cle-A | 7 | 13 | 1 | 3 | 0 | 0 | 0 | 0 | 0 | 0 | .231 | .231 | .231 | 31 | -1 | 0 | 0 | 0 | .947 | 8 | /S-4 | 0.0 |

■ **JOE PRICE**   Price, Joseph Preston "Lumber"   b: 4/10/1897, Milligan College, Tenn.   d: 1/15/61, Washington, D.C.   BR/TR, 6'1.5", 187 lbs.   Deb: 9/5/28

| 1928 | NY-N | 1 | 1 | 0 | 0 | 0 | 0 | 0 | 0 | 0 | 1 | .000 | .000 | .000 | -99 | -0 | 0 | | | .000 | -1 | /O-1 | -0.1 |

■ **BOB PRICHARD**   Prichard, Robert Alexander   b: 10/21/17, Paris, Tex.   d: 9/25/91, Abilene, Tex.   BL/TL, 6'1", 195 lbs.   Deb: 6/14/39

| 1939 | Was-A | 26 | 85 | 8 | 20 | 5 | 0 | 0 | 8 | 19 | 16 | .235 | .375 | .294 | 79 | -2 | 0 | 2 | -1 | .992 | -1 | 1-26 | -0.6 |

■ **JERRY PRIDDY**   Priddy, Gerald Edward   b: 11/9/19, Los Angeles, Cal.   d: 3/3/80, N.Hollywood, Cal.   BR/TR, 5'11.5", 180 lbs.   Deb: 4/17/41

1941	NY-A	56	174	18	37	7	0	1	26	18	16	.213	.290	.270	50	-13	4	2	0	.968	9	2-31,3-14,1-10	-0.2
1942	*NY-A	59	189	23	53	9	2	2	28	31	27	.280	.385	.381	118	6	0	1	-1	.944	5	3-35,1-11/2-8,S-3	1.1
1943	Was-A	149	560	68	152	31	3	4	62	67	76	.271	.350	.359	112	9	5	5	-2	.971	4	*2-134,S-15/3-1	2.2
1946	Was-A	138	511	54	130	22	8	6	58	57	73	.254	.332	.364	100	-0	9	3	1	.962	2	*2-138	1.2
1947	Was-A	147	505	42	108	20	3	3	49	62	79	.214	.301	.283	65	-24	7	6	-2	.980	-2	*2-146	-1.8
1948	StL-A	151	560	96	166	40	9	8	79	86	71	.296	.391	.443	118	16	6	5	-1	.968	24	*2-146	4.4
1949	StL-A	145	544	83	158	26	4	11	63	80	81	.290	.382	.414	106	5	5	3	-0	.968	-3	*2-145	0.8
1950	Det-A	157	618	104	171	26	6	13	75	95	95	.277	.376	.401	98	-3	2	7	-4	.981	31	*2-157	3.0
1951	Det-A	154	584	73	152	22	6	8	57	69	73	.260	.338	.360	88	-9	4	3	-1	.980	10	*2-154/S-1	0.7
1952	Det-A	75	279	37	79	23	3	4	20	42	29	.283	.379	.430	124	10	1	8	-5	.968	-1	2-75	0.8
1953	Det-A	65	196	14	46	6	2	1	24	17	19	.235	.299	.301	63	-10	1	1	-0	.977	-2	2-45,1-11/3-2	-0.5
Total	11	1296	4720	612	1252	232	46	61	541	624	639	.265	.353	.373	97	-13	44	44	-13	.973	82	*2-1179/3-52,1-32,S	11.7

■ **CURTIS PRIDE**   Pride, Curtis John   b: 12/17/68, Washington, D.C.   BL/TR, 6', 205 lbs.   Deb: 9/14/93

1993	Mon-N	10	9	3	4	1	1	1	5	0	3	.444	.444	1.111	288	2	1	0	0	1.000	-0	/O-2	0.2
1995	Mon-N	48	63	10	11	1	0	0	2	5	16	.175	.235	.190	13	-8	3	2	-0	.920	-4	O-24	-1.2
1996	Det-A	95	267	52	80	17	5	10	31	31	63	.300	.372	.513	121	8	11	6	-0	.967	-3	O-48,D-31	0.2
1997	Det-A	79	162	21	34	4	4	2	19	24	45	.210	.316	.321	67	-8	6	4	-1	.980	-6	O-35,D-23	-1.5
	Bos-A	2	2	1	1	0	0	1	1	0	1	.500	.500	2.000	502	1	0	0	0	.000	-0	/H	0.1
	Yr	81	164	22	35	4	4	3	20	24	46	.213	.317	.341	73	-6	6	4	-1	.980	-6	O-35,D-23	-1.4
1998	Atl-N	70	107	19	27	6	1	3	9	9	29	.252	.328	.411	88	-2	4	0	1	1.000	1	O-22/D-2	0.0
Total	5	304	610	106	157	29	11	17	67	69	157	.257	.337	.425	94	-5	25	12	0	.971	-13	O-131/D-56	-2.2

■ **JOHNNY PRIEST**   Priest, John Gooding   b: 6/23/1886, St.Joseph, Mo.   d: 11/4/79, Washington, D.C.   BR/TR, 5'11", 170 lbs.   Deb: 5/30/11

1911	NY-A	8	21	2	3	0	0	0	2	2		.143	.250	.143	10	-2	3			.824	-3	/2-5,3-2	-0.6
1912	NY-A	2	2	1	1	0	0	0	1	0		.500	.500	.500	176	-0				.000	0	H	0.0
Total	2	10	23	3	4	0	0	0	3	2		.174	.269	.174	23	-2	3			.824	-3	/2-5,3-2	-0.6

■ **TOM PRINCE**   Prince, Thomas Albert   b: 8/13/64, Kankakee, Ill.   BR/TR, 5'11", 185 lbs.   Deb: 9/22/87

1987	Pit-N	4	9	1	2	1	0	1	2	0	2	.222	.222	.667	123	0	0	0		1.000	1	/C-4	0.1
1988	Pit-N	29	74	3	13	2	0	0	6	4	15	.176	.218	.203	22	-7	0	0	0	.983	-2	C-28	-0.9
1989	Pit-N	21	52	1	7	4	0	0	5	6	12	.135	.224	.212	26	-5	1	1	-0	.960	-3	C-21	-0.5
1990	Pit-N	4	10	1	1	0	0	0	0	1	2	.100	.182	.100	-21	-2	0	1	-1	1.000	0	/C-3	-0.2
1991	Pit-N	26	34	4	9	3	0	1	2	7	3	.265	.405	.441	140	2	0	0	0	.984	1	C-19/1-1	0.4
1992	Pit-N	27	44	1	4	2	0	0	5	6	9	.091	.200	.136	-3	-6	1	1	-0	.977	3	C-19/3-1	-0.3
1993	Pit-N	66	179	14	35	14	0	2	24	13	38	.196	.276	.307	56	-11	1	1	-0	.984	-1	C-59	-0.9
1994	LA-N	3	6	2	2	0	0	0	1	1	3	.333	.429	.333	109	0	0	0		1.000	0	/C-3	0.0
1995	LA-N	18	40	3	8	2	1	0	4	4	10	.200	.273	.375	75	-2	0	0	0	.988	0	C-17	-0.1
1996	LA-N	40	64	6	19	6	0	1	11	6	15	.297	.375	.438	123	2	0	0	0	.994	9	C-35	1.1
1997	LA-N	47	100	17	22	5	0	3	14	5	15	.220	.278	.360	71	-5	0	0	0	.996	10	C-45	0.7
1998	LA-N	37	81	7	15	5	1	0	5	7	24	.185	.267	.272	44	-7	0	0	0	1.000	5	C-32	-0.1
Total	12	322	693	60	137	44	2	9	79	60	148	.198	.276	.306	59	-40	3	4	-2	.988	26	C-285/3-1,1-1	-0.7

■ **WALTER PRINCE**   Prince, Walter Farr   b: 5/9/1861, Amherst, N.H.   d: 3/2/38, Bristol, N.H.   BL/TR, 5'9", 150 lbs.   Deb: 8/7/1883

1883	Lou-a	4	11	1	2	0	0	0				.182	.182	.182	19	-1				.500	-2	/O-2,1-2,S-1	-0.3
1884	Det-N	7	21	0	3	0	0	0	1	3	4	.143	.250	.143	29	-2				.375	-3	/O-7	-0.5
	Was-a	43	166	22	36	3	2	1			13	.217	.286	.277	95	0				.940	-6	1-43	-0.9
	Was-U	1	4	0	1	0	0	0				.250	.250	.250	54	0				.818	-0	/1-1	-0.1
Total	2	55	202	23	42	3	2	1	1	16	4	.208	.276	.257	83	-2				.935	-11	/1-46,O-9,S-1	-1.8

■ **BUDDY PRITCHARD**   Pritchard, Harold William   b: 1/25/36, South Gate, Cal.   BR/TR, 6'1", 195 lbs.   Deb: 4/21/57

| 1957 | Pit-N | 23 | 11 | 1 | 1 | 0 | 0 | 0 | 0 | 0 | 3 | .091 | .091 | .091 | -53 | -2 | 0 | 0 | 0 | .947 | 5 | S-10/2-3 | 0.2 |

■ **CHRIS PRITCHETT**   Pritchett, Christopher Davis   b: 1/31/70, Merced, Cal.   BL/TR, 6'4", 185 lbs.   Deb: 9/6/96

1996	Cal-A	5	13	0	2	0	0	0	0	0	3	.154	.154	.154	-22	-2	0	0	0	1.000	-0	/1-5	-0.3
1998	Ana-A	31	80	12	23	2	1	2	8	4	16	.287	.321	.412	88	-1	2	0	1	.995	4	1-29/D-1	0.1
Total	2	36	93	13	25	2	1	2	9	4	19	.269	.299	.376	73	-4	2	0	1	.996	3	/1-34,D-1	-0.2

■ **GEORGE PROESER**   Proeser, George "Yatz"   b: 5/30/1864, Cincinnati, Ohio   d: 10/13/41, New Burlington, O.   BL/TL, 5'10", 190 lbs.   Deb: 9/15/1888

1888	Cle-a	7	23	5	7	2	0	0	1	1		.304	.333	.391	136	1	0			.846	-1	/P-7	0.0
1890	Syr-a	13	53	11	13	1	1	0	6	10		.245	.365	.358	126	2	1			.895	-2	O-13	0.0
Total	2	20	76	16	20	3	1	1	7	11		.263	.356	.368	129	3	1			.895	-3	/O-13,P-7	0.0

■ **JAKE PROPST**   Propst, William Jacob   b: 3/10/1895, Kennedy, Ala.   d: 2/24/67, Columbus, Miss.   BL/TL, 5'10", 165 lbs.   Deb: 8/7/23

| 1923 | Was-A | 1 | 1 | 0 | 0 | 0 | 0 | 0 | 0 | 0 | 0 | .000 | .000 | .000 | -99 | -0 | 0 | 0 | 0 | .000 | 0 | H | 0.0 |

■ **DOC PROTHRO**   Prothro, James Thompson   b: 7/16/1893, Memphis, Tenn.   d: 10/14/71, Memphis, Tenn.   BR/TR, 5'10.5", 170 lbs.   Deb: 9/26/20

1920	Was-A	6	13	2	5	0	0	0	2	0	4	.385	.385	.385	107	0	0	0	0	1.000	0	/S-2,3-2	0.0
1923	Was-A	6	8	2	2	0	1	0	3	1	3	.250	.333	.500	124	0	0	0	0	1.000	3	/3-6	0.3
1924	Was-A	46	159	17	53	11	5	0	24	15	11	.333	.394	.465	125	6	4	4	-1	.915	-11	3-45	-0.3
1925	Bos-A	119	415	44	130	23	3	0	51	52	21	.313	.390	.383	97	-0	9	11	-4	.945	-6	*3-108/S-3	-0.2
1926	Cin-N	3	5	1	1	0	0	0	1	0	1	.200	.333	.600	151	0	0	0	0	1.000	0	/3-2	0.0
Total	5	180	600	66	191	34	10	0	81	68	40	.318	.390	.408	105	6	13	15		.940	-14	3-163/S-5	-0.2

■ **EARL PRUESS**   Pruess, Earl Henry "Gibby"   b: 4/2/1895, Chicago, Ill.   d: 8/28/79, Branson, Mo.   BR/TR, 5'10.5", 170 lbs.   Deb: 9/15/20

| 1920 | StL-A | 1 | 0 | 1 | 0 | 0 | 0 | 0 | 0 | 1 | 0 | — | 1.000 | — | 176 | 0 | 1 | 0 | 0 | 1.000 | 0 | /O-1 | 0.1 |

■ **JIM PRUETT**   Pruett, James Calvin   b: 12/16/17, Nashville, Tenn.   BR/TR, 5'10", 178 lbs.   Deb: 9/26/44

1944	Phi-A	3	4	1	1	0	0	0	0	1	0	.250	.500	.250	119	0	0	0	0	1.000	1	/C-2	0.1
1945	Phi-A	6	9	1	2	0	0	0	0	1	2	.222	.300	.222	53	-1	0	1	-1	1.000	1	/C-4	-0.1
Total	2	9	13	2	3	0	0	0	0	2	2	.231	.375	.231	77	-0	0	1	-1	1.000	1	/C-6	0.0

■ **RON PRUITT**   Pruitt, Ronald Ralph   b: 10/21/51, Flint, Mich.   BR/TR, 6', 185 lbs.   Deb: 6/25/75

1975	Tex-A	14	17	2	3	0	0	0	0	1	3	.176	.222	.176	14	-2	0	0		1.000	-1	C-13/O-1	-0.3
1976	Cle-A	47	86	7	23	1	1	0	5	16	8	.267	.382	.302	103	1	2	3	-1	1.000	2	O-26/C-6,3-6,1-1,D	0.2
1977	Cle-A	78	219	29	63	10	2	6	32	28	22	.288	.373	.379	109	4	2	3	-1	.972	-8	O-69/C-4,3-1,D-4	-0.7
1978	Cle-A	71	187	17	44	6	1	6	17	16	20	.235	.296	.374	88	-3	2	1	-0	.984	-6	C-48,O-16/3-2,D-5	-1.0
1979	Cle-A	64	166	23	47	7	0	2	21	19	21	.283	.357	.361	94	-1	0	0	0	.957	-5	O-29,D-14,C-11/3-3	-0.6
1980	Cle-A	23	36	1	11	0	0	0	4	4	6	.306	.375	.333	95	-0	0	0	0	1.000		/O-6,3-2,D-2	0.0
	Chi-A	33	70	8	21	2	0	2	11	8	7	.300	.372	.414	116	2	0	0	0	1.000	-1	O-11/C-5,3-3,1-1,D	0.0
	Yr	56	106	9	32	2	0	2	15	12	13	.302	.373	.387	109	2	0	0	0	1.000		O-17/D-9,3-5,C-5,1	0.0
1981	Cle-A	5	9	0	0	0	0	0	0	1	2	.000	.100	.000	-70	-2	0	0		1.000	-1	/O-3,C-1,D-1	-0.3

YEAR	TM/L	G	AB	R	H	2B	3B	HR	RBI	BB	SO	AVG	OBP	SLG	PRO+	BR/A	SB	CS	SBR	FA	FR	G/POS	TPR
1982	SF-N	5	4	1	2	1	0	0	2	1	1	.500	.600	.750	276	1	0	0	0	1.000	0	/C-1,O-1	0.1
1983	SF-N	1	1	0	0	0	0	0	0	0	0	.000	.000	.000	-99	-0	0	0	0	.000	0	/H	0.0
Total	9	341	795	88	214	28	4	12	92	94	90	.269	.348	.360	97	-1	8	7	-2	.977	-20	O-162/C-89,D-37,31	-2.6
■ GREG PRYOR	Pryor, Gregory Russell b: 10/2/49, Marietta, Ohio BR/TR, 6', 186 lbs. Deb: 6/4/76																						
1976	Tex-A	5	8	2	3	0	0	0	1	0	1	.375	.375	.375	118	0	0	0	0	1.000	0	/2-3,S-1,3-1	0.1
1978	Chi-A	82	222	27	58	11	0	2	15	11	18	.261	.299	.338	78	-7	3	1	0	.966	6	2-35,S-28,3-20	0.4
1979	Chi-A	143	476	60	131	23	3	3	34	35	41	.275	.327	.355	84	-10	3	4	-2	.961	-5	*S-119,2-25,3-22	-0.3
1980	Chi-A	122	338	32	81	18	4	1	29	12	35	.240	.270	.325	63	-18	2	2	-1	.975	22	S-76,3-41/2-5,D-1	1.1
1981	Chi-A	47	76	4	17	1	0	0	6	6	8	.224	.298	.237	57	-4	0	0	0	.931	4	3-27,S-13/2-5	0.0
1982	KC-A	73	152	23	41	10	1	2	12	10	20	.270	.315	.388	92	-2	2	0	1	.951	8	3-40,2-15,1-14,/S-7	0.6
1983	KC-A	68	115	9	25	4	0	1	14	7	8	.217	.262	.278	49	-8	0	0	0	.958	11	3-60/1-6,2-3	0.2
1984	*KC-A	123	270	32	71	11	1	4	25	12	28	.263	.302	.356	80	-7	0	3	-2	.970	17	*3-105,2-22/S-2,1D	0.8
1985	*KC-A	63	114	8	25	3	0	1	3	8	12	.219	.270	.272	49	-8	0	1	-1	.946	2	3-26,2-20,S-13,/1D	-0.5
1986	KC-A	63	112	7	19	4	0	0	7	3	14	.170	.191	.205	8	-14	1	1	-0	.935	6	3-35,S-17,2-12,/1-1	-0.9
Total	10	789	1883	204	471	85	9	14	146	104	185	.250	.293	.327	70	-78	11	12	-4	.952	71	3-377,S-276,2/1D	1.5
■ GEORGE PUCCINELLI	Puccinelli, George Lawrence "Pooch" or "Count" b: 6/22/07, San Francisco, Cal. d: 4/16/56, San Francisco, Cal BR/TR, 6'0.5", 190 lbs. Deb: 7/17/30																						
1930	*StL-N	11	16	5	9	1	0	3	8	0	1	.563	.563	1.188	298	5	0			1.000	-1	/O-3	0.3
1932	StL-N	31	108	17	30	8	0	3	11	12	13	.278	.350	.435	107	1	1			.942	2	O-30	0.2
1934	StL-A	10	26	4	6	1	0	2	5	1	8	.231	.286	.500	92	-1	0	0	0	.941	1	/O-6	0.0
1936	Phi-A	135	457	83	127	30	3	11	78	65	70	.278	.369	.429	98	-1	2	3	-1	.948	0	*O-117	-0.6
Total	4	187	607	109	172	40	3	19	102	78	92	.283	.367	.453	105	4	3	3		.947	2	O-156	-0.1
■ KIRBY PUCKETT	Puckett, Kirby b: 3/14/61, Chicago, Ill. BR/TR, 5'8", 210 lbs. Deb: 5/8/84																						
1984	Min-A	128	557	63	165	12	5	0	31	16	69	.296	.321	.336	78	-16	14	7	0	.993	30	*O-128	1.0
1985	Min-A	161	691	80	199	29	13	4	74	41	87	.288	.332	.385	90	-9	21	12	-1	.984	21	*O-161	0.6
1986	Min-A★	161	680	119	223	37	6	31	96	34	99	.328	.366	.537	138	34	20	12	-1	.986	11	*O-160	3.8
1987	*Min-A★	157	624	96	**207**	32	5	28	99	32	91	.332	.370	.534	131	26	12	7	-1	.986	5	*O-147/D-8	2.5
1988	Min-A★	158	657	109	**234**	42	5	24	121	23	83	.356	.380	.545	151	42	6	7	-2	.994	20	*O-158	5.4
1989	Min-A★	159	635	75	**215**	45	4	9	85	41	59	**.339**	.381	.465	129	23	11	4	1	.991	18	*O-157/D-2	3.9
1990	Min-A★	146	551	82	164	40	3	12	80	57	73	.298	.367	.446	119	14	5	4	-1	.989	8	*O-141/2-1,3-1,SD	1.7
1991	*Min-A★	152	611	92	195	29	6	15	89	31	78	.319	.356	.460	118	14	11	5	0	.985	4	*O-152	1.5
1992	Min-A★	160	639	104	**210**	38	4	19	110	44	97	.329	.377	.490	137	30	17	7	1	.993	6	*O-149/2-2,3-2,SD	3.4
1993	Min-A★	156	622	89	184	39	3	22	89	47	93	.296	.352	.474	119	16	8	6	-1	.994	4	*O-139,D-17	1.4
1994	Min-A★	108	439	79	139	32	3	20	**112**	28	47	.317	.367	.540	130	18	6	3	0	.986	8	O-95,D-13	2.1
1995	Min-A★	137	538	83	169	39	0	23	99	56	89	.314	.382	.515	130	24	3	2	-0	.981	1	*O-109,D-28/2-1,3S	1.8
Total	12	1783	7244	1071	2304	414	57	207	1085	450	965	.318	.363	.477	123	216	134	76	-5	.989	137	*O-1696/D-81,32S	29.1
■ JOHN PUHL	Puhl, John G. b: 1/10/1876, Brooklyn, N.Y. d: 8/24/1900, Bayonne, N.J. Deb: 10/13/1898																						
1898	NY-N	2	9	1	2	0	0	0	1	0		.222	.222	.222	28	-1	0			.667	-1	/3-2	-0.1
1899	NY-N	1	2	0	0	0	0	0	0	0		.000	.333	.000	-6	-0	0			.667	-0	/3-1	0.0
Total	2	3	11	1	2	0	0	0	1	0		.182	.250	.182	24	-1	0			.667	-1	/3-3	-0.1
■ TERRY PUHL	Puhl, Terry Stephen b: 7/8/56, Melville, Sask., Can BL/TR, 6'2", 200 lbs. Deb: 7/12/77																						
1977	Hou-N	60	229	40	69	13	5	0	10	30	31	.301	.385	.402	122	8	10	1	2	.992	3	O-59	1.1
1978	Hou-N☆	149	585	87	169	25	6	3	35	48	46	.289	.347	.368	108	6	32	14	1	.992	15	*O-148	1.6
1979	Hou-N	157	600	87	172	22	4	8	49	58	46	.287	.353	.377	105	5	30	22	-4	**1.000**	3	*O-152	-0.3
1980	*Hou-N	141	535	75	151	24	5	13	55	60	52	.282	.359	.419	126	19	27	11	2	.991	14	*O-135	3.0
1981	*Hou-N	96	350	43	88	19	4	3	28	31	49	.251	.319	.354	96	-2	22	4	4	**1.000**	5	O-88	0.3
1982	Hou-N	145	507	64	133	17	9	8	50	51	49	.262	.332	.379	106	4	17	9	-0	.989	-6	*O-138	-0.7
1983	Hou-N	137	465	66	136	25	7	8	44	36	48	.292	.346	.428	121	12	24	11	1	.991	-4	*O-124	0.5
1984	Hou-N	132	449	66	135	19	7	9	55	59	45	.301	.383	.434	139	24	13	8	-1	.986	-2	*O-126	1.9
1985	Hou-N	57	194	34	55	14	3	2	23	18	23	.284	.347	.418	116	4	6	2	1	1.000	0	O-53	0.3
1986	*Hou-N	81	172	17	42	10	0	3	14	15	24	.244	.305	.355	84	-4	3	2	-0	1.000	-4	O-47	-1.0
1987	Hou-N	90	122	9	28	5	0	2	15	11	16	.230	.293	.320	65	-6	1	1	-0	.980	-6	O-40	-1.3
1988	Hou-N	113	234	42	71	7	2	3	19	35	30	.303	.396	.389	131	11	22	4	4	.983	-7	O-78	0.7
1989	Hou-N	121	354	41	96	25	4	0	27	45	39	.271	.355	.364	110	6	9	8	-2	1.000	-2	*O-103/1-3	-0.1
1990	Hou-N	37	41	5	12	1	0	0	8	5	7	.293	.383	.317	98	0	1	2	-1	1.000	-2	/O-8,1-1	-0.3
1991	KC-A	15	18	0	4	0	0	0	3	3	2	.222	.333	.222	57	-1	0	0	0	.000	-0	/O-1,D-2	-0.1
Total	15	1531	4855	676	1361	226	56	62	435	505	507	.280	.351	.388	113	84	217	99	6	.993	8	*O-1300/1-4,D-2	5.6
■ RICH PUIG	Puig, Richard Gerald b: 3/16/53, Tampa, Fla. BL/TR, 5'10", 165 lbs. Deb: 9/13/74																						
1974	NY-N	4	10	0	0	0	0	0	0	1	2	.000	.091	.000	-74	-2	0	0	0	.923	-0	/2-3,3-1	-0.3
■ LUIS PUJOLS	Pujols, Luis Bienvenido (Toribio) b: 11/18/55, Santiago, D.R. BR/TR, 6'1", 195 lbs. Deb: 9/22/77 C																						
1977	Hou-N	6	15	0	1	0	0	0	0	0	5	.067	.067	.067	-70	-4	0	0	0	1.000	0	/C-6	-0.4
1978	Hou-N	56	153	11	20	8	1	1	11	12	45	.131	.199	.216	17	-18	0	0	0	.981	0	C-55/1-1	-1.8
1979	Hou-N	26	75	7	17	2	1	0	8	2	14	.227	.247	.280	46	-6	0	0	0	.993	1	C-26	-0.4
1980	*Hou-N	78	221	15	44	6	1	0	20	13	29	.199	.247	.235	38	-19	0	0	0	.990	-3	C-75/3-1	-2.1
1981	*Hou-N	40	117	5	28	3	1	1	14	10	17	.239	.299	.308	76	-4	1	0	0	.995	-1	C-39	-0.3
1982	Hou-N	65	176	8	35	6	2	4	15	10	40	.199	.242	.324	62	-10	0	3	-2	.991	5	C-64	-0.5
1983	Hou-N	40	87	4	17	2	0	0	12	5	14	.195	.239	.218	29	-8	0	0	0	.971	5	C-39	-0.3
1984	KC-A	4	5	0	1	0	0	0	1	0	0	.200	.200	.200	11	-1	0	0	0	1.000	0	/C-4	0.0
1985	Tex-A	1	1	0	1	0	0	0	0	0	0	1.000	1.000	1.000	444	0	0	0	0	1.000	-0	/C-1	0.0
Total	9	316	850	50	164	27	6	6	81	52	164	.193	.241	.260	43	-68	1	3	-2	.987	7	C-309/3-1,1-1	-5.8
■ HARVEY PULLIAM	Pulliam, Harvey Jerome b: 10/20/67, San Francisco, Cal. BR/TR, 6', 205 lbs. Deb: 8/10/91																						
1991	KC-A	18	33	4	9	1	0	3	4	3	9	.273	.333	.576	146	2	0	0	0	.917	-2	O-15	0.0
1992	KC-A	4	5	2	1	1	0	0	0	1	3	.200	.333	.400	102	0	0	0	0	1.000	0	/O-1,D-2	0.0
1993	KC-A	27	62	7	16	5	0	1	6	2	14	.258	.292	.387	76	-2	0	0	0	.971	-5	O-26	-0.8
1995	Col-N	5	5	1	2	1	0	1	3	0	2	.400	.400	1.200	234	1	0	0	0	.000	-0	/O-1	0.1
1996	Col-N	10	15	2	2	0	0	0	0	2	6	.133	.235	.133	0	-2	0	0	0	1.000	-0	/O-3	-0.2
1997	Col-N	59	67	15	19	3	0	3	9	5	15	.284	.333	.463	86	-2	0	1	-1	.962	-7	O-33	-1.0
Total	6	123	187	31	49	11	0	8	22	13	49	.262	.313	.449	89	-3	0	1	-1	.956	-14	/O-79,D-2	-1.9
■ BLONDIE PURCELL	Purcell, William Aloysius b: Paterson, N.J. BR/TR, 5'9.5", 159 lbs. Deb: 5/1/1879 M																						
1879	Syr-N	63	277	32	72	6	3	0	25	3	13	.260	.268	.303	99	0				.773	-13	O-47,P-22/C-1	-1.2
	Cin-N	12	50	10	11	0	0	0	4	0	3	.220	.220	.220	48	-3				.750	1	O-10/P-2	-0.2
	Yr	75	327	42	83	6	3	0	29	3	16	.254	.261	.291	91	-3				.767	-13	O-57,P-24/C-1	-1.4
1880	Cin-N	77	325	48	95	13	6	1	24	5	13	.292	.303	.378	131	10				.814	-2	O-55,P-25/S-1	0.4
1881	Cle-N	20	80	3	14	2	1	0	4	5	8	.175	.224	.225	44	-5				.786	-2	O-20	-0.7
	Buf-N	30	113	15	33	7	2	0	17	8	8	.292	.339	.389	130	4				.706	-6	O-25/P-9	-0.3
	Yr	50	193	18	47	9	3	0	21	13	16	.244	.291	.321	95	-1				.748	-8	O-45/P-9	-1.0
1882	Buf-N	84	380	79	105	18	6	2	40	14	27	.276	.302	.371	113	5				.820	-5	*O-82/P-6	-0.1
1883	Phi-N	97	425	70	114	20	5	1	32	13	26	.268	.290	.346	101	2				.777	5	3-46,O-44,P-11,M	0.4
1884	Phi-N	103	428	67	108	11	7	1	31	29	30	.252	.300	.318	99	1				.874	-0	*O-103/P-1	-0.1
1885	Phi-a	66	304	71	90	15	5	0	22	16		.296	.337	.378	119	5				.858	-1	O-66/P-1	0.2
	Bos-N	21	87	9	19	1	1	0	3	3	15	.218	.244	.253	63	-3				.840	-3	O-21	-0.7
1886	Bal-a	26	85	17	19	0	1	0	8	17		.224	.365	.247	96	1	13			.867	-1	O-26/S-1,P-1	0.0

YEAR	TM/L	G	AB	R	H	2B	3B	HR	RBI	BB	SO	AVG	OBP	SLG	PRO+	BR/A	SB	CS	SBR	FA	FR	G/POS	TPR
1887	Bal-a	140	567	101	142	25	8	4	96	46		.250	.318	.344	90	-7	88			.925	-4	*O-140/P-1	-1.0
1888	Bal-a	101	406	53	96	9	4	2	39	27		.236	.289	.293	89	-5	16			.906	-6	*O-100/S-2,1-1	-1.2
	Phi-a	18	66	10	11	3	1	0	6	5		.167	.236	.242	54	-3	10			.903	0	O-17/3-1	-0.3
	Yr	119	472	63	107	12	5	2	45	32		.227	.281	.286	84	-8	26			.905	-6	*O-117/S-2,1-1,3-1	-1.5
1889	Phi-a	129	507	72	160	19	7	0	85	50	27	.316	.383	.381	119	14	22			.903	-10	*O-129	0.1
1890	Phi-a	110	463	110	128	28	3	2	59	43		.276	.343	.363	111	6	48			.949	-1	*O-110	0.1
Total	12	1097	4563	767	1217	177	60	13	495	284	170	.267	.314	.340	103	22	197			.869	-49	O-995/P-79,3S1C	-4.6

■ PID PURDY Purdy, Everett Virgil b: 6/15/04, Beatrice, Neb. d: 1/16/51, Beatrice, Neb. BL/TR, 5′6″, 150 lbs. Deb: 9/7/26

YEAR	TM/L	G	AB	R	H	2B	3B	HR	RBI	BB	SO	AVG	OBP	SLG	PRO+	BR/A	SB	CS	SBR	FA	FR	G/POS	TPR
1926	Chi-A	11	33	5	6	2	1	0	6	2	1	.182	.229	.303	39	-3	0	1	-1	1.000	0	/O-9	-0.4
1927	Cin-N	18	62	15	22	2	4	1	12	4	3	.355	.412	.565	164	5	0			.946	-3	O-16	0.1
1928	Cin-N	70	223	32	69	11	1	0	25	23	13	.309	.377	.368	97	-0	1			.966	0	O-61	-0.4
1929	Cin-N	82	181	22	49	7	5	1	16	19	8	.271	.350	.381	85	-4	2			.978	-1	O-42	-0.7
Total	4	181	499	74	146	22	11	2	59	48	25	.293	.362	.393	97	-2	3	1		.969	-4	O-128	-1.4

■ JESSE PURNELL Purnell, Jesse Rhoades b: 5/11/1881, Glenside, Pa. d: 7/4/66, Philadelphia, Pa. BL/TR, 5′5.5″, 140 lbs. Deb: 10/1/04

YEAR	TM/L	G	AB	R	H	2B	3B	HR	RBI	BB	SO	AVG	OBP	SLG	PRO+	BR/A	SB	CS	SBR	FA	FR	G/POS	TPR
1904	Phi-N	7	19	2	2	0	0	0	1	4		.105	.292	.105	25	-1	1			.864	-1	/3-7	-0.2

■ BILLY PURTELL Purtell, William Patrick b: 1/6/1886, Columbus, Ohio d: 3/17/62, Bradenton, Fla. BR/TR, 5′9″, 170 lbs. Deb: 4/16/08

YEAR	TM/L	G	AB	R	H	2B	3B	HR	RBI	BB	SO	AVG	OBP	SLG	PRO+	BR/A	SB	CS	SBR	FA	FR	G/POS	TPR
1908	Chi-A	26	69	3	9	2	0	0	3	2		.130	.155	.159	2	-7	2			.940	6	3-25	0.0
1909	Chi-A	103	361	34	93	9	3	0	40	19		.258	.302	.299	94	-3	14			.929	5	3-71,2-32	0.4
1910	Chi-A	102	368	21	82	5	3	1	36	21		.223	.272	.261	70	-13	5			.907	4	*3-102	-0.7
	Bos-A	49	168	15	35	1	2	1	15	18		.208	.289	.256	69	-6	2			.908	-5	3-41/S-8	-1.0
	Yr	151	536	36	117	6	5	2	51	39		.218	.278	.259	70	-19	7			.907	-1	*3-143/S-8	-1.7
1911	Bos-A	27	82	5	23	5	3	0	7	1		.280	.298	.415	99	-1	1			.867	-1	3-15/2-3,S-3,O-1	-0.1
1914	Det-A	28	76	4	13	4	0	0	3	2	7	.171	.203	.224	27	-7	0	2	-1	.946	-1	3-16/S-2,2-1	-0.9
Total	5	335	1124	82	255	26	11	2	104	63	7	.227	.275	.275	73	-37	24	2		.915	9	3-270/2-36,S-13,O-1	-2.3

■ ED PUTMAN Putman, Eddy William b: 9/25/53, Los Angeles, Cal. BR/TR, 6′1″, 190 lbs. Deb: 9/7/76

YEAR	TM/L	G	AB	R	H	2B	3B	HR	RBI	BB	SO	AVG	OBP	SLG	PRO+	BR/A	SB	CS	SBR	FA	FR	G/POS	TPR
1976	Chi-N	5	7	0	3	0	0	0	0	0	0	.429	.429	.429	132	0	0	0	0	1.000	0	/C-3,1-1	0.0
1978	Chi-N	17	25	2	5	0	0	0	3	4	6	.200	.310	.200	40	-2	0	0	0	.950	-0	/3-8,1-3,C-2	-0.2
1979	Det-A	21	39	4	9	3	0	2	4	4	12	.231	.302	.462	99	-0	0	1	-1	1.000	1	C-16/1-5	0.0
Total	3	43	71	6	17	3	0	2	7	8	18	.239	.316	.366	81	-2	0	1	-1	1.000	1	/C-21,1-9,3-8	-0.2

■ PAT PUTNAM Putnam, Patrick Edward b: 12/3/53, Bethel, Vt. BL/TR, 6′1″, 214 lbs. Deb: 9/2/77

YEAR	TM/L	G	AB	R	H	2B	3B	HR	RBI	BB	SO	AVG	OBP	SLG	PRO+	BR/A	SB	CS	SBR	FA	FR	G/POS	TPR
1977	Tex-A	11	26	3	8	4	0	0	3	1	4	.308	.333	.462	113	0	0	1	-1	1.000	-1	/1-7,D-3	-0.1
1978	Tex-A	20	46	4	7	1	0	1	2	2	5	.152	.188	.239	19	-5	0	0	0	1.000	0	D-12/1-4	-0.6
1979	Tex-A	139	426	57	118	19	2	18	64	23	50	.277	.323	.458	109	4	1	6	-3	.994	0	1-96,D-32	-0.5
1980	Tex-A	147	410	42	108	16	2	13	55	36	49	.263	.323	.407	102	0	0	2	-1	.992	5	*1-137/3-1,D-1	-0.3
1981	Tex-A	95	297	33	79	17	2	8	35	17	38	.266	.306	.418	113	3	4	2	0	.993	3	1-94/O-3	0.2
1982	Tex-A	43	122	14	28	8	0	2	9	10	18	.230	.293	.344	78	-4	0	2	-1	.990	1	1-39/3-1,O-1	-0.6
1983	Sea-A	144	469	58	126	23	2	19	67	39	57	.269	.329	.448	107	4	2	1	0	.994	4	*1-125,D-11	0.0
1984	Sea-A	64	155	11	31	6	0	2	16	12	27	.200	.257	.277	49	-11	3	0	1	1.000	-1	D-30,O-13/1-6	-1.3
	Min-A	14	38	1	3	1	0	0	4	4	12	.079	.167	.105	-22	-6	0	0	0	.000	0	D-11	-0.7
	Yr	78	193	12	34	7	0	2	20	16	39	.176	.239	.244	34	-17	3	0	1	1.000	-1	D-41,O-13/1-6	-2.0
Total	8	677	1989	223	508	95	8	63	255	144	260	.255	.309	.406	96	-14	10	14	-5	.993	10	1-508,D-100/O-17,3	-3.9

■ JIM PYBURN Pyburn, James Edward b: 11/1/32, Fairfield, Ala. BR/TR, 6′, 190 lbs. Deb: 4/17/55

YEAR	TM/L	G	AB	R	H	2B	3B	HR	RBI	BB	SO	AVG	OBP	SLG	PRO+	BR/A	SB	CS	SBR	FA	FR	G/POS	TPR
1955	Bal-A	39	98	5	20	2	2	0	7	8	24	.204	.271	.265	48	-7	1	1	-0	1.000	-5	3-33/O-1	-1.3
1956	Bal-A	84	156	23	27	3	3	2	11	17	26	.173	.254	.269	41	-14	4	1	1	.975	-11	O-77	-2.6
1957	Bal-A	35	40	8	9	0	0	1	2	9	6	.225	.367	.300	90	-0	1	0	0	1.000	-2	O-28/C-1	-0.3
Total	3	158	294	36	56	5	5	3	20	34	56	.190	.277	.272	51	-21	6	2	1	.982	-18	O-106/3-33,C-1	-4.2

■ EDDIE PYE Pye, Robert Edward b: 2/13/67, Columbia, Tenn. BR/TR, 5′10″, 175 lbs. Deb: 6/3/94

YEAR	TM/L	G	AB	R	H	2B	3B	HR	RBI	BB	SO	AVG	OBP	SLG	PRO+	BR/A	SB	CS	SBR	FA	FR	G/POS	TPR
1994	LA-N	7	10	2	1	0	0	0	0	1	4	.100	.182	.100	-26	-2	0	0	0	1.000	2	/2-3,S-3	0.1
1995	LA-N	7	8	0	0	0	0	0	0	0	4	.000	.000	.000	-99	-2	0	0	0	.000	0	/3-2	-0.2
Total	2	14	18	2	1	0	0	0	0	1	8	.056	.105	.056	-61	-4	0	0	0	1.000	2	/S-3,2-3,3-2	-0.1

■ FRANKIE PYTLAK Pytlak, Frank Anthony b: 7/30/08, Buffalo, N.Y. d: 5/8/77, Buffalo, N.Y. BR/TR, 5′7.5″, 160 lbs. Deb: 4/22/32

YEAR	TM/L	G	AB	R	H	2B	3B	HR	RBI	BB	SO	AVG	OBP	SLG	PRO+	BR/A	SB	CS	SBR	FA	FR	G/POS	TPR
1932	Cle-A	12	29	5	7	1	1	0	4	3	2	.241	.333	.345	71	-1	0	0	0	1.000	3	C-12	0.2
1933	Cle-A	80	248	36	77	10	6	2	33	17	10	.310	.355	.423	101	-0	3	4	-2	1.000	11	C-69	1.2
1934	Cle-A	91	289	46	75	12	4	0	35	36	11	.260	.352	.329	75	-10	11	2	2	.989	-10	C-88	-1.3
1935	Cle-A	55	149	14	44	6	1	1	12	11	4	.295	.348	.369	84	-3	3	2	-0	.984	-1	C-48	-0.2
1936	Cle-A	75	224	35	72	15	4	0	31	24	11	.321	.394	.424	101	1	5	2	0	.996	-6	C-58	-0.1
1937	Cle-A	125	397	60	125	15	6	1	44	52	15	.315	.404	.390	100	3	16	5	2	.986	10	*C-115	1.9
1938	Cle-A	113	364	46	112	14	7	1	43	36	15	.308	.376	.393	95	-2	9	5	-0	.987	-8	C-99	-0.4
1939	Cle-A	63	183	20	49	2	5	0	14	20	5	.268	.343	.333	76	-6	4	1	1	1.000	3	C-51	0.0
1940	Cle-A	62	149	16	21	2	1	0	16	17	5	.141	.234	.168	6	-21	0	1	-1	.996	7	C-58/O-1	-1.0
1941	Bos-A	106	336	36	91	23	1	2	39	28	19	.271	.329	.363	81	-9	5	7	-3	.991	1	C-91	-0.4
1945	Bos-A	9	17	1	2	0	0	0	0	3	0	.118	.250	.118	8	-2	0	0	0	1.000	1	/C-6	-0.1
1946	Bos-A	4	14	1	2	0	0	0	1	0	0	.143	.143	.143	-19	-2	0	0	0	1.000	2	/C-4	0.0
Total	12	795	2399	316	677	100	36	7	272	247	97	.282	.355	.363	84	-53	56	29	-1	.991	12	C-699/O-1	-0.2

■ TIM PYZNARSKI Pyznarski, Timothy Matthew b: 2/4/60, Chicago, Ill. BR/TR, 6′2″, 195 lbs. Deb: 9/14/86

YEAR	TM/L	G	AB	R	H	2B	3B	HR	RBI	BB	SO	AVG	OBP	SLG	PRO+	BR/A	SB	CS	SBR	FA	FR	G/POS	TPR
1986	SD-N	15	42	3	10	1	0	0	0	4	11	.238	.319	.262	63	-2	2	0	1	.977	-0	1-13	-0.3

■ JIM QUALLS Qualls, James Robert b: 10/9/46, Exeter, Cal. BB/TR, 5′10″, 158 lbs. Deb: 4/10/69

YEAR	TM/L	G	AB	R	H	2B	3B	HR	RBI	BB	SO	AVG	OBP	SLG	PRO+	BR/A	SB	CS	SBR	FA	FR	G/POS	TPR
1969	Chi-N	43	120	12	30	5	3	0	9	2	14	.250	.268	.342	62	-6	2	1	0	1.000	-3	O-35/2-4	-1.2
1970	Mon-N	9	9	1	1	0	0	0	1	0	0	.111	.111	.111	-40	-2	0	0	0	1.000	-1	/2-2,O-2	-0.3
1972	Chi-A	11	10	0	0	0	0	0	0	0	2	.000	.000	.000	-98	-2	0	0	0	1.000	0	/O-1	-0.3
Total	3	63	139	13	31	5	3	0	10	2	16	.223	.239	.302	46	-10	2	1	0	1.000	-4	/O-38,2-6	-1.8

■ MEL QUEEN Queen, Melvin Douglas b: 3/26/42, Johnson City, N.Y. BL/TR, 6′1″, 197 lbs. Deb: 4/13/64 FMC

YEAR	TM/L	G	AB	R	H	2B	3B	HR	RBI	BB	SO	AVG	OBP	SLG	PRO+	BR/A	SB	CS	SBR	FA	FR	G/POS	TPR
1964	Cin-N	48	95	7	19	2	0	2	12	4	19	.200	.232	.284	43	-7	0	1	-1	.977	1	O-20	-0.8
1965	Cin-N	5	3	0	0	0	0	0	0	0	1	.000	.000	.000	-94	-1	0	0	0	1.000	-0	/O-1	-0.1
1966	Cin-N	56	55	4	7	1	0	0	5	10	12	.127	.262	.145	16	-6	0	0	0	1.000	-4	O-32/P-7	-1.1
1967	Cin-N	49	81	6	17	4	0	0	5	4	10	.210	.247	.259	40	-6	2	0	1	.941	-2	P-31	0.0
1968	Cin-N	10	8	2	1	0	0	0	0	1	3	.125	.222	.125	6	-1	0	0	0	1.000	0	/P-5	0.0
1969	Cin-N	2	6	0	1	0	0	0	1	0	2	.167	.167	.167	-6	-1	0	0	0	1.000	-0	/P-2	0.0
1970	Cal-A	37	16	1	4	0	0	0	1	0	2	.250	.250	.250	40	-1	0	0	0	1.000	-1	P-34	0.0
1971	Cal-A	45	8	0	0	0	0	0	1	1	0	.000	.111	.000	-71	-2	0	0	0	.900	-1	P-44	0.0
1972	Cal-A	17	2	0	0	0	0	0	0	1	1	.000	.333	.000	5	-0	0	0	0	1.000	-0	P-17	0.0
Total	9	269	274	20	49	7	0	2	25	21	50	.179	.237	.226	30	-25	2	1	0	.951	-7	P-140/O-53	-2.0

■ BILLY QUEEN Queen, William Eddleman "Doc" b: 11/28/28, Gastonia, N.C. BR/TR, 6′1″, 185 lbs. Deb: 4/13/54

YEAR	TM/L	G	AB	R	H	2B	3B	HR	RBI	BB	SO	AVG	OBP	SLG	PRO+	BR/A	SB	CS	SBR	FA	FR	G/POS	TPR
1954	Mil-N	3	2	0	0	0	0	0	0	0	2	.000	.000	.000	-99	-1	0	0	0	1.000	-0	/O-1	-0.1

■ GEORGE QUELLICH Quellich, George William b: 2/10/06, Johnsville, Cal. d: 8/31/58, Johnsville, Cal. BR/TR, 6′1″, 180 lbs. Deb: 8/1/31

YEAR	TM/L	G	AB	R	H	2B	3B	HR	RBI	BB	SO	AVG	OBP	SLG	PRO+	BR/A	SB	CS	SBR	FA	FR	G/POS	TPR
1931	Det-A	13	54	6	12	5	0	1	11	3	4	.222	.263	.370	63	-3	1	0	0	1.000	1	O-13	-0.2

■ JOE QUEST Quest, Joseph L. b: 11/16/1852, New Castle, Pa. d: 11/14/24, San Diego, Cal. BR/TR, 5′6″, 150 lbs. Deb: 8/30/1871 U

YEAR	TM/L	G	AB	R	H	2B	3B	HR	RBI	BB	SO	AVG	OBP	SLG	PRO+	BR/A	SB	CS	SBR	FA	FR	G/POS	TPR
1871	Cle-n	3	13	1	3	1	0	0	2	1	0	.231	.286	.308	75	-0	0	0	0	.571	-2	/2-2,S-1	-0.2

YEAR	TM/L	G	AB	R	H	2B	3B	HR	RBI	BB	SO	AVG	OBP	SLG	PRO+	BR/A	SB	CS	SBR	FA	FR	G/POS	TPR
1878	Ind-N	62	278	45	57	3	2	0	13	12	24	.205	.238	.230	63	-10				.876	2	*2-62	-0.4
1879	Chi-N	83	334	38	69	16	1	0	22	9	33	.207	.227	.260	57	-16				**.925**	14	*2-83	0.4
1880	Chi-N	82	300	37	71	12	1	0	27	8	16	.237	.256	.283	78	-7				.895	4	*2-80/S-2,3-1	0.1
1881	Chi-N	78	293	35	72	6	0	1	26	2	29	.246	.251	.276	63	-13				**.929**	6	*2-77/S-1	-0.4
1882	Chi-N	42	159	24	32	5	2	0	15	8	16	.201	.240	.258	57	-8				.879	-5	2-41/S-1	-1.1
1883	Det-N	37	137	22	32	8	2	0	15	10	18	.234	.286	.321	88	-1				.897	0	2-37	-0.1
	StL-a	19	78	12	20	3	1	0	10	1		.256	.266	.321	83	-2				.890	-6	2-19	-0.7
1884	StL-a	81	310	46	64	9	5	0		19		.206	.257	.268	69	-11				.894	-9	*2-81	-1.7
	Pit-a	12	43	2	9	3	0	0		0		.209	.227	.279	63	-2				.938	0	/2-7,S-5	-0.1
	Yr	93	353	48	73	12	5	0		19		.207	.253	.269	68	-12				.898	-9	2-88/S-5	-1.8
1885	Det-N	55	200	24	39	8	2	0	21	14	25	.195	.248	.255	63	-8				.898	-2	2-39,S-15/O-1	-0.8
1886	Phi-a	42	150	14	31	4	1	0	10	20		.207	.300	.247	71	-4	5			.847	2	S-41/2-2	-0.2
Total	9	593	2282	299	496	77	17	1	159	103	161	.217	.252	.267	67	-81	5	0		.902	5	2-528/S-65,O-1,3-1	-5.0

■ HAL QUICK Quick, James Harold "Blondie" b: 10/4/17, Rome, Ga. d: 3/9/74, Swansea, Ill. BR/TR, 5'10.5", 163 lbs. Deb: 9/7/39

YEAR	TM/L	G	AB	R	H	2B	3B	HR	RBI	BB	SO	AVG	OBP	SLG	PRO+	BR/A	SB	CS	SBR	FA	FR	G/POS	TPR
1939	Was-A	12	41	3	10	1	0	0	2	1	1	.244	.279	.268	44	-4	1	0	0	.927	1	S-10	-0.1

■ FRANK QUILICI Quilici, Francis Ralph "Guido" b: 5/11/39, Chicago, Ill. BR/TR, 6', 175 lbs. Deb: 7/18/65 MC

YEAR	TM/L	G	AB	R	H	2B	3B	HR	RBI	BB	SO	AVG	OBP	SLG	PRO+	BR/A	SB	CS	SBR	FA	FR	G/POS	TPR
1965	*Min-A	56	149	16	31	5	1	0	7	15	33	.208	.280	.255	51	-9	1	1	-0	.990	3	2-52/S-4	-0.3
1967	Min-A	23	19	2	2	1	0	0	0	3	4	.105	.227	.158	14	-2	0	0	0	1.000	1	2-13/3-8,S-1	-0.1
1968	Min-A	97	229	22	56	11	4	1	22	21	45	.245	.311	.341	93	-2	0	0	0	1.000	17	2-48,3-40/S-6,1-1	2.0
1969	Min-A	118	144	19	25	3	1	2	12	12	22	.174	.237	.250	36	-13	2	0	1	.935	24	3-84,2-36/S-1	1.5
1970	*Min-A	111	141	19	32	3	0	2	12	15	16	.227	.301	.291	63	-7	0	2	-1	.987	15	2-73,3-27/S-1	1.0
Total	5	405	682	78	146	23	6	5	53	66	120	.214	.284	.287	63	-33	3	3	-1	.993	60	2-222,3-159/S-13,1	4.1

■ LEE QUILLEN Quillen, Leon Abner b: 5/5/1882, North Branch, Minn. d: 5/14/65, St.Paul, Minn. BR/TR, 5'10", 165 lbs. Deb: 9/30/06

YEAR	TM/L	G	AB	R	H	2B	3B	HR	RBI	BB	SO	AVG	OBP	SLG	PRO+	BR/A	SB	CS	SBR	FA	FR	G/POS	TPR
1906	Chi-A	4	9	1	3	0	0	0	0	0		.333	.333	.333	112	0	1			.600	-2	/S-3	-0.2
1907	Chi-A	49	151	17	29	5	0	0	14	10		.192	.256	.225	56	-7	8			.871	0	3-48	-0.6
Total	2	53	160	18	32	5	0	0	14	10		.200	.260	.231	59	-7	9			.871	-2	/3-48,S-3	-0.8

■ QUINLAN Quinlan Deb: 9/7/1874

YEAR	TM/L	G	AB	R	H	2B	3B	HR	RBI	BB	SO	AVG	OBP	SLG	PRO+	BR/A	SB	CS	SBR	FA	FR	G/POS	TPR
1874	Phi-n	1	4	0	1	0	0	0	1	0	0	.250	.250	.250	59	-0	0	0	0	1.000	0	/S-1	0.0

■ FRANK QUINLAN Quinlan, Francis Patrick b: 3/9/1869, Marlborough, Mass. d: 5/4/04, Brockton, Mass. 5'9", 180 lbs. Deb: 10/5/1891

YEAR	TM/L	G	AB	R	H	2B	3B	HR	RBI	BB	SO	AVG	OBP	SLG	PRO+	BR/A	SB	CS	SBR	FA	FR	G/POS	TPR
1891	Bos-a	2	5	0	0	0	0	0	0	0	2	.000	.000	.000	-99	-1	0			1.000	-1	/C-1,O-1	-0.2

■ FINNERS QUINLAN Quinlan, Thomas Finners b: 10/21/1887, Scranton, Pa. d: 2/17/66, Scranton, Pa. BL/TL, 5'8", 154 lbs. Deb: 9/6/13

YEAR	TM/L	G	AB	R	H	2B	3B	HR	RBI	BB	SO	AVG	OBP	SLG	PRO+	BR/A	SB	CS	SBR	FA	FR	G/POS	TPR
1913	StL-N	13	50	1	8	0	0	0	1	1	9	.160	.176	.160	-4	-7	0			.897	2	O-12	-0.6
1915	Chi-A	42	114	11	22	3	0	0	7	4	11	.193	.270	.219	45	-8	3	4	-2	1.000	-2	O-32	-1.3
Total	2	55	164	12	30	3	0	0	8	5	20	.183	.243	.201	31	-14	3	4		.961	0	/O-44	-1.9

■ TOM QUINLAN Quinlan, Thomas Raymond b: 3/27/68, St.Paul, Minn. BR/TR, 6'3", 200 lbs. Deb: 9/4/90

YEAR	TM/L	G	AB	R	H	2B	3B	HR	RBI	BB	SO	AVG	OBP	SLG	PRO+	BR/A	SB	CS	SBR	FA	FR	G/POS	TPR
1990	Tor-A	1	2	0	1	0	0	0	0	0	1	.500	.667	.500	227	1	0	0	0	1.000	-0	/3-1	0.0
1992	Tor-A	13	15	2	1	1	0	0	2	2	9	.067	.176	.133	-12	-2	0	0	0	.909	-1	3-13	-0.3
1994	Phi-N	24	35	6	7	2	0	1	3	3	13	.200	.263	.343	55	-2	0	0	0	.966	2	3-20	-0.1
1996	Min-A	4	6	0	0	0	0	0	0	0	3	.000	.000	.000	-99	-2	0	0	0	.667	-1	/3-4	-0.2
Total	4	42	58	8	9	3	0	1	5	5	26	.155	.234	.259	30	-6	0	0	0	.932	0	/3-38	-0.6

■ FRANK QUINN Quinn, Frank J. b: 1876, Grand Rapids, Mich. d: 2/17/20, Camden, Ind. 5'8", Deb: 8/9/1899

YEAR	TM/L	G	AB	R	H	2B	3B	HR	RBI	BB	SO	AVG	OBP	SLG	PRO+	BR/A	SB	CS	SBR	FA	FR	G/POS	TPR
1899	Chi-N	12	34	6	6	0	1	0	1	6		.176	.300	.235	49	-2	1			.909	-4	O-10/2-1	-0.6

■ JOHN QUINN Quinn, John Edward "Pick" b: 9/12/1885, Framingham, Mass. d: 4/9/56, Marlboro, Mass. BR/TR, 5'11", 150 lbs. Deb: 10/9/11

YEAR	TM/L	G	AB	R	H	2B	3B	HR	RBI	BB	SO	AVG	OBP	SLG	PRO+	BR/A	SB	CS	SBR	FA	FR	G/POS	TPR
1911	Phi-N	1	2	0	0	0	0	0	0	0	0	.000	.000	.000	-99	-1	0			1.000	-0	/C-1	-0.1

■ JOE QUINN Quinn, Joseph C. b: 8/1849, Chicago, Ill. d: 1/2/09, Chicago, Ill. 5'8.5", 148 lbs. Deb: 7/26/1871

YEAR	TM/L	G	AB	R	H	2B	3B	HR	RBI	BB	SO	AVG	OBP	SLG	PRO+	BR/A	SB	CS	SBR	FA	FR	G/POS	TPR
1871	Kek-n	5	17	8	4	0	0	0	2	4	0	.235	.381	.235	81	-0	3	1	0	.964	2	/C-5	0.1
1877	Chi-N	4	14	1	1	0	0	0	0	1	0	.071	.133	.071	-30	-2				.667	0	/O-4	-0.2

■ JOE QUINN Quinn, Joseph J. b: 12/25/1864, Sydney, Australia d: 11/12/40, St.Louis, Mo. BR/TR, 5'7", 158 lbs. Deb: 4/26/1884 M

YEAR	TM/L	G	AB	R	H	2B	3B	HR	RBI	BB	SO	AVG	OBP	SLG	PRO+	BR/A	SB	CS	SBR	FA	FR	G/POS	TPR
1884	StL-U	103	429	74	116	21	1	0		9		.270	.285	.324	81	-22				.945	-1	*1-100/O-3,S-1	-3.1
1885	StL-N	97	343	27	73	8	2	0	15	9	38	.213	.233	.248	59	-15				.875	-6	O-57,3-31,1-11	-2.2
1886	StL-N	75	271	33	63	11	3	1	21	8	31	.232	.254	.306	75	-8	12			.895	-1	O-48,2-15/1-7,3S	-0.9
1888	Bos-N	38	156	19	47	8	3	4	29	2	5	.301	.310	.468	143	7	12			.914	-7	2-38	0.1
1889	Bos-N	112	444	57	116	13	5	2	69	25	21	.261	.308	.327	73	-17	24			.860	-29	S-63,2-47/3-2	-3.5
1890	Bos-P	130	509	87	153	19	8	7	82	44	24	.301	.359	.411	99	-4	29			**.942**	15	*2-130	1.5
1891	Bos-N	124	508	70	122	8	10	3	63	28	28	.240	.288	.313	67	-25	24			.938	-23	*2-124	-3.8
1892	*Bos-N	143	532	63	116	14	1	1	59	35	40	.218	.275	.254	55	-30	17			**.951**	2	*2-143	-2.4
1893	StL-N	135	547	68	126	18	6	0	71	33	7	.230	.279	.285	50	-41	24			.942	-30	*2-135	-5.6
1894	StL-N	106	405	59	116	18	1	4	61	24	8	.286	.328	.365	67	-23	25			.952	21	*2-106	0.3
1895	StL-N	134	543	84	169	19	9	2	74	36	6	.311	.356	.390	94	-5	22			.946	-2	*2-134,M	0.0
1896	StL-N	48	191	19	40	6	1	1	17	9	5	.209	.252	.267	39	-17	8			.956	2	2-48	-1.1
	*Bal-N	24	82	22	27	1	1	0	5	6	1	.329	.375	.366	94	-1	6			.951	-3	/2-8,O-8,3-5,S-1	-0.3
	Yr	72	273	41	67	7	2	1	22	15	6	.245	.290	.297	56	-18	14			.955	-1	2-56/O-8,3-5,S-1	-1.4
1897	Bal-N	75	285	33	74	11	4	1	45	13		.260	.299	.337	68	-14	12			.946	9	3-37,S-21,2-11,/O1	-0.3
1898	Bal-N	12	32	5	8	1	0	0	5	1		.250	.273	.281	58	-2	0			.893	0	/3-8,2-1,O-1	-0.1
	StL-N	103	375	35	94	10	5	0	36	24		.251	.301	.304	72	-14	13			.962	-1	2-62,S-41/O-1	-0.8
	Yr	115	407	40	102	11	5	0	41	25		.251	.299	.302	71	-16	13			.960	-0	2-63,S-41/3-8,O-2	-0.9
1899	Cle-N	147	615	73	176	24	6	0	72	21		.286	.312	.345	86	-13	22			**.962**	3	*2-147,M	-0.2
1900	StL-N	22	80	12	21	2	0	1	11	10		.262	.344	.325	86	-1	4			.933	-8	2-14/S-6,3-1	-0.8
	Cin-N	74	266	18	73	5	2	0	25	16		.274	.316	.308	74	-9	7			.950	-18	2-74	-2.2
	Yr	96	346	30	94	7	2	1	36	26		.272	.323	.312	77	-10	11			.947	-26	2-88/S-6,3-1	-3.0
1901	Was-A	66	266	33	67	11	2	2	34	11		.252	.287	.331	72	-10	7			.954	-14	2-66	-2.0
Total	17	1768	6879	891	1797	228	70	29	794	364	214	.261	.302	.327	74	-265	268			.946	-91	*2-1303,S-135,O1/3	-27.4

■ PADDY QUINN Quinn, Paddy Deb: 5/4/1875

YEAR	TM/L	G	AB	R	H	2B	3B	HR	RBI	BB	SO	AVG	OBP	SLG	PRO+	BR/A	SB	CS	SBR	FA	FR	G/POS	TPR
1875	Wes-n	11	43	4	14	1	0	0	5	0	1	.326	.326	.349	127	1	0	1	-1	.861	1	C-10/O-1	0.1
	Har-n	5	13	1	3	0	0	0	1	1	3	.231	.200	.231	78	-0	0	1	-1	.833	-0	/C-3,O-3	-0.1
	Chi-n	17	61	12	14	0	0	0	1	0	2	.230	.230	.230	59	-2	1	1	-0	.778	-5	C-11,O-10	-0.7
	Yr	33	117	17	31	1	0	0	7	1	6	.265	.271	.274	87	-2	1	3	-2	.826	-5	C-24,O-14	-0.7

■ PADDY QUINN Quinn, Patrick b: Boston, Mass. d: 3/1893, 5'8", 162 lbs. Deb: 9/9/1875

YEAR	TM/L	G	AB	R	H	2B	3B	HR	RBI	BB	SO	AVG	OBP	SLG	PRO+	BR/A	SB	CS	SBR	FA	FR	G/POS	TPR
1875	Atl-n	2	8	2	1	0	0	0	0	0	0	.125	.125	.125	-15	-1	0	0	0	.800	-3	/O-2,S-1	-0.3
1881	Bos-N	1	4	0	0	0	0	0	0	0	0	.000	.000	.000	-99	-1				1.000	-0	/1-1	-0.1
	Wor-N	2	7	0	1	0	0	0	1	1	2	.143	.250	.143	25	-1				.714	-3	/C-2	-0.3
	Yr	3	11	0	1	0	0	0	1	1	2	.091	.167	.091	-16	-1				.714	-3	/C-2,1-1	-0.4

■ TOM QUINN Quinn, Thomas Oscar b: 4/25/1864, Annapolis, Md. d: 7/24/32, Pittsburgh, Pa. BR/TR, 5'8", 180 lbs. Deb: 9/2/1886

YEAR	TM/L	G	AB	R	H	2B	3B	HR	RBI	BB	SO	AVG	OBP	SLG	PRO+	BR/A	SB	CS	SBR	FA	FR	G/POS	TPR
1886	Pit-a	3	11	1	0	0	0	0	0	0		.000	.000	.000	-99	-2	1			.929	-2	/C-3	-0.3
1889	Bal-a	55	194	18	34	2	1	1	15	19	22	.175	.252	.211	32	-17	6			.925	8	C-55	-0.4
1890	Pit-P	55	207	23	44	4	3	1	15	17	8	.213	.282	.275	54	-13	1			.888	-4	C-55	-1.0
Total	3	113	412	42	78	6	4	2	30	36	30	.189	.261	.238	40	-33	8			.910	2	C-113	-1.7

■ LUIS QUINONES

Quinones, Luis Raul b: 4/28/62, Ponce, P.R. BB/TR, 5′11″, 175 lbs. Deb: 5/27/83

YEAR	TM/L	G	AB	R	H	2B	3B	HR	RBI	BB	SO	AVG	OBP	SLG	PRO+	BR/A	SB	CS	SBR	FA	FR	G/POS	TPR
1983	Oak-A	19	42	5	8	2	1	0	4	1	4	.190	.209	.286	37	-4	1	1	-0	1.000	1	/2-6,3-4,O-4,S-3,D	-0.3
1986	SF-N	71	106	13	19	1	3	0	11	3	17	.179	.209	.245	26	-11	3	1	0	.922	-7	S-33,3-31/2-8	-1.7
1987	Chi-N	49	101	12	22	6	0	0	8	10	16	.218	.288	.277	49	-7	0	0	0	.965	-7	S-28/2-4,3-1	-1.2
1988	Cin-N	23	52	4	12	3	0	1	11	2	11	.231	.259	.346	70	-2	1	1	-0	.974	1	S-10/2-4,3-4	-0.1
1989	Cin-N	97	340	43	83	13	4	12	34	25	46	.244	.302	.412	99	-1	2	4	-2	.979	-5	2-53,3-50/S-5	-0.7
1990	*Cin-N	83	145	10	35	7	0	2	17	13	29	.241	.308	.331	73	-5	1	0	0	.981	9	3-22,2-13/S-9,1-1	0.5
1991	Cin-N	97	212	15	47	4	3	4	20	21	31	.222	.298	.325	72	-8	1	2	-1	.975	-4	2-33,3-19/S-5	-1.2
1992	Min-A	3	5	0	1	0	0	0	1	0	0	.200	.200	.200	12	-1	0	0	0	.714	-0	/3-1,S-1,D-1	-0.1
Total	8	442	1003	102	227	36	11	19	106	75	154	.226	.285	.341	72	-39	9	9	-3	.937	-11	3-132,2-121/SDO1	-4.8

■ REY QUINONES

Quinones, Rey Francisco (Santiago) b: 11/11/63, Rio Piedras, P.R. BR/TR, 5′11″, 160 lbs. Deb: 5/17/86

YEAR	TM/L	G	AB	R	H	2B	3B	HR	RBI	BB	SO	AVG	OBP	SLG	PRO+	BR/A	SB	CS	SBR	FA	FR	G/POS	TPR
1986	Bos-A	62	190	26	45	12	1	2	15	19	26	.237	.316	.342	79	-5	3	2	-0	.940	-8	S-62	-0.8
	Sea-A	36	122	6	23	4	0	0	7	5	31	.189	.220	.221	21	-13	1	1	-0	.945	1	S-36	-1.0
	Yr	98	312	32	68	16	1	2	22	24	57	.218	.280	.295	56	-19	4	3	-1	.942	-7	S-98	-1.8
1987	Sea-A	135	478	55	132	18	2	12	56	26	71	.276	.319	.397	84	-11	1	3	-2	.959	-10	*S-135	-1.0
1988	Sea-A	140	499	63	124	30	3	12	52	23	71	.248	.286	.393	84	-12	0	3	-2	.963	3	*S-135/D-4	0.0
1989	Sea-A	7	19	2	2	0	0	0	0	1	1	.105	.150	.105	-26	-3	0	0	0	.889	-2	/S-7	-0.5
	Pit-N	71	225	21	47	11	0	3	29	15	40	.209	.261	.298	62	-12	0	2	-1	.934	-11	S-69	-2.0
Total	4	451	1533	173	373	75	6	29	159	89	240	.243	.290	.357	74	-56	5	11	-5	.952	-27	S-444/D-4	-5.3

■ CARLOS QUINTANA

Quintana, Carlos Narcis (Hernandez) b: 8/26/65, Estado Miranda, Venez. BR/TR, 6′2″, 195 lbs. Deb: 9/16/88

YEAR	TM/L	G	AB	R	H	2B	3B	HR	RBI	BB	SO	AVG	OBP	SLG	PRO+	BR/A	SB	CS	SBR	FA	FR	G/POS	TPR
1988	Bos-A	5	6	1	2	0	0	0	2	2	3	.333	.500	.333	133	0	0	0	0	1.000	-0	/O-3,D-1	0.0
1989	Bos-A	34	77	6	16	5	0	0	6	7	12	.208	.274	.273	51	-5	0	0	0	.926	-5	O-21/1-1,D-7	-1.0
1990	*Bos-A	149	512	56	147	28	0	7	67	52	74	.287	.355	.383	102	2	1	2	-1	.987	15	*1-148/O-3	0.5
1991	Bos-A	149	478	69	141	21	1	11	71	61	66	.295	.377	.412	113	10	1	0	0	.993	7	*1-138,O-13/D-1	0.9
1993	Bos-A	101	303	31	74	5	0	1	19	31	52	.244	.318	.271	57	-18	1	0	0	.991	-1	1-53,O-51	-2.2
Total	5	438	1376	163	380	59	1	19	165	153	207	.276	.351	.362	93	-11	3	2	-0	.990	15	1-340/O-91,D-9	-1.8

■ MARSHALL QUINTON

Quinton, Marshall J. b: Philadelphia, Pa. 5′11″, 190 lbs. Deb: 8/7/1884

YEAR	TM/L	G	AB	R	H	2B	3B	HR	RBI	BB	SO	AVG	OBP	SLG	PRO+	BR/A	SB	CS	SBR	FA	FR	G/POS	TPR
1884	Ric-a	26	94	12	22	5	0	0		0		.234	.242	.287	73	-3				.878	-9	C-14,O-10/S-2	-1.0
1885	Phi-a	7	29	6	6	1	0	0	4	1		.207	.258	.241	55	-2				.869	-2	/C-7	-0.3
Total	2	33	123	18	28	6	0	0	4	1		.228	.246	.276	68	-4				.874	-11	/C-21,O-10,S-2	-1.3

■ JAMIE QUIRK

Quirk, James Patrick b: 10/22/54, Whittier, Cal. BL/TR, 6′4″, 200 lbs. Deb: 9/4/75 C

YEAR	TM/L	G	AB	R	H	2B	3B	HR	RBI	BB	SO	AVG	OBP	SLG	PRO+	BR/A	SB	CS	SBR	FA	FR	G/POS	TPR
1975	KC-A	14	39	2	10	0	0	1	5	2	7	.256	.293	.333	75	-1	0	0	0	.909	0	O-10/3-2,D-1	-0.1
1976	*KC-A	64	114	11	28	6	0	1	15	2	22	.246	.259	.325	70	-5	0	0	0	1.000	-1	D-19,S-12,3-11,/1-2	-0.6
1977	Mil-A	93	221	16	48	14	1	3	13	8	47	.217	.251	.330	57	-14	0	1	-1	.950	0	D-53,O-10/3-8	-1.6
1978	KC-A	17	29	3	6	2	0	0	2	5	4	.207	.324	.276	68	-1	0	0	0	.926	2	3-10/S-2,D-1	0.1
1979	KC-A	51	79	8	24	6	1	1	11	5	13	.304	.353	.443	111	1	0	0	0	.944	-1	/C-9,S-5,3-3,D-9	0.1
1980	KC-A	62	163	13	45	5	0	5	21	7	24	.276	.310	.399	92	-2	3	2	-0	.929	-1	3-28,C-15/O-7,1D	-0.3
1981	KC-A	46	100	8	25	7	0	0	10	6	17	.250	.299	.320	79	-3	0	2	-1	.985	-3	C-22/3-8,2-1,O-1	-0.7
1982	KC-A	36	78	8	18	3	0	1	5	3	15	.231	.259	.308	55	-5	0	0	0	1.000	2	C-29/1-6,3-1,O-1	-0.3
1983	StL-N	48	86	3	18	2	1	2	11	6	27	.209	.269	.326	64	-4	0	0	0	.929	-5	C-22/3-7,S-1	-0.9
1984	Chi-A	3	2	0	0	0	0	0	1	0	2	.000	.000	.000	-96	-1	0	0	0	1.000	0	/3-1	-0.1
	Cle-A	1	1	1	1	0	0	1	1	0	0	1.000	1.000	4.000	1189	1	0	0	0	.000	0	/C-1	0.1
	Yr	4	3	1	1	0	0	1	2	0	2	.333	.333	1.333	324	1	0	0	0	1.000	0	/3-1,C-1	0.0
1985	*KC-A	19	57	3	16	3	1	0	4	2	9	.281	.305	.368	83	-1	0	0	0	.986	-3	C-17/1-1	-0.3
1986	KC-A	80	219	24	47	10	0	8	26	17	41	.215	.274	.370	72	-9	0	1	-1	.989	11	C-41,3-24/1-6,O-1	0.3
1987	KC-A	109	296	24	70	17	0	5	33	28	56	.236	.311	.345	72	-12	1	0	0	.986	-4	*C-108/S-1	-0.8
1988	KC-A	84	196	22	47	7	1	8	25	28	41	.240	.338	.408	107	2	1	5	-3	.982	14	C-79/1-1,3-1	1.8
1989	NY-A	13	24	0	2	0	0	0	0	3	5	.083	.185	.083	-22	-4	0	1	-1	1.000	1	/C-6,S-1,D-1	-0.3
	Oak-A	9	10	1	2	0	0	1	1	0	4	.200	.200	.500	95	-0	0	0	0	.500	-0	/3-3,C-2,1-1,O-1	-0.1
	Bal-A	25	51	5	11	2	0	0	9	9	11	.216	.333	.255	70	-2	0	1	-1	1.000	5	C-24	0.4
	Yr	47	85	6	15	2	0	1	10	12	20	.176	.278	.235	47	-6	0	2	-1	1.000	6	C-32/3-3,S-1,D1O	0.0
1990	*Oak-A	56	121	12	34	5	1	3	26	14	34	.281	.360	.413	121	4	0	0	0	.977	-2	C-37/1-8,3-8,O-1,D	0.4
1991	Oak-A	76	203	16	53	4	0	1	17	16	28	.261	.321	.296	76	-6	0	3	-2	.982	6	C-54/1-8,3-1,D-1	0.0
1992	*Oak-A	78	177	13	39	7	1	2	11	16	28	.220	.296	.305	72	-7	0	0	0	.973	5	C-59/1-9,3-2,D-1	0.1
Total	18	984	2266	193	544	100	7	43	247	177	435	.240	.300	.347	78	-68	5	16	-8	.982	28	C-525,3-118/D1OS2	-2.8

■ BRIAN RAABE

Raabe, Brian Charles b: 11/5/67, New Ulm, Minn. BR/TR, 5′9″, 177 lbs. Deb: 9/17/95

YEAR	TM/L	G	AB	R	H	2B	3B	HR	RBI	BB	SO	AVG	OBP	SLG	PRO+	BR/A	SB	CS	SBR	FA	FR	G/POS	TPR
1995	Min-A	6	14	4	3	0	0	0	1	1	0	.214	.267	.214	27	-1	0	0	0	1.000	-1	/2-4,3-2	-0.2
1996	Min-A	7	9	0	2	0	0	0	1	0	1	.222	.222	.222	13	-1	0	0	0	.857	-1	/3-6,2-1	-0.2
1997	Sea-A	2	3	0	0	0	0	0	0	1	2	.000	.250	.000	-28	-1	0	0	0	1.000	-1	/3-2,2-1	-0.1
	Col-N	2	3	0	1	0	0	0	0	0	1	.333	.333	.333	61	-0	0	0	0	1.000	0	/2-1	0.0
Total	3	17	29	4	6	0	0	0	2	2	4	.207	.258	.207	21	-3	0	0	0	.889	-2	/3-10,2-7	-0.5

■ JOHN RABB

Rabb, John Andrew b: 6/23/60, Los Angeles, Cal. BR/TR, 6′1″, 180 lbs. Deb: 9/4/82

YEAR	TM/L	G	AB	R	H	2B	3B	HR	RBI	BB	SO	AVG	OBP	SLG	PRO+	BR/A	SB	CS	SBR	FA	FR	G/POS	TPR
1982	SF-N	2	2	0	1	0	1	0	0	0	1	.500	.500	1.500	441	1	0	0	0	1.000	-0	/O-1	0.1
1983	SF-N	40	104	10	24	9	0	1	14	9	17	.231	.292	.346	79	-3	1	0	0	.973	4	C-31/O-2	0.3
1984	SF-N	54	82	10	16	1	0	3	9	10	33	.195	.283	.317	71	-3	1	1	-0	.988	-2	1-13/O-8,C-6	-0.6
1985	Atl-N	3	2	0	0	0	0	0	0	0	1	.000	.000	.000	-94	-1	0	0	0	.000	-0	/O-1	-0.1
1988	Sea-A	9	14	2	5	2	0	0	4	0	1	.357	.357	.500	131	1	0	0	0	1.000	0	/O-2,1-1,D-5	0.1
Total	5	108	204	22	46	12	1	4	27	19	53	.225	.291	.353	81	-6	2	1	0	.966	2	/C-37,1-14,O-14,D-5	-0.2

■ JOE RABBITT

Rabbitt, Joseph Patrick b: 1/16/1900, Frontenac, Kan. d: 12/5/69, Norwalk, Conn. BL/TR, 5′10″, 165 lbs. Deb: 9/15/22

YEAR	TM/L	G	AB	R	H	2B	3B	HR	RBI	BB	SO	AVG	OBP	SLG	PRO+	BR/A	SB	CS	SBR	FA	FR	G/POS	TPR
1922	Cle-A	2	3	1	1	0	0	0	0	0	0	.333	.333	.333	74	-0	0	0	0	.000	-1	/O-1	-0.1

■ MARV RACKLEY

Rackley, Marvin Eugene b: 7/25/21, Seneca, S.C. BL/TL, 5′10″, 170 lbs. Deb: 4/15/47

YEAR	TM/L	G	AB	R	H	2B	3B	HR	RBI	BB	SO	AVG	OBP	SLG	PRO+	BR/A	SB	CS	SBR	FA	FR	G/POS	TPR
1947	Bro-N	18	9	2	2	0	0	0	2	1	0	.222	.300	.222	39	-1	0			1.000	0	/O-2	0.0
1948	Bro-N	88	281	55	92	13	5	0	15	19	25	.327	.370	.409	107	3	8			.949	-5	O-74	-0.6
1949	*Bro-N	9	9	2	4	1	0	0	1	1	0	.444	.500	.556	175	1	0			1.000	-0	/O-3	0.1
	Pit-N	11	35	5	11	2	0	0	2	2	3	.314	.351	.371	92	-0	1			1.000	0	/O-8	-0.1
	*Bro-N	54	141	23	41	4	1	1	14	13	8	.291	.351	.355	86	-2	1			.986	-8	O-44	-1.2
	Yr	74	185	30	56	7	1	1	17	16	11	.303	.358	.368	91	-2	2			.990	-8	O-55	-1.2
1950	Cin-N	5	2	0	1	0	0	0	1	0	0	.500	.500	.500	163	0	0			.000	0	H	0.0
Total	4	185	477	87	151	20	6	1	35	36	36	.317	.365	.390	100	0	10			.966	-13	O-131	-1.8

■ CHARLEY RADBOURN

Radbourn, Charles Gardner "Old Hoss"
b: 12/11/1854, Rochester, N.Y. d: 2/5/1897, Bloomington, Ill. BR/TR, 5′9″, 168 lbs. Deb: 5/5/1880 H

YEAR	TM/L	G	AB	R	H	2B	3B	HR	RBI	BB	SO	AVG	OBP	SLG	PRO+	BR/A	SB	CS	SBR	FA	FR	G/POS	TPR
1880	Buf-N	6	21	1	3	0	0	0	1	0	1	.143	.143	.143	-3	-2				.900	4	/O-3,2-3	0.2
1881	Pro-N	72	270	27	59	9	0	0	28	10	15	.219	.246	.252	58	-12				.906	-2	P-41,O-25,S-13	-0.9
1882	Pro-N	83	326	30	78	11	0	1	32	12	22	.239	.266	.282	76	-8				.912	1	P-55,O-31/S-1	-0.2
1883	Pro-N	89	381	59	108	11	3	3	48	14	16	.283	.309	.352	98	-1				.920	2	*P-76,O-20/1-2	-0.3
1884	*Pro-N	87	361	48	83	7	1	1	37	26	42	.230	.282	.263	74	-10				.892	-6	*P-75/O-7,1-5,S2	-0.3
1885	Pro-N	66	249	34	58	9	2	0	22	36	27	.233	.330	.285	103	3				.937	0	P-49,O-16/2-2	-0.3
1886	Bos-N	66	253	30	60	5	1	2	22	17	36	.237	.285	.289	78	-6	5			.924	1	P-58/O-6	-0.2
1887	Bos-N	51	175	25	40	2	2	1	24	18	21	.229	.308	.280	64	-8	6			.848	-4	P-50/O-2	-0.1
1888	Bos-N	24	79	6	17	1	0	0	6	3	14	.215	.262	.228	56	-4	4			.895	-1	P-24	0.0
1889	Bos-N	35	122	17	23	1	0	1	13	9	19	.189	.256	.221	32	-11	3			.975	1	P-33/O-2,3-1	-0.1
1890	Bos-P	45	154	20	39	6	0	0	16	9	20	.253	.299	.292	55	-11	7			.935	0	P-41/O-4,1-1	-0.2

YEAR	TM/L	G	AB	R	H	2B	3B	HR	RBI	BB	SO	AVG	OBP	SLG	PRO+	BR/A	SB	CS	SBR	FA	FR	G/POS	TPR
1891	Cin-N	29	96	11	17	2	2	0	10	4	11	.177	.225	.240	35	-8	1			.880	-3	P-26/O-2,3-1	-0.1
Total	12	653	2487	308	585	64	11	9	259	158	244	.235	.283	.281	72	-79	26			.913	-6	P-528,O-118/S123	-2.5

■ JOHN RADCLIFF
Radcliff, John Y. b: 6/29/1848, Philadelphia, Pa. d: 7/26/11, Ocean City, N.J. 5'6", 140 lbs. Deb: 5/20/1871

YEAR	TM/L	G	AB	R	H	2B	3B	HR	RBI	BB	SO	AVG	OBP	SLG	PRO+	BR/A	SB	CS	SBR	FA	FR	G/POS	TPR
1871	Ath-n	28	145	47	44	7	5	0	22	6	1	.303	.331	.421	116	3	5	1	1	.804	3	*S-28	0.4
1872	Bal-n	56	297	71	86	13	4	1	44	0	2	.290	.290	.370	97	-3	3	3	-1	.771	-4	*S-50/3-6,2-1	-0.6
1873	Bal-n	45	245	59	70	7	0	0	33	3	2	.286	.294	.314	81	-5	0	0	0	.762	-1	3-24,S-23/2-1	-0.5
1874	Phi-n	23	103	20	25	7	0	1	14	2	0	.243	.257	.340	87	-2	1	1	-0	.800	-3	O-15/2-4,S-3,3-3,1	-0.4
1875	Cen-n	5	23	2	4	0	0	0	0	1	0	.174	.208	.174	37	-1	0	0	0	.651	-1	/S-5	-0.2
Total	5 n	157	813	199	229	34	9	2	113	12	5	.282	.292	.353	93	-8	9	5	-0	.764	-5	S-109/3-33,O-15,21	-1.3

■ RIP RADCLIFF
Radcliff, Raymond Allen b: 1/19/06, Kiowa, Okla. d: 5/23/62, Enid, Okla. BL/TL, 5'10", 170 lbs. Deb: 9/17/34

YEAR	TM/L	G	AB	R	H	2B	3B	HR	RBI	BB	SO	AVG	OBP	SLG	PRO+	BR/A	SB	CS	SBR	FA	FR	G/POS	TPR
1934	Chi-A	14	56	7	15	2	1	0	5	0	2	.268	.268	.339	54	-4	1	0	0	.946	1	O-14	-0.3
1935	Chi-A	146	623	95	178	28	8	10	68	53	21	.286	.346	.404	91	-9	4	4	-1	.968	-18	*O-142	-3.1
1936	Chi-A★	138	618	120	207	31	7	8	82	44	12	.335	.381	.447	100	-0	6	3	0	.936	-17	*O-132	-2.0
1937	Chi-A	144	584	105	190	38	10	4	79	53	25	.325	.383	.445	108	8	6	1	1	.966	-4	*O-139	0.0
1938	Chi-A	129	503	64	166	23	6	5	81	36	17	.330	.376	.429	99	-1	5	7	-3	.979	-1	O-99,1-23	-0.9
1939	Chi-A	113	397	49	105	25	2	2	53	26	21	.264	.313	.353	68	-20	6	4	-1	.970	-10	O-78,1-20	-3.3
1940	StL-A	150	584	83	**200**	33	9	7	81	47	20	.342	.392	.466	119	17	6	4	-1	.973	-6	*O-139/1-4	0.2
1941	StL-A	19	71	12	20	2	2	2	14	10	1	.282	.370	.451	112	1	1	1	-0	1.000	-2	O-14/1-3	-0.2
	Det-A	96	379	47	120	14	5	3	40	19	13	.317	.351	.404	90	-6	4	4	-1	.970	-5	O-87	-1.7
	Yr	115	450	59	140	16	7	5	54	29	14	.311	.354	.411	94	-5	5	5	-2	.974	-8	*O-101/1-3	-1.9
1942	Det-A	62	144	13	36	5	0	1	20	9	6	.250	.294	.306	64	-7	0	1	-1	.978	-0	O-24/1-4	-1.0
1943	Det-A	70	115	3	30	4	0	0	10	13	3	.261	.341	.296	81	-2	1	1	-0	1.000	0	O-19/1-1	-0.4
Total	10	1081	4074	598	1267	205	50	42	533	310	141	.311	.362	.417	96	-23	40	30	-6	.967	-62	O-887/1-55	-12.7

■ DAVE RADER
Rader, David Martin b: 12/26/48, Claremore, Okla. BL/TR, 5'11", 165 lbs. Deb: 9/5/71

YEAR	TM/L	G	AB	R	H	2B	3B	HR	RBI	BB	SO	AVG	OBP	SLG	PRO+	BR/A	SB	CS	SBR	FA	FR	G/POS	TPR
1971	SF-N	3	4	0	0	0	0	0	0	0	0	.000	.000	.000	-99	-1	0	0	0	1.000	-0	/C-1	-0.1
1972	SF-N	133	459	44	119	14	1	6	41	29	31	.259	.308	.333	81	-12	1	2	-1	.985	-13	*C-127	-2.2
1973	SF-N	148	462	59	106	15	4	9	41	63	22	.229	.330	.338	82	-10	0	0	0	.991	-12	*C-148	-1.7
1974	SF-N	113	323	26	94	16	2	1	26	31	21	.291	.353	.362	96	-1	1	0	0	.984	-9	*C-109	-0.6
1975	SF-N	98	292	39	85	15	0	5	31	32	30	.291	.363	.394	106	3	1	0	0	.984	-3	C-94	0.4
1976	SF-N	88	255	25	67	15	0	1	22	27	21	.263	.333	.333	87	-4	2	0	1	.984	-9	C-81	-1.0
1977	StL-N	66	114	15	30	7	1	1	16	9	10	.263	.317	.368	85	-3	1	0	0	.976	4	C-38	0.2
1978	Chi-N	116	305	29	62	13	3	3	36	34	26	.203	.285	.295	56	-18	1	1	-0	.977	-13	*C-114	-3.1
1979	Phi-N	31	54	3	11	1	1	1	5	6	7	.204	.283	.315	61	-3	0	0	0	.932	-4	C-25	-0.6
1980	Bos-A	50	137	14	45	11	0	3	17	14	12	.328	.391	.474	129	6	1	1	-0	.981	3	C-34/D-9	0.9
Total	10	846	2405	254	619	107	12	30	235	245	180	.257	.329	.349	86	-43	8	4	0	.983	-56	C-771/D-9	-7.8

■ DON RADER
Rader, Donald Russell b: 9/5/1893, Wolcott, Ind. d: 6/26/83, Walla Walla, Wash BL/TR, 5'10", 164 lbs. Deb: 7/25/13

YEAR	TM/L	G	AB	R	H	2B	3B	HR	RBI	BB	SO	AVG	OBP	SLG	PRO+	BR/A	SB	CS	SBR	FA	FR	G/POS	TPR
1913	Chi-A	4	3	1	1	1	0	0	0	0	0	.333	.333	.667	193	0	0			.000	-1	/3-1,O-1	0.0
1921	Phi-N	9	32	4	9	2	0	0	3	3	5	.281	.343	.344	76	-1	0	0	0	1.000	-6	/S-9	-0.6
Total	2	13	35	5	10	3	0	0	3	3	5	.286	.342	.371	84	-1	0	0		1.000	-6	/S-9,O-1,3-1	-0.6

■ DOUG RADER
Rader, Douglas Lee "Rojo" or "The Red Rooster" b: 7/30/44, Chicago, Ill. BR/TR, 6'3", 215 lbs. Deb: 7/31/67 MC

YEAR	TM/L	G	AB	R	H	2B	3B	HR	RBI	BB	SO	AVG	OBP	SLG	PRO+	BR/A	SB	CS	SBR	FA	FR	G/POS	TPR
1967	Hou-N	47	162	24	54	10	4	2	26	7	31	.333	.368	.481	146	9	0	3	-2	.972	-1	1-36/3-7	0.5
1968	Hou-N	98	333	42	89	16	4	6	43	31	51	.267	.332	.393	119	8	2	2	-1	.930	1	3-86/1-5	0.9
1969	Hou-N	155	569	62	140	25	3	11	83	62	103	.246	.327	.359	94	-5	1	5	-3	.945	14	*3-154/1-4	0.8
1970	Hou-N	156	576	90	145	25	3	25	87	57	102	.252	.323	.436	106	3	3	2	-0	**.966**	24	*3-154/1-1	2.5
1971	Hou-N	135	484	51	118	21	4	12	56	40	112	.244	.306	.378	95	-4	5	1	1	.946	2	*3-135	-0.3
1972	Hou N	152	553	70	131	24	7	22	90	57	120	.237	.314	.425	110	6	5	5	-2	.958	18	*3-152	2.2
1973	Hou-N	154	574	79	146	26	0	21	89	46	97	.254	.313	.409	99	-2	4	3	-1	.945	-5	*3-152	-0.9
1974	Hou-N	152	533	61	137	27	3	17	78	60	131	.257	.337	.415	114	9	7	2	1	.965	5	*3-152	1.4
1975	Hou-N	129	448	41	100	23	2	12	48	42	101	.223	.297	.364	89	-9	5	4	-1	**.971**	8	*3-124/S-2	-0.2
1976	SD-N	139	471	45	121	22	4	9	55	55	102	.257	.338	.378	112	7	3	4	-2	.955	14	*3-137	1.9
1977	SD-N	52	170	19	46	8	3	5	27	33	40	.271	.392	.441	137	10	0	1	-1	.961	1	3-51	1.0
	Tor-A	96	313	47	75	18	2	13	40	38	65	.240	.328	.435	104	2	2	1	0	.966	1	3-45,D-34/1-7,O-1	0.0
Total	11	1465	5186	631	1302	245	39	155	722	528	1055	.251	.325	.403	106	34	37	33	-9	.956	82	*3-1349/1-53,DSO	9.8

■ PAUL RADFORD
Radford, Paul Revere "Shorty" b: 10/14/1861, Roxbury, Mass. d: 2/21/45, Boston, Mass. BR/TR, 5'6", 148 lbs. Deb: 5/1/1883

YEAR	TM/L	G	AB	R	H	2B	3B	HR	RBI	BB	SO	AVG	OBP	SLG	PRO+	BR/A	SB	CS	SBR	FA	FR	G/POS	TPR
1883	Bos-N	72	258	46	53	6	3	0	14	9	26	.205	.232	.252	46	-16				.836	-5	*O-72	-1.9
1884	*Pro-N	97	355	56	70	11	2	1	29	25	43	.197	.250	.248	58	-16				.882	5	*O-96/P-2	-1.1
1885	Pro-N	105	371	55	90	12	5	0	32	33	43	.243	.304	.302	99	1				.852	1	*O-88,S-16/P-3,2-1	0.0
1886	KC-N	122	493	78	113	17	5	0	20	58	48	.229	.310	.284	77	-13	39			.890	10	*O-92,S-30/2-1	-0.5
1887	NY-a	128	486	127	129	15	5	4	45	**106**		.265	.403	.342	114	17	73			.833	-2	S-76,O-37,2-18,/P-2	1.3
1888	Bro-a	90	308	48	67	9	3	2	29	35		.218	.305	.286	90	-2	33			.944	9	O-88/2-2	0.4
1889	Cle-N	136	487	94	116	21	5	1	46	91	37	.238	.365	.308	91	-1	30			.942	-0	*O-136/3-1	-0.4
1890	Cle-P	122	466	98	136	24	12	2	62	82	28	.292	.406	.408	128	24	25			.895	8	O-80,S-36/3-7,2P	2.5
1891	Bos-a	133	456	102	118	11	5	0	65	96	36	.259	.393	.305	102	7	55			.906	20	*S-131/O-4,P-1	2.9
1892	Was-N	137	510	93	130	19	4	1	37	86	47	.255	.366	.314	109	10	35			.933	-7	O-62,3-54,S-20,/2-2	0.3
1893	Was-N	124	464	87	106	18	3	2	34	104	42	.228	.378	.293	82	-6	32			.901	7	*O-123/2-1,P-1	-0.4
1894	Was-N	95	325	61	78	13	5	0	49	65	23	.240	.378	.311	70	-13	24			.852	-0	S-47,2-25,O-24	-0.8
Total	12	1361	4979	945	1206	176	57	13	462	790	373	.242	.351	.308	92	-9	346			.901	46	O-902,S-356/32P	2.3

■ RYAN RADMANOVICH
Radmanovich, Ryan Ashley b: 8/9/71, Calgary, Alb., Can. BL/TR, 6'2", 200 lbs. Deb: 4/13/98

YEAR	TM/L	G	AB	R	H	2B	3B	HR	RBI	BB	SO	AVG	OBP	SLG	PRO+	BR/A	SB	CS	SBR	FA	FR	G/POS	TPR
1998	Sea-A	25	69	5	15	4	0	2	10	4	25	.217	.260	.362	60	-4	1	1	-0	1.000	-1	O-24/1-1	-0.6

■ JACK RADTKE
Radtke, Jack William b: 4/14/13, Denver, Colo. BB/TR, 5'7", 160 lbs. Deb: 8/1/36

YEAR	TM/L	G	AB	R	H	2B	3B	HR	RBI	BB	SO	AVG	OBP	SLG	PRO+	BR/A	SB	CS	SBR	FA	FR	G/POS	TPR
1936	Bro-N	33	31	8	3	0	0	0	2	4	9	.097	.200	.097	-18	-5	3			1.000	5	2-14/3-5,S-4	0.0

■ JACK RAFTER
Rafter, John Cornelius b: 2/20/1875, Troy, N.Y. d: 1/5/43, Troy, N.Y. BR/TR, 5'8", 165 lbs. Deb: 9/24/04

YEAR	TM/L	G	AB	R	H	2B	3B	HR	RBI	BB	SO	AVG	OBP	SLG	PRO+	BR/A	SB	CS	SBR	FA	FR	G/POS	TPR
1904	Pit-N	1	3	0	0	0	0	0	0	0		.000	.000	.000	-97	-1	0			1.000	0	/C-1	-0.1

■ TOM RAFTERY
Raftery, Thomas Francis b: 10/5/1881, Boston, Mass. d: 12/31/54, Boston, Mass. BR/TR, 5'10.5", 175 lbs. Deb: 4/18/09

YEAR	TM/L	G	AB	R	H	2B	3B	HR	RBI	BB	SO	AVG	OBP	SLG	PRO+	BR/A	SB	CS	SBR	FA	FR	G/POS	TPR
1909	Cle-A	8	32	6	7	2	1	0	0	4		.219	.306	.344	101	0	1			1.000	-1	/O-8	-0.1

■ TOM RAGLAND
Ragland, Thomas b: 6/16/46, Talladega, Ala. BR/TR, 5'10", 155 lbs. Deb: 4/5/71

YEAR	TM/L	G	AB	R	H	2B	3B	HR	RBI	BB	SO	AVG	OBP	SLG	PRO+	BR/A	SB	CS	SBR	FA	FR	G/POS	TPR
1971	Was-A	10	23	1	4	0	0	0	0	0	5	.174	.208	.174	10	-3	0	0	0	1.000	-1	2-10	-0.3
1972	Tex-A	25	58	3	10	2	0	0	2	5	11	.172	.238	.207	35	-5	0	1	-1	.982	-3	2-13/3-5,S-3	-0.9
1973	Cle-A	67	183	16	47	7	1	0	12	8	31	.257	.292	.306	67	-8	2	3	-1	.984	13	2-65/S-2	0.7
Total	3	102	264	20	61	9	1	0	14	13	47	.231	.272	.273	56	-15	2	4	-2	.985	10	/2-88,S-5,3-5	-0.5

■ LARRY RAINES
Raines, Lawrence Glenn Hope b: 3/9/30, St.Albans, W.Va. d: 1/28/78, Lansing, Mich. BR/TR, 5'10", 165 lbs. Deb: 4/16/57

YEAR	TM/L	G	AB	R	H	2B	3B	HR	RBI	BB	SO	AVG	OBP	SLG	PRO+	BR/A	SB	CS	SBR	FA	FR	G/POS	TPR
1957	Cle-A	96	244	39	64	14	0	2	16	19	40	.262	.318	.344	82	-6	5	2	0	.922	-5	3-27,S-25,2-10,/O-8	-0.9
1958	Cle-A	7	9	1	0	0	0	0	0	0	5	.000	.000	.000	-99	-2	0	1	-1	.933	4	/2-2	0.0
Total	2	103	253	40	64	14	0	2	16	19	45	.253	.308	.332	76	-9	5	3	-0	.963	-2	/3-27,S-25,2-12,O-8	-0.9

■ TIM RAINES
Raines, Timothy "Rock" b: 9/16/59, Sanford, Fla. BB/TR, 5'8", 178 lbs. Deb: 9/11/79

YEAR	TM/L	G	AB	R	H	2B	3B	HR	RBI	BB	SO	AVG	OBP	SLG	PRO+	BR/A	SB	CS	SBR	FA	FR	G/POS	TPR
1979	Mon-N	6	0	3	0	0	0	0	0	0	0	—	—	—	—	0	2	0	1	.000	0	/R	0.0
1980	Mon-N	15	20	5	1	0	0	0	0	6	3	.050	.269	.050	-6	-3	5	0	2	1.000	2	/2-7,O-1	0.1
1981	*Mon-N★	88	313	61	95	13	7	5	37	45	31	.304	.394	.438	134	15	**71**	11	**15**	.976	2	O-81/2-1	3.1
1982	Mon-N★	156	647	90	179	32	8	4	43	75	83	.277	.354	.369	101	2	**78**	16	**14**	.992	3	*O-120,2-36	1.8

YEAR	TM/L	G	AB	R	H	2B	3B	HR	RBI	BB	SO	AVG	OBP	SLG	PRO+	BR/A	SB	CS	SBR	FA	FR	G/POS	TPR
1983	Mon-N★	156	615	**133**	183	32	8	11	71	97	70	.298	.395	.429	129	27	**90**	14	**19**	.988	16	*O-154/2-7	5.8
1984	Mon-N★	160	622	106	192	**38**	9	8	60	87	69	.309	.395	.437	140	35	**75**	10	**17**	.988	10	*O-160/2-2	5.8
1985	Mon-N★	150	575	115	184	30	13	11	41	81	60	.320	.407	.475	155	44	70	9	16	.993	10	*O-146	**6.6**
1986	Mon-N★	151	580	91	194	35	10	9	62	78	60	**.334**	**.415**	.476	146	39	70	9	16	.979	11	*O-147	**6.2**
1987	Mon-N★	139	530	**123**	175	34	8	18	68	90	52	.330	.431	.526	148	40	50	5	12	.987	16	*O-139	6.1
1988	Mon-N	109	429	66	116	19	7	12	48	53	44	.270	.353	.431	119	11	33	7	6	.988	7	*O-108	2.2
1989	Mon-N	145	517	76	148	29	6	9	60	93	48	.286	.398	.418	132	25	41	9	7	.996	3	*O-139	3.3
1990	Mon-N	130	457	65	131	11	5	9	62	70	43	.287	.385	.392	119	14	49	16	5	.976	-1	*O-123	1.6
1991	Chi-A	155	609	102	163	20	6	5	50	83	68	.268	.360	.345	98	2	51	15	6	.990	10	*O-133,D-19	1.4
1992	Chi-A	144	551	102	162	22	9	7	54	81	48	.294	.384	.405	123	19	45	6	10	.994	14	*O-129,D-14	4.0
1993	*Chi-A	115	415	75	127	16	4	16	54	64	35	.306	.402	.480	139	25	21	7	2	**1.000**	-1	*O-112	2.3
1994	Chi-A	101	384	80	102	15	5	10	52	61	43	.266	.368	.409	102	2	13	0	4	.981	4	O-96	0.7
1995	Chi-A	133	502	81	143	25	4	12	67	70	52	.285	.376	.422	112	11	13	2	3	.980	1	*O-107,D-22	0.9
1996	*NY-A	59	201	45	57	10	0	9	33	34	29	.284	.390	.468	116	6	10	1	2	.988	-1	O-50/D-2	0.5
1997	*NY-A	74	271	56	87	20	2	4	38	41	34	.321	.410	.454	126	12	8	5	-1	.988	-6	O-57,D-13	0.3
1998	*NY-A	109	321	53	93	13	1	5	47	55	49	.290	.398	.383	125	6	8	3	1	.985	-4	D-56,O-47	-0.1
Total	20	2295	8559	1528	2532	414	112	164	947	1264	921	.296	.389	.428	125	334	803	145	154	.988	96	*O-2049,D-126/2-53	52.6
■ JOHN RAINEY	Rainey, John Paul b: 7/26/1864, Birmingham, Mich. d: 11/11/12, Detroit, Mich. BL/TR, 5'10", 164 lbs. Deb: 8/25/1887																						
1887	NY-N	17	58	6	17	3	0	0	12	5	6	.293	.349	.345	98	0	0			.818	-3	3-17	-0.2
1890	Buf-P	42	166	29	39	5	1	1	20	24	15	.235	.349	.295	79	-3	12			.870	0	O-28/S-7,3-6,2-2	-0.3
Total	2	59	224	35	56	8	1	1	32	29	21	.250	.349	.308	84	-3	12			.827	-3	/O-28,3-23,S-7,2-2	-0.5
■ GARY RAJSICH	Rajsich, Gary Louis b: 10/28/54, Youngstown, Ohio BL/TL, 6'2", 210 lbs. Deb: 4/9/82 F																						
1982	NY-N	80	162	17	42	8	3	2	12	17	40	.259	.333	.383	100	0	1	3	-2	1.000	-2	O-35/1-2	-0.5
1983	NY-N	11	36	5	12	3	0	1	3	3	1	.333	.400	.500	149	2	0	0	0	1.000	-0	1-10	0.2
1984	StL-N	7	7	1	1	0	0	0	2	2	1	.143	.333	.143	39	-0	0	0	0	1.000	-0	/1-3	-0.1
1985	SF-N	51	91	5	15	6	0	0	10	17	22	.165	.296	.231	52	-5	0	1	-1	.990	-1	1-23	-0.9
Total	4	149	296	28	70	17	3	3	27	39	64	.236	.329	.345	90	-3	1	4	-2	.994	-4	/1-38,O-35	-1.3
■ DOC RALSTON	Ralston, Samuel Beryl b: 8/3/1885, Pierpont, Ohio d: 8/29/50, Lancaster, Pa. BR/TR, 6', 185 lbs. Deb: 9/8/10																						
1910	Was-A	21	73	4	15	1	0	0	3	3		.205	.256	.219	51	-4	2			.976	2	O-21	-0.4
■ BOB RAMAZZOTTI	Ramazzotti, Robert Louis b: 1/16/17, Elanora, Pa. BR/TR, 5'8.5", 175 lbs. Deb: 4/20/46																						
1946	Bro-N	62	120	10	25	4	0	0	7	9	13	.208	.264	.242	43	-9	0			.939	5	3-30,2-16	-0.3
1948	Bro-N	4	3	0	0	0	0	0	0	0	1	.000	.000	.000	-97	-1	0			1.000	0	/3-2,2-1	-0.1
1949	Bro-N	5	13	1	2	0	0	1	3	0	3	.154	.154	.385	38	-1	0			.833	-1	/3-3	-0.2
	Chi-N	65	190	14	34	3	1	0	6	5	33	.179	.200	.205	9	-24	9			.972	6	3-36,S-12/2-4	-1.8
	Yr	70	203	15	36	3	1	1	9	5	36	.177	.197	.217	11	-26	9			.965	5	3-39,S-12/2-4	-2.0
1950	Chi-N	61	145	19	38	3	3	1	6	4	16	.262	.287	.345	66	-7	3			.961	-2	2-31,3-10/S-3	-0.8
1951	Chi-N	73	158	13	39	5	2	1	15	10	23	.247	.292	.323	64	-8	0	0	0	.950	13	S-51/2-6,3-1	0.7
1952	Chi-N	50	183	26	52	5	3	1	12	14	14	.284	.338	.361	93	-2	3	1	0	.979	-2	2-50	-0.1
1953	Chi-N	26	39	3	6	2	0	0	4	3	4	.154	.214	.205	10	-5	0	0	0	.911	-0	2-18	-0.5
Total	7	346	851	86	196	22	9	4	53	45	107	.230	.271	.291	52	-58	15	1		.966	18	2-126/3-82,S-66	-3.1
■ ALEX RAMIREZ	Ramirez, Alexander Ramon b: 10/3/74, Caracas, Venez. BR/TR, 5'11", 180 lbs. Deb: 9/19/98																						
1998	Cle-A	3	8	1	1	0	0	0	0	0	3	.125	.125	.125	-34	-2	0	0	0	.833	-0	/O-3	-0.2
■ ARAMIS RAMIREZ	Ramirez, Aramis (Nin) b: 6/25/78, Santo Domingo, D.R. BR/TR, 6'1", 190 lbs. Deb: 5/26/98																						
1998	Pit-N	72	251	23	59	9	1	6	24	18	72	.235	.297	.351	66	-13	0	1	-1	.941	-14	3-71	-2.6
■ MANNY RAMIREZ	Ramirez, Manuel Aristides (Onelcida) b: 5/30/72, Brooklyn, N.Y. BR/TR, 6', 190 lbs. Deb: 9/2/93																						
1993	Cle-A	22	53	5	9	1	0	2	5	2	8	.170	.200	.302	33	-5	0	0	0	1.000	0	D-20/O-1	-0.6
1994	Cle-A	91	290	51	78	22	0	17	60	42	72	.269	.361	.521	124	10	4	2	0	.994	-1	O-84/D-5	0.7
1995	*Cle-A★	137	484	85	149	26	1	31	107	75	112	.308	.406	.558	146	33	6	6	-2	.978	-4	*O-131/D-5	2.2
1996	*Cle-A	152	550	94	170	45	3	33	112	85	104	.309	.404	.582	146	39	8	5	-1	.970	8	*O-149/D-3	3.9
1997	*Cle-A	150	561	99	184	40	0	26	88	79	115	.328	.417	.538	142	37	2	3	-1	.975	-0	*O-146/D-4	3.0
1998	*Cle-A★	150	571	108	168	35	2	45	145	76	121	.294	.383	.599	145	37	5	3	-0	.977	3	*O-148/D-2	3.4
Total	6	702	2509	442	758	169	6	154	517	359	532	.302	.394	.558	140	151	25	19	-4	.977	6	O-659/D-39	12.6
■ MARIO RAMIREZ	Ramirez, Mario (Torres) b: 9/12/57, Yauco, P.R. BR/TR, 5'9", 159 lbs. Deb: 4/25/80																						
1980	NY-N	18	24	2	5	0	0	0	0	1	7	.208	.240	.208	27	-2	0	0	0	1.000	3	/S-7/2-4,3-3	0.1
1981	SD-N	13	13	1	1	0	0	0	1	2	5	.077	.200	.077	-21	-2	0	0	0	1.000	4	/S-2,3-2	0.2
1982	SD-N	13	23	1	4	1	0	0	1	2	4	.174	.240	.217	30	-2	0	0	0	.963	2	/S-8,2-1,3-1	0.0
1983	SD-N	55	107	11	21	6	3	0	12	20	23	.196	.328	.308	80	-2	0	0	0	.985	-2	S-38/3-1	-0.2
1984	*SD-N	48	59	12	7	1	0	2	9	13	14	.119	.278	.237	46	-4	0	0	0	.971	-1	S-33/3-6,2-2	-0.3
1985	SD-N	37	60	6	17	0	0	2	5	3	11	.283	.317	.383	97	-0	0	0	0	.918	-5	S-27/2-7	-0.4
Total	6	184	286	33	55	8	3	4	28	41	64	.192	.296	.283	64	-13	0	0	0	.970	1	S-115/2-14,3-13	-0.6
■ MILT RAMIREZ	Ramirez, Milton (Barboza) b: 4/2/50, Mayaguez, P.R. BR/TR, 5'9", 150 lbs. Deb: 4/11/70																						
1970	StL-N	62	79	8	15	2	1	0	3	8	9	.190	.264	.241	36	-7	0	1	-1	.923	10	S-59/3-1	0.5
1971	StL-N	4	11	2	3	0	0	0	0	2	1	.273	.385	.273	86	-0	0	0	0	.947	-1	/S-4	-0.1
1979	Oak-A	28	62	4	10	1	1	0	3	3	8	.161	.200	.210	11	-8	0	0	0	.923	-5	3-12,2-11/S-8	-1.2
Total	3	94	152	14	28	3	2	0	6	13	18	.184	.248	.230	30	-15	0	1	-1	.920	4	/S-71,3-13,2-11	-0.8
■ ORLANDO RAMIREZ	Ramirez, Orlando (Leal) b: 12/18/51, Cartagena, Colombia BR/TR, 5'10", 175 lbs. Deb: 7/6/74																						
1974	Cal-A	31	86	4	14	0	0	0	7	6	23	.163	.217	.163	11	-10	2	1	0	.956	5	S-31	-0.1
1975	Cal-A	44	100	10	24	4	1	0	4	11	22	.240	.315	.300	80	-2	9	6	-1	.905	0	S-40	0.0
1976	Cal-A	30	70	3	14	1	0	0	5	6	11	.200	.263	.214	44	-5	3	2	-0	.966	4	S-30	0.1
1977	Cal-A	25	13	6	1	0	0	0	0	0	3	.077	.077	.077	-60	-3	1	0	0	1.000	8	/2-5,S-3,D-1	0.6
1979	Cal-A	13	12	1	0	0	0	0	0	1	6	.000	.143	.000	-60	-3	1	0	0	.844	4	S-10/D-1	0.2
Total	5	143	281	24	53	5	1	0	16	24	65	.189	.255	.214	37	-23	16	9	-1	.931	22	S-114/2-5,D-2	0.8
■ RAFAEL RAMIREZ	Ramirez, Rafael Emilio (Peguero) b: 2/18/58, San Pedro De Macoris, D.R. BR/TR, 6', 185 lbs. Deb: 8/4/80																						
1980	Atl-N	50	165	17	44	6	1	2	11	2	33	.267	.292	.352	76	-5	2	1	0	.949	-10	S-46	-1.1
1981	Atl-N	95	307	30	67	16	2	2	20	24	47	.218	.277	.303	63	-15	7	3	0	.942	-2	S-95	-0.8
1982	*Atl-N	157	609	74	169	24	4	10	52	36	49	.278	.321	.379	91	-7	27	14	-0	.956	17	*S-157	2.4
1983	Atl-N	152	622	82	185	13	5	7	58	36	48	.297	.338	.368	89	-9	16	12	-2	.949	8	*S-152	1.2
1984	Atl-N☆	145	591	51	157	22	4	2	48	26	70	.266	.298	.327	70	-23	14	17	-6	.959	-3	*S-145	-2.0
1985	Atl-N	138	568	54	141	25	4	5	58	20	63	.248	.274	.333	65	-27	2	6	-3	.954	9	*S-133	-0.9
1986	Atl-N	134	496	57	119	21	1	8	33	21	60	.240	.275	.335	64	-25	19	8	1	.952	13	S-86,3-57/O-3	-0.4
1987	Atl-N	56	179	22	47	12	0	1	21	8	16	.263	.302	.346	68	-8	6	3	0	.946	-6	S-38,3-12	-1.1
1988	Hou-N	155	566	51	156	30	5	6	59	18	61	.276	.302	.378	98	-4	3	2	-0	.965	-10	*S-154	-0.2
1989	Hou-N	151	537	46	132	20	2	6	54	29	64	.246	.284	.324	76	-18	3	1	0	.945	-41	*S-149	-5.1
1990	Hou-N	132	445	44	116	19	3	2	37	24	46	.261	.300	.330	75	-15	10	5	0	.953	-18	*S-129	-2.5
1991	Hou-N	101	233	17	55	10	0	1	20	13	40	.236	.276	.292	64	-12	3	3	-1	.953	-14	S-45,2-27/3-2	-2.5
1992	Hou-N	73	176	17	44	6	0	1	13	7	24	.250	.283	.301	68	-8	0	0	0	.961	-6	S-57/3-1	-1.1
Total	13	1539	5494	562	1432	224	31	53	484	264	621	.261	.297	.342	77	-177	112	75	-11	.953	-64	*S-1386/3-72,2-27,O	-14.1
■ DOMINGO RAMOS	Ramos, Domingo Antonio (De Ramos) b: 3/29/58, Santiago, D.R. BR/TR, 5'10", 155 lbs. Deb: 9/8/78																						
1978	NY-A	1	0	0	0	0	0	0	0	0	0	—	—	—	—	0	0	0	0	.000	0	/S-1	0.0
1980	Tor-A	5	16	0	2	0	0	0	0	2	5	.125	.222	.125	-2	-2	0	0	0	1.000	-0	/2-2,S-2,D-1	-0.2

YEAR	TM/L	G	AB	R	H	2B	3B	HR	RBI	BB	SO	AVG	OBP	SLG	PRO+	BR/A	SB	CS	SBR	FA	FR	G/POS	TPR
1982	Sea-A	8	26	3	4	2	0	0	1	3	2	.154	.241	.231	30	-3	0	0	0	.920	-5	/S-8	-0.8
1983	Sea-A	53	127	14	36	4	0	2	10	7	12	.283	.326	.362	86	-2	3	1	0	.948	8	S-28/2-8,3-8,D-2	0.8
1984	Sea-A	59	81	6	15	2	0	0	2	5	12	.185	.233	.210	24	-8	2	2	-1	.911	4	3-38,S-13/1-5,2-3	-0.5
1985	Sea-A	75	168	19	33	6	0	1	15	17	23	.196	.270	.250	43	-13	0	1	-1	.951	-8	S-36,2-20,1-14,/3-7	-1.8
1986	Sea-A	49	99	8	18	2	0	0	5	8	13	.182	.250	.202	25	-10	0	1	-1	.966	13	S-21,2-16/3-8,D-2	0.3
1987	Sea-A	42	103	9	32	6	0	2	11	3	12	.311	.336	.427	96	-1	0	1	-1	.953	7	S-25/3-7,2-6,D-2	0.7
1988	Cle-A	22	46	7	12	1	0	0	5	3	7	.261	.320	.283	68	-2	0	0	0	1.000	2	2-11/1-5,S-4,3-2	0.0
	Cal-A	10	15	3	2	0	0	0	0	0	0	.133	.133	.133	-26	-2	0	0	0	1.000	-0	/3-8,O-1	-0.3
	Yr	32	61	10	14	1	0	0	5	3	7	.230	.277	.246	47	-4	0	0	0	1.000	2	2-11,3-10/1-5,SO	-0.3
1989	*Chi-N	85	179	18	47	6	2	1	19	17	23	.263	.333	.335	85	-3	1	1	-0	.959	3	S-42,3-30	0.2
1990	Chi-N	98	226	22	60	5	0	2	17	27	29	.265	.346	.314	77	-6	0	2	-1	.932	-15	3-66,S-21/2-1	-2.1
Total	11	507	1086	109	261	34	2	8	85	92	138	.240	.304	.297	64	-53	6	9	-4	.955	7	S-201,3-174/21DO	-3.7

■ CHUCHO RAMOS

Ramos, Jesus Manuel (Garcia) b: 4/12/18, Maturin, Venez. d: 9/2/77, Caracas, Venez. BR/TL, 5′10.5″, 167 lbs. Deb: 5/7/44

YEAR	TM/L	G	AB	R	H	2B	3B	HR	RBI	BB	SO	AVG	OBP	SLG	PRO+	BR/A	SB	CS	SBR	FA	FR	G/POS	TPR
1944	Cin-N	4	10	1	5	1	0	0	0	0	0	.500	.500	.600	217	1	0			1.000	-1	/O-3	0.0

■ JOHN RAMOS

Ramos, John Joseph b: 8/6/65, Tampa, Fla. BR/TR, 6′, 190 lbs. Deb: 9/18/91

YEAR	TM/L	G	AB	R	H	2B	3B	HR	RBI	BB	SO	AVG	OBP	SLG	PRO+	BR/A	SB	CS	SBR	FA	FR	G/POS	TPR
1991	NY-A	10	26	4	8	1	0	0	3	1	3	.308	.333	.346	88	-0	0	0	0	1.000	0	/C-5,D-4	0.0

■ KEN RAMOS

Ramos, Kenneth Cecil b: 6/6/67, Sidney, Neb. BL/TL, 6′1″, 185 lbs. Deb: 5/16/97

YEAR	TM/L	G	AB	R	H	2B	3B	HR	RBI	BB	SO	AVG	OBP	SLG	PRO+	BR/A	SB	CS	SBR	FA	FR	G/POS	TPR
1997	Hou-N	14	12	0	0	0	0	0	1	2	0	.000	.143	.000	-61	-3	0	0	0	.000	-1	/O-2	-0.4

■ PEDRO RAMOS

Ramos, Pedro (Guerra) "Pete" b: 4/28/35, Pinar Del Rio, Cuba BB/TR, 6′, 185 lbs. Deb: 4/11/55

YEAR	TM/L	G	AB	R	H	2B	3B	HR	RBI	BB	SO	AVG	OBP	SLG	PRO+	BR/A	SB	CS	SBR	FA	FR	G/POS	TPR
1955	Was-A	59	38	6	3	0	0	0	0	2	18	.079	.125	.079	-47	-8	0	1	-1	.964	-1	P-45	0.0
1956	Was-A	56	44	9	9	0	2	0	2	2	16	.205	.239	.295	40	-4	0	1	-1	1.000	-0	P-37	0.0
1957	Was-A	56	76	6	13	0	0	1	10	2	27	.171	.192	.211	10	-9	0	0	0	**1.000**	-0	P-43	0.0
1958	Was-A	53	88	9	21	1	0	0	10	0	33	.239	.239	.250	35	-8	0	0	0	.982	-1	P-43	0.0
1959	Was-A☆	45	75	7	11	1	1	1	2	4	38	.147	.190	.227	14	-9	1	0	0	**1.000**	-1	P-37	0.0
1960	Was-A	53	86	6	10	3	0	2	4	1	36	.116	.126	.221	-8	-13	0	0	0	**1.000**	0	P-43	0.0
1961	Min-A	53	93	8	16	1	0	3	11	3	42	.172	.206	.280	27	-10	0	0	0	.955	-3	P-42	0.0
1962	Cle-A	39	68	6	10	3	0	3	8	1	29	.147	.171	.324	31	-7	0	0	0	.962	0	P-37	0.0
1963	Cle-A	54	55	13	6	0	0	3	7	3	32	.109	.155	.273	17	-6	0	0	0	.963	-2	P-36	0.0
1964	Cle-A	44	39	6	7	0	0	2	2	2	22	.179	.220	.333	52	-3	0	0	0	.960	-1	P-36	0.0
	NY-A	13	5	0	0	0	0	0	0	0	2	.000	.000	.000	-98	-1	0	0	0	.000	-1	P-13	0.0
	Yr	57	44	6	7	0	0	2	2	2	24	.159	.196	.295	34	-4	0	0	0	.960	-2	P-49	0.0
1965	NY-A	65	12	0	1	0	0	0	0	0	8	.083	.083	.083	-53	-2	1	0	0	.895	-1	P-65	0.0
1966	NY-A	52	13	0	2	0	0	0	0	0	8	.154	.154	.154	-12	-2	0	0	0	.952	-0	P-52	0.0
1967	Phi-N	6	1	0	0	0	0	0	0	0	0	.000	.000	.000	-99	-0	0	0	0	1.000	1	/P-6	0.0
1969	Pit-N	5	1	0	0	0	0	0	0	0	1	.000	.000	.000	-99	-0	0	0	0	1.000	0	/P-5	0.0
	Cin-N	38	8	0	0	0	0	0	0	1	4	.000	.111	.000	-63	-2	0	0	0	1.000	-0	P-38	0.0
	Yr	43	9	0	0	0	0	0	0	1	5	.000	.100	.000	-67	-2	0	0	0	1.000	-0	P-43	0.0
1970	Was-A	5	1	0	0	0	0	0	0	1	0	.000	.500	.000	52	0	0	0	0	1.000	0	/P-4	0.0
Total	15	696	703	76	109	9	3	15	56	22	316	.155	.183	.240	14	-85	2	2	-1	.977	-9	P-582	0.0

■ BOBBY RAMOS

Ramos, Roberto b: 11/5/55, Havana, Cuba BR/TR, 5′11″, 208 lbs. Deb: 9/26/78

YEAR	TM/L	G	AB	R	H	2B	3B	HR	RBI	BB	SO	AVG	OBP	SLG	PRO+	BR/A	SB	CS	SBR	FA	FR	G/POS	TPR
1978	Mon-N	2	4	0	0	0	0	0	0	0	1	.000	.000	.000	-99	-1	0	0	0	1.000	0	/C-1	-0.1
1980	Mon-N	13	32	5	5	2	0	0	2	5	5	.156	.270	.219	38	-3	0	0	0	.964	0	C-12	-0.2
1981	Mon-N	26	41	4	8	1	0	1	3	3	5	.195	.250	.293	53	-3	0	0	0	.974	4	C-23	0.1
1982	NY-A	4	11	1	1	0	0	1	2	0	3	.091	.091	.364	18	-1	0	0	0	1.000	1	/C-4	0.0
1983	Mon-N	27	61	2	14	3	1	0	5	8	11	.230	.329	.311	79	-2	0	0	0	.984	4	C-25	0.4
1984	Mon-N	31	83	8	16	1	0	2	5	6	13	.193	.247	.277	49	-6	0	0	0	.982	7	C-31	0.2
Total	6	103	232	20	44	7	1	4	17	22	38	.190	.263	.280	53	-15	0	0	0	.980	15	/C-96	0.4

■ FERNANDO RAMSEY

Ramsey, Fernando David (Ramsey) b: 12/20/65, Rainbow, Panama BR/TR, 6′1″, 175 lbs. Deb: 9/7/92

YEAR	TM/L	G	AB	R	H	2B	3B	HR	RBI	BB	SO	AVG	OBP	SLG	PRO+	BR/A	SB	CS	SBR	FA	FR	G/POS	TPR
1992	Chi-N	18	25	0	3	0	0	0	2	0	6	.120	.120	.120	-31	-4	0	0	0	1.000	-4	O-15	-1.0

■ MIKE RAMSEY

Ramsey, Michael James b: 7/8/60, Thomson, Ga. BB/TL, 6′ ″, 170 lbs. Deb: 4/6/87

YEAR	TM/L	G	AB	R	H	2B	3B	HR	RBI	BB	SO	AVG	OBP	SLG	PRO+	BR/A	SB	CS	SBR	FA	FR	G/POS	TPR
1987	LA-N	48	125	18	29	4	2	0	12	10	32	.232	.289	.296	57	-8	2	4	-2	.973	-3	O-43	-1.4

■ MIKE RAMSEY

Ramsey, Michael Jeffrey b: 3/29/54, Roanoke, Va. BB/TR, 6′1″, 170 lbs. Deb: 9/4/78

YEAR	TM/L	G	AB	R	H	2B	3B	HR	RBI	BB	SO	AVG	OBP	SLG	PRO+	BR/A	SB	CS	SBR	FA	FR	G/POS	TPR
1978	StL-N	12	5	4	1	0	0	0	0	0	1	.200	.200	.200	12	-1	0	0	0	.909	4	/S-4	0.3
1980	StL-N	59	126	11	33	8	1	0	8	3	17	.262	.279	.341	70	-5	0	0	0	.960	0	2-24,S-20/3-8	-0.3
1981	StL-N	47	124	19	32	3	0	0	9	8	16	.258	.303	.282	65	-5	4	0	1	.966	13	S-35/3-5,2-1,O-1	1.1
1982	*StL-N	112	256	18	59	8	2	1	21	22	34	.230	.294	.289	63	-12	6	5	-1	.963	8	2-43,3-28,S-22,/O-2	-0.2
1983	StL-N	97	175	25	46	4	3	1	16	12	23	.263	.314	.337	80	-5	4	2	0	.968	3	2-66,S-20/3-8,O-1	0.0
1984	StL-N	21	15	1	1	1	0	0	0	1	3	.067	.125	.133	-28	-3	0	0	0	1.000	4	/2-7,S-7,3-1	0.2
	Mon-N	37	70	2	15	1	0	0	3	0	13	.214	.214	.229	26	-7	0	0	0	.975	1	S-26,2-12	-0.4
	Yr	58	85	3	16	2	0	0	3	1	16	.188	.198	.212	16	-10	0	0	0	.978	5	S-33,2-19/3-1	-0.2
1985	LA-N	9	15	1	2	1	0	0	0	2	4	.133	.235	.200	24	-2	0	0	0	.923	-0	/S-4,2-2	-0.1
Total	7	394	786	81	189	26	6	2	57	48	111	.240	.286	.296	63	-39	14	7	0	.964	33	2-155,S-138/3-50,O	0.6

■ BILL RAMSEY

Ramsey, William Thrace "Square Jaw" b: 10/20/20, Osceola, Ark. BR/TR, 6′, 175 lbs. Deb: 4/19/45

YEAR	TM/L	G	AB	R	H	2B	3B	HR	RBI	BB	SO	AVG	OBP	SLG	PRO+	BR/A	SB	CS	SBR	FA	FR	G/POS	TPR
1945	Bos-N	78	137	16	40	8	0	1	12	4	22	.292	.326	.372	93	-2	1			.963	-7	O-43	-1.0

■ DICK RAND

Rand, Richard Hilton b: 3/7/31, South Gate, Cal. d: 1/22/96, Moreno Valley, Cal. BR/TR, 6′2″, 185 lbs. Deb: 9/16/53

YEAR	TM/L	G	AB	R	H	2B	3B	HR	RBI	BB	SO	AVG	OBP	SLG	PRO+	BR/A	SB	CS	SBR	FA	FR	G/POS	TPR
1953	StL-N	9	31	3	9	1	0	0	1	2	6	.290	.333	.323	72	-1	0	0	0	.984	3	/C-9	0.2
1955	StL-N	3	10	1	3	0	0	1	3	1	1	.300	.364	.600	150	1	0	1	-1	1.000	-2	/C-3	-0.1
1957	Pit-N	60	105	7	23	2	1	1	9	11	24	.219	.293	.286	58	-6	0	0	0	.973	0	C-57	-0.5
Total	3	72	146	11	35	3	1	2	13	14	31	.240	.306	.315	68	-7	0	1	-1	.977	2	/C-69	-0.4

■ JOE RANDA

Randa, Joseph Gregory b: 12/18/69, Milwaukee, Wis. BR/TR, 5′11″, 190 lbs. Deb: 4/30/95

YEAR	TM/L	G	AB	R	H	2B	3B	HR	RBI	BB	SO	AVG	OBP	SLG	PRO+	BR/A	SB	CS	SBR	FA	FR	G/POS	TPR
1995	KC-A	34	70	6	12	2	0	1	5	6	17	.171	.237	.243	25	-8	0	1	-1	.949	2	3-22/2-9,D-2	-0.6
1996	KC-A	110	337	36	102	24	1	6	47	26	47	.303	.354	.433	98	-1	13	4	2	.951	-4	3-92,2-15/1-7,D-1	-0.3
1997	Pit-N	126	443	58	134	27	9	7	60	41	64	.302	.369	.451	112	8	4	2	0	.937	20	*3-120,2-13	2.8
1998	Det-A	138	460	56	117	21	2	9	50	41	70	.254	.325	.367	79	-14	8	7	-2	.976	9	*3-118,2-20/1-1,D-1	-0.6
Total	4	408	1310	156	365	74	12	23	162	114	198	.279	.343	.406	92	-15	25	14	-1	.954	27	3-352/2-57,1-8,D-4	1.3

■ SAP RANDALL

Randall, James Odell b: 8/19/60, Mobile, Ala. BB/TR, 5′11″, 195 lbs. Deb: 8/2/88

YEAR	TM/L	G	AB	R	H	2B	3B	HR	RBI	BB	SO	AVG	OBP	SLG	PRO+	BR/A	SB	CS	SBR	FA	FR	G/POS	TPR
1988	Chi-A	4	12	1	0	0	0	0	1	2	3	.000	.143	.000	-57	-3	0	0	0	1.000	0	/1-2,O-1,D-1	-0.3

■ NEWT RANDALL

Randall, Newton J. b: 2/3/1880, New Lowell, Ont., Canada d: 5/3/55, Duluth, Minn. BR/TR, 5′10″, Deb: 4/18/07

YEAR	TM/L	G	AB	R	H	2B	3B	HR	RBI	BB	SO	AVG	OBP	SLG	PRO+	BR/A	SB	CS	SBR	FA	FR	G/POS	TPR
1907	Chi-N	22	78	6	16	4	2	0	4	8		.205	.279	.308	79	-2	2			.904	1	O-21	-0.2
	Bos-N	75	258	16	55	6	3	0	15	19		.213	.285	.260	71	-8	4			.920	-8	O-73	-2.1
	Yr	97	336	22	71	10	5	0	19	27		.211	.284	.271	73	-10	6			.915	-7	O-94	-2.3

■ BOB RANDALL

Randall, Robert Lee b: 6/10/48, Norton, Kan. BR/TR, 6′3″, 180 lbs. Deb: 4/13/76 C

YEAR	TM/L	G	AB	R	H	2B	3B	HR	RBI	BB	SO	AVG	OBP	SLG	PRO+	BR/A	SB	CS	SBR	FA	FR	G/POS	TPR
1976	Min-A	153	475	55	127	18	4	1	34	28	38	.267	.319	.328	88	-7	3	5	-2	.969	-4	*2-153	-0.4
1977	Min-A	103	306	36	73	13	2	0	22	15	25	.239	.290	.294	60	-17	1	4	-2	.985	10	*2-101/1-1,3-1,D-1	-0.2
1978	Min-A	119	330	36	89	11	3	0	21	24	22	.270	.331	.321	82	-7	5	3	-0	.983	10	*2-116/3-2,D-1	1.0
1979	Min-A	80	199	25	49	7	0	0	14	15	17	.246	.299	.281	55	-12	2	2	-1	.983	7	2-71/3-7,S-1,O-1	-0.3
1980	Min-A	5	15	2	3	1	0	0	0	1	0	.200	.250	.267	39	-1	0	0	0	.909	0	/3-4,2-1	-0.1
Total	5	460	1325	154	341	50	9	1	91	83	102	.257	.311	.311	74	-44	11	14	-5	.979	22	2-442/3-14,D-2,OS1	-0.0

YEAR	TM/L	G	AB	R	H	2B	3B	HR	RBI	BB	SO	AVG	OBP	SLG	PRO+	BR/A	SB	CS	SBR	FA	FR	G/POS	TPR
■ **LEN RANDLE**	Randle, Leonard Shenoff b: 2/12/49, Long Beach, Cal. BB/TR, 5'10", 169 lbs. Deb: 6/16/71																						
1971	Was-A	75	215	27	47	11	0	2	13	24	56	.219	.300	.298	74	-7	1	1	-0	.967	5	2-66	0.3
1972	Tex-A	74	249	23	48	13	0	2	21	13	51	.193	.236	.269	52	-15	4	5	-2	.952	1	2-65/S-4,O-2	-1.5
1973	Tex-A	10	29	3	6	1	1	1	1	0	2	.207	.207	.414	74	-1	0	2	-1	.964	-2	/2-5,O-2	-0.5
1974	Tex-A	151	520	65	157	17	4	1	49	29	43	.302	.341	.356	103	2	26	17	-2	.935	1	3-89,2-40,O-21,/SD	0.1
1975	Tex-A	156	601	85	166	24	7	4	57	57	80	.276	.343	.359	99	0	16	19	-7	.973	15	2-79,O-66,3/CSD	1.0
1976	Tex-A	142	539	53	121	11	6	1	51	46	63	.224	.288	.273	63	-24	30	15	0	.971	-4	*2-113,O-30/3-2,D-1	-2.3
1977	NY-N	136	513	78	156	22	7	5	27	65	70	.304	.384	.404	117	14	33	21	-3	.961	-7	*3-110,2-20/O-6,S-1	0.5
1978	NY-N	132	437	53	102	16	8	2	35	64	57	.233	.333	.320	86	-7	14	11	-2	.967	-7	*3-124/2-5	-1.8
1979	NY-A	20	39	2	7	0	0	0	3	3	2	.179	.238	.179	15	-5	0	0	0	1.000	-0	O-11/D-2	-0.5
1980	Chi-N	130	489	67	135	19	6	5	39	50	55	.276	.344	.370	93	-4	19	13	-2	.929	-7	*3-111,2-17/O-6	-1.4
1981	Sea-A	82	273	22	63	9	1	4	25	17	22	.231	.278	.315	68	-11	11	6	-0	.986	7	3-59,2-21/O-5,S-3	-0.4
1982	Sea-A	30	46	10	8	2	0	0	1	4	4	.174	.240	.217	26	-5	2	2	-1	.964	6	D-13/3-9,2-6	0.0
Total	12	1138	3950	488	1016	145	40	27	322	372	505	.257	.323	.335	87	-63	156	112	-20	.953	9	3-521,2-437,O/DSC	-6.5
■ **WILLIE RANDOLPH**	Randolph, Willie Larry b: 7/6/54, Holly Hill, S.C. BR/TR, 5'11", 166 lbs. Deb: 7/29/75 C																						
1975	*Pit-N	30	61	9	10	1	0	0	3	7	6	.164	.250	.180	21	-6	1	0	0	.962	4	2-14/3-1	-0.2
1976	*NY-A†	125	430	59	115	15	4	1	40	58	39	.267	.358	.328	103	4	37	12	4	.974	15	*2-124	3.2
1977	*NY-A★	147	551	91	151	28	11	4	40	64	53	.274	.351	.387	102	3	13	6	0	.980	6	*2-147	1.9
1978	NY-A	134	499	87	139	18	6	3	42	82	51	.279	.385	.357	112	12	36	7	7	.978	-8	*2-134	2.1
1979	NY-A	153	574	98	155	15	13	5	61	95	39	.270	.376	.368	104	7	33	12	3	.985	9	*2-153	2.9
1980	*NY-A★	138	513	99	151	23	7	7	46	**119**	45	.294	.429	.407	133	31	30	5	6	.976	-7	*2-138	3.8
1981	*NY-A★	93	357	59	83	14	3	2	24	57	24	.232	.338	.305	88	-4	14	5	1	.977	-2	2-93	0.1
1982	NY-A	144	553	85	155	21	4	3	36	75	35	.280	.369	.349	100	3	16	9	-1	.981	-3	*2-142/D-1	0.7
1983	NY-A	104	420	73	117	21	1	2	38	53	32	.279	.361	.348	100	2	12	4	1	.979	3	*2-104	1.1
1984	NY-A	142	564	86	162	24	2	2	31	86	42	.287	.382	.348	108	10	10	6	-1	.983	11	*2-142	2.5
1985	NY-A	143	497	75	137	21	2	5	40	85	39	.276	.386	.356	107	9	16	9	-1	.985	-3	*2-143	1.1
1986	NY-A	141	492	76	136	15	2	5	50	94	49	.276	.396	.346	105	9	15	2	3	.972	-12	*2-139/D-1	0.5
1987	NY-A★	120	449	96	137	24	2	7	67	82	25	.305	.415	.414	122	19	11	1	3	.981	-2	*2-119/D-1	2.4
1988	NY-A	110	404	43	93	20	1	2	34	55	39	.230	.325	.300	77	-11	8	4	0	.988	8	*2-110	0.1
1989	LA-N★	145	549	62	155	18	0	2	36	71	51	.282	.369	.326	102	4	7	6	-2	.987	-1	*2-140	0.7
1990	LA-N	26	96	15	26	4	0	1	9	13	9	.271	.364	.344	98	0	1	0	0	.969	-2	2-26	-0.1
	*Oak-A	93	292	37	75	9	3	1	21	32	25	.257	.332	.318	86	-5	6	1	1	.982	-12	2-84/D-6	-1.4
1991	Mil-A	124	431	60	141	14	3	0	54	75	38	.327	.427	.374	127	20	4	2	0	.969	10	*2-121/D-2	3.3
1992	NY-N	90	286	29	72	11	1	2	15	40	34	.252	.352	.318	92	-1	1	3	-2	.977	-14	2-79	-1.6
Total	18	2202	8018	1239	2210	316	65	54	687	1243	675	.276	.375	.351	105	105	271	94	25	.980	0	*2-2152/D-11,3-1	23.1
■ **MERRITT RANEW**	Ranew, Merritt Thomas b: 5/10/38, Albany, Ga. BL/TR, 5'10", 180 lbs. Deb: 4/13/62																						
1962	Hou-N	71	218	26	51	6	8	4	24	14	43	.234	.289	.390	87	-5	2	2	-1	.980	-6	C-58	-0.9
1963	Chi-N	78	154	18	52	8	1	3	15	9	32	.338	.382	.461	134	7	1	0	0	.980	-5	C-37/1-9	0.3
1964	Chi-N	16	33	0	3	0	0	0	1	2	6	.091	.167	.091	-24	-5	0	0	0	1.000	2	/C-9	-0.3
	Mil-N	9	17	1	2	0	0	0	0	0	3	.118	.118	.118	-33	-3	0	1	-1	1.000	-1	/C-3	-0.5
	Yr	25	50	1	5	0	0	0	1	2	9	.100	.151	.100	-27	-8	0	1	-1	1.000	1	C-12	-0.8
1965	Cal-A	41	91	12	19	4	0	1	10	7	22	.209	.265	.286	58	-5	0	0	0	.988	-10	C-24	-1.5
1969	Sea-A	54	81	11	20	2	0	0	4	10	14	.247	.330	.272	71	-3	0	0	0	.969	-6	C-13/O-3,3-1	-0.9
Total	5	269	594	68	147	20	9	8	54	42	120	.247	.304	.352	83	-14	3	3	-1	.982	-25	C-144/1-9,O-3,3-1	-3.8
■ **JEFF RANSOM**	Ransom, Jeffrey Dean b: 11/11/60, Fresno, Cal. BR/TR, 5'11", 185 lbs. Deb: 9/5/81																						
1981	SF-N	5	15	2	4	1	0	0	0	1	1	.267	.313	.333	85	-0	0	0	0	1.000	2	/C-5	0.2
1982	SF-N	15	44	5	7	0	0	0	3	6	7	.159	.260	.159	20	-5	0	0	0	.988	2	C-14	-0.3
1983	SF-N	6	20	3	4	0	0	1	3	4	7	.200	.333	.350	92	-0	0	0	0	.946	-2	/C-6	-0.1
Total	3	26	79	10	15	1	0	1	6	11	15	.190	.289	.241	50	-5	0	0	0	.980	2	/C-25	-0.2
■ **EARL RAPP**	Rapp, Earl Wellington b: 5/20/21, Corunna, Mich. d: 2/13/92, Swedesboro, N.J. BL/TR, 6'2", 185 lbs. Deb: 4/28/49																						
1949	Det-A	1	0	0	0	0	0	0	0	1	0	—	1.000	—	175	0	0	0	0	.000	0	H	0.0
	Chi-A	19	54	3	14	1	1	0	11	5	6	.259	.322	.315	71	-2	1	1	-0	.974	2	O-13	-0.1
	Yr	20	54	3	14	1	1	0	11	6	6	.259	.333	.315	74	-2	1	1	-0	.974	2	O-13	-0.1
1951	NY-N	13	11	0	1	0	0	0	1	2	3	.091	.231	.091	-10	-2	0	0	0	.000	0	H	-0.2
	StL-A	26	98	14	32	5	3	2	14	11	11	.327	.394	.500	137	5	1	0	0	.979	0	O-25	0.4
1952	StL-A	30	49	3	7	4	0	0	4	0	8	.143	.143	.224	1	-7	0	0	0	1.000	-1	/O-7	-0.8
	Was-A	46	67	7	19	6	0	0	9	6	13	.284	.351	.373	105	0	0	0	0	.917	-2	O-10	-0.2
	Yr	76	116	10	26	10	0	0	13	6	21	.224	.268	.310	61	-6	0	0	0	.958	-3	O-17	-1.0
Total	3	135	279	27	73	16	4	2	39	25	41	.262	.325	.369	89	-5	2	1	0	.973	-0	/O-55	-0.9
■ **GOLDIE RAPP**	Rapp, Joseph Aloysius b: 2/6/1892, Cincinnati, Ohio d: 7/1/66, LaMesa, Cal. BB/TR, 5'10", 165 lbs. Deb: 4/13/21																						
1921	NY-N	58	181	21	39	9	1	0	15	15	13	.215	.276	.276	46	-14	3	11	-6	.941	13	3-56	-0.3
	Phi-N	52	202	28	56	7	1	1	10	14	8	.277	.324	.337	70	-9	6	7	-2	.950	-2	3-50/2-1	-1.0
	Yr	110	383	49	95	16	2	1	25	29	21	.248	.301	.308	59	-22	9	18	-8	.945	10	*3-106/2-1	-1.3
1922	Phi-N	119	502	58	127	26	3	0	38	32	29	.253	.299	.317	54	-35	6	12	-5	.948	5	*3-117/S-2	-2.5
1923	Phi-N	47	179	27	47	5	0	1	10	14	14	.263	.320	.307	59	-10	1	1	-0	.947	-1	3-45	-0.7
Total	3	276	1064	134	269	47	5	2	73	75	64	.253	.303	.312	57	-68	16	31	-14	.947	14	3-268/S-2,2-1	-4.5
■ **BILL RARIDEN**	Rariden, William Angel "Bedford Bill" b: 2/4/1888, Bedford, Ind. d: 8/28/42, Bedford, Ind. BR/TR, 5'10", 168 lbs. Deb: 8/12/09																						
1909	Bos-N	13	42	1	6	1	0	0	1	4		.143	.217	.167	18	-4	1			.912	-3	C-13	-0.7
1910	Bos-N	49	137	15	31	5	1	1	14	12	22	.226	.293	.299	70	-5	1			.962	3	C-49	0.2
1911	Bos-N	70	246	22	56	9	0	0	21	21	18	.228	.288	.264	51	-16	3			.952	1	C-65/3-3,2-1	-0.8
1912	Bos-N	79	247	27	55	3	1	1	14	18	35	.223	.281	.255	46	-18	3			.964	-5	C-73	-1.6
1913	Bos-N	95	246	31	58	9	2	3	30	30	21	.236	.324	.325	84	-5	5			.976	-0	C-87	0.2
1914	Ind-F	131	396	44	93	15	5	0	47	61	43	.235	.337	.298	67	-23	12			.981	20	*C-130	0.9
1915	New-F	142	444	49	120	30	7	0	40	60	29	.270	.361	.369	112	1	8			.978	23	*C-142	3.8
1916	NY-N	120	351	23	78	9	3	1	29	55	32	.222	.333	.274	92	-1	4			.972	-9	*C-119	-0.1
1917	*NY-N	101	266	20	72	10	1	0	25	42	17	.271	.372	.316	116	7	3			.971	-17	*C-100	-0.3
1918	NY-N	69	183	15	41	5	1	0	17	15	15	.224	.283	.262	68	-7	1			**.984**	-9	C-63	-1.3
1919	*Cin-N	74	218	16	47	6	3	1	24	17	19	.216	.275	.284	70	-8	4			.983	3	C-70	0.1
1920	Cin-N	39	101	9	25	3	0	0	10	5	0	.248	.283	.277	62	-5	2	0	1	.972	-0	C-37	-0.3
Total	12	982	2877	272	682	105	24	7	272	340	251	.237	.320	.298	78	-83	47	0		.973	8	C-948/3-3,2-1	0.1
■ **MORRIE RATH**	Rath, Morris Charles b: 12/25/1886, Mobeetie, Tex. d: 11/18/45, Upper Darby, Pa. BL/TR, 5'8.5", 160 lbs. Deb: 9/28/09																						
1909	Phi-A	7	26	4	7	1	0	0	3	2		.269	.387	.308	117	1	1			.846	2	/S-4,3-2	0.3
1910	Phi-A	18	26	3	4	0	0	0	1	5		.154	.290	.154	40	-2	0			.950	-2	3-11/2-3	-0.4
	Cle-A	24	67	5	13	3	0	0	0	10		.194	.299	.239	68	-2	2			.950	2	3-22/S-1	0.1
	Yr	42	93	8	17	3	0	0	1	15		.183	.296	.215	60	-4	2			.950	0	3-33/2-3,S-1	-0.3
1912	Chi-A	157	591	104	161	10	2	1	19	95		.272	.380	.301	98	5	30			**.963**	18	*2-157	1.9
1913	Chi-A	92	295	37	59	2	0	0	12	46	22	.200	.310	.207	52	-16	22			.962	-2	2-86	-2.0
1919	*Cin-N	138	537	77	142	13	1	1	29	64	24	.264	.343	.298	96	0	17			.974	13	*2-138	2.2
1920	Cin-N	129	506	61	135	7	4	2	28	36	24	.267	.319	.308	82	-11	10	11	-4	**.977**	-7	*2-126/3-1,O-1	-1.9
Total	6	565	2048	291	521	36	7	4	92	258	70	.254	.342	.285	86	-25	82	11		.970	25	2-510/3-36,S-5,O-1	0.2
■ **GENE RATLIFF**	Ratliff, Kelly Eugene b: 9/28/45, Macon, Ga. BR/TR, 6'5", 185 lbs. Deb: 5/15/65																						
1965	Hou-N	4	4	0	0	0	0	0	0	0	4	.000	.000	.000	-99	-1	0	0	0	.000	0	H	-0.1

YEAR	TM/L	G	AB	R	H	2B	3B	HR	RBI	BB	SO	AVG	OBP	SLG	PRO+	BR/A	SB	CS	SBR	FA	FR	G/POS	TPR
■ PAUL RATLIFF	Ratliff, Paul Hawthorne b: 1/23/44, San Diego, Cal. BL/TR, 6'2", 190 lbs. Deb: 4/14/63																						
1963	Min-A	10	21	2	4	1	0	1	3	2	7	.190	.292	.381	85	-0	0	0	0	.976	2	/C-7	0.2
1970	*Min-A	69	149	19	40	7	2	5	22	15	51	.268	.363	.443	119	4	0	0	0	.980	-15	C-53	-1.0
1971	Min-A	21	44	3	7	1	0	2	6	4	17	.159	.229	.318	52	-3	0	0	0	1.000	1	C-15	-0.2
	Mil-A	23	41	3	7	1	0	3	7	5	21	.171	.277	.415	95	-0	0	0	0	.966	-1	C-13	-0.1
	Yr	44	85	6	14	2	0	5	13	9	38	.165	.253	.365	72	-3	0	0	0	.985	0	C-28	-0.3
1972	Mil-A	22	42	1	3	0	0	1	4	2	23	.071	.114	.143	-25	-6	0	0	0	1.000	-2	C-13	-1.0
Total	4	145	297	28	61	10	2	12	42	28	119	.205	.293	.374	86	-6	0	0	0	.983	-16	C-101	-2.1
■ TOMMY RAUB	Raub, Thomas Jefferson b: 12/1/1870, Raubsville, Pa. d: 2/15/49, Phillipsburg, N.J. BR/TR, 5'10", 155 lbs. Deb: 5/3/03																						
1903	Chi-N	36	84	6	19	3	2	0	7	5		.226	.278	.310	69	-4	3			.900	-4	C-12/1-6,O-5,3-4	-0.7
1906	StL-N	24	78	9	22	2	4	0	2	4		.282	.325	.410	135	3	2			.957	-4	C-22	0.1
Total	2	60	162	15	41	5	6	0	9	9		.253	.301	.358	99	-1	5			.940	-8	/C-34,1-6,O-5,3-4	-0.6
■ BOB RAUDMAN	Raudman, Robert Joyce "Shorty" b: 3/14/42, Erie, Pa. BL/TL, 5'9.5", 185 lbs. Deb: 9/13/66																						
1966	Chi-N	8	29	1	7	2	0	0	2	1	4	.241	.267	.310	59	-2	0	0	0	.909	0	/O-8	-0.2
1967	Chi-N	8	26	0	4	0	0	0	1	1	4	.154	.185	.154	-2	-3	0	0	0	.875	0	/O-8	-0.4
Total	2	16	55	1	11	2	0	0	3	2	8	.200	.228	.236	30	-5	0	0	0	.889	0	/O-16	-0.6
■ JOHNNY RAWLINGS	Rawlings, John William "Red" b: 8/17/1892, Bloomfield, Iowa d: 10/16/72, Inglewood, Cal. BR/TR, 5'8", 158 lbs. Deb: 4/14/14																						
1914	Cin-N	33	60	9	13	1	0	0	8	6	8	.217	.288	.233	54	-3	1			.885	0	3-10/2-7,S-5	-0.3
	KC-F	61	193	19	41	3	0	0	15	22	25	.212	.296	.228	46	-17	6			.937	17	S-61	0.5
1915	KC-F	120	399	40	86	9	2	2	24	27	40	.216	.269	.263	52	-32	17			.926	-4	*S-120	-3.0
1917	Bos-N	122	371	37	95	9	4	2	31	38	32	.256	.337	.318	107	4	12			.977	11	2-96,S-17/3-1,O-1	2.3
1918	Bos-N	111	410	32	85	7	3	0	21	30	31	.207	.265	.239	56	-21	10			.956	2	S-71,2-20,O-18	-1.8
1919	Bos-N	77	275	30	70	8	2	1	16	16	20	.255	.298	.309	86	-5	10			.961	-12	2-58,O-10/S-5	-1.7
1920	Bos-N	5	3	0	0	0	0	0	2	0	1	.000	.000	.000	-99	-1	0	0	0	1.000	-1	/2-1	-0.1
	Phi-N	98	384	39	90	19	2	3	30	22	25	.234	.278	.318	67	-16	9	6	-1	.970	-2	2-97	-1.7
	Yr	103	387	39	90	19	2	3	32	22	26	.233	.276	.315	67	-17	9	6	-1	.970	-2	2-98	-1.8
1921	Phi-N	60	254	20	74	14	2	1	16	8	12	.291	.318	.374	76	-9	4	5	-2	.954	5	2-60	-0.4
	*NY-N	86	307	40	82	8	1	1	30	18	19	.267	.316	.309	66	-14	4	4	-1	.970	-1	2-86/S-1	-1.5
	Yr	146	561	60	156	22	3	2	46	26	31	.278	.317	.339	71	-23	8	9	-3	.963	3	*2-146/S-1	-1.9
1922	NY-N	88	308	46	87	13	8	1	30	23	15	.282	.342	.386	87	-6	7	6	-2	.984	-4	2-77/3-5	-0.9
1923	Pit-N	119	461	53	131	18	4	1	45	25	29	.284	.322	.347	75	-17	9	0	3	.958	-8	*2-119	-2.0
1924	Pit-N	3	3	0	1	0	0	0	2	0	0	.333	.333	.333	78	-0	0	0	0	.000	0	H	0.0
1925	Pit-N	36	110	17	31	7	0	2	13	8	8	.282	.336	.400	82	-3	0	1	-1	.981	3	2-29	0.0
1926	Pit-N	61	181	27	42	6	0	0	20	14	10	.232	.287	.265	47	-13	3			.970	-3	2-59	-1.5
Total	12	1080	3719	409	928	122	28	14	303	257	275	.250	.303	.309	71	-153	92	22		.968	3	2-709,S-280/O-29,3	-12.1
■ IRV RAY	Ray, Irving Burton "Stubby" b: 1/22/1864, Harrington, Me. d: 2/21/48, Harrington, Me. BL/TR, 5'6", 165 lbs. Deb: 7/7/1888																						
1888	Bos-N	50	206	26	51	2	3	2	26	6	11	.248	.272	.316	85	-4	7			.879	-11	S-48/2-3	-1.4
1889	Bos-N	9	33	8	10	1	0	0	2	4	0	.303	.378	.333	94	-0	1			.875	-4	/S-5,3-4	-0.4
	Bal-a	26	106	20	36	4	1	0	17	7	6	.340	.397	.396	124	3	12			.784	-7	S-20/O-6	-0.3
1890	Bal-a	38	139	28	50	6	2	1	20	15		.360	.433	.453	154	9	11			.894	-10	S-38	0.2
1891	Bal-a	103	418	72	116	17	5	0	58	54	18	.278	.366	.342	102	2	28			.885	-14	O-64,S-40	-1.0
Total	4	226	902	154	263	30	11	3	123	86	35	.292	.360	.359	109	11	59			.863	-46	S-151/O-70,3-4,2-3	-2.9
■ JOHNNY RAY	Ray, John Cornelius b: 3/1/57, Chouteau, Okla. BB/TR, 5'11", 185 lbs. Deb: 9/2/81																						
1981	Pit-N	31	102	10	25	11	0	0	6	6	9	.245	.287	.353	78	-3	0	0	0	.987	2	2-31	0.0
1982	Pit-N	162	647	79	182	30	7	7	63	36	34	.281	.320	.382	93	-7	16	7	1	.977	8	*2-162	1.1
1983	Pit-N	151	576	68	163	**38**	7	5	53	35	26	.283	.324	.399	97	-3	18	9	0	.983	17	*2-151	2.2
1984	Pit-N	155	555	75	173	**38**	6	6	67	37	31	.312	.358	.434	122	15	11	6	-0	.984	-9	*2-149	1.1
1985	Pit-N	154	594	67	163	33	3	7	70	46	24	.274	.328	.375	97	-3	13	9	-2	.976	-15	*2-151	-1.4
1986	Pit-N	155	579	67	174	33	0	7	78	58	47	.301	.367	.394	107	7	6	9	-4	.993	5	*2-151	1.5
1987	Pit-N	123	472	48	129	19	3	5	54	41	36	.273	.331	.358	82	-12	4	2	0	.981	4	*2-119	-0.2
	Cal-A	30	127	16	44	11	0	0	15	3	10	.346	.362	.433	113	2	0	0	0	.986	-1	2-29/D-1	0.3
1988	Cal-A★	153	602	75	184	42	7	6	83	36	38	.306	.349	.429	120	15	4	1	1	.972	-7	*2-104,O-40/D-6	1.1
1989	Cal-A	134	530	52	153	16	3	5	62	36	30	.289	.334	.358	97	-2	6	3	0	.984	4	*2-130	0.6
1990	Cal-A	105	404	47	112	23	0	5	43	19	44	.277	.310	.371	91	-6	2	3	-1	.987	12	*2-100/D-1	0.7
Total	10	1353	5188	604	1502	294	36	53	594	353	329	.290	.336	.391	101	4	80	49	-5	.982	20	*2-1277/O-40,D-8	7.0
■ LARRY RAY	Ray, Larry Dale b: 3/11/58, Madison, Ind. BL/TR, 6'1", 195 lbs. Deb: 9/10/82																						
1982	Hou-N	5	6	0	1	0	0	0	1	0	4	.167	.167	.167	-7	-1	0	0	0	1.000	-0	/O-1	-0.1
■ FLOYD RAYFORD	Rayford, Floyd Kinnard b: 7/27/57, Memphis, Tenn. BR/TR, 5'10", 195 lbs. Deb: 4/17/80																						
1980	Bal-A	8	18	1	4	0	0	0	1	0	5	.222	.222	.222	22	-2	0	0	0	.900	0	/3-4,2-1,D-1	-0.2
1982	Bal-A	34	53	7	7	0	0	3	5	6	14	.132	.220	.302	42	-4	0	1	-1	.898	5	3-27/C-2,D-2	-0.1
1983	StL-N	56	104	5	22	4	0	3	14	10	27	.212	.281	.337	70	-4	1	0	0	.883	-4	3-33	-0.9
1984	Bal-A	86	250	24	64	14	0	4	27	12	51	.256	.298	.360	83	-6	0	3	-2	.991	11	C-66,3-22/1-1	0.5
1985	Bal-A	105	359	55	110	21	1	18	48	10	69	.306	.325	.521	131	13	3	1	0	.972	-2	3-78,C-29/D-1	1.2
1986	Bal-A	81	210	15	37	4	0	8	19	15	50	.176	.231	.310	46	-16	0	0	0	.912	4	3-72,C-10/D-1	-1.3
1987	Bal-A	20	50	5	11	0	0	2	3	2	9	.220	.250	.340	56	-3	0	0	0	.980	6	C-17/3-1,D-1	0.4
Total	7	390	1044	112	255	43	1	38	117	55	225	.244	.284	.397	86	-23	4	5	-2	.931	21	3-237,C-124/D-6,12	-0.4
■ FRED RAYMER	Raymer, Frederick Charles b: 11/12/1875, Leavenworth, Kan. d: 6/11/57, Los Angeles, Cal. BR/TR, 5'11", 185 lbs. Deb: 4/24/01																						
1901	Chi-N	120	463	41	108	14	2	0	43	11		.233	.257	.272	56	-27	18			.881	-17	3-82,S-29/1-5,2-3	-4.1
1904	Bos-N	114	419	28	88	12	3	1	27	13		.210	.236	.260	55	-23	17			**.958**	7	*2-114	-1.4
1905	Bos-N	137	498	26	105	14	2	0	31	8		.211	.232	.247	44	-35	15			.949	-18	*2-134/1-1,O-1	-5.5
Total	3	371	1380	95	301	40	7	1	101	32		.218	.242	.259	51	-85	50			.954	-28	2-251/3-82,S-29,1O	-11.0
■ HARRY RAYMOND	Raymond, Harry H. "Jack" b: 2/20/1862, Utica, N.Y. d: 3/21/25, San Diego, Cal. 5'9", 179 lbs. Deb: 9/9/1888																						
1888	Lou-a	32	123	8	26	2	0	0	13	1		.211	.218	.228	44	-8	7			.884	-1	3-31/O-1	-0.8
1889	Lou-a	130	515	58	123	12	9	0	47	19	45	.239	.270	.297	63	-26	19			.886	-1	*3-129/O-1,P-1	-1.9
1890	*Lou-a	123	521	91	135	7	4	2	51	22		.259	.293	.299	76	-17	18			.874	-2	*3-119/S-4	-1.3
1891	Lou-a	14	59	4	12	2	0	0	2	5	6	.203	.288	.237	51	-4	3			.898	5	S-14	0.2
1892	Pit-N	12	49	4	4	0	1	0	2	4	8	.082	.151	.122	-17	-7	1			.867	-2	3-12	-0.8
	Was-N	4	15	2	1	0	0	0	0	3	2	.067	.222	.067	-12	-2	1			.783	1	/3-4	-0.1
	Yr	16	64	6	5	0	1	0	2	7	10	.078	.169	.109	-15	-9	2			.838	-1	3-16	-0.9
Total	5	315	1282	167	301	23	14	2	115	54	61	.235	.270	.279	62	-63	49			.878	1	3-295/S-18,O-2,P-1	-4.7
■ LOU RAYMOND	Raymond, Louis Anthony (b: Louis Anthony Raymondjack) b: 12/11/1894, Buffalo, N.Y. d: 5/2/79, Rochester, N.Y. BR/TR, 5'10.5", 187 lbs. Deb: 5/2/19																						
1919	Phi-N	1	2	0	1	0	0	0	0	0	0	.500	.500	.500	188	0	0			.000	0	/2-1	0.0
■ AL REACH	Reach, Alfred James b: 5/25/1840, London, England d: 1/14/28, Atlantic City, N.J BL/TL, 5'6", 155 lbs. Deb: 5/20/1871 FM																						
1871	Ath-n	26	133	43	47	7	6	0	34	5	6	.353	.377	.496	150	9	2	0	1	.844	-0	*2-26	0.4
1872	Ath-n	24	118	21	23	0	0	0	11	4	0	.195	.221	.195	29	-9	1	1	-0	.943	4	O-20/1-4	-0.3
1873	Ath-n	13	73	13	16	5	1	0	9	0	0	.219	.219	.315	53	-5	2	0	1	.881	5	/2-9,O-7	0.0
1874	Ath-n	14	55	8	7	2	0	0	2	0	4	.127	.127	.164	-7	-7	0	0	0	.732	4	O-14	-0.2
1875	Ath-n	3	14	4	4	1	0	0	1	0	0	.286	.286	.357	110	0	2	1	0	1.000	-2	/O-2,2-1	-0.1
Total	5 n	80	393	89	97	15	7	0	57	9	10	.247	.264	.321	73	-12	7	2	1	.857	11	/O-43,2-36,1-4	-0.2

YEAR	TM/L	G	AB	R	H	2B	3B	HR	RBI	BB	SO	AVG	OBP	SLG	PRO+	BR/A	SB	CS	SBR	FA	FR	G/POS	TPR
■ BOB REACH	Reach, Robert b: 8/28/1843, Williamsburg, N.Y. d: 5/19/22, Springfield, Mass. 5'5", 155 lbs. Deb: 4/23/1872 F																						
1872	Oly-n	2	8	1	2	0	0	0	0	0	0	.250	.250	.250	57	-0	0	0	0	.727	-1	/S-2	-0.1
1873	Was-n	1	5	1	1	0	0	0	0	0	0	.200	.200	.200	20	-0	0	0	0	.500	-1	/S-1	-0.1
Total	2 n	3	13	2	3	0	0	0	0	0	0	.231	.231	.231	42	-1	0	0	0	.632	-2	/S-3	-0.2
■ RANDY READY	Ready, Randy Max b: 1/8/60, Fremont, Cal. BR/TR, 5'11", 180 lbs. Deb: 9/4/83																						
1983	Mil-A	12	37	8	15	3	2	1	6	6	3	.405	.488	.676	234	7	0	1	-1	1.000	0	/3-4,D-6	0.6
1984	Mil-A	37	123	13	23	6	1	3	13	14	18	.187	.270	.325	66	-6	0	0	0	.946	3	3-36	-0.3
1985	Mil-A	48	181	29	48	9	5	1	21	14	23	.265	.321	.387	93	-2	0	0	0	.989	4	O-37/3-7,2-3,D-2	0.1
1986	Mil-A	23	79	8	15	4	0	1	4	9	9	.190	.273	.278	49	-6	2	0	1	.950	-4	O-11/2-7,3-3,D-1	-0.9
	SD-N	1	3	0	0	0	0	0	0	0	1	.000	.000	.000	-99	-1	0	0	0	.667	-0	/3-1	-0.1
1987	SD-N	124	350	69	108	26	6	12	54	67	44	.309	.424	.520	154	30	7	3	0	.912	2	3-52,2-51,O-16	3.2
1988	SD-N	114	331	43	88	16	2	7	39	39	38	.266	.349	.390	114	6	6	2	1	.952	-10	3-57,2-26,O-16	-0.3
1989	SD-N	28	67	4	17	2	1	0	5	11	6	.254	.359	.313	94	-0	0	0	0	.963	1	3-18/2-2,O-1	0.2
	Phi-N	72	187	33	50	11	1	8	21	31	31	.267	.377	.465	140	10	4	3	-1	.962	-6	O-36,3-14/2-7	0.4
	Yr	100	254	37	67	13	2	8	26	42	37	.264	.372	.425	127	10	4	3	-1	.962	-4	O-37,3-32/2-9	0.6
1990	Phi-N	101	217	26	53	9	1	1	26	29	35	.244	.336	.309	79	-5	3	2	-0	1.000	-6	O-30,2-28	-1.2
1991	Phi-N	76	205	32	51	10	1	1	20	47	25	.249	.391	.322	104	4	2	1	0	.989	-7	2-66	-0.2
1992	*Oak-A	61	125	17	25	2	0	3	17	25	23	.200	.333	.288	80	-3	1	0	0	1.000	-3	O-24,D-24/3-7,12	-0.7
1993	Mon-N	40	134	22	34	8	1	1	10	23	8	.254	.367	.351	89	-1	2	1	0	.968	3	2-28,1-13/3-3	0.2
1994	Phi-N	17	42	5	16	1	0	1	3	8	6	.381	.480	.476	147	3	0	1	-1	1.000	-3	2-11/3-1	0.0
1995	Phi-N	23	29	3	4	0	0	0	0	3	6	.138	.219	.138	-3	-4	0	1	-1	.967	-0	/1-3,2-1	-0.6
Total	13	777	2110	312	547	107	21	40	239	326	276	.259	.362	.387	108	33	27	15	-1	.979	-27	2-234,3-203,O/D1	0.4
■ LEROY REAMS	Reams, Leroy b: 8/11/43, Pine Bluff, Ark. BL/TR, 6'2", 175 lbs. Deb: 6/7/69																						
1969	Phi-N	1	1	0	0	0	0	0	0	0	1	.000	.000	.000	-99	-0	0	0	0	.000	0	H	0.0
■ PHIL REARDON	Reardon, Philip Michael b: 10/3/1883, Brooklyn, N.Y. d: 9/28/20, Brooklyn, N.Y. BR/TR, Deb: 9/19/06																						
1906	Bro-N	5	14	0	1	0	0	0	0	0		.071	.133	.071	-39	-2	0			.917	1	/O-4	-0.2
■ ART REBEL	Rebel, Arthur Anthony b: 3/4/15, Cincinnati, Ohio BL/TL, 5'8", 180 lbs. Deb: 4/19/38																						
1938	Phi-N	7	9	2	2	0	0	0	1	1	1	.222	.300	.222	47	-1	0			1.000	-1	/O-3	-0.1
1945	StL-N	26	72	12	25	4	0	0	5	6	4	.347	.397	.403	120	2	1			.976	2	O-18	0.3
Total	2	33	81	14	27	4	0	0	6	7	5	.333	.386	.383	112	1	1			.978	1	/O-21	0.2
■ JEFF REBOULET	Reboulet, Jeffrey Allen b: 4/30/64, Dayton, Ohio BR/TR, 6', 169 lbs. Deb: 5/12/92																						
1992	Min-A	73	137	15	26	7	1	1	16	23	26	.190	.311	.277	64	-6	3	2	-0	.971	21	S-36,3-22,2-13,/OD	1.6
1993	Min-A	109	240	33	62	8	0	1	15	35	37	.258	.357	.304	79	-5	5	5	-2	.982	13	S-62,3-35,2-11,/OD	0.9
1994	Min-A	74	189	28	49	11	1	3	23	18	23	.259	.327	.376	81	-5	0	0	0	.963	-7	S-42,2-14,1/3OD	-0.9
1995	Min-A	87	216	39	63	11	0	4	23	27	34	.292	.373	.398	101	1	1	2	-1	.993	10	S-39,3-22,1-17,2/C	1.1
1996	Min-A	107	234	20	52	9	0	0	23	25	34	.222	.300	.261	43	-20	4	2	0	.987	-5	S-37,3-36,21/OD	-2.2
1997	*Bal-A	99	228	26	54	9	0	4	27	23	44	.237	.310	.329	69	-10	3	0	1	.977	-3	2-63,S-22,3-12,/OD	-0.9
1998	Bal-A	79	126	20	31	6	0	1	8	19	34	.246	.354	.317	77	-4	0	1	-1	.974	3	2-28,S-28,3-23	0.2
Total	7	628	1370	181	337	61	2	14	135	170	232	.246	.333	.324	73	-50	16	12	-2	.977	30	S-266,2-166,3/1ODC	-0.2
■ JOHN RECCIUS	Reccius, John b: 10/29/1859, Louisville, Ky. d: 9/1/30, Louisville, Ky. 5'6.5", Deb: 5/2/1882 F																						
1882	Lou-a	74	266	46	63	12	3	1		23		.237	.298	.316	113	5				.857	-3	*O-65,P-13	0.2
1883	Lou-a	18	63	10	9	2	0	0	3	7		.143	.229	.175	34	-4				.833	-1	O-18/P-1	-0.5
Total	2	92	329	56	72	14	3	1	3	30		.219	.284	.289	98	1				.851	-4	/O-83,P-14	-0.3
■ PHIL RECCIUS	Reccius, Phillip b: 6/7/1862, Louisville, Ky. d: 2/15/03, Louisville, Ky. 5'9", 163 lbs. Deb: 9/25/1882 F																						
1882	Lou-a	4	15	0	2	0	0	0		0		.133	.133	.133	-10	-2				.778	-0	/O-4	-0.2
1883	Lou-a	1	3	1	1	1	0	0		0		.333	.333	.667	231	0				1.000	-0	/O-1	0.0
1884	Lou-a	73	263	23	63	9	2	3	21	5		.240	.267	.323	96	-1				.845	-2	3-51,P-18,S-10	-0.2
1885	Lou-a	102	402	57	97	8	10	1	38	13		.241	.267	.318	84	-8				.829	-2	*3-97/P-7	-0.7
1886	Lou-a	5	13	4	4	1	1	0	2	3		.308	.471	.538	204	2	0			.889	1	/O-5,P-1	0.2
1887	Lou-a	11	37	9	9	2	0	0	4	8		.243	.391	.297	92	0	3			.926	2	O-10/S-1	0.1
	Cle-a	62	229	23	47	6	3	0	29	24		.205	.295	.258	56	-12	9			.877	8	3-62/P-1	-0.3
	Yr	73	266	32	56	8	3	0	33	32		.211	.309	.263	62	-12	12			.877	10	3-62,O-10/S-1,P-1	-0.2
1888	Lou-a	2	9	0	2	1	0	0	4	1		.222	.300	.333	105	0	0			.750	-2	/3-2	-0.1
1890	Roc-a	1	4	0	0	0	0	0	1	0		.000	.000	.000	-99	-1	0			.000	-0	/O-1	-0.1
Total	8	261	975	117	225	28	16	4	99	54		.231	.280	.305	81	-21	12			.848	5	3-212/P-27,O-21,S	-1.3
■ JOHNNY REDER	Reder, John Anthony b: 9/24/09, Lublin, Poland d: 4/12/90, Fall River, Mass. BR/TR, 6', 184 lbs. Deb: 4/16/32																						
1932	Bos-A	17	37	4	5	1	0	0	3	6	6	.135	.256	.162	11	-5	0	0	0	.990	0	1-10/3-1	-0.5
■ BUCK REDFERN	Redfern, George Howard b: 4/7/02, Asheville, N.C. d: 9/8/64, Asheville, N.C. BR/TR, 5'11", 165 lbs. Deb: 4/11/28																						
1928	Chi-A	86	261	22	61	6	3	0	35	12	19	.234	.267	.280	44	-21	8	2	1	.953	6	2-45,S-33/3-1	-0.9
1929	Chi-A	21	46	0	6	0	0	0	3	3	3	.130	.184	.130	-18	-8	1	1	-0	.967	-5	2-11/3-5,S-4	-1.2
Total	2	107	307	22	67	6	3	0	38	15	22	.218	.255	.257	35	-29	9	3	1	.955	1	/2-56,S-37,3-6	-2.1
■ JOE REDFIELD	Redfield, Joseph Randall b: 1/14/61, Doylestown, Pa. BR/TR, 6'2", 190 lbs. Deb: 6/4/88																						
1988	Cal-A	1	2	0	0	0	0	0	0	0	0	.000	.000	.000	-99	-1	0	0	0	1.000	0	/3-1	0.0
1991	Pit-N	11	18	1	2	0	0	0	0	4	1	.111	.273	.111	12	-2	0	1	-1	.917	-1	/3-9	-0.3
Total	2	12	20	1	2	0	0	0	0	4	1	.100	.250	.100	2	-3	0	1	-1	.923	-0	/3-10	-0.3
■ GLENN REDMON	Redmon, Glenn Vincent b: 1/11/48, Detroit, Mich. BR/TR, 5'11", 180 lbs. Deb: 9/8/74																						
1974	SF-N	7	17	0	4	3	0	0	4	1	3	.235	.278	.412	87	-0	0	0	0	.955	-1	/2-4	-0.1
■ BILLY REDMON	Redmon, William T. b: Brooklyn, N.Y. BL/TL, Deb: 5/4/1875																						
1875	RS-n	19	82	12	16	2	0	0	1	2	7	.195	.214	.220	56	-3	3	0	1	.837	5	S-19/C-2	0.2
1877	Cin-N	3	12	1	3	1	0	0	3	1	1	.250	.308	.333	115	0				.833	2	/S-3	0.2
1878	Mil-N	48	187	16	43	8	0	0	21	8	13	.230	.262	.273	71	-6				.785	-17	S-39/O-7,3-3,C-1	-2.1
Total	2	51	199	17	46	9	0	0	24	9	14	.231	.264	.276	73	-6				.791	-16	/S-42,O-7,3-3,C-1	-1.9
■ HARRY REDMOND	Redmond, Harry John b: 9/13/1887, Cleveland, Ohio d: 7/10/60, Cleveland, Ohio BR/TR, 5'8", 170 lbs. Deb: 9/7/09																						
1909	Bro-N	6	19	3	0	0	0	0	1	0		.000	.000	.000	-99	-4	0			.892	3	/2-5	-0.1
■ WAYNE REDMOND	Redmond, Howard Wayne b: 11/25/45, Athens, Ala. BR/TR, 5'10", 165 lbs. Deb: 9/7/65																						
1965	Det-A	4	4	1	0	0	0	0	0	1	1	.000	.200	.000	-38	-1	0	0	0	1.000	-0	/O-2	-0.1
1969	Det-A	5	3	0	0	0	0	0	0	0	2	.000	.000	.000	-96	-1	0	0	0	.000	0	H	-0.1
Total	2	9	7	1	0	0	0	0	0	1	3	.000	.125	.000	-60	-1	0	0	0	1.000	-0	/O-2	-0.2
■ JACK REDMOND	Redmond, John McKittrick "Red" (b: Jackson Mc Kittrick Redmond) b: 9/3/10, Florence, Ariz. d: 7/27/68, Garland, Tex. BL/TR, 5'11", 185 lbs. Deb: 4/22/35																						
1935	Was-A	22	34	8	6	1	0	1	7	3	1	.176	.243	.294	40	-3	0	0	0	.978	2	C-15	-0.1
■ MIKE REDMOND	Redmond, Michael Patrick b: 5/5/71, Seattle, Wash. BR/TR, 6'1", 185 lbs. Deb: 5/31/98																						
1998	Fla-N	37	118	10	39	9	0	2	12	5	16	.331	.368	.458	117	3	0	0	0	.992	1	C-37	0.6
■ GARY REDUS	Redus, Gary Eugene b: 11/1/56, Athens, Ala. BR/TR, 6'1", 185 lbs. Deb: 9/7/82																						
1982	Cin-N	20	83	12	18	3	2	1	7	5	21	.217	.261	.337	65	-4	11	2	2	.970	1	O-20	-0.2
1983	Cin-N	125	453	90	112	20	9	17	51	71	111	.247	.353	.444	115	10	39	14	3	.972	9	*O-120	1.9

YEAR	TM/L	G	AB	R	H	2B	3B	HR	RBI	BB	SO	AVG	OBP	SLG	PRO+	BR/A	SB	CS	SBR	FA	FR	G/POS	TPR
1984	Cin-N	123	394	69	100	21	3	7	22	52	71	.254	.342	.376	97	-1	48	11	8	.967	-2	*O-114	0.3
1985	Cin-N	101	246	51	62	14	4	6	28	44	52	.252	.368	.415	113	5	48	12	7	.986	-10	O-85	0.1
1986	Phi-N	90	340	62	84	22	4	11	33	47	78	.247	.344	.432	109	4	25	7	3	.980	10	O-89	1.5
1987	Chi-A	130	475	78	112	26	6	12	48	69	90	.236	.333	.392	89	-7	52	11	9	.979	4	*O-123/D-4	0.1
1988	Chi-A	77	262	42	69	10	4	6	34	33	52	.263	.350	.401	110	4	26	2	7	.987	1	O-68/D-2	0.9
	Pit-N	30	71	12	14	2	0	2	4	15	19	.197	.345	.310	90	-0	5	2	0	.957	2	O-19	0.1
1989	Pit-N	98	279	42	79	18	7	6	33	40	51	.283	.375	.462	143	16	25	6	4	.987	0	1-72,O-16	1.5
1990	*Pit-N	96	227	32	56	15	3	6	23	33	38	.247	.347	.419	114	5	11	5	0	.988	-2	1-72/O-7	-0.1
1991	*Pit-N	98	252	45	62	12	2	7	24	28	39	.246	.329	.393	104	1	17	3	3	.990	-11	1-47,O-33	-1.1
1992	*Pit-N	76	176	26	45	7	3	3	12	17	25	.256	.321	.381	99	-0	11	4	1	1.000	-4	1-36,O-15	-0.6
1993	Tex-A	77	222	28	64	12	4	6	31	23	35	.288	.355	.459	122	7	4	4	-1	.981	-8	O-61/1-5,2-1,D-1	-0.4
1994	Tex-A	18	33	2	9	1	0	0	2	4	6	.273	.351	.303	71	-1	0	0	0	1.000	-2	/O-7,1-5	-0.3
Total	13	1159	3513	591	886	183	51	90	352	481	688	.252	.345	.410	107	39	322	83	47	.974	-12	O-777,1-237/D-7,2-1	3.7

■ BOB REECE
Reece, Robert Scott b: 1/5/51, Sacramento, Cal. BR/TR, 6'1", 190 lbs. Deb: 4/22/78

YEAR	TM/L	G	AB	R	H	2B	3B	HR	RBI	BB	SO	AVG	OBP	SLG	PRO+	BR/A	SB	CS	SBR	FA	FR	G/POS	TPR
1978	Mon-N	9	11	2	2	1	0	0	3	0	4	.182	.182	.273	26	-1	0	0	0	.947	1	/C-9	0.0

■ DARREN REED
Reed, Darren A. Douglas b: 10/16/65, Ojai, Cal. BR/TR, 6'1", 190 lbs. Deb: 5/1/90

YEAR	TM/L	G	AB	R	H	2B	3B	HR	RBI	BB	SO	AVG	OBP	SLG	PRO+	BR/A	SB	CS	SBR	FA	FR	G/POS	TPR
1990	NY-N	26	39	5	8	4	1	1	2	3	11	.205	.262	.436	89	-1	1	0	0	.955	-1	O-14	-0.2
1992	Mon-N	42	81	10	14	2	0	5	10	6	23	.173	.239	.383	74	-3	0	0	0	1.000	-3	O-29	-0.7
	Min-A	14	33	2	6	2	0	0	4	2	11	.182	.229	.242	31	-3	0	0	0	1.000	-2	O-13/D-1	-0.6
Total	2	82	153	17	28	8	1	6	16	11	45	.183	.242	.366	68	-7	1	0	0	.987	-6	/O-56,D-1	-1.5

■ HUGH REED
Reed, Hugh b: 1837, Chicago, Ill. d: 11/3/1883, Chicago, Ill. Deb: 8/26/1874

YEAR	TM/L	G	AB	R	H	2B	3B	HR	RBI	BB	SO	AVG	OBP	SLG	PRO+	BR/A	SB	CS	SBR	FA	FR	G/POS	TPR
1874	Bal-n	1	4	0	0	0	0	0	0	0	0	.000	.000	.000	-99	-1	0	0	0	1.000	-0	/O-1	-0.1

■ JEFF REED
Reed, Jeffrey Scott b: 11/12/62, Joliet, Ill. BL/TR, 6'2", 190 lbs. Deb: 4/5/84

YEAR	TM/L	G	AB	R	H	2B	3B	HR	RBI	BB	SO	AVG	OBP	SLG	PRO+	BR/A	SB	CS	SBR	FA	FR	G/POS	TPR
1984	Min-A	18	21	3	3	3	0	0	1	2	6	.143	.217	.286	36	-2	0	0	0	.977	2	C-18	0.1
1985	Min-A	7	10	2	2	0	0	0	0	0	3	.200	.200	.200	9	-1	0	0	0	1.000	-0	/C-7	-0.1
1986	Min-A	68	165	13	39	6	1	2	9	16	19	.236	.308	.321	70	-7	1	0	0	.994	8	C-64	0.5
1987	Mon-N	75	207	15	44	11	0	1	21	12	20	.213	.259	.280	42	-17	0	1	-1	.970	-4	C-74	-1.8
1988	Mon-N	43	123	10	27	3	2	0	9	13	22	.220	.294	.276	62	-6	1	0	0	.995	2	C-39	-0.1
	Cin-N	49	142	10	33	6	0	1	7	15	19	.232	.306	.296	71	-5	0	0	0	.993	5	C-49	0.4
	Yr	92	265	20	60	9	2	1	16	28	41	.226	.300	.287	66	-11	1	0	0	.994	8	C-88	0.3
1989	Cin-N	102	287	16	64	11	0	3	23	34	46	.223	.310	.293	71	-10	0	0	0	.988	-5	C-99	-1.1
1990	*Cin-N	72	175	12	44	8	1	3	16	24	26	.251	.342	.360	89	-2	0	0	0	.987	2	C-70	0.3
1991	Cin-N	91	270	20	72	15	2	3	31	23	38	.267	.327	.370	92	-3	0	1	-1	.991	-2	C-89	0.0
1992	Cin-N	15	25	2	4	0	0	0	2	1	4	.160	.192	.160	1	-3	0	0	0	1.000	-0	/C-6	-0.3
1993	SF-N	66	119	10	31	3	0	6	12	16	22	.261	.348	.437	112	2	0	1	-1	1.000	3	C-37	0.6
1994	SF-N	50	103	11	18	3	0	1	7	11	21	.175	.254	.233	30	-11	0	0	0	.993	-4	C-33	-1.3
1995	SF-N	66	113	12	30	2	0	0	9	20	17	.265	.376	.283	79	-2	0	0	0	.995	3	C-42	0.3
1996	Col-N	116	341	34	97	20	1	8	37	43	65	.284	.368	.419	87	-8	2	2	-1	.982	-12	*C-111	-1.4
1997	Col-N	90	256	43	76	10	0	17	47	35	55	.297	.386	.535	112	3	2	1	0	.987	4	C-78	1.2
1998	Col-N	113	259	43	75	17	1	9	39	37	57	.290	.380	.467	99	-0	0	0	0	.986	-4	C-99	0.1
Total	15	1041	2616	256	659	118	8	54	270	302	440	.252	.332	.365	81	-72	6	6	-2	.988	-0	C-915	-2.6

■ JODY REED
Reed, Jody Eric b: 7/26/62, Tampa, Fla. BR/TR, 5'9", 165 lbs. Deb: 9/12/87

YEAR	TM/L	G	AB	R	H	2B	3B	HR	RBI	BB	SO	AVG	OBP	SLG	PRO+	BR/A	SB	CS	SBR	FA	FR	G/POS	TPR
1987	Bos-A	9	30	4	9	1	1	0	8	4	0	.300	.382	.400	105	0	1	1	-0	1.000	5	/S-4,2-2,3-1	0.5
1988	*Bos-A	109	338	60	99	23	1	1	28	45	21	.293	.382	.376	109	6	1	3	-2	.971	3	S-94,2-11/3-4,D-1	1.5
1989	Bos-A	146	524	76	151	42	2	3	40	73	44	.288	.379	.393	111	10	4	5	-2	.967	1	S-77,2-70/3-4,OD	1.7
1990	*Bos-A	155	598	70	173	**45**	0	5	51	75	65	.289	.372	.390	108	9	4	4	-1	.990	-6	*2-119,S-50/D-1	0.8
1991	Bos-A	153	618	87	175	42	2	5	60	60	53	.283	.350	.382	98	-1	6	5	-1	.982	1	*2-152/S-6	0.2
1992	Bos-A	143	550	64	136	27	1	3	40	62	44	.247	.324	.316	75	-17	7	8	-3	.982	**24**	*2-142/D-1	0.7
1993	LA-N	132	445	48	123	21	2	2	31	38	40	.276	.335	.346	88	-7	1	3	-2	**.993**	19	*2-132	1.4
1994	Mil-A	108	399	48	108	22	0	2	37	57	34	.271	.365	.341	80	-10	5	4	-1	**.995**	11	*2-106	0.4
1995	SD-N	131	445	58	114	18	1	4	40	59	38	.256	.350	.328	83	-9	6	4	-1	.994	18	*2-130/S-5	1.5
1996	*SD-N	146	495	45	121	20	0	2	49	59	53	.244	.329	.297	71	-20	2	5	-2	.987	4	*2-145	-0.9
1997	Det-A	52	112	6	22	2	0	0	8	10	15	.196	.280	.214	32	-11	3	2	-0	.987	13	2-41/D-5	0.3
Total	11	1284	4554	566	1231	263	10	27	392	542	407	.270	.352	.350	90	-52	40	44	-14	.988	94	*2-1050,S-236/D3O	8.1

■ JACK REED
Reed, John Burwell b: 2/2/33, Silver City, Miss. BR/TR, 6', 185 lbs. Deb: 4/23/61

YEAR	TM/L	G	AB	R	H	2B	3B	HR	RBI	BB	SO	AVG	OBP	SLG	PRO+	BR/A	SB	CS	SBR	FA	FR	G/POS	TPR
1961	*NY-A	28	13	4	2	0	0	0	1	1	1	.154	.214	.154	0	-2	0	0	0	.933	-9	O-27	-1.1
1962	NY-A	88	43	17	13	2	1	1	4	4	7	.302	.362	.465	125	1	2	1	0	.941	-23	O-75	-2.2
1963	NY-A	106	73	18	15	3	1	0	1	9	14	.205	.293	.274	60	-4	5	1	1	1.000	-21	O-89	-2.6
Total	3	222	129	39	30	5	2	1	6	14	22	.233	.308	.326	76	-4	7	2	1	.972	-53	O-191	-5.9

■ MILT REED
Reed, Milton D. b: 7/4/1890, Atlanta, Ga. d: 7/27/38, Atlanta, Ga. BL/TR, 5'9.5", 150 lbs. Deb: 9/9/11

YEAR	TM/L	G	AB	R	H	2B	3B	HR	RBI	BB	SO	AVG	OBP	SLG	PRO+	BR/A	SB	CS	SBR	FA	FR	G/POS	TPR
1911	StL-N	1	1	0	0	0	0	0	0	0	0	.000	.000	.000	-99	-0	0			.000	0	H	0.0
1913	Phi-N	13	24	4	6	1	0	0	0	1	5	.250	.280	.292	61	-1	1			.900	-4	/S-9,2-3	-0.5
1914	Phi-N	44	107	10	22	2	1	0	2	10	13	.206	.280	.243	52	-6	4			.887	-17	S-22,2-11/3-1	-2.5
1915	Bro-F	10	31	2	9	1	1	0	8	2	0	.290	.353	.387	109	-0	2			.864	-5	S-10	-0.5
Total	4	68	163	16	37	4	2	0	10	13	18	.227	.292	.276	63	-8	7			.880	-26	/S-41,2-14,3-1	-3.5

■ TED REED
Reed, Ralph Edwin b: 10/18/1890, Beaver, Pa. d: 2/16/59, Beaver, Pa. BR/TR, 5'11", 190 lbs. Deb: 9/10/15

YEAR	TM/L	G	AB	R	H	2B	3B	HR	RBI	BB	SO	AVG	OBP	SLG	PRO+	BR/A	SB	CS	SBR	FA	FR	G/POS	TPR
1915	New-F	20	77	5	20	1	2	0	4	2	7	.260	.287	.325	76	-4	1			.863	-3	3-20	-0.7

■ BILLY REED
Reed, William Joseph b: 11/12/22, Shawano, Wis. BL/TR, 5'10.5", 175 lbs. Deb: 4/15/52

YEAR	TM/L	G	AB	R	H	2B	3B	HR	RBI	BB	SO	AVG	OBP	SLG	PRO+	BR/A	SB	CS	SBR	FA	FR	G/POS	TPR
1952	Bos-N	15	52	4	13	0	0	0	0	0	5	.250	.264	.250	45	-4	0	0	0	.931	-7	2-14	-1.0

■ ICICLE REEDER
Reeder, James Edward b: 1865, Cincinnati, Ohio BR, 6', Deb: 6/24/1884

YEAR	TM/L	G	AB	R	H	2B	3B	HR	RBI	BB	SO	AVG	OBP	SLG	PRO+	BR/A	SB	CS	SBR	FA	FR	G/POS	TPR
1884	Cin-a	3	14	0	2	0	0	0		0		.143	.143	.143	-6	-2				1.000	-0	/O-3	-0.2
	Was-U	3	12	0	2	0	0	0		0		.167	.167	.167	1	-2				.500	-1	/O-3	-0.3
Total	1	6	26	0	4	0	0	0		0		.154	.154	.154	-3	-3				.714	-1	/O-6	-0.5

■ NICK REEDER
Reeder, Nicholas (b: Nicholas Herchenroeder) b: 3/22/1867, Louisville, Ky. d: 9/26/1894, Louisville, Ky. BR/TR, 5'9", 189 lbs. Deb: 4/11/1891

YEAR	TM/L	G	AB	R	H	2B	3B	HR	RBI	BB	SO	AVG	OBP	SLG	PRO+	BR/A	SB	CS	SBR	FA	FR	G/POS	TPR
1891	Lou-a	1	2	0	0	0	0	0	0	0	1	.000	.000	.000	-99	-1	0			1.000	-0	/3-1	-0.1

■ RANDY REESE
Reese, Andrew Jackson b: 2/7/04, Tupelo, Miss. d: 1/10/66, Tupelo, Miss. BR/TR, 5'11", 180 lbs. Deb: 4/15/27

YEAR	TM/L	G	AB	R	H	2B	3B	HR	RBI	BB	SO	AVG	OBP	SLG	PRO+	BR/A	SB	CS	SBR	FA	FR	G/POS	TPR
1927	NY-N	97	355	43	94	14	2	4	21	13	52	.265	.298	.349	73	-14	5			.912	-1	3-64,O-16/1-1	-1.3
1928	NY-N	109	406	61	125	18	4	6	44	13	24	.308	.331	.416	94	-5	7			.941	-10	O-64,2-26/1-6,S3	-1.7
1929	NY-N	58	209	36	55	11	3	0	21	15	19	.263	.316	.344	64	-12	8			.960	1	2-44/O-8,3-4	-0.9
1930	NY-N	67	172	26	47	4	2	4	25	10	12	.273	.313	.390	70	-9	1			.957	-3	O-32,3-10/1-1	-1.2
Total	4	331	1142	166	321	47	11	14	111	51	107	.281	.315	.378	78	-39	21			.954	-14	O-120/3-84,2-70,1S	-5.1

■ POKEY REESE
Reese, Calvin b: 6/10/73, Columbia, S.C. BR/TR, 5'11", 180 lbs. Deb: 4/1/97

YEAR	TM/L	G	AB	R	H	2B	3B	HR	RBI	BB	SO	AVG	OBP	SLG	PRO+	BR/A	SB	CS	SBR	FA	FR	G/POS	TPR
1997	Cin-N	128	397	48	87	15	0	4	26	31	82	.219	.284	.287	49	-29	25	7	3	.966	-2	*S-110/2-8,3-8	-1.9
1998	Cin-N	59	133	20	34	2	2	1	16	14	28	.256	.327	.323	68	-6	3	2	-0	.985	3	3-32,S-18/2-3	-0.2
Total	2	187	530	68	121	17	2	5	42	45	110	.228	.295	.296	54	-35	28	9	3	.956	1	S-128/3-40,2-11	-2.1

■ PEE WEE REESE
Reese, Harold Henry b: 7/23/18, Ekron, Ky. BR/TR, 5'9", 175 lbs. Deb: 4/23/40 CH

YEAR	TM/L	G	AB	R	H	2B	3B	HR	RBI	BB	SO	AVG	OBP	SLG	PRO+	BR/A	SB	CS	SBR	FA	FR	G/POS	TPR
1940	Bro-N	84	312	58	85	8	4	5	28	45	42	.272	.366	.372	98	0	15			.960	-14	S-83	-0.7
1941	*Bro-N	152	595	76	136	23	5	2	46	68	56	.229	.311	.294	68	-24	10			.946	8	*S-151	-0.5

YEAR	TM/L	G	AB	R	H	2B	3B	HR	RBI	BB	SO	AVG	OBP	SLG	PRO+	BR/A	SB	CS	SBR	FA	FR	G/POS	TPR
1942	Bro-N★	151	564	87	144	24	5	3	53	82	55	.255	.350	.332	98	1	15			.959	17	*S-151	2.9
1946	Bro-N†	152	542	79	154	16	10	5	60	87	71	.284	.384	.378	116	14	10			.966	-4	*S-152	2.1
1947	*Bro-N★	142	476	81	135	24	4	12	73	**104**	67	.284	.414	.426	119	17	7			.966	-2	*S-142	2.2
1948	Bro-N★	151	566	96	155	31	4	9	75	79	63	.274	.363	.390	100	2	25			.962	10	*S-149	2.1
1949	*Bro-N★	155	617	**132**	172	27	3	16	73	116	59	.279	.396	.410	112	15	26			**.977**	2	*S-155	2.7
1950	Bro-N★	141	531	97	138	21	5	11	52	91	62	.260	.369	.380	96	-1	17			.963	2	*S-134/3-7	1.1
1951	Bro-N★	154	616	94	176	20	8	10	84	81	57	.286	.371	.393	103	5	20	14	-2	.953	-8	*S-154	0.6
1952	*Bro-N★	149	559	94	152	18	8	6	58	86	59	.272	.369	.365	103	5	**30**	5	**6**	.969	-11	*S-145	1.1
1953	*Bro-N★	140	524	108	142	25	7	13	61	82	61	.271	.374	.420	104	5	22	6	**3**	.966	-1	*S-135	1.7
1954	Bro-N☆	141	554	98	171	35	8	10	69	90	62	.309	.408	.455	121	20	8	5	-1	.965	-4	*S-140	2.7
1955	*Bro-N	145	553	99	156	29	4	10	61	78	60	.282	.374	.403	103	5	8	7	-2	.965	-13	*S-142	0.2
1956	*Bro-N	147	572	85	147	19	2	9	46	56	69	.257	.324	.344	74	-20	13	4	2	.965	-9	*S-136,3-12	-1.7
1957	Bro-N	103	330	33	74	3	1	1	29	39	32	.224	.308	.248	47	-23	5	2	0	.943	10	3-75,S-23	-1.0
1958	LA-N	59	147	21	33	7	2	4	17	26	15	.224	.341	.381	88	-2	1	2	-1	.929	-8	S-22,3-21	-0.9
Total	16	2166	8058	1338	2170	330	80	126	885	1210	890	.269	.366	.377	98	19	232	45		.962	-25	*S-2014,3-115	14.6
■ **JIMMIE REESE**	Reese, James Herman (b: James Herman Soloman) b: 10/1/01, New York, N.Y. d: 7/13/94, Santa Ana, Cal. BL/TR, 5′11.5″, 165 lbs. Deb: 4/19/30 C																						
1930	NY-A	77	188	44	65	14	2	3	18	11	8	.346	.382	.489	125	7	1	1	-0	.974	-9	2-48/3-5	-0.1
1931	NY-A	65	245	41	59	10	2	3	26	17	10	.241	.293	.335	68	-12	2	3	-1	.972	5	2-61	-0.4
1932	StL-N	90	309	38	82	15	0	2	26	20	19	.265	.314	.333	72	-12	4			.979	9	2-77	0.1
Total	3	232	742	123	206	39	4	8	70	48	37	.278	.324	.373	84	-17	7	4		.975	4	2-186/3-5	-0.4
■ **RICH REESE**	Reese, Richard Benjamin b: 9/29/41, Leipsic, Ohio BL/TL, 6′3″, 200 lbs. Deb: 9/4/64																						
1964	Min-A	10	7	0	0	0	0	0	0	0	1	.000	.000	.000	-99	-2	0	0	0	1.000	0	/1-1	-0.2
1965	Min-A	14	7	0	2	1	0	0	0	2	2	.286	.444	.429	143	1	0	0	0	1.000	-0	/1-6,O-1	0.0
1966	Min-A	3	2	0	0	0	0	0	0	1	2	.000	.333	.000	5	-0	0	0	0	.000	0	H	0.0
1967	Min-A	95	101	13	25	5	0	4	20	8	17	.248	.303	.416	102	0	0	0	0	.990	-1	1-36,O-10	-0.2
1968	Min-A	126	332	40	86	15	2	4	28	18	36	.259	.303	.352	93	-3	3	1	0	.991	-2	1-87,O-15	-1.2
1969	*Min-A	132	419	52	135	24	4	16	69	23	57	.322	.365	.513	140	21	1	5	-3	.993	-4	*1-117/O-5	0.6
1970	*Min-A	153	501	63	131	15	5	10	56	48	70	.261	.335	.371	93	-4	5	4	-1	.992	-2	*1-146	-1.9
1971	Min-A	120	329	40	72	8	3	10	39	20	35	.219	.274	.353	74	-12	7	4	-0	.994	-3	1-95/O-9	-2.4
1972	Min-A	132	197	23	43	3	2	5	26	25	27	.218	.306	.330	85	-3	0	1	-1	.988	3	1-98,O-13	-0.5
1973	Det-A	59	102	10	14	1	0	2	4	7	17	.137	.193	.206	11	-12	0	0	0	1.000	-3	1-37,O-21	-1.8
	Min-A	22	23	7	4	1	1	1	3	6	6	.174	.345	.435	114	1	0	0	0	1.000	1	1-17	0.1
	Yr	81	125	17	18	2	1	3	7	13	23	.144	.225	.248	31	-12	0	0	0	1.000	-2	1-54,O-21	-1.7
Total	10	866	2020	248	512	73	17	52	245	158	270	.253	.314	.384	95	-15	16	15	-4	.992	-10	1-640/O-74	-7.5
■ **BOBBY REEVES**	Reeves, Robert Edwin "Gunner" b: 6/24/04, Hill City, Tenn. d: 6/4/93, Chattanooga, Tenn. BR/TR, 5′11″, 170 lbs. Deb: 6/9/26																						
1926	Was-A	20	49	4	11	0	1	0	7	6	9	.224	.321	.265	56	-3	1	1	-0	.940	1	3-16/2-1,S-1	-0.1
1927	Was-A	112	380	37	97	11	5	1	39	21	53	.255	.296	.318	60	-23	3	1	0	.923	-7	S-96,3-12/2-2	-1.8
1928	Was-A	102	353	44	107	16	8	3	42	24	47	.303	.351	.419	102	1	4	8	-4	.908	-4	S-66,2-22/3-8,O-1	0.2
1929	Bos-A	140	460	66	114	19	2	2	28	60	57	.248	.343	.311	71	-18	7	8	-3	.912	1	*3-131/2-2,S-2,1-1	-1.4
1930	Bos-A	92	272	41	59	7	4	2	18	50	36	.217	.345	.294	66	-12	6	2	1	.895	5	3-62,S-15,2-11	-0.2
1931	Bos-A	36	84	11	14	2	2	0	1	14	16	.167	.293	.238	43	-7	0	1	-1	.912	-8	2-29/P-1	-1.3
Total	6	502	1598	203	402	55	22	8	135	175	218	.252	.331	.329	73	-62	21	21	-6	.906	-11	3-229,S-180/2P1O	-4.6
■ **RUDY REGALADO**	Regalado, Rudolph Valentino b: 5/21/30, Los Angeles, Cal. BR/TR, 6′1″, 185 lbs. Deb: 4/13/54																						
1954	*Cle-A	65	180	21	45	5	0	2	24	19	16	.250	.335	.311	76	-5	0	2	-1	.967	-5	3-50/2-2	-1.3
1955	Cle-A	10	26	2	7	2	0	0	5	2	4	.269	.321	.346	77	-1	0	0	0	.955	2	/3-8,2-1	0.1
1956	Cle-A	16	47	4	11	1	0	0	2	4	1	.234	.308	.255	49	-3	0	0	0	.783	-7	3-14/1-1	-1.0
Total	3	91	253	27	63	8	0	2	31	25	21	.249	.329	.304	71	-10	0	2	-1	.944	-10	/3-72,2-3,1-1	-2.2
■ **JOE REGAN**	Regan, Joseph Charles b: 7/12/1872, Seymour, Conn. d: 11/18/48, Hartford, Conn. BR/TR, 6′1″, Deb: 9/21/1898																						
1898	NY-N	2	5	1	1	0	0	0	2	0		.200	.200	.200	15	-1	0			1.000	-1	/O-2	-0.1
■ **BILL REGAN**	Regan, William Wright b: 1/23/1899, Pittsburgh, Pa. d: 6/11/68, Pittsburgh, Pa. BR/TR, 5′10″, 155 lbs. Deb: 6/2/26																						
1926	Bos-A	108	403	40	106	21	3	4	34	23	37	.263	.309	.360	76	-15	6	3	0	.965	17	*2-106	0.5
1927	Bos-A	129	468	43	128	37	10	2	66	26	51	.274	.315	.408	88	-10	10	10	-3	.960	3	*2-121	-0.6
1928	Bos-A	138	511	53	135	30	6	7	75	21	40	.264	.296	.387	80	-17	9	6	-1	.963	15	*2-137/O-1	0.0
1929	Bos-A	104	371	38	107	27	7	1	54	22	38	.288	.328	.407	90	-6	7	5	-1	.962	-16	2-91,3-10/1-1	-1.8
1930	Bos-A	134	507	54	135	35	10	3	53	25	60	.266	.303	.393	78	-19	4	2	0	.963	-10	*2-127/3-2	-2.0
1931	Pit-N	28	104	8	21	8	0	1	10	5	19	.202	.239	.308	46	-8	2			.944	-0	2-28	-0.7
Total	6	641	2364	236	632	158	36	18	292	122	245	.267	.306	.387	81	-75	38	26		.962	8	2-610/3-12,1-1,O-1	-4.6
■ **TONY REGO**	Rego, Antone (b: Antone De Rego) b: 10/31/1897, Wailuku, Hawaii d: 1/6/78, Tulsa, Okla. BR/TR, 5′4″, 165 lbs. Deb: 6/21/24																						
1924	StL-A	24	59	5	13	1	0	0	5	1	3	.220	.233	.237	20	-7	0	0	0	.972	0	C-23	-0.6
1925	StL-A	20	32	5	13	2	1	0	3	3	2	.406	.472	.531	147	2	0	0	0	.979	2	C-19	0.5
Total	2	44	91	10	26	3	1	0	8	4	5	.286	.323	.341	66	-5	0	0	0	.975	2	/C-42	-0.1
■ **WALLY REHG**	Rehg, Walter Phillip b: 8/31/1888, Summerfield, Ill. d: 4/5/46, Burbank, Cal. BR/TR, 5′8″, 160 lbs. Deb: 4/14/12																						
1912	Pit-N	8	9	1	0	0	0	0	0	0	1	.000	.000	.000	-99	-2	0			1.000	-1	/O-2	-0.3
1913	Bos-A	30	101	13	28	3	2	0	9	2	7	.277	.291	.347	84	-2	4			.943	-3	O-26	-0.7
1914	Bos-A	88	151	14	33	4	2	0	11	18	11	.219	.306	.272	74	-5	5	8	-3	.980	-5	O-43	-1.6
1915	Bos-A	5	5	2	1	0	0	0	0	0	1	.200	.200	.200	20	-1	1			1.000	-0	/O-1	0.0
1917	Bos-N	87	341	48	92	12	6	1	31	24	32	.270	.320	.349	111	4	13			.956	-5	O-86	-0.6
1918	Bos-N	40	133	6	32	5	1	1	12	5	14	.241	.268	.316	81	-3	3			.988	2	O-38	-0.4
1919	Cin-N	5	12	1	2	0	0	0	3	1	0	.167	.231	.167	21	-1	0			.875	0	/O-5	-0.1
Total	7	263	752	85	188	24	11	2	66	50	66	.250	.299	.319	90	-11	26	8		.965	-12	O-201	-3.7
■ **FRANK REIBER**	Reiber, Frank Bernard "Tubby" b: 9/19/09, Huntington, W.Va. BR/TR, 5′8.5″, 169 lbs. Deb: 4/13/33																						
1933	Det-A	13	18	3	5	0	1	1	3	2	3	.278	.350	.556	134	1	0	0	0	.929	-2	/C-6	-0.1
1934	Det-A	3	1	0	0	0	0	0	0	2	0	.000	.667	.000	84	0	0	0	0	.000	0	H	0.0
1935	Det-A	8	11	3	3	0	0	0	1	3	3	.273	.429	.273	88	0	0	0	0	1.000	-1	/C-5	0.0
1936	Det-A	20	55	7	15	2	0	1	5	5	7	.273	.333	.364	72	-2	0	1	-1	.982	-4	C-17/O-1	-0.5
Total	4	44	85	13	23	2	1	2	9	12	13	.271	.361	.388	89	-1	0	1	-1	.975	-6	/C-28,O-1	-0.6
■ **HERMAN REICH**	Reich, Herman Charles b: 11/23/17, Bell, Cal. BR/TL, 6′2″, 200 lbs. Deb: 5/3/49																						
1949	Was-A	2	2	0	0	0	0	0	0	0	1	.000	.000	.000	-99	-1	0	0	0	.000	0	H	-0.1
	Cle-A	1	2	0	1	0	0	0	0	1	0	.500	.667	.500	215	1	0	0	0	.000	-0	/O-1	0.0
	Yr	3	4	0	1	0	0	0	0	1	1	.250	.400	.250	75	-0	0	0	0	.000	-0	/O-1	-0.1
	Chi-N	108	386	43	108	18	2	3	34	13	32	.280	.305	.360	80	-12	4			.989	14	1-85,O-16	0.1
Total	1	111	390	43	109	18	2	3	34	14	33	.279	.306	.359	80	-12	4	0		.969	14	/1-85,O-17	0.0
■ **RICK REICHARDT**	Reichardt, Frederic Carl b: 3/16/43, Madison, Wis. BR/TR, 6′3″, 215 lbs. Deb: 9/1/64																						
1964	LA-A	11	37	0	6	0	0	0	0	1	12	.162	.184	.162	-3	-5	1	0	0	1.000	0	O-11	-0.6
1965	Cal-A	20	75	8	20	4	0	1	6	5	12	.267	.321	.360	95	-0	4	1	1	.975	1	O-20	0.0
1966	Cal-A	89	319	48	92	5	4	16	44	27	61	.288	.368	.480	145	19	8	4	0	.976	-1	O-87	1.4
1967	Cal-A	146	498	56	132	14	2	17	69	35	90	.265	.322	.404	118	10	5	3	-0	.974	10	*O-138	1.4
1968	Cal-A	151	534	62	136	20	3	21	73	42	118	.255	.330	.421	131	19	8	7	-2	.989	9	*O-148	2.2
1969	Cal-A	137	493	60	125	11	4	13	68	43	100	.254	.324	.371	99	-2	3	6	-3	.981	8	*O-136/1-3	-0.4
1970	Cal-A	9	6	1	1	0	0	0	1	3	0	.167	.444	.167	78	0	0	0	0	1.000	-0	/O-1	0.0
	Was-A	107	277	42	70	14	2	15	46	23	69	.253	.330	.480	127	9	2	4	-2	.985	-8	O-79/3-1	-0.5

YEAR	TM/L	G	AB	R	H	2B	3B	HR	RBI	BB	SO	AVG	OBP	SLG	PRO+	BR/A	SB	CS	SBR	FA	FR	G/POS	TPR
	Yr	116	283	43	71	14	2	15	47	26	69	.251	.333	.473	126	9	2	4	-2	.985	-8	O-80/3-1	-0.5
1971	Chi-A	138	496	53	138	14	2	19	62	37	90	.278	.336	.429	112	7	5	10	-5	.981	-7	*O-128/1-9	-1.3
1972	Chi-A	101	291	31	73	14	4	8	43	28	63	.251	.323	.409	114	5	2	2	-1	.981	-10	O-90	-1.1
1973	Chi-A	46	153	15	42	8	1	3	16	8	29	.275	.315	.399	96	-1	2	3	-1	1.000	-2	O-37/D-6	-0.6
	KC-A	41	127	15	28	5	2	3	17	11	28	.220	.283	.362	75	-5	0	1	-1	1.000	-1	D-31/O-7	-0.7
	Yr	87	280	30	70	13	3	6	33	19	57	.250	.300	.382	86	-6	2	4	-2	1.000	-3	O-44,D-37	-1.3
1974	KC-A	1	1	0	1	0	0	0	0	0	0	1.000	1.000	1.000	451	0	0	0	0	.000	0	H	0.0
Total	11	997	3307	391	864	109	24	116	445	263	672	.261	.328	.414	115	56	40	41	-13	.982	-2	O-882/D-37,1-12,3-1	-0.2

■ DICK REICHLE
Reichle, Richard Wendell b: 11/23/1896, Lincoln, Ill. d: 6/13/67, St.Louis, Mo. BL/TR, 6', 185 lbs. Deb: 9/19/22

YEAR	TM/L	G	AB	R	H	2B	3B	HR	RBI	BB	SO	AVG	OBP	SLG	PRO+	BR/A	SB	CS	SBR	FA	FR	G/POS	TPR
1922	Bos-A	6	24	3	6	1	0	0	0	0	2	.250	.280	.292	50	-2	0	0	0	1.000	-0	/O-6	-0.3
1923	Bos-A	122	361	40	93	17	3	1	39	22	34	.258	.315	.330	69	-16	3	6	-3	.976	-7	O-93/1-2	-3.1
Total	2	128	385	43	99	18	3	1	39	22	36	.257	.313	.327	68	-18	3	6	-3	.977	-7	/O-99,1-2	-3.4

■ JESSIE REID
Reid, Jessie Thomas b: 6/1/62, Honolulu, Hawaii BL/TL, 6'1", 200 lbs. Deb: 9/9/87

YEAR	TM/L	G	AB	R	H	2B	3B	HR	RBI	BB	SO	AVG	OBP	SLG	PRO+	BR/A	SB	CS	SBR	FA	FR	G/POS	TPR
1987	SF-N	6	8	1	1	0	0	1	1	1	5	.125	.222	.500	89	-0	0	0	0	1.000	-1	/O-3	-0.1
1988	SF-N	2	2	0	0	0	0	0	0	0	1	.000	.000	.000	-99	-1	0	0	0	.000	0	H	-0.1
Total	2	8	10	1	1	0	0	1	1	1	6	.100	.182	.400	54	-1	0	0	0	1.000	-1	/O-3	-0.2

■ SCOTT REID
Reid, Scott Donald b: 1/7/47, Chicago, Ill. BL/TR, 6'1", 195 lbs. Deb: 9/10/69

YEAR	TM/L	G	AB	R	H	2B	3B	HR	RBI	BB	SO	AVG	OBP	SLG	PRO+	BR/A	SB	CS	SBR	FA	FR	G/POS	TPR
1969	Phi-N	13	19	5	4	0	0	0	0	7	5	.211	.423	.211	85	0	0	1	-1	1.000	-1	/O-5	-0.2
1970	Phi-N	25	49	5	6	1	0	0	1	11	22	.122	.283	.143	18	-5	0	0	0	1.000	3	O-18	-0.3
Total	2	38	68	10	10	1	0	0	1	18	27	.147	.326	.162	37	-5	0	1	-1	1.000	2	/O-23	-0.5

■ BILLY REID
Reid, William Alexander b: 5/17/1857, London, Ont., Can. d: 6/26/40, London, Ont., Can. BL/TR, 6', 170 lbs. Deb: 5/1/1883

YEAR	TM/L	G	AB	R	H	2B	3B	HR	RBI	BB	SO	AVG	OBP	SLG	PRO+	BR/A	SB	CS	SBR	FA	FR	G/POS	TPR
1883	Bal-a	24	97	14	27	3	0	0		4		.278	.307	.309	96	-1				.842	-8	2-23/S-1	-0.7
1884	Pit-a	19	70	11	17	2	0	0		4		.243	.293	.271	84	-1				.724	-4	O-17/3-1,2-1	-0.5
Total	2	43	167	25	44	5	0	0		8		.263	.301	.293	91	-2				.839	-12	/2-24,O-17,3-1,S-1	-1.2

■ DUKE REILLEY
Reilley, Alexander Aloysius "Midget" b: 8/25/1884, Chicago, Ill. d: 3/4/68, Indianapolis, Ind. BB/TR, 5'4.5", 148 lbs. Deb: 8/28/09

YEAR	TM/L	G	AB	R	H	2B	3B	HR	RBI	BB	SO	AVG	OBP	SLG	PRO+	BR/A	SB	CS	SBR	FA	FR	G/POS	TPR
1909	Cle-A	20	62	10	13	0	0	0	0	4		.210	.258	.210	46	-4	5			.979	2	O-18	-0.3

■ CHARLIE REILLEY
Reilley, Charles E. b: 1856, Hartford, Conn. BR/TR, 5'10", 165 lbs. Deb: 5/1/1879

YEAR	TM/L	G	AB	R	H	2B	3B	HR	RBI	BB	SO	AVG	OBP	SLG	PRO+	BR/A	SB	CS	SBR	FA	FR	G/POS	TPR
1879	Tro-N	62	236	17	54	5	1	0	19	1	20	.229	.232	.258	66	-8				.867	-16	C-49,1-11/O-2	-2.2
1880	Cin-N	30	103	8	21	1	0	0	9	0	5	.204	.204	.214	42	-6				.759	-5	O-16,C-13/3-4	-1.1
1881	Det-N	19	70	8	12	2	0	0	3	0	10	.171	.171	.200	16	-7				.889	-4	C-10/O-4,S-3,3-1	-0.9
	Wor-N	2	8	2	3	0	0	0	1	0	1	.375	.375	.375	129	0				1.000	-2	/C-2	-0.2
	Yr	21	78	10	15	2	0	0	4	0	11	.192	.192	.218	28	-6				.897	-6	C-12/O-4,S-3,3-1	-1.1
1882	Pro-N	3	11	0	2	0	0	0	2	1	2	.182	.250	.182	41	-1				.714	-2	/C-3	-0.3
1884	Bos-U	3	11	1	0	0	0	0		1		.000	.083	.000	-74	-3				1.000	-1	/O-2,3-1	-0.3
Total	5	119	439	36	92	8	1	0	34	3	38	.210	.215	.232	48	-24				.867	-30	/C-77,O-24,1-12,3S	-5.0

■ ARCH REILLY
Reilly, Archer Edwin b: 8/17/1891, Alton, Ill. d: 11/29/63, Columbus, Ohio BR/TR, 5'10", 163 lbs. Deb: 6/1/17

YEAR	TM/L	G	AB	R	H	2B	3B	HR	RBI	BB	SO	AVG	OBP	SLG	PRO+	BR/A	SB	CS	SBR	FA	FR	G/POS	TPR
1917	Pit-N	1	0	0	0	0	0	0	0	0	0	—	—	—	—	0	0			1.000	0	/3-1	0.0

■ BARNEY REILLY
Reilly, Bernard Eugene b: 2/7/1885, Brockton, Mass. d: 11/15/34, St.Joseph, Mo. BR/TR, 6' ", 175 lbs. Deb: 7/2/09

YEAR	TM/L	G	AB	R	H	2B	3B	HR	RBI	BB	SO	AVG	OBP	SLG	PRO+	BR/A	SB	CS	SBR	FA	FR	G/POS	TPR
1909	Chi-A	12	25	3	5	0	0	0	3	3		.200	.286	.200	56	-1	2			.962	4	2-11/O-1	0.2

■ JOSH REILLY
Reilly, Charles b: 1868, San Francisco, Cal. d: 6/13/38, San Francisco, Cal. Deb: 5/2/1896

YEAR	TM/L	G	AB	R	H	2B	3B	HR	RBI	BB	SO	AVG	OBP	SLG	PRO+	BR/A	SB	CS	SBR	FA	FR	G/POS	TPR
1896	Chi-N	9	42	6	9	1	0	0	2	1	1	.214	.233	.238	23	-5	2			.857	-1	/2-8,S-1	-0.4

■ CHARLIE REILLY
Reilly, Charles Thomas "Princeton Charlie" (b: Charles Thomas O'Reilly)
b: 2/15/1867, Princeton, N.J. d: 12/16/37, Los Angeles, Cal. BB/TR, 5'11", 190 lbs. Deb: 10/9/1889

YEAR	TM/L	G	AB	R	H	2B	3B	HR	RBI	BB	SO	AVG	OBP	SLG	PRO+	BR/A	SB	CS	SBR	FA	FR	G/POS	TPR
1889	Col-a	6	23	5	11	1	0	3	6	2	2	.478	.538	.913	326	7	9			.923	2	/3-6	0.7
1890	Col-a	137	530	75	141	23	3	4	77	35		.266	.319	.343	102	1	43			**.893**	28	*3-137	2.9
1891	Pit-N	114	415	43	91	8	5	3	44	29	58	.219	.277	.284	65	-19	20			.857	2	*3-99,S-11/O-4	-1.1
1892	Phi-N	91	331	42	65	7	3	1	24	18	43	.196	.242	.245	47	-21	13			.905	10	3-70,O-15/2-4	-0.9
1893	Phi-N	104	416	64	102	16	7	4	56	33	36	.245	.314	.346	76	-16	13			.895	-1	*3-104	-1.2
1894	Phi-N	39	135	21	40	1	2	0	19	16	10	.296	.383	.333	76	-4	9			.874	2	3-28/O-5,2-4,S-1,1	-0.2
1895	Phi-N	49	179	28	48	6	1	0	25	13	12	.268	.335	.313	67	-8	7			.900	-3	S-34,3-11/2-3,O-1	-0.8
1897	Was-N	101	351	64	97	18	3	2	60	34		.276	.359	.362	91	-4	18			.905	18	*3-101	1.4
Total	8	641	2380	342	595	80	24	17	311	180	161	.250	.314	.325	80	-65	132			.890	59	3-556/S-46,O-25,21	0.8

■ HAL REILLY
Reilly, Harold John b: 4/1/1894, Oshkosh, Wis. d: 12/24/57, Chicago, Ill. BR/TR, 6', 180 lbs. Deb: 6/19/19

YEAR	TM/L	G	AB	R	H	2B	3B	HR	RBI	BB	SO	AVG	OBP	SLG	PRO+	BR/A	SB	CS	SBR	FA	FR	G/POS	TPR
1919	Chi-N	1	3	0	0	0	0	0	0	0	1	.000	.000	.000	-99	-1	0			.000	-1	/O-1	-0.1

■ JOHN REILLY
Reilly, John Good "Long Jong" b: 10/5/1858, Cincinnati, Ohio d: 5/31/37, Cincinnati, Ohio BR/TR, 6'3", 178 lbs. Deb: 5/18/1880

YEAR	TM/L	G	AB	R	H	2B	3B	HR	RBI	BB	SO	AVG	OBP	SLG	PRO+	BR/A	SB	CS	SBR	FA	FR	G/POS	TPR
1880	Cin-N	73	272	21	56	8	4	0	16	3	36	.206	.215	.265	62	-10				.947	-4	*1-72/O-3	-2.0
1883	Cin-a	98	437	103	136	21	14	9	79	9		.311	.325	.485	149	21				.961	-1	*1-98/O-1	0.9
1884	Cin-a	105	448	114	152	24	19	**11**	91	5		.339	.366	**.551**	186	39				.971	-2	*1-103/O-3,S-1	2.3
1885	Cin-a	111	482	92	143	18	11	5	60	11		.297	.322	.411	128	13				.963	-5	*1-107/O-7	-0.4
1886	Cin-a	115	441	92	117	12	11	6	79	31		.265	.321	.383	116	7	19			.967	-1	*1-110/O-6	-0.7
1887	Cin-a	134	551	106	170	35	14	10	96	22		.309	.352	.477	127	17	50			.980	-0	*1-127/O-9	0.2
1888	Cin-a	127	527	112	169	28	14	**13**	**103**	17		.321	.363	**.501**	**167**	36	82			.977	-0	*1-117,O-10	2.2
1889	Cin-a	111	427	84	111	24	13	5	66	34	37	.260	.340	.412	110	4	43			**.984**	-2	*1-109/O-2	-0.4
1890	Cin-N	133	553	114	166	25	**26**	6	86	16	41	.300	.328	.472	133	18	29			.977	-3	*1-132/O-1	0.7
1891	Cin-N	135	546	60	132	20	13	4	64	9	42	.242	.267	.348	78	-18	22			.982	-7	*1-100,O-36	-2.8
Total	10	1142	4684	898	1352	215	139	69	740	157	156	.289	.325	.438	128	127	245			.972	-25	*1-1075/O-78,S-1	0.0

■ JOE REILLY
Reilly, Joseph J. b: 1861, New York, N.Y. 5'10", 140 lbs. Deb: 6/8/1885

YEAR	TM/L	G	AB	R	H	2B	3B	HR	RBI	BB	SO	AVG	OBP	SLG	PRO+	BR/A	SB	CS	SBR	FA	FR	G/POS	TPR
1885	NY-a	10	40	6	7	3	0	0	3	2		.175	.214	.250	50	-2				.848	1	/2-8,3-2	0.0

■ TOM REILLY
Reilly, Thomas Henry b: 8/3/1884, St.Louis, Mo. d: 10/18/18, New Orleans, La. BR/TR, 5'10", Deb: 7/27/08

YEAR	TM/L	G	AB	R	H	2B	3B	HR	RBI	BB	SO	AVG	OBP	SLG	PRO+	BR/A	SB	CS	SBR	FA	FR	G/POS	TPR
1908	StL-N	29	81	5	14	1	0	1	3	2		.173	.193	.222	34	-6	4			.866	-6	S-29	-1.4
1909	StL-N	5	7	0	2	0	1	0	2	0		.286	.286	.571	176	0	0			1.000	0	/S-5	0.1
1914	Cle-A	1	1	0	0	0	0	0	0	0	0	.000	.000	.000	-96	-0	0			.000	0	H	0.0
Total	3	35	89	5	16	1	1	1	5	2	0	.180	.198	.247	44	-6	4			.875	-6	/S-34	-1.3

■ KEVIN REIMER
Reimer, Kevin Michael b: 6/28/64, Macon, Ga. BL/TR, 6'2", 225 lbs. Deb: 9/13/88

YEAR	TM/L	G	AB	R	H	2B	3B	HR	RBI	BB	SO	AVG	OBP	SLG	PRO+	BR/A	SB	CS	SBR	FA	FR	G/POS	TPR
1988	Tex-A	12	25	2	3	0	0	1	2	0	6	.120	.120	.240	-2	-3	0	0	0	.000	-0	/O-1,D-7	-0.4
1989	Tex-A	3	5	0	0	0	0	0	0	0	1	.000	.000	.000	-98	-1	0	0	0	.000	0	/D-1	-0.1
1990	Tex-A	64	100	5	26	9	1	2	15	10	22	.260	.333	.430	112	1	0	1	-1	.857	-2	D-21/O-9	-0.2
1991	Tex-A	136	394	46	106	22	0	20	69	33	93	.269	.336	.477	125	12	0	3	-2	.948	-5	O-66,D-56	0.1
1992	Tex-A	148	494	56	132	32	2	16	58	42	103	.267	.337	.437	120	12	2	4	-2	.949	-3	*O-110,D-32	0.5
1993	Mil-A	125	437	53	109	22	1	13	60	30	72	.249	.305	.394	88	-9	5	4	-1	.962	-1	D-83,O-37	-1.4
Total	6	488	1455	162	376	85	4	52	204	115	297	.258	.323	.430	108	12	7	12	-5	.948	-11	O-223,D-200	-1.5

■ MIKE REINBACH
Reinbach, Michael Wayne b: 8/6/49, San Diego, Cal. BL/TR, 6'2", 195 lbs. Deb: 4/7/74

YEAR	TM/L	G	AB	R	H	2B	3B	HR	RBI	BB	SO	AVG	OBP	SLG	PRO+	BR/A	SB	CS	SBR	FA	FR	G/POS	TPR
1974	Bal-A	12	20	2	5	1	0	0	2	2	5	.250	.318	.300	81	-0	0	0	0	1.000	-1	/O-3,D-3	-0.1

■ WALLY REINECKER
Reinecker, Walter (b: Walter Joseph Smith) b: 4/21/1890, Pittsburgh, Pa. d: 4/18/57, Pittsburgh, Pa. BR/TR, 5'6", 150 lbs. Deb: 9/17/15

YEAR	TM/L	G	AB	R	H	2B	3B	HR	RBI	BB	SO	AVG	OBP	SLG	PRO+	BR/A	SB	CS	SBR	FA	FR	G/POS	TPR
1915	Bal-F	3	8	0	1	0	0	0	0	0	0	.125	.222	.125	-1	-1	0			.571	-2	/3-3	-0.3

YEAR	TM/L	G	AB	R	H	2B	3B	HR	RBI	BB	SO	AVG	OBP	SLG	PRO+	BR/A	SB	CS	SBR	FA	FR	G/POS	TPR
■ **ART REINHOLZ**	Reinholz, Arthur August b: 1/27/03, Detroit, Mich. d: 12/29/80, New Port Richey, Fla. BR/TR, 5'10.5", 175 lbs. Deb: 9/27/28																						
1928	Cle-A	2	3	0	1	0	0	0	0	1	0	.333	.500	.333	122	0	0	0	0	.833	1	/3-2	0.1
■ **CHARLIE REIPSCHLAGER**	Reipschlager, Charles W. BR/TR, 5'6.5", 160 lbs. Deb: 5/2/1883																						
1883	NY-a	37	145	8	27	4	2	0		4		.186	.208	.241	42	-9				.936	5	C-29/O-8	-0.3
1884	*NY-a	59	233	21	56	13	2	0		1		.240	.250	.313	85	-4				.925	19	C-51/O-8	1.7
1885	NY-a	72	268	29	65	11	1	0	21	9		.243	.270	.291	84	-4				.879	-8	C-59/O-6,3-6,S-1,2	-0.6
1886	NY-a	65	232	21	49	4	6	0	25	9		.211	.244	.280	67	-9	2			.880	-6	C-57/O-9	-0.8
1887	Cle-a	63	231	20	49	8	3	0	17	11		.212	.251	.273	47	-16	7			.888	3	C-48,1-16	-0.8
Total	5	296	1109	99	246	40	14	0	63	34		.222	.248	.283	66	-43	9			.900	12	C-244/O-31,132S	-0.8
■ **BOBBY REIS**	Reis, Robert Joseph Thomas b: 1/2/09, Woodside, N.Y. d: 5/1/73, St.Paul, Minn. BR/TR, 6'1", 175 lbs. Deb: 9/19/31																						
1931	Bro-N	6	17	3	5	0	0	0	2	2	0	.294	.368	.294	81	-0	0			.933	-1	/3-6	-0.1
1932	Bro-N	1	4	0	1	0	0	0	0	0	1	.250	.250	.250	36	-0	0			.500	-1	/3-1	-0.1
1935	Bro-N	52	85	10	21	3	2	0	4	6	13	.247	.297	.329	70	-4	2			.950	2	O-21,P-14/2-4,13	-0.2
1936	Bos-N	37	60	3	13	2	0	0	5	3	6	.217	.254	.250	39	-5	0			1.000	3	P-35/O-2	-0.1
1937	Bos-N	45	86	10	21	5	0	0	6	13	12	.244	.343	.302	84	-2	2			1.000	-4	O-18/P-4,1-4	-0.6
1938	Bos-N	34	49	6	9	0	0	0	4	1	3	.184	.200	.184	7	-6	1			1.000	-3	P-16,O-10/S-3,C2	-0.7
Total	6	175	301	32	70	10	2	0	21	25	35	.233	.291	.279	59	-17	5			1.000	-2	/P-69,O-51,312SC	-1.8
■ **PETE REISER**	Reiser, Harold Patrick b: 3/17/19, St.Louis, Mo. d: 10/25/81, Palm Springs, Cal. BL/TR, 5'10.5", 185 lbs. Deb: 7/23/40 C																						
1940	Bro-N	58	225	34	66	11	4	3	20	15	33	.293	.338	.418	101	0	2			.960	-4	3-30,O-17/S-5	-0.3
1941	*Bro-N★	137	536	**117**	184	**39**	**17**	14	76	46	71	**.343**	.406	**.558**	**163**	43	4			.981	12	*O-133	**4.7**
1942	Bro-N★	125	480	89	149	33	5	10	64	48	45	.310	.375	.463	142	25	**20**			.969	-2	*O-125	1.8
1946	Bro-N☆	122	423	75	117	21	5	11	73	55	58	.277	.361	.428	122	12	**34**			.978	7	O-97,3-15	1.6
1947	*Bro-N	110	388	68	120	23	2	5	46	68	41	.309	.415	.418	117	13	14			.988	-5	*O-108	0.2
1948	Bro-N	64	127	17	30	8	2	1	19	29	21	.236	.382	.354	97	1	4			.981	-5	O-30/3-4	-0.6
1949	Bos-N	84	221	32	60	8	3	8	40	33	42	.271	.369	.443	123	8	3			.980	-1	O-63/3-4	0.4
1950	Bos-N	53	78	12	16	2	0	1	10	18	22	.205	.367	.269	75	-2	1			.979	-2	O-24/3-1	-0.4
1951	Pit-N	74	140	22	38	9	3	2	13	27	20	.271	.389	.421	115	4	4	2	0	.982	-2	O-27/3-5	0.1
1952	Cle-A	34	44	7	6	1	0	3	7	4	16	.136	.208	.364	61	-3	1	1	-0	1.000	-1	O-10	-0.5
Total	10	861	2662	473	786	155	41	58	368	343	369	.295	.380	.450	127	100	87	3		.979	-1	O-634/3-59,S-5	7.0
■ **CHARLIE REISING**	Reising, Charles "Pop" b: 8/28/1861, Lanesville, Ind. d: 7/26/15, Louisville, Ky. Deb: 7/19/1884																						
1884	Ind-a	2	8	0	0	0	0	0		1		.000	.111	.000	-62	-1				.400	-1	/O-2	-0.3
■ **AL REISS**	Reiss, Albert Allen b: 1/8/09, Elizabeth, N.J. d: 5/13/89, Red Bank, N.J. BB/TR, 5'10.5", 165 lbs. Deb: 6/22/32																						
1932	Phi-A	9	5	0	1	0	0	0	1	1	1	.200	.333	.200	40	-0	0	0	0	1.000	0	/S-6	0.0
■ **HEINIE REITZ**	Reitz, Henry P. b: 6/29/1867, Chicago, Ill. d: 11/10/14, Sacramento, Cal BL/TR, 5'7", 158 lbs. Deb: 4/27/1893																						
1893	Bal-N	130	490	90	140	17	13	1	76	65	32	.286	.377	.380	100	1	24			.939	-1	*2-130	0.3
1894	*Bal-N	108	446	86	135	22	**31**	2	105	42	24	.303	.372	.504	105	0	18			**.968**	27	*2-97,3-12	2.4
1895	Bal-N	71	245	45	72	15	5	0	29	18	11	.294	.350	.396	90	-4	15			.938	-5	2-48,3-18/S-1	-0.5
1896	*Bal-N	120	464	76	133	15	6	4	106	49	32	.287	.357	.371	91	-6	28			.952	-18	*2-118/S-3	-1.4
1897	*Bal-N	128	477	76	138	15	6	2	84	50		.289	.370	.358	93	-3	23			**.962**	22	*2-128	2.1
1898	Was-N	132	489	62	148	20	2	2	47	32		.303	.357	.364	107	4	11			**.959**	6	*2-132	1.8
1899	Pit-N	34	130	11	34	4	2	0	15	10		.262	.314	.323	75	-4	3			.975	1	2-34	-0.1
Total	7	723	2741	446	800	108	65	11	462	266	99	.292	.363	.391	97	-13	122			.955	33	2-687/3-30,S-4	4.6
■ **KEN REITZ**	Reitz, Kenneth John b: 6/24/51, San Francisco, Cal BR/TR, 6', 185 lbs. Deb: 9/5/72																						
1972	StL-N	21	78	5	28	4	0	0	10	2	4	.359	.375	.410	125	2	0	1	-1	.956	-4	3-20	-0.2
1973	StL-N	147	426	40	100	20	2	6	42	9	25	.235	.257	.333	63	-23	0	1	-1	**.974**	-6	*3-135/S-1	-3.2
1974	StL-N	154	579	48	157	28	2	7	54	23	63	.271	.301	.363	86	-13	0	0	0	**.974**	-17	*3-151/S-2,2-1	-3.3
1975	StL-N	161	592	43	159	25	1	5	63	22	54	.269	.300	.340	75	-21	1	1	-0	.946	-21	*3-160	-4.5
1976	SF-N	155	577	40	154	21	1	5	66	24	48	.267	.297	.333	76	-19	5	4	-1	.959	2	*3-155/S-1	-2.0
1977	StL-N	157	587	58	153	36	1	17	79	19	74	.261	.292	.412	88	-12	2	6	-3	**.980**	-2	*3-157	-1.9
1978	StL-N	150	540	41	133	26	2	10	75	23	61	.246	.283	.357	79	-17	1	0	0	**.973**	1	*3-150	-1.9
1979	StL-N	159	605	42	162	41	2	8	73	25	85	.268	.301	.382	84	-14	1	0	0	.972	-13	*3-158	-2.9
1980	StL-N★	151	523	39	141	33	0	8	58	22	44	.270	.303	.379	86	-10	0	1	-1	**.979**	-4	*3-150	-1.9
1981	Chi-N	82	260	10	56	9	1	2	28	15	56	.215	.266	.281	53	-16	0	0	0	**.977**	5	3-81	-1.3
1982	Pit-N	7	10	0	0	0	0	0	0	0	4	.000	.091	.000	-70	-2	0	0	0	1.000	1	/3-4	-0.2
Total	11	1344	4777	366	1243	243	12	68	548	184	518	.260	.293	.359	79	-144	10	14	-5	.970	-58	*3-1321/S-4,2-1	-23.3
■ **DESI RELAFORD**	Relaford, Desmond Lamont b: 9/16/73, Valdosta, Ga. BB/TR, 5'8", 155 lbs. Deb: 8/1/96																						
1996	Phi-N	15	40	2	7	2	0	0	1	3	9	.175	.233	.225	21	-5	1	0	0	.933	-1	/S-9,2-4	-0.4
1997	Phi-N	15	38	3	7	1	2	0	6	5	6	.184	.279	.316	55	-3	3	0	1	.977	-1	S-12	-0.2
1998	Phi-N	142	494	45	121	25	3	5	41	33	87	.245	.296	.338	63	-27	9	5	-0	.960	-9	*S-137	-2.2
Total	3	172	572	50	135	28	5	5	48	41	102	.236	.291	.329	60	-34	13	5	1	.960	-11	S-158/2-4	-2.8
■ **BUTCH REMENTER**	Rementer, Willis J. H. b: 3/14/1878, Philadelphia, Pa. d: 9/23/22, Philadelphia, Pa. TR , Deb: 10/8/04																						
1904	Phi-N	1	2	0	0	0	0	0	0	0		.000	.000	.000	-99	-0	0			1.000	-0	/C-1	-0.1
■ **JACK REMSEN**	Remsen, John Jay b: 4/1850, Brooklyn, N.Y. BR/TR, 5'11", 189 lbs. Deb: 5/2/1872																						
1872	Atl-n	37	164	25	40	4	5	0	13	2	6	.244	.253	.329	66	-10	1	2	-1	.792	2	*O-37	-0.5
1873	Atl-n	50	207	29	61	4	6	1	29	2	2	.295	.301	.386	115	5	1	2	-1	.811	0	*O-50	0.4
1874	Mut-n	64	284	52	65	9	3	2	38	0	5	.229	.229	.303	67	-11	6	0	2	.864	5	*O-63/1-3	-0.2
1875	Har-n	86	358	70	96	10	4	0	34	5	4	.268	.278	.318	102	-1	6	3	0	.887	5	*O-86	0.4
1876	Har-N	69	324	62	89	12	5	1	30	1	15	.275	.277	.352	100	-2				.887	8	*O-69	0.5
1877	StL-N	33	123	14	32	3	4	0	13	4	3	.260	.283	.350	104	1				.906	2	O-33	0.1
1878	Chi-N	56	224	32	52	11	1	1	19	**17**	33	.232	.286	.304	88	-3				**.944**	6	*O-56	0.0
1879	Chi-N	42	152	14	33	4	2	0	8	2	23	.217	.227	.270	60	-7				.862	-2	O-31,1-11	-1.0
1881	Cle-N	48	172	14	30	4	3	0	13	9	31	.174	.215	.233	43	-11				.873	-1	O-48	-1.2
1884	Phi-N	12	43	9	9	2	0	0	3	6	9	.209	.306	.256	83	-1				.952	0	O-12	-0.1
	Bro-a	81	301	45	67	6	6	3		23		.223	.278	.312	91	-2				.914	4	*O-81	0.0
Total	4 n	237	1013	176	262	27	18	3	114	9	17	.259	.265	.330	88	-16	14	7	0	.845	12	O-236/1-3	0.1
Total	6	341	1339	190	312	42	21	5	86	62	114	.233	.267	.307	84	-24				.900	17	O-330/1-11	-1.7
■ **JERRY REMY**	Remy, Gerald Peter b: 11/8/52, Fall River, Mass. BL/TR, 5'9", 165 lbs. Deb: 4/7/75																						
1975	Cal-A	147	569	82	147	17	5	1	46	45	55	.258	.313	.311	82	-13	34	21	-2	.982	10	*2-147	0.2
1976	Cal-A	143	502	64	132	14	3	0	28	38	43	.263	.315	.303	87	-8	35	16	1	.977	15	*2-133/D-5	1.7
1977	Cal-A	154	575	74	145	19	10	4	44	59	59	.252	.324	.341	85	-11	41	17	2	.975	-12	*2-152/3-1	-1.0
1978	Bos-A☆	148	583	87	162	24	6	2	44	40	55	.278	.324	.350	81	-15	30	13	1	.983	2	*2-140/S-1,D-4	-0.1
1979	Bos-A	80	306	49	91	11	2	0	29	26	25	.297	.352	.346	85	-6	14	9	-1	.970	-21	2-76	-2.3
1980	Bos-A	63	230	24	72	7	2	0	9	10	14	.313	.342	.361	88	-4	14	6	1	.977	-3	2-60/O-1	-0.3
1981	Bos-A	88	358	55	110	9	1	0	31	36	30	.307	.371	.338	99	1	9	2	2	.984	-7	2-87	0.0
1982	Bos-A	155	636	89	178	22	3	0	47	55	77	.280	.339	.324	79	-17	16	9	-1	.982	-16	*2-154	-2.6
1983	Bos-A	146	592	73	163	16	5	0	43	40	35	.275	.321	.319	72	-22	11	3	2	.990	-31	*2-144	-4.5
1984	Bos-A	30	104	8	26	1	1	0	8	7	11	.250	.297	.279	58	-6	4	3	-1	.973	-3	2-24	-0.9
Total	10	1154	4455	605	1226	140	38	7	329	356	404	.275	.329	.328	82	-101	208	99	3	.981	-67	*2-1117/D-9,O-1,S3	-9.8
■ **RICK RENICK**	Renick, Warren Richard b: 3/16/44, London, Ohio BR/TR, 6', 190 lbs. Deb: 7/11/68 C																						
1968	Min-A	42	97	16	21	5	2	3	13	9	42	.216	.283	.402	101	-0	0	0	0	.946	-0	S-40	0.3

YEAR	TM/L	G	AB	R	H	2B	3B	HR	RBI	BB	SO	AVG	OBP	SLG	PRO+	BR/A	SB	CS	SBR	FA	FR	G/POS	TPR
1969	*Min-A	71	139	21	34	3	0	5	17	12	32	.245	.309	.374	88	-2	0	1	-1	.913	-8	3-30,O-10/S-6	-1.1
1970	*Min-A	81	179	20	41	8	0	7	25	22	29	.229	.317	.391	93	-2	0	2	-1	.987	-3	3-30,O-25/S-1	-0.8
1971	Min-A	27	45	4	10	2	0	1	8	5	14	.222	.314	.333	81	-1	0	0	0	.846	-3	/3-7,O-7	-0.5
1972	Min-A	55	93	10	16	2	0	4	8	15	25	.172	.287	.323	77	-2	0	1	-1	1.000	-4	O-21/1-6,3-4,S-1	-0.9
Total	5	276	553	71	122	20	2	20	71	63	142	.221	.304	.373	89	-8	0	4	-2	.940	-18	/3-71,O-63,S-48,1-6	-3.0
■ BILL RENNA Renna, William Beneditto "Big Bill" b: 10/14/24, Hanford, Cal. BR/TR, 6'3", 218 lbs. Deb: 4/14/53																							
1953	NY-A	61	121	19	38	6	3	2	13	13	31	.314	.385	.463	133	6	0	1	-1	.983	-6	O-40	-0.2
1954	Phi-A	123	422	52	98	15	4	13	53	41	60	.232	.305	.379	86	-9	1	3	-2	.972	6	*O-115	-1.0
1955	KC-A	100	249	33	53	7	3	7	28	31	42	.213	.305	.349	75	-9	0	3	-2	.992	-6	O-79	-2.1
1956	KC-A	33	48	12	13	3	0	2	5	3	10	.271	.314	.458	101	-0	1	0	0	.950	-6	O-25	-0.6
1958	Bos-A	39	56	5	15	5	0	4	18	6	14	.268	.339	.571	136	3	0	0	0	1.000	-1	O-11	0.1
1959	Bos-A	14	22	2	2	0	0	0	2	5	9	.091	.259	.091	0	-3	0	0	0	1.000	-2	/O-7	-0.5
Total	6	370	918	123	219	36	10	28	119	99	166	.239	.317	.391	91	-14	2	7	-4	.979	-15	O-277	-4.3
■ TONY RENSA Rensa, George Anthony "Pug" b: 9/29/01, Parsons, Pa. d: 1/4/87, Wilkes-Barre, Pa. BR/TR, 5'10", 180 lbs. Deb: 5/5/30																							
1930	Det-A	20	37	6	10	2	1	1	3	6	7	.270	.386	.459	111	1	1	0	0	.964	-1	C-18	0.1
	Phi-N	54	172	31	49	11	2	3	31	10	18	.285	.328	.424	75	-7	0			.932	-11	C-49	-1.3
1931	Phi-N	19	29	2	3	1	0	0	2	6	2	.103	.257	.138	8	-4	0			.958	2	C-17	-0.1
1933	NY-A	8	29	4	9	2	1	0	3	1	3	.310	.333	.448	112	0	0	1	-1	.977	-1	/C-8	-0.1
1937	Chi-A	26	57	10	17	5	1	0	5	8	6	.298	.385	.421	103	0	3	0	1	.975	1	C-23	0.3
1938	Chi-A	59	165	15	41	5	0	3	19	25	16	.248	.351	.333	71	-7	1	1	-0	.982	6	C-57	0.1
1939	Chi-A	14	25	3	5	0	0	0	2	1	2	.200	.231	.200	11	-3	0	0	0	.972	1	C-13	-0.2
Total	6	200	514	71	134	26	5	7	65	57	54	.261	.338	.372	74	-20	5	*2*		.965	-4	C-185	-1.2
■ EDGAR RENTERIA Renteria, Edgar Enrique b: 8/7/76, Barranquilla, Colombia BR/TR, 6'1", 172 lbs. Deb: 5/10/96																							
1996	Fla-N	106	431	68	133	18	3	5	31	33	68	.309	.361	.399	103	3	16	2	4	.979	12	*S-106	2.6
1997	*Fla-N	154	617	90	171	21	3	4	52	45	108	.277	.330	.340	80	-18	32	15	1	.975	-4	*S-153	-0.8
1998	Fla-N★	133	517	79	146	18	2	3	31	48	78	.282	.348	.342	84	-11	41	22	-1	.966	-8	*S-130	-0.6
Total	3	393	1565	237	450	57	8	12	114	126	254	.288	.345	.357	88	-27	89	39	3	.973	0	S-389	1.2
■ RICH RENTERIA Renteria, Richard Avina b: 12/25/61, Harbor City, Cal. BR/TR, 5'9", 172 lbs. Deb: 9/14/86																							
1986	Pit-N	10	12	2	3	1	0	0	1	0	4	.250	.250	.333	58	-1	0	0	0	.600	0	/3-1	-0.1
1987	Sea-A	12	10	2	1	1	0	0	0	1	2	.100	.182	.200	1	-1	1	0	0	.833	1	/2-4,S-1,D-4	0.0
1988	Sea-A	31	88	6	18	9	0	0	6	2	8	.205	.222	.307	45	-7	1	3	-2	.958	4	D-12,S-11/3-5,2-4	-0.3
1993	Fla-N	103	263	27	67	9	2	2	30	21	31	.255	.315	.327	68	-11	0	2	-1	.989	-4	2-45,3-25/O-1	-1.6
1994	Fla-N	28	49	5	11	0	0	2	4	1	4	.224	.269	.347	57	-3	0	1	-1	.929	-1	3-14/2-6,O-2	-0.4
Total	5	184	422	42	100	20	2	4	41	25	49	.237	.286	.322	61	-23	2	6	-3	.986	1	/2-59,3-45,D-16,SO	-2.4
■ BOB REPASS Repass, Robert Willis b: 11/6/17, W.Pittston, Pa. BR/TR, 6'1", 185 lbs. Deb: 9/18/39																							
1939	StL-N	3	6	0	2	1	0	0	1	0	2	.333	.333	.500	114	0	0			1.000	0	/2-2	0.1
1942	Was-A	81	259	30	62	11	1	2	23	33	30	.239	.328	.313	81	-6	6	1	1	.973	-3	2-33,3-29,S-11	-0.4
Total	2	84	265	30	64	12	1	2	24	33	32	.242	.328	.317	82	-6	6	*1*		.973	-2	/2-35,3-29,S-11	-0.3
■ ROGER REPOZ Repoz, Roger Allen b: 8/3/40, Bellingham, Wash. BL/TL, 6'3", 195 lbs. Deb: 9/11/64																							
1964	NY-A	11	1	1	0	0	0	0	0	1	1	.000	.500	.000	52	0	0	0	0	1.000	-3	/O-9	-0.3
1965	NY-A	79	218	34	48	7	4	12	28	25	57	.220	.300	.454	112	3	1	1	-0	.993	-2	O-69	-0.2
1966	NY-A	37	43	4	15	4	1	0	9	4	8	.349	.404	.488	161	3	0	0	0	1.000	-10	O-30	-0.8
	KC-A	101	319	40	69	10	3	11	34	44	80	.216	.315	.370	99	0	3	3	-1	.991	-3	O-52,1-45	-1.0
	Yr	138	362	44	84	14	4	11	43	48	88	.232	.325	.384	106	3	3	3	-1	.992	-13	O-82,1-45	-1.8
1967	KC-A	40	87	9	21	6	1	2	8	12	20	.241	.340	.402	122	3	4	2	0	1.000	1	O-31	0.3
	Cal-A	74	176	25	44	9	1	5	20	19	37	.250	.323	.398	116	3	2	2	-1	.959	-3	O-63	-0.3
	Yr	114	263	34	65	15	2	7	28	31	57	.247	.329	.399	118	6	6	4	-1	.972	-1	O-94	0.0
1968	Cal-A	133	375	30	90	8	1	13	54	38	83	.240	.315	.371	111	5	8	7	-2	.987	-5	*O-114	-0.8
1969	Cal-A	103	219	25	36	1	1	8	19	32	52	.164	.271	.288	59	-12	1	3	-2	.985	-5	O-48,1-31	-2.4
1970	Cal-A	137	407	50	97	17	6	18	47	45	90	.238	.319	.442	112	5	4	2	0	.995	-4	*O-110,1-18	-0.6
1971	Cal-A	113	297	39	59	11	1	13	41	60	69	.199	.335	.374	108	4	3	5	-2	1.000	-4	O-97,1-13	-0.8
1972	Cal-A	3	3	0	1	0	0	0	0	0	2	.333	.333	.333	105	0	0	0	0	.000	0	H	0.0
Total	9	831	2145	257	480	73	19	82	260	280	499	.224	.316	.390	106	14	26	25	-7	.989	-39	O-623,1-107	-6.9
■ RIP REPULSKI Repulski, Eldon John b: 10/4/27, Sauk Rapids, Minn. d: 2/10/93, Waite Park, Minn. BR/TR, 6', 195 lbs. Deb: 4/14/53																							
1953	StL-N	153	567	75	156	25	4	15	66	33	71	.275	.325	.413	91	-8	3	6	-3	.987	-7	*O-153	-2.3
1954	StL-N	152	619	99	175	39	5	19	79	43	75	.283	.333	.454	102	0	8	10	-4	.975	-5	*O-152	-1.5
1955	StL-N	147	512	64	138	28	2	23	73	49	66	.270	.338	.467	111	7	5	7	-3	.974	-5	*O-141	-0.7
1956	StL-N★	112	376	44	104	18	3	11	55	24	46	.277	.332	.428	102	1	2	2	-1	.974	-0	*O-100	-0.5
1957	Phi-N	134	516	65	134	23	4	20	68	19	74	.260	.293	.436	95	-5	7	1	2	.968	3	*O-130	-0.9
1958	Phi-N	85	238	33	58	9	4	13	40	15	47	.244	.300	.479	103	-0	0	0	0	.949	-2	O-56	-0.5
1959	*LA-N	53	94	11	24	4	0	2	14	13	23	.255	.346	.362	83	-2	0	1	-1	1.000	-5	O-31	-0.9
1960	LA-N	4	5	0	1	0	0	0	0	0	1	.200	.200	.200	9	-1	0	0	0	1.000	-1	/O-2	-0.1
	Bos-A	73	136	14	33	6	1	3	20	10	25	.243	.295	.368	75	-5	0	0	0	1.000	-2	O-33	-0.8
1961	Bos-A	15	25	2	7	1	0	0	1	1	5	.280	.308	.320	66	-1	0	2	-1	1.000	-1	/O-4	-0.3
Total	9	928	3088	407	830	153	23	106	416	207	433	.269	.322	.436	98	-14	25	29	-10	.976	-24	O-802	-8.5
■ LARRY RESSLER Ressler, Lawrence P. b: 8/10/1848, France d: 6/12/18, Reading, Pa. Deb: 4/26/1875																							
1875	Was-n	27	108	17	21	1	0	0	5	0	4	.194	.194	.204	40	-6	4	0	1	.831	6	O-20/2-7	0.1
■ DINO RESTELLI Restelli, Dino Paul "Dingo" b: 9/23/24, St.Louis, Mo. BR/TR, 6'1.5", 191 lbs. Deb: 6/14/49																							
1949	Pit-N	72	232	41	58	11	0	12	40	35	26	.250	.358	.453	113	4	3			.961	5	O-61/1-1	0.6
1951	Pit-N	21	38	1	7	1	0	1	3	2	4	.184	.225	.289	36	-3	0	0	0	.920	-1	O-11	-0.5
Total	2	93	270	42	65	12	0	13	43	37	30	.241	.341	.430	103	1	3	*0*		.956	4	/O-72,1-1	0.1
■ MERV RETTENMUND Rettenmund, Mervin Weldon b: 6/6/43, Flint, Mich. BR/TR, 5'10", 195 lbs. Deb: 4/14/68 C																							
1968	Bal-A	31	64	10	19	5	0	2	7	18	20	.297	.458	.469	181	8	1	1	-0	1.000	-5	O-23	0.1
1969	*Bal-A	95	190	27	47	10	3	4	25	28	28	.247	.344	.395	105	2	6	1	1	.991	-10	O-78	-1.1
1970	*Bal-A	106	338	60	109	17	2	18	58	38	59	.322	.396	.544	155	25	13	7	-0	.976	-1	O-93	2.0
1971	*Bal-A	141	491	81	156	23	4	11	75	87	60	.318	.424	.448	149	36	15	6	1	.977	-3	*O-134	2.8
1972	Bal-A	102	301	40	70	10	2	6	21	41	37	.233	.325	.339	95	-1	6	4	-1	.989	-6	O-98	-1.3
1973	*Bal-A	95	321	59	84	17	2	9	44	57	38	.262	.380	.411	124	12	11	2	2	.985	3	O-90	1.4
1974	Cin-N	80	208	30	45	6	0	6	28	37	39	.216	.340	.332	90	-2	5	1	1	1.000	-5	O-69	-0.9
1975	*Cin-N	93	188	24	45	6	1	2	19	35	22	.239	.359	.314	86	-2	5	0	2	1.000	-5	O-61/3-1	-0.8
1976	SD-N	86	140	16	32	7	0	2	11	29	23	.229	.361	.321	103	2	4	1	1	.977	2	O-43	0.3
1977	SD-N	107	126	23	36	6	1	4	17	33	28	.286	.438	.444	153	12	1	2	-1	1.000	-4	O-27/3-1	0.6
1978	Cal-A	50	108	16	29	5	1	1	14	30	13	.269	.436	.361	131	7	0	3	-2	.968	-3	O-22,D-18	0.1
1979	*Cal-A	35	76	7	20	2	0	1	10	11	14	.263	.364	.329	91	-0	1	0	0	1.000	-3	D-17/O-9	-0.3
1980	Cal-A	2	4	0	1	0	0	0	0	1	1	.250	.400	.250	84	-0	0	0	0	.000	0	/D-1	0.0
Total	13	1023	2555	393	693	114	16	66	329	445	382	.271	.383	.406	124	97	68	28	4	.985	-41	O-747/D-36,3-2	2.9
■ KEN RETZER Retzer, Kenneth Leo b: 4/30/34, Wood River, Ill. BL/TR, 6', 185 lbs. Deb: 9/9/61																							
1961	Was-A	16	53	7	18	4	0	1	3	4	5	.340	.386	.472	130	2	1	0	0	.988	1	C-16	0.4
1962	Was-A	109	340	36	97	11	2	8	37	26	21	.285	.336	.400	98	-1	2	0	1	.985	0	C-99	0.3
1963	Was-A	95	265	21	64	10	0	5	31	17	20	.242	.292	.336	76	-9	2	0	1	.981	-11	C-81	-1.7

YEAR	TM/L	G	AB	R	H	2B	3B	HR	RBI	BB	SO	AVG	OBP	SLG	PRO+	BR/A	SB	CS	SBR	FA	FR	G/POS	TPR
1964	Was-A	17	32	1	3	0	0	0	1	5	4	.094	.237	.094	-4	-4	0	0	0	.971	4	C-13	0.0
Total	4	237	690	65	182	25	2	14	72	52	50	.264	.318	.367	87	-12	5	0	2	.983	-6	C-209	-1.0

■ DAVE REVERING

Revering, David Alvin b: 2/12/53, Roseville, Cal. BL/TR, 6′4″, 210 lbs. Deb: 4/8/78

YEAR	TM/L	G	AB	R	H	2B	3B	HR	RBI	BB	SO	AVG	OBP	SLG	PRO+	BR/A	SB	CS	SBR	FA	FR	G/POS	TPR
1978	Oak-A	152	521	49	141	21	3	16	46	26	55	.271	.305	.415	106	2	0	1	-1	.989	9	*1-138/D-3	0.3
1979	Oak-A	125	472	63	136	25	5	19	77	34	65	.288	.337	.483	125	15	1	4	-2	.986	2	*1-104,D-18	0.7
1980	Oak-A	106	376	48	109	21	5	15	62	32	37	.290	.346	.492	136	17	1	0	0	.989	3	1-95/D-5	1.5
1981	Oak-A	31	87	12	20	1	1	2	10	11	12	.230	.323	.333	94	-0	0	1	-1	.995	-1	1-29/D-2	-0.4
	*NY-A	45	119	8	28	4	1	2	7	11	20	.235	.300	.336	84	-2	0	1	-1	.994	3	1-44	-0.2
	Yr	76	206	20	48	5	2	4	17	22	32	.233	.310	.335	88	-3	0	2	-1	.994	2	1-73/D-2	-0.6
1982	NY-A	14	40	2	6	2	0	0	2	3	4	.150	.209	.200	13	-5	0	0	0	1.000	-2	1-13/D-1	-0.7
	Tor-A	55	135	15	29	6	0	5	18	22	30	.215	.325	.370	83	-3	0	3	-2	1.000	-0	D-49/1-4	-0.7
	Sea-A	29	82	8	17	3	1	3	12	9	17	.207	.286	.378	78	-3	0	0	0	.986	-1	1-27	-0.5
	Yr	98	257	25	52	11	1	8	32	34	51	.202	.296	.346	71	-10	0	3	-2	.992	-3	D-50,1-44	-1.9
Total	5	557	1832	205	486	83	16	62	234	148	240	.265	.321	.430	110	20	2	10	-5	.989	13	1-454/D-78	-0.0

■ HENRY REVILLE

Reville, Henry b: Baltimore, Md. Deb: 10/14/1874

YEAR	TM/L	G	AB	R	H	2B	3B	HR	RBI	BB	SO	AVG	OBP	SLG	PRO+	BR/A	SB	CS	SBR	FA	FR	G/POS	TPR
1874	Bal-n	1	4	0	0	0	0	0	0	0	0	.000	.000	.000	-99	-1	0	0	0	1.000	1	/O-1	0.0

■ WILLIAM REXTER

Rexter, William H. b: Brooklyn, N.Y. Deb: 9/25/1875

YEAR	TM/L	G	AB	R	H	2B	3B	HR	RBI	BB	SO	AVG	OBP	SLG	PRO+	BR/A	SB	CS	SBR	FA	FR	G/POS	TPR
1875	Atl-n	1	4	0	0	0	0	0	0	0	0	.000	.000	.000	-99	-1	0	0	0	1.000	-0	/O-1	-0.1

■ GILBERTO REYES

Reyes, Gilberto Rolando (Polanco) b: 12/10/63, Santo Domingo, D.R. BR/TR, 6′2″, 203 lbs. Deb: 6/11/83

YEAR	TM/L	G	AB	R	H	2B	3B	HR	RBI	BB	SO	AVG	OBP	SLG	PRO+	BR/A	SB	CS	SBR	FA	FR	G/POS	TPR
1983	LA-N	19	31	1	5	2	0	0	0	0	5	.161	.188	.226	14	-4	0	0	0	.944	2	C-19	-0.1
1984	LA-N	4	5	0	0	0	0	0	0	0	3	.000	.000	.000	-99	-1	0	0	0	1.000	-0	/C-2	-0.2
1985	LA-N	6	1	0	0	0	0	0	0	1	1	.000	.667	.000	105	0	0	0	0	1.000	2	/C-6	0.2
1987	LA-N	1	0	0	0	0	0	0	0	0	0	—	—	—	—	0	0	0	0	.000	-0	/C-1	0.0
1988	LA-N	5	9	1	1	0	0	0	0	0	3	.111	.111	.111	-37	-2	0	0	0	1.000	0	/C-5	-0.1
1989	Mon-N	4	5	0	1	0	0	0	1	0	1	.200	.200	.200	14	-1	0	0	0	1.000	1	/C-4	0.0
1991	Mon-N	83	207	11	45	9	0	0	13	19	51	.217	.286	.261	56	-12	2	4	-2	.975	14	C-80	0.4
Total	7	122	258	13	52	11	0	0	14	20	64	.202	.267	.244	45	-19	2	4	-2	.973	17	C-117	0.2

■ NAP REYES

Reyes, Napoleon Aguilera b: 11/24/19, Santiago De Cuba, Cuba d: 9/15/95, Miami, Fla. BR/TR, 6′1″, 205 lbs. Deb: 5/19/43

YEAR	TM/L	G	AB	R	H	2B	3B	HR	RBI	BB	SO	AVG	OBP	SLG	PRO+	BR/A	SB	CS	SBR	FA	FR	G/POS	TPR
1943	NY-N	40	125	13	32	4	2	0	13	4	12	.256	.290	.320	76	-4	2			.994	-5	1-38/3-1	-1.2
1944	NY-N	116	374	38	108	16	5	8	53	15	24	.289	.325	.422	109	3	2			.990	2	1-63,3-37/O-3	0.3
1945	NY-N	122	431	39	124	15	4	5	44	25	26	.288	.338	.376	97	-2	1			.961	-4	*3-115/1-5	-0.3
1950	NY-N	1	1	0	0	0	0	0	0	0	0	.000	.000	.000	-99	-0	0			.667	-0	/1-1	-0.1
Total	4	279	931	90	264	35	11	13	110	44	62	.284	.326	.387	99	-3	5			.960	-7	3-153,1-107/O-3	-1.3

■ CARL REYNOLDS

Reynolds, Carl Nettles b: 2/1/03, LaRue, Tex. d: 5/29/78, Houston, Tex. BR/TR, 6′, 194 lbs. Deb: 9/1/27

YEAR	TM/L	G	AB	R	H	2B	3B	HR	RBI	BB	SO	AVG	OBP	SLG	PRO+	BR/A	SB	CS	SBR	FA	FR	G/POS	TPR
1927	Chi-A	14	42	5	9	3	0	1	7	5	7	.214	.313	.357	75	-2	1	2	-1	1.000	2	O-13	-0.1
1928	Chi-A	84	291	51	94	21	11	2	36	17	13	.323	.371	.491	126	10	15	3	3	.979	-2	O-74	0.6
1929	Chi-A	131	517	81	164	24	12	11	67	20	37	.317	.348	.474	111	6	19	9	0	.949	-2	*O-130	-0.4
1930	Chi-A	138	563	103	202	25	18	22	104	20	39	.359	.388	.584	148	38	16	4	2	.975	10	*O-132	3.6
1931	Chi-A	118	462	71	134	24	14	6	77	24	26	.290	.333	.442	108	4	17	6	2	.949	-4	*O-109	-0.6
1932	Was-A	102	406	53	124	28	7	9	63	13	19	.305	.332	.475	108	3	8	4	0	.983	5	O-95	0.1
1933	StL-A	135	475	81	136	26	14	8	71	49	25	.286	.357	.451	106	3	5	4	-1	.965	-2	*O-124	-0.5
1934	Bos-A	113	413	61	125	26	9	4	86	27	28	.303	.350	.438	95	-4	5	3	-0	.977	3	*O-100	-0.5
1935	Bos-A	78	244	33	66	13	4	6	35	24	20	.270	.336	.430	91	-4	4	1	1	.975	6	O-64	0.0
1936	Was-A	89	293	41	81	18	2	4	41	21	22	.276	.329	.392	82	-9	8	4	0	.968	-0	O-72	-1.1
1937	Chi-N	7	11	0	3	1	0	0	1	2	2	.273	.385	.364	100	0	0			.800	-0	/O-2	0.0
1938	*Chi-N	125	497	59	150	28	10	3	67	22	32	.302	.335	.416	103	1	9			.983	-3	*O-125	-0.5
1939	Chi-N	88	281	33	69	10	6	4	44	16	38	.246	.298	.367	76	-10	5			.972	2	O-72	-1.1
Total	13	1222	4495	672	1357	247	107	80	699	260	308	.302	.346	.458	107	36	112	40		.970	15	*O-1112	-0.5

■ CHARLIE REYNOLDS

Reynolds, Charles Lawrence b: 5/1/1865, Williamsburg, Ind. d: 7/3/44, Denver, Colo. 5′9″, 175 lbs. Deb: 5/8/1889

YEAR	TM/L	G	AB	R	H	2B	3B	HR	RBI	BB	SO	AVG	OBP	SLG	PRO+	BR/A	SB	CS	SBR	FA	FR	G/POS	TPR
1889	KC-a	1	4	1	1	0	0	0	1	0	1	.250	.250	.250	40	-0	0			1.000	-1	/C-1	-0.1
	Bro-a	12	42	5	9	1	1	0	3	1	6	.214	.233	.286	47	-3	2			.892	1	C-12	-0.1
	Yr	13	46	6	10	1	1	0	4	1	7	.217	.234	.283	46	-3	2			.893	-1	C-13	-0.2

■ DANNY REYNOLDS

Reynolds, Daniel Vance "Squirrel" b: 11/27/19, Stony Point, N.C. BR/TR, 5′11″, 158 lbs. Deb: 5/26/45

YEAR	TM/L	G	AB	R	H	2B	3B	HR	RBI	BB	SO	AVG	OBP	SLG	PRO+	BR/A	SB	CS	SBR	FA	FR	G/POS	TPR
1945	Chi-A	29	72	6	12	2	1	0	4	3	8	.167	.200	.222	23	-7	1	2	-1	.947	2	S-14,2-11	-0.5

■ DON REYNOLDS

Reynolds, Donald Edward b: 4/16/53, Arkadelphia, Ark. BR/TR, 5′8″, 178 lbs. Deb: 4/7/78 F

YEAR	TM/L	G	AB	R	H	2B	3B	HR	RBI	BB	SO	AVG	OBP	SLG	PRO+	BR/A	SB	CS	SBR	FA	FR	G/POS	TPR
1978	SD-N	57	87	8	22	2	0	0	10	15	14	.253	.363	.276	87	-1	1	0	0	.923	-4	O-25	-0.6
1979	SD-N	30	45	6	10	1	2	0	6	7	6	.222	.327	.333	86	-1	0	1	-1	.950	-1	O-14	-0.3
Total	2	87	132	14	32	3	2	0	16	22	20	.242	.351	.295	87	-2	1	1	-0	.935	-5	/O-39	-0.9

■ CRAIG REYNOLDS

Reynolds, Gordon Craig b: 12/27/52, Houston, Tex. BL/TR, 6′1″, 175 lbs. Deb: 8/1/75

YEAR	TM/L	G	AB	R	H	2B	3B	HR	RBI	BB	SO	AVG	OBP	SLG	PRO+	BR/A	SB	CS	SBR	FA	FR	G/POS	TPR
1975	*Pit-N	31	76	8	17	3	0	0	4	3	5	.224	.253	.263	44	-6	0	1	-1	.969	4	S-30	0.0
1976	Pit-N	7	4	1	1	0	0	1	1	0	0	.250	.250	1.000	241	1	0	0	0	.889	2	/S-4,2-1	0.2
1977	Sea-A	135	420	41	104	12	3	4	28	15	23	.248	.279	.319	63	-22	6	6	-2	.955	8	*S-134	-0.2
1978	Sea-A☆	148	548	57	160	16	7	5	44	36	41	.292	.339	.374	101	1	9	6	-1	.960	4	*S-146	2.2
1979	Hou-N★	146	555	63	147	20	9	0	39	21	49	.265	.294	.333	75	-20	12	6	0	.965	-15	*S-143	-2.0
1980	*Hou-N	137	381	34	86	9	6	3	28	20	39	.226	.264	.304	63	-20	2	1	0	.969	12	*S-135	0.4
1981	*Hou-N	87	323	43	84	10	**12**	4	31	12	31	.260	.287	.402	99	-3	3	3	-1	.973	-5	S-85	0.1
1982	Hou-N	54	118	16	30	2	3	1	7	11	9	.254	.323	.347	95	-1	3	1	0	.958	2	S-35/3-7	0.4
1983	Hou-N	65	98	10	21	3	0	1	6	6	10	.214	.260	.276	52	-7	0	1	-1	.956	-4	2-26,3-15/S-8,O-1	-1.1
1984	Hou-N	146	527	61	137	15	11	6	60	22	53	.260	.290	.364	89	-10	7	1	2	.965	18	*S-143/3-1	2.3
1985	Hou-N	107	379	43	103	18	8	4	32	12	30	.272	.294	.393	93	-5	4	4	-1	.977	10	*S-102/2-1	1.4
1986	*Hou-N	114	313	32	78	7	3	6	41	12	31	.249	.277	.348	73	-12	3	1	0	.978	-12	S-98/1-5,3-4,O-2,P	-1.7
1987	Hou-N	135	374	35	95	17	3	4	28	30	44	.254	.309	.348	77	-13	5	1	1	.970	-12	*S-129/3-2	-1.4
1988	Hou-N	78	161	20	41	7	0	1	14	8	23	.255	.290	.317	77	-5	3	0	1	.970	-5	S-22,3-19,2-11,1-10	-0.8
1989	Hou-N	101	189	16	38	4	0	2	14	19	18	.201	.274	.254	54	-11	1	0	0	.979	8	2-29,S-26,3/1PO	-0.1
Total	15	1491	4466	480	1142	143	65	42	377	227	406	.256	.293	.345	80	-133	58	32	-2	.966	17	*S-1240/2-68,31OP	-0.3

■ HAROLD REYNOLDS

Reynolds, Harold Craig b: 11/26/60, Eugene, Ore. BB/TR, 5′11″, 165 lbs. Deb: 9/2/83 F

YEAR	TM/L	G	AB	R	H	2B	3B	HR	RBI	BB	SO	AVG	OBP	SLG	PRO+	BR/A	SB	CS	SBR	FA	FR	G/POS	TPR
1983	Sea-A	20	59	8	12	4	1	0	1	2	9	.203	.230	.305	44	-5	0	2	-1	.975	-1	2-18	-0.6
1984	Sea-A	10	10	3	3	0	0	0	0	0	1	.300	.364	.300	87	-0	1	1	-0	1.000	4	/2-6	0.4
1985	Sea-A	67	104	15	15	3	1	0	6	17	14	.144	.264	.192	27	-10	3	2	-0	.960	19	2-61	1.0
1986	Sea-A	126	445	46	99	19	4	1	24	29	42	.222	.275	.290	53	-29	30	12	2	.977	29	*2-126	0.7
1987	Sea-A★	160	530	73	146	31	8	1	35	39	34	.275	.327	.370	80	-15	**60**	20	6	.977	19	*2-160	1.7
1988	Sea-A★	158	598	61	169	26	**11**	4	41	51	51	.283	.341	.383	98	-1	35	29	-7	.977	6	*2-158	0.5
1989	Sea-A	153	613	87	184	24	9	0	43	55	45	.300	.361	.369	103	3	25	18	-3	.980	**27**	*2-151/D-1	3.2
1990	Sea-A	160	642	100	162	36	5	5	55	81	52	.252	.339	.347	91	-6	31	16	-0	.978	15	*2-160	1.3
1991	Sea-A	161	631	95	160	34	6	3	57	72	63	.254	.335	.341	87	-9	28	8	4	.978	5	*2-159/D-1	0.3
1992	Sea-A	140	458	55	113	23	3	3	33	45	41	.247	.318	.330	81	-11	15	12	-3	.982	2	*2-134/O-1,D-1	-0.9
1993	Bal-A	145	485	64	122	20	4	4	47	66	47	.252	.346	.334	80	-12	12	11	-3	.986	3	*2-141/D-1	-0.7
1994	Cal-A	74	207	33	48	10	1	0	11	23	18	.232	.312	.290	56	-13	10	7	-1	.996	-13	2-65/D-3	-2.3
Total	12	1374	4782	640	1233	230	53	21	353	480	417	.258	.329	.341	83	-107	250	138	-8	.979	116	*2-1339/D-7,O-1	4.6

■ R. J. REYNOLDS
Reynolds, Robert James b: 4/19/59, Sacramento, Cal. BB/TR, 6', 190 lbs. Deb: 9/1/83

YEAR	TM/L	G	AB	R	H	2B	3B	HR	RBI	BB	SO	AVG	OBP	SLG	PRO+	BR/A	SB	CS	SBR	FA	FR	G/POS	TPR
1983	LA-N	24	55	5	13	0	0	2	11	3	11	.236	.276	.345	72	-2	5	0	2	.931	-2	O-18	-0.3
1984	LA-N	73	240	24	62	12	2	2	24	14	38	.258	.302	.350	84	-6	7	5	-1	.973	-7	O-63	-1.6
1985	LA-N	73	207	22	55	10	4	0	25	13	31	.266	.312	.353	88	-4	6	3	0	.970	-2	O-54	-0.7
	Pit-N	31	130	22	40	5	3	3	17	9	18	.308	.357	.462	129	5	12	2	2	.958	1	O-31	0.7
	Yr	104	337	44	95	15	7	3	42	22	49	.282	.330	.395	104	1	18	5	2	.965	-1	O-85	0.0
1986	Pit-N	118	402	63	108	30	2	9	48	40	78	.269	.336	.420	105	2	16	9	-1	.955	-15	*O-112	-1.7
1987	Pit-N	117	335	47	87	24	1	7	51	34	80	.260	.328	.400	91	-4	14	1	4	.993	-6	O-99	-1.0
1988	Pit-N	130	323	35	80	14	2	6	51	20	62	.248	.292	.359	87	-6	15	2	3	.974	-6	O-95	-1.2
1989	Pit-N	125	363	45	98	16	2	6	48	34	66	.270	.334	.375	106	3	22	5	4	.990	-1	O-98	0.4
1990	*Pit-N	95	215	25	62	10	1	0	19	23	35	.288	.357	.344	98	-0	12	2	2	.972	-6	O-59	-0.5
Total	8	786	2270	288	605	121	17	35	294	190	419	.267	.325	.381	97	-12	109	29	15	.973	-44	O-629	-5.9

■ RONN REYNOLDS
Reynolds, Ronn Dwayne b: 9/28/58, Wichita, Kan. BR/TR, 6', 200 lbs. Deb: 9/29/82

YEAR	TM/L	G	AB	R	H	2B	3B	HR	RBI	BB	SO	AVG	OBP	SLG	PRO+	BR/A	SB	CS	SBR	FA	FR	G/POS	TPR
1982	NY-N	2	4	0	0	0	0	0	0	1	1	.000	.200	.000	-40	-1	0	0	0	1.000	-1	/C-2	-0.2
1983	NY-N	24	66	4	13	1	0	0	2	8	12	.197	.284	.212	40	-5	0	0	0	.942	-1	C-24	-0.5
1985	NY-N	28	43	4	9	2	0	0	1	0	18	.209	.227	.256	36	-4	0	0	0	.990	6	C-25	0.3
1986	Phi-N	43	126	8	27	4	0	3	10	5	30	.214	.244	.317	52	-8	0	0	0	.991	1	C-42	-0.5
1987	Hou-N	38	102	5	17	4	0	1	7	3	29	.167	.190	.235	12	-13	0	1	-1	.975	4	C-38	-0.8
1990	SD-N	8	15	1	1	1	0	0	1	1	6	.067	.125	.133	-29	-3	0	0	0	1.000	1	/C-8	-0.2
Total	6	143	356	22	67	12	0	4	21	18	96	.188	.229	.256	32	-34	0	1	-1	.977	10	C-139	-1.9

■ TOMMIE REYNOLDS
Reynolds, Tommie D b: 8/15/41, Arizona, La. BR/TR, 6'2", 190 lbs. Deb: 9/5/63 C

YEAR	TM/L	G	AB	R	H	2B	3B	HR	RBI	BB	SO	AVG	OBP	SLG	PRO+	BR/A	SB	CS	SBR	FA	FR	G/POS	TPR
1963	KC-A	8	19	1	1	1	0	0	0	1	7	.053	.143	.105	-28	-3	0	0	0	.800	-1	/O-5	-0.5
1964	KC-A	31	94	11	19	1	0	2	9	10	22	.202	.292	.277	58	-5	0	0	0	.976	-0	O-25/3-3	-0.7
1965	KC-A	90	270	34	64	11	3	1	22	36	41	.237	.327	.311	83	-5	9	2	2	.982	7	O-83/3-1	0.0
1967	NY-N	101	136	16	28	1	0	2	9	11	26	.206	.280	.257	56	-8	1	1	-0	.971	-13	O-72/3-5,C-1	-2.5
1969	Oak-A	107	315	51	81	10	0	2	20	34	29	.257	.345	.308	87	-4	1	3	-2	.979	6	O-89	-0.5
1970	Cal-A	59	120	11	30	3	1	1	6	6	10	.250	.291	.317	70	-5	1	1	-0	.969	0	O-32/3-1	-0.7
1971	Cal-A	45	86	4	16	3	0	2	8	9	6	.186	.286	.291	68	-4	0	1	-1	.978	-2	O-26/3-1	-0.7
1972	Mil-A	72	130	13	26	5	1	2	13	10	25	.200	.262	.300	68	-5	0	0	0	.961	-1	O-41/1-1,3-1	-0.9
Total	8	513	1170	141	265	35	5	12	87	117	166	.226	.307	.296	73	-39	12	8	-1	.973	-4	O-373/3-12,1-1,C-1	-6.5

■ BILL REYNOLDS
Reynolds, William Dee b: 8/14/1884, Eastland, Tex. d: 6/5/24, Carnegie, Okla. BR/TR, 6', 185 lbs. Deb: 9/15/13

YEAR	TM/L	G	AB	R	H	2B	3B	HR	RBI	BB	SO	AVG	OBP	SLG	PRO+	BR/A	SB	CS	SBR	FA	FR	G/POS	TPR
1913	NY-A	5	5	0	0	0	0	0	0	0	1	.000	.000	.000	-99	-1	0			.917	0	/C-5	-0.1
1914	NY-A	4	5	0	2	0	0	0	0	0	3	.400	.400	.400	141	0	0			1.000	0	/C-1	0.1
Total	2	9	10	0	2	0	0	0	0	0	4	.200	.200	.200	19	-1	0			.941	0	/C-6	0.0

■ BOBBY RHAWN
Rhawn, Robert John "Rocky" b: 2/13/19, Catawissa, Pa. d: 6/9/84, Danville, Pa. BR/TR, 5'8", 180 lbs. Deb: 9/17/47

YEAR	TM/L	G	AB	R	H	2B	3B	HR	RBI	BB	SO	AVG	OBP	SLG	PRO+	BR/A	SB	CS	SBR	FA	FR	G/POS	TPR
1947	NY-N	13	45	7	14	3	0	1	3	8	1	.311	.415	.444	128	2	0			.913	0	/2-8,3-5	0.3
1948	NY-N	36	44	11	12	2	1	1	8	8	6	.273	.385	.432	120	1	3			.872	1	S-14/3-7	0.2
1949	NY-N	14	29	8	5	0	0	0	2	7	2	.172	.333	.172	40	-2	1			.959	4	/2-8	0.2
	Pit-N	3	7	0	1	0	0	0	0	0	0	.143	.143	.143	-23	-1	0			.889	1	/3-2	0.0
	Yr	17	36	8	6	0	0	0	2	7	2	.167	.302	.167	29	-3	1			.959	4	/2-8,3-2	0.2
	Chi-A	24	73	12	15	4	1	0	5	12	8	.205	.318	.288	63	-4	0	1	-1	.959	3	3-19/S-3	-0.2
Total	3	90	198	38	47	9	2	2	18	35	17	.237	.352	.333	84	-4	4	1		.963	8	/3-33,S-17,2-16	0.5

■ CY RHEAM
Rheam, Kenneth Johnston b: 9/28/1893, Pittsburgh, Pa. d: 10/23/47, Pittsburgh, Pa. BR/TR, 6' ", 175 lbs. Deb: 5/20/14

YEAR	TM/L	G	AB	R	H	2B	3B	HR	RBI	BB	SO	AVG	OBP	SLG	PRO+	BR/A	SB	CS	SBR	FA	FR	G/POS	TPR
1914	Pit-F	73	214	15	45	5	3	0	20	9	33	.210	.242	.262	38	-22	6			.976	-5	1-43,3-13,2-11,/O-1	-2.9
1915	Pit-F	34	69	10	12	0	0	1	5	1	7	.174	.186	.217	13	-9	4			.959	0	O-22/1-1	-1.1
Total	2	107	283	25	57	5	3	1	25	10	40	.201	.229	.251	32	-32	10			.976	-5	/1-44,O-23,3-13,2	-4.0

■ BILLY RHIEL
Rhiel, William Joseph b: 8/16/1900, Youngstown, Ohio d: 8/16/46, Youngstown, Ohio BR/TR, 5'11", 175 lbs. Deb: 4/20/29

YEAR	TM/L	G	AB	R	H	2B	3B	HR	RBI	BB	SO	AVG	OBP	SLG	PRO+	BR/A	SB	CS	SBR	FA	FR	G/POS	TPR
1929	Bro-N	76	205	27	57	9	4	4	25	19	25	.278	.339	.420	89	-4	0			.979	1	2-47/3-7,S-2	-0.1
1930	Bos-N	20	47	3	8	4	0	0	4	2	5	.170	.204	.255	11	-7	0			.947	-4	3-13/2-2	-0.9
1932	Det-A	85	250	30	70	13	3	3	38	17	23	.280	.328	.392	82	-7	2	0	1	.956	-5	3-37,1-12/O-8,2-1	-1.0
1933	Det-A	19	17	1	3	0	1	0	1	5	4	.176	.364	.294	75	-0	0	0	0	1.000	0	/O-1	0.0
Total	4	200	519	61	138	26	8	7	68	43	57	.266	.323	.387	78	-18	2	0		.949	-8	/3-57,2-50,1-12,OS	-2.0

■ DUSTY RHODES
Rhodes, James Lamar b: 5/13/27, Mathews, Ala. BL/TR, 6', 180 lbs. Deb: 7/15/52

YEAR	TM/L	G	AB	R	H	2B	3B	HR	RBI	BB	SO	AVG	OBP	SLG	PRO+	BR/A	SB	CS	SBR	FA	FR	G/POS	TPR
1952	NY-N	67	176	34	44	8	1	10	36	23	33	.250	.340	.477	123	5	1	0	0	.917	-4	O-56	0.0
1953	NY-N	76	163	18	38	7	0	11	30	10	28	.233	.277	.479	91	-3	0	1	-1	.965	1	O-47	-0.4
1954	*NY-N	82	164	31	56	7	3	15	50	18	25	.341	.410	.695	181	19	1	0	0	.984	-3	O-37	1.5
1955	NY-N	94	187	22	57	5	2	6	32	27	26	.305	.393	.449	122	7	1	1	-0	.986	-4	O-45	0.1
1956	NY-N	111	244	20	53	10	3	8	33	30	41	.217	.303	.381	83	-6	0	0	0	.958	-5	O-68	-1.4
1957	NY-N	92	190	20	39	5	1	4	19	18	34	.205	.278	.305	57	-12	0	0	0	1.000	-6	O-44	-2.0
1959	SF-N	54	48	1	9	2	0	0	7	5	9	.188	.264	.229	34	-5	0	0	0	.000	0	H	-0.5
Total	7	576	1172	146	296	44	10	54	207	131	196	.253	.329	.445	104	5	3	2	-0	.963	-20	O-297	-2.7

■ KARL RHODES
Rhodes, Karl Derrick "Tuffy" b: 8/21/68, Cincinnati, Ohio BL/TL, 5'11", 170 lbs. Deb: 8/7/90

YEAR	TM/L	G	AB	R	H	2B	3B	HR	RBI	BB	SO	AVG	OBP	SLG	PRO+	BR/A	SB	CS	SBR	FA	FR	G/POS	TPR
1990	Hou-N	38	86	12	21	6	1	1	3	13	12	.244	.343	.372	100	0	4	1	1	.955	-1	O-30	-0.1
1991	Hou-N	44	136	7	29	3	1	1	12	14	26	.213	.291	.272	63	-7	2	2	-1	.958	3	O-44	-0.5
1992	Hou-N	5	4	0	0	0	0	0	0	0	2	.000	.000	.000	-99	-1	0	0	0	.000	-1	/O-1	-0.2
1993	Hou-N	5	2	0	0	0	0	0	0	0	0	.000	.000	.000	-99	-1	0	0	0	1.000	-1	/O-4	-0.2
	Chi-N	15	52	12	15	2	1	3	7	11	9	.288	.413	.538	155	4	2	0	1	.970	-3	O-14	0.2
	Yr	20	54	12	15	2	1	3	7	11	9	.278	.400	.519	147	4	2	0	1	.971	-4	O-18	0.0
1994	Chi-N	95	269	39	63	17	0	8	19	33	64	.234	.320	.387	84	-6	6	4	-1	.967	-8	O-76	-1.6
1995	Chi-N	13	16	2	2	0	0	0	2	0	4	.125	.125	.125	-34	-3	0	0	0	.889	-2	O-11	-0.5
	Bos-A	10	25	2	2	1	0	0	1	3	4	.080	.179	.120	-20	-4	0	0	0	.947	-1	/O-9	-0.6
Total	6	225	590	74	132	29	3	13	44	74	121	.224	.312	.349	79	-18	14	7	0	.960	-14	O-189	-3.5

■ KEVIN RHOMBERG
Rhomberg, Kevin Jay b: 11/22/55, Dubuque, Iowa BR/TR, 6', 175 lbs. Deb: 9/1/82

YEAR	TM/L	G	AB	R	H	2B	3B	HR	RBI	BB	SO	AVG	OBP	SLG	PRO+	BR/A	SB	CS	SBR	FA	FR	G/POS	TPR
1982	Cle-A	16	18	3	6	0	0	1	1	2	4	.333	.400	.500	146	1	0	2	-1	.900	-0	/O-7,3-1,D-4	0.0
1983	Cle-A	12	21	2	10	0	0	0	2	2	4	.476	.522	.476	170	2	1	1	-0	1.000	-2	/O-9,D-1	0.0
1984	Cle-A	13	8	0	2	0	0	0	0	0	3	.250	.250	.250	38	-1	0	0	0	1.000	-2	/O-7,1-1,2-1,D-1	-0.2
Total	3	41	47	5	18	0	0	1	3	4	11	.383	.431	.447	140	3	1	3	2	.963	4	/O-23,D-6,2-1,1-3	-0.2

■ HAL RHYNE
Rhyne, Harold J. b: 3/30/1899, Paso Robles, Cal. d: 1/7/71, Orangevale, Cal. BR/TR, 5'8.5", 163 lbs. Deb: 4/18/26

YEAR	TM/L	G	AB	R	H	2B	3B	HR	RBI	BB	SO	AVG	OBP	SLG	PRO+	BR/A	SB	CS	SBR	FA	FR	G/POS	TPR
1926	Pit-N	109	366	46	92	14	3	2	39	35	21	.251	.327	.322	71	-14	1			.967	8	2-66,S-44/3-1	0.0
1927	*Pit-N	62	168	21	46	5	0	0	17	14	9	.274	.330	.304	66	-8	0			.963	-7	2-45,3-10/S-7	-1.2
1929	Bos-A	120	346	41	87	24	5	0	38	25	14	.251	.309	.350	71	-15	4	1	1	.935	-3	*S-113/3-1,O-1	-0.5
1930	Bos-A	107	296	34	60	8	5	0	23	25	19	.203	.269	.264	37	-28	1	4	-2	.944	4	*S-107	-1.5
1931	Bos-A	147	565	75	154	34	3	0	51	57	41	.273	.341	.343	85	-11	3	3	-1	**.963**	17	*S-147	1.7
1932	Bos-A	71	207	26	47	12	5	0	14	23	14	.227	.310	.333	69	-10	3	2	-0	.966	-2	S-55/3-4,2-1	-0.6
1933	Chi-A	39	83	9	22	1	1	0	10	5	9	.265	.315	.301	67	-4	1	1	-0	.955	5	2-19,3-13/S-2	0.2
Total	7	655	2031	252	508	98	22	2	192	184	127	.250	.318	.323	69	-91	13	11		.950	23	S-475,2-131/3-29,O	-1.9

■ DEL RICE
Rice, Delbert b: 10/27/22, Portsmouth, Ohio d: 1/26/83, Buena Park, Cal. BR/TR, 6'2", 190 lbs. Deb: 5/2/45 MC

YEAR	TM/L	G	AB	R	H	2B	3B	HR	RBI	BB	SO	AVG	OBP	SLG	PRO+	BR/A	SB	CS	SBR	FA	FR	G/POS	TPR
1945	StL-N	83	253	27	66	17	3	1	28	16	33	.261	.313	.364	86	-5	0			.994	9	C-77	0.7
1946	*StL-N	55	139	10	38	8	1	1	12	8	16	.273	.313	.367	89	-2	0			.977	-0	C-53	0.0
1947	StL-N	97	261	28	57	7	3	12	44	36	40	.218	.315	.406	87	-6	1			.981	4	C-94	0.3

YEAR	TM/L	G	AB	R	H	2B	3B	HR	RBI	BB	SO	AVG	OBP	SLG	PRO+	BR/A	SB	CS	SBR	FA	FR	G/POS	TPR
1948	StL-N	100	290	24	57	10	1	4	34	37	46	.197	.298	.279	54	-18	1			**.996**	8	C-99	-0.4
1949	StL-N	92	284	25	67	16	1	4	29	30	40	.236	.320	.342	74	-10	0			.992	-3	C-92	-0.8
1950	StL-N	130	414	39	101	20	3	9	54	43	65	.244	.323	.372	78	-13	0			.984	6	*C-130	-0.1
1951	StL-N	122	374	34	94	13	1	9	47	34	26	.251	.319	.364	83	-9	0	0	0	.985	2	*C-120	-0.2
1952	StL-N	147	495	43	128	27	2	11	65	33	38	.259	.313	.388	93	-6	0	1	-1	.992	-4	*C-147	-0.4
1953	StL-N†	135	419	32	99	22	1	6	37	48	49	.236	.323	.337	72	-16	0	0	0	.988	-5	*C-135	-1.5
1954	StL-N	56	147	13	37	10	1	2	16	16	21	.252	.325	.374	81	-4	0	1	-1	.985	6	C-52	0.3
1955	StL-N	20	59	6	12	3	0	1	7	7	6	.203	.288	.305	58	-4	0	0	0	.964	-5	C-18	-0.8
	Mil-N	27	71	5	14	0	1	2	7	6	12	.197	.260	.310	53	-5	0	0	0	.981	1	C-22	-0.4
	Yr	47	130	11	26	3	1	3	14	13	18	.200	.273	.308	55	-9	0	0	0	.973	-5	C-40	-1.2
1956	Mil-N	71	188	15	40	9	1	3	17	18	34	.213	.282	.319	65	-10	0	0	0	.983	2	C-65	-0.5
1957	*Mil-N	54	144	15	33	1	1	9	20	17	37	.229	.311	.438	106	1	0	0	0	.992	6	C-48	0.9
1958	Mil-N	43	121	10	27	7	0	1	8	8	30	.223	.271	.306	57	-8	0	0	0	.995	-0	C-38	-0.6
1959	Mil-N	13	29	3	6	0	0	0	1	2	3	.207	.258	.207	28	-3	0	0	0	.956	-0	/C-9	-0.3
1960	Chi-N	18	52	2	12	3	0	0	4	2	7	.231	.259	.288	50	-4	0	0	0	.968	-2	C-18	-0.5
	StL-N	1	2	0	0	0	0	0	0	1	0	.000	.333	.000	1	-0	0	0	0	1.000	-0	/C-1	-0.1
	Yr	19	54	2	12	3	0	0	4	3	7	.222	.263	.278	49	-4	0	0	0	.970	-2	C-19	-0.6
	Bal-A	1	1	0	0	0	0	0	0	0	0	.000	.000	.000	-99	-0	0	0	0	1.000	-0	/C-1	0.0
1961	LA-A	44	83	11	20	4	0	4	11	20	19	.241	.388	.434	107	1	0	1	-1	.994	2	C-30	0.3
Total	17	1309	3826	342	908	177	20	79	441	382	522	.237	.312	.356	78	-122	2	3		.987	25	*C-1249	-4.1

■ SAM RICE

Rice, Edgar Charles b: 2/20/1890, Morocco, Ind. d: 10/13/74, Rossmoor, Md. BL/TR, 5'9", 150 lbs. Deb: 8/7/15 H

YEAR	TM/L	G	AB	R	H	2B	3B	HR	RBI	BB	SO	AVG	OBP	SLG	PRO+	BR/A	SB	CS	SBR	FA	FR	G/POS	TPR
1915	Was-A	4	8	0	3	0	0	0	0	0	1	.375	.375	.375	122	0	0			.889	0	/P-4	0.0
1916	Was-A	58	197	26	59	8	3	1	17	15	13	.299	.352	.386	123	5	4			.957	2	O-46/P-5	0.5
1917	Was-A	155	586	77	177	25	7	0	69	50	41	.302	.360	.369	124	16	35			.960	8	*O-155	1.8
1918	Was-A	7	23	3	8	1	0	0	3	2	0	.348	.400	.391	141	1	1			1.000	3	/O-6	0.4
1919	Was-A	141	557	80	179	23	9	3	71	42	26	.321	.376	.411	122	16	26			.962	8	*O-141	1.5
1920	Was-A	153	624	83	211	29	9	3	80	39	23	.338	.381	.428	117	15	**63**	30	1	.960	21	*O-153	2.5
1921	Was-A	143	561	83	185	39	13	4	79	38	10	.330	.382	.467	121	17	26	12	1	.964	11	*O-141	1.6
1922	Was-A	154	633	91	187	37	13	6	69	48	13	.295	.347	.423	105	3	20	9	1	.951	9	*O-154	0.1
1923	Was-A	148	595	117	188	35	**18**	3	75	57	12	.316	.381	.450	125	20	20	8	1	.970	8	*O-147	1.9
1924	*Was-A	154	646	106	**216**	39	14	1	76	46	24	.334	.382	.443	116	14	24	13	-1	.967	4	*O-154	0.6
1925	*Was-A	152	649	111	227	31	13	1	87	37	10	.350	.388	.442	113	12	26	11	1	.968	9	*O-152	1.1
1926	Was-A	152	641	98	**216**	32	14	3	76	42	20	.337	.380	.445	117	15	24	23	-7	.961	7	*O-152	0.5
1927	Was-A	142	603	98	179	33	14	2	65	36	11	.297	.336	.408	93	-7	19	6	2	.975	-0	*O-139	-1.4
1928	Was-A	148	616	95	202	32	15	2	55	49	15	.328	.379	.438	115	14	16	3	**3**	.973	-8	*O-147	-0.2
1929	Was-A	150	616	119	199	39	10	1	62	55	9	.323	.382	.424	106	7	16	8	0	.970	7	*O-147	0.3
1930	Was-A	147	593	121	207	35	13	1	73	55	14	.349	.407	.457	118	18	13	8	-1	.963	4	*O-145	1.0
1931	Was-A	120	413	81	128	21	8	0	42	35	11	.310	.365	.400	100	1	6	5	-1	.970	1	*O-105	-0.6
1932	Was-A	106	288	58	93	16	7	1	34	32	6	.323	.391	.438	116	7	7	4	-0	.972	-3	O-69	0.0
1933	*Was-A	73	85	19	25	4	3	1	12	2	7	.294	.326	.447	104	0	0	2	-1	1.000	-8	O-39	-0.9
1934	Cle-A	97	335	48	98	19	1	1	33	28	9	.293	.351	.364	83	-8	5	1	1	.963	-7	O-78	-1.6
Total	20	2404	9269	1514	2987	498	184	34	1078	708	275	.322	.374	.427	113	166	351	143		.965	75	*O-2270/P-9	9.1

■ HAL RICE

Rice, Harold Housten "Hoot" b: 2/11/24, Morganette, W.Va. d: 12/22/97, St.Augustine, Fla. BL/TR, 6'1", 195 lbs. Deb: 9/25/48

YEAR	TM/L	G	AB	R	H	2B	3B	HR	RBI	BB	SO	AVG	OBP	SLG	PRO+	BR/A	SB	CS	SBR	FA	FR	G/POS	TPR
1948	StL-N	8	31	3	10	1	2	0	3	2	4	.323	.364	.484	121	1	0			1.000	-1	/O-8	0.0
1949	StL-N	40	46	3	9	2	1	1	9	3	7	.196	.245	.348	55	-3	0			1.000	-2	O-10	-0.6
1950	StL-N	44	128	12	27	3	1	2	11	10	10	.211	.268	.297	46	-10	0			.972	-1	O-37	-1.3
1951	StL-N	69	236	20	60	12	1	4	38	24	22	.254	.323	.364	84	-5	0	1	-1	.953	-3	O-63	-1.1
1952	StL-N	98	295	37	85	14	5	7	45	16	26	.288	.325	.441	110	3	1	3	-2	.972	-5	O-81	-0.7
1953	StL-N	8	8	0	2	0	0	0	0	0	3	.250	.250	.250	31	-1	0	0	0	.000	0	H	-0.1
	Pit-N	78	286	39	89	16	1	4	42	17	22	.311	.350	.416	99	-0	0	1	-1	.973	14	O-70	1.0
	Yr	86	294	39	91	16	1	4	42	17	25	.310	.347	.412	97	-1	0	1	-1	.973	14	O-70	0.9
1954	Pit-N	28	81	10	14	4	1	1	9	14	24	.173	.295	.284	52	-6	0	2	-1	1.000	3	O-24	-0.5
	Chi-N	51	72	5	11	0	0	0	5	8	15	.153	.237	.153	4	-10	0	0	0	.897	-4	O-24	-1.5
	Yr	79	153	15	25	4	1	1	14	22	39	.163	.269	.222	29	-16	0	2	-1	.966	-2	O-48	-2.0
Total	7	424	1183	129	307	52	12	19	162	94	133	.260	.314	.372	82	-32	1	7		.969	0	O-317	-4.8

■ HARRY RICE

Rice, Harry Francis b: 11/22/01, Ware Station, Ill. d: 1/1/71, Portland, Ore. BL/TR, 5'9", 185 lbs. Deb: 4/18/23

YEAR	TM/L	G	AB	R	H	2B	3B	HR	RBI	BB	SO	AVG	OBP	SLG	PRO+	BR/A	SB	CS	SBR	FA	FR	G/POS	TPR
1923	StL-A	4	3	0	0	0	0	0	0	0	0	.000	.000	.000	-95	-1	0	0	0	.000	0	H	-0.1
1924	StL-A	54	93	19	26	7	0	0	15	7	5	.280	.350	.355	77	-3	1	3	-2	.917	-0	3-15/2-4,1-2,S-2,O	-0.4
1925	StL-A	103	354	87	127	25	8	11	47	54	15	.359	.450	.568	149	28	8	7	-2	.984	6	O-85/1-3,C-1,2-1,3	2.4
1926	StL-A	148	578	86	181	27	10	9	59	63	40	.313	.384	.441	110	9	10	11	-4	.970	7	*O-133/3-8,2-4,S-2	0.3
1927	StL-A	137	520	90	149	26	9	7	68	50	21	.287	.351	.412	94	-5	5	4	-1	.938	12	*O-130/3-7	-0.2
1928	Det-A	131	510	87	154	21	12	6	81	44	27	.302	.360	.425	104	3	20	13	-2	.962	1	*O-129/3-2	-0.7
1929	Det-A	130	536	97	163	33	7	6	69	61	23	.304	.379	.425	106	6	6	10	-4	.960	6	*O-127/3-3	-0.1
1930	Det-A	37	128	16	39	6	0	2	24	19	8	.305	.403	.398	102	1	0	3	-2	.944	-0	O-35	-0.3
	NY-A	100	346	62	103	17	5	7	74	31	21	.298	.361	.436	106	3	3	3	-1	.969	8	O-87/1-6,3-1	0.4
	Yr	137	474	78	142	23	5	9	98	50	29	.300	.372	.426	105	4	3	6	-3	.964	7	*O-122/1-6,3-1	0.1
1931	Was-A	47	162	32	43	5	6	0	15	12	10	.265	.320	.370	81	-5	2	1	0	.968	-1	O-42	-0.8
1933	Cin-N	143	510	44	133	19	6	0	54	35	24	.261	.316	.322	84	-10	4			**.991**	3	*O-141/3-1	-1.6
Total	10	1034	3740	620	1118	186	63	48	506	376	194	.299	.368	.421	104	25	59	55		.966	39	O-911/3-38,12SC	-1.1

■ JIM RICE

Rice, James Edward b: 3/8/53, Anderson, S.C. BR/TR, 6'2", 205 lbs. Deb: 8/19/74 C

YEAR	TM/L	G	AB	R	H	2B	3B	HR	RBI	BB	SO	AVG	OBP	SLG	PRO+	BR/A	SB	CS	SBR	FA	FR	G/POS	TPR
1974	Bos-A	24	67	6	18	2	1	1	13	4	12	.269	.319	.373	92	-1	0	0	0	.800	-1	D-16/O-3	-0.2
1975	Bos-A	144	564	92	174	29	4	22	102	36	122	.309	.354	.491	126	17	10	5	0	1.000	-1	O-90,D-54	1.2
1976	Bos-A	153	581	75	164	25	8	25	85	28	123	.282	.320	.482	118	10	8	5	-1	.967	0	O-98,D-54	0.5
1977	Bos-A★	160	644	104	206	29	15	**39**	114	53	120	.320	.379	**.593**	143	36	5	4	-1	.956	1	*D-116,O-44	3.0
1978	Bos-A★	163	677	121	**213**	25	**15**	**46**	**139**	58	126	.315	.373	**.600**	153	**44**	7	5	-1	.989	10	*O-114,D-49	4.8
1979	Bos-A★	158	619	117	201	39	6	39	130	57	97	.325	.385	.596	152	43	9	4	0	.984	2	*O-125,D-33	3.7
1980	Bos-A†	124	504	81	148	22	6	24	86	30	87	.294	.338	.504	121	13	8	3	1	.988	7	*O-109,D-15	1.5
1981	Bos-A	108	451	51	128	18	1	17	62	34	76	.284	.338	.441	116	8	2	2	-1	.988	5	*O-108	0.9
1982	Bos-A	145	573	86	177	24	5	24	97	55	98	.309	.376	.494	129	23	0	1	-1	.969	-1	*O-145	1.8
1983	Bos-A★	155	626	90	191	34	1	**39**	**126**	52	102	.305	.364	.550	137	30	0	2	-1	.984	17	*O-151/D-4	4.1
1984	Bos-A★	159	657	98	184	25	7	28	122	44	102	.280	.326	.467	111	9	4	0	1	.989	12	*O-157/D-2	1.7
1985	Bos-A★	140	546	85	159	20	3	27	103	51	75	.291	.354	.487	122	16	2	0	1	.964	0	*O-130/D-7	1.2
1986	*Bos-A★	157	618	98	200	39	2	20	110	62	78	.324	.389	.490	137	32	0	1	-1	.977	17	*O-156/D-1	4.2
1987	Bos-A	108	404	66	112	14	0	13	62	45	77	.277	.360	.408	100	1	1	1	-0	.977	4	O-94,D-12	0.1
1988	*Bos-A	135	485	57	128	18	3	15	72	48	89	.264	.334	.406	102	1	1	1	-0	.968	-2	*D-112,O-19	-0.4
1989	Bos-A	56	209	22	49	10	2	3	28	13	39	.234	.283	.344	71	-8	1	0	0	.000	0	D-55	-0.9
Total	16	2089	8225	1249	2452	373	79	382	1451	670	1423	.298	.356	.502	127	275	58	34	-3	.980	71	*O-1543,D-530	27.2

■ LEN RICE

Rice, Leonard Oliver b: 9/2/18, Lead, S.Dak. d: 6/13/92, Sonora, Cal. BR/TR, 6', 175 lbs. Deb: 4/26/44

YEAR	TM/L	G	AB	R	H	2B	3B	HR	RBI	BB	SO	AVG	OBP	SLG	PRO+	BR/A	SB	CS	SBR	FA	FR	G/POS	TPR
1944	Cin-N	10	4	1	0	0	0	0	0	0	0	.000	.000	.000	-99	-1	0			1.000	1	/C-5	0.0
1945	Chi-N	32	99	10	23	3	0	0	7	5	8	.232	.269	.263	49	-7	2			.976	-1	C-29	-0.6
Total	2	42	103	11	23	3	0	0	7	5	8	.223	.259	.252	44	-8	2			.977	0	/C-34	-0.6

■ BOB RICE

Rice, Robert Turnbull b: 5/28/1899, Philadelphia, Pa. d: 2/20/86, Elizabethtown, Pa BR/TR, 5'10", 170 lbs. Deb: 9/1/26

YEAR	TM/L	G	AB	R	H	2B	3B	HR	RBI	BB	SO	AVG	OBP	SLG	PRO+	BR/A	SB	CS	SBR	FA	FR	G/POS	TPR
1926	Phi-N	19	54	3	8	0	1	0	10	3	4	.148	.193	.185	2	-7	0			.864	1	3-15/2-2,S-2	-0.6

■ LEE RICHARD
Richard, Lee Edward "Bee Bee" b: 9/18/48, Lafayette, La. BR/TR, 5'11", 165 lbs. Deb: 4/7/71

YEAR	TM/L	G	AB	R	H	2B	3B	HR	RBI	BB	SO	AVG	OBP	SLG	PRO+	BR/A	SB	CS	SBR	FA	FR	G/POS	TPR
1971	Chi-A	87	260	38	60	7	3	2	17	20	46	.231	.288	.304	66	-12	8	9	-3	.920	-0	S-68,O-16	-0.8
1972	Chi-A	11	29	5	7	0	0	0	1	0	7	.241	.241	.241	43	-2	1	0	0	1.000	-0	/O-6,S-1	-0.2
1974	Chi-A	32	67	5	11	1	0	0	1	5	8	.164	.222	.179	16	-7	0	0	0	.821	3	3-12/S-6,2-3,O-1,D	-0.4
1975	Chi-A	43	45	11	9	0	1	0	5	4	7	.200	.265	.244	44	-3	2	3	-1	1.000	6	3-12/S-9,2-5,D-5	0.2
1976	StL-N	66	91	12	16	4	2	0	5	4	9	.176	.211	.264	34	-8	1	0	0	.975	12	2-26,S-12/3-1	0.5
Total	5	239	492	71	103	12	6	2	29	33	77	.209	.260	.270	50	-32	12	12	-4	.923	20	/S-96,2-34,3-25,OD	-0.7

■ GENE RICHARDS
Richards, Eugene b: 9/29/53, Monticello, S.C. BL/TL, 6', 175 lbs. Deb: 4/6/77

YEAR	TM/L	G	AB	R	H	2B	3B	HR	RBI	BB	SO	AVG	OBP	SLG	PRO+	BR/A	SB	CS	SBR	FA	FR	G/POS	TPR
1977	SD-N	146	525	79	152	16	11	5	32	60	80	.290	.365	.390	114	11	56	12	10	.963	1	*O-109,1-32	1.6
1978	SD-N	154	555	90	171	26	12	4	45	64	80	.308	.384	.420	135	26	37	17	1	.965	-12	*O-124,1-26	0.9
1979	SD-N	150	545	77	152	17	9	4	41	47	62	.279	.345	.365	100	0	24	8	2	.973	4	*O-132	0.1
1980	SD-N	158	642	91	193	26	8	4	41	61	73	.301	.363	.385	116	14	61	16	9	.979	15	*O-156	3.3
1981	SD-N	104	393	47	113	14	**12**	3	42	53	44	.288	.374	.407	131	17	20	8	1	.975	3	*O-102	1.8
1982	SD-N	132	521	63	149	13	8	3	28	36	52	.286	.335	.359	99	-1	30	20	-3	.977	0	*O-103/1-25	-0.8
1983	SD-N	95	233	37	64	11	3	3	22	17	17	.275	.327	.386	100	-0	14	5	1	.980	-1	O-54	-0.2
1984	SF-N	87	135	18	34	4	0	0	4	18	28	.252	.340	.281	79	-3	5	3	-0	.940	-1	O-26	-0.5
Total	8	1026	3549	502	1028	127	63	26	255	356	436	.290	.358	.383	113	63	247	89	21	.972	10	O-806/1-83	6.2

■ FRED RICHARDS
Richards, Fred Charles "Fuzzy" b: 11/3/27, Warren, Ohio BL/TL, 6'1.5", 185 lbs. Deb: 9/15/51

YEAR	TM/L	G	AB	R	H	2B	3B	HR	RBI	BB	SO	AVG	OBP	SLG	PRO+	BR/A	SB	CS	SBR	FA	FR	G/POS	TPR
1951	Chi-N	10	27	1	8	2	0	0	4	2	3	.296	.345	.370	91	-0	0	0	0	1.000	1	/1-9	0.1

■ PAUL RICHARDS
Richards, Paul Rapier b: 11/21/08, Waxahachie, Tex. d: 5/4/86, Waxahachie, Tex. BR/TR, 6'1.5", 180 lbs. Deb: 4/17/32 M

YEAR	TM/L	G	AB	R	H	2B	3B	HR	RBI	BB	SO	AVG	OBP	SLG	PRO+	BR/A	SB	CS	SBR	FA	FR	G/POS	TPR
1932	Bro-N	3	8	0	0	0	0	0	0	0	2	.000	.000	.000	-99	-2	0			1.000	4	/C-3	0.1
1933	NY-N	51	87	4	17	3	0	0	10	3	12	.195	.222	.230	30	-8	0			.989	1	C-36	-0.6
1934	NY-N	42	75	10	12	1	0	0	3	13	8	.160	.284	.173	26	-7	0			1.000	2	C-37	-0.4
1935	NY-N	7	4	0	1	0	0	0	0	2	1	.250	.500	.250	110	0	0			1.000	1	/C-4	0.2
	Phi-A	85	257	31	63	10	1	4	29	24	12	.245	.310	.339	68	-12	0	0	0	.977	-3	C-79	-1.1
1943	Det-A	100	313	32	69	7	1	5	33	38	35	.220	.307	.297	71	-11	1	0	0	**.986**	21	*C-100	1.8
1944	Det-A	95	300	24	71	13	0	3	37	35	30	.237	.318	.310	76	-9	8	3	1	.979	16	C-90	1.3
1945	*Det-A	83	234	26	60	12	1	3	32	19	31	.256	.315	.355	88	-4	4	0	1	**.995**	12	C-83	1.4
1946	Det-A	57	139	13	28	5	2	0	11	23	18	.201	.315	.266	60	-7	2	0	1	.997	15	C-54	1.2
Total	8	523	1417	140	321	51	5	15	155	157	149	.227	.305	.301	68	-60	15	3		.987	69	C-486	3.9

■ RICHARDSON
Richardson b: Boston, Mass. 5'4", 136 lbs. Deb: 7/10/1884

YEAR	TM/L	G	AB	R	H	2B	3B	HR	RBI	BB	SO	AVG	OBP	SLG	PRO+	BR/A	SB	CS	SBR	FA	FR	G/POS	TPR
1884	CP-U	1	4	0	0	0	0	0		0		.000	.000	.000	-99	-1				.667	-1	/2-1	-0.2

■ HARDY RICHARDSON
Richardson, Abram Harding "Old True Blue"
b: 4/21/1855, Clarksboro, N.J. d: 1/14/31, Utica, N.Y. BR/TR, 5'9.5", 170 lbs. Deb: 5/1/1879

YEAR	TM/L	G	AB	R	H	2B	3B	HR	RBI	BB	SO	AVG	OBP	SLG	PRO+	BR/A	SB	CS	SBR	FA	FR	G/POS	TPR
1879	Buf-N	79	336	54	95	18	10	0	37	16	30	.283	.315	.396	130	10				.843	-6	*3-78/C-1	0.6
1880	Buf-N	83	343	48	89	18	8	0	17	14	37	.259	.289	.359	116	5				.848	-7	*3-81/C-5	0.1
1881	Buf-N	83	344	62	100	18	9	2	53	12	27	.291	.315	.413	129	11				.914	25	*O-79/2-5,S-1,3-1	3.1
1882	Buf-N	83	354	61	96	20	8	2	57	11	33	.271	.293	.390	115	5				.898	16	*2-83	2.1
1883	Buf-N	92	399	73	124	34	7	1	56	22	20	.311	.347	.439	134	16				.903	19	*2-92	3.1
1884	Buf-N	102	439	85	132	27	9	6	60	22	41	.301	.334	.444	138	18				.897	8	2-71,O-24/3-5,1-3	2.3
1885	Buf-N	96	426	90	136	19	11	6	44	20	22	.319	.350	.458	154	24				.905	13	2-50,O-48/S-1,P-1	3.4
1886	Det-N	125	538	125	**189**	27	11	**11**	61	46	27	.351	.402	.504	169	44	42			.899	10	O-80,2-42/P-4,S3	4.8
1887	*Det-N	120	543	131	178	25	18	8	94	31	40	.328	.366	.484	130	20	29			.941	17	2-64,O-59	3.2
1888	Det-N	58	266	60	77	18	2	6	32	17	23	.289	.335	.440	145	13	13			.925	4	2-58	1.9
1889	Bos-N	132	536	122	163	33	10	6	79	48	44	.304	.367	.437	117	10	47			.924	13	2-86,O-46	2.3
1890	Bos-P	130	555	126	181	26	14	13	**146**	52	46	.326	.384	.494	125	16	42			.950	2	*O-124/S-6,1-1	1.1
1891	Bos-a	74	278	45	71	9	4	7	52	40	26	.255	.351	.392	114	5	16			.955	-0	O-60/3-9,S-4,1-3	0.3
1892	Was-N	10	37	2	4	0	0	0	0	5	3	.108	.214	.108	-2	-4	2			.941	-0	/O-7,3-2,2-1	-0.4
	NY-N	64	248	36	53	11	5	2	34	21	26	.214	.278	.323	83	-6	14			.931	-1	2-33,O-17/1-9,S-6	-0.6
	Yr	74	285	38	57	11	5	2	34	26	29	.200	.269	.295	72	-10	16			.933	-1	2-34,O-24/1-9,S3	-1.0
Total	14	1331	5642	1120	1688	303	126	70	822	377	445	.299	.344	.435	130	186	205			.915	113	2-585,O-544,3/S1CP	27.3

■ NOLEN RICHARDSON
Richardson, Clifford Nolen b: 1/18/03, Chattanooga, Tenn. d: 9/25/51, Athens, Ga. BR/TR, 6'1.5", 170 lbs. Deb: 4/16/29

YEAR	TM/L	G	AB	R	H	2B	3B	HR	RBI	BB	SO	AVG	OBP	SLG	PRO+	BR/A	SB	CS	SBR	FA	FR	G/POS	TPR
1929	Det-A	13	21	2	4	0	0	0	2	2	1	.190	.261	.190	18	-3	1	1	-0	.839	-4	S-13	-0.6
1931	Det-A	38	148	13	40	9	2	0	16	6	3	.270	.299	.358	70	-7	2	1	0	.946	-2	3-38	-0.6
1932	Det-A	69	155	13	34	5	2	0	12	9	13	.219	.262	.277	38	-14	5	2	0	.986	11	3-65/S-4	0.0
1935	NY-A	12	46	3	10	1	1	0	5	3	1	.217	.265	.283	44	-4	0	0	0	.922	-6	S-12	-0.9
1938	Cin-N	35	100	8	29	4	0	0	10	3	4	.290	.311	.330	78	-3	0			.966	-1	S-35	-0.2
1939	Cin-N	1	3	0	0	0	0	0	0	0	0	.000	.000	.000	-99	-1	0			1.000	1	/S-1	0.0
Total	6	168	473	39	117	19	5	0	45	23	22	.247	.282	.309	55	-31	8	4		.969	-2	3-103/S-65	-2.3

■ DANNY RICHARDSON
Richardson, Daniel b: 1/25/1863, Elmira, N.Y. d: 9/12/26, New York, N.Y. BR/TR, 5'8", 165 lbs. Deb: 5/22/1884 M

YEAR	TM/L	G	AB	R	H	2B	3B	HR	RBI	BB	SO	AVG	OBP	SLG	PRO+	BR/A	SB	CS	SBR	FA	FR	G/POS	TPR
1884	NY-N	74	277	36	70	8	1	1	27	16	17	.253	.294	.300	85	-5				.907	2	O-55,S-19	-0.4
1885	NY-N	49	198	26	52	9	3	0	25	10	14	.263	.298	.338	107	1				.950	-1	O-22,3-21/P-9	0.1
1886	NY-N	68	237	43	55	9	1	1	27	17	21	.232	.283	.291	74	-7	12			.953	-0	O-64/P-5,S-1,3-1,2	-0.9
1887	NY-N	122	450	79	125	19	10	3	62	36	25	.278	.337	.384	105	4	41			.928	15	*2-108,3-14/P-1	1.8
1888	*NY-N	135	561	82	127	16	7	8	61	15	35	.226	.248	.323	82	-12	35			**.942**	9	*2-135	0.2
1889	*NY-N	125	497	88	139	22	8	7	100	46	37	.280	.342	.398	106	3	32			.934	13	*2-125	2.0
1890	NY-P	123	528	102	135	12	9	4	80	37	19	.256	.307	.335	66	-29	37			.900	25	S-68,2-56	0.3
1891	NY-N	123	516	85	139	18	5	4	51	33	27	.269	.313	.347	96	-4	28			.952	**49**	*2-114/S-9	**4.5**
1892	Was-N	142	551	48	132	13	4	3	58	25	45	.240	.274	.294	74	-19	25			.931	**58**	S-93,2-49/3-1,M	4.0
1893	Bro-N	54	206	36	46	6	2	0	27	13	18	.223	.279	.272	49	-15	7			.949	-17	2-46/3-5,S-3	-2.6
1894	Lou-N	116	430	51	109	17	2	1	40	35	31	.253	.317	.309	55	-31	8			.916	3	*S-107,2-10	-1.7
Total	11	1131	4451	676	1129	149	52	32	558	283	289	.254	.301	.332	82	-113	225			.940	156	2-644,S-300,O/3P	7.3

■ JEFF RICHARDSON
Richardson, Jeffrey Scott b: 8/26/65, Grand Island, Neb. BR/TR, 6'2", 175 lbs. Deb: 7/14/89

YEAR	TM/L	G	AB	R	H	2B	3B	HR	RBI	BB	SO	AVG	OBP	SLG	PRO+	BR/A	SB	CS	SBR	FA	FR	G/POS	TPR
1989	Cin-N	53	125	10	21	4	0	2	11	10	23	.168	.235	.248	37	-10	1	0	0	.969	-2	S-39/3-8	-1.0
1991	Pit-N	6	4	0	1	0	0	0	0	0	3	.250	.250	.250	42	-0	0	0	0	.000	-1	/3-3,S-2	-0.1
1993	Bos-A	15	24	3	5	2	0	0	2	1	3	.208	.240	.292	40	-2	0	0	0	1.000	6	/2-8,S-5,3-1,D-2	0.4
Total	3	74	153	13	27	6	0	2	13	11	29	.176	.236	.255	38	-13	1	0	0	.971	3	/S-46,3-12,2-8,D-2	-0.7

■ KEN RICHARDSON
Richardson, Kenneth Franklin b: 5/2/15, Orleans, Ind. d: 12/7/87, Woodland Hills, Cal BR/TR, 5'10.5", 187 lbs. Deb: 4/14/42

YEAR	TM/L	G	AB	R	H	2B	3B	HR	RBI	BB	SO	AVG	OBP	SLG	PRO+	BR/A	SB	CS	SBR	FA	FR	G/POS	TPR
1942	Phi-A	6	15	1	1	0	0	0	0	2	0	.067	.176	.067	-30	-3	0	0	0	1.000	0	/O-3,1-1,3-1	-0.3
1946	Phi-N	6	20	1	3	1	0	0	2	0	2	.150	.150	.200	-1	-3	0			.939	-0	/2-6	-0.3
Total	2	12	35	2	4	1	0	0	2	2	2	.114	.162	.143	-14	-5	0	0		.939	-0	/2-6,O-3,3-1,1-1	-0.6

■ BOBBY RICHARDSON
Richardson, Robert Clinton b: 8/19/35, Sumter, S.C. BR/TR, 5'9", 170 lbs. Deb: 8/5/55

YEAR	TM/L	G	AB	R	H	2B	3B	HR	RBI	BB	SO	AVG	OBP	SLG	PRO+	BR/A	SB	CS	SBR	FA	FR	G/POS	TPR
1955	NY-A	11	26	2	4	0	0	0	3	2	0	.154	.214	.154	0	-4	1	1	-0	.864	-5	/2-6,S-4	-0.9
1956	NY-A	5	7	1	1	0	0	0	0	0	1	.143	.143	.143	-25	-1	0	0	0	1.000	2	/2-5	0.1
1957	*NY-A☆	97	305	36	78	11	1	0	19	9	26	.256	.277	.298	58	-18	1	3	-2	.979	5	2-93	-0.8
1958	*NY-A	73	182	18	45	6	2	0	14	8	5	.247	.279	.302	62	-10	1	3	-2	.973	8	2-51,3-13/S-2	0.0
1959	NY-A☆	134	469	53	141	18	6	2	33	26	20	.301	.337	.377	99	-1	5	5	-2	.970	2	*2-109,S-14,3-12	0.9
1960	*NY-A	150	460	45	116	12	3	1	26	35	19	.252	.305	.298	68	-21	6	6	-2	.973	-4	*2-141,3-11	-1.5
1961	*NY-A	162	662	80	173	17	5	3	49	30	23	.261	.295	.316	67	-32	9	7	-2	.978	-9	*2-161	-2.6
1962	*NY-A★	161	692	99	**209**	38	5	8	59	37	24	.302	.338	.406	103	1	11	9	-2	.982	-3	*2-161	1.3
1963	*NY-A★	151	630	72	167	20	6	3	48	25	22	.265	.295	.330	76	-21	15	1	4	.984	7	*2-150	0.5

YEAR	TM/L	G	AB	R	H	2B	3B	HR	RBI	BB	SO	AVG	OBP	SLG	PRO+	BR/A	SB	CS	SBR	FA	FR	G/POS	TPR
1964	*NY-A★	159	679	90	181	25	4	4	50	28	36	.267	.296	.333	73	-25	11	2	2	.982	-14	*2-157/S-1	-2.4
1965	NY-A★	160	664	76	164	28	2	6	47	37	39	.247	.288	.322	74	-24	7	5	-1	.981	-3	*2-158	-1.4
1966	NY-A★	149	610	71	153	21	3	7	42	25	28	.251	.281	.330	78	-19	6	6	-2	.980	3	*2-147/3-2	-0.8
Total	12	1412	5386	643	1432	196	37	34	390	262	243	.266	.301	.335	77	-173	73	48	-7	.979	-11	*2-1339/3-38,S-21	-7.6
■ TOM RICHARDSON Richardson, Thomas Mitchell b: 8/7/1883, Louisville, Ill. d: 11/15/39, Onawa, Iowa BR/TR, 6', 190 lbs. Deb: 8/2/17																							
1917	StL-A	1	1	0	0	0	0	0	0	0	0	.000	.000	.000	-99	-0	0			.000	0	H	0.0
■ BILL RICHARDSON Richardson, William Henry b: 9/24/1878, Salem, Ind. d: 11/6/49, Sullivan, Ind. BR/TR, 5'11", 200 lbs. Deb: 9/20/01																							
1901	StL-N	15	52	7	11	2	0	2	7	6		.212	.293	.365	95	-0	1			.981	-1	1-15	-0.2
■ MIKE RICHARDT Richardt, Michael Anthony b: 5/24/58, Los Angeles, Cal. BR/TR, 6', 170 lbs. Deb: 8/30/80																							
1980	Tex-A	22	71	2	16	2	0	0	8	1	7	.225	.236	.254	35	-6	0	0	0	.978	-1	2-20/D-1	-0.6
1982	Tex-A	119	402	34	97	10	0	3	43	23	42	.241	.284	.289	61	-22	9	1	2	.988	4	2-98,D-15/O-6	-1.1
1983	Tex-A	22	83	9	13	2	1	1	7	2	11	.157	.176	.241	14	-10	2	1	0	.992	2	2-20	-0.7
1984	Tex-A	6	9	0	1	0	0	0	0	1	1	.111	.200	.111	-11	-1	0	1	-1	1.000	1	/2-4	-0.1
	Hou-N	16	15	1	4	1	0	0	2	0	1	.267	.267	.333	73	-1	0	0	0	.000	0	H	-0.1
Total	4	185	580	46	131	15	1	4	60	27	62	.226	.262	.276	50	-40	11	3	2	.988	6	2-142/D-16,O-6	-2.6
■ LANCE RICHBOURG Richbourg, Lance Clayton b: 12/18/1897, DeFuniak Springs, Fla. d: 9/10/75, Crestview, Fla. BL/TR, 5'10.5", 160 lbs. Deb: 7/4/21																							
1921	Phi-N	10	5	2	1	1	0	0	0	0	3	.200	.200	.400	51	-0	1	1	-0	1.000	2	/2-4	0.1
1924	Was-A	15	32	3	9	2	1	0	1	2	0	.281	.324	.406	90	-1	0	0	0	1.000	1	/O-7	0.0
1927	Bos-N	115	450	57	139	12	9	2	34	22	30	.309	.342	.389	104	1	24			.953	-4	*O-110	-1.0
1928	Bos-N	148	612	105	206	26	12	2	52	62	39	.337	.399	.428	123	22	11			.972	7	*O-148	1.8
1929	Bos-N	139	557	76	170	24	13	3	56	42	26	.305	.355	.411	93	-6	7			.971	5	*O-134	-1.0
1930	Bos-N	130	529	81	161	23	8	3	54	19	31	.304	.331	.395	77	-20	13			.971	-3	*O-128	-2.8
1931	Bos-N	97	286	32	82	11	6	2	29	19	14	.287	.331	.388	96	-2	9			.981	-3	O-71	-1.0
1932	Chi-N	44	148	22	38	2	2	1	21	8	4	.257	.295	.318	65	-7	0			.986	-1	O-33	-1.0
Total	8	698	2619	378	806	101	51	13	247	174	147	.308	.352	.400	97	-14	65	1		.970	4	O-631/2-4	-4.9
■ ROB RICHIE Richie, Robert Eugene b: 9/5/65, Reno, Nev. BL/TR, 6'2", 190 lbs. Deb: 8/19/89																							
1989	Det-A	19	49	6	13	4	2	1	10	5	10	.265	.333	.490	132	2	0	1	-1	.917	-1	O-13/D-4	0.0
■ DON RICHMOND Richmond, Donald Lester b: 10/27/19, Gillett, Pa. d: 5/24/81, Elmira, N.Y. BL/TR, 6'1", 175 lbs. Deb: 9/16/41																							
1941	Phi-A	9	35	3	7	1	1	0	5	0	1	.200	.200	.286	28	-4	0	2	-1	.957	-2	/3-9	-0.7
1946	Phi-A	16	62	3	18	3	0	1	9	0	10	.290	.290	.387	89	-1	1	0	0	.940	-3	3-16	-0.4
1947	Phi-A	19	21	2	4	1	1	0	4	3	3	.190	.292	.333	72	-1	0	0	0	.500	-3	/3-4,2-1	-0.4
1951	StL-N	12	34	3	3	1	0	1	4	3	3	.088	.162	.206	-2	-5	0	1	-1	1.000	5	3-11	-0.1
Total	4	56	152	11	32	6	2	2	22	6	17	.211	.241	.316	51	-11	1	3	-2	.957	-4	/3-40,2-1	-1.6
■ LEE RICHMOND Richmond, J Lee b: 5/5/1857, Sheffield, Ohio d: 10/1/29, Toledo, Ohio TL, 5'10", 155 lbs. Deb: 9/27/1879																							
1879	Bos-N	1	6	0	2	0	0	0	1	0	1	.333	.333	.333	118	0				1.000	0	/P-1	0.0
1880	Wor-N	77	309	44	70	8	4	0	34	9	32	.227	.248	.278	72	-10				.827	-13	*P-74,O-20	-0.7
1881	Wor-N	61	252	31	63	5	1	0	28	10	10	.250	.279	.278	71	-8				.937	-1	P-53,O-11	-0.4
1882	Wor-N	55	228	50	64	8	9	2	28	9	11	.281	.308	.421	128	7				.889	2	P-48,O-11	0.0
1883	Pro-N	49	194	41	55	8	6	1	19	15	19	.284	.335	.402	120	5				.714	-10	O-41,P-12	-0.6
1886	Cin-a	8	29	3	8	0	0	0	3	3		.276	.344	.276	92	-0	0			.400	-4	/O-7,P-3	-0.3
Total	6	251	1018	169	262	29	20	3	113	46	73	.257	.289	.334	94	-7	0			.886	-26	P-191/O-90	-2.0
■ JOHN RICHMOND Richmond, John H. b: 1854, Pennsylvania TR, 5'9", 170 lbs. Deb: 4/22/1875																							
1875	Ath-n	29	125	29	25	2	0	0	12	1	4	.200	.206	.216	42	-8	1	0	0	.814	-2	2-17,O-11/C-3	-0.9
1879	Syr-N	62	254	31	54	8	4	1	23	4	24	.213	.225	.287	76	-6				.874	-7	O-35,S-28/C-2	-1.2
1880	Bos-N	32	129	12	32	3	1	0	9	2	18	.248	.260	.287	88	-2				.844	-12	S-31/O-1	-1.1
1881	Bos-N	27	98	13	27	2	2	1	12	6	7	.276	.317	.367	120	2				.969	-0	O-25/S-2	0.2
1882	Cle-N	41	140	12	24	6	2	0	11	11	27	.171	.232	.243	54	-7				.917	3	O-41	-0.4
	Phi-a	18	65	8	12	2	2	0	4	11		.185	.303	.277	87	-1				.892	0	O-18	-0.1
1883	Col-a	92	385	63	109	7	8	0		25		.283	.327	.343	126	13				**.877**	26	*S-91/O-2	**3.5**
1884	Col-a	105	398	57	100	13	7	3		35		.251	.317	.342	125	13				.866	-9	*S-105	0.4
1885	Pit-a	34	131	14	27	2	2	0	12	8		.206	.262	.252	64	-5				.849	-10	S-23,O-11	-1.3
Total	7	411	1600	210	385	43	28	5	71	102	76	.241	.288	.312	101	8				.866	-10	S-280,O-133/C-2	-0.0
■ AL RICHTER Richter, Allen Gordon b: 2/7/27, Norfolk, Va. BR/TR, 5'11", 165 lbs. Deb: 9/23/51																							
1951	Bos-A	5	11	1	1	0	0	0	0	3	0	.091	.286	.091	5	-1	0	0	0	1.000	2	/S-3	0.1
1953	Bos-A	1	0	0	0	0	0	0	0	0	0	—	—	—	—	0	0	0	0	1.000	0	/S-1	0.0
Total	2	6	11	1	1	0	0	0	0	3	0	.091	.286	.091	5	-1	0	0	0	1.000	3	/S-4	0.1
■ JOHN RICHTER Richter, John M. b: 2/8/1873, Louisville, Ky. d: 10/4/27, Louisville, Ky. 6', 178 lbs. Deb: 10/6/1898																							
1898	Lou-N	3	13	1	2	0	0	0	0	0		.154	.154	.154	-12	-2	0			.929	0	/3-3	-0.1
■ JOE RICKERT Rickert, Joseph Francis "Diamond Joe" b: 12/12/1876, London, Ohio d: 10/15/43, Springfield, Ohio BR/TR, 5'10.5", 165 lbs. Deb: 10/12/1898																							
1898	Pit-N	2	6	0	1	0	0	0	0	0		.167	.167	.167	-5	-1	0			1.000	1	/O-2	0.0
1901	Bos-N	13	60	6	10	1	2	0	1	3		.167	.206	.250	29	-6	1			.974	2	O-13	-0.4
Total	2	15	66	6	11	1	2	0	1	3		.167	.203	.242	27	-6	1			.979	3	/O-15	-0.4
■ MARV RICKERT Rickert, Marvin August "Twitch" b: 1/8/21, Longbranch, Wash. d: 6/3/78, Oakville, Wash. BL/TR, 6'2", 195 lbs. Deb: 9/10/42																							
1942	Chi-N	8	26	5	7	0	0	0	1	1	5	.269	.296	.269	69	-1	0			1.000	1	/O-6	0.0
1946	Chi-N	111	392	44	103	18	3	7	47	28	54	.263	.314	.378	98	-3	3			.972	-6	*O-104	-1.4
1947	Chi-N	71	137	7	20	0	0	2	15	15	17	.146	.230	.190	13	-17	0			.982	-1	O-30/1-7	-2.0
1948	Cin-N	8	6	0	1	0	0	0	0	0	0	.167	.167	.167	-10	-1	0			.000	0	H	-0.1
	*Bos-N	3	13	1	3	0	1	0	2	0	1	.231	.286	.385	81	-0	0			1.000	1	/O-3	0.1
	Yr	11	19	1	4	0	1	0	2	0	1	.211	.250	.316	54	-1	0			1.000	1	/O-3	0.0
1949	Bos-N	100	277	44	81	18	3	6	49	23	38	.292	.347	.444	117	6	1			.981	-0	O-75,1-12	0.2
1950	Pit-N	17	20	0	3	0	0	0	4	0	4	.150	.150	.150	-20	-3	0			.000	-1	/O-3	-0.5
	Chi-A	84	278	38	66	9	2	4	27	21	42	.237	.291	.327	60	-18	0	1	-1	.968	-6	O-78/1-1	-2.6
Total	6	402	1149	139	284	45	9	19	145	88	161	.247	.302	.352	79	-38	4	1		.976	-12	O-299/1-20	-6.3
■ DAVE RICKETTS Ricketts, David William b: 7/12/35, Pottstown, Pa. BB/TR, 6'2", 195 lbs. Deb: 9/25/63 FC																							
1963	StL-N	3	8	0	2	0	0	0	0	0	2	.250	.250	.250	41	-1	0	0	0	1.000	-0	/C-3	-0.1
1965	StL-N	11	29	1	7	0	0	0	0	1	3	.241	.267	.241	40	-2	0	0	0	.977	-2	C-11	-0.4
1967	*StL-N	52	99	11	27	8	0	1	14	4	7	.273	.301	.384	96	-1	0	0	0	1.000	-0	C-21	0.0
1968	*StL-N	20	22	1	3	0	0	0	1	0	3	.136	.136	.136	-18	-3	0	0	0	1.000	-0	/C-1	-0.4
1969	StL-N	30	44	2	12	1	0	0	5	4	5	.273	.333	.295	77	-1	0	0	0	.983	1	/C-8	0.0
1970	Pit-N	14	11	0	2	0	0	0	0	1	3	.182	.250	.182	18	-1	0	0	0	.909	1	/C-7	-0.1
Total	6	130	213	15	53	9	0	1	20	10	23	.249	.283	.305	67	-9	0	0	0	.988	-1	/C-51	-1.0
■ BRANCH RICKEY Rickey, Wesley Branch "The Mahatma" b: 12/20/1881, Flat, Ohio d: 12/9/65, Columbia, Mo. BL/TR, 5'9", 175 lbs. Deb: 6/16/05 MH																							
1905	StL-A	1	3	0	0	0	0	0	0	0		.000	.000	.000	-99	-1	0			1.000	-0	/C-1	-0.1
1906	StL-A	65	201	22	57	7	3	3	24	16		.284	.345	.393	137	8	4			.954	-8	C-55/O-1	0.7
1907	NY-A	52	137	16	25	1	3	0	15	11		.182	.253	.234	51	-7	4			.846	-5	O-22,C-11/1-9	-1.4
1914	StL-A	2	2	0	0	0	0	0	0	0	1	.000	.000	.000	-99	-0	0			.000	0	HM	-0.1
Total	4	120	343	38	82	8	6	3	39	27	1	.239	.304	.324	97	-0	8			.940	-13	/C-67,O-23,1-9	-0.9

YEAR	TM/L	G	AB	R	H	2B	3B	HR	RBI	BB	SO	AVG	OBP	SLG	PRO+	BR/A	SB	CS	SBR	FA	FR	G/POS	TPR

■ CHRIS RICKLEY — Rickley, Christian b: 10/7/1859, Philadelphia, Pa. d: 10/25/11, Philadelphia, Pa. 5'8", 160 lbs. Deb: 6/9/1884

| 1884 | Phi-U | 6 | 25 | 5 | 5 | 2 | 0 | 0 | | | 2 | .200 | .259 | .280 | 68 | -2 | | | | .757 | 0 | /S-6 | -0.1 |

■ JOHN RICKS — Ricks, John Deb: 9/21/1891

1891	StL-a	5	18	3	3	0	0	0	0	0	2	.167	.167	.167	-4	-3	0			.810	-1	/3-5	-0.3
1894	StL-N	1	1	0	0	0	0	0	0	0	0	.000	.000	.000	-99	-0	0			.250	-1	/3-1	-0.1
Total	2	6	19	3	3	0	0	0	0	0	2	.158	.158	.158	-9	-3	0			.720	-2	/3-6	-0.4

■ FRED RICO — Rico, Alfredo (Cruz) b: 7/4/44, Jerome, Ariz. BR/TR, 5'10", 180 lbs. Deb: 9/1/69

| 1969 | KC-A | 12 | 26 | 4 | 6 | 2 | 0 | 0 | 2 | 9 | 10 | .231 | .429 | .308 | 108 | 1 | 0 | 1 | -1 | 1.000 | 4 | /O-9,3-1 | 0.4 |

■ ART RICO — Rico, Arthur Raymond b: 7/23/1896, Roxbury, Mass. d: 1/3/19, Boston, Mass. BR/TR, 5'9.5", 185 lbs. Deb: 7/31/16

1916	Bos-N	4	4	0	0	0	0	0	0	0	0	.000	.000	.000	-99	-1	0			1.000	-0	/C-4	-0.1
1917	Bos-N	13	14	1	4	1	0	0	2	0	2	.286	.286	.357	102	-0	0			.950	-2	C-11,O-2	-0.1
Total	2	17	18	1	4	1	0	0	2	0	2	.222	.222	.278	56	-1	0			.962	-2	/C-15,O-2	-0.2

■ HARRY RICONDA — Riconda, Henry Paul b: 3/17/1897, New York, N.Y. d: 11/15/58, Mahopac, N.Y. BR/TR, 5'10", 175 lbs. Deb: 4/19/23

1923	Phi-A	55	175	23	46	11	4	0	12	12	18	.263	.317	.371	80	-6	4	2	0	.911	4	3-47/S-2	0.2
1924	Phi-A	83	281	34	71	16	3	1	21	27	43	.253	.323	.342	71	-13	3	4	-2	.927	1	3-73/S-2	-0.7
1926	Bos-N	4	12	1	2	0	0	0	0	2	2	.167	.286	.167	27	-1	0			.818	-1	/3-4	-0.2
1928	Bro-N	92	281	22	63	15	4	3	35	20	28	.224	.285	.338	63	-16	6			.957	3	2-53,3-21,S-16	-0.9
1929	Pit-N	8	15	3	7	2	0	0	2	0	0	.467	.467	.600	158	1	0			.840	-0	/S-4	0.1
1930	Cin-N	1	1	0	0	0	0	0	0	0	0	.000	.000	.000	-99	-0	0			.000	0	H	0.0
Total	6	243	765	83	189	44	11	4	70	61	91	.247	.309	.349	71	-34	13	6		.922	7	3-145/2-53,S-24	-1.5

■ JOHN RIDDLE — Riddle, John H. b: 2/1864, Pennsylvania BR/TR, Deb: 9/18/1889

1889	Was-N	11	37	3	8	3	0	0	3	2	8	.216	.256	.297	58	-2	0			.841	1	/C-9,O-2	-0.1
1890	Phi-a	27	85	7	7	0	1	0	2	17		.082	.243	.106	3	-10	4			.914	-2	C-13,O-12/2-2,3-1	-1.0
Total	2	38	122	10	15	3	1	0	5	19	8	.123	.246	.164	20	-12	4			.880	-2	/C-22,O-14,2-2,3-1	-1.1

■ JOHNNY RIDDLE — Riddle, John Ludy "Mutt" b: 10/3/05, Clinton, S.C. BR/TR, 5'11", 190 lbs. Deb: 4/17/30 FC

1930	Chi-A	25	58	7	14	3	1	4	3	6		.241	.290	.328	58	-4	0	0	0	1.000	-3	C-25	-0.4
1937	Was-A	8	26	2	7	0	0	0	3	0	2	.269	.296	.269	46	-2	0	0	0	.971	0	/C-8	-0.1
	Bos-N	3	3	0	0	0	0	0	0	0	0	.000	.250	.000	-29	-1	0			1.000	1	/C-2	0.0
1938	Bos-N	19	57	6	16	1	0	0	2	4	2	.281	.328	.298	81	-1	0			.951	4	C-19	0.3
1941	Cin-N	10	10	2	3	0	0	0	0	0	0	.300	.300	.300	69	-0	0			1.000	1	C-10	0.1
1944	Cin-N	1	0	0	0	0	0	0	0	0	0	—	—	—	—	0	0			.000	0	/C-1	0.0
1945	Cin-N	23	45	0	8	0	0	0	2	4	6	.178	.245	.178	23	-5	0			1.000	4	C-23	-0.1
1948	Pit-N	10	15	1	3	0	0	0	0	1	2	.200	.250	.200	23	-2	0			1.000	0	C-10	-0.1
Total	7	98	214	18	51	4	1	0	11	13	19	.238	.288	.266	51	-15	0	0		.983	7	/C-98	-0.3

■ HANK RIEBE — Riebe, Harvey Donald b: 10/10/21, Cleveland, Ohio BR/TR, 5'9.5", 175 lbs. Deb: 8/26/42

1942	Det-A	11	35	1	11	2	0	0	2	0	6	.314	.314	.371	85	-1	0	0	0	1.000	-1	C-11	-0.1
1947	Det-A	8	7	0	0	0	0	0	2	0	2	.000	.000	.000	-97	-2	0	0	0	1.000	-0	C-3	-0.2
1948	Det-A	25	62	0	12	0	0	0	5	3	5	.194	.231	.194	13	-8	0	1	-1	1.000	0	C-24	-0.7
1949	Det-A	17	33	1	6	2	0	0	2	0	5	.182	.182	.242	12	-4	1	0	0	.960	-2	C-11	-0.5
Total	4	61	137	2	29	4	0	0	11	3	18	.212	.229	.241	26	-15	1	1	0	.994	-3	/C-49	-1.5

■ NIKCO RIESGO — Riesgo, Damon Nikco b: 1/11/67, Long Beach, Cal. BR/TR, 6'2", 185 lbs. Deb: 4/20/91

| 1991 | Mon-N | 4 | 7 | 1 | 1 | 0 | 0 | 0 | 0 | 3 | 1 | .143 | .400 | .143 | 60 | -0 | 0 | 0 | 0 | .500 | -0 | /O-2 | 0.0 |

■ JOE RIGGERT — Riggert, Joseph Aloysius b: 12/11/1886, Janesville, Wis. d: 12/10/73, Kansas City, Mo. BR/TR, 5'9.5", 170 lbs. Deb: 5/12/11

1911	Bos-A	50	146	19	31	4	4	2	13	12		.212	.290	.336	75	-5	5			.929	-4	O-39	-1.1
1914	Bro-N	27	83	6	16	1	3	2	6	4	20	.193	.230	.349	70	-4	2			.972	-1	O-20	-0.5
	StL-N	34	89	9	19	5	2	0	8	5	14	.213	.255	.315	70	-4	4			.961	-3	O-30	-0.9
	Yr	61	172	15	35	6	5	2	14	9	34	.203	.243	.331	70	-7	6			.966	-4	O-50	-1.4
1919	Bos-N	63	240	34	68	8	5	4	17	25	30	.283	.356	.408	135	10	9			.950	2	O-61	0.9
Total	3	174	558	68	134	18	14	8	44	46	64	.240	.305	.366	98	-2	20			.950	-6	O-150	-1.6

■ ADAM RIGGS — Riggs, Adam David b: 10/4/72, Steubenville, O. BR/TR, 6', 195 lbs. Deb: 8/7/97

| 1997 | LA-N | 9 | 20 | 3 | 4 | 1 | 0 | 0 | 1 | 4 | 3 | .200 | .333 | .250 | 60 | -1 | 1 | 0 | 0 | 1.000 | 0 | /2-8 | 0.0 |

■ LEW RIGGS — Riggs, Lewis Sidney b: 4/22/10, Mebane, N.C. d: 8/12/75, Durham, N.C. BL/TR, 6', 175 lbs. Deb: 4/28/34

1934	StL-N	2	1	0	0	0	0	0	0	0	1	.000	.000	.000	-94	-0	0			.000	0	H	0.0
1935	Cin-N	142	532	73	148	26	8	5	46	43	32	.278	.334	.385	96	-3	8			.928	3	*3-135	1.0
1936	Cin-N★	141	538	69	138	20	12	6	57	38	33	.257	.314	.372	90	-9	5			.968	12	*3-140	0.8
1937	Cin-N	122	384	43	93	17	5	6	45	24	17	.242	.289	.359	79	-13	4			.941	20	*3-100/2-4,S-1	1.0
1938	Cin-N	142	531	53	134	21	13	2	55	40	28	.252	.311	.352	84	-12	3			.947	-1	*3-140	-1.1
1939	Cin-N	22	38	5	6	1	0	0	1	5	4	.158	.256	.184	20	-4	1			.957	-1	3-11	-0.5
1940	*Cin-N	41	72	8	21	7	1	1	9	2	4	.292	.311	.458	109	0	0			.943	2	3-11	0.2
1941	*Bro-N	77	197	27	60	13	4	5	36	16	12	.305	.357	.487	131	7	1			.932	-7	3-43/1-1,2-1	0.1
1942	Bro-N	70	180	20	50	5	0	3	22	13	9	.278	.333	.356	100	-0	0			.944	-6	3-46/1-1	-0.6
1946	Bro-N	1	4	0	0	0	0	0	0	0	0	.000	.000	.000	-99	-1	0			1.000	0	/3-1	-0.1
Total	10	760	2477	298	650	110	43	28	271	181	140	.262	.317	.375	91	-35	22			.945	27	3-627/2-5,1-2,S-1	0.8

■ TOPPER RIGNEY — Rigney, Emory Elmo b: 1/7/1897, Groveton, Tex. d: 6/6/72, San Antonio, Tex. BR/TR, 5'9", 150 lbs. Deb: 4/12/22

1922	Det-A	155	536	68	161	17	7	2	63	68	44	.300	.380	.369	99	2	17	8	0	.938	-13	*S-155	0.5
1923	Det-A	129	470	63	148	24	11	3	74	55	35	.315	.389	.419	115	11	7	5	-1	.944	-16	*S-129	0.7
1924	Det-A	147	499	81	144	29	9	4	94	102	39	.289	.410	.407	113	14	11	11	-3	.967	10	*S-146	3.4
1925	Det-A	62	146	21	36	5	2	2	18	21	15	.247	.341	.349	77	-5	2	2	-1	.934	-14	S-51/3-4	-1.5
1926	Bos-A	148	525	71	142	32	6	4	53	108	31	.270	.395	.377	105	9	6	8	-3	.969	20	*S-146	3.9
1927	Bos-A	8	18	0	2	1	0	0	0	1	2	.111	.158	.167	-16	-3	0	0	0	1.000	-1	/3-4,S-1	-0.4
	Was-A	45	132	20	36	5	4	0	13	22	10	.273	.381	.371	97	0	1	2	-1	.929	-3	S-32/3-6	0.0
	Yr	53	150	20	38	6	4	0	13	23	12	.253	.356	.347	84	-3	1	2	-1	.932	-4	S-33,3-10	-0.4
Total	6	694	2326	324	669	113	39	13	315	377	176	.288	.388	.387	104	28	44	36	-8	.953	-18	S-660/3-14	6.6

■ BILL RIGNEY — Rigney, William Joseph "Specs" or "The Cricket" b: 1/29/18, Alameda, Cal. BR/TR, 6'1", 178 lbs. Deb: 4/16/46 MC

1946	NY-N	110	360	38	85	9	1	3	31	36	29	.236	.307	.292	70	-14	9			.965	3	3-73,S-33	-0.9
1947	NY-N	130	531	84	142	24	3	17	59	51	54	.267	.337	.420	99	-1	7			.974	-7	2-72,3-41,S-24	0.5
1948	NY-N★	113	424	72	112	17	3	10	43	47	54	.264	.342	.389	97	-2	4			.967	-11	*2-105/S-7	-0.7
1949	NY-N	122	389	53	108	19	6	6	47	47	38	.278	.356	.404	103	2	3			.928	-17	S-81,2-26,3-14	-0.8
1950	NY-N	56	83	18	15	2	0	0	8	8	6	.181	.253	.205	22	-9	0			.966	6	2-23,3-11	-0.3
1951	*NY-N	44	69	9	16	2	0	4	9	8	7	.232	.321	.435	100	-0	0	1	-1	.953	5	3-12/2-9	0.5
1952	NY-N	60	90	15	27	5	1	1	14	11	6	.300	.388	.411	121	3	2	3	-1	.889	-1	3-10/2-9,S-4,1-1	0.1
1953	NY-N	19	20	2	5	0	0	0	1	0	3	.250	.250	.250	30	-2	0			1.000	0	/3-2,2-1	-0.2
Total	8	654	1966	281	510	78	14	41	212	208	206	.259	.334	.376	91	-23	25	4		.971	-13	2-245,3-163,S/1	-1.8

■ CULLEY RIKARD — Rikard, Culley b: 5/9/14, Oxford, Miss. BL/TR, 5'11", 183 lbs. Deb: 9/20/41

1941	Pit-N	6	20	1	4	1	0	0	1	1	1	.200	.238	.250	38	-2	0			1.000	1	/O-5	-0.1
1942	Pit-N	38	52	6	10	2	1	0	5	7	8	.192	.288	.269	62	-2	0			.958	-4	O-16	-0.7
1947	Pit-N	109	324	57	93	16	4	4	32	50	39	.287	.384	.398	105	4	1			.978	-1	O-79	-0.1
Total	3	153	396	64	107	19	5	4	37	58	48	.270	.365	.374	97	-0	1			.978	-4	O-100	-0.9

■ ERNEST RILES Riles, Ernest b: 10/2/60, Cairo, Ga. BL/TR, 6'1", 180 lbs. Deb: 5/14/85

YEAR	TM/L	G	AB	R	H	2B	3B	HR	RBI	BB	SO	AVG	OBP	SLG	PRO+	BR/A	SB	CS	SBR	FA	FR	G/POS	TPR
1985	Mil-A	116	448	54	128	12	7	5	45	36	54	.286	.342	.377	97	-1	2	2	-1	.957	-19	*S-115/D-1	-0.9
1986	Mil-A	145	524	69	132	24	2	9	47	54	80	.252	.323	.357	82	-12	7	7	-2	.964	-30	*S-142	-3.1
1987	Mil-A	83	276	38	72	11	1	4	38	30	47	.261	.336	.351	80	-7	3	4	-2	.935	-6	3-65,S-21	-1.3
1988	Mil-A	41	127	7	32	6	1	1	9	7	26	.252	.291	.339	75	-4	2	2	-1	.958	1	3-28/S-9,D-5	-0.3
	SF-N	79	187	26	55	7	2	3	28	10	33	.294	.330	.401	114	3	1	2	-1	.975	8	3-30,2-17,S-16	1.2
1989	*SF-N	122	302	43	84	13	2	7	40	28	50	.278	.343	.404	116	6	0	6	-4	.962	-10	3-83,2-18/S-7,O-5	-0.7
1990	SF-N	92	155	22	31	2	1	8	21	26	26	.200	.315	.381	94	-1	0	0	0	.986	-4	S-26,2-24,3-10	-0.4
1991	Oak-A	108	281	30	60	8	4	5	32	31	42	.214	.294	.324	75	-10	3	2	-0	.939	-10	3-69,S-20/2-7,1-5	-1.9
1992	Hou-N	39	61	5	16	1	0	1	4	2	11	.262	.286	.328	77	-2	1	0	0	1.000	-2	/S-6,3-5,1-4,2-2	-0.4
1993	Bos-A	94	143	15	27	8	0	5	20	20	40	.189	.297	.350	69	-7	1	3	-2	1.000	5	2-20,D-15,3-11,/1-1	-0.4
Total	9	919	2504	309	637	92	20	48	284	244	409	.254	.323	.365	89	-36	20	28	-11	.964	-67	S-362,3-301/2D1O	-8.2

■ JIM RILEY Riley, James Joseph b: 11/10/1886, Buffalo, N.Y. d: 3/25/49, Buffalo, N.Y. BR/TR, 6', 165 lbs. Deb: 8/2/10

YEAR	TM/L	G	AB	R	H	2B	3B	HR	RBI	BB	SO	AVG	OBP	SLG	PRO+	BR/A	SB	CS	SBR	FA	FR	G/POS	TPR
1910	Bos-N	1	1	0	0	0	0	0	0	1	1	.000	.500	.000	46	0	0			.600	-0	/O-1	0.0

■ JIM RILEY Riley, James Norman b: 5/25/1895, Bayfield, N.B., Can d: 5/25/69, Seguin, Tex. BL/TR, 5'10.5", 185 lbs. Deb: 7/3/21

YEAR	TM/L	G	AB	R	H	2B	3B	HR	RBI	BB	SO	AVG	OBP	SLG	PRO+	BR/A	SB	CS	SBR	FA	FR	G/POS	TPR
1921	StL-A	4	11	0	0	0	0	0	0	1	3	.000	.083	.000	-73	-3	0	0	0	.818	-3	/2-4	-0.6
1923	Was-A	2	3	1	0	0	0	0	0	2	0	.000	.400	.000	12	-0	0	0	0	.882	-1	/1-2	-0.1
Total	2	6	14	1	0	0	0	0	0	3	3	.000	.176	.000	-50	-3	0	0	0	.818	-4	/2-4,1-2	-0.7

■ LEE RILEY Riley, Leon Francis b: 8/20/06, Princeton, Neb. d: 9/13/70, Schenectady, N.Y. BL/TR, 6'1", 185 lbs. Deb: 4/19/44

YEAR	TM/L	G	AB	R	H	2B	3B	HR	RBI	BB	SO	AVG	OBP	SLG	PRO+	BR/A	SB	CS	SBR	FA	FR	G/POS	TPR
1944	Phi-N	4	12	1	1	1	0	0	1	0	0	.083	.083	.167	-32	-2	0			1.000	-1	/O-3	-0.4

■ BILLY RILEY Riley, William James "Pigtail Billy" b: 1855, Cincinnati, Ohio d: 11/9/1887, Cincinnati, Ohio BR/TR, 5'10", 160 lbs. Deb: 5/5/1875

YEAR	TM/L	G	AB	R	H	2B	3B	HR	RBI	BB	SO	AVG	OBP	SLG	PRO+	BR/A	SB	CS	SBR	FA	FR	G/POS	TPR
1875	Wes-n	8	33	4	5	1	0	0	1	1	1	.152	.176	.182	23	-3	0	0	0	.667	-0	/O-8	-0.2
1879	Cle-N	43	161	14	23	2	0	0	9	2	26	.143	.153	.155	2	-16				.850	5	O-43	-1.2

■ FRANK RINGO Ringo, Frank C. b: 10/12/1860, Parkville, Mo. d: 4/12/1889, Kansas City, Mo. BR , 5'11", 175 lbs. Deb: 5/1/1883

YEAR	TM/L	G	AB	R	H	2B	3B	HR	RBI	BB	SO	AVG	OBP	SLG	PRO+	BR/A	SB	CS	SBR	FA	FR	G/POS	TPR
1883	Phi-N	60	221	24	42	10	1	0	12	6	34	.190	.211	.244	42	-14				.847	-9	C-39,O-11/S-6,32	-1.8
1884	Phi-N	26	91	4	12	2	0	0	6	3	19	.132	.160	.154	-1	-10				.783	-16	C-26	-2.2
	Phi-a	2	6	0	0	0	0	0		0		.000	.000	.000	-94	-1				.762	1	/C-2	0.0
1885	Det-N	17	65	12	16	3	0	0	2	0	7	.246	.246	.292	73	-2				.852	2	/C-8,3-8,O-1	0.1
	Pit-a	3	11	0	2	0	0	0	0	0		.182	.182	.182	15	-1				.941	3	/C-3	0.2
1886	Pit-a	15	56	3	12	2	2	0	5	1		.214	.228	.321	72	-2	0			.934	-0	/1-9,C-6	-0.2
	KC-N	16	56	6	13	7	0	0	7	5	10	.232	.295	.357	92	-1	0			.904	-6	C-13/O-2,3-1	-0.4
Total	4	139	506	49	97	24	3	0	32	15	70	.192	.215	.251	46	-32	0			.844	-24	/C-97,3-14,O1S2	-4.3

■ BOB RINKER Rinker, Robert John b: 4/21/21, Audenried, Pa. BR/TR, 6', 190 lbs. Deb: 9/6/50

YEAR	TM/L	G	AB	R	H	2B	3B	HR	RBI	BB	SO	AVG	OBP	SLG	PRO+	BR/A	SB	CS	SBR	FA	FR	G/POS	TPR
1950	Phi-A	3	3	0	1	0	0	0	0	0	0	.333	.333	.333	72	-0	0	0	0	.000	0	/C-1	0.0

■ ARMANDO RIOS Rios, Armando b: 9/13/71, Santurce, P.R. BL/TL, 5'9", 180 lbs. Deb: 9/1/98

YEAR	TM/L	G	AB	R	H	2B	3B	HR	RBI	BB	SO	AVG	OBP	SLG	PRO+	BR/A	SB	CS	SBR	FA	FR	G/POS	TPR
1998	SF-N	12	7	3	4	0	0	2	3	3	2	.571	.700	1.429	449	4	0	0	0	1.000	-1	/O-5	0.3

■ JUAN RIOS Rios, Juan Onofre Velez (b: Juan Onofre Velez (Rios)) b: 6/14/42, Mayaguez, P.R. d: 8/28/95, Mayaguez, P.R. BR/TR, 6'3", 185 lbs. Deb: 4/9/69

YEAR	TM/L	G	AB	R	H	2B	3B	HR	RBI	BB	SO	AVG	OBP	SLG	PRO+	BR/A	SB	CS	SBR	FA	FR	G/POS	TPR
1969	KC-A	87	196	20	44	5	1	1	5	7	19	.224	.262	.276	50	-13	1	3	-2	.967	-16	2-46,S-32/3-4	-2.8

■ CAL RIPKEN Ripken, Calvin Edwin Jr. b: 8/24/60, Havre De Grace, Md. BR/TR, 6'4", 225 lbs. Deb: 8/10/81 F

YEAR	TM/L	G	AB	R	H	2B	3B	HR	RBI	BB	SO	AVG	OBP	SLG	PRO+	BR/A	SB	CS	SBR	FA	FR	G/POS	TPR
1981	Bal-A	23	39	1	5	0	0	0	0	1	8	.128	.150	.128	-19	-6	0	0	0	.946	0	S-12/3-6	-0.6
1982	Bal-A	160	598	90	158	32	5	28	93	46	95	.264	.320	.475	115	11	3	3	-1	.972	-7	S-94,3-71	1.0
1983	*Bal-A★	162	663	**121**	**211**	**47**	2	27	102	58	97	.318	.373	.517	145	39	0	4	-2	.970	16	*S-162	**6.7**
1984	Bal-A★	162	641	103	195	37	7	27	86	71	89	.304	.375	.510	146	39	2	1	0	.971	**39**	*S-162	**9.1**
1985	Bal-A★	161	642	116	181	32	5	26	110	67	68	.282	.351	.469	125	22	2	3	-1	.967	7	*S-161	4.3
1986	Bal-A★	162	627	98	177	35	1	25	81	70	60	.282	.358	.461	123	20	4	2	0	.982	10	*S-162	4.4
1987	Bal-A★	162	624	97	157	28	3	27	98	81	77	.252	.339	.436	106	6	3	5	-2	.973	-4	*S-162	1.3
1988	Bal-A★	161	575	87	152	25	1	23	81	102	69	.264	.377	.431	129	26	2	2	-1	.973	-2	*S-161	3.7
1989	Bal-A★	162	646	80	166	30	0	21	93	57	72	.257	.320	.401	105	3	3	2	-0	.990	4	*S-162	2.0
1990	Bal-A★	161	600	78	150	28	4	21	84	82	66	.250	.345	.415	115	13	3	1	0	**.996**	-29	*S-161	-0.3
1991	Bal-A★	162	650	99	210	46	5	34	114	53	46	.323	.379	.566	164	54	6	1	1	**.986**	18	*S-162	**8.3**
1992	Bal-A★	162	637	73	160	29	1	14	72	64	50	.251	.326	.366	91	-7	4	3	-1	.984	-13	*S-162	-0.9
1993	Bal-A★	162	641	87	165	26	3	24	90	65	58	.257	.331	.420	96	-4	1	4	-2	.977	-5	*S-162	0.2
1994	Bal-A★	112	444	71	140	19	3	13	75	32	41	.315	.367	.459	106	4	1	0	0	**.985**	-13	*S-112	0.1
1995	Bal-A★	144	550	71	144	33	2	17	88	52	59	.262	.328	.422	92	-7	0	1	-1	**.989**	-1	*S-144	0.4
1996	*Bal-A★	163	640	94	178	40	1	26	102	59	78	.278	.343	.466	102	1	1	2	-1	.980	0	*S-158/3-6	1.3
1997	*Bal-A★	162	615	79	166	30	0	17	84	56	73	.270	.336	.402	94	-5	1	0	0	.949	6	*3-162/S-3	0.2
1998	Bal-A★	161	601	65	163	27	1	14	61	51	68	.271	.332	.389	89	-10	0	2	-1	**.979**	-3	*3-161	-1.3
Total	18	2704	10433	1510	2878	544	44	384	1514	1067	1174	.276	.346	.447	114	198	36	36	-11	.979	23	*S-2302,3-406	39.9

■ BILLY RIPKEN Ripken, William Oliver b: 12/16/64, Havre De Grace, Md. BR/TR, 6'1", 186 lbs. Deb: 7/11/87 F

YEAR	TM/L	G	AB	R	H	2B	3B	HR	RBI	BB	SO	AVG	OBP	SLG	PRO+	BR/A	SB	CS	SBR	FA	FR	G/POS	TPR
1987	Bal-A	58	234	27	72	9	0	2	20	21	23	.308	.365	.372	99	0	4	1	1	.990	-3	2-58	0.0
1988	Bal-A	150	512	52	106	18	1	2	34	33	63	.207	.262	.258	47	-36	8	2	1	.984	2	*2-149/3-2,D-1	-2.7
1989	Bal-A	115	318	31	76	11	2	2	26	22	53	.239	.288	.305	69	-13	1	2	-1	.985	13	*2-114/D-1	0.2
1990	Bal-A	129	406	48	118	28	1	3	38	28	43	.291	.342	.387	107	4	5	2	0	.987	-9	*2-127	-0.2
1991	Bal-A	104	287	24	62	11	1	0	14	15	31	.216	.255	.261	45	-22	0	1	-1	.986	4	*2-103	-1.6
1992	Bal-A	111	330	35	76	15	0	4	36	18	26	.230	.276	.312	63	-17	2	3	-1	**.993**	0	*2-108/D-2	-1.6
1993	Tex-A	50	132	12	25	4	0	0	11	11	19	.189	.272	.220	35	-12	0	2	-1	.992	4	2-34,S-18/3-1	-0.7
1994	Tex-A	32	81	9	25	5	0	0	6	3	11	.309	.333	.370	81	-2	2	0	1	.970	2	3-18,2-12/S-2,1-1	0.0
1995	Cle-A	8	17	4	7	0	0	2	3	0	3	.412	.412	.765	195	2	0	0	0	1.000	-3	/2-7,3-1	0.0
1996	Bal-A	57	135	19	31	8	0	2	12	9	18	.230	.283	.333	55	-9	0	0	0	.968	6	2-30,3-25/1-1	-0.3
1997	Tex-A	71	203	18	56	9	1	3	24	9	32	.276	.307	.374	73	-8	0	1	-1	.971	6	S-31,2-25,3-13,/1-9	0.0
1998	Det-A	27	74	8	20	3	0	0	5	5	10	.270	.325	.311	66	-4	3	2	-0	.926	-2	S-21/1-2,2-2,3-2,D	-0.4
Total	12	912	2729	287	674	121	6	20	229	174	332	.247	.296	.318	69	-116	25	16	-2	.987	20	2-769/S-72,3-62,1D	-7.3

■ JIMMY RIPPLE Ripple, James Albert b: 10/14/09, Export, Pa. d: 7/16/59, Greensburg, Pa. BL/TR, 5'10", 170 lbs. Deb: 4/20/36

YEAR	TM/L	G	AB	R	H	2B	3B	HR	RBI	BB	SO	AVG	OBP	SLG	PRO+	BR/A	SB	CS	SBR	FA	FR	G/POS	TPR
1936	*NY-N	96	311	42	95	17	2	7	47	28	15	.305	.365	.441	117	7	1			.980	-0	O-76	0.4
1937	*NY-N	121	426	70	135	23	3	5	66	29	20	.317	.362	.420	110	6	3			.980	-9	*O-111	-0.7
1938	NY-N	134	501	68	131	21	3	10	60	49	21	.261	.333	.375	94	-4	2			.976	-3	*O-131	-1.1
1939	NY-N	66	123	10	28	4	0	1	12	8	7	.228	.286	.285	53	-8	0			1.000	-2	O-23	-1.0
	Bro-N	28	106	18	35	8	4	0	22	11	8	.330	.398	.481	131	5	0			1.000	-2	O-28	0.2
	Yr	94	229	28	63	12	4	1	34	19	15	.275	.339	.376	90	-3	0			1.000	-3	O-51	-0.8
1940	Bro-N	7	13	0	3	0	0	0	0	2	2	.231	.333	.231	55	-1	0			1.000	1	/O-3	0.0
	*Cin-N	32	101	15	31	10	0	4	20	13	5	.307	.397	.525	151	7	1			1.000	-5	O-30	0.1
	Yr	39	114	15	34	10	0	4	20	15	7	.298	.389	.491	139	6	1			1.000	-4	O-33	0.1
1941	Cin-N	38	102	10	22	6	1	1	9	9	4	.216	.279	.324	69	-4	0			1.000	-2	O-25	-0.9
1943	Phi-A	32	126	8	30	3	1	0	15	7	7	.238	.284	.278	65	-6	0	0	0	1.000	-4	O-31	-1.3
Total	7	554	1809	241	510	92	14	28	251	156	89	.282	.343	.395	101	2	7	0		.984	-27	O-458	-4.3

■ SWEDE RISBERG Risberg, Charles August b: 10/13/1894, San Francisco, Cal d: 10/13/75, Red Bluff, Cal. BR/TR, 6', 175 lbs. Deb: 4/11/17

YEAR	TM/L	G	AB	R	H	2B	3B	HR	RBI	BB	SO	AVG	OBP	SLG	PRO+	BR/A	SB	CS	SBR	FA	FR	G/POS	TPR
1917	*Chi-A	149	474	59	96	20	8	1	45	59	65	.203	.297	.285	76	-13	16			.913	-39	*S-146	-5.1
1918	Chi-A	82	273	36	70	12	3	1	27	23	32	.256	.321	.333	97	-1	5			.944	-8	S-30,3-24,2-12,/1O	-0.8
1919	*Chi-A	119	414	48	106	19	6	2	38	35	38	.256	.317	.345	86	-8	19			.934	-13	S-97,1-22	-1.7

YEAR	TM/L	G	AB	R	H	2B	3B	HR	RBI	BB	SO	AVG	OBP	SLG	PRO+	BR/A	SB	CS	SBR	FA	FR	G/POS	TPR
1920	Chi-A	126	458	53	122	21	10	2	65	31	45	.266	.316	.369	81	-14	12	10	-2	.934	-4	*S-124	-0.9
Total	4	476	1619	196	394	72	27	6	175	148	180	.243	.311	.332	83	-36	52	10		.928	-64	S-397/1-29,3-24,2O	-8.5
■ POP RISING Rising, Percival Sumner b: 1/2/1872, Industry, Pa. d: 1/28/38, Rochester, Pa. Deb: 8/10/05																							
1905	Bos-A	11	29	2	3	1	1	0	2	2		.103	.161	.207	16	-3	0			1.000	0	/O-6,3-1	-0.3
■ CLAUDE RITCHEY Ritchey, Claude Cassius "Little All Right" b: 10/5/1873, Emlenton, Pa. d: 11/8/51, Emlenton, Pa. BB/TR, 5'6.5", 167 lbs. Deb: 4/22/1897																							
1897	Cin-N	101	337	58	95	12	4	0	41	42		.282	.370	.341	83	-8	11			.897	-16	S-70,O-22/2-8	-2.0
1898	Lou-N	151	551	65	140	10	4	5	51	46		.254	.322	.314	84	-11	19			.919	-16	S-80,2-71	-1.8
1899	Lou-N	147	536	65	161	15	7	4	71	49		.300	.370	.377	105	5	21			.938	-6	*2-137,S-11	0.6
1900	*Pit-N	123	476	62	139	17	8	1	67	29		.292	.339	.368	94	-4	18			.952	7	*2-123	0.8
1901	Pit-N	140	540	66	160	20	4	1	74	47		.296	.358	.354	104	4	15			.941	2	*2-139/S-1	1.1
1902	Pit-N	115	405	54	112	13	1	2	55	53		.277	.370	.328	112	8	10			**.966**	6	*2-114/O-1	1.9
1903	*Pit-N	138	506	66	145	28	10	0	59	55		.287	.360	.381	108	6	15			**.961**	19	*2-137	2.8
1904	Pit-N	156	544	79	143	22	12	0	51	59		.263	.338	.347	109	7	12			.958	-2	*2-156/S-2	0.9
1905	Pit-N	153	533	54	136	29	6	0	52	51		.255	.324	.332	93	-4	12			**.961**	-5	*2-153/S-2	-0.8
1906	Pit-N	152	484	46	130	21	5	1	62	68		.269	.369	.339	116	11	6			**.966**	1	*2-151	1.5
1907	Bos-N	144	499	45	127	17	4	2	51	50		.255	.329	.317	103	2	8			**.971**	14	*2-144	1.7
1908	Bos-N	121	421	44	115	10	3	2	36	50		.273	.361	.325	121	12	7			.967	16	*2-120	3.1
1909	Bos-N	30	87	4	15	1	0	0	3	8		.172	.242	.184	31	-7	1			.959	0	2-25	-0.8
Total	13	1671	5919	708	1618	215	68	18	673	607		.273	.348	.342	101	21	155			.957	19	*2-1478,S-166/O-23	9.0
■ CHARLIE RITTER Ritter, Charles J. Deb: 9/21/1885																							
1885	Buf-N	2	6	0	1	0	0	0	0	0	2	.167	.167	.167	8	-1				.813	0	/2-2	0.0
■ FLOYD RITTER Ritter, Floyd Alexander b: 6/1/1870, Dorset, Ohio d: 2/7/43, Stevenson, Wash. BR/TR, 5'8", 155 lbs. Deb: 6/4/1890																							
1890	Tol-a	1	3	0	0	0	0	0	0	0		.000	.000	.000	-97	-1	0			.778	0	/C-1	-0.1
■ LEW RITTER Ritter, Lewis Elmer "Old Dog" b: 9/7/1875, Liverpool, Pa. d: 5/27/52, Harrisburg, Pa. BR/TR, 5'9", 150 lbs. Deb: 9/10/02																							
1902	Bro-N	16	57	5	12	1	0	0	2	1		.211	.237	.228	43	-4	2			.973	3	C-16	0.1
1903	Bro-N	78	259	26	61	9	6	0	37	19		.236	.290	.317	75	-9	9			.940	-17	C-74/O-2	-1.8
1904	Bro-N	72	214	23	53	4	1	0	19	20		.248	.318	.276	86	-3	17			.966	5	C-57/2-5,3-1	0.9
1905	Bro-N	92	311	32	68	10	5	1	28	15		.219	.255	.293	68	-13	16			.951	-14	C-84/O-4,3-2	-2.0
1906	Bro-N	73	226	22	47	1	3	0	15	16		.208	.263	.239	61	-10	6			.978	-8	C-53/O-9,1-3,3-2	-1.6
1907	Bro-N	93	271	15	55	6	1	0	17	18		.203	.255	.232	57	-14	5			.969	-1	C-89	-0.8
1908	Bro-N	38	99	6	19	2	1	0	2	7		.192	.245	.232	55	-5	0			.961	-3	C-37	-0.6
Total	7	462	1437	129	315	33	17	1	120	96		.219	.271	.268	67	-58	55			.960	-36	C-410/O-15,3-5,2-1	-5.8
■ WHITEY RITTERSON Ritterson, Edward West b: 4/26/1855, Philadelphia, Pa. d: 7/28/17, Sellersville, Pa. BR/TR, 5'8", Deb: 5/3/1876																							
1876	Phi-N	16	52	8	13	3	0	0	4	0	2	.250	.250	.308	86	-1				.671	-8	C-14/O-4,3-1	-0.7
■ JIM RITZ Ritz, James L. b: 1874, Pittsburgh, Pa. d: 11/10/1896, Pittsburgh, Pa. Deb: 7/20/1894																							
1894	Pit-N	1	4	1	0	0	0	0	0	0	0	.000	.200	.000	-49	-1	1			.750	-0	/3-1	-0.1
■ GERMAN RIVERA Rivera, German (Diaz) b: 7/6/60, Santurce, P.R. BR/TR, 6'2", 195 lbs. Deb: 9/2/83																							
1983	LA-N	13	17	1	6	1	0	0	0	2	2	.353	.421	.412	132	1	0	1	-1	.929	2	/3-8	0.2
1984	LA-N	94	227	20	59	12	2	2	17	21	30	.260	.325	.357	92	-2	1	0	0	.937	16	3-90	1.4
1985	Hou-N	13	36	3	7	2	1	0	2	4	8	.194	.275	.306	64	-2	0	0	0	.941	3	3-11	0.1
Total	3	120	280	24	72	15	3	2	19	27	40	.257	.325	.354	91	-3	1	1	-0	.937	20	3-109	1.7
■ BOMBO RIVERA Rivera, Jesus Manuel (Torres) b: 8/2/52, Ponce, P.R. BR/TR, 5'10", 187 lbs. Deb: 4/17/75																							
1975	Mon-N	5	9	1	1	0	0	0	0	2	3	.111	.273	.111	9	-1	0	0	0	.889	-1	/O-5	-0.2
1976	Mon-N	68	185	22	51	11	4	2	19	13	32	.276	.323	.411	103	0	1	0	0	.950	-0	O-56	-0.1
1978	Min-A	101	251	35	68	8	2	3	23	35	47	.271	.365	.355	101	2	5	3	-0	.982	-9	O-94/D-1	-1.1
1979	Min-A	112	263	37	74	13	5	2	31	17	40	.281	.325	.392	89	-4	5	5	-2	.989	-4	*O-105/D-2	-1.3
1980	Min-A	44	113	13	25	7	0	3	10	4	20	.221	.248	.363	61	-6	0	0	0	.922	-4	O-37/D-1	-1.2
1982	KC-A	5	10	1	1	0	0	0	0	0	2	.100	.100	.100	-45	-2	0	0	0	1.000	-1	/O-3	-0.3
Total	6	335	831	109	220	39	11	10	83	71	144	.265	.324	.374	90	-12	11	8	-2	.970	-19	O-300/D-4	-4.2
■ LUIS RIVERA Rivera, Luis Antonio (Pedraza) b: 1/3/64, Cidra, P.R. BR/TR, 5'9", 170 lbs. Deb: 8/3/86																							
1986	Mon-N	55	166	20	34	11	1	0	13	17	33	.205	.286	.283	58	-9	1	1	-0	.953	-9	S-55	-1.5
1987	Mon-N	18	32	0	5	2	0	0	1	1	8	.156	.182	.219	5	-4	0	0	0	.923	2	S-15	-0.2
1988	Mon-N	123	371	35	83	17	3	4	30	24	69	.224	.273	.318	66	-16	3	4	-2	.962	-6	*S-116	-1.6
1989	Bos-A	93	323	35	83	17	1	5	29	20	60	.257	.302	.362	81	-8	2	3	-1	.958	-3	S-90/2-1,D-1	-0.6
1990	*Bos-A	118	346	38	78	20	0	7	45	25	58	.225	.280	.344	70	-14	4	3	-1	.965	11	*S-112/2-3,3-1	0.4
1991	Bos-A	129	414	64	107	22	3	8	40	35	86	.258	.321	.384	90	-6	4	4	-1	.959	3	*S-129	0.6
1992	Bos-A	102	288	17	62	11	1	0	29	26	56	.215	.287	.260	51	-18	4	3	-1	.966	14	S-93/2-1,3-1,O-1,D	0.1
1993	Bos-A	62	130	13	27	8	1	1	7	11	36	.208	.275	.308	53	-9	1	2	-1	.969	12	2-27,S-27/3-2,D-7	0.4
1994	NY-N	32	43	11	12	2	1	3	5	4	14	.279	.367	.581	144	3	0	1	-1	.971	5	S-11/2-5	0.7
1997	Hou-N	7	13	2	3	0	1	0	3	1	6	.231	.286	.385	76	-0	0	0	0	.875	0	/S-6,2-1	0.0
1998	KC-A	42	89	14	22	4	0	0	7	7	17	.247	.302	.292	53	-6	1	1	-0	.961	6	S-30/2-6,3-6	0.2
Total	11	781	2215	249	516	114	12	28	209	171	443	.233	.292	.333	70	-90	20	22	-7	.961	35	S-684/2-44,3-10,DO	-1.5
■ JIM RIVERA Rivera, Manuel Joseph "Jungle Jim" b: 7/22/22, New York, N.Y. BL/TL, 6', 196 lbs. Deb: 4/15/52																							
1952	StL-A	97	336	45	86	13	6	4	30	29	59	.256	.319	.366	88	-6	8	7	-2	.976	9	O-88	-0.3
	Chi-A	53	201	27	50	7	3	3	18	21	27	.249	.320	.358	88	-4	13	2	3	.988	4	O-53	0.1
	Yr	150	537	72	136	20	9	7	48	50	86	.253	.319	.363	88	-10	21	9	1	.980	12	*O-141	-0.2
1953	Chi-A	156	567	79	147	26	**16**	11	78	53	70	.259	.329	.420	98	-3	22	15	-2	.976	-1	*O-156	-1.2
1954	Chi-A	145	490	62	140	16	8	13	61	49	68	.286	.358	.431	111	7	18	10	-1	.959	-17	*O-143	-1.6
1955	Chi-A	147	454	71	120	24	4	10	52	62	59	.264	.354	.401	100	0	**25**	16	-2	.981	2	*O-143	-0.6
1956	Chi-A	139	491	76	125	23	5	12	66	49	75	.255	.326	.395	88	-9	20	9	1	.976	1	*O-134	-1.4
1957	Chi-A	125	402	51	103	21	6	14	52	40	80	.256	.328	.443	108	4	18	2	**4**	.974	-7	O-86,1-31	-0.6
1958	Chi-A	116	276	37	62	8	4	9	35	24	49	.225	.289	.380	84	-7	21	3	5	.994	-3	O-99	-1.0
1959	*Chi-A	80	177	18	39	9	4	4	19	11	19	.220	.270	.384	78	-6	5	3	-0	.976	-8	O-69	-1.6
1960	Chi-A	48	17	17	5	0	0	1	1	3	3	.294	.400	.471	136	1	4	0	1	1.000	-6	O-24	-0.4
1961	Chi-A	1	0	0	0	0	0	0	0	0	0	—	—	—	—	0	0	1	-1	.000	0	H	-0.1
	KC-A	64	141	20	34	8	0	2	10	24	14	.241	.352	.340	84	-3	6	2	1	.981	-9	O-43	1.3
	Yr	65	141	20	34	8	0	2	10	24	14	.241	.352	.340	84	-3	6	3	0	.981	-9	O-43	-1.4
Total	10	1171	3552	503	911	155	56	83	422	365	523	.256	.330	.402	96	-25	160	70	6	.977	-36	*O-1038/1-31	-10.0
■ RUBEN RIVERA Rivera, Ruben (Moreno) b: 11/14/73, Chorrera, Panama BR/TR, 6'3", 200 lbs. Deb: 9/3/95																							
1995	NY-A	5	1	0	0	0	0	0	0	0	1	.000	.000	.000	-99	-0	0	0	0	1.000	-1	/O-4	-0.1
1996	*NY-A	46	88	17	25	6	1	2	16	13	26	.284	.388	.443	110	2	6	2	1	1.000	-2	O-45	0.0
1997	SD-N	17	20	2	5	1	0	0	1	2	9	.250	.318	.300	68	-1	2	1	0	1.000	-1	/O-7	-0.2
1998	*SD-N	95	172	31	36	7	2	6	29	28	52	.209	.327	.378	91	-2	5	1	1	.973	-14	O-91	-1.5
Total	4	163	281	50	66	14	3	8	46	43	88	.235	.345	.391	95	-2	13	4	2	.985	-18	O-147	-1.8
■ MICKEY RIVERS Rivers, John Milton b: 10/31/48, Miami, Fla. BL/TL, 5'10", 165 lbs. Deb: 8/4/70																							
1970	Cal-A	17	25	6	8	2	0	0	3	3	5	.320	.414	.400	130	1	1	0	0	1.000	0	/O-5	0.1
1971	Cal-A	79	268	31	71	12	2	1	12	19	38	.265	.316	.336	91	-4	13	1	3	.976	-3	O-76	-0.7
1972	Cal-A	58	159	18	34	6	2	0	7	8	26	.214	.256	.277	62	-8	4	3	-1	.981	-1	O-48	-1.3
1973	Cal-A	30	129	26	45	6	4	0	16	8	11	.349	.391	.457	150	8	8	3	1	.909	-4	O-29	0.4

YEAR	TM/L	G	AB	R	H	2B	3B	HR	RBI	BB	SO	AVG	OBP	SLG	PRO+	BR/A	SB	CS	SBR	FA	FR	G/POS	TPR
1974	Cal-A	118	466	69	133	19	**11**	3	31	39	47	.285	.342	.393	118	10	30	13	1	.994	10	*O-116	1.7
1975	Cal-A	155	616	70	175	17	**13**	1	53	43	42	.284	.333	.359	103	1	**70**	14	**13**	.977	11	*O-152/D-1	1.9
1976	*NY-A★	137	590	95	184	31	8	8	67	13	51	.312	.330	.432	123	14	43	7	9	.986	9	*O-136	2.8
1977	*NY-A	138	565	79	184	18	5	12	69	18	45	.326	.351	.439	115	11	22	14	-2	.982	13	*O-136/D-1	1.6
1978	*NY-A	141	559	78	148	25	8	11	48	29	51	.265	.305	.397	98	-3	25	5	5	.980	10	*O-138	0.5
1979	NY-A	74	286	37	82	18	5	3	25	13	21	.287	.320	.416	99	-1	3	7	-3	.974	-6	O-69/D-1	-1.3
	Tex-A	58	247	35	74	9	3	6	25	9	18	.300	.327	.433	104	1	7	2	1	.981	3	O-57	0.2
	Yr	132	533	72	156	27	8	9	50	22	39	.293	.323	.424	101	-0	10	9	-2	.978	-3	*O-126/D-1	-1.1
1980	Tex-A	147	630	96	210	32	6	7	60	20	34	.333	.355	.437	119	15	18	7	1	.978	10	*O-141/D-4	2.0
1981	Tex-A	99	399	62	114	21	2	3	26	24	31	.286	.328	.371	107	3	9	5	-0	.996	4	O-97	0.3
1982	Tex-A	19	68	6	16	1	1	1	4	0	7	.235	.235	.324	54	-4	0	0	0	.000	0	D-16	-0.5
1983	Tex-A	96	309	37	88	17	0	1	20	11	21	.285	.312	.350	83	-7	9	4	0	.980	0	D-53,O-23	-0.9
1984	Tex-A	102	313	40	94	13	1	4	33	9	23	.300	.320	.387	91	-4	5	5	-2	1.000	-0	D-48,O-30	-0.8
Total	15	1468	5629	785	1660	247	71	61	499	266	471	.295	.329	.397	106	32	267	90	26	.982	57	*O-1253,D-124	6.0
■ **JOHNNY RIZZO**	Rizzo, John Costa b: 7/30/12, Houston, Tex. d: 12/4/77, Houston, Tex. BR/TR, 6′, 190 lbs. Deb: 4/19/38																						
1938	Pit-N	143	555	97	167	31	9	23	111	54	61	.301	.368	.514	139	28	1			.951	-8	*O-140	1.6
1939	Pit-N	94	330	49	86	23	3	6	55	42	27	.261	.349	.403	103	2	0			.974	-0	O-86	-0.2
1940	Pit-N	9	28	1	5	1	0	0	2	5	5	.179	.324	.214	51	-2	0			.818	-2	/O-7	-0.4
	Cin-N	31	110	17	31	6	0	4	17	14	14	.282	.363	.445	121	3	1			.974	5	O-30	0.6
	Phi-N	103	367	53	107	12	2	20	53	37	31	.292	.358	.499	139	19	2			.968	6	O-91/3-7	2.0
	Yr	143	505	71	143	19	2	24	72	56	50	.283	.357	.471	130	20	3			.964	9	*O-128/3-7	2.2
1941	Phi-N	99	235	20	51	9	2	4	24	24	34	.217	.295	.323	77	-7	1			.968	0	O-62/3-2	-1.1
1942	Bro-N	78	217	31	50	8	0	4	27	24	25	.230	.307	.323	83	-5	2			.977	-2	O-70	-1.0
Total	5	557	1842	268	497	90	16	61	289	200	197	.270	.345	.435	116	38	7			.964	-1	O-486/3-9	1.5
■ **PHIL RIZZUTO**	Rizzuto, Philip Francis "Scooter" (b: Fiero Francis Rizzuto) b: 9/25/17, Brooklyn, N.Y. BR/TR, 5′6″, 160 lbs. Deb: 4/14/41 H																						
1941	*NY-A	133	515	65	158	20	9	3	46	27	36	.307	.343	.398	97	-3	14	5	1	.957	16	*S-128	2.2
1942	*NY-A☆	144	553	79	157	24	7	4	68	44	40	.284	.343	.374	104	2	22	6	3	.962	**25**	*S-144	4.0
1946	NY-A	126	471	53	121	17	1	2	38	34	39	.257	.315	.310	74	-16	14	7	0	.961	13	*S-125	0.5
1947	*NY-A	153	549	78	150	26	9	2	60	57	31	.273	.350	.364	100	0	11	6	-0	.969	16	*S-151	2.5
1948	NY-A	128	464	65	117	13	2	6	50	60	24	.252	.340	.328	79	-13	6	5	-1	.973	-11	*S-128	-1.8
1949	*NY-A	153	614	110	169	22	7	5	65	72	34	.275	.352	.358	88	-10	18	6	**2**	**.971**	3	*S-152	0.5
1950	*NY-A★	155	617	125	200	36	7	7	66	92	39	.324	.418	.439	123	25	12	8	-1	**.982**	9	*S-155	**4.1**
1951	*NY-A★	144	540	87	148	21	6	2	43	58	27	.274	.350	.346	92	-5	18	3	**4**	.968	6	*S-144	1.5
1952	*NY-A★	152	578	89	147	24	10	2	43	67	42	.254	.337	.341	95	-4	17	6	2	.976	19	*S-152	2.8
1953	*NY-A★	134	413	54	112	21	3	2	54	71	39	.271	.383	.351	103	5	4	3	-1	.963	-3	*S-133	1.1
1954	NY-A	127	307	47	60	11	0	2	15	41	23	.195	.292	.251	51	-20	3	2	-0	.968	-1	*S-126/2-1	-1.3
1955	*NY-A	81	143	19	37	4	1	1	9	22	18	.259	.369	.322	88	-1	7	1	2	.957	-9	S-79/2-1	-0.5
1956	NY-A	31	52	6	12	0	0	0	6	6	6	.231	.310	.231	46	-4	3	0	1	.934	3	S-30	0.2
Total	13	1661	5816	877	1588	239	62	38	563	651	398	.273	.351	.355	93	-44	149	58	10	.968	86	*S-1647/2-2	15.8
■ **MEL ROACH**	Roach, Melvin Earl b: 1/25/33, Richmond, Va. BR/TR, 6′1″, 190 lbs. Deb: 7/31/53																						
1953	Mil-N	5	2	1	0	0	0	0	0	0	1	.000	.000	.000	-99	-1	0	0	0	.000	0	/2-1	-0.1
1954	Mil-N	3	4	0	0	0	0	0	0	0	1	.000	.000	.000	-99	-1	0	0	0	1.000	-0	/1-1	-0.1
1957	Mil-N	7	6	1	1	0	0	0	0	0	3	.167	.167	.167	-11	-1	0	0	0	1.000	0	/2-5	-0.1
1958	Mil-N	44	136	14	42	7	0	3	10	6	15	.309	.338	.426	110	1	0	0	0	.993	-2	2-27/O-7,1-1	0.2
1959	Mil-N	19	31	1	3	0	0	0	0	2	4	.097	.152	.097	-35	-6	0	0	0	.880	1	/2-8,O-4,3-1	-0.5
1960	Mil-N	48	140	12	42	12	0	3	18	6	19	.300	.333	.450	121	3	0	0	0	.975	-8	O-21,2-20/1-1,3-1	-0.4
1961	Mil-N	13	36	3	6	0	0	1	6	2	4	.167	.250	.250	35	-3	0	0	0	1.000	-2	/O-9,1-2	-0.6
	Chi-N	23	39	1	5	2	0	0	1	3	9	.128	.190	.179	-1	-6	1	0	0	.981	-1	/1-7,2-7	-0.7
	Yr	36	75	4	11	2	0	1	7	5	13	.147	.220	.213	16	-9	1	0	0	1.000	-3	/O-9,1-9,2-7	-1.3
1962	Phi-N	65	105	9	20	4	0	0	8	5	19	.190	.227	.229	23	-11	0	0	0	.951	-1	3-26/2-9,1-4,O-3	-1.2
Total	8	227	499	42	119	25	0	7	43	24	75	.238	.278	.331	66	-24	1	0	0	.969	-12	/2-77,O-44,3-28,1	-3.5
■ **MIKE ROACH**	Roach, Michael Stephen b: 12/23/1873, New York, N.Y. d: 11/12/16, New York, N.Y. Deb: 8/10/1899																						
1899	Was-N	24	78	7	17	1	0	0	7	3		.218	.265	.231	37	-7	3			.964	-5	C-20/1-3	-0.9
■ **ROXEY ROACH**	Roach, Wilbur Charles b: 11/28/1882, Anita, Pa. d: 12/26/47, Bay City, Mich. BR/TR, 5′11″, 160 lbs. Deb: 5/2/10																						
1910	NY-A	70	220	27	47	9	2	0	20	29		.214	.313	.273	79	-5	15			.913	-7	S-58/O-9	-1.1
1911	NY-A	13	40	4	10	2	1	0	2	6		.250	.348	.350	89	-1	0			.891	-1	/S-8,2-5	-0.1
1912	Was-A	2	2	1	1	0	0	1	1	0		.500	.500	2.000	600	1	0			.500	-1	/S-2	0.0
1915	Buf-F	92	346	35	93	20	3	2	31	17	34	.269	.303	.361	85	-13	11			.959	15	S-92	1.0
Total	4	177	608	67	151	31	6	3	54	52	34	.248	.311	.334	85	-17	26			.938	7	S-160/O-9,2-5	-0.2
■ **MIKE ROARKE**	Roarke, Michael Thomas b: 11/8/30, West Warwick, R.I. BR/TR, 6′2″, 195 lbs. Deb: 4/19/61 C																						
1961	Det-A	86	229	21	51	6	1	2	22	20	31	.223	.285	.284	51	-16	0	0	0	.988	4	C-85	-0.9
1962	Det-A	56	136	11	29	4	1	4	14	13	17	.213	.287	.346	67	-6	0	0	0	.982	6	C-53	0.1
1963	Det-A	23	44	5	14	0	0	0	1	2	3	.318	.362	.318	89	-0	0	0	0	.986	1	C-16	0.1
1964	Det-A	29	82	4	19	1	0	0	7	10	10	.232	.315	.244	57	-4	0	0	0	.994	3	C-27	0.0
Total	4	194	491	41	113	11	2	6	44	45	61	.230	.297	.297	60	-27	0	0	0	.987	14	C-181	-0.7
■ **FRED ROAT**	Roat, Frederick R. b: 11/10/1867, Oregon, Ill. d: 9/24/13, Oregon, Ill. TR, Deb: 5/10/1890																						
1890	Pit-N	57	215	18	48	2	0	2	17	16	22	.223	.286	.260	67	-8	7			.847	2	3-44/1-9,O-4	-0.5
1892	Chi-N	8	31	4	6	0	1	0	2	2	3	.194	.242	.258	51	-2	2			.897	-3	/2-8	-0.5
Total	2	65	246	22	54	2	1	2	19	18	25	.220	.281	.260	65	-10	9			.847	-1	/3-44,1-9,2-8,O-4	-1.0
■ **TONY ROBELLO**	Robello, Thomas Vardasco b: 2/9/13, San Leandro, Cal. d: 12/25/94, Fort Worth, Tex. BR/TR, 5′10.5″, 175 lbs. Deb: 8/13/33																						
1933	Cin-N	14	30	1	7	3	0	0	3	1	5	.233	.258	.333	69	-1	0			1.000	2	2-11/3-2	0.1
1934	Cin-N	2	2	0	0	0	0	0	0	0	1	.000	.000	.000	-99	-1	0			.000	0	H	-0.1
Total	2	16	32	1	7	3	0	0	3	1	6	.219	.242	.313	58	-2	0			1.000	2	/2-11,3-2	0.0
■ **SKIPPY ROBERGE**	Roberge, Joseph Albert Armand b: 5/19/17, Lowell, Mass. d: 6/7/93, Lowell, Mass. BR/TR, 5′11″, 185 lbs. Deb: 7/18/41																						
1941	Bos-N	55	167	12	36	6	0	0	15	9	18	.216	.256	.251	45	-12	0			.978	5	2-46/3-5,S-2	-0.5
1942	Bos-N	74	172	10	37	7	0	1	12	9	19	.215	.258	.273	57	-10	1			.977	8	2-29,3-27/S-6	0.0
1946	Bos-N	48	169	13	39	6	2	2	20	7	12	.231	.270	.325	68	-8	1			.973	2	3-48	-0.5
Total	3	177	508	35	112	19	2	3	47	25	49	.220	.261	.283	57	-30	2			.967	15	/3-80,2-75,S-8	-1.0
■ **KEVIN ROBERSON**	Roberson, Kevin Lynn b: 1/29/68, Decatur, Ill. BB/TR, 6′4″, 210 lbs. Deb: 7/15/93																						
1993	Chi-N	62	180	23	34	4	1	9	27	12	48	.189	.251	.372	65	-10	0	1	-1	.963	-6	O-51	-1.8
1994	Chi-N	44	55	8	12	4	0	4	9	2	14	.218	.271	.509	99	-1	0	0	0	.800	-2	/O-9	-0.2
1995	Chi-N	32	38	5	7	1	0	4	6	6	14	.184	.311	.526	118	1	0	1	-1	1.000	-2	O-11	-0.2
1996	NY-N	27	36	8	8	1	0	3	9	7	17	.222	.364	.500	131	2	0	0	0	1.000	-2	O-10	0.0
Total	4	165	309	44	61	10	1	20	51	27	93	.197	.277	.430	86	-8	0	2	-1	.955	-12	/O-81	-2.2
■ **RED ROBERTS**	Roberts, Charles Emory b: 8/8/18, Carrollton, Ga. BR/TR, 6′, 170 lbs. Deb: 9/3/43																						
1943	Was-A	9	23	1	6	1	0	1	3	4	2	.261	.370	.435	140	1	0	0	0	.778	-5	/S-6,3-1	-0.3
■ **SKIPPER ROBERTS**	Roberts, Clarence Ashley b: 1/11/1888, Wardner, Idaho d: 12/24/63, Long Beach, Cal. BL/TR, 5′10.5″, 175 lbs. Deb: 6/12/13																						
1913	StL-N	26	41	4	6	2	0	0	3	3	13	.146	.205	.195	15	-5	1			.859	-2	C-16	-0.6
1914	Pit-F	33	55	7	12	2	1	0	4	1	11	.218	.246	.291	46	-5	2			.941	-1	C-14	-0.6
	Chi-F	4	3	0	1	0	0	0	1	1	1	.333	.500	.333	138	0	0			.000	0	H	0.0

YEAR	TM/L	G	AB	R	H	2B	3B	HR	RBI	BB	SO	AVG	OBP	SLG	PRO+	BR/A	SB	CS	SBR	FA	FR	G/POS	TPR
	Pit-F	19	39	5	10	2	1	1	4	1	8	.256	.293	.436	98	-1	1			.923	-4	/C-9,O-1	-0.4
	Yr	56	97	12	23	4	2	1	9	3	20	.237	.275	.351	70	-6	3			.935	-5	C-23/O-1	-1.0
Total	2	82	138	16	29	6	2	1	12	6	33	.210	.253	.304	54	-11	4			.906	-7	/C-39,O-1	-1.6

■ CURT ROBERTS

Roberts, Curtis Benjamin b: 8/16/29, Pineland, Tex. d: 11/14/69, Oakland, Cal. BR/TR, 5'8", 165 lbs. Deb: 4/13/54

YEAR	TM/L	G	AB	R	H	2B	3B	HR	RBI	BB	SO	AVG	OBP	SLG	PRO+	BR/A	SB	CS	SBR	FA	FR	G/POS	TPR
1954	Pit-N	134	496	47	115	18	7	1	36	55	49	.232	.311	.302	62	-27	6	3	0	.969	2	*2-131	-1.6
1955	Pit-N	6	17	1	2	1	0	0	0	2	1	.118	.211	.176	4	-2	0	0	0	.913	-1	/2-6	-0.3
1956	Pit-N	31	62	6	11	5	2	0	4	5	12	.177	.239	.323	50	-5	1	0	0	.988	-2	2-27	-0.4
Total	3	171	575	54	128	24	9	1	40	62	62	.223	.300	.301	59	-34	7	3	0	.969	0	2-164	-2.3

■ DAVE ROBERTS

Roberts, David Leonard b: 6/30/33, Panama City, Pan. BL/TL, 6', 172 lbs. Deb: 9/5/62

YEAR	TM/L	G	AB	R	H	2B	3B	HR	RBI	BB	SO	AVG	OBP	SLG	PRO+	BR/A	SB	CS	SBR	FA	FR	G/POS	TPR
1962	Hou-N	16	53	3	13	3	0	1	10	8	8	.245	.355	.358	99	0	0	0	0	1.000	-1	O-12/1-6	-0.2
1964	Hou-N	61	125	9	23	4	1	1	7	14	28	.184	.271	.256	52	-8	0	1	-1	.983	4	1-34/O-4	-0.6
1966	Pit-N	14	16	3	2	1	0	0	0	0	7	.125	.125	.188	-15	-2	0	0	0	.950	0	/1-2	-0.2
Total	3	91	194	15	38	8	1	2	17	22	43	.196	.284	.278	60	-10	0	1	-1	.983	3	/1-42,O-16	-1.0

■ DAVE ROBERTS

Roberts, David Wayne b: 2/17/51, Lebanon, Ore. BR/TR, 6'3", 215 lbs. Deb: 6/7/72 C

YEAR	TM/L	G	AB	R	H	2B	3B	HR	RBI	BB	SO	AVG	OBP	SLG	PRO+	BR/A	SB	CS	SBR	FA	FR	G/POS	TPR
1972	SD-N	100	418	38	102	17	0	5	33	18	64	.244	.275	.321	74	-16	7	2	1	.931	-6	3-84,2-20/S-3,C-1	-2.3
1973	SD-N	127	479	56	137	20	3	21	64	17	83	.286	.312	.472	124	12	11	2	2	.942	3	*3-111,2-12	1.7
1974	SD-N	113	318	26	53	10	1	5	18	32	69	.167	.247	.252	41	-26	2	0	1	.955	-4	*3-103/S-3,O-1	-3.1
1975	SD-N	33	113	7	32	2	0	2	12	13	19	.283	.367	.354	107	2	3	1	0	.925	-4	3-30/2-5	-0.2
1977	SD-N	82	186	15	41	14	1	1	23	11	32	.220	.268	.323	64	-10	2	1	0	.982	-4	C-63/2-2,3-2,S-1	-1.3
1978	SD-N	54	97	7	21	4	1	1	7	12	25	.216	.309	.309	79	-3	0	0	0	.980	-1	C-41/1-8,O-2	-0.4
1979	Tex-A	44	84	12	22	2	1	3	14	7	17	.262	.319	.417	98	-0	1	0	0	.980	2	C-14,O-11/2-8,13D	0.3
1980	Tex-A	101	235	27	56	4	0	10	30	13	38	.238	.281	.383	83	-6	0	1	-1	.930	-21	3-37,S-33,C/O12	-2.6
1981	*Hou-N	27	54	4	13	3	0	1	5	3	6	.241	.281	.352	83	-1	1	0	0	.958	0	1-10/3-7,2-3,C-1	-0.2
1982	Phi-N	28	33	2	6	1	0	0	2	2	8	.182	.229	.212	23	-3	0	1	-1	.818	1	3-11,C-10/2-7	-0.3
Total	10	709	2017	194	483	77	7	49	208	128	361	.239	.288	.357	83	-53	27	8	3	.939	-35	3-386,C-152/2S1OD	-8.4

■ BIP ROBERTS

Roberts, Leon Joseph b: 10/27/63, Berkeley, Cal. BB/TR, 5'7", 165 lbs. Deb: 4/7/86

YEAR	TM/L	G	AB	R	H	2B	3B	HR	RBI	BB	SO	AVG	OBP	SLG	PRO+	BR/A	SB	CS	SBR	FA	FR	G/POS	TPR
1986	SD-N	101	241	34	61	5	2	1	12	14	29	.253	.294	.303	66	-11	14	12	-3	.971	4	2-87	-0.8
1988	SD-N	5	9	1	3	0	0	0	0	1	2	.333	.400	.333	115	0	0	2	-1	.500	-1	/3-2,2-1	-0.2
1989	SD-N	117	329	81	99	15	8	3	25	49	45	.301	.393	.422	133	16	21	11	-0	.976	-8	O-54,3-37,S-14,/2-9	0.8
1990	SD-N	149	556	104	172	36	3	9	44	55	65	.309	.378	.433	122	17	46	12	7	.982	-1	O-75,3-56,S-18,/2-8	2.4
1991	SD-N	117	424	66	119	13	3	3	32	37	71	.281	.344	.347	92	-4	26	11	1	.978	-7	2-68,O-46	-0.9
1992	Cin-N★	147	532	92	172	34	6	4	45	62	54	.323	.396	.432	131	24	44	16	4	.993	-14	O-79,2-42,3-36	1.4
1993	Cin-N	83	292	46	70	13	0	1	18	38	46	.240	.333	.295	70	-11	26	6	4	.984	-9	2-64,O-11/3-3,S-1	-1.5
1994	SD-N	105	403	52	129	15	5	2	31	39	57	.320	.384	.397	107	6	21	7	2	.976	-15	2-90,O-20	-0.4
1995	SD-N	73	296	40	90	14	0	2	25	17	36	.304	.346	.372	92	-3	20	2	5	.989	4	O-50,2-25/S-7	0.6
1996	KC-A	90	339	39	96	21	2	0	52	25	38	.283	.336	.357	76	-12	12	9	-2	.986	-6	2-63,D-16,O-11	-1.6
1997	KC-A	97	346	44	107	17	2	1	36	21	53	.309	.351	.379	88	-5	15	3	3	.981	-4	O-84,3-10	-0.8
	*Cle-A	23	85	19	23	3	0	3	8	7	14	.271	.340	.412	92	-1	3	0	1	.932	-3	2-13,O-10	-0.2
	Yr	120	431	63	130	20	2	4	44	28	67	.302	.348	.385	89	-6	18	3	4	.982	-6	O-94,2-13,3-10	-1.0
1998	Det-A	34	113	17	28	6	0	0	9	16	14	.248	.351	.301	71	-4	6	1	1	1.000	-0	D-29/O-2,2-1	-0.5
	Oak-A	61	182	28	51	11	0	1	15	15	24	.280	.342	.357	85	-4	10	3	1	.970	-10	2-30,O-22/3-3	-1.1
	Yr	95	295	45	79	17	0	1	24	31	38	.268	.345	.336	80	-8	16	4	2	.971	-11	2-31,D-29,O-24,/3-3	-1.6
Total	12	1202	4147	663	1220	203	31	30	352	396	548	.294	.360	.380	100	7	264	95	22	.977	-70	2-501,O-464,3/DS	-2.8

■ LEON ROBERTS

Roberts, Leon Kauffman b: 1/22/51, Vicksburg, Mich. BR/TR, 6'3", 200 lbs. Deb: 9/3/74

YEAR	TM/L	G	AB	R	H	2B	3B	HR	RBI	BB	SO	AVG	OBP	SLG	PRO+	BR/A	SB	CS	SBR	FA	FR	G/POS	TPR
1974	Det-A	17	63	5	17	3	2	0	7	3	10	.270	.303	.381	92	-1	0	2	-1	.926	-3	O-17	-0.6
1975	Det-A	129	447	51	115	17	5	10	38	36	94	.257	.318	.385	94	-4	3	7	-3	.982	8	*O-127/D-1	-0.5
1976	Hou-N	87	235	31	68	11	2	7	33	19	43	.289	.350	.443	136	10	1	0	0	.980	-4	O-60	0.5
1977	Hou-N	19	27	1	2	0	0	0	2	1	8	.074	.107	.074	-55	-6	0	0	0	1.000	-2	/O-9	-0.8
1978	Sea-A	134	472	78	142	21	7	22	92	41	52	.301	.367	.515	146	28	6	3	0	.975	10	*O-128/D-2	3.3
1979	Sea-A	140	450	61	122	24	6	15	54	56	64	.271	.354	.451	114	9	3	3	-1	.983	4	*O-136/D-1	0.7
1980	Sea-A	119	374	48	94	18	3	10	33	43	59	.251	.330	.396	97	-1	8	4	0	.984	3	*O-104/D-4	-0.2
1981	Tex-A	72	233	26	65	17	2	4	31	25	38	.279	.351	.421	128	8	3	4	-2	.992	-4	O-71	0.0
1982	Tex-A	31	73	7	17	3	0	1	6	4	14	.233	.282	.315	67	-3	0	0	0	1.000	-5	O-28/D-1	-0.9
	Tor-A	40	105	6	24	4	0	1	5	7	16	.229	.277	.295	52	-7	1	1	-0	1.000	-2	D-21,O-16	-1.0
	Yr	71	178	13	41	7	0	2	11	11	30	.230	.279	.303	58	-10	1	1	-0	1.000	-7	O-44,D-22	-1.9
1983	KC-A	84	213	24	55	7	0	8	24	17	27	.258	.316	.404	96	-1	1	1	-0	.979	-6	O-76/D-1	-1.0
1984	KC-A	29	45	4	10	1	1	0	3	4	3	.222	.300	.289	63	-2	0	0	0	1.000	-3	O-16/P-1,D-3	-0.5
Total	11	901	2737	342	731	126	28	78	328	256	428	.267	.335	.419	108	29	26	25	-7	.982	-3	O-788/D-34,P-1	-1.0

■ JIM ROBERTSON

Robertson, Alfred James b: 1/29/28, Chicago, Ill. BR/TR, 5'9", 183 lbs. Deb: 4/15/54

YEAR	TM/L	G	AB	R	H	2B	3B	HR	RBI	BB	SO	AVG	OBP	SLG	PRO+	BR/A	SB	CS	SBR	FA	FR	G/POS	TPR
1954	Phi-A	63	147	9	27	8	0	0	8	23	25	.184	.298	.238	48	-10	0	0	0	.974	-2	C-50	-1.0
1955	KC-A	6	8	1	2	0	0	0	0	1	2	.250	.333	.250	58	-0	0	0	0	1.000	0	/C-4	0.0
Total	2	69	155	10	29	8	0	0	8	24	27	.187	.300	.239	49	-10	0	0	0	.975	-2	/C-54	-1.0

■ ANDRE ROBERTSON

Robertson, Andre Levett b: 10/2/57, Orange, Tex. BR/TR, 5'10", 160 lbs. Deb: 9/3/81

YEAR	TM/L	G	AB	R	H	2B	3B	HR	RBI	BB	SO	AVG	OBP	SLG	PRO+	BR/A	SB	CS	SBR	FA	FR	G/POS	TPR
1981	*NY-A	10	19	1	5	1	0	0	0	0	3	.263	.263	.316	67	-1	1	1	-0	1.000	4	/S-8,2-3	0.3
1982	NY-A	44	118	16	26	5	0	2	9	8	19	.220	.270	.314	61	-6	0	0	0	.966	8	S-27,2-15/3-2	0.4
1983	NY-A	98	322	37	80	16	3	1	22	8	54	.248	.273	.326	67	-15	2	4	-2	.960	22	S-78,2-29	1.2
1984	NY-A	52	140	10	30	5	1	0	6	4	20	.214	.236	.264	40	-12	0	1	-1	.930	11	S-49/2-6	0.2
1985	NY-A	50	125	16	41	5	0	2	17	6	24	.328	.364	.416	116	3	1	2	-1	.867	-6	3-33,S-14/2-2	-0.4
Total	5	254	724	80	182	32	4	5	54	26	120	.251	.281	.327	69	-31	4	8	-4	.953	38	S-176/2-55,3-35	1.7

■ DARYL ROBERTSON

Robertson, Daryl Berdene b: 1/5/36, Cripple Creek, Colo BR/TR, 6', 184 lbs. Deb: 5/4/62

YEAR	TM/L	G	AB	R	H	2B	3B	HR	RBI	BB	SO	AVG	OBP	SLG	PRO+	BR/A	SB	CS	SBR	FA	FR	G/POS	TPR
1962	Chi-N	9	19	0	2	0	0	0	2	2	10	.105	.190	.105	-18	-3	0	0	0	1.000	-1	/S-6,3-1	-0.4

■ DAVE ROBERTSON

Robertson, Davis Aydelotte b: 9/25/1889, Portsmouth, Va. d: 11/5/70, Virginia Beach, Va. BL/TL, 6', 186 lbs. Deb: 6/5/12

YEAR	TM/L	G	AB	R	H	2B	3B	HR	RBI	BB	SO	AVG	OBP	SLG	PRO+	BR/A	SB	CS	SBR	FA	FR	G/POS	TPR
1912	NY-N	3	2	0	1	0	0	0	1	0	1	.500	.500	.500	169	0	1			1.000	-1	/1-1,O-1	0.0
1914	NY-N	82	256	25	68	12	3	2	32	10	26	.266	.299	.359	99	-2	9			.950	-2	O-71	-0.7
1915	NY-N	141	544	72	160	17	10	3	58	22	52	.294	.326	.379	120	11	22	10	1	.956	-1	*O-138	0.4
1916	NY-N	150	587	88	180	18	8	**12**	69	14	56	.307	.326	.426	137	22	21	17	-4	.960	5	*O-144	1.7
1917	*NY-N	142	532	64	138	16	9	**12**	54	10	47	.259	.276	.391	107	1	17			.942	1	*O-140	-0.7
1919	NY-N	1	0	0	0	0	0	0	0	0	0	—	—	—	—	0	0			.000	0	R	0.0
	Chi-N	27	96	8	20	2	0	1	10	1	10	.208	.224	.260	45	-6	3			.932	-2	O-25	-1.2
	Yr	28	96	8	20	2	0	1	10	1	10	.208	.224	.260	45	-6	3			.932	-2	O-25	-1.2
1920	Chi-N	134	500	68	150	29	11	10	75	40	44	.300	.353	.462	130	18	17	23	-9	.968	-9	*O-134	-0.9
1921	Chi-N	22	36	7	8	3	0	0	14	1	3	.222	.243	.306	44	-3	0	2	-1	1.000	-2	/O-7	-0.7
	Pit-N	60	230	29	74	18	3	6	48	12	16	.322	.361	.504	123	7	4	5	-2	.960	-4	O-58	-0.3
	Yr	82	266	36	82	21	3	6	62	13	19	.308	.345	.477	113	4	4	7	-3	.962	-6	O-65	-1.0
1922	NY-N	42	47	5	13	2	0	1	3	3	7	.277	.320	.383	80	-1	0	0	0	.909	-2	/O-8	-0.3
Total	9	804	2830	366	812	117	44	47	364	113	262	.287	.318	.409	117	46	94	57		.955	-16	O-726/1-1	-2.7

■ DON ROBERTSON

Robertson, Donald Alexander b: 10/15/30, Harvey, Ill. BL/TL, 5'10", 180 lbs. Deb: 4/13/54

YEAR	TM/L	G	AB	R	H	2B	3B	HR	RBI	BB	SO	AVG	OBP	SLG	PRO+	BR/A	SB	CS	SBR	FA	FR	G/POS	TPR
1954	Chi-N	14	6	2	0	0	0	0	0	0	2	.000	.000	.000	-99	-2	0	0	0	1.000	-2	/O-6	-0.4

■ GENE ROBERTSON

Robertson, Eugene Edward b: 12/25/1898, St.Louis, Mo. d: 10/21/81, Fallon, Nev. BL/TR, 5'7", 152 lbs. Deb: 7/4/19

YEAR	TM/L	G	AB	R	H	2B	3B	HR	RBI	BB	SO	AVG	OBP	SLG	PRO+	BR/A	SB	CS	SBR	FA	FR	G/POS	TPR
1919	StL-A	5	7	1	1	0	0	0	0	1	2	.143	.250	.143	11	-1	0			.750	-2	/S-2	-0.2
1922	StL-A	18	27	2	8	2	1	0	1	1	1	.296	.321	.444	95	-0	1	0	0	.875	1	/3-7,S-6,2-1	0.1

YEAR	TM/L	G	AB	R	H	2B	3B	HR	RBI	BB	SO	AVG	OBP	SLG	PRO+	BR/A	SB	CS	SBR	FA	FR	G/POS	TPR
1923	StL-A	78	251	36	62	10	1	0	17	21	7	.247	.310	.295	57	-16	4	2	0	.935	-14	3-74/2-1	-2.4
1924	StL-A	121	439	70	140	25	4	4	52	36	14	.319	.373	.421	99	-1	3	5	-2	.958	-11	*3-111/2-2	-0.5
1925	StL-A	154	582	97	158	26	5	14	76	81	30	.271	.364	.405	90	-8	10	7	-1	.939	-2	*3-154/S-1	-0.1
1926	StL-A	78	247	23	62	12	6	1	19	17	10	.251	.302	.360	69	-12	5	1	1	.924	-5	3-55,S-10/2-3	-1.1
1928	*NY-A	83	251	29	73	9	0	1	36	14	6	.291	.328	.339	78	-8	2	4	-2	.926	-8	3-70/2-3	-1.4
1929	NY-A	90	309	45	92	15	6	0	35	28	6	.298	.358	.385	98	-1	3	3	-1	.966	-11	3-77	-1.0
	Bos-N	8	28	1	8	0	0	0	6	1	0	.286	.310	.286	51	-2	1			.875	-2	/3-6,S-1	-0.3
1930	Bos-N	21	59	7	11	1	0	0	7	5	3	.186	.250	.203	12	-8	0			.949	-2	3-17	-0.9
Total	9	656	2200	311	615	100	23	20	249	205	79	.280	.344	.373	83	-58	29	22		.941	-56	3-571/S-20,2-10	-7.8

■ **MIKE ROBERTSON** Robertson, Michael Francis b: 10/9/70, Norwich, Conn. BL/TL, 6', 180 lbs. Deb: 9/6/96

YEAR	TM/L	G	AB	R	H	2B	3B	HR	RBI	BB	SO	AVG	OBP	SLG	PRO+	BR/A	SB	CS	SBR	FA	FR	G/POS	TPR
1996	Chi-A	6	7	0	1	1	0	0	0	0	1	.143	.143	.286	5	-1	0	0	0	1.000	0	/1-2,D-2	-0.1
1997	Phi-N	22	38	3	8	2	1	0	4	0	6	.211	.268	.316	52	-3	1	0	0	1.000	-0	/1-5,O-5,D-1	-0.3
1998	Ari-N	11	13	0	2	0	0	0	0	0	2	.154	.154	.154	-20	-2	0	0	0	.000	0	/D-2	-0.2
Total	3	39	58	3	11	3	1	0	4	0	9	.190	.230	.276	31	-6	1	0	0	1.000	-0	/1-7,O-5,D-5	-0.6

■ **BOB ROBERTSON** Robertson, Robert Eugene b: 10/2/46, Frostburg, Md. BR/TR, 6'1", 210 lbs. Deb: 9/18/67

YEAR	TM/L	G	AB	R	H	2B	3B	HR	RBI	BB	SO	AVG	OBP	SLG	PRO+	BR/A	SB	CS	SBR	FA	FR	G/POS	TPR
1967	Pit-N	9	35	4	6	0	0	2	4	3	12	.171	.237	.343	64	-2	0	0	0	.990	-0	/1-9	-0.3
1969	Pit-N	32	96	7	20	4	1	1	9	8	30	.208	.269	.302	61	-5	1	0	0	.996	1	1-26	-0.6
1970	*Pit-N	117	390	69	112	19	4	27	82	51	98	.287	.372	.564	150	27	4	1	1	.995	3	1-99/3-5,O-3	2.1
1971	*Pit-N	131	469	65	127	18	2	26	72	60	101	.271	.358	.484	137	23	1	2	-1	.993	15	*1-126	2.6
1972	*Pit-N	115	306	25	59	11	0	12	41	41	84	.193	.294	.346	83	-7	1	1	-0	.993	9	1-89,O-23,3-11	-0.4
1973	Pit-N	119	397	43	95	16	0	14	40	55	77	.239	.333	.385	101	1	0	4	-2	.995	5	*1-107	-0.5
1974	*Pit-N	91	236	25	54	11	0	16	48	33	48	.229	.323	.479	127	7	0	0	0	.991	-1	1-63	0.3
1975	*Pit-N	75	124	17	34	4	0	6	18	23	25	.274	.396	.452	136	7	0	0	0	.996	1	1-27	0.7
1976	Pit-N	61	129	10	28	5	1	2	25	16	23	.217	.303	.318	76	-4	0	1	-1	.996	-0	1-29	-0.7
1978	Sea-A	64	174	17	40	5	2	8	28	24	39	.230	.327	.420	109	2	0	0	0	1.000	-1	D-29,1-18	-0.1
1979	Tor-A	15	29	1	3	0	0	1	1	3	9	.103	.188	.207	6	-4	0	0	0	1.000	2	/1-9,D-4	-0.3
Total	11	829	2385	283	578	93	10	115	368	317	546	.242	.334	.434	115	45	7	9	-3	.994	34	1-602/D-33,O-26,3	2.8

■ **SHERRY ROBERTSON** Robertson, Sherrard Alexander b: 1/1/19, Montreal, Que., Can. d: 10/23/70, Houghton, S.Dak. BL/TR, 6', 180 lbs. Deb: 9/8/40 C

YEAR	TM/L	G	AB	R	H	2B	3B	HR	RBI	BB	SO	AVG	OBP	SLG	PRO+	BR/A	SB	CS	SBR	FA	FR	G/POS	TPR
1940	Was-A	10	33	4	7	0	1	0	0	5	6	.212	.316	.273	58	-2	0	0	0	.940	1	S-10	0.0
1941	Was-A	1	3	0	0	0	0	0	0	0	3	.000	.000	.000	-99	-1	0	0	0	.750	0	/3-1	-0.1
1943	Was-A	59	120	22	26	4	1	3	14	17	19	.217	.319	.342	97	-0	0	2	-1	.897	-4	3-27/S-1	-0.6
1946	Was-A	74	230	30	46	6	3	6	19	30	42	.200	.292	.330	78	-7	6	2	1	.902	-6	3-38,2-14,S-12,/O-1	-1.1
1947	Was-A	95	266	25	62	9	3	1	23	32	52	.233	.318	.301	74	-9	4	5	-2	.949	0	O-55,3-10/2-4	-1.4
1948	Was-A	71	187	19	46	11	3	2	22	24	26	.246	.335	.369	90	-3	8	0	**2**	.939	-1	O-51	-0.4
1949	Was-A	110	374	59	94	17	3	11	42	42	35	.251	.329	.401	95	-5	10	3	1	.947	-8	2-71,3-19,O-13	-0.9
1950	Was-A	71	123	19	32	3	3	2	16	22	18	.260	.372	.382	98	0	1	1	-0	.952	-9	O-14,2-12/3-1	-0.8
1951	Was-A	62	111	14	21	2	1	1	10	9	22	.189	.256	.252	38	-10	2	1	0	.949	3	O-22	-0.7
1952	Was-A	1	0	0	0	0	0	0	0	0	0	—	—	—	—	0	0	0	0	.000	0	R	0.0
	Phi-A	43	60	8	12	3	0	0	5	21	15	.200	.407	.250	81	-0	1	2	-1	.958	-3	/2-8,O-7,3-2	-0.5
	Yr	44	60	8	12	3	0	0	5	21	15	.200	.407	.250	81	-0	1	2	-1	.958	-3	/2-8,O-7,3-2	-0.5
Total	10	597	1507	200	346	55	18	26	151	202	238	.230	.323	.342	83	-37	32	16	0	.946	-27	O-163,2-109/3-98,S	-6.5

■ **BILLY JO ROBIDOUX** Robidoux, William Joseph b: 1/13/64, Ware, Mass. BL/TR, 6'1", 200 lbs. Deb: 9/11/85

YEAR	TM/L	G	AB	R	H	2B	3B	HR	RBI	BB	SO	AVG	OBP	SLG	PRO+	BR/A	SB	CS	SBR	FA	FR	G/POS	TPR
1985	Mil-A	18	51	5	9	2	0	3	8	12	16	.176	.333	.392	98	0	0	0	0	1.000	-1	O-11/1-6,D-1	-0.1
1986	Mil-A	56	181	15	41	8	0	1	21	33	36	.227	.346	.287	72	-6	0	0	0	.986	-2	1-43,D-10	-1.1
1987	Mil-A	23	62	9	12	0	0	0	4	8	17	.194	.286	.194	30	-6	0	1	-1	.983	-0	1-10,D-10	-0.7
1988	Mil-A	33	91	9	23	5	0	0	5	8	14	.253	.313	.308	74	-3	1	1	-0	.983	2	1-30/D-1	-0.3
1989	Chi-A	16	39	2	5	2	0	0	1	4	9	.128	.209	.179	11	-5	0	0	0	.990	-1	1-15/O-1	-0.6
1990	Bos-A	27	44	3	8	4	0	1	4	6	14	.182	.294	.341	74	-2	0	0	0	.981	-0	1-11/D-4	-0.2
Total	6	173	468	43	98	21	0	5	43	71	106	.209	.315	.286	65	-21	1	2	-1	.986	-1	1-115/D-26,O-12	-3.0

■ **AARON ROBINSON** Robinson, Aaron Andrew b: 6/23/15, Lancaster, S.C. d: 3/9/66, Lancaster, S.C. BL/TR, 6'2", 205 lbs. Deb: 5/6/43

YEAR	TM/L	G	AB	R	H	2B	3B	HR	RBI	BB	SO	AVG	OBP	SLG	PRO+	BR/A	SB	CS	SBR	FA	FR	G/POS	TPR
1943	NY-A	1	1	0	0	0	0	0	0	0	0	.000	.000	.000	-99	-0	0	0	0	.000	0	H	0.0
1945	NY-A	50	160	19	45	6	1	8	24	21	23	.281	.368	.481	139	8	0	0	0	1.000	-3	C-45	0.8
1946	NY-A	100	330	32	98	17	2	16	64	48	39	.297	.388	.506	146	21	0	1	-1	.983	-11	C-95	1.5
1947	*NY-A☆	82	252	23	68	11	5	5	36	40	26	.270	.370	.413	119	7	0	1	-1	.997	-0	C-74	1.1
1948	Chi-A	98	326	47	82	14	2	8	39	46	30	.252	.344	.380	96	-2	0	1	-1	.989	-5	C-92	-0.1
1949	Det-A	110	331	38	89	12	0	13	56	73	21	.269	.402	.423	118	11	0	2	-1	.986	-1	*C-108	1.4
1950	Det-A	107	283	37	64	7	0	9	37	75	35	.226	.388	.346	86	-3	0	1	-1	.993	-3	*C-103	-0.2
1951	Det-A	36	82	3	17	6	0	0	9	17	9	.207	.343	.280	70	-3	0	0	0	1.000	-2	C-35	-0.4
	Bos-A	26	74	9	15	1	1	2	7	17	10	.203	.352	.324	76	-2	0	0	0	.983	-1	C-25	-0.2
	Yr	62	156	12	32	7	1	2	16	34	19	.205	.347	.301	73	-5	0	0	0	.991	-3	C-60	-0.6
Total	8	610	1839	208	478	74	11	61	272	337	194	.260	.375	.412	112	35	0	6	-4	.990	-26	C-577	3.9

■ **VAL ROBINSON** Robinson, Alfred Valentine Deb: 5/1/1872

YEAR	TM/L	G	AB	R	H	2B	3B	HR	RBI	BB	SO	AVG	OBP	SLG	PRO+	BR/A	SB	CS	SBR	FA	FR	G/POS	TPR
1872	Oly-n	7	30	6	6	0	0	0	4	1	1	.200	.226	.200	34	-2	0	0	0	.750	-0	/O-7	-0.1

■ **BROOKS ROBINSON** Robinson, Brooks Calbert b: 5/18/37, Little Rock, Ark. BR/TR, 6'1", 190 lbs. Deb: 9/17/55 CH

YEAR	TM/L	G	AB	R	H	2B	3B	HR	RBI	BB	SO	AVG	OBP	SLG	PRO+	BR/A	SB	CS	SBR	FA	FR	G/POS	TPR
1955	Bal-A	6	22	0	2	0	0	0	1	0	10	.091	.091	.091	-55	-5	0	0	0	.833	-2	/3-6	-0.7
1956	Bal-A	15	44	5	10	4	0	1	1	1	5	.227	.244	.386	70	-2	0	0	0	.944	0	3-14/2-1	-0.2
1957	Bal-A	50	117	13	28	6	1	2	14	7	10	.239	.288	.359	81	-4	1	0	0	.971	4	3-47	0.1
1958	Bal-A	145	463	31	110	16	3	3	32	31	51	.238	.293	.305	68	-21	1	2	-1	.953	10	*3-140,2-16	-1.0
1959	Bal-A	88	313	29	89	15	2	4	24	17	37	.284	.325	.383	96	-2	2	2	-1	.955	7	3-87/2-1	0.4
1960	Bal-A★	152	595	74	175	27	9	14	88	35	49	.294	.333	.440	109	5	2	2	-1	**.977**	12	*3-152/2-3	1.6
1961	Bal-A★	163	668	89	192	38	7	7	61	47	57	.287	.338	.397	99	-2	1	3	-2	**.972**	-6	*3-163/2-2,S-1	-0.7
1962	Bal-A★	162	634	77	192	29	9	23	86	42	70	.303	.347	.486	129	23	3	1	0	**.979**	7	*3-162/S-3,2-2	3.2
1963	Bal-A★	161	589	67	148	26	4	11	67	46	84	.251	.307	.365	91	-8	2	3	-1	**.976**	9	*3-160/S-1	0.0
1964	Bal-A★	163	612	82	194	35	3	28	**118**	51	64	.317	.373	.521	146	37	1	0	0	**.972**	-2	*3-163	3.5
1965	Bal-A★	144	559	81	166	25	2	18	80	47	47	.297	.354	.445	123	16	3	0	1	.967	-6	*3-143	0.9
1966	*Bal-A★	157	620	91	167	35	2	23	100	56	36	.269	.335	.444	123	18	2	3	-1	**.976**	4	*3-157	1.9
1967	Bal-A★	158	610	88	164	25	5	22	77	54	54	.269	.332	.434	126	19	1	3	-2	**.980**	**31**	*3-158	5.0
1968	Bal-A★	162	608	65	154	36	6	17	75	44	55	.253	.308	.416	118	11	1	1	-0	**.970**	17	*3-162	3.2
1969	*Bal-A★	156	598	73	140	21	3	23	84	56	55	.234	.303	.395	93	-7	2	1	0	**.976**	19	*3-156	1.3
1970	*Bal-A★	158	608	84	168	31	4	18	94	53	53	.276	.338	.429	109	7	1	1	-0	.966	-1	*3-156	0.4
1971	*Bal-A★	156	589	67	160	21	1	20	92	63	50	.272	.345	.413	115	11	0	0	0	.968	7	*3-156	1.8
1972	Bal-A★	153	556	48	139	23	2	8	64	43	45	.250	.306	.342	90	-7	1	0	0	**.977**	6	*3-152	-0.3
1973	*Bal-A★	155	549	53	141	17	2	9	72	55	50	.257	.328	.344	90	-7	2	0	1	.970	9	*3-154	0.2
1974	*Bal-A★	153	553	46	159	27	0	7	59	56	47	.288	.356	.374	114	11	2	0	1	.967	21	*3-153	3.2
1975	Bal-A	144	482	50	97	15	1	6	53	44	33	.201	.269	.274	57	-28	0	0	0	**.979**	4	*3-143	-2.5
1976	Bal-A	71	218	16	46	8	2	3	11	8	24	.211	.242	.307	64	-11	0	0	0	.969	0	3-71	-1.2
1977	Bal-A	24	47	3	7	2	0	1	4	4	4	.149	.216	.255	30	-5	0	0	0	1.000	2	3-15	-0.3
Total	23	2896	10654	1232	2848	482	68	268	1357	860	990	.267	.325	.401	105	52	28	22	-5	.971	151	*3-2870/2-25,S-5	19.8

■ **BRUCE ROBINSON** Robinson, Bruce Philip b: 4/16/54, LaJolla, Cal. BL/TR, 6'1", 185 lbs. Deb: 8/19/78 F

YEAR	TM/L	G	AB	R	H	2B	3B	HR	RBI	BB	SO	AVG	OBP	SLG	PRO+	BR/A	SB	CS	SBR	FA	FR	G/POS	TPR
1978	Oak-A	28	84	5	21	3	1	0	8	3	8	.250	.276	.310	68	-4	0	0	0	.965	7	C-28	0.4
1979	NY-A	6	12	0	2	0	0	0	2	1	0	.167	.231	.167	9	-2	0	0	0	.943	2	/C-6	0.1
1980	NY-A	4	5	0	0	0	0	0	0	0	4	.000	.000	.000	-99	-1	0	0	0	1.000	-0	/C-3	-0.2
Total	3	38	101	5	23	3	1	0	10	4	12	.228	.257	.277	52	-7	0	0	0	.962	9	/C-37	0.3

YEAR	TM/L	G	AB	R	H	2B	3B	HR	RBI	BB	SO	AVG	OBP	SLG	PRO+	BR/A	SB	CS	SBR	FA	FR	G/POS	TPR
■ CHARLIE ROBINSON	Robinson, Charles Henry b: 7/27/1856, Westerly, R.I. d: 5/18/13, BL/TR, Deb: 8/2/1884																						
1884	Ind-a	20	80	11	23	2	0	0		3		.287	.313	.313	108	1				.967	-1	C-17/S-3,O-1	0.1
1885	Bro-a	11	40	5	6	2	1	0	4	3		.150	.209	.250	44	-3				.840	-4	C-11	-0.5
Total	2	31	120	16	29	4	1	0	4	6		.242	.278	.292	85	-2				.919	-5	/C-28,S-3,O-1	-0.4
■ RABBIT ROBINSON	Robinson, Clyde b: 3/5/1882, Wellsburg, W.Va. d: 4/9/15, Waterbury, Conn. BR/TR, 5'6", 148 lbs. Deb: 4/22/03																						
1903	Was-A	103	373	41	79	10	8	1	20	33		.212	.279	.290	69	-13	16			.917	2	2-45,O-30,S-24,/3-5	-1.1
1904	Det-A	101	320	30	77	13	6	0	37	29		.241	.314	.319	103	2	14			.925	1	S-30,3-26,O-20,2-19	0.5
1910	Cin-N	2	7	0	0	0	0	0	1	1	0	.000	.125	.000	-66	-1	0			1.000	-1	/3-2	-0.3
Total	3	206	700	71	156	23	14	1	58	63	0	.223	.294	.300	83	-13	30			.940	2	/2-64,S-54,O-50,3	-0.9
■ CRAIG ROBINSON	Robinson, Craig George b: 8/21/48, Abington, Pa. BR/TR, 5'10", 165 lbs. Deb: 9/9/72																						
1972	Phi-N	5	15	0	3	1	0	0	0	1	2	.200	.250	.267	46	-1	0	0	0	1.000	2	/S-4	0.2
1973	Phi-N	46	146	11	33	7	0	0	7	0	25	.226	.226	.274	37	-12	1	1	-0	.945	1	S-42/2-4	-0.8
1974	Atl-N	145	452	52	104	4	6	0	29	30	57	.230	.282	.265	52	-29	11	2	2	.956	-17	*S-142	-2.8
1975	Atl-N	10	17	1	1	0	0	0	0	0	5	.059	.059	.059	-65	-4	0	0	0	1.000	1	/S-7	-0.2
	SF-N	29	29	4	2	1	0	0	0	2	6	.069	.129	.103	-34	-5	0	0	0	.941	5	S-12/2-9	0.0
	Yr	39	46	5	3	1	0	0	0	2	11	.065	.104	.087	-45	-9	0	0	0	.967	6	S-19/2-9	-0.2
1976	SF-N	15	13	4	4	1	0	0	2	3	4	.308	.438	.385	131	1	0	1	-1	.952	4	/2-7,3-2,S-1	0.4
	Atl-N	15	17	4	4	0	0	0	3	5	2	.235	.409	.235	81	-0	0	0	0	.952	2	/2-5,S-2,3-1	0.2
	Yr	30	30	8	8	1	0	0	5	8	6	.267	.421	.300	102	1	0	1	-1	.952	6	2-12/3-3,S-3	0.6
1977	Atl-N	27	29	4	6	1	0	0	1	1	6	.207	.233	.241	25	-3	0	0	0	1.000	6	S-23	0.3
Total	6	292	718	80	157	15	6	0	42	42	107	.219	.265	.256	44	-54	12	4	1	.956	3	S-233/2-25,3-3	-2.7
■ DAVE ROBINSON	Robinson, David Tanner b: 5/22/46, Minneapolis, Minn. BB/TL, 6'1", 186 lbs. Deb: 9/10/70 F																						
1970	SD-N	15	38	5	12	2	0	2	6	5	4	.316	.395	.526	151	3	2	0	1	1.000	1	O-13	0.4
1971	SD-N	7	6	0	0	0	0	0	0	1	3	.000	.143	.000	-61	-1	0	0	0	.000	0	H	-0.1
Total	2	22	44	5	12	2	0	2	6	6	7	.273	.360	.455	124	1	2	0	1	1.000	1	/O-13	0.3
■ EARL ROBINSON	Robinson, Earl John b: 11/3/36, New Orleans, La. BR/TR, 6'1", 190 lbs. Deb: 9/10/58																						
1958	LA-N	8	15	3	3	0	0	0	0	1	4	.200	.250	.200	20	-2	0	0	0	1.000	1	/3-6	0.0
1961	Bal-A	96	222	37	59	12	3	8	30	31	54	.266	.356	.455	119	6	4	3	-1	.973	-3	O-82	-0.1
1962	Bal-A	29	63	12	18	3	1	1	4	8	10	.286	.366	.413	116	2	2	0	1	1.000	0	O-17	0.2
1964	Bal-A	37	121	11	33	5	1	3	10	7	24	.273	.313	.405	98	-1	1	2	-1	.986	1	O-34	-0.2
Total	4	170	421	63	113	20	5	12	44	47	92	.268	.342	.425	109	5	7	5	-1	.980	-1	O-133/3-6	-0.1
■ FLOYD ROBINSON	Robinson, Floyd Andrew b: 5/9/36, Prescott, Ark. BL/TR, 5'9", 175 lbs. Deb: 8/10/60																						
1960	Chi-A	22	46	7	13	0	0	0	1	11	8	.283	.431	.283	98	1	2	3	-1	.960	-2	O-17	-0.4
1961	Chi-A	132	432	69	134	20	7	11	59	52	32	.310	.389	.465	129	19	7	4	-0	.991	4	*O-106	1.6
1962	Chi-A	156	600	89	187	**45**	10	11	109	72	47	.312	.387	.475	131	27	4	2	0	.973	-10	*O-155	0.8
1963	Chi-A	146	527	71	149	21	6	13	71	62	43	.283	.363	.419	120	15	4	3	-1	.984	-7	*O-137	0.1
1964	Chi-A	141	525	83	158	17	3	11	59	70	41	.301	.388	.408	125	20	9	5	-0	.987	-12	*O-138	0.1
1965	Chi-A	156	577	70	153	15	6	14	66	76	51	.265	.356	.385	117	15	4	1	1	.985	-4	*O-153	0.4
1966	Chi-A	127	342	44	81	11	2	5	35	44	32	.237	.332	.325	96	-1	8	2	1	.962	-14	*O-113	-1.9
1967	Cin-N	55	130	19	31	6	2	1	10	14	14	.238	.313	.338	77	-4	3	1	0	.981	-4	O-39	-1.0
1968	Oak-A	53	81	5	20	5	0	1	14	4	10	.247	.282	.346	94	-1	0	0	0	1.000	-1	O-18	-0.3
	Bos-A	23	24	1	3	0	0	0	2	3	4	.125	.250	.125	15	-2	1	0	0	.833	-3	O-10	-0.6
	Yr	76	105	6	23	5	0	1	16	7	14	.219	.274	.295	74	-3	1	0	0	.963	-4	O-28	-0.9
Total	9	1011	3284	458	929	140	36	67	426	408	282	.283	.367	.409	118	90	42	21	0	.981	-53	O-886	-1.2
■ FRANK ROBINSON	Robinson, Frank b: 8/31/35, Beaumont, Tex. BR/TR, 6'1", 195 lbs. Deb: 4/17/56 MCH																						
1956	Cin-N★	152	572	**122**	166	27	6	38	83	64	95	.290	.381	.558	139	32	8	4	0	.976	6	*O-152	3.0
1957	Cin-N★	150	611	97	197	29	5	29	75	44	92	.322	.379	.529	131	27	10	2	2	.989	19	*O-136,1-24	3.8
1958	Cin-N	148	554	90	149	25	6	31	83	62	80	.269	.350	.504	116	12	10	1	2	.991	9	*O-138,3-11	1.7
1959	Cin-N★	146	540	106	168	31	4	36	125	69	93	.311	.397	.583	152	41	18	8	1	.984	-9	*1-125,O-40	2.3
1960	Cin-N	139	464	86	138	33	6	31	83	82	67	.297	.413	**.595**	169	46	13	6	0	.993	7	1-78,O-51/3-1	4.5
1961	*Cin-N★	153	545	117	176	32	7	37	124	71	64	.323	.411	**.611**	164	51	22	3	**5**	.990	10	*O-150/3-1	5.5
1962	Cin-N★	162	609	**134**	208	**51**	2	39	136	76	62	.342	**.424**	**.624**	**172**	**62**	18	9	0	.994	9	*O-161	6.0
1963	Cin-N	140	482	79	125	19	3	21	91	81	69	.259	.381	.442	132	23	26	10	2	.984	9	*O-139/1-1	2.9
1964	Cin-N	156	568	103	174	38	6	29	96	79	67	.306	.399	.548	158	45	23	5	4	.986	2	*O-156	4.6
1965	Cin-N★	156	582	109	172	33	5	33	113	70	100	.296	.388	.540	148	38	13	9	-2	.990	2	*O-155	3.3
1966	*Bal-A★	155	576	**122**	182	34	2	**49**	**122**	87	90	**.316**	**.415**	**.637**	**200**	**76**	8	5	-1	.985	-4	*O-151/1-3	**6.7**
1967	Bal-A†	129	479	83	149	23	7	30	94	71	84	.311	.408	.576	189	54	2	3	-1	.990	-2	*O-126/1-2	4.8
1968	Bal-A	130	421	69	113	27	1	15	52	73	84	.268	.391	.444	153	30	11	2	2	.962	-8	*O-117/1-3	2.0
1969	*Bal-A★	148	539	111	166	19	5	32	100	88	62	.308	.417	.540	164	49	9	3	1	.987	-1	*O-134,1-19	4.2
1970	*Bal-A★	132	471	88	144	24	1	25	78	69	70	.306	.402	.520	151	34	2	1	0	.987	6	*O-120/1-7	3.4
1971	*Bal-A★	133	455	82	128	16	2	28	99	72	62	.281	.390	.510	154	34	3	0	1	.973	-4	O-92,1-37	2.4
1972	LA-N	103	342	41	86	6	1	19	59	55	76	.251	.358	.442	129	14	2	3	-1	.967	-1	O-95	0.8
1973	Cal-A	147	534	85	142	29	0	30	97	82	93	.266	.374	.489	153	38	1	1	-0	.976	4	*D-127,O-17	3.8
1974	Cal-A★	129	427	75	107	26	2	20	63	75	85	.251	.375	.461	148	28	5	1	1	.000	-0	*D-123/O-1	2.7
	Cle-A	15	50	6	10	1	1	2	5	10	10	.200	.333	.380	106	1	0	1	-1	.958	-1	D-11/1-4	-0.1
	Yr	144	477	81	117	27	3	22	68	85	95	.245	.371	.453	143	29	5	2	0	.906	-1	*D-134/1-4,O-1	2.6
1975	Cle-A	49	118	19	28	5	0	9	24	29	15	.237	.388	.508	152	9	0	0	0	.000	0	D-42,M	0.8
1976	Cle-A	36	67	5	15	0	0	3	10	11	12	.224	.333	.358	104	1	0	0	0	1.000	-1	D-18/1-2,O-1,M	-0.1
Total	21	2808	10006	1829	2943	528	72	586	1812	1420	1532	.294	.392	.537	154	744	204	77	15	.984	52	*O-2132,D-321,1/3	69.0
■ FRED ROBINSON	Robinson, Frederic Henry b: 7/6/1856, South Acton, Mass. d: 12/18/33, Hudson, Mass. BR/TR, Deb: 4/17/1884 F																						
1884	Cin-U	3	13	1	3	0	0	0		0		.231	.231	.231	37	-1				.727	-3	/2-3	-0.4
■ JACKIE ROBINSON	Robinson, Jack Roosevelt b: 1/31/19, Cairo, Ga. d: 10/24/72, Stamford, Conn. BR/TR, 5'11", 204 lbs. Deb: 4/15/47 H																						
1947	*Bro-N	151	590	125	175	31	5	12	48	74	36	.297	.383	.427	111	11	**29**			.989	-3	*1-151	0.2
1948	Bro-N	147	574	108	170	38	8	12	85	57	37	.296	.367	.453	117	13	22			**.980**	1	*2-116,1-30/3-6	2.0
1949	*Bro-N★	156	593	122	203	38	12	16	124	86	27	**.342**	.432	.528	150	45	**37**			.981	-1	*2-156	4.9
1950	Bro-N★	144	518	99	170	39	4	14	81	80	24	.328	.423	.500	139	32	12			**.986**	11	*2-144	**4.7**
1951	Bro-N★	153	548	106	185	33	7	19	88	79	27	.338	.429	.527	153	43	25	8	3	**.992**	17	*2-150	**6.8**
1952	*Bro-N★	149	510	104	157	17	3	19	75	106	40	.308	**.440**	.465	149	41	24	7	3	.974	4	*2-146	**5.6**
1953	*Bro-N★	136	484	109	159	34	7	12	95	74	30	.329	.425	.502	137	30	17	4	3	.981	8	O-76,3-44/2-9,1S	3.5
1954	Bro-N★	124	386	62	120	22	4	15	59	63	20	.311	.417	.505	135	22	7	3	0	1.000	-9	O-74,3-50/2-4	1.0
1955	*Bro-N	105	317	51	81	6	2	8	36	61	18	.256	.381	.363	96	1	12	3	2	.966	7	3-84,O-10/1-1,2-1	0.9
1956	*Bro-N	117	357	61	98	15	2	10	43	60	32	.275	.383	.412	106	5	12	5	1	.967	15	3-72,2-22/1-9,O-2	2.2
Total	10	1382	4877	947	1518	273	54	137	734	740	291	.311	.410	.474	131	241	197	30		.983	49	2-748,3-256,1O/S	31.8
■ JACK ROBINSON	Robinson, John W. "Bridgeport" b: 7/15/1880, Portland, Maine d: 7/22/21, Macon, Ga. TR , Deb: 9/6/02																						
1902	NY-N	4	9	0	0	0	0	0	0	0		.000	.000	.000	-99	-2	0			1.000	1	/C-3	-0.1
■ KERRY ROBINSON	Robinson, Kerry Keith b: 10/3/73, St.Louis, Mo. BL/TL, 6', 175 lbs. Deb: 9/22/98																						
1998	TB-A	2	3	0	0	0	0	0	0	0	1	.000	.000	.000	-96	-1	0	0	0	1.000	0	/O-2	-0.1
■ WILBERT ROBINSON	Robinson, Wilbert "Uncle Robby" b: 6/29/1863, Bolton, Mass. d: 8/8/34, Atlanta, Ga. BR/TR, 5'8.5", 215 lbs. Deb: 4/19/1886 FMCH																						
1886	Phi-a	87	342	57	69	11	3	1	30	21		.202	.254	.260	61	-16	33			.893	-10	C-61,1-22/O-5	-1.9
1887	Phi-a	68	264	28	60	6	2	1	24	14		.227	.269	.277	52	-17	15			.901	1	C-67/1-3,O-1	-0.8

YEAR	TM/L	G	AB	R	H	2B	3B	HR	RBI	BB	SO	AVG	OBP	SLG	PRO+	BR/A	SB	CS	SBR	FA	FR	G/POS	TPR
1888	Phi-a	66	254	32	62	7	2	1	31	9		.244	.270	.299	83	-5	11			.938	25	C-65/1-1	2.4
1889	Phi-a	69	264	31	61	13	2	0	28	6	34	.231	.251	.295	56	-16	9			.943	4	C-69	-0.5
1890	Phi-a	82	329	32	78	13	4	4	42	16		.237	.279	.337	83	-9	20			.930	-9	C-82	-0.9
	Bal-a	14	48	7	13	1	0	0	4	3		.271	.314	.292	75	-2	1			.989	6	C-11/1-3	0.5
	Yr	96	377	39	91	14	4	4	46	19		.241	.283	.332	82	-10	21			.938	-3	C-93/1-3	-0.4
1891	Bal-a	93	334	25	72	8	5	2	46	16	37	.216	.251	.287	54	-22	18			.954	3	C-92/O-1	-0.9
1892	Bal-N	90	330	36	88	14	4	2	57	15	35	.267	.303	.352	95	-3	5			.921	-18	C-87/1-2,O-1	-1.4
1893	Bal-N	95	359	49	120	21	3	3	57	26	22	.334	.382	.435	115	7	17			.942	-8	*C-93/1-1	0.6
1894	*Bal-N	109	414	69	146	21	4	1	98	46	18	.353	.421	.430	101	2	12			.944	-5	*C-109	0.5
1895	*Bal-N	77	282	38	74	19	1	0	48	12	19	.262	.295	.337	61	-17	11			**.979**	14	C-75	0.3
1896	*Bal-N	67	245	43	85	9	6	2	38	14	13	.347	.385	.457	120	6	9			.948	3	C-67	1.4
1897	Bal-N	48	181	25	57	9	0	0	23	8		.315	.347	.365	88	-3	0			.965	-2	C-48	0.0
1898	Bal-N	79	289	29	80	12	2	0	38	16		.277	.317	.332	84	-6	3			.965	-5	C-77	-0.4
1899	Bal-N	108	356	40	101	15	2	0	47	31		.284	.344	.337	83	-8	5			.949	-18	*C-105	-1.7
1900	StL-N	60	210	26	52	5	1	0	28	11		.248	.291	.281	59	-12	7			.974	-1	C-54	-0.7
1901	Bal-A	68	239	32	72	12	3	0	26	10		.301	.335	.377	93	-3	9			.949	-2	C-67	0.2
1902	Bal-A	91	335	38	98	16	7	1	57	12		.293	.321	.391	93	-4	11			.949	-15	C-87,M	-1.0
Total	17	1371	5075	637	1388	212	51	18	722	286	178	.273	.316	.346	83	-129	196			.941	-36	*C-1316/1-32,O-8	-4.3

■ EDDIE ROBINSON

Robinson, William Edward b: 12/15/20, Paris, Tex. BL/TR, 6'2.5", 210 lbs. Deb: 9/9/42 C

YEAR	TM/L	G	AB	R	H	2B	3B	HR	RBI	BB	SO	AVG	OBP	SLG	PRO+	BR/A	SB	CS	SBR	FA	FR	G/POS	TPR
1942	Cle-A	8	8	1	1	0	0	0	2	1	0	.125	.222	.125	-1	-1	0	0	0	1.000	-0	/1-1	-0.1
1946	Cle-A	8	30	6	12	1	0	3	4	2	4	.400	.438	.733	238	5	0	0	0	.988	-2	/1-8	0.3
1947	Cle-A	95	318	52	78	10	1	14	52	30	18	.245	.314	.415	105	0	1	0	0	.994	-2	1-87	-0.4
1948	*Cle-A	134	493	53	125	18	5	16	83	36	42	.254	.307	.408	91	-9	1	0	0	**.995**	-1	*1-131	-1.0
1949	Was-A★	143	527	66	155	27	3	18	78	67	30	.294	.381	.459	125	18	3	4	-2	.987	-2	*1-143	1.3
1950	Was-A	36	129	21	30	4	2	1	13	25	4	.233	.365	.318	80	-3	0	0	0	1.000	0	1-36	-0.4
	Chi-A	119	424	62	133	11	2	20	73	60	28	.314	.405	.491	132	21	0	0	0	.987	-7	*1-119	1.1
	Yr	155	553	83	163	15	4	21	86	85	32	.295	.395	.450	120	18	0	0	0	.990	-7	*1-155	0.7
1951	Chi-A★	151	564	85	159	23	5	29	117	77	54	.282	.371	.495	135	27	2	5	-2	.988	-6	*1-147	1.1
1952	Chi-A★	155	594	79	176	33	1	22	104	70	49	.296	.382	.466	134	27	2	0	1	.990	-8	*1-155	1.5
1953	Phi-A★	156	615	64	152	28	4	22	102	63	56	.247	.322	.413	94	-7	1	2	-1	.988	-14	*1-155	-2.8
1954	NY-A	85	142	11	37	9	0	3	27	19	21	.261	.348	.387	105	1	0	0	0	.980	1	1-29	0.0
1955	*NY-A	88	173	25	36	1	0	16	42	36	26	.208	.360	.491	129	7	0	0	0	.995	-2	1-46	0.3
1956	NY-A	26	54	7	12	1	0	5	11	5	3	.222	.323	.519	123	1	0	1	-1	1.000	-0	1-14	0.0
	KC-A	75	172	13	34	5	1	2	12	26	20	.198	.310	.273	55	-11	0	0	0	.977	-4	1-47	-1.7
	Yr	101	226	20	46	6	1	7	23	31	23	.204	.313	.332	71	-10	0	1	-1	.983	-4	1-61	-1.7
1957	Det-A	13	9	0	0	0	0	0	0	3	0	.000	.308	.000	-9	-1	0	0	0	1.000	0	/1-1	-0.1
	Cle-A	19	27	1	6	1	0	1	3	0	3	.222	.250	.370	68	-1	0	0	0	1.000	0	/1-7	-0.1
	Bal-A	4	3	0	0	0	0	0	0	1	1	.000	.250	.000	-28	-1	0	0	0	.000	0	H	-0.1
	Yr	36	39	1	6	1	0	1	3	4	4	.154	.267	.256	44	-3	0	0	0	1.000	1	/1-8	-0.3
Total	13	1315	4282	546	1146	172	24	172	723	521	359	.268	.354	.440	113	73	10	12	-4	.990	-45	*1-1126	-1.1

■ YANK ROBINSON

Robinson, William H. b: 9/19/1859, Philadelphia, Pa. d: 8/25/1894, St.Louis, Mo. BR/TR, 5'6.5", 170 lbs. Deb: 8/24/1882

YEAR	TM/L	G	AB	R	H	2B	3B	HR	RBI	BB	SO	AVG	OBP	SLG	PRO+	BR/A	SB	CS	SBR	FA	FR	G/POS	TPR
1882	Det-N	11	39	1	7	1	0	0	2	1	13	.179	.200	.205	30	-3				.800	-4	S-10/O-1,P-1	-0.6
1884	Bal-U	102	415	101	111	24	4	3		**37**		.267	.327	.366	100	-13				.831	16	3-71,S-14,C-11,P/2	0.7
1885	*StL-a	78	287	63	75	8	8	0	35	29		.261	.344	.345	113	5				.862	-6	O-52,2-19/C-5,31	-0.1
1886	*StL-a	133	481	89	132	26	9	3	71	64		.274	.377	.385	132	19	51			.888	-4	*2-125/3-6,O-1,SP	1.8
1887	*StL-a	125	430	102	131	32	4	1	74	92		.305	.445	.405	125	17	75			.899	-13	*2-117/3-6,O-2,SCP	0.6
1888	*StL-a	134	455	111	105	17	6	3	53	**116**		.231	**.400**	.314	117	13	56			.895	-44	*2-102,S-34	-2.4
1889	StL-a	132	452	97	94	17	3	5	70	**118**	55	.208	.378	.292	81	-10	39			.887	-35	*2-132	-3.3
1890	Pit-P	98	306	59	70	10	3	0	38	101	33	.229	.434	.281	101	12	17			.887	-19	*2-98	-0.1
1891	Cin-a	97	342	48	61	9	4	1	37	68	51	.178	.328	.237	57	-19	23			.867	-11	*2-97	-2.2
	StL-a	1	3	0	0	0	0	0	0	0	0	.000	.000	.000	-87	-1	0			.750	-1	/2-1	-0.1
	Yr	98	345	48	61	9	4	1	37	68	51	.177	.325	.235	56	-19	23			.866	-12	2-98	-2.3
1892	Was-N	67	218	26	39	4	3	0	19	38	28	.179	.301	.225	61	-9	11			.852	-4	3-58/S-5,2-4	-1.0
Total	10	978	3428	697	825	148	44	16	399	664	180	.241	.375	.324	101	12	272			.887	-124	2-698,3-143/SOCP1	-6.7

■ BILL ROBINSON

Robinson, William Henry b: 6/26/43, McKeesport, Pa. BR/TR, 6'3", 205 lbs. Deb: 9/20/66 C

YEAR	TM/L	G	AB	R	H	2B	3B	HR	RBI	BB	SO	AVG	OBP	SLG	PRO+	BR/A	SB	CS	SBR	FA	FR	G/POS	TPR
1966	Atl-N	6	11	1	3	0	1	0	3	0	1	.273	.273	.455	96	-0	0	0	0	.800	-1	/O-5	-0.2
1967	NY-A	116	342	31	67	6	1	7	29	28	56	.196	.261	.281	62	-16	2	2	-1	.968	-2	*O-102	-2.6
1968	NY-A	107	342	34	82	16	7	6	40	26	54	.240	.297	.380	107	2	7	6	-2	.985	-3	O-98	-0.8
1969	NY-A	87	222	23	38	11	2	3	21	16	39	.171	.227	.279	42	-18	3	1	0	.963	-3	O-62/1-1	-2.6
1972	Phi-N	82	188	19	45	9	1	8	21	5	30	.239	.259	.426	89	-4	2	3	-1	.982	-8	O-72	-1.6
1973	Phi-N	124	452	62	130	32	1	25	65	27	91	.288	.329	.529	131	16	5	4	-1	.979	-7	*O-113,3-14	0.4
1974	Phi-N	100	280	32	66	14	1	5	29	17	61	.236	.282	.346	72	-11	5	3	-0	.971	-3	O-87	-1.9
1975	*Pit-N	92	200	26	56	12	2	6	33	11	36	.280	.318	.450	112	2	3	1	0	.991	-2	O-57	-0.1
1976	Pit-N	122	393	55	119	22	3	21	64	16	73	.303	.332	.534	142	18	2	4	-2	.993	-12	O-78,3-37/1-3	0.2
1977	Pit-N	137	507	74	154	32	1	26	104	25	92	.304	.340	.525	125	16	12	6	0	.992	-14	1-86,O-43,3-17	-0.5
1978	Pit-N	136	499	70	123	36	2	14	80	35	105	.246	.302	.411	93	-6	14	11	-2	.988	-4	*O-127,3-29/1-3	-1.8
1979	*Pit-N	148	421	59	111	17	6	24	75	24	81	.264	.305	.504	111	4	13	2	3	.982	-13	*O-125,1-28/3-3	-1.1
1980	Pit-N	100	272	28	78	10	1	12	36	15	45	.287	.324	.463	116	5	1	4	-2	.985	-10	1-49,O-41	-1.2
1981	Pit-N	39	88	8	19	3	0	2	8	5	18	.216	.258	.318	61	-5	1	0	0	1.000	-0	1-23/O-7,3-1	-0.6
1982	Pit-N	31	71	8	17	3	0	4	12	5	19	.239	.289	.451	101	-0	0	1	-1	1.000	-1	O-22	-0.2
	Phi-N	35	69	6	18	6	0	3	19	7	15	.261	.329	.478	121	2	1	1	-0	.960	-1	O-19/1-5	0.0
	Yr	66	140	14	35	9	0	7	31	12	34	.250	.309	.464	111	1	1	2	-1	.984	-1	O-41/1-5	-0.2
1983	Phi-N	10	7	0	1	0	0	0	2	1	4	.143	.250	.143	12	-1	0	0	0	1.000	-1	/1-3,3-2,O-1	-0.2
Total	16	1472	4364	536	1127	229	29	166	641	263	820	.258	.303	.438	104	4	71	49	-8	.979	-84	*O-1059,1-201,3-103	-14.8

■ RAFAEL ROBLES

Robles, Rafael Orlando (Natera) b: 10/20/47, San Pedro De Macoris, D.R. d: 8/13/98, New York, N.Y. BR/TR, 6', 170 lbs. Deb: 4/8/69

YEAR	TM/L	G	AB	R	H	2B	3B	HR	RBI	BB	SO	AVG	OBP	SLG	PRO+	BR/A	SB	CS	SBR	FA	FR	G/POS	TPR
1969	SD-N	6	20	1	2	0	0	0	0	1	3	.100	.143	.100	-32	-4	1	1	-0	.895	-4	/S-6	-0.8
1970	SD-N	23	89	5	19	1	0	0	3	5	11	.213	.263	.225	33	-8	3	0	1	.968	2	S-23	-0.3
1972	SD-N	18	24	1	4	0	0	0	0	0	3	.167	.167	.167	-5	-3	0	0	0	.952	-2	S-15/3-1	-0.5
Total	3	47	133	7	25	1	0	0	3	6	17	.188	.229	.195	17	-15	4	1	1	.958	-4	/S-44,3-1	-1.6

■ SERGIO ROBLES

Robles, Sergio (Valenzuela) b: 4/16/46, Magdalena, Mexico BR/TR, 6'2", 190 lbs. Deb: 8/27/72

YEAR	TM/L	G	AB	R	H	2B	3B	HR	RBI	BB	SO	AVG	OBP	SLG	PRO+	BR/A	SB	CS	SBR	FA	FR	G/POS	TPR
1972	Bal-A	2	5	0	1	0	0	0	0	0	0	.200	.200	.200	19	-0	0	0	0	1.000	-1	/C-1	-0.2
1973	Bal-A	8	13	0	1	0	0	0	0	3	1	.077	.250	.077	-4	-2	0	0	0	1.000	3	/C-8	0.1
1976	LA-N	6	3	0	0	0	0	0	0	0	2	.000	.000	.000	-99	-1	0	0	0	1.000	1	/C-6	0.0
Total	3	16	21	0	2	0	0	0	0	3	3	.095	.208	.095	-11	-3	0	0	0	1.000	2	/C-15	-0.1

■ TOM ROBSON

Robson, Thomas James b: 1/15/46, Rochester, N.Y. BR/TR, 6'3", 215 lbs. Deb: 9/14/74 C

YEAR	TM/L	G	AB	R	H	2B	3B	HR	RBI	BB	SO	AVG	OBP	SLG	PRO+	BR/A	SB	CS	SBR	FA	FR	G/POS	TPR
1974	Tex-A	6	13	2	3	1	0	0	2	4	3	.231	.412	.308	112	0	0	0	0	1.000	-0	/1-1,D-5	0.0
1975	Tex-A	17	35	3	7	0	0	0	2	1	3	.200	.222	.200	20	-4	0	0	0	1.000	-0	/1-5,D-4	-0.4
Total	2	23	48	5	10	1	0	0	4	5	6	.208	.283	.229	48	-3	0	0	0	1.000	-0	/D-9,1-6	-0.4

■ ADAM ROCAP

Rocap, Adam b: 1854, Philadelphia, Pa. d: 3/29/1892, Philadelphia, Pa. 5'9", 170 lbs. Deb: 5/5/1875

YEAR	TM/L	G	AB	R	H	2B	3B	HR	RBI	BB	SO	AVG	OBP	SLG	PRO+	BR/A	SB	CS	SBR	FA	FR	G/POS	TPR
1875	Ath-n	16	69	13	12	1	0	0	4	1	7	.174	.186	.188	27	-5	3	2	-0	.839	-1	O-12/2-4	-0.6

■ MICKEY ROCCO

Rocco, Michael Dominick b: 3/2/16, St.Paul, Minn. d: 6/1/97, St.Paul, Minn. BL/TL, 5'11", 188 lbs. Deb: 6/5/43

YEAR	TM/L	G	AB	R	H	2B	3B	HR	RBI	BB	SO	AVG	OBP	SLG	PRO+	BR/A	SB	CS	SBR	FA	FR	G/POS	TPR
1943	Cle-A	108	405	43	97	14	4	5	46	51	40	.240	.328	.331	99	-0	1	2	-1	**.995**	-5	*1-108	-1.4
1944	Cle-A	155	653	87	174	29	7	13	70	56	51	.266	.325	.392	108	5	4	8	-4	.993	17	*1-155	1.1

YEAR	TM/L	G	AB	R	H	2B	3B	HR	RBI	BB	SO	AVG	OBP	SLG	PRO+	BR/A	SB	CS	SBR	FA	FR	G/POS	TPR
1945	Cle-A	143	565	81	149	28	6	10	56	52	40	.264	.326	.388	111	6	0	4	-2	**.992**	4	*1-141	-0.2
1946	Cle-A	34	98	8	24	2	0	2	14	15	15	.245	.345	.327	94	-0	1	1	-0	.996	5	1-27	0.3
Total	4	440	1721	219	444	73	17	30	186	174	146	.258	.327	.372	106	11	6	15	-7	.994	21	1-431	-0.2

■ JACK ROCHE Roche, John Joseph "Red" b: 11/22/1890, Los Angeles, Cal. d: 3/30/83, Peoria, Ariz. BR/TR, 6'1", 178 lbs. Deb: 5/24/14

YEAR	TM/L	G	AB	R	H	2B	3B	HR	RBI	BB	SO	AVG	OBP	SLG	PRO+	BR/A	SB	CS	SBR	FA	FR	G/POS	TPR
1914	StL-N	12	9	1	6	2	1	0	3	0	1	.667	.700	1.111	441	4	1			.667	-2	/C-9	0.2
1915	StL-N	46	39	2	8	0	1	0	6	4	8	.205	.295	.256	68	-1	1			1.000	0	/C-4	-0.1
1917	StL-N	1	1	0	0	0	0	0	0	0	0	.000	.000	.000	-99	-0	0			.000	-1	/C-1	-0.1
Total	3	59	49	3	14	2	2	0	9	4	9	.286	.364	.408	133	2	2			.750	-2	/C-14	0.0

■ BEN ROCHEFORT Rochefort, Bennett Harold (b: Bennett Harold Rochefort Gilbert) b: 8/15/1896, Camden, N.J. d: 4/2/81, Red Bank, N.J. BL/TR, 6'2", 185 lbs. Deb: 10/3/14

YEAR	TM/L	G	AB	R	H	2B	3B	HR	RBI	BB	SO	AVG	OBP	SLG	PRO+	BR/A	SB	CS	SBR	FA	FR	G/POS	TPR
1914	Phi-A	1	2	0	1	0	0	0	0	0	1	.500	.500	.500	209	0	0			1.000	0	/1-1	0.1

■ LOU ROCHELLI Rochelli, Louis Joseph b: 1/11/19, Staunton, Ill. d: 10/23/92, Victoria, Tex. BR/TR, 6'1", 175 lbs. Deb: 8/25/44

YEAR	TM/L	G	AB	R	H	2B	3B	HR	RBI	BB	SO	AVG	OBP	SLG	PRO+	BR/A	SB	CS	SBR	FA	FR	G/POS	TPR
1944	Bro-N	5	17	0	3	0	1	0	2	2	6	.176	.263	.294	58	-1	0			.964	-0	/2-5	-0.1

■ LES ROCK Rock, Lester Henry (b: Lester Henry Schwarzrock) b: 8/19/12, Springfield, Minn. d: 9/9/91, Davis, Cal. BL/TR, 6'2", 184 lbs. Deb: 9/11/36

YEAR	TM/L	G	AB	R	H	2B	3B	HR	RBI	BB	SO	AVG	OBP	SLG	PRO+	BR/A	SB	CS	SBR	FA	FR	G/POS	TPR
1936	Chi-A	2	1	0	0	0	0	0	1	0	0	.000	.000	.000	-97	-0	0	0	0	.000	0	/1-2	0.0

■ IKE ROCKENFIELD Rockenfield, Isaac Broc b: 11/3/1876, Omaha, Neb. d: 2/21/27, San Diego, Cal. BR/TR, 5'7", 150 lbs. Deb: 5/5/05

YEAR	TM/L	G	AB	R	H	2B	3B	HR	RBI	BB	SO	AVG	OBP	SLG	PRO+	BR/A	SB	CS	SBR	FA	FR	G/POS	TPR
1905	StL-A	95	322	40	70	12	0	0	16	46		.217	.340	.255	95	2	11			.926	-8	2-95	-0.6
1906	StL-A	27	89	3	21	4	0	0	8	1		.236	.277	.281	78	-2	0			.956	-5	2-26	-0.8
Total	2	122	411	43	91	16	0	0	24	47		.221	.328	.260	91	-1	11			.933	-14	2-121	-1.4

■ PAT ROCKETT Rockett, Patrick Edward b: 1/9/55, San Antonio, Tex. BR/TR, 5'11", 170 lbs. Deb: 9/17/76

YEAR	TM/L	G	AB	R	H	2B	3B	HR	RBI	BB	SO	AVG	OBP	SLG	PRO+	BR/A	SB	CS	SBR	FA	FR	G/POS	TPR
1976	Atl-N	4	5	0	1	0	0	0	0	0	1	.200	.200	.200	13	-1	0	0	0	1.000	-1	/S-2	-0.2
1977	Atl-N	93	264	27	67	10	0	1	24	27	32	.254	.330	.303	64	-13	1	2	-1	.940	-11	S-84	-1.6
1978	Atl-N	55	142	6	20	2	0	0	4	13	12	.141	.213	.155	4	-18	1	2	-1	.970	-10	S-51	-2.6
Total	3	152	411	33	88	12	0	1	28	40	45	.214	.289	.251	43	-32	2	4	-2	.949	-21	S-137	-4.4

■ ANDRE RODGERS Rodgers, Kenneth Andre Ian "Andy" b: 12/2/34, Nassau, Bahamas BR/TR, 6'3", 200 lbs. Deb: 4/16/57

YEAR	TM/L	G	AB	R	H	2B	3B	HR	RBI	BB	SO	AVG	OBP	SLG	PRO+	BR/A	SB	CS	SBR	FA	FR	G/POS	TPR
1957	NY-N	32	86	8	21	2	1	3	9	9	21	.244	.323	.395	92	-1	0	0	0	.950	5	S-20/3-8	0.6
1958	SF-N	22	63	7	13	3	1	2	11	4	14	.206	.254	.381	67	-3	0	0	0	.972	-3	S-18	-0.5
1959	SF-N	71	228	32	57	12	1	6	24	32	50	.250	.345	.390	98	-0	2	1	0	.933	-9	S-66	-0.4
1960	SF-N	81	217	22	53	8	5	2	22	24	44	.244	.328	.355	92	-2	1	1	-0	.953	-4	S-41,3-21/1-6,O-2	-0.4
1961	Chi-N	73	214	27	57	17	0	6	23	25	54	.266	.346	.430	103	1	1	1	-0	.983	1	1-42,S-24/O-2,2-1	0.0
1962	Chi-N	138	461	40	128	20	8	5	44	44	93	.278	.344	.388	93	-4	5	6	-2	.960	7	*S-133/1-1	1.3
1963	Chi-N	150	516	51	118	17	4	5	33	65	90	.229	.325	.306	79	-12	5	7	-3	.954	-3	*S-150	-0.7
1964	Chi-N	129	448	50	107	17	3	12	46	53	88	.239	.319	.371	90	-5	5	1	1	.965	19	*S-126	2.4
1965	Pit-N	75	178	17	51	12	0	2	25	18	28	.287	.352	.388	108	2	2	1	0	.950	-6	S-33,3-15/1-6,2-1	-0.2
1966	Pit-N	36	49	6	9	1	0	0	4	8	7	.184	.298	.204	43	-4	0	1	-1	.913	-1	/S-5,3-3,O-3,1-2	-0.5
1967	Pit-N	47	61	8	14	3	0	2	4	8	18	.230	.319	.377	98	-0	1	1	-0	1.000	2	/1-9,3-5,S-3,2-2	0.2
Total	11	854	2521	268	628	112	23	45	245	290	507	.249	.331	.365	90	-29	22	20	-5	.956	9	S-619/1-66,3-52,O2	1.8

■ BUCK RODGERS Rodgers, Robert Leroy b: 8/16/38, Delaware, Ohio BB/TR, 6'2", 195 lbs. Deb: 9/8/61 MC

YEAR	TM/L	G	AB	R	H	2B	3B	HR	RBI	BB	SO	AVG	OBP	SLG	PRO+	BR/A	SB	CS	SBR	FA	FR	G/POS	TPR
1961	LA-A	16	56	8	18	2	0	2	13	1	6	.321	.333	.464	99	-0	0	0	0	.965	-1	C-14	0.0
1962	LA-A	155	565	65	146	34	6	6	61	45	68	.258	.313	.372	86	-12	1	8	-5	.989	1	*C-150	-1.0
1963	LA-A	100	300	24	70	6	0	4	23	29	35	.233	.305	.293	73	-11	2	2	-1	.979	-14	C-85	-2.4
1964	LA-A	148	514	38	125	18	3	4	54	40	71	.243	.303	.313	80	-15	4	3	-1	.987	14	*C-146	0.5
1965	Cal-A	132	411	33	86	14	3	1	32	35	61	.209	.276	.265	56	-23	4	5	-2	.991	6	*C-128	-1.4
1966	Cal-A	133	454	45	107	20	3	7	48	29	57	.236	.285	.339	81	-12	3	4	-2	.992	-4	*C-133	-1.1
1967	Cal-A	139	429	29	94	13	3	6	41	34	55	.219	.280	.305	76	-13	1	4	-2	.991	2	*C-134/O-1	-0.7
1968	Cal-A	91	258	13	49	6	0	1	14	16	48	.190	.245	.225	45	-17	2	1	0	.985	0	C-87	-1.4
1969	Cal-A	18	46	4	9	1	0	0	2	5	8	.196	.288	.217	46	-3	0	0	0	1.000	-0	C-18	-0.3
Total	9	932	3033	259	704	114	18	31	288	234	409	.232	.291	.312	74	-107	17	27	-11	.988	3	C-895/O-1	-7.8

■ BILL RODGERS Rodgers, Wilbur Kincaid "Rawmeat Bill" b: 4/18/1887, Pleasant Ridge, O. d: 12/24/78, Goliad, Tex. BL/TR, 5'9.5", 170 lbs. Deb: 4/15/15

YEAR	TM/L	G	AB	R	H	2B	3B	HR	RBI	BB	SO	AVG	OBP	SLG	PRO+	BR/A	SB	CS	SBR	FA	FR	G/POS	TPR
1915	Cle-A	16	45	8	14	2	0	0	7	8	7	.311	.415	.356	128	2	3	3	-1	.945	-4	2-13	-0.3
	Bos-A	11	6	2	0	0	0	0	0	3	2	.000	.333	.000	-0	-1	0			.900	1	/2-6	0.1
	Yr	27	51	10	14	2	0	0	7	11	9	.275	.403	.314	115	2	3	3	-1	.938	-3	2-19	-0.2
	Cin-N	72	213	20	51	13	4	0	12	11	29	.239	.299	.338	91	-3	8	5	-1	.947	5	2-56/S-6,3-1,O-1	0.3
1916	Cin-N	3	4	0	0	0	0	0	0	0	2	.000	.000	.000	-99	-1	0			1.000	-0	/S-1	-0.2
Total	2	102	268	30	65	15	4	0	19	22	40	.243	.316	.328	93	-2	11	8		.945	2	/2-75,S-7,O-1,3-1	-0.1

■ BILL RODGERS Rodgers, William Sherman b: 12/5/22, Harrisburg, Pa. BL/TL, 6', 162 lbs. Deb: 9/27/44

YEAR	TM/L	G	AB	R	H	2B	3B	HR	RBI	BB	SO	AVG	OBP	SLG	PRO+	BR/A	SB	CS	SBR	FA	FR	G/POS	TPR
1944	Pit-N	2	4	1	1	0	0	0	0	0	1	.250	.250	.250	39	-0	0			.000	-1	/O-1	-0.1
1945	Pit-N	1	1	0	1	0	0	0	0	0	0	1.000	1.000	1.000	440	0	0			.000	0	H	0.0
Total	2	3	5	1	2	0	0	0	0	0	1	.400	.400	.400	120	0	0			—	-1	/O-1	-0.1

■ ERIC RODIN Rodin, Eric Chapman b: 2/5/30, Orange, N.J. d: 1/4/91, Somerville, N.J. BR/TR, 6'2", 215 lbs. Deb: 9/7/54

YEAR	TM/L	G	AB	R	H	2B	3B	HR	RBI	BB	SO	AVG	OBP	SLG	PRO+	BR/A	SB	CS	SBR	FA	FR	G/POS	TPR
1954	NY-N	5	6	0	0	0	0	0	0	0	2	.000	.000	.000	-99	-2	0	0	0	1.000	-1	/O-3	-0.3

■ ALEX RODRIGUEZ Rodriguez, Alexander Emmanuel b: 7/27/75, New York, N.Y. BR/TR, 6'3", 190 lbs. Deb: 7/8/94

YEAR	TM/L	G	AB	R	H	2B	3B	HR	RBI	BB	SO	AVG	OBP	SLG	PRO+	BR/A	SB	CS	SBR	FA	FR	G/POS	TPR
1994	Sea-A	17	54	4	11	0	0	0	2	3	20	.204	.246	.204	17	-7	3	0	1	.915	1	S-17	-0.3
1995	*Sea-A	48	142	15	33	6	2	5	19	6	42	.232	.264	.408	71	-7	4	2	0	.953	-2	S-46/D-1	-0.5
1996	Sea-A★	146	601	**141**	215	**54**	1	36	123	59	104	**.358**	.419	.631	160	55	15	4	2	.977	-10	*S-146	5.4
1997	*Sea-A★	141	587	100	176	40	3	23	84	41	99	.300	.351	.496	119	15	29	6	5	.962	-1	*S-140/D-1	3.0
1998	Sea-A★	161	686	123	**213**	35	5	42	124	45	121	.310	.362	.560	135	33	46	13	6	.975	-0	*S-160/D-1	4.9
Total	5	513	2070	383	648	135	11	106	352	154	386	.313	.366	.543	131	89	97	25	14	.969	-12	S-509/D-3	12.5

■ AURELIO RODRIGUEZ Rodriguez, Aurelio (Ituarte) b: 12/28/47, Cananea, Mexico BR/TR, 5'10", 180 lbs. Deb: 9/1/67

YEAR	TM/L	G	AB	R	H	2B	3B	HR	RBI	BB	SO	AVG	OBP	SLG	PRO+	BR/A	SB	CS	SBR	FA	FR	G/POS	TPR
1967	Cal-A	29	130	14	31	3	1	1	8	2	21	.238	.250	.300	64	-6	1	0	0	.989	5	3-29	-0.2
1968	Cal-A	76	223	14	54	10	1	1	16	17	36	.242	.299	.309	88	-3	0	2	-1	.921	-7	3-70/2-2	-1.3
1969	Cal-A	159	561	47	130	17	2	7	49	32	88	.232	.276	.307	66	-27	5	3	-0	.954	8	*3-159	-2.0
1970	Cal-A	17	63	6	17	2	2	0	7	3	6	.270	.313	.365	90	-1	0	1	-1	1.000	4	3-17	0.2
	Was-A	142	547	64	135	31	5	19	76	37	81	.247	.303	.426	104	0	15	5	2	.961	13	*3-136/S-7	1.4
	Yr	159	610	70	152	33	7	19	83	40	87	.249	.304	.420	102	-1	15	6	1	.965	17	*3-153/S-7	1.6
1971	Det-A	154	604	68	153	30	7	15	39	27	93	.253	.289	.401	90	-10	4	6	-2	.953	15	*3-153/S-1	0.1
1972	*Det-A	153	601	65	142	23	5	13	56	28	104	.236	.273	.356	83	-14	2	3	-1	.969	24	*3-153/S-2	0.9
1973	Det-A	160	555	46	123	27	3	9	58	31	85	.222	.267	.330	63	-28	3	1	0	.971	10	*3-160/S-1	-1.9
1974	Det-A	159	571	54	127	23	5	5	49	26	70	.222	.258	.306	60	-30	2	0	1	.961	22	*3-159	-1.0
1975	Det-A	151	507	47	124	20	6	13	60	30	63	.245	.287	.385	85	-12	1	1	-0	.953	21	*3-151	0.8
1976	Det-A	128	480	40	115	13	2	8	50	19	61	.240	.270	.325	71	-19	0	4	-2	**.978**	13	*3-128	-0.9
1977	Det-A	96	306	30	67	14	1	10	32	16	36	.219	.258	.369	65	-15	1	1	-0	.972	16	3-95/S-1	-0.1
1978	Det-A	134	385	40	102	25	2	7	43	19	37	.265	.305	.395	93	-5	0	1	-1	**.987**	2	*3-131	-0.5
1979	Det-A	106	343	27	87	18	0	5	36	11	40	.254	.279	.350	66	-17	0	2	-1	.956	5	*3-106/1-1	-1.4
1980	SD-N	89	175	7	35	7	2	2	13	6	26	.200	.227	.297	48	-13	1	1	-0	.965	10	3-88/S-2	-0.4
	*NY-A	52	164	14	36	6	1	3	14	7	35	.220	.251	.323	57	-10	0	0	0	.954	-5	3-49/2-6	-1.6
1981	*NY-A	27	52	4	18	2	0	2	8	2	10	.346	.370	.500	151	3	0	0	0	.951	4	3-20/2-3,1-1,D-2	0.7
1982	Chi-A	118	257	24	62	15	1	3	31	11	35	.241	.275	.342	68	-11	0	0	0	.969	19	*3-112/2-3,S-2	0.6
1983	Bal-A	45	67	0	8	0	0	0	2	0	13	.119	.132	.119	-31	-12	0	0	0	.969	2	3-45	-1.1

YEAR	TM/L	G	AB	R	H	2B	3B	HR	RBI	BB	SO	AVG	OBP	SLG	PRO+	BR/A	SB	CS	SBR	FA	FR	G/POS	TPR
	*Chi-A	22	20	1	4	1	0	1	1	0	3	.200	.200	.400	58	-1	0	0	0	1.000	4	3-22	0.3
	Yr	67	87	1	12	1	0	1	3	0	16	.138	.148	.184	-9	-13	0	0	0	.978	6	3-67	-0.8
Total	17	2017	6611	612	1570	287	46	124	648	324	943	.237	.276	.351	75	-232	35	31	-8	.964	183	*3-1983/S-16,2D1	-7.4
■ CARLOS RODRIGUEZ	Rodriguez, Carlos (Marquez) b: 11/1/67, Mexico City, Mexico BB/TR, 5'9", 160 lbs. Deb: 6/16/91																						
1991	NY-A	15	37	1	7	0	0	0	2	1	2	.189	.211	.189	11	-4	0	0	0	.957	1	S-11/2-3	-0.3
1994	Bos-A	57	174	15	50	14	1	1	13	11	13	.287	.330	.397	82	-5	1	0	0	.973	2	S-32,2-20/3-4	0.1
1995	Bos-A	13	30	5	10	2	0	0	5	2	2	.333	.394	.400	104	0	0	0	0	.960	3	/2-7,S-6,3-1	0.4
Total	3	85	241	21	67	16	1	1	20	14	17	.278	.320	.365	75	-9	1	0	0	.972	6	/S-49,2-30,3-5	0.2
■ EDWIN RODRIGUEZ	Rodriguez, Edwin (Morales) b: 8/14/60, Ponce, P.R. BR/TR, 5'11", 175 lbs. Deb: 9/28/82																						
1982	NY-A	3	9	2	3	0	0	0	1	1	1	.333	.400	.333	106	0	0	0	0	.875	1	/2-3	0.1
1983	SD-N	7	12	1	2	1	0	0	0	1	3	.167	.231	.250	34	-1	0	0	0	1.000	-1	/2-5,S-2,3-1	-0.2
1985	SD-N	1	1	0	0	0	0	0	0	0	0	.000	.000	.000	-99	-0	0	0	0	.000	0	/H	0.0
Total	3	11	22	3	5	1	0	0	1	2	4	.227	.292	.273	58	-1	0	0	0	.935	0	/2-8,S-2,3-1	-0.1
■ ELLIE RODRIGUEZ	Rodriguez, Eliseo (Delgado) b: 5/24/46, Fajardo, P.R. BR/TR, 5'11", 185 lbs. Deb: 5/26/68																						
1968	NY-A	9	24	1	5	0	0	0	1	3	3	.208	.296	.208	57	-1	0	0	0	1.000	0	/C-9	0.0
1969	KC-A☆	95	267	27	63	10	0	2	20	31	26	.236	.333	.296	77	-7	3	2	-0	.990	-8	C-90	-1.2
1970	KC-A	80	231	25	52	8	2	1	15	27	35	.225	.317	.290	68	-9	2	1	0	.988	12	C-75	0.6
1971	Mil-A	115	319	28	67	10	1	1	30	41	51	.210	.315	.257	64	-13	1	1	-0	.992	6	*C-114	-0.4
1972	Mil-A☆	116	355	31	101	14	2	2	35	52	43	.285	.386	.352	123	13	1	4	-2	.983	-11	*C-114	0.5
1973	Mil-A	94	290	30	78	8	1	0	30	41	28	.269	.378	.303	96	1	4	3	-1	.986	4	C-75,D-14	0.7
1974	Cal-A	140	395	48	100	20	0	7	36	69	56	.253	.376	.357	119	13	4	5	-2	.992	-10	*C-137/D-1	0.8
1975	Cal-A	90	226	20	53	6	0	3	27	49	37	.235	.384	.301	103	4	2	2	-1	.991	-7	C-90	0.0
1976	LA-N	36	66	10	14	0	0	0	9	19	12	.212	.409	.212	82	0	0	0	0	.986	4	C-33	0.6
Total	9	775	2173	220	533	76	6	16	203	332	291	.245	.359	.308	94	0	17	18	-6	.989	-10	C-737/D-15	1.6
■ HECTOR RODRIGUEZ	Rodriguez, Hector Antonio (Ordenana) b: 6/13/20, Alquizar, Cuba BR/TR, 5'8", 165 lbs. Deb: 4/15/52																						
1952	Chi-A	124	407	55	108	14	0	1	40	47	22	.265	.346	.307	82	-8	7	6	-2	.959	2	*3-113	-1.0
■ HENRY RODRIGUEZ	Rodriguez, Henry Anderson (Lorenzo) b: 11/8/67, Santo Domingo, D.R. BL/TL, 6'1", 200 lbs. Deb: 7/5/92																						
1992	LA-N	53	146	11	32	7	0	3	14	8	30	.219	.260	.329	67	-7	0	0	0	.960	1	O-48/1-1	-0.7
1993	LA-N	76	176	20	39	10	0	8	23	11	39	.222	.267	.415	84	-5	1	0	0	.984	-6	O-48,1-13	-1.2
1994	LA-N	104	306	33	82	14	2	8	49	17	58	.268	.311	.405	91	-5	0	1	-1	.986	0	O-86,1-17	-0.8
1995	LA-N	21	80	6	21	4	1	1	10	5	17	.262	.306	.375	86	-2	0	1	-1	1.000	-1	O-20/1-1	-0.4
	Mon-N	24	58	7	12	0	0	1	5	6	11	.207	.281	.259	42	-5	0	0	0	1.000	-2	1-10/O-8	-0.8
	Yr	45	138	13	33	4	1	2	15	11	28	.239	.295	.326	65	-7	0	1	-1	.977	-2	O-28,1-11	-1.2
1996	Mon-N★	145	532	81	147	42	1	36	103	37	160	.276	.327	.562	126	17	2	0	1	.947	-9	O-89,1-51	0.1
1997	Mon-N	132	476	55	116	28	3	26	83	42	149	.244	.308	.479	103	-1	3	3	-1	.985	-2	*O-126/1-3	-0.6
1998	*Chi-N	128	415	56	104	21	1	31	85	54	113	.251	.337	.530	117	9	1	3	-2	.996	12	*O-114/D-5	1.8
Total	7	683	2189	269	553	126	8	114	372	180	577	.253	.311	.474	104	2	7	8	-3	.980	-6	O-539/1-96,D-5	-2.6
■ IVAN RODRIGUEZ	Rodriguez, Ivan (Torres) "Pudge" b: 11/27/71, Manati, P.R. BR/TR, 5'9", 205 lbs. Deb: 6/20/91																						
1991	Tex-A	88	280	24	74	16	0	3	27	5	42	.264	.277	.354	75	-10	0	1	-1	.983	14	C-88	0.7
1992	Tex-A★	123	420	39	109	16	1	8	37	24	73	.260	.301	.360	87	-8	0	0	0	.983	8	*C-116/D-2	0.7
1993	Tex-A★	137	473	56	129	28	4	10	66	29	70	.273	.320	.412	99	-2	8	7	-2	.991	6	*C-134/D-1	0.9
1994	Tex-A★	99	363	56	108	19	1	16	57	31	42	.298	.364	.488	117	9	6	3	0	.992	-4	C-99	1.0
1995	Tex-A★	130	492	56	149	32	2	12	67	16	48	.303	.330	.449	98	-3	0	2	-1	.990	-2	*C-127/D-1	0.3
1996	*Tex-A★	153	639	116	192	47	3	19	86	38	55	.300	.344	.473	98	-3	5	0	2	.989	10	*C-146/D-6	1.6
1997	Tex-A★	150	597	98	187	34	4	20	77	38	89	.313	.362	.484	112	10	7	3	0	.992	4	*C-143/D-5	2.2
1998	*Tex-A★	145	579	88	186	40	4	21	91	32	88	.321	.360	.513	118	15	9	0	3	.994	-3	*C-139/D-6	2.2
Total	8	1025	3843	533	1134	232	19	109	508	213	507	.295	.337	.450	103	8	35	16	1	.989	33	C-992/D-21	9.6
■ JOSE RODRIGUEZ	Rodriguez, Jose "El Hombre Goma" b: 2/23/1894, Havana, Cuba d: 1/21/53, Havana, Cuba BR/TR, 5'8", 150 lbs. Deb: 10/5/16																						
1916	NY-N	1	0	0	0	0	0	0	0	0	0	—	—	—	—	0	0			.000	0	R	0.0
1917	NY-N	7	20	2	4	0	1	0	2	2	1	.200	.273	.300	78	-1	2			1.000	-1	/1-7	-0.2
1918	NY-N	50	125	15	20	0	2	0	15	12	3	.160	.239	.192	33	-10	6			.978	4	2-40/1-8,3-2	-0.4
Total	3	58	145	17	24	0	3	0	17	14	4	.166	.244	.207	39	-10	8			.989	3	/2-40,1-15,3-2	-0.6
■ TONY RODRIGUEZ	Rodriguez, Luis Antonio b: 8/15/70, Rio Piedras, P.R. BR/TR, 5'11", 165 lbs. Deb: 7/6/96																						
1996	Bos-A	27	67	7	16	1	0	1	9	4	8	.239	.292	.299	49	-5	0	0	0	.979	5	S-21/3-5	0.2
■ RUBEN RODRIGUEZ	Rodriguez, Ruben Dario (Martinez) b: 8/4/64, Cabrera, D.R. BR/TR, 6'3", 190 lbs. Deb: 9/17/86																						
1986	Pit-N	2	3	0	0	0	0	0	0	0	1	.000	.000	.000	-98	-1	0	0	0	1.000	1	/C-2	0.0
1988	Pit-N	2	5	1	1	0	1	0	1	0	2	.200	.200	.600	123	0	0	0	0	1.000	0	/C-2	0.0
Total	2	4	8	1	1	0	1	0	1	0	3	.125	.125	.375	36	-1	0	0	0	1.000	1	/C-4	0.0
■ STEVE RODRIGUEZ	Rodriguez, Steven James b: 11/29/70, Las Vegas, Nev. BR/TR, 5'8", 170 lbs. Deb: 4/30/95																						
1995	Bos-A	6	8	1	1	0	0	0	0	1	1	.125	.222	.125	-6	-1	1	0	0	.667	-2	/S-4,2-1,D-1	-0.2
	Det-A	12	31	4	6	1	0	0	0	5	9	.194	.306	.226	41	-3	1	2	-1	.982	4	2-12/S-1	0.1
	Yr	18	39	5	7	1	0	0	0	6	10	.179	.289	.205	31	-4	2	2	-1	.983	2	2-13/S-5,D-1	-0.1
■ VIC RODRIGUEZ	Rodriguez, Victor Manuel (Rivera) b: 7/14/61, New York, N.Y. BR/TR, 5'11", 173 lbs. Deb: 9/5/84																						
1984	Bal-A	11	17	4	7	3	0	0	2	0	2	.412	.412	.588	177	2	0	0	0	.958	2	/2-7,D-1	0.3
1989	Min-A	6	11	2	5	2	0	0	0	0	1	.455	.455	.636	191	1	0	0	0	.900	1	/3-5,D-1	0.2
Total	2	17	28	6	12	5	0	0	2	0	3	.429	.429	.607	183	3	0	0	0	.958	3	/2-7,3-5,D-2	0.5
■ GARY ROENICKE	Roenicke, Gary Steven b: 12/5/54, Covina, Cal. BR/TR, 6'3", 205 lbs. Deb: 6/8/76 F																						
1976	Mon-N	29	90	9	20	3	1	2	5	4	18	.222	.263	.344	69	-4	0	0	0	.955	-1	O-25	-0.6
1978	Bal-A	27	58	5	15	3	0	3	15	8	3	.259	.358	.466	138	3	0	1	-1	1.000	-3	O-20	-0.1
1979	*Bal-A	133	376	60	98	16	1	25	64	61	74	.261	.381	.508	143	24	1	3	-2	.981	-8	*O-130/D-2	0.9
1980	Bal-A	118	297	40	71	13	0	10	28	41	49	.239	.343	.384	100	1	2	0	1	**1.000**	-13	*O-113	-1.5
1981	Bal-A	85	219	31	59	16	0	3	20	23	29	.269	.344	.384	110	3	1	2	-1	.983	-13	O-83	-1.4
1982	Bal-A	137	393	58	106	25	1	21	74	70	73	.270	.392	.499	143	25	6	7	-2	.990	-9	*O-125,1-10	1.1
1983	*Bal-A	115	323	45	84	13	0	19	64	30	35	.260	.331	.477	121	9	2	2	-1	.982	-14	*O-100/1-7,3-2,D-2	-0.8
1984	Bal-A	121	326	36	73	19	1	10	44	58	43	.224	.348	.380	104	3	1	2	-1	.995	-10	*O-117	-1.1
1985	Bal-A	114	225	36	49	9	0	15	43	44	36	.218	.346	.458	121	7	2	2	-1	.993	-8	O-89,D-17	-0.4
1986	NY-A	69	136	11	36	5	0	3	18	27	30	.265	.390	.368	109	3	1	1	-0	1.000	-6	O-37,D-15/3-3,1-2	-0.4
1987	Atl-N	67	151	25	33	8	0	9	28	32	23	.219	.359	.450	107	2	0	0	0	.968	-4	O-44/1-9	-0.3
1988	Atl-N	49	114	11	26	5	0	1	7	8	15	.228	.279	.298	63	-5	0	0	0	1.000	-4	O-35/1-1	-1.1
Total	12	1064	2708	367	670	135	4	121	410	406	428	.247	.354	.434	117	70	16	20	-7	.988	-92	O-918/D-36,1-29,3-5	-5.7
■ RON ROENICKE	Roenicke, Ronald Jon b: 8/19/56, Covina, Cal. BB/TL, 6', 180 lbs. Deb: 9/2/81 F																						
1981	LA-N	22	47	6	11	0	0	0	0	6	8	.234	.321	.234	62	-2	1	1	-0	1.000	-0	O-20	-0.3
1982	LA-N	109	143	18	37	8	0	1	12	21	32	.259	.361	.336	99	1	5	0	2	.984	-19	O-72	-1.9
1983	LA-N	81	145	12	32	4	0	2	12	14	26	.221	.289	.290	61	-8	3	2	-0	.987	-12	O-62	-2.2
	Sea-A	59	198	23	50	12	0	4	23	33	22	.253	.365	.374	100	1	6	2	1	.993	7	O-54/1-8,D-1	0.6
1984	*SD-N	12	20	4	6	1	0	1	2	2	5	.300	.364	.500	141	1	0	0	0	1.000	-2	O-10	-0.2
1985	SF-N	65	133	23	34	9	1	3	13	35	27	.256	.411	.406	136	8	6	2	1	.984	-1	O-35	0.7
1986	Phi-N	102	275	42	68	13	1	5	42	61	52	.247	.384	.356	102	3	2	2	-1	.989	-2	O-83	-0.2
1987	Phi-N	63	78	9	13	3	1	1	4	14	15	.167	.293	.269	49	-6	1	0	0	.964	-6	O-26	-1.2

YEAR	TM/L	G	AB	R	H	2B	3B	HR	RBI	BB	SO	AVG	OBP	SLG	PRO+	BR/A	SB	CS	SBR	FA	FR	G/POS	TPR
1988	Cin-N	14	37	4	5	1	0	0	5	4	8	.135	.238	.162	16	-4	0	0	0	1.000	-2	O-14	-0.7
Total	8	527	1076	141	256	51	3	17	113	190	195	.238	.355	.338	92	-5	24	9	2	.989	-37	O-376/1-8,D-1	-5.4
■ **OSCAR ROETTGER**	Roettger, Oscar Frederick Louis "Okkie" b: 2/19/1900, St.Louis, Mo. d: 7/4/86, St.Louis, Mo. BR/TR, 6', 170 lbs. Deb: 7/7/23 F																						
1923	NY-A	5	2	0	0	0	0	0	0	0	0	.000	.000	.000	-98	-1	0	0	0	1.000	0	/P-5	0.0
1924	NY-A	1	0	0	0	0	0	0	0	0	0	—	—	—	—	0	0	0	0	.000	0	/P-1	0.0
1927	Bro-N	5	4	0	0	0	0	0	0	1	1	.000	.333	.000	-4	-0	0			.000	-1	/O-1	-0.1
1932	Phi-A	26	60	7	14	1	0	0	6	5	4	.233	.292	.250	40	-5	0	0	0	.978	-2	1-15	-0.7
Total	4	37	66	7	14	1	0	0	6	6	5	.212	.288	.227	34	-6	0	0	0	1.000	-2	/1-15,P-6,O-1	-0.8
■ **WALLY ROETTGER**	Roettger, Walter Henry b: 8/28/02, St.Louis, Mo. d: 9/14/51, Champaign, Ill. BR/TR, 6'1.5", 190 lbs. Deb: 5/1/27 F																						
1927	StL-N	5	1	0	0	0	0	0	0	1	0	.000	.500	.000	42	0	0			.500	-1	/O-3	-0.1
1928	StL-N	68	261	27	89	17	4	6	44	10	22	.341	.372	.506	125	9	2			.981	-1	O-66	0.4
1929	StL-N	79	269	27	68	11	3	3	42	13	27	.253	.287	.349	56	-19	0			.993	-4	O-69	-2.5
1930	NY-N	121	420	51	119	15	5	5	51	25	29	.283	.330	.379	72	-19	1			**.992**	-6	*O-114	-2.9
1931	Cin-N	44	185	25	65	11	4	1	20	7	9	.351	.378	.470	135	8	1			.990	-1	O-44	0.4
	*StL-N	45	151	16	43	12	2	0	17	9	14	.285	.337	.391	92	-2	0			.974	-6	O-42	-1.1
	Yr	89	336	41	108	23	6	1	37	16	23	.321	.360	.435	114	6	1			.983	-7	O-86	-0.7
1932	Cin-N	106	347	26	96	18	3	3	43	23	24	.277	.323	.372	89	-5	0			.991	-1	O-94	-1.2
1933	Cin-N	84	209	13	50	7	1	1	17	8	10	.239	.267	.297	62	-11	0			.977	0	O-55	-1.4
1934	Pit-N	47	106	7	26	5	1	0	11	3	8	.245	.266	.311	53	-7	0			1.000	1	O-23	-0.7
Total	8	599	1949	192	556	96	23	19	245	99	143	.285	.324	.387	85	-46	4			.986	-19	O-510	-9.1
■ **ED ROETZ**	Roetz, Edward Bernard b: 8/6/05, Philadelphia, Pa. d: 3/16/65, Philadelphia, Pa. BR/TR, 5'10", 160 lbs. Deb: 5/26/29																						
1929	StL-A	16	45	7	11	4	1	0	5	4	6	.244	.306	.378	72	-2	0	0	0	.909	-1	/S-8,1-5,2-2,3-1	-0.2
■ **BILLY ROGELL**	Rogell, William George b: 11/24/04, Springfield, Ill. BB/TR, 5'10.5", 163 lbs. Deb: 4/14/25																						
1925	Bos-A	58	169	12	33	5	1	0	17	11	17	.195	.244	.237	22	-20	0	3	-2	.935	6	2-49/S-6	-1.4
1927	Bos-A	82	207	35	55	14	6	2	28	24	28	.266	.342	.420	99	-1	3	1	0	.966	6	3-53/2-2,O-2	0.7
1928	Bos-A	102	296	33	69	10	4	0	29	22	47	.233	.295	.294	56	-19	2	6	-3	.935	-13	S-67,2-22/O-6,3-3	-2.7
1930	Det-A	54	144	20	24	4	2	0	9	15	23	.167	.250	.222	20	-18	1	2	-1	.938	4	S-33,3-13/O-1	-1.0
1931	Det-A	48	185	21	56	12	3	2	24	24	17	.303	.383	.432	110	3	8	8	-2	.958	11	S-48	1.5
1932	Det-A	144	554	88	150	29	6	9	61	50	38	.271	.332	.394	84	-14	14	6	1	.944	8	*S-139/3-4	0.6
1933	Det-A	155	587	67	173	42	11	0	57	79	33	.295	.381	.404	106	7	6	9	-4	.944	20	*S-155	3.2
1934	*Det-A	154	592	114	175	32	8	3	100	74	36	.296	.374	.392	97	-1	13	3	2	.962	9	*S-154	1.8
1935	*Det-A	150	560	88	154	23	11	6	71	80	29	.275	.367	.387	99	0	3	6	-3	**.971**	12	*S-150	1.7
1936	Det-A	146	585	85	160	27	5	6	68	73	41	.274	.357	.368	79	-19	14	10	-2	**.965**	-1	*S-146/3-1	-1.1
1937	Det-A	146	536	85	148	30	7	8	64	83	48	.276	.376	.403	94	-3	5	5	-2	**.967**	2	*S-146	0.7
1938	Det-A	136	501	76	130	22	8	3	55	86	37	.259	.373	.353	78	-15	9	2	2	.959	8	*S-134	0.4
1939	Det-A	74	174	24	40	6	3	2	23	26	14	.230	.330	.333	65	-9	3	1	0	.931	2	S-43,3-21/2-2	-0.3
1940	Chi-N	33	59	7	8	0	0	1	3	2	8	.136	.164	.186	-4	-8	1			.900	-5	S-14/3-9,2-3	-1.3
Total	14	1482	5149	755	1375	256	75	42	609	649	416	.267	.351	.370	84	-115	82	62		.956	68	*S-1235,3-104/2O	2.8
■ **EMMETT ROGERS**	Rogers, Emmett b: 1865, Rome, N.Y. BB, 5'10", 165 lbs. Deb: 4/19/1890																						
1890	Tol-a	35	110	18	19	3	3	0		7	14	.173	.266	.255	52	-7	2			.924	5	C-34/O-1	0.1
■ **FRALEY ROGERS**	Rogers, Fraley W. b: 1850, Brooklyn, N.Y. d: 5/10/1881, New York, N.Y. 5'8", 184 lbs. Deb: 4/30/1872																						
1872	Bos-n	45	204	39	56	7	1	1	28	1	4	.275	.278	.333	83	-5	2	0	1	.790	-2	*O-41/1-6	-0.3
1873	Bos-n	1	6	1	2	1	0	0	2	0	1	.333	.333	.500	133	0	0	0	0	.813	-1	/1-1	0.0
Total	2 n	46	210	40	58	8	1	1	30	1	5	.276	.280	.338	84	-5	2	0	1	.893	-2	/O-41,1-7	-0.3
■ **JIM ROGERS**	Rogers, James F. b: 4/9/1872, Hartford, Conn. 5'7.5", 180 lbs. Deb: 4/17/1896 M																						
1896	Was-N	38	154	21	43	6	4	1	30	10	9	.279	.323	.390	87	-3	3			.882	-6	3-32/2-6,O-1	-0.7
	Lou-N	72	290	39	75	8	6	0	38	15	14	.259	.297	.328	67	-14	13			.971	-2	1-60,S-12	-1.3
	Yr	110	444	60	118	14	10	1	68	25	23	.266	.306	.349	74	-17	16			.971	-8	1-60,3-32,S-12,/2O	-2.0
1897	Lou-N	41	150	22	22	3	2	2	22	22		.147	.260	.233	32	-15	4			.933	-4	2-39/1-3,M	-1.5
Total	2	151	594	82	140	17	12	3	90	47	23	.236	.294	.320	64	-32	20			.970	-12	/1-63,2-45,3-32,SO	-3.5
■ **JAY ROGERS**	Rogers, Jay Lewis b: 8/3/1888, Sandusky, N.Y. d: 7/1/64, Carlisle, N.Y. BR/TR, 5'11.5", 178 lbs. Deb: 5/22/14																						
1914	NY-A	5	8	0	0	0	0	0	0	0	4	.000	.000	.000	-99	-2	0			.923	-0	/C-4	-0.2
■ **PACKY ROGERS**	Rogers, Stanley Frank (b: Stanley Frank Hazinski) b: 4/26/13, Swoyersville, Pa. d: 5/15/98, Elmira, N.Y. BR/TR, 5'8", 175 lbs. Deb: 7/12/38																						
1938	Bro-N	23	37	3	7	1	1	0	5	6	6	.189	.302	.270	57	-2	0			1.000	-1	/S-9,3-8,2-3,O-1	-0.2
■ **MIKE ROGODZINSKI**	Rogodzinski, Michael George b: 2/22/48, Evanston, Ill. BL/TR, 6', 185 lbs. Deb: 5/4/73																						
1973	Phi-N	66	80	13	19	3	0	2	7	12	19	.237	.337	.350	88	-1	0	0	0	.947	-3	O-16	-0.4
1974	Phi-N	17	15	1	1	0	0	0	1	2	3	.067	.176	.067	-29	-3	0	0	0	.000	-1	/O-1	-0.3
1975	Phi-N	16	19	3	5	1	0	0	4	3	2	.263	.364	.316	86	-0	0	1	-1	.667	-1	/O-2	-0.2
Total	3	99	114	17	25	4	0	2	12	17	24	.219	.321	.307	73	-4	0	1	-1	.909	-4	/O-19	-0.9
■ **DAVE ROHDE**	Rohde, David Grant b: 5/8/64, Los Altos, Cal. BB/TR, 6'2", 180 lbs. Deb: 4/9/90																						
1990	Hou-N	59	98	8	18	4	0	0	5	9	20	.184	.286	.224	44	-7	0	0	0	1.000	-0	2-32/3-4,S-2	-0.7
1991	Hou-N	29	41	3	5	0	0	0	0	5	8	.122	.217	.122	-2	-6	0	0	0	1.000	1	/2-4,3-3,S-3,1-1	-0.5
1992	Cle-A	5	7	0	0	0	0	0	0	2	3	.000	.222	.000	-34	-1	0	0	0	.900	1	/3-5	-0.1
Total	3	93	146	11	23	4	0	0	5	16	31	.158	.263	.185	27	-14	0	0	0	1.000	2	/2-36,3-12,S-5,1-1	-1.3
■ **GEORGE ROHE**	Rohe, George Anthony "Whitey" b: 9/15/1875, Cincinnati, Ohio d: 6/10/57, Cincinnati, Ohio BR/TR, 5'9", 165 lbs. Deb: 5/7/01																						
1901	Bal-A	14	36	7	10	2	0	0	4	5		.278	.381	.333	95	-0	1			.912	-3	/1-8,3-6	-0.2
1905	Chi-A	34	113	14	24	1	0	1	12	12		.212	.310	.248	81	-2	2			.934	-4	2-17,3-17	-0.5
1906	*Chi-A	77	225	14	58	5	1	0	25	16		.258	.316	.289	92	-2	8			.926	2	3-57/2-5,O-1	0.2
1907	Chi-A	144	494	46	105	11	2	2	51	39		.213	.274	.255	71	-15	16			.898	-5	3-76,2-39,S-30	-1.9
Total	4	269	868	81	197	19	3	3	92	72		.227	.294	.266	79	-19	27			.917	-9	3-156/2-61,S-30,1O	-2.4
■ **DAN ROHN**	Rohn, Daniel Jay b: 1/10/56, Alpena, Mich. BL/TR, 5'7", 165 lbs. Deb: 9/2/83																						
1983	Chi-N	23	31	3	12	3	2	0	6	2	2	.387	.424	.613	176	3	1	0	0	.923	-0	/2-6,S-1	0.3
1984	Chi-N	25	31	1	4	0	0	1	3	1	6	.129	.156	.226	6	-4	0	0	0	1.000	0	/3-7,2-5,S-5	-0.4
1986	Cle-A	6	10	1	2	0	0	0	2	1	1	.200	.273	.200	32	-1	0	0	0	.900	1	/2-2,3-2,S-1	0.0
Total	3	54	72	5	18	3	2	1	11	4	9	.250	.289	.389	82	-2	1	0	0	.930	1	/2-13,3-9,S-7	-0.1
■ **DAN ROHRMEIER**	Rohrmeier, Daniel b: 9/27/65, Cincinnati, O. BR/TR, 6', 185 lbs. Deb: 9/3/97																						
1997	Sea-A	7	9	4	3	0	0	0	2	2	4	.333	.455	.333	111	0	0	0	0	1.000	0	/1-3,D-4	0.1
■ **RAY ROHWER**	Rohwer, Ray b: 6/5/1895, Dixon, Cal. d: 1/24/88, Davis, Cal. BL/TL, 5'10", 155 lbs. Deb: 4/13/21																						
1921	Pit-N	30	40	6	10	3	2	0	6	4	8	.250	.318	.425	93	-1	0	1	-1	.842	-1	O-10	-0.3
1922	Pit-N	53	129	19	38	6	3	3	22	10	17	.295	.350	.457	105	1	1	0	0	.938	0	O-30	-0.1
Total	2	83	169	25	48	9	5	3	28	14	25	.284	.342	.450	102	0	1	1	-0	.917	-1	/O-40	-0.4
■ **TONY ROIG**	Roig, Anton Ambrose b: 12/23/27, New Orleans, La. BR/TR, 6'1", 180 lbs. Deb: 9/13/53																						
1953	Was-A	3	8	0	1	1	0	0	0	0	1	.125	.125	.250	-1	-1	0	0	0	1.000	2	/2-2	0.0
1955	Was-A	29	57	3	13	1	1	0	4	2	15	.228	.254	.281	46	-5	0	0	0	.932	1	S-21/3-8,2-1	-0.3
1956	Was-A	44	119	11	25	5	2	0	7	20	29	.210	.324	.286	62	-6	2	0	1	.973	7	2-27,S-19	0.4
Total	3	76	184	14	39	7	3	0	11	22	45	.212	.296	.283	55	-12	2	0	1	.927	9	/S-40,2-30,3-8	0.1

YEAR	TM/L	G	AB	R	H	2B	3B	HR	RBI	BB	SO	AVG	OBP	SLG	PRO+	BR/A	SB	CS	SBR	FA	FR	G/POS	TPR
■ **COOKIE ROJAS**		Rojas, Octavio Victor (Rivas) b: 3/6/39, Havana, Cuba BR/TR, 5'10", 170 lbs. Deb: 4/10/62 MC																					
1962	Cin-N	39	86	9	19	2	0	0	6	9	4	.221	.302	.244	47	-6	1	1	-0	.949	-2	2-30/3-1	-0.6
1963	Phi-N	64	77	18	17	0	1	1	2	3	8	.221	.259	.286	57	-4	4	1	1	.991	16	2-25/O-1	1.5
1964	Phi-N	109	340	58	99	19	5	2	31	22	17	.291	.338	.394	107	3	1	3	-2	.967	-11	O-70,2-20,S-18,/C3	-1.1
1965	Phi-N★	142	521	78	158	25	3	3	42	42	33	.303	.359	.380	110	8	5	5	-2	.986	-3	2-84,O-55,S-11,/C1	0.9
1966	Phi-N	156	626	77	168	18	1	6	55	35	46	.268	.311	.329	78	-18	4	6	-2	.983	-9	*2-106,O-56/S-2	-2.6
1967	Phi-N	147	528	60	137	21	2	4	45	30	58	.259	.299	.330	79	-14	8	4	0	.977	-4	*2-137/O-9,C-3,SP3	-1.1
1968	Phi-N	152	621	53	144	19	0	9	48	16	55	.232	.251	.306	67	-26	4	8	-4	**.987**	11	*2-150/C-1	-1.2
1969	Phi-N	110	391	35	89	11	1	4	30	23	28	.228	.272	.292	60	-22	1	6	-3	.980	-3	2-95/O-2	-2.2
1970	StL-N	23	47	2	5	0	0	0	2	3	4	.106	.176	.106	-22	-8	0	0	0	1.000	0	2-10/O-3,S-2	-0.7
	KC-A	98	384	36	100	13	3	2	28	20	29	.260	.297	.326	72	-15	3	7	-3	.982	-1	2-97	-1.1
1971	KC-A★	115	414	56	124	22	2	6	59	39	35	.300	.363	.406	118	10	8	3	1	**.991**	-12	*2-111/S-2,O-1	0.9
1972	KC-A★	137	487	49	127	25	0	3	53	41	35	.261	.319	.331	94	-3	2	8	-4	.986	-2	*2-131/3-6,S-2	-0.2
1973	KC-A★	139	551	78	152	29	3	6	69	37	38	.276	.323	.372	88	-9	18	4	3	.982	9	*2-137	1.1
1974	KC-A☆	144	542	52	147	17	1	6	60	30	43	.271	.313	.339	83	-12	8	4	0	**.987**	-24	*2-141	-3.1
1975	KC-A	120	406	34	103	18	2	2	37	30	24	.254	.305	.323	75	-13	4	5	-2	.980	-15	*2-117/D-1	-2.5
1976	*KC-A	63	132	11	32	6	0	0	16	8	15	.242	.286	.288	68	-5	2	0	1	1.000	-13	2-40/3-6,1-1,D-9	-1.7
1977	*KC-A	64	156	8	39	9	1	0	10	8	17	.250	.287	.321	65	-8	1	3	-2	.944	3	3-31,2-16/D-6	-0.5
Total	16	1822	6309	714	1660	254	25	54	593	396	489	.263	.309	.337	83	-144	74	68	-19	.984	-60	*2-1447,O-197/3SDC1P	-14.2
■ **STAN ROJEK**		Rojek, Stanley Andrew b: 4/21/19, N.Tonawanda, N.Y. d: 7/9/97, N.Tonawanda, N.Y. BR/TR, 5'10", 170 lbs. Deb: 9/22/42																					
1942	Bro-N	1	0	1	0	0	0	0	0	0	0	—	—	—	—	0	0			.000	0	R	0.0
1946	Bro-N	45	47	11	13	2	1	0	2	4	1	.277	.333	.362	96	-0	1			.974	5	S-15/2-6,3-4	0.6
1947	Bro-N	32	80	7	21	0	1	0	7	7	3	.262	.322	.287	61	-4	1			.971	8	S-17/3-9,2-7	0.4
1948	Pit-N	156	641	85	186	27	5	4	51	61	41	.290	.355	.367	94	-4	24			.962	-9	*S-156	-0.4
1949	Pit-N	144	557	72	136	19	2	0	31	50	31	.244	.309	.285	59	-31	4			.966	1	*S-144	-2.0
1950	Pit-N	76	230	28	59	12	1	0	17	18	13	.257	.313	.317	64	-12	2			.967	-15	S-68/2-3	-2.2
1951	Pit-N	8	16	0	3	0	0	0	0	0	1	.188	.188	.188	1	-2	0	0	0	.900	-1	/S-8	-0.3
	StL-N	51	186	21	51	7	3	0	14	10	10	.274	.318	.344	78	-6	0	3	-2	.974	1	S-51	-0.4
	Yr	59	202	21	54	7	3	0	14	10	11	.267	.308	.332	72	-8	0	3	-2	.968	-1	S-59	-0.7
1952	StL-A	9	7	0	1	0	0	0	0	2	0	.143	.333	.143	35	-1	0	0	0	1.000	2	/S-4,2-1	0.1
Total	8	522	1764	225	470	67	13	4	122	152	100	.266	.327	.326	74	-61	32	3		.965	-9	S-463/2-17,3-13	-4.2
■ **SCOTT ROLEN**		Rolen, Scott Bruce b: 4/4/75, Evansville, Ind. BR/TR, 6'4", 210 lbs. Deb: 8/1/96																					
1996	Phi-N	37	130	10	33	7	0	4	18	13	27	.254	.326	.400	89	-2	0	2	-1	.954	-7	3-37	-1.0
1997	Phi-N	156	561	93	159	35	3	21	92	76	138	.283	.382	.469	121	19	16	6	1	.948	13	*3-155	3.3
1998	Phi-N	160	601	120	174	45	4	31	110	93	141	.290	.394	.532	135	33	14	7	0	.970	13	*3-159	4.8
Total	3	353	1292	223	366	87	7	56	220	182	306	.283	.382	.491	125	50	30	15	0	.959	19	3-351	7.1
■ **RED ROLFE**		Rolfe, Robert Abial b: 10/17/08, Penacook, N.H. d: 7/8/69, Gilford, N.H. BL/TR, 5'11.5", 170 lbs. Deb: 6/29/31 MC																					
1931	NY-A	1	0	0	0	0	0	0	0	0	0	—	—	—	—	0	0	0	0	1.000	-0	/S-1	0.0
1934	NY-A	89	279	54	80	13	2	0	18	26	16	.287	.348	.348	86	-6	2	3	-1	.944	4	S-46,3-26	0.0
1935	NY-A	149	639	108	192	33	9	5	67	57	39	.300	.361	.404	103	3	7	3	0	**.964**	-7	*3-136,S-17	0.2
1936	*NY-A	135	568	116	181	39	**15**	10	70	68	38	.319	.392	.493	121	18	3	0	1	**.957**	3	*3-133	2.4
1937	*NY-A★	154	648	143	179	34	10	4	62	90	53	.276	.365	.378	87	-11	4	2	0	.962	5	*3-154	-0.2
1938	*NY-A☆	151	631	132	196	36	8	10	80	74	44	.311	.386	.441	107	8	13	1	3	.959	-7	*3-151	0.6
1939	*NY-A★	152	648	**139**	**213**	**46**	10	14	80	81	41	.329	.404	.495	131	31	7	6	-2	.958	-15	*3-152	1.5
1940	NY-A†	139	588	102	147	26	6	10	53	50	48	.250	.311	.366	78	-20	4	2	0	.949	-1	*3-138	-1.7
1941	*NY-A	136	561	106	148	22	5	8	42	57	38	.264	.332	.364	85	-12	3	2	-0	.946	-10	*3-134	-1.9
1942	*NY-A	69	265	42	58	8	2	8	25	23	18	.219	.281	.355	80	-8	1	1	-0	.959	5	3-60	-0.3
Total	10	1175	4827	942	1394	257	67	69	497	526	335	.289	.360	.413	100	2	44	20	1	.956	-22	*3-1084/S-64	0.6
■ **RAY ROLLING**		Rolling, Raymond Copeland b: 9/8/1886, Martinsburg, Mo. d: 8/25/66, St.Paul, Minn. BR/TR, 5'10.5", 160 lbs. Deb: 9/6/12																					
1912	StL-N	5	15	0	3	0	0		0	0	5	.200	.200	.200	10	-2	0			.947	-0	/2-4	-0.2
■ **RED ROLLINGS**		Rollings, William Russell b: 3/21/04, Mobile, Ala. d: 12/31/64, Mobile, Ala. BL/TR, 5'11", 167 lbs. Deb: 4/17/27																					
1927	Bos-A	82	184	19	49	4	1	0	9	12	10	.266	.325	.299	64	-9	3	1	0	.938	-5	3-44,1-10/2-2	-1.2
1928	Bos-A	50	48	7	11	3	1	0	9	6	8	.229	.315	.333	72	-2	0	0	0	1.000	-2	/1-5,2-4,O-4,3-1	-0.4
1930	Bos-N	52	123	10	29	6	0	0	10	9	5	.236	.288	.285	40	-12	2			.973	3	3-28,2-10	-0.7
Total	3	184	355	36	89	13	2	0	28	27	23	.251	.311	.299	57	-23	5	1		.947	-5	/3-73,2-16,1-15,O-4	-2.3
■ **RICH ROLLINS**		Rollins, Richard John "Red" b: 4/16/38, Mount Pleasant, Pa. BR/TR, 5'10", 185 lbs. Deb: 6/16/61																					
1961	Min-A	13	17	3	5	1	0	0	3	2	2	.294	.400	.353	98	0	0	0	0	1.000	1	/2-5,3-4	0.1
1962	Min-A★	159	624	96	186	23	5	16	96	75	61	.298	.379	.428	112	13	3	1	0	.943	-5	*3-159/S-1	1.0
1963	Min-A	136	531	75	163	23	1	16	61	36	59	.307	.360	.444	122	15	2	0	1	.935	-7	*3-132/2-1	1.0
1964	Min-A	148	596	87	161	25	**10**	12	68	53	80	.270	.335	.406	104	3	2	5	-2	.947	-2	*3-146	-0.3
1965	*Min-A	140	469	59	117	22	1	5	32	37	54	.249	.310	.333	79	-12	4	0	1	.958	-4	*3-112,2-16	-1.7
1966	Min-A	90	269	30	66	7	1	10	40	13	34	.245	.290	.390	88	-5	0	2	-1	.953	-4	3-65/2-2,O-1	-1.2
1967	Min-A	109	339	31	83	11	2	6	39	27	58	.245	.306	.342	84	-6	1	1	-0	.963	-10	3-97	-1.9
1968	Min-A	93	203	14	49	5	0	6	30	10	34	.241	.287	.355	89	-3	3	1	0	.931	-2	3-56	-0.5
1969	Sea-A	58	187	15	42	7	0	4	21	7	19	.225	.271	.326	68	-9	2	0	1	.948	3	3-47/S-1	-0.5
1970	Mil-A	14	25	3	5	1	0	0	5	3	4	.200	.286	.240	46	-2	0	0	0	1.000	1	/3-7	-0.1
	Cle-A	42	43	6	10	0	0	2	4	3	5	.233	.283	.372	75	-2	0	0	0	.600	-1	/3-5	-0.3
	Yr	56	68	9	15	1	0	2	9	6	9	.221	.284	.324	65	-3	0	0	0	.900	-0	3-12	-0.4
Total	10	1002	3303	419	887	125	20	77	399	266	410	.269	.330	.388	98	-7	17	10	-1	.947	-30	3-830/2-24,S-2,O-1	-4.4
■ **BILL ROLLINSON**		Rollinson, William (b: William Henry Winslow) b: 6/10/1856, Fairfield, Maine d: 9/28/38, Bristow, Va. Deb: 6/17/1884																					
1884	Was-U	1	3	0	0	0	0	0		0		.000	.000	.000	-99	-1				.714	0	/C-1	0.0
■ **BILL ROMAN**		Roman, William Anthony b: 10/11/38, Detroit, Mich. BL/TL, 6'4", 190 lbs. Deb: 9/30/64																					
1964	Det-A	3	8	2	3	0	0	1	1	0	2	.375	.375	.750	201	1	0	0	0	1.000	0	/1-2	0.1
1965	Det-A	21	27	0	2	0	0	0	0	2	7	.074	.138	.074	-38	-5	0	0	0	1.000	-0	/1-6	-0.6
Total	2	24	35	2	5	0	0	1	1	2	9	.143	.189	.229	17	-4	0	0	0	1.000	-0	/1-8	-0.5
■ **JOHNNY ROMANO**		Romano, John Anthony "Honey" b: 8/23/34, Hoboken, N.J. BR/TR, 5'11", 205 lbs. Deb: 9/12/58																					
1958	Chi-A	4	7	1	2	0	0	0	1	1	0	.286	.375	.286	86	-0	0	0	0	1.000	1	/C-2	0.1
1959	*Chi-A	53	126	20	37	5	1	5	25	23	18	.294	.407	.468	141	8	0	1	-1	.979	1	C-38	1.0
1960	Cle-A	108	316	40	86	12	2	16	52	37	50	.272	.354	.475	126	11	0	0	0	.988	-11	C-99	0.6
1961	Cle-A★	142	509	76	152	29	1	21	80	61	60	.299	.379	.483	132	24	0	0	0	.989	-9	*C-141	2.2
1962	Cle-A★	135	459	71	120	19	3	25	81	73	64	.261	.369	.479	130	20	0	1	-1	.990	-9	*C-130	1.6
1963	Cle-A	89	255	28	55	5	2	10	34	38	49	.216	.322	.369	94	-2	4	3	-1	.993	-11	C-71/O-4	-1.1
1964	Cle-A	106	352	46	85	18	1	19	47	51	83	.241	.349	.460	124	12	2	2	-1	.991	-5	C-96/1-1	1.2
1965	Chi-A	122	356	39	86	11	0	18	48	59	74	.242	.357	.424	129	15	0	2	-1	.992	4	*C-111/O-4,1-2	2.4
1966	Chi-A	122	329	33	76	12	0	15	47	58	72	.231	.348	.404	124	11	0	0	0	.993	3	*C-102	2.2
1967	StL-N	24	58	1	7	1	0	0	2	13	15	.121	.282	.138	24	-5	1	0	0	.983	-1	C-20	-0.5
Total	10	905	2767	355	706	112	10	129	417	414	485	.255	.358	.443	123	93	7	9	-3	.990	-36	C-810/O-8,1-3	9.7
■ **TOM ROMANO**		Romano, Thomas Michael b: 10/25/58, Syracuse, N.Y. BR/TR, 5'10", 170 lbs. Deb: 9/1/87																					
1987	Mon-N	7	3	1	0	0	0	0	0	0	1	.000	.000	.000	-97	-1	0	0	0	.000	-1	/O-3	-0.2

YEAR	TM/L	G	AB	R	H	2B	3B	HR	RBI	BB	SO	AVG	OBP	SLG	PRO+	BR/A	SB	CS	SBR	FA	FR	G/POS	TPR
■ MANDY ROMERO	Romero, Armando b: 10/29/67, Miami, Fla. BB/TR, 5′11″, 200 lbs. Deb: 7/15/97																						
1997	SD-N	21	48	7	10	0	0	2	4	2	18	.208	.240	.333	52	-4	1	0	0	1.000	3	C-19	0.0
1998	SD-N	6	9	1	0	0	0	0	0	1	3	.000	.100	.000	-78	-2	0	0	0	.963	1	/C-6	-0.1
	Bos-A	12	13	2	3	1	0	0	1	3	3	.231	.375	.308	80	-0	0	0	0	1.000	0	/C-4,D-3	0.0
Total	2	39	70	10	13	1	0	2	5	6	24	.186	.250	.286	42	-6	1	0	0	.993	4	/C-29,D-3	-0.1
■ ED ROMERO	Romero, Edgardo Ralph (Rivera) b: 12/9/57, Santurce, P.R. BR/TR, 5′11″, 175 lbs. Deb: 7/16/77																						
1977	Mil-A	10	25	4	7	1	0	0	2	4	3	.280	.379	.320	93	-0	0	0	0	.971	0	S-10	0.1
1980	Mil-A	42	104	20	27	7	0	1	10	9	11	.260	.319	.356	87	-2	2	0	1	.894	4	S-22,2-15/3-3	0.6
1981	*Mil-A	44	91	6	18	3	0	1	10	4	9	.198	.232	.264	45	-7	0	2	-1	.949	10	S-22,2-18/3-3	0.5
1982	Mil-A	52	144	18	36	8	0	1	7	8	16	.250	.289	.326	73	-5	0	0	0	.975	-1	2-39,S-10/3-2,O-1	-0.5
1983	Mil-A	59	145	17	46	7	0	1	18	8	8	.317	.353	.386	112	2	1	0	0	.962	-10	S-22,O-15/3-5,2D	-0.6
1984	Mil-A	116	357	36	90	12	0	1	31	29	25	.252	.310	.294	71	-13	3	3	-1	.943	2	3-59,S-39,2/1OD	-1.0
1985	Mil-A	88	251	24	63	11	1	0	21	26	20	.251	.321	.303	72	-9	1	1	-0	.977	8	S-43,2-31,O-14,/3-1	0.4
1986	*Bos-A	100	233	41	49	11	0	2	23	18	16	.210	.273	.283	51	-16	2	0	1	.959	-8	S-75,3-18/2-4,O-1	-1.7
1987	Bos-A	88	235	23	64	5	0	0	14	18	22	.272	.324	.294	64	-12	0	2	-1	.973	2	2-29,S-24,3-24,/1-8	-0.8
1988	*Bos-A	31	75	3	18	3	0	0	5	3	8	.240	.278	.280	55	-5	0	0	0	1.000	-1	3-15/S-8/2-5,1-1,D	-0.4
1989	Bos-A	46	113	14	24	4	0	0	6	7	7	.212	.264	.248	42	-9	0	2	-1	.983	13	2-22,3-14,S-10	0.4
	Atl-N	7	19	1	5	1	0	1	1	0	0	.263	.263	.474	104	-0	0	0	0	.947	5	/2-4,S-2,3-1	0.5
	Mil-A	15	50	3	10	3	0	0	3	0	10	.200	.200	.260	29	-5	0	0	0	1.000	0	2-11/3-4,S-1,D-2	-0.4
1990	Det-A	32	70	8	16	3	0	0	4	6	4	.229	.289	.271	57	-4	0	0	0	.982	6	3-27/D-3	0.2
Total	12	730	1912	218	473	79	1	8	155	140	159	.247	.300	.302	67	-83	9	10	-3	.958	30	S-288,2-192,3/O1D	-2.7
■ KEVIN ROMINE	Romine, Kevin Andrew b: 5/23/61, Exeter, N.H. BR/TR, 5′11″, 185 lbs. Deb: 9/5/85																						
1985	Bos-A	24	28	3	6	2	0	0	1	1	4	.214	.241	.286	42	-2	1	0	0	1.000	-5	O-23/D-1	-0.8
1986	Bos-A	35	35	6	9	2	0	0	2	3	9	.257	.316	.314	72	-1	2	0	1	1.000	-6	O-33	-0.7
1987	Bos-A	9	24	5	7	2	0	0	2	2	6	.292	.346	.375	89	-0	0	0	0	1.000	-0	/O-7,D-2	-0.1
1988	*Bos-A	57	78	17	15	2	1	1	6	7	15	.192	.259	.282	49	-5	2	0	1	.957	-13	O-45/D-5	-1.8
1989	Bos-A	92	274	30	75	13	0	1	23	21	53	.274	.330	.332	82	-6	1	1	-0	.982	-2	O-89/D-2	-1.0
1990	Bos-A	70	136	21	37	7	0	2	14	12	27	.272	.336	.368	92	-1	4	0	1	.976	-11	O-64/D-1	-1.2
1991	Bos-A	44	55	7	9	2	0	1	7	3	10	.164	.207	.255	26	-6	1	1	-0	.964	-4	O-23,D-14	-1.1
Total	7	331	630	89	158	30	1	5	55	49	124	.251	.308	.325	73	-22	11	2	2	.980	-41	O-284/D-25	-6.7
■ MARC RONAN	Ronan, Edward Marcus b: 9/19/69, Ozark, Ala. BL/TR, 6′2″, 190 lbs. Deb: 9/21/93																						
1993	StL-N	6	12	0	1	0	0	0	0	0	5	.083	.083	.083	-56	-3	0	0	0	1.000	2	/C-6	-0.1
■ HENRI RONDEAU	Rondeau, Henri Joseph b: 5/7/1887, Danielson, Conn. d: 5/28/43, Woonsocket, R.I. BR/TR, 5′11″, 175 lbs. Deb: 4/11/13																						
1913	Det-A	35	70	5	13	2	0	0	5	14	16	.186	.321	.214	58	-3	1			1.000	-2	C-16/1-6	-0.4
1915	Was-A	14	40	3	7	0	0	0	4	4	3	.175	.250	.175	27	-4	1	2	-1	1.000	3	O-11	-0.3
1916	Was-A	50	162	20	36	5	3	1	28	18	18	.222	.311	.309	87	-2	7			.958	3	O-48	-0.2
Total	3	99	272	28	56	7	3	1	37	36	37	.206	.305	.265	71	-9	9	2		.967	4	/O-59,C-16,1-6	-0.9
■ GENE ROOF	Roof, Eugene Lawrence b: 1/13/58, Paducah, Ky. BB/TR, 6′2″, 180 lbs. Deb: 9/3/81 F																						
1981	StL-N	23	60	11	18	6	0	0	3	12	16	.300	.417	.400	129	3	5	1	1	.950	-2	O-20	0.2
1982	StL-N	11	15	3	4	0	0	0	2	1	4	.267	.313	.267	63	-1	2	0	1	1.000	-1	/O-5	-0.2
1983	StL-N	6	3	1	0	0	0	0	0	0	0	.000	.000	.000	-99	-1	0	0	0	.000	-0	/O-1	-0.1
	Mon-N	8	12	2	2	2	0	0	1	1	3	.167	.231	.333	55	-1	0	0	0	1.000	-1	/O-5	-0.2
	Yr	14	15	3	2	2	0	0	1	1	3	.133	.188	.267	25	-2	0	0	0	1.000	-2	/O-6	-0.3
Total	3	48	90	17	24	8	0	0	6	14	23	.267	.365	.356	102	1	7	1	2	.958	-5	/O-31	-0.3
■ PHIL ROOF	Roof, Phillip Anthony b: 3/5/41, Paducah, Ky. BR/TR, 6′3″, 210 lbs. Deb: 4/29/61 FC																						
1961	Mil-N	1	0	0	0	0	0	0	0	0	0	—	—	—	—	0	0	0	0	1.000	0	/C-1	0.0
1964	Mil-N	1	2	0	0	0	0	0	0	0	1	.000	.000	.000	-99	-1	0	0	0	1.000	1	/C-1	0.1
1965	Cal-A	9	22	1	3	0	0	0	0	0	6	.136	.136	.136	-23	-3	0	0	0	.983	6	/C-9	0.2
	Cle-A	43	52	3	9	1	0	0	3	5	13	.173	.259	.192	30	-5	0	0	0	.994	13	C-41	1.0
	Yr	52	74	4	12	1	0	0	3	5	19	.162	.225	.176	15	-8	0	0	0	.992	19	C-50	1.2
1966	KC-A	127	369	33	77	14	3	7	44	37	95	.209	.286	.320	76	-11	2	5	-2	.985	-1	*C-123/1-2	-0.7
1967	KC-A	114	327	23	67	14	5	6	24	23	85	.205	.268	.333	79	-9	4	1	1	.991	-1	*C-113	-0.5
1968	Oak-A	34	64	5	12	0	0	1	2	2	15	.188	.212	.234	37	-5	1	0	0	.968	-1	C-32	-0.5
1969	Oak-A	106	247	19	58	6	1	2	19	33	55	.235	.337	.291	81	-5	1	0	0	.983	-1	*C-106	-0.2
1970	Mil-A	110	321	39	73	7	1	13	37	32	72	.227	.307	.377	87	-6	3	2	-0	.988	8	*C-107/1-1	0.6
1971	Mil-A	41	114	6	22	2	1	1	10	8	28	.193	.252	.254	44	-8	0	0	0	.975	3	C-39	-0.4
	Min-A	31	87	6	21	4	0	0	6	8	18	.241	.305	.287	67	-4	0	1	-1	.985	8	C-29	0.5
	Yr	72	201	12	43	6	1	1	16	16	46	.214	.275	.269	54	-12	0	1	-1	.980	11	C-68	0.1
1972	Min-A	61	146	16	30	11	1	3	12	6	27	.205	.237	.356	71	-6	0	1	-1	.978	-2	C-61	-0.8
1973	Min-A	47	117	10	23	4	1	1	15	13	27	.197	.277	.274	53	-7	0	0	0	.992	6	C-47	0.1
1974	Min-A	44	97	10	19	1	0	2	13	6	24	.196	.257	.268	50	-6	0	0	0	1.000	7	C-44	0.3
1975	Min-A	63	126	18	38	2	0	7	21	9	28	.302	.353	.484	133	5	0	0	0	.989	6	C-63	1.3
1976	Min-A	18	46	1	10	3	0	0	4	2	6	.217	.250	.283	55	-3	0	0	0	.962	5	C-12/D-1	0.3
	Chi-A	4	9	0	1	0	0	0	0	0	3	.111	.111	.111	-35	-2	0	0	0	1.000	-0	/C-4	-0.2
	Yr	22	55	1	11	3	0	0	4	2	9	.200	.228	.255	40	-4	0	0	0	.967	5	C-16/D-1	0.1
1977	Tor-A	3	5	0	0	0	0	0	0	0	1	.000	.000	.000	-99	-1	0	0	0	1.000	1	/C-3	0.0
Total	15	857	2151	190	463	69	13	43	210	184	504	.215	.284	.319	73	-77	11	10	-3	.986	58	C-835/1-3,D-1	1.1
■ GEORGE ROOKS	Rooks, George Brinton McClellan (b: George Brinton Mc Clellan Ruckser) b: 10/21/1863, Chicago, Ill. d: 3/11/35, Chicago, Ill. BR/TR, 5′11″, 170 lbs. Deb: 5/12/1891 F																						
1891	Bos-N	5	16	1	2	0	0	0	0	4	1	.125	.300	.125	23	-2	0			1.000	1	/O-5	-0.1
■ ROLANDO ROOMES	Roomes, Rolando Audley b: 2/15/62, Kingston, Jamaica BR/TR, 6′3″, 180 lbs. Deb: 4/12/88																						
1988	Chi-N	17	16	3	3	0	0	0	0	0	4	.188	.188	.188	8	-2	0	1	-1	.833	-1	/O-5	-0.4
1989	Cin-N	107	315	36	83	18	5	7	34	13	100	.263	.299	.419	100	-1	12	8	-1	.981	-3	*O-100	-0.7
1990	Cin-N	30	61	5	13	0	0	2	7	0	20	.213	.213	.311	41	-5	0	0	0	1.000	-0	O-19	-0.6
	Mon-N	16	14	1	4	0	1	0	1	1	6	.286	.333	.429	112	0	0	2	-1	1.000	-1	/O-6	-0.3
	Yr	46	75	6	17	0	1	2	8	1	26	.227	.237	.333	54	-5	0	2	-1	1.000	-2	O-25	-0.9
Total	3	170	406	45	103	18	6	9	42	14	130	.254	.284	.394	88	-8	12	11	-3	.980	-5	O-130	-2.0
■ FRANK ROONEY	Rooney, Frank (b: Frank Rovny) b: 10/12/1884, Podebrady, Bohemia (Austria-Hungary) d: 4/6/77, Bessemer, Mich. Dob: 4/18/14																						
1914	Ind-F	12	35	1	7	0	1	1	8	1	0	.200	.222	.343	47	-3	2			.980	-1	/1-9	-0.5
■ PAT ROONEY	Rooney, Patrick Eugene b: 11/28/57, Chicago, Ill. BR/TR, 6′1″, 190 lbs. Deb: 9/9/81																						
1981	Mon-N	4	5	0	0	0	0	0	0	0	3	.000	.000	.000	-99	-1	0	0	0	1.000	-1	/O-2	-0.2
■ JORGE ROQUE	Roque, Jorge (Vargas) b: 4/28/50, Ponce, P.R. BR/TR, 5′10″, 158 lbs. Deb: 9/4/70																						
1970	StL-N	5	1	2	0	0	0	0	0	0	1	.000	.500	.000	45	0	0	0	0	.000	-0	/O-1	0.0
1971	StL-N	3	10	2	3	0	0	0	1	0	3	.300	.300	.300	68	-0	1	0	0	1.000	-0	/O-3	0.0
1972	StL-N	32	67	3	7	2	1	1	5	6	19	.104	.178	.209	10	-8	1	1	-0	.980	-1	O-24	-1.1
1973	Mon-N	25	61	7	9	2	0	1	6	4	17	.148	.212	.230	22	-7	2	2	-1	.878	-3	O-24	-1.1
Total	4	65	139	14	19	4	1	2	12	10	40	.137	.205	.223	20	-15	4	3	-1	.934	-4	/O-52	-2.2
■ LUIS ROSADO	Rosado, Luis (Robles) b: 12/6/55, Santurce, P.R. BR/TR, 6′, 180 lbs. Deb: 9/8/77																						
1977	NY-N	9	24	1	5	1	0	0	3	1	3	.208	.269	.250	42	-2	0	0	0	.980	-0	/1-7,C-1	-0.3

YEAR	TM/L	G	AB	R	H	2B	3B	HR	RBI	BB	SO	AVG	OBP	SLG	PRO+	BR/A	SB	CS	SBR	FA	FR	G/POS	TPR
1980	NY-N	2	4	0	0	0	0	0	0	0	1	.000	.000	.000	-99	-1	0	0	0	1.000	-0	/1-1	-0.1
Total	2	11	28	1	5	1	0	0	3	1	4	.179	.233	.214	23	-3	0	0	0	.983	-0	/1-8,C-1	-0.4

■ BUDDY ROSAR Rosar, Warren Vincent b: 7/3/14, Buffalo, N.Y. d: 3/13/94, Rochester, N.Y. BR/TR, 5'9", 190 lbs. Deb: 4/29/39

YEAR	TM/L	G	AB	R	H	2B	3B	HR	RBI	BB	SO	AVG	OBP	SLG	PRO+	BR/A	SB	CS	SBR	FA	FR	G/POS	TPR
1939	NY-A	43	105	18	29	5	1	0	12	13	10	.276	.356	.343	81	-3	4	0	1	.980	4	C-35	0.4
1940	NY-A	73	228	34	68	11	3	4	37	19	11	.298	.357	.425	106	2	7	1	2	.983	1	C-63	0.8
1941	*NY-A	67	209	25	60	17	2	1	36	22	10	.287	.355	.402	101	0	0	0	0	.996	0	C-60	0.5
1942	*NY-A☆	69	209	18	48	10	0	2	34	17	20	.230	.288	.306	68	-9	1	2	-1	.996	4	C-58	-0.2
1943	Cle-A☆	115	382	53	108	17	1	1	41	33	12	.283	.340	.340	106	2	0	4	-2	.983	7	*C-114	1.5
1944	Cle-A	99	331	29	87	9	3	0	30	34	17	.263	.339	.308	89	-4	1	2	-1	**.989**	4	C-98	0.5
1945	Phi-A	92	300	23	63	12	1	1	25	20	16	.210	.262	.267	54	-18	2	1	0	.987	-0	C-85	-1.5
1946	Phi-A★	121	424	34	120	22	2	2	47	36	17	.283	.339	.358	96	-3	1	3	-2	**1.000**	7	*C-117	1.0
1947	Phi-A★	102	359	40	93	20	2	1	33	40	13	.259	.335	.334	85	-7	1	3	-2	**.996**	13	*C-102	1.2
1948	Phi-A★	90	302	30	77	13	0	4	41	39	12	.255	.344	.338	82	-7	0	2	-1	**.997**	-3	C-90	-0.5
1949	Phi-A	32	95	7	19	2	0	0	6	16	5	.200	.315	.221	45	-7	0	0	0	.992	-2	C-31	-0.8
1950	Bos-A	27	84	13	25	2	0	1	12	7	4	.298	.352	.357	75	-3	0	0	0	.991	-1	C-25	-0.3
1951	Bos-A	58	170	11	39	7	0	1	13	19	14	.229	.307	.288	56	-10	0	0	0	.996	0	C-56	-0.8
Total	13	988	3198	335	836	147	15	18	367	315	161	.261	.330	.334	84	-67	17	18	-6	.992	33	C-934	1.8

■ JIMMY ROSARIO Rosario, Angel Ramon (Ferrer) b: 5/5/45, Bayamon, P.R. BB/TR, 5'10", 155 lbs. Deb: 4/8/71

YEAR	TM/L	G	AB	R	H	2B	3B	HR	RBI	BB	SO	AVG	OBP	SLG	PRO+	BR/A	SB	CS	SBR	FA	FR	G/POS	TPR
1971	*SF-N	92	192	26	43	6	1	0	13	33	35	.224	.341	.266	75	-5	7	4	-0	1.000	-1	O-67	-0.9
1972	SF-N	7	2	1	0	0	0	0	0	0	0	.000	.000	.000	-99	-1	0	1	-1	.000	-1	/O-1	-0.2
1976	Mil-A	15	37	4	7	0	0	1	5	3	8	.189	.250	.270	53	-2	1	3	-2	1.000	-2	O-12/D-2	-0.7
Total	3	114	231	31	50	6	1	1	18	36	43	.216	.325	.264	70	-8	8	8	-2	1.000	-4	/O-80,D-2	-1.8

■ MEL ROSARIO Rosario, Melvin Gregorio b: 5/25/73, Santo Domingo, D.R. BB/TR, 6', 191 lbs. Deb: 9/11/97

YEAR	TM/L	G	AB	R	H	2B	3B	HR	RBI	BB	SO	AVG	OBP	SLG	PRO+	BR/A	SB	CS	SBR	FA	FR	G/POS	TPR
1997	Bal-A	4	3	0	0	0	0	0	0	0	1	.000	.000	.000	-99	-1	0	0	0	.875	0	/C-4	-0.1

■ SANTIAGO ROSARIO Rosario, Santiago b: 7/25/39, Guayanilla, P.R. BL/TL, 5'11", 165 lbs. Deb: 6/23/65

YEAR	TM/L	G	AB	R	H	2B	3B	HR	RBI	BB	SO	AVG	OBP	SLG	PRO+	BR/A	SB	CS	SBR	FA	FR	G/POS	TPR
1965	KC-A	81	85	8	20	3	0	2	8	6	16	.235	.293	.341	81	-2	0	0	0	.991	-1	1-31/O-3	-0.4

■ VICTOR ROSARIO Rosario, Victor Manuel (Rivera) b: 8/26/66, Hato Mayor Del Rey, D.R. BR/TR, 5'11", 155 lbs. Deb: 9/6/90

YEAR	TM/L	G	AB	R	H	2B	3B	HR	RBI	BB	SO	AVG	OBP	SLG	PRO+	BR/A	SB	CS	SBR	FA	FR	G/POS	TPR
1990	Atl-N	9	7	3	1	0	0	0	0	1	1	.143	.250	.143	10	-1	0	0	0	1.000	1	/S-3,2-1	0.0

■ PETE ROSE Rose, Peter Edward Jr. b: 11/16/69, Cincinnati, O. BL/TR, 6'1", 180 lbs. Deb: 9/1/97 F

YEAR	TM/L	G	AB	R	H	2B	3B	HR	RBI	BB	SO	AVG	OBP	SLG	PRO+	BR/A	SB	CS	SBR	FA	FR	G/POS	TPR
1997	Cin-N	11	14	2	2	0	0	0	0	2	9	.143	.250	.143	6	-2	0	0	0	.600	-1	/3-2,1-1	-0.2

■ PETE ROSE Rose, Peter Edward Sr. "Charlie Hustle" b: 4/14/41, Cincinnati, Ohio BB/TR, 5'11", 200 lbs. Deb: 4/8/63 FM

YEAR	TM/L	G	AB	R	H	2B	3B	HR	RBI	BB	SO	AVG	OBP	SLG	PRO+	BR/A	SB	CS	SBR	FA	FR	G/POS	TPR
1963	Cin-N	157	623	101	170	25	9	6	41	55	72	.273	.337	.371	101	1	13	15	-5	.971	-23	*2-157/O-1	-1.3
1964	Cin-N	136	516	64	139	13	2	4	34	36	51	.269	.319	.326	79	-13	4	10	-5	.979	-14	*2-128	-2.3
1965	Cin-N★	162	670	117	**209**	35	11	11	81	69	76	.312	.383	.446	124	23	8	3	1	.975	-18	*2-162	2.1
1966	Cin-N	156	654	97	205	38	5	16	70	37	61	.313	.351	.460	113	11	4	9	-4	.981	-8	*2-140,3-16	1.0
1967	Cin-N★	148	585	86	176	32	8	12	76	56	66	.301	.365	.444	117	13	11	6	-0	.982	-4	*O-123,2-35	0.6
1968	Cin-N†	149	626	94	**210**	42	6	10	49	56	76	**.335**	**.394**	.470	149	38	3	7	-3	.990	7	*O-148/2-3,1-1	3.8
1969	Cin-N★	156	627	**120**	218	33	11	16	82	88	65	**.348**	.432	.512	155	49	7	10	-4	.988	5	*O-156/2-2	4.3
1970	*Cin-N★	159	649	120	**205**	37	9	15	52	73	64	.316	.387	.470	128	26	12	7	-1	**.997**	5	*O-159	2.2
1971	Cin-N★	160	632	86	192	27	4	13	44	68	50	.304	.374	.421	127	24	13	9	-2	.994	4	*O-158	1.9
1972	*Cin-N	154	645	107	**198**	31	11	6	57	73	46	.307	.383	.417	135	31	10	3	1	.994	16	*O-154	4.3
1973	*Cin-N★	160	680	115	**230**	36	8	5	64	65	42	**.338**	.401	.437	139	37	10	7	-1	.992	17	*O-159	4.6
1974	Cin-N★	163	652	**110**	185	**45**	7	3	51	106	54	.284	.388	.388	119	21	2	4	-2	**.997**	18	*O-163	3.0
1975	*Cin-N★	162	662	**112**	210	**47**	4	7	74	89	50	.317	.407	.432	130	31	0	1	-1	.963	-36	*3-137,O-35	-0.7
1976	*Cin-N★	162	665	**130**	**215**	**42**	6	10	63	86	54	.323	.406	.450	139	37	9	5	-0	**.969**	-12	*3-159/O-1	2.5
1977	Cin-N★	162	655	95	204	38	7	9	64	66	42	.311	.379	.432	115	15	16	4	2	.958	-24	*3-161	-0.8
1978	Cin-N★	159	655	103	198	**51**	3	7	52	62	30	.302	.365	.421	119	17	13	9	-2	.961	-26	*3-156/O-7,1-2	-1.3
1979	Phi-N★	163	628	90	208	40	5	4	59	95	32	.331	.421	.430	128	29	20	11	-1	.995	-5	*1-159/3-5,2-1	1.4
1980	*Phi-N★	162	655	95	185	**42**	1	1	64	66	33	.282	.354	.354	93	-4	12	8	-1	**.997**	9	*1-162	-0.6
1981	*Phi-N★	107	431	73	**140**	18	5	0	33	46	26	.325	.394	.390	118	12	4	4	-1	.996	9	*1-107	1.4
1982	Phi-N★	162	634	80	172	25	4	3	54	66	32	.271	.347	.338	90	-6	8	8	-2	.995	6	*1-162	-1.3
1983	*Phi-N	151	493	52	121	14	3	0	45	52	28	.245	.320	.286	70	-19	7	7	-2	.990	-2	*1-112,O-35	-3.0
1984	Mon-N	95	278	34	72	6	2	0	23	31	20	.259	.335	.295	82	-6	1	1	-0	.988	8	1-40,O-28	-0.2
	Cin-N	26	96	9	35	9	0	0	11	9	7	.365	.430	.458	143	6	0	0	0	.990	-3	1-23/M	0.2
	Yr	121	374	43	107	15	2	0	34	40	27	.286	.360	.337	99	1	1	1	-0	.989	5	1-63,O-28	0.0
1985	Cin-N★	119	405	60	107	12	2	2	46	86	35	.264	.398	.319	98	4	8	1	2	.995	0	*1-110/M	-0.1
1986	Cin-N	72	237	15	52	8	2	0	25	30	31	.219	.317	.270	61	-12	3	0	1	.990	-1	1-61/M	-1.7
Total	24	3562	14053	2165	4256	746	135	160	1314	1566	1143	.303	.377	.409	117	366	198	149	-30	.991	-71	*O-1327,1-939,32	20.0

■ BOBBY ROSE Rose, Robert Richard b: 3/15/67, Covina, Cal. BR/TR, 5'11", 170 lbs. Deb: 8/12/89

YEAR	TM/L	G	AB	R	H	2B	3B	HR	RBI	BB	SO	AVG	OBP	SLG	PRO+	BR/A	SB	CS	SBR	FA	FR	G/POS	TPR
1989	Cal-A	14	38	4	8	1	2	1	3	2	10	.211	.268	.421	93	-1	0	0	0	.920	-1	3-10/2-3	-0.1
1990	Cal-A	7	13	5	5	0	0	1	2	2	1	.385	.467	.615	204	2	0	0	0	1.000	-1	/2-4,3-3	0.1
1991	Cal-A	22	65	5	18	5	1	1	8	3	13	.277	.309	.431	102	-0	0	0	0	1.000	-1	/2-8,O-7,3-4,1-3	-0.1
1992	Cal-A	30	84	10	18	5	0	2	10	8	9	.214	.298	.345	79	-2	1	1	-0	.953	8	2-28/1-2	0.6
Total	4	73	200	24	49	11	3	5	23	15	33	.245	.307	.405	98	-1	1	1	-0	.965	6	/2-43,3-17,O-7,1-5	0.5

■ JOHNNY ROSEBORO Roseboro, John Junior b: 5/13/33, Ashland, Ohio BL/TR, 5'11.5", 190 lbs. Deb: 6/14/57 C

YEAR	TM/L	G	AB	R	H	2B	3B	HR	RBI	BB	SO	AVG	OBP	SLG	PRO+	BR/A	SB	CS	SBR	FA	FR	G/POS	TPR
1957	Bro-N	35	69	6	10	2	0	2	6	10	20	.145	.253	.261	35	-6	0	0	0	.972	3	C-19/1-5	-0.3
1958	LA-N☆	114	384	52	104	11	9	14	43	36	56	.271	.336	.456	104	2	11	8	-2	.987	-16	*C-104/O-5	-1.0
1959	*LA-N	118	397	39	92	14	7	10	38	52	69	.232	.325	.378	81	-11	7	5	-1	.991	6	*C-117	0.2
1960	LA-N	103	287	22	61	15	3	8	42	44	53	.213	.325	.369	84	-6	7	6	-2	.993	3	C-87/1-1,3-1	0.1
1961	LA-N★	128	394	59	99	16	6	18	59	56	62	.251	.350	.459	104	2	6	4	-1	.986	7	*C-125	1.4
1962	LA-N★	128	389	45	97	16	7	7	55	50	60	.249	.345	.380	101	1	12	3	2	.985	-2	*C-128	0.6
1963	*LA-N	135	470	50	111	13	7	9	49	36	50	.236	.295	.351	91	-6	7	6	-2	.992	-10	*C-134	-1.4
1964	LA-N	134	414	42	119	24	1	3	45	44	61	.287	.361	.372	115	9	3	3	-1	.993	1	*C-128	1.6
1965	*LA-N	136	437	42	102	10	0	8	57	34	51	.233	.292	.311	75	-15	1	6	-3	.994	-2	*C-131/3-1	-1.5
1966	*LA-N	142	445	47	123	23	2	9	53	44	51	.276	.346	.398	115	9	3	2	-0	.993	6	*C-138	2.4
1967	LA-N	116	334	37	91	18	2	4	24	38	33	.272	.350	.374	117	8	2	4	-2	.984	-11	*C-107	0.0
1968	Min-A	135	380	31	82	12	0	8	39	46	57	.216	.304	.311	82	-7	2	3	-1	.991	-5	*C-117	-0.6
1969	*Min-A★	115	361	33	95	12	0	3	32	39	44	.263	.335	.321	83	-8	5	5	-2	.980	0	*C-111	-0.4
1970	Was-A	46	86	7	20	4	0	1	6	18	10	.233	.365	.314	94	-0	1	1	-0	1.000	-3	C-30	-0.2
Total	14	1585	4847	512	1206	190	44	104	548	547	677	.249	.329	.371	95	-28	67	56	-14	.989	-22	*C-1476/1-6,O-5,3-2	0.9

■ BOB ROSELLI Roselli, Robert Edward b: 12/10/31, San Francisco, Cal. BR/TR, 5'11", 185 lbs. Deb: 8/16/55

YEAR	TM/L	G	AB	R	H	2B	3B	HR	RBI	BB	SO	AVG	OBP	SLG	PRO+	BR/A	SB	CS	SBR	FA	FR	G/POS	TPR
1955	Mil-N	6	9	1	2	1	0	0	0	1	4	.222	.364	.333	91	-0	0	0	0	.917	0	/C-2	0.0
1956	Mil-N	4	2	1	1	0	0	1	1	0	1	.500	.500	2.000	564	1	0	0	0	1.000	2	/C-3	0.3
1958	Mil-N	1	1	0	0	0	0	0	0	0	0	.000	.000	.000	-99	-0	0	0	0	.000	0	H	0.0
1961	Chi-A	22	38	2	10	3	0	0	4	0	11	.263	.263	.342	61	-2	0	0	0	1.000	-1	C-10	-0.3
1962	Chi-A	35	64	4	12	3	1	1	5	11	15	.188	.316	.313	70	-3	1	0	0	.988	-1	C-20	-0.3
Total	5	68	114	8	25	7	1	2	10	12	31	.219	.305	.351	76	-4	1	0	0	.986	-1	/C-35	-0.3

■ DAVE ROSELLO Rosello, David (Rodriguez) b: 6/26/50, Mayaguez, P.R. BR/TR, 5'11", 160 lbs. Deb: 9/10/72

YEAR	TM/L	G	AB	R	H	2B	3B	HR	RBI	BB	SO	AVG	OBP	SLG	PRO+	BR/A	SB	CS	SBR	FA	FR	G/POS	TPR
1972	Chi-N	5	12	2	3	0	0	1	3	3	2	.250	.400	.500	139	1	0	0	0	.846	1	/S-5	0.2
1973	Chi-N	16	38	4	10	2	0	0	2	2	4	.263	.300	.316	66	-2	2	2	-1	.964	3	2-13/S-1	0.1
1974	Chi-N	62	148	9	30	7	0	0	10	10	28	.203	.253	.250	39	-12	1	1	-0	.972	3	2-49,S-12	-0.7

YEAR	TM/L	G	AB	R	H	2B	3B	HR	RBI	BB	SO	AVG	OBP	SLG	PRO+	BR/A	SB	CS	SBR	FA	FR	G/POS	TPR
1975	Chi-N	19	58	7	15	2	0	1	8	9	8	.259	.358	.345	92	-0	0	1	-1	.952	1	S-19	0.2
1976	Chi-N	91	227	27	55	5	1	1	11	41	33	.242	.361	.286	78	-5	1	2	-1	.966	-7	S-86/2-1	-0.4
1977	Chi-N	56	82	18	18	2	1	1	9	12	12	.220	.319	.305	62	-4	0	0	0	.938	-3	3-21,S-10/2-3	-0.7
1979	Cle-A	59	107	20	26	6	1	3	14	15	27	.243	.336	.402	98	-0	1	0	0	.976	-5	2-33,3-14,S-11	-0.3
1980	Cle-A	71	117	16	29	3	0	2	12	9	19	.248	.302	.325	71	-5	0	0	0	.980	3	2-43,3-22/S-3,D-1	0.0
1981	Cle-A	43	84	11	20	4	0	1	7	7	12	.238	.297	.321	79	-2	0	1	-1	.979	3	2-26/3-8,S-4,D-4	0.1
Total	9	422	873	114	206	31	3	10	76	108	145	.236	.321	.313	73	-29	5	7	-3	.975	0	2-168,S-151/3-65,D	-1.5

■ CHIEF ROSEMAN

Roseman, James John b: 1856, New York, N.Y. d: 7/4/38, Brooklyn, N.Y. BR/TR, 5'7", 167 lbs. Deb: 5/1/1882 M

YEAR	TM/L	G	AB	R	H	2B	3B	HR	RBI	BB	SO	AVG	OBP	SLG	PRO+	BR/A	SB	CS	SBR	FA	FR	G/POS	TPR
1882	Tro-N	82	331	41	78	21	6	1	29	3	41	.236	.243	.344	90	-3				.853	-3	*O-82	-0.6
1883	NY-a	93	398	48	100	13	6	0		11		.251	.271	.314	84	-8				.855	-3	*O-91/1-2	-1.1
1884	*NY-a	107	436	97	130	16	11	4		21		.298	.339	.413	148	23				.885	-2	*O-107	1.7
1885	NY-a	101	410	72	114	13	14	4	46	25		.278	.335	.407	145	22				.865	-7	*O-101/P-1	1.1
1886	NY-a	134	559	90	127	19	10	5	53	24		.227	.269	.324	89	-8	6			.891	-3	*O-134/P-1	-1.2
1887	Phi-a	21	73	16	16	2	1	0	8	10		.219	.352	.274	76	-2	3			.821	-0	O-21	-0.2
	NY-a	60	241	30	55	10	1	1	27	9		.228	.265	.290	57	-14	3			.868	-8	O-59/1-3,P-2	-1.8
	Bro-a	1	3	2	1	0	0	0	1	0		.333	.500	.333	133	0	0			1.000	-3	/O-1	-0.3
	Yr	82	317	48	72	12	2	1	36	19		.227	.290	.287	63	-15	6			.856	-11	O-81/1-3,P-2	-2.3
1890	StL-a	80	302	47	103	26	0	2	58	30		.341	.449	.447	144	16	7			.819	-8	O-58,1-22,M	0.4
	Lou-a	2	8	0	2	0	0	0	0	0		.250	.250	.250	48	-1	0			.864	-1	/1-2	-0.1
	Yr	82	310	47	105	26	0	2	58	30		.339	.444	.442	142	16	7			.819	-9	O-58,1-24	0.3
Total	7	681	2761	443	726	120	49	17	222	133	41	.263	.312	.360	109	27	19			.866	-37	O-654/1-29,P-4	-2.1

■ AL ROSEN

Rosen, Albert Leonard "Flip" b: 2/29/24, Spartanburg, S.C. BR/TR, 5'10.5", 180 lbs. Deb: 9/10/47

YEAR	TM/L	G	AB	R	H	2B	3B	HR	RBI	BB	SO	AVG	OBP	SLG	PRO+	BR/A	SB	CS	SBR	FA	FR	G/POS	TPR
1947	Cle-A	7	9	1	1	0	0	0	0	0	3	.111	.111	.111	-39	-2	0	0	0	.000	1	/3-2,O-1	-0.1
1948	*Cle-A	5	5	0	1	0	0	0	0	0	2	.200	.200	.200	7	-1	0	0	0	1.000	0	/3-2	-0.1
1949	Cle-A	23	44	3	7	2	0	0	5	7	4	.159	.275	.205	28	-5	0	1	-1	1.000	-1	3-10	-0.6
1950	Cle-A	155	554	100	159	23	4	**37**	116	100	72	.287	.405	.543	146	38	5	7	-3	.969	1	*3-154	3.1
1951	Cle-A	154	573	82	152	30	1	24	102	85	71	.265	.362	.447	125	19	7	5	-1	.958	-15	*3-154	0.1
1952	Cle-A★	148	567	101	171	32	5	28	**105**	75	54	.302	.387	.524	162	46	8	6	-1	.958	-20	*3-147/1-4,S-3	2.3
1953	Cle-A★	155	599	**115**	201	27	5	**43**	**145**	85	48	.336	.422	**.613**	**181**	**67**	8	7	-2	.964	1	*3-154/1-1,S-1	**6.2**
1954	*Cle-A★	137	466	76	140	20	2	24	102	85	43	.300	.412	.506	148	33	6	2	1	.959	-14	3-87,1-46/2-1,S-1	1.6
1955	Cle-A★	139	492	61	120	13	1	21	81	92	44	.244	.367	.402	103	4	4	2	0	.963	3	*3-106,1-41	0.4
1956	Cle-A	121	416	64	111	18	2	15	61	58	44	.267	.357	.428	104	2	1	3	-2	.945	-8	*3-116	-0.5
Total	10	1044	3725	603	1063	165	20	192	717	587	385	.285	.386	.495	138	202	39	33	-8	.961	-52	3-932/1-92,S-5,2O	12.4

■ GOODY ROSEN

Rosen, Goodwin George b: 8/28/12, Toronto, Ont., Can. d: 4/6/94, Toronto, Ont., Can. BL/TL, 5'10", 155 lbs. Deb: 9/14/37

YEAR	TM/L	G	AB	R	H	2B	3B	HR	RBI	BB	SO	AVG	OBP	SLG	PRO+	BR/A	SB	CS	SBR	FA	FR	G/POS	TPR
1937	Bro-N	22	77	10	24	5	1	0	6	6	6	.312	.361	.403	106	1	2			.981	1	O-21	0.1
1938	Bro-N	138	473	75	133	17	11	4	51	65	43	.281	.368	.389	106	5	0			**.989**	13	*O-113	1.5
1939	Bro-N	54	183	22	46	6	4	1	12	23	21	.251	.335	.344	80	-5	4			1.000	-3	O-47	-1.0
1944	Bro-N	89	264	38	69	8	3	0	23	26	27	.261	.330	.314	83	-5	0			.991	12	O-65	0.4
1945	Bro-N†	145	606	126	197	24	11	12	75	50	36	.325	.379	.460	134	26	4			.993	2	*O-141	2.1
1946	Bro-N	3	3	0	1	0	0	0	0	0	1	.333	.333	.333	89	-0	0			.000	-1	/O-1	-0.1
	NY-N	100	310	39	87	11	4	5	30	48	32	.281	.377	.390	117	8	2			.976	4	O-84	0.8
	Yr	103	313	39	88	11	4	5	30	48	33	.281	.377	.390	117	8	2			.976	3	O-85	0.7
Total	6	551	1916	310	557	71	34	22	197	218	166	.291	.364	.398	111	31	12			.989	28	O-472	3.8

■ HARRY ROSENBERG

Rosenberg, Harry b: 6/22/09, San Francisco, Cal. d: 4/13/97, San Mateo, Cal. BR/TR, 5'9.5", 160 lbs. Deb: 7/15/30 F

YEAR	TM/L	G	AB	R	H	2B	3B	HR	RBI	BB	SO	AVG	OBP	SLG	PRO+	BR/A	SB	CS	SBR	FA	FR	G/POS	TPR
1930	NY-N	9	5	1	0	0	0	0	0	1	4	.000	.167	.000	-56	-1	0			1.000	-1	/O-3	-0.2

■ LOU ROSENBERG

Rosenberg, Louis b: 3/5/04, San Francisco, Cal. d: 9/8/91, Daly City, Cal. BR/TR, 5'7", 155 lbs. Deb: 5/22/23 F

YEAR	TM/L	G	AB	R	H	2B	3B	HR	RBI	BB	SO	AVG	OBP	SLG	PRO+	BR/A	SB	CS	SBR	FA	FR	G/POS	TPR
1923	Chi-A	3	4	0	1	0	0	0	0	0	1	.250	.250	.250	32	-0	0	1	-1	1.000	-1	/2-2	-0.2

■ MAX ROSENFELD

Rosenfeld, Max b: 12/23/02, New York, N.Y. d: 3/10/69, Miami, Fla. BR/TR, 5'8", 175 lbs. Deb: 4/21/31

YEAR	TM/L	G	AB	R	H	2B	3B	HR	RBI	BB	SO	AVG	OBP	SLG	PRO+	BR/A	SB	CS	SBR	FA	FR	G/POS	TPR
1931	Bro-N	3	9	0	2	1	0	0	0	1	1	.222	.300	.333	70	-0	0			1.000	-1	/O-3	-0.1
1932	Bro-N	34	39	8	14	3	0	2	7	0	10	.359	.359	.590	153	3	2			.970	-9	O-30	-0.7
1933	Bro-N	5	9	0	1	0	0	0	0	1	1	.111	.200	.111	-10	-1	0			1.000	0	/O-2	-0.1
Total	3	42	57	8	17	4	0	2	7	2	12	.298	.322	.474	115	1	2			.978	-9	/O-35	-0.9

■ LARRY ROSENTHAL

Rosenthal, Lawrence John b: 5/21/10, St.Paul, Minn. d: 3/4/92, Woodbury, Minn. BL/TL, 6'0.5", 190 lbs. Deb: 6/20/36

YEAR	TM/L	G	AB	R	H	2B	3B	HR	RBI	BB	SO	AVG	OBP	SLG	PRO+	BR/A	SB	CS	SBR	FA	FR	G/POS	TPR
1936	Chi-A	85	317	71	89	15	8	3	46	59	37	.281	.394	.407	95	-1	2	0	1	.977	6	O-80	0.2
1937	Chi-A	58	97	20	28	5	3	0	9	9	20	.289	.355	.402	90	-1	1	0	0	.980	-3	O-25	-0.4
1938	Chi-A	61	105	14	30	5	1	1	12	12	13	.286	.359	.381	83	-3	0	1	-1	.959	-3	O-22	-0.6
1939	Chi-A	107	324	50	86	21	5	10	51	53	46	.265	.369	.454	106	3	6	4	-1	.990	-3	O-93	-0.3
1940	Chi-A	107	276	46	83	14	5	6	42	64	32	.301	.432	.453	128	15	2	3	-1	.977	-3	O-92	0.6
1941	Chi-A	20	59	9	14	4	0	0	1	12	5	.237	.366	.305	80	-1	0	0	0	.938	-1	O-18	-0.3
	Cle-A	45	75	10	14	3	1	1	8	9	10	.187	.274	.293	53	-5	1	0	0	1.000	0	O-14/1-1	-0.5
	Yr	65	134	19	28	7	1	1	9	21	15	.209	.316	.299	66	-6	1	0	0	.971	-1	O-32/1-1	-0.8
1944	NY-A	36	101	9	20	3	0	0	9	19	15	.198	.325	.228	57	-5	1	0	0	.986	3	O-26	-0.3
	Phi-A	32	54	5	11	2	0	1	6	5	9	.204	.271	.296	63	-3	0	0	0	.960	-4	O-19	-0.8
	Yr	68	155	14	31	5	0	1	15	24	24	.200	.307	.252	60	-7	1	0	0	.979	-2	O-45	-1.1
1945	Phi-A	28	75	6	15	3	2	0	5	9	8	.200	.286	.293	68	-3	0	1	-1	1.000	-2	O-21	-0.8
Total	8	579	1483	240	390	75	25	22	189	251	195	.263	.370	.392	96	-5	13	9	-2	.979	-11	O-410/1-1	-3.2

■ SI ROSENTHAL

Rosenthal, Simon b: 11/13/03, Boston, Mass. d: 4/7/69, Boston, Mass. BL/TL, 5'9", 165 lbs. Deb: 9/8/25

YEAR	TM/L	G	AB	R	H	2B	3B	HR	RBI	BB	SO	AVG	OBP	SLG	PRO+	BR/A	SB	CS	SBR	FA	FR	G/POS	TPR
1925	Bos-A	19	72	6	19	5	2	0	8	7	3	.264	.329	.389	82	-2	1	0	0	.919	0	O-17	-0.3
1926	Bos-A	104	285	34	76	12	3	4	34	19	18	.267	.317	.372	82	-9	4	1	1	.962	-13	O-67	-2.5
Total	2	123	357	40	95	17	5	4	42	26	21	.266	.319	.375	82	-11	5	1	1	.950	-13	/O-84	-2.8

■ BUNNY ROSER

Roser, John William Joseph "Jack" b: 11/15/01, St.Louis, Mo. d: 5/6/79, Rocky Hill, Conn. BL/TL, 5'11", 175 lbs. Deb: 8/24/22

YEAR	TM/L	G	AB	R	H	2B	3B	HR	RBI	BB	SO	AVG	OBP	SLG	PRO+	BR/A	SB	CS	SBR	FA	FR	G/POS	TPR
1922	Bos-N	32	113	13	27	3	4	0	16	10	19	.239	.306	.336	69	-5	2	1	0	.915	-2	O-32	-1.0

■ JOHNNY ROSKOS

Roskos, John Edward b: 11/19/74, Victorville, Cal. BR/TR, 5'11", 198 lbs. Deb: 4/20/98

YEAR	TM/L	G	AB	R	H	2B	3B	HR	RBI	BB	SO	AVG	OBP	SLG	PRO+	BR/A	SB	CS	SBR	FA	FR	G/POS	TPR
1998	Fla-N	10	10	1	1	0	0	0	0	0	5	.100	.100	.100	-50	-2	0	0	0	1.000	-0	/1-1	-0.2

■ CHET ROSS

Ross, Chester James b: 4/1/17, Buffalo, N.Y. d: 2/21/89, Buffalo, N.Y. BR/TR, 6'1", 195 lbs. Deb: 9/15/39

YEAR	TM/L	G	AB	R	H	2B	3B	HR	RBI	BB	SO	AVG	OBP	SLG	PRO+	BR/A	SB	CS	SBR	FA	FR	G/POS	TPR
1939	Bos-N	11	31	4	10	1	1	0	0	2	10	.323	.364	.419	118	1	0			1.000	1	/O 8	0.1
1940	Bos-N	149	569	84	160	23	14	17	89	59	127	.281	.352	.460	130	22	4			.962	7	*O-149	2.1
1941	Bos-N	29	50	1	6	1	0	0	4	9	17	.120	.254	.140	14	-6	0			1.000	-1	O-12	-0.7
1942	Bos-N	76	220	20	43	7	2	5	19	16	37	.195	.250	.314	66	-10	0			.992	-1	O-57	-1.5
1943	Bos-N	94	285	27	62	12	2	7	32	26	67	.218	.285	.347	84	-7	1			.977	3	O-73	-0.8
1944	Bos-N	54	154	20	35	9	2	5	26	12	23	.227	.287	.409	91	-3	1			1.000	3	O-38	-0.2
Total	6	413	1309	156	316	53	21	34	170	124	281	.241	.309	.392	100	-3	6			.976	11	O-337	-1.0

■ DON ROSS

Ross, Donald Raymond b: 7/16/14, Pasadena, Cal. d: 4/4/96, Arcadia, Cal. BR/TR, 6'2", 200 lbs. Deb: 4/19/38

YEAR	TM/L	G	AB	R	H	2B	3B	HR	RBI	BB	SO	AVG	OBP	SLG	PRO+	BR/A	SB	CS	SBR	FA	FR	G/POS	TPR
1938	Det-A	77	265	22	69	7	1	1	30	29	11	.260	.333	.306	58	-17	1	0	0	.946	4	3-75	-1.0
1940	Bro-N	10	38	4	11	2	0	1	8	3	3	.289	.341	.421	103	0	1			.879	-0	3-10	0.0
1942	Det-A	87	226	29	62	10	2	3	30	36	16	.274	.379	.376	104	2	2	1	0	.964	-3	O-38,3-20	-0.3
1943	Det-A	89	247	19	66	13	0	0	18	20	3	.267	.325	.320	82	-5	2	0	1	.985	-8	O-38,S-18/2-7,3-1	-1.4
1944	Det-A	66	167	14	35	5	0	2	15	14	9	.210	.275	.275	54	-10	2	1	0	.958	-1	O-37/S-2,1-1	-1.4
1945	Det-A	8	29	3	11	4	0	0	4	5	1	.379	.471	.517	175	3	2	0	1	.960	-0	/3-8	0.4
	Cle-A	106	363	26	95	15	1	2	43	42	15	.262	.340	.325	97	-1	0	4	-2	.958	-13	*3-106	-1.5

YEAR	TM/L	G	AB	R	H	2B	3B	HR	RBI	BB	SO	AVG	OBP	SLG	PRO+	BR/A	SB	CS	SBR	FA	FR	G/POS	TPR
	Yr	114	392	29	106	19	1	2	47	47	16	.270	.350	.339	104	3	2	4	-2	.958	-14	*3-114	-1.1
1946	Cle-A	55	153	12	41	7	0	3	14	17	12	.268	.341	.373	106	1	0	0	0	.944	-12	3-41/O-2	-1.1
Total	7	498	1488	129	390	63	4	12	162	166	70	.262	.338	.334	86	-26	10	6		.946	-33	3-261,O-115/S21	-6.3

■ JOE ROSSI
Rossi, Joseph Anthony b: 3/13/23, Oakland, Cal. BR/TR, 6'1", 205 lbs. Deb: 4/20/52

YEAR	TM/L	G	AB	R	H	2B	3B	HR	RBI	BB	SO	AVG	OBP	SLG	PRO+	BR/A	SB	CS	SBR	FA	FR	G/POS	TPR
1952	Cin-N	55	145	14	32	0	1	1	6	20	20	.221	.319	.255	61	-7	1	0	0	.982	2	C-46	-0.3

■ CLAUDE ROSSMAN
Rossman, Claude R. b: 6/17/1881, Philmont, N.Y. d: 1/16/28, Poughkeepsie, N.Y. BL/TL, 6', 188 lbs. Deb: 9/16/04

YEAR	TM/L	G	AB	R	H	2B	3B	HR	RBI	BB	SO	AVG	OBP	SLG	PRO+	BR/A	SB	CS	SBR	FA	FR	G/POS	TPR
1904	Cle-A	18	62	5	13	5	0	0	6	0		.210	.210	.290	58	-3	0			.933	-4	O-17	-0.9
1906	Cle-A	118	396	49	122	13	2	1	53	17		.308	.338	.359	120	8	11			.984	-8	*1-105/O-1	-0.3
1907	*Det-A	153	571	60	158	21	8	0	69	33		.277	.318	.342	107	3	20			.981	-14	*1-153	-1.6
1908	*Det-A	138	524	45	154	33	13	2	71	27		.294	.330	.418	137	19	8			.981	6	*1-138	2.5
1909	Det-A	82	287	16	75	8	3	0	39	13		.261	.293	.310	87	-5	10			.981	-6	1-75	-1.3
	StL-A	2	8	0	1	0	0	0	0	0		.125	.125	.125	-23	-1	0			1.000	-0	/O-2	-0.2
	Yr	84	295	16	76	8	3	0	39	13		.258	.289	.305	84	-6	10			.981	-6	1-75/O-2	-1.5
Total	5	511	1848	175	523	80	26	3	238	90		.283	.318	.359	113	21	49			.982	-26	1-471/O-20	-1.8

■ RICO ROSSY
Rossy, Elam Jose (Ramos) b: 2/16/64, San Juan, P.R. BR/TR, 5'10", 175 lbs. Deb: 9/11/91

YEAR	TM/L	G	AB	R	H	2B	3B	HR	RBI	BB	SO	AVG	OBP	SLG	PRO+	BR/A	SB	CS	SBR	FA	FR	G/POS	TPR
1991	Atl-N	5	1	0	0	0	0	0	0	0	1	.000	.000	.000	-94	-0	0	0	0	.000	0	/S-1	0.0
1992	KC-A	59	149	21	32	8	1	1	12	20	20	.215	.312	.302	71	-5	0	3	-2	.961	5	S-51/3-9,2-3	0.1
1993	KC-A	46	86	10	19	4	0	2	12	9	11	.221	.302	.337	68	-4	0	0	0	.987	1	2-24,3-16,S-11	-0.2
1998	Sea-A	37	81	12	16	6	0	1	4	6	13	.198	.253	.309	45	-7	0	0	0	1.000	9	3-25/2-6,S-4,D-1	0.2
Total	4	147	317	43	67	18	1	4	28	35	45	.211	.294	.312	63	-16	0	3	-2	.967	15	/S-67,3-50,2-33,D-1	0.1

■ FRANK ROTH
Roth, Francis Charles b: 10/11/1878, Chicago, Ill. d: 3/27/55, Burlington, Wis. BR/TR, 5'10", 160 lbs. Deb: 4/18/03 FC

YEAR	TM/L	G	AB	R	H	2B	3B	HR	RBI	BB	SO	AVG	OBP	SLG	PRO+	BR/A	SB	CS	SBR	FA	FR	G/POS	TPR
1903	Phi-N	68	220	27	60	11	4	0	22	9		.273	.304	.359	92	-3	3			.935	-7	C-60/3-1	-0.3
1904	Phi-N	81	229	28	59	8	1	1	20	12		.258	.298	.314	92	-2	8			.958	-11	C-67/1-1,2-1	-0.7
1905	StL-A	35	107	9	25	3	0	0	7	6		.234	.274	.262	74	-3	1			.962	-6	C-29	-0.7
1906	Chi-A	16	51	4	10	1	1	0	7	3		.196	.241	.255	57	-3	1			.990	3	C-15	0.2
1909	Cin-N	56	147	12	35	7	2	0	16	6		.238	.287	.313	87	-3	5			.967	-3	C-54	-0.2
1910	Cin-N	26	29	3	7	2	0	0	3	0	2	.241	.267	.310	71	-1	1			.938	-0	/C-4,O-1	-0.1
Total	6	282	783	83	196	32	8	1	75	36	2	.250	.289	.315	86	-15	19			.956	-24	C-229/O-1,2-1,13	-1.8

■ BRAGGO ROTH
Roth, Robert Frank b: 8/28/1892, Burlington, Wis. d: 9/11/36, Chicago, Ill. BR/TR, 5'7.5", 170 lbs. Deb: 9/1/14 F

YEAR	TM/L	G	AB	R	H	2B	3B	HR	RBI	BB	SO	AVG	OBP	SLG	PRO+	BR/A	SB	CS	SBR	FA	FR	G/POS	TPR
1914	Chi-A	34	126	14	37	4	6	1	10	8	25	.294	.355	.444	142	6	3	3	-1	.924	2	O-34	0.5
1915	Chi-A	70	240	44	60	6	10	3	35	29	50	.250	.338	.396	116	4	12	6	0	.837	-15	3-35,O-30	-1.2
	Cle-A	39	144	23	43	4	7	4	20	22	22	.299	.399	.507	168	12	14	4	2	.878	-6	O-39	0.6
	Yr	109	384	67	103	10	17	**7**	55	51	72	.268	.361	.438	135	16	26	10	2	.906	-21	O-69,3-35	-0.6
1916	Cle-A	125	409	50	117	19	7	4	72	38	48	.286	.350	.396	117	8	29	14	0	.954	3	*O-112	0.6
1917	Cle-A	145	495	69	141	30	9	1	72	52	73	.285	.355	.388	118	10	51			.957	-0	*O-135	0.3
1918	Cle-A	106	375	53	106	21	12	1	59	53	41	.283	.383	.411	127	13	35			.936	-3	*O-106	0.4
1919	Phi-A	48	195	33	63	13	8	5	29	15	21	.323	.377	.549	156	13	11			.975	-5	O-48	0.6
	Bos-A	63	227	32	58	9	4	0	23	24	32	.256	.337	.330	93	-2	9			.943	-4	O-58	-1.0
	Yr	111	422	65	121	22	12	5	52	39	53	.287	.355	.431	124	12	20			.955	-9	*O-106	-0.4
1920	Was-A	138	468	80	136	23	8	9	92	75	57	.291	.395	.432	122	17	24	12	0	.952	-10	*O-128	-0.2
1921	NY-A	43	152	29	43	9	2	2	10	19	20	.283	.370	.408	96	-1	1	2	-1	.923	-3	O-37	-0.7
Total	8	811	2831	427	804	138	73	30	422	335	389	.284	.367	.416	122	81	189	41		.944	-42	O-727/3-35	-0.1

■ BOB ROTHEL
Rothel, Robert Burton b: 9/17/23, Columbia Station, Ohio d: 3/21/84, Huron, Ohio BR/TR, 5'10.5", 170 lbs. Deb: 4/22/45

YEAR	TM/L	G	AB	R	H	2B	3B	HR	RBI	BB	SO	AVG	OBP	SLG	PRO+	BR/A	SB	CS	SBR	FA	FR	G/POS	TPR
1945	Cle-A	4	10	0	2	0	0	0	0	3	1	.200	.385	.200	75	-0	0	0	0	.875	-1	/3-4	-0.1

■ BOBBY ROTHERMEL
Rothermel, Edward Hill b: 12/18/1870, Fleetwood, Pa. d: 2/11/27, Detroit, Mich. Deb: 6/18/1899

YEAR	TM/L	G	AB	R	H	2B	3B	HR	RBI	BB	SO	AVG	OBP	SLG	PRO+	BR/A	SB	CS	SBR	FA	FR	G/POS	TPR
1899	Bal-N	10	21	1	2	0	0	0	3	1		.095	.136	.095	-34	-4	0			.867	-2	/2-5,3-2,S-1	-0.6

■ JACK ROTHFUSS
Rothfuss, John Albert b: 4/18/1872, Newark, N.J. d: 4/20/47, Basking Ridge, N.J BR/TR, 5'11.5", 195 lbs. Deb: 8/2/1897

YEAR	TM/L	G	AB	R	H	2B	3B	HR	RBI	BB	SO	AVG	OBP	SLG	PRO+	BR/A	SB	CS	SBR	FA	FR	G/POS	TPR
1897	Pit-N	35	115	20	36	3	1	2	18	5		.313	.352	.409	104	1	3			.984	-1	1-32	0.0

■ CLAUDE ROTHGEB
Rothgeb, Claude James b: 1/1/1880, Milford, Ill. d: 7/6/44, Manitowoc, Wis. BB , 6'0.5", 200 lbs. Deb: 6/17/05

YEAR	TM/L	G	AB	R	H	2B	3B	HR	RBI	BB	SO	AVG	OBP	SLG	PRO+	BR/A	SB	CS	SBR	FA	FR	G/POS	TPR
1905	Was-A	7	16	2	2	0	0	0	0	0		.125	.125	.125	-22	-2	1			.833	-0	/O-4	-0.3

■ JACK ROTHROCK
Rothrock, John Huston b: 3/14/05, Long Beach, Cal. d: 2/2/80, San Bernardino, Cal BB/TR, 5'11.5", 165 lbs. Deb: 7/28/25

YEAR	TM/L	G	AB	R	H	2B	3B	HR	RBI	BB	SO	AVG	OBP	SLG	PRO+	BR/A	SB	CS	SBR	FA	FR	G/POS	TPR
1925	Bos-A	22	55	6	19	3	3	0	7	3	7	.345	.379	.509	124	2	0	0	0	.893	-4	S-22	0.0
1926	Bos-A	15	17	3	5	1	0	0	2	3	1	.294	.400	.353	101	0	0	0	0	.692	-2	/S-2	-0.1
1927	Bos-A	117	428	61	111	24	8	1	36	24	46	.259	.302	.360	73	-19	5	5	-2	.953	4	S-40,2-36,3-20,1-13	-1.1
1928	Bos-A	117	344	52	92	9	4	3	22	33	40	.267	.333	.343	79	-10	12	6	0	.979	-17	O-53,3-17,1S/2PC	-2.9
1929	Bos-A	143	473	70	142	19	7	6	59	43	47	.300	.361	.408	100	0	23	13	-1	.970	2	*O-128	-0.7
1930	Bos-A	45	65	4	18	3	1	0	4	2	9	.277	.299	.354	67	-3	0	2	-1	.947	1	/O-9,3-1	-0.4
1931	Bos-A	133	475	81	132	32	3	4	42	47	48	.278	.343	.383	96	-3	13	7	-0	.982	-1	O-79,2-23/1-8,3S	-0.8
1932	Bos-A	12	48	3	10	1	0	0	0	5	5	.208	.283	.229	35	-5	3	0	1	.973	2	O-12	-0.2
	Chi-A	39	64	8	12	2	1	0	6	5	9	.188	.246	.250	31	-7	1	0	0	.929	-9	O-19/3-8,1-1	-1.4
	Yr	51	112	11	22	3	1	0	6	10	14	.196	.262	.241	33	-11	4	0	1	.961	-7	O-31/3-8,1-1	-1.6
1934	*StL-N	154	647	106	184	35	3	11	72	49	56	.284	.336	.399	90	-9	10			.975	5	*O-154/2-1	-1.1
1935	StL-N	129	502	76	137	18	5	3	56	57	29	.273	.347	.347	84	-10	7			.980	1	*O-127	-1.4
1937	Phi-A	88	232	28	62	15	0	0	21	28	15	.267	.346	.332	73	-9	1	0	0	.992	-6	O-58/2-1	-1.5
Total	11	1014	3350	498	924	162	35	28	327	299	312	.276	.336	.370	85	-73	75	33		.976	-24	O-639/S-78,231CP	-11.6

■ EDD ROUSH
Roush, Edd J b: 5/8/1893, Oakland City, Ind. d: 3/21/88, Bradenton, Fla. BL/TL, 5'11", 170 lbs. Deb: 8/20/13 CH

YEAR	TM/L	G	AB	R	H	2B	3B	HR	RBI	BB	SO	AVG	OBP	SLG	PRO+	BR/A	SB	CS	SBR	FA	FR	G/POS	TPR
1913	Chi-A	9	10	2	1	0	0	0	0	0	2	.100	.100	.100	-42	-2	0			1.000	-0	/O-2	-0.2
1914	Ind-F	74	166	26	54	8	4	1	30	6	20	.325	.353	.440	104	-2	12			.989	2	O-43/1-2	-0.2
1915	New-F	145	551	73	164	20	11	3	60	38	25	.298	.350	.390	115	1	28			.972	4	*O-144	-0.2
1916	NY-N	39	69	4	13	0	1	0	5	1	4	.188	.200	.217	30	-6	4			.952	-1	O-15	-0.9
	Cin-N	69	272	34	78	7	14	0	15	13	19	.287	.336	.415	133	10	15			.971	6	O-69	1.4
	Yr	108	341	38	91	7	15	0	20	14	23	.267	.309	.375	114	4	19			.969	5	O-84	0.5
1917	Cin-N	136	522	82	178	19	14	4	67	27	24	**.341**	.379	.454	162	36	21			.962	2	*O-134	3.4
1918	Cin-N	113	435	61	145	18	10	5	62	22	10	.333	.368	**.455**	**153**	26	24			.960	8	*O-113	3.0
1919	*Cin-N	133	504	73	162	19	12	4	71	42	19	**.321**	.380	.431	147	29	20			.989	10	*O-133	3.3
1920	Cin-N	149	579	81	196	22	16	4	90	42	22	.339	.386	.453	142	31	36	24	-4	.975	16	*O-139,1-11/2-1	3.4
1921	Cin-N	112	418	68	147	27	12	4	71	31	8	.352	.403	.502	145	27	19	17	-5	.980	2	*O-108	1.6
1922	Cin-N	49	165	29	58	7	4	1	24	19	5	.352	.428	.461	132	9	5	3	-0	.990	1	O-43	0.6
1923	Cin-N	138	527	88	185	**41**	18	6	88	46	16	.351	.406	.531	149	36	10	15	-6	.970	-4	*O-137	1.7
1924	Cin-N	121	483	67	168	23	**21**	3	72	22	11	.348	.376	.501	135	22	17	13	-3	.959	-5	*O-119	0.7
1925	Cin-N	134	540	91	183	28	16	8	83	35	14	.339	.383	.494	125	20	22	20	-5	.978	1	*O-134	0.6
1926	Cin-N	144	563	95	182	37	10	7	79	38	17	.323	.366	.462	125	18	8			.955	-12	*O-143/1-1	-0.4
1927	NY-N	140	570	83	173	27	4	7	58	26	15	.304	.335	.402	97	-4	18			.975	-4	*O-138	-1.6
1928	NY-N	46	163	20	41	5	3	2	13	14	8	.252	.315	.356	75	-6	1			.955	2	O-39	-0.7
1929	NY-N	115	450	76	146	19	7	8	52	45	16	.324	.390	.451	108	6	6			.982	-1	*O-107	-0.2
1931	Cin-N	101	376	46	102	12	5	1	41	17	5	.271	.308	.338	78	-12	2			.981	-4	O-88	-2.2
Total	18	1967	7363	1099	2376	339	182	68	981	484	260	.323	.369	.446	126	240	268	92		.972	23	*O-1848/1-14,2-1	13.1

■ PHIL ROUTCLIFFE
Routcliffe, Philip John "Chicken" b: 10/24/1870, Oswego, N.Y. d: 10/4/18, Oswego, N.Y. BR/TR, 6', 175 lbs. Deb: 4/21/1890

YEAR	TM/L	G	AB	R	H	2B	3B	HR	RBI	BB	SO	AVG	OBP	SLG	PRO+	BR/A	SB	CS	SBR	FA	FR	G/POS	TPR
1890	Pit-N	1	4	1	1	0	0	0	1	0	0	.250	.400	.250	102	0	1			1.000	0	/O-1	0.0

YEAR	TM/L	G	AB	R	H	2B	3B	HR	RBI	BB	SO	AVG	OBP	SLG	PRO+	BR/A	SB	CS	SBR	FA	FR	G/POS	TPR
■ DAVE ROWAN	Rowan, David (b: David Drohan) b: 12/6/1882, Elora, Ont., Canada d: 7/30/55, Toronto, Ont., Can BL/TL, 5′11″, 175 lbs. Deb: 5/27/11																						
1911	StL-A	18	65	7	25	1	1	0	11	4		.385	.420	.431	143	4	0			.945	-2	1-18	0.2
■ WADE ROWDON	Rowdon, Wade Lee b: 9/7/60, Riverhead, N.Y. BR/TR, 6′2″, 180 lbs. Deb: 9/8/84																						
1984	Cin-N	4	7	0	2	0	0	0	0	0	1	.286	.286	.286	58	-0	0	0	0	1.000	1	/S-1,3-1	0.1
1985	Cin-N	5	9	2	2	0	0	0	2	2	1	.222	.364	.222	64	-0	0	0	0	.667	-1	/3-4	-0.2
1986	Cin-N	38	80	9	20	5	1	0	10	9	17	.250	.333	.338	82	-2	2	0	1	.889	-7	/3-7,S-6,O-5,2-3	-0.8
1987	Chi-N	11	31	2	7	1	1	1	4	3	10	.226	.294	.419	83	-1	0	2	-1	.818	-1	/3-9	-0.4
1988	Bal-A	20	30	1	3	0	0	0	0	0	6	.100	.100	.100	-45	-6	1	1	-0	.947	1	/3-8,O-5,D-5	-0.5
Total	5	78	157	14	34	6	2	1	16	14	35	.217	.285	.299	59	-9	3	3	-1	.866	-7	/3-29,O-10,S-7,D2	-1.8
■ DAVE ROWE	Rowe, David Elwood b: 10/9/1854, Harrisburg, Pa. d: 12/9/30, Glendale, Cal. BR/TR, 5′9″, 180 lbs. Deb: 5/30/1877 FM																						
1877	Chi-N	2	7	0	2	0	0	0	0	0	3	.286	.286	.286	72	-0				.667	-1	/O-2,P-1	-0.1
1882	Cle-N	24	97	13	25	4	3	1	17	4	9	.258	.287	.392	119	2				.837	-3	O-23/P-1	-0.1
1883	Bal-a	59	256	40	80	11	6	0		2		.313	.318	.402	127	6				.798	-9	O-50/S-7,1-3,P-1	-0.3
1884	StL-U	109	485	95	142	32	11	4		10		.293	.307	.429	117	-5				**.947**	-2	*O-92,S-14/2-2,1P	-0.8
1885	StL-N	16	62	8	10	3	0	0	3	5	8	.161	.224	.210	44	-4				.906	-2	O-16	-0.5
1886	KC-N	105	429	53	103	24	8	3	57	15	43	.240	.266	.354	82	-11	2			.851	-5	*O-90,S-11/2-4,M	-1.6
1888	KC-a	32	122	14	21	3	4	0	13	6		.172	.217	.262	50	-7	2			.914	2	O-32,M	-0.6
Total	7	347	1458	223	383	77	32	8	90	42	63	.263	.284	.376	99	-19	4			.878	-19	O-305/S-32,2-6,1P	-4.0
■ HARLAND ROWE	Rowe, Harland Stimson "Hypie" b: 4/20/1896, Springvale, Me. d: 5/26/69, Springvale, Maine BL/TR, 6′1″, 170 lbs. Deb: 6/23/16																						
1916	Phi-A	17	36	2	5	1	0	0	3	2	8	.139	.184	.167	6	-4	0			.842	-3	/3-8,O-1	-0.7
■ JACK ROWE	Rowe, John Charles b: 12/8/1856, Hamburg, Pa. d: 4/25/11, St.Louis, Mo. BL/TR, 5′8″, 170 lbs. Deb: 9/6/1879 FM																						
1879	Buf-N	8	34	8	12	1	0	0	8	0	1	.353	.353	.382	139	1				.905	2	/C-6,O-2	0.3
1880	Buf-N	79	326	43	82	10	6	1	36	6	17	.252	.265	.328	98	-1				.897	-19	*C-60,O-25/3-3	-2.0
1881	Buf-N	64	246	30	82	11	**11**	1	43	1	12	.333	.336	.480	156	15				.900	-7	C-46/S-7,3-7,O-5	0.9
1882	Buf-N	75	308	43	82	14	5	1	42	12	0	.266	.294	.354	105	1				.950	-13	C-46,S-22/3-7,O-1	-0.9
1883	Buf-N	87	374	65	104	18	7	1	38	15	14	.278	.306	.372	102	1				.899	-17	C-49,O-28,S-18,/3-3	-1.2
1884	Buf-N	93	400	85	126	14	14	4	61	23	14	.315	.352	.450	146	20				**.943**	-10	C-65,O-30/S-6	1.3
1885	Buf-N	98	421	62	122	28	8	2	51	13	19	.290	.311	.409	127	11				.834	-14	S-65,C-23,O-12	-0.1
1886	Det-N	111	468	97	142	21	9	6	87	26	27	.303	.340	.425	128	14	12			.880	-21	*S-110/C-3	-0.5
1887	*Det-N	124	537	135	171	30	10	6	96	39	11	.318	.368	.445	121	14	22			.907	-27	*S-124	-1.0
1888	Det-N	105	451	62	125	19	8	2	74	19	28	.277	.311	.368	116	7	10			.861	-9	*S-105	0.1
1889	Pit-N	75	317	57	82	14	3	2	32	22	16	.259	.313	.341	91	-4	5			.896	-10	S-75	-0.8
1890	Buf-P	125	504	77	126	22	7	2	76	48	18	.250	.324	.333	83	-11	10			**.901**	-2	*S-125,M	-0.4
Total	12	1044	4386	764	1256	202	88	28	644	224	177	.286	.323	.392	115	68	59			.882	-147	S-657,C-298,O/3	-4.3
■ SCHOOLBOY ROWE	Rowe, Lynwood Thomas b: 1/11/10, Waco, Tex. d: 1/8/61, ElDorado, Ark. BR/TR, 6′4.5″, 210 lbs. Deb: 4/15/33 C																						
1933	Det-A	21	50	6	11	1	0	0	6	1	4	.220	.235	.240	26	-5	0	0	0	1.000	2	P-19	0.0
1934	*Det-A	51	109	15	33	8	1	2	22	6	20	.303	.339	.450	102	-0	0	0	0	**1.000**	-0	P-45	0.0
1935	*Det-A☆	45	109	19	34	3	2	3	28	12	12	.312	.380	.459	120	3	0	0	0	.981	-2	P-42	0.0
1936	Det-A★	45	90	16	23	2	1	1	12	13	15	.256	.356	.333	71	-4	0	0	0	.984	2	P-41	0.0
1937	Det-A	10	10	2	2	0	0	0	1	1	4	.200	.273	.200	21	-1	0	0	0	1.000	0	P-10	0.0
1938	Det-A	4	6	1	1	1	0	0	0	0	1	.167	.167	.333	21	-1	0	0	0	.889	1	/P-4	0.0
1939	Det-A	31	61	7	15	0	1	1	12	5	7	.246	.303	.328	57	-4	1	1	-0	.947	0	P-28	0.0
1940	*Det-A	27	67	7	18	6	1	1	18	5	13	.269	.319	.433	85	-2	1	1	-0	**1.000**	-0	P-27	0.0
1941	Det-A	32	55	10	15	0	3	1	12	5	8	.273	.333	.436	93	-1	0	0	0	.927	1	P-27	0.0
1942	Det-A	2	4	0	0	0	0	0	0	0	0	.000	.000	.000	-93	-1	0	0	0	1.000	0	/P-2	0.0
	Bro-N	14	19	2	4	0	0	0	2	1	4	.211	.250	.211	35	-2	0			1.000	0	/P-9	0.0
1943	Phi-N	82	120	14	36	7	0	4	18	15	21	.300	.382	.458	148	7	0			.981	0	P-27	0.0
1946	Phi-N	30	61	4	11	5	0	1	6	3	16	.180	.219	.311	51	-4	0			1.000	-2	P-17	0.0
1947	Phi-N★	43	79	9	22	2	0	2	11	13	18	.278	.380	.380	106	1	0			.974	-1	P-31	0.0
1948	Phi-N	31	52	3	10	0	0	1	4	4	10	.192	.250	.250	36	-5	1			.976	1	P-30	0.0
1949	Phi-N	23	17	1	4	1	0	1	1	2	4	.235	.316	.471	111	0	0			.870	1	P-23	0.0
Total	15	491	909	116	239	36	9	18	153	86	157	.263	.328	.382	87	-17	3	2		.974	2	P-382	0.0
■ BAMA ROWELL	Rowell, Carvel William b: 1/13/16, Citronelle, Ala. d: 8/16/93, Citronelle, Ala. BL/TR, 5′11″, 185 lbs. Deb: 9/4/39																						
1939	Bos-N	21	59	5	11	2	2	0	6	1	4	.186	.200	.288	32	-6	0			.853	-2	O-16	-0.9
1940	Bos-N	130	486	46	148	19	8	3	58	18	22	.305	.331	.395	105	2	12			.953	-3	*2-115/O-7	0.6
1941	Bos-N	138	483	49	129	23	6	7	60	39	36	.267	.322	.383	102	0	11			.935	-10	*2-112,O-14/3-2	-0.3
1946	Bos-N	95	293	37	82	12	6	3	31	29	15	.280	.345	.392	108	3	5			.978	-0	O-85	-0.1
1947	Bos-N	113	384	48	106	23	2	5	40	18	14	.276	.310	.385	86	-9	7			.945	-8	*O-100/2-7,3-4	-2.1
1948	Phi-N	77	196	15	47	16	2	1	22	8	14	.240	.270	.357	70	-9	2			.821	-12	3-18,O-17,2-12	-2.1
Total	6	574	1901	200	523	95	26	19	217	113	105	.275	.316	.382	95	-20	37			.945	-35	2-246,O-239/3-24	-4.9
■ ED ROWEN	Rowen, W. Edward b: 10/22/1857, Bridgeport, Conn. d: 2/22/1892, Bridgeport, Conn. 5′6″, 155 lbs. Deb: 5/1/1882																						
1882	Bos-N	83	327	36	81	7	4	1	43	19	18	.248	.289	.303	90	-3				.885	-12	O-48,C-34/S-6,3-1	-1.3
1883	Phi-a	49	196	28	43	10	1	0	21	11		.219	.261	.281	69	-7				.855	-2	C-44/O-8,3-1,2-1	-0.6
1884	Phi-a	4	15	4	6	1	0	0	1	1		.400	.471	.467	194	2				.806	-3	/C-4	-0.1
Total	3	136	538	68	130	18	5	1	65	31	18	.242	.284	.299	85	-9				.866	-17	/C-82,O-56,S-6,32	-2.0
■ CHUCK ROWLAND	Rowland, Charlie Leland b: 7/23/1899, Warrenton, N.C. d: 1/21/92, Raleigh, N.C. BR/TR, 6′1″, 185 lbs. Deb: 5/11/23																						
1923	Phi-A	5	6	0	0	0	0	0	0	0	2	.000	.000	.000	-99	-2	0	0	0	1.000	0	/C-4	-0.1
■ RICH ROWLAND	Rowland, Richard Garnet b: 2/25/64, Cloverdale, Cal. BR/TR, 6′1″, 215 lbs. Deb: 9/7/90																						
1990	Det-A	7	19	3	3	1	0	0	0	2	4	.158	.238	.211	26	-2	0	0	0	.967	-0	/C-5,D-2	-0.2
1991	Det-A	4	4	0	1	0	0	0	1	1	2	.250	.400	.250	83	-0	0	0	0	1.000	0	/C-2,D-1	0.0
1992	Det-A	6	14	2	3	0	0	0	0	3	3	.214	.353	.214	62	-1	0	0	0	1.000	0	/C-3,1-1,3-1,D-2	-0.1
1993	Det-A	21	46	2	10	3	0	0	4	5	16	.217	.294	.283	56	-3	0	0	0	.988	5	C-17/D-3	0.2
1994	Bos-A	46	118	14	27	3	0	9	20	11	35	.229	.295	.483	92	-2	0	0	0	.972	-1	C-39/1-1,D-4	-0.1
1995	Bos-A	14	29	1	5	1	0	0	1	0	11	.172	.172	.207	-2	-4	0	0	0	.977	2	C-11/D-3	-0.2
Total	6	98	230	22	49	8	0	9	26	22	71	.213	.282	.365	67	-12	0	0	0	.976	5	/C-77,D-15,1-2,3-1	-0.4
■ JIM ROXBURGH	Roxburgh, James A. b: 1/17/1858, San Francisco, Cal d: 2/21/34, San Francisco, Cal BR/TR, 5′10″, 170 lbs. Deb: 5/30/1884																						
1884	Bal-a	2	4	1	2	0	0	0		1		.500	.667	.500	275	1				.824	-0	/C-2	0.1
1887	Phi-a	2	8	0	1	0	0	0	0	0		.125	.125	.125	-30	-1	0			.875	-2	/C-2,2-1	-0.2
Total	2	4	12	1	3	0	0	0	0	1		.250	.357	.250	81	-0	0			.840	-2	/C-4,2-1	-0.1
■ STAN ROYER	Royer, Stanley Dean b: 8/31/67, Olney, Ill. BR/TR, 6′3″, 195 lbs. Deb: 9/11/91																						
1991	StL-N	9	21	1	6	1	0	0	1	1	2	.286	.318	.333	83	-0	0	0	0	1.000	-2	/3-5	-0.2
1992	StL-N	13	31	6	10	2	0	2	9	1	4	.323	.344	.581	162	2	0	0	0	.900	-0	/3-5,1-4	0.2
1993	StL-N	24	46	4	14	2	0	1	8	2	14	.304	.333	.413	100	-0	0	1	-1	.857	-0	3-10/1-2	-0.1
1994	StL-N	39	57	3	10	5	0	1	2	0	18	.175	.175	.316	25	-6	0	0	0	.972	-1	1-11/3-5	-0.7
	Bos-A	4	9	0	1	0	0	0	1	0	3	.111	.111	.111	-41	-2	0	0	0	.833	-0	/3-3,1-1	-0.2
Total	4	89	164	14	41	10	0	4	21	4	41	.250	.268	.384	74	-7	0	1	-1	.895	-3	/3-28,1-18	-1.0
■ JERRY ROYSTER	Royster, Jeron Kennis b: 10/18/52, Sacramento, Cal. BR/TR, 6′, 165 lbs. Deb: 8/14/73 C																						
1973	LA-N	10	19	1	4	0	0	0	2	0	5	.211	.211	.211	18	-2	1	0	0	.842	2	/3-6,2-1	0.0
1974	LA-N	6	0	2	0	0	0	0	0	0	0	—	—	—	—	0	0	0	0	1.000	1	/2-1,3-1,O-1	0.1
1975	LA-N	13	36	2	9	2	1	0	1	1	3	.250	.270	.361	77	-1	1	0	0	1.000	-3	/O-7,2-4,3-3,S-1	-0.4

YEAR	TM/L	G	AB	R	H	2B	3B	HR	RBI	BB	SO	AVG	OBP	SLG	PRO+	BR/A	SB	CS	SBR	FA	FR	G/POS	TPR
1976	Atl-N	149	533	65	132	13	1	5	45	52	53	.248	.316	.304	72	-19	24	13	-1	.962	17	*3-148/S-2	-0.4
1977	Atl-N	140	445	64	96	10	2	6	28	38	67	.216	.279	.288	47	-33	28	10	2	.953	-29	3-56,S-51,2-38,/O-1	-5.5
1978	Atl-N	140	529	67	137	17	8	2	35	56	49	.259	.333	.333	78	-15	27	17	-2	.974	-13	2-75,S-60/3-1	-1.7
1979	Atl-N	154	601	103	164	25	6	3	51	62	59	.273	.341	.349	83	-13	35	8	6	.948	13	3-80,2-77	1.0
1980	Atl-N	123	392	42	95	17	5	1	20	37	48	.242	.309	.319	73	-14	22	13	-1	.948	-11	2-49,3-48,O-41	-2.6
1981	Atl-N	64	93	13	19	4	1	0	9	7	14	.204	.260	.269	49	-6	7	5	-1	.950	3	3-24,2-13	-0.4
1982	*Atl-N	108	261	43	77	13	2	2	25	22	36	.295	.354	.383	102	1	14	6	1	.943	-2	3-62,O-25,2-16,S-10	-0.1
1983	Atl-N	91	268	32	63	10	3	3	30	28	35	.235	.307	.328	71	-10	11	7	-1	.940	7	3-47,2-26,O-18,S-13	-0.4
1984	Atl-N	81	227	22	47	13	2	1	21	15	41	.207	.259	.295	52	-15	6	4	-1	.973	5	2-29,3-17,S-16,O-11	-0.9
1985	SD-N	90	249	31	70	13	2	5	31	32	31	.281	.365	.410	118	7	6	5	-1	.975	2	2-58,3-29/S-7,O-2	1.0
1986	SD-N	118	257	31	66	12	0	5	26	32	45	.257	.339	.362	95	-1	3	5	-2	.931	-4	3-59,S-24,2-21,/O-7	-0.6
1987	Chi-A	55	154	25	37	11	0	7	23	19	28	.240	.328	.448	101	-0	2	1	0	.969	-8	3-30,O-13/2-5,D-4	-0.8
	NY-A	18	42	1	15	2	0	0	4	4	4	.357	.413	.405	120	1	2	1	0	.909	2	3-13/2-1,S-1,O-1	0.3
	Yr	73	196	26	52	13	0	7	27	23	32	.265	.345	.439	104	1	4	2	0	.954	-5	3-43,O-14/2-6,DS	-0.5
1988	Atl-N	68	102	8	18	3	0	0	1	6	16	.176	.222	.206	22	-10	0	0	0	1.000	-2	O-26,3-10/2-2,S-2	-1.3
Total	16	1428	4208	552	1049	165	33	40	352	411	534	.249	.318	.333	76	-130	189	95	-0	.951	-19	3-634,2-416,SO/D	-12.7

■ **WILLIE ROYSTER** Royster, Willie Arthur b: 4/11/54, Clarksville, Va. BR/TR, 5'11", 180 lbs. Deb: 9/3/81

YEAR	TM/L	G	AB	R	H	2B	3B	HR	RBI	BB	SO	AVG	OBP	SLG	PRO+	BR/A	SB	CS	SBR	FA	FR	G/POS	TPR
1981	Bal-A	4	4	0	0	0	0	0	0	0	2	.000	.000	.000	-99	-1	0	0	0	1.000	-0	/C-4	-0.1

■ **VIC ROZNOVSKY** Roznovsky, Victor Joseph b: 10/19/38, Shiner, Tex. BL/TR, 6'1", 180 lbs. Deb: 6/28/64

YEAR	TM/L	G	AB	R	H	2B	3B	HR	RBI	BB	SO	AVG	OBP	SLG	PRO+	BR/A	SB	CS	SBR	FA	FR	G/POS	TPR
1964	Chi-N	35	76	2	15	1	0	0	2	5	18	.197	.247	.211	29	-7	0	1	-1	.976	-6	C-26	-1.3
1965	Chi-N	71	172	9	38	4	1	3	15	16	30	.221	.298	.308	70	-7	1	0	0	.984	2	C-63	-0.2
1966	Bal-A	41	97	4	23	5	0	1	10	9	11	.237	.308	.320	82	-2	0	0	0	.995	-3	C-34	-0.3
1967	Bal-A	45	97	7	20	5	0	0	10	1	20	.206	.214	.258	39	-7	0	0	0	.993	-2	C-23	-0.9
1969	Phi-N	13	13	0	3	0	0	0	1	1	4	.231	.286	.231	47	-1	0	0	0	1.000	0	/C-2	-0.1
Total	5	205	455	22	99	15	1	4	38	32	83	.218	.275	.281	59	-24	1	1	-0	.988	-9	C-148	-2.8

■ **AL RUBELING** Rubeling, Albert William b: 5/10/13, Baltimore, Md. d: 1/28/88, Baltimore, Md. BR/TR, 6', 185 lbs. Deb: 4/16/40

YEAR	TM/L	G	AB	R	H	2B	3B	HR	RBI	BB	SO	AVG	OBP	SLG	PRO+	BR/A	SB	CS	SBR	FA	FR	G/POS	TPR
1940	Phi-A	108	376	49	92	16	6	4	38	48	58	.245	.330	.351	78	-12	4	5	-2	.933	-7	3-98,2-10	-1.7
1941	Phi-A	6	19	0	5	0	0	0	2	2	1	.263	.333	.263	61	-1	0	0	0	.833	-2	/3-6	-0.2
1943	Pit-N	47	168	23	44	8	4	0	9	8	17	.262	.295	.357	85	-4	0			.974	-1	2-44/3-1	-0.2
1944	Pit-N	92	184	22	45	7	2	4	30	19	19	.245	.322	.370	90	-2	4			1.000	-1	O-18,2-17,3-16	-0.3
Total	4	253	747	94	186	31	12	8	79	77	95	.249	.321	.355	82	-19	8	5		.939	-10	3-121/2-71,O-18	-2.4

■ **SONNY RUBERTO** Ruberto, John Edward b: 1/2/46, Staten Island, N.Y. BR/TR, 5'11", 175 lbs. Deb: 5/25/69 C

YEAR	TM/L	G	AB	R	H	2B	3B	HR	RBI	BB	SO	AVG	OBP	SLG	PRO+	BR/A	SB	CS	SBR	FA	FR	G/POS	TPR
1969	SD-N	19	21	3	3	0	0	0	0	1	7	.143	.182	.143	-8	-3	0	0	0	1.000	4	C-15	0.1
1972	Cin-N	2	3	0	0	0	0	0	0	0	1	.000	.250	.000	-25	-0	0	0	0	1.000	-0	/C-2	-0.1
Total	2	21	24	3	3	0	0	0	0	1	8	.125	.192	.125	-10	-3	0	0	0	1.000	4	/C-17	0.0

■ **ART RUBLE** Ruble, William Arthur "Speedy" b: 3/11/03, Knoxville, Tenn. d: 11/1/83, Maryville, Tenn. BL/TR, 5'10.5", 168 lbs. Deb: 4/18/27

YEAR	TM/L	G	AB	R	H	2B	3B	HR	RBI	BB	SO	AVG	OBP	SLG	PRO+	BR/A	SB	CS	SBR	FA	FR	G/POS	TPR
1927	Det-A	56	91	16	15	4	2	0	11	14	15	.165	.283	.253	39	-8	2	2	-1	.970	-7	O-43	-1.7
1934	Phi-N	19	54	7	15	4	0	0	8	7	3	.278	.361	.352	81	-1	0			.839	-2	O-14	-0.3
Total	2	75	145	23	30	8	2	0	19	21	18	.207	.311	.290	55	-10	2	2		.929	-9	/O-57	-2.0

■ **JOHNNY RUCKER** Rucker, John Joel b: 1/15/17, Crabapple, Ga. d: 8/7/85, Moultrie, Ga. BL/TR, 6'2", 175 lbs. Deb: 4/16/40

YEAR	TM/L	G	AB	R	H	2B	3B	HR	RBI	BB	SO	AVG	OBP	SLG	PRO+	BR/A	SB	CS	SBR	FA	FR	G/POS	TPR
1940	NY-N	86	277	38	82	7	5	4	23	7	32	.296	.313	.401	95	-3	4			.954	-3	O-57	-0.9
1941	NY-N	143	622	95	179	38	9	1	42	29	61	.288	.320	.383	95	-6	8			.967	5	*O-142	-0.9
1943	NY-N	132	505	56	138	19	4	2	46	22	44	.273	.304	.339	85	-11	4			.969	3	*O-117	-1.6
1944	NY-N	144	587	79	143	14	8	6	39	24	48	.244	.275	.325	69	-26	8			.985	-6	*O-139	-4.1
1945	NY-N	105	429	58	117	19	11	7	51	20	36	.273	.305	.417	98	-3	7			.978	-1	O-98	-1.0
1946	NY-N	95	197	28	52	8	2	1	13	7	27	.264	.300	.340	81	-5	4			.948	-10	O-54	-1.8
Total	6	705	2617	354	711	105	39	21	214	109	248	.272	.302	.366	87	-54	35			.971	-12	O-607	-10.3

■ **JOHN RUDDERHAM** Rudderham, John Edmund b: 8/30/1863, Quincy, Mass. d: 4/3/42, Randolph, Mass. BR/TR, 5'8", 170 lbs. Deb: 9/18/1884

YEAR	TM/L	G	AB	R	H	2B	3B	HR	RBI	BB	SO	AVG	OBP	SLG	PRO+	BR/A	SB	CS	SBR	FA	FR	G/POS	TPR
1884	Bos-U	1	4	0	1	0	0	0	0			.250	.250	.250	53	-0				.000	-1	/O-1	-0.1

■ **JOE RUDI** Rudi, Joseph Oden b: 9/7/46, Modesto, Cal. BR/TR, 6'2", 200 lbs. Deb: 4/11/67 C

YEAR	TM/L	G	AB	R	H	2B	3B	HR	RBI	BB	SO	AVG	OBP	SLG	PRO+	BR/A	SB	CS	SBR	FA	FR	G/POS	TPR
1967	KC-A	19	43	4	8	2	0	0	1	3	7	.186	.239	.233	41	-3	0	0	0	.984	-2	/1-9,O-6	-0.6
1968	Oak-A	68	181	10	32	5	1	1	12	12	32	.177	.236	.232	44	-12	1	1	-0	.987	-3	O-56	-2.2
1969	Oak-A	35	122	10	23	3	1	2	6	5	16	.189	.220	.279	41	-10	1	1	-0	1.000	2	O-18,1-11	-1.1
1970	Oak-A	106	350	40	108	23	2	11	42	16	61	.309	.342	.480	129	12	3	1	0	.982	-2	O-63,1-28	0.4
1971	*Oak-A	127	513	62	137	23	4	10	52	28	62	.267	.306	.386	97	-4	3	2	-0	.996	7	*O-121/1-5	-0.4
1972	*Oak-A★	147	593	94	**181**	32	**9**	19	75	37	62	.305	.348	.486	154	36	3	4	-2	.992	-1	*O-147/3-1	3.0
1973	*Oak-A	120	437	53	118	25	1	12	66	30	72	.270	.320	.414	111	5	0	0	0	.992	4	*O-117/1-1,D-1	0.3
1974	*Oak-A★	158	593	73	174	**39**	4	22	99	34	92	.293	.337	.484	143	29	2	3	-1	.984	-7	*O-140,1-27/D-2	1.5
1975	*Oak-A★	126	468	66	130	26	6	21	75	40	56	.278	.339	.494	136	20	2	1	0	.991	-12	1-91,O-44/D-2	0.0
1976	Oak-A	130	500	54	135	32	3	13	94	41	71	.270	.329	.424	124	14	6	1	1	.989	-1	*O-126/1-2,D-2	0.9
1977	Cal-A	64	242	48	64	13	2	13	53	22	48	.264	.336	.496	128	9	1	0	0	1.000	5	O-61/D-3	1.2
1978	Cal-A	133	497	58	127	27	1	17	79	28	82	.256	.298	.416	103	-0	2	1	0	.992	7	*O-111,D-11,1-10	0.1
1979	Cal-A	90	330	35	80	11	3	11	61	24	61	.242	.296	.394	87	-7	0	0	0	.989	6	O-80/1-5,D-3	-0.5
1980	Cal-A	104	372	42	88	17	1	16	53	17	84	.237	.279	.417	90	-7	1	0	0	.991	8	O-90/1-6,D-3	-0.2
1981	Bos-A	49	122	14	22	3	0	6	24	8	29	.180	.242	.352	66	-6	0	0	0	1.000	-1	D-21/1-5,O-1	-0.9
1982	Oak-A	71	193	21	41	6	1	5	18	24	35	.212	.303	.332	77	-6	0	0	0	.991	-7	1-49,O-14/D-3	-1.5
Total	16	1547	5556	684	1468	287	39	179	810	369	870	.264	.314	.427	112	69	25	15	-1	.991	3	*O-1195,1-249/D3	-0.0

■ **DUTCH RUDOLPH** Rudolph, John Herman b: 7/10/1882, Natrona, Pa. d: 4/17/67, Natrona, Pa. BL/TL, 5'10", 160 lbs. Deb: 7/3/03

YEAR	TM/L	G	AB	R	H	2B	3B	HR	RBI	BB	SO	AVG	OBP	SLG	PRO+	BR/A	SB	CS	SBR	FA	FR	G/POS	TPR
1903	Phi-N	1	1	0	0	0	0	0	0	0		.000	.000	.000	-99	-0	0			.000	0	H	0.0
1904	Chi-N	2	3	0	1	0	0	0	0	0		.333	.333	.333	106	0	0			1.000	-1	/O-2	-0.1
Total	2	3	4	0	1	0	0	0	0	0		.250	.250	.250	52	-0	0			1.000	-1	/O-2	-0.1

■ **KEN RUDOLPH** Rudolph, Kenneth Victor b: 12/29/46, Rockford, Ill. BR/TR, 6'1", 185 lbs. Deb: 4/20/69

YEAR	TM/L	G	AB	R	H	2B	3B	HR	RBI	BB	SO	AVG	OBP	SLG	PRO+	BR/A	SB	CS	SBR	FA	FR	G/POS	TPR
1969	Chi-N	27	34	7	7	1	0	1	6	6	11	.206	.325	.324	73	-1	0	0	0	.977	0	C-11/O-3	-0.1
1970	Chi-N	20	40	1	4	1	0	0	2	1	12	.100	.122	.125	-30	-7	0	0	0	1.000	1	C-16	-0.5
1971	Chi-N	25	76	5	15	3	0	0	7	6	20	.197	.265	.237	38	-6	0	0	0	1.000	7	C-25	0.2
1972	Chi-N	42	106	10	25	1	1	2	9	6	14	.236	.283	.321	64	-5	1	2	-1	.966	5	C-41	0.1
1973	Chi-N	64	170	12	35	8	1	2	17	7	25	.206	.242	.300	46	-13	1	4	-2	.970	-3	C-64	-1.6
1974	SF-N	57	158	11	41	3	0	0	10	21	15	.259	.350	.278	74	-5	0	0	0	.996	3	C-56	0.0
1975	StL-N	44	80	5	16	2	0	1	6	3	10	.200	.229	.262	35	-7	0	0	0	.972	2	C-31	-0.5
1976	StL-N	27	50	1	8	3	0	0	5	1	7	.160	.176	.220	12	-6	0	0	0	.940	2	C-14	-0.4
1977	SF-N	11	15	1	3	0	0	0	0	1	3	.200	.250	.200	22	-2	0	0	0	.946	3	C-11	0.1
	Bal-A	11	14	2	4	1	0	0	2	0	4	.286	.286	.357	79	-0	0	0	0	1.000	5	C-11	0.4
Total	9	328	743	55	158	23	2	6	64	52	121	.213	.268	.273	48	-52	2	6	-3	.980	24	C-280/O-3	-2.3

■ **MUDDY RUEL** Ruel, Herold Dominic b: 2/20/1896, St.Louis, Mo. d: 11/13/63, Palo Alto, Cal. BR/TR, 5'9", 150 lbs. Deb: 5/29/15 MC

YEAR	TM/L	G	AB	R	H	2B	3B	HR	RBI	BB	SO	AVG	OBP	SLG	PRO+	BR/A	SB	CS	SBR	FA	FR	G/POS	TPR
1915	StL-A	10	14	0	0	0	0	0	1	5	5	.000	.263	.000	-22	-2	0			.958	-1	/C-6	-0.3
1917	NY-A	6	17	1	2	0	0	0	1	2	2	.118	.211	.118	0	-2	1			1.000	-1	/C-6	-0.3
1918	NY-A	3	6	0	2	0	0	0	0	2	1	.333	.500	.333	148	1	1			1.000	0	/C-2	0.1
1919	NY-A	79	233	18	56	6	0	0	31	34	26	.240	.340	.266	71	-8	4			.975	2	C-79	0.1
1920	NY-A	82	261	30	70	14	1	1	15	15	18	.268	.310	.341	70	-12	4	2	0	.984	0	C-80	-0.6
1921	Bos-A	113	358	41	99	21	1	1	45	41	15	.277	.352	.349	82	-9	2	7	-4	.977	-10	*C-109	-1.6
1922	Bos-A	116	361	34	92	15	1	0	28	41	26	.255	.333	.302	67	-17	4	2	0	.978	-2	*C-112	-1.2

YEAR	TM/L	G	AB	R	H	2B	3B	HR	RBI	BB	SO	AVG	OBP	SLG	PRO+	BR/A	SB	CS	SBR	FA	FR	G/POS	TPR
1923	Was-A	136	449	63	142	24	3	0	54	55	21	.316	.394	.383	111	9	4	6	-2	.980	19	*C-133	3.0
1924	*Was-A	149	501	50	142	20	2	0	57	62	20	.283	.370	.331	84	-9	7	11	-5	.980	14	*C-147	0.9
1925	*Was-A	127	393	55	122	9	2	0	54	63	16	.310	.411	.344	95	1	4	5	-2	.982	12	*C-126/1-1	1.6
1926	Was-A	117	368	42	110	22	4	1	53	61	14	.299	.401	.389	109	8	7	6	-2	**.989**	2	*C-117	1.4
1927	Was-A	131	428	61	132	16	5	1	52	63	18	.308	.403	.376	104	6	9	6	-1	.988	-3	*C-128	1.1
1928	Was-A	108	350	31	90	18	2	0	55	44	14	.257	.342	.320	75	-11	12	10	-2	**.989**	7	*C-101/1-2	0.1
1929	Was-A	69	188	16	46	4	2	0	20	31	7	.245	.352	.287	66	-8	0	4	-2	.990	9	C-62	0.3
1930	Was-A	66	198	18	50	3	4	0	26	24	13	.253	.342	.308	66	-9	1	0	0	.986	4	C-60	0.0
1931	Bos-A	33	83	6	25	5	0	0	6	9	6	.301	.370	.361	98	0	0	0	0	.945	1	C-30	0.3
	Det-A	14	50	1	6	1	0	0	3	5	1	.120	.200	.140	-9	-8	0	0	0	.975	3	C-14	-0.4
	Yr	47	133	7	31	6	0	0	9	14	7	.233	.306	.278	56	-8	0	0	0	.958	4	C-44	-0.1
1932	Det-A	51	136	10	32	4	2	0	18	17	6	.235	.320	.294	58	-8	1	0	0	.989	-2	C-49	-0.7
1933	StL-A	36	63	13	12	2	0	0	8	24	4	.190	.414	.222	68	-1	0	0	0	1.000	3	C-28	0.2
1934	Chi-A	22	57	4	12	3	0	0	7	8	5	.211	.308	.263	47	-4	0	0	0	.976	-2	C-21	-0.5
Total	19	1468	4514	494	1242	187	29	4	534	606	238	.275	.365	.332	83	-84	61	59		.982	53	*C-1410/1-3	3.5

■ DUTCH RUETHER

Ruether, Walter Henry b: 9/13/1893, Alameda, Cal. d: 5/16/70, Phoenix, Ariz. BL/TL, 6'1.5", 180 lbs. Deb: 4/13/17

YEAR	TM/L	G	AB	R	H	2B	3B	HR	RBI	BB	SO	AVG	OBP	SLG	PRO+	BR/A	SB	CS	SBR	FA	FR	G/POS	TPR
1917	Chi-N	31	44	3	12	1	3	0	11	8	11	.273	.385	.432	139	2	0			1.000	1	P-10/1-5	0.1
	Cin-N	19	24	1	5	2	0	0	1	3	6	.208	.296	.292	84	-0	1			.833	-0	/P-7	0.0
	Yr	50	68	4	17	3	3	0	12	11	17	.250	.354	.382	122	2	1			.920	0	P-17/1-5	0.1
1918	Cin-N	2	3	0	0	0	0	0	0	0	2	.000	.000	.000	-99	-1	0			1.000	-0	/P-2	0.0
1919	*Cin-N	42	92	8	24	2	3	0	6	4	18	.261	.292	.348	94	-1	1			.971	-3	P-33	0.0
1920	Cin-N	45	104	3	20	4	0	0	10	5	24	.192	.229	.231	33	-9	0	0	0	.952	0	P-37/1-1	0.0
1921	Bro-N	49	97	12	34	5	2	2	13	4	9	.351	.376	.505	127	3	1	0	0	.966	-1	P-36	0.0
1922	Bro-N	67	125	12	26	6	1	2	20	12	11	.208	.283	.320	56	-9	0	0	0	**1.000**	-0	P-35	0.0
1923	Bro-N	49	117	6	32	1	0	0	10	12	12	.274	.341	.282	68	-5	0	0	0	.968	-2	P-34/1-1	0.0
1924	Bro-N	34	62	5	15	1	1	0	4	5	2	.242	.299	.290	60	-3	0	0	0	.981	1	P-30	0.0
1925	*Was-A	55	108	18	36	3	2	1	15	10	8	.333	.390	.426	109	2	0	1	-1	.962	-3	P-30/1-1	0.0
1926	Was-A	47	92	6	23	2	0	1	11	6	10	.250	.296	.304	58	-6	0	0	0	.974	-2	P-23	0.0
	*NY-A	13	21	2	2	0	0	0	0	0	1	.095	.136	.095	-39	-4	0	0	0	.875	-1	/P-5	0.0
	Yr	60	113	8	25	2	0	1	11	6	11	.221	.267	.265	40	-10	0	0	0	.957	-3	P-28	0.0
1927	NY-A	35	80	7	21	3	0	1	10	8	15	.262	.330	.338	76	-3	0	0	0	**1.000**	0	P-27	0.0
Total	11	488	969	83	250	30	12	7	111	77	129	.258	.314	.335	76	-33	3	1		.970	-9	P-309/1-8	0.1

■ RUDY RUFER

Rufer, Rudolph Joseph b: 10/28/26, Ridgewood, N.Y. BR/TR, 6'0.5", 165 lbs. Deb: 9/22/49

YEAR	TM/L	G	AB	R	H	2B	3B	HR	RBI	BB	SO	AVG	OBP	SLG	PRO+	BR/A	SB	CS	SBR	FA	FR	G/POS	TPR
1949	NY-N	7	15	1	1	0	0	0	2	2	0	.067	.176	.067	-32	-3	0			.957	-1	/S-7	-0.3
1950	NY-N	15	11	1	1	0	0	0	0	0	1	.091	.091	.091	-52	-2	1			.889	1	/S-8	-0.1
Total	2	22	26	2	2	0	0	0	2	2	1	.077	.143	.077	-40	-5	1			.938	1	/S-15	-0.4

■ RED RUFFING

Ruffing, Charles Herbert b: 5/3/04, Granville, Ill. d: 2/17/86, Mayfield Hts., O. BR/TR, 6'1.5", 205 lbs. Deb: 5/31/24 CH

YEAR	TM/L	G	AB	R	H	2B	3B	HR	RBI	BB	SO	AVG	OBP	SLG	PRO+	BR/A	SB	CS	SBR	FA	FR	G/POS	TPR
1924	Bos-A	8	7	0	1	0	1	0	0	0	1	.143	.143	.429	44	-1	0	0	0	1.000	-1	/P-8	0.0
1925	Bos-A	37	79	6	17	4	2	0	11	1	22	.215	.235	.316	39	-8	0	0	0	.983	-1	P-37	0.0
1926	Bos-A	37	51	8	10	1	0	1	5	2	12	.196	.226	.275	31	-5	0	1	-1	.978	-1	P-37	0.0
1927	Bos-A	29	55	5	14	3	1	0	4	0	6	.255	.268	.345	59	-4	0	0	0	.978	0	P-26	0.0
1928	Bos-A	60	121	12	38	13	1	2	19	3	12	.314	.331	.488	115	2	0	0	0	.951	-3	P-42	0.0
1929	Bos-A	60	114	9	35	9	0	2	17	2	13	.307	.325	.439	97	-1	0	0	0	.946	-2	P-35/O-2	-0.1
1930	Bos-A	6	11	2	3	2	0	0	1	0	1	.273	.273	.455	84	-0	0	0	0	.667	-1	/P-4	0.0
	NY-A	52	99	15	37	6	2	4	21	7	7	.374	.415	.596	160	9	0	0	0	.938	-2	P-34	0.0
	Yr	58	110	17	40	8	2	4	22	7	8	.364	.402	.582	153	8	0	0	0	.914	-3	P-38	0.0
1931	NY-A	48	109	14	36	8	1	3	12	1	13	.330	.336	.505	125	3	0	0	0	**1.000**	-3	P-37/O-1	0.0
1932	*NY-A	55	124	20	38	6	1	3	19	6	10	.306	.338	.444	106	1	0	0	0	.955	-2	P-35	0.0
1933	NY-A	55	115	10	29	3	1	2	13	7	15	.252	.295	.348	74	-5	0	0	0	.964	-0	P-35	0.0
1934	NY-A★	45	113	11	28	3	0	2	13	3	17	.248	.274	.327	58	-8	0	0	0	.933	-3	P-36	0.0
1935	NY-A	50	109	13	37	10	0	2	18	3	9	.339	.363	.486	125	3	0	0	0	**1.000**	-2	P-30	0.0
1936	*NY-A	53	127	14	37	5	0	5	22	11	12	.291	.348	.449	99	-1	0	0	0	.986	2	P-33	0.0
1937	*NY-A	54	129	11	26	3	0	1	10	13	24	.202	.275	.248	32	-13	0	0	0	.974	-4	P-31	0.0
1938	*NY-A☆	45	107	12	24	4	1	3	17	17	21	.224	.331	.364	74	-4	0	0	0	**1.000**	-2	P-31	0.0
1939	*NY-A★	44	114	12	35	1	0	1	20	7	18	.307	.347	.342	78	-4	1	0	0	.952	-2	P-28	0.0
1940	NY-A★	33	89	8	11	4	0	1	7	3	9	.124	.152	.202	-9	-15	0	0	0	.947	-3	P-30	0.0
1941	*NY-A☆	38	89	10	27	8	1	2	22	4	12	.303	.333	.483	115	1	0	0	0	**1.000**	-3	P-23	0.0
1942	*NY-A☆	30	80	8	20	4	0	1	13	5	13	.250	.302	.338	81	-2	0	0	0	.974	-2	P-24	0.0
1945	NY-A	21	46	4	10	0	1	1	5	0	8	.217	.217	.326	54	-3	0	0	0	.929	-2	P-11	0.0
1946	NY-A	8	25	1	3	1	0	0	1	1	8	.120	.154	.160	-12	-4	0	0	0	1.000	-1	/P-8	0.0
1947	Chi-A	14	24	2	5	0	0	0	3	1	3	.208	.240	.208	26	-2	0	0	0	1.000	-0	/P-9	0.0
Total	22	882	1937	207	521	98	13	36	273	97	266	.269	.306	.389	81	-60	1	1	-0	.968	-35	P-624/O-3	-0.1

■ CHICO RUIZ

Ruiz, Hiraldo (Sablon) b: 12/5/38, Santo Domingo, Cuba d: 2/9/72, San Diego, Cal. BB/TR, 6', 173 lbs. Deb: 4/13/64

YEAR	TM/L	G	AB	R	H	2B	3B	HR	RBI	BB	SO	AVG	OBP	SLG	PRO+	BR/A	SB	CS	SBR	FA	FR	G/POS	TPR
1964	Cin-N	77	311	33	76	13	2	2	16	7	41	.244	.270	.318	63	-15	11	3	2	.942	-10	3-49,2-30	-2.4
1965	Cin-N	29	18	7	2	1	0	0	1	0	5	.111	.111	.167	-21	-3	1	2	-1	.875	2	/3-4,S-3	-0.2
1966	Cin-N	82	110	13	28	2	1	0	5	5	14	.255	.287	.291	56	-6	1	2	-1	.927	-1	3-27/O-8,S-6	-0.9
1967	Cin-N	105	250	32	55	12	4	0	13	11	35	.220	.259	.300	53	-15	9	4	0	.969	0	2-56,3-13,S-11,/O-5	-1.2
1968	Cin-N	85	139	15	36	2	1	0	9	12	18	.259	.318	.288	78	-3	4	3	-1	.979	8	2-34,1-16/3-5,S-3	0.6
1969	Cin-N	88	196	19	48	4	1	0	13	14	28	.245	.295	.276	58	-11	4	2	0	.949	-7	2-39,S-29/3-7,1O	-1.3
1970	Cal-A	68	107	10	26	3	1	0	12	7	16	.243	.296	.290	64	-5	3	0	1	.985	0	3-27/2-3,S-3,1-2,C	-0.4
1971	Cal-A	31	19	4	5	0	0	0	0	2	7	.263	.333	.263	76	-1	1	0	0	1.000	2	/3-3,2-2	0.2
Total	8	565	1150	133	276	37	10	2	69	58	164	.240	.281	.295	60	-59	34	16	1	.966	-6	2-164,3-135/S1OC	-5.6

■ CHICO RUIZ

Ruiz, Manuel (Cruz) b: 11/1/51, Santurce, P.R. BR/TR, 5'11.5", 170 lbs. Deb: 7/29/78

YEAR	TM/L	G	AB	R	H	2B	3B	HR	RBI	BB	SO	AVG	OBP	SLG	PRO+	BR/A	SB	CS	SBR	FA	FR	G/POS	TPR
1978	Atl-N	18	46	3	13	3	0	0	2	2	4	.283	.313	.348	76	-1	0	0	0	.984	1	2-14/3-1	0.1
1980	Atl-N	25	26	3	8	2	1	0	2	3	7	.308	.379	.462	129	1	0	1	-1	.875	2	3-16/S-4,2-2	0.2
Total	2	43	72	6	21	5	1	0	4	5	11	.292	.338	.389	95	-0	0	1	-1	.880	3	/3-17,2-16,S-4	0.3

■ JOE RULLO

Rullo, Joseph Vincent b: 6/16/16, New York, N.Y. d: 10/28/69, Philadelphia, Pa. BR/TR, 5'11", 168 lbs. Deb: 9/22/43

YEAR	TM/L	G	AB	R	H	2B	3B	HR	RBI	BB	SO	AVG	OBP	SLG	PRO+	BR/A	SB	CS	SBR	FA	FR	G/POS	TPR
1943	Phi-A	16	55	2	16	3	0	0	6	8	7	.291	.381	.345	114	1	0	0	0	.963	-1	2-16	0.2
1944	Phi-A	35	96	5	16	0	0	0	5	6	19	.167	.223	.167	12	-11	1	0	0	.954	3	2-33/1-1,O-1	-0.6
Total	2	51	151	7	32	3	0	0	11	14	26	.212	.283	.232	50	-10	1	0	0	.957	2	/2-49,O-1,1-1	-0.4

■ WILLIAM RUMLER

Rumler, William George b: 3/27/1891, Milford, Neb. d: 5/26/66, Lincoln, Neb. BR/TR, 6'1", 190 lbs. Deb: 5/4/14

YEAR	TM/L	G	AB	R	H	2B	3B	HR	RBI	BB	SO	AVG	OBP	SLG	PRO+	BR/A	SB	CS	SBR	FA	FR	G/POS	TPR
1914	StL-A	34	46	2	8	1	0	0	6	3	12	.174	.240	.196	32	-4	2	2	-1	1.000	-3	C-10/O-6	-0.8
1916	StL-A	27	37	6	12	3	0	0	10	3	7	.324	.375	.405	141	2	0			.971	0	/C-9	0.3
1917	StL-A	78	88	7	23	3	4	1	16	8	9	.261	.323	.420	132	3	2			.938	-0	/O-9	0.3
Total	3	139	171	15	43	7	4	1	32	14	28	.251	.312	.357	107	1	4	2		.986	-3	/C-19,O-15	-0.2

■ PAUL RUNGE

Runge, Paul William b: 5/21/58, Kingston, N.Y. BR/TR, 6', 175 lbs. Deb: 9/25/81

YEAR	TM/L	G	AB	R	H	2B	3B	HR	RBI	BB	SO	AVG	OBP	SLG	PRO+	BR/A	SB	CS	SBR	FA	FR	G/POS	TPR
1981	Atl-N	10	27	2	7	1	0	0	2	4	4	.259	.355	.296	84	-0	0	0	0	.911	-1	S-10	-0.1
1982	Atl-N	4	2	0	0	0	0	0	0	0	0	.000	.000	.000	-96	-1	0	0	0	.000	0	/H	-0.1
1983	Atl-N	5	8	0	2	0	0	0	1	1	4	.250	.333	.250	59	-0	0	0	0	1.000	-1	/2-2	-0.1
1984	Atl-N	28	90	5	24	3	1	0	3	10	14	.267	.340	.322	81	-2	5	3	-0	.970	10	2-22/S-7,3-3	0.9
1985	Atl-N	50	87	15	19	3	0	1	5	18	18	.218	.352	.287	76	-2	0	1	-1	.929	4	3-28/S-5,2-2	0.1
1986	Atl-N	7	8	1	2	0	0	0	0	2	4	.250	.400	.250	79	-0	0	0	0	1.000	2	/2-5	0.2
1987	Atl-N	27	47	9	10	1	0	3	8	5	10	.213	.288	.426	82	-1	0	1	-1	.923	1	3-10/S-9,2-2	-0.1

YEAR	TM/L	G	AB	R	H	2B	3B	HR	RBI	BB	SO	AVG	OBP	SLG	PRO+	BR/A	SB	CS	SBR	FA	FR	G/POS	TPR
1988	Atl-N	52	76	11	16	5	0	0	7	14	21	.211	.333	.276	73	-2	0	0	0	1.000	-1	3-19/2-7,S-6	-0.4
Total	8	183	345	43	80	13	1	4	26	54	75	.232	.336	.310	77	-9	5	5	-2	.941	13	/3-60,2-40,S-37	0.4

■ TOM RUNNELLS

Runnells, Thomas William b: 4/17/55, Greeley, Colo. BB/TR, 6', 175 lbs. Deb: 8/9/85 MC

YEAR	TM/L	G	AB	R	H	2B	3B	HR	RBI	BB	SO	AVG	OBP	SLG	PRO+	BR/A	SB	CS	SBR	FA	FR	G/POS	TPR
1985	Cin-N	28	35	3	7	1	0	0	0	3	4	.200	.263	.229	37	-3	0	0	0	1.000	1	S-11/2-1	-0.2
1986	Cin-N	12	11	1	1	1	0	0	0	0	2	.091	.091	.182	-26	-2	0	0	0	1.000	1	/2-4,3-3	-0.1
Total	2	40	46	4	8	2	0	0	0	3	6	.174	.224	.217	23	-5	0	0	0	1.000	2	/S-11,2-5,3-3	-0.3

■ PETE RUNNELS

Runnels, James Edward (b: James Edward Runnells) b: 1/28/28, Lufkin, Tex. d: 5/20/91, Pasadena, Tex. BL/TR, 6', 170 lbs. Deb: 7/1/51 MC

YEAR	TM/L	G	AB	R	H	2B	3B	HR	RBI	BB	SO	AVG	OBP	SLG	PRO+	BR/A	SB	CS	SBR	FA	FR	G/POS	TPR
1951	Was-A	78	273	31	76	12	2	0	25	31	24	.278	.354	.337	89	-3	0	3	-2	.949	-21	S-73	-2.1
1952	Was-A	152	555	70	158	18	3	1	64	72	55	.285	.368	.333	99	2	0	10	-6	.966	-15	*S-147/2-1	-0.8
1953	Was-A	137	486	64	125	15	5	2	50	64	36	.257	.347	.321	83	-10	3	4	-2	.958	-33	*S-121,2-11	-3.5
1954	Was-A	139	488	75	131	17	15	3	56	78	60	.268	.369	.383	112	10	2	3	-1	.953	-19	*S-107,2-27/O-1	0.0
1955	Was-A	134	503	66	143	16	4	2	49	55	51	.284	.356	.344	94	-3	3	9	-5	.976	-3	*2-132/S-2	0.0
1956	Was-A	147	578	72	179	29	9	8	76	58	64	.310	.375	.433	113	11	5	5	-2	.995	0	1-81,2-69/S-3	1.0
1957	Was-A	134	473	53	109	18	4	2	35	55	51	.230	.313	.298	69	-20	2	3	-1	.995	2	1-72,3-32,2-23	-2.2
1958	Bos-A	147	568	103	183	32	5	8	59	87	49	.322	.418	.438	127	25	1	2	-1	.985	8	*2-106,1-42	3.8
1959	Bos-A★	147	560	95	176	33	6	6	57	95	48	.314	.415	.427	126	24	6	5	-1	.982	6	*2-101,1-44/S-9	3.3
1960	Bos-A★	143	528	80	169	29	2	2	35	71	51	**.320**	.403	.394	112	12	5	2	0	**.986**	9	*2-129,1-57/3-3	3.2
1961	Bos-A	143	360	49	114	20	3	3	38	46	32	.317	.399	.414	115	9	5	1	1	**.995**	1	*1-113,3-11/2-7,S-1	0.5
1962	Bos-A★	152	562	80	183	33	5	10	60	79	57	**.326**	.411	.456	129	26	3	4	-2	.993	-1	*1-151	1.3
1963	Hou-N	124	388	35	98	9	1	2	23	45	42	.253	.335	.296	89	-4	2	0	1	.993	-10	1-70,2-36/3-3	-1.5
1964	Hou-N	22	51	3	10	1	0	0	3	8	7	.196	.305	.216	53	-3	0	0	0	.986	-2	1-14	-0.6
Total	14	1799	6373	876	1854	282	64	49	630	844	627	.291	.376	.378	106	76	37	51	-20	.994	-78	1-644,2-642,S/30	2.4

■ JOHN RUSS

Russ, John b: 4/1/1858, Cannelton, Ind. d: 1/18/12, Louisville, Ky. Deb: 7/4/1882

YEAR	TM/L	G	AB	R	H	2B	3B	HR	RBI	BB	SO	AVG	OBP	SLG	PRO+	BR/A	SB	CS	SBR	FA	FR	G/POS	TPR
1882	Bal-a	1	3	0	1	0	0	0		0		.333	.333	.333	136	0				.000	-1	/O-1,P-1	0.0

■ REB RUSSELL

Russell, Ewell Albert b: 4/12/1889, Jackson, Miss. d: 9/30/73, Indianapolis, Ind BL/TL, 5'11", 185 lbs. Deb: 4/18/13

YEAR	TM/L	G	AB	R	H	2B	3B	HR	RBI	BB	SO	AVG	OBP	SLG	PRO+	BR/A	SB	CS	SBR	FA	FR	G/POS	TPR
1913	Chi-A	52	106	9	20	5	3	1	7	1	29	.189	.204	.321	54	-7	0			.952	-5	P-52	0.0
1914	Chi-A	46	64	6	17	1	1	0	7	1	14	.266	.277	.313	78	-2	0			.946	0	P-38	0.0
1915	Chi-A	45	86	11	21	2	3	0	7	4	14	.244	.293	.337	86	-2	1			.971	-2	P-41	0.0
1916	Chi-A	56	91	9	13	2	0	0	6	0	18	.143	.152	.165	-5	-12	1			.974	-2	P-56	0.0
1917	*Chi-A	39	68	5	19	3	3	0	9	2	10	.279	.300	.412	115	1	0			.984	-1	P-35/O-1	0.0
1918	Chi-A	27	50	2	7	3	0	0	3	0	6	.140	.157	.200	8	-6	0			1.000	-2	P-19/O-1	0.0
1919	Chi-A	1	0	0	0	0	0	0	0	0	0	—	—	—	—	0	0			.000	0	/P-1	0.0
1922	Pit-N	60	220	51	81	14	8	12	75	14	18	.368	.423	.668	175	23	4	2	0	.968	-2	O-60	1.6
1923	Pit-N	94	291	49	84	18	7	9	58	20	21	.289	.341	.491	115	5	3	1	0	.970	-2	O-76	-0.2
Total	9	420	976	142	262	48	25	22	172	42	130	.268	.309	.436	104	0	9	3		.968	-15	P-242,O-138	1.4

■ RIP RUSSELL

Russell, Glen David b: 1/26/15, Los Angeles, Cal. d: 9/26/76, Los Alamitos, Cal BR/TR, 6'1", 180 lbs. Deb: 5/5/39

YEAR	TM/L	G	AB	R	H	2B	3B	HR	RBI	BB	SO	AVG	OBP	SLG	PRO+	BR/A	SB	CS	SBR	FA	FR	G/POS	TPR
1939	Chi-N	143	542	55	148	24	5	9	79	36	56	.273	.318	.386	87	-11	2			.988	-5	*1-143	-3.1
1940	Chi-N	68	215	15	53	7	2	5	33	8	23	.247	.277	.367	78	-7	1			.982	-6	1-51/3-3	-1.8
1941	Chi-N	6	17	1	5	1	0	0	1	1	5	.294	.333	.353	97	-0	0			.975	0	/1-5	0.0
1942	Chi-N	102	302	32	73	9	0	8	41	17	21	.242	.282	.351	88	-6	0			.974	-12	1-35,2-24,3-10,/O-3	-2.0
1946	*Bos-A	80	274	22	57	10	1	6	35	13	30	.208	.247	.318	54	-18	1	1	-0	.942	-1	3-70/2-3	-1.9
1947	Bos-A	26	52	8	8	1	0	1	3	8	7	.154	.267	.231	36	-4	0	0	0	.923	1	3-13	-0.3
Total	6	425	1402	133	344	52	8	29	192	83	142	.245	.289	.356	77	-46	4	1		.984	-22	1-234/3-96,2-27,O-3	-9.1

■ HARVEY RUSSELL

Russell, Harvey Holmes b: 1/10/1887, Marshall, Va. d: 1/8/80, Alexandria, Va. BL/TR, 5'9.5", 163 lbs. Deb: 4/17/14

YEAR	TM/L	G	AB	R	H	2B	3B	HR	RBI	BB	SO	AVG	OBP	SLG	PRO+	BR/A	SB	CS	SBR	FA	FR	G/POS	TPR
1914	Bal-F	81	168	18	39	3	2	0	13	18	17	.232	.310	.274	58	-12	2			.956	-17	C-47/S-1,O-1	-2.7
1915	Bal-F	53	73	5	19	1	2	0	11	14	5	.260	.407	.329	105	1	1			.989	-4	C-21	-0.2
Total	2	134	241	23	58	4	4	0	24	32	22	.241	.342	.290	73	-11	3			.965	-22	/C-68,O-1,S-1	-2.9

■ JIM RUSSELL

Russell, James William b: 10/1/18, Fayette City, Pa. d: 11/24/87, Pittsburgh, Pa. BB/TR, 6'1", 181 lbs. Deb: 9/12/42

YEAR	TM/L	G	AB	R	H	2B	3B	HR	RBI	BB	SO	AVG	OBP	SLG	PRO+	BR/A	SB	CS	SBR	FA	FR	G/POS	TPR
1942	Pit-N	5	14	2	1	0	0	0	0	1	4	.071	.133	.071	-38	-2	0			1.000	1	/O-3	-0.2
1943	Pit-N	146	533	79	138	19	11	4	44	77	67	.259	.354	.358	102	3	12			.990	2	*O-134/1-6	-0.2
1944	Pit-N	152	580	109	181	34	14	8	66	79	63	.312	.399	.460	136	29	6			.986	13	*O-149	3.5
1945	Pit-N	146	510	88	145	24	8	12	77	71	40	.284	.377	.433	120	15	15			.973	3	*O-140	1.1
1946	Pit-N	146	516	68	143	29	6	8	50	67	54	.277	.362	.403	114	10	11			.966	-2	*O-134/1-5	0.1
1947	Pit-N	128	478	68	121	21	8	8	51	63	58	.253	.343	.381	89	-7	7			.980	11	*O-119	-0.2
1948	Bos-N	89	322	44	85	18	1	9	54	46	31	.264	.361	.410	110	5	4			.992	6	O-84	0.6
1949	Bos-N	130	415	57	96	22	1	8	54	64	68	.231	.337	.347	88	-6	3			.975	-9	*O-120	-2.1
1950	Bro-N	77	214	37	49	8	2	10	32	31	36	.229	.329	.425	95	-2	1			.993	4	O-55	0.0
1951	Bro-N	16	13	2	0	0	0	0	0	4	6	.000	.278	.000	-18	-2	0	0	0	1.000	-1	/O-4	-0.3
Total	10	1035	3595	554	959	175	51	67	428	503	427	.267	.360	.400	108	44	59	0		.981	27	O-942/1-11	2.3

■ JOHN RUSSELL

Russell, John William b: 1/5/61, Oklahoma City, Okla. BR/TR, 6', 200 lbs. Deb: 6/22/84

YEAR	TM/L	G	AB	R	H	2B	3B	HR	RBI	BB	SO	AVG	OBP	SLG	PRO+	BR/A	SB	CS	SBR	FA	FR	G/POS	TPR
1984	Phi-N	39	99	11	28	8	1	2	11	12	33	.283	.360	.444	123	3	0	1	-1	1.000	-1	O-29/C-2	0.1
1985	Phi-N	81	216	22	47	12	0	9	23	18	72	.218	.278	.398	85	-5	2	0	1	1.000	-6	O-49,1-18	-1.4
1986	Phi-N	93	315	35	76	21	2	13	60	25	103	.241	.303	.444	100	-1	0	1	-1	.976	-5	C-89	-0.1
1987	Phi-N	24	62	5	9	1	0	3	8	3	17	.145	.185	.306	26	-7	0	1	-1	.955	0	O-10/C-7	-0.7
1988	Phi-N	22	49	5	12	1	0	3	4	3	15	.245	.302	.388	95	-0	0	0	0	.945	3	C-15	0.3
1989	Atl-N	74	159	14	29	2	0	2	9	8	53	.182	.226	.233	31	-14	0	0	0	.990	-7	C-45,O-14/1-2,3P	-2.1
1990	Tex-A	68	128	16	35	4	0	2	8	11	41	.273	.331	.352	91	-1	1	0	0	.980	2	C-31,D-19/O-6,13	0.1
1991	Tex-A	22	27	3	3	0	0	0	1	1	7	.111	.143	.111	-29	-5	0	0	0	1.000	-0	/O-8,C-5,D-5	-0.5
1992	Tex-A	7	10	1	1	0	0	0	2	1	4	.100	.250	.100	2	-1	0	0	0	1.000	1	/C-4,O-2,D-1	0.0
1993	Tex-A	18	22	1	5	1	0	1	3	2	10	.227	.292	.409	90	-0	0	0	0	1.000	-2	C-11/1-1,3-1,O-1	-0.2
Total	10	448	1087	113	245	50	3	34	129	84	355	.225	.285	.371	79	-32	3	3	-1	.979	-16	C-209,O-119/D13P	-4.5

■ LLOYD RUSSELL

Russell, Lloyd Opal b: 4/10/13, Atoka, Okla. d: 5/24/68, Waco, Tex. BR/TR, 5'11", 166 lbs. Deb: 4/26/38

YEAR	TM/L	G	AB	R	H	2B	3B	HR	RBI	BB	SO	AVG	OBP	SLG	PRO+	BR/A	SB	CS	SBR	FA	FR	G/POS	TPR
1938	Cle-A	2	0	0	0	0	0	0	0	0	0	—	—	—	—	0	0	0	0	.000	0	R	0.0

■ PAUL RUSSELL

Russell, Paul A. b: 1870, Reading, Pa. d: Pottstown, Pa. Deb: 7/29/1894

YEAR	TM/L	G	AB	R	H	2B	3B	HR	RBI	BB	SO	AVG	OBP	SLG	PRO+	BR/A	SB	CS	SBR	FA	FR	G/POS	TPR
1894	StL-N	3	10	1	1	0	0	0	0	0	2	.100	.100	.100	-52	-2	0			1.000	0	/O-1,3-1,2-1	-0.2

■ BILL RUSSELL

Russell, William Ellis b: 10/21/48, Pittsburg, Kan. BR/TR, 6', 175 lbs. Deb: 4/7/69 MC

YEAR	TM/L	G	AB	R	H	2B	3B	HR	RBI	BB	SO	AVG	OBP	SLG	PRO+	BR/A	SB	CS	SBR	FA	FR	G/POS	TPR
1969	LA-N	98	212	35	48	6	2	5	15	22	45	.226	.302	.344	87	-4	4	1	1	.978	-7	O-86	-1.4
1970	LA-N	81	278	30	72	11	9	0	28	16	28	.259	.306	.363	82	-8	9	1	2	.983	6	O-79/S-1	-0.3
1971	LA-N	91	211	29	48	7	4	2	15	11	39	.227	.266	.327	71	-9	6	3	0	.964	-6	2-41,O-40/S-6	-1.4
1972	LA-N	129	434	47	118	19	5	4	34	34	64	.272	.328	.366	99	-1	14	7	0	.949	15	*S-121/O-6	3.3
1973	LA-N★	162	615	55	163	26	3	4	56	34	63	.265	.305	.337	81	-17	15	7	0	.963	9	*S-162	1.4
1974	*LA-N	160	553	61	149	18	6	5	65	53	53	.269	.338	.351	97	-2	14	5	1	.946	-19	*S-160/O-1	0.1
1975	LA-N	84	252	24	52	9	2	0	14	23	28	.206	.278	.258	52	-17	5	0	2	.967	-21	S-83	-3.0
1976	LA-N★	149	554	53	152	17	3	5	65	21	46	.274	.304	.343	85	-12	15	5	2	.963	-14	*S-149	-0.7
1977	*LA-N	153	634	84	176	28	6	4	51	24	43	.278	.306	.360	78	-20	16	7	1	.963	10	*S-153	0.8
1978	*LA-N	155	625	72	179	32	4	3	46	30	34	.286	.321	.365	92	-8	10	6	-1	.962	12	*S-155	2.5
1979	LA-N	153	627	72	170	26	4	7	56	24	43	.271	.299	.359	80	-19	6	9	-4	.957	-26	*S-150	-3.3
1980	LA-N★	130	466	38	123	23	2	3	34	18	44	.264	.296	.341	79	-14	13	2	3	.968	-22	*S-129	-1.9
1981	*LA-N	82	262	20	61	9	2	0	22	19	20	.233	.287	.282	64	-12	2	1	0	.965	10	S-80	0.5
1982	LA-N	153	497	64	136	20	2	3	46	63	30	.274	.360	.340	99	2	10	2	2	.961	-4	*S-150	1.4
1983	*LA-N	131	451	47	111	13	1	1	30	33	31	.246	.303	.286	64	-21	13	9	-2	.964	1	*S-127	-1.0

YEAR	TM/L	G	AB	R	H	2B	3B	HR	RBI	BB	SO	AVG	OBP	SLG	PRO+	BR/A	SB	CS	SBR	FA	FR	G/POS	TPR
1984	LA-N	89	262	25	70	12	1	0	19	25	24	.267	.331	.321	85	-5	4	4	-1	.965	-4	S-65,O-18/2-5	-0.6
1985	LA-N	76	169	19	44	6	1	0	13	18	9	.260	.335	.308	83	-3	4	0	1	.919	-7	S-23,O-21/2-8,3-5	-0.7
1986	LA-N	105	216	21	54	11	0	0	18	15	23	.250	.305	.301	73	-8	7	0	2	1.000	-7	O-48,S-32/2-8,3-1	-1.2
Total	18	2181	7318	796	1926	293	57	46	627	483	667	.263	.312	.338	83	-177	167	69	9	.960	-74	*S-1746,O-299/23	-5.5

■ HANK RUSZKOWSKI

Ruszkowski, Henry Alexander b: 11/10/25, Cleveland, Ohio BR/TR, 6′, 190 lbs. Deb: 9/26/44

YEAR	TM/L	G	AB	R	H	2B	3B	HR	RBI	BB	SO	AVG	OBP	SLG	PRO+	BR/A	SB	CS	SBR	FA	FR	G/POS	TPR
1944	Cle-A	3	8	1	3	0	0	0	1	0	1	.375	.375	.375	119	0	0	0	0	1.000	-0	/C-2	0.0
1945	Cle-A	14	49	2	10	0	0	0	5	4	9	.204	.264	.204	38	-4	0	0	0	.975	3	C-14	0.0
1947	Cle-A	23	27	5	7	2	0	3	4	2	6	.259	.310	.667	172	2	0	0	0	1.000	-2	C-16	0.1
Total	3	40	84	8	20	2	0	3	10	6	16	.238	.289	.369	91	-2	0	0	0	.981	1	/C-32	0.1

■ BABE RUTH

Ruth, George Herman "The Bambino" or "The Sultan Of Swat"
b: 2/6/1895, Baltimore, Md. d: 8/16/48, New York, N.Y. BL/TL, 6′2″, 215 lbs. Deb: 7/11/14 CH

YEAR	TM/L	G	AB	R	H	2B	3B	HR	RBI	BB	SO	AVG	OBP	SLG	PRO+	BR/A	SB	CS	SBR	FA	FR	G/POS	TPR
1914	Bos-A	5	10	1	2	1	0	0	2	0	4	.200	.200	.300	50	-1	0			1.000	-0	/P-4	0.0
1915	*Bos-A	42	92	16	29	10	1	4	21	9	23	.315	.376	.576	191	9	0			.976	1	P-32	0.0
1916	*Bos-A	67	136	18	37	5	3	3	15	10	23	.272	.322	.419	122	3	0			.973	0	P-44	0.0
1917	Bos-A	52	123	14	40	6	3	2	12	12	18	.325	.385	.472	163	9	0			.984	2	P-41	0.0
1918	*Bos-A	95	317	50	95	26	11	**11**	66	57	58	.300	.410	**.555**	194	36	6			.949	3	O-59,P-20,1-13	2.6
1919	Bos-A	130	432	**103**	139	34	12	**29**	**114**	101	58	.322	**.456**	**.657**	**224**	**74**	7			**.996**	5	*O-111,P-17/1-5	**6.3**
1920	NY-A	142	458	**158**	172	36	9	**54**	**137**	**148**	80	.376	**.530**	**.847**	**252**	**107**	14	14	-4	.936	-0	*O-141/1-2,P-1	**8.6**
1921	*NY-A	152	540	**177**	204	44	16	**59**	**171**	**144**	81	.378	**.512**	**.846**	**236**	**115**	17	13	-3	.966	4	*O-152/P-2,1-2	**9.4**
1922	*NY-A	110	406	94	128	24	8	35	99	84	80	.315	.434	**.672**	**181**	48	2	5	-2	.964	1	*O-110/1-1	3.7
1923	*NY-A	152	522	**151**	205	45	13	**41**	**131**	**170**	93	.393	**.545**	**.764**	**238**	**116**	17	21	-8	.973	16	*O-148/1-4	**10.6**
1924	NY-A	153	529	**143**	200	39	7	**46**	121	**142**	81	**.378**	**.513**	**.739**	**221**	**101**	9	13	-5	.962	7	*O-152	**8.5**
1925	NY-A	98	359	61	104	12	2	25	66	59	68	.290	.393	.543	138	20	2	4	-2	.974	9	O-98	1.9
1926	*NY-A	152	495	**139**	184	30	5	**47**	**146**	**144**	76	.372	**.516**	**.737**	**228**	**100**	11	9	-2	.979	1	*O-149/1-2	**8.4**
1927	*NY-A	151	540	**158**	192	29	8	**60**	164	**138**	89	.356	**.487**	**.772**	**229**	106	7	6	-2	.963	5	*O-151	**9.2**
1928	*NY-A	154	536	**163**	173	29	8	**54**	**142**	**135**	87	.323	.461	**.709**	**210**	**89**	4	5	-2	.975	-3	*O-154	**7.0**
1929	NY-A	135	499	121	172	26	6	**46**	154	72	60	.345	.430	**.697**	**199**	**71**	5	3	-0	.984	-9	*O-133	**5.0**
1930	NY-A	145	518	150	186	28	9	**49**	153	**136**	61	.359	**.493**	**.732**	**216**	**98**	10	10	-3	.965	-0	*O-144/P-1	**7.3**
1931	NY-A	145	534	149	199	31	3	**46**	163	**128**	51	.373	**.495**	**.700**	**223**	**102**	5	4	-1	.972	-12	*O-142/1-1	**7.3**
1932	*NY-A	133	457	120	156	13	5	41	137	**130**	62	.341	**.489**	.661	**206**	79	2	2	-1	.961	-7	*O-128/1-1	5.8
1933	NY-A★	137	459	97	138	21	3	34	103	**114**	90	.301	.442	.582	180	57	4	5	-2	.970	-7	*O-132/P-1,1-1	3.8
1934	NY-A★	125	365	78	105	17	4	22	84	103	63	.288	.447	.537	164	40	1	3	-2	.962	-6	*O-111	2.5
1935	Bos-N	28	72	13	13	0	0	6	12	20	24	.181	.359	.431	121	3	0			.952	-4	O-26	-0.2
Total	22	2503	8399	2174	2873	506	136	714	2213	2056	1330	.342	.474	.690	209	1382	123	117		.968	5	*O-2241,P-163/1-32	107.7

■ JIM RUTHERFORD

Rutherford, James Hollis b: 9/26/1886, Stillwater, Minn. d: 9/18/56, Cleveland, Ohio BL/TR, 6′1″, 180 lbs. Deb: 7/12/10

YEAR	TM/L	G	AB	R	H	2B	3B	HR	RBI	BB	SO	AVG	OBP	SLG	PRO+	BR/A	SB	CS	SBR	FA	FR	G/POS	TPR
1910	Cle-A	1	2	0	1	0	0	0	0	0		.500	.500	.500	210	0	0			1.000	-0	/O-1	0.0

■ MICKEY RUTNER

Rutner, Milton b: 3/18/20, Hempstead, N.Y. BR/TR, 5′11″, 190 lbs. Deb: 9/11/47

YEAR	TM/L	G	AB	R	H	2B	3B	HR	RBI	BB	SO	AVG	OBP	SLG	PRO+	BR/A	SB	CS	SBR	FA	FR	G/POS	TPR
1947	Phi-A	12	48	4	12	1	0	1	4	3	2	.250	.294	.333	73	-2	0	0	0	.885	-3	3-11	-0.5

■ MARK RYAL

Ryal, Mark Dwayne b: 4/28/60, Henryetta, Okla. BL/TL, 6′1″, 185 lbs. Deb: 9/7/82

YEAR	TM/L	G	AB	R	H	2B	3B	HR	RBI	BB	SO	AVG	OBP	SLG	PRO+	BR/A	SB	CS	SBR	FA	FR	G/POS	TPR
1982	KC-A	6	13	0	1	0	0	0	0	1	3	.077	.143	.077	-38	-2	0	0	0	.900	-1	/O-5	-0.3
1985	Chi-A	12	33	4	5	3	0	0	3	3	3	.152	.222	.242	26	-3	0	0	0	1.000	-1	O-12	-0.5
1986	Cal-A	13	32	6	12	0	0	2	5	2	4	.375	.412	.563	164	3	1	0	0	.900	-1	/O-6,1-4,D-2	0.2
1987	Cal-A	58	100	7	20	6	0	5	18	3	15	.200	.223	.410	65	-5	0	0	0	.955	-6	O-21/1-4,D-5	-1.1
1989	Phi-N	29	33	2	8	2	0	0	5	1	6	.242	.265	.303	62	-2	0	0	0	1.000	-1	/1-4,O-4	-0.3
1990	Pit-N	9	12	0	1	0	0	0	0	0	3	.083	.083	.083	-56	-3	0	0	0	1.000	-1	/O-4	-0.4
Total	6	127	223	19	47	11	0	7	31	10	34	.211	.245	.354	61	-13	1	0	0	.957	-11	/O-52,1-12,D-7	-2.4

■ CONNIE RYAN

Ryan, Cornelius Joseph b: 2/27/20, New Orleans, La. d: 1/3/96, Metairie, La. BR/TR, 5′11″, 175 lbs. Deb: 4/14/42 MC

YEAR	TM/L	G	AB	R	H	2B	3B	HR	RBI	BB	SO	AVG	OBP	SLG	PRO+	BR/A	SB	CS	SBR	FA	FR	G/POS	TPR
1942	NY-N	11	27	4	5	0	0	0	2	4	3	.185	.290	.185	40	-2	1			.944	7	2-11	0.5
1943	Bos-N	132	457	52	97	10	2	1	24	58	56	.212	.301	.249	61	-22	7			.962	-20	*2-100,3-30	-3.8
1944	Bos-N★	88	332	56	98	18	5	4	25	36	40	.295	.364	.416	114	7	13			.974	13	2-80,3-14	2.4
1946	Bos-N	143	502	55	121	28	8	1	48	55	63	.241	.317	.335	84	-11	7			.968	-2	*2-120,3-24	-0.5
1947	Bos-N	150	544	60	144	33	5	5	69	71	60	.265	.351	.371	94	-4	5			.973	-7	*2-150/S-1	0.0
1948	*Bos-N	51	122	14	26	3	0	0	10	21	16	.213	.333	.238	58	-6	0			.966	4	2-40/3-4	0.0
1949	Bos-N	85	208	28	52	13	1	6	20	21	30	.250	.319	.409	99	-1	1			.973	6	3-25,S-18,2-16,/1-3	0.6
1950	Bos-N	20	72	12	14	2	0	3	6	12	9	.194	.326	.347	82	-2	0			1.000	1	2-20	0.0
	Cin-N	106	367	45	95	18	5	3	43	52	46	.259	.352	.360	87	-5	4			.973	11	*2-103	0.9
	Yr	126	439	57	109	20	5	6	49	64	55	.248	.348	.358	87	-7	4			.978	12	*2-123	0.9
1951	Cin-N	136	473	75	112	17	4	16	53	79	72	.237	.350	.391	97	-0	11	6	-0	.970	-3	*2-121/3-3,1-2,O-1	0.2
1952	Phi-N	154	577	81	139	24	6	12	49	69	72	.241	.327	.366	93	-5	13	5	1	.972	-5	*2-154	-0.1
1953	Phi-N	90	247	47	73	14	6	5	26	30	35	.296	.372	.462	116	6	5	1	1	.958	-5	2-65/1-2	0.5
	Chi-A	17	54	6	12	1	0	0	6	9	12	.222	.333	.241	55	-3	2	0	1	.927	-1	3-16	-0.4
1954	Cin-N	1	0	0	0	0	0	0	0	1	0	—	1.000	—	182	0	0	0	0	.000	0	H	0.0
Total	12	1184	3982	535	988	181	42	56	381	518	514	.248	.337	.357	90	-48	69	12		.970	-1	2-980,3-116/S10	0.3

■ CYCLONE RYAN

Ryan, Daniel R. b: 1866, Cappagh White, Ireland d: 1/30/17, Medfield, Mass. TR , 6′, 200 lbs. Deb: 8/8/1887

YEAR	TM/L	G	AB	R	H	2B	3B	HR	RBI	BB	SO	AVG	OBP	SLG	PRO+	BR/A	SB	CS	SBR	FA	FR	G/POS	TPR
1887	NY-a	8	32	4	7	1	0	0	3	3		.219	.286	.250	52	-2	1			.938	-0	/1-8,P-2	-0.2
1891	Bos-N	1	1	0	0	0	0	0	0	0	0	.000	.000	.000	-89	-0	0			1.000	0	/P-1	0.0
Total	2	9	33	4	7	1	0	0	3	3	0	.212	.278	.242	48	-2	1			1.000	0	/1-8,P-3	-0.2

■ MIKE RYAN

Ryan, J. b: St.Louis, Mo. Deb: 7/25/1895

YEAR	TM/L	G	AB	R	H	2B	3B	HR	RBI	BB	SO	AVG	OBP	SLG	PRO+	BR/A	SB	CS	SBR	FA	FR	G/POS	TPR
1895	StL-N	2	2	0	0	0	0	0	0	0	0	.000	.000	.000	-99	-1	0			.000	-1	/3-2	-0.1

■ JIMMY RYAN

Ryan, James Edward "Pony" b: 2/11/1863, Clinton, Mass. d: 10/26/23, Chicago, Ill. BR/TL, 5′9″, 162 lbs. Deb: 10/8/1885

YEAR	TM/L	G	AB	R	H	2B	3B	HR	RBI	BB	SO	AVG	OBP	SLG	PRO+	BR/A	SB	CS	SBR	FA	FR	G/POS	TPR
1885	Chi-N	3	13	2	6	1	0	0	2	1	1	.462	.500	.538	207	1				.737	1	/S-2,O-1	0.2
1886	*Chi-N	84	327	58	100	17	6	4	53	12	28	.306	.330	.431	114	2	10			.828	1	O-70/S-6,3-6,2-5,P	0.1
1887	Chi-N	126	508	117	145	23	10	11	74	53	19	.285	.360	.435	106	1	50			.857	-2	*O-122/P-8,2-3	-0.5
1888	Chi-N	129	549	115	**182**	**33**	10	**16**	64	35	50	.332	.377	**.515**	170	41	60			.878	4	*O-128/P-8	3.8
1889	Chi-N	135	576	140	177	31	14	17	72	70	62	.307	.388	.498	140	29	45			.926	6	*O-106,S-29	2.9
1890	Chi-P	118	486	99	165	32	5	6	89	60	36	.340	.416	.463	129	20	30			.919	2	*O-118	1.5
1891	Chi-N	118	505	110	140	22	15	9	66	53	38	.277	.355	.434	129	18	27			.905	5	*O-117/S-2,P-2	1.7
1892	Chi-N	128	505	105	148	21	11	10	65	61	41	.293	.375	.438	144	27	27			.921	5	*O-120/S-9	2.5
1893	Chi-N	83	341	82	102	21	7	3	30	59	25	.299	.407	.428	124	14	8			.908	-1	O-73,S-10/P-1	0.7
1894	Chi-N	108	474	132	171	37	7	3	62	50	23	.361	.425	.487	113	10	11			.910	9	*O-108	0.9
1895	Chi-N	108	438	83	139	22	8	6	49	48	22	.317	.392	.445	109	5	18			.937	2	*O-108	-0.1
1896	Chi-N	128	489	83	149	24	10	3	86	46	16	.305	.369	.413	102	1	29			.912	-0	*O-128	-0.9
1897	Chi-N	136	520	103	156	33	17	5	85	50		.300	.369	.458	113	8	27			.945	7	*O-136	0.4
1898	Chi-N	144	572	122	185	32	13	4	79	73		.323	.405	.446	144	34	29			.914	-7	*O-144	1.6
1899	Chi-N	125	525	91	158	20	10	3	68	43		.301	.357	.394	109	6	9			.956	-1	*O-125	-0.4
1900	Chi-N	105	415	66	115	25	4	5	59	29		.277	.329	.393	102	0	19			.913	-11	*O-105	-1.7
1902	Was-A	120	484	92	155	32	6	6	44	43		.320	.384	.448	129	19	10			.949	3	*O-120	1.3
1903	Was-A	114	437	42	109	25	4	7	46	17		.249	.290	.373	96	-3	9			.970	3	*O-114	-0.7
Total	18	2012	8164	1642	2502	451	157	118	1093	803	361	.306	.374	.444	123	233	418			.918	25	*O-1943/S-58,P23	13.3

■ JACK RYAN

Ryan, John Bernard b: 11/12/1868, Haverhill, Mass. d: 8/21/52, Boston, Mass. BR/TR, 5′10.5″, 165 lbs. Deb: 9/2/1889 C

YEAR	TM/L	G	AB	R	H	2B	3B	HR	RBI	BB	SO	AVG	OBP	SLG	PRO+	BR/A	SB	CS	SBR	FA	FR	G/POS	TPR
1889	Lou-a	21	79	8	14	1	0	0	2	3	17	.177	.207	.190	14	-9	2			.864	-6	C-15/O-4,3-2	-1.2
1890	*Lou-a	93	337	43	73	16	4	0	35	12		.217	.244	.288	58	-19	6			.932	5	C-89/O-3,S-1,1-1	-0.6

YEAR	TM/L	G	AB	R	H	2B	3B	HR	RBI	BB	SO	AVG	OBP	SLG	PRO+	BR/A	SB	CS	SBR	FA	FR	G/POS	TPR
1891	Lou-a	75	253	24	57	5	4	2	25	15	40	.225	.271	.300	64	-13	3			.930	-1	C-56,1-11/3-6,O2	-0.8
1894	Bos-N	53	201	39	54	12	7	1	29	13	16	.269	.316	.413	69	-12	3			.911	0	C-51/1-2	-0.5
1895	Bos-N	49	189	22	55	7	0	0	18	6	6	.291	.313	.328	61	-12	3			.951	1	C-43/2-5,O-1	-0.5
1896	Bos-N	8	32	2	3	1	0	0	0	0	1	.094	.094	.125	-40	-7	0			.911	2	/C-8	-0.3
1898	Bro-N	87	301	39	57	11	4	0	24	15		.189	.233	.252	39	-24	5			.960	3	C-84/3-4,1-1	-1.3
1899	Bal-N	2	4	0	2	1	0	0	1	0		.500	.500	.750	229	1	1			1.000	1	/C-2	0.2
1901	StL-N	83	300	27	59	6	5	0	31	7		.197	.218	.250	37	-24	5			.982	5	C-65/2-9,1-5,O-3	-1.3
1902	StL-N	76	267	23	48	4	4	0	14	4		.180	.195	.225	31	-22	2			.966	-7	C-66/1-4,3-4,2-2,S	-2.4
1903	StL-N	67	227	18	54	5	1	1	10	10		.238	.273	.282	60	-12	2			.971	-9	C-47,1-18/S-2	-1.6
1912	Was-A	1	1	0	0	0	0	0	0	0		.000	.000	.000	-99	-0	0			1.000	0	/3-1	0.0
1913	Was-A	1	1	0	0	0	0	0	0	0	0	.000	.000	.000	-98	-0	0			1.000	0	/C-1	0.0
Total	13	616	2192	245	476	69	29	4	189	85	80	.217	.249	.281	50	-154	32			.947	-6	C-527/1-42,23OS	-10.3

■ BUDDY RYAN
Ryan, John Budd b: 10/6/1885, Denver, Colo. d: 7/9/56, Sacramento, Cal. BL/TR, 5'9.5", 172 lbs. Deb: 4/11/12

YEAR	TM/L	G	AB	R	H	2B	3B	HR	RBI	BB	SO	AVG	OBP	SLG	PRO+	BR/A	SB	CS	SBR	FA	FR	G/POS	TPR
1912	Cle-A	93	328	53	89	12	9	1	31	30		.271	.343	.372	101	0	12			.963	5	O-90	0.0
1913	Cle-A	73	243	26	72	6	1	0	32	11	13	.296	.332	.329	91	-3	9			.986	-2	O-68/1-1	-0.8
Total	2	166	571	79	161	18	10	1	63	41	13	.282	.339	.354	97	-3	21			.973	3	O-158/1-1	-0.8

■ BLONDY RYAN
Ryan, John Collins b: 1/4/06, Lynn, Mass d: 11/28/59, Swampscott, Mass. BR/TR, 6'1", 178 lbs. Deb: 7/13/30

YEAR	TM/L	G	AB	R	H	2B	3B	HR	RBI	BB	SO	AVG	OBP	SLG	PRO+	BR/A	SB	CS	SBR	FA	FR	G/POS	TPR
1930	Chi-A	28	87	9	18	0	4	1	10	6	13	.207	.258	.333	50	-7	2	0	1	.875	-1	3-23/S-2,2-1	-0.6
1933	*NY-N	146	525	47	125	10	5	3	48	15	62	.238	.259	.293	58	-29	0			.950	17	*S-146	-0.2
1934	NY-N	110	385	35	93	19	0	2	41	19	68	.242	.277	.306	57	-23	3			.953	12	3-65,S-30,2-25	-0.6
1935	Phi-N	39	129	13	34	3	0	1	10	7	20	.264	.312	.310	61	-7	1			.912	2	S-35/2-1,3-1	-0.3
	NY-A	30	105	12	25	1	3	0	11	3	10	.238	.259	.305	48	-8	0	0	0	.908	-4	S-30	-1.1
1937	*NY-N	21	75	10	18	3	1	1	13	6	8	.240	.296	.347	73	-3	0			.941	1	S-19/2-1,3-1	-0.1
1938	NY-N	12	24	1	5	0	0	0	0	1	3	.208	.240	.208	24	-2	0			1.000	-1	/2-5,3-3,S-2	-0.3
Total	6	386	1330	127	318	36	13	8	133	57	184	.239	.271	.304	57	-80	6	0		.936	26	S-264/3-93,2-33	-3.2

■ JACK RYAN
Ryan, John Francis b: 5/5/05, West Mineral, Kan. d: 9/2/67, Rochester, Minn. BR/TR, 6', 185 lbs. Deb: 6/18/29

YEAR	TM/L	G	AB	R	H	2B	3B	HR	RBI	BB	SO	AVG	OBP	SLG	PRO+	BR/A	SB	CS	SBR	FA	FR	G/POS	TPR
1929	Bos-A	2	3	0	0	0	0	0	0	0	0	.000	.000	.000	-99	-1	0	0	0	1.000	-1	/O-2	-0.2

■ JOHNNY RYAN
Ryan, John Joseph b: 10/1853, Philadelphia, Pa. d: 3/22/02, Philadelphia, Pa. 5'7.5", 150 lbs. Deb: 8/19/1873

YEAR	TM/L	G	AB	R	H	2B	3B	HR	RBI	BB	SO	AVG	OBP	SLG	PRO+	BR/A	SB	CS	SBR	FA	FR	G/POS	TPR
1873	Phi-n	2	8	1	2	0	0	0	1	0	0	.250	.250	.250	47	-1	0	0	0	.800	0	/1-1,O-1	0.0
1874	Bal-n	47	181	29	35	8	1	0	19	5	13	.193	.215	.249	49	-10	3	0	1	.862	13	*O-47/P-1	0.4
1875	NH-n	37	146	17	23	2	2	0	8	3	12	.158	.174	.199	34	-8	10	4	1	.796	-8	O-30,P-10/C-4,S-1	-1.1
1876	Lou-N	64	241	32	61	5	1	1	18	6	23	.253	.271	.295	75	-9				.886	-7	*O-64/P-1	-1.5
1877	Cin-N	6	26	2	4	0	1	0	2	1	5	.154	.185	.231	34	-2				.769	-1	/O-6	-0.3
Total	3 n	86	335	47	60	10	3	0	28	8	25	.179	.198	.227	43	-19	13	4	2	.850	5	/O-78,P-11,C-4,S1	-0.7
Total	2	70	267	34	65	5	2	1	20	7	28	.243	.263	.288	72	-11				.877	-9	/O-70,P-1	-1.8

■ JOHN RYAN
Ryan, John M. (Played 1 Game Under Real Name Of Daniel Sheehan) b: Washington, D.C. Deb: 6/11/1884

YEAR	TM/L	G	AB	R	H	2B	3B	HR	RBI	BB	SO	AVG	OBP	SLG	PRO+	BR/A	SB	CS	SBR	FA	FR	G/POS	TPR
1884	Was-U	7	28	2	4	0	1	0		1		.143	.172	.214	17	-4				.667	-1	/O-7,3-1	-0.5
	Wil-U	2	6	0	1	0	0	0		1		.167	.286	.167	39	-1				.800	-0	/O-2	-0.1
	Yr	9	34	2	5	0	1	0		2		.147	.194	.206	22	-4				.706	-1	/O-9,3-1	-0.6

■ MIKE RYAN
Ryan, Michael James b: 11/25/41, Haverhill, Mass. BR/TR, 6'2", 205 lbs. Deb: 10/3/64 C

YEAR	TM/L	G	AB	R	H	2B	3B	HR	RBI	BB	SO	AVG	OBP	SLG	PRO+	BR/A	SB	CS	SBR	FA	FR	G/POS	TPR
1964	Bos-A	1	3	0	1	0	0	0	2	1	0	.333	.500	.333	131	0	0	0	0	1.000	-1	/C-1	0.0
1965	Bos-A	33	107	7	17	0	1	3	9	5	19	.159	.196	.262	27	-10	0	0	0	.981	0	C-33	-0.9
1966	Bos-A	116	369	27	79	15	3	2	32	29	68	.214	.271	.287	55	-21	1	0	0	.992	1	*C-114	-1.4
1967	*Bos-A	79	226	21	45	4	2	2	27	26	42	.199	.285	.261	58	-11	2	0	1	.988	1	C-79	-0.6
1968	Phi-N	96	296	12	53	6	1	1	15	15	59	.179	.219	.216	31	-25	0	3	-2	.991	-4	C-96	-2.8
1969	Phi-N	133	446	41	91	17	2	12	44	30	66	.204	.257	.332	66	-22	1	1	-0	.991	2	*C-132	-1.4
1970	Phi-N	46	134	14	24	8	0	2	11	16	24	.179	.267	.284	49	-10	0	0	0	.992	-12	C-46	-2.1
1971	Phi-N	43	134	9	22	5	1	3	6	10	32	.164	.222	.284	42	-10	0	0	0	1.000	12	C-43	0.3
1972	Phi-N	46	106	6	19	4	0	2	10	10	25	.179	.256	.274	49	-7	0	0	0	.992	6	C-46	0.0
1973	Phi-N	28	69	7	16	1	2	1	5	6	19	.232	.293	.348	75	-2	0	0	0	.992	1	C-27	-0.1
1974	Pit-N	15	30	2	3	0	0	0	0	4	16	.100	.206	.100	-13	-5	0	0	0	1.000	3	C-15	-0.1
Total	11	636	1920	146	370	60	12	28	161	152	370	.193	.253	.280	51	-124	4	4	-1	.991	10	C-632	-9.1

■ TOM RYDER
Ryder, Thomas BL, Deb: 7/22/1884

YEAR	TM/L	G	AB	R	H	2B	3B	HR	RBI	BB	SO	AVG	OBP	SLG	PRO+	BR/A	SB	CS	SBR	FA	FR	G/POS	TPR
1884	StL-U	8	28	4	7	1	0	0		2		.250	.300	.286	76	-2				.650	-0	/O-8	-0.2

■ GENE RYE
Rye, Eugene Rudolph "Half-Pint" (b: Eugene Rudolph Mercantelli)
b: 11/15/06, Chicago, Ill. d: 1/21/80, Park Ridge, Ill. BL/TR, 5'6", 165 lbs. Deb: 4/22/31

YEAR	TM/L	G	AB	R	H	2B	3B	HR	RBI	BB	SO	AVG	OBP	SLG	PRO+	BR/A	SB	CS	SBR	FA	FR	G/POS	TPR
1931	Bos-A	17	39	3	7	0	0	0	1	2	5	.179	.220	.179	6	-5	0	0	0	.944	-1	O-10	-0.7

■ ALEX SABO
Sabo, Alexander "Giz" (b: Alexsander Szabo) b: 2/14/10, New Brunswick, N.J BR/TR, 6', 192 lbs. Deb: 8/1/36

YEAR	TM/L	G	AB	R	H	2B	3B	HR	RBI	BB	SO	AVG	OBP	SLG	PRO+	BR/A	SB	CS	SBR	FA	FR	G/POS	TPR
1936	Was-A	4	8	1	3	0	0	0	1	0	2	.375	.375	.375	91	-0	0	0	0	.923	1	/C-4	0.1
1937	Was-A	1	0	0	0	0	0	0	0	0	0	—	—	—	—	0	0	0	0	1.000	-0	/C-1	0.0
Total	2	5	8	1	3	0	0	0	1	0	2	.375	.375	.375	91	-0	0	0	0	.929	1	/C-5	0.1

■ CHRIS SABO
Sabo, Christopher Andrew b: 1/19/62, Detroit, Mich. BR/TR, 6', 185 lbs. Deb: 4/4/88

YEAR	TM/L	G	AB	R	H	2B	3B	HR	RBI	BB	SO	AVG	OBP	SLG	PRO+	BR/A	SB	CS	SBR	FA	FR	G/POS	TPR
1988	Cin-N★	137	538	74	146	40	2	11	44	29	52	.271	.316	.414	104	2	46	14	5	**.966**	19	*3-135/S-2	2.7
1989	Cin-N	82	304	40	79	21	1	6	29	25	33	.260	.318	.395	99	-1	14	9	-1	.943	-3	3-76	-0.5
1990	*Cin-N★	148	567	95	153	38	2	25	71	61	58	.270	.345	.476	118	14	25	10	2	**.966**	-6	*3-146	1.1
1991	Cin-N★	153	582	91	175	35	3	26	88	44	79	.301	.356	.505	134	25	19	6	2	.966	-15	*3-151	1.3
1992	Cin-N	96	344	42	84	19	3	12	43	30	54	.244	.307	.422	102	-0	4	5	-2	.961	-1	3-93	-0.3
1993	Cin-N	148	552	86	143	33	2	21	82	43	105	.259	.319	.440	101	-1	6	4	-1	.967	-15	*3-148	-1.6
1994	Bal-A	68	258	41	66	15	3	11	42	20	38	.256	.322	.465	95	-3	1	1	-0	.958	-11	3-37,O-22,D-10	-1.4
1995	Chi-A	20	71	10	18	5	0	1	8	3	12	.254	.303	.366	76	-3	2	0	1	.909	-1	D-15/1-1,3-1	-0.3
	StL-N	5	13	0	2	1	0	0	3	1	2	.154	.214	.231	17	-2	1	0	0	.929	-1	/1-2,3-1	-0.2
1996	Cin-N	54	125	15	32	7	1	3	16	18	27	.256	.354	.400	98	-0	2	0	1	.961	6	3-43	0.6
Total	9	911	3354	494	898	214	17	116	426	274	460	.268	.329	.445	109	32	120	49	7	.963	-28	3-831/D-25,O-22,1S	1.4

■ FRANK SACKA
Sacka, Frank b: 8/30/24, Romulus, Mich. d: 12/7/94, Dearborn, Mich. BR/TR, 6', 195 lbs. Deb: 4/29/51

YEAR	TM/L	G	AB	R	H	2B	3B	HR	RBI	BB	SO	AVG	OBP	SLG	PRO+	BR/A	SB	CS	SBR	FA	FR	G/POS	TPR
1951	Was-A	7	16	1	4	0	0	0	3	0	5	.250	.250	.250	36	-1	0	0	0	.962	2	/C-6	0.0
1953	Was-A	7	18	2	5	0	0	0	3	3	1	.278	.381	.278	82	-0	0	0	0	1.000	2	/C-6	0.2
Total	2	14	34	3	9	0	0	0	6	3	6	.265	.324	.265	62	-2	0	0	0	.982	3	/C-12	0.2

■ MIKE SADEK
Sadek, Michael George b: 5/30/46, Minneapolis, Minn. BR/TR, 5'9", 165 lbs. Deb: 4/13/73

YEAR	TM/L	G	AB	R	H	2B	3B	HR	RBI	BB	SO	AVG	OBP	SLG	PRO+	BR/A	SB	CS	SBR	FA	FR	G/POS	TPR
1973	SF-N	39	66	6	11	1	1	0	4	11	8	.167	.286	.212	38	-5	1	0	0	.981	7	C-35	0.3
1975	SF-N	42	106	14	25	5	2	0	9	14	14	.236	.325	.321	76	-3	1	0	0	.995	7	C-38	0.5
1976	SF-N	55	93	8	19	2	0	0	7	11	10	.204	.295	.226	48	-6	0	0	0	.985	8	C-51	0.3
1977	SF-N	61	126	12	29	7	0	1	15	12	5	.230	.297	.310	63	-6	2	1	0	.992	10	C-57	0.4
1978	SF-N	40	109	15	26	3	0	2	9	10	11	.239	.303	.321	77	-3	1	0	0	.975	2	C-37	-0.1
1979	SF-N	63	126	14	30	5	0	1	11	15	24	.238	.324	.302	77	-4	1	0	0	.993	1	C-60/O-1	-0.1
1980	SF-N	64	151	14	38	4	1	1	16	27	18	.252	.365	.311	93	-0	0	0	0	.974	4	C-59	0.6
1981	SF-N	19	36	5	6	3	0	0	3	8	7	.167	.318	.250	64	-1	0	0	0	.979	7	C-19	0.6
Total	8	383	813	88	184	30	4	5	74	108	97	.226	.319	.292	70	-30	6	1	1	.985	45	C-356/O-1	2.5

■ DONNIE SADLER
Sadler, Donnie Lamont b: 6/17/75, Clifton, Tex. BR/TR, 5'6", 165 lbs. Deb: 4/1/98

YEAR	TM/L	G	AB	R	H	2B	3B	HR	RBI	BB	SO	AVG	OBP	SLG	PRO+	BR/A	SB	CS	SBR	FA	FR	G/POS	TPR
1998	*Bos-A	58	124	21	28	4	4	3	15	6	28	.226	.278	.395	72	-5	4	0	1	.971	0	2-50/S-4,D-4	-0.2

YEAR	TM/L	G	AB	R	H	2B	3B	HR	RBI	BB	SO	AVG	OBP	SLG	PRO+	BR/A	SB	CS	SBR	FA	FR	G/POS	TPR
■ ED SADOWSKI	Sadowski, Edward Roman b: 1/19/31, Pittsburgh, Pa. d: 11/6/93, Garden Grove, Cal. BR/TR, 5'11", 175 lbs. Deb: 4/20/60 F																						
1960	Bos-A	38	93	10	20	2	0	3	8	8	13	.215	.284	.333	64	-5	0	0	0	.995	6	C-36	0.2
1961	LA-A	69	164	16	38	13	0	4	12	11	33	.232	.280	.384	68	-8	2	3	-1	.987	8	C-56	0.1
1962	LA-A	27	55	4	11	4	0	1	3	2	14	.200	.228	.327	49	-4	1	0	0	.968	3	C-18	-0.1
1963	LA-A	80	174	24	30	1	1	4	15	17	33	.172	.246	.259	44	-13	2	1	0	.997	20	C-68	0.9
1966	Atl-N	3	9	1	1	0	0	0	1	1	1	.111	.200	.111	-10	-1	0	0	0	1.000	1	/C-3	-0.1
Total	5	217	495	55	100	20	1	12	39	39	94	.202	.262	.319	56	-31	5	4	-1	.991	37	C-181	1.0
■ BOB SADOWSKI	Sadowski, Robert Frank "Sid" b: 1/15/37, St.Louis, Mo. BL/TR, 6', 175 lbs. Deb: 9/16/60																						
1960	StL-N	1	1	0	0	0	0	0	0	1	0	.000	.500	.000	47	0	0	0	0	.000	-1	/2-1	-0.1
1961	Phi-N	16	54	4	7	0	0	0	0	4	7	.130	.203	.130	-9	-8	1	0	0	.971	-1	3-14	-0.9
1962	Chi-A	79	130	22	30	3	3	6	24	13	22	.231	.301	.438	97	-1	0	0	0	.955	5	3-16,2-12	0.5
1963	LA-A	88	144	12	36	6	0	1	22	15	34	.250	.321	.313	83	-3	2	1	0	1.000	-3	O-25/3-6,2-4	-0.7
Total	4	184	329	38	73	9	3	7	46	33	63	.222	.295	.331	73	-13	3	1	0	.953	-0	/3-36,O-25,2-17	-1.2
■ OLMEDO SAENZ	Saenz, Olmedo (Sanchez) b: 10/8/70, Chitre Herrera, Pan. BR/TR, 6'2", 185 lbs. Deb: 5/28/94																						
1994	Chi-A	5	14	2	2	0	1	0	0	0	5	.143	.143	.286	7	-2	0	0	0	1.000	-0	/3-5	-0.2
■ TOM SAFFELL	Saffell, Thomas Judson b: 7/26/21, Etowah, Tenn. BL/TR, 5'11", 170 lbs. Deb: 7/2/49																						
1949	Pit-N	73	205	36	66	7	1	2	25	21	27	.322	.385	.395	107	3	5			.992	-3	O-53	-0.3
1950	Pit-N	67	182	18	37	7	0	2	6	14	34	.203	.264	.275	41	-16	1			.993	6	O-43	-1.1
1951	Pit-N	49	65	11	13	0	0	1	5	5	18	.200	.257	.246	35	-6	1	1	-0	.929	-4	O-17	-1.0
1955	Pit-N	73	113	21	19	1	0	1	3	15	22	.168	.266	.204	27	-12	1	0	0	.964	-7	O-47	-2.0
	KC-A	9	37	5	8	0	0	0	1	4	7	.216	.293	.216	38	-3	1	0	0	.962	-0	/O-9	-0.3
Total	4	271	602	91	143	15	1	6	40	59	108	.238	.307	.296	60	-34	9	1		.980	-8	O-169	-4.7
■ HARRY SAGE	Sage, Harry "Doc" b: 3/16/1864, Rock Island, Ill. d: 5/27/47, Rock Island, Ill. BR/TR, 5'10", 185 lbs. Deb: 4/17/1890																						
1890	Tol-a	81	275	40	41	8	4	2	25	29		.149	.235	.229	36	-23	10			.948	8	C-80/O-1	-0.7
■ PONY SAGER	Sager, Samuel B. b: 1847, Marshalltown, Iowa 140 lbs. Deb: 5/6/1871																						
1871	Rok-n	8	39	9	11	0	0	0	5	2	2	.282	.317	.282	78	-1	5	1	1	.643	-4	/S-4,O-4	-0.2
■ MARC SAGMOEN	Sagmoen, Marc Richard b: 4/16/71, Seattle, Wash. BL/TL, 5'11", 185 lbs. Deb: 4/15/97																						
1997	Tex-A	21	43	2	6	2	0	1	4	2	13	.140	.178	.256	11	-6	0	0	0	1.000	-3	O-17/1-1,D-1	-0.8
■ VIC SAIER	Saier, Victor Sylvester b: 5/4/1891, Lansing, Mich. d: 5/14/67, E.Lansing, Mich. BL/TR, 5'11", 185 lbs. Deb: 5/3/11																						
1911	Chi-N	86	259	42	67	15	1	1	37	25	37	.259	.340	.336	89	-3	11			.980	-4	1-73	-0.8
1912	Chi-N	122	451	74	130	25	14	2	61	34	65	.288	.340	.419	107	3	11			.992	-5	*1-120	-0.4
1913	Chi-N	149	519	94	150	15	**21**	14	92	62	62	.289	.370	.480	141	27	26			.983	-5	*1-149	2.1
1914	Chi-N	153	537	87	129	24	8	18	72	94	61	.240	.357	.415	130	21	19			.986	-11	*1-153	0.8
1915	Chi-N	144	497	74	131	35	11	11	64	64	62	.264	.350	.445	140	23	29	9	3	.985	-5	*1-139	2.0
1916	Chi-N	147	498	60	126	25	3	7	50	79	68	.253	.356	.357	108	7	20	17	-4	.984	-0	*1-147	-0.3
1917	Chi-N	6	21	5	5	1	0	0	2	2	1	.238	.304	.286	75	-1	0			1.000	2	/1-6	0.1
1919	Pit-N	58	166	19	37	3	3	2	17	18	13	.223	.306	.313	83	-3	5			.985	-5	1-51	-1.0
Total	8	865	2948	455	775	143	61	55	395	378	369	.263	.351	.409	119	75	121	26		.986	-33	1-838	2.5
■ EBBA ST.CLAIRE	St.Claire, Edward Joseph b: 8/5/21, Whitehall, N.Y. d: 8/22/82, Whitehall, N.Y. BB/TR, 6'1", 219 lbs. Deb: 4/17/51 F																						
1951	Bos-N	72	220	22	62	17	2	1	25	12	24	.282	.322	.391	98	-2	2	0	1	.977	3	C-62	0.4
1952	Bos-N	39	108	5	23	2	0	2	4	8	12	.213	.267	.287	56	-7	0	1	-1	.972	4	C-34	-0.2
1953	Mil-N	33	80	7	16	3	0	2	5	3	9	.200	.229	.313	42	-7	0	0	0	.992	3	C-27	-0.3
1954	NY-N	20	42	5	11	1	0	2	6	12	7	.262	.436	.429	126	2	0	0	0	.975	2	C-16	0.5
Total	4	164	450	39	112	23	2	7	40	35	52	.249	.306	.356	81	-13	2	1	0	.978	12	C-139	0.4
■ LENN SAKATA	Sakata, Lenn Haruki b: 6/8/54, Honolulu, Hawaii BR/TR, 5'9", 160 lbs. Deb: 7/21/77																						
1977	Mil-A	53	154	13	25	2	0	2	12	9	22	.162	.209	.214	16	-18	1	3	-2	.985	17	2-53	0.1
1978	Mil-A	30	78	8	15	4	0	0	3	8	11	.192	.267	.244	44	-6	1	0	0	.975	0	2-29	-0.4
1979	Mil-A	4	14	1	7	2	0	0	1	0	1	.500	.500	.643	206	2	0	0	0	1.000	2	/2-4	0.4
1980	Bal-A	43	83	12	16	3	2	1	9	6	10	.193	.247	.313	53	-6	2	1	0	.984	6	2-34/S-4,D-1	0.2
1981	Bal-A	61	150	19	34	4	0	5	15	11	18	.227	.284	.353	83	-4	4	0	1	.963	2	S-42,2-20	0.4
1982	Bal-A	136	343	40	89	18	1	6	31	30	39	.259	.326	.370	91	-4	7	4	-0	.977	-6	2-83,S-56	-0.3
1983	*Bal-A	66	134	23	34	7	0	3	12	16	17	.254	.338	.373	97	-0	8	4	0	.990	4	2-60/C-1,D-1	0.6
1984	Bal-A	81	157	23	30	1	0	3	11	6	15	.191	.221	.255	32	-15	4	1	1	.988	5	2-76/O-1	-0.7
1985	Bal-A	55	97	15	22	3	0	3	6	6	15	.227	.279	.351	73	-4	3	2	-0	.960	-1	2-50/D-1	-0.4
1986	Oak-A	17	34	4	12	2	0	0	5	3	6	.353	.405	.412	133	2	0	1	-1	.984	5	2-16/D-1	0.6
1987	NY-A	19	45	5	12	0	1	2	4	2	4	.267	.313	.444	99	-0	0	1	-1	.929	1	3-12/2-6	0.0
Total	11	565	1289	163	296	46	4	25	109	97	158	.230	.288	.330	71	-52	30	17	-1	.982	36	2-431,S-102/3DOC	0.5
■ MARK SALAS	Salas, Mark Bruce b: 3/8/61, Montebello, Cal. BL/TR, 6', 205 lbs. Deb: 6/19/84																						
1984	StL-N	14	20	1	2	1	0	0	1	0	3	.100	.100	.150	-31	-3	0	0	0	1.000	-1	/C-4,O-3	-0.5
1985	Min-A	120	360	51	108	20	5	9	41	18	37	.300	.335	.458	108	3	0	1	-1	.991	2	*C-115/D-3	1.0
1986	Min-A	91	258	28	60	7	4	8	33	18	32	.233	.285	.384	78	-8	3	1	0	.980	-6	C-69/D-8	-1.0
1987	Min-A	22	45	8	17	2	0	3	9	5	6	.378	.440	.622	171	5	0	1	-1	.989	1	C-14	0.5
	NY-A	50	115	13	23	4	0	3	12	10	17	.200	.281	.313	58	-7	0	0	0	1.000	-3	C-41/O-1,D-4	-0.7
	Yr	72	160	21	40	6	0	6	21	15	23	.250	.326	.400	91	-2	0	1	-1	.996	-2	C-55/D-4,O-1	-0.2
1988	Chi-A	75	196	17	49	7	0	3	9	12	17	.250	.303	.332	78	-6	0	0	0	.979	0	C-69/D-1	-0.2
1989	Cle-A	30	77	4	17	4	1	2	7	5	13	.221	.277	.377	81	-2	0	0	0	1.000	-0	D-20/C-5	-0.3
1990	Det-A	74	164	18	38	3	0	9	24	21	28	.232	.323	.415	104	1	0	0	0	.988	-4	C-57/3-1,D-3	-0.1
1991	Det-A	33	57	2	5	1	0	1	7	0	10	.088	.119	.158	-24	-10	0	0	0	1.000	0	C-11/1-5,D-8	-1.0
Total	8	509	1292	142	319	49	10	38	143	89	163	.247	.302	.389	86	-27	3	3	-1	.987	-11	C-385/D-47,1-5,O3	-2.3
■ ANGEL SALAZAR	Salazar, Argenis Antonio (Yepez) b: 11/4/61, Anaco, Venez. BR/TR, 6', 173 lbs. Deb: 8/10/83																						
1983	Mon-N	36	37	5	8	1	1	0	1	1	8	.216	.237	.297	47	-3	0	0	0	.966	2	S-34	0.1
1984	Mon-N	80	174	12	27	4	2	0	12	4	38	.155	.179	.201	7	-22	1	1	-0	.960	-3	S-80	-2.1
1986	KC-A	117	298	24	73	20	2	0	24	7	47	.245	.267	.326	59	-17	1	1	-0	.978	-5	*S-115/2-1	-1.3
1987	KC-A	116	317	24	65	7	0	2	21	6	46	.205	.220	.246	23	-35	4	4	-1	.981	22	*S-116	-0.6
1988	Chi-N	34	60	4	15	1	1	0	1	1	11	.250	.262	.300	58	-3	0	0	0	.966	7	S-29/2-2,3-1	0.5
Total	5	383	886	69	188	33	6	2	59	19	150	.212	.231	.270	36	-80	6	6	-2	.974	23	S-374/2-3,3-1	-3.4
■ LUIS SALAZAR	Salazar, Luis Ernesto (Garcia) b: 5/19/56, Barcelona, Venez. BR/TR, 5'9", 180 lbs. Deb: 8/15/80																						
1980	SD-N	44	169	28	57	4	7	1	25	9	25	.337	.374	.462	140	8	11	2	2	.944	-2	3-42/O-4	0.8
1981	SD-N	109	400	37	121	19	6	3	38	16	72	.303	.331	.403	116	6	11	8	-2	.955	-1	3-94,O-23	0.2
1982	SD-N	145	524	55	127	15	5	8	62	23	80	.242	.277	.336	75	-20	32	9	4	.938	16	*3-129,S-18/O-1	-0.1
1983	SD-N	134	481	52	124	16	2	14	45	17	80	.258	.286	.387	88	-10	24	9	2	.949	10	*3-118,S-19	0.2
1984	*SD-N	93	228	20	55	7	2	3	17	6	38	.241	.261	.329	65	-11	11	7	-1	.970	5	3-58,O-24/S-4	-0.9
1985	Chi-A	122	327	39	80	18	2	10	45	12	60	.245	.271	.404	79	-10	14	4	2	.968	-19	O-84,3-39/1-6,D-8	-3.0
1986	Chi-A	4	7	1	1	0	0	0	0	1	3	.143	.250	.143	10	-1	0	0	0	.000	0	/D-2	-0.1
1987	SD-N	84	189	13	48	5	0	3	17	14	30	.254	.305	.328	70	-8	3	3	-1	.957	-9	3-38,S-22,O-10,/P1	-1.7
1988	Det-A	130	452	61	122	14	1	12	62	21	70	.270	.307	.385	96	-4	6	0	2	.992	-10	O-68,S-37,3-31,/21	-1.1
1989	SD-N	95	246	27	66	7	2	8	22	11	44	.268	.302	.411	102	-0	1	3	-2	.968	7	3-72,O-14/S-9,1-2	0.6
	*Chi-N	26	80	7	26	5	0	1	12	4	13	.325	.357	.425	114	1	0	1	-1	.921	-6	3-25/O-2	-0.5
	Yr	121	326	34	92	12	2	9	34	15	57	.282	.316	.414	105	1	1	4	-2	.959	1	3-97,O-16/S-9,1-2	0.1
1990	Chi-N	115	410	44	104	13	3	12	47	19	59	.254	.293	.388	80	-12	3	1	0	.950	-20	3-91,O-28	-3.3

YEAR	TM/L	G	AB	R	H	2B	3B	HR	RBI	BB	SO	AVG	OBP	SLG	PRO+	BR/A	SB	CS	SBR	FA	FR	G/POS	TPR
1991	Chi-N	103	333	34	86	14	1	14	38	15	45	.258	.292	.432	97	-3	0	3	-2	.956	-7	3-86/1-7,O-1	-1.2
1992	Chi-N	98	255	20	53	7	2	5	25	11	34	.208	.241	.310	53	-16	1	1	-0	.935	3	3-40,O-34,S-12,/1-5	-1.5
Total	13	1302	4101	438	1070	144	33	94	455	179	653	.261	.294	.381	88	-79	117	51	5	.950	-33	3-863,O-293,S/1D2P	-11.6

■ **ED SALES** Sales, Edward A. b: 1861, Harrisburg, Pa. d: 8/10/12, New Haven, Conn. BL/TR, Deb: 7/15/1890

YEAR	TM/L	G	AB	R	H	2B	3B	HR	RBI	BB	SO	AVG	OBP	SLG	PRO+	BR/A	SB	CS	SBR	FA	FR	G/POS	TPR
1890	Pit-N	51	189	19	43	7	3	1	23	16	15	.228	.298	.312	88	-3	3			.871	-14	S-51	-1.2

■ **BILL SALKELD** Salkeld, William Franklin b: 3/8/17, Pocatello, Idaho d: 4/22/67, Los Angeles, Cal. BL/TR, 5'10", 190 lbs. Deb: 4/18/45 F

YEAR	TM/L	G	AB	R	H	2B	3B	HR	RBI	BB	SO	AVG	OBP	SLG	PRO+	BR/A	SB	CS	SBR	FA	FR	G/POS	TPR
1945	Pit-N	95	267	45	83	16	1	15	52	50	16	.311	.420	.547	161	23	2			.973	-9	C-86	1.9
1946	Pit-N	69	160	18	47	8	0	3	19	39	16	.294	.432	.400	133	9	2			.972	-1	C-51	1.2
1947	Pit-N	47	61	5	13	2	0	0	8	6	8	.213	.284	.246	41	-5	0			.971	-3	C-15	-0.7
1948	*Bos-N	78	198	26	48	8	1	8	28	42	37	.242	.378	.414	116	6	1			.990	5	C-59	1.5
1949	Bos-N	66	161	17	41	5	0	5	25	44	24	.255	.417	.379	121	8	1			.980	-4	C-63	0.7
1950	Chi-A	1	3	0	0	0	0	0	0	1	0	.000	.250	.000	-33	-1	0	0	0	1.000	-0	/C-1	-0.1
Total	6	356	850	111	232	39	2	31	132	182	101	.273	.402	.433	129	40	6	0		.979	-11	C-275	4.5

■ **CHICO SALMON** Salmon, Ruthford Eduardo b: 12/3/40, Colon, Panama BR/TR, 5'10", 170 lbs. Deb: 6/28/64

YEAR	TM/L	G	AB	R	H	2B	3B	HR	RBI	BB	SO	AVG	OBP	SLG	PRO+	BR/A	SB	CS	SBR	FA	FR	G/POS	TPR
1964	Cle-A	86	283	43	87	17	2	4	25	13	37	.307	.342	.424	113	4	10	6	-1	1.000	-8	O-53,2-32,1-13	-0.4
1965	Cle-A	79	120	20	29	8	0	3	12	5	19	.242	.283	.383	87	-2	7	4	-0	.985	-6	1-28,O-17/2-5,3-5	-1.0
1966	Cle-A	126	422	46	108	13	2	7	40	21	41	.256	.291	.346	82	-10	10	1	2	.958	-18	S-61,2-28,1-24,O/3	-2.2
1967	Cle-A	90	203	19	46	13	1	2	19	17	29	.227	.290	.330	82	-5	10	4	1	1.000	1	O-28,1-24,2-24,S/3	-0.2
1968	Cle-A	103	276	24	59	8	1	3	12	12	30	.214	.254	.283	63	-13	7	7	-2	.971	-15	2-45,3-18,S-15,O1	-3.1
1969	*Bal-A	52	91	18	27	5	0	3	12	10	22	.297	.379	.451	130	4	0	0	0	1.000	-5	1-17/2-9,S-9,3-3,O	-0.1
1970	*Bal-A	63	172	19	43	4	0	7	22	8	30	.250	.287	.395	85	-4	2	2	-1	.946	-20	S-33,2-12,3-11,/1-2	-2.2
1971	Bal-A	42	84	11	15	1	0	2	7	3	21	.179	.207	.262	32	-8	0	0	0	1.000	-3	/1-9,2-9,3-6,S-5	-1.1
1972	Bal-A	17	16	2	1	1	0	0	0	0	4	.063	.063	.125	-44	-3	0	0	0	1.000	0	/1-2,3-1	-0.3
Total	9	658	1667	202	415	70	6	31	149	89	233	.249	.291	.354	84	-36	46	24	-1	.959	-75	2-164,S-137,1O/3	-10.6

■ **TIM SALMON** Salmon, Timothy James b: 8/24/68, Long Beach, Cal. BR/TR, 6'3", 220 lbs. Deb: 8/21/92

YEAR	TM/L	G	AB	R	H	2B	3B	HR	RBI	BB	SO	AVG	OBP	SLG	PRO+	BR/A	SB	CS	SBR	FA	FR	G/POS	TPR
1992	Cal-A	23	79	8	14	1	0	2	6	11	23	.177	.286	.266	55	-5	1	1	-0	.953	-0	O-21	-0.6
1993	Cal-A	142	515	93	146	35	1	31	95	82	135	.283	.387	.536	141	30	5	6	-2	.980	15	*O-140/D-1	3.8
1994	Cal-A	100	373	67	107	18	2	23	70	54	102	.287	.384	.531	131	17	1	3	-2	.966	8	O-99	2.0
1995	Cal-A	143	537	111	177	34	3	34	105	91	111	.330	.432	.594	165	54	5	5	-2	.988	16	*O-142/D-1	**5.9**
1996	Cal-A	156	581	90	166	27	4	30	98	93	125	.286	.388	.501	122	21	4	2	0	.975	8	*O-153/D-3	2.3
1997	Ana-A	157	582	95	172	28	1	33	129	95	142	.296	.401	.517	138	34	9	12	-5	.971	19	*O-153/D-4	4.2
1998	Ana-A	136	463	84	139	28	1	26	88	90	100	.300	.417	.533	143	33	0	1	-1	.959	2	*D-111,O-19	2.5
Total	7	857	3130	548	921	171	12	179	591	516	738	.294	.399	.528	138	185	25	30	-11	.975	66	O-727,D-120	20.1

■ **JACK SALTZGAVER** Saltzgaver, Otto Hamlin b: 1/23/03, Croton, Iowa d: 2/1/78, Keokuk, Iowa BL/TR, 5'11", 165 lbs. Deb: 4/12/32

YEAR	TM/L	G	AB	R	H	2B	3B	HR	RBI	BB	SO	AVG	OBP	SLG	PRO+	BR/A	SB	CS	SBR	FA	FR	G/POS	TPR
1932	NY-A	20	47	10	6	2	1	0	5	10	10	.128	.281	.213	31	-5	1	1	-0	.958	-3	2-16	-0.7
1934	NY-A	94	350	64	95	8	1	6	36	48	28	.271	.359	.351	90	-4	8	1	2	.953	-16	3-84/1-4	-1.4
1935	NY-A	61	149	17	39	6	0	3	18	23	12	.262	.368	.362	95	-1	0	2	-1	.937	-13	2-25,3-18/1-6	-1.2
1936	NY-A	34	90	14	19	5	0	1	13	13	18	.211	.311	.300	53	-7	0	0	0	.972	-5	3-16/2-6,1-4	-0.9
1937	NY-A	17	11	6	2	0	0	0	0	3	4	.182	.357	.182	40	-1	0	0	0	1.000	-0	/1-4	-0.1
1945	Pit-N	52	117	20	38	5	3	0	10	8	8	.325	.368	.419	114	2	0			.963	-4	2-31/3-1	0.0
Total	6	278	764	131	199	26	5	10	82	105	80	.260	.351	.347	85	-15	9	4		.957	-40	3-119/2-78,1-18	-4.3

■ **ED SAMCOFF** Samcoff, Edward William b: 9/1/24, Sacramento, Cal. BR/TR, 5'10", 165 lbs. Deb: 4/21/51

YEAR	TM/L	G	AB	R	H	2B	3B	HR	RBI	BB	SO	AVG	OBP	SLG	PRO+	BR/A	SB	CS	SBR	FA	FR	G/POS	TPR
1951	Phi-A	4	11	0	0	0	0	0	0	1	2	.000	.083	.000	-75	-3	0	0	0	1.000	-2	/2-3	-0.4

■ **RON SAMFORD** Samford, Ronald Edward b: 2/28/30, Dallas, Tex. BR/TR, 5'11", 156 lbs. Deb: 4/15/54

YEAR	TM/L	G	AB	R	H	2B	3B	HR	RBI	BB	SO	AVG	OBP	SLG	PRO+	BR/A	SB	CS	SBR	FA	FR	G/POS	TPR
1954	NY-N	12	5	2	0	0	0	0	0	0	1	.000	.000	.000	-99	-1	0	1	-1	1.000	1	/2-3	-0.1
1955	Det-A	1	1	0	0	0	0	0	0	0	1	.000	.000	.000	-99	-0	0	0	0	1.000	0	/S-1	0.0
1957	Det-A	54	91	6	20	1	2	0	5	6	15	.220	.276	.275	49	-6	1	0	0	.964	13	S-35,2-11/3-4	0.9
1959	Was-A	91	237	23	53	13	0	5	22	11	29	.224	.264	.342	65	-12	1	0	0	.947	0	S-64,2-23	-0.6
Total	4	158	334	31	73	14	2	5	27	17	46	.219	.263	.317	58	-20	2	1	0	.952	15	S-100/2-37,3-4	0.2

■ **BILL SAMPLE** Sample, William Amos b: 4/2/55, Roanoke, Va. BR/TR, 5'9", 175 lbs. Deb: 9/2/78

YEAR	TM/L	G	AB	R	H	2B	3B	HR	RBI	BB	SO	AVG	OBP	SLG	PRO+	BR/A	SB	CS	SBR	FA	FR	G/POS	TPR
1978	Tex-A	8	15	2	7	2	0	0	3	0	3	.467	.467	.600	197	2	0	0	0	.000	-1	/O-2,D-3	0.1
1979	Tex-A	128	325	60	95	21	2	5	35	37	28	.292	.368	.415	112	6	8	6	-1	1.000	-4	*O-103/D-9	-0.2
1980	Tex-A	99	204	29	53	10	0	4	19	18	15	.260	.338	.368	96	-1	8	5	-1	.973	-9	O-72/D-4	-1.3
1981	Tex-A	66	230	36	65	16	0	3	25	17	21	.283	.350	.391	120	6	4	1	1	.993	-1	O-64	0.4
1982	Tex-A	97	360	56	94	14	2	10	29	27	35	.261	.318	.394	99	-1	10	2	2	.981	2	O-91/D-1	0.0
1983	Tex-A	147	554	80	152	28	3	12	57	44	46	.274	.333	.401	103	2	44	8	8	.988	6	*O-146	1.2
1984	Tex-A	130	489	67	121	20	2	5	33	29	46	.247	.290	.327	68	-21	18	6	2	.986	0	*O-122/D-2	-2.3
1985	NY-A	59	139	18	40	5	0	1	15	9	10	.288	.340	.345	90	-2	2	1	0	.989	-4	O-55	-0.7
1986	Atl-N	92	200	23	57	11	0	6	14	14	26	.285	.341	.430	105	1	4	2	0	.986	-8	O-56/2-1	-0.8
Total	9	826	2516	371	684	127	9	46	230	195	230	.272	.331	.384	98	-7	98	31	11	.987	-19	O-711/D-19,2-1	-3.6

■ **AMADO SAMUEL** Samuel, Amado Ruperto b: 12/6/38, San Pedro De Macoris, D.R. BR/TR, 6'1", 170 lbs. Deb: 4/10/62

YEAR	TM/L	G	AB	R	H	2B	3B	HR	RBI	BB	SO	AVG	OBP	SLG	PRO+	BR/A	SB	CS	SBR	FA	FR	G/POS	TPR
1962	Mil-N	76	209	16	43	10	0	3	20	12	54	.206	.249	.297	47	-16	0	2	-1	.958	-4	S-36,2-28/3-3	-1.7
1963	Mil-N	15	17	0	3	1	0	0	0	0	4	.176	.176	.235	18	-2	0	1	-1	.786	2	/S-7,2-4	0.0
1964	NY-N	53	142	7	33	7	0	0	5	4	24	.232	.264	.282	55	-9	0	1	-1	.945	6	S-34,3-17/2-3	-0.2
Total	3	144	368	23	79	18	0	3	25	16	82	.215	.251	.288	49	-26	0	4	-2	.942	4	/S-77,2-35,3-20	-1.9

■ **JUAN SAMUEL** Samuel, Juan Milton b: 12/9/60, San Pedro De Macoris, D.R. BR/TR, 5'11", 170 lbs. Deb: 8/24/83

YEAR	TM/L	G	AB	R	H	2B	3B	HR	RBI	BB	SO	AVG	OBP	SLG	PRO+	BR/A	SB	CS	SBR	FA	FR	G/POS	TPR
1983	*Phi-N	18	65	14	18	1	2	2	5	4	16	.277	.329	.446	114	1	3	2	-0	.916	3	2-18	0.5
1984	Phi-N☆	160	701	105	191	36	**19**	15	69	28	168	.272	.307	.442	107	3	72	15	13	.962	-22	*2-160	-0.1
1985	Phi-N	161	663	101	175	31	13	19	74	33	141	.264	.305	.436	102	-0	53	19	5	.983	-2	*2-159	0.8
1986	Phi-N	145	591	90	157	36	12	16	78	26	142	.266	.306	.448	102	-1	42	14	4	.967	-9	*2-143	0.0
1987	Phi-N★	160	655	113	178	37	**15**	28	100	60	162	.272	.338	.502	115	12	35	15	2	.978	-19	*2-160	0.3
1988	Phi-N	157	629	68	153	32	9	12	67	39	151	.243	.300	.380	92	-7	33	10	4	.978	-26	*2-152/O-3,3-1	-2.5
1989	Phi-N	51	199	32	49	3	1	8	20	18	45	.246	.312	.392	100	-0	11	3	2	.993	5	O-50	0.5
	NY-N	86	333	37	76	13	1	3	28	24	75	.228	.300	.300	76	-10	31	9	4	.986	7	O-84	-0.2
	Yr	137	532	69	125	16	2	11	48	42	120	.235	.304	.335	85	-10	42	12	5	.989	11	*O-134	0.3
1990	LA-N	143	492	62	119	24	3	13	52	51	126	.242	.319	.382	95	-4	38	20	-1	.972	-5	*2-108,O-31	-0.9
1991	LA-N★	153	594	74	161	22	6	12	58	49	133	.271	.330	.389	104	2	23	8	2	.978	4	*2-152	1.2
1992	LA-N	47	122	7	32	3	1	0	15	7	22	.262	.308	.303	75	-4	2	2	-1	.974	-2	2-38/O-1	-0.6
	KC-A	29	102	15	29	5	3	0	8	7	27	.284	.336	.392	101	0	6	1	1	.903	-3	O-18,2-10	-0.2
1993	Cin-N	103	261	31	60	10	4	4	26	23	53	.230	.300	.345	72	-11	9	7	-2	.971	3	2-70/1-6,3-4,O-3	-0.7
1994	Det-A	59	136	32	42	9	5	5	21	10	26	.309	.369	.559	134	7	5	2	0	1.000	3	O-27,D-10/2-8,1-2	0.8
1995	Det-A	76	171	28	48	10	1	10	34	24	38	.281	.376	.526	132	8	5	4	-1	.983	-1	1-37,D-16/O-9,2-6	0.3
	KC-A	15	34	3	6	0	0	2	5	5	11	.176	.282	.353	63	-2	1	0	0	1.000	-2	/O-5,1-1,D-7	-0.3
	Yr	91	205	31	54	10	1	12	39	29	49	.263	.360	.498	121	6	6	4	-1	.984	-3	1-38,D-23,O-14,/2-6	0.0
1996	Tor-A	69	188	34	48	8	3	8	26	15	65	.255	.320	.457	94	-2	9	1	2	1.000	-8	O-24,D-24,1-17	-1.0
1997	Tor-A	45	95	13	27	5	4	3	15	10	28	.284	.364	.516	126	3	5	3	-0	1.000	-1	D-15/3-9,1-7,2-4,O	0.1
1998	Tor-A	43	50	14	9	2	0	1	2	7	13	.180	.293	.280	50	-4	13	8	-1	.882	-0	D-11,O-10/1-3,2-2	-0.5
Total	16	1720	6081	873	1578	287	102	161	703	440	1442	.259	.317	.420	101	-8	396	143	33	.973	-76	*2-1190,O-267/D13	-2.5

■ **IKE SAMULS** Samuls, Samuel Earl b: 2/20/1876, Chicago, Ill. d: 1/1/42, Los Angeles, Cal. BR/TR, Deb: 8/3/1895

YEAR	TM/L	G	AB	R	H	2B	3B	HR	RBI	BB	SO	AVG	OBP	SLG	PRO+	BR/A	SB	CS	SBR	FA	FR	G/POS	TPR
1895	StL-N	24	74	5	17	2	0	0	5	5	7	.230	.278	.257	39	-7	5			.750	-3	3-21/S-3	-0.8

■ GUS SANBERG
Sanberg, Gustave E. b: 2/23/1896, Long Island City, N.Y. d: 2/3/30, Los Angeles, Cal. BR/TR, 6′1″, 189 lbs. Deb: 5/11/23

YEAR	TM/L	G	AB	R	H	2B	3B	HR	RBI	BB	SO	AVG	OBP	SLG	PRO+	BR/A	SB	CS	SBR	FA	FR	G/POS	TPR
1923	Cin-N	7	17	1	3	1	0	0	1	1	1	.176	.222	.235	21	-2	0	0	0	1.000	-1	/C-5	-0.3
1924	Cin-N	24	52	1	9	0	0	0	3	2	7	.173	.204	.173	2	-7	0	0	0	1.000	0	C-24	-0.6
Total	2	31	69	2	12	1	0	0	4	3	8	.174	.208	.188	7	-9	0	0	0	1.000	-1	/C-29	-0.9

■ ALEJANDRO SANCHEZ
Sanchez, Alejandro (Pimentel) b: 2/14/59, San Pedro De Macoris, D.R. BR/TR, 6′, 185 lbs. Deb: 9/6/82

YEAR	TM/L	G	AB	R	H	2B	3B	HR	RBI	BB	SO	AVG	OBP	SLG	PRO+	BR/A	SB	CS	SBR	FA	FR	G/POS	TPR
1982	Phi-N	7	14	3	4	1	0	2	4	0	4	.286	.286	.786	186	1	0	0	0	1.000	-0	/O-4	0.1
1983	Phi-N	8	7	2	2	0	0	0	2	0	2	.286	.286	.286	59	-0	0	0	0	.500	-1	/O-2	-0.1
1984	SF-N	13	41	3	8	0	1	0	2	0	12	.195	.195	.244	23	-4	2	3	-1	.952	0	O-11	-0.6
1985	Det-A	71	133	19	33	6	2	6	12	0	39	.248	.248	.459	89	-3	2	2	-1	.923	-6	O-31,D-28	-1.0
1986	Min-A	8	16	1	2	0	0	0	1	1	8	.125	.176	.125	-16	-3	0	0	0	.000	-0	/O-1,D-3	-0.3
1987	Oak-A	2	3	0	0	0	0	0	0	0	1	.000	.000	.000	-99	-1	0	0	0	1.000	-0	/O-1,D-1	-0.1
Total	6	109	214	28	49	7	3	8	21	1	66	.229	.233	.402	71	-9	4	5	-2	.929	-7	/O-50,D-32	-2.0

■ CELERINO SANCHEZ
Sanchez, Celerino (Perez) b: 2/3/44, Veracruz, Mexico d: 5/1/92, Leon, Mexico BR/TR, 5′11″, 160 lbs. Deb: 6/13/72

YEAR	TM/L	G	AB	R	H	2B	3B	HR	RBI	BB	SO	AVG	OBP	SLG	PRO+	BR/A	SB	CS	SBR	FA	FR	G/POS	TPR
1972	NY-A	71	250	18	62	8	3	0	22	12	30	.248	.293	.304	81	-6	0	0	0	.939	4	3-68	-0.4
1973	NY-A	34	64	12	14	3	0	1	9	2	12	.219	.242	.313	57	-4	1	1	-0	1.000	1	3-11,D-11/S-2,O-2	-0.3
Total	2	105	314	30	76	11	3	1	31	14	42	.242	.283	.306	76	-10	1	1	-0	.943	5	/3-79,D-11,O-2,S-2	-0.7

■ ORLANDO SANCHEZ
Sanchez, Orlando (Marquez) b: 9/7/56, Canovanas, P.R. BL/TR, 6′1″, 195 lbs. Deb: 5/6/81

YEAR	TM/L	G	AB	R	H	2B	3B	HR	RBI	BB	SO	AVG	OBP	SLG	PRO+	BR/A	SB	CS	SBR	FA	FR	G/POS	TPR
1981	StL-N	27	49	5	14	2	1	0	6	2	6	.286	.314	.367	90	-1	1	0	0	.926	-2	C-18	-0.2
1982	StL-N	26	37	6	7	0	1	0	3	5	5	.189	.286	.243	49	-2	0	0	0	1.000	-1	C-15	-0.3
1983	StL-N	6	6	0	0	0	0	0	0	0	4	.000	.000	.000	-99	-2	0	0	0	1.000	-0	/C-1	-0.2
1984	KC-A	10	10	0	1	1	0	0	2	0	2	.100	.100	.200	-19	-2	0	0	0	1.000	-0	/C-1	-0.2
	Bal-A	4	8	0	2	0	0	0	1	0	2	.250	.250	.250	40	-1	0	0	0	1.000	-0	/C-4	-0.1
	Yr	14	18	0	3	1	0	0	3	0	4	.167	.167	.222	7	-2	0	0	0	1.000	-0	/C-5	-0.3
Total	4	73	110	11	24	3	2	0	12	7	19	.218	.265	.282	53	-7	1	0	0	.962	-3	/C-39	-1.0

■ REY SANCHEZ
Sanchez, Rey Francisco (Guadalupe) b: 10/5/67, Rio Piedras, P.R. BR/TR, 5′9″, 170 lbs. Deb: 9/8/91

YEAR	TM/L	G	AB	R	H	2B	3B	HR	RBI	BB	SO	AVG	OBP	SLG	PRO+	BR/A	SB	CS	SBR	FA	FR	G/POS	TPR
1991	Chi-N	13	23	1	6	0	0	0	2	4	3	.261	.370	.261	77	-0	0	0	0	1.000	2	S-10/2-2	0.2
1992	Chi-N	74	255	24	64	14	3	1	19	10	17	.251	.287	.341	75	-9	2	1	0	.974	14	S-68/2-4	1.1
1993	Chi-N	105	344	35	97	11	2	0	28	15	22	.282	.318	.326	74	-13	1	1	-0	.969	27	S-98	2.1
1994	Chi-N	96	291	26	83	13	1	0	24	20	29	.285	.346	.337	80	-8	2	5	-2	.993	**29**	2-50,S-30,3-17	2.1
1995	Chi-N	114	428	57	119	22	2	3	27	14	48	.278	.302	.360	75	-16	6	4	-1	.987	4	*2-111/S-4	-0.6
1996	Chi-N	95	289	28	61	9	0	1	12	22	42	.211	.274	.253	39	-25	7	1	2	.977	22	S-92	0.6
1997	Chi-N	97	205	14	51	9	0	1	12	11	26	.249	.287	.307	54	-14	4	2	0	.964	-0	S-63,2-32/3-1	-1.0
	*NY-A	38	138	21	43	12	0	1	15	5	21	.312	.340	.420	98	-1	0	4	-2	.976	-1	2-37/S-6	-0.2
1998	SF-N	109	316	44	90	14	2	2	30	16	47	.285	.327	.361	81	-9	0	0	0	.977	15	S-76,2-36	1.4
Total	8	741	2289	250	614	104	10	9	169	117	255	.268	.310	.334	71	-93	22	18	-4	.973	111	S-447,2-272/3-18	5.7

■ HEINIE SAND
Sand, John Henry b: 7/3/1897, San Francisco, Cal d: 11/3/58, San Francisco, Cal. BR/TR, 5′8″, 160 lbs. Deb: 4/17/23

YEAR	TM/L	G	AB	R	H	2B	3B	HR	RBI	BB	SO	AVG	OBP	SLG	PRO+	BR/A	SB	CS	SBR	FA	FR	G/POS	TPR
1923	Phi-N	132	470	85	107	16	5	4	32	82	56	.228	.347	.309	67	-21	7	3	0	.934	-2	*S-120,3-11	-1.0
1924	Phi-N	137	539	79	132	21	6	6	40	52	57	.245	.316	.340	67	-25	5	4	-1	**.959**	2	*S-137	-0.9
1925	Phi-N	148	496	69	138	30	7	3	55	64	65	.278	.364	.385	84	-11	1	1	-0	.928	-6	*S-143	-0.2
1926	Phi-N	149	567	99	154	30	5	4	37	66	56	.272	.350	.363	88	-9	2			.939	-3	*S-149	0.3
1927	Phi-N	141	535	87	160	22	8	1	49	58	59	.299	.369	.376	98	0	5			.949	-15	S-86,3-58	-0.3
1928	Phi-N	141	426	38	90	26	1	0	38	60	47	.211	.310	.277	53	-29	1			.951	-1	*S-137	-1.4
Total	6	848	3033	457	781	145	32	18	251	382	340	.258	.343	.344	77	-94	21	8		.943	-25	S-772/3-69	-3.5

■ RYNE SANDBERG
Sandberg, Ryne Dee b: 9/18/59, Spokane, Wash. BR/TR, 6′2″, 180 lbs. Deb: 9/2/81

YEAR	TM/L	G	AB	R	H	2B	3B	HR	RBI	BB	SO	AVG	OBP	SLG	PRO+	BR/A	SB	CS	SBR	FA	FR	G/POS	TPR
1981	Phi-N	13	6	2	1	0	0	0	0	0	1	.167	.167	.167	-5	-1	0	0	0	1.000	4	/S-5,2-1	0.3
1982	Chi-N	156	635	103	172	33	5	7	54	36	90	.271	.314	.372	89	-10	32	12	2	.970	5	*3-133,2-24	-0.5
1983	Chi-N	158	633	94	165	25	4	8	48	51	79	.261	.319	.351	81	-16	37	11	5	**.986**	**41**	*2-157/S-1	3.8
1984	*Chi-N★	156	636	**114**	200	36	**19**	19	84	52	101	.314	.369	.520	135	28	32	7	5	**.993**	23	*2-156	**6.4**
1985	Chi-N★	153	609	113	186	31	6	26	83	57	97	.305	.366	.504	127	21	54	11	10	.986	8	*2-153/S-1	4.6
1986	Chi-N★	154	627	68	178	28	5	14	76	46	79	.284	.333	.411	97	-4	34	11	4	**.994**	5	*2-153	1.2
1987	Chi-N★	132	523	81	154	25	2	16	59	59	79	.294	.368	.442	109	8	21	2	5	.985	1	*2-131	2.0
1988	Chi-N★	155	618	77	163	23	8	19	69	54	91	.264	.324	.419	107	5	25	10	2	.987	11	*2-153	2.5
1989	*Chi-N★	157	606	**104**	176	25	5	30	76	59	85	.290	.357	.497	132	24	15	5	2	.992	1	*2-155	3.3
1990	Chi-N★	155	615	**116**	188	30	3	**40**	100	50	84	.306	.359	.559	138	30	25	7	3	.989	7	*2-154	4.3
1991	Chi-N★	158	585	104	170	32	2	26	100	87	89	.291	.384	.485	137	30	22	8	2	**.995**	11	*2-157	4.7
1992	Chi-N★	158	612	100	186	32	8	26	87	68	73	.304	.374	.510	145	35	17	6	2	.990	14	*2-157	5.7
1993	Chi-N★	117	456	67	141	20	0	9	45	37	62	.309	.364	.412	109	6	9	2	2	.988	-4	*2-115	0.7
1994	Chi-N	57	223	36	53	9	5	5	24	23	40	.238	.312	.390	83	-6	2	3	-1	.987	3	2-57	-0.1
1996	Chi-N	150	554	85	135	28	4	25	92	54	116	.244	.319	.444	96	-4	12	8	-1	.991	-12	*2-146	-0.8
1997	Chi-N	135	447	54	118	26	0	12	64	28	94	.264	.310	.403	83	-12	7	4	-0	.984	-25	*2-126/D-1	-3.0
Total	16	2164	8385	1318	2386	403	76	282	1061	761	1260	.285	.347	.452	113	134	344	107	39	.989	93	*2-1995,3-133/S-7,D	35.1

■ BEN SANDERS
Sanders, Alexander Bennett b: 2/16/1865, Catharpin, Va. d: 8/29/30, Memphis, Tenn. BR/TR, 6′, 210 lbs. Deb: 6/6/1888

YEAR	TM/L	G	AB	R	H	2B	3B	HR	RBI	BB	SO	AVG	OBP	SLG	PRO+	BR/A	SB	CS	SBR	FA	FR	G/POS	TPR
1888	Phi-N	57	236	26	58	11	2	1	25	8	12	.246	.276	.322	86	-4	13			.929	3	P-31,O-25/3-1	-0.3
1889	Phi-N	44	169	21	47	8	2	0	21	6	11	.278	.307	.349	76	-6	4			.879	-3	P-44/O-3	-0.1
1890	Phi-P	52	189	31	59	6	6	0	30	10	10	.312	.347	.407	99	-1	2			.924	1	P-43,O-10	-0.1
1891	Phi-a	40	156	24	39	6	4	1	19	7	12	.250	.291	.359	83	-5	2			.839	-6	O-22,P-19	-0.7
1892	Lou-N	54	198	30	54	12	2	3	18	16	17	.273	.330	.399	131	7	6			.930	-3	P-31,1-15/O-9	0.0
Total	5	247	948	132	257	43	16	5	113	47	62	.271	.310	.366	95	-9	27			.916	-8	P-168/O-69,1-15,3-1	-1.2

■ DEION SANDERS
Sanders, Deion Luwynn b: 8/9/67, Ft.Myers, Fla. BL/TL, 6′1″, 195 lbs. Deb: 5/31/89

YEAR	TM/L	G	AB	R	H	2B	3B	HR	RBI	BB	SO	AVG	OBP	SLG	PRO+	BR/A	SB	CS	SBR	FA	FR	G/POS	TPR
1989	NY-A	14	47	7	11	2	0	2	7	3	8	.234	.280	.404	92	-1	1	0	0	.969	-0	O-14	-0.1
1990	NY-A	57	133	24	21	2	2	3	9	13	27	.158	.238	.271	42	-11	8	2	1	.973	-4	O-42/D-4	-1.5
1991	Atl-N	54	110	16	21	1	2	4	13	12	23	.191	.270	.345	68	-5	11	3	2	.952	-5	O-44	-0.9
1992	*Atl-N	97	303	54	92	6	**14**	8	28	18	52	.304	.347	.495	128	10	26	9	2	.983	-1	O-75	1.1
1993	*Atl-N	95	272	42	75	18	6	6	28	16	42	.276	.323	.452	104	1	19	7	2	.986	-0	O-60	0.1
1994	Atl-N	46	191	32	55	10	0	4	21	16	28	.288	.346	.403	93	-2	19	7	2	.980	-2	O-46	-0.3
	Cin-N	46	184	26	51	7	4	0	7	16	35	.277	.342	.359	84	-4	19	9	0	1.000	2	O-45	-0.3
	Yr	92	375	58	106	17	4	4	28	32	63	.283	.344	.381	88	-6	38	16	2	.991	0	O-91	-0.6
1995	Cin-N	33	129	19	31	2	3	1	10	9	18	.240	.300	.326	65	-6	16	3	3	.968	4	O-33	0.0
	SF-N	52	214	29	61	9	5	5	18	18	42	.285	.345	.444	110	3	8	6	-1	.981	1	O-52	0.1
	Yr	85	343	48	92	11	8	6	28	27	60	.268	.329	.399	93	-4	24	9	2	.977	5	O-85	0.1
1997	Cin-N	115	465	53	127	13	7	5	23	34	67	.273	.331	.363	81	-13	56	13	9	.984	6	*O-113	0.0
Total	8	609	2048	302	545	70	43	38	164	155	342	.266	.324	.398	91	-28	183	59	20	.981	0	O-524/D-4	-1.8

■ JOHN SANDERS
Sanders, John Frank b: 11/20/45, Grand Island, Neb. BR/TR, 6′2″, 200 lbs. Deb: 4/13/65

YEAR	TM/L	G	AB	R	H	2B	3B	HR	RBI	BB	SO	AVG	OBP	SLG	PRO+	BR/A	SB	CS	SBR	FA	FR	G/POS	TPR
1965	KC-A	1	0	0	0	0	0	0	0	0	0	—	—	—	—	0	0	0	0	.000	0	R	0.0

■ RAY SANDERS
Sanders, Raymond Floyd b: 12/4/16, Bonne Terre, Mo. d: 10/28/83, Washington, Mo. BL/TR, 6′2″, 185 lbs. Deb: 4/14/42

YEAR	TM/L	G	AB	R	H	2B	3B	HR	RBI	BB	SO	AVG	OBP	SLG	PRO+	BR/A	SB	CS	SBR	FA	FR	G/POS	TPR
1942	*StL-N	95	282	37	71	17	2	5	39	42	31	.252	.351	.379	106	3	2			.991	-4	1-77	-0.6
1943	*StL-N	144	478	69	134	21	5	11	73	77	33	.280	.381	.414	124	17	1			.995	-7	*1-141	-0.2
1944	*StL-N	154	601	87	177	34	9	12	102	71	50	.295	.371	.441	126	21	2			**.994**	-13	*1-152	0.0
1945	StL-N	143	537	85	148	29	3	8	78	83	55	.276	.375	.385	109	9	3			.986	-5	*1-142	-0.5
1946	Bos-N	80	259	43	63	12	0	6	35	50	38	.243	.368	.359	105	3	0			.988	4	1-77	0.3
1948	*Bos-N	5	4	0	1	0	0	0	2	1	0	.250	.400	.250	81	-0	0			.000	0	H	0.0

YEAR	TM/L	G	AB	R	H	2B	3B	HR	RBI	BB	SO	AVG	OBP	SLG	PRO+	BR/A	SB	CS	SBR	FA	FR	G/POS	TPR
1949	Bos-N	9	21	0	3	1	0	0	0	4	9	.143	.280	.190	30	-2	0			.984	2	/1-7	0.0
Total	7	630	2182	321	597	114	19	42	329	328	216	.274	.370	.401	115	50	8			.991	-22	1-596	-0.6
■ REGGIE SANDERS	Sanders, Reginald Jerome b: 9/9/49, Birmingham, Ala. BR/TR, 6'2", 205 lbs. Deb: 9/1/74																						
1974	Det-A	26	99	12	27	7	0	3	10	5	20	.273	.308	.434	108	1	1	0	0	.987	1	1-25/D-1	0.0
■ REGGIE SANDERS	Sanders, Reginald Laverne b: 12/1/67, Florence, S.C. BR/TR, 6'1", 186 lbs. Deb: 8/22/91																						
1991	Cin-N	9	40	6	8	0	0	1	3	0	9	.200	.200	.275	31	-4	1	1	-0	1.000	1	/O-9	-0.4
1992	Cin-N	116	385	62	104	26	6	12	36	48	98	.270	.357	.462	127	14	16	7	1	.978	5	*O-110	1.9
1993	Cin-N	138	496	90	136	16	4	20	83	51	118	.274	.348	.444	110	7	27	10	2	.975	8	*O-137	1.4
1994	Cin-N	107	400	66	105	20	8	17	62	41	114	.262	.334	.480	110	5	21	9	1	.975	12	*O-104	1.5
1995	*Cin-N★	133	484	91	148	36	6	28	99	69	122	.306	.401	.579	155	39	36	12	4	.983	5	*O-130	4.3
1996	Cin-N	81	287	49	72	17	1	14	33	44	86	.251	.354	.463	113	6	24	8	2	.988	7	O-80	1.3
1997	Cin-N	86	312	52	79	19	2	19	56	42	93	.253	.347	.510	119	8	13	7	-0	.974	8	O-85	1.3
1998	Cin-N	135	481	83	129	18	6	14	59	51	137	.268	.347	.418	96	-3	20	9	1	.978	-6	*O-131	-0.8
Total	8	805	2885	499	781	152	33	125	431	346	777	.271	.355	.476	118	72	158	63	10	.979	39	O-786	10.5
■ MIKE SANDLOCK	Sandlock, Michael Joseph b: 10/17/15, Old Greenwich, Conn. BB/TR, 6'1", 185 lbs. Deb: 9/19/42																						
1942	Bos-N	2	1	1	1	0	0	0	0	0	0	1.000	1.000	1.000	496	0	0			.000	0	/S-2	0.1
1944	Bos-N	30	30	1	3	0	0	0	2	5	3	.100	.250	.100	1	-4	0			.956	7	3-22/S-7	0.3
1945	Bro-N	80	195	21	55	14	2	2	17	18	19	.282	.346	.405	109	2	2			.991	1	C-47,S-22/2-4,3-2	0.6
1946	Bro-N	19	34	1	5	0	0	0	0	3	4	.147	.216	.147	4	-4	0			.973	6	C-17/3-1	0.3
1953	Pit-N	64	186	10	43	5	0	0	12	12	19	.231	.281	.258	42	-16	0	0	0	.991	16	C-64	0.3
Total	5	195	446	34	107	19	2	2	31	38	45	.240	.304	.305	66	-21	2	0		.989	30	C-128/S-31,3-25,2-4	1.6
■ CHARLIE SANDS	Sands, Charles Duane b: 12/17/47, Newport News, Va. BL/TR, 6'2", 215 lbs. Deb: 6/21/67																						
1967	NY-A	1	1	0	0	0	0	0	0	0	1	.000	.000	.000	-99	-0	0	0	0	.000	0	H	0.0
1971	*Pit-N	28	25	4	5	2	0	1	5	7	6	.200	.375	.400	120	1	0	0	0	1.000	0	/C-3	0.1
1972	Pit-N	1	1	0	0	0	0	0	0	0	0	.000	.000	.000	-99	-0	0	0	0	.000	0	H	0.0
1973	Cal-A	17	33	5	9	2	1	1	5	5	10	.273	.368	.485	150	2	0	0	0	.917	-8	C-10	-0.5
1974	Cal-A	43	83	6	16	2	0	4	13	23	17	.193	.374	.361	119	3	0	0	0	1.000	-1	D-21/C-5	0.2
1975	Oak-A	3	2	0	1	0	0	0	0	1	1	.500	.667	.500	239	1	0	0	0	.000	0	/D-1	0.1
Total	6	93	145	15	31	6	1	6	23	36	35	.214	.374	.393	125	6	0	0	0	.955	-8	/D-22,C-18	-0.1
■ TOMMY SANDT	Sandt, Thomas James b: 12/22/50, Brooklyn, N.Y. BR/TR, 5'11", 175 lbs. Deb: 6/29/75 C																						
1975	Oak-A	1	0	0	0	0	0	0	0	0	0	—	—	—	—	0	0	0	0	.000	0	/2-1	0.0
1976	Oak-A	41	67	6	14	1	0	0	3	7	9	.209	.284	.224	52	-4	0	0	0	.966	3	S-29/2-9,3-2	0.1
Total	2	42	67	6	14	1	0	0	3	7	9	.209	.284	.224	52	-4	0	0	0	1.000	3	/S-29,2-10,3-2	0.1
■ CHANCE SANFORD	Sanford, Chance Steven b: 6/2/72, Houston, Tex. BL/TR, 5'10", 165 lbs. Deb: 4/30/98																						
1998	Pit-N	14	28	3	4	1	1	0	3	1	6	.143	.172	.250	8	-4	0	0	0	.900	-3	/3-5,2-1,S-1	-0.7
■ JACK SANFORD	Sanford, John Doward b: 6/23/17, Chatham, Va. BR/TR, 6'3", 195 lbs. Deb: 8/24/40																						
1940	Was-A	34	122	5	24	4	2	0	10	6	17	.197	.234	.262	30	-13	0	0	0	.993	-2	1-34	-1.7
1941	Was-A	3	5	1	2	0	1	0	0	1	1	.400	.500	.800	251	1	0	0	0	1.000	-0	/1-1	0.1
1946	Was-A	10	26	7	6	0	1	0	1	2	6	.231	.286	.308	70	-1	0	0	0	.971	-2	/1-6	-0.3
Total	3	47	153	13	32	4	4	0	11	9	24	.209	.253	.288	44	-13	0	0	0	.989	-4	/1-41	-1.9
■ MANNY SANGUILLEN	Sanguillen, Manuel De Jesus (Magan) b: 3/21/44, Colon, Panama BR/TR, 6', 193 lbs. Deb: 7/23/67																						
1967	Pit-N	30	96	6	26	4	0	0	8	4	12	.271	.300	.313	75	-3	0	1	-1	.986	-5	C-28	-0.8
1969	Pit-N	129	459	62	139	21	6	5	57	12	48	.303	.325	.407	106	2	8	4	0	.981	4	*C-113	1.3
1970	*Pit-N	128	486	63	158	19	9	7	61	17	45	.325	.348	.444	113	7	2	3	-1	.988	1	*C-125	1.3
1971	*Pit-N☆	138	533	60	170	26	5	7	81	19	32	.319	.346	.426	118	11	6	4	-1	.994	5	*C-135	2.2
1972	*Pit-N★	136	520	55	155	18	8	7	71	21	38	.298	.325	.404	108	4	1	2	-1	.988	-3	*C-127/O-2	0.6
1973	Pit-N	149	589	64	166	26	7	12	65	17	29	.282	.305	.411	99	-3	2	5	-2	.983	4	C-89,O-59	-0.1
1974	*Pit-N	151	596	77	171	21	4	7	68	21	27	.287	.317	.371	95	-6	2	2	-1	.985	-6	*C-151	-0.7
1975	*Pit-N☆	133	481	60	158	24	4	9	58	48	31	.328	.393	.451	135	23	5	4	-1	.987	-5	*C-132	2.4
1976	Pit-N	114	389	52	113	16	6	2	36	28	18	.290	.341	.378	103	1	2	4	-2	.978	-7	*C-111	-0.4
1977	Oak-A	152	571	42	157	17	5	6	58	22	35	.275	.304	.354	80	-16	2	5	-2	.985	-8	C-77,D-58/O-9,1-7	-2.7
1978	Pit-N	85	220	15	58	5	1	3	16	9	10	.264	.299	.336	74	-8	2	2	-1	1.000	-2	1-40,C-18	-1.3
1979	*Pit-N	56	74	8	17	5	2	0	4	2	5	.230	.250	.351	59	-4	0	0	0	.947	0	/C-8,1-5	-0.4
1980	Pit-N	47	48	2	12	3	0	0	2	3	1	.250	.294	.313	68	-2	3	2	-0	.956	0	/1-5	-0.2
Total	13	1448	5062	566	1500	205	57	65	585	223	331	.296	.329	.398	103	6	35	38	-12	.986	-23	*C-1114/O-70,D-58,1	1.2
■ ED SANICKI	Sanicki, Edward Robert "Butch" b: 7/7/23, Wallington, N.J. d: 7/6/98, Old Bridge, N.J. BR/TR, 5'9", 175 lbs. Deb: 9/14/49																						
1949	Phi-N	7	13	4	3	0	0	3	7	1	4	.231	.286	.923	217	2	0			1.000	-1	/O-6	0.1
1951	Phi-N	13	4	1	2	1	0	0	1	1	1	.500	.600	.750	265	1	1	0	0	1.000	-4	O-10	-0.3
Total	2	20	17	5	5	1	0	3	8	2	5	.294	.368	.882	231	3	1	0		1.000	-5	/O-16	-0.2
■ BEN SANKEY	Sankey, Benjamin Turner b: 9/2/07, Nauvoo, Ala. BR/TR, 5'10", 155 lbs. Deb: 10/5/29																						
1929	Pit-N	2	7	1	1	0	0	0	0	0	1	.143	.143	.143	-28	-1	0			.909	-0	/S-2	-0.1
1930	Pit-N	13	30	6	5	0	0	0	0	2	3	.167	.219	.167	-5	-5	0			.871	-0	/S-6,2-4	-0.4
1931	Pit-N	57	132	14	30	2	5	0	14	14	10	.227	.301	.318	67	-6	0			.920	-9	S-49/2-2,3-2	-1.1
Total	3	72	169	21	36	2	5	0	14	16	14	.213	.281	.284	49	-13	0			.914	-10	/S-57,2-6,3-2	-1.6
■ ANDRES SANTANA	Santana, Andres Confesor (Belonis) b: 2/5/68, San Pedro De Macoris, D.R. BB/TR, 5'11", 160 lbs. Deb: 9/16/90																						
1990	SF-N	6	2	0	0	0	0	0	1	0	0	.000	.000	.000	-99	-1	0	0	0	1.000	1	/S-3	0.0
■ RAFAEL SANTANA	Santana, Rafael Francisco (De La Cruz) b: 1/31/58, LaRomana, D.R. BR/TR, 6'1", 165 lbs. Deb: 4/5/83																						
1983	StL-N	30	14	1	3	0	0	0	2	2	2	.214	.353	.214	61	-1	0	1	-1	.857	2	/2-9,S-6,3-4	0.1
1984	NY-N	51	152	14	42	11	1	1	12	9	17	.276	.317	.382	97	-1	0	3	-2	.970	-3	S-50	-0.1
1985	NY-N	154	529	41	136	19	1	1	29	29	54	.257	.296	.302	69	-22	1	0	0	.965	-11	*S-153	-1.9
1986	*NY-N	139	394	38	86	11	0	1	28	36	43	.218	.287	.254	52	-25	0	0	0	.973	17	*S-137/2-1	0.2
1987	NY-N	139	439	41	112	21	2	5	44	29	57	.255	.303	.346	75	-16	1	1	-0	.973	15	*S-138	0.9
1988	NY-A	148	480	50	115	12	1	4	38	33	61	.240	.290	.294	64	-23	1	2	-1	.966	-9	*S-148	-2.1
1990	Cle-A	7	13	3	3	0	0	1	3	0	0	.231	.231	.462	89	-0	0	0	0	1.000	-2	/S-7	-0.2
Total	7	668	2021	188	497	74	5	13	156	138	234	.246	.296	.307	68	-88	3	7	-3	.969	9	S-639/2-10,3-4	-3.1
■ F. P. SANTANGELO	Santangelo, Frank-Paul b: 10/24/67, Livonia, Mich. BB/TR, 5'10", 165 lbs. Deb: 8/2/95																						
1995	Mon-N	35	98	11	29	5	1	1	9	12	9	.296	.384	.398	103	1	1	1	-0	.979	-1	O-25/2-5	-0.1
1996	Mon-N	152	393	54	109	20	5	7	56	49	61	.277	.373	.407	103	3	5	2	0	.983	5	*O-124,3-23/2-5,S-1	0.5
1997	Mon-N	130	350	56	87	19	5	5	31	50	73	.249	.381	.374	99	2	8	5	-1	1.000	-7	O-99,3-32/2-7,S-1	-0.6
1998	Mon-N	122	383	53	82	18	0	4	23	44	72	.214	.331	.292	66	-18	7	3	0	.983	-11	O-92,2-35/3-1	-2.7
Total	4	439	1224	174	307	62	11	17	119	155	215	.251	.363	.361	91	-11	21	11	-0	.987	-14	O-340/3-56,2-52,S-2	-2.9
■ BENITO SANTIAGO	Santiago, Benito (Rivera) b: 3/9/65, Ponce, P.R. BR/TR, 6'1", 182 lbs. Deb: 9/14/86																						
1986	SD-N	17	62	10	18	2	0	3	6	2	12	.290	.313	.468	115	1	0	1	-1	.946	-6	C-17	-0.5
1987	SD-N	146	546	64	164	33	2	18	79	16	112	.300	.326	.467	111	6	21	12	-1	.976	-7	*C-146	0.8
1988	SD-N	139	492	49	122	22	2	10	46	24	82	.248	.284	.362	86	-10	15	7	0	.985	-5	*C-136	-0.5
1989	SD-N★	129	462	50	109	16	3	16	62	26	89	.236	.278	.387	88	-9	11	6	-0	.975	-6	*C-127	-0.8
1990	SD-N†	100	344	42	93	8	5	11	53	27	55	.270	.329	.419	103	1	5	5	-2	.980	-5	C-98	0.1
1991	SD-N★	152	580	60	155	22	3	17	87	23	114	.267	.300	.403	93	-7	8	10	-4	.985	-1	*C-151/O-1	-0.2

YEAR	TM/L	G	AB	R	H	2B	3B	HR	RBI	BB	SO	AVG	OBP	SLG	PRO+	BR/A	SB	CS	SBR	FA	FR	G/POS	TPR
1992	SD-N★	106	386	37	97	21	0	10	42	21	52	.251	.290	.383	88	-7	2	5	-2	.982	-11	*C-103	-1.6
1993	Fla-N	139	469	49	108	19	6	13	50	37	88	.230	.294	.380	74	-18	10	7	-1	.987	-6	*C-136/O-1	-1.7
1994	Fla-N	101	337	35	92	14	2	11	41	25	57	.273	.325	.424	91	-5	1	2	-1	.991	3	C-97	0.3
1995	*Cin-N	81	266	40	76	20	0	11	44	24	48	.286	.354	.485	119	7	2	2	-1	.996	2	C-75/1-8	1.3
1996	Phi-N	136	481	71	127	21	2	30	85	49	104	.264	.333	.503	116	9	2	0	1	.987	-7	*C-114,1-14	0.8
1997	Tor-A	97	341	31	83	10	0	13	42	17	80	.243	.283	.387	72	-15	1	0	1	.997	-3	C-95/D-1	-1.1
1998	Tor-A	15	29	3	9	5	0	0	4	1	6	.310	.333	.483	109	0	0	0	0	1.000	-2	C-15	-0.1
Total	13	1358	4795	541	1253	213	25	163	641	292	899	.261	.307	.418	95	-45	78	57	-11	.985	-52	*C-1310/1-22,O-2,D	-3.2

■ RON SANTO
Santo, Ronald Edward b: 2/25/40, Seattle, Wash. BR/TR, 6', 190 lbs. Deb: 6/26/60

YEAR	TM/L	G	AB	R	H	2B	3B	HR	RBI	BB	SO	AVG	OBP	SLG	PRO+	BR/A	SB	CS	SBR	FA	FR	G/POS	TPR
1960	Chi-N	95	347	44	87	24	2	9	44	31	44	.251	.312	.409	97	-2	0	3	-2	.945	-19	3-94	-2.4
1961	Chi-N	154	578	84	164	32	6	23	83	73	77	.284	.364	.479	120	17	2	3	-1	.937	5	*3-153	2.2
1962	Chi-N	162	604	44	137	20	4	17	83	65	94	.227	.304	.358	74	-22	4	1	1	.955	11	*3-157/S-8	-0.8
1963	Chi-N★	162	630	79	187	29	6	25	99	42	92	.297	.345	.481	128	22	6	4	-1	.951	13	*3-162	3.6
1964	Chi-N☆	161	592	94	185	33	**13**	30	114	**86**	96	.313	**.401**	.564	162	50	3	4	-2	.963	17	*3-161	**6.5**
1965	Chi-N★	164	608	88	173	30	4	33	101	88	109	.285	.379	.510	144	37	3	1	0	.957	19	*3-164	5.4
1966	Chi-N★	155	561	93	175	21	8	30	94	**95**	78	.312	**.417**	.538	161	50	4	5	-2	.956	29	*3-152/S-8	**7.5**
1967	Chi-N	161	586	107	176	23	4	31	98	**96**	103	.300	.401	.512	153	43	1	5	-3	.957	**31**	*3-161	**7.3**
1968	Chi-N★	162	577	86	142	17	3	26	98	**96**	106	.246	.357	.421	124	20	3	4	-2	**.971**	17	*3-162	4.0
1969	Chi-N★	160	575	97	166	18	4	29	123	96	97	.289	.392	.485	128	23	1	3	-2	.947	6	*3-160	2.9
1970	Chi-N	154	555	83	148	30	4	26	114	92	108	.267	.372	.476	112	9	2	0	1	.945	13	*3-152/O-1	2.1
1971	Chi-N★	154	555	77	148	22	1	21	88	79	95	.267	.358	.423	105	4	4	0	1	.958	-3	*3-149/O-6	0.2
1972	Chi-N★	133	464	68	140	25	5	17	74	69	75	.302	.397	.487	135	23	1	4	-2	.948	6	*3-129/2-3,S-1,O-1	2.7
1973	Chi-N★	149	536	65	143	29	2	20	77	63	97	.267	.348	.440	109	7	1	2	-1	.950	-12	*3-146	-0.7
1974	Chi-A	117	375	29	83	12	1	5	41	37	72	.221	.295	.299	69	-14	0	2	-1	.970	6	D-47,2-39,3-28,/1S	-1.0
Total	15	2243	8143	1138	2254	365	67	342	1331	1108	1343	.277	.366	.464	123	264	35	41	-14	.954	138	*3-2130/D-47,2SO1	39.5

■ RAFAEL SANTO DOMINGO
Santo Domingo, Rafael (Molina) b: 11/24/55, Orocovis, P.R. BB/TR, 6', 160 lbs. Deb: 9/7/79

YEAR	TM/L	G	AB	R	H	2B	3B	HR	RBI	BB	SO	AVG	OBP	SLG	PRO+	BR/A	SB	CS	SBR	FA	FR	G/POS	TPR
1979	Cin-N	7	6	0	1	0	0	0	0	1	3	.167	.286	.167	26	-1	0	0	0	.000	0	/H	-0.1

■ NELSON SANTOVENIA
Santovenia, Nelson Gil (Mayol) b: 7/27/61, Pinar Del Rio, Cuba BR/TR, 6'3", 215 lbs. Deb: 9/16/87

YEAR	TM/L	G	AB	R	H	2B	3B	HR	RBI	BB	SO	AVG	OBP	SLG	PRO+	BR/A	SB	CS	SBR	FA	FR	G/POS	TPR
1987	Mon-N	2	1	0	0	0	0	0	0	0	0	.000	.000	.000	-97	-0	0	0	0	1.000	-0	/C-1	0.0
1988	Mon-N	92	309	26	73	20	2	8	41	24	77	.236	.298	.392	92	-4	2	3	-1	.983	2	C-86/1-1	0.4
1989	Mon-N	97	304	30	76	14	1	5	31	24	37	.250	.311	.352	88	-5	2	1	0	.981	12	C-89/1-1	1.3
1990	Mon-N	59	163	13	31	3	1	6	28	8	31	.190	.228	.331	54	-11	0	3	-2	.980	2	C-51	-0.9
1991	Mon-N	41	96	7	24	5	0	2	14	2	18	.250	.265	.365	76	-3	0	0	0	.976	-4	C-30/1-7	-0.6
1992	Chi-A	2	3	1	1	0	0	1	2	0	0	.333	.333	1.333	352	1	0	0	0	1.000	-0	/C-2	0.1
1993	KC-A	4	8	0	1	0	0	0	0	1	2	.125	.222	.125	-4	-1	0	0	0	1.000	0	/C-4	-0.1
Total	7	297	884	77	206	42	4	22	116	59	165	.233	.286	.364	82	-23	4	7	-3	.981	12	C-263/1-9	0.2

■ EDWARD SANTRY
Santry, Edward b: Chicago, Ill. d: 3/6/1899, Chicago, Ill. Deb: 8/7/1884

YEAR	TM/L	G	AB	R	H	2B	3B	HR	RBI	BB	SO	AVG	OBP	SLG	PRO+	BR/A	SB	CS	SBR	FA	FR	G/POS	TPR
1884	Det-N	6	22	1	4	0	0	0	0	1	2	.182	.217	.182	29	-2				.821	-0	/S-5,2-1	-0.2

■ JOE SARGENT
Sargent, Joseph Alexander "Horse Belly" b: 9/24/1893, Rochester, N.Y. d: 7/5/50, Rochester, N.Y. BR/TR, 5'10", 165 lbs. Deb: 4/27/21

YEAR	TM/L	G	AB	R	H	2B	3B	HR	RBI	BB	SO	AVG	OBP	SLG	PRO+	BR/A	SB	CS	SBR	FA	FR	G/POS	TPR
1921	Det-A	66	178	21	45	8	5	2	22	24	26	.253	.342	.388	87	-4	2	3	-1	.927	3	2-24,3-23,S-19	0.1

■ BILL SARNI
Sarni, William Florine b: 9/19/27, Los Angeles, Cal. d: 4/15/83, Creve Coeur, Mo. BR/TR, 5'11", 187 lbs. Deb: 5/9/51 C

YEAR	TM/L	G	AB	R	H	2B	3B	HR	RBI	BB	SO	AVG	OBP	SLG	PRO+	BR/A	SB	CS	SBR	FA	FR	G/POS	TPR
1951	StL-N	36	86	7	15	1	0	0	2	9	13	.174	.253	.186	20	-10	1	0	0	.984	0	C-35	-0.8
1952	StL-N	3	5	0	1	0	0	0	0	0	1	.200	.200	.200	11	-1	0	0	0	1.000	2	/C-3	0.2
1954	StL-N	123	380	40	114	18	4	9	70	25	42	.300	.343	.439	101	0	3	3	-1	**.996**	-13	*C-118	-0.8
1955	StL-N	107	325	32	83	15	2	3	34	27	33	.255	.314	.342	74	-12	1	1	-0	.987	-6	C-99	-1.5
1956	StL-N	43	148	12	43	7	2	5	22	8	15	.291	.331	.466	111	2	1	0	0	.992	3	C-41	0.7
	NY-N	78	238	16	55	9	3	5	23	20	31	.231	.293	.357	74	-9	0	1	-1	.993	-6	C-78	-1.3
	Yr	121	386	28	98	16	5	10	45	28	46	.254	.308	.399	88	-7	1	1	-0	.992	-3	*C-119	-0.6
Total	5	390	1182	107	311	50	11	22	151	89	135	.263	.316	.380	84	-29	6	5	-1	.991	-19	C-374	-3.5

■ MACKEY SASSER
Sasser, Mack Daniel b: 8/3/62, Fort Gaines, Ga. BL/TR, 6'1", 210 lbs. Deb: 7/17/87

YEAR	TM/L	G	AB	R	H	2B	3B	HR	RBI	BB	SO	AVG	OBP	SLG	PRO+	BR/A	SB	CS	SBR	FA	FR	G/POS	TPR
1987	SF-N	2	4	0	0	0	0	0	0	0	0	.000	.000	.000	-99	-1	0	0	0	1.000	0	/C-1	-0.1
	Pit-N	12	23	2	5	0	0	0	2	0	2	.217	.217	.217	16	-3	0	0	0	1.000	-1	/C-5	-0.4
	Yr	14	27	2	5	0	0	0	2	0	2	.185	.185	.185	-2	-4	0	0	0	1.000	-1	/C-6	-0.5
1988	*NY-N	60	123	9	35	10	1	1	17	6	9	.285	.318	.407	112	1	0	0	0	.977	9	C-42/3-1,O-1	1.3
1989	NY-N	72	182	17	53	14	2	1	22	7	15	.291	.317	.407	111	2	0	1	-1	.992	0	C-62/3-1	0.4
1990	NY-N	100	270	31	83	14	0	6	41	15	19	.307	.346	.426	111	4	0	0	0	.975	-9	C-87/1-1	0.0
1991	NY-N	96	228	18	62	14	2	5	35	9	19	.272	.303	.417	101	-1	0	2	-1	.994	-9	C-43,O-21,1-10	-1.0
1992	NY-N	92	141	7	34	6	0	2	18	3	10	.241	.257	.326	65	-7	0	0	0	.989	-11	C-27,1-12/O-9	-1.9
1993	Sea-A	83	188	18	41	10	2	1	21	15	30	.218	.279	.309	57	-12	1	0	0	.946	-3	O-37,D-19/C-4,1-1	-1.5
1994	Sea-A	3	4	0	0	0	0	0	0	0	0	.000	.000	.000	-98	-1	0	0	0	.000	-0	/C-1,O-1	-0.1
1995	Pit-N	14	26	1	4	1	0	0	0	0	0	.154	.154	.192	-9	-4	0	0	0	1.000	-1	C-11	-0.4
Total	9	534	1189	103	317	69	7	16	156	55	104	.267	.301	.377	89	-21	1	3	-2	.983	-24	C-283/O-69,1-24,D3	-3.7

■ ROB SASSER
Sasser, Robert Doffell b: 3/9/75, Philadelphia, Pa. BR/TR, 6'3", 205 lbs. Deb: 7/31/98

YEAR	TM/L	G	AB	R	H	2B	3B	HR	RBI	BB	SO	AVG	OBP	SLG	PRO+	BR/A	SB	CS	SBR	FA	FR	G/POS	TPR
1998	Tex-A	1	1	0	0	0	0	0	0	0	0	.000	.000	.000	-96	-0	0	0	0	.000	0	/H	0.0

■ TOM SATRIANO
Satriano, Thomas Victor Nicholas b: 8/28/40, Pittsburgh, Pa. BL/TR, 6'1", 190 lbs. Deb: 7/23/61

YEAR	TM/L	G	AB	R	H	2B	3B	HR	RBI	BB	SO	AVG	OBP	SLG	PRO+	BR/A	SB	CS	SBR	FA	FR	G/POS	TPR
1961	LA-A	35	96	15	19	5	1	1	8	12	16	.198	.294	.302	53	-6	2	0	1	.915	0	3-23,2-10/S-1	-0.5
1962	LA-A	10	19	4	8	2	0	2	6	0	1	.421	.421	.842	238	3	0	0	0	.833	-0	/3-5	0.3
1963	LA-A	23	50	1	9	1	0	0	2	9	10	.180	.305	.200	48	-3	0	0	0	.952	3	3-13/C-2,1-1	0.0
1964	LA-A	108	255	18	51	9	0	1	17	30	37	.200	.284	.247	55	-16	0	2	-1	.917	-2	3-38,1-32,C-25,/S2	-2.0
1965	Cal-A	47	79	8	13	2	0	1	4	10	10	.165	.258	.228	40	-6	1	1	-0	1.000	0	3-15,C-12,2-12,/1-3	-0.6
1966	Cal-A	103	226	16	54	5	3	0	24	27	32	.239	.320	.288	78	-6	3	3	-1	.991	-9	C-43,1-36,3-25,/2-4	-1.5
1967	Cal-A	90	201	13	45	7	0	4	21	28	25	.224	.319	.318	92	-1	1	0	0	.962	-7	3-38,C-23,2-15,/1-5	-0.8
1968	Cal-A	111	297	20	75	9	0	8	35	37	44	.253	.337	.364	117	6	0	0	0	.989	-9	C-85,2-14,3-11,/1-1	0.3
1969	Cal-A	41	108	5	28	2	0	1	16	18	15	.259	.370	.306	95	0	0	2	-1	1.000	-1	C-36/1-5,2-2	0.0
	Bos-A	47	127	9	24	2	0	0	11	22	12	.189	.318	.205	46	-8	0	0	0	.978	-2	C-44	-0.8
	Yr	88	235	14	52	4	0	1	27	40	27	.221	.342	.251	68	-8	0	2	-1	.987	-2	C-80/1-5,2-2	-0.8
1970	Bos-A	59	165	21	39	9	1	3	13	21	23	.236	.326	.358	83	-4	0	0	0	.985	0	C-51	-0.1
Total	10	674	1623	130	365	53	5	21	157	214	225	.225	.317	.303	79	-41	7	8	-3	.987	-26	C-321,3-168/12S	-5.7

■ FRANK SAUCIER
Saucier, Francis Field b: 5/28/26, Leslie, Mo. BL/TR, 6'1", 180 lbs. Deb: 7/21/51

YEAR	TM/L	G	AB	R	H	2B	3B	HR	RBI	BB	SO	AVG	OBP	SLG	PRO+	BR/A	SB	CS	SBR	FA	FR	G/POS	TPR
1951	StL-A	18	14	4	1	1	0	0	1	3	4	.071	.278	.143	16	-2	0	0	0	.714	-1	/O-3	-0.2

■ ED SAUER
Sauer, Edward "Horn" b: 1/3/19, Pittsburgh, Pa. d: 7/1/88, Thousand Oaks, Cal BR/TR, 6'1", 188 lbs. Deb: 9/17/43 F

YEAR	TM/L	G	AB	R	H	2B	3B	HR	RBI	BB	SO	AVG	OBP	SLG	PRO+	BR/A	SB	CS	SBR	FA	FR	G/POS	TPR
1943	Chi-N	14	55	3	15	3	0	0	9	3	6	.273	.322	.327	89	-1	1			1.000	2	O-13	0.1
1944	Chi-N	23	50	3	11	4	0	0	5	2	6	.220	.250	.300	55	-3	0			.960	-0	O-12	-0.4
1945	*Chi-N	49	93	8	24	4	1	2	11	8	23	.258	.317	.387	97	-1	2			1.000	-2	O-26	-0.4
1949	StL-N	24	45	5	10	2	1	0	1	3	8	.222	.271	.311	53	-3	0			1.000	-2	O-10	-0.5
	Bos-N	79	214	26	57	12	0	3	31	17	34	.266	.323	.364	89	-4	0			.972	-7	O-71	-1.4
	Yr	103	259	31	67	14	1	3	32	20	42	.259	.314	.355	82	-7	0			.974	-9	O-81	-1.9
Total	4	189	457	45	117	25	2	5	57	33	77	.256	.309	.352	83	-11	3			.981	-9	O-132	-2.6

■ HANK SAUER
Sauer, Henry John b: 3/17/17, Pittsburgh, Pa. BR/TR, 6'4", 199 lbs. Deb: 9/9/41 FC

YEAR	TM/L	G	AB	R	H	2B	3B	HR	RBI	BB	SO	AVG	OBP	SLG	PRO+	BR/A	SB	CS	SBR	FA	FR	G/POS	TPR
1941	Cin-N	9	33	4	10	4	0	0	5	1	4	.303	.324	.424	109	0	0			.957	1	/O-8	0.1

YEAR	TM/L	G	AB	R	H	2B	3B	HR	RBI	BB	SO	AVG	OBP	SLG	PRO+	BR/A	SB	CS	SBR	FA	FR	G/POS	TPR
1942	Cin-N	7	20	4	5	0	0	2	4	2	2	.250	.318	.550	152	1	0			.976	0	/1-4	0.1
1945	Cin-N	31	116	18	34	1	0	5	20	6	16	.293	.328	.431	112	1	2			.972	1	O-28/1-3	0.1
1948	Cin-N	145	530	78	138	22	1	35	97	60	85	.260	.340	.504	130	20	2			.973	4	*O-132,1-12	1.6
1949	Cin-N	42	152	22	36	6	0	4	16	18	19	.237	.318	.355	79	-4	0			.956	5	O-39/1-1	-0.1
	Chi-N	96	357	59	104	17	1	27	83	37	47	.291	.363	.571	151	24	0			.981	2	O-96	2.0
	Yr	138	509	81	140	23	1	31	99	55	66	.275	.349	.507	129	19	0			.972	7	*O-135/1-1	1.9
1950	Chi-N★	145	540	85	148	32	2	32	103	60	67	.274	.350	.519	127	19	1			.965	-1	*O-125,1-18	1.2
1951	Chi-N	141	525	77	138	19	4	30	89	45	77	.263	.325	.486	113	7	2	1	0	.981	10	*O-132	1.3
1952	Chi-N★	151	567	89	153	31	3	**37**	**121**	77	92	.270	.361	.531	143	32	1	2	-1	.983	17	*O-151	4.2
1953	Chi-N	108	395	61	104	16	5	19	60	50	56	.263	.349	.473	109	5	0	0	0	.970	3	*O-105	0.4
1954	Chi-N	142	520	98	150	18	1	41	103	70	68	.288	.379	.563	140	30	2	1	0	.963	-2	*O-141	2.2
1955	Chi-N	79	261	29	55	8	1	12	28	26	47	.211	.287	.387	77	-9	0	0	0	.984	-1	O-68	-1.4
1956	StL-N	75	151	11	45	4	0	5	24	25	31	.298	.408	.424	124	6	0	0	0	1.000	-1	O-37	0.3
1957	NY-N	127	378	46	98	14	1	26	76	49	59	.259	.344	.508	126	13	1	0	0	.992	-12	O-98	-0.4
1958	SF-N	88	236	27	59	8	0	12	46	35	37	.250	.356	.436	111	4	0	0	0	.950	-4	O-67	-0.3
1959	SF-N	13	15	1	1	0	0	1	1	0	7	.067	.067	.267	-17	-3	0	0	0	.000	-0	/O-1	-0.3
Total	15	1399	4796	709	1278	200	19	288	876	561	714	.266	.347	.496	123	146	11	4		.974	22	*O-1228/1-38	11.0

■ **DOUG SAUNDERS** Saunders, Douglas Long b: 12/13/69, Yorba Linda, Cal. BR/TR, 6′, 172 lbs. Deb: 6/13/93

YEAR	TM/L	G	AB	R	H	2B	3B	HR	RBI	BB	SO	AVG	OBP	SLG	PRO+	BR/A	SB	CS	SBR	FA	FR	G/POS	TPR
1993	NY-N	28	67	8	14	2	0	0	0	3	4	.209	.243	.239	30	-7	0	0	0	.956	1	2-22/3-4,S-1	-0.5

■ **RUSTY SAUNDERS** Saunders, Russell Collier b: 3/12/06, Trenton, N.J. d: 11/24/67, Trenton, N.J. BR/TR, 6′2″, 205 lbs. Deb: 9/24/27

YEAR	TM/L	G	AB	R	H	2B	3B	HR	RBI	BB	SO	AVG	OBP	SLG	PRO+	BR/A	SB	CS	SBR	FA	FR	G/POS	TPR
1927	Phi-A	5	15	2	2	1	0	0	2	3	2	.133	.278	.200	24	-2	0	0	0	.818	0	/O-4	-0.2

■ **AL SAUTERS** Sauters, Al b: Philadelphia, Pa. Deb: 9/8/1890

YEAR	TM/L	G	AB	R	H	2B	3B	HR	RBI	BB	SO	AVG	OBP	SLG	PRO+	BR/A	SB	CS	SBR	FA	FR	G/POS	TPR
1890	Phi-a	14	41	1	4	0	0	0	0	11		.098	.288	.098	14	-4	0			.850	-4	3-11/O-2,2-2	-0.7

■ **DON SAVAGE** Savage, Donald Anthony b: 3/5/19, Bloomfield, N.J. d: 12/25/61, Montclair, N.J. BR/TR, 6′, 180 lbs. Deb: 4/18/44

YEAR	TM/L	G	AB	R	H	2B	3B	HR	RBI	BB	SO	AVG	OBP	SLG	PRO+	BR/A	SB	CS	SBR	FA	FR	G/POS	TPR
1944	NY-A	71	239	31	63	7	5	4	24	20	41	.264	.323	.385	98	-1	1	1	-0	.946	-10	3-60	-1.2
1945	NY-A	34	58	5	13	1	0	0	3	3	14	.224	.262	.241	44	-4	1	0	0	.891	1	3-14/O-2	-0.3
Total	2	105	297	36	76	8	5	4	27	23	55	.256	.312	.357	88	-5	2	1	0	.935	-10	/3-74,O-2	-1.5

■ **JIMMIE SAVAGE** Savage, James Harold b: 8/29/1883, Southington, Conn. d: 6/26/40, New Castle, Pa. BB/TR, 5′5″, 150 lbs. Deb: 9/3/12

YEAR	TM/L	G	AB	R	H	2B	3B	HR	RBI	BB	SO	AVG	OBP	SLG	PRO+	BR/A	SB	CS	SBR	FA	FR	G/POS	TPR
1912	Phi-N	2	3	1	0	0	0	0	0	1	0	.000	.250	.000	-27	-1	0			.750	-0	/2-1	-0.1
1914	Pit-F	132	479	81	136	9	9	1	26	67	32	.284	.372	.347	97	-7	17			.963	-9	O-93,3-29,S-11,/2-3	-1.8
1915	Pit-F	14	21	0	3	0	0	0	0	1	0	.143	.182	.143	-8	-3	0			1.000	-1	/O-3,3-1	-0.5
Total	3	148	503	82	139	9	9	1	26	69	32	.276	.364	.336	92	-10	17			.964	-10	/O-96,3-30,S-11,2-4	-2.4

■ **TED SAVAGE** Savage, Theodore Edmund (b: Ephesian Savage) b: 2/21/36, Venice, Ill. BR/TR, 6′1″, 185 lbs. Deb: 4/9/62

YEAR	TM/L	G	AB	R	H	2B	3B	HR	RBI	BB	SO	AVG	OBP	SLG	PRO+	BR/A	SB	CS	SBR	FA	FR	G/POS	TPR
1962	Phi-N	127	335	54	89	11	2	7	39	40	66	.266	.347	.373	96	-1	16	5	2	.974	1	*O-109	-0.4
1963	Pit-N	85	149	22	29	2	1	5	14	14	31	.195	.268	.322	69	-6	4	3	-1	.943	-5	O-47	-1.5
1965	StL-N	30	63	7	10	3	0	1	4	6	9	.159	.232	.254	34	-6	1	1	-0	.938	-2	O-20	-0.9
1966	StL-N	16	29	4	5	2	1	0	3	4	7	.172	.273	.310	61	-2	4	0	1	1.000	-1	/O-7	-0.2
1967	StL-N	9	8	1	1	0	0	0	0	1	3	.125	.222	.125	2	-1	0	0	0	.000	0	H	-0.1
	Chi-N	96	225	40	49	10	1	5	33	40	54	.218	.348	.338	93	-1	7	6	-2	.979	-5	O-86/3-1	-1.2
	Yr	105	233	41	50	10	1	5	33	41	57	.215	.344	.330	90	-1	7	6	-2	.979	-5	O-86/3-1	-1.3
1968	Chi-N	3	8	0	2	0	0	0	0	0	1	.250	.250	.250	47	-1	0	1	-1	1.000	-1	/O-2	-0.2
	LA-N	61	126	7	26	6	1	2	7	10	20	.206	.270	.317	82	-3	1	2	-1	.985	0	O-39	-0.6
	Yr	64	134	7	28	6	1	2	7	10	21	.209	.269	.313	80	-4	1	3	-2	.986	-1	O-41	-0.8
1969	Cin-N	68	110	20	25	7	0	2	11	20	27	.227	.346	.345	90	-1	3	0	1	.983	-6	O-42/2-1	-0.7
1970	Mil-A	114	276	43	77	10	5	12	50	57	44	.279	.406	.482	143	18	10	6	-1	.953	-10	O-82/1-1	0.4
1971	Mil-A	14	17	2	3	0	0	0	1	5	4	.176	.364	.176	58	-1	1	0	0	1.000	-2	/O-6	-0.3
	KC-A	19	29	2	5	0	0	0	1	3	6	.172	.250	.172	22	-3	2	0	1	1.000	-2	/O-9	-0.5
	Yr	33	46	4	8	0	0	0	2	8	10	.174	.296	.174	36	-4	3	0	1	1.000	-3	O-15	-0.8
Total	9	642	1375	202	321	51	11	34	163	200	272	.233	.335	.361	94	-6	49	24	0	.970	-32	O-449/1-1,2-1,3-1	-6.2

■ **BOB SAVERINE** Saverine, Robert Paul "Rabbit" b: 6/2/41, Norwalk, Conn. BB/TR, 5′9″, 165 lbs. Deb: 9/12/59

YEAR	TM/L	G	AB	R	H	2B	3B	HR	RBI	BB	SO	AVG	OBP	SLG	PRO+	BR/A	SB	CS	SBR	FA	FR	G/POS	TPR
1959	Bal-A	1	0	1	0	0	0	0	0	0	0	—	—	—	—	0	0	0	0	.000	0	R	0.0
1962	Bal-A	8	21	2	5	2	0	0	3	1	3	.238	.273	.333	66	-1	0	2	-1	1.000	2	/2-7	0.0
1963	Bal-A	115	167	21	39	1	2	1	12	25	44	.234	.333	.281	77	-4	8	3	1	.976	-9	O-59,2-19,S-13	-1.2
1964	Bal-A	46	34	14	5	1	0	0	0	3	6	.147	.216	.176	11	-4	3	1	0	1.000	5	S-15/O-2	0.1
1966	Was-A	120	406	54	102	10	4	5	24	27	62	.251	.301	.333	83	-9	4	3	-1	.972	-19	2-70,3-26,S-11,/O-9	-2.5
1967	Was-A	89	233	22	55	13	0	0	8	17	34	.236	.288	.292	75	-7	8	0	2	.957	-20	2-48,S-10/3-8,O-2	-2.4
Total	6	379	861	114	206	27	6	6	47	73	149	.239	.300	.305	76	-26	23	9	2	.971	-40	2-144/O-72,S-49,3	-6.0

■ **CARL SAWATSKI** Sawatski, Carl Ernest "Swats" b: 11/4/27, Shickshinny, Pa. d: 11/24/91, Little Rock, Ark. BL/TR, 5′10″, 210 lbs. Deb: 9/29/48

YEAR	TM/L	G	AB	R	H	2B	3B	HR	RBI	BB	SO	AVG	OBP	SLG	PRO+	BR/A	SB	CS	SBR	FA	FR	G/POS	TPR
1948	Chi-N	2	2	0	0	0	0	0	0	0	0	.000	.000	.000	-99	-1	0			.000	0	H	-0.1
1950	Chi-N	38	103	4	18	1	0	1	7	11	19	.175	.254	.214	25	-11	0			.983	-1	C-32	-1.1
1953	Chi-N	43	59	5	13	3	0	1	5	7	7	.220	.303	.322	62	-3	0	0	0	.943	-1	C-15	-0.3
1954	Chi-A	43	109	6	20	3	3	1	12	15	20	.183	.282	.294	56	-7	0	0	0	.987	0	C-33	-0.5
1957	*Mil-N	58	105	13	25	4	0	6	17	10	15	.238	.316	.448	110	1	0	0	0	.986	6	C-28	0.8
1958	Mil-N	10	10	1	1	0	0	0	1	2	5	.100	.250	.100	-3	-1	0	0	0	1.000	1	/C-3	-0.1
	Phi-N	60	183	12	42	4	1	5	12	16	42	.230	.302	.344	72	-8	0	0	0	.986	-3	C-53	-0.8
	Yr	70	193	13	43	4	1	5	13	18	47	.223	.299	.332	68	-9	0	0	0	.987	-3	C-56	-0.9
1959	Phi-N	74	198	15	58	10	0	9	43	32	36	.293	.394	.480	129	9	0	0	0	.979	-14	C-69	-0.1
1960	StL-N	78	179	16	41	4	0	6	27	22	24	.229	.313	.352	75	-6	0	0	0	.993	-7	C-67	-1.0
1961	StL-N	86	174	23	52	8	0	10	33	25	17	.299	.387	.517	125	6	0	0	0	.996	-7	C-60/O-1	0.2
1962	StL-N	85	222	26	56	9	1	13	42	36	38	.252	.357	.477	111	3	0	0	0	.997	-1	C-70	0.5
1963	StL-N	56	105	12	25	0	0	6	14	15	28	.238	.333	.410	103	1	2	0	1	.986	-5	C-27	-0.3
Total	11	633	1449	133	351	46	5	58	213	191	251	.242	.333	.401	92	-16	2	0		.988	-32	C-457/O-1	-2.8

■ **CARL SAWYER** Sawyer, Carl Everett "Huck" b: 10/19/1890, Seattle, Wash. d: 1/17/57, Los Angeles, Cal. BR/TR, 5′11″, 160 lbs. Deb: 9/11/15

YEAR	TM/L	G	AB	R	H	2B	3B	HR	RBI	BB	SO	AVG	OBP	SLG	PRO+	BR/A	SB	CS	SBR	FA	FR	G/POS	TPR
1915	Was-A	10	32	8	8	1	0	0	3	4	5	.250	.351	.281	88	-0	2			.964	-2	/2-6,S-4	-0.2
1916	Was-A	16	31	3	6	1	0	0	2	4	4	.194	.306	.226	60	-1	3			.963	2	/2-6,S-5,3-1	0.1
Total	2	26	63	11	14	2	0	0	5	8	9	.222	.329	.254	74	-2	5			.964	-1	/2-12,S-9,3-1	-0.1

■ **DAVE SAX** Sax, David John b: 9/22/58, Sacramento, Cal. BR/TR, 6′, 185 lbs. Deb: 9/1/82 F

YEAR	TM/L	G	AB	R	H	2B	3B	HR	RBI	BB	SO	AVG	OBP	SLG	PRO+	BR/A	SB	CS	SBR	FA	FR	G/POS	TPR
1982	LA-N	2	2	0	0	0	0	0	0	0	0	.000	.000	.000	-99	-1	0	0	0	1.000	-0	/O-1	-0.1
1983	LA-N	7	8	0	0	0	0	0	1	0	0	.000	.000	.000	-99	-2	0	0	0	.917	-0	/C-4	-0.2
1985	Bos-A	22	36	2	11	3	0	0	6	3	3	.306	.359	.389	101	0	0	1	-1	.985	-2	C-16/O-4	-0.2
1986	Bos-A	4	11	1	5	1	0	1	1	0	1	.455	.455	.818	237	2	0	0	0	1.000	-1	/C-2,1-1	0.1
1987	Bos-A	2	3	0	0	0	0	0	0	0	1	.000	.000	.000	-97	-1	0	0	0	1.000	1	/C-2	0.0
Total	5	37	60	3	16	4	0	1	8	3	5	.267	.302	.383	84	-1	0	1	-1	.980	-2	/C-24,O-5,1-1	-0.4

■ **OLLIE SAX** Sax, Erik Oliver b: 11/5/04, Branford, Conn. d: 3/21/82, Newark, N.J. BR/TR, 5′8″, 164 lbs. Deb: 4/13/28

YEAR	TM/L	G	AB	R	H	2B	3B	HR	RBI	BB	SO	AVG	OBP	SLG	PRO+	BR/A	SB	CS	SBR	FA	FR	G/POS	TPR
1928	StL-A	16	17	4	3	0	0	0	0	5	3	.176	.364	.176	45	-1	0	0	0	.955	3	/3-9	0.2

■ **STEVE SAX** Sax, Stephen Louis b: 1/29/60, Sacramento, Cal. BR/TR, 5′11″, 185 lbs. Deb: 8/18/81 F

YEAR	TM/L	G	AB	R	H	2B	3B	HR	RBI	BB	SO	AVG	OBP	SLG	PRO+	BR/A	SB	CS	SBR	FA	FR	G/POS	TPR
1981	*LA-N	31	119	15	33	2	0	2	9	7	14	.277	.317	.345	91	-2	5	7	-3	.975	2	2-29	-0.1
1982	LA-N★	150	638	88	180	23	7	4	47	49	53	.282	.335	.359	97	-3	49	19	3	.977	-9	*2-149	0.0
1983	*LA-N★	155	623	94	175	18	5	5	41	58	73	.281	.343	.350	93	-5	56	30	-1	.961	-30	*2-152	-3.0
1984	LA-N	145	569	70	138	24	4	1	35	47	53	.243	.301	.304	71	-21	34	19	-1	.973	12	*2-141	-0.6

YEAR	TM/L	G	AB	R	H	2B	3B	HR	RBI	BB	SO	AVG	OBP	SLG	PRO+	BR/A	SB	CS	SBR	FA	FR	G/POS	TPR
1985	*LA-N	136	488	62	136	8	4	1	42	54	43	.279	.354	.318	92	-3	27	11	2	.969	-9	*2-135/3-1	-0.6
1986	LA-N★	157	633	91	210	43	4	6	56	59	58	.332	.391	.441	139	33	40	17	2	.980	-5	*2-154	3.7
1987	LA-N	157	610	84	171	22	7	6	46	44	61	.280	.332	.369	88	-11	37	11	5	.982	1	*2-152/3-1,O-1	0.3
1988	*LA-N	160	632	70	175	19	4	5	57	45	51	.277	.326	.343	95	-4	42	12	5	.981	-19	*2-158	-1.2
1989	NY-A★	158	651	88	205	26	3	5	63	52	44	.315	.366	.387	114	13	43	17	3	**.987**	-10	*2-158	1.1
1990	NY-A★	155	615	70	160	24	2	4	42	49	46	.260	.319	.325	80	-16	43	9	8	.987	-13	*2-154	-1.9
1991	NY-A	158	652	85	198	38	2	10	56	41	38	.304	.348	.414	110	8	31	11	3	.990	-7	*2-149/3-5,D-4	0.7
1992	Chi-A	143	567	74	134	26	4	4	47	43	42	.236	.292	.317	72	-22	30	12	2	.972	-28	*2-141/D-1	-4.6
1993	Chi-A	57	119	20	28	5	0	1	8	8	6	.235	.283	.303	59	-7	7	3	0	1.000	-5	O-32,D-21/2-1	-1.2
1994	Oak-A	7	24	2	6	0	1	0	1	0	2	.250	.250	.333	53	-2	0	0	0	1.000	2	/2-6	0.1
Total	14	1769	6940	913	1949	278	47	54	550	556	584	.281	.336	.358	95	-41	444	178	26	.978	-117	*2-1679/O-33,D-26,3	-7.3

■ JIMMY SAY
Say, James I. b: 1862, Baltimore, Md. d: 6/23/1894, Baltimore, Md. Deb: 7/22/1882 F

YEAR	TM/L	G	AB	R	H	2B	3B	HR	RBI	BB	SO	AVG	OBP	SLG	PRO+	BR/A	SB	CS	SBR	FA	FR	G/POS	TPR
1882	Lou-a	1	4	1	1	0	0	0		0		.250	.250	.250	73	-0				.333	-1	/3-1	-0.1
	Phi-a	22	82	12	17	2	0	1		1		.207	.217	.268	56	-4				.884	1	S-22	-0.2
	Yr	23	86	13	18	2	0	1		1		.209	.218	.267	57	-4				.884	0	S-22/3-1	-0.3
1884	Wil-U	16	59	3	13	1	2	0		1		.220	.233	.305	60	-5				.733	-3	3-16	-0.7
	KC-U	2	8	0	2	0	0	0		0		.250	.250	.250	60	-1				.200	-2	/3-2	-0.3
	Yr	18	67	3	15	1	2	0		1		.224	.235	.299	60	-5				.680	-5	3-18	-1.0
1887	Cle-a	16	64	9	24	5	3	0	12	1		.375	.385	.547	163	5	0			.714	-4	3-16	0.1
Total	3	57	217	25	57	8	5	1	12	3		.263	.273	.359	90	-5	0			.690	-9	/3-35,S-22	-1.2

■ LOU SAY
Say, Louis I. b: 2/4/1854, Baltimore, Md. d: 6/5/30, Fallston, Md. BR/TR, 5'7", 145 lbs. Deb: 4/14/1873 F

YEAR	TM/L	G	AB	R	H	2B	3B	HR	RBI	BB	SO	AVG	OBP	SLG	PRO+	BR/A	SB	CS	SBR	FA	FR	G/POS	TPR
1873	Mar-n	3	12	1	2	0	0	0	2	0	0	.167	.167	.167	-1	-1	0	0	0	.667	1	/S-2,O-1	0.0
1874	Bal-n	18	66	4	14	3	0	0	5	0	1	.212	.212	.258	50	-3	0	0	0	.786	12	S-18	0.6
1875	Was-n	11	38	4	10	0	0	0	2	0	7	.263	.263	.263	87	-0	0	0	0	.698	-1	/S-8,2-2,O-1	-0.2
1880	Cin-N	48	191	14	38	8	1	0	15	4	31	.199	.215	.251	58	-8				.832	1	S-48	-0.4
1882	Phi-a	49	199	35	45	4	3	1	28	8		.226	.256	.291	75	-6				.867	6	S-49	0.2
1883	Bal-a	74	324	52	83	13	2	1		10		.256	.278	.318	89	-5				.794	7	*S-74	0.4
1884	Bal-U	78	339	65	81	14	2	2		11		.239	.263	.310	66	-25				.795	2	*S-78	-2.0
	KC-U	17	70	6	14	2	0	1		2		.200	.222	.271	56	-6				.860	9	S-16/2-1	0.2
	Yr	95	409	71	95	16	2	3		13		.232	.256	.303	65	-30				.808	10	S-94/2-1	-1.8
Total	3 n	32	116	9	26	3	0	0	9	0	8	.224	.224	.250	57	-5	0	0	0	.750	12	/S-28,2-2,O-2	0.4
Total	4	266	1123	172	261	41	8	5	43	35	31	.232	.256	.297	72	-49				.820	24	S-265/2-1	-1.6

■ JERRY SCALA
Scala, Gerard Michael b: 9/27/24, Bayonne, N.J. d: 12/14/93, Fallston, Md. BL/TR, 5'11", 178 lbs. Deb: 4/22/48

YEAR	TM/L	G	AB	R	H	2B	3B	HR	RBI	BB	SO	AVG	OBP	SLG	PRO+	BR/A	SB	CS	SBR	FA	FR	G/POS	TPR
1948	Chi-A	3	6	1	0	0	0	0	0	0	3	.000	.000	.000	-99	-2	0	0	0	1.000	-0	/O-2	-0.2
1949	Chi-A	37	120	17	30	7	1	1	13	17	19	.250	.348	.350	88	-2	3	3	-1	.988	-3	O-37	-0.8
1950	Chi-A	40	67	8	13	2	1	0	6	10	10	.194	.299	.254	44	-6	0	0	0	1.000	-4	O-23	-1.0
Total	3	80	193	26	43	9	2	1	19	27	32	.223	.321	.306	67	-9	3	3	-1	.993	-7	/O-62	-2.0

■ SKEETER SCALZI
Scalzi, Frank John b: 6/16/13, Lafferty, Ohio d: 8/25/84, Pittsburgh, Pa. BR/TR, 5'6", 160 lbs. Deb: 7/21/39

YEAR	TM/L	G	AB	R	H	2B	3B	HR	RBI	BB	SO	AVG	OBP	SLG	PRO+	BR/A	SB	CS	SBR	FA	FR	G/POS	TPR
1939	NY-N	11	18	3	6	0	0	0	0	3	2	.333	.429	.333	106	0	1			.875	2	/S-5,3-1	0.3

■ JOHNNY SCALZI
Scalzi, John Anthony b: 3/22/07, Stamford, Conn. d: 9/27/62, Port Chester, N.Y BR/TR, 5'7", 170 lbs. Deb: 6/19/31

YEAR	TM/L	G	AB	R	H	2B	3B	HR	RBI	BB	SO	AVG	OBP	SLG	PRO+	BR/A	SB	CS	SBR	FA	FR	G/POS	TPR
1931	Bos-N	2	1	0	0	0	0	0	0	0	1	.000	.000	.000	-99	-0	0			.000	0	H	0.0

■ MORT SCANLAN
Scanlan, Mortimer J. b: 3/18/1861, Chicago, Ill. d: 12/29/28, Chicago, Ill. 6'1", 186 lbs. Deb: 4/21/1890

YEAR	TM/L	G	AB	R	H	2B	3B	HR	RBI	BB	SO	AVG	OBP	SLG	PRO+	BR/A	SB	CS	SBR	FA	FR	G/POS	TPR
1890	NY-N	3	10	0	0	0	0	0	0	2	5	.000	.167	.000	-50	-2	1			1.000	-0	/1-3	-0.2

■ PATRICK SCANLAN
Scanlan, Patrick J. b: 3/25/1861, Nova Scotia, Can. d: 7/17/13, Springfield, Mass. Deb: 7/4/1884

YEAR	TM/L	G	AB	R	H	2B	3B	HR	RBI	BB	SO	AVG	OBP	SLG	PRO+	BR/A	SB	CS	SBR	FA	FR	G/POS	TPR
1884	Bos-U	6	24	2	7	1	0	0		0		.292	.292	.333	90	-1				.800	0	/O-6	-0.1

■ PAT SCANLON
Scanlon, James Patrick b: 9/23/52, Minneapolis, Minn. BL/TR, 6', 180 lbs. Deb: 9/27/74

YEAR	TM/L	G	AB	R	H	2B	3B	HR	RBI	BB	SO	AVG	OBP	SLG	PRO+	BR/A	SB	CS	SBR	FA	FR	G/POS	TPR
1974	Mon-N	2	4	1	1	0	0	0	0	0	1	.250	.250	.250	38	-0	0	0	0	1.000	1	/3-1	0.0
1975	Mon-N	60	109	5	20	3	1	2	15	17	25	.183	.294	.284	58	-6	0	1	-1	.957	2	3-28/1-1	-0.5
1976	Mon-N	11	27	2	5	1	0	1	2	2	5	.185	.241	.333	59	-2	0	0	0	.842	-1	/3-7,1-1	-0.3
1977	SD-N	47	79	9	15	3	0	1	11	12	20	.190	.297	.266	58	-5	0	0	0	.957	-5	2-15,3-11/O-1	-0.9
Total	4	120	219	17	41	7	1	4	28	31	51	.187	.288	.283	58	-13	0	1	-1	.938	-3	/3-47,2-15,1-2,O-1	-1.7

■ RUSS SCARRITT
Scarritt, Stephen Russell Mallory b: 1/14/03, Pensacola, Fla. d: 12/4/94, Pensacola, Fla. BL/TR, 5'10.5", 165 lbs. Deb: 4/18/29

YEAR	TM/L	G	AB	R	H	2B	3B	HR	RBI	BB	SO	AVG	OBP	SLG	PRO+	BR/A	SB	CS	SBR	FA	FR	G/POS	TPR
1929	Bos-A	151	540	69	159	26	17	1	71	34	38	.294	.337	.411	94	-6	13	11	-3	.944	1	*O-145	-1.7
1930	Bos-A	113	447	48	129	17	8	2	48	12	49	.289	.312	.376	76	-17	4	7	-3	.967	4	*O-110	-2.1
1931	Bos-A	10	39	2	6	1	0	0	1	2	2	.154	.195	.179	-1	-6	0	0	0	1.000	1	/O-9	-0.5
1932	Phi-N	11	11	0	2	0	0	0	0	1	2	.182	.250	.182	16	-1	0			1.000	-0	/O-1	-0.1
Total	4	285	1037	119	296	44	25	3	120	49	91	.285	.320	.385	82	-30	17	18		.956	6	O-265	-4.4

■ LES SCARSELLA
Scarsella, Leslie George b: 11/23/13, Santa Cruz, Cal. d: 12/17/58, San Francisco, Cal BL/TL, 5'11", 185 lbs. Deb: 9/15/35

YEAR	TM/L	G	AB	R	H	2B	3B	HR	RBI	BB	SO	AVG	OBP	SLG	PRO+	BR/A	SB	CS	SBR	FA	FR	G/POS	TPR
1935	Cin-N	6	10	4	2	1	0	0	0	3	1	.200	.385	.300	89	0	0			1.000	1	/1-2	0.0
1936	Cin-N	115	485	63	152	21	9	3	65	14	36	.313	.335	.412	107	3	6			.989	2	*1-115	-0.7
1937	Cin-N	110	329	35	81	11	4	3	34	17	26	.246	.285	.331	70	-14	5			.984	-5	1-65,O-14	-2.7
1939	Cin-N	16	14	0	2	0	0	0	2	0	2	.143	.143	.143	-23	-2	0			.000	0	H	-0.2
1940	Bos-N	18	60	7	18	1	3	0	8	3	5	.300	.344	.417	115	1	2			.986	-1	1-15	-0.1
Total	5	265	898	109	255	34	16	6	109	37	70	.284	.315	.378	92	-13	13			.988	-4	1-197/O-14	-3.7

■ STEVE SCARSONE
Scarsone, Steven Wayne b: 4/11/66, Anaheim, Cal. BR/TR, 6'2", 195 lbs. Deb: 5/15/92

YEAR	TM/L	G	AB	R	H	2B	3B	HR	RBI	BB	SO	AVG	OBP	SLG	PRO+	BR/A	SB	CS	SBR	FA	FR	G/POS	TPR
1992	Phi-N	7	13	1	2	0	0	0	0	1	6	.154	.214	.154	6	-2	0	0	0	1.000	-2	/2-3	-0.4
	Bal-A	11	17	2	3	0	0	0	0	1	6	.176	.222	.176	13	-2	0	0	0	.889	-1	/2-5,3-2,S-1	-0.3
1993	SF-N	44	103	16	26	9	0	2	15	4	32	.252	.280	.398	82	-3	0	1	-1	1.000	-5	2-20/3-8,1-6	-0.8
1994	SF-N	52	103	21	28	8	0	2	13	10	20	.272	.336	.408	97	-0	0	2	-1	.990	9	2-22/3-8,1-6,S-1	0.8
1995	SF-N	80	233	33	62	10	3	11	29	18	82	.266	.335	.476	114	4	3	2	-0	.927	-5	3-50,2-13,1-11	-0.2
1996	SF-N	105	283	28	62	12	1	5	23	25	91	.219	.287	.322	63	-16	2	3	-1	.973	-4	2-74,3-14/1-1,S-1	-1.6
1997	StL-N	5	10	0	1	0	0	0	0	2	5	.100	.250	.100	-4	-2	1	0	1	1.000	-3	/2-2,O-2,3-1	-0.4
Total	6	304	762	101	184	39	4	20	80	61	242	.241	.304	.382	83	-20	6	8	-3	.977	-11	2-139/3-83,1-24,SO	-2.9

■ PAUL SCHAAL
Schaal, Paul b: 3/3/43, Pittsburgh, Pa. BR/TR, 5'11", 180 lbs. Deb: 9/3/64

YEAR	TM/L	G	AB	R	H	2B	3B	HR	RBI	BB	SO	AVG	OBP	SLG	PRO+	BR/A	SB	CS	SBR	FA	FR	G/POS	TPR
1964	LA-A	17	32	3	4	0	0	0	0	2	5	.125	.176	.125	-16	-5	0	1	-1	1.000	-1	/2-9,3-9	-0.7
1965	Cal-A	155	483	48	108	12	2	9	45	61	88	.224	.312	.313	80	-12	6	3	0	.970	-10	*3-153/2-1	-2.8
1966	Cal-A	138	386	59	94	15	7	6	24	68	56	.244	.364	.365	113	9	6	4	-1	.948	-2	*3-131	0.4
1967	Cal-A	99	272	31	51	9	1	6	20	38	39	.188	.289	.294	76	-8	2	2	-1	.970	-2	3-88/S-2,2-1	-1.2
1968	Cal-A	60	219	22	46	7	1	2	16	29	25	.210	.308	.279	82	-4	5	7	-3	.958	9	3-58	0.3
1969	KC-A	61	205	22	54	6	0	1	13	25	27	.263	.339	.307	84	-3	2	1	0	.897	-19	3-49/2-6,S-6	-2.2
1970	KC-A	124	380	50	102	12	3	5	35	43	39	.268	.344	.355	93	-3	7	4	-0	.938	-16	3-97,S-10/2-6	-2.0
1971	KC-A	161	548	80	150	31	6	11	63	103	51	.274	.391	.412	129	25	7	5	-1	.940	-12	*3-161	1.1
1972	KC-A	127	435	47	99	19	3	6	41	61	59	.228	.325	.326	95	-1	1	3	-2	.947	-16	*3-123/S-1	-2.3
1973	KC-A	121	396	61	114	14	3	8	42	63	45	.288	.392	.399	114	10	5	6	-2	.913	-12	*3-121	-0.5
1974	KC-A	12	34	3	6	2	0	1	4	5	5	.176	.300	.324	75	-1	0	0	0	.949	1	3-12	-0.1
	Cal-A	53	165	10	41	5	0	2	20	18	27	.248	.322	.315	89	-2	2	2	-1	.903	-10	3-51	-1.4
	Yr	65	199	13	47	7	0	3	24	23	32	.236	.318	.317	86	-3	2	2	-1	.914	-9	3-63	-1.5
Total	11	1128	3555	436	869	132	26	57	323	516	466	.244	.344	.344	98	4	43	38	-10	.943	-91	*3-1053/2-23,S-19	-11.4

■ GERMANY SCHAEFER
Schaefer, Herman A. b: 2/4/1877, Chicago, Ill. d: 5/16/19, Saranac Lake, N.Y. BR/TR, 5'9", 175 lbs. Deb: 10/5/01

YEAR	TM/L	G	AB	R	H	2B	3B	HR	RBI	BB	SO	AVG	OBP	SLG	PRO+	BR/A	SB	CS	SBR	FA	FR	G/POS	TPR
1901	Chi-N	2	5	0	3	1	0	0	0	2		.600	.714	.800	352	2	0			1.000	1	/2-1,3-1	0.3
1902	Chi-N	81	291	32	57	2	3	0	14	19		.196	.250	.223	48	-18	12			.864	-9	3-75/1-3,O-2,S-1	-2.8
1905	Det-A	153	554	64	135	17	9	2	47	45		.244	.302	.318	96	-3	19			.955	8	*2-151/S-3	0.7
1906	Det-A	124	446	48	106	14	3	2	42	32		.238	.290	.296	81	-10	31			.948	9	*2-114/S-7	0.0
1907	*Det-A	109	372	45	96	12	3	1	32	30		.258	.313	.315	97	-1	21			.961	-5	2-74,S-18,3-14,/O-1	-0.7
1908	*Det-A	153	584	96	151	20	10	3	52	37		.259	.304	.342	106	2	40			.918	4	S-68,2-58,3-29	0.9
1909	Det-A	87	280	26	70	12	0	0	22	14		.250	.286	.293	79	-7	12			.966	14	2-86/O-1	0.6
	Was-A	37	128	13	31	5	1	1	4	6		.242	.281	.320	94	-1	2			.941	0	2-32/3-1	-0.2
	Yr	124	408	39	101	17	1	1	26	20		.248	.284	.301	84	-8	14			.960	14	*2-118/O-1,3-1	0.4
1910	Was-A	74	229	27	63	6	5	0	14	25		.275	.352	.345	124	7	17			.953	-1	2-35,O-26/3-2	0.5
1911	Was-A	125	440	74	147	14	7	0	45	57		.334	.412	.398	129	19	22			.980	0	*1-108/O-7	1.8
1912	Was-A	60	166	21	41	7	3	0	19	23		.247	.342	.325	90	-2	11			.900	-11	O-19,1-15,2-15,/P-1	-1.4
1913	Was-A	54	100	17	32	1	1	0	7	15	12	.320	.419	.350	123	4	6			.926	-2	2-16/1-6,3-2,P-1,O	0.1
1914	Was-A	30	29	6	7	1	0	0	2	3	5	.241	.313	.276	74	-1	4	1	1	1.000	0	/2-3,O-3	0.0
1915	New-F	59	154	26	33	5	3	0	8	25	11	.214	.328	.286	78	-6	3			.952	-1	O-17,1-13/3-9,2-2	-0.9
1916	NY-A	1	1	0	0	0	0	0	0	0	0	.000	.000	.000	-98	-0	0			.000	0	/O-1	0.0
1918	Cle-A	1	5	2	0	0	0	0	0	0	0	.000	.000	.000	-91	-1	1			1.000	-0	/2-1	-0.2
Total	15	1150	3784	497	972	117	48	9	308	333	28	.257	.319	.320	96	-15	201	1		.954	5	2-588,1-145,3/SOP	-1.3

■ JEFF SCHAEFER
Schaefer, Jeffrey Scott b: 5/31/60, Patchogue, N.Y. BR/TR, 5'10", 170 lbs. Deb: 4/7/89

YEAR	TM/L	G	AB	R	H	2B	3B	HR	RBI	BB	SO	AVG	OBP	SLG	PRO+	BR/A	SB	CS	SBR	FA	FR	G/POS	TPR
1989	Chi-A	15	10	2	1	0	0	0	0	0	2	.100	.100	.100	-45	-2	1	1	-0	.900	1	/S-5,2-4,3-4,D-1	-0.1
1990	Sea-A	55	107	11	22	3	0	0	6	3	11	.206	.241	.234	33	-10	4	1	1	.933	11	3-26,S-24/2-3	0.4
1991	Sea-A	84	164	19	41	7	1	1	11	5	25	.250	.272	.323	64	-8	3	1	0	.968	2	S-46,3-30,2-11,/D-1	-0.3
1992	Sea-A	65	70	5	8	2	0	1	3	2	10	.114	.139	.186	-10	-10	0	1	-1	.922	14	S-33,3-21/2-7,D-2	0.5
1994	Oak-A	6	8	0	1	0	0	0	0	0	1	.125	.125	.125	-39	-2	0	0	0	.800	-1	/3-3,S-2,1-1	-0.2
Total	5	225	359	37	73	12	1	2	20	10	49	.203	.229	.259	35	-32	8	4	0	.957	28	S-110/3-84,2-25,D1	0.3

■ HARRY SCHAFER
Schafer, Harry C. "Silk Stocking" b: 8/14/1846, Philadelphia, Pa. d: 2/28/35, Philadelphia, Pa. BR/TR, 5'9.5", 143 lbs. Deb: 5/5/1871

YEAR	TM/L	G	AB	R	H	2B	3B	HR	RBI	BB	SO	AVG	OBP	SLG	PRO+	BR/A	SB	CS	SBR	FA	FR	G/POS	TPR
1871	Bos-n	31	149	38	42	7	5	0	28	3	1	.282	.296	.396	94	-2	13	4	2	.684	3	*3-31	0.0
1872	Bos-n	48	225	51	65	10	4	1	37	0	8	.289	.289	.382	99	-2	2	0	1	.795	4	*3-43/O-5,C-2	0.0
1873	Bos-n	60	295	65	79	12	3	2	46	3	1	.268	.275	.349	78	-10	3	4	-2	.732	-15	*3-47,O-13	-2.1
1874	Bos-n	71	327	69	87	10	2	1	45	1	5	.266	.268	.318	83	-8	2	4	-2	.785	6	*3-71/S-1	-0.3
1875	Bos-n	52	222	49	64	9	0	0	17	1	8	.288	.291	.329	111	2	3	2	-0	.795	3	*3-51/O-1	0.4
1876	Bos-N	70	286	47	72	11	0	0	35	4	11	.252	.262	.290	82	-5				.810	3	*3-70	0.0
1877	Bos-N	33	141	20	39	5	2	0	13	0	7	.277	.277	.340	90	-2				.621	-12	O-23/3-9,S-1	-1.3
1878	Bos-N	2	8	0	1	0	0	0	0	0	1	.125	.125	.125	-16	-1				1.000	-1	/O-2	-0.2
Total	5 n	262	1218	272	337	48	14	4	173	8	23	.277	.281	.349	91	-20	23	14	-2	.764	0	3-243/O-19,C-2,S-1	-2.0
Total	3	105	435	67	112	16	2	0	48	4	19	.257	.264	.303	83	-8				.810	-9	/3-79,O-25,S-1	-1.5

■ JIMMIE SCHAFFER
Schaffer, Jimmie Ronald b: 4/5/36, Limeport, Pa. BR/TR, 5'9", 185 lbs. Deb: 5/20/61 C

YEAR	TM/L	G	AB	R	H	2B	3B	HR	RBI	BB	SO	AVG	OBP	SLG	PRO+	BR/A	SB	CS	SBR	FA	FR	G/POS	TPR
1961	StL-N	68	153	15	39	7	0	1	16	9	29	.255	.301	.320	59	-9	0	0	0	.996	4	C-68	-0.3
1962	StL-N	70	66	7	16	2	1	0	6	6	16	.242	.306	.303	58	-4	1	0	0	.993	7	C-69	0.4
1963	Chi-N	57	142	17	34	7	0	7	19	11	35	.239	.294	.437	102	0	0	0	0	.996	1	C-54	0.3
1964	Chi-N	54	122	9	25	6	1	2	9	17	17	.205	.307	.320	74	-4	2	4	-2	.970	-8	C-43	-1.2
1965	Chi-A	17	31	2	6	3	1	0	1	3	4	.194	.265	.355	79	-1	0	0	0	1.000	3	C-14	0.2
	NY-N	24	37	0	5	2	0	0	0	1	15	.135	.158	.189	-3	-5	0	0	0	.968	-1	C-21	-0.5
1966	Phi-N	8	15	2	2	1	0	1	4	1	7	.133	.188	.400	58	-1	0	0	0	.952	-1	/C-6	-0.1
1967	Phi-N	2	2	1	0	0	0	0	0	1	1	.000	.333	.000	3	-0	0	0	0	1.000	0	/C-1	0.0
1968	Cin-N	4	6	0	1	0	0	0	1	0	3	.167	.167	.167	0	-1	0	0	0	1.000	-1	/C-2	-0.2
Total	8	304	574	53	128	28	3	11	56	49	127	.223	.286	.340	69	-24	3	4	-2	.989	5	C-278	-1.4

■ JOHNNY SCHAIVE
Schaive, John Edward b: 2/25/34, Springfield, Ill. BR/TR, 5'8", 175 lbs. Deb: 9/19/58

YEAR	TM/L	G	AB	R	H	2B	3B	HR	RBI	BB	SO	AVG	OBP	SLG	PRO+	BR/A	SB	CS	SBR	FA	FR	G/POS	TPR
1958	Was-A	7	24	1	6	0	0	0	1	1	4	.250	.280	.250	48	-2	0	0	0	1.000	-1	/2-6	-0.2
1959	Was-A	16	59	3	9	2	0	0	2	0	7	.153	.167	.186	-3	-8	0	0	0	.977	4	2-16	-0.3
1960	Was-A	6	12	1	3	1	0	0	0	0	3	.250	.250	.333	57	-1	0	0	0	.917	-0	/2-4	-0.1
1962	Was-A	82	225	20	57	15	1	6	29	6	25	.253	.273	.409	81	-7	0	1	-1	.967	4	3-49/2-6	-0.3
1963	Was-A	3	3	0	0	0	0	0	0	0	1	.000	.000	.000	-99	-1	0	0	0	.000	0	H	-0.1
Total	5	114	323	25	75	18	1	6	32	7	40	.232	.251	.350	61	-18	0	1	-1	.980	7	/3-49,2-32	-1.0

■ ROY SCHALK
Schalk, Le Roy John b: 11/9/08, Chicago, Ill. d: 3/11/90, Gainesville, Tex. BR/TR, 5'10", 168 lbs. Deb: 9/17/32

YEAR	TM/L	G	AB	R	H	2B	3B	HR	RBI	BB	SO	AVG	OBP	SLG	PRO+	BR/A	SB	CS	SBR	FA	FR	G/POS	TPR
1932	NY-A	3	12	3	3	1	0	0	0	2	2	.250	.357	.333	84	-0	0	0	0	.867	-2	/2-3	-0.1
1944	Chi-A	146	587	47	129	14	4	1	44	45	52	.220	.276	.262	55	-34	5	4	-1	.964	-14	*2-142/S-5	-4.4
1945	Chi-A	133	513	50	127	23	1	1	65	32	41	.248	.293	.302	75	-17	3	6	-3	.977	6	*2-133	-0.6
Total	3	282	1112	100	259	38	5	2	109	79	95	.233	.285	.281	64	-52	8	10	-4	.970	-9	2-278/S-5	-5.1

■ RAY SCHALK
Schalk, Raymond William "Cracker" b: 8/12/1892, Harvey, Ill. d: 5/19/70, Chicago, Ill. BR/TR, 5'9", 165 lbs. Deb: 8/11/12 MCH

YEAR	TM/L	G	AB	R	H	2B	3B	HR	RBI	BB	SO	AVG	OBP	SLG	PRO+	BR/A	SB	CS	SBR	FA	FR	G/POS	TPR
1912	Chi-A	23	63	7	18	2	0	0	8	3		.286	.357	.317	96	-0	2			.917	4	C-23	0.6
1913	Chi-A	129	401	38	98	15	5	1	38	27	36	.244	.297	.314	80	-11	14			.980	-0	*C-125	-0.1
1914	Chi-A	136	392	30	106	13	2	0	36	38	24	.270	.347	.314	100	1	24	11	1	.974	6	*C-125	2.0
1915	Chi-A	135	413	46	110	14	4	1	54	62	21	.266	.366	.327	104	4	15	18	-6	**.984**	-3	*C-134	0.6
1916	Chi-A	129	410	36	95	12	9	0	41	41	31	.232	.311	.305	84	-8	30	13	1	**.988**	9	*C-124	1.3
1917	*Chi-A	140	424	48	96	12	5	2	51	59	27	.226	.331	.292	88	-4	19			.981	5	*C-139	1.4
1918	Chi-A	108	333	35	73	6	3	0	22	36	22	.219	.301	.255	67	-12	12			.978	-4	*C-106	-0.9
1919	*Chi-A	131	394	57	111	9	3	0	34	51	25	.282	.367	.320	93	-1	11			.981	1	*C-129	1.0
1920	Chi-A	151	485	64	131	25	5	1	61	68	19	.270	.362	.348	89	-6	10	4	1	**.986**	-1	*C-151	0.4
1921	Chi-A	128	416	32	105	24	4	0	47	40	36	.252	.328	.329	69	-19	3	4	-2	**.985**	8	*C-126	-0.6
1922	Chi-A	142	442	57	124	22	3	4	60	67	36	.281	.379	.371	97	0	12	4	1	**.989**	20	*C-142	2.8
1923	Chi-A	123	382	42	87	12	2	1	44	39	28	.228	.306	.277	55	-25	7	4	-0	.983	5	*C-121	-1.3
1924	Chi-A	57	153	15	30	4	2	1	11	21	10	.196	.301	.268	49	-12	1	5	-3	.959	6	C-56	-0.5
1925	Chi-A	125	343	44	94	18	1	0	52	57	27	.274	.382	.332	87	-4	11	5	0	.983	3	*C-125	0.5
1926	Chi-A	82	226	26	60	9	1	0	32	27	11	.265	.349	.314	77	-7	5	1	1	.977	-6	C-80	-0.8
1927	Chi-A	16	26	2	6	2	0	0	2	2	1	.231	.286	.308	55	-2	0	0	0	1.000	1	C-15,M	0.0
1928	Chi-A	2	1	0	1	0	0	0	1	0	0	1.000	1.000	1.000	433	0	1	0	0	1.000	1	/C-1,M	0.1
1929	NY-N	5	2	0	0	0	0	0	0	0	1	.000	.000	.000	-99	-1	0			1.000	1	/C-5	0.0
Total	18	1762	5306	579	1345	199	49	11	594	638	355	.253	.340	.316	83	-105	177	69		.981	55	*C-1727	6.5

■ GENE SCHALL
Schall, Eugene David b: 6/5/70, Abington, Pa. BR/TR, 6'3", 190 lbs. Deb: 6/16/95

YEAR	TM/L	G	AB	R	H	2B	3B	HR	RBI	BB	SO	AVG	OBP	SLG	PRO+	BR/A	SB	CS	SBR	FA	FR	G/POS	TPR
1995	Phi-N	24	65	2	15	2	0	0	5	6	16	.231	.306	.262	51	-4	0	0	0	.984	-1	1-14/O-4	-0.6
1996	Phi-N	28	66	7	18	5	1	2	10	12	15	.273	.392	.470	125	3	0	0	0	.986	-2	1-19	-0.1
Total	2	52	131	9	33	7	1	2	15	18	31	.252	.351	.366	89	-2	0	0	0	.985	-2	/1-33,O-4	-0.7

■ BIFF SCHALLER
Schaller, Walter b: 9/23/1889, Chicago, Ill. d: 10/9/39, Emeryville, Cal. BL/TR, 5'11", 168 lbs. Deb: 4/30/11

YEAR	TM/L	G	AB	R	H	2B	3B	HR	RBI	BB	SO	AVG	OBP	SLG	PRO+	BR/A	SB	CS	SBR	FA	FR	G/POS	TPR
1911	Det-A	40	60	8	8	0	1	1	7	4		.133	.200	.217	15	-7	1			1.000	-1	O-16/1-1	-0.8
1913	Chi-A	36	96	12	21	3	0	0	4	20	16	.219	.353	.250	78	-2	5			.918	-6	O-32	-1.0
Total	2	76	156	20	29	3	1	1	11	24	16	.186	.298	.237	54	-9	6			.949	-7	/O-48,1-1	-1.8

■ BOBBY SCHANG
Schang, Robert Martin b: 12/7/1886, Wales Center, N.Y. d: 8/29/66, Sacramento, Cal. BR/TR, 5'7", 165 lbs. Deb: 9/23/14 F

YEAR	TM/L	G	AB	R	H	2B	3B	HR	RBI	BB	SO	AVG	OBP	SLG	PRO+	BR/A	SB	CS	SBR	FA	FR	G/POS	TPR
1914	Pit-N	11	35	0	8	1	1	0	1	0	10	.229	.229	.314	64	-2	0			.964	-2	C-10	-0.3
1915	Pit-N	56	125	13	23	6	3	0	4	14	32	.184	.271	.280	68	-5	2	2	-1	.974	-7	C-45	-1.0
	NY-N	12	21	1	3	0	0	0	1	4	5	.143	.280	.143	31	-2	1			.875	-3	/C-6	-0.4

YEAR	TM/L	G	AB	R	H	2B	3B	HR	RBI	BB	SO	AVG	OBP	SLG	PRO+	BR/A	SB	CS	SBR	FA	FR	G/POS	TPR
	Yr	68	146	14	26	6	3	0	5	18	37	.178	.273	.260	63	-6	3	2	-0	.960	-9	C-51	-1.4
1927	StL-N	3	5	0	1	0	0	0	0	0	0	.200	.200	.200	7	-1	0			1.000	-0	/C-3	-0.1
Total	3	82	186	14	35	7	4	0	6	18	47	.188	.263	.269	62	-9	3	2		.962	-11	/C-64	-1.8

■ **WALLY SCHANG** Schang, Walter Henry b: 8/22/1889, S.Wales, N.Y. d: 3/6/65, St.Louis, Mo. BB/TR, 5'10", 180 lbs. Deb: 5/9/13 FC

YEAR	TM/L	G	AB	R	H	2B	3B	HR	RBI	BB	SO	AVG	OBP	SLG	PRO+	BR/A	SB	CS	SBR	FA	FR	G/POS	TPR
1913	*Phi-A	79	207	32	55	16	3	3	30	34	44	.266	.392	.415	139	12	4			.967	-5	C-72	1.4
1914	*Phi-A	107	307	44	88	11	8	3	45	32	33	.287	.371	.404	138	15	7	7	-2	.956	1	*C-100	2.3
1915	Phi-A	116	359	64	89	9	11	1	44	66	47	.248	.385	.343	122	14	18	3	4	.890	-1	3-43,O-41,C-26	1.9
1916	Phi-A	110	338	41	90	15	8	7	38	38	44	.266	.358	.420	140	16	14			.966	5	O-61,C-36	2.2
1917	Phi-A	118	316	41	90	14	9	3	36	29	24	.285	.362	.415	139	14	6			.956	-10	C-80,3-12/O-6	1.2
1918	*Bos-A	88	225	36	55	7	1	0	20	46	35	.244	.377	.284	101	3	4			.962	-13	C-57,O-16/3-5,S-1	-0.7
1919	Bos-A	113	330	43	101	16	3	0	55	71	42	.306	.436	.373	136	21	15			.972	-4	*C-103	2.7
1920	Bos-A	122	387	58	118	30	7	4	51	64	37	.305	.413	.450	134	22	7	7	-2	.958	-3	C-73,O-40	1.8
1921	*NY-A	134	424	77	134	30	5	6	55	78	35	.316	.428	.453	122	18	7	4	-0	.969	-6	*C-132	1.8
1922	*NY-A	124	408	46	130	21	7	1	53	53	36	.319	.405	.412	111	9	12	6	0	.976	0	*C-119	1.5
1923	*NY-A	84	272	39	75	8	2	2	29	27	17	.276	.360	.342	84	-5	5	2	0	.970	-8	C-81	-0.9
1924	NY-A	114	356	46	104	19	7	5	52	48	43	.292	.382	.427	109	5	2	6	-3	.972	-2	*C-108	0.7
1925	NY-A	73	167	17	40	8	1	2	24	17	9	.240	.310	.335	65	-9	2	1	0	.974	2	C-58	-0.4
1926	StL-A	103	285	36	94	19	5	8	50	32	20	.330	.405	.516	133	13	5	5	-2	.968	-1	C-82/O-3	1.5
1927	StL-A	97	264	40	84	15	2	5	42	41	33	.318	.414	.447	119	9	3	2	-0	.976	-9	C-75	0.5
1928	StL-A	91	245	41	70	10	5	3	39	68	26	.286	.448	.404	121	12	8	2	1	.984	-12	C-82	0.8
1929	StL-A	94	249	43	59	10	5	5	36	74	22	.237	.424	.378	104	6	1	4	-2	**.988**	-6	C-85	0.5
1930	Phi-A	45	92	16	16	4	1	1	9	17	15	.174	.309	.272	47	-7	0	0	0	.973	2	C-36	-0.3
1931	Det-A	30	76	9	14	2	0	0	2	14	11	.184	.311	.211	38	-6	1	0	0	.965	-0	C-30	-0.4
Total	19	1842	5307	769	1506	264	90	59	710	849	573	.284	.393	.401	117	160	121	49		.967	-69	*C-1435,O-167/3S	18.1

■ **ART SCHAREIN** Scharein, Arthur Otto "Scoop" b: 6/30/05, Decatur, Ill. d: 7/2/69, San Antonio, Tex. BR/TR, 5'11", 155 lbs. Deb: 7/6/32 F

YEAR	TM/L	G	AB	R	H	2B	3B	HR	RBI	BB	SO	AVG	OBP	SLG	PRO+	BR/A	SB	CS	SBR	FA	FR	G/POS	TPR
1932	StL-A	81	303	43	92	19	2	0	42	25	10	.304	.363	.380	87	-5	4	8	-4	.965	18	3-77/S-3,2-2	1.4
1933	StL-A	123	471	49	96	13	3	0	26	41	21	.204	.269	.244	35	-44	7	9	-3	.949	14	3-95,S-24/2-7	-2.5
1934	StL-A	1	2	0	1	0	0	0	2	0	0	.500	.500	.500	146	0	0	0	0	.000	0	H	0.0
Total	3	205	776	92	189	32	5	0	70	66	31	.244	.306	.298	56	-49	11	17	-7	.956	32	3-172/S-27,2-9	-1.1

■ **GEORGE SCHAREIN** Scharein, George Albert "Tom" b: 11/21/14, Decatur, Ill. d: 12/23/81, Decatur, Ill. BR/TR, 6'1", 174 lbs. Deb: 4/19/37 F

YEAR	TM/L	G	AB	R	H	2B	3B	HR	RBI	BB	SO	AVG	OBP	SLG	PRO+	BR/A	SB	CS	SBR	FA	FR	G/POS	TPR
1937	Phi-N	146	511	44	123	20	1	0	57	36	47	.241	.293	.284	53	-33	13			.947	9	*S-146	-1.4
1938	Phi-N	117	390	47	93	16	4	1	29	16	33	.238	.268	.308	60	-22	11			.921	-2	S-77,2-39/3-1	-1.7
1939	Phi-N	118	399	35	95	17	1	1	33	13	40	.238	.262	.293	50	-28	4			.958	-9	*S-117	-2.9
1940	Phi-N	7	17	0	5	0	0	0	0	0	3	.294	.294	.294	65	-1	0			.839	-1	/S-7	-0.1
Total	4	388	1317	126	316	53	6	2	119	65	123	.240	.277	.294	54	-84	28			.943	-3	S-347/2-39,3-1	-6.1

■ **NICK SCHARF** Scharf, Edward T. b: 7/1858, Baltimore, Md. d: 5/12/37, Baltimore, Md. TR , Deb: 5/18/1882

YEAR	TM/L	G	AB	R	H	2B	3B	HR	RBI	BB	SO	AVG	OBP	SLG	PRO+	BR/A	SB	CS	SBR	FA	FR	G/POS	TPR
1882	Bal-a	10	39	4	8	1	1	1		0		.205	.205	.359	94	-0				.727	-2	/O-9,3-1	-0.2
1883	Bal-a	3	13	1	2	1	0	0		1		.154	.214	.231	42	-1				.643	-3	/S-3	-0.3
Total	2	13	52	5	10	2	1	1		1		.192	.208	.327	79	-1				.727	-4	/O-9,S-3,3-1	-0.5

■ **AL SCHEER** Scheer, Allan G. b: 10/21/1888, Dayton, Ohio d: 5/6/59, Logansport, Ind. BL/TR, 5'9", 165 lbs. Deb: 8/2/13

YEAR	TM/L	G	AB	R	H	2B	3B	HR	RBI	BB	SO	AVG	OBP	SLG	PRO+	BR/A	SB	CS	SBR	FA	FR	G/POS	TPR
1913	Bro-N	6	22	3	5	0	0	0	0	2	4	.227	.292	.227	48	-1	1			.800	-1	/O-6	-0.3
1914	Ind-F	120	363	63	111	23	6	3	45	49	39	.306	.396	.427	112	2	9			.926	-5	*O-102/2-4,S-1	-0.7
1915	New-F	155	546	75	146	25	14	2	60	65	38	.267	.353	.375	111	0	31			.971	-2	*O-155	-1.0
Total	3	281	931	141	262	48	20	5	105	116	81	.281	.368	.392	110	1	41			.953	-9	O-263/2-4,S-1	-2.0

■ **HEINIE SCHEER** Scheer, Henry b: 7/31/1900, New York, N.Y. d: 3/21/76, New Haven, Conn. BR/TR, 5'8", 146 lbs. Deb: 4/20/22

YEAR	TM/L	G	AB	R	H	2B	3B	HR	RBI	BB	SO	AVG	OBP	SLG	PRO+	BR/A	SB	CS	SBR	FA	FR	G/POS	TPR
1922	Phi-A	51	135	10	23	3	0	4	12	3	25	.170	.188	.281	21	-16	1	0	0	.976	9	2-30,3-10	-0.6
1923	Phi-A	69	210	26	50	8	1	2	21	17	41	.238	.301	.314	61	-12	3	4	-2	.971	-9	2-61	-2.1
Total	2	120	345	36	73	11	1	6	33	20	66	.212	.259	.301	46	-28	4	4	-1	.973	0	/2-91,3-10	-2.7

■ **FRITZ SCHEEREN** Scheeren, Frederick "Dutch" b: 9/8/1891, Kokomo, Ind. d: 6/17/73, Oil City, Pa. BR/TR, 6', 180 lbs. Deb: 9/14/14

YEAR	TM/L	G	AB	R	H	2B	3B	HR	RBI	BB	SO	AVG	OBP	SLG	PRO+	BR/A	SB	CS	SBR	FA	FR	G/POS	TPR
1914	Pit-N	11	31	4	9	0	1	1	2	1	6	.290	.313	.452	132	1	1			.824	-3	O-10	-0.3
1915	Pit-N	4	3	0	0	0	0	0	0	0	0	.000	.000	.000	-99	-1	0			.000	-1	/O-1	-0.1
Total	2	15	34	4	9	0	1	1	2	1	6	.265	.286	.412	111	0	1			.824	-4	/O-11	-0.4

■ **BOB SCHEFFING** Scheffing, Robert Boden b: 8/11/13, Overland, Mo. d: 10/26/85, Phoenix, Ariz. BR/TR, 6'2", 189 lbs. Deb: 4/27/41 MC

YEAR	TM/L	G	AB	R	H	2B	3B	HR	RBI	BB	SO	AVG	OBP	SLG	PRO+	BR/A	SB	CS	SBR	FA	FR	G/POS	TPR
1941	Chi-N	51	132	9	32	8	0	1	20	5	19	.242	.270	.326	70	-6	2			.966	-3	C-34	-0.7
1942	Chi-N	44	102	7	20	3	0	2	12	7	11	.196	.248	.284	58	-6	2			.986	4	C-32	0.0
1946	Chi-N	63	115	8	32	4	1	0	18	12	18	.278	.346	.330	94	-1	0			1.000	-7	C-40	-0.6
1947	Chi-N	110	363	33	96	11	5	5	50	25	25	.264	.312	.364	82	-10	2			.984	-6	C-97	-1.0
1948	Chi-N	102	293	23	88	18	2	5	45	22	27	.300	.351	.427	114	5	0			.989	-5	C-78	0.6
1949	Chi-N	55	149	12	40	6	1	3	19	9	9	.268	.314	.383	88	-3	0			.977	-3	C-40	-0.4
1950	Chi-N	12	16	0	3	1	0	0	1	0	2	.188	.188	.250	14	-2	0			.917	0	/C-3	-0.2
	Cin-N	21	47	4	13	0	0	2	6	4	2	.277	.333	.404	93	-1	0			1.000	-4	C-11	-0.4
	Yr	33	63	4	16	1	0	2	7	4	4	.254	.299	.365	74	-3	0			.982	-3	C-14	-0.6
1951	Cin-N	47	122	9	31	2	0	2	14	16	9	.254	.345	.320	79	-3	0	0	0	.976	-4	C-41	-0.5
	StL-N	12	18	0	2	0	0	0	2	3	5	.111	.238	.111	-3	-3	0	0	0	1.000	1	C-11	-0.1
	Yr	59	140	9	33	2	0	2	16	19	14	.236	.331	.293	68	-6	0	0	0	.980	-2	C-52	-0.6
Total	8	517	1357	105	357	53	9	20	187	103	127	.263	.316	.360	86	-28	6	0		.984	-25	C-387	-3.3

■ **TED SCHEFFLER** Scheffler, Theodore J. b: 4/5/1864, New York, N.Y. d: 2/24/49, Jamaica, N.Y. BR/TR, 5'10", 160 lbs. Deb: 8/7/1888

YEAR	TM/L	G	AB	R	H	2B	3B	HR	RBI	BB	SO	AVG	OBP	SLG	PRO+	BR/A	SB	CS	SBR	FA	FR	G/POS	TPR
1888	Det-N	27	94	17	19	3	1	0	4	9	9	.202	.286	.255	74	-2	4			.847	-4	O-27	-0.7
1890	Roc-a	119	445	111	109	12	6	3	34	78		.245	.374	.319	113	13	77			.911	9	*O-119/C-1	1.6
Total	2	146	539	128	128	15	7	3	38	87	9	.237	.360	.308	106	11	81			.899	5	O-146/C-1	0.9

■ **FRANK SCHEIBECK** Scheibeck, Frank S. b: 6/28/1865, Detroit, Mich. d: 10/22/56, Detroit, Mich. BR/TR, 5'7", 145 lbs. Deb: 5/9/1887

YEAR	TM/L	G	AB	R	H	2B	3B	HR	RBI	BB	SO	AVG	OBP	SLG	PRO+	BR/A	SB	CS	SBR	FA	FR	G/POS	TPR
1887	Cle-a	3	9	2	2	0	0	0	0	2		.222	.364	.222	67	-0	0			.500	-2	/S-1,3-1,P-1	-0.1
1888	Det-N	1	4	0	0	0	0	0	0	0	0	.000	.000	.000	-99	-1	0			.500	-1	/S-1	-0.3
1890	Tol-a	134	485	72	117	13	5	1	49	76		.241	.350	.295	88	-5	57			.883	1	*S-134	0.3
1894	Pit-N	28	102	20	36	2	3	1	10	11	9	.353	.416	.461	112	2	7			.891	-8	S-11/O-9,3-3,2-2	-0.4
	Was-N	52	196	49	45	2	4	0	17	45	24	.230	.384	.281	64	-9	11			.876	5	S-52	-0.1
	Yr	80	298	69	81	4	7	1	27	56	33	.272	.394	.342	81	-7	18			.878	-3	S-63/O-9,3-3,2-2	-0.5
1895	Was-N	48	167	17	31	5	2	0	25	17	21	.186	.265	.240	31	-17	5			.888	2	S-44/3-2,2-2	1.4
1899	Was-N	27	94	19	27	4	1	0	9	11		.287	.368	.351	99	0	5			.877	-11	S-27	-0.8
1901	Cle-A	93	329	33	70	11	3	0	38	18		.213	.258	.264	47	-24	3			.897	-14	S-92	-2.7
1906	Det-A	3	10	1	1	0	0	0	0	2		.100	.250	.100	11	-1	0			.889	-1	/2-3	-0.2
Total	8	389	1396	213	329	37	18	2	148	182	54	.236	.329	.292	70	-55	88			.884	-33	S-362/O-9,2-7,3P	-5.7

■ **RICHIE SCHEINBLUM** Scheinblum, Richard Alan b: 11/5/42, New York, N.Y. BB/TR, 6'1", 180 lbs. Deb: 9/1/65

YEAR	TM/L	G	AB	R	H	2B	3B	HR	RBI	BB	SO	AVG	OBP	SLG	PRO+	BR/A	SB	CS	SBR	FA	FR	G/POS	TPR
1965	Cle-A	4	1	1	0	0	0	0	0	0	0	.000	.000	.000	-99	-0	0	0	0	.000	0	H	0.0
1967	Cle-A	18	66	8	21	4	2	0	6	5	10	.318	.366	.439	136	3	0	2	-1	.943	-0	O-18	0.1
1968	Cle-A	19	55	3	12	5	0	0	5	5	8	.218	.295	.309	84	-1	0	0	0	1.000	1	O-16	-0.1
1969	Cle-A	102	199	13	37	5	1	1	13	19	30	.186	.257	.236	37	-17	0	2	-1	.974	-1	O-50	-2.3
1971	Was-A	27	49	5	7	3	0	0	4	5	5	.143	.263	.204	36	-4	0	0	0	.933	0	O-13	-0.2
1972	KC-A★	134	450	60	135	21	4	8	66	58	40	.300	.385	.418	139	23	0	1	-1	.965	-3	*O-119	1.7
1973	Cin-N	29	54	5	12	2	0	1	8	10	4	.222	.344	.315	88	-1	0	0	0	.960	-2	O-19	-0.4
	Cal-A	77	229	28	75	10	2	3	21	35	27	.328	.419	.428	150	17	0	0	0	.969	-0	O-54/D-7	1.4

YEAR	TM/L	G	AB	R	H	2B	3B	HR	RBI	BB	SO	AVG	OBP	SLG	PRO+	BR/A	SB	CS	SBR	FA	FR	G/POS	TPR
1974	Cal-A	10	26	1	4	0	0	0	2	1	2	.154	.185	.154	-2	-3	0	0	0	.929	-1	/O-8,D-1	-0.5
	KC-A	36	83	7	15	2	0	0	2	8	8	.181	.253	.205	31	-7	0	1	-1	.000	-1	D-17/O-2	-1.0
	Yr	46	109	8	19	2	0	0	4	9	10	.174	.237	.193	24	-10	0	1	-1	.929	-2	D-18,O-10	-1.5
	StL-N	6	6	0	2	0	0	0	0	0	1	.333	.333	.333	88	-0	0	0	0	.000	0	H	0.0
Total	8	462	1218	131	320	52	9	13	127	149	135	.263	.346	.352	104	10	0	6	-4	.965	-4	O-299/D-25	-1.3

■ DANNY SCHELL Schell, Clyde Daniel b: 12/26/27, Fostoria, Mich. d: 5/11/72, Mayville, Mich. BR/TR, 6′1″, 195 lbs. Deb: 4/13/54

YEAR	TM/L	G	AB	R	H	2B	3B	HR	RBI	BB	SO	AVG	OBP	SLG	PRO+	BR/A	SB	CS	SBR	FA	FR	G/POS	TPR
1954	Phi-N	92	272	25	77	14	3	7	33	17	31	.283	.330	.434	97	-2	0	3	-2	.974	1	O-69	-0.6
1955	Phi-N	2	2	0	0	0	0	0	0	0	1	.000	.000	.000	-99	-1	0	0	0	.000	0	H	-0.1
Total	2	94	274	25	77	14	3	7	33	17	32	.281	.328	.431	96	-2	0	3	-2	.974	1	/O-69	-0.7

■ AL SCHELLHASE Schellhase, Albert Herman "Schelley" b: 9/13/1864, Evansville, Ind. d: 1/3/19, Evansville, Ind. BR/TR, 5′8″, 148 lbs. Deb: 5/7/1890

YEAR	TM/L	G	AB	R	H	2B	3B	HR	RBI	BB	SO	AVG	OBP	SLG	PRO+	BR/A	SB	CS	SBR	FA	FR	G/POS	TPR
1890	Bos-N	9	29	1	4	0	0	0	1	1	10	.138	.167	.138	-10	-4	0			.778	-1	/O-5,C-2,S-1,3-1	-0.4
1891	Lou-a	7	20	4	3	0	0	0	1	1	2	.150	.190	.150	-2	-3	3			.943	0	/C-7	-0.2
Total	2	16	49	5	7	0	0	0	2	2	12	.143	.176	.143	-7	-7	3			.922	-1	/C-9,O-5,3-1,S-1	-0.6

■ FRED SCHEMANSKE Schemanske, Frederick George "Buck" b: 4/28/03, Detroit, Mich. d: 2/18/60, Detroit, Mich. BR/TR, 6′2″, 190 lbs. Deb: 9/15/23

YEAR	TM/L	G	AB	R	H	2B	3B	HR	RBI	BB	SO	AVG	OBP	SLG	PRO+	BR/A	SB	CS	SBR	FA	FR	G/POS	TPR
1923	Was-A	2	2	0	2	0	0	0	2	1	0	1.000	1.000	1.000	450	1	0	0	0	.000	-0	/P-1	0.0

■ MIKE SCHEMER Schemer, Michael "Lefty" b: 11/20/17, Baltimore, Md. d: 4/22/83, Miami, Fla. BL/TL, 6′, 180 lbs. Deb: 8/8/45

YEAR	TM/L	G	AB	R	H	2B	3B	HR	RBI	BB	SO	AVG	OBP	SLG	PRO+	BR/A	SB	CS	SBR	FA	FR	G/POS	TPR
1945	NY-N	31	108	10	36	3	1	1	10	6	1	.333	.368	.407	114	2	2			.993	4	1-27	0.4
1946	NY-N	1	1	0	0	0	0	0	0	0	0	.000	.000	.000	-99	-0	0			.000	0	H	0.0
Total	2	32	109	10	36	3	1	1	10	6	1	.330	.365	.404	112	2	2			.993	4	/1-27	0.4

■ BILL SCHENCK Schenck, William G. b: 7/1854, Brooklyn, N.Y. d: 1/29/34, Brooklyn, N.Y. 5′7″, 171 lbs. Deb: 5/29/1882

YEAR	TM/L	G	AB	R	H	2B	3B	HR	RBI	BB	SO	AVG	OBP	SLG	PRO+	BR/A	SB	CS	SBR	FA	FR	G/POS	TPR
1882	Lou-a	60	231	37	60	11	3	0		8		.260	.285	.333	114	4				.814	-7	*3-58/S-2,P-2	-0.1
1884	Ric-a	42	151	14	31	4	0	3		1		.205	.216	.291	65	-6				.836	-5	S-40/2-2	-1.0
1885	Bro-a	1	4	0	0	0	0	0	0	0		.000	.000	.000	-99	-1				1.000	0	/3-1	-0.1
Total	3	103	386	51	91	15	3	3	0	9		.236	.255	.313	92	-3				.817	-12	/3-59,S-42,2-2,P-2	-1.2

■ HANK SCHENZ Schenz, Henry Leonard b: 4/11/19, New Richmond, Ohio d: 5/12/88, Cincinnati, Ohio BR/TR, 5′9.5″, 175 lbs. Deb: 9/18/46

YEAR	TM/L	G	AB	R	H	2B	3B	HR	RBI	BB	SO	AVG	OBP	SLG	PRO+	BR/A	SB	CS	SBR	FA	FR	G/POS	TPR
1946	Chi-N	6	11	0	2	0	0	0	1	0	0	.182	.182	.182	3	-1	1			1.000	0	/3-5	-0.1
1947	Chi-N	7	14	2	1	0	0	0	0	2	1	.071	.235	.071	-16	-2	0			.917	0	/3-5	-0.2
1948	Chi-N	96	337	43	88	17	1	1	14	18	15	.261	.306	.326	74	-12	3			.974	-5	2-78/3-5	-1.4
1949	Chi-N	7	14	2	6	0	0	0	1	1	0	.429	.467	.429	146	1	2			1.000	1	/3-5	0.2
1950	Pit-N	58	101	17	23	4	2	1	5	6	7	.228	.271	.337	57	-6	0			.987	3	2-21,3-12/S-4	-0.3
1951	Pit-N	25	61	5	13	1	0	0	3	0	2	.213	.226	.230	22	-7	0	2	-1	.961	-3	2-19/3-2	-1.0
	*NY-N	8	0	1	0	0	0	0	0	0	0	—	—	—	—	0	0	0	0	.000	0	R	0.0
	Yr	33	61	6	13	1	0	0	3	0	2	.213	.226	.230	22	-7	0	2	-1	.961	-3	2-19/3-2	-1.0
Total	6	207	538	70	133	22	3	2	24	27	25	.247	.291	.310	63	-28	6	2		.974	-5	2-118/3-34,S-4	-2.8

■ JOE SCHEPNER Schepner, Joseph Maurice "Gentleman Joe" b: 8/10/1895, Aliquippa, Pa. d: 7/25/59, Mobile, Ala. BR/TR, 5′10″, 160 lbs. Deb: 9/11/19

YEAR	TM/L	G	AB	R	H	2B	3B	HR	RBI	BB	SO	AVG	OBP	SLG	PRO+	BR/A	SB	CS	SBR	FA	FR	G/POS	TPR
1919	StL-A	14	48	2	10	4	0	0	6	1	5	.208	.224	.292	43	-4	0			.947	-1	3-13	-0.5

■ BOB SCHERBARTH Scherbarth, Robert Elmer b: 1/18/26, Milwaukee, Wis. BR/TR, 6′, 180 lbs. Deb: 4/23/50

YEAR	TM/L	G	AB	R	H	2B	3B	HR	RBI	BB	SO	AVG	OBP	SLG	PRO+	BR/A	SB	CS	SBR	FA	FR	G/POS	TPR
1950	Bos-A	1	0	0	0	0	0	0	0	0	0	—	—	—	—	0	0	0	0	.000	0	/C-1	0.0

■ HARRY SCHERER Scherer, Harry Deb: 7/24/1889

YEAR	TM/L	G	AB	R	H	2B	3B	HR	RBI	BB	SO	AVG	OBP	SLG	PRO+	BR/A	SB	CS	SBR	FA	FR	G/POS	TPR
1889	Lou-a	1	3	0	1	0	0	0	0	0	0	.333	.333	.333	92	-0	0			.500	-1	/O-1	-0.1

■ LOU SCHIAPPACASSE Schiappacasse, Louis Joseph b: 3/29/1881, Ann Arbor, Mich. d: 9/20/10, Ann Arbor, Mich. BR/TR, Deb: 9/7/02

YEAR	TM/L	G	AB	R	H	2B	3B	HR	RBI	BB	SO	AVG	OBP	SLG	PRO+	BR/A	SB	CS	SBR	FA	FR	G/POS	TPR
1902	Det-A	2	5	0	0	0	0	0	1	1		.000	.167	.000	-50	-1	0			.000	-1	/O-2	-0.2

■ MORRIE SCHICK Schick, Maurice Francis b: 4/17/1892, Chicago, Ill. d: 10/25/79, Hazel Crest, Ill. BR/TR, 5′11″, 170 lbs. Deb: 4/15/17

YEAR	TM/L	G	AB	R	H	2B	3B	HR	RBI	BB	SO	AVG	OBP	SLG	PRO+	BR/A	SB	CS	SBR	FA	FR	G/POS	TPR
1917	Chi-N	14	34	3	5	0	0	0	3	3	10	.147	.216	.147	11	-3	0			.960	0	O-12	-0.4

■ CHUCK SCHILLING Schilling, Charles Thomas b: 10/25/37, Brooklyn, N.Y. BR/TR, 5′11″, 170 lbs. Deb: 4/11/61

YEAR	TM/L	G	AB	R	H	2B	3B	HR	RBI	BB	SO	AVG	OBP	SLG	PRO+	BR/A	SB	CS	SBR	FA	FR	G/POS	TPR
1961	Bos-A	158	646	87	167	25	2	5	62	78	77	.259	.340	.327	77	-19	7	6	-2	**.991**	15	*2-158	1.2
1962	Bos-A	119	413	48	95	17	1	7	35	29	48	.230	.287	.327	63	-22	1	0	0	.985	13	*2-118	0.4
1963	Bos-A	146	576	63	135	25	0	8	33	41	72	.234	.291	.319	69	-24	3	2	-0	.985	-14	*2-143	-2.6
1964	Bos-A	47	163	18	32	6	0	0	7	15	22	.196	.264	.233	38	-13	0	1	-1	.974	-0	2-42	-1.2
1965	Bos-A	71	171	14	41	3	2	3	9	13	17	.240	.293	.333	73	-6	0	1	-1	.976	10	2-41	0.7
Total	5	541	1969	230	470	76	5	23	146	176	236	.239	.305	.317	68	-84	11	10	-3	.985	24	2-502	-1.5

■ BILL SCHINDLER Schindler, William Gibbons b: 7/10/1896, Perryville, Mo. d: 2/6/79, Perryville, Mo. BR/TR, 5′11″, 160 lbs. Deb: 9/3/20

YEAR	TM/L	G	AB	R	H	2B	3B	HR	RBI	BB	SO	AVG	OBP	SLG	PRO+	BR/A	SB	CS	SBR	FA	FR	G/POS	TPR
1920	StL-N	1	2	0	0	0	0	0	0	0	1	.000	.000	.000	-99	-1	0	0	0	1.000	-0	/C-1	-0.1

■ DUTCH SCHIRICK Schirick, Harry Ernest b: 6/15/1890, Ruby, N.Y. d: 11/12/68, Kingston, N.Y. BR/TR, 5′8″, 160 lbs. Deb: 9/17/14

YEAR	TM/L	G	AB	R	H	2B	3B	HR	RBI	BB	SO	AVG	OBP	SLG	PRO+	BR/A	SB	CS	SBR	FA	FR	G/POS	TPR
1914	StL-A	1	0	0	0	0	0	0	0	1	0	—	1.000	—	212	0	2			.000	0	H	0.1

■ LARRY SCHLAFLY Schlafly, Harry Linton b: 9/20/1878, Port Washington, Ohio d: 6/27/19, Canton, Ohio BR/TR, 5′11″, 182 lbs. Deb: 9/18/02 M

YEAR	TM/L	G	AB	R	H	2B	3B	HR	RBI	BB	SO	AVG	OBP	SLG	PRO+	BR/A	SB	CS	SBR	FA	FR	G/POS	TPR
1902	Chi-N	10	31	5	10	0	3	0	5	6		.323	.432	.516	198	4	2			1.000	-4	/O-5,2-4,3-2	0.0
1906	Was-A	123	426	60	105	13	8	2	30	50		.246	.345	.329	117	11	29			.961	15	*2-123	2.8
1907	Was-A	24	74	10	10	0	0	1	4	22		.135	.354	.176	75	0	7			.928	-9	2-24	-1.1
1914	Buf-F	51	127	16	33	7	1	2	19	12	22	.260	.338	.378	93	-3	3			.951	2	2-23/1-7,C-1,3OM	-0.2
Total	4	208	658	91	158	20	12	5	58	90	22	.240	.349	.330	111	11	41			.954	4	2-174/1-7,O-6,3C	1.5

■ ADMIRAL SCHLEI Schlei, George Henry b: 1/12/1878, Cincinnati, Ohio d: 1/24/58, Huntington, W.Va. BR/TR, 5′8.5″, 179 lbs. Deb: 4/24/04

YEAR	TM/L	G	AB	R	H	2B	3B	HR	RBI	BB	SO	AVG	OBP	SLG	PRO+	BR/A	SB	CS	SBR	FA	FR	G/POS	TPR
1904	Cin-N	97	291	25	69	8	3	0	32	17		.237	.297	.285	74	-9	7			.977	10	C-88	1.1
1905	Cin-N	99	314	32	71	8	3	1	36	22		.226	.285	.280	62	-15	9			.962	16	C-89/1-6	1.0
1906	Cin-N	116	388	44	95	13	8	4	54	29		.245	.304	.351	100	-1	7			.961	9	C-91,1-21	1.8
1907	Cin-N	84	246	28	67	3	2	0	27	28		.272	.347	.301	99	1	5			.980	7	C-67/1-3,O-2	1.5
1908	Cin-N	92	300	31	66	6	4	1	22	22		.220	.278	.277	79	-7	2			.962	-8	C-88	-0.8
1909	NY-N	92	279	25	68	12	0	0	30	40		.244	.343	.287	94	-0	4			.963	3	C-89	1.2
1910	NY-N	55	99	10	19	2	1	0	8	14	10	.192	.304	.232	57	-5	4			.986	0	C-49	-0.2
1911	NY-N	1	1	0	0	0	0	0	0	0	1	.000	.000	.000	-97	-0	0			.000	0	H	0.0
Total	8	636	1918	195	455	52	21	6	209	172	11	.237	.307	.296	83	-37	38			.968	36	C-561/1-30,O-2	5.6

■ RUDY SCHLESINGER Schlesinger, William Cordes b: 11/5/41, Cincinnati, Ohio BR/TR, 6′2″, 175 lbs. Deb: 5/4/65

YEAR	TM/L	G	AB	R	H	2B	3B	HR	RBI	BB	SO	AVG	OBP	SLG	PRO+	BR/A	SB	CS	SBR	FA	FR	G/POS	TPR
1965	Bos-A	1	1	0	0	0	0	0	0	0	0	.000	.000	.000	-94	-0	0	0	0	.000	0	H	0.0

■ DUTCH SCHLIEBNER Schliebner, Frederick Paul b: 5/19/1891, Charlottenburg, Germany d: 4/15/75, Toledo, Ohio BR/TR, 5′10″, 180 lbs. Deb: 4/17/23

YEAR	TM/L	G	AB	R	H	2B	3B	HR	RBI	BB	SO	AVG	OBP	SLG	PRO+	BR/A	SB	CS	SBR	FA	FR	G/POS	TPR
1923	Bro-N	19	76	11	19	4	0	0	4	5	7	.250	.296	.303	60	-4	1	0	0	.981	3	1-19	-0.3
	StL-A	127	444	50	122	19	6	4	52	39	60	.275	.339	.372	82	-12	3	2	-0	.989	-0	*1-127	-1.9
Total	1	146	520	61	141	23	6	4	56	44	67	.271	.333	.362	79	-16	4	2	0	.988	2	1-146	-2.2

■ JAY SCHLUETER Schlueter, Jay D b: 7/31/49, Phoenix, Ariz. BR/TR, 6′, 182 lbs. Deb: 6/18/71

YEAR	TM/L	G	AB	R	H	2B	3B	HR	RBI	BB	SO	AVG	OBP	SLG	PRO+	BR/A	SB	CS	SBR	FA	FR	G/POS	TPR
1971	Hou-N	7	3	1	1	0	0	0	0	0	1	.333	.333	.333	92	-0	0	0	0	1.000	-0	/O-2	0.0

■ NORM SCHLUETER Schlueter, Norman John "Duke" b: 9/25/16, Belleville, Ill. BR/TR, 5′10″, 175 lbs. Deb: 5/28/38

YEAR	TM/L	G	AB	R	H	2B	3B	HR	RBI	BB	SO	AVG	OBP	SLG	PRO+	BR/A	SB	CS	SBR	FA	FR	G/POS	TPR
1938	Chi-A	35	118	11	27	5	1	0	7	4	15	.229	.254	.288	35	-12	1	0	0	.952	-3	C-34	-1.2
1939	Chi-A	34	56	5	13	2	1	0	8	1	11	.232	.246	.304	39	-5	2	0	1	.988	1	C-32	-0.3
1944	Cle-A	49	122	2	15	4	0	0	11	12	22	.123	.201	.156	3	-15	0	2	-1	.985	-8	C-43	-2.4
Total	3	118	296	18	55	11	2	0	26	17	48	.186	.230	.236	24	-33	3	2	-0	.974	-10	C-109	-3.9

YEAR	TM/L	G	AB	R	H	2B	3B	HR	RBI	BB	SO	AVG	OBP	SLG	PRO+	BR/A	SB	CS	SBR	FA	FR	G/POS	TPR
■ **RAY SCHMANDT**	Schmandt, Raymond Henry b: 1/25/1896, St.Louis, Mo. d: 2/2/69, St.Louis, Mo. BR/TR, 6′1″, 175 lbs. Deb: 6/24/15																						
1915	StL-A	3	4	0	0	0	0	0	0	0	1	.000	.000	.000	-99	-1	0			1.000	-0	/1-1	-0.1
1918	Bro-N	34	114	11	35	5	4	0	18	7	7	.307	.347	.421	134	4	1			.934	-4	2-34	0.3
1919	Bro-N	47	127	8	21	4	0	0	10	4	13	.165	.191	.197	16	-13	0			.911	0	2-18,1-12/3-6	-1.3
1920	*Bro-N	28	63	7	15	2	1	0	7	3	4	.238	.273	.302	63	-3	1	1	-0	.995	3	1-20	0.0
1921	Bro-N	95	350	42	107	8	5	1	43	11	22	.306	.329	.366	81	-10	3	4	-2	.989	0	1-92	-1.3
1922	Bro-N	110	396	54	106	17	3	2	44	21	28	.268	.306	.341	67	-20	6	6	-2	.989	5	*1-110	-2.0
Total	6	317	1054	122	284	36	13	3	122	46	75	.269	.301	.337	72	-42	11	11		.990	5	1-235/2-52,3-6	-4.4
■ **GEORGE SCHMEES**	Schmees, George Edward "Rocky" b: 9/6/24, Cincinnati, Ohio d:10/30/98, San Jose, Cal. BL/TL, 6′, 190 lbs. Deb: 4/15/52																						
1952	StL-A	34	61	9	8	1	1	0	3	2	18	.131	.159	.180	-6	-9	0	0	0	.932	-1	O-19/1-2	-1.0
	Bos-A	42	64	8	13	3	0	0	3	10	11	.203	.311	.250	53	-4	0	1	-1	1.000	-7	O-29/P-2,1-2	-1.4
	Yr	76	125	17	21	4	1	0	6	12	29	.168	.241	.216	26	-12	0	1	-1	.960	-8	O-48/1-4,P-2	-2.4
■ **BOSS SCHMIDT**	Schmidt, Charles b: 9/12/1880, Coal Hill, Ark. d: 11/14/32, Clarksville, Ark. BB/TR, 5′11″, 200 lbs. Deb: 4/30/06 F																						
1906	Det-A	68	216	13	47	4	3	0	10	6		.218	.242	.264	57	-11	1			.958	7	C-67	0.3
1907	*Det-A	104	349	32	85	6	6	0	23	5		.244	.269	.295	77	-10	8			.944	3	*C-103	0.3
1908	*Det-A	122	419	45	111	14	3	1	38	16		.265	.297	.320	96	-3	5			.951	8	*C-121	1.9
1909	*Det-A	84	253	21	53	8	2	1	28	7		.209	.240	.269	58	-13	7			.955	-6	C-81/O-1	-1.4
1910	Det-A	71	197	22	51	7	7	1	23	2		.259	.277	.381	99	-2	2			.973	-8	C-66	-0.4
1911	Det-A	28	46	4	13	2	1	0	2	0		.283	.298	.370	82	-1	0			1.000	-2	/C-9,O-1	-0.3
Total	6	477	1480	137	360	41	22	3	124	36		.243	.270	.307	79	-39	23			.955	3	C-447/O-2	0.4
■ **BUTCH SCHMIDT**	Schmidt, Charles John "Butcher Boy" b: 7/19/1886, Baltimore, Md. d: 9/4/52, Baltimore, Md. BL/TL, 6′1.5″, 200 lbs. Deb: 5/11/09																						
1909	NY-A	1	2	0	0	0	0	0	0	0		.000	.000	.000	-99	-0	0			.500	-0	/P-1	0.0
1913	Bos-N	22	78	6	24	2	2	1	14	2	5	.308	.333	.423	113	1	1			.983	1	1-22	0.1
1914	*Bos-N	147	537	67	153	17	9	1	71	43	55	.285	.350	.356	111	8	14			.990	3	*1-147	0.7
1915	Bos-N	127	458	46	115	26	7	2	60	36	59	.251	.318	.352	107	4	3	10	-5	.987	-4	*1-127	-1.0
Total	4	297	1075	119	292	45	18	4	145	81	119	.272	.335	.358	109	12	18	10		.988	-1	1-296/P-1	-0.2
■ **DAVE SCHMIDT**	Schmidt, David Frederick b: 12/22/56, Mesa, Ariz. BR/TR, 6′1″, 190 lbs. Deb: 4/28/81																						
1981	Bos-A	15	42	6	10	1	0	2	3	7	17	.238	.347	.405	109	1	0	0	0	1.000	-4	C-15	-0.3
■ **MIKE SCHMIDT**	Schmidt, Michael Jack b: 9/27/49, Dayton, Ohio BR/TR, 6′2″, 203 lbs. Deb: 9/12/72 H																						
1972	Phi-N	13	34	2	7	0	0	1	3	5	15	.206	.325	.294	75	-1	0	0	0	.964	2	3-11/2-1	0.1
1973	Phi-N	132	367	43	72	11	0	18	52	62	136	.196	.326	.373	91	-4	8	2	1	.954	**21**	*3-125/2-4,1-2,S-2	1.9
1974	Phi-N★	162	568	108	160	28	7	**36**	116	106	138	.282	.398	**.546**	156	43	23	12	-0	.954	26	*3-162	**6.9**
1975	Phi-N	158	562	93	140	34	3	**38**	95	101	180	.249	.367	.523	139	29	29	12	2	.954	**24**	*3-151,S-10	5.7
1976	*Phi-N★	160	584	112	153	31	4	**38**	107	100	149	.262	.380	.524	150	39	14	9	-1	.961	**25**	*3-160	**6.4**
1977	*Phi-N★	154	544	114	149	27	11	38	101	104	122	.274	.399	.574	151	40	15	8	-0	.964	29	*3-149/S-2,2-1	**6.7**
1978	*Phi-N	145	513	93	129	27	2	21	78	91	103	.251	.368	.435	122	17	19	6	2	.963	10	*3-139/S-1	2.9
1979	Phi-N★	160	541	109	137	25	4	45	114	**120**	115	.253	.392	.564	153	41	9	5	-0	.954	18	*3-157/S-2	5.8
1980	*Phi-N†	150	548	104	157	25	8	**48**	**121**	89	119	.286	.388	**.624**	**169**	**50**	12	5	1	.946	23	*3-149	**7.3**
1981	*Phi-N★	102	354	**78**	112	19	2	**31**	**91**	**73**	71	.316	**.439**	**.644**	**195**	**46**	12	4	1	.956	23	*3-101	**7.0**
1982	Phi-N★	148	514	108	144	26	3	35	87	**107**	131	.280	**.407**	**.547**	**161**	**45**	14	7	0	.950	19	*3-148	**6.1**
1983	*Phi-N★	154	534	104	136	16	4	**40**	109	**128**	148	.255	**.402**	.524	**156**	**45**	7	8	-3	.959	23	*3-153/S-2	**6.4**
1984	Phi-N★	151	528	93	146	23	3	**36**	**106**	92	116	.277	.388	.536	**155**	**39**	5	7	-3	.941	12	*3-145/1-2,S-1	4.8
1985	Phi-N	158	549	89	152	31	5	33	93	87	117	.277	.379	.532	148	36	1	3	-2	.993	5	*1-106,3-54/S-1	3.3
1986	Phi-N★	160	552	97	160	29	1	**37**	**119**	89	84	.290	.395	**.547**	**152**	**40**	1	2	-1	**.980**	-7	*3-124,1-35	2.8
1987	Phi-N★	147	522	88	153	28	0	35	113	83	80	.293	.392	.548	141	32	2	1	0	.971	13	*3-138/1-9,S-3	4.1
1988	Phi-N	108	390	52	97	21	2	12	62	49	42	.249	.342	.405	111	6	3	0	1	.939	3	*3-104/1-3	1.0
1989	Phi-N†	42	148	19	30	7	0	6	28	21	17	.203	.302	.372	91	-2	0	1	-1	.918	-5	3-42	-0.8
Total	18	2404	8352	1506	2234	408	59	548	1595	1507	1883	.267	.384	.527	147	543	174	92	-3	.955	265	*3-2212,1-157/S2	78.4
■ **BOB SCHMIDT**	Schmidt, Robert Benjamin b: 4/22/33, St.Louis, Mo. BR/TR, 6′2″, 205 lbs. Deb: 4/16/58																						
1958	SF-N☆	127	393	46	96	20	2	14	54	33	59	.244	.308	.412	90	-6	0	1	-1	.982	-3	*C-123	-0.3
1959	SF-N	71	181	17	44	7	1	5	20	13	24	.243	.297	.376	80	-6	0	2	-1	1.000	-0	C-70	-0.4
1960	SF-N	110	344	31	92	12	1	8	37	26	51	.267	.319	.378	96	-3	0	3	-2	.981	-3	*C-108	-0.2
1961	SF-N	2	6	0	1	0	0	0	1	0	1	.167	.167	.167	-12	-1	0	0	0	1.000	1	/C-2	0.0
	Cin-N	27	70	4	9	0	0	1	4	8	14	.129	.218	.171	5	-10	0	0	0	.993	1	C-27	-0.7
	Yr	29	76	4	10	0	0	1	5	8	15	.132	.214	.171	4	-10	0	0	0	.994	3	C-29	-0.7
1962	Was-A	88	256	28	62	14	0	10	31	14	37	.242	.284	.414	86	-6	0	0	0	**.997**	-2	C-88	-0.5
1963	Was-A	9	15	3	3	1	0	0	0	3	5	.200	.333	.267	71	-0	0	0	0	1.000	-1	/C-6	-0.2
1965	NY-A	20	40	4	10	1	0	1	3	3	8	.250	.302	.350	85	-1	0	0	0	.990	2	C-20	0.2
Total	7	454	1305	133	317	55	4	39	150	100	199	.243	.299	.381	84	-33	0	6	-4	.988	-5	C-444	-2.1
■ **WALTER SCHMIDT**	Schmidt, Walter Joseph b: 3/20/1887, Coal Hill, Ark. d: 7/4/73, Modesto, Cal. BR/TR, 5′9″, 159 lbs. Deb: 4/13/16 F																						
1916	Pit-N	64	184	16	35	1	2	2	15	10	13	.190	.236	.250	49	-11	3			.976	0	C-57	-0.8
1917	Pit-N	72	183	9	45	7	0	0	17	11	11	.246	.296	.284	76	-5	4			.978	8	C-61	0.8
1918	Pit-N	105	323	31	77	6	3	0	27	17	19	.238	.281	.276	68	-12	7			.981	16	*C-104	1.3
1919	Pit-N	85	267	23	67	9	2	0	29	23	9	.251	.310	.300	81	-6	5			.982	1	C-85	0.3
1920	Pit-N	94	310	22	86	8	4	0	20	24	15	.277	.337	.329	89	-4	9	3	1	.971	-5	C-92	-0.1
1921	Pit-N	114	393	30	111	9	3	0	38	12	13	.282	.307	.321	65	-20	10	6	-1	**.986**	7	*C-111	-0.7
1922	Pit-N	40	152	21	50	11	1	0	22	1	5	.329	.333	.414	91	-2	2	1	0	.995	-6	C-40	-0.6
1923	Pit-N	97	335	39	83	7	2	0	37	22	12	.248	.300	.281	53	-22	10	5	0	.981	-9	C-96	-2.6
1924	Pit-N	58	177	16	43	3	2	1	20	13	5	.243	.295	.299	59	-10	6	1	1	.986	2	C-57	-0.4
1925	StL-N	37	87	9	22	2	1	0	9	4	3	.253	.293	.299	51	-6	1	0	0	.967	6	C-31	0.1
Total	10	766	2411	216	619	63	20	3	234	137	105	.257	.301	.303	68	-99	57	16		.980	20	C-734	-2.7
■ **HANK SCHMULBACH**	Schmulbach, Henry Alrives b: 1/17/25, E.St.Louis, Ill. BL/TR, 5′11″, 165 lbs. Deb: 9/27/43																						
1943	StL-A	1	0	1	0	0	0	0	0	0	0	—	—	—	—	0	0	0	0	.000	0	R	0.0
■ **DAVE SCHNECK**	Schneck, David Lee b: 6/18/49, Allentown, Pa. BL/TL, 5′10″, 200 lbs. Deb: 7/14/72																						
1972	NY-N	37	123	7	23	3	2	3	10	10	26	.187	.254	.317	63	-6	0	1	-1	.985	-1	O-33	-1.0
1973	NY-N	13	36	2	7	0	1	0	0	1	4	.194	.216	.250	29	-3	0	0	0	1.000	0	O-12	-0.4
1974	NY-N	93	254	23	52	11	1	5	25	16	43	.205	.255	.315	60	-15	4	1	1	.974	0	O-84	-1.7
Total	3	143	413	32	82	14	4	8	35	27	73	.199	.251	.310	58	-24	4	2	0	.979	-0	O-129	-3.1
■ **RED SCHOENDIENST**	Schoendienst, Albert Fred b: 2/2/23, Germantown, Ill. BB/TR, 6′, 170 lbs. Deb: 4/17/45 MCH																						
1945	StL-N	137	565	89	157	22	6	1	47	21	17	.278	.305	.343	78	-18	**26**			.983	3	*O-118,S-10/2-1	-2.1
1946	*StL-N★	142	606	94	170	28	5	0	34	37	27	.281	.322	.343	85	-12	12			**.984**	-1	*2-128,3-12/S-4	-0.4
1947	StL-N	151	659	91	167	25	9	3	48	48	27	.253	.304	.332	66	-32	6			.976	-2	*2-142/3-5,O-1	-2.4
1948	StL-N★	119	408	64	111	21	4	4	36	28	16	.272	.319	.373	82	-11	1			.980	1	2-96	-0.5
1949	StL-N★	151	640	102	190	25	2	3	54	51	18	.297	.351	.356	86	-11	8			**.987**	24	*2-138,S-14/3-6,O-2	1.9
1950	StL-N★	153	642	81	177	**43**	9	7	63	33	32	.276	.313	.403	83	-17	3			.985	8	*2-143,S-10/3-1	-0.2
1951	StL-N★	135	553	88	160	32	7	6	54	35	23	.289	.335	.405	98	-3	0	1	-1	.990	16	*2-124/S-8	1.9
1952	StL-N☆	152	620	91	188	40	7	7	67	42	30	.303	.347	.424	113	10	9	6	-1	.977	**33**	*2-142,3-11/S-3	4.9
1953	StL-N★	146	564	107	193	35	5	15	79	60	23	.342	.405	.502	135	30	3	3	-1	**.983**	25	*2-140	**5.8**
1954	StL-N★	148	610	98	192	38	8	5	79	54	22	.315	.371	.428	107	7	4	2	0	.980	**33**	*2-144	4.8
1955	StL-N★	145	553	68	148	21	3	11	51	54	28	.268	.337	.376	89	-8	7	7	-2	**.985**	-15	*2-142	-1.4
1956	StL-N	40	153	22	48	9	0	0	15	13	5	.314	.367	.373	100	0	0	1	-1	.995	-2	2-36	0.1

YEAR	TM/L	G	AB	R	H	2B	3B	HR	RBI	BB	SO	AVG	OBP	SLG	PRO+	BR/A	SB	CS	SBR	FA	FR	G/POS	TPR
	NY-N	92	334	39	99	12	3	2	14	28	10	.296	.354	.368	95	-1	1	2	-1	.993	-11	2-85	-0.6
	Yr	132	487	61	147	21	3	2	29	41	15	.302	.358	.370	97	-1	1	3	-2	**.993**	-12	*2-121	-0.5
1957	NY-N	57	254	35	78	8	4	9	33	10	8	.307	.338	.476	116	5	2	1	0	.984	-2	2-57	0.8
	*Mil-N★	93	394	56	122	23	4	6	32	23	7	.310	.349	.434	117	8	2	3	-1	.987	4	2-92/O-2	1.9
	Yr	150	648	91	**200**	31	8	15	65	33	15	.309	.345	.451	117	14	4	4	-1	.986	3	*2-149/O-2	2.7
1958	*Mil-N	106	427	47	112	23	1	1	24	31	21	.262	.314	.328	77	-15	3	1	0	**.987**	3	*2-105	-0.7
1959	Mil-N	5	3	0	0	0	0	0	0	0	0	.000	.000	.000	-99	-1	0	0	0	.667	-0	/2-4	-0.1
1960	Mil-N	68	226	21	58	9	1	1	19	17	13	.257	.311	.319	79	-7	1	0	0	.964	-17	2-62	-1.9
1961	StL-N	72	120	9	36	9	0	1	12	12	6	.300	.364	.400	93	-1	1	0	0	.955	-11	2-32	-0.9
1962	StL-N	98	143	21	43	4	0	2	12	9	12	.301	.346	.371	84	-3	0	0	0	.986	-0	2-21/3-4	-0.2
1963	StL-N	6	5	0	0	0	0	0	0	0	1	.000	.000	.000	-91	-1	0	0	0	.000	0	H	-0.1
Total	19	2216	8479	1223	2449	427	78	84	773	606	346	.289	.338	.387	93	-82	89	27		.983	88	*2-1834,O-123/S3	10.6

■ JUMBO SCHOENECK Schoeneck, Louis N. b: 3/3/1862, Chicago, Ill. d: 1/20/30, Chicago, Ill. BR/TR, 6′3″, 223 lbs. Deb: 4/20/1884

YEAR	TM/L	G	AB	R	H	2B	3B	HR	RBI	BB	SO	AVG	OBP	SLG	PRO+	BR/A	SB	CS	SBR	FA	FR	G/POS	TPR
1884	CP-U	90	366	56	116	22	2	2		8		.317	.332	.404	123	-1				.956	0	*1-90	-1.0
	Bal-U	16	60	5	15	2	0	0		0		.250	.250	.283	56	-5				.962	2	1-16	-0.5
	Yr	106	426	61	131	24	2	2		8		.308	.320	.387	112	-6				**.957**	2	*1-106	-1.5
1888	Ind-N	48	169	15	40	4	0	0	20	9	24	.237	.283	.260	73	-5	11			.974	-1	1-48/P-2	-1.0
1889	Ind-N	16	62	3	15	2	2	0	8	3	3	.242	.299	.339	76	-2	1			.978	2	1-16	-0.1
Total	3	170	657	79	186	30	4	2	28	20	27	.283	.308	.350	99	-13	12			.964	3	1-170/P-2	-2.6

■ DICK SCHOFIELD Schofield, John Richard "Ducky" b: 1/7/35, Springfield, Ill. BB/TR, 5′9″, 165 lbs. Deb: 7/3/53 F

YEAR	TM/L	G	AB	R	H	2B	3B	HR	RBI	BB	SO	AVG	OBP	SLG	PRO+	BR/A	SB	CS	SBR	FA	FR	G/POS	TPR
1953	StL-N	33	39	9	7	0	0	2	4	2	11	.179	.220	.333	42	-3	0	0	0	.917	10	S-15	0.6
1954	StL-N	43	7	17	1	0	1	0	1	0	3	.143	.143	.429	42	-1	1	1	-0	1.000	2	S-11	0.1
1955	StL-N	12	4	3	0	0	0	0	0	0	1	.000	.000	.000	-99	-1	0	0	0	1.000	1	/S-3	-0.1
1956	StL-N	16	30	3	3	2	0	0	1	0	6	.100	.100	.167	-30	-5	0	0	0	.923	-1	/S-9	-0.6
1957	StL-N	65	56	10	9	0	0	0	1	7	13	.161	.254	.161	14	-7	1	3	-2	.948	10	S-23	0.2
1958	StL-N	39	108	16	23	4	0	1	8	23	15	.213	.351	.278	67	-4	0	2	-1	.932	-5	S-27	-0.8
	Pit-N	26	27	4	4	0	1	0	2	3	6	.148	.233	.222	22	-3	0	1	-1	1.000	0	/S-5,3-2	-0.3
	Yr	65	135	20	27	4	1	1	10	26	21	.200	.329	.267	59	-7	0	3	-2	.943	-5	S-32/3-2	-1.1
1959	Pit-N	81	145	21	34	10	1	1	9	16	22	.234	.311	.338	73	-5	1	1	-0	.980	10	2-28/S-8,O-3	0.7
1960	*Pit-N	65	102	9	34	4	1	0	10	16	20	.333	.429	.392	126	5	0	1	-1	.947	8	S-23,2-10/3-1	1.4
1961	Pit-N	60	78	16	15	2	1	0	2	10	19	.192	.284	.244	42	-6	0	1	-1	.923	9	3-11/S-9,2-5,O-3	0.3
1962	Pit-N	54	104	19	30	3	0	2	10	17	22	.288	.388	.375	106	2	0	1	-1	.933	-6	3-20/2-2,S-1	-0.4
1963	Pit-N	138	541	54	133	18	2	3	32	69	83	.246	.334	.303	84	-8	2	4	-2	.966	10	*S-117,2-20/3-1	1.1
1964	Pit-N	121	398	50	98	22	5	3	36	54	60	.246	.346	.349	97	0	1	2	-1	.950	2	*S-111	0.9
1965	Pit-N	31	109	13	25	5	0	0	6	15	19	.229	.323	.275	70	-4	1	0	0	.974	4	S-28	0.3
	SF-N	101	379	39	77	10	1	2	19	33	50	.203	.272	.251	47	-26	2	4	-2	.984	-6	S-93	-2.9
	Yr	132	488	52	102	15	1	2	25	48	69	.209	.284	.256	52	-30	3	4	-2	**.981**	-2	*S-121	-2.6
1966	SF-N	11	16	4	1	0	0	0	0	2	2	.063	.167	.063	-32	-3	0	0	0	1.000	2	/S-8	-0.1
	NY-A	25	58	5	9	2	0	0	2	9	8	.155	.269	.190	36	-5	0	0	0	.909	5	S-19	0.2
	LA-N	20	70	10	18	2	0	0	4	8	8	.257	.350	.257	78	-2	1	1	-0	.923	-3	3-19/S-3	-0.5
1967	LA-N	84	232	23	50	10	1	2	15	31	40	.216	.308	.293	79	-6	1	2	-1	.976	-0	S-69/2-4,3-2	-0.1
1968	*StL-N	69	127	14	28	7	1	1	8	13	31	.220	.303	.315	87	-2	1	2	-1	.973	9	S-43,2-23	1.0
1969	Bos-A	94	226	30	58	9	3	2	20	29	44	.257	.351	.350	92	-2	0	2	-1	.981	2	2-37,S-11/3-9,O-5	0.3
1970	Bos-A	76	139	16	26	1	2	1	14	21	26	.187	.298	.245	48	-9	0	1	-1	.969	-4	2-15,3-15/S-3	-1.4
1971	Mil-A	23	28	2	3	2	0	0	1	2	8	.107	.194	.179	6	-4	0	0	0	1.000	-2	3-12/S-4,2-2	-0.5
	StL-N	34	60	7	13	2	0	1	6	10	9	.217	.347	.300	82	-1	0	0	0	.935	2	S-17,2-13/3-3	0.3
Total	19	1321	3083	394	699	113	20	21	211	390	526	.227	.319	.297	73	-101	12	29	-14	.961	58	S-660,2-159/3-95,O	-0.3

■ DICK SCHOFIELD Schofield, Richard Craig b: 11/21/62, Springfield, Ill. BR/TR, 5′10″, 178 lbs. Deb: 9/8/83 F

YEAR	TM/L	G	AB	R	H	2B	3B	HR	RBI	BB	SO	AVG	OBP	SLG	PRO+	BR/A	SB	CS	SBR	FA	FR	G/POS	TPR
1983	Cal-A	21	54	4	11	2	0	3	4	6	8	.204	.295	.407	92	-1	0	0	0	.929	5	S-21	0.5
1984	Cal-A	140	400	39	77	10	3	4	21	33	79	.192	.264	.262	47	-29	5	2	0	**.982**	3	*S-140	-1.2
1985	Cal-A	147	438	50	96	19	3	8	41	35	70	.219	.289	.331	70	-18	11	4	1	.963	1	*S-147	-0.3
1986	*Cal-A	139	458	67	114	17	6	13	57	48	55	.249	.327	.397	97	-2	23	5	4	.972	15	*S-137	2.9
1987	Cal-A	134	479	52	120	17	3	9	46	37	63	.251	.307	.355	78	-16	19	3	4	**.984**	-18	*S-131/2-2,D-1	-1.8
1988	Cal-A	155	527	61	126	11	6	6	34	40	57	.239	.304	.317	76	-16	20	5	3	**.983**	23	*S-155	2.3
1989	Cal-A	91	302	42	69	11	2	4	26	28	47	.228	.300	.318	76	-10	9	3	1	.983	-8	S-90	-0.9
1990	Cal-A	99	310	41	79	8	1	1	18	52	61	.255	.365	.297	89	-2	3	4	-2	.966	12	S-99	1.6
1991	Cal-A	134	427	44	96	9	3	0	31	50	69	.225	.310	.260	60	-22	8	4	0	.975	12	*S-133	0.0
1992	Cal-A	1	3	0	1	0	0	0	0	1	0	.333	.500	.333	137	0	0	0	0	1.000	-1	/S-1	-0.1
	NY-N	142	420	52	86	18	2	4	36	60	82	.205	.311	.286	71	-14	11	4	1	**.988**	13	*S-141	1.0
1993	Tor-A	36	110	11	21	1	2	0	5	16	25	.191	.294	.236	44	-8	3	0	1	.977	5	S-36	-0.2
1994	Tor-A	95	325	38	83	14	1	4	32	34	62	.255	.333	.342	74	-12	7	7	-2	.972	-9	S-95	-1.4
1995	LA-N	9	10	0	1	0	0	0	0	1	3	.100	.182	.100	-25	-2	0	0	0	1.000	3	/S-3,3-1	0.1
	Cal-A	12	20	1	5	0	0	0	2	4	2	.250	.375	.250	67	-1	0	0	0	1.000	1	S-12	0.1
1996	Cal-A	13	16	3	4	0	0	0	0	1	1	.250	.294	.250	39	-1	1	0	0	.889	1	/S-7,2-2,3-1,D-1	0.0
Total	14	1368	4299	505	989	137	32	56	353	446	684	.230	.309	.316	73	-154	120	41	11	.976	56	*S-1348/2-4,3-2,D-2	2.6

■ OTTO SCHOMBERG Schomberg, Otto H. (b: Otto H. Shambrick) b: 11/14/1864, Milwaukee, Wis. d: 5/3/27, Ottawa, Kan. BL/TL, Deb: 7/7/1886

YEAR	TM/L	G	AB	R	H	2B	3B	HR	RBI	BB	SO	AVG	OBP	SLG	PRO+	BR/A	SB	CS	SBR	FA	FR	G/POS	TPR
1886	Pit-a	72	246	53	67	6	6	1	29	57		.272	.417	.358	144	17	7			.966	-7	1-72	0.1
1887	Ind-N	112	419	91	129	18	16	5	83	56	32	.308	.397	.463	143	27	21			.958	-10	*1-112/O-1	0.4
1888	Ind-N	30	112	11	24	5	1	1	10	10	12	.214	.290	.304	88	-1	6			.857	-5	O-15,1-15	-0.8
Total	3	214	777	155	220	29	23	7	122	123	44	.283	.389	.407	136	43	34			.961	-22	1-199/O-16	-0.3

■ JERRY SCHOONMAKER Schoonmaker, Jerald Lee b: 12/14/33, Seymour, Mo. BR/TR, 5′11″, 190 lbs. Deb: 6/11/55

YEAR	TM/L	G	AB	R	H	2B	3B	HR	RBI	BB	SO	AVG	OBP	SLG	PRO+	BR/A	SB	CS	SBR	FA	FR	G/POS	TPR
1955	Was-A	20	46	5	7	0	1	1	4	5	11	.152	.235	.261	35	-4	1	0	0	.960	-1	O-15	-0.6
1957	Was-A	30	23	5	2	1	0	0	0	2	11	.087	.160	.130	-20	-4	0	0	0	1.000	-3	O-13	-0.7
Total	2	50	69	10	9	1	1	1	4	7	22	.130	.211	.217	16	-8	1	0	0	.975	-4	/O-28	-1.3

■ GENE SCHOTT Schott, Arthur Eugene b: 7/14/13, Batavia, Ohio d: 11/16/92, Sun City Center, Fla. BR/TR, 6′2″, 185 lbs. Deb: 4/16/35

YEAR	TM/L	G	AB	R	H	2B	3B	HR	RBI	BB	SO	AVG	OBP	SLG	PRO+	BR/A	SB	CS	SBR	FA	FR	G/POS	TPR
1935	Cin-N	36	60	6	12	2	0	0	2	3	13	.200	.238	.233	28	-6	0			.965	3	P-33	0.0
1936	Cin-N	39	60	10	18	3	1	1	8	5	18	.300	.354	.433	118	1	0			.947	1	P-31	0.0
1937	Cin-N	50	49	5	7	2	0	0	4	1	14	.143	.160	.184	-7	-7	0			.961	1	P-37	0.0
1938	Cin-N	31	24	3	3	0	0	0	0	1	4	.125	.160	.125	-21	-4	0			1.000	1	P-31	0.0
1939	Phi-N	8	6	3	2	0	1	0	0	0	0	.333	.333	.667	168	0	0			.500	-1	/P-4	0.0
	Bro-N	1	0	0	0	0	0	0	0	0	0	—	—	—	—	0	0			.000	0	R	0.0
	Yr	9	6	3	2	0	1	0	0	0	0	.333	.333	.667	166	0	0			.500	-1	/P-4	0.0
Total	5	165	199	27	42	7	2	1	14	10	49	.211	.249	.281	45	-15	0			.959	6	P-136	0.0

■ PAUL SCHRAMKA Schramka, Paul Edward b: 3/22/28, Milwaukee, Wis. BL/TL, 6′, 185 lbs. Deb: 4/14/53

YEAR	TM/L	G	AB	R	H	2B	3B	HR	RBI	BB	SO	AVG	OBP	SLG	PRO+	BR/A	SB	CS	SBR	FA	FR	G/POS	TPR
1953	Chi-N	2	0	0	0	0	0	0	0	0	0	—	—	—	—	0	0	0	0	.000	-0	/O-1	0.0

■ OSSEE SCHRECKENGOST Schreckengost, Ossee Freeman (a.k.a. Ossee Schreck)
b: 4/11/1875, New Bethlehem, Pa. d: 7/9/14, Philadelphia, Pa. BR/TR, 5′10″, 180 lbs. Deb: 9/8/1897

YEAR	TM/L	G	AB	R	H	2B	3B	HR	RBI	BB	SO	AVG	OBP	SLG	PRO+	BR/A	SB	CS	SBR	FA	FR	G/POS	TPR
1897	Lou-N	1	3	0	0	0	0	0	0	0		.000	.000	.000	-99	-1	0			1.000	-0	/C-1	-0.1
1898	Cle-N	10	35	5	11	2	3	0	10	0		.314	.314	.543	146	2	1			.860	0	/C-9	0.2
1899	StL-N	6	8	0	0	0	0	0	0	1		.000	.111	.000	-67	-2	0			1.000	-1	/1-1,O-1	-0.2
	Cle-N	43	150	15	47	8	3	0	10	6		.313	.348	.407	115	3	4			.911	-5	C-39/1-1,S-1,O-1	0.0
	StL-N	66	269	42	77	12	2	2	37	14		.286	.324	.368	88	-5	14			.963	-3	1-41,C-25/2-1	-0.6
	Yr	115	427	57	124	20	5	2	47	21		.290	.328	.375	94	-5	18			.927	-9	C-64,1-43/O-2,S2	-0.8

YEAR	TM/L	G	AB	R	H	2B	3B	HR	RBI	BB	SO	AVG	OBP	SLG	PRO+	BR/A	SB	CS	SBR	FA	FR	G/POS	TPR
1901	Bos-A	86	280	37	85	13	5	0	38	19		.304	.356	.386	108	3	6			.926	2	C-72/1-4	1.1
1902	Cle-A	18	74	5	25	0	0	0	9	0		.338	.338	.338	91	-1	2			.975	-1	1-17	-0.2
	Phi-A	79	284	45	92	17	2	2	43	9		.324	.347	.419	107	2	3			.960	22	C-71/1-7,O-1	2.9
	Yr	97	358	50	117	17	2	2	52	9		.327	.345	.402	104	1	5			.960	21	C-71,1-24/O-1	2.7
1903	Phi-A	92	306	26	78	13	4	3	30	11		.255	.285	.353	87	-5	0			.975	18	C-77,1-10	2.1
1904	Phi-A	95	311	23	58	9	1	1	21	5		.186	.199	.232	34	-23	3			.979	5	C-84/1-9	-1.0
1905	*Phi-A	123	420	30	114	19	6	0	45	3		.271	.278	.345	96	-4	9			**.984**	12	*C-114/1-2	2.1
1906	Phi-A	98	338	29	96	20	1	1	41	10		.284	.305	.358	104	0	5			.971	8	C-89/1-4	1.9
1907	Phi-A	101	356	30	97	16	3	0	38	17		.272	.306	.334	102	-0	4			**.985**	16	C-99/1-2	2.7
1908	Phi-A	71	207	16	46	7	1	0	16	6		.222	.248	.266	63	-9	1			.978	9	C-65/1-1	0.6
	Chi-A	6	16	1	3	0	0	0	0	1		.188	.235	.188	38	-1	0			.982	4	/C-6	0.4
	Yr	77	223	17	49	7	1	0	16	7		.220	.247	.260	61	-10	1			.978	13	C-71/1-1	1.0
Total	11	895	3057	304	829	136	31	9	338	102		.271	.297	.345	90	-42	52			.970	86	C-751/1-99,O-3,2S	11.9
■ HANK SCHREIBER	Schreiber, Henry Walter b: 7/12/1891, Cleveland, Ohio d: 2/23/68, Indianapolis, Ind. BR/TR, 5′11″, 165 lbs. Deb: 4/14/14																						
1914	Chi-A	1	2	0	0	0	0	0	0	0	1	.000	.000	.000	-99	-0	0			.000	-1	/O-1	-0.1
1917	Bos-N	2	7	1	2	0	0	0	0	0	1	.286	.286	.286	80	-0	0			1.000	-1	/S-1,3-1	-0.1
1919	Cin-N	19	58	5	13	4	0	0	4	0	12	.224	.224	.293	56	-3	0			.984	7	3-17/S-2	0.4
1921	NY-N	4	6	2	2	0	0	0	2	1	1	.333	.429	.333	104	0	0	0	0	.500	-0	/2-2,S-2,3-1	0.0
1926	Chi-N	10	18	2	1	1	0	0	0	0	1	.056	.056	.111	-55	-4	0			1.000	1	/S-3,3-3,2-1	-0.3
Total	5	36	91	10	18	5	0	0	6	1	16	.198	.207	.253	34	-8	0	0		.986	6	/3-22,S-8,2-3,O-1	-0.1
■ TED SCHREIBER	Schreiber, Theodore Henry b: 7/11/38, Brooklyn, N.Y. BR/TR, 5′11″, 175 lbs. Deb: 4/14/63																						
1963	NY-N	39	50	1	8	0	0	0	2	4	14	.160	.236	.160	16	-5	0	1	-1	.977	8	3-17/S-9,2-3	0.2
■ POP SCHRIVER	Schriver, William Frederick b: 7/11/1865, Brooklyn, N.Y. d: 12/27/32, Brooklyn, N.Y. BR/TR, 5′9.5″, 172 lbs. Deb: 4/29/1886																						
1886	Bro-a	8	21	2	1	0	0	0	0	2		.048	.130	.048	-43	-3	0			.667	0	/O-5,C-3	-0.3
1888	Phi-N	40	134	15	26	5	2	1	23	7	21	.194	.250	.284	66	-5	2			.870	-3	C-27/S-6,3-6,O-1	-0.6
1889	Phi-N	55	211	24	56	10	0	1	19	16	8	.265	.323	.327	75	-8	5			.920	3	C-48/2-6,3-1	0.0
1890	Phi-N	57	223	37	61	9	6	0	35	22	15	.274	.339	.368	103	0	9			.916	-3	C-34,1-10/3-8,2O	0.1
1891	Chi-N	27	90	15	30	1	4	1	21	10	9	.333	.412	.467	156	7	1			.964	2	C-27/1-2	0.9
1892	Chi-N	92	326	40	73	10	6	1	34	27	25	.224	.297	.301	80	-8	4			.929	-9	C-82,O-10	-1.1
1893	Chi-N	64	229	49	65	8	3	4	34	14	9	.284	.336	.397	96	-2	4			.926	2	C-56/O-5	0.4
1894	Chi-N	96	349	55	96	12	3	3	47	29	21	.275	.341	.352	64	-21	9			.923	-0	*C-88/S-3,3-3,1-2	-1.0
1895	NY-N	24	92	16	29	2	1	1	16	9	10	.315	.382	.391	102	1	3			.898	-3	C-18/1-6	0.0
1897	Cin-N	61	178	29	54	12	4	1	30	19		.303	.374	.433	105	1	3			.959	-4	C-53	0.2
1898	Pit-N	95	315	25	72	15	3	0	32	23		.229	.287	.295	68	-13	0			.957	-5	C-92/1-1	-0.8
1899	Pit-N	91	301	31	85	19	5	1	49	23		.282	.343	.389	101	0	4			.958	5	C-78/1-8	1.0
1900	*Pit-N	37	92	12	27	7	0	1	12	10		.293	.381	.402	115	2	0			.959	-4	C-24/1-1	0.0
1901	StL-N	53	166	17	45	7	3	1	23	12		.271	.335	.367	109	2	2			.971	4	C-24,1-19	0.8
Total	14	800	2727	367	720	117	40	16	375	223	118	.264	.329	.354	88	-48	46			.934	-15	C-654/1-49,O32S	-0.4
■ BOB SCHRODER	Schroder, Robert James b: 12/30/44, Ridgefield, N.J. BL/TR, 6′, 175 lbs. Deb: 4/20/65																						
1965	SF-N	31	9	4	2	0	0	0	1	1	1	.222	.300	.222	48	-1	0	0	0	1.000	3	/2-4,3-1	0.3
1966	SF-N	10	33	0	8	0	0	0	2	0	2	.242	.242	.242	34	-3	0	0	0	.963	-5	/S-9	-0.8
1967	SF-N	62	135	20	31	4	0	0	7	15	15	.230	.307	.259	64	-6	1	0	0	.993	-10	2-45/3-4	-1.5
1968	SF-N	35	44	5	7	1	1	0	2	7	3	.159	.288	.227	56	-2	0	0	0	.960	-3	2-12/S-4,3-2	-0.6
Total	4	138	221	29	48	5	1	0	12	23	21	.217	.294	.249	58	-11	1	0	0	.989	-15	/2-61,S-13,3-7	-2.6
■ BILL SCHROEDER	Schroeder, Alfred William b: 9/7/58, Baltimore, Md. BR/TR, 6′2″, 200 lbs. Deb: 7/13/83																						
1983	Mil-A	23	73	7	13	2	1	3	7	3	23	.178	.221	.356	60	-4	0	1	-1	.980	-3	C-23	-0.7
1984	Mil-A	61	210	29	54	6	0	14	25	8	54	.257	.291	.486	115	3	0	1	-1	.987	-5	C-58/1-1,D-3	0.0
1985	Mil-A	53	194	18	47	8	0	8	25	12	61	.242	.293	.407	90	-3	0	1	-1	.987	-7	C-48/1-1,D-4	-0.9
1986	Mil-A	64	217	32	46	14	0	7	19	9	59	.212	.263	.373	69	-10	1	0	0	.995	-4	C-35,1-19,D-10	-1.2
1987	Mil-A	75	250	35	83	12	0	14	42	16	56	.332	.379	.548	138	13	5	2	0	.995	-6	C-67/1-4,D-2	1.1
1988	Mil-A	41	122	9	19	2	0	5	10	6	36	.156	.208	.295	39	-10	0	0	0	1.000	5	C-30,1-10/D-1	-0.4
1989	Cal-A	41	138	16	28	2	0	6	15	3	44	.203	.220	.348	59	-8	0	0	0	.991	10	C-33/1-8	0.3
1990	Cal-A	18	58	7	13	3	0	4	9	1	10	.224	.237	.483	98	-1	0	0	0	1.000	2	C-15/1-3	0.2
Total	8	376	1262	153	303	49	1	61	152	58	343	.240	.282	.426	91	-20	6	5	-1	.992	-8	C-309/1-46,D-20	-1.6
■ RICK SCHU	Schu, Richard Spencer b: 1/26/62, Philadelphia, Pa. BR/TR, 6′, 170 lbs. Deb: 9/1/84																						
1984	Phi-N	17	29	12	8	2	1	2	5	6	6	.276	.400	.621	180	3	0	0	0	.952	-0	3-15	0.3
1985	Phi-N	112	416	54	105	21	4	7	24	38	78	.252	.318	.373	90	-6	8	6	-1	.933	-10	*3-111	-2.0
1986	Phi-N	92	208	32	57	10	1	8	25	18	44	.274	.338	.447	111	3	2	2	-1	.913	1	3-58	0.3
1987	Phi-N	92	196	24	46	6	3	7	23	20	36	.235	.312	.403	85	-4	0	2	-1	.905	-1	3-45,1-28	-0.9
1988	Bal-A	89	270	22	69	9	4	4	20	21	49	.256	.316	.363	92	-3	6	4	-1	.937	-12	3-72/1-4,D-9	-1.6
1989	Bal-A	1	0	0	0	0	0	0	0	0	0	—	—	—	—	0	0	0	0	1.000	-0	/2-1	0.0
	Det-A	98	266	25	57	11	0	7	21	24	37	.214	.279	.335	74	-10	1	2	-1	.934	-2	3-83/2-5,1-3,S-3,D	-1.2
	Yr	99	266	25	57	11	0	7	21	24	37	.214	.279	.335	74	-10	1	2	-1	.934	-2	3-83/D-9,2-6,1-3,S	-1.2
1990	Cal-A	61	157	19	42	8	0	6	14	11	25	.268	.315	.433	110	1	0	0	0	.918	0	3-38,1-15/O-4,2-1	0.1
1991	Phi-N	17	22	1	2	0	0	0	2	1	7	.091	.130	.091	-37	-4	0	0	0	.667	-1	/3-3,1-1	-0.5
1996	Mon-N	1	4	0	0	0	0	0	0	0	0	.000	.000	.000	-98	-1	0	0	0	.667	-0	/3-1	-0.2
Total	9	580	1568	189	386	67	13	41	134	139	282	.246	.311	.384	91	-20	17	16	-5	.926	-25	3-426/1-51,D2OS	-5.7
■ HEINIE SCHUBLE	Schuble, Henry George b: 11/1/06, Houston, Tex. d: 10/2/90, Baytown, Tex. BR/TR, 5′9″, 152 lbs. Deb: 7/8/27																						
1927	StL-N	65	218	29	56	6	2	4	28	7	27	.257	.283	.358	69	-10	0			.915	-7	S-65	-1.0
1929	Det-A	92	258	35	60	11	7	2	28	19	23	.233	.288	.353	64	-15	3	2	-0	.886	-10	S-86/3-2	-1.5
1932	Det-A	102	340	58	92	20	6	5	52	24	37	.271	.319	.409	84	-9	14	5	1	.941	8	3-76,S-16	0.6
1933	Det-A	49	96	12	21	4	1	0	6	5	17	.219	.257	.281	42	-8	2	0	1	.951	1	3-23/S-2,2-1	-0.5
1934	Det-A	11	15	2	4	2	0	0	2	1	4	.267	.313	.400	83	-0	0	0	0	1.000	0	/S-3,3-2,2-1	0.0
1935	Det-A	11	8	3	2	0	0	0	0	1	0	.250	.333	.250	55	-0	0	0	0	.714	1	/3-2,2-1	0.1
1936	StL-N	2	0	0	0	0	0	0	0	0	0	—	—	—	—	0	0			.000	0	/3-1	0.0
Total	7	332	935	139	235	43	16	11	116	57	108	.251	.296	.367	70	-43	19	7		.906	-6	S-172,3-106/2-3	-2.3
■ WES SCHULMERICH	Schulmerich, Edward Wesley b: 8/21/01, Hillsboro, Ore. d: 6/26/85, Corvallis, Ore. BR/TR, 5′11″, 210 lbs. Deb: 5/1/31																						
1931	Bos-N	95	327	36	101	17	7	2	43	28	30	.309	.363	.422	115	7	0			.966	-4	O-87	-0.3
1932	Bos-N	119	404	47	105	22	5	11	57	27	61	.260	.314	.421	99	-1	5			.968	3	*O-101	-0.5
1933	Bos-N	29	85	10	21	6	1	1	13	5	10	.247	.289	.376	97	-1	0			.980	1	O-21	-0.1
	Phi-N	97	365	53	122	19	4	8	59	32	45	.334	.394	.474	130	15	1			.977	-2	O-97	0.8
	Yr	126	450	63	143	25	5	9	72	37	55	.318	.375	.456	126	15	1			.978	-1	*O-118	0.7
1934	Phi-N	15	52	2	13	1	0	0	1	4	8	.250	.316	.269	51	-3	0			.963	-1	O-13	-0.4
	Cin-N	74	209	21	55	8	3	5	19	22	43	.263	.333	.402	98	-1	1			.976	-2	O-56	-0.5
	Yr	89	261	23	68	9	3	5	20	26	51	.261	.330	.375	88	-4	1			.974	-3	O-69	-0.9
Total	4	429	1442	169	417	73	20	27	192	118	197	.289	.347	.424	109	15	7			.971	-6	O-375	-1.0
■ ART SCHULT	Schult, Arthur William "Dutch" b: 6/20/28, Brooklyn, N.Y. BR/TR, 6′4″, 220 lbs. Deb: 5/17/53																						
1953	NY-A	7	0	3	0	0	0	0	0	0	0	—	—	—	—	0	0	0	0	.000	0	R	0.0
1956	Cin-N	5	7	3	3	0	0	0	2	1	1	.429	.500	.429	144	1	0	0	0	.000	-0	/O-1	0.0
1957	Cin-N	21	34	4	9	2	0	0	4	0	2	.265	.286	.324	59	-2	0	0	0	1.000	1	/O-5	-0.2
	Was-A	77	247	30	65	14	0	4	35	14	30	.263	.305	.368	84	-6	0	1	-1	.987	-1	1-35,O-31	-1.1
1959	Chi-N	42	118	17	32	7	0	2	14	7	14	.271	.323	.381	88	-2	0	0	0	.985	-4	1-23,O-15	-0.8

YEAR	TM/L	G	AB	R	H	2B	3B	HR	RBI	BB	SO	AVG	OBP	SLG	PRO+	BR/A	SB	CS	SBR	FA	FR	G/POS	TPR
1960	Chi-N	12	15	1	2	1	0	0	1	1	3	.133	.188	.200	6	-2	0	0	0	1.000	-1	/O-4,1-1	-0.3
Total	5	164	421	58	111	24	0	6	56	23	50	.264	.308	.363	81	-11	0	1	-1	.987	-5	/1-59,O-56	-2.4

■ FRANK SCHULTE

Schulte, Frank M. "Wildfire" b: 9/17/1882, Cohocton, N.Y. d: 10/2/49, Oakland, Cal. BL/TR, 5'11", 170 lbs. Deb: 9/21/04

YEAR	TM/L	G	AB	R	H	2B	3B	HR	RBI	BB	SO	AVG	OBP	SLG	PRO+	BR/A	SB	CS	SBR	FA	FR	G/POS	TPR
1904	Chi-N	20	84	16	24	4	3	2	13	2		.286	.310	.476	141	3	1			.949	0	O-20	0.3
1905	Chi-N	123	493	67	135	15	14	1	47	32		.274	.326	.367	102	0	16			.981	-7	*O-123	-1.3
1906	*Chi-N	146	563	77	158	18	**13**	7	60	31		.281	.324	.396	118	9	25			.975	0	*O-146	0.2
1907	*Chi-N	97	342	44	98	14	7	2	32	22		.287	.339	.386	120	7	7			.973	-3	O-92	0.0
1908	*Chi-N	102	386	42	91	20	2	1	43	29		.236	.294	.306	88	-5	15			.994	-6	*O-102	-1.8
1909	Chi-N	140	538	57	142	16	11	4	60	24		.264	.298	.357	101	-2	23			.968	-13	*O-140	-2.4
1910	*Chi-N	151	559	93	168	29	15	**10**	68	39	57	.301	.349	.460	137	22	22			.968	-6	*O-150	0.9
1911	Chi-N	154	577	105	173	30	21	**21**	**107**	76	71	.300	.384	**.534**	**156**	**40**	23			.971	-5	*O-154	2.7
1912	Chi-N	139	553	90	146	27	11	12	64	53	70	.264	.336	.418	106	3	17			.952	-4	*O-139	-0.8
1913	Chi-N	132	497	85	138	28	6	9	68	39	68	.278	.336	.412	113	7	21			.956	-8	*O-130	-0.7
1914	Chi-N	137	465	54	112	22	7	5	61	39	55	.241	.306	.351	95	-3	16			.954	-10	*O-134	-2.1
1915	Chi-N	151	550	66	137	20	6	12	62	49	68	.249	.313	.373	107	4	19	17	-5	.962	4	*O-147	-0.4
1916	Chi-N	72	230	31	68	11	1	5	27	20	35	.296	.352	.417	123	6	9			.951	-3	O-67	0.0
	Pit-N	55	177	12	45	5	3	0	14	17	19	.254	.323	.316	96	-0	5			.968	-2	O-48	-0.5
	Yr	127	407	43	113	16	4	5	41	37	54	.278	.339	.373	111	6	14			.958	-5	*O-115	-0.5
1917	Pit-N	30	103	11	22	5	1	0	7	10	14	.214	.283	.282	71	-3	5			.963	-0	O-28	-0.6
	Phi-N	64	149	21	32	10	0	1	15	16	22	.215	.299	.302	81	-3	4			.923	-10	O-42	-1.7
	Yr	94	252	32	54	15	1	1	22	26	36	.214	.293	.294	77	-6	9			.943	-10	O-70	-2.3
1918	Was-A	93	267	35	77	14	3	0	44	47	36	.288	.406	.363	135	14	5			.969	1	O-75	1.2
Total	15	1806	6533	906	1766	288	124	92	792	545	515	.270	.332	.395	114	98	233	17		.966	-70	*O-1737	-7.0

■ FRED SCHULTE

Schulte, Fred William "Fritz" (b: Fred William Schult)
b: 1/13/01, Belvidere, Ill. d: 5/20/83, Belvidere, Ill. BR/TR, 6'1", 183 lbs. Deb: 4/15/27

YEAR	TM/L	G	AB	R	H	2B	3B	HR	RBI	BB	SO	AVG	OBP	SLG	PRO+	BR/A	SB	CS	SBR	FA	FR	G/POS	TPR
1927	StL-A	60	189	32	60	16	5	3	34	20	14	.317	.383	.503	124	6	5	3	-0	.916	-3	O-49	0.0
1928	StL-A	146	556	90	159	44	6	7	85	51	60	.286	.347	.424	99	-2	6	5	-1	.973	17	*O-143	0.5
1929	StL-A	121	446	63	137	24	5	3	71	59	44	.307	.389	.404	101	2	8	3	1	**.989**	13	*O-116	0.7
1930	StL-A	113	392	59	109	23	5	5	62	41	44	.278	.348	.401	86	-8	12	8	-1	.966	-2	O-98/1-5	-1.7
1931	StL-A	134	553	100	168	32	7	9	65	56	49	.304	.369	.436	107	6	6	8	-3	.971	6	*O-134	-0.1
1932	StL-A	146	565	106	166	35	6	9	73	71	44	.294	.373	.425	100	1	5	9	-4	.986	0	*O-129/1-5	-1.1
1933	*Was-A	144	550	98	162	30	7	5	87	61	27	.295	.366	.402	104	4	10	12	-4	.980	16	*O-142	0.8
1934	Was-A	136	524	72	156	32	6	3	73	53	34	.298	.363	.399	100	0	3	7	-3	.986	-1	*O-134	-0.8
1935	Was-A	76	226	33	60	6	4	2	23	26	22	.265	.344	.354	83	-5	0	3	-2	.980	-8	O-56	-1.6
1936	Pit-N	74	238	28	62	7	3	1	17	20	20	.261	.320	.328	73	-9	1			.977	-3	O-55	-1.4
1937	Pit-N	29	20	5	2	0	0	0	3	4	3	.100	.280	.100	7	-2	0			.800	-1	/O-4	-0.4
Total	11	1179	4259	686	1241	249	54	47	593	462	361	.291	.362	.408	98	-7	56	58		.976	35	*O-1060/1-10	-5.1

■ HAM SCHULTE

Schulte, Herman Joseph (b: Herman Joseph Schultehenrich)
b: 9/1/12, St.Louis, Mo. d: 12/21/93, St.Charles, Mo. BR/TR, 5'8.5", 158 lbs. Deb: 4/16/40 F

YEAR	TM/L	G	AB	R	H	2B	3B	HR	RBI	BB	SO	AVG	OBP	SLG	PRO+	BR/A	SB	CS	SBR	FA	FR	G/POS	TPR
1940	Phi-N	120	436	44	103	18	2	1	21	32	30	.236	.288	.294	63	-22	3			**.980**	-10	*2-119/S-1	-2.5

■ JOHNNY SCHULTE

Schulte, John Clement b: 9/8/1896, Fredericktown, Mo. d: 6/28/78, St.Louis, Mo. BL/TR, 5'11", 190 lbs. Deb: 4/18/23 C

YEAR	TM/L	G	AB	R	H	2B	3B	HR	RBI	BB	SO	AVG	OBP	SLG	PRO+	BR/A	SB	CS	SBR	FA	FR	G/POS	TPR
1923	StL-A	7	3	1	0	0	0	0	1	4	0	.000	.571	.000	56	0	0	0	0	1.000	1	/C-1,1-1	0.1
1927	StL-N	64	156	35	45	8	2	9	32	47	19	.288	.456	.538	160	16	1			.956	3	C-59	2.1
1928	Phi-N	65	113	14	28	2	2	4	17	15	12	.248	.336	.407	90	-2	0			.949	-5	C-34	-0.5
1929	Chi-N	31	69	6	18	3	0	0	9	7	11	.261	.329	.304	58	-4	0			.978	-0	C-30	-0.2
1932	StL-A	15	24	2	5	2	0	0	3	1	6	.208	.240	.292	35	-2	0	0	0	.864	-1	/C-6	-0.2
	Bos-N	10	9	1	2	0	0	1	2	2	1	.222	.364	.556	149	1	0			1.000	1	C-10	0.2
Total	5	192	374	59	98	15	4	14	64	76	49	.262	.388	.436	112	8	1	0		.957	-2	C-140/1-1	1.5

■ JACK SCHULTE

Schulte, John Herman Frank b: 11/15/1881, Cincinnati, Ohio d: 8/17/75, Roseville, Mich. BR/TR, 5'9", 180 lbs. Deb: 8/19/06

YEAR	TM/L	G	AB	R	H	2B	3B	HR	RBI	BB	SO	AVG	OBP	SLG	PRO+	BR/A	SB	CS	SBR	FA	FR	G/POS	TPR
1906	Bos-N	2	7	0	0	0	0	0	0	0		.000	.000	.000	-99	-2	0			1.000	-1	/S-2	-0.3

■ LEN SCHULTE

Schulte, Leonard Bernard (b: Leonard Bernard Schultehenrich)
b: 12/5/16, St.Charles, Mo. d: 5/6/86, Orlando, Fla. BR/TR, 5'10", 160 lbs. Deb: 9/27/44 F

YEAR	TM/L	G	AB	R	H	2B	3B	HR	RBI	BB	SO	AVG	OBP	SLG	PRO+	BR/A	SB	CS	SBR	FA	FR	G/POS	TPR
1944	StL-A	1	0	0	0	0	0	0	0	1	0	—	1.000	—	188	0	0	0	0	.000	0	H	0.0
1945	StL-A	119	430	37	106	16	1	0	36	24	35	.247	.286	.288	64	-20	0	3	-2	.961	-8	3-71,2-37,S-14	-2.8
1946	StL-A	4	5	1	2	0	0	0	2	0	0	.400	.400	.400	118	0	0	0	0	1.000	1	/2-1,3-1	0.1
Total	3	124	435	38	108	16	1	0	38	25	35	.248	.289	.290	65	-20	0	3	-2	.962	-7	/3-72,2-38,S-14	-2.7

■ HOWIE SCHULTZ

Schultz, Howard Henry "Stretch" or "Steeple" b: 7/3/22, St.Paul, Minn. BR/TR, 6'6", 200 lbs. Deb: 8/16/43

YEAR	TM/L	G	AB	R	H	2B	3B	HR	RBI	BB	SO	AVG	OBP	SLG	PRO+	BR/A	SB	CS	SBR	FA	FR	G/POS	TPR
1943	Bro-N	45	182	20	49	12	0	1	34	6	24	.269	.300	.352	88	-3	3			.986	2	1-45	-0.5
1944	Bro-N	138	526	59	134	32	3	11	83	24	67	.255	.290	.390	92	-8	6			.988	-0	*1-136	-1.6
1945	Bro-N	39	142	18	34	8	2	1	19	10	14	.239	.294	.345	78	-5	2			.984	3	1-38	-0.4
1946	Bro-N	90	249	27	63	14	1	3	27	16	34	.253	.298	.353	84	-6	2			.989	5	1-87	-0.5
1947	Bro-N	2	1	0	0	0	0	0	0	0	0	.000	.000	.000	-96	-0	0			1.000	-0	/1-1	0.0
	Phi-N	114	403	30	90	19	1	6	35	21	70	.223	.264	.320	56	-27	0			.993	-1	*1-114	-3.1
	Yr	116	404	30	90	19	1	6	35	21	70	.223	.263	.319	56	-27	0			.993	-1	*1-115	-3.1
1948	Phi-N	6	13	0	1	0	0	0	1	1	2	.077	.143	.077	-40	-3	0			1.000	0	/1-3	-0.2
	Cin-N	36	72	9	12	0	0	2	9	4	7	.167	.211	.250	25	-8	2			.982	-3	1-26	-1.1
	Yr	42	85	9	13	0	0	2	10	5	9	.153	.200	.224	15	-10	2			.984	-3	1-29	-1.3
Total	6	470	1588	163	383	85	7	24	208	82	218	.241	.281	.349	75	-60	15			.989	6	1-450	-7.4

■ JOHN SCHULTZ

Schultz, John b: St.Louis, Mo. Deb: 8/7/1891

YEAR	TM/L	G	AB	R	H	2B	3B	HR	RBI	BB	SO	AVG	OBP	SLG	PRO+	BR/A	SB	CS	SBR	FA	FR	G/POS	TPR
1891	StL-a	1	2	0	0	0	0	0	0	0	0	.000	.000	.000	-87	-0	0			1.000	0	/C-1	0.0

■ JOE SCHULTZ

Schultz, Joseph Charles Jr. "Dode" b: 8/29/18, Chicago, Ill. d: 1/10/96, St.Louis, Mo. BL/TR, 5'11", 184 lbs. Deb: 9/27/39 FMC

YEAR	TM/L	G	AB	R	H	2B	3B	HR	RBI	BB	SO	AVG	OBP	SLG	PRO+	BR/A	SB	CS	SBR	FA	FR	G/POS	TPR
1939	Pit-N	4	14	3	4	2	0	0	2	2	0	.286	.375	.429	117	0	0			1.000	1	/C-4	0.1
1940	Pit-N	16	36	2	7	0	1	0	4	2	1	.194	.237	.250	35	-3	0			.917	-3	C-13	-0.6
1941	Pit-N	2	2	1	1	0	0	0	0	0	0	.500	.500	.500	183	0	0			.000	0	/C-2	0.0
1943	StL-A	46	92	6	22	5	0	0	8	9	8	.239	.307	.293	74	-3	0	1	-1	.979	-5	C-26	-0.8
1944	StL-A	3	8	1	2	0	0	0	0	0	0	.250	.250	.250	41	-1	0			.000	0	H	-0.1
1945	StL-A	41	44	1	13	2	0	0	8	3	1	.295	.340	.341	93	-1	0	0	0	.818	-1	/C-3	-0.1
1946	StL-A	42	57	1	22	4	0	0	14	11	2	.386	.485	.456	156	5	0	0	0	.941	0	/C-4	0.0
1947	StL-A	43	38	3	7	0	0	1	1	4	5	.184	.262	.263	45	-3	0	0	0	1.000	-5	C-17	0.1
1948	StL-A	43	37	0	7	0	0	0	9	6	3	.189	.302	.189	32	-3	0	0	0	.000	0	H	-0.3
Total	9	240	328	18	85	13	1	1	46	37	21	.259	.334	.314	81	-8	0	1		.964	-12	/C-69	-1.9

■ JOE SCHULTZ

Schultz, Joseph Charles Sr. "Germany" b: 7/24/1893, Pittsburgh, Pa. d: 4/13/41, Columbia, S.C. BR/TR, 5'11.5", 172 lbs. Deb: 9/28/12 F

YEAR	TM/L	G	AB	R	H	2B	3B	HR	RBI	BB	SO	AVG	OBP	SLG	PRO+	BR/A	SB	CS	SBR	FA	FR	G/POS	TPR
1912	Bos-N	4	12	1	3	1	0	0	4	0	2	.250	.250	.333	58	-1	0			.824	-0	/2-4	-0.1
1913	Bos-N	9	18	2	4	0	0	0	1	2	7	.222	.333	.222	59	-1	0			1.000	0	/O-5,2-1	-0.1
1915	Bro-N	56	120	13	35	3	2	0	4	10	18	.292	.346	.350	109	1	3	4	-2	.894	-4	3-27/S-1	-0.3
	Chi-N	7	8	1	2	0	0	0	3	0	2	.250	.250	.250	51	-0	0			.857	0	/2-2	0.0
	Yr	63	128	14	37	3	2	0	7	10	20	.289	.341	.344	106	1	3	4	-2	.894	-3	3-27/2-2,S-1	-0.3
1916	Pit-N	77	204	18	53	8	2	0	22	7	14	.260	.298	.319	88	-3	6			.840	-15	2-24,3-24/O-6,S-1	-1.9
1919	StL-N	88	229	24	58	9	1	2	21	11	7	.253	.287	.328	90	-3	4			1.000	-7	O-49/2-6,3-1	-1.4
1920	StL-N	99	320	38	84	5	5	0	32	21	11	.262	.308	.309	81	-8	5	4	-1	.945	-4	O-80	-2.0
1921	StL-N	92	275	37	85	20	3	6	45	15	11	.309	.347	.469	116	6	4	3	-1	.977	-2	O-67/3-3,1-2	-0.1
1922	StL-N	112	344	50	108	13	4	2	64	19	10	.314	.350	.392	96	-3	3	1	0	.976	2	O-89	-0.6

YEAR	TM/L	G	AB	R	H	2B	3B	HR	RBI	BB	SO	AVG	OBP	SLG	PRO+	BR/A	SB	CS	SBR	FA	FR	G/POS	TPR
1923	StL-N	2	7	0	2	0	0	0	1	1	0	.286	.375	.286	78	-0	0	0	0	1.000	0	/O-2	0.0
1924	StL-N	12	12	0	2	0	0	0	2	3	0	.167	.333	.167	39	-1	0	0	0	1.000	-1	/O-2	-0.2
	Phi-N	88	284	35	80	15	1	5	29	20	18	.282	.329	.394	83	-7	6	2	1	.960	-6	O-76	-1.8
	Yr	100	296	35	82	15	1	5	31	23	18	.277	.329	.385	82	-8	6	2	1	.960	-7	O-78	-2.0
1925	Phi-N	24	64	10	22	6	0	0	8	4	1	.344	.382	.438	100	0	1	1	-0	.923	-2	O-20	-0.3
	Cin-N	33	62	6	20	3	1	0	13	3	1	.323	.354	.403	95	-0	3	1	0	.950	-4	O-15/2-1	-0.5
	Yr	57	126	16	42	9	1	0	21	7	2	.333	.368	.421	99	-0	4	2	0	.932	-6	O-35/2-1	-0.8
Total	11	703	1959	235	558	83	19	15	249	116	102	.285	.327	.370	93	-21	35	16		.966	-42	O-411/3-55,2-38,1S	-9.3

■ JEFF SCHULZ Schulz, Jeffrey Alan b: 6/2/61, Evansville, Ind. BL/TR, 6′1″, 190 lbs. Deb: 9/2/89

YEAR	TM/L	G	AB	R	H	2B	3B	HR	RBI	BB	SO	AVG	OBP	SLG	PRO+	BR/A	SB	CS	SBR	FA	FR	G/POS	TPR
1989	KC-A	7	9	0	2	0	0	0	1	0	2	.222	.222	.222	26	-1	0	0	0	1.000	-0	/O-5	-0.1
1990	KC-A	30	66	5	17	5	1	0	6	6	13	.258	.319	.364	92	-1	0	0	0	.943	-3	O-22/D-1	-0.4
1991	Pit-N	3	3	0	0	0	0	0	0	0	2	.000	.000	.000	-99	-1	0	0	0	.000	0	/H	-0.1
Total	3	40	78	5	19	5	1	0	7	6	17	.244	.298	.333	77	-2	0	0	0	.951	-4	/O-27,D-1	-0.6

■ BILL SCHUSTER Schuster, William Charles "Broadway Bill" b: 8/4/12, Buffalo, N.Y. d: 6/28/87, ElMonte, Cal. BR/TR, 5′9″, 164 lbs. Deb: 9/29/37

YEAR	TM/L	G	AB	R	H	2B	3B	HR	RBI	BB	SO	AVG	OBP	SLG	PRO+	BR/A	SB	CS	SBR	FA	FR	G/POS	TPR
1937	Pit-N	3	6	2	3	0	0	0	1	1	0	.500	.571	.500	193	1	0			1.000	1	/S-2	0.2
1939	Bos-N	2	3	0	0	0	0	0	0	0	1	.000	.000	.000	-99	-1	0			.833	-0	/S-1,3-1	-0.1
1943	Chi-N	13	51	3	15	2	1	0	0	3	2	.294	.333	.373	105	0	0			.977	7	S-13	0.8
1944	Chi-N	60	154	14	34	7	1	1	14	12	16	.221	.277	.299	62	-8	4			.946	-4	S-38/2-6	-1.0
1945	*Chi-N	45	47	8	9	2	1	0	2	7	4	.191	.296	.277	61	-2	2			.949	8	S-22/2-3,3-1	0.7
Total	5	123	261	27	61	11	3	1	17	23	23	.234	.296	.310	72	-10	6			.954	11	/S-76,2-9,3-2	0.6

■ RANDY SCHWARTZ Schwartz, Douglas Randall b: 2/9/44, Los Angeles, Cal. BL/TL, 6′3″, 230 lbs. Deb: 9/8/65

YEAR	TM/L	G	AB	R	H	2B	3B	HR	RBI	BB	SO	AVG	OBP	SLG	PRO+	BR/A	SB	CS	SBR	FA	FR	G/POS	TPR
1965	KC-A	6	7	0	2	0	0	0	1	0	4	.286	.286	.286	64	-0	0	0	0	1.000	1	/1-2	0.0
1966	KC-A	10	11	0	1	0	0	0	1	1	3	.091	.167	.091	-24	-2	0	0	0	1.000	-0	/1-2	-0.2
Total	2	16	18	0	3	0	0	0	2	1	7	.167	.211	.167	10	-2	0	0	0	1.000	0	/1-4	-0.2

■ BILL SCHWARTZ Schwartz, William August "Pop" or "Scooper Bill" b: 4/3/1864, Jamestown, Ky. d: 12/22/40, Newport, Ky. BR/TR, 6′1″, 195 lbs. Deb: 5/3/1883

YEAR	TM/L	G	AB	R	H	2B	3B	HR	RBI	BB	SO	AVG	OBP	SLG	PRO+	BR/A	SB	CS	SBR	FA	FR	G/POS	TPR
1883	Col-a	2	4	0	1	0	0	0		0		.250	.250	.250	67	-0				.600	-1	/1-1,C-1	-0.1
1884	Cin-U	29	106	14	25	4	0	1		3		.236	.257	.302	64	-8				.837	-4	C-25/O-3,3-1	-0.9
Total	2	31	110	14	26	4	0	1		3		.236	.257	.300	64	-8				.828	-6	/C-26,O-3,3-1,1-1	-1.0

■ BILL SCHWARTZ Schwartz, William Charles "Blab" b: 4/22/1884, Cleveland, Ohio d: 8/29/61, Nashville, Tenn. BR/TR, 6′2″, 185 lbs. Deb: 5/2/04

YEAR	TM/L	G	AB	R	H	2B	3B	HR	RBI	BB	SO	AVG	OBP	SLG	PRO+	BR/A	SB	CS	SBR	FA	FR	G/POS	TPR
1904	Cle-A	24	86	5	13	2	0	0	0	0		.151	.151	.174	3	-9	4			.980	-4	1-22/3-1	-1.6

■ BILL SCHWARZ Schwarz, William De Witt b: 1/30/1891, Birmingham, Ala. d: 6/24/49, Jacksonville, Fla TR, Deb: 8/20/14

YEAR	TM/L	G	AB	R	H	2B	3B	HR	RBI	BB	SO	AVG	OBP	SLG	PRO+	BR/A	SB	CS	SBR	FA	FR	G/POS	TPR
1914	NY-A	1	1	0	0	0	0	0	0	0	1	.000	.000	.000	-99	-0	0			1.000	0	/C-1	0.0

■ AL SCHWEITZER Schweitzer, Albert Caspar "Cheese" b: 12/23/1882, Cleveland, Ohio d: 1/27/69, Newark, Ohio BR/TR, 5′6″, 170 lbs. Deb: 4/30/08

YEAR	TM/L	G	AB	R	H	2B	3B	HR	RBI	BB	SO	AVG	OBP	SLG	PRO+	BR/A	SB	CS	SBR	FA	FR	G/POS	TPR
1908	StL-A	64	182	22	53	4	2	1	14	20		.291	.374	.352	135	8	6			.952	5	O-55	1.2
1909	StL-A	27	76	7	17	2	0	0	2	5		.224	.298	.250	79	-2	3			.933	-3	O-22	-0.6
1910	StL-A	113	379	37	87	11	2	2	37	36		.230	.303	.285	90	-4	26			.937	-4	*O-109	-1.5
1911	StL-A	76	237	31	51	11	4	0	34	43		.215	.338	.295	80	-5	12			.934	-1	O-68	-0.9
Total	4	280	874	97	208	28	8	3	87	104		.238	.327	.299	95	-3	47			.940	-3	O-254	-1.8

■ PI SCHWERT Schwert, Pius Louis b: 11/22/1892, Angola, N.Y. d: 3/11/41, Washington, D.C. BR/TR, 5′10.5″, 160 lbs. Deb: 10/6/14

YEAR	TM/L	G	AB	R	H	2B	3B	HR	RBI	BB	SO	AVG	OBP	SLG	PRO+	BR/A	SB	CS	SBR	FA	FR	G/POS	TPR
1914	NY-A	2	5	0	0	0	0	0	0	2	2	.000	.286	.000	-13	-1	0			.909	1	/C-2	0.0
1915	NY-A	9	18	6	5	3	0	0	6	1	6	.278	.316	.444	128	0	0			.972	0	/C-9	0.1
Total	2	11	23	6	5	3	0	0	6	3	8	.217	.308	.348	97	-0	0			.957	1	/C-11	0.1

■ ART SCHWIND Schwind, Arthur Edwin b: 11/4/1889, Ft.Wayne, Ind. d: 1/13/68, Sullivan, Ill. BB/TR, 5′8″, 150 lbs. Deb: 10/3/12

YEAR	TM/L	G	AB	R	H	2B	3B	HR	RBI	BB	SO	AVG	OBP	SLG	PRO+	BR/A	SB	CS	SBR	FA	FR	G/POS	TPR
1912	Bos-N	1	2	0	1	0	0	0	0	0	0	.500	.500	.500	171	0	0			.000	0	/3-1	0.0

■ JERRY SCHYPINSKI Schypinski, Gerald Albert b: 9/16/31, Detroit, Mich. BL/TR, 5′10″, 170 lbs. Deb: 8/31/55

YEAR	TM/L	G	AB	R	H	2B	3B	HR	RBI	BB	SO	AVG	OBP	SLG	PRO+	BR/A	SB	CS	SBR	FA	FR	G/POS	TPR
1955	KC-A	22	69	7	15	2	0	0	5	1	6	.217	.229	.246	27	-7	0	0	0	.932	-2	S-21/2-2	-0.8

■ MIKE SCIOSCIA Scioscia, Michael Lorri b: 11/27/58, Upper Darby, Pa. BL/TR, 6′2″, 220 lbs. Deb: 4/20/80 C

YEAR	TM/L	G	AB	R	H	2B	3B	HR	RBI	BB	SO	AVG	OBP	SLG	PRO+	BR/A	SB	CS	SBR	FA	FR	G/POS	TPR
1980	LA-N	54	134	8	34	5	1	1	8	12	9	.254	.315	.328	81	-3	1	0	0	.992	3	C-54	0.2
1981	*LA-N	93	290	27	80	10	0	2	29	36	18	.276	.358	.331	100	1	0	2	-1	.987	-3	C-91	0.0
1982	LA-N	129	365	31	80	11	1	5	38	44	31	.219	.305	.296	70	-14	2	0	1	.986	-7	*C-123	-1.7
1983	LA-N	12	35	3	11	3	0	1	7	5	2	.314	.400	.486	145	2	0	0	0	1.000	-3	C-11	0.0
1984	LA-N	114	341	29	93	18	0	5	38	52	26	.273	.371	.370	110	6	2	1	0	.985	14	*C-112	2.6
1985	*LA-N	141	429	47	127	26	3	7	53	77	21	.296	.409	.420	136	25	3	3	-1	.986	2	*C-139	3.4
1986	LA-N	122	374	36	94	18	1	5	26	62	23	.251	.362	.345	103	4	3	3	-1	.982	-1	*C-119	1.0
1987	LA-N	142	461	44	122	26	1	6	38	55	23	.265	.344	.364	90	-6	7	4	-0	.989	11	*C-138	1.4
1988	*LA-N	130	408	29	105	18	0	3	35	38	31	.257	.321	.324	88	-6	0	3	-2	.991	8	*C-123	1.0
1989	LA-N★	133	408	40	102	16	0	10	44	52	29	.250	.339	.363	102	2	0	2	-1	.988	18	*C-130	2.7
1990	LA-N★	135	435	46	115	25	0	12	66	55	31	.264	.351	.405	110	7	4	1	1	.989	5	*C-132	2.1
1991	LA-N	119	345	39	91	16	2	8	40	47	32	.264	.357	.391	113	7	4	3	-1	.990	9	*C-115	2.1
1992	LA-N	117	348	19	77	6	3	3	24	32	31	.221	.289	.282	63	-17	3	2	-0	.988	11	*C-108	0.0
Total	13	1441	4373	398	1131	198	12	68	446	567	307	.259	.347	.356	99	9	29	24	-6	.988	67	*C-1395	14.8

■ LOU SCOFFIC Scoffic, Louis "Weaser" b: 5/20/13, Herrin, Ill. d: 8/28/97, Herrin, Ill. BR/TR, 5′10″, 182 lbs. Deb: 4/16/36

YEAR	TM/L	G	AB	R	H	2B	3B	HR	RBI	BB	SO	AVG	OBP	SLG	PRO+	BR/A	SB	CS	SBR	FA	FR	G/POS	TPR
1936	StL-N	4	7	2	3	0	0	0	2	1	2	.429	.500	.429	153	1	0			.875	-0	/O-3	0.0

■ DARYL SCONIERS Sconiers, Daryl Anthony b: 10/3/58, San Bernardino, Cal. BL/TL, 6′2″, 195 lbs. Deb: 9/13/81

YEAR	TM/L	G	AB	R	H	2B	3B	HR	RBI	BB	SO	AVG	OBP	SLG	PRO+	BR/A	SB	CS	SBR	FA	FR	G/POS	TPR
1981	Cal-A	15	52	6	14	1	1	1	7	1	10	.269	.283	.385	91	-1	0	0	0	1.000	1	1-12/D-3	-0.1
1982	Cal-A	12	13	0	2	0	0	0	2	2	1	.154	.267	.154	19	-1	0	0	0	1.000	0	/1-3,D-1	-0.1
1983	Cal-A	106	314	49	86	19	3	8	46	17	41	.274	.311	.430	102	0	4	2	0	.986	-5	1-57,D-27/O-1	-0.8
1984	Cal-A	57	160	14	39	4	0	4	17	13	17	.244	.301	.344	78	-5	1	2	-1	.990	-1	1-41/D-1	-0.9
1985	Cal-A	44	98	14	28	6	1	2	12	15	18	.286	.381	.429	122	3	2	1	0	.973	-1	D-20/1-6	0.2
Total	5	234	637	83	169	30	5	15	84	48	87	.265	.317	.399	97	-3	7	5	-1	.989	-6	1-119/D-52,O-1	-1.7

■ SCOTT Scott Deb: 7/16/1884

YEAR	TM/L	G	AB	R	H	2B	3B	HR	RBI	BB	SO	AVG	OBP	SLG	PRO+	BR/A	SB	CS	SBR	FA	FR	G/POS	TPR
1884	Bal-U	13	53	10	12	1	1	1		2		.226	.255	.340	71	-4				.909	-2	O-13/3-1	-0.5

■ TONY SCOTT Scott, Anthony b: 9/18/51, Cincinnati, Ohio BB/TR, 6′, 175 lbs. Deb: 9/1/73

YEAR	TM/L	G	AB	R	H	2B	3B	HR	RBI	BB	SO	AVG	OBP	SLG	PRO+	BR/A	SB	CS	SBR	FA	FR	G/POS	TPR
1973	Mon-N	11	1	2	0	0	0	0	0	0	1	.000	.000	.000	-97	-0	0	0	0	.000	-2	/O-3	-0.2
1974	Mon-N	19	7	2	2	0	0	0	1	1	3	.286	.375	.286	82	-0	1	1	-0	1.000	-5	O-16	-0.6
1975	Mon-N	92	143	19	26	4	2	0	11	12	38	.182	.259	.238	37	-12	5	6	-2	.962	-9	O-71	-2.6
1977	StL-N	95	292	38	85	16	3	3	41	33	48	.291	.369	.397	107	4	13	10	-2	.996	5	O-89	0.3
1978	StL-N	96	219	28	50	5	2	1	14	14	41	.228	.281	.283	59	-12	5	6	-2	.946	-9	O-77	-2.7
1979	StL-N	153	587	69	152	22	10	6	68	34	92	.259	.305	.361	80	-16	37	17	1	.984	17	*O-151	-0.5
1980	StL-N	143	415	51	104	19	3	0	28	35	68	.251	.310	.311	72	-15	22	10	1	**.997**	1	*O-134	-2.0
1981	StL-N	45	176	21	40	5	2	2	17	5	22	.227	.253	.313	58	-10	10	7	-1	1.000	1	O-44	-1.3
	*Hou-N	55	225	28	66	13	2	2	22	15	32	.293	.338	.396	113	3	8	3	1	.985	1	O-55	0.3
	Yr	100	401	49	106	18	4	4	39	20	54	.264	.301	.359	88	-7	18	10	-1	.992	2	O-99	-1.0
1982	Hou-N	132	460	43	110	16	3	1	29	15	56	.239	.265	.293	61	-26	18	4	3	.982	-3	*O-129	-3.1
1983	Hou-N	80	186	20	42	6	1	2	17	11	39	.226	.269	.301	62	-10	5	4	-1	1.000	-12	O-61	-2.6
1984	Hou-N	25	21	2	4	1	0	0	0	4	3	.190	.320	.238	63	-1	0	0	0	1.000	-1	/O-6	-0.2
	Mon-N	45	71	8	18	4	0	0	5	7	21	.254	.321	.310	81	-2	1	1	-0	1.000	-2	O-17	-0.4

YEAR	TM/L	G	AB	R	H	2B	3B	HR	RBI	BB	SO	AVG	OBP	SLG	PRO+	BR/A	SB	CS	SBR	FA	FR	G/POS	TPR
	Yr	70	92	10	22	5	0	0	5	11	24	.239	.320	.293	78	-3	1	1	-0	1.000	-3	O-23	-0.6
Total	11	991	2803	331	699	111	28	17	253	186	464	.249	.300	.327	75	-97	125	69	-4	.986	-18	O-853	-15.6
■ **DONNIE SCOTT**	Scott, Donald Malcolm b: 8/16/61, Dunedin, Fla. BB/TR, 5'11", 185 lbs. Deb: 9/30/83																						
1983	Tex-A	2	4	0	0	0	0	0	0	0	0	.000	.000	.000	-99	-1	0	0	0	1.000	1	/C-2	0.0
1984	Tex-A	81	235	16	52	9	0	3	20	20	44	.221	.282	.298	59	-13	0	1	-1	.974	4	C-80	-0.6
1985	Sea-A	80	185	18	41	13	0	4	23	15	41	.222	.280	.357	72	-7	1	1	-0	.981	-7	C-74	-1.2
1991	Cin-N	10	19	0	3	0	0	0	0	0	2	.158	.158	.158	-11	-3	0	0	0	1.000	-3	/C-8	-0.6
Total	4	173	443	34	96	22	0	7	43	35	87	.217	.274	.314	60	-24	1	2	-1	.977	-5	C-164	-2.4
■ **PETE SCOTT**	Scott, Floyd John b: 12/21/1898, Woodland, Cal. d: 5/3/53, Daly City, Cal. BR/TR, 5'11.5", 175 lbs. Deb: 4/13/26																						
1926	Chi-N	77	189	34	54	13	1	3	34	22	31	.286	.363	.413	107	2	3			.968	-2	O-59/3-1	-0.2
1927	Chi-N	71	156	28	49	18	1	0	21	19	18	.314	.392	.442	123	5	1			.986	-2	O-36	0.1
1928	Pit-N	60	177	33	55	10	4	5	33	18	14	.311	.378	.497	122	5	1			.979	2	O-42/1-8	0.4
Total	3	208	522	95	158	41	6	8	88	59	63	.303	.377	.450	117	13	5			.976	-1	O-137/1-8,3-1	0.3
■ **GARY SCOTT**	Scott, Gary Thomas b: 8/22/68, New Rochelle, N.Y. BR/TR, 6', 175 lbs. Deb: 4/9/91																						
1991	Chi-N	31	79	8	13	3	0	1	5	13	14	.165	.305	.241	53	-5	0	1	-1	.969	2	3-31	-0.4
1992	Chi-N	36	96	8	15	2	0	2	11	5	14	.156	.198	.240	23	-10	0	1	-1	.922	-2	3-29/S-2	-1.4
Total	2	67	175	16	28	5	0	3	16	18	28	.160	.250	.240	38	-14	0	2	-1	.946	-0	/3-60,S-2	-1.8
■ **GEORGE SCOTT**	Scott, George Charles "Boomer" b: 3/23/44, Greenville, Miss. BR/TR, 6'2", 215 lbs. Deb: 4/12/66																						
1966	Bos-A★	162	601	73	147	18	7	27	90	65	152	.245	.326	.433	105	4	4	0	1	.991	3	*1-158/3-5	-0.3
1967	*Bos-A	159	565	74	171	21	7	19	82	63	119	.303	.377	.465	136	26	10	8	-2	.987	-5	*1-152/3-2	1.1
1968	Bos-A	124	350	23	60	14	0	3	25	26	88	.171	.239	.237	42	-24	3	5	-2	.987	1	*1-112/3-6	-3.7
1969	Bos-A	152	549	63	139	14	5	16	52	61	74	.253	.332	.384	95	-4	4	3	-1	.954	-6	*3-109,1-53	-1.4
1970	Bos-A	127	480	50	142	24	5	16	63	44	95	.296	.357	.467	117	11	4	11	-5	.934	-8	3-68,1-59	-0.9
1971	Bos-A	146	537	72	141	16	4	24	78	41	102	.263	.321	.441	106	3	0	3	-2	.992	-7	*1-143	-2.1
1972	Mil-A	152	578	71	154	24	4	20	88	43	130	.266	.322	.426	123	15	16	4	2	.992	-5	*1-139,3-23	0.0
1973	Mil-A	158	604	98	185	30	4	24	107	61	94	.306	.372	.488	144	34	9	5	-0	.994	7	*1-157/D-1	2.8
1974	Mil-A	158	604	74	170	36	2	17	82	59	90	.281	.348	.432	124	18	9	9	-3	**.992**	8	*1-148/D-9	1.3
1975	Mil-A★	158	617	86	176	26	4	**36**	**109**	51	97	.285	.343	.515	139	29	6	5	-1	.989	3	*1-144,D-12/3-5	2.1
1976	Mil-A	156	606	73	166	21	5	18	77	53	118	.274	.337	.414	122	15	0	1	-1	.991	-2	*1-155	0.2
1977	Bos-A★	157	584	103	157	26	5	33	95	57	112	.269	.340	.500	112	8	1	1	-0	.985	0	*1-157	-0.1
1978	Bos-A	120	412	51	96	16	4	12	54	44	86	.233	.307	.379	83	-10	1	1	-0	.991	-8	*1-113/D-7	-2.6
1979	Bos-A	45	156	18	35	9	1	4	23	17	22	.224	.301	.372	76	-5	0	0	0	.986	-2	1-41	-1.0
	KC-A	44	146	19	39	8	2	1	20	12	32	.267	.331	.370	87	-3	1	1	-0	.989	-3	1-41/3-1,D-2	-0.8
	NY-A	16	44	9	14	3	1	1	6	2	7	.318	.348	.500	128	2	1	0	0	1.000	-0	D-15/1-1	0.1
	Yr	105	346	46	88	20	4	6	49	31	61	.254	.319	.387	87	-6	2	1	0	.987	-5	1-83,D-17/3-1	-1.7
Total	14	2034	7433	957	1992	306	60	271	1051	699	1418	.268	.335	.435	113	119	69	57	-14	.990	-25	*1-1773,3-219/D-46	-5.3
■ **JIM SCOTT**	Scott, James Walter b: 9/22/1888, Shenandoah, Pa. d: 5/12/72, S.Pasadena, Fla. BR/TR, 5'9.5", 165 lbs. Deb: 4/22/14																						
1914	Pit-F	8	24	2	6	1	0	0	1	5	0	.250	.379	.292	85	-1	1			.800	-3	/S-8	-0.3
■ **JOHN SCOTT**	Scott, John Henry b: 1/24/52, Jackson, Miss. BR/TR, 6'2", 165 lbs. Deb: 9/7/74																						
1974	SD-N	14	15	3	1	0	0	0	0	0	4	.067	.067	.067	-65	-3	1	0	0	1.000	-1	/O-8	-0.4
1975	SD-N	25	9	6	0	0	0	0	0	0	2	.000	.000	.000	-99	-2	2	0	1	.000	-1	/O-1	-0.3
1977	Tor-A	79	233	26	56	9	0	2	15	8	39	.240	.266	.305	54	-15	10	8	-2	.963	-5	O-67/D-2	-2.4
Total	3	118	257	35	57	9	0	2	15	8	45	.222	.245	.280	43	-21	13	8	-1	.965	-6	/O-76,D-2	-3.1
■ **LE GRANT SCOTT**	Scott, Le Grant Edward b: 7/25/10, Cleveland, Ohio d: 11/12/93, Birmingham, Ala. BL/TL, 5'8.5", 170 lbs. Deb: 4/19/39																						
1939	Phi-N	76	232	31	65	15	1	1	26	22	14	.280	.343	.366	93	-2	5			.959	1	O-55	-0.3
■ **EVERETT SCOTT**	Scott, Lewis Everett "Deacon" b: 11/19/1892, Bluffton, Ind. d: 11/2/60, Fort Wayne, Ind. BR/TR, 5'8", 148 lbs. Deb: 4/14/14																						
1914	Bos-A	144	539	66	129	15	6	2	37	32	43	.239	.286	.301	76	-17	9	14	-6	.949	-11	*S-143	-2.4
1915	*Bos-A	100	359	25	72	11	0	0	28	17	21	.201	.237	.231	41	-27	4	7	-3	.961	4	*S-100	-2.0
1916	*Bos-A	123	366	37	85	19	2	0	27	23	24	.232	.283	.295	73	-13	8			**.967**	7	*S-121/2-1,3-1	0.0
1917	Bos-A	157	528	40	127	24	7	0	50	20	46	.241	.268	.313	78	-16	12			**.953**	8	*S-157	-0.1
1918	*Bos-A	126	443	40	98	11	5	0	43	12	16	.221	.242	.269	55	-26	11			**.976**	18	*S-126	-0.3
1919	Bos-A	138	507	41	141	19	0	0	38	19	26	.278	.306	.316	79	-15	8			**.976**	7	*S-138	0.0
1920	Bos-A	154	569	41	153	21	12	4	61	21	15	.269	.300	.369	80	-19	4	11	-5	**.973**	17	*S-154	0.6
1921	Bos-A	154	576	65	151	21	9	1	62	27	21	.262	.295	.335	62	-34	5	9	-4	**.972**	**38**	*S-154	1.4
1922	*NY-A	154	557	64	150	23	5	3	45	23	22	.269	.304	.345	67	-27	2	3	-1	**.966**	17	*S-154	0.5
1923	*NY-A	152	533	48	131	16	4	6	60	13	19	.246	.266	.325	54	-37	1	3	-2	**.961**	-11	*S-152	-3.5
1924	NY-A	153	548	56	137	12	6	4	64	21	15	.250	.278	.316	53	-40	3	7	-3	.966	10	*S-153	-1.6
1925	NY-A	22	60	3	13	0	0	0	4	2	2	.217	.242	.217	17	-8	0	1	-1	.988	3	S-18	-0.3
	Was-A	33	103	10	28	6	1	0	18	4	4	.272	.299	.350	65	-6	1	2	-1	.932	3	S-30/3-2	-0.1
	Yr	55	163	13	41	6	1	0	22	6	6	.252	.278	.301	48	-13	1	3	-2	.952	6	S-48/3-2	-0.4
1926	Chi-A	40	143	15	36	10	1	0	13	9	8	.252	.296	.336	67	-7	1	3	-2	.955	5	S-39	0.0
	Cin-N	4	6	1	4	0	0	0	1	0	0	.667	.667	.667	267	1	0			.875	0	/S-4	0.2
Total	13	1654	5837	552	1455	208	58	20	551	243	282	.249	.281	.315	65	-291	69	60		.965	115	*S-1643/3-3,2-1	-7.6
■ **MILT SCOTT**	Scott, Milton Parker "Mikado Milt" b: 1/17/1866, Chicago, Ill. d: 11/3/38, Baltimore, Md. BR, 5'9", 160 lbs. Deb: 9/30/1882																						
1882	Chi-N	1	5	1	2	0	0	0	0	0	0	.400	.400	.400	151	0				1.000	0	/1-1	0.0
1884	Det-N	110	438	29	108	17	5	3	50	9	62	.247	.262	.329	90	-5				.968	-1	*1-110	-1.7
1885	Det-N	38	148	14	39	7	0	0	12	4	16	.264	.283	.311	92	-2				.967	2	1-38	-0.4
	Pit-a	55	210	15	52	7	1	0	18	5		.248	.272	.290	79	-5				.986	3	1-55	-0.8
1886	Bal-a	137	484	48	92	11	4	2	52	22		.190	.239	.242	52	-26	11			.974	8	*1-137/P-1	-3.0
Total	4	341	1285	107	293	42	10	5	132	40	78	.228	.257	.288	74	-38	11			.973	12	1-341/P-1	-5.9
■ **DICK SCOTT**	Scott, Richard Edward b: 7/19/62, Ellsworth, Maine BR/TR, 6'1", 170 lbs. Deb: 5/19/89																						
1989	Oak-A	3	2	0	0	0	0	0	1	0	0	.000	.000	.000	-99	-1	0	0	0	.000	0	/S-3	-0.1
■ **RODNEY SCOTT**	Scott, Rodney Darrell b: 10/16/53, Indianapolis, Ind. BB/TR, 6', 160 lbs. Deb: 4/11/75																						
1975	KC-A	48	15	13	1	0	0	0	0	1	3	.067	.125	.067	-43	-3	4	2	0	1.000	6	D-22/2-9,S-8,R-0	0.2
1976	Mon-N	7	10	3	4	0	0	0	0	1	1	.400	.455	.400	138	1	2	0	1	1.000	-0	/2-6,S-3	0.1
1977	Oak-A	133	364	56	95	4	4	0	20	43	50	.261	.344	.294	77	-10	33	18	-1	.963	-30	2-71,S-70/3-5,OD	-3.2
1978	Chi-N	78	227	41	64	5	1	0	15	43	41	.282	.403	.313	91	-0	27	10	2	.929	-9	3-59,O-10/2-6,S-6	-0.8
1979	Mon-N	151	562	69	134	12	5	3	42	66	82	.238	.321	.294	69	-22	39	12	5	.980	-15	*2-113,S-39	-2.2
1980	Mon-N	154	567	84	127	13	**13**	0	46	70	75	.224	.310	.293	69	-22	63	13	11	.982	-16	*2-129,S-21	-1.7
1981	*Mon-N	95	336	43	69	9	3	0	26	50	35	.205	.310	.250	60	-16	30	7	5	.983	-15	2-93	-2.2
1982	Mon-N	14	25	2	5	0	0	0	1	3	2	.200	.286	.200	37	-2	5	0	2	.971	-1	2-12	-0.1
	NY-A	10	26	5	5	0	0	0	0	4	2	.192	.300	.192	39	-2	2	0	1	.963	1	/S-6,2-4	0.0
Total	8	690	2132	316	504	43	26	3	150	281	291	.236	.328	.285	71	-77	205	62	24	.979	-81	2-443,S-153/3DO	-9.9
■ **JIM SCRANTON**	Scranton, James Dean b: 4/5/60, Torrance, Cal. BR/TR, 6', 175 lbs. Deb: 9/5/84																						
1984	KC-A	2	2	0	0	0	0	0	0	0	0	.000	.000	.000	-99	-1	0	0	0	1.000	-1	/S-1,3-1	-0.1
1985	KC-A	6	4	1	0	0	0	0	0	0	0	.000	.000	.000	-99	-1	0	0	0	1.000	2	/S-5	0.1
Total	2	8	6	1	0	0	0	0	0	0	0	.000	.000	.000	-99	-2	0	0	0	1.000	2	/S-6,3-1	0.0
■ **CHUCK SCRIVENER**	Scrivener, Wayne Allison b: 10/3/47, Alexandria, Va. BR/TR, 5'9", 170 lbs. Deb: 9/18/75																						
1975	Det-A	4	16	0	4	1	0	0	0	0	1	.250	.250	.313	56	-1	1	0	0	1.000	-2	/3-3,S-2	-0.3

YEAR	TM/L	G	AB	R	H	2B	3B	HR	RBI	BB	SO	AVG	OBP	SLG	PRO+	BR/A	SB	CS	SBR	FA	FR	G/POS	TPR
1976	Det-A	80	222	28	49	7	1	2	16	19	34	.221	.282	.288	65	-10	1	0	0	.976	7	2-43,S-37/3-5	0.4
1977	Det-A	61	72	10	6	0	0	0	2	5	9	.083	.143	.083	-35	-13	0	0	0	.981	10	S-50/2-8,3-3	-0.1
Total	3	145	310	38	59	8	1	2	18	24	44	.190	.249	.242	40	-24	2	0	1	.970	15	/S-89,2-51,3-11	-0.0
■ **TONY SCRUGGS**	Scruggs, Anthony Raymond b: 3/19/66, Riverside, Cal. BR/TR, 6'1", 210 lbs. Deb: 4/8/91																						
1991	Tex-A	5	6	1	0	0	0	0	0	0	1	.000	.000	.000	-99	-2	0	0	0	1.000	-1	/O-5	-0.3
■ **KEN SEARS**	Sears, Kenneth Eugene "Ziggy" b: 7/6/17, Streator, Ill. d: 7/17/68, Bridgeport, Tex. BL/TR, 6'1", 200 lbs. Deb: 5/2/43																						
1943	NY-A	60	187	22	52	7	0	2	22	11	18	.278	.328	.348	97	-1	1	3	-2	.974	1	C-50	0.2
1946	StL-A	7	15	1	5	0	0	0	1	3	0	.333	.444	.333	114	1	0	0	0	1.000	-3	/C-4	-0.2
Total	2	67	202	23	57	7	0	2	23	14	18	.282	.338	.347	99	-0	1	3	-2	.975	-2	/C-54	0.0
■ **JIMMY SEBRING**	Sebring, James Dennison b: 3/22/1882, Liberty, Pa. d: 12/22/09, Williamsport, Pa. BL/TR, 6', 180 lbs. Deb: 9/8/02																						
1902	Pit-N	19	80	15	26	4	4	0	15	5		.325	.365	.475	153	5	2			.974	4	O-19	0.7
1903	*Pit-N	124	506	71	140	16	13	4	64	32		.277	.325	.383	98	-3	20			.927	7	*O-124	-0.3
1904	Pit-N	80	305	28	82	11	7	0	32	17		.269	.307	.351	100	-1	8			.959	9	O-80	0.3
	Cin-N	56	222	22	50	9	2	0	24	14		.225	.271	.284	65	-9	8			1.000	4	O-56	-1.0
	Yr	136	527	50	132	20	9	0	56	31		.250	.292	.323	85	-10	16			.974	12	*O-136	-0.7
1905	Cin-N	58	217	31	62	10	5	2	28	14		.286	.329	.406	107	1	11			.885	-6	O-56	-0.8
1909	Bro-N	25	81	11	8	1	1	0	5	11		.099	.207	.136	7	-9	3			.951	-2	O-25	-1.3
	Was-A	1	0	0	0	0	0	0	0	0		—	—	—	—	0	0			.000	-1	/O-1	-0.1
Total	5	363	1411	178	368	51	32	6	168	93		.261	.308	.355	93	-16	52			.945	14	O-361	-2.5
■ **FRANK SECORY**	Secory, Frank Edward b: 8/24/12, Mason City, Iowa d: 4/7/95, Port Huron, Mich. BR/TR, 6'1", 200 lbs. Deb: 4/28/40 U																						
1940	Det-A	1	1	0	0	0	0	0	0	0	1	.000	.000	.000	-91	-0	0	0	0	.000	0	H	0.0
1942	Cin-N	2	5	1	0	0	0	0	1	3	2	.000	.375	.000	14	-0	0			.857	0	/O-2	0.0
1944	Chi-N	22	56	10	18	1	0	4	17	6	8	.321	.387	.554	163	5	1			1.000	0	O-17	0.4
1945	*Chi-N	35	57	4	9	1	0	0	6	2	7	.158	.186	.175	1	-8	0			1.000	-1	O-12	-1.0
1946	Chi-N	33	43	6	10	3	0	3	12	6	6	.233	.327	.512	139	2	0			.833	-3	/O-9	-0.1
Total	5	93	162	21	37	5	0	7	36	17	24	.228	.302	.389	95	-2	1	0		.964	-4	/O-40	-0.7
■ **CHARLIE SEE**	See, Charles Henry "Chad" b: 10/13/1896, Pleasantville, N.Y d: 7/19/48, Bridgeport, Conn. BL/TR, 5'10.5", 175 lbs. Deb: 8/6/19																						
1919	Cin-N	8	14	1	4	0	0	0	1	1	0	.286	.333	.286	89	-0	0			.833	-1	/O-4	-0.2
1920	Cin-N	47	82	9	25	4	0	0	15	1	7	.305	.329	.354	97	-0	2	4	-2	1.000	3	O-17/P-1	-0.1
1921	Cin-N	37	106	11	26	5	1	1	7	7	5	.245	.298	.340	72	-4	3	2	-0	.954	-0	O-30	-0.7
Total	3	92	202	21	55	9	1	1	23	9	12	.272	.313	.342	83	-5	5	6		.967	1	/O-51,P-1	-1.0
■ **LARRY SEE**	See, Ralph Laurence b: 6/20/60, Norwalk, Cal. BR/TR, 6'1", 195 lbs. Deb: 9/3/86																						
1986	LA-N	13	20	1	5	2	0	0	2	2	7	.250	.318	.350	90	-0	0	0	0	.979	1	/1-9	0.0
1988	Tex-A	13	23	0	3	0	0	0	0	1	8	.130	.167	.130	-15	-3	0	0	0	1.000	-0	/C-2,1-2/3-1,D-7	-0.4
Total	2	26	43	1	8	2	0	0	2	3	15	.186	.239	.233	32	-4	0	0	0	.967	1	/1-11,D-7,C-2,3-1	-0.4
■ **BOB SEEDS**	Seeds, Ira Robert "Suitcase Bob" b: 2/24/07, Ringgold, Tex. d: 10/28/93, Erick, Okla. BR/TR, 6', 180 lbs. Deb: 4/19/30																						
1930	Cle-A	85	277	37	79	11	3	3	32	12	22	.285	.315	.379	72	-12	1	3	-2	.953	2	O-70	-1.5
1931	Cle-A	48	134	26	41	4	1	1	10	11	11	.306	.359	.373	88	-2	1	0	0	.966	-2	O-33/1-2	-0.6
1932	Cle-A	2	4	0	0	0	0	0	0	0	0	.000	.000	.000	-94	-1	0	0	0	.000	-0	/O-1	-0.2
	Chi-A	116	434	53	126	18	6	2	45	31	37	.290	.342	.373	91	-6	5	7	-3	.964	-9	*O-112	-2.2
	Yr	118	438	53	126	18	6	2	45	31	37	.288	.339	.370	89	-7	5	7	-3	.964	-9	*O-113	-2.4
1933	Bos-A	82	230	26	56	13	4	0	23	21	20	.243	.310	.335	71	-10	1	3	-2	.985	-5	1-41,O-32	-2.0
1934	Bos-A	8	6	0	1	0	0	0	1	0	1	.167	.167	.167	-13	-1	0	0	0	.000	-0	/O-1	-0.1
	Cle-A	61	186	28	46	8	1	0	18	21	13	.247	.327	.301	62	-10	2	1	0	.977	-4	O-48	-1.5
	Yr	69	192	28	47	8	1	0	19	21	14	.245	.322	.297	59	-11	2	1	0	.977	-4	O-49	-1.6
1936	*NY-A	13	42	12	11	1	0	4	10	5	3	.262	.340	.571	126	1	3	1	0	1.000	1	/O-9,3-3	0.2
1938	NY-N	81	296	35	86	12	3	9	52	20	33	.291	.338	.443	112	4	0			.987	-5	O-76	-0.3
1939	NY-N	63	173	33	46	5	1	5	26	22	31	.266	.352	.393	99	0	1			.975	-8	O-50	-0.9
1940	NY-N	56	155	18	45	5	2	4	16	17	19	.290	.371	.426	118	4	0			.985	-4	O-40	-0.2
Total	9	615	1937	268	537	77	21	28	233	160	190	.277	.336	.382	89	-32	14	15		.970	-35	O-472/1-43,3-3	-9.3
■ **PAT SEEREY**	Seerey, James Patrick b: 3/17/23, Wilburton, Okla. d: 4/28/86, Jennings, Mo. BR/TR, 5'10", 200 lbs. Deb: 6/9/43																						
1943	Cle-A	26	72	8	16	3	0	1	5	4	19	.222	.263	.306	70	-3	0	0	0	.974	1	O-16	-0.3
1944	Cle-A	101	342	39	80	16	0	15	39	19	99	.234	.276	.412	99	-3	0	2	-1	.986	1	O-86	-0.8
1945	Cle-A	126	414	56	98	22	2	14	56	66	97	.237	.342	.401	120	11	1	2	-1	.975	-15	*O-117	-1.2
1946	Cle-A	117	404	57	91	17	2	26	62	65	101	.225	.334	.470	131	15	2	3	-1	.981	-5	*O-115	0.4
1947	Cle-A	82	216	24	37	4	1	11	29	34	66	.171	.284	.352	78	-7	0	1	-1	.957	-8	O-68	-1.9
1948	Cle-A	10	23	7	6	0	0	1	6	7	8	.261	.433	.391	123	1	0	0	0	1.000	-2	/O-7	-0.1
	Chi-A	95	340	44	78	11	0	18	64	61	94	.229	.347	.421	107	3	0	0	0	.981	-0	O-93	-0.2
	Yr	105	363	51	84	11	0	19	70	68	102	.231	.353	.419	108	4	0	0	0	.982	-2	*O-100	-0.3
1949	Chi-A	4	4	1	0	0	0	0	0	3	1	.000	.429	.000	19	-0	0	0	0	1.000	-1	/O-2	-0.1
Total	7	561	1815	236	406	73	5	86	261	259	485	.224	.321	.412	109	16	3	8	-4	.978	-27	O-504	-4.2
■ **EMMETT SEERY**	Seery, John Emmett b: 2/13/1861, Princeville, Ill. d: 8/7/30, Saranac Lake, N.Y. BL/TR, Deb: 4/17/1884																						
1884	Bal-U	105	463	113	144	25	7	2		20		.311	.340	.408	114	-7				.828	7	*O-103/C-3,3-2	-0.1
	KC-U	1	4	2	2	1	0	0		1		.500	.600	.750	353	1				.000	-0	/O-1	0.1
	Yr	106	467	115	146	26	7	2		21		.313	.342	.411	116	-6				.828	6	*O-104/C-3,3-2	0.0
1885	StL-N	59	216	20	35	7	0	1	14	16	37	.162	.220	.208	42	-13				.874	5	O-59/3-1	-0.9
1886	StL-N	126	453	73	108	22	6	2	48	57	82	.238	.324	.327	105	5	24			.883	-5	*O-126/P-2	-0.2
1887	Ind-N	122	465	104	104	18	15	4	28	71	68	.224	.331	.353	93	-2	48			.891	7	*O-122/S-1	0.2
1888	Ind-N	133	500	87	110	20	10	5	50	64	73	.220	.316	.330	104	4	80			.939	8	*O-133/S-1	0.9
1889	Ind-N	127	526	123	165	26	12	8	59	67	59	.314	.401	.454	136	27	19			.909	1	*O-127	2.1
1890	Bro-P	104	394	78	88	12	7	1	50	70	36	.223	.348	.297	69	-17	44			.894	7	*O-104	-1.1
1891	Cin-a	97	372	77	106	15	10	4	36	81	52	.285	.423	.411	128	15	19			.898	3	*O-97	1.3
1892	Lou-N	42	154	18	31	6	1	0	15	24	19	.201	.309	.253	77	-3	6			.961	3	O-42	-0.2
Total	9	916	3547	695	893	152	68	27	300	471	426	.252	.345	.356	104	11	240			.896	36	O-914/3-3,C-3,SP	2.1
■ **KEVIN SEFCIK**	Sefcik, Kevin John b: 2/10/71, Tinley Park, Ill. BR/TR, 5'11", 175 lbs. Deb: 9/8/95																						
1995	Phi-N	5	4	1	0	0	0	0	0	0	2	.000	.000	.000	-99	-1	0	0	0	1.000	0	/3-2	-0.1
1996	Phi-N	44	116	10	33	5	3	0	9	9	16	.284	.346	.379	90	-1	3	0	1	.986	1	S-21,3-20/2-1	0.1
1997	Phi-N	61	119	11	32	3	0	2	6	4	9	.269	.290	.345	68	-6	1	2	-1	.961	-3	2-22,S-10/3-4	-0.8
1998	Phi-N	104	169	27	53	7	2	3	20	25	32	.314	.423	.432	121	7	4	2	0	.989	-6	O-60/3-2,2-1	0.0
Total	4	214	408	49	118	15	5	5	35	38	59	.289	.364	.387	96	-1	8	4	0	.979	-9	/O-60,S-31,3-28,2	-0.8
■ **KAL SEGRIST**	Segrist, Kal Hill b: 4/14/31, Greenville, Tex. BR/TR, 6', 180 lbs. Deb: 7/16/52																						
1952	NY-A	13	23	3	1	0	0	0	1	3	1	.043	.154	.043	-46	-5	0	0	0	.971	0	2-11/3-1	-0.4
1955	Bal-A	7	9	1	3	0	0	0	0	2	0	.333	.455	.333	123	0	0	0	0	1.000	0	/3-3,1-1,2-1	0.1
Total	2	20	32	4	4	0	0	0	1	5	1	.125	.243	.125	4	-4	0	0	0	.971	1	/2-12,3-4,1-1	-0.3
■ **DAVID SEGUI**	Segui, David Vincent b: 7/19/66, Kansas City, Kan. BB/TL, 6'1", 202 lbs. Deb: 5/8/90 F																						
1990	Bal-A	40	123	14	30	7	0	2	15	11	15	.244	.311	.350	87	-2	0	0	0	.990	1	1-36/D-4	-0.3
1991	Bal-A	86	212	15	59	7	0	2	22	12	19	.278	.317	.340	85	-4	1	1	-0	.996	1	1-42,O-33/D-4	-0.6
1992	Bal-A	115	189	21	44	9	0	1	17	20	23	.233	.306	.296	68	-8	1	0	0	.998	2	1-95,O-18	-0.8
1993	Bal-A	146	450	54	123	27	0	10	60	58	53	.273	.356	.400	99	-0	2	1	0	.996	4	*1-144/D-1	-0.7
1994	NY-N	92	336	46	81	17	1	10	43	33	43	.241	.311	.387	81	-10	0	0	0	.996	-3	1-78,O-21	-1.9

YEAR	TM/L	G	AB	R	H	2B	3B	HR	RBI	BB	SO	AVG	OBP	SLG	PRO+	BR/A	SB	CS	SBR	FA	FR	G/POS	TPR
1995	NY-N	33	73	9	24	3	1	2	11	12	9	.329	.430	.479	144	5	1	3	-2	1.000	-2	O-18/1-7	0.1
	Mon-N	97	383	59	117	22	3	10	57	28	38	.305	.356	.457	109	5	1	4	-2	.997	0	1-97/O-2	-0.6
	Yr	130	456	68	141	25	4	12	68	40	47	.309	.369	.461	115	10	2	7	-4	.997	-2	*1-104,O-20	-0.5
1996	Mon-N	115	416	69	119	30	1	11	58	60	54	.286	.376	.442	112	8	4	4	-1	.993	6	*1-113	0.2
1997	Mon-N	125	459	75	141	22	3	21	68	57	66	.307	.385	.505	131	21	0	1	-1	.995	-1	*1-125	0.9
1998	Sea-A	143	522	79	159	36	1	19	84	49	80	.305	.364	.487	119	14	3	1	0	**.999**	14	*1-134/O-1	1.4
Total	9	992	3163	441	897	180	10	88	435	340	400	.284	.354	.430	106	30	14	14	-4	.996	23	1-871/O-93,D-9	-2.3

■ **FERNANDO SEGUIGNOL** Seguignol, Fernando Alfredo b: 1/19/75, Bocas Del Toro, Panama BB/TR, 6'5", 190 lbs. Deb: 9/5/98

YEAR	TM/L	G	AB	R	H	2B	3B	HR	RBI	BB	SO	AVG	OBP	SLG	PRO+	BR/A	SB	CS	SBR	FA	FR	G/POS	TPR
1998	Mon-N	16	42	6	11	4	0	2	3	3	15	.262	.311	.500	110	0	0	0	0	1.000	2	/O-9,1-7	0.2

■ **KURT SEIBERT** Seibert, Kurt Elliott b: 10/16/55, Cheverly, Md. BB/TR, 6', 165 lbs. Deb: 9/3/79

YEAR	TM/L	G	AB	R	H	2B	3B	HR	RBI	BB	SO	AVG	OBP	SLG	PRO+	BR/A	SB	CS	SBR	FA	FR	G/POS	TPR
1979	Chi-N	7	2	2	0	0	0	0	0	0	1	.000	.000	.000	-91	-1	0	0	0	1.000	0	/2-1	0.0

■ **SOCKS SEIBOLD** Seibold, Harry b: 4/3/1896, Philadelphia, Pa. d: 9/21/65, Philadelphia, Pa. BR/TR, 5'8.5", 162 lbs. Deb: 9/18/15

YEAR	TM/L	G	AB	R	H	2B	3B	HR	RBI	BB	SO	AVG	OBP	SLG	PRO+	BR/A	SB	CS	SBR	FA	FR	G/POS	TPR
1915	Phi-A	10	26	3	3	1	0	0	2	4	4	.115	.233	.154	16	-3	0			.714	-4	/S-7	-0.7
1916	Phi-A	5	12	0	2	1	0	0	1	0	4	.167	.167	.250	26	-1	0			1.000	2	/P-3,O-1	0.0
1917	Phi-A	36	59	6	13	1	1	0	5	4	8	.220	.281	.271	70	-2	1			.978	-2	P-33/O-2	-0.1
1919	Phi-A	15	13	1	2	0	0	0	1	0	4	.154	.154	.154	-13	-2	0			.941	0	P-14	0.0
1929	Bos-N	33	70	6	20	2	0	0	9	6	6	.286	.342	.314	67	-3	0			**1.000**	-1	P-33	0.0
1930	Bos-N	36	90	6	19	2	0	1	5	6	6	.211	.260	.267	29	-11	0			.941	-3	P-36	0.0
1931	Bos-N	33	70	3	9	0	0	0	2	1	9	.129	.141	.129	-28	-13	0			**1.000**	0	P-33	0.0
1932	Bos-N	28	46	2	7	0	0	0	2	2	0	.152	.188	.152	-8	-7	0			1.000	2	P-28	0.0
1933	Bos-N	11	9	0	1	0	0	0	0	2	2	.111	.273	.111	14	-1	0			1.000	0	P-11	0.0
Total	9	207	395	27	76	7	1	1	27	25	43	.192	.242	.223	25	-42	1			.982	-5	P-191/S-7,O-3	-0.8

■ **RICKY SEILHEIMER** Seilheimer, Ricky Allen b: 8/30/60, Brenham, Tex. BL/TR, 5'11", 185 lbs. Deb: 7/5/80

YEAR	TM/L	G	AB	R	H	2B	3B	HR	RBI	BB	SO	AVG	OBP	SLG	PRO+	BR/A	SB	CS	SBR	FA	FR	G/POS	TPR
1980	Chi-A	21	52	4	11	3	1	1	3	4	15	.212	.268	.365	72	-2	1	0	0	.946	-3	C-21	-0.4

■ **KEVIN SEITZER** Seitzer, Kevin Lee b: 3/26/62, Springfield, Ill. BR/TR, 5'11", 190 lbs. Deb: 9/3/86

YEAR	TM/L	G	AB	R	H	2B	3B	HR	RBI	BB	SO	AVG	OBP	SLG	PRO+	BR/A	SB	CS	SBR	FA	FR	G/POS	TPR
1986	KC-A	28	96	16	31	4	1	2	11	19	14	.323	.440	.448	140	6	0	0	0	.987	1	1-22/O-5,3-3	0.6
1987	KC-A★	161	641	105	**207**	33	8	15	83	80	85	.323	.400	.470	126	26	12	7	-1	.947	8	*3-141,1-25/O-3,D-1	2.9
1988	KC-A	149	559	90	170	32	5	5	60	72	64	.304	.389	.406	122	19	10	8	-2	.938	3	*3-147/O-1,D-1	1.9
1989	KC-A	160	597	78	168	17	2	4	48	102	76	.281	.391	.337	107	11	17	8	0	.950	-11	*3-159/S-6,O-3,1-2	0.3
1990	KC-A	158	622	91	171	31	5	6	38	67	66	.275	.347	.370	102	3	7	5	-1	.953	-9	*3-152,2-10	-0.6
1991	KC-A	85	234	28	62	11	3	1	25	29	21	.265	.351	.350	94	-1	4	1	1	.940	0	3-68/D-3	0.0
1992	Mil-A	148	540	74	146	35	1	5	71	57	44	.270	.342	.367	101	1	13	11	-3	**.969**	-13	*3-146/2-2,1-1	-1.5
1993	Oak-A	73	255	24	65	10	2	4	27	27	33	.255	.329	.357	90	-4	4	7	-3	.933	-9	3-46,1-24/O-3,2PDS	-1.7
	Mil-A	47	162	21	47	6	0	7	30	17	15	.290	.361	.457	120	5	3	0	1	.942	-2	3-33/1-7,2-1,O-1,D	0.3
	Yr	120	417	45	112	16	2	11	57	44	48	.269	.341	.396	102	1	7	7	-2	.937	-11	3-79,1-31/D-6,O2PS	-1.4
1994	Mil-A	80	309	44	97	24	2	5	49	30	38	.314	.378	.453	108	4	2	1	0	.924	-4	3-43,1-35/D-4	-0.3
1995	Mil-A★	132	492	56	153	33	3	5	69	64	57	.311	.397	.421	107	7	2	0	1	.968	-1	3-88,1-36,D-14	0.3
1996	Mil-A	132	490	74	155	25	3	12	62	73	68	.316	.409	.453	113	13	6	1	1	.996	0	1-65,D-56,3-12	0.4
	*Cle-A	22	83	11	32	10	0	1	16	14	11	.386	.480	.542	159	8	0	0	0	1.000	2	D-17/1-5	0.8
	Yr	154	573	85	187	35	3	13	78	87	79	.326	.420	.466	120	21	6	1	1	.997	3	D-73,1-70,3-12	1.2
1997	*Cle-A	64	198	27	53	14	0	2	24	18	25	.268	.329	.369	79	-6	0	0	0	1.000	1	D-24,1-19,3-13	-0.8
Total	12	1439	5278	739	1557	285	35	74	613	669	617	.295	.378	.404	110	94	80	49	-5	.949	-33	*3-1051,1-241,D/O2SP	2.6

■ **KIP SELBACH** Selbach, Albert Karl b: 3/24/1872, Columbus, Ohio d: 2/17/56, Columbus, Ohio BR/TR, 5'7", 190 lbs. Deb: 4/24/1894

YEAR	TM/L	G	AB	R	H	2B	3B	HR	RBI	BB	SO	AVG	OBP	SLG	PRO+	BR/A	SB	CS	SBR	FA	FR	G/POS	TPR
1894	Was-N	97	372	69	114	21	17	7	71	51	20	.306	.390	.511	120	11	21			.915	-9	O-80,S-19	-0.2
1895	Was-N	129	516	115	166	21	**22**	6	55	69	28	.322	.403	.483	129	23	31			.912	16	*O-118/S-6,2-5	2.4
1896	Was-N	127	487	100	148	17	13	5	100	76	28	.304	.405	.423	119	16	49			.946	7	*O-126	1.1
1897	Was-N	124	486	113	152	25	16	5	59	80		.313	.414	.461	131	24	46			.955	13	*O-124	2.4
1898	Was-N	132	515	88	156	28	11	3	60	64		.303	.383	.417	130	21	25			.948	20	*O-131/S-1	2.9
1899	Cin-N	140	521	104	154	27	11	3	87	70		.296	.384	.407	115	12	38			.953	17	*O-140	1.6
1900	NY-N	141	523	98	176	29	12	4	68	72		.337	.425	.461	151	40	36			.951	10	*O-141	3.5
1901	NY-N	125	502	89	145	29	6	1	56	45		.289	.350	.376	115	10	8			.942	-10	*O-125	-0.9
1902	Bal-A	128	503	86	161	27	9	3	60	58		.320	.393	.427	122	16	22			.941	9	*O-127	1.6
1903	Was-A	140	533	68	134	23	12	3	49	41		.251	.305	.356	96	-3	20			.956	-3	*O-140/3-1	-1.5
1904	Was-A	48	178	15	49	8	4	0	14	24		.275	.361	.365	132	7	9			.931	3	O-48	0.8
	Bos-A	98	376	50	97	19	8	0	30	48		.258	.347	.351	114	8	10			.961	1	O-98	0.3
	Yr	146	554	65	146	27	12	0	44	72		.264	.351	.356	120	15	19			.950	4	*O-146	1.1
1905	Bos-A	121	418	54	103	16	6	4	47	67		.246	.355	.342	120	12	12			.928	-1	*O-112	0.6
1906	Bos-A	60	228	15	48	9	2	0	23	18		.211	.277	.268	71	-7	7			.966	1	O-58	-1.0
Total	13	1610	6158	1064	1803	299	149	44	779	783	76	.293	.376	.411	121	190	334			.944	74	*O-1568/S-26,2-5,3	13.6

■ **BILL SELBY** Selby, William Frank b: 6/11/70, Monroeville, Ala. BL/TR, 5'9", 190 lbs. Deb: 4/19/96

YEAR	TM/L	G	AB	R	H	2B	3B	HR	RBI	BB	SO	AVG	OBP	SLG	PRO+	BR/A	SB	CS	SBR	FA	FR	G/POS	TPR
1996	Bos-A	40	95	12	26	4	0	3	6	9	11	.274	.337	.411	86	-2	1	1	-0	.980	-6	2-14,3-14/O-6	-0.7

■ **GEORGE SELKIRK** Selkirk, George Alexander "Twinkletoes"
b: 1/4/08, Huntsville, Ont., Canada d: 1/19/87, Ft.Lauderdale, Fla BL/TR, 6'1", 182 lbs. Deb: 8/12/34

YEAR	TM/L	G	AB	R	H	2B	3B	HR	RBI	BB	SO	AVG	OBP	SLG	PRO+	BR/A	SB	CS	SBR	FA	FR	G/POS	TPR
1934	NY-A	46	176	23	55	7	1	5	38	15	17	.313	.370	.449	118	4	1	1	-0	.989	-2	O-46	0.1
1935	NY-A	128	491	64	153	29	12	11	94	44	36	.312	.372	.487	128	18	2	7	-4	.975	6	*O-127	1.5
1936	*NY-A★	137	493	93	152	28	9	18	107	94	60	.308	.420	.511	133	28	13	7	-0	.974	3	*O-135	2.2
1937	*NY-A	78	256	49	84	13	5	18	68	34	24	.328	.411	.629	157	22	8	2	1	.987	5	O-69	2.3
1938	*NY-A	99	335	58	85	12	5	10	62	68	52	.254	.384	.409	99	1	9	4	0	.973	-3	O-95	-0.4
1939	*NY-A★	128	418	103	128	17	4	21	101	103	49	.306	.452	.517	149	37	12	5	1	**.989**	-4	*O-124	2.6
1940	NY-A	118	379	68	102	17	5	19	71	84	43	.269	.406	.491	137	23	3	6	-3	.962	-3	*O-111	1.2
1941	*NY-A	70	164	30	36	5	0	6	25	28	30	.220	.340	.360	86	-3	1	0	0	.967	-2	O-47	-0.7
1942	*NY-A	42	78	15	15	3	0	0	10	16	8	.192	.330	.231	60	-3	0	0	0	1.000	-1	O-19	-0.6
Total	9	846	2790	503	810	131	41	108	576	486	319	.290	.400	.483	128	127	49	32	-5	.977	-1	O-773	8.2

■ **RUBE SELLERS** Sellers, Oliver b: 3/7/1881, Duquesne, Pa. d: 1/14/52, Pittsburgh, Pa. BR/TR, 5'10", 180 lbs. Deb: 8/12/10

YEAR	TM/L	G	AB	R	H	2B	3B	HR	RBI	BB	SO	AVG	OBP	SLG	PRO+	BR/A	SB	CS	SBR	FA	FR	G/POS	TPR
1910	Bos-N	12	32	3	5	0	0	0	2	6	5	.156	.289	.156	29	-3	1			1.000	-2	/O-9	-0.6

■ **FRANK SELMAN** Selman, Frank C. (a.k.a. Frank C. Williams 1871-75) b: Baltimore, Md. Deb: 5/4/1871

YEAR	TM/L	G	AB	R	H	2B	3B	HR	RBI	BB	SO	AVG	OBP	SLG	PRO+	BR/A	SB	CS	SBR	FA	FR	G/POS	TPR
1871	Kek-n	14	65	14	15	3	0	1	10	4	0	.231	.275	.323	70	-3	1	0	0	.711	-3	3-14/C-5,S-2	-0.4
1872	Oly-n	9	42	3	10	2	0	0	1	0	1	.238	.238	.286	64	-2	0	2	-1	.788	-3	/C-7,3-2	-0.4
1873	Mar-n	1	3	1	1	0	0	0	0	0	0	.333	.333	.333	129	0	0	0	0	.000	-0	/P-1	0.0
1874	Bal-n	12	54	9	16	3	2	0	7	0	2	.296	.296	.426	130	2	2	0	1	.304	-18	/C-6,S-6,2-2,3-2,O	-1.2
1875	Was-n	1	3	0	1	0	0	0	0	0	0	.333	.333	.333	137	0	0	0	0	1.000	0	/1-1	0.0
Total	5 n	37	167	27	43	8	2	1	18	4	3	.257	.275	.347	88	-2	3	2	-0	.657	-23	/C-18,3-18,SO21P	-2.0

■ **CAREY SELPH** Selph, Carey Isom b: 12/5/01, Donaldson, Ark. d: 2/24/76, Houston, Tex. BR/TR, 5'9.5", 175 lbs. Deb: 5/25/29

YEAR	TM/L	G	AB	R	H	2B	3B	HR	RBI	BB	SO	AVG	OBP	SLG	PRO+	BR/A	SB	CS	SBR	FA	FR	G/POS	TPR
1929	StL-N	25	51	8	12	1	1	0	7	6	4	.235	.316	.294	52	-4	1			.981	-5	2-16	-0.7
1932	Chi-A	116	396	50	112	19	8	0	51	31	9	.283	.341	.371	90	-6	7	6	-2	.910	-6	3-71,2-26	-0.7
Total	2	141	447	58	124	20	9	0	58	37	13	.277	.338	.362	85	-10	8	6		.955	-11	/3-71,2-42	-1.4

■ **MIKE SEMBER** Sember, Michael David b: 2/24/53, Hammond, Ind. BR/TR, 6', 185 lbs. Deb: 8/18/77

YEAR	TM/L	G	AB	R	H	2B	3B	HR	RBI	BB	SO	AVG	OBP	SLG	PRO+	BR/A	SB	CS	SBR	FA	FR	G/POS	TPR
1977	Chi-N	3	4	0	1	0	0	0	0	0	2	.250	.250	.250	31	-0	0	0	0	1.000	1	/2-1	0.0
1978	Chi-N	9	3	2	1	0	0	0	0	1	1	.333	.500	.333	122	0	0	0	0	.667	1	/3-7,S-1	0.1
Total	2	12	7	2	2	0	0	0	0	1	3	.286	.375	.286	74	-0	0	0	0	.667	1	/3-7,S-1,2-1	0.1

YEAR	TM/L	G	AB	R	H	2B	3B	HR	RBI	BB	SO	AVG	OBP	SLG	PRO+	BR/A	SB	CS	SBR	FA	FR	G/POS	TPR
■ ANDY SEMINICK Seminick, Andrew Wasil b: 9/12/20, Pierce, W.Va. BR/TR, 5′11″, 187 lbs. Deb: 9/14/43 C																							
1943	Phi-N	22	72	9	13	2	0	2	5	7	22	.181	.253	.292	60	-4	0			.930	1	C-22/O-1	-0.2
1944	Phi-N	22	63	9	14	2	1	0	4	6	17	.222	.300	.286	68	-3	2			.963	1	C-11/O-7	-0.2
1945	Phi-N	80	188	18	45	7	2	6	26	18	38	.239	.313	.394	98	-1	3			.979	-0	C-70/3-4,O-1	0.2
1946	Phi-N	124	406	55	107	15	5	12	52	39	86	.264	.334	.414	115	7	2			.974	-6	*C-118	0.8
1947	Phi-N	111	337	48	85	16	2	13	50	58	69	.252	.370	.427	115	8	4			.978	7	*C-107	2.1
1948	Phi-N	125	391	49	88	11	3	13	44	58	68	.225	.328	.368	90	-5	4			.965	6	*C-124	0.9
1949	Phi-N★	109	334	52	81	11	2	24	68	69	74	.243	.380	.503	138	19	0			.975	7	C-98	3.1
1950	*Phi-N	130	393	55	113	15	3	24	68	68	50	.288	.400	.524	143	26	0			.976	4	*C-124	3.5
1951	Phi-N	101	291	42	66	8	1	11	37	63	67	.227	.370	.375	102	3	1	0	0	.979	-3	C-91	0.4
1952	Cin-N	108	336	38	86	16	1	14	50	35	65	.256	.330	.435	111	4	1	3	-2	.973	-4	C-99	0.4
1953	Cin-N	119	387	46	91	12	0	19	64	49	82	.235	.323	.413	90	-6	2	2	-1	.982	-5	*C-112	-0.6
1954	Cin-N	86	247	25	58	9	4	7	30	48	39	.235	.364	.389	93	-1	0	0	0	.989	3	C-82	0.6
1955	Cin-N	6	15	1	2	0	0	1	1	0	3	.133	.133	.333	18	-2	0	0	0	1.000	2	/C-5	0.0
	Phi-N	93	289	32	71	12	1	11	34	32	59	.246	.333	.408	97	-1	1	2	-1	.994	10	C-88	1.1
	Yr	99	304	33	73	12	1	12	35	32	62	.240	.325	.405	93	-3	1	2	-1	**.994**	12	C-93	1.1
1956	Phi-N	60	161	16	32	3	1	7	23	31	38	.199	.332	.360	88	-2	3	0	1	.976	-8	C-54	-0.7
1957	Phi-N	8	11	0	1	0	0	0	0	1	3	.091	.167	.091	-29	-2	0	0	0	1.000	1	/C-8	-0.1
Total	15	1304	3921	495	953	139	26	164	556	582	780	.243	.347	.417	107	40	23	7		.977	15	*C-1213/O-9,3-4	11.3
■ SONNY SENERCHIA Senerchia, Emanuel Robert b: 4/6/31, Newark, N.J. BR/TR, 6′1″, 195 lbs. Deb: 8/22/52																							
1952	Pit-N	29	100	5	22	5	0	3	11	4	21	.220	.250	.360	66	-5	0	3	-2	.953	-8	3-28	-1.7
■ COUNT SENSENDERFER Sensenderfer, John Phillips Jenkins b: 12/28/1847, Philadelphia, Pa. d: 5/3/03, Philadelphia, Pa. 5′9″, 170 lbs. Deb: 5/20/1871																							
1871	Ath-n	25	127	38	41	5	2	0	23	0	1	.323	.323	.394	106	1	5	3	-0	.814	-1	*O-25	0.1
1872	Ath-n	1	5	2	2	0	0	0	1	0	0	.400	.400	.400	146	0	0	1	-1	.000	-0	/O-1	0.0
1873	Ath-n	20	86	12	24	1	0	0	8	0	2	.279	.279	.291	65	-4	0	2	-1	.827	0	O-19/1-1	-0.3
1874	Ath-n	5	16	3	3	0	0	0	2	0	0	.188	.188	.188	19	-1	0	0	0	.625	-1	/O-5	-0.2
Total	4 n	51	234	55	70	6	2	0	34	0	3	.299	.299	.342	85	-5	5	6	-2	.807	-2	/O-50,1-1	-0.4
■ PAUL SENTELL Sentell, Leopold Theodore b: 8/27/1879, New Orleans, La. d: 4/27/23, Cincinnati, Ohio BR/TR, 5′9″, 176 lbs. Deb: 4/12/06 U																							
1906	Phi-N	63	192	19	44	5	1	1	14	14		.229	.292	.281	79	-5	15			.887	-9	3-33,2-19/O-2,S-1	-1.4
1907	Phi-N	3	3	0	0	0	0	0	0	1		.000	.250	.000	-22	-0	0			1.000	-2	/S-2,O-1	-0.3
Total	2	66	195	19	44	5	1	1	14	15		.226	.291	.277	77	-5	15			1.000	-11	/3-33,2-19,S-3,O-3	-1.7
■ TED SEPKOWSKI Sepkowski, Theodore Walter (b: Theodore Walter Sczepkowski) b: 11/9/23, Baltimore, Md. BL/TR, 5′11″, 190 lbs. Deb: 9/9/42																							
1942	Cle-A	5	10	0	1	0	0	0	0	0	3	.100	.100	.100	-46	-2	0	0	0	.824	0	/2-2	-0.1
1946	Cle-A	2	8	2	4	1	0	0	1	0	0	.500	.500	.625	228	1	0	0	0	.833	-1	/3-2	0.1
1947	Cle-A	10	8	0	1	1	0	0	0	1	1	.125	.222	.250	32	-1	0	0	0	.000	-0	/O-1	-0.1
	NY-A	2	0	1	0	0	0	0	0	0	0	—	—	—	—	0	0	1	-1	.000	0	R	-0.1
	Yr	12	8	1	1	1	0	0	0	1	1	.125	.222	.250	32	-1	0	1	-1	.000	-0	/O-1	-0.2
Total	3	19	26	3	6	2	0	0	1	1	4	.231	.259	.308	61	-1	0	1	-1	.833	-1	/3-2,2-2,O-1	-0.2
■ BILL SERENA Serena, William Robert b: 10/2/24, Alameda, Cal. d: 4/17/96, Hayward, Cal. BR/TR, 5′9.5″, 175 lbs. Deb: 9/16/49																							
1949	Chi-N	12	37	3	8	3	0	1	7	7	9	.216	.341	.378	95	-0	0			.923	-4	3-11	-0.5
1950	Chi-N	127	435	56	104	20	4	17	61	65	75	.239	.339	.421	100	-0	1			.945	-2	*3-125	-0.4
1951	Chi-N	13	39	8	13	3	1	1	4	11	4	.333	.490	.538	173	5	0	2	-1	.941	-4	3-12	0.0
1952	Chi-N	122	390	49	107	21	5	15	61	39	83	.274	.345	.469	122	11	1	0	0	.971	-1	3-58,2-49	1.1
1953	Chi-N	93	275	30	69	10	5	10	52	41	46	.251	.350	.433	100	0	0	0	0	.983	-15	2-49,3-28	-1.2
1954	Chi-N	41	63	8	10	0	1	4	13	14	18	.159	.321	.381	81	-2	0	0	0	.933	-3	3-12/2-2	-0.5
Total	6	408	1239	154	311	57	16	48	198	177	235	.251	.348	.439	108	14	2	2		.951	-30	3-246,2-100	-1.5
■ PAUL SERNA Serna, Paul David b: 11/16/58, ElCentro, Cal. BR/TR, 5′8″, 170 lbs. Deb: 9/1/81																							
1981	Sea-A	30	94	11	24	2	0	4	9	3	11	.255	.293	.404	95	-1	2	3	-1	.954	-3	S-23/2-7	-0.2
1982	Sea-A	65	169	15	38	3	0	3	8	4	13	.225	.247	.296	47	-12	0	5	-3	.936	3	S-31,2-18,3-15,/D-2	-1.0
Total	2	95	263	26	62	5	0	7	17	7	24	.236	.264	.335	64	-13	2	8	-4	.945	1	/S-54,2-25,3-15,D-2	-1.2
■ SCOTT SERVAIS Servais, Scott Daniel b: 6/4/67, LaCrosse, Wis. BR/TR, 6′2″, 195 lbs. Deb: 7/12/91																							
1991	Hou-N	16	37	0	6	3	0	0	6	4	8	.162	.244	.243	40	-3	0	0	0	.988	2	C-14	0.0
1992	Hou-N	77	205	12	49	9	0	0	15	11	25	.239	.294	.283	67	-9	0	0	0	.995	-2	C-73	-0.8
1993	Hou-N	85	258	24	63	11	0	11	32	22	45	.244	.316	.415	97	-2	0	0	0	.996	2	C-82	-0.4
1994	Hou-N	78	251	27	49	15	1	9	41	10	44	.195	.238	.371	58	-17	0	0	0	.996	1	C-78	-1.2
1995	Hou-N	28	89	7	20	10	0	1	12	9	15	.225	.303	.371	82	-3	0	1	-1	.977	5	C-28	0.4
	Chi-N	52	175	31	50	12	0	12	35	23	37	.286	.375	.560	145	11	2	1	0	.981	-2	C-52	1.3
	Yr	80	264	38	70	22	0	13	47	32	52	.265	.351	.496	125	9	2	2	-1	.980	3	C-80	1.7
1996	Chi-N	129	445	42	118	20	0	11	63	30	75	.265	.331	.384	86	-9	0	2	-1	.988	0	*C-128/1-1	-0.2
1997	Chi-N	122	385	36	100	21	0	6	45	24	56	.260	.313	.361	74	-15	0	1	-1	.990	2	*C-118/1-1,D-2	-0.6
1998	*Chi-N	113	325	35	72	15	1	7	36	26	51	.222	.289	.338	61	-19	1	0	0	.994	-6	*C-110/1-1	-1.7
Total	8	700	2170	214	527	116	2	57	285	159	356	.243	.307	.377	80	-64	3	5	-2	.991	2	C-683/1-3,D-2	-2.4
■ WALTER SESSI Sessi, Walter Anthony "Watsie" b: 7/23/18, Finleyville, Pa. d:4/18/98, Mobile, Ala. BL/TL, 6′3″, 225 lbs. Deb: 9/18/41																							
1941	StL-N	5	13	2	0	0	0	0	0	1	2	.000	.071	.000	-74	-3	0			.750	-1	/O-3	-0.4
1946	StL-N	15	14	2	2	0	0	1	2	1	4	.143	.200	.357	54	-1	0			.000	0	H	-0.1
Total	2	20	27	4	2	0	0	1	2	2	6	.074	.138	.185	-9	-4	0			.750	-1	/O-3	-0.5
■ JOHN SEVCIK Sevcik, John Joseph b: 7/11/42, Oak Park, Ill. BR/TR, 6′2″, 205 lbs. Deb: 4/24/65																							
1965	Min-A	12	16	1	1	1	0	0	0	1	5	.063	.118	.125	-30	-3	0	0	0	1.000	3	C-11	0.0
■ HANK SEVEREID Severeid, Henry Levai b: 6/1/1891, Story City, Iowa d: 12/17/68, San Antonio, Tex. BR/TR, 6′, 175 lbs. Deb: 5/15/11																							
1911	Cin-N	37	56	5	17	6	1	0	10	3	6	.304	.350	.446	127	2	0			.913	-3	C-22	0.0
1912	Cin-N	50	114	10	27	0	3	0	13	8	11	.237	.287	.289	60	-6	0			.943	-9	C-20/1-7,O-6	-1.4
1913	Cin-N	8	6	0	0	0	0	0	0	1	1	.000	.143	.000	-58	-1	0			1.000	-1	/C-2,O-1	-0.2
1915	StL-A	80	203	12	45	6	1	1	22	16	25	.222	.279	.276	69	-8	2	1	0	.966	-10	C-64	-1.5
1916	StL-A	100	293	23	80	8	2	0	34	26	17	.273	.341	.314	102	1	3			.976	-16	C-89/1-1,3-1	-1.0
1917	StL-A	143	501	45	133	23	4	1	57	28	20	.265	.306	.333	99	-3	6			.966	-19	*C-139/1-1	-1.2
1918	StL-A	51	133	8	34	4	0	0	11	18	4	.256	.357	.286	97	0	4			.946	-5	C-42	-0.2
1919	StL-A	112	351	16	87	12	2	0	36	21	13	.248	.298	.293	65	-16	2			.983	-5	*C-103	-1.3
1920	StL-A	123	422	46	117	14	5	2	49	33	11	.277	.336	.348	79	-13	5	3	-0	.983	3	*C-117	-0.2
1921	StL-A	143	472	66	153	23	7	2	78	42	9	.324	.379	.415	97	2	7	2	1	.972	-3	*C-126	0.3
1922	StL-A	137	517	49	166	32	7	3	78	28	12	.321	.356	.427	100	-1	1	4	-2	.984	7	*C-133	1.1
1923	StL-A	122	432	50	133	27	6	3	51	31	11	.308	.356	.419	98	-2	3	0	1	**.993**	10	*C-116	1.3
1924	StL-A	137	432	37	133	23	2	4	48	36	15	.308	.362	.398	90	-7	1	6	-3	**.989**	-2	*C-130	-0.4
1925	StL-A	34	109	15	40	9	0	1	21	11	2	.367	.425	.477	122	4	0	2	-1	.993	-0	C-31	0.4
	*Was-A	50	110	11	39	8	1	0	14	13	6	.355	.423	.445	123	4	0	0	0	.986	2	C-35	0.7
	Yr	84	219	26	79	17	1	1	35	24	8	.361	.424	.461	123	9	0	2	-1	.990	1	C-66	1.1
1926	Was-A	22	34	2	7	1	0	0	4	3	2	.206	.270	.235	33	-3	0	0	0	.977	0	C-16	-0.2
	*NY-A	41	127	13	34	8	1	0	13	13	4	.268	.336	.346	79	-4	1	1	-0	.988	-3	C-40	-0.5
	Yr	63	161	15	41	9	1	0	17	16	6	.255	.322	.323	70	-7	1	1	-0	.985	-3	C-56	-0.7
Total	15	1390	4312	408	1245	204	42	17	539	331	169	.289	.342	.367	91	-55	35	19		.978	-56	*C-1225/1-9,O-7,3-1	-4.3

■ RICH SEVERSON
Severson, Richard Allen b: 1/18/45, Artesia, Cal. BR/TR, 6', 174 lbs. Deb: 4/10/70

YEAR	TM/L	G	AB	R	H	2B	3B	HR	RBI	BB	SO	AVG	OBP	SLG	PRO+	BR/A	SB	CS	SBR	FA	FR	G/POS	TPR
1970	KC-A	77	240	22	60	11	1	1	22	16	33	.250	.300	.317	70	-10	0	0	0	.962	1	S-50,2-25	-0.2
1971	KC-A	16	30	4	9	0	2	0	1	3	5	.300	.364	.433	126	1	0	0	0	1.000	6	/2-6,S-6,3-1	0.8
Total	2	93	270	26	69	11	3	1	23	19	38	.256	.307	.330	76	-9	0	0	0	.958	7	/S-56,2-31,3-1	0.6

■ ED SEWARD
Seward, Edward William (b: Edward William Sourhardt) b: 6/29/1867, Cleveland, Ohio d: 7/30/47, Cleveland, Ohio TR, 5'7", 175 lbs. Deb: 9/30/1885 U

YEAR	TM/L	G	AB	R	H	2B	3B	HR	RBI	BB	SO	AVG	OBP	SLG	PRO+	BR/A	SB	CS	SBR	FA	FR	G/POS	TPR
1885	Pro-N	1	3	0	0	0	0	0	0	0	2	.000	.000	.000	-99	-1				1.000	1	/P-1	0.0
1887	Phi-a	74	266	31	50	10	0	5	28	16		.188	.239	.282	45	-20	14			.901	-3	P-55,O-21	-0.5
1888	Phi-a	64	225	27	32	3	3	2	14	18		.142	.215	.209	36	-16	12			.887	4	P-57/O-7	-0.1
1889	Phi-a	46	143	22	31	5	3	2	17	22	19	.217	.333	.336	92	-1	6			.885	-4	P-39/O-8,2-1	-0.2
1890	Phi-a	26	72	7	10	4	0	0	2	8		.139	.244	.194	30	-6	3			.811	-2	P-21/O-6	-0.2
1891	Cle-N	7	19	2	4	2	0	0	1	3	4	.211	.318	.316	81	-0	0			1.000	-2	/O-3,P-3,1-1	-0.2
Total	6	218	728	89	127	24	6	9	62	67	25	.174	.253	.261	52	-44	35			.882	-7	P-176/O-45,1-1,2-1	-1.2

■ GEORGE SEWARD
Seward, George E. b: St.Louis, Mo. 5'7.5", 145 lbs. Deb: 5/19/1875

YEAR	TM/L	G	AB	R	H	2B	3B	HR	RBI	BB	SO	AVG	OBP	SLG	PRO+	BR/A	SB	CS	SBR	FA	FR	G/POS	TPR
1875	StL-n	25	96	12	24	2	0	0	8	1	1	.250	.258	.271	92	-0	1	0	0	.817	-2	C-18/O-7,2-2	-0.1
1876	NY-N	1	3	0	0	0	0	0	0	0	0	.000	.000	.000	-99	-1				1.000	1	/2-1	0.0
1882	StL-a	38	144	23	31	1	1	0		12		.215	.276	.236	71	-4				.776	-0	O-35/C-5	-0.4
Total	2	39	147	23	31	1	1	0	0	12	0	.211	.270	.231	68	-5				.776	0	/O-35,C-5,2-1	-0.4

■ LUKE SEWELL
Sewell, James Luther b: 1/5/01, Titus, Ala. d: 5/14/87, Akron, Ohio BR/TR, 5'9", 160 lbs. Deb: 6/30/21 FMC

YEAR	TM/L	G	AB	R	H	2B	3B	HR	RBI	BB	SO	AVG	OBP	SLG	PRO+	BR/A	SB	CS	SBR	FA	FR	G/POS	TPR
1921	Cle-A	3	6	0	0	0	0	0	1	0	3	.000	.000	.000	-99	-2	0	0	0	1.000	1	/C-3	-0.1
1922	Cle-A	41	87	14	23	5	0	0	10	5	8	.264	.312	.322	65	-4	1	1	-0	.963	0	C-39	-0.3
1923	Cle-A	10	10	2	2	0	1	0	1	1	0	.200	.273	.400	76	-0	0	0	0	.833	0	/C-7	0.0
1924	Cle-A	63	165	27	48	9	1	0	17	22	13	.291	.387	.358	92	-1	1	0	0	.959	5	C-57	0.7
1925	Cle-A	74	220	30	51	10	2	0	18	33	18	.232	.337	.295	61	-12	6	2	1	.971	7	C-66/O-2	-0.2
1926	Cle-A	126	433	41	103	16	4	0	46	36	27	.238	.302	.293	55	-28	9	3	1	.983	2	*C-125	-1.7
1927	Cle-A	128	470	52	138	27	6	0	53	20	23	.294	.328	.377	82	-13	4	8	-4	.963	-2	*C-126	-0.9
1928	Cle-A	122	411	52	111	16	9	3	52	26	27	.270	.318	.375	81	-12	3	4	-2	.972	13	*C-118	0.9
1929	Cle-A	124	406	41	96	16	3	1	39	29	26	.236	.287	.298	49	-31	6	6	-2	.966	4	*C-124	-1.6
1930	Cle-A	76	292	40	75	21	2	1	43	14	9	.257	.293	.353	61	-18	5	2	0	.974	-2	C-76	-1.1
1931	Cle-A	108	375	45	103	30	4	1	53	36	17	.275	.341	.384	86	-8	1	1	-0	.980	-8	*C-104	-0.8
1932	Cle-A	87	300	36	76	20	2	2	52	38	24	.253	.337	.353	74	-11	4	5	-2	.978	4	C-84	-0.4
1933	*Was-A	141	474	65	125	30	4	2	61	48	24	.264	.335	.357	84	-10	7	2	1	.990	-6	*C-141	-0.7
1934	Was-A	72	207	21	49	7	3	2	21	22	10	.237	.313	.329	68	-10	0	1	-1	.994	-1	C-50/O-7,1-6,2-1,3	-0.9
1935	Chi-A	118	421	52	120	19	3	2	67	32	18	.285	.336	.359	78	-14	3	2	-0	.988	6	*C-112	-0.2
1936	Chi-A	128	451	59	113	20	5	5	73	54	16	.251	.332	.350	66	-24	11	2	2	.984	12	*C-126	-0.4
1937	Chi-A☆	122	412	51	111	21	6	1	61	46	18	.269	.343	.357	77	-14	4	5	-2	.985	6	*C-118	-0.3
1938	Chi-A	65	211	23	45	4	1	0	27	20	20	.213	.284	.242	32	-22	0	0	0	.985	7	C-65	-1.1
1939	Cle-A	16	20	1	3	1	0	0	1	3	1	.150	.261	.200	20	-2	0	0	0	.966	-1	C-15/1-1	-0.2
1942	StL-A	6	12	1	1	0	0	0	0	1	5	.083	.154	.083	-32	-2	0	0	0	.944	1	/C-6,M	-0.1
Total	20	1630	5383	653	1393	272	56	20	696	486	307	.259	.323	.341	70	-242	65	44	-7	.978	48	*C-1562/O-9,1-7,32	-9.4

■ JOE SEWELL
Sewell, Joseph Wheeler b: 10/9/1898, Titus, Ala. d: 3/6/90, Mobile, Ala. BL/TR, 5'6.5", 155 lbs. Deb: 9/10/20 FCH

YEAR	TM/L	G	AB	R	H	2B	3B	HR	RBI	BB	SO	AVG	OBP	SLG	PRO+	BR/A	SB	CS	SBR	FA	FR	G/POS	TPR
1920	*Cle-A	22	70	14	23	4	1	0	12	9	4	.329	.412	.414	116	2	1	0	0	.884	3	S-22	0.6
1921	Cle-A	154	572	101	182	36	12	4	93	80	17	.318	.412	.444	117	17	7	6	-2	.944	-3	*S-154	2.5
1922	Cle-A	153	558	80	167	28	7	2	83	73	20	.299	.386	.385	101	3	10	12	-4	.939	12	*S-139,2-12	2.5
1923	Cle-A	153	553	98	195	41	10	3	109	98	12	.353	.456	.479	147	43	9	6	-1	.930	6	*S-151	6.0
1924	Cle-A	153	594	99	188	**45**	5	4	106	67	13	.316	.388	.429	109	9	3	3	-1	.960	**21**	*S-153	4.3
1925	Cle-A	155	608	78	204	37	7	1	98	64	4	.336	.402	.424	109	10	7	6	-2	**.967**	16	*S-153/2-3	3.8
1926	Cle-A	154	578	91	187	41	5	4	85	65	6	.324	.399	.433	116	15	17	7	1	.955	3	*S-154	3.3
1927	Cle-A	153	569	83	180	48	5	1	92	51	7	.316	.382	.424	108	7	3	16	-9	**.962**	6	*S-153	1.9
1928	Cle-A	155	588	79	190	40	2	4	70	58	9	.323	.391	.418	111	11	7	1	2	**.963**	27	*S-137,3-19	5.4
1929	Cle-A	152	578	90	182	38	3	7	73	48	4	.315	.372	.427	102	2	6	6	-2	.975	15	*3-152	2.0
1930	Cle-A	109	353	44	102	17	6	0	48	41	3	.289	.374	.371	86	-6	1	4	-2	.950	0	3-97	-0.2
1931	NY-A	130	484	102	146	22	1	6	64	61	8	.302	.390	.388	111	11	1	1	-0	.952	-2	*3-121/2-1	1.5
1932	*NY-A	125	503	95	137	21	3	11	68	56	3	.272	.349	.392	96	-2	0	2	-1	.974	2	*3-123	0.6
1933	NY-A	135	524	87	143	18	1	2	54	71	4	.273	.361	.323	87	-7	2	2	-1	.964	3	*3-131	0.3
Total	14	1903	7132	1141	2226	436	68	49	1055	842	114	.312	.391	.413	109	116	74	72	-21	.951	107	*S-1216,3-643/2-16	34.5

■ TOMMY SEWELL
Sewell, Thomas Wesley b: 4/16/06, Titus, Ala. d: 7/30/56, Montgomery, Ala. BL/TR, 5'7.5", 155 lbs. Deb: 6/21/27 F

YEAR	TM/L	G	AB	R	H	2B	3B	HR	RBI	BB	SO	AVG	OBP	SLG	PRO+	BR/A	SB	CS	SBR	FA	FR	G/POS	TPR
1927	Chi-N	1	1	0	0	0	0	0	0	0	0	.000	.000	.000	-99	-0	0			.000	0	H	0.0

■ RICHIE SEXSON
Sexson, Richard Lockwood b: 12/29/74, Portland, Ore. BR/TR, 6'6", 205 lbs. Deb: 9/14/97

YEAR	TM/L	G	AB	R	H	2B	3B	HR	RBI	BB	SO	AVG	OBP	SLG	PRO+	BR/A	SB	CS	SBR	FA	FR	G/POS	TPR
1997	Cle-A	5	11	1	3	0	0	0	0	0	2	.273	.273	.273	41	-1	0	0	0	1.000	0	/1-2,D-1	-0.1
1998	*Cle-A	49	174	28	54	14	1	11	35	6	42	.310	.344	.592	133	7	1	1	-0	.984	4	1-45/O-3,D-2	0.6
Total	2	54	185	29	57	14	1	11	35	6	44	.308	.340	.573	127	7	1	1	-0	.984	4	/1-47,O-3,D-3	0.5

■ JIMMY SEXTON
Sexton, Jimmy Dale b: 12/15/51, Mobile, Ala. BR/TR, 5'10", 175 lbs. Deb: 9/2/77

YEAR	TM/L	G	AB	R	H	2B	3B	HR	RBI	BB	SO	AVG	OBP	SLG	PRO+	BR/A	SB	CS	SBR	FA	FR	G/POS	TPR
1977	Sea-A	14	37	5	8	1	1	1	3	2	6	.216	.256	.378	71	-2	1	1	-0	.929	3	S-12	0.2
1978	Hou-N	88	141	17	29	3	2	2	6	13	28	.206	.273	.298	64	-7	16	2	4	.981	-3	S-58/3-8,2-3	-0.2
1979	Hou-N	52	43	8	9	0	0	0	1	7	7	.209	.320	.209	50	-3	1	3	-2	.943	7	S-11/3-4,2-2	0.3
1981	Oak-A	7	3	3	0	0	0	0	0	0	2	.000	.000	.000	-99	-1	2	0	1	1.000	1	/3-1,D-1	0.1
1982	Oak-A	69	139	19	34	4	0	2	14	9	24	.245	.295	.317	71	-6	16	0	5	.957	-3	S-47/3-8,D-5	-0.1
1983	StL-N	6	9	1	1	1	0	0	0	1	4	.111	.200	.222	17	-1	0	0	0	1.000	1	/S-4,3-2	0.0
Total	6	236	372	53	81	9	3	5	24	32	71	.218	.281	.298	64	-19	36	6	7	.962	5	S-132/3-23,D-6,2-5	0.3

■ TOM SEXTON
Sexton, Thomas William b: 3/14/1865, Rock Island, Ill. d: 2/8/34, Rock Island, Ill. Deb: 9/27/1884

YEAR	TM/L	G	AB	R	H	2B	3B	HR	RBI	BB	SO	AVG	OBP	SLG	PRO+	BR/A	SB	CS	SBR	FA	FR	G/POS	TPR
1884	Mil-U	12	47	9	11	2	0	0		4		.234	.294	.277	136	-1				.853	-1	S-12	-0.2

■ SOCKS SEYBOLD
Seybold, Ralph Orlando b: 11/23/1870, Washingtonville, O d: 12/22/21, Greensburg, Pa. BR/TR, 5'11", 175 lbs. Deb: 8/20/1899

YEAR	TM/L	G	AB	R	H	2B	3B	HR	RBI	BB	SO	AVG	OBP	SLG	PRO+	BR/A	SB	CS	SBR	FA	FR	G/POS	TPR
1899	Cin-N	22	85	13	19	5	1	0	8	6		.224	.283	.306	60	-5	2			.917	1	O-22	-0.5
1901	Phi-A	114	449	74	150	24	14	8	90	40		.334	.397	.503	142	25	15			.954	-5	*O-100,1-14	1.0
1902	Phi-A	137	522	91	165	27	12	**16**	97	43		.316	.375	.506	137	24	6			.963	2	*O-136	1.6
1903	Phi-A	137	522	76	156	**45**	8	8	84	38		.299	.353	.462	137	23	5			.964	-2	*O-120,1-18	1.4
1904	Phi-A	143	510	56	149	26	9	3	64	42		.292	.351	.396	129	17	12			.975	1	*O-129,1-13	1.2
1905	*Phi-A	133	492	64	135	37	4	6	59	42		.274	.341	.402	133	18	5			.983	9	*O-133	2.3
1906	Phi-A	116	411	41	130	23	2	5	59	30		.316	.367	.418	141	19	9			.925	-5	*O-114	0.9
1907	Phi-A	147	564	58	153	29	4	5	92	40		.271	.324	.363	116	10	10			.973	1	*O-147	0.5
1908	Phi-A	48	130	5	28	2	0	0	3	12		.215	.287	.231	64	-5	2			.921	-4	O-34	-1.1
Total	9	997	3685	478	1085	218	54	51	556	293		.294	.353	.424	129	126	66			.961	-3	O-935/1-45	7.3

■ CY SEYMOUR
Seymour, James Bentley b: 12/9/1872, Albany, N.Y. d: 9/20/19, New York, N.Y. BL/TL, 6', 200 lbs. Deb: 4/22/1896

YEAR	TM/L	G	AB	R	H	2B	3B	HR	RBI	BB	SO	AVG	OBP	SLG	PRO+	BR/A	SB	CS	SBR	FA	FR	G/POS	TPR
1896	NY-N	12	32	2	7	0	0	0	0	0	7	.219	.219	.219	16	-4	0			.857	0	P-11/O-1	-0.1
1897	NY-N	44	137	13	33	5	1	2	14	4		.241	.262	.336	59	-9	3			.850	7	P-38/O-6	-0.2
1898	NY-N	80	297	41	82	5	2	4	23	9		.276	.300	.347	88	-6	8			.887	7	P-45,O-35/2-1	-0.7
1899	NY-N	50	159	25	52	3	2	2	27	4		.327	.344	.409	110	1	2			.839	3	P-32/O-8,1-3,3-1	-0.2
1900	NY-N	23	40	9	12	0	0	0	2	3		.300	.349	.300	84	-1	0			.828	-0	P-13/O-3,1-1	-0.2
1901	Bal-A	134	547	84	166	19	8	1	77	28		.303	.337	.373	93	-6	38			.945	14	*O-133/1-1	-0.2
1902	Bal-A	72	280	38	75	8	8	3	41	18		.268	.317	.386	90	-4	12			.956	1	O-72	-0.8
	Cin-N	62	244	27	83	8	2	2	37	12		.340	.378	.414	132	8	8			.920	4	O-61/P-1,3-1	0.9

YEAR	TM/L	G	AB	R	H	2B	3B	HR	RBI	BB	SO	AVG	OBP	SLG	PRO+	BR/A	SB	CS	SBR	FA	FR	G/POS	TPR
1903	Cin-N	135	558	85	191	25	15	7	72	33		.342	.382	.478	130	18	25			.902	5	*O-135	1.4
1904	Cin-N	131	531	71	166	26	13	5	58	29		.313	.352	.439	132	17	11			.951	13	*O-130	2.4
1905	Cin-N	149	581	95	**219**	**40**	**21**	8	**121**	51		**.377**	.429	**.559**	**175**	**51**	21			.947	12	*O-149	5.7
1906	Cin-N	79	307	35	79	7	2	4	38	24		.257	.317	.332	98	-1	9			.968	10	O-79	0.6
	NY-N	72	269	35	86	12	3	4	42	18		.320	.365	.431	145	13	20			.978	-2	O-72	0.8
	Yr	151	576	70	165	19	5	8	80	42		.286	.339	.378	120	12	29			.972	8	*O-151	1.4
1907	NY-N	131	473	46	139	25	8	3	75	36		.294	.350	.400	131	16	21			.975	3	*O-126	1.6
1908	NY-N	156	587	60	157	23	2	5	92	30		.267	.306	.339	101	-1	18			.949	11	*O-155	0.5
1909	NY-N	80	280	37	87	12	5	1	30	25		.311	.369	.400	137	12	14			.968	0	O-74	1.0
1910	NY-N	79	287	32	76	9	4	1	40	23	18	.265	.324	.334	92	-3	10			.936	-6	O-76	-1.4
1913	Bos-N	39	73	2	13	2	0	0	10	7	7	.178	.259	.205	33	-6	2			.950	0	O-18	-0.7
Total	16	1528	5682	737	1723	229	96	52	799	354	32	.303	.347	.405	117	95	222			.945	81	*O-1333,P-140/132	10.4

■ TILLIE SHAFER

Shafer, Arthur Joseph b: 3/22/1889, Los Angeles, Cal. d: 1/10/62, Los Angeles, Cal. BB/TR, 5'10", 165 lbs. Deb: 4/24/09

YEAR	TM/L	G	AB	R	H	2B	3B	HR	RBI	BB	SO	AVG	OBP	SLG	PRO+	BR/A	SB	CS	SBR	FA	FR	G/POS	TPR
1909	NY-N	38	84	11	15	2	1	0	7	14		.179	.296	.226	61	-3	6			.750	-0	3-16,2-13/O-2	-0.4
1910	NY-N	29	21	5	4	1	0	0	1	0	6	.190	.190	.238	25	-2	0			.889	5	/3-8,2-2,S-2	0.3
1912	*NY-N	78	163	48	47	4	1	0	23	30	19	.288	.408	.325	99	2	22			.879	-7	S-31,3-16,2-15	-0.3
1913	*NY-N	138	508	74	146	17	12	5	52	61	55	.287	.369	.398	118	13	32			.923	-9	3-79,2-25,S-16,O-15	0.6
Total	4	283	776	138	212	24	14	5	83	105	80	.273	.366	.360	106	10	60			.903	-12	3-119/2-55,S-49,O	0.2

■ RALPH SHAFER

Shafer, Ralph Newton b: 3/17/1894, Cincinnati, Ohio d: 2/5/50, Akron, Ohio 5'11", Deb: 7/25/14

YEAR	TM/L	G	AB	R	H	2B	3B	HR	RBI	BB	SO	AVG	OBP	SLG	PRO+	BR/A	SB	CS	SBR	FA	FR	G/POS	TPR
1914	Pit-N	1	0	0	0	0	0	0	0	0	0	—	—	—	—	0	0			.000	0	H	0.0

■ SHAFFER

Shaffer Deb: 9/15/1875

YEAR	TM/L	G	AB	R	H	2B	3B	HR	RBI	BB	SO	AVG	OBP	SLG	PRO+	BR/A	SB	CS	SBR	FA	FR	G/POS	TPR
1875	Atl-n	1	4	0	0	0	0	0	0	0	0	.000	.000	.000	-99	-1	0	0	0	.500	-0	/O-1	-0.1

■ FRANK SHAFFER

Shaffer, Frank Deb: 4/24/1884

YEAR	TM/L	G	AB	R	H	2B	3B	HR	RBI	BB	SO	AVG	OBP	SLG	PRO+	BR/A	SB	CS	SBR	FA	FR	G/POS	TPR
1884	Alt-U	19	74	11	21	2	0	0		3		.284	.312	.311	88	-3				.889	-3	O-17/C-2,3-1	-0.6
	KC-U	44	164	18	28	3	2	0		15		.171	.240	.213	44	-16				.768	-3	O-41/C-2,2-1,S-1,3	-1.7
	Bal-U	3	13	1	1	0	0	0		0		.077	.077	.077	-48	-3				.750	-1	/O-3	-0.3
	Yr	66	251	30	50	5	2	0		18		.199	.253	.235	53	-21				.796	-6	O-61/C-4,3-2,2-1,S	-2.6

■ ORATOR SHAFFER

Shaffer, George b: 1852, Philadelphia, Pa. BL/TR, 5'9", 165 lbs. Deb: 5/23/1874 F

YEAR	TM/L	G	AB	R	H	2B	3B	HR	RBI	BB	SO	AVG	OBP	SLG	PRO+	BR/A	SB	CS	SBR	FA	FR	G/POS	TPR
1874	Har-n	9	35	6	8	0	0	1	3	0	4	.229	.229	.314	69	-1	0	0	0	.710	-1	/O-9	-0.2
	Mut-n	1	5	1	1	0	0	0	0	0	0	.200	.200	.200	28	-0	0	0	0	.000	-0	/O-1	-0.1
	Yr	10	40	7	9	0	0	1	3	0	4	.225	.225	.300	64	-2	0	0	0	.710	-2	O-10	-0.3
1875	Phi-n	19	70	10	17	2	1	0	6	0	4	.243	.243	.300	84	-1	2	0	1	.769	-2	O-12/3-5,1-2	-0.2
1877	Lou-N	61	260	38	74	9	5	3	34	9	17	.285	.309	.392	101	-2				.835	14	*O-60/1-1	0.8
1878	Ind-N	63	266	48	90	19	6	0	30	13	20	.338	.369	.455	**196**	**28**				.842	8	*O-63	**2.9**
1879	Chi-N	73	316	53	96	13	0	0	35	6	28	.304	.317	.345	111	3				.801	20	*O-72/3-1	1.8
1880	Cle-N	83	338	62	90	14	9	0	21	17	36	.266	.301	.361	126	9				.901	17	*O-83	2.3
1881	Cle-N	85	343	48	88	13	6	1	34	23	20	.257	.303	.338	107	4				.880	2	*O-85	0.4
1882	Cle-N	84	313	37	67	14	2	3	28	27	27	.214	.276	.300	88	-3				.805	-9	*O-84	-1.2
1883	Buf-N	95	401	67	117	11	3	0	41	27	39	.292	.336	.334	103	2				.861	20	*O-95	1.8
1884	StL-U	106	467	130	168	**40**	10	2		30		.360	.398	.501	165	24				.870	-3	*O-100/2-7,1-1	1.7
1885	StL-N	69	257	30	50	11	2	0	18	19	31	.195	.250	.253	67	-8				.918	11	O-69	0.1
	Phi-a	2	9	1	2	0	1	0	1	1		.222	.300	.444	125	0				1.000	-1	/O-2	0.0
1886	Phi-a	21	82	15	22	3	3	0	8	8		.268	.333	.378	121	2	3			.815	0	O-21	0.2
1890	Phi-a	100	390	55	110	15	5	1	58	47		.282	.367	.354	115	9	29			**.958**	2	*O-98/1-3	0.6
Total	2 n	29	110	17	26	2	1	1	9	0	8	.236	.236	.300	76	-3	2	0	1	.737	-4	/O-22,3-5,1-2	-0.5
Total	11	842	3442	584	974	162	52	10	308	227	218	.283	.328	.369	119	66	32			.865	81	O-832/2-7,1-5,3-1	11.4

■ TAYLOR SHAFFER

Shaffer, Taylor b: 7/1870, Philadelphia, Pa. Deb: 4/17/1890 F

YEAR	TM/L	G	AB	R	H	2B	3B	HR	RBI	BB	SO	AVG	OBP	SLG	PRO+	BR/A	SB	CS	SBR	FA	FR	G/POS	TPR
1890	Phi-a	69	261	28	45	3	4	0	21	28		.172	.258	.215	40	-19	19			.921	4	2-69	-1.0

■ ART SHAMSKY

Shamsky, Arthur Louis b: 10/14/41, St.Louis, Mo. BL/TL, 6'1", 175 lbs. Deb: 4/17/65

YEAR	TM/L	G	AB	R	H	2B	3B	HR	RBI	BB	SO	AVG	OBP	SLG	PRO+	BR/A	SB	CS	SBR	FA	FR	G/POS	TPR
1965	Cin-N	64	96	13	25	4	3	2	10	10	29	.260	.330	.427	104	1	1	0	0	.966	0	O-18/1-1	0.0
1966	Cin-N	96	234	41	54	5	0	21	47	32	45	.231	.323	.521	120	6	0	2	-1	.973	-3	O-74	-0.1
1967	Cin-N	76	147	6	29	3	1	3	13	15	34	.197	.276	.293	56	-8	0	1	-1	.984	-2	O-40	-1.4
1968	NY-N	116	345	30	82	14	4	12	48	21	58	.238	.295	.406	108	3	1	0	0	.993	1	O-82,1-17	-0.2
1969	*NY-N	100	303	42	91	9	3	14	47	36	32	.300	.380	.488	139	16	1	2	-1	.992	-6	O-78/1-9	0.4
1970	NY-N	122	403	48	118	19	2	11	49	49	33	.293	.374	.432	115	9	1	1	-0	1.000	1	O-58,1-56	0.2
1971	NY-N	68	135	13	25	6	2	5	18	21	18	.185	.299	.370	90	-2	1	1	-0	.984	2	O-38/1-1	-0.2
1972	Chi-N	15	16	1	2	0	0	0	1	3	3	.125	.263	.125	12	-2	0	0	0	1.000	0	/1-4	-0.2
	Oak-A	8	7	0	0	0	0	0	0	1	2	.000	.125	.000	-64	-1	0	0	0	.000	0	H	-0.2
Total	8	665	1686	194	426	60	15	68	233	188	254	.253	.333	.427	109	21	5	7	-3	.987	-8	O-388/1-88	-1.7

■ JIM SHANDLEY

Shandley, James H. b: New York d: 11/4/04, Brooklyn, N.Y. Deb: 5/3/1876

YEAR	TM/L	G	AB	R	H	2B	3B	HR	RBI	BB	SO	AVG	OBP	SLG	PRO+	BR/A	SB	CS	SBR	FA	FR	G/POS	TPR
1876	NY-N	2	8	0	1	0	0	0	0	0	0	.125	.125	.125	-19	-1				.600	-1	/O-2	-0.1

■ WALLY SHANER

Shaner, Walter Dedaker "Skinny" b: 5/24/1900, Lynchburg, Va. d: 11/13/92, Las Vegas, Nev. BR/TR, 6'2", 195 lbs. Deb: 5/4/23

YEAR	TM/L	G	AB	R	H	2B	3B	HR	RBI	BB	SO	AVG	OBP	SLG	PRO+	BR/A	SB	CS	SBR	FA	FR	G/POS	TPR
1923	Cle-A	3	4	1	1	0	0	0	0	1	1	.250	.400	.250	74	-0	0	0	0	1.000	-1	/O-2,3-1	-0.1
1926	Bos-A	69	191	20	54	12	2	0	21	17	13	.283	.348	.366	89	-3	1	0	0	.965	0	O-48	-0.6
1927	Bos-A	122	406	54	111	33	6	3	49	21	35	.273	.311	.406	87	-10	11	4	1	.955	-8	*O-108/1-1	-2.2
1929	Cin-N	13	28	5	9	0	0	1	4	4	5	.321	.406	.429	112	1	1			1.000	-1	/1-8,O-2	-0.1
Total	4	207	629	80	175	45	8	4	74	43	54	.278	.327	.394	89	-12	13	4		.959	-9	O-160/1-9,3-1	-3.0

■ HOWIE SHANKS

Shanks, Howard Samuel "Hank" b: 7/21/1890, Chicago, Ill. d: 7/30/41, Monaca, Pa. BR/TR, 5'11", 170 lbs. Deb: 5/9/12 C

YEAR	TM/L	G	AB	R	H	2B	3B	HR	RBI	BB	SO	AVG	OBP	SLG	PRO+	BR/A	SB	CS	SBR	FA	FR	G/POS	TPR
1912	Was-A	116	399	52	92	14	7	1	48	40		.231	.305	.308	75	-13	21			.962	-2	*O-114	-2.1
1913	Was-A	109	390	38	99	11	5	1	37	15	40	.254	.287	.315	75	-14	24			.978	3	*O-109	-1.6
1914	Was-A	143	500	44	112	22	10	4	64	29	51	.224	.269	.332	78	-16	18	16	-4	.954	-0	*O-139	-3.0
1915	Was-A	141	492	52	123	19	8	0	47	30	42	.250	.297	.321	83	-12	12	14	-5	.982	7	O-80,3-49,2-10	-1.2
1916	Was-A	140	471	51	119	15	7	1	48	41	34	.253	.317	.321	92	-5	23	12	-0	.987	10	O-88,3-31/S-8,1-7	0.2
1917	Was-A	126	430	45	87	15	5	0	28	33	37	.202	.269	.260	62	-20	15			.929	13	S-90,O-26/1-2	-0.5
1918	Was-A	120	436	42	112	19	4	1	56	31	21	.257	.312	.326	94	-4	23			.957	1	O-64,2-48/3-3	-0.4
1919	Was-A	135	491	33	122	8	7	1	54	25	48	.248	.289	.299	66	-23	13			.922	-11	S-94,2-34/O-6	-2.9
1920	Was-A	128	444	56	119	16	7	4	37	29	43	.268	.316	.363	82	-13	11	6	-0	.951	-6	3-63,O-35,1-14,/2S	-1.8
1921	Was-A	154	562	81	170	24	**18**	7	69	57	30	.302	.370	.447	113	10	11	10	-3	**.960**	5	*3-154/2-1	2.2
1922	Was-A	84	272	35	77	10	9	1	32	25	25	.283	.352	.397	100	-0	6	0	2	.920	7	3-54,O-27	1.0
1923	Bos-A	131	464	38	118	19	5	3	57	19	37	.254	.285	.336	63	-26	6	6	-2	.939	-19	3-83,2-38/O-6,S-1	-3.9
1924	Bos-A	72	193	22	50	16	3	0	25	21	12	.259	.332	.373	81	-6	1	0	0	.972	7	S-41,3-22/O-4,12	0.6
1925	NY-A	66	155	15	40	3	1	1	18	20	15	.258	.343	.310	68	-7	1	0	0	.938	-6	3-26,2-21/O-4	-1.0
Total	14	1665	5699	604	1440	211	96	25	620	415	443	.253	.308	.337	82	-148	185	64		.971	10	O-702,3-485,S2/1	-14.4

■ DOC SHANLEY

Shanley, Harry Root b: 1890, Granbury, Tex. d: 12/13/34, St.Petersburg, Fla BR/TR, 6', 174 lbs. Deb: 9/15/12

YEAR	TM/L	G	AB	R	H	2B	3B	HR	RBI	BB	SO	AVG	OBP	SLG	PRO+	BR/A	SB	CS	SBR	FA	FR	G/POS	TPR
1912	StL-A	5	8	1	0	0	0	0	1	2		.000	.200	.000	-43	-1	0			.833	-2	/S-4	-0.3

■ WARREN SHANNABROOK

Shannabrook, Warren H. b: 11/30/1880, Massillon, Ohio d: 3/10/64, N.Canton, Ohio BR/TR, 6', 170 lbs. Deb: 8/13/06

YEAR	TM/L	G	AB	R	H	2B	3B	HR	RBI	BB	SO	AVG	OBP	SLG	PRO+	BR/A	SB	CS	SBR	FA	FR	G/POS	TPR
1906	Was-A	1	2	0	0	0	0	0	0	0		.000	.000	.000	-99	-0	0			1.000	-1	/3-1	-0.1

■ DAN SHANNON

Shannon, Daniel Webster b: 3/23/1865, Bridgeport, Conn. d: 10/25/13, Bridgeport, Conn. 5'9", 175 lbs. Deb: 4/17/1889 M

YEAR	TM/L	G	AB	R	H	2B	3B	HR	RBI	BB	SO	AVG	OBP	SLG	PRO+	BR/A	SB	CS	SBR	FA	FR	G/POS	TPR
1889	Lou-a	121	498	90	128	22	12	4	48	42	52	.257	.315	.373	97	-3	26			.910	7	*2-121,M	0.9

YEAR	TM/L	G	AB	R	H	2B	3B	HR	RBI	BB	SO	AVG	OBP	SLG	PRO+	BR/A	SB	CS	SBR	FA	FR	G/POS	TPR
1890	Phi-P	19	75	15	18	5	1	1	16	4	12	.240	.278	.373	72	-4	4			.926	-4	2-19	-0.6
	NY-P	83	324	59	70	7	8	3	44	25	34	.216	.274	.315	53	-25	21			.908	1	2-77/S-6	-1.5
	Yr	102	399	74	88	12	9	4	60	29	46	.221	.275	.326	56	-28	25			.911	-3	2-96/S-6	-2.1
1891	Was-a	19	67	7	9	2	0	0	3	6	9	.134	.205	.164	6	-8	3			.878	1	S-14/2-5,M	-0.6
Total	3	242	964	171	225	36	21	8	111	77	107	.233	.291	.339	73	-39	54			.911	5	2-222/S-20	-1.8

■ FRANK SHANNON Shannon, John Francis b: 12/3/1873, San Francisco, Cal. d: 2/27/34, Boston, Mass. 5′3″, 155 lbs. Deb: 10/1/1892

YEAR	TM/L	G	AB	R	H	2B	3B	HR	RBI	BB	SO	AVG	OBP	SLG	PRO+	BR/A	SB	CS	SBR	FA	FR	G/POS	TPR
1892	Was-N	1	4	0	1	0	0	0	2	0	2	.250	.250	.250	53	-0	0			.625	-1	/S-1	-0.1
1896	Lou-N	31	115	14	18	1	1	1	15	13	15	.157	.248	.209	22	-13	3			.830	-13	S-28/3-3	-2.2
Total	2	32	119	14	19	1	1	1	17	13	17	.160	.248	.210	23	-13	3			.820	-14	/S-29,3-3	-2.3

■ JOE SHANNON Shannon, Joseph Aloysius b: 2/11/1897, Jersey City, N.J. d: 7/28/55, Jersey City, N.J. BR/TR, 5′11″, 170 lbs. Deb: 7/7/15 F

YEAR	TM/L	G	AB	R	H	2B	3B	HR	RBI	BB	SO	AVG	OBP	SLG	PRO+	BR/A	SB	CS	SBR	FA	FR	G/POS	TPR
1915	Bos-N	5	10	3	2	0	0	0	1	0	3	.200	.200	.200	22	-1	0			.750	-0	/O-4,2-1	-0.1

■ RED SHANNON Shannon, Maurice Joseph b: 2/11/1897, Jersey City, N.J. d: 4/12/70, Jersey City, N.J. BB/TR, 5′11″, 170 lbs. Deb: 10/7/15 F

YEAR	TM/L	G	AB	R	H	2B	3B	HR	RBI	BB	SO	AVG	OBP	SLG	PRO+	BR/A	SB	CS	SBR	FA	FR	G/POS	TPR
1915	Bos-N	1	3	0	0	0	0	0	0	0	0	.000	.000	.000	-99	-1	0			.857	1	/2-1	0.0
1917	Phi-A	11	35	8	10	0	0	0	7	6	9	.286	.390	.286	108	1	2			.875	-0	S-10	0.1
1918	Phi-A	72	225	23	54	6	5	0	16	42	52	.240	.367	.311	103	3	5			.898	-4	S-45,2-26	0.3
1919	Phi-A	39	155	14	42	7	2	0	14	12	28	.271	.331	.342	88	-2	4			.948	-5	2-37	-0.6
	Bos-A	80	290	36	75	11	7	0	17	17	42	.259	.313	.345	90	-5	7			.973	-4	2-79	-0.6
	Yr	119	445	50	117	18	9	0	31	29	70	.263	.320	.344	89	-7	11			.965	-9	*2-116	-1.2
1920	Was-A	63	222	30	64	8	7	0	30	22	32	.288	.352	.387	99	-0	2	5	-2	.919	-19	S-31,2-16,3-15	-1.8
	Phi-A	24	88	4	15	1	1	0	3	4	12	.170	.207	.205	9	-12	1	1	-0	.945	-1	S-24	-1.1
	Yr	87	310	34	79	9	8	0	33	26	44	.255	.313	.335	73	-12	3	6	-3	.931	-21	S-55,2-16,3-15	-2.9
1921	Phi-A	1	1	0	0	0	0	0	0	0	0	.000	.000	.000	-99	-0	0	0	0	.000	0	H	0.0
1926	Chi-N	19	51	9	17	5	0	0	4	6	3	.333	.414	.431	126	2	0			.957	-2	S-13	0.1
Total	7	310	1070	124	277	38	22	0	91	109	178	.259	.334	.336	89	-14	21	6		.957	-35	2-159,S-123/3-15	-3.6

■ OWEN SHANNON Shannon, Owen Dennis Ignatius b: 12/22/1879, Omaha, Neb. d: 4/10/18, Omaha, Neb. BR/TR, Deb: 9/6/03

YEAR	TM/L	G	AB	R	H	2B	3B	HR	RBI	BB	SO	AVG	OBP	SLG	PRO+	BR/A	SB	CS	SBR	FA	FR	G/POS	TPR
1903	StL-A	9	28	1	6	2	0	0	3	1		.214	.241	.286	59	-1	0			.957	-0	/C-8,1-1	-0.1
1907	Was-A	4	7	0	1	0	0	0	0	0		.143	.143	.143	-10	-1	0			1.000	3	/C-4	0.2
Total	2	13	35	1	7	2	0	0	3	1		.200	.222	.257	47	-2	0			.970	2	/C-12,1-1	0.1

■ MIKE SHANNON Shannon, Thomas Michael "Moonman" b: 7/5/39, St.Louis, Mo. BR/TR, 6′3″, 195 lbs. Deb: 9/11/62

YEAR	TM/L	G	AB	R	H	2B	3B	HR	RBI	BB	SO	AVG	OBP	SLG	PRO+	BR/A	SB	CS	SBR	FA	FR	G/POS	TPR
1962	StL-N	10	15	3	2	0	0	0	0	1	3	.133	.188	.133	-11	-2	0	0	0	1.000	-0	/O-7	-0.3
1963	StL-N	32	26	3	8	0	0	1	2	0	6	.308	.333	.423	106	0	0	1	-1	.944	-5	O-26	-0.6
1964	*StL-N	88	253	30	66	8	2	9	43	19	54	.261	.313	.415	95	-2	4	0	1	.983	-6	O-88	-1.1
1965	StL-N	124	244	32	54	17	3	3	25	28	46	.221	.307	.352	78	-7	2	1	0	.994	-1	*O-101/C-4	-1.1
1966	StL-N	137	459	61	132	20	6	16	64	37	106	.288	.341	.462	120	12	8	4	0	.985	6	*O-129/C-1	1.3
1967	*StL-N	130	482	53	118	18	3	12	77	37	89	.245	.304	.369	93	-5	2	4	-2	.919	-11	*3-122/O-6	-2.1
1968	*StL-N	156	576	62	153	29	2	15	79	37	114	.266	.312	.401	114	9	1	2	-1	.952	-7	*3-156	0.1
1969	StL-N	150	551	51	140	15	5	12	55	49	87	.254	.316	.365	90	-8	1	4	-2	.945	-19	*3-149	-3.0
1970	StL-N	55	174	18	37	9	2	0	22	16	20	.213	.279	.287	51	-12	1	1	-0	.919	-13	3-51	-2.7
Total	9	882	2780	313	710	116	23	68	367	224	525	.255	.313	.387	96	-16	19	17	-5	.938	-57	3-478,O-357/C-5	-9.5

■ WALLY SHANNON Shannon, Walter Charles b: 1/23/33, Cleveland, Ohio d: 2/8/92, Creve Coeur, Mo. BL/TR, 6′, 178 lbs. Deb: 7/9/59

YEAR	TM/L	G	AB	R	H	2B	3B	HR	RBI	BB	SO	AVG	OBP	SLG	PRO+	BR/A	SB	CS	SBR	FA	FR	G/POS	TPR
1959	StL-N	47	95	5	27	5	0	0	5	0	12	.284	.292	.337	63	-5	0	0	0	1.000	-11	S-21,2-10	-1.4
1960	StL-N	18	23	2	4	0	0	0	1	3	6	.174	.296	.174	30	-2	0	0	0	1.000	2	2-15/S-1	0.1
Total	2	65	118	7	31	5	0	0	6	3	18	.263	.293	.305	56	-7	0	0	0	.955	-9	/2-25,S-22	-1.3

■ SPIKE SHANNON Shannon, William Porter b: 2/7/1878, Pittsburgh, Pa. d: 5/16/40, Minneapolis, Minn. BB/TR, 5′11″, 180 lbs. Deb: 4/15/04 U

YEAR	TM/L	G	AB	R	H	2B	3B	HR	RBI	BB	SO	AVG	OBP	SLG	PRO+	BR/A	SB	CS	SBR	FA	FR	G/POS	TPR
1904	StL-N	134	500	84	140	10	3	1	26	50		.280	.349	.318	111	9	34			**.978**	9	*O-133	1.0
1905	StL-N	140	544	73	146	16	3	0	41	47		.268	.327	.309	92	-4	27			**.984**	0	*O-140	-1.1
1906	StL-N	80	302	36	78	4	0	0	25	36		.258	.337	.272	94	-1	15			.972	6	O-80	0.1
	NY-N	76	287	42	73	5	1	0	25	34		.254	.342	.279	91	-1	18			.958	-7	O-76	-1.3
	Yr	156	589	78	151	9	1	0	50	70		.256	.339	.275	93	-2	33			.966	-1	*O-156	-1.2
1907	NY-N	155	585	**104**	155	12	5	1	33	82		.265	.363	.308	107	9	33			.977	2	*O-155	0.5
1908	NY-N	77	268	34	60	2	1	1	21	28		.224	.314	.250	77	-6	13			.976	-3	O-74	-1.4
	Pit-N	32	127	10	25	0	2	0	12	9		.197	.250	.228	53	-7	5			.947	1	O-32	-0.8
	Yr	109	395	44	85	2	3	1	33	37		.215	.294	.243	69	-12	18			.964	-2	*O-106	-2.2
Total	5	694	2613	383	677	49	15	3	183	286		.259	.337	.293	96	-1	145			.974	8	O-690	-3.0

■ BILLY SHANTZ Shantz, Wilmer Ebert b: 7/31/27, Pottstown, Pa. d: 12/13/93, Lauderhill, Fla. BR/TR, 6′1″, 160 lbs. Deb: 4/13/54 F

YEAR	TM/L	G	AB	R	H	2B	3B	HR	RBI	BB	SO	AVG	OBP	SLG	PRO+	BR/A	SB	CS	SBR	FA	FR	G/POS	TPR
1954	Phi-A	51	164	13	42	9	3	1	17	17	23	.256	.326	.366	89	-3	0	0	0	.975	-13	C-51	-1.4
1955	KC-A	79	217	18	56	4	1	1	12	11	14	.258	.294	.300	59	-13	0	0	0	.990	-10	C-78	-2.1
1960	NY-A	1	0	0	0	0	0	0	0	0	0	—	—	—	—	0	0	0	0	1.000	-0	/C-1	0.0
Total	3	131	381	31	98	13	4	2	29	28	37	.257	.308	.328	72	-15	0	0	0	.984	-23	C-130	-3.5

■ RALPH SHARMAN Sharman, Ralph Edward "Bally" b: 4/11/1895, Cleveland, Ohio d: 5/24/18, Camp Sheridan, Ala BR/TR, 5′11″, 176 lbs. Deb: 9/10/17

YEAR	TM/L	G	AB	R	H	2B	3B	HR	RBI	BB	SO	AVG	OBP	SLG	PRO+	BR/A	SB	CS	SBR	FA	FR	G/POS	TPR
1917	Phi-A	13	37	2	11	2	1	0	2	3	2	.297	.366	.405	137	2	1			.941	-1	O-10	0.0

■ DICK SHARON Sharon, Richard Louis b: 4/15/50, San Mateo, Cal. BR/TR, 6′2″, 195 lbs. Deb: 5/13/73

YEAR	TM/L	G	AB	R	H	2B	3B	HR	RBI	BB	SO	AVG	OBP	SLG	PRO+	BR/A	SB	CS	SBR	FA	FR	G/POS	TPR
1973	Det-A	91	178	20	43	9	0	7	16	10	31	.242	.282	.410	87	-4	2	0	1	.970	-10	O-91	-1.5
1974	Det-A	60	129	12	28	4	0	2	10	14	29	.217	.294	.295	67	-5	4	4	-1	.989	-5	O-56	-1.4
1975	SD-N	91	160	14	31	7	0	4	20	26	35	.194	.306	.313	77	-5	0	2	-1	.948	-7	O-57	-1.6
Total	3	242	467	46	102	20	0	13	46	50	95	.218	.294	.345	79	-14	6	6	-2	.969	-22	O-204	-4.5

■ BILL SHARP Sharp, William Howard b: 1/18/50, Lima, Ohio BL/TL, 5′10″, 178 lbs. Deb: 5/26/73

YEAR	TM/L	G	AB	R	H	2B	3B	HR	RBI	BB	SO	AVG	OBP	SLG	PRO+	BR/A	SB	CS	SBR	FA	FR	G/POS	TPR
1973	Chi-A	77	196	23	54	8	3	4	22	19	28	.276	.349	.408	109	2	2	3	-1	.981	2	O-70/D-1	0.1
1974	Chi-A	100	320	45	81	13	2	4	24	25	37	.253	.311	.344	86	-6	0	3	-2	.986	-1	O-99	-1.3
1975	Chi-A	18	35	1	7	0	0	0	4	2	3	.200	.243	.200	26	-3	0	0	0	.941	-3	O-14	-0.7
	Mil-A	125	373	37	95	27	3	1	34	19	26	.255	.293	.351	81	-10	0	3	-2	.994	-3	*O-124	-2.0
	Yr	143	408	38	102	27	3	1	38	21	29	.250	.288	.338	76	-14	0	3	-2	.991	-6	*O-138	-2.7
1976	Mil-A	78	180	16	44	4	0	0	11	10	15	.244	.288	.267	64	-8	1	3	-2	.975	0	O-56/D-7	-1.2
Total	4	398	1104	122	281	52	8	9	95	75	109	.255	.306	.341	83	-25	3	12	-6	.985	-5	O-363/D-8	-5.1

■ BUD SHARPE Sharpe, Bayard Heston b: 8/6/1881, West Chester, Pa. d: 5/31/16, Haddock, Ga. BL/TR, Deb: 4/14/05

YEAR	TM/L	G	AB	R	H	2B	3B	HR	RBI	BB	SO	AVG	OBP	SLG	PRO+	BR/A	SB	CS	SBR	FA	FR	G/POS	TPR
1905	Bos-N	46	170	8	31	3	2	0	11	7		.182	.215	.224	31	-15	0			.904	2	O-42/C-3,1-1	-1.5
1910	Bos-N	115	439	30	105	14	3	0	29	14	31	.239	.264	.285	58	-25	4			.987	7	*1-113	-1.9
	Pit-N	4	16	2	3	0	1	0	1	0	2	.188	.188	.313	43	-1	0			1.000	0	/1-4	-0.1
	Yr	119	455	32	108	14	4	0	30	14	33	.237	.262	.286	57	-26	4			.987	8	*1-117	-2.0
Total	2	165	625	40	139	17	6	0	41	21	33	.222	.249	.269	50	-41	4			.987	9	1-118/O-42,C-3	-3.5

■ MIKE SHARPERSON Sharperson, Michael Tyrone b: 10/4/61, Orangeburg, S.C. d: 5/26/96, Las Vegas, Nev. BR/TR, 6′3″, 191 lbs. Deb: 4/6/87

YEAR	TM/L	G	AB	R	H	2B	3B	HR	RBI	BB	SO	AVG	OBP	SLG	PRO+	BR/A	SB	CS	SBR	FA	FR	G/POS	TPR
1987	Tor-A	32	96	4	20	4	1	0	9	7	15	.208	.269	.271	43	-8	2	1	0	.971	-5	2-32	-1.1
	LA-N	10	33	7	9	2	0	0	1	4	5	.273	.351	.333	85	-1	0	0	0	1.000	2	/3-7,2-6	0.1
1988	*LA-N	46	59	8	16	1	0	0	4	1	12	.271	.295	.288	70	-2	0	1	-1	.949	-0	2-20/3-6,S-4	-0.3
1989	LA-N	27	28	2	7	3	0	0	5	4	7	.250	.344	.357	102	0	0	1	-1	1.000	-0	/2-4,1-2,3-2,S-1	0.0
1990	LA-N	129	357	42	106	14	2	3	36	46	39	.297	.379	.373	111	7	15	6	1	.949	6	*3-106,S-15/2-9,1-6	1.4
1991	LA-N	105	216	24	60	11	2	2	20	25	24	.278	.355	.375	108	3	1	3	-2	.981	-5	3-68,S-16,1-10,/2-5	-0.3
1992	LA-N★	128	317	48	95	21	0	3	36	47	33	.300	.390	.394	125	12	2	2	-1	.979	1	2-63,3-60/S-2	1.4
1993	LA-N	73	90	13	23	4	0	2	10	5	17	.256	.302	.367	83	-2	2	0	1	.945	1	2-17/3-6,S-3,1-1,O	0.0

YEAR	TM/L	G	AB	R	H	2B	3B	HR	RBI	BB	SO	AVG	OBP	SLG	PRO+	BR/A	SB	CS	SBR	FA	FR	G/POS	TPR
1995	Atl-N	7	7	1	1	1	0	0	2	0	2	.143	.143	.286	9	-1	0	0	0	.000	0	/3-1	-0.1
Total	8	557	1203	149	337	61	5	10	123	139	154	.280	.357	.364	103	8	22	14	-2	.952	-0	3-256,2-156/S10	1.1

■ JACK SHARROTT Sharrott, John Henry b: 8/13/1869, Bangor, Me. d: 12/31/27, Los Angeles, Cal. BR/TR, 5′9″, 165 lbs. Deb: 4/22/1890

YEAR	TM/L	G	AB	R	H	2B	3B	HR	RBI	BB	SO	AVG	OBP	SLG	PRO+	BR/A	SB	CS	SBR	FA	FR	G/POS	TPR
1890	NY-N	32	109	16	22	3	2	0	14	0	14	.202	.202	.266	36	-9	6			.932	-2	P-25/O-9	-0.6
1891	NY-N	10	30	5	10	2	0	1	7	1	2	.333	.355	.500	154	2	3			.950	1	P-10	0.0
1892	NY-N	4	8	1	1	0	0	0	0	0	1	.125	.125	.125	-25	-1	0			.333	-1	/O-3,P-1	-0.2
1893	Phi-N	50	152	25	38	4	3	1	22	8	14	.250	.287	.336	66	-8	6			.824	-8	O-33,P-12	-1.3
Total	4	96	299	47	71	9	5	2	43	9	31	.237	.260	.321	61	-17	15			.927	-10	/P-48,O-45	-2.1

■ SHAG SHAUGHNESSY Shaughnessy, Francis Joseph b: 4/8/1883, Amboy, Ill. d: 5/15/69, Montreal, Que., Can BR/TR, 6′1.5″, 185 lbs. Deb: 4/17/05 C

YEAR	TM/L	G	AB	R	H	2B	3B	HR	RBI	BB	SO	AVG	OBP	SLG	PRO+	BR/A	SB	CS	SBR	FA	FR	G/POS	TPR
1905	Was-A	1	3	0	0	0	0	0	0	0		.000	.250	.000	-19	-0	0			.667	-0	/O-1	-0.1
1908	Phi-A	8	29	2	9	0	0	0	1	2		.310	.355	.310	109	0	3			1.000	-1	/O-8	-0.1
Total	2	9	32	2	9	0	0	0	1	2		.281	.343	.281	97	-0	3			.938	-1	/O-9	-0.2

■ JON SHAVE Shave, Jonathan Taylor b: 11/4/67, Waycross, Ga. BR/TR, 6′, 185 lbs. Deb: 5/15/93

YEAR	TM/L	G	AB	R	H	2B	3B	HR	RBI	BB	SO	AVG	OBP	SLG	PRO+	BR/A	SB	CS	SBR	FA	FR	G/POS	TPR
1993	Tex-A	17	47	3	15	2	0	0	7	0	8	.319	.319	.362	86	-1	1	3	-2	.917	-2	/S-9,2-8	-0.4
1998	Min-A	19	40	7	10	3	0	1	5	3	10	.250	.302	.400	80	-1	1	2	-1	1.000	1	3-15/1-1,S-1,D-1	-0.1
Total	2	36	87	10	25	5	0	1	12	3	18	.287	.311	.379	83	-2	2	5	-2	.917	-1	/3-15,S-10,2-8,D1	-0.5

■ AL SHAW Shaw, Albert Simpson b: 3/1/1881, Toledo, Ill. d: 12/30/74, Danville, Ill. BL/TR, 5′8.5″, 165 lbs. Deb: 9/28/07

YEAR	TM/L	G	AB	R	H	2B	3B	HR	RBI	BB	SO	AVG	OBP	SLG	PRO+	BR/A	SB	CS	SBR	FA	FR	G/POS	TPR
1907	StL-N	9	25	2	7	0	0	0	1	3		.280	.379	.280	110	1	1			.947	-1	/O-9	0.0
1908	StL-N	107	367	40	97	13	4	1	19	25		.264	.311	.330	110	3	9			.931	7	O-91/S-4,3-1	0.7
1909	StL-N	114	331	45	82	12	7	2	34	55		.248	.355	.344	125	11	15			.940	-1	O-92	0.7
1914	Bro-F	112	376	81	122	27	7	5	49	44	59	.324	.395	.473	137	14	24			.955	1	*O-102	1.1
1915	KC-F	132	448	67	126	22	10	6	67	46	45	.281	.348	.415	119	4	15			.942	-14	*O-124	-1.8
Total	5	474	1547	235	434	74	28	14	170	173	104	.281	.353	.392	123	33	64			.942	-8	O-418/S-4,3-1	0.7

■ AL SHAW Shaw, Alfred "Shoddy" b: 10/3/1874, Burslem, England d: 3/25/58, Uhrichsville, Ohio BR/TR, 5′8″, 170 lbs. Deb: 6/8/01

YEAR	TM/L	G	AB	R	H	2B	3B	HR	RBI	BB	SO	AVG	OBP	SLG	PRO+	BR/A	SB	CS	SBR	FA	FR	G/POS	TPR
1901	Det-A	55	171	20	46	7	0	1	23	10		.269	.321	.327	76	-6	2			.938	-0	C-42/1-9,3-2,S-1	-0.2
1907	Bos-A	76	198	10	38	1	3	0	7	18		.192	.269	.227	59	-9	4			.971	15	C-73/1-1	1.3
1908	Chi-A	32	49	0	4	1	0	0	2	2		.082	.118	.102	-29	-7	0			.953	2	C-29	-0.4
1909	Bos-N	18	41	1	4	0	0	0	0	5		.098	.213	.098	-3	-5	0			.975	4	C-14	0.0
Total	4	181	459	31	92	9	3	1	32	35		.200	.267	.240	53	-26	6			.961	20	C-158/1-10,3-2,S-1	0.7

■ BEN SHAW Shaw, Benjamin Nathaniel b: 6/18/1893, LaCenter, Ky. d: 3/16/59, Cleveland, Ohio BR/TR, 5′11.5″, 190 lbs. Deb: 4/11/17

YEAR	TM/L	G	AB	R	H	2B	3B	HR	RBI	BB	SO	AVG	OBP	SLG	PRO+	BR/A	SB	CS	SBR	FA	FR	G/POS	TPR
1917	Pit-N	2	2	0	0	0	0	0	0	0	0	.000	.000	.000	-97	-0	0			.000	0	H	-0.1
1918	Pit-N	21	36	5	7	1	0	0	2	2	2	.194	.275	.222	51	-2	0			.981	-2	/1-9,C-5	-0.4
Total	2	23	38	5	7	1	0	0	2	2	2	.184	.262	.211	43	-2	0			.981	-2	/1-9,C-5	-0.5

■ HUNKY SHAW Shaw, Royal N b: 9/29/1884, Yakima, Wash. d: 7/3/69, Yakima, Wash. BB/TR, 5′8″, 165 lbs. Deb: 5/16/08

YEAR	TM/L	G	AB	R	H	2B	3B	HR	RBI	BB	SO	AVG	OBP	SLG	PRO+	BR/A	SB	CS	SBR	FA	FR	G/POS	TPR
1908	Pit-N	1	1	0	0	0	0	0	0	0		.000	.000	.000	-99	-0	0			.000	0	H	0.0

■ MARTY SHAY Shay, Arthur Joseph b: 4/25/1896, Boston, Mass. d: 2/20/51, Worcester, Mass. BR/TR, 5′7.5″, 148 lbs. Deb: 9/16/16

YEAR	TM/L	G	AB	R	H	2B	3B	HR	RBI	BB	SO	AVG	OBP	SLG	PRO+	BR/A	SB	CS	SBR	FA	FR	G/POS	TPR
1916	Chi-N	2	7	0	2	0	0	0	0	0	1	.286	.286	.286	68	-0	0			.917	0	/S-2	0.0
1924	Bos-N	19	68	4	16	3	1	0	2	5	5	.235	.297	.309	65	-3	2	1	0	.950	-12	2-19/S-1	-1.5
Total	2	21	75	4	18	3	1	0	2	5	6	.240	.296	.307	66	-4	2	1		.929	-12	/2-19,S-3	-1.5

■ DANNY SHAY Shay, Daniel C. b: 11/8/1876, Springfield, Ohio d: 12/1/27, Kansas City, Mo. TR , 5′10″, Deb: 4/30/01

YEAR	TM/L	G	AB	R	H	2B	3B	HR	RBI	BB	SO	AVG	OBP	SLG	PRO+	BR/A	SB	CS	SBR	FA	FR	G/POS	TPR
1901	Cle-A	19	75	4	17	2	2	0	10	2		.227	.266	.307	61	-4	0			.901	-4	S-19	-0.6
1904	StL-N	99	340	45	87	11	1	1	18	39		.256	.338	.303	103	3	36			.911	-7	S-97/2-2	-0.2
1905	StL-N	78	281	30	67	12	1	0	28	35		.238	.331	.288	88	-3	11			.953	-13	2-39,S-39	-1.6
1907	NY-N	35	79	10	15	1	1	1	6	12		.190	.304	.266	76	-2	5			.931	-7	2-13/S-9,O-2	-1.1
Total	4	231	775	89	186	26	5	2	62	88		.240	.325	.294	90	-6	52			.902	-31	S-164/2-54,O-2	-3.5

■ GERRY SHEA Shea, Gerald J. b: 7/26/1881, St.Louis, Mo. d: 5/3/64, Berkeley, Mo. TR , 5′7″, 160 lbs. Deb: 10/1/05

YEAR	TM/L	G	AB	R	H	2B	3B	HR	RBI	BB	SO	AVG	OBP	SLG	PRO+	BR/A	SB	CS	SBR	FA	FR	G/POS	TPR
1905	StL-N	2	6	0	2	0	0	0	0	0		.333	.333	.333	102	-0	0			.917	1	/C-2	0.1

■ NAP SHEA Shea, John Edward "Napoleon" b: 5/23/1874, Ware, Mass. d: 7/8/68, Bloomfield Hills, Mich. BR/TR, 5′5″, 155 lbs. Deb: 9/11/02

YEAR	TM/L	G	AB	R	H	2B	3B	HR	RBI	BB	SO	AVG	OBP	SLG	PRO+	BR/A	SB	CS	SBR	FA	FR	G/POS	TPR
1902	Phi-N	3	8	1	1	0	0	0	0	1		.125	.300	.125	32	-1	0			1.000	-0	/C-3	-0.1

■ MERV SHEA Shea, Mervyn David John b: 9/5/1900, San Francisco, Cal d: 1/27/53, Sacramento, Cal. BR/TR, 5′11″, 175 lbs. Deb: 4/23/27 C

YEAR	TM/L	G	AB	R	H	2B	3B	HR	RBI	BB	SO	AVG	OBP	SLG	PRO+	BR/A	SB	CS	SBR	FA	FR	G/POS	TPR
1927	Det-A	34	85	5	15	6	3	0	9	7	15	.176	.239	.318	43	-8	0	0	0	.949	-1	C-31	-0.6
1928	Det-A	39	85	8	20	2	3	0	9	9	11	.235	.316	.329	69	-4	2	2	-1	.951	4	C-30	0.1
1929	Det-A	50	162	23	47	6	0	3	24	19	18	.290	.365	.383	92	-1	2	1	0	.964	-6	C-46	-0.3
1933	Bos-A	16	56	1	8	3	0	0	8	4	7	.143	.200	.196	5	-8	0	0	0	1.000	-2	C-16	-0.8
	StL-A	94	279	26	73	11	1	1	27	43	26	.262	.360	.319	76	-8	2	0	1	.995	9	C-85	0.6
	Yr	110	335	27	81	14	1	1	35	47	33	.242	.335	.299	65	-16	2	0	1	**.996**	7	*C-101	-0.2
1934	Chi-A	62	176	8	28	3	0	0	5	24	19	.159	.260	.176	14	-22	0	1	-1	.972	1	C-60	-1.8
1935	Chi-A	46	122	8	28	2	0	0	13	30	9	.230	.382	.246	64	-5	0	0	0	.990	8	C-43	0.5
1936	Chi-A	14	24	3	3	0	0	0	2	6	5	.125	.300	.125	8	-3	0	0	0	1.000	1	C-14	-0.2
1937	Chi-A	25	71	7	15	1	0	0	5	15	10	.211	.349	.225	48	-5	1	0	0	.966	3	C-25	-0.1
1938	Bro-N	48	120	14	22	5	0	0	12	28	20	.183	.338	.225	56	-6	1			.977	-1	C-47	-0.5
1939	Det-A	4	2	0	0	0	0	0	0	0	1	.000	.000	.000	-93	-1	0	0	0	.500	-1	/C-4	-0.1
1944	Phi-N	7	15	2	4	0	0	1	1	4	4	.267	.421	.467	155	1	0			.952	-0	/C-6	0.1
Total	11	439	1197	105	263	39	7	5	115	189	145	.220	.327	.277	58	-70	8	4		.976	16	C-407	-3.1

■ DANNY SHEAFFER Sheaffer, Danny Todd b: 8/2/61, Jacksonville, Fla. BR/TR, 6′, 202 lbs. Deb: 4/9/87

YEAR	TM/L	G	AB	R	H	2B	3B	HR	RBI	BB	SO	AVG	OBP	SLG	PRO+	BR/A	SB	CS	SBR	FA	FR	G/POS	TPR
1987	Bos-A	25	66	5	8	1	0	1	5	0	14	.121	.121	.182	-21	-11	0	0	0	.977	-3	C-25	-1.2
1989	Cle-A	7	16	1	1	0	0	0	0	2	2	.063	.167	.063	-32	-3	0	0	0	.000	0	/3-2,O-1,D-3	-0.3
1993	Col-N	82	216	26	60	9	1	4	32	8	15	.278	.307	.384	72	-9	2	3	-1	.994	-2	C-65/1-7,O-2,3-1	-0.9
1994	Col-N	44	110	11	24	4	0	1	12	10	11	.218	.283	.282	41	-10	0	2	-1	.995	4	C-30/1-2,O-1	-0.6
1995	StL-N	76	208	24	48	10	1	5	30	23	38	.231	.307	.361	76	-7	0	0	0	.993	11	C-67/1-3,3-1	0.7
1996	*StL-N	79	198	10	45	9	3	2	20	9	25	.227	.271	.333	59	-12	3	3	-1	.983	1	C-47,3-17/1-6,O-3	-0.9
1997	StL-N	76	132	10	33	5	0	0	11	8	17	.250	.298	.288	55	-9	1	0	0	.957	-10	3-30,O-22/C-9,2-3	-1.8
Total	7	389	946	87	219	38	5	13	110	60	122	.232	.281	.323	56	-61	6	8	-3	.990	2	C-243/3-51,O12D	-5.0

■ DAVE SHEAN Shean, David William b: 7/9/1883, Arlington, Mass. d: 5/22/63, Boston, Mass. BR/TR, 5′11″, 175 lbs. Deb: 9/10/06

YEAR	TM/L	G	AB	R	H	2B	3B	HR	RBI	BB	SO	AVG	OBP	SLG	PRO+	BR/A	SB	CS	SBR	FA	FR	G/POS	TPR
1906	Phi-A	22	75	7	16	3	2	0	3	5		.213	.280	.307	81	2	6			.980	-2	2-22	-0.4
1908	Phi-N	14	48	4	7	2	0	0	2	1		.146	.180	.188	17	-5	1			.871	-6	S-14	-1.3
1909	Phi-N	36	112	14	26	2	2	0	4	14		.232	.323	.286	88	-1	3			.982	-2	2-14,1-11/O-3,S-1	-0.4
	Bos-N	75	267	32	66	11	4	1	29	17		.247	.297	.330	90	-4	14			.956	8	2-72	0.3
	Yr	111	379	46	92	13	6	1	33	31		.243	.305	.317	90	-5	17			.960	6	2-86,1-11/O-3,S-1	-0.1
1910	Bos-N	150	543	52	130	12	7	3	36	42	45	.239	.294	.304	71	-21	16			.953	**43**	*2-148	2.0
1911	Chi-N	54	145	17	28	4	0	0	15	8	15	.193	.240	.221	29	-14	4			.947	1	2-23,S-19/3-1	-1.2
1912	Bos-N	4	10	1	3	0	0	0	0	1	2	.300	.417	.300	96	0	0			.917	-1	/S-4	-0.1
1917	Cin-N	131	442	36	93	9	5	2	35	22	39	.210	.249	.267	61	-21	10			.961	19	*2-131	0.4
1918	*Bos-A	115	425	58	112	16	3	0	34	40	25	.264	.331	.315	97	-1	11			.967	-9	*2-115	-0.3
1919	Bos-A	29	100	4	14	0	0	0	8	5	7	.140	.189	.140	-7	-14	1			.981	4	2-29	-0.9
Total	9	630	2167	225	495	59	23	6	166	155	133	.228	.284	.285	70	-82	66			.961	55	2-554/S-38,1-11,O3	-1.9

■ RAY SHEARER Shearer, Ray Solomon b: 9/19/29, Jacobus, Pa. d: 2/21/82, York, Pa. BR/TR, 6′, 200 lbs. Deb: 9/18/57

YEAR	TM/L	G	AB	R	H	2B	3B	HR	RBI	BB	SO	AVG	OBP	SLG	PRO+	BR/A	SB	CS	SBR	FA	FR	G/POS	TPR
1957	Mil-N	2	2	1	1	0	0	0	0	1	1	.500	.667	.500	237	1	0	0	0	.000	-0	/O-1	0.0

YEAR	TM/L	G	AB	R	H	2B	3B	HR	RBI	BB	SO	AVG	OBP	SLG	PRO+	BR/A	SB	CS	SBR	FA	FR	G/POS	TPR
■ **JOHN SHEARON**	Shearon, John M. b: 1870, Pittsburgh, Pa. d: 2/1/23, Bradford, Pa. Deb: 7/28/1891																						
1891	Cle-N	30	124	10	30	1	1	0	13	1	15	.242	.248	.266	48	-9	6			.814	-4	O-25/P-6	-1.1
1896	Cle-N	16	64	6	11	0	1	0	3	4	6	.172	.221	.203	11	-8	3			.818	-4	O-16	-1.2
Total	2	46	188	16	41	1	2	0	16	5	21	.218	.238	.245	34	-17	9			.815	-9	/O-41,P-6	-2.3
■ **JIMMY SHECKARD**	Sheckard, Samuel James Tilden b: 11/23/1878, Upper Chanceford, Pa. d: 1/15/47, Lancaster, Pa. BL/TR, 5'9", 175 lbs. Deb: 9/14/1897																						
1897	Bro-N	13	49	12	14	3	2	3	14	6		.286	.364	.612	164	4	5			.753	-5	S-11/O-2	0.0
1898	Bro-N	105	408	51	113	17	9	4	64	37		.277	.349	.392	113	6	8			.926	-4	*O-105/3-1	-0.5
1899	Bal-N	147	536	104	158	18	10	3	75	56		.295	.380	.382	104	4	**77**			.943	21	*O-146/1-1	1.3
1900	Bro-N	85	273	74	82	19	10	1	39	42		.300	.416	.454	132	13	30			.925	2	O-78	0.9
1901	Bro-N	133	554	116	196	29	**19**	11	104	47		.354	.409	**.534**	168	46	35			.944	7	*O-121,3-12	4.3
1902	Bal-A	4	15	3	4	1	0	0	0	1		.267	.313	.333	76	-0	2			1.000	-1	/O-4	-0.2
	Bro-N	123	486	86	129	20	10	4	37	57		.265	.349	.372	122	13	23			.964	8	*O-123	1.4
1903	Bro-N	139	515	99	171	29	9	**9**	75	75		.332	.423	.476	161	**43**	**67**			.951	23	*O-139	5.5
1904	Bro-N	143	507	70	121	23	6	1	46	56		.239	.317	.314	97	0	21			.956	7	*O-141/2-2	-0.1
1905	Bro-N	130	480	58	140	20	11	3	41	61		.292	.380	.398	142	27	23			.967	15	*O-129	3.7
1906	*Chi-N	149	549	90	144	27	10	1	45	67		.262	.349	.353	112	9	30			.986	0	*O-149	0.2
1907	*Chi-N	143	484	76	129	23	1	1	36	76		.267	.373	.324	112	10	31			.975	-10	*O-142	-0.7
1908	*Chi-N	115	403	54	93	18	3	2	22	62		.231	.336	.305	101	3	18			.955	-2	*O-115	-0.5
1909	Chi-N	148	525	81	134	29	5	1	43	72		.255	.346	.335	109	7	15			.967	-3	*O-148	-0.2
1910	*Chi-N	144	507	82	130	27	6	5	51	83	53	.256	.366	.363	114	11	22			.976	7	*O-143	1.2
1911	Chi-N	156	539	**121**	149	26	11	4	50	**147**	58	.276	**.434**	.388	130	32	32			.963	15	*O-156	3.8
1912	Chi-N	146	523	85	128	22	10	3	47	**122**	81	.245	.392	.342	102	8	15			.962	8	*O-146	0.8
1913	StL-N	52	136	18	27	2	1	0	17	41	25	.199	.388	.228	79	-1	5			.953	-3	O-46	-0.6
	Cin-N	47	116	16	22	1	3	0	7	27	16	.190	.343	.250	71	-3	6			.969	-3	O-38	-0.8
	Yr	99	252	34	49	3	4	0	24	68	41	.194	.368	.238	76	-4	11			.960	-6	O-84	-1.4
Total	17	2122	7605	1296	2084	354	136	56	813	1135	233	.274	.375	.378	120	232	465			.958	82	*O-2071/3-13,S21	19.5
■ **JIM SHEEHAN**	Sheehan, James Thomas "Big Jim" b: 6/3/13, New Haven, Conn. BR/TR, 6'2", 196 lbs. Deb: 9/26/36																						
1936	NY-N	1	4	0	0	0	0	0	0	0	2	.000	.000	.000	-99	-1	0			.833	-0	/C-1	-0.1
■ **JACK SHEEHAN**	Sheehan, John Thomas b: 4/15/1893, Chicago, Ill. d: 5/29/87, W.Palm Beach, Fla. BB/TR, 5'8.5", 165 lbs. Deb: 9/11/20																						
1920	*Bro-N	3	5	0	2	1	0	0	0	1	0	.400	.500	.600	208	1	0	0	0	.875	0	/S-2,3-1	0.1
1921	Bro-N	5	12	2	0	0	0	0	0	0	1	.000	.000	.000	-97	-3	0	0	0	.900	-0	/2-2,S-1,3-1	-0.3
Total	2	8	17	2	2	1	0	0	0	1	1	.118	.167	.176	-7	-3	0	0	0	.909	0	/S-3,2-2,3-2	-0.2
■ **TOMMY SHEEHAN**	Sheehan, Thomas H. b: 11/6/1877, Sacramento, Cal. d: 5/22/59, Panama City, Pan. BR/TR, 5'8", 160 lbs. Deb: 8/2/00																						
1900	NY-N	1	2	0	0	0	0	0	0	0		.000	.000	.000	-99	-1	0			.000	0	/S-1	-0.1
1906	Pit-N	95	315	28	76	6	3	1	34	18		.241	.284	.289	75	-9	13			.947	-5	3-90	-1.3
1907	Pit-N	75	226	23	62	2	3	0	25	23		.274	.341	.310	103	1	10			.941	-1	3-57,S-10	0.3
1908	Bro-N	146	468	45	100	18	2	0	29	53		.214	.302	.261	83	-7	9			.930	-6	*3-145	-0.9
Total	4	317	1011	96	238	26	8	1	88	94		.235	.305	.280	85	-16	32			.938	-12	3-292/S-11	-2.0
■ **BIFF SHEEHAN**	Sheehan, Timothy James b: 2/13/1868, Hartford, Conn. d: 10/21/23, Hartford, Conn. TR , 5'9", 165 lbs. Deb: 7/22/1895																						
1895	StL-N	52	180	24	57	3	6	1	18	20	6	.317	.394	.417	111	3	7			.940	-2	O-41,1-11	-0.1
1896	StL-N	6	19	0	3	0	0	0	1	4	0	.158	.304	.158	25	-2	0			1.000	-1	/O-6	-0.3
Total	2	58	199	24	60	3	6	1	19	24	6	.302	.385	.392	103	2	7			.948	-3	/O-47,1-11	-0.4
■ **EARL SHEELY**	Sheely, Earl Homer "Whitey" b: 2/12/1893, Bushnell, Ill. d: 9/16/52, Seattle, Wash. BR/TR, 6'3.5", 195 lbs. Deb: 4/14/21 F																						
1921	Chi-A	154	563	68	171	25	6	11	95	57	34	.304	.375	.428	106	5	4	9	-4	.988	5	*1-154	0.2
1922	Chi-A	149	526	72	167	37	4	6	80	60	27	.317	.393	.437	117	14	4	6	-2	.993	2	*1-149	0.7
1923	Chi-A	156	570	74	169	25	3	4	88	79	30	.296	.387	.372	102	4	5	5	-2	.992	-1	*1-156	-0.6
1924	Chi-A	146	535	84	171	34	3	3	103	95	28	.320	.426	.411	120	21	7	4	-0	.991	-10	*1-146	0.2
1925	Chi-A	153	600	93	189	43	3	9	111	68	23	.315	.389	.442	117	16	3	3	-1	.988	-5	*1-153	0.1
1926	Chi-A	145	525	77	157	40	2	6	89	75	13	.299	.394	.417	116	14	3	1	0	**.995**	0	*1-144	0.6
1927	Chi-A	45	129	11	27	3	0	2	16	20	5	.209	.320	.279	58	-8	1	3	-2	.982	-4	1-36	-1.5
1929	Pit-N	139	485	63	142	22	4	6	88	75	24	.293	.392	.392	93	-3	6			**.996**	-0	*1-139	-1.6
1931	Bos-N	147	538	30	147	15	2	1	77	34	21	.273	.319	.314	73	-20	0			.992	-3	*1-143	-3.6
Total	9	1234	4471	572	1340	244	27	48	747	563	205	.300	.383	.399	104	45	33	31		.991	-14	*1-1220	-5.5
■ **BUD SHEELY**	Sheely, Hollis Kimball b: 11/26/20, Spokane, Wash. d: 10/17/85, Sacramento, Cal. BL/TR, 6'1", 200 lbs. Deb: 7/26/51 F																						
1951	Chi-A	34	89	2	16	2	0	0	7	6	7	.180	.240	.202	21	-10	0	0	0	.986	3	C-33	-0.5
1952	Chi-A	36	75	1	18	2	0	0	3	12	7	.240	.352	.267	73	-2	0	1	-1	.992	-2	C-31	-0.3
1953	Chi-A	31	46	4	10	1	0	0	2	9	8	.217	.345	.239	58	-2	0	0	0	1.000	0	C-17	-0.1
Total	3	101	210	7	44	5	0	0	12	27	22	.210	.305	.233	49	-14	0	1	-1	.991	2	/C-81	-0.9
■ **CHUCK SHEERIN**	Sheerin, Charles Joseph b: 4/17/09, Brooklyn, N.Y. d: 9/27/86, Valley Stream, N.Y. BR/TR, 5'11.5", 198 lbs. Deb: 4/21/36																						
1936	Phi-N	39	72	4	19	4	0	0	4	7	18	.264	.329	.319	68	-3	0			.942	-3	2-17,3-13/S-5	-0.5
■ **ANDY SHEETS**	Sheets, Andrew Mark b: 11/19/71, Baton Rouge, La. BR/TR, 6'2", 180 lbs. Deb: 4/22/96																						
1996	Sea-A	47	110	18	21	8	0	0	9	10	41	.191	.264	.264	34	-11	2	0	1	.947	8	3-25,2-18/S-7	-0.2
1997	*Sea-A	32	89	18	22	3	0	4	9	7	34	.247	.302	.416	86	-2	2	0	1	.872	-1	3-21/S-9,2-2	-0.1
1998	*SD-N	88	194	31	47	5	3	7	29	21	62	.242	.319	.407	96	-2	7	2	1	.964	5	S-39,3-23,2-22,/1-2	0.8
Total	3	167	393	67	90	16	3	11	47	38	137	.229	.300	.369	75	-15	11	2	2	.913	13	/3-69,S-55,2-42,1-2	0.5
■ **LARRY SHEETS**	Sheets, Larry Kent b: 12/6/59, Staunton, Va. BL/TR, 6'3", 225 lbs. Deb: 9/18/84																						
1984	Bal-A	8	16	3	7	1	0	1	2	1	3	.438	.471	.688	221	3	0	0	0	1.000	0	/O-7	0.3
1985	Bal-A	113	328	43	86	8	0	17	50	28	52	.262	.324	.442	110	4	0	1	-1	.875	-2	D-93/O-9,1-1	-0.1
1986	Bal-A	112	338	42	92	17	1	18	60	21	56	.272	.319	.488	117	7	2	0	1	.984	-0	D-58,O-32/C-6,13	0.5
1987	Bal-A	135	469	74	148	23	0	31	94	31	67	.316	.362	.563	144	28	1	1	-0	.975	-4	*O-124/1-3,D-7	1.8
1988	Bal-A	136	452	38	104	19	1	10	47	42	72	.230	.304	.343	83	-10	1	6	-3	.974	1	O-76,D-50/1-3	-1.6
1989	Bal-A	102	304	33	74	12	1	7	33	26	58	.243	.309	.359	90	-4	1	1	-0	.000	0	D-88	-0.7
1990	Det-A	131	360	40	94	17	2	10	52	24	42	.261	.311	.403	97	-2	1	3	-2	.981	-7	O-79,D-44	-1.4
1993	Sea-A	11	17	0	2	1	0	0	1	2	1	.118	.250	.176	17	-2	0	0	0	1.000	-0	/O-1,D-5	-0.2
Total	8	748	2284	273	607	98	5	94	339	175	351	.266	.323	.437	109	23	6	12	-5	.976	-12	D-345,O-328/1C3	-1.4
■ **GARY SHEFFIELD**	Sheffield, Gary Antonian b: 11/18/68, Tampa, Fla. BR/TR, 5'11", 190 lbs. Deb: 9/3/88																						
1988	Mil-A	24	80	12	19	1	0	4	12	7	7	.237	.299	.400	93	-1	3	1	0	.967	-10	S-24	-0.9
1989	Mil-A	95	368	34	91	18	0	5	32	27	33	.247	.306	.337	82	-9	10	6	-1	.959	-17	S-70,3-21/D-4	-2.2
1990	Mil-A	125	487	67	143	30	1	10	67	44	41	.294	.356	.421	117	11	25	10	2	.934	-4	*3-125	0.9
1991	Mil-A	50	175	25	34	12	2	2	22	19	15	.194	.284	.320	69	-8	5	5	-2	.922	-12	3-43/D-5	-2.1
1992	SD-N★	146	557	87	184	34	3	33	100	48	40	**.330**	.390	.580	168	48	5	6	-2	.961	10	*3-144	5.8
1993	SD-N	68	258	34	76	12	2	10	36	18	30	.295	.348	.473	115	5	5	1	1	.905	-11	3-67	-0.5
	Fla-N★	72	236	33	69	8	3	10	37	29	34	.292	.384	.479	122	8	12	4	1	.894	-4	3-66	0.5
	Yr	140	494	67	145	20	5	20	73	47	64	.294	.365	.476	119	13	17	5	2	.899	-16	*3-133	0.0
1994	Fla-N	87	322	61	89	16	1	27	78	51	50	.276	.380	.584	144	21	12	6	0	.970	0	O-87	1.9
1995	Fla-N	63	213	46	69	8	0	16	46	55	45	.324	.471	.587	176	27	19	4	3	.942	0	O-61	2.8
1996	Fla-N★	161	519	118	163	33	1	42	120	142	66	.314	**.469**	.624	**192**	**77**	16	9	-1	.976	-9	*O-161	6.1
1997	*Fla-N	135	444	86	111	22	1	21	71	121	79	.250	.426	.446	135	30	11	7	-1	.980	8	*O-132/D-1	3.3
1998	Fla-N	40	136	21	37	11	1	6	28	26	16	.272	.396	.500	136	8	4	2	0	.986	2	O-37	0.9
	LA-N★	90	301	52	95	16	1	16	57	69	30	.316	.452	.535	167	34	18	5	2	.994	2	O-89	3.7

YEAR	TM/L	G	AB	R	H	2B	3B	HR	RBI	BB	SO	AVG	OBP	SLG	PRO+	BR/A	SB	CS	SBR	FA	FR	G/POS	TPR
	Yr	130	437	73	132	27	2	22	85	95	46	.302	.435	.524	158	42	22	7	2	.991	4	*O-126	4.6
Total	11	1156	4096	676	1180	221	16	202	706	656	486	.288	.395	.498	141	252	145	66	4	.975	-46	O-567,3-466/S-94,D	20.2
■ **JOHN SHELBY** Shelby, John T. b: 2/23/58, Lexington, Ky. BB/TR, 6'1", 175 lbs. Deb: 9/15/81 C																							
1981	Bal-A	7	2	2	0	0	0	0	0	0	1	.000	.000	.000	-99	-1	2	0	1	1.000	-2	/O-4	-0.2
1982	Bal-A	26	35	8	11	3	0	1	2	0	5	.314	.314	.486	116	1	0	1	-1	1.000	-8	O-24	-0.8
1983	*Bal-A	126	325	52	84	15	2	5	27	18	64	.258	.297	.363	82	-8	15	2	3	.981	-14	*O-115/D-1	-2.2
1984	Bal-A	128	383	44	80	12	5	6	30	20	71	.209	.248	.313	55	-24	12	4	1	.993	-10	*O-124	-3.6
1985	Bal-A	69	205	28	58	6	2	7	27	7	44	.283	.307	.434	103	0	5	1	1	.981	0	O-59/2-1,D-3	0.0
1986	Bal-A	135	404	54	92	14	4	11	49	18	75	.228	.264	.364	70	-18	18	6	2	.978	-12	*O-121/D-2	-3.1
1987	Bal-A	21	32	4	6	0	0	1	3	1	13	.188	.212	.281	30	-3	0	1	-1	1.000	-3	O-19/D-1	-0.7
	LA-N	120	476	61	132	26	0	21	69	31	97	.277	.323	.464	108	4	16	6	1	.972	11	*O-117	1.2
1988	*LA-N	140	494	65	130	23	6	10	64	44	128	.263	.323	.395	109	5	16	5	2	.982	7	*O-140	1.0
1989	LA-N	108	345	28	63	11	1	1	12	25	92	.183	.238	.229	35	-29	10	7	-1	.991	0	O-98	-3.5
1990	LA-N	25	24	2	6	1	0	0	2	0	7	.250	.250	.292	50	-2	1	0	0	1.000	-3	O-12	-0.5
	Det-A	78	222	22	55	9	3	4	20	10	51	.248	.280	.369	80	-7	3	5	-2	.973	-1	O-68/D-5	-1.1
1991	Det-A	53	143	19	22	8	1	3	8	8	23	.154	.204	.287	34	-13	0	2	-1	.982	-1	O-47/D-4	-1.6
Total	11	1036	3090	389	739	128	24	70	313	182	671	.239	.282	.364	79	-96	98	40	5	.982	-36	O-948/D-16,2-1	-15.1
■ **BOB SHELDON** Sheldon, Bob Mitchell b: 11/27/50, Montebello, Cal. BL/TR, 6', 170 lbs. Deb: 4/10/74																							
1974	Mil-A	10	17	4	2	1	1	0	0	4	2	.118	.286	.294	67	-1	0	1	-1	1.000	-1	/2-3,D-4	-0.2
1975	Mil-A	53	181	17	52	3	3	0	14	13	14	.287	.342	.337	92	-2	0	3	-2	.977	-8	2-44/D-6	-1.0
1977	Mil-A	31	64	9	13	4	1	0	3	6	9	.203	.271	.297	55	-4	0	0	0	1.000	1	D-17/2-5	-0.4
Total	3	94	262	30	67	8	5	0	17	23	25	.256	.321	.324	81	-6	0	4	-2	.979	-9	/2-52,D-27	-1.6
■ **SCOTT SHELDON** Sheldon, Scott Patrick b: 11/28/68, Hammond, Ind. BR/TR, 6'3", 185 lbs. Deb: 5/18/97																							
1997	Oak-A	13	24	2	6	0	0	1	2	1	6	.250	.308	.375	78	-1	0	0	0	.939	-1	S-12/2-1,3-1	-0.1
1998	Tex-A	7	16	0	2	0	0	0	1	1	6	.125	.176	.125	-19	-3	0	0	0	1.000	2	/3-3,S-2,1-1,D-1	0.0
Total	2	20	40	2	8	0	0	1	3	2	12	.200	.256	.275	38	-4	0	0	0	.938	2	/S-14,3-4,D-1,12	-0.1
■ **HUGH SHELLEY** Shelley, Hubert Leneirre b: 10/26/10, Rogers, Tex. d: 6/16/78, Beaumont, Tex. BR/TR, 6', 170 lbs. Deb: 6/25/35																							
1935	Det-A	7	8	1	2	0	0	0	1	2	1	.250	.400	.250	74	-0	0	0	0	1.000	-1	/O-5	-0.2
■ **SKEETER SHELTON** Shelton, Andrew Kemper b: 6/29/1888, Huntington, W.Va. d: 1/9/54, Huntington, W.Va. BR/TR, 5'11", 175 lbs. Deb: 8/25/15																							
1915	NY-A	10	40	1	1	0	0	0	0	2	10	.025	.071	.025	-71	-8	0			1.000	0	O-10	-1.0
■ **BEN SHELTON** Shelton, Benjamin Davis b: 9/21/69, Chicago, Ill. BR/TL, 6'3", 210 lbs. Deb: 6/16/93																							
1993	Pit-N	15	24	3	6	1	0	2	7	3	3	.250	.333	.542	130	1	0	0	0	.889	-0	/O-6,1-2	0.0
■ **STEVE SHEMO** Shemo, Stephen Michael b: 4/9/15, Swoyersville, Pa. d: 4/13/92, Eden, N.C. BR/TR, 5'11", 175 lbs. Deb: 4/18/44																							
1944	Bos-N	18	31	3	9	2	0	0	1	1	3	.290	.313	.355	84	-1	0			.966	3	2-16/3-2	0.3
1945	Bos-N	17	46	4	11	1	0	0	7	1	3	.239	.255	.261	43	-4	0			.921	-6	2-12/3-3,S-1	-0.9
Total	2	35	77	7	20	3	0	0	8	2	6	.260	.278	.299	60	-4	0			.948	-3	/2-28,3-5,S-1	-0.6
■ **JACK SHEPARD** Shepard, Jack Leroy b: 5/13/32, Clovis, Cal. d: 12/31/94, Atherton, Cal. BR/TR, 6'2", 195 lbs. Deb: 6/19/53																							
1953	Pit-N	2	4	0	1	0	0	0	0	0	2	.250	.250	.250	31	-0	0	0	0	.750	-0	/C-2	-0.1
1954	Pit-N	82	227	24	69	8	2	3	22	26	33	.304	.375	.396	103	2	0	0	0	.977	2	C-67	0.6
1955	Pit-N	94	264	24	63	10	2	2	23	33	25	.239	.323	.314	71	-10	1	0	0	.982	-10	C-77	-1.8
1956	Pit-N	100	256	24	62	11	2	7	30	25	37	.242	.310	.383	87	-5	1	1	-0	.990	1	C-86/1-2	-0.1
Total	4	278	751	72	195	29	6	12	75	84	97	.260	.334	.362	86	-14	2	1	0	.982	-8	C-232/1-2	-1.4
■ **RAY SHEPARDSON** Shepardson, Raymond Francis b: 5/3/1897, Little Falls, N.Y. d: 11/8/75, Little Falls, N.Y. BR/TR, 5'11.5", 170 lbs. Deb: 9/19/24																							
1924	StL-N	3	6	1	0	0	0	0	0	0	3	.000	.000	.000	-99	-2	0	0	0	1.000	0	/C-3	-0.2
■ **RON SHEPHERD** Shepherd, Ronald Wayne b: 10/27/60, Longview, Tex. BR/TR, 6'4", 175 lbs. Deb: 9/5/84																							
1984	Tor-A	12	4	0	0	0	0	0	0	0	3	.000	.000	.000	-97	-1	0	1	-1	1.000	-1	/O-5,D-4	-0.3
1985	Tor-A	38	35	7	4	2	0	0	1	2	12	.114	.162	.171	-8	-5	3	0	1	1.000	-4	O-16,D-15	-0.9
1986	Tor-A	65	69	16	14	4	0	2	4	3	22	.203	.236	.348	55	-4	0	0	0	1.000	-8	O-32,D-16	-1.3
Total	3	115	108	23	18	6	0	2	5	5	37	.167	.204	.278	29	-11	3	1	0	1.000	-13	/O-53,D-35	-2.5
■ **JOHN SHEPPARD** Sheppard, John b: Baltimore, Md. Deb: 6/27/1873																							
1873	Mar-n	3	11	1	0	0	0	0	0	0	1	.000	.000	.000	-99	-3	0	0	0	.500	-1	/O-2,C-1	-0.3
■ **SHERIDAN** Sheridan Deb: 10/9/1875																							
1875	Atl-n	1	4	0	0	0	0	0	0	0	1	.000	.000	.000	-99	-1	0	0	0	.000	-0	/O-1	-0.1
■ **RED SHERIDAN** Sheridan, Eugene Anthony b: 11/14/1896, Brooklyn, N.Y. d: 11/25/75, Queens Village, N.Y. BR/TR, 5'10.5", 160 lbs. Deb: 7/3/18																							
1918	Bro-N	2	4	0	1	0	0	0	0	1	0	.250	.400	.250	100	0	1			1.000	-1	/2-2	-0.1
1920	Bro-N	3	2	0	0	0	0	0	0	0	1	.000	.000	.000	-97	-0	0	0	0	1.000	1	/S-3	0.1
Total	2	5	6	0	1	0	0	0	0	1	1	.167	.286	.167	37	-0	1	0		1.000	1	/S-3,2-2	0.0
■ **NEILL SHERIDAN** Sheridan, Neill Rawlins "Wild Horse" b: 11/20/21, Sacramento, Cal. BR/TR, 6'1.5", 195 lbs. Deb: 9/19/48																							
1948	Bos-A	2	1	0	0	0	0	0	0	0	1	.000	.000	.000	-95	-0	0	0	0	.000	0	H	0.0
■ **PAT SHERIDAN** Sheridan, Patrick Arthur b: 12/4/57, Ann Arbor, Mich. BL/TR, 6'3", 175 lbs. Deb: 9/16/81																							
1981	KC-A	3	1	0	0	0	0	0	0	0	1	.000	.000	.000	-99	-0	0	0	0	1.000	-1	/O-3	-0.1
1983	KC-A	109	333	43	90	12	2	7	36	20	64	.270	.312	.381	89	-5	12	3	2	.988	-2	*O-100	-0.8
1984	*KC-A	138	481	64	136	24	4	8	53	41	91	.283	.340	.399	103	2	19	6	2	.986	-3	*O-134	-0.3
1985	*KC-A	78	206	18	47	9	2	3	17	23	38	.228	.309	.335	76	-7	11	3	2	.983	-4	O-69/D-1	-1.1
1986	Det-A	98	236	41	56	9	1	6	19	21	57	.237	.302	.360	80	-7	9	2	2	.977	-10	O-90/D-5	-1.7
1987	*Det-A	141	421	57	109	19	3	6	49	44	90	.259	.330	.361	87	-7	18	13	-2	.976	-12	*O-137	-2.4
1988	Det-A	127	347	47	88	9	5	11	47	44	64	.254	.341	.403	112	6	8	6	-1	.981	-6	*O-111/D-3	-0.4
1989	Det-A	50	120	16	29	3	0	3	15	17	21	.242	.336	.342	93	-1	4	0	1	.982	-3	O-35/D-8	-0.4
	*SF-N	70	161	20	33	3	4	3	14	13	45	.205	.264	.329	71	-7	4	1	1	.983	-4	O-66	-1.2
1991	NY-A	62	113	13	23	3	0	4	7	13	30	.204	.286	.336	71	-5	1	1	-0	1.000	-3	O-34/D-2	-0.8
Total	9	876	2419	319	611	91	21	51	257	236	501	.253	.321	.371	91	-30	86	35	5	.983	-48	O-779/D-19	-9.2
■ **ED SHERLING** Sherling, Edward Creech "Shine" b: 7/17/1897, Coalburg, Ala. d: 11/16/65, Enterprise, Cal. BR/TR, 6'1", 185 lbs. Deb: 8/13/24																							
1924	Phi-A	4	2	2	1	1	0	0	0	0	0	.500	.500	1.000	278	0	0	0	0	.000	0	H	0.0
■ **MONK SHERLOCK** Sherlock, John Clinton b: 10/26/04, Buffalo, N.Y. d: 11/26/85, Buffalo, N.Y. BR/TR, 5'10", 175 lbs. Deb: 4/20/30 F																							
1930	Phi-N	92	299	51	97	18	2	0	38	27	28	.324	.380	.398	83	-8	0			.990	4	1-70/2-5,O-1	-0.9
■ **VINCE SHERLOCK** Sherlock, Vincent Thomas "Baldy" b: 3/27/10, Buffalo, N.Y. d: 5/11/97, Cheektowaga, N.Y. BR/TR, 6', 180 lbs. Deb: 9/18/35 F																							
1935	Bro-N	9	26	4	12	1	0	0	6	1	2	.462	.481	.500	168	3	1			.907	-1	/2-8	0.2
■ **DARRELL SHERMAN** Sherman, Darrell Edward b: 12/4/67, Los Angeles, Cal. BL/TL, 5'9", 160 lbs. Deb: 4/8/93																							
1993	SD-N	37	63	8	14	1	0	0	2	6	8	.222	.319	.238	51	-4	2	1	0	1.000	-3	O-26	-0.8
■ **DENNIS SHERRILL** Sherrill, Dennis Lee b: 3/3/56, Miami, Fla. BR/TR, 6', 165 lbs. Deb: 9/4/78																							
1978	NY-A	2	1	1	0	0	0	0	0	0	1	.000	.000	.000	-99	-0	0	0	0	.000	-0	/3-1,D-1	-0.1
1980	NY-A	3	4	0	1	0	0	0	0	0	1	.250	.250	.250	38	-0	0	0	0	1.000	-0	/S-2,2-1	-0.1
Total	2	5	5	1	1	0	0	0	0	0	2	.200	.200	.200	11	-1	0	0	0	1.000	-1	/S-2,2-1,D-1,3-1	-0.2

■ NORM SHERRY
Sherry, Norman Burt b: 7/16/31, New York, N.Y. BR/TR, 5′11″, 181 lbs. Deb: 4/12/59 FMC

YEAR	TM/L	G	AB	R	H	2B	3B	HR	RBI	BB	SO	AVG	OBP	SLG	PRO+	BR/A	SB	CS	SBR	FA	FR	G/POS	TPR
1959	LA-N	2	3	0	1	0	0	0	2	0	0	.333	.500	.333	119	0	0	0	0	1.000	-1	/C-2	-0.1
1960	LA-N	47	138	22	39	4	1	8	19	12	29	.283	.353	.500	122	4	0	0	0	.993	-4	C-44	0.2
1961	LA-N	47	121	10	31	2	0	5	21	9	30	.256	.308	.397	78	-4	0	0	0	.993	4	C-45	0.1
1962	LA-N	35	88	7	16	2	0	3	16	6	17	.182	.242	.307	49	-7	0	0	0	.992	9	C-34	0.3
1963	NY-N	63	147	6	20	1	0	2	11	10	26	.136	.206	.184	13	-16	1	0	0	.980	3	C-61	-1.2
Total	5	194	497	45	107	9	1	18	69	37	102	.215	.280	.346	69	-23	1	0	0	.989	11	C-186	-0.7

■ BARRY SHETRONE
Shetrone, Barry Stevan b: 7/6/38, Baltimore, Md. BL/TR, 6′2″, 190 lbs. Deb: 7/27/59

YEAR	TM/L	G	AB	R	H	2B	3B	HR	RBI	BB	SO	AVG	OBP	SLG	PRO+	BR/A	SB	CS	SBR	FA	FR	G/POS	TPR
1959	Bal-A	33	79	8	16	1	1	0	5	5	9	.203	.250	.241	36	-7	3	0	1	.947	-4	O-23	-1.2
1960	Bal-A	1	0	1	0	0	0	0	0	0	0	—	—	—	—	0	0	0	0	.000	0	R	0.0
1961	Bal-A	3	7	0	1	0	0	0	1	0	2	.143	.143	.143	-24	-1	0	0	0	1.000	-0	/O-2	-0.2
1962	Bal-A	21	24	3	6	1	0	1	1	0	5	.250	.250	.417	81	-1	0	0	0	1.000	-0	/O-6	-0.1
1963	Was-A	2	2	0	0	0	0	0	0	0	0	.000	.000	.000	-99	-1	0	0	0	.000	0	H	-0.1
Total	5	60	112	12	23	2	1	1	7	5	16	.205	.239	.268	39	-9	3	0	1	.962	-5	/O-31	-1.6

■ JOHN SHETZLINE
Shetzline, John Henry b: 1850, Philadelphia, Pa. d: 12/15/1892, Philadelphia, Pa. 5′11.5″, 190 lbs. Deb: 5/2/1882

YEAR	TM/L	G	AB	R	H	2B	3B	HR	RBI	BB	SO	AVG	OBP	SLG	PRO+	BR/A	SB	CS	SBR	FA	FR	G/POS	TPR
1882	Bal-a	73	282	23	62	8	3	0		5		.220	.233	.270	75	-7				.800	3	3-52,2-20/O-1,S-1	-0.2

■ JIMMY SHEVLIN
Shevlin, James Cornelius b: 7/9/09, Cincinnati, Ohio d: 10/30/74, Ft.Lauderdale, Fla BL/TL, 5′10.5″, 155 lbs. Deb: 6/29/30

YEAR	TM/L	G	AB	R	H	2B	3B	HR	RBI	BB	SO	AVG	OBP	SLG	PRO+	BR/A	SB	CS	SBR	FA	FR	G/POS	TPR
1930	Det-A	28	14	4	2	0	0	0	2	2	3	.143	.250	.143	2	-2	0	0	0	1.000	1	1-25	-0.2
1932	Cin-N	7	24	3	5	2	0	0	4	4	0	.208	.345	.292	76	-1	4			.985	-0	/1-7	-0.2
1934	Cin-N	18	39	6	12	2	0	0	6	6	5	.308	.400	.359	107	1	0			1.000	0	1-10	0.0
Total	3	53	77	13	19	4	0	0	12	12	8	.247	.356	.299	77	-2	4	0		.995	1	/1-42	-0.4

■ PETE SHIELDS
Shields, Francis Leroy b: 9/21/1891, Swiftwater, Miss. d: 2/11/61, Jackson, Miss. BR/TR, 6′, 175 lbs. Deb: 4/14/15

YEAR	TM/L	G	AB	R	H	2B	3B	HR	RBI	BB	SO	AVG	OBP	SLG	PRO+	BR/A	SB	CS	SBR	FA	FR	G/POS	TPR
1915	Cle-A	23	72	4	15	6	0	0	6	4	14	.208	.250	.292	61	-4	3	3	-1	.974	0	1-23	-0.6

■ TOMMY SHIELDS
Shields, Thomas Charles b: 8/14/64, Fairfax, Va. BL/TR, 6′, 180 lbs. Deb: 7/25/92

YEAR	TM/L	G	AB	R	H	2B	3B	HR	RBI	BB	SO	AVG	OBP	SLG	PRO+	BR/A	SB	CS	SBR	FA	FR	G/POS	TPR
1992	Bal-A	2	0	0	0	0	0	0	0	0	0	—	—	—	—	0	0	0	0	.000	0	/R	0.0
1993	Chi-N	20	34	4	6	1	0	0	1	2	10	.176	.222	.206	16	-4	0	0	0	1.000	2	/2-7,3-7,1-1,O-1	-0.2
Total	2	22	34	4	6	1	0	0	1	2	10	.176	.222	.206	16	-4	0	0	0	1.000	2	/3-7,2-7,O-1,1-1	-0.2

■ JIM SHILLING
Shilling, James Robert b: 5/14/14, Tulsa, Okla. d: 9/12/86, Tulsa, Okla. BR/TR, 5′11″, 175 lbs. Deb: 4/21/39

YEAR	TM/L	G	AB	R	H	2B	3B	HR	RBI	BB	SO	AVG	OBP	SLG	PRO+	BR/A	SB	CS	SBR	FA	FR	G/POS	TPR
1939	Cle-A	31	98	8	27	7	2	0	12	7	9	.276	.324	.388	84	-3	1	0	0	.935	4	2-27/S-3	0.2
	Phi-N	11	33	3	10	1	3	0	4	1	4	.303	.324	.515	126	1	0			.944	-2	/2-5,S-3,3-3,O-1	0.0
Total	1	42	131	11	37	8	5	0	16	8	13	.282	.324	.420	94	-2	1	0		.936	2	/2-32,S-6,3-3,O-1	0.2

■ GINGER SHINAULT
Shinault, Enoch Erskine b: 9/7/1892, Benton, Ark. d: 12/29/30, Denver, Colo. BR/TR, 5′11″, 170 lbs. Deb: 7/4/21

YEAR	TM/L	G	AB	R	H	2B	3B	HR	RBI	BB	SO	AVG	OBP	SLG	PRO+	BR/A	SB	CS	SBR	FA	FR	G/POS	TPR
1921	Cle-A	22	29	5	11	1	0	0	4	6	5	.379	.486	.414	129	2	1	0	0	.917	2	C-20	0.4
1922	Cle-A	13	15	1	2	1	0	0	0	0	2	.133	.133	.200	-14	-3	0	0	0	.400	-4	C-11	-0.6
Total	2	35	44	6	13	2	0	0	4	6	7	.295	.380	.341	85	-1	1	0	0	.868	-2	/C-31	-0.2

■ BILLY SHINDLE
Shindle, William b: 12/5/1860, Gloucester, N.J. d: 6/3/36, Lakeland, N.J. BR/TR, 5′8.5″, 155 lbs. Deb: 10/5/1886

YEAR	TM/L	G	AB	R	H	2B	3B	HR	RBI	BB	SO	AVG	OBP	SLG	PRO+	BR/A	SB	CS	SBR	FA	FR	G/POS	TPR
1886	Det-N	7	26	4	7	0	0	0	4	0	5	.269	.269	.269	62	-1	2			.900	1	/S-7	0.0
1887	Det-N	22	84	17	24	3	2	0	12	7	10	.286	.341	.369	94	-1	13			.818	-5	3-21/O-1	-0.4
1888	Bal-a	135	514	61	107	14	8	1	53	20		.208	.249	.272	69	-18	52			**.922**	**37**	*3-135	1.9
1889	Bal-a	138	567	122	178	24	7	3	64	42	37	.314	.369	.397	116	11	56			.862	20	*3-138	3.0
1890	Phi-P	132	584	127	189	21	21	10	90	40	30	.324	.371	.483	124	17	51			.856	8	*S-130/3-2	2.6
1891	Phi-N	103	415	68	87	13	1	0	38	33	39	.210	.278	.246	51	-26	17			.874	6	*3-100/S-3	-1.3
1892	Bal-N	143	619	100	156	20	18	3	50	35	34	.252	.301	.357	96	-6	24			.882	36	*3-134/S-9	3.2
1893	Bal-N	125	521	100	136	22	11	1	75	66	17	.261	.353	.351	86	-10	17			.885	8	*3-125	0.0
1894	Bro-N	116	476	94	141	22	9	4	96	29	20	.296	.344	.405	86	-11	19			.897	1	*3-116	-0.8
1895	Bro-N	116	477	91	133	21	2	3	69	47	28	.279	.357	.350	90	-5	17			.897	0	*3-116	-0.2
1896	Bro-N	131	516	75	144	24	9	1	61	24	20	.279	.316	.366	84	-13	24			.912	-12	*3-131	-1.9
1897	Bro-N	134	542	83	154	32	6	4	105	35		.284	.336	.387	96	-4	23			.904	-12	*3-134	-1.1
1898	Bro-N	120	466	50	105	10	3	1	41	10		.225	.249	.266	48	-32	3			.911	7	*3-120	-2.3
Total	13	1422	5807	992	1561	226	97	31	758	388	240	.269	.323	.357	88	-99	318			.892	95	*3-1272,S-149/O-1	2.7

■ RAZOR SHINES
Shines, Anthony Raymond "Ray" b: 7/18/56, Durham, N.C. BB/TR, 6′1″, 210 lbs. Deb: 9/9/83

YEAR	TM/L	G	AB	R	H	2B	3B	HR	RBI	BB	SO	AVG	OBP	SLG	PRO+	BR/A	SB	CS	SBR	FA	FR	G/POS	TPR
1983	Mon-N	3	2	0	1	0	0	0	0	0	0	.500	.500	.500	179	0	0	0	0	.000	-0	/O-1	0.0
1984	Mon-N	12	20	0	6	1	0	0	2	0	3	.300	.300	.350	86	-0	0	0	0	1.000	-1	/1-3,3-1	-0.2
1985	Mon-N	47	50	0	6	0	0	0	3	4	9	.120	.185	.120	-14	-8	0	1	-1	.950	0	/1-5,P-1	-0.8
1987	Mon-N	6	9	0	2	0	0	0	0	1	0	.222	.364	.222	58	-0	1	0	0	1.000	-0	/1-2	0.0
Total	4	68	81	0	15	1	0	0	5	5	12	.185	.241	.198	24	-8	1	1	-0	.975	-1	/1-10,P-1,3-1,O-1	-1.0

■ RALPH SHINNERS
Shinners, Ralph Peter b: 10/4/1895, Monches, Wis. d: 7/23/62, Milwaukee, Wis. BR/TR, 6′, 180 lbs. Deb: 4/12/22

YEAR	TM/L	G	AB	R	H	2B	3B	HR	RBI	BB	SO	AVG	OBP	SLG	PRO+	BR/A	SB	CS	SBR	FA	FR	G/POS	TPR
1922	NY-N	56	135	16	34	4	2	0	15	5	22	.252	.308	.311	60	-8	3	5	-2	.915	-4	O-37	-1.5
1923	NY-N	33	13	5	2	1	0	0	0	2	1	.154	.267	.231	33	-1	0	0	0	1.000	-1	/O-6	-0.2
1925	StL-N	74	251	39	74	9	2	7	36	12	19	.295	.330	.430	90	-4	8	5	-1	.982	-3	O 66	-1.1
Total	3	163	399	60	110	14	4	7	51	19	42	.276	.320	.383	78	-13	11	10	-3	.959	-8	O-109	-2.8

■ TIM SHINNICK
Shinnick, Timothy James "Dandy" or "Good Eye" b: 11/6/1867, Exeter, N.H. d: 5/18/44, Exeter, N.H. BB/TR, 5′9″, 150 lbs. Deb: 4/19/1890

YEAR	TM/L	G	AB	R	H	2B	3B	HR	RBI	BB	SO	AVG	OBP	SLG	PRO+	BR/A	SB	CS	SBR	FA	FR	G/POS	TPR
1890	*Lou-a	133	493	87	126	16	11	1	82	62		.256	.348	.339	105	4	62			.925	-25	*2-130/3-3	-1.1
1891	Lou-a	128	443	79	98	10	11	1	54	54	47	.221	.314	.300	77	-13	36			.915	-21	*2-120/3-7,S-1	-2.5
Total	2	261	936	166	224	26	22	2	136	116	47	.239	.332	.321	91	-9	98			.920	-45	2-250/3-10,S-1	-3.6

■ BILL SHIPKE
Shipke, William Martin "Skipper Bill" or "Muskrat Bill" (b: William Martin Shipkrethaver)
b: 11/18/1882, St.Louis, Mo. d: 9/10/40, Omaha, Neb. BR/TR, 5′7″, 145 lbs. Deb: 4/23/06

YEAR	TM/L	G	AB	R	H	2B	3B	HR	RBI	BB	SO	AVG	OBP	SLG	PRO+	BR/A	SB	CS	SBR	FA	FR	G/POS	TPR
1906	Cle-A	2	6	0	0	0	0	0	0	0		.000	.000	.000	-99	-1	0			.933	2	/2-2	0.0
1907	Was-A	64	189	17	37	3	2	1	9	15		.196	.262	.249	68	-7	6			.944	7	3-63	0.3
1908	Was-A	111	341	40	71	7	8	0	20	38		.208	.297	.276	94	-1	15			.932	-7	*3-110/2-1	-0.5
1909	Was-A	9	16	2	2	1	0	0	0	2		.125	.222	.188	31	-1	0			.905	2	/3-6,S-2	0.1
Total	4	186	552	59	110	11	10	1	29	55		.199	.280	.261	81	-10	21			.935	4	3-179/2-3,S-2	-0.1

■ CRAIG SHIPLEY
Shipley, Craig Barry b: 1/7/63, Parramatta, Australia BR/TR, 6′1″, 185 lbs. Deb: 6/22/86

YEAR	TM/L	G	AB	R	H	2B	3B	HR	RBI	BB	SO	AVG	OBP	SLG	PRO+	BR/A	SB	CS	SBR	FA	FR	G/POS	TPR
1986	LA-N	12	27	3	3	1	0	0	4	2	5	.111	.200	.148	-3	-4	0	0	0	.914	-1	S-10/2-1,3-1	-0.4
1987	LA-N	26	35	3	9	1	0	0	2	0	6	.257	.257	.286	45	-3	0	0	0	.949	3	S-18/3-6	0.0
1989	NY-N	4	7	3	1	0	0	0	0	0	1	.143	.143	.143	-19	-1	0	0	0	1.000	-0	/S-3,3-2	-0.1
1991	SD-N	37	91	6	25	3	0	1	6	2	14	.275	.298	.341	77	-3	0	1	-1	.902	-1	S-19,2-14	-0.3
1992	SD-N	52	105	7	26	6	0	0	7	2	21	.248	.262	.305	59	-6	1	1	-0	.986	10	S-23,2-11/3-8	0.5
1993	SD-N	105	230	25	54	9	0	4	22	10	31	.235	.276	.326	59	-13	12	3	2	.964	-8	S-38,3-37,2-12,/O-5	-1.7
1994	SD-N	81	240	32	80	14	4	4	30	9	28	.333	.365	.475	120	7	6	6	-2	.936	-8	3-53,S-14,2-13,/O1	-0.2
1995	Hou-N	92	232	23	61	8	1	3	24	8	28	.263	.293	.345	73	-10	6	1	1	.982	-2	3-65,S-11/2-4,1-1	-1.0
1996	SD-N	33	92	13	29	5	0	1	7	2	15	.315	.344	.402	102	0	7	0	2	.985	0	2-17/S-7,3-4,O-3	0.3
1997	SD-N	63	139	22	38	9	0	5	19	7	20	.273	.308	.446	102	-0	1	1	-0	.947	-6	S-21,2-16/1-4,3-2	-0.5
1998	Ana-A	77	147	18	38	7	1	2	17	5	22	.259	.306	.361	72	-6	0	4	-2	.963	1	3-48,2-11/1-8,SO	-0.6
Total	11	582	1345	155	364	63	6	20	138	47	191	.271	.304	.371	80	-39	33	17	-0	.963	-13	3-226,S-169/21O	-4.0

■ ART SHIRES
Shires, Charles Arthur "Art The Great" b: 8/13/07, Italy, Tex. d: 7/13/67, Italy, Tex. BL/TR, 6′1″, 195 lbs. Deb: 8/20/28

YEAR	TM/L	G	AB	R	H	2B	3B	HR	RBI	BB	SO	AVG	OBP	SLG	PRO+	BR/A	SB	CS	SBR	FA	FR	G/POS	TPR
1928	Chi-A	33	123	20	42	6	1	1	11	13	10	.341	.409	.431	122	5	0	3	-2	.990	3	1-32	0.3
1929	Chi-A	100	353	41	110	20	7	3	41	32	20	.312	.370	.433	108	4	4	5	-2	.991	0	1-90/2-3	-0.6

YEAR	TM/L	G	AB	R	H	2B	3B	HR	RBI	BB	SO	AVG	OBP	SLG	PRO+	BR/A	SB	CS	SBR	FA	FR	G/POS	TPR
1930	Chi-A	37	128	14	33	5	1	1	18	6	6	.258	.291	.336	61	-8	2	0	1	.979	-2	1-33	-1.2
	Was-A	38	84	11	31	5	0	1	19	5	5	.369	.404	.464	119	3	1	3	-2	.982	0	1-21	0.0
	Yr	75	212	25	64	10	1	2	37	11	11	.302	.336	.387	84	-5	3	3	-1	.980	-2	1-54	-1.2
1932	Bos-N	82	298	32	71	9	3	5	30	25	21	.238	.299	.339	74	-11	1			.988	-2	1-80	-2.0
Total	4	290	986	118	287	45	12	11	119	81	62	.291	.347	.395	95	-8	8	11		.988	-1	1-256/2-3	-3.5

■ **BART SHIRLEY** Shirley, Barton Arvin b: 1/4/40, Corpus Christi, Tex. BR/TR, 5'10", 183 lbs. Deb: 9/14/64

YEAR	TM/L	G	AB	R	H	2B	3B	HR	RBI	BB	SO	AVG	OBP	SLG	PRO+	BR/A	SB	CS	SBR	FA	FR	G/POS	TPR
1964	LA-N	18	62	6	17	1	1	0	7	4	8	.274	.318	.323	87	-1	0	0	0	.900	1	3-10/S-8	0.0
1966	LA-N	12	5	2	1	0	0	0	0	0	2	.200	.200	.200	13	-1	0	0	0	1.000	1	/S-5	0.1
1967	NY-N	6	12	1	0	0	0	0	0	0	5	.000	.000	.000	-99	-3	0	0	0	.917	0	/2-3	-0.3
1968	LA-N	39	83	6	15	3	0	0	4	10	13	.181	.269	.217	51	-5	0	1	-1	.903	3	S-21,2-18	-0.1
Total	4	75	162	15	33	4	1	0	11	14	28	.204	.267	.241	53	-10	0	1	-1	.936	5	/S-34,2-21,3-10	-0.3

■ **MULE SHIRLEY** Shirley, Ernest Raeford b: 5/24/01, Snow Hill, N.C. d: 8/4/55, Goldsboro, N.C. BL/TL, 5'11", 180 lbs. Deb: 5/6/24

YEAR	TM/L	G	AB	R	H	2B	3B	HR	RBI	BB	SO	AVG	OBP	SLG	PRO+	BR/A	SB	CS	SBR	FA	FR	G/POS	TPR
1924	*Was-A	30	77	12	18	2	2	0	16	3	7	.234	.262	.312	49	-6	0	0	0	.984	0	1-25	-0.7
1925	Was-A	14	23	2	3	1	0	0	2	1	7	.130	.167	.174	-14	-4	0	0	0	1.000	0	/1-9	-0.4
Total	2	44	100	14	21	3	2	0	18	4	14	.210	.240	.280	34	-10	0	0	0	.988	0	/1-34	-1.1

■ **IVEY SHIVER** Shiver, Ivey Merwin "Chick" b: 1/22/06, Sylvester, Ga. d: 8/31/72, Savannah, Ga. BR/TR, 6'1.5", 190 lbs. Deb: 4/14/31

YEAR	TM/L	G	AB	R	H	2B	3B	HR	RBI	BB	SO	AVG	OBP	SLG	PRO+	BR/A	SB	CS	SBR	FA	FR	G/POS	TPR
1931	Det-A	2	9	2	1	0	0	0	0	0	3	.111	.111	.111	-40	-2	0	0	0	1.000	-1	/O-2	-0.2
1934	Cin-N	19	59	6	12	1	0	2	6	3	15	.203	.242	.322	51	-4	1			1.000	-2	O-15	-0.7
Total	2	21	68	8	13	1	0	2	6	3	18	.191	.225	.294	38	-6	1	0		1.000	-3	/O-17	-0.9

■ **GEORGE SHOCH** Shoch, George Quintus b: 1/6/1859, Philadelphia, Pa. d: 9/30/37, Philadelphia, Pa. BR/TR, 5'6", 158 lbs. Deb: 9/10/1886

YEAR	TM/L	G	AB	R	H	2B	3B	HR	RBI	BB	SO	AVG	OBP	SLG	PRO+	BR/A	SB	CS	SBR	FA	FR	G/POS	TPR
1886	Was-N	26	95	11	28	2	1	1	18	2	13	.295	.309	.368	112	1	2			.882	-5	O-25/S-1	-0.4
1887	Was-N	70	264	47	63	9	1	1	18	21	16	.239	.304	.292	70	-10	29			.897	7	O-63/S-6,2-1	-0.3
1888	Was-N	90	317	46	58	6	3	2	24	25	22	.183	.262	.240	64	-11	23			.900	4	S-52,O-35/2-1,P-1	-0.7
1889	Was-N	30	109	12	26	2	0	0	11	20	5	.239	.385	.257	86	0	9			.905	3	O-29/S-1	0.2
1891	Mil-a	34	127	29	40	7	1	1	16	18	5	.315	.435	.409	118	2	12			.932	3	S-25/3-9	0.6
1892	Bal-N	76	308	42	85	15	3	1	50	24	19	.276	.340	.354	107	2	14			.872	0	S-57,O-12/3-7	0.4
1893	Bro-N	94	327	53	86	17	1	2	54	48	13	.263	.366	.339	92	-2	9			.892	-3	O-46,3-37,S-11,/2-3	-0.5
1894	Bro-N	64	239	47	77	6	5	1	37	26	6	.322	.400	.402	101	2	16			.926	-1	O-35,3-14/2-9,S-6	-0.1
1895	Bro-N	61	216	49	56	9	7	0	29	32	6	.259	.368	.366	97	1	7			.952	-6	O-39,2-13/S-6,3-3	-0.6
1896	Bro-N	76	250	36	73	7	4	1	28	33	10	.292	.381	.364	103	3	11			.941	-13	2-62,O-10/3-3,S-1	-0.6
1897	Bro-N	85	284	42	79	9	2	0	38	49		.278	.393	.324	96	2	6			.941	5	2-68,S-13/O-4	0.9
Total	11	706	2536	414	671	89	28	10	323	298	115	.265	.355	.334	94	-10	138			.912	-6	O-298,S-179,2/3P	-1.1

■ **COSTEN SHOCKLEY** Shockley, John Costen b: 2/8/42, Georgetown, Del. BL/TL, 6'2", 200 lbs. Deb: 7/17/64

YEAR	TM/L	G	AB	R	H	2B	3B	HR	RBI	BB	SO	AVG	OBP	SLG	PRO+	BR/A	SB	CS	SBR	FA	FR	G/POS	TPR
1964	Phi-N	11	35	4	8	0	0	1	2	2	8	.229	.270	.314	65	-2	0	0	0	.968	-1	/1-9	-0.3
1965	Cal-A	40	107	5	20	2	0	2	17	9	16	.187	.256	.262	49	-7	0	0	0	.996	0	1-31/O-1	-0.9
Total	2	51	142	9	28	2	0	3	19	11	24	.197	.260	.275	53	-9	0	0	0	.991	-1	/1-40,O-1	-1.2

■ **CHARLIE SHOEMAKER** Shoemaker, Charles Landis b: 8/10/39, Los Angeles, Cal. d: 5/31/90, Mount Penn, Pa. BL/TR, 5'10", 155 lbs. Deb: 9/9/61

YEAR	TM/L	G	AB	R	H	2B	3B	HR	RBI	BB	SO	AVG	OBP	SLG	PRO+	BR/A	SB	CS	SBR	FA	FR	G/POS	TPR
1961	KC-A	7	26	5	10	2	0	0	1	2	2	.385	.429	.462	135	1	0	0	0	1.000	0	/2-6	0.2
1962	KC-A	5	11	1	2	0	0	0	0	0	2	.182	.182	.182	-2	-2	0	0	0	1.000	1	/2-4	0.0
1964	KC-A	16	52	6	11	2	2	0	3	0	9	.212	.212	.327	46	-4	0	0	0	.964	-5	2-14	-0.8
Total	3	28	89	12	23	4	2	0	4	2	13	.258	.275	.348	67	-4	0	0	0	.981	-3	/2-24	-0.6

■ **STRICK SHOFNER** Shofner, Frank Strickland b: 7/23/19, Crawford, Tex. d: 10/10/98, Crawford, Tex. BL/TR, 5'10.5", 187 lbs. Deb: 4/19/47

YEAR	TM/L	G	AB	R	H	2B	3B	HR	RBI	BB	SO	AVG	OBP	SLG	PRO+	BR/A	SB	CS	SBR	FA	FR	G/POS	TPR
1947	Bos-A	5	13	1	2	0	1	0	0	0	3	.154	.154	.308	25	-1	0	0	0	1.000	1	/3-4	-0.1

■ **EDDIE SHOKES** Shokes, Edward Christopher b: 1/27/20, Charleston, S.C. BL/TL, 6', 170 lbs. Deb: 6/9/41

YEAR	TM/L	G	AB	R	H	2B	3B	HR	RBI	BB	SO	AVG	OBP	SLG	PRO+	BR/A	SB	CS	SBR	FA	FR	G/POS	TPR
1941	Cin-N	1	1	0	0	0	0	0	0	0	1	.000	.000	.000	-99	-0	0			.000	0	H	0.0
1946	Cin-N	31	83	3	10	1	0	0	5	18	21	.120	.277	.133	19	-8	1			.996	-1	1-29	-1.2
Total	2	32	84	3	10	1	0	0	5	18	22	.119	.275	.131	18	-9	1			.996	-1	/1-29	-1.2

■ **RAY SHOOK** Shook, Raymond Curtis b: 11/18/1889, Perry, Ohio d: 9/16/70, South Bend, Ind. BR/TR, 5'7.5", 155 lbs. Deb: 4/16/16

YEAR	TM/L	G	AB	R	H	2B	3B	HR	RBI	BB	SO	AVG	OBP	SLG	PRO+	BR/A	SB	CS	SBR	FA	FR	G/POS	TPR
1916	Chi-A	1	0	0	0	0	0	0	0	0	0	—	—	—	—	0	0			.000	0	R	0.0

■ **RON SHOOP** Shoop, Ronald Lee b: 9/19/31, Rural Valley, Pa. BR/TR, 5'11", 180 lbs. Deb: 8/22/59

YEAR	TM/L	G	AB	R	H	2B	3B	HR	RBI	BB	SO	AVG	OBP	SLG	PRO+	BR/A	SB	CS	SBR	FA	FR	G/POS	TPR
1959	Det-A	3	7	1	1	0	0	0	1	0	1	.143	.143	.143	-20	-1	0	0	0	1.000	-1	/C-3	-0.2

■ **TOM SHOPAY** Shopay, Thomas Michael b: 2/21/45, Bristol, Conn. BL/TR, 5'9.5", 160 lbs. Deb: 9/17/67

YEAR	TM/L	G	AB	R	H	2B	3B	HR	RBI	BB	SO	AVG	OBP	SLG	PRO+	BR/A	SB	CS	SBR	FA	FR	G/POS	TPR
1967	NY-A	8	27	2	8	1	0	2	6	1	5	.296	.321	.556	161	2	2	0	1	.917	1	/O-7	0.3
1969	NY-A	28	48	2	4	0	1	0	0	2	10	.083	.120	.125	-33	-9	0	1	-1	1.000	1	O-11	-1.0
1971	*Bal-A	47	74	10	19	2	0	0	5	3	7	.257	.286	.284	62	-4	2	1	0	1.000	-1	O-13	-0.5
1972	Bal-A	49	40	3	9	0	0	0	2	5	12	.225	.311	.225	60	-2	0	0	0	1.000	-0	/O-3	-0.2
1975	Bal-A	40	31	4	5	1	0	0	2	4	7	.161	.257	.194	31	-3	3	0	1	1.000	-3	O-13/C-1,D-3	-0.5
1976	Bal-A	14	20	4	4	0	0	0	1	3	3	.200	.304	.200	53	-1	1	0	0	1.000	-4	O-11/C-1	-0.5
1977	Bal-A	67	69	15	13	3	0	1	4	8	7	.188	.273	.275	53	-4	3	3	-1	1.000	-18	O-52/D-2	-2.5
Total	7	253	309	40	62	7	1	3	20	26	51	.201	.263	.259	50	-21	11	5	0	.993	-24	O-110/D-5,C-2	-4.9

■ **DAVE SHORT** Short, David Orvis b: 5/11/17, Magnolia, Ark. d: 11/22/83, Shreveport, La. BL/TR, 5'11.5", 162 lbs. Deb: 9/16/40

YEAR	TM/L	G	AB	R	H	2B	3B	HR	RBI	BB	SO	AVG	OBP	SLG	PRO+	BR/A	SB	CS	SBR	FA	FR	G/POS	TPR
1940	Chi-A	4	3	1	1	0	0	0	0	1	2	.333	.500	.333	119	0	0	0	0	.000	0	H	0.0
1941	Chi-A	3	8	0	0	0	0	0	0	2	1	.000	.200	.000	-44	-2	0	0	0	.800	-0	/O-2	-0.2
Total	2	7	11	1	1	0	0	0	0	3	3	.091	.286	.091	3	-1	0	0	0	.800	-0	/O-2	-0.2

■ **CHICK SHORTEN** Shorten, Charles Henry b: 4/19/1892, Scranton, Pa. d: 10/23/65, Scranton, Pa. BL/TL, 6', 175 lbs. Deb: 9/22/15

YEAR	TM/L	G	AB	R	H	2B	3B	HR	RBI	BB	SO	AVG	OBP	SLG	PRO+	BR/A	SB	CS	SBR	FA	FR	G/POS	TPR
1915	Bos-A	6	14	1	3	1	0	0	0	0	2	.214	.214	.286	51	-1	0			1.000	-1	/O-5	-0.2
1916	*Bos-A	53	112	14	33	2	1	0	11	10	8	.295	.352	.330	105	1	1			1.000	-8	O-33	-0.9
1917	Bos-A	69	168	12	30	4	2	0	16	10	10	.179	.229	.226	39	-12	2			.977	-5	O-43	-2.2
1919	Det-A	95	270	37	85	9	3	0	22	22	13	.315	.366	.370	110	4	5			.973	-6	O-75	-0.8
1920	Det-A	116	364	35	105	9	6	1	40	28	14	.288	.339	.354	86	-7	2	4	-2	.989	-1	O-99	-1.7
1921	Det-A	92	217	33	59	11	3	0	23	20	11	.272	.333	.350	75	-8	2	3	-1	.981	-4	O-51	-1.6
1922	StL-A	55	131	22	36	12	5	2	16	16	8	.275	.354	.489	114	2	0	1	-1	1.000	-2	O-31	-0.3
1924	Cin-N	41	69	7	19	3	0	0	6	4	2	.275	.315	.319	71	-3	0	0	0	1.000	-4	O-15	-0.7
Total	8	527	1345	161	370	51	20	3	134	110	68	.275	.330	.349	87	-25	12	8		.985	-31	O-352	-8.4

■ **BURT SHOTTON** Shotton, Burton Edwin "Barney" b: 10/18/1884, Brownhelm, Ohio d: 7/29/62, Lake Wales, Fla. BL/TR, 5'11", 175 lbs. Deb: 9/13/09 MC

YEAR	TM/L	G	AB	R	H	2B	3B	HR	RBI	BB	SO	AVG	OBP	SLG	PRO+	BR/A	SB	CS	SBR	FA	FR	G/POS	TPR
1909	StL-A	17	61	5	16	0	1	0	0	5		.262	.328	.295	104	0	3			.915	1	O-17	0.1
1911	StL-A	139	572	84	146	11	8	0	36	51		.255	.317	.302	76	-18	26			.950	7	*O-139	-1.8
1912	StL-A	154	580	87	168	15	8	2	40	86		.290	.390	.353	117	18	35			.941	7	*O-154	1.6
1913	StL-A	147	549	105	163	23	8	1	28	**99**	63	.297	.405	.373	132	27	43			.951	13	*O-146	3.5
1914	StL-A	154	579	82	156	19	9	0	38	64	66	.269	.344	.333	108	6	40	29	-5	.940	2	*O-152	-0.5
1915	StL-A	156	559	93	158	18	11	1	30	118	62	.283	.409	.360	135	31	43	32	-6	.931	-3	*O-154	1.5
1916	StL-A	156	614	97	174	23	6	1	36	**110**	65	.283	.392	.345	128	26	41	28	-5	.950	10	*O-156	2.5
1917	StL-A	118	398	47	89	9	1	1	20	62	47	.224	.330	.259	83	-6	16			.923	-12	*O-107	-2.6
1918	Was-A	126	505	68	132	16	7	0	21	67	28	.261	.349	.321	104	4	25			.942	6	*O-122	0.3
1919	StL-N	85	270	35	77	13	5	1	20	22	25	.285	.341	.381	125	8	16			.927	-5	O-67	-0.1
1920	StL-N	62	180	28	41	5	0	1	12	18	14	.228	.305	.272	69	-7	5	1	1	.959	1	O-51	-0.9
1921	StL-N	38	48	9	12	1	1	1	7	7	4	.250	.357	.375	96	-0	0	2	-1	.958	-0	O-11	-0.2
1922	StL-N	34	30	5	6	1	0	0	2	4	6	.200	.294	.233	39	-3	0	1	-1	1.000	-1	/O-3	-0.4

YEAR	TM/L	G	AB	R	H	2B	3B	HR	RBI	BB	SO	AVG	OBP	SLG	PRO+	BR/A	SB	CS	SBR	FA	FR	G/POS	TPR
1923	StL-N	1	0	1	0	0	0	0	0	0	0	—	—	—	—	0	0	0	0	.000	0	R	0.0
Total	14	1387	4945	746	1338	154	65	9	290	713	380	.271	.365	.333	110	88	293	93		.942	25	*O-1279	3.0

■ **JOHN SHOUPE** Shoupe, John F. b: 9/30/1851, Cincinnati, Ohio d: 2/13/20, Cincinnati, Ohio BL/TL, 5'7", 140 lbs. Deb: 5/3/1879

YEAR	TM/L	G	AB	R	H	2B	3B	HR	RBI	BB	SO	AVG	OBP	SLG	PRO+	BR/A	SB	CS	SBR	FA	FR	G/POS	TPR
1879	Tro-N	11	44	5	4	0	0	0	1	0	3	.091	.091	.091	-43	-6				.820	-3	S-10/2-1	-0.8
1882	StL-a	2	7	1	0	0	0	0		0		.000	.000	.000	-96	-1				1.000	1	/2-2	0.0
1884	Was-U	1	4	1	3	0	0	0		0		.750	.750	.750	368	1				.857	2	/O-1	0.2
Total	3	14	55	7	7	0	0	0	1	0	3	.127	.127	.127	-17	-7				.857	-0	/S-10,2-3,O-1	-0.6

■ **JOHN SHOVLIN** Shovlin, John Joseph "Brode" b: 1/14/1891, Drifton, Pa. d: 2/16/76, Bethesda, Md. BR/TR, 5'7", 163 lbs. Deb: 6/21/11

YEAR	TM/L	G	AB	R	H	2B	3B	HR	RBI	BB	SO	AVG	OBP	SLG	PRO+	BR/A	SB	CS	SBR	FA	FR	G/POS	TPR
1911	Pit-N	2	1	1	0	0	0	0	0	0	1	.000	.000	.000	-96	-0	0			.000	0	H	0.0
1919	StL-A	9	35	4	7	0	0	0	1	5	2	.200	.300	.200	41	-3	0			.936	-2	/2-9	-0.4
1920	StL-A	7	7	2	2	0	0	0	2	0	0	.286	.286	.286	50	-0	0	0	0	1.000	1	/S-5	0.0
Total	3	18	43	7	9	0	0	0	3	5	3	.209	.292	.209	39	-3	0	0		.936	-1	/2-9,S-5	-0.4

■ **GEORGE SHUBA** Shuba, George Thomas "Shotgun" b: 12/13/24, Youngstown, Ohio BL/TR, 5'11", 180 lbs. Deb: 7/2/48

YEAR	TM/L	G	AB	R	H	2B	3B	HR	RBI	BB	SO	AVG	OBP	SLG	PRO+	BR/A	SB	CS	SBR	FA	FR	G/POS	TPR
1948	Bro-N	63	161	21	43	6	0	4	32	34	31	.267	.395	.379	107	3	1			.936	-10	O-56	-0.9
1949	Bro-N	1	1	0	0	0	0	0	0	0	0	.000	.000	.000	-96	-0	0			.000	0	H	0.0
1950	Bro-N	34	111	15	23	8	2	3	12	13	22	.207	.302	.396	80	-3	2			.984	3	O-27	-0.2
1952	*Bro-N	94	256	40	78	12	1	9	40	38	29	.305	.395	.465	136	13	1	3	-2	.992	-2	O-67	0.7
1953	*Bro-N	74	169	19	43	12	1	5	23	17	20	.254	.326	.426	92	-2	1	2	-1	.984	-5	O-44	-1.0
1954	Bro-N	45	65	3	10	5	0	2	10	7	10	.154	.247	.323	46	-5	0	0	0	.913	-1	O-13	-0.7
1955	*Bro-N	44	51	8	14	2	0	1	8	11	10	.275	.422	.373	110	1	0	0	0	.909	-2	/O-9	-0.1
Total	7	355	814	106	211	45	4	24	125	120	122	.259	.359	.413	104	6	5	5		.967	-18	O-216	-2.2

■ **FRANK SHUGART** Shugart, Frank Harry (b: Frank Harry Shugarts)
b: 12/10/1866, Luthersburg, Pa. d: 9/9/44, Clearfield, Pa. BL/TR, 5'8", 170 lbs. Deb: 8/23/1890

YEAR	TM/L	G	AB	R	H	2B	3B	HR	RBI	BB	SO	AVG	OBP	SLG	PRO+	BR/A	SB	CS	SBR	FA	FR	G/POS	TPR
1890	Chi-P	29	106	8	20	5	5	0	15	5	13	.189	.232	.330	47	-9	5			.881	-5	S-25/O-5	-1.0
1891	Pit-N	75	320	57	88	19	8	3	33	20	26	.275	.324	.412	117	5	21			.902	4	S-75	1.2
1892	Pit-N	137	554	94	148	19	14	0	62	47	48	.267	.329	.352	106	3	28			.886	9	*S-134/C-2,O-1	1.6
1893	Pit-N	52	210	37	55	7	3	1	32	19	15	.262	.332	.338	80	-6	12			.882	-3	S-51	-0.5
	StL-N	59	246	41	69	10	4	0	28	22	10	.280	.354	.354	88	-4	13			.907	-3	O-28,S-23/3-9	-0.6
	Yr	111	456	78	124	17	7	1	60	41	25	.272	.344	.346	84	-10	25			.868	-6	S-74,O-28/3-9	-1.1
1894	StL-N	133	527	103	154	19	18	7	72	38	37	.292	.350	.436	89	-12	21			.912	-3	*O-122/S-7,3-7	-1.8
1895	Lou-N	113	473	61	125	14	13	4	70	31	25	.264	.315	.374	82	-13	14			.874	-17	*S-88,O-27	-2.3
1897	Phi-N	40	163	20	41	8	2	5	25	8	8	.252	.287	.417	87	-4	5			.872	-4	S-40	-0.7
1901	Chi-A	107	415	62	104	9	12	2	47	28		.251	.301	.345	81	-11	12			.885	-8	*S-107	-0.9
Total	8	745	3014	483	804	110	79	22	384	218	174	.267	.323	.378	90	-51	131			.883	-30	S-550,O-183/3-16,C	-5.0

■ **TERRY SHUMPERT** Shumpert, Terrance Darnell b: 8/16/66, Paducah, Ky. BR/TR, 5'11", 185 lbs. Deb: 5/1/90

YEAR	TM/L	G	AB	R	H	2B	3B	HR	RBI	BB	SO	AVG	OBP	SLG	PRO+	BR/A	SB	CS	SBR	FA	FR	G/POS	TPR
1990	KC-A	32	91	7	25	6	1	0	8	2	17	.275	.298	.363	85	-2	3	3	-1	.977	2	2-27/D-3	0.0
1991	KC-A	144	369	45	80	16	4	5	34	30	75	.217	.285	.322	67	-17	17	11	-2	.975	3	*2-144	-1.3
1992	KC-A	36	94	6	14	5	1	1	11	3	17	.149	.175	.255	19	-10	2	2	-1	.969	1	2-33/S-1,D-1	-1.0
1993	KC-A	8	10	0	1	0	0	0	0	2	2	.100	.250	.100	-2	-1	1	0	0	1.000	2	/2-8	0.1
1994	KC-A	64	183	28	44	6	2	8	24	13	39	.240	.291	.426	79	-7	18	3	4	.964	-8	2-38,3-24/S-1,D-2	-0.8
1995	Bos-A	21	47	6	11	3	0	0	3	4	13	.234	.294	.298	53	-3	3	1	0	1.000	3	/2-8,3-5,S-3,D-1	0.1
1996	Chi-N	27	31	5	7	1	0	2	6	2	11	.226	.294	.452	91	-1	0	1	-1	.923	-0	3-10/2-4,S-1	-0.1
1997	SD-N	13	33	4	9	3	0	1	6	3	4	.273	.333	.455	112	0	0	0	0	.973	-1	/2-7,O-3,3-2	0.0
1998	Col-N	23	26	3	6	1	0	1	2	2	8	.231	.286	.385	60	-2	0	0	0	1.000	2	/2-6	0.1
Total	9	368	884	104	197	41	8	18	94	61	186	.223	.278	.348	67	-42	44	21	1	.974	3	2-275/3-41,D-7,SO	-2.9

■ **VINCE SHUPE** Shupe, Vincent William b: 9/5/21, E.Canton, Ohio d: 4/5/62, Canton, Ohio BL/TL, 5'11", 180 lbs. Deb: 7/7/45

YEAR	TM/L	G	AB	R	H	2B	3B	HR	RBI	BB	SO	AVG	OBP	SLG	PRO+	BR/A	SB	CS	SBR	FA	FR	G/POS	TPR
1945	Bos-N	78	283	22	76	8	0	0	15	17	16	.269	.312	.297	69	-11	3			.989	1	1-77	-1.5

■ **ED SICKING** Sicking, Edward Joseph b: 3/30/1897, St.Bernard, Ohio d: 8/30/78, Madeira, Ohio BR/TR, 5'9.5", 165 lbs. Deb: 8/26/16

YEAR	TM/L	G	AB	R	H	2B	3B	HR	RBI	BB	SO	AVG	OBP	SLG	PRO+	BR/A	SB	CS	SBR	FA	FR	G/POS	TPR
1916	Chi-N	1	1	0	0	0	0	0	0	0	0	.000	.000	.000	-90	-0	0			.000	0	H	0.0
1918	NY-N	46	132	9	33	4	0	0	12	6	11	.250	.283	.280	73	-4	2			.917	-8	3-24,2-18/S-3	-1.3
1919	NY-N	6	15	2	5	0	0	0	3	1	0	.333	.412	.333	127	1	0			.971	3	/S-6	0.4
	Phi-N	61	185	16	40	2	1	0	15	8	17	.216	.253	.238	45	-12	4			.925	5	S-35,2-22	-0.5
	Yr	67	200	18	45	2	1	0	18	9	17	.225	.265	.245	51	-12	4			.933	8	S-41,2-22	-0.1
1920	NY-N	46	134	11	23	3	1	0	9	10	10	.172	.234	.209	28	-12	6	2	1	.915	4	3-28,2-15/S-3	-0.7
	Cin-N	37	123	12	33	3	0	0	17	13	5	.268	.338	.293	83	-2	2	3	-1	.955	1	2-25/S-9,3-2	-0.1
	Yr	83	257	23	56	6	1	0	26	23	15	.218	.285	.249	55	-14	8	5	-1	.952	4	2-40,3-30,S-12	-0.8
1927	Pit-N	6	7	1	1	1	0	0	3	1	0	.143	.250	.286	40	-1	0			1.000	2	/2-5	0.1
Total	5	203	597	51	135	13	2	0	59	39	43	.226	.277	.255	57	-31	14	5		.965	5	/2-85,S-56,3-54	-2.1

■ **JOE SIDDALL** Siddall, Joseph Todd b: 10/25/67, Windsor, Ont., Can. BL/TR, 6'1", 197 lbs. Deb: 7/28/93

YEAR	TM/L	G	AB	R	H	2B	3B	HR	RBI	BB	SO	AVG	OBP	SLG	PRO+	BR/A	SB	CS	SBR	FA	FR	G/POS	TPR
1993	Mon-N	19	20	0	2	1	0	0	1	1	5	.100	.143	.150	-21	-3	0	0	0	1.000	2	C-15/1-1,O-1	-0.1
1995	Mon-N	7	10	4	3	0	0	0	1	3	3	.300	.500	.300	113	1	0	0	0	.882	-3	/C-7	-0.2
1996	Fla-N	18	47	0	7	1	0	0	3	2	8	.149	.184	.170	-6	-7	0	0	0	.977	-1	C-18	-0.8
1998	Det-A	29	65	3	12	3	0	1	6	7	25	.185	.264	.277	41	-6	0	0	0	.994	8	C-27/O-1	0.3
Total	4	73	142	7	24	5	0	1	11	13	41	.169	.244	.225	24	-16	0	0	0	.983	6	/C-67,O-2,1-1	-0.8

■ **NORM SIEBERN** Siebern, Norman Leroy b: 7/26/33, St.Louis, Mo. BL/TR, 6'3", 205 lbs. Deb: 6/15/56

YEAR	TM/L	G	AB	R	H	2B	3B	HR	RBI	BB	SO	AVG	OBP	SLG	PRO+	BR/A	SB	CS	SBR	FA	FR	G/POS	TPR
1956	*NY-A	54	162	27	33	1	4	4	21	19	38	.204	.287	.333	66	-9	1	1	-0	.971	0	O-51	-1.1
1958	*NY-A	134	460	79	138	19	5	14	55	66	87	.300	.389	.454	136	24	5	8	-3	.982	5	*O-133	2.0
1959	NY-A	120	380	52	103	17	0	11	53	41	71	.271	.345	.403	108	4	3	1	0	.989	-2	O-93/1-2	-0.2
1960	KC-A	144	520	69	145	31	6	19	69	72	68	.279	.369	.471	125	18	0	0	0	.987	-1	O-75,1-69	0.9
1961	KC-A	153	560	68	166	36	5	18	98	82	91	.296	.387	.475	127	23	2	4	-2	.989	-1	*1-109,O-47	0.9
1962	KC-A★	162	600	114	185	25	6	25	117	110	88	.308	.416	.495	138	35	3	1	0	.994	5	*1-162	2.9
1963	KC-A☆	152	556	80	151	25	2	16	83	79	82	.272	.362	.410	110	9	1	4	-2	.991	4	*1-131,O-16	0.4
1964	Bal-A★	150	478	92	117	24	2	12	56	**106**	87	.245	.384	.379	114	13	2	3	-1	.995	4	*1-149	1.0
1965	Bal-A	106	297	44	76	13	4	8	32	50	49	.256	.365	.407	117	8	1	2	-1	.991	1	1-76	0.4
1966	Cal-A	125	336	29	83	14	1	5	41	63	61	.247	.366	.339	107	6	0	1	-1	.992	1	1-99	0.0
1967	SF-N	46	58	6	9	1	1	0	4	14	13	.155	.319	.207	54	-3	0	0	0	1.000	-0	1-15/O-2	-0.4
	*Bos-A	33	44	2	9	0	2	0	7	6	8	.205	.300	.295	71	-1	0	0	0	.981	1	1-13/O-1	-0.2
1968	Bos-A	27	30	0	2	0	0	0	0	0	5	.067	.067	.067	-56	-5	0	0	0	1.000	-1	/1-2,O-2	-0.7
Total	12	1406	4481	662	1217	206	38	132	636	708	748	.272	.372	.423	117	122	18	25	-10	.992	17	1-827,O-420	5.9

■ **DICK SIEBERT** Siebert, Richard Walther b: 2/19/12, Fall River, Mass. d: 12/9/78, Minneapolis, Minn. BL/TL, 6', 170 lbs. Deb: 9/7/32 F

YEAR	TM/L	G	AB	R	H	2B	3B	HR	RBI	BB	SO	AVG	OBP	SLG	PRO+	BR/A	SB	CS	SBR	FA	FR	G/POS	TPR
1932	Bro-N	6	7	1	2	0	0	0	0	2	2	.286	.444	.286	104	0	0			1.000	-0	/1-2	0.0
1936	Bro-N	2	2	0	0	0	0	0	0	0	0	.000	.000	.000	-99	-1	0			1.000	0	/O-1	0.0
1937	StL-N	22	38	3	7	2	0	0	2	4	8	.184	.279	.237	47	-3	1			.979	-1	/1-7	-0.4
1938	StL-N	1	1	0	1	0	0	0	0	0	0	1.000	1.000	1.000	427	0	0			.000	0	H	0.0
	Phi-A	48	194	24	55	8	3	0	28	10	8	.284	.329	.356	73	-8	2	3	-1	1.000	5	1-46	-0.9
1939	Phi-A	101	402	58	118	28	3	6	47	21	22	.294	.329	.423	93	-6	4	1	1	.991	5	1-99	-1.0
1940	Phi-A	154	595	69	170	31	6	5	77	33	34	.286	.325	.383	85	-14	8	6	-1	.985	8	*1-154	-2.1
1941	Phi-A	123	467	63	156	28	8	5	79	37	22	.334	.385	.460	126	17	1	3	-2	.990	6	*1-123	1.2
1942	Phi-A	153	612	57	159	25	7	2	74	24	17	.260	.291	.333	76	-21	4	5	-2	.989	-2	*1-152	-3.6
1943	Phi-A★	146	558	50	140	26	7	1	72	33	21	.251	.295	.328	83	-14	6	7	-2	.990	4	*1-145	-2.2
1944	Phi-A	132	468	52	143	27	5	6	52	62	17	.306	.387	.423	133	21	2	0	1	.993	-4	1-74,O-58	1.2

YEAR	TM/L	G	AB	R	H	2B	3B	HR	RBI	BB	SO	AVG	OBP	SLG	PRO+	BR/A	SB	CS	SBR	FA	FR	G/POS	TPR
1945	Phi-A	147	573	62	153	29	1	7	51	50	33	.267	.328	.358	99	-1	2	7	-4	.991	10	*1-147	-0.5
Total	11	1035	3917	439	1104	204	40	32	482	276	185	.282	.332	.379	96	-29	30	32		.990	31	1-949/O-59	-8.3

■ FRED SIEFKE

Siefke, Frederick Edwin b: 3/27/1870, New York, N.Y. d: 4/18/1893, New York, N.Y. 5'11", 168 lbs. Deb: 5/2/1890

YEAR	TM/L	G	AB	R	H	2B	3B	HR	RBI	BB	SO	AVG	OBP	SLG	PRO+	BR/A	SB	CS	SBR	FA	FR	G/POS	TPR
1890	Bro-a	16	58	1	8	2	0	0	3	5		.138	.206	.172	12	-6	2			.811	0	3-16	-0.5

■ JOHN SIEGEL

Siegel, John b: York, Pa. Deb: 6/9/1884

YEAR	TM/L	G	AB	R	H	2B	3B	HR	RBI	BB	SO	AVG	OBP	SLG	PRO+	BR/A	SB	CS	SBR	FA	FR	G/POS	TPR
1884	Phi-U	8	31	4	7	2	0	0		1		.226	.250	.290	68	-2				.533	-5	/3-8	-0.6

■ JOHNNY SIEGLE

Siegle, John Herbert b: 7/8/1874, Urbana, Ohio d: 2/12/68, Urbana, Ohio BR/TR, 5'10", 165 lbs. Deb: 9/15/05

YEAR	TM/L	G	AB	R	H	2B	3B	HR	RBI	BB	SO	AVG	OBP	SLG	PRO+	BR/A	SB	CS	SBR	FA	FR	G/POS	TPR
1905	Cin-N	17	56	9	17	1	2	1	8	7		.304	.391	.446	135	2	0			.960	-1	O-16	0.0
1906	Cin-N	22	68	4	8	2	2	0	7	3		.118	.178	.206	19	-7	0			.959	0	O-21	-0.8
Total	2	39	124	13	25	3	4	1	15	10		.202	.277	.315	75	-4	0			.959	-1	/O-37	-0.8

■ OSCAR SIEMER

Siemer, Oscar Sylvester "Cotton" b: 8/14/01, St.Louis, Mo. d: 12/5/59, St.Louis, Mo. BR/TR, 5'9", 162 lbs. Deb: 5/20/25

YEAR	TM/L	G	AB	R	H	2B	3B	HR	RBI	BB	SO	AVG	OBP	SLG	PRO+	BR/A	SB	CS	SBR	FA	FR	G/POS	TPR
1925	Bos-N	16	46	5	14	0	1	1	6	1	0	.304	.319	.413	94	-1	0	0	0	.900	-2	C-16	-0.2
1926	Bos-N	31	73	3	15	1	0	0	5	2	7	.205	.227	.219	22	-8	0			.920	-2	C-30	-0.9
Total	2	47	119	8	29	1	1	1	11	3	7	.244	.262	.294	51	-9	0	0		.913	-4	/C-46	-1.1

■ RUBEN SIERRA

Sierra, Ruben Angel (Garcia) b: 10/6/65, Rio Piedras, P.R. BB/TR, 6'1", 200 lbs. Deb: 6/1/86

YEAR	TM/L	G	AB	R	H	2B	3B	HR	RBI	BB	SO	AVG	OBP	SLG	PRO+	BR/A	SB	CS	SBR	FA	FR	G/POS	TPR
1986	Tex-A	113	382	50	101	13	10	16	55	22	65	.264	.306	.476	106	2	7	8	-3	.972	-10	*O-107/D-3	-1.4
1987	Tex-A	158	643	97	169	35	4	30	109	39	114	.263	.307	.470	102	-0	16	11	-2	.963	5	*O-157	-0.2
1988	Tex-A	156	615	77	156	32	2	23	91	44	91	.254	.305	.424	99	-2	18	4	3	.979	6	*O-153/D-1	0.2
1989	Tex-A★	162	634	101	194	35	**14**	29	**119**	43	82	.306	.352	**.543**	146	36	8	2	1	.973	6	*O-162	3.9
1990	Tex-A	159	608	70	170	37	2	16	96	49	86	.280	.334	.426	111	8	9	0	3	.967	0	*O-151/D-7	0.7
1991	Tex-A★	161	661	110	203	44	5	25	116	56	91	.307	.361	.502	139	33	16	4	2	.979	5	*O-161	3.6
1992	Tex-A★	124	500	66	139	30	6	14	70	31	59	.278	.320	.446	117	9	12	4	1	.970	0	*O-119/D-4	0.8
	*Oak-A	27	101	17	28	4	1	3	17	14	9	.277	.365	.426	128	4	2	0	1	1.000	1	O-25/D-2	0.5
	Yr	151	601	83	167	34	7	17	87	45	68	.278	.328	.443	119	13	14	4	2	.976	1	*O-144/D-6	1.3
1993	Oak-A	158	630	77	147	23	5	22	101	52	97	.233	.292	.390	87	-14	25	5	5	.977	7	*O-133,D-25	-0.7
1994	Oak-A★	110	426	71	114	21	1	23	92	23	64	.268	.305	.484	108	2	8	5	-1	.948	-4	O-98,D-10	-0.5
1995	Oak-A	70	264	40	70	17	0	12	42	24	42	.265	.326	.466	109	2	4	4	-1	.957	-5	O-62/D-7	-0.5
	*NY-A	56	215	33	56	15	0	7	44	22	34	.260	.329	.428	96	-2	1	0	0	.950	1	D-46,O-10	-0.4
	Yr	126	479	73	126	32	0	19	86	46	76	.263	.328	.449	103	1	5	4	-1	.956	-5	O-72,D-53	-0.9
1996	NY-A	96	360	39	93	17	1	11	52	40	58	.258	.333	.403	85	-9	1	3	-2	.984	2	D-61,O-33	-1.1
	Det-A	46	158	22	35	9	1	1	20	20	25	.222	.309	.310	57	-10	3	1	0	.914	1	O-23,D-20	-1.0
	Yr	142	518	61	128	26	2	12	72	60	83	.247	.325	.375	76	-19	4	4	-1	.950	4	D-81,O-56	-2.1
1997	Cin-N	25	90	6	22	5	1	2	7	6	21	.244	.292	.389	75	-3	0	0	0	1.000	1	O-24	-0.3
	Tor-A	14	48	4	10	0	2	1	5	3	13	.208	.255	.354	56	-3	0	0	0	.929	-1	/O-7,D-6	-0.4
1998	Chi-A	27	74	7	16	4	1	4	11	3	11	.216	.247	.459	80	-3	2	0	1	1.000	-1	O-14/D-5	-0.3
Total	13	1662	6409	887	1723	341	56	239	1047	491	962	.269	.322	.451	108	49	132	51	9	.971	14	*O-1439,D-197	2.9

■ ROY SIEVERS

Sievers, Roy Edward "Squirrel" b: 11/18/26, St.Louis, Mo. BR/TR, 6'1", 195 lbs. Deb: 4/21/49 C

YEAR	TM/L	G	AB	R	H	2B	3B	HR	RBI	BB	SO	AVG	OBP	SLG	PRO+	BR/A	SB	CS	SBR	FA	FR	G/POS	TPR
1949	StL-A	140	471	84	144	28	1	16	91	70	75	.306	.398	.471	124	16	1	5	-3	.973	6	*O-125/3-7	1.3
1950	StL-A	113	370	46	88	20	4	10	57	34	42	.238	.305	.395	75	-16	1	3	-2	.983	6	O-78,3-21	-1.4
1951	StL-A	31	89	10	20	2	1	1	11	9	21	.225	.303	.303	62	-5	0	0	0	.985	-2	O-25	-0.7
1952	StL-A	11	30	3	6	3	0	0	5	1	4	.200	.226	.300	44	-2	0	0	0	.968	-1	/1-7	-0.4
1953	StL-A	92	285	37	77	15	0	8	35	32	47	.270	.344	.407	100	-0	0	1	-1	.992	-6	1-76	-1.0
1954	Was-A	145	514	75	119	26	6	24	102	80	77	.232	.337	.446	120	12	2	1	0	.971	9	*O-133/1-8	1.5
1955	Was-A	144	509	74	138	20	8	25	106	73	66	.271	.367	.489	136	24	1	2	-1	.988	-1	*O-129,1-17/3-2	1.6
1956	Was-A★	152	550	92	139	27	2	29	95	100	88	.253	.373	.467	121	17	0	0	0	.987	2	O-78,1-76	1.0
1957	Was-A☆	152	572	99	172	23	5	**42**	**114**	76	55	.301	.389	.579	163	49	1	1	-0	.985	4	*O-130,1-21	4.4
1958	Was-A	148	550	85	162	18	1	39	108	53	63	.295	.361	.544	148	34	3	1	0	.991	5	*O-114,1-33	3.1
1959	Was-A★	115	385	55	93	19	0	21	49	53	62	.242	.336	.455	116	8	1	1	-0	.989	5	1-93,O-13	0.5
1960	Chi-A	127	444	87	131	22	0	28	93	74	69	.295	.399	.534	152	33	1	1	-0	.993	-7	*1-114/O-6	1.7
1961	Chi-A★	141	492	76	145	26	6	27	92	61	62	.295	.379	.537	144	30	1	0	0	.993	0	*1-132	1.9
1962	Phi-N	144	477	61	125	19	5	21	80	56	80	.262	.348	.455	117	11	2	1	0	.991	1	*1-130/O-7	0.4
1963	Phi-N	138	450	46	108	19	2	19	82	43	72	.240	.313	.418	110	5	0	2	-1	.989	-1	*1-126	-0.2
1964	Phi-N	49	120	7	22	3	1	4	16	13	20	.183	.269	.325	67	-5	0	0	0	.992	-1	1-33	-0.8
	Was-A	33	58	5	10	1	0	4	11	9	14	.172	.284	.397	87	-1	0	0	0	1.000	1	1-15	0.0
1965	Was-A	12	21	3	4	1	0	0	0	4	3	.190	.320	.238	62	-1	0	0	0	1.000	-1	/1-7	-0.2
Total	17	1887	6387	945	1703	292	42	318	1147	841	920	.267	.357	.475	124	210	14	19	-7	.991	19	1-888,O-838/3-30	12.7

■ FRANK SIFFELL

Siffell, Frank b: 1860, Germany d: 10/26/09, Philadelphia, Pa. Deb: 6/14/1884

YEAR	TM/L	G	AB	R	H	2B	3B	HR	RBI	BB	SO	AVG	OBP	SLG	PRO+	BR/A	SB	CS	SBR	FA	FR	G/POS	TPR
1884	Phi-a	7	17	3	3	1	0	0	3	0		.176	.222	.235	46	-1				.875	-3	/C-7	-0.3
1885	Phi-a	3	10	0	1	0	0	0	0	0		.100	.100	.100	-35	-2				.750	-3	/C-2,O-1	-0.4
Total	2	10	27	3	4	1	0	0	3	0		.148	.179	.185	16	-3				.841	-6	/C-9,O-1	-0.7

■ FRANK SIGAFOOS

Sigafoos, Francis Leonard b: 3/21/04, Easton, Pa. d: 4/12/68, Indianapolis, Ind. BR/TR, 5'9", 170 lbs. Deb: 9/3/26

YEAR	TM/L	G	AB	R	H	2B	3B	HR	RBI	BB	SO	AVG	OBP	SLG	PRO+	BR/A	SB	CS	SBR	FA	FR	G/POS	TPR
1926	Phi-A	13	43	4	11	0	0	0	2	0	3	.256	.256	.256	32	-4	0	0	0	.915	-3	S-12	-0.6
1929	Det-A	14	23	3	4	1	0	0	2	5	4	.174	.321	.217	41	-2	0	2	-1	.909	-2	/3-6,S-5	-0.4
	Chi-A	7	3	1	1	0	0	0	1	2	1	.333	.600	.333	148	1	0	0	0	1.000	1	/2-6	0.2
	Yr	21	26	4	5	1	0	0	3	7	5	.192	.364	.231	56	-1	0	2	-1	.909	-1	/3-6,2-6,S-5	-0.2
1931	Cin-N	21	65	6	11	2	0	0	8	0	6	.169	.182	.200	3	-9	0			.881	-3	3-15/S-2	-1.1
Total	3	55	134	14	27	3	0	0	13	7	14	.201	.246	.224	25	-15	0	2		.887	-7	/3-21,S-19,2-6	-1.9

■ PADDY SIGLIN

Siglin, Wesley Peter b: 9/24/1891, Aurelia, Iowa d: 8/5/56, Oakland, Cal. BR/TR, 5'10", 160 lbs. Deb: 9/12/14

YEAR	TM/L	G	AB	R	H	2B	3B	HR	RBI	BB	SO	AVG	OBP	SLG	PRO+	BR/A	SB	CS	SBR	FA	FR	G/POS	TPR
1914	Pit-N	14	39	4	6	0	0	0	2	4	6	.154	.233	.154	16	-4	1			.911	-6	2-11	-1.1
1915	Pit-N	6	7	1	2	0	0	0	0	1	2	.286	.375	.286	103	0	1			.800	-0	/2-1	0.0
1916	Pit-N	3	4	0	1	0	0	0	0	0	2	.250	.250	.250	53	-0	0			.857	0	/2-3	0.0
Total	3	23	50	5	9	0	0	0	2	5	10	.180	.255	.180	32	-4	2			.895	-5	/2-15	-1.1

■ TRIPP SIGMAN

Sigman, Wesley Triplett b: 1/17/1899, Mooresville, N.C. d: 3/8/71, Augusta, Ga. BL/TR, 6', 180 lbs. Deb: 9/18/29

YEAR	TM/L	G	AB	R	H	2B	3B	HR	RBI	BB	SO	AVG	OBP	SLG	PRO+	BR/A	SB	CS	SBR	FA	FR	G/POS	TPR
1929	Phi-N	10	29	8	15	1	0	2	9	3	1	.517	.563	.759	210	5	0			.944	-2	O-10	0.2
1930	Phi-N	52	100	15	27	4	1	4	6	6	9	.270	.324	.450	79	-4	1			.932	-1	O-19	-0.6
Total	2	62	129	23	42	5	1	6	15	9	10	.326	.379	.519	108	1	1			.935	-3	/O-29	-0.4

■ EDDIE SILBER

Silber, Edward James b: 6/6/14, Philadelphia, Pa. d: 10/26/76, Dunedin, Fla. BR/TR, 5'11", 170 lbs. Deb: 9/3/37

YEAR	TM/L	G	AB	R	H	2B	3B	HR	RBI	BB	SO	AVG	OBP	SLG	PRO+	BR/A	SB	CS	SBR	FA	FR	G/POS	TPR
1937	StL-A	22	83	10	26	2	0	0	4	5	13	.313	.352	.337	74	-3	0	2	-1	.871	-7	O-21	-1.1
1939	StL-A	1	1	0	0	0	0	0	0	0	1	.000	.000	.000	-98	-0	0	0	0	.000	0	H	0.0
Total	2	23	84	10	26	2	0	0	4	5	14	.310	.348	.333	72	-3	0	2	-1	.871	-7	/O-21	-1.1

■ ED SILCH

Silch, Edward "Baldy" b: 2/22/1865, St.Louis, Mo. d: 1/15/1895, St.Louis, Mo. TR , 6'2", 180 lbs. Deb: 4/29/1888

YEAR	TM/L	G	AB	R	H	2B	3B	HR	RBI	BB	SO	AVG	OBP	SLG	PRO+	BR/A	SB	CS	SBR	FA	FR	G/POS	TPR
1888	Bro-a	14	48	5	13	4	0	0	3	4		.271	.327	.354	118	1	4			.870	-2	O-14	-0.1

■ DANNY SILVA

Silva, Daniel James b: 10/5/1896, Everett, Mass. d: 4/4/74, Hyannis, Mass. BR/TR, 6', 170 lbs. Deb: 8/11/19

YEAR	TM/L	G	AB	R	H	2B	3B	HR	RBI	BB	SO	AVG	OBP	SLG	PRO+	BR/A	SB	CS	SBR	FA	FR	G/POS	TPR
1919	Was-A	1	4	0	1	0	0	0	0	0	0	.250	.250	.250	41	-0	0			1.000	1	/3-1	0.0

■ AL SILVERA

Silvera, Aaron Albert b: 8/26/35, San Diego, Cal. BR/TR, 6', 180 lbs. Deb: 6/12/55

YEAR	TM/L	G	AB	R	H	2B	3B	HR	RBI	BB	SO	AVG	OBP	SLG	PRO+	BR/A	SB	CS	SBR	FA	FR	G/POS	TPR
1955	Cin-N	13	7	3	1	0	0	0	2	0	1	.143	.143	.143	-23	-1	0	0	0	.000	-0	/O-1	-0.2
1956	Cin-N	1	0	0	0	0	0	0	0	0	0	—	—	—	—	0	0	0	0	.000	0	R	0.0
Total	2	14	7	3	1	0	0	0	2	0	1	.143	.143	.143	-23	-1	0	0	0	—	-0	/O-1	-0.2

■ CHARLIE SILVERA Silvera, Charles Anthony Ryan "Swede" b: 10/13/24, San Francisco, Cal BR/TR, 5'10", 175 lbs. Deb: 9/29/48 C

YEAR	TM/L	G	AB	R	H	2B	3B	HR	RBI	BB	SO	AVG	OBP	SLG	PRO+	BR/A	SB	CS	SBR	FA	FR	G/POS	TPR
1948	NY-A	4	14	1	8	0	1	0	1	0	1	.571	.571	.714	243	3	0	0	0	1.000	0	/C-4	0.3
1949	*NY-A	58	130	8	41	2	0	0	13	18	5	.315	.403	.331	95	0	2	1	0	.985	4	C-51	0.6
1950	NY-A	18	25	2	4	0	0	0	1	1	2	.160	.192	.160	-9	-4	0	0	0	.959	3	C-15	-0.1
1951	NY-A	18	51	5	14	3	0	1	7	5	3	.275	.339	.392	101	-0	0	0	0	1.000	0	C-18	0.1
1952	NY-A	20	55	4	18	3	0	0	11	5	2	.327	.383	.382	121	2	0	3	-2	1.000	-3	C-20	-0.2
1953	NY-A	42	82	11	23	3	1	0	12	9	5	.280	.352	.341	91	-1	0	1	-1	.992	6	C-39/3-1	0.6
1954	NY-A	20	37	1	10	1	0	0	4	3	2	.270	.341	.297	79	-1	0	1	-1	.962	5	C-18	0.4
1955	NY-A	14	26	1	5	0	0	0	1	6	4	.192	.344	.192	48	-2	0	0	0	1.000	3	C-11	0.2
1956	NY-A	7	9	0	2	0	0	0	0	2	3	.222	.364	.222	60	-0	0	0	0	.909	-1	/C-7	-0.1
1957	Chi-N	26	53	1	11	3	0	0	2	4	5	.208	.263	.264	43	-4	0	0	0	.982	3	C-26	-0.1
Total	10	227	482	34	136	15	2	1	52	53	32	.282	.356	.328	86	-8	2	6	-3	.985	21	C-209/3-1	1.7

■ LUIS SILVERIO Silverio, Luis Pascual (Delmonte) b: 10/23/56, Villa Gonzalez, D.R. BR/TR, 5'11", 165 lbs. Deb: 9/9/78

YEAR	TM/L	G	AB	R	H	2B	3B	HR	RBI	BB	SO	AVG	OBP	SLG	PRO+	BR/A	SB	CS	SBR	FA	FR	G/POS	TPR
1978	KC-A	8	11	7	6	2	1	0	3	2	3	.545	.615	.909	315	3	1	1	-0	.833	-2	/O-6,D-2	0.1

■ TOM SILVERIO Silverio, Tomas Roberto (Veloz) b: 10/14/45, Santiago, D.R. BL/TL, 5'10", 170 lbs. Deb: 4/30/70

YEAR	TM/L	G	AB	R	H	2B	3B	HR	RBI	BB	SO	AVG	OBP	SLG	PRO+	BR/A	SB	CS	SBR	FA	FR	G/POS	TPR
1970	Cal-A	15	15	1	0	0	0	0	0	2	4	.000	.118	.000	-67	-3	0	1	-1	1.000	-2	/O-5,1-1	-0.7
1971	Cal-A	3	3	0	1	0	0	0	0	0	0	.333	.333	.333	96	-0	0	0	0	.000	-1	/O-1	-0.1
1972	Cal-A	13	12	1	2	0	0	0	0	0	5	.167	.167	.167	-1	-1	0	0	0	1.000	-1	/O-4	-0.3
Total	3	31	30	2	3	0	0	0	0	2	9	.100	.156	.100	-27	-5	0	1	-1	1.000	-4	/O-10,1-1	-1.1

■ DAVE SILVESTRI Silvestri, David Joseph b: 9/29/67, St.Louis, Mo. BR/TR, 6', 196 lbs. Deb: 4/27/92

YEAR	TM/L	G	AB	R	H	2B	3B	HR	RBI	BB	SO	AVG	OBP	SLG	PRO+	BR/A	SB	CS	SBR	FA	FR	G/POS	TPR
1992	NY-A	7	13	3	4	0	2	0	1	0	3	.308	.308	.615	154	1	0	0	0	.889	1	/S-6	0.2
1993	NY-A	7	21	4	6	1	0	1	4	5	3	.286	.423	.476	146	2	0	0	0	.955	2	/S-4,3-3	0.3
1994	NY-A	12	18	3	2	0	1	1	2	4	9	.111	.273	.389	71	-1	0	1	-1	1.000	1	/2-9,3-2,S-1	-0.1
1995	NY-A	17	21	4	2	0	0	1	4	4	9	.095	.269	.238	34	-2	0	0	0	1.000	2	/2-7,1-4,S-1,D-4	0.0
	Mon-N	39	72	12	19	6	0	2	7	9	27	.264	.346	.431	100	-0	2	0	1	1.000	-3	/S-9,3-8,1-4,2-3,O	-0.2
1996	Mon-N	86	162	16	33	4	0	1	17	34	41	.204	.342	.247	57	-9	2	1	0	.913	-2	3-47,S-10/O-2,12	-1.1
1997	Tex-A	2	4	0	0	0	0	0	0	0	1	.000	.000	.000	-95	-1	0	0	0	.000	-1	/3-1,S-1	-0.2
1998	TB-A	8	14	0	1	0	0	0	0	0	2	.071	.071	.071	-60	-3	0	0	0	1.000	1	/3-3,2-2,S-1,D-2	-0.2
Total	7	178	325	42	67	11	3	6	35	56	95	.206	.325	.314	68	-14	4	2	0	.912	-0	/3-64,S-33,21DO	-1.3

■ KEN SILVESTRI Silvestri, Kenneth Joseph "Hawk" b: 5/3/16, Chicago, Ill. d: 3/31/92, Tallahassee, Fla. BB/TR, 6'1", 200 lbs. Deb: 4/18/39 MC

YEAR	TM/L	G	AB	R	H	2B	3B	HR	RBI	BB	SO	AVG	OBP	SLG	PRO+	BR/A	SB	CS	SBR	FA	FR	G/POS	TPR
1939	Chi-A	22	75	6	13	3	0	2	5	6	13	.173	.244	.293	36	-8	0	1	-1	.947	-0	C-20	-0.7
1940	Chi-A	28	24	5	6	2	0	2	10	4	7	.250	.357	.583	138	1	0	0	0	1.000	-0	/C-1	0.1
1941	NY-A	17	40	6	10	5	0	1	4	7	6	.250	.362	.450	115	1	0	0	0	1.000	0	C-13	0.2
1946	NY-A	13	21	4	6	1	0	0	1	3	7	.286	.375	.333	98	0	0	0	0	.977	2	C-12	0.3
1947	NY-A	3	10	0	2	0	0	0	0	2	2	.200	.333	.200	51	-1	0	0	0	1.000	-2	/C-3	-0.2
1949	Phi-N	4	4	1	0	0	0	0	0	2	1	.000	.333	.000	-3	-0	0			1.000	0	/C-1,2-1,S-1	0.0
1950	*Phi-N	11	20	2	5	0	1	0	4	4	3	.250	.400	.350	101	0	0			1.000	-1	/C-9	-0.1
1951	Phi-N	4	9	2	2	0	0	0	1	3	2	.222	.417	.222	78	-0	0	0	0	1.000	-3	/C-3,2-1	-0.3
Total	8	102	203	26	44	11	1	5	25	31	41	.217	.326	.355	78	-6	0	1		.974	-3	/C-62,2-2,S-1	-0.7

■ AL SIMMONS Simmons, Aloysius Harry "Bucketfoot Al" (b: Aloys Szymanski)
b: 5/22/02, Milwaukee, Wis. d: 5/26/56, Milwaukee, Wis. BR/TR, 5'11", 190 lbs. Deb: 4/15/24 CH

YEAR	TM/L	G	AB	R	H	2B	3B	HR	RBI	BB	SO	AVG	OBP	SLG	PRO+	BR/A	SB	CS	SBR	FA	FR	G/POS	TPR
1924	Phi-A	152	594	69	183	31	9	8	102	30	60	.308	.343	.431	98	-4	16	15	-4	.976	7	*O-152	-1.1
1925	Phi-A	153	654	122	**253**	43	12	24	129	35	41	.387	.419	.599	146	42	7	14	-6	.966	5	*O-153	2.8
1926	Phi-A	147	583	90	199	53	10	19	109	48	49	.341	.392	.564	139	31	11	3	2	.975	-4	*O-147	1.7
1927	Phi-A	106	406	86	159	36	11	15	108	31	30	.392	.436	.645	168	39	10	2	2	.985	3	*O-105	3.4
1928	Phi-A	119	464	78	163	33	9	15	107	31	30	.351	.396	.558	144	28	1	4	-2	.988	2	*O-114	1.9
1929	*Phi-A	143	581	114	212	41	9	34	**157**	31	38	.365	.398	.642	158	46	4	2	0	.989	17	*O-142	4.9
1930	*Phi-A	138	554	**152**	211	41	16	36	165	39	34	**.381**	.423	.708	173	58	9	2	2	**.990**	6	*O-136	4.9
1931	*Phi-A	128	513	105	200	37	13	22	128	47	45	**.390**	.444	.641	172	52	3	3	-1	.987	8	*O-128	4.6
1932	Phi-A	154	670	144	**216**	28	9	35	151	47	76	.322	.368	.548	129	26	4	2	0	.980	-5	*O-154	1.0
1933	Chi-A★	146	605	85	200	29	10	14	119	39	49	.331	.373	.481	130	24	5	1	1	.990	14	*O-145	3.0
1934	Chi-A★	138	558	102	192	36	7	18	104	53	58	.344	.403	.530	135	28	3	2	-0	.987	5	*O-138	2.5
1935	Chi-A★	128	525	68	140	22	7	16	79	33	43	.267	.313	.427	87	-12	4	6	-2	.981	1	*O-126	-1.8
1936	Det-A	143	568	96	186	38	6	13	112	49	35	.327	.383	.484	112	10	6	4	-1	**.986**	-4	*O-138/1-1	0.0
1937	Was-A	103	419	60	117	21	10	8	84	27	35	.279	.329	.434	95	-5	3	2	-0	.984	5	*O-102	-0.4
1938	Was-A	125	470	79	142	23	6	21	95	38	40	.302	.357	.511	123	14	2	1	0	.983	-8	*O-117	0.2
1939	Bos-N	93	330	39	93	17	5	7	43	22	40	.282	.331	.427	110	3	0			.982	-0	O-82	0.0
	*Cin-N	9	21	0	3	0	0	0	1	2	3	.143	.217	.143	-1	-3	0			.938	1	/O-5	-0.2
	Yr	102	351	39	96	17	5	7	44	24	43	.274	.324	.410	103	-0	0			.978	1	O-87	-0.2
1940	Phi-A	37	81	7	25	4	0	1	19	4	8	.309	.341	.395	92	-1	0	0	0	.963	2	O-18	0.0
1941	Phi-A	9	24	1	3	1	0	0	1	1	2	.125	.160	.167	-14	-4	0	0	0	1.000	1	/O-5	-0.4
1943	Bos-A	40	133	9	27	5	0	1	12	8	21	.203	.248	.263	49	-9	0	1	-1	.986	-2	O-33	-1.4
1944	Phi-A	4	6	1	3	0	0	0	2	0	0	.500	.500	.500	189	1	0	0	0	1.000	-0	/O-2	0.0
Total	20	2215	8759	1507	2927	539	149	307	1827	615	737	.334	.380	.535	132	361	88	64		.982	53	*O-2142/1-1	25.6

■ BRIAN SIMMONS Simmons, Brian Lee b: 9/4/73, Lebanon, Pa. BB/TR, 6'2", 185 lbs. Deb: 9/21/98

YEAR	TM/L	G	AB	R	H	2B	3B	HR	RBI	BB	SO	AVG	OBP	SLG	PRO+	BR/A	SB	CS	SBR	FA	FR	G/POS	TPR
1998	Chi-A	5	19	4	7	0	0	2	6	0	2	.368	.368	.684	170	2	0	1	-1	1.000	-0	/O-5	0.1

■ HACK SIMMONS Simmons, George Washington b: 1/29/1885, Brooklyn, N.Y. d: 4/26/42, Arverne, N.Y. BR/TR, 5'8", 179 lbs. Deb: 4/15/10

YEAR	TM/L	G	AB	R	H	2B	3B	HR	RBI	BB	SO	AVG	OBP	SLG	PRO+	BR/A	SB	CS	SBR	FA	FR	G/POS	TPR
1910	Det-A	42	110	12	25	3	1	0	9	10		.227	.303	.273	75	-3	1			.984	-0	1-22/3-7,O-2	-0.3
1912	NY-A	110	401	45	96	17	2	0	41	33		.239	.308	.292	68	-17	19			.946	-21	2-88,1-13/S-4	-4.0
1914	Bal-F	114	352	50	95	16	5	1	38	32	26	.270	.341	.352	86	-11	7			.894	-8	O-73,2-26/1-4,S3	-2.4
1915	Bal-F	39	88	8	18	7	1	1	14	10	9	.205	.293	.341	76	-4	1			1.000	-3	2-13,O-13	-0.9
Total	4	305	951	115	234	43	9	2	102	85	35	.246	.318	.317	76	-36	28			.953	-32	2-127/O-88,1-39,3S	-7.6

■ JOHN SIMMONS Simmons, John Earl b: 7/7/24, Birmingham, Ala. BR/TR, 6'1.5", 192 lbs. Deb: 4/22/49

YEAR	TM/L	G	AB	R	H	2B	3B	HR	RBI	BB	SO	AVG	OBP	SLG	PRO+	BR/A	SB	CS	SBR	FA	FR	G/POS	TPR
1949	Was-A	62	93	12	20	0	0	0	5	11	6	.215	.298	.215	38	-8	0	0	0	1.000	-5	O-26	-1.4

■ JOE SIMMONS Simmons, Joseph S. b: 6/13/1845, New York, N.Y. 5'9", 166 lbs. Deb: 5/8/1871 M

YEAR	TM/L	G	AB	R	H	2B	3B	HR	RBI	BB	SO	AVG	OBP	SLG	PRO+	BR/A	SB	CS	SBR	FA	FR	G/POS	TPR
1871	Chi-n	27	129	29	28	6	1	0	17	1	0	.217	.223	.279	39	-12	4	1	1	.894	-1	*O-25/1-2	-0.7
1872	Cle-n	18	90	11	23	5	1	0	9	1	2	.256	.264	.333	87	-1	1	0	0	.938	0	1-15/O-3	0.0
1875	Wes-n	13	53	5	9	1	0	0	4	0	2	.170	.170	.189	23	-4	1	2	-1	.733	-1	O-10/1-3,M	-0.5
Total	3 n	58	272	45	60	12	2	0	30	2	4	.221	.226	.279	51	-17	6	3	0	.855	-1	/O-38,1-20	-1.2

■ NELSON SIMMONS Simmons, Nelson Bernard b: 6/27/63, Washington, D.C. BB/TR, 6'1", 185 lbs. Deb: 9/4/84

YEAR	TM/L	G	AB	R	H	2B	3B	HR	RBI	BB	SO	AVG	OBP	SLG	PRO+	BR/A	SB	CS	SBR	FA	FR	G/POS	TPR
1984	Det-A	9	30	4	13	2	0	0	3	2	5	.433	.469	.500	169	3	1	0	0	1.000	-1	/O-5,D-4	0.2
1985	Det-A	75	251	31	60	11	0	10	33	26	41	.239	.310	.402	94	-2	1	0	0	.945	-1	O-38,D-31	-0.5
1987	Bal-A	16	49	3	13	1	1	1	4	3	8	.265	.308	.388	85	-1	0	1	-1	1.000	1	O-13/D-1	-0.1
Total	3	100	330	38	86	14	1	11	40	31	54	.261	.324	.409	99	-1	2	1	0	.963	-1	/O-56,D-36	-0.4

■ TED SIMMONS Simmons, Ted Lyle b: 8/9/49, Highland Park, Mich. BB/TR, 6', 200 lbs. Deb: 9/21/68

YEAR	TM/L	G	AB	R	H	2B	3B	HR	RBI	BB	SO	AVG	OBP	SLG	PRO+	BR/A	SB	CS	SBR	FA	FR	G/POS	TPR
1968	StL-N	2	3	0	1	0	0	0	0	1	1	.333	.500	.333	156	0	0	0	0	1.000	-1	/C-2	0.0
1969	StL-N	5	14	0	3	0	1	0	3	1	1	.214	.267	.357	73	-1	0	0	0	.957	-1	/C-4	-0.2
1970	StL-N	82	284	29	69	8	2	3	24	37	37	.243	.334	.317	74	-10	2	2	-1	.990	-3	C-79	-0.9
1971	StL-N	133	510	64	155	32	4	7	77	36	50	.304	.353	.424	115	10	1	3	-2	.989	-13	*C-130	0.0
1972	StL-N☆	152	594	70	180	36	6	16	96	29	57	.303	.338	.465	127	19	1	3	-2	.991	6	*C-135,1-15	3.0
1973	StL-N★	161	619	62	192	36	2	13	91	61	47	.310	.374	.438	124	21	2	2	-1	.987	10	*C-153/1-6,O-2	3.7

YEAR	TM/L	G	AB	R	H	2B	3B	HR	RBI	BB	SO	AVG	OBP	SLG	PRO+	BR/A	SB	CS	SBR	FA	FR	G/POS	TPR
1974	StL-N☆	152	599	66	163	33	6	20	103	47	35	.272	.331	.447	117	11	0	0	0	.986	-4	*C-141,1-12	1.3
1975	StL-N	157	581	80	193	32	3	18	100	63	35	.332	.398	.491	141	32	1	3	-2	.983	-6	*C-154/1-2,O-2	3.2
1976	StL-N	150	546	60	159	35	3	5	75	73	35	.291	.375	.394	117	14	0	7	-4	.993	-9	*C-113,1-30/O-7,3-2	0.2
1977	StL-N★	150	516	82	164	25	3	21	95	79	37	.318	.410	.500	145	35	2	6	-3	.987	-14	*C-143/O-1	2.2
1978	StL-N★	152	516	71	148	40	5	22	80	77	39	.287	.383	.512	150	35	1	1	-0	.988	-6	*C-134,O-23	3.3
1979	StL-N†	123	448	68	127	22	0	26	87	61	34	.283	.374	.507	137	23	0	1	-1	.985	-5	*C-122	2.2
1980	StL-N	145	495	84	150	33	2	21	98	59	45	.303	.379	.505	140	27	1	0	0	.985	-9	*C-129/O-5	2.4
1981	*Mil-A★	100	380	45	82	13	3	14	61	23	32	.216	.266	.376	88	-8	0	1	-1	.980	-9	C-75,D-22/1-4	-1.6
1982	*Mil-A	137	539	73	145	29	0	23	97	32	40	.269	.312	.451	114	8	0	0	0	**.995**	-1	*C-121,D-15	1.1
1983	Mil-A★	153	600	76	185	39	3	13	108	41	51	.308	.355	.448	129	22	4	2	0	.975	-4	C-86,D-66	2.0
1984	Mil-A	132	497	44	110	23	2	4	52	30	40	.221	.270	.300	60	-28	3	0	1	.995	-1	D-77,1-37,3-14	-3.3
1985	Mil-A	143	528	60	144	28	2	12	76	57	32	.273	.345	.402	104	4	1	1	-0	.992	-3	D-99,1-28,C-15,/3-2	-0.3
1986	Atl-N	76	127	14	32	5	0	4	25	12	14	.252	.321	.386	89	-2	1	0	0	.964	-3	1-14,C-10/3-9	-0.5
1987	Atl-N	73	177	20	49	8	0	4	30	21	23	.277	.354	.390	92	-2	1	1	-0	.984	-1	1-28,C-15/3-2	-0.4
1988	Atl-N	78	107	6	21	6	0	2	11	15	9	.196	.295	.308	70	-4	0	0	0	.993	-1	1-19,C-10	-0.6
Total	21	2456	8680	1074	2472	483	47	248	1389	855	694	.285	.352	.437	118	208	21	33	-14	.987	-79	*C-1771,D-279,1/O3	16.8

■ MIKE SIMMS

Simms, Michael Howard b: 1/12/67, Orange, Cal. BR/TR, 6'4", 185 lbs. Deb: 9/5/90

YEAR	TM/L	G	AB	R	H	2B	3B	HR	RBI	BB	SO	AVG	OBP	SLG	PRO+	BR/A	SB	CS	SBR	FA	FR	G/POS	TPR
1990	Hou-N	12	13	3	4	1	0	1	2	0	4	.308	.308	.615	152	1	0	0	0	1.000	-0	/1-6	0.1
1991	Hou-N	49	123	18	25	5	0	3	16	18	38	.203	.305	.317	80	-3	1	0	0	.889	-5	O-41	-0.9
1992	Hou-N	15	24	1	6	1	0	1	3	2	9	.250	.333	.417	116	0	0	0	0	1.000	-1	/O-9,1-1	-0.1
1994	Hou-N	6	12	1	1	1	0	0	0	0	5	.083	.083	.167	-39	-2	1	0	0	.857	-0	/O-3	-0.2
1995	Hou-N	50	121	14	31	4	0	9	24	13	28	.256	.343	.512	131	5	1	2	-1	.995	-1	1-25,O-12	0.1
1996	Hou-N	49	68	6	12	2	1	1	8	4	16	.176	.233	.279	37	-6	1	0	0	1.000	-1	O-12/1-5	-0.7
1997	Tex-A	59	111	13	28	8	0	5	22	8	27	.252	.303	.459	90	-2	0	1	-1	.958	-4	D-28,O-19/1-2	-0.8
1998	*Tex-A	86	186	36	55	11	0	16	46	24	47	.296	.385	.613	148	13	0	1	-1	1.000	-8	O-43,D-26,1-16	0.1
Total	8	326	658	92	162	33	1	36	121	69	174	.246	.325	.464	108	5	4	4	-1	.954	-20	O-139/1-55,D-54	-2.4

■ HANK SIMON

Simon, Henry Joseph b: 8/25/1862, Hawkinsville, N.Y. d: 1/1/25, Albany, N.Y. BR/TR, Deb: 10/7/1887

YEAR	TM/L	G	AB	R	H	2B	3B	HR	RBI	BB	SO	AVG	OBP	SLG	PRO+	BR/A	SB	CS	SBR	FA	FR	G/POS	TPR
1887	Cle-a	3	10	1	1	0	0	0	0	0		.100	.100	.100	-45	-2	0			1.000	-1	/O-3	-0.2
1890	Bro-a	89	373	66	96	17	11	0	38	34		.257	.323	.362	105	2	23			.951	6	O-89	0.4
	Syr-a	38	156	33	47	5	3	2	23	17		.301	.370	.410	145	9	12			.941	-3	O-38	0.4
	Yr	127	529	99	143	22	14	2	61	51		.270	.337	.376	116	10	35			.948	3	*O-127	0.8
Total	2	130	539	100	144	22	14	2	61	51		.267	.333	.371	113	9	35			.949	3	O-130	0.6

■ MIKE SIMON

Simon, Michael Edward b: 4/13/1883, Hayden, Ind. d: 6/10/63, Los Angeles, Cal. BR/TR, 5'11", 188 lbs. Deb: 6/27/09

YEAR	TM/L	G	AB	R	H	2B	3B	HR	RBI	BB	SO	AVG	OBP	SLG	PRO+	BR/A	SB	CS	SBR	FA	FR	G/POS	TPR
1909	Pit-N	12	18	2	3	0	0	0	2	1		.167	.211	.167	16	-2	0			.917	0	/C-9	-0.1
1910	Pit-N	22	50	3	10	0	1	0	5	1	2	.200	.216	.240	31	-4	1			1.000	-4	C-14	-0.8
1911	Pit-N	71	215	19	49	4	3	0	22	10	14	.228	.275	.274	52	-14	1			.968	0	C-68	-0.8
1912	Pit-N	42	113	10	34	2	1	0	11	5	9	.301	.331	.336	84	-3	1			.991	3	C-40	0.4
1913	Pit-N	92	255	23	63	6	2	1	17	10	15	.247	.281	.298	68	-11	3			.975	19	C-92	1.5
1914	StL-F	93	276	21	57	11	2	0	21	18	21	.207	.263	.261	41	-27	2			.984	12	C-78	-0.9
1915	Bro-F	47	142	7	25	5	1	0	12	9	12	.176	.225	.225	27	-16	1			.992	-0	C-45	-1.4
Total	7	379	1069	85	241	28	10	1	90	54	73	.225	.269	.273	51	-77	9			.979	30	C-346	-2.1

■ RANDALL SIMON

Simon, Randall Carlito b: 5/26/75, Willemstad, Curacao BL/TL, 6', 180 lbs. Deb: 9/1/97

YEAR	TM/L	G	AB	R	H	2B	3B	HR	RBI	BB	SO	AVG	OBP	SLG	PRO+	BR/A	SB	CS	SBR	FA	FR	G/POS	TPR
1997	Atl-N	13	14	2	6	1	0	0	1	1	2	.429	.467	.500	151	1	0	0	0	1.000	0	/1-6	0.1
1998	Atl-N	7	16	2	3	0	0	0	4	0	1	.188	.188	.188	-2	-2	0	0	0	1.000	-0	/1-4	-0.3
Total	2	20	30	4	9	1	0	0	5	1	3	.300	.323	.333	70	-1	0	0	0	1.000	-0	/1-10	-0.2

■ SYL SIMON

Simon, Sylvester Adam "Sammy" b: 12/14/1897, Evansville, Ind. d: 2/28/73, Chandler, Ind. BR/TR, 5'10.5", 170 lbs. Deb: 10/1/23

YEAR	TM/L	G	AB	R	H	2B	3B	HR	RBI	BB	SO	AVG	OBP	SLG	PRO+	BR/A	SB	CS	SBR	FA	FR	G/POS	TPR
1923	StL-A	1	1	0	0	0	0	0	0	0	0	.000	.000	.000	-95	-0	0	0	0	.000	0	H	0.0
1924	StL-A	23	32	5	8	1	1	0	6	3	5	.250	.314	.344	66	-2	0	0	0	.889	-0	/3-6,S-5	-0.1
Total	2	24	33	5	8	1	1	0	6	3	5	.242	.306	.333	61	-2	0	0	0	.889	-0	/3-6,S-5	-0.1

■ MEL SIMONS

Simons, Melbern Ellis "Butch" b: 7/1/1900, Carlyle, Ill. d: 11/10/74, Paducah, Ky. BL/TR, 5'10", 175 lbs. Deb: 4/14/31

YEAR	TM/L	G	AB	R	H	2B	3B	HR	RBI	BB	SO	AVG	OBP	SLG	PRO+	BR/A	SB	CS	SBR	FA	FR	G/POS	TPR
1931	Chi-A	68	189	24	52	9	0	0	12	12	17	.275	.318	.323	73	-7	1	1	-0	.950	-9	O-59	-1.8
1932	Chi-A	7	5	0	0	0	0	0	0	0	1	.000	.000	.000	-99	-2	0	0	0	1.000	-3	/O-6	-0.4
Total	2	75	194	24	52	9	0	0	12	12	18	.268	.311	.314	69	-9	1	1	-0	.951	-12	/O-65	-2.2

■ HARRY SIMPSON

Simpson, Harry Leon "Suitcase" or "Goody" b: 12/3/25, Atlanta, Ga. d: 4/3/79, Akron, Ohio BL/TR, 6'1", 180 lbs. Deb: 4/21/51

YEAR	TM/L	G	AB	R	H	2B	3B	HR	RBI	BB	SO	AVG	OBP	SLG	PRO+	BR/A	SB	CS	SBR	FA	FR	G/POS	TPR
1951	Cle-A	122	332	51	76	7	0	7	24	45	48	.229	.325	.313	77	-10	6	4	-1	.971	-4	O-68,1-50	-1.8
1952	Cle-A	146	545	66	145	21	10	10	65	56	82	.266	.337	.396	111	6	5	3	-0	.988	-4	*O-127,1-28	-0.4
1953	Cle-A	82	242	25	55	3	1	7	22	18	27	.227	.284	.335	68	-11	0	0	0	.968	-6	O-69/1-2	-2.0
1955	Cle-A	3	1	1	0	0	0	0	0	2	0	.000	.667	.000	88	0	0	0	0	.000	0	H	0.0
	KC-A	112	396	42	119	16	7	5	52	34	61	.301	.359	.414	106	3	3	5	-2	.978	1	*O-100/1-3	-0.2
	Yr	115	397	43	119	16	7	5	52	36	61	.300	.361	.413	106	3	3	5	-2	.978	1	*O-100/1-3	-0.2
1956	KC-A★	141	543	76	159	22	**11**	21	105	47	82	.293	.350	.490	119	13	2	3	-1	.965	-15	*O-111,1-32	-1.1
1957	KC-A	50	179	24	53	9	6	6	24	12	28	.296	.340	.514	128	6	0	1	-1	.996	1	1-27,O-21	0.3
	*NY-A	75	224	27	56	7	3	7	39	19	36	.250	.309	.402	94	-2	1	0	0	.952	-2	O-42,1-21	-0.8
	Yr	125	403	51	109	16	**9**	13	63	31	64	.270	.323	.452	110	4	1	1	-0	.957	-2	O-63,1-48	-0.5
1958	NY-A	24	51	1	11	2	1	0	6	6	12	.216	.310	.294	70	-2	0	0	0	1.000	-3	O-15	-0.5
	KC-A	78	212	21	56	7	1	7	27	26	33	.264	.345	.406	104	1	0	2	-1	.990	-3	1-43,O-11	-0.6
	Yr	102	263	22	67	9	2	7	33	32	45	.255	.338	.384	98	-0	0	2	-1	.990	-5	1-43,O-26	-1.1
1959	KC-A	8	14	1	4	0	0	1	2	2	4	.286	.412	.500	146	1	0	0	0	1.000	0	/1-4	0.1
	Chi-A	38	75	5	14	5	1	2	13	4	14	.187	.228	.360	59	-5	0	0	0	.947	-2	O-12/1-1	-0.7
	Yr	46	89	6	18	5	1	3	15	6	18	.202	.260	.382	75	-3	0	0	0	.947	-2	O-12/1-5	-0.6
	Pit-N	9	15	3	4	2	0	0	2	0	2	.267	.267	.400	75	-1	0	0	0	1.000	-0	/O-3	-0.1
Total	8	888	2829	343	752	101	41	73	381	271	429	.266	.332	.408	102	-1	17	18	-6	.974	-37	O-579,1-211	-7.8

■ JOE SIMPSON

Simpson, Joe Allen b: 12/31/51, Purcell, Okla. BL/TL, 6'3", 175 lbs. Deb: 9/2/75

YEAR	TM/L	G	AB	R	H	2B	3B	HR	RBI	BB	SO	AVG	OBP	SLG	PRO+	BR/A	SB	CS	SBR	FA	FR	G/POS	TPR
1975	LA-N	9	6	3	2	0	0	0	0	0	2	.333	.333	.333	89	-0	0	0	0	1.000	-2	/O-6	-0.2
1976	LA-N	23	30	2	4	1	0	0	0	1	6	.133	.161	.167	-7	-4	0	1	-1	1.000	-4	O-20	-1.0
1977	LA-N	29	23	2	4	0	0	0	1	2	6	.174	.240	.174	13	-3	1	1	-0	.957	-6	O-28/1-1	-1.0
1978	LA-N	10	5	1	2	0	0	0	1	0	2	.400	.400	.400	125	0	0	0	0	1.000	-3	O-10	-0.3
1979	Sea-A	120	265	29	75	11	0	2	27	11	21	.283	.314	.347	77	-9	6	3	0	.966	-5	*O-105/D-3	-1.6
1980	Sea-A	129	365	42	91	15	3	3	34	28	43	.249	.306	.332	74	13	17	4	3	.977	-8	*O-119/1-3	-2.3
1981	Sea-A	91	288	32	64	11	3	2	30	15	41	.222	.263	.302	60	-15	12	3	2	.978	-0	O-88	-1.7
1982	Sea-A	105	296	39	76	14	4	2	23	22	48	.257	.313	.351	80	-8	8	14	-6	.984	-7	O-97	-2.3
1983	KC-A	91	119	16	20	2	2	0	8	11	21	.168	.250	.218	30	-11	1	1	-0	.995	-0	1-54,O-38/P-2,D-1	-1.3
Total	9	607	1397	166	338	54	12	9	124	90	190	.242	.291	.317	67	-63	45	27	-3	.978	-35	O-511/1-58,D-4,P-2	-11.7

■ MARTY SIMPSON

Simpson, Martin b: Baltimore, Md. Deb: 5/14/1873

YEAR	TM/L	G	AB	R	H	2B	3B	HR	RBI	BB	SO	AVG	OBP	SLG	PRO+	BR/A	SB	CS	SBR	FA	FR	G/POS	TPR
1873	Mar-n	4	15	4	2	0	0	0	2	0	0	.133	.133	.133	-27	-2	0	0	0	.792	0	/2-3,C-1	-0.1

■ DICK SIMPSON

Simpson, Richard Charles b: 7/28/43, Washington, D.C. BR/TR, 6'4", 176 lbs. Deb: 9/21/62

YEAR	TM/L	G	AB	R	H	2B	3B	HR	RBI	BB	SO	AVG	OBP	SLG	PRO+	BR/A	SB	CS	SBR	FA	FR	G/POS	TPR
1962	LA-A	6	8	1	2	1	0	0	1	2	3	.250	.400	.375	114	0	0	0	0	1.000	-1	/O-4	0.0
1964	LA-A	21	50	11	7	1	0	2	4	8	15	.140	.259	.280	55	-3	2	2	-1	1.000	-2	O-16	-0.7
1965	Cal-A	8	27	2	6	1	0	0	3	2	8	.222	.276	.259	54	-2	1	0	0	.875	-1	/O-8	-0.3
1966	Cin-N	92	84	26	20	2	0	4	14	10	32	.238	.333	.405	96	-0	0	1	-1	.921	-18	O-64	-2.1
1967	Cin-N	44	54	8	14	3	0	1	6	7	11	.259	.344	.370	94	-0	0	1	-1	.973	-2	O-26	-0.3
1968	StL-N	26	56	11	13	0	0	3	8	8	21	.232	.328	.393	117	1	0	1	-1	1.000	-3	O-22	-0.4

YEAR	TM/L	G	AB	R	H	2B	3B	HR	RBI	BB	SO	AVG	OBP	SLG	PRO+	BR/A	SB	CS	SBR	FA	FR	G/POS	TPR
	Hou-N	59	177	25	33	7	2	3	11	20	61	.186	.284	.299	77	-5	4	4	-1	.970	-6	O-49	-1.7
	Yr	85	233	36	46	7	2	6	19	28	82	.197	.294	.322	86	-4	4	5	-2	.979	-9	O-71	-2.1
1969	NY-A	6	11	2	3	2	0	0	4	3	6	.273	.429	.455	153	1	0	0	0	1.000	-1	/O-5	0.0
	Sea-A	26	51	8	9	2	0	2	5	4	17	.176	.236	.333	59	-3	3	1	0	1.000	-3	O-17	-0.7
	Yr	32	62	10	12	4	0	2	9	7	23	.194	.275	.355	77	-2	3	1	0	1.000	-4	O-22	-0.7
Total	7	288	518	94	107	19	2	15	56	64	174	.207	.301	.338	84	-11	10	10	-3	.967	-35	O-211	-6.2

■ DUKE SIMS

Sims, Duane B b: 6/5/41, Salt Lake City, Ut. BL/TR, 6'2", 205 lbs. Deb: 9/22/64

YEAR	TM/L	G	AB	R	H	2B	3B	HR	RBI	BB	SO	AVG	OBP	SLG	PRO+	BR/A	SB	CS	SBR	FA	FR	G/POS	TPR
1964	Cle-A	2	6	0	0	0	0	0	0	0	2	.000	.000	.000	-99	-2	0	0	0	1.000	1	/C-1	-0.1
1965	Cle-A	48	118	9	21	0	0	6	15	15	33	.178	.271	.331	69	-5	0	0	0	.980	-2	C-40	-0.5
1966	Cle-A	52	133	12	35	2	2	6	19	11	31	.263	.338	.444	122	4	0	1	-1	.975	-5	C-48	0.1
1967	Cle-A	88	272	25	55	8	2	12	37	30	64	.202	.295	.379	97	-1	3	3	-1	.989	-3	C-85	0.0
1968	Cle-A	122	361	48	90	21	0	11	44	62	68	.249	.367	.399	134	17	1	3	-2	.983	-1	C-84,1-31/O-4	2.0
1969	Cle-A	114	326	40	77	8	0	18	45	66	80	.236	.374	.426	120	10	1	2	-1	.991	-4	*C-102/O-3,1-1	1.2
1970	Cle-A	110	345	46	91	12	0	23	56	46	59	.264	.360	.499	128	13	0	4	-2	.993	-2	C-39,O-36,1-29	0.8
1971	LA-N	90	230	23	63	7	2	6	25	30	39	.274	.360	.400	122	7	0	1	-1	.992	0	C-74	1.0
1972	LA-N	51	151	7	29	7	0	2	11	17	23	.192	.278	.278	60	-8	0	0	0	.989	-1	C-48	-0.8
	*Det-A	38	98	11	31	4	0	4	19	19	18	.316	.432	.480	166	9	0	0	0	.994	-3	C-25/O-4	0.8
1973	Det-A	80	252	31	61	10	0	8	30	30	36	.242	.327	.377	92	-3	1	2	-1	.979	2	C-68/O-6	0.1
	NY-A	4	9	3	3	0	0	1	1	3	1	.333	.500	.667	234	2	0	0	0	1.000	1	/C-1,D-2	0.2
	Yr	84	261	34	64	10	0	9	31	33	37	.245	.334	.387	97	-1	1	2	-1	.979	2	C-69/O-6,D-2	0.3
1974	NY-A	5	15	1	2	1	0	0	2	1	5	.133	.188	.200	12	-2	0	0	0	1.000	-0	/C-1,D-3	-0.2
	Tex-A	39	106	7	22	0	0	3	6	8	24	.208	.282	.292	67	-4	0	0	0	.970	-3	C-30/O-1,D-2	-0.7
	Yr	44	121	8	24	1	0	3	8	9	29	.198	.271	.281	60	-6	0	0	0	.971	-3	C-31/D-5,O-1	-0.9
Total	11	843	2422	263	580	80	6	100	310	338	483	.239	.341	.401	111	38	6	16	-8	.986	-20	C-646/1-61,O-54,D-7	3.9

■ GREG SIMS

Sims, Gregory Emmett b: 6/28/46, San Francisco, Cal BB/TR, 6', 190 lbs. Deb: 4/15/66

YEAR	TM/L	G	AB	R	H	2B	3B	HR	RBI	BB	SO	AVG	OBP	SLG	PRO+	BR/A	SB	CS	SBR	FA	FR	G/POS	TPR
1966	Hou-N	7	6	1	1	0	0	0	0	1	3	.167	.286	.167	32	-1	0	0	0	.500	-0	/O-1	-0.1

■ MATT SINATRO

Sinatro, Matthew Stephen b: 3/22/60, Hartford, Conn. BR/TR, 5'9", 175 lbs. Deb: 9/22/81

YEAR	TM/L	G	AB	R	H	2B	3B	HR	RBI	BB	SO	AVG	OBP	SLG	PRO+	BR/A	SB	CS	SBR	FA	FR	G/POS	TPR
1981	Atl-N	12	32	4	9	1	1	0	4	5	4	.281	.378	.375	111	1	1	0	0	1.000	4	C-12	0.6
1982	Atl-N	37	81	10	11	2	0	1	4	4	9	.136	.176	.198	4	-10	0	1	-1	1.000	4	C-35	-0.7
1983	Atl-N	7	12	0	2	0	0	0	2	2	1	.167	.286	.167	26	-1	0	0	0	.967	2	/C-7	0.0
1984	Atl-N	2	4	0	0	0	0	0	0	0	0	.000	.000	.000	-93	-1	0	0	0	1.000	-0	/C-2	-0.2
1987	Oak-A	6	3	0	0	0	0	0	0	0	1	.000	.000	.000	-99	-1	0	0	0	1.000	-0	/C-6	-0.1
1988	Oak-A	10	9	1	3	2	0	0	5	0	1	.333	.333	.556	149	1	0	0	0	1.000	2	/C-9	0.3
1989	Det-A	13	25	2	3	0	0	0	1	1	3	.120	.185	.120	-13	-4	0	0	0	1.000	0	C-13	-0.3
1990	Sea-A	30	50	2	15	1	0	0	4	4	10	.300	.352	.320	88	-1	1	0	0	.992	7	C-28	0.7
1991	Sea-A	5	8	1	2	0	0	0	1	1	1	.250	.333	.250	64	-0	0	0	0	1.000	1	/C-5	0.1
1992	Sea-A	18	28	0	3	0	0	0	0	0	5	.107	.107	.107	-40	-5	0	0	0	1.000	0	C-18	-0.5
Total	10	140	252	20	48	6	1	1	21	17	35	.190	.244	.234	34	-22	2	1	0	.996	19	C-135	-0.1

■ HOSEA SINER

Siner, Hosea John b: 3/20/1885, Shelburn, Ind. d: 6/10/48, Sullivan, Ind. BR/TR, 5'10.5", 185 lbs. Deb: 7/28/09

YEAR	TM/L	G	AB	R	H	2B	3B	HR	RBI	BB	SO	AVG	OBP	SLG	PRO+	BR/A	SB	CS	SBR	FA	FR	G/POS	TPR
1909	Bos-N	10	23	1	3	0	0	0	1	2		.130	.200	.130	3	-3	0			.909	-1	/3-5,2-1,S-1	-0.4

■ DUANE SINGLETON

Singleton, Duane Earl b: 8/6/72, Staten Island, N.Y. BL/TR, 6'1", 170 lbs. Deb: 8/4/94

YEAR	TM/L	G	AB	R	H	2B	3B	HR	RBI	BB	SO	AVG	OBP	SLG	PRO+	BR/A	SB	CS	SBR	FA	FR	G/POS	TPR
1994	Mil-A	2	0	0	0	0	0	0	0	0	0	—	—	—	—	0	0	0	0	1.000	-1	/O-2	-0.1
1995	Mil-A	13	31	0	2	0	0	0	0	1	10	.065	.094	.065	-55	-7	1	0	0	1.000	-1	O-11	-0.7
1996	Det-A	18	56	5	9	1	0	0	3	4	15	.161	.230	.179	5	-8	0	2	-1	1.000	0	O-15	-0.9
Total	3	33	87	5	11	1	0	0	3	5	25	.126	.183	.138	-16	-15	1	2	-1	1.000	-2	/O-28	-1.7

■ KEN SINGLETON

Singleton, Kenneth Wayne b: 6/10/47, New York, N.Y. BB/TR, 6'4", 213 lbs. Deb: 6/24/70

YEAR	TM/L	G	AB	R	H	2B	3B	HR	RBI	BB	SO	AVG	OBP	SLG	PRO+	BR/A	SB	CS	SBR	FA	FR	G/POS	TPR
1970	NY-N	69	198	22	52	8	0	5	26	30	48	.263	.362	.379	99	0	1	1	-0	.968	-0	O-51	-0.3
1971	NY-N	115	298	34	73	5	0	13	46	61	64	.245	.377	.393	120	10	0	1	-1	.974	-5	O-96	0.0
1972	Mon-N	142	507	77	139	23	2	14	50	70	99	.274	.364	.410	118	13	5	10	-5	.972	-0	*O-137	0.2
1973	Mon-N	162	560	100	169	26	2	23	103	123	91	.302	**.429**	.479	146	41	2	8	-4	.983	3	*O-161	3.3
1974	Mon-N	148	511	68	141	20	2	9	74	93	84	.276	.387	.376	108	9	5	2	0	.955	-9	*O-143	-0.6
1975	Bal-A	155	586	88	176	37	4	15	55	118	82	.300	.418	.454	156	49	3	5	-2	.990	-6	*O-155	3.5
1976	Bal-A	154	544	62	151	25	2	13	70	79	76	.278	.369	.403	134	25	2	2	-1	.983	-3	*O-134,D-19	1.6
1977	Bal-A★	152	536	90	176	24	0	24	99	107	101	.328	.442	.507	168	57	0	1	-1	.986	1	*O-150/D-1	4.9
1978	Bal-A	149	502	67	147	21	2	20	81	98	94	.293	.410	.462	**154**	40	0	0	0	.976	-13	*O-140/D-5	2.2
1979	*Bal-A★	159	570	93	168	29	1	35	111	109	118	.295	.409	.533	158	49	3	1	0	.981	-6	*O-143,D-16	3.6
1980	Bal-A	156	583	85	177	28	3	24	104	92	94	.304	.399	.485	143	37	0	2	-1	.984	-10	*O-151/D-5	1.9
1981	Bal-A★	103	363	48	101	16	1	13	49	61	59	.278	.382	.435	135	18	0	0	0	**1.000**	-3	O-72,D-30	1.2
1982	Bal-A	156	561	71	141	27	2	14	77	86	93	.251	.353	.381	102	4	0	1	-1	1.000	-0	*D-148/O-5	-0.3
1983	*Bal-A	151	507	52	140	21	3	18	84	99	83	.276	.395	.436	131	25	0	2	-1	.000	0	*D-150	1.9
1984	Bal-A	111	363	28	78	7	1	6	36	37	60	.215	.287	.289	61	-19	0	0	0	.000	0	*D-103	-2.2
Total	15	2082	7189	985	2029	317	25	246	1065	1263	1246	.282	.391	.436	132	359	21	36	-15	.980	-52	*O-1538,D-477	20.9

■ FRED SINGTON

Sington, Frederic William b: 2/24/10, Birmingham, Ala. BR/TR, 6'2", 215 lbs. Deb: 9/23/34

YEAR	TM/L	G	AB	R	H	2B	3B	HR	RBI	BB	SO	AVG	OBP	SLG	PRO+	BR/A	SB	CS	SBR	FA	FR	G/POS	TPR
1934	Was-A	9	35	2	10	2	0	0	6	4	3	.286	.359	.343	85	-1	0	1	-1	.933	-1	/O-9	-0.2
1935	Was-A	20	22	1	4	0	0	0	3	5	1	.182	.333	.182	38	-2	0	0	0	.889	0	/O-4	-0.2
1936	Was-A	25	94	13	30	8	0	1	28	15	9	.319	.413	.436	116	3	0	0	0	.946	-1	O-25	0.1
1937	Was-A	78	228	27	54	15	4	3	36	37	33	.237	.348	.377	87	-4	1	1	-0	.961	-3	O-64	-0.9
1938	Bro-N	17	53	10	19	6	1	2	5	13	5	.358	.493	.623	200	8	1			1.000	-2	O-17	0.6
1939	Bro-N	32	84	13	23	5	0	1	7	15	15	.274	.384	.369	100	1	0			.978	-1	O-22	-0.1
Total	6	181	516	66	140	36	5	7	85	89	66	.271	.382	.401	104	5	2	2		.961	-7	O-141	-0.7

■ DICK SIPEK

Sipek, Richard Francis b: 1/16/23, Chicago, Ill. BL/TR, 5'9", 170 lbs. Deb: 4/28/45

YEAR	TM/L	G	AB	R	H	2B	3B	HR	RBI	BB	SO	AVG	OBP	SLG	PRO+	BR/A	SB	CS	SBR	FA	FR	G/POS	TPR
1945	Cin-N	82	156	14	38	6	2	0	13	9	15	.244	.302	.308	71	-6	0			.972	-0	O-31	-0.8

■ JOHN SIPIN

Sipin, John White b: 8/29/46, Watsonville, Cal. BR/TR, 6'1.5", 175 lbs. Deb: 5/24/69

YEAR	TM/L	G	AB	R	H	2B	3B	HR	RBI	BB	SO	AVG	OBP	SLG	PRO+	BR/A	SB	CS	SBR	FA	FR	G/POS	TPR
1969	SD-N	68	229	22	51	12	2	2	9	8	44	.223	.252	.319	61	-13	2	0	1	.976	-2	2-60	-1.0

■ GEORGE SISLER

Sisler, George Harold "Georgeous George"
b: 3/24/1893, Manchester, Ohio d: 3/26/73, Richmond Heights, Mo. BL/TL, 5'11", 170 lbs. Deb: 6/28/15 FMCH

YEAR	TM/L	G	AB	R	H	2B	3B	HR	RBI	BB	SO	AVG	OBP	SLG	PRO+	BR/A	SB	CS	SBR	FA	FR	G/POS	TPR
1915	StL-A	81	274	28	78	10	2	3	29	7	27	.285	.307	.369	106	0	10	9	-2	.989	-3	1-36,O-29,P-15	-0.8
1916	StL-A	151	580	83	177	21	11	4	76	40	37	.305	.355	.400	133	21	34	26	-5	.985	-2	*1-141/P-3,O-3,3-2	0.8
1917	StL-A	135	539	60	190	30	9	2	52	30	19	.353	.390	.453	163	38	37			.985	4	*1-133/2-2	4.0
1918	StL-A	114	452	69	154	21	9	2	41	40	17	.341	.400	.440	159	31	**45**			.990	9	*1-114/P-2	3.8
1919	StL-A	132	511	96	180	31	15	10	83	27	20	.352	.390	.530	153	33	28			.991	13	*1-131	4.3
1920	StL-A	154	631	137	**257**	49	18	19	122	46	19	**.407**	.449	.632	179	68	42	17	**2**	.990	15	*1-154/P-1	7.8
1921	StL-A	138	582	125	216	38	**18**	12	104	34	27	.371	.411	.560	137	31	**35**	11	**4**	.993	8	*1-138	3.6
1922	StL-A	142	586	**134**	**246**	42	**18**	8	105	49	14	**.420**	.467	.594	169	**59**	**51**	19	**4**	.988	12	*1-141	**6.6**
1924	StL-A	151	636	94	194	27	10	9	74	31	29	.305	.340	.421	90	-12	19	17	-5	.984	1	*1-151,M	-2.3
1925	StL-A	150	649	100	224	21	15	12	105	27	24	.345	.371	.479	109	6	11	12	-4	.983	11	*1-150/P-1,M	0.4
1926	StL-A	150	613	78	178	21	12	7	71	30	30	.290	.327	.398	84	-16	12	8	-1	.987	-4	*1-149/P-1,M	-3.0
1927	StL-A	149	614	87	201	32	8	5	97	24	15	.327	.357	.430	100	-1	**27**	7	**4**	.984	11	*1-149	0.3
1928	Was-A	20	49	1	12	1	0	0	2	1	2	.245	.260	.265	39	-4	0	1	-1	1.000	-2	/1-5,O-5	-0.8
	Bos-N	118	491	71	167	26	4	4	68	30	15	.340	.380	.434	119	13	11			.988	7	*1-118/P-1	0.9
1929	Bos-N	154	629	67	205	40	8	2	79	33	17	.326	.363	.424	98	-2	6			.982	3	*1-154	-1.3

YEAR	TM/L	G	AB	R	H	2B	3B	HR	RBI	BB	SO	AVG	OBP	SLG	PRO+	BR/A	SB	CS	SBR	FA	FR	G/POS	TPR
1930	Bos-N	116	431	54	133	15	7	3	67	23	15	.309	.346	.397	82	-12	7			.987	5	*1-107	-1.6
Total	15	2055	8267	1284	2812	425	164	102	1175	472	327	.340	.379	.468	124	254	375	127		.987	88	*1-1971/O-37,P23	22.7

■ DICK SISLER Sisler, Richard Allan b: 11/2/20, St.Louis, Mo. d: 11/21/98, Nashville, Tenn. BL/TR, 6'2", 205 lbs. Deb: 4/16/46 FMC

YEAR	TM/L	G	AB	R	H	2B	3B	HR	RBI	BB	SO	AVG	OBP	SLG	PRO+	BR/A	SB	CS	SBR	FA	FR	G/POS	TPR
1946	*StL-N	83	235	17	61	11	2	3	42	14	28	.260	.307	.362	86	-5	0			.988	-2	1-37,O-29	-1.1
1947	StL-N	46	74	4	15	2	1	0	9	3	8	.203	.234	.257	29	-8	0			.976	-0	1-10/O-5	-0.8
1948	Phi-N	121	446	60	122	21	3	11	56	47	46	.274	.344	.408	105	3	1			.983	-4	*1-120	-0.2
1949	Phi-N	121	412	42	119	19	6	7	50	25	38	.289	.333	.415	102	0	0			.987	-9	1-96	-0.9
1950	*Phi-N★	141	523	79	155	29	4	13	83	64	50	.296	.373	.442	115	12	1			.987	2	*O-137	0.8
1951	Phi-N	125	428	46	123	20	5	8	52	40	39	.287	.351	.414	107	4	1	0	0	.968	0	*O-111	0.1
1952	Cin-N	11	27	3	5	1	1	0	4	3	5	.185	.267	.296	56	-2	0	0	0	1.000	-1	/O-7	-0.3
	StL-N	119	418	48	109	14	5	13	60	29	35	.261	.312	.411	99	-2	3	3	-1	.985	2	*1-114	-0.5
	Yr	130	445	51	114	15	6	13	64	32	40	.256	.309	.404	96	-3	3	3	-1	.985	1	*1-114/O-7	-0.8
1953	StL-N	32	43	3	11	1	1	0	4	1	4	.256	.273	.326	55	-3	0	0	0	1.000	1	1-10	-0.2
Total	8	799	2606	302	720	118	28	55	360	226	253	.276	.336	.406	101	-0	6	3		.985	-10	1-387,O-289	-3.1

■ SIBBY SISTI Sisti, Sebastian Daniel b: 7/26/20, Buffalo, N.Y. BR/TR, 5'11", 175 lbs. Deb: 7/21/39 C

YEAR	TM/L	G	AB	R	H	2B	3B	HR	RBI	BB	SO	AVG	OBP	SLG	PRO+	BR/A	SB	CS	SBR	FA	FR	G/POS	TPR
1939	Bos-N	63	215	19	49	7	1	1	11	12	38	.228	.269	.284	52	-15	4			.994	0	2-34,3-17,S-10	-1.2
1940	Bos-N	123	459	73	115	19	5	6	34	36	64	.251	.311	.353	87	-9	4			.936	-2	*3-102,2-16	-0.8
1941	Bos-N	140	541	72	140	24	3	1	45	38	76	.259	.309	.320	81	-15	7			.916	-8	*3-137/2-2,S-2	-2.0
1942	Bos-N	129	407	50	86	11	4	4	35	45	55	.211	.296	.287	73	-14	5			.970	-4	*2-124/O-1	-1.1
1946	Bos-N	1	0	0	0	0	0	0	0	0	0	—	—	—	—	0	0			.000	0	/3-1	0.0
1947	Bos-N	56	153	22	43	8	0	2	15	20	17	.281	.371	.373	100	1	2			.947	-9	S-51/2-1	-0.6
1948	*Bos-N	83	221	30	54	6	2	0	21	31	34	.244	.340	.290	73	-7	0			.972	-5	2-44,S-26	-0.9
1949	Bos-N	101	268	39	69	12	0	5	22	34	42	.257	.343	.358	93	-2	1			.989	-13	O-48,2-21,S-18,/3-1	-1.5
1950	Bos-N	69	105	21	18	3	1	2	11	16	19	.171	.287	.276	52	-7	1			.931	0	S-23,2-19,3-13,/1O	-0.6
1951	Bos-N	114	362	46	101	20	2	2	38	32	50	.279	.341	.362	96	-2	4	5	-2	.944	-23	S-55,2-52/3-6,1O	-2.2
1952	Bos-N	90	245	19	52	10	1	4	24	14	43	.212	.255	.310	58	-15	2	0	1	.966	-12	2-33,O-23,S-18,/3-9	-2.5
1953	Mil-N	38	23	8	5	1	0	0	4	5	2	.217	.357	.261	69	-1	0	0	0	1.000	4	2-13/S-6,3-4	0.3
1954	Mil-N	9	0	2	0	0	0	0	0	0	0	—	—	—	—	0	0	0	0	.000	0	R	0.0
Total	13	1016	2999	401	732	121	19	27	260	283	440	.244	.313	.324	79	-85	30	5		.973	-72	2-359,3-290,S/O1	-13.1

■ ED SIXSMITH Sixsmith, Edward b: 2/26/1863, Philadelphia, Pa. d: 12/12/26, Philadelphia, Pa. BR/TR, Deb: 9/11/1884

YEAR	TM/L	G	AB	R	H	2B	3B	HR	RBI	BB	SO	AVG	OBP	SLG	PRO+	BR/A	SB	CS	SBR	FA	FR	G/POS	TPR
1884	Phi-N	1	2	0	0	0	0	0	0	0	0	.000	.000	.000	-99	-0				1.000	-1	/C-1	-0.1

■ TED SIZEMORE Sizemore, Theodore Crawford b: 4/15/45, Gadsden, Ala. BR/TR, 5'10", 165 lbs. Deb: 4/7/69

YEAR	TM/L	G	AB	R	H	2B	3B	HR	RBI	BB	SO	AVG	OBP	SLG	PRO+	BR/A	SB	CS	SBR	FA	FR	G/POS	TPR
1969	LA-N	159	590	69	160	20	5	4	46	45	40	.271	.328	.342	95	-5	5	5	-2	.979	-6	*2-118,S-46/O-1	0.3
1970	LA-N	96	340	40	104	10	1	1	34	34	19	.306	.369	.350	98	0	5	1	1	.984	-7	2-86/O-9,S-2	0.1
1971	StL-N	135	478	53	126	14	5	3	42	42	26	.264	.324	.333	83	-10	4	6	-2	.976	-3	2-93,S-39,O-15,/3-1	-0.4
1972	StL-N	120	439	53	116	17	4	2	38	37	36	.264	.327	.335	90	-6	8	3	1	.976	0	*2-111	0.2
1973	StL-N	142	521	69	147	22	1	1	54	68	34	.282	.367	.334	96	-0	6	4	-1	.981	9	*2-139/3-3	1.8
1974	StL-N	129	504	68	126	17	0	2	47	70	37	.250	.341	.296	80	-11	8	4	0	.980	13	*2-128/S-1,O-1	0.9
1975	StL-N	153	562	56	135	23	1	3	49	45	37	.240	.299	.301	64	-27	1	5	-3	.972	-25	*2-153	-4.9
1976	LA-N	84	266	18	64	8	1	0	18	15	22	.241	.281	.278	60	-14	2	3	-1	.986	2	2-71/3-3,C-2	-1.0
1977	*Phi-N	152	519	64	146	20	3	4	47	52	40	.281	.348	.355	85	-9	8	11	-4	.986	9	*2-152	0.6
1978	*Phi-N	108	351	38	77	12	0	0	25	25	29	.219	.273	.254	48	-24	8	1	2	.978	4	*2-107	-1.1
1979	Chi-N	98	330	36	82	17	0	2	24	32	25	.248	.321	.318	68	-14	3	3	-1	.973	15	2-96	0.8
	Bos-A	26	88	12	23	7	0	1	6	4	5	.261	.301	.375	77	-3	1	0	0	.993	9	2-26/C-2	0.7
1980	Bos-A	9	23	1	5	1	0	0	0	0	0	.217	.217	.261	29	-2	0	0	0	.927	3	/2-8	0.2
Total	12	1411	5011	577	1311	188	21	23	430	469	350	.262	.327	.321	80	-125	59	46	-10	.979	25	*2-1288/S-88,O3C	-1.8

■ FRANK SKAFF Skaff, Francis Michael b: 9/30/13, LaCrosse, Wis. d: 4/12/88, Towson, Md. BR/TR, 5'10", 185 lbs. Deb: 9/11/35 MC

YEAR	TM/L	G	AB	R	H	2B	3B	HR	RBI	BB	SO	AVG	OBP	SLG	PRO+	BR/A	SB	CS	SBR	FA	FR	G/POS	TPR
1935	Bro-N	6	11	4	6	1	1	0	3	0	2	.545	.545	.818	267	2	0			.857	-0	/3-3	0.2
1943	Phi-A	32	64	8	18	2	1	1	8	6	11	.281	.343	.391	115	1	0	0	0	.976	1	1-18/3-3,S-1	0.2
Total	2	38	75	12	24	3	2	1	11	6	13	.320	.370	.453	138	4	0	0		.900	1	/1-18,3-6,S-1	0.4

■ DAVE SKAGGS Skaggs, David Lindsey b: 6/12/51, Santa Monica, Cal. BR/TR, 6'2", 200 lbs. Deb: 4/17/77

YEAR	TM/L	G	AB	R	H	2B	3B	HR	RBI	BB	SO	AVG	OBP	SLG	PRO+	BR/A	SB	CS	SBR	FA	FR	G/POS	TPR
1977	Bal-A	80	216	22	62	9	1	1	24	20	34	.287	.347	.352	97	-0	0	0	0	.995	-1	C-80	0.1
1978	Bal-A	36	86	6	13	1	1	0	2	9	14	.151	.232	.186	20	-9	0	1	-1	.988	5	C-35	-0.5
1979	*Bal-A	63	137	9	34	8	0	1	14	13	14	.248	.313	.328	76	-4	0	0	0	.984	2	C-63	0.0
1980	Bal-A	2	5	0	1	0	0	0	0	0	1	.200	.200	.200	10	-1	0	0	0	1.000	1	/C-2	0.0
	Cal-A	24	66	7	13	0	0	1	9	9	13	.197	.293	.242	50	-4	0	0	0	.968	-10	C-24	-1.4
	Yr	26	71	7	14	0	0	1	9	9	14	.197	.287	.239	47	-5	0	0	0	.971	-9	C-26	-1.4
Total	4	205	510	44	123	18	2	3	49	51	76	.241	.310	.302	72	-19	0	1	-1	.988	-3	C-204	-1.8

■ BUD SKETCHLEY Sketchley, Harry Clement b: 3/30/19, Virden, Man., Can. d: 12/19/79, Los Angeles, Cal. BL/TL, 5'10", 180 lbs. Deb: 4/14/42

YEAR	TM/L	G	AB	R	H	2B	3B	HR	RBI	BB	SO	AVG	OBP	SLG	PRO+	BR/A	SB	CS	SBR	FA	FR	G/POS	TPR
1942	Chi-A	13	36	1	7	1	0	0	3	7	4	.194	.326	.222	57	-2	0	1	-1	.952	-1	O-12	-0.4

■ ROE SKIDMORE Skidmore, Robert Roe b: 10/30/45, Decatur, Ill. BR/TR, 6'3", 188 lbs. Deb: 9/17/70

YEAR	TM/L	G	AB	R	H	2B	3B	HR	RBI	BB	SO	AVG	OBP	SLG	PRO+	BR/A	SB	CS	SBR	FA	FR	G/POS	TPR
1970	Chi-N	1	1	0	1	0	0	0	0	0	0	1.000	1.000	1.000	390	0	0	0	0	.000	0	H	0.0

■ BILL SKIFF Skiff, William Franklin b: 10/16/1895, New Rochelle, N.Y. d: 12/25/76, Bronxville, N.Y. BR/TR, 5'10", 170 lbs. Deb: 5/17/21

YEAR	TM/L	G	AB	R	H	2B	3B	HR	RBI	BB	SO	AVG	OBP	SLG	PRO+	BR/A	SB	CS	SBR	FA	FR	G/POS	TPR
1921	Pit-N	16	45	7	13	2	0	0	11	0	4	.289	.289	.333	63	-2	1	1	-0	.982	-2	C-13	-0.4
1926	NY-A	6	11	0	1	0	0	0	0	0	1	.091	.091	.091	-53	-2	0	0	0	1.000	-1	/C-6	-0.3
Total	2	22	56	7	14	2	0	0	11	0	5	.250	.250	.286	40	-5	1	1	-0	.984	-3	/C-19	-0.7

■ ALEXANDER SKINNER Skinner, Alexander b: 8/14/1856, Chicago, Ill. d: 3/5/01, Washington, Mass. Deb: 7/12/1884

YEAR	TM/L	G	AB	R	H	2B	3B	HR	RBI	BB	SO	AVG	OBP	SLG	PRO+	BR/A	SB	CS	SBR	FA	FR	G/POS	TPR
1884	Bal-U	1	3	0	1	0	0	0		0		.333	.333	.333	93	-0				1.000	0	/O-1	0.0
	CP-U	1	3	1	1	0	0	0		0		.333	.333	.333	103	-0				.000	-0	/O-1	0.0
	Yr	2	6	1	2	0	0	0		0		.333	.333	.333	98	-0				1.000	-0	/O-2	0.0

■ CAMP SKINNER Skinner, Elisha Harrison b: 6/25/1897, Douglasville, Ga. d: 8/4/44, Douglasville, Ga. BL/TR, 5'11", 165 lbs. Deb: 5/2/22

YEAR	TM/L	G	AB	R	H	2B	3B	HR	RBI	BB	SO	AVG	OBP	SLG	PRO+	BR/A	SB	CS	SBR	FA	FR	G/POS	TPR
1922	NY-A	27	33	1	6	0	0	0	2	0	4	.182	.206	.182	2	-5	1	0	0	1.000	-0	/O-4	-0.5
1923	Bos-A	7	13	1	3	2	0	0	1	0	0	.231	.231	.385	60	-1	0	0	0	.000	-1	/O-2	-0.2
Total	2	34	46	2	9	2	0	0	3	0	4	.196	.213	.239	18	-6	1	0	0	1.000	-2	/O-6	-0.7

■ JOEL SKINNER Skinner, Joel Patrick b: 2/21/61, LaJolla, Cal. BR/TR, 6'4", 204 lbs. Deb: 6/12/83 F

YEAR	TM/L	G	AB	R	H	2B	3B	HR	RBI	BB	SO	AVG	OBP	SLG	PRO+	BR/A	SB	CS	SBR	FA	FR	G/POS	TPR
1983	Chi-A	6	11	2	3	0	0	0	1	0	1	.273	.273	.273	49	-1	0	0	0	.960	2	/C-6	0.2
1984	Chi-A	43	80	4	17	2	0	0	3	7	19	.213	.276	.237	42	-6	1	0	0	.989	10	C-43	0.6
1985	Chi-A	22	44	9	15	4	1	1	5	5	13	.341	.408	.545	153	3	0	0	0	.971	4	C-21	0.8
1986	Chi-A	60	149	17	30	5	1	4	20	9	43	.201	.252	.329	55	-10	1	0	0	.988	-7	C-60	-1.3
	NY-A	54	166	6	43	4	0	1	17	7	40	.259	.289	.301	62	-9	0	4	-2	.981	6	C-54	-0.3
	Yr	114	315	23	73	9	1	5	37	16	83	.232	.271	.314	58	-18	1	4	-2	.984	-1	*C-114	-1.6
1987	NY-A	64	139	9	19	4	0	3	14	8	46	.137	.189	.230	11	-18	0	0	0	.984	-3	C-64	-1.7
1988	NY-A	88	251	23	57	15	0	4	23	14	72	.227	.268	.335	68	-11	0	0	0	.990	-7	C-85/O-2,1-1	-1.3
1989	Cle-A	79	178	10	41	10	0	1	13	9	42	.230	.271	.303	61	-9	1	1	-0	.990	-4	C-79	-1.1
1990	Cle-A	49	139	16	35	4	1	2	16	7	44	.252	.288	.338	75	-5	0	0	0	.996	0	C-49	-0.2
1991	Cle-A	99	284	23	69	14	0	1	24	14	67	.243	.281	.303	61	-15	0	2	-1	.991	1	C-99	-1.0
Total	9	564	1441	119	329	62	3	17	136	80	387	.228	.271	.311	60	-81	3	7	-3	.988	3	C-560/O-2,1-1	-5.3

■ BOB SKINNER Skinner, Robert Ralph b: 10/3/31, LaJolla, Cal. BL/TR, 6'4", 190 lbs. Deb: 4/13/54 FMC

YEAR	TM/L	G	AB	R	H	2B	3B	HR	RBI	BB	SO	AVG	OBP	SLG	PRO+	BR/A	SB	CS	SBR	FA	FR	G/POS	TPR
1954	Pit-N	132	470	67	117	15	9	8	46	47	59	.249	.317	.370	80	-15	4	0	1	.986	-3	*1-118/O-2	-2.2

YEAR	TM/L	G	AB	R	H	2B	3B	HR	RBI	BB	SO	AVG	OBP	SLG	PRO+	BR/A	SB	CS	SBR	FA	FR	G/POS	TPR
1956	Pit-N	113	233	29	47	8	3	5	29	26	50	.202	.285	.326	65	-12	1	1	-0	.977	-9	O-36,1-23/3-1	-2.5
1957	Pit-N	126	387	58	118	12	6	13	45	38	50	.305	.370	.468	127	15	10	4	1	.963	3	O-93/1-9,3-1	1.3
1958	Pit-N★	144	529	93	170	33	9	13	70	58	55	.321	.390	.491	135	27	12	4	1	.977	9	*O-141	3.0
1959	Pit-N	143	547	78	153	18	4	13	61	67	65	.280	.358	.399	102	3	10	7	-1	.964	6	*O-142/1-1	0.1
1960	*Pit-N★	145	571	83	156	33	6	15	86	59	86	.273	.342	.431	109	7	11	8	-2	.981	7	*O-141	0.6
1961	Pit-N	119	381	61	102	20	3	3	42	51	49	.268	.360	.360	91	-3	3	5	-2	.973	3	O-97	-0.8
1962	Pit-N	144	510	87	154	29	7	20	75	76	89	.302	.397	.504	140	30	10	4	1	.960	1	*O-139	2.3
1963	Pit-N	34	122	18	33	5	5	0	8	13	22	.270	.341	.393	110	2	4	1	1	.983	2	O-32	0.2
	Cin-N	72	194	25	49	10	2	3	17	21	42	.253	.332	.371	99	0	1	2	-1	1.000	2	O-51	-0.2
	Yr	106	316	43	82	15	7	3	25	34	64	.259	.335	.380	103	2	5	3	-0	.993	3	O-83	0.0
1964	Cin-N	25	59	6	13	3	0	3	5	4	12	.220	.270	.424	89	-1	0	0	0	.913	1	O-12	-0.1
	*StL-N	55	118	10	32	5	0	1	16	11	20	.271	.333	.339	83	-2	0	0	0	.938	-1	O-31	-0.5
	Yr	80	177	16	45	8	0	4	21	15	32	.254	.313	.367	85	-3	0	0	0	.930	-0	O-43	-0.6
1965	StL-N	80	152	25	47	5	4	5	26	12	30	.309	.360	.493	126	5	1	0	0	.935	-4	O-33	0.0
1966	StL-N	49	45	2	7	1	0	1	5	2	17	.156	.208	.244	25	-5	0	0	0	.000	0	H	-0.5
Total	12	1381	4318	642	1198	197	58	103	531	485	646	.277	.353	.421	108	52	67	36	-2	.969	14	O-950,1-151/3-2	0.7
■ LOU SKIZAS	Skizas, Louis Peter "The Nervous Greek" b: 6/2/32, Chicago, Ill. BR/TR, 5'11", 175 lbs. Deb: 4/19/56																						
1956	NY-A	6	6	0	1	0	0	0	1	0	2	.167	.167	.167	-12	-1	0	0	0	.000	0	H	-0.1
	KC-A	83	297	39	94	11	3	11	39	15	17	.316	.349	.485	118	6	3	1	0	.975	5	O-74	0.8
	Yr	89	303	39	95	11	3	11	40	15	19	.314	.346	.479	116	5	3	1	0	.975	5	O-74	0.7
1957	KC-A	119	376	34	92	14	1	18	44	27	15	.245	.299	.431	95	-4	5	2	0	.976	-9	O-76,3-32	-1.6
1958	Det-A	23	33	4	8	2	0	1	2	5	1	.242	.342	.394	95	-0	0	0	0	.750	-3	/O-5,3-4	-0.3
1959	Chi-A	8	13	3	1	0	0	0	0	3	2	.077	.250	.077	-6	-2	0	0	0	1.000	-0	/O-6	-0.2
Total	4	239	725	80	196	27	4	30	86	50	37	.270	.319	.443	102	-1	8	3	1	.973	-7	O-161/3-36	-1.4
■ BILL SKOWRON	Skowron, William Joseph "Moose" b: 12/18/30, Chicago, Ill. BR/TR, 5'11", 195 lbs. Deb: 4/13/54																						
1954	NY-A	87	215	37	73	12	9	7	41	19	18	.340	.396	.577	170	19	2	1	0	.986	-1	1-61/3-5,2-2	1.7
1955	*NY-A	108	288	46	92	17	3	12	61	21	32	.319	.372	.524	141	15	1	1	-0	.989	-3	1-74/3-3	0.8
1956	*NY-A	134	464	78	143	21	6	23	90	50	60	.308	.383	.528	143	27	4	4	-1	.993	3	*1-120/3-2	2.1
1957	*NY-A★	122	457	54	139	15	5	17	88	31	60	.304	.352	.470	125	14	3	2	-0	.992	6	*1-115	1.3
1958	*NY-A★	126	465	61	127	22	3	14	73	28	69	.273	.320	.424	107	3	1	1	-0	**.993**	-2	*1-118/3-2	-0.8
1959	NY-A★	74	282	39	84	13	5	15	59	20	47	.298	.351	.539	145	16	1	0	0	.991	0	1-72	1.2
1960	*NY-A★	146	538	63	166	34	3	26	91	38	95	.309	.356	.528	144	30	2	3	-1	.991	9	*1-142	2.6
1961	*NY-A☆	150	561	76	150	23	4	28	89	35	108	.267	.320	.472	115	8	0	0	0	.993	-1	*1-149	-0.5
1962	*NY-A	140	478	63	129	16	6	23	80	36	99	.270	.328	.473	116	9	0	1	-1	.991	-5	*1-135	-0.5
1963	*LA-N	89	237	19	48	8	0	4	19	13	49	.203	.253	.287	59	-13	0	1	-1	.991	-1	1-66/3-1	-1.9
1964	Was-A	73	262	28	71	10	0	13	41	11	56	.271	.308	.458	110	3	0	0	0	.994	-2	1-66	-0.2
	Chi-A	73	273	19	80	11	3	4	38	19	36	.293	.341	.399	108	3	0	0	0	.998	-1	1-70	-0.1
	Yr	146	535	47	151	21	3	17	79	30	92	.282	.325	.428	109	5	0	0	0	.996	-3	*1-136	-0.3
1965	Chi-A†	146	559	63	153	24	3	18	78	32	77	.274	.319	.424	116	9	1	3	-2	.994	-6	*1-145	-0.5
1966	Chi-A	120	337	27	84	15	2	6	29	26	45	.249	.309	.359	98	-2	1	1	-0	.991	1	1-98	-0.7
1967	Chi-A	8	8	0	0	0	0	0	1	0	1	.000	.000	.000	-99	-2	0	0	0	.000	0	H	-0.2
	Cal-A	62	123	8	27	2	1	1	10	4	18	.220	.267	.276	63	-6	0	0	0	.988	-1	1-32	-0.9
	Yr	70	131	8	27	2	1	1	11	4	19	.206	.252	.260	53	-8	0	0	0	.988	-1	1-32	-1.1
Total	14	1658	5547	681	1566	243	53	211	888	383	870	.282	.335	.459	121	134	16	18	-6	.992	-3	*1-1463/3-13,2-2	3.4
■ BOB SKUBE	Skube, Robert Jacob b: 10/8/57, Northridge, Cal. BL/TL, 6', 180 lbs. Deb: 9/17/82																						
1982	Mil-A	4	3	0	2	0	0	0	0	0	0	.667	.667	.667	285	1	0	0	0	.000	-1	/O-1,D-1	0.0
1983	Mil-A	12	25	2	5	1	1	0	9	4	7	.200	.310	.320	80	-1	0	0	0	1.000	-1	/O-8,1-1,D-2	-0.1
Total	2	16	28	2	7	1	1	0	9	4	7	.250	.344	.357	101	0	0	0	0	1.000	-1	/O-9,D-3,1-1	-0.1
■ GORDON SLADE	Slade, Gordon Leigh "Oskie" b: 10/9/04, Salt Lake City, Utah d: 1/2/74, Long Beach, Cal. BR/TR, 5'10.5", 160 lbs. Deb: 4/21/30																						
1930	Bro-N	25	37	8	8	2	0	1	2	3	5	.216	.275	.351	51	-3	0			.938	10	S-21	0.7
1931	Bro-N	85	272	27	65	13	2	1	29	23	28	.239	.310	.313	68	-12	2			.947	11	S-82/3-2	0.7
1932	Bro-N	79	250	23	60	15	1	1	23	11	26	.240	.280	.320	62	-13	3			.943	11	S-55,3-23	0.2
1933	StL-N	39	62	6	7	1	0	0	3	6	7	.113	.191	.129	-7	-8	1			.941	3	S-31/2-1	-0.5
1934	Cin-N	138	555	61	158	19	8	4	52	25	34	.285	.320	.369	86	-11	6			.952	2	S-97,2-39	-0.1
1935	Cin-N	71	196	22	55	10	0	1	14	16	16	.281	.341	.347	88	-3	0			.927	-12	S-30,2-19/O-8,3-7	-1.2
Total	6	437	1372	147	353	60	11	8	123	84	116	.257	.307	.335	73	-51	12			.945	25	S-316/2-59,3-32,O-8	-0.2
■ ART SLADEN	Sladen, Arthur b: 10/28/1860, Dracut, Mass. d: 2/28/14, Dracut, Mass. Deb: 4/22/1884																						
1884	Bos-U	2	7	0	0	0	0	0		0		.000	.000	.000	-99	-2				1.000	-1	/O-2	-0.2
■ JIMMY SLAGLE	Slagle, James Franklin "Rabbit" or "Shorty" b: 7/11/1873, Worthville, Pa. d: 5/10/56, Chicago, Ill. BL/TR, 5'7", 144 lbs. Deb: 4/17/1899																						
1899	Was-N	147	599	92	163	15	8	0	41	55		.272	.338	.324	83	-13	22			.953	20	*O-146	-0.3
1900	Phi-N	141	574	115	165	16	9	0	45	60		.287	.358	.347	96	-2	34			.922	1	*O-141	-1.1
1901	Phi-N	48	183	20	37	6	2	1	20	16		.202	.277	.273	59	-10	5			.930	6	O-48	-0.7
	Bos-N	66	255	35	69	7	0	0	7	34		.271	.359	.298	84	-4	14			.935	-2	O-66	-1.1
	Yr	114	438	55	106	13	2	1	27	50		.242	.325	.288	74	-13	19			.932	4	*O-114	-1.8
1902	Chi-N	115	454	64	143	11	4	0	28	53		.315	.387	.357	133	20	40			.965	7	*O-113	2.1
1903	Chi-N	139	543	104	162	20	6	0	44	81		.298	.393	.357	118	17	33			.936	2	*O-139	1.0
1904	Chi-N	120	481	73	125	12	10	1	31	41		.260	.322	.333	102	1	28			.921	-3	*O-120	-0.9
1905	Chi-N	155	568	96	153	19	4	0	37	97		.269	.379	.317	104	8	27			.962	3	*O-155	0.4
1906	Chi-N	127	498	71	119	8	6	0	33	63		.239	.324	.279	83	-8	25			.976	2	*O-127	-1.3
1907	*Chi-N	136	489	71	126	6	6	0	32	76		.258	.359	.294	99	3	28			.962	-10	*O-136	-1.4
1908	Chi-N	104	352	38	78	4	1	0	26	43		.222	.306	.239	71	-10	17			.976	-6	*O-101	-2.3
Total	10	1298	4996	779	1340	124	56	2	344	619		.268	.352	.317	97	3	273			.950	22	*O-1292	-5.6
■ JACK SLATTERY	Slattery, John Terrence b: 1/6/1878, S.Boston, Mass. d: 7/17/49, Boston, Mass. BR/TR, 6'2", 191 lbs. Deb: 9/28/01 MC																						
1901	Bos-A	1	3	1	1	0	0	0	1	1		.333	.500	.333	137	0	0			1.000	0	/C-1	0.0
1903	Cle-A	4	11	1	0	0	0	0	0	0		.000	.000	.000	-99	-3	0			.885	-1	/1-2	-0.4
	Chi-A	63	211	8	46	3	2	0	20	2		.218	.233	.251	47	-14	2			.974	-8	C-56/1-5	-1.7
	Yr	67	222	9	46	3	2	0	20	2		.207	.221	.239	40	-16	2			.974	-9	C-56/1-7	-2.1
1906	StL-N	3	7	0	2	0	0	0	0	1		.286	.375	.286	111	0	0			1.000	-1	/C-2	0.0
1909	Was-A	32	56	4	12	2	0	0	6	2		.214	.254	.250	62	-2	1			.953	-1	1-11/C-6	-0.3
Total	4	103	288	14	61	5	2	0	27	6		.212	.236	.243	47	-18	3			.974	-10	/C-65,1-18	-2.4
■ MIKE SLATTERY	Slattery, Michael J. b: 11/26/1866, Boston, Mass. d: 10/16/04, Boston, Mass. BL/TL, 6'2", 210 lbs. Deb: 4/17/1884																						
1884	Bos-U	106	413	60	86	6	2	0		4		.208	.216	.232	36	-44				.802	6	*O-96,1-11	-3.6
1888	*NY-N	103	391	50	96	12	6	1	35	13	28	.246	.272	.315	87	-6	26			.919	1	*O-103	-0.8
1889	*NY-N	12	48	7	14	2	0	1	12	4	3	.292	.346	.396	107	0	2			.852	-1	O-12	0.0
1890	NY-P	97	411	80	126	20	11	5	67	27	25	.307	.352	.445	103	-2	18			.905	-14	*O-97	-1.5
1891	Cin-N	41	158	24	33	3	2	1	16	10	10	.209	.256	.272	53	-10	1			.941	-0	O-41	-1.0
	Was-a	15	60	8	17	1	0	0	5	4	5	.283	.358	.300	93	-0	6			.862	-2	O-15	-0.2
Total	5	374	1481	229	372	44	21	8	135	62	71	.251	.284	.325	77	-61	53			.883	-11	O-364/1-11	-7.1
■ DON SLAUGHT	Slaught, Donald Martin b: 9/11/58, Long Beach, Cal. BR/TR, 6'1", 190 lbs. Deb: 7/6/82																						
1982	KC-A	43	115	14	32	6	0	3	8	9	12	.278	.331	.409	102	0	0	0	0	.994	2	C-43	0.4
1983	KC-A	83	276	21	86	13	4	0	28	11	27	.312	.338	.388	99	-1	3	1	0	.964	-7	C-79/D-1	-0.4
1984	*KC-A	124	409	48	108	27	4	4	42	20	55	.264	.302	.379	86	-8	0	0	0	.982	-10	*C-123/D-1	-1.2

YEAR	TM/L	G	AB	R	H	2B	3B	HR	RBI	BB	SO	AVG	OBP	SLG	PRO+	BR/A	SB	CS	SBR	FA	FR	G/POS	TPR
1985	Tex-A	102	343	34	96	17	4	8	35	20	41	.280	.331	.423	103	1	5	4	-1	.990	-11	*C-102	-0.6
1986	Tex-A	95	314	39	83	17	1	13	46	16	59	.264	.310	.449	101	-0	3	2	-0	.993	-6	C-91/D-2	-0.1
1987	Tex-A	95	237	25	53	15	2	8	16	24	51	.224	.298	.405	84	-6	0	3	-2	.985	-0	C-85/D-5	-0.4
1988	NY-A	97	322	33	91	25	1	9	43	24	54	.283	.338	.450	120	8	1	0	0	.979	-12	C-94/D-1	0.3
1989	NY-A	117	350	34	88	21	3	5	38	30	57	.251	.319	.371	95	-2	1	1	-0	.991	-5	*C-105/D-3	-0.2
1990	*Pit-N	84	230	27	69	18	3	4	29	27	27	.300	.381	.457	134	11	0	1	-1	.979	-3	C-78	1.2
1991	*Pit-N	77	220	19	65	17	1	1	29	21	32	.295	.365	.395	116	5	1	0	0	.987	-5	C-69/3-1	0.4
1992	*Pit-N	87	255	26	88	17	3	4	37	17	23	.345	.391	.482	147	16	2	2	-1	.988	-4	C-79	1.7
1993	Pit-N	116	377	34	113	19	2	10	55	29	56	.300	.359	.440	113	7	2	1	0	.993	-10	*C-105	0.3
1994	Pit-N	76	240	21	69	7	0	2	21	34	31	.287	.383	.342	90	-2	0	0	0	.994	-1	C-74	0.2
1995	Pit-N	35	112	13	34	6	0	0	13	9	8	.304	.361	.357	88	-2	0	0	0	.996	2	C-33	0.2
1996	Cal-A	62	207	23	67	9	0	6	32	13	20	.324	.369	.454	106	2	0	0	0	.992	-8	C-59/D-1	-0.3
	Chi-A	14	36	2	9	1	0	0	4	2	2	.250	.289	.278	47	-3	0	0	0	.986	1	C-12/D-1	-0.1
	Yr	76	243	25	76	10	0	6	36	15	22	.313	.358	.428	98	-1	0	0	0	.991	-7	C-71/D-2	-0.4
1997	SD-N	20	20	2	0	0	0	0	0	5	4	.000	.200	.000	-45	-4	0	0	0	1.000	-1	/C-6	-0.5
Total	16	1327	4063	415	1151	235	28	77	476	311	559	.283	.341	.412	104	22	18	15	-4	.987	-79	*C-1237/D-15,3-1	0.9

■ ENOS SLAUGHTER

Slaughter, Enos Bradsher "Country" b: 4/27/16, Roxboro, N.C. BL/TR, 5'9", 192 lbs. Deb: 4/19/38 H

YEAR	TM/L	G	AB	R	H	2B	3B	HR	RBI	BB	SO	AVG	OBP	SLG	PRO+	BR/A	SB	CS	SBR	FA	FR	G/POS	TPR
1938	StL-N	112	395	59	109	20	10	8	58	32	38	.276	.330	.438	104	1	1			.970	-2	O-92	-0.4
1939	StL-N	149	604	95	193	**52**	5	12	86	44	53	.320	.371	.482	120	16	2			.968	**16**	*O-149	2.6
1940	StL-N	140	516	96	158	25	13	17	73	50	35	.306	.370	.504	131	21	8			.989	3	*O-132	1.8
1941	StL-N★	113	425	71	132	22	9	13	76	53	28	.311	.390	.496	139	22	4			.947	-8	*O-108	0.7
1942	*StL-N★	152	591	100	**188**	31	**17**	13	98	88	30	.318	.412	.494	153	41	9			.987	4	*O-151	3.9
1946	*StL-N★	156	609	100	183	30	8	18	**130**	69	41	.300	.374	.465	131	24	9			.981	6	*O-156	2.4
1947	StL-N★	147	551	100	162	31	13	10	86	59	27	.294	.366	.452	111	9	4			.982	9	*O-142	1.0
1948	StL-N★	146	549	91	176	27	11	11	90	81	29	.321	.409	.470	130	25	4			.971	6	*O-146	2.2
1949	StL-N★	151	568	92	191	34	**13**	13	96	79	37	.336	.418	.511	141	35	3			.983	1	*O-150	2.8
1950	StL-N★	148	556	82	161	26	7	10	101	66	33	.290	.367	.415	100	1	3			.978	-1	*O-145	-0.6
1951	StL-N★	123	409	48	115	17	8	4	64	67	25	.281	.386	.391	109	8	7	2	1	.995	-0	*O-106	0.5
1952	StL-N★	140	510	73	153	17	12	11	101	70	25	.300	.386	.445	130	22	6	1	1	.989	2	*O-137	2.0
1953	StL-N★	143	492	64	143	34	9	6	89	80	28	.291	.395	.433	116	14	4	4	-1	**.996**	-6	*O-137	0.2
1954	NY-A	69	125	19	31	4	2	1	19	28	8	.248	.386	.336	102	2	0	2	-1	.974	-6	O-30	-0.7
1955	NY-A	10	9	1	1	0	0	0	1	1	1	.111	.200	.111	-15	-1	0	0	0	.000	0	H	-0.1
	KC-A	108	267	49	86	12	4	5	34	40	17	.322	.414	.453	132	13	2	3	-1	.985	-4	O-77	0.5
	Yr	118	276	50	87	12	4	5	35	41	18	.315	.408	.442	127	12	2	3	-1	.985	-4	O-77	0.4
1956	KC-A	91	223	37	62	14	3	2	23	29	20	.278	.364	.395	100	0	1	0	0	.981	-3	O-56	-0.5
	*NY-A	24	83	15	24	4	2	0	4	5	6	.289	.330	.386	91	-1	1	1	-0	1.000	-2	O-20	-0.4
	Yr	115	306	52	86	18	5	2	27	34	26	.281	.355	.392	97	-1	2	1	0	.985	-5	O-76	-0.9
1957	*NY-A	96	209	24	53	7	1	5	34	40	19	.254	.373	.368	105	3	0	2	-1	1.000	-3	O-64	-0.5
1958	*NY-A	77	138	21	42	4	1	4	19	21	16	.304	.396	.435	133	7	2	0	1	.957	-5	O-35	0.1
1959	NY-A	74	99	10	17	2	0	6	21	13	19	.172	.268	.374	77	-4	1	0	0	.964	-5	O-26	-0.9
	Mil-N	11	18	0	3	0	0	0	1	3	3	.167	.286	.167	27	-2	0	0	0	1.000	-1	/O-5	-0.3
Total	19	2380	7946	1247	2383	413	148	169	1304	1018	538	.300	.382	.453	122	256	71	15		.980	-0	*O-2064	16.3

■ SCOTTIE SLAYBACK

Slayback, Elbert b: 10/5/01, Paducah, Ky. d: 11/30/79, Cincinnati, Ohio BR/TR, 5'8", 165 lbs. Deb: 9/26/26

YEAR	TM/L	G	AB	R	H	2B	3B	HR	RBI	BB	SO	AVG	OBP	SLG	PRO+	BR/A	SB	CS	SBR	FA	FR	G/POS	TPR
1926	NY-N	2	8	0	0	0	0	0	0	0	0	.000	.000	.000	-99	-2	0			.889	-1	/2-2	-0.4

■ BRUCE SLOAN

Sloan, Bruce Adams "Fatso" b: 10/4/14, McAlester, Okla. d: 9/24/73, Oklahoma City, Okla. BL/TL, 5'9", 195 lbs. Deb: 4/29/44

YEAR	TM/L	G	AB	R	H	2B	3B	HR	RBI	BB	SO	AVG	OBP	SLG	PRO+	BR/A	SB	CS	SBR	FA	FR	G/POS	TPR
1944	NY-N	59	104	7	28	4	1	1	9	13	8	.269	.350	.356	99	0	0			.935	-4	O-21	-0.5

■ TOD SLOAN

Sloan, Yale Yeastman b: 12/24/1890, Madisonville, Tenn d: 9/12/56, Akron, Ohio BL/TR, 6', 175 lbs. Deb: 9/22/13

YEAR	TM/L	G	AB	R	H	2B	3B	HR	RBI	BB	SO	AVG	OBP	SLG	PRO+	BR/A	SB	CS	SBR	FA	FR	G/POS	TPR
1913	StL-A	7	26	2	7	1	0	0	2	1	9	.269	.321	.308	87	-0	1			.950	2	/O-7	0.1
1917	StL-A	109	313	32	72	6	2	2	25	28	34	.230	.307	.281	83	-6	8			.963	-3	O-77	-1.5
1919	StL-A	27	63	9	15	1	3	0	6	12	3	.238	.368	.349	99	0	0			.933	-1	O-20	-0.1
Total	3	143	402	43	94	8	5	2	33	41	46	.234	.319	.294	86	-6	9			.957	-1	O-104	-1.5

■ RON SLOCUM

Slocum, Ronald Reece b: 7/2/45, Modesto, Cal. BR/TR, 6'2", 185 lbs. Deb: 9/8/69

YEAR	TM/L	G	AB	R	H	2B	3B	HR	RBI	BB	SO	AVG	OBP	SLG	PRO+	BR/A	SB	CS	SBR	FA	FR	G/POS	TPR
1969	SD-N	13	24	6	7	1	0	1	5	0	5	.292	.292	.458	112	0	0	0	0	.938	-1	/2-4,3-4,S-1	-0.1
1970	SD-N	60	71	8	10	2	2	1	11	8	24	.141	.237	.268	37	-7	0	1	-1	.978	13	C-19,S-17,3-11,/2-9	0.6
1971	SD-N	7	18	1	0	0	0	0	0	0	8	.000	.053	.000	-90	-5	0	0	0	.905	1	/3-6	-0.3
Total	3	80	113	15	17	3	2	2	16	8	37	.150	.220	.265	33	-11	0	1	-1	.887	13	/3-21,C-19,S-18,2	0.2

■ CRAIG SMAJSTRLA

Smajstrla, Craig Lee b: 6/19/62, Houston, Tex. BB/TR, 5'9", 165 lbs. Deb: 9/6/88

YEAR	TM/L	G	AB	R	H	2B	3B	HR	RBI	BB	SO	AVG	OBP	SLG	PRO+	BR/A	SB	CS	SBR	FA	FR	G/POS	TPR
1988	Hou-N	8	3	2	0	0	0	0	0	0	1	.000	.000	.000	-99	-1	0	0	0	1.000	0	/2-2	-0.1

■ CHARLIE SMALL

Small, Charles Albert b: 10/24/05, Auburn, Me. d: 1/14/53, Auburn, Me. BL/TR, 5'11", 180 lbs. Deb: 7/7/30

YEAR	TM/L	G	AB	R	H	2B	3B	HR	RBI	BB	SO	AVG	OBP	SLG	PRO+	BR/A	SB	CS	SBR	FA	FR	G/POS	TPR
1930	Bos-A	25	18	1	3	1	0	0	0	2	5	.167	.250	.222	22	-2	1	0	0	1.000	-0	/O-1	-0.2

■ HANK SMALL

Small, George Henry b: 7/31/53, Atlanta, Ga. BR/TR, 6'3", 205 lbs. Deb: 9/27/78

YEAR	TM/L	G	AB	R	H	2B	3B	HR	RBI	BB	SO	AVG	OBP	SLG	PRO+	BR/A	SB	CS	SBR	FA	FR	G/POS	TPR
1978	Atl-N	1	4	0	0	0	0	0	0	0	0	.000	.000	.000	-90	-1	0	0	0	1.000	0	/1-1	-0.1

■ JIM SMALL

Small, James Arthur b: 3/8/37, Portland, Ore. BL/TL, 6'1.5", 180 lbs. Deb: 6/22/55

YEAR	TM/L	G	AB	R	H	2B	3B	HR	RBI	BB	SO	AVG	OBP	SLG	PRO+	BR/A	SB	CS	SBR	FA	FR	G/POS	TPR
1955	Det-A	12	4	2	0	0	0	0	0	1	1	.000	.200	.000	-44	-1	0	0	0	1.000	-1	/O-4	-0.1
1956	Det-A	58	91	13	29	4	2	0	10	6	10	.319	.361	.407	102	0	0	0	0	.940	-3	O-26	-0.3
1957	Det-A	36	42	7	9	2	0	0	0	2	11	.214	.250	.262	39	-4	0	2	-1	1.000	-3	O-14	-0.8
1958	KC-A	2	4	0	0	0	0	0	0	1	0	.000	.200	.000	-39	-1	0	0	0	1.000	0	/O-1	-0.1
Total	4	108	141	22	38	6	2	0	10	10	22	.270	.318	.340	75	-5	0	2	-1	.957	-6	/O-45	-1.3

■ ROY SMALLEY

Smalley, Roy Frederick Jr. b: 10/25/52, Los Angeles, Cal. BB/TR, 6'1", 185 lbs. Deb: 4/30/75 F

YEAR	TM/L	G	AB	R	H	2B	3B	HR	RBI	BB	SO	AVG	OBP	SLG	PRO+	BR/A	SB	CS	SBR	FA	FR	G/POS	TPR
1975	Tex-A	78	250	22	57	8	0	3	33	30	42	.228	.311	.296	73	-8	4	0	1	.941	4	S-59,2-19/C-1	0.3
1976	Tex-A	41	129	15	29	2	0	1	8	29	27	.225	.367	.264	85	-1	2	0	1	.963	-6	2-38/S-5	-0.3
	Min-A	103	384	46	104	16	3	2	36	47	79	.271	.353	.344	103	3	0	4	-2	.967	5	*S-103	1.9
	Yr	144	513	61	133	18	3	3	44	76	106	.259	.357	.324	98	2	2	4	-2	.966	-1	*S-108,2-38	1.6
1977	Min-A	150	584	93	135	21	5	6	56	74	89	.231	.319	.315	75	-19	5	5	-2	.958	19	*S-150	1.5
1978	Min-A	158	586	80	160	31	3	19	77	85	70	.273	.366	.433	122	18	2	8	-4	.970	18	*S-157	**5.3**
1979	Min-A★	162	621	94	168	28	3	24	95	80	80	.271	.357	.441	110	9	2	3	-1	.968	**33**	*S-161/1-1	**5.6**
1980	Min-A	133	486	64	135	24	1	12	63	65	63	.278	.365	.405	103	3	3	3	-1	.975	21	*S-125/1-3,D-3	3.7
1981	Min-A	56	167	24	44	7	1	7	22	31	24	.263	.379	.443	128	7	0	0	0	.946	-17	S-37,D-15/1-1	-0.8
1982	Min-A	4	13	2	2	1	0	0	0	3	4	.154	.313	.231	51	-1	0	0	0	1.000	1	/S-4	0.0
	NY-A	142	486	55	125	14	2	20	67	68	100	.257	.348	.418	111	8	0	1	-1	.977	-19	S-89,3-53/2-1,D-4	-0.4
	Yr	146	499	57	127	15	2	20	67	71	104	.255	.347	.413	109	7	0	1	-1	.979	-18	S-93,3-53/D-4,2-1	-0.4
1983	NY-A	130	451	70	124	24	1	18	62	58	68	.275	.360	.452	127	17	3	3	-1	.959	-16	S-91,3-26,1-22	0.7
1984	NY-A	67	209	17	50	8	1	7	26	15	35	.239	.290	.388	89	-4	2	1	0	.905	0	3-35,S-13/1-5,D-5	-0.4
	Chi-A	47	135	15	23	4	0	4	13	22	30	.170	.287	.289	57	-8	1	1	-0	.947	-8	3-38/S-3,1-1,D-2	-1.6
	Yr	114	344	32	73	12	1	11	39	37	65	.212	.289	.349	76	-12	3	2	-0	.923	-7	3-73,S-16/D-7,1-6	-2.0
1985	Min-A	129	388	57	100	20	0	12	45	60	65	.258	.359	.402	102	2	0	2	-1	.987	-15	D-56,S-49,3-14,/1-1	-1.1
1986	Min-A	143	459	59	113	20	4	20	57	68	80	.246	.343	.438	108	6	1	3	-2	.963	-4	*D-114,S-19/3-8	-0.1
1987	*Min-A	110	309	32	85	16	1	8	34	36	52	.275	.353	.411	98	-0	2	0	1	.850	-3	D-73,3-14/S-4	-0.5
Total	13	1653	5657	745	1454	244	25	163	694	771	908	.257	.348	.395	103	32	27	34	-12	.966	14	*S-1069,D-272,3/21C	13.8

■ ROY SMALLEY

Smalley, Roy Frederick Sr. b: 6/9/26, Springfield, Mo. BR/TR, 6'3", 190 lbs. Deb: 4/20/48 F

YEAR	TM/L	G	AB	R	H	2B	3B	HR	RBI	BB	SO	AVG	OBP	SLG	PRO+	BR/A	SB	CS	SBR	FA	FR	G/POS	TPR
1948	Chi-N	124	361	25	78	11	4	4	36	23	76	.216	.265	.302	55	-23	0			.941	9	*S-124	-0.8

YEAR	TM/L	G	AB	R	H	2B	3B	HR	RBI	BB	SO	AVG	OBP	SLG	PRO+	BR/A	SB	CS	SBR	FA	FR	G/POS	TPR
1949	Chi-N	135	477	57	117	21	10	8	35	36	77	.245	.304	.382	85	-12	2			.947	14	*S-132	1.2
1950	Chi-N	154	557	58	128	21	9	21	85	49	114	.230	.297	.413	85	-14	2			.945	**21**	*S-154	1.9
1951	Chi-N	79	238	24	55	7	4	8	31	25	53	.231	.304	.395	85	-6	0	0	0	.953	-13	S-74	-1.3
1952	Chi-N	87	261	36	58	14	1	5	30	29	58	.222	.305	.341	78	-8	0	0	0	.952	-11	S-82	-1.4
1953	Chi-N	82	253	20	63	9	0	6	25	28	57	.249	.329	.356	77	-8	0	0	0	.932	-6	S-77	-0.9
1954	Mil-N	25	36	5	8	0	0	1	7	4	9	.222	.317	.306	67	-2	0	0	0	.950	4	/S-9,2-7,1-2	0.3
1955	Phi-N	92	260	33	51	11	1	7	39	39	58	.196	.306	.327	69	-11	0	0	0	.974	-16	S-87/2-1,3-1	-2.0
1956	Phi-N	65	168	14	38	9	3	0	16	23	29	.226	.323	.315	74	-6	0	0	0	.949	-1	S-60	-0.3
1957	Phi-N	28	31	5	5	0	1	1	1	1	9	.161	.212	.323	42	-3	0	0	0	.941	1	S-20	-0.1
1958	Phi-N	1	2	0	0	0	0	0	0	0	1	.000	.000	.000	-99	-1	0	0	0	.714	0	/S-1	0.0
Total	11	872	2644	277	601	103	33	61	305	257	541	.227	.300	.360	77	-93	4	0		.947	3	S-820/2-8,1-2,3-1	-3.4
■ WILL SMALLEY	Smalley, William Darwin "Deacon" b: 6/27/1871, Oakland, Cal. d: 10/11/1891, Bay City, Mich. BR/TR, Deb: 4/19/1890																						
1890	Cle-N	136	502	62	107	11	1	0	42	60	44	.213	.303	.239	60	-23	10			.895	17	*3-136	-0.2
1891	Was-a	11	38	5	6	0	1	0	3	5	2	.158	.256	.211	35	-3	0			.762	-2	/3-9,2-2	-0.4
Total	2	147	540	67	113	11	2	0	45	65	46	.209	.300	.237	58	-27	10			.887	15	3-145/2-2	-0.6
■ JOE SMAZA	Smaza, Joseph Paul b: 7/7/23, Detroit, Mich. d: 5/30/79, Royal Oak, Mich. BL/TL, 5'11", 175 lbs. Deb: 9/18/46																						
1946	Chi-A	2	5	2	1	0	0	0	0	0	0	.200	.200	.200	12	-1	0	0	0	.000	-1	/O-1	-0.1
■ BILL SMILEY	Smiley, William B. b: 1856, Baltimore, Md. d: 7/11/1884, Baltimore, Md. Deb: 10/13/1874																						
1874	Bal-n	2	7	0	0	0	0	0	0	0	0	.000	.000	.000	-99	-1	0	0	0	.786	1	/3-2	-0.1
1882	StL-a	59	240	30	51	4	2	0		6		.213	.232	.246	59	-10				.885	-7	*2-57/O-2	-1.5
	Bal-a	16	61	3	9	0	0	0		0		.148	.148	.148	-0	-6				.843	2	2-16/S-2	-0.4
	Yr	75	301	33	60	4	2	0		6		.199	.215	.226	48	-16				.874	-5	2-73/O-2,S-2	-1.9
■ EDGAR SMITH	Smith, Albert Edgar b: 10/15/1860, North Haven, Conn. TR, 6', 200 lbs. Deb: 6/20/1883																						
1883	Bos-N	30	115	10	25	5	3	0	16	5	11	.217	.250	.313	68	-4				.905	-0	O-30/C-1	-0.4
■ ALECK SMITH	Smith, Alexander Benjamin "Broadway Aleck" b: 1871, New York, N.Y. d: 7/9/19, New York, N.Y. TR, Deb: 4/23/1897																						
1897	Bro-N	66	237	36	71	13	1	1	39	4		.300	.317	.376	87	-5	12			.903	-6	C-43,O-18/1-6	-0.7
1898	Bro-N	52	199	25	52	6	5	0	23	3		.261	.276	.342	77	-7	7			.909	-10	O-26,C-20/3-2,21	-1.6
1899	Bro-N	17	61	6	11	0	1	0	6	2		.180	.206	.213	15	-7	0			.917	-3	C-17	-0.8
	Bal-N	41	120	17	46	6	4	0	25	4		.383	.417	.500	144	7	7			.951	-4	C-36/O-2,1-1	0.5
	Yr	58	181	23	57	6	5	0	31	6		.315	.347	.403	101	-0	7			.939	-7	C-53/O-2,1-1	-0.3
1900	Bro-N	7	25	2	6	0	0	0	3	1		.240	.269	.240	39	-2	2			.875	-2	/3-6,C-1	-0.4
1901	NY-N	26	78	5	11	0	0	0	6	0		.141	.141	.141	-19	-12	2			.962	-2	C-24	-1.1
1902	Bal-A	41	145	10	34	3	0	0	21	8		.234	.275	.255	45	-11	5			.947	-6	C-27/1-7,O-4,2-3,3	-1.3
1903	Bos-A	11	33	4	10	1	0	0	4	0		.303	.303	.333	86	-1	0			.932	0	C-10	0.0
1904	Chi-N	10	29	2	6	1	0	0	1	3		.207	.281	.241	62	-1	1			.778	-2	/O-6,C-1,3-1	-0.3
1906	NY-N	16	28	0	5	0	0	0	2	1		.179	.207	.179	20	-3	1			1.000	-1	/C-8,1-3,O-1	-0.3
Total	9	287	955	107	252	30	11	1	130	26		.264	.288	.321	69	-41	37			.933	-35	C-187/O-57,1-18,32	-6.0
■ AL SMITH	Smith, Alphonse Eugene "Fuzzy" b: 2/7/28, Kirkwood, Mo. BR/TR, 6', 191 lbs. Deb: 7/10/53																						
1953	Cle-A	47	150	28	36	9	0	3	14	20	25	.240	.341	.360	92	-1	2	0	1	.920	-3	O-39/3-2	-0.6
1954	*Cle-A	131	481	101	135	29	6	11	50	88	65	.281	.399	.435	126	20	2	9	-5	.984	-3	*O-109,3-21/S-4	0.8
1955	Cle-A★	154	607	**123**	186	27	4	22	77	93	77	.306	.411	.473	132	30	11	6	-0	.977	-17	*O-120,3-45/S-5,2-1	0.7
1956	Cle-A	141	526	87	144	26	5	16	71	84	72	.274	.382	.433	112	11	6	3	0	.981	-7	*O-122,3-28/2-1	-0.2
1957	Cle-A	135	507	78	125	23	5	11	49	79	70	.247	.353	.377	100	2	12	6	0	.913	-16	3-84,O-58	-1.6
1958	Chi-A	139	480	61	121	23	5	12	58	48	77	.252	.326	.396	100	-0	3	3	-1	.970	-1	*O-138/3-1	-1.0
1959	*Chi-A	129	472	65	112	16	4	17	55	46	74	.237	.312	.396	94	-5	7	5	-1	.980	10	*O-128/3-1	-0.2
1960	Chi-A★	142	536	80	169	31	3	12	72	50	65	.315	.377	.451	124	18	8	3	1	.966	-5	*O-141	0.7
1961	Chi-A	147	532	88	148	29	4	28	93	56	67	.278	.352	.506	128	20	4	4	-1	.948	-11	3-80,O-71	0.5
1962	Chi-A	142	511	62	149	23	8	16	82	57	60	.292	.366	.462	122	16	3	3	-1	.935	-23	*3-105,O-39	-0.8
1963	Bal-A	120	368	45	100	17	1	10	39	32	74	.272	.335	.405	110	5	9	0	3	.971	-4	O-97	-0.1
1964	Cle-A	61	136	15	22	1	1	4	9	8	32	.162	.214	.272	34	-12	0	1	-1	1.000	-3	O-48/3-1	-1.9
	Bos-A	29	51	10	11	4	0	2	7	13	10	.216	.385	.412	116	2	0	0	0	.917	-2	3-10/O-8	0.0
	Yr	90	187	25	33	5	1	6	16	21	42	.176	.267	.310	59	-10	0	1	-1	.987	-4	O-56,3-11	-1.9
Total	12	1517	5357	843	1458	258	46	164	676	674	768	.272	.360	.429	113	105	67	43	-6	.974	-84	*O-1118,3-378/S-9,2	-3.7
■ TONY SMITH	Smith, Anthony b: 5/14/1884, Chicago, Ill. d: 2/27/64, Galveston, Tex. BR/TR, 5'9", 150 lbs. Deb: 8/12/07																						
1907	Was-A	51	139	12	26	1	1	0	8	18		.187	.285	.209	63	-5	3			.920	-9	S-51	-1.5
1910	Bro-N	106	321	31	58	10	1	1	16	69	53	.181	.329	.227	65	-11	9			.941	12	*S-101/3-6	0.6
1911	Bro-N	13	40	3	6	1	0	0	2	8	7	.150	.292	.175	33	-3	1			.870	0	S-10/2-3	-0.3
Total	3	170	500	46	90	12	2	1	26	95	60	.180	.314	.218	62	-19	13			.931	3	S-162/3-6,2-3	-1.2
■ KLONDIKE SMITH	Smith, Armstrong Frederick b: 1/4/1887, London, England d: 11/15/59, Springfield, Mass. BL/TL, 5'9", 160 lbs. Deb: 9/28/12																						
1912	NY-A	7	27	0	5	1	0	0	0	0		.185	.185	.222	15	-3	1			1.000	-1	/O-7	-0.5
■ BILLY SMITH	Smith, Billy Edward b: 7/14/53, Jonesboro, La. BB/TR, 6'2.5", 185 lbs. Deb: 4/13/75																						
1975	Cal-A	59	143	10	29	5	1	0	14	12	27	.203	.265	.252	50	-10	1	3	-2	.932	-9	S-50/1-6,3-2,D-4	-1.6
1976	Cal-A	13	8	0	3	0	0	0	0	0	2	.375	.375	.375	128	0	0	0	0	.625	-1	S-10/D-1	0.0
1977	Bal-A	109	367	44	79	12	2	5	29	33	71	.215	.282	.300	62	-19	3	2	-0	.991	4	*2-104/S-5,1-2,3-1	-0.8
1978	Bal-A	85	250	29	65	12	2	5	30	27	40	.260	.335	.384	108	3	3	0	1	.986	-1	2-83/S-2	0.8
1979	*Bal-A	68	189	18	47	9	4	6	33	15	33	.249	.311	.434	102	-0	1	0	0	.980	-8	2-63/S-5	-0.4
1981	SF-N	36	61	6	11	0	0	1	5	9	16	.180	.286	.230	48	-4	0	0	0	.971	-0	S-21/2-5,3-3	-0.3
Total	6	370	1018	107	234	38	9	17	111	96	189	.230	.299	.335	79	-30	8	5	-1	.987	-15	2-255/S-93,1-8,3D	-2.3
■ BOBBY GENE SMITH	Smith, Bobby Gene b: 5/28/34, Hood River, Ore. BR/TR, 5'11", 185 lbs. Deb: 4/16/57																						
1957	StL-N	93	185	24	39	7	1	3	18	13	35	.211	.263	.308	52	-13	1	1	-0	.973	-8	O-79	-2.5
1958	StL-N	28	88	8	25	3	0	2	5	2	18	.284	.308	.386	79	-3	1	0	0	1.000	-1	O-27	-0.5
1959	StL-N	43	60	11	13	1	1	1	7	1	9	.217	.230	.317	41	-5	0	0	0	.971	-4	O-32	-1.0
1960	Phi-N	98	217	24	62	5	2	4	27	10	28	.286	.317	.382	90	-3	2	3	-1	1.000	1	O-70/3-1	-0.6
1961	Phi-N	79	174	16	44	7	0	2	18	15	32	.253	.316	.328	72	-7	0	1	-1	.971	6	O-47	-0.4
1962	NY-N	8	22	1	3	0	1	0	2	3	2	.136	.240	.227	26	-2	0	1	-1	1.000	-1	/O-6	-0.4
	Chi-N	13	29	3	5	0	0	1	2	2	6	.172	.226	.276	33	-3	0	1	-1	1.000	-1	/O-7	-0.5
	StL-N	91	130	13	30	9	0	0	12	7	14	.231	.270	.300	48	-10	1	1	-0	1.000	-14	O-80	-2.6
	Yr	112	181	17	38	9	1	1	16	12	22	.210	.259	.287	43	-15	1	3	-2	1.000	-15	O-93	-3.5
1965	Cal-A	23	57	4	13	3	0	0	5	2	10	.228	.267	.281	57	-3	0	1	-1	1.000	-0	O-15	-0.5
Total	7	476	962	101	234	35	5	13	96	55	154	.243	.286	.331	64	-48	5	9	-4	.986	-22	O-363/3-1	-9.0
■ BRICK SMITH	Smith, Brick Dudley b: 5/2/59, Charlotte, N.C. BR/TR, 6'4", 225 lbs. Deb: 9/13/87																						
1987	Sea-A	5	8	1	1	0	0	0	0	2	4	.125	.300	.125	18	-1	0	0	0	.963	0	/1-3,D-1	-0.1
1988	Sea-A	4	10	1	1	0	0	0	1	0	1	.100	.100	.100	-42	-2	0	0	0	1.000	1	/1-4	-0.1
Total	2	9	18	2	2	0	0	0	1	2	5	.111	.200	.111	-12	-3	0	0	0	.983	1	/1-7,D-1	-0.2
■ BERNIE SMITH	Smith, Calvin Bernard b: 9/4/41, Ponchatoula, La. BR/TR, 5'9", 164 lbs. Deb: 7/31/70																						
1970	Mil-A	44	76	8	21	3	1	1	6	11	12	.276	.382	.382	110	2	1	3	-2	.979	-7	O-39	-0.8
1971	Mil-A	15	36	1	5	1	0	1	3	0	5	.139	.162	.250	15	-4	0	0	0	.923	-3	O-12	-0.8
Total	2	59	112	9	26	4	1	2	9	11	17	.232	.317	.339	83	-3	1	3	-2	.967	-9	/O-51	-1.6

YEAR	TM/L	G	AB	R	H	2B	3B	HR	RBI	BB	SO	AVG	OBP	SLG	PRO+	BR/A	SB	CS	SBR	FA	FR	G/POS	TPR
■ REGGIE SMITH	Smith, Carl Reginald b: 4/2/45, Shreveport, La. BB/TR, 6', 195 lbs. Deb: 9/18/66 C																						
1966	Bos-A	6	26	1	4	1	0	0	0	0	5	.154	.154	.192	-1	-3	0	0	0	.944	1	/O-6	-0.3
1967	*Bos-A	158	565	78	139	24	6	15	61	57	95	.246	.316	.389	99	-1	16	6	1	.983	17	*O-144/2-6	1.2
1968	Bos-A	155	558	78	148	**37**	5	15	69	64	77	.265	.345	.430	125	17	22	18	-4	.985	10	*O-155	1.7
1969	Bos-A★	143	543	87	168	29	7	25	93	54	67	.309	.373	.527	142	29	7	13	-6	.959	6	*O-139	2.2
1970	Bos-A	147	580	109	176	32	7	22	74	51	60	.303	.364	.497	126	20	10	7	-1	.977	16	*O-145	2.7
1971	Bos-A	159	618	85	175	**33**	2	30	96	63	82	.283	.354	.489	128	21	11	3	2	.966	16	*O-159	3.2
1972	Bos-A★	131	467	75	126	25	4	21	74	68	63	.270	.367	.475	142	25	15	4	2	.981	5	*O-129	2.9
1973	Bos-A	115	423	79	128	23	2	21	69	68	49	.303	.400	.515	148	28	3	2	-0	.983	7	*O-104/1-1,D-8	2.9
1974	StL-N★	143	517	79	160	26	9	23	100	71	70	.309	.394	.528	158	39	4	3	-1	.976	6	*O-132/1-1	4.0
1975	StL-N★	135	477	67	144	26	3	19	76	63	59	.302	.387	.488	137	24	9	7	-2	.963	-5	O-69,1-66/3-1	1.1
1976	StL-N	47	170	20	37	7	1	8	23	14	28	.218	.281	.412	94	-2	1	2	-1	.986	7	1-17,O-16,3-13	0.2
	LA-N	65	225	35	63	8	4	10	26	18	42	.280	.336	.484	133	9	2	0	1	.985	3	O-58/3-1	1.0
	Yr	112	395	55	100	15	5	18	49	32	70	.253	.312	.453	116	6	3	2	-0	.989	10	O-74,1-17,3-14	1.2
1977	*LA-N★	148	488	104	150	27	4	32	87	104	76	.307	**.432**	.576	**168**	51	7	5	-1	.980	-7	*O-140	3.7
1978	*LA-N★	128	447	82	132	27	2	29	93	70	90	.295	.392	.559	**164**	38	12	5	1	.950	-4	*O-126	3.1
1979	LA-N	68	234	41	64	13	1	10	32	31	50	.274	.363	.466	126	9	6	5	-1	.988	8	O-62	1.3
1980	LA-N★	92	311	47	100	13	0	15	55	41	63	.322	.402	.508	155	24	5	6	-2	.994	6	O-84	2.6
1981	*LA-N	41	35	5	7	1	0	1	8	7	8	.200	.333	.314	88	-0	0	0	0	1.000	0	/1-2	0.0
1982	SF-N	106	349	51	99	11	0	18	56	46	46	.284	.367	.470	133	15	7	0	2	.982	2	1-99	1.5
Total	17	1987	7033	1123	2020	363	57	314	1092	890	1030	.287	.370	.489	136	342	137	86	-11	.976	93	*O-1668,1-186/3D2	35.0
■ CHARLIE SMITH	Smith, Charles J. b: 12/11/1840, Brooklyn, N.Y. d: 11/15/1897, Great Neck, N.Y. 5'10.5", 150 lbs. Deb: 5/18/1871																						
1871	Mut-n	14	72	15	19	2	1	0	5	1	1	.264	.274	.319	77	-1	6	0	2	.688	-1	3-12/2-3	-0.1
■ POP SMITH	Smith, Charles Marvin b: 10/12/1856, Digby, N.S., Canada d: 4/18/27, Boston, Mass. BR/TR, 5'11", 170 lbs. Deb: 5/1/1880 U																						
1880	Cin-N	83	334	35	69	10	9	0	27	6	36	.207	.221	.290	72	-9				.855	-11	*2-83	-1.6
1881	Cle-N	10	34	1	4	0	0	0	3	0	8	.118	.118	.118	-27	-5				.838	-2	3-10	-0.6
	Buf-N	3	11	3	0	0	0	0	1	3	5	.000	.214	.000	-27	-1				.840	-1	/2-3	-0.2
	Wor-N	11	41	1	3	0	0	0	2	3	5	.073	.136	.073	-31	-6				.955	2	/O-8,2-3	-0.4
	Yr	24	86	5	7	0	0	0	6	6	18	.081	.141	.081	-28	-12				.838	-1	3-10/O-8,2-6	-1.2
1882	Phi-a	20	65	10	6	0	0	0	2	12		.092	.234	.092	12	-6				.732	2	3-11/S-4,O-3,2-2	-0.3
	Lou-a	3	11	1	2	0	0	0		0		.182	.182	.182	24	-1				.778	-0	/S-3	-0.1
	Yr	23	76	11	8	0	0	0	2	12		.105	.227	.105	14	-7				.732	2	3-11/S-7,O-3,2-2	-0.4
1883	Col-a	97	405	82	106	14	**17**	4		22		.262	.300	.410	137	18				.889	18	*2-73,3-24/P-3	3.1
1884	Col-a	108	445	78	106	18	10	6		20		.238	.289	.364	122	12				.905	29	*2-108	3.9
1885	Pit-a	106	453	85	113	11	13	0	35	25		.249	.293	.331	98	-1				.922	33	*2-106	3.2
1886	Pit-a	126	483	75	105	20	9	2	57	42		.217	.288	.308	87	-7	38			**.895**	21	*S-98,2-28/C-1	1.4
1887	Pit-N	122	456	69	98	12	7	2	54	30	48	.215	.283	.285	62	-22	30			.914	-6	*2-89,S-33	-2.2
1888	Pit-N	131	481	61	99	15	2	4	52	22	78	.206	.248	.270	71	-15	37			.901	-2	S-75,2-56	-1.3
1889	Pit-N	72	258	26	54	10	2	5	27	24	38	.209	.292	.322	79	-7	12			.897	-0	S-58/2-9,3-3,O-3	-0.3
	Bos-N	59	208	21	54	13	4	0	32	23	30	.260	.345	.361	92	-3	11			.890	-0	S-59	0.1
	Yr	131	466	47	108	23	6	5	59	47	68	.232	.315	.339	85	-9	23			.894	-0	*S-117/2-9,3-3,O-3	-0.2
1890	Bos-N	134	463	82	106	16	12	1	53	80	81	.229	.353	.322	90	-5	39			.918	-20	*2-134/S-1	-1.5
1891	Was-a	27	90	13	16	2	2	0	13	13	16	.178	.295	.244	57	-5	2			.919	7	2-19/S-5,3-4	0.3
Total	12	1112	4238	643	941	141	87	24	358	325	345	.222	.287	.313	86	-64	169			.903	70	2-713,S-336/3OPC	3.5
■ CHARLEY SMITH	Smith, Charles William b: 9/15/37, Charleston, S.C. d: 11/29/94, Reno, Nev. BR/TR, 6', 177 lbs. Deb: 9/8/60																						
1960	LA-N	18	60	2	10	1	1	0	5	1	15	.167	.180	.217	8	-8	0	0	0	.953	0	3-18	-0.8
1961	LA-N	9	24	4	6	1	0	2	3	1	6	.250	.280	.542	103	-0	0	0	0	1.000	-0	/3-4,S-3	0.0
	Phi-N	112	411	43	102	13	4	9	47	23	76	.248	.296	.365	75	-15	3	4	-2	.924	-2	3-94,S-14	-1.7
	Yr	121	435	47	108	14	4	11	50	24	82	.248	.295	.375	77	-15	3	4	-2	.926	-3	3-98,S-17	-1.7
1962	Chi-A	65	145	11	30	4	0	2	17	9	32	.207	.258	.276	44	-12	0	1	-1	.944	2	3-54	-1.0
1963	Chi-A	4	7	0	2	0	1	0	1	0	2	.286	.286	.571	136	0	0	0	0	1.000	2	/S-1	0.2
1964	Chi-A	2	7	1	1	0	0	1	1	0	1	.143	.250	.429	87	-0	0	0	0	1.000	3	/3-2	0.3
	NY-N	127	443	44	106	12	0	20	58	19	101	.239	.275	.402	90	-7	2	2	-1	.917	-12	3-85,S-36,O-13	-2.1
1965	NY-N	135	499	49	122	20	3	16	62	17	123	.244	.275	.393	89	-9	2	1	0	.957	10	*3-131/S-6,2-1	-0.2
1966	StL-N	116	391	34	104	13	4	10	43	22	81	.266	.305	.396	93	-4	0	2	-1	.964	-1	*3-107/S-1	-0.9
1967	NY-A	135	425	38	95	15	3	9	38	32	110	.224	.279	.336	84	-9	0	2	-1	.947	11	*3-115	-0.1
1968	NY-A	46	70	2	16	4	1	1	7	5	18	.229	.280	.357	95	-1	0	0	0	.961	4	3-13	0.3
1969	Chi-N	2	2	0	0	0	0	0	0	0	0	.000	.000	.000	-89	-0	0	0	0	.000	0	H	-0.1
Total	10	771	2484	228	594	83	18	69	281	130	565	.239	.281	.370	82	-65	7	12	-5	.945	16	3-623/S-61,O-13,2-1	-6.1
■ CHRIS SMITH	Smith, Christopher William b: 7/18/57, Torrance, Cal. BB/TR, 6', 185 lbs. Deb: 5/14/81																						
1981	Mon-N	7	7	0	0	0	0	0	0	0	2	.000	.000	.000	-99	-2	0	0	0	1.000	0	/2-1	-0.2
1982	Mon-N	2	2	0	0	0	0	0	0	0	1	.000	.000	.000	-98	-1	0	0	0	.000	0	/H	-0.1
1983	SF-N	22	67	13	22	6	1	1	11	7	12	.328	.408	.493	153	5	0	0	0	.976	-2	1-15/O-4,3-1	0.2
Total	3	31	76	13	22	6	1	1	11	7	15	.289	.365	.434	124	3	0	0	0	.976	-2	/1-15,O-4,3-1,2-1	-0.1
■ EARL SMITH	Smith, Earl Calvin b: 3/14/28, Sunnyside, Wash. BR/TR, 6', 185 lbs. Deb: 4/14/55																						
1955	Pit-N	5	16	1	1	0	0	0	0	4	2	.063	.286	.063	-1	-2	0	0	0	1.000	-0	/O-5	-0.3
■ EARL SMITH	Smith, Earl Leonard "Sheriff" b: 1/20/1891, Oak Hill, Ohio d: 3/14/43, Portsmouth, Ohio BB/TR, 5'11", 170 lbs. Deb: 9/12/16																						
1916	Chi-N	14	27	2	7	1	1	0	4	2	5	.259	.310	.370	98	-0	1			.800	-3	/O-7	-0.3
1917	StL-A	52	199	31	56	7	7	0	10	15	21	.281	.332	.387	124	5	5			.977	5	O-51	0.8
1918	StL-A	89	286	28	77	10	5	0	32	13	16	.269	.303	.339	97	-3	13			.952	1	O-81	-0.6
1919	StL-A	88	252	21	63	12	5	1	36	18	27	.250	.300	.349	80	-7	1			.971	10	O-68	-0.2
1920	StL-A	103	353	45	108	21	8	3	55	13	18	.306	.336	.436	100	-1	11	4	1	.916	-5	3-70,O-15	-0.3
1921	StL-A	25	78	7	26	4	2	2	14	3	4	.333	.366	.513	115	1	0	0	0	.878	-3	3-13/O-4	-0.1
	Was-A	59	180	20	39	5	2	2	12	10	19	.217	.266	.300	46	-15	1	0	0	.949	4	O-43/3-1	-1.3
	Yr	84	258	27	65	9	4	4	26	13	23	.252	.296	.364	69	-13	1	0	0	.944	0	O-47,3-14	-1.4
1922	Was-A	65	205	22	53	12	2	1	23	8	17	.259	.293	.351	71	-10	4	4	-1	.917	1	O-49/3-2	-1.3
Total	7	495	1580	176	429	72	32	9	186	82	127	.272	.311	.375	90	-30	36	8		.952	10	O-318/3-86	-3.3
■ EARL SMITH	Smith, Earl Sutton "Oil" b: 2/14/1897, Hot Springs, Ark. d: 6/8/63, Little Rock, Ark. BL/TR, 5'10.5", 180 lbs. Deb: 4/24/19																						
1919	NY-N	21	36	5	9	2	1	0	8	3	3	.250	.308	.361	102	0	1			.973	-3	C-14/2-1	-0.2
1920	NY-N	91	262	20	77	7	1	1	30	18	16	.294	.344	.340	98	-0	5	2	0	.976	-5	C-82	0.0
1921	*NY-N	89	229	35	77	8	4	10	51	27	8	.336	.409	.537	148	16	4	3	-1	.965	-10	C-78	0.9
1922	*NY-N	90	234	29	65	11	4	9	39	37	12	.278	.383	.474	119	7	1	1	-0	.978	-2	C-75	0.8
1923	NY-N	24	34	2	7	1	1	1	4	4	1	.206	.289	.382	77	-1	0	0	0	.975	2	C-12	0.1
	Bos-N	72	191	22	55	15	1	3	19	22	10	.288	.364	.424	112	3	0	1	-1	.975	-4	C-54	0.2
	Yr	96	225	24	62	16	2	4	23	26	11	.276	.353	.418	106	2	0	1	-1	.975	-2	C-66	0.3
1924	Bos-N	33	59	1	16	3	0	0	8	6	3	.271	.338	.322	81	-1	0	1	-1	.946	-1	C-13	-0.2
	Pit-N	39	111	12	41	10	1	4	21	13	4	.369	.435	.586	168	11	2	0	1	.974	0	C-35	1.3
	Yr	72	170	13	57	13	1	4	29	19	7	.335	.402	.494	140	10	2	1	0	.967	-1	C-48	1.1
1925	*Pit-N	109	329	34	103	22	3	8	64	31	13	.313	.374	.471	107	3	4	1	1	.968	11	C-96	1.9
1926	Pit-N	105	292	29	101	17	2	2	46	28	7	.346	.407	.438	121	9	1			.964	4	C-98	1.9
1927	*Pit-N	66	189	16	51	3	1	5	25	21	11	.270	.346	.376	87	-3	0			.986	-4	C-61	-0.4
1928	Pit-N	32	85	8	21	6	0	2	11	11	7	.247	.333	.388	85	-2	0			.967	-4	C-28	-0.3
	*StL-N	24	58	3	13	2	0	0	7	5	4	.224	.286	.259	42	-5	0			1.000	-1	C-18	-0.4
	Yr	56	143	11	34	8	0	2	18	16	11	.238	.314	.336	68	-7	0			.980	-5	C-46	-0.7

YEAR	TM/L	G	AB	R	H	2B	3B	HR	RBI	BB	SO	AVG	OBP	SLG	PRO+	BR/A	SB	CS	SBR	FA	FR	G/POS	TPR
1929	StL-N	57	145	9	50	8	0	1	22	18	6	.345	.417	.421	107	3	0			.962	-5	C-50	0.1
1930	StL-N	8	10	0	0	0	0	0	0	3	1	.000	.231	.000	-36	-2	0			.913	1	/C-6	-0.1
Total	12	860	2264	225	686	115	19	46	355	247	106	.303	.374	.432	111	37	18	9		.971	-20	C-720/2-1	5.6

■ EDGAR SMITH Smith, Edgar Eugene b: 6/12/1862, Providence, R.I. d: 11/3/1892, Providence, R.I. BR/TR, 5'10", 160 lbs. Deb: 5/25/1883

YEAR	TM/L	G	AB	R	H	2B	3B	HR	RBI	BB	SO	AVG	OBP	SLG	PRO+	BR/A	SB	CS	SBR	FA	FR	G/POS	TPR
1883	Pro-N	2	9	2	2	1	0	0	1	0	2	.222	.222	.333	64	-0				1.000	-0	/1-2,O-2	-0.1
	Phi-N	1	4	1	3	0	0	0	1	0	0	.750	.750	.750	393	1				.000	-1	/P-1,O-1	0.0
	Yr	3	13	3	5	1	0	0	2	0	2	.385	.385	.462	158	1				1.000	-1	/O-3,1-2,P-1	-0.1
1884	Was-a	14	57	5	5	0	1	0		1		.088	.103	.123	-30	-8				.794	5	O-12/P-3	-0.2
1885	Pro-N	1	4	0	1	0	0	0	0	0	0	.250	.250	.250	64	-0				.750	0	/P-1	0.0
1890	Cle-N	8	24	2	7	0	1	0	4	4	1	.292	.393	.375	126	1	0			.900	1	/P-6,O-2	0.0
Total	4	26	98	10	18	1	2	0	6	5	3	.184	.223	.235	47	-6	0			.821	5	/O-17,P-11,1-2	-0.3

■ MAYO SMITH Smith, Edward Mayo b: 1/17/15, New London, Mo. d: 11/24/77, Boynton Beach, Fla BL/TR, 6', 183 lbs. Deb: 6/24/45 M

YEAR	TM/L	G	AB	R	H	2B	3B	HR	RBI	BB	SO	AVG	OBP	SLG	PRO+	BR/A	SB	CS	SBR	FA	FR	G/POS	TPR
1945	Phi-A	73	203	18	43	5	0	0	11	36	13	.212	.333	.236	67	-7	0	1	-1	.976	-8	O-65	-2.0

■ ELMER SMITH Smith, Elmer Ellsworth b: 3/23/1868, Pittsburgh, Pa. d: 11/3/45, Pittsburgh, Pa. BL/TL, 5'11", 178 lbs. Deb: 9/10/1886

YEAR	TM/L	G	AB	R	H	2B	3B	HR	RBI	BB	SO	AVG	OBP	SLG	PRO+	BR/A	SB	CS	SBR	FA	FR	G/POS	TPR
1886	Cin-a	9	28	6	8	1	1	0	2	9		.286	.459	.393	163	3	0			.600	-2	P-9/O-1	0.0
1887	Cin-a	52	186	26	47	10	6	0	23	11		.253	.298	.371	84	-5	5			.851	-6	P-52/O-2	-0.1
1888	Cin-a	40	129	15	29	4	1	0	9	20		.225	.329	.271	88	-1	2			.838	-6	P-40/O-2	-0.1
1889	Cin-a	29	83	12	23	3	1	2	17	7	18	.277	.348	.410	112	1	1			.821	-4	P-29	0.0
1892	Pit-N	138	511	86	140	16	14	4	63	82	43	.274	.375	.384	129	20	22			.885	-5	*O-124,P-17	0.8
1893	Pit-N	128	518	121	179	26	23	7	103	77	23	.346	.435	.525	158	44	26			.921	3	*O-128	3.3
1894	Pit-N	125	489	128	174	33	19	6	72	65	12	.356	.436	.538	135	29	33			.933	4	*O-125/P-1	1.9
1895	Pit-N	124	480	88	145	14	12	1	81	55	25	.302	.381	.387	104	5	34			.896	-3	*O-123	-0.6
1896	Pit-N	122	484	121	175	21	14	6	94	74	18	.362	.454	.500	158	45	33			.946	9	*O-122	3.6
1897	Pit-N	123	467	99	145	19	17	6	54	70		.310	.408	.463	135	26	25			.904	3	*O-123	1.6
1898	Cin-N	123	486	79	166	21	10	1	66	69		.342	.425	.432	136	25	20			.949	4	*O-123/P-1	1.8
1899	Cin-N	87	339	65	101	13	6	1	24	47		.298	.385	.381	108	5	10			.922	-1	O-87	-0.2
1900	Cin-N	29	111	14	31	4	4	1	18	18		.279	.389	.414	125	4	5			.930	0	O-27	0.2
	NY-N	85	312	47	81	9	7	2	34	24		.260	.317	.353	89	-5	14			.953	-8	O-83	-1.8
	Yr	114	423	61	112	13	11	3	52	42		.265	.337	.369	99	-1	19			.944	-8	*O-110	-1.6
1901	Pit-N	4	4	0	0	0	0	0	0	2		.000	.333	.000	1	-0	0			1.000	-0	/O-1	-0.1
	Bos-N	16	57	5	10	2	1	0	3	6		.175	.254	.246	41	-4	2			.833	-3	O-15	-0.8
	Yr	20	61	5	10	2	1	0	3	8		.164	.261	.230	40	-5	2			.846	-3	O-16	-0.9
Total	14	1234	4684	912	1454	196	136	37	663	636	139	.310	.398	.434	126	191	232			.921	-17	*O-1086,P-149	9.5

■ ELMER SMITH Smith, Elmer John b: 9/21/1892, Sandusky, Ohio d: 8/3/84, Columbia, Ky. BL/TR, 5'10", 165 lbs. Deb: 9/20/14

YEAR	TM/L	G	AB	R	H	2B	3B	HR	RBI	BB	SO	AVG	OBP	SLG	PRO+	BR/A	SB	CS	SBR	FA	FR	G/POS	TPR
1914	Cle-A	13	53	5	17	3	0	0	8	2	11	.321	.345	.377	113	1	1	1	-0	1.000	1	O-13	0.1
1915	Cle-A	144	476	37	118	23	12	3	67	36	75	.248	.301	.366	97	-4	10	11	-4	.923	0	*O-123	-1.4
1916	Cle-A	79	213	25	59	15	3	3	40	18	35	.277	.336	.418	119	4	3			.966	-2	O-57	0.0
	Was-A	45	168	12	36	10	3	2	27	18	28	.214	.298	.345	94	-2	4			.988	1	O-45	-0.3
	Yr	124	381	37	95	25	6	5	67	36	63	.249	.319	.386	108	2	7			.976	-1	*O-102	-0.3
1917	Was-A	35	117	8	26	4	3	0	17	5	14	.222	.260	.308	74	-4	1			.901	-0	O-29	-0.7
	Cle-A	64	161	21	42	5	1	3	22	13	18	.261	.316	.360	99	-1	6			.986	-1	O-40	-0.4
	Yr	99	278	29	68	9	4	3	39	18	32	.245	.293	.338	89	-5	7			.943	-1	O-69	-1.1
1919	Cle-A	114	395	60	110	24	6	9	54	41	30	.278	.354	.438	115	7	15			.957	-6	*O-111	-0.7
1920	*Cle-A	129	456	82	144	37	10	12	103	53	35	.316	.391	.520	135	22	5	4	-1	.970	-8	*O-129	0.5
1921	Cle-A	129	431	98	125	28	9	16	85	56	46	.290	.374	.508	121	13	0	2	-1	.971	-8	*O-127	-0.4
1922	Bos-A	73	231	43	66	13	6	6	32	25	21	.286	.358	.472	116	5	0	3	-2	.947	2	O-58	0.1
	*NY-A	21	27	1	5	0	0	1	5	3	5	.185	.267	.296	46	-2	0	0	0	.933	-2	O-11	-0.4
	Yr	94	258	44	71	13	6	7	37	28	26	.275	.348	.453	108	2	0	3	-2	.945	1	O-69	-0.3
1923	NY-A	70	183	30	56	6	2	7	35	21	21	.306	.377	.475	121	5	3	1	0	.948	-2	O-47	0.1
1925	Cin-N	96	284	47	77	13	7	8	46	28	20	.271	.339	.451	102	0	6	5	-1	.967	-5	O-80	-1.0
Total	10	1012	3195	469	881	181	62	70	541	319	359	.276	.344	.437	112	44	54	27		.957	-29	O-870	-4.5

■ MIKE SMITH Smith, Elwood Hope b: 11/16/04, Norfolk, Va. d: 5/31/81, Chesapeake, Va. BL/TR, 5'11.5", 170 lbs. Deb: 9/4/26

YEAR	TM/L	G	AB	R	H	2B	3B	HR	RBI	BB	SO	AVG	OBP	SLG	PRO+	BR/A	SB	CS	SBR	FA	FR	G/POS	TPR
1926	NY-N	4	7	0	1	0	0	0	0	0	2	.143	.143	.143	-23	-1	0			1.000	0	/O-1	-0.1

■ CARR SMITH Smith, Emanuel Carr b: 4/8/01, Kernersville, N.C. d: 4/14/89, Miami, Fla. BR/TR, 6'1", 175 lbs. Deb: 9/23/23

YEAR	TM/L	G	AB	R	H	2B	3B	HR	RBI	BB	SO	AVG	OBP	SLG	PRO+	BR/A	SB	CS	SBR	FA	FR	G/POS	TPR
1923	Was-A	5	9	0	1	1	0	0	1	0	0	.111	.111	.222	-14	-2	0	0	0	1.000	-1	/O-4	-0.3
1924	Was-A	5	10	1	2	0	0	0	0	0	3	.200	.200	.200	3	-1	0	0	0	1.000	-1	/O-4	-0.3
Total	2	10	19	1	3	1	0	0	1	0	3	.158	.158	.211	-5	-3	0	0	0	1.000	-3	/O-8	-0.6

■ ERNIE SMITH Smith, Ernest Henry "Kansas City Kid" b: 10/11/1899, Totowa, N.J. d: 4/6/73, Brooklyn, N.Y. BR/TR, 5'8", 155 lbs. Deb: 4/17/30

YEAR	TM/L	G	AB	R	H	2B	3B	HR	RBI	BB	SO	AVG	OBP	SLG	PRO+	BR/A	SB	CS	SBR	FA	FR	G/POS	TPR
1930	Chi-A	24	79	5	19	3	0	0	3	5	6	.241	.286	.278	45	-7	2	0	1	.920	0	S-21	-0.3

■ FRANK SMITH Smith, Frank L. b: 11/24/1857, Canada d: 10/11/28, Canandaigua, N.Y. Deb: 8/6/1884

YEAR	TM/L	G	AB	R	H	2B	3B	HR	RBI	BB	SO	AVG	OBP	SLG	PRO+	BR/A	SB	CS	SBR	FA	FR	G/POS	TPR
1884	Pit-a	10	36	3	9	0	1	0		0		.250	.250	.306	79	-1				.930	-3	/C-7,O-3	-0.3

■ FRED SMITH Smith, Fred Vincent b: 7/29/1886, Cleveland, Ohio d: 5/28/61, Cleveland, Ohio BR/TR, 5'11.5", 185 lbs. Deb: 4/17/13 F

YEAR	TM/L	G	AB	R	H	2B	3B	HR	RBI	BB	SO	AVG	OBP	SLG	PRO+	BR/A	SB	CS	SBR	FA	FR	G/POS	TPR
1913	Bos-N	92	285	35	65	9	3	0	27	29	55	.228	.302	.281	65	-12	7			.920	-14	3-59,2-14,S-11,/O-4	-2.7
1914	Buf-F	145	473	48	104	12	10	2	45	49	78	.220	.297	.300	62	-33	24			.930	-0	*3-127,S-19/1-1	-2.8
1915	Buf-F	35	114	8	27	2	4	0	11	13	15	.237	.320	.325	80	-5	2			.920	3	S-32/3-1	0.1
	Bro-F	110	385	41	95	16	6	5	58	25	49	.247	.298	.358	85	-15	21			.920	1	S-94,3-15	-0.6
	Yr	145	499	49	122	18	10	5	69	38	64	.244	.303	.351	84	-19	23			.920	5	*S-126,3-16	-0.5
1917	StL-N	56	165	11	30	0	2	1	17	17	22	.182	.262	.224	51	-9	4			.950	7	3-51/2-2,S-1	-0.2
Total	4	438	1422	143	321	39	25	8	158	133	219	.226	.296	.305	69	-73	58			.932	-3	3-253,S-157/2O1	-6.2

■ GEORGE SMITH Smith, George Cornelius b: 7/7/37, St.Petersburg, Fla. d: 6/15/87, St.Petersburg, Fla. BR/TR, 5'10", 170 lbs. Deb: 8/4/63

YEAR	TM/L	G	AB	R	H	2B	3B	HR	RBI	BB	SO	AVG	OBP	SLG	PRO+	BR/A	SB	CS	SBR	FA	FR	G/POS	TPR
1963	Det-A	52	171	16	37	8	2	0	17	18	34	.216	.298	.287	63	-8	4	0	1	.982	11	2-52	0.9
1964	Det-A	5	7	1	2	0	0	0	2	1	4	.286	.375	.286	86	-0	1	0	0	1.000	1	/2-3	0.1
1965	Det-A	32	53	6	5	0	0	1	1	3	18	.094	.143	.151	-16	-8	0	0	0	.984	3	2-22/S-3,3-3	-0.5
1966	Bos-A	128	403	41	86	19	4	8	37	37	86	.213	.284	.340	71	-15	4	0	1	.969	16	*2-109,S-19	1.1
Total	4	217	634	64	130	27	6	9	57	59	142	.205	.278	.309	62	-31	9	0	3	.974	30	2-186/S-22,3-3	1.6

■ HEINIE SMITH Smith, George Henry b: 10/24/1871, Pittsburgh, Pa. d: 6/25/39, Buffalo, N.Y. BR/TR, 5'9.5", 160 lbs. Deb: 9/8/1897 M

YEAR	TM/L	G	AB	R	H	2B	3B	HR	RBI	BB	SO	AVG	OBP	SLG	PRO+	BR/A	SB	CS	SBR	FA	FR	G/POS	TPR
1897	Lou-N	21	76	7	20	3	0	1	7	3		.263	.300	.342	72	-3	1			.928	-3	2-21	-0.4
1898	Lou-N	35	121	14	23	4	0	0	13	6		.190	.246	.223	35	-10	6			.910	-6	2-33	-1.3
1899	Pit-N	15	53	9	15	3	1	0	12	5		.283	.345	.377	98	-0	2			.851	-3	2-15/S-1	-0.2
1901	NY-N	9	29	5	6	2	1	1	4	1		.207	.233	.448	99	-0	1			.969	-1	/2-7,P-2	-0.1
1902	NY-N	138	511	46	129	19	2	0	33	17		.252	.278	.297	78	-14	32			.953	4	*2-138,M	-0.6
1903	Det-A	93	336	36	75	11	3	1	22	19		.223	.271	.283	68	-13	12			.928	-2	2-93	-1.2
Total	6	311	1126	117	268	42	7	3	91	51		.238	.276	.296	71	-41	54			.934	-11	2-307/P-2,S-1	-3.8

■ GERMANY SMITH Smith, George J. b: 4/21/1863, Pittsburgh, Pa. d: 12/1/27, Altoona, Pa. BR/TR, 6', 175 lbs. Deb: 4/17/1884

YEAR	TM/L	G	AB	R	H	2B	3B	HR	RBI	BB	SO	AVG	OBP	SLG	PRO+	BR/A	SB	CS	SBR	FA	FR	G/POS	TPR
1884	Alt-U	25	108	9	34	8	1	0		1		.315	.321	.407	118	-1				.871	6	S-25/P-1	0.5
	Cle-N	72	291	31	74	14	4	4	26	2	45	.254	.259	.371	93	-3				.879	9	2-42,S-30	0.7
1885	Bro-a	108	419	63	108	17	11	4	62	10		.258	.275	.379	105	1				.884	**40**	*S-108	3.7
1886	Bro-a	105	426	66	105	17	6	2	45	19		.246	.279	.329	89	-7	22			.860	13	*S-105/O-1,C-1	0.6
1887	Bro-a	103	435	79	128	19	16	4	72	13		.294	.316	.439	108	2	26			**.886**	**32**	*S-101/3-2	2.8
1888	Bro-a	103	402	47	86	10	7	3	61	22		.214	.255	.296	76	-11	27			.844	6	*S-103/2-1	-0.3

YEAR	TM/L	G	AB	R	H	2B	3B	HR	RBI	BB	SO	AVG	OBP	SLG	PRO+	BR/A	SB	CS	SBR	FA	FR	G/POS	TPR
1889	*Bro-a	121	446	89	103	22	3	3	53	40	42	.231	.296	.314	73	-16	35			.899	-4	*S-120/O-1	-1.1
1890	*Bro-N	129	481	76	92	6	5	1	47	42	23	.191	.260	.231	43	-35	24			.904	4	*S-129	-2.1
1891	Cin-N	138	512	50	103	11	5	3	53	38	32	.201	.258	.260	50	-33	16			.909	11	*S-138	-1.2
1892	Cin-N	139	506	58	121	13	6	8	63	42	52	.239	.297	.336	93	-6	19			.920	25	*S-139	2.3
1893	Cin-N	130	500	63	118	18	6	4	56	38	20	.236	.293	.320	61	-30	14			**.934**	20	*S-130	-0.4
1894	Cin-N	127	482	73	127	33	5	3	76	41	28	.263	.324	.371	65	-30	15			.911	20	*S-127	-0.3
1895	Cin-N	127	503	75	151	23	6	4	74	34	24	.300	.345	.394	87	-12	13			.923	2	*S-127	-0.3
1896	Cin-N	120	456	65	131	21	9	3	71	28	22	.287	.330	.393	84	-13	22			.926	-10	*S-120	-1.6
1897	Bro-N	112	428	47	86	17	3	0	29	14		.201	.233	.255	30	-44	1			.908	-11	*S-112	-4.6
1898	StL-N	51	157	16	25	2	1	1	9	24		.159	.275	.204	37	-12	1			.904	-5	S-51	-1.5
Total	15	1710	6552	907	1592	251	94	47	797	408	288	.243	.289	.332	74	-249	235			.902	157	*S-1665/2-43,3OCP	-2.8

■ **JUD SMITH** Smith, Grant Judson b: 1/13/1869, Green Oak, Mich. d: 12/7/47, Los Angeles, Cal. BR/TR, Deb: 5/21/1893

YEAR	TM/L	G	AB	R	H	2B	3B	HR	RBI	BB	SO	AVG	OBP	SLG	PRO+	BR/A	SB	CS	SBR	FA	FR	G/POS	TPR
1893	Cin-N	17	43	7	10	1	0	1	5	9	5	.233	.365	.326	82	-1	1			.750	-2	/O-9,3-6,S-1	-0.3
	StL-N	4	13	1	1	0	0	0	0	1	2	.077	.200	.077	-25	-2	0			.889	1	/3-4	-0.1
	Yr	21	56	8	11	1	0	1	5	10	7	.196	.328	.268	58	-3	1			.844	-1	3-10/O-9,S-1	-0.4
1896	Pit-N	10	35	6	12	2	1	0	4	2	2	.343	.395	.457	129	1	3			.909	2	3-10	0.3
1898	Was-N	66	234	33	71	7	5	3	28	22		.303	.378	.415	127	8	11			.903	-10	3-47,S-10/1-7,2-1	0.0
1901	Pit-N	6	21	1	3	1	0	0	0	3		.143	.250	.190	28	-2	0			.947	0	/3-6	-0.2
Total	4	103	346	48	97	11	6	4	37	37	9	.280	.363	.382	109	5	15			.900	-9	/3-73,S-11,O-9,12	-0.3

■ **GREG SMITH** Smith, Gregory Alan b: 4/5/67, Baltimore, Md. BB/TR, 5′11″, 170 lbs. Deb: 9/2/89

YEAR	TM/L	G	AB	R	H	2B	3B	HR	RBI	BB	SO	AVG	OBP	SLG	PRO+	BR/A	SB	CS	SBR	FA	FR	G/POS	TPR
1989	Chi-N	4	5	1	2	0	0	0	2	0	0	.400	.500	.400	149	0	0	0	0	.778	0	/2-2	0.1
1990	Chi-N	18	44	4	9	2	1	0	5	2	5	.205	.239	.295	43	-3	1	0	0	1.000	4	/2-7,S-7	0.1
1991	LA-N	5	3	1	0	0	0	0	0	0	2	.000	.000	.000	-99	-1	0	0	0	.000	0	/2-1	-0.1
Total	3	27	52	6	11	2	1	0	7	2	7	.212	.255	.288	47	-4	1	0	0	.944	4	/2-10,S-7	0.1

■ **HAL SMITH** Smith, Harold Raymond "Cura" b: 6/1/31, Barling, Ark. BR/TR, 5′11″, 189 lbs. Deb: 5/2/56 C

YEAR	TM/L	G	AB	R	H	2B	3B	HR	RBI	BB	SO	AVG	OBP	SLG	PRO+	BR/A	SB	CS	SBR	FA	FR	G/POS	TPR
1956	StL-N	75	227	27	64	12	0	5	23	15	22	.282	.326	.401	94	-2	1	0	0	.982	-2	C-66	-0.1
1957	StL-N☆	100	333	25	93	12	3	2	37	18	18	.279	.316	.351	78	-10	2	2	-1	.990	-1	C-97	-0.8
1958	StL-N	77	220	13	50	4	1	1	24	14	14	.227	.274	.268	42	-18	0	0	0	.989	-1	C-71	-1.6
1959	StL-N★	142	452	35	122	15	3	13	50	15	28	.270	.295	.403	78	-14	2	6	-3	.989	5	*C-141	-0.6
1960	StL-N	127	337	20	77	16	0	2	28	29	33	.228	.292	.294	56	-20	1	0	0	.990	18	*C-124	0.5
1961	StL-N	45	125	6	31	4	1	0	10	11	12	.248	.314	.296	57	-7	0	0	0	.993	17	C-45	1.2
1965	Pit-N	4	3	0	0	0	0	0	0	0	1	.000	.000	.000	-99	-1	0	0	0	1.000	2	/C-4	0.1
Total	7	570	1697	126	437	63	8	23	172	102	128	.258	.301	.345	69	-73	6	8	-3	.989	38	C-548	-1.3

■ **HAL SMITH** Smith, Harold Wayne b: 12/7/30, W.Frankfort, Ill. BR/TR, 6′, 195 lbs. Deb: 4/11/55

YEAR	TM/L	G	AB	R	H	2B	3B	HR	RBI	BB	SO	AVG	OBP	SLG	PRO+	BR/A	SB	CS	SBR	FA	FR	G/POS	TPR
1955	Bal-A	135	424	41	115	23	4	4	52	30	21	.271	.322	.373	93	-6	1	3	-2	.986	-3	*C-125	-0.6
1956	Bal-A	77	229	16	60	14	0	3	18	17	22	.262	.316	.362	85	-6	1	0	0	.994	3	C-71	0.0
	KC-A	37	142	15	39	9	2	2	24	3	12	.275	.290	.408	82	-4	1	1	-0	.986	1	C-37	-0.2
	Yr	114	371	31	99	23	2	5	42	20	34	.267	.306	.380	85	-10	2	1	0	.991	5	*C-108	-0.2
1957	KC-A	107	360	41	109	26	0	13	41	14	44	.303	.331	.483	118	7	2	2	-1	.983	-1	*C-103	0.9
1958	KC-A	99	315	32	86	19	2	5	46	25	47	.273	.330	.394	97	-2	0	0	0	.949	-1	3-43,C-31,1-14	-0.1
1959	KC-A	108	292	36	84	12	0	5	31	34	39	.288	.368	.380	104	3	0	3	-2	.953	7	3-77,C-22	0.9
1960	*Pit-N	77	258	37	76	18	2	11	45	22	48	.295	.355	.508	132	11	1	1	-0	.985	-6	C-71	0.9
1961	Pit-N	67	193	12	43	10	0	3	26	11	38	.223	.268	.321	55	-13	0	0	0	.990	-1	C-65	-1.0
1962	Hou-N	109	345	32	81	14	0	12	35	24	55	.235	.288	.380	84	-9	0	0	0	.986	2	C-92/3-6,1-2	-0.4
1963	Hou-N	31	58	1	14	2	0	0	2	4	15	.241	.290	.276	68	-2	0	0	0	.985	-3	C-11	-0.5
1964	Cin-N	32	66	6	8	1	0	0	3	12	20	.121	.256	.136	14	-7	1	0	0	.983	-3	C-20	-1.0
Total	10	879	2682	269	715	148	10	58	323	196	361	.267	.320	.394	94	-29	7	10	-4	.986	-3	C-648,3-126/1-16	-1.1

■ **HARRY SMITH** Smith, Harry Thomas b: 10/31/1874, Yorkshire, England d: 2/17/33, Salem, N.J. BR/TR, Deb: 7/11/01 M

YEAR	TM/L	G	AB	R	H	2B	3B	HR	RBI	BB	SO	AVG	OBP	SLG	PRO+	BR/A	SB	CS	SBR	FA	FR	G/POS	TPR
1901	Phi-A	11	34	3	11	1	0	0	3	2		.324	.378	.353	99	0	1			.969	-3	/C-9,O-1	-0.2
1902	Pit-N	50	185	14	35	4	1	0	12	4		.189	.211	.222	32	-15	4			.972	-2	C-50	-1.2
1903	*Pit-N	61	212	15	37	3	2	0	19	12		.175	.222	.208	22	-22	2			.974	-4	C-60/O-1	-1.9
1904	Pit-N	47	141	17	35	3	1	0	18	16		.248	.346	.284	92	-0	5			.964	-4	C-44/O-3	0.1
1905	Pit-N	1	3	0	0	0	0	0	1	0		.000	.000	.000	-98	-1	1			1.000	0	/C-1	-0.1
1906	Pit-N	1	1	0	0	0	0	0	0	0		.000	.000	.000	-96	-0	0			.800	0	/C-1	0.0
1907	Pit-N	18	38	4	10	1	0	0	1	4		.263	.364	.289	103	0	0			.939	-3	C-18	-0.1
1908	Bos-N	41	130	13	32	2	2	1	16	7		.246	.295	.315	96	-1	2			.975	0	C-38	0.3
1909	Bos-N	43	113	9	19	4	1	0	4	5		.168	.203	.221	30	-9	3			.972	2	C-31,M	-0.5
1910	Bos-N	70	147	8	35	4	0	1	15	5	14	.238	.263	.286	57	-8	5			.949	3	C-38	-0.2
Total	10	343	1004	83	214	22	7	2	89	55	14	.213	.262	.255	54	-56	23			.967	-9	C-290/O-5	-3.8

■ **HARRY SMITH** Smith, Harry W. b: 2/5/1856, N.Vernon, Ind. d: 6/4/1898, Queensville, Ind. BR/TR, 6′, 175 lbs. Deb: 5/8/1877

YEAR	TM/L	G	AB	R	H	2B	3B	HR	RBI	BB	SO	AVG	OBP	SLG	PRO+	BR/A	SB	CS	SBR	FA	FR	G/POS	TPR
1877	Chi-N	24	94	7	19	1	0	0	3	4	6	.202	.235	.213	37	-7				.853	-7	2-14,O-10	-1.3
	Cin-N	10	36	4	9	2	1	0	3	1	5	.250	.270	.361	109	0				.879	1	/C-8,2-3,O-3	0.1
	Yr	34	130	11	28	3	1	0	6	5	11	.215	.244	.254	54	-7				.837	-7	2-17,O-13/C-8	-1.2
1889	Lou-a	1	2	0	1	0	0	0	1	0	1	.500	.500	.500	189	0	0			.000	-2	/O-1,C-1	-0.1
Total	2	35	132	11	29	3	1	0	7	5	12	.220	.248	.258	56	-6	0			.720	-8	/2-17,O-14,C-9	-1.3

■ **HARVEY SMITH** Smith, Harvey Fetterhoff b: 7/24/1871, Union Deposit, Pa d: 11/12/62, Harrisburg, Pa. BL/TR, 5′8″, 160 lbs. Deb: 8/19/1896

YEAR	TM/L	G	AB	R	H	2B	3B	HR	RBI	BB	SO	AVG	OBP	SLG	PRO+	BR/A	SB	CS	SBR	FA	FR	G/POS	TPR
1896	Was-N	36	131	21	36	7	2	0	17	12	7	.275	.345	.359	86	-3	9			.861	3	3-36	0.1

■ **HAPPY SMITH** Smith, Henry Joseph b: 7/14/1883, Coquille, Ore. d: 2/26/61, San Jose, Cal. BL/TR, 6′, 185 lbs. Deb: 4/15/10

YEAR	TM/L	G	AB	R	H	2B	3B	HR	RBI	BB	SO	AVG	OBP	SLG	PRO+	BR/A	SB	CS	SBR	FA	FR	G/POS	TPR
1910	Bro-N	35	76	6	18	2	0	0	5	4	14	.237	.275	.263	59	-4	4			.974	2	O-16	-0.3

■ **JACK SMITH** Smith, Jack b: 6/23/1895, Chicago, Ill. d: 5/2/72, Westchester, Ill. BL/TL, 5′8″, 165 lbs. Deb: 9/30/15

YEAR	TM/L	G	AB	R	H	2B	3B	HR	RBI	BB	SO	AVG	OBP	SLG	PRO+	BR/A	SB	CS	SBR	FA	FR	G/POS	TPR
1915	StL-N	4	16	2	3	0	1	0	0	1	5	.188	.235	.313	65	-1	0			1.000	-1	/O-4	-0.2
1916	StL-N	130	357	43	87	6	5	6	34	20	50	.244	.291	.339	94	-3	24	16	-2	.949	-11	*O-120	-2.5
1917	StL-N	137	462	64	137	16	11	3	34	38	65	.297	.351	.398	133	18	25			.961	-10	*O-128	0.2
1918	StL-N	42	166	24	35	2	1	0	4	7	21	.211	.260	.235	53	-9	5			.941	1	O-42	-1.3
1919	StL-N	119	408	47	91	16	3	0	15	26	29	.223	.271	.277	69	-16	30			.960	-0	*O-111	-2.6
1920	StL-N	91	313	53	104	22	5	1	28	25	23	.332	.385	.444	143	17	14	9	-1	.963	-10	O-83	0.1
1921	StL-N	116	411	86	135	22	9	7	33	21	24	.328	.361	.477	122	12	11	6	-0	.955	-6	*O-103	-0.2
1922	StL-N	143	510	117	158	23	12	8	46	50	30	.310	.375	.449	117	13	18	7	1	.951	-8	*O-136	-0.3
1923	StL-N	124	407	98	126	16	6	5	41	27	20	.310	.356	.415	105	3	32	11	3	.974	4	*O-109	0.3
1924	StL-N	124	459	91	130	18	6	2	33	33	27	.283	.333	.362	88	-8	24	16	-2	.968	10	*O-114	-0.8
1925	StL-N	80	243	53	61	11	4	4	31	19	13	.251	.308	.379	73	-10	20	2	5	.958	-3	O-64	-1.2
1926	StL-N	1	1	0	0	0	0	0	0	0	1	.000	.000	.000	-96	-0	0			.000	0	H	0.0
	Bos-N	96	322	46	100	15	2	2	25	28	12	.311	.369	.388	114	7	11			.973	2	O-83	0.3
	Yr	97	323	46	100	15	2	2	25	28	13	.310	.368	.387	113	6	11			.973	2	O-83	0.3
1927	Bos-N	84	183	27	58	6	4	1	24	16	12	.317	.375	.410	119	5	8			.950	-0	O-48	0.2
1928	Bos-N	96	254	30	71	9	2	1	32	21	14	.280	.335	.343	82	-7	6			.988	1	O-65	-1.0
1929	Bos-N	19	20	2	5	0	0	0	2	2	2	.250	.318	.250	45	-2	0			.833	-3	/O-9	-0.5
Total	15	1406	4532	783	1301	182	71	40	382	334	348	.287	.339	.385	103	18	228	67		.961	-36	*O-1219	-9.5

■ **STUB SMITH** Smith, James A. b: 11/26/1876, Elmwood, Ill. BL/TR, 5′6″, 145 lbs. Deb: 9/10/1898

YEAR	TM/L	G	AB	R	H	2B	3B	HR	RBI	BB	SO	AVG	OBP	SLG	PRO+	BR/A	SB	CS	SBR	FA	FR	G/POS	TPR
1898	Bos-N	3	10	1	1	0	0	0	0	0		.100	.100	.100	-41	-2	0			.933	1	/S-3	-0.1

YEAR	TM/L	G	AB	R	H	2B	3B	HR	RBI	BB	SO	AVG	OBP	SLG	PRO+	BR/A	SB	CS	SBR	FA	FR	G/POS	TPR
■ RED SMITH	Smith, James Carlisle b: 4/6/1890, Greenville, S.C. d: 10/11/66, Atlanta, Ga. BR/TR, 5′11″, 165 lbs. Deb: 9/5/11																						
1911	Bro-N	28	111	10	29	6	1	0	19	5	13	.261	.299	.333	80	-3	5			.900	-2	3-28	-0.5
1912	Bro-N	128	486	75	139	28	6	4	57	54	51	.286	.362	.393	111	8	22			.938	5	*3-125	1.3
1913	Bro-N	151	540	70	160	**40**	10	6	76	45	67	.296	.358	.441	124	16	22			.933	-1	*3-151	1.7
1914	Bro-N	90	330	39	81	10	8	4	48	30	26	.245	.310	.361	97	-2	11			.937	12	3-90	1.4
	Bos-N	60	207	30	65	17	1	3	37	28	24	.314	.401	.449	153	14	4			.937	10	3-60	2.8
	Yr	150	537	69	146	27	9	7	85	58	50	.272	.346	.395	119	12	15			.937	23	*3-150	4.2
1915	Bos-N	157	549	66	145	34	4	2	65	67	49	.264	.345	.352	116	12	10	5	0	.947	-6	*3-157	1.4
1916	Bos-N	150	509	48	132	16	10	3	60	53	55	.259	.333	.348	114	9	13			.928	-4	*3-150	1.1
1917	Bos-N	147	505	60	149	31	6	2	62	53	61	.295	.369	.392	142	26	16			.925	-21	*3-147	0.9
1918	Bos-N	119	429	55	128	20	3	2	65	45	47	.298	.373	.373	133	18	8			.922	4	*3-119	2.7
1919	Bos-N	87	241	24	59	6	0	1	25	40	22	.245	.359	.282	98	2	6			.981	-0	O-48,3-23	0.0
Total	9	1117	3907	477	1087	208	49	27	514	420	415	.278	.353	.377	120	100	117	5		.932	-2	*3-1050/O-48	12.8
■ HARRY SMITH	Smith, James Harry b: 5/15/1890, Baltimore, Md. d: 4/1/22, Charlotte, N.C. BR/TR, 5′10″, 180 lbs. Deb: 9/21/14																						
1914	NY-N	5	7	0	3	0	0	0	2	3	1	.429	.600	.429	215	1	1			1.000	2	/C-4	0.3
1915	NY-N	21	32	1	4	0	1	0	3	6	12	.125	.263	.188	40	-2	0	1	-1	.967	-3	C-18	-0.5
	Bro-F	28	65	5	13	0	0	1	4	7	16	.200	.278	.246	48	-5	2			.967	-5	C-19/O-1	-1.0
1917	Cin-N	8	17	0	2	0	0	0	1	2	7	.118	.211	.118	2	-2	0			.978	4	/C-7	0.3
1918	Cin-N	13	27	4	5	1	2	0	4	3	6	.185	.267	.370	95	-0	1			1.000	-2	/C-6,O-1	-0.2
Total	4	75	148	10	27	1	3	1	14	21	42	.182	.284	.250	59	-8	4	1		.975	-4	/C-54,O-2	-1.1
■ JIMMY SMITH	Smith, James Lawrence "Greenfield Jimmy" b: 5/15/1895, Pittsburgh, Pa. d: 1/1/74, Pittsburgh, Pa. BB/TR, 5′9″, 152 lbs. Deb: 9/26/14																						
1914	Chi-F	3	6	1	3	1	0	0	1	0	0	.500	.500	.667	229	1	0			1.000	1	/S-3	0.2
1915	Chi-F	95	318	32	69	11	4	4	30	14	65	.217	.250	.314	62	-23	4			.904	-14	S-92/2-1	-3.3
	Bal-F	33	108	9	19	1	1	1	11	11	23	.176	.258	.231	37	-11	3			.883	-4	S-33	-1.3
	Yr	128	426	41	88	12	5	5	41	25	88	.207	.252	.293	55	-34	7			.898	-18	*S-125/2-1	-4.6
1916	Pit-N	36	96	4	18	1	1	0	5	6	22	.188	.257	.219	46	-6	0			.929	1	S-27/3-6	-0.4
1917	NY-N	36	96	12	22	5	1	0	9	9	18	.229	.295	.302	86	-2	6			.971	-2	2-29/S-7	-0.3
1918	Bos-N	34	102	8	23	3	4	1	14	3	13	.225	.255	.363	91	-2	1			1.000	-1	2-10/S-9,O-6,3-5	-0.2
1919	*Cin-N	28	40	9	11	1	3	1	10	4	8	.275	.341	.525	163	3	1			1.000	-2	/3-6,S-5,2-4,O-4	0.2
1921	Phi-N	67	247	31	57	8	1	4	22	11	28	.231	.266	.320	50	-18	2	8	-4	.971	8	2-66	-1.3
1922	Phi-N	38	114	13	25	1	0	1	6	5	9	.219	.258	.254	30	-12	1	3	-2	.952	-3	S-23,2-13/3-1	-1.4
Total	8	370	1127	119	247	32	15	12	108	63	186	.219	.265	.306	60	-69	18	11		.910	-16	S-199,2-123/3-18,O	-7.8
■ JIM SMITH	Smith, James Lorne b: 9/8/54, Santa Monica, Cal. BR/TR, 6′3″, 185 lbs. Deb: 4/12/82																						
1982	Pit-N	42	42	5	10	2	1	0	4	5	7	.238	.319	.333	80	-1	0	1	-1	.929	8	S-29/2-3,3-1	0.8
■ JOHN SMITH	Smith, John b: Baltimore, Md. Deb: 4/14/1873																						
1873	Mar-n	5	19	2	2	0	0	0	1	0	1	.105	.105	.105	-49	-3	0	0	0	.773	-2	/S-3,O-2	-0.3
1874	Bal-n	6	21	2	4	1	0	0	1	0	1	.190	.190	.238	37	-1	0	0	0	.731	-10	/S-6	-1.0
1875	NH-n	1	3	0	0	0	0	0	0	1	0	.000	.250	.000	-6	-0	0	0	0	.500	-1	/S-1	-0.1
Total	3 n	12	43	4	6	1	0	0	2	1	2	.140	.159	.163	1	-5	0	0	0	.722	-12	/S-10,O-2	-1.4
■ DWIGHT SMITH	Smith, John Dwight b: 11/8/63, Tallahassee, Fla. BL/TR, 5′11″, 175 lbs. Deb: 5/1/89																						
1989	*Chi-N	109	343	52	111	19	6	9	52	31	51	.324	.383	.493	138	17	9	4	0	.975	1	*O-102	1.7
1990	Chi-N	117	290	34	76	15	0	6	27	28	46	.262	.331	.376	88	-5	11	6	-0	.986	-4	O-81	-1.1
1991	Chi-N	90	167	16	38	7	2	3	21	11	32	.228	.279	.347	72	-6	2	3	-1	.962	-3	O-42	-1.1
1992	Chi-N	109	217	28	60	10	3	3	24	13	40	.276	.320	.392	98	-1	9	8	-2	.979	-10	O-63	-1.5
1993	Chi-N	111	310	51	93	17	5	11	35	25	51	.300	.358	.494	127	11	8	6	-1	.955	-8	O-89	0.1
1994	Cal-A	45	122	19	32	5	1	5	18	7	20	.262	.302	.443	88	-3	2	3	-1	.912	-2	O-31/D-2	-0.6
	Bal-A	28	74	12	23	2	1	3	12	5	17	.311	.363	.486	111	1	0	1	-1	.939	-4	O-22/D-3	-0.4
	Yr	73	196	31	55	7	2	8	30	12	37	.281	.325	.459	97	-1	2	4	-2	.922	-6	O-53/D-5	-1.0
1995	*Atl-N	103	131	16	33	8	2	3	21	13	35	.252	.329	.412	91	-2	0	3	-2	.923	-4	O-25	-0.8
1996	Atl-N	101	153	16	31	5	0	3	16	17	42	.203	.287	.294	51	-11	1	3	-2	.962	-0	O-29	-1.3
Total	8	813	1807	244	497	88	20	46	226	150	334	.275	.335	.422	101	2	42	37	-10	.964	-34	O-484/D-5	-5.0
■ JOHN SMITH	Smith, John J. b: 1858, New York, N.Y. 5′11″, 210 lbs. Deb: 5/1/1882																						
1882	Tro-N	35	149	27	36	4	3	0	14	3	24	.242	.257	.309	84	-2				.960	-0	1-35	-0.6
	Wor-N	19	70	10	17	3	2	0	5	5	10	.243	.293	.343	101	0				.939	1	1-19	-0.1
	Yr	54	219	37	53	7	5	0	19	8	34	.242	.269	.320	90	-2				.952	1	1-54	-0.7
■ JACK SMITH	Smith, John Joseph (b: John Joseph Coffey) b: 8/8/1893, Oswayo, Pa. d: 12/4/62, New York, N.Y. BR/TR, 5′9″, Deb: 5/18/12																						
1912	Det-A	1	0	0	0	0	0	0	0	0		—	—	—	—	0	0			1.000	1	/3-1	0.1
■ JOHN SMITH	Smith, John Marshall b: 9/27/06, Washington, D.C. d: 5/9/82, Silver Spring, Md. BB/TR, 6′1″, 180 lbs. Deb: 9/17/31																						
1931	Bos-A	4	15	2	2	0	0	0	1	2	1	.133	.235	.133	-1	-2	1	0	0	1.000	-1	/1-4	-0.3
■ KEITH SMITH	Smith, Keith Lavarne b: 5/3/53, Palmetto, Fla. BR/TR, 5′9″, 178 lbs. Deb: 8/2/77																						
1977	Tex-A	23	67	13	16	4	0	2	6	4	7	.239	.301	.388	85	-1	2	0	1	.975	-1	O-22	-0.2
1979	StL-N	6	13	1	3	0	0	0	0	0	1	.231	.231	.231	26	-1	0	1	-1	1.000	2	/O-5	0.0
1980	StL-N	24	31	3	4	1	0	0	2	2	2	.129	.182	.161	-3	-4	0	0	0	1.000	-1	/O-7	-0.6
Total	3	53	111	17	23	5	0	2	8	6	10	.207	.261	.306	54	-7	2	1	0	.985	0	/O-34	-0.8
■ KEN SMITH	Smith, Kenneth Earl b: 2/12/58, Youngstown, Ohio BL/TR, 6′1″, 195 lbs. Deb: 9/22/81																						
1981	Atl-N	5	3	0	1	1	0	0	0	0	1	.333	.333	.667	174	0	0	0	0	1.000	0	/1-4	0.1
1982	Atl-N	48	41	6	12	1	0	0	3	6	13	.293	.383	.317	94	-0	0	0	0	1.000	-1	/1-6,O-3	-0.2
1983	Atl-N	30	12	2	2	0	0	1	2	1	5	.167	.231	.417	71	-1	1	0	0	1.000	2	1-13	0.2
Total	3	83	56	8	15	2	0	1	5	7	19	.268	.349	.357	93	-0	1	0	0	1.000	1	/1-23,O-3	0.1
■ L. SMITH	Smith, L. Deb: 9/7/1882																						
1882	Bal-a	1	3	0	0	0	0	0		0		.000	.000	.000	-99	-1				1.000	-0	/O-1	-0.1
■ PADDY SMITH	Smith, Lawrence Patrick b: 5/16/1894, Pelham, N.Y. d: 12/2/90, New Rochelle, N.Y. BL/TR, 6′, 195 lbs. Deb: 7/6/20																						
1920	Bos-A	2	2	0	0	0	0	0	0	0	1	.000	.000	.000	-99	-1	0	0	0	.000	0	/C-1	-0.1
■ BULL SMITH	Smith, Lewis Oscar b: 8/20/1880, Plum, W.Va. d: 5/1/28, Charleston, W.Va. BR/TR, 6′, 180 lbs. Deb: 8/30/04																						
1904	Pit-N	13	42	2	6	0	1	0	0	1		.143	.163	.190	9	-5	0			.857	-0	O-13	-0.6
1906	Chi-N	1	1	0	0	0	0	0	0	0		.000	.000	.000	-95	-0	0			.000	0	H	0.0
1911	Was-A	1	0	0	0	0	0	0	0	0		—	—	—	—	0	0			.000	0	R	0.0
Total	3	15	43	2	6	0	1	0	0	1		.140	.159	.186	6	-5	0			.857	-0	/O-13	-0.6
■ LEO SMITH	Smith, Lionel H. b: 5/13/1859, Brooklyn, N.Y. d: 8/30/35, Brooklyn, N.Y. 5′6″, 142 lbs. Deb: 8/28/1890																						
1890	Roc-a	35	112	11	21	1	3	0	11	14		.188	.283	.250	62	-5	1			.948	8	S-35	0.5
■ LONNIE SMITH	Smith, Lonnie b: 12/22/55, Chicago, Ill. BR/TR, 5′9″, 170 lbs. Deb: 9/2/78																						
1978	Phi-N	17	4	6	0	0	0	0	0	4	3	.000	.500	.000	50	0	4	0	1	1.000	-3	O-11	-0.2
1979	Phi-N	17	30	4	5	2	0	0	3	1	7	.167	.194	.233	15	-4	2	1	0	1.000	-1	O-11	-0.5
1980	*Phi-N	100	298	69	101	14	4	3	20	26	48	.339	.399	.443	128	12	33	13	2	.969	-9	O-82	0.2
1981	*Phi-N	62	176	40	57	14	3	2	11	18	14	.324	.402	.472	141	10	21	10	0	.971	2	O-51	1.1
1982	*StL-N★	156	592	**120**	182	35	8	8	69	64	74	.307	.383	.434	127	23	68	26	5	.970	-1	*O-149	2.3
1983	StL-N	130	492	83	158	31	5	8	45	41	55	.321	.384	.453	131	21	43	18	2	.941	3	*O-126	2.3

YEAR	TM/L	G	AB	R	H	2B	3B	HR	RBI	BB	SO	AVG	OBP	SLG	PRO+	BR/A	SB	CS	SBR	FA	FR	G/POS	TPR
1984	StL-N	145	504	77	126	20	4	6	49	70	90	.250	.352	.341	98	1	50	13	7	.948	-3	*O-140	0.1
1985	StL-N	28	96	15	25	2	2	0	7	15	20	.260	.377	.323	98	1	12	6	0	1.000	-1	O-28	-0.2
	*KC-A	120	448	77	115	23	4	6	41	41	69	.257	.325	.366	88	-7	40	7	8	.958	-3	*O-119	-0.6
1986	KC-A	134	508	80	146	25	7	8	44	46	78	.287	.358	.411	107	6	26	9	2	.965	4	*O-118,D-10	0.7
1987	KC-A	48	167	26	42	7	1	3	8	24	31	.251	.359	.359	89	-2	9	4	0	.915	-2	O-32,D-15	-0.4
1988	Atl-N	43	114	14	27	3	0	3	9	10	25	.237	.298	.342	79	-3	4	2	0	.968	-1	O-35	-0.6
1989	Atl-N	134	482	89	152	34	4	21	79	76	95	.315	**.420**	.533	166	44	25	12	0	.993	9	*O-132	5.2
1990	Atl-N	135	466	72	142	27	9	9	42	58	69	.305	.389	.459	125	17	10	10	-3	.956	5	*O-122	1.7
1991	*Atl-N	122	353	58	97	19	1	7	44	50	64	.275	.379	.394	111	7	9	5	-0	.965	-8	O-99	-0.3
1992	*Atl-N	84	158	23	39	8	2	6	33	17	37	.247	.331	.437	109	2	4	0	1	.954	0	O-35	0.3
1993	Pit-N	94	199	35	57	5	4	6	24	43	42	.286	.425	.442	133	12	9	4	0	.981	-4	O-60	0.7
	Bal-A	9	24	8	5	1	0	2	3	8	10	.208	.406	.500	136	1	0	0	0	1.000	0	/O-4,D-5	0.2
1994	Bal-A	35	59	13	12	3	0	0	2	11	18	.203	.338	.254	53	-4	1	0	0	1.000	0	D-30/O-2	-0.4
Total	17	1613	5170	909	1488	273	58	98	533	623	849	.288	.374	.420	117	138	370	140	27	.964	-12	*O-1356/D-60	11.6

■ MARK SMITH
Smith, Mark Edward b: 5/7/70, Pasadena, Cal. BR/TR, 6'3", 205 lbs. Deb: 5/14/94

YEAR	TM/L	G	AB	R	H	2B	3B	HR	RBI	BB	SO	AVG	OBP	SLG	PRO+	BR/A	SB	CS	SBR	FA	FR	G/POS	TPR
1994	Bal-A	3	7	0	1	0	0	0	2	0	2	.143	.143	.143	-25	-1	0	0	0	1.000	0	/O-3	-0.1
1995	Bal-A	37	104	11	24	5	0	3	15	12	22	.231	.316	.365	76	-4	3	0	1	1.000	2	O-32/D-3	-0.2
1996	Bal-A	27	78	9	19	2	0	4	10	3	20	.244	.298	.423	80	-3	0	2	-1	.980	2	O-20/D-6	-0.2
1997	Pit-N	71	193	29	55	13	1	9	35	28	36	.285	.376	.503	125	7	3	1	0	1.000	-2	O-42/1-9,D-5	0.4
1998	Pit-N	59	128	18	25	6	0	2	13	10	26	.195	.270	.289	44	-11	7	0	2	.977	-0	O-24/1-6,D-3	-0.9
Total	5	197	510	67	124	26	1	18	75	53	106	.243	.323	.404	86	-11	13	3	2	.991	2	O-121/D-17,1-15	-1.0

■ RED SMITH
Smith, Marvin Harold b: 7/17/1900, Ashley, Ill. d: 2/19/61, Los Angeles, Cal. BL/TR, 5'7", 165 lbs. Deb: 4/14/25

YEAR	TM/L	G	AB	R	H	2B	3B	HR	RBI	BB	SO	AVG	OBP	SLG	PRO+	BR/A	SB	CS	SBR	FA	FR	G/POS	TPR
1925	Phi-A	20	14	1	4	0	0	0	1	2	5	.286	.375	.286	65	-1	0	0	0	.864	1	S-16/3-2	0.1

■ MILT SMITH
Smith, Milton b: 3/27/29, Columbus, Ga. d: 4/11/97, San Diego, Cal. BR/TR, 5'10", 165 lbs. Deb: 7/21/55

YEAR	TM/L	G	AB	R	H	2B	3B	HR	RBI	BB	SO	AVG	OBP	SLG	PRO+	BR/A	SB	CS	SBR	FA	FR	G/POS	TPR
1955	Cin-N	36	102	15	20	3	1	3	8	13	24	.196	.293	.333	62	-6	2	2	-1	.915	-2	3-28/2-5	-0.8

■ NATE SMITH
Smith, Nathaniel Beverly b: 4/26/35, Chicago, Ill. BR/TR, 5'11", 170 lbs. Deb: 9/19/62

YEAR	TM/L	G	AB	R	H	2B	3B	HR	RBI	BB	SO	AVG	OBP	SLG	PRO+	BR/A	SB	CS	SBR	FA	FR	G/POS	TPR
1962	Bal-A	5	9	3	2	1	0	0	0	1	4	.222	.364	.333	95	0	0	0	0	1.000	1	/C-3	0.1

■ OLLIE SMITH
Smith, Oliver H. b: 1868, Mt.Vernon, Ohio BL/TL, Deb: 7/11/1894

YEAR	TM/L	G	AB	R	H	2B	3B	HR	RBI	BB	SO	AVG	OBP	SLG	PRO+	BR/A	SB	CS	SBR	FA	FR	G/POS	TPR
1894	Lou-N	38	134	26	40	6	1	3	20	27	15	.299	.427	.425	114	5	13			.883	-2	O-38	0.0

■ OZZIE SMITH
Smith, Osborne Earl b: 12/26/54, Mobile, Ala. BB/TR, 5'11", 150 lbs. Deb: 4/7/78

YEAR	TM/L	G	AB	R	H	2B	3B	HR	RBI	BB	SO	AVG	OBP	SLG	PRO+	BR/A	SB	CS	SBR	FA	FR	G/POS	TPR
1978	SD-N	159	590	69	152	17	6	1	46	47	43	.258	.312	.312	81	-15	40	12	5	.970	26	*S-159	3.6
1979	SD-N	156	587	77	124	18	6	0	27	37	37	.211	.260	.262	46	-45	28	7	4	.976	21	*S-155	-0.3
1980	SD-N	158	609	67	140	18	5	0	35	71	49	.230	.315	.276	70	-23	57	15	8	.974	**41**	*S-158	4.7
1981	SD-N★	110	450	53	100	11	2	0	21	41	37	.222	.294	.256	62	-22	22	12	-1	**.976**	**26**	*S-110	1.5
1982	*StL-N★	140	488	58	121	24	1	2	43	68	32	.248	.342	.314	84	-8	25	5	5	**.984**	**33**	*S-139	4.4
1983	StL-N★	159	552	69	134	30	6	3	50	64	36	.243	.323	.335	82	-12	34	7	6	.975	18	*S-158	2.7
1984	StL-N★	124	412	53	106	20	5	1	44	56	17	.257	.349	.337	96	-0	35	7	6	**.982**	**26**	*S-124	4.5
1985	*StL-N★	158	537	70	148	22	3	6	54	65	27	.276	.356	.361	102	3	31	8	5	**.983**	16	*S-158	4.0
1986	StL-N★	153	514	67	144	19	4	0	54	79	27	.280	.378	.333	99	3	31	7	5	**.978**	-9	*S-144	1.3
1987	*StL-N★	158	600	104	182	40	4	0	75	89	36	.303	.394	.383	105	8	43	9	8	**.987**	19	*S-158	4.7
1988	StL-N★	153	575	80	155	27	1	3	51	74	43	.270	.354	.336	98	1	57	9	**12**	.972	**23**	*S-150	5.1
1989	StL-N★	155	593	82	162	30	8	2	50	55	37	.273	.337	.361	96	-2	29	7	5	.976	6	*S-153	2.2
1990	StL-N★	143	512	61	130	21	1	1	50	61	33	.254	.336	.305	77	-14	32	6	6	.980	-13	*S-140	-1.0
1991	StL-N★	150	550	96	157	30	3	3	50	83	36	.285	.380	.367	110	11	35	9	5	**.987**	-21	*S-150	0.6
1992	StL-N★	132	518	73	153	20	2	0	31	59	34	.295	.367	.342	105	6	43	9	8	.985	8	*S-132	3.3
1993	StL-N	141	545	75	157	22	6	1	53	43	18	.288	.341	.356	89	-8	21	8	2	.974	18	*S-134	2.2
1994	StL-N★	98	381	51	100	18	3	3	30	38	26	.262	.329	.349	79	-12	6	3	0	.982	-2	S-96	-0.5
1995	StL-N†	44	156	16	31	5	1	0	11	17	12	.199	.286	.244	41	-13	4	3	-1	.964	1	S-41	-0.8
1996	*StL-N★	82	227	36	64	10	2	2	18	25	9	.282	.358	.370	93	-1	7	5	-1	.969	6	S-52	0.8
Total	19	2573	9396	1257	2460	402	69	28	793	1072	589	.262	.339	.328	87	-145	580	148	85	.978	243	*S-2511	43.0

■ KEITH SMITH
Smith, Patrick Keith b: 10/20/61, Los Angeles, Cal. BB/TR, 6'1", 175 lbs. Deb: 4/12/84

YEAR	TM/L	G	AB	R	H	2B	3B	HR	RBI	BB	SO	AVG	OBP	SLG	PRO+	BR/A	SB	CS	SBR	FA	FR	G/POS	TPR
1984	NY-A	2	4	0	0	0	0	0	0	0	2	.000	.200	.000	-41	-1	0	0	0	.923	2	/S-2	0.2
1985	NY-A	4	0	1	0	0	0	0	0	0	0	—	—	—	—	0	0	0	0	1.000	0	/S-3	0.0
Total	2	6	4	1	0	0	0	0	0	0	2	.000	.200	.000	-41	-1	0	0	0	.929	3	/S-5	0.2

■ PAUL SMITH
Smith, Paul Leslie b: 3/19/31, New Castle, Pa. BL/TL, 5'8", 165 lbs. Deb: 4/14/53

YEAR	TM/L	G	AB	R	H	2B	3B	HR	RBI	BB	SO	AVG	OBP	SLG	PRO+	BR/A	SB	CS	SBR	FA	FR	G/POS	TPR
1953	Pit-N	118	389	41	110	12	7	4	44	24	23	.283	.329	.380	85	-9	3	0	1	.985	-2	1-74,O-19	-1.3
1957	Pit-N	81	150	12	38	4	0	3	11	12	17	.253	.313	.340	78	-5	0	2	-1	1.000	-3	O-33/1-1	-1.1
1958	Pit-N	6	3	0	1	0	0	0	0	3	0	.333	.667	.333	180	1	0	0	0	.000	0	H	0.1
	Chi-N	18	20	1	3	0	0	0	1	3	4	.150	.261	.150	13	-2	0	0	0	.941	0	/1-4	-0.3
	Yr	24	23	1	4	0	0	0	1	6	4	.174	.345	.174	44	-2	0	0	0	.941	0	/1-4	-0.2
Total	3	223	562	54	152	16	7	7	56	42	44	.270	.326	.361	81	-15	3	2	-0	.984	-5	/1-79,O-52	-2.6

■ PAUL SMITH
Smith, Paul Stoner b: 5/7/1888, Mt.Zion, Ill. d: 7/3/58, Decatur, Ill. BL/TR, 6'1", 190 lbs. Deb: 9/19/16

YEAR	TM/L	G	AB	R	H	2B	3B	HR	RBI	BB	SO	AVG	OBP	SLG	PRO+	BR/A	SB	CS	SBR	FA	FR	G/POS	TPR
1916	Cin-N	10	44	5	10	0	1	0	1	1	8	.227	.244	.273	60	-2	3			1.000	-1	O-10	-0.4

■ RAY SMITH
Smith, Raymond Edward b: 9/18/55, Glendale, Cal. BR/TR, 6'1", 185 lbs. Deb: 4/9/81

YEAR	TM/L	G	AB	R	H	2B	3B	HR	RBI	BB	SO	AVG	OBP	SLG	PRO+	BR/A	SB	CS	SBR	FA	FR	G/POS	TPR
1981	Min-A	15	40	4	8	1	0	1	1	0	3	.200	.200	.300	40	-3	0	0	0	1.000	1	C-15	-0.1
1982	Min-A	9	23	1	5	0	1	0	1	1	3	.217	.250	.304	50	-2	0	0	0	1.000	1	/C-9	0.0
1983	Min-A	59	152	11	34	5	0	0	8	10	12	.224	.276	.257	46	-11	1	0	0	.984	11	C-59	0.2
Total	3	83	215	16	47	6	1	1	10	11	18	.219	.260	.270	45	-16	1	0	0	.988	14	/C-83	0.1

■ DICK SMITH
Smith, Richard Arthur b: 5/17/39, Lebanon, Ore. BR/TR, 6'2", 205 lbs. Deb: 7/20/63

YEAR	TM/L	G	AB	R	H	2B	3B	HR	RBI	BB	SO	AVG	OBP	SLG	PRO+	BR/A	SB	CS	SBR	FA	FR	G/POS	TPR
1963	NY-N	20	42	4	10	0	1	0	3	5	10	.238	.319	.286	74	-1	3	2	-0	1.000	-2	O-10/1-2	-0.4
1964	NY-N	46	94	14	21	6	1	0	3	1	29	.223	.247	.309	57	-6	6	2	1	.987	-3	1-18,O-13	-1.0
1965	LA-N	10	6	0	0	0	0	0	1	0	3	.000	.000	.000	-99	-2	0	0	0	1.000	-3	/O-9	-0.6
Total	3	76	142	18	31	6	2	0	7	6	42	.218	.260	.289	56	-8	9	4	0	1.000	-8	/O-32,1-20	-2.0

■ DICK SMITH
Smith, Richard Harrison b: 7/21/27, Blandburg, Pa. BR/TR, 5'8", 160 lbs. Deb: 9/14/51

YEAR	TM/L	G	AB	R	H	2B	3B	HR	RBI	BB	SO	AVG	OBP	SLG	PRO+	BR/A	SB	CS	SBR	FA	FR	G/POS	TPR
1951	Pit-N	12	46	2	8	0	0	0	4	8	8	.174	.296	.174	29	-4	0	2	-1	.936	2	3-12	-0.3
1952	Pit-N	29	66	8	7	1	0	0	5	9	3	.106	.213	.121	-5	-9	0	0	0	.958	5	3-16/2-4,S-4	-0.5
1953	Pit-N	13	43	4	7	0	1	0	2	6	6	.163	.265	.209	26	-5	0	1	-1	.961	5	S-13	0.1
1954	Pit-N	12	31	2	3	1	1	0	0	6	5	.097	.243	.194	16	-4	0	0	0	.933	2	/3-9	-0.2
1955	Pit-N	4	0	1	0	0	0	0	0	1	0	—	1.000	—	198	0	0	0	0	.000	0	/S-1	0.0
Total	5	70	186	17	25	2	2	0	11	30	22	.134	.255	.167	15	-22	0	3	-2	.944	14	/3-37,S-18,2-4	-0.9

■ DICK SMITH
Smith, Richard Kelly b: 8/25/44, Lincolnton, N.C. BR/TR, 6'5", 200 lbs. Deb: 8/20/69

YEAR	TM/L	G	AB	R	H	2B	3B	HR	RBI	BB	SO	AVG	OBP	SLG	PRO+	BR/A	SB	CS	SBR	FA	FR	G/POS	TPR
1969	Was-A	21	28	2	3	0	0	0	0	4	7	.107	.242	.107	1	-4	0	0	0	.909	-2	/O-9	-0.6

■ RED SMITH
Smith, Richard Paul b: 5/18/04, Brokaw, Wis. d: 3/8/78, Sylvania, Ohio BR/TR, 5'10", 185 lbs. Deb: 5/31/27 C

YEAR	TM/L	G	AB	R	H	2B	3B	HR	RBI	BB	SO	AVG	OBP	SLG	PRO+	BR/A	SB	CS	SBR	FA	FR	G/POS	TPR
1927	NY-N	1	0	0	0	0	0	0	0	0	0	—	—	—	—	0	0			1.000	-0	/C-1	0.0

■ BOB SMITH
Smith, Robert Eldridge b: 4/22/1895, Rogersville, Tenn. d: 7/19/87, Waycross, Ga. BR/TR, 5'10", 175 lbs. Deb: 4/19/23

YEAR	TM/L	G	AB	R	H	2B	3B	HR	RBI	BB	SO	AVG	OBP	SLG	PRO+	BR/A	SB	CS	SBR	FA	FR	G/POS	TPR
1923	Bos-N	115	375	30	94	16	3	0	40	17	35	.251	.285	.309	59	-23	4	9	-4	.944	14	*S-101/2-8	-0.3
1924	Bos-N	106	347	32	79	12	3	2	38	15	26	.228	.260	.297	51	-25	5	2	0	.958	8	S-80,3-23	-0.6
1925	Bos-N	58	174	17	49	9	4	0	23	5	6	.282	.302	.379	80	-6	2	2	-1	.906	3	S-21,2-15,P-13,/O-1	0.0

YEAR	TM/L	G	AB	R	H	2B	3B	HR	RBI	BB	SO	AVG	OBP	SLG	PRO+	BR/A	SB	CS	SBR	FA	FR	G/POS	TPR
1926	Bos-N	40	84	10	25	6	2	0	13	2	4	.298	.314	.417	105	-0	0			.972	2	P-33	0.0
1927	Bos-N	54	109	10	27	3	1	1	10	2	4	.248	.261	.321	60	-7	0			.966	2	P-41	0.0
1928	Bos-N	39	92	11	23	2	0	1	8	1	6	.250	.258	.304	49	-7	2			.965	3	P-38	0.0
1929	Bos-N	39	99	12	17	4	2	1	8	2	8	.172	.188	.283	16	-14	1			.986	4	P-34/S-5	0.2
1930	Bos-N	39	81	7	19	2	0	0	4	0	5	.235	.235	.259	20	-10	0			.984	2	P-38	0.0
1931	Chi-N	36	87	7	19	2	0	0	4	5	2	.218	.261	.241	35	-8	0			**1.000**	1	P-36	0.0
1932	*Chi-N	36	42	5	10	4	1	0	4	0	2	.238	.238	.381	64	-2	1			1.000	3	P-34/2-2	0.2
1933	Cin-N	23	25	2	5	1	0	0	1	1	0	.200	.231	.240	35	-2	1			.882	-1	P-16/S-1	0.0
	Bos-N	14	20	1	4	0	1	0	2	0	1	.200	.200	.300	45	-2	0			1.000	1	P-14	0.0
	Yr	37	45	3	9	1	1	0	3	1	1	.200	.217	.267	39	-4	1			.946	0	P-30/S-1	0.0
1934	Bos-N	42	36	5	9	1	0	0	3	0	1	.250	.250	.278	44	-3	0			1.000	1	P-39	0.0
1935	Bos-N	47	63	3	17	0	0	0	4	1	5	.270	.281	.270	53	-4	0			.980	-1	P-46	0.0
1936	Bos-N	35	45	1	10	2	0	0	4	0	4	.222	.222	.267	33	-4	0			1.000	1	P-35	0.0
1937	Bos-N	19	10	1	2	0	0	0	0	1	1	.200	.273	.200	33	-1	0			1.000	-1	P-18	0.0
Total	15	742	1689	154	409	64	17	5	166	52	110	.242	.265	.309	53	-117	16	13		.981	42	P-435,S-208/23O	-0.5

■ BOBBY SMITH
Smith, Robert Eugene b: 4/10/74, Oakland, Cal. BR/TR, 6'3", 190 lbs. Deb: 4/3/98

YEAR	TM/L	G	AB	R	H	2B	3B	HR	RBI	BB	SO	AVG	OBP	SLG	PRO+	BR/A	SB	CS	SBR	FA	FR	G/POS	TPR
1998	TB-A	117	370	44	102	15	3	11	55	34	110	.276	.346	.422	94	-3	5	3	-0	.963	11	3-97/S-7,2-6,D-7	0.8

■ JOE SMITH
Smith, Salvatore (b: Salvatore Persico) b: 12/29/1893, New York, N.Y. d: 1/12/74, Yonkers, N.Y. BR/TR, 5'7", 170 lbs. Deb: 7/7/13

YEAR	TM/L	G	AB	R	H	2B	3B	HR	RBI	BB	SO	AVG	OBP	SLG	PRO+	BR/A	SB	CS	SBR	FA	FR	G/POS	TPR
1913	NY-A	14	32	1	5	0	0	0	2	1	14	.156	.182	.156	-1	-4	1			.952	0	C-14	-0.3

■ SKYROCKET SMITH
Smith, Samuel J. b: 3/19/1868, St.Louis, Mo. d: 4/26/16, St.Louis, Mo. BR , 6'2", 170 lbs. Deb: 4/18/1888

YEAR	TM/L	G	AB	R	H	2B	3B	HR	RBI	BB	SO	AVG	OBP	SLG	PRO+	BR/A	SB	CS	SBR	FA	FR	G/POS	TPR
1888	Lou-a	58	206	27	49	9	4	1	31	24		.238	.349	.335	122	7	5			.970	-0	1-58	0.1

■ SYD SMITH
Smith, Sydney E. b: 8/31/1883, Smithville, S.C. d: 6/5/61, Orangeburg, S.C. BR/TR, 5'10", 190 lbs. Deb: 4/14/08

YEAR	TM/L	G	AB	R	H	2B	3B	HR	RBI	BB	SO	AVG	OBP	SLG	PRO+	BR/A	SB	CS	SBR	FA	FR	G/POS	TPR
1908	Phi-A	46	128	8	26	8	0	1	10	4		.203	.233	.289	65	-5	0			.975	-0	C-31/1-6,O-1	-0.3
	StL-A	27	76	6	14	4	0	0	5	4		.184	.225	.237	50	-4	2			.977	8	C-24	0.7
	Yr	73	204	14	40	12	0	1	15	8		.196	.230	.270	60	-9	2			.976	8	C-55/1-6,O-1	0.4
1910	Cle-A	9	27	1	9	1	0	0	3	3		.333	.400	.370	140	1	0			.958	0	/C-9	0.2
1911	Cle-A	58	154	8	46	8	1	1	21	11		.299	.353	.383	104	1	0			.979	9	C-48/1-1,3-1	1.3
1914	Pit-N	5	11	1	3	0	0	0	1	0	1	.273	.273	.273	65	-1	0			1.000	-0	/C-3	0.0
1915	Pit-N	1	1	0	0	0	0	0	0	0	0	.000	.000	.000	-99	-0	0			.000	0	H	0.0
Total	5	146	397	24	98	21	1	2	40	22	1	.247	.291	.320	83	-8	2			.977	16	C-115/1-7,3-1,O-1	1.9

■ TOM SMITH
Smith, Thomas N. b: 1851, Guelph, Ontario, Canada d: 3/28/1889, Detroit, Mich. 5'8", 141 lbs. Deb: 9/15/1875

YEAR	TM/L	G	AB	R	H	2B	3B	HR	RBI	BB	SO	AVG	OBP	SLG	PRO+	BR/A	SB	CS	SBR	FA	FR	G/POS	TPR
1875	Atl-n	3	13	0	1	0	0	0	1	0	0	.077	.077	.077	-53	-2	0	0	0	.783	0	/2-3	-0.1

■ TOMMY SMITH
Smith, Tommy Alexander b: 8/1/48, Albemarle, N.C. BL/TR, 6'3", 215 lbs. Deb: 9/6/73

YEAR	TM/L	G	AB	R	H	2B	3B	HR	RBI	BB	SO	AVG	OBP	SLG	PRO+	BR/A	SB	CS	SBR	FA	FR	G/POS	TPR
1973	Cle-A	14	41	6	10	2	0	2	3	1	2	.244	.262	.439	93	-1	1	0	0	1.000	-1	O-13	-0.2
1974	Cle-A	23	31	4	3	1	0	0	0	2	7	.097	.176	.129	-11	-4	0	0	0	.938	-2	O-17/D-1	-0.7
1975	Cle-A	8	8	0	1	0	0	0	2	0	1	.125	.125	.125	-29	-1	0	0	0	1.000	-1	/O-3,D-3	-0.2
1976	Cle-A	55	164	17	42	3	1	2	12	8	8	.256	.291	.323	80	-4	8	0	2	.979	-0	O-50/D-2	-0.4
1977	Sea-A	21	27	1	7	1	1	0	4	0	6	.259	.259	.370	70	-1	0	1	-1	1.000	-2	O-14	-0.4
Total	5	121	271	28	63	7	2	4	21	11	24	.232	.265	.317	68	-12	9	1	2	.977	-5	/O-97,D-6	-1.9

■ VINNIE SMITH
Smith, Vincent Ambrose b: 12/7/15, Richmond, Va. d: 12/14/79, Virginia Beach, Va BR/TR, 6'1", 176 lbs. Deb: 9/10/41 U

YEAR	TM/L	G	AB	R	H	2B	3B	HR	RBI	BB	SO	AVG	OBP	SLG	PRO+	BR/A	SB	CS	SBR	FA	FR	G/POS	TPR
1941	Pit-N	9	33	3	10	1	0	0	5	1	5	.303	.324	.333	86	-1	0			.941	-2	/C-9	-0.2
1946	Pit-N	7	21	2	4	0	0	0	0	1	5	.190	.227	.190	19	-2	0			.967	1	/C-7	-0.1
Total	2	16	54	5	14	1	0	0	5	2	10	.259	.286	.278	59	-3	0			.953	-1	/C-16	-0.3

■ WALLY SMITH
Smith, Wallace H. b: 3/13/1889, Philadelphia, Pa. d: 6/10/30, Florence, Ariz. BR/TR, 5'11.5", 180 lbs. Deb: 4/17/11

YEAR	TM/L	G	AB	R	H	2B	3B	HR	RBI	BB	SO	AVG	OBP	SLG	PRO+	BR/A	SB	CS	SBR	FA	FR	G/POS	TPR
1911	StL-N	81	194	23	42	6	5	2	19	21	33	.216	.303	.330	79	-6	5			.936	2	3-26,S-25/2-8,O-1	-0.2
1912	StL-N	75	219	22	56	5	5	0	26	29	27	.256	.351	.324	87	-3	4			.949	-1	3-32,S-22/1-6	-0.2
1914	Was-A	45	97	11	19	4	1	0	8	3	12	.196	.235	.258	46	-7	3	4	-2	.955	-4	2-12/1-7,S-7,3-5,O	-1.3
Total	3	201	510	56	117	15	11	2	53	53	72	.229	.312	.314	77	-15	12	4		.947	-3	/3-63,S-54,2-20,1O	-1.7

■ WIB SMITH
Smith, Wilbur Floyd b: 8/30/1886, Evart, Mich. d: 11/18/59, Fargo, N.D. BL/TR, 5'10.5", 165 lbs. Deb: 5/31/09

YEAR	TM/L	G	AB	R	H	2B	3B	HR	RBI	BB	SO	AVG	OBP	SLG	PRO+	BR/A	SB	CS	SBR	FA	FR	G/POS	TPR
1909	StL-A	17	42	3	8	0	0	0	2	0		.190	.190	.190	22	-4	0			.836	-9	C-13/1-1	-1.4

■ RED SMITH
Smith, Willard Jehu b: 4/11/1892, Logansport, Ind. d: 7/17/72, Noblesville, Ind. BR/TR, 5'8", 165 lbs. Deb: 9/17/17

YEAR	TM/L	G	AB	R	H	2B	3B	HR	RBI	BB	SO	AVG	OBP	SLG	PRO+	BR/A	SB	CS	SBR	FA	FR	G/POS	TPR
1917	Pit-N	11	21	1	3	1	0	0	2	3	4	.143	.250	.190	35	-2	1			1.000	2	/C-6	0.0
1918	Pit-N	15	24	1	4	1	0	0	3	3	0	.167	.259	.208	42	-2	0			.939	-1	C-10	-0.2
Total	2	26	45	2	7	2	0	0	5	6	4	.156	.255	.200	39	-3	1			.969	1	/C-16	-0.2

■ BILL SMITH
Smith, William E. b: Cleveland, Ohio d: 8/9/1886, Toronto, Ont., Can. 5'11", 178 lbs. Deb: 9/17/1884

YEAR	TM/L	G	AB	R	H	2B	3B	HR	RBI	BB	SO	AVG	OBP	SLG	PRO+	BR/A	SB	CS	SBR	FA	FR	G/POS	TPR
1884	Cle-N	1	3	0	0	0	0	0	0	0	2	.000	.000	.000	-97	-1				.000	-0	/O-1	-0.1

■ BILL SMITH
Smith, William J. b: Baltimore, Md. d: 8/9/1886, Deb: 4/14/1873 M

YEAR	TM/L	G	AB	R	H	2B	3B	HR	RBI	BB	SO	AVG	OBP	SLG	PRO+	BR/A	SB	CS	SBR	FA	FR	G/POS	TPR
1873	Mar-n	6	23	2	4	0	0	0	1	0	0	.174	.174	.174	5	-2	0	0	0	.500	-3	/O-3,C-2,2-1,M	-0.4

■ WILLIE SMITH
Smith, Willie b: 2/11/39, Anniston, Ala. BL/TL, 6', 190 lbs. Deb: 6/18/63

YEAR	TM/L	G	AB	R	H	2B	3B	HR	RBI	BB	SO	AVG	OBP	SLG	PRO+	BR/A	SB	CS	SBR	FA	FR	G/POS	TPR
1963	Det-A	17	8	2	1	0	0	0	0	0	1	.125	.125	.125	-29	-1	0	0	0	1.000	0	P-11	0.0
1964	LA-A	118	359	46	108	14	6	11	51	8	39	.301	.320	.465	128	11	7	5	-1	.977	-6	O-87,P-15	-0.1
1965	Cal-A	136	459	52	120	14	9	14	57	32	60	.261	.311	.423	109	4	9	8	-2	.980	-0	*O-123/1-2	-0.4
1966	Cal-A	90	195	18	36	3	2	1	20	12	37	.185	.243	.236	39	-15	1	0	0	.974	-3	O-52	-2.2
1967	Cle-A	21	32	0	7	2	0	0	2	1	10	.219	.242	.281	54	-2	0	2	-1	.800	-1	/O-4,1-3	-0.5
1968	Cle-A	33	42	1	6	2	0	0	3	3	14	.143	.217	.190	25	-4	0	0	0	1.000	-0	/1-7,P-2,O-1	-0.5
	Chi-N	55	142	13	39	8	2	5	25	12	33	.275	.335	.465	129	5	0	0	0	1.000	-3	O-38/1-4,P-1	-0.1
1969	Chi-N	103	195	21	48	9	1	9	25	25	49	.246	.332	.441	102	0	1	0	0	.929	-7	O-33,1-24	-1.0
1970	Chi-N	87	167	15	36	9	1	5	24	11	32	.216	.268	.371	62	-10	2	1	0	.994	-5	1-43/O-1	-1.8
1971	Cin-N	31	55	3	9	2	0	1	4	3	9	.164	.207	.255	31	-5	0	0	0	1.000	1	1-10	-0.5
Total	9	691	1654	171	410	63	21	46	211	107	284	.248	.297	.395	94	-18	20	16	-4	.975	-24	O-339/1-93,P-29	-7.1

■ HOMER SMOOT
Smoot, Homer Vernon "Doc" b: 3/23/1878, Galestown, Md. d: 3/25/28, Salisbury, Md. BL/TR, 5'10", 180 lbs. Deb: 4/17/02

YEAR	TM/L	G	AB	R	H	2B	3B	HR	RBI	BB	SO	AVG	OBP	SLG	PRO+	BR/A	SB	CS	SBR	FA	FR	G/POS	TPR
1902	StL-N	129	518	58	161	19	4	3	48	23		.311	.350	.380	130	17	20			.931	-1	*O-129	0.9
1903	StL-N	129	500	67	148	22	8	4	49	32		.296	.342	.396	114	8	17			.942	-7	*O-129	-0.7
1904	StL-N	137	520	58	146	23	6	3	66	37		.281	.331	.365	120	12	23			.966	2	*O-137	0.6
1905	StL-N	139	534	73	166	21	16	4	58	33		.311	.359	.433	140	24	21			.975	1	*O-138	1.9
1906	StL-N	86	343	41	85	9	10	0	31	11		.248	.289	.332	98	-2	3			.953	2	O-86	-0.6
	Cin-N	60	220	11	57	8	1	1	17	13		.259	.315	.318	93	-2	0			.944	1	O-59	-0.4
	Yr	146	563	52	142	17	11	1	48	24		.252	.300	.327	96	-4	3			.950	2	*O-145	-1.0
Total	5	680	2635	308	763	102	45	15	269	149		.290	.336	.380	120	57	84			.953	-2	O-678	1.7

■ HENRY SMOYER
Smoyer, Henry Neitz "Hennie" (b: Henry Neitz Smowery) b: 4/24/1890, Fredericksburg, Pa. d: 2/28/58, DuBois, Pa. BR/TR, 5'6", Deb: 8/14/12

YEAR	TM/L	G	AB	R	H	2B	3B	HR	RBI	BB	SO	AVG	OBP	SLG	PRO+	BR/A	SB	CS	SBR	FA	FR	G/POS	TPR
1912	StL-A	6	14	1	3	0	0	0	0	2		.214	.313	.214	53	-1	0			1.000	-0	/S-4,3-2	-0.1

■ FRANK SMYKAL
Smykal, Frank John (b: Frank John Smejkal) b: 10/13/1889, Chicago, Ill. d: 8/11/50, Chicago, Ill. BR/TR, 5'7", 150 lbs. Deb: 8/30/16

YEAR	TM/L	G	AB	R	H	2B	3B	HR	RBI	BB	SO	AVG	OBP	SLG	PRO+	BR/A	SB	CS	SBR	FA	FR	G/POS	TPR
1916	Pit-N	6	10	1	3	0	0	0	2	3	1	.300	.500	.300	147	1	1			.842	-1	/S-5,3-1	0.1

■ CLANCY SMYRES
Smyres, Clarence Melvin b: 5/24/22, Culver City, Cal. BB/TR, 5'11.5", 175 lbs. Deb: 4/18/44

YEAR	TM/L	G	AB	R	H	2B	3B	HR	RBI	BB	SO	AVG	OBP	SLG	PRO+	BR/A	SB	CS	SBR	FA	FR	G/POS	TPR
1944	Bro-N	5	2	1	0	0	0	0	0	0	0	.000	.000	.000	-99	-1	0			.000	0	H	-0.1

■ RED SMYTH Smyth, James Daniel b: 1/30/1893, Holly Springs, Miss. d: 4/14/58, Inglewood, Cal. BL/TR, 5'9", 152 lbs. Deb: 8/11/15

YEAR	TM/L	G	AB	R	H	2B	3B	HR	RBI	BB	SO	AVG	OBP	SLG	PRO+	BR/A	SB	CS	SBR	FA	FR	G/POS	TPR
1915	Bro-N	19	22	3	3	1	0	0	3	4	2	.136	.269	.182	37	-2	1	2	-1	1.000	-1	/O-9	-0.4
1916	Bro-N	2	5	0	0	0	0	0	0	0	3	.000	.000	.000	-97	-1	0			1.000	-0	/2-2	-0.2
1917	Bro-N	29	24	5	3	0	0	0	1	4	6	.125	.250	.125	16	-2	0			.667	-1	/3-4,O-2	-0.3
	StL-N	38	72	5	15	0	2	0	4	4	9	.208	.269	.264	66	-3	3			.889	-5	O-23	-1.0
	Yr	67	96	10	18	0	2	0	5	8	15	.188	.264	.229	52	-5	3			.871	-6	O-25/3-4	-1.3
1918	StL-N	40	113	19	24	1	2	0	4	16	11	.212	.315	.257	78	-2	3			.956	-0	O-25,2-11	-0.4
Total	4	128	236	32	45	2	4	0	12	28	31	.191	.285	.233	60	-10	7	2		.934	-7	/O-59,2-13,3-4	-2.3

■ JOHN SNEED Sneed, Jonathon L. b: Columbus, Ohio d: 1/4/1899, Memphis, Tenn. 5'8", 160 lbs. Deb: 5/1/1884

YEAR	TM/L	G	AB	R	H	2B	3B	HR	RBI	BB	SO	AVG	OBP	SLG	PRO+	BR/A	SB	CS	SBR	FA	FR	G/POS	TPR
1884	Ind-a	27	102	14	22	4	0	1		6		.216	.259	.284	79	-2				.817	-0	O-27	-0.3
1890	Tol-a	9	30	3	6	0	0	0	4	8		.200	.368	.200	66	-1	5			.889	2	/O-9	0.1
	Col-a	128	484	114	141	13	15	2	65	63		.291	.383	.393	138	26	39			.883	-8	*O-126/S-2	1.2
	Yr	137	514	117	147	13	15	2	69	71		.286	.382	.381	133	25	44			.883	-5	*O-135/S-2	1.3
1891	Col-a	99	366	66	94	9	6	1	61	55	29	.257	.366	.322	103	4	24			.894	-4	*O-99	-0.3
Total	3	263	982	197	263	26	21	4	130	132	29	.268	.364	.349	117	27	68			.879	-10	O-261/S-2	0.7

■ CHARLIE SNELL Snell, Charles Anthony (b: Charles Anthony Schnell)
b: 11/29/1893, Hampstead, Md. d: 4/4/88, Reading, Pa. BR/TR, 5'11", 160 lbs. Deb: 7/19/12

YEAR	TM/L	G	AB	R	H	2B	3B	HR	RBI	BB	SO	AVG	OBP	SLG	PRO+	BR/A	SB	CS	SBR	FA	FR	G/POS	TPR
1912	StL-A	8	19	0	4	1	0	0	0	3		.211	.348	.263	78	-0	0			.941	2	/C-8	0.2

■ WALLY SNELL Snell, Walter Henry "Doc" b: 5/19/1889, W.Bridgewater, Mass. d: 7/23/80, Providence, R.I. BR/TR, 5'10", 170 lbs. Deb: 8/1/13

YEAR	TM/L	G	AB	R	H	2B	3B	HR	RBI	BB	SO	AVG	OBP	SLG	PRO+	BR/A	SB	CS	SBR	FA	FR	G/POS	TPR
1913	Bos-A	6	12	1	3	0	0	0	0	0	1	.250	.250	.250	45	-1	1			.923	0	/C-2	0.0

■ DUKE SNIDER Snider, Edwin Donald "The Silver Fox" b: 9/19/26, Los Angeles, Cal. BL/TR, 6', 190 lbs. Deb: 4/17/47 CH

YEAR	TM/L	G	AB	R	H	2B	3B	HR	RBI	BB	SO	AVG	OBP	SLG	PRO+	BR/A	SB	CS	SBR	FA	FR	G/POS	TPR
1947	Bro-N	40	83	6	20	3	1	0	5	3	24	.241	.276	.301	51	-6	2			.980	-2	O-25	-0.9
1948	Bro-N	53	160	22	39	6	6	5	21	12	27	.244	.297	.450	96	-2	4			.989	-3	O-47	-0.7
1949	*Bro-N	146	552	100	161	28	7	23	92	56	92	.292	.361	.493	122	16	12			.984	4	*O-145	1.2
1950	Bro-N★	152	620	109	**199**	31	10	31	107	58	79	.321	.379	.553	139	33	16			.983	9	*O-151	3.4
1951	Bro-N★	150	606	96	168	26	6	29	101	62	97	.277	.344	.483	118	14	14	10	-2	.987	3	*O-150	0.9
1952	*Bro-N☆	144	534	80	162	25	7	21	92	55	77	.303	.368	.494	136	25	7	4	-0	.992	1	*O-141	2.1
1953	*Bro-N★	153	590	**132**	198	38	4	42	126	82	90	.336	.419	**.627**	165	56	16	7	1	.987	-3	*O-151	4.6
1954	Bro-N★	149	584	**120**	199	39	10	40	130	84	96	.341	.427	.647	170	60	6	6	-2	.981	-5	*O-148	4.6
1955	*Bro-N★	148	538	**126**	166	34	6	42	**136**	104	87	.309	.421	.628	169	55	9	7	-2	.989	1	*O-146	4.7
1956	*Bro-N★	151	542	112	158	33	2	**43**	101	**99**	101	.292	**.402**	**.598**	152	41	3	3	-1	.984	-0	*O-150	3.2
1957	Bro-N	139	508	91	139	25	7	40	92	77	104	.274	.370	.587	139	27	3	4	-2	.990	-6	*O-136	1.1
1958	LA-N	106	327	45	102	12	3	15	58	32	49	.312	.375	.505	126	12	2	2	-1	.987	-13	O-92	-0.6
1959	*LA-N	126	370	59	114	11	2	23	88	58	71	.308	.402	.535	137	20	1	5	-3	.975	-17	*O-107	-0.4
1960	LA-N	101	235	38	57	13	5	14	36	46	54	.243	.369	.519	131	11	1	0	0	.965	-12	O-75	-0.4
1961	LA-N	85	233	35	69	8	3	16	56	29	43	.296	.376	.562	133	11	1	1	-0	.975	-2	O-66	0.6
1962	LA-N	80	158	28	44	11	3	5	30	36	32	.278	.418	.481	150	13	2	0	1	.967	-1	O-39	1.0
1963	NY-N★	129	354	44	86	8	3	14	45	56	74	.243	.348	.401	113	7	0	1	-1	.986	-10	*O-106	-0.8
1964	SF-N	91	167	16	35	7	0	4	17	22	40	.210	.302	.323	74	-5	0	0	0	.979	-5	O-43	-1.3
Total	18	2143	7161	1259	2116	358	85	407	1333	971	1237	.295	.381	.540	138	388	99	50		.985	-62	*O-1918	22.3

■ VAN SNIDER Snider, Van Voorhees b: 8/11/63, Birmingham, Ala. BL/TR, 6'3", 185 lbs. Deb: 9/2/88

YEAR	TM/L	G	AB	R	H	2B	3B	HR	RBI	BB	SO	AVG	OBP	SLG	PRO+	BR/A	SB	CS	SBR	FA	FR	G/POS	TPR
1988	Cin-N	11	28	4	6	1	0	1	6	0	13	.214	.214	.357	59	-2	0	1	-1	1.000	-1	/O-8	-0.3
1989	Cin-N	8	7	1	1	0	0	0	0	0	5	.143	.143	.143	-17	-1	0	0	0	1.000	-2	/O-6	-0.3
Total	2	19	35	5	7	1	0	1	6	0	18	.200	.200	.314	44	-3	0	1	-1	1.000	-2	/O-14	-0.6

■ ROXY SNIPES Snipes, Wyatt Eure "Rock" b: 10/28/1896, Marion, S.C. d: 5/1/41, Fayetteville, N.C. BL/TR, 6', 185 lbs. Deb: 7/15/23

YEAR	TM/L	G	AB	R	H	2B	3B	HR	RBI	BB	SO	AVG	OBP	SLG	PRO+	BR/A	SB	CS	SBR	FA	FR	G/POS	TPR
1923	Chi-A	1	1	0	0	0	0	0	0	0	0	.000	.000	.000	-99	-0	0	0	0	.000	0	H	0.0

■ CHAPPIE SNODGRASS Snodgrass, Amzie Beal b: 3/18/1870, Springfield, Ohio d: 9/9/51, New York, N.Y. BR/TR, 5'10", 165 lbs. Deb: 5/15/01

YEAR	TM/L	G	AB	R	H	2B	3B	HR	RBI	BB	SO	AVG	OBP	SLG	PRO+	BR/A	SB	CS	SBR	FA	FR	G/POS	TPR
1901	Bal-A	3	10	0	1	0	0	0	1	0		.100	.100	.100	-43	-2	0			.500	-1	/O-2	-0.3

■ FRED SNODGRASS Snodgrass, Frederick Carlisle "Snow" b: 10/19/1887, Ventura, Cal. d: 4/5/74, Ventura, Cal. BR/TR, 5'11.5", 175 lbs. Deb: 6/4/08

YEAR	TM/L	G	AB	R	H	2B	3B	HR	RBI	BB	SO	AVG	OBP	SLG	PRO+	BR/A	SB	CS	SBR	FA	FR	G/POS	TPR
1908	NY-N	6	4	2	1	0	0	0	1	0		.250	.250	.250	57	-0	1			1.000	1	/C-3	0.1
1909	NY-N	28	70	10	21	5	0	1	6	7		.300	.387	.414	146	4	10			.921	-1	O-20/C-2,1-1	0.3
1910	NY-N	123	396	69	127	22	8	2	44	71	52	.321	.440	.432	154	32	33			.970	-8	*O-101/1-9,C-1,3-1	2.0
1911	*NY-N	151	534	83	157	27	10	1	77	72	59	.294	.393	.388	115	13	51			.973	9	*O-149/1-1,3-1	1.4
1912	*NY-N	146	535	91	144	24	9	3	69	70	65	.269	.362	.364	96	-1	43			.948	-3	*O-116,1-27/2-1	-1.1
1913	*NY-N	141	457	65	133	21	6	3	49	53	44	.291	.373	.383	115	11	27			.968	6	*O-133/1-3,2-1	1.1
1914	NY-N	113	392	54	103	20	4	0	44	37	43	.263	.336	.334	103	2	25			.977	5	O-96,1-14/2-1,3-1	0.2
1915	NY-N	80	252	36	49	9	0	0	20	35	33	.194	.307	.230	68	-8	11	12	-4	.935	4	O-75	-1.3
	Bos-N	23	79	10	22	2	0	0	9	7	9	.278	.352	.304	104	1	0	4	-2	.938	-2	O-18/1-5	-0.5
	Yr	103	331	46	71	11	0	0	29	42	42	.215	.318	.248	76	-7	11	16	-6	.935	2	O-93/1-5	-1.8
1916	Bos-N	112	382	33	95	13	5	1	32	34	54	.249	.318	.317	100	0	14			.983	13	*O-110	0.9
Total	9	923	3101	453	852	143	42	11	351	386	359	.275	.367	.359	110	53	215	16		.965	24	O-818/1-60,C-6,23	3.1

■ CHRIS SNOPEK Snopek, Christopher Charles b: 9/20/70, Cynthiana, Ky. BR/TR, 6'1", 185 lbs. Deb: 7/31/95

YEAR	TM/L	G	AB	R	H	2B	3B	HR	RBI	BB	SO	AVG	OBP	SLG	PRO+	BR/A	SB	CS	SBR	FA	FR	G/POS	TPR
1995	Chi-A	22	68	12	22	4	0	1	7	9	12	.324	.403	.426	121	2	1	0	0	1.000	-0	3-17/S-6	0.3
1996	Chi-A	46	104	18	27	6	1	6	18	6	16	.260	.306	.510	106	0	0	1	-1	.939	4	3-27,S-12/D-3	0.4
1997	Chi-A	86	298	27	65	15	0	5	35	18	51	.218	.265	.319	54	-21	3	2	-0	.915	-15	3-82/S-4	-3.4
1998	Chi-A	53	125	17	26	2	0	1	4	14	24	.208	.293	.248	44	-10	3	0	1	.972	6	S-33,2-12/3-3,1OD	0.0
	Bos-A	8	12	2	2	0	0	0	2	2	5	.167	.286	.167	22	-1	0	0	0	.750	-2	/2-3,3-3,D-2	-0.3
	Yr	61	137	19	28	2	0	1	6	16	29	.204	.292	.241	42	-11	3	0	1	.972	5	S-33,2-15/3-6,D1O	-0.3
Total	4	215	607	76	142	27	1	13	66	49	108	.234	.294	.346	68	-29	7	3	0	.928	-6	3-132/S-55,2DO1	-3.0

■ CHARLIE SNOW Snow, Charles M. b: 8/3/1849, Lowell, Mass. Deb: 10/1/1874

YEAR	TM/L	G	AB	R	H	2B	3B	HR	RBI	BB	SO	AVG	OBP	SLG	PRO+	BR/A	SB	CS	SBR	FA	FR	G/POS	TPR
1874	Atl-n	1	1	0	1	0	0	0	0	0	0	1.000	1.000	1.000	615	1	0	0	0	.000	-1	/C-1	0.0

■ J. T. SNOW Snow, Jack Thomas b: 2/26/68, Long Beach, Cal. BB/TL, 6'2", 202 lbs. Deb: 9/20/92

YEAR	TM/L	G	AB	R	H	2B	3B	HR	RBI	BB	SO	AVG	OBP	SLG	PRO+	BR/A	SB	CS	SBR	FA	FR	G/POS	TPR
1992	NY-A	7	14	1	2	1	0	0	2	5	5	.143	.368	.214	67	-0	0	0	0	1.000	-0	/1-6,D-1	-0.1
1993	Cal-A	129	419	60	101	18	2	16	57	55	88	.241	.332	.408	95	-3	3	0	1	.995	-2	*1-129	-1.5
1994	Cal-A	61	223	22	49	4	0	8	30	19	48	.220	.290	.345	62	-13	0	1	-1	.996	-1	1-61	-1.9
1995	Cal-A	143	544	80	157	22	1	24	102	52	91	.289	.354	.465	112	9	2	1	0	.997	-17	*1-143	-2.0
1996	Cal-A	155	575	69	148	20	1	17	67	56	96	.257	.329	.384	79	-18	1	6	-3	.993	1	*1-154	-3.3
1997	*SF-N	157	531	81	149	36	1	28	104	96	124	.281	.392	.510	137	30	6	4	-1	.995	-2	*1-156	1.2
1998	SF-N	138	435	65	108	29	1	15	79	58	84	.248	.337	.423	99	-1	1	2	-1	**.999**	4	*1-136	-0.7
Total	7	790	2741	378	714	130	6	108	441	341	536	.260	.345	.430	101	4	13	14	-5	.996	-17	1-785/D-1	-8.3

■ BERNIE SNYDER Snyder, Bernard Austin b: 8/25/13, Philadelphia, Pa. BR/TR, 6', 165 lbs. Deb: 9/15/35

YEAR	TM/L	G	AB	R	H	2B	3B	HR	RBI	BB	SO	AVG	OBP	SLG	PRO+	BR/A	SB	CS	SBR	FA	FR	G/POS	TPR
1935	Phi-A	10	32	5	11	1	0	0	3	1	2	.344	.364	.375	92	-0	0	0	0	.880	-3	/2-5,S-4	-0.2

■ CHARLES SNYDER Snyder, Charles b: Camden, N.J. d: 3/3/01, Philadelphia, Pa. BR/TR, Deb: 9/19/1890

YEAR	TM/L	G	AB	R	H	2B	3B	HR	RBI	BB	SO	AVG	OBP	SLG	PRO+	BR/A	SB	CS	SBR	FA	FR	G/POS	TPR
1890	Phi-a	9	33	5	9	1	0	0	4	2		.273	.314	.303	84	-1	0			.583	-3	/O-5,C-5	-0.4

■ POP SNYDER Snyder, Charles N. b: 10/6/1854, Washington, D.C. d: 10/29/24, Washington, D.C. BR/TR, 5'11.5", 184 lbs. Deb: 6/16/1873 MU

YEAR	TM/L	G	AB	R	H	2B	3B	HR	RBI	BB	SO	AVG	OBP	SLG	PRO+	BR/A	SB	CS	SBR	FA	FR	G/POS	TPR
1873	Was-n	28	108	16	21	2	0	0	4	3	3	.194	.216	.213	29	-9	0	1	-1	.848	-1	C-28/O-3	-0.7
1874	Bal-n	39	151	24	33	4	0	1	17	1	2	.219	.224	.265	56	-7	0	0	0	.789	-0	C-39	-0.5
1875	Phi-n	66	263	38	64	8	2	1	25	4	4	.243	.255	.300	89	-3	3	8	-4	.825	4	*C-66/1-1	-0.1

YEAR	TM/L	G	AB	R	H	2B	3B	HR	RBI	BB	SO	AVG	OBP	SLG	PRO+	BR/A	SB	CS	SBR	FA	FR	G/POS	TPR
1876	Lou-N	56	224	21	44	4	1	1	9	2	7	.196	.204	.237	39	-16				.833	11	*C-55/O-4	-0.3
1877	Lou-N	61	248	23	64	7	2	2	28	3	14	.258	.267	.327	73	-10				**.910**	15	*C-61/O-1,S-1	0.7
1878	Bos-N	60	226	21	48	5	0	0	14	1	19	.212	.216	.235	44	-14				**.912**	5	*C-58/O-2	-0.7
1879	Bos-N	81	329	42	78	16	3	2	35	5	31	.237	.249	.322	85	-6				**.925**	**24**	*C-80/O-2	1.9
1881	Bos-N	62	219	14	50	8	0	0	16	3	23	.228	.239	.265	61	-9				.897	3	*C-60/O-1,S-1,2-1	-0.4
1882	Cin-a	72	309	49	90	12	2	1	50	9		.291	.311	.353	117	4				.916	19	*C-70/1-2,O-1,M	2.3
1883	Cin-a	58	250	38	64	14	6	0	34	8		.256	.279	.360	99	-1				.919	14	C-57/S-2,M	1.4
1884	Cin-a	67	268	32	69	9	9	0	39	7		.257	.276	.358	101	-1				.922	27	C-65/1-2,O-1,M	2.9
1885	Cin-a	39	152	13	36	4	3	1	19	6		.237	.270	.322	85	-3				.880	3	C-38/1-1	0.3
1886	Cin-a	60	220	33	41	8	3	0	28	13		.186	.242	.250	52	-13	11			.874	-5	C-41,1-19/O-1	-1.3
1887	Cle-a	74	282	33	72	12	6	0	27	9		.255	.281	.340	75	-10	5			.905	19	C-63,1-13	1.1
1888	Cle-a	64	237	22	51	7	3	0	14	6		.215	.238	.270	64	-10	9			.901	8	C-58/1-4,O-3	0.3
1889	Cle-N	22	83	5	16	3	0	0	12	2	12	.193	.221	.229	26	-8	4			.907	2	C-22	-0.4
1890	Cle-P	13	48	5	9	1	0	0	12	1	9	.188	.220	.208	16	-6	1			.958	3	C-13	-0.1
1891	Was-a	8	27	4	5	0	1	0	2	0	3	.185	.241	.259	45	-2	0			1.000	0	/1-4,C-3,O-1,M	-0.2
Total	3 n	133	522	78	118	14	2	2	46	8	9	.226	.238	.272	66	-19	3	9	-5	.819	3	C-133/O-3,1-1	-1.3
Total	15	797	3122	355	737	110	39	7	339	75	118	.236	.256	.303	73	-104	30			.904	148	C-744/1-45,O-17,S2	7.5

■ REDLEG SNYDER

Snyder, Emanuel Sebastian (b: Emanuel Sebastian Schneider)
b: 12/12/1854, Camden, N.J. d: 11/24/32, Camden, N.J. BR/TR, 5′10″, 175 lbs. Deb: 4/25/1876

YEAR	TM/L	G	AB	R	H	2B	3B	HR	RBI	BB	SO	AVG	OBP	SLG	PRO+	BR/A	SB	CS	SBR	FA	FR	G/POS	TPR
1876	Cin-N	55	205	10	31	3	1	0	12	1	19	.151	.155	.176	12	-17				.825	5	*O-55	-1.2
1884	Wil-U	17	52	4	10	0	0	0		1		.192	.208	.192	21	-6				.976	1	1-16/O-1	-0.7
Total	2	72	257	14	41	3	1	0	12	2	19	.160	.166	.179	14	-24				.825	6	/O-56,1-16	-1.9

■ COONEY SNYDER

Snyder, Frank C. b: Toronto, Ontario, Canada d: 3/9/17, Toronto, Ont., Can. 6′3″, 180 lbs. Deb: 5/19/1898

YEAR	TM/L	G	AB	R	H	2B	3B	HR	RBI	BB	SO	AVG	OBP	SLG	PRO+	BR/A	SB	CS	SBR	FA	FR	G/POS	TPR
1898	Lou-N	17	61	4	10	0	0	0	6	3		.164	.215	.164	9	-7	0			.935	-6	C-17	-1.1

■ FRANK SNYDER

Snyder, Frank Elton "Pancho" b: 5/27/1893, San Antonio, Tex. d: 1/5/62, San Antonio, Tex. BR/TR, 6′2″, 185 lbs. Deb: 8/25/12 C

YEAR	TM/L	G	AB	R	H	2B	3B	HR	RBI	BB	SO	AVG	OBP	SLG	PRO+	BR/A	SB	CS	SBR	FA	FR	G/POS	TPR
1912	StL-N	11	18	2	2	0	0	0	0	2	7	.111	.200	.111	-14	-3	1			.919	0	C-11	-0.2
1913	StL-N	7	21	1	4	0	1	0	2	0	4	.190	.190	.286	35	-2	0			.956	2	/C-7	0.0
1914	StL-N	100	326	19	75	15	4	1	25	13	28	.230	.262	.310	71	-13	1			**.979**	5	C-98	0.0
1915	StL-N	144	473	41	141	22	7	2	55	39	49	.298	.353	.387	124	13	3	6	-3	.983	7	*C-142	3.1
1916	StL-N	132	406	23	105	12	4	0	39	18	31	.259	.290	.308	84	-8	7			.973	9	C-72,1-46/S-1	0.5
1917	StL-N	115	313	18	74	9	2	1	33	27	43	.236	.301	.288	83	-6	4			.975	0	C-94/2-1	0.2
1918	StL-N	39	112	5	28	7	1	0	10	6	13	.250	.288	.330	92	-1	4			.959	2	C-27/1-3	0.3
1919	StL-N	50	154	7	28	4	2	0	14	5	13	.182	.213	.234	36	-12	2			.983	5	C-48/1-1	-0.4
	NY-N	32	92	7	21	6	0	0	11	8	9	.228	.297	.293	79	-2	1			.983	-4	C-31	-0.5
	Yr	82	246	14	49	10	2	0	25	13	22	.199	.245	.256	53	-14	3			.983	1	C-79/1-1	-0.9
1920	NY-N	87	264	26	66	13	4	3	27	17	18	.250	.295	.364	89	-4	2	2	-1	.978	1	C-84	0.2
1921	*NY-N	108	309	36	99	13	2	8	45	27	24	.320	.382	.453	120	9	3	4	-2	.985	5	*C-101	1.7
1922	*NY-N	104	318	34	109	21	5	5	51	23	25	.343	.387	.487	123	11	1	5	-3	.980	-3	C-97	0.9
1923	*NY-N	120	402	37	103	13	6	5	63	24	29	.256	.298	.356	73	-17	5	3	-0	**.990**	3	*C-112	-0.9
1924	*NY-N	118	354	37	107	18	3	5	53	30	43	.302	.357	.412	109	4	3	0	1	.987	-16	*C-110	-0.4
1925	NY-N	107	325	21	78	9	1	11	51	20	49	.240	.286	.375	70	-16	0	0	0	**.985**	2	C-96	-0.8
1926	NY-N	55	148	10	32	3	2	5	16	13	13	.216	.280	.365	73	-6	0			.981	-0	C-55	-0.3
1927	StL-N	63	194	7	50	5	0	1	30	9	18	.258	.291	.299	56	-12	0			.981	0	C-62	-0.8
Total	16	1392	4229	331	1122	170	44	47	525	281	416	.265	.313	.360	90	-65	37	20		.981	16	*C-1247/1-50,2-1,S	2.6

■ JERRY SNYDER

Snyder, Gerald George b: 7/21/29, Jenks, Okla. BR/TR, 6′, 170 lbs. Deb: 5/8/52

YEAR	TM/L	G	AB	R	H	2B	3B	HR	RBI	BB	SO	AVG	OBP	SLG	PRO+	BR/A	SB	CS	SBR	FA	FR	G/POS	TPR
1952	Was-A	36	57	5	9	2	0	0	2	5	8	.158	.226	.193	18	-6	1	0	0	.965	7	2-19/S-4	0.2
1953	Was-A	29	62	10	21	4	0	0	4	5	8	.339	.388	.403	117	2	1	1	-0	.988	7	S-17/2-4	0.9
1954	Was-A	64	154	17	36	3	1	0	17	15	18	.234	.302	.266	60	-8	3	0	1	.978	9	S-48/2-3	0.5
1955	Was-A	46	107	7	24	5	0	0	5	6	6	.224	.265	.271	47	-8	1	1	-0	.977	1	2-22,S-20	-0.5
1956	Was-A	43	148	14	40	3	1	2	14	10	9	.270	.321	.345	76	-5	1	0	0	.968	-5	S-35/2-7	-0.6
1957	Was-A	42	93	6	14	1	0	1	4	4	9	.151	.186	.194	4	-12	0	1	-1	.966	1	S-15,2-13/3-1	-1.1
1958	Was-A	6	9	1	1	0	0	0	1	1	1	.111	.200	.111	-12	-1	0	0	0	1.000	-1	/2-2,S-1	-0.2
Total	7	266	630	60	145	18	2	3	47	46	59	.230	.284	.279	54	-41	7	3	0	.971	20	S-140/2-70,3-1	-0.8

■ JIM SNYDER

Snyder, James C. A. b: 9/15/1847, Brooklyn, N.Y. d: 12/1/22, Rockaway Beach, N.Y 5′7″, 130 lbs. Deb: 5/7/1872

YEAR	TM/L	G	AB	R	H	2B	3B	HR	RBI	BB	SO	AVG	OBP	SLG	PRO+	BR/A	SB	CS	SBR	FA	FR	G/POS	TPR
1872	Eck-n	26	107	16	28	2	2	0	11	0	1	.262	.262	.318	91	0	0	0	0	.763	4	S-25/C-1,O-1	0.3

■ CORY SNYDER

Snyder, James Cory b: 11/11/62, Inglewood, Cal. BR/TR, 6′3″, 185 lbs. Deb: 6/13/86

YEAR	TM/L	G	AB	R	H	2B	3B	HR	RBI	BB	SO	AVG	OBP	SLG	PRO+	BR/A	SB	CS	SBR	FA	FR	G/POS	TPR
1986	Cle-A	103	416	58	113	21	1	24	69	16	123	.272	.299	.500	115	6	2	3	-1	.987	-7	O-74,S-34,3-11,/D-1	-0.2
1987	Cle-A	157	577	74	136	24	2	33	82	31	166	.236	.276	.456	89	-12	5	1	1	.971	2	*O-139,S-18	-1.2
1988	Cle-A	142	511	71	139	24	3	26	75	42	101	.272	.329	.483	121	13	5	1	1	.985	14	*O-141/D-1	2.3
1989	Cle-A	132	489	49	105	17	0	18	59	23	134	.215	.253	.360	70	-21	6	5	-1	**.997**	19	*O-125/S-7,D-2	-0.7
1990	Cle-A	123	438	46	102	27	3	14	55	21	118	.233	.271	.404	87	-10	1	4	-2	.975	2	*O-120/S-5	-1.3
1991	Chi-A	50	117	10	22	4	0	3	11	6	41	.188	.228	.299	46	-9	0	0	0	.981	-2	O-29,1-18	-1.2
	Tor-A	21	49	4	7	0	1	0	6	3	19	.143	.192	.184	4	-6	0	0	0	1.000	-3	O-14/1-4,3-3,D-3	-0.9
	Yr	71	166	14	29	4	1	3	17	9	60	.175	.217	.265	33	-15	0	0	0	.985	-5	O-43,1-22/3-3,D-3	-2.1
1992	SF-N	124	390	48	105	22	2	14	57	23	96	.269	.313	.444	119	7	4	4	-1	.992	-5	O-70,1-27,3-14,/2S	-0.1
1993	LA-N	143	516	61	137	33	1	11	56	47	147	.266	.332	.397	100	-1	4	1	1	.979	-8	*O-115,3-23,1-12,/S	-1.0
1994	LA-N	73	153	18	36	6	0	6	18	14	47	.235	.304	.392	85	-4	1	0	0	.967	-8	O-50/1-9,3-6,S-4,2	-1.2
Total	9	1068	3656	439	902	178	13	149	488	226	992	.247	.293	.425	95	-36	28	19	-3	.983	3	O-877/S-73,132D	-5.5

■ JIM SNYDER

Snyder, James Robert b: 8/15/32, Dearborn, Mich. BR/TR, 6′1″, 185 lbs. Deb: 9/15/61 MC

YEAR	TM/L	G	AB	R	H	2B	3B	HR	RBI	BB	SO	AVG	OBP	SLG	PRO+	BR/A	SB	CS	SBR	FA	FR	G/POS	TPR
1961	Min-A	3	5	0	0	0	0	0	0	0	1	.000	.000	.000	-95	-1	0	0	0	1.000	0	/2-3	-0.1
1962	Min-A	12	10	1	1	0	0	0	1	0	0	.100	.100	.100	-44	-2	0	1	-1	.941	-6	/2-5,1-1	-0.8
1964	Min-A	26	71	3	11	2	0	1	9	4	11	.155	.211	.225	21	-8	0	0	0	.990	-4	2-25	-1.0
Total	3	41	86	4	12	2	0	1	10	4	12	.140	.187	.198	6	-11	0	1	-1	.984	-10	/2-33,1-1	-1.9

■ JACK SNYDER

Snyder, John William b: 10/6/1886, Lincoln, Pa. d: 12/13/81, Brownsville, Pa. BR/TR, 5′9″, 168 lbs. Deb: 6/13/14

YEAR	TM/L	G	AB	R	H	2B	3B	HR	RBI	BB	SO	AVG	OBP	SLG	PRO+	BR/A	SB	CS	SBR	FA	FR	G/POS	TPR
1914	Buf-F	1	0	0	0	0	0	0	0	1	0	—	1.000	—	183	0	0			.000	0	/C-1	0.0
1917	Bro-N	7	11	1	3	0	0	0	1	0	2	.273	.273	.273	66	-0	0			1.000	0	/C-5	0.0
Total	2	8	11	1	3	0	0	0	1	1	2	.273	.333	.273	84	-0	0			1.000	0	/C-6	0.0

■ JOSH SNYDER

Snyder, Joshua M. b: 3/1844, Brooklyn, N.Y. d: 4/21/1881, Brooklyn, N.Y. Deb: 5/18/1872

YEAR	TM/L	G	AB	R	H	2B	3B	HR	RBI	BB	SO	AVG	OBP	SLG	PRO+	BR/A	SB	CS	SBR	FA	FR	G/POS	TPR
1872	Eck-n	9	37	2	6	2	0	0	1	1	1	.162	.184	.216	27	-3	0	0	0	.778	2	/O-9	0.0

■ RUSS SNYDER

Snyder, Russell Henry b: 6/22/34, Oak, Neb. BL/TR, 6′1″, 190 lbs. Deb: 4/18/59

YEAR	TM/L	G	AB	R	H	2B	3B	HR	RBI	BB	SO	AVG	OBP	SLG	PRO+	BR/A	SB	CS	SBR	FA	FR	G/POS	TPR
1959	KC-A	73	243	41	76	13	2	3	21	19	29	.313	.367	.420	113	5	6	2	1	.986	3	O-64	0.5
1960	KC-A	125	304	45	79	10	5	4	26	20	28	.260	.308	.365	81	-9	7	3	0	.986	-10	O-91	-2.2
1961	Bal-A	115	312	46	91	13	5	1	13	20	32	.292	.334	.375	92	-4	5	3	-0	.966	-16	*O-108	-2.5
1962	Bal-A	139	416	47	127	19	4	9	40	17	46	.305	.336	.435	113	6	7	4	-0	.974	-3	*O-121	-0.4
1963	Bal-A	148	429	51	110	21	2	7	36	40	48	.256	.323	.364	95	-3	18	5	2	.988	-18	*O-130	-2.5
1964	Bal-A	56	93	11	27	3	0	1	7	11	22	.290	.365	.355	102	1	0	2	-1	.971	-9	O-40	-1.1
1965	Bal-A	132	345	49	93	11	2	1	29	27	38	.270	.324	.322	83	-7	3	4	-2	1.000	-7	*O-106	-2.2
1966	*Bal-A	117	373	66	114	21	5	3	41	38	37	.306	.370	.413	127	13	2	1	0	.986	-13	*O-104	-0.5
1967	Bal-A	108	275	40	65	8	2	4	23	32	48	.236	.318	.324	91	-3	5	2	0	.985	-1	O-69	-0.8
1968	Chi-A	38	82	2	11	2	0	1	5	4	16	.134	.174	.195	12	-9	0	0	0	1.000	-5	O-22	-1.8
	Cle-A	68	217	30	61	8	2	2	23	25	21	.281	.355	.364	120	6	1	1	-0	.991	4	O-54/1-1	0.7
	Yr	106	299	32	72	10	2	3	28	29	37	.241	.308	.318	90	-3	1	1	-0	.992	-1	O-76/1-1	-1.1

YEAR	TM/L	G	AB	R	H	2B	3B	HR	RBI	BB	SO	AVG	OBP	SLG	PRO+	BR/A	SB	CS	SBR	FA	FR	G/POS	TPR
1969	Cle-A	122	266	26	66	10	0	2	24	25	33	.248	.313	.308	72	-10	3	2	-0	.961	-4	O-84	-1.8
1970	Mil-A	124	276	34	64	11	0	4	31	16	40	.232	.274	.315	62	-15	1	3	-2	.966	-16	*O-106	-3.7
Total	12	1365	3631	488	984	150	29	42	319	294	438	.271	.327	.363	94	-28	58	32	-2	.981	-96	*O-1099/1-1	-18.3

■ CHIEF SOCKALEXIS Sockalexis, Louis M. b: 10/24/1871, Old Town, Maine d: 12/24/13, Burlington, Maine BL/TR, 5′11″, 185 lbs. Deb: 4/22/1897

YEAR	TM/L	G	AB	R	H	2B	3B	HR	RBI	BB	SO	AVG	OBP	SLG	PRO+	BR/A	SB	CS	SBR	FA	FR	G/POS	TPR
1897	Cle-N	66	278	43	94	9	8	3	42	18		.338	.385	.460	116	5	16			.888	1	O-66	0.1
1898	Cle-N	21	67	11	15	2	0	0	10	1		.224	.246	.254	44	-5	0			.964	2	O-16	-0.4
1899	Cle-N	7	22	0	6	1	0	0	3	1		.273	.304	.318	76	-1	0			.818	1	/O-5	0.0
Total	3	94	367	54	115	12	8	3	55	20		.313	.355	.414	103	-0	16			.896	4	/O-87	-0.3

■ BILL SODD Sodd, William b: 9/18/14, Ft.Worth, Tex. d: 5/14/98, Fort Worth, Tex. BR/TR, 6′2″, 210 lbs. Deb: 9/27/37

YEAR	TM/L	G	AB	R	H	2B	3B	HR	RBI	BB	SO	AVG	OBP	SLG	PRO+	BR/A	SB	CS	SBR	FA	FR	G/POS	TPR
1937	Cle-A	1	1	0	0	0	0	0	0	0	1	.000	.000	.000	-99	-0	0	0	0	.000	0	H	0.0

■ ERIC SODERHOLM Soderholm, Eric Thane b: 9/24/48, Cortland, N.Y. BR/TR, 5′11″, 187 lbs. Deb: 9/3/71

YEAR	TM/L	G	AB	R	H	2B	3B	HR	RBI	BB	SO	AVG	OBP	SLG	PRO+	BR/A	SB	CS	SBR	FA	FR	G/POS	TPR
1971	Min-A	21	64	9	10	4	0	1	4	10	17	.156	.299	.266	59	-3	0	1	-1	.942	3	3-20	-0.1
1972	Min-A	93	287	28	54	10	0	13	39	19	48	.188	.246	.359	75	-10	3	3	-1	.942	2	3-79	-1.1
1973	Min-A	35	111	22	33	7	2	1	9	21	16	.297	.414	.423	131	6	1	2	-1	.921	0	3-33/S-1	0.5
1974	Min-A	141	464	63	128	18	3	10	51	48	68	.276	.350	.392	110	6	7	3	0	.956	-4	*3-130/S-1	0.2
1975	Min-A	117	419	62	120	17	2	11	58	53	66	.286	.367	.415	119	11	3	5	-2	.969	12	*3-113/D-3	2.1
1977	Chi-A	130	460	77	129	20	3	25	67	47	47	.280	.352	.500	129	18	2	4	-2	**.978**	0	*3-126/D-3	1.5
1978	Chi-A	143	457	57	118	17	1	20	67	39	44	.258	.322	.431	109	4	2	2	-1	.964	0	*3-128,D-11/2-1	0.2
1979	Chi-A	56	210	31	53	8	2	6	34	19	19	.252	.314	.395	90	-3	0	1	-1	.986	15	3-56	1.0
	Tex-A	63	147	15	40	6	0	4	19	12	9	.272	.331	.395	96	-1	0	0	0	.944	0	3-37,D-14/1-2	-0.1
	Yr	119	357	46	93	14	2	10	53	31	28	.261	.321	.395	93	-4	0	1	-1	.975	15	3-93,D-14/1-2	0.9
1980	*NY-A	95	275	38	79	13	1	11	35	27	25	.287	.353	.462	123	9	0	0	0	.952	-1	D-51,3-37	0.5
Total	9	894	2894	402	764	120	14	102	383	295	359	.264	.337	.421	110	37	18	21	-7	.962	27	3-759/D-82,1-2,S2	4.7

■ RICK SOFIELD Sofield, Richard Michael b: 12/16/56, Cheyenne, Wyo. BL/TR, 6′1″, 195 lbs. Deb: 4/6/79

YEAR	TM/L	G	AB	R	H	2B	3B	HR	RBI	BB	SO	AVG	OBP	SLG	PRO+	BR/A	SB	CS	SBR	FA	FR	G/POS	TPR
1979	Min-A	35	93	8	28	5	0	0	12	12	27	.301	.381	.355	96	-0	2	3	-1	.954	-3	O-35	-0.5
1980	Min-A	131	417	52	103	18	4	9	49	24	92	.247	.291	.374	75	-15	4	5	-2	.979	-5	*O-126/D-2	-2.6
1981	Min-A	41	102	9	18	2	0	0	5	8	22	.176	.236	.196	24	-10	3	2	-0	.983	-1	O-34	-1.2
Total	3	207	612	69	149	25	4	9	66	44	141	.243	.296	.342	71	-25	9	10	-3	.975	-8	O-195/D-2	-4.3

■ LUIS SOJO Sojo, Luis Beltran (Sojo) b: 1/3/66, Caracas, Venez. BR/TR, 5′11″, 174 lbs. Deb: 7/14/90

YEAR	TM/L	G	AB	R	H	2B	3B	HR	RBI	BB	SO	AVG	OBP	SLG	PRO+	BR/A	SB	CS	SBR	FA	FR	G/POS	TPR
1990	Tor-A	33	80	14	18	3	0	1	9	5	5	.225	.271	.300	58	-4	1	1	-0	.969	-3	2-15/S-5,O-5,3-4,D	-0.8
1991	Cal-A	113	364	38	94	14	1	3	20	14	26	.258	.295	.327	72	-14	4	2	0	.981	20	*2-107/S-2,3-1,OD	0.8
1992	Cal-A	106	368	37	100	12	3	7	43	14	24	.272	.300	.378	88	-7	7	11	-5	.985	2	2-96/3-9,S-5	-0.7
1993	Tor-A	19	47	5	8	2	0	0	6	4	2	.170	.235	.213	21	-5	0	0	0	1.000	-1	/2-8,S-8,3-3	-0.6
1994	Sea-A	63	213	32	59	9	2	6	22	8	25	.277	.309	.423	85	-5	2	1	0	.973	18	2-40,S-24/3-1,D-2	1.4
1995	*Sea-A	102	339	50	98	18	2	7	39	23	19	.289	.336	.416	93	-4	4	2	0	.983	-14	S-80,2-19/O-6	-1.0
1996	Sea-A	77	247	20	52	8	1	1	16	10	13	.211	.244	.263	28	-27	2	2	-1	.940	10	3-33,2-27,S-19	-1.4
	*NY-A	18	40	3	11	2	0	0	5	1	4	.275	.293	.325	56	-3	0	0	0	1.000	3	2-14/S-4,3-1	0.1
	Yr	95	287	23	63	10	1	1	21	11	17	.220	.251	.272	32	-30	2	2	-1	.986	13	2-41,3-34,S-23	-1.3
1997	NY-A	77	215	27	66	6	1	2	25	16	14	.307	.358	.372	92	-2	3	1	0	.982	-5	2-72/S-4,3-3,1-2	-0.3
1998	*NY-A	54	147	16	34	3	1	0	14	4	15	.231	.252	.265	35	-14	1	0	0	.973	4	S-20,1-19/2-8,3D	-0.8
Total	9	662	2060	242	540	77	11	27	199	99	147	.262	.300	.350	72	-85	24	20	-5	.981	34	2-406,S-171/31OD	-3.3

■ TONY SOLAITA Solaita, Tolia b: 1/15/47, Nuuuli, Amer.Samoa d: 2/10/90, Tafuna, Amer.Samoa BL/TL, 6′, 215 lbs. Deb: 9/16/68

YEAR	TM/L	G	AB	R	H	2B	3B	HR	RBI	BB	SO	AVG	OBP	SLG	PRO+	BR/A	SB	CS	SBR	FA	FR	G/POS	TPR
1968	NY-A	1	1	0	0	0	0	0	0	0	1	.000	.000	.000	-99	-0	0	0	0	1.000	-0	/1-1	0.0
1974	KC-A	96	239	31	64	12	0	7	30	35	70	.268	.364	.406	115	5	0	3	-2	.991	3	1-65,D-14/O-1	0.3
1975	KC-A	93	231	35	60	11	0	16	44	39	79	.260	.371	.515	145	14	0	1	-1	.994	3	D-37,1-35	1.4
1976	KC-A	31	68	4	16	4	0	0	9	6	17	.235	.297	.294	73	-2	0	0	0	.974	0	D-14/1-5	-0.3
	Cal-A	63	215	25	58	9	0	9	33	34	44	.270	.369	.437	145	13	1	1	-0	.998	8	1-54/D-7	1.7
	Yr	94	283	29	74	13	0	9	42	40	61	.261	.353	.403	126	10	1	1	-0	.996	8	1-59,D-21	1.4
1977	Cal-A	116	324	40	78	15	0	14	53	56	77	.241	.353	.417	113	7	1	3	-2	.990	1	1-91/D-6	0.2
1978	Cal-A	60	94	10	21	3	0	1	14	16	25	.223	.336	.287	80	-2	0	0	0	1.000	1	D-18,1-11	-0.2
1979	Mon-N	29	42	5	12	4	0	1	7	11	16	.286	.434	.452	143	3	0	0	0	.989	0	1-13	0.3
	Tor-A	36	102	14	27	8	1	2	13	17	16	.265	.370	.422	112	2	0	0	0	1.000	0	D-26/1-6	0.1
Total	7	525	1316	164	336	66	1	50	203	214	345	.255	.361	.421	120	39	2	8	-4	.993	17	1-281,D-122/O-1	3.5

■ MOSE SOLOMON Solomon, Mose Hirsch "The Rabbi Of Swat" b: 12/8/1900, New York, N.Y. d: 6/25/66, Miami, Fla. BL/TL, 5′9.5″, 180 lbs. Deb: 9/30/23

YEAR	TM/L	G	AB	R	H	2B	3B	HR	RBI	BB	SO	AVG	OBP	SLG	PRO+	BR/A	SB	CS	SBR	FA	FR	G/POS	TPR
1923	NY-N	2	8	0	3	1	0	0	1	0	1	.375	.375	.500	131	0	0	0	0	.833	-0	/O-2	0.0

■ MOOSE SOLTERS Solters, Julius Joseph (b: Julius Joseph Soltesz) b: 3/22/06, Pittsburgh, Pa. d: 9/28/75, Pittsburgh, Pa. BR/TR, 6′, 190 lbs. Deb: 4/17/34

YEAR	TM/L	G	AB	R	H	2B	3B	HR	RBI	BB	SO	AVG	OBP	SLG	PRO+	BR/A	SB	CS	SBR	FA	FR	G/POS	TPR
1934	Bos-A	101	365	61	109	25	4	7	58	18	50	.299	.333	.447	93	-5	9	4	0	.933	2	O-89	-0.6
1935	Bos-A	24	79	15	19	6	1	0	8	2	7	.241	.268	.342	53	-6	1	1	-0	.966	3	O-21	-0.4
	StL-A	127	552	79	182	39	6	18	104	34	35	.330	.369	.520	122	15	10	1	2	.989	16	*O-127	2.7
	Yr	151	631	94	201	45	7	18	112	36	42	.319	.356	.498	113	9	11	2	2	.985	19	*O-148	2.3
1936	StL-A	152	628	100	183	45	7	17	134	41	76	.291	.336	.467	93	-10	3	0	1	.956	12	*O-147	-0.3
1937	Cle-A	152	589	90	190	42	11	20	109	42	56	.323	.372	.533	125	19	6	9	-4	.953	2	*O-149	1.2
1938	Cle-A	67	199	30	40	6	3	2	22	13	28	.201	.250	.291	36	-21	4	1	1	.969	1	O-46	-1.8
1939	Cle-A	41	102	19	28	7	2	2	19	9	15	.275	.333	.441	100	-0	2	1	0	.915	-3	O-25	-0.4
	StL-A	40	131	14	27	6	1	0	14	10	20	.206	.262	.267	35	-13	1	0	0	.935	0	O-30	-1.2
	Yr	81	233	33	55	13	3	2	33	19	35	.236	.294	.343	63	-14	3	1	0	.927	-3	O-55	-1.6
1940	Chi-A	116	428	65	132	28	3	12	80	27	54	.308	.351	.472	110	5	3	3	-1	.971	5	*O-107	0.4
1941	Chi-A	76	251	24	65	9	4	4	43	18	31	.259	.311	.375	82	-7	3	2	-0	.966	1	O-63	-1.0
1943	Chi-A	42	97	6	15	0	0	1	8	7	5	.155	.212	.186	17	-10	0	1	-1	.941	-3	O-21	-1.7
Total	9	938	3421	503	990	213	42	83	599	221	377	.289	.334	.449	96	-32	42	23	-1	.960	36	O-825	-3.1

■ JOCK SOMERLOTT Somerlott, John Wesley b: 10/26/1882, Flint, Ind. d: 4/21/65, Butler, Ind. BR/TR, 6′, 160 lbs. Deb: 9/19/10

YEAR	TM/L	G	AB	R	H	2B	3B	HR	RBI	BB	SO	AVG	OBP	SLG	PRO+	BR/A	SB	CS	SBR	FA	FR	G/POS	TPR
1910	Was-A	16	63	6	14	0	0	0	2	3		.222	.258	.222	53	-3	2			.994	0	1-16	-0.4
1911	Was-A	13	40	2	7	0	0	0	2	0		.175	.195	.175	4	-5	2			.992	2	1-12	-0.4
Total	2	29	103	8	21	0	0	0	4	3		.204	.234	.204	32	-9	4			.993	2	/1-28	-0.8

■ ED SOMERVILLE Somerville, Edward G. b: 3/1/1853, Philadelphia, Pa. d: 10/1/1877, London, Ont., Canada BR/TR, 5′7″, 158 lbs. Deb: 4/30/1875

YEAR	TM/L	G	AB	R	H	2B	3B	HR	RBI	BB	SO	AVG	OBP	SLG	PRO+	BR/A	SB	CS	SBR	FA	FR	G/POS	TPR
1875	Cen-n	14	57	6	13	3	0	0	6	1	3	.228	.241	.281	88	-0	1	0	0	.771	-6	2-14/S-1	-0.5
	NH-n	33	136	14	29	5	0	0	7	1	3	.213	.219	.250	72	-3	1	2	-1	.802	13	2-29/3-2,1-1,S-1	0.7
	Yr	47	193	20	42	8	0	0	13	2	6	.218	.226	.259	77	-3	2	2	-1	.794	7	2-43/S-2,3-2,1-1	0.2
1876	Lou-N	64	256	29	48	5	1	0	14	1	6	.188	.191	.215	30	-21				.870	**30**	*2-64	0.8

■ JOE SOMMER Sommer, Joseph John b: 11/20/1858, Covington, Ky. d: 1/16/38, Cincinnati, Ohio BR/TR, Deb: 7/8/1880

YEAR	TM/L	G	AB	R	H	2B	3B	HR	RBI	BB	SO	AVG	OBP	SLG	PRO+	BR/A	SB	CS	SBR	FA	FR	G/POS	TPR
1880	Cin-N	24	88	10	16	1	0	0	6	0	2	.182	.182	.193	28	-6				.913	-1	O-22/S-1,3-1,C-1	-0.7
1882	Cin-a	80	354	82	102	12	6	1	29	24		.288	.333	.364	128	10				**.925**	4	*O-80	1.2
1883	Cin-a	97	413	79	115	5	7	3	52	20		.278	.312	.346	106	2				.854	-1	*O-94/3-3,P-1	0.0
1884	Bal-a	107	479	96	129	11	10	4		8		.269	.293	.359	107	2				.841	6	*3-97/O-9,2-1	0.8
1885	Bal-a	110	471	84	118	23	6	1	44	24		.251	.291	.331	98	-1				.921	12	*O-107/S-2,3-2,P1	0.7
1886	Bal-a	139	560	79	117	18	4	1	52	24		.209	.245	.261	60	-26	31			.900	13	*O-95,2-32,3/SP	-1.2
1887	Bal-a	131	463	88	123	11	5	0	65	63		.266	.358	.311	93	0	29			.902	0	*O-110,2-13,3/SP	-0.1
1888	Bal-a	79	297	31	65	10	0	0	35	18		.219	.266	.253	68	-10	13			.871	-4	O-44,S-34/2-2,1-1	-1.3
1889	Bal-a	106	386	51	85	13	2	1	36	42	49	.220	.298	.272	62	-19	18			.929	9	*O-105/S-1	-1.1
1890	Cle-N	9	35	4	8	1	0	0	0	2	2	.229	.270	.257	55	-2	0			.789	-2	/O-9,P-1	-0.4

YEAR	TM/L	G	AB	R	H	2B	3B	HR	RBI	BB	SO	AVG	OBP	SLG	PRO+	BR/A	SB	CS	SBR	FA	FR	G/POS	TPR
	Bal-a	38	129	13	33	4	2	0	23	13		.256	.324	.318	85	-3	10			.892	1	O-38	-0.3
Total	10	920	3675	617	911	109	42	11	342	238	53	.248	.297	.309	88	-54	101			.901	38	O-713,3-124/2SP1C	-2.4
■ **PETE SOMMERS** Sommers, Joseph Andrews b: 10/26/1866, Cleveland, Ohio d: 7/22/08, Cleveland, Ohio BR/TR, 5′11.5″, 181 lbs. Deb: 4/27/1887																							
1887	NY-a	33	116	9	21	3	0	1	12	7		.181	.234	.233	32	-11	6			.830	-8	C-31/O-1,1-1	-1.3
1888	Bos-N	4	13	1	3	1	0	0	0	0	3	.231	.231	.308	69	-0	0			.880	-0	/C-4	-0.1
1889	Chi-N	12	45	5	10	5	0	0	8	2	8	.222	.271	.333	65	-2	0			.836	-5	C-11/O-1	-0.6
	Ind-N	23	84	12	21	2	2	2	14	1	16	.250	.267	.393	82	-3	2			.905	-2	C-21/O-2	-0.3
	Yr	35	129	17	31	7	2	2	22	3	24	.240	.269	.372	76	-5	2			.882	-7	C-32/O-3	-0.9
1890	NY-N	17	47	4	5	1	1	0	1	4	13	.106	.192	.170	6	-6	0			.837	1	C-11/1-5,O-2	-0.4
	Cle-N	9	34	4	7	1	1	0	1	2	3	.206	.250	.294	60	-2	0			.906	1	/C-8,O-1	-0.1
	Yr	26	81	8	12	2	2	0	2	6	16	.148	.216	.222	28	-8	0			.865	1	C-19/1-5,O-3	-0.5
Total	4	98	339	35	67	13	4	3	36	16	43	.198	.242	.286	50	-24	8			.860	-15	/C-86,O-7,1-6	-2.8
■ **BILL SOMMERS** Sommers, William Dunn b: 2/17/23, Brooklyn, N.Y. BR/TR, 6′, 180 lbs. Deb: 4/25/50																							
1950	StL-A	65	137	24	35	5	1	0	14	25	14	.255	.370	.307	72	-5	0	1	-1	.917	-9	3-37,2-21	-1.4
■ **BILL SORRELL** Sorrell, William b: 10/14/40, Morehead, Ky. BL/TR, 6′, 190 lbs. Deb: 9/2/65																							
1965	Phi-N	10	13	2	5	0	0	1	2	2	1	.385	.467	.615	206	2	0	0	0	.000	0	/3-1	0.2
1967	SF-N	18	17	1	3	1	0	0	1	3	2	.176	.300	.235	56	-1	0	0	0	1.000	-2	/O-5	-0.3
1970	KC-A	57	135	12	36	2	0	4	14	10	13	.267	.317	.370	89	-2	1	0	0	.873	-6	3-29/O-4,1-3	-0.9
Total	3	85	165	15	44	3	0	5	17	15	16	.267	.328	.376	95	-1	1	0	0	.873	-8	/3-30,O-9,1-3	-1.0
■ **CHICK SORRELLS** Sorrells, Raymond Edwin b: 7/31/1896, Stringtown, Okla. d: 7/20/83, Terrell, Tex. BR/TR, 5′9″, 155 lbs. Deb: 9/18/22																							
1922	Cle-A	2	1	0	0	0	0	0	0	0	0	.000	.000	.000	-99	-0	0	0	0	1.000	1	/S-1	0.1
■ **PAUL SORRENTO** Sorrento, Paul Anthony b: 11/17/65, Somerville, Mass. BL/TR, 6′2″, 200 lbs. Deb: 9/8/89																							
1989	Min-A	14	21	2	5	0	0	0	1	5	4	.238	.385	.238	74	-0	0	0	0	1.000	-0	/1-5,D-5	-0.1
1990	Min-A	41	121	11	25	4	1	5	13	12	31	.207	.284	.380	79	-4	1	1	-0	.992	-1	D-23,1-15	-0.7
1991	*Min-A	26	47	6	12	2	0	4	13	4	11	.255	.314	.553	129	2	0	0	0	1.000	1	1-13/D-2	0.2
1992	Cle-A	140	458	52	123	24	1	18	60	51	89	.269	.343	.443	121	12	0	3	-2	.993	-1	*1-121,D-11	0.1
1993	Cle-A	148	463	75	119	26	1	18	65	58	121	.257	.342	.434	108	5	3	1	0	.995	-0	*1-144/O-3,D-1	-0.5
1994	Cle-A	95	322	43	90	14	0	14	62	34	68	.280	.348	.453	104	2	0	1	-1	.995	1	1-86/D-8	-0.5
1995	*Cle-A	104	323	50	76	14	0	25	79	51	71	.235	.340	.511	116	7	1	1	-0	.992	-2	1-91,D-11	-0.4
1996	Sea-A	143	471	67	136	32	1	23	93	57	103	.289	.374	.507	120	14	0	2	-1	.990	-2	*1-138	-0.1
1997	*Sea-A	146	457	68	123	19	0	31	80	51	112	.269	.346	.514	122	14	0	2	-1	.996	5	*1-139/D-1	0.5
1998	TB-A	137	435	40	98	27	0	17	57	54	133	.225	.315	.405	82	-12	2	3	-1	1.000	2	D-86,1-27,O-18	-1.9
Total	10	994	3118	414	807	162	4	155	523	377	743	.259	.342	.462	109	38	7	14	-6	.994	3	1-779,D-148/O-21	-3.4
■ **SAMMY SOSA** Sosa, Samuel Peralta b: 11/12/68, San Pedro De Macoris, D.R. BR/TR, 6′, 185 lbs. Deb: 6/16/89																							
1989	Tex-A	25	84	8	20	3	0	1	3	0	20	.238	.238	.310	52	-5	0	2	-1	.944	-2	O-19	-0.9
	Chi-A	33	99	19	27	5	0	3	10	11	27	.273	.357	.414	120	3	7	3	0	.969	-5	O-33/D-6	-0.2
	Yr	58	183	27	47	8	0	4	13	11	47	.257	.306	.366	89	-3	7	5	-1	.960	-7	O-52/D-6	-1.1
1990	Chi-A	153	532	72	124	26	10	15	70	33	150	.233	.285	.404	93	-7	32	16	0	.962	9	*O-152	-0.2
1991	Chi-A	116	316	39	64	10	1	10	33	14	98	.203	.241	.335	59	-19	13	6	0	.973	-3	*O-111/D-2	-2.3
1992	Chi-N	67	262	41	68	7	2	8	25	19	63	.260	.319	.393	98	-1	15	7	0	.961	-3	O-67	-0.6
1993	Chi-N	159	598	92	156	25	5	33	93	38	135	.261	.309	.485	111	6	36	11	4	.976	0	*O-158	0.7
1994	Chi-N	105	426	59	128	17	6	25	70	25	92	.300	.342	.545	128	16	22	13	-1	.973	5	*O-105	1.7
1995	Chi-N★	144	564	89	151	17	3	36	119	58	134	.268	.341	.500	121	15	34	7	6	.962	14	*O-143	3.1
1996	Chi-N	124	498	84	136	21	2	40	100	34	134	.273	.326	.564	126	16	18	5	2	.964	12	*O-124	2.6
1997	Chi-N	162	642	90	161	31	4	36	119	45	174	.251	.302	.480	98	-5	22	12	-1	.977	17	*O-161	0.8
1998	*Chi-N†	159	643	**134**	198	20	0	66	**158**	73	171	.308	.379	.647	155	50	18	9	0	.975	16	*O-159	6.3
Total	10	1247	4664	727	1233	182	33	273	800	350	1198	.264	.320	.493	113	69	217	91	11	.969	61	*O-1232/D-8	11.0
■ **DENNY SOTHERN** Sothern, Dennis Elwood b: 1/20/04, Washington, D.C. d: 12/7/77, Durham, N.C. BR/TR, 5′11″, 175 lbs. Deb: 9/10/26																							
1926	Phi-N	14	53	5	13	1	0	3	10	4	10	.245	.310	.434	94	-1	0			.975	2	O-13	0.0
1928	Phi-N	141	579	82	165	27	5	5	38	34	53	.285	.327	.375	80	-17	17			.964	8	*O-136	-1.8
1929	Phi-N	76	294	52	90	21	3	5	27	16	24	.306	.346	.449	90	-5	13			.967	3	O-71	-0.6
1930	Phi-N	90	347	66	97	26	1	5	36	22	37	.280	.326	.403	70	-17	6			.967	8	O-84	-1.3
	Pit-N	17	51	4	9	4	0	1	4	3	4	.176	.222	.314	28	-6	2			.971	-1	O-13	-0.7
	Yr	107	398	70	106	30	1	6	40	25	41	.266	.313	.392	65	-23	8			.967	8	O-97	-2.0
1931	Bro-N	19	31	10	5	1	0	0	0	4	8	.161	.257	.194	23	-3	0			.958	-1	O-10	-0.5
Total	5	357	1355	219	379	80	9	19	115	83	136	.280	.325	.394	77	-50	38			.966	20	O-327	-4.9
■ **STEVE SOUCHOCK** Souchock, Stephen "Bud" b: 3/3/19, Yatesboro, Pa. BR/TR, 6′2.5″, 203 lbs. Deb: 5/25/46																							
1946	NY-A	47	86	15	26	3	3	2	10	7	13	.302	.362	.477	131	3	0	3	-2	.964	-2	1-20	-0.1
1948	NY-A	44	118	11	24	3	1	3	11	7	13	.203	.248	.322	51	-9	3	0	1	.988	-2	1-32	-1.0
1949	Chi-A	84	252	29	59	13	5	7	37	25	38	.234	.303	.409	90	-6	5	2	0	.951	2	O-39,1-30	-0.6
1951	Det-A	91	188	33	46	10	3	11	28	18	27	.245	.314	.505	118	3	0	2	-1	.941	-6	O-59/3-3,1-1,2-1	-0.6
1952	Det-A	92	265	40	66	16	4	13	45	21	28	.249	.304	.487	117	4	1	0	0	.964	1	O-56,3-13/1-9	0.2
1953	Det-A	89	278	29	84	13	3	11	46	8	35	.302	.326	.489	119	5	5	1	1	.962	-1	O-80/1-1	0.2
1954	Det-A	25	39	6	7	0	1	3	8	2	10	.179	.220	.462	84	-1	1	1	-0	1.000	-1	/O-9,3-2	-0.3
1955	Det-A	1	1	0	1	0	0	0	1	0	0	1.000	1.000	1.000	449	0	0	0	0	.000	0	H	0.0
Total	8	473	1227	163	313	58	20	50	186	88	164	.255	.307	.457	106	1	15	9	-1	.957	-10	O-243/1-93,3-18,2-1	-2.2
■ **CLYDE SOUTHWICK** Southwick, Clyde Aubra b: 11/3/1886, Maxwell, Iowa d: 10/14/61, Freeport, Ill. BL/TR, 6′, 180 lbs. Deb: 8/22/11																							
1911	StL-A	4	12	3	3	0	0	0	0	1		.250	.308	.250	58	-1	0			.938	-1	/C-4	-0.1
■ **BILL SOUTHWORTH** Southworth, William Frederick b: 11/10/45, Madison, Wis. BR/TR, 6′2″, 205 lbs. Deb: 10/2/64																							
1964	Mil-N	3	7	2	2	0	0	1	2	0	3	.286	.444	.714	219	1	0	0	0	1.000	-1	/3-2	0.0
■ **BILLY SOUTHWORTH** Southworth, William Harrison b: 3/9/1893, Harvard, Neb. d: 11/15/69, Columbus, Ohio BL/TR, 5′9″, 170 lbs. Deb: 8/4/13 MC																							
1913	Cle-A	1	0	0	0	0	0	0	0	0	0	—	—	—	—	0	0			.000	0	/O-1	0.0
1915	Cle-A	60	177	25	39	2	5	0	8	36	12	.220	.352	.288	90	-1	2	4	-2	.942	1	O-44	-0.4
1918	Pit-N	64	246	37	84	5	7	2	43	26	9	.341	.409	.443	154	17	19			.980	9	O-64	2.4
1919	Pit-N	121	453	56	127	14	**14**	4	61	32	22	.280	.329	.400	114	7	23			.968	5	*O-121	0.5
1920	Pit-N	146	546	64	155	17	13	2	53	52	20	.284	.348	.374	104	4	23	25	-8	**.991**	10	*O-142	-0.5
1921	Bos-N	141	569	86	175	25	15	7	79	36	13	.308	.351	.441	115	11	22	20	-5	.975	9	*O-141	0.4
1922	Bos-N	43	158	27	51	4	4	4	18	18	1	.323	.392	.475	128	7	4	1	1	.955	5	O-41	0.9
1923	Bos-N	153	611	95	195	29	16	6	78	61	23	.319	.383	.448	124	21	14	16	-5	.943	6	*O-151/2-2	1.1
1924	*NY-N	94	281	40	72	13	0	3	36	32	16	.256	.332	.335	81	-7	1	6	-3	.935	-3	O-75	-1.7
1925	NY-N	123	473	79	138	19	5	6	44	51	11	.292	.363	.391	97	-1	6	13	-6	.964	-8	*O-119	-2.2
1926	NY-N	36	116	23	38	6	1	5	30	7	1	.328	.366	.526	139	6	1			.970	-2	O-29	0.2
	*StL-N	99	391	76	124	22	6	11	69	26	9	.317	.364	.488	123	11	13			.971	-3	O-99	0.2
	Yr	135	507	99	162	28	7	16	99	33	10	.320	.365	.497	127	17	14			.971	-5	*O-128	0.4
1927	StL-N	92	306	52	92	15	5	2	39	23	7	.301	.350	.402	98	-1	10			.970	-7	O-83	-1.3
1929	StL-N	19	32	1	6	2	0	0	3	2	4	.188	.235	.250	20	-4	0			1.000	-0	/O-5,M	-0.4
Total	13	1192	4359	661	1296	173	91	52	561	402	148	.297	.359	.415	111	69	138	85		.965	23	*O-1115/2-2	-0.8
■ **JOHN SOWDERS** Sowders, John b: 12/10/1866, Louisville, Ky. d: 7/29/39, Indianapolis, Ind BR/TL, 6′, Deb: 6/28/1887 F																							
1887	Ind-N	1	2	0	0	0	0	0	0	0	1	.000	.000	.000	-99	-1	0			1.000	-1	/O-1,P-1	0.0
1889	KC-a	28	87	11	19	3	0	0	6	4	20	.218	.269	.253	46	-6	1			.842	-3	P-25/O-3	-0.1

YEAR	TM/L	G	AB	R	H	2B	3B	HR	RBI	BB	SO	AVG	OBP	SLG	PRO+	BR/A	SB	CS	SBR	FA	FR	G/POS	TPR
1890	Bro-P	40	132	14	25	3	0	1	20	10	12	.189	.246	.235	27	-14	0			.921	-2	P-39/O-3	-0.1
Total	3	69	221	25	44	6	0	1	26	14	33	.199	.253	.240	33	-21	1			.884	-6	/P-65,O-7	-0.2

■ LEN SOWDERS
Sowders, Leonard b: 6/29/1861, Louisville, Ky. d: 11/19/1888, Indianapolis, Ind. 5′11.5″, 172 lbs. Deb: 9/10/1886 F

YEAR	TM/L	G	AB	R	H	2B	3B	HR	RBI	BB	SO	AVG	OBP	SLG	PRO+	BR/A	SB	CS	SBR	FA	FR	G/POS	TPR
1886	Bal-a	23	76	10	20	3	1	0	14	12		.263	.364	.329	121	2	6			.889	-1	O-23/1-1	0.1

■ AL SPALDING
Spalding, Albert Goodwill b: 9/2/1850, Byron, Ill. d: 9/9/15, San Diego, Cal. BR/TR, 6′1″, 170 lbs. Deb: 5/5/1871 MH

YEAR	TM/L	G	AB	R	H	2B	3B	HR	RBI	BB	SO	AVG	OBP	SLG	PRO+	BR/A	SB	CS	SBR	FA	FR	G/POS	TPR
1871	Bos-n	31	144	43	39	10	1	1	31	8	1	.271	.309	.375	93	-2	2	0	1	.776	-3	*P-31/O-9	-0.2
1872	Bos-n	48	237	60	84	11	5	0	47	3	1	.354	.363	.443	139	9	3	0	1	**.902**	5	*P-48/O-7	-0.2
1873	Bos-n	60	322	83	106	18	2	1	60	3	1	.329	.335	.407	110	1	1	0	0	.855	6	*P-60,O-13	-0.3
1874	Bos-n	71	362	80	119	13	1	0	54	3	0	.329	.334	.370	119	6	2	1	0	**.854**	5	*P-71/O-6	-0.1
1875	Bos-n	74	343	68	107	15	3	0	56	3	3	.312	.318	.373	134	10	2	2	-1	.906	-1	*P-72,O-18/1-4	-0.3
1876	Chi-N	66	292	54	91	14	2	0	44	6	3	.312	.326	.373	118	3				.951	1	*P-61,O-10/1-3,SM	-0.2
1877	Chi-N	60	254	29	65	7	6	0	35	3	16	.256	.265	.331	77	-8				.959	6	*1-45,2-13/P-4,3M	-0.2
1878	Chi-N	1	4	0	2	0	0	0	0	0	0	.500	.500	.500	215	0				.429	-2	/2-1	-0.1
Total	5 n	284	1408	334	455	67	12	2	248	20	6	.323	.333	.392	121	24	10	3	1	.868	13	P-282/O-53,1-4	-1.1
Total	3	127	550	83	158	21	8	0	79	9	19	.287	.299	.355	99	-4				.948	5	/P-65,1-48,2O3S	-0.5

■ DICK SPALDING
Spalding, Charles Harry b: 10/13/1893, Philadelphia, Pa. d: 2/3/50, Philadelphia, Pa. BL/TL, 5′11″, 185 lbs. Deb: 4/18/27 C

YEAR	TM/L	G	AB	R	H	2B	3B	HR	RBI	BB	SO	AVG	OBP	SLG	PRO+	BR/A	SB	CS	SBR	FA	FR	G/POS	TPR
1927	Phi-N	115	442	68	131	16	3	0	25	38	40	.296	.352	.346	86	-7	5			**.992**	3	*O-113	-1.1
1928	Was-A	16	23	1	8	0	0	0	0	0	4	.348	.348	.348	84	-1	0	2	-1	1.000	-3	O-11	-0.5
Total	2	131	465	69	139	16	3	0	25	38	44	.299	.352	.346	86	-8	5	2		.993	-0	O-124	-1.6

■ AL SPANGLER
Spangler, Albert Donald b: 7/8/33, Philadelphia, Pa. BL/TL, 6′, 175 lbs. Deb: 9/16/59 C

YEAR	TM/L	G	AB	R	H	2B	3B	HR	RBI	BB	SO	AVG	OBP	SLG	PRO+	BR/A	SB	CS	SBR	FA	FR	G/POS	TPR
1959	Mil-N	6	12	3	5	0	1	0	0	1	1	.417	.462	.583	192	2	1	0	0	1.000	-1	/O-4	0.1
1960	Mil-N	101	105	26	28	5	2	0	6	14	17	.267	.358	.352	103	1	6	2	1	.989	-14	O-92	-1.4
1961	Mil-N	68	97	23	26	2	0	0	6	28	9	.268	.432	.289	102	2	4	2	0	1.000	-7	O-44	-0.6
1962	Hou-N	129	418	51	119	10	9	5	35	70	46	.285	.391	.388	119	14	7	6	-2	.960	-0	*O-121	0.5
1963	Hou-N	120	430	52	121	25	4	4	27	50	38	.281	.358	.386	122	13	5	8	-3	.987	3	*O-113	0.6
1964	Hou-N	135	449	51	110	18	5	4	38	41	43	.245	.314	.334	88	-7	7	8	-3	.964	-5	*O-127	-2.3
1965	Hou-N	38	112	18	24	1	1	1	7	14	8	.214	.302	.268	66	-5	1	1	-0	.956	-1	O-33	-0.8
	Cal-A	51	96	17	25	1	0	0	1	8	9	.260	.317	.271	70	-4	4	0	1	.973	-4	O-24	-0.8
1966	Cal-A	6	9	2	6	0	0	0	0	2	2	.667	.727	.667	312	3	0	0	0	1.000	-1	/O-3	0.2
1967	Chi-N	62	130	18	33	7	0	0	13	23	17	.254	.366	.308	91	-1	2	2	-1	.986	-3	O-41	-0.6
1968	Chi-N	88	177	21	48	9	3	2	18	20	24	.271	.348	.390	114	3	0	1	-1	.973	-5	O-48	-0.5
1969	Chi-N	82	213	23	45	8	1	4	23	21	16	.211	.285	.315	60	-11	0	2	-1	.950	-7	O-58	-2.4
1970	Chi-N	21	14	2	2	1	0	1	1	3	3	.143	.294	.429	81	-0	0	0	0	1.000	-1	/O-6	-0.2
1971	Chi-N	5	5	0	2	0	0	0	0	0	1	.400	.400	.400	111	0	0	0	0	.000	0	H	0.0
Total	13	912	2267	307	594	87	26	21	175	295	234	.262	.350	.351	100	10	37	32	-8	.973	-45	O-714	-8.2

■ BOB SPEAKE
Speake, Robert Charles "Spook" b: 8/22/30, Springfield, Mo. BL/TL, 6′1″, 178 lbs. Deb: 4/16/55

YEAR	TM/L	G	AB	R	H	2B	3B	HR	RBI	BB	SO	AVG	OBP	SLG	PRO+	BR/A	SB	CS	SBR	FA	FR	G/POS	TPR
1955	Chi-N	95	261	36	57	9	5	12	43	28	71	.218	.301	.429	91	-4	3	4	-2	.959	-3	O-55/1-8	-1.2
1957	Chi-N	129	418	65	97	14	5	16	50	38	68	.232	.301	.404	89	-8	5	6	-2	.974	6	O-60,1-39	-1.0
1958	SF-N	66	71	9	15	3	0	3	10	13	15	.211	.333	.380	90	-1	0	1	-1	.938	0	O-10	-0.1
1959	SF-N	15	11	0	1	0	0	0	1	1	4	.091	.167	.091	-30	-2	0	0	0	.000	0	H	-0.2
Total	4	305	761	110	170	26	10	31	104	80	158	.223	.302	.406	88	-14	8	11	-4	.966	3	O-125/1-47	-2.5

■ TRIS SPEAKER
Speaker, Tristram E "The Grey Eagle" b: 4/4/1888, Hubbard, Tex. d: 12/8/58, Lake Whitney, Tex. BL/TL, 5′11.5″, 193 lbs. Deb: 9/14/07 MH

YEAR	TM/L	G	AB	R	H	2B	3B	HR	RBI	BB	SO	AVG	OBP	SLG	PRO+	BR/A	SB	CS	SBR	FA	FR	G/POS	TPR
1907	Bos-A	7	19	0	3	0	0	0	1	1		.158	.200	.158	14	-2	0			1.000	1	/O-4	-0.1
1908	Bos-A	31	116	12	26	2	2	0	9	4		.224	.262	.276	73	-4	3			1.000	5	O-31	0.0
1909	Bos-A	143	544	73	168	26	13	7	77	38		.309	.362	.443	151	30	35			.973	**23**	*O-142	5.2
1910	Bos-A	141	538	92	183	20	14	7	65	52		.340	.404	.468	169	42	35			.957	15	*O-140	5.5
1911	Bos-A	141	500	88	167	34	13	8	70	59		.334	.418	.502	158	39	25			.956	6	*O-138	3.7
1912	*Bos-A	153	580	136	222	**53**	12	**10**	90	82		.383	**.464**	.567	185	65	52			.958	22	*O-153	**7.7**
1913	Bos-A	141	520	94	189	35	22	3	71	65	22	.363	.441	.533	180	53	46			.942	24	*O-139	**7.3**
1914	Bos-A	158	571	101	**193**	**46**	18	4	90	77	25	.338	.423	.503	178	55	42	29	-5	.968	28	*O-156/P-1,1-1	**7.6**
1915	*Bos-A	150	547	108	176	25	12	0	69	81	14	.322	.416	.411	152	38	29	25	-6	.976	13	*O-150	4.0
1916	Cle-A	151	546	102	**211**	**41**	8	2	79	82	20	**.386**	**.470**	**.502**	**181**	**57**	35	27	-6	.975	9	*O-151	**5.7**
1917	Cle-A	142	523	90	184	42	11	2	60	67	14	.352	.432	.486	168	43	30			.980	8	*O-142	4.7
1918	Cle-A	127	471	73	150	**33**	11	0	61	64	9	.318	.403	.435	140	23	27			.973	11	*O-127	3.0
1919	Cle-A	134	494	83	146	38	12	2	63	73	12	.296	.395	.433	125	18	15			.983	19	*O-134,M	2.9
1920	*Cle-A	150	552	137	214	**50**	11	8	107	97	13	.388	.483	.562	171	61	10	13	-5	.977	10	*O-148,M	5.2
1921	Cle-A	132	506	107	183	**52**	14	3	75	68	12	.362	.439	.538	146	37	2	4	-2	**.984**	10	*O-128,M	3.3
1922	Cle-A	131	426	85	161	**48**	8	11	71	77	11	.378	**.474**	.606	178	52	8	3	1	**.983**	8	*O-109,M	5.0
1923	Cle-A	150	574	133	218	**59**	11	17	130	93	15	.380	.469	.610	183	71	8	9	-3	.968	10	*O-150,M	6.4
1924	Cle-A	135	486	94	167	36	9	9	65	72	13	.344	.432	.510	141	31	5	7	-3	.963	5	*O-128,M	2.3
1925	Cle-A	117	429	79	167	35	5	12	87	70	12	.389	**.479**	.578	166	46	5	2	0	.967	10	*O-109,M	**4.5**
1926	Cle-A	150	539	96	164	52	8	7	86	94	15	.304	.408	.469	127	23	6	1	1	.981	10	*O-149,M	2.4
1927	Was-A	141	523	71	171	43	6	2	73	55	8	.327	.395	.444	119	15	9	8	-2	.967	1	*O-120,1-17	0.6
1928	Phi-A	64	191	28	51	22	2	3	30	10	5	.267	.310	.450	95	-2	5	1	1	.975	1	O-50	-0.4
Total	22	2789	10195	1882	3514	792	222	117	1529	1381	220	.345	.428	.500	156	793	432	129		.970	248	*O-2698/1-18,P-1	86.5

■ HORACE SPEED
Speed, Horace Arthur b: 10/4/51, Los Angeles, Cal. BR/TR, 6′1″, 180 lbs. Deb: 4/10/75

YEAR	TM/L	G	AB	R	H	2B	3B	HR	RBI	BB	SO	AVG	OBP	SLG	PRO+	BR/A	SB	CS	SBR	FA	FR	G/POS	TPR
1975	SF-N	17	15	2	2	1	0	0	1	1	8	.133	.235	.200	21	-2	0	0	0	.900	-2	/O-9	-0.4
1978	Cle-A	70	106	13	24	4	1	0	4	14	31	.226	.322	.283	72	-3	2	4	-2	.977	-12	O-61/D-3	-1.9
1979	Cle-A	26	14	6	2	0	0	0	1	5	7	.143	.368	.143	44	-1	2	1	0	.875	-5	O-16/D-4	-0.5
Total	3	113	135	21	28	5	1	0	6	20	46	.207	.318	.259	63	-6	4	5	-2	.956	-19	/O-86,D-7	-2.8

■ TIM SPEHR
Spehr, Timothy Joseph b: 7/2/66, Excelsior Springs, Mo. BR/TR, 6′2″, 200 lbs. Deb: 7/18/91

YEAR	TM/L	G	AB	R	H	2B	3B	HR	RBI	BB	SO	AVG	OBP	SLG	PRO+	BR/A	SB	CS	SBR	FA	FR	G/POS	TPR
1991	KC-A	37	74	7	14	5	0	3	14	9	18	.189	.286	.378	82	-2	1	0	0	.986	12	C-37	1.1
1993	Mon-N	53	87	14	20	6	0	2	10	6	20	.230	.287	.368	71	-4	2	0	1	.954	9	C-49	0.7
1994	Mon-N	52	36	8	9	3	1	0	5	4	11	.250	.325	.389	84	-1	2	0	1	1.000	10	C-46/O-2	1.0
1995	Mon-N	41	35	4	9	5	0	1	3	6	7	.257	.366	.486	118	1	0	0	0	.990	8	C-38	0.9
1996	Mon-N	63	44	4	4	1	0	1	3	3	15	.091	.167	.182	-8	-7	1	0	0	.985	8	C-58/O-1	0.1
1997	KC-A	17	35	3	6	0	0	1	2	2	12	.171	.237	.257	28	-4	0	0	0	1.000	4	C-17	0.1
	Atl-N	8	14	2	3	1	0	1	4	0	4	.214	.214	.500	79	-1	1	0	0	.947	3	/C-7	0.2
1998	NY-N	21	51	3	7	1	0	0	3	7	16	.137	.267	.157	14	-6	1	0	0	1.000	5	C-21/1-1	0.0
	KC-A	11	25	5	6	2	0	1	2	8	3	.240	.457	.440	129	2	0	0	0	1.000	-1	C-11	0.1
Total	7	303	401	50	78	24	1	10	46	45	106	.195	.289	.334	63	-22	8	0	2	.984	56	C-284/O-3,1-1	4.2

■ CHRIS SPEIER
Speier, Chris Edward b: 6/28/50, Alameda, Cal. BR/TR, 6′1″, 182 lbs. Deb: 4/7/71 F

YEAR	TM/L	G	AB	R	H	2B	3B	HR	RBI	BB	SO	AVG	OBP	SLG	PRO+	BR/A	SB	CS	SBR	FA	FR	G/POS	TPR
1971	*SF-N	157	601	74	141	17	6	8	46	56	90	.235	.307	.323	80	-16	4	7	-3	.958	-12	*S-156	-1.1
1972	SF-N★	150	562	74	151	25	2	15	71	82	92	.269	.365	.400	116	14	9	4	0	.974	-5	*S-150	3.3
1973	SF-N★	153	542	58	135	17	4	11	71	66	69	.249	.333	.356	87	-8	4	5	-2	.956	-10	*S-150/2-1	0.0
1974	SF-N☆	141	501	55	125	19	5	9	53	62	64	.250	.337	.361	91	-5	3	2	-0	.969	3	*S-135/2-4	1.6
1975	SF-N	141	487	60	132	30	5	10	69	70	50	.271	.364	.415	111	8	4	5	-2	**.982**	1	*S-136/3-1	2.3
1976	SF-N	145	495	51	112	18	4	3	40	60	52	.226	.315	.297	72	-17	2	2	-1	.974	-1	*S-135/2-7,3-5,1-1	-0.2
1977	SF-N	6	17	1	3	1	0	0	0	0	3	.176	.176	.235	9	-2	0	0	0	.920	2	/S-5	0.0
	Mon-N	139	531	58	125	30	6	5	38	67	78	.235	.322	.343	81	-14	1	2	-1	.970	-12	*S-138	-1.1
	Yr	145	548	59	128	31	6	5	38	67	81	.234	.318	.339	79	-16	1	2	-1	.968	-10	*S-143	-1.1
1978	Mon-N	150	501	47	126	18	3	5	51	60	75	.251	.333	.329	87	-8	1	0	0	.975	1	*S-148	1.3

YEAR	TM/L	G	AB	R	H	2B	3B	HR	RBI	BB	SO	AVG	OBP	SLG	PRO+	BR/A	SB	CS	SBR	FA	FR	G/POS	TPR
1979	Mon-N	113	344	31	78	13	1	7	26	43	45	.227	.318	.331	78	-10	0	0	0	.970	4	*S-112	0.6
1980	Mon-N	128	388	35	103	14	4	1	32	52	38	.265	.352	.330	91	-3	0	3	-2	.965	-0	*S-127/3-1	0.9
1981	*Mon-N	96	307	33	69	10	2	2	25	38	29	.225	.310	.290	70	-11	1	2	-1	.964	-11	S-96	-1.4
1982	Mon-N	156	530	41	136	26	4	7	60	47	67	.257	.318	.360	88	-9	1	6	-3	.982	-21	*S-155	-1.9
1983	Mon-N	88	261	31	67	12	2	2	22	29	37	.257	.336	.341	88	-4	2	1	0	.962	-11	S-74,3-12/2-2	-0.8
1984	Mon-N	25	40	1	6	0	0	0	1	1	8	.150	.171	.150	-10	-6	0	0	0	.960	-2	S-13/3-4	-0.7
	StL-N	38	118	9	21	7	1	3	8	9	19	.178	.242	.331	61	-7	0	0	0	.983	10	S-34/3-2	0.6
	Yr	63	158	10	27	7	1	3	9	10	27	.171	.225	.285	44	-12	0	0	0	.980	8	S-47/3-6	-0.1
	Min-A	12	33	2	7	0	0	0	1	3	7	.212	.278	.212	36	-3	0	0	0	.977	-3	S-12	-0.5
1985	Chi-N	106	218	16	53	11	0	4	24	17	34	.243	.298	.349	72	-8	1	3	-2	.964	2	S-58,3-31,2-13	-0.4
1986	Chi-N	95	155	21	44	8	0	6	23	15	32	.284	.351	.452	111	2	2	2	-1	.984	9	3-53,S-23/2-7	1.2
1987	*SF-N	111	317	39	79	13	0	11	39	42	51	.249	.343	.394	99	-0	4	7	-3	.989	2	2-55,3-44,S-22	0.1
1988	SF-N	82	171	26	37	9	1	3	18	23	39	.216	.313	.333	89	-2	3	3	-1	.985	3	2-45,3-22,S-12	0.2
1989	SF-N	28	37	7	9	4	0	0	2	5	9	.243	.333	.351	99	0	0	0	0	1.000	-2	/3-9,S-9,2-4,1-1	-0.2
Total	19	2260	7156	770	1759	302	50	112	720	847	988	.246	.329	.349	88	-107	42	54	-20	.970	-52	*S-1900,3-184,2/1	3.8

■ BOB SPENCE
Spence, John Robert b: 2/10/46, San Diego, Cal. BL/TR, 6'4", 215 lbs. Deb: 9/5/69

YEAR	TM/L	G	AB	R	H	2B	3B	HR	RBI	BB	SO	AVG	OBP	SLG	PRO+	BR/A	SB	CS	SBR	FA	FR	G/POS	TPR
1969	Chi-A	12	26	0	4	1	0	0	3	0	9	.154	.154	.192	-4	-4	0	0	0	1.000	-0	/1-6	-0.5
1970	Chi-A	46	130	11	29	4	1	4	15	11	32	.223	.289	.362	75	-5	0	0	0	.994	3	1-37	-0.5
1971	Chi-A	14	27	2	4	0	0	0	1	5	6	.148	.281	.148	24	-3	0	0	0	.986	-1	/1-7	-0.4
Total	3	72	183	13	37	5	1	4	19	16	47	.202	.270	.306	57	-11	0	0	0	.993	2	/1-50	-1.4

■ STAN SPENCE
Spence, Stanley Orville b: 3/20/15, S.Portsmouth, Ky. d: 1/9/83, Kinston, N.C. BL/TL, 5'10.5", 180 lbs. Deb: 6/8/40

YEAR	TM/L	G	AB	R	H	2B	3B	HR	RBI	BB	SO	AVG	OBP	SLG	PRO+	BR/A	SB	CS	SBR	FA	FR	G/POS	TPR
1940	Bos-A	51	68	5	19	2	1	2	13	4	9	.279	.319	.426	88	-1	0	1	-1	1.000	-4	O-15	-0.6
1941	Bos-A	86	203	22	47	10	3	2	28	18	14	.232	.304	.340	68	-10	1	0	0	1.000	-1	O-52/1-1	-1.3
1942	Was-A☆	149	629	94	203	27	**15**	4	79	62	16	.323	.384	.432	131	26	5	2	0	.973	-3	*O-149	1.6
1943	Was-A	149	570	72	152	23	10	12	88	84	39	.267	.366	.405	130	23	8	1	2	.983	3	*O-148	2.1
1944	Was-A★	153	592	83	187	31	8	18	100	69	28	.316	.391	.486	157	43	3	7	-3	.989	19	*O-150/1-3	5.2
1946	Was-A★	152	578	83	169	50	10	16	87	62	31	.292	.365	.497	148	34	1	7	-4	.982	8	*O-150	3.3
1947	Was-A★	147	506	62	141	22	6	16	73	81	41	.279	.378	.441	131	22	2	2	-1	.984	8	*O-142	2.2
1948	Bos-A	114	391	71	92	17	4	12	61	82	33	.235	.368	.391	97	-1	0	2	-1	.977	-1	O-92,1-14	-0.7
1949	Bos-A	7	20	3	3	1	0	0	1	6	1	.150	.346	.200	43	-1	0	0	0	1.000	1	/O-5	-0.1
	StL-A	104	314	46	77	13	3	13	45	52	36	.245	.356	.430	103	1	1	1	-0	.995	3	O-87/1-1	-0.1
	Yr	111	334	49	80	14	3	13	46	58	37	.240	.355	.416	99	-1	1	1	-0	.996	4	O-92/1-1	-0.2
Total	9	1112	3871	541	1090	196	60	95	575	520	248	.282	.369	.437	126	135	21	23	-8	.984	34	O-990/1-19	11.6

■ SPENCER
Spencer Deb: 6/3/1872

YEAR	TM/L	G	AB	R	H	2B	3B	HR	RBI	BB	SO	AVG	OBP	SLG	PRO+	BR/A	SB	CS	SBR	FA	FR	G/POS	TPR
1872	Nat-n	1	4	1	0	0	0	0	0	0	0	.000	.000	.000	-86	-1	0	0	0	.429	-1	/S-1	-0.1

■ CHET SPENCER
Spencer, Chester Arthur b: 3/4/1883, S.Webster, Ohio d: 11/10/38, Portsmouth, Ohio BL/TR, 6', 180 lbs. Deb: 8/22/06

YEAR	TM/L	G	AB	R	H	2B	3B	HR	RBI	BB	SO	AVG	OBP	SLG	PRO+	BR/A	SB	CS	SBR	FA	FR	G/POS	TPR
1906	Bos-N	8	27	1	4	1	0	0	0	0		.148	.148	.185	4	-3	0			.875	-1	/O-8	-0.5

■ DARYL SPENCER
Spencer, Daryl Dean "Big Dee" b: 7/13/29, Wichita, Kan. BR/TR, 6'2", 190 lbs. Deb: 9/17/52

YEAR	TM/L	G	AB	R	H	2B	3B	HR	RBI	BB	SO	AVG	OBP	SLG	PRO+	BR/A	SB	CS	SBR	FA	FR	G/POS	TPR
1952	NY-N	7	17	0	5	0	1	0	3	1	4	.294	.333	.412	105	0	0	0	0	1.000	1	/S-3,3-3	0.2
1953	NY-N	118	408	55	85	18	5	20	56	42	74	.208	.287	.424	81	-13	0	1	-1	.927	-10	S-53,3-36,2-32	-1.8
1956	NY-N	146	489	46	108	13	2	14	42	35	65	.221	.277	.342	66	-24	1	3	-2	.974	-2	2-70,S-66,3-12	-1.8
1957	NY-N	148	534	65	133	31	2	11	50	50	50	.249	.315	.376	85	-11	3	1	0	.950	14	*S-110,2-36/3-6	1.6
1958	SF-N	148	539	71	138	20	5	17	74	73	60	.256	.348	.406	101	2	1	0	0	.955	-1	*S-134,2-17	1.4
1959	SF-N	152	555	59	147	20	1	12	62	58	67	.265	.334	.369	89	-8	5	0	2	.970	-4	*2-151/S-4	0.1
1960	StL-N	148	507	70	131	20	3	16	58	81	74	.258	.366	.404	102	3	1	1	-0	.946	-24	*S-138,2-16	-1.0
1961	StL-N	37	130	19	33	4	0	4	21	23	17	.254	.366	.377	89	-2	1	0	0	.956	-1	S-37	0.1
	LA-N	60	189	27	46	7	0	8	27	20	35	.243	.329	.407	86	-4	0	1	-1	.964	5	3-57/S-3	0.1
	Yr	97	319	46	79	11	0	12	48	43	52	.248	.344	.395	88	-5	1	1	-0	.964	4	3-57,S-40	0.2
1962	LA-N	77	157	24	37	5	1	2	12	32	31	.236	.365	.318	91	-1	0	0	0	.925	7	3-57,S-10	0.7
1963	LA-N	7	9	0	1	0	0	0	0	3	2	.111	.333	.111	37	-1	0	0	0	1.000	-0	/3-3	-0.1
	Cin-N	50	155	21	37	7	0	1	23	31	37	.239	.369	.303	93	0	1	0	0	.979	3	3-48	0.3
	Yr	57	164	21	38	7	0	1	23	34	39	.232	.367	.293	91	-0	1	0	0	.979	2	3-51	0.2
Total	10	1098	3689	457	901	145	20	105	428	449	516	.244	.329	.380	88	-59	13	7	-0	.953	-13	S-558,2-322,3-222	-0.2

■ TUBBY SPENCER
Spencer, Edward Russell b: 1/26/1884, Oil City, Pa. d: 2/1/45, San Francisco, Cal. BR/TR, 5'10", 215 lbs. Deb: 7/23/05

YEAR	TM/L	G	AB	R	H	2B	3B	HR	RBI	BB	SO	AVG	OBP	SLG	PRO+	BR/A	SB	CS	SBR	FA	FR	G/POS	TPR
1905	StL-A	35	115	6	27	1	2	0	11	7		.235	.285	.278	83	-2	2			.962	-6	C-34	-0.5
1906	StL-A	58	188	15	33	6	1	0	17	7		.176	.205	.218	34	-15	4			.935	-5	C-54	-1.6
1907	StL-A	71	230	27	61	11	1	1	25	7		.265	.299	.335	102	-0	1			.957	-2	C-63	0.4
1908	StL-A	91	286	19	60	6	1	0	28	17		.210	.254	.238	60	-13	1			.983	-1	C-88	-0.6
1909	Bos-A	28	74	6	12	1	0	0	9	6		.162	.225	.176	26	-6	2			.992	-4	C-26	-0.9
1911	Phi-N	11	32	2	5	1	0	1	3	3	7	.156	.229	.281	42	-3	0			.925	-1	C-11	-0.3
1916	Det-A	19	54	7	20	1	1	1	10	6	6	.370	.443	.481	172	5	2			.988	-7	C-19	0.0
1917	Det-A	70	192	13	46	8	3	0	22	15	15	.240	.324	.313	95	-1	0			.978	-2	C-62	0.1
1918	Det-A	66	155	11	34	8	1	0	8	19	18	.219	.313	.284	83	-3	1			.966	-12	C-48/1-1	-1.3
Total	9	449	1326	106	298	43	10	3	133	87	46	.225	.281	.279	76	-37	13			.966	-40	C-405/1-1	-4.7

■ TOM SPENCER
Spencer, Hubert Thomas b: 2/28/51, Gallipolis, Ohio BR/TR, 6', 170 lbs. Deb: 7/17/78 C

YEAR	TM/L	G	AB	R	H	2B	3B	HR	RBI	BB	SO	AVG	OBP	SLG	PRO+	BR/A	SB	CS	SBR	FA	FR	G/POS	TPR
1978	Chi-A	29	65	3	12	1	0	0	4	2	9	.185	.209	.200	15	-7	0	1	-1	1.000	-1	O-27/D-2	-1.0

■ JIM SPENCER
Spencer, James Lloyd b: 7/30/47, Hanover, Pa. BL/TL, 6'2", 195 lbs. Deb: 9/7/68 F

YEAR	TM/L	G	AB	R	H	2B	3B	HR	RBI	BB	SO	AVG	OBP	SLG	PRO+	BR/A	SB	CS	SBR	FA	FR	G/POS	TPR
1968	Cal-A	19	68	2	13	1	0	0	5	3	10	.191	.236	.206	36	-5	0	0	0	.994	3	1-19	-0.4
1969	Cal-A	113	386	39	98	14	3	10	31	26	53	.254	.304	.383	96	-4	1	0	0	.991	-1	*1-107	-1.4
1970	Cal-A	146	511	61	140	20	4	12	68	28	61	.274	.312	.399	98	-3	0	2	-1	**.995**	-1	*1-142	-1.8
1971	Cal-A	148	510	50	121	21	2	18	59	48	63	.237	.307	.392	104	1	0	1	-1	**.996**	2	*1-145	-1.2
1972	Cal-A	82	212	13	47	5	0	1	14	12	25	.222	.263	.259	59	-11	0	1	-1	.990	-2	1-35,O-24	-2.0
1973	Cal-A	29	87	10	21	4	2	2	11	9	9	.241	.320	.402	111	1	0	0	0	1.000	-2	1-26/D-2	-0.3
	Tex-A★	102	352	35	94	12	3	4	43	34	41	.267	.333	.352	97	-1	0	3	-2	.999	5	1-99/D-1	-0.5
	Yr	131	439	45	115	16	5	6	54	43	50	.262	.331	.362	100	-0	0	3	-2	**.999**	3	*1-125/D-3	-0.8
1974	Tex-A	118	352	36	98	11	4	7	44	22	27	.278	.326	.392	109	3	1	2	-1	.998	1	1-60,D-54	-0.1
1975	Tex-A	132	403	50	107	18	1	11	47	35	43	.266	.327	.397	105	2	0	1	-1	.995	5	1-99,D-25	0.1
1976	Chi-A	150	518	53	131	13	2	14	70	49	52	.253	.319	.367	100	-0	6	4	-1	**.998**	8	*1-143/D-2	-0.3
1977	Chi-A	128	470	56	116	16	1	18	69	36	50	.247	.303	.400	90	-7	1	2	-1	.991	2	*1-125	-1.3
1978	*NY-A	71	150	12	34	9	1	7	24	15	32	.227	.297	.440	107	1	0	1	-1	1.000	1	D-35,1-15	-0.1
1979	NY-A	106	295	60	85	15	3	23	53	38	25	.288	.369	.593	158	23	0	2	-1	.992	-0	D-71,1-26	1.8
1980	*NY-A	97	259	38	61	9	0	13	43	30	44	.236	.317	.421	102	0	1	0	0	.990	2	1-75,D-15	-0.2
1981	NY-A	25	63	6	9	2	0	2	4	9	7	.143	.250	.270	50	-4	0	0	0	1.000	2	1-25	-0.3
	*Oak-A	54	171	14	35	6	0	2	9	10	20	.205	.249	.275	53	-11	1	0	0	.997	2	1-48	-1.1
	Yr	79	234	20	44	8	0	4	13	19	27	.188	.249	.274	52	-15	1	0	0	.998	5	1-73	-1.4
1982	Oak-A	33	101	6	17	3	1	2	5	3	20	.168	.192	.277	28	-10	0	0	0	.992	2	1-32	-1.0
Total	15	1553	4908	541	1227	179	27	146	599	407	582	.250	.310	.387	98	-26	11	19	-8	.995	30	*1-1221,D-205/O-24	-10.1

■ BEN SPENCER
Spencer, Lloyd Benjamin b: 5/15/1890, Patapsco, Md. d: 9/1/70, Finksburg, Md. BL/TL, 5'8", 160 lbs. Deb: 9/8/13 F

YEAR	TM/L	G	AB	R	H	2B	3B	HR	RBI	BB	SO	AVG	OBP	SLG	PRO+	BR/A	SB	CS	SBR	FA	FR	G/POS	TPR
1913	Was-A	8	21	2	6	1	1	0	2	2	4	.286	.348	.429	124	1	0			.917	-1	/O-8	-0.1

■ SHANE SPENCER
Spencer, Michael Shane b: 2/20/72, Key West, Fla. BR/TR, 5'11", 210 lbs. Deb: 4/10/98

YEAR	TM/L	G	AB	R	H	2B	3B	HR	RBI	BB	SO	AVG	OBP	SLG	PRO+	BR/A	SB	CS	SBR	FA	FR	G/POS	TPR
1998	*NY-A	27	67	18	25	6	0	10	27	5	12	.373	.417	.910	237	13	0	1	-1	1.000	-4	O-22/1-1,D-4	0.8

YEAR	TM/L	G	AB	R	H	2B	3B	HR	RBI	BB	SO	AVG	OBP	SLG	PRO+	BR/A	SB	CS	SBR	FA	FR	G/POS	TPR
■ **ROY SPENCER**	Spencer, Roy Hampton b: 2/22/1900, Scranton, N.C. d: 2/8/73, Port Charlotte, Fla BR/TR, 5'10", 168 lbs. Deb: 4/19/25																						
1925	Pit-N	14	28	1	6	1	0	0	2	1	3	.214	.241	.250	24	-3	1	0	0	.905	-2	C-11	-0.4
1926	Pit-N	28	43	5	17	3	0	0	4	1	0	.395	.409	.465	128	2	0			.970	-1	C-12	0.2
1927	*Pit-N	38	92	9	26	3	1	0	13	3	3	.283	.305	.337	67	-4	0			.974	2	C-34	-0.1
1929	Was-A	50	116	18	18	4	0	1	9	8	15	.155	.222	.216	13	-15	0	0	0	.967	-2	C-41	-1.3
1930	Was-A	93	321	32	82	11	4	0	36	18	27	.255	.303	.315	57	-21	3	0	1	.989	5	C-93	-0.7
1931	Was-A	145	483	48	133	16	3	1	60	35	21	.275	.327	.327	72	-19	0	0	0	.985	7	*C-145	-0.2
1932	Was-A	102	317	28	78	9	0	1	41	24	17	.246	.301	.284	53	-22	0	1	-1	.978	-10	C-98	-2.5
1933	Cle-A	75	227	26	46	5	2	0	23	23	17	.203	.282	.242	38	-20	0	0	0	.990	5	C-72	-1.0
1934	Cle-A	5	7	0	1	1	0	0	2	0	1	.143	.143	.286	8	-1	0	0	0	1.000	1	/C-4	0.0
1936	NY-N	19	18	3	5	1	0	0	3	2	3	.278	.350	.333	86	-0	0			1.000	1	C-14	0.1
1937	Bro-N	51	117	5	24	2	2	0	4	8	17	.205	.256	.256	39	-10	0			1.000	9	C-45	0.1
1938	Bro-N	16	45	2	12	1	1	0	6	5	6	.267	.340	.333	84	-1	0			.968	-0	C-16	-0.1
Total	12	636	1814	177	448	57	13	3	203	128	130	.247	.301	.298	56	-115	4	1		.984	16	C-585	-5.9
■ **VERN SPENCER**	Spencer, Vernon Murray b: 2/4/1894, Wixom, Mich. d: 6/3/71, Wixom, Mich. BL/TR, 5'7", 165 lbs. Deb: 7/4/20																						
1920	NY-N	45	140	15	28	2	3	0	19	11	17	.200	.258	.257	49	-9	4	3	-1	.932	-1	O-40	-1.4
■ **PAUL SPERAW**	Speraw, Paul Bachman "Polly" or "Birdie" b: 10/5/1893, Annville, Pa. d: 2/22/62, Cedar Rapids, Iowa BR/TR, 5'8.5", 145 lbs. Deb: 9/15/20																						
1920	StL-A	1	2	0	0	0	0	0	0	0	0	.000	.000	.000	-97	-1	0	0	0	1.000	0	/3-1	0.0
■ **ED SPERBER**	Sperber, Edwin George b: 1/21/1895, Cincinnati, Ohio d: 1/5/76, Cincinnati, Ohio BL/TL, 5'11", 175 lbs. Deb: 4/16/24																						
1924	Bos-N	24	59	8	17	2	0	1	12	10	9	.288	.400	.373	113	2	3	1	0	.897	-3	O-17	-0.2
1925	Bos-N	2	2	0	0	0	0	0	0	0	0	.000	.000	.000	-99	-1	0	0	0	.000	0	H	-0.1
Total	2	26	61	8	17	2	0	1	12	10	9	.279	.389	.361	106	1	3	1	0	.897	-3	/O-17	-0.3
■ **ROB SPERRING**	Sperring, Robert Walter b: 10/10/49, San Francisco, Cal. BR/TR, 6'1", 185 lbs. Deb: 8/11/74																						
1974	Chi-N	42	107	9	22	3	0	1	5	9	28	.206	.267	.262	46	-8	1	2	-1	.952	5	2-35/S-8	-0.2
1975	Chi-N	65	144	25	30	4	1	1	9	16	31	.208	.292	.271	54	-9	0	2	-1	.946	12	3-22,2-17,S-16,/O-8	0.3
1976	Chi-N	43	93	8	24	3	0	0	7	9	25	.258	.324	.290	69	-4	0	2	-1	.955	-9	3-20,S-15/2-4,O-3	-1.3
1977	Hou-N	58	129	6	24	3	0	1	9	12	23	.186	.255	.233	35	-12	0	0	0	.940	-2	S-22,2-20,3-11	-1.2
Total	4	208	473	48	100	13	1	3	30	46	107	.211	.283	.262	51	-32	1	6	-3	.964	6	/2-76,S-61,3-53,O	-2.4
■ **STAN SPERRY**	Sperry, Stanley Kenneth b: 2/19/14, Evansville, Wis. d: 9/27/62, Evansville, Wis. BL/TR, 5'10.5", 164 lbs. Deb: 7/28/36																						
1936	Phi-N	20	37	2	5	3	0	0	4	3	5	.135	.200	.216	11	-5	0			.900	-4	2-15	-0.8
1938	Phi-A	60	253	28	69	6	3	0	27	15	9	.273	.313	.320	61	-15	1	2	-1	.959	-8	2-60	-1.9
Total	2	80	290	30	74	9	3	0	31	18	14	.255	.299	.307	54	-20	1	2		.951	-12	/2-75	-2.7
■ **BILL SPIERS**	Spiers, William James b: 6/5/66, Orangeburg, S.C. BL/TR, 6'2", 190 lbs. Deb: 4/7/89																						
1989	Mil-A	114	345	44	88	9	3	4	33	21	63	.255	.300	.333	79	-10	10	2	2	.962	14	S-89,3-12/2-4,1D	1.2
1990	Mil-A	112	363	44	88	15	3	2	36	16	45	.242	.276	.317	66	-17	11	6	-0	.976	-7	*S-111	-1.6
1991	Mil-A	133	414	71	117	13	6	8	54	34	55	.283	.340	.401	107	4	14	8	-1	.970	-11	*S-128/O-1,D-2	0.1
1992	Mil-A	12	16	2	5	2	0	0	2	1	4	.313	.353	.438	123	0	1	1	-0	1.000	-2	/S-5,2-4,3-1,D-1	-0.2
1993	Mil-A	113	340	43	81	8	4	2	36	29	51	.238	.306	.303	65	-16	9	8	-2	.971	-24	*2-104/O-7,S-4,D-1	-3.9
1994	Mil-A	73	214	27	54	10	1	0	17	19	42	.252	.316	.308	59	-13	7	1	2	.947	-4	3-35,S-35/O-2,1D	-1.2
1995	NY-N	63	72	5	15	2	1	0	11	12	15	.208	.321	.264	58	-4	0	1	-1	.794	3	3-11/2-6	-0.1
1996	Hou-N	122	218	27	55	10	1	6	26	20	34	.252	.321	.390	94	-3	7	0	2	.959	4	3-77/2-7,1-4,S-4,O	0.4
1997	*Hou-N	132	291	51	93	27	4	4	48	61	42	.320	.439	.481	146	23	10	5	0	.935	11	3-84,S-28/1-8,2-4	3.5
1998	*Hou-N	123	384	66	105	27	4	4	43	45	62	.273	.357	.396	97	-1	11	2	2	.966	-6	3-99/2-9,1-7,S-2	-0.3
Total	10	997	2657	380	701	123	27	30	306	258	413	.264	.333	.364	89	-36	80	34	4	.968	-22	S-406,3-319,2/1OD	-2.1
■ **HARRY SPIES**	Spies, Henry b: 6/12/1866, New Orleans, La. d: 7/7/42, Los Angeles, Cal. BL/TR, 5'9", 170 lbs. Deb: 4/20/1895																						
1895	Cin-N	14	50	2	11	0	1	0	5	3	2	.220	.264	.260	34	-5	0			.867	2	C-12/1-2	-0.2
	Lou-N	72	276	42	74	14	7	2	35	11	19	.268	.313	.391	86	-7	4			.981	-3	1-47,C-26/S-1	-0.5
	Yr	86	326	44	85	14	8	2	40	14	21	.261	.305	.371	78	-12	4			.979	-2	1-49,C-38/S-1	-0.7
■ **ED SPIEZIO**	Spiezio, Edward Wayne b: 10/31/41, Joliet, Ill. BR/TR, 5'11", 180 lbs. Deb: 7/23/64 F																						
1964	StL-N	12	12	0	4	0	0	0	0	0	1	.333	.333	.333	81	-0	0	0	0	.000	0	H	0.0
1965	StL-N	10	18	0	3	0	0	0	5	1	4	.167	.250	.167	18	-2	0	0	0	1.000	0	/3-3	-0.2
1966	StL-N	26	73	4	16	5	1	2	10	5	11	.219	.269	.397	82	-2	1	0	0	.885	-4	3-19	-0.6
1967	*StL-N	55	105	9	22	2	0	3	10	7	18	.210	.265	.314	66	-5	2	1	0	.962	-0	3-19/O-7	-0.6
1968	*StL-N	29	51	1	8	0	0	0	2	5	6	.157	.232	.157	19	-5	1	1	-0	1.000	0	O-11/3-2	-0.6
1969	SD-N	121	355	29	83	9	0	13	43	38	64	.234	.315	.369	95	-3	1	2	-1	.939	1	3-98/O-1	-0.3
1970	SD-N	110	316	45	90	18	1	12	42	43	42	.285	.377	.462	129	13	4	0	1	.953	2	3-93	1.5
1971	SD-N	97	308	16	71	10	1	7	36	22	50	.231	.290	.338	83	-8	6	5	-1	.962	1	3-91/O-1	-1.0
1972	SD-N	20	29	2	4	2	0	0	4	1	6	.138	.167	.207	6	-4	1	0	0	1.000	-2	/3-5	-0.6
	Chi-A	74	277	20	66	10	1	2	22	13	43	.238	.277	.303	71	-10	0	1	-1	.952	7	3-74	-0.5
Total	9	554	1544	126	367	56	4	39	174	135	245	.238	.306	.355	88	-25	16	10	-1	.949	4	3-404/O-20	-2.9
■ **SCOTT SPIEZIO**	Spiezio, Scott Edward b: 9/21/72, Joliet, Ill. BB/TR, 6'2", 205 lbs. Deb: 9/14/96 F																						
1996	Oak-A	9	29	6	9	2	0	2	8	4	4	.310	.394	.586	146	2	0	1	-1	.846	-1	/3-5,D-4	0.0
1997	Oak-A	147	538	58	131	28	4	14	65	44	75	.243	.302	.388	80	-17	9	3	1	**.990**	0	*2-146/3-1	-0.7
1998	Oak-A	114	406	54	105	19	1	9	50	44	56	.259	.334	.377	87	-7	1	3	-2	.975	-7	*2-112/D-1	-0.9
Total	3	270	973	118	245	49	5	25	123	92	135	.252	.318	.390	85	-22	10	7	-1	.984	-8	2-258/3-6,D-5	-1.6
■ **CHARLIE SPIKES**	Spikes, Leslie Charles b: 1/23/51, Bogalusa, La. BR/TR, 6'3", 220 lbs. Deb: 9/1/72																						
1972	NY-A	14	34	2	5	1	0	0	3	1	13	.147	.171	.176	4	-4	0	1	-1	1.000	0	/O-9	-0.6
1973	Cle-A	140	506	68	120	12	3	23	73	45	103	.237	.306	.409	98	-3	5	3	-0	.964	5	*O-111,D-26	-0.4
1974	Cle-A	155	568	63	154	23	1	22	80	34	100	.271	.320	.431	116	9	10	7	-1	.968	0	*O-154	0.2
1975	Cle-A	111	345	41	79	13	3	11	33	30	51	.229	.291	.380	88	-6	7	6	-2	.974	1	*O-103/D-2	-1.1
1976	Cle-A	101	334	34	79	11	5	3	31	23	50	.237	.296	.326	83	-7	5	6	-2	.985	1	O-98/D-2	-1.3
1977	Cle-A	32	95	13	22	2	0	3	11	11	17	.232	.324	.347	86	-2	0	2	-1	.972	-3	O-27/D-2	-0.7
1978	Det-A	10	28	1	7	1	0	0	2	2	6	.250	.344	.286	77	-1	0	0	0	.909	-1	/O-9	-0.3
1979	Atl-N	66	93	12	26	8	0	3	21	5	30	.280	.316	.462	102	-0	0	0	0	.842	-3	O-15	-0.4
1980	Atl-N	41	36	6	10	1	0	0	2	3	18	.278	.350	.306	82	-1	0	0	0	1.000	-2	/O-7	-0.3
Total	9	670	2039	240	502	72	12	65	256	154	388	.246	.306	.389	96	-14	27	25	-7	.969	-2	O-533/D-32	-4.9
■ **HARRY SPILMAN**	Spilman, William Harry b: 7/18/54, Albany, Ga. BL/TR, 6'1", 190 lbs. Deb: 9/11/78																						
1978	Cin-N	4	4	1	1	0	0	0	0	0	1	.250	.250	.250	40	-0	0	0	0	.000	0	H	0.0
1979	*Cin-N	43	56	7	12	3	0	0	5	7	5	.214	.323	.268	63	-3	0	0	0	1.000	-0	1-12/3-4	-0.3
1980	Cin-N	65	101	14	27	4	0	4	19	9	19	.267	.333	.426	110	1	0	0	0	.986	0	1-18/O-2,C-1,3-1	0.0
1981	Cin-N	23	24	4	4	1	0	0	3	3	7	.167	.259	.208	33	-2	0	0	0	1.000	0	/3-3,1-2	-0.2
	*Hou-N	28	34	5	10	0	0	0	1	2	3	.294	.333	.294	83	-1	0	1	-1	1.000	-0	1-13	-0.2
	Yr	51	58	9	14	1	0	0	4	5	10	.241	.302	.259	61	-3	0	1	-1	.984	-0	1-15/3-3	-0.4
1982	Hou-N	38	61	7	17	2	0	3	11	5	10	.279	.333	.459	129	2	0	0	0	.989	-1	1-11	0.1
1983	Hou-N	42	78	7	13	3	0	1	9	5	12	.167	.217	.244	29	-8	0	0	0	1.000	-2	1-19/C-6	-1.1
1984	Hou-N	32	72	14	19	2	0	2	15	12	10	.264	.369	.375	118	2	0	0	0	.978	-3	1-18/C-8	-0.2
1985	Hou-N	44	66	3	9	1	0	1	4	3	7	.136	.174	.197	4	-9	0	0	0	1.000	-1	1-19/C-2	-1.1
1986	Det-A	24	49	6	12	2	0	3	8	3	8	.245	.288	.469	102	-0	0	0	0	1.000	0	D-11/3-2,C-1,1-1	0.0
	SF-N	58	94	12	27	7	0	2	22	12	13	.287	.368	.426	124	3	0	0	0	.994	0	1-19/3-5,C-1,2-1,O	0.2
1987	*SF-N	83	90	5	24	5	0	1	14	9	20	.267	.333	.356	87	-2	1	1	-0	.875	-2	3-10/1-9,C-1	-0.5

YEAR	TM/L	G	AB	R	H	2B	3B	HR	RBI	BB	SO	AVG	OBP	SLG	PRO+	BR/A	SB	CS	SBR	FA	FR	G/POS	TPR
1988	SF-N	40	40	4	7	1	1	1	3	4	6	.175	.250	.325	67	-2	0	0	0	1.000	1	/1-6,C-2,O-1	-0.2
	Hou-N	7	5	0	0	0	0	0	0	0	3	.000	.000	.000	-99	-1	0	0	0	1.000	0	/1-1	-0.1
	Yr	47	45	4	7	1	1	1	3	4	9	.156	.224	.289	48	-3	0	0	0	1.000	1	/1-7,C-2,O-1	-0.3
1989	Hou-N	32	36	7	10	3	0	0	3	7	2	.278	.395	.361	122	1	0	0	0	1.000	0	/1-9,C-1	0.1
Total	12	563	810	96	192	34	1	18	117	81	126	.237	.309	.348	85	-17	1	2	-1	.991	-8	1-157/3-25,CDO2	-3.5
■ HAL SPINDEL Spindel, Harold Stewart b: 5/27/13, Chandler, Okla. BR/TR, 6', 185 lbs. Deb: 4/23/39																							
1939	StL-A	48	119	13	32	3	1	0	11	8	7	.269	.315	.311	59	-7	0	2	-1	.993	-0	C-32	-0.6
1945	Phi-N	36	87	7	20	3	0	0	8	6	7	.230	.280	.264	53	-6	0			.964	0	C-31	-0.4
1946	Phi-N	1	3	0	1	0	0	0	1	0	0	.333	.333	.333	92	-0	0			1.000	-0	/C-1	0.0
Total	3	85	209	20	53	6	1	0	20	14	14	.254	.300	.292	57	-13	0	2		.980	0	/C-64	-1.0
■ ANDY SPOGNARDI Spognardi, Andrea Ettore b: 10/18/08, Boston, Mass. BR/TR, 5'9.5", 160 lbs. Deb: 9/2/32																							
1932	Bos-A	17	34	9	10	1	0	0	1	6	6	.294	.400	.324	92	-0	0	0	0	.979	3	/2-9,S-3,3-2	0.3
■ AL SPOHRER Spohrer, Alfred Ray b: 12/3/02, Philadelphia, Pa. d: 7/17/72, Plymouth, N.H. BR/TR, 5'10.5", 175 lbs. Deb: 4/13/28																							
1928	NY-N	2	2	0	0	0	0	0	0	0	0	.000	.000	.000	-99	-1	0			1.000	0	/C-2	-0.1
	Bos-N	51	124	15	27	3	0	0	9	5	11	.218	.254	.242	32	-12	1			.976	-5	C-48	-1.5
	Yr	53	126	15	27	3	0	0	9	5	11	.214	.250	.238	30	-13	1			.977	-5	C-50	-1.6
1929	Bos-N	114	342	42	93	21	8	2	48	26	35	.272	.327	.398	82	-11	1			.954	-10	*C-109	-1.0
1930	Bos-N	112	356	44	113	22	8	2	37	22	24	.317	.361	.441	96	-3	3			.957	-18	*C-108	-1.0
1931	Bos-N	114	350	23	84	17	5	0	27	22	27	.240	.285	.317	64	-18	2			.982	-0	*C-111	-1.1
1932	Bos-N	104	335	31	90	12	2	0	33	15	26	.269	.300	.316	69	-15	2			.991	10	*C-100	0.1
1933	Bos-N	67	184	11	46	6	1	1	12	11	13	.250	.292	.310	78	-6	3			.972	-6	C-65	-0.9
1934	Bos-N	100	265	25	59	15	0	0	17	14	18	.223	.262	.279	49	-20	1			.977	0	C-98	-1.5
1935	Bos-N	92	260	22	63	7	1	1	16	9	12	.242	.273	.288	55	-17	0			.958	-10	C-90	-2.3
Total	8	756	2218	213	575	103	25	6	199	124	166	.259	.301	.336	70	-101	13			.972	-39	C-731	-9.3
■ JIM SPOTTS Spotts, James Russell b: 4/10/09, Honey Brook, Pa. d: 6/15/64, Medford, N.J. BR/TR, 5'10.5", 175 lbs. Deb: 4/23/30																							
1930	Phi-N	3	2	1	0	0	0	0	0	0	1	.000	.000	.000	-93	-1	0			1.000	0	/C-2	0.0
■ CHARLIE SPRAGUE Sprague, Charles Wellington b: 10/10/1864, Cleveland, Ohio d: 12/31/12, Des Moines, Iowa BL/TL, 5'11", 150 lbs. Deb: 9/17/1887																							
1887	Chi-N	3	13	0	2	0	0	0	0	0	2	.154	.154	.154	-13	-2	0			.667	-1	/P-3,O-1	-0.1
1889	Cle-N	2	7	2	1	0	0	0	1	1	0	.143	.250	.143	11	-1	1			.857	1	/P-2	0.0
1890	Tol-a	55	199	25	47	5	6	1	19	16		.236	.303	.337	86	-4	10			.892	-6	O-40,P-19	-0.7
Total	3	60	219	27	50	5	6	1	20	17	2	.228	.293	.320	77	-7	11			.892	-6	/O-41,P-24	-0.8
■ ED SPRAGUE Sprague, Edward Nelson Jr. b: 7/25/67, Castro Valley, Cal. BR/TR, 6'2", 210 lbs. Deb: 5/8/91 F																							
1991	Tor-A	61	160	17	44	7	0	4	20	19	43	.275	.363	.394	105	2	0	3	-2	.870	-1	3-35,1-22/C-2,D-2	-0.2
1992	*Tor-A	22	47	6	11	2	0	1	7	3	7	.234	.280	.340	70	-2	0	0	0	.985	1	C-15/1-4,3-1,D-2	-0.1
1993	*Tor-A	150	546	50	142	31	1	12	73	32	85	.260	.313	.386	86	-11	1	0	0	.955	-9	*3-150	-1.9
1994	Tor-A	109	405	38	97	19	1	11	44	23	95	.240	.298	.373	71	-18	1	0	0	.946	-12	*3-107/1-3	-2.8
1995	Tor-A	144	521	77	127	27	2	18	74	58	96	.244	.337	.407	93	-5	0	0	0	.958	-1	*3-139/1-7,D-2	-0.6
1996	Tor-A	159	591	88	146	35	2	36	101	60	146	.247	.329	.496	105	2	0	0	0	.956	-14	*3-148,D-10	-1.2
1997	Tor-A	138	504	63	115	29	4	14	48	51	102	.228	.307	.385	79	-16	0	1	-1	.945	-12	*3-129/D-8	-2.8
1998	Tor-A	105	382	49	91	20	0	17	51	24	73	.238	.302	.424	86	-9	0	2	-1	.924	-9	*3-105	-1.7
	Oak-A	27	87	8	13	5	0	3	7	2	17	.149	.187	.310	27	-10	1	0	0	.909	0	3-23/1-1	-0.9
	Yr	132	469	57	104	25	0	20	58	26	90	.222	.281	.403	76	-18	1	2	-1	.921	-9	*3-128/1-1	-2.6
Total	8	915	3243	396	786	175	10	116	425	272	664	.242	.315	.410	87	-67	3	6	-3	.944	-58	3-837/1-37,D-24,C	-12.2
■ HARRY SPRATT Spratt, Henry Lee b: 7/10/1887, Broadford, Va. d: 7/3/69, Washington, D.C. BL/TR, 5'8.5", 175 lbs. Deb: 4/13/11																							
1911	Bos-N	62	154	22	37	4	4	2	13	13	25	.240	.299	.357	77	-5	1			.892	-8	S-26/2-5,3-4,O-4	-1.2
1912	Bos-N	27	89	6	23	3	2	3	15	7	11	.258	.313	.438	102	-0	2			.842	-13	S-23	-1.2
Total	2	89	243	28	60	7	6	5	28	20	36	.247	.304	.387	86	-6	3			.871	-22	/S-49,2-5,O-4,3-4	-2.4
■ GEORGE SPRIGGS Spriggs, George Herman b: 5/22/41, Jewell, Md. BL/TR, 5'11", 175 lbs. Deb: 9/15/65																							
1965	Pit-N	9	2	5	1	0	0	0	0	0	0	.500	.500	.500	182	0	2	0	1	.000	-0	/O-1	0.0
1966	Pit-N	9	7	0	1	0	0	0	0	0	3	.143	.143	.143	-20	-1	0	0	0	.000	0	H	-0.1
1967	Pit-N	38	57	14	10	1	1	0	5	6	20	.175	.254	.228	39	-4	3	0	1	1.000	-2	O-13	-0.6
1969	KC-A	23	29	4	4	2	1	0	0	3	8	.138	.242	.276	44	-2	0	0	0	1.000	-1	/O-6	-0.4
1970	KC-A	51	130	12	27	2	3	1	7	14	32	.208	.285	.292	59	-7	4	3	-1	.953	1	O-36	-0.9
Total	5	130	225	35	43	5	5	1	12	23	63	.191	.269	.271	51	-15	9	3	1	.965	-3	/O-56	-2.0
■ STEVE SPRINGER Springer, Steven Michael b: 2/11/61, Long Beach, Cal. BR/TR, 6', 190 lbs. Deb: 5/22/90																							
1990	Cle-A	4	12	1	2	0	0	0	1	0	6	.167	.167	.167	-7	-2	0	0	0	1.000	-1	/3-3,D-1	-0.2
1992	NY-N	4	5	0	2	1	0	0	0	0	1	.400	.400	.600	182	0	0	0	0	1.000	-0	/2-1,3-1	0.0
Total	2	8	17	1	4	1	0	0	1	0	7	.235	.235	.294	48	-1	0	0	0	1.000	-1	/3-4,2-1,D-1	-0.2
■ JOE SPRINZ Sprinz, Joseph Conrad "Mule" b: 8/3/02, St.Louis, Mo. d: 1/11/94, Fremont, Cal. BR/TR, 5'11", 185 lbs. Deb: 7/16/30																							
1930	Cle-A	17	45	5	8	1	0	0	2	4	4	.178	.245	.200	14	-6	0	0	0	1.000	6	C-17	0.1
1931	Cle-A	1	3	0	0	0	0	0	0	0	0	.000	.000	.000	-95	-1	0	0	0	1.000	0	/C-1	-0.1
1933	StL-N	3	5	1	1	0	0	0	0	1	1	.200	.333	.200	53	-0	0			1.000	2	/C-3	0.2
Total	3	21	53	6	9	1	0	0	2	5	5	.170	.241	.189	12	-7	0	0		1.000	8	/C-21	0.2
■ FREDDY SPURGEON Spurgeon, Fred b: 10/9/1900, Wabash, Ind. d: 11/5/70, Kalamazoo, Mich. BR/TR, 5'11.5", 160 lbs. Deb: 9/19/24																							
1924	Cle-A	3	7	0	1	1	0	0	0	0	0	.143	.250	.286	37	-1	0	0	0	.882	1	/2-3	0.0
1925	Cle-A	107	376	50	108	9	3	0	32	15	21	.287	.315	.327	62	-22	8	5	-1	.927	-4	3-56,2-46/S-3	-2.0
1926	Cle-A	149	614	101	181	31	3	0	49	27	36	.295	.327	.355	77	-21	7	2	1	.962	-8	*2-149	-2.3
1927	Cle-A	57	179	30	45	6	1	1	19	18	14	.251	.323	.313	65	-9	8	1	2	.938	-8	2-52	-1.3
Total	4	316	1176	181	335	47	7	1	100	60	71	.285	.322	.339	70	-53	23	8	2	.958	-19	2-250/3-56,S-3	-5.6
■ ED SPURNEY Spurney, Edward Frederick b: 1/19/1872, Cleveland, Ohio d: 10/12/32, Cleveland, Ohio Deb: 6/26/1891																							
1891	Pit-N	3	7	2	2	1	0	0	0	2	1	.286	.444	.429	158	1	0			.889	-1	/S-3	0.0
■ MIKE SQUIRES Squires, Michael Lynn b: 3/5/52, Kalamazoo, Mich. BL/TL, 5'11", 185 lbs. Deb: 9/1/75 C																							
1975	Chi-A	20	65	5	15	0	0	0	4	8	5	.231	.315	.231	55	-3	3	0	1	.988	0	1-20	-0.4
1977	Chi-A	3	3	0	0	0	0	0	0	0	1	.000	.000	.000	-99	-1	0	0	0	1.000	0	/1-1	0.0
1978	Chi-A	46	150	25	42	9	2	0	19	16	21	.280	.349	.367	101	0	4	4	-1	.997	-2	1-45	-0.6
1979	Chi-A	122	295	44	78	10	1	2	22	22	9	.264	.320	.325	74	-10	15	5	2	.995	4	*1-110/O-1	-0.9
1980	Chi-A	131	343	38	97	11	3	2	33	33	24	.283	.347	.350	92	-3	8	9	-3	.995	4	*1-114/C-2	-0.7
1981	Chi-A	92	294	35	78	9	0	0	25	22	17	.265	.316	.296	79	-8	7	2	1	.992	2	1-88/O-1	-0.9
1982	Chi-A	116	195	33	52	9	3	1	21	14	13	.267	.316	.359	85	-4	3	3	-1	.995	7	*1-109	-0.1
1983	*Chi-A	143	153	21	34	4	1	1	11	22	11	.222	.328	.281	67	-6	3	3	-1	**.996**	6	*1-124/3-1,D-5	-0.4
1984	Chi-A	104	82	9	15	1	0	0	6	6	7	.183	.239	.195	21	-9	2	2	-1	1.000	4	1-77,3-13/O-3,P-1	-0.6
1985	Chi-A	2	0	1	0	0	0	0	0	0	0	—	—	—	—	0	0	0	0	.000	0	/R	0.0
Total	10	779	1580	211	411	53	10	6	141	143	108	.260	.323	.318	78	-43	45	28	-3	.995	25	1-688/3-14,D-5,OCP	-4.6
■ MARV STAEHLE Staehle, Marvin Gustave b: 3/13/42, Oak Park, Ill. BL/TR, 5'10", 172 lbs. Deb: 9/15/64																							
1964	Chi-A	6	5	0	2	0	0	0	2	0	0	.400	.400	.400	127	0	1	0	0	.000	0	H	0.0
1965	Chi-A	7	7	0	3	0	0	0	2	0	0	.429	.429	.429	154	0	0	0	0	.000	0	H	0.0
1966	Chi-A	8	15	2	2	0	0	0	0	4	2	.133	.316	.133	37	-1	1	0	0	1.000	1	/2-6	0.0
1967	Chi-A	32	54	1	6	1	0	0	1	4	8	.111	.172	.130	-10	-7	1	1	-0	1.000	1	2-17/S-5	-0.7

YEAR	TM/L	G	AB	R	H	2B	3B	HR	RBI	BB	SO	AVG	OBP	SLG	PRO+	BR/A	SB	CS	SBR	FA	FR	G/POS	TPR
1969	Mon-N	6	17	4	7	2	0	1	1	2	0	.412	.474	.706	226	3	0	0	0	.944	-1	/2-4	0.3
1970	Mon-N	104	321	41	70	9	1	0	26	39	21	.218	.309	.252	52	-21	1	3	-2	.963	-13	2-91/S-1	-2.9
1971	Atl-N	22	36	5	4	0	0	0	1	5	4	.111	.238	.111	2	-5	0	0	0	1.000	4	/2-7,3-1	0.0
Total	7	185	455	53	94	12	1	1	33	54	35	.207	.296	.244	50	-30	4	4	-1	.971	-8	2-125/S-6,3-1	-3.3
■ HEINIE STAFFORD	Stafford, Henry Alexander b: 11/1/1891, Orleans, Vt. d: 1/29/72, Lake Worth, Fla. BR/TR, 5'7", 160 lbs. Deb: 10/5/16																						
1916	NY-N	1	1	0	0	0	0	0	0	0	0	.000	.000	.000	-99	-0	0			.000	0	H	0.0
■ GENERAL STAFFORD	Stafford, James Joseph "Jamsey" b: 7/9/1868, Webster, Mass. d: 9/18/23, Worcester, Mass. BR/TR, 5'8", 165 lbs. Deb: 8/27/1890 F																						
1890	Buf-P	15	49	11	7	1	0	0	3	7	8	.143	.250	.163	13	-6	2			.893	-2	P-12/O-4	-0.2
1893	NY-N	67	281	58	79	7	4	5	27	25	31	.281	.344	.388	94	-3	19			.901	-7	O-67	-1.1
1894	NY-N	14	46	10	10	1	1	0	4	10	7	.217	.368	.283	59	-3	2			.750	-3	/3-6,O-5,2-1,1-1	-0.5
1895	NY-N	123	463	79	129	12	5	3	73	40	32	.279	.344	.346	80	-13	42			.911	-9	*2-109,O-12/3-2	-1.3
1896	NY-N	59	230	28	66	9	1	0	40	13	18	.287	.333	.335	79	-7	15			.897	-5	O-53/S-6	-1.3
1897	NY-N	7	23	0	2	0	0	0	3	3		.087	.192	.087	-26	-4	0			1.000	-3	/O-5,S-2	-0.7
	Lou-N	111	432	68	120	16	5	7	53	31		.278	.330	.387	92	-6	14			.887	-12	*S-103/O-7,3-1	-1.4
	Yr	118	455	68	122	16	5	7	56	34		.268	.323	.371	86	-10	14			.882	-16	*S-105,O-12/3-1	-2.1
1898	Lou-N	49	181	26	54	3	0	1	25	19		.298	.368	.331	103	1	7			.901	-8	2-28,O-22/3-1	-0.6
	Bos-N	37	123	21	32	2	0	1	8	4		.260	.289	.301	66	-6	3			.909	-3	O-35/1-1	-1.1
	Yr	86	304	47	86	5	0	2	33	23		.283	.337	.319	87	-5	10			.924	-12	O-57,2-28/3-1,1-1	-1.7
1899	Bos-N	55	182	29	55	4	2	3	40	7		.302	.328	.396	89	-4	9			.956	-9	O-41/2-5,S-5	-1.4
	Was-N	31	118	11	29	5	1	1	14	5		.246	.276	.331	67	-6	4			.951	-5	2-17,S-13/3-2	-0.9
	Yr	86	300	40	84	9	3	4	54	12		.280	.308	.370	81	-9	13			.956	-14	O-41,2-22,S-18,/3-2	-2.3
Total	8	568	2128	341	583	60	19	21	290	164	96	.274	.331	.350	82	-56	117			.911	-67	O-251,2-160,S/3P1	-10.5
■ BOB STAFFORD	Stafford, Robert M. b: 6/26/1872, Oak Ridge, N.C. d: 8/20/16, Moores Springs, N.C. Deb: 10/12/1890																						
1890	Phi-a	1	2	0	0	0	0	0	0	0		.000	.000	.000	-99	-1	0			1.000	1	/O-1	0.0
■ STEVE STAGGS	Staggs, Stephen Robert b: 5/6/51, Anchorage, Alaska BR/TR, 5'9", 150 lbs. Deb: 7/1/77																						
1977	Tor-A	72	290	37	75	11	6	2	28	36	38	.259	.340	.359	90	-3	5	9	-4	.965	-14	2-72	-1.6
1978	Oak-A	47	78	10	19	2	2	0	0	19	17	.244	.392	.321	108	2	2	3	-1	.976	-3	2-40/S-2,3-2,D-2	0.0
Total	2	119	368	47	94	13	8	2	28	55	55	.255	.352	.351	94	-2	7	12	-5	.968	-17	2-112/D-2,3-2,S-2	-1.6
■ CHICK STAHL	Stahl, Charles Sylvester b: 1/10/1873, Avilla, Ind. d: 3/28/07, W.Baden, Ind. BL/TL, 5'10", 160 lbs. Deb: 4/19/1897 M																						
1897	*Bos-N	114	469	112	166	30	13	4	97	38		.354	.406	.499	130	19	18			.928	-3	*O-111	0.6
1898	Bos-N	125	467	72	144	21	8	3	52	46		.308	.375	.407	118	10	6			.968	-2	*O-125	0.0
1899	Bos-N	148	576	122	202	23	19	7	52	72		.351	.426	.493	139	30	33			.969	6	*O-148/P-1	2.2
1900	Bos-N	136	553	88	163	23	16	5	82	34		.295	.336	.421	96	-7	27			**.968**	9	*O-135	-0.7
1901	Bos-A	131	515	105	156	20	16	6	72	54		.303	.377	.439	128	20	29			.957	-1	*O-131	0.9
1902	Bos-A	127	508	92	164	22	11	2	58	37		.323	.375	.421	117	12	24			.953	-5	*O-125	-0.1
1903	*Bos-A	77	299	60	82	12	6	2	44	28		.274	.338	.375	108	3	10			.961	-2	O-74	-0.4
1904	Bos-A	157	587	83	170	27	**19**	3	67	64		.290	.366	.416	139	27	11			.961	-14	*O-157	0.4
1905	Bos-A	134	500	61	129	17	4	0	47	50		.258	.332	.308	102	3	18			.977	-6	*O-134	-1.1
1906	Bos-A	155	595	63	170	24	6	4	51	47		.286	.346	.366	123	16	13			.961	10	*O-155,M	2.0
Total	10	1304	5069	858	1546	219	118	36	622	470		.305	.369	.416	121	133	189			.961	-8	*O-1295/P-1	3.8
■ JAKE STAHL	Stahl, Garland b: 4/13/1879, Elkhart, Ill. d: 9/18/22, Monrovia, Cal. BR/TR, 6'2", 195 lbs. Deb: 4/20/03 M																						
1903	Bos-A	40	92	14	22	3	5	2	8	4		.239	.286	.446	111	1	1			.956	-2	C-28/O-1	0.1
1904	Was-A	142	520	54	136	29	12	3	50	21		.262	.309	.381	119	10	25			.978	6	*1-119,O-23	1.3
1905	Was-A	141	501	66	125	22	12	5	66	28		.250	.311	.371	121	11	41			.986	2	*1-140,M	0.9
1906	Was-A	137	482	38	107	9	8	0	51	21		.222	.266	.274	73	-16	30			.983	-2	*1-136,M	-2.4
1908	NY-A	75	274	34	70	18	5	2	42	11		.255	.304	.380	120	5	17			.933	4	O-68/1-6	0.7
	Bos-A	78	262	29	64	9	11	0	23	20		.244	.333	.363	123	7	13			.984	-2	1-78	0.4
	Yr	153	536	63	134	27	16	2	65	31		.250	.319	.371	122	12	30			.984	2	1-84,O-68	1.1
1909	Bos-A	127	435	62	128	19	12	6	60	43		.294	.377	.434	153	27	16			.986	-11	*1-126	1.6
1910	Bos-A	144	531	68	144	19	16	**10**	77	42		.271	.334	.424	134	19	22			.985	-7	*1-142	1.3
1912	*Bos-A	95	326	40	98	21	6	3	60	31		.301	.372	.429	123	9	13			.980	-2	1-92,M	0.6
1913	Bos-A	2	2	0	0	0	0	0	0	0	1	.000	.000	.000	-98	-0	0			.000	0	HM	-0.1
Total	9	981	3425	405	894	149	87	31	437	221	1	.261	.323	.382	120	73	178			.983	-14	1-839/O-92,C-28	4.4
■ LARRY STAHL	Stahl, Larry Floyd b: 6/29/41, Belleville, Ill. BL/TL, 6'1", 185 lbs. Deb: 9/11/64																						
1964	KC-A	15	46	7	12	1	0	3	6	1	10	.261	.277	.478	102	-0	0	0	0	.955	1	O-10	0.0
1965	KC-A	28	81	9	16	2	1	4	14	5	16	.198	.253	.395	82	-2	1	0	0	1.000	1	O-21	-0.2
1966	KC-A	119	312	37	78	11	5	5	34	17	63	.250	.291	.365	90	-5	5	3	-0	.980	-4	O-94	-1.3
1967	NY-N	71	155	9	37	5	0	1	18	8	25	.239	.285	.290	66	-7	2	2	-1	.969	3	O-43	-0.7
1968	NY-N	53	183	15	43	7	2	3	10	21	38	.235	.314	.344	97	-0	3	0	1	.983	1	O-47/1-9	-0.2
1969	SD-N	95	162	10	32	6	2	3	10	17	31	.198	.278	.315	68	-7	3	3	-1	.981	2	O-37,1-13	-0.9
1970	SD-N	52	66	5	12	2	0	0	3	2	14	.182	.206	.212	13	-8	2	2	-1	1.000	-3	O-20	-1.3
1971	SD-N	114	308	27	78	13	4	8	36	26	59	.253	.311	.399	107	2	4	3	-1	.987	6	O-75/1-7	0.3
1972	SD-N	107	297	31	67	9	3	7	20	31	67	.226	.299	.347	89	-5	1	3	-2	.986	-1	O-76/1-1	-1.1
1973	*Cin-N	76	111	17	25	2	2	2	12	14	34	.225	.317	.333	85	-2	1	0	0	1.000	-6	O-29/1-2	-0.9
Total	10	730	1721	167	400	58	19	36	163	142	357	.232	.293	.351	86	-35	22	16	-3	.983	-1	O-452/1-32	-6.3
■ SCOTT STAHOVIAK	Stahoviak, Scott Edmund b: 3/6/70, Waukegan, Ill. BL/TR, 6'5", 210 lbs. Deb: 9/10/93																						
1993	Min-A	20	57	1	11	4	0	0	1	3	22	.193	.233	.263	33	-5	0	2	-1	.922	3	3-19	-0.4
1995	Min-A	94	263	28	70	19	0	3	23	30	61	.266	.344	.373	86	-5	5	1	1	.998	7	1-69,3-22/D-1	-0.2
1996	Min-A	130	405	72	115	30	3	13	61	59	114	.284	.378	.469	111	7	3	3	-1	.994	10	*1-114/D-9	0.6
1997	Min-A	91	275	33	63	17	0	10	33	24	73	.229	.305	.400	81	-8	5	2	0	.990	4	1-81/D-5	-1.0
1998	Min-A	9	19	1	2	0	0	1	1	0	7	.105	.105	.263	-8	-3	0	0	0	.975	0	/1-4,O-1	-0.3
Total	5	344	1019	135	261	70	3	27	119	116	277	.256	.337	.410	91	-14	13	8	-1	.994	24	1-268/3-41,D-15,O-1	-1.3
■ ROY STAIGER	Staiger, Roy Joseph b: 1/6/50, Tulsa, Okla. BR/TR, 6', 195 lbs. Deb: 9/12/75																						
1975	NY-N	13	19	2	3	1	0	0	0	0	4	.158	.158	.211	2	-3	0	0	0	1.000	1	3-13	-0.1
1976	NY-N	95	304	23	67	8	1	2	26	25	35	.220	.282	.273	62	-16	3	3	-1	.967	19	3-93/S-1	0.2
1977	NY-N	40	123	16	31	9	0	2	11	4	20	.252	.276	.374	76	-5	1	0	0	.934	6	3-36/S-1	0.1
1979	NY-A	4	11	1	3	1	0	0	1	1	0	.273	.333	.364	90	-0	0	0	0	1.000	0	/3-4	0.0
Total	4	152	457	42	104	19	1	4	38	30	59	.228	.277	.300	64	-23	4	3	-1	.960	26	3-146/S-2	0.2
■ TUCK STAINBACK	Stainback, George Tucker b: 8/4/11, Los Angeles, Cal. d: 11/29/92, Camarillo, Cal. BR/TR, 5'11.5", 175 lbs. Deb: 4/17/34																						
1934	Chi-N	104	359	47	110	14	3	2	46	8	42	.306	.327	.379	90	-5	7			.955	-6	O-96/3-1	-1.5
1935	Chi-N	47	94	16	24	4	0	3	11	0	13	.255	.271	.394	76	-4	1			.932	-5	O-28	-0.9
1936	Chi-N	44	75	13	13	3	0	1	5	6	14	.173	.235	.253	31	-7	1			1.000	-4	O-26	-1.2
1937	Chi-N	72	160	18	37	7	1	0	14	7	16	.231	.268	.287	49	-11	3			.981	-2	O-49	-1.4
1938	StL-N	6	10	2	0	0	0	0	0	0	3	.000	.000	.000	-95	-3	0			1.000	1	/O-2	-0.2
	Phi-N	30	81	9	21	3	0	1	11	3	3	.259	.294	.333	74	-3	1			.980	-2	O-25	-0.6
	Bro-N	35	104	15	34	6	3	0	20	2	4	.327	.346	.442	113	1	1			.981	-1	O-23	0.0
	Yr	71	195	26	55	9	3	1	31	5	10	.282	.307	.374	86	-4	2			.982	-3	O-50	-0.8
1939	Bro-N	68	201	22	54	7	0	3	19	4	23	.269	.290	.348	68	-9	0			.938	-5	O-55	-1.6
1940	Det-A	15	40	4	9	2	0	0	1	1	9	.225	.262	.275	36	-4	0	0	0	.968	4	/O-9	-0.1
1941	Det-A	94	200	19	49	8	1	2	10	3	21	.245	.260	.325	49	-15	6	3	0	.948	-15	O-80	-3.2
1942	*NY-A	15	10	0	2	0	0	0	0	0	2	.200	.200	.200	13	-1	0	0	0	1.000	-0	/O-3	-0.1
1943	*NY-A	71	231	31	60	11	2	0	10	7	16	.260	.285	.325	77	-7	3	3	-1	.993	-1	O-60	-1.3

YEAR	TM/L	G	AB	R	H	2B	3B	HR	RBI	BB	SO	AVG	OBP	SLG	PRO+	BR/A	SB	CS	SBR	FA	FR	G/POS	TPR
1944	NY-A	30	78	13	17	3	0	0	5	3	7	.218	.247	.256	42	-6	1	0	0	.957	-3	O-24	-1.0
1945	NY-A	95	327	40	84	12	2	5	32	13	20	.257	.289	.352	82	-9	0	4	-2	.968	9	O-83	-0.7
1946	Phi-A	91	291	35	71	10	2	0	20	7	20	.244	.264	.292	56	-18	3	2	-0	.963	3	O-66	-2.0
Total	13	817	2261	284	585	90	14	17	204	64	213	.259	.284	.333	68	-101	27	12		.965	-29	O-629/3-1	-15.8

■ MATT STAIRS Stairs, Matthew Wade b: 2/27/68, St.John, N.B., Canada BL/TR, 5′9″, 175 lbs. Deb: 5/29/92

YEAR	TM/L	G	AB	R	H	2B	3B	HR	RBI	BB	SO	AVG	OBP	SLG	PRO+	BR/A	SB	CS	SBR	FA	FR	G/POS	TPR
1992	Mon-N	13	30	2	5	2	0	0	5	7	7	.167	.324	.233	61	-1	0	0	0	.933	-1	O-10	-0.3
1993	Mon-N	6	8	1	3	1	0	0	2	0	1	.375	.375	.500	126	0	0	0	0	1.000	-0	/O-1	0.0
1995	*Bos-A	39	88	8	23	7	1	1	17	4	14	.261	.301	.398	77	-3	0	1	-1	.913	-4	O-23/D-2	-0.8
1996	Oak-A	61	137	21	38	5	1	10	23	19	23	.277	.369	.547	130	6	1	1	-0	.985	1	O-44/1-1,D-5	0.5
1997	Oak-A	133	352	62	105	19	0	27	73	50	60	.298	.390	.582	152	27	3	2	-0	.977	-9	O-89,D-16/1-7	1.4
1998	Oak-A	149	523	88	154	33	1	26	106	59	93	.294	.372	.511	130	23	8	3	1	1.000	3	*D-120,O-12/1-6	1.8
Total	6	401	1138	182	328	67	3	64	226	139	198	.288	.371	.521	131	52	12	7	-1	.973	-11	O-179,D-143/1-14	2.6

■ GALE STALEY Staley, George Gaylord b: 5/2/1899, DePere, Wis. d: 4/19/89, Walnut Creek, Cal. BL/TR, 5′8.5″, 167 lbs. Deb: 9/16/25

YEAR	TM/L	G	AB	R	H	2B	3B	HR	RBI	BB	SO	AVG	OBP	SLG	PRO+	BR/A	SB	CS	SBR	FA	FR	G/POS	TPR
1925	Chi-N	7	26	2	11	2	0	0	3	2	1	.423	.464	.500	144	2	0	1	-1	.979	4	/2-7	0.5

■ VIRGIL STALLCUP Stallcup, Thomas Virgil "Red" b: 1/3/22, Ravensford, N.C. d: 5/2/89, Greenville, S.C. BR/TR, 6′3″, 185 lbs. Deb: 4/18/47

YEAR	TM/L	G	AB	R	H	2B	3B	HR	RBI	BB	SO	AVG	OBP	SLG	PRO+	BR/A	SB	CS	SBR	FA	FR	G/POS	TPR
1947	Cin-N	8	1	1	0	0	0	0	0	0	1	.000	.000	.000	-99	-0	0			.000	0	/S-1	0.0
1948	Cin-N	149	539	40	123	30	4	3	65	18	52	.228	.253	.315	55	-36	2			.956	-0	*S-148	-2.8
1949	Cin-N	141	575	49	146	28	5	3	45	9	44	.254	.268	.336	60	-33	1			.962	-10	*S-141	-3.3
1950	Cin-N	136	483	44	121	23	2	8	54	17	39	.251	.276	.356	65	-26	4			**.973**	-5	*S-136	-2.1
1951	Cin-N	121	428	33	103	17	2	8	49	6	40	.241	.251	.346	58	-26	2	4	-2	**.969**	-8	*S-117	-2.8
1952	Cin-N	2	1	0	0	0	0	0	0	0	0	.000	.000	.000	-99	-0	0	0	0	.000	0	/S-1	0.0
	StL-N	29	31	4	4	1	0	0	1	1	5	.129	.156	.161	-12	-5	0	0	0	1.000	2	S-12	-0.3
	Yr	31	32	4	4	1	0	0	1	1	5	.125	.152	.156	-15	-5	0	0	0	1.000	2	S-13	-0.3
1953	StL-N	1	1	0	0	0	0	0	0	0	0	.000	.000	.000	-99	-0	0	0	0	.000	0	H	0.0
Total	7	587	2059	171	497	99	13	22	214	51	181	.241	.260	.334	58	-127	9	4		.965	-21	S-556	-11.3

■ GEORGE STALLER Staller, George Walborn "Stopper" b: 4/1/16, Rutherford Heights, Pa. d: 7/3/92, Harrisburg, Pa. BL/TL, 5′11″, 190 lbs. Deb: 9/14/43 C

YEAR	TM/L	G	AB	R	H	2B	3B	HR	RBI	BB	SO	AVG	OBP	SLG	PRO+	BR/A	SB	CS	SBR	FA	FR	G/POS	TPR
1943	Phi-A	21	85	14	23	1	3	3	12	5	6	.271	.326	.459	129	3	1	0	0	.977	-1	O-20	0.1

■ GEORGE STALLINGS Stallings, George Tweedy "Gentleman George" b: 11/17/1867, Augusta, Ga. d: 5/13/29, Haddock, Ga. BR/TR, 6′1″, 187 lbs. Deb: 5/22/1890 M

YEAR	TM/L	G	AB	R	H	2B	3B	HR	RBI	BB	SO	AVG	OBP	SLG	PRO+	BR/A	SB	CS	SBR	FA	FR	G/POS	TPR
1890	Bro-N	4	11	1	0	0	0	0	0	1	3	.000	.154	.000	-54	-2	0			.933	-1	/C-4	-0.3
1897	Phi-N	2	9	1	2	1	0	0	0	0		.222	.222	.333	47	-1	0			1.000	1	/O-1,1-1,M	0.0
1898	Phi-N	1	0	1	0	0	0	0	0	0		—	—	—	—	0	0			.000	0	/HM	0.0
Total	3	7	20	3	2	1	0	0	0	1	3	.100	.182	.150	-7	-3	0			.933	-1	/C-4,1-1,O-1	-0.3

■ OSCAR STANAGE Stanage, Oscar Harland b: 3/17/1883, Tulare, Cal. d: 11/11/64, Detroit, Mich. BR/TR, 5′9.5″, 185 lbs. Deb: 5/19/06 C

YEAR	TM/L	G	AB	R	H	2B	3B	HR	RBI	BB	SO	AVG	OBP	SLG	PRO+	BR/A	SB	CS	SBR	FA	FR	G/POS	TPR
1906	Cin-N	1	1	0	0	0	0	0	0	0		.000	.000	.000	-96	-0	0			1.000	-0	/C-1	0.0
1909	*Det-A	77	252	17	66	8	6	0	21	11		.262	.298	.341	98	-1	2			.964	-8	C-77	-0.3
1910	Det-A	88	275	24	57	7	4	2	25	20		.207	.266	.284	68	-11	1			.952	-4	C-84	-0.7
1911	Det-A	141	503	45	133	13	7	3	51	20		.264	.297	.336	73	-20	3			.952	-13	*C-141	-1.8
1912	Det-A	121	394	35	103	9	4	0	41	34		.261	.326	.305	83	-8	3			.950	-28	*C-120	-2.5
1913	Det-A	80	241	19	54	13	2	0	21	21	35	.224	.292	.295	73	-9	5			.960	-8	C-77	-1.1
1914	Det-A	122	400	16	77	8	4	0	25	24	58	.192	.242	.233	41	-29	2	1	0	.960	-6	*C-122	-2.7
1915	Det-A	100	300	27	67	9	2	1	31	20	41	.223	.274	.277	62	-15	5	1	1	.964	-9	*C-100	-1.7
1916	Det-A	94	291	16	69	17	3	0	30	17	48	.237	.286	.316	78	-9	3			.969	-9	C-94	-1.2
1917	Det-A	99	297	19	61	14	1	0	30	20	35	.205	.262	.259	59	-15	3			.977	-4	C-95	-1.3
1918	Det-A	54	186	9	47	4	0	1	14	11	18	.253	.294	.290	80	-5	2			.980	-8	C-47/1-5,S-1	-1.1
1919	Det-A	38	120	9	29	4	1	1	15	7	12	.242	.295	.317	73	-4	1			.974	1	C-36/1-1	-0.1
1920	Det-A	78	238	12	55	17	0	0	17	14	21	.231	.277	.303	55	-16	0	0	0	.958	-10	C-77	-2.0
1925	Det-A	3	5	0	1	0	0	0	0	0	0	.200	.200	.200	2	-1	0	0	0	1.000	-1	/C-3	-0.2
Total	14	1096	3503	248	819	123	34	8	321	219	268	.234	.284	.295	69	-142	30	2		.961	-107	*C-1074/1-6,S-1	-16.7

■ JERRY STANDAERT Standaert, Jerome John b: 11/2/01, Chicago, Ill. d: 8/4/64, Chicago, Ill. BR/TR, 5′10″, 168 lbs. Deb: 4/16/25

YEAR	TM/L	G	AB	R	H	2B	3B	HR	RBI	BB	SO	AVG	OBP	SLG	PRO+	BR/A	SB	CS	SBR	FA	FR	G/POS	TPR
1925	Bro-N	1	1	0	0	0	0	0	0	0	1	.000	.000	.000	-99	-0	0	0	0	.000	0	H	0.0
1926	Bro-N	66	113	13	39	8	2	0	14	5	7	.345	.378	.451	124	4	0			.918	-11	2-21,3-14/S-6	-0.6
1929	Bos-A	19	18	1	3	2	0	0	4	3	2	.167	.286	.278	47	-1	0	0	0	.958	-0	1-10	-0.2
Total	3	86	132	14	42	10	2	0	18	8	10	.318	.362	.424	111	2	0	0		.918	-11	/2-21,3-14,1-10,S-6	-0.8

■ PETE STANICEK Stanicek, Peter Louis b: 4/18/63, Harvey, Ill. BB/TR, 5′11″, 175 lbs. Deb: 9/1/87 F

YEAR	TM/L	G	AB	R	H	2B	3B	HR	RBI	BB	SO	AVG	OBP	SLG	PRO+	BR/A	SB	CS	SBR	FA	FR	G/POS	TPR
1987	Bal-A	30	113	9	31	3	0	0	9	8	19	.274	.333	.301	72	-4	8	1	2	.975	-6	2-19,D-10/3-2	-0.7
1988	Bal-A	83	261	29	60	7	1	4	17	28	45	.230	.314	.310	78	-7	12	6	0	.985	-5	O-65,2-16/D-1	-1.3
Total	2	113	374	38	91	10	1	4	26	36	64	.243	.320	.307	76	-11	20	7	2	.967	-10	/O-65,2-35,D-11,3-2	-2.0

■ STEVE STANICEK Stanicek, Stephen Blair b: 6/19/61, Lake Forest, Ill. BR/TR, 6′, 190 lbs. Deb: 9/16/87 F

YEAR	TM/L	G	AB	R	H	2B	3B	HR	RBI	BB	SO	AVG	OBP	SLG	PRO+	BR/A	SB	CS	SBR	FA	FR	G/POS	TPR
1987	Mil-A	4	7	2	2	0	0	0	0	0	2	.286	.286	.286	51	-0	0	0	0	.000	0	/D-1	0.0
1989	Phi-N	9	9	0	1	0	0	0	1	0	3	.111	.111	.111	-36	-2	0	0	0	.000	0	H	-0.2
Total	2	13	16	2	3	0	0	0	1	0	5	.188	.188	.188	4	-2	0	0	0		0	/D-1	-0.2

■ TOM STANKARD Stankard, Thomas Francis b: 3/20/1882, Waltham, Mass. d: 6/13/58, Waltham, Mass. BR/TR, 6′, 190 lbs. Deb: 7/2/04

YEAR	TM/L	G	AB	R	H	2B	3B	HR	RBI	BB	SO	AVG	OBP	SLG	PRO+	BR/A	SB	CS	SBR	FA	FR	G/POS	TPR
1904	Pit-N	2	2	0	0	0	0	0	0	0		.000	.000	.000	-97	-0	0			1.000	-1	/S-1,3-1	-0.1

■ ANDY STANKIEWICZ Stankiewicz, Andrew Neal b: 8/10/64, Inglewood, Cal. BR/TR, 5′9″, 165 lbs. Deb: 4/11/92

YEAR	TM/L	G	AB	R	H	2B	3B	HR	RBI	BB	SO	AVG	OBP	SLG	PRO+	BR/A	SB	CS	SBR	FA	FR	G/POS	TPR
1992	NY-A	116	400	52	107	22	2	2	25	38	42	.268	.339	.348	93	-3	9	5	-0	.973	6	S-81,2-34/D-1	0.9
1993	NY-A	16	9	5	0	0	0	0	0	1	1	.000	.100	.000	-73	-2	0	0	0	1.000	6	/2-6,3-4,S-1,D-1	0.4
1994	Hou-N	37	54	10	14	3	0	1	5	12	12	.259	.403	.370	109	1	1	1	-0	1.000	-0	S-17/2-6,3-1	0.2
1995	Hou-N	43	52	6	6	1	0	0	7	12	19	.115	.281	.135	15	-6	4	2	0	.985	12	S-14/2-6,3-3	0.6
1996	Mon-N	64	77	12	22	5	1	0	9	6	12	.286	.360	.377	92	-1	1	0	0	.969	1	2-19,S-13/3-1	0.2
1997	Mon-N	76	107	11	24	9	0	1	5	4	22	.224	.252	.336	53	-8	1	1	-0	.957	6	2-25,S-14/3-3,D-2	-0.1
1998	Ari-N	77	145	9	30	5	0	0	8	7	33	.207	.253	.241	29	-15	1	0	0	.994	-4	2-61	-1.6
Total	7	429	844	105	203	45	3	4	59	80	141	.241	.314	.315	71	-33	17	9	-0	.986	27	2-157,S-140/3-12,D	0.6

■ EDDIE STANKY Stanky, Edward Raymond "The Brat" or "Muggsy" b: 9/3/16, Philadelphia, Pa. BR/TR, 5′8″, 170 lbs. Deb: 4/21/43 MC

YEAR	TM/L	G	AB	R	H	2B	3B	HR	RBI	BB	SO	AVG	OBP	SLG	PRO+	BR/A	SB	CS	SBR	FA	FR	G/POS	TPR
1943	Chi-N	142	510	92	125	15	1	0	47	92	42	.245	.363	.278	88	-3	4			.966	12	*2-131,S-12/3-2	1.8
1944	Chi-N	13	25	4	6	0	1	0	0	2	2	.240	.296	.320	74	-1	1			.875	2	/2-3,S-3,3-3	0.1
	Bro-N	89	261	32	72	9	2	0	16	44	13	.276	.382	.326	102	3	3			.961	-18	2-58,S-35/3-1	-1.0
	Yr	102	286	36	78	9	3	0	16	46	15	.273	.375	.325	100	2	4			.958	-16	2-61,S-38/3-4	-0.9
1945	Bro-N	153	555	**128**	143	29	5	1	39	**148**	42	.258	.417	.333	111	18	6			.962	9	*2-153/S-1	3.6
1946	Bro-N	144	483	98	132	24	7	0	36	**137**	56	.273	**.436**	.352	124	25	8			.977	-5	*2-141	3.1
1947	*Bro-N★	146	559	97	141	24	5	3	53	103	39	.252	.373	.329	85	-8	3			**.985**	7	*2-146	0.8
1948	*Bos-N†	67	247	49	79	14	2	2	29	61	13	.320	.455	.417	140	18	3			.981	5	2-66	2.6
1949	Bos-N	138	506	90	144	24	5	1	42	113	41	.285	.417	.358	116	19	3			.979	-9	*2-135	1.6
1950	NY-N☆	152	527	115	158	25	5	8	51	**144**	50	.300	**.460**	.412	131	35	9			.976	2	*2-151	4.1
1951	*NY-N	145	515	88	127	17	2	14	43	127	63	.247	.401	.369	108	12	8	5	-1	.977	-1	*2-140	1.7
1952	StL-N	53	83	13	19	4	0	0	7	19	9	.229	.373	.277	83	-1	0	0	0	1.000	-1	2-20,M	-0.1
1953	StL-N	17	30	5	8	0	0	0	1	6	4	.267	.405	.267	80	-0	0	0	0	1.000	1	/2-8,M	0.1
Total	11	1259	4301	811	1154	185	35	29	364	996	374	.268	.410	.348	109	116	48	5		.975	4	*2-1152/S-51,3-6	18.4

■ FRED STANLEY
Stanley, Frederick Blair b: 8/13/47, Farnhamville, Iowa BR/TR, 5'10", 167 lbs. Deb: 9/11/69 C

YEAR	TM/L	G	AB	R	H	2B	3B	HR	RBI	BB	SO	AVG	OBP	SLG	PRO+	BR/A	SB	CS	SBR	FA	FR	G/POS	TPR
1969	Sea-A	17	43	2	12	2	1	0	4	3	8	.279	.326	.372	96	-0	1	0	0	.962	-4	S-15/2-1	-0.3
1970	Mil-A	6	0	1	0	0	0	0	0	0	0	—	—	—	—	0	0	0	0	1.000	1	/2-2	0.1
1971	Cle-A	60	129	14	29	4	0	2	12	27	25	.225	.363	.302	83	-2	1	0	0	.971	7	S-55/2-3	1.1
1972	Cle-A	6	12	1	2	1	0	0	0	2	3	.167	.286	.250	58	-1	0	0	0	.917	-3	/S-5,2-1	-0.4
	SD-N	39	85	15	17	2	0	0	2	12	19	.200	.306	.224	57	-4	1	0	0	.989	3	2-21,S-17/3-4	0.1
1973	NY-A	26	66	6	14	0	1	1	5	7	16	.212	.288	.288	65	-3	0	0	0	.981	3	S-21/2-3	0.3
1974	NY-A	33	38	2	7	0	0	0	3	3	2	.184	.244	.184	25	-4	1	2	-1	.973	12	S-19,2-15	0.9
1975	NY-A	117	252	34	56	5	1	0	15	21	27	.222	.285	.250	53	-15	3	1	0	.977	4	S-83,2-33/3-1	-0.4
1976	*NY-A	110	260	32	62	2	2	1	20	34	29	.238	.329	.273	78	-6	1	0	0	.983	-24	*S-110/2-3	-1.9
1977	*NY-A	48	46	6	12	0	0	1	7	8	6	.261	.370	.326	93	-0	1	1	-0	.958	3	S-42/3-3,2-2	0.4
1978	*NY-A	81	160	14	35	7	0	1	9	25	31	.219	.324	.281	73	-5	0	0	0	.959	-5	S-71,2-11/3-4	-0.3
1979	NY-A	57	100	9	20	1	0	2	14	5	17	.200	.238	.270	38	-9	0	1	-1	.978	13	S-31,3-16/2-8,1O	0.5
1980	NY-A	49	86	13	18	3	0	0	5	5	5	.209	.269	.244	42	-7	0	0	0	.923	7	S-19,2-17,3-12	0.2
1981	*Oak-A	66	145	15	28	4	0	0	7	15	23	.193	.269	.221	44	-10	2	0	1	.986	-17	S-62/2-6	-2.2
1982	Oak-A	101	228	33	44	7	0	2	17	29	32	.193	.287	.250	51	-15	0	1	-1	.963	-20	S-98/2-2	-2.8
Total	14	816	1650	197	356	38	5	10	120	196	243	.216	.302	.263	62	-80	11	6	-0	.971	-19	S-648,2-128/3O1	-4.7

■ JIM STANLEY
Stanley, James F. b: 1889, BB/TR, 5'6", 148 lbs. Deb: 4/19/14

YEAR	TM/L	G	AB	R	H	2B	3B	HR	RBI	BB	SO	AVG	OBP	SLG	PRO+	BR/A	SB	CS	SBR	FA	FR	G/POS	TPR
1914	Chi-F	54	98	13	19	3	0	0	4	19	14	.194	.347	.224	61	-6	2			.878	-10	S-40/3-3,2-1,O-1	-1.5

■ JOE STANLEY
Stanley, Joseph b: New Jersey Deb: 4/24/1884

YEAR	TM/L	G	AB	R	H	2B	3B	HR	RBI	BB	SO	AVG	OBP	SLG	PRO+	BR/A	SB	CS	SBR	FA	FR	G/POS	TPR
1884	Bal-U	6	21	3	5	1	0	0		0		.238	.238	.286	53	-2				.444	-2	/O-6	-0.4

■ JOE STANLEY
Stanley, Joseph Bernard b: 4/2/1881, Washington, D.C. d: 9/13/67, Detroit, Mich. BB/TR, 5'9.5", 150 lbs. Deb: 9/11/1897 F

YEAR	TM/L	G	AB	R	H	2B	3B	HR	RBI	BB	SO	AVG	OBP	SLG	PRO+	BR/A	SB	CS	SBR	FA	FR	G/POS	TPR
1897	Was-N	1	1	0	0	0	0	0	0	0		.000	.000	.000	-99	-0	0			.000	-0	/P-1	0.0
1902	Was-A	3	12	2	4	0	0	0	1	0		.333	.333	.333	85	-0	0			.833	-1	/O-3	-0.1
1903	Bos-N	86	308	40	77	12	5	1	47	18		.250	.306	.331	85	-6	10			.902	3	O-77/P-1,S-1	-0.7
1904	Bos-N	3	8	0	0	0	0	0	0	0		.000	.000	.000	-99	-2	0			.800	1	/O-3	-0.2
1905	Was-A	28	92	13	24	2	1	1	17	7		.261	.313	.337	111	1	4			.944	0	O-27	0.0
1906	Was-A	73	221	18	36	0	4	0	9	20		.163	.236	.199	38	-15	6			.934	-5	O-63/P-1	-2.6
1909	Chi-N	22	52	4	7	1	0	0	2	6		.135	.224	.154	17	-5	0			.947	-4	O-16	-1.1
Total	7	216	694	77	148	15	10	2	76	51		.213	.275	.272	66	-28	20			.918	-6	O-189/P-3,S-1	-4.7

■ MICKEY STANLEY
Stanley, Mitchell Jack b: 7/20/42, Grand Rapids, Mich BR/TR, 6'1", 195 lbs. Deb: 9/13/64

YEAR	TM/L	G	AB	R	H	2B	3B	HR	RBI	BB	SO	AVG	OBP	SLG	PRO+	BR/A	SB	CS	SBR	FA	FR	G/POS	TPR
1964	Det-A	4	11	3	3	0	0	0	1	0	1	.273	.273	.273	52	-1	0	0	0	1.000	-1	/O-4	-0.2
1965	Det-A	30	117	14	28	6	0	3	13	3	12	.239	.258	.368	75	-4	1	0	0	.986	3	O-29	-0.3
1966	Det-A	92	235	28	68	15	4	3	19	17	20	.289	.337	.426	115	4	2	1	0	1.000	2	O-82	0.4
1967	Det-A	145	333	38	70	7	3	7	24	29	46	.210	.273	.312	71	-12	9	2	2	.982	-8	*O-129/1-8	-2.6
1968	*Det-A	153	583	88	151	16	6	11	60	42	57	.259	.313	.364	102	1	4	3	-1	**1.000**	3	*O-130,1-15/S-9,2-1	-0.4
1969	Det-A	149	592	73	139	28	1	16	70	52	56	.235	.299	.367	82	-15	8	4	0	.985	-19	*O-101,S-59/1-4	-3.6
1970	Det-A	142	568	83	143	21	11	13	47	45	56	.252	.307	.396	92	-8	10	1	2	**1.000**	6	*O-132/1-9	-0.7
1971	Det-A	139	401	43	117	14	5	7	41	24	44	.292	.332	.404	103	1	1	3	-2	.988	6	*O-139	0.1
1972	*Det-A	142	435	45	102	16	6	14	55	29	49	.234	.282	.395	97	-3	1	0	0	.994	6	*O-139	-0.3
1973	Det-A	157	602	81	147	23	5	17	57	48	65	.244	.300	.384	86	-13	0	4	-2	.993	13	*O-157	-1.0
1974	Det-A	99	394	40	87	13	2	8	34	26	63	.221	.271	.325	68	-17	5	3	-0	.992	6	O-91,1-12/2-1	-1.7
1975	Det-A	52	164	26	42	7	3	3	19	15	27	.256	.322	.390	96	-1	1	1	-0	.983	-1	O-28,1-14/3-7,D-1	-0.5
1976	Det-A	84	214	34	55	17	1	4	29	14	19	.257	.303	.402	101	-0	2	0	1	.969	-2	O-38,1-17,3/S2D	-0.4
1977	Det-A	75	222	30	51	9	1	8	23	18	30	.230	.287	.387	78	-7	0	0	0	.972	-6	O-57/1-3,S-3,D-2	-1.5
1978	Det-A	53	151	15	40	9	0	3	8	9	19	.265	.306	.384	90	-2	0	1	-1	.960	-6	O-34,1-12	-1.1
Total	15	1516	5022	641	1243	201	48	117	500	371	564	.248	.300	.377	89	-77	44	23	-1	.991	2	*O-1290/1-94,S3D2	-13.8

■ MIKE STANLEY
Stanley, Robert Michael b: 6/25/63, Ft.Lauderdale, Fla BR/TR, 6'1", 185 lbs. Deb: 6/24/86

YEAR	TM/L	G	AB	R	H	2B	3B	HR	RBI	BB	SO	AVG	OBP	SLG	PRO+	BR/A	SB	CS	SBR	FA	FR	G/POS	TPR
1986	Tex-A	15	30	4	10	3	0	1	1	3	7	.333	.394	.533	146	2	1	0	0	.857	-1	/3-7,C-4,O-1,D-3	0.1
1987	Tex-A	78	216	34	59	8	1	6	37	31	48	.273	.367	.403	104	2	3	0	1	.980	-11	C-61,1-12/O-1,D-5	-0.5
1988	Tex-A	94	249	21	57	8	0	3	27	37	62	.229	.329	.297	75	-7	0	0	0	.991	-3	C-64,D-18/1-6,3-2	-0.7
1989	Tex-A	67	122	9	30	3	1	1	11	12	29	.246	.324	.311	78	-3	1	0	0	.978	-4	C-25,D-21/1-7,3-3	-0.7
1990	Tex-A	103	189	21	47	8	1	2	19	30	25	.249	.352	.333	92	-1	1	0	0	.985	-3	C-63,D-14/3-8,1-6	-0.2
1991	Tex-A	95	181	25	45	13	1	3	25	34	44	.249	.373	.381	111	4	0	0	0	.980	-10	C-58,1-12/3-6,OD	-0.4
1992	NY-A	68	173	24	43	7	0	8	27	33	45	.249	.372	.428	124	7	0	0	0	.980	5	C-55/1-4,D-6	1.4
1993	NY-A	130	423	70	129	17	1	26	84	57	85	.305	.394	.534	152	31	1	1	-0	**.996**	-9	*C-122/D-2	2.8
1994	NY-A	82	290	54	87	20	0	17	57	39	56	.300	.387	.545	142	18	0	0	0	.993	-0	C-72/1-7,D-4	2.0
1995	*NY-A★	118	399	63	107	29	1	18	83	57	106	.268	.367	.481	120	12	1	1	-0	.993	-4	*C-107,D-10	1.3
1996	Bos-A	121	397	73	107	20	1	24	69	69	62	.270	.384	.506	120	13	2	0	1	.985	-27	*C-105,D-10	-0.7
1997	Bos-A	97	260	45	78	17	0	13	53	39	50	.300	.403	.515	135	14	0	1	-1	.996	-1	D-53,1-31,C-15	0.8
	*NY-A	28	87	16	25	8	0	3	12	15	22	.287	.392	.483	128	4	0	0	0	1.000	-1	D-16,1-12	0.1
	Yr	125	347	61	103	25	0	16	65	54	72	.297	.400	.507	133	18	0	1	-1	.997	-1	D-69,1-43,C-15	0.9
1998	Tor-A	98	341	49	82	13	0	22	47	56	86	.240	.356	.472	113	7	2	1	0	.995	-1	D-73,1-22/O-1	0.0
	*Bos-A	47	156	25	45	12	0	7	32	26	43	.288	.397	.500	131	8	1	0	0	1.000	-1	D-34,1-13	0.4
	Yr	145	497	74	127	25	0	29	79	82	129	.256	.369	.481	119	15	3	1	0	.997	-2	*D-107,1-35/O-1	0.4
Total	13	1241	3513	533	951	186	7	154	584	538	770	.271	.373	.459	120	110	13	4	2	.988	-70	C-751,D-275,1/3O	5.7

■ JACK STANSBURY
Stansbury, John James b: 12/6/1885, Phillipsburg, N.J. d: 12/26/70, Easton, Pa. BR/TR, 5'9", 165 lbs. Deb: 6/30/18

YEAR	TM/L	G	AB	R	H	2B	3B	HR	RBI	BB	SO	AVG	OBP	SLG	PRO+	BR/A	SB	CS	SBR	FA	FR	G/POS	TPR
1918	Bos-A	20	47	3	6	1	0	0	2	6	3	.128	.241	.149	18	-5	0			.980	2	3-18/O-2	-0.2

■ BUCK STANTON
Stanton, George Washington b: 6/19/06, Stantonsburg, N.C d: 1/1/92, San Antonio, Tex. BL/TL, 5'10", 150 lbs. Deb: 9/5/31

YEAR	TM/L	G	AB	R	H	2B	3B	HR	RBI	BB	SO	AVG	OBP	SLG	PRO+	BR/A	SB	CS	SBR	FA	FR	G/POS	TPR
1931	StL-A	13	15	3	3	2	0	0	0	0	6	.200	.200	.333	37	-1	0	0	0	.750	-0	/O-1	-0.1

■ HARRY STANTON
Stanton, Harry Andrew b: St.Louis, Mo. TR , Deb: 10/14/00

YEAR	TM/L	G	AB	R	H	2B	3B	HR	RBI	BB	SO	AVG	OBP	SLG	PRO+	BR/A	SB	CS	SBR	FA	FR	G/POS	TPR
1900	StL-N	1	0	0	0	0	0	0	0	0		—	—	—	—	0	0			.000	0	/C-1	0.0

■ LEROY STANTON
Stanton, Leroy Bobby b: 4/10/46, Latta, S.C. BR/TR, 6'1", 195 lbs. Deb: 9/10/70

YEAR	TM/L	G	AB	R	H	2B	3B	HR	RBI	BB	SO	AVG	OBP	SLG	PRO+	BR/A	SB	CS	SBR	FA	FR	G/POS	TPR
1970	NY-N	4	4	0	1	0	1	0	0	0	0	.250	.250	.750	157	0	0	0	0	1.000	-0	/O-1	0.0
1971	NY-N	5	21	2	4	1	0	0	2	2	4	.190	.261	.238	43	-2	0	0	0	1.000	-0	/O-5	-0.2
1972	Cal-A	127	402	44	101	15	3	12	39	22	100	.251	.297	.393	110	3	2	3	-1	.983	2	*O-124	-0.2
1973	Cal-A	119	306	41	72	9	2	8	34	27	88	.235	.301	.356	92	-4	3	3	-1	.965	-7	*O-107	-1.6
1974	Cal-A	118	415	48	111	21	2	11	62	33	107	.267	.329	.407	117	8	10	8	-2	.975	4	*O-114	0.6
1975	Cal-A	137	440	67	115	20	3	14	82	52	85	.261	.347	.416	124	14	18	6	2	.961	2	*O-131/D-1	1.3
1976	Cal-A	93	231	12	44	13	1	2	25	24	57	.190	.270	.281	66	-10	2	6	-3	.985	-15	O-79/D-4	-3.3
1977	Sea-A	133	454	56	125	24	1	27	90	42	115	.275	.343	.511	131	18	0	1	-1	.953	5	O-91,D-33	1.7
1978	Sea-A	93	302	24	55	11	0	3	24	34	80	.182	.267	.248	46	-21	1	0	0	1.000	-0	D-59,O-30	-2.5
Total	9	829	2575	294	628	114	13	77	358	236	636	.244	.313	.388	103	6	36	27	-5	.972	-9	O-682/D-97	-4.2

■ TOM STANTON
Stanton, Thomas Patrick b: 10/25/1874, St.Louis, Mo. d: 1/17/57, St.Louis, Mo. BB/TR, 5'10", 175 lbs. Deb: 4/19/04

YEAR	TM/L	G	AB	R	H	2B	3B	HR	RBI	BB	SO	AVG	OBP	SLG	PRO+	BR/A	SB	CS	SBR	FA	FR	G/POS	TPR
1904	Chi-N	1	3	0	0	0	0	0	0	0		.000	.000	.000	-99	-1	0			1.000	-0	/C-1	-0.1

■ JOE STAPLES
Staples, Joseph F. b: Buffalo, N.Y. Deb: 9/19/1885

YEAR	TM/L	G	AB	R	H	2B	3B	HR	RBI	BB	SO	AVG	OBP	SLG	PRO+	BR/A	SB	CS	SBR	FA	FR	G/POS	TPR
1885	Buf-N	7	22	0	1	0	0	0	0	0	9	.045	.045	.045	-68	-4				.545	-3	/O-6,2-1	-0.7

■ DAVE STAPLETON
Stapleton, David Leslie b: 1/16/54, Fairhope, Ala. BR/TR, 6'1", 178 lbs. Deb: 5/30/80

YEAR	TM/L	G	AB	R	H	2B	3B	HR	RBI	BB	SO	AVG	OBP	SLG	PRO+	BR/A	SB	CS	SBR	FA	FR	G/POS	TPR
1980	Bos-A	106	449	61	144	33	5	7	45	13	32	.321	.341	.463	112	6	3	2	-0	.979	10	2-94/1-8,O-6,3-2,D	2.1
1981	Bos-A	93	355	45	101	17	1	10	42	21	22	.285	.326	.423	108	3	0	4	-2	.948	-7	S-33,3-25,2-23,1/D	-0.4

YEAR	TM/L	G	AB	R	H	2B	3B	HR	RBI	BB	SO	AVG	OBP	SLG	PRO+	BR/A	SB	CS	SBR	FA	FR	G/POS	TPR
1982	Bos-A	150	538	66	142	28	1	14	65	31	40	.264	.308	.398	87	-10	2	4	-2	.991	2	*1-106,S-27/23OD	-1.3
1983	Bos-A	151	542	54	134	31	1	10	66	40	44	.247	.301	.363	76	-18	1	1	-0	.993	-2	*1-145/2-5	-2.9
1984	Bos-A	13	39	4	9	2	0	0	1	3	3	.231	.286	.282	55	-2	0	0	0	1.000	1	1-10/D-1	-0.2
1985	Bos-A	30	66	4	15	6	0	0	2	4	11	.227	.271	.318	58	-4	0	0	0	1.000	1	2-14/1-8,D-5	-0.2
1986	*Bos-A	39	39	4	5	1	0	0	3	2	10	.128	.171	.154	-11	-6	0	0	0	1.000	3	1-29/2-6,3-2	-0.4
Total	7	582	2028	238	550	118	8	41	224	114	162	.271	.312	.398	90	-31	6	11	-5	.993	7	1-318,2-151/S3DO	-3.3
■ WILLIE STARGELL Stargell, Wilver Dornel b: 3/6/40, Earlsboro, Okla. BL/TL, 6'2.5", 225 lbs. Deb: 9/16/62 CH																							
1962	Pit-N	10	31	1	9	3	1	0	4	3	10	.290	.353	.452	114	1	0	1	-1	.929	-0	/O-9	-0.1
1963	Pit-N	108	304	34	74	11	6	11	47	19	85	.243	.292	.428	104	1	0	2	-1	.953	-8	O-65,1-16	-1.3
1964	Pit-N★	117	421	53	115	19	7	21	78	17	92	.273	.305	.501	123	11	1	1	-0	.900	-7	O-59,1-50	-0.2
1965	Pit-N★	144	533	68	145	25	8	27	107	39	127	.272	.330	.501	130	19	1	1	-0	.965	0	*O-137/1-7	1.3
1966	Pit-N★	140	485	84	153	30	0	33	102	48	109	.315	.384	.581	164	41	2	3	-1	.945	-4	*O-127,1-15	3.0
1967	Pit-N	134	462	54	125	18	6	20	73	67	103	.271	.367	.465	136	23	1	0	0	.938	-2	O-98,1-37	1.5
1968	Pit-N	128	435	57	103	15	1	24	67	47	105	.237	.320	.441	129	14	5	0	2	.945	-3	*O-113,1-13	0.7
1969	Pit-N	145	522	89	160	31	6	29	92	61	120	.307	.385	.556	164	44	1	0	0	.970	-2	*O-116,1-23	3.4
1970	*Pit-N	136	474	70	125	18	3	31	85	44	119	.264	.333	.511	125	14	0	1	-1	.976	7	*O-125/1-1	1.5
1971	*Pit-N★	141	511	104	151	26	0	**48**	125	83	154	.295	.401	.628	188	**59**	0	0	0	.984	3	*O-138	**5.8**
1972	*Pit-N★	138	495	75	145	28	2	33	112	65	129	.293	.377	.558	166	42	1	1	-0	.984	-13	*1-101,O-32	2.0
1973	Pit-N★	148	522	106	156	**43**	3	**44**	**119**	80	129	.299	.395	**.646**	**189**	**61**	0	0	0	.975	7	*O-142	**6.3**
1974	*Pit-N	140	508	90	153	37	4	25	96	87	106	.301	.409	.537	**169**	**49**	0	2	-1	.967	2	*O-135/1-1	4.5
1975	*Pit-N	124	461	71	136	32	2	22	90	58	109	.295	.377	.516	147	29	0	0	0	.992	-10	*1-122	1.1
1976	Pit-N	117	428	54	110	20	3	20	65	50	101	.257	.342	.458	124	13	2	0	1	.988	-10	*1-111	-0.5
1977	Pit-N	63	186	29	51	12	0	13	35	31	55	.274	.386	.548	144	12	0	1	-1	.986	-1	1-55	0.7
1978	Pit-N★	122	390	60	115	18	2	28	97	50	93	.295	.385	.567	156	29	3	2	-0	.994	-2	*1-112	2.2
1979	*Pit-N	126	424	60	119	19	0	32	82	47	105	.281	.357	.552	138	21	0	1	-1	**.997**	-6	*1-113	0.8
1980	Pit-N	67	202	28	53	10	1	11	38	26	52	.262	.352	.485	129	8	0	0	0	.992	0	1-54	0.5
1981	Pit-N	38	60	2	17	4	0	0	9	5	9	.283	.338	.350	93	-1	0	0	0	1.000	-2	/1-9	-0.4
1982	Pit-N	74	73	6	17	4	0	3	17	10	24	.233	.325	.411	102	0	0	0	0	1.000	0	/1-8	0.0
Total	21	2360	7927	1195	2232	423	55	475	1540	937	1936	.282	.363	.529	147	488	17	16	-5	.961	-51	*O-1296,1-848	32.8
■ MATT STARK Stark, Matthew Scott b: 1/21/65, Whittier, Cal. BR/TR, 6'4", 225 lbs. Deb: 4/8/87																							
1987	Tor-A	5	12	0	1	0	0	0	0	0	0	.083	.083	.083	-55	-3	0	0	0	1.000	1	/C-5	-0.2
1990	Chi-A	8	16	0	4	1	0	0	3	1	6	.250	.294	.313	71	-1	0	0	0	.000	0	/D-6	-0.1
Total	2	13	28	0	5	1	0	0	3	1	6	.179	.207	.214	15	-3	0	0	0	1.000	1	/D-6,C-5	-0.3
■ DOLLY STARK Stark, Monroe Randolph b: 1/19/1885, Ripley, Miss. d: 12/1/24, Memphis, Tenn. BR/TR, 5'9", 160 lbs. Deb: 9/12/09																							
1909	Cle-A	19	60	4	12	0	0	0	1	6		.200	.273	.200	48	-3	4			.875	-10	S-19	-1.5
1910	Bro-N	30	103	7	17	3	0	0	8	7	19	.165	.225	.194	23	-10	2			.893	-1	S-30	-1.1
1911	Bro-N	70	193	25	57	4	1	0	19	20	24	.295	.370	.326	100	1	6			.910	-3	S-34,2-18/3-3	-0.1
1912	Bro-N	8	22	2	4	0	0	0	2	1	3	.182	.217	.182	10	-3	2			.892	0	/S-7	-0.2
Total	4	127	378	38	90	7	1	0	30	34	46	.238	.308	.262	66	-15	14			.896	-14	/S-90,2-18,3-3	-2.9
■ GEORGE STARNAGLE Starnagle, George Henry (b: George Henry Steuernagel) b: 10/6/1873, Belleville, Ill. d: 2/15/46, Belleville, Ill. BR/TR, 5'11", 175 lbs. Deb: 9/14/02																							
1902	Cle-A	1	3	0	0	0	0	0	0	0		.000	.000	.000	-99	-1	0			.667	-1	/C-1	-0.1
■ CHARLIE STARR Starr, Charles Watkin b: 8/30/1878, Pike Co., Ohio d: 10/18/37, Pasadena, Cal. TR, 5'10.5", 165 lbs. Deb: 4/29/05																							
1905	StL-A	26	97	9	20	0	0	0	6	7		.206	.260	.206	51	-5	0			.938	-4	2-18/3-6	-1.0
1908	Pit-N	20	59	8	11	2	0	0	8	13		.186	.342	.220	80	-0	6			.926	-5	2-12/S-5,3-2	-0.7
1909	Bos-N	61	216	16	48	2	3	0	6	31		.222	.333	.259	80	-4	7			.931	-9	2-54/S-6,3-3	-1.5
	Phi-N	3	3	0	0	0	0	0	0	0		.000	.000	.000	-99	-1	0			.000	0	H	-0.1
	Yr	64	219	16	48	2	3	0	6	31		.219	.329	.256	78	-4	7			.931	-9	2-54/S-6,3-3	-1.6
Total	3	110	375	33	79	4	3	0	20	51		.211	.315	.237	72	-10	13			.931	-18	/2-84,S-11,3-11	-3.3
■ BILL STARR Starr, William b: 2/26/11, Brooklyn, N.Y. d: 8/12/91, LaJolla, Cal. BR/TR, 6'1", 175 lbs. Deb: 8/23/35																							
1935	Was-A	12	24	1	5	0	0	0	1	0	1	.208	.208	.208	8	-3	0	0	0	.971	2	C-12	-0.1
1936	Was-A	1	0	0	0	0	0	0	0	0	0	—	—	—	—	0	0	0	0	.000	0	/C-1	0.0
Total	2	13	24	1	5	0	0	0	1	0	1	.208	.208	.208	8	-3	0	0	0	.971	2	/C-13	-0.1
■ JOE START Start, Joseph "Old Reliable" or "Rocks" b: 10/14/1842, New York, N.Y. d: 3/27/27, Providence, R.I. BL/TL, 5'9", 165 lbs. Deb: 5/18/1871 M																							
1871	Mut-n	33	161	35	58	5	1	1	34	3	0	.360	.372	.422	140	10	4	2	0	.921	-2	*1-33	0.6
1872	Mut-n	55	282	62	76	4	0	0	50	0	0	.270	.270	.284	75	-6	3	3	-1	**.955**	2	*1-55	-0.2
1873	Mut-n	53	251	42	67	8	3	1	28	4	0	.267	.278	.335	82	-5	1	0	0	.943	5	*1-53/O-2,M	0.2
1874	Mut-n	63	306	67	96	13	3	2	46	4	0	.314	.323	.395	125	7	5	0	2	**.961**	4	*1-63/O-2	1.0
1875	Mut-n	69	314	58	90	10	5	4	30	3	0	.287	.293	.389	128	7	1	4	-2	.948	2	*1-69	0.6
1876	NY-N	56	264	40	73	6	0	0	21	1	2	.277	.279	.299	107	3				**.964**	3	*1-56	0.4
1877	Har-N	60	271	55	90	3	6	1	21	6	2	.332	.347	.399	150	16				**.964**	-2	*1-60	1.2
1878	Chi-N	61	285	58	**100**	12	5	1	27	2	3	.351	.355	.439	150	14				.957	-2	*1-61	0.9
1879	Pro-N	66	317	70	101	11	5	2	37	7	4	.319	.333	.404	144	15				**.973**	0	*1-65/O-1	1.2
1880	Pro-N	82	345	53	96	14	6	0	27	13	20	.278	.304	.354	126	10				.971	-3	*1-82	-0.1
1881	Pro-N	79	348	56	114	12	6	0	29	9	7	.328	.345	.397	135	13				.963	-4	*1-79	0.2
1882	Pro-N	82	356	58	117	8	10	0	48	11	7	.329	.349	.407	142	16				.974	2	*1-82	0.8
1883	Pro-N	87	370	63	105	16	7	1	57	22	16	.284	.324	.373	108	4				.957	-1	*1-87	-0.5
1884	*Pro-N	93	381	80	105	10	5	2	32	35	25	.276	.337	.344	117	8				**.980**	1	*1-93	-0.1
1885	Pro-N	101	374	47	103	11	4	0	41	39	10	.275	.344	.326	121	10				.972	1	*1-101	-0.1
1886	Was-N	31	122	10	27	4	1	0	17	5	13	.221	.252	.270	63	-5	4			.973	-2	1-31	-1.0
Total	5 n	273	1314	264	387	40	12	8	188	14	0	.295	.302	.361	108	13	14	9	-1	.948	11	1-273/O-4	2.2
Total	11	798	3433	590	1031	107	55	7	357	150	109	.300	.330	.370	127	103	4			.968	-7	1-797/O-1	2.9
■ DAVE STATON Staton, David Alan b: 4/12/68, Seattle, Wash. BR/TR, 6'5", 215 lbs. Deb: 9/8/93																							
1993	SD-N	17	42	7	11	3	0	5	9	3	12	.262	.326	.690	161	3	0	0	0	1.000	3	1-12	0.5
1994	SD-N	29	66	6	12	2	0	4	6	10	18	.182	.289	.394	78	-2	0	0	0	1.000	4	1-20	0.0
Total	2	46	108	13	23	5	0	9	15	13	30	.213	.303	.509	110	1	0	0	0	1.000	7	/1-32	0.5
■ JOE STATON Staton, Joseph b: 3/8/48, Seattle, Wash. BL/TL, 6'3", 175 lbs. Deb: 9/5/72																							
1972	Det-A	6	2	1	0	0	0	0	0	0	1	.000	.000	.000	-97	-0	0	1	-1	1.000	0	/1-2	-0.1
1973	Det-A	9	17	2	4	0	0	0	3	0	3	.235	.235	.235	31	-2	1	0	0	.969	2	/1-5	0.0
Total	2	15	19	3	4	0	0	0	3	0	4	.211	.211	.211	18	-2	1	1	-0	.973	2	/1-7	-0.1
■ JIGGER STATZ Statz, Arnold John b: 10/20/1897, Waukegan, Ill. d: 3/16/88, Corona Del Mar, Cal. BR/TR, 5'7.5", 150 lbs. Deb: 7/30/19																							
1919	NY-N	21	60	7	18	2	1	0	6	3	8	.300	.333	.367	112	1	2			.977	-1	O-18/2-5	-0.1
1920	NY-N	16	30	0	4	0	1	0	5	2	9	.133	.188	.200	11	-3	0	1	-1	.944	-3	O-12	-0.8
	Bos-A	2	3	0	0	0	0	0	0	0	0	.000	.000	.000	-99	-1	0	0	0	1.000	-1	/O-2	-0.2
1922	Chi-N	110	462	77	137	19	5	1	34	41	31	.297	.355	.366	85	-10	16	13	-3	.959	9	*O-110	-1.1
1923	Chi-N	154	655	110	209	33	8	10	70	56	42	.319	.375	.440	114	14	29	23	-5	.975	18	*O-154	1.5
1924	Chi-N	135	549	69	152	22	5	3	49	37	50	.277	.325	.352	80	-15	13	9	-2	.961	15	*O-131/2-1	-1.1
1925	Chi-N	38	148	21	38	6	3	2	14	11	16	.257	.317	.378	76	-6	4	0	1	.943	2	O-37	-0.5
1927	Bro-N	130	507	64	139	24	7	1	21	26	43	.274	.310	.355	77	-17	10			.990	15	*O-122/2-1	-0.9
1928	Bro-N	77	171	28	40	8	1	0	16	18	12	.234	.311	.292	59	-10	3			.965	-6	O-52/2-1	-1.8
Total	8	683	2585	376	737	114	31	17	215	194	211	.285	.337	.373	87	-47	77	46		.969	48	O-638/2-8	-5.0

■ RUSTY STAUB
Staub, Daniel Joseph b: 4/1/44, New Orleans, La. BL/TR, 6'2", 200 lbs. Deb: 4/9/63 C

YEAR	TM/L	G	AB	R	H	2B	3B	HR	RBI	BB	SO	AVG	OBP	SLG	PRO+	BR/A	SB	CS	SBR	FA	FR	G/POS	TPR
1963	Hou-N	150	513	43	115	17	4	6	45	59	58	.224	.310	.308	84	-10	0	0	0	.989	-1	*1-109,O-49	-1.9
1964	Hou-N	89	292	26	63	10	2	8	35	21	31	.216	.275	.346	78	-9	1	1	-0	.992	-1	1-49,O-38	-1.5
1965	Hou-N	131	410	43	105	20	1	14	63	52	57	.256	.343	.412	120	11	3	0	1	.951	4	*O-112/1-1	1.1
1966	Hou-N	153	554	60	155	28	3	13	81	58	61	.280	.349	.412	119	14	2	1	0	.962	9	*O-148/1-1	1.7
1967	Hou-N★	149	546	71	182	**44**	1	10	74	60	47	.333	.402	.473	155	40	0	4	-2	.962	7	*O-144	3.9
1968	Hou-N★	161	591	54	172	37	1	6	72	73	57	.291	.376	.387	132	26	2	0	1	.992	-1	*1-147,O-15	1.5
1969	Mon-N☆	158	549	89	166	26	5	29	79	110	61	.302	.427	.526	165	52	3	4	-2	.966	7	*O-156	5.0
1970	Mon-N★	160	569	98	156	23	7	30	94	112	93	.274	.396	.497	138	33	12	11	-3	.985	11	*O-160	3.3
1971	Mon-N☆	162	599	94	186	34	6	19	97	74	42	.311	.394	.482	147	38	9	5	-0	.945	5	*O-162	3.6
1972	NY-N	66	239	32	70	11	0	9	38	31	13	.293	.379	.452	139	13	0	1	-1	.982	0	O-65	1.0
1973	*NY-N	152	585	77	163	36	1	15	76	74	52	.279	.363	.421	118	15	1	1	-0	.978	11	*O-152	1.9
1974	NY-N	151	561	65	145	22	2	19	78	77	39	.258	.351	.406	113	10	2	1	0	.983	9	*O-147	1.3
1975	NY-N	155	574	93	162	30	4	19	105	77	55	.282	.376	.448	134	27	2	0	1	.986	8	*O-153	3.0
1976	Det-A★	161	589	73	176	28	3	15	96	83	49	.299	.392	.433	136	29	3	1	0	.970	-6	*O-126,D-36	1.8
1977	Det-A	158	623	84	173	34	3	22	101	59	47	.278	.341	.448	107	6	1	1	-0	.000	0	*D-156	0.1
1978	Det-A	162	642	75	175	30	1	24	121	76	35	.273	.352	.435	117	15	3	1	0	.000	0	*D-162	1.0
1979	Det-A	68	246	32	58	12	1	9	40	32	18	.236	.336	.402	95	-2	1	0	0	.000	0	D-66	-0.3
	Mon-N	38	86	9	23	3	0	3	14	14	10	.267	.370	.407	113	2	0	0	0	.994	-2	1-22/O-1	-0.2
1980	Tex-A	109	340	42	102	23	2	9	55	39	18	.300	.375	.459	131	15	1	1	-0	.977	-2	D-57,1-30,O-14	0.8
1981	NY-N	70	161	9	51	9	0	5	21	22	12	.317	.402	.466	148	11	1	0	0	.989	-2	1-41	0.7
1982	NY-N	112	219	11	53	9	0	3	27	24	10	.242	.317	.324	80	-5	0	0	0	.959	2	O-27,1-18	-0.5
1983	NY-N	104	115	5	34	6	0	3	28	14	10	.296	.377	.426	123	4	0	0	0	.976	-1	/1-5,O-5	0.3
1984	NY-N	78	72	2	19	4	0	1	18	4	9	.264	.303	.361	87	-1	0	0	0	1.000	-0	/1-3	-0.2
1985	NY-N	54	45	2	12	3	0	1	8	10	4	.267	.400	.400	128	2	0	0	0	1.000	-0	/O-1	0.2
Total	23	2951	9720	1189	2716	499	47	292	1466	1255	888	.279	.366	.431	125	334	47	33	-6	.969	55	*O-1675,D-477,1-426	27.6

■ ECKY STEARNS
Stearns, Daniel Eckford b: 10/17/1861, Buffalo, N.Y. d: 6/28/44, Glendale, Cal. BL/TR, 6'1", 185 lbs. Deb: 8/17/1880

YEAR	TM/L	G	AB	R	H	2B	3B	HR	RBI	BB	SO	AVG	OBP	SLG	PRO+	BR/A	SB	CS	SBR	FA	FR	G/POS	TPR
1880	Buf-N	28	104	8	19	6	1	0	13	3	23	.183	.206	.260	55	-5				.774	-9	O-20/C-8,3-5,S-1	-1.4
1881	Det-N	3	11	1	1	1	0	0	0	0	2	.091	.091	.182	-16	-1				.714	-1	/S-3	-0.2
1882	Cin-a	49	214	28	55	10	2	0	35	6		.257	.277	.322	96	-1				.931	-2	1-35,O-12/2-2,S-1	-0.7
1883	Bal-a	93	382	54	94	10	9	1		**34**		.246	.308	.327	101	1				.947	3	*1-92/O-1	-0.5
1884	Bal-a	100	396	61	94	12	3	3		28		.237	.298	.306	94	-3				.949	4	*1-100/2-1	-1.0
1885	Bal-a	67	253	40	47	3	8	1	29	38		.186	.306	.273	85	-2				.973	1	1-63/O-3,C-2	-0.8
	Buf-N	30	105	7	21	6	1	0	9	8	23	.200	.257	.276	70	-3				.821	-7	S-19,1-12/C-2	-1.1
1889	KC-a	139	560	96	160	24	12	3	87	56	69	.286	.351	.387	104	1	67			.967	0	*1-135/3-4	-0.7
Total	7	509	2025	295	491	72	36	8	173	173	117	.242	.306	.325	94	-14	67			.956	-10	1-437/O-36,SC32	-6.4

■ JOHN STEARNS
Stearns, John Hardin b: 8/21/51, Denver, Col. BR/TR, 6', 185 lbs. Deb: 9/22/74 C

YEAR	TM/L	G	AB	R	H	2B	3B	HR	RBI	BB	SO	AVG	OBP	SLG	PRO+	BR/A	SB	CS	SBR	FA	FR	G/POS	TPR
1974	Phi-N	1	2	0	1	0	0	0	0	0	0	.500	.500	.500	173	0	0	0	0	1.000	-1	/C-1	0.0
1975	NY-N	59	169	25	32	5	1	3	10	17	15	.189	.271	.284	57	-10	4	1	1	.994	6	C-54	-0.1
1976	NY-N	32	103	13	27	6	0	2	10	16	11	.262	.367	.379	119	3	1	2	-1	.987	3	C-30	0.7
1977	NY-N★	139	431	52	108	25	1	12	55	77	76	.251	.373	.397	112	10	9	8	-2	.982	4	*C-127/1-6	1.5
1978	NY-N	143	477	65	126	24	1	15	73	70	57	.264	.368	.413	122	16	25	13	-0	.985	-3	*C-141/3-1	1.7
1979	NY-N☆	155	538	58	131	29	2	9	66	52	57	.243	.315	.355	86	-11	15	15	-5	.983	5	*C-121,1-16,3-11,/O	-0.8
1980	NY-N★	91	319	42	91	25	1	0	45	33	24	.285	.354	.370	105	3	7	3	0	.985	5	C-74,1-16/3-1	1.0
1981	NY-N	80	273	25	74	12	1	1	24	24	17	.271	.330	.333	90	-3	12	2	2	.983	-2	C-66/1-9,3-4	-0.2
1982	NY-N★	98	352	46	103	25	3	4	28	30	35	.293	.352	.415	114	7	17	7	1	.987	-7	C-81,3-12	0.4
1983	NY-N	4	0	2	0	0	0	0	0	0	0	—	—	—	—	0	0	0	0	.000	0	/R	0.0
1984	NY-N	8	17	6	3	1	0	0	1	4	2	.176	.333	.235	63	-1	1	0	0	1.000	-1	/C-4,1-2	-0.1
Total	11	810	2681	334	696	152	10	46	312	323	294	.260	.345	.375	102	13	91	51	-3	.985	10	C-699/1-49,3-29,O-6	4.1

■ JOHN STEDRONSKY
Stedronsky, John b: Troy, N.Y. Deb: 9/25/1879

YEAR	TM/L	G	AB	R	H	2B	3B	HR	RBI	BB	SO	AVG	OBP	SLG	PRO+	BR/A	SB	CS	SBR	FA	FR	G/POS	TPR
1879	Chi-N	4	12	0	1	0	0	0	0	0	3	.083	.083	.083	-42	-2				.789	1	/3-4	0.0

■ FARMER STEELMAN
Steelman, Morris James b: 6/29/1875, Millville, N.J. d: 9/16/44, Merchantville, N.J. TR , Deb: 9/15/1899

YEAR	TM/L	G	AB	R	H	2B	3B	HR	RBI	BB	SO	AVG	OBP	SLG	PRO+	BR/A	SB	CS	SBR	FA	FR	G/POS	TPR
1899	Lou-N	4	15	2	1	0	1	0	2	2		.067	.176	.200	3	-2	0			.929	-2	/C-4	-0.3
1900	Bro-N	1	4	0	0	0	0	0	0	0		.000	.000	.000	-94	-1	0			1.000	0	/C-1	-0.1
1901	Bro-N	1	3	0	1	0	0	0	0	0		.333	.333	.333	91	-0	0			.875	1	/C-1	0.1
	Phi-A	27	88	5	23	2	0	0	7	10		.261	.350	.284	74	-3	4			1.000	2	C-14,O-12	0.0
1902	Phi-A	10	32	1	6	1	0	0	6	2		.188	.235	.219	25	-3	2			1.000	1	/C-5,O-5	-0.2
Total	4	43	142	8	31	3	1	0	15	14		.218	.297	.254	52	-9	6			.985	2	/C-25,O-17	-0.5

■ JIM STEELS
Steels, James Earl b: 5/30/61, Jackson, Miss. BL/TL, 5'10", 185 lbs. Deb: 4/6/87

YEAR	TM/L	G	AB	R	H	2B	3B	HR	RBI	BB	SO	AVG	OBP	SLG	PRO+	BR/A	SB	CS	SBR	FA	FR	G/POS	TPR
1987	SD-N	62	68	9	13	1	1	0	6	11	14	.191	.304	.235	47	-5	3	2	-0	.960	-6	O-28	-1.2
1988	Tex-A	36	53	4	10	1	0	0	5	0	15	.189	.189	.208	11	-6	2	0	1	1.000	-5	O-17/1-7,D-7	-1.1
1989	SF-N	13	12	0	1	0	0	0	0	2	4	.083	.214	.083	-12	-2	0	0	0	1.000	0	/1-3,O-1	-0.2
Total	3	111	133	13	24	2	1	0	11	13	33	.180	.253	.211	28	-13	5	2	0	.973	-11	/O-46,1-10,D-7	-2.5

■ GENE STEERE
Steere, Frederick Eugene b: 8/16/1872, S.Scituate, R.I. d: 3/13/42, San Francisco, Cal Deb: 8/29/1894

YEAR	TM/L	G	AB	R	H	2B	3B	HR	RBI	BB	SO	AVG	OBP	SLG	PRO+	BR/A	SB	CS	SBR	FA	FR	G/POS	TPR
1894	Pit-N	10	39	3	8	0	0	0	4	2	1	.205	.244	.205	9	-6	2			.896	-2	S-10	-0.6

■ JOHN STEFERO
Stefero, John Robert b: 9/22/59, Sumter, S.C. BL/TR, 5'8", 185 lbs. Deb: 6/24/83

YEAR	TM/L	G	AB	R	H	2B	3B	HR	RBI	BB	SO	AVG	OBP	SLG	PRO+	BR/A	SB	CS	SBR	FA	FR	G/POS	TPR
1983	Bal-A	9	11	2	5	1	0	0	4	3	2	.455	.571	.545	213	2	0	0	0	.920	0	/C-9	0.2
1986	Bal-A	52	120	14	28	2	0	2	13	16	25	.233	.324	.300	72	-4	0	1	-1	.984	-2	C-50/2-1	-0.4
1987	Mon-N	18	56	4	11	0	0	1	3	3	17	.196	.237	.250	28	-6	0	0	0	.981	-0	C-17	-0.5
Total	3	79	187	20	44	3	0	3	20	22	44	.235	.316	.299	67	-8	0	1	-1	.979	-2	/C-76,2-1	-0.7

■ DAVE STEGMAN
Stegman, David William b: 1/30/54, Inglewood, Cal. BR/TR, 5'11", 190 lbs. Deb: 9/4/78

YEAR	TM/L	G	AB	R	H	2B	3B	HR	RBI	BB	SO	AVG	OBP	SLG	PRO+	BR/A	SB	CS	SBR	FA	FR	G/POS	TPR
1978	Det-A	8	14	3	4	2	0	1	3	1	2	.286	.333	.643	164	1	0	0	0	1.000	-2	/O-7	-0.1
1979	Det-A	12	31	6	6	0	0	3	5	2	3	.194	.242	.484	88	-1	1	1	-0	1.000	1	O-12	-0.1
1980	Det-A	65	130	12	23	5	0	2	9	14	23	.177	.257	.262	41	-10	1	1	-0	.988	-13	O-57/D-2	-2.6
1982	NY-A	2	0	0	0	0	0	0	0	0	0	—	—	—	—	0	0	0	0	.000	0	/D-1	0.0
1983	Chi-A	30	53	5	9	2	0	0	4	10	9	.170	.302	.208	42	-4	0	1	-1	1.000	-7	O-29	-1.2
1984	Chi-A	55	92	13	24	1	2	2	11	4	18	.261	.306	.380	85	-2	3	0	1	.985	-9	O-46/D-3	-1.1
Total	6	172	320	39	66	10	2	8	32	31	55	.206	.280	.325	64	-16	5	3	-0	.991	-31	O-151/D-6	-5.1

■ JUSTIN STEIN
Stein, Justin Marion "Ott" b: 8/9/11, St.Louis, Mo. d: 5/1/92, Crove Coeur, Mo. BR/TR, 5'11", 180 lbs. Deb: 5/28/38

YEAR	TM/L	G	AB	R	H	2B	3B	HR	RBI	BB	SO	AVG	OBP	SLG	PRO+	BR/A	SB	CS	SBR	FA	FR	G/POS	TPR
1938	Phi-N	11	39	6	10	0	1	0	2	2	4	.256	.293	.308	67	-2	0			.880	0	/3-7,2-3	-0.2
	Cin-N	11	18	3	6	1	0	0	1	0	1	.333	.333	.389	101	-0	0			.857	1	/S-7,2-2	0.1
	Yr	22	57	9	16	1	1	0	3	2	5	.281	.305	.333	78	-2	0			.857	1	/3-7,S-7,2-5	-0.1

■ BILL STEIN
Stein, William Allen b: 1/21/47, Battle Creek, Mich. BR/TR, 5'10", 170 lbs. Deb: 9/6/72

YEAR	TM/L	G	AB	R	H	2B	3B	HR	RBI	BB	SO	AVG	OBP	SLG	PRO+	BR/A	SB	CS	SBR	FA	FR	G/POS	TPR
1972	StL-N	14	35	2	11	0	1	2	3	0	7	.314	.314	.543	141	2	1	0	0	1.000	-3	/3-4,O-4	-0.2
1973	StL-N	32	55	4	12	2	0	0	2	7	18	.218	.306	.255	57	-3	0	0	0	1.000	-2	O-10/1-2,3-1	-0.5
1974	Chi-A	13	43	5	12	1	0	0	5	7	8	.279	.380	.302	96	0	0	0	0	.871	-2	3-11/D-2	-0.2
1975	Chi-A	76	226	23	61	7	1	3	21	18	32	.270	.327	.350	90	-3	2	2	-1	.974	3	2-28,3-24,D-18,/O-1	0.1
1976	Chi-A	117	392	32	105	15	2	4	36	22	67	.268	.310	.347	92	-5	4	2	0	.960	-11	2-58,3-58/1-1,SOD	-1.3
1977	Sea-A	151	556	53	144	26	5	13	67	29	79	.259	.302	.394	89	-10	3	4	-2	.964	-11	*3-147/S-2,D-3	-2.4
1978	Sea-A	114	403	41	105	24	4	4	37	37	56	.261	.323	.370	95	-3	1	0	0	.929	-6	*3-111/D-1	-1.0
1979	Sea-A	88	250	28	62	9	2	7	27	17	28	.248	.301	.384	82	-7	1	2	-1	.959	11	3-67,2-17/S-3	0.3

YEAR	TM/L	G	AB	R	H	2B	3B	HR	RBI	BB	SO	AVG	OBP	SLG	PRO+	BR/A	SB	CS	SBR	FA	FR	G/POS	TPR
1980	Sea-A	67	198	16	53	5	1	5	27	16	25	.268	.326	.379	92	-2	1	1	-0	.972	5	3-34,2-14/1-8,D-5	0.3
1981	Tex-A	53	115	21	38	6	0	2	22	7	15	.330	.369	.435	138	5	1	2	-1	1.000	1	1-20/O-8,3-7,2-3,S	0.4
1982	Tex-A	85	184	14	44	8	0	1	16	12	23	.239	.293	.299	66	-8	0	0	0	.957	3	2-34,3-28/S-6,1OD	-0.5
1983	Tex-A	78	232	21	72	15	1	2	33	8	31	.310	.333	.409	105	1	2	3	-1	.975	0	2-32,1-23,3-10,/D-6	0.0
1984	Tex-A	27	43	3	12	1	0	0	3	5	9	.279	.354	.302	81	-1	0	0	0	.967	-3	2-11/1-3,3-3,D-4	-0.3
1985	Tex-A	44	79	5	20	3	1	1	12	1	15	.253	.272	.354	69	-3	0	0	0	.952	1	3-11/1-8,2-3,O-3,D	-0.3
Total	14	959	2811	268	751	122	18	44	311	186	413	.267	.316	.370	91	-37	16	16	-5	.950	-13	3-516,2-200/1DOS	-5.6

■ **TERRY STEINBACH** Steinbach, Terry Lee b: 3/2/62, New Ulm, Minn. BR/TR, 6'1", 195 lbs. Deb: 9/12/86

YEAR	TM/L	G	AB	R	H	2B	3B	HR	RBI	BB	SO	AVG	OBP	SLG	PRO+	BR/A	SB	CS	SBR	FA	FR	G/POS	TPR
1986	Oak-A	6	15	3	5	0	0	2	4	1	0	.333	.375	.733	208	2	0	0	0	.962	-0	/C-5	0.2
1987	Oak-A	122	391	66	111	16	3	16	56	32	66	.284	.352	.463	122	12	1	2	-1	.986	-12	*C-107,3-10/1-1,D-8	0.6
1988	*Oak-A★	104	351	42	93	19	1	9	51	33	47	.265	.338	.402	110	5	3	0	1	.983	5	C-84/3-9,1-8,O-1,D	1.6
1989	*Oak-A★	130	454	37	124	13	1	7	42	30	66	.273	.321	.352	93	-5	1	2	-1	.985	-7	*C-103,O-14,1/3D	-0.7
1990	*Oak-A	114	379	32	95	15	2	9	57	19	66	.251	.294	.372	89	-7	0	1	-1	.988	-4	C-83,D-25/1-3	-0.7
1991	Oak-A	129	456	50	125	31	1	6	67	22	70	.274	.318	.386	99	-2	2	2	-1	.980	-24	*C-117/1-9,D-2	-2.0
1992	*Oak-A	128	438	48	122	20	1	12	53	45	58	.279	.347	.411	118	10	2	3	-1	.985	-4	*C-124/1-5,D-2	1.2
1993	Oak-A★	104	389	47	111	19	1	10	43	25	65	.285	.333	.416	107	3	3	3	-1	.989	-22	C-86,1-15/D-6	-1.6
1994	Oak-A	103	369	51	105	21	2	11	57	26	62	.285	.332	.442	106	2	2	1	0	**.998**	-2	C-93/1-6,D-6	0.5
1995	Oak-A	114	406	43	113	26	1	15	65	25	74	.278	.325	.458	107	2	1	3	-2	.993	-2	*C-111/1-2	0.6
1996	Oak-A	145	514	79	140	25	1	35	100	49	115	.272	.343	.529	118	12	0	1	-1	.991	-10	*C-137/1-1,D-4	0.8
1997	Min-A	122	447	60	111	27	1	12	54	35	106	.248	.304	.394	79	-14	6	1	1	.993	-9	*C-116/1-2,D-1	-1.4
1998	Min-A	124	422	45	102	25	2	14	54	38	89	.242	.310	.410	85	-10	0	1	-1	.990	-10	*C-119/D-3	-1.3
Total	13	1445	5031	603	1357	257	17	158	703	380	884	.270	.327	.422	103	11	21	20	-6	.989	-102	*C-1285/D-68,13O	-2.2

■ **HANK STEINBACHER** Steinbacher, Henry John b: 3/22/13, Sacramento, Cal. d: 4/3/77, Sacramento, Cal. BL/TR, 5'11", 180 lbs. Deb: 4/21/37

YEAR	TM/L	G	AB	R	H	2B	3B	HR	RBI	BB	SO	AVG	OBP	SLG	PRO+	BR/A	SB	CS	SBR	FA	FR	G/POS	TPR
1937	Chi-A	26	73	13	19	4	1	1	9	4	7	.260	.299	.384	71	-4	2	0	1	.960	-2	O-15	-0.5
1938	Chi-A	106	399	59	132	23	8	4	61	41	19	.331	.393	.459	110	7	1	3	-2	.963	-4	*O-101	-0.2
1939	Chi-A	71	111	16	19	2	1	1	15	21	8	.171	.303	.234	38	-10	0	0	0	1.000	-2	O-22	-1.2
Total	3	203	583	88	170	29	10	6	85	66	34	.292	.364	.407	92	-7	3	3	-1	.968	-8	O-138	-1.9

■ **GENE STEINBRENNER** Steinbrenner, Eugene Gass b: 11/17/1892, Pittsburgh, Pa. d: 4/25/70, Pittsburgh, Pa. BR/TR, 5'8.5", 155 lbs. Deb: 4/25/12

YEAR	TM/L	G	AB	R	H	2B	3B	HR	RBI	BB	SO	AVG	OBP	SLG	PRO+	BR/A	SB	CS	SBR	FA	FR	G/POS	TPR
1912	Phi-N	3	9	0	2	1	0	0	1	0	3	.222	.222	.333	48	-1	0			.900	-1	/2-3	-0.1

■ **BILL STEINECKE** Steinecke, William Robert b: 2/7/07, Cincinnati, Ohio d: 7/20/86, St.Augustine, Fla BR/TR, 5'8.5", 175 lbs. Deb: 9/16/31

YEAR	TM/L	G	AB	R	H	2B	3B	HR	RBI	BB	SO	AVG	OBP	SLG	PRO+	BR/A	SB	CS	SBR	FA	FR	G/POS	TPR
1931	Pit-N	4	4	0	0	0	0	0	0	0	1	.000	.000	.000	-99	-1	0			.000	0	/C-1	-0.1

■ **BEN STEINER** Steiner, Benjamin Saunders b: 7/28/21, Alexandria, Va. d: 10/27/88, Venice, Fla. BL/TR, 5'11", 165 lbs. Deb: 4/17/45

YEAR	TM/L	G	AB	R	H	2B	3B	HR	RBI	BB	SO	AVG	OBP	SLG	PRO+	BR/A	SB	CS	SBR	FA	FR	G/POS	TPR
1945	Bos-A	78	304	39	78	8	3	3	20	31	29	.257	.327	.332	89	-4	10	6	-1	.967	-4	2-77	-0.4
1946	Bos-A	3	4	1	1	0	0	0	0	0	0	.250	.250	.250	38	-0	0	0	0	.750	0	/3-1	0.0
1947	Det-A	1	0	1	0	0	0	0	0	0	0	—	—	—	—	0	0	0	0	.000	0	R	0.0
Total	3	82	308	41	79	8	3	3	20	31	29	.256	.326	.331	89	-4	10	6	-1	.967	-4	/2-77,3-1	-0.4

■ **RED STEINER** Steiner, James Harry b: 1/7/15, Los Angeles, Cal. BL/TR, 6', 185 lbs. Deb: 5/11/45

YEAR	TM/L	G	AB	R	H	2B	3B	HR	RBI	BB	SO	AVG	OBP	SLG	PRO+	BR/A	SB	CS	SBR	FA	FR	G/POS	TPR
1945	Cle-A	12	20	0	3	0	0	0	2	1	4	.150	.190	.150	-1	-3	0	0	0	1.000	1	/C-4	-0.2
	Bos-A	26	59	6	12	1	0	0	4	14	2	.203	.356	.220	67	-2	0	0	0	.986	-5	C-24	-0.6
	Yr	38	79	6	15	1	0	0	6	15	6	.190	.319	.203	52	-4	0	0	0	.989	-4	C-28	-0.8

■ **HARRY STEINFELDT** Steinfeldt, Harry M. b: 9/29/1877, St.Louis, Mo. d: 8/17/14, Bellevue, Ky. BR/TR, 5'9.5", 180 lbs. Deb: 4/22/1898

YEAR	TM/L	G	AB	R	H	2B	3B	HR	RBI	BB	SO	AVG	OBP	SLG	PRO+	BR/A	SB	CS	SBR	FA	FR	G/POS	TPR
1898	Cin-N	88	308	47	91	18	6	0	43	27		.295	.354	.393	107	2	9			.917	-1	2-31,O-29,3-22,/S1	0.1
1899	Cin-N	107	386	62	94	16	8	0	43	40		.244	.324	.326	77	-12	19			.885	-6	3-59,2-40/S-8,O-2	-1.4
1900	Cin-N	134	510	57	125	29	7	2	66	27		.245	.292	.341	76	-18	14			.922	**36**	3-67,2-64/O-2,S-2	1.9
1901	Cin-N	105	382	40	95	18	7	6	47	28		.249	.303	.380	104	1	10			.886	10	3-55,2-50	1.3
1902	Cin-N	129	479	53	133	20	7	1	49	24		.278	.316	.355	98	-3	12			.912	22	*3-129/O-1	2.1
1903	Cin-N	118	439	71	137	**32**	12	6	83	47		.312	.386	.481	132	16	6			.937	7	*3-104,S-14	2.4
1904	Cin-N	99	349	35	85	11	6	1	52	29		.244	.313	.318	87	-5	16			.887	-7	3-98	-1.0
1905	Cin-N	114	384	49	104	16	9	1	39	30		.271	.329	.367	97	-3	15			.919	14	*3-103/1-1,2-1,O-1	1.6
1906	*Chi-N	151	539	81	**176**	27	10	3	**83**	47		.327	.395	.430	149	31	29			**.954**	-17	*3-150/2-1	2.0
1907	*Chi-N	152	542	52	144	25	5	1	70	37		.266	.323	.336	100	-0	19			**.967**	-5	*3-151	-0.1
1908	*Chi-N	150	539	63	130	20	6	1	62	36		.241	.294	.306	88	-8	12			.940	-12	*3-150	-1.6
1909	Chi-N	151	528	73	133	27	6	2	59	57		.252	.331	.337	105	3	22			.940	2	*3-151	1.1
1910	*Chi-N	129	448	70	113	21	1	2	58	36	29	.252	.323	.317	88	-7	10			**.946**	0	*3-128	-0.4
1911	Bos-N	19	63	5	16	4	0	1	8	6	3	.254	.338	.365	89	-1	1			.810	-5	3-19	-0.6
Total	14	1646	5896	758	1576	284	90	27	762	471	32	.267	.330	.360	101	-4	194			.926	38	*3-1386,2-187/OS1	7.4

■ **BILL STELLBAUER** Stellbauer, William Jennings b: 3/20/1894, Bremond, Tex. d: 2/16/74, New Braunfels, Tex BR/TR, 5'10", 175 lbs. Deb: 4/12/16

YEAR	TM/L	G	AB	R	H	2B	3B	HR	RBI	BB	SO	AVG	OBP	SLG	PRO+	BR/A	SB	CS	SBR	FA	FR	G/POS	TPR
1916	Phi-A	25	48	2	13	2	1	0	5	6	7	.271	.352	.354	118	1	2			.857	-4	O-14	-0.3

■ **RICK STELMASZEK** Stelmaszek, Richard Francis b: 10/8/48, Chicago, Ill. BL/TR, 6'1", 195 lbs. Deb: 6/25/71 C

YEAR	TM/L	G	AB	R	H	2B	3B	HR	RBI	BB	SO	AVG	OBP	SLG	PRO+	BR/A	SB	CS	SBR	FA	FR	G/POS	TPR
1971	Was-A	6	9	0	0	0	0	0	0	0	3	.000	.000	.000	-99	-2	0	0	0	1.000	-1	/C-3	-0.3
1973	Tex-A	7	9	0	1	0	0	0	0	1	2	.111	.200	.111	-11	-1	0	0	0	1.000	-0	/C-7	-0.1
	Cal-A	22	26	2	4	1	0	0	3	6	7	.154	.313	.192	49	-2	0	0	0	1.000	-2	C-22	-0.3
	Yr	29	35	2	5	1	0	0	3	7	9	.143	.286	.171	34	-3	0	0	0	1.000	-2	C-29	-0.4
1974	Chi-N	25	44	2	10	2	0	1	7	10	6	.227	.370	.341	96	0	0	0	0	.983	-6	C-16	-0.5
Total	3	60	88	4	15	3	0	1	10	17	18	.170	.305	.239	55	-5	0	0	0	.993	-9	/C-48	-1.2

■ **FRED STEM** Stem, Frederick Boothe b: 9/22/1885, Oxford, N.C. d: 9/5/64, Darlington, S.C. BL/TR, 6'2", 160 lbs. Deb: 9/15/08

YEAR	TM/L	G	AB	R	H	2B	3B	HR	RBI	BB	SO	AVG	OBP	SLG	PRO+	BR/A	SB	CS	SBR	FA	FR	G/POS	TPR
1908	Bos-N	20	72	9	20	0	1	0	3	2		.278	.297	.306	94	-1	1			.995	-1	1-19	-0.2
1909	Bos-N	73	245	13	51	2	3	0	11	12		.208	.254	.241	51	-14	5			.989	10	1-68	-0.5
Total	2	93	317	22	71	2	4	0	14	14		.224	.263	.256	60	-15	6			.990	10	/1-87	-0.7

■ **CASEY STENGEL** Stengel, Charles Dillon "The Old Professor"
b: 7/30/1890, Kansas City, Mo. d: 9/29/75, Glendale, Cal. BL/TL, 5'11", 175 lbs. Deb: 9/17/12 MCH

YEAR	TM/L	G	AB	R	H	2B	3B	HR	RBI	BB	SO	AVG	OBP	SLG	PRO+	BR/A	SB	CS	SBR	FA	FR	G/POS	TPR
1912	Bro-N	17	57	9	18	1	0	1	13	15	9	.316	.466	.386	140	5	5			.902	-2	O-17	0.2
1913	Bro-N	124	438	60	119	16	8	7	43	56	58	.272	.356	.393	110	7	19			.960	2	*O-119	0.3
1914	Bro-N	126	412	55	130	13	10	4	60	56	55	.316	**.404**	.425	143	24	19			.964	-8	*O-121	1.1
1915	Bro-N	132	459	52	109	20	12	3	50	34	46	.237	.294	.353	94	-4	5	10	-5	.959	0	*O-129	-1.6
1916	*Bro-N	127	462	66	129	27	8	8	53	33	51	.279	.329	.424	127	13	11			.965	3	*O-121	1.1
1917	Bro-N	150	549	69	141	23	12	6	73	60	62	.257	.336	.375	115	10	18			.969	13	*O-150	1.6
1918	Pit-N	39	122	18	30	4	1	1	12	16	14	.246	.343	.320	99	0	11			.973	2	O-37	0.1
1919	Pit-N	89	321	38	94	10	10	4	43	35	35	.293	.364	.424	131	13	12			.957	3	O-87	1.0
1920	Phi-N	129	445	53	130	25	6	9	50	38	35	.292	.356	.436	121	12	7	13	-6	.954	-3	*O-118	-0.5
1921	Phi-N	24	59	7	18	3	1	0	4	6	7	.305	.369	.390	94	-0	1	1	-0	.969	2	O-15	0.1
	NY-N	18	22	4	5	1	0	0	2	1	5	.227	.261	.273	41	-2	0	1	-1	.875	-3	/O-8	-0.6
	Yr	42	81	11	23	4	1	0	6	7	12	.284	.341	.358	81	-2	1	2	-1	.950	-0	O-23	-0.5
1922	*NY-N	84	250	48	92	8	10	7	48	21	17	.368	.436	.564	155	21	4	2	0	.969	-4	O-77	1.1
1923	*NY-N	75	218	39	74	11	5	5	43	20	18	.339	.400	.505	139	12	6	2	1	.983	-7	O-57	0.3
1924	Bos-N	131	461	57	129	20	6	5	39	45	39	.280	.348	.382	100	0	13	13	-4	.978	-7	*O-126	-1.9
1925	Bos-N	12	13	0	1	0	0	0	2	1	2	.077	.143	.077	-46	-3	0	1	-1	1.000	-0	/O-1	-0.4
Total	14	1277	4288	575	1219	182	89	60	535	437	453	.284	.356	.410	119	107	131	43		.964	-9	*O-1183	1.9

■ **MIKE STENHOUSE** Stenhouse, Michael Steven b: 5/29/58, Pueblo, Colo. BL/TR, 6'1", 195 lbs. Deb: 10/3/82 F

YEAR	TM/L	G	AB	R	H	2B	3B	HR	RBI	BB	SO	AVG	OBP	SLG	PRO+	BR/A	SB	CS	SBR	FA	FR	G/POS	TPR
1982	Mon-N	1	1	0	0	0	0	0	0	0	1	.000	.000	.000	-98	-0	0	0	0	.000	0	/H	0.0

YEAR	TM/L	G	AB	R	H	2B	3B	HR	RBI	BB	SO	AVG	OBP	SLG	PRO+	BR/A	SB	CS	SBR	FA	FR	G/POS	TPR
1983	Mon-N	24	40	2	5	1	0	0	2	4	10	.125	.205	.150	-0	-5	0	0	0	1.000	-3	/O-9,1-5	-0.9
1984	Mon-N	80	175	14	32	8	0	4	16	26	32	.183	.292	.297	69	-7	0	0	0	.986	-3	O-48,1-14	-1.2
1985	Min-A	81	179	23	40	5	0	5	21	29	18	.223	.332	.335	79	-5	1	0	0	.929	0	D-27,O-16/1-8	-0.6
1986	Bos-A	21	21	1	2	1	0	0	1	12	5	.095	.424	.143	63	-0	0	0	0	1.000	-0	/O-4,1-3	-0.1
Total	5	207	416	40	79	15	0	9	40	71	66	.190	.309	.291	67	-18	1	0	0	.973	-5	/O-77,1-30,D-27	-2.8

■ RENNIE STENNETT

Stennett, Renaldo Antonio (Porte) b: 4/5/51, Colon, Panama BR/TR, 5'11", 175 lbs. Deb: 7/10/71

YEAR	TM/L	G	AB	R	H	2B	3B	HR	RBI	BB	SO	AVG	OBP	SLG	PRO+	BR/A	SB	CS	SBR	FA	FR	G/POS	TPR
1971	Pit-N	50	153	24	54	5	4	1	15	7	9	.353	.381	.458	137	7	1	1	-0	.954	2	2-36	1.2
1972	*Pit-N	109	370	43	106	14	5	3	30	9	43	.286	.307	.376	95	-4	4	3	-1	.977	6	2-49,O-41/S-6	0.4
1973	Pit-N	128	466	45	113	18	3	10	55	16	63	.242	.268	.358	74	-18	2	3	-1	.981	-0	2-84,S-43/O-5	-1.0
1974	*Pit-N	157	673	84	196	29	3	7	56	32	51	.291	.325	.374	99	-3	8	9	-3	.980	13	*2-154/O-2	1.5
1975	*Pit-N	148	616	89	176	25	7	7	62	33	42	.286	.326	.383	97	-4	5	4	-1	.979	13	*2-144	1.6
1976	Pit-N	157	654	59	168	31	9	2	60	19	32	.257	.279	.341	75	-23	18	6	2	.981	17	*2-157/S-4	0.6
1977	Pit-N	116	453	53	152	20	4	5	51	29	24	.336	.378	.430	113	9	28	18	-2	.982	-7	*2-113	0.8
1978	Pit-N	106	333	30	81	9	2	3	35	13	22	.243	.276	.309	60	-18	2	1	0	.971	-12	2-80/3-6	-2.5
1979	*Pit-N	108	319	31	76	13	2	0	24	24	25	.238	.292	.292	57	-19	1	4	-2	.974	6	*2-102	-0.9
1980	SF-N	120	397	34	97	13	2	2	37	22	31	.244	.287	.302	66	-18	4	4	-1	.973	-13	*2-111	-2.8
1981	SF-N	38	87	8	20	0	0	1	7	3	6	.230	.264	.264	51	-6	2	1	0	1.000	-2	2-19	-0.7
Total	11	1237	4521	500	1239	177	41	41	432	207	348	.274	.308	.359	85	-96	75	54	-10	.978	23	*2-1049/S-53,O-48,3	-1.8

■ JAKE STENZEL

Stenzel, Jacob Charles (b: Jacob Charles Stelzle)
b: 6/24/1867, Cincinnati, Ohio d: 1/6/19, Cincinnati, Ohio BR/TR, 5'10", 168 lbs. Deb: 6/16/1890

YEAR	TM/L	G	AB	R	H	2B	3B	HR	RBI	BB	SO	AVG	OBP	SLG	PRO+	BR/A	SB	CS	SBR	FA	FR	G/POS	TPR
1890	Chi-N	11	41	3	11	1	0	0	3	1	0	.268	.286	.293	66	-2	0			.857	-4	/O-6,C-6	-0.4
1892	Pit-N	3	9	0	0	0	0	0	0	1	3	.000	.100	.000	-69	-2	1			1.000	0	/O-2,C-1	-0.1
1893	Pit-N	60	224	57	81	13	4	4	37	24	17	.362	.423	.509	150	16	16			.905	-9	O-45,C-12/S-1,2-1	0.4
1894	Pit-N	131	522	148	185	39	20	13	121	75	13	.354	.441	.580	146	40	61			.925	-1	*O-131	2.2
1895	Pit-N	129	514	114	192	38	13	7	97	57	25	.374	.447	.539	162	50	53			.912	-5	*O-129	2.8
1896	Pit-N	114	479	104	173	26	14	2	82	32	13	.361	.410	.486	141	28	57			.922	-3	*O-114/1-1	1.3
1897	*Bal-N	131	536	113	189	**43**	7	4	116	36		.353	.404	.481	133	25	69			.932	-11	*O-131	0.4
1898	Bal-N	35	138	33	35	5	2	0	22	12		.254	.340	.319	87	-2	4			.926	-2	O-35	-0.6
	StL-N	108	404	64	114	15	11	1	33	41		.282	.367	.381	112	7	21			.943	0	*O-108	-0.1
	Yr	143	542	97	149	20	13	1	55	53		.275	.360	.365	106	5	25			.940	-2	*O-143	-0.7
1899	StL-N	35	128	21	35	9	0	1	19	16		.273	.367	.367	99	0	8			.949	-1	O-33	-0.3
	Cin-N	9	29	5	9	1	0	0	3	4		.310	.412	.345	106	1	2			1.000	-1	/O-7	-0.1
	Yr	44	157	26	44	10	0	1	22	20		.280	.376	.363	101	1	10			.957	-2	O-40	-0.4
Total	9	766	3024	662	1024	190	71	32	533	299	71	.339	.408	.480	135	161	292			.927	-36	O-741/C-19,1-1,2S	5.5

■ RAY STEPHENS

Stephens, Carl Ray b: 9/22/62, Houston, Tex. BR/TR, 6', 190 lbs. Deb: 9/20/90

YEAR	TM/L	G	AB	R	H	2B	3B	HR	RBI	BB	SO	AVG	OBP	SLG	PRO+	BR/A	SB	CS	SBR	FA	FR	G/POS	TPR
1990	StL-N	5	15	2	2	1	0	1	1	0	3	.133	.133	.400	41	-1	0	0	0	1.000	2	/C-5	0.1
1991	StL-N	6	7	0	2	0	0	0	0	1	3	.286	.375	.286	88	-0	0	0	0	1.000	1	/C-6	0.1
1992	Tex-A	8	13	0	2	0	0	0	0	0	5	.154	.154	.154	-14	-2	0	0	0	1.000	-0	/C-6,D-1	-0.2
Total	3	19	35	2	6	1	0	1	1	1	11	.171	.194	.286	32	-3	0	0	0	1.000	3	/C-17,D-1	0.0

■ GENE STEPHENS

Stephens, Glen Eugene b: 1/20/33, Gravette, Ark. BL/TR, 6'3.5", 175 lbs. Deb: 4/16/52

YEAR	TM/L	G	AB	R	H	2B	3B	HR	RBI	BB	SO	AVG	OBP	SLG	PRO+	BR/A	SB	CS	SBR	FA	FR	G/POS	TPR
1952	Bos-A	21	53	10	12	5	0	0	5	3	8	.226	.268	.321	59	-3	4	2	0	.962	0	O-13	-0.4
1953	Bos-A	78	221	30	45	6	2	3	18	29	56	.204	.302	.290	57	-13	3	3	-1	.966	-7	O-72	-2.3
1955	Bos-A	109	157	25	46	9	4	3	18	20	34	.293	.380	.459	114	3	0	0	0	.947	-11	O-75	-0.9
1956	Bos-A	104	63	22	17	2	0	1	7	12	12	.270	.387	.349	85	-1	0	1	-1	.983	-17	O-71	-1.8
1957	Bos-A	120	173	25	46	6	4	3	26	26	20	.266	.362	.399	102	1	0	2	-1	.987	-19	O-90	-2.2
1958	Bos-A	134	270	38	59	10	1	9	25	22	46	.219	.280	.363	71	-11	1	2	-1	.975	-16	*O-110	-3.3
1959	Bos-A	92	270	34	75	13	1	3	39	29	33	.278	.356	.367	95	-1	5	2	0	.981	1	O-85	-0.3
1960	Bos-A	35	109	9	25	4	0	2	11	14	22	.229	.317	.321	71	-4	5	1	1	.951	-1	O-31	-0.6
	Bal-A	84	193	38	46	11	0	5	11	25	25	.238	.329	.373	91	-2	4	2	0	.992	-10	O-77	-1.6
	Yr	119	302	47	71	15	0	7	22	39	47	.235	.325	.354	83	-7	9	3	1	.979	-11	*O-108	-2.2
1961	Bal-A	32	58	4	11	2	0	0	2	14	7	.190	.347	.224	58	-3	1	1	-0	1.000	-6	O-30	-1.0
	KC-A	62	183	22	38	6	1	4	26	16	27	.208	.279	.317	58	-11	3	2	-0	.968	1	O-54	-1.3
	Yr	94	241	26	49	8	1	4	28	30	34	.203	.297	.295	59	-14	4	3	-1	.975	-5	O-84	-2.3
1962	KC-A	5	4	0	0	0	0	0	0	1	1	.000	.200	.000	-39	-1	0	0	0	.000	0	H	-0.1
1963	Chi-A	6	18	5	7	0	0	1	2	1	3	.389	.421	.556	174	2	0	0	0	.909	1	/O-5	0.3
1964	Chi-A	82	141	21	33	4	2	3	17	21	28	.234	.341	.355	97	-0	1	2	-1	.969	-5	O-59	-0.9
Total	12	964	1913	283	460	78	15	37	207	233	322	.240	.327	.355	82	-45	27	20	-4	.973	-87	O-772	-16.4

■ JIM STEPHENS

Stephens, James Walter "Little Nemo" b: 12/10/1883, Salineville, Ohio d: 1/2/65, Oxford, Ala. BR/TR, 5'6.5", 157 lbs. Deb: 4/11/07

YEAR	TM/L	G	AB	R	H	2B	3B	HR	RBI	BB	SO	AVG	OBP	SLG	PRO+	BR/A	SB	CS	SBR	FA	FR	G/POS	TPR
1907	StL-A	58	173	15	35	6	3	0	11	15		.202	.270	.272	73	-5	3			.967	-4	C-56	-0.5
1908	StL-A	47	150	14	30	4	1	0	6	9		.200	.255	.240	61	-6	0			.960	-0	C-45	-0.3
1909	StL-A	79	223	18	49	5	0	3	18	13		.220	.278	.283	83	-5	5			.980	3	C-72	0.5
1910	StL-A	99	289	24	62	3	7	0	23	16		.215	.261	.273	72	-10	2			.971	2	C-96	0.1
1911	StL-A	70	212	11	49	5	5	0	17	17		.231	.300	.302	71	-8	1			.949	-2	C-66	-0.4
1912	StL-A	75	205	13	51	7	5	0	22	7		.249	.274	.332	76	-8	3			.954	4	C-66	0.2
Total	6	428	1252	95	276	30	21	3	97	77		.220	.273	.285	73	-42	14			.965	3	C-401	-0.4

■ VERN STEPHENS

Stephens, Vernon Decatur "Junior" or "Buster"
b: 10/23/20, McAlister, N.Mex. d: 11/3/68, Long Beach, Cal. BR/TR, 5'10", 185 lbs. Deb: 9/13/41

YEAR	TM/L	G	AB	R	H	2B	3B	HR	RBI	BB	SO	AVG	OBP	SLG	PRO+	BR/A	SB	CS	SBR	FA	FR	G/POS	TPR
1941	StL-A	3	2	0	1	0	0	0	0	0	0	.500	.500	.500	160	0	0	0	0	.500	-0	/S-1	0.0
1942	StL-A	145	575	84	169	26	6	14	92	41	53	.294	.341	.433	115	9	1	3	-2	.944	-10	*S-144	0.7
1943	StL-A★	137	512	75	148	27	3	22	91	54	73	.289	.357	.482	142	25	3	2	-0	.943	-25	*S-123,O-11	0.8
1944	*StL-A★	145	559	91	164	32	1	20	**109**	62	54	.293	.365	.462	128	19	2	2	-1	.954	-4	*S-143	2.7
1945	StL-A†	149	571	90	165	27	3	**24**	89	55	70	.289	.352	.473	132	21	2	1	0	**.961**	-17	*S-144/3-4	1.7
1946	StL-A★	115	450	67	138	19	4	14	64	35	49	.307	.357	.460	121	11	0	1	-1	.950	0	*S-112	1.8
1947	StL-A	150	562	74	157	18	4	15	83	70	61	.279	.359	.406	110	8	8	4	0	.970	12	*S-149	2.9
1948	Bos-A★	155	635	114	171	25	8	29	137	77	56	.269	.350	.471	112	7	1	0	0	.971	10	*S-155	2.6
1949	Bos-A★	155	610	113	177	31	2	39	**159**	101	73	.290	.391	.539	135	28	2	2	-1	.966	4	*S-155	4.1
1950	Bos-A☆	149	628	125	185	34	6	30	**144**	65	43	.295	.361	.511	110	6	1	0	0	.981	-0	*S-146	1.6
1951	Bos-A★	109	377	62	113	21	2	17	78	38	33	.300	.364	.501	120	9	1	2	-1	.978	14	3-89/S-2	2.1
1952	Bos-A	92	295	35	75	13	2	7	44	39	31	.254	.343	.383	95	-2	2	2	-1	.957	4	S-53,3-29	0.5
1953	Chi-A	44	129	14	24	6	0	1	14	13	18	.186	.261	.256	39	-11	2	0	1	.990	-3	3-38/S-3	-1.4
	StL-A	46	165	16	53	8	0	4	17	18	24	.321	.388	.442	121	5	0	0	0	.954	-2	3-46	0.2
	Yr	90	294	30	77	14	0	5	31	31	42	.262	.332	.361	85	-6	2	0	1	.968	-5	3-84/S-3	-1.2
1954	Bal-A	101	365	31	104	17	1	8	46	17	36	.285	.317	.403	104	-1	0	3	-2	.966	-6	3-96	-1.1
1955	Bal-A	3	6	0	1	0	0	0	0	0	0	.167	.286	.167	26	-1	0	0	0	1.000	-1	/3-2	-0.1
	Chi-A	22	56	10	14	3	0	3	7	7	11	.250	.333	.464	110	1	0	0	0	1.000	4	3-18	0.5
	Yr	25	62	10	15	3	0	3	7	7	11	.242	.329	.435	102	0	0	0	0	1.000	4	3-20	0.4
Total	15	1720	6497	1001	1859	307	42	247	1174	692	685	.286	.355	.460	118	137	25	22	-6	.960	-20	*S-1330,3-322/O-11	19.6

■ RIGGS STEPHENSON

Stephenson, Jackson Riggs "Old Hoss" b: 1/5/1898, Akron, Ala. d: 11/15/85, Tuscaloosa, Ala. BR/TR, 5'10", 185 lbs. Deb: 4/13/21

YEAR	TM/L	G	AB	R	H	2B	3B	HR	RBI	BB	SO	AVG	OBP	SLG	PRO+	BR/A	SB	CS	SBR	FA	FR	G/POS	TPR
1921	Cle-A	65	206	45	68	17	2	2	34	23	15	.330	.408	.461	119	7	4	1	1	.942	-1	2-54/3-2	0.7
1922	Cle-A	86	233	47	79	24	5	2	32	27	18	.339	.421	.511	141	15	3	0	1	.952	-6	3-34,2-25/O-3	1.2
1923	Cle-A	91	301	48	96	20	6	5	65	15	25	.319	.357	.475	118	6	5	5	-2	.970	11	2-66/O-3,3-2	1.6
1924	Cle-A	71	240	33	89	20	0	4	44	27	10	.371	.439	.504	141	15	1	2	-1	.961	-13	2-58/O-7	0.1
1925	Cle-A	19	54	8	16	3	1	1	9	7	3	.296	.387	.444	110	1	1	1	-0	.946	1	O-16	0.1
1926	Chi-N	82	281	40	95	18	3	3	44	31	16	.338	.404	.456	129	12	2			.950	-4	O-74	0.4

YEAR	TM/L	G	AB	R	H	2B	3B	HR	RBI	BB	SO	AVG	OBP	SLG	PRO+	BR/A	SB	CS	SBR	FA	FR	G/POS	TPR
1927	Chi-N	152	579	101	199	**46**	9	7	82	65	28	.344	.415	.491	142	36	8			.975	4	*O-146/3-6	3.0
1928	Chi-N	137	512	75	166	36	9	8	90	68	29	.324	.407	.477	132	25	8			.982	0	*O-135	1.6
1929	*Chi-N	136	495	91	179	36	6	17	110	67	21	.362	.445	.562	147	39	10			.984	-0	*O-130	2.7
1930	Chi-N	109	341	56	125	21	1	5	68	32	20	.367	.421	.478	116	10	2			.958	-5	O-80	0.0
1931	Chi-N	80	263	34	84	14	4	1	52	37	14	.319	.405	.414	119	9	1			.985	-2	O-66	0.2
1932	*Chi-N	147	583	86	189	49	4	4	85	54	27	.324	.383	.443	123	20	3			.984	-5	*O-147	0.5
1933	Chi-N	97	346	45	114	17	4	4	51	34	16	.329	.397	.436	138	18	5			.985	-2	O-91	1.2
1934	Chi-N	38	74	5	16	0	0	0	7	7	5	.216	.293	.216	39	-6	0			1.000	1	O-15	-0.5
Total	14	1310	4508	714	1515	321	54	63	773	494	247	.336	.407	.473	130	206	53	9		.978	-21	O-913,2-203/3-44	12.8

■ JOHN STEPHENSON Stephenson, John Herman b: 4/13/41, S.Portsmouth, Ky. BL/TR, 5'11", 180 lbs. Deb: 4/14/64

YEAR	TM/L	G	AB	R	H	2B	3B	HR	RBI	BB	SO	AVG	OBP	SLG	PRO+	BR/A	SB	CS	SBR	FA	FR	G/POS	TPR
1964	NY-N	37	57	2	9	0	0	1	2	4	18	.158	.226	.211	24	-6	0	0	0	.800	-4	3-14/O-8	-1.1
1965	NY-N	62	121	9	26	5	0	4	15	8	19	.215	.264	.355	75	-4	0	1	-1	.981	-9	C-47/O-2	-1.3
1966	NY-N	63	143	17	28	1	1	1	11	8	28	.196	.248	.238	37	-12	0	0	0	.973	-1	C-52/O-1	-1.2
1967	Chi-N	18	49	3	11	3	1	0	5	1	6	.224	.255	.327	62	-2	0	0	0	1.000	1	C-13	-0.1
1968	Chi-N	2	2	0	0	0	0	0	0	0	0	.000	.000	.000	-94	-0	0	0	0	.000	0	H	-0.1
1969	SF-N	22	27	2	6	2	0	0	3	0	4	.222	.222	.296	45	-2	0	0	0	.941	-3	/C-9,3-1	-0.5
1970	SF-N	23	43	3	3	1	0	0	6	2	7	.070	.111	.093	-45	-9	0	0	0	1.000	2	/C-9,O-1	-0.6
1971	Cal-A	98	279	24	61	17	0	3	25	22	21	.219	.283	.312	74	-10	0	0	0	.992	-9	C-88	-1.7
1972	Cal-A	66	146	14	40	3	1	2	17	11	8	.274	.342	.349	112	2	0	0	0	.993	-7	C-56	-0.4
1973	Cal-A	60	122	9	30	5	0	1	9	7	7	.246	.292	.311	76	-4	0	0	0	.980	-8	C-56	-1.1
Total	10	451	989	83	214	37	3	12	93	63	118	.216	.272	.296	64	-48	0	1	-1	.986	-38	C-330/3-15,O-12	-8.1

■ JOE STEPHENSON Stephenson, Joseph Chester b: 6/30/21, Detroit, Mich. BR/TR, 6'2", 185 lbs. Deb: 9/19/43 F

YEAR	TM/L	G	AB	R	H	2B	3B	HR	RBI	BB	SO	AVG	OBP	SLG	PRO+	BR/A	SB	CS	SBR	FA	FR	G/POS	TPR
1943	NY-N	9	24	4	6	1	0	0	1	0	5	.250	.250	.292	56	-1	0			.973	2	/C-6	0.1
1944	Chi-N	4	8	1	1	0	0	0	0	1	3	.125	.222	.125	-1	-1	1			1.000	1	/C-3	0.0
1947	Chi-A	16	35	3	5	0	0	0	3	1	7	.143	.211	.143	-1	-5	0	0	0	.959	0	C-13	-0.4
Total	3	29	67	8	12	1	0	0	4	2	15	.179	.225	.194	19	-7	1	0		.970	3	/C-22	-0.3

■ PHIL STEPHENSON Stephenson, Phillip Raymond b: 9/19/60, Guthrie, Okla. BL/TL, 6'1", 195 lbs. Deb: 4/5/89

YEAR	TM/L	G	AB	R	H	2B	3B	HR	RBI	BB	SO	AVG	OBP	SLG	PRO+	BR/A	SB	CS	SBR	FA	FR	G/POS	TPR
1989	Chi-N	17	21	0	3	0	0	0	0	2	3	.143	.217	.143	5	-3	1	0	0	1.000	-1	/O-3	-0.3
	SD-N	10	17	4	6	0	0	2	2	3	2	.353	.450	.706	225	3	0	0	0	.977	0	/1-8	0.3
	Yr	27	38	4	9	0	0	2	2	5	5	.237	.326	.395	100	0	1	0	0	.977	-0	/1-8,O-3	0.0
1990	SD-N	103	182	26	38	9	1	4	19	30	43	.209	.321	.335	80	-5	2	1	0	.997	3	1-60	-0.5
1991	SD-N	11	7	0	2	0	0	0	0	2	3	.286	.444	.286	106	0	0	0	0	.000	0	/H	0.0
1992	SD-N	53	71	5	11	2	1	0	8	10	11	.155	.259	.211	34	-6	0	0	0	1.000	-3	O-15/1-7	-1.0
Total	4	194	298	35	60	11	2	6	29	47	62	.201	.310	.312	73	-10	3	1	0	.993	-1	/1-75,O-18	-1.5

■ DUMMY STEPHENSON Stephenson, Reuben Crandol b: 9/22/1869, Petersburg, N.J. d: 12/1/24, Trenton, N.J. BR/TR, 5'11.5", 180 lbs. Deb: 9/9/1892

YEAR	TM/L	G	AB	R	H	2B	3B	HR	RBI	BB	SO	AVG	OBP	SLG	PRO+	BR/A	SB	CS	SBR	FA	FR	G/POS	TPR
1892	Phi-N	8	37	4	10	3	0	0	5	0	2	.270	.289	.351	94	-0	0			.800	-2	/O-8	-0.2

■ BOB STEPHENSON Stephenson, Robert Lloyd b: 8/11/28, Blair, Okla. BR/TR, 6', 165 lbs. Deb: 4/14/55

YEAR	TM/L	G	AB	R	H	2B	3B	HR	RBI	BB	SO	AVG	OBP	SLG	PRO+	BR/A	SB	CS	SBR	FA	FR	G/POS	TPR
1955	StL-N	67	111	19	27	3	0	0	6	5	18	.243	.276	.270	46	-9	2	1	0	.938	-1	S-48/2-7,3-1	-0.7

■ WALTER STEPHENSON Stephenson, Walter McQueen "Tarzan" b: 3/27/11, Saluda, N.C. d: 7/4/93, Shreveport, La. BR/TR, 6', 180 lbs. Deb: 4/29/35

YEAR	TM/L	G	AB	R	H	2B	3B	HR	RBI	BB	SO	AVG	OBP	SLG	PRO+	BR/A	SB	CS	SBR	FA	FR	G/POS	TPR
1935	*Chi-N	16	26	2	10	1	1	0	2	1	5	.385	.407	.500	142	1	0			1.000	2	/C-6	0.3
1936	Chi-N	6	12	0	1	0	0	0	1	0	5	.083	.083	.083	-54	-3	0			1.000	-0	/C-4	-0.3
1937	Phi-N	10	23	1	6	0	0	0	2	2	3	.261	.320	.261	55	-1	0			.967	0	/C-7	-0.1
Total	3	32	61	3	17	1	1	0	5	3	13	.279	.313	.328	70	-2	0			.984	2	/C-17	-0.1

■ DUTCH STERRETT Sterrett, Charles Hurlbut b: 10/1/1889, Milroy, Pa. d: 12/9/65, Baltimore, Md. BR/TR, 5'11.5", 165 lbs. Deb: 6/20/12

YEAR	TM/L	G	AB	R	H	2B	3B	HR	RBI	BB	SO	AVG	OBP	SLG	PRO+	BR/A	SB	CS	SBR	FA	FR	G/POS	TPR
1912	NY-A	66	230	30	61	4	7	1	32	11		.265	.310	.357	85	-5	8			.972	-7	O-37,1-17,C-10,/2-1	-1.3
1913	NY-A	21	35	0	6	0	0	0	3	1	5	.171	.216	.171	14	-4	1			1.000	-1	/1-6,C-1	-0.5
Total	2	87	265	30	67	4	7	1	35	12	5	.253	.298	.332	77	-9	9			.986	-8	/O-37,1-23,C-11,2-1	-1.8

■ CHUCK STEVENS Stevens, Charles Augustus b: 7/10/18, Van Houten, N.Mex BB/TL, 6'1", 180 lbs. Deb: 9/16/41

YEAR	TM/L	G	AB	R	H	2B	3B	HR	RBI	BB	SO	AVG	OBP	SLG	PRO+	BR/A	SB	CS	SBR	FA	FR	G/POS	TPR
1941	StL-A	4	13	2	2	0	0	0	2	0	1	.154	.154	.154	-18	-2	0	0	0	.966	-1	/1-4	-0.3
1946	StL-A	122	432	53	107	17	4	3	27	47	62	.248	.324	.326	78	-12	4	6	-2	**.995**	3	*1-120	-1.9
1948	StL-A	85	287	34	75	12	4	1	26	41	26	.261	.354	.341	83	-6	2	2	-1	.991	1	1-85	-0.7
Total	3	211	732	89	184	29	8	4	55	88	89	.251	.333	.329	79	-20	6	8	-3	.993	3	1-209	-2.9

■ LEE STEVENS Stevens, De Wain Lee b: 7/10/67, Kansas City, Mo. BL/TL, 6'4", 219 lbs. Deb: 7/16/90

YEAR	TM/L	G	AB	R	H	2B	3B	HR	RBI	BB	SO	AVG	OBP	SLG	PRO+	BR/A	SB	CS	SBR	FA	FR	G/POS	TPR
1990	Cal-A	67	248	28	53	10	0	7	32	22	75	.214	.278	.339	73	-9	1	1	-0	.994	-4	1-67	-1.9
1991	Cal-A	18	58	8	17	7	0	0	9	6	12	.293	.359	.414	113	1	1	2	-1	.989	-1	1-11/O-9	-0.1
1992	Cal-A	106	312	25	69	19	0	7	37	29	64	.221	.289	.349	78	-10	1	4	-2	.995	-4	1-91/D-2	-2.2
1996	Tex-A	27	78	6	18	2	3	3	12	6	22	.231	.294	.449	80	-3	0	0	0	.994	0	1-18/O-5	-0.4
1997	Tex-A	137	426	58	128	24	2	21	74	23	83	.300	.338	.514	112	6	1	3	-2	.994	-5	1-62,D-38,O-22	-0.8
1998	*Tex-A	120	344	52	91	17	4	20	59	31	93	.265	.325	.512	108	3	0	2	-1	.996	-1	D-72,1-37/O-7	-0.5
Total	6	475	1466	177	376	79	9	58	223	117	349	.256	.313	.441	97	-12	4	12	-6	.994	-13	1-286,D-112/O-43	-5.9

■ ED STEVENS Stevens, Edward Lee "Big Ed" b: 1/12/25, Galveston, Tex. BL/TL, 6'1", 190 lbs. Deb: 8/9/45 C

YEAR	TM/L	G	AB	R	H	2B	3B	HR	RBI	BB	SO	AVG	OBP	SLG	PRO+	BR/A	SB	CS	SBR	FA	FR	G/POS	TPR
1945	Bro-N	55	201	29	55	14	3	4	29	32	20	.274	.376	.433	125	7	0			.987	0	1-55	0.4
1946	Bro-N	103	310	34	75	13	7	10	60	27	44	.242	.303	.426	104	0	2			.986	-4	1-99	-0.9
1947	Bro-N	5	13	0	2	1	0	0	0	1	5	.154	.214	.231	18	-2	0			.971	1	/1-4	-0.1
1948	Pit-N	128	429	47	109	19	6	10	69	35	53	.254	.313	.396	89	-8	4			**.996**	5	*1-117	-0.3
1949	Pit-N	67	221	22	58	10	1	4	32	22	24	.262	.332	.371	86	-4	1			.995	10	1-58	0.5
1950	Pit-N	17	46	2	9	2	0	0	3	4	5	.196	.260	.239	31	-5	0			1.000	1	1-12	-0.4
Total	6	375	1220	134	308	59	17	28	193	121	151	.252	.322	.398	95	-10	7			.992	13	1-345	-0.8

■ R C STEVENS Stevens, R C b: 7/22/34, Moultrie, Ga. BL/TR, 6'5", 219 lbs. Deb: 4/15/58

YEAR	TM/L	G	AB	R	H	2B	3B	HR	RBI	BB	SO	AVG	OBP	SLG	PRO+	BR/A	SB	CS	SBR	FA	FR	G/POS	TPR
1958	Pit-N	59	90	16	24	3	1	7	18	5	25	.267	.320	.556	129	3	0	0	0	.991	3	1-52	0.4
1959	Pit-N	3	7	2	2	0	0	1	1	0	0	.286	.286	.714	157	0	0	0	0	1.000	0	/1-1	0.0
1960	Pit-N	9	3	1	0	0	0	0	0	0	1	.000	.000	.000	-99	-1	0	0	0	1.000	1	/1-7	0.0
1961	Was-A	33	62	2	8	1	0	0	2	7	15	.129	.217	.145	-1	-9	1	0	0	1.000	4	1-25	-0.6
Total	4	104	162	21	34	4	1	8	21	12	41	.210	.273	.395	77	-6	1	0	0	.995	7	/1-85	-0.2

■ ROBERT STEVENS Stevens, Robert Deb: 5/4/1875

YEAR	TM/L	G	AB	R	H	2B	3B	HR	RBI	BB	SO	AVG	OBP	SLG	PRO+	BR/A	SB	CS	SBR	FA	FR	G/POS	TPR
1875	Was-n	1	4	0	1	0	0	0	0	0	0	.250	.250	.250	77	-0	0	0	0	.000	-1	/O-1	-0.1

■ BOBBY STEVENS Stevens, Robert Jordan b: 4/17/07, Chevy Chase, Md. BL/TR, 5'8", 149 lbs. Deb: 7/3/31

YEAR	TM/L	G	AB	R	H	2B	3B	HR	RBI	BB	SO	AVG	OBP	SLG	PRO+	BR/A	SB	CS	SBR	FA	FR	G/POS	TPR
1931	Phi-N	12	35	3	12	0	0	0	4	2	2	.343	.410	.343	97	0	0			.870	-5	S-10	-0.4

■ TODD STEVERSON Steverson, Todd Anthony b: 11/15/71, Los Angeles, Cal. BR/TR, 6'2", 195 lbs. Deb: 4/28/95

YEAR	TM/L	G	AB	R	H	2B	3B	HR	RBI	BB	SO	AVG	OBP	SLG	PRO+	BR/A	SB	CS	SBR	FA	FR	G/POS	TPR
1995	Det-A	30	42	11	11	0	0	2	6	6	10	.262	.354	.405	97	-0	2	0	1	1.000	-6	O-27/D-1	-0.6
1996	SD-N	1	1	0	0	0	0	0	0	0	1	.000	.000	.000	-99	-0	0	0	0	.000	0	/H	0.0
Total	2	31	43	11	11	0	0	2	6	6	11	.256	.347	.395	93	-0	2	0	1	1.000	-6	/O-27,D-1	-0.6

■ ANDY STEWART Stewart, Andrew David b: 12/5/70, Oshawa, Ont., Canada BR/TR, 5'11", 205 lbs. Deb: 9/6/97

YEAR	TM/L	G	AB	R	H	2B	3B	HR	RBI	BB	SO	AVG	OBP	SLG	PRO+	BR/A	SB	CS	SBR	FA	FR	G/POS	TPR
1997	KC-A	5	8	1	2	1	0	0	0	0	0	.250	.250	.375	59	-0	0	0	0	1.000	1	/C-4,D-1	0.0

■ ACE STEWART Stewart, Asa b: 2/14/1869, Terre Haute, Ind. d: 4/17/12, Terre Haute, Ind. BR/TR, 5'10", 176 lbs. Deb: 4/18/1895

YEAR	TM/L	G	AB	R	H	2B	3B	HR	RBI	BB	SO	AVG	OBP	SLG	PRO+	BR/A	SB	CS	SBR	FA	FR	G/POS	TPR
1895	Chi-N	97	365	52	88	8	10	8	76	39	40	.241	.314	.384	75	-16	14			.911	-8	*2-97	-1.6

YEAR	TM/L	G	AB	R	H	2B	3B	HR	RBI	BB	SO	AVG	OBP	SLG	PRO+	BR/A	SB	CS	SBR	FA	FR	G/POS	TPR
■ TUFFY STEWART	Stewart, Charles Eugene b: 7/31/1883, Chicago, Ill. d: 11/18/34, Chicago, Ill. BL/TL, 5'10", 167 lbs. Deb: 8/8/13																						
1913	Chi-N	9	8	1	1	1	0	0	2	2	5	.125	.300	.250	58	-0	1			1.000	0	/O-1	0.0
1914	Chi-N	2	1	0	0	0	0	0	0	0	0	.000	.000	.000	-99	-0	0			.000	0	H	0.0
Total	2	11	9	1	1	1	0	0	2	2	5	.111	.273	.222	43	-1	1			1.000	0	/O-1	0.0
■ BUD STEWART	Stewart, Edward Perry b: 6/15/16, Sacramento, Cal. BL/TR, 5'11", 170 lbs. Deb: 4/19/41																						
1941	Pit-N	73	172	27	46	7	0	0	10	12	17	.267	.315	.308	76	-5	3			.962	-2	O-41	-0.9
1942	Pit-N	82	183	21	40	8	4	0	20	22	16	.219	.302	.306	76	-5	2			1.000	-4	O-34,3-10/2-6	-1.1
1948	NY-A	6	5	1	1	1	0	0	0	0	0	.200	.200	.400	58	-0	0	0	0	.000	0	H	0.0
	Was-A	118	401	56	112	17	13	7	69	49	27	.279	.361	.439	115	8	8	9	-3	.975	-4	*O-114	-0.5
	Yr	124	406	57	113	18	13	7	69	49	27	.278	.359	.438	115	7	8	9	-3	.975	-4	*O-114	-0.5
1949	Was-A	118	388	58	110	23	4	8	43	49	33	.284	.368	.425	112	6	6	4	-1	.982	-7	*O-105	-0.6
1950	Was-A	118	378	46	101	15	6	4	35	46	33	.267	.348	.370	88	-7	5	4	-1	.991	-3	*O-100	-1.4
1951	Chi-A	95	217	40	60	13	5	6	40	29	9	.276	.367	.465	127	8	1	6	-3	.983	-7	O-63	-0.4
1952	Chi-A	92	225	23	60	10	0	5	30	28	17	.267	.350	.378	102	1	3	0	1	.982	-4	O-60	-0.5
1953	Chi-A	53	59	16	16	2	0	2	13	14	3	.271	.411	.407	118	2	1	0	0	1.000	-4	O-16	-0.2
1954	Chi-A	18	13	0	1	0	0	0	0	3	2	.077	.250	.077	-7	-2	0	0	0	1.000	-0	/O-2	-0.2
Total	9	773	2041	288	547	96	32	32	260	252	157	.268	.351	.393	102	5	29	23		.982	-35	O-535/3-10,2-6	-5.8
■ GLEN STEWART	Stewart, Glen Weldon "Gabby" b: 9/29/12, Tullahoma, Tenn. d: 2/11/97, Memphis, Tenn. BR/TR, 6', 175 lbs. Deb: 6/26/40																						
1940	NY-N	15	29	1	4	1	0	0	0	1	2	.138	.167	.172	-6	-4	0			.875	1	/3-6,S-5	-0.3
1943	Phi-N	110	336	23	71	10	1	2	24	32	41	.211	.284	.265	61	-17	1			.947	-9	S-77,2-18/1-8,C-1	-2.1
1944	Phi-N	118	377	32	83	11	5	0	29	28	40	.220	.274	.276	57	-22	0			.963	5	3-83,S-32/2-1	-1.5
Total	3	243	742	56	158	22	6	2	53	61	83	.213	.275	.267	56	-42	1			.953	-4	S-114/3-89,2-19,1C	-3.9
■ JIMMY STEWART	Stewart, James Franklin b: 6/11/39, Opelika, Ala. BB/TR, 6', 165 lbs. Deb: 9/3/63																						
1963	Chi-N	13	37	1	11	2	0	0	1	1	7	.297	.316	.351	87	-1	1	1	-0	.973	1	/S-9,2-1	0.0
1964	Chi-N	132	415	59	105	17	0	3	33	49	61	.253	.335	.316	81	-9	10	8	-2	.981	-7	2-61,S-45/O-4,3-1	-1.0
1965	Chi-N	116	282	26	63	9	4	0	19	30	53	.223	.303	.284	65	-12	13	3	2	.955	-11	O-55,S-48	-2.3
1966	Chi-N	57	90	4	16	4	1	0	4	7	12	.178	.253	.244	38	-7	1	1	-0	1.000	-1	O-15/2-4,S-2,3-2	-1.0
1967	Chi-N	6	6	1	1	0	0	0	1	0	0	.167	.167	.167	-4	-1	0	0	0	.000	0	H	-0.1
	Chi-A	24	18	5	3	0	0	0	1	1	6	.167	.211	.167	13	-2	1	0	0	1.000	0	/O-6,2-5,S-2	-0.2
1969	Cin-N	119	221	26	56	3	4	4	24	19	33	.253	.313	.357	83	-5	4	2	0	.973	-9	O-66,2-18/3-6,S-1	-1.6
1970	*Cin-N	101	105	15	28	3	1	1	8	8	13	.267	.325	.343	79	-3	5	3	-0	1.000	-11	O-48,2-18/3-9,C1	-1.4
1971	Cin-N	80	82	7	19	2	2	0	9	9	12	.232	.308	.305	76	-3	3	1	0	1.000	-10	O-19/3-9,2-6	-1.3
1972	Hou-N	68	96	14	21	5	2	0	9	6	9	.219	.265	.313	65	-5	0	1	-1	1.000	-5	O-11/1-9,2-8,3-2	-1.2
1973	Hou-N	61	68	6	13	0	0	0	3	9	12	.191	.295	.191	37	-5	0	0	0	1.000	0	/3-8,O-3,2-1	-0.6
Total	10	777	1420	164	336	45	14	8	112	139	218	.237	.308	.305	71	-53	38	20	-1	.969	-53	O-227,2-122,S/31C	-10.7
■ STUFFY STEWART	Stewart, John Franklin b: 1/31/1894, Jasper, Fla. d: 12/30/80, Lake City, Fla. BR/TR, 5'9.5", 160 lbs. Deb: 9/3/16																						
1916	StL-N	9	17	0	3	0	0	0	1	0	3	.176	.176	.176	9	-2	0			.833	-2	/2-8	-0.4
1917	StL-N	13	9	4	0	0	0	0	0	0	4	.000	.000	.000	-99	-2	0			1.000	-3	/O-7,2-2	-0.5
1922	Pit-N	3	13	3	2	0	0	0	0	0	1	.154	.154	.154	-20	-2	0	0	0	.875	-1	/2-3	-0.3
1923	Bro-N	4	11	3	4	1	0	1	1	1	1	.364	.417	.727	202	2	0	0	0	.786	-1	/2-3	0.0
1925	Was-A	7	17	3	6	1	0	0	3	1	2	.353	.389	.412	105	0	1	0	0	.929	1	/3-5,2-1	0.1
1926	Was-A	62	63	27	17	6	1	0	9	6	6	.270	.333	.397	92	-1	8	4	0	.975	7	2-25/3-1	0.6
1927	Was-A	56	129	24	31	6	2	0	4	8	15	.240	.285	.318	57	-8	12	2	2	.939	1	2-37/3-2	-0.4
1929	Was-A	22	6	10	0	0	0	0	0	1	0	.000	.143	.000	-60	-1	0	1	-1	1.000	2	/2-3	0.0
Total	8	176	265	74	63	14	3	1	18	17	32	.238	.284	.325	61	-15	21	7		.932	4	/2-82,3-8,O-7	-0.9
■ MARK STEWART	Stewart, Mark "Big Slick" b: 10/11/1889, Whitlock, Tenn. d: 1/17/32, Memphis, Tenn. BL/TR, 6'1", 180 lbs. Deb: 10/4/13																						
1913	Cin-N	1	1	0	0	0	0	0	0	0	0	.000	.000	.000	-99	-0	0			.000	0	/C-1	0.0
■ SHANNON STEWART	Stewart, Shannon Harold b: 2/25/74, Cincinnati, Ohio BR/TR, 6', 175 lbs. Deb: 9/2/95																						
1995	Tor-A	12	38	2	8	0	0	0	1	5	5	.211	.318	.211	41	-3	2	0	1	.955	-1	O-12	-0.4
1996	Tor-A	7	17	2	3	1	0	0	2	1	4	.176	.222	.235	16	-2	1	0	0	.800	-2	/O-6	-0.4
1997	Tor-A	44	168	25	48	13	7	0	22	19	24	.286	.372	.446	112	3	10	3	1	.980	1	O-41/D-1	0.4
1998	Tor-A	144	516	90	144	29	3	12	55	67	77	.279	.378	.417	107	7	51	18	5	.980	-2	*O-144	0.6
Total	4	207	739	119	203	43	10	12	80	92	110	.275	.370	.409	102	5	64	21	7	.977	-5	O-203/D-1	0.2
■ NEB STEWART	Stewart, Walter Nesbitt b: 5/21/18, S.Charleston, Ohio d: 6/8/90, London, Ohio BR/TR, 6'1", 195 lbs. Deb: 9/8/40																						
1940	Phi-N	10	31	3	4	0	0	0	0	1	5	.129	.156	.129	-21	-5	0			.944	0	/O-9	-0.5
■ BILL STEWART	Stewart, William Wayne b: 4/15/28, Bay City, Mich. BR/TR, 5'11", 200 lbs. Deb: 4/17/55																						
1955	KC-A	11	18	2	2	1	0	0	0	1	6	.111	.158	.167	-13	-3	0	0	0	1.000	-0	/O-6	-0.3
■ ROYLE STILLMAN	Stillman, Royle Eldon b: 1/2/51, Santa Monica, Cal. BL/TR, 5'11", 180 lbs. Deb: 6/22/75																						
1975	Bal-A	13	14	1	6	0	0	0	1	1	3	.429	.467	.429	165	1	0	0	0	1.000	-0	/O-2	0.1
1976	Bal-A	20	22	0	2	0	0	0	1	3	4	.091	.200	.091	-14	-3	0	0	0	1.000	-0	/1-2,D-5	-0.3
1977	Chi-A	56	119	18	25	7	1	3	13	17	21	.210	.309	.361	82	-3	2	1	0	.977	-3	O-26,D-13/1-1	-0.7
Total	3	89	155	19	33	7	1	3	15	21	28	.213	.307	.329	77	-5	2	1	0	.978	-3	/O-28,D-18,1-3	-0.9
■ KURT STILLWELL	Stillwell, Kurt Andrew b: 6/4/65, Glendale, Cal. BB/TR, 5'11", 175 lbs. Deb: 4/13/86 F																						
1986	Cin-N	104	279	31	64	6	1	0	26	30	47	.229	.309	.258	56	-16	6	2	1	.951	-2	S-80	-1.2
1987	Cin-N	131	395	54	102	20	7	4	33	32	50	.258	.317	.375	79	-12	4	6	-2	.914	-21	S-51,2-37,3-20	-3.1
1988	KC-A★	128	459	63	115	28	5	10	53	47	76	.251	.324	.399	100	0	6	5	-1	.976	-18	*S-124	-0.8
1989	KC-A	130	463	52	121	20	7	7	54	42	64	.261	.327	.380	99	-1	9	6	-1	.970	-32	*S-130	-2.4
1990	KC-A	144	506	60	126	35	4	3	51	39	60	.249	.308	.352	85	-10	0	2	-1	.957	-20	*S-141	-2.1
1991	KC-A	122	385	44	102	17	1	6	51	33	56	.265	.325	.361	89	-6	3	4	-2	.959	-25	*S-118	-2.4
1992	SD-N	114	379	35	86	15	3	2	24	26	58	.227	.278	.298	62	-19	4	1	1	.970	-14	*2-111	-3.3
1993	SD-N	57	121	9	26	4	0	1	11	11	22	.215	.286	.273	49	-9	4	3	-1	.921	-5	S-30/3-3	-1.2
	Cal-A	22	61	2	16	2	2	0	3	4	11	.262	.308	.361	76	-2	2	0	1	.952	-4	2-18/S-7	-0.5
1996	Tex-A	46	77	12	21	4	0	1	4	10	11	.273	.364	.364	81	-2	0	0	0	.964	-9	2-21/S-9,3-6,1-1,D	-0.9
Total	9	998	3125	362	779	151	30	34	310	274	455	.249	.313	.349	82	-76	38	29	-6	.958	-151	S-690,2-187/3D1	-17.9
■ RON STILLWELL	Stillwell, Ronald Roy b: 12/3/39, Los Angeles, Cal. BR/TR, 5'11", 165 lbs. Deb: 7/3/61 F																						
1961	Was-A	8	16	3	2	1	0	0	1	1	4	.125	.176	.188	-3	-2	0	0	0	.929	-1	/S-5	-0.3
1962	Was-A	6	22	5	6	0	0	0	2	2	2	.273	.333	.273	66	-1	0	0	0	1.000	-2	/2-6,S-1	-0.3
Total	2	14	38	8	8	1	0	0	3	3	6	.211	.268	.237	37	-3	0	0	0	.929	-3	/2-6,S-6	-0.6
■ CRAIG STIMAC	Stimac, Craig Steven b: 11/18/54, Oak Park, Ill. BR/TR, 6'2", 185 lbs. Deb: 8/12/80																						
1980	SD-N	20	50	5	11	2	0	0	7	1	6	.220	.235	.260	40	-4	0	0	0	.982	4	C-11/3-2	0.0
1981	SD-N	9	9	0	1	0	0	0	0	0	3	.111	.111	.111	-40	-2	0	0	0	.000	0	/H	-0.2
Total	2	29	59	5	12	2	0	0	7	1	9	.203	.217	.237	29	-6	0	0	0	.982	4	/C-11,3-2	-0.2
■ KELLY STINNETT	Stinnett, Kelly Lee b: 2/14/70, Lawton, Okla. BR/TR, 5'11", 195 lbs. Deb: 4/5/94																						
1994	NY-N	47	150	20	38	6	2	2	14	11	28	.253	.325	.360	79	-4	2	0	1	.979	-5	C-44	-0.6
1995	NY-N	77	196	23	43	8	1	4	18	29	65	.219	.338	.332	80	-5	2	0	1	.983	1	C-67	0.1
1996	Mil-A	14	26	1	2	0	0	0	0	2	11	.077	.172	.077	-33	-5	0	0	0	.960	1	C-14/D-1	-0.4
1997	Mil-A	30	36	2	9	4	0	0	3	3	9	.250	.308	.361	73	-1	0	0	0	.989	5	C-25/D-1	0.4
1998	Ari-N	92	274	35	71	14	1	11	34	35	74	.259	.356	.438	104	2	0	1	-1	.984	-6	C-86/D-1	0.1
Total	5	260	682	81	163	32	4	17	69	80	187	.239	.335	.372	85	-14	4	1	1	.982	-4	C-236/D-3	-0.4

■ BOB STINSON Stinson, Gorrell Robert b: 10/11/45, Elkin, N.C. BB/TR, 5′11.5″, 185 lbs. Deb: 9/23/69

YEAR	TM/L	G	AB	R	H	2B	3B	HR	RBI	BB	SO	AVG	OBP	SLG	PRO+	BR/A	SB	CS	SBR	FA	FR	G/POS	TPR
1969	LA-N	4	8	1	3	0	0	0	2	0	2	.375	.375	.375	119	0	0	1	-1	.952	1	/C-4	0.0
1970	LA-N	4	3	1	0	0	0	0	0	0	1	.000	.000	.000	-99	-1	0	0	0	1.000	-0	/C-3	-0.1
1971	StL-N	17	19	3	4	1	0	0	1	1	7	.211	.250	.263	44	-1	0	0	0	.971	2	/C-6,O-3	0.1
1972	Hou-N	27	35	3	6	1	0	0	2	1	6	.171	.216	.200	19	-4	0	0	0	.964	-4	C-12/O-3	-0.9
1973	Mon-N	48	111	12	29	6	1	3	12	17	15	.261	.374	.414	114	3	0	1	-1	.979	-3	C-35/3-1	0.0
1974	Mon-N	38	87	4	15	2	0	1	6	15	16	.172	.294	.230	45	-6	1	1	-0	1.000	1	C-29	-0.5
1975	KC-A	63	147	18	39	9	1	1	9	18	29	.265	.349	.361	98	0	1	0	0	.993	7	C-59/1-1,2-1,O-1,D	1.0
1976	*KC-A	79	209	26	55	7	1	2	25	25	29	.263	.345	.335	99	0	3	1	0	.979	-6	C-79	-0.4
1977	Sea-A	105	297	27	80	11	1	8	32	37	50	.269	.362	.394	107	4	0	3	-2	.984	-7	C-99/D-1	-0.2
1978	Sea-A	124	364	46	94	14	3	11	55	45	42	.258	.349	.404	112	6	2	1	0	.987	-18	*C-123/D-1	-0.9
1979	Sea-A	95	247	19	60	8	0	6	28	33	38	.243	.342	.348	85	-4	1	2	-1	.978	-7	C-91	-0.9
1980	Sea-A	48	107	6	23	2	0	1	8	9	19	.215	.282	.262	50	-7	0	0	0	.979	-9	C-45	-1.5
Total	12	652	1634	166	408	61	7	33	180	201	254	.250	.340	.356	93	-10	8	10	-4	.984	-44	C-585/O-7,D-3,213	-4.3

■ GAT STIRES Stires, Garrett b: 10/13/1849, Hunterdon Co., N.J d: 6/13/33, Byron, Ill. BL/TR, 5′8″, 180 lbs. Deb: 5/6/1871

YEAR	TM/L	G	AB	R	H	2B	3B	HR	RBI	BB	SO	AVG	OBP	SLG	PRO+	BR/A	SB	CS	SBR	FA	FR	G/POS	TPR
1871	Rok-n	25	110	23	30	4	6	2	24	7	5	.273	.316	.473	129	5	3	0	1	.837	1	*O-25	0.4

■ SNUFFY STIRNWEISS Stirnweiss, George Henry b: 10/26/18, New York, N.Y. d: 9/15/58, Newark Bay, N.J. BR/TR, 5′8.5″, 175 lbs. Deb: 4/22/43

YEAR	TM/L	G	AB	R	H	2B	3B	HR	RBI	BB	SO	AVG	OBP	SLG	PRO+	BR/A	SB	CS	SBR	FA	FR	G/POS	TPR
1943	*NY-A	83	274	34	60	8	4	1	25	47	37	.219	.333	.288	82	-5	11	9	-2	.938	-6	S-68/2-4	-0.9
1944	NY-A	154	643	**125**	**205**	35	**16**	8	43	73	87	.319	.389	.460	137	32	**55**	11	**10**	**.982**	19	*2-154	7.1
1945	NY-A†	152	632	**107**	**195**	32	**22**	10	64	78	62	**.309**	.385	**.476**	**143**	**34**	**33**	17	-0	.970	26	*2-152	**7.2**
1946	NY-A★	129	487	75	122	19	7	0	37	66	58	.251	.340	.318	83	-9	18	6	**2**	.991	-6	3-79,2-46/S-4	-0.9
1947	*NY-A	148	571	102	146	18	8	5	41	89	47	.256	.358	.342	96	-1	5	3	-0	.983	-11	*2-148	-0.1
1948	NY-A	141	515	90	130	20	7	3	32	86	62	.252	.360	.336	87	-8	5	4	-1	**.993**	-11	*2-141	-1.1
1949	*NY-A	70	157	29	41	8	2	0	11	29	20	.261	.380	.338	90	-1	3	2	-0	.974	4	2-51/3-4	0.4
1950	NY-A	7	2	0	0	0	0	0	0	0	0	.000	.000	.000	-99	-1	0	0	0	1.000	1	/2-4	0.0
	StL-A	93	326	32	71	16	2	1	24	51	49	.218	.324	.288	56	-21	3	3	-1	.975	-24	2-62,3-31/S-5	-4.2
	Yr	100	328	32	71	16	2	1	24	51	49	.216	.322	.287	55	-22	3	3	-1	.975	-23	2-66,3-31/S-5	-4.2
1951	Cle-A	50	88	10	19	1	0	1	4	22	25	.216	.373	.261	78	-2	1	0	0	.992	7	2-25/3-2	0.7
1952	Cle-A	1	0	0	0	0	0	0	0	0	0	—	—	—	—	0	0	0	0	.000	0	/3-1	0.0
Total	10	1028	3695	604	989	157	68	29	281	541	447	.268	.362	.371	102	19	134	55	7	.980	-1	2-787,3-117/S-77	8.2

■ JACK STIVETTS Stivetts, John Elmer "Happy Jack" b: 3/31/1868, Ashland, Pa. d: 4/18/30, Ashland, Pa. BR/TR, 6′2″, 185 lbs. Deb: 6/26/1889

YEAR	TM/L	G	AB	R	H	2B	3B	HR	RBI	BB	SO	AVG	OBP	SLG	PRO+	BR/A	SB	CS	SBR	FA	FR	G/POS	TPR
1889	StL-a	27	79	12	18	2	2	0	7	3	13	.228	.265	.304	55	-5	0			.896	-1	P-26/O-1	-0.1
1890	StL-a	67	226	36	65	15	6	7	43	16		.288	.337	.500	128	4	2			.894	4	P-54,O-10/1-3	0.1
1891	StL-a	85	302	45	92	10	2	7	54	10	32	.305	.331	.421	100	-4	4			.898	3	P-64,O-24	-0.2
1892	*Bos-N	71	240	40	71	14	2	3	36	27	28	.296	.369	.408	124	6	8			.904	-0	P-54,O-18/1-1	0.0
1893	Bos-N	50	172	32	51	5	6	3	25	12	14	.297	.342	.448	101	-1	6			.955	-4	P-38/O-8,3-3	-0.2
1894	Bos-N	68	244	55	80	12	7	8	64	16	21	.328	.369	.533	107	0	3			.943	-4	P-45,O-16/1-4	-0.1
1895	Bos-N	46	158	20	30	6	4	0	24	6	18	.190	.220	.278	26	-19	1			.961	-1	P-38/1-5,O-2	-0.3
1896	Bos-N	67	222	43	77	9	6	3	49	12	10	.347	.383	.482	120	5	4			.946	-6	P-42,O-12/1-5,3-1	-0.2
1897	*Bos-N	61	199	41	73	9	9	2	37	15		.367	.417	.533	141	11	2			.926	-3	O-29,P-18/2-2,1-2	0.1
1898	Bos-N	41	111	16	28	1	1	2	16	10		.252	.314	.333	81	-3	1			.909	-5	O-14,1-10/S-4,2P	-0.8
1899	Cle-N	18	39	8	8	1	1	0	2	6		.205	.326	.282	73	-1	0			1.000	1	/O-7,P-7,S-1,3-1	-0.2
Total	11	601	1992	348	593	84	46	35	357	133	136	.298	.344	.439	104	-7	31			.924	-17	P-388,O-141/1S32	-1.9

■ MILT STOCK Stock, Milton Joseph b: 7/11/1893, Chicago, Ill. d: 7/16/77, Fairhope, Ala. BR/TR, 5′8″, 154 lbs. Deb: 9/29/13 C

YEAR	TM/L	G	AB	R	H	2B	3B	HR	RBI	BB	SO	AVG	OBP	SLG	PRO+	BR/A	SB	CS	SBR	FA	FR	G/POS	TPR
1913	NY-N	7	17	2	3	1	0	0	1	2	1	.176	.263	.235	43	-1	2			.838	2	/S-7	0.1
1914	NY-N	115	365	52	96	17	1	3	41	34	21	.263	.333	.340	103	2	11			.939	15	*3-113/S-1	2.2
1915	*Phi-N	69	227	37	59	7	3	1	15	22	26	.260	.325	.330	98	-0	6	2	1	.971	2	3-55/S-4	0.5
1916	Phi-N	132	509	61	143	25	6	1	43	27	33	.281	.320	.360	105	2	21	26	-9	.955	-6	*3-117,S-15	-1.0
1917	Phi-N	150	564	76	149	27	6	3	53	51	34	.264	.326	.349	103	2	25			.942	-9	*3-133,S-19	-0.4
1918	Phi-N	123	481	62	132	14	1	1	42	35	22	.274	.325	.314	89	-6	20			.946	-5	*3-123	-0.9
1919	StL-N	135	492	56	151	16	4	0	52	49	21	.307	.371	.356	127	17	17			.966	17	2-77,3-58	4.3
1920	StL-N	155	639	85	204	28	6	0	76	40	27	.319	.360	.382	117	14	15	17	-6	.939	-8	*3-155	0.9
1921	StL-N	149	587	96	180	27	6	3	84	48	26	.307	.360	.388	100	1	11	3	2	.940	-22	*3-149	-0.9
1922	StL-N	151	581	85	177	33	9	5	79	42	29	.305	.352	.418	103	1	7	12	-5	.950	-9	*3-149/S-1	-0.1
1923	StL-N	151	603	63	174	33	3	2	96	40	21	.289	.334	.363	86	-13	9	6	-1	.955	-14	*3-150/2-1	-1.4
1924	Bro-N	142	561	66	136	14	4	2	52	26	32	.242	.277	.292	54	-36	3	8	-4	.931	-23	*3-142	-5.2
1925	Bro-N	146	615	98	202	28	9	1	62	38	28	.328	.368	.408	101	1	8	1	2	.978	1	*2-141/3-5	0.6
1926	Bro-N	3	8	0	0	0	0	0	0	1	0	.000	.111	.000	-69	-2	0			.923	-1	/2-3	-0.2
Total	14	1628	6249	839	1806	270	58	22	696	455	321	.289	.339	.361	98	-17	155	75		.945	-59	*3-1349,2-222/S-47	-1.5

■ KEVIN STOCKER Stocker, Kevin Douglas b: 2/13/70, Spokane, Wash. BB/TR, 6′1″, 175 lbs. Deb: 7/7/93

YEAR	TM/L	G	AB	R	H	2B	3B	HR	RBI	BB	SO	AVG	OBP	SLG	PRO+	BR/A	SB	CS	SBR	FA	FR	G/POS	TPR
1993	*Phi-N	70	259	46	84	12	3	2	31	30	43	.324	.411	.417	124	11	5	0	2	.958	-1	S-70	1.7
1994	Phi-N	82	271	38	74	11	2	2	28	44	41	.273	.388	.351	92	-1	2	2	-1	.959	-2	S-82	0.4
1995	Phi-N	125	412	42	90	14	3	1	32	43	75	.218	.306	.274	54	-26	6	1	1	.969	8	*S-125	-0.7
1996	Phi-N	119	394	46	100	22	6	5	41	43	89	.254	.339	.378	88	-6	6	4	-1	.975	5	*S-119	0.8
1997	Phi-N	149	504	51	134	23	5	4	40	51	91	.266	.336	.355	81	-13	11	6	-0	.981	-18	*S-147	-1.8
1998	TB-A	112	336	37	70	11	3	6	25	27	80	.208	.283	.313	53	-24	5	3	-0	.979	20	*S-110	0.5
Total	6	657	2176	260	552	93	22	20	197	238	419	.254	.339	.344	79	-60	35	16	1	.972	12	S-653	0.9

■ LEN STOCKWELL Stockwell, Leonard Clark b: 8/25/1859, Cordova, Ill. d: 1/28/05, Niles, Cal. BR/TR, 5′11″, 165 lbs. Deb: 5/17/1879

YEAR	TM/L	G	AB	R	H	2B	3B	HR	RBI	BB	SO	AVG	OBP	SLG	PRO+	BR/A	SB	CS	SBR	FA	FR	G/POS	TPR
1879	Cle-N	2	6	0	0	0	0	0	0	0	2	.000	.000	.000	-99	-1				1.000	1	/O-2	0.0
1884	Lou-a	2	9	0	1	0	0	0		0		.111	.111	.111	-29	-1				.667	-1	/O-2,C-1	-0.2
1890	Cle-N	2	7	2	2	1	0	0	0	0	3	.286	.286	.429	110	0	0			1.000	0	/O-1,1-1	0.0
Total	3	6	22	2	3	1	0	0	0	0	5	.136	.136	.182	-1	-2	0			.900	1	/O-5,1-1,C-1	-0.2

■ STODDARD Stoddard Deb: 9/25/1875

YEAR	TM/L	G	AB	R	H	2B	3B	HR	RBI	BB	SO	AVG	OBP	SLG	PRO+	BR/A	SB	CS	SBR	FA	FR	G/POS	TPR
1875	Atl-n	2	9	1	1	1	0	0	0	0	1	.111	.111	.222	15	-1	0	0	0	.800	-0	/O-2	-0.1

■ AL STOKES Stokes, Albert John (b: Albert John Stocek) b: 1/1/1900, Chicago, Ill. d: 12/19/86, Grantham, N.H. BR/TR, 5′9″, 175 lbs. Deb: 5/10/25

YEAR	TM/L	G	AB	R	H	2B	3B	HR	RBI	BB	SO	AVG	OBP	SLG	PRO+	BR/A	SB	CS	SBR	FA	FR	G/POS	TPR
1925	Bos-A	17	52	7	11	0	1	0	1	4	8	.212	.268	.250	32	-5	0	0	0	.969	3	C-17	-0.2
1926	Bos-A	30	86	7	14	3	3	0	6	8	28	.163	.234	.267	32	-9	0	0	0	.931	-4	C-29	-1.1
Total	2	47	138	14	25	3	4	0	7	12	36	.181	.247	.261	32	-15	0	0	0	.946	-1	/C-46	-1.3

■ GENE STONE Stone, Eugene Daniel b: 1/16/44, Burbank, Cal. BL/TL, 5′11″, 190 lbs. Deb: 5/13/69

YEAR	TM/L	G	AB	R	H	2B	3B	HR	RBI	BB	SO	AVG	OBP	SLG	PRO+	BR/A	SB	CS	SBR	FA	FR	G/POS	TPR
1969	Phi-N	18	28	4	6	0	1	0	0	4	9	.214	.313	.286	70	-1	0	0	0	1.000	-1	/1-5	-0.2

■ GEORGE STONE Stone, George Robert b: 9/3/1877, Lost Nation, Iowa d: 1/3/45, Clinton, Iowa BL/TL, 5′9″, 175 lbs. Deb: 4/20/03

YEAR	TM/L	G	AB	R	H	2B	3B	HR	RBI	BB	SO	AVG	OBP	SLG	PRO+	BR/A	SB	CS	SBR	FA	FR	G/POS	TPR
1903	Bos-A	2	2	0	0	0	0	0	0	0		.000	.000	.000	-95	-0	0			.000	0	H	0.0
1905	StL-A	154	632	76	**187**	25	13	7	52	44		.296	.347	.410	147	32	26			.954	2	*O-154	2.9
1906	StL-A	154	581	91	208	25	20	6	71	52		**.358**	**.417**	**.501**	**195**	**63**	35			.968	-1	*O-154	5.9
1907	StL-A	155	596	77	191	13	11	4	59	59		.320	.387	.399	151	36	23			.970	-3	*O-155	2.9
1908	StL-A	148	588	89	165	21	8	5	31	55		.281	.345	.369	131	21	20			.947	-0	*O-148	1.6
1909	StL-A	83	310	33	89	5	4	1	15	24		.287	.340	.339	123	8	8			.928	2	O-81	0.7
1910	StL-A	152	562	60	144	17	12	0	40	48		.256	.315	.329	108	5	20			.972	-2	*O-145	-0.5
Total	7	848	3271	426	984	106	68	23	268	282		.301	.360	.396	145	164	132			.958	-3	O-837	13.5

■ **RON STONE** Stone, Harry Ronald b: 9/9/42, Corning, Cal. BL/TL, 6'2", 195 lbs. Deb: 4/13/66

YEAR	TM/L	G	AB	R	H	2B	3B	HR	RBI	BB	SO	AVG	OBP	SLG	PRO+	BR/A	SB	CS	SBR	FA	FR	G/POS	TPR
1966	KC-A	26	22	2	6	1	0	0	0	0	2	.273	.273	.318	71	-1	1	1	-0	1.000	-1	/O-4,1-3	-0.3
1969	Phi-N	103	222	22	53	7	1	1	24	29	28	.239	.335	.293	79	-5	3	1	0	.978	-3	O-69	-1.2
1970	Phi-N	123	321	30	84	12	5	3	39	38	45	.262	.342	.358	90	-4	5	6	-2	.968	-3	O-99/1-6	-1.4
1971	Phi-N	95	185	16	42	8	1	2	23	25	36	.227	.319	.314	80	-4	2	2	-1	.964	-4	O-51/1-3	-1.2
1972	Phi-N	41	54	3	9	0	1	0	3	9	11	.167	.286	.204	40	-4	0	0	0	1.000	1	O-15	-0.4
Total	5	388	804	73	194	28	8	6	89	101	122	.241	.329	.318	81	-18	11	10	-3	.973	-11	O-238/1-12	-4.5

■ **JEFF STONE** Stone, Jeffrey Glen b: 12/26/60, Kennett, Mo. BL/TR, 6', 175 lbs. Deb: 9/9/83

YEAR	TM/L	G	AB	R	H	2B	3B	HR	RBI	BB	SO	AVG	OBP	SLG	PRO+	BR/A	SB	CS	SBR	FA	FR	G/POS	TPR
1983	Phi-N	9	4	2	3	0	2	0	3	0	1	.750	.750	1.750	580	2	4	0	1	.000	-0	/O-1	0.3
1984	Phi-N	51	185	27	67	4	6	1	15	9	26	.362	.398	.465	139	10	27	5	5	.916	-2	O-46	1.1
1985	Phi-N	88	264	36	70	4	3	3	11	15	50	.265	.307	.337	78	-8	15	5	2	.966	-6	O-69	-1.5
1986	Phi-N	82	249	32	69	6	4	6	19	20	52	.277	.341	.406	101	0	19	6	2	.982	2	O-58	0.3
1987	Phi-N	66	125	19	32	7	1	1	16	8	38	.256	.316	.352	74	-5	3	1	0	1.000	-1	O-25	-0.6
1988	Bal-A	26	61	4	10	1	0	0	1	4	11	.164	.215	.180	12	-7	4	1	1	.963	-2	O-21/D-1	-0.9
1989	Tex-A	22	36	5	6	1	2	0	5	3	5	.167	.250	.306	55	-2	2	1	0	.000	-1	D-15/O-3	-0.4
	Bos-A	18	15	3	3	0	0	0	1	1	2	.200	.250	.200	27	-1	1	0	0	1.000	-3	O-11/D-3	-0.5
	Yr	40	51	8	9	1	2	0	6	4	7	.176	.250	.275	46	-4	3	1	0	1.000	-5	D-18,O-14	-0.9
1990	Bos-A	10	2	1	1	0	0	0	1	0	1	.500	.500	.500	173	0	0	1	-1	.000	0	/D-2	0.0
Total	8	372	941	129	261	23	18	11	72	60	186	.277	.328	.375	92	-10	75	20	11	.963	-14	O-234/D-21	-2.2

■ **JOHN STONE** Stone, John Thomas "Rocky" b: 10/10/05, Mulberry, Tenn. d: 11/30/55, Shelbyville, Tenn. BL/TR, 6'1", 178 lbs. Deb: 8/31/28

YEAR	TM/L	G	AB	R	H	2B	3B	HR	RBI	BB	SO	AVG	OBP	SLG	PRO+	BR/A	SB	CS	SBR	FA	FR	G/POS	TPR
1928	Det-A	26	113	20	40	10	3	2	21	5	8	.354	.387	.549	141	6	1	0	0	.962	-1	O-26	0.3
1929	Det-A	51	150	23	39	11	2	2	15	11	13	.260	.311	.400	81	-5	1	1	-0	.986	-1	O-36	-0.8
1930	Det-A	127	425	60	132	29	11	3	56	32	49	.311	.360	.452	102	1	6	9	-4	.966	0	*O-109	-0.9
1931	Det-A	147	584	86	191	28	11	10	76	56	48	.327	.388	.464	119	16	13	13	-4	.959	4	*O-147	0.6
1932	Det-A	145	582	106	173	35	12	17	108	58	64	.297	.361	.486	113	10	2	1	0	.961	3	*O-142	0.3
1933	Det-A	148	574	86	161	33	11	11	80	54	37	.280	.344	.434	103	1	1	4	-2	.970	1	*O-141	-0.7
1934	Was-A	113	419	77	132	28	7	7	67	52	26	.315	.395	.465	126	17	1	2	-1	.966	7	*O-112	1.7
1935	Was-A	125	455	78	143	27	18	1	78	39	29	.314	.372	.459	118	11	4	5	-2	.955	0	*O-114	0.5
1936	Was-A	123	437	95	149	22	11	15	90	60	26	.341	.421	.545	145	31	8	0	2	.967	7	*O-114	3.1
1937	Was-A	139	542	84	179	33	15	6	88	66	36	.330	.403	.480	127	23	6	4	-1	.984	7	*O-137	2.2
1938	Was-A	56	213	24	52	12	4	3	28	30	16	.244	.337	.380	85	-5	2	1	0	.974	-2	O-53	-0.8
Total	11	1200	4494	739	1391	268	105	77	707	463	352	.310	.376	.467	116	106	45	40	-10	.967	24	*O-1131	5.5

■ **TIGE STONE** Stone, William Arthur b: 9/18/01, Macon, Ga. d: 1/1/60, Jacksonville, Fla. BR/TR, 5'8", 145 lbs. Deb: 8/23/23

YEAR	TM/L	G	AB	R	H	2B	3B	HR	RBI	BB	SO	AVG	OBP	SLG	PRO+	BR/A	SB	CS	SBR	FA	FR	G/POS	TPR
1923	StL-N	5	1	0	1	0	0	0	0	2	0	1.000	1.000	1.000	438	1	0	0	0	.000	-2	/O-4,P-1	-0.2

■ **JOHN STONEHAM** Stoneham, John Andrew b: 11/8/08, Wood River, Ill. BL/TR, 5'9.5", 168 lbs. Deb: 9/18/33

YEAR	TM/L	G	AB	R	H	2B	3B	HR	RBI	BB	SO	AVG	OBP	SLG	PRO+	BR/A	SB	CS	SBR	FA	FR	G/POS	TPR
1933	Chi-A	10	25	4	3	0	0	1	3	2	2	.120	.185	.240	12	-3	0	0	0	1.000	-2	/O-9	-0.5

■ **HOWIE STORIE** Storie, Howard Edward "Sponge" b: 5/15/11, Pittsfield, Mass. d: 7/27/68, Pittsfield, Mass. BR/TR, 5'10", 175 lbs. Deb: 9/7/31

YEAR	TM/L	G	AB	R	H	2B	3B	HR	RBI	BB	SO	AVG	OBP	SLG	PRO+	BR/A	SB	CS	SBR	FA	FR	G/POS	TPR
1931	Bos-A	6	17	2	2	0	0	0	0	3	2	.118	.250	.118	-1	-2	0	0	0	1.000	0	/C-6	-0.2
1932	Bos-A	6	8	0	3	0	0	0	0	0	0	.375	.375	.375	98	-0	0	0	0	1.000	0	/C-5	0.0
Total	2	12	25	2	5	0	0	0	0	3	2	.200	.286	.200	31	-2	0	0	0	1.000	1	/C-11	-0.2

■ **ALAN STORKE** Storke, Alan Marshall b: 9/27/1884, Auburn, N.Y. d: 3/18/10, Newton, Mass. BR/TR, 6'1", Deb: 9/24/06

YEAR	TM/L	G	AB	R	H	2B	3B	HR	RBI	BB	SO	AVG	OBP	SLG	PRO+	BR/A	SB	CS	SBR	FA	FR	G/POS	TPR
1906	Pit-N	5	12	1	3	1	0	0	1	1		.250	.308	.333	96	-0	1			1.000	0	/3-2,S-1	0.0
1907	Pit-N	112	357	24	92	6	6	1	39	16		.258	.295	.317	90	-5	6			.925	-13	3-67,1-23/2-7,S-5	-1.8
1908	Pit-N	64	202	20	51	5	3	1	12	9		.252	.284	.322	93	-2	4			.988	-6	1-49/3-6,2-1	-1.0
1909	Pit-N	37	118	12	30	5	2	0	12	7		.254	.302	.331	89	-2	1			.994	-0	1-18,3-14	-0.2
	StL-N	48	174	11	49	5	0	0	10	12		.282	.328	.310	105	1	5			.958	-1	S-44/2-4,1-1	0.0
	Yr	85	292	23	79	10	2	0	22	19		.271	.317	.318	97	-1	6			.958	-2	S-44,1-19,3-14,/2-4	-0.2
Total	4	266	863	68	225	22	11	2	74	45		.261	.300	.319	94	-8	17			.990	-20	/1-91,3-89,S-50,2	-3.0

■ **LIN STORTI** Storti, Lindo Ivan b: 12/5/06, Santa Monica, Cal. d: 7/24/82, Ontario, Cal. BB/TR, 5'11", 165 lbs. Deb: 9/18/30

YEAR	TM/L	G	AB	R	H	2B	3B	HR	RBI	BB	SO	AVG	OBP	SLG	PRO+	BR/A	SB	CS	SBR	FA	FR	G/POS	TPR
1930	StL-A	7	28	6	9	1	1	0	2	2	6	.321	.367	.429	98	-0	0	0	0	.975	1	/2-6	0.1
1931	StL-A	86	273	32	60	15	4	3	26	15	50	.220	.263	.337	55	-19	0	2	-1	.926	9	3-67/2-7	-0.7
1932	StL-A	53	193	19	50	11	2	3	26	5	20	.259	.278	.383	66	-10	1	0	0	.956	-4	3-51	-1.0
1933	StL-A	70	210	26	41	7	4	3	21	25	31	.195	.281	.310	53	-15	2	2	-1	.934	-2	3-32,2-24	-1.4
Total	4	216	704	83	160	34	11	9	75	47	107	.227	.277	.345	59	-44	3	4	-2	.936	4	3-150/2-37	-3.0

■ **TOM STOUCH** Stouch, Thomas Carl b: 12/2/1869, Perrysville, Ohio d: 10/7/56, Lancaster, Pa. BR/TR, 6'2", 165 lbs. Deb: 7/7/1898

YEAR	TM/L	G	AB	R	H	2B	3B	HR	RBI	BB	SO	AVG	OBP	SLG	PRO+	BR/A	SB	CS	SBR	FA	FR	G/POS	TPR
1898	Lou-N	4	16	4	5	1	0	0	6	1		.313	.353	.375	110	0	0			.850	-2	/2-4	-0.2

■ **DA ROND STOVALL** Stovall, Da Rond Tyrone b: 1/3/73, St.Louis, Mo. BB/TL, 6'1", 185 lbs. Deb: 4/1/98

YEAR	TM/L	G	AB	R	H	2B	3B	HR	RBI	BB	SO	AVG	OBP	SLG	PRO+	BR/A	SB	CS	SBR	FA	FR	G/POS	TPR
1998	Mon-N	62	78	11	16	2	1	2	6	6	29	.205	.262	.333	55	-5	1	0	0	.925	-10	O-47	-1.5

■ **GEORGE STOVALL** Stovall, George Thomas "Firebrand" b: 11/23/1878, Leeds, Mo. d: 11/5/51, Burlington, Iowa BR/TR, 6'2", 180 lbs. Deb: 7/4/04 FM

YEAR	TM/L	G	AB	R	H	2B	3B	HR	RBI	BB	SO	AVG	OBP	SLG	PRO+	BR/A	SB	CS	SBR	FA	FR	G/POS	TPR
1904	Cle-A	52	181	18	54	10	1	1	31	2		.298	.317	.381	121	4	3			.978	-2	1-38/2-9,O-3,3-1	0.1
1905	Cle-A	112	423	41	115	31	1	1	47	13		.272	.295	.357	105	1	13			.973	-5	1-60,2-46/O-4	-0.7
1906	Cle-A	116	443	54	121	19	5	0	37	8		.273	.288	.339	97	-3	15			.985	-5	1-55,3-30,2-19	-1.0
1907	Cle-A	124	466	38	110	17	6	1	36	18		.236	.267	.305	82	-11	13			.983	-4	*1-122/3-2	-2.0
1908	Cle-A	138	534	71	156	29	6	2	45	17		.292	.316	.380	126	13	14			**.990**	3	*1-132/O-5,S-1	1.5
1909	Cle-A	145	565	60	139	17	10	2	49	6		.246	.259	.322	80	-15	25			**.988**	10	*1-145	-0.8
1910	Cle-A	142	521	49	136	19	4	0	52	14		.261	.284	.313	86	-10	16			**.988**	7	*1-132/2-2	-0.4
1911	Cle-A	126	458	48	124	17	7	0	79	21		.271	.306	.338	79	-14	11			**.986**	7	*1-118/2-2,M	-0.8
1912	StL-A	116	398	35	101	17	5	0	45	14		.254	.286	.322	76	-14	11			.983	5	1-94,M	-1.0
1913	StL-A	89	303	34	87	14	3	1	24	7	23	.287	.305	.363	98	-3	7			.988	8	1-76,M	0.4
1914	KC-F	124	450	51	128	20	5	7	75	23	35	.284	.325	.398	100	-9	6			.989	4	*1-116/3-1,M	-0.8
1915	KC-F	130	480	48	111	21	3	0	44	29	36	.231	.283	.287	63	-32	8			.987	5	*1-129,M	-3.3
Total	12	1414	5222	547	1382	231	56	15	564	172	94	.265	.292	.339	91	-93	142			.986	32	*1-1217/2-78,3OS	-8.8

■ **HARRY STOVEY** Stovey, Harry Duffield (b: Harry Duffield Stowe)
b: 12/20/1856, Philadelphia, Pa. d: 9/20/37, New Bedford, Mass BR/TR, 5'11.5", 175 lbs. Deb: 5/1/1880 M

YEAR	TM/L	G	AB	R	H	2B	3B	HR	RBI	BB	SO	AVG	OBP	SLG	PRO+	BR/A	SB	CS	SBR	FA	FR	G/POS	TPR
1880	Wor-N	83	355	76	94	21	**14**	**6**	28	12	46	.265	.289	.454	136	11				.860	-5	O-46,1-37/P-2	0.2
1881	Wor-N	75	341	57	92	25	7	2	30	12	23	.270	.295	.402	111	3				.955	-5	*1-57,O-18,M	-0.7
1882	Wor-N	84	360	90	104	13	10	5	26	22	34	.289	.330	.422	136	14				.956	4	1-43,O-41	1.2
1883	Phi-a	94	421	**110**	128	**31**	6	**14**	66	27		.304	.346	**.506**	158	25				**.965**	0	*1-93/O-3,P-1	1.4
1884	Phi-a	104	448	**124**	146	22	**23**	10	83	26		.326	.368	.545	182	38				.960	-1	*1-104	2.3
1885	Phi-a	112	486	**130**	153	27	9	**13**	75	39		.315	.371	.488	160	31				.967	4	*1-82,O-30,M	2.2
1886	Phi-a	123	489	115	144	28	11	7	59	64		.294	.377	.440	154	31	**68**			.870	3	O-63,1-62/P-1	2.2
1887	Phi-a	124	497	125	142	31	12	4	77	56		.286	.366	.421	119	13	74			.902	12	O-80,1-46	1.5
1888	Phi-a	130	530	127	152	25	**20**	9	65	62		.287	.365	.460	165	**39**	87			.943	4	*O-118,1-13	3.5
1889	Phi-a	137	556	**152**	171	38	13	**19**	**119**	77	68	.308	.393	**.525**	162	45	63			.897	18	*O-137/1-1	**4.9**
1890	Bos-P	118	481	142	144	25	11	12	84	81	38	.299	.406	.472	126	17	**97**			.921	2	*O-117/1-1	1.2
1891	Bos-N	134	544	118	152	31	**20**	**16**	95	79	69	.279	.373	**.498**	137	21	57			.910	9	*O-134/1-1	2.2
1892	Bos-N	38	146	21	24	8	1	0	12	14	19	.164	.252	.233	43	-11	20			.901	0	O-38	-1.1
	Bal-N	74	283	58	77	14	11	4	55	40	32	.272	.364	.442	140	13	20			.913	-3	O-64,1-10	0.6
	Yr	112	429	79	101	22	12	4	67	54	51	.235	.326	.371	106	2	40			.908	-3	*O-102,1-10	-0.5
1893	Bal-N	8	26	4	4	2	0	0	5	8	3	.154	.353	.231	55	-1	1			.864	0	/O-7	-0.1
	Bro-N	48	175	43	44	6	6	1	29	44	11	.251	.402	.371	111	5	22			.901	-3	O-48	0.0

YEAR	TM/L	G	AB	R	H	2B	3B	HR	RBI	BB	SO	AVG	OBP	SLG	PRO+	BR/A	SB	CS	SBR	FA	FR	G/POS	TPR
	Yr	56	201	47	48	8	6	1	34	52	14	.239	.395	.353	103	4	23			.895	-2	O-55	-0.1
Total	14	1486	6138	1492	1771	347	174	122	908	663	343	.289	.361	.461	142	294	509			.896	40	O-944,1-550/P-4	21.5

■ RAY STOVIAK

Stoviak, Raymond Thomas b: 6/6/15, Scottdale, Pa. BL/TL, 6'1", 195 lbs. Deb: 6/5/38

YEAR	TM/L	G	AB	R	H	2B	3B	HR	RBI	BB	SO	AVG	OBP	SLG	PRO+	BR/A	SB	CS	SBR	FA	FR	G/POS	TPR
1938	Phi-N	10	10	1	0	0	0	0	0	0	3	.000	.000	.000	-99	-3	0			1.000	-1	/O-4	-0.4

■ JOE STRAIN

Strain, Joseph Allan b: 4/30/54, Denver, Colo. BR/TR, 5'10", 169 lbs. Deb: 6/28/79

YEAR	TM/L	G	AB	R	H	2B	3B	HR	RBI	BB	SO	AVG	OBP	SLG	PRO+	BR/A	SB	CS	SBR	FA	FR	G/POS	TPR
1979	SF-N	67	257	27	62	8	1	1	12	13	21	.241	.286	.292	62	-14	8	4	0	.982	-1	2-67/3-1	-1.1
1980	SF-N	77	189	26	54	6	0	0	16	10	10	.286	.322	.317	81	-5	1	2	-1	.989	-11	2-42/3-6,S-1	-1.5
1981	Chi-N	25	74	7	14	1	0	0	1	5	7	.189	.250	.203	28	-7	0	0	0	.975	7	2-20	0.2
Total	3	169	520	60	130	15	1	1	29	28	38	.250	.293	.288	64	-25	9	6	-1	.983	-5	2-129/3-7,S-1	-2.4

■ PAUL STRAND

Strand, Paul Edward b: 12/19/1893, Carbonado, Wash. d: 7/2/74, Salt Lake City, Utah BR/TL, 6'0.5", 190 lbs. Deb: 5/15/13

YEAR	TM/L	G	AB	R	H	2B	3B	HR	RBI	BB	SO	AVG	OBP	SLG	PRO+	BR/A	SB	CS	SBR	FA	FR	G/POS	TPR
1913	Bos-N	7	6	0	1	0	0	0	0	0	0	.167	.167	.167	-5	-1	0			.875	0	/P-7	0.0
1914	Bos-N	18	24	2	8	2	0	0	3	0	2	.333	.333	.417	123	1	0			.813	-0	P-16	0.0
1915	Bos-N	24	22	3	2	0	0	0	2	0	4	.091	.091	.091	-47	-4	0			.750	-1	/P-6,O-5	-0.2
1924	Phi-A	47	167	15	38	9	4	0	13	4	9	.228	.254	.329	49	-13	3	3	-1	.988	-6	O-44	-2.2
Total	4	96	219	20	49	11	4	0	18	4	15	.224	.244	.311	47	-18	3	3		.989	-7	/O-49,P-29	-2.4

■ LARRY STRANDS

Strands, John Lawrence b: 12/5/1885, Chicago, Ill. d: 1/19/57, Forest Park, Ill. BR/TR, 5'10.5", 165 lbs. Deb: 4/25/15

YEAR	TM/L	G	AB	R	H	2B	3B	HR	RBI	BB	SO	AVG	OBP	SLG	PRO+	BR/A	SB	CS	SBR	FA	FR	G/POS	TPR
1915	New-F	35	75	7	14	3	1	1	11	6	11	.187	.247	.293	55	-6	1			.852	-7	3-12/2-9,O-2	-1.3

■ SAMMY STRANG

Strang, Samuel Nicklin "The Dixie Thrush" (b: Samuel Strang Nicklin)
b: 12/16/1876, Chattanooga, Tenn. d: 3/13/32, Chattanooga, Tenn. BB/TR, 5'8", 160 lbs. Deb: 7/10/1896

YEAR	TM/L	G	AB	R	H	2B	3B	HR	RBI	BB	SO	AVG	OBP	SLG	PRO+	BR/A	SB	CS	SBR	FA	FR	G/POS	TPR
1896	Lou-N	14	46	6	12	0	0	0	7	6	6	.261	.346	.261	64	-2	4			.803	-8	S-14	-0.8
1900	Chi-N	27	102	15	29	3	0	0	9	8		.284	.348	.314	86	-1	1			.887	-11	3-16/S-9,2-2	-1.1
1901	NY-N	135	493	55	139	14	6	1	34	59		.282	.364	.341	109	9	40			.877	2	3-91,2-37/O-5,S-4	1.2
1902	Chi-A	137	536	108	158	18	5	3	46	76		.295	.387	.364	114	14	38			.890	5	*3-137	2.0
	Chi-N	3	11	1	4	0	0	0	0	0		.364	.364	.364	128	0	1			1.000	-1	/2-2,3-2	0.0
1903	Bro-N	135	508	101	138	21	5	0	38	75		.272	.376	.333	106	8	46			.914	-7	*3-124/O-8,2-3	0.2
1904	Bro-N	77	271	28	52	11	0	1	9	45		.192	.316	.244	75	-6	16			.910	-32	2-63,3-12/S-1	-3.9
1905	*NY-N	111	294	51	76	9	4	3	29	58		.259	.389	.347	117	10	23			.915	-17	2-47,O-38/S-9,13	-0.9
1906	NY-N	113	313	50	100	16	4	4	49	54		.319	.423	.435	164	25	21			.944	3	2-57,O-39/S-4,31	3.0
1907	NY-N	123	306	56	77	20	4	4	30	60		.252	.388	.382	137	16	21			.947	-1	O-70,2-13/3-7,1S	1.4
1908	NY-N	28	53	8	5	0	0	0	2	23		.094	.385	.094	52	-1	5			.863	-3	2-14/O-5,S-3	-0.5
Total	10	903	2933	479	790	112	28	16	253	464	6	.269	.377	.343	113	72	216			.891	-70	3-393,2-238,O/S1	0.6

■ ALAN STRANGE

Strange, Alan Cochrane "Inky" b: 11/7/06, Philadelphia, Pa. d: 6/27/94, Seattle, Wash. BR/TR, 5'9", 162 lbs. Deb: 4/17/34

YEAR	TM/L	G	AB	R	H	2B	3B	HR	RBI	BB	SO	AVG	OBP	SLG	PRO+	BR/A	SB	CS	SBR	FA	FR	G/POS	TPR
1934	StL-A	127	430	39	100	17	2	1	45	48	28	.233	.310	.288	51	-31	3	1	0	.955	4	*S-125	-1.9
1935	StL-A	49	147	8	34	6	1	0	17	17	7	.231	.311	.286	53	-10	0	0	0	.960	2	S-49	-0.6
	Was-A	20	54	3	10	2	1	0	5	4	1	.185	.241	.259	30	-6	0	0	0	.974	3	S-16	-0.2
	Yr	69	201	11	44	8	2	0	22	21	8	.219	.293	.279	47	-16	0	0	0	.963	5	S-65	-0.8
1940	StL-A	54	167	26	31	8	3	0	6	22	12	.186	.284	.269	43	-14	2	1	0	.962	3	S-35/2-4	-0.7
1941	StL-A	45	112	14	26	4	0	0	11	15	5	.232	.323	.268	56	-7	1	0	0	.973	2	S-32/1-2,3-1	-0.3
1942	StL-A	19	37	3	10	2	0	0	5	3	1	.270	.325	.324	82	-1	0	1	-1	.935	5	3-10/S-3,2-1	0.3
Total	5	314	947	93	211	39	7	1	89	109	54	.223	.304	.282	50	-69	6	3	0	.959	18	S-260/3-11,2-5,1-2	-3.4

■ DOUG STRANGE

Strange, Joseph Douglas b: 4/13/64, Greenville, S.C. BB/TR, 6'1", 185 lbs. Deb: 7/13/89

YEAR	TM/L	G	AB	R	H	2B	3B	HR	RBI	BB	SO	AVG	OBP	SLG	PRO+	BR/A	SB	CS	SBR	FA	FR	G/POS	TPR
1989	Det-A	64	196	16	42	4	1	1	14	17	36	.214	.280	.260	54	-12	3	3	-1	.878	1	3-54/2-9,S-9,D-1	-1.1
1991	Chi-N	3	9	0	4	1	0	0	1	0	1	.444	.500	.556	188	1	1	0	0	.800	-1	/3-3	0.0
1992	Chi-N	52	94	7	15	1	0	1	5	10	15	.160	.240	.202	26	-9	1	0	0	.900	-0	3-33,2-12	-1.0
1993	Tex-A	145	484	58	124	29	0	7	60	43	69	.256	.321	.360	86	-10	6	4	-1	.980	-9	*2-135/3-9,S-1	-1.5
1994	Tex-A	73	226	26	48	12	1	5	26	15	38	.212	.270	.341	56	-15	1	3	-2	.970	7	2-53,3-13/O-3	-0.7
1995	*Sea-A	74	155	19	42	9	2	2	21	10	25	.271	.323	.394	85	-4	0	3	-2	.948	6	3-41/2-5,O-4,D-1	0.1
1996	Sea-A	88	183	19	43	7	1	3	23	14	31	.235	.293	.333	58	-12	1	0	0	.961	-7	3-39,O-11,D-10/12	-1.8
1997	Mon-N	118	327	40	84	16	2	12	47	36	76	.257	.334	.428	98	-1	0	2	-1	.947	2	*3-105/2-3,O-2,1-1	0.0
1998	Pit-N	90	185	9	32	8	0	0	14	10	39	.173	.219	.216	14	-24	1	0	0	.940	-3	3-42/2-9,1-3	-2.6
Total	9	707	1859	194	434	87	7	31	211	155	330	.233	.297	.338	68	-85	14	15	-5	.927	-6	3-339,2-229/ODS1	-8.6

■ ASA STRATTON

Stratton, Asa Evans b: 2/10/1853, Grafton, Mass. d: 8/14/25, Fitchburg, Mass. Deb: 6/17/1881

YEAR	TM/L	G	AB	R	H	2B	3B	HR	RBI	BB	SO	AVG	OBP	SLG	PRO+	BR/A	SB	CS	SBR	FA	FR	G/POS	TPR
1881	Wor-N	1	4	0	1	0	0	0	0	0	2	.250	.250	.250	55	-0				.333	-1	/S-1	-0.2

■ SCOTT STRATTON

Stratton, C. Scott b: 10/2/1869, Campbellsburg, Ky. d: 3/8/39, Louisville, Ky. BL/TR, 6', 180 lbs. Deb: 4/21/1888

YEAR	TM/L	G	AB	R	H	2B	3B	HR	RBI	BB	SO	AVG	OBP	SLG	PRO+	BR/A	SB	CS	SBR	FA	FR	G/POS	TPR
1888	Lou-a	67	249	35	64	8	1	1	29	12		.257	.310	.309	101	0	10			.821	-5	O-38,P-33	-0.5
1889	Lou-a	62	229	30	66	7	5	4	34	13	36	.288	.332	.415	114	3	10			.915	5	O-29,P-19,1-17	0.3
1890	*Lou-a	55	189	29	61	3	5	0	24	16		.323	.385	.392	132	8	8			**.977**	5	P-50/O-5	0.0
1891	Pit-N	2	8	1	1	0	0	0	0	0	3	.125	.125	.125	-28	-1	0			.900	1	/P-2	0.0
	Lou-a	34	115	9	27	2	0	0	8	11	13	.235	.307	.252	61	-6	8			.939	2	P-20/1-8,O-6	-0.3
1892	Lou-N	63	219	22	56	2	9	0	23	17	21	.256	.318	.347	110	2	9			.915	1	P-42,O-17/1-6	-0.1
1893	Lou-N	60	217	34	49	8	5	0	16	25	15	.226	.309	.309	70	-9	6			.975	6	P-37,O-24/1-1	-0.4
1894	Lou-N	13	37	9	12	1	2	0	4	4	2	.324	.390	.459	112	1	1			.929	2	/P-7,O-5	0.1
	Chi-N	23	96	29	36	5	4	3	23	6	1	.375	.417	.604	136	5	3			.933	-1	P-15/O-5,1-2	0.0
	Yr	36	133	38	48	6	6	3	27	10	3	.361	.410	.564	131	6	4			.932	1	P-22,O-10/1-2	0.1
1895	Chi-N	10	24	3	7	1	1	0	2	4	2	.292	.393	.417	102	0	1			.833	-1	/P-5,O-4	-0.1
Total	8	389	1383	201	379	37	32	8	163	108	93	.274	.335	.364	103	4	56			.938	15	P-230,O-133/1-34	-1.0

■ JOE STRAUB

Straub, Joseph b: 1/19/1858, Germany d: 2/13/29, Pueblo, Colo. BR/TR, 5'10", 160 lbs. Deb: 6/24/1880

YEAR	TM/L	G	AB	R	H	2B	3B	HR	RBI	BB	SO	AVG	OBP	SLG	PRO+	BR/A	SB	CS	SBR	FA	FR	G/POS	TPR
1880	Tro-N	3	12	1	3	0	0	0	3	1	3	.250	.308	.250	87	-0				.815	0	/C-3	0.0
1882	Phi-a	8	32	2	6	2	0	0	1	1		.188	.212	.250	50	-2				.830	-1	/C-7,O-1	-0.2
1883	Col-a	27	100	4	13	0	0	0		4		.130	.163	.130	-5	-11				.860	-3	C-14,1-12/O-1	-1.3
Total	3	38	144	7	22	2	0	0	4	6	3	.153	.187	.167	17	-13				.843	-4	/C-24,1-12,O-2	-1.5

■ JOE STRAUSS

Strauss, Joseph "Dutch" or "The Socker" (b: Joseph Strasser)
b: 11/16/1858, Cincinnati, Ohio d: 6/24/06, Cincinnati, Ohio BR/TR, Deb: 7/27/1884

YEAR	TM/L	G	AB	R	H	2B	3B	HR	RBI	BB	SO	AVG	OBP	SLG	PRO+	BR/A	SB	CS	SBR	FA	FR	G/POS	TPR
1884	KC-U	16	60	4	12	3	0	0		1		.200	.213	.250	46	-6				.833	-1	O-10/C-3,2-2,3-1	-0.6
1885	Lou-a	2	6	0	1	0	0	0	0	0		.167	.167	.167	6	-1				.000	-2	/O-1,C-1	-0.2
1886	Lou-a	74	297	36	64	5	6	1	31	8		.215	.239	.283	60	-15	25			.857	4	O-73/P-2,C-1	-1.1
	Bro-a	9	36	6	9	1	1	0	5	1		.250	.270	.333	88	-1	4			1.000	1	/O-7,C-2	0.0
	Yr	83	333	42	73	6	7	1	36	9		.219	.242	.288	63	-16	29			.866	5	O-80/C-3,P-2	-1.1
Total	3	101	399	46	86	9	7	1	36	10		.216	.237	.281	59	-22	29			.861	2	/O-91,C-7,P-2,23	-1.9

■ DARRYL STRAWBERRY

Strawberry, Darryl Eugene b: 3/12/62, Los Angeles, Cal. BL/TL, 6'6", 200 lbs. Deb: 5/6/83

YEAR	TM/L	G	AB	R	H	2B	3B	HR	RBI	BB	SO	AVG	OBP	SLG	PRO+	BR/A	SB	CS	SBR	FA	FR	G/POS	TPR
1983	NY-N	122	420	63	108	15	7	26	74	47	128	.257	.338	.512	134	17	19	6	2	.984	6	*O-117	2.3
1984	NY-N★	147	522	75	131	27	4	26	97	75	131	.251	.345	.467	128	19	27	8	3	.980	4	*O-146	2.3
1985	NY-N★	111	393	78	109	15	4	29	79	73	96	.277	.392	.557	167	36	26	11	1	.991	-4	*O-110	3.0
1986	*NY-N★	136	475	76	123	27	5	27	93	72	141	.259	.363	.507	142	27	28	12	1	.975	2	*O-131	2.7
1987	NY-N★	154	532	108	151	32	5	39	104	97	122	.284	.401	.583	165	51	36	12	4	.972	1	*O-151	5.0
1988	*NY-N★	153	543	101	146	27	3	**39**	101	85	127	.269	.371	**.545**	**168**	47	29	14	0	.971	7	*O-150	**5.2**
1989	NY-N†	134	476	69	107	26	1	29	77	61	105	.225	.314	.466	126	15	11	4	1	.972	9	*O-131	2.2
1990	NY-N★	152	542	92	150	18	1	37	108	70	110	.277	.364	.518	140	29	15	8	-0	.989	6	*O-149	3.2
1991	LA-N†	139	505	86	134	22	4	28	99	75	125	.265	.364	.491	141	28	10	8	-2	.978	-2	*O-136	2.1
1992	LA-N	43	156	20	37	8	0	5	25	19	34	.237	.324	.385	101	0	3	1	0	.986	-1	O-42	-0.1

YEAR	TM/L	G	AB	R	H	2B	3B	HR	RBI	BB	SO	AVG	OBP	SLG	PRO+	BR/A	SB	CS	SBR	FA	FR	G/POS	TPR
1993	LA-N	32	100	12	14	2	0	5	12	16	19	.140	.271	.310	59	-6	1	0	0	.905	-4	O-29	-1.1
1994	SF-N	29	92	13	22	3	1	4	17	19	22	.239	.369	.424	111	2	0	3	-2	.969	2	O-27	0.1
1995	*NY-A	32	87	15	24	4	1	3	13	10	22	.276	.364	.448	111	1	0	0	0	.909	1	D-15,O-11	0.1
1996	*NY-A	63	202	35	53	13	0	11	36	31	55	.262	.363	.490	113	4	6	5	-1	1.000	-3	O-34,D-26	-0.3
1997	NY-A	11	29	1	3	1	0	0	2	3	9	.103	.188	.138	-13	-5	0	0	0	1.000	-1	/O-4,D-4	-0.5
1998	NY-A	101	295	44	73	11	2	24	57	46	90	.247	.355	.542	132	13	8	7	-2	.905	-3	D-81,O-16	0.3
Total	16	1559	5369	888	1385	251	38	332	994	799	1336	.258	.358	.504	139	279	219	99	6	.977	20	*O-1384,D-126	26.5

■ GABBY STREET Street, Charles Evard "Old Sarge" b: 9/30/1882, Huntsville, Ala. d: 2/6/51, Joplin, Mo. BR/TR, 5'11", 180 lbs. Deb: 9/13/04 MC

YEAR	TM/L	G	AB	R	H	2B	3B	HR	RBI	BB	SO	AVG	OBP	SLG	PRO+	BR/A	SB	CS	SBR	FA	FR	G/POS	TPR
1904	Cin-N	11	33	1	4	1	0	0	0	1		.121	.147	.152	-7	-4	2			.973	4	C-11	0.1
1905	Cin-N	2	2	0	0	0	0	0	0	2		.000	.500	.000	48	0	0			1.000	1	/C-1	0.1
	Bos-N	3	12	0	2	0	0	0	0	0		.167	.167	.167	-1	-1	1			.778	-2	/C-3	-0.4
	Cin-N	29	91	8	23	5	1	0	8	6		.253	.306	.330	81	-2	1			.975	3	C-26	0.4
	Yr	34	105	8	25	5	1	0	8	8		.238	.298	.305	73	-4	2			.957	2	C-30	0.1
1908	Was-A	131	394	31	81	12	7	1	32	40		.206	.289	.279	92	-3	5			.973	-1	*C-128	0.8
1909	Was-A	137	407	25	86	12	1	0	29	26		.211	.262	.246	63	-17	2			.981	11	*C-137	0.7
1910	Was-A	89	257	13	52	6	0	1	16	23		.202	.273	.237	63	-11	1			**.978**	9	C-86	0.7
1911	Was-A	72	216	16	48	7	1	0	14	14		.222	.279	.264	53	-14	4			.973	7	C-71	0.0
1912	NY-A	29	88	4	16	1	1	0	6	7		.182	.258	.216	34	-8	1			.958	0	C-29	-0.5
1931	StL-N	1	1	0	0	0	0	0	0	0	0	.000	.000	.000	-96	-0	0			1.000	0	/C-1,M	0.0
Total	8	504	1501	98	312	44	11	2	105	119	0	.208	.273	.256	66	-60	17			.974	32	C-493	1.9

■ WALT STREULI Streuli, Walter Herbert b: 9/26/35, Memphis, Tenn. BR/TR, 6'2", 195 lbs. Deb: 9/25/54

YEAR	TM/L	G	AB	R	H	2B	3B	HR	RBI	BB	SO	AVG	OBP	SLG	PRO+	BR/A	SB	CS	SBR	FA	FR	G/POS	TPR
1954	Det-A	1	0	0	0	0	0	0	0	1	0	—	1.000	—	195	0	0	0	0	1.000	-0	/C-1	0.0
1955	Det-A	2	4	1	1	1	0	0	1	0	0	.250	.250	.500	100	-0	0	0	0	1.000	0	/C-2	0.0
1956	Det-A	3	8	0	2	1	0	0	1	1	2	.250	.333	.375	87	-0	0	0	0	.933	0	/C-3	0.0
Total	3	6	12	1	3	2	0	0	2	2	2	.250	.357	.417	106	0	0	0	0	.957	0	/C-6	0.0

■ JOHN STRICK Strick, John Quincy Adams Deb: 5/18/1882

YEAR	TM/L	G	AB	R	H	2B	3B	HR	RBI	BB	SO	AVG	OBP	SLG	PRO+	BR/A	SB	CS	SBR	FA	FR	G/POS	TPR
1882	Lou-a	32	110	17	18	6	1	0		9		.164	.227	.236	60	-4				.898	-0	C-21/O-6,2-6,S-1,1	-0.3

■ CUB STRICKER Stricker, John A. (b: John A. Streaker) b: 2/15/1860, Philadelphia, Pa. d: 11/19/37, Philadelphia, Pa. BR/TR, 5'3", 138 lbs. Deb: 5/2/1882 M

YEAR	TM/L	G	AB	R	H	2B	3B	HR	RBI	BB	SO	AVG	OBP	SLG	PRO+	BR/A	SB	CS	SBR	FA	FR	G/POS	TPR
1882	Phi-a	72	272	34	59	6	1	0	18	15		.217	.258	.246	63	-12				.904	**23**	*2-72/P-2,O-1	1.2
1883	Phi-a	89	330	67	90	8	0	1	40	19		.273	.312	.306	93	-4				.837	-20	*2-88/C-2	-2.0
1884	Phi-a	107	399	59	92	16	11	1		19		.231	.267	.333	89	-6				.870	-34	*2-107/O-1,C-1,P-1	-3.5
1885	Phi-a	106	398	71	93	9	3	1	41	21		.234	.284	.279	74	-12				.879	-13	*2-106	-2.0
1887	Cle-a	131	534	122	141	19	4	2	53	53		.264	.334	.326	87	-8	86			.912	10	*2-126/S-6,P-3	0.5
1888	Cle-a	127	493	80	115	13	6	1	33	50		.233	.311	.290	96	-0	60			.929	23	*2-122/O-6,P-2	2.5
1889	Cle-N	136	566	83	142	10	4	1	47	58	18	.251	.323	.288	73	-19	32			.932	7	*2-135/S-1	-0.4
1890	Cle-P	127	544	93	133	19	8	2	65	54	16	.244	.318	.320	77	-17	24			.905	5	*2-109,S-20	-0.3
1891	Bos-a	139	514	96	111	15	4	0	46	63	34	.216	.309	.261	64	-23	54			.942	**24**	*2-139	0.7
1892	StL-N	28	98	12	20	1	0	0	11	10	7	.204	.297	.214	58	-4	5			.939	-4	2-27/S-1,M	-0.8
	Bal-N	75	269	45	71	5	5	3	37	32	18	.264	.344	.353	108	3	13			.918	3	2-75	0.6
	Yr	103	367	57	91	6	5	3	48	42	25	.248	.332	.316	96	-1	18			.923	-2	*2-102/S-1	-0.2
1893	Was-N	59	218	28	39	7	1	0	20	20	12	.179	.248	.220	25	-24	4			.903	7	2-39,O-12/S-4,3-4	-1.4
Total	11	1196	4635	790	1106	128	47	12	411	414	105	.239	.306	.294	78	-125	278			.907	30	*2-1145/S-32,OP3C	-4.9

■ GEORGE STRICKLAND Strickland, George Bevan "Bo" b: 1/10/26, New Orleans, La. BR/TR, 6'1", 180 lbs. Deb: 5/7/50 MC

YEAR	TM/L	G	AB	R	H	2B	3B	HR	RBI	BB	SO	AVG	OBP	SLG	PRO+	BR/A	SB	CS	SBR	FA	FR	G/POS	TPR
1950	Pit-N	23	27	0	3	0	0	0	2	3	8	.111	.226	.111	-8	-4	0			.978	3	S-19/3-1	-0.1
1951	Pit-N	138	454	59	98	12	7	9	47	65	83	.216	.318	.333	73	-17	4	2	0	.943	12	*S-125,2-13	0.5
1952	Pit-N	76	232	17	41	6	2	5	22	21	45	.177	.248	.284	46	-17	4	2	0	.953	15	2-45,S-28/1-1,3-1	0.2
	Cle-A	31	88	8	19	4	0	1	8	14	15	.216	.324	.295	78	-2	0	0	0	.964	10	S-30/2-1	0.9
1953	Cle-A	123	419	43	119	17	4	5	47	51	52	.284	.362	.379	103	3	0	0	0	.974	16	*S-122/1-1	2.7
1954	*Cle-A	112	361	42	77	12	3	6	37	55	62	.213	.319	.313	72	-13	2	1	0	.961	-12	*S-112	-1.6
1955	Cle-A	130	388	34	81	9	5	2	34	49	60	.209	.302	.273	54	-25	1	0	0	**.976**	8	*S-128	-0.6
1956	Cle-A	85	171	22	36	1	2	3	17	22	27	.211	.301	.292	56	-11	0	1	-1	.986	16	2-28,S-28,3-26	0.8
1957	Cle-A	89	201	21	47	8	2	1	19	26	29	.234	.325	.308	75	-7	0	3	-2	.980	15	2-48,S-23,3-19	1.1
1959	Cle-A	132	441	55	105	15	2	3	48	51	64	.238	.317	.302	74	-15	1	1	-0	.971	-9	3-80,S-50/2-4	-2.0
1960	Cle-A	32	42	4	7	0	0	1	3	4	8	.167	.255	.238	35	-4	0	0	0	.962	1	S-14,3-12/2-2	-0.3
Total	10	971	2824	305	633	84	27	36	284	361	453	.224	.314	.311	70	-112	12	10	0	.963	74	S-679,2-141,3/1	1.6

■ GEORGE STRIEF Strief, George Andrew b: 10/16/1856, Cincinnati, Ohio d: 4/1/46, Cleveland, Ohio BR/TR, 5'7", 172 lbs. Deb: 5/1/1879 U

YEAR	TM/L	G	AB	R	H	2B	3B	HR	RBI	BB	SO	AVG	OBP	SLG	PRO+	BR/A	SB	CS	SBR	FA	FR	G/POS	TPR
1879	Cle-N	71	264	24	46	7	1	0	15	10	23	.174	.204	.208	37	-17				.918	-9	O-55,2-16	-2.6
1882	Pit-a	79	297	45	58	9	6	2		13		.195	.229	.286	76	-7				.917	0	*2-78/S-1	-0.4
1883	StL-a	82	302	22	68	9	0	1	22	12		.225	.255	.265	64	-13				.899	6	*2-67,O-15	-0.5
1884	StL-a	48	184	22	37	5	2	2		13		.201	.254	.283	72	-6				.848	-3	O-44/2-3,1-1	-0.9
	KC-U	15	56	5	6	5	0	0		4		.107	.167	.196	11	-8				.900	8	2-15	0.1
	CP-U	15	53	6	11	5	0	0		3		.208	.250	.302	67	-4				.905	-2	2-15	-0.5
	Yr	30	109	11	17	10	0	0		7		.156	.207	.248	40	-11				.902	7	2-30	-0.4
	Cle-N	8	29	2	7	2	0	0	0	0	5	.241	.241	.310	70	-1				1.000	-0	/O-6,3-2	-0.1
1885	Phi-a	44	175	19	48	8	5	0	27	9		.274	.310	.377	110	1				.828	-2	3-19,S-10/O-8,2-7	-0.1
Total	5	362	1360	145	281	50	14	5	64	64	28	.207	.242	.275	67	-53				.899	-1	2-201,O-128/3S1	-5.0

■ LOU STRINGER Stringer, Louis Bernard b: 5/13/17, Grand Rapids, Mich BR/TR, 5'11", 173 lbs. Deb: 4/15/41

YEAR	TM/L	G	AB	R	H	2B	3B	HR	RBI	BB	SO	AVG	OBP	SLG	PRO+	BR/A	SB	CS	SBR	FA	FR	G/POS	TPR
1941	Chi-N	145	512	59	126	31	4	5	53	59	86	.246	.324	.352	94	-4	3			.960	20	*2-137/S-7	2.6
1942	Chi-N	121	406	45	96	10	5	9	41	31	55	.236	.292	.352	92	-6	3			.955	2	*2-113/3-1	0.3
1946	Chi-N	80	209	26	51	3	1	3	19	26	34	.244	.328	.311	83	-4	0			.956	-5	2-62/S-1,3-1	-0.5
1948	Bos-A	4	11	1	1	0	0	1	1	0	3	.091	.091	.364	17	-1	0	0	0	.947	2	/2-2	0.1
1949	Bos-A	35	41	10	11	4	0	1	6	5	10	.268	.348	.439	100	-0	0	0	0	.978	3	/2-9	0.3
1950	Bos-A	24	17	7	5	1	0	0	2	0	4	.294	.294	.353	59	-1	1	0	0	.778	3	/3-3,2-1,S-1	0.2
Total	6	409	1196	148	290	49	10	19	122	121	192	.242	.313	.348	90	-17	7	0	0	.958	25	2-324/S-9,3-5	3.0

■ JOE STRIPP Stripp, Joseph Valentine "Jersey Joe" b: 2/3/03, Harrison, N.J. d: 6/10/89, Orlando, Fla. BR/TR, 5'11.5", 175 lbs. Deb: 7/2/28

YEAR	TM/L	G	AB	R	H	2B	3B	HR	RBI	BB	SO	AVG	OBP	SLG	PRO+	BR/A	SB	CS	SBR	FA	FR	G/POS	TPR
1928	Cin-N	42	139	18	40	7	3	1	17	8	8	.288	.340	.403	95	-1	0			.931	-7	O-21,3-17/S-1	-0.8
1929	Cin-N	64	187	24	40	3	2	3	20	24	15	.214	.313	.299	55	-13	2			.960	8	3-55/2-2	-0.2
1930	Cin-N	130	464	74	142	37	6	3	64	51	37	.306	.377	.431	100	1	15			.996	0	1-75,3-48	-0.4
1931	Cin-N	105	426	71	138	26	2	3	42	21	31	.324	.359	.415	114	8	5			.957	4	3-96/1-9	1.6
1932	Bro-N	138	534	94	162	36	9	6	64	36	30	.303	.350	.438	113	9	14			.954	16	3-93,1-43	2.7
1933	Bro-N	141	537	69	149	20	7	1	51	26	23	.277	.312	.346	92	-7	5			.967	5	*3-140	0.7
1934	Bro-N	104	384	50	121	19	6	1	40	22	20	.315	.354	.404	108	4	2			.941	-6	3-96/1-7,S-1	0.1
1935	Bro-N	109	373	44	114	13	5	3	43	22	15	.306	.344	.391	99	-0	2			.962	7	3-88,1-15/O-1	0.8
1936	Bro-N	110	439	51	139	31	1	1	60	22	12	.317	.351	.399	100	0	2			**.968**	8	*3-106	1.1
1937	Bro-N	90	300	37	73	10	2	1	26	20	18	.243	.291	.300	60	-17	1			.971	-6	3-66,1-14/S-3	-2.3
1938	StL-N	54	199	24	57	7	0	0	18	18	10	.286	.349	.322	81	-5	0			.977	-8	3-51	-1.2
	Bos-N	59	229	19	63	10	0	1	19	10	7	.275	.305	.332	84	-6	2			.966	1	3-58	-0.4
	Yr	113	428	43	120	17	0	1	37	28	17	.280	.326	.327	82	-10	2			**.971**	-7	*3-109	-1.6
Total	11	1146	4211	575	1238	219	43	24	464	280	226	.294	.340	.384	96	-27	50			.961	21	3-914,1-163/OS2	1.7

■ MARK STRITTMATTER Strittmatter, Mark Arthur b: 4/4/69, Huntington, N.Y. BR/TR, 6'1", 210 lbs. Deb: 9/3/98

YEAR	TM/L	G	AB	R	H	2B	3B	HR	RBI	BB	SO	AVG	OBP	SLG	PRO+	BR/A	SB	CS	SBR	FA	FR	G/POS	TPR
1998	Col-N	4	4	0	0	0	0	0	0	0	3	.000	.000	.000	-84	-1	0	0	0	1.000	1	/C-3	0.0

■ ALLIE STROBEL
Strobel, Albert Irving b: 6/11/1884, Boston, Mass. d: 2/10/55, Hollywood, Fla. BR/TR, 6', 160 lbs. Deb: 8/29/05

YEAR	TM/L	G	AB	R	H	2B	3B	HR	RBI	BB	SO	AVG	OBP	SLG	PRO+	BR/A	SB	CS	SBR	FA	FR	G/POS	TPR
1905	Bos-N	5	19	1	2	0	0	0	2	0		.105	.105	.105	-38	-3	0			1.000	-0	/3-4,O-1	-0.4
1906	Bos-N	100	317	28	64	10	3	1	24	29		.202	.273	.262	69	-12	2			.946	-6	2-93/S-6,O-1	-1.8
Total	2	105	336	29	66	10	3	1	26	29		.196	.264	.253	63	-15	2			1.000	-6	/2-93,S-6,3-4,O-2	-2.2

■ JIM STRONER
Stroner, James Melvin b: 5/29/01, Chicago, Ill. d: 12/6/75, Tarboro, N.C. BR/TR, 5'10", 175 lbs. Deb: 5/1/29

YEAR	TM/L	G	AB	R	H	2B	3B	HR	RBI	BB	SO	AVG	OBP	SLG	PRO+	BR/A	SB	CS	SBR	FA	FR	G/POS	TPR
1929	Pit-N	6	8	0	3	1	0	0	0	1	0	.375	.444	.500	130	0	0			.571	-0	/3-2	0.0

■ ED STROUD
Stroud, Edwin Marvin b: 10/31/39, Lapine, Ala. BL/TR, 5'11", 180 lbs. Deb: 9/11/66

YEAR	TM/L	G	AB	R	H	2B	3B	HR	RBI	BB	SO	AVG	OBP	SLG	PRO+	BR/A	SB	CS	SBR	FA	FR	G/POS	TPR
1966	Chi-A	12	36	3	6	2	0	0	1	2	8	.167	.231	.222	33	-3	3	0	1	1.000	-0	O-11	-0.3
1967	Chi-A	20	27	6	8	0	1	0	3	1	5	.296	.345	.370	116	0	7	2	1	1.000	-1	O-12	0.0
	Was-A	87	204	36	41	5	3	1	10	25	29	.201	.291	.270	69	-7	8	6	-1	.983	-13	O-79	-2.7
	Yr	107	231	42	49	5	4	1	13	26	34	.212	.297	.281	75	-7	15	8	-0	.985	-14	O-91	-2.7
1968	Was-A	105	306	41	73	10	10	4	23	20	50	.239	.285	.376	102	-0	9	3	1	.979	-4	O-84	-0.9
1969	Was-A	123	206	35	52	5	6	4	29	30	33	.252	.353	.393	114	4	12	2	2	.982	-11	O-85	-0.8
1970	Was-A	129	433	69	115	11	5	5	32	40	79	.266	.332	.349	92	-5	29	8	4	.993	2	*O-118	-0.4
1971	Chi-A	53	141	19	25	4	3	0	2	11	20	.177	.237	.248	36	-12	4	5	-2	1.000	-11	O-44	-2.9
Total	6	529	1353	209	320	37	28	14	100	129	224	.237	.307	.336	87	-22	72	26	6	.988	-38	O-433	-8.0

■ STEVE STROUGHTER
Stroughter, Stephen Lewis b: 3/15/52, Visalia, Cal. BL/TR, 6'2", 190 lbs. Deb: 4/7/82

YEAR	TM/L	G	AB	R	H	2B	3B	HR	RBI	BB	SO	AVG	OBP	SLG	PRO+	BR/A	SB	CS	SBR	FA	FR	G/POS	TPR
1982	Sea-A	26	47	4	8	1	0	1	3	3	9	.170	.235	.255	34	-4	0	0	0	1.000	1	/O-3,D-9	-0.3

■ AMOS STRUNK
Strunk, Amos Aaron b: 1/22/1889, Philadelphia, Pa. d: 7/22/79, Llanerch, Pa. BL/TL, 5'11.5", 175 lbs. Deb: 9/24/08

YEAR	TM/L	G	AB	R	H	2B	3B	HR	RBI	BB	SO	AVG	OBP	SLG	PRO+	BR/A	SB	CS	SBR	FA	FR	G/POS	TPR
1908	Phi-A	12	34	4	8	1	0	0	0	4		.235	.316	.265	83	-1	0			.903	1	O-11	0.0
1909	Phi-A	11	35	1	4	0	0	0	2	1		.114	.139	.114	-20	-5	2			1.000	-1	/O-9	-0.7
1910	*Phi-A	16	48	9	16	0	1	0	2	3		.333	.373	.375	135	2	4			1.000	1	O-14	0.2
1911	*Phi-A	74	215	42	55	7	2	1	21	35		.256	.363	.321	93	-1	13			.958	1	O-62/1-2	-0.2
1912	Phi-A	122	412	58	119	13	12	3	63	47		.289	.366	.400	123	13	29			**.990**	11	*O-116	1.8
1913	*Phi-A	94	292	30	89	11	12	0	46	29	23	.305	.368	.425	135	12	14			.962	-2	O-81	0.8
1914	*Phi-A	122	404	58	111	15	3	2	45	57	38	.275	.364	.342	117	10	25	22	-6	**.987**	9	*O-120	0.8
1915	Phi-A	132	485	76	144	28	16	1	45	56	45	.297	.371	.427	144	25	17	19	-6	.980	12	*O-111,1-19	2.6
1916	Phi-A	150	544	71	172	30	9	3	49	66	59	.316	.393	.421	152	35	21	23	-8	.978	2	*O-143/1-7	2.3
1917	Phi-A	148	540	83	152	26	7	1	45	68	37	.281	.363	.361	123	16	16			**.986**	-2	*O-146	0.6
1918	*Bos-A	114	413	50	106	18	9	0	35	36	13	.257	.316	.344	101	-1	20			**.988**	-5	*O-113	-1.3
1919	Bos-A	48	184	27	50	11	3	0	17	13	13	.272	.323	.364	98	-1	3			.968	-1	O-48	-0.6
	Phi-A	60	194	15	41	6	4	0	13	23	15	.211	.298	.284	63	-9	3			.981	1	O-52	-1.3
	Yr	108	378	42	91	17	7	0	30	36	28	.241	.310	.323	79	-11	6			.974	-1	*O-100	-1.9
1920	Phi-A	58	202	23	60	9	3	0	20	21	9	.297	.363	.371	94	-1	0	6	-4	.990	-4	O-54	-1.3
	Chi-A	53	188	33	45	8	1	1	16	28	15	.239	.338	.309	72	-7	1	0	0	.981	-1	O-49	-1.0
	Yr	111	390	56	105	17	4	1	36	49	24	.269	.351	.341	83	-8	1	6	-3	.985	-5	*O-103	-2.3
1921	Chi-A	121	401	68	133	19	10	3	69	38	27	.332	.391	.451	116	10	7	10	-4	.970	-8	*O-111	-0.9
1922	Chi-A	92	311	36	90	11	4	0	33	33	28	.289	.358	.350	85	-6	9	6	-1	.989	2	O-74/1-7	-1.0
1923	Chi-A	54	54	7	17	0	0	0	8	8	5	.315	.403	.315	92	-0	1	0	0	1.000	-0	/O-5,1-2	0.0
1924	Chi-A	1	1	0	0	0	0	0	0	0	0	.000	.000	.000	-99	-0	0	0	0	.000	0	H	0.0
	Phi-A	30	42	5	6	0	0	0	1	7	4	.143	.265	.143	7	-6	0	0	0	1.000	-3	/O-8	-0.8
	Yr	31	43	5	6	0	0	0	1	7	4	.140	.260	.140	5	-6	0	0	0	1.000	-3	/O-8	-0.8
Total	17	1512	4999	696	1418	213	96	15	530	573	331	.284	.359	.374	112	86	185	86		.980	13	*O-1327/1-37	0.0

■ AL STRUVE
Struve, Albert b: St.Louis, Mo. Deb: 6/22/1884

YEAR	TM/L	G	AB	R	H	2B	3B	HR	RBI	BB	SO	AVG	OBP	SLG	PRO+	BR/A	SB	CS	SBR	FA	FR	G/POS	TPR
1884	StL-a	2	7	2	2	0	0	0		0		.286	.286	.286	84	-0				.000	1	/O-1,C-1	0.1

■ LUKE STUART
Stuart, Luther Lane b: 5/23/1892, Alamance Co., N.C. d: 6/15/47, Winston-Salem, N.C. BR/TR, 5'8", 165 lbs. Deb: 7/28/21

YEAR	TM/L	G	AB	R	H	2B	3B	HR	RBI	BB	SO	AVG	OBP	SLG	PRO+	BR/A	SB	CS	SBR	FA	FR	G/POS	TPR
1921	StL-A	3	3	2	1	0	0	1	2	0	1	.333	.333	1.333	291	1	0	0	0	1.000	-1	/2-3	0.0

■ DICK STUART
Stuart, Richard Lee "Dr. Strangeglove" b: 11/7/32, San Francisco, Cal. BR/TR, 6'4", 212 lbs. Deb: 7/10/58

YEAR	TM/L	G	AB	R	H	2B	3B	HR	RBI	BB	SO	AVG	OBP	SLG	PRO+	BR/A	SB	CS	SBR	FA	FR	G/POS	TPR
1958	Pit-N	67	254	38	68	12	5	16	48	11	75	.268	.311	.543	124	7	0	0	0	.973	1	1-64	0.3
1959	Pit-N	118	397	64	118	15	2	27	78	42	86	.297	.367	.549	141	22	1	1	-0	.976	1	*1-105/O-1	1.6
1960	*Pit-N	122	438	48	114	17	5	23	83	39	107	.260	.321	.479	115	8	0	0	0	.986	-1	*1-108	-0.3
1961	Pit-N★	138	532	83	160	28	8	35	117	34	121	.301	.347	.581	140	28	0	3	-2	.983	-2	*1-132/O-1	1.3
1962	Pit-N	114	394	52	90	11	4	16	64	32	94	.228	.290	.398	83	-11	0	1	-1	.982	2	*1-101	-1.7
1963	Bos-A	157	612	81	160	25	4	42	**118**	44	144	.261	.312	.521	125	18	0	0	0	.979	8	*1-155	2.0
1964	Bos-A	156	603	73	168	27	1	33	114	37	130	.279	.323	.491	117	12	0	0	0	.981	1	*1-155	0.7
1965	Phi-N	149	538	53	126	19	1	28	95	39	136	.234	.290	.429	101	-1	1	0	0	.986	3	*1-143/3-1	-0.5
1966	NY-N	31	87	7	19	0	0	4	13	9	26	.218	.292	.356	81	-2	0	1	-1	.974	-1	1-23	-0.6
	*LA-N	38	91	4	24	1	0	3	9	11	17	.264	.356	.374	112	2	0	1	-1	.991	3	1-25	0.3
	Yr	69	178	11	43	1	0	7	22	20	43	.242	.325	.365	97	-1	0	2	-1	.982	2	1-48	-0.3
1969	Cal-A	22	51	3	8	2	0	1	4	3	21	.157	.204	.255	29	-5	0	0	0	.991	-1	1-13	-0.8
Total	10	1112	3997	506	1055	157	30	228	743	301	957	.264	.319	.489	117	77	2	7	-4	.982	13	*1-1024/O-2,3-1	2.3

■ BILL STUART
Stuart, William Alexander "Chauncey" b: 8/28/1873, Boalsburg, Pa. d: 10/14/28, Fort Worth, Tex. 5'11", 170 lbs. Deb: 8/15/1895

YEAR	TM/L	G	AB	R	H	2B	3B	HR	RBI	BB	SO	AVG	OBP	SLG	PRO+	BR/A	SB	CS	SBR	FA	FR	G/POS	TPR
1895	Pit-N	19	77	5	19	3	0	0	10	2	6	.247	.275	.286	47	-6	2			.913	-1	S-17/2-2	-0.5
1899	NY-N	1	3	0	0	0	0	0	0	0		.000	.000	.000	-99	-1	0			1.000	-0	/2-1	-0.1
Total	2	20	80	5	19	3	0	0	10	2	6	.237	.265	.275	42	-7	2			.909	-1	/S-17,2-3	-0.6

■ FRANKLIN STUBBS
Stubbs, Franklin Lee b: 10/21/60, Richlands, N.C. BL/TL, 6'2", 215 lbs. Deb: 4/28/84

YEAR	TM/L	G	AB	R	H	2B	3B	HR	RBI	BB	SO	AVG	OBP	SLG	PRO+	BR/A	SB	CS	SBR	FA	FR	G/POS	TPR
1984	LA-N	87	217	22	42	2	3	8	17	24	63	.194	.274	.341	73	-8	2	2	-1	.993	-1	1-51,O-20	-1.3
1985	LA-N	10	9	0	2	0	0	0	2	0	3	.222	.222	.222	25	-1	0	0	0	1.000	-0	/1-4	-0.1
1986	LA-N	132	420	55	95	11	1	23	58	37	107	.226	.292	.421	101	-2	7	1	2	.969	-4	*O-124,1-13	-0.9
1987	LA-N	129	386	48	90	16	3	16	52	31	85	.233	.292	.415	87	-9	8	1	2	**.994**	7	*1-111,O-18	-0.8
1988	*LA-N	115	242	30	54	13	0	8	34	23	61	.223	.293	.376	94	-2	11	3	2	.978	2	1-84,O-13	-0.4
1989	LA-N	69	103	11	30	6	0	4	15	16	27	.291	.387	.466	145	6	3	2	-0	.948	1	O-28/1-7	0.7
1990	Hou-N	146	448	59	117	23	2	23	71	48	114	.261	.335	.475	124	13	19	6	2	.991	-9	1-72,O-71	0.0
1991	Mil-A	103	362	48	77	16	2	11	38	35	71	.213	.286	.359	79	-11	13	4	2	.991	5	1-92/O-4,D-4	-1.1
1992	Mil-A	92	288	37	66	11	1	9	42	27	68	.229	.297	.368	87	-5	11	8	-2	.987	6	1-68,D-16/O-1	-0.7
1995	Det-A	62	116	13	29	11	0	2	19	19	27	.250	.360	.397	97	-0	0	1	-1	.972	-7	1-20,O-20/D-3	-0.9
Total	10	945	2591	323	602	109	12	104	348	260	626	.232	.305	.404	97	-19	74	28	5	.989	-1	1-522,O-299/D-23	-5.5

■ MOOSE STUBING
Stubing, Lawrence George b: 3/31/38, Bronx, N.Y. BL/TL, 6'3", 220 lbs. Deb: 4/14/67 MC

YEAR	TM/L	G	AB	R	H	2B	3B	HR	RBI	BB	SO	AVG	OBP	SLG	PRO+	BR/A	SB	CS	SBR	FA	FR	G/POS	TPR
1967	Cal-A	5	5	0	0	0	0	0	0	0	4	.000	.000	.000	-99	-1	0	0	0	.000	0	H	-0.1

■ SEEM STUDLEY
Studley, Seymour L. "Warhorse" b: Washington, D.C. d: 1874, Washington, D.C. Deb: 4/20/1872

YEAR	TM/L	G	AB	R	H	2B	3B	HR	RBI	BB	SO	AVG	OBP	SLG	PRO+	BR/A	SB	CS	SBR	FA	FR	G/POS	TPR
1872	Nat-n	5	21	3	2	0	0	0	2	0	1	.095	.095	.095	-35	-4	0	0	0	.571	-1	/O-5	-0.3

■ GEORGE STUMPF
Stumpf, George Frederick b: 12/15/10, New Orleans, La. d: 3/6/93, Metairie, La. BL/TL, 5'8", 155 lbs. Deb: 9/19/31

YEAR	TM/L	G	AB	R	H	2B	3B	HR	RBI	BB	SO	AVG	OBP	SLG	PRO+	BR/A	SB	CS	SBR	FA	FR	G/POS	TPR
1931	Bos-A	7	28	2	7	1	1	0	4	1	2	.250	.276	.357	69	-1	0	0	0	1.000	-1	/O-7	-0.3
1932	Bos-A	79	169	18	34	2	2	1	18	18	21	.201	.278	.254	40	-15	1	1	-0	.952	-7	O-51	-2.3
1933	Bos-A	22	41	8	14	3	0	0	5	4	2	.341	.400	.415	117	1	4	0	1	1.000	-3	O-15	-0.1
1936	Chi-A	10	22	3	6	1	0	0	5	2	1	.273	.333	.318	59	-1	0	0	0	1.000	1	/O-4	-0.1
Total	4	118	260	31	61	7	3	1	32	25	26	.235	.302	.296	57	-17	5	1	1	.969	-11	/O-77	-2.8

■ BILL STUMPF
Stumpf, William Frederick b: 3/21/1892, Baltimore, Md. d: 2/14/66, Crownsville, Md. BR/TR, 6'0.5", 175 lbs. Deb: 5/11/12

YEAR	TM/L	G	AB	R	H	2B	3B	HR	RBI	BB	SO	AVG	OBP	SLG	PRO+	BR/A	SB	CS	SBR	FA	FR	G/POS	TPR
1912	NY-A	42	129	8	31	0	0	0	10	6		.240	.279	.240	46	-9	5			.892	-6	S-26/2-8,3-5,1-1,O	-1.3

YEAR	TM/L	G	AB	R	H	2B	3B	HR	RBI	BB	SO	AVG	OBP	SLG	PRO+	BR/A	SB	CS	SBR	FA	FR	G/POS	TPR
1913	NY-A	12	29	5	6	1	0	0	1	3	3	.207	.281	.241	53	-2	0			.818	-3	/S-6,2-4,O-1	-0.5
Total	2	54	158	13	37	1	0	0	11	9	3	.234	.280	.241	47	-11	5			.877	-9	/S-32,2-12,3-5,O1	-1.8

■ GUY STURDY
Sturdy, Guy R. b: 8/7/1899, Sherman, Tex. d: 5/4/65, Marshall, Tex. BL/TL, 6'0.5", 180 lbs. Deb: 9/30/27

YEAR	TM/L	G	AB	R	H	2B	3B	HR	RBI	BB	SO	AVG	OBP	SLG	PRO+	BR/A	SB	CS	SBR	FA	FR	G/POS	TPR
1927	StL-A	5	21	5	9	1	0	0	5	1	0	.429	.455	.476	137	1	2	0	1	.974	-1	/1-5	0.1
1928	StL-A	54	45	3	10	1	0	1	8	8	4	.222	.340	.311	70	-2	1	0	0	1.000	-0	/1-1	-0.2
Total	2	59	66	8	19	2	0	1	13	9	4	.288	.373	.364	91	-1	3	0	1	.975	-1	/1-6	-0.1

■ BOBBY STURGEON
Sturgeon, Robert Howard b: 8/6/19, Clinton, Ind. BR/TR, 6', 175 lbs. Deb: 4/16/40

YEAR	TM/L	G	AB	R	H	2B	3B	HR	RBI	BB	SO	AVG	OBP	SLG	PRO+	BR/A	SB	CS	SBR	FA	FR	G/POS	TPR
1940	Chi-N	7	21	1	4	1	0	0	2	0	1	.190	.190	.238	18	-2	0			.848	2	/S-7	0.0
1941	Chi-N	129	433	45	106	15	3	0	25	9	30	.245	.260	.293	58	-25	5			.956	-4	*S-126/2-1,3-1	-2.1
1942	Chi-N	63	162	8	40	7	1	0	7	4	13	.247	.269	.302	70	-7	2			.988	21	2-32,S-29/3-2	1.7
1946	Chi-N	100	294	26	87	12	2	1	21	10	18	.296	.319	.361	94	-3	0			.934	-13	S-72,2-21	-1.3
1947	Chi-N	87	232	16	59	10	5	0	21	7	12	.254	.276	.341	66	-12	0			.975	13	S-45,2-30/3-5	0.4
1948	Bos-N	34	78	10	17	3	1	0	4	4	5	.218	.256	.282	46	-6	0			.938	-3	2-18/S-4,3-4	-0.9
Total	6	420	1220	106	313	48	12	1	80	34	79	.257	.277	.318	68	-56	7			.951	14	S-283,2-102/3-12	-2.2

■ DEAN STURGIS
Sturgis, Dean Donnell b: 12/1/1892, Beloit, Kan. d: 6/4/50, Uniontown, Pa. BR/TR, 6'1", 180 lbs. Deb: 5/1/14

YEAR	TM/L	G	AB	R	H	2B	3B	HR	RBI	BB	SO	AVG	OBP	SLG	PRO+	BR/A	SB	CS	SBR	FA	FR	G/POS	TPR
1914	Phi-A	4	4	1	1	0	0	0	0	1	2	.250	.400	.250	100	0	0			1.000	0	/C-1	0.0

■ JOHNNY STURM
Sturm, John Peter Joseph b: 1/23/16, St.Louis, Mo. BL/TL, 6'1", 185 lbs. Deb: 4/14/41

YEAR	TM/L	G	AB	R	H	2B	3B	HR	RBI	BB	SO	AVG	OBP	SLG	PRO+	BR/A	SB	CS	SBR	FA	FR	G/POS	TPR
1941	*NY-A	124	524	58	125	17	3	3	36	37	50	.239	.293	.300	58	-32	3	5	-2	.990	-2	*1-124	-4.5

■ GEORGE STUTZ
Stutz, George "Kid" or "Satan" b: 2/12/1893, Philadelphia, Pa. d: 12/29/30, Philadelphia, Pa. BL/TR, 5'5", 150 lbs. Deb: 8/17/26

YEAR	TM/L	G	AB	R	H	2B	3B	HR	RBI	BB	SO	AVG	OBP	SLG	PRO+	BR/A	SB	CS	SBR	FA	FR	G/POS	TPR
1926	Phi-N	6	9	0	0	0	0	0	0	0	2	.000	.000	.000	-95	-2	0			.938	1	/S-5	-0.1

■ LENA STYLES
Styles, William Graves b: 11/27/1899, Gurley, Ala. d: 3/14/56, Hunstville, Ala. BR/TR, 6'1", 185 lbs. Deb: 9/10/19

YEAR	TM/L	G	AB	R	H	2B	3B	HR	RBI	BB	SO	AVG	OBP	SLG	PRO+	BR/A	SB	CS	SBR	FA	FR	G/POS	TPR
1919	Phi-A	8	22	0	6	1	0	0	5	1	6	.273	.304	.318	74	-1	0			.974	0	/C-8	0.0
1920	Phi-A	24	50	5	13	3	1	0	5	6	7	.260	.339	.360	84	-1	1	0	0	.966	2	/C-9,1-7	0.1
1921	Phi-A	4	5	0	1	0	0	0	0	0	2	.200	.200	.200	2	-1	0	0	0	.333	-1	/C-2	-0.2
1930	Cin-N	7	12	2	3	0	1	0	1	1	2	.250	.357	.417	91	-0	0			.875	0	/C-5,1-1	0.0
1931	Cin-N	34	87	7	21	3	0	0	5	8	7	.241	.313	.276	63	-4	0			.949	-7	C-31	-0.9
Total	5	77	176	14	44	7	2	0	16	16	24	.250	.320	.313	71	-7	1	0		.929	-6	/C-55,1-8	-1.0

■ CHRIS STYNES
Stynes, Christopher Desmond b: 1/19/73, Queens, N.Y. BR/TR, 5'9", 170 lbs. Deb: 5/19/95

YEAR	TM/L	G	AB	R	H	2B	3B	HR	RBI	BB	SO	AVG	OBP	SLG	PRO+	BR/A	SB	CS	SBR	FA	FR	G/POS	TPR
1995	KC-A	22	35	7	6	1	0	0	2	4	3	.171	.256	.200	20	-4	0	0	0	.982	6	2-17/D-2	0.2
1996	KC-A	36	92	8	27	6	0	0	6	2	5	.293	.309	.359	68	-4	5	2	0	.939	-2	O-19/2-5,3-2,D-3	-0.6
1997	Cin-N	49	198	31	69	7	1	6	28	11	13	.348	.394	.485	127	8	11	2	2	.976	5	O-38/2-8,3-3	1.4
1998	Cin-N	123	347	52	88	10	1	6	27	32	36	.254	.324	.340	71	-14	15	1	4	1.000	-8	O-80,3-22,2-11,/S-2	-1.7
Total	4	230	672	98	190	24	2	12	63	49	57	.283	.339	.378	84	-15	31	5	6	.984	1	O-137/2-41,3-27,DS	-0.7

■ NEIL STYNES
Stynes, Cornelius William b: 12/10/1868, Arlington, Mass. d: 3/26/44, Somerville, Mass. BR/TR, 6', 165 lbs. Deb: 9/8/1890

YEAR	TM/L	G	AB	R	H	2B	3B	HR	RBI	BB	SO	AVG	OBP	SLG	PRO+	BR/A	SB	CS	SBR	FA	FR	G/POS	TPR
1890	Cle-P	2	8	0	0	0	0	0	0	0	0	.000	.000	.000	-99	-2	0			.846	-0	/C-2	-0.2

■ KEN SUAREZ
Suarez, Kenneth Raymond b: 4/12/43, Tampa, Fla. BR/TR, 5'9", 175 lbs. Deb: 4/14/66

YEAR	TM/L	G	AB	R	H	2B	3B	HR	RBI	BB	SO	AVG	OBP	SLG	PRO+	BR/A	SB	CS	SBR	FA	FR	G/POS	TPR
1966	KC-A	35	69	5	10	0	1	0	2	15	26	.145	.298	.174	41	-5	2	0	1	.954	5	C-34	0.3
1967	KC-A	39	63	7	15	5	0	2	9	16	21	.238	.392	.413	143	4	1	0	0	.979	7	C-36	1.3
1968	Cle-A	17	10	1	1	0	0	0	0	1	3	.100	.182	.100	-13	-1	0	0	0	1.000	1	C-12/2-1,3-1,O-1	0.0
1969	Cle-A	36	85	7	25	5	0	1	9	15	12	.294	.400	.388	117	3	1	0	0	.991	6	C-36	1.0
1971	Cle-A	50	123	10	25	7	0	1	9	18	15	.203	.315	.285	65	-5	0	1	-1	.993	9	C-48	0.4
1972	Tex-A	25	33	2	5	1	0	0	4	1	4	.152	.176	.182	7	-4	0	0	0	.965	1	C-17	-0.3
1973	Tex-A	93	278	25	69	11	0	1	27	33	16	.248	.339	.299	84	-5	1	2	-1	.989	3	C-90	0.1
Total	7	295	661	57	150	29	1	5	60	99	97	.227	.334	.297	81	-13	5	3	-0	.984	31	C-273/O-1,3-1,2-1	2.8

■ LUIS SUAREZ
Suarez, Luis Abelardo b: 8/24/16, Alto Songo, Cuba d: 6/5/91, Havana, Cuba BR/TR, 5'11", 170 lbs. Deb: 5/28/44

YEAR	TM/L	G	AB	R	H	2B	3B	HR	RBI	BB	SO	AVG	OBP	SLG	PRO+	BR/A	SB	CS	SBR	FA	FR	G/POS	TPR
1944	Was-A	1	2	0	0	0	0	0	0	0	0	.000	.000	.000	-99	-1	0	0	0	1.000	0	/3-1	0.0

■ TONY SUCK
Suck, Anthony (b: Charles Anthony Zuck) b: 6/11/1858, Chicago, Ill. d: 1/29/1895, Chicago, Ill. 5'9", 164 lbs. Deb: 8/9/1883

YEAR	TM/L	G	AB	R	H	2B	3B	HR	RBI	BB	SO	AVG	OBP	SLG	PRO+	BR/A	SB	CS	SBR	FA	FR	G/POS	TPR
1883	Buf-N	2	7	1	0	0	0	0	0	1	4	.000	.125	.000	-56	-1				.000	-2	/O-1,C-1	-0.3
1884	CP-U	53	188	18	28	2	0	0		13		.149	.204	.160	12	-26				.904	-5	C-28,S-15,O-12,/3-1	-2.5
	Bal-U	3	10	2	3	0	0	0		0		.300	.300	.300	75	-1				.882	2	/C-3	0.1
	Yr	56	198	20	31	2	0	0		13		.157	.209	.167	15	-26				.901	-3	C-31,S-15,O-12,/3-1	-2.4
Total	2	58	205	21	31	2	0	0	0	14	4	.151	.205	.161	12	-27				.894	-5	/C-32,S-15,O-13,3-1	-2.7

■ BILL SUDAKIS
Sudakis, William Paul "Suds" b: 3/27/46, Joliet, Ill. BB/TR, 6'1", 190 lbs. Deb: 9/3/68

YEAR	TM/L	G	AB	R	H	2B	3B	HR	RBI	BB	SO	AVG	OBP	SLG	PRO+	BR/A	SB	CS	SBR	FA	FR	G/POS	TPR
1968	LA-N	24	87	11	24	4	2	3	12	15	14	.276	.382	.471	168	7	1	0	0	.953	4	3-24	1.3
1969	LA-N	132	462	50	108	17	5	14	53	40	94	.234	.296	.383	96	-5	3	2	-0	.946	11	*3-121	0.7
1970	LA-N	94	269	37	71	11	0	14	44	35	46	.264	.355	.461	122	8	4	0	1	.983	-6	C-38,3-37/O-3,1-1	0.5
1971	LA-N	41	83	10	16	3	0	3	7	12	22	.193	.302	.337	86	-2	0	1	-1	1.000	1	C-19/3-3,1-1,O-1	-0.1
1972	NY-N	18	49	3	7	0	0	1	7	6	14	.143	.236	.204	27	-5	0	0	0	.967	1	/1-7,C-5	-0.5
1973	Tex-A	82	235	32	60	11	0	15	43	23	53	.255	.322	.494	132	9	0	1	-1	.962	-4	3-29,1-24/C-9,OD	0.3
1974	NY-A	89	259	26	60	8	0	7	39	25	48	.232	.302	.344	87	-5	0	0	0	.990	2	D-39,1-33/3-3,C-1	-0.6
1975	Cal-A	30	58	4	7	2	0	1	6	12	15	.121	.282	.207	43	-4	1	1	-0	.941	-1	D-13/C-5,1-2	-0.6
	Cle-A	20	46	4	9	0	0	1	3	4	7	.196	.260	.261	48	-3	0	1	-1	1.000	-1	1-12/C-6	-0.5
	Yr	50	104	8	16	2	0	2	9	16	22	.154	.273	.231	45	-7	1	2	-1	1.000	-2	1-14,D-13,C-11	-1.1
Total	8	530	1548	177	362	56	7	59	214	172	313	.234	.313	.393	102	2	9	6	-1	.942	6	3-217/C-83,1-80,DO	0.5

■ PETE SUDER
Suder, Peter "Pecky" b: 4/16/16, Aliquippa, Pa. BR/TR, 6', 175 lbs. Deb: 4/15/41

YEAR	TM/L	G	AB	R	H	2B	3B	HR	RBI	BB	SO	AVG	OBP	SLG	PRO+	BR/A	SB	CS	SBR	FA	FR	G/POS	TPR
1941	Phi-A	139	531	45	130	20	9	4	52	19	47	.245	.271	.339	62	-31	1	3	-2	.957	-7	*3-136/S-3	-3.6
1942	Phi-A	128	476	46	122	20	4	4	54	24	39	.256	.293	.340	78	-15	4	4	-1	.954	3	S-69,3-34,2-31	-0.8
1943	Phi-A	131	475	30	105	14	5	3	41	14	40	.221	.243	.291	56	-28	1	1	-0	.971	-8	2-95,3-32/S-5	-3.3
1946	Phi-A	128	455	38	128	20	3	2	50	18	37	.281	.309	.352	85	-10	1	1	-0	.959	1	S-67,3-33,2-12,/1O	-0.5
1947	Phi-A	145	528	45	127	28	4	5	60	35	44	.241	.290	.337	73	-21	0	3	-2	**.986**	-17	*2-140/S-3,3-2	-3.1
1948	Phi-A	148	519	64	125	23	5	7	60	60	60	.241	.321	.345	77	-18	1	3	-2	.988	-1	*2-148	-1.2
1949	Phi-A	118	445	44	119	24	6	10	75	23	35	.267	.306	.416	93	-8	0	1	-1	.975	7	2-89,3-36/S-2	0.2
1950	Phi-A	77	248	34	61	10	0	8	35	23	31	.246	.310	.383	78	-9	2	2	-1	.979	1	2-47,3-11,S-10,/1-4	-0.7
1951	Phi-A	123	440	46	108	18	1	1	42	30	42	.245	.295	.298	59	-25	5	5	-2	**.987**	10	*2-103,S-18/3-3	-1.1
1952	Phi-A	74	228	22	55	7	2	1	20	16	17	.241	.291	.303	61	-12	1	1	-0	.991	3	2-43,S-17,3-16	-0.7
1953	Phi-A	115	454	44	130	11	3	4	35	17	35	.286	.312	.350	76	-16	3	3	-1	.974	4	3-72,2-38/S-7	-1.2
1954	Phi-A	69	205	8	41	11	1	0	16	7	16	.200	.226	.263	34	-19	0	0	0	.961	9	2-35,3-20/S-2	-1.0
1955	KC-A	26	81	3	17	4	1	0	1	2	13	.210	.229	.284	37	-7	0	1	-1	.990	-3	2-24	-1.0
Total	13	1421	5085	469	1268	210	44	49	541	288	456	.249	.291	.337	71	-220	19	28	-11	.982	2	2-805,3-395,S/1O	-18.0

■ WILLIAM SUERO
Suero, Williams (Urban) b: 11/7/66, Santo Domingo, D.R. d: 11/30/95, Santo Domingo, D.R. BR/TR, 5'9", 175 lbs. Deb: 4/9/92

YEAR	TM/L	G	AB	R	H	2B	3B	HR	RBI	BB	SO	AVG	OBP	SLG	PRO+	BR/A	SB	CS	SBR	FA	FR	G/POS	TPR
1992	Mil-A	18	16	4	3	1	0	0	0	2	1	.188	.316	.250	62	-1	1	1	-0	.971	4	2-15/S-1,D-2	0.3
1993	Mil-A	15	14	0	4	0	0	0	0	1	3	.286	.333	.286	69	-1	0	1	-1	.944	3	/2-8,3-1	0.2
Total	2	33	30	4	7	1	0	0	0	3	4	.233	.324	.267	65	-1	1	2	-1	.962	7	/2-23,D-2,3-1,S-1	0.5

■ JOE SUGDEN
Sugden, Joseph b: 7/31/1870, Philadelphia, Pa. d: 6/28/59, Philadelphia, Pa. BB/TR, 5'10", 180 lbs. Deb: 7/20/1893 C

YEAR	TM/L	G	AB	R	H	2B	3B	HR	RBI	BB	SO	AVG	OBP	SLG	PRO+	BR/A	SB	CS	SBR	FA	FR	G/POS	TPR
1893	Pit-N	27	92	20	24	4	3	0	12	10	11	.261	.340	.370	90	-1	1			.956	-0	C-27	0.0
1894	Pit-N	39	139	23	46	13	2	2	23	14	2	.331	.404	.496	117	4	3			.910	-5	C-31/3-4,S-3,O-1	0.1
1895	Pit-N	49	155	28	48	4	1	1	17	16	12	.310	.385	.368	100	1	4			.903	3	C-49	0.7
1896	Pit-N	80	301	42	89	5	7	0	36	19	9	.296	.348	.359	90	-4	5			.952	1	C-70/1-7,O-4	0.4

YEAR	TM/L	G	AB	R	H	2B	3B	HR	RBI	BB	SO	AVG	OBP	SLG	PRO+	BR/A	SB	CS	SBR	FA	FR	G/POS	TPR
1897	Pit-N	84	288	31	64	6	4	0	38	18		.222	.275	.271	46	-22	9			.941	-4	C-81/1-3	-1.5
1898	StL-N	89	289	29	73	7	1	0	34	23		.253	.314	.284	70	-11	5			.937	0	C-60,O-15/1-8	-0.5
1899	Cle-N	76	250	19	69	5	1	0	14	11		.276	.307	.304	73	-9	2			.935	-0	C-66/O-4,1-3,3-1	-0.4
1901	Chi-A	48	153	21	42	7	1	0	19	13		.275	.339	.333	89	-2	4			.970	4	C-42/1-5	0.6
1902	StL-A	68	200	25	50	7	2	0	15	20		.250	.330	.305	78	-5	2			.956	-2	C-61/1-4,P-1	-0.1
1903	StL-A	79	241	18	51	4	0	0	22	25		.212	.288	.228	58	-11	4			.983	6	C-66/1-8	0.2
1904	StL-A	105	348	25	93	6	3	0	30	28		.267	.331	.302	107	4	6			**.989**	-1	C-79,1-28	1.3
1905	StL-A	90	266	21	46	4	0	0	23	23		.173	.247	.188	41	-17	3			.983	19	C-76/1-9	1.0
1912	Det-A	1	4	1	1	0	0	0	0	0		.250	.250	.250	44	-0	0			.941	1	/1-1	0.0
Total	13	835	2726	303	696	72	25	3	283	220	34	.255	.319	.303	78	-75	48			.957	22	C-708/1-76,O3SP	1.8

■ **GUS SUHR** Suhr, August Richard b: 1/3/06, San Francisco, Cal. BL/TR, 6', 180 lbs. Deb: 4/15/30

YEAR	TM/L	G	AB	R	H	2B	3B	HR	RBI	BB	SO	AVG	OBP	SLG	PRO+	BR/A	SB	CS	SBR	FA	FR	G/POS	TPR
1930	Pit-N	151	542	93	155	26	14	17	107	80	56	.286	.380	.480	106	5	11			.992	-7	*1-151	-1.5
1931	Pit-N	87	270	26	57	13	4	4	32	38	25	.211	.308	.333	73	-10	4			.993	0	1-76	-1.6
1932	Pit-N	154	581	78	153	31	16	5	81	63	39	.263	.337	.398	99	-1	7			.988	-10	*1-154	-2.3
1933	Pit-N	154	566	72	151	31	11	10	75	72	52	.267	.350	.413	117	14	2			.991	-4	*1-154	-0.5
1934	Pit-N	151	573	67	162	36	13	13	103	66	52	.283	.360	.459	115	12	4			.994	-5	*1-151	-0.6
1935	Pit-N	153	529	68	144	33	12	10	81	70	54	.272	.357	.437	109	7	6			.989	-7	*1-149/O-2	-1.5
1936	Pit-N☆	156	583	111	182	33	12	11	118	95	34	.312	.410	.467	133	30	8			**.993**	-4	*1-156	1.1
1937	Pit-N	151	575	69	160	28	14	5	97	83	42	.278	.369	.402	109	9	2			.993	-4	*1-151	-1.2
1938	Pit-N	145	530	82	156	35	14	3	64	87	37	.294	.394	.430	126	21	4			.993	-8	*1-145	-0.4
1939	Pit-N	63	204	23	59	10	2	1	31	25	23	.289	.367	.373	101	1	4			.993	-4	1-52	-0.9
	Phi-N	60	198	21	63	12	2	3	24	34	14	.318	.421	.444	137	12	1			.995	1	1-60	0.7
	Yr	123	402	44	122	22	4	4	55	59	37	.303	.394	.408	118	13	5			.994	-4	*1-112	-0.2
1940	Phi-N	10	25	4	4	0	0	2	5	5	5	.160	.300	.400	95	-0	0			.967	-2	/1-7	-0.2
Total	11	1435	5176	714	1446	288	114	84	818	718	433	.279	.368	.428	112	101	53			.992	-53	*1-1406/O-2	-8.9

■ **CLYDE SUKEFORTH** Sukeforth, Clyde Leroy "Sukey" b: 11/30/01, Washington, Me. BL/TR, 5'10", 155 lbs. Deb: 5/23/26 MC

YEAR	TM/L	G	AB	R	H	2B	3B	HR	RBI	BB	SO	AVG	OBP	SLG	PRO+	BR/A	SB	CS	SBR	FA	FR	G/POS	TPR
1926	Cin-N	1	1	0	0	0	0	0	0	0	1	.000	.000	.000	-99	-0	0			.000	0	H	0.0
1927	Cin-N	38	58	12	11	2	0	0	2	7	2	.190	.277	.224	37	-5	2			.970	1	C-24	-0.3
1928	Cin-N	33	53	5	7	2	1	0	3	3	5	.132	.179	.208	1	-8	0			.966	1	C-26	-0.6
1929	Cin-N	84	237	31	84	16	2	1	33	17	6	.354	.398	.451	115	6	8			.981	-8	C-76	0.4
1930	Cin-N	94	296	30	84	9	3	1	19	17	12	.284	.325	.345	65	-17	1			.976	-3	C-82	-1.1
1931	Cin-N	112	351	22	90	15	4	0	25	38	13	.256	.334	.322	82	-8	0			.965	-8	*C-106	-0.8
1932	Bro-N	59	111	14	26	4	4	0	12	6	10	.234	.280	.342	68	-5	1			.991	-3	C-36	-0.7
1933	Bro-N	20	36	1	2	0	0	0	0	2	1	.056	.105	.056	-55	-7	0			.983	3	C-18	-0.4
1934	Bro-N	27	43	5	7	1	0	0	1	1	6	.163	.182	.186	-1	-6	0			1.000	-1	C-18	-0.6
1945	Bro-N	18	51	2	15	1	0	0	1	4	1	.294	.345	.314	85	-1	0			.947	-3	C-13	-0.3
Total	10	486	1237	122	326	50	14	2	96	95	57	.264	.319	.331	71	-51	12			.974	-20	C-399	-4.4

■ **GUY SULARZ** Sularz, Guy Patrick b: 11/7/55, Minneapolis, Minn. BR/TR, 5'11", 165 lbs. Deb: 9/2/80

YEAR	TM/L	G	AB	R	H	2B	3B	HR	RBI	BB	SO	AVG	OBP	SLG	PRO+	BR/A	SB	CS	SBR	FA	FR	G/POS	TPR
1980	SF-N	25	65	3	16	1	1	0	3	9	6	.246	.338	.292	79	-2	1	0	0	.975	12	2-21/3-5	1.2
1981	SF-N	10	20	0	4	0	0	0	2	2	4	.200	.304	.200	46	-1	0	1	-1	1.000	4	/2-6,3-1	0.3
1982	SF-N	63	101	15	23	3	0	1	7	9	11	.228	.291	.287	62	-5	3	0	1	.961	10	S-37,3-14/2-9	0.9
1983	SF-N	10	20	3	2	0	0	0	0	3	2	.100	.217	.100	-10	-3	0	0	0	.917	3	/S-6,3-4	0.0
Total	4	108	206	21	45	4	1	1	12	23	23	.218	.300	.262	59	-11	4	1	1	.954	29	/S-43,2-36,3-24	2.4

■ **ERNIE SULIK** Sulik, Ernest Richard "Dave" b: 7/7/10, San Francisco, Cal. d: 5/31/63, Oakland, Cal. BL/TL, 5'10", 178 lbs. Deb: 4/15/36

YEAR	TM/L	G	AB	R	H	2B	3B	HR	RBI	BB	SO	AVG	OBP	SLG	PRO+	BR/A	SB	CS	SBR	FA	FR	G/POS	TPR
1936	Phi-N	122	404	69	116	14	4	6	36	40	22	.287	.353	.386	90	-6	4			.971	-6	*O-105	-1.5

■ **SULLIVAN** Sullivan b: Bristol, R.I. Deb: 5/14/1875

YEAR	TM/L	G	AB	R	H	2B	3B	HR	RBI	BB	SO	AVG	OBP	SLG	PRO+	BR/A	SB	CS	SBR	FA	FR	G/POS	TPR
1875	NH-n	2	8	3	3	0	0	0	2	0	1	.375	.375	.375	185	1	1	0	0	1.000	-1	/O-2	0.0

■ **ANDY SULLIVAN** Sullivan, Andrew R. b: 8/30/1884, Southborough, Mass d: 2/14/20, Framingham, Mass. TR , Deb: 9/13/04

YEAR	TM/L	G	AB	R	H	2B	3B	HR	RBI	BB	SO	AVG	OBP	SLG	PRO+	BR/A	SB	CS	SBR	FA	FR	G/POS	TPR
1904	Bos-N	1	1	0	0	0	0	0	0	1		.000	.500	.000	61	0	0			1.000	-0	/S-1	0.0

■ **JACKIE SULLIVAN** Sullivan, Carl Mancel b: 2/22/18, Princeton, Tex. d: 10/15/92, Dallas, Tex. BR/TR, 5'11", 172 lbs. Deb: 7/6/44

YEAR	TM/L	G	AB	R	H	2B	3B	HR	RBI	BB	SO	AVG	OBP	SLG	PRO+	BR/A	SB	CS	SBR	FA	FR	G/POS	TPR
1944	Det-A	1	1	0	0	0	0	0	0	0	0	.000	.000	.000	-95	-0	0	0	0	1.000	-0	/2-1	0.0

■ **DAN SULLIVAN** Sullivan, Daniel C. "Link" b: 5/9/1857, Providence, R.I. d: 10/26/1893, Providence, R.I. TR , 5'11", 194 lbs. Deb: 5/2/1882

YEAR	TM/L	G	AB	R	H	2B	3B	HR	RBI	BB	SO	AVG	OBP	SLG	PRO+	BR/A	SB	CS	SBR	FA	FR	G/POS	TPR
1882	Lou-a	67	286	44	78	8	2	0		9		.273	.295	.315	112	4				.878	7	*C-54,3-10/O-4,S-1	1.2
1883	Lou-a	36	145	8	31	5	2	0		3		.214	.230	.276	67	-5				.900	-6	C-31/O-2,3-2,S-1	-0.8
1884	Lou-a	63	247	27	59	8	6	0	26	9		.239	.268	.320	95	-1				.930	-15	C-63/O-1	-0.9
1885	Lou-a	13	44	3	8	1	0	0	4	2		.182	.234	.205	40	-3				.948	-3	C-13	-0.4
	StL-a	17	60	4	7	2	0	0	3	6		.117	.197	.150	10	-6				.956	1	C-13/1-4	-0.4
	Yr	30	104	7	15	3	0	0	7	8		.144	.212	.173	22	-9				.952	-2	C-26/1-4	-0.8
1886	Pit-a	1	4	0	0	0	0	0	0	0		.000	.000	.000	-99	-1	0			.600	-1	/C-1	-0.2
Total	5	197	786	86	183	24	10	0	33	29		.233	.262	.289	84	-12	0			.909	-17	C-175/3-12,O-7,1S	-1.5

■ **DENNY SULLIVAN** Sullivan, Dennis J. b: 6/26/1858, Boston, Mass. d: 12/31/25, Boston, Mass. TR , 5'9", 170 lbs. Deb: 8/25/1879

YEAR	TM/L	G	AB	R	H	2B	3B	HR	RBI	BB	SO	AVG	OBP	SLG	PRO+	BR/A	SB	CS	SBR	FA	FR	G/POS	TPR
1879	Pro-N	5	19	5	5	2	0	0	2	1	1	.263	.300	.368	121	0				.429	-4	/3-4,O-1	-0.3
1880	Bos-N	1	4	1	1	0	0	0	1	0	1	.250	.250	.250	72	-0				.857	-1	/C-1	-0.1
Total	2	6	23	6	6	2	0	0	3	1	2	.261	.292	.348	113	0				.429	-4	/3-4,C-1,O-1	-0.4

■ **DENNY SULLIVAN** Sullivan, Dennis William b: 9/28/1882, Hillsboro, Wis. d: 6/2/56, W.Los Angeles, Cal BL/TR, 5'10", Deb: 4/22/05

YEAR	TM/L	G	AB	R	H	2B	3B	HR	RBI	BB	SO	AVG	OBP	SLG	PRO+	BR/A	SB	CS	SBR	FA	FR	G/POS	TPR
1905	Was-A	3	11	0	0	0	0	0	0	1		.000	.083	.000	-76	-2	0			1.000	-1	/O-3	-0.3
1907	Bos-A	144	551	73	135	18	0	1	26	44		.245	.315	.283	92	-4	16			.975	1	*O-143	-0.9
1908	Bos-A	101	355	33	85	7	8	0	25	14		.239	.276	.304	86	-6	14			.981	7	O-97	-0.3
	Cle-A	4	6	0	0	0	0	0	0	0		.000	.000	.000	-99	-1	0			1.000	-0	/O-2	-0.2
	Yr	105	361	33	85	7	8	0	25	14		.235	.272	.299	83	-7	14			.982	7	O-99	-0.5
1909	Cle-A	3	2	0	1	0	0	0	0	0		.500	.500	.500	207	0	0			.000	-1	/O-2	-0.1
Total	4	255	925	106	221	25	8	1	51	59		.239	.296	.286	87	-13	30			.978	7	O-247	-1.8

■ **HAYWOOD SULLIVAN** Sullivan, Haywood Cooper b: 12/15/30, Donalsonville, Ga. BR/TR, 6'4", 215 lbs. Deb: 9/20/55 FM

YEAR	TM/L	G	AB	R	H	2B	3B	HR	RBI	BB	SO	AVG	OBP	SLG	PRO+	BR/A	SB	CS	SBR	FA	FR	G/POS	TPR
1955	Bos-A	2	6	1	0	0	0	0	0	0	1	.000	.000	.000	-92	-2	0	0	0	1.000	1	/C-2	-0.1
1957	Bos-A	2	1	0	0	0	0	0	0	0	0	.000	.000	.000	-95	-0	0	0	0	1.000	0	/C-1	0.0
1959	Bos-A	4	2	0	0	0	0	0	0	1	1	.000	.333	.000	-0	-0	0	0	0	1.000	1	/C-2	0.0
1960	Bos-A	52	124	9	20	1	0	3	10	16	24	.161	.257	.242	35	-11	0	0	0	.992	6	C-50	-0.4
1961	KC-A	117	331	42	80	16	2	6	40	46	45	.242	.334	.356	83	-7	1	0	0	.984	-6	C-88,1-16/O-5	-0.9
1962	KC-A	95	274	33	68	7	2	4	29	31	54	.248	.327	.332	74	-9	1	0	0	.980	-9	C-94/1-1	-1.5
1963	KC-A	40	113	9	24	6	1	0	8	15	15	.212	.305	.283	62	-5	0	0	0	.992	8	C-37	0.4
Total	7	312	851	94	192	30	5	13	87	109	140	.226	.314	.318	69	-36	2	0	1	.985	1	C-274/1-17,O-5	-2.5

■ **JOHN SULLIVAN** Sullivan, John Eugene b: 2/16/1873, Illinois d: 6/5/24, St.Paul, Minn. BR/TR, 5'10", 170 lbs. Deb: 4/19/05

YEAR	TM/L	G	AB	R	H	2B	3B	HR	RBI	BB	SO	AVG	OBP	SLG	PRO+	BR/A	SB	CS	SBR	FA	FR	G/POS	TPR
1905	Det-A	13	32	4	5	0	0	0	4	4		.156	.250	.156	29	-2	0			.964	4	C-12	0.3
1908	Pit-N	1	1	0	0	0	0	0	0	0		.000	.000	.000	-99	-0	0			1.000	0	/C-1	0.0
Total	2	14	33	4	5	0	0	0	4	4		.152	.243	.152	26	-3	0			.965	4	/C-13	0.3

■ **CHUB SULLIVAN** Sullivan, John Frank b: 1/12/1856, Boston, Mass. d: 9/12/1881, Boston, Mass. BR/TR, 6', 164 lbs. Deb: 9/24/1877

YEAR	TM/L	G	AB	R	H	2B	3B	HR	RBI	BB	SO	AVG	OBP	SLG	PRO+	BR/A	SB	CS	SBR	FA	FR	G/POS	TPR
1877	Cin-N	8	32	4	8	0	0	0	4	1	0	.250	.273	.250	74	-1				.944	-1	/1-8	-0.1
1878	Cin-N	61	244	29	63	4	2	0	20	2	9	.258	.264	.291	91	-2				**.975**	5	*1-61	0.1

YEAR	TM/L	G	AB	R	H	2B	3B	HR	RBI	BB	SO	AVG	OBP	SLG	PRO+	BR/A	SB	CS	SBR	FA	FR	G/POS	TPR
1880	Wor-N	43	166	22	43	6	3	0	0	4	6	.259	.276	.331	97	-1				.983	3	1-43	-0.2
Total	3	112	442	55	114	10	5	0	24	7	15	.258	.269	.303	92	-4				.976	7	1-112	-0.2

■ JOHN SULLIVAN

Sullivan, John Lawrence b: 3/21/1890, Williamsport, Pa. d: 4/1/66, Milton, Pa. BR/TR, 5′11″, 180 lbs. Deb: 4/18/20

YEAR	TM/L	G	AB	R	H	2B	3B	HR	RBI	BB	SO	AVG	OBP	SLG	PRO+	BR/A	SB	CS	SBR	FA	FR	G/POS	TPR
1920	Bos-N	81	250	36	74	14	4	1	28	29	29	.296	.374	.396	126	9	3	2	-0	.977	-2	O-66/1-6	0.3
1921	Bos-N	5	5	0	0	0	0	0	0	0	0	.000	.000	.000	-99	-1	0	0	0	.000	0	H	-0.1
	Chi-N	76	240	28	79	14	4	4	41	19	26	.329	.381	.471	124	8	3	5	-2	.962	-7	O-66	-0.5
	Yr	81	245	28	79	14	4	4	41	19	26	.322	.374	.461	120	7	3	5	-2	.962	-7	O-66	-0.6
Total	2	162	495	64	153	28	8	5	69	48	55	.309	.374	.428	123	16	6	7	-2	.969	-9	O-132/1-6	-0.3

■ JOHN SULLIVAN

Sullivan, John Paul b: 11/2/20, Chicago, Ill. BR/TR, 5′10″, 170 lbs. Deb: 6/7/42 C

YEAR	TM/L	G	AB	R	H	2B	3B	HR	RBI	BB	SO	AVG	OBP	SLG	PRO+	BR/A	SB	CS	SBR	FA	FR	G/POS	TPR
1942	Was-A	94	357	38	84	16	1	0	42	25	30	.235	.285	.286	61	-19	2	0	1	.936	-11	S-92	-2.4
1943	Was-A	134	456	49	95	12	2	1	55	57	59	.208	.298	.250	63	-20	6	2	1	.946	11	*S-133	0.1
1944	Was-A	138	471	49	118	12	1	0	30	52	43	.251	.325	.280	77	-13	3	3	-1	.934	-14	*S-138	-1.7
1947	Was-A	49	133	13	34	0	1	0	5	22	14	.256	.361	.271	79	-3	0	2	-1	.963	8	S-40/2-1	0.6
1948	Was-A	85	173	25	36	4	1	0	12	22	25	.208	.297	.243	46	-13	2	2	-1	.951	2	S-57/2-4	-0.8
1949	StL-A	105	243	29	55	8	3	0	18	38	35	.226	.331	.284	61	-13	5	2	0	.942	-9	S-71,3-23/2-6	-1.8
Total	6	605	1833	203	422	52	9	1	162	216	206	.230	.312	.270	66	-80	18	11	-1	.942	-13	S-531/3-23,2-11	-6.0

■ JOHN SULLIVAN

Sullivan, John Peter b: 1/3/41, Somerville, N.J. BL/TR, 6′, 195 lbs. Deb: 9/20/63

YEAR	TM/L	G	AB	R	H	2B	3B	HR	RBI	BB	SO	AVG	OBP	SLG	PRO+	BR/A	SB	CS	SBR	FA	FR	G/POS	TPR
1963	Det-A	3	5	0	0	0	0	0	0	2	1	.000	.286	.000	-11	-1	0	0	0	1.000	0	/C-2	0.0
1964	Det-A	2	3	0	0	0	0	0	0	0	1	.000	.000	.000	-99	-1	0	0	0	1.000	0	/C-2	-0.1
1965	Det-A	34	86	5	23	0	0	2	11	9	13	.267	.344	.337	93	-0	0	0	0	.994	1	C-29	0.2
1967	NY-N	65	147	4	32	5	0	0	6	6	26	.218	.248	.252	44	-11	0	2	-1	.991	-11	C-57	-2.3
1968	Phi-N	12	18	0	4	0	0	0	1	2	4	.222	.300	.222	59	-1	0	0	0	.967	-0	/C-8	-0.1
Total	5	116	259	9	59	5	0	2	18	19	45	.228	.283	.270	59	-13	0	2	-1	.991	-10	/C-98	-2.3

■ JOE SULLIVAN

Sullivan, Joseph Daniel b: 1/6/1870, Charlestown, Mass. d: 11/2/1897, Charlestown, Mass. 5′10″, 178 lbs. Deb: 4/27/1893

YEAR	TM/L	G	AB	R	H	2B	3B	HR	RBI	BB	SO	AVG	OBP	SLG	PRO+	BR/A	SB	CS	SBR	FA	FR	G/POS	TPR
1893	Was-N	128	508	72	134	16	13	2	64	36	24	.264	.322	.358	83	-14	7			.860	-29	*S-128	-3.0
1894	Was-N	17	60	7	15	3	0	0	5	6	2	.250	.357	.300	62	-3	3			.900	-3	/2-8,S-6,3-1,O-1	-0.4
	Phi-N	75	304	63	107	10	8	3	63	23	10	.352	.407	.467	113	7	10			.887	-16	S-75	-0.4
	Yr	92	364	70	122	13	8	3	68	29	12	.335	.398	.440	105	4	13			.884	-19	S-81/2-8,3-1,O-1	-0.8
1895	Phi-N	94	373	75	126	7	3	2	50	24	20	.338	.395	.389	102	2	15			.879	-16	*S-89/O-6	-0.9
1896	Phi-N	48	191	45	48	5	3	2	24	18	12	.251	.347	.340	83	-4	9			.962	-4	O-45/S-2,3-2	-1.0
	StL-N	51	212	25	62	4	2	2	21	9	12	.292	.351	.358	91	-3	5			.955	-6	O-45/2-7	-1.0
	Yr	99	403	70	110	9	5	4	45	27	24	.273	.349	.350	87	-7	14			.959	-10	O-90/2-7,S-2,3-2	-2.0
Total	4	413	1648	287	492	45	29	11	227	116	80	.299	.362	.381	93	-14	49			.872	-73	S-300/O-97,2-15,3-3	-6.7

■ MARC SULLIVAN

Sullivan, Marc Cooper b: 7/25/58, Quincy, Mass. BR/TR, 6′4″, 205 lbs. Deb: 10/1/82 F

YEAR	TM/L	G	AB	R	H	2B	3B	HR	RBI	BB	SO	AVG	OBP	SLG	PRO+	BR/A	SB	CS	SBR	FA	FR	G/POS	TPR
1982	Bos-A	2	6	0	2	0	0	0	0	0	2	.333	.333	.333	79	-0	0	0	0	1.000	1	/C-2	0.1
1984	Bos-A	2	6	1	3	0	0	0	1	1	0	.500	.571	.500	191	1	0	0	0	.950	1	/C-2	0.2
1985	Bos-A	32	69	10	12	2	0	2	3	6	15	.174	.240	.290	43	-6	0	0	0	.993	4	C-32	-0.1
1986	Bos-A	41	119	15	23	4	0	1	14	7	32	.193	.262	.252	40	-10	0	0	0	.986	-5	C-41	-1.2
1987	Bos-A	60	160	11	27	5	0	2	10	4	43	.169	.199	.237	15	-20	0	0	0	.994	0	C-60	-1.6
Total	5	137	360	37	67	11	0	5	28	18	92	.186	.237	.258	33	-34	0	0	0	.990	1	C-137	-2.6

■ MARTY SULLIVAN

Sullivan, Martin C. b: 10/20/1862, Lowell, Mass. d: 1/6/1894, Lowell, Mass. BR/TR, Deb: 4/30/1887

YEAR	TM/L	G	AB	R	H	2B	3B	HR	RBI	BB	SO	AVG	OBP	SLG	PRO+	BR/A	SB	CS	SBR	FA	FR	G/POS	TPR
1887	Chi-N	115	472	98	134	13	16	7	77	36	53	.284	.340	.424	98	-5	35			.847	-7	*O-115/P-1	-1.2
1888	Chi-N	75	314	40	74	12	6	7	39	15	32	.236	.273	.379	99	-2	9			.927	3	O-75	-0.1
1889	Ind-N	69	256	45	73	11	3	4	35	50	31	.285	.404	.398	122	10	15			.910	-5	O-64/1-5	0.2
1890	Bos-N	121	505	82	144	19	7	6	61	56	48	.285	.357	.386	108	3	33			.951	4	*O-120/3-1	0.3
1891	Bos-N	17	67	15	15	1	0	2	7	5	3	.224	.288	.328	71	-3	7			.926	-2	O-17	-0.5
	Cle-N	1	4	0	1	0	0	0	1	0	1	.250	.250	.250	44	-0	0			.000	-0	/O-1	-0.1
	Yr	18	71	15	16	1	0	2	8	5	4	.225	.286	.324	69	-3	7			.926	-3	O-18	-0.6
Total	5	398	1618	280	441	56	32	26	220	162	168	.273	.341	.395	104	3	99			.909	-8	O-392/1-5,3-1,P-1	-1.4

■ MIKE SULLIVAN

Sullivan, Michael Joseph b: 6/10/1860, Webster, Mass. d: 6/16/29, Webster, Mass. BR/TR, 5′8.5″, 165 lbs. Deb: 4/26/1888

YEAR	TM/L	G	AB	R	H	2B	3B	HR	RBI	BB	SO	AVG	OBP	SLG	PRO+	BR/A	SB	CS	SBR	FA	FR	G/POS	TPR
1888	Phi-a	28	112	20	31	5	6	1	19	3		.277	.296	.455	140	4	10			.742	-6	O-18,3-10	-0.2

■ PAT SULLIVAN

Sullivan, Patrick J. b: 12/22/1862, Milwaukee, Wis. TR , 5′11″, 165 lbs. Deb: 8/30/1884

YEAR	TM/L	G	AB	R	H	2B	3B	HR	RBI	BB	SO	AVG	OBP	SLG	PRO+	BR/A	SB	CS	SBR	FA	FR	G/POS	TPR
1884	KC-U	31	114	15	22	3	1	0		4		.193	.220	.237	44	-11				.767	1	3-21/O-9,C-1,P-1	-0.9

■ RUSS SULLIVAN

Sullivan, Russell Guy b: 2/19/23, Fredericksburg, Va BL/TR, 6′, 196 lbs. Deb: 9/8/51

YEAR	TM/L	G	AB	R	H	2B	3B	HR	RBI	BB	SO	AVG	OBP	SLG	PRO+	BR/A	SB	CS	SBR	FA	FR	G/POS	TPR
1951	Det-A	7	26	2	5	1	0	1	1	2	1	.192	.250	.346	60	-2	0	0	0	.938	0	/O-7	-0.2
1952	Det-A	15	52	7	17	2	1	3	5	3	5	.327	.375	.577	161	4	1	0	0	.826	-2	O-14	0.2
1953	Det-A	23	72	7	18	5	1	1	6	13	5	.250	.379	.389	109	1	0	0	0	.958	3	O-20	0.4
Total	3	45	150	16	40	8	2	5	12	18	11	.267	.357	.447	118	4	1	0	0	.920	1	/O-41	0.4

■ SUTER SULLIVAN

Sullivan, Suter G. b: 10/14/1872, Baltimore, Md. d: 4/19/25, Baltimore, Md. 6′, 170 lbs. Deb: 7/24/1898

YEAR	TM/L	G	AB	R	H	2B	3B	HR	RBI	BB	SO	AVG	OBP	SLG	PRO+	BR/A	SB	CS	SBR	FA	FR	G/POS	TPR
1898	StL-N	42	144	10	32	3	0	0	12	13		.222	.300	.243	55	-8	1			.875	-13	S-23,O-10/2-6,1P	-1.9
1899	Cle-N	127	473	37	116	16	3	0	55	25		.245	.297	.292	67	-22	16			.938	5	*3-101,O-20/S-3,12	-1.6
Total	2	169	617	47	148	19	3	0	67	38		.240	.298	.280	64	-30	17			.889	-8	3-101/O-30,S21P	-3.5

■ TOM SULLIVAN

Sullivan, Thomas Brandon b: 12/19/06, Nome, Alaska d: 8/16/44, Seattle, Wash. BR/TR, 6′, 190 lbs. Deb: 6/14/25

YEAR	TM/L	G	AB	R	H	2B	3B	HR	RBI	BB	SO	AVG	OBP	SLG	PRO+	BR/A	SB	CS	SBR	FA	FR	G/POS	TPR
1925	Cin-N	1	1	0	0	0	0	0	0	0	0	.000	.000	.000	-99	-0	0	0	0	1.000	-0	/C-1	0.0

■ SLEEPER SULLIVAN

Sullivan, Thomas Jefferson "Old Iron Hands" b: St.Louis, Mo. d: 9/25/1899, Camden, N.J. BR/TR, 175 lbs. Deb: 5/3/1881

YEAR	TM/L	G	AB	R	H	2B	3B	HR	RBI	BB	SO	AVG	OBP	SLG	PRO+	BR/A	SB	CS	SBR	FA	FR	G/POS	TPR
1881	Buf-N	35	121	13	23	4	0	0	15	1	21	.190	.197	.223	32	-9				.853	-12	C-31/O-5	-2.0
1882	StL-a	51	188	24	34	3	3	0		3		.181	.194	.229	40	-12				.840	-18	C-51	-2.7
1883	StL-a	8	27	2	6	0	1	0		0		.222	.222	.296	62	-1				.939	5	/C-6,O-2	0.3
	Lou-a	1	2	0	0	0	0	0		0		.000	.000	.000	-99	-0				.667	-1	/C-1	-0.1
	Yr	9	29	2	6	0	1	0		0		.207	.207	.276	52	-2				.923	5	/C-7,O-2	0.2
1884	StL-U	2	9	0	1	0	0	0		0		.111	.111	.111	-31	-2				.000	-1	/O-1,C-1,P-1	-0.2
Total	4	97	347	39	64	7	4	0	15	4	21	.184	.194	.228	36	-24				.851	-27	/C-90,O-8,P-1	-4.7

■ TED SULLIVAN

Sullivan, Timothy Paul b: 1851, County Clare, Ireland d: 7/5/29, Washington, D.C. Deb: 9/9/1884 MU

YEAR	TM/L	G	AB	R	H	2B	3B	HR	RBI	BB	SO	AVG	OBP	SLG	PRO+	BR/A	SB	CS	SBR	FA	FR	G/POS	TPR
1884	KC-U	3	9	0	3	0	0	0		1		.333	.400	.333	143	0				1.000	-2	/O-2,S-1,M	-0.1

■ BILL SULLIVAN

Sullivan, William b: 7/4/1853, Holyoke, Mass. d: 11/13/1884, Holyoke, Mass. Deb: 8/9/1878

YEAR	TM/L	G	AB	R	H	2B	3B	HR	RBI	BB	SO	AVG	OBP	SLG	PRO+	BR/A	SB	CS	SBR	FA	FR	G/POS	TPR
1878	Chl-N	2	6	1	1	0	0	0	0	0	0	.167	.167	.167	9	-1				1.000	-1	/O-2	-0.1

■ BILLY SULLIVAN

Sullivan, William Joseph Jr. b: 10/23/10, Chicago, Ill. d: 1/4/94, Sarasota, Fla. BL/TR, 6′, 170 lbs. Deb: 6/9/31 F

YEAR	TM/L	G	AB	R	H	2B	3B	HR	RBI	BB	SO	AVG	OBP	SLG	PRO+	BR/A	SB	CS	SBR	FA	FR	G/POS	TPR
1931	Chi-A	92	363	48	100	16	5	2	33	20	14	.275	.315	.364	83	-10	4	4	-1	.912	-9	3-83/O-2,1-1	-1.4
1932	Chi-A	93	307	31	97	16	1	1	45	20	9	.316	.358	.384	99	-1	1	3	-2	.990	-3	1-52,3-17/C-5,O-3	-0.8
1933	Chi-A	54	125	9	24	0	1	0	13	10	5	.192	.252	.208	24	-14	0	0	0	.982	-3	1-22/C-8	-1.7
1935	Cin-N	85	241	29	64	9	4	2	36	19	16	.266	.324	.361	87	-4	4			.992	2	1-40,3-15/2-6	-0.5
1936	Cle-A	93	319	39	112	32	6	2	48	16	9	.351	.382	.508	117	7	5	2	0	.968	-2	C-72/3-5,1-3,O-1	0.8
1937	Cle-A	72	168	26	48	12	3	3	22	17	7	.286	.355	.446	100	-0	1	4	-2	.949	-6	C-38/1-5,3-1	-0.6
1938	StL-A	111	375	35	104	16	1	7	49	20	10	.277	.316	.381	74	-16	8	5	-1	**.990**	-1	C-99/1-6	-1.2
1939	StL-A	118	332	53	96	17	5	5	50	34	18	.289	.362	.416	96	-2	3	3	-1	.954	4	O-59,C-19/1-4	0.0
1940	*Det-A	78	220	36	68	14	4	3	41	31	11	.309	.399	.450	109	4	2	0	1	.976	1	C-57/3-6	0.9
1941	Det-A	85	234	29	66	15	1	3	29	35	11	.282	.375	.393	94	-1	0	3	-2	.976	5	C-63	0.7
1942	Bro-N	43	101	11	27	2	1	1	14	12	6	.267	.345	.337	98	0	1			.962	-0	C-41	0.2

YEAR	TM/L	G	AB	R	H	2B	3B	HR	RBI	BB	SO	AVG	OBP	SLG	PRO+	BR/A	SB	CS	SBR	FA	FR	G/POS	TPR
1947	Pit-N	38	55	1	14	3	0	0	8	6	3	.255	.328	.309	68	-2	1			1.000	1	C-12	-0.1
Total	12	962	2840	347	820	152	32	29	388	240	119	.289	.346	.395	91	-40	30	24		.972	-11	C-414,1-133,3/O2	-3.7

■ BILLY SULLIVAN Sullivan, William Joseph Sr. b: 2/1/1875, Oakland, Wis. d: 1/28/65, Newberg, Ore. BR/TR, 5'9", 155 lbs. Deb: 9/13/1899 FM

YEAR	TM/L	G	AB	R	H	2B	3B	HR	RBI	BB	SO	AVG	OBP	SLG	PRO+	BR/A	SB	CS	SBR	FA	FR	G/POS	TPR
1899	Bos-N	22	74	10	20	2	0	2	12	1		.270	.308	.378	80	-2	2			.952	5	C-22	0.4
1900	Bos-N	72	238	36	65	6	0	8	41	9		.273	.302	.399	83	-7	4			.974	0	C-66/S-1,2-1	-0.1
1901	Chi-A	98	367	54	90	15	6	4	56	10		.245	.271	.351	74	-14	12			**.967**	-1	C-97/3-1	-0.5
1902	Chi-A	76	263	36	64	12	3	1	26	6		.243	.268	.323	66	-13	11			.967	-3	C-70/1-2,O-2	-0.8
1903	Chi-A	32	111	10	21	4	0	1	7	5		.189	.224	.252	45	-8	3			.988	-2	C-31	-0.7
1904	Chi-A	108	371	29	85	18	4	1	44	12		.229	.255	.307	81	-9	11			.964	2	*C-107	0.5
1905	Chi-A	98	323	25	65	10	3	2	26	13		.201	.239	.269	64	-14	14			.974	-4	C-92/1-2,3-1	-1.0
1906	*Chi-A	118	387	37	83	18	4	2	33	22		.214	.262	.297	77	-11	10			**.974**	-4	*C-118	-0.4
1907	Chi-A	112	329	30	59	8	4	0	36	21		.179	.235	.228	49	-19	6			.983	-1	*C-108/2-1	-1.2
1908	Chi-A	137	430	40	82	8	4	0	29	22		.191	.235	.228	51	-23	15			**.985**	-20	*C-137	-3.6
1909	Chi-A	97	265	11	43	3	0	0	16	17		.162	.226	.174	28	-21	9			.983	5	C-97,M	-1.0
1910	Chi-A	45	142	10	26	4	1	0	6	7		.183	.227	.225	43	-10	0			.976	12	C-45	0.8
1911	Chi-A	89	256	26	55	9	3	0	31	16		.215	.266	.273	52	-17	1			**.986**	1	C-89	-0.7
1912	Chi-A	41	91	9	19	2	1	0	15	9		.209	.287	.253	57	-5	0			.975	1	C-41	-0.1
1914	Chi-A	1	0	0	0	0	0	0	0	0	0	—	—	—	—	0	0			1.000	-0	/C-1	0.0
1916	Det-A	1	0	0	0	0	0	0	0	0	0	—	—	—	—	0	0			.000	0	/C-1	0.0
Total	16	1147	3647	363	777	119	33	21	378	170	0	.213	.254	.281	63	-172	98			.976	-8	*C-1122/1-4,O32S	-8.4

■ HOMER SUMMA Summa, Homer Wayne b: 11/3/1898, Gentry, Mo. d: 1/29/66, Los Angeles, Cal. BL/TR, 5'10.5", 170 lbs. Deb: 9/13/20

YEAR	TM/L	G	AB	R	H	2B	3B	HR	RBI	BB	SO	AVG	OBP	SLG	PRO+	BR/A	SB	CS	SBR	FA	FR	G/POS	TPR
1920	Pit-N	10	22	1	7	1	1	0	1	3	1	.318	.400	.455	141	1	1	0	0	.950	1	/O-6	0.2
1922	Cle-A	12	46	9	16	3	3	1	6	1	1	.348	.400	.609	159	4	1	2	-1	1.000	0	O-12	0.2
1923	Cle-A	137	525	92	172	27	6	3	69	33	20	.328	.374	.419	109	6	9	13	-5	.951	-13	*O-136	-1.9
1924	Cle-A	111	390	55	113	21	6	2	38	11	16	.290	.311	.390	79	-14	4	2	0	.941	-6	O-95	-2.4
1925	Cle-A	75	224	28	74	10	1	0	25	13	6	.330	.375	.384	92	-2	3	2	-0	.966	-9	O-54/3-2	-1.3
1926	Cle-A	154	581	74	179	31	6	4	76	47	9	.308	.368	.403	100	0	15	8	-0	.975	7	*O-154	-0.3
1927	Cle-A	145	574	73	164	41	7	4	74	32	18	.286	.331	.402	89	-11	6	5	-1	.955	-8	*O-145	-2.8
1928	Cle-A	134	504	60	143	26	3	3	57	20	15	.284	.319	.365	78	-16	4	2	0	.971	-4	*O-132	-2.9
1929	*Phi-A	37	81	12	22	4	0	0	10	2	1	.272	.298	.321	57	-5	1	1	-0	.980	-5	O-24	-1.1
1930	Phi-A	25	54	10	15	2	1	1	5	4	1	.278	.339	.407	85	-1	0	0	0	.938	0	O-15	-0.2
Total	10	840	3001	414	905	166	34	18	361	166	88	.302	.346	.398	92	-38	44	35	-8	.961	-36	O-773/3-2	-12.5

■ CHAMP SUMMERS Summers, John Junior b: 6/15/46, Bremerton, Wash. BL/TR, 6'2", 205 lbs. Deb: 5/4/74 C

YEAR	TM/L	G	AB	R	H	2B	3B	HR	RBI	BB	SO	AVG	OBP	SLG	PRO+	BR/A	SB	CS	SBR	FA	FR	G/POS	TPR
1974	Oak-A	20	24	2	3	1	0	0	3	1	5	.125	.160	.167	-6	-3	0	0	0	1.000	-4	O-12/D-2	-0.8
1975	Chi-N	76	91	14	21	5	1	1	16	10	13	.231	.314	.341	78	-3	0	0	0	.889	-4	O-18	-0.8
1976	Chi-N	83	126	11	26	2	0	3	13	13	31	.206	.286	.294	59	-7	1	0	0	.964	-5	O-26,1-10/C-1	-1.4
1977	Cin-N	59	76	11	13	4	0	3	6	6	16	.171	.241	.342	53	-5	0	0	0	1.000	-1	O-16/3-1	-0.6
1978	Cin-N	13	35	4	9	2	0	1	3	7	4	.257	.381	.400	118	1	2	1	0	.933	-2	O-12	-0.2
1979	Cin-N	27	60	10	12	2	1	1	11	13	15	.200	.351	.317	83	-1	0	1	-1	.941	-2	O-13/1-6	-0.4
	Det-A	90	246	47	77	12	1	20	51	40	33	.313	.415	.614	168	24	7	6	-2	.989	-10	O-69,D-10/1-4	1.0
1980	Det-A	120	347	61	103	19	1	17	60	52	52	.297	.396	.504	142	21	4	3	-1	.953	-8	D-64,O-47/1-1	0.9
1981	Det-A	64	165	16	42	8	0	3	21	19	35	.255	.342	.358	98	0	1	1	-0	.964	-2	D-37,O-18	-0.4
1982	SF-N	70	125	15	31	5	0	4	19	16	17	.248	.347	.384	105	1	0	1	-1	.913	-3	O-31/1-3	-0.4
1983	SF-N	29	22	3	3	0	0	0	3	7	8	.136	.345	.136	39	-1	0	0	0	1.000	0	/O-1	-0.1
1984	*SD-N	47	54	5	10	3	0	1	12	4	15	.185	.254	.296	54	-3	0	0	0	1.000	-1	/1-8	-0.5
Total	11	698	1371	199	350	63	4	54	218	188	244	.255	.353	.425	111	24	15	13	-3	.959	-41	O-263,D-113/13C	-3.7

■ KID SUMMERS Summers, William b: Toronto, Ont., Canada d: 10/16/1895, Toronto, Ont., Can. TR, Deb: 8/5/1893

YEAR	TM/L	G	AB	R	H	2B	3B	HR	RBI	BB	SO	AVG	OBP	SLG	PRO+	BR/A	SB	CS	SBR	FA	FR	G/POS	TPR
1893	StL-N	2	1	1	0	0	0	0	0	0	0	.000	.500	.000	37	0	0			.500	-0	/O-1,C-1	0.0

■ CARL SUMNER Sumner, Carl Ringdahl "Lefty" b: 9/28/08, Cambridge, Mass. BL/TL, 5'8", 170 lbs. Deb: 7/28/28

YEAR	TM/L	G	AB	R	H	2B	3B	HR	RBI	BB	SO	AVG	OBP	SLG	PRO+	BR/A	SB	CS	SBR	FA	FR	G/POS	TPR
1928	Bos-A	16	29	6	8	1	1	0	3	5	6	.276	.382	.379	103	0	0	0	0	.923	-3	O-10	-0.3

■ ART SUNDAY Sunday, Arthur (b: August Wacher) b: 1/21/1862, Springfield, Ohio BL/TL, 5'9", 193 lbs. Deb: 5/5/1890

YEAR	TM/L	G	AB	R	H	2B	3B	HR	RBI	BB	SO	AVG	OBP	SLG	PRO+	BR/A	SB	CS	SBR	FA	FR	G/POS	TPR
1890	Bro-P	24	83	26	22	5	1	0	13	15	9	.265	.419	.349	100	1	0			.909	-5	O-24	-0.4

■ BILLY SUNDAY Sunday, William Ashley "Parson" or "The Evangelist" b: 11/19/1862, Ames, Iowa d: 11/6/35, Chicago, Ill. BL/TR, 5'10", 160 lbs. Deb: 5/22/1883

YEAR	TM/L	G	AB	R	H	2B	3B	HR	RBI	BB	SO	AVG	OBP	SLG	PRO+	BR/A	SB	CS	SBR	FA	FR	G/POS	TPR
1883	Chi-N	14	54	6	13	4	0	0	5	1	18	.241	.255	.315	68	-2				.647	-5	O-14	-0.6
1884	Chi-N	43	176	25	39	4	1	4	28	4	36	.222	.239	.324	70	-7				.663	-9	O-43	-1.5
1885	*Chi-N	46	172	36	44	3	3	2	20	12	33	.256	.304	.343	96	-2				.825	-9	O-46	-1.1
1886	Chi-N	28	103	16	25	2	2	0	6	7	26	.243	.291	.301	70	-4	10			.914	-0	O-28	-0.5
1887	Chi-N	50	199	41	58	6	6	3	32	21	20	.291	.362	.427	105	0	34			.766	-8	O-50	-0.7
1888	Pit-N	120	505	69	119	14	3	0	15	12	36	.236	.256	.275	75	-14	71			.939	17	*O-120	-0.1
1889	Pit-N	81	321	62	77	10	6	2	25	27	33	.240	.307	.327	85	-6	47			.946	8	O-81	0.0
1890	Pit-N	86	358	58	92	9	2	1	33	32	20	.257	.327	.302	94	-1	56			.883	11	O-86/P-1	0.6
	Phi-N	31	119	26	31	3	1	0	6	18	7	.261	.367	.303	93	-0	28			.950	3	O-31	0.2
	Yr	117	477	84	123	12	3	1	39	50	27	.258	.337	.302	94	-1	84			.900	15	*O-117/P-1	0.8
Total	8	499	2007	339	498	55	24	12	170	134	229	.248	.300	.317	86	-37	246			.883	9	O-499/P-1	-3.7

■ JIM SUNDBERG Sundberg, James Howard b: 5/18/51, Galesburg, Ill. BR/TR, 6', 195 lbs. Deb: 4/4/74

YEAR	TM/L	G	AB	R	H	2B	3B	HR	RBI	BB	SO	AVG	OBP	SLG	PRO+	BR/A	SB	CS	SBR	FA	FR	G/POS	TPR
1974	Tex-A☆	132	368	45	91	13	3	3	36	62	61	.247	.356	.323	99	2	2	4	-2	.990	6	*C-132	1.2
1975	Tex-A	155	472	45	94	9	0	6	36	51	77	.199	.283	.256	54	-28	3	1	0	.981	5	*C-155	-1.6
1976	Tex-A	140	448	33	102	24	2	3	34	37	61	.228	.287	.310	73	-15	0	0	0	**.991**	17	*C-140	0.6
1977	Tex-A	149	453	61	132	20	3	6	65	53	77	.291	.368	.389	105	5	2	3	-1	**.994**	23	*C-149	3.0
1978	Tex-A★	149	518	54	144	23	6	6	58	64	70	.278	.361	.380	108	7	2	5	-2	**.997**	16	*C-148/D-1	2.5
1979	Tex-A	150	495	50	136	23	4	5	64	51	51	.275	.348	.368	94	-3	3	3	-1	**.995**	9	*C-150	1.1
1980	Tex-A	151	505	59	138	24	1	10	63	64	67	.273	.356	.384	106	6	2	2	-1	.993	6	*C-151	1.6
1981	Tex-A	102	339	42	94	17	2	3	28	50	48	.277	.372	.366	120	10	2	5	-2	.996	-3	C-98/O-2	0.9
1982	Tex-A	139	470	37	118	22	5	10	47	49	57	.251	.323	.383	98	-2	2	6	-3	.991	-2	*C-132/O-1	-0.2
1983	Tex-A	131	378	30	76	14	0	2	28	35	64	.201	.272	.254	47	-27	0	4	-2	.993	5	*C-131	-1.9
1984	Mil-A★	110	348	43	91	19	4	7	43	38	63	.261	.334	.399	106	3	1	1	-0	**.995**	7	*C-109	1.4
1985	*KC-A	115	367	38	90	12	4	10	35	33	67	.245	.309	.381	88	-6	0	2	-1	.992	1	*C-112	-0.1
1986	KC-A	140	429	41	91	9	1	12	42	57	91	.212	.305	.322	69	-18	1	1	-0	**.995**	-1	*C-134	-1.1
1987	Chi-N	61	139	9	28	2	0	4	15	19	40	.201	.306	.302	60	-8	0	0	0	.994	9	C-57	0.3
1988	Chi-N	24	54	8	13	1	0	2	9	8	15	.241	.339	.370	99	0	0	0	0	1.000	-1	C-20	0.0
	Tex-A	38	91	13	26	4	0	4	13	5	17	.286	.323	.462	114	1	0	0	0	1.000	0	C-36	0.3
1989	Tex-A	76	147	13	29	7	1	2	8	23	37	.197	.306	.299	70	-5	0	0	0	.992	1	C-73/D-1	-0.1
Total	16	1962	6021	621	1493	243	36	95	624	699	963	.248	.328	.348	89	-78	20	37	-16	.993	96	*C-1927/O-3,D-2	7.9

■ B.J. SURHOFF Surhoff, William James b: 8/4/64, Bronx, N.Y. BL/TR, 6'1", 200 lbs. Deb: 4/8/87 F

YEAR	TM/L	G	AB	R	H	2B	3B	HR	RBI	BB	SO	AVG	OBP	SLG	PRO+	BR/A	SB	CS	SBR	FA	FR	G/POS	TPR
1987	Mil-A	115	395	50	118	22	3	7	68	36	30	.299	.357	.423	103	2	11	10	-3	.984	6	C-98,3-10/1-1,D-7	1.1
1988	Mil-A	139	493	47	121	21	0	5	38	31	49	.245	.294	.318	71	-19	21	6	3	.990	-8	*C-106,3-31/1-2,SO	-1.7
1989	Mil-A	126	436	42	108	17	4	5	55	25	29	.248	.293	.339	79	-13	14	12	-3	.985	-5	*C-106,D-12/3-6	-1.6
1990	Mil-A	135	474	55	131	21	4	6	59	41	37	.276	.335	.376	99	-0	18	7	1	.985	-6	*C-125,3-11	0.3
1991	Mil-A	143	505	57	146	19	4	5	68	26	33	.289	.324	.372	94	-4	5	8	-3	.995	-4	*C-127/3-5,O-2,2D	-0.4
1992	Mil-A	139	480	63	121	19	1	4	62	46	41	.252	.320	.321	82	-11	14	8	-1	.990	6	*C-109,1-17/O-7,3D	-0.1
1993	Mil-A	148	552	66	151	38	3	7	79	36	47	.274	.320	.391	92	-7	12	9	-2	.949	-7	*3-121,O-24/1-8,CD	-1.6
1994	Mil-A	40	134	20	35	11	2	5	22	16	14	.261	.340	.485	105	1	0	1	-1	.923	-4	3-18,C-12/1-8,OD	-0.4

YEAR	TM/L	G	AB	R	H	2B	3B	HR	RBI	BB	SO	AVG	OBP	SLG	PRO+	BR/A	SB	CS	SBR	FA	FR	G/POS	TPR
1995	Mil-A	117	415	72	133	26	3	13	73	37	43	.320	.382	.492	118	11	7	3	0	.993	3	O-60,1-55,C-18,/D-3	0.9
1996	*Bal-A	143	537	74	157	27	6	21	82	47	79	.292	.353	.482	109	6	0	1	-1	.948	-7	*3-106,O-27,D-10,/1	-0.3
1997	*Bal-A	147	528	80	150	30	4	18	88	49	60	.284	.351	.458	112	9	1	1	-0	.992	7	*O-133/1-3,3-3,D-9	1.2
1998	Bal-A	162	573	79	160	34	1	22	92	49	81	.279	.337	.457	106	4	9	7	-2	.989	-0	*O-157/1-1	-0.1
Total	12	1554	5522	705	1531	285	35	118	786	439	543	.277	.333	.406	98	-22	112	73	-10	.988	-19	C-704,O-414,3/1D2S	-2.7

■ GEORGE SUSCE Susce, George Cyril Methodius "Good Kid" b: 8/13/07, Pittsburgh, Pa. d: 2/25/86, Sarasota, Fla. BR/TR, 5'11.5", 200 lbs. Deb: 4/23/29 FC

YEAR	TM/L	G	AB	R	H	2B	3B	HR	RBI	BB	SO	AVG	OBP	SLG	PRO+	BR/A	SB	CS	SBR	FA	FR	G/POS	TPR
1929	Phi-N	17	17	5	5	3	0	1	1	1	2	.294	.368	.647	137	1	0			.900	-2	C-11	-0.1
1932	Det-A	2	0	0	0	0	0	0	0	0	0	—	—	—	—	0	0	0	0	1.000	-0	/C-2	0.0
1939	Pit-N	31	75	8	17	3	1	1	4	12	5	.227	.333	.333	81	-2	0			.984	2	C-31	0.2
1940	StL-A	61	113	6	24	4	0	0	13	9	9	.212	.282	.248	38	-10	1	0	0	.984	6	C-61	-0.1
1941	Cle-A	1	0	0	0	0	0	0	0	0	0	—	—	—	—	0	0	0	0	1.000	-0	/C-1	0.0
1942	Cle-A	2	1	1	1	0	0	0	0	1	0	1.000	1.000	1.000	492	1	0	0	0	1.000	-0	/C-2	0.1
1943	Cle-A	3	1	0	0	0	0	0	0	0	0	.000	.000	.000	-99	-0	0	0	0	1.000	1	/C-3	0.0
1944	Cle-A	29	61	3	14	1	0	0	4	2	5	.230	.254	.246	45	-4	0	0	0	.948	1	C-29	-0.2
Total	8	146	268	23	61	11	1	2	22	25	21	.228	.301	.299	60	-15	1	0		.974	8	C-140	-0.1

■ PETE SUSKO Susko, Peter Jonathan b: 7/2/04, Laura, Ohio d: 5/22/78, Jacksonville, Fla. BL/TL, 5'11", 172 lbs. Deb: 8/1/34

YEAR	TM/L	G	AB	R	H	2B	3B	HR	RBI	BB	SO	AVG	OBP	SLG	PRO+	BR/A	SB	CS	SBR	FA	FR	G/POS	TPR
1934	Was-A	58	224	25	64	5	3	2	25	18	10	.286	.342	.362	85	-5	3	4	-2	.988	3	1-58	-0.9

■ BUTCH SUTCLIFFE Sutcliffe, Charles Inigo b: 7/22/15, Fall River, Mass. d: 3/2/94, Fall River, Mass. BR/TR, 5'8.5", 165 lbs. Deb: 8/28/38

YEAR	TM/L	G	AB	R	H	2B	3B	HR	RBI	BB	SO	AVG	OBP	SLG	PRO+	BR/A	SB	CS	SBR	FA	FR	G/POS	TPR
1938	Bos-N	4	4	1	1	0	0	0	2	2	1	.250	.500	.250	124	0	0			.800	0	/C-3	0.1

■ SY SUTCLIFFE Sutcliffe, Elmer Ellsworth b: 4/15/1862, Wheaton, Ill. d: 2/13/1893, Wheaton, Ill. BL/TL, 6'2", 170 lbs. Deb: 10/2/1884

YEAR	TM/L	G	AB	R	H	2B	3B	HR	RBI	BB	SO	AVG	OBP	SLG	PRO+	BR/A	SB	CS	SBR	FA	FR	G/POS	TPR
1884	Chi-N	4	15	4	3	1	0	0	2	2	4	.200	.294	.267	72	-0				.976	2	/C-4	0.2
1885	Chi-N	11	43	5	8	1	1	0	4	2	5	.186	.222	.256	48	-3				.838	-5	C-11/O-1	-0.6
	StL-N	16	49	2	6	1	0	0	4	5	10	.122	.204	.143	15	-4				.881	-2	C-14/O-2	-0.5
	Yr	27	92	7	14	2	1	0	8	7	15	.152	.212	.196	32	-7				.862	-7	C-25/O-3	-1.1
1888	Det-N	49	191	17	49	5	3	0	23	5	14	.257	.276	.314	88	-3	6			.901	7	S-24,C-14/1-5,O2	0.6
1889	Cle-N	46	161	17	40	3	2	1	21	14	6	.248	.309	.311	75	-5	5			.892	9	C-37/1-8,O-1	0.6
1890	Cle-P	99	386	62	127	14	8	2	60	33	16	.329	.382	.422	125	14	10			.883	-5	C-84,O-15/S-4,3-2	1.3
1891	Was-a	53	201	29	71	8	3	2	33	17	17	.353	.409	.453	153	14	8			.918	-4	O-35,C-22/S-3,3-1	0.9
1892	Bal-N	66	276	41	77	10	7	1	27	14	15	.279	.316	.377	107	1	12			.958	-7	1-66	-0.9
Total	7	344	1322	177	381	43	24	6	174	92	87	.288	.336	.371	107	13	41			.887	-5	C-186/1-79,OS32	1.6

■ GARY SUTHERLAND Sutherland, Gary Lynn b: 9/27/44, Glendale, Cal. BR/TR, 6', 185 lbs. Deb: 9/17/66 F

YEAR	TM/L	G	AB	R	H	2B	3B	HR	RBI	BB	SO	AVG	OBP	SLG	PRO+	BR/A	SB	CS	SBR	FA	FR	G/POS	TPR
1966	Phi-N	3	3	0	0	0	0	0	0	0	0	.000	.000	.000	-99	-1	0	0	0	1.000	1	/S-1	0.0
1967	Phi-N	103	231	23	57	12	1	1	19	17	22	.247	.298	.320	76	-7	0	3	-2	.928	-16	S-66,O-25	-2.3
1968	Phi-N	67	138	16	38	7	0	0	15	8	15	.275	.315	.326	93	-1	0	0	0	.968	-3	2-17,S-10,3-10,/O-7	-0.3
1969	Mon-N	141	544	63	130	26	1	3	35	37	31	.239	.290	.307	67	-24	5	7	-3	.971	10	*2-139,S-15/O-1	-0.5
1970	Mon-N	116	359	37	74	10	0	3	26	31	22	.206	.273	.259	43	-29	2	2	-1	.975	3	2-97,S-15/3-1	-1.8
1971	Mon-N	111	304	25	78	7	2	4	26	18	12	.257	.302	.332	79	-8	3	4	-2	.963	-1	2-56,S-46/O-4,3-2	-0.3
1972	Hou-N	5	8	0	1	0	0	0	1	0	0	.125	.125	.125	-29	-1	0	0	0	.000	-1	/2-1,3-1	-0.2
1973	Hou-N	16	54	8	14	5	0	0	3	3	5	.259	.298	.352	80	-2	0	0	0	.971	-4	2-14/S-1	-0.5
1974	Det-A	149	619	60	157	20	1	5	49	26	37	.254	.284	.313	69	-25	1	3	-2	.976	-23	*2-147,S-10/3-4	-4.4
1975	Det-A	129	503	51	130	12	3	6	39	45	41	.258	.323	.330	81	-12	0	2	-1	.968	-7	*2-128	-1.4
1976	Det-A	42	117	10	24	5	2	0	6	7	12	.205	.250	.282	53	-7	0	1	-1	.984	1	2-42	-0.4
	Mil-A	59	115	9	25	2	0	1	9	8	7	.217	.274	.261	58	-6	0	2	-1	.955	-0	2-45/1-2,D-8	-0.6
	Yr	101	232	19	49	7	2	1	15	15	19	.211	.262	.272	56	-13	0	3	-2	.970	1	2-87/D-8,1-2	-1.0
1977	SD-N	80	103	5	25	3	0	1	11	7	15	.243	.291	.301	66	-5	0	0	0	.943	-4	2-30,3-21/1-4	-0.8
1978	StL-N	10	6	1	1	0	0	0	0	0	0	.167	.167	.167	-7	-1	0	0	0	1.000	1	/2-1	0.0
Total	13	1031	3104	308	754	109	10	24	239	207	219	.243	.292	.308	69	-129	11	24	-11	.971	-42	2-717,S-164/3OD1	-13.5

■ LEO SUTHERLAND Sutherland, Leonardo (Cantin) b: 4/6/58, Santiago De Cuba, Cuba BL/TL, 5'10", 165 lbs. Deb: 8/11/80

YEAR	TM/L	G	AB	R	H	2B	3B	HR	RBI	BB	SO	AVG	OBP	SLG	PRO+	BR/A	SB	CS	SBR	FA	FR	G/POS	TPR
1980	Chi-A	34	89	9	23	3	0	0	5	1	11	.258	.267	.292	53	-6	4	1	1	.943	-1	O-23	-0.7
1981	Chi-A	11	12	6	2	0	0	0	0	3	1	.167	.333	.167	49	-1	2	1	0	1.000	-3	/O-7	-0.4
Total	2	45	101	15	25	3	0	0	5	4	12	.248	.276	.277	53	-6	6	2	1	.949	-4	/O-30	-1.1

■ GLENN SUTKO Sutko, Glenn Edward b: 5/9/68, Atlanta, Ga. BR/TR, 6'3", 225 lbs. Deb: 10/3/90

YEAR	TM/L	G	AB	R	H	2B	3B	HR	RBI	BB	SO	AVG	OBP	SLG	PRO+	BR/A	SB	CS	SBR	FA	FR	G/POS	TPR
1990	Cin-N	1	1	0	0	0	0	0	0	0	1	.000	.000	.000	-96	-0	0	0	0	1.000	0	/C-1	0.0
1991	Cin-N	10	10	0	1	0	0	0	1	2	6	.100	.250	.100	2	-1	0	0	0	.875	0	/C-9	-0.1
Total	2	11	11	0	1	0	0	0	1	2	7	.091	.231	.091	-6	-2	0	0	0	.889	0	/C-10	-0.1

■ EZRA SUTTON Sutton, Ezra Ballou b: 9/17/1850, Palmyra, N.Y. d: 6/20/07, Braintree, Mass. BR/TR, 5'8.5", 153 lbs. Deb: 5/4/1871

YEAR	TM/L	G	AB	R	H	2B	3B	HR	RBI	BB	SO	AVG	OBP	SLG	PRO+	BR/A	SB	CS	SBR	FA	FR	G/POS	TPR
1871	Cle-n	29	128	35	45	3	7	3	23	1	0	.352	.357	.555	166	11	3	1	0	**.795**	-1	*3-29/O-2,C-1	0.6
1872	Cle-n	22	107	30	30	6	1	0	10	1	1	.280	.287	.355	102	1	1	0	0	.718	-5	3-22	-0.4
1873	Ath-n	51	242	51	81	7	6	0	33	2	2	.335	.340	.413	114	2	1	3	-2	.806	1	*3-43/S-8,2-2	0.0
1874	Ath-n	55	243	54	71	10	3	0	28	0	2	.292	.292	.358	99	-2	6	4	-1	.827	-1	3-36,S-20	-0.4
1875	Ath-n	75	358	83	116	11	7	1	59	1	3	.324	.326	.402	136	9	13	10	-2	.803	14	*3-73/P-2,1-2,SO	1.8
1876	Phi-N	54	236	45	70	12	7	1	31	3	2	.297	.305	.419	141	10				.915	-4	1-29,2-15/3-8,O-4	0.5
1877	Bos-N	58	253	43	74	10	6	0	39	4	10	.292	.304	.379	110	2				.882	-9	S-36,3-22	-0.4
1878	Bos-N	60	239	31	54	9	3	1	29	2	14	.226	.232	.301	69	-9				.888	-1	*3-59/S-1	-0.7
1879	Bos-N	84	339	54	84	13	4	0	34	2	18	.248	.252	.310	82	-7				.884	-12	S-51,3-33	-1.4
1880	Bos-N	76	288	41	72	9	2	0	25	7	7	.250	.268	.295	94	-2				.896	4	S-39,3-37	0.6
1881	Bos-N	83	333	43	97	12	4	0	31	13	9	.291	.318	.351	116	6				.877	-3	*3-81/S-2	0.4
1882	Bos-N	81	319	44	80	8	1	2	38	24	25	.251	.303	.301	94	-1				.856	-5	*3-77/S-4	-0.3
1883	Bos-N	94	414	101	134	28	15	3	73	17	12	.324	.350	.486	147	22				.866	-1	*3-93/O-1,S-1	1.8
1884	Bos-N	110	468	102	**162**	28	7	3	61	29	22	.346	.384	.455	164	34				**.908**	-4	*3-110	2.7
1885	Bos-N	110	457	78	143	23	8	4	47	17	25	.313	.338	.425	151	24				.875	-0	*3-91,S-16/2-2,1-1	2.4
1886	Bos-N	116	499	83	138	21	6	3	48	26	21	.277	.312	.361	108	5	18			.859	-5	O-43,S-28,3-28,2-18	0.0
1887	Bos-N	77	326	58	99	14	9	3	46	13	6	.304	.342	.429	113	5	17			.875	15	S-37,O-18,2-13,3-11	1.7
1888	Bos-N	28	110	16	24	3	1	1	16	7	3	.218	.277	.291	80	-2	10			.859	-5	3-27/S-1	-0.7
Total	5 n	232	1078	253	343	37	24	4	153	5	8	.318	.321	.408	122	21	24	18	-4	.796	7	3-203/S-29,O1P2C	1.6
Total	13	1031	4281	739	1231	190	73	21	518	164	174	.288	.315	.381	118	88	45			.871	-30	3-677,S-216/O21	6.6

■ LARRY SUTTON Sutton, Larry James b: 5/14/70, West Covina, Cal. BL/TL, 5'11", 175 lbs. Deb: 8/17/97

YEAR	TM/L	G	AB	R	H	2B	3B	HR	RBI	BB	SO	AVG	OBP	SLG	PRO+	BR/A	SB	CS	SBR	FA	FR	G/POS	TPR
1997	KC-A	27	69	9	20	2	0	2	8	5	12	.290	.338	.406	91	-1	0	0	0	1.000	-0	1-12/O-1,D-3	-0.2
1998	KC-A	111	310	29	76	14	2	5	42	29	46	.245	.316	.352	70	-13	3	3	-1	.987	-3	O-79/1-6,D-3	-1.8
Total	2	138	379	38	96	16	2	7	50	34	58	.253	.320	.361	74	-14	3	3	-1	.987	-3	/O-80,1-18,D-6	-2.0

■ DALE SVEUM Sveum, Dale Curtis b: 11/23/63, Richmond, Cal. BB/TR, 6'3", 185 lbs. Deb: 5/12/86

YEAR	TM/L	G	AB	R	H	2B	3B	HR	RBI	BB	SO	AVG	OBP	SLG	PRO+	BR/A	SB	CS	SBR	FA	FR	G/POS	TPR
1986	Mil-A	91	317	35	78	13	2	7	35	32	63	.246	.317	.366	83	-8	4	3	-1	.865	-8	3-65,2-13,S-13	-1.6
1987	Mil-A	153	535	86	135	27	3	25	95	40	133	.252	.306	.454	95	-5	2	6	-3	.965	-13	*S-142,2-13	-0.8
1988	Mil-A	129	467	41	113	14	4	9	51	21	122	.242	.276	.347	73	-18	1	0	0	.955	-6	*S-127/2-1,D-1	-1.3
1990	Mil-A	48	117	15	23	7	0	1	12	12	30	.197	.282	.282	59	-6	0	1	-1	.918	-6	3-22,2-16/1-5,S-5	-1.3
1991	Mil-A	90	266	33	64	19	1	4	43	32	78	.241	.324	.365	93	-2	2	4	-2	.968	-7	S-51,3-38/2-2,D-3	-0.8
1992	Phi-N	54	135	13	24	4	0	2	16	16	39	.178	.265	.252	47	-9	0	0	0	.948	2	S-34/3-5,1-4	-0.6
	Chi-A	40	114	15	25	9	0	2	12	12	29	.219	.294	.351	81	-3	1	1	-0	.944	-10	S-37/1-2,3-2	-1.1
1993	Oak-A	30	79	12	14	2	1	2	6	16	21	.177	.316	.304	72	-3	0	0	0	.976	-4	1-14/3-7,2-4,SOD	-0.8
1994	Sea-A	10	27	3	5	0	0	1	2	2	10	.185	.241	.296	37	-3	0	0	0	.909	1	/3-3,D-4	-0.2
1996	Pit-N	12	34	9	12	5	0	1	5	6	6	.353	.450	.588	167	3	0	0	0	.913	-1	3-10	0.3
1997	Pit-N	126	306	30	80	20	1	12	47	27	81	.261	.321	.451	98	-2	0	3	-2	.941	-7	3-47,S-28,1-21,/2-2	-0.9

YEAR	TM/L	G	AB	R	H	2B	3B	HR	RBI	BB	SO	AVG	OBP	SLG	PRO+	BR/A	SB	CS	SBR	FA	FR	G/POS	TPR
1998	NY-A	30	58	6	9	0	0	0	3	4	16	.155	.210	.155	-3	-9	0	0	0	.975	1	1-21/3-6,D-3	-0.9
Total	11	813	2455	298	582	120	12	66	327	220	628	.237	.301	.376	82	-64	10	18	-8	.959	-58	S-438,3-205/12DO	-10.0

■ HARRY SWACINA Swacina, Harry Joseph "Swats" b: 8/22/1881, St.Louis, Mo. d: 6/21/44, Birmingham, Ala. BR/TR, 6'2", 190 lbs. Deb: 9/13/07

YEAR	TM/L	G	AB	R	H	2B	3B	HR	RBI	BB	SO	AVG	OBP	SLG	PRO+	BR/A	SB	CS	SBR	FA	FR	G/POS	TPR
1907	Pit-N	26	95	9	19	1	1	0	10	4		.200	.240	.232	47	-6	1			.996	-1	1-26	-0.9
1908	Pit-N	53	176	7	38	6	1	0	13	5		.216	.238	.261	59	-8	4			.983	-5	1-50	-1.7
1914	Bal-F	158	617	70	173	26	8	0	90	14	23	.280	.297	.348	73	-33	15			.985	10	*1-158	-2.9
1915	Bal-F	85	301	24	74	13	1	1	38	9	11	.246	.268	.306	59	-21	9			.986	6	1-75/2-1	-1.9
Total	4	322	1189	110	304	46	11	1	151	32	34	.256	.276	.315	66	-69	29			.986	10	1-309/2-1	-7.4

■ ANDY SWAN Swan, Andrew J. Deb: 7/23/1884

YEAR	TM/L	G	AB	R	H	2B	3B	HR	RBI	BB	SO	AVG	OBP	SLG	PRO+	BR/A	SB	CS	SBR	FA	FR	G/POS	TPR
1884	Was-a	5	21	3	3	1	0	0			0	.143	.143	.190	9	-2				.824	-3	/1-3,3-2	-0.5
	Ric-a	3	10	2	5	0	0	0			0	.500	.500	.500	230	1				1.000	-0	/1-3	0.1
	Yr	8	31	5	8	1	0	0			0	.258	.258	.290	85	-0				.902	-3	/1-6,3-2	-0.4

■ MARTY SWANDELL Swandell, John Martin (b: Martin Schwendel) b: 1841, Baden, Germany d: 10/25/06, Brooklyn, N.Y. TL, 5'10.5", 146 lbs. Deb: 5/7/1872 U

YEAR	TM/L	G	AB	R	H	2B	3B	HR	RBI	BB	SO	AVG	OBP	SLG	PRO+	BR/A	SB	CS	SBR	FA	FR	G/POS	TPR
1872	Eck-n	14	55	7	11	0	0	0	4	2	1	.200	.228	.200	38	-3	0	0	0	.625	-2	/3-8,O-4,1-1,2-1	-0.4
1873	Res-n	2	9	1	1	0	0	0	1	0	0	.111	.111	.111	-37	-1	0	0	0	.909	-0	/1-2	-0.1
Total	2 n	16	64	8	12	0	0	0	5	2	1	.188	.212	.188	27	-4	0	0	0	.944	-3	/3-8,O-4,1-3,2-1	-0.5

■ PINKY SWANDER Swander, Edward O. b: 7/4/1880, Portsmouth, Ohio d: 10/24/44, Springfield, Mass. BL/TL, 5'9", 180 lbs. Deb: 9/18/03

YEAR	TM/L	G	AB	R	H	2B	3B	HR	RBI	BB	SO	AVG	OBP	SLG	PRO+	BR/A	SB	CS	SBR	FA	FR	G/POS	TPR
1903	StL-A	14	51	9	14	2	2	0	6	10		.275	.413	.392	146	4	0			.833	-2	O-14	0.1
1904	StL-A	1	1	0	0	0	0	0	0	0		.000	.000	.000	-99	-0	0			.000	0	H	0.0
Total	2	15	52	9	14	2	2	0	6	10		.269	.406	.385	142	3	0			.833	-2	/O-14	0.1

■ EVAR SWANSON Swanson, Ernest Evar b: 10/15/02, DeKalb, Ill. d: 7/17/73, Galesburg, Ill. BR/TR, 5'9", 170 lbs. Deb: 4/18/29

YEAR	TM/L	G	AB	R	H	2B	3B	HR	RBI	BB	SO	AVG	OBP	SLG	PRO+	BR/A	SB	CS	SBR	FA	FR	G/POS	TPR
1929	Cin-N	148	574	100	172	35	12	4	43	41	47	.300	.353	.423	96	-5	33			.970	-3	*O-142	-1.6
1930	Cin-N	95	301	43	93	15	3	2	22	11	17	.309	.335	.399	81	-10	4			.963	0	O-71	-1.3
1932	Chi-A	14	52	9	16	3	1	0	8	8	3	.308	.400	.404	116	2	3	1	0	.960	-2	O-14	-0.1
1933	Chi-A	144	539	102	165	25	7	1	63	93	35	.306	.411	.384	117	18	19	11	-1	.973	-5	*O-139	0.4
1934	Chi-A	117	426	71	127	9	5	0	34	59	31	.298	.385	.343	86	-6	10	3	1	.980	-3	*O-105	-1.2
Total	5	518	1892	325	573	87	28	7	170	212	133	.303	.376	.390	98	-1	69	15		.971	-14	O-471	-3.8

■ KARL SWANSON Swanson, Karl Edward b: 12/17/03, N.Henderson, Ill. BL/TR, 5'10", 155 lbs. Deb: 8/12/28

YEAR	TM/L	G	AB	R	H	2B	3B	HR	RBI	BB	SO	AVG	OBP	SLG	PRO+	BR/A	SB	CS	SBR	FA	FR	G/POS	TPR
1928	Chi-A	22	64	2	9	1	0	0	6	4	7	.141	.191	.156	-8	-10	3	0	1	.943	1	2-21	-0.7
1929	Chi-A	2	1	0	0	0	0	0	0	0	0	.000	.000	.000	-99	-0	0	0	0	.000	0	H	0.0
Total	2	24	65	2	9	1	0	0	6	4	7	.138	.188	.154	-9	-10	3	0	1	.943	1	/2-21	-0.7

■ STAN SWANSON Swanson, Stanley Lawrence b: 5/19/44, Yuba City, Cal. BR/TR, 5'11", 168 lbs. Deb: 6/23/71

YEAR	TM/L	G	AB	R	H	2B	3B	HR	RBI	BB	SO	AVG	OBP	SLG	PRO+	BR/A	SB	CS	SBR	FA	FR	G/POS	TPR
1971	Mon-N	49	106	14	26	3	0	2	11	10	13	.245	.310	.330	81	-3	1	3	-2	1.000	-6	O-38	-1.2

■ BILL SWANSON Swanson, William Andrew b: 10/12/1888, New York, N.Y. d: 10/14/54, New York, N.Y. BB/TR, 5'6", 156 lbs. Deb: 9/2/14

YEAR	TM/L	G	AB	R	H	2B	3B	HR	RBI	BB	SO	AVG	OBP	SLG	PRO+	BR/A	SB	CS	SBR	FA	FR	G/POS	TPR
1914	Bos-A	11	20	0	4	2	0	0	0	3	4	.200	.304	.300	82	-0	0	1	-1	.875	-3	/2-6,3-3,S-1	-0.5

■ ED SWARTWOOD Swartwood, Cyrus Edward b: 1/12/1859, Rockford, Ill. d: 5/15/24, Pittsburgh, Pa. BL/TR, 5'11", 198 lbs. Deb: 8/11/1881 U

YEAR	TM/L	G	AB	R	H	2B	3B	HR	RBI	BB	SO	AVG	OBP	SLG	PRO+	BR/A	SB	CS	SBR	FA	FR	G/POS	TPR
1881	Buf-N	1	3	0	1	0	0	0	0	1	0	.333	.500	.333	170	0				.500	-1	/O-1	0.0
1882	Pit-a	76	325	**86**	107	**18**	11	4		21		.329	.370	.489	197	33				.788	-8	*O-73/1-4	2.2
1883	Pit-a	94	412	86	**147**	24	8	3		25		**.357**	**.394**	.476	**187**	**40**				.936	2	1-60,O-37/C-3	3.1
1884	Pit-a	102	399	74	115	19	6	0		33		.288	.365	.366	137	18				.804	-3	*O-79,1-22/3-1,P-1	0.9
1885	Bro-a	99	399	80	106	8	9	0	49	36		.266	.334	.331	110	6				.851	-10	*O-95/1-4,S-1,C-1	-0.7
1886	Bro-a	122	471	95	132	13	10	3	58	**70**		.280	.377	.369	133	20	37			.884	7	*O-122/C-1	2.2
1887	Bro-a	91	363	72	92	14	8	1	54	46		.253	.342	.344	91	-4	29			.835	2	O-91	-0.3
1890	Tol-a	126	462	106	151	23	11	3	64	80		.327	.444	.444	157	37	53			.925	8	*O-126/P-1	3.5
1892	Pit-N	13	42	8	10	1	0	0	4	13	11	.238	.418	.262	106	1	1			.933	4	O-13	0.4
Total	9	724	2876	607	861	120	63	14	229	325	11	.299	.379	.400	142	152	120			.856	0	O-637/1-90,C-5,PS3	11.3

■ CHARLIE SWEASY Sweasy, Charles James (b: Charles James Swasey) b: 11/2/1847, Newark, N.J. d: 3/30/08, Newark, N.J. BR/TR, 5'9", 172 lbs. Deb: 5/19/1871 M

YEAR	TM/L	G	AB	R	H	2B	3B	HR	RBI	BB	SO	AVG	OBP	SLG	PRO+	BR/A	SB	CS	SBR	FA	FR	G/POS	TPR
1871	Oly-n	5	19	5	4	1	0	0	4	1	0	.211	.250	.263	50	-1	0	0	0	.788	-1	/2-5	-0.1
1872	Cle-n	12	57	8	16	0	0	0	6	2	1	.281	.305	.281	86	-0	1	0	0	.833	3	2-11/O-1	0.1
1873	Bos-n	1	4	0	1	0	0	0	0	0	0	.250	.250	.250	45	-0	0	0	0	.714	-1	/2-1	-0.1
1874	Bal-n	8	33	2	8	0	0	0	4	2	0	.242	.286	.242	72	-1	0	0	0	.646	-6	/2-8,O-1	-0.6
	Atl-n	10	44	4	5	1	0	0	3	0	0	.114	.114	.136	-23	-5	0	0	0	.879	5	2-10	-0.1
	Yr	18	77	6	13	1	0	0	7	2	0	.169	.190	.182	21	-6	0	0	0	.781	-1	2-18/O-1	-0.7
1875	RS-n	19	76	7	13	1	0	0	4	3	1	.171	.203	.184	39	-4	2	4	-2	.828	-5	2-19,M	-0.9
1876	Cin-N	56	225	18	46	5	2	0	10	2	5	.204	.211	.244	60	-8				.864	2	*2-55/O-1	-0.5
1878	Pro-N	55	212	23	37	3	0	0	8	7	23	.175	.201	.189	29	-16				.846	-9	*2-55	-1.9
Total	5 n	55	233	26	47	3	0	0	21	8	2	.202	.228	.215	47	-12	3	4	-2	.808	-4	/2-54,O-2	-1.7
Total	2	111	437	41	83	8	2	0	18	9	28	.190	.206	.217	44	-24				.855	-6	2-110/O-1	-2.4

■ BUCK SWEENEY Sweeney, Charles Francis b: 4/15/1890, Pittsburgh, Pa. d: 3/13/55, Pittsburgh, Pa. Deb: 9/28/14

YEAR	TM/L	G	AB	R	H	2B	3B	HR	RBI	BB	SO	AVG	OBP	SLG	PRO+	BR/A	SB	CS	SBR	FA	FR	G/POS	TPR
1914	Phi-A	1	1	0	0	0	0	0	0	0	1	.000	.000	.000	-99	-0	0			1.000	-0	/O-1	-0.1

■ CHARLIE SWEENEY Sweeney, Charles J. b: 4/13/1863, San Francisco, Cal d: 4/4/02, San Francisco, Cal. BR/TR, 5'10.5", 181 lbs. Deb: 5/11/1882

YEAR	TM/L	G	AB	R	H	2B	3B	HR	RBI	BB	SO	AVG	OBP	SLG	PRO+	BR/A	SB	CS	SBR	FA	FR	G/POS	TPR
1882	Pro-N	1	4	0	0	0	0	0	0	0	1	.000	.000	.000	-99	-1				.500	0	/O-1	-0.1
1883	Pro-N	22	87	9	19	3	0	0	15	2	10	.218	.236	.253	47	-5				.863	3	P-20/O-7	0.0
1884	Pro-N	41	168	24	50	9	0	1	19	11	17	.298	.341	.369	125	5				.940	-2	P-27,O-17/1-1	-0.2
	StL-U	45	171	31	54	14	2	1		10		.316	.354	.439	134	2				**.943**	4	P-33,O-13/1-1	-0.1
1885	StL-N	71	267	27	55	7	1	0	24	12	33	.206	.240	.240	59	-11				.827	-3	O-39,P-35	-1.0
1886	StL-N	17	64	4	16	2	0	0	7	3	10	.250	.284	.281	77	-2	0			.929	-0	P-11/O-4,S-2	-0.1
1887	Cle-a	36	133	22	30	4	4	0	19	21		.226	.331	.316	83	-2	11			.936	-4	1-20,O-10/P-3,S3	-0.7
Total	6	233	894	117	224	39	7	2	84	59	71	.251	.297	.317	90	-14	11			.909	-3	P-129/O-91,1-22,S3	-2.2

■ DAN SWEENEY Sweeney, Daniel J. b: 1/28/1868, Philadelphia, Pa. d: 7/13/13, Louisville, Ky. 5'5", 160 lbs. Deb: 4/18/1895

YEAR	TM/L	G	AB	R	H	2B	3B	HR	RBI	BB	SO	AVG	OBP	SLG	PRO+	BR/A	SB	CS	SBR	FA	FR	G/POS	TPR
1895	Lou-N	22	90	18	24	5	0	1	16	17	2	.267	.389	.356	99	1	2			.794	-4	O-22	-0.4

■ JEFF SWEENEY Sweeney, Edward Francis "Ed" b: 7/19/1888, Chicago, Ill. d: 7/4/47, Chicago, Ill. BR/TR, 6'1", 200 lbs. Deb: 5/16/08

YEAR	TM/L	G	AB	R	H	2B	3B	HR	RBI	BB	SO	AVG	OBP	SLG	PRO+	BR/A	SB	CS	SBR	FA	FR	G/POS	TPR
1908	NY-A	32	82	4	12	2	0	0	2	5		.146	.195	.171	19	-7	0			.955	-0	C-25/1-1,O-1	-0.6
1909	NY-A	67	176	19	47	3	0	0	21	16		.267	.328	.284	93	-1	3			.947	3	C-62/1-3	0.8
1910	NY-A	78	215	25	43	4	4	0	13	17		.200	.271	.256	62	-10	12			.974	5	C-77	0.2
1911	NY-A	83	229	17	53	6	5	0	18	14		.231	.299	.301	63	-12	8			.964	-3	C-83	-0.7
1912	NY-A	110	351	37	94	12	1	0	30	27		.268	.325	.308	77	-11	6			.955	-1	*C-108	-0.1
1913	NY-A	117	351	35	93	10	2	2	40	37	41	.265	.348	.322	96	-1	11			.964	9	*C-112/1-1,O-1	1.9
1914	NY-A	87	258	25	55	8	1	1	22	35	30	.213	.316	.264	75	-7	19	6	2	.980	2	C-78	0.4
1915	NY-A	53	137	12	26	2	0	0	5	25	12	.190	.319	.204	57	-6	3	3	-1	.975	-6	C-53	-0.9
1919	Pit-N	17	42	0	4	1	0	0	0	5	6	.095	.191	.119	-5	-5	1			.944	-3	C-15	-0.8
Total	9	644	1841	174	427	48	13	3	151	181	89	.232	.310	.277	73	-59	63	9		.964	6	C-613/1-5,O-2	0.2

■ HANK SWEENEY Sweeney, Henry Leon b: 12/28/15, Franklin, Tenn. d: 5/6/80, Columbia, Tenn. BL/TL, 6', 185 lbs. Deb: 10/1/44

YEAR	TM/L	G	AB	R	H	2B	3B	HR	RBI	BB	SO	AVG	OBP	SLG	PRO+	BR/A	SB	CS	SBR	FA	FR	G/POS	TPR
1944	Pit-N	1	2	0	0	0	0	0	0	0	1	.000	.000	.000	-96	-1	0			1.000	0	/1-1	0.0

■ JERRY SWEENEY Sweeney, Jeremiah H. b: 1860, Boston, Mass. d: 8/25/1891, Boston, Mass. 5'9.5", 157 lbs. Deb: 8/22/1884

YEAR	TM/L	G	AB	R	H	2B	3B	HR	RBI	BB	SO	AVG	OBP	SLG	PRO+	BR/A	SB	CS	SBR	FA	FR	G/POS	TPR
1884	KC-U	31	129	16	34	3	0	0		4		.264	.286	.287	85	-6				.958	3	1-31	-0.7

YEAR	TM/L	G	AB	R	H	2B	3B	HR	RBI	BB	SO	AVG	OBP	SLG	PRO+	BR/A	SB	CS	SBR	FA	FR	G/POS	TPR

■ ROONEY SWEENEY   Sweeney, John J.   b: 1860, New York, N.Y.   5'8", 155 lbs.   Deb: 7/25/1883

1883	Bal-a	25	101	13	21	5	2	0		4		.208	.238	.297	69	-4				.878	-1	C-23/O-3	-0.3
1884	Bal-U	48	186	37	42	7	1	0		15		.226	.284	.274	63	-14				.917	-8	C-33,O-16/3-1	-1.7
1885	StL-N	3	11	1	1	0	0	0	0	0	4	.091	.091	.091	-44	-2				.750	-0	/O-2,C-1	-0.2
Total	3	76	298	51	64	12	3	0	0	19	4	.215	.262	.262	62	-19				.905	-9	/C-57,O-21,3-1	-2.2

■ MARK SWEENEY   Sweeney, Mark Patrick   b: 10/26/69, Framingham, Mass.   BL/TL, 6'1", 195 lbs.   Deb: 8/4/95

1995	StL-N	37	77	5	21	2	0	2	13	10	15	.273	.356	.377	94	-0	1	1	-0	.994	-1	1-19/O-1	-0.3
1996	*StL-N	98	170	32	45	9	0	3	22	33	29	.265	.387	.371	102	2	3	0	1	.984	-5	O-43,1-15	-0.3
1997	StL-N	44	61	5	13	3	0	0	4	9	14	.213	.324	.262	56	-4	0	1	-1	1.000	-5	O-25/1-4	-0.9
	SD-N	71	103	11	33	4	0	2	19	11	18	.320	.386	.417	119	3	2	2	-1	.944	-5	O-20/1-7	-0.3
	Yr	115	164	16	46	7	0	2	23	20	32	.280	.362	.360	94	-1	2	3	-1	.976	-9	O-45,1-11	-1.2
1998	*SD-N	122	192	17	45	8	3	2	15	26	37	.234	.329	.339	82	-5	1	2	-1	1.000	-0	O-34,1-21/D-1	-1.4
Total	4	372	603	70	157	26	3	9	73	89	113	.260	.358	.358	93	-4	7	6	-2	.979	-21	O-123/1-66,D-1	-3.2

■ MIKE SWEENEY   Sweeney, Michael John   b: 7/22/73, Orange, Cal.   BR/TR, 6'1", 195 lbs.   Deb: 9/14/95

1995	KC-A	4	4	1	1	0	0	0	0	0	0	.250	.250	.250	30	-0	0	0	0	.875	-0	/C-4	-0.1
1996	KC-A	50	165	23	46	10	0	4	24	18	21	.279	.364	.412	96	-1	1	2	-1	.994	-0	C-26,D-22	-0.1
1997	KC-A	84	240	30	58	8	0	7	31	17	33	.242	.308	.363	72	-10	3	2	-0	.993	5	C-76/D-3	0.0
1998	KC-A	92	282	32	73	18	0	8	35	24	38	.259	.321	.408	84	-7	2	3	-1	.984	-7	C-91	-0.9
Total	4	230	691	86	178	36	0	19	90	59	92	.258	.327	.392	83	-18	6	7	-2	.988	-2	C-197/D-25	-1.1

■ PETE SWEENEY   Sweeney, Peter Jay   b: 12/31/1863, California   d: 8/22/01, San Francisco, Cal   BR/TR,   Deb: 9/28/1888

1888	Was-N	11	44	3	8	0	1	0	5	0	4	.182	.182	.227	32	-3	0			.784	-0	/3-8,O-3	-0.4
1889	Was-N	49	193	13	44	7	3	1	23	11	26	.228	.284	.311	70	-8	8			.802	-10	3-47/2-1,O-1	-1.5
	StL-a	9	38	8	14	2	0	0	8	1	5	.368	.415	.421	122	1	8			.780	-1	/3-8,O-1	0.0
1890	StL-a	49	190	23	34	3	2	0	10	17		.179	.271	.216	38	-16	8			.880	-5	2-23,3-21/1-3,O-2	-1.7
	Lou-a	2	7	1	1	0	0	0	1	1		.143	.250	.286	59	-0	1			.889	-1	/S-2	-0.2
	Phi-a	14	49	5	8	1	1	0	0	7		.163	.281	.224	50	-3	0			.915	-6	/2-9,O-4,3-2	-0.7
	Yr	65	246	29	43	5	3	0	11	25		.175	.272	.220	41	-19	9			.889	-12	2-32,3-23/O-6,1S	-2.6
Total	3	134	521	53	109	14	7	1	47	37	35	.209	.280	.269	57	-30	19			.799	-24	/3-86,2-33,O-11,1S	-4.5

■ BILL SWEENEY   Sweeney, William John   b: 3/6/1886, Covington, Ky.   d: 5/26/48, Cambridge, Mass.   BR/TR, 5'11", 175 lbs.   Deb: 6/14/07

1907	Chi-N	3	10	1	1	0	0	0	1	1		.100	.182	.100	-11	-1	1			.571	-4	/S-3	-0.7
	Bos-N	58	191	24	50	2	0	0	18	15		.262	.316	.272	85	-3	8			.871	0	3-23,S-15,O-11,/21	-0.3
	Yr	61	201	25	51	2	0	0	19	16		.254	.309	.264	79	-4	9			.871	-4	3-23,S-18,O-11,/21	-1.0
1908	Bos-N	127	418	44	102	15	3	0	40	45		.244	.317	.294	97	-0	17			.930	12	*3-123/S-3,2-1	1.8
1909	Bos-N	138	493	44	120	19	3	1	36	37		.243	.296	.300	81	-11	25			.903	8	*3-112,S-26	0.1
1910	Bos-N	150	499	43	133	22	4	5	46	61	28	.267	.349	.357	101	1	25			.903	-1	*S-110,3-21,1-17	0.5
1911	Bos-N	137	523	92	164	33	6	3	63	77	26	.314	.404	.417	120	15	33			.944	11	*2-136	2.4
1912	Bos-N	153	593	84	204	31	13	1	100	68	34	.344	.416	.445	133	29	27			.959	27	*2-153	5.0
1913	Bos-N	139	502	65	129	17	6	0	47	66	50	.257	.347	.315	88	-6	18			.939	1	*2-137	-0.7
1914	Chi-N	134	463	45	101	14	5	1	38	53	15	.218	.298	.276	71	-15	18			.954	15	*2-134	-0.2
Total	8	1039	3692	442	1004	153	40	11	389	423	153	.272	.349	.344	100	8	172			.949	69	2-566,3-279,S/10	7.9

■ BILL SWEENEY   Sweeney, William Joseph   b: 12/29/04, Cleveland, Ohio   d: 4/18/57, San Diego, Cal.   BR/TR, 5'11", 180 lbs.   Deb: 4/13/28

1928	Det-A	89	309	47	78	15	5	0	19	15	28	.252	.287	.333	62	-18	12	9	-2	.993	4	1-75/O-3	-2.1
1930	Bos-A	88	243	32	75	13	0	4	30	9	15	.309	.333	.412	91	-4	5	3	-0	.997	-1	1-56/3-1	-0.9
1931	Bos-A	131	498	48	147	30	3	1	58	20	30	.295	.322	.373	87	-10	5	12	-6	.993	10	*1-124	-1.6
Total	3	308	1050	127	300	58	8	5	107	44	73	.286	.314	.370	80	-32	22	24	-8	.994	13	1-255/O-3,3-1	-4.6

■ RICK SWEET   Sweet, Ricky Joe   b: 9/7/52, Longview, Wash.   BB/TR, 6'1", 200 lbs.   Deb: 4/8/78   C

1978	SD-N	88	226	15	50	8	0	1	11	27	22	.221	.307	.270	68	-9	1	4	-2	.984	3	C-76	-0.8
1982	NY-N	3	3	0	1	0	0	0	0	0	1	.333	.333	.333	88	-0	0	0	0	.000	0	/H	0.0
	Sea-A	88	258	29	66	6	1	4	24	20	24	.256	.314	.333	76	-8	3	0	1	.993	-6	C-83	-1.1
1983	Sea-A	93	249	18	55	9	0	1	22	13	26	.221	.260	.269	44	-19	2	2	-1	.987	-3	C-85	-1.9
Total	3	272	736	62	172	23	1	6	57	60	73	.234	.294	.292	63	-37	6	6	-2	.988	-7	C-244	-3.8

■ HAM SWEIGERT   Sweigert, Hampton   Deb: 10/12/1890

| 1890 | Phi-a | 1 | 1 | 0 | 0 | 0 | 0 | 0 | 0 | 0 | 1 | .000 | .500 | .000 | 49 | 0 | 1 | | | .000 | -0 | /O-1 | 0.0 |

■ AUGIE SWENTOR   Swentor, August William   b: 11/21/1899, Seymour, Conn.   d: 11/10/69, Waterbury, Conn.   BR/TR, 6', 185 lbs.   Deb: 9/12/22

| 1922 | Chi-A | 1 | 1 | 0 | 0 | 0 | 0 | 0 | 0 | 0 | 1 | .000 | .000 | .000 | -99 | -0 | 0 | 0 | 0 | .000 | 0 | H | 0.0 |

■ STEVE SWETONIC   Swetonic, Stephen Albert   b: 8/13/03, Mt.Pleasant, Pa.   d: 4/22/74, Canonsburg, Pa.   BR/TR, 5'11", 185 lbs.   Deb: 4/17/29

1929	Pit-N	42	48	11	13	3	1	0	4	1		.271	.314	.375	68	-2	0			.960	2	P-41	0.0
1930	Pit-N	23	36	2	4	0	0	0	2	1	5	.111	.135	.167	-27	-8	0			1.000	-0	P-23	0.0
1931	Pit-N	14	7	0	1	0	0	0	0	1	3	.143	.250	.143	8	-1	0			1.000	-0	P-14	0.0
1932	Pit-N	24	54	1	5	1	0	0	2	1	7	.093	.125	.111	-37	-10	0			1.000	-1	P-24	0.0
1933	Pit-N	31	55	3	11	0	2	0	4	1	7	.200	.214	.273	38	-4	0			.950	-1	P-31	0.0
1935	Pit-N	1	0	1	0	0	0	0	0	0			—	—		-0	0			.000	0	R	0.0
Total	6	135	200	18	34	6	3	0	10	7	28	.170	.202	.230	13	-26	0			.973	-2	P-133	0.0

■ POP SWETT   Swett, William E.   b: 4/16/1870, San Francisco, Cal   d: 11/22/34, San Francisco, Cal   6', 175 lbs.   Deb: 5/3/1890

| 1890 | Bos-P | 37 | 94 | 16 | 18 | 4 | 3 | 1 | 12 | 16 | 26 | .191 | .321 | .330 | 69 | -4 | 4 | | | .820 | -8 | C-34/O-3 | -0.8 |

■ BOB SWIFT   Swift, Robert Virgil   b: 3/6/15, Salina, Kan.   d: 10/17/66, Detroit, Mich.   BR/TR, 5'11.5", 180 lbs.   Deb: 4/16/40   MC

1940	StL-A	130	398	37	97	20	1	0	39	28	39	.244	.295	.299	53	-27	1	0	0	.980	-20	*C-128	-3.6
1941	StL-A	63	170	13	44	7	0	0	21	22	11	.259	.344	.300	69	-7	2	0	1	.985	-4	C-58	-0.6
1942	StL-A	29	76	3	15	4	0	0	8	3	5	.197	.228	.289	44	-6	0	2	-1	1.000	-1	C-28	-0.7
	Phi-A	60	192	9	44	3	0	0	15	13	17	.229	.278	.245	48	-13	1	2	-1	.970	2	C-60	-0.8
	Yr	89	268	12	59	7	0	0	23	16	22	.220	.264	.257	47	-19	1	4	-2	.977	1	C-88	-1.5
1943	Phi-A	77	224	16	43	5	1	1	11	35	16	.192	.301	.237	58	-11	1	0	0	.976	-3	C-77	-0.9
1944	Det-A	80	247	16	63	11	1	1	19	27	27	.255	.331	.320	82	-5	0	1	-1	.982	1	C-76	0.1
1945	*Det-A	95	279	19	65	5	0	0	24	26	22	.233	.298	.251	56	-15	1	0	0	.988	1	C-94	-0.9
1946	Det-A	42	107	13	25	2	0	2	10	14	7	.234	.322	.308	72	-4	0	0	0	.980	-4	C-42	-0.7
1947	Det-A	97	279	23	70	11	0	1	33	36	16	.251	.330	.301	74	9	2	2	-1	.989	-0	C-97	-0.4
1948	Det-A	113	292	23	65	6	0	4	33	51	29	.223	.338	.284	65	-14	1	0	0	.991	6	*C-112	-0.1
1949	Det-A	74	189	16	45	6	0	2	18	26	20	.238	.330	.302	68	-9	0	0	0	.989	1	C-69	-0.5
1950	Det-A	67	132	14	30	4	0	2	9	25	6	.227	.350	.303	66	-6	0	0	0	.995	8	C-63	0.3
1951	Det-A	44	104	8	20	2	0	0	5	12	10	.192	.276	.192	28	-10	0	0	0	.982	2	C-43	-0.7
1952	Det-A	28	58	3	8	1	0	0	4	7	7	.138	.242	.155	12	-7	0	0	0	.977	6	C-28	-0.7
1953	Det-A	2	3	0	1	0	0	0	0	0	0	.333	.600	.667	245	-0	0	0	0	1.000	1	/C-2	0.2
Total	14	1001	2750	212	635	86	3	14	238	324	233	.231	.313	.280	61	-141	10	6	-1	.985	-5	C-980	-9.3

■ JOSH SWINDELL   Swindell, Joshua Ernest   b: 7/5/1883, Rose Hill, Kan.   d: 3/19/69, Fruita, Colo.   BR/TR, 6', 180 lbs.   Deb: 9/16/11

1911	Cle-A	4	4	0	1	0	0	0	0	0	0	.250	.250	.250	39	-0	0			.800	-0	/P-4	0.0
1913	Cle-A	1	0	0	0	0	0	0	0	0	0	—	—	—	—	-0	0			.000	-0	R	0.0
Total	2	5	4	0	1	0	0	0	0	0	0	.250	.250	.250	39	-0	0			.800	-0	/P-4	0.0

■ CHARLIE SWINDELLS   Swindells, Charles Jay "Swin"   b: 10/26/1878, Rockford, Ill.   d: 7/22/40, Portland, Ore.   BR/TR, 5'11.5", 180 lbs.   Deb: 9/7/04

| 1904 | StL-N | 3 | 8 | 0 | 1 | 0 | 0 | 0 | 0 | 0 | | .125 | .125 | .125 | -24 | -1 | 0 | | | 1.000 | -0 | /C-3 | -0.1 |

■ STEVE SWISHER Swisher, Steven Eugene b: 8/9/51, Parkersburg, W.Va. BR/TR, 6'2", 205 lbs. Deb: 6/14/74

YEAR	TM/L	G	AB	R	H	2B	3B	HR	RBI	BB	SO	AVG	OBP	SLG	PRO+	BR/A	SB	CS	SBR	FA	FR	G/POS	TPR
1974	Chi-N	90	280	21	60	5	0	5	27	37	63	.214	.310	.286	65	-12	0	3	-2	.987	-1	C-90	-1.2
1975	Chi-N	93	254	20	54	16	2	1	22	30	57	.213	.306	.303	66	-11	1	0	0	.979	-8	C-93	-1.6
1976	Chi-N☆	109	377	25	89	13	3	5	42	20	82	.236	.278	.326	65	-18	2	1	0	.983	-3	*C-107	-1.9
1977	Chi-N	74	205	21	39	7	0	5	15	9	47	.190	.231	.298	37	-19	0	0	0	.976	-3	C-72	-2.0
1978	StL-N	45	115	11	32	5	1	1	10	8	14	.278	.331	.365	96	-1	1	0	0	.991	6	C-42	0.7
1979	StL-N	38	73	4	11	1	1	1	3	6	17	.151	.215	.233	22	-8	0	0	0	.974	1	C-33	-0.6
1980	StL-N	18	24	2	6	1	0	0	2	1	7	.250	.280	.292	58	-1	0	0	0	.957	0	/C-8	-0.1
1981	SD-N	16	28	2	4	0	0	0	0	2	11	.143	.200	.143	-2	-4	0	0	0	.971	-0	C-10	-0.4
1982	SD-N	26	58	2	10	1	0	2	3	5	24	.172	.238	.293	50	-4	0	0	0	.981	1	C-26	-0.2
Total	9	509	1414	108	305	49	7	20	124	118	322	.216	.281	.303	59	-78	4	4	-1	.982	-5	C-481	-7.3

■ RON SWOBODA Swoboda, Ronald Alan "Rocky" b: 6/30/44, Baltimore, Md. BR/TR, 6'2", 205 lbs. Deb: 4/12/65

YEAR	TM/L	G	AB	R	H	2B	3B	HR	RBI	BB	SO	AVG	OBP	SLG	PRO+	BR/A	SB	CS	SBR	FA	FR	G/POS	TPR
1965	NY-N	135	399	52	91	15	3	19	50	33	102	.228	.292	.424	102	-0	2	3	-1	.947	1	*O-112	-0.5
1966	NY-N	112	342	34	76	9	4	8	50	31	76	.222	.296	.342	79	-10	4	2	0	.987	0	O-97	-1.4
1967	NY-N	134	449	47	126	17	3	13	53	41	96	.281	.342	.419	119	11	3	1	0	.957	3	*O-108,1-20	0.8
1968	NY-N	132	450	46	109	14	6	11	59	52	113	.242	.326	.373	109	6	8	1	2	.975	4	*O-125	0.6
1969	*NY-N	109	327	38	77	10	2	9	52	43	90	.235	.328	.361	91	-3	1	1	-0	.988	0	O-97	-0.9
1970	NY-N	115	245	29	57	8	2	9	40	40	72	.233	.343	.392	96	-1	2	4	-2	.984	-12	*O-100	-1.8
1971	Mon-N	39	75	7	19	4	3	0	6	11	16	.253	.364	.387	112	2	0	1	-1	.977	-3	O-26	-0.3
	NY-A	54	138	17	36	2	1	2	20	27	35	.261	.393	.333	114	4	0	0	0	.965	-3	O-47	-0.1
1972	NY-A	63	113	9	28	8	0	1	12	17	29	.248	.346	.345	110	2	0	1	-1	.983	-5	O-35/1-2	-0.5
1973	NY-A	35	43	6	5	0	0	1	2	4	18	.116	.191	.186	7	-5	0	0	0	1.000	-4	O-20/D-4	-1.0
Total	9	928	2581	285	624	87	24	73	344	299	647	.242	.325	.379	101	4	20	14	-2	.972	-18	O-767/1-22,D-4	-5.1

■ LOU SYLVESTER Sylvester, Louis J. b: 2/14/1855, Springfield, Ill. BR/TR, 5'3", 165 lbs. Deb: 4/18/1884

YEAR	TM/L	G	AB	R	H	2B	3B	HR	RBI	BB	SO	AVG	OBP	SLG	PRO+	BR/A	SB	CS	SBR	FA	FR	G/POS	TPR
1884	Cin-U	82	333	67	89	13	8	2		18		.267	.305	.372	97	-12				.792	0	*O-81/P-6,S-2	-1.0
1886	Lou-a	45	154	41	35	5	3	0	17	29		.227	.350	.299	98	0	3			.913	-0	O-45	-0.1
	Cin-a	17	55	10	10	0	0	3	8	7		.182	.286	.345	94	-0	2			.909	1	O-17	0.0
	Yr	62	209	51	45	5	3	3	25	36		.215	.333	.311	97	-0	5			.912	1	O-62	-0.1
1887	StL-a	29	112	20	25	4	3	1	18	13		.223	.310	.339	73	-5	13			.923	2	O-29/2-1	-0.3
Total	3	173	654	138	159	22	14	6	43	67		.243	.315	.347	93	-17	18			.854	3	O-172/P-6,S-2,2-1	-1.4

■ JOE SZEKELY Szekely, Joseph b: 2/2/25, Cleveland, Ohio BR/TR, 5'11", 180 lbs. Deb: 9/13/53

YEAR	TM/L	G	AB	R	H	2B	3B	HR	RBI	BB	SO	AVG	OBP	SLG	PRO+	BR/A	SB	CS	SBR	FA	FR	G/POS	TPR
1953	Cin-N	5	13	0	1	0	0	0	0	0	3	.077	.077	.077	-59	-3	0	0	0	1.000	1	/O-3	-0.2

■ KEN SZOTKIEWICZ Szotkiewicz, Kenneth John b: 2/25/47, Wilmington, Del. BL/TR, 6', 165 lbs. Deb: 4/7/70

YEAR	TM/L	G	AB	R	H	2B	3B	HR	RBI	BB	SO	AVG	OBP	SLG	PRO+	BR/A	SB	CS	SBR	FA	FR	G/POS	TPR
1970	Det-A	47	84	9	9	1	0	3	9	12	29	.107	.219	.226	23	-9	0	0	0	.971	9	S-44	0.4

■ JERRY TABB Tabb, Jerry Lynn b: 3/17/52, Altus, Okla. BL/TR, 6'2", 195 lbs. Deb: 9/8/76

YEAR	TM/L	G	AB	R	H	2B	3B	HR	RBI	BB	SO	AVG	OBP	SLG	PRO+	BR/A	SB	CS	SBR	FA	FR	G/POS	TPR
1976	Chi-N	11	24	2	7	0	0	0	0	3	2	.292	.370	.292	82	-0	0	0	0	1.000	-1	/1-6	-0.1
1977	Oak-A	51	144	8	32	3	0	6	19	10	26	.222	.273	.368	74	-6	0	1	-1	.993	-2	1-36/D-5	-1.0
1978	Oak-A	12	9	0	1	0	0	0	1	2	5	.111	.273	.111	12	-1	0	0	0	1.000	-0	/1-2,D-2	-0.1
Total	3	74	177	10	40	3	0	6	20	15	33	.226	.286	.345	72	-7	0	1	-1	.994	-3	/1-44,D-7	-1.2

■ PAT TABLER Tabler, Patrick Sean b: 2/2/58, Hamilton, Ohio BR/TR, 6'2", 200 lbs. Deb: 8/21/81

YEAR	TM/L	G	AB	R	H	2B	3B	HR	RBI	BB	SO	AVG	OBP	SLG	PRO+	BR/A	SB	CS	SBR	FA	FR	G/POS	TPR
1981	Chi-N	35	101	11	19	3	1	1	5	13	26	.188	.281	.267	54	-6	0	1	-1	.982	1	2-35	-0.4
1982	Chi-N	25	85	9	20	4	2	1	7	6	20	.235	.293	.365	81	-2	0	0	0	.949	-5	3-25	-0.8
1983	Cle-A	124	430	56	125	23	5	6	65	56	63	.291	.374	.409	111	8	2	4	-2	.948	-3	O-88,3-25/2-2,D-6	0.0
1984	Cle-A	144	473	66	137	21	3	10	68	47	62	.290	.358	.410	110	7	3	1	0	.998	-13	1-67,O-43,3-36,/2D	-1.1
1985	Cle-A	117	404	47	111	18	3	5	59	27	55	.275	.323	.371	90	-5	0	6	-4	.983	1	1-92,D-18/3-4,2-1	-1.4
1986	Cle-A	130	473	61	154	29	2	6	48	29	75	.326	.368	.433	119	13	3	1	0	.990	1	*1-107,D-18	0.6
1987	Cle-A★	151	553	66	170	34	3	11	86	51	84	.307	.372	.439	113	12	5	2	0	.984	5	1-82,D-66	0.9
1988	Cle-A	41	143	16	32	5	1	1	17	23	27	.224	.335	.294	76	-4	1	0	0	1.000	-1	D-29,1-10	-0.6
	KC-A	89	301	37	93	17	2	1	49	23	41	.309	.362	.389	109	4	2	3	-1	.986	-2	D-40,O-37/1-7,3-1	-0.1
	Yr	130	444	53	125	22	3	2	66	46	68	.282	.353	.358	98	0	3	3	-1	.986	-2	D-69,O-37,1-17,/3-1	-0.7
1989	KC-A	123	390	36	101	11	1	2	42	37	42	.259	.326	.308	80	-9	0	0	0	.970	2	O-55,D-39,1-20,/23	-1.1
1990	KC-A	75	195	12	53	14	0	1	19	20	21	.272	.343	.359	98	-0	0	2	-1	.986	-0	O-42,D-15/3-6,1-5	-0.3
	NY-N	17	43	6	12	1	1	1	10	3	8	.279	.340	.419	108	0	0	0	0	1.000	1	O-10	0.1
1991	*Tor-A	82	185	20	40	5	1	1	21	29	21	.216	.326	.270	64	-8	0	0	0	.985	0	D-57,1-20/O-1	-1.2
1992	*Tor-A	49	135	11	34	5	0	0	16	11	14	.252	.308	.289	65	-6	0	0	0	1.000	-1	1-34/O-8,3-1,D-2	-1.0
Total	12	1202	3911	454	1101	190	25	47	512	375	559	.282	.348	.379	99	3	16	20	-7	.988	-14	1-444,D-291,O/32	-6.4

■ GREG TABOR Tabor, Gregory Steven b: 5/21/61, Castro Valley, Cal. BR/TR, 6' ", 165 lbs. Deb: 9/10/87

YEAR	TM/L	G	AB	R	H	2B	3B	HR	RBI	BB	SO	AVG	OBP	SLG	PRO+	BR/A	SB	CS	SBR	FA	FR	G/POS	TPR
1987	Tex-A	9	9	4	1	1	0	0	1	0	4	.111	.111	.222	-15	-1	0	0	0	.938	4	/2-4,D-1	0.2

■ JIM TABOR Tabor, James Reubin "Rawhide" b: 11/5/16, New Hope, Ala. d: 8/22/53, Sacramento, Cal. BR/TR, 6'2", 175 lbs. Deb: 8/2/38

YEAR	TM/L	G	AB	R	H	2B	3B	HR	RBI	BB	SO	AVG	OBP	SLG	PRO+	BR/A	SB	CS	SBR	FA	FR	G/POS	TPR
1938	Bos-A	19	57	8	18	3	2	1	8	1	6	.316	.328	.491	98	-1	0	1	-1	.889	1	3-11/S-2	0.0
1939	Bos-A	149	577	76	167	33	8	14	95	40	54	.289	.337	.447	95	-6	16	10	-1	.923	7	*3-148	0.1
1940	Bos-A	120	459	73	131	28	6	21	81	42	58	.285	.345	.510	114	8	14	10	-2	.926	5	*3-120	1.3
1941	Bos-A	126	498	65	139	29	3	16	101	36	48	.279	.328	.446	100	-2	17	9	-0	.930	2	*3-125	0.3
1942	Bos-A	139	508	56	128	18	2	12	75	37	47	.252	.303	.366	85	-12	6	13	-6	.924	-9	*3-138	-2.5
1943	Bos-A	137	537	57	130	26	3	13	85	43	54	.242	.299	.374	95	-5	7	7	-2	.938	-8	*3-133/O-2	-1.5
1944	Bos-A	116	438	58	125	25	3	13	72	31	38	.285	.334	.445	123	11	4	4	-1	.950	3	*3-114	1.5
1946	Phi-N	124	463	53	124	15	2	10	50	36	51	.268	.322	.374	100	-1	3			.954	-3	*3-124	-0.3
1947	Phi-N	75	251	27	59	14	0	4	31	20	21	.235	.297	.339	71	-11	2			.916	-17	3-67	-2.8
Total	9	1005	3788	473	1021	191	29	104	598	286	377	.270	.322	.418	99	-20	69	54		.933	-19	3-980/O-2,S-2	-3.9

■ JEFF TACKETT Tackett, Jeffrey Wilson b: 12/1/65, Fresno, Cal. BR/TR, 6'2", 200 lbs. Deb: 9/11/91

YEAR	TM/L	G	AB	R	H	2B	3B	HR	RBI	BB	SO	AVG	OBP	SLG	PRO+	BR/A	SB	CS	SBR	FA	FR	G/POS	TPR
1991	Bal-A	6	8	1	1	0	0	0	0	2	2	.125	.300	.125	23	-1	0	0	0	1.000	0	/C-6	0.0
1992	Bal-A	65	179	21	43	8	1	5	24	17	28	.240	.313	.380	91	-2	0	0	0	.997	6	C-64/3-1	0.7
1993	Bal-A	39	87	8	15	3	0	0	9	13	28	.172	.280	.207	32	-8	0	0	0	.989	5	C-38/P-1	-0.2
1994	Bal-A	26	53	5	12	3	1	2	9	5	13	.226	.317	.434	87	-1	0	0	0	.980	2	C-26	0.1
Total	4	136	327	35	71	14	2	7	42	37	71	.217	.304	.336	72	-12	0	0	0	.992	13	C-134/P-1,3-1	0.6

■ DOUG TAITT Taitt, Douglas John "Poco" b: 8/3/02, Bay City, Mich. d: 12/12/70, Portland, Ore. BL/TR, 6', 176 lbs. Deb: 4/10/28

YEAR	TM/L	G	AB	R	H	2B	3B	HR	RBI	BB	SO	AVG	OBP	SLG	PRO+	BR/A	SB	CS	SBR	FA	FR	G/POS	TPR
1928	Bos-A	143	482	51	144	28	14	3	61	36	32	.299	.350	.434	107	4	13	6	0	.975	5	*O-139/P-1	0.0
1929	Bos-A	26	65	6	18	4	0	0	6	8	5	.277	.365	.338	84	-1	0	1	-1	.955	-0	O-21	-0.3
	Chi-A	47	124	11	21	7	0	0	12	8	13	.169	.220	.226	15	-16	0	0	0	.966	0	O-30	-1.7
	Yr	73	189	17	39	11	0	0	18	16	18	.206	.272	.265	39	-17	0	1	-1	.961	0	O-51	-2.0
1931	Phi-N	38	151	13	34	4	2	1	15	4	14	.225	.245	.298	42	-12	0			.990	5	O-38	-1.0
1932	Phi-N	4	2	0	0	0	0	0	1	2	0	.000	.500	.000	43	0	0			.000	0	H	0.0
Total	4	258	824	81	217	43	16	4	95	58	64	.263	.314	.369	79	-26	13	7		.975	10	O-228/P-1	-3.0

■ BOB TALBOT Talbot, Robert Dale b: 6/6/27, Visalia, Cal. BR/TR, 6', 170 lbs. Deb: 9/16/53

YEAR	TM/L	G	AB	R	H	2B	3B	HR	RBI	BB	SO	AVG	OBP	SLG	PRO+	BR/A	SB	CS	SBR	FA	FR	G/POS	TPR
1953	Chi-N	8	30	5	10	0	1	0	0	0	4	.333	.333	.400	88	-1	1	0	0	1.000	3	/O-7	0.2
1954	Chi-N	114	403	45	97	15	4	1	19	16	25	.241	.275	.305	50	-29	3	6	-3	.985	-6	*O-111	-4.3
Total	2	122	433	50	107	15	5	1	19	16	29	.247	.279	.312	53	-30	4	6	-2	.986	-4	O-118	-4.1

■ TIM TALTON Talton, Marion Lee b: 1/14/39, Pikeville, N.C. BL/TR, 6'3", 200 lbs. Deb: 7/8/66

YEAR	TM/L	G	AB	R	H	2B	3B	HR	RBI	BB	SO	AVG	OBP	SLG	PRO+	BR/A	SB	CS	SBR	FA	FR	G/POS	TPR
1966	KC-A	37	53	8	18	3	1	2	6	1	5	.340	.364	.547	163	4	0	1	-1	1.000	-1	C-14/1-9	0.3

YEAR	TM/L	G	AB	R	H	2B	3B	HR	RBI	BB	SO	AVG	OBP	SLG	PRO+	BR/A	SB	CS	SBR	FA	FR	G/POS	TPR
1967	KC-A	46	59	7	15	3	1	0	5	7	13	.254	.333	.339	102	0	0	0	0	.971	-5	C-22/1-1	-0.4
Total	2	83	112	15	33	6	2	2	11	8	18	.295	.347	.438	131	4	0	1	-1	.980	-6	/C-36,1-10	-0.1
■ JOHN TAMARGO		Tamargo, John Felix b: 11/7/51, Tampa, Fla. BB/TR, 5'10", 180 lbs. Deb: 9/3/76																					
1976	StL-N	10	10	2	3	0	0	0	1	3	0	.300	.462	.300	118	1	0	0	0	1.000	-1	/C-1	0.0
1977	StL-N	4	4	0	0	0	0	0	0	0	2	.000	.000	.000	-99	-1	0	0	0	1.000	-1	/C-1	-0.1
1978	StL-N	6	6	0	0	0	0	0	0	0	2	.000	.000	.000	-99	-2	0	0	0	.000	0	/C-1	-0.2
	SF-N	36	92	6	22	4	1	1	8	18	7	.239	.364	.337	101	1	1	1	-0	.965	-2	C-31	-0.1
	Yr	42	98	6	22	4	1	1	8	18	9	.224	.345	.316	89	-1	1	1	-0	.965	-2	C-32	-0.3
1979	SF-N	30	60	7	12	3	0	2	6	4	8	.200	.250	.350	66	-3	0	0	0	.985	-6	C-17	-0.9
	Mon-N	12	21	0	8	2	0	0	5	3	3	.381	.458	.476	157	2	0	0	0	1.000	-1	/C-4	0.1
	Yr	42	81	7	20	5	0	2	11	7	11	.247	.307	.383	92	-1	0	0	0	.989	-7	C-21	-0.8
1980	Mon-N	37	51	4	14	3	0	1	13	6	5	.275	.351	.392	107	1	0	0	0	.975	-2	C-12	-0.1
Total	5	135	244	19	59	12	1	4	33	34	27	.242	.335	.348	92	-2	1	1	-0	.974	-12	/C-67	-1.3
■ LEO TANKERSLEY		Tankersley, Lawrence William b: 6/8/01, Terrell, Tex. d: 9/18/80, Dallas, Tex. BR/TR, 6', 176 lbs. Deb: 7/2/25																					
1925	Chi-A	1	3	0	0	0	0	0	0	0	0	.000	.000	.000	-99	-1	0	0	0	1.000	-1	/C-1	-0.2
■ JESSE TANNEHILL		Tannehill, Jesse Niles "Powder" b: 7/14/1874, Dayton, Ky. d: 9/22/56, Dayton, Ky. BB/TL, 5'8", 150 lbs. Deb: 6/17/1894 FC																					
1894	Cin-N	5	11	0	0	0	0	0	1	1	2	.000	.083	.000	-76	-3	0			.600	-1	/P-5	0.0
1897	Pit-N	56	184	22	49	8	2	0	22	18		.266	.338	.332	80	-5	4			.900	7	O-33,P-21	-0.1
1898	Pit-N	60	152	25	44	9	3	1	17	7		.289	.321	.408	111	1	4			.956	4	P-43/O-7	0.0
1899	Pit-N	47	132	17	34	5	3	0	10	8		.258	.310	.341	79	-4	2			.954	3	P-40/O-1	-0.1
1900	Pit-N	34	110	19	37	7	0	0	17	5		.336	.365	.400	110	1	2			.924	1	P-29/O-4	0.0
1901	Pit-N	42	135	19	33	3	3	1	12	6		.244	.277	.333	74	-5	0			.917	-2	P-32,O-10	-0.1
1902	Pit-N	44	148	27	43	6	1	1	17	12		.291	.348	.365	116	3	3			.969	-3	P-26,O-16	-0.2
1903	NY-A	40	111	18	26	6	2	1	13	8		.234	.292	.351	87	-2	1			.969	1	P-32/O-5	-0.2
1904	Bos-A	45	122	14	24	2	6	0	6	9		.197	.252	.311	73	-4	1			.991	2	P-33/O-2	-0.1
1905	Bos-A	37	93	11	21	2	0	1	12	16		.226	.339	.280	96	0	1			.946	2	P-37	0.0
1906	Bos-A	31	79	12	22	2	2	0	4	6		.278	.329	.354	114	1	1			.948	0	P-27	0.0
1907	Bos-A	21	51	2	10	3	1	0	6	2		.196	.241	.294	71	-2	0			.981	0	P-18	0.0
1908	Bos-A	1	2	0	1	0	0	0	0	0		.500	.500	.500	219	0	0			1.000	0	/P-1	0.0
	Was-A	26	43	[illegible]	11	1	0	0	3	2		.256	.289	.279	92	-0	0			.897	1	P-10	0.0
	Yr	27	45	1	12	1	0	0	3	2		.267	.298	.289	99	-0	0			.907	2	P-11	0.0
1909	Was-A	16	36	2	6	1	0	0	1	5		.167	.286	.194	55	-2	0			1.000	-0	/O-9,P-3	-0.3
1911	Cin-N	1	1	0	0	0	0	0	0	0	1	.000	.000	.000	-99	-0	0			1.000	0	/P-1	0.0
Total	15	506	1410	189	361	55	23	5	141	105	3	.256	.311	.338	90	-20	19			.953	16	P-358/O-87	-1.1
■ LEE TANNEHILL		Tannehill, Lee Ford b: 10/26/1880, Dayton, Ky. d: 2/16/38, Live Oak, Fla. BR/TR, 5'11", 170 lbs. Deb: 4/22/03 F																					
1903	Chi-A	138	503	48	113	14	3	2	50	25		.225	.263	.276	65	-22	10			.908	-5	*S-138	-2.1
1904	Chi-A	153	547	50	125	31	5	0	61	20		.229	.260	.303	81	-13	14			.947	**28**	*3-153	2.2
1905	Chi-A	142	480	38	96	17	2	0	39	45		.200	.274	.244	67	-17	8			.931	28	*3-142	1.8
1906	*Chi-A	116	378	26	69	8	3	0	33	31		.183	.254	.220	50	-21	7			.951	**39**	3-99,S-17	2.4
1907	Chi-A	33	108	9	26	2	0	0	11	8		.241	.293	.259	79	-2	3			.912	5	3-31/S-2	0.4
1908	Chi-A	141	482	44	104	15	3	0	35	25		.216	.257	.259	69	-17	6			.935	18	*3-136/S-5	0.7
1909	Chi-A	155	531	39	118	21	5	0	47	31		.222	.269	.281	77	-15	12			.941	7	3-91,S-64	-0.5
1910	Chi-A	67	230	17	51	10	0	1	21	11		.222	.263	.278	73	-8	3			.947	3	S-38,1-23/3-6	-0.4
1911	Chi-A	141	516	60	131	17	6	0	49	32		.254	.300	.310	73	-20	0			.957	**43**	*S-102,2-27/3-7,1-5	2.8
1912	Chi-A	4	3	0	0	0	0	0	0	1		.000	.400	.000	18	-0	0			.667	-1	/3-3,S-1	-0.1
Total	10	1090	3778	331	833	135	27	3	346	229		.220	.269	.273	70	-134	63			.938	165	3-668,S-367/1-28,2	7.2
■ CHUCK TANNER		Tanner, Charles William b: 7/4/29, New Castle, Pa. BL/TL, 6', 185 lbs. Deb: 4/12/55 FM																					
1955	Mil-N	97	243	27	60	9	3	6	27	27	32	.247	.322	.383	91	-3	0	0	0	.981	-4	O-62	-1.0
1956	Mil-N	60	63	6	15	2	0	1	4	10	10	.238	.342	.317	84	-1	0	0	0	.800	-3	/O-8	-0.4
1957	Mil-N	22	69	5	17	3	0	2	6	5	4	.246	.297	.377	86	-2	0	0	0	1.000	-0	O-18	-0.3
	Chi-N	95	318	42	91	16	2	7	42	23	20	.286	.338	.415	103	1	0	2	-1	.988	-1	O-82	-0.6
	Yr	117	387	47	108	19	2	9	48	28	24	.279	.331	.408	100	-0	0	2	-1	.990	-1	*O-100	-0.9
1958	Chi-N	73	103	10	27	6	0	4	17	9	10	.262	.321	.437	100	-0	1	0	0	.955	-2	O-15	-0.3
1959	Cle-A	14	48	6	12	2	0	1	5	2	9	.250	.280	.354	76	-2	0	0	0	1.000	-1	O-10	-0.3
1960	Cle-A	21	25	2	7	1	0	0	4	4	6	.280	.379	.320	94	-0	1	0	0	1.000	-1	/O-4	0.0
1961	LA-A	7	8	0	1	0	0	0	0	2	2	.125	.300	.125	16	-1	0	0	0	.000	-0	/O-1	-0.1
1962	LA-A	7	8	0	1	0	0	0	0	0	0	.125	.125	.125	-34	-1	0	0	0	.000	-1	/O-2	-0.2
Total	8	396	885	98	231	39	5	21	105	82	93	.261	.325	.388	93	-10	2	2	-1	.983	-13	O-202	-3.2
■ WALTER TAPPAN		Tappan, Walter Van Dorn "Tap" b: 10/8/1890, Carlinville, Ill. d: 12/19/67, Lynwood, Cal. BR/TR, 5'8", 158 lbs. Deb: 4/16/14																					
1914	KC-F	18	39	1	8	1	0	1	3	1	0	.205	.225	.308	46	-4	1			.875	-3	/S-8,3-6,2-1	-0.7
■ EL TAPPE		Tappe, Elvin Walter b: 5/21/27, Quincy, Ill. d: 10/11/98, Quincy, Ill. BR/TR, 5'11", 180 lbs. Deb: 4/24/54 MC																					
1954	Chi-N	46	119	5	22	3	0	0	4	10	9	.185	.248	.210	21	-14	0	0	0	.986	6	C-46	-0.6
1955	Chi-N	2	0	0	0	0	0	0	0	0	0	—	—	—	—	0	0	0	0	1.000	1	/C-2	0.1
1956	Chi-N	3	1	0	0	0	0	0	0	1	0	.000	.500	.000	51	0	0	0	0	1.000	0	/C-3	0.0
1958	Chi-N	17	28	2	6	0	0	0	4	3	1	.214	.290	.214	37	-2	0	0	0	.962	-1	C-16	-0.3
1960	Chi-N	51	103	11	24	7	0	0	3	11	12	.233	.313	.301	70	-4	0	1	-1	.992	9	C-49	0.6
1962	Chi-N	26	53	3	11	0	0	0	6	4	3	.208	.288	.208	34	-5	0	0	0	1.000	4	C-26,M	0.0
Total	6	145	304	21	63	10	0	0	17	29	25	.207	.283	.240	41	-25	0	1	-1	.989	19	C-142	-0.2
■ TED TAPPE		Tappe, Theodore Nash b: 2/2/31, Seattle, Wash. BL/TR, 6'3", 185 lbs. Deb: 9/14/50																					
1950	Cin-N	7	5	1	1	0	0	1	1	1	1	.200	.333	.800	187	1	0			.000	0	H	0.1
1951	Cin-N	4	3	0	1	0	0	0	0	0	0	.333	.333	.333	79	-0	0			.000	0	H	0.0
1955	Chi-N	23	50	12	13	2	0	4	10	11	11	.260	.413	.540	151	4	0	0	0	1.000	-2	O-15	0.1
Total	3	34	58	13	15	2	0	5	11	12	12	.259	.403	.552	151	5	0	0		1.000	-2	/O-15	0.2
■ TONY TARASCO		Tarasco, Anthony Giacinto b: 12/9/70, New York, N.Y. BL/TR, 6'1", 205 lbs. Deb: 4/30/93																					
1993	*Atl-N	24	35	6	8	2	0	0	2	0	5	.229	.250	.286	43	-3	0	1	-1	1.000	-3	O-12	-0.6
1994	Atl-N	87	132	16	36	6	0	5	19	9	17	.273	.319	.432	91	-2	5	0	2	1.000	-8	O-45	-0.8
1995	Mon-N	126	438	64	109	18	4	14	40	51	78	.249	.330	.404	89	-7	24	3	5	.979	6	*O-116	0.1
1996	*Bal-A	31	84	14	20	3	0	1	9	7	15	.238	.297	.310	54	-6	5	3	-0	1.000	1	O-23/D-6	-0.5
1997	Bal-A	100	166	26	34	8	1	7	26	25	33	.205	.313	.392	85	-4	2	2	-1	.991	-10	O-81/D-2	-1.4
1998	Cin-N	15	24	5	5	2	0	1	4	3	5	.208	.296	.417	81	-1	0	0	0	1.000	-1	/O-7	-0.1
Total	6	383	879	131	212	39	5	28	100	95	153	.241	.318	.392	83	-22	36	9	5	.987	-13	O-284/D-8	-3.3
■ ARLIE TARBERT		Tarbert, Wilbur Arlington b: 9/10/04, Cleveland, Ohio d: 11/27/46, Cleveland, Ohio BR/TR, 6', 160 lbs. Deb: 6/18/27																					
1927	Bos-A	33	69	5	13	1	0	0	5	3	12	.188	.253	.203	20	-8	0	0	0	.944	-4	O-27	-1.3
1928	Bos-A	6	17	1	3	1	0	0	2	1	1	.176	.222	.235	21	-2	1	0	0	.900	-0	/O-6	-0.2
Total	2	39	86	6	16	2	0	0	7	4	13	.186	.247	.209	20	-10	1	0	0	.935	-5	/O-33	-1.5
■ DANNY TARTABULL		Tartabull, Danilo (Mora) b: 10/30/62, San Juan, P.R. BR/TR, 6'1", 205 lbs. Deb: 9/7/84 F																					
1984	Sea-A	10	20	3	6	1	0	2	7	2	3	.300	.391	.650	185	2	0	0	0	.931	2	/S-8,2-1	0.4
1985	Sea-A	19	61	8	20	7	1	1	7	8	14	.328	.406	.525	152	4	1	0	0	.940	-3	S-16/3-4	0.3
1986	Sea-A	137	511	76	138	25	6	25	96	61	157	.270	.349	.489	124	17	4	8	-4	.953	1	*O-101,2-31/3-1,D-3	1.2
1987	KC-A	158	582	95	180	27	3	34	101	79	136	.309	.393	.541	141	35	9	4	0	.976	-6	*O-149/D-6	2.2
1988	KC-A	146	507	80	139	38	3	26	102	76	119	.274	.373	.515	145	31	8	5	-1	.963	-4	*O-130,D-13	2.2

YEAR	TM/L	G	AB	R	H	2B	3B	HR	RBI	BB	SO	AVG	OBP	SLG	PRO+	BR/A	SB	CS	SBR	FA	FR	G/POS	TPR
1989	KC-A	133	441	54	118	22	0	18	62	69	123	.268	.370	.440	128	18	4	2	0	.982	-7	O-71,D-55	0.8
1990	KC-A	88	313	41	84	19	0	15	60	36	93	.268	.344	.473	128	11	1	1	-0	.965	-4	O-52,D-32	0.5
1991	KC-A★	132	484	78	153	35	3	31	100	65	121	.316	.400	**.593**	170	46	6	3	0	.965	-10	*O-124/D-6	3.2
1992	NY-A	123	421	72	112	19	0	25	85	103	115	.266	.410	.489	152	33	2	2	-1	.980	1	O-69,D-53	3.1
1993	NY-A	138	513	87	128	33	2	31	102	92	156	.250	.366	.503	135	26	0	0	0	.978	-1	D-88,O-50	1.9
1994	NY-A	104	399	68	102	24	1	19	67	66	111	.256	.363	.464	115	10	1	1	-0	1.000	-2	D-78,O-26	0.3
1995	NY-A	59	192	25	43	12	0	6	28	33	54	.224	.341	.380	88	-3	0	0	0	1.000	-0	D-39,O-18	-0.6
	Oak-A	24	88	9	23	4	0	2	7	10	28	.261	.337	.375	90	-1	0	2	-1	1.000	-0	D-22/O-1	-0.4
	Yr	83	280	34	66	16	0	8	35	43	82	.236	.340	.379	89	-4	0	2	-1	1.000	-1	D-61,O-19	-1.0
1996	Chi-A	132	472	58	120	23	3	27	101	64	128	.254	.343	.487	112	8	1	2	-1	.973	3	*O-122,D-10	0.6
1997	Phi-N	3	7	2	0	0	0	0	0	4	4	.000	.364	.000	5	-1	0	0	0	1.000	-1	/O-3	-0.2
Total	14	1406	5011	756	1366	289	22	262	925	768	1362	.273	.371	.496	133	236	37	30	-7	.971	-32	O-916,D-405/2S3	15.5

■ **JOSE TARTABULL** Tartabull, Jose Milages (Guzman) b: 11/27/38, Cienfuegos, Cuba BL/TL, 5′11″, 165 lbs. Deb: 4/10/62 F

YEAR	TM/L	G	AB	R	H	2B	3B	HR	RBI	BB	SO	AVG	OBP	SLG	PRO+	BR/A	SB	CS	SBR	FA	FR	G/POS	TPR
1962	KC-A	107	310	49	86	6	5	0	22	20	19	.277	.323	.329	73	-12	19	5	3	.974	4	O-85	-1.0
1963	KC-A	79	242	27	58	8	5	1	19	17	17	.240	.290	.326	68	-10	16	1	4	.986	-3	O-71	-1.3
1964	KC-A	104	100	9	20	2	0	0	3	5	12	.200	.238	.220	28	-10	4	0	1	.978	-12	O-59	-2.2
1965	KC-A	68	218	28	68	11	4	1	19	18	20	.312	.364	.413	122	6	11	5	0	.986	7	O-54	1.1
1966	KC-A	37	127	13	30	2	3	0	4	11	13	.236	.297	.299	74	-4	8	1	2	1.000	0	O-32	-0.4
	Bos-A	68	195	28	54	7	4	0	11	6	11	.277	.299	.354	79	-6	11	3	2	.989	-2	O-47	-0.9
	Yr	105	322	41	84	9	7	0	15	17	24	.261	.298	.332	77	-10	19	4	3	.994	-2	O-79	-1.3
1967	*Bos-A	115	247	36	55	1	2	0	10	23	26	.223	.289	.243	54	-13	6	6	-2	.989	-12	O-83	-3.4
1968	Bos-A	72	139	24	39	6	0	0	6	6	5	.281	.310	.324	87	-2	2	3	-1	.984	-4	O-43	-1.0
1969	Oak-A	75	266	28	71	11	1	0	11	9	11	.267	.291	.316	73	-10	3	4	-2	.993	1	O-63	-1.5
1970	Oak-A	24	13	5	3	2	0	0	2	0	2	.231	.231	.385	69	-1	1	0	0	1.000	-2	/O-6	-0.2
Total	9	749	1857	247	484	56	24	2	107	115	136	.261	.304	.320	74	-61	81	28	8	.986	-24	O-543	-10.8

■ **LA SCHELLE TARVER** Tarver, La Schelle b: 1/30/59, Modesto, Cal. BL/TL, 5′11″, 165 lbs. Deb: 7/12/86

YEAR	TM/L	G	AB	R	H	2B	3B	HR	RBI	BB	SO	AVG	OBP	SLG	PRO+	BR/A	SB	CS	SBR	FA	FR	G/POS	TPR
1986	Bos-A	13	25	3	3	0	0	0	1	1	4	.120	.154	.120	-24	-4	0	1	-1	1.000	-1	/O-9	-0.6

■ **WILLIE TASBY** Tasby, Willie b: 1/8/33, Shreveport, La. BR/TR, 5′11″, 175 lbs. Deb: 9/9/58

YEAR	TM/L	G	AB	R	H	2B	3B	HR	RBI	BB	SO	AVG	OBP	SLG	PRO+	BR/A	SB	CS	SBR	FA	FR	G/POS	TPR
1958	Bal-A	18	50	6	10	3	0	1	1	7	15	.200	.310	.320	78	-1	1	1	-0	1.000	-4	O-16	-0.7
1959	Bal-A	142	505	69	126	16	5	13	48	34	80	.250	.305	.378	88	-9	3	5	-2	.968	3	*O-137	-1.5
1960	Bal-A	39	85	9	18	2	1	0	3	9	12	.212	.295	.259	52	-6	1	0	0	.980	-8	O-36	-1.4
	Bos-A	105	385	68	108	17	1	7	37	51	54	.281	.372	.384	101	2	3	1	0	.979	3	*O-102	0.0
	Yr	144	470	77	126	19	2	7	40	60	66	.268	.358	.362	93	-3	4	1	1	.979	-5	*O-138	-1.4
1961	Was-A	141	494	54	124	13	2	17	63	58	94	.251	.332	.389	93	-5	4	10	-5	.985	2	*O-139	-1.5
1962	Was-A	11	34	4	7	0	0	0	0	2	6	.206	.250	.206	24	-4	0	0	0	.933	-2	O-10	-0.6
	Cle-A	75	199	25	48	7	0	4	17	25	41	.241	.326	.337	81	-5	0	2	-1	1.000	-12	O-66/3-1	-2.2
	Yr	86	233	29	55	7	0	4	17	27	47	.236	.315	.318	73	-9	0	2	-1	.992	-14	O-76/3-1	-2.8
1963	Cle-A	52	116	11	26	3	1	4	5	15	25	.224	.318	.371	93	-1	0	1	-1	.981	-5	O-37/2-1	-0.8
Total	6	583	1868	246	467	61	10	46	174	201	327	.250	.328	.367	89	-28	12	20	-8	.980	-22	O-543/2-1,3-1	-8.7

■ **POP TATE** Tate, Edward Christopher "Dimples" b: 12/22/1860, Richmond, Va. d: 6/25/32, Richmond, Va. BR/TL, 5′10″, 178 lbs. Deb: 9/26/1885

YEAR	TM/L	G	AB	R	H	2B	3B	HR	RBI	BB	SO	AVG	OBP	SLG	PRO+	BR/A	SB	CS	SBR	FA	FR	G/POS	TPR
1885	Bos-N	4	13	1	2	0	0	0	2	1	3	.154	.214	.154	21	-1				.865	1	/C-4	0.0
1886	Bos-N	31	106	13	24	3	1	0	3	7	17	.226	.274	.274	70	-4	0			.885	-4	C-31	-0.3
1887	Bos-N	60	231	34	60	5	3	0	27	8	9	.260	.296	.307	68	-10	7			.924	13	C-53/O-8	0.7
1888	Bos-N	41	148	18	34	7	1	1	6	8	7	.230	.278	.311	86	-2	3			.854	-3	C-41/O-1	-0.1
1889	Bal-a	72	253	28	46	6	3	1	27	13	37	.182	.236	.241	35	-22	4			.938	-3	C-62,1-10	-1.7
1890	Bal-a	19	71	7	13	1	1	0	6	4		.183	.284	.225	48	-5	3			.923	-2	C-11/1-8	-0.5
Total	6	227	822	101	179	22	9	2	71	41	73	.218	.269	.274	58	-43	17			.905	3	C-202/1-18,O-9	-1.9

■ **BENNIE TATE** Tate, Henry Bennett b: 12/3/01, Whitwell, Tenn. d: 10/27/73, W.Frankfort, Ill. BL/TR, 5′8″, 165 lbs. Deb: 4/29/24

YEAR	TM/L	G	AB	R	H	2B	3B	HR	RBI	BB	SO	AVG	OBP	SLG	PRO+	BR/A	SB	CS	SBR	FA	FR	G/POS	TPR
1924	*Was-A	21	43	2	13	2	0	0	7	1	2	.302	.318	.349	74	-2	0	0	0	.841	-3	C-14	-0.4
1925	Was-A	16	27	0	13	3	0	0	7	2	2	.481	.517	.593	185	4	0	0	0	.955	2	C-14	0.5
1926	Was-A	59	142	17	38	5	2	1	13	15	1	.268	.338	.352	82	-4	0	0	0	.960	-5	C-45	-0.6
1927	Was-A	61	131	12	41	5	1	1	24	8	4	.313	.357	.389	95	-1	0	3	-2	.977	4	C-39	0.4
1928	Was-A	57	122	10	30	6	0	0	15	10	4	.246	.303	.295	58	-7	0	4	-2	.985	2	C-30	-0.5
1929	Was-A	81	265	26	78	12	3	0	30	16	8	.294	.335	.362	79	-8	2	5	-2	.971	-2	C-74	-0.6
1930	Was-A	14	20	1	5	0	0	0	2	0	1	.250	.250	.250	27	-2	0	0	0	.933	-1	/C-9	-0.2
	Chi-A	72	230	26	73	11	2	0	27	18	10	.317	.367	.383	94	-2	2	1	0	.981	-10	C-70	-0.5
	Yr	86	250	27	78	11	2	0	29	18	11	.312	.358	.372	88	-4	2	1	0	.978	-11	C-79	-0.7
1931	Chi-A	89	273	27	73	12	3	0	22	26	10	.267	.331	.333	80	-8	1	1	-0	.987	7	C-85	0.4
1932	Chi-A	4	10	1	1	0	0	0	0	1	0	.100	.182	.100	-27	-2	0	0	0	1.000	0	/C-4	-0.1
	Bos-A	81	273	21	67	12	5	2	26	20	6	.245	.297	.348	68	-13	0	1	-1	.974	-5	C-76	-1.4
	Yr	85	283	22	68	12	5	2	26	21	6	.240	.293	.339	65	-15	0	1	-1	.975	-5	C-80	-1.5
1934	Chi-N	11	24	1	3	0	0	0	0	1	3	.125	.160	.125	-23	-4	0			1.000	-3	/C-8	-0.7
Total	10	566	1560	144	435	68	16	4	173	118	51	.279	.330	.351	78	-50	5	15		.974	-14	C-468	-3.7

■ **HUGHIE TATE** Tate, Hugh Henry b: 5/19/1880, Everett, Pa. d: 8/7/56, Greenville, Pa. BR/TR, 5′11″, 190 lbs. Deb: 9/21/05

YEAR	TM/L	G	AB	R	H	2B	3B	HR	RBI	BB	SO	AVG	OBP	SLG	PRO+	BR/A	SB	CS	SBR	FA	FR	G/POS	TPR
1905	Was-A	4	13	1	4	0	1	0	2	0		.308	.308	.462	149	1	1			1.000	0	/O-3	0.1

■ **LEE TATE** Tate, Lee Willie "Skeeter" b: 3/18/32, Black Rock, Ark. BR/TR, 5′10″, 165 lbs. Deb: 9/12/58

YEAR	TM/L	G	AB	R	H	2B	3B	HR	RBI	BB	SO	AVG	OBP	SLG	PRO+	BR/A	SB	CS	SBR	FA	FR	G/POS	TPR
1958	StL-N	10	35	4	7	2	0	0	1	4	3	.200	.282	.257	42	-3	0	0	0	.950	-4	/S-9	-0.6
1959	StL-N	41	50	5	7	1	1	1	4	5	7	.140	.232	.260	29	-5	0	0	0	.927	1	S-39/2-2,3-2	-0.3
Total	2	51	85	9	14	3	1	1	5	9	10	.165	.253	.259	34	-8	0	0	0	.934	-4	/S-48,3-2,2-2	-0.9

■ **FERNANDO TATIS** Tatis, Fernando b: 1/1/75, San Pedro De Macoris, D.R. BR/TR, 6′1″, 175 lbs. Deb: 7/26/97

YEAR	TM/L	G	AB	R	H	2B	3B	HR	RBI	BB	SO	AVG	OBP	SLG	PRO+	BR/A	SB	CS	SBR	FA	FR	G/POS	TPR
1997	Tex-A	60	223	29	57	9	0	8	29	14	42	.256	.300	.404	77	-8	3	0	1	.951	-11	3-60	-1.7
1998	Tex-A	95	330	41	89	17	2	3	32	12	66	.270	.303	.361	69	-15	6	2	1	.945	10	3-94	-0.4
	StL-N	55	202	28	58	16	2	8	26	24	57	.287	.368	.505	125	7	7	3	0	.927	-1	3-55/S-3	0.8
Total	2	210	755	98	204	42	4	19	87	50	165	.270	.321	.412	86	-16	16	5	2	.941	-2	3-209/S-3	-1.3

■ **JIM TATUM** Tatum, James Ray b: 10/9/67, Grossmont, Cal. BR/TR, 6′2″, 200 lbs. Deb: 9/18/92

YEAR	TM/L	G	AB	R	H	2B	3B	HR	RBI	BB	SO	AVG	OBP	SLG	PRO+	BR/A	SB	CS	SBR	FA	FR	G/POS	TPR
1992	Mil-A	5	8	0	1	0	0	0	0	1	2	.125	.222	.125	-0	-1	0	0	0	1.000	-0	/3-5	-0.1
1993	Col-N	92	98	7	20	5	0	1	12	5	27	.204	.250	.286	37	-9	0	0	0	.978	-2	1-12/3-6,O-3	-1.1
1995	Col-N	34	34	4	8	1	1	0	4	1	7	.235	.257	.324	40	-3	0	0	0	1.000	-1	/O-2,C-1	-0.4
1996	Bos-A	2	8	1	1	0	0	0	0	0	2	.125	.125	.125	-36	-2	0	0	0	1.000	-0	/3-2	-0.2
	SD-N	5	3	0	0	0	0	0	0	0	1	.000	.000	.000	-99	-1	0	0	0	.000	0	/3-1	-0.1
1998	NY-N	35	50	4	9	1	2	2	13	3	19	.180	.226	.400	58	-3	0	0	0	1.000	-1	/1-9,C-4,O-4,3-3,D	-0.4
Total	5	173	201	16	39	7	3	3	29	10	58	.194	.236	.303	37	-19	0	0	0	.987	-4	/1-21,3-17,O-9,CD	-2.3

■ **JARVIS TATUM** Tatum, Jarvis b: 10/11/46, Fresno, Cal. BR/TR, 6′, 185 lbs. Deb: 9/7/68

YEAR	TM/L	G	AB	R	H	2B	3B	HR	RBI	BB	SO	AVG	OBP	SLG	PRO+	BR/A	SB	CS	SBR	FA	FR	G/POS	TPR
1968	Cal-A	17	51	7	9	1	0	0	2	0	9	.176	.176	.196	13	-5	0	0	0	1.000	-0	O-11	-0.7
1969	Cal-A	10	22	2	7	0	0	0	0	0	6	.318	.318	.318	83	-1	0	1	-1	.857	-1	/O-5	-0.2
1970	Cal-A	75	181	28	43	7	0	0	6	17	35	.238	.303	.276	63	-9	1	0	0	.982	-5	O-58	-1.7
Total	3	102	254	37	59	8	0	0	8	17	50	.232	.280	.264	56	-15	1	1	-0	.979	-6	/O-74	-2.6

■ **TOMMY TATUM** Tatum, V T b: 7/16/19, Decatur, Tex. d: 11/7/89, Oklahoma City, Okla BR/TR, 6′, 185 lbs. Deb: 8/1/41

YEAR	TM/L	G	AB	R	H	2B	3B	HR	RBI	BB	SO	AVG	OBP	SLG	PRO+	BR/A	SB	CS	SBR	FA	FR	G/POS	TPR
1941	Bro-N	8	12	1	2	1	0	0	1	1	3	.167	.231	.250	34	-1	0			1.000	-1	/O-4	-0.2
1947	Bro-N	4	6	0	0	0	0	0	0	0	1	.000	.000	.000	-96	-2	0			1.000	-1	/O-3	-0.3
	Cin-N	69	176	19	48	5	2	1	16	16	16	.273	.333	.341	80	-5	7			1.000	4	O-49/2-1	-0.3

YEAR	TM/L	G	AB	R	H	2B	3B	HR	RBI	BB	SO	AVG	OBP	SLG	PRO+	BR/A	SB	CS	SBR	FA	FR	G/POS	TPR
	Yr	73	182	19	48	5	2	1	16	16	17	.264	.323	.330	74	-7	7			1.000	3	O-52/2-1	-0.6
Total	2	81	194	20	50	6	2	1	17	17	20	.258	.318	.325	72	-8	7			1.000	2	/O-56,2-1	-0.8

■ EDDIE TAUBENSEE

Taubensee, Edward Kenneth b: 10/31/68, Beeville, Tex. BL/TR, 6′4″, 205 lbs. Deb: 5/18/91

YEAR	TM/L	G	AB	R	H	2B	3B	HR	RBI	BB	SO	AVG	OBP	SLG	PRO+	BR/A	SB	CS	SBR	FA	FR	G/POS	TPR
1991	Cle-A	26	66	5	16	2	1	0	8	5	16	.242	.296	.303	66	-3	0	0	0	.979	-7	C-25	-0.9
1992	Hou-N	104	297	23	66	15	0	5	28	31	78	.222	.300	.323	80	-8	2	1	0	.992	4	*C-103	0.1
1993	Hou-N	94	288	26	72	11	1	9	42	21	44	.250	.301	.389	86	-6	1	0	0	.992	4	C-90	0.3
1994	Hou-N	5	10	0	1	0	0	0	0	0	3	.100	.100	.100	-50	-2	0	0	0	1.000	1	/C-5	-0.1
	Cin-N	61	177	29	52	8	2	8	21	15	28	.294	.349	.497	118	4	2	0	1	.990	-1	C-61	0.7
	Yr	66	187	29	53	8	2	8	21	15	31	.283	.337	.476	110	2	2	0	1	.990	-0	C-66	0.6
1995	*Cin-N	80	218	32	62	14	2	9	44	22	52	.284	.355	.491	121	6	2	2	-1	.983	-9	C-65/1-3	0.0
1996	Cin-N	108	327	46	95	20	0	12	48	26	64	.291	.343	.462	109	4	3	4	-2	.981	-11	C-94	-0.3
1997	Cin-N	108	254	26	68	18	0	10	34	22	66	.268	.329	.457	102	0	0	1	-1	.987	-8	C-64,O-11/1-7,D-3	-0.6
1998	Cin-N	130	431	61	120	27	0	11	72	52	93	.278	.356	.418	98	-0	1	0	0	.988	-15	*C-126	-0.6
Total	8	716	2068	248	552	115	6	64	297	194	444	.267	.331	.421	99	-5	11	8	-2	.988	-42	C-633/O-11,1-10,D-3	-1.4

■ FRED TAUBY

Tauby, Frederick Joseph (b: Frederick Joseph Taubensee) b: 3/27/06, Canton, Ohio d: 11/23/55, Concord, Cal. BR/TR, 5′9.5″, 168 lbs. Deb: 9/1/35

YEAR	TM/L	G	AB	R	H	2B	3B	HR	RBI	BB	SO	AVG	OBP	SLG	PRO+	BR/A	SB	CS	SBR	FA	FR	G/POS	TPR
1935	Chi-A	13	32	5	4	1	0	0	2	2	3	.125	.176	.156	-13	-5	0	0	0	1.000	2	/O-7	-0.4
1937	Phi-N	11	20	2	0	0	0	0	3	0	5	.000	.000	.000	-93	-5	1			1.000	-2	/O-7	-0.7
Total	2	24	52	7	4	1	0	0	5	2	8	.077	.111	.096	-43	-11	1	0		1.000	-0	/O-14	-1.1

■ DON TAUSSIG

Taussig, Donald Franklin b: 2/19/32, New York, N.Y. BR/TR, 6′, 180 lbs. Deb: 4/23/58

YEAR	TM/L	G	AB	R	H	2B	3B	HR	RBI	BB	SO	AVG	OBP	SLG	PRO+	BR/A	SB	CS	SBR	FA	FR	G/POS	TPR
1958	SF-N	39	50	10	10	0	0	1	4	3	8	.200	.245	.260	35	-5	0	0	0	1.000	-9	O-36	-1.4
1961	StL-N	98	188	27	54	14	5	2	25	16	34	.287	.343	.447	98	-1	2	2	-1	.992	-9	O-87	-1.3
1962	Hou-N	16	25	1	5	0	0	1	1	2	11	.200	.259	.320	59	-2	0	0	0	1.000	1	/O-4	-0.1
Total	3	153	263	38	69	14	5	4	30	21	53	.262	.317	.399	84	-7	2	2	-1	.994	-17	O-127	-2.8

■ JESUS TAVAREZ

Tavarez, Jesus Rafael (Alcantaras) b: 3/26/71, Santo Domingo, D.R. BB/TR, 6′, 170 lbs. Deb: 5/23/94

YEAR	TM/L	G	AB	R	H	2B	3B	HR	RBI	BB	SO	AVG	OBP	SLG	PRO+	BR/A	SB	CS	SBR	FA	FR	G/POS	TPR
1994	Fla-N	17	39	4	7	0	0	0	4	1	5	.179	.200	.179	-0	-6	1	1	-0	1.000	2	O-11	-0.4
1995	Fla-N	63	190	31	55	6	2	2	13	16	27	.289	.348	.374	90	-2	7	5	-1	1.000	-10	O-61	-1.4
1996	Fla-N	98	114	14	25	3	0	0	6	7	18	.219	.264	.246	37	-10	5	1	1	1.000	-15	O-65	-2.4
1997	Bos-A	42	69	12	12	3	1	0	9	4	9	.174	.219	.246	21	-8	0	0	0	.980	-7	O-35/D-2	-1.5
1998	Bal-A	8	11	2	2	0	0	1	1	2	3	.182	.308	.455	97	-0	0	1	-1	1.000	-3	/O-8	-0.3
Total	5	228	423	63	101	12	3	3	33	30	62	.239	.291	.303	56	-27	13	8	-1	.996	-32	O-180/D-2	-6.0

■ JACKIE TAVENER

Tavener, John Adam "Rabbit" b: 12/27/1897, Celina, Ohio d: 9/14/69, Fort Worth, Tex. BL/TR, 5′5″, 138 lbs. Deb: 9/24/21

YEAR	TM/L	G	AB	R	H	2B	3B	HR	RBI	BB	SO	AVG	OBP	SLG	PRO+	BR/A	SB	CS	SBR	FA	FR	G/POS	TPR
1921	Det-A	2	4	0	0	0	0	0	0	0	1	.000	.000	.000	-99	-1	0	0	0	1.000	1	/S-2	0.0
1925	Det-A	134	453	45	111	11	11	0	47	39	60	.245	.309	.318	60	-28	5	4	-1	.963	7	*S-134	-0.8
1926	Det-A	156	532	65	141	22	14	1	58	52	53	.265	.332	.365	80	-16	8	7	-2	.952	9	*S-156	0.8
1927	Det-A	116	419	60	115	22	9	5	59	36	38	.274	.333	.406	90	-7	19	8	1	.948	4	*S-114	0.9
1928	Det-A	132	473	59	123	24	15	5	52	33	51	.260	.314	.406	86	-11	13	8	-1	.944	14	*S-131	1.7
1929	Cle-A	92	250	25	53	9	4	2	27	26	28	.212	.289	.304	51	-19	1	4	-2	.945	23	S-89	1.1
Total	6	632	2131	254	543	88	53	13	243	186	231	.255	.318	.364	75	-82	46	31	-5	.951	58	S-626	3.7

■ ALEX TAVERAS

Taveras, Alejandro Antonio (Betances) b: 10/9/55, Santiago, D.R. BR/TR, 5′10″, 155 lbs. Deb: 9/9/76

YEAR	TM/L	G	AB	R	H	2B	3B	HR	RBI	BB	SO	AVG	OBP	SLG	PRO+	BR/A	SB	CS	SBR	FA	FR	G/POS	TPR
1976	Hou-N	14	46	3	10	0	0	0	2	2	1	.217	.250	.217	37	-4	1	2	-1	.923	1	/2-7,S-7	-0.3
1982	LA-N	11	3	1	1	1	0	0	2	0	1	.333	.333	.667	178	0	0	0	0	1.000	4	/2-4,3-4,S-2	0.4
1983	LA-N	10	4	0	0	0	0	0	0	0	1	.000	.000	.000	-99	-1	0	0	0	.000	2	/S-3,2-2,3-1	0.1
Total	3	35	53	4	11	1	0	0	4	2	3	.208	.236	.226	34	-5	1	2	-1	.938	7	/2-13,S-12,3-5	0.2

■ FRANK TAVERAS

Taveras, Franklin Crisostomo (Fabian) b: 12/24/49, Las Matas De Santa Cruz, D.R. BR/TR, 6′, 168 lbs. Deb: 9/25/71

YEAR	TM/L	G	AB	R	H	2B	3B	HR	RBI	BB	SO	AVG	OBP	SLG	PRO+	BR/A	SB	CS	SBR	FA	FR	G/POS	TPR
1971	Pit-N	1	0	0	0	0	0	0	0	0	0	—	—	—	—	0	0	0	0	.000	0	R	0.0
1972	Pit-N	4	3	0	0	0	0	0	0	1	1	.000	.250	.000	-24	-0	0	0	0	1.000	-1	/S-4	-0.1
1974	*Pit-N	126	333	33	82	4	2	0	26	25	41	.246	.303	.270	63	-16	13	4	2	.941	-17	*S-124	-1.9
1975	*Pit-N	134	378	44	80	9	4	0	23	37	42	.212	.285	.257	52	-24	17	6	2	.953	-15	*S-132	-2.5
1976	Pit-N	144	519	76	134	8	6	0	24	44	79	.258	.321	.297	75	-16	58	11	11	.952	-5	*S-141	0.8
1977	Pit-N	147	544	72	137	20	10	1	29	38	71	.252	.308	.331	69	-23	**70**	18	**10**	.962	-22	*S-146	-2.0
1978	Pit-N	157	654	81	182	31	9	0	38	29	60	.278	.314	.353	82	-16	46	25	-1	.946	-29	*S-157	-2.8
1979	Pit-N	11	45	4	11	3	0	0	1	0	2	.244	.244	.311	48	-3	2	1	0	.935	-4	S-11	-0.7
	NY-N	153	635	89	167	26	9	1	33	33	72	.263	.301	.337	77	-21	42	19	1	.966	-21	*S-153	-2.5
	Yr	164	680	93	178	29	9	1	34	33	74	.262	.298	.335	75	-25	44	20	1	.964	-25	*S-164	-3.2
1980	NY-N	141	562	65	157	27	0	0	25	23	64	.279	.309	.327	80	-16	32	18	-1	.959	-39	*S-140	-4.3
1981	NY-N	84	283	30	65	11	3	0	11	12	36	.230	.266	.290	58	-16	16	4	2	.931	-22	S-79	-3.0
1982	Mon-N	48	87	9	14	5	1	0	4	7	6	.161	.223	.241	29	-8	4	0	1	.947	-1	S-26,2-19	-0.7
Total	11	1150	4043	503	1029	144	44	2	214	249	474	.255	.302	.313	71	-159	300	106	26	.953	-175	*S-1113/2-19	-19.7

■ TONY TAYLOR

Taylor, Antonio Nemesio (Sanchez) b: 12/19/35, Central Alara, Cuba BR/TR, 5′9″, 179 lbs. Deb: 4/15/58 C

YEAR	TM/L	G	AB	R	H	2B	3B	HR	RBI	BB	SO	AVG	OBP	SLG	PRO+	BR/A	SB	CS	SBR	FA	FR	G/POS	TPR
1958	Chi-N	140	497	63	117	15	3	6	27	40	93	.235	.301	.314	64	-25	21	6	3	.968	9	*2-137/3-1	-0.4
1959	Chi-N	150	624	96	175	30	8	8	38	45	86	.280	.335	.393	94	-5	23	9	2	.970	10	*2-149/S-2	1.7
1960	Chi-N	19	76	14	20	3	3	1	9	8	12	.263	.341	.421	108	1	2	0	1	.977	-2	2-19	0.1
	Phi-N★	127	505	66	145	22	4	4	35	33	86	.287	.333	.370	92	-5	24	11	1	.968	-6	*2-123/3-4	0.2
	Yr	146	581	80	165	25	7	5	44	41	98	.284	.334	.377	94	-4	26	11	1	.969	-8	*2-142/3-4	0.3
1961	Phi-N	106	400	47	100	17	3	2	26	29	59	.250	.304	.322	67	-19	11	5	0	.980	0	2-91/3-3	-0.8
1962	Phi-N	152	625	87	162	21	5	7	43	68	82	.259	.337	.342	85	-12	20	9	1	.972	-15	*2-150/S-2	-1.1
1963	Phi-N	157	640	102	180	20	10	5	49	42	99	.281	.332	.367	102	2	23	9	2	**.986**	-9	*2-149,3-13	1.0
1964	Phi-N	154	570	62	143	13	6	4	46	46	74	.251	.321	.316	81	-13	13	7	-0	.977	-21	*2-150	-2.3
1965	Phi-N	106	323	41	74	14	3	3	27	22	58	.229	.303	.319	77	-10	5	4	-1	.958	-2	2-86/3-5	-0.6
1966	Phi-N	125	434	47	105	14	8	5	40	31	56	.242	.294	.346	77	-14	8	4	0	.988	4	2-68,3-52	-0.6
1967	Phi-N	132	462	55	110	16	6	2	34	42	74	.238	.308	.312	77	-13	10	9	-2	.991	-8	1-58,3-44,2-42,/S-3	-2.7
1968	Phi-N	145	547	59	137	20	2	3	38	39	60	.250	.304	.311	85	-10	22	5	4	.966	16	*3-138/2-5,1-1	1.2
1969	Phi-N	138	557	68	146	24	5	3	30	42	62	.262	.318	.339	87	-10	19	10	-0	.967	-2	3-71,2-57,1-10	-0.9
1970	Phi-N	124	439	74	132	26	9	9	55	50	67	.301	.376	.462	127	17	9	11	-4	.996	0	2-59,3-38,O-18,/S-1	1.6
1971	Phi-N	36	107	9	25	2	1	1	5	9	10	.234	.293	.299	68	-4	2	2	-1	1.000	5	2-14,3-11/1-2	0.0
	Det-A	55	181	27	52	10	2	3	19	12	11	.287	.335	.414	107	1	5	1	1	.995	1	2-51/3-3	0.7
1972	*Det-A	78	228	33	69	12	4	1	20	14	34	.303	.348	.404	119	5	5	1	1	.966	-8	2-67/3-8,1-1	0.1
1973	Det-A	84	275	35	63	9	3	5	24	17	29	.229	.276	.338	68	-12	9	5	-0	.987	-14	2-72/1-6,3-4,O-1,D	-2.3
1974	Phi-N	62	64	5	21	4	0	2	13	6	6	.328	.394	.484	139	3	0	0	0	1.000	-1	/1-7,3-5,2-4	0.2
1975	Phi-N	79	103	13	25	5	1	1	17	17	18	.243	.355	.340	90	-1	3	3	-1	.913	1	3-16/1-4,2-3	-0.1
1976	Phi-N	26	23	2	6	1	0	0	3	1	7	.261	.320	.304	76	-1	0	0	0	.000	-0	/2-2,3-1	-0.1
Total	19	2195	7680	1005	2007	298	86	75	598	613	1083	.261	.322	.352	88	-123	234	111	4	.976	-41	*2-1498,3-417/1OSD	-5.1

■ BEN TAYLOR

Taylor, Benjamin Eugene b: 9/30/24, Metropolis, Ill. BL/TL, 6′, 185 lbs. Deb: 7/29/51

YEAR	TM/L	G	AB	R	H	2B	3B	HR	RBI	BB	SO	AVG	OBP	SLG	PRO+	BR/A	SB	CS	SBR	FA	FR	G/POS	TPR
1951	StL-A	33	93	14	24	2	1	3	6	9	22	.258	.337	.398	95	-1	1	1	-0	.972	-2	1-25	-0.4
1952	Det-A	7	18	0	3	0	0	0	0	0	5	.167	.167	.167	-7	-3	0	0	0	1.000	-0	/1-4	-0.3
1955	Mil-N	12	10	2	1	0	0	0	0	2	4	.100	.250	.100	-3	-1	0	0	0	1.000	-0	/1-1	-0.2
Total	3	52	121	16	28	2	1	3	6	11	31	.231	.306	.339	73	-5	1	1	-0	.976	-2	/1-30	-0.9

■ CHINK TAYLOR

Taylor, C L b: 2/9/1898, Burnet, Tex. d: 7/7/80, Temple, Tex. BR/TR, 5′9″, 160 lbs. Deb: 4/18/25

YEAR	TM/L	G	AB	R	H	2B	3B	HR	RBI	BB	SO	AVG	OBP	SLG	PRO+	BR/A	SB	CS	SBR	FA	FR	G/POS	TPR
1925	Chi-N	8	6	2	0	0	0	0	0	0	0	.000	.000	.000	-99	-2	0	0	0	1.000	-1	/O-2	-0.2

■ CARL TAYLOR

Taylor, Carl Means b: 1/20/44, Sarasota, Fla. BR/TR, 6′2″, 207 lbs. Deb: 4/11/68

YEAR	TM/L	G	AB	R	H	2B	3B	HR	RBI	BB	SO	AVG	OBP	SLG	PRO+	BR/A	SB	CS	SBR	FA	FR	G/POS	TPR
1968	Pit-N	44	71	5	15	1	0	0	7	10	10	.211	.309	.225	63	-3	1	0	0	.979	-6	C-29/O-2	-0.8

YEAR	TM/L	G	AB	R	H	2B	3B	HR	RBI	BB	SO	AVG	OBP	SLG	PRO+	BR/A	SB	CS	SBR	FA	FR	G/POS	TPR
1969	Pit-N	104	221	30	77	10	1	4	33	31	36	.348	.435	.457	153	17	0	1	-1	.914	-1	O-36,1-24	1.3
1970	StL-N	104	245	39	61	12	2	6	45	41	30	.249	.359	.388	98	0	5	2	0	.986	-4	O-46,1-15/3-1	-0.6
1971	Pit-N	7	12	1	2	0	1	0	0	0	5	.167	.167	.333	39	-1	0	0	0	1.000	0	/O-1	-0.1
	KC-A	20	39	3	7	0	0	0	3	5	13	.179	.273	.179	30	-3	0	1	-1	.964	1	O-12	-0.4
1972	KC-A	63	113	17	30	2	1	0	11	17	16	.265	.366	.301	101	1	4	1	1	.982	-5	C-21/O-7,1-6,3-5	-0.4
1973	KC-A	69	145	18	33	6	1	0	16	32	20	.228	.367	.283	79	-3	2	2	-1	.980	2	C-63/1-2,D-1	0.0
Total	6	411	846	113	225	31	6	10	115	136	130	.266	.371	.352	103	9	12	7	-1	.980	-14	C-113,O-104/13D	-1.0

■ **DANNY TAYLOR** Taylor, Daniel Turney b: 12/23/1900, Lash, Pa. d: 10/11/72, Latrobe, Pa. BR/TR, 5'10", 190 lbs. Deb: 6/30/26

YEAR	TM/L	G	AB	R	H	2B	3B	HR	RBI	BB	SO	AVG	OBP	SLG	PRO+	BR/A	SB	CS	SBR	FA	FR	G/POS	TPR
1926	Was-A	21	50	10	15	0	1	1	5	5	7	.300	.364	.400	102	0	1	2	-1	1.000	-1	O-12	-0.3
1929	Chi-N	2	3	0	0	0	0	0	0	1	1	.000	.250	.000	-32	-1	0			1.000	-0	/O-1	-0.1
1930	Chi-N	74	219	43	62	14	3	2	37	27	34	.283	.364	.402	84	-5	6			.971	-1	O-52	-0.9
1931	Chi-N	88	270	48	81	13	6	5	41	31	46	.300	.372	.448	117	7	4			.989	4	O-67	0.6
1932	Chi-N	6	22	3	5	2	0	0	3	3	1	.227	.320	.318	73	-1	1			.900	-0	/O-6	-0.1
	Bro-N	105	395	84	128	22	7	11	48	33	41	.324	.378	.499	136	20	13			.989	4	O-96	1.7
	Yr	111	417	87	133	24	7	11	51	36	42	.319	.374	.489	133	19	14			.983	4	*O-102	1.6
1933	Bro-N	103	358	75	102	21	9	9	40	47	45	.285	.368	.469	144	21	11			.977	2	O-91	1.8
1934	Bro-N	120	405	62	121	24	6	7	57	63	47	.299	.396	.440	130	19	12			.975	-8	*O-108	0.7
1935	Bro-N	112	352	51	102	19	5	7	59	46	32	.290	.372	.432	118	10	6			.970	-6	O-99	0.0
1936	Bro-N	43	116	12	34	6	0	2	15	11	14	.293	.359	.397	102	1	2			.981	-3	O-31	-0.3
Total	9	674	2190	388	650	121	37	44	305	267	268	.297	.374	.446	121	71	56	2		.979	-10	O-563	3.1

■ **DWIGHT TAYLOR** Taylor, Dwight Bernard b: 3/24/60, Los Angeles, Cal. BL/TL, 5'9", 166 lbs. Deb: 4/14/86

YEAR	TM/L	G	AB	R	H	2B	3B	HR	RBI	BB	SO	AVG	OBP	SLG	PRO+	BR/A	SB	CS	SBR	FA	FR	G/POS	TPR
1986	KC-A	4	2	1	0	0	0	0	0	0	0	.000	.000	.000	-98	-1	0	0	0	.000	-1	/O-1,D-2	-0.1

■ **ED TAYLOR** Taylor, Edward James b: 11/17/01, Chicago, Ill. d: 1/30/92, Chula Vista, Cal. BR/TR, 5'6.5", 160 lbs. Deb: 4/14/26

YEAR	TM/L	G	AB	R	H	2B	3B	HR	RBI	BB	SO	AVG	OBP	SLG	PRO+	BR/A	SB	CS	SBR	FA	FR	G/POS	TPR
1926	Bos-N	92	272	37	73	8	2	0	33	38	26	.268	.368	.313	93	-1	4			.945	-1	3-62,S-33	0.4

■ **LIVE OAK TAYLOR** Taylor, Edward S. Deb: 8/21/1877

YEAR	TM/L	G	AB	R	H	2B	3B	HR	RBI	BB	SO	AVG	OBP	SLG	PRO+	BR/A	SB	CS	SBR	FA	FR	G/POS	TPR
1877	Har-N	2	8	0	3	0	0	0	0	0	2	.375	.375	.375	153	0				1.000	-1	/O-2	0.0
1884	Pit-a	41	152	22	32	4	1	0		6		.211	.255	.250	64	-6				.798	-1	O-41	-0.7
Total	2	43	160	22	35	4	1	0	0	6	2	.219	.260	.256	68	-5				.802	-1	/O-43	-0.7

■ **FRED TAYLOR** Taylor, Frederick Rankin b: 12/3/24, Zanesville, Ohio BL/TR, 6'3", 201 lbs. Deb: 9/12/50

YEAR	TM/L	G	AB	R	H	2B	3B	HR	RBI	BB	SO	AVG	OBP	SLG	PRO+	BR/A	SB	CS	SBR	FA	FR	G/POS	TPR
1950	Was-A	6	16	1	2	0	0	0	0	1	2	.125	.176	.125	-23	-3	0	0	0	.968	0	/1-3	-0.3
1951	Was-A	6	12	1	2	1	0	0	0	0	4	.167	.167	.250	12	-2	0	0	0	.962	-0	/1-2	-0.2
1952	Was-A	10	19	3	5	1	0	0	4	3	2	.263	.364	.316	93	-0	0	0	0	1.000	1	/1-5	0.1
Total	3	22	47	5	9	2	0	0	4	4	8	.191	.255	.234	33	-5	0	0	0	.979	1	/1-10	-0.4

■ **HARRY TAYLOR** Taylor, Harry Leonard b: 4/4/1866, Halsey Valley, N.Y. d: 7/12/55, Buffalo, N.Y. BL , 6'2", 160 lbs. Deb: 4/18/1890

YEAR	TM/L	G	AB	R	H	2B	3B	HR	RBI	BB	SO	AVG	OBP	SLG	PRO+	BR/A	SB	CS	SBR	FA	FR	G/POS	TPR
1890	*Lou-a	134	553	115	169	7	7	0	53	68		.306	.383	.344	117	14	45			.982	5	*1-118,S-12/2-4,C-1	1.2
1891	Lou-a	93	356	81	105	7	4	2	37	55	33	.295	.397	.354	116	10	15			.979	3	1-92/3-1,2-1,C-1	0.7
1892	Lou-N	125	493	66	128	7	1	0	34	58	23	.260	.342	.278	96	1	24			.923	-8	O-73,1-34,2-14,/3S	-1.0
1893	Bal-N	88	360	50	102	9	1	1	54	32	11	.283	.347	.322	77	-12	24			.976	-3	*1-88	-1.4
Total	4	440	1762	312	504	30	13	3	178	213	67	.286	.367	.323	102	14	108			.979	-2	1-332/O-73,2S3C	-0.5

■ **HARRY TAYLOR** Taylor, Harry Warren b: 12/26/07, McKeesport, Pa. d: 4/27/69, Toledo, Ohio BL/TL, 6'1.5", 185 lbs. Deb: 4/14/32

YEAR	TM/L	G	AB	R	H	2B	3B	HR	RBI	BB	SO	AVG	OBP	SLG	PRO+	BR/A	SB	CS	SBR	FA	FR	G/POS	TPR
1932	Chi-N	10	8	1	1	0	0	0	0	1	1	.125	.222	.125	-4	-1	0			1.000	-0	/1-1	-0.1

■ **SANDY TAYLOR** Taylor, James B. 5'10.5", 175 lbs. Deb: 8/11/1879

YEAR	TM/L	G	AB	R	H	2B	3B	HR	RBI	BB	SO	AVG	OBP	SLG	PRO+	BR/A	SB	CS	SBR	FA	FR	G/POS	TPR
1879	Tro-N	24	97	10	21	4	0	0	8	1	8	.216	.224	.258	63	-4				.765	-3	O-24	-0.8

■ **ZACK TAYLOR** Taylor, James Wren b: 7/27/1898, Yulee, Fla. d: 9/19/74, Orlando, Fla. BR/TR, 5'11.5", 180 lbs. Deb: 6/15/20 MC

YEAR	TM/L	G	AB	R	H	2B	3B	HR	RBI	BB	SO	AVG	OBP	SLG	PRO+	BR/A	SB	CS	SBR	FA	FR	G/POS	TPR
1920	Bro-N	9	13	3	5	2	0	0	5	0	2	.385	.385	.538	158	1	0	1	-1	.882	-1	/C-9	-0.1
1921	Bro-N	30	102	6	20	0	2	0	8	1	8	.196	.212	.235	17	-12	2	0	1	.965	0	C-30	-1.0
1922	Bro-N	7	14	0	3	0	0	0	2	1	1	.214	.267	.214	26	-2	0	0	0	.950	-1	/C-6	-0.2
1923	Bro-N	96	337	29	97	11	6	0	46	9	13	.288	.312	.356	78	-11	2	5	-2	.967	14	C-84	0.4
1924	Bro-N	99	345	36	100	9	4	1	39	14	14	.290	.319	.348	81	-9	0	1	-1	**.988**	-8	C-93	-1.2
1925	Bro-N	109	352	33	109	16	4	3	44	17	19	.310	.343	.403	92	-4	0	0	0	.959	-9	C-96	-0.8
1926	Bos-N	125	432	36	110	22	3	0	42	28	27	.255	.303	.319	74	-17	1			.985	2	*C-123	-0.7
1927	Bos-N	30	96	8	23	2	1	1	14	8	5	.240	.298	.313	69	-4	0			.988	12	C-27	0.9
	NY-N	83	258	18	60	7	3	0	21	17	20	.233	.283	.283	52	-17	2			.972	-4	C-81	-1.6
	Yr	113	354	26	83	9	4	1	35	25	25	.234	.287	.291	56	-22	2			.978	8	*C-108	-0.7
1928	Bos-N	125	399	36	100	15	1	2	30	33	29	.251	.313	.308	66	-20	2			.985	-12	*C-124	-2.1
1929	Bos-N	34	101	8	25	7	0	0	10	7	9	.248	.303	.317	56	-7	0			.965	6	C-31	0.2
	*Chi-N	64	215	29	59	16	3	1	31	19	18	.274	.336	.391	79	-7	0			.979	-1	C-64	-0.2
	Yr	98	316	37	84	23	3	1	41	26	27	.266	.326	.367	72	-14	0			.974	5	C-95	0.0
1930	Chi-N	32	95	12	22	2	1	1	11	2	12	.232	.255	.305	34	-10	0			1.000	-1	C-28	-0.8
1931	Chi-N	8	4	0	1	0	0	0	0	2	1	.250	.500	.250	106	0	0			1.000	1	/C-5	0.1
1932	Chi-N	21	30	2	6	1	0	0	3	1	4	.200	.226	.233	24	-3	0			1.000	3	C-14	0.0
1933	Chi-N	16	11	0	0	0	0	0	0	0	1	.000	.000	.000	-99	-3	0			1.000	-0	C-12	-0.3
1934	NY-A	4	7	0	1	0	0	0	0	0	1	.143	.143	.143	-28	-1	0	0	0	1.000	-0	/C-3	-0.2
1935	Bro-N	26	54	2	7	3	0	0	5	2	8	.130	.175	.185	-3	-8	0			.970	0	C-26	-0.7
Total	16	918	2865	258	748	113	28	9	311	161	192	.261	.304	.329	68	-135	9	7		.977	1	C-856	-8.3

■ **JOE TAYLOR** Taylor, Joe Cephus b: 3/2/26, Chapman, Ala. d: 3/18/93, Pittsburgh, Pa. BR/TR, 6'1", 185 lbs. Deb: 8/26/54

YEAR	TM/L	G	AB	R	H	2B	3B	HR	RBI	BB	SO	AVG	OBP	SLG	PRO+	BR/A	SB	CS	SBR	FA	FR	G/POS	TPR
1954	Phi-A	18	58	5	13	1	1	1	8	2	9	.224	.250	.328	57	-4	0	1	-1	.943	-0	O-16	-0.6
1957	Cin-N	33	107	14	28	7	0	4	9	6	24	.262	.301	.439	89	-2	0	1	-1	.971	4	O-27	0.0
1958	StL-N	18	23	2	7	3	0	1	3	2	4	.304	.360	.565	135	1	0	0	0	1.000	-0	/O-5	0.1
	Bal-A	36	77	11	21	4	0	2	9	7	19	.273	.333	.403	107	1	0	0	0	.972	-2	O-21	-0.2
1959	Bal-A	14	32	2	5	1	0	1	2	11	5	.156	.372	.281	84	-0	0	0	0	1.000	-3	O-12	-0.3
Total	4	119	297	34	74	16	1	9	31	28	61	.249	.314	.401	92	-4	0	2	-1	.969	-1	/O-81	-1.0

■ **LEO TAYLOR** Taylor, Leo Thomas "Chink" b: 5/13/01, Walla Walla, Wash. d: 5/20/82, Seattle, Wash. BR/TR, 5'10.5", 150 lbs. Deb: 5/3/23

YEAR	TM/L	G	AB	R	H	2B	3B	HR	RBI	BB	SO	AVG	OBP	SLG	PRO+	BR/A	SB	CS	SBR	FA	FR	G/POS	TPR
1923	Chi-A	1	0	0	0	0	0	0	0	0	0	—	—	—	—	0	0	0	0	.000	0	R	0.0

■ **HAWK TAYLOR** Taylor, Robert Dale b: 4/3/39, Metropolis, Ill. BR/TR, 6'2", 190 lbs. Deb: 6/9/57

YEAR	TM/L	G	AB	R	H	2B	3B	HR	RBI	BB	SO	AVG	OBP	SLG	PRO+	BR/A	SB	CS	SBR	FA	FR	G/POS	TPR
1957	Mil-N	7	1	2	0	0	0	0	0	0	0	.000	.000	.000	-99	-0	0	0	0	.000	0	/C-1	0.0
1958	Mil-N	4	8	1	1	1	0	0	0	0	3	.125	.125	.250	-4	-1	0	0	0	1.000	-0	/O-4	-0.2
1961	Mil-N	20	26	1	5	0	0	1	1	3	11	.192	.276	.308	58	-2	0	1	-1	1.000	0	/O-5,C-1	-0.2
1962	Mil-N	20	47	3	12	0	0	0	2	2	10	.255	.286	.255	48	-3	0	1	-1	.960	1	O-11	-0.3
1963	Mil-N	16	29	1	2	0	0	0	0	1	12	.069	.100	.069	-51	-6	0	0	0	1.000	-0	/O-8	-0.7
1964	NY-N	92	225	20	54	8	0	4	23	8	33	.240	.272	.329	70	-9	0	0	0	.981	1	C-45,O-16	-0.8
1965	NY-N	25	46	5	7	0	0	4	10	1	8	.152	.170	.413	61	-3	0	0	0	.962	-2	C-15/1-1	-0.5
1966	NY-N	53	109	5	19	2	0	3	12	3	19	.174	.204	.275	32	-10	0	1	-1	1.000	-4	C-29,1-13	-1.5
1967	NY-N	13	37	3	9	3	0	0	4	2	8	.243	.282	.324	74	-1	0	0	0	.955	5	C-12	0.4
	Cal-A	23	52	5	16	3	0	1	3	4	8	.308	.357	.423	135	2	0	0	0	1.000	2	C-19	0.5
1969	KC-A	64	89	7	24	5	0	3	21	6	18	.270	.316	.427	105	0	0	0	0	.909	-4	O-18/C-6	-0.4
1970	KC-A	57	55	3	9	3	0	0	6	6	16	.164	.258	.218	33	-5	0	0	0	1.000	0	/C-3,1-1	-0.5
Total	11	394	724	56	158	25	0	16	82	36	146	.218	.259	.319	62	-38	0	3	-2	.984	-1	C-131/O-62,1-15	-4.2

YEAR	TM/L	G	AB	R	H	2B	3B	HR	RBI	BB	SO	AVG	OBP	SLG	PRO+	BR/A	SB	CS	SBR	FA	FR	G/POS	TPR
■ BOB TAYLOR	Taylor, Robert Lee b: 3/20/44, Leland, Miss. BL/TR, 5'9", 170 lbs. Deb: 4/9/70																						
1970	SF-N	63	84	12	16	0	0	2	10	12	13	.190	.320	.262	58	-5	0	0	0	1.000	-3	O-26/C-1	-0.9
■ SAMMY TAYLOR	Taylor, Samuel Douglas b: 2/27/33, Woodruff, S.C. BL/TR, 6'2", 185 lbs. Deb: 4/27/58																						
1958	Chi-N	96	301	30	78	12	2	6	36	27	46	.259	.320	.372	84	-7	2	1	0	.988	-11	C-87	-1.3
1959	Chi-N	110	353	41	95	13	2	13	43	35	47	.269	.337	.428	103	1	1	0	0	.982	-15	*C-109	-0.8
1960	Chi-N	74	150	14	31	9	0	3	17	6	18	.207	.242	.327	55	-10	0	1	-1	.978	-9	C-43	-1.8
1961	Chi-N	89	235	26	56	8	2	8	23	23	39	.238	.317	.391	86	-5	0	0	0	.989	-8	C-75	-1.0
1962	Chi-N	7	15	0	2	1	0	0	1	3	3	.133	.278	.200	30	-1	0	0	0	1.000	-1	/C-6	-0.3
	NY-N	68	158	12	35	4	2	3	20	23	17	.222	.328	.329	76	-5	0	0	0	.991	-9	C-50	-1.2
	Yr	75	173	12	37	5	2	3	21	26	20	.214	.323	.318	72	-6	0	0	0	.992	-10	C-56	-1.5
1963	NY-N	22	35	3	9	0	1	0	6	5	7	.257	.350	.314	91	-0	0	0	0	1.000	0	C-13	0.0
	Cin-N	3	6	0	0	0	0	0	0	0	2	.000	.000	.000	-97	-1	0	0	0	.833	-1	/C-2	-0.3
	Yr	25	41	3	9	0	1	0	6	5	9	.220	.304	.268	65	-2	0	0	0	.984	-1	C-15	-0.3
	Cle-A	4	10	1	3	0	0	0	1	0	2	.300	.300	.300	69	-0	0	0	0	1.000	-1	/C-2	-0.1
Total	6	473	1263	127	309	47	9	33	147	122	181	.245	.315	.375	84	-29	3	2	-0	.986	-55	C-387	-6.8
■ TOMMY TAYLOR	Taylor, Thomas Livingstone Carlton b: 9/17/1892, Mexia, Tex. d: 4/5/56, Greenville, Miss. BR/TR, 5'8.5", 160 lbs. Deb: 7/9/24																						
1924	*Was-A	26	73	11	19	3	1	0	10	2	8	.260	.289	.329	61	-4	2	0	1	.923	-5	3-16/2-2,O-1	-0.8
■ BILLY TAYLOR	Taylor, William H. b: 12/1870, Butler, Ky. d: 9/12/05, Cincinnati, Ohio 5'10", 160 lbs. Deb: 9/19/1898																						
1898	Lou-N	9	24	2	6	1	0	0	2	1		.250	.308	.292	73	-1	1			.909	-1	/3-7,2-1	-0.2
■ BILLY TAYLOR	Taylor, William Henry "Bollicky Bill" b: 1855, Washington, D.C. d: 5/14/1900, Jacksonville, Fla. BR/TR, 5'11.5", 204 lbs. Deb: 5/21/1881																						
1881	Wor-N	6	28	3	3	1	0	0	2	0	2	.107	.107	.143	-21	-4				.882	1	/O-5,P-1	-0.2
	Det-N	1	4	0	2	2	0	0	1	0	0	.500	.500	1.000	346	1				.750	-0	/3-1	0.1
	Cle-N	24	103	6	25	1	0	0	12	0	8	.243	.243	.252	59	-5				.859	-1	O-23/P-1,3-1	-0.6
	Yr	31	135	9	30	4	0	0	15	0	10	.222	.222	.252	50	-7				.864	-0	O-28/P-2,3-2	-0.7
1882	Pit-a	70	299	40	84	16	13	3		7		.281	.297	.452	157	17				.862	-11	C-27,1-23,3-14,/OP	0.5
1883	Pit-a	83	369	43	96	13	7	2		9		.260	.278	.350	106	3				.747	-15	O-37,C-33,P-19,/1-9	-0.9
1884	StL-U	43	186	44	68	23	1	3		7		.366	.389	.548	175	11				.872	1	P-33,1-10/O-4	0.4
	Phi-a	30	111	8	28	6	2	0		2		.252	.272	.342	93	-1				.784	2	P-30	0.0
1885	Phi-a	6	21	0	4	0	0	0	2	0		.190	.190	.190	19	-2				.556	-1	/P-6	0.0
1886	Bal-a	10	39	4	12	0	1	0	8	1		.308	.325	.359	117	1	1			.800	-1	/P-8,1-1,C-1	0.0
1887	Phi-a	1	4	0	1	0	0	0	1	0		.250	.250	.250	40	-0	0			1.000	-0	/P-1	0.0
Total	7	274	1164	148	323	62	24	8	26	26	10	.277	.294	.393	121	21	1			.820	-26	P-100/O-77,C-61,13	-0.7
■ BILL TAYLOR	Taylor, William Michael b: 12/30/29, Alhambra, Cal. BL/TR, 6'3", 212 lbs. Deb: 4/14/54																						
1954	NY-N	55	65	4	12	1	0	2	10	3	15	.185	.243	.292	38	-6	0	0	0	1.000	-3	/O-9	-0.9
1955	NY-N	65	64	9	17	4	0	4	12	1	16	.266	.277	.516	104	-0	0	0	0	.000	-1	/O-2	-0.1
1956	NY-N	1	4	0	1	1	0	0	0	0	1	.250	.250	.500	96	-0	0	0	0	1.000	-0	/O-1	0.0
1957	NY-N	11	9	0	0	0	0	0	0	1	2	.000	.100	.000	-70	-2	0	0	0	.000	0	H	-0.2
	Det-A	9	23	4	8	2	0	1	3	0	3	.348	.348	.565	142	1	0	0	0	1.000	-1	/O-5	0.0
1958	Det-A	8	8	0	3	0	0	0	1	0	2	.375	.375	.375	100	-0	0	0	0	1.000	-0	/O-1	0.0
Total	5	149	173	17	41	8	0	7	26	5	39	.237	.267	.405	74	-7	0	0	0	1.000	-5	/O-18	-1.2
■ ZACHARY TAYLOR	Taylor, Zachary H. Deb: 9/10/1874																						
1874	Bal-n	13	48	3	12	0	0	0	3	0	1	.250	.250	.250	61	-2	0	0	0	.914	-1	1-13	-0.2
■ BIRDIE TEBBETTS	Tebbetts, George Robert b: 11/10/12, Burlington, Vt. BR/TR, 5'11.5", 170 lbs. Deb: 9/16/36 M																						
1936	Det-A	10	33	7	10	1	2	1	4	5	3	.303	.395	.545	129	1	0	0	0	.982	2	C-10	0.4
1937	Det-A	50	162	15	31	4	3	2	16	10	13	.191	.238	.290	32	-18	0	0	0	.963	-4	C-48	-1.8
1938	Det-A	53	143	16	42	6	2	1	25	12	13	.294	.348	.385	79	-5	1	2	-1	.985	-5	C-53	-0.7
1939	Det-A	106	341	37	89	22	2	4	53	25	20	.261	.315	.372	70	-16	2	1	0	.970	15	*C-100	0.3
1940	*Det-A	111	379	46	112	24	4	4	46	35	14	.296	.357	.412	90	-6	4	5	-2	.975	18	*C-107	1.8
1941	Det-A☆	110	359	28	102	19	4	2	47	38	29	.284	.354	.376	85	-8	1	2	-1	.977	7	C-98	0.6
1942	Det-A★	99	308	24	76	11	0	1	27	39	17	.247	.335	.292	71	-11	4	0	1	.977	7	C-97	0.5
1946	Det-A	87	280	20	68	11	2	1	34	28	23	.243	.312	.307	69	-11	1	3	-2	.982	-1	C-87	-1.0
1947	Det-A	20	53	1	5	1	0	0	2	3	3	.094	.143	.113	-27	-9	0	1	-1	1.000	8	C-20	-0.1
	Bos-A	90	291	22	87	10	0	1	28	21	30	.299	.346	.344	86	-5	2	4	-2	.974	-3	C-89	-0.4
	Yr	110	344	23	92	11	0	1	30	24	33	.267	.315	.308	69	-14	2	5	-2	.980	5	*C-109	-0.5
1948	Bos-A★	128	446	54	125	26	2	5	68	62	32	.280	.371	.381	95	-2	5	2	0	.981	-9	*C-126	-0.2
1949	Bos-A★	122	403	42	109	14	0	5	48	62	22	.270	.369	.342	83	-9	8	1	**2**	.980	-6	*C-118	-0.5
1950	Bos-A	79	268	33	83	10	1	8	45	29	26	.310	.377	.444	100	-0	1	1	-0	.988	-6	C-74	-0.3
1951	Cle-A	55	137	8	36	6	0	2	18	8	7	.263	.308	.350	82	-4	0	0	0	.977	-1	C-44	-0.3
1952	Cle-A	42	101	4	25	4	0	1	8	12	9	.248	.339	.317	89	-1	0	1	-1	.986	-4	C-37	-0.4
Total	14	1162	3704	357	1000	169	22	38	469	389	261	.270	.341	.358	81	-103	29	23	-5	.978	19	*C-1108	-2.1
■ PUSSY TEBEAU	Tebeau, Charles Alston b: 2/22/1870, Worcester, Mass. d: 3/25/50, Pittsfield, Mass. BR/TR, 5'10", 175 lbs. Deb: 7/22/1895																						
1895	Cle-N	2	6	3	3	0	0	0	1	2	1	.500	.625	.500	182	1	1			1.000	1	/O-2	0.1
■ GEORGE TEBEAU	Tebeau, George E. "White Wings" b: 12/26/1861, St.Louis, Mo. d: 2/4/23, Denver, Colo. BR/TR, 5'9", 175 lbs. Deb: 4/16/1887 F																						
1887	Cin-a	85	318	57	94	12	5	4	33	31		.296	.364	.403	111	4	37			.887	4	O-84/P-1	0.5
1888	Cin-a	121	411	72	94	12	12	3	51	61		.229	.338	.338	111	6	37			.911	4	*O-121	0.6
1889	Cin-a	135	496	110	125	21	11	7	70	69	62	.252	.350	.381	105	3	61			.887	-5	*O-134/1-1	-0.5
1890	Tol-a	94	381	71	102	16	10	1	36	51		.268	.359	.370	112	6	55			.951	3	*O-94/P-1	0.4
1894	Was-N	61	222	41	50	10	6	0	28	37	20	.225	.341	.324	63	-13	17			.857	-9	O-61	-2.0
	Cle-N	40	150	32	47	9	4	0	25	25	18	.313	.411	.427	99	0	9			.928	-5	O-27,1-12/3-1	-0.5
	Yr	101	372	73	97	19	10	0	53	62	38	.261	.369	.366	78	-12	26			.880	-14	O-88,1-12/3-1	-2.5
1895	Cle-N	91	337	57	110	16	6	0	68	50	28	.326	.415	.409	107	5	12			.873	-9	O-49,1-42	-0.5
Total	6	627	2315	440	622	96	54	15	311	324	128	.269	.364	.376	103	11	228			.900	-19	O-570/1-55,P-2,3-1	-2.0
■ PATSY TEBEAU	Tebeau, Oliver Wendell b: 12/5/1864, St.Louis, Mo. d: 5/15/18, St.Louis, Mo. BR/TR, 5'8", 163 lbs. Deb: 9/20/1887 FM																						
1887	Chi-N	20	68	8	11	3	0	0	10	4	4	.162	.208	.206	14	-8	8			.855	-3	3-20	-1.0
1889	Cle-N	136	521	72	147	20	6	8	76	37	41	.282	.332	.390	103	1	26			.897	0	*3-136	0.5
1890	Cle-P	110	450	86	134	26	6	5	74	34	20	.298	.351	.416	114	8	14			**.872**	13	*3-110,M	2.0
1891	Cle-N	61	249	38	65	8	3	1	41	16	13	.261	.313	.329	84	-6	12			.884	6	3-61/O-1,M	0.3
1892	*Cle-N	86	340	47	83	13	3	2	49	23	34	.244	.307	.318	86	-7	6			.911	-2	3-74/2-5,1-4,S-3,M	-0.5
1893	Cle-N	116	486	90	160	32	8	2	102	32	11	.329	.375	.440	110	4	19			.980	6	1-57,3-56/2-3,M	0.8
1894	Cle-N	125	523	82	158	23	7	3	89	35	35	.302	.347	.390	75	-23	30			.977	-5	*1-115,2-10/3-2,SM	-2.1
1895	*Cle-N	63	264	50	84	13	2	2	52	16	18	.318	.362	.405	92	-4	8			.992	6	1-49/2-9,3-6,M	0.3
1896	*Cle-N	132	543	56	146	22	6	2	94	21	22	.269	.300	.343	65	-29	20			.985	7	*1-122/3-7,2-5,SPM	-1.8
1897	Cle-N	109	412	62	110	15	9	0	59	30		.267	.323	.347	73	-17	11			**.994**	0	*1-92,2-18/3-2,SM	-1.4
1898	Cle-N	131	477	53	123	11	4	1	63	53		.258	.341	.304	86	-7	5			.984	3	1-91,2-34/S-7,3M	-0.2
1899	StL-N	77	281	27	69	10	3	1	26	18		.246	.303	.313	67	-13	5			.980	-3	1-65,S-11/3-1,2M	-1.3
1900	StL-N	1	4	0	0	0	0	0	0	0		.000	.000	.000	-99	-1	0			.700	-1	/S-1,M	-0.1
Total	13	1167	4618	671	1290	196	57	27	735	319	198	.279	.332	.364	86	-101	164			.984	28	1-595,3-478/2SPO	-4.5
■ DICK TEED	Teed, Richard Leroy b: 3/8/26, Springfield, Mass. BB/TR, 5'11", 180 lbs. Deb: 7/24/53																						
1953	Bro-N	1	1	0	0	0	0	0	0	0	1	.000	.000	.000	-98	-0	0	0	0	.000	0	H	0.0

YEAR	TM/L	G	AB	R	H	2B	3B	HR	RBI	BB	SO	AVG	OBP	SLG	PRO+	BR/A	SB	CS	SBR	FA	FR	G/POS	TPR
■ MIGUEL TEJADA	Tejada, Miguel Odalis (Martinez) b: 5/25/76, Bani, D.R. BR/TR, 5'10", 170 lbs. Deb: 8/27/97																						
1997	Oak-A	26	99	10	20	3	2	2	10	2	22	.202	.240	.333	48	-8	2	0	1	.968	-2	S-26	-0.6
1998	Oak-A	105	365	53	85	20	1	11	45	28	86	.233	.300	.384	78	-12	5	6	-2	.950	1	*S-104	-0.4
Total	2	131	464	63	105	23	3	13	55	30	108	.226	.288	.373	72	-20	7	6	-2	.954	-1	S-130	-1.0
■ WILFREDO TEJADA	Tejada, Wilfredo Aristides (Andujar) b: 11/12/62, Santo Domingo, D.R. BR/TR, 6', 175 lbs. Deb: 9/9/86																						
1986	Mon-N	10	25	1	6	1	0	0	2	2	8	.240	.296	.280	60	-1	0	0	0	1.000	-1	C-10	-0.1
1988	Mon-N	8	15	1	4	2	0	0	2	0	4	.267	.267	.400	85	-0	0	0	0	1.000	3	/C-7	0.3
Total	2	18	40	2	10	3	0	0	4	2	12	.250	.286	.325	70	-2	0	0	0	1.000	2	/C-17	0.2
■ JOHNNY TEMPLE	Temple, John Ellis b: 8/8/27, Lexington, N.C. d: 1/9/94, Anderson, S.C. BR/TR, 5'11", 175 lbs. Deb: 4/15/52 C																						
1952	Cin-N	30	97	8	19	3	0	1	5	5	1	.196	.235	.258	37	-8	2	1	0	.984	-1	2-22	-0.8
1953	Cin-N	63	110	14	29	4	0	1	9	7	12	.264	.314	.327	67	-5	1	0	0	.964	10	2-44	0.6
1954	Cin-N	146	505	60	155	14	8	0	44	62	24	.307	.385	.366	94	-1	21	7	2	.973	-10	*2-144	0.0
1955	Cin-N	150	588	94	165	20	3	0	50	80	32	.281	.368	.325	81	-13	19	4	3	.971	-3	*2-149/S-1	-0.1
1956	Cin-N★	154	632	88	180	18	3	2	41	58	40	.285	.346	.332	78	-17	14	4	2	.981	-7	*2-154/O-1	-1.0
1957	Cin-N★	145	557	85	158	24	4	0	37	**94**	34	.284	.391	.341	92	-2	19	5	**3**	.974	-21	*2-145	-0.8
1958	Cin-N	141	542	82	166	31	6	3	47	91	41	.306	.406	.402	109	11	15	8	-0	.979	-19	*2-141/1-1	0.2
1959	Cin-N★	149	598	102	186	35	6	8	67	72	40	.311	.387	.430	114	14	14	3	2	.974	-26	*2-149	0.2
1960	Cle-A	98	381	50	102	13	1	2	19	32	20	.268	.326	.323	79	-11	11	5	0	.974	-30	2-77,3-17	-3.4
1961	Cle-A★	129	518	73	143	22	3	3	30	61	36	.276	.352	.347	90	-6	9	5	-0	.969	-30	*2-129	-2.2
1962	Bal-A	78	270	28	71	8	1	1	17	36	22	.263	.352	.311	85	-4	7	4	-0	.981	-19	2-71	-1.6
	Hou-N	31	95	14	25	4	0	0	12	7	11	.263	.314	.305	72	-4	1	0	0	.941	-8	2-26/3-1	-0.9
1963	Hou-N	100	322	22	85	12	1	1	17	41	24	.264	.347	.317	99	1	7	2	1	.970	-20	2-61,3-29	-1.4
1964	Cin-N	6	3	0	0	0	0	0	0	2	1	.000	.400	.000	23	-0	0	0	0	.000	0	H	0.0
Total	13	1420	5218	720	1484	208	36	22	395	648	338	.284	.365	.351	91	-46	140	48	13	.974	-183	*2-1312/3-47,1OS	-11.2
■ GARRY TEMPLETON	Templeton, Garry Lewis b: 3/24/56, Lockney, Tex. BB/TR, 5'11", 190 lbs. Deb: 8/9/76																						
1976	StL-N	53	213	32	62	8	2	1	17	7	33	.291	.317	.362	91	-3	11	7	-1	.922	1	S-53	0.4
1977	StL-N★	153	621	94	200	19	**18**	8	79	15	70	.322	.339	.449	111	8	28	24	-6	.958	-3	*S-151	1.6
1978	StL-N	155	647	82	181	31	**13**	2	47	22	87	.280	.304	.377	91	-10	34	11	4	.953	23	*S-155	3.8
1979	StL-N†	154	672	105	**211**	32	**19**	9	62	18	91	.314	.333	.458	113	9	26	10	2	.960	18	*S-150	4.7
1980	StL-N	118	504	83	161	19	9	4	43	18	43	.319	.343	.417	108	4	31	15	0	.959	28	*S-115	4.7
1981	StL-N	80	333	47	96	16	8	1	33	14	55	.288	.317	.393	98	-2	8	12	-5	.960	5	S-76	0.7
1982	SD-N	141	563	76	139	25	8	6	64	26	82	.247	.281	.352	80	-17	27	16	-2	.961	-24	*S-136	-3.2
1983	SD-N	126	460	39	121	20	2	3	40	21	57	.263	.295	.335	77	-15	16	6	1	.960	-14	*S-123	-1.7
1984	*SD-N	148	493	40	127	19	3	2	35	39	81	.258	.313	.320	79	-14	8	3	1	.960	-23	*S-146	-2.4
1985	SD-N★	148	546	63	154	30	2	6	55	41	88	.282	.333	.377	100	-0	16	6	1	.968	-7	*S-148	0.9
1986	SD-N	147	510	42	126	21	2	2	44	35	86	.247	.297	.308	68	-22	10	5	0	.966	-28	*S-144	-3.9
1987	SD-N	148	510	42	113	13	5	5	48	42	92	.222	.282	.296	55	-33	14	3	2	.972	9	*S-146	-1.0
1988	SD-N	110	362	35	90	15	7	3	36	20	50	.249	.288	.354	85	-8	8	2	1	.968	15	*S-105/3-2	1.7
1989	SD-N	142	506	43	129	26	3	6	40	23	80	.255	.287	.354	82	-13	1	3	-2	.970	13	*S-140	1.0
1990	SD-N	144	505	45	125	25	3	9	59	24	59	.248	.282	.362	75	-18	1	4	-2	.957	-9	*S-135	-1.9
1991	SD-N	32	57	5	11	1	1	1	6	1	9	.193	.207	.298	39	-5	0	1	-1	.950	-3	3-15/S-1	-0.8
	NY-N	80	219	20	50	9	1	2	20	9	29	.228	.259	.306	59	-12	3	1	0	.963	5	S-40,1-25/3-2,O-2	-0.6
	Yr	112	276	25	61	10	2	3	26	10	38	.221	.248	.304	54	-17	3	2	-0	.963	3	S-41,1-25,3-17,/O-2	-1.4
Total	16	2079	7721	893	2096	329	106	70	728	375	1092	.271	.306	.369	87	-150	242	129	-5	.961	7	*S-1964/1-25,3-19,O	4.0
■ GENE TENACE	Tenace, Fury Gene (b: Fiore Gino Tennaci) b: 10/10/46, Russellton, Pa. BR/TR, 6', 190 lbs. Deb: 5/29/69 MC																						
1969	Oak-A	16	38	1	6	0	0	1	2	1	15	.158	.200	.237	23	-4	0	0	0	1.000	-0	C-13	-0.4
1970	Oak-A	38	105	19	32	6	0	7	20	23	30	.305	.430	.562	178	12	0	2	-1	.990	4	C-30	1.6
1971	*Oak-A	65	179	26	49	7	0	7	25	29	34	.274	.381	.430	132	8	2	1	0	.994	-6	C-52/O-1	0.4
1972	*Oak-A	82	227	22	51	5	3	5	32	24	42	.225	.307	.339	97	-1	0	0	0	.979	-8	C-49/O-9,1-7,2-2,3	-0.9
1973	*Oak-A	160	510	83	132	18	2	24	84	101	94	.259	.391	.443	142	32	2	2	-1	.989	-11	*1-134,C-33/2-1,D-3	1.2
1974	*Oak-A	158	484	71	102	17	1	26	73	**110**	105	.211	.370	.411	133	25	2	9	-5	.995	-9	*1-106,C-79/2-3	0.9
1975	*Oak-A★	158	498	83	127	17	0	29	87	106	127	.255	.398	.464	146	35	7	4	-0	.984	-16	*C-125,1-68/D-1	2.2
1976	Oak-A	128	417	64	104	19	1	22	66	81	91	.249	.376	.458	150	28	5	4	-1	.995	-20	1-70,C-65/D-2	0.5
1977	SD-N	147	437	66	102	24	4	15	61	**125**	119	.233	.417	.410	137	31	5	3	-0	.980	-7	C-99,1-36,3-14	2.5
1978	SD-N	142	401	60	90	18	4	16	61	101	98	.224	.394	.409	135	24	6	5	-1	.993	-3	1-80,C-71/3-1	1.8
1979	SD-N	151	463	61	122	16	4	20	67	105	106	.263	.407	.445	141	31	2	6	-3	**.998**	-3	C-94,1-72	2.5
1980	SD-N	133	316	46	70	11	1	17	50	92	63	.222	.403	.424	139	21	4	4	-1	.979	-7	*C-104,1-19	1.7
1981	StL-N	58	129	26	30	7	0	5	22	38	26	.233	.421	.403	131	8	0	0	0	.980	-6	C-38/1-7	0.3
1982	*StL-N	66	124	18	32	9	0	7	18	36	31	.258	.439	.500	160	12	1	1	-0	.994	1	C-37/1-7	1.5
1983	Pit-N	53	62	7	11	5	0	0	6	12	17	.177	.346	.258	68	-2	0	1	-1	.989	-2	1-19/C-3,O-1	-0.5
Total	15	1555	4390	653	1060	179	20	201	674	984	998	.241	.391	.429	137	261	36	42	-14	.986	-92	C-892,1-625/3OD2	15.3
■ JOHN TENER	Tener, John Kinley b: 7/25/1863, County Tyrone, Ireland d: 5/19/46, Pittsburgh, Pa. BR/TR, 6'4", 180 lbs. Deb: 6/8/1885																						
1885	Bal-a	1	4	0	0	0	0	0	0	0		.000	.000	.000	-99	-1				.000	-1	/O-1	-0.2
1888	Chi-N	12	46	4	9	1	0	0	1	1	15	.196	.229	.217	40	-3	1			.892	0	P-12/O-1	0.0
1889	Chi-N	42	150	18	41	4	2	1	19	7	22	.273	.306	.347	78	-5	2			.929	3	P-35/O-6,1-2	-0.1
1890	Pit-P	18	63	7	12	0	0	2	5	7	10	.190	.301	.286	62	-3	1			.966	2	P-14/O-2,3-2	-0.2
Total	4	73	263	29	62	5	2	3	25	15	47	.236	.287	.304	66	-12	4			.933	4	/P-61,O-10,3-2,1-2	-0.5
■ TOM TENNANT	Tennant, Thomas Francis b: 7/3/1882, Monroe, Wis. d: 2/15/55, San Carlos, Cal. BL/TL, 5'11", 165 lbs. Deb: 4/18/12																						
1912	StL-A	2	2	1	0	0	0	0	0	0		.000	.000	.000	-99	-1	0			.000	0	H	-0.1
■ FRED TENNEY	Tenney, Fred Clay b: 7/9/1859, Marlborough, N.H. d: 6/15/19, Fall River, Mass. Deb: 4/28/1884																						
1884	Was-U	32	119	17	28	3	1	0		6		.235	.272	.277	69	-8				.867	-1	O-27/1-6	-0.8
	Bos-U	4	17	1	2	0	0	0		0		.118	.118	.118	-29	-3				.750	-1	/P-4	0.0
	Wil-U	1	3	0	0	0	0	0		0		.000	.000	.000	-97	-1				1.000	0	/P-1	0.0
	Yr	37	139	18	30	3	1	0		6		.216	.248	.252	53	-12				.867	-1	O-27/1-6,P-5	-0.8
■ FRED TENNEY	Tenney, Frederick b: 11/26/1871, Georgetown, Mass. d: 7/3/52, Boston, Mass. BL/TL, 5'9", 155 lbs. Deb: 6/16/1894 M																						
1894	Bos-N	27	86	23	34	7	1	2	21	12	9	.395	.469	.570	139	5	6			.893	-0	C-20/O-6,1-1	0.5
1895	Bos-N	49	173	35	47	9	1	1	21	24	5	.272	.360	.353	78	-6	6			.885	-4	O-28,C-21	-0.8
1896	Bos-N	88	348	64	117	14	3	2	49	36	12	.336	.400	.411	108	4	18			.957	1	O-60,C-27	0.3
1897	*Bos-N	132	566	125	180	24	3	1	85	49		.318	.376	.376	93	-6	34			.988	5	*1-128/O-4	0.0
1898	Bos-N	117	488	106	160	25	5	0	62	33		.328	.370	.400	114	8	23			.980	5	*1-117/C-1	1.1
1899	Bos-N	150	603	115	209	19	17	1	67	63		.347	.411	.439	122	17	28			.978	10	*1-150	2.5
1900	Bos-N	112	437	77	122	13	5	1	56	39		.279	.346	.339	80	-13	17			.981	9	*1-111	-0.4
1901	Bos-N	115	451	66	127	13	1	1	22	37		.282	.340	.322	85	-9	15			.976	7	*1-113/C-2	-0.2
1902	Bos-N	134	489	88	154	18	3	2	30	73		.315	.409	.376	141	28	21			**.985**	13	*1-134	3.9
1903	Bos-N	122	447	79	140	22	3	3	41	70		.313	.415	.396	137	26	21			.974	8	*1-122	3.1
1904	Bos-N	147	533	76	144	17	9	1	37	57		.270	.351	.341	118	13	17			.986	8	*1-144/O-4	1.9
1905	Bos-N	149	549	84	158	18	3	0	28	67		.288	.368	.332	111	11	17			.982	22	*1-148/P-1,M	2.9
1906	Bos-N	143	544	61	154	12	8	1	28	58		.283	.357	.340	121	15	17			.983	10	*1-143,M	2.2
1907	Bos-N	150	554	83	151	18	8	0	26	82		.273	.371	.334	121	17	15			.989	9	*1-149,M	2.5
1908	NY-N	156	583	**101**	149	20	1	2	49	72		.256	.344	.304	102	4	17			.990	10	*1-156	1.4
1909	NY-N	101	375	43	88	8	2	3	30	52		.235	.333	.291	92	-2	8			.986	8	1-98	0.6
1911	Bos-N	102	369	52	97	13	4	1	36	50	17	.263	.352	.328	84	-7	5			.985	2	1-96/O-2,M	-0.5
Total	17	1994	7595	1278	2231	270	77	22	688	874	43	.294	.371	.358	109	107	285			.983	124	*1-1810,O-104/CP	21.0

YEAR	TM/L	G	AB	R	H	2B	3B	HR	RBI	BB	SO	AVG	OBP	SLG	PRO+	BR/A	SB	CS	SBR	FA	FR	G/POS	TPR
■ **FRANK TEPEDINO** Tepedino, Frank Ronald b: 11/23/47, Brooklyn, N.Y. BL/TL, 5′11″, 192 lbs. Deb: 5/12/67																							
1967	NY-A	9	5	0	2	0	0	0	0	1	1	.400	.500	.400	175	1	0	0	0	1.000	0	/1-1	0.1
1969	NY-A	13	39	6	9	0	0	0	4	4	4	.231	.302	.231	53	-2	1	0	0	.950	-1	O-13	-0.4
1970	NY-A	16	19	2	6	2	0	0	2	1	2	.316	.350	.421	118	0	0	1	-1	1.000	-1	/1-1,O-1	-0.1
1971	NY-A	6	6	0	0	0	0	0	0	0	0	.000	.000	.000	-99	-2	0	0	0	1.000	-0	/O-1	-0.2
	Mil-A	53	106	11	21	1	0	2	7	4	17	.198	.234	.264	41	-8	2	2	-1	.986	3	1-28	-0.8
	Yr	59	112	11	21	1	0	2	7	4	17	.188	.222	.250	34	-10	2	2	-1	.986	3	1-28/O-1	-1.0
1972	NY-A	8	8	0	0	0	0	0	0	0	1	.000	.000	.000	-99	-2	0	0	0	.000	0	H	-0.2
1973	Atl-N	74	148	20	45	5	0	4	29	13	21	.304	.360	.419	107	1	0	0	0	.992	2	1-58	0.1
1974	Atl-N	78	169	11	39	5	1	0	16	9	13	.231	.274	.272	51	-11	1	2	-1	.988	1	1-46	-1.4
1975	Atl-N	8	7	0	0	0	0	0	0	1	2	.000	.125	.000	-61	-2	0	0	0	.000	0	H	-0.2
Total	8	265	507	50	122	13	1	6	58	33	61	.241	.290	.306	65	-24	4	5	-2	.989	4	1-134/O-15	-3.1
■ **JOE TEPSIC** Tepsic, Joseph John b: 9/18/23, Slovan, Pa. BR/TR, 5′9″, 170 lbs. Deb: 7/12/46																							
1946	Bro-N	15	5	2	0	0	0	0	0	1	1	.000	.167	.000	-50	-1	0			1.000	-0	/O-1	-0.1
■ **JERRY TERRELL** Terrell, Jerry Wayne b: 7/13/46, Waseca, Minn. BR/TR, 6′, 170 lbs. Deb: 4/14/73																							
1973	Min-A	124	438	43	116	15	2	1	32	21	56	.265	.300	.315	71	-17	13	7	-0	.962	-14	S-81,3-30,2-14,/OD	-2.2
1974	Min-A	116	229	43	56	4	6	0	19	11	27	.245	.279	.314	68	-10	3	2	-0	.960	**23**	S-34,2-26,3D/O1	1.7
1975	Min-A	108	385	48	110	16	2	1	36	19	27	.286	.324	.345	88	-6	4	4	-1	.947	-3	S-41,2-39,13/OD	-0.6
1976	Min-A	89	171	29	42	3	1	0	8	9	15	.246	.287	.275	64	-8	11	2	2	.988	7	2-31,3-26,S-16,D/O	0.3
1977	Min-A	93	214	32	48	6	0	1	20	11	21	.224	.265	.266	46	-16	10	4	1	.953	5	3-59,2-14/S-7,1OD	-1.0
1978	KC-A	73	133	14	27	1	0	0	8	4	13	.203	.226	.211	23	-13	8	4	0	1.000	6	2-31,3-25,S-11,/1-5	-0.6
1979	KC-A	31	40	5	12	3	0	1	2	1	1	.300	.317	.450	102	-0	1	0	0	.963	3	3-19/2-7,P-1,S-1,D	0.3
1980	KC-A	23	16	4	1	0	0	0	0	0	0	.063	.063	.063	-65	-4	0	0	0	1.000	2	/O-7,1-3,2-3,P-1,D	-0.2
Total	8	657	1626	218	412	48	11	4	125	76	160	.253	.289	.304	66	-73	50	23	1	.961	28	3-192,S-191,2/D1OP	-2.3
■ **TOM TERRELL** Terrell, John Thomas b: 6/19/1867, Louisville, Ky. d: 7/9/1893, Louisville, Ky. Deb: 10/5/1886																							
1886	Lou-a	1	4	0	1	0	0	0	0	0		.250	.250	.250	54	-0	0			.000	-2	/O-1,C-1	-0.2
■ **TERRY** Terry b: Attleborough, Pa. Deb: 4/26/1875																							
1875	Was-n	6	22	0	4	0	1	0	2	0	1	.182	.182	.273	58	-1	0	0	0	.810	-3	/1-4,O-3	-0.3
■ **ADONIS TERRY** Terry, William H b: 8/7/1864, Westfield, Mass. d: 2/24/15, Milwaukee, Wis. BR/TR, 5′11.5″, 168 lbs. Deb: 5/1/1884 U																							
1884	Bro-a	67	236	15	55	10	3	0		8		.233	.258	.301	81	-5				.764	-1	P-56,O-13	0.1
1885	Bro-a	71	264	23	45	1	3	1	20	10		.170	.201	.208	29	-21				.883	2	O-47,P-25/3-1	-1.3
1886	Bro-a	75	299	34	71	8	9	2	39	10		.237	.265	.344	89	-5	17			.934	4	P-34,O-32,S-13	-0.4
1887	Bro-a	86	352	56	103	6	10	3	65	16		.293	.323	.392	98	-2	27			.895	3	O-49,P-40/S-2	-0.4
1888	Bro-a	30	115	13	29	6	0	0	8	5		.252	.283	.304	89	-2	7			.909	1	P-23/O-7,1-2	0.0
1889	*Bro-a	49	160	29	48	6	6	2	26	14	14	.300	.356	.450	129	5	8			.963	5	P-41,1-10	0.0
1890	*Bro-N	99	363	63	101	17	9	4	59	40	34	.278	.356	.408	122	10	32			.930	-1	O-54,P-46/1-1	0.2
1891	Bro-N	30	91	10	19	7	1	0	6	9	26	.209	.301	.308	78	-3	4			.957	-2	P-25/O-5	-0.1
1892	Bal-N	1	4	0	0	0	0	0	0	0	1	.000	.000	.000	-97	-1	0			1.000	0	/P-1	0.0
	Pit-N	31	100	10	16	0	4	2	11	10	11	.160	.236	.300	62	-5	2			.938	-0	P-30/O-1	-0.1
	Yr	32	104	10	16	0	4	2	11	10	12	.154	.228	.288	56	-6	2			.940	-0	P-31/O-1	-0.1
1893	Pit-N	26	71	9	18	4	3	0	11	3	12	.254	.293	.394	84	-2	1			.920	0	P-26	0.0
1894	Pit-N	1	0	0	0	0	0	0	0	0	0	—	—	—	—	0	0			.000	0	/P-1	0.0
	Chi-N	30	95	19	33	4	2	0	17	11	12	.347	.415	.432	99	-0	3			.875	-2	P-23/O-7,1-2	-0.1
	Yr	31	95	19	33	4	2	0	17	11	12	.347	.415	.432	99	0	3			.875	-2	P-24/O-7,1-2	-0.1
1895	Chi-N	40	137	18	30	3	2	1	10	2	17	.219	.236	.292	33	-14	1			.895	2	P-38/O-1,S-1	-0.1
1896	Chi-N	30	99	14	26	4	2	0	15	8	12	.263	.324	.343	73	-4	4			.968	-2	P-30	0.0
1897	Chi-N	1	3	1	0	0	0	0	0	0		.000	.000	.000	-96	-1	0			.750	0	/P-1	0.0
Total	14	667	2389	314	594	76	54	15	287	146	139	.249	.295	.344	85	-50	106			.903	10	P-440,O-216/S13	-2.2
■ **BILL TERRY** Terry, William Harold "Memphis Bill" b: 10/30/1898, Atlanta, Ga. d: 1/9/89, Jacksonville, Fla. BL/TL, 6′1″, 200 lbs. Deb: 9/24/23 MH																							
1923	NY-N	3	7	1	1	0	0	0	0	2	2	.143	.333	.143	30	-1	0	0	0	1.000	0	/1-2	-0.1
1924	*NY-N	77	163	26	39	7	2	5	24	17	18	.239	.311	.399	91	-2	1	1	-0	.988	-2	1-35	-0.6
1925	NY-N	133	489	75	156	31	6	11	70	42	52	.319	.374	.474	120	14	4	5	-2	.990	4	*1-126	0.8
1926	NY-N	98	225	26	65	12	5	5	43	22	17	.289	.352	.453	117	5	3			.979	4	1-38,O-14	0.5
1927	NY-N	150	580	101	189	32	13	20	121	46	53	.326	.377	.529	141	31	1			.993	5	*1-150	2.6
1928	NY-N	149	568	100	185	36	11	17	101	64	36	.326	.394	.518	136	29	7			.993	-2	*1-149	1.4
1929	NY-N	150	607	103	226	39	5	14	117	48	35	.372	.418	.522	132	31	10			.994	7	*1-149/O-1	2.0
1930	NY-N	154	633	139	**254**	39	15	23	129	57	33	**.401**	.452	.619	159	61	8			.990	13	*1-154	5.0
1931	NY-N	153	611	**121**	213	43	**20**	9	112	47	36	.349	.397	.529	150	**42**	8			.990	9	*1-153	3.6
1932	NY-N	154	643	124	225	42	11	28	117	32	23	.350	.382	.580	158	49	4			.991	14	*1-154,M	4.9
1933	*NY-N★	123	475	68	153	20	5	6	58	40	23	.322	.375	.423	129	19	3			.992	1	*1-117,M	0.9
1934	NY-N★	153	602	109	213	30	6	8	83	60	47	.354	.414	.463	138	34	0			**.994**	6	*1-153,M	2.6
1935	NY-N★	145	596	91	203	32	8	6	64	41	55	.341	.383	.451	126	22	7			**.996**	6	*1-143,M	1.2
1936	*NY-N	79	229	36	71	10	5	2	39	19	19	.310	.363	.424	112	4	0			.996	3	1-56,M	0.1
Total	14	1721	6428	1120	2193	373	112	154	1078	537	449	.341	.393	.506	137	338	56	6		.992	67	*1-1579/O-15	24.9
■ **ZEB TERRY** Terry, Zebulon Alexander b: 6/17/1891, Denison, Tex. d: 3/14/88, Los Angeles, Cal. BR/TR, 5′8″, 129 lbs. Deb: 4/12/16																							
1916	Chi-A	94	269	20	51	8	4	0	17	33	36	.190	.292	.249	62	-12	4			.935	-10	S-93	-1.9
1917	Chi-A	2	1	0	0	0	0	0	0	2	0	.000	.667	.000	102	0	0			1.000	-1	/S-1	0.0
1918	Bos-N	28	105	17	32	2	2	0	8	8	14	.305	.360	.362	125	3	1			.977	8	S-27	1.4
1919	Pit-N	129	472	46	107	12	6	0	27	31	26	.227	.280	.278	65	-19	12			**.960**	-31	*S-127	-4.8
1920	Chi-N	133	496	56	139	26	9	0	52	44	22	.280	.341	.369	102	2	12	16	-6	.962	14	S-70,2-63	1.9
1921	Chi-N	123	488	59	134	18	1	2	45	27	19	.275	.318	.328	71	-20	1	13	-8	.972	6	*2-122	-1.9
1922	Chi-N	131	496	56	142	24	2	0	67	34	16	.286	.335	.343	74	-19	2	11	-6	.964	9	*2-125/S-4,3-3	-1.2
Total	7	640	2327	254	605	90	24	2	216	179	133	.260	.318	.322	78	-64	32	40		.956	-5	S-322,2-310/3-3	-6.5
■ **WAYNE TERWILLIGER** Terwilliger, Willard Wayne "Twig" b: 6/27/25, Clare, Mich. BR/TR, 5′11″, 170 lbs. Deb: 8/6/49 C																							
1949	Chi-N	36	112	11	25	2	1	2	10	16	22	.223	.326	.313	74	-4	0			.978	4	2-34	0.2
1950	Chi-N	133	480	63	116	22	3	10	32	43	63	.242	.311	.363	77	-16	13			.967	-9	*2-126/1-1,3-1,O-1	-1.9
1951	Chi-N	50	192	26	41	6	0	0	10	29	21	.214	.317	.245	52	-12	3	1	0	.969	-4	2-49	-1.3
	Bro-N	37	50	11	14	1	0	0	4	8	7	.280	.390	.300	87	-0	1	0	0	.949	6	2-24/3-1	0.7
	Yr	87	242	37	55	7	0	0	14	37	28	.227	.332	.256	59	-12	4	1	1	.964	3	2-73/3-1	-0.6
1953	Was-A	134	464	62	117	24	4	4	46	64	65	.252	.343	.347	89	-6	7	4	-0	.982	5	*2-133	0.6
1954	Was-A	106	337	42	70	10	1	3	24	32	40	.208	.282	.270	55	-21	3	3	-1	.972	13	2-90,3-10/S-3	-0.4
1955	NY-N	80	257	29	66	16	1	1	18	36	42	.257	.350	.339	84	-5	2	4	-2	.985	26	2-78/S-1,3-1	2.4
1956	NY-N	14	18	0	4	1	0	0	0	0	5	.222	.222	.278	34	-2	0	0	0	.958	2	/2-6	0.1
1959	KC-A	74	180	27	48	11	0	2	18	19	31	.267	.337	.361	90	-2	2	2	-1	.972	20	2-63/S-2,3-1	2.0
1960	KC-A	2	1	0	0	0	0	0	0	0	0	.000	.000	.000	-99	-0	0	0	0	1.000	0	/2-2	0.0
Total	9	666	2091	271	501	93	10	22	162	247	296	.240	.323	.325	76	-69	31	14		.974	64	2-605/3-14,S-6,O1	2.4
■ **AL TESCH** Tesch, Albert John "Tiny" b: 1/27/1891, Jersey City, N.J. d: 8/3/47, Jersey City, N.J. BB/TR, 5′10″, 155 lbs. Deb: 8/21/15																							
1915	Bro-F	8	7	2	2	1	0	0	2	0	0	.286	.286	.429	100	-0	0			.867	3	/2-3	0.3
■ **NICK TESTA** Testa, Nicholas b: 6/29/28, New York, N.Y. BR/TR, 5′8″, 180 lbs. Deb: 4/23/58 C																							
1958	SF-N	1	0	0	0	0	0	0	0	0	0	—	—	—	—	0	0	0	0	.000	-1	/C-1	0.0

■ DICK TETTELBACH

Tettelbach, Richard Morley "Tut" b: 6/26/29, New Haven, Conn. d: 1/26/95, E.Harwich, Mass. BR/TR, 6', 195 lbs. Deb: 9/25/55

YEAR	TM/L	G	AB	R	H	2B	3B	HR	RBI	BB	SO	AVG	OBP	SLG	PRO+	BR/A	SB	CS	SBR	FA	FR	G/POS	TPR
1955	NY-A	2	5	0	0	0	0	0	0	0	0	.000	.000	.000	-99	-1	0	0	0	1.000	0	/O-2	-0.2
1956	Was-A	18	64	10	10	1	2	1	9	14	15	.156	.308	.281	56	-4	0	1	-1	1.000	2	O-18	-0.4
1957	Was-A	9	11	2	2	0	0	0	1	4	2	.182	.400	.182	65	-0	0	0	0	.900	-0	/O-3	-0.1
Total	3	29	80	12	12	1	2	1	10	18	17	.150	.306	.250	49	-6	0	1	-1	.980	2	/O-23	-0.7

■ MICKEY TETTLETON

Tettleton, Mickey Lee b: 9/16/60, Oklahoma City, Okla. BB/TR, 6'2", 212 lbs. Deb: 6/30/84

YEAR	TM/L	G	AB	R	H	2B	3B	HR	RBI	BB	SO	AVG	OBP	SLG	PRO+	BR/A	SB	CS	SBR	FA	FR	G/POS	TPR
1984	Oak-A	33	76	10	20	2	1	1	5	11	21	.263	.356	.355	105	1	0	0	0	.992	0	C-32	0.2
1985	Oak-A	78	211	23	53	12	0	3	15	28	59	.251	.344	.351	98	0	2	2	-1	.989	-1	C-76/D-1	0.2
1986	Oak-A	90	211	26	43	9	0	10	35	39	51	.204	.331	.389	103	1	7	1	2	.984	-2	C-89	0.5
1987	Oak-A	82	211	19	41	3	0	8	26	30	65	.194	.295	.322	68	-10	1	1	-0	.987	4	C-80/1-1,D-1	-0.2
1988	Bal-A	86	283	31	74	11	1	11	37	28	70	.261	.332	.424	113	5	0	1	-1	.992	-10	C-80	0.1
1989	Bal-A★	117	411	72	106	21	2	26	65	73	117	.258	.371	.509	150	28	3	2	-0	.994	-7	C-75,D-43	2.4
1990	Bal-A	135	444	68	99	21	2	15	51	106	160	.223	.378	.381	117	14	2	4	-2	.991	-13	C-90,D-40/1-5,O-1	0.4
1991	Det-A	154	501	85	132	17	2	31	89	101	131	.263	.389	.491	140	30	3	3	-1	.990	-15	*C-125,D-24/O-3,1-1	2.0
1992	Det-A	157	525	82	125	25	0	32	83	**122**	137	.238	.383	.469	137	29	0	6	-4	**.996**	-18	*C-113,D-40/1-3,O-2	1.2
1993	Det-A	152	522	79	128	25	4	32	110	109	139	.245	.376	.492	132	25	3	7	-3	.992	-17	1-59,C-56,O-55,/D-4	0.3
1994	Det-A★	107	339	57	84	18	2	17	51	97	98	.248	.422	.463	127	18	0	1	-1	.992	-15	C-53,1-24,D-22,O-18	0.3
1995	Tex-A	134	429	76	102	19	1	32	78	107	110	.238	.398	.510	131	22	0	0	0	.972	-3	O-63,D-58/1-9,C-3	1.2
1996	*Tex-A	143	491	78	121	26	1	24	83	95	137	.246	.372	.450	101	2	2	1	0	.977	-2	*D-115,1-23	-0.9
1997	Tex-A	17	44	5	4	1	0	3	4	3	12	.091	.167	.318	22	-5	0	0	0	.000	0	D-13	-0.6
Total	14	1485	4698	711	1132	210	16	245	732	949	1307	.241	.372	.449	122	161	23	29	-11	.991	-100	C-872,D-361,O1	7.1

■ TIM TEUFEL

Teufel, Timothy Shawn b: 7/7/58, Greenwich, Conn. BR/TR, 6', 175 lbs. Deb: 9/3/83

YEAR	TM/L	G	AB	R	H	2B	3B	HR	RBI	BB	SO	AVG	OBP	SLG	PRO+	BR/A	SB	CS	SBR	FA	FR	G/POS	TPR
1983	Min-A	21	78	11	24	7	1	3	6	2	8	.308	.325	.538	128	3	0	0	0	.990	-1	2-18/S-1,D-1	0.2
1984	Min-A	157	568	76	149	30	3	14	61	76	73	.262	.351	.400	103	3	1	3	-2	.984	-12	*2-157	-0.4
1985	Min-A	138	434	58	113	24	3	10	50	48	70	.260	.338	.399	95	-2	4	2	0	.980	-33	*2-137/D-1	-3.1
1986	*NY-N	93	279	35	69	20	1	4	31	32	42	.247	.327	.369	94	-2	1	2	-1	.971	-18	2-84/1-3,3-1	-1.9
1987	NY-N	97	299	55	92	29	0	14	61	44	53	.308	.400	.545	155	24	3	2	-0	.972	-11	2-92/1-1	1.6
1988	*NY-N	90	273	35	64	20	0	4	31	29	41	.234	.310	.352	94	-2	0	1	-1	.981	12	2-84/1-3	1.2
1989	NY-N	83	219	27	56	7	2	2	15	32	50	.256	.353	.333	102	2	1	3	-2	.960	-1	2-40,1-33	-0.2
1990	NY-N	80	175	28	43	11	0	10	24	15	33	.246	.305	.480	113	2	0	0	0	.991	-4	1-24,2-24,3-10	-0.3
1991	NY-N	20	34	2	4	0	0	1	2	2	8	.118	.167	.206	4	-4	1	1	-0	1.000	0	/1-6,3-5,2-1	-0.5
	SD-N	97	307	39	70	16	0	11	42	49	69	.228	.336	.388	100	1	8	2	1	.987	-14	2-65,3-48	-1.2
	Yr	117	341	41	74	16	0	12	44	51	77	.217	.321	.370	91	-3	9	3	1	.987	-14	2-66,3-53/1-6	-1.7
1992	SD-N	101	246	23	55	10	0	6	25	31	45	.224	.313	.337	83	-5	2	1	0	.987	-3	2-52,3-26/1-5	-0.8
1993	SD-N	96	200	26	50	11	2	7	31	27	39	.250	.339	.430	102	1	2	2	-1	.990	-3	2-52/3-9,1-8	-0.1
Total	11	1073	3112	415	789	185	12	86	379	387	531	.254	.338	.404	104	19	23	19	-5	.980	-88	2-806/3-99,1-83,DS	-5.5

■ GEORGE TEXTOR

Textor, George Bernhardt b: 12/27/1888, Newport, Ky. d: 3/10/54, Massillon, Ohio BB/TR, 5'10.5", 174 lbs. Deb: 4/19/14

YEAR	TM/L	G	AB	R	H	2B	3B	HR	RBI	BB	SO	AVG	OBP	SLG	PRO+	BR/A	SB	CS	SBR	FA	FR	G/POS	TPR
1914	Ind-F	22	57	2	10	0	0	0	4	2	9	.175	.230	.175	10	-8	0			.955	2	C-21	-0.5
1915	New-F	3	6	1	2	0	0	0	0	0	0	.333	.333	.333	93	-0	0			1.000	-1	/C-3	-0.1
Total	2	25	63	3	12	0	0	0	4	2	9	.190	.239	.190	17	-8	0			.957	1	/C-24	-0.6

■ MOE THACKER

Thacker, Morris Benton b: 5/21/34, Louisville, Ky. d: 11/13/97, Louisville, Ky. BR/TR, 6'3", 210 lbs. Deb: 4/20/58

YEAR	TM/L	G	AB	R	H	2B	3B	HR	RBI	BB	SO	AVG	OBP	SLG	PRO+	BR/A	SB	CS	SBR	FA	FR	G/POS	TPR
1958	Chi-N	11	24	4	6	1	0	2	3	1	7	.250	.280	.542	113	0	0	0	0	.952	1	/C-9	0.1
1960	Chi-N	54	90	5	14	1	0	0	6	14	20	.156	.269	.167	23	-9	1	1	-0	.980	5	C-50	-0.3
1961	Chi-N	25	35	3	6	0	0	0	2	11	11	.171	.383	.171	53	-2	0	0	0	.973	-1	C-25	-0.2
1962	Chi-N	65	107	8	20	5	0	0	9	14	40	.187	.287	.234	40	-9	0	1	-1	.996	13	C-65	0.5
1963	StL-N	3	4	0	0	0	0	0	0	0	3	.000	.000	.000	-91	-1	0	0	0	1.000	1	/C-3	0.0
Total	5	158	260	20	46	7	0	2	20	40	81	.177	.291	.227	41	-20	1	2	-1	.984	18	C-152	0.1

■ AL THAKE

Thake, Albert b: 9/21/1849, Wymondham, England d: 9/1/1872, Brooklyn, N.Y. 6', Deb: 6/13/1872

YEAR	TM/L	G	AB	R	H	2B	3B	HR	RBI	BB	SO	AVG	OBP	SLG	PRO+	BR/A	SB	CS	SBR	FA	FR	G/POS	TPR
1872	Atl-n	18	78	14	23	2	2	0	15	0	2	.295	.295	.372	89	-3	2	0	1	.808	-1	O-18/2-1	-0.2

■ RON THEOBALD

Theobald, Ronald Merrill b: 7/28/43, Oakland, Cal. BR/TR, 5'8", 165 lbs. Deb: 4/12/71

YEAR	TM/L	G	AB	R	H	2B	3B	HR	RBI	BB	SO	AVG	OBP	SLG	PRO+	BR/A	SB	CS	SBR	FA	FR	G/POS	TPR
1971	Mil-A	126	388	50	107	12	2	1	23	38	39	.276	.345	.325	92	-3	11	8	-2	.973	1	*2-111/S-1,3-1	0.6
1972	Mil-A	125	391	45	86	11	0	1	19	68	38	.220	.343	.256	81	-5	0	7	-4	.988	-13	*2-113	-1.9
Total	2	251	779	95	193	23	2	2	42	106	77	.248	.344	.290	87	-9	11	15	-6	.980	-12	2-224/3-1,S-1	-1.3

■ GEORGE THEODORE

Theodore, George Basil b: 11/13/47, Salt Lake City, Ut. BR/TR, 6'4", 190 lbs. Deb: 4/14/73

YEAR	TM/L	G	AB	R	H	2B	3B	HR	RBI	BB	SO	AVG	OBP	SLG	PRO+	BR/A	SB	CS	SBR	FA	FR	G/POS	TPR
1973	*NY-N	45	116	14	30	4	0	1	15	10	13	.259	.323	.319	80	-3	1	0	0	.984	2	O-33/1-4	-0.2
1974	NY-N	60	76	7	12	1	0	1	1	8	14	.158	.247	.211	29	-7	0	0	0	.990	-5	1-14,O-12	-1.4
Total	2	105	192	21	42	5	0	2	16	18	27	.219	.292	.276	60	-10	1	0	0	.958	-3	/O-45,1-18	-1.6

■ TOMMY THEVENOW

Thevenow, Thomas Joseph b: 9/6/03, Madison, Ind. d: 7/29/57, Madison, Ind. BR/TR, 5'10", 155 lbs. Deb: 9/4/24

YEAR	TM/L	G	AB	R	H	2B	3B	HR	RBI	BB	SO	AVG	OBP	SLG	PRO+	BR/A	SB	CS	SBR	FA	FR	G/POS	TPR
1924	StL-N	23	89	4	18	4	1	0	7	1	6	.202	.211	.270	28	-9	1	3	-2	.951	8	S-23	0.0
1925	StL-N	50	175	17	47	7	2	0	17	7	12	.269	.301	.331	60	-11	3	0	1	.950	3	S-50	-0.2
1926	*StL-N	156	563	64	144	15	5	2	63	27	26	.256	.291	.311	60	-32	8			.956	18	*S-156	0.3
1927	StL-N	59	191	23	37	6	1	0	4	14	8	.194	.249	.236	29	-19	2			.945	7	S-59	-0.6
1928	*StL-N	69	171	11	35	8	3	0	13	20	12	.205	.288	.287	50	-13	0			.931	-4	S-64/3-3,1-1	-1.1
1929	Phi-N	90	317	30	72	11	0	0	35	25	25	.227	.288	.262	35	-32	3			.953	3	S-90	-1.7
1930	Phi-N	156	573	57	164	21	1	0	78	23	26	.286	.316	.326	52	-44	1			.941	-2	*S-156	-2.6
1931	Pit-N	120	404	35	86	12	1	0	38	28	22	.213	.266	.248	39	-34	0			.964	9	*S-120	-1.4
1932	Pit-N	59	194	12	46	3	3	0	26	7	12	.237	.264	.284	48	-14	0			.918	-1	S-29,3-22	-1.1
1933	Pit-N	73	253	20	79	5	1	0	34	3	5	.312	.320	.340	89	-4	2			.975	-13	2-61/S-3,3-1	-1.4
1934	Pit-N	122	446	37	121	16	2	0	54	20	20	.271	.306	.316	65	-21	0			.969	-18	2-75,3-44/S-1	-3.3
1935	Pit-N	110	408	38	97	9	9	0	47	12	23	.238	.261	.304	50	-29	1			.951	4	3-82,S-13/2-8	-2.0
1936	Cin-N	106	321	25	75	7	2	0	36	15	23	.234	.268	.268	48	-24	2			.945	-9	S-68,2-33,3-12	-2.7
1937	Bos-N	21	34	5	4	0	1	0	2	4	2	.118	.211	.176	7	-4	0			.969	1	S-12/3-6,2-2	-0.3
1938	Pit-N	15	25	2	5	0	0	0	2	4	0	.200	.333	.200	49	-1	0			1.000	3	/2-9,S-4,3-1	0.2
Total	15	1229	4164	380	1030	124	32	2	456	210	222	.247	.285	.294	52	-292	23	3		.950	9	S-848,2-188,3/1	-17.9

■ HENRY THIELMAN

Thielman, Henry Joseph b: 10/3/1880, St.Cloud, Minn. d: 9/2/42, New York, N.Y. BR/TR, 5'11", 175 lbs. Deb: 4/17/02 F

YEAR	TM/L	G	AB	R	H	2B	3B	HR	RBI	BB	SO	AVG	OBP	SLG	PRO+	BR/A	SB	CS	SBR	FA	FR	G/POS	TPR
1902	NY-N	6	9	0	1	0	0	0	0	2		.111	.273	.111	19	-1	1			.800	1	/P-2,O-3	-0.1
	Cin-N	28	91	6	12	0	2	0	4	5		.132	.177	.176	8	-10	0			.910	-2	P-25/O-3	-0.2
	Yr	34	100	6	13	0	2	0	4	7		.130	.187	.170	9	-11	1			.903	-1	P-27/O-6	-0.3
1903	Bro-N	9	23	3	5	1	0	1	2	5		.217	.357	.391	117	1	0			.750	-0	/O-5,P-4	-0.1
Total	2	43	123	9	18	1	2	1	6	12		.146	.222	.211	30	-10	1			.918	-1	/P-31,O-11	-0.4

■ ANDRES THOMAS

Thomas, Andres Perez (b: Andres Perez (Thomas)) b: 11/10/63, Boca Chica, D.R. BR/TR, 6'1", 185 lbs. Deb: 9/3/85

YEAR	TM/L	G	AB	R	H	2B	3B	HR	RBI	BB	SO	AVG	OBP	SLG	PRO+	BR/A	SB	CS	SBR	FA	FR	G/POS	TPR
1985	Atl-N	15	18	6	5	0	0	0	2	0	2	.278	.278	.278	53	-1	0	0	0	.920	3	S-10	0.2
1986	Atl-N	102	323	26	81	17	2	6	32	8	49	.251	.269	.372	71	-14	4	6	-2	.958	26	S-97	1.8
1987	Atl-N	82	324	29	75	11	0	5	39	14	50	.231	.268	.312	50	-23	6	5	-1	.953	9	S-81	-0.8
1988	Atl-N	153	606	54	153	22	2	13	68	14	95	.252	.271	.360	76	-20	7	3	0	.959	-8	*S-150	-1.7
1989	Atl-N	141	554	41	118	18	0	13	57	12	62	.213	.230	.316	53	-35	3	3	-1	.956	6	*S-138	-2.0
1990	Atl-N	84	278	26	61	8	0	5	30	11	43	.219	.249	.302	48	-20	2	1	0	.967	3	S-72/3-5	-1.2
Total	6	577	2103	182	493	76	4	42	228	59	301	.234	.256	.334	61	-113	22	18	-4	.958	38	S-548/3-5	-3.7

■ PINCH THOMAS

Thomas, Chester David b: 1/24/1888, Camp Point, Ill. d: 12/24/53, Modesto, Cal. BL/TR, 5'9.5", 173 lbs. Deb: 4/24/12

YEAR	TM/L	G	AB	R	H	2B	3B	HR	RBI	BB	SO	AVG	OBP	SLG	PRO+	BR/A	SB	CS	SBR	FA	FR	G/POS	TPR
1912	Bos-A	13	30	0	6	0	0	0	5	2		.200	.250	.200	28	-3	1			.966	2	/C-8	0.0

YEAR	TM/L	G	AB	R	H	2B	3B	HR	RBI	BB	SO	AVG	OBP	SLG	PRO+	BR/A	SB	CS	SBR	FA	FR	G/POS	TPR
1913	Bos-A	38	91	6	26	1	2	1	15	2	11	.286	.309	.374	97	-1	1			.983	1	C-31	0.3
1914	Bos-A	66	130	9	25	1	0	0	5	18	17	.192	.291	.200	48	-8	1			.966	-2	C-64/1-1	-0.6
1915	*Bos-A	86	203	21	48	4	4	0	21	13	20	.236	.286	.296	76	-7	3	2	-0	.969	4	C-82	0.3
1916	*Bos-A	99	216	21	57	10	1	1	21	33	13	.264	.364	.333	109	4	4			.981	-8	C-90	0.2
1917	Bos-A	83	202	24	48	7	0	0	24	27	9	.238	.333	.272	86	-2	2			**.986**	3	C-77	0.7
1918	Cle-A	32	73	2	18	0	1	0	5	6	6	.247	.304	.274	68	-3	0			.948	1	C-24	-0.1
1919	Cle-A	34	46	2	5	0	0	0	2	4	3	.109	.180	.109	-17	-7	0			.980	-2	C-21	-0.8
1920	*Cle-A	9	9	2	3	1	0	0	0	3	1	.333	.500	.444	147	1	0	0	0	1.000	1	/C-7	0.2
1921	Cle-A	21	35	1	9	3	0	0	4	10	2	.257	.422	.343	96	0	0	0	0	.882	-6	C-19	-0.5
Total	10	481	1035	88	245	27	8	2	102	118	82	.237	.318	.284	78	-25	12	2		.973	-5	C-423/1-1	-0.3

■ DAN THOMAS

Thomas, Danny Lee b: 5/9/51, Birmingham, Ala. d: 6/12/80, Mobile, Ala. BR/TR, 6′2″, 190 lbs. Deb: 9/2/76

YEAR	TM/L	G	AB	R	H	2B	3B	HR	RBI	BB	SO	AVG	OBP	SLG	PRO+	BR/A	SB	CS	SBR	FA	FR	G/POS	TPR
1976	Mil-A	32	105	13	29	5	1	4	15	14	28	.276	.372	.457	145	6	1	2	-1	.955	-0	O-32	0.4
1977	Mil-A	22	70	11	19	3	2	2	11	8	11	.271	.354	.457	119	2	0	2	-1	1.000	1	/O-9,D-9	0.1
Total	2	54	175	24	48	8	3	6	26	22	39	.274	.365	.457	134	8	1	4	-2	.966	0	/O-41,D-9	0.5

■ DERREL THOMAS

Thomas, Derrel Osbon b: 1/14/51, Los Angeles, Cal. BB/TR, 6′, 160 lbs. Deb: 9/14/71

YEAR	TM/L	G	AB	R	H	2B	3B	HR	RBI	BB	SO	AVG	OBP	SLG	PRO+	BR/A	SB	CS	SBR	FA	FR	G/POS	TPR
1971	Hou-N	5	5	0	0	0	0	0	0	0	2	.000	.000	.000	-99	-1	0	1	-1	1.000	1	/2-1	-0.1
1972	SD-N	130	500	48	115	15	5	5	36	41	73	.230	.291	.310	76	-17	9	9	-3	.967	-18	2-83,S-49/O-3	-2.8
1973	SD-N	113	404	41	96	7	1	0	22	34	52	.238	.300	.260	61	-21	15	5	2	.914	-14	S-74,2-47	-2.3
1974	SD-N	141	523	48	129	24	6	3	41	51	58	.247	.315	.333	85	-11	7	8	-3	.976	6	*2-104,3-22,O-20,/S	-0.4
1975	SF-N	144	540	99	149	21	9	6	48	57	56	.276	.348	.381	98	-1	28	13	1	.974	-7	*2-141/O-1	0.0
1976	SF-N	81	272	38	63	5	4	2	19	29	26	.232	.315	.301	73	-9	10	11	-4	.964	2	2-69/O-2,S-1,3-1	-0.7
1977	SF-N	148	506	75	135	13	10	8	44	46	70	.267	.330	.379	90	-7	15	13	-3	.991	10	O-78,2-27,S-26,/31	0.0
1978	SD-N	128	352	36	80	10	2	3	26	35	37	.227	.303	.293	73	-13	11	6	-0	.991	3	O-77,2-40,3-26,1-14	-1.1
1979	LA-N	141	406	47	104	15	4	5	44	41	49	.256	.332	.350	87	-6	18	5	2	.996	2	*O-119,3-18/2-5,S1	-0.6
1980	LA-N	117	297	32	79	18	3	1	22	26	48	.266	.327	.357	93	-3	7	9	-3	.987	-1	O-52,S-49,2-18,/C3	-0.4
1981	*LA-N	80	218	25	54	4	0	4	24	25	23	.248	.325	.321	87	-3	7	2	1	.986	-10	2-30,S-26,O-18,3-10	-1.0
1982	LA-N	66	98	13	26	2	1	0	2	10	12	.265	.333	.306	82	-2	2	3	-1	1.000	-7	O-28,2-18,3-14,/S-6	-1.0
1983	*LA-N	118	192	38	48	6	6	2	8	27	36	.250	.348	.375	101	1	9	3	1	.990	-12	O-82,S-13/2-9,3-7	-1.1
1984	Mon-N	108	243	26	62	12	2	0	20	20	33	.255	.312	.321	82	-6	0	4	-2	.963	-38	S-62,O-48,2-15,/31	-4.4
	Cal-A	14	29	3	4	0	1	0	2	3	4	.138	.219	.207	19	-3	0	0	0	.889	-5	/O-7,S-4,3-3	-0.8
1985	Phi-N	63	92	16	19	2	0	4	12	11	14	.207	.291	.359	79	-3	2	0	1	.906	-8	S-21/O-7,C-1,2-1,3	-0.9
Total	15	1597	4677	585	1163	154	54	43	370	456	593	.249	.319	.332	83	-105	140	92	-13	.970	-94	2-608,O-542,S3/1C	-17.6

■ FRANK THOMAS

Thomas, Frank Edward "The Big Hurt" b: 5/27/68, Columbus, Ga. BR/TR, 6′5″, 257 lbs. Deb: 8/2/90

YEAR	TM/L	G	AB	R	H	2B	3B	HR	RBI	BB	SO	AVG	OBP	SLG	PRO+	BR/A	SB	CS	SBR	FA	FR	G/POS	TPR
1990	Chi-A	60	191	39	63	11	3	7	31	44	54	.330	.460	.529	180	23	0	1	-1	.989	-5	1-51/D-8	1.4
1991	Chi-A	158	559	104	178	31	2	32	109	**138**	112	.318	**.454**	.553	**181**	**69**	1	2	-1	.996	-4	*D-101,1-56	5.5
1992	Chi-A	160	573	108	185	**46**	2	24	115	**122**	88	.323	**.446**	.536	176	**64**	6	3	0	.992	-10	*1-158/D-2	4.3
1993	*Chi-A★	153	549	106	174	36	0	41	128	112	54	.317	.434	.607	180	66	4	2	0	.989	-9	*1-150/D-4	4.3
1994	Chi-A★	113	399	**106**	141	34	1	38	101	**109**	61	.353	**.494**	**.729**	**214**	**74**	2	3	-1	.991	-8	1-99,D-13	**5.0**
1995	Chi-A★	145	493	102	152	27	0	40	111	**136**	74	.308	.463	.606	184	69	3	2	-0	.991	-13	1-90,D-54	4.0
1996	Chi-A†	141	527	110	184	26	0	40	134	109	70	.349	.465	.626	181	**71**	1	1	-0	.992	-4	*1-139	4.7
1997	Chi-A†	146	530	110	184	35	0	35	125	109	69	**.347**	**.461**	.611	**184**	**71**	1	1	-0	.986	-7	1-97,D-49	4.7
1998	Chi-A	160	585	109	155	35	2	29	109	110	93	.265	.387	.480	127	26	7	0	2	.984	-2	*D-146,1-14	1.6
Total	9	1236	4406	894	1416	281	10	286	963	989	675	.321	.449	.584	177	533	25	15	-1	.991	-61	1-854,D-377	35.5

■ FRANK THOMAS

Thomas, Frank Joseph b: 6/11/29, Pittsburgh, Pa. BR/TR, 6′3″, 205 lbs. Deb: 8/17/51

YEAR	TM/L	G	AB	R	H	2B	3B	HR	RBI	BB	SO	AVG	OBP	SLG	PRO+	BR/A	SB	CS	SBR	FA	FR	G/POS	TPR
1951	Pit-N	39	148	21	39	9	2	2	16	9	15	.264	.306	.392	84	-4	0	2	-1	1.000	1	O-37	-0.5
1952	Pit-N	6	21	1	2	0	0	0	0	1	1	.095	.136	.095	-34	-4	0	0	0	1.000	-0	/O-5	-0.5
1953	Pit-N	128	455	68	116	22	1	30	102	50	93	.255	.331	.505	115	8	1	2	-1	.976	10	*O-118	1.2
1954	Pit-N★	153	577	81	172	32	7	23	94	51	74	.298	.365	.497	124	19	3	2	-0	.989	12	*O-153	2.4
1955	Pit-N★	142	510	72	125	16	2	25	72	60	76	.245	.327	.431	101	-0	2	0	1	.984	-0	*O-139	-0.6
1956	Pit-N	157	588	69	166	24	3	25	80	36	61	.282	.329	.461	112	8	0	5	-3	.942	-8	*3-111,O-56/2-4	-0.3
1957	Pit-N	151	594	72	172	30	1	23	89	44	66	.290	.342	.460	116	12	3	1	0	.977	-1	1-71,O-59,3-31	0.5
1958	Pit-N★	149	562	89	158	26	4	35	109	42	79	.281	.339	.528	129	21	0	1	-1	.926	-32	*3-139/O-8,1-2	-1.1
1959	Cin-N	108	374	41	84	18	2	12	47	27	56	.225	.282	.380	72	-16	0	2	-1	.927	-13	3-64,O-33,1-14	-3.3
1960	Chi-N	135	479	54	114	12	1	21	64	28	74	.238	.280	.399	84	-12	1	0	0	.983	-10	1-50,O-49,3-33	-2.8
1961	Chi-N	15	50	7	13	2	0	2	6	2	8	.260	.288	.420	84	-1	0	0	0	1.000	-1	O-10/1-6	-0.3
	Mil-N	124	423	58	120	13	3	25	67	29	70	.284	.338	.506	128	15	2	4	-2	.954	-0	*O-109,1-11	0.7
	Yr	139	473	65	133	15	3	27	73	31	78	.281	.333	.497	123	14	2	4	-2	.956	-1	*O-119,1-17	0.4
1962	NY-N	156	571	69	152	23	3	34	94	48	95	.266	.332	.496	117	12	2	1	0	.962	8	*O-126,1-11,3-10	1.1
1963	NY-N	126	420	34	109	9	1	15	60	33	48	.260	.318	.393	102	1	0	0	0	.988	5	O-96,1-15/3-1	0.0
1964	NY-N	60	197	19	50	6	1	3	19	10	29	.254	.297	.340	81	-5	1	1	-0	1.000	4	O-31,1-19/3-2	-0.4
	Phi-N	39	143	20	42	11	0	7	26	5	12	.294	.318	.517	132	5	0	1	-1	.976	1	1-36	0.4
	Yr	99	340	39	92	17	1	10	45	15	41	.271	.305	.415	103	0	1	2	-1	.982	5	1-55,O-31/3-2	0.0
1965	Phi-N	35	77	7	20	4	0	1	7	4	10	.260	.296	.351	83	-2	0	0	0	1.000	-3	O-12,1-11/3-1	-0.6
	Hou-N	23	58	7	10	2	0	3	9	3	15	.172	.213	.362	63	-3	0	0	0	.984	-2	1-16/3-2,O-1	-0.6
	Mil-N	15	33	3	7	3	0	0	1	2	11	.212	.257	.303	57	-2	0	0	0	.979	-1	/1-6,O-3	-0.3
	Yr	73	168	17	37	9	0	4	17	9	36	.220	.260	.345	71	-7	0	0	0	.985	-6	1-33,O-16/3-3	-1.5
1966	Chi-N	5	5	0	0	0	0	0	0	0	1	.000	.000	.000	-99	-1	0	0	0	.000	0	H	-0.1
Total	16	1766	6285	792	1671	262	31	286	962	484	894	.266	.323	.454	108	52	15	22	-9	.978	-31	*O-1045,3-394,1/2	-5.1

■ FRED THOMAS

Thomas, Frederick Harvey "Tommy" b: 12/19/1892, Milwaukee, Wis. d: 1/15/86, Rice Lake, Wis. BR/TR, 5′10″, 160 lbs. Deb: 4/22/18

YEAR	TM/L	G	AB	R	H	2B	3B	HR	RBI	BB	SO	AVG	OBP	SLG	PRO+	BR/A	SB	CS	SBR	FA	FR	G/POS	TPR
1918	*Bos-A	44	144	19	37	2	1	1	11	15	20	.257	.331	.306	94	-1	4			.968	5	3-41/S-1	0.6
1919	Phi-A	124	453	42	96	11	10	2	23	43	52	.212	.283	.294	61	-24	12			.945	-5	*3-124	-2.5
1920	Phi-A	76	255	27	59	6	3	1	11	26	17	.231	.307	.290	58	-15	8	4	0	.960	1	3-61,S-12	-1.0
	Was-A	3	7	0	1	0	0	0	0	0	1	.143	.143	.143	-25	-1	0	1	-1	1.000	2	/3-2	0.0
	Yr	79	262	27	60	6	3	1	11	26	18	.229	.303	.286	56	-16	8	5	-1	.962	3	3-63,S-12	-1.0
Total	3	247	859	88	193	19	14	4	45	84	90	.225	.297	.293	65	-41	24	5		.954	3	3-228/S-13	-2.9

■ GEORGE THOMAS

Thomas, George Edward b: 11/29/37, Minneapolis, Minn. BR/TR, 6′3.5″, 190 lbs. Deb: 9/11/57 C

YEAR	TM/L	G	AB	R	H	2B	3B	HR	RBI	BB	SO	AVG	OBP	SLG	PRO+	BR/A	SB	CS	SBR	FA	FR	G/POS	TPR
1957	Det-A	1	1	0	0	0	0	0	0	0	1	.000	.000	.000	-97	-0	0	0	0	.000	-0	/3-1	-0.1
1958	Det-A	1	0	0	0	0	0	0	0	0	0	—	—	—	—	0	0	0	0	.000	-0	/O-1	0.0
1961	Det-A	17	6	2	0	0	0	0	0	0	4	.000	.000	.000	-97	-2	0	0	0	.000	0	/O-2,S-1	-0.1
	LA-A	79	282	39	79	12	1	13	59	21	66	.280	.337	.468	101	-0	3	6	-3	.986	-11	O-45,3-38	-1.6
	Yr	90	200	41	79	12	1	13	59	21	70	.274	.330	.458	99	-1	3	6	-3	.986	-10	O-47,3-38/S-1	-1.7
1962	LA-A	56	181	13	43	10	2	4	12	21	37	.238	.320	.381	91	2	0	0	0	.957	1	O-51	-0.4
1963	LA-A	53	167	14	35	7	1	4	15	9	32	.210	.254	.335	68	-8	0	0	0	.941	-2	O-39,3-10/1-4	-1.2
	Det-A	49	109	13	26	4	1	1	11	11	22	.239	.314	.321	76	-3	2	1	0	1.000	-2	O-40/2-1	-0.7
	Yr	102	276	27	61	11	2	5	26	20	54	.221	.279	.330	71	-11	2	1	0	.974	-4	O-79,3-10/1-4,2-1	-1.9
1964	Det-A	105	308	39	88	15	2	12	44	18	53	.286	.331	.464	117	6	4	1	1	.988	-2	O-90/3-1	0.1
1965	Det-A	79	169	19	36	5	1	3	10	12	39	.213	.273	.308	64	-8	2	3	-1	.948	-3	O-59/2-1	-1.5
1966	Bos-A	69	173	25	41	4	0	5	20	23	33	.237	.333	.347	87	-2	1	0	0	1.000	0	O-48/3-6,C-2,1-2	-0.4
1967	*Bos-A	65	89	10	19	2	0	1	6	3	23	.213	.255	.270	51	-5	0	1	-1	.973	-8	O-43/1-3,C-1	-1.7
1968	Bos-A	12	10	3	2	0	0	1	1	1	3	.200	.273	.500	122	0	1	0	0	1.000	-2	/O-9	-0.1
1969	Bos-A	29	51	9	18	3	1	0	8	3	11	.353	.400	.451	131	2	0	0	0	1.000	-4	O-12,1-10/C-1,3-1	-0.2
1970	Bos-A	38	99	13	34	8	0	2	13	11	12	.343	.420	.485	139	6	0	0	0	.972	-5	O-26/3-6	0.0
1971	Bos-A	9	13	0	1	0	0	0	1	1	4	.077	.143	.077	-34	-2	0	0	0	1.000	-2	/O-5	-0.4
	Min-A	23	30	4	8	1	0	0	2	4	3	.267	.353	.300	84	-0	0	0	0	1.000	-4	O-11/1-1,3-1	-0.5

YEAR	TM/L	G	AB	R	H	2B	3B	HR	RBI	BB	SO	AVG	OBP	SLG	PRO+	BR/A	SB	CS	SBR	FA	FR	G/POS	TPR
	Yr	32	43	4	9	1	0	0	3	5	7	.209	.292	.233	48	-3	0	0	0	1.000	-5	O-16/1-1,3-1	-0.9
Total	13	685	1688	203	430	71	9	46	202	138	343	.255	.318	.389	92	-20	13	12	-3	.976	-42	O-481/3-64,1C2S	-8.8
■ HERB THOMAS	Thomas, Herbert Mark b: 5/26/02, Sampson City, Fla. d: 12/4/91, Starke, Fla. BR/TR, 5′4.5″, 157 lbs. Deb: 8/28/24																						
1924	Bos-N	32	127	12	28	4	1	1	8	9	8	.220	.288	.291	58	-8	5	2	0	.983	8	O-32	-0.1
1925	Bos-N	5	17	2	4	0	1	0	0	2	0	.235	.350	.353	88	-0	0	1	-1	.963	-1	/2-5	-0.2
1927	Bos-N	24	74	11	17	6	1	0	6	3	9	.230	.269	.338	67	-4	2			.972	-11	2-17/S-2	-1.4
	NY-N	13	17	2	3	1	1	0	1	1	1	.176	.263	.353	64	-1	0			.900	0	/O-3,S-1	-0.1
	Yr	37	91	13	20	7	2	0	7	4	10	.220	.268	.341	65	-5	2			.972	-11	2-17/S-3,O-3	-1.5
Total	3	74	235	27	52	11	4	1	15	15	18	.221	.285	.315	63	-13	7	3		.976	-4	/O-35,2-22,S-3	-1.8
■ IRA THOMAS	Thomas, Ira Felix b: 1/22/1881, Ballston Spa, N.Y. d: 10/11/58, Philadelphia, Pa. BR/TR, 6′2″, 200 lbs. Deb: 5/18/06 C																						
1906	NY-A	44	115	12	23	1	2	0	15	8		.200	.258	.243	52	-6	2			.938	-5	C-42	-0.8
1907	NY-A	80	208	20	40	5	4	1	24	10		.192	.240	.269	58	-10	5			.953	8	C-61/1-2	0.3
1908	*Det-A	40	101	6	31	1	0	0	8	5		.307	.346	.317	111	1	0			.972	-5	C-29	-0.2
1909	Phi-A	84	256	22	57	9	3	0	31	18		.223	.292	.281	79	-6	4			**.985**	12	C-84	1.5
1910	*Phi-A	60	180	14	50	8	2	1	19	6		.278	.301	.361	108	1	2			.967	8	C-60	1.5
1911	*Phi-A	103	297	33	81	14	3	0	39	23		.273	.341	.340	92	-3	4			.974	6	*C-103	1.2
1912	Phi-A	48	139	14	30	4	2	1	13	8		.216	.268	.295	63	-7	3			.971	-1	C-48	-0.4
1913	Phi-A	22	53	3	15	4	1	0	6	4	8	.283	.333	.396	116	1	0			.983	3	C-21	0.5
1914	Phi-A	2	3	0	0	0	0	0	0	0	0	.000	.000	.000	-99	-1	0			1.000	0	/C-1	0.0
1915	Phi-A	1	0	0	0	0	0	0	0	0	0	—	—	—	—	0	0			1.000	0	/C-1	0.0
Total	10	484	1352	124	327	46	17	3	155	82	8	.242	.296	.308	82	-30	20			.970	26	C-450/1-2	3.6
■ GORMAN THOMAS	Thomas, James Gorman b: 12/12/50, Charleston, S.C. BR/TR, 6′2″, 210 lbs. Deb: 4/6/73																						
1973	Mil-A	59	155	16	29	7	1	2	11	14	61	.187	.254	.284	53	-10	5	5	-2	.957	-4	O-50/3-1,D-3	-1.7
1974	Mil-A	17	46	10	12	4	0	2	11	8	15	.261	.370	.478	143	3	4	0	1	1.000	-1	O-13/D-2	0.3
1975	Mil-A	121	240	34	43	12	2	10	28	31	84	.179	.273	.371	80	-7	4	2	0	.961	-13	*O-113/D-6	-2.4
1976	Mil-A	99	227	27	45	9	2	8	36	31	67	.198	.297	.361	94	-2	2	3	-1	.986	-5	O-94/3-1,D-1	-1.2
1978	Mil-A	137	452	70	111	24	1	32	86	73	133	.246	.353	.515	141	24	3	4	-2	.983	-4	*O-137	1.4
1979	Mil-A	156	557	97	136	29	0	**45**	123	98	175	.244	.359	.539	138	30	1	5	-3	.991	4	*O-152/D-4	2.3
1980	Mil-A	162	628	78	150	26	3	38	105	58	170	.239	.305	.471	113	8	8	5	-1	.985	3	*O-160/D-2	0.5
1981	*Mil-A★	103	363	54	94	22	0	21	65	50	85	.259	.352	.493	149	22	4	5	-2	.979	3	O-97/D-6	2.1
1982	*Mil-A	158	567	96	139	29	1	**39**	112	84	143	.245	.347	.506	139	30	3	7	-3	.991	10	*O-157	3.2
1983	Mil-A	46	164	21	30	6	1	5	18	23	50	.183	.287	.323	73	-6	2	1	0	.992	-0	O-46	-0.8
	Cle-A	106	371	51	82	17	0	17	51	57	98	.221	.326	.404	96	-2	8	3	1	.982	12	*O-106	0.7
	Yr	152	535	72	112	23	1	22	69	80	148	.209	.314	.379	90	-7	10	4	1	.985	11	*O-152	-0.1
1984	Sea-A	35	108	6	17	3	0	1	13	28	27	.157	.336	.213	56	-5	0	3	-2	1.000	-3	O-34/D-1	-1.1
1985	Sea-A	135	484	76	104	16	1	32	87	84	126	.215	.332	.450	111	8	3	2	-0	.000	0	*D-133	0.5
1986	Sea-A	57	170	24	33	4	0	10	26	27	55	.194	.308	.394	89	-3	1	2	-1	.000	0	D-52	-0.5
	Mil-A	44	145	21	26	4	1	6	10	31	50	.179	.324	.345	80	-4	2	2	-1	.980	-1	D-36/1-6	-0.6
	Yr	101	315	45	59	8	1	16	36	58	105	.187	.316	.371	85	-6	3	4	-2	.980	-1	D-88/1-6	-1.1
Total	13	1435	4677	681	1051	212	13	268	782	697	1339	.225	.328	.448	114	86	50	49	-14	.984	1	*O-1159,D-246/1-6,3	2.7
■ LEE THOMAS	Thomas, James Leroy b: 2/5/36, Peoria, Ill. BL/TR, 6′2″, 198 lbs. Deb: 4/22/61 C																						
1961	NY-A	2	2	0	1	0	0	0	0	0	0	.500	.500	.500	177	0	0	0	0	.000	0	H	0.0
	LA-A	130	450	77	128	11	5	24	70	47	74	.284	.355	.491	111	6	0	5	-3	.966	-3	O-86,1-34	-0.7
	Yr	132	452	77	129	11	5	24	70	47	74	.285	.355	.491	111	6	0	5	-3	.966	-3	O-86,1-34	-0.7
1962	LA-A★	160	583	88	169	21	2	26	104	55	74	.290	.357	.467	124	19	6	1	1	.982	-10	1-90,O-74	0.0
1963	LA-A	149	528	52	116	12	6	9	55	53	82	.220	.302	.316	78	-15	6	0	2	.996	3	*1-104,O-43	-1.8
1964	LA-A	47	172	14	47	8	1	2	24	18	22	.273	.342	.366	108	2	1	0	0	.949	-1	O-47/1-1	-0.1
	Bos-A	107	401	44	103	19	2	13	42	34	29	.257	.321	.411	97	-2	2	1	0	.995	3	*O-107/1-1	-0.4
	Yr	154	573	58	150	27	3	15	66	52	51	.262	.328	.398	100	0	3	1	0	.981	3	*O-154/1-2	-0.5
1965	Bos-A	151	521	74	141	27	4	22	75	72	42	.271	.362	.464	126	18	6	2	1	.984	5	*1-127,O-20	1.7
1966	Atl-N	39	126	11	25	1	1	6	15	10	15	.198	.263	.365	71	-5	1	1	-0	.987	2	1-36	-0.6
	Chi-N	75	149	15	36	4	0	1	9	14	15	.242	.319	.289	70	-6	0	0	0	.992	-1	1-20,O-17	-0.9
	Yr	114	275	26	61	5	1	7	24	24	30	.222	.294	.324	71	-11	1	1	-0	.989	1	1-56,O-17	-1.5
1967	Chi-N	77	191	16	42	4	1	2	23	15	22	.220	.287	.283	61	-9	1	0	0	.969	-4	O-43,1-10	-1.7
1968	Hou-N	90	201	14	39	4	0	1	11	14	22	.194	.250	.229	45	-13	2	1	0	.973	-1	O-48/1-2	-1.9
Total	8	1027	3324	405	847	111	22	106	428	332	397	.255	.328	.397	99	-6	25	11	1	.975	-7	O-485,1-425	-6.4
■ BUD THOMAS	Thomas, John Tillman b: 3/10/29, Sedalia, Mo. BR/TR, 6′, 180 lbs. Deb: 9/2/51																						
1951	StL-A	14	20	3	7	0	0	1	1	0	3	.350	.350	.500	124	1	2	0	1	1.000	1	S-14	0.3
■ KITE THOMAS	Thomas, Keith Marshall b: 4/27/23, Kansas City, Kan. d: 1/7/95, Rocky Mount, N.C. BR/TR, 6′1.5″, 195 lbs. Deb: 4/19/52																						
1952	Phi-A	75	116	24	29	6	1	6	18	20	27	.250	.365	.474	124	4	0	1	-1	.957	-3	O-29	-0.1
1953	Phi-A	24	49	1	6	0	0	0	2	3	6	.122	.173	.122	-18	-8	0	0	0	1.000	-0	O-15	-0.9
	Was-A	38	58	10	17	3	2	1	12	11	7	.293	.414	.466	141	4	0	0	0	1.000	-2	/O-8,C-1	0.2
	Yr	62	107	11	23	3	2	1	14	14	13	.215	.311	.308	68	-5	0	0	0	1.000	-2	O-23/C-1	-0.7
Total	2	137	223	35	52	9	3	7	32	34	40	.233	.340	.395	98	-1	0	1	-1	.978	-5	/O-52,C-1	-0.8
■ LEO THOMAS	Thomas, Leo Raymond "Tommy" b: 7/26/23, Turlock, Cal. BR/TR, 5′11.5″, 178 lbs. Deb: 4/29/50																						
1950	StL-A	35	121	19	24	6	0	1	9	20	14	.198	.312	.273	49	-9	0	1	-1	.964	-4	3-35	-1.3
1952	StL-A	41	124	12	29	5	1	0	12	17	7	.234	.336	.290	73	-4	2	0	1	.934	4	3-37/S-3,2-1	0.0
	Chi-A	19	24	1	4	0	0	0	6	6	4	.167	.333	.167	42	-2	0	0	0	.952	1	/3-9	-0.1
	Yr	60	148	13	33	5	1	0	18	23	11	.223	.335	.270	68	-5	2	0	1	.936	4	3-46/S-3,2-1	-0.1
Total	2	95	269	32	57	11	1	1	27	43	25	.212	.325	.271	59	-15	2	1	0	.948	1	/3-81,S-3,2-1	-1.4
■ RAY THOMAS	Thomas, Raymond Joseph b: 7/9/10, Dover, N.H. d: 12/6/93, Wilson, N.C. BR/TR, 5′10.5″, 175 lbs. Deb: 7/21/38																						
1938	Bro-N	1	3	1	1	0	0	0	0	0	0	.333	.333	.333	82	-0	0			1.000	0	/C-1	0.0
■ RED THOMAS	Thomas, Robert William b: 4/25/1898, Hargrove, Ala. d: 3/29/62, Fremont, Ohio BR/TR, 5′11″, 165 lbs. Deb: 9/13/21																						
1921	Chi-N	8	30	5	8	3	0	1	5	4	5	.267	.371	.467	120	1	0	1	-1	.962	1	/O-8	0.1
■ ROY THOMAS	Thomas, Roy Allen b: 3/24/1874, Norristown, Pa. d: 11/20/59, Norristown, Pa. BL/TL, 5′11″, 150 lbs. Deb: 4/14/1899 FC																						
1899	Phi-N	150	547	137	178	12	4	0	47	115		.325	.457	.362	130	35	42			.952	4	*O-135,1-14	2.6
1900	Phi-N	140	531	**132**	168	4	3	0	33	**115**		.316	.451	.335	119	26	37			.958	-2	*O-139/P-1	1.2
1901	Phi-N	129	479	102	148	5	2	1	28	**100**		.309	.437	.334	123	22	27			.967	-2	*O-129	1.0
1902	Phi-N	138	500	89	143	4	7	0	24	**107**		.286	**.414**	.322	127	24	17			.974	5	*O-138	2.2
1903	Phi-N	130	477	88	156	11	2	1	27	**107**		.327	**.453**	.365	139	34	17			.963	14	*O-130	3.8
1904	Phi-N	139	496	92	144	6	6	3	29	**102**		.290	.416	.345	141	32	28			.974	15	*O-139	4.0
1905	Phi-N	147	562	118	178	11	6	0	31	93		.317	.417	.358	137	32	23			.983	19	*O-147	4.5
1906	Phi-N	142	493	81	125	10	7	0	16	**107**		.254	.393	.302	117	17	22			**.986**	10	*O-142	2.2
1907	Phi-N	121	419	70	102	15	3	1	23	**83**		.243	.374	.301	113	11	11			.980	5	*O-121	1.3
1908	Phi-N	6	24	2	4	0	0	0	0	2		.167	.231	.167	26	-2	0			1.000	-1	/O-6	-0.3
	Pit-N	102	386	52	99	11	10	1	24	49		.256	.348	.345	121	11	11			.975	5	*O-101	1.3
	Yr	108	410	54	103	11	10	1	24	51		.251	.341	.334	116	9	11			.976	4	*O-107	1.0
1909	Bos-N	82	281	36	74	9	1	0	11	47		.263	.369	.302	104	3	5			.976	-2	O-76	-0.1
1910	Phi-N	23	71	7	13	0	2	0	4	7	5	.183	.266	.239	46	-5	4			.952	-2	O-20	-0.8
1911	Phi-N	21	30	5	5	2	0	0	2	8	6	.167	.342	.233	61	-1	0			1.000	1	O-11	-0.1
Total	13	1470	5296	1011	1537	100	53	7	299	1042	11	.290	.413	.333	124	240	244			.972	71	*O-1434/1-14,P-1	22.8

YEAR	TM/L	G	AB	R	H	2B	3B	HR	RBI	BB	SO	AVG	OBP	SLG	PRO+	BR/A	SB	CS	SBR	FA	FR	G/POS	TPR

■ VALMY THOMAS Thomas, Valmy b: 10/21/28, Santurce, P.R. BR/TR, 5'9", 165 lbs. Deb: 4/16/57

1957	NY-N	88	241	30	60	10	3	6	31	16	29	.249	.298	.390	83	-6	0	0	0	.991	2	C-88	-0.1
1958	SF-N	63	143	14	37	5	0	3	16	13	24	.259	.325	.357	82	-4	1	0	0	.992	2	C-61	0.1
1959	Phi-N	66	140	5	28	2	0	1	7	9	19	.200	.253	.236	31	-14	1	0	0	.980	15	C-65/3-1	0.4
1960	Bal-A	8	16	0	1	0	0	0	0	1	0	.063	.118	.063	-51	-3	0	1	-1	1.000	1	/C-8	-0.3
1961	Cle-A	27	86	7	18	3	0	2	6	6	7	.209	.261	.314	54	-6	0	0	0	.988	9	C-27	0.4
Total	5	252	626	56	144	20	3	12	60	45	79	.230	.285	.329	64	-33	2	1	0	.988	29	C-249/3-1	0.5

■ BILL THOMAS Thomas, William Miskey b: 12/8/1877, Norristown, Pa. d: 1/14/50, Evansburg, Pa. BR/TR, 5'10", 190 lbs. Deb: 5/1/02 F

| 1902 | Phi-N | 6 | 17 | 1 | 2 | 0 | 0 | 0 | | 0 | 1 | .118 | .167 | .118 | -12 | -2 | 0 | | | .500 | -1 | /O-3,1-1,2-1 | -0.4 |

■ WALT THOMAS Thomas, William Walter "Tommy" b: 4/28/1884, Foot Of Ten, Pa. d: 6/6/50, Altoona, Pa. BR/TR, 5'8", Deb: 9/18/08

| 1908 | Bos-N | 5 | 13 | 2 | 2 | 0 | 0 | 0 | | 1 | | .154 | .313 | .154 | 51 | -1 | 1 | 2 | | .864 | -1 | /S-5 | -0.2 |

■ ART THOMASON Thomason, Arthur Wilson b: 2/12/1889, Liberty, Mo. d: 5/2/44, Kansas City, Mo. BL/TL, 5'8", 150 lbs. Deb: 8/10/10

| 1910 | Cle-A | 20 | 70 | 4 | 12 | 0 | 1 | 0 | 2 | 5 | | .171 | .227 | .200 | 33 | -5 | 3 | | | .944 | 2 | O-20 | -0.5 |

■ GARY THOMASSON Thomasson, Gary Leah b: 7/29/51, San Diego, Cal. BL/TL, 6'1", 180 lbs. Deb: 9/5/72

1972	SF-N	10	27	5	9	1	1	0	1	1	7	.333	.357	.444	125	1	0	0	0	1.000	-2	/1-7,O-2	-0.1
1973	SF-N	112	235	35	67	10	4	4	30	22	43	.285	.346	.413	105	2	2	0	1	.992	-3	1-47,O-43	-0.4
1974	SF-N	120	315	41	77	14	3	2	29	38	56	.244	.326	.327	79	-8	7	1	2	.981	1	O-76,1-19	-1.0
1975	SF-N	114	326	44	74	12	3	7	32	37	48	.227	.308	.347	78	-10	9	3	1	.978	7	O-74,1-17	-0.5
1976	SF-N	103	328	45	85	20	5	8	38	30	45	.259	.323	.424	107	2	8	3	1	.959	-7	O-54,1-39	-0.9
1977	SF-N	145	446	63	114	24	6	17	71	75	102	.256	.364	.451	118	12	16	4	2	.959	-5	*O-113,1-31	0.5
1978	Oak-A	47	154	17	31	4	1	5	16	15	44	.201	.272	.338	74	-6	4	1	1	.969	-2	O-44/1-5	-0.5
	*NY-A	55	116	20	32	4	1	3	20	13	22	.276	.349	.405	114	2	0	2	-1	.972	0	O-50/D-1	0.0
	Yr	102	270	37	63	8	2	8	36	28	66	.233	.305	.367	92	-3	4	3	-1	.971	2	O-94/1-5,D-1	-0.5
1979	LA-N	115	315	39	78	11	1	14	45	43	70	.248	.340	.422	108	4	4	2	0	.980	-12	*O-100/1-1	-1.2
1980	LA-N	80	111	6	24	3	0	1	12	17	26	.216	.326	.270	69	-4	0	0	0	.974	-6	O-31/1-1	-1.2
Total	9	901	2373	315	591	103	25	61	294	291	463	.249	.332	.391	98	-5	50	16	5	.970	-24	O-587,1-163/D-1	-5.3

■ JIM THOME Thome, James Howard b: 8/27/70, Peoria, Ill. BL/TR, 6'4", 220 lbs. Deb: 9/4/91

1991	Cle-A	27	98	7	25	4	2	1	9	5	16	.255	.298	.367	82	-2	1	1	-0	.900	1	3-27	-0.2
1992	Cle-A	40	117	8	24	3	1	2	12	10	34	.205	.279	.299	63	-6	2	0	1	.882	-6	3-40	-1.2
1993	Cle-A	47	154	28	41	11	0	7	22	29	36	.266	.396	.474	133	8	2	1	0	.950	-2	3-47	0.6
1994	Cle-A	98	321	58	86	20	1	20	52	46	84	.268	.360	.523	124	11	3	1	0	.940	-1	3-94	0.9
1995	*Cle-A	137	452	92	142	29	3	25	73	97	113	.314	.440	.558	155	41	4	3	-1	.948	-14	*3-134/D-1	2.5
1996	*Cle-A	151	505	122	157	28	5	38	116	123	141	.311	.451	.612	166	56	2	2	-1	.953	-6	*3-150/D-1	4.4
1997	*Cle-A★	147	496	104	142	25	0	40	102	**120**	146	.286	.428	.579	154	43	1	1	-0	.993	1	*1-145	2.8
1998	*Cle-A★	123	440	89	129	34	2	30	85	90	141	.293	.417	.584	151	35	1	0	0	.991	0	*1-117/D-6	2.3
Total	8	770	2583	508	746	154	14	163	471	520	711	.289	.413	.549	146	186	16	11	-2	.940	-25	3-492,1-262/D-8	12.1

■ ANDREW THOMPSON Thompson, Andrew M. b: 1845, Illinois Deb: 4/26/1875 M

| 1875 | Was-n | 11 | 41 | 3 | 4 | 0 | 1 | 0 | 3 | 0 | 1 | .098 | .098 | .146 | -17 | -4 | 0 | 0 | 0 | .624 | -7 | C-11/O-1 | -1.0 |

■ BOBBY THOMPSON Thompson, Bobby La Rue b: 11/3/53, Charlotte, N.C. BB/TR, 5'11", 175 lbs. Deb: 4/16/78

| 1978 | Tex-A | 64 | 120 | 23 | 27 | 3 | 3 | 2 | 12 | 9 | 26 | .225 | .290 | .350 | 79 | -3 | 7 | 2 | 1 | .982 | -5 | O-52/D-3 | -0.9 |

■ TIM THOMPSON Thompson, Charles Lemoine b: 3/1/24, Coalport, Pa. BL/TR, 5'11", 190 lbs. Deb: 4/28/54 C

1954	Bro-N	10	13	2	2	1	0	0	1	1	1	.154	.214	.231	15	-1	0	0	0	.909	-1	/C-2,O-1	-0.2
1956	KC-A	92	268	21	73	13	2	1	27	17	23	.272	.321	.347	76	-9	2	4	-2	.981	2	C-68	-0.6
1957	KC-A	81	230	25	47	10	0	7	19	18	26	.204	.262	.339	62	-13	0	0	0	.993	-3	C-62	-1.3
1958	Det-A	4	6	1	1	0	0	0	0	3	2	.167	.444	.167	70	0	0	0	0	1.000	-1	/C-4	-0.1
Total	4	187	517	49	123	24	2	8	47	39	52	.238	.294	.338	68	-24	2	4	-2	.986	-3	C-136/O-1	-2.2

■ DANNY THOMPSON Thompson, Danny Leon b: 2/1/47, Wichita, Kan. d: 12/10/76, Rochester, Minn. BR/TR, 6', 183 lbs. Deb: 6/25/70

1970	*Min-A	96	302	25	66	9	0	0	22	7	39	.219	.236	.248	33	-27	0	1	0	.986	-12	2-81,3-37/S-6	-3.5
1971	Min-A	48	57	10	15	2	0	0	7	7	12	.263	.344	.298	81	-1	0	0	0	.897	1	3-17/2-3,S-1	0.0
1972	Min-A	144	573	54	158	22	6	4	48	34	57	.276	.319	.356	96	-3	3	4	-2	.957	-9	*S-144	0.8
1973	Min-A	99	347	29	78	13	2	1	36	16	41	.225	.263	.282	52	-22	1	0	0	.950	7	S-95/3-1,D-1	-0.4
1974	Min-A	97	264	25	66	6	1	4	25	22	29	.250	.313	.326	81	-6	1	1	-0	.963	-14	S-88/3-5,D-1	-1.8
1975	Min-A	112	355	25	96	11	2	5	37	18	30	.270	.306	.355	85	-8	0	0	0	.941	-17	*S-100/3-7,2-1,D-3	-1.7
1976	Min-A	34	124	9	29	4	0	0	6	3	8	.234	.258	.266	53	-7	1	1	0	.988	-1	S-34	-0.5
	Tex-A	64	196	12	42	3	0	1	13	13	19	.214	.267	.245	49	-12	2	2	-1	.976	-7	3-39,2-14,S-10,/D-1	-2.0
	Yr	98	320	21	71	7	0	1	19	16	27	.222	.263	.253	51	-20	3	3	-1	.981	-9	S-44,3-39,2-14,/D-1	-2.5
Total	7	694	2218	189	550	70	11	15	194	120	235	.248	.289	.310	70	-88	8	11	-4	.956	-60	S-478,3-106/2-99,D	-9.1

■ DON THOMPSON Thompson, Donald Newlin b: 12/28/23, Swepsonville, N.C. BL/TL, 6', 185 lbs. Deb: 4/24/49

1949	Bos-N	7	11	0	2	0	0	0	0	0	2	.182	.182	.182	-2	-2	0			.800	-0	/O-2	-0.2
1951	Bro-N	80	118	25	27	3	0	0	6	12	12	.229	.305	.254	51	-8	2	8	-4	.987	-11	O-61	-2.5
1953	*Bro-N	96	153	25	37	5	0	1	12	14	13	.242	.310	.294	57	-9	2	3	-1	.989	-14	O-81	-2.6
1954	Bro-N	34	25	2	1	0	0	0	1	5	5	.040	.226	.040	-25	-5	0	0	0	1.000	-9	O-29	-1.4
Total	4	217	307	52	67	8	0	1	19	31	32	.218	.296	.254	46	-23	4	11		.984	-35	O-173	-6.7

■ FRANK THOMPSON Thompson, Frank Deb: 9/11/1875

| 1875 | Atl-n | 1 | 5 | 1 | 2 | 0 | 0 | 0 | | 0 | 0 | .400 | .400 | .400 | 205 | 1 | 0 | 0 | 0 | .000 | -1 | /O-1 | 0.0 |

■ FRANK THOMPSON Thompson, Frank E b: 7/2/1895, Springfield, Mo. d: 6/27/40, Jasper Co., Mo. BR/TR, 5'8", 155 lbs. Deb: 5/6/20

| 1920 | StL-A | 22 | 53 | 7 | 9 | 0 | 0 | 0 | 5 | 13 | 10 | .170 | .343 | .170 | 38 | -4 | 1 | 1 | -0 | .878 | -4 | 3-14/2-2 | -0.8 |

■ HANK THOMPSON Thompson, Henry Curtis b: 12/8/25, Oklahoma City, Okla d: 9/30/69, Fresno, Cal. BL/TR, 5'9", 174 lbs. Deb: 7/17/47

1947	StL-A	27	78	10	20	1	1	0	5	10	7	.256	.341	.295	76	-2	2	1	0	.957	1	2-19	0.0
1949	NY-N	75	275	51	77	10	4	9	34	42	30	.280	.377	.444	120	8	5			.961	-8	2-69/3-1	0.4
1950	NY-N	148	512	82	148	17	6	20	91	81	60	.289	.391	.463	123	19	8			.944	5	*3-138,O-10	2.1
1951	*NY-N	87	264	37	62	8	4	8	33	43	23	.235	.342	.386	95	-1	1	2	-1	.925	-14	3-71	-1.8
1952	NY-N	128	423	67	110	13	9	17	67	50	38	.260	.344	.454	119	10	4	4	-1	.979	9	O-72,3-46/2-4	1.4
1953	NY-N	114	388	80	117	15	8	24	74	60	39	.302	.400	.567	146	27	6	5	-1	.956	-3	*3-101/O-9,2-1	1.9
1954	*NY-N	136	448	76	118	18	1	26	86	90	58	.263	.392	.482	126	19	3	0	1	.945	-4	*3-130/O-2,2-1	1.3
1955	NY-N	135	432	65	106	13	1	17	63	84	56	.245	.373	.398	105	5	2	2	-1	.943	-5	*3-124/O-2-7,S-1	0.7
1956	NY-N	83	183	24	43	9	0	8	29	31	26	.235	.349	.415	105	2	2	1	0	.908	3	3-44,O-10/S-1	0.2
Total	9	933	3003	492	801	104	34	129	482	493	337	.267	.374	.453	118	87	33	15		.941	-13	3-655,O-102,2/S	6.2

■ HOMER THOMPSON Thompson, Homer Thomas b: 6/1/1891, Spring City, Tenn. d: 9/12/57, Atlanta, Ga. BR/TR, 5'9", 160 lbs. Deb: 10/5/12 F

| 1912 | NY-A | 1 | 0 | 0 | 0 | 0 | 0 | 0 | 0 | 0 | 0 | — | — | — | | 0 | 0 | | | .500 | -0 | /C-1 | 0.0 |

■ SHAG THOMPSON Thompson, James Alfred b: 4/29/1893, Haw River, N.C. d: 1/7/90, Black Mountain, N.C BL/TR, 5'8.5", 165 lbs. Deb: 6/8/14

1914	Phi-A	16	29	3	5	0	1	0	2	7	8	.172	.351	.241	82	-0	1			.941	1	/O-8	0.1
1915	Phi-A	17	33	5	11	2	0	0	2	5	5	.333	.405	.394	144	2	0	1		1.000	-1	/O-7	0.1
1916	Phi-A	15	17	4	0	0	0	0	0	6	5	.000	.292	.000	-12	-2	1			1.000	-1	/O-8	-0.3
Total	3	48	79	12	16	2	1	0	4	18	20	.203	.357	.253	87	-0	2	1		.978	1	/O-23	-0.1

■ JASON THOMPSON Thompson, Jason Dolph b: 7/6/54, Hollywood, Cal. BL/TL, 6'3", 210 lbs. Deb: 4/23/76

| 1976 | Det-A | 123 | 412 | 45 | 90 | 12 | 1 | 17 | 54 | 68 | 72 | .218 | .331 | .376 | 103 | 2 | 2 | 4 | -2 | .994 | 2 | *1-117 | -0.7 |

YEAR	TM/L	G	AB	R	H	2B	3B	HR	RBI	BB	SO	AVG	OBP	SLG	PRO+	BR/A	SB	CS	SBR	FA	FR	G/POS	TPR
1977	Det-A☆	158	585	87	158	24	5	31	105	73	91	.270	.352	.487	120	15	0	1	-1	.991	-7	*1-158	-0.2
1978	Det-A★	153	589	79	169	25	3	26	96	74	96	.287	.367	.472	130	24	0	0	0	.993	-5	*1-151	1.0
1979	Det-A	145	492	58	121	16	1	20	79	70	90	.246	.341	.404	97	-2	2	0	1	.994	0	*1-140/D-2	-0.9
1980	Det-A	36	126	10	27	5	0	4	20	13	26	.214	.293	.349	73	-5	0	1	-1	1.000	4	1-36	-0.4
	Cal-A	102	312	59	99	14	0	17	70	70	60	.317	.442	.526	168	33	2	0	1	1.000	-3	1-47,D-45	2.6
	Yr	138	438	69	126	19	0	21	90	83	86	.288	.402	.475	141	28	2	1	0	1.000	1	1-83,D-45	2.2
1981	Pit-N	86	223	36	54	13	0	15	42	59	49	.242	.401	.502	150	17	0	0	0	.989	-1	1-78	1.3
1982	Pit-N★	156	550	87	156	32	0	31	101	101	107	.284	.397	.511	148	37	1	0	0	.993	-1	*1-155	2.9
1983	Pit-N	152	517	70	134	20	1	18	76	99	128	.259	.379	.406	115	14	1	0	0	.993	-6	*1-151	-0.1
1984	Pit-N	154	543	61	138	22	0	17	74	87	73	.254	.359	.389	110	9	0	0	0	.990	-10	*1-152	-1.1
1985	Pit-N	123	402	42	97	17	1	12	61	84	58	.241	.372	.378	111	9	0	0	0	.992	2	*1-114	0.5
1986	Mon-N	30	51	6	10	4	0	0	4	18	12	.196	.406	.275	92	1	0	1	-1	.962	-3	1-15	-0.4
Total	11	1418	4802	640	1253	204	12	208	782	816	862	.261	.369	.438	121	155	8	7	-2	.992	-28	*1-1314/D-47	4.5

■ JASON THOMPSON

Thompson, Jason Michael b: 6/13/71, Orlando, Fla. BL/TL, 6'4", 200 lbs. Deb: 6/9/96

YEAR	TM/L	G	AB	R	H	2B	3B	HR	RBI	BB	SO	AVG	OBP	SLG	PRO+	BR/A	SB	CS	SBR	FA	FR	G/POS	TPR
1996	SD-N	13	49	4	11	4	0	2	6	1	14	.224	.240	.429	76	-2	0	0	0	.964	1	1-13	-0.2

■ TUG THOMPSON

Thompson, John P. b: London, Ontario, Canada BL/TR, 5'8", 160 lbs. Deb: 8/31/1882

YEAR	TM/L	G	AB	R	H	2B	3B	HR	RBI	BB	SO	AVG	OBP	SLG	PRO+	BR/A	SB	CS	SBR	FA	FR	G/POS	TPR
1882	Cin-a	1	5	0	1	0	0	0		0		.200	.200	.200	33	-0				.000	-1	/O-1	-0.1
1884	Ind-a	24	97	10	20	3	0	0		2		.206	.222	.237	51	-5				.429	-11	O-12,C-12	-1.4
Total	2	25	102	10	21	3	0	0		2		.206	.221	.235	50	-5				.409	-11	/O-13,C-12	-1.5

■ FRESCO THOMPSON

Thompson, Lafayette Fresco "Tommy" b: 6/6/02, Centreville, Ala. d: 11/20/68, Fullerton, Cal. BR/TR, 5'8", 150 lbs. Deb: 9/5/25

YEAR	TM/L	G	AB	R	H	2B	3B	HR	RBI	BB	SO	AVG	OBP	SLG	PRO+	BR/A	SB	CS	SBR	FA	FR	G/POS	TPR
1925	Pit-N	14	37	4	9	2	1	0	8	4	1	.243	.317	.351	66	-2	2	1	0	.977	-2	2-12	-0.4
1926	NY-N	2	8	1	5	0	0	0	1	2	0	.625	.700	.625	262	2	1			1.000	-1	/2-2	0.1
1927	Phi-N	153	597	78	181	32	14	1	70	34	36	.303	.343	.409	99	-1	19			.963	-5	*2-153	-0.1
1928	Phi-N	152	634	99	182	34	11	3	50	42	27	.287	.332	.390	85	-14	19			.966	9	*2-152	-0.1
1929	Phi-N	148	623	115	202	41	3	4	53	75	34	.324	.398	.419	96	-1	16			.965	12	*2-148	1.5
1930	Phi-N	122	478	77	135	34	4	4	46	35	29	.282	.331	.395	70	-24	7			.955	1	*2-112	-1.5
1931	Bro-N	74	181	26	48	6	1	1	21	23	16	.265	.351	.326	84	-3	5			.946	-3	2-43,S-10/3-5	-0.4
1932	Bro-N	3	1	0	0	0	0	0	0	0	0	.000	.000	.000	-99	-0	0			.000	0	H	0.0
1934	NY-N	1	1	0	0	0	0	0	0	0	0	.000	.000	.000	-99	-0	0			.000	0	H	0.0
Total	9	669	2560	400	762	149	34	13	249	215	143	.298	.353	.398	88	-45	69	1		.962	10	2-622/S-10,3-5	-0.9

■ MILT THOMPSON

Thompson, Milton Bernard b: 1/5/59, Washington, D.C. BL/TR, 5'11", 170 lbs. Deb: 9/4/84

YEAR	TM/L	G	AB	R	H	2B	3B	HR	RBI	BB	SO	AVG	OBP	SLG	PRO+	BR/A	SB	CS	SBR	FA	FR	G/POS	TPR
1984	Atl-N	25	99	16	30	1	0	2	4	11	11	.303	.373	.374	103	1	14	2	3	.956	3	O-25	0.6
1985	Atl-N	73	182	17	55	7	2	0	6	7	36	.302	.339	.363	91	-2	9	4	0	.964	-5	O-49	-0.9
1986	Phi-N	96	299	38	75	7	1	6	23	26	62	.251	.313	.341	78	-9	19	4	3	.991	4	O-89	-0.5
1987	Phi-N	150	527	86	159	26	9	7	43	42	87	.302	.353	.425	102	2	46	10	8	.989	9	*O-146	1.3
1988	Phi-N	122	378	53	109	16	2	2	33	39	59	.288	.356	.357	103	3	17	9	-0	.983	5	*O-112	0.4
1989	StL-N	155	545	60	158	28	8	4	68	39	91	.290	.342	.393	106	4	27	8	3	.978	2	*O-147	0.7
1990	StL-N	135	418	42	91	14	7	6	30	39	60	.218	.292	.328	70	-17	25	5	5	.971	-4	*O-116	-2.0
1991	StL-N	115	326	55	100	16	5	6	34	32	53	.307	.369	.442	126	11	16	9	-1	.991	9	O-91	1.9
1992	StL-N	109	208	31	61	9	1	4	17	16	39	.293	.350	.404	116	4	18	6	2	.974	-3	O-45	0.2
1993	*Phi-N	129	340	42	89	14	2	4	44	40	57	.262	.343	.350	87	-5	9	4	0	.994	-3	*O-106	-1.0
1994	Phi-N	87	220	29	60	7	0	3	30	23	28	.273	.350	.345	80	-6	7	2	1	1.000	-6	O-79	-1.2
	Hou-N	9	21	5	6	0	0	1	3	1	2	.286	.318	.429	97	-0	2	0	1	1.000	-0	/O-6	0.0
	Yr	96	241	34	66	7	0	4	33	24	30	.274	.347	.353	82	-6	9	2	2	1.000	-6	O-85	-1.2
1995	Hou-N	92	132	14	29	9	0	2	19	14	37	.220	.299	.333	71	-6	4	2	0	.979	-3	O-34	-0.9
1996	LA-N	48	51	2	6	1	0	0	1	6	10	.118	.211	.137	-6	-8	1	1	-0	1.000	-3	O-17	-1.1
	Col-N	14	15	1	1	1	0	0	2	1	3	.067	.125	.133	-26	-3	0	0	0	1.000	0	/O-1	-0.3
	Yr	62	66	3	7	2	0	0	3	7	13	.106	.192	.136	-12	-11	1	1	-0	1.000	-3	O-18	-1.4
Total	13	1359	3761	491	1029	156	37	47	357	336	635	.274	.337	.372	94	-31	214	66	25	.984	4	*O-1063	-2.8

■ ROBBY THOMPSON

Thompson, Robert Randall b: 5/10/62, W.Palm Beach, Fla. BR/TR, 5'11", 170 lbs. Deb: 4/8/86

YEAR	TM/L	G	AB	R	H	2B	3B	HR	RBI	BB	SO	AVG	OBP	SLG	PRO+	BR/A	SB	CS	SBR	FA	FR	G/POS	TPR
1986	SF-N	149	549	73	149	27	3	7	47	42	112	.271	.329	.370	97	-3	12	15	-5	.976	1	*2-149/S-1	-0.2
1987	*SF-N	132	420	62	110	26	5	10	44	40	91	.262	.338	.419	104	2	16	11	-2	.972	6	*2-126	1.2
1988	SF-N†	138	477	66	126	24	6	7	48	40	111	.264	.326	.384	108	4	14	5	1	.978	-9	*2-134	0.2
1989	*SF-N	148	547	91	132	26	**11**	13	50	51	133	.241	.321	.400	108	5	12	2	2	.989	5	*2-148	1.8
1990	SF-N	144	498	67	122	22	3	15	56	34	96	.245	.301	.392	92	-7	14	4	2	.989	**28**	*2-142	2.6
1991	SF-N	144	492	74	129	24	5	19	48	63	95	.262	.353	.447	128	18	14	7	0	.985	10	*2-144	3.2
1992	SF-N	128	443	54	115	25	1	14	49	43	75	.260	.336	.415	118	10	5	9	-4	.978	20	*2-120	3.1
1993	SF-N†	128	494	85	154	30	2	19	65	45	97	.312	.377	.496	136	25	10	4	1	.988	11	*2-128	3.9
1994	SF-N	35	129	13	27	8	2	2	7	15	32	.209	.292	.349	69	-6	3	1	0	.989	4	2-35	0.0
1995	SF-N	95	336	51	75	15	0	8	23	42	76	.223	.317	.339	75	-12	1	2	-1	.993	-16	2-91	-2.3
1996	SF-N	63	227	35	48	11	1	5	21	24	69	.211	.301	.335	70	-10	2	2	-1	.976	-10	2-62	-1.6
Total	11	1304	4612	671	1187	238	39	119	458	439	987	.257	.331	.403	105	27	103	62	-6	.983	50	*2-1279/S-1	11.9

■ TOMMY THOMPSON

Thompson, Rupert Lockhart b: 5/19/10, Elkhart, Ill. d: 5/24/71, Auburn, Cal. BL/TR, 5'9.5", 155 lbs. Deb: 9/3/33

YEAR	TM/L	G	AB	R	H	2B	3B	HR	RBI	BB	SO	AVG	OBP	SLG	PRO+	BR/A	SB	CS	SBR	FA	FR	G/POS	TPR
1933	Bos-N	24	97	6	18	1	0	0	6	4	6	.186	.218	.196	21	-10	0			1.000	2	O-24	-1.0
1934	Bos-N	105	343	40	91	12	3	0	37	13	19	.265	.300	.318	71	-15	2			.964	10	O-82	-0.8
1935	Bos-N	112	297	34	81	7	1	4	30	36	17	.273	.353	.343	96	-1	2			.965	1	O-85	-0.2
1936	Bos-N	106	266	37	76	9	0	4	36	31	12	.286	.362	.365	103	2	3			1.000	0	O-39,1-25	-0.2
1938	Chi-A	19	18	2	2	0	0	0	2	1	2	.111	.158	.111	-31	-4	0	0	0	1.000	-0	/1-1	-0.3
1939	Chi-A	1	0	0	0	0	0	0	1	0	0	—	—	—	—	-0	0	0	0	.000	0	H	0.0
	StL-A	30	86	23	26	5	0	1	7	23	7	.302	.455	.395	117	4	0	0	0	.977	-0	O-23	0.3
	Yr	31	86	23	26	5	0	1	8	23	7	.302	.455	.395	117	4	0	0	0	.977	-0	O-23	0.3
Total	6	397	1107	142	294	34	4	9	119	108	63	.266	.335	.328	84	-23	7	0		.975	13	O-253/1-26	-2.2

■ RYAN THOMPSON

Thompson, Ryan Orlando b: 11/4/67, Chestertown, Md. BR/TR, 6'3", 200 lbs. Deb: 9/1/92

YEAR	TM/L	G	AB	R	H	2B	3B	HR	RBI	BB	SO	AVG	OBP	SLG	PRO+	BR/A	SB	CS	SBR	FA	FR	G/POS	TPR
1992	NY-N	30	108	15	24	7	1	3	10	8	24	.222	.276	.389	88	-2	2	2	-1	.988	0	O-29	-0.3
1993	NY-N	80	288	34	72	19	2	11	26	19	81	.250	.303	.444	98	-2	2	7	-4	.987	10	O-76	0.3
1994	NY-N	98	334	39	75	14	1	18	59	28	94	.225	.304	.434	90	-6	1	1	-0	.989	8	O-98	0.0
1995	NY-N	75	267	39	67	13	0	7	31	19	77	.251	.310	.378	83	-7	3	1	0	.985	8	O-74	0.0
1996	Cle-A	8	22	2	7	0	0	1	5	1	6	.318	.348	.455	101	0	0	0	0	1.000	-3	/O-8	-0.3
Total	5	291	1019	129	245	53	4	40	131	75	282	.240	.303	.418	91	-17	8	11	-4	.988	24	O-285	-0.3

■ SAM THOMPSON

Thompson, Samuel Luther "Big Sam" b: 3/5/1860, Danville, Ind. d: 11/7/22, Detroit, Mich. BL/TL, 6'2", 207 lbs. Deb: 7/2/1885 H

YEAR	TM/L	G	AB	R	H	2B	3B	HR	RBI	BB	SO	AVG	OBP	SLG	PRO+	BR/A	SB	CS	SBR	FA	FR	G/POS	TPR
1885	Det-N	63	254	58	77	11	9	7	44	16	22	.303	.344	.500	170	19				.885	7	O-62/3-1	2.2
1886	Det-N	122	503	101	156	18	13	8	89	35	31	.310	.355	.445	138	22	13			.945	10	*O-122	2.6
1887	*Det-N	127	545	118	**203**	29	**23**	10	**166**	32	19	.372	.416	**.565**	165	46	22			.909	7	*O-127	**4.2**
1888	Det-N	56	238	51	67	10	8	6	40	23	10	.282	.352	.466	159	16	5			.882	-7	O-56	0.7
1889	Phi-N	128	533	103	158	36	4	**20**	111	36	22	.296	.348	.492	123	11	24			.901	-7	*O-128	0.1
1890	Phi-N	132	549	116	**172**	**41**	9	4	102	42	29	.313	.371	.443	133	21	25			.939	2	*O-132	1.7
1891	Phi-N	133	554	108	163	23	10	7	90	52	20	.294	.363	.410	122	15	29			.937	19	*O-133	2.6
1892	Phi-N	153	609	109	186	28	11	9	104	59	19	.305	.377	.432	145	33	28			.937	4	*O-153	2.8
1893	Phi-N	131	600	130	**222**	**37**	13	11	126	50	17	.370	.424	.530	153	44	18			.931	-11	*O-131/1-1	2.2
1894	Phi-N	99	437	108	178	29	27	13	141	40	13	.407	.458	.686	177	53	24			**.977**	-4	*O-99	3.2
1895	Phi-N	119	538	131	211	45	21	**18**	**165**	31	11	.392	.430	**.654**	177	56	27			.943	12	*O-118	4.7
1896	Phi-N	119	517	103	154	28	7	12	100	28	13	.298	.341	.449	109	4	12			**.974**	18	*O-119	1.0
1897	Phi-N	3	13	2	3	0	1	0	3	1		.231	.286	.385	78	-0	0			.833	0	/O-3	-0.1

YEAR	TM/L	G	AB	R	H	2B	3B	HR	RBI	BB	SO	AVG	OBP	SLG	PRO+	BR/A	SB	CS	SBR	FA	FR	G/POS	TPR
1898	Phi-N	14	63	14	22	5	3	1	15	4		.349	.388	.571	182	6	2			1.000	2	O-14	0.7
1906	Det-A	8	31	4	7	0	1	0	3	1		.226	.250	.290	67	-1	0			1.000	-0	/O-8	-0.2
Total	15	1407	5984	1256	1979	340	160	126	1299	450	226	.331	.384	.504	146	343	229			.935	53	*O-1405/1-1,3-1	28.4

■ SCOT THOMPSON

Thompson, Vernon Scot b: 12/7/55, Grove City, Pa. BL/TL, 6'3", 195 lbs. Deb: 9/3/78

YEAR	TM/L	G	AB	R	H	2B	3B	HR	RBI	BB	SO	AVG	OBP	SLG	PRO+	BR/A	SB	CS	SBR	FA	FR	G/POS	TPR
1978	Chi-N	19	36	7	15	3	0	0	2	2	4	.417	.447	.500	147	2	0	0	0	1.000	-2	/O-5,1-2	0.0
1979	Chi-N	128	346	36	100	13	5	2	29	17	37	.289	.324	.373	82	-9	4	3	-1	.971	-9	*O-100	-2.3
1980	Chi-N	102	226	26	48	10	1	2	13	28	31	.212	.302	.292	62	-11	6	6	-2	.963	-6	O-66,1-12	-2.2
1981	Chi-N	57	115	8	19	5	0	0	8	7	8	.165	.213	.209	19	-12	2	0	1	.980	-5	O-30/1-3	-1.9
1982	Chi-N	49	74	11	27	5	1	0	7	5	4	.365	.405	.459	138	4	0	1	-1	1.000	-1	O-23/1-4	0.2
1983	Chi-N	53	88	4	17	3	1	0	10	3	14	.193	.220	.250	28	-9	0	0	0	1.000	-5	O-29/1-1	-1.5
1984	SF-N	120	245	30	75	7	1	1	31	30	26	.306	.382	.355	112	5	5	3	-0	.998	-1	1-87/O-6	0.0
1985	SF-N	64	111	8	23	5	0	0	6	2	10	.207	.221	.252	34	-10	0	0	0	.995	2	1-24	-1.0
	Mon-N	34	32	2	9	1	0	0	4	3	7	.281	.343	.313	90	-0	0	0	0	1.000	-0	/1-3,O-3	-0.1
	Yr	98	143	10	32	6	0	0	10	5	17	.224	.250	.266	47	-10	0	0	0	.995	2	1-27/O-3	-1.1
Total	8	626	1273	132	333	52	9	5	110	97	141	.262	.315	.328	76	-40	17	13	-3	.973	-27	O-262,1-136	-8.8

■ BOBBY THOMSON

Thomson, Robert Brown "The Staten Island Scot" b: 10/25/23, Glasgow, Scotland BR/TR, 6'2", 185 lbs. Deb: 9/9/46

YEAR	TM/L	G	AB	R	H	2B	3B	HR	RBI	BB	SO	AVG	OBP	SLG	PRO+	BR/A	SB	CS	SBR	FA	FR	G/POS	TPR
1946	NY-N	18	54	8	17	4	1	2	9	4	5	.315	.362	.537	152	3	0			.935	0	3-16	0.4
1947	NY-N	138	545	105	154	26	5	29	85	40	78	.283	.336	.508	121	13	1			.980	9	*O-127/2-9	1.5
1948	NY-N★	138	471	75	117	20	2	16	63	30	77	.248	.296	.401	87	-11	2			.970	6	*O-125	-1.1
1949	NY-N★	156	641	99	198	35	9	27	109	44	45	.309	.355	.518	132	26	10			.982	20	*O-156	3.6
1950	NY-N	149	563	79	142	22	7	25	85	55	45	.252	.324	.449	101	-1	3			.978	10	*O-149	0.3
1951	*NY-N	148	518	89	152	27	8	32	101	73	57	.293	.385	.562	150	36	5	5	-2	.966	-11	O-77,3-69	2.0
1952	NY-N★	153	608	89	164	29	**14**	24	108	52	74	.270	.331	.482	122	16	5	2	0	.940	-7	3-91,O-63	0.5
1953	NY-N	154	608	80	175	22	6	26	106	43	57	.288	.338	.472	106	4	4	2	0	.983	3	*O-154	0.1
1954	Mil-N	43	99	7	23	3	0	2	15	12	29	.232	.315	.323	71	-4	0	0	0	.980	1	O-26	-0.5
1955	Mil-N	101	343	40	88	12	3	12	56	34	52	.257	.324	.414	99	-1	2	1	0	.969	0	O-91	-0.5
1956	Mil-N	142	451	59	106	10	4	20	74	43	75	.235	.304	.408	95	-5	2	4	-2	.974	-4	*O-136/3-3	-1.7
1957	Mil-N	41	148	15	35	5	3	4	23	8	27	.236	.285	.392	86	-4	2	1	0	.988	-1	O-38	-0.7
	NY-N	81	215	24	52	7	4	8	38	19	39	.242	.303	.423	93	-3	1	2	-1	.992	-4	O-71/3-1	-1.1
	Yr	122	363	39	87	12	7	12	61	27	66	.240	.296	.410	90	-6	3	3	-1	.990	-5	*O-109/3-1	-1.8
1958	Chi-N	152	547	67	155	27	5	21	82	56	76	.283	.354	.466	117	13	0	2	-1	.989	4	*O-148/3-4	0.8
1959	Chi-N	122	374	55	97	15	2	11	52	35	50	.259	.326	.398	93	-4	1	0	0	.987	-7	*O-116	-1.6
1960	Bos-A	40	114	12	30	3	1	5	20	11	15	.263	.328	.439	102	0	0	1	-1	.971	2	O-27/1-1	0.0
	Bal-A	3	6	0	0	0	0	0	0	0	3	.000	.000	.000	-99	-2	0	0	0	.000	-1	/O-2	-0.3
	Yr	43	120	12	30	3	1	5	20	11	18	.250	.313	.417	93	-2	0	1	-1	.971	1	O-29/1-1	-0.3
Total	15	1779	6305	903	1705	267	74	264	1026	559	804	.270	.333	.462	111	77	38	20		.980	20	*O-1506,3-184/2-9,1	1.7

■ DICKIE THON

Thon, Richard William b: 6/20/58, South Bend, Ind. BR/TR, 5'11", 175 lbs. Deb: 5/22/79

YEAR	TM/L	G	AB	R	H	2B	3B	HR	RBI	BB	SO	AVG	OBP	SLG	PRO+	BR/A	SB	CS	SBR	FA	FR	G/POS	TPR
1979	*Cal-A	35	56	6	19	3	0	0	8	5	10	.339	.393	.393	117	2	0	0	0	.923	3	2-24/S-8,3-1,D-1	0.5
1980	Cal-A	80	267	32	68	12	2	0	15	10	28	.255	.284	.315	65	-13	7	5	-1	.928	-12	S-22,2-21,D-15,3/1	-2.3
1981	*Hou-N	49	95	13	26	6	0	0	3	9	13	.274	.337	.337	96	-0	6	1	1	.950	-5	2-28,S-13/3-5	-0.3
1982	Hou-N	136	496	73	137	31	**10**	3	36	37	48	.276	.328	.397	110	5	37	8	6	.975	5	*S-119/3-8,2-1	2.9
1983	Hou-N★	154	619	81	177	28	9	20	79	54	73	.286	.345	.457	128	21	34	16	1	.966	21	*S-154	5.9
1984	Hou-N	5	17	3	6	0	1	0	1	0	4	.353	.389	.471	151	1	0	1	-1	1.000	-0	/S-5	0.1
1985	Hou-N	84	251	26	63	6	1	6	29	18	50	.251	.301	.355	85	-5	8	3	1	.967	7	S-79	0.9
1986	*Hou-N	106	278	24	69	13	1	3	21	29	49	.248	.319	.335	83	-6	6	5	-1	.972	-2	*S-104	-0.3
1987	Hou-N	32	66	6	14	1	0	1	3	16	13	.212	.366	.273	75	-2	3	0	1	.925	-8	S-31	-0.7
1988	SD-N	95	258	36	68	12	2	1	18	33	49	.264	.349	.337	100	1	19	4	3	.954	-20	S-70/2-2,3-1	-1.1
1989	Phi-N	136	435	45	118	18	4	15	60	33	81	.271	.323	.434	115	7	6	3	0	.972	16	*S-129	3.4
1990	Phi-N	149	552	54	141	20	4	8	48	37	77	.255	.306	.350	80	-15	12	5	1	.964	3	*S-148	0.0
1991	Phi-N	146	539	44	136	18	4	9	44	25	84	.252	.285	.351	79	-16	11	5	0	.969	-8	*S-146	-1.4
1992	Tex-A	95	275	30	68	15	3	4	37	20	40	.247	.298	.367	89	-5	12	2	2	.958	0	S-87	0.3
1993	Mil-A	85	245	23	66	10	1	1	33	22	39	.269	.330	.331	79	-7	6	5	-1	.966	-11	S-28,3-25,2-22,D-14	-1.7
Total	15	1387	4449	496	1176	193	42	71	435	348	658	.264	.319	.374	95	-33	167	63	12	.965	-13	*S-1143/2-98,3D1	6.2

■ JACK THONEY

Thoney, John "Bullet Jack" (b: John Thoeny) b: 12/8/1879, Ft.Thomas, Ky. d: 10/24/48, Covington, Ky. BR/TR, 5'10", 175 lbs. Deb: 4/26/02

YEAR	TM/L	G	AB	R	H	2B	3B	HR	RBI	BB	SO	AVG	OBP	SLG	PRO+	BR/A	SB	CS	SBR	FA	FR	G/POS	TPR
1902	Cle-A	28	105	14	30	7	1	0	11	9		.286	.342	.371	102	0	4			.891	-15	2-14,S-11/O-2	-1.3
	Bal-A	3	11	1	0	0	0	0	0	1		.000	.083	.000	-72	-3	1			.778	-2	/3-3	-0.4
	Yr	31	116	15	30	7	1	0	11	10		.259	.317	.336	84	-2	5			.891	-17	2-14,S-11/3-3,O-2	-1.7
1903	Cle-A	32	122	10	25	3	0	1	9	2		.205	.218	.254	42	-9	7			.889	1	O-24/2-5,3-2	-0.9
1904	Was-A	17	70	6	21	3	0	0	6	1		.300	.310	.343	108	0	2			.860	2	O-17	0.1
	NY-A	36	128	17	24	4	2	0	12	8		.188	.241	.250	53	-7	9			.826	1	3-26,O-10	-0.7
	Yr	53	198	23	45	7	2	0	18	9		.227	.264	.283	71	-7	11			.886	3	O-27,3-26	-0.6
1908	Bos-A	109	416	58	106	5	9	2	30	13		.255	.282	.325	94	-4	16			.948	8	*O-101	0.0
1909	Bos-A	13	40	1	5	1	0	0	3	2		.125	.167	.150	0	-5	2			.960	1	O-10	-0.4
1911	Bos-A	26	20	5	5	0	0	0	2	0		.250	.250	.250	40	-2	1			.000	0	H	-0.2
Total	6	264	912	112	216	23	12	3	73	36		.237	.269	.298	75	-27	42			.929	-4	O-164/3-31,2-19,S	-3.8

■ ANDY THORNTON

Thornton, Andre b: 8/13/49, Tuskegee, Ala. BR/TR, 6'2", 205 lbs. Deb: 7/28/73

YEAR	TM/L	G	AB	R	H	2B	3B	HR	RBI	BB	SO	AVG	OBP	SLG	PRO+	BR/A	SB	CS	SBR	FA	FR	G/POS	TPR
1973	Chi-N	17	35	3	7	3	0	0	2	7	9	.200	.333	.286	68	-1	0	0	0	.989	2	/1-9	0.0
1974	Chi-N	107	303	41	79	16	4	10	46	48	50	.261	.369	.439	120	9	2	1	0	.992	8	1-90/3-1	1.2
1975	Chi-N	120	372	70	109	21	4	18	60	88	63	.293	.433	.516	156	32	3	2	-0	.988	3	*1-113/3-2	2.8
1976	Chi-N	27	85	8	17	6	0	2	14	20	14	.200	.364	.341	93	-0	2	0	1	.987	1	1-25	0.0
	Mon-N	69	183	20	35	5	2	9	24	28	32	.191	.308	.388	93	-2	2	1	0	.994	-0	1-43,O-11	-0.6
	Yr	96	268	28	52	11	2	11	38	48	46	.194	.327	.373	93	-2	4	1	1	.991	1	1-68,O-11	-0.6
1977	Cle-A	131	433	77	114	20	5	28	70	70	82	.263	.379	.527	149	30	3	4	-2	.995	-3	*1-117/D-9	1.9
1978	Cle-A	145	508	97	133	22	4	33	105	93	72	.262	.382	.516	152	37	4	7	-3	.995	5	*1-145	3.0
1979	Cle-A	143	515	89	120	31	1	26	93	90	93	.233	.351	.449	114	11	5	4	-1	.994	-3	*1-130,D-13	-0.1
1981	Cle-A	69	226	22	54	12	0	6	30	23	37	.239	.309	.372	97	-1	3	1	0	.986	-1	D-53,1-11	-0.4
1982	Cle-A★	161	589	90	161	26	1	32	116	109	81	.273	.389	.484	139	34	6	7	-2	1.000	0	*D-152/1-8	2.5
1983	Cle-A	141	508	78	143	27	1	17	77	87	72	.281	.389	.439	123	18	4	2	0	.991	2	*D-114,1-27	1.4
1984	Cle-A★	155	587	91	159	26	0	33	99	91	79	.271	.371	.484	132	27	6	5	-1	.979	0	*D-144,1-11	2.1
1985	Cle-A	124	461	49	109	13	0	22	88	47	75	.236	.307	.408	94	-4	3	2	-0	.000	0	*D-122	-0.7
1986	Cle-A	120	401	49	92	14	0	17	66	65	67	.229	.338	.392	100	1	4	1	1	.000	0	*D-110	0.1
1987	Cle-A	36	85	8	10	2	0	0	5	10	25	.118	.211	.141	-4	-13	1	0	0	.000	0	D-21	-1.3
Total	14	1565	5291	792	1342	244	22	253	895	876	851	.254	.364	.452	123	177	48	37	-8	.992	14	D-738,1-729/O-11,3	11.7

■ JOHN THORNTON

Thornton, John b: 1870, Washington, D.C. 5'10.5", 175 lbs. Deb: 8/14/1889

YEAR	TM/L	G	AB	R	H	2B	3B	HR	RBI	BB	SO	AVG	OBP	SLG	PRO+	BR/A	SB	CS	SBR	FA	FR	G/POS	TPR
1889	Was-N	1	4	0	0	0	0	0	1	0	1	.000	.000	.000	-99	-1	0			1.000	-0	/P-1	0.0
1891	Phi-N	39	123	7	17	3	0	0	6	2	10	.138	.152	.163	-8	-17	1			.881	-0	P-37/O-3	-0.2
1892	Phi-N	5	13	1	5	0	0	0	2	0	0	.385	.385	.385	133	0	0			.857	-1	/P-3,O-2	-0.1
	StL-N	1	3	0	0	0	0	0	0	0	2	.000	.000	.000	-99	-1	0			.000	-0	/O-1	-0.1
	Yr	6	16	1	5	0	0	0	2	0	2	.313	.313	.313	90	-0	0			.500	-1	/P-3,O-3	-0.2
Total	3	46	143	8	22	3	0	0	9	2	13	.154	.166	.175	-1	-18	1			.881	-1	/P-41,O-6	-0.4

■ LOU THORNTON

Thornton, Louis b: 4/26/63, Montgomery, Ala. BL/TR, 6'2", 185 lbs. Deb: 4/8/85

YEAR	TM/L	G	AB	R	H	2B	3B	HR	RBI	BB	SO	AVG	OBP	SLG	PRO+	BR/A	SB	CS	SBR	FA	FR	G/POS	TPR
1985	*Tor-A	56	72	18	17	1	1	1	8	2	24	.236	.267	.319	58	-4	1	0	0	.957	-7	O-35,D-16	-1.1
1987	Tor-A	12	2	5	1	0	0	0	0	1	0	.500	.667	.500	212	0	0	1	-1	.000	-2	/O-4,D-6	-0.2
1988	Tor-A	11	2	1	0	0	0	0	0	0	0	.000	.000	.000	-99	-1	0	0	0	1.000	-4	O-10/D-1	-0.5

YEAR	TM/L	G	AB	R	H	2B	3B	HR	RBI	BB	SO	AVG	OBP	SLG	PRO+	BR/A	SB	CS	SBR	FA	FR	G/POS	TPR
1989	NY-N	13	13	5	4	1	0	0	1	0	1	.308	.308	.385	102	-0	2	0	1	1.000	-1	/O-6	0.0
1990	NY-N	3	0	0	0	0	0	0	0	0	0	—	—	—	—	0	0	0	0	1.000	0	/O-2	-0.1
Total	5	95	89	29	22	2	1	1	9	3	25	.247	.280	.326	65	-4	3	1	0	.965	-13	/O-57,D-23	-1.9

■ OTIS THORNTON
Thornton, Otis Benjamin b: 6/30/45, Docena, Ala. BR/TR, 6'1", 186 lbs. Deb: 7/6/73

YEAR	TM/L	G	AB	R	H	2B	3B	HR	RBI	BB	SO	AVG	OBP	SLG	PRO+	BR/A	SB	CS	SBR	FA	FR	G/POS	TPR
1973	Hou-N	2	3	0	0	0	0	0	1	0	2	.000	.000	.000	-99	-1	0	0	0	1.000	0	/C-2	-0.1

■ WALTER THORNTON
Thornton, Walter Miller b: 2/18/1875, Lewiston, Maine d: 7/14/60, Los Angeles, Cal. BL/TL, 6'1", 180 lbs. Deb: 7/1/1895

YEAR	TM/L	G	AB	R	H	2B	3B	HR	RBI	BB	SO	AVG	OBP	SLG	PRO+	BR/A	SB	CS	SBR	FA	FR	G/POS	TPR
1895	Chi-N	8	22	4	7	1	0	1	7	3	1	.318	.400	.500	123	1	0			.900	-1	/P-7,1-1	0.0
1896	Chi-N	9	22	6	8	0	1	0	1	5	2	.364	.481	.455	142	2	2			.800	-1	/P-5,O-3	0.0
1897	Chi-N	75	265	39	85	9	6	0	55	30		.321	.402	.400	108	4	13			.781	-11	O-59,P-16	-1.0
1898	Chi-N	62	210	34	62	5	2	0	14	22		.295	.362	.338	101	1	8			.877	-3	O-34,P-28	-0.3
Total	4	154	519	83	162	15	9	1	77	60	3	.312	.390	.382	108	7	23			.821	-15	/O-96,P-56,1-1	-1.3

■ BOB THORPE
Thorpe, Benjamin Robert b: 11/19/26, Caryville, Fla. d: 10/30/96, Waveland, Miss. BR/TR, 6'1.5", 190 lbs. Deb: 4/19/51

YEAR	TM/L	G	AB	R	H	2B	3B	HR	RBI	BB	SO	AVG	OBP	SLG	PRO+	BR/A	SB	CS	SBR	FA	FR	G/POS	TPR
1951	Bos-N	2	2	1	1	0	1	0	1	0	0	.500	.500	1.500	448	1	0	0	0	.000	0	H	0.1
1952	Bos-N	81	292	20	76	8	2	3	26	5	42	.260	.275	.332	70	-13	3	1	0	.972	0	O-72	-1.6
1953	Mil-N	27	37	1	6	1	0	0	5	1	6	.162	.184	.189	-3	-6	0	1	-1	1.000	-5	O-18	-1.1
Total	3	110	331	22	83	9	3	3	32	6	48	.251	.266	.323	64	-17	3	2	-0	.975	-5	/O-90	-2.6

■ JIM THORPE
Thorpe, James Francis b: 5/28/1887, Prague, Okla. d: 3/28/53, Long Beach, Cal. BR/TR, 6'1", 185 lbs. Deb: 4/14/13

YEAR	TM/L	G	AB	R	H	2B	3B	HR	RBI	BB	SO	AVG	OBP	SLG	PRO+	BR/A	SB	CS	SBR	FA	FR	G/POS	TPR
1913	NY-N	19	35	6	5	0	0	1	2	1	9	.143	.167	.229	12	-4	2			.944	-1	/O-9	-0.5
1914	NY-N	30	31	5	6	1	0	0	2	0	4	.194	.194	.226	25	-3	1			.750	-2	/O-4	-0.5
1915	NY-N	17	52	8	12	3	1	0	1	2	16	.231	.259	.327	82	-1	4	2	0	.933	-2	O-15	-0.5
1917	Cin-N	77	251	29	62	2	8	4	36	6	35	.247	.267	.367	98	-2	11			.962	2	O-69	-0.5
	*NY-N	26	57	12	11	3	2	0	4	8	10	.193	.303	.316	93	-0	1			.939	-3	O-18	-0.5
	Yr	103	308	41	73	5	10	4	40	14	45	.237	.275	.357	97	-2	12			.958	-1	O-87	-1.0
1918	NY-N	58	113	15	28	4	4	1	11	4	18	.248	.286	.381	105	0	3			.983	-12	O-44	-1.5
1919	NY-N	2	3	0	1	0	0	0	1	0	0	.333	.333	.333	102	-0	0			1.000	-1	/O-2	-0.1
	Bos-N	60	156	16	51	7	3	1	25	6	30	.327	.360	.429	143	7	7			.926	-7	O-38/1-2	-0.2
	Yr	62	159	16	52	7	3	1	26	6	30	.327	.359	.428	142	7	7			.928	-7	O-40/1-2	-0.3
Total	6	289	698	91	176	20	18	7	82	27	122	.252	.286	.362	99	-3	29	2		.951	-25	O-199/1-2	-4.3

■ BUCK THRASHER
Thrasher, Frank Edward b: 8/6/1889, Watkinsville, Ga. d: 6/12/38, Cleveland, Ohio BL/TR, 5'11", 182 lbs. Deb: 9/27/16

YEAR	TM/L	G	AB	R	H	2B	3B	HR	RBI	BB	SO	AVG	OBP	SLG	PRO+	BR/A	SB	CS	SBR	FA	FR	G/POS	TPR
1916	Phi-A	7	29	4	9	2	1	0	4	2	1	.310	.355	.448	148	1	0			1.000	-1	/O-7	0.0
1917	Phi-A	23	77	5	18	2	1	0	2	3	12	.234	.272	.286	71	-3	0			.938	-3	O-22	-0.8
Total	2	30	106	9	27	4	2	0	6	5	13	.255	.295	.330	92	-1	0			.951	-4	/O-29	-0.8

■ MARV THRONEBERRY
Throneberry, Marvin Eugene "Marvelous Marv"
b: 9/2/33, Collierville, Tenn. d: 6/23/94, Fisherville, Tenn. BL/TL, 6', 197 lbs. Deb: 9/25/55 F

YEAR	TM/L	G	AB	R	H	2B	3B	HR	RBI	BB	SO	AVG	OBP	SLG	PRO+	BR/A	SB	CS	SBR	FA	FR	G/POS	TPR
1955	NY-A	1	2	1	2	1	0	0	3	0	0	1.000	1.000	1.500	574	1	1	0	0	1.000	0	/1-1	0.2
1958	*NY-A	60	150	30	34	5	2	7	19	19	40	.227	.318	.427	107	1	1	1	-0	.991	-1	1-40/O-5	-0.3
1959	NY-A	80	192	27	46	5	0	8	22	18	51	.240	.305	.391	93	-2	0	0	0	.989	-1	1-54,O-13	-0.6
1960	KC-A	104	236	29	59	9	2	11	41	23	60	.250	.317	.445	103	0	0	0	0	.991	1	1-71	-0.4
1961	KC-A	40	130	17	31	2	1	6	24	19	30	.238	.336	.408	96	-1	0	0	0	.996	1	1-30,O-10	-0.2
	Bal-A	56	96	9	20	3	0	5	11	12	20	.208	.296	.396	86	-2	0	0	0	.923	-3	O-15,1-11	-0.6
	Yr	96	226	26	51	5	1	11	35	31	50	.226	.319	.403	93	-3	0	0	0	.991	-2	1-41,O-25	-0.8
1962	Bal-A	9	9	1	0	0	0	0	0	4	6	.000	.308	.000	-9	-1	0	0	0	1.000	-0	/O-2	-0.2
	NY-N	116	357	29	87	11	3	16	49	34	83	.244	.309	.426	94	-4	1	3	-2	.981	4	1-97	-0.8
1963	NY-N	14	14	0	2	1	0	0	1	1	5	.143	.200	.214	19	-1	0	0	0	1.000	-0	/1-3	-0.2
Total	7	480	1186	143	281	37	8	53	170	130	295	.237	.313	.416	96	-10	3	4	-2	.987	1	1-307/O-45	-3.1

■ FAYE THRONEBERRY
Throneberry, Maynard Faye b: 6/22/31, Fisherville, Tenn. BL/TR, 6', 190 lbs. Deb: 4/15/52 F

YEAR	TM/L	G	AB	R	H	2B	3B	HR	RBI	BB	SO	AVG	OBP	SLG	PRO+	BR/A	SB	CS	SBR	FA	FR	G/POS	TPR
1952	Bos-A	98	310	38	80	11	3	5	23	33	67	.258	.331	.361	86	-6	16	7	1	.955	-0	O-86	-0.9
1955	Bos-A	60	144	20	37	7	3	6	27	14	31	.257	.327	.472	104	-0	0	0	0	.960	1	O-34	-0.1
1956	Bos-A	24	50	6	11	2	0	1	3	3	16	.220	.264	.320	48	-4	0	0	0	.909	-2	O-13	-0.6
1957	Bos-A	1	1	0	0	0	0	0	0	0	1	.000	.000	.000	-95	-0	0	0	0	.000	0	H	0.0
	Was-A	68	195	21	36	8	2	2	12	17	37	.185	.254	.277	45	-15	0	1	-1	.983	-6	O-58	-2.6
	Yr	69	196	21	36	8	2	2	12	17	38	.184	.252	.276	45	-15	0	1	-1	.983	-6	O-58	-2.6
1958	Was-A	44	87	12	16	1	1	4	7	4	28	.184	.245	.356	64	-5	0	1	-1	1.000	-3	O-26	-1.0
1959	Was-A	117	327	36	82	11	2	10	42	33	61	.251	.325	.388	95	-2	6	4	-1	.953	-2	O-86	-0.8
1960	Was-A	85	157	18	39	7	1	1	23	18	33	.248	.330	.325	78	-4	1	1	-0	.947	-3	O-34	-1.0
1961	LA-A	24	31	1	6	1	0	0	0	5	10	.194	.306	.226	40	-3	0	0	0	1.000	1	/O-5	-0.2
Total	8	521	1302	152	307	48	12	29	137	127	284	.236	.309	.358	79	-39	23	14	-2	.962	-15	O-342	-7.2

■ GARY THURMAN
Thurman, Gary Montez b: 11/12/64, Indianapolis, Ind. BR/TR, 5'10", 175 lbs. Deb: 8/30/87

YEAR	TM/L	G	AB	R	H	2B	3B	HR	RBI	BB	SO	AVG	OBP	SLG	PRO+	BR/A	SB	CS	SBR	FA	FR	G/POS	TPR
1987	KC-A	27	81	12	24	2	0	0	5	8	20	.296	.360	.321	81	-2	7	2	1	.971	4	O-27	0.3
1988	KC-A	35	66	6	11	1	0	0	2	4	20	.167	.214	.182	12	-8	5	1	1	.949	-7	O-32/D-1	-1.5
1989	KC-A	72	87	24	17	2	1	0	5	15	26	.195	.314	.241	59	-4	16	0	5	.949	-17	O-60/D-4	-1.8
1990	KC-A	23	60	5	14	3	0	0	3	2	12	.233	.258	.283	52	-4	1	1	-0	1.000	-2	O-21	-0.7
1991	KC-A	80	184	24	51	9	0	2	13	11	42	.277	.321	.359	87	-3	15	5	2	.970	-5	O-72	-0.7
1992	KC-A	88	200	25	49	6	3	0	20	9	34	.245	.281	.305	62	-10	9	6	-1	.986	2	O-67/D-9	-1.0
1993	Det-A	75	89	22	19	2	2	0	13	11	30	.213	.300	.281	58	-5	7	0	2	.950	-12	O-53/D-9	-1.5
1995	Sea-A	13	25	3	8	2	0	0	3	1	3	.320	.346	.400	93	-0	5	2	0	1.000	-1	/O-9	-0.1
1997	NY-N	11	6	0	1	0	0	0	0	0	0	.167	.167	.167	-13	-1	0	1	-1	1.000	-3	/O-7	-0.4
Total	9	424	798	121	194	27	6	2	64	61	187	.243	.298	.299	65	-38	65	18	9	.971	-40	O-348/D-23	-7.4

■ BOB THURMAN
Thurman, Robert Burns b: 5/14/17, Wichita, Kan. BL/TL, 6'1", 205 lbs. Deb: 4/14/55

YEAR	TM/L	G	AB	R	H	2B	3B	HR	RBI	BB	SO	AVG	OBP	SLG	PRO+	BR/A	SB	CS	SBR	FA	FR	G/POS	TPR
1955	Cin-N	82	152	19	33	2	3	7	22	17	26	.217	.296	.408	80	-5	0	2	-1	.949	-4	O-36	-1.1
1956	Cin-N	80	139	25	41	5	2	8	22	10	14	.295	.342	.532	123	4	0	0	0	.953	-3	O-29	0.0
1957	Cin-N	74	190	38	47	4	2	16	40	15	33	.247	.306	.542	114	3	0	0	0	.987	-0	O-44	0.0
1958	Cin-N	94	178	23	41	7	4	4	20	20	38	.230	.322	.382	81	-5	1	2	-1	.976	2	O-41	-0.6
1959	Cin-N	4	4	1	1	0	0	0	2	0	1	.250	.250	.250	33	-0	0	0	0	.000	0	H	0.0
Total	5	334	663	106	163	18	11	35	106	62	112	.246	.315	.465	99	-3	1	4	-2	.970	-5	O-150	-1.7

■ EDDIE TIEMEYER
Tiemeyer, Edward Carl b: 5/9/1885, Cincinnati, Ohio d: 9/27/46, Cincinnati, Ohio BR/TR, 5'11.5", 185 lbs. Deb: 8/19/06

YEAR	TM/L	G	AB	R	H	2B	3B	HR	RBI	BB	SO	AVG	OBP	SLG	PRO+	BR/A	SB	CS	SBR	FA	FR	G/POS	TPR
1906	Cin-N	5	11	3	2	0	0	0	0	1		.182	.250	.182	33	-1	0			1.000	0	/3-3,P-1	0.0
1907	Cin-N	1	0	1	0	0	0	0	0	1		—	1.000	—	206	0	0			.000	0	H	0.0
1909	NY-A	3	8	1	3	1	0	0	0	1		.375	.444	.500	197	1	0			.962	-1	/1-3	0.0
Total	3	9	19	5	5	1	0	0	0	3		.263	.364	.316	110	0	0			.962	-0	/1-3,3-3,P-1	0.0

■ MIKE TIERNAN
Tiernan, Michael Joseph "Silent Mike" b: 1/21/1867, Trenton, N.J. d: 11/9/18, New York, N.Y. BL/TL, 5'11", 165 lbs. Deb: 4/30/1887

YEAR	TM/L	G	AB	R	H	2B	3B	HR	RBI	BB	SO	AVG	OBP	SLG	PRO+	BR/A	SB	CS	SBR	FA	FR	G/POS	TPR
1887	NY-N	103	407	82	117	13	12	10	62	32	31	.287	.344	.452	125	14	28			.865	-9	*O-103/P-5	0.3
1888	*NY-N	113	443	75	130	16	8	9	52	42	42	.293	.364	.427	153	28	52			**.960**	-0	*O-113	2.3
1889	*NY-N	122	499	**147**	167	23	14	10	73	**96**	32	.335	.447	.497	163	47	33			.896	-3	*O-122	3.5
1890	NY-N	133	553	132	168	25	21	**13**	59	68	53	.304	.385	**.495**	**156**	**38**	56			.896	-15	*O-133	1.6
1891	NY-N	134	542	111	166	30	12	**16**	73	69	32	.306	.388	.494	**163**	**43**	53			.901	-9	*O-134	2.7
1892	NY-N	116	450	79	129	16	10	5	66	57	46	.287	.369	.400	135	20	20			.899	-3	*O-116	1.0
1893	NY-N	125	511	114	158	19	12	14	102	72	24	.309	.399	.476	131	23	26			.927	-9	*O-125	0.6
1894	*NY-N	112	424	84	117	19	13	5	77	54	21	.276	.359	.417	87	-9	28			.922	-11	*O-111	-2.1
1895	NY-N	120	476	127	165	23	21	7	70	66	19	.347	.427	.527	149	36	36			.946	-5	*O-119	1.7
1896	NY-N	133	521	132	192	24	16	7	89	77	18	.369	.452	.516	159	48	35			.970	-2	*O-133	2.9

YEAR	TM/L	G	AB	R	H	2B	3B	HR	RBI	BB	SO	AVG	OBP	SLG	PRO+	BR/A	SB	CS	SBR	FA	FR	G/POS	TPR
1897	NY-N	127	528	123	174	29	10	5	72	61		.330	.400	.451	128	22	40			.931	-11	*O-127	0.2
1898	NY-N	103	415	90	116	15	11	5	49	43		.280	.357	.405	122	12	19			.973	-12	*O-103	-0.7
1899	NY-N	35	137	17	35	4	2	0	7	10		.255	.306	.314	73	-5	2			.938	-4	O-35	-1.1
Total	13	1476	5906	1313	1834	256	162	106	851	747	318	.311	.392	.463	138	314	428			.924	-92	*O-1474/P-5	12.9
■ **COTTON TIERNEY** Tierney, James Arthur b: 2/10/1894, Kansas City, Kan. d: 4/18/53, Kansas City, Mo. BR/TR, 5'8", 175 lbs. Deb: 9/23/20																							
1920	Pit-N	12	46	4	11	5	0	0	8	3	4	.239	.286	.348	79	-1	1	1	-0	.964	-2	2-10/S-2	-0.3
1921	Pit-N	117	442	49	132	22	8	3	52	24	31	.299	.338	.405	93	-5	4	6	-2	.965	-27	2-72,3-32/O-4,S-3	-3.0
1922	Pit-N	122	441	58	152	26	14	7	86	22	40	.345	.378	.515	127	16	7	8	-3	.964	-37	*2-105/O-2,S-1,3-1	-2.0
1923	Pit-N	29	120	22	35	5	2	2	23	2	10	.292	.309	.417	88	-3	2	1	0	.941	-3	2-29	-0.5
	Phi-N	121	480	68	152	31	1	11	65	24	42	.317	.352	.454	100	-2	3	4	-2	.975	18	*2-115/O-7,3-2	1.5
	Yr	150	600	90	187	36	3	13	88	26	52	.312	.343	.447	97	-4	5	5	-2	.968	15	*2-144/O-7,3-2	1.0
1924	Bos-N	136	505	38	131	16	1	6	58	22	37	.259	.296	.331	71	-22	11	8	-2	.964	-2	*2-115,3-22	-2.2
1925	Bro-N	93	265	27	68	14	4	2	39	12	23	.257	.294	.362	68	-13	0	3	-2	.963	-1	3-61/1-1,2-1	-1.1
Total	6	630	2299	266	681	119	30	31	331	109	187	.296	.332	.415	93	-29	28	31	-10	.966	-54	2-447,3-118/OS1	-7.6
■ **BILL TIERNEY** Tierney, William J. b: 5/14/1858, Boston, Mass. d: 9/21/1898, Boston, Mass. Deb: 5/2/1882																							
1882	Cin-a	1	5	1	0	0	0	0		0		.000	.000	.000	-95	-1				.917	0	/1-1	-0.1
1884	Bal-U	1	3	0	1	0	0	0		1		.333	.500	.333	142	0				1.000	-0	/O-1	0.0
Total	2	2	8	1	1	0	0	0		1		.125	.222	.125	13	-1				1.000	0	/O-1,1-1	-0.1
■ **JOHN TILLEY** Tilley, John C. b: New York, N.Y. BR , 5'7", 154 lbs. Deb: 8/23/1882																							
1882	Cle-N	15	56	2	5	1	1	0	4	2	11	.089	.121	.143	-16	-7				.857	2	O-15	-0.5
1884	Tol-a	17	56	5	10	2	0	0		4		.179	.246	.214	50	-3				.632	-4	O-17	-0.7
	StP-U	9	26	2	4	1	0	0		3		.154	.241	.192	61	-3				.938	0	/O-9	-0.3
Total	2	41	138	9	19	4	1	0	4	9	11	.138	.196	.181	23	-13				.818	-2	/O-41	-1.5
■ **BOB TILLMAN** Tillman, John Robert b: 3/24/37, Nashville, Tenn. BR/TR, 6'4", 205 lbs. Deb: 4/15/62																							
1962	Bos-A	81	249	28	57	6	4	14	38	19	65	.229	.286	.454	93	-4	0	0	0	.983	-4	C-66	-0.5
1963	Bos-A	96	307	24	69	10	2	8	32	34	64	.225	.304	.349	80	-8	0	0	0	.992	1	C-95	-0.4
1964	Bos-A	131	425	43	118	18	1	17	61	49	74	.278	.352	.445	114	9	0	0	0	.989	-8	*C-131	0.7
1965	Bos-A	111	368	20	79	10	3	6	35	40	69	.215	.292	.307	66	-16	0	0	0	.988	-7	*C-106	-1.8
1966	Bos-A	78	204	12	47	8	0	3	24	22	35	.230	.305	.314	71	-7	0	0	0	.990	-3	C-72	-0.7
1967	Bos-A	30	64	4	12	1	0	1	4	3	18	.188	.224	.250	37	-5	0	0	0	.977	2	C-26	-0.3
	NY-A	22	63	5	16	1	0	2	9	7	17	.254	.329	.365	109	1	0	0	0	.970	0	C-15	0.2
	Yr	52	127	9	28	2	0	3	13	10	35	.220	.277	.307	70	-5	0	0	0	.974	2	C-41	-0.1
1968	Atl-N	86	236	16	52	4	0	5	20	16	55	.220	.278	.301	74	-8	1	0	0	.990	-1	C-75	-0.4
1969	*Atl-N	69	190	18	37	5	0	12	29	18	47	.195	.264	.411	86	-4	0	0	0	.988	-10	C-69	-1.2
1970	Atl-N	71	223	19	53	5	0	11	30	20	66	.238	.300	.408	83	-6	0	0	0	.988	-2	C-70	-0.5
Total	9	775	2329	189	540	68	10	79	282	228	510	.232	.302	.371	85	-49	1	0	0	.988	-31	C-725	-4.9
■ **RUSTY TILLMAN** Tillman, Kerry Jerome b: 8/29/60, Jacksonville, Fla. BR/TR, 6', 185 lbs. Deb: 6/6/82																							
1982	NY-N	12	13	4	2	1	0	0	0	0	4	.154	.154	.231	6	-2	1	0	0	1.000	-1	/O-3	-0.2
1986	Oak-A	22	39	6	10	1	0	1	6	3	11	.256	.310	.359	88	-1	2	0	1	.952	-3	O-17	-0.4
1988	SF-N	4	4	1	1	0	0	1	3	2	1	.250	.500	1.000	335	1	0	0	0	1.000	-0	/O-1	0.1
Total	3	38	56	11	13	2	0	2	9	5	16	.232	.295	.375	88	-1	3	0	1	.958	-4	/O-21	-0.5
■ **OZZIE TIMMONS** Timmons, Osborne Llewellyn b: 9/18/70, Tampa, Fla. BR/TR, 6'2", 205 lbs. Deb: 4/26/95																							
1995	Chi-N	77	171	30	45	10	1	8	28	13	32	.263	.315	.474	107	1	3	0	1	.970	-6	O-55	-0.5
1996	Chi-N	65	140	18	28	4	0	7	16	15	30	.200	.282	.379	70	-6	1	0	0	1.000	-3	O-47	-1.0
1997	Cin-N	6	9	1	3	1	0	0	0	0	1	.333	.333	.444	100	-0	0	0	0	.000	-1	/O-1	-0.1
Total	3	148	320	49	76	15	1	15	44	28	63	.237	.301	.431	90	-5	4	0	1	.977	-10	O-103	-1.6
■ **BEN TINCUP** Tincup, Austin Ben b: 12/14/1890, Adair, Okla. d: 7/5/80, Claremore, Okla. BL/TR, 6'1", 180 lbs. Deb: 5/22/14 C																							
1914	Phi-N	31	53	3	9	1	1	0	1	0	18	.170	.170	.226	16	-6	0			.926	1	P-28	0.0
1915	Phi-N	11	9	1	0	0	0	0	0	0	3	.000	.000	.000	-99	-2	0			1.000	0	P-10	0.0
1916	Phi-N	1	1	0	0	0	0	0	0	0	0	.000	.000	.000	-97	-0	0			.000	0	H	0.0
1918	Phi-N	11	8	0	1	1	0	0	0	0	4	.125	.125	.250	13	-1	0			.800	1	/P-8,O-1	0.0
1928	Chi-N	2	3	0	0	0	0	0	0	0	0	.000	.000	.000	-99	-1	0			1.000	0	/P-2	0.0
Total	5	56	74	4	10	2	1	0	1	0	25	.135	.135	.189	-4	-10	0			.917	2	/P-48,O-1	0.0
■ **RON TINGLEY** Tingley, Ronald Irvin b: 5/27/59, Presque Isle, Maine BR/TR, 6'2", 194 lbs. Deb: 9/25/82																							
1982	SD-N	8	20	0	2	0	0	0	0	0	7	.100	.100	.100	-46	-4	0	0	0	.957	3	/C-8	-0.1
1988	Cle-A	9	24	1	4	0	0	1	2	2	8	.167	.231	.292	44	-2	0	0	0	1.000	3	/C-9	0.2
1989	Cal-A	4	3	0	1	0	0	0	0	1	0	.333	.500	.333	142	0	0	0	0	.889	0	/C-4	0.1
1990	Cal-A	5	3	0	0	0	0	0	0	1	1	.000	.250	.000	-25	-0	0	0	0	1.000	1	/C-5	0.0
1991	Cal-A	45	115	11	23	7	0	1	13	8	34	.200	.258	.287	51	-8	1	1	-0	.988	10	C-45	0.4
1992	Cal-A	71	127	15	25	2	1	3	8	13	35	.197	.282	.299	62	-6	0	1	-1	.987	11	C-69	0.7
1993	Cal-A	58	90	7	18	7	0	0	12	9	22	.200	.280	.278	49	-6	1	2	-1	.995	9	C-58	0.4
1994	Fla-N	19	52	4	9	3	1	1	2	5	18	.173	.246	.327	46	-4	0	0	0	.990	2	C-18	-0.1
	Chi-A	5	5	0	0	0	0	0	0	0	2	.000	.000	.000	-99	-1	0	0	0	1.000	1	/C-5	0.0
1995	Det-A	54	124	14	28	8	1	4	18	15	38	.226	.309	.403	84	-3	0	1	-1	.991	-5	C-53/1-1	-0.5
Total	9	278	563	52	110	27	3	10	55	54	165	.195	.271	.307	56	-35	2	5	-2	.989	37	C-274/1-1	1.1
■ **JOE TINKER** Tinker, Joseph Bert b: 7/27/1880, Muscotah, Kan. d: 7/27/48, Orlando, Fla. BR/TR, 5'9", 175 lbs. Deb: 4/17/02 MH																							
1902	Chi-N	131	494	55	129	19	5	2	54	26		.261	.298	.332	97	-3	27			.906	4	*S-124/3-8	0.9
1903	Chi-N	124	460	67	134	21	7	2	70	37		.291	.345	.380	110	5	27			.906	0	*S-107,3-19	1.0
1904	Chi-N	141	488	55	108	12	13	3	41	29		.221	.268	.318	80	-12	41			.925	19	*S-140/O-1	1.1
1905	Chi-N	149	547	70	135	18	8	2	66	34		.247	.292	.320	79	-15	31			.940	17	*S-149	0.5
1906	*Chi-N	148	523	75	122	18	4	1	64	43		.233	.293	.289	77	-14	30			**.944**	4	*S-147/3-1	-0.6
1907	*Chi-N	117	402	36	89	11	3	1	36	25		.221	.269	.271	65	-17	20			.939	16	*S-113	0.2
1908	*Chi-N	157	548	67	146	22	14	6	68	32		.266	.307	.391	117	8	30			**.958**	30	*S-157	4.8
1909	Chi-N	143	516	56	132	26	11	4	57	17		.256	.280	.372	100	-4	23			**.940**	20	*S-143	2.1
1910	*Chi-N	134	473	48	136	25	9	3	69	24	35	.288	.322	.397	110	3	20			.942	16	*S-132	2.5
1911	Chi-N	144	536	61	149	24	12	4	69	39	31	.278	.327	.390	100	-2	30			**.937**	**23**	*S-143	3.1
1912	Chi-N	142	550	80	155	24	7	0	75	38	21	.282	.331	.351	87	-11	25			.943	25	*S-142	2.6
1913	Cin-N	110	382	47	121	20	13	1	57	20	26	.317	.352	.445	127	12	10			.968	17	*S 101/3 9,M	**3.9**
1914	Chi-F	126	438	50	112	21	7	2	46	38	30	.256	.317	.349	86	-16	19			.947	19	*S-125,M	1.3
1915	Chi-F	31	67	7	18	2	1	0	9	13	5	.269	.387	.328	109	0	3			.914	-2	S-16/2-5,3-4,M	-0.1
1916	Chi-N	7	10	0	1	0	0	0	1	1	1	.100	.182	.100	-11	-1	0			.909	-0	/S-4,3-2,M	-0.2
Total	15	1804	6434	774	1687	263	114	31	782	416	149	.262	.308	.353	95	-66	336			.938	208	*S-1743/3-43,2-5,O	23.1
■ **LEE TINSLEY** Tinsley, Lee Owen b: 3/4/69, Shelbyville, Ky. BB/TR, 5'10", 185 lbs. Deb: 4/6/93																							
1993	Sea-A	11	19	2	3	1	0	1	2	2	9	.158	.238	.368	60	-1	0	0	0	.900	-1	/O-6,D-2	-0.2
1994	Bos-A	78	144	27	32	4	0	2	14	19	36	.222	.317	.292	56	-9	13	0	4	.991	-5	O-60,D-10	-1.1
1995	*Bos-A	100	341	61	97	17	1	7	41	39	74	.284	.360	.402	95	-2	18	8	1	.979	0	O-97	-0.4
1996	Phi-N	31	52	1	7	0	0	0	2	4	22	.135	.196	.135	-11	-8	2	4	-2	.960	-4	O-22	-1.5
	Bos-A	92	192	28	47	6	1	3	14	13	56	.245	.300	.333	59	-12	6	8	-3	.993	-6	O-83	-2.1
1997	Sea-A	49	122	12	24	6	2	0	6	11	34	.197	.263	.279	42	-10	2	0	1	1.000	-1	O-41/D-5	-1.1
Total	5	361	870	131	210	34	4	13	79	88	231	.241	.314	.334	66	-44	41	20	0	.985	-18	O-309/D-17	-6.4

YEAR	TM/L	G	AB	R	H	2B	3B	HR	RBI	BB	SO	AVG	OBP	SLG	PRO+	BR/A	SB	CS	SBR	FA	FR	G/POS	TPR
■ JIM TIPPER	Tipper, James b: 6/18/1849, Middletown, Conn. d: 4/21/1895, New Haven, Conn. 5'5.5", 148 lbs. Deb: 4/26/1872																						
1872	Man-n	24	112	23	31	5	1	0	15	0	0	.277	.277	.339	94	-0	0	0	0	.778	-1	O-19/3-5	0.0
1874	Har-n	45	197	36	60	8	0	0	19	1	7	.305	.308	.345	104	-0	0	1	-1	.812	-1	*O-45	0.0
1875	NH-n	41	159	10	25	1	0	0	4	1	6	.157	.162	.164	16	-12	1	0	0	.790	-3	O-41	-1.3
Total	3 n	110	468	69	116	14	1	0	38	2	13	.248	.251	.282	76	-12	1	1	-0	.799	-5	O-105/3-5	-1.3
■ ERIC TIPTON	Tipton, Eric Gordon "Dukie" or "Blue Devil" b: 4/20/15, Petersburg, Va. BR/TR, 5'11", 190 lbs. Deb: 6/9/39																						
1939	Phi-A	47	104	12	24	4	2	1	14	13	7	.231	.316	.337	68	-5	2	0	1	.942	-5	O-34	-1.0
1940	Phi-A	2	8	2	1	0	1	0	0	1	1	.125	.222	.375	53	-1	0	0	0	1.000	-0	/O-2	-0.1
1941	Phi-A	1	4	0	2	0	0	0	0	0	0	.500	.500	.500	169	0	0	0	0	1.000	-0	/O-1	0.0
1942	Cin-N	63	207	22	46	5	5	4	18	25	14	.222	.309	.353	94	-2	1			.977	-1	O-58	-0.6
1943	Cin-N	140	493	82	142	26	7	9	49	85	36	.288	.395	.424	138	27	1			.984	-1	*O-139	2.0
1944	Cin-N	140	479	62	144	28	3	3	36	59	32	.301	.380	.390	121	15	5			.983	3	*O-139	1.1
1945	Cin-N	108	331	32	80	17	1	5	34	40	37	.242	.327	.344	89	-5	11			.970	-1	O-83	-1.0
Total	7	501	1626	212	439	80	19	22	151	223	127	.270	.360	.383	112	30	20	0		.977	-6	O-456	0.4
■ JOE TIPTON	Tipton, Joe Hicks b: 2/18/22, McCaysville, Ga. d: 3/1/94, Birmingham, Ala. BR/TR, 5'11", 185 lbs. Deb: 5/2/48																						
1948	*Cle-A	47	90	11	26	3	0	1	13	4	10	.289	.333	.356	85	-2	0	0	0	.971	0	C-40	0.0
1949	Chi-A	67	191	20	39	5	3	3	19	27	17	.204	.306	.309	65	-10	1	1	-0	.992	2	C-53	-0.5
1950	Phi-A	64	184	15	49	5	1	6	20	19	16	.266	.335	.402	90	-3	0	0	0	.987	-4	C-59	-0.5
1951	Phi-A	72	213	23	51	9	0	3	20	51	25	.239	.389	.324	92	0	1	1	-0	.969	2	C-72	0.5
1952	Phi-A	23	68	6	13	4	0	3	8	15	10	.191	.337	.382	94	-0	0	0	0	.990	-2	C-23	-0.2
	Cle-A	43	105	15	26	2	0	6	22	21	21	.248	.383	.438	137	6	1	0	0	.971	-8	C-35	-0.1
	Yr	66	173	21	39	6	0	9	30	36	31	.225	.365	.416	119	5	1	0	0	.979	-11	C-58	-0.3
1953	Cle-A	47	109	17	25	2	0	6	13	19	13	.229	.359	.413	111	2	0	0	0	1.000	-7	C-46	-0.4
1954	Was-A	54	157	9	35	6	1	1	10	30	30	.223	.354	.293	83	-2	0	1	-1	.992	3	C-52	0.3
Total	7	417	1117	116	264	36	5	29	125	186	142	.236	.351	.355	91	-11	3	3	-1	.984	-14	C-380	-0.9
■ TOM TISCHINSKI	Tischinski, Thomas Arthur b: 7/12/44, Kansas City, Mo. BR/TR, 5'10", 190 lbs. Deb: 4/11/69																						
1969	Min-A	37	47	2	9	0	0	0	2	8	8	.191	.309	.191	42	-3	0	0	0	1.000	0	C-32	-0.3
1970	Min-A	24	46	6	9	0	0	1	2	9	6	.196	.327	.261	63	-2	0	0	0	.990	1	C-22	0.0
1971	Min-A	21	23	0	3	2	0	0	2	1	4	.130	.200	.217	18	-3	0	0	0	.982	3	C-21	0.1
Total	3	82	116	8	21	2	0	1	6	18	18	.181	.296	.224	46	-8	0	0	0	.992	4	/C-75	-0.2
■ JOHN TITUS	Titus, John Franklin "Silent John" b: 2/21/1876, St.Clair, Pa. d: 1/8/43, St.Clair, Pa. BL/TL, 5'9", 156 lbs. Deb: 6/8/03																						
1903	Phi-N	72	280	38	80	15	6	2	34	19		.286	.340	.404	115	5	5			.952	3	O-72	0.3
1904	Phi-N	146	504	60	148	25	5	4	55	46		.294	.362	.387	136	22	15			.952	8	*O-140	2.3
1905	Phi-N	147	548	99	169	36	14	2	89	69		.308	.397	.436	154	39	11			.962	9	*O-147	4.1
1906	Phi-N	145	484	67	129	22	5	1	57	78		.267	.378	.339	124	17	12			.974	7	*O-142	2.0
1907	Phi-N	145	523	72	144	23	12	3	63	47		.275	.345	.382	130	18	9			.928	-5	*O-142	0.9
1908	Phi-N	149	539	75	154	24	5	2	48	53		.286	.365	.360	127	18	27			.963	-3	*O-149	1.1
1909	Phi-N	151	540	69	146	22	6	3	46	66		.270	.367	.350	121	16	23			.971	5	*O-149	1.7
1910	Phi-N	143	535	91	129	26	5	3	35	93	44	.241	.358	.325	96	0	20			.976	1	*O-142	-0.6
1911	Phi-N	76	236	35	67	14	1	8	26	32	16	.284	.372	.453	129	9	3			.979	-1	O-60	0.5
1912	Phi-N	45	157	43	43	9	5	3	22	33	14	.274	.403	.452	125	6	6			.917	-7	O-42	-0.3
	Bos-N	96	345	56	112	23	6	2	48	49	20	.325	.422	.443	134	19	5			.965	-5	O-96	0.9
	Yr	141	502	99	155	32	11	5	70	82	34	.309	.416	.446	131	25	11			.952	-12	*O-138	0.6
1913	Bos-N	87	269	33	80	14	2	5	38	35	22	.297	.392	.420	129	12	4			.919	-7	O-75	0.2
Total	11	1402	4960	738	1401	253	72	38	561	620	116	.282	.373	.385	127	181	140			.959	7	*O-1356	13.1
■ JIM TOBIN	Tobin, James Anthony "Abba Dabba" b: 12/27/12, Oakland, Cal. d: 5/19/69, Oakland, Cal. BR/TR, 6', 185 lbs. Deb: 4/30/37 F																						
1937	Pit-N	21	34	7	15	4	0	0	6	4	3	.441	.500	.559	187	4	0			.938	-2	P-20	0.0
1938	Pit-N	56	103	8	25	6	1	0	11	9	12	.243	.310	.320	73	-4	0			**1.000**	-2	P-40	0.0
1939	Pit-N	43	74	9	18	3	1	2	11	2	12	.243	.263	.392	75	-3	0			1.000	-1	P-25	0.0
1940	Bos-N	20	43	5	12	3	0	0	3	1	10	.279	.295	.349	82	-1	0			.957	-1	P-15	0.0
1941	Bos-N	43	103	6	19	5	0	0	9	10	31	.184	.257	.233	40	-8	1			.966	4	P-33	0.0
1942	Bos-N	47	114	14	28	2	0	6	15	16	23	.246	.344	.421	126	4	0			.947	6	P-37	0.0
1943	Bos-N	46	107	8	30	4	0	2	12	6	16	.280	.319	.374	101	-0	0			.927	2	P-33/1-1	0.0
1944	Bos-N★	62	116	13	22	5	1	2	18	16	28	.190	.288	.302	63	-6	0			.972	7	P-43	0.0
1945	Bos-N	41	77	9	11	3	0	3	12	15	22	.143	.290	.299	64	-4	0			**1.000**	2	P-27	0.0
	*Det-A	17	25	2	3	0	0	2	5	1	5	.120	.154	.360	44	-2	0	0	0	.950	1	P-14	0.0
Total	9	396	796	81	183	35	3	17	102	80	162	.230	.303	.345	82	-20	1	0		.965	17	P-287/1-1	0.0
■ JOHNNY TOBIN	Tobin, John Martin "Tip" b: 9/15/06, Jamaica Plain, Mass. d: 8/6/83, Rhinebeck, N.Y. BR/TR, 6'3", 187 lbs. Deb: 9/22/32																						
1932	NY-N	1	1	0	0	0	0	0	0	0	0	.000	.000	.000	-99	-0	0			.000	0	H	0.0
■ JOHNNY TOBIN	Tobin, John Patrick "Jackie" b: 1/8/21, Oakland, Cal. d: 1/18/82, Oakland, Cal. BL/TR, 6', 165 lbs. Deb: 4/20/45 F																						
1945	Bos-A	84	278	25	70	6	2	0	21	26	24	.252	.320	.288	75	-8	2	6	-3	.951	9	3-72/2-5,O-1	0.0
■ JACK TOBIN	Tobin, John Thomas b: 5/4/1892, St.Louis, Mo. d: 12/10/69, St.Louis, Mo. BL/TL, 5'8", 142 lbs. Deb: 4/16/14 C																						
1914	StL-F	139	529	81	143	24	10	7	35	51	53	.270	.340	.393	94	-12	20			.952	5	*O-132	-1.4
1915	StL-F	158	625	92	**184**	26	13	6	51	68	42	.294	.366	.406	111	2	31			.965	3	*O-158	-0.3
1916	StL-A	77	150	16	32	4	1	0	10	12	13	.213	.272	.253	61	-7	7			.842	-9	O-41	-2.0
1918	StL-A	122	480	59	133	19	5	0	36	48	26	.277	.349	.338	111	7	13			.971	-1	*O-122	-0.1
1919	StL-A	127	486	54	159	22	7	6	57	36	24	.327	.376	.438	125	15	8			.953	2	*O-123	0.9
1920	StL-A	147	593	94	202	34	10	4	62	39	23	.341	.383	.452	117	14	21	13	-2	.960	5	*O-147	0.6
1921	StL-A	150	671	132	236	31	**18**	8	59	45	22	.352	.395	.487	117	16	7	12	-5	.956	8	*O-150	0.8
1922	StL-A	146	625	122	207	34	8	13	66	56	22	.331	.388	.474	119	17	7	9	-3	.940	-8	*O-145	-0.4
1923	StL-A	151	637	91	202	32	15	13	73	42	13	.317	.363	.476	113	10	8	7	-2	.969	-8	*O-151	-1.0
1924	StL-A	136	569	87	170	30	8	2	48	50	12	.299	.357	.390	87	-11	6	10	-4	.957	2	*O-132	-2.1
1925	StL-A	77	193	25	58	11	0	2	27	9	5	.301	.335	.389	79	-6	8	2	1	1.000	-5	O-39/1-3	-1.2
1926	Was-A	27	33	5	7	0	1	0	3	0	0	.212	.212	.273	26	-4	0	0	0	1.000	-2	/O-7	-0.5
	Bos-A	51	209	26	57	9	0	1	14	16	3	.273	.324	.330	73	-8	6	5	-1	.966	-3	O-51	-1.6
	Yr	78	242	31	64	9	1	1	17	16	3	.264	.310	.322	67	-12	6	5	-1	.970	-5	O-58	-2.1
1927	Bos-A	111	374	52	116	18	3	2	40	36	9	.310	.371	.390	100	0	5	4	-1	.947	-5	O-93	-1.1
Total	13	1619	6174	936	1906	294	99	64	581	508	267	.309	.364	.420	106	33	147	62		.957	-14	*O-1491/1-3	-9.4
■ BILL TOBIN	Tobin, William F. b: 10/10/1854, Hartford, Conn. d: 10/10/12, Hartford, Conn. BL , Deb: 7/21/1880																						
1880	Wor-N	5	16	1	2	0	0	0	3	0	5	.125	.125	.125	-14	-2				1.000	-0	/1-5	-0.2
	Tro-N	33	136	14	22	1	1	0	8	4	20	.162	.186	.184	24	-11				.950	-1	1-33	-1.4
	Yr	38	152	15	24	1	1	0	11	4	25	.158	.179	.178	20	-12				.958	-1	1-38	-1.6
■ AL TODD	Todd, Alfred Chester b: 1/7/02, Troy, N.Y. d: 3/8/85, Elmira, N.Y. BR/TR, 6'1", 198 lbs. Deb: 4/25/32																						
1932	Phi-N	33	70	8	16	5	0	0	9	1	9	.229	.260	.300	45	-5	1			.899	-4	C-25	-0.9
1933	Phi-N	73	136	13	28	4	0	0	10	4	18	.206	.239	.235	32	-12	1			.983	5	C-34/O-2	-0.6
1934	Phi-N	91	302	33	96	22	2	4	41	10	39	.318	.344	.444	96	-2	3			.976	-2	C-82	-0.1
1935	Phi-N	107	328	40	95	18	3	3	42	19	35	.290	.334	.390	85	-7	3			.968	-12	C-87	-1.4
1936	Pit-N	76	267	28	73	10	5	2	28	11	24	.273	.307	.371	80	-8	4			.976	1	C-70	-0.3
1937	Pit-N	133	514	51	158	18	10	8	86	16	36	.307	.330	.428	104	1	2			.972	-2	*C-128	0.7
1938	Pit-N	133	491	52	130	19	7	7	75	18	31	.265	.296	.375	83	-13	2			.985	10	*C-132	0.4
1939	Bro-N	86	245	28	68	10	0	5	32	13	16	.278	.317	.380	83	-6	1			.985	8	C-73	0.5

YEAR	TM/L	G	AB	R	H	2B	3B	HR	RBI	BB	SO	AVG	OBP	SLG	PRO+	BR/A	SB	CS	SBR	FA	FR	G/POS	TPR
1940	Chi-N	104	381	31	97	13	2	6	42	11	29	.255	.283	.346	74	-14	1			.984	-6	*C-104	-1.2
1941	Chi-N	6	6	1	1	0	0	0	0	0	1	.167	.167	.167	-6	-1	0			.000	0	H	-0.1
1943	Chi-N	21	45	1	6	0	0	0	1	1	5	.133	.152	.133	-17	-7	0			.986	4	C-17	-0.3
Total	11	863	2785	286	768	119	29	35	366	104	243	.276	.307	.377	82	-74	18			.977	1	C-752/O-2	-3.3
■ PHIL TODT	Todt, Philip Julius "Hook" b: 8/9/01, St.Louis, Mo. d: 11/15/73, St.Louis, Mo. BL/TL, 6', 175 lbs. Deb: 4/25/24																						
1924	Bos-A	52	103	17	27	8	2	1	14	6	9	.262	.309	.408	84	-3	0	1	-1	.983	-3	1-18/O-4	-0.7
1925	Bos-A	141	544	62	151	29	13	11	75	44	29	.278	.343	.439	97	-4	3	2	-0	.991	3	*1-140	-0.9
1926	Bos-A	154	599	56	153	19	12	7	69	40	38	.255	.306	.362	76	-23	3	2	-0	.988	10	*1-154	-2.2
1927	Bos-A	140	516	55	122	22	6	6	52	28	23	.236	.280	.337	61	-32	6	2	1	.991	9	*1-139	-3.0
1928	Bos-A	144	539	61	136	31	8	12	73	26	47	.252	.290	.406	83	-16	6	5	-1	**.997**	3	*1-144	-2.6
1929	Bos-A	153	534	49	140	38	10	4	64	31	28	.262	.305	.393	80	-17	6	7	-2	.991	3	*1-153	-3.0
1930	Bos-A	111	383	49	103	22	5	11	62	24	33	.269	.312	.439	92	-7	4	1	1	.993	3	*1-104	-1.2
1931	*Phi-A	62	197	23	48	14	2	5	44	8	22	.244	.273	.411	73	-9	1	1	-0	.995	-4	1-52	-1.7
Total	8	957	3415	372	880	183	58	57	453	207	229	.258	.305	.395	81	-111	29	21	-4	.992	24	1-904/O-4	-15.3
■ BOBBY TOLAN	Tolan, Robert b: 11/19/45, Los Angeles, Cal. BL/TL, 5'11", 170 lbs. Deb: 9/3/65 C																						
1965	StL-N	17	69	8	13	2	0	0	6	0	4	.188	.200	.217	16	-8	2	1	0	.970	-1	O-17	-1.0
1966	StL-N	43	93	10	16	5	1	1	6	6	15	.172	.238	.280	43	-7	1	2	-1	.952	-1	O-26/1-1	-1.1
1967	*StL-N	110	265	35	67	7	3	6	32	19	43	.253	.313	.370	96	-2	12	7	-1	.992	-9	O-80,1-13	-1.6
1968	*StL-N	92	278	28	64	12	1	5	17	13	42	.230	.272	.335	82	-7	9	5	-0	.967	-2	O-67/1-9	-1.4
1969	Cin-N	152	637	104	194	25	10	21	93	27	92	.305	.348	.474	122	17	26	12	1	.974	11	*O-150	2.0
1970	*Cin-N	152	589	112	186	34	6	16	80	62	94	.316	.388	.475	130	25	**57**	20	5	.978	8	*O-150	3.0
1972	*Cin-N	149	604	88	171	28	5	8	82	44	88	.283	.338	.386	112	8	42	15	4	.990	13	*O-149	1.9
1973	Cin-N	129	457	42	94	14	2	9	51	27	68	.206	.255	.304	57	-28	15	10	-2	.966	-4	*O-120	-4.1
1974	SD-N	95	357	45	95	16	1	8	40	20	41	.266	.321	.384	101	-1	7	9	-3	.971	-2	O-88	-1.0
1975	SD-N	147	506	58	129	19	4	5	43	28	45	.255	.307	.338	84	-12	11	13	-5	.971	-2	*O-120,1-27	-2.6
1976	*Phi-N	110	272	32	71	7	0	5	35	7	39	.261	.290	.342	76	-9	10	5	0	.992	-12	1-50,O-35	-2.6
1977	Phi-N	15	16	1	2	0	0	0	1	1	4	.125	.176	.125	-17	-3	0	0	0	.944	-0	/1-5	-0.3
	Pit-N	49	74	7	15	4	0	2	9	4	10	.203	.244	.338	53	-5	1	1	-0	1.000	-0	/1-20/O-2	-0.6
	Yr	64	90	8	17	4	0	2	10	5	14	.189	.232	.300	40	-8	1	1	-0	.992	-0	1-25/O-2	-0.9
1979	SD-N	22	21	2	4	0	1	0	2	0	2	.190	.190	.286	30	-2	0	0	0	1.000	-0	/1-5,O-1	-0.2
Total	13	1282	4238	572	1121	173	34	86	497	258	587	.265	.317	.382	96	-32	193	100	-2	.976	-1	*O-1005,1-130	-9.6
■ JOSE TOLENTINO	Tolentino, Jose (Franco) b: 6/3/61, Mexico City, Mexico BL/TL, 6'1", 195 lbs. Deb: 7/28/91																						
1991	Hou-N	44	54	6	14	4	0	1	6	4	9	.259	.310	.389	101	-0	0	0	0	.982	1	1-10/O-1	0.1
■ WAYNE TOLLESON	Tolleson, Jimmy Wayne b: 11/22/55, Spartanburg, S.C. BB/TR, 5'9", 160 lbs. Deb: 9/1/81																						
1981	Tex-A	14	24	6	4	0	0	0	1	1	5	.167	.200	.167	7	-3	2	0	1	1.000	-1	/3-6,S-2	-0.3
1982	Tex-A	38	70	6	8	1	0	0	2	5	14	.114	.173	.129	-16	-11	1	1	-0	.958	5	S-26/3-4,2-1	-0.5
1983	Tex-A	134	470	64	122	13	2	3	20	40	68	.260	.320	.315	77	-14	33	10	4	.972	-10	*2-112,S-26/D-1	-1.3
1984	Tex-A	118	338	35	72	9	2	0	9	27	47	.213	.277	.251	46	-24	22	4	4	.979	-7	*2-109/S-7,3-5,OD	-2.3
1985	Tex-A	123	323	45	101	9	5	1	18	21	46	.313	.355	.381	100	0	21	12	-1	.972	-4	S-81,2-29,3-12,/D-6	0.3
1986	Chi-A	81	260	39	65	7	3	3	29	38	43	.250	.346	.335	84	-5	13	6	0	.955	-10	3-65,S-18/O-2,D-2	-1.5
	NY-A	60	215	22	61	9	2	0	14	14	33	.284	.333	.344	86	-4	4	4	-1	.981	6	S-56/3-7,2-3	0.6
	Yr	141	475	61	126	16	5	3	43	52	76	.265	.340	.339	85	-9	17	10	-1	.981	-4	S-74,3-72/2-3,OD	-0.9
1987	NY-A	121	349	48	77	4	0	1	22	43	72	.221	.306	.241	48	-25	5	3	-0	.970	-3	*S-119/3-3	-1.7
1988	NY-A	21	59	8	15	2	0	0	5	8	12	.254	.343	.288	79	-1	1	0	0	.981	6	2-12,3-10/S-1	0.5
1989	NY-A	80	140	16	23	5	2	1	9	16	23	.164	.255	.250	43	-10	5	1	1	.912	10	3-28,S-28,2-13,D-10	0.1
1990	NY-A	73	74	12	11	1	1	0	4	6	21	.149	.213	.189	13	-9	1	0	0	.983	15	S-45,2-13/3-3,D-5	0.8
Total	10	863	2322	301	559	60	17	9	133	219	384	.241	.308	.293	66	-106	108	41	8	.974	7	S-409,2-292,3/DO	-5.3
■ TIM TOLMAN	Tolman, Timothy Lee b: 4/20/56, Santa Monica, Cal. BR/TR, 6', 195 lbs. Deb: 9/9/81																						
1981	Hou-N	4	8	0	1	0	0	0	0	0	0	.125	.125	.125	-30	-1	0	0	0	1.000	-1	/O-3	-0.3
1982	Hou-N	15	26	4	5	2	0	1	3	4	3	.192	.300	.385	98	-0	0	0	0	1.000	-0	/O-5,1-1	-0.1
1983	Hou-N	43	56	4	11	4	0	2	10	6	9	.196	.274	.375	83	-2	0	1	-1	1.000	-2	/1-7,O-3	-0.4
1984	Hou-N	14	17	2	3	1	0	0	0	0	3	.176	.176	.235	16	-2	0	0	0	1.000	-0	/O-3,1-1	-0.3
1985	Hou-N	31	43	4	6	1	0	2	8	1	10	.140	.178	.302	33	-4	0	1	-1	1.000	-1	/O-9,1-6	-0.6
1986	Det-A	16	34	4	6	1	0	0	2	6	4	.176	.300	.206	41	-3	1	1	-0	1.000	-1	/O-4,1-3,D-9	-0.4
1987	Det-A	9	12	3	1	1	0	0	1	7	2	.083	.450	.167	77	0	0	0	0	1.000	-1	/O-7,D-2	-0.1
Total	7	132	196	21	33	10	0	5	24	24	31	.168	.266	.296	58	-11	1	3	-2	1.000	-6	/O-34,1-18,D-11	-2.2
■ CHICK TOLSON	Tolson, Charles Julius "Toby" b: 11/6/1898, Washington, D.C. d: 4/16/65, Washington, D.C. BR/TR, 6', 185 lbs. Deb: 7/3/25																						
1925	Cle-A	3	12	0	3	0	0	0	0	2	1	.250	.357	.250	56	-1	0	0	0	1.000	0	/1-3	-0.1
1926	Chi-N	57	80	4	25	6	1	1	8	5	8	.313	.353	.450	113	1	0			.991	0	1-13	0.1
1927	Chi-N	39	54	6	16	4	0	2	17	4	9	.296	.345	.481	119	1	0			1.000	0	/1-8	0.1
1929	*Chi-N	32	109	13	28	5	0	1	19	9	16	.257	.325	.330	63	-6	0			.978	-2	1-31	-1.0
1930	Chi-N	13	20	0	6	1	0	0	1	6	5	.300	.462	.350	99	0	1			.979	1	/1-5	0.0
Total	5	144	275	23	78	16	1	4	45	26	39	.284	.350	.393	90	-4	1	0		.985	-1	/1-60	-0.9
■ ANDY TOMBERLIN	Tomberlin, Andy Lee b: 11/7/66, Monroe, N.C. BL/TL, 5'11", 160 lbs. Deb: 8/12/93																						
1993	Pit-N	27	42	4	12	0	1	1	5	2	14	.286	.333	.405	97	-0	0	0	0	1.000	-0	/O-7	-0.1
1994	Bos-A	18	36	1	7	0	1	1	1	6	12	.194	.310	.333	63	-2	1	0	0	1.000	-0	O-11/P-1,D-5	-0.2
1995	Oak-A	46	85	15	18	0	0	4	10	5	22	.212	.256	.353	60	-5	4	1	1	.979	-9	O-42/D-2	-1.3
1996	NY-N	63	66	12	17	4	0	3	10	9	27	.258	.355	.455	117	2	0	0	0	1.000	-4	O-17/1-1	-0.2
1997	NY-N	6	7	0	2	0	0	0	0	1	3	.286	.375	.286	79	-0	0	0	0	1.000	-0	/O-2	-0.1
1998	Det-A	32	69	8	15	2	0	2	12	3	25	.217	.280	.333	58	-4	1	0	0	1.000	-1	D-22/O-5	-0.6
Total	6	192	305	40	71	6	2	11	38	26	103	.233	.304	.374	77	-10	6	1	1	.989	-15	/O-84,D-29,1-1,P-1	-2.5
■ GEORGE TOMER	Tomer, George Clarence b: 11/26/1895, Perry, Iowa d: 12/15/84, Perry, Iowa BL/TR, 6', 180 lbs. Deb: 9/17/13																						
1913	StL-A	1	1	0	0	0	0	0	0	0	1	.000	.000	.000	-99	-0	0			.000	0	H	0.0
■ PHIL TOMNEY	Tomney, Philip Howard "Buster" b: 7/17/1863, Reading, Pa. d: 3/18/1892, Reading, Pa. BR/TR, 5'7", 155 lbs. Deb: 9/7/1888																						
1888	Lou-a	34	120	15	18	3	0	0	4	7		.150	.197	.175	20	-11	11			.882	6	S-34	-0.3
1889	Lou-a	112	376	61	80	8	5	4	38	46	47	.213	.304	.293	71	-13	26			.857	27	*S-112	1.7
1890	*Lou-a	108	386	72	107	21	7	1	58	43		.277	.357	.376	119	9	27			**.902**	18	*S-108	2.9
Total	3	254	882	148	205	32	12	5	100	96	47	.232	.313	.313	86	-15	61			.878	50	S 254	4.3
■ TONY TONNEMAN	Tonneman, Charles Richard b: 9/10/1881, Chicago, Ill. d: 8/7/51, Prescott, Ariz. BR/TR, 5'10.5", 175 lbs. Deb: 9/19/11																						
1911	Bos-A	2	5	0	1	1	0	0	3	1		.200	.333	.400	105	0	0			.900	1	/C-2	0.1
■ BERT TOOLEY	Tooley, Albert R. b: 8/30/1886, Howell, Mich. d: 8/17/76, Marshall, Mich. BR/TR, 5'10", 155 lbs. Deb: 4/12/11																						
1911	Bro-N	119	433	55	89	11	3	1	29	53	63	.206	.295	.252	56	-25	18			.925	-8	*S-114	-2.6
1912	Bro-N	77	265	34	62	6	5	2	37	19	21	.234	.285	.317	67	-13	12			.885	-15	S-76	-2.1
Total	2	196	698	89	151	17	8	3	66	72	84	.216	.291	.277	60	-37	30			.909	-24	S-190	-4.7
■ SPECS TOPORCER	Toporcer, George b: 2/9/1899, New York, N.Y. d: 5/17/89, Huntington Station, N.Y. BL/TR, 5'10.5", 165 lbs. Deb: 4/13/21																						
1921	StL-N	22	53	4	14	1	0	0	2	3	4	.264	.304	.283	57	-3	1	0	0	.938	0	2-12/S-2	-0.2
1922	StL-N	116	352	56	114	25	6	3	36	24	18	.324	.370	.455	117	8	2	1	0	.939	-23	S-91/3-6,2-1,O-1	-0.5
1923	StL-N	97	303	45	77	11	3	3	35	41	14	.254	.349	.340	84	-6	4	3	-1	.945	-13	2-52,S-33/1-1,3-1	-1.5
1924	StL-N	70	198	30	62	10	3	1	24	11	14	.313	.362	.409	108	2	2	3	-1	.974	-16	3-33,S-25/2-3	-1.0
1925	StL-N	83	268	38	76	13	4	2	26	36	15	.284	.373	.384	92	-2	7	2	1	.960	-3	S-66/2-7	0.3

YEAR	TM/L	G	AB	R	H	2B	3B	HR	RBI	BB	SO	AVG	OBP	SLG	PRO+	BR/A	SB	CS	SBR	FA	FR	G/POS	TPR
1926	*StL-N	64	88	13	22	3	2	0	9	8	9	.250	.327	.330	74	-3	1			.983	-9	2-27/S-5,3-1	-1.2
1927	StL-N	86	290	37	72	13	4	0	19	27	16	.248	.314	.321	68	-13	5			.980	-11	3-54,S-27/2-2,1-1	-1.9
1928	StL-N	8	14	0	0	0	0	0	0	0	3	.000	.000	.000	-98	-4	0			1.000	0	/1-1,2-1	-0.4
Total	8	546	1566	223	437	76	22	9	151	150	93	.279	.347	.373	90	-20	22	9		.946	-74	S-249,2-105/310	-6.4

■ JEFF TORBORG Torborg, Jeffrey Allen b: 11/26/41, Plainfield, N.J. BR/TR, 6'0.5", 195 lbs. Deb: 5/10/64 MC

YEAR	TM/L	G	AB	R	H	2B	3B	HR	RBI	BB	SO	AVG	OBP	SLG	PRO+	BR/A	SB	CS	SBR	FA	FR	G/POS	TPR
1964	LA-N	28	43	4	10	1	1	0	4	3	8	.233	.298	.302	75	-1	0	0	0	.977	-2	C-27	-0.3
1965	LA-N	56	150	8	36	5	1	3	13	10	26	.240	.292	.347	85	-3	0	0	0	.991	4	C-53	0.3
1966	LA-N	46	120	4	27	3	0	1	13	10	23	.225	.285	.275	61	-6	0	0	0	.986	6	C-45	0.2
1967	LA-N	76	196	11	42	4	1	2	12	13	31	.214	.267	.276	60	-10	1	3	-2	.989	12	C-75	0.3
1968	LA-N	37	93	2	15	2	0	0	4	6	10	.161	.212	.183	21	-9	0	0	0	.991	10	C-37	0.3
1969	LA-N	51	124	7	23	4	0	0	7	9	17	.185	.241	.218	31	-12	1	0	0	.996	11	C-50	0.1
1970	LA-N	64	134	11	31	8	0	1	17	14	15	.231	.304	.313	69	-6	1	1	-0	.983	10	C-63	0.5
1971	Cal-A	55	123	6	25	5	0	0	5	3	6	.203	.222	.244	34	-11	0	0	0	.987	5	C-49	-0.6
1972	Cal-A	59	153	5	32	3	0	0	8	14	21	.209	.280	.229	56	-8	0	0	0	.998	16	C-58	1.1
1973	Cal-A	102	255	20	56	7	0	1	18	21	32	.220	.279	.259	57	-15	0	2	-1	.991	8	*C-102	-0.4
Total	10	574	1391	78	297	42	3	8	101	103	189	.214	.270	.265	56	-82	3	6	-3	.990	79	C-559	1.5

■ EARL TORGESON Torgeson, Clifford Earl "The Earl Of Snohomish" b: 1/1/24, Snohomish, Wash. d: 11/8/90, Everett, Wash. BL/TL, 6'3", 180 lbs. Deb: 4/15/47 C

YEAR	TM/L	G	AB	R	H	2B	3B	HR	RBI	BB	SO	AVG	OBP	SLG	PRO+	BR/A	SB	CS	SBR	FA	FR	G/POS	TPR
1947	Bos-N	128	399	73	112	20	6	16	78	82	59	.281	.403	.481	137	24	11			.984	-1	*1-117	1.9
1948	*Bos-N	134	438	70	111	23	5	10	67	81	54	.253	.372	.397	110	9	19			.993	1	*1-129	0.9
1949	Bos-N	25	100	17	26	5	1	4	19	13	4	.260	.345	.450	118	2	4			.988	-3	1-25	-0.1
1950	Bos-N	156	576	**120**	167	30	3	23	87	119	69	.290	.412	.472	141	39	15			.986	-0	*1-156	3.4
1951	Bos-N	155	581	99	153	21	4	24	92	102	70	.263	.375	.437	127	24	20	11	-1	.988	-1	*1-155	1.5
1952	Bos-N	122	382	49	88	17	0	5	34	81	38	.230	.366	.314	94	0	11	7	-1	.989	-1	*1-105/O-5	-0.6
1953	Phi-N	111	379	58	104	25	8	11	64	53	57	.274	.366	.470	117	10	7	1	2	.987	-3	*1-105	0.4
1954	Phi-N	135	490	63	133	22	6	5	54	75	52	.271	.368	.371	93	-3	7	1	2	.990	-10	*1-133	-1.8
1955	Phi-N	47	150	29	40	5	3	1	17	32	20	.267	.396	.360	104	2	2	3	-1	.995	-1	1-43	-0.3
	Det-A	89	300	58	85	10	1	9	50	61	29	.283	.404	.413	123	12	9	0	**3**	.992	-0	1-83	1.0
1956	Det-A	117	318	61	84	9	3	12	42	78	47	.264	.409	.425	120	12	6	4	-1	.992	-7	1-83	0.0
1957	Det-A	30	50	5	12	2	1	1	5	12	10	.240	.387	.380	108	1	0	0	0	1.000	0	1-17	0.0
	Chi-A	86	251	53	74	11	2	7	46	49	44	.295	.410	.438	131	13	7	3	0	.998	-5	1-70/O-1	0.4
	Yr	116	301	58	86	13	3	8	51	61	54	.286	.406	.429	127	14	7	3	0	.999	-5	1-87/O-1	0.4
1958	Chi-A	96	188	37	50	8	0	10	30	48	29	.266	.415	.468	146	14	7	2	1	.978	-2	1-73	1.0
1959	*Chi-A	127	277	40	61	5	3	9	45	62	55	.220	.363	.357	100	2	7	6	-2	.983	-6	*1-103	-1.1
1960	Chi-A	68	57	12	15	2	0	2	9	21	8	.263	.462	.404	137	5	1	0	0	.983	0	1-10	0.5
1961	Chi-A	20	15	1	1	0	0	0	1	3	5	.067	.222	.067	-19	-3	0	0	0	1.000	-0	/1-1	-0.3
	NY-A	22	18	3	2	0	0	0	0	8	3	.111	.385	.111	42	-1	0	1	-1	.969	-0	/1-8	-0.2
	Yr	42	33	4	3	0	0	0	1	11	8	.091	.318	.091	16	-4	0	1	-1	.970	-0	/1-9	-0.5
Total	15	1668	4969	848	1318	215	46	149	740	980	653	.265	.387	.417	118	162	133	39		.989	-39	*1-1416/O-6	6.6

■ RED TORPHY Torphy, Walter Anthony b: 11/6/1891, Fall River, Mass. d: 2/11/80, Fall River, Mass. BR/TR, 5'11", 169 lbs. Deb: 9/25/20

YEAR	TM/L	G	AB	R	H	2B	3B	HR	RBI	BB	SO	AVG	OBP	SLG	PRO+	BR/A	SB	CS	SBR	FA	FR	G/POS	TPR
1920	Bos-N	3	15	1	3	2	0	0	2	0	1	.200	.200	.333	54	-1	0	0	0	.969	-1	/1-3	-0.2

■ FRANK TORRE Torre, Frank Joseph b: 12/30/31, Brooklyn, N.Y. BL/TL, 6'3", 205 lbs. Deb: 4/20/56 F

YEAR	TM/L	G	AB	R	H	2B	3B	HR	RBI	BB	SO	AVG	OBP	SLG	PRO+	BR/A	SB	CS	SBR	FA	FR	G/POS	TPR
1956	Mil-N	111	159	17	41	6	0	0	16	11	4	.258	.306	.296	67	-7	1	0	0	.993	6	1-89	-0.4
1957	*Mil-N	129	364	46	99	19	5	5	40	29	19	.272	.341	.393	104	2	0	0	0	**.996**	1	*1-117	-0.3
1958	*Mil-N	138	372	41	115	22	5	6	55	42	14	.309	.390	.444	131	17	2	0	1	**.994**	6	*1-122	1.8
1959	Mil-N	115	263	23	60	15	1	1	33	35	12	.228	.326	.304	75	-9	0	0	0	.994	-0	1-87	-1.4
1960	Mil-N	21	44	2	9	1	0	0	5	3	2	.205	.255	.227	36	-4	0	0	0	1.000	-1	1-17	-0.6
1962	Phi-N	108	168	13	52	8	2	0	20	24	6	.310	.408	.381	117	5	1	1	-0	.980	3	1-76	0.6
1963	Phi-N	92	112	8	28	7	2	1	10	11	7	.250	.333	.375	105	1	0	0	0	.989	5	1-56	0.5
Total	7	714	1482	150	404	78	15	13	179	155	64	.273	.352	.372	101	5	4	1	1	.993	19	1-564	0.2

■ JOE TORRE Torre, Joseph Paul b: 7/18/40, Brooklyn, N.Y. BR/TR, 6'2", 212 lbs. Deb: 9/25/60 FM

YEAR	TM/L	G	AB	R	H	2B	3B	HR	RBI	BB	SO	AVG	OBP	SLG	PRO+	BR/A	SB	CS	SBR	FA	FR	G/POS	TPR
1960	Mil-N	2	2	0	1	0	0	0	0	0	1	.500	.500	.500	189	0	0	0	0	.000	0	H	0.0
1961	Mil-N	113	406	40	113	21	4	10	42	28	60	.278	.331	.424	105	2	3	5	-2	.982	-8	*C-112	-0.3
1962	Mil-N	80	220	23	62	8	1	5	26	24	24	.282	.358	.395	105	2	1	0	0	.986	6	C-63	1.0
1963	Mil-N☆	142	501	57	147	19	4	14	71	42	79	.293	.354	.431	126	17	1	5	-3	.994	-7	*C-105,1-37/O-2	1.0
1964	Mil-N★	154	601	87	193	36	5	20	109	36	67	.321	.366	.498	140	31	2	4	-2	**.995**	-8	C-96,1-70	2.4
1965	Mil-N★	148	523	68	152	21	1	27	80	61	79	.291	.373	.489	140	28	0	1	-1	.991	-6	*C-100,1-49	2.6
1966	Atl-N★	148	546	83	172	20	3	36	101	60	61	.315	.385	.560	157	41	0	4	-2	.984	-3	*C-114,1-36	4.2
1967	Atl-N★	135	477	67	132	18	1	20	68	49	75	.277	.348	.444	127	16	2	2	-1	.991	-5	*C-114,1-23	1.7
1968	Atl-N	115	424	45	115	11	2	10	55	34	72	.271	.333	.377	112	7	1	0	0	**.996**	-11	C-92,1-29	0.1
1969	StL-N	159	602	72	174	29	6	18	101	66	85	.289	.364	.447	126	21	0	0	0	.996	-3	*1-144,C-17	0.7
1970	StL-N★	161	624	89	203	27	9	21	100	70	91	.325	.399	.498	136	33	2	2	-1	.987	-8	C-90,3-73/1-1	2.8
1971	StL-N★	161	634	97	**230**	34	8	24	**137**	63	70	**.363**	.424	.555	169	57	4	1	1	.951	-17	*3-161	4.1
1972	StL-N★	149	544	71	157	26	6	11	81	54	64	.289	.361	.419	123	17	3	0	1	.963	-15	*3-117,1-27	-0.1
1973	StL-N★	141	519	67	149	17	2	13	69	65	78	.287	.377	.403	116	14	2	0	1	.993	-12	*1-114,3-58	-0.6
1974	StL-N	147	529	59	149	28	1	11	70	69	88	.282	.373	.401	117	14	1	2	-1	.992	3	*1-139,3-18	0.8
1975	NY-N	114	361	33	89	16	3	6	35	35	55	.247	.317	.357	91	-5	0	0	0	.950	-1	3-83,1-24	-0.7
1976	NY-N	114	310	36	95	10	3	5	31	21	35	.306	.360	.406	124	9	1	3	-2	.989	3	1-78/3-4	0.6
1977	NY-N	26	51	2	9	3	0	1	9	2	10	.176	.208	.294	34	-5	0	0	0	.988	-1	1-16/3-1,M	-0.7
Total	18	2209	7874	996	2342	344	59	252	1185	779	1094	.297	.367	.452	129	299	23	29	-11	.990	-93	C-903,1-787,3/O	19.6

■ GIL TORRES Torres, Don Gilberto (Nunez) b: 8/23/15, Regla, Cuba d: 1/10/83, Regla, Cuba BR/TR, 6', 155 lbs. Deb: 4/25/40

YEAR	TM/L	G	AB	R	H	2B	3B	HR	RBI	BB	SO	AVG	OBP	SLG	PRO+	BR/A	SB	CS	SBR	FA	FR	G/POS	TPR
1940	Was-A	2	0	0	0	0	0	0	0	0	0	—	—	—	—	0	0	0	0	1.000	0	/P-2	0.0
1944	Was-A	134	524	42	140	20	6	0	58	21	24	.267	.297	.328	82	-14	10	7	-1	.952	9	*3-123,2-10/1-4	-0.5
1945	Was-A	147	562	39	133	12	5	0	48	21	29	.237	.264	.276	62	-30	7	4	-0	.953	-21	*S-145/3-2	-4.3
1946	Was-A	63	185	18	47	8	0	0	13	11	12	.254	.296	.297	70	-8	3	2	-0	.939	2	S-31,3-18/2-7,P-3	-0.4
Total	4	346	1271	99	320	40	11	0	119	53	65	.252	.282	.301	72	-51	20	13	-2	.951	-11	S-176,3-143/2P1	-5.2

■ FELIX TORRES Torres, Felix (Sanchez) b: 5/1/32, Ponce, P.R. BR/TR, 5'11", 165 lbs. Deb: 4/10/62

YEAR	TM/L	G	AB	R	H	2B	3B	HR	RBI	BB	SO	AVG	OBP	SLG	PRO+	BR/A	SB	CS	SBR	FA	FR	G/POS	TPR
1962	LA-A	127	451	44	117	19	4	11	74	28	73	.259	.308	.392	90	-7	0	0	0	.938	-3	*3-123	-1.0
1963	LA-A	138	463	40	121	32	1	4	51	30	73	.261	.310	.361	93	-5	1	0	0	.939	-4	*3-122/1-2	-1.0
1964	LA-A	100	277	25	64	10	0	12	28	13	56	.231	.268	.397	91	-5	1	3	-2	.970	-0	3-72/1-3	-0.8
Total	3	365	1191	109	302	61	5	27	153	71	202	.254	.300	.381	91	-18	2	3	-1	.945	-8	3-317/1-5	-2.8

■ HECTOR TORRES Torres, Hector Epitacio (Marroquin) b: 9/16/45, Monterrey, Mexico BR/TR, 6', 175 lbs. Deb: 4/10/68 C

YEAR	TM/L	G	AB	R	H	2B	3B	HR	RBI	BB	SO	AVG	OBP	SLG	PRO+	BR/A	SB	CS	SBR	FA	FR	G/POS	TPR
1968	Hou-N	128	466	44	104	11	1	1	24	18	64	.223	.252	.258	54	-26	2	3	-1	.958	-4	*S-127/2-1	-2.2
1969	Hou-N	34	69	5	11	1	0	1	8	2	12	.159	.183	.217	12	-8	0	0	0	.944	0	S-22	-0.7
1970	Hou-N	31	65	6	16	1	2	0	5	6	8	.246	.310	.323	73	-3	0	0	0	.947	1	S-22/2-6	0.0
1971	Chi-N	31	58	4	13	3	0	0	2	4	10	.224	.274	.276	49	-4	0	0	0	.962	1	S-18/2-4	-0.2
1972	Mon-N	83	181	14	28	4	1	2	7	13	26	.155	.215	.221	24	-18	0	2	-1	.965	14	2-60,S-16/O-2,P3	-0.2
1973	Hou-N	38	66	3	6	1	0	0	2	7	13	.091	.189	.106	-16	-10	0	1	-1	.952	7	S-22,2-13	-0.2
1975	SD-N	112	352	31	91	12	0	5	26	22	32	.259	.302	.335	82	-10	2	3	-1	.971	11	S-75,3-42,2-16	0.8
1976	SD-N	74	215	8	42	6	0	4	15	16	31	.195	.254	.279	56	-13	2	1	0	.949	-16	S-63/3-4,2-3	-2.5
1977	Tor-A	91	266	33	64	7	3	5	26	16	33	.241	.286	.346	70	-11	1	1	-0	.980	-2	S-68,2-23/3-2	-0.6
Total	9	622	1738	148	375	46	7	18	115	104	229	.216	.262	.281	55	-103	7	11	-5	.962	11	S-433,2-126/3OP	-5.8

■ RICARDO TORRES
Torres, Ricardo J. (Martinez) b: 4/16/1891, Regla, Cuba d: 4/17/60, Regla, Cuba BR/TR, 5'11", 160 lbs. Deb: 5/18/20 F

YEAR	TM/L	G	AB	R	H	2B	3B	HR	RBI	BB	SO	AVG	OBP	SLG	PRO+	BR/A	SB	CS	SBR	FA	FR	G/POS	TPR
1920	Was-A	16	30	8	10	1	0	0	3	1	4	.333	.355	.367	94	-0	0	0	0	1.000	-1	/1-7,C-5	-0.1
1921	Was-A	2	3	1	1	0	0	0	0	1	1	.333	.500	.333	122	0	0	0	0	.750	-1	/C-2	-0.1
1922	Was-A	4	4	0	0	0	0	0	0	0	1	.000	.000	.000	-99	-1	0	0	0	1.000	1	/C-3	0.0
Total	3	22	37	9	11	1	0	0	3	2	6	.297	.333	.324	76	-1	0	0	0	.955	-1	/C-10,1-7	-0.2

■ RUSTY TORRES
Torres, Rosendo (Hernandez) b: 9/30/48, Aguadilla, P.R. BB/TR, 5'10", 180 lbs. Deb: 9/20/71

YEAR	TM/L	G	AB	R	H	2B	3B	HR	RBI	BB	SO	AVG	OBP	SLG	PRO+	BR/A	SB	CS	SBR	FA	FR	G/POS	TPR
1971	NY-A	9	26	5	10	3	0	2	3	0	8	.385	.385	.731	223	4	0	1	-1	1.000	0	/O-5	0.3
1972	NY-A	80	199	15	42	7	0	3	13	18	44	.211	.280	.291	73	-7	0	4	-2	.978	-6	O-62	-2.1
1973	Cle-A	122	312	31	64	8	1	7	28	50	62	.205	.321	.304	76	-9	6	5	-1	.976	-5	*O-114	-2.0
1974	Cle-A	108	150	19	28	2	0	3	12	13	24	.187	.252	.260	48	-10	2	1	0	.959	-19	O-94/D-1	-3.3
1976	Cal-A	120	264	37	54	16	3	6	27	36	39	.205	.300	.356	98	-1	4	4	-1	.990	-11	*O-105/3-1,D-6	-1.7
1977	Cal-A	58	77	9	12	1	1	3	10	10	18	.156	.253	.312	55	-5	0	1	-1	.984	-12	O-54	-1.9
1978	Chi-A	16	44	7	14	3	0	3	6	6	7	.318	.400	.591	174	4	0	1	-1	.964	-2	O-14	0.1
1979	Chi-A	90	170	26	43	5	0	8	24	23	37	.253	.349	.424	107	2	0	0	0	.976	-13	O-85	-1.3
1980	KC-A	51	72	10	12	0	0	0	3	8	7	.167	.250	.167	16	-8	1	3	-2	.973	-4	O-40/D-1	-1.4
Total	9	654	1314	159	279	45	5	35	126	164	246	.212	.303	.334	82	-30	13	20	-8	.977	-73	O-573/D-8,3-1	-13.3

■ KELVIN TORVE
Torve, Kelvin Curtis b: 1/10/60, Rapid City, S.Dak. BL/TR, 6'3", 205 lbs. Deb: 6/25/88

YEAR	TM/L	G	AB	R	H	2B	3B	HR	RBI	BB	SO	AVG	OBP	SLG	PRO+	BR/A	SB	CS	SBR	FA	FR	G/POS	TPR
1988	Min-A	12	16	1	3	0	0	1	2	1	2	.188	.235	.375	66	-1	0	1	-1	1.000	0	/1-4,D-1	-0.1
1990	NY-N	20	38	0	11	4	0	0	2	4	9	.289	.386	.395	116	1	0	0	0	1.000	-2	/1-9,O-1	-0.2
1991	NY-N	10	8	0	0	0	0	0	0	0	1	.000	.000	.000	-99	-2	0	0	0	1.000	1	/1-1	-0.1
Total	3	42	62	1	14	4	0	1	4	5	12	.226	.304	.339	78	-2	0	1	-1	1.000	-2	/1-14,O-1,D-1	-0.4

■ CESAR TOVAR
Tovar, Cesar Leonardo "Pepito" (b: Cesar Leonard Perez (Tovar))
b: 7/3/40, Caracas, Venez. d: 7/14/94, Caracas, Venez. BR/TR, 5'9", 155 lbs. Deb: 4/12/65

YEAR	TM/L	G	AB	R	H	2B	3B	HR	RBI	BB	SO	AVG	OBP	SLG	PRO+	BR/A	SB	CS	SBR	FA	FR	G/POS	TPR
1965	Min-A	18	25	3	5	1	0	0	2	2	3	.200	.259	.240	41	-2	2	0	1	.800	1	/2-4,3-2,O-2,S-1	-0.1
1966	Min-A	134	465	57	121	19	5	2	41	44	50	.260	.329	.335	86	-7	16	6	1	.978	-8	2-76,S-31,O-24	-0.8
1967	Min-A	164	649	98	173	32	7	6	47	46	51	.267	.328	.365	97	-2	19	11	-1	.994	-4	O-74,3-70,2-36,/S-9	-1.1
1968	Min-A	157	613	89	167	31	6	6	47	34	41	.272	.328	.372	106	5	35	13	3	.966	-2	O-78,3-75,S2/PC1	0.6
1969	*Min-A	158	535	99	154	25	5	11	52	37	37	.288	.344	.415	109	6	45	12	6	.983	9	*O-113,2-41,3-20	1.9
1970	*Min-A	161	650	120	195	**36**	**13**	10	54	52	47	.300	.359	.442	118	15	30	15	0	.977	0	*O-151/2-8,3-4	0.8
1971	Min-A	157	657	94	**204**	29	3	1	45	45	39	.311	.357	.368	103	3	18	14	-3	.986	4	*O-154/3-7,2-2	-0.4
1972	Min-A	141	548	86	145	20	6	2	31	39	39	.265	.329	.334	93	-4	21	10	0	.983	7	*O-139	-0.4
1973	Phi-N	97	328	49	88	18	4	1	21	29	35	.268	.337	.357	90	-4	6	4	-1	.928	-15	3-46,O-24,2-22	-2.1
1974	Tex-A	138	562	78	164	24	6	4	58	47	33	.292	.356	.377	114	11	13	9	-2	.980	-1	*O-135/D-3	0.3
1975	Tex-A	102	427	53	110	16	0	3	28	27	25	.258	.306	.316	77	-13	16	11	-2	.919	-3	D-66,O-31/2-1	-2.2
	*Oak-A	19	26	5	6	1	0	0	3	3	3	.231	.310	.269	66	-1	4	0	1	1.000	-0	/2-4,3-3,S-1,D-7	0.0
	Yr	121	453	58	116	17	0	3	31	30	28	.256	.307	.313	76	-14	20	11	-1	.919	-3	D-73,O-31/2-5,3S	-2.2
1976	Oak-A	29	45	1	8	0	0	0	4	4	4	.178	.275	.178	36	-3	1	2	-1	.958	-5	O-20/D-4	-1.0
	NY-A	13	39	2	6	1	0	0	2	4	3	.154	.250	.179	27	-3	0	1	-1	1.000	1	D-10/2-3	-0.4
	Yr	42	84	3	14	1	0	0	6	8	7	.167	.263	.179	32	-7	1	3	-2	.958	-4	O-20,D-14/2-3	-1.4
Total	12	1488	5569	834	1546	253	55	46	435	413	410	.278	.337	.368	99	-0	226	108	3	.980	-18	O-945,3-227,2/DS1CP	-4.9

■ BABE TOWNE
Towne, Jay King b: 3/12/1880, Coon Rapids, Iowa d: 10/29/38, Des Moines, Iowa BR/TR, 5'10", 180 lbs. Deb: 8/1/06

YEAR	TM/L	G	AB	R	H	2B	3B	HR	RBI	BB	SO	AVG	OBP	SLG	PRO+	BR/A	SB	CS	SBR	FA	FR	G/POS	TPR
1906	*Chi-A	14	36	3	10	0	0	0	6	7		.278	.395	.278	115	1	0			.923	-4	C-13	-0.2

■ GEORGE TOWNSEND
Townsend, George Hodgson "Sleepy" b: 6/4/1867, Hartsdale, N.Y. d: 3/15/30, New Haven, Conn. BR/TR, 5'7.5", 180 lbs. Deb: 6/25/1887

YEAR	TM/L	G	AB	R	H	2B	3B	HR	RBI	BB	SO	AVG	OBP	SLG	PRO+	BR/A	SB	CS	SBR	FA	FR	G/POS	TPR
1887	Phi-a	31	109	12	21	3	0	0	14	3		.193	.214	.220	21	-12	8			.865	-7	C-28/O-3	-1.3
1888	Phi-a	42	161	13	25	6	0	0	12	4		.155	.181	.193	20	-14	2			.912	-2	C-42	-1.1
1890	Bal-a	18	67	6	16	4	1	0	9	4		.239	.282	.328	76	-2	3			.930	2	C-18	0.1
1891	Bal-a	61	204	29	39	5	4	0	18	20	21	.191	.279	.255	52	-13	3			.909	-11	C-58/O-3	-1.6
Total	4	152	541	60	101	18	5	0	53	31	21	.187	.239	.238	40	-41	16			.905	-17	C-146/O-6	-3.9

■ JIM TOY
Toy, James Madison b: 2/20/1858, Beaver Falls, Pa. d: 3/13/19, Cresson, Pa. 5'6", 160 lbs. Deb: 4/20/1887

YEAR	TM/L	G	AB	R	H	2B	3B	HR	RBI	BB	SO	AVG	OBP	SLG	PRO+	BR/A	SB	CS	SBR	FA	FR	G/POS	TPR
1887	Cle-a	109	423	56	94	20	5	1	56	17		.222	.256	.300	56	-25	8			.975	3	1-82,O-11,C-10,/3S	-2.5
1890	Bro-a	44	160	11	29	3	0	0	7	11		.181	.238	.200	30	-14	2			.867	-1	C-44	-0.9
Total	2	153	583	67	123	23	5	1	63	28		.211	.251	.273	50	-39	10			.859	3	/1-82,C-54,O-11,3S	-3.4

■ JIM TRABER
Traber, James Joseph b: 12/26/61, Columbus, Ohio BL/TL, 6', 194 lbs. Deb: 9/21/84

YEAR	TM/L	G	AB	R	H	2B	3B	HR	RBI	BB	SO	AVG	OBP	SLG	PRO+	BR/A	SB	CS	SBR	FA	FR	G/POS	TPR
1984	Bal-A	10	21	3	5	0	0	0	2	2	4	.238	.304	.238	54	-1	0	0	0	.000	0	/D-9	-0.1
1986	Bal-A	65	212	28	54	7	0	13	44	18	31	.255	.328	.472	116	4	0	0	0	.988	1	1-29,D-21/O-8	0.3
1988	Bal-A	103	352	25	78	6	0	10	45	19	42	.222	.263	.324	65	-17	1	2	-1	.990	8	1-57,D-30,O-11	-1.6
1989	Bal-A	86	234	14	49	8	0	4	26	19	41	.209	.269	.295	61	-12	4	3	-1	.998	5	1-69/D-5	-1.3
Total	4	264	819	70	186	21	0	27	117	58	118	.227	.283	.352	77	-26	5	5	-2	.993	15	1-155/D-65,O-19	-2.7

■ DICK TRACEWSKI
Tracewski, Richard Joseph b: 2/3/35, Eynon, Pa. BR/TR, 5'11", 167 lbs. Deb: 4/12/62 MC

YEAR	TM/L	G	AB	R	H	2B	3B	HR	RBI	BB	SO	AVG	OBP	SLG	PRO+	BR/A	SB	CS	SBR	FA	FR	G/POS	TPR
1962	LA-N	15	2	3	0	0	0	0	0	2	0	.000	.500	.000	50	0	0	0	0	1.000	2	/S-4	0.2
1963	*LA-N	104	217	23	49	2	1	1	10	19	39	.226	.288	.258	63	-10	2	3	-1	.957	19	S-81,2-23	1.3
1964	LA-N	106	304	31	75	13	4	1	26	31	61	.247	.316	.326	88	-5	3	3	-1	.970	-0	2-56,3-30,S-19	-0.1
1965	*LA-N	78	186	17	40	6	0	1	20	25	30	.215	.315	.263	69	-7	2	6	-3	.950	8	3-53,2-14/S-7	-0.2
1966	Det-A	81	124	15	24	1	1	0	7	10	32	.194	.254	.218	36	-10	1	1	-0	.947	11	2-70/S-3	0.3
1967	Det-A	74	107	19	30	4	2	1	9	8	20	.280	.330	.383	107	1	1	1	-0	.965	9	S-44,2-12,3-10	1.3
1968	*Det-A	90	212	30	33	3	1	4	15	24	51	.156	.242	.236	44	-14	3	0	1	.982	-5	S-51,3-16,2-14	-1.6
1969	Det-A	66	79	10	11	2	0	0	4	15	20	.139	.277	.165	25	-8	3	0	1	.957	16	S-41,2-13/3-6	1.2
Total	8	614	1231	148	262	31	9	8	91	134	253	.213	.291	.272	65	-53	15	14	-4	.958	60	S-250,2-202,3-115	2.4

■ JIM TRACY
Tracy, James Edwin b: 12/31/55, Hamilton, Ohio BL/TR, 6', 185 lbs. Deb: 7/20/80

YEAR	TM/L	G	AB	R	H	2B	3B	HR	RBI	BB	SO	AVG	OBP	SLG	PRO+	BR/A	SB	CS	SBR	FA	FR	G/POS	TPR
1980	Chi-N	42	122	12	31	3	3	3	9	13	37	.254	.326	.402	95	-1	2	2	-1	.950	-7	O-31/1-1	-1.0
1981	Chi-N	45	63	6	15	2	1	0	5	12	14	.238	.360	.302	85	-1	1	0	0	1.000	-1	O-11	-0.2
Total	2	87	185	18	46	5	4	3	14	25	51	.249	.338	.368	92	-2	3	2	-0	.964	-8	/O-42,1-1	-1.2

■ JOHN TRAFFLEY
Traffley, John M. b: 1862, Chicago, Ill. d: 5/15/1900, Baltimore, Md. 5'9", 180 lbs. Deb: 6/15/1889 F

YEAR	TM/L	G	AB	R	H	2B	3B	HR	RBI	BB	SO	AVG	OBP	SLG	PRO+	BR/A	SB	CS	SBR	FA	FR	G/POS	TPR
1889	Lou-a	1	2	0	1	0	0	0	0	0	0	.500	.500	.500	189	0	0			.000	-1	/O-1	0.0

■ BILL TRAFFLEY
Traffley, William Franklin b: 12/21/1859, Staten Island, N.Y d: 6/23/08, Des Moines, Iowa BR/TR, 5'11.5", 185 lbs. Deb: 7/27/1878 F

YEAR	TM/L	G	AB	R	H	2B	3B	HR	RBI	BB	SO	AVG	OBP	SLG	PRO+	BR/A	SB	CS	SBR	FA	FR	G/POS	TPR
1878	Chi-N	2	9	1	1	0	0	0	1	0	1	.111	.111	.111	-25	-1				1.000	-1	/C-2	-0.2
1883	Cin-a	30	105	17	21	5	0	0	8	4		.200	.229	.248	51	-6				.851	2	C-29/S-2	-0.2
1884	Bal-a	53	210	25	37	4	6	0		3		.176	.192	.252	42	-13				.926	-8	C-47/O-6,1-1	-1.6
1885	Bal-a	69	254	27	39	4	5	1	20	17		.154	.215	.220	38	-17				**.943**	2	C-61,O-10/2-3	-0.9
1886	Bal-a	25	85	15	18	0	1	0	7	10		.212	.295	.235	68	-3	8			.952	-3	C-25	-0.2
Total	5	179	663	85	116	13	12	1	36	34	1	.175	.220	.235	45	-40	8			.927	-8	C-164/O-16,2-3,S1	-3.1

■ WALT TRAGESSER
Tragesser, Walter Joseph b: 6/14/1887, Lafayette, Ind. d: 12/14/70, Lafayette, Ind. BR/TR, 6', 175 lbs. Deb: 7/30/13

YEAR	TM/L	G	AB	R	H	2B	3B	HR	RBI	BB	SO	AVG	OBP	SLG	PRO+	BR/A	SB	CS	SBR	FA	FR	G/POS	TPR
1913	Bos-N	2	0	0	0	0	0	0	0	0	0	—	—	—	—	0	0			1.000	-0	/C-2	0.0
1915	Bos-N	7	7	1	0	0	0	0	0	0	2	.000	.000	.000	-99	-2	0			.944	1	/C-7	-0.1
1916	Bos-N	41	54	3	11	1	0	0	4	5	10	.204	.283	.222	59	-2	0			.971	4	C-29	0.3
1917	Bos-N	98	297	23	66	10	2	0	25	15	36	.222	.264	.269	68	-12	5			.971	-2	C-94	-0.7
1918	Bos-N	7	1	0	0	0	0	0	0	0	0	.000	.000	.000	-99	-0	0			.833	1	/C-7	0.0
1919	Bos-N	20	40	3	7	2	0	0	3	2	10	.175	.233	.225	39	-3	1			.959	-0	C-14	-0.3
	Phi-N	35	114	7	27	7	0	0	8	9	31	.237	.298	.298	74	-3	4			.953	4	C-34	0.4
	Yr	55	154	10	34	9	0	0	11	11	41	.221	.281	.279	67	-6	5			.954	4	C-48	0.1

YEAR	TM/L	G	AB	R	H	2B	3B	HR	RBI	BB	SO	AVG	OBP	SLG	PRO+	BR/A	SB	CS	SBR	FA	FR	G/POS	TPR
1920	Phi-N	62	176	17	37	11	1	6	26	4	36	.210	.236	.386	73	-7	4	0	1	.944	-13	C-52	-1.6
Total	7	272	689	54	148	31	3	6	66	35	125	.215	.260	.295	67	-29	14	0		.961	-6	C-239	-2.0
■ **RED TRAMBACK** Tramback, Stephen Joseph b: 11/1/15, Iselin, Pa. d: 12/28/79, Buffalo, N.Y. BL/TL, 6', 175 lbs. Deb: 9/15/40																							
1940	NY-N	2	4	0	1	0	0	0	0	1	1	.250	.400	.250	82	-0	1			.667	-0	/O-1	0.0
■ **ALAN TRAMMELL** Trammell, Alan Stuart b: 2/21/58, Garden Grove, Cal. BR/TR, 6', 175 lbs. Deb: 9/9/77																							
1977	Det-A	19	43	6	8	0	0	0	0	4	12	.186	.255	.186	21	-5	0	0	0	.961	-7	S-19	-1.0
1978	Det-A	139	448	49	120	14	6	2	34	45	56	.268	.337	.339	88	-6	3	1	0	.979	6	*S-139	1.7
1979	Det-A	142	460	68	127	11	4	6	50	43	55	.276	.338	.357	85	-9	17	14	-3	.961	-14	*S-142	-1.1
1980	Det-A★	146	560	107	168	21	5	9	65	69	63	.300	.380	.404	112	11	12	12	-4	.980	-27	*S-144	-0.3
1981	Det-A	105	392	52	101	15	3	2	31	49	31	.258	.345	.327	91	-3	10	3	1	.983	6	*S-105	1.5
1982	Det-A	157	489	66	126	34	3	9	57	52	47	.258	.329	.395	97	-2	19	8	1	.978	-8	*S-157	0.6
1983	Det-A	142	505	83	161	31	2	14	66	57	64	.319	.388	.471	139	28	30	10	3	.979	-18	*S-140	2.6
1984	*Det-A†	139	555	85	174	34	5	14	69	60	63	.314	.383	.468	135	27	19	13	-2	.980	-12	*S-114,D-22	2.4
1985	Det-A★	149	605	79	156	21	7	13	57	50	71	.258	.317	.380	90	-8	14	5	1	.977	-16	*S-149	-0.8
1986	Det-A	151	574	107	159	33	7	21	75	59	57	.277	.350	.469	121	16	25	12	0	.969	6	*S-149/D-2	3.5
1987	*Det-A★	151	597	109	205	34	3	28	105	60	47	.343	.406	.551	157	49	21	2	5	.971	-10	*S-149	5.4
1988	Det-A†	128	466	73	145	24	1	15	69	46	46	.311	.378	.464	140	25	7	4	-0	.980	-7	*S-125	2.8
1989	Det-A	121	449	54	109	20	3	5	43	45	45	.243	.317	.334	86	-8	10	2	2	.985	12	*S-117/D-2	1.6
1990	Det-A★	146	559	71	170	37	1	14	89	68	55	.304	.381	.449	130	24	12	10	-2	.979	1	*S-142/D-3	3.3
1991	Det-A	101	375	57	93	20	0	9	55	37	39	.248	.320	.373	90	-5	11	2	2	.979	4	S-92/D-6	0.8
1992	Det-A	29	102	11	28	7	1	1	11	15	4	.275	.373	.392	114	2	2	2	-1	.977	-1	S-27/D-1	0.3
1993	Det-A	112	401	72	132	25	3	12	60	38	38	.329	.390	.496	137	21	12	8	-1	.989	-13	S-63,3-35/O-8,D-6	1.1
1994	Det-A	76	292	38	78	17	1	8	28	16	35	.267	.307	.414	84	-8	3	0	1	.968	-4	S-63,D-11	-0.6
1995	Det-A	74	223	28	60	12	0	2	23	27	19	.269	.348	.350	83	-5	3	1	0	.980	-6	S-60/D-6	-0.6
1996	Det-A	66	193	16	45	2	0	1	16	10	27	.233	.271	.259	35	-19	6	0	2	.976	-4	S-43,2-11/3-8,O-1	-1.6
Total	20	2293	8288	1231	2365	412	55	185	1003	850	874	.285	.354	.415	110	126	236	109	5	.977	-111	*S-2139/D-59,32O	21.6
■ **BUBBA TRAMMELL** Trammell, Thomas Bubba b: 11/6/71, Knoxville, Tenn. BR/TR, 6'3", 205 lbs. Deb: 4/1/97																							
1997	Det-A	44	123	14	28	5	0	4	13	15	35	.228	.312	.366	77	-4	3	1	0	1.000	-1	O-28,D-15	-0.6
1998	TB-A	59	199	28	57	18	1	12	35	16	45	.286	.340	.568	125	6	0	2	-1	1.000	-3	O-37,D-19	0.0
Total	2	103	322	42	85	23	1	16	48	31	80	.264	.329	.491	107	2	3	3	-1	1.000	-4	/O-65,D-34	-0.6
■ **CECIL TRAVIS** Travis, Cecil Howell b: 8/8/13, Riverdale, Ga. BL/TR, 6'1.5", 185 lbs. Deb: 5/16/33																							
1933	Was-A	18	43	7	13	1	0	0	2	2	5	.302	.348	.326	80	-1	0	0	0	.974	4	3-15	0.3
1934	Was-A	109	392	48	125	22	4	1	53	24	37	.319	.361	.403	101	0	1	5	-3	.937	3	3-99	0.4
1935	Was-A	138	534	85	170	27	8	0	61	41	28	.318	.377	.399	104	4	4	2	0	.963	21	*3-114,O-16	2.7
1936	Was-A	138	517	77	164	34	10	2	92	39	21	.317	.366	.433	102	1	4	4	-1	.938	-13	S-71,O-53/2-4,3-2	-0.9
1937	Was-A	135	526	72	181	27	7	3	66	39	34	.344	.395	.439	115	13	3	2	-0	.965	-11	*S-129	1.0
1938	Was-A☆	146	567	96	190	30	5	5	67	58	22	.335	.401	.432	117	16	6	5	-1	.950	3	*S-143	2.6
1939	Was-A	130	476	55	139	20	9	5	63	34	25	.292	.342	.403	97	-3	0	3	-2	.958	-4	*S-118	0.1
1940	Was-A★	136	528	60	170	37	11	2	76	48	23	.322	.381	.445	121	16	0	1	-1	.934	16	*3-113,S-23	3.3
1941	Was-A★	152	608	106	**218**	39	19	7	101	52	25	.359	.410	.520	152	44	2	2	-1	.964	2	*S-136,3-16	5.3
1945	Was-A	15	54	4	13	2	1	0	10	4	5	.241	.293	.315	83	-1	0	1	-1	.920	0	3-14	-0.1
1946	Was-A	137	465	45	117	22	3	1	56	45	47	.252	.323	.318	85	-10	2	4	-2	.959	-19	S-75,3-56	-2.7
1947	Was-A	74	204	10	44	4	1	1	10	16	19	.216	.273	.260	50	-14	1	3	-2	.932	-2	3-39,S-15	-1.8
Total	12	1328	4914	665	1544	265	78	27	657	402	291	.314	.370	.416	109	64	23	32	-12	.955	0	S-710,3-468/O-69,2	10.2
■ **BRIAN TRAXLER** Traxler, Brian Lee b: 9/26/67, Waukegan, Ill. BL/TL, 5'10", 200 lbs. Deb: 4/24/90																							
1990	LA-N	9	11	0	1	1	0	0	0	0	4	.091	.091	.182	-28	-2	0	0	0	1.000	1	/1-3	-0.2
■ **JIM TRAY** Tray, James (b: James Trahey) b: 2/14/1860, Jackson, Mich. d: 7/28/05, Jackson, Mich. 5'11", 180 lbs. Deb: 9/6/1884																							
1884	Ind-a	6	21	2	6	0	0	0		2		.286	.348	.286	112	0				.857	-2	/C-4,1-2	-0.1
■ **PIE TRAYNOR** Traynor, Harold Joseph b: 11/11/1899, Framingham, Mass. d: 3/16/72, Pittsburgh, Pa. BR/TR, 6', 170 lbs. Deb: 9/15/20 MH																							
1920	Pit-N	17	52	6	11	3	1	0	2	3	6	.212	.268	.308	63	-3	1	3	-2	.860	-6	S-17	-0.9
1921	Pit-N	7	19	0	5	0	0	0	2	1	2	.263	.300	.263	49	-1	0	0	0	.917	1	/3-3,S-1	0.0
1922	Pit-N	142	571	89	161	17	12	4	81	27	28	.282	.319	.375	77	-20	17	3	3	.945	-6	*3-124,S-18	-1.0
1923	Pit-N	153	616	108	208	19	**19**	12	101	34	19	.338	.377	.489	124	20	28	13	1	.950	8	*3-152/S-1	4.0
1924	Pit-N	142	545	86	160	26	13	5	82	37	26	.294	.340	.417	100	-1	24	18	-4	.968	9	*3-141	1.5
1925	*Pit-N	150	591	114	189	39	14	6	106	52	19	.320	.377	.464	106	5	15	9	-1	**.957**	23	*3-150/S-1	3.5
1926	Pit-N	152	574	83	182	25	17	3	92	38	14	.317	.361	.436	108	5	8			.952	7	*3-148/S-3	2.1
1927	*Pit-N	149	573	93	196	32	9	5	106	22	11	.342	.370	.455	112	8	11			.962	13	*3-143/S-9	2.8
1928	Pit-N	144	569	91	192	38	12	3	124	28	10	.337	.370	.462	112	9	12			.946	4	*3-144	2.0
1929	Pit-N	130	540	94	192	27	12	4	108	30	7	.356	.393	.472	111	9	13			.951	-1	*3-130	1.2
1930	Pit-N	130	497	90	182	22	11	9	119	48	19	.366	.423	.509	124	21	7			.941	5	*3-130	2.9
1931	Pit-N	155	615	81	183	37	15	2	103	54	28	.298	.354	.416	107	6	6			.925	-9	*3-155	0.7
1932	Pit-N	135	513	74	169	27	10	2	68	32	20	.329	.373	.433	118	13	6			.936	-3	*3-127	1.9
1933	Pit-N★	154	624	85	190	27	6	1	82	35	24	.304	.342	.372	104	3	5			.946	-1	*3-154	1.3
1934	Pit-N★	119	444	62	137	22	10	1	61	21	27	.309	.341	.410	98	-2	3			.954	-10	*3-110,M	-0.7
1935	Pit-N	57	204	24	57	10	3	1	36	10	17	.279	.323	.373	84	-5	2			.888	-3	3-49/1-1,M	-0.6
1937	Pit-N	5	12	3	2	0	0	0	0	0	1	.167	.167	.167	-9	-2	0			1.000	1	/3-3,M	0.0
Total	17	1941	7559	1183	2416	371	164	58	1273	472	278	.320	.362	.435	107	68	158	46		.947	31	*3-1863/S-50,1-1	20.7
■ **FRED TREACEY** Treacey, Frederick S. b: 1847, Brooklyn, N.Y. 5'9.5", 145 lbs. Deb: 5/16/1871 F																							
1871	Chi-n	25	124	39	42	7	5	**4**	33	2	5	.339	.349	.573	144	5	13	5	1	**.918**	7	*O-25	0.9
1872	Ath-n	47	236	53	65	7	3	2	29	5	10	.275	.290	.356	97	-1	7	5	-1	.814	-2	*O-47	-0.1
1873	Phi-n	51	243	49	62	7	2	1	32	5	6	.255	.270	.313	70	-10	2	3	-1	.771	3	*O-51	-0.4
1874	Chi-n	35	148	18	28	5	0	0	12	2	6	.189	.200	.223	35	-10	4	4	-1	.790	7	O-35	-0.3
1875	Cen-n	11	46	9	12	3	0	0	2	2	0	.261	.292	.326	124	1	1	0	0	.848	1	O-11	0.3
	Phi-n	43	179	23	38	3	3	0	15	1	3	.212	.217	.263	63	-7	6	3	0	.858	2	O-43	-0.3
	Yr	54	225	32	50	6	3	0	17	3	3	.222	.232	.276	75	-6	7	3	0	.856	4	O-54	0.0
1876	NY-N	57	256	47	54	5	1	0	18	1	5	.211	.214	.238	58	-10				.844	12	*O-57	0.1
Total	5 n	212	976	191	247	32	13	7	123	17	30	.253	.266	.334	84	-21	33	20	-2	.826	20	O-212	0.1
■ **PETE TREACEY** Treacey, Peter b: 1852, Brooklyn, N.Y. Deb: 8/5/1876 F																							
1876	NY-N	2	5	1	0	0	0	0	0	1	0	.000	.167	.000	-46	-1				.750	-1	/S-2	-0.2
■ **RAY TREADAWAY** Treadaway, Edgar Raymond b: 10/31/07, Ragland, Ala. d: 10/12/35, Chattanooga, Tenn. BL/TR, 5'7", 150 lbs. Deb: 9/17/30																							
1930	Was-A	6	19	1	4	2	0	0	1	0	3	.211	.211	.316	31	-2	0	0	0	.833	-1	/3-4	-0.3
■ **GEORGE TREADWAY** Treadway, George B. BL/TL, 6', 185 lbs. Deb: 4/27/1893																							
1893	Bal-N	115	458	78	119	16	17	1	67	58	50	.260	.348	.376	91	-7	24			.901	9	*O-115	-0.3
1894	Bro-N	123	479	124	157	27	26	4	102	72	43	.328	.418	.518	134	28	27			.892	1	*O-122/1-1	1.6
1895	Bro-N	86	339	54	87	14	3	7	54	33	22	.257	.326	.378	88	-6	9			.886	-9	O-86	-1.8
1896	Lou-N	2	7	0	1	0	0	0	1	1	0	.143	.250	.143	5	-1	0			.500	-1	/O-1,1-1	-0.2
Total	4	326	1283	256	364	57	46	12	224	164	115	.284	.368	.428	106	14	60			.891	-1	O-324/1-2	-0.7
■ **JEFF TREADWAY** Treadway, Hugh Jeffery b: 1/22/63, Columbus, Ga. BL/TR, 5'11", 170 lbs. Deb: 9/4/87																							
1987	Cin-N	23	84	9	28	4	0	2	4	2	6	.333	.356	.452	108	1	1	0	0	.958	-7	2-21	-0.5
1988	Cin-N	103	301	30	76	19	4	2	23	27	30	.252	.320	.362	92	-3	2	0	1	.984	3	2-97/3-2	0.4

YEAR	TM/L	G	AB	R	H	2B	3B	HR	RBI	BB	SO	AVG	OBP	SLG	PRO+	BR/A	SB	CS	SBR	FA	FR	G/POS	TPR
1989	Atl-N	134	473	58	131	18	3	8	40	30	38	.277	.320	.378	96	-3	3	2	-0	.981	3	*2-123/3-6	0.5
1990	Atl-N	128	474	56	134	20	2	11	59	25	42	.283	.323	.403	93	-5	3	4	-2	.976	10	*2-122	0.6
1991	*Atl-N	106	306	41	98	17	2	3	32	23	19	.320	.372	.418	115	6	2	2	-1	.960	-8	2-93	0.0
1992	*Atl-N	61	126	5	28	6	1	0	5	9	16	.222	.274	.286	55	-7	1	2	-1	.993	0	2-45/3-1	-0.8
1993	Cle-A	97	221	25	67	14	1	2	27	14	21	.303	.350	.403	102	1	1	1	-0	.933	1	3-42,2-19/D-4	0.2
1994	LA-N	52	67	14	20	3	0	0	5	5	8	.299	.356	.343	89	-1	1	1	-0	.950	-1	2-24/3-3	-0.1
1995	LA-N	17	17	2	2	0	1	0	3	0	2	.118	.118	.235	-11	-3	0	0	0	.000	-1	/3-2,2-1	-0.3
	Mon-N	41	50	4	12	2	0	0	10	5	2	.240	.309	.280	55	-3	0	1	-1	1.000	-2	2-11/3-1	-0.5
	Yr	58	67	6	14	2	1	0	13	5	4	.209	.264	.269	41	-6	0	1	-1	1.000	-2	2-12/3-3	-0.8
Total	9	762	2119	244	596	103	14	28	208	140	184	.281	.329	.383	94	-17	14	13	-4	.975	-1	2-556/3-57,D-4	-0.5

■ RED TREADWAY Treadway, Thadford Leon b: 4/28/20, Athlone, N.C. d: 5/26/94, Atlanta, Ga. BL/TR, 5'10", 175 lbs. Deb: 7/25/44

YEAR	TM/L	G	AB	R	H	2B	3B	HR	RBI	BB	SO	AVG	OBP	SLG	PRO+	BR/A	SB	CS	SBR	FA	FR	G/POS	TPR
1944	NY-N	50	170	23	51	5	2	0	5	13	11	.300	.350	.353	98	-0	2			.957	1	O-38	-0.1
1945	NY-N	88	224	31	54	4	2	4	23	20	13	.241	.303	.330	75	-8	3			.940	-9	O-60	-2.0
Total	2	138	394	54	105	9	4	4	28	33	24	.266	.323	.340	85	-8	5			.948	-8	/O-98	-2.1

■ FRANK TRECHOCK Trechock, Frank Adam b: 12/24/15, Windber, Pa. d: 1/16/89, Minneapolis, Minn. BR/TR, 5'10", 175 lbs. Deb: 9/19/37

YEAR	TM/L	G	AB	R	H	2B	3B	HR	RBI	BB	SO	AVG	OBP	SLG	PRO+	BR/A	SB	CS	SBR	FA	FR	G/POS	TPR
1937	Was-A	1	4	0	2	0	0	0	0	0	1	.500	.500	.500	160	0	0	0	0	.750	0	/S-1	0.1

■ NICK TREMARK Tremark, Nicholas Joseph b: 10/15/12, Yonkers, N.Y. BL/TL, 5'5", 150 lbs. Deb: 8/9/34

YEAR	TM/L	G	AB	R	H	2B	3B	HR	RBI	BB	SO	AVG	OBP	SLG	PRO+	BR/A	SB	CS	SBR	FA	FR	G/POS	TPR
1934	Bro-N	17	28	3	7	1	0	0	6	2	2	.250	.300	.286	61	-2	0			1.000	-1	/O-9	-0.3
1935	Bro-N	10	13	1	3	1	0	0	3	1	1	.231	.286	.308	61	-1	0			1.000	-1	/O-4	-0.1
1936	Bro-N	8	32	6	8	2	0	0	1	3	2	.250	.333	.313	74	-1	0			1.000	1	/O-8	0.0
Total	3	35	73	10	18	4	0	0	10	6	5	.247	.313	.301	67	-3	0			1.000	-0	/O-21	-0.4

■ CHRIS TREMIE Tremie, Christopher James b: 10/17/69, Houston, Tex. BR/TR, 6', 200 lbs. Deb: 7/1/95

YEAR	TM/L	G	AB	R	H	2B	3B	HR	RBI	BB	SO	AVG	OBP	SLG	PRO+	BR/A	SB	CS	SBR	FA	FR	G/POS	TPR
1995	Chi-A	10	24	0	4	0	0	0	0	1	2	.167	.200	.167	-3	-4	0	0	0	.976	-1	/C-9,D-1	-0.4
1998	Tex-A	2	3	2	1	1	0	0	0	1	1	.333	.500	.667	192	0	0	0	0	.000	0	/D-2	0.0
Total	2	12	27	2	5	1	0	0	0	2	3	.185	.241	.222	22	-3	0	0	0	.976	-1	/C-9,D-3	-0.4

■ OVERTON TREMPER Tremper, Carlton Overton b: 3/22/06, Brooklyn, N.Y. d: 1/9/96, Clearwater, Fla. BR/TR, 5'10", 163 lbs. Deb: 6/16/27

YEAR	TM/L	G	AB	R	H	2B	3B	HR	RBI	BB	SO	AVG	OBP	SLG	PRO+	BR/A	SB	CS	SBR	FA	FR	G/POS	TPR
1927	Bro-N	26	60	4	14	0	0	0	4	0	2	.233	.246	.233	29	-6	0			1.000	-4	O-18	-1.1
1928	Bro-N	10	31	1	6	2	1	0	1	0	1	.194	.194	.323	33	-3	0			1.000	-0	/O-9	-0.4
Total	2	36	91	5	20	2	1	0	5	0	3	.220	.228	.264	30	-9	0			1.000	-4	/O-27	-1.5

■ GEORGE TRENWITH Trenwith, George b: Ireland d: 2/1/1890, Philadelphia, Pa. Deb: 4/30/1875

YEAR	TM/L	G	AB	R	H	2B	3B	HR	RBI	BB	SO	AVG	OBP	SLG	PRO+	BR/A	SB	CS	SBR	FA	FR	G/POS	TPR
1875	Cen-n	10	45	5	8	2	0	0	4	1	2	.178	.196	.222	49	-2	0	0	0	.583	-6	3-10	-0.7
	NH-n	6	25	1	6	2	0	0	3	0	1	.240	.240	.320	106	0	0	0	0	.692	-2	/3-6	-0.1
	Yr	16	70	6	14	4	0	0	7	1	3	.200	.211	.257	69	-2	0	0	0	.629	-8	3-16	-0.8

■ MIKE TRESH Tresh, Michael b: 2/23/14, Hazleton, Pa. d: 10/4/66, Detroit, Mich. BR/TR, 5'11", 170 lbs. Deb: 9/4/38 F

YEAR	TM/L	G	AB	R	H	2B	3B	HR	RBI	BB	SO	AVG	OBP	SLG	PRO+	BR/A	SB	CS	SBR	FA	FR	G/POS	TPR
1938	Chi-A	10	29	3	7	2	0	0	2	8	4	.241	.405	.310	80	-1	0	0	0	.978	2	C-10	0.1
1939	Chi-A	119	352	49	91	5	2	0	38	64	30	.259	.377	.284	70	-13	3	2	-0	.985	2	*C-119	-0.5
1940	Chi-A	135	480	62	135	15	5	1	64	49	40	.281	.349	.340	78	-14	3	10	-5	.983	7	*C-135	-0.1
1941	Chi-A	115	390	38	98	10	1	0	33	38	27	.251	.319	.282	61	-21	1	0	0	.981	10	*C-115	-0.1
1942	Chi-A	72	233	21	54	8	1	0	15	28	24	.232	.314	.275	68	-9	2	0	1	.977	-6	C-72	-0.9
1943	Chi-A	86	279	20	60	3	0	0	20	37	20	.215	.307	.226	57	-14	2	1	0	.982	-1	C-85	-0.9
1944	Chi-A	93	312	22	81	8	1	0	25	37	15	.260	.342	.292	83	-5	0	3	-2	.981	-3	C-93	-0.5
1945	Chi-A†	150	458	50	114	12	0	0	47	65	37	.249	.342	.275	82	-8	6	3	0	.984	-2	*C-150	-0.1
1946	Chi-A	80	217	28	47	5	2	0	21	36	24	.217	.336	.258	70	-7	0	2	-1	.995	14	C-79	1.0
1947	Chi-A	90	274	19	66	6	2	0	20	26	26	.241	.311	.277	67	-12	2	0	1	.975	-7	C-89	-1.3
1948	Chi-A	39	108	10	27	1	0	1	11	9	9	.250	.308	.287	61	-6	0	0	0	.983	-1	C-34	-0.5
1949	Cle-A	38	37	4	8	0	0	0	1	5	7	.216	.310	.216	41	-3	0	0	0	1.000	6	C-38	0.3
Total	12	1027	3169	326	788	75	14	2	297	402	263	.249	.335	.283	71	-113	19	21	-7	.983	22	*C-1019	-3.5

■ TOM TRESH Tresh, Thomas Michael b: 9/20/37, Detroit, Mich. BB/TR, 6', 191 lbs. Deb: 9/3/61 F

YEAR	TM/L	G	AB	R	H	2B	3B	HR	RBI	BB	SO	AVG	OBP	SLG	PRO+	BR/A	SB	CS	SBR	FA	FR	G/POS	TPR
1961	NY-A	9	8	1	2	0	0	0	0	0	1	.250	.250	.250	36	-1	0	0	0	1.000	3	/S-3	0.2
1962	*NY-A★	157	622	94	178	26	5	20	93	67	74	.286	.363	.441	119	17	4	8	-4	.970	-11	*S-111,O-43	1.0
1963	*NY-A★	145	520	91	140	28	5	25	71	83	79	.269	.374	.487	140	29	3	3	-1	.981	2	*O-144	2.4
1964	*NY-A	153	533	75	131	25	5	16	73	73	110	.246	.344	.402	105	5	13	0	4	**.996**	-14	*O-146	-1.3
1965	NY-A	156	602	94	168	29	6	26	74	59	92	.279	.348	.477	133	25	5	2	0	.970	-21	*O-154	-0.3
1966	NY-A	151	537	76	125	12	4	27	68	86	89	.233	.345	.421	123	18	5	4	-1	.985	28	O-84,3-64	4.1
1967	NY-A	130	448	45	98	23	3	14	53	50	86	.219	.303	.377	104	2	1	0	0	.972	4	*O-118	-0.1
1968	NY-A	152	507	60	99	18	3	11	52	76	97	.195	.305	.308	89	-5	10	5	0	.951	9	*S-119,O-27	1.7
1969	NY-A	45	143	13	26	5	2	1	9	17	23	.182	.269	.266	52	-9	2	1	0	.980	0	S-41	-0.5
	Det-A	94	331	46	74	13	1	13	37	39	47	.224	.309	.387	90	-5	2	2	-1	.965	-18	S-77,O-11/3-1	-1.7
	Yr	139	474	59	100	18	3	14	46	56	70	.211	.297	.350	79	-14	4	3	-1	.971	-18	*S-118,O-11/3-1	-2.2
Total	9	1192	4251	595	1041	179	34	153	530	550	698	.245	.337	.411	113	75	45	25	-2	.979	-19	O-727,S-351/3-65	5.5

■ ALEX TREVINO Trevino, Alejandro (Castro) b: 8/26/57, Monterrey, Mex. BR/TR, 5'11", 170 lbs. Deb: 9/11/78 F

YEAR	TM/L	G	AB	R	H	2B	3B	HR	RBI	BB	SO	AVG	OBP	SLG	PRO+	BR/A	SB	CS	SBR	FA	FR	G/POS	TPR
1978	NY-N	6	12	3	3	0	0	0	0	1	2	.250	.308	.250	60	-1	0	0	0	1.000	0	/C-5,3-1	-0.1
1979	NY-N	79	207	24	56	11	1	0	20	20	27	.271	.338	.333	87	-3	2	2	-1	.976	10	C-36,3-27/2-8	0.7
1980	NY-N	106	355	26	91	11	2	0	37	13	41	.256	.285	.299	65	-17	0	3	-2	.977	-5	C-86,3-14/2-1	-2.2
1981	NY-N	56	149	17	39	2	0	0	10	13	19	.262	.325	.275	73	-5	3	0	1	.963	2	C-45/2-4,O-2,3-1	0.0
1982	Cin-N	120	355	24	89	10	3	1	33	34	34	.251	.321	.304	74	-11	3	1	0	.979	4	*C-116/3-2	-0.3
1983	Cin-N	74	167	14	36	8	1	1	13	17	20	.216	.288	.293	59	-9	0	0	0	.987	11	C-63/3-4,2-1	0.4
1984	Cin-N	6	6	0	1	0	0	0	0	0	2	.167	.167	.167	-6	-1	0	0	0	1.000	-0	/C-4	-0.1
	Atl-N	79	266	36	65	16	0	3	28	16	27	.244	.290	.338	71	-10	5	2	0	.989	7	C-79	0.0
	Yr	85	272	36	66	16	0	3	28	16	29	.243	.287	.335	69	-11	5	2	0	.989	6	C-83	-0.1
1985	SF-N	57	157	17	34	10	1	6	19	20	24	.217	.305	.408	103	0	0	0	0	.978	-0	C-55/3-1	0.2
1986	LA-N	89	202	31	53	13	0	4	26	27	35	.262	.352	.386	111	3	0	0	0	.969	-4	C-63/1-1	0.3
1987	LA-N	72	144	16	32	7	1	3	16	6	28	.222	.273	.347	65	-8	1	0	0	.987	-3	C-45/O-2,3-1	-0.8
1988	Hou-N	78	193	19	48	17	0	2	13	24	29	.249	.341	.368	108	2	5	2	0	.977	-9	C-74/O-1	-0.2
1989	Hou-N	59	131	15	38	7	1	2	16	7	18	.290	.331	.405	113	2	0	0	0	.989	-3	C-32/1-2,3-2	0.0
1990	Hou-N	42	69	3	13	3	0	1	10	6	11	.188	.273	.275	53	-4	0	1	-1	.992	6	C-30/1-1	0.2
	NY-N	9	10	0	3	1	0	0	2	1	0	.300	.364	.400	110	0	0	0	0	.929	0	/C-7	0.1
	Cin-N	7	7	0	3	1	0	0	1	0	0	.429	.500	.571	186	1	0	0	0	1.000	1	/C-2	0.2
	Yr	58	86	3	19	5	0	1	13	7	11	.221	.302	.314	71	-3	0	1	-1	.982	7	C-39/1-1	0.5
Total	13	939	2430	245	604	117	10	23	244	205	317	.249	.312	.333	81	-61	19	11	-1	.979	16	C-742/3-53,2-14,O1	-1.6

■ BOBBY TREVINO Trevino, Carlos (Castro) b: 8/15/43, Monterrey, Mexico BR/TR, 6'2", 185 lbs. Deb: 5/22/68 F

YEAR	TM/L	G	AB	R	H	2B	3B	HR	RBI	BB	SO	AVG	OBP	SLG	PRO+	BR/A	SB	CS	SBR	FA	FR	G/POS	TPR
1968	Cal-A	17	40	1	9	1	0	0	1	2	9	.225	.262	.250	58	-2	0	1	-1	.962	-0	O-11	-0.4

■ GUS TRIANDOS Triandos, Gus b: 7/30/30, San Francisco, Cal BR/TR, 6'3", 215 lbs. Deb: 8/13/53

YEAR	TM/L	G	AB	R	H	2B	3B	HR	RBI	BB	SO	AVG	OBP	SLG	PRO+	BR/A	SB	CS	SBR	FA	FR	G/POS	TPR
1953	NY-A	18	51	5	8	2	0	1	6	3	9	.157	.204	.255	24	-6	0	0	0	.991	0	1-12/C-5	-0.6
1954	NY-A	2	1	0	0	0	0	0	0	0	1	.000	.000	.000	-99	-0	0	0	0	.000	0	/C-1	0.0
1955	Bal-A	140	481	47	133	17	3	12	65	40	55	.277	.335	.399	104	1	0	0	0	.989	0	*1-103,C-36/3-1	-0.4
1956	Bal-A	131	452	47	126	18	1	21	88	48	73	.279	.351	.462	122	12	0	0	0	.989	10	C-89,1-52	2.2
1957	Bal-A☆	129	418	44	106	21	1	19	72	38	73	.254	.320	.445	114	6	0	0	0	.992	-2	*C-120	0.9
1958	Bal-A★	137	474	59	116	10	0	30	79	60	65	.245	.331	.456	120	12	1	0	0	.987	1	*C-132	2.2
1959	Bal-A★	126	393	43	85	7	1	25	73	65	56	.216	.332	.430	110	5	0	0	0	.981	2	*C-125	1.4
1960	Bal-A	109	364	36	98	18	0	12	54	41	62	.269	.345	.418	107	3	0	0	0	.989	-7	*C-105	0.2

YEAR	TM/L	G	AB	R	H	2B	3B	HR	RBI	BB	SO	AVG	OBP	SLG	PRO+	BR/A	SB	CS	SBR	FA	FR	G/POS	TPR
1961	Bal-A	115	397	35	97	21	0	17	63	44	60	.244	.321	.426	101	-0	0	0	0	.989	4	*C-114	0.9
1962	Bal-A	66	207	20	33	7	0	6	23	29	43	.159	.263	.280	49	-15	0	0	0	.985	-2	C-63	-1.5
1963	Det-A	106	327	28	78	13	0	14	41	32	67	.239	.318	.407	98	-1	0	0	0	**.998**	-6	C-90	-0.3
1964	Phi-N	73	188	17	47	9	0	8	33	26	41	.250	.344	.426	117	5	0	0	0	.985	2	C-64/1-1	1.0
1965	Phi-N	30	82	3	14	2	0	0	4	9	17	.171	.253	.195	29	-8	0	0	0	.975	-5	C-28	-1.3
	Hou-N	24	72	5	13	2	0	2	7	5	14	.181	.244	.292	54	-5	0	0	0	.970	-2	C-20	-0.6
	Yr	54	154	8	27	4	0	2	11	14	31	.175	.249	.240	40	-12	0	0	0	.973	-7	C-48	-1.9
Total	13	1206	3907	389	954	147	6	167	608	440	636	.244	.324	.413	103	10	1	0	0	.987	-4	C-992,1-168/3-1	4.1

■ MANNY TRILLO

Trillo, Jesus Manuel Marcano (b: Jesus Manuel Marcano (Trillo)) b: 12/25/50, Caripito, Ven. BR/TR, 6'1", 164 lbs. Deb: 6/28/73

YEAR	TM/L	G	AB	R	H	2B	3B	HR	RBI	BB	SO	AVG	OBP	SLG	PRO+	BR/A	SB	CS	SBR	FA	FR	G/POS	TPR
1973	Oak-A	17	12	0	3	2	0	0	3	0	4	.250	.250	.417	90	-0	0	0	0	.941	5	2-16	0.5
1974	*Oak-A	21	33	3	5	0	0	0	2	2	8	.152	.222	.152	10	-4	0	0	0	.949	6	2-21	0.2
1975	Chi-N	154	545	55	135	12	2	7	70	45	78	.248	.309	.316	70	-21	1	7	-4	.967	16	*2-153/S-1	-0.1
1976	Chi-N	158	582	42	139	24	3	4	59	53	70	.239	.306	.311	69	-23	17	6	2	.981	18	*2-156/S-1	0.7
1977	Chi-N★	152	504	51	141	18	5	7	57	44	58	.280	.344	.377	84	-11	3	5	-2	.970	30	*2-149	2.7
1978	Chi-N	152	552	53	144	17	5	4	55	50	67	.261	.325	.332	75	-18	0	7	-4	.978	**29**	*2-149	1.8
1979	Phi-N	118	431	40	112	22	1	6	42	20	59	.260	.299	.357	76	-15	4	7	-3	.985	6	*2-118	-0.4
1980	*Phi-N	141	531	68	155	25	9	7	43	32	46	.292	.336	.412	102	1	8	3	1	.987	19	*2-140	3.1
1981	*Phi-N★	94	349	37	100	14	3	6	36	26	37	.287	.341	.395	104	2	10	4	1	.987	11	2-94	2.0
1982	Phi-N★	149	549	52	149	24	1	0	39	33	53	.271	.316	.319	76	-17	8	10	-4	**.994**	5	*2-149	-0.8
1983	Cle-A★	88	320	33	87	13	1	1	29	21	46	.272	.317	.328	75	-11	1	3	-2	.989	3	2-87	-0.5
	Mon-N	31	121	16	32	8	0	2	16	10	18	.264	.331	.380	97	-0	0	0	0	.979	-6	2-31	-0.5
1984	SF-N	98	401	45	102	21	1	4	36	25	55	.254	.303	.342	84	-9	0	0	0	.988	-8	2-96/3-4	-1.5
1985	SF-N	125	451	36	101	16	2	3	25	40	44	.224	.289	.288	65	-21	2	0	1	.981	4	*2-120/3-1	-1.4
1986	Chi-N	81	152	22	45	10	0	1	19	16	21	.296	.363	.382	98	-0	0	2	-1	.949	-0	3-53,1-11/2-6	-0.2
1987	Chi-N	108	214	27	63	8	0	8	26	25	37	.294	.368	.444	110	3	0	3	-2	.994	-4	1-47,3-35,2-10,/S-6	-0.6
1988	Chi-N	76	164	15	41	5	0	1	14	8	32	.250	.285	.299	65	-7	2	0	1	.994	1	1-24,3-17,2-13,/S-7	-0.7
1989	Cin-N	17	39	3	8	0	0	0	0	2	9	.205	.262	.205	34	-3	0	0	0	1.000	-4	2-10/1-3,S-1	-0.8
Total	17	1780	5950	598	1562	239	33	61	571	452	742	.263	.318	.345	80	-155	56	57	-17	.981	129	*2-1518,3-110/1S	3.5

■ COAKER TRIPLETT

Triplett, Herman Coaker b: 12/18/11, Boone, N.C. d: 1/30/92, Boone, N.C. BR/TR, 5'11", 185 lbs. Deb: 4/19/38

YEAR	TM/L	G	AB	R	H	2B	3B	HR	RBI	BB	SO	AVG	OBP	SLG	PRO+	BR/A	SB	CS	SBR	FA	FR	G/POS	TPR
1938	Chi-N	12	36	4	9	2	1	0	2	0	1	.250	.250	.361	65	-2	0			1.000	-1	/O-9	-0.3
1941	StL-N	76	185	29	53	6	3	3	21	18	27	.286	.350	.400	104	1	0			.965	-3	O-46	-0.4
1942	StL-N	64	154	18	42	7	4	1	23	17	15	.273	.345	.390	107	1	1			.966	-3	O-46	-0.4
1943	StL-N	9	25	1	2	0	0	1	4	1	6	.080	.115	.200	-9	-4	0			1.000	-1	/O-6	-0.4
	Phi-N	105	360	45	98	16	4	14	52	28	28	.272	.325	.456	129	11	2			.970	2	O-90	0.8
	Yr	114	385	46	100	16	4	15	56	29	34	.260	.312	.439	120	7	2			.972	1	O-96	0.4
1944	Phi-N	84	184	15	43	5	1	1	25	19	10	.234	.305	.288	70	-7	1			.989	-1	O-44	-1.0
1945	Phi-N	120	363	36	87	11	1	7	46	40	27	.240	.315	.333	83	-9	6			.945	-3	O-92	-1.7
Total	6	470	1307	148	334	47	14	27	173	123	114	.256	.320	.375	97	-8	10			.965	-9	O-333	-3.4

■ HAL TROSKY

Trosky, Harold Arthur Sr. (b: Harold Arthur Troyavesky Sr.)
b: 11/11/12, Norway, Iowa d: 6/18/79, Cedar Rapids, Ia. BL/TR, 6'2", 207 lbs. Deb: 9/11/33 F

YEAR	TM/L	G	AB	R	H	2B	3B	HR	RBI	BB	SO	AVG	OBP	SLG	PRO+	BR/A	SB	CS	SBR	FA	FR	G/POS	TPR
1933	Cle-A	11	44	6	13	1	2	1	8	2	12	.295	.340	.477	110	0	0	0	0	.990	-1	1-11	-0.1
1934	Cle-A	154	625	117	206	45	9	35	142	58	49	.330	.388	.598	149	42	2	2	-1	.986	0	*1-154	2.5
1935	Cle-A	154	632	84	171	33	7	26	113	46	60	.271	.321	.468	100	-4	1	2	-1	.993	1	*1-153	-1.9
1936	Cle-A	151	629	124	216	45	9	42	**162**	36	58	.343	.382	.644	148	41	6	5	-1	.985	1	*1-151/2-1	2.3
1937	Cle-A	153	601	104	179	36	9	32	128	65	60	.298	.367	.547	127	21	3	1	0	.993	-2	*1-152	0.2
1938	Cle-A	150	554	106	185	40	9	19	110	67	40	.334	.407	.542	138	32	5	1	1	.993	4	*1-148	1.8
1939	Cle-A	122	448	89	150	31	4	25	104	52	28	.335	.405	.589	157	37	2	3	-1	.992	11	*1-118	3.1
1940	Cle-A	140	522	85	154	39	4	25	93	79	45	.295	.392	.529	140	31	1	2	-1	.991	-7	*1-139	1.0
1941	Cle-A	89	310	43	91	17	0	11	51	44	21	.294	.383	.455	127	12	1	2	-1	.989	-3	1-85	0.3
1944	Chi-A	135	497	55	120	32	2	10	70	62	30	.241	.327	.374	101	1	3	2	-0	.993	-9	*1-130	-1.7
1946	Chi-A	88	299	22	76	12	3	2	31	34	37	.254	.330	.334	89	-4	4	3	-1	.991	-8	1-80	-1.8
Total	11	1347	5161	835	1561	331	58	228	1012	545	440	.302	.371	.522	130	210	28	23	-5	.991	-12	*1-1321/2-1	5.7

■ MIKE TROST

Trost, Michael J. b: 1866, Philadelphia, Pa. d: 3/24/01, Philadelphia, Pa. TR , 6'0.5", 180 lbs. Deb: 8/21/1890

YEAR	TM/L	G	AB	R	H	2B	3B	HR	RBI	BB	SO	AVG	OBP	SLG	PRO+	BR/A	SB	CS	SBR	FA	FR	G/POS	TPR
1890	StL-a	17	51	10	13	2	0	1	7	6		.255	.345	.353	93	-1	4			.890	1	C-13/O-4	0.0
1895	Lou-N	3	12	1	1	0	0	0	1	0	1	.083	.083	.083	-61	-3	1			1.000	-1	/1-3	-0.3
Total	2	20	63	11	14	2	0	1	8	6	1	.222	.300	.302	66	-4	5			.890	0	/C-13,O-4,1-3	-0.3

■ SAM TROTT

Trott, Samuel W. b: 3/1859, Maryland d: 6/5/25, Catonsville, Md. BL/TL, 5'9", 190 lbs. Deb: 5/29/1880 M

YEAR	TM/L	G	AB	R	H	2B	3B	HR	RBI	BB	SO	AVG	OBP	SLG	PRO+	BR/A	SB	CS	SBR	FA	FR	G/POS	TPR
1880	Bos-N	39	125	14	26	4	1	0	9	3	5	.208	.227	.256	65	-4				.893	6	C-36/O-4	0.2
1881	Det-N	6	25	3	5	2	1	0	2	1	3	.200	.231	.360	80	-1				.868	-2	/C-6	-0.3
1882	Det-N	32	129	11	31	7	1	0	12	0	13	.240	.240	.310	75	-4				.890	7	C-23/S-3,2-3,1O3	0.3
1883	Det-N	75	295	27	72	14	1	0	29	10	23	.244	.269	.298	76	-8				.882	-17	2-42,C-34/O-6,1-1	-2.0
1884	Bal-a	71	284	36	73	17	9	3		4		.257	.272	.412	116	4				.931	16	C-60/2-6,O-5	2.3
1885	Bal-a	21	88	12	24	2	2	0	12	5		.273	.312	.341	108	1				.882	-5	C-17/O-4,2-2,S-1	-0.2
1887	Bal-a	85	300	44	77	16	3	0	37	27		.257	.322	.330	87	-4	8			.915	5	C-69,2-11/O-3,1S	0.6
1888	Bal-a	31	108	19	30	11	4	0	22	4		.278	.304	.454	145	5	1			.908	-4	C-27/O-3,2-1,1-1	0.3
Total	8	360	1354	166	338	73	22	3	123	54	44	.250	.280	.343	93	-11	9			.906	6	C-272/2-65,O1S3	1.2

■ QUINCY TROUPPE

Trouppe, Quincy Thomas b: 12/25/12, Dublin, Ga. d: 8/12/93, Creve Coeur, Mo. BB/TR, 6'2.5", 225 lbs. Deb: 4/30/52

YEAR	TM/L	G	AB	R	H	2B	3B	HR	RBI	BB	SO	AVG	OBP	SLG	PRO+	BR/A	SB	CS	SBR	FA	FR	G/POS	TPR
1952	Cle-A	6	10	1	1	0	0	0	0	1	3	.100	.182	.100	-22	-2	0	0	0	1.000	2	/C-6	0.1

■ DASHER TROY

Troy, John Joseph b: 5/8/1856, New York, N.Y. d: 3/30/38, Ozone Park, N.Y. BR/TR, 5'5", 154 lbs. Deb: 8/23/1881

YEAR	TM/L	G	AB	R	H	2B	3B	HR	RBI	BB	SO	AVG	OBP	SLG	PRO+	BR/A	SB	CS	SBR	FA	FR	G/POS	TPR
1881	Det-N	11	44	2	15	3	0	0	4	3	8	.341	.383	.409	143	2				.792	-4	/3-7,2-4	-0.1
1882	Det-N	40	152	22	37	7	2	0	14	5	10	.243	.268	.316	86	-2				.847	-19	2-31,S-11	-1.9
	Pro-N	4	17	1	4	0	0	0	1	0	1	.235	.235	.235	52	-1				.750	-1	/S-4	-0.2
	Yr	44	169	23	41	7	2	0	15	5	11	.243	.264	.308	83	-3				.847	-21	2-31,S-15	-2.1
1883	NY-N	85	316	37	68	7	5	0	20	9	33	.215	.237	.269	54	-17				.879	-14	*2-73,S-12	-2.6
1884	*NY-a	107	421	80	111	22	10	2		19		.264	.300	.378	123	11				.879	-21	*2-107	-0.7
1885	NY-a	45	177	24	39	3	3	2	12	5		.220	.258	.305	84	-3				.866	-13	2-42/O-2,S-1	-1.3
Total	5	292	1127	166	274	42	20	4	51	41	52	.243	.274	.327	92	-10				.873	-72	2-257/S-28,3-7,O-2	-6.8

■ FRED TRUAX

Truax, Frederick W. b: 1868, d: 12/18/1899, Omaha, Neb. Deb: 8/18/1890

YEAR	TM/L	G	AB	R	H	2B	3B	HR	RBI	BB	SO	AVG	OBP	SLG	PRO+	BR/A	SB	CS	SBR	FA	FR	G/POS	TPR
1890	Pit-N	1	3	0	1	0	0	0	1	1	1	.333	.500	.333	163	0	0			1.000	0	/O-1	0.0

■ HARRY TRUBY

Truby, Harry Garvin "Bird Eye" b: 5/12/1870, Ironton, Ohio d: 3/21/53, Ironton, Ohio TR , 5'11", 185 lbs. Deb: 8/21/1895 U

YEAR	TM/L	G	AB	R	H	2B	3B	HR	RBI	BB	SO	AVG	OBP	SLG	PRO+	BR/A	SB	CS	SBR	FA	FR	G/POS	TPR
1895	Chi-N	33	119	17	40	3	0	0	16	10	7	.336	.402	.361	92	-1	7			.950	0	2-33	0.1
1896	Chi-N	29	109	13	28	2	2	2	31	6	5	.257	.314	.367	76	-4	4			.935	1	2-28	-0.2
	Pit-N	8	32	1	5	0	0	0	3	2	4	.156	.206	.156	-4	-5	1			.949	-4	/2-8	-0.7
	Yr	37	141	14	33	2	2	2	34	8	9	.234	.289	.319	59	-9	5			.938	-3	2-36	-0.9
Total	2	70	260	31	73	5	2	2	50	18	16	.281	.342	.338	75	-10	12			.944	-3	/2-69	-0.8

■ FRANK TRUESDALE

Truesdale, Frank Day b: 3/31/1884, St.Louis, Mo. d: 8/27/43, Albuquerque, N.Mex. BB/TR, 5'8", 145 lbs. Deb: 4/27/10

YEAR	TM/L	G	AB	R	H	2B	3B	HR	RBI	BB	SO	AVG	OBP	SLG	PRO+	BR/A	SB	CS	SBR	FA	FR	G/POS	TPR
1910	StL-A	123	415	39	91	7	2	1	25	48		.219	.303	.253	79	-9	29			.914	-5	*2-122	-1.7
1911	StL-A	1	0	1	0	0	0	0	0	0		—	—	—	—	0	0			.000	0	R	0.0
1914	NY-A	77	217	22	46	4	0	0	13	39	35	.212	.340	.230	72	-5	11	11	-3	.947	-2	2-67/3-4	-1.2
1918	Bos-A	15	36	6	10	1	0	0	2	4	5	.278	.350	.306	100	0	1			.913	-1	2-10	0.0
Total	4	216	668	68	147	12	2	1	40	91	40	.220	.318	.249	78	-14	41	11		.924	-7	2-199/3-4	-2.9

YEAR	TM/L	G	AB	R	H	2B	3B	HR	RBI	BB	SO	AVG	OBP	SLG	PRO+	BR/A	SB	CS	SBR	FA	FR	G/POS	TPR
■ ED TRUMBULL	Trumbull, Edward J. (b: Edward J. Trembly) b: 11/3/1860, Chicopee, Mass. d: 1/14/37, Kingston, Pa. Deb: 5/10/1884																						
1884	Was-a	25	86	5	10	2	0	0		2		.116	.136	.140	-11	-10				.828	-0	O-15,P-10	-0.5
■ GREG TUBBS	Tubbs, Gregory Alan b: 8/31/62, Smithville, Tenn. BR/TR, 5'9", 185 lbs. Deb: 8/1/93																						
1993	Cin-N	35	59	10	11	0	0	1	2	14	10	.186	.351	.237	61	-3	3	1	0	.975	-4	O-21	-0.6
■ EDDIE TUCKER	Tucker, Eddie Jack "Scooter" b: 11/18/66, Greenville, Miss. BR/TR, 6'2", 205 lbs. Deb: 6/14/92																						
1992	Hou-N	20	50	5	6	1	0	0	3	3	13	.120	.200	.140	-2	-7	1	1	-0	.976	-6	C-19	-1.3
1993	Hou-N	9	26	1	5	1	0	0	3	2	3	.192	.250	.231	31	-3	0	0	0	1.000	2	/C-8	0.0
1995	Hou-N	5	7	1	2	0	0	1	1	0	0	.286	.286	.714	164	1	0	0	0	1.000	-0	/C-3	0.0
	Cle-A	17	20	2	0	0	0	0	0	5	4	.000	.231	.000	-33	-4	0	0	0	.982	1	C-17	-0.2
Total	3	51	103	9	13	2	0	1	7	10	20	.126	.224	.175	11	-13	1	1	-0	.986	-3	/C-47	-1.5
■ MICHAEL TUCKER	Tucker, Michael Anthony b: 6/25/71, S.Boston, Va. BL/TR, 6'2", 185 lbs. Deb: 4/26/95																						
1995	KC-A	62	177	23	46	10	0	4	17	18	51	.260	.332	.384	84	-4	2	3	-1	.986	1	O-36,D-22	-0.7
1996	KC-A	108	339	55	88	18	4	12	53	40	69	.260	.350	.442	99	-1	10	4	1	.989	-2	O-98/1-9,D-5	-0.4
1997	*Atl-N	138	499	80	141	25	7	14	56	44	116	.283	.348	.445	104	3	12	7	-1	.980	-5	*O-129	-0.5
1998	*Atl-N	130	414	54	101	27	3	13	46	49	112	.244	.328	.418	90	-6	8	3	1	.995	1	*O-118	-0.5
Total	4	438	1429	212	376	80	14	43	172	151	348	.263	.341	.429	96	-8	32	17	-1	.987	-5	O-381/D-27,1-9	-2.1
■ OLLIE TUCKER	Tucker, Oliver Dinwiddie b: 1/27/02, Radiant, Va. d: 7/13/40, Radiant, Va. BL/TR, 5'11", 180 lbs. Deb: 4/17/27																						
1927	Was-A	20	24	1	5	2	0	0	8	4	2	.208	.321	.292	61	-1	0	0	0	1.000	-0	/O-5	-0.2
1928	Cle-A	14	47	5	6	0	0	1	2	7	3	.128	.255	.191	19	-6	0	2	-1	1.000	-0	O-14	-0.8
Total	2	34	71	6	11	2	0	1	10	11	5	.155	.277	.225	33	-7	0	2	-1	1.000	-1	/O-19	-1.0
■ TOMMY TUCKER	Tucker, Thomas Joseph "Foghorn" b: 10/28/1863, Holyoke, Mass. d: 10/22/35, Montague, Mass. BB/TR, 5'11", 165 lbs. Deb: 4/16/1887																						
1887	Bal-a	136	524	114	144	15	9	6	84	29		.275	.347	.372	107	7	85			.976	4	*1-136	-0.3
1888	Bal-a	136	520	74	149	17	12	6	61	16		.287	.330	.400	137	21	43			.975	4	*1-129/O-7,P-1	1.1
1889	Bal-a	134	527	103	**196**	22	11	5	99	42	26	**.372**	**.450**	.484	**163**	**46**	63			.964	-1	*1-123,O-12	3.0
1890	Bos-N	132	539	104	159	17	8	1	62	56	22	.295	.387	.362	110	7	43			**.979**	-2	*1-132	-0.1
1891	Bos-N	140	548	103	148	16	5	2	69	37	30	.270	.349	.328	87	-10	26			.976	-3	*1-140/P-1	-1.9
1892	*Bos-N	149	542	85	153	15	7	1	62	45	35	.282	.365	.341	104	3	22			.972	-12	*1-149	-1.5
1893	Bos-N	121	486	83	138	13	2	7	91	27	31	.284	.347	.362	82	-15	8			.980	-11	*1-121	-2.4
1894	Bos-N	123	500	112	165	24	6	3	100	53	21	.330	.412	.420	94	-5	18			**.985**	2	*1-123/O-1	-0.2
1895	Bos-N	125	462	87	115	19	6	3	73	61	29	.249	.360	.335	74	-18	15			.978	6	*1-125	-0.8
1896	Bos-N	122	474	74	144	27	5	2	72	30	29	.304	.363	.395	94	-5	6			.985	3	*1-122	0.0
1897	Bos-N	4	14	0	3	2	0	0	4	2		.214	.313	.357	72	-1	0			.957	1	/1-4	0.0
	Was-N	93	352	52	119	18	5	5	61	27		.338	.403	.460	128	14	18			.984	-3	*1-93	1.0
	Yr	97	366	52	122	20	5	5	65	29		.333	.399	.456	126	14	18			.982	-2	1-97	1.0
1898	Bro-N	73	283	35	79	9	4	1	34	12		.279	.325	.350	94	-3	1			.991	7	1-73	0.4
	StL-N	72	252	18	60	7	2	0	20	18		.238	.319	.282	71	-9	1			.973	-0	1-72	-0.9
	Yr	145	535	53	139	16	6	1	54	30		.260	.322	.318	83	-12	2			.982	7	*1-145	-0.5
1899	Cle-N	127	456	40	110	19	3	0	40	24		.241	.297	.296	68	-20	3			.977	-1	*1-127	-1.9
Total	13	1687	6479	1084	1882	240	85	42	932	479	223	.290	.364	.373	101	12	352			.978	-8	*1-1669/O-20,P-2	-4.5
■ THURMAN TUCKER	Tucker, Thurman Lowell "Joe E." b: 9/26/17, Gordon, Tex. d: 5/7/93, Oklahoma City, Okla. BL/TR, 5'11", 170 lbs. Deb: 4/14/42																						
1942	Chi-A	7	24	2	3	0	1	0	1	0	4	.125	.125	.208	-7	-3	0	0	0	.900	-1	/O-5	-0.5
1943	Chi-A	139	528	81	124	15	6	3	39	79	72	.235	.336	.303	87	-6	29	17	-2	.988	15	*O-132	0.0
1944	Chi-A★	124	446	59	128	15	6	2	46	57	40	.287	.368	.361	110	7	13	12	-3	**.991**	18	*O-120	1.6
1946	Chi-A	121	438	62	126	20	3	1	36	54	45	.288	.367	.354	106	5	9	10	-3	.990	2	*O-110	-0.2
1947	Chi-A	89	254	28	60	9	4	1	17	38	25	.236	.336	.315	85	-5	10	4	1	.978	-1	O-65	-0.9
1948	*Cle-A	83	242	52	63	13	2	1	19	31	17	.260	.347	.343	86	-5	11	2	2	1.000	-1	O-66	-0.6
1949	Cle-A	80	197	28	48	5	2	0	14	18	19	.244	.307	.289	59	-12	4	2	0	.984	2	O-42	-1.1
1950	Cle-A	57	101	13	18	2	0	1	7	14	14	.178	.284	.228	34	-10	1	0	0	.968	-5	O-34	-1.5
1951	Cle-A	1	1	0	0	0	0	0	0	0	1	.000	.000	.000	-99	-0	0	0	0	.000	0	H	0.0
Total	9	701	2231	325	570	79	24	9	179	291	237	.255	.342	.325	89	-28	77	47	-5	.988	29	O-574	-3.2
■ BRIAN TURANG	Turang, Brian Craig b: 6/14/67, Long Beach, Cal. BR/TR, 5'10", 170 lbs. Deb: 8/13/93																						
1993	Sea-A	40	140	22	35	11	1	0	7	17	20	.250	.340	.343	83	-3	6	2	1	.986	-2	O-38/3-2,2-1,D-1	-0.5
1994	Sea-A	38	112	9	21	5	1	1	8	7	25	.188	.242	.277	33	-11	3	1	0	.978	-4	O-30/2-5,D-4	-1.5
Total	2	78	252	31	56	16	2	1	15	24	45	.222	.297	.313	60	-14	9	3	1	.983	-6	/O-68,2-6,D-5,3-2	-2.0
■ JERRY TURBIDY	Turbidy, Jeremiah b: 7/4/1852, Dudley, Mass. d: 9/5/20, Webster, Mass. 5'8", 165 lbs. Deb: 7/27/1884																						
1884	KC-U	13	49	5	11	4	0	0		3		.224	.269	.306	85	-2				.830	6	S-13	0.3
■ EDDIE TURCHIN	Turchin, Edward Lawrence "Smiley" b: 2/10/17, New York, N.Y. d: 2/8/82, Brookhaven, N.Y. BR/TR, 5'10", 165 lbs. Deb: 5/9/43																						
1943	Cle-A	11	13	4	3	0	0	0	1	3	1	.231	.375	.231	84	-0	0	0	0	1.000	1	/3-4,S-2	0.2
■ PETE TURGEON	Turgeon, Eugene Joseph b: 1/3/1897, Minneapolis, Minn. d: 1/24/77, Wichita Falls, Tex BR/TR, 5'6", 145 lbs. Deb: 9/20/23																						
1923	Chi-N	3	6	1	1	0	0	0	0	0	0	.167	.167	.167	-12	-1	0	0	0	.875	0	/S-2	-0.1
■ CHRIS TURNER	Turner, Christopher Wan b: 3/23/69, Bowling Green, Ky. BR/TR, 6'1", 190 lbs. Deb: 8/27/93																						
1993	Cal-A	25	75	9	21	5	0	1	13	9	16	.280	.365	.387	99	0	1	1	-0	.992	-4	C-25	-0.2
1994	Cal-A	58	149	23	36	7	1	1	12	10	29	.242	.294	.322	58	-9	3	0	1	.997	4	C-57	-0.2
1995	Cal-A	5	10	0	1	0	0	0	1	0	3	.100	.100	.100	-48	-2	0	0	0	1.000	1	/C-4,D-1	-0.1
1996	Cal-A	4	3	1	1	0	0	0	1	1	0	.333	.500	.333	116	0	0	0	0	1.000	-0	/C-3,O-1	0.0
1997	Ana-A	13	23	4	6	1	1	1	2	5	8	.261	.393	.522	136	1	0	0	0	1.000	-2	/C-8,1-2,O-1,D-1	0.0
1998	KC-A	4	9	0	0	0	0	0	0	0	4	.000	.100	.000	-68	-2	0	0	0	1.000	-1	/C-4	-0.3
Total	6	109	269	37	65	13	2	3	29	25	60	.242	.313	.338	69	-12	4	1	1	.996	-1	C-101/1-2,O-2,D-2	-0.8
■ EARL TURNER	Turner, Earl Edwin b: 5/6/23, Pittsfield, Mass. BR/TR, 5'9", 170 lbs. Deb: 9/25/48																						
1948	Pit-N	2	1	0	0	0	0	0	0	0	0	.000	.000	.000	-98	-0	0			.000	0	/C-1	0.0
1950	Pit-N	40	74	10	18	0	0	3	5	4	13	.243	.282	.365	66	-4	1			.974	2	C-34	-0.1
Total	2	42	75	10	18	0	0	3	5	4	13	.240	.278	.360	64	-4	1			.974	2	/C-35	-0.1
■ TUCK TURNER	Turner, George A. b: 2/13/1873, W.New Brighton, N.Y. d: 7/16/45, Staten Island, N.Y. BB/TL, 5'6.5", 155 lbs. Deb: 8/18/1893																						
1893	Phi-N	36	155	32	50	4	3	1	13	9	19	.323	.364	.406	105	1	7			.933	-2	O-36	-0.2
1894	Phi-N	80	339	91	141	21	9	1	82	23	13	.416	.456	.540	143	24	11			.916	-9	O-78/P-1	0.8
1895	Phi-N	59	210	51	81	8	6	2	43	25	11	.386	.453	.510	147	16	14			.847	-8	O-55	0.3
1896	Phi-N	13	32	12	7	2	0	0	0	8	5	.219	.375	.281	75	-1	6			.905	2	/O-8	0.0
	StL-N	51	203	30	50	7	8	1	27	14	21	.246	.298	.374	80	-7	6			.961	-5	O-51	-1.4
	Yr	64	235	42	57	9	8	1	27	22	26	.243	.310	.362	79	-8	12			.948	-4	O-59	-1.4
1897	StL-N	103	416	58	121	17	12	2	41	35		.291	.350	.404	101	-0	8			.945	-7	*O-102	-1.3
1898	StL-N	35	141	20	28	8	0	0	7	14		.199	.280	.255	52	-9	1			.929	-3	O-34	-1.3
Total	6	377	1496	294	478	67	38	7	213	128	69	.320	.377	.429	111	24	53			.920	-32	O-364/P-1	-3.1
■ JERRY TURNER	Turner, John Webber b: 1/17/54, Texarkana, Ark. BL/TL, 5'9", 180 lbs. Deb: 9/2/74																						
1974	SD-N	17	48	4	14	1	0	0	2	3	5	.292	.333	.313	85	-1	2	1	0	1.000	-1	O-13	-0.3
1975	SD-N	11	22	1	6	0	0	0	0	2	1	.273	.333	.273	74	-1	0	0	0	.909	0	/O-4	-0.1
1976	SD-N	105	281	41	75	16	5	5	37	32	38	.267	.342	.413	123	8	12	6	0	.960	-2	O-74	0.3
1977	SD-N	118	289	43	71	16	1	10	48	31	43	.246	.319	.412	105	1	12	4	1	.947	3	O-69	0.3
1978	SD-N	106	225	28	63	9	1	8	37	21	32	.280	.349	.436	128	8	6	4	-1	.970	-7	O-58	-0.2

YEAR	TM/L	G	AB	R	H	2B	3B	HR	RBI	BB	SO	AVG	OBP	SLG	PRO+	BR/A	SB	CS	SBR	FA	FR	G/POS	TPR
1979	SD-N	138	448	55	111	23	2	9	61	34	58	.248	.304	.368	88	-9	4	2	0	.958	-1	*O-115	-1.5
1980	SD-N	85	153	22	44	5	0	3	18	10	18	.288	.339	.379	106	1	8	3	1	1.000	-4	O-34	-0.4
1981	SD-N	33	31	5	7	0	0	2	6	4	3	.226	.314	.419	115	0	0	1	-1	.833	-1	/O-4	-0.1
	Chi-A	10	12	1	2	0	0	0	2	1	2	.167	.231	.167	16	-1	0	0	0	1.000	0	/O-1	-0.1
1982	Det-A	85	210	21	52	3	0	8	27	20	37	.248	.313	.376	88	-4	1	3	-2	.909	-4	D-50,O-13	-1.1
1983	SD-N	25	23	1	3	0	0	0	0	1	8	.130	.167	.130	-17	-4	0	0	0	.000	-0	/O-1	-0.4
Total	10	733	1742	222	448	73	9	45	238	159	245	.257	.322	.387	101	-1	45	24	-1	.959	-18	O-386/D-50	-3.6

■ SHANE TURNER
Turner, Shane Lee b: 1/8/63, Los Angeles, Cal. BL/TR, 5'10", 180 lbs. Deb: 8/19/88

YEAR	TM/L	G	AB	R	H	2B	3B	HR	RBI	BB	SO	AVG	OBP	SLG	PRO+	BR/A	SB	CS	SBR	FA	FR	G/POS	TPR
1988	Phi-N	18	35	1	6	0	0	0	1	5	9	.171	.275	.171	30	-3	0	0	0	.941	-2	/3-8,S-5	-0.6
1991	Bal-A	4	1	0	0	0	0	0	0	0	0	.000	.000	.000	-99	-0	0	0	0	1.000	-0	/2-1,D-1	0.0
1992	Sea-A	34	74	8	20	5	0	0	5	9	15	.270	.349	.338	93	-0	2	1	0	.881	-5	3-18,O-15	-0.6
Total	3	56	110	9	26	5	0	0	6	14	24	.236	.323	.282	71	-4	2	1	0	.898	-7	/3-26,O-15,S-5,D2	-1.2

■ TERRY TURNER
Turner, Terrence Lamont "Cotton Top" b: 2/28/1881, Sandy Lake, Pa. d: 7/18/60, Cleveland, Ohio BR/TR, 5'8", 149 lbs. Deb: 8/25/01 C

YEAR	TM/L	G	AB	R	H	2B	3B	HR	RBI	BB	SO	AVG	OBP	SLG	PRO+	BR/A	SB	CS	SBR	FA	FR	G/POS	TPR
1901	Pit-N	2	7	0	3	0	0	0	1	0		.429	.429	.429	145	0	0			.833	1	/3-2	0.2
1904	Cle-A	111	404	41	95	9	6	1	45	11		.235	.255	.295	74	-13	5			.940	3	*S-111	-0.7
1905	Cle-A	155	586	49	155	16	14	4	72	14		.265	.289	.360	104	0	17			.946	-26	*S-155	-2.5
1906	Cle-A	147	584	85	170	27	7	2	62	35		.291	.338	.372	124	15	27			**.960**	23	*S-147	4.6
1907	Cle-A	140	524	57	127	20	7	0	46	19		.242	.272	.307	84	-11	27			**.950**	-4	*S-139	-1.3
1908	Cle-A	60	201	21	48	11	1	0	19	15		.239	.298	.303	95	-1	18			.952	-4	O-36,S-17	-0.7
1909	Cle-A	53	208	25	52	7	4	0	16	14		.250	.304	.322	94	-2	14			.969	10	2-26,S-26	0.9
1910	Cle-A	150	574	71	132	14	6	0	33	53		.230	.301	.275	79	-13	31			.973	2	S-94,3-46/2-9	-0.7
1911	Cle-A	117	417	59	105	16	9	0	28	34		.252	.310	.333	78	-13	29			.970	2	3-94,2-14,S-10	-0.9
1912	Cle-A	103	370	54	114	14	4	0	33	31		.308	.363	.368	106	3	19			**.951**	-2	*3-103	0.1
1913	Cle-A	120	388	60	96	13	4	0	44	55	35	.247	.348	.302	88	-4	13			.954	16	3-71,2-25,S-21	1.5
1914	Cle-A	121	428	43	105	14	9	1	33	44	36	.245	.319	.327	91	-5	17	13	-3	**.963**	21	*3-104,2-17	1.8
1915	Cle-A	75	262	35	66	14	1	0	14	29	13	.252	.329	.313	90	-3	12	11	-3	.965	-9	2-51,3-20	-1.4
1916	Cle-A	124	428	52	112	15	3	0	38	40	29	.262	.325	.311	86	-7	15			.963	5	3-77,2-42	0.2
1917	Cle-A	69	180	16	37	7	0	0	15	14	19	.206	.263	.244	51	-11	4			.980	-2	3-40,2-23/S-1	-1.3
1918	Cle-A	74	233	24	58	7	2	0	23	22	15	.249	.316	.296	77	-6	6			.969	-4	3-46,2-26/S-1	-0.8
1919	Phi-A	38	127	7	24	3	0	0	6	5	9	.189	.220	.213	21	-13	2			.946	1	S-19,2-17/3-1	-1.1
Total	17	1659	5921	699	1499	207	77	8	528	435	156	.253	.308	.318	89	-83	256	24		.952	34	S-741,3-604,2/O	-2.1

■ TOM TURNER
Turner, Thomas Richard b: 9/8/16, Custer Co., Okla. d: 5/14/86, Kennewick, Wash. BR/TR, 6'2", 195 lbs. Deb: 4/25/40

YEAR	TM/L	G	AB	R	H	2B	3B	HR	RBI	BB	SO	AVG	OBP	SLG	PRO+	BR/A	SB	CS	SBR	FA	FR	G/POS	TPR
1940	Chi-A	37	96	11	20	1	2	0	6	3	12	.208	.240	.260	29	-10	1	0	0	.969	2	C-29	-0.6
1941	Chi-A	38	126	7	30	5	0	0	8	9	15	.238	.289	.278	51	-9	2	0	1	.979	5	C-35	0.0
1942	Chi-A	56	182	18	44	9	1	3	21	19	15	.242	.313	.352	89	-3	0	1	-1	.971	-1	C-54	0.0
1943	Chi-A	51	154	16	37	7	1	2	11	13	21	.240	.299	.338	86	-3	1	0	0	.978	4	C-49	0.5
1944	Chi-A	36	113	9	26	6	0	2	13	5	16	.230	.263	.336	71	-5	0	1	-1	.958	-2	C-36	-0.6
	*StL-A	15	25	2	8	1	0	0	4	2	5	.320	.370	.360	103	0	0	0	0	.969	-1	C-11	0.0
	Yr	51	138	11	34	7	0	2	17	7	21	.246	.283	.341	77	-5	0	1	-1	.960	-3	C-47	-0.6
Total	5	233	696	63	165	29	4	7	63	51	84	.237	.290	.320	70	-29	4	2	0	.972	7	C-214	-0.7

■ BILL TUTTLE
Tuttle, William Robert b: 7/4/29, Elwood, Ill. d: 7/27/98, Anoka, Minn. BR/TR, 6', 190 lbs. Deb: 9/10/52

YEAR	TM/L	G	AB	R	H	2B	3B	HR	RBI	BB	SO	AVG	OBP	SLG	PRO+	BR/A	SB	CS	SBR	FA	FR	G/POS	TPR
1952	Det-A	7	25	2	6	0	0	0	2	0	1	.240	.240	.240	34	-2	0	0	0	1.000	1	/O-6	-0.2
1954	Det-A	147	530	64	141	20	11	7	58	62	60	.266	.345	.385	102	1	5	8	-3	.985	4	*O-145	-0.5
1955	Det-A	154	603	102	168	23	4	14	78	76	54	.279	.360	.400	107	6	6	3	0	.985	15	*O-154	1.4
1956	Det-A	140	546	61	138	22	4	9	65	38	48	.253	.303	.357	73	-22	5	4	-1	.976	10	*O-137	-2.0
1957	Det-A	133	451	49	113	12	4	5	47	44	41	.251	.319	.328	75	-15	2	6	-3	.982	4	*O-128	-2.1
1958	KC-A	148	511	77	118	14	9	11	51	74	58	.231	.329	.358	88	-8	7	9	-3	.988	1	*O-145	-1.8
1959	KC-A	126	463	74	139	19	6	7	43	48	38	.300	.371	.413	113	9	10	6	-1	.984	12	*O-121	1.4
1960	KC-A	151	559	75	143	21	3	8	40	66	52	.256	.337	.347	85	-11	1	5	-3	.988	17	*O-148	-0.4
1961	KC-A	25	84	15	22	2	2	0	8	9	9	.262	.333	.333	77	-3	0	0	0	.951	-1	O-25	-0.5
	Min-A	113	370	38	91	12	3	5	38	43	41	.246	.324	.335	73	-14	1	3	-2	.943	-13	3-85,O-64/2-2	-3.0
	Yr	138	454	53	113	14	5	5	46	52	50	.249	.326	.335	73	-16	1	3	-2	.970	-14	O-89,3-85/2-2	-3.5
1962	Min-A	110	123	21	26	4	1	1	13	19	14	.211	.322	.285	62	-6	1	0	0	.973	-31	*O-104	-3.9
1963	Min-A	16	3	0	0	0	0	0	0	1	0	.000	.250	.000	-22	-0	0	0	0	1.000	-4	O-14	-0.5
Total	11	1270	4268	578	1105	149	47	67	443	480	416	.259	.336	.363	88	-65	38	44	-15	.983	14	*O-1191/3-85,2-2	-12.1

■ GUY TUTWILER
Tutwiler, Guy Isbell "King Tut" b: 7/17/1889, Coalburg, Ala. d: 8/15/30, Birmingham, Ala. BL/TR, 6', 175 lbs. Deb: 8/29/11

YEAR	TM/L	G	AB	R	H	2B	3B	HR	RBI	BB	SO	AVG	OBP	SLG	PRO+	BR/A	SB	CS	SBR	FA	FR	G/POS	TPR
1911	Det-A	13	32	3	6	2	0	0	3	2		.188	.235	.250	34	-3	0			.778	-4	/2-6,O-3	-0.7
1913	Det-A	14	47	4	10	0	1	0	7	4	12	.213	.275	.255	56	-3	2			.987	1	1-14	-0.2
Total	2	27	79	7	16	2	1	0	10	6	12	.203	.259	.253	47	-6	2			.987	-3	/1-14,2-6,O-3	-0.9

■ ART TWINEHAM
Twineham, Arthur W. "Old Hoss" b: 11/26/1866, Galesburg, Ill. BL/TL, 6'1.5", 190 lbs. Deb: 9/11/1893

YEAR	TM/L	G	AB	R	H	2B	3B	HR	RBI	BB	SO	AVG	OBP	SLG	PRO+	BR/A	SB	CS	SBR	FA	FR	G/POS	TPR
1893	StL-N	14	48	8	15	2	0	0	11	1	2	.313	.340	.354	84	-1	0			.928	2	C-14	0.2
1894	StL-N	38	127	22	40	4	1	1	16	9	11	.315	.387	.386	87	-2	2			.939	4	C-38	0.4
Total	2	52	175	30	55	6	1	1	27	10	13	.314	.375	.377	86	-3	2			.936	7	/C-52	0.6

■ LARRY TWITCHELL
Twitchell, Lawrence Grant b: 2/18/1864, Cleveland, Ohio d: 8/23/30, Cleveland, Ohio BR/TR, 6', 185 lbs. Deb: 4/30/1886

YEAR	TM/L	G	AB	R	H	2B	3B	HR	RBI	BB	SO	AVG	OBP	SLG	PRO+	BR/A	SB	CS	SBR	FA	FR	G/POS	TPR
1886	Det-N	4	16	0	1	0	0	0	0	0	2	.063	.063	.063	-60	-3	0			1.000	0	/P-4,O-2	-0.1
1887	*Det-N	65	264	44	88	14	6	0	51	8	19	.333	.358	.432	115	4	12			.871	-6	O-53,P-15	-0.2
1888	Det-N	131	524	71	128	19	4	5	67	28	45	.244	.286	.324	95	-3	14			.885	-9	*O-131/P-2	-1.6
1889	Cle-N	134	549	73	151	16	11	4	95	29	37	.275	.315	.366	92	-7	17			.916	-10	*O-134/P-1	-1.8
1890	Cle-P	56	233	33	52	6	3	2	36	17	17	.223	.279	.300	60	-14	4			.821	-9	O-56	-2.0
	Buf-P	44	172	24	38	3	1	2	17	23	12	.221	.316	.285	67	-7	4			.918	-1	O-32,P-13/1-3	-0.7
	Yr	100	405	57	90	9	4	4	53	40	29	.222	.295	.294	63	-21	8			.857	-10	O-88,P-13/1-3	-2.7
1891	Col-a	57	224	32	62	9	4	2	35	20	28	.277	.341	.379	113	3	10			.887	-10	O-56/P-6	-0.7
1892	Was-N	51	192	20	42	9	5	0	20	11	31	.219	.275	.318	82	-5	8			.897	-5	O-48/S-3,3-1	-1.1
1893	Lou-N	45	187	37	58	11	3	2	31	17	20	.310	.377	.433	125	7	7			.874	-2	O-45	0.2
1894	Lou-N	52	210	28	56	16	3	2	32	15	20	.267	.316	.400	77	-9	8			.908	6	O-51/P-1	-0.5
Total	9	639	2571	362	676	103	40	19	384	168	231	.263	.313	.356	91	-34	84			.890	-45	O-608/P-42,S-3,13	-8.5

■ BABE TWOMBLY
Twombly, Clarence Edward b: 1/18/1896, Jamaica Plain, Mass. d: 11/23/74, San Clemente, Cal. BL/TR, 5'10", 165 lbs. Deb: 4/14/20 F

YEAR	TM/L	G	AB	R	H	2B	3B	HR	RBI	BB	SO	AVG	OBP	SLG	PRO+	BR/A	SB	CS	SBR	FA	FR	G/POS	TPR
1920	Chi-N	78	183	25	43	1	1	2	14	17	20	.235	.303	.284	68	-7	5	9	-4	.970	0	O-45/2-2	-1.5
1921	Chi-N	87	175	22	66	8	1	1	18	11	10	.377	.414	.451	129	8	4	6	-2	.968	0	O-45	0.3
Total	2	165	358	47	109	9	2	3	32	28	30	.304	.357	.366	98	0	9	15	-6	.969	1	/O-90,2-2	-1.2

■ GEORGE TWOMBLY
Twombly, George Frederick "Silent George" b: 6/4/1892, Boston, Mass. d: 2/17/75, Lexington, Mass. BR/TR, 5'9", 165 lbs. Deb: 7/9/14 F

YEAR	TM/L	G	AB	R	H	2B	3B	HR	RBI	BB	SO	AVG	OBP	SLG	PRO+	BR/A	SB	CS	SBR	FA	FR	G/POS	TPR
1914	Cin-N	68	240	22	56	0	5	0	19	14	27	.233	.284	.275	64	-11	12			.968	1	O-68	-1.4
1915	Cin-N	46	66	5	13	0	1	0	5	8	8	.197	.293	.227	57	-3	5	3	-0	1.000	-4	O-24	-0.9
1916	Cin-N	3	5	0	0	0	0	0	0	1	1	.000	.167	.000	-48	-1	0			1.000	-0	/O-1	-0.1
1917	Bos-N	32	102	8	19	1	1	0	9	18	5	.186	.314	.216	68	-3	4			.943	-5	O-29/1-1	-1.1
1919	Was-A	1	4	0	0	0	0	0	0	0	0	.000	.000	.000	-99	-1	0			.000	-1	/O-1	-0.2
Total	5	150	417	35	88	1	7	0	33	41	41	.211	.289	.247	62	-18	21	3		.967	-9	O-123/1-1	-3.7

■ JIM TYACK
Tyack, James Frederick b: 1/9/11, Florence, Mont. d: 1/3/95, Bakersfield, Cal. BL/TR, 6'2", 195 lbs. Deb: 4/20/43

YEAR	TM/L	G	AB	R	H	2B	3B	HR	RBI	BB	SO	AVG	OBP	SLG	PRO+	BR/A	SB	CS	SBR	FA	FR	G/POS	TPR
1943	Phi-A	54	155	11	40	8	1	0	23	14	9	.258	.320	.323	88	-2	1	1	-0	.977	1	O-38	-0.4

■ FRED TYLER
Tyler, Frederick Franklin "Clancy" b: 12/16/1891, Derry, N.H. d: 10/14/45, E.Derry, N.H. BR/TR, 5'10.5", 180 lbs. Deb: 4/14/14 F

YEAR	TM/L	G	AB	R	H	2B	3B	HR	RBI	BB	SO	AVG	OBP	SLG	PRO+	BR/A	SB	CS	SBR	FA	FR	G/POS	TPR
1914	Bos-N	6	19	2	2	0	0	0	2	1	5	.105	.150	.105	-24	-3	0			1.000	-1	/C-6	-0.3

YEAR	TM/L	G	AB	R	H	2B	3B	HR	RBI	BB	SO	AVG	OBP	SLG	PRO+	BR/A	SB	CS	SBR	FA	FR	G/POS	TPR
■ **JOHNNIE TYLER**	Tyler, John Anthony "Ty Ty" or "Katz" (b: John Tylka) b: 7/30/06, Mt.Pleasant, Pa. d: 7/11/72, Mt.Pleasant, Pa. BB/TR, 6', 175 lbs. Deb: 9/16/34																						
1934	Bos-N	3	6	0	1	0	0	0	1	0	3	.167	.167	.167	-11	-1	0			1.000	1	/O-1	0.0
1935	Bos-N	13	47	7	16	2	1	2	11	4	3	.340	.404	.553	168	4	0			.893	-0	O-11	0.4
Total	2	16	53	7	17	2	1	2	12	4	6	.321	.379	.509	148	3	0			.906	1	/O-12	0.4
■ **EARL TYREE**	Tyree, Earl Carlton "Ty" b: 3/4/1890, Huntsville, Ill. d: 5/17/54, Rushville, Ill. BR/TR, 5'8", 160 lbs. Deb: 10/5/14																						
1914	Chi-N	1	4	1	0	0	0	0	0	0	0	.000	.000	.000	-99	-1	0			1.000	-1	/C-1	-0.2
■ **JIM TYRONE**	Tyrone, James Vernon b: 1/29/49, Alice, Tex. BR/TR, 6'1", 185 lbs. Deb: 8/27/72 F																						
1972	Chi-N	13	8	1	0	0	0	0	0	0	3	.000	.000	.000	-90	-2	1	0	0	1.000	0	/O-4	-0.1
1974	Chi-N	57	81	19	15	0	1	3	3	6	8	.185	.241	.321	54	-5	1	1	-0	.962	-8	O-32/3-1	-1.5
1975	Chi-N	11	22	0	5	0	1	0	3	1	4	.227	.261	.318	58	-1	1	1	-0	1.000	-1	/O-8	-0.3
1977	Oak-A	96	294	32	72	11	1	5	26	25	62	.245	.304	.340	76	-10	3	1	0	.950	1	O-81/1-1,S-1,D-4	-1.1
Total	4	177	405	52	92	11	3	8	32	32	77	.227	.284	.328	67	-18	6	3	0	.955	-7	O-125/D-4,S-1,13	-3.0
■ **WAYNE TYRONE**	Tyrone, Oscar Wayne b: 8/1/50, Alice, Tex. BR/TR, 6'1", 185 lbs. Deb: 7/15/76 F																						
1976	Chi-N	30	57	3	13	1	0	1	8	3	21	.228	.267	.298	55	-3	0	0	0	1.000	-3	/O-7,1-5,3-5	-0.7
■ **TY TYSON**	Tyson, Albert Thomas b: 6/1/1892, Wilkes-Barre, Pa. d: 8/16/53, Buffalo, N.Y. BR/TR, 5'11", 169 lbs. Deb: 4/13/26																						
1926	NY-N	97	335	40	98	16	1	3	35	15	28	.293	.329	.373	90	-5	6			.980	3	O-92	-0.8
1927	NY-N	43	159	24	42	7	2	1	17	10	19	.264	.308	.352	76	-5	5			.929	-3	O-41	-1.1
1928	Bro-N	59	210	25	57	11	1	1	21	10	14	.271	.317	.348	75	-8	3			.965	0	O-55	-1.1
Total	3	199	704	89	197	34	4	5	73	35	61	.280	.320	.361	82	-19	14			.966	0	O-188	-3.0
■ **TURKEY TYSON**	Tyson, Cecil Washington "Slim" b: 12/6/14, Elm City, N.C. BL/TR, 6'5.5", 225 lbs. Deb: 4/23/44																						
1944	Phi-N	1	1	0	0	0	0	0	0	0	0	.000	.000	.000	-99	-0	0			.000	0	H	0.0
■ **MIKE TYSON**	Tyson, Michael Ray b: 1/13/50, Rocky Mount, N.C. BR/TR, 5'9", 170 lbs. Deb: 9/5/72																						
1972	StL-N	13	37	1	7	1	0	0	0	1	9	.189	.211	.216	22	-4	0	1	-1	.981	4	2-11/S-2	0.0
1973	StL-N	144	469	48	114	15	4	1	33	23	66	.243	.281	.299	61	-25	2	5	-2	.944	-19	*S-128,2-16	-3.0
1974	StL-N	151	422	35	94	14	5	1	37	22	70	.223	.266	.287	55	-26	4	2	0	.955	15	*S-143,2-12	0.6
1975	StL-N	122	368	45	98	16	3	2	37	24	39	.266	.316	.342	80	-10	5	2	0	.971	-12	S-95,2-24/3-5	-1.3
1976	StL-N	76	245	26	70	12	9	3	28	16	34	.286	.330	.445	117	5	3	1	0	.971	8	2-74	1.8
1977	StL-N	138	418	42	103	15	2	7	57	30	48	.246	.300	.342	73	-16	3	4	-2	.979	22	*2-135	1.3
1978	StL-N	125	377	26	88	16	0	3	26	24	41	.233	.279	.300	63	-19	2	0	1	.977	0	*2-124	-1.1
1979	StL-N	75	190	18	42	8	2	5	20	13	28	.221	.275	.363	72	-8	2	1	0	.975	8	2-71	0.4
1980	Chi-N	123	341	34	81	19	3	3	23	15	61	.238	.274	.337	65	-16	1	2	-1	.968	9	*2-117	-0.1
1981	Chi-N	50	92	6	17	2	0	2	8	7	15	.185	.250	.272	46	-7	1	0	0	.940	0	2-36/S-1	-0.5
Total	10	1017	2959	281	714	118	28	27	269	175	411	.241	.287	.327	69	-126	23	18	-4	.973	36	2-620,S-369/3-5	-1.9
■ **BOB UECKER**	Uecker, Robert George b: 1/26/35, Milwaukee, Wis. BR/TR, 6'1", 190 lbs. Deb: 4/13/62																						
1962	Mil-N	33	64	5	16	2	0	1	8	7	15	.250	.324	.328	78	-2	0	0	0	.982	4	C-24	0.3
1963	Mil-N	13	16	3	4	2	0	0	0	2	5	.250	.333	.375	105	0	0	0	0	.958	1	/C-6	0.1
1964	StL-N	40	106	8	21	1	0	1	6	17	24	.198	.315	.236	53	-6	0	1	-1	.987	5	C-40	-0.1
1965	StL-N	53	145	17	33	7	0	2	10	24	27	.228	.345	.317	80	-3	0	1	-1	.985	-1	C-49	-0.3
1966	Phi-N	78	207	15	43	6	0	7	30	22	36	.208	.284	.338	72	-8	0	0	0	.985	1	C-76	-0.3
1967	Phi-N	18	35	3	6	2	0	0	7	5	9	.171	.275	.229	45	-2	0	0	0	.973	0	C-17	-0.2
	Atl-N	62	158	14	23	2	0	3	13	19	51	.146	.237	.215	31	-14	0	1	-1	.972	5	C-59	-0.8
	Yr	80	193	17	29	4	0	3	20	24	60	.150	.244	.218	33	-16	0	1	-1	.972	5	C-76	-1.0
Total	6	297	731	65	146	22	0	14	74	96	167	.200	.295	.287	63	-35	0	3	-2	.981	14	C-271	-1.3
■ **FRENCHY UHALT**	Uhalt, Bernard Bartholomew b: 4/27/10, Bakersfield, Cal. BL/TR, 5'10", 180 lbs. Deb: 4/17/34																						
1934	Chi-A	57	165	28	40	5	1	0	16	29	12	.242	.359	.285	66	-7	6	5	-1	.935	-1	O-40	-1.0
■ **TED UHLAENDER**	Uhlaender, Theodore Otto b: 10/21/40, Chicago Heights, Ill. BL/TR, 6'2", 190 lbs. Deb: 9/4/65																						
1965	Min-A	13	22	1	4	0	0	0	1	0	2	.182	.182	.182	3	-3	1	0	0	1.000	1	/O-4	-0.2
1966	Min-A	105	367	39	83	12	2	2	22	27	33	.226	.281	.286	60	-19	10	2	2	.985	12	*O-100	-1.0
1967	Min-A	133	415	41	107	19	7	6	49	13	45	.258	.285	.381	88	-7	4	4	-1	**.996**	7	*O-118	-0.7
1968	Min-A	140	488	52	138	21	5	7	52	28	46	.283	.326	.389	110	5	16	7	1	.986	-2	*O-129	-0.3
1969	*Min-A	152	554	93	151	18	2	8	62	44	52	.273	.331	.356	90	-7	15	9	-1	.997	-6	*O-150	-2.2
1970	Cle-A	141	473	56	127	21	2	11	46	39	44	.268	.326	.391	92	-5	3	6	-3	.991	-14	*O-134	-3.0
1971	Cle-A	141	500	52	144	20	3	2	47	38	44	.288	.338	.352	88	-7	3	6	-3	.992	1	*O-131	-1.7
1972	*Cin-N	73	113	9	18	3	0	0	6	13	11	.159	.246	.186	26	-11	0	1	-1	.976	-2	O-27	-1.6
Total	8	898	2932	343	772	114	21	36	285	202	277	.263	.313	.353	86	-54	52	35	-5	.991	-3	O-793	-10.7
■ **GEORGE UHLE**	Uhle, George Ernest "The Bull" b: 9/18/1898, Cleveland, Ohio d: 2/26/85, Lakewood, Ohio BR/TR, 6', 190 lbs. Deb: 4/30/19 C																						
1919	Cle-A	26	43	7	13	2	1	0	6	1	5	.302	.318	.395	94	-1	0			.915	0	P-26	0.0
1920	*Cle-A	27	32	4	11	0	0	0	2	2	2	.344	.382	.344	91	-0	1	0	0	1.000	0	P-27	0.0
1921	Cle-A	48	94	21	23	2	3	1	18	6	9	.245	.290	.362	64	-5	0	0	0	.938	-3	P-41	0.0
1922	Cle-A	56	109	21	29	8	2	0	14	13	6	.266	.350	.376	88	-2	1	2	-1	.932	-3	P-50	0.0
1923	Cle-A	58	144	23	52	10	3	0	22	7	10	.361	.391	.472	127	5	2	1	0	.982	0	P-54	0.0
1924	Cle-A	59	107	10	33	6	1	1	19	4	8	.308	.339	.411	92	-2	0	1	-1	**1.000**	1	P-28	0.0
1925	Cle-A	55	101	10	29	3	3	0	13	7	7	.287	.339	.376	81	-3	0	0	0	.943	-3	P-29	0.0
1926	Cle-A	50	132	16	30	3	0	1	11	10	12	.227	.287	.273	46	-10	2	2	-1	.933	-0	P-39	0.0
1927	Cle-A	43	79	4	21	7	1	0	14	5	12	.266	.310	.380	78	-3	0	1	-1	.974	-1	P-25	0.0
1928	Cle-A	55	98	9	28	3	2	1	17	8	4	.286	.340	.388	90	-2	0	0	0	.972	3	P-31	0.0
1929	Det-A	40	108	18	37	1	1	0	13	6	6	.343	.377	.370	93	-1	0	0	0	.929	-3	P-32	0.0
1930	Det-A	59	117	15	36	4	2	2	21	8	13	.308	.352	.427	95	-1	0	0	0	.975	-3	P-33	0.0
1931	Det-A	53	90	8	22	6	0	2	7	8	8	.244	.306	.378	76	-3	0	1	-1	**1.000**	-1	P-29	0.0
1932	Det-A	38	55	2	10	3	1	0	4	6	5	.182	.262	.273	37	-5	0	0	0	1.000	-1	P-33	0.0
1933	Det-A	1	0	0	0	0	0	0	0	0	0	—	—	—	—	0	0	0	0	.000	0	/P-1	0.0
	NY-N	8	5	1	0	0	0	0	0	1	3	.000	.167	.000	-50	-1	0			1.000	0	/P-6	0.0
	NY-A	12	20	1	8	1	0	0	1	4	2	.400	.500	.450	163	2	0	0	0	1.000	-1	P-12	0.0
1934	NY-A	10	5	1	3	0	1	0	1	0	0	.600	.600	1.000	329	2	0	0	0	1.000	-0	P-10	0.0
1936	Cle-A	24	21	1	8	1	0	1	4	2	0	.381	.435	.571	145	1	0	0	0	.000	-1	/P-7	0.0
Total	17	722	1360	172	393	60	21	9	187	98	112	.289	.339	.384	86	-29	6	8		.960	-15	P-513	0.0
■ **MAURY UHLER**	Uhler, Maurice William b: 12/14/1886, Pikesville, Md. d: 5/4/18, Baltimore, Md. BR/TR, 5'11", 165 lbs. Deb: 4/14/14																						
1914	Cin-N	46	56	12	12	2	0	0	3	5	11	.214	.279	.250	56	-3	4			.932	-8	O-36	-1.3
■ **CHARLIE UHLIR**	Uhlir, Charles Karel b: 7/30/12, Chicago, Ill. d: 7/9/84, Spirit Lake, Iowa BL/TL, 5'7.5", 150 lbs. Deb: 8/3/34																						
1934	Chi-A	14	27	3	4	0	0	0	3	2	6	.148	.207	.148	-7	-4	0	0	0	1.000	-1	/O-6	-0.5
■ **MIKE ULISNEY**	Ulisney, Michael Edward "Slugs" b: 9/28/17, Greenwald, Pa. BR/TR, 5'9", 165 lbs. Deb: 5/5/45																						
1945	Bos-N	11	18	4	7	1	0	1	4	1	0	.389	.421	.611	184	2	0			.714	-2	/C-4	0.0
■ **SCOTT ULLGER**	Ullger, Scott Matthew b: 6/10/56, New York, N.Y. BR/TR, 6'2", 186 lbs. Deb: 4/17/83																						
1983	Min-A	35	79	8	15	4	0	0	5	5	21	.190	.247	.241	34	-7	0	2	-1	.990	-2	1-30/3-3,D-1	-1.1
■ **GEORGE ULRICH**	Ulrich, George T. b: 6/5/1869, Philadelphia, Pa. Deb: 5/1/1892																						
1892	Was-N	6	24	1	7	1	0	0	0	0	4	.292	.292	.333	92	-0	2			.889	-1	/3-3,S-2,C-2	-0.1

YEAR	TM/L	G	AB	R	H	2B	3B	HR	RBI	BB	SO	AVG	OBP	SLG	PRO+	BR/A	SB	CS	SBR	FA	FR	G/POS	TPR
1893	Cin-N	1	3	0	0	0	0	0	0	0	0	.000	.250	.000	-31	-1	1			1.000	-0	/O-1	-0.1
1896	NY-N	14	45	4	8	1	0	0	1	1	1	.178	.229	.200	14	-6	0			.920	0	O-11/3-3	-0.5
Total	3	21	72	5	15	2	0	0	1	1	5	.208	.250	.236	35	-7	3			.923	-1	/O-12,3-6,C-2,S-2	-0.7
■ **TOM UMPHLETT**	Umphlett, Thomas Mullen b: 5/12/30, Scotland Neck, N.C BR/TR, 6'2", 180 lbs. Deb: 4/16/53																						
1953	Bos-A	137	495	53	140	27	5	3	59	34	30	.283	.331	.376	86	-10	4	2	0	.983	6	*O-136	-0.9
1954	Was-A	114	342	21	75	8	3	1	33	17	42	.219	.256	.269	46	-26	1	2	-1	.989	0	*O-101	-3.2
1955	Was-A	110	323	34	70	10	0	2	19	24	35	.217	.271	.266	47	-25	2	1	0	.988	4	*O-103	-2.5
Total	3	361	1160	108	285	45	8	6	111	75	107	.246	.293	.314	65	-61	7	5	-1	.986	10	O-340	-6.6
■ **BOB UNGLAUB**	Unglaub, Robert Alexander b: 7/31/1881, Baltimore, Md. d: 11/29/16, Baltimore, Md. BR/TR, 5'11", 178 lbs. Deb: 4/15/04 M																						
1904	NY-A	6	19	2	4	0	0	0	2	0		.211	.211	.211	32	-1	0			.786	-1	/3-4,S-1	-0.3
	Bos-A	9	13	1	2	1	0	0	2	1		.154	.214	.231	39	-1	0			.625	-2	/2-3,3-2,S-1	-0.3
	Yr	15	32	3	6	1	0	0	4	1		.188	.212	.219	35	-2	0			.842	-3	/3-6,2-3,S-2	-0.6
1905	Bos-A	43	121	18	27	5	1	0	11	6		.223	.260	.281	71	-4	2			.928	1	3-21/2-7,1-2	-0.3
1907	Bos-A	139	544	49	138	17	13	1	62	23		.254	.284	.338	99	-3	14			.986	-1	*1-139,M	-0.9
1908	Bos-A	72	266	23	70	11	3	1	25	7		.263	.287	.338	100	-1	6			.980	2	1-72	-0.1
	Was-A	72	276	23	85	10	5	0	29	8		.308	.327	.380	142	11	8			.928	11	3-39,2-27/1-4	2.5
	Yr	144	542	46	155	21	8	1	54	15		.286	.308	.360	120	9	14			.981	12	1-76,3-39,2-27	2.4
1909	Was-A	130	480	43	127	14	9	3	41	22		.265	.301	.350	111	4	15			.992	1	1-57,O-42,2-25,/3-4	0.3
1910	Was-A	124	431	29	101	9	4	0	44	21		.234	.270	.274	74	-14	21			.985	6	*1-124	-1.0
Total	6	595	2150	188	554	67	35	5	216	88		.258	.288	.328	99	-10	66			.986	15	1-398/3-70,2-62,OS	-0.1
■ **TIM UNROE**	Unroe, Timothy Brian b: 10/7/70, Round Lake Beach, Ill. BR/TR, 6'3", 200 lbs. Deb: 5/30/95																						
1995	Mil-A	2	4	0	1	0	0	0	0	0	0	.250	.250	.250	29	-0	0	0	0	1.000	-0	/1-2	-0.1
1996	Mil-A	14	16	5	3	0	0	0	0	4	5	.188	.350	.188	40	-1	0	1	-1	.976	1	1-11/3-3,O-1,D-1	-0.1
1997	Mil-A	32	16	3	4	1	0	2	5	2	9	.250	.333	.688	156	1	2	0	1	.969	2	1-23/3-2,O-2,2-1	0.3
Total	3	48	36	8	8	1	0	2	5	6	14	.222	.333	.417	89	-1	2	1	0	.975	2	/1-36,3-5,O-3,2D	0.1
■ **AL UNSER**	Unser, Albert Bernard b: 10/12/12, Morrisonville, Ill. d: 7/7/95, Decatur, Ill. BR/TR, 6'1", 175 lbs. Deb: 9/14/42 F																						
1942	Det-A	4	8	2	3	0	0	0	0	0	2	.375	.375	.375	103	0	0	0	0	1.000	1	/C-4	0.1
1943	Det-A	38	101	14	25	5	0	0	4	15	15	.248	.350	.297	84	-2	0	1	-1	.982	-3	C-37	-0.3
1944	Det-A	11	25	2	3	0	1	1	5	3	2	.120	.214	.320	49	-2	0	0	0	.864	-4	/2-5,C-1	-0.6
1945	Cin-N	67	204	23	54	10	3	3	21	14	24	.265	.318	.387	98	-1	0			.956	0	C-61	0.2
Total	4	120	338	41	85	15	4	4	30	32	43	.251	.322	.355	90	-5	0	1		.967	-7	C-103/2-5	-0.6
■ **DEL UNSER**	Unser, Delbert Bernard b: 12/9/44, Decatur, Ill. BL/TL, 6'1", 180 lbs. Deb: 4/10/68 FC																						
1968	Was-A	156	635	66	146	13	7	1	30	46	66	.230	.284	.277	73	-21	11	6	-0	.988	19	*O-156/1-1	-1.2
1969	Was-A	153	581	69	166	19	**8**	7	57	58	54	.286	.351	.382	111	8	8	10	-4	.972	6	*O-149	0.2
1970	Was-A	119	322	37	83	5	1	5	30	30	29	.258	.321	.326	83	-7	1	1	-0	.984	-3	*O-103	-1.6
1971	Was-A	153	581	63	148	19	6	9	41	59	68	.255	.326	.355	98	-2	11	6	-0	.981	3	*O-151	-0.7
1972	Cle-A	132	383	29	91	12	0	1	17	28	46	.238	.291	.277	67	-15	5	9	-4	.989	2	*O-119	-2.5
1973	Phi-N	136	440	64	127	20	4	11	52	47	55	.289	.359	.427	114	9	5	8	-3	.988	17	*O-132	1.7
1974	Phi-N	142	454	72	120	18	5	11	61	50	62	.264	.339	.399	101	1	6	4	-1	.981	6	*O-135	0.0
1975	NY-N	147	531	65	156	18	2	10	53	37	76	.294	.340	.392	107	4	4	3	-1	.987	12	*O-144	1.1
1976	NY-N	77	276	28	63	13	2	5	25	18	40	.228	.278	.344	80	-8	4	4	-1	.995	4	O-77	-0.9
	Mon-N	69	220	29	50	6	2	7	15	11	44	.227	.264	.368	75	-8	3	3	-1	.983	-6	O-65	-1.9
	Yr	146	496	57	113	19	4	12	40	29	84	.228	.272	.355	78	-16	7	7	-2	.990	-3	*O-142	-2.8
1977	Mon-N	113	289	33	79	14	1	12	40	33	41	.273	.348	.453	116	6	2	5	-2	.976	-7	O-72,1-27	-0.6
1978	Mon-N	130	179	16	35	5	0	2	15	24	29	.196	.294	.257	56	-10	2	0	1	.994	1	1-64,O-33	-1.1
1979	Phi-N	95	141	26	42	8	0	6	29	14	33	.298	.361	.482	124	5	2	0	1	.978	-4	O-30,1-22	-0.1
1980	*Phi-N	96	110	15	29	6	4	0	10	10	21	.264	.325	.391	94	-1	0	1	-1	1.000	3	1-31,O-23	0.0
1981	Phi-N	62	59	5	9	3	0	0	6	13	9	.153	.306	.203	45	-4	0	0	0	1.000	-3	1-18,O-16	-0.7
1982	Phi-N	19	14	0	0	0	0	0	0	3	2	.000	.176	.000	-46	-3	0	0	0	1.000	-1	/1-5,O-2	-0.4
Total	15	1799	5215	617	1344	179	42	87	481	481	675	.258	.321	.358	93	-47	64	60	-17	.984	48	*O-1407,1-168	-8.7
■ **JOHN UPHAM**	Upham, John Leslie b: 12/29/41, Windsor, Ont., Can. BL/TL, 6', 180 lbs. Deb: 4/16/67																						
1967	Chi-N	8	3	1	2	0	0	0	0	0	0	.667	.667	.667	270	1	0	0	0	.000	0	/P-5	0.0
1968	Chi-N	13	10	0	2	0	0	0	0	0	3	.200	.200	.200	19	-1	0	0	0	1.000	-1	/P-2,O-2	-0.1
Total	2	21	13	1	4	0	0	0	0	0	3	.308	.308	.308	78	-0	0	0	0	1.000	-1	/P-7,O-2	-0.1
■ **DIXIE UPRIGHT**	Upright, Roy T. b: 5/30/26, Kannapolis, N.C. d: 11/13/86, Concord, N.C. BL/TL, 6', 175 lbs. Deb: 4/18/53																						
1953	StL-A	9	8	3	2	0	0	1	1	1	3	.250	.333	.625	151	0	0	0	0	.000	0	H	0.0
■ **WILLIE UPSHAW**	Upshaw, Willie Clay b: 4/27/57, Blanco, Tex. BL/TL, 6', 185 lbs. Deb: 4/9/78 C																						
1978	Tor-A	95	224	26	53	8	2	1	17	21	35	.237	.302	.304	69	-9	4	6	-2	.943	-6	O-52,D-18,1-10	-2.0
1980	Tor-A	34	61	10	13	3	1	1	5	6	14	.213	.284	.344	68	-3	1	0	0	.983	1	1-14,D-12/O-1	-0.2
1981	Tor-A	61	111	15	19	3	1	4	10	11	16	.171	.252	.324	61	-6	2	1	0	1.000	-2	D-15,1-14,O-14	-0.9
1982	Tor-A	160	580	77	155	25	7	21	75	52	91	.267	.329	.443	100	-1	8	8	-2	.989	-1	*1-155/D-5	-1.3
1983	Tor-A	160	579	99	177	26	7	27	104	61	98	.306	.377	.515	134	27	10	7	-1	.985	3	*1-159/D-1	1.9
1984	Tor-A	152	569	79	158	31	9	19	84	55	86	.278	.347	.464	118	13	10	4	1	.990	-3	*1-151/D-1	0.1
1985	*Tor-A	148	501	79	138	31	5	15	65	48	71	.275	.344	.447	112	8	8	8	-2	.992	1	*1-147/D-1	-0.1
1986	Tor-A	155	573	85	144	28	6	9	60	78	87	.251	.343	.368	91	-5	23	5	4	.992	5	*1-154/D-1	-0.8
1987	Tor-A	150	512	68	125	22	4	15	58	58	78	.244	.325	.391	87	-10	10	11	-4	.993	12	*1-146	-1.1
1988	Cle-A	149	493	58	121	22	3	11	50	62	66	.245	.332	.369	94	-3	12	9	-2	.991	1	*1-144	-1.6
Total	10	1264	4203	596	1103	199	45	123	528	452	642	.262	.337	.419	102	12	88	59	-9	.990	11	*1-1094/O-67,D-54	-6.0
■ **TOM UPTON**	Upton, Thomas Herbert "Muscles" b: 12/29/26, Esther, Mo. BR/TR, 6', 160 lbs. Deb: 4/19/50 F																						
1950	StL-A	124	389	50	92	5	6	2	30	52	45	.237	.328	.296	58	-24	7	2	1	.946	-10	*S-115/2-2,3-1	-2.3
1951	StL-A	52	131	9	26	4	3	0	12	12	22	.198	.271	.275	46	-10	1	1	-0	.949	-4	S-47	-1.2
1952	Was-A	5	5	1	0	0	0	0	0	1	0	.000	.167	.000	-53	-1	0	0	0	1.000	2	/S-3	0.1
Total	3	181	525	60	118	9	9	2	42	65	67	.225	.313	.288	55	-35	8	3	1	.948	-13	S-165/2-2,3-1	-3.4
■ **LUKE URBAN**	Urban, Louis John b: 3/22/1898, Fall River, Mass. d: 12/7/80, Somerset, Mass. BR/TR, 5'8", 168 lbs. Deb: 7/19/27																						
1927	Bos-N	35	111	11	32	5	0	0	10	3	6	.288	.313	.333	79	-4	1			.947	-8	C-34	-0.9
1928	Bos-N	15	17	0	3	0	0	0	2	0	1	.176	.222	.176	6	-2	0			1.000	1	C-10	-0.1
Total	2	50	128	11	35	5	0	0	12	3	7	.273	.301	.313	69	-6	1			.955	-7	/C-44	-1.0
■ **BILLY URBANSKI**	Urbanski, William Michael b: 6/5/03, Linoleumville, N.Y d: 7/12/73, Perth Amboy, N.J. BR/TR, 5'8", 165 lbs. Deb: 7/4/31																						
1931	Bos-N	82	303	22	72	13	4	0	17	10	32	.238	.274	.307	58	-18	3			.961	11	3-68,S-19	-0.2
1932	Bos-N	136	563	80	153	25	8	8	46	28	60	.272	.307	.387	89	-10	8			.946	1	*S-136	0.3
1933	Bos-N	144	566	65	142	21	4	0	35	33	48	.251	.298	.302	78	-17	4			.953	-4	*S-143	-1.1
1934	Bos-N	146	605	104	177	30	6	7	53	56	37	.293	.357	.397	110	9	4			**.961**	-10	*S-146	0.7
1935	Bos-N	132	514	53	118	17	0	4	30	40	32	.230	.286	.286	59	-30	3			.939	-27	*S-129	-5.0
1936	Bos-N	122	494	55	129	17	5	0	26	31	42	.261	.310	.316	74	-18	2			.937	-18	S-80,3-38	-3.0
1937	Bos-N	1	1	0	0	0	0	0	0	0	1	.000	.000	.000	-99	-0	0			.000	0	H	0.0
Total	7	763	3046	379	791	123	27	19	207	198	252	.260	.309	.337	81	-85	24			.949	-47	S-653,3-106	-8.3
■ **JOSE URIBE**	Uribe, Jose Altagracia (Played Under Real Name Of Jose Altagracia Gonzalez (Uribe) In 1984) b: 1/21/59, San Cristobal, D.R. BB/TR, 5'10", 165 lbs. Deb: 9/13/84																						
1984	StL-N	8	19	4	4	0	0	0	3	0	2	.211	.211	.211	19	-2	1	0	0	.955	0	/S-5,2-1	-0.1
1985	SF-N	147	476	46	113	20	4	3	26	30	57	.237	.285	.315	71	-19	8	2	1	.961	-2	*S-145/2-1	-0.7

YEAR	TM/L	G	AB	R	H	2B	3B	HR	RBI	BB	SO	AVG	OBP	SLG	PRO+	BR/A	SB	CS	SBR	FA	FR	G/POS	TPR
1986	SF-N	157	453	46	101	15	1	3	43	61	76	.223	.315	.280	69	-18	22	11	0	.977	12	*S-156	0.8
1987	*SF-N	95	309	44	90	16	5	5	30	24	35	.291	.344	.424	107	3	12	2	2	.971	11	S-95	2.3
1988	SF-N	141	493	47	124	10	7	3	35	36	69	.252	.302	.318	82	-12	14	10	-2	.970	-3	*S-140	-0.6
1989	*SF-N	151	453	34	100	12	6	1	30	34	74	.221	.275	.280	61	-23	6	6	-2	.973	8	*S-150	-0.6
1990	SF-N	138	415	35	103	8	6	1	24	29	49	.248	.297	.304	68	-18	5	9	-4	.965	16	*S-134	0.3
1991	SF-N	90	231	23	51	8	4	1	12	20	33	.221	.283	.303	67	-10	3	4	-2	.966	6	S-87	-0.1
1992	SF-N	66	162	24	39	9	1	2	13	14	25	.241	.301	.346	88	-3	2	2	-1	.971	9	S-62	0.9
1993	Hou-N	45	53	4	13	1	0	0	3	8	5	.245	.355	.264	71	-2	1	0	0	.944	6	S-41	0.6
Total	10	1038	3064	307	738	99	34	19	219	256	425	.241	.300	.314	75	-105	74	46	-5	.969	62	*S-1015/2-2	2.8

■ **LON URY** Ury, Louis Newton "Old Sleep" b: 1877, Ft.Scott, Kan. d: 3/4/18, Kansas City, Mo. TR, 6', Deb: 9/9/03

YEAR	TM/L	G	AB	R	H	2B	3B	HR	RBI	BB	SO	AVG	OBP	SLG	PRO+	BR/A	SB	CS	SBR	FA	FR	G/POS	TPR
1903	StL-N	2	7	0	1	0	0	0	0	0		.143	.143	.143	-19	-1	0			1.000	0	/1-2	-0.1

■ **BOB USHER** Usher, Robert Royce b: 3/1/25, San Diego, Cal. BR/TR, 6'1.5", 180 lbs. Deb: 4/16/46

YEAR	TM/L	G	AB	R	H	2B	3B	HR	RBI	BB	SO	AVG	OBP	SLG	PRO+	BR/A	SB	CS	SBR	FA	FR	G/POS	TPR
1946	Cin-N	92	152	16	31	5	1	1	14	13	27	.204	.271	.270	56	-9	2			.982	-12	O-80/3-1	-2.5
1947	Cin-N	9	22	2	4	0	0	1	1	2	2	.182	.250	.318	50	-2	0			1.000	0	/O-8	-0.2
1950	Cin-N	106	321	51	83	17	0	6	35	27	38	.259	.316	.368	79	-10	3			.985	-5	O-93	-1.8
1951	Cin-N	114	303	27	63	12	2	5	25	19	36	.208	.257	.310	51	-21	4	5	-2	.974	-3	O-98	-3.0
1952	Chi-N	1	0	0	0	0	0	0	0	1	0	—	1.000	—	197	0	0	0	0	.000	0	H	0.0
1957	Cle-A	10	8	1	1	0	0	0	0	1	3	.125	.222	.125	-3	-1	0	0	0	1.000	-2	/O-4,3-1	-0.3
	Was-A	96	295	36	77	7	1	5	27	27	30	.261	.327	.342	84	-6	0	0	0	.979	3	O-95	-0.8
	Yr	106	303	37	78	7	1	5	27	28	33	.257	.324	.337	82	-7	0	0	0	.979	2	O-99/3-1	-1.1
Total	6	428	1101	133	259	41	4	18	102	90	136	.235	.295	.329	69	-49	9	5		.980	-19	O-378/3-2	-8.6

■ **DUTCH USSAT** Ussat, William August b: 4/11/04, Dayton, Ohio d: 5/29/59, Dayton, Ohio BR/TR, 6'1", 170 lbs. Deb: 9/13/25

YEAR	TM/L	G	AB	R	H	2B	3B	HR	RBI	BB	SO	AVG	OBP	SLG	PRO+	BR/A	SB	CS	SBR	FA	FR	G/POS	TPR
1925	Cle-A	1	1	0	0	0	0	0	0	0	0	.000	.000	.000	-99	-0	0	0	0	1.000	0	/2-1	0.0
1927	Cle-A	4	16	4	3	0	1	0	2	0	1	.188	.278	.313	53	-1	0	0	0	1.000	-1	/3-4	-0.2
Total	2	5	17	4	3	0	1	0	2	0	1	.176	.263	.294	44	-1	0	0	0	1.000	-1	/3-4,2-1	-0.2

■ **TEX VACHE** Vache, Ernest Lewis b: 11/17/1894, Santa Monica, Cal. d: 6/11/53, Los Angeles, Cal. BR/TR, 6'1", 200 lbs. Deb: 4/16/25

YEAR	TM/L	G	AB	R	H	2B	3B	HR	RBI	BB	SO	AVG	OBP	SLG	PRO+	BR/A	SB	CS	SBR	FA	FR	G/POS	TPR
1925	Bos-A	110	252	41	79	15	7	3	48	21	33	.313	.382	.464	114	5	2	2	-1	.908	-12	O-53	-1.0

■ **GENE VADEBONCOEUR** Vadeboncoeur, Onesime Eugene
b: 7/15/1858, Louiseville, Que., Can. d: 10/16/35, Haverhill, Mass. BR/TR, 5'6", 150 lbs. Deb: 7/11/1884

YEAR	TM/L	G	AB	R	H	2B	3B	HR	RBI	BB	SO	AVG	OBP	SLG	PRO+	BR/A	SB	CS	SBR	FA	FR	G/POS	TPR
1884	Phi-N	4	14	1	3	0	0	0	3	1	2	.214	.267	.214	56	-1				.846	-1	/C-4	-0.1

■ **HARRY VAHRENHORST** Vahrenhorst, Harry Henry "Van" b: 2/13/1885, St.Louis, Mo. d: 10/10/43, St.Louis, Mo. BR/TR, 6'1", 175 lbs. Deb: 9/21/04

YEAR	TM/L	G	AB	R	H	2B	3B	HR	RBI	BB	SO	AVG	OBP	SLG	PRO+	BR/A	SB	CS	SBR	FA	FR	G/POS	TPR
1904	StL-A	1	1	0	0	0	0	0	0	0		.000	.000	.000	-99	-0	0			.000	0	H	0.0

■ **MIKE VAIL** Vail, Michael Lewis b: 11/10/51, San Francisco, Cal. BR/TR, 6', 185 lbs. Deb: 8/18/75

YEAR	TM/L	G	AB	R	H	2B	3B	HR	RBI	BB	SO	AVG	OBP	SLG	PRO+	BR/A	SB	CS	SBR	FA	FR	G/POS	TPR
1975	NY-N	38	162	17	49	8	1	3	17	9	37	.302	.339	.420	115	3	0	0	0	.971	11	O-36	1.3
1976	NY-N	53	143	8	31	5	1	0	9	6	19	.217	.248	.266	49	-10	0	1	-1	.941	-1	O-35	-1.4
1977	NY-N	108	279	29	73	12	1	8	35	19	58	.262	.313	.398	94	-3	0	7	-4	.965	2	O-85	-0.8
1978	Cle-A	14	34	2	8	2	1	0	2	1	9	.235	.257	.353	71	-1	1	1	-0	1.000	-0	/O-9,D-1	-0.2
	Chi-N	74	180	15	60	6	2	4	33	3	24	.333	.344	.456	109	2	0	1	-1	.981	-9	O-45/3-1	-1.0
1979	Chi-N	87	179	28	60	8	2	7	35	14	27	.335	.383	.520	131	7	0	2	-1	.964	-4	O-39/3-2	0.1
1980	Chi-N	114	312	30	93	17	2	6	47	14	77	.298	.330	.423	101	0	2	5	-2	.963	-4	O-77	-0.9
1981	Cin-N	31	31	1	5	0	0	0	3	0	9	.161	.161	.161	-8	-4	0	0	0	1.000	-1	/O-3	-0.5
1982	Cin-N	78	189	9	48	10	1	4	29	6	33	.254	.277	.381	81	-5	0	0	0	.988	0	O-52	-0.6
1983	SF-N	18	26	1	4	1	0	0	3	0	7	.154	.185	.192	5	-3	0	0	0	1.000	-1	/1-4,O-2	-0.5
	Mon-N	34	53	5	15	2	0	2	4	8	10	.283	.387	.434	128	2	0	0	0	.958	1	O-15/1-1,3-1	0.3
	Yr	52	79	6	19	3	0	2	7	8	17	.241	.326	.354	90	-1	0	0	0	.960	-0	O-17/1-5,3-1	-0.2
1984	LA-N	16	16	1	1	0	0	0	2	1	7	.063	.118	.063	-49	-3	0	0	0	.000	-0	/O-1	-0.4
Total	10	665	1604	146	447	71	11	34	219	81	317	.279	.315	.400	95	-17	3	17	-9	.968	-5	O-399/1-5,3-4,D-1	-4.6

■ **PEDRO VALDES** Valdes, Pedro Jose (Manzo) b: 6/29/73, Fajardo, P.R. BL/TL, 6'1", 180 lbs. Deb: 5/15/96

YEAR	TM/L	G	AB	R	H	2B	3B	HR	RBI	BB	SO	AVG	OBP	SLG	PRO+	BR/A	SB	CS	SBR	FA	FR	G/POS	TPR
1996	Chi-N	9	8	2	1	1	0	0	1	1	5	.125	.222	.250	24	-1	0	0	0	1.000	-1	/O-2	-0.1
1998	Chi-N	14	23	1	5	1	1	0	2	1	3	.217	.250	.348	51	-2	0	1	-1	1.000	-0	/O-7	-0.3
Total	2	23	31	3	6	2	1	0	3	2	8	.194	.242	.323	44	-3	0	1	-1	1.000	-1	/O-9	-0.4

■ **ROY VALDES** Valdes, Rogelio Lazaro (Rojas) b: 2/20/20, Havana, Cuba BR/TR, 5'11", 185 lbs. Deb: 5/3/44

YEAR	TM/L	G	AB	R	H	2B	3B	HR	RBI	BB	SO	AVG	OBP	SLG	PRO+	BR/A	SB	CS	SBR	FA	FR	G/POS	TPR
1944	Was-A	1	1	0	0	0	0	0	0	0	0	.000	.000	.000	-99	-0	0	0	0	.000	0	H	0.0

■ **SANDY VALDESPINO** Valdespino, Hilario (Borroto) b: 1/14/39, San Jose De Las Lajas, Cuba BL/TL, 5'8", 170 lbs. Deb: 4/12/65

YEAR	TM/L	G	AB	R	H	2B	3B	HR	RBI	BB	SO	AVG	OBP	SLG	PRO+	BR/A	SB	CS	SBR	FA	FR	G/POS	TPR
1965	*Min-A	108	245	38	64	8	2	1	22	20	28	.261	.322	.322	80	-6	7	4	-0	.990	0	O-57	-0.9
1966	Min-A	52	108	11	19	1	1	2	9	4	24	.176	.212	.259	33	-9	2	2	-1	1.000	-1	O-23	-1.3
1967	Min-A	99	97	9	16	2	0	1	3	5	22	.165	.206	.216	23	-9	3	1	0	.977	-11	O-65	-2.4
1968	Atl-N	36	86	8	20	1	0	1	4	10	20	.233	.320	.279	81	-2	0	0	0	.976	1	O-20	-0.2
1969	Hou-N	41	119	17	29	4	0	0	12	15	19	.244	.328	.277	73	-4	2	2	-1	.976	1	O-29	-0.5
	Sea-A	20	38	3	8	1	0	0	2	1	7	.211	.250	.237	37	-3	0	1	-1	.889	2	/O-7	-0.2
1970	Mil-A	8	9	0	0	0	0	0	0	0	4	.000	.000	.000	-99	-2	0	0	0	.000	-0	/O-1	-0.3
1971	KC-A	18	63	10	20	6	0	2	15	2	5	.317	.338	.508	138	3	0	0	0	.950	-2	O-15	0.0
Total	7	382	765	96	176	23	3	7	67	57	129	.230	.288	.295	66	-33	14	10	-2	.974	-10	O-217	-5.8

■ **JULIO VALDEZ** Valdez, Julio Julian (b: Julio Julian Castillo (Valdez)) b: 6/3/56, San Cristobal, D.R. BB/TR, 6'2", 160 lbs. Deb: 9/2/80

YEAR	TM/L	G	AB	R	H	2B	3B	HR	RBI	BB	SO	AVG	OBP	SLG	PRO+	BR/A	SB	CS	SBR	FA	FR	G/POS	TPR
1980	Bos-A	8	19	4	5	1	0	1	4	0	5	.263	.300	.474	103	-0	2	0	1	.935	7	/S-8	0.8
1981	Bos-A	17	23	1	5	0	0	0	3	0	2	.217	.217	.217	24	-2	0	1	-1	.955	3	S-17	0.1
1982	Bos-A	28	20	3	5	1	0	0	1	0	7	.250	.250	.300	48	-1	1	0	0	.976	7	S-22/D-3	0.6
1983	Bos-A	12	25	3	3	0	0	0	0	1	4	.120	.185	.120	-13	-4	0	0	0	.939	-1	/2-9,S-2,D-1	-0.5
Total	4	65	87	11	18	2	0	1	8	1	18	.207	.233	.264	36	-8	3	1	0	.955	16	/S-49,2-9,D-4	1.0

■ **MARIO VALDEZ** Valdez, Mario A. b: 11/19/74, Obregon, Mex. BL/TL, 6'2", 190 lbs. Deb: 6/15/97

YEAR	TM/L	G	AB	R	H	2B	3B	HR	RBI	BB	SO	AVG	OBP	SLG	PRO+	BR/A	SB	CS	SBR	FA	FR	G/POS	TPR
1997	Chi-A	54	115	11	28	7	0	1	13	17	39	.243	.356	.330	84	-2	1	0	0	1.000	-3	1-47/3-1,D-2	-0.7

■ **JOSE VALDIVIELSO** Valdivielso, Jose (Lopez) (b: Jose Martinez De Valdivielso (Lopez)) b: 5/22/34, Matanzas, Cuba BR/TR, 6'1", 175 lbs. Deb: 6/21/55

YEAR	TM/L	G	AB	R	H	2B	3B	HR	RBI	BB	SO	AVG	OBP	SLG	PRO+	BR/A	SB	CS	SBR	FA	FR	G/POS	TPR
1955	Was-A	94	294	32	65	12	5	2	28	21	38	.221	.280	.316	63	-16	1	2	-1	.956	9	S-94	0.0
1956	Was-A	90	246	18	58	8	2	4	29	29	36	.236	.319	.333	72	-10	3	1	0	.947	16	S-90	1.3
1959	Was-A	24	14	1	4	0	0	0	0	1	3	.286	.333	.286	72	-0	0	0	0	1.000	5	S-21	0.5
1960	Was-A	117	268	23	57	1	1	2	19	20	36	.213	.277	.246	43	-21	1	2	-1	.954	9	*S-115/3-1	-0.7
1961	Min-A	76	149	15	29	5	0	1	9	8	19	.195	.236	.248	28	-15	1	1	-0	.971	-2	S-43,2-15,3-14	-1.4
Total	5	401	971	89	213	26	8	9	85	79	132	.219	.284	.290	55	-63	6	6	-2	.955	37	S-363/2-15,3-15	-0.3

■ **JOHN VALENTIN** Valentin, John William b: 2/18/67, Mineola, N.Y. BR/TR, 6', 185 lbs. Deb: 7/27/92

YEAR	TM/L	G	AB	R	H	2B	3B	HR	RBI	BB	SO	AVG	OBP	SLG	PRO+	BR/A	SB	CS	SBR	FA	FR	G/POS	TPR
1992	Bos-A	58	185	21	51	13	0	5	25	20	17	.276	.353	.427	110	3	1	0	0	.963	5	S-58	1.1
1993	Bos-A	144	468	50	130	40	3	11	66	49	77	.278	.349	.447	106	3	3	4	-2	.971	5	*S-144	1.7
1994	Bos-A	84	301	53	95	26	2	9	49	42	38	.316	.405	.505	127	13	3	1	0	.979	1	S-83/D-1	2.0
1995	*Bos-A	135	520	108	155	37	2	27	102	81	67	.298	.403	.533	136	29	20	5	3	.973	6	*S-135	4.6
1996	Bos-A	131	527	84	156	29	3	13	59	63	59	.296	.379	.436	103	4	9	10	-3	.971	6	*S-118,3-12/D-1	1.5
1997	Bos-A	143	575	95	176	**47**	5	18	77	58	66	.306	.375	.499	123	19	7	4	-0	.976	18	2-79,3-64	3.9
1998	*Bos-A	153	588	113	145	44	1	23	73	77	82	.247	.343	.442	102	2	4	5	-2	.965	13	*3-153/2-1	1.3
Total	7	848	3164	524	908	236	16	106	451	390	406	.287	.372	.472	115	73	47	29	-3	.972	52	S-538,3-229/2-80,D	16.1

YEAR	TM/L	G	AB	R	H	2B	3B	HR	RBI	BB	SO	AVG	OBP	SLG	PRO+	BR/A	SB	CS	SBR	FA	FR	G/POS	TPR
■ JAVIER VALENTIN Valentin, Jose (Rosario) b: 9/19/75, Manati, P.R. BB/TR, 5'10", 198 lbs. Deb: 9/13/97 F																							
1997	Min-A	4	7	1	2	0	0	0	0	0	3	.286	.286	.286	49	-1	0	0	0	1.000	1	/C-4	0.0
1998	Min-A	55	162	11	32	7	1	3	18	11	30	.198	.249	.309	44	-14	0	0	0	.983	-1	C-53/D-1	-1.1
Total	2	59	169	12	34	7	1	3	18	11	33	.201	.250	.308	44	-14	0	0	0	.984	-0	/C-57,D-1	-1.1
■ JOSE VALENTIN Valentin, Jose Antonio b: 10/12/69, Manati, P.R. BB/TR, 5'10", 175 lbs. Deb: 9/17/92 F																							
1992	Mil-A	4	3	1	0	0	0	0	1	0	0	.000	.000	.000	-99	-1	0	0	0	.667	-1	/2-1,S-1	-0.2
1993	Mil-A	19	53	10	13	1	2	1	7	7	16	.245	.344	.396	100	0	1	0	0	.922	-0	S-19	0.1
1994	Mil-A	97	285	47	68	19	0	11	46	38	75	.239	.332	.421	89	-5	12	3	2	.954	**28**	S-83,2-18/3-1	2.9
1995	Mil-A	112	338	62	74	23	3	11	49	37	83	.219	.296	.402	75	-13	16	8	0	.971	20	*S-104/3-1,D-4	1.4
1996	Mil-A	154	552	90	143	33	7	24	95	66	145	.259	.338	.475	99	-2	17	4	3	.950	-3	*S-151	0.9
1997	Mil-A	136	494	58	125	23	1	17	58	39	109	.253	.313	.407	85	-11	19	8	1	.967	1	*S-134/D-1	0.2
1998	Mil-N	151	428	65	96	24	0	16	49	63	105	.224	.325	.393	84	-10	10	7	-1	.963	0	*S-139/1-2,D-1	0.2
Total	7	673	2153	333	519	123	13	80	305	250	533	.241	.322	.422	88	-43	75	30	5	.960	45	S-631/2-19,D-6,13	5.5
■ ELLIS VALENTINE Valentine, Ellis Clarence b: 7/30/54, Helena, Ark. BR/TR, 6'4", 207 lbs. Deb: 9/3/75																							
1975	Mon-N	12	33	2	12	4	0	1	3	2	4	.364	.400	.576	161	3	0	0	0	.867	-1	O-11	0.1
1976	Mon-N	94	305	36	85	15	2	7	39	30	51	.279	.343	.410	108	3	14	1	4	.972	0	O-88	0.4
1977	Mon-N★	127	508	63	149	28	2	25	76	30	58	.293	.333	.504	124	15	13	5	1	.972	1	*O-126	1.1
1978	Mon-N	151	570	75	165	35	2	25	76	35	88	.289	.333	.489	129	19	13	8	-1	.970	14	*O-146	2.7
1979	Mon-N	146	548	73	151	29	3	21	82	22	74	.276	.305	.454	105	1	11	9	-2	.983	1	*O-144	-0.6
1980	Mon-N	86	311	40	98	22	2	13	67	25	44	.315	.372	.524	147	19	5	5	-2	.970	1	O-83	1.6
1981	Mon-N	22	76	8	16	3	0	3	15	6	11	.211	.268	.368	78	-2	0	1	-1	1.000	-0	O-21	-0.4
	NY-N	48	169	15	35	8	1	5	21	5	38	.207	.230	.355	65	-9	0	3	-2	.957	3	O-47	-1.0
	Yr	70	245	23	51	11	1	8	36	11	49	.208	.242	.359	69	-11	0	4	-2	.969	3	O-68	-1.4
1982	NY-N	111	337	33	97	14	1	8	48	5	38	.288	.300	.407	97	-3	1	3	-2	.983	1	O-98	-0.6
1983	Cal-A	86	271	30	65	10	2	13	43	18	48	.240	.287	.435	97	-2	2	1	0	.963	-7	O-85	-1.2
1985	Tex-A	11	38	5	8	1	0	2	4	2	8	.211	.250	.395	72	-2	0	1	-1	1.000	-1	/O-7,D-4	-0.4
Total	10	894	3166	380	881	169	15	123	474	180	462	.278	.319	.458	113	42	59	37	-5	.972	10	O-856/D-4	1.7
■ FRED VALENTINE Valentine, Fred Lee "Squeaky" b: 1/19/35, Clarksdale, Miss. BB/TR, 6'1", 190 lbs. Deb: 9/7/59																							
1959	Bal-A	12	19	0	6	0	0	0	1	3	4	.316	.409	.316	104	0	0	1	-1	.889	-2	/O-8	-0.2
1963	Bal-A	26	41	5	11	1	0	0	1	8	5	.268	.388	.293	98	0	0	0	0	1.000	-1	O-10	-0.2
1964	Was-A	102	212	20	48	5	0	4	20	21	44	.226	.305	.307	71	-8	4	2	0	.978	-4	O-57	-1.5
1965	Was-A	12	29	6	7	0	0	0	1	4	5	.241	.353	.241	73	-1	3	0	1	1.000	-0	O-11	0.0
1966	Was-A	146	508	77	140	29	7	16	59	51	63	.276	.353	.455	132	21	22	10	1	.980	-4	*O-138/1-2	1.2
1967	Was-A	151	457	52	107	16	1	11	44	56	76	.234	.331	.346	104	4	17	3	3	.989	-6	*O-136	-0.6
1968	Was-A	37	101	11	24	2	0	3	7	6	11	.238	.294	.347	96	-1	1	0	0	1.000	-1	O-27	-0.3
	Bal-A	47	91	9	17	3	2	2	5	7	20	.187	.253	.330	75	-3	0	0	0	.972	-1	O-26	-0.6
	Yr	84	192	20	41	5	2	5	12	13	31	.214	.274	.339	86	-4	1	0	0	.986	-3	O-53	-0.9
Total	7	533	1458	180	360	56	10	36	138	156	228	.247	.331	.373	106	13	47	16	5	.983	-20	O-413/1-2	-2.2
■ BOB VALENTINE Valentine, Robert Deb: 5/20/1876																							
1876	NY-N	1	3	0	0	0	0	0	0	0	0	.000	.000	.000	-99	-1				.400	-0	/C-1	-0.1
■ BOBBY VALENTINE Valentine, Robert John b: 5/13/50, Stamford, Conn. BR/TR, 5'10", 189 lbs. Deb: 9/2/69 MC																							
1969	LA-N	5	0	3	0	0	0	0	0	0	0	—	—	—	—	0	0	0	0	.000	0	R	0.0
1971	LA-N	101	281	32	70	10	2	1	25	15	20	.249	.292	.310	75	-10	5	3	-0	.961	-1	S-37,3-23,2-21,O-11	-0.7
1972	LA-N	119	391	42	107	11	2	3	32	27	33	.274	.324	.335	90	-5	5	5	-2	.976	0	2-49,3-39,O-16,S-10	-0.4
1973	Cal-A	32	126	12	38	5	2	1	13	5	9	.302	.328	.397	112	1	6	1	1	.948	0	S-25/O-8	0.6
1974	Cal-A	117	371	39	97	10	3	3	39	25	25	.261	.313	.329	90	-5	8	5	-1	.950	-8	O-62,S-36,3-15,/2D	-1.3
1975	Cal-A	26	57	5	16	2	0	0	5	4	3	.281	.339	.316	92	-0	0	2	-1	.958	-2	D-13/1-3,3-2,O-2	-0.4
	SD-N	7	15	1	2	0	0	1	1	4	0	.133	.316	.333	86	-0	1	0	0	1.000	-1	/O-4	-0.1
1976	SD-N	15	49	3	18	4	0	0	4	6	2	.367	.436	.449	165	4	0	1	-1	1.000	1	O-10/1-4	0.4
1977	SD-N	44	67	5	12	3	0	1	10	7	10	.179	.257	.269	46	-5	0	0	0	.962	-1	S-10,3-10/1-1	-0.6
	NY-N	42	83	8	11	1	0	1	3	6	9	.133	.191	.181	0	-12	0	0	0	1.000	-1	1-15,S-14/3-4	-1.2
	Yr	86	150	13	23	4	0	2	13	13	19	.153	.221	.220	20	-17	0	0	0	.969	-2	S-24,1-16,3-14	-1.8
1978	NY-N	69	160	17	43	7	0	1	18	19	18	.269	.350	.331	95	-1	1	1	-0	.977	-9	2-45/3-9	-0.8
1979	Sea-A	62	98	9	27	6	0	0	7	22	5	.276	.408	.337	102	2	1	2	-1	.971	-6	S-29,O-15/2-4,3CD	-0.5
Total	10	639	1698	176	441	59	9	12	157	140	134	.260	.319	.326	86	-31	27	20	-4	.957	-27	S-161,O-128,23/1DC	-5.0
■ BENNY VALENZUELA Valenzuela, Benjamin Beltran "Papelero" b: 6/2/33, Los Mochis, Mexico BR/TR, 5'10", 175 lbs. Deb: 4/27/58																							
1958	StL-N	10	14	0	3	1	0	0	0	1	0	.214	.267	.286	45	-1	0	0	0	.875	0	/3-3	-0.1
■ DAVE VALLE Valle, David b: 10/30/60, Bayside, N.Y. BR/TR, 6'2", 200 lbs. Deb: 9/7/84																							
1984	Sea-A	13	27	4	8	1	0	1	4	1	5	.296	.321	.444	111	0	0	0	0	1.000	2	C-13	0.3
1985	Sea-A	31	70	2	11	1	0	0	4	1	17	.157	.181	.171	-3	-10	0	0	0	.976	-1	C-31	-1.0
1986	Sea-A	22	53	10	18	3	0	5	15	7	7	.340	.417	.679	191	7	0	0	0	.982	-4	C-12/1-4	0.3
1987	Sea-A	95	324	40	83	16	3	12	53	15	46	.256	.295	.435	86	-7	2	0	1	.989	1	C-75,D-14/1-2,O-1	-0.1
1988	Sea-A	93	290	29	67	15	2	10	50	18	38	.231	.297	.400	89	-5	0	1	-1	.989	6	C-84/1-1,D-3	0.7
1989	Sea-A	94	316	32	75	10	3	7	34	29	32	.237	.313	.354	85	-6	0	0	0	.993	-3	C-93	-0.3
1990	Sea-A	107	308	37	66	15	0	7	33	45	48	.214	.328	.331	84	-6	1	2	-1	**.997**	-0	*C-104/1-1	-0.1
1991	Sea-A	132	324	38	63	8	1	8	32	34	49	.194	.289	.299	63	-16	0	2	-1	.992	9	*C-129/1-2	-0.2
1992	Sea-A	124	367	39	88	16	1	9	30	27	58	.240	.306	.362	86	-7	0	0	0	.990	-3	*C-122	-0.4
1993	Sea-A	135	423	48	109	19	0	13	63	48	56	.258	.357	.395	100	1	1	0	0	.995	9	*C-135	1.7
1994	Bos-A	30	76	6	12	2	1	1	5	9	18	.158	.256	.250	30	-8	0	1	-1	.982	-1	C-28/1-2	-0.8
	Mil-A	16	36	8	14	6	0	1	5	9	4	.389	.522	.639	189	5	0	1	-1	1.000	0	C-12/D-2	0.5
	Yr	46	112	14	26	8	1	2	10	18	22	.232	.348	.375	83	-3	0	2	-1	.986	-1	C-40/1-2,D-2	-0.3
1995	Tex-A	36	75	7	18	3	0	0	5	6	18	.240	.305	.280	52	-5	1	0	0	.993	7	C-29/1-7	0.3
1996	Tex-A	42	86	14	26	6	1	3	17	9	17	.302	.368	.500	111	1	0	0	0	.994	8	C-35/1-5,D-1	1.0
Total	13	970	2775	314	658	121	12	77	350	258	413	.237	.316	.373	86	-55	5	7	-3	.992	29	C-902/1-24,D-20,O-1	1.9
■ HECTOR VALLE Valle, Hector Jose b: 10/27/40, Vega Baja, P.R. BR/TR, 5'9", 180 lbs. Deb: 6/6/65																							
1965	LA-N	9	13	1	4	0	0	0	2	2	3	.308	.400	.308	110	0	0	0	0	1.000	-0	/C-6	0.0
■ ELMER VALO Valo, Elmer William b: 3/5/21, Ribnik, Czech. d: 7/19/98, Palmerton, Pa. BL/TR, 5'11", 190 lbs. Deb: 9/22/40 C																							
1940	Phi-A	6	23	6	8	0	0	0	0	3	0	.348	.423	.348	104	0	2	0	1	1.000	1	/O-6	0.1
1941	Phi-A	15	50	13	21	0	1	2	6	4	2	.420	.463	.580	179	6	0	0	0	1.000	-1	O-10	0.4
1942	Phi-A	133	459	64	115	13	10	2	40	70	21	.251	.355	.336	95	-1	13	8	-1	.964	1	*O-122	-0.8
1943	Phi-A	77	249	31	55	6	2	3	18	35	13	.221	.319	.297	81	-5	2	6	-3	.986	-1	O-63	-1.3
1946	Phi-A	108	348	59	107	21	6	1	31	60	18	.307	.411	.411	131	17	9	8	-2	.974	1	O-90	1.2
1947	Phi-A	112	370	60	111	12	6	5	36	64	21	.300	.406	.405	123	14	11	3	2	.973	-1	*O-104	1.0
1948	Phi-A	113	383	72	117	17	4	3	46	81	13	.305	.432	.394	120	16	10	6	-1	.983	-1	*O-109	0.9
1949	Phi-A	150	547	86	155	27	12	5	85	119	32	.283	.413	.404	121	21	14	11	-2	.981	10	*O-150	2.1
1950	Phi-A	129	446	62	125	16	5	10	46	82	22	.280	.400	.406	109	9	12	7	-1	.982	4	*O-117	0.6
1951	Phi-A	123	444	75	134	27	8	7	55	75	20	.302	.412	.446	129	21	11	6	-0	.981	-0	*O-116	1.6
1952	Phi-A	129	388	69	109	26	4	5	47	101	16	.281	.432	.407	126	19	12	11	-3	.962	-3	*O-121	1.0
1953	Phi-A	50	85	15	19	3	0	0	9	22	7	.224	.383	.259	73	-2	0	1	-1	1.000	-1	O-25	-0.4
1954	Phi-A	95	224	28	48	11	6	1	33	51	18	.214	.360	.330	90	-1	2	1	0	.965	2	O-62	-0.3
1955	KC-A	112	283	50	103	17	4	3	37	52	18	.364	.463	.484	153	24	5	3	-0	.987	2	O-72	2.2
1956	KC-A	9	9	1	2	0	0	0	2	1	1	.222	.300	.222	40	-1	0	0	0	.000	-0	/O-1	-0.1

YEAR	TM/L	G	AB	R	H	2B	3B	HR	RBI	BB	SO	AVG	OBP	SLG	PRO+	BR/A	SB	CS	SBR	FA	FR	G/POS	TPR
	Phi-N	98	291	40	84	13	3	5	37	48	21	.289	.395	.405	118	9	7	6	-2	.966	-0	O-87	0.4
1957	Bro-N	81	161	14	44	10	1	4	26	25	16	.273	.374	.422	104	1	0	1	-1	1.000	-4	O-36	-0.5
1958	LA-N	65	101	9	25	2	1	1	14	12	11	.248	.327	.317	69	-4	0	1	-1	1.000	-6	O-26	-1.2
1959	Cle-A	34	24	3	7	0	0	0	5	7	0	.292	.452	.292	113	1	0	0	0	1.000	-1	/O-2	0.1
1960	NY-A	8	5	1	0	0	0	0	0	2	1	.000	.286	.000	-17	-1	0	0	0	.000	-1	/O-2	-0.2
	Was-A	76	64	6	18	3	0	0	16	17	4	.281	.439	.328	112	2	0	0	0	1.000	-1	/O-6	0.2
	Yr	84	69	7	18	3	0	0	16	19	5	.261	.427	.304	103	2	0	0	0	1.000	-1	/O-8	0.0
1961	Min-A	33	32	0	5	2	0	0	4	3	3	.156	.250	.219	25	-3	0	0	0	1.000	0	/O-1	-0.3
	Phi-N	50	43	4	8	2	0	1	8	8	6	.186	.327	.302	69	-2	0	0	0	.000	-0	/O-1	-0.2
Total	20	1806	5029	768	1420	228	73	58	601	942	284	.282	.399	.391	114	142	110	79	-14	.977	1	*O-1329	6.5

■ **DEACON Van BUREN** Van Buren, Edward Eugene b: 12/14/1870, LaSalle Co., Ill. d: 6/29/57, Portland, Ore. BL/TR, 5′10″, 175 lbs. Deb: 4/21/04

YEAR	TM/L	G	AB	R	H	2B	3B	HR	RBI	BB	SO	AVG	OBP	SLG	PRO+	BR/A	SB	CS	SBR	FA	FR	G/POS	TPR
1904	Bro-N	1	1	0	1	0	0	0	0	0		1.000	1.000	1.000	531	0	0			.000	0	H	0.0
	Phi-N	12	43	2	10	2	0	0	3	3		.233	.283	.279	76	-1	2			.962	1	O-12	-0.1
	Yr	13	44	2	11	2	0	0	3	3		.250	.298	.295	86	-1	2			.962	1	O-12	-0.1

■ **TY Van BURKLEO** Van Burkleo, Tyler Lee b: 10/7/63, Oakland, Cal. BL/TL, 6′5″, 225 lbs. Deb: 7/28/93

YEAR	TM/L	G	AB	R	H	2B	3B	HR	RBI	BB	SO	AVG	OBP	SLG	PRO+	BR/A	SB	CS	SBR	FA	FR	G/POS	TPR
1993	Cal-A	12	33	2	5	3	0	1	1	6	9	.152	.282	.333	63	-2	1	0	0	1.000	-2	1-12	-0.4
1994	Col-N	2	5	0	0	0	0	0	0	0	1	.000	.000	.000	-86	-1	0	0	0	1.000	0	/1-2	-0.1
Total	2	14	38	2	5	3	0	1	1	6	10	.132	.250	.289	42	-3	1	0	0	1.000	-1	/1-14	-0.5

■ **AL Van CAMP** Van Camp, Albert Joseph b: 9/7/03, Moline, Ill. d: 2/2/81, Davenport, Iowa BR/TR, 5′11.5″, 175 lbs. Deb: 9/11/28

YEAR	TM/L	G	AB	R	H	2B	3B	HR	RBI	BB	SO	AVG	OBP	SLG	PRO+	BR/A	SB	CS	SBR	FA	FR	G/POS	TPR
1928	Cle-A	5	17	0	4	1	0	0	2	0	1	.235	.235	.294	38	-2	1	0	0	.980	-1	/1-5	-0.2
1931	Bos-A	101	324	34	89	15	4	0	33	20	24	.275	.319	.346	79	-10	3	2	-0	.973	-5	O-59,1-25	-2.0
1932	Bos-A	34	103	10	23	4	2	0	6	4	17	.223	.252	.301	44	-9	0	0	0	.985	1	1-25	-1.0
Total	3	140	444	44	116	20	6	0	41	24	42	.261	.301	.333	69	-21	4	2	0	.991	-5	/O-59,1-55	-3.2

■ **CARL VANDAGRIFT** Vandagrift, Carl William b: 4/22/1883, Cantrall, Ill. d: 10/9/20, Fort Wayne, Ind. BR/TR, 5′8″, 155 lbs. Deb: 5/19/14

YEAR	TM/L	G	AB	R	H	2B	3B	HR	RBI	BB	SO	AVG	OBP	SLG	PRO+	BR/A	SB	CS	SBR	FA	FR	G/POS	TPR
1914	Ind-F	43	136	25	34	4	0	0	9	9	15	.250	.301	.279	53	-11	7			.925	-6	2-28,3-12/S-5	-1.8

■ **JOHN VANDER WAL** Vander Wal, John Henry b: 4/29/66, Grand Rapids, Mich. BL/TL, 6′2″, 190 lbs. Deb: 9/6/91

YEAR	TM/L	G	AB	R	H	2B	3B	HR	RBI	BB	SO	AVG	OBP	SLG	PRO+	BR/A	SB	CS	SBR	FA	FR	G/POS	TPR
1991	Mon-N	21	61	4	13	4	1	1	8	1	18	.213	.226	.361	63	-3	0	0	0	1.000	-1	O-17	-0.5
1992	Mon-N	105	213	21	51	8	2	4	20	24	36	.239	.316	.352	90	-3	3	0	1	.981	0	O-57/1-7	-0.3
1993	Mon-N	106	215	34	50	7	4	5	30	27	30	.233	.321	.372	81	-6	6	3	0	.988	-12	1-42,O-38	-2.1
1994	Col-N	91	110	12	27	3	1	5	15	16	31	.245	.341	.427	85	-3	2	1	0	1.000	-2	1-14/O-7	-0.5
1995	*Col-N	105	101	15	35	8	1	5	21	16	23	.347	.436	.594	131	4	1	1	-0	.957	-1	1-10,O-10	0.2
1996	Col-N	104	151	20	38	6	2	5	31	19	38	.252	.339	.417	79	-5	2	2	-1	1.000	-3	O-26,1-10	-0.9
1997	Col-N	76	92	7	16	2	0	1	11	10	33	.174	.255	.228	23	-11	1	1	-0	.923	-2	/O-9,1-5,D-2	-1.3
1998	Col-N	89	104	18	30	10	1	5	20	16	29	.288	.383	.548	115	2	0	0	0	1.000	-4	O-25/1-2	-0.1
	*SD-N	20	25	3	6	3	0	0	0	6	5	.240	.387	.360	106	0	0	0	0	1.000	0	/O-5,1-3,D-3	0.0
	Yr	109	129	21	36	13	1	5	20	22	34	.279	.384	.512	114	3	0	0	0	1.000	-4	O-30/1-5,D-3	-0.1
Total	8	717	1072	134	266	51	12	31	156	135	243	.248	.333	.405	86	-24	15	8	-0	.985	-24	O-194/1-93,D-5	-5.5

■ **FRED Van DUSEN** Van Dusen, Frederick William b: 7/31/37, Jackson Heights, N.Y. BL/TL, 6′3″, 180 lbs. Deb: 9/11/55

YEAR	TM/L	G	AB	R	H	2B	3B	HR	RBI	BB	SO	AVG	OBP	SLG	PRO+	BR/A	SB	CS	SBR	FA	FR	G/POS	TPR
1955	Phi-N	1	0	0	0	0	0	0	0	0	0	—	1.000	—	199	0	0	0	0	.000	0	H	0.0

■ **BILL Van DYKE** Van Dyke, William Jennings b: 12/15/1863, Paris, Ill. d: 5/5/33, ElPaso, Tex. BR/TR, 5′8″, 170 lbs. Deb: 4/17/1890

YEAR	TM/L	G	AB	R	H	2B	3B	HR	RBI	BB	SO	AVG	OBP	SLG	PRO+	BR/A	SB	CS	SBR	FA	FR	G/POS	TPR
1890	Tol-a	129	502	74	129	14	11	2	54	25		.257	.296	.341	85	-12	73			.924	-7	*O-110,3-18/2-2,C-1	-1.9
1892	StL-N	4	16	2	2	0	0	0	1	0	1	.125	.125	.125	-26	-2	0			.875	-1	/O-4	-0.3
1893	Bos-N	3	12	2	3	1	0	0	1	0	1	.250	.250	.333	50	-1	1			1.000	-1	/O-3	-0.1
Total	3	136	530	78	134	15	11	2	56	25	2	.253	.290	.334	81	-16	74			.924	-8	O-117/3-18,2-2,C-1	-2.3

■ **DAVE Van GORDER** Van Gorder, David Thomas b: 3/27/57, Los Angeles, Cal. BR/TR, 6′2″, 205 lbs. Deb: 6/15/82

YEAR	TM/L	G	AB	R	H	2B	3B	HR	RBI	BB	SO	AVG	OBP	SLG	PRO+	BR/A	SB	CS	SBR	FA	FR	G/POS	TPR
1982	Cin-N	51	137	4	25	3	1	0	7	14	19	.182	.263	.219	35	-12	1	0	0	.986	-2	C-51	-1.2
1984	Cin-N	38	101	10	23	2	0	0	6	12	17	.228	.310	.248	56	-6	0	0	0	1.000	2	C-36/1-1	-0.3
1985	Cin-N	73	151	12	36	7	0	2	24	9	19	.238	.286	.325	67	-7	0	0	0	.989	-3	C-70	-0.8
1986	Cin-N	9	10	0	0	0	0	0	0	1	2	.000	.091	.000	-70	-2	0	0	0	1.000	1	/C-7	-0.2
1987	Bal-A	12	21	4	5	0	0	1	1	3	6	.238	.333	.381	91	-0	0	0	0	.978	1	C-12	0.1
Total	5	183	420	30	89	12	1	3	38	39	63	.212	.282	.267	52	-26	1	0	0	.990	-2	C-176/1-1	-2.4

■ **GEORGE Van HALTREN** Van Haltren, George Edward Martin "Rip"
b: 3/30/1866, St.Louis, Mo. d: 9/29/45, Oakland, Cal. BL/TL, 5′11″, 170 lbs. Deb: 6/27/1887 M

YEAR	TM/L	G	AB	R	H	2B	3B	HR	RBI	BB	SO	AVG	OBP	SLG	PRO+	BR/A	SB	CS	SBR	FA	FR	G/POS	TPR
1887	Chi-N	45	172	30	35	4	0	3	17	15	15	.203	.271	.279	47	-13	12			.927	-3	O-27,P-20	-0.9
1888	Chi-N	81	318	46	90	9	14	4	34	22	34	.283	.329	.437	133	11	21			.872	-2	O-57,P-30	0.1
1889	Chi-N	134	543	126	168	20	10	9	81	82	41	.309	.405	.433	128	21	28			.898	-3	*O-130/S-3,2-1	1.3
1890	Bro-P	92	376	84	126	8	9	5	54	41	23	.335	.405	.444	119	10	35			.896	5	O-67,P-28/S-3	0.5
1891	Bal-a	139	566	136	180	14	15	9	83	71	46	.318	.398	.443	139	29	75			.882	-12	O-81,S-59/P-6,2-2	1.5
1892	Bal-N	135	556	105	168	20	12	7	57	70	34	.302	.382	.419	139	26	49			.850	0	*O-129/P-4,3-3,1SM	1.9
	Pit-N	13	55	10	11	2	2	0	5	6	0	.200	.279	.309	77	-2	6			.905	-2	O-13	-0.4
	Yr	148	611	115	179	22	14	7	62	76	34	.293	.373	.409	133	25	55			.854	-2	*O-142/P-4,3-3,1S	1.5
1893	Pit-N	124	529	129	179	14	11	3	79	75	25	.338	.422	.423	127	24	37			.869	-6	*O-111,S-12/2-2	1.0
1894	*NY-N	137	519	109	172	22	4	7	104	55	22	.331	.400	.430	101	2	43			.914	-2	*O-137	-0.7
1895	NY-N	131	521	113	177	23	19	8	103	57	29	.340	.408	.503	137	29	32			.914	-3	*O-131/P-1	1.3
1896	NY-N	133	562	136	197	18	**21**	5	74	55	36	.351	.410	.484	139	32	39			.952	4	*O-133/P-2	2.1
1897	NY-N	129	564	117	186	22	9	3	64	40		.330	.375	.417	112	10	50			.937	9	*O-129	0.8
1898	NY-N	156	654	129	204	28	16	2	68	59		.312	.372	.413	129	24	36			.917	-2	*O-156	1.0
1899	NY-N	151	604	117	182	21	3	2	58	74		.301	.378	.356	106	8	31			.932	3	*O-151	-0.1
1900	NY-N	141	571	114	180	30	7	1	51	50		.315	.371	.398	118	14	**45**			.939	10	*O-141/P-1	1.2
1901	NY-N	135	543	82	182	23	6	1	47	51		.335	.396	.405	138	28	24			.941	4	*O-135/P-1	2.1
1902	NY-N	24	88	14	23	1	2	0	7	17		.261	.381	.318	117	3	6			.925	2	O-24	0.3
1903	NY-N	84	280	42	72	6	1	0	28	28		.257	.327	.286	72	-9	14			.959	-6	O-75	-1.9
Total	17	1984	8021	1639	2532	285	161	69	1014	868	305	.316	.385	.417	121	245	583			.915	-6	*O-1827/P-93,S231	11.1

■ **JOHN VANN** Vann, John Silas b: 6/7/1893, Fairland, Okla. d: 6/10/58, Shreveport, La. BR/TR, Deb: 6/11/13

YEAR	TM/L	G	AB	R	H	2B	3B	HR	RBI	BB	SO	AVG	OBP	SLG	PRO+	BR/A	SB	CS	SBR	FA	FR	G/POS	TPR
1913	StL-N	1	1	0	0	0	0	0	0	0	1	.000	.000	.000	-99	-0	0			.000	0	H	0.0

■ **JAY Van NOY** Van Noy, Jay Lowell b: 11/4/28, Garland, Utah BL/TR, 6′1″, 200 lbs. Deb: 6/18/51

YEAR	TM/L	G	AB	R	H	2B	3B	HR	RBI	BB	SO	AVG	OBP	SLG	PRO+	BR/A	SB	CS	SBR	FA	FR	G/POS	TPR
1951	StL-N	6	7	1	0	0	0	0	0	1	6	.000	.125	.000	-63	-2	0	0	0	1.000	-0	/O-1	-0.2

■ **MAURICE Van ROBAYS** Van Robays, Maurice Rene "Bomber" b: 11/15/14, Detroit, Mich. d: 3/1/65, Detroit, Mich. BR/TR, 6′0.5″, 190 lbs. Deb: 9/7/39

YEAR	TM/L	G	AB	R	H	2B	3B	HR	RBI	BB	SO	AVG	OBP	SLG	PRO+	BR/A	SB	CS	SBR	FA	FR	G/POS	TPR
1939	Pit-N	27	105	13	33	9	0	2	16	6	10	.314	.351	.457	118	2	0			.919	-4	O-25/3-1	-0.2
1940	Pit-N	145	572	82	156	27	7	11	116	33	58	.273	.316	.402	98	-3	2			.963	-4	*O-143/1-1	-1.5
1941	Pit-N	129	457	62	129	23	5	4	78	41	29	.282	.343	.381	104	2	0			.974	7	*O-121	0.2
1942	Pit-N	100	328	29	76	13	5	1	46	30	24	.232	.298	.311	76	-10	0			.986	5	O-84	-1.0
1943	Pit-N	69	236	32	68	17	7	1	35	18	19	.288	.344	.432	119	5	0			.940	-3	O-60	-0.1
1946	Pit-N	59	146	14	31	5	3	1	12	11	15	.212	.272	.308	63	-7	0			.955	-5	O-37/1-2	-1.5
Total	6	529	1844	232	493	94	27	20	303	139	155	.267	.321	.380	97	-11	2			.966	-3	O-470/1-3,3-1	-4.1

■ **ANDY Van SLYKE** Van Slyke, Andrew James b: 12/21/60, Utica, N.Y. BL/TR, 6′2″, 192 lbs. Deb: 6/17/83

YEAR	TM/L	G	AB	R	H	2B	3B	HR	RBI	BB	SO	AVG	OBP	SLG	PRO+	BR/A	SB	CS	SBR	FA	FR	G/POS	TPR
1983	StL-N	101	309	51	81	15	5	8	38	46	64	.262	.360	.421	115	7	21	7	2	.974	-10	O-69,3-30/1-9	-0.3
1984	StL-N	137	361	45	88	16	4	7	50	63	71	.244	.356	.368	107	5	28	5	5	1.000	-12	O-81,3-32,1-30	-0.5
1985	*StL-N	146	424	61	110	25	6	13	55	47	54	.259	.336	.439	116	9	34	6	7	.996	-2	*O-142/1-2	1.0

YEAR	TM/L	G	AB	R	H	2B	3B	HR	RBI	BB	SO	AVG	OBP	SLG	PRO+	BR/A	SB	CS	SBR	FA	FR	G/POS	TPR
1986	StL-N	137	418	48	113	23	7	13	61	47	85	.270	.345	.452	119	10	21	8	2	.969	3	*O-110,1-38	1.1
1987	Pit-N	157	564	93	165	36	11	21	82	56	122	.293	.361	.507	126	20	34	8	5	.988	10	*O-150/1-1	3.0
1988	Pit-N★	154	587	101	169	23	**15**	25	100	57	126	.288	.352	.506	146	33	30	9	4	.991	17	*O-152	5.1
1989	Pit-N	130	476	64	113	18	9	9	53	47	100	.237	.310	.370	97	-2	16	4	2	.989	14	*O-123/1-2	1.1
1990	*Pit-N	136	493	67	140	26	6	17	77	66	89	.284	.370	.465	133	23	14	4	2	.976	3	*O-133	2.5
1991	*Pit-N	138	491	87	130	24	7	17	83	71	85	.265	.362	.446	128	19	10	3	1	.996	1	*O-135	1.9
1992	*Pit-N★	154	614	103	**199**	**45**	12	14	89	58	99	.324	.386	.505	152	41	12	3	2	.989	11	*O-154	5.4
1993	Pit-N†	83	323	42	100	13	4	8	50	24	40	.310	.361	.449	116	7	11	2	2	.995	3	O-78	1.0
1994	Pit-N	105	374	41	92	18	3	6	30	52	72	.246	.341	.358	82	-9	7	0	2	.992	6	O-99	-0.4
1995	Bal-A	17	63	6	10	1	0	3	8	5	15	.159	.221	.317	37	-6	0	0	0	.978	2	O-17	-0.4
	Phi-N	63	214	26	52	10	2	3	16	28	41	.243	.336	.350	81	-5	7	0	2	.984	3	O-56	-0.2
Total	13	1658	5711	835	1562	293	91	164	792	667	1063	.274	.352	.443	120	151	245	59	38	.988	48	*O-1499/1-82,3-62	20.3

■ **IKE Van ZANDT** Van Zandt, Charles Isaac b: 2/1876, Brooklyn, N.Y. d: 9/14/08, Nashua, N.H. BL, Deb: 8/5/01

YEAR	TM/L	G	AB	R	H	2B	3B	HR	RBI	BB	SO	AVG	OBP	SLG	PRO+	BR/A	SB	CS	SBR	FA	FR	G/POS	TPR
1901	NY-N	3	6	1	1	0	0	0	0	0		.167	.167	.167	-3	-1	0			.333	-2	/P-2,O-1	-0.1
1904	Chi-N	3	11	0	0	0	0	0	0	0		.000	.000	.000	-99	-3	0			1.000	0	/O-3	-0.3
1905	StL-A	94	322	31	75	15	1	1	20	7		.233	.252	.295	77	-10	7			.874	-13	O-75/P-1,1-1	-2.9
Total	3	100	339	32	76	15	1	1	20	7		.224	.242	.283	69	-13	7			.868	-14	/O-79,P-3,1-1	-3.3

■ **DICK Van ZANT** Van Zant, Richard "Foghorn Dick" b: 11/1864, Indiana d: 8/6/12, Wayne Co., Ind. Deb: 10/4/1888

YEAR	TM/L	G	AB	R	H	2B	3B	HR	RBI	BB	SO	AVG	OBP	SLG	PRO+	BR/A	SB	CS	SBR	FA	FR	G/POS	TPR
1888	Cle-a	10	31	1	8	1	0	0	1	1		.258	.303	.290	93	-0	1			.784	0	3-10	0.0

■ **EDDIE VARGAS** Vargas, Hediberto (Rodriguez) b: 2/23/59, Guanica, P.R. BR/TR, 6'4", 205 lbs. Deb: 9/8/82

YEAR	TM/L	G	AB	R	H	2B	3B	HR	RBI	BB	SO	AVG	OBP	SLG	PRO+	BR/A	SB	CS	SBR	FA	FR	G/POS	TPR
1982	Pit-N	8	8	1	3	1	0	0	3	0	2	.375	.375	.500	139	0	0	0	0	1.000	0	/1-5	0.0
1984	Pit-N	18	31	3	7	2	0	0	2	3	5	.226	.294	.290	65	-1	0	0	0	.982	-0	1-13	-0.2
Total	2	26	39	4	10	3	0	0	5	3	7	.256	.310	.333	80	-1	0	0	0	.986	-0	/1-18	-0.2

■ **JASON VARITEK** Varitek, Jason A. b: 4/11/72, Rochester, Minn. BB/TR, 6'2", 210 lbs. Deb: 9/24/97

YEAR	TM/L	G	AB	R	H	2B	3B	HR	RBI	BB	SO	AVG	OBP	SLG	PRO+	BR/A	SB	CS	SBR	FA	FR	G/POS	TPR
1997	Bos-A	1	1	0	1	0	0	0	0	0	0	1.000	1.000	1.000	416	0	0	0	0	1.000	-0	/C-1	0.0
1998	*Bos-A	86	221	31	56	13	0	7	33	17	45	.253	.313	.407	85	-5	2	2	-1	.988	0	C-75/D-3	-0.2
Total	2	87	222	31	57	13	0	7	33	17	45	.257	.315	.410	87	-5	2	2	-1	.988	0	/C-76,D-3	-0.2

■ **BUCK VARNER** Varner, Glen Gann b: 8/17/30, Hixson, Tenn. BL/TR, 5'10", 170 lbs. Deb: 9/19/52

YEAR	TM/L	G	AB	R	H	2B	3B	HR	RBI	BB	SO	AVG	OBP	SLG	PRO+	BR/A	SB	CS	SBR	FA	FR	G/POS	TPR
1952	Was-A	2	4	0	0	0	0	0	0	1	1	.000	.200	.000	-43	-1	0	0	0	1.000	-0	/O-1	-0.1

■ **PETE VARNEY** Varney, Richard Fred b: 4/10/49, Roxbury, Mass. BR/TR, 6'3", 235 lbs. Deb: 8/26/73

YEAR	TM/L	G	AB	R	H	2B	3B	HR	RBI	BB	SO	AVG	OBP	SLG	PRO+	BR/A	SB	CS	SBR	FA	FR	G/POS	TPR
1973	Chi-A	5	4	0	0	0	0	0	0	1	0	.000	.200	.000	-38	-1	0	0	0	1.000	0	/C-5	0.0
1974	Chi-A	9	28	1	7	0	0	0	2	1	8	.250	.276	.250	51	-2	0	0	0	.981	1	/C-9	0.0
1975	Chi-A	36	107	12	29	5	1	2	8	6	28	.271	.316	.393	98	-1	2	0	1	.988	-1	C-34/D-2	0.0
1976	Chi-A	14	41	5	10	2	0	3	5	2	9	.244	.279	.512	128	1	0	0	0	.988	1	C-14	0.3
	Atl-N	5	10	0	1	0	0	0	0	0	2	.100	.100	.100	-41	-2	0	0	0	1.000	-1	/C-5	-0.2
Total	4	69	190	18	47	7	1	5	15	10	47	.247	.289	.374	86	-4	2	0	1	.988	1	/C-67,D-2	0.1

■ **GARY VARSHO** Varsho, Gary Andrew b: 6/20/61, Marshfield, Wis. BL/TR, 5'11", 190 lbs. Deb: 7/6/88

YEAR	TM/L	G	AB	R	H	2B	3B	HR	RBI	BB	SO	AVG	OBP	SLG	PRO+	BR/A	SB	CS	SBR	FA	FR	G/POS	TPR
1988	Chi-N	46	73	6	20	3	0	0	5	1	6	.274	.284	.315	69	-3	5	0	2	.906	-2	O-18	-0.4
1989	Chi-N	61	87	10	16	4	2	0	6	4	13	.184	.220	.276	38	-7	3	0	1	.929	-3	O-21	-1.0
1990	Chi-N	46	48	10	12	4	0	0	1	1	6	.250	.265	.333	59	-3	2	0	1	1.000	-1	/O-3	-0.3
1991	*Pit-N	99	187	23	51	11	2	4	23	19	34	.273	.346	.417	115	4	9	2	2	.989	-4	O-54/1-3	0.0
1992	*Pit-N	103	162	22	36	6	3	4	22	10	32	.222	.267	.370	80	-5	5	2	0	.984	-5	O-44	-1.1
1993	Cin-N	77	95	8	22	6	0	2	11	9	19	.232	.305	.358	77	-3	1	0	0	1.000	-2	O-22	-0.5
1994	Pit-N	67	82	15	21	6	3	0	5	4	19	.256	.307	.402	82	-2	0	1	-1	.926	-10	O-36/1-1	-1.3
1995	Phi-N	72	103	7	26	1	1	0	11	7	17	.252	.313	.282	58	-6	2	0	1	.939	-4	O-25	-0.9
Total	8	571	837	101	204	41	11	10	84	55	146	.244	.296	.355	78	-25	27	5	5	.963	-30	O-223/1-4	-5.5

■ **JIM VATCHER** Vatcher, James Ernest b: 5/27/66, Santa Monica, Cal. BR/TR, 5'9", 165 lbs. Deb: 5/30/90

YEAR	TM/L	G	AB	R	H	2B	3B	HR	RBI	BB	SO	AVG	OBP	SLG	PRO+	BR/A	SB	CS	SBR	FA	FR	G/POS	TPR
1990	Phi-N	36	46	5	12	1	0	1	4	4	6	.261	.320	.348	84	-1	0	0	0	1.000	-6	O-24	-0.8
	Atl-N	21	27	2	7	1	1	0	3	1	9	.259	.286	.370	75	-1	0	0	0	1.000	-1	/O-6	-0.2
	Yr	57	73	7	19	2	1	1	7	5	15	.260	.308	.356	80	-2	0	0	0	1.000	-7	O-30	-1.0
1991	SD-N	17	20	3	4	0	0	0	2	4	6	.200	.333	.200	52	-1	1	0	0	.900	-2	O-11	-0.3
1992	SD-N	13	16	1	4	1	0	0	2	3	6	.250	.368	.313	93	-0	0	0	0	1.000	-2	O-13	-0.2
Total	3	87	109	11	27	3	1	1	11	12	27	.248	.322	.321	77	-3	1	0	0	.980	-11	/O-54	-1.5

■ **GLENN VAUGHAN** Vaughan, Glenn Edward "Sparky" b: 2/15/44, Compton, Cal. BB/TR, 5'11", 170 lbs. Deb: 9/20/63

YEAR	TM/L	G	AB	R	H	2B	3B	HR	RBI	BB	SO	AVG	OBP	SLG	PRO+	BR/A	SB	CS	SBR	FA	FR	G/POS	TPR
1963	Hou-N	9	30	1	5	0	0	0	0	2	5	.167	.219	.167	14	-3	1	0	0	.914	-3	/S-9,3-1	-0.7

■ **ARKY VAUGHAN** Vaughan, Joseph Floyd b: 3/9/12, Clifty, Ark. d: 8/30/52, Eagleville, Cal. BL/TR, 5'10.5", 175 lbs. Deb: 4/17/32 H

YEAR	TM/L	G	AB	R	H	2B	3B	HR	RBI	BB	SO	AVG	OBP	SLG	PRO+	BR/A	SB	CS	SBR	FA	FR	G/POS	TPR
1932	Pit-N	129	497	71	158	15	10	4	61	39	26	.318	.375	.412	113	11	10			.934	-20	*S-128	0.1
1933	Pit-N	152	573	85	180	29	**19**	9	97	64	23	.314	.388	.478	146	35	3			.945	-9	*S-152	3.8
1934	Pit-N★	149	558	115	186	41	11	12	94	**94**	38	.333	**.431**	.511	148	41	10			.952	3	*S-149	**5.1**
1935	Pit-N★	137	499	108	192	34	10	19	99	**97**	18	**.385**	**.491**	**.607**	**187**	**67**	4			.950	-11	*S-137	**6.1**
1936	Pit-N☆	156	568	**122**	190	30	11	9	78	**118**	21	.335	**.453**	.474	146	44	6			.945	-11	*S-156	4.1
1937	Pit-N★	126	469	71	151	17	**17**	5	72	54	22	.322	.394	.463	132	22	7			.956	0	*S-108,O-12	2.8
1938	Pit-N☆	148	541	88	174	35	5	7	68	104	21	.322	.433	.444	140	36	14			.961	18	*S-147	**6.4**
1939	Pit-N★	152	595	94	182	30	11	6	62	70	20	.306	.385	.424	119	18	12			.962	9	*S-152	3.9
1940	Pit-N★	156	594	**113**	178	40	**15**	7	95	88	25	.300	.393	.453	134	30	12			.942	8	*S-155/3-2	**5.1**
1941	Pit-N★	106	374	69	118	20	7	6	38	50	13	.316	.399	.455	141	21	8			.958	-12	S-97/3-3	1.7
1942	Bro-N★	128	495	82	137	18	4	2	49	51	17	.277	.348	.341	100	1	8			.959	-10	*3-119/S-5,2-1	-0.8
1943	Bro-N	149	610	**112**	186	39	6	5	66	60	13	.305	.370	.413	126	20	**20**			.965	-24	S-99,3-55	0.4
1947	*Bro-N	64	126	24	41	5	2	2	25	27	11	.325	.444	.444	132	7	4			1.000	1	O-22,3-10	0.7
1948	Bro-N	65	123	19	30	3	0	3	22	21	8	.244	.354	.341	86	-2	0			1.000	1	O-26/3-8	-0.2
Total	14	1817	6622	1173	2103	356	128	96	926	937	276	.318	.406	.453	136	352	118			.951	-59	*S-1485,3-197/O2	39.2

■ **FRED VAUGHN** Vaughn, Frederick Thomas "Muscles" b: 10/18/18, Coalinga, Cal. d: 3/2/64, Near Lake Wales, Fla. BR/TR, 5'10", 185 lbs. Deb: 8/20/44

YEAR	TM/L	G	AB	R	H	2B	3B	HR	RBI	BB	SO	AVG	OBP	SLG	PRO+	BR/A	SB	CS	SBR	FA	FR	G/POS	TPR
1944	Was-A	30	109	10	28	2	1	1	21	9	24	.257	.319	.321	87	-2	2	2	-1	.942	-2	2-26/3-3	-0.3
1945	Was-A	80	268	28	63	7	4	1	25	23	48	.235	.298	.302	81	-7	0	3	-2	.946	-5	2-76/S-1	-1.0
Total	2	110	377	38	91	9	5	2	46	32	72	.241	.304	.308	83	-9	2	5	-2	.945	-6	2-102/3-3,S-1	-1.3

■ **GREG VAUGHN** Vaughn, Gregory Lamont b: 7/3/65, Sacramento, Cal. BR/TR, 6', 193 lbs. Deb: 8/10/89

YEAR	TM/L	G	AB	R	H	2B	3B	HR	RBI	BB	SO	AVG	OBP	SLG	PRO+	BR/A	SB	CS	SBR	FA	FR	G/POS	TPR
1989	Mil-A	38	113	18	30	3	0	5	23	13	23	.265	.341	.425	116	2	4	1	1	.943	-3	O-24,D-13	-0.1
1990	Mil-A	120	382	51	84	26	2	17	61	33	91	.220	.284	.432	98	-3	7	4	-0	.967	-1	*O-106/D-8	-0.6
1991	Mil-A	145	542	81	132	24	5	27	98	62	125	.244	.322	.456	116	10	2	2	-1	.994	13	*O-135,D-10	1.8
1992	Mil-A	141	501	77	114	18	2	23	78	60	123	.228	.316	.409	104	2	15	15	-5	.990	3	*O-131/D-7	-0.2
1993	Mil-A★	154	569	97	152	28	2	30	97	89	118	.267	.371	.482	129	24	10	7	-1	.986	4	O-94,D-58	2.1
1994	Mil-A	95	370	59	94	24	1	19	55	51	93	.254	.346	.478	105	2	9	5	-0	.982	-0	O-81,D-14	-0.1
1995	Mil-A	108	392	67	88	19	1	17	59	55	89	.224	.320	.408	83	-10	10	4	1	.000	0	*D-104	-1.6
1996	Mil-A☆	102	375	78	105	16	0	31	95	58	99	.280	.382	.571	132	18	5	2	0	.980	-2	*O-100/D-1	1.3
	*SD-N	43	141	20	29	3	1	10	22	24	31	.206	.329	.454	110	2	4	1	1	.974	3	O-39	0.4
1997	SD-N	120	361	60	78	10	0	18	57	56	110	.216	.325	.393	94	-4	7	4	-0	.994	2	O-94/D-3	-0.4
1998	*SD-N★	158	573	112	156	28	4	50	119	79	121	.272	.365	.597	159	47	11	4	1	.993	10	*O-151/D-4	5.5
Total	10	1224	4319	720	1062	199	18	247	764	580	1023	.246	.339	.472	116	90	84	49	-4	.985	29	O-955,D-222	8.1

■ FARMER VAUGHN
Vaughn, Harry Francis b: 3/1/1864, Ruraldale, Ohio d: 2/21/14, Cincinnati, Ohio BR/TR, 6'3", 177 lbs. Deb: 10/7/1886

YEAR	TM/L	G	AB	R	H	2B	3B	HR	RBI	BB	SO	AVG	OBP	SLG	PRO+	BR/A	SB	CS	SBR	FA	FR	G/POS	TPR
1886	Cin-a	1	3	0	0	0	0	0	0	0		.000	.250	.000	-19	-0	0			.917	1	/C-1	0.0
1888	Lou-a	51	189	15	37	4	2	1	21	4		.196	.216	.254	52	-10	4			.863	-2	O-28,C-25	-1.0
1889	Lou-a	90	360	39	86	11	5	3	45	7	41	.239	.253	.322	65	-18	13			.900	3	C-54,O-20,1-18,/3-3	-1.0
1890	NY-P	44	166	27	44	7	0	1	22	10	9	.265	.307	.325	63	-10	6			.877	-12	C-30,O-12/3-1,2-1	-1.6
1891	Cin-a	51	175	21	45	7	1	1	14	14	15	.257	.316	.326	77	-6	7			.923	7	C-44/O-6,1-2,3-2,P	0.3
	Mil-a	25	99	13	33	7	0	0	9	4	5	.333	.359	.404	98	-2	1			.924	2	C-20/1-4,O-1	0.2
	Yr	76	274	34	78	14	1	1	23	18	20	.285	.331	.354	85	-8	8			.923	9	C-64/O-7,1-6,3-2,P	0.5
1892	Cin-N	91	346	45	88	10	5	2	50	16	13	.254	.295	.329	90	-5	10			.929	-13	C-67,1-14,O-11,/3-6	-1.3
1893	Cin-N	121	483	68	135	17	12	1	108	35	17	.280	.332	.371	85	-12	16			**.969**	1	C-80,O-23,1-21	-0.5
1894	Cin-N	72	284	50	88	15	5	8	64	12	11	.310	.338	.482	92	-6	5			.918	-1	C-43,1-27/O-8,S-3	-0.2
1895	Cin-N	92	334	60	102	23	5	1	48	17	10	.305	.339	.413	90	-7	15			.934	11	C-77,1-15/3-1,2-1	0.9
1896	Cin-N	114	433	71	127	20	9	2	66	16	7	.293	.320	.395	82	-14	7			.984	3	1-57,C-57	-0.3
1897	Cin-N	54	199	21	58	13	5	0	30	2		.291	.299	.407	80	-7	2			.986	-0	1-35,C-15	-0.5
1898	Cin-N	78	275	35	84	12	4	1	46	11		.305	.339	.389	101	-1	4			.979	-3	1-39,C-33	0.0
1899	Cin-N	31	108	9	19	1	0	0	2	3		.176	.198	.185	5	-14	2			.982	3	1-21/C-7,O-1	-0.9
Total	13	915	3454	474	946	147	53	21	525	151	128	.274	.307	.365	80	-112	92			.926	-0	C-553,1-253,O/3S2P	-5.9

■ MO VAUGHN
Vaughn, Maurice Samuel b: 12/15/67, Norwalk, Conn. BL/TR, 6'1", 230 lbs. Deb: 6/27/91

YEAR	TM/L	G	AB	R	H	2B	3B	HR	RBI	BB	SO	AVG	OBP	SLG	PRO+	BR/A	SB	CS	SBR	FA	FR	G/POS	TPR
1991	Bos-A	74	219	21	57	12	0	4	32	26	43	.260	.344	.370	93	-2	2	1	0	.985	-2	1-49,D-16	-0.7
1992	Bos-A	113	355	42	83	16	2	13	57	47	67	.234	.328	.400	97	-2	3	3	-1	.982	-2	1-85,D-20	-1.1
1993	Bos-A	152	539	86	160	34	1	29	101	79	130	.297	.395	.525	136	28	4	3	-1	.987	-9	*1-131,D-19	0.7
1994	Bos-A	111	394	65	122	25	1	26	82	57	112	.310	.410	.576	144	26	4	4	-1	.989	-5	*1-106/D-1	1.0
1995	*Bos-A★	140	550	98	165	28	3	39	**126**	68	150	.300	.391	.575	142	34	11	4	1	.992	-3	*1-138/D-2	1.8
1996	Bos-A★	161	635	118	207	29	1	44	143	95	154	.326	.425	.583	148	49	2	0	1	.988	-10	*1-146,D-15	2.2
1997	Bos-A	141	527	91	166	24	0	35	96	86	154	.315	.422	.560	151	42	2	2	-1	.988	-6	*1-131/D-9	2.1
1998	*Bos-A†	154	609	107	205	31	2	40	115	61	144	.337	.404	.591	154	49	0	0	0	.991	-2	*1-142,D-12	2.9
Total	8	1046	3828	628	1165	199	10	230	752	519	954	.304	.397	.542	139	225	28	17	-2	.988	-38	1-928/D-94	8.9

■ BOBBY VAUGHN
Vaughn, Robert b: 6/4/1885, Stamford, N.Y. d: 4/11/65, Seattle, Wash. BR/TR, 5'9", 150 lbs. Deb: 6/12/09

YEAR	TM/L	G	AB	R	H	2B	3B	HR	RBI	BB	SO	AVG	OBP	SLG	PRO+	BR/A	SB	CS	SBR	FA	FR	G/POS	TPR
1909	NY-A	5	14	1	2	0	0	0	0	1		.143	.200	.143	8	-1	1			.882	-3	/2-4,S-1	-0.5
1915	StL-F	144	521	69	146	19	9	0	32	58	38	.280	.356	.351	94	-10	24			.953	-8	*2-127,S-12/3-8	-1.7
Total	2	149	535	70	148	19	9	0	32	59	38	.277	.352	.346	92	-11	25			.951	-11	2-131/S-13,3-8	-2.2

■ BOBBY VEACH
Veach, Robert Hayes b: 6/29/1888, Island, Ky. d: 8/7/45, Detroit, Mich. BL/TR, 5'11", 160 lbs. Deb: 8/6/12

YEAR	TM/L	G	AB	R	H	2B	3B	HR	RBI	BB	SO	AVG	OBP	SLG	PRO+	BR/A	SB	CS	SBR	FA	FR	G/POS	TPR
1912	Det-A	23	79	8	27	5	1	0	15	5		.342	.388	.430	138	4	2			.927	2	O-22	0.5
1913	Det-A	137	491	54	132	22	10	0	64	53	31	.269	.346	.354	107	4	22			.917	-5	*O-135	-0.7
1914	Det-A	149	531	56	146	19	14	1	72	50	29	.275	.341	.369	110	6	20	20	-6	.965	3	*O-145	-0.4
1915	Det-A	152	569	81	178	**40**	10	3	**112**	68	43	.313	.390	.434	140	27	16	19	-7	.975	2	*O-152	1.6
1916	Det-A	150	566	92	173	33	15	3	91	52	41	.306	.367	.433	135	23	24	15	-2	.967	4	*O-150	1.9
1917	Det-A	154	571	79	182	31	12	8	**103**	61	44	.319	.393	.457	160	40	21			.956	5	*O-154	4.0
1918	Det-A	127	499	59	139	21	13	3	**78**	35	23	.279	.331	.391	123	11	21			.977	3	*O-127/P-1	0.8
1919	Det-A	139	538	87	**191**	**45**	**17**	3	101	33	33	.355	.398	.519	160	40	19			.967	11	*O-138	4.3
1920	Det-A	154	612	92	188	39	15	11	113	36	22	.307	.353	.474	121	15	11	7	-1	.967	15	*O-154	1.6
1921	Det-A	150	612	110	207	43	13	16	128	48	31	.338	.387	.529	133	28	14	10	-2	.974	15	*O-149	2.8
1922	Det-A	155	618	96	202	34	13	9	126	42	27	.327	.377	.468	123	20	9	1	2	.982	8	*O-154	1.8
1923	Det-A	114	293	45	94	13	3	2	39	29	21	.321	.388	.406	111	5	10	3	1	.943	-14	O-85	-1.2
1924	Bos-A	142	519	77	153	35	9	5	99	47	18	.295	.359	.426	102	0	5	5	-2	.956	-1	*O-130	-1.1
1925	Bos-A	1	5	0	1	0	0	0	2	1	1	.200	.333	.200	38	-0	0	0	0	1.000	0	/O-1	0.0
	NY-A	56	116	13	41	10	2	0	15	8	0	.353	.400	.474	123	4	1	4	-2	.957	-7	O-33	-0.6
	*Was-A	18	37	4	9	3	0	0	8	3	3	.243	.300	.324	60	-2	0	0	0	.923	-3	O-11	-0.5
	Yr	75	158	17	51	13	2	0	25	12	4	.323	.374	.430	106	1	1	4	-2	.952	-10	O-45	-1.1
Total	14	1821	6656	953	2063	393	147	64	1166	571	367	.310	.370	.442	127	225	195	84		.964	38	*O-1740/P-1	14.8

■ PEEK-A-BOO VEACH
Veach, William Walter b: 6/15/1862, Indianapolis, Ind d: 11/12/37, Indianapolis, Ind. Deb: 8/24/1884

YEAR	TM/L	G	AB	R	H	2B	3B	HR	RBI	BB	SO	AVG	OBP	SLG	PRO+	BR/A	SB	CS	SBR	FA	FR	G/POS	TPR
1884	KC-U	27	82	9	11	1	0	1		9		.134	.220	.183	27	-10				.833	-1	O-14,P-12/2-1,1-1	-0.6
1887	Lou-a	1	3	0	0	0	0	0	0	1		.000	.250	.000	-26	-0	0			.750	-0	/P-1	0.0
1890	Cle-N	64	238	24	56	10	5	0	32	33	28	.235	.336	.319	93	-1	9			.971	6	1-64	0.1
	Pit-N	8	30	6	9	1	1	2	5	8	3	.300	.447	.600	231	5	0			.968	0	/1-8	0.5
	Yr	72	268	30	65	11	6	2	37	41	31	.243	.349	.351	107	4	9			.971	7	1-72	0.6
Total	3	100	353	39	76	12	6	3	37	51	31	.215	.319	.309	90	-6	9			.971	6	/1-73,O-14,P-13,2-1	0.0

■ COOT VEAL
Veal, Orville Inman b: 7/9/32, Sandersville, Ga. BR/TR, 6'1", 165 lbs. Deb: 7/30/58

YEAR	TM/L	G	AB	R	H	2B	3B	HR	RBI	BB	SO	AVG	OBP	SLG	PRO+	BR/A	SB	CS	SBR	FA	FR	G/POS	TPR
1958	Det-A	58	207	29	53	10	2	0	16	14	21	.256	.306	.324	69	-9	1	1	-0	.981	-8	S-58	-1.3
1959	Det-A	77	89	12	18	1	0	1	15	8	7	.202	.276	.247	42	-7	0	0	0	.962	10	S-72	0.5
1960	Det-A	27	64	8	19	5	1	0	8	11	7	.297	.400	.406	115	2	0	0	0	.988	-2	S-22/3-3,2-1	0.1
1961	Was-A	69	218	21	44	10	0	0	8	19	29	.202	.275	.248	41	-18	1	8	-5	.974	0	S-63	-1.7
1962	Pit-N	1	1	0	0	0	0	0	0	0	1	.000	.000	.000	-99	-0	0	0	0	.000	0	H	0.0
1963	Det-A	15	32	5	7	0	0	0	4	4	4	.219	.306	.219	48	-2	0	0	0	.980	4	S-12	0.2
Total	6	247	611	75	141	26	3	1	51	56	69	.231	.301	.288	59	-34	2	9	-5	.976	4	S-227/3-3,2-1	-2.2

■ JESUS VEGA
Vega, Jesus Anthony (Morales) b: 10/14/55, Bayamon, P.R. BR/TR, 6'1", 176 lbs. Deb: 9/5/79

YEAR	TM/L	G	AB	R	H	2B	3B	HR	RBI	BB	SO	AVG	OBP	SLG	PRO+	BR/A	SB	CS	SBR	FA	FR	G/POS	TPR
1979	Min-A	4	7	0	0	0	0	0	0	0	2	.000	.000	.000	-96	-2	0	0	0	.000	0	/D-3	-0.2
1980	Min-A	12	30	3	5	0	0	0	4	3	7	.167	.242	.167	13	-4	1	0	0	1.000	0	/1-2,D-9	-0.3
1982	Min-A	71	199	23	53	6	0	5	29	8	19	.266	.295	.372	80	-6	6	1	1	.974	-1	D-39,1-18/O-1	-0.8
Total	3	87	236	26	58	6	0	5	33	11	28	.246	.279	.335	65	-11	7	1	2	.975	-1	/D-51,1-20,O-1	-1.3

■ JORGE VELANDIA
Velandia, Jorge Luis (Macias) b: 1/12/75, Caracas, Venez. BR/TR, 5'9", 160 lbs. Deb: 6/20/97

YEAR	TM/L	G	AB	R	H	2B	3B	HR	RBI	BB	SO	AVG	OBP	SLG	PRO+	BR/A	SB	CS	SBR	FA	FR	G/POS	TPR
1997	SD-N	14	29	0	3	2	0	0	0	1	7	.103	.133	.172	-22	-5	0	0	0	.941	2	/S-6,2-5,3-3	-0.3
1998	Oak-A	8	4	0	1	0	0	0	0	0	1	.250	.250	.250	32	-0	0	0	0	.909	3	/S-7,2-1	0.3
Total	2	22	33	0	4	2	0	0	0	1	8	.121	.147	.182	-16	-6	0	0	0	.929	5	/S-13,2-6,3-3	0.0

■ RANDY VELARDE
Velarde, Randy Lee b: 11/24/62, Midland, Tex. BR/TR, 6', 190 lbs. Deb: 8/20/87

YEAR	TM/L	G	AB	R	H	2B	3B	HR	RBI	BB	SO	AVG	OBP	SLG	PRO+	BR/A	SB	CS	SBR	FA	FR	G/POS	TPR
1987	NY-A	8	22	1	4	0	0	0	1	0	6	.182	.182	.182	-3	-3	0	0	0	.933	0	/S-8	-0.3
1988	NY-A	48	115	18	20	6	0	5	12	8	24	.174	.240	.357	65	-6	1	1	-0	.967	8	2-24,S-14,3-11	0.4
1989	NY-A	33	100	12	34	4	2	2	11	7	14	.340	.389	.480	145	6	0	3	-2	.954	2	3-27/S-9	0.6
1990	NY-A	95	229	21	48	6	2	5	19	20	53	.210	.276	.319	66	-11	0	3	-2	.945	9	3-74,S-15/O-5,2D	-0.2
1991	NY-A	80	184	19	45	11	1	1	15	18	43	.245	.322	.332	81	-4	3	1	0	.935	7	3-50,S-31/O-2	0.4
1992	NY-A	121	412	57	112	24	1	7	46	38	78	.272	.336	.386	103	1	7	2	1	.974	-8	S-75,3-26,O-23,/2-3	-0.1
1993	NY-A	85	226	28	68	13	2	7	24	18	39	.301	.363	.469	126	8	2	2	-1	.932	-1	O-50,S-26,3-16,/D-1	0.7
1994	NY-A	77	280	47	78	16	1	9	34	22	61	.279	.340	.439	103	1	4	2	0	.944	1	S-49,3-27/O-7,2-5	0.5
1995	*NY-A	111	367	60	102	19	1	7	46	55	64	.278	.378	.392	102	3	5	1	1	.976	-15	2-62,S-28,O-20,3-19	-0.5
1996	Cal-A	136	530	82	151	27	3	14	54	70	118	.285	.374	.426	101	3	7	7	-2	.982	-26	*2-114,3-28/S-7	-1.7
1997	Ana-A	1	0	0	0	0	0	0	0	0	0	—	—	—	—	0	0	0	0	.000	0	/R	0.0
1998	Ana-A	51	188	29	49	13	1	4	26	34	42	.261	.377	.404	102	2	7	2	1	.982	-8	2-51	-0.2
Total	12	846	2653	374	711	139	14	61	288	290	542	.268	.346	.400	99	-1	36	24	-4	.934	-30	3-278,2-262,SO/D	-0.4

■ GUILLERMO VELASQUEZ
Velasquez, Guillermo (Burgara) b: 4/23/68, Mexicali, Mexico BL/TR, 6'3", 220 lbs. Deb: 9/14/92

YEAR	TM/L	G	AB	R	H	2B	3B	HR	RBI	BB	SO	AVG	OBP	SLG	PRO+	BR/A	SB	CS	SBR	FA	FR	G/POS	TPR
1992	SD-N	15	23	1	7	0	0	1	5	1	7	.304	.333	.435	114	0	0	0	0	.933	-1	/1-3,O-2	-0.1
1993	SD-N	79	143	7	30	2	0	3	20	13	35	.210	.276	.287	50	-10	0	0	0	.984	-1	1-38/O-6	-1.4
Total	2	94	166	8	37	2	0	4	25	14	42	.223	.283	.307	58	-10	0	0	0	.981	-2	/1-41,O-8	-1.5

■ FREDDIE VELAZQUEZ Velazquez, Federico Antonio (Velasquez) b: 12/6/37, Santo Domingo, D.R. BR/TR, 6′1″, 185 lbs. Deb: 4/20/69

YEAR	TM/L	G	AB	R	H	2B	3B	HR	RBI	BB	SO	AVG	OBP	SLG	PRO+	BR/A	SB	CS	SBR	FA	FR	G/POS	TPR
1969	Sea-A	6	16	1	2	2	0	0	2	1	3	.125	.176	.250	18	-2	0	0	0	1.000	-1	/C-5	-0.2
1973	Atl-N	15	23	2	8	1	0	0	3	1	3	.348	.375	.391	105	0	0	0	0	.975	2	C-11	0.2
Total	2	21	39	3	10	3	0	0	5	2	6	.256	.293	.333	71	-2	0	0	0	.985	1	/C-16	0.0

■ OTTO VELEZ Velez, Otoniel (Franceschi) b: 11/29/50, Ponce, P.R. BR/TR, 6′, 195 lbs. Deb: 9/4/73

YEAR	TM/L	G	AB	R	H	2B	3B	HR	RBI	BB	SO	AVG	OBP	SLG	PRO+	BR/A	SB	CS	SBR	FA	FR	G/POS	TPR
1973	NY-A	23	77	9	15	4	0	2	7	15	24	.195	.326	.325	87	-1	0	1	-1	.959	1	O-23	-0.2
1974	NY-A	27	67	9	14	1	1	2	10	15	24	.209	.354	.343	103	1	0	0	0	.986	-4	1-21/O-3,3-2	-0.4
1975	NY-A	6	8	0	2	0	0	0	1	2	0	.250	.400	.250	89	0	0	0	0	1.000	-0	/1-1,D-1	0.0
1976	*NY-A	49	94	11	25	6	0	2	10	23	26	.266	.410	.394	137	6	0	0	0	.979	-3	O-24/1-8,3-1,D-5	0.2
1977	Tor-A	120	360	50	92	19	3	16	62	65	87	.256	.371	.458	123	13	4	2	0	.973	0	O-79,D-28	0.9
1978	Tor-A	91	248	29	66	14	2	9	38	45	41	.266	.383	.448	130	11	1	3	-2	.982	7	O-74/1-1,D-9	1.4
1979	Tor-A	99	274	45	79	21	0	15	48	46	45	.288	.396	.529	145	18	0	1	-1	.971	-5	O-73/1-6,D-9	0.9
1980	Tor-A	104	357	54	96	12	3	20	62	54	86	.269	.368	.487	126	13	0	0	0	.975	0	D-97/1-3	1.0
1981	Tor-A	80	240	32	51	9	2	11	28	55	60	.213	.366	.404	114	6	0	3	-2	1.000	-0	D-74/1-1	0.1
1982	Tor-A	28	52	4	10	1	0	1	5	13	15	.192	.354	.269	68	-2	1	0	0	.000	0	D-24	-0.3
1983	Cle-A	10	25	1	2	0	0	0	1	3	6	.080	.179	.080	-25	-4	0	0	0	.000	0	/D-8	-0.5
Total	11	637	1802	244	452	87	11	78	272	336	414	.251	.372	.441	122	61	6	10	-4	.973	-4	O-276,D-255/1-41,3	3.1

■ PAT VELTMAN Veltman, Arthur Patrick b: 3/24/06, Mobile, Ala. d: 10/1/80, San Antonio, Tex. BR/TR, 6′, 175 lbs. Deb: 4/17/26

YEAR	TM/L	G	AB	R	H	2B	3B	HR	RBI	BB	SO	AVG	OBP	SLG	PRO+	BR/A	SB	CS	SBR	FA	FR	G/POS	TPR
1926	Chi-A	5	4	1	1	0	0	0	0	1	1	.250	.400	.250	75	-0	0	0	0	1.000	0	/S-1	0.0
1928	NY-N	1	3	1	1	0	1	0	0	1	0	.333	.500	1.000	282	1	0			1.000	0	/O-1	0.1
1929	NY-N	2	1	1	0	0	0	0	0	2	0	.000	.667	.000	81	0	0			1.000	-0	/C-1	0.0
1931	Bos-N	1	1	0	0	0	0	0	0	0	0	.000	.000	.000	-99	-0	0			.000	0	H	0.0
1932	NY-N	2	1	0	0	0	0	0	0	0	1	.000	.000	.000	-99	-0	0			.000	0	H	0.0
1934	Pit-N	12	28	1	3	0	0	0	2	0	1	.107	.107	.107	-41	-6	0			1.000	-2	C-11	-0.7
Total	6	23	38	4	5	0	1	0	2	4	3	.132	.214	.184	7	-5	0	0		1.000	-2	/C-12,O-1,S-1	-0.6

■ MAX VENABLE Venable, William McKinley b: 6/6/57, Phoenix, Ariz. BL/TR, 5′10″, 185 lbs. Deb: 4/8/79

YEAR	TM/L	G	AB	R	H	2B	3B	HR	RBI	BB	SO	AVG	OBP	SLG	PRO+	BR/A	SB	CS	SBR	FA	FR	G/POS	TPR
1979	SF-N	55	85	12	14	1	1	0	3	10	18	.165	.260	.200	29	-8	3	3	-1	.914	-5	O-25	-1.5
1980	SF-N	64	138	13	37	5	0	0	10	15	22	.268	.340	.304	83	-3	8	2	1	1.000	-5	O-40	-0.9
1981	SF-N	18	32	2	6	0	2	0	1	4	3	.188	.278	.313	68	-1	3	1	0	1.000	0	/O-5	-0.1
1982	SF-N	71	125	17	28	2	1	1	7	7	16	.224	.265	.280	53	-8	9	3	1	.986	-4	O-53	-1.2
1983	SF-N	94	228	28	50	7	4	6	27	22	34	.219	.296	.364	85	-5	15	2	3	.993	3	O-66	-0.1
1984	Mon-N	38	71	7	17	2	0	2	7	3	7	.239	.280	.352	80	-2	1	0	0	1.000	-4	O-27	-0.7
1985	Cin-N	77	135	21	39	12	3	0	10	6	17	.289	.319	.422	101	-0	11	3	2	1.000	-1	O-39	-0.1
1986	Cin-N	108	147	17	31	7	1	2	15	17	24	.211	.293	.313	64	-7	7	2	1	.969	-10	O-57	-1.8
1987	Cin-N	7	7	2	1	0	0	0	2	0	0	.143	.143	.143	-23	-1	0	0	0	1.000	-1	/O-4	-0.2
1989	Cal-A	20	53	7	19	4	0	0	4	1	16	.358	.370	.434	128	2	0	0	0	1.000	-3	O-13	-0.1
1990	Cal-A	93	189	26	49	9	3	4	21	24	31	.259	.343	.402	110	3	5	1	1	.975	-12	O-77/D-1	-1.0
1991	Cal-A	82	187	24	46	8	2	3	21	11	30	.246	.295	.358	80	-5	2	1	0	.967	-11	O-65/D-3	-1.8
Total	12	727	1397	176	337	57	17	18	128	120	218	.241	.304	.345	81	-37	64	18	8	.982	-54	O-471/D-4	-9.5

■ ROBIN VENTURA Ventura, Robin Mark b: 7/14/67, Santa Maria, Cal. BL/TR, 6′1″, 198 lbs. Deb: 9/12/89

YEAR	TM/L	G	AB	R	H	2B	3B	HR	RBI	BB	SO	AVG	OBP	SLG	PRO+	BR/A	SB	CS	SBR	FA	FR	G/POS	TPR
1989	Chi-A	16	45	5	8	3	0	0	7	8	6	.178	.315	.244	61	-2	0	0	0	.962	2	3-16	0.0
1990	Chi-A	150	493	48	123	17	1	5	54	55	53	.249	.326	.318	83	-10	1	4	-2	.939	-0	*3-147/1-1	-1.2
1991	Chi-A	157	606	92	172	25	1	23	100	80	67	.284	.371	.442	127	24	2	4	-2	.959	1	*3-151,1-31	2.3
1992	Chi-A★	157	592	85	167	38	1	16	93	93	71	.282	.380	.431	128	25	2	4	-2	.957	24	*3-157/1-2	4.6
1993	*Chi-A	157	554	85	145	27	1	22	94	105	82	.262	.382	.433	121	20	1	6	-3	.965	-5	*3-155/1-4	1.2
1994	Chi-A	109	401	57	113	15	1	18	78	61	69	.282	.379	.459	117	11	3	1	0	.935	-4	*3-108/1-3,S-1	0.7
1995	Chi-A	135	492	79	145	22	0	26	93	75	98	.295	.389	.498	135	26	4	3	-1	.948	-3	*3-121,1-18/D-1	2.0
1996	Chi-A	158	586	96	168	31	2	34	105	78	81	.287	.372	.520	129	25	1	3	-2	.974	-0	*3-150,1-14	2.0
1997	Chi-A	54	183	27	48	10	1	6	26	34	21	.262	.378	.426	114	5	0	0	0	.956	1	3-54	0.5
1998	Chi-A	161	590	84	155	31	4	21	91	79	111	.263	.351	.436	106	5	1	1	-0	.966	19	*3-161	2.3
Total	10	1254	4542	658	1244	219	12	171	741	668	659	.274	.369	.440	118	128	15	26	-11	.957	34	*3-1220/1-73,D-1,S	14.4

■ VINCE VENTURA Ventura, Vincent b: 4/18/17, New York, N.Y. BR/TR, 6′1.5″, 190 lbs. Deb: 5/8/45

YEAR	TM/L	G	AB	R	H	2B	3B	HR	RBI	BB	SO	AVG	OBP	SLG	PRO+	BR/A	SB	CS	SBR	FA	FR	G/POS	TPR
1945	Was-A	18	58	4	12	0	0	0	2	4	4	.207	.258	.207	39	-5	0	0	0	.886	-1	O-15	-0.7

■ QUILVIO VERAS Veras, Quilvio Alberto (Perez) b: 4/3/71, Santo Domingo, D.R. BB/TR, 5′9″, 170 lbs. Deb: 4/25/95

YEAR	TM/L	G	AB	R	H	2B	3B	HR	RBI	BB	SO	AVG	OBP	SLG	PRO+	BR/A	SB	CS	SBR	FA	FR	G/POS	TPR
1995	Fla-N	124	440	86	115	20	7	5	32	80	68	.261	.386	.373	101	4	**56**	21	4	.986	7	*2-122/O-2	2.2
1996	Fla-N	73	253	40	64	8	1	4	14	51	42	.253	.382	.340	96	1	8	8	-2	.986	6	2-67	0.9
1997	SD-N	145	539	74	143	23	1	3	45	72	84	.265	.359	.328	88	-7	33	12	3	.984	-6	*2-142	-0.2
1998	*SD-N	138	517	79	138	24	2	6	45	84	78	.267	.376	.356	101	3	24	9	2	.987	13	*2-131	2.8
Total	4	480	1749	279	460	75	11	18	136	287	272	.263	.374	.349	96	1	121	50	6	.986	21	2-462/O-2	5.7

■ EMIL VERBAN Verban, Emil Matthew "Dutch" or "Antelope" b: 8/27/15, Lincoln, Ill. d: 6/8/89, Quincy, Ill. BR/TR, 5′11″, 165 lbs. Deb: 4/18/44

YEAR	TM/L	G	AB	R	H	2B	3B	HR	RBI	BB	SO	AVG	OBP	SLG	PRO+	BR/A	SB	CS	SBR	FA	FR	G/POS	TPR
1944	*StL-N	146	498	51	128	14	2	0	43	19	14	.257	.287	.293	62	-25	0			.968	-6	*2-146	-2.4
1945	StL-N†	155	597	59	166	22	8	0	72	19	15	.278	.304	.342	77	-19	4			**.978**	-19	*2-155	-2.9
1946	StL-N	1	1	0	0	0	0	0	0	0	0	.000	.000	.000	-96	-0	0			.000	0	H	0.0
	Phi-N★	138	473	44	130	17	5	0	34	21	18	.275	.306	.332	83	-12	5			.963	-3	*2-138	-0.6
	Yr	139	474	44	130	17	5	0	34	21	18	.274	.305	.331	83	-12	5			.963	-3	*2-138	-0.6
1947	Phi-N★	155	540	50	154	14	8	0	42	23	8	.285	.316	.341	77	-16	5			.982	17	*2-155	0.9
1948	Phi-N	55	169	14	39	5	1	0	11	11	5	.231	.282	.272	51	-11	0			.975	-4	2-54	-1.3
	Chi-N	56	248	37	73	15	1	1	16	4	7	.294	.308	.375	88	-5	4			.964	6	2-56	0.4
	Yr	111	417	51	112	20	2	1	27	15	12	.269	.297	.333	72	-17	4			.969	2	*2-110	-0.9
1949	Chi-N	98	343	38	99	11	1	0	22	8	2	.289	.309	.327	72	-14	3			.965	3	2-88	-0.7
1950	Chi-N	45	37	7	4	1	0	0	1	3	5	.108	.175	.135	-17	-6	0			.966	6	/2-8,S-3,3-1,O-1	-0.1
	Bos-N	4	5	1	0	0	0	0	0	0	0	.000	.000	.000	-99	-1	0			.833	1	/2-2	0.0
	Yr	49	42	8	4	1	0	0	1	3	5	.095	.156	.119	-27	-8	0			.927	7	2-10/S-3,3-1,O-1	-0.1
Total	7	853	2911	301	793	99	26	1	241	108	74	.272	.301	.325	73	-113	21			.971	1	2-802/S-3,O-1,3-1	-6.7

■ GENE VERBLE Verble, Gene Kermit "Satchel" b: 6/29/28, Concord, N.C. BR/TR, 5′10″, 163 lbs. Deb: 4/17/51

YEAR	TM/L	G	AB	R	H	2B	3B	HR	RBI	BB	SO	AVG	OBP	SLG	PRO+	BR/A	SB	CS	SBR	FA	FR	G/POS	TPR
1951	Was-A	68	177	16	36	3	2	0	15	18	10	.203	.277	.243	42	-14	1	1	-0	.978	-2	S-28,2-19/3-1	-1.3
1953	Was-A	13	21	4	4	0	0	0	2	2	1	.190	.261	.190	24	-2	0	0	0	1.000	2	/S-8	0.0
Total	2	81	198	20	40	3	2	0	17	20	11	.202	.275	.237	40	-16	1	1	-0	.981	1	/S-36,2-19,3-1	-1.3

■ FRANK VERDI Verdi, Frank Michael b: 6/2/26, Brooklyn, N.Y. BR/TR, 5′10.5″, 170 lbs. Deb: 5/10/53

YEAR	TM/L	G	AB	R	H	2B	3B	HR	RBI	BB	SO	AVG	OBP	SLG	PRO+	BR/A	SB	CS	SBR	FA	FR	G/POS	TPR
1953	NY-A	1	0	0	0	0	0	0	0	0	0	—	—	—	—	0	0	0	0	.000	0	/S-1	0.0

■ JOHNNY VERGEZ Vergez, John Louis b: 7/9/06, Oakland, Cal. d: 7/15/91, Davis, Cal. BR/TR, 5′8″, 165 lbs. Deb: 4/14/31

YEAR	TM/L	G	AB	R	H	2B	3B	HR	RBI	BB	SO	AVG	OBP	SLG	PRO+	BR/A	SB	CS	SBR	FA	FR	G/POS	TPR
1931	NY-N	152	565	67	157	24	2	13	81	29	65	.278	.320	.396	94	-6	11			.932	-3	*3-152	0.0
1932	NY-N	118	376	42	98	21	3	6	43	25	36	.261	.310	.380	86	-8	1			.935	5	*3-111/S-1	0.5
1933	NY-N	123	458	57	124	21	6	16	72	39	66	.271	.332	.448	123	13	1			.928	-14	*3-123	0.7
1934	NY-N	108	320	31	64	18	1	7	27	28	55	.200	.269	.328	60	-19	1			.943	10	*3-104	-0.5
1935	Phi-N	148	546	56	136	27	4	9	63	46	67	.249	.312	.363	73	-21	8			**.953**	-7	*3-148/S-2	-2.2
1936	Phi-N	15	40	4	11	2	0	1	5	3	11	.275	.326	.400	86	-1	0			.964	0	3-12	0.0
	StL-N	8	18	1	3	1	0	0	1	1	3	.167	.211	.222	17	-2	0			.929	0	/3-8	-0.2
	Yr	23	58	5	14	3	0	1	6	4	14	.241	.290	.345	66	-3	0			.952	0	3-20	-0.2
Total	6	672	2323	258	593	114	16	52	292	171	303	.255	.311	.385	87	-44	22			.939	-8	3-658/S-3	-1.7

■ **MICKEY VERNON** Vernon, James Barton b: 4/22/18, Marcus Hook, Pa. BL/TL, 6'2", 180 lbs. Deb: 7/8/39 MC

YEAR	TM/L	G	AB	R	H	2B	3B	HR	RBI	BB	SO	AVG	OBP	SLG	PRO+	BR/A	SB	CS	SBR	FA	FR	G/POS	TPR
1939	Was-A	76	276	23	71	15	4	1	30	24	28	.257	.317	.351	76	-10	1	1	-0	.985	-3	1-75	-2.0
1940	Was-A	5	19	0	3	0	0	0	0	0	3	.158	.158	.158	-19	-3	0	0	0	1.000	-0	/1-4	-0.4
1941	Was-A	138	531	73	159	27	11	9	93	43	51	.299	.352	.443	114	9	9	3	1	.992	-6	*1-132	-0.6
1942	Was-A	151	621	76	168	34	6	9	86	59	63	.271	.337	.388	104	3	25	6	4	.982	-8	*1-151	-1.1
1943	Was-A	145	553	89	148	29	8	7	70	67	55	.268	.357	.387	122	16	24	8	2	.990	-11	*1-143	0.0
1946	Was-A★	148	587	88	207	**51**	8	8	85	49	64	**.353**	.403	.508	163	47	14	10	-2	.990	-1	*1-147	3.6
1947	Was-A	154	600	77	159	29	12	7	85	49	42	.265	.320	.388	99	-3	12	12	-4	.987	-4	*1-154	-1.7
1948	Was-A★	150	558	78	135	27	7	3	48	54	43	.242	.310	.332	73	-23	15	11	-2	.989	5	*1-150	-2.1
1949	Cle-A	153	584	72	170	27	4	18	83	58	51	.291	.357	.443	113	9	9	7	-2	.991	19	*1-153	2.4
1950	Cle-A	28	90	8	17	0	0	0	10	12	10	.189	.284	.189	24	-10	2	0	1	.996	1	1-25	-0.8
	Was-A	90	327	47	100	17	3	9	65	50	29	.306	.404	.459	127	14	6	1	1	.990	1	1-85	1.3
	Yr	118	417	55	117	17	3	9	75	62	39	.281	.379	.400	104	4	8	1	2	**.991**	3	*1-110	0.5
1951	Was-A	141	546	69	160	30	7	9	87	53	45	.293	.358	.423	112	9	7	6	-2	**.994**	-4	*1-137	-0.3
1952	Was-A	154	569	71	143	33	9	10	80	89	66	.251	.353	.394	111	9	7	7	-2	**.993**	1	*1-153	0.2
1953	Was-A★	152	608	101	205	**43**	11	15	115	63	57	**.337**	.403	.518	151	43	4	6	-2	.992	-3	*1-152	3.1
1954	Was-A★	151	597	90	173	**33**	14	20	97	61	61	.290	.360	.492	140	29	1	4	-2	**.992**	-9	*1-148	1.1
1955	Was-A★	150	538	74	162	23	8	14	85	74	50	.301	.389	.452	133	25	0	4	-2	.994	-8	*1-144	0.6
1956	Bos-A★	119	403	67	125	28	4	15	84	57	40	.310	.405	.511	125	15	1	0	0	.989	-3	*1-108	0.5
1957	Bos-A	102	270	36	65	18	1	7	38	41	35	.241	.351	.393	97	-0	0	0	0	.992	4	1-70	-0.1
1958	Cle-A★	119	355	49	104	22	3	8	55	44	56	.293	.374	.439	126	13	0	4	-2	.987	-2	1-96	0.4
1959	Mil-N	74	91	8	20	4	0	3	14	7	20	.220	.283	.363	77	-3	0	0	0	.983	1	1-10/O-4	-0.3
1960	Pit-N	9	8	0	1	0	0	0	1	1	0	.125	.222	.125	-2	-1	0	0	0	.000	0	H	-0.1
Total	20	2409	8731	1196	2495	490	120	172	1311	955	869	.286	.359	.428	116	186	137	90	-13	.990	-32	*1-2237/O-4	3.7

■ **ZOILO VERSALLES** Versalles, Zoilo Casanova (Rodriguez) "Zorro" b: 12/18/39, Veldado, Cuba d: 6/9/95, Bloomington, Minn. BR/TR, 5'10", 150 lbs. Deb: 8/1/59

YEAR	TM/L	G	AB	R	H	2B	3B	HR	RBI	BB	SO	AVG	OBP	SLG	PRO+	BR/A	SB	CS	SBR	FA	FR	G/POS	TPR
1959	Was-A	29	59	4	9	0	0	1	1	4	15	.153	.219	.203	17	-7	1	0	0	.943	3	S-29	-0.2
1960	Was-A	15	45	2	6	2	2	0	4	2	5	.133	.170	.267	16	-5	0	0	0	.935	-1	S-15	-0.6
1961	Min-A	129	510	65	143	25	5	7	53	25	61	.280	.315	.390	83	-13	16	9	-1	.952	-2	*S-129	-0.5
1962	Min-A	160	568	69	137	18	3	17	67	37	71	.241	.290	.373	74	-22	5	5	-2	.970	32	*S-160	2.3
1963	Min-A★	159	621	74	162	31	**13**	10	54	33	66	.261	.303	.401	94	-6	7	4	-0	.961	-2	*S-159	0.3
1964	Min-A	160	659	94	171	33	**10**	20	64	42	88	.259	.312	.431	103	2	14	4	2	.957	-17	*S-160	-0.2
1965	*Min-A★	160	666	**126**	182	**45**	**12**	19	77	41	122	.273	.322	.462	115	11	27	5	**5**	.950	2	*S-160	3.1
1966	Min-A	137	543	73	135	20	6	7	36	40	85	.249	.308	.346	82	-12	10	12	-4	.942	-17	*S-135	-2.2
1967	Min-A	160	581	63	116	16	7	6	50	33	113	.200	.250	.282	53	-34	5	3	-0	.958	2	*S-159	-1.9
1968	LA-N	122	403	29	79	16	3	2	24	26	84	.196	.245	.266	57	-22	6	4	-1	.954	8	*S-119	-0.3
1969	Cle-A	72	217	21	49	11	1	1	13	21	47	.226	.300	.300	66	-10	3	1	0	.975	-11	2-46,3-30/S-3	-1.8
	Was-A	31	75	9	20	2	1	0	6	3	13	.267	.304	.320	79	-2	1	0	0	.935	-1	S-13/2-6,3-5	-0.2
	Yr	103	292	30	69	13	2	1	19	24	60	.236	.301	.305	69	-12	4	1	1	.978	-12	2-52,3-35,S-16	-2.0
1971	Atl-N	66	194	21	37	11	0	5	22	11	40	.191	.234	.325	53	-12	2	1	0	.902	-14	3-30,S-24/2-1	-2.6
Total	12	1400	5141	650	1246	230	63	95	471	318	810	.242	.292	.367	82	-133	97	48	0	.956	-20	*S-1265/3-65,2-53	-4.8

■ **TOM VERYZER** Veryzer, Thomas Martin b: 2/11/53, Port Jefferson, N.Y BR/TR, 6'1", 185 lbs. Deb: 8/14/73

YEAR	TM/L	G	AB	R	H	2B	3B	HR	RBI	BB	SO	AVG	OBP	SLG	PRO+	BR/A	SB	CS	SBR	FA	FR	G/POS	TPR
1973	Det-A	18	20	1	6	0	1	0	2	2	4	.300	.364	.400	108	0	0	0	0	.857	-5	S-18	-0.4
1974	Det-A	22	55	4	13	2	0	2	9	5	8	.236	.300	.382	92	-1	1	0	0	.927	-10	S-20	-0.9
1975	Det-A	128	404	37	102	13	1	5	48	23	76	.252	.301	.327	74	-14	2	6	-3	.960	-4	*S-128	-0.8
1976	Det-A	97	354	31	83	8	2	1	25	21	44	.234	.289	.277	64	-16	1	4	-2	.966	-1	S-97	-0.8
1977	Det-A	125	350	31	69	12	1	2	28	16	44	.197	.232	.254	31	-33	0	1	-1	.969	10	*S-124	-1.1
1978	Cle-A	130	421	48	114	18	4	1	32	13	36	.271	.301	.340	81	-11	1	2	-1	.963	-4	*S-129	-0.1
1979	Cle-A	149	449	41	99	9	3	0	34	34	54	.220	.281	.254	45	-34	2	5	-2	.974	4	*S-148	-1.6
1980	Cle-A	109	358	28	97	12	0	2	28	10	25	.271	.306	.321	72	-14	0	5	-3	.971	-1	*S-108	-0.5
1981	Cle-A	75	221	13	54	4	0	0	14	10	10	.244	.280	.262	58	-12	1	0	0	.970	-7	S-75	-1.1
1982	NY-N	40	54	6	18	2	0	0	4	3	4	.333	.368	.370	108	1	1	0	0	.962	-1	2-26,S-16	0.1
1983	Chi-N	59	88	5	18	3	0	1	3	3	13	.205	.231	.273	37	-8	0	0	0	.978	7	S-28,3-17	0.1
1984	*Chi-N	44	74	5	14	1	0	0	4	3	11	.189	.259	.203	29	-7	0	0	0	.966	-2	S-36/3-5,2-4	-0.7
Total	12	996	2848	250	687	84	12	14	231	143	329	.241	.285	.294	61	-148	9	23	-11	.966	-14	S-927/2-30,3-22	-7.8

■ **ERNIE VICK** Vick, Henry Arthur b: 7/2/1900, Toledo, Ohio d: 7/16/80, Ann Arbor, Mich. BR/TR, 5'9.5", 185 lbs. Deb: 6/29/22

YEAR	TM/L	G	AB	R	H	2B	3B	HR	RBI	BB	SO	AVG	OBP	SLG	PRO+	BR/A	SB	CS	SBR	FA	FR	G/POS	TPR
1922	StL-N	3	6	1	2	2	0	0	0	0	0	.333	.333	.667	159	0	0	0	0	.875	-0	/C-3	0.0
1924	StL-N	16	23	2	8	1	0	0	0	3	3	.348	.423	.391	122	1	0	0	0	.974	3	C-16	0.4
1925	StL-N	14	32	3	6	2	1	0	3	3	1	.188	.257	.313	44	-3	0	0	0	.929	0	/C-9	-0.2
1926	StL-N	24	51	6	10	2	0	0	4	3	4	.196	.241	.235	27	-5	0			.944	-1	C-23	-0.5
Total	4	57	112	12	26	7	1	0	7	9	8	.232	.289	.313	58	-7	0	0		.944	2	/C-51	-0.3

■ **SAMMY VICK** Vick, Samuel Bruce b: 4/12/1895, Batesville, Miss. d: 8/17/86, Memphis, Tenn. BR/TR, 5'10.5", 163 lbs. Deb: 9/20/17

YEAR	TM/L	G	AB	R	H	2B	3B	HR	RBI	BB	SO	AVG	OBP	SLG	PRO+	BR/A	SB	CS	SBR	FA	FR	G/POS	TPR
1917	NY-A	10	36	4	10	3	0	0	2	1	6	.278	.297	.361	100	-0	2			.882	-1	O-10	-0.2
1918	NY-A	2	3	1	2	0	0	0	1	0	0	.667	.667	.667	296	1	0			.000	-1	/O-1	0.0
1919	NY-A	106	407	59	101	15	9	2	27	35	55	.248	.308	.344	82	-10	9			.952	-4	*O-100	-2.3
1920	NY-A	51	118	21	26	7	1	0	11	14	20	.220	.313	.297	60	-7	1	1	-0	.949	-4	O-33	-1.3
1921	Bos-A	44	77	5	20	3	1	0	9	1	10	.260	.269	.325	52	-6	0	1	-1	1.000	-1	O-14	-0.8
Total	5	213	641	90	159	28	11	2	50	51	91	.248	.305	.335	76	-22	12	2		.951	-11	O-158	-4.6

■ **GEORGE VICO** Vico, George Steve "Sam" b: 8/9/23, San Fernando, Cal. d: 1/13/94, Redondo Beach, Cal. BL/TR, 6'4", 200 lbs. Deb: 4/20/48

YEAR	TM/L	G	AB	R	H	2B	3B	HR	RBI	BB	SO	AVG	OBP	SLG	PRO+	BR/A	SB	CS	SBR	FA	FR	G/POS	TPR
1948	Det-A	144	521	50	139	23	9	8	58	39	39	.267	.326	.392	88	-11	2	2	-1	.988	-3	*1-142	-1.5
1949	Det-A	67	142	15	27	5	2	4	18	21	17	.190	.311	.338	72	-6	0	0	0	.985	2	1-53	-0.4
Total	2	211	663	65	166	28	11	12	76	60	56	.250	.323	.380	85	-17	2	2	-1	.987	-1	1-195	-1.9

■ **JOSE VIDAL** Vidal, Jose (Nicolas) "Papito" b: 4/3/40, Batey Lechugas, D.R. BR/TR, 6', 190 lbs. Deb: 9/5/66

YEAR	TM/L	G	AB	R	H	2B	3B	HR	RBI	BB	SO	AVG	OBP	SLG	PRO+	BR/A	SB	CS	SBR	FA	FR	G/POS	TPR
1966	Cle-A	17	32	4	6	1	1	0	3	5	11	.188	.297	.281	67	-1	0	1	-1	1.000	-1	O-11	-0.3
1967	Cle-A	16	34	4	4	0	0	0	0	7	12	.118	.268	.118	17	-3	0	1	-1	1.000	-1	O-10	-0.6
1968	Cle-A	37	54	5	9	0	0	2	5	2	15	.167	.196	.278	43	-4	3	0	1	1.000	-5	O-26/1-1	-1.0
1969	Sea-A	18	26	7	5	0	1	1	2	4	8	.192	.323	.385	99	-0	1	1	-0	.917	-0	/O-6	-0.1
Total	4	88	146	20	24	1	2	3	10	18	46	.164	.261	.260	53	-8	4	3	-1	.985	-7	/O-53,1-1	-2.0

■ **JOSE VIDRO** Vidro, Jose Angel (Cetty) b: 8/27/74, Mayaguez, P.R. BB/TR, 5'11", 175 lbs. Deb: 6/8/97

YEAR	TM/L	G	AB	R	H	2B	3B	HR	RBI	BB	SO	AVG	OBP	SLG	PRO+	BR/A	SB	CS	SBR	FA	FR	G/POS	TPR
1997	Mon-N	67	169	19	42	12	1	2	17	11	20	.249	.302	.367	74	-7	1	0	0	.958	-6	3-36/2-5,D-5	-1.2
1998	Mon-N	83	205	24	45	12	0	0	18	27	33	.220	.322	.278	60	-11	2	2	-1	.975	-17	2-56/3-7	-2.5
Total	2	150	374	43	87	24	1	2	35	38	53	.233	.313	.318	67	-18	3	2	-0	.973	-23	/2-61,3-43,D-5	-3.7

■ **HECTOR VILLANUEVA** Villanueva, Hector (Balasquide) b: 10/2/64, Rio Piedras, P.R. BR/TR, 6'1", 220 lbs. Deb: 6/1/90

YEAR	TM/L	G	AB	R	H	2B	3B	HR	RBI	BB	SO	AVG	OBP	SLG	PRO+	BR/A	SB	CS	SBR	FA	FR	G/POS	TPR
1990	Chi-N	52	114	14	31	4	1	7	18	4	27	.272	.308	.509	112	1	1	0	0	.991	-4	C-23,1-14	-0.2
1991	Chi-N	71	192	23	53	10	1	13	32	21	30	.276	.347	.542	140	9	0	0	0	.979	-9	C-55/1-6	0.4
1992	Chi-N	51	112	9	17	6	0	2	13	11	24	.152	.228	.259	37	-9	0	0	0	.978	6	C-28/1-6	-0.2
1993	StL-N	17	55	7	8	1	0	3	9	4	17	.145	.203	.327	40	-5	0	0	0	1.000	-1	C-17	-0.5
Total	4	191	473	53	109	21	2	25	72	40	98	.230	.293	.442	98	-4	1	0	0	.984	-7	C-123/1-26	-0.5

■ **FERNANDO VINA** Vina, Fernando b: 4/16/69, Sacramento, Cal. BL/TR, 5'9", 170 lbs. Deb: 4/10/93

YEAR	TM/L	G	AB	R	H	2B	3B	HR	RBI	BB	SO	AVG	OBP	SLG	PRO+	BR/A	SB	CS	SBR	FA	FR	G/POS	TPR
1993	Sea-A	24	45	5	10	2	0	0	2	4	3	.222	.327	.267	61	-2	6	0	2	1.000	6	2-16/S-4,D-2	0.6
1994	NY-N	79	124	20	31	6	0	0	6	12	11	.250	.372	.298	78	-3	3	1	0	.979	2	2-13,3-12/S-9,O-6	0.0
1995	Mil-A	113	288	46	74	7	7	3	29	22	28	.257	.329	.361	75	-10	6	3	0	.983	10	2-99/S-6,3-2	0.4

YEAR	TM/L	G	AB	R	H	2B	3B	HR	RBI	BB	SO	AVG	OBP	SLG	PRO+	BR/A	SB	CS	SBR	FA	FR	G/POS	TPR
1996	Mil-A	140	554	94	157	19	10	7	46	38	35	.283	.344	.392	82	-15	16	7	1	.979	8	*2-137	0.3
1997	Mil-A	79	324	37	89	12	2	4	28	12	23	.275	.315	.361	75	-12	8	7	-2	.982	2	2-77/D-1	-0.7
1998	Mil-N★	159	637	101	198	39	7	7	45	54	46	.311	.387	.427	110	12	22	16	-3	.986	29	*2-158	4.8
Total	6	594	1972	303	559	85	26	21	156	142	146	.283	.353	.385	88	-30	61	34	-2	.983	57	2-500/S-19,3-14,OD	5.4

■ CHARLIE VINSON Vinson, Charles Anthony "Chuck" b: 1/5/44, Washington, D.C. BL/TL, 6'3", 207 lbs. Deb: 9/19/66

YEAR	TM/L	G	AB	R	H	2B	3B	HR	RBI	BB	SO	AVG	OBP	SLG	PRO+	BR/A	SB	CS	SBR	FA	FR	G/POS	TPR
1966	Cal-A	13	22	3	4	2	0	1	6	5	9	.182	.357	.409	123	1	0	0	0	1.000	-1	1-11	0.0

■ RUBE VINSON Vinson, Ernest Augustus b: 3/20/1879, Dover, Del. d: 10/12/51, Chester, Pa. 5'9", 168 lbs. Deb: 9/27/04

YEAR	TM/L	G	AB	R	H	2B	3B	HR	RBI	BB	SO	AVG	OBP	SLG	PRO+	BR/A	SB	CS	SBR	FA	FR	G/POS	TPR
1904	Cle-A	15	49	12	15	1	0	0	2	10		.306	.433	.327	143	3	2			1.000	3	O-15	0.6
1905	Cle-A	39	134	12	26	3	1	0	9	7		.194	.245	.231	51	-7	4			.930	-3	O-36	-1.4
1906	Chi-A	10	24	2	6	0	0	0	3	2		.250	.308	.250	77	-1	1			.600	-3	/O-7	-0.4
Total	3	64	207	26	47	4	1	0	14	19		.227	.301	.256	77	-5	7			.919	-3	/O-58	-1.2

■ JIM VIOX Viox, James Harry b: 12/30/1890, Lockland, Ohio d: 1/6/69, Erlanger, Ky. BR/TR, 5'7", 150 lbs. Deb: 5/9/12

YEAR	TM/L	G	AB	R	H	2B	3B	HR	RBI	BB	SO	AVG	OBP	SLG	PRO+	BR/A	SB	CS	SBR	FA	FR	G/POS	TPR
1912	Pit-N	33	70	8	13	2	3	1	7	3	9	.186	.219	.343	53	-5	2			.957	-4	3-10/S-8,O-3,2-1	-0.9
1913	Pit-N	137	492	86	156	32	8	2	65	64	28	.317	.399	.427	142	29	14			.959	-43	*2-124,S-10	-1.6
1914	Pit-N	143	506	52	134	18	5	1	57	63	33	.265	.351	.326	106	6	9			.939	-25	*2-138/S-2,O-2	-2.2
1915	Pit-N	150	503	56	129	17	8	2	45	75	31	.256	.357	.334	111	10	12	8	-1	.954	-23	*2-134,3-13/O-2	-1.4
1916	Pit-N	43	132	12	33	7	0	1	17	17	11	.250	.340	.326	104	1	2			.937	-16	2-25,3-11	-1.6
Total	5	506	1703	214	465	76	24	7	191	222	112	.273	.361	.358	116	41	39	8		.949	-111	2-422/3-34,S-20,O-7	-7.7

■ BILL VIRDON Virdon, William Charles b: 6/9/31, Hazel Park, Mich. BL/TR, 6', 175 lbs. Deb: 4/12/55 MC

YEAR	TM/L	G	AB	R	H	2B	3B	HR	RBI	BB	SO	AVG	OBP	SLG	PRO+	BR/A	SB	CS	SBR	FA	FR	G/POS	TPR
1955	StL-N	144	534	58	150	18	6	17	68	36	64	.281	.327	.433	100	-1	2	4	-2	.966	-0	*O-142	-1.0
1956	StL-N	24	71	10	15	2	0	2	9	5	8	.211	.273	.324	60	-4	0	1	-1	.982	-1	O-24	-0.7
	Pit-N	133	509	67	170	21	10	8	37	33	63	.334	.376	.462	126	19	6	6	-2	.989	4	*O-130	1.4
	Yr	157	580	77	185	23	10	10	46	38	71	.319	.363	.445	118	14	6	7	-2	.988	3	*O-154	0.7
1957	Pit-N	144	561	59	141	28	11	8	50	33	69	.251	.293	.383	82	-15	3	3	-1	.986	12	*O-141	-1.3
1958	Pit-N	144	604	75	161	24	11	9	46	52	70	.267	.326	.387	90	-9	5	3	-0	.993	11	*O-143	-0.6
1959	Pit-N	144	519	67	132	24	2	8	41	55	65	.254	.328	.355	83	-12	7	4	-0	.979	**24**	*O-144	0.4
1960	*Pit-N	120	409	60	108	16	9	8	40	40	44	.264	.330	.406	99	-0	8	2	1	.983	7	*O-109	0.3
1961	Pit-N	146	599	81	156	22	8	9	58	49	45	.260	.316	.369	81	-16	5	8	-3	.985	11	*O-145	-1.7
1962	Pit-N	156	663	82	164	27	**10**	6	47	36	65	.247	.287	.345	69	-30	5	13	-6	.976	6	*O-156	-4.0
1963	Pit-N	142	554	58	149	22	6	8	53	43	55	.269	.322	.374	99	-1	1	2	-1	.988	6	*O-142	-0.4
1964	Pit-N	145	473	59	115	11	3	3	27	30	48	.243	.288	.298	66	-21	1	5	-3	.976	-7	*O-134	-3.9
1965	Pit-N	135	481	58	134	22	5	4	24	30	49	.279	.322	.370	94	-4	4	3	-1	.970	-2	*O-128	-1.3
1968	Pit-N	6	3	1	1	0	0	1	2	0	2	.333	.333	1.333	388	1	0	0	0	1.000	-1	/O-4	-0.1
Total	12	1583	5980	735	1596	237	81	91	502	442	647	.267	.318	.379	89	-95	47	54	-18	.982	69	*O-1542	-12.9

■ OZZIE VIRGIL Virgil, Osvaldo Jose Jr. b: 12/7/56, Mayaguez, P.R. BR/TR, 6'1", 205 lbs. Deb: 10/5/80 F

YEAR	TM/L	G	AB	R	H	2B	3B	HR	RBI	BB	SO	AVG	OBP	SLG	PRO+	BR/A	SB	CS	SBR	FA	FR	G/POS	TPR
1980	Phi-N	1	5	1	1	1	0	0	0	0	1	.200	.200	.400	60	-0	0	0	0	1.000	-1	/C-1	-0.1
1981	Phi-N	6	6	0	0	0	0	0	0	0	2	.000	.000	.000	-96	-2	0	0	0	1.000	0	/C-1	-0.2
1982	Phi-N	49	101	11	24	6	0	3	8	10	26	.238	.306	.386	91	-1	0	1	-1	.964	4	C-35	0.3
1983	*Phi-N	55	140	11	30	7	0	6	23	8	34	.214	.272	.393	83	-4	0	2	-1	.966	-5	C-51	-0.8
1984	Phi-N	141	456	61	119	21	2	18	68	45	91	.261	.334	.434	113	7	1	1	-0	.992	-3	*C-137	1.0
1985	Phi-N★	131	426	47	105	16	3	19	55	49	85	.246	.331	.432	109	5	0	0	0	**.994**	-4	*C-120	0.7
1986	Atl-N	114	359	45	80	9	0	15	48	63	73	.223	.345	.373	93	-2	1	0	0	.984	14	*C-111	2.0
1987	Atl-N★	123	429	57	106	13	1	27	72	47	81	.247	.331	.471	104	2	0	1	-1	.989	-2	*C-122	0.8
1988	Atl-N	107	320	23	82	10	0	9	31	22	54	.256	.314	.372	92	-3	2	0	1	.990	-11	C-96	-0.8
1989	Tor-A	9	11	2	2	1	0	1	2	4	3	.182	.400	.545	167	1	0	0	0	1.000	-0	/C-1,D-6	0.1
1990	Tor-A	3	5	0	0	0	0	0	0	0	3	.000	.000	.000	-98	-1	0	0	0	1.000	-0	/C-2,D-1	-0.1
Total	11	739	2258	258	549	84	6	98	307	248	453	.243	.326	.416	101	1	4	5	-2	.987	-8	C-677/D-7	2.9

■ OZZIE VIRGIL Virgil, Osvaldo Jose Sr. (Pichardo) b: 5/17/33, Monte Cristi, D.R. BR/TR, 6', 175 lbs. Deb: 9/23/56 FC

YEAR	TM/L	G	AB	R	H	2B	3B	HR	RBI	BB	SO	AVG	OBP	SLG	PRO+	BR/A	SB	CS	SBR	FA	FR	G/POS	TPR
1956	NY-N	3	12	2	5	1	1	0	2	0	0	.417	.417	.667	186	1	1	0	0	.800	-2	/3-3	0.0
1957	NY-N	96	226	26	53	0	2	4	24	14	27	.235	.279	.305	57	-14	2	3	-1	.926	9	3-62,O-24/S-1	-0.6
1958	Det-A	49	193	19	47	10	2	3	19	8	20	.244	.274	.363	69	-9	1	0	0	.981	3	3-49	-0.5
1960	Det-A	62	132	16	30	4	2	3	13	4	14	.227	.250	.356	60	-8	1	1	-0	.974	8	3-42/2-8,S-5,C-1	0.1
1961	Det-A	20	30	1	4	0	0	1	1	1	5	.133	.161	.233	4	-4	0	0	0	.938	-1	/3-9,C-3,2-1,S-1	-0.5
	KC-A	11	21	1	3	0	0	0	0	0	3	.143	.143	.143	-23	-4	0	0	0	.818	0	/3-4,C-3	-0.3
	Yr	31	51	2	7	0	0	1	1	1	8	.137	.154	.196	-7	-8	0	0	0	.889	-1	3-13/C-6,2-1,S-1	-0.8
1962	Bal-A	1	0	0	0	0	0	0	0	1	0	—	1.000	—	209	0	0	0	0	.000	0	H	0.0
1965	Pit-N	39	49	3	13	2	0	1	5	2	10	.265	.294	.367	85	-1	0	0	0	1.000	2	C-15/3-7,2-5	0.1
1966	SF-N	42	89	7	19	2	0	2	9	4	12	.213	.247	.303	51	-6	1	1	-0	.984	0	C-13,3-13/1-5,2O	-0.6
1969	SF-N	1	1	0	0	0	0	0	0	0	0	.000	.000	.000	-99	-0	0	0	0	.000	0	H	0.0
Total	9	324	753	75	174	19	7	14	73	34	91	.231	.264	.331	59	-43	6	5	-1	.951	19	3-189/C-35,O2S1	-2.3

■ JAKE VIRTUE Virtue, Jacob Kitchline "Guesses" b: 3/2/1865, Philadelphia, Pa. d: 2/3/43, Camden, N.J. BB/TL, 5'9.5", 165 lbs. Deb: 7/21/1890

YEAR	TM/L	G	AB	R	H	2B	3B	HR	RBI	BB	SO	AVG	OBP	SLG	PRO+	BR/A	SB	CS	SBR	FA	FR	G/POS	TPR
1890	Cle-N	62	223	39	68	6	5	2	25	49	15	.305	.432	.404	147	16	9			.982	0	1-62	1.2
1891	Cle-N	139	517	82	135	19	14	2	72	75	40	.261	.363	.364	107	6	15			.972	-10	*1-139	-1.0
1892	*Cle-N	147	557	98	157	15	20	2	89	84	68	.282	.380	.391	128	20	14			.984	-4	*1-147	0.8
1893	Cle-N	97	378	87	100	16	10	1	60	54	14	.265	.358	.368	88	-7	11			.975	1	1-73,O-13/S-5,3P	-0.7
1894	Cle-N	29	89	15	23	4	1	0	10	13	3	.258	.359	.326	64	-5	1			.885	-2	O-21/2-3,1-2,P-1	-0.6
Total	5	474	1764	321	483	60	50	7	256	275	140	.274	.376	.376	111	30	50			.978	-15	1-423/O-34,3-5,S2P	-0.3

■ JOE VISNER Visner, Joseph Paul (b: Joseph Paul Vezina) b: 9/27/1859, Minneapolis, Minn. d: 6/17/45, Fosston, Minn. BL/TR, 5'11", 180 lbs. Deb: 7/4/1885

YEAR	TM/L	G	AB	R	H	2B	3B	HR	RBI	BB	SO	AVG	OBP	SLG	PRO+	BR/A	SB	CS	SBR	FA	FR	G/POS	TPR
1885	Bal-a	4	13	2	3	0	0	0	2	2		.231	.333	.231	82	-0				.750	-1	/O-4	-0.1
1889	*Bro-a	80	295	56	76	12	10	8	68	36	36	.258	.346	.447	125	9	13			.871	-16	C-53,O-29	-0.2
1890	Pit-P	127	521	110	139	15	**22**	3	71	76	44	.267	.369	.397	114	13	18			.893	-6	*O-127	0.2
1891	Was-a	18	68	13	19	2	3	1	7	8	7	.279	.355	.441	134	3	2			.806	-2	O-17/C-1,3-1	0.0
	StL-a	6	27	2	4	0	1	0	1	0	3	.148	.148	.222	5	-4	0			1.000	0	/O-6	-0.3
	Yr	24	95	15	23	2	4	1	8	8	10	.242	.301	.379	94	-1	2			.846	-2	O-23/C-1,3-1	-0.3
Total	4	235	924	183	241	29	36	12	149	122	90	.261	.354	.409	115	21	33			.892	-25	O-183/C-54,3-1	-0.4

■ JOE VITELLI Vitelli, Antonio Joseph b: 4/12/08, McKees Rocks, Pa. d: 2/7/67, Pittsburgh, Pa. BR/TR, 6'1", 195 lbs. Deb: 5/30/44

YEAR	TM/L	G	AB	R	H	2B	3B	HR	RBI	BB	SO	AVG	OBP	SLG	PRO+	BR/A	SB	CS	SBR	FA	FR	G/POS	TPR
1944	Pit-N	4	3	0	0	0	0	0	0	0	0	.000	.000	.000	-96	-1	0			.750	0	/P-4	0.0
1945	Pit-N	1	0	1	0	0	0	0	0	0	0	—	—	—	—	0	0			.000	0	R	0.0
Total	2	5	3	1	0	0	0	0	0	0	0	.000	.000	.000	-96	-1	0			.750	0	/P-4	0.0

■ JOE VITIELLO Vitiello, Joseph David b: 4/11/70, Cambridge, Mass. BR/TR, 6'2", 215 lbs. Deb: 4/29/95

YEAR	TM/L	G	AB	R	H	2B	3B	HR	RBI	BB	SO	AVG	OBP	SLG	PRO+	BR/A	SB	CS	SBR	FA	FR	G/POS	TPR
1995	KC-A	53	130	13	33	4	0	7	21	8	25	.254	.317	.446	95	-1	0	0	0	.982	-0	D-38/1-8	-0.5
1996	KC-A	85	257	29	62	15	1	8	40	38	69	.241	.346	.401	88	-4	2	0	1	1.000	0	D-70/1-9,O-1	-0.8
1997	KC-A	51	130	11	31	6	0	5	18	14	37	.238	.322	.400	85	-3	0	0	0	.980	-3	O-28,D-12/1-1	-0.6
1998	KC-A	3	7	0	1	0	0	0	0	1	2	.143	.250	.143	6	-1	0	0	0	.000	0	/D-2	-0.1
Total	4	192	524	53	127	25	1	20	79	61	133	.242	.332	.408	88	-10	2	0	1	.980	-3	D-122/O-29,1-18	-2.0

■ OSSIE VITT Vitt, Oscar Joseph b: 1/4/1890, San Francisco, Cal. d: 1/31/63, Oakland, Cal. BR/TR, 5'10", 150 lbs. Deb: 4/11/12 M

YEAR	TM/L	G	AB	R	H	2B	3B	HR	RBI	BB	SO	AVG	OBP	SLG	PRO+	BR/A	SB	CS	SBR	FA	FR	G/POS	TPR
1912	Det-A	76	273	39	67	4	4	0	19	18		.245	.297	.289	70	-11	17			.929	0	O-28,3-24,2-15	-1.2
1913	Det-A	99	359	45	86	11	3	2	33	31	18	.240	.304	.304	79	-10	5			.960	5	2-78,3-17/O-2	-0.6
1914	Det-A	66	195	35	49	7	0	0	8	31	8	.251	.354	.287	90	-1	10	8	-2	.964	2	2-36,3-16/O-2,S-1	-0.1
1915	Det-A	152	560	116	140	18	13	1	48	80	22	.250	.348	.334	99	0	26	18	-3	**.964**	14	*3-151/2-2	1.9
1916	Det-A	153	597	88	135	17	12	0	42	75	28	.226	.314	.295	80	-14	18			**.964**	28	*3-151/S-2	2.1

YEAR	TM/L	G	AB	R	H	2B	3B	HR	RBI	BB	SO	AVG	OBP	SLG	PRO+	BR/A	SB	CS	SBR	FA	FR	G/POS	TPR
1917	Det-A	140	512	65	130	13	6	0	47	56	15	.254	.329	.303	93	-3	18			.940	-17	*3-140	-2.0
1918	Det-A	81	267	29	64	5	2	0	17	32	6	.240	.321	.273	83	-5	5			.953	4	3-66/2-9,O-3	0.1
1919	Bos-A	133	469	64	114	10	3	0	40	44	11	.243	.309	.277	69	-18	9			**.970**	14	*3-133	0.1
1920	Bos-A	87	296	50	65	10	4	1	28	43	10	.220	.321	.291	66	-14	5	4	-1	.986	-6	3-64,2-21	-1.7
1921	Bos-A	78	232	29	44	11	1	0	13	45	13	.190	.321	.246	48	-17	1	2	-1	.962	-4	3-71/O-3,1-2	-1.6
Total	10	1065	3760	560	894	106	48	4	295	455	131	.238	.322	.295	80	-93	114	32		.960	40	3-833,2-161/OS1	-3.0

■ **JOSE VIZCAINO** Vizcaino, Jose Luis (Pimental) b: 3/26/68, San Cristobal, D.R. BB/TR, 6'1", 180 lbs. Deb: 9/10/89

YEAR	TM/L	G	AB	R	H	2B	3B	HR	RBI	BB	SO	AVG	OBP	SLG	PRO+	BR/A	SB	CS	SBR	FA	FR	G/POS	TPR
1989	LA-N	7	10	2	2	0	0	0	0	0	1	.200	.200	.200	15	-1	0	0	0	.882	2	/S-5	0.1
1990	LA-N	37	51	3	14	1	1	0	2	4	8	.275	.327	.333	85	-1	1	1	-0	.956	3	S-11/2-6	0.2
1991	Chi-N	93	145	7	38	5	0	0	10	5	18	.262	.287	.297	61	-7	2	1	0	.947	7	3-57,S-33/2-9	0.1
1992	Chi-N	86	285	25	64	10	4	1	17	14	35	.225	.261	.298	57	-16	3	0	1	.969	2	S-50,3-29/2-5	-1.1
1993	Chi-N	151	551	74	158	19	4	4	54	46	71	.287	.345	.358	90	-7	12	9	-2	.968	8	S-81,3-44,2-34	0.6
1994	NY-N	103	410	47	105	13	3	3	33	33	62	.256	.315	.324	68	-19	1	11	-6	.970	-12	*S-102	-2.8
1995	NY-N	135	509	66	146	21	5	3	56	35	76	.287	.334	.365	87	-9	8	3	1	**.984**	10	*S-134/2-1	1.3
1996	NY-N	96	363	47	110	12	6	1	32	28	58	.303	.358	.377	99	-0	9	5	-0	.986	2	2-93	0.6
	*Cle-A	48	179	23	51	5	2	0	13	7	24	.285	.312	.335	64	-10	6	2	1	.981	2	2-45/S-4,D-1	-0.4
1997	*SF-N	151	568	77	151	19	7	5	50	48	87	.266	.323	.350	78	-18	8	8	-2	.976	7	*S-147/2-5	0.0
1998	LA-N	67	237	30	62	9	0	3	29	17	35	.262	.314	.338	75	-9	7	3	0	.985	-6	S-66	-0.8
Total	10	974	3308	401	901	114	32	20	296	237	475	.272	.323	.344	79	-98	57	43	-9	.975	24	S-633,2-198,3/D	-2.2

■ **OMAR VIZQUEL** Vizquel, Omar Enrique (Gonzalez) b: 4/24/67, Caracas, Venez. BB/TR, 5'9", 165 lbs. Deb: 4/3/89

YEAR	TM/L	G	AB	R	H	2B	3B	HR	RBI	BB	SO	AVG	OBP	SLG	PRO+	BR/A	SB	CS	SBR	FA	FR	G/POS	TPR
1989	Sea-A	143	387	45	85	7	3	1	20	28	40	.220	.274	.261	50	-25	1	4	-2	.971	11	*S-143	-0.7
1990	Sea-A	81	255	19	63	3	2	2	18	18	22	.247	.297	.298	66	-11	4	1	1	.980	-3	S-81	-0.7
1991	Sea-A	142	426	42	98	16	4	1	41	45	37	.230	.304	.293	66	-19	7	2	1	.980	24	*S-138/2-1	1.5
1992	Sea-A	136	483	49	142	20	4	0	21	32	38	.294	.340	.352	94	-4	15	13	-3	**.989**	0	*S-136	0.3
1993	Sea-A	158	560	68	143	14	2	2	31	50	71	.255	.321	.298	67	-25	12	14	-5	.980	**23**	*S-155/D-2	0.5
1994	Cle-A	69	286	39	78	10	1	1	33	23	23	.273	.327	.325	69	-13	13	4	2	.981	-1	S-69	-0.5
1995	*Cle-A	136	542	87	144	28	0	6	56	59	59	.266	.339	.351	79	-16	29	11	2	.986	-3	*S-136	-0.4
1996	*Cle-A	151	542	98	161	36	1	9	64	56	42	.297	.367	.417	98	-0	35	9	5	.971	-1	*S-150	1.6
1997	*Cle-A	153	565	89	158	23	6	5	49	57	58	.280	.348	.368	84	-12	43	12	6	.985	5	*S-152	1.2
1998	*Cle-A★	151	576	86	166	30	6	2	50	62	64	.288	.361	.372	88	-8	37	12	4	**.993**	6	*S-151	1.4
Total	10	1320	4622	622	1238	187	29	29	383	430	454	.268	.333	.340	78	-134	196	82	10	.982	61	*S-1311/D-2,2-1	4.2

■ **OTTO VOGEL** Vogel, Otto Henry b: 10/26/1899, Mendota, Ill. d: 7/19/69, Iowa City, Iowa BR/TR, 6', 195 lbs. Deb: 6/5/23

YEAR	TM/L	G	AB	R	H	2B	3B	HR	RBI	BB	SO	AVG	OBP	SLG	PRO+	BR/A	SB	CS	SBR	FA	FR	G/POS	TPR
1923	Chi-N	41	81	10	17	0	1	1	6	7	11	.210	.297	.272	51	-6	2	3	-1	.929	-2	O-24/3-1	-1.0
1924	Chi-N	70	172	28	46	11	2	1	24	10	26	.267	.319	.372	84	-4	4	4	-1	.956	1	O-53/3-2	-0.7
Total	2	111	253	38	63	11	3	2	30	17	37	.249	.312	.340	73	-10	6	7	-2	.948	-1	/O-77,3-3	-1.7

■ **JACK VOIGT** Voigt, John David b: 5/17/66, Sarasota, Fla. BR/TR, 6'1", 175 lbs. Deb: 8/3/92

YEAR	TM/L	G	AB	R	H	2B	3B	HR	RBI	BB	SO	AVG	OBP	SLG	PRO+	BR/A	SB	CS	SBR	FA	FR	G/POS	TPR
1992	Bal-A	1	0	0	0	0	0	0	0	0	0	—	—	—	—	0	0	0	0	.000	0	/R	0.0
1993	Bal-A	64	152	32	45	11	1	6	23	25	33	.296	.395	.500	133	8	1	0	0	.987	-1	O-43/1-5,3-3,D-9	0.5
1994	Bal-A	59	141	15	34	5	0	3	20	18	25	.241	.331	.340	70	-6	0	0	0	.989	-4	O-54/1-6,D-2	-1.0
1995	Bal-A	3	1	1	1	0	0	0	0	0	0	1.000	1.000	1.000	416	0	0	0	0	1.000	0	/1-1,D-1	0.1
	Tex-A	33	62	8	10	3	0	2	8	10	14	.161	.278	.306	51	-5	0	0	0	1.000	-2	O-25/1-5,D-2	-0.7
	Yr	36	63	9	11	3	0	2	8	10	14	.175	.288	.317	56	-4	0	0	0	1.000	-2	O-25/1-6,D-3	-0.6
1996	Tex-A	5	9	1	1	0	0	0	0	0	2	.111	.111	.111	-41	-2	0	0	0	1.000	0	/O-3,3-1	-0.2
1997	Mil-A	72	151	20	37	9	2	8	22	19	36	.245	.333	.490	110	2	1	2	-1	.985	-2	O-40,1-19/3-6,D-1	-0.2
1998	Oak-A	57	72	7	10	4	0	1	10	6	19	.139	.205	.236	15	-9	5	1	1	.987	-3	1-27,O-20/3-2,D-3	-1.1
Total	7	294	588	84	138	32	3	20	83	78	129	.235	.326	.401	87	-12	7	3	0	.990	-12	O-185/1-63,D-18,3	-2.6

■ **CLYDE VOLLMER** Vollmer, Clyde Frederick b: 9/24/21, Cincinnati, Ohio BR/TR, 6'1", 190 lbs. Deb: 5/31/42

YEAR	TM/L	G	AB	R	H	2B	3B	HR	RBI	BB	SO	AVG	OBP	SLG	PRO+	BR/A	SB	CS	SBR	FA	FR	G/POS	TPR
1942	Cin-N	12	43	2	4	0	0	1	4	1	5	.093	.114	.163	-20	-7	0			1.000	1	O-11	-0.6
1946	Cin-N	9	22	1	4	0	0	0	1	1	3	.182	.217	.182	14	-2	2			1.000	-3	/O-7	-0.6
1947	Cin-N	78	155	19	34	10	0	1	13	9	18	.219	.267	.303	51	-11	0			.984	-7	O-66	-2.0
1948	Cin-N	7	9	0	1	0	0	0	0	1	1	.111	.200	.111	-14	-1	0			.000	-1	/O-2	-0.2
	Was-A	1	5	1	2	0	0	0	0	0	1	.400	.400	.400	116	0	0	0	0	1.000	0	/O-1	0.0
1949	Was-A	129	443	58	112	17	1	14	59	53	62	.253	.335	.391	94	-6	1	2	-1	.982	4	*O-114	-0.7
1950	Was-A	6	14	4	4	0	0	0	1	2	3	.286	.375	.286	75	-0	1	0	0	1.000	0	/O-3	0.0
	Bos-A	57	169	35	48	10	0	7	37	21	35	.284	.363	.467	102	-0	1	0	0	.954	-2	O-39	-0.3
	Yr	63	183	39	52	10	0	7	38	23	38	.284	.364	.454	100	-0	2	0	1	.957	-1	O-42	-0.3
1951	Bos-A	115	386	66	97	9	2	22	85	55	66	.251	.346	.456	105	2	0	0	0	.986	0	*O-106	-0.2
1952	Bos-A	90	250	35	66	12	4	11	50	39	47	.264	.370	.476	124	8	2	2	-1	1.000	-1	O-70	0.4
1953	Bos-A	1	0	0	0	0	0	0	0	1	0	—	1.000	—	180	0	0	0	0	.000	0	H	0.0
	Was-A	118	408	54	106	15	3	11	74	48	59	.260	.342	.392	100	0	0	2	-1	.979	7	*O-106	0.2
	Yr	119	408	54	106	15	3	11	74	49	59	.260	.343	.392	101	0	0	2	-1	.979	7	*O-106	0.2
1954	Was-A	62	117	8	30	4	0	2	15	12	28	.256	.331	.342	89	-2	0	0	0	1.000	-3	O-26	-0.6
Total	10	685	2021	283	508	77	10	69	339	243	328	.251	.335	.402	95	-19	7	6		.984	-3	O-551	-4.6

■ **FRITZ Von KOLNITZ** Von Kolnitz, Alfred Holmes b: 5/20/1893, Charleston, S.C. d: 3/18/48, Mount Pleasant, S.C. BR/TR, 5'10.5", 175 lbs. Deb: 4/18/14

YEAR	TM/L	G	AB	R	H	2B	3B	HR	RBI	BB	SO	AVG	OBP	SLG	PRO+	BR/A	SB	CS	SBR	FA	FR	G/POS	TPR
1914	Cin-N	41	104	8	23	2	0	0	6	6	16	.221	.270	.240	51	-6	4			.914	-4	3-20,O-11/C-2,1-1	-1.1
1915	Cin-N	50	78	6	15	4	1	0	6	7	11	.192	.259	.269	59	-4	1	3	-2	.933	-6	3-18/S-6,1-3,C-2,O	-1.2
1916	Chi-A	24	44	1	10	3	0	0	7	2	6	.227	.261	.295	66	-2	0			.909	-5	3-13	-0.7
Total	3	115	226	15	48	9	1	0	19	15	33	.212	.264	.261	56	-12	5	3		.918	-15	/3-51,O-12,S-6,1C	-3.0

■ **JOE VOSMIK** Vosmik, Joseph Franklin b: 4/4/10, Cleveland, Ohio d: 1/27/62, Cleveland, Ohio BR/TR, 6', 185 lbs. Deb: 9/13/30

YEAR	TM/L	G	AB	R	H	2B	3B	HR	RBI	BB	SO	AVG	OBP	SLG	PRO+	BR/A	SB	CS	SBR	FA	FR	G/POS	TPR
1930	Cle-A	9	26	1	6	2	0	0	4	1	1	.231	.259	.308	42	-2	0	0	0	.933	1	/O-5	-0.2
1931	Cle-A	149	591	80	189	36	14	7	117	38	30	.320	.363	.464	110	7	7	7	-2	.970	6	*O-147	0.1
1932	Cle-A	153	621	106	194	39	12	10	97	58	42	.312	.376	.462	109	8	2	3	-1	**.989**	24	*O-153	1.9
1933	Cle-A	119	438	53	115	20	10	4	56	42	13	.263	.331	.381	84	-10	0	2	-1	.985	6	*O-113	-1.1
1934	Cle-A	104	405	71	138	33	2	6	78	35	10	.341	.393	.477	122	13	1	1	-0	.976	-2	*O-104	0.6
1935	Cle-A★	152	620	93	**216**	**47**	**20**	10	110	59	30	.348	.408	.537	140	36	2	1	0	.986	1	*O-150	2.9
1936	Cle-A	138	506	76	145	29	7	7	94	79	21	.287	.383	.413	96	-2	5	1	1	.978	-1	*O-136	-0.6
1937	StL-A	144	594	81	193	47	9	4	93	49	38	.325	.377	.455	108	7	2	3	-1	.972	8	*O-143	0.8
1938	Bos-A	146	621	121	**201**	37	6	9	86	59	26	.324	.384	.446	103	3	0	3	-2	.978	3	*O-146	-0.1
1939	Bos-A	145	554	89	153	29	6	7	84	66	33	.276	.356	.388	87	-10	4	3	-1	.974	-4	*O-144	-1.9
1940	Bro-N	116	404	45	114	14	6	1	42	22	21	.282	.321	.354	81	-10	0			.976	0	O-99	-1.5
1941	Bro-N	25	56	0	11	0	0	0	4	4	4	.196	.250	.196	26	-5	0			1.000	-5	O-18	-1.2
1944	Was-A	14	36	2	7	2	0	0	9	2	3	.194	.237	.250	41	-3	0	0	0	1.000	-2	O-12	-0.6
Total	13	1414	5472	818	1682	335	92	65	874	514	272	.307	.369	.438	104	29	23	24		.979	34	*O-1370	-0.9

■ **ALEX VOSS** Voss, Alexander b: 5/16/1858, Roswell, Ga. d: 8/31/06, Cincinnati, Ohio BR/TR, 6'1", 180 lbs. Deb: 4/17/1884

YEAR	TM/L	G	AB	R	H	2B	3B	HR	RBI	BB	SO	AVG	OBP	SLG	PRO+	BR/A	SB	CS	SBR	FA	FR	G/POS	TPR
1884	Was-U	63	245	33	47	9	0	0		5		.192	.208	.229	33	-27				.848	4	P-27,3-16,1-15,O/S	-1.6
	KC-U	14	45	1	4	0	0	0		0		.089	.089	.089	-53	-10				.867	1	/O-8,P-7	-0.4
	Yr	77	290	34	51	9	0	0		5		.176	.190	.207	21	-36				.859	5	P-34,O-21,3-16,1/S	-2.0

■ **BILL VOSS** Voss, William Edward b: 10/31/43, Glendale, Cal. BL/TL, 6'2", 160 lbs. Deb: 9/14/65

YEAR	TM/L	G	AB	R	H	2B	3B	HR	RBI	BB	SO	AVG	OBP	SLG	PRO+	BR/A	SB	CS	SBR	FA	FR	G/POS	TPR
1965	Chi-A	11	33	4	6	0	1	1	3	3	5	.182	.250	.333	68	-1	0	0	0	1.000	-1	O-10	-0.4
1966	Chi-A	2	2	0	0	0	0	0	0	0	2	.000	.000	.000	-99	-1	0	0	0	1.000	-0	/O-1	-0.1
1967	Chi-A	13	22	4	2	0	0	0	0	0	1	.091	.091	.091	-48	-4	1	1	-0	1.000	-2	O-11	-0.7
1968	Chi-A	61	167	14	26	2	1	2	15	16	34	.156	.238	.216	38	-12	5	3	-0	.963	-4	O-55	-2.2

YEAR	TM/L	G	AB	R	H	2B	3B	HR	RBI	BB	SO	AVG	OBP	SLG	PRO+	BR/A	SB	CS	SBR	FA	FR	G/POS	TPR
1969	Cal-A	133	349	33	91	11	4	2	40	35	40	.261	.328	.332	90	-5	5	3	-0	.995	1	*O-111/1-2	-0.9
1970	Cal-A	80	181	21	44	4	3	3	30	23	18	.243	.335	.348	92	-2	2	1	0	.979	2	O-55	-0.2
1971	Mil-A	97	275	31	69	4	0	10	30	24	45	.251	.313	.375	95	-2	2	2	-1	.987	-4	O-79	-1.1
1972	Mil-A	27	36	1	3	1	0	0	1	5	4	.083	.195	.111	-7	-5	0	1	-1	.929	-3	O-11	-0.9
	Oak-A	40	97	10	22	5	1	1	5	9	16	.227	.299	.330	92	-1	0	0	0	1.000	-1	O-34	-0.4
	Yr	67	133	11	25	6	1	1	6	14	20	.188	.270	.271	64	-6	0	1	-1	.987	-4	O-45	-1.3
	StL-N	11	15	1	4	2	0	0	3	2	2	.267	.353	.400	115	0	0	0	0	1.000	-0	/O-2	0.0
Total	8	475	1177	119	267	29	10	19	127	117	167	.227	.300	.317	78	-33	15	11	-2	.986	-11	O-369/1-2	-6.9

■ **PHIL VOYLES** Voyles, Philip Vance b: 5/12/1900, Murphy, N.C. d: 11/3/72, Marlborough, Mass. BL/TR, 5′11.5″, 175 lbs. Deb: 9/4/29

YEAR	TM/L	G	AB	R	H	2B	3B	HR	RBI	BB	SO	AVG	OBP	SLG	PRO+	BR/A	SB	CS	SBR	FA	FR	G/POS	TPR
1929	Bos-N	20	68	9	16	0	2	0	14	6	8	.235	.297	.294	49	-5	0			.922	-2	O-20	-0.8

■ **GEORGE VUKOVICH** Vukovich, George Stephen b: 6/24/56, Chicago, Ill. BL/TR, 6′, 198 lbs. Deb: 4/13/80

YEAR	TM/L	G	AB	R	H	2B	3B	HR	RBI	BB	SO	AVG	OBP	SLG	PRO+	BR/A	SB	CS	SBR	FA	FR	G/POS	TPR
1980	*Phi-N	78	58	6	13	1	1	0	8	6	9	.224	.297	.276	58	-3	0	0	0	.933	-9	O-28	-1.3
1981	*Phi-N	20	26	5	10	0	0	1	4	1	0	.385	.407	.500	150	2	1	0	0	1.000	-2	/O-9	0.0
1982	Phi-N	123	335	41	91	18	2	6	42	32	47	.272	.335	.391	100	0	2	9	-5	.977	-6	*O-102	-1.3
1983	Cle-A	124	312	31	77	13	2	3	44	24	37	.247	.305	.330	72	-12	3	4	-2	.986	-13	*O-122	-2.9
1984	Cle-A	134	437	38	133	22	5	9	60	34	61	.304	.356	.439	117	10	1	4	-2	.994	14	*O-130	1.8
1985	Cle-A	149	434	43	106	22	0	8	45	30	75	.244	.295	.350	76	-14	2	2	-1	.988	-7	*O-137	-2.6
Total	6	628	1602	164	430	76	10	27	203	127	229	.268	.324	.379	92	-18	9	19	-9	.987	-22	O-528	-6.3

■ **JOHN VUKOVICH** Vukovich, John Christopher b: 7/31/47, Sacramento, Cal. BR/TR, 6′1″, 190 lbs. Deb: 9/11/70 MC

YEAR	TM/L	G	AB	R	H	2B	3B	HR	RBI	BB	SO	AVG	OBP	SLG	PRO+	BR/A	SB	CS	SBR	FA	FR	G/POS	TPR
1970	Phi-N	3	8	1	1	0	0	0	0	1	0	.125	.222	.125	-5	-1	0	0	0	.778	1	/S-2,3-1	0.0
1971	Phi-N	74	217	11	36	5	0	0	14	12	34	.166	.213	.189	15	-24	2	1	0	.956	10	3-74	-1.6
1973	Mil-A	55	128	10	16	3	0	2	9	9	40	.125	.182	.195	7	-16	0	2	-1	.948	-4	3-40,1-13/S-1	-2.2
1974	Mil-A	38	80	5	15	1	0	3	11	1	16	.188	.198	.313	45	-6	2	1	0	.945	2	S-12,3-12,2-11,/1-4	-0.2
1975	Cin-N	31	38	4	8	3	0	0	2	4	5	.211	.286	.289	59	-2	0	0	0	.925	7	3-31	0.5
1976	Phi-N	4	8	2	1	0	0	1	2	0	2	.125	.125	.500	69	-0	0	0	0	1.000	-0	/3-4,1-1	-0.1
1977	Phi-N	2	2	0	0	0	0	0	0	0	1	.000	.000	.000	-96	-1	0	0	0	.000	0	H	-0.1
1979	Phi-N	10	15	0	3	1	0	0	1	0	3	.200	.200	.267	25	-2	0	0	0	1.000	2	/3-7,2-3	0.0
1980	Phi-N	49	62	4	10	1	1	0	5	2	7	.161	.200	.210	14	-7	0	1	-1	.958	0	3-34/2-9,S-5,1-1	-0.8
1981	Phi-N	11	1	0	0	0	0	0	0	0	1	.000	.000	.000	-96	-0	0	0	0	.800	1	/3-9,1-1,2-1	0.0
Total	10	277	559	37	90	14	1	6	44	29	109	.161	.205	.222	20	-59	4	5	-2	.951	18	3-212/2-24,1-20,S	-4.5

■ **FRANK WADDEY** Waddey, Frank Orum b: 8/21/05, Memphis, Tenn. d: 10/21/90, Knoxville, Tenn. BL/TL, 5′10.5″, 185 lbs. Deb: 4/16/31

YEAR	TM/L	G	AB	R	H	2B	3B	HR	RBI	BB	SO	AVG	OBP	SLG	PRO+	BR/A	SB	CS	SBR	FA	FR	G/POS	TPR
1931	StL-A	14	22	3	6	1	0	0	2	2	3	.273	.333	.318	70	-1	0	0	0	1.000	-3	/O-7	-0.4

■ **HAM WADE** Wade, Abraham Lincoln b: 12/20/1880, Spring City, Pa. d: 7/21/68, Riverside, N.J. BR/TR, 5′8″, 155 lbs. Deb: 9/9/07

YEAR	TM/L	G	AB	R	H	2B	3B	HR	RBI	BB	SO	AVG	OBP	SLG	PRO+	BR/A	SB	CS	SBR	FA	FR	G/POS	TPR
1907	NY-N	1	0	0	0	0	0	0	0	0		—	1.000	—	208	0	0			1.000	0	/O-1	0.0

■ **GALE WADE** Wade, Galeard Lee b: 1/20/29, Hollister, Mo. BL/TR, 6′1.5″, 185 lbs. Deb: 4/11/55

YEAR	TM/L	G	AB	R	H	2B	3B	HR	RBI	BB	SO	AVG	OBP	SLG	PRO+	BR/A	SB	CS	SBR	FA	FR	G/POS	TPR
1955	Chi-N	9	33	5	6	1	0	1	1	4	3	.182	.270	.303	52	-2	0	0	0	.867	-2	/O-9	-0.5
1956	Chi-N	10	12	0	0	0	0	0	0	1	0	.000	.077	.000	-78	-3	0	0	0	.875	-0	/O-3	-0.4
Total	2	19	45	5	6	1	0	1	1	5	3	.133	.220	.222	18	-5	0	0	0	.870	-2	/O-12	-0.9

■ **RIP WADE** Wade, Richard Frank b: 1/12/1898, Duluth, Minn. d: 7/15/57, Duluth, Minn. BL/TR, 5′11″, 174 lbs. Deb: 4/19/23

YEAR	TM/L	G	AB	R	H	2B	3B	HR	RBI	BB	SO	AVG	OBP	SLG	PRO+	BR/A	SB	CS	SBR	FA	FR	G/POS	TPR
1923	Was-A	33	69	8	16	2	2	2	14	5	10	.232	.284	.406	84	-2	0	0	0	.967	-2	O-19	-0.5

■ **WOODY WAGENHORST** Wagenhorst, Ellwood Otto b: 6/3/1863, Kutztown, Pa. d: 2/12/46, Washington, D.C. 5′11″, 165 lbs. Deb: 6/25/1888

YEAR	TM/L	G	AB	R	H	2B	3B	HR	RBI	BB	SO	AVG	OBP	SLG	PRO+	BR/A	SB	CS	SBR	FA	FR	G/POS	TPR
1888	Phi-N	2	8	2	1	0	0	0	0	0	1	.125	.125	.125	-19	-1	0			.800	-1	/3-2	-0.2

■ **BUTTS WAGNER** Wagner, Albert b: 9/17/1871, Chartiers, Pa. d: 11/26/28, Pittsburgh, Pa. BR/TR, 5′10″, 170 lbs. Deb: 4/27/1898 F

YEAR	TM/L	G	AB	R	H	2B	3B	HR	RBI	BB	SO	AVG	OBP	SLG	PRO+	BR/A	SB	CS	SBR	FA	FR	G/POS	TPR
1898	Was-N	63	223	20	50	11	2	1	31	14		.224	.279	.305	67	-10	4			.833	-11	3-39,O-10/S-8,2-5	-1.9
	Bro-N	11	38	2	9	1	1	0	3	2		.237	.275	.316	69	-2	0			.813	-3	3-11	-0.4
	Yr	74	261	22	59	12	3	1	34	16		.226	.279	.307	68	-12	4			.828	-14	3-50,O-10/S-8,2-5	-2.3

■ **HEINIE WAGNER** Wagner, Charles F. b: 9/23/1880, New York, N.Y. d: 3/20/43, New Rochelle, N.Y. BR/TR, 5′9″, 183 lbs. Deb: 7/1/02 MC

YEAR	TM/L	G	AB	R	H	2B	3B	HR	RBI	BB	SO	AVG	OBP	SLG	PRO+	BR/A	SB	CS	SBR	FA	FR	G/POS	TPR
1902	NY-N	17	56	4	12	1	0	0	2	0		.214	.214	.232	38	-4	3			.862	-3	S-17	-0.6
1906	Bos-A	9	32	1	9	0	0	0	4	1		.281	.303	.281	83	-1	2			.943	1	/2-9	0.1
1907	Bos-A	111	385	29	82	10	4	2	21	31		.213	.275	.275	76	-10	20			.931	2	*S-109/2-1,3-1	-0.6
1908	Bos-A	153	526	62	130	11	5	1	46	27		.247	.288	.293	86	-8	20			.939	32	*S-153	3.0
1909	Bos-A	124	430	53	110	16	7	1	49	35		.256	.316	.333	103	1	18			.933	14	*S-123/2-1	2.0
1910	Bos-A	142	491	61	134	26	7	1	52	44		.273	.335	.360	115	8	26			.927	-12	*S-140	0.2
1911	Bos-A	80	261	34	67	13	8	1	38	29		.257	.340	.379	101	0	15			.946	-4	2-40,S-32	-0.2
1912	*Bos-A	144	504	75	138	25	6	2	68	62		.274	.358	.359	100	1	21			.922	-13	*S-144	0.0
1913	Bos-A	110	365	43	83	14	8	2	34	40	29	.227	.316	.326	86	-7	9			.937	4	*S-103/2-5,3-1	0.7
1915	Bos-A	84	267	38	64	11	2	0	29	37	34	.240	.339	.296	93	-1	8	4	0	.927	-16	2-79/3-1,O-1	-1.7
1916	Bos-A	6	8	2	4	1	0	0	0	3	0	.500	.636	.625	278	2	2			1.000	2	/3-4,2-1,S-1	0.5
1918	Bos-A	3	8	0	1	0	0	0	0	1	0	.125	.222	.125	5	-1	0			.900	-0	/2-2,3-1	-0.1
Total	12	983	3333	402	834	128	47	10	343	310	63	.250	.319	.326	95	-19	144	4		.928	8	S-822,2-138/3-8,O-1	3.3

■ **HAL WAGNER** Wagner, Harold Edward b: 7/2/15, E.Riverton, N.J. d: 8/7/79, Riverside, N.J. BL/TR, 6′, 165 lbs. Deb: 10/3/37

YEAR	TM/L	G	AB	R	H	2B	3B	HR	RBI	BB	SO	AVG	OBP	SLG	PRO+	BR/A	SB	CS	SBR	FA	FR	G/POS	TPR
1937	Phi-A	1	0	0	0	0	0	0	0	0	0	—	—	—	—	0	0	0	0	1.000	0	/C-1	0.0
1938	Phi-A	33	88	10	20	2	1	0	8	8	9	.227	.299	.273	45	-7	0	0	0	.972	-1	C-30	-0.7
1939	Phi-A	5	8	0	1	0	0	0	0	0	3	.125	.125	.125	-37	-2	0	0	0	1.000	2	/C-5	0.0
1940	Phi-A	34	75	9	19	5	1	0	10	11	6	.253	.356	.347	85	-1	0	0	0	.964	3	C-28	0.3
1941	Phi-A	46	131	18	29	8	2	1	15	19	9	.221	.320	.336	75	-5	1	0	0	.976	2	C-42	0.1
1942	Phi-A☆	104	288	26	68	17	1	1	30	24	29	.236	.304	.313	74	-10	1	0	0	.986	-2	C-94	-0.6
1943	Phi-A	111	289	22	69	17	1	1	26	36	17	.239	.327	.315	89	-4	3	3	-1	.980	-8	C-99	-0.7
1944	Phi-A	5	4	0	1	0	0	0	0	0	0	.250	.250	.250	44	-0	0	0	0	1.000	0	/C-1	0.0
	Bos-A	66	223	21	74	13	4	1	38	29	14	.332	.418	.439	147	15	1	1	-0	.970	0	C-64	1.9
	Yr	71	227	21	75	13	4	1	38	29	14	.330	.415	.436	145	15	1	1	-0	.971	0	C-65	1.9
1946	*Bos-A★	117	370	39	85	12	2	6	52	69	32	.230	.354	.322	85	-5	3	1	0	.983	-7	*C-116	-0.6
1947	Bos-A	21	65	5	15	3	0	0	6	9	5	.231	.324	.277	63	-3	0	0	0	.978	-1	C-21	-0.3
	Det-A	71	191	19	55	10	0	5	33	28	16	.288	.382	.419	119	5	0	1	-1	.990	-4	C-71	0.5
	Yr	92	256	24	70	13	0	5	39	37	21	.273	.367	.383	105	2	0	1	-1	.987	-5	C-92	0.2
1948	Det-A	54	109	10	22	3	0	0	10	20	11	.202	.326	.229	48	-8	1	0	0	.989	-4	C-52	-0.8
	Phi-N	3	4	0	0	0	0	0	0	0	0	.000	.000	.000	-99	-1	0			1.000	1	/C-1	0.0
1949	Phi-N	1	4	0	0	0	0	0	0	0	1	.000	.000	.000	-99	-1	0			.750	-1	/C-1	-0.2
Total	12	672	1849	179	458	90	12	15	228	253	152	.248	.343	.334	87	-27	10	6		.981	-21	C-626	-1.1

■ **HONUS WAGNER** Wagner, John Peter "The Flying Dutchman" b: 2/24/1874, Chartiers, Pa. d: 12/6/55, Carnegie, Pa. BR/TR, 5′11″, 200 lbs. Deb: 7/19/1897 FMCH

YEAR	TM/L	G	AB	R	H	2B	3B	HR	RBI	BB	SO	AVG	OBP	SLG	PRO+	BR/A	SB	CS	SBR	FA	FR	G/POS	TPR
1897	Lou-N	61	237	37	80	17	4	2	39	15		.338	.379	.468	127	9	19			.908	3	O-52/2-9	0.7
1898	Lou-N	151	588	80	176	29	3	10	105	31		.299	.341	.410	117	10	27			.972	-4	1-75,3-65,2-10	0.7
1899	Lou-N	147	571	98	192	43	13	7	113	40		.336	.391	.494	142	31	37			.928	1	3-75,O-61/2-7,1-4	2.6
1900	*Pit-N	135	527	107	201	**45**	**22**	4	100	41		**.381**	.434	**.573**	**175**	52	38			.965	-8	*O-118/3-9,2-7,1P	3.3
1901	Pit-N	140	549	101	194	37	11	6	**126**	53		.353	.417	.494	159	41	**49**			.918	10	S-61,O-54,3-24,/2-1	5.1
1902	Pit-N	136	534	**105**	176	**30**	16	3	**91**	43		.330	.394	**.463**	**159**	**36**	**42**			1.000	8	O-61,S-44,1-32,/P2	4.4
1903	*Pit-N	129	512	97	182	30	**19**	5	101	44		**.355**	.414	.518	160	39	46			.933	25	*S-111,O-12/1-6	**6.3**
1904	Pit-N	132	490	97	171	**44**	14	4	75	59		**.349**	**.423**	**.520**	**186**	**50**	**53**			.929	-6	*S-121/O-8,1-3,2-2	**4.8**
1905	Pit-N	147	548	114	199	32	14	6	101	54		.363	.427	.505	173	49	57			.935	20	*S-145/O-2	**7.3**
1906	Pit-N	142	516	**103**	175	**38**	9	2	71	58		**.339**	.416	.459	166	40	53			.941	24	*S-137/O-2,3-1	**7.3**

YEAR	TM/L	G	AB	R	H	2B	3B	HR	RBI	BB	SO	AVG	OBP	SLG	PRO+	BR/A	SB	CS	SBR	FA	FR	G/POS	TPR
1907	Pit-N	142	515	98	180	**38**	14	6	82	46		**.350**	**.408**	**.513**	**186**	**49**	**61**			.938	4	*S-138/1-4	**6.3**
1908	Pit-N	151	568	100	**201**	**39**	**19**	10	**109**	54		**.354**	**.415**	**.542**	**205**	**65**	**53**			.943	-7	*S-151	**7.0**
1909	*Pit-N	137	495	92	168	**39**	10	5	**100**	66		**.339**	**.420**	**.489**	**168**	**39**	35			.940	6	*S-136/O-1	**5.2**
1910	Pit-N	150	556	90	**178**	34	8	4	81	59	47	.320	.390	.432	132	22	24			.935	3	*S-138,1-11/2-2	3.2
1911	Pit-N	130	473	87	158	23	16	9	89	67	34	**.334**	.423	.507	154	35	20			.932	4	*S-101,1-28/O-1	**4.4**
1912	Pit-N	145	558	91	181	35	20	7	**102**	59	38	.324	.395	.496	145	34	26			**.962**	23	*S-143	**6.6**
1913	Pit-N	114	413	51	124	18	4	3	56	26	40	.300	.349	.385	114	7	21			**.962**	13	*S-105	3.1
1914	Pit-N	150	552	60	139	15	9	1	50	51	51	.252	.317	.317	93	-5	23			**.950**	7	*S-132,3-17/1-1	1.4
1915	Pit-N	156	566	68	155	32	17	6	78	39	64	.274	.325	.422	127	16	22	15	-2	**.948**	-5	*S-131,2-12,1-10	2.0
1916	Pit-N	123	432	45	124	15	9	1	39	34	36	.287	.350	.370	120	11	11			.942	-15	S-92,1-24/2-4	0.1
1917	Pit-N	74	230	15	61	7	1	0	24	24	17	.265	.337	.304	94	-1	5			.985	-4	1-47,3-18/2-2,SM	-0.7
Total	21	2792	10430	1736	3415	640	252	101	1732	963	327	.327	.391	.466	150	631	722	15		.940	101	*S-1887,O-372,13/2P	81.1

■ **JOE WAGNER** Wagner, Joseph Bernard b: 4/24/1889, New York, N.Y. d: 11/15/48, Bronx, N.Y. BR/TR, 5'11", 165 lbs. Deb: 4/25/15

1915	Cin-N	75	197	17	35	5	2	0	13	8	35	.178	.210	.223	31	-17	4	6	-2	.961	6	2-46,S-12/3-2	-1.4

■ **LEON WAGNER** Wagner, Leon Lamar "Daddy Wags" b: 5/13/34, Chattanooga, Tenn. BL/TR, 6'1", 195 lbs. Deb: 6/22/58

1958	SF-N	74	221	31	70	9	0	13	35	18	34	.317	.371	.534	139	12	1	0	0	.949	-0	O-57	0.9
1959	SF-N	87	129	20	29	4	3	5	22	25	24	.225	.363	.419	110	2	0	0	0	.941	-2	O-28	0.0
1960	StL-N	39	98	12	21	2	0	4	11	17	17	.214	.336	.357	83	-2	0	1	-1	.963	1	O-32	-0.4
1961	LA-A	133	453	74	127	19	2	28	79	48	65	.280	.353	.517	116	9	5	1	1	.971	2	*O-116	0.5
1962	LA-A★	160	612	96	164	21	5	37	107	50	87	.268	.328	.500	123	17	7	5	-1	.972	-7	*O-156	0.0
1963	LA-A★	149	550	73	160	11	1	26	90	49	73	.291	.356	.456	134	24	5	7	-3	.960	-2	*O-141	1.3
1964	Cle-A	163	641	94	162	19	2	31	100	56	121	.253	.319	.434	108	6	14	2	3	.959	-1	*O-163	0.0
1965	Cle-A	144	517	91	152	18	1	28	79	60	52	.294	.371	.495	143	29	12	2	2	.957	-9	*O-134	1.7
1966	Cle-A	150	549	70	153	20	0	23	66	46	69	.279	.336	.441	121	14	5	2	0	.990	-8	*O-139	0.0
1967	Cle-A	135	433	56	105	15	1	15	54	37	76	.242	.320	.386	107	4	3	3	-1	.980	-7	*O-117	-1.1
1968	Cle-A	38	49	5	9	4	0	0	6	6	6	.184	.273	.265	65	-2	0	0	0	.500	-3	O-10	-0.7
	Chi-A	69	162	14	46	8	0	1	18	21	31	.284	.366	.352	117	4	2	1	0	.941	-8	O-46	-0.7
	Yr	107	211	19	55	12	0	1	24	27	37	.261	.345	.332	106	2	2	1	0	.895	-11	O-56	-1.4
1969	SF-N	11	12	0	4	0	0	0	2	2	1	.333	.467	.333	130	1	0	0	0	1.000	0	/O-1	0.1
Total	12	1352	4426	636	1202	150	15	211	669	435	656	.272	.343	.455	121	117	54	24	2	.964	-44	*O-1140	1.6

■ **MARK WAGNER** Wagner, Mark Duane b: 3/4/54, Conneaut, Ohio BR/TR, 6'1", 175 lbs. Deb: 8/20/76

1976	Det-A	39	115	9	30	2	3	0	12	6	18	.261	.298	.330	81	-3	0	2	-1	.947	10	S-39	1.0
1977	Det-A	22	48	4	7	0	1	1	3	4	12	.146	.226	.250	28	-5	0	1	-1	.923	-1	S-21/2-1	-0.5
1978	Det-A	39	109	10	26	1	2	0	6	3	11	.239	.272	.284	55	-6	1	0	0	.964	-6	S-35/2-4	-0.9
1979	Det-A	75	146	16	40	3	0	1	13	16	25	.274	.346	.315	77	-4	3	2	-0	.974	8	S-41,2-29/3-2,D-1	0.7
1980	Det-A	45	72	5	17	1	0	0	3	7	11	.236	.304	.250	52	-4	0	1	-1	.935	2	S-28/3-9,2-6	-0.1
1981	Tex-A	50	85	15	22	4	1	1	14	8	13	.259	.323	.365	103	0	1	1	-0	.964	2	S-43/2-4,3-2	0.5
1982	Tex-A	60	179	14	43	4	1	0	8	10	28	.240	.280	.274	56	-11	1	0	0	.955	-0	S-60	-0.5
1983	Tex-A	2	2	0	0	0	0	0	0	0	1	.000	.000	.000	-99	-1	0	0	0	1.000	1	/S-2	0.1
1984	Oak-A	82	87	8	20	5	1	0	12	7	11	.230	.287	.310	70	-4	2	0	1	.951	12	S-57,3-15/2-8,PD	1.0
Total	9	414	843	81	205	20	9	3	71	61	130	.243	.297	.299	66	-38	8	7	-2	.953	26	S-326/2-52,3-28,DP	1.3

■ **BILL WAGNER** Wagner, William Joseph b: 1/2/1894, Jesup, Iowa d: 1/11/51, Waterloo, Iowa BR/TR, 6', 187 lbs. Deb: 7/16/14

1914	Pit-N	3	1	0	0	0	0	0	0	0	0	.000	.000	.000	-99	-0	0			1.000	0	/C-3	0.0
1915	Pit-N	5	5	0	0	0	0	0	0	1	2	.000	.167	.000	-48	-1	0			1.000	2	/C-3	0.1
1916	Pit-N	19	38	2	9	0	2	0	2	5	8	.237	.326	.342	104	0	0			.936	2	C-15	0.3
1917	Pit-N	53	151	15	31	7	2	0	9	11	22	.205	.264	.278	64	-6	1			.958	-4	C-37,1-12	-0.9
1918	Bos-N	13	47	2	10	0	0	1	7	4	5	.213	.275	.277	71	-2	0			.917	-5	C-13	-0.6
Total	5	93	242	19	50	7	4	1	18	21	37	.207	.273	.281	69	-9	1			.947	-5	/C-71,1-12	-1.1

■ **KERMIT WAHL** Wahl, Kermit Emerson b: 11/18/22, Columbia, S.Dak. d: 9/16/87, Tucson, Ariz. BR/TR, 5'11", 170 lbs. Deb: 6/23/44

1944	Cin-N	4	1	0	0	0	0	0	0	0	0	.000	.000	.000	-99	-0	0			.000	0	/3-1	0.0
1945	Cin-N	71	194	18	39	8	2	0	10	23	22	.201	.286	.263	54	-12	2			.948	5	2-32,S-31/3-7	-0.3
1947	Cin-N	39	81	8	14	0	0	1	4	6	12	.173	.239	.210	20	-9	0			.964	6	3-20/S-9,2-2	-0.3
1950	Phi-A	89	280	26	72	12	3	2	27	30	30	.257	.331	.343	74	-11	1	1	-0	.946	11	3-61,S-18/2-2	0.0
1951	Phi-A	20	59	4	11	2	0	0	6	9	5	.186	.294	.220	40	-5	0	0	0	.967	2	3-18	-0.3
	StL-A	8	27	2	9	1	1	0	3	0	3	.333	.333	.444	106	0	0	0	0	.950	1	/3-6	0.0
	Yr	28	86	6	20	3	1	0	9	9	8	.233	.305	.291	60	-5	0	0	0	.962	3	3-24	-0.3
Total	5	231	642	58	145	23	6	3	50	68	72	.226	.302	.294	60	-37	3	1		.949	25	3-113/S-58,2-36	-0.9

■ **EDDIE WAITKUS** Waitkus, Edward Stephen b: 9/4/19, Cambridge, Mass. d: 9/15/72, Jamaica Plain, Mass. BL/TL, 6'1", 175 lbs. Deb: 4/15/41

1941	Chi-N	12	28	1	5	0	0	0	0	0	3	.179	.207	.179	10	-3	0			.949	-1	/1-9	-0.5
1946	Chi-N	113	441	50	134	24	5	4	55	23	14	.304	.340	.408	114	6	3			.996	4	*1-106	0.4
1947	Chi-N	130	514	60	150	28	6	2	35	32	17	.292	.336	.381	94	-5	3			.994	8	*1-126	-0.2
1948	Chi-N★	139	562	87	166	27	10	7	44	43	19	.295	.348	.416	110	7	11			.992	7	*1-116,O-20	1.1
1949	Phi-N†	54	209	41	64	16	3	1	28	33	12	.306	.403	.426	126	9	3			.994	1	1-54	0.9
1950	*Phi-N	154	641	102	182	32	5	2	44	55	29	.284	.341	.359	86	-12	3			.993	-2	*1-154	-1.8
1951	Phi-N	145	610	65	157	27	4	1	46	53	22	.257	.317	.320	73	-23	0	3	-2	.992	-2	*1-144	-3.4
1952	Phi-N	146	499	51	144	29	4	2	49	64	23	.289	.371	.375	108	7	2	2	-1	.991	-2	*1-146	0.0
1953	Phi-N	81	247	24	72	9	2	1	16	13	23	.291	.330	.356	79	-7	1	1	-0	.989	-1	1-59	-1.1
1954	Bal-A	95	311	35	88	17	4	2	33	28	25	.283	.344	.383	107	2	0	1	-1	1.000	1	1-78	-0.2
1955	Bal-A	38	85	2	22	1	1	0	9	11	10	.259	.344	.294	78	-2	2	0	1	.974	-2	1-26	-0.5
	Phi-N	33	107	10	30	5	0	2	14	17	7	.280	.379	.383	105	1	0	1	-1	.996	0	1-31	-0.1
Total	11	1140	4254	528	1214	215	44	24	373	372	204	.285	.344	.374	96	-21	28	8		.993	10	*1-1049/O-20	-5.4

■ **CHARLIE WAITT** Waitt, Charles C. b: 10/14/1853, Hallowell, Me. d: 10/21/12, San Francisco, Cal. TR, 5'11", 165 lbs. Deb: 5/25/1875

1875	StL-n	30	113	14	23	10	0	0	12	2	7	.204	.217	.292	83	-1	3	2	-0	.787	-3	O-28/1-4	-0.4
1877	Chi-N	10	41	2	4	0	0	0	2	0	3	.098	.098	.098	-34	-6				.793	2	O-10	-0.4
1882	Bal-a	72	250	19	39	4	0	0		13		.156	.198	.172	28	-17				.874	0	*O-72	-1.6
1883	Phi-N	1	3	0	1	0	0	0	0	0	1	.333	.333	.333	114	0				.333	-1	/O-1	-0.1
Total	3	83	294	21	44	4	0	0	2	13	4	.150	.186	.163	18	-24				.855	1	/O-83	-2.1

■ **DON WAKAMATSU** Wakamatsu, Wilbur Donald b: 2/22/63, Hood River, Ore. BR/TR, 6'2", 200 lbs. Deb: 5/22/91

1991	Chi-A	18	31	2	7	0	0	0	0	1	6	.226	.250	.226	33	-3	0	0	0	1.000	-0	C-18	-0.3

■ **HOWARD WAKEFIELD** Wakefield, Howard John b: 4/2/1884, Ducyrus, Ohio d: 4/16/41, Chicago, Ill. BR/TR, 6'1", 185 lbs. Deb: 9/18/05 F

1905	Cle-A	10	26	3	4	0	0	0	1	0		.154	.185	.154	8	-3	0			.926	-3	/C-8	-0.5
1906	Was-A	77	211	17	59	9	2	1	21	7		.280	.303	.355	111	2	6			.946	-15	C-60	-0.8
1907	Cle-A	26	37	4	5	2	0	0	3	3		.135	.200	.189	24	-3	0			.930	-0	C-11	-0.3
Total	3	113	274	24	68	11	2	1	25	10		.248	.277	.314	89	-4	6			.943	-18	/C-79	-1.6

■ **DICK WAKEFIELD** Wakefield, Richard Cummings b: 5/6/21, Chicago, Ill. d: 8/26/85, Redford, Mich. BL/TR, 6'4", 210 lbs. Deb: 6/26/41 F

1941	Det-A	7	7	0	1	0	0	0	0	0	1	.143	.143	.143	-22	-1	0	0	0	1.000	-0	/O-1	-0.1
1943	Det-A★	155	633	91	**200**	**38**	8	7	79	62	60	.316	.377	.434	127	21	4	5	-2	.959	-6	*O-155	0.6
1944	Det-A	78	276	53	98	15	5	12	53	55	29	.355	.464	.576	186	33	2	2	-1	.963	-4	O-78	2.5
1946	Det-A	111	396	64	106	11	5	12	59	59	55	.268	.364	.412	110	6	3	5	-2	.964	0	*O-104	-0.1
1947	Det-A	112	368	59	104	15	5	8	51	80	44	.283	.412	.416	127	17	1	4	-2	.950	-2	*O-101	0.7
1948	Det-A	110	322	50	89	20	5	11	53	70	55	.276	.406	.472	129	15	0	1	-1	.948	0	O-86	1.0
1949	Det-A	59	126	17	26	3	1	6	19	32	24	.206	.367	.389	100	0	0	0	0	1.000	2	O-32	0.0

YEAR	TM/L	G	AB	R	H	2B	3B	HR	RBI	BB	SO	AVG	OBP	SLG	PRO+	BR/A	SB	CS	SBR	FA	FR	G/POS	TPR
1950	NY-A	3	2	0	1	0	0	0	1	1	1	.500	.667	.500	208	1	0	0	0	.000	0	H	0.0
1952	NY-N	3	2	0	0	0	0	0	0	1	1	.000	.333	.000	-0	-0	0	0	0	.000	0	H	0.0
Total	9	638	2132	334	625	102	29	56	315	360	270	.293	.396	.447	130	92	10	17	-7	.959	-11	O-557	4.6

■ MATT WALBECK
Walbeck, Matthew Lovick b: 10/2/69, Sacramento, Cal. BB/TR, 5′11″, 190 lbs. Deb: 4/7/93

YEAR	TM/L	G	AB	R	H	2B	3B	HR	RBI	BB	SO	AVG	OBP	SLG	PRO+	BR/A	SB	CS	SBR	FA	FR	G/POS	TPR
1993	Chi-N	11	30	2	6	2	0	1	6	1	6	.200	.226	.367	56	-2	0	0	0	1.000	-0	C-11	-0.2
1994	Min-A	97	338	31	69	12	0	5	35	17	37	.204	.246	.284	36	-32	1	1	-0	.993	-7	C-95/D-1	-3.2
1995	Min-A	115	393	40	101	18	1	1	44	25	71	.257	.303	.316	61	-22	3	1	0	.991	-15	*C-113	-2.8
1996	Min-A	63	215	25	48	10	0	2	24	9	34	.223	.254	.298	38	-20	3	1	0	.994	-5	C-61	-2.0
1997	Det-A	47	137	18	38	3	0	3	10	12	19	.277	.336	.365	83	-3	3	3	-1	.988	-2	C-44	-0.3
1998	Ana-A	108	338	41	87	15	2	6	46	30	68	.257	.322	.367	78	-11	1	1	-0	.990	7	*C-104/D-2	0.2
Total	6	441	1451	157	349	60	3	18	165	94	235	.241	.289	.323	58	-91	11	7	-1	.991	-22	C-428/D-3	-8.3

■ ED WALCZAK
Walczak, Edwin Joseph "Husky" b: 9/21/18, Arctic, R.I. d: 3/10/98, Norwich, Conn. BR/TR, 5′11″, 180 lbs. Deb: 9/3/45

YEAR	TM/L	G	AB	R	H	2B	3B	HR	RBI	BB	SO	AVG	OBP	SLG	PRO+	BR/A	SB	CS	SBR	FA	FR	G/POS	TPR
1945	Phi-N	20	57	6	12	3	0	0	2	6	9	.211	.286	.263	55	-3	0			.966	1	2-17/S-2	-0.2

■ FRED WALDEN
Walden, Thomas Fred b: 6/25/1890, Fayette, Mo. d: 9/27/55, Jefferson Barracks, Mo. BR/TR, Deb: 6/3/12

YEAR	TM/L	G	AB	R	H	2B	3B	HR	RBI	BB	SO	AVG	OBP	SLG	PRO+	BR/A	SB	CS	SBR	FA	FR	G/POS	TPR
1912	StL-A	1	0	0	0	0	0	0	0	0		—	—	—	—	0	0			.000	-1	/C-1	-0.1

■ IRV WALDRON
Waldron, Irving J. b: 1/21/1876, Hillside, N.Y. d: 7/22/44, Worcester, Mass. BR/TR, Deb: 4/25/01

YEAR	TM/L	G	AB	R	H	2B	3B	HR	RBI	BB	SO	AVG	OBP	SLG	PRO+	BR/A	SB	CS	SBR	FA	FR	G/POS	TPR
1901	Mil-A	62	266	48	79	8	6	0	29	16		.297	.342	.372	103	1	12			.883	-2	O-62	-0.5
	Was-A	79	332	54	107	14	3	0	23	22		.322	.368	.383	110	5	8			.955	-5	O-78	-0.5
	Yr	141	598	102	186	22	9	0	52	38		.311	.356	.378	107	6	20			.923	-7	*O-140	-1.0

■ JIM WALEWANDER
Walewander, James b: 5/2/62, Chicago, Ill. BB/TR, 5′10″, 160 lbs. Deb: 5/31/87

YEAR	TM/L	G	AB	R	H	2B	3B	HR	RBI	BB	SO	AVG	OBP	SLG	PRO+	BR/A	SB	CS	SBR	FA	FR	G/POS	TPR
1987	Det-A	53	54	24	13	3	1	1	4	7	6	.241	.328	.389	93	-0	2	1	0	1.000	15	2-24,3-17/S-3,D-8	1.4
1988	Det-A	88	175	23	37	5	0	0	6	12	26	.211	.262	.240	43	-13	11	4	1	.977	14	2-61/S-8,3-3,D-9	0.4
1990	NY-A	9	5	1	1	1	0	0	1	0	0	.200	.200	.400	64	-0	1	1	-0	1.000	1	/2-2,3-2,S-1,D-2	0.1
1993	Cal-A	12	8	2	1	0	0	0	3	5	1	.125	.462	.125	64	0	1	1	-0	1.000	6	/S-6,2-2,D-3	0.5
Total	4	162	242	50	52	9	1	1	14	24	33	.215	.286	.273	57	-14	15	7	0	.982	37	/2-89,D-22,3-22,S	2.4

■ RUBE WALKER
Walker, Albert Bluford b: 5/16/26, Lenoir, N.C. d: 12/12/92, Morganton, N.C. BL/TR, 6′1″, 185 lbs. Deb: 4/20/48 C

YEAR	TM/L	G	AB	R	H	2B	3B	HR	RBI	BB	SO	AVG	OBP	SLG	PRO+	BR/A	SB	CS	SBR	FA	FR	G/POS	TPR
1948	Chi-N	79	171	17	47	8	0	5	26	24	17	.275	.371	.409	115	4	0			.980	-3	C-44	0.4
1949	Chi-N	56	172	11	42	4	1	3	22	9	18	.244	.282	.331	66	-9	0			.964	-5	C-43	-1.1
1950	Chi-N	74	213	19	49	7	1	6	16	18	34	.230	.290	.357	70	-10	0			.975	1	C-62	-0.6
1951	Chi-N	37	107	9	25	4	0	2	5	12	13	.234	.311	.327	71	-4	0			.969	-4	C-31	-0.7
	Bro-N	36	74	6	18	4	0	2	9	6	14	.243	.300	.378	80	-2	0	0	0	.972	-5	C-23	-0.6
	Yr	73	181	15	43	8	0	4	14	18	27	.238	.307	.348	74	-7	0	0	0	.970	-9	C-54	-1.3
1952	Bro-N	46	139	9	36	8	0	1	19	8	17	.259	.304	.338	77	-4	0	0	0	.987	5	C-40	0.3
1953	Bro-N	43	95	5	23	6	0	3	9	7	11	.242	.301	.400	79	-3	0	0	0	.978	1	C-28	-0.1
1954	Bro-N	50	155	12	28	7	0	5	23	24	17	.181	.294	.323	59	-10	0	0	0	.996	1	C-47	-0.6
1955	Bro-N	48	103	6	26	5	0	2	13	15	11	.252	.347	.359	86	-2	1	0	0	.987	2	C-35	0.1
1956	*Bro-N	54	146	5	31	6	1	3	20	7	18	.212	.248	.329	50	-10	0	1	-1	.986	-1	C-43	-1.1
1957	Bro-N	60	166	12	30	8	0	2	23	15	33	.181	.249	.265	35	-15	2	0	1	.992	-6	C-50	-1.9
1958	LA-N	25	44	3	5	2	0	1	7	5	10	.114	.204	.227	14	-6	0	0	0	.985	-2	C-20	-0.7
Total	11	608	1585	114	360	69	3	35	192	150	213	.227	.296	.341	68	-71	3	1		.982	-15	C-466	-6.6

■ TONY WALKER
Walker, Anthony Bruce b: 7/1/59, San Diego, Cal. BR/TR, 6′2″, 205 lbs. Deb: 4/8/86

YEAR	TM/L	G	AB	R	H	2B	3B	HR	RBI	BB	SO	AVG	OBP	SLG	PRO+	BR/A	SB	CS	SBR	FA	FR	G/POS	TPR
1986	Hou-N	84	90	19	20	7	0	2	10	11	15	.222	.307	.367	87	-2	11	3	2	.986	-14	O-68	-1.5

■ FRANK WALKER
Walker, Charles Franklin b: 9/22/1894, Enoree, S.C. d: 9/16/74, Bristol, Tenn. BR/TR, 5′11″, 165 lbs. Deb: 9/6/17

YEAR	TM/L	G	AB	R	H	2B	3B	HR	RBI	BB	SO	AVG	OBP	SLG	PRO+	BR/A	SB	CS	SBR	FA	FR	G/POS	TPR
1917	Det-A	2	2	0	0	0	0	0	0	0	1	.000	.000	.000	-99	-0	0			.000	0	H	-0.1
1918	Det-A	55	167	10	33	10	3	1	20	7	29	.198	.234	.311	67	-8	3			.922	-2	O-45	-1.4
1920	Phi-A	24	91	10	21	2	2	0	10	5	14	.231	.286	.297	54	-6	0	2	-1	.983	-1	O-24	-1.0
1921	Phi-A	19	66	6	15	3	0	1	6	8	11	.227	.311	.318	60	-4	1	0	0	.961	1	O-19	-0.4
1925	NY-N	39	81	12	18	1	0	1	5	9	11	.222	.308	.272	51	-6	1	1	-0	.960	-2	O-21	-0.8
Total	5	139	407	38	87	16	5	3	41	29	66	.214	.273	.300	58	-24	5	3		.949	-4	O-109	-3.7

■ TILLY WALKER
Walker, Clarence William b: 9/4/1887, Telford, Tenn. d: 9/20/59, Unicoi, Tenn BR/TR, 5′11″, 165 lbs. Deb: 4/12/11

YEAR	TM/L	G	AB	R	H	2B	3B	HR	RBI	BB	SO	AVG	OBP	SLG	PRO+	BR/A	SB	CS	SBR	FA	FR	G/POS	TPR
1911	Was-A	95	356	44	99	6	4	2	39	15		.278	.311	.334	82	-10	12			.917	-1	O-94	-1.6
1912	Was-A	39	110	22	30	2	1	0	9	8		.273	.333	.309	83	-2	11			.837	-3	O-34/2-1	-0.6
1913	StL-A	23	85	7	25	4	1	0	11	2	9	.294	.310	.365	100	-0	5			.911	-0	O-23	-0.2
1914	StL-A	151	517	67	154	24	16	6	78	51	72	.298	.365	.441	148	28	29	17	-2	.972	16	*O-145	3.9
1915	StL-A	144	510	53	137	20	7	5	49	36	77	.269	.323	.365	110	4	20	17	-4	.940	15	*O-139	0.8
1916	*Bos-A	128	467	68	124	29	11	3	46	23	45	.266	.303	.394	109	2	14			.959	-4	*O-128	-0.9
1917	Bos-A	106	337	41	83	18	7	2	37	25	38	.246	.300	.359	102	-1	6			.972	6	O-96	0.0
1918	Phi-A	114	414	56	122	20	0	**11**	48	41	44	.295	.360	.423	135	16	8			.953	5	*O-109	1.6
1919	Phi-A	125	456	47	133	30	6	10	64	26	41	.292	.330	.450	116	7	8			.933	-4	*O-115	-0.4
1920	Phi-A	149	585	79	157	23	7	17	82	41	59	.268	.321	.419	94	-8	8	3	1	.940	6	*O-149	-1.2
1921	Phi-A	142	556	89	169	32	5	23	101	73	41	.304	.389	.504	125	21	3	5	-2	.955	9	*O-142	1.6
1922	Phi-A	153	565	111	160	31	4	37	99	61	67	.283	.357	.549	130	21	4	3	-1	.956	-2	*O-148	0.8
1923	Phi-A	52	109	12	30	5	2	2	16	14	11	.275	.368	.413	104	1	1	2	-1	1.000	-2	O-26	-0.3
Total	13	1421	5067	696	1423	244	71	118	679	416	504	.281	.339	.427	115	80	129	47		.949	41	*O-1348/2-1	3.5

■ CHICO WALKER
Walker, Cleotha b: 11/25/58, Jackson, Miss. BB/TR, 5′9″, 179 lbs. Deb: 9/2/80

YEAR	TM/L	G	AB	R	H	2B	3B	HR	RBI	BB	SO	AVG	OBP	SLG	PRO+	BR/A	SB	CS	SBR	FA	FR	G/POS	TPR
1980	Bos-A	19	57	3	12	0	0	1	5	6	10	.211	.297	.263	52	-4	3	2	-0	.958	1	2-11/D-7	-0.3
1981	Bos-A	6	17	3	6	0	0	0	2	1	2	.353	.389	.353	108	0	0	2	-1	1.000	-2	/2-5	-0.3
1983	Bos-A	4	5	2	2	0	2	0	1	0	0	.400	.400	1.200	299	1	0	0	0	1.000	0	/O-3	0.1
1984	Bos-A	3	2	0	0	0	0	0	1	0	1	.000	.000	.000	-96	-1	0	0	0	1.000	0	/2-1	-0.1
1985	Chi-N	21	12	3	1	0	0	0	0	0	5	.083	.083	.083	-48	-2	1	0	0	1.000	-2	/O-6,2-2	-0.4
1986	Chi-N	28	101	21	28	3	2	1	7	10	20	.277	.342	.376	91	-1	15	4	2	.956	-5	O-26	-0.5
1987	Chi-N	47	105	15	21	4	0	0	7	12	23	.200	.282	.238	38	-9	11	4	1	.974	-5	O-33/3-2	-1.4
1988	Cal-A	33	78	8	12	1	0	0	2	6	15	.154	.214	.167	8	-9	2	1	0	.933	-2	O-17/2-7,3-2	-1.2
1991	Chi-N	124	374	51	96	10	1	6	34	33	57	.257	.317	.337	80	-9	13	5	1	.929	-23	3-57,O-53/2-6	-3.4
1992	Chi-N	19	26	2	3	0	0	0	2	3	4	.115	.207	.115	-6	-4	1	0	0	1.000	0	/O-6,2-2,3-2	-0.4
	NY-N	107	227	24	70	12	1	4	36	24	46	.308	.375	.423	127	8	14	1	4	.971	-7	3-36,2-16,O-15	0.5
	Yr	126	253	26	73	12	1	4	38	27	50	.289	.357	.391	113	5	15	1	4	.960	-7	3-38,O-21,2-18	0.1
1993	NY-N	115	213	18	48	7	1	5	19	14	29	.225	.273	.338	63	-11	7	0	2	.976	-4	2-24,3-23,O-15	-1.3
Total	11	526	1217	150	299	37	7	17	116	109	212	.246	.308	.329	75	-41	67	19	9	.968	-49	O-174,3-122/2-74,D	-8.7

■ DUANE WALKER
Walker, Duane Allen b: 3/13/57, Pasadena, Tex. BL/TL, 6′, 185 lbs. Deb: 5/25/82

YEAR	TM/L	G	AB	R	H	2B	3B	HR	RBI	BB	SO	AVG	OBP	SLG	PRO+	BR/A	SB	CS	SBR	FA	FR	G/POS	TPR
1982	Cin-N	86	239	26	52	10	0	5	22	27	58	.218	.302	.322	73	-8	9	3	1	.992	0	O-69	-0.9
1983	Cin-N	109	225	14	53	12	1	2	29	20	43	.236	.298	.324	70	-9	6	3	0	.956	0	O-60	-1.1
1984	Cin-N	83	195	35	57	10	3	10	28	33	35	.292	.395	.528	150	14	7	3	0	.950	-5	O-68	0.8
1985	Cin-N	37	48	5	8	2	1	2	6	6	18	.167	.259	.375	72	-2	1	0	0	.882	-1	O-10	-0.3
	Tex-A	53	132	14	23	2	0	5	11	15	29	.174	.264	.303	54	-8	2	1	0	1.000	1	O-32,D-10	-0.8
1988	StL-N	24	22	1	4	1	0	0	3	2	7	.182	.250	.227	38	-2	0	0	0	.000	-2	/O-4,1-1	-0.4
Total	5	392	861	95	197	37	5	24	99	103	190	.229	.313	.367	86	-16	25	10	2	.967	-6	O-243/D-10,1-1	-2.7

■ ERNIE WALKER
Walker, Ernest Robert b: 9/17/1890, Blossburg, Ala. d: 4/1/65, Pell City, Ala. BL/TR, 6′, 165 lbs. Deb: 4/13/13 F

YEAR	TM/L	G	AB	R	H	2B	3B	HR	RBI	BB	SO	AVG	OBP	SLG	PRO+	BR/A	SB	CS	SBR	FA	FR	G/POS	TPR
1913	StL-A	7	14	0	3	0	0	0	2	0	5	.214	.214	.214	26	-1	0			1.000	-0	/O-2	-0.2
1914	StL-A	74	131	19	39	5	3	1	14	13	26	.298	.366	.405	137	6	6	4	-1	.960	-6	O-38	-0.3

YEAR	TM/L	G	AB	R	H	2B	3B	HR	RBI	BB	SO	AVG	OBP	SLG	PRO+	BR/A	SB	CS	SBR	FA	FR	G/POS	TPR
1915	StL-A	50	109	15	23	4	2	0	9	23	32	.211	.348	.284	93	0	5	8	-3	.881	-6	O-33	-1.1
Total	3	131	254	34	65	9	5	1	25	36	63	.256	.351	.343	112	4	11	12		.928	-12	/O-73	-1.6

■ DIXIE WALKER Walker, Fred "The People's Cherce" b: 9/24/10, Villa Rica, Ga. d: 5/17/82, Birmingham, Ala. BL/TR, 6'1", 175 lbs. Deb: 4/28/31 FC

YEAR	TM/L	G	AB	R	H	2B	3B	HR	RBI	BB	SO	AVG	OBP	SLG	PRO+	BR/A	SB	CS	SBR	FA	FR	G/POS	TPR
1931	NY-A	2	10	1	3	2	0	0	1	0	4	.300	.300	.500	113	0	0	0	0	1.000	-0	/O-2	0.0
1933	NY-A	98	328	68	90	15	7	15	51	26	28	.274	.330	.500	125	9	2	2	-1	.962	5	O-77	0.9
1934	NY-A	17	17	2	2	0	0	0	0	1	3	.118	.167	.118	-27	-3	0	0	0	1.000	-0	/O-1	-0.3
1935	NY-A	8	13	1	2	1	0	0	1	0	1	.154	.154	.231	-2	-2	0	0	0	.750	-1	/O-2	-0.2
1936	NY-A	6	20	3	7	0	2	1	5	1	3	.350	.381	.700	167	2	1	1	-0	1.000	-1	/O-5	0.0
	Chi-A	26	70	12	19	2	0	0	11	14	6	.271	.400	.300	73	-2	1	0	0	1.000	1	O-17	-0.2
	Yr	32	90	15	26	2	2	1	16	15	9	.289	.396	.389	92	-1	2	1	0	1.000	-0	O-22	-0.2
1937	Chi-A	154	593	105	179	28	**16**	9	95	78	26	.302	.383	.449	109	9	1	2	-1	.952	-10	*O-154	-0.6
1938	Det-A	127	454	84	140	27	6	6	43	65	32	.308	.396	.434	102	3	5	4	-1	.979	-9	*O-114	-1.0
1939	Det-A	43	154	30	47	4	5	4	19	15	8	.305	.367	.474	106	1	4	1	1	.970	4	O-37	0.4
	Bro-N	61	225	27	63	6	4	2	38	20	10	.280	.339	.369	87	-4	1			.968	2	O-59	-0.4
1940	Bro-N	143	556	75	171	37	8	6	66	42	21	.308	.357	.435	111	8	3			.973	2	*O-136	0.3
1941	*Bro-N	148	531	88	165	32	8	9	71	70	18	.311	.391	.452	131	23	4			.976	11	*O-146	2.7
1942	Bro-N	118	393	57	114	28	1	6	54	47	15	.290	.367	.412	126	13	1			.986	-1	*O-110	0.7
1943	Bro-N★	138	540	83	163	32	6	5	71	49	24	.302	.363	.411	123	16	3			.969	3	*O-136	1.2
1944	Bro-N★	147	535	77	191	37	8	13	91	72	27	**.357**	.434	.529	173	53	6			.962	-3	*O-140	4.4
1945	Bro-N†	154	607	102	182	42	9	8	**124**	75	16	.300	.381	.438	128	24	6			.992	12	*O-153	2.8
1946	Bro-N★	150	576	80	184	29	9	9	116	67	28	.319	.391	.448	136	28	14			.969	-8	*O-149	1.4
1947	*Bro-N★	148	529	77	162	31	3	9	94	97	26	.306	.415	.427	119	19	6			.964	-8	*O-147	0.3
1948	Pit-N	129	408	39	129	19	3	2	54	52	18	.316	.393	.392	111	8	1			.977	-12	*O-112	-1.0
1949	Pit-N	88	181	26	51	4	1	1	18	26	11	.282	.372	.331	88	-2	0			.984	-4	O-39/1-3	-0.8
Total	18	1905	6740	1037	2064	376	96	105	1023	817	325	.306	.383	.437	121	202	59	10		.972	-16	*O-1736/1-3	10.6

■ GEE WALKER Walker, Gerald Holmes b: 3/19/08, Gulfport, Miss. d: 3/20/81, Whitfield, Miss. BR/TR, 5'11", 188 lbs. Deb: 4/14/31 FC

YEAR	TM/L	G	AB	R	H	2B	3B	HR	RBI	BB	SO	AVG	OBP	SLG	PRO+	BR/A	SB	CS	SBR	FA	FR	G/POS	TPR
1931	Det-A	59	189	20	56	17	2	1	28	14	21	.296	.345	.423	98	-1	10	7	-1	.953	-3	O-44	-0.8
1932	Det-A	127	480	71	155	32	6	8	78	13	38	.323	.345	.465	104	1	30	6	**5**	.949	4	*O-116	0.3
1933	Det-A	127	483	68	135	29	7	9	64	15	49	.280	.304	.424	89	-10	26	9	**2**	.942	-1	*O-113	-1.3
1934	*Det-A	98	347	54	104	19	2	6	39	19	20	.300	.340	.418	94	-4	20	9	1	.947	2	O-80	-0.4
1935	*Det-A	98	362	52	109	22	6	7	53	15	21	.301	.329	.453	104	0	6	4	-1	.954	-3	O-85	-0.6
1936	Det-A	134	550	105	194	55	5	12	93	23	30	.353	.387	.536	125	19	17	8	0	.948	5	*O-125	1.7
1937	Det-A†	151	635	105	213	42	4	18	113	41	74	.335	.380	.499	117	15	23	7	3	.956	-6	*O-151	0.6
1938	Chi-A	120	442	69	135	23	6	16	87	38	32	.305	.360	.493	109	5	9	4	0	.958	-5	*O-107	-0.4
1939	Chi-A	149	598	95	174	30	11	13	111	28	43	.291	.330	.443	94	-8	17	6	2	.967	9	*O-147	-0.2
1940	Was-A	140	595	87	175	29	7	13	96	24	58	.294	.325	.432	101	-2	21	4	4	.967	-2	*O-140	-0.7
1941	Cle-A	121	445	56	126	26	11	6	48	18	46	.283	.313	.431	100	-3	12	6	0	.982	8	*O-105	-0.2
1942	Cin-N	119	422	40	97	20	2	5	50	31	44	.230	.290	.322	79	-12	11			.973	4	*O-110	-1.4
1943	Cin-N	114	429	48	105	23	2	3	54	12	38	.245	.270	.329	74	-16	6			.980	-5	*O-106	-2.9
1944	Cin-N	121	478	56	133	21	3	5	62	23	48	.278	.318	.366	96	-4	7			.967	-7	*O-117	-1.8
1945	Cin-N	106	316	28	80	11	2	2	21	16	38	.253	.289	.320	71	-13	8			.962	-7	O-67/3-3	-2.4
Total	15	1784	6771	954	1991	399	76	124	997	330	600	.294	.331	.430	99	-32	223	70		.961	-7	*O-1613/3-3	-10.5

■ GREG WALKER Walker, Gregory Lee b: 10/6/59, Douglas, Ga. BL/TR, 6'3", 210 lbs. Deb: 9/18/82

YEAR	TM/L	G	AB	R	H	2B	3B	HR	RBI	BB	SO	AVG	OBP	SLG	PRO+	BR/A	SB	CS	SBR	FA	FR	G/POS	TPR
1982	Chi-A	11	17	3	7	2	1	2	7	2	3	.412	.474	1.000	292	4	0	0	0	.000	0	/D-4	0.4
1983	*Chi-A	118	307	32	83	16	3	10	55	28	57	.270	.335	.440	107	3	2	1	0	.985	-7	1-59,D-21	-0.8
1984	Chi-A	136	442	62	130	29	2	24	75	35	66	.294	.349	.532	134	19	8	5	-1	.995	-5	*1-101,D-21	0.7
1985	Chi-A	163	601	77	155	38	4	24	92	44	100	.258	.311	.454	102	0	5	2	0	.994	-3	*1-151/D-7	-1.1
1986	Chi-A	78	282	37	78	10	6	13	51	29	44	.277	.348	.493	122	8	1	2	-1	.993	-1	1-77/D-1	0.1
1987	Chi-A	157	566	85	145	33	2	27	94	75	112	.256	.348	.465	110	9	2	1	0	.994	-14	*1-154/D-3	-1.6
1988	Chi-A	99	377	45	93	22	1	8	42	29	77	.247	.306	.374	90	-6	0	1	-1	.993	-14	1-98	-2.9
1989	Chi-A	77	233	25	49	14	0	5	26	23	50	.210	.290	.335	77	-7	0	0	0	.987	-6	1-48,D-23	-1.7
1990	Chi-A	2	5	0	1	0	0	0	0	0	2	.200	.200	.200	12	-1	0	0	0	1.000	0	/1-1,D-1	0.0
	Bal-A	14	34	2	5	0	0	0	2	3	9	.147	.237	.147	10	-4	1	0	0	.000	0	D-11	-0.4
	Yr	16	39	2	6	0	0	0	2	3	11	.154	.233	.154	10	-5	1	0	0	1.000	0	D-12/1-1	-0.4
Total	9	855	2864	368	746	164	19	113	444	268	520	.260	.328	.449	108	26	19	12	-2	.993	-49	1-689/D-92	-7.3

■ HARRY WALKER Walker, Harry William "Harry The Hat" b: 10/22/16, Pascagoula, Miss. BL/TR, 6'2", 190 lbs. Deb: 9/25/40 FMC

YEAR	TM/L	G	AB	R	H	2B	3B	HR	RBI	BB	SO	AVG	OBP	SLG	PRO+	BR/A	SB	CS	SBR	FA	FR	G/POS	TPR
1940	StL-N	7	27	2	5	2	0	0	6	0	2	.185	.185	.259	20	-3	0			1.000	2	/O-7	-0.1
1941	StL-N	7	15	3	4	1	0	0	1	2	1	.267	.353	.333	88	-0	0			.875	-1	/O-5	-0.2
1942	*StL-N	74	191	38	60	12	2	0	16	11	14	.314	.355	.398	112	2	2			.968	-1	O-56/2-2	-0.1
1943	*StL-N★	148	564	76	166	28	6	2	53	40	24	.294	.341	.376	102	1	5			.965	-5	*O-144/2-1	-1.3
1946	*StL-N	112	346	53	82	14	6	3	27	30	29	.237	.300	.338	77	-11	12			.974	5	O-92/1-8	-1.1
1947	StL-N	10	25	2	5	1	0	0	0	4	2	.200	.310	.240	46	-2	0			.938	-2	O-10	-0.4
	Phi-N★	130	488	79	181	28	16	1	41	59	37	.371	.443	.500	156	41	13			.966	14	*O-127/1-4	4.6
	Yr	140	513	81	186	29	**16**	1	41	63	39	**.363**	.436	.487	150	39	13			.964	12	*O-137/1-4	4.2
1948	Phi-N	112	332	34	97	11	2	2	23	33	30	.292	.358	.355	95	-1	4			.981	2	O-81/1-4,3-1	-0.4
1949	Chi-N	42	159	20	42	6	3	1	14	11	6	.264	.312	.358	81	-4	2			.947	-3	O-39	-1.0
	Cin-N	86	314	53	100	15	2	1	23	34	17	.318	.385	.389	107	4	4			.963	2	O-77/1-1	0.2
	Yr	128	473	73	142	21	5	2	37	45	23	.300	.361	.378	99	-0	6			.959	-2	*O-116/1-1	-0.8
1950	StL-N	60	150	17	31	5	0	0	7	18	12	.207	.292	.240	40	-13	0			.969	-1	O-46/1-2	-1.5
1951	StL-N	8	26	6	8	1	0	0	2	2	1	.308	.357	.346	90	-0	0	0	0	1.000	-1	/O-6,1-1	-0.2
1955	StL-N	11	14	2	5	2	0	0	1	1	0	.357	.400	.500	137	1	0	0	0	1.000	1	/O-1,M	0.2
Total	11	807	2651	385	786	126	37	10	214	245	175	.296	.358	.383	103	15	42	0		.968	10	O-691/1-20,2-3,3-1	-1.3

■ HUB WALKER Walker, Harvey Willos b: 8/17/06, Gulfport, Miss. d: 11/26/82, San Jose, Cal. BL/TR, 5'10.5", 175 lbs. Deb: 4/15/31 F

YEAR	TM/L	G	AB	R	H	2B	3B	HR	RBI	BB	SO	AVG	OBP	SLG	PRO+	BR/A	SB	CS	SBR	FA	FR	G/POS	TPR
1931	Det-A	90	252	27	72	13	1	0	16	23	25	.286	.355	.345	82	-6	10	1	2	.961	-0	O-66	-0.7
1935	Det-A	9	25	4	4	3	0	0	1	3	4	.160	.250	.280	38	-2	0	0	0	1.000	-0	/O-7	-0.3
1936	Cin-N	92	258	49	71	18	1	4	23	35	32	.275	.366	.399	113	5	8			.970	-4	O-73/C-1,1-1	-0.1
1937	Cin-N	78	221	33	55	9	4	1	19	34	24	.249	.349	.339	92	-1	7			.993	4	O-58/2-3	0.0
1945	*Det-A	28	23	4	3	0	0	0	1	9	4	.130	.375	.130	46	-1	1	0	0	1.000	-2	/O-7	-0.3
Total	5	297	779	117	205	43	6	5	60	104	89	.263	.354	.353	92	-5	26	1		.975	-4	O-211/2-3,1-1,C-1	-1.4

■ JOHNNY WALKER Walker, John Miles b: 12/11/1896, Toulon, Ill. d: 8/19/76, Hollywood, Fla. BR/TR, 6', 175 lbs. Deb: 9/19/19

YEAR	TM/L	G	AB	R	H	2B	3B	HR	RBI	BB	SO	AVG	OBP	SLG	PRO+	BR/A	SB	CS	SBR	FA	FR	G/POS	TPR
1919	Phi-A	3	9	0	0	0	0	0	0	0	2	.000	.000	.000	-99	-2	0			.941	-0	/C-3	-0.2
1920	Phi-A	9	22	0	5	1	0	0	5	0	1	.227	.227	.273	32	-2	0	0	0	.960	-1	/C-6	-0.2
1921	Phi-A	113	423	41	109	14	5	2	46	9	29	.258	.278	.329	54	-30	5	0	2	.989	-6	1-99/C-7	-3.5
Total	3	125	454	41	114	15	5	2	51	9	32	.251	.270	.319	50	-35	5	0		.968	-7	/1-99,C-16	-3.9

■ SPEED WALKER Walker, Joseph Richard b: 1/23/1898, Munhall, Pa. d: 6/20/59, W.Mifflin, Pa. BR/TR, 6', 170 lbs. Deb: 9/15/23

YEAR	TM/L	G	AB	R	H	2B	3B	HR	RBI	BB	SO	AVG	OBP	SLG	PRO+	BR/A	SB	CS	SBR	FA	FR	G/POS	TPR
1923	StL-N	2	7	1	2	0	0	0	0	0	1	.286	.286	.286	52	-0	0	0	0	1.000	-0	/1-2	-0.1

■ LARRY WALKER Walker, Larry Kenneth Robert b: 12/1/66, Maple Ridge, B.C., Canada BL/TR, 6'3", 215 lbs. Deb: 8/16/89

YEAR	TM/L	G	AB	R	H	2B	3B	HR	RBI	BB	SO	AVG	OBP	SLG	PRO+	BR/A	SB	CS	SBR	FA	FR	G/POS	TPR
1989	Mon-N	20	47	4	8	0	0	0	4	5	13	.170	.264	.170	26	-4	1	1	-0	1.000	0	O-15	-0.5
1990	Mon-N	133	419	59	101	18	3	19	51	49	112	.241	.328	.434	112	6	21	7	2	.985	9	*O-124	1.5
1991	Mon-N	137	487	59	141	30	2	16	64	42	102	.290	.352	.458	128	17	14	9	-1	.991	9	*O-102,1-39	2.1
1992	Mon-N★	143	528	85	159	31	4	23	93	41	97	.301	.358	.506	143	28	18	6	2	.993	14	*O-139	4.4
1993	Mon-N	138	490	85	130	24	5	22	86	80	76	.265	.375	.469	119	15	29	7	5	.979	10	*O-132/1-4	2.6
1994	Mon-N	103	395	76	127	**44**	2	19	86	47	74	.322	.399	.587	151	30	15	5	2	.973	4	O-68,1-35	2.9

YEAR	TM/L	G	AB	R	H	2B	3B	HR	RBI	BB	SO	AVG	OBP	SLG	PRO+	BR/A	SB	CS	SBR	FA	FR	G/POS	TPR
1995	*Col-N	131	494	96	151	31	5	36	101	49	72	.306	.384	.607	121	11	16	3	3	.988	1	*O-129	1.1
1996	Col-N	83	272	58	75	18	4	18	58	20	58	.276	.346	.570	110	2	18	2	4	.994	-3	O-83	0.1
1997	Col-N★	153	568	143	208	46	4	**49**	130	78	90	.366	**.455**	**.720**	164	51	33	8	5	.992	-4	*O-151/1-3,D-1	4.7
1998	Col-N★	130	454	113	165	46	3	23	67	64	61	**.363**	.446	.630	147	32	14	4	2	.984	2	*O-123/2-1,3-1,D-1	3.3
Total	10	1171	4154	778	1265	288	32	225	740	475	755	.305	.385	.552	134	187	179	52	23	.987	41	*O-1066/1-81,D32	22.2

■ FLEET WALKER
Walker, Moses Fleetwood b: 10/7/1856, Mt.Pleasant, Ohio d: 5/11/24, Cleveland, Ohio BR/TR, 159 lbs. Deb: 5/1/1884 F

YEAR	TM/L	G	AB	R	H	2B	3B	HR	RBI	BB	SO	AVG	OBP	SLG	PRO+	BR/A	SB	CS	SBR	FA	FR	G/POS	TPR
1884	Tol-a	42	152	23	40	2	3	0		8		.263	.325	.316	106	1				.887	-6	C-41/O-1	-0.1

■ OSCAR WALKER
Walker, Oscar b: 3/18/1854, Brooklyn, N.Y. d: 5/20/1889, Brooklyn, N.Y. BL/TL, 5'10", 166 lbs. Deb: 9/17/1875

YEAR	TM/L	G	AB	R	H	2B	3B	HR	RBI	BB	SO	AVG	OBP	SLG	PRO+	BR/A	SB	CS	SBR	FA	FR	G/POS	TPR
1875	Atl-n	1	2	0	0	0	0	0	0	1	0	.000	.333	.000	30	-0	0	0	0	.400	-0	/1-1,O-1	0.0
1879	Buf-N	72	287	35	79	15	6	1	35	8	38	.275	.295	.380	118	5				.946	3	*1-72	0.5
1880	Buf-N	34	126	12	29	4	2	1	15	6	18	.230	.265	.317	95	-1				.917	-2	1-24,O-11	-0.4
1882	StL-a	76	318	48	76	15	7	**7**		10		.239	.262	.396	115	4				.846	8	*O-75/2-1,1-1	1.0
1884	Bro-a	95	382	59	103	12	8	2		9		.270	.292	.359	110	4				.868	0	O-59,1-36	-0.1
1885	Bal-a	4	13	1	0	0	0	0	1	0		.000	.000	.000	-99	-3				.667	-1	/O-4	-0.4
Total	5	281	1126	155	287	46	23	11	51	33	56	.255	.278	.366	109	9				.850	8	O-149,1-133/2-1	0.6

■ TODD WALKER
Walker, Todd Arthur b: 5/25/73, Bakersfield, Cal. BL/TR, 6', 180 lbs. Deb: 8/30/96

YEAR	TM/L	G	AB	R	H	2B	3B	HR	RBI	BB	SO	AVG	OBP	SLG	PRO+	BR/A	SB	CS	SBR	FA	FR	G/POS	TPR
1996	Min-A	25	82	8	21	6	0	0	6	4	13	.256	.291	.329	55	-6	2	0	1	.956	-0	3-20/2-4,D-1	-0.5
1997	Min-A	52	156	15	37	7	1	3	16	11	30	.237	.292	.353	66	-8	7	0	2	.969	2	3-40/2-8,D-2	-0.3
1998	Min-A	143	528	85	167	41	3	12	62	47	65	.316	.374	.473	118	15	19	7	2	.978	-23	*2-140/D-1	0.1
Total	3	220	766	108	225	54	4	15	84	62	108	.294	.349	.433	101	1	28	7	4	.978	-21	2-152/3-60,D-4	-0.7

■ WALT WALKER
Walker, Walter S. b: 3/12/1860, Berlin, Mich. d: 2/28/22, Pontiac, Mich. TR, 5'10.5", 162 lbs. Deb: 5/8/1884

YEAR	TM/L	G	AB	R	H	2B	3B	HR	RBI	BB	SO	AVG	OBP	SLG	PRO+	BR/A	SB	CS	SBR	FA	FR	G/POS	TPR
1884	Det-N	1	4	1	1	0	0	0	0	0	0	.250	.250	.250	61	-0				.750	-1	C-1	-0.1

■ WELDAY WALKER
Walker, Welday Wilberforce b: 6/1859, Steubenville, Ohio d: 11/23/37, Steubenville, Ohio Deb: 7/15/1884 F

YEAR	TM/L	G	AB	R	H	2B	3B	HR	RBI	BB	SO	AVG	OBP	SLG	PRO+	BR/A	SB	CS	SBR	FA	FR	G/POS	TPR
1884	Tol-a	5	18	1	4	1	0	0	2	0		.222	.222	.278	60	-1				.667	-1	/O-5	-0.2

■ CURT WALKER
Walker, William Curtis b: 7/3/1896, Beeville, Tex. d: 12/9/55, Beeville, Tex. BL/TR, 5'9.5", 170 lbs. Deb: 9/17/19

YEAR	TM/L	G	AB	R	H	2B	3B	HR	RBI	BB	SO	AVG	OBP	SLG	PRO+	BR/A	SB	CS	SBR	FA	FR	G/POS	TPR
1919	NY-A	1	1	0	0	0	0	0	0	0	0	.000	.000	.000	-99	-0	0			.000	0	H	0.0
1920	NY-N	8	14	0	1	0	0	0	0	1	3	.071	.133	.071	-41	-3	0	0	0	1.000	-1	/O-4	-0.4
1921	NY-N	64	192	30	55	13	5	3	35	15	8	.286	.338	.453	107	2	4	3	-1	.978	1	O-58	-0.2
	Phi-N	21	77	11	26	2	1	0	8	5	5	.338	.378	.390	96	-0	0	2	-1	.970	-5	O-21	-0.8
	Yr	85	269	41	81	15	6	3	43	20	13	.301	.349	.435	104	1	4	5	-2	.976	-4	O-79	-1.0
1922	Phi-N	148	581	102	196	36	11	12	89	56	46	.337	.399	.499	119	16	11	4	1	.955	6	*O-147	1.1
1923	Phi-N	140	527	66	148	26	5	5	66	45	31	.281	.337	.378	79	-16	12	12	-4	.947	5	*O-137/1-1	-2.3
1924	Phi-N	24	71	11	21	6	1	1	8	7	4	.296	.359	.451	103	0	0	1	-1	.900	-4	O-20	-0.5
	Cin-N	109	397	55	119	21	10	4	46	44	15	.300	.371	.433	117	10	7	5	-1	.978	0	*O-109	0.2
	Yr	133	468	66	140	27	11	5	54	51	19	.299	.369	.436	114	10	7	6	-2	.969	-4	*O-129	-0.3
1925	Cin-N	145	509	86	162	22	16	6	71	57	31	.318	.387	.460	118	15	14	11	-2	**.983**	2	*O-141	0.5
1926	Cin-N	155	571	83	175	24	20	6	78	60	31	.306	.372	.450	124	19	3			.961	4	*O-152	1.2
1927	Cin-N	146	527	60	154	16	10	6	80	47	19	.292	.350	.395	102	2	5			.957	3	*O-141	-0.5
1928	Cin-N	123	427	64	119	15	12	6	73	49	14	.279	.354	.412	101	1	19			.955	4	*O-122	-0.3
1929	Cin-N	141	492	76	154	28	15	7	83	85	17	.313	.416	.474	126	23	17			.969	-6	*O-138	0.7
1930	Cin-N	134	472	74	145	26	11	8	51	64	30	.307	.391	.460	110	9	4			.965	-6	*O-120	-0.5
Total	12	1359	4858	718	1475	235	117	64	688	535	254	.304	.374	.440	110	77	96	38		.963	2	*O-1310/1-1	-1.8

■ HOWARD WALL
Wall, Howard Deb: 9/13/1873

YEAR	TM/L	G	AB	R	H	2B	3B	HR	RBI	BB	SO	AVG	OBP	SLG	PRO+	BR/A	SB	CS	SBR	FA	FR	G/POS	TPR
1873	Was-n	1	4	1	1	0	0	0	0	0	0	.250	.250	.250	51	-0	0	0	0	.000	0	/S-1	0.0

■ JOE WALL
Wall, Joseph Francis "Gummy" b: 7/24/1873, Brooklyn, N.Y. d: 7/17/36, Brooklyn, N.Y. BL/TL, Deb: 9/22/01

YEAR	TM/L	G	AB	R	H	2B	3B	HR	RBI	BB	SO	AVG	OBP	SLG	PRO+	BR/A	SB	CS	SBR	FA	FR	G/POS	TPR
1901	NY-N	4	8	0	4	0	0	0	1	0		.500	.500	.500	198	1	0			1.000	-3	/C-2,O-1	-0.1
1902	NY-N	6	14	2	5	2	0	0	0	2		.357	.438	.500	191	2	0			1.000	-0	/O-3	0.1
	Bro-N	5	18	0	3	0	0	0	0	3		.167	.318	.167	50	-1	0			.893	-3	/C-5	-0.4
	Yr	11	32	2	8	2	0	0	0	5		.250	.368	.313	110	1	0			.893	-3	/C-5,O-3	-0.3
Total	2	15	40	2	12	2	0	0	1	5		.300	.391	.350	127	2	0			.903	-6	/C-7,O-4	-0.4

■ JACK WALLACE
Wallace, Clarence Eugene b: 8/6/1890, Winnfield, La. d: 10/15/60, Winnfield, La. BR/TR, 5'10.5", 175 lbs. Deb: 9/27/15

YEAR	TM/L	G	AB	R	H	2B	3B	HR	RBI	BB	SO	AVG	OBP	SLG	PRO+	BR/A	SB	CS	SBR	FA	FR	G/POS	TPR
1915	Chi-N	2	7	1	2	0	0	0	1	0	2	.286	.375	.286	101	0	0			1.000	2	/C-2	0.2

■ DON WALLACE
Wallace, Donald Allen b: 8/25/40, Sapulpa, Okla. BL/TR, 5'8", 165 lbs. Deb: 4/12/67

YEAR	TM/L	G	AB	R	H	2B	3B	HR	RBI	BB	SO	AVG	OBP	SLG	PRO+	BR/A	SB	CS	SBR	FA	FR	G/POS	TPR
1967	Cal-A	23	6	2	0	0	0	0	0	3	2	.000	.333	.000	6	-1	0	1	-1	1.000	2	/2-4,1-1,3-1	0.1

■ DOC WALLACE
Wallace, Frederick Renshaw "Jesse" b: 9/30/1893, Church Hill, Md. d: 12/31/64, Haverford, Pa. BR/TR, 5'6.5", 135 lbs. Deb: 5/2/19

YEAR	TM/L	G	AB	R	H	2B	3B	HR	RBI	BB	SO	AVG	OBP	SLG	PRO+	BR/A	SB	CS	SBR	FA	FR	G/POS	TPR
1919	Phi-N	2	4	0	1	0	0	0	0	0	1	.250	.250	.250	47	-0	0			.875	0	/S-2	0.0

■ JIM WALLACE
Wallace, James L. b: 11/14/1881, Boston, Mass. d: 5/16/53, Revere, Mass. BL/TL, 5'9", 150 lbs. Deb: 8/24/05

YEAR	TM/L	G	AB	R	H	2B	3B	HR	RBI	BB	SO	AVG	OBP	SLG	PRO+	BR/A	SB	CS	SBR	FA	FR	G/POS	TPR
1905	Pit-N	7	29	3	6	1	0	0	3	3		.207	.281	.241	55	-2	2			.929	1	/O-7	-0.1

■ BOBBY WALLACE
Wallace, Rhoderick John b: 11/4/1873, Pittsburgh, Pa. d: 11/3/60, Torrance, Cal. BR/TR, 5'8", 170 lbs. Deb: 9/15/1894 MUCH

YEAR	TM/L	G	AB	R	H	2B	3B	HR	RBI	BB	SO	AVG	OBP	SLG	PRO+	BR/A	SB	CS	SBR	FA	FR	G/POS	TPR
1894	Cle-N	4	13	0	2	1	0	0	1	0	1	.154	.154	.231	-8	-2	0			1.000	1	/P-4	0.0
1895	Cle-N	30	98	16	21	2	3	0	10	6	17	.214	.274	.296	44	-9	0			.910	3	P-30	0.0
1896	*Cle-N	45	149	19	35	6	3	1	17	11	21	.235	.287	.336	60	-9	2			.950	-2	O-23,P-22/1-1	-0.8
1897	Cle-N	130	516	99	173	33	21	4	112	48		.335	.394	.504	129	19	14			.928	3	*3-130/O-1	2.2
1898	Cle-N	154	593	81	160	25	13	3	99	63		.270	.344	.371	106	5	7			.936	17	*3-141,2-13	2.3
1899	StL-N	151	577	91	170	28	14	12	108	54		.295	.357	.454	119	13	17			.919	39	*S-100,3-52	5.3
1900	StL-N	126	485	70	130	25	9	4	70	40		.268	.328	.381	96	-4	7			.934	3	*S-126/3-1	0.8
1901	StL-N	134	550	69	178	34	15	2	91	20		.324	.351	.451	138	24	15			.929	**30**	*S-134	**6.2**
1902	StL-A	133	494	71	141	32	9	1	63	45		.285	.350	.393	107	5	18			.948	11	*S-131/P-1,O-1	2.2
1903	StL-A	135	511	63	136	21	7	1	54	28		.266	.309	.341	97	-2	10			.924	18	*S-135	2.3
1904	StL-A	139	541	57	149	29	4	2	69	42		.275	.330	.355	124	15	20			**.947**	8	*S-139	3.0
1905	StL-A	156	587	67	159	25	9	1	59	45		.271	.324	.349	120	12	13			.935	20	*S-156	3.9
1906	StL-A	139	476	64	123	21	7	2	67	58		.258	.344	.345	121	13	24			.949	3	*S-138	2.2
1907	StL-A	147	538	56	138	20	7	0	70	54		.257	.328	.320	107	5	16			.941	7	*S-147	1.7
1908	StL-A	137	487	59	123	24	4	1	60	52		.253	.327	.324	111	7	5			**.951**	18	*S-137	3.1
1909	StL-A	116	403	36	96	12	2	0	35	38		.238	.310	.278	92	-3	7			.946	11	S-87,3-29	1.2
1910	StL-A	138	508	47	131	19	7	0	37	49		.258	.324	.323	110	6	12			.948	22	S-99,3-39	3.6
1911	StL-A	125	410	35	95	12	2	0	31	46		.232	.312	.271	66	-18	8			.943	2	*S-124/2-1,M	-0.8
1912	StL-A	100	323	39	78	14	5	0	31	43		.241	.332	.316	89	-4	3			.942	8	S-87,3-10/2-2,M	1.2
1913	StL-A	55	147	11	31	5	0	0	21	14	16	.211	.293	.245	59	-7	1			.931	-5	S-39/3-7	-1.0
1914	StL-A	26	73	3	16	2	1	0	5	5	13	.219	.269	.274	66	-3	1	1	-0	.889	-11	S-19/3-2	-1.5
1915	StL-A	9	13	1	3	0	1	0	4	5	0	.231	.444	.385	154	1	0	1	-1	.848	1	/S-9	0.2
1916	StL-A	14	18	0	5	0	0	0	1	2	1	.278	.350	.278	93	-0	0			.958	5	/3-9,S-5	0.6
1917	StL-N	8	10	0	1	0	0	0	2	0	1	.100	.100	.100	-40	-2	0			1.000	-1	/3-5,S-2	-0.3
1918	StL-N	32	98	3	15	1	0	0	4	6	9	.153	.202	.163	12	-10	1			.959	2	2-17,S-12/3-1	-0.8
Total	25	2383	8618	1057	2309	391	143	34	1121	774	79	.268	.332	.358	106	53	201	2		.938	211	*S-1826,3-426/P2O1	36.8

■ TIM WALLACH
Wallach, Timothy Charles b: 9/14/57, Huntington Park, Cal. BR/TR, 6'3", 200 lbs. Deb: 9/6/80

YEAR	TM/L	G	AB	R	H	2B	3B	HR	RBI	BB	SO	AVG	OBP	SLG	PRO+	BR/A	SB	CS	SBR	FA	FR	G/POS	TPR
1980	Mon-N	5	11	1	2	0	0	1	2	1	5	.182	.250	.455	93	-0	0	0	0	1.000	-1	/O-3,1-1	-0.2
1981	*Mon-N	71	212	19	50	9	1	4	13	15	37	.236	.299	.344	81	-5	0	1	-1	1.000	-4	O-35,1-16,3-15	-1.3

YEAR	TM/L	G	AB	R	H	2B	3B	HR	RBI	BB	SO	AVG	OBP	SLG	PRO+	BR/A	SB	CS	SBR	FA	FR	G/POS	TPR
1982	Mon-N	158	596	89	160	31	3	28	97	36	81	.268	.314	.471	115	9	6	4	-1	.948	-6	*3-156/O-2,1-1	-0.1
1983	Mon-N	156	581	54	156	33	3	19	70	55	97	.269	.338	.434	113	9	0	3	-2	.956	-7	*3-156	-0.2
1984	Mon-N★	160	582	55	143	25	4	18	72	50	101	.246	.313	.395	102	0	3	7	-3	.959	16	*3-160/S-1	1.1
1985	Mon-N★	155	569	70	148	36	3	22	81	38	79	.260	.312	.450	117	10	9	9	-3	.967	37	*3-154	4.3
1986	Mon-N	134	480	50	112	22	1	18	71	44	72	.233	.311	.396	94	-5	8	4	0	.958	15	*3-132	0.8
1987	Mon-N★	153	593	89	177	**42**	4	26	123	37	98	.298	.347	.514	121	16	9	5	-0	.952	-0	*3-150/P-1	1.3
1988	Mon-N	159	592	52	152	32	5	12	69	38	88	.257	.305	.389	93	-6	2	6	-3	.962	12	*3-153/2-1	0.2
1989	Mon-N★	154	573	76	159	**42**	0	13	77	58	81	.277	.345	.419	116	12	3	7	-3	.958	6	*3-153/P-1	1.7
1990	Mon-N★	161	626	69	185	37	5	21	98	42	80	.296	.343	.471	126	20	6	9	-4	.954	4	*3-161	2.2
1991	Mon-N	151	577	60	130	22	1	13	73	50	100	.225	.294	.334	77	-18	2	4	-2	**.968**	6	*3-149	-1.3
1992	Mon-N	150	537	53	120	29	1	9	59	50	90	.223	.299	.331	79	-15	2	2	-1	.964	18	3-85,1-71	-0.2
1993	LA-N	133	477	42	106	19	1	12	62	32	70	.222	.275	.342	68	-23	0	2	-1	.958	0	*3-130/1-1	-2.4
1994	LA-N	113	414	68	116	21	1	23	78	46	80	.280	.358	.502	130	17	0	2	-1	.959	-10	*3-113	0.6
1995	*LA-N	97	327	24	87	22	2	9	38	27	69	.266	.330	.428	107	2	0	0	0	.976	-11	3-96/1-1	-0.8
1996	Cal-A	57	190	23	45	7	0	8	20	18	47	.237	.306	.400	76	-7	1	0	0	.941	2	3-46/1-3,D-8	-0.5
	*LA-N	45	162	14	37	3	1	4	22	12	32	.228	.286	.333	68	-8	0	1	-1	.971	-7	3-45	-1.6
Total	17	2212	8099	908	2085	432	36	260	1125	649	1307	.257	.319	.416	103	9	51	66	-24	.959	71	*3-2054/1-94,ODP2S	3.6

■ JACK WALLAESA

Wallaesa, John b: 8/31/19, Easton, Pa. d: 12/27/86, Easton, Pa. BB/TR, 6'3", 191 lbs. Deb: 9/22/40

1940	Phi-A	6	20	0	3	0	0	0	2	0	2	.150	.150	.150	-22	-4	0	0	0	.903	1	/S-6	-0.2
1942	Phi-A	36	117	13	30	4	1	2	13	8	26	.256	.315	.359	90	-2	0	1	-1	.920	-7	S-36	-0.8
1946	Phi-A	63	194	16	38	4	2	5	11	14	47	.196	.250	.314	57	-12	1	0	0	.916	-16	S-59	-2.6
1947	Chi-A	81	205	25	40	9	1	7	32	23	51	.195	.279	.351	78	-7	2	2	-1	.968	13	S-27,O-22/3-1	0.6
1948	Chi-A	33	48	2	9	0	0	1	3	1	12	.188	.204	.250	21	-6	0	0	0	1.000	-0	/S-5,O-1	-0.5
Total	5	219	584	56	120	17	4	15	61	46	138	.205	.267	.325	65	-30	3	3	-1	.933	-10	S-133/O-23,3-1	-3.5

■ NORM WALLEN

Wallen, Norman Edward (b: Norman Edward Walentoski) b: 2/13/17, Milwaukee, Wis. BR/TR, 5'11.5", 175 lbs. Deb: 4/20/45

1945	Bos-N	4	15	1	2	0	1	0	1	1	1	.133	.188	.267	25	-2	0			.800	-2	/3-4	-0.3

■ TY WALLER

Waller, Elliott Tyrone b: 3/14/57, Fresno, Cal. BR/TR, 6', 180 lbs. Deb: 9/6/80 C

1980	StL-N	5	12	3	1	0	0	0	0	1	5	.083	.154	.083	-31	-2	0	0	0	1.000	-2	/3-5	-0.5
1981	Chi-N	30	71	10	19	2	1	3	13	4	18	.268	.307	.451	108	0	2	0	1	.978	-2	3-22/2-3,O-3	-0.2
1982	Chi-N	17	21	4	5	0	0	0	1	2	5	.238	.304	.238	52	-1	0	0	0	1.000	-2	/O-7,3-1	-0.3
1987	Hou-N	11	6	1	1	1	0	0	0	0	3	.167	.167	.333	30	-1	0	0	0	1.000	-1	/O-3	-0.1
Total	4	63	110	18	26	3	1	3	14	7	31	.236	.282	.364	78	-4	2	0	1	.961	-7	/3-28,O-13,2-3	-1.1

■ DENNY WALLING

Walling, Dennis Martin b: 4/17/54, Neptune, N.J. BL/TR, 6'1", 185 lbs. Deb: 9/7/75 C

1975	Oak-A	6	8	0	1	1	0	0	2	0	4	.125	.125	.250	4	-1	0	0	0	1.000	-1	/O-3	-0.2
1976	Oak-A	3	11	1	3	0	0	0	0	0	3	.273	.273	.273	63	-1	0	0	0	.889	-1	/O-3	-0.1
1977	Hou-N	6	21	1	6	0	1	0	6	2	4	.286	.348	.381	105	0	0	1	-1	1.000	1	/O-5	0.0
1978	Hou-N	120	247	30	62	11	3	3	36	30	24	.251	.335	.356	101	0	9	2	2	.980	2	O-78	0.1
1979	Hou-N	82	147	21	48	8	4	3	31	17	21	.327	.396	.497	151	10	3	2	-0	.985	-3	O-42	0.6
1980	*Hou-N	100	284	30	85	6	5	3	29	35	26	.299	.376	.387	123	9	4	3	-1	.989	-7	1-63,O-19	-0.2
1981	*Hou-N	65	158	23	37	6	0	5	23	28	17	.234	.349	.367	109	2	2	1	0	.990	-5	1-27,O-27	-0.4
1982	Hou-N	85	146	22	30	4	1	1	14	23	19	.205	.314	.267	69	-6	4	2	0	1.000	-4	O-32,1-20	-1.1
1983	Hou-N	100	135	24	40	5	3	3	19	15	16	.296	.367	.444	132	6	2	2	-1	.992	-4	1-42,3-13,O-13	0.0
1984	Hou-N	87	249	37	70	11	5	3	31	16	28	.281	.327	.402	112	3	7	1	2	.956	-1	3-52,1-16/O-6	0.2
1985	Hou-N	119	345	44	93	20	1	7	45	25	26	.270	.319	.394	101	-0	5	2	0	.938	-2	3-51,1-46,O-13	-0.5
1986	*Hou-N	130	382	54	119	23	1	13	58	36	31	.312	.371	.479	136	18	1	1	-0	.960	2	*3-102,O-11/1-4	1.8
1987	Hou-N	110	325	45	92	21	4	5	33	39	37	.283	.360	.418	110	5	5	1	1	.948	-4	3-79,1-16/O-7	-0.1
1988	Hou-N	65	176	19	43	10	2	1	20	15	18	.244	.304	.341	88	-3	1	0	0	.950	9	3-51/1-3,O-1	0.6
	StL-N	19	58	3	13	3	0	0	1	2	7	.224	.250	.276	50	-4	1	0	0	1.000	-2	O-11/3-5,1-1	-0.7
	Yr	84	234	22	56	13	2	1	21	17	25	.239	.291	.325	79	-7	2	0	1	.941	6	3-56,O-12/1-4	-0.1
1989	StL-N	69	79	9	24	7	0	1	11	14	12	.304	.409	.430	136	4	0	0	0	.969	-2	1-20/3-9,O-6	0.2
1990	StL-N	78	127	7	28	5	0	1	19	8	15	.220	.267	.283	51	-8	0	0	0	1.000	1	1-15,3-11/O-8	-0.9
1991	Tex-A	24	44	1	4	1	0	0	2	3	8	.091	.184	.114	-16	-7	0	0	0	.950	-3	3-14/O-5	-1.0
1992	Hou-N	3	3	1	1	0	0	0	0	0	0	.333	.333	.333	94	-0	0	0	0	.000	0	/H	0.0
Total	18	1271	2945	372	799	142	30	49	380	308	316	.271	.341	.390	107	29	44	18	2	.947	-25	3-387,O-290,1-273	-1.7

■ JOE WALLIS

Wallis, Harold Joseph b: 1/9/52, E.St.Louis, Ill. BB/TR, 5'10", 195 lbs. Deb: 9/2/75

1975	Chi-N	16	56	9	16	2	2	1	4	5	14	.286	.344	.446	113	1	2	0	1	1.000	-0	O-15	0.1
1976	Chi-N	121	338	51	86	11	5	5	21	33	62	.254	.323	.361	86	-6	3	9	-5	.976	2	O-90	-1.3
1977	Chi-N	56	80	14	20	3	0	2	8	16	25	.250	.375	.363	89	-1	0	1	-1	.974	-8	O-35	-1.0
1978	Chi-N	28	55	7	17	2	1	1	6	5	13	.309	.367	.436	110	1	0	2	-1	1.000	-4	O-25	-0.5
	Oak-A	85	279	28	66	16	1	6	26	26	42	.237	.302	.366	91	-4	1	4	-2	.980	3	O-80/D-1	-0.7
1979	Oak-A	23	78	6	11	2	0	1	3	10	18	.141	.247	.205	25	-8	1	0	0	1.000	-1	O-23	-1.0
Total	5	329	886	115	216	36	9	16	68	95	174	.244	.318	.359	86	-17	7	16	-8	.982	-9	O-268/D-1	-4.4

■ LEE WALLS

Walls, Ray Lee b: 1/6/33, San Diego, Cal. d: 10/11/93, Los Angeles, Cal. BR/TR, 6'3", 205 lbs. Deb: 4/21/52 C

1952	Pit-N	32	80	6	15	0	1	2	5	8	22	.188	.261	.287	51	-5	0	0	0	1.000	0	O-19	-0.6
1956	Pit-N	143	474	72	130	20	11	11	54	50	83	.274	.346	.432	110	7	3	5	-2	.967	6	*O-133/3-1	0.4
1957	Pit-N	8	22	3	4	1	0	0	0	2	5	.182	.250	.227	30	-2	1	0	0	1.000	1	/O-7	-0.2
	Chi-N	117	366	42	88	10	5	6	33	27	67	.240	.294	.344	72	-15	5	3	-0	.984	-5	O-94/3-1	-2.6
	Yr	125	388	45	92	11	5	6	33	29	72	.237	.292	.338	70	-17	6	3	0	.985	-4	*O-101/3-1	-2.8
1958	Chi-N★	136	513	80	156	19	3	24	72	47	62	.304	.371	.493	128	21	4	4	-1	.992	5	*O-132	1.8
1959	Chi-N	120	354	43	91	18	3	8	33	42	73	.257	.344	.393	97	-1	0	2	-1	.967	-8	*O-119	-1.5
1960	Cin-N	29	84	12	23	3	2	1	7	17	20	.274	.396	.393	115	2	2	0	1	.960	1	O-24/1-2	0.2
	Phi-N	65	181	19	36	6	1	3	19	14	32	.199	.256	.293	50	-13	3	2	-0	.947	-9	3-34,O-13/1-7	-2.4
	Yr	94	265	31	59	9	3	4	26	31	52	.223	.304	.325	72	-10	5	2	0	.958	-8	O-37,3-34/1-9	-2.2
1961	Phi-N	91	261	32	73	6	4	8	30	19	48	.280	.329	.425	99	-1	2	2	-1	.987	-6	1-28,3-26,O-17	-1.0
1962	LA-N	60	109	9	29	3	1	0	17	10	21	.266	.328	.312	77	-3	1	0	0	.929	-4	O-17,1-11/3-4	-0.8
1963	LA-N	64	86	12	20	1	0	3	11	7	25	.233	.290	.349	89	-1	0	0	0	1.000	-2	O-18/1-5,3-2	-0.4
1964	LA-N	37	28	1	5	1	0	0	3	2	12	.179	.233	.214	29	-3	0	0	0	1.000	-2	/O-6,C-1	-0.5
Total	10	902	2558	331	670	88	31	66	284	245	470	.262	.330	.398	96	-14	21	18	-5	.977	-23	O-599/3-68,1-53,C-1	-7.6

■ AUSTIN WALSH

Walsh, Austin Edward b: 9/1/1891, Cambridge, Mass. d: 1/26/55, Glendale, Cal. BL/TL, 5'11", 175 lbs. Deb: 4/19/14

1914	Chi-F	57	121	14	29	6	1	1	10	4	25	.240	.264	.331	65	-9	0			1.000	-3	O-30	-1.3

■ JIMMY WALSH

Walsh, James Charles b: 9/22/1885, Kallila, Ireland d: 7/3/62, Syracuse, N.Y. BL/TR, 5'10.5", 170 lbs. Deb: 8/26/12

1912	Phi-A	31	107	11	27	8	2	0	15	12		.252	.328	.364	101	0	7			.947	0	O-30	-0.1
1913	Phi-A	97	303	56	77	16	5	0	27	38	40	.254	.341	.340	102	1	15			.961	1	O-90	-0.2
1914	NY-A	43	136	13	26	1	3	1	11	29	21	.191	.333	.265	80	-2	6	9	-4	.977	-1	O-41	-0.9
	*Phi-A	68	216	35	51	11	6	3	36	30	27	.236	.340	.384	123	6	6	12	-5	.966	-0	O-56/1-3,3-3,S-1	-0.2
	Yr	111	352	48	77	12	9	4	47	59	48	.219	.337	.338	106	4	12	21	-9	.971	-1	O-97/1-3,3-3,S-1	-1.1
1915	Phi-A	117	417	48	86	15	6	1	20	57	64	.206	.306	.278	78	-11	22	12	-1	.976	7	*O-109/3-2,1-1	-1.0
1916	Phi-A	114	390	42	91	13	6	1	27	54	36	.233	.330	.305	95	-1	27	14	-0	.939	-0	*O-113/1-1	-0.9
	*Bos-A	14	17	5	3	1	0	0	2	4	2	.176	.333	.235	71	-0	3	2	-0	1.000	-3	/O-6,3-2	-0.4
	Yr	128	407	47	94	14	6	1	29	58	38	.231	.330	.302	94	-2	30	16	-1	.940	-3	*O-119/3-2,1-1	-1.3
1917	Bos-A	57	185	25	49	6	3	0	12	25	14	.265	.352	.330	109	3	6			.982	-0	O-47	0.0
Total	6	541	1771	235	410	71	31	6	150	249	204	.232	.330	.317	96	-4	92	49		.964	5	O-492/3-7,1-5,S-1	-3.7

YEAR	TM/L	G	AB	R	H	2B	3B	HR	RBI	BB	SO	AVG	OBP	SLG	PRO+	BR/A	SB	CS	SBR	FA	FR	G/POS	TPR
■ **JOHN WALSH** Walsh, John Gabriel b: 3/25/1879, Wilkes-Barre, Pa. d: 4/25/47, Jamaica, N.Y. BR/TR, 5'8.5", 162 lbs. Deb: 6/22/03																							
1903	Phi-N	1	3	0	0	0	0	0	0	0	0	.000	.000	.000	-99	-1	0			1.000	-0	/3-1	-0.1
■ **JOE WALSH** Walsh, Joseph Francis b: 10/14/1886, Minersville, Pa. d: 1/6/67, Buffalo, N.Y. BR/TR, 6'2", 170 lbs. Deb: 10/8/10																							
1910	NY-A	1	4	0	2	1	0	0	2	0		.500	.500	.750	275	1	0			1.000	-1	/C-1	0.0
1911	NY-A	4	9	2	2	1	0	0	0	0		.222	.222	.333	51	-1	0			1.000	-3	/C-4	-0.3
Total	2	5	13	2	4	2	0	0	2	0		.308	.308	.462	114	0	0			1.000	-4	/C-5	-0.3
■ **JOE WALSH** Walsh, Joseph Patrick "Tweet" b: 3/13/17, Boston, Mass. d: 10/5/96, Boston, Mass. BR/TR, 5'10", 155 lbs. Deb: 7/1/38																							
1938	Bos-N	4	8	0	0	0	0	0	0	0	2	.000	.000	.000	-99	-2	0			.900	-2	/S-4	-0.4
■ **JOE WALSH** Walsh, Joseph R. "Reddy" b: 11/5/1864, Chicago, Ill. d: 8/8/11, Omaha, Neb. BL/TR, Deb: 9/3/1891																							
1891	Bal-a	26	100	14	21	0	1	1	10	6	18	.210	.255	.260	47	-7	4			.865	6	S-13,2-13	0.0
■ **DEE WALSH** Walsh, Leo Thomas b: 3/28/1890, St.Louis, Mo. d: 7/14/71, St.Louis, Mo. BB/TR, 5'9.5", 165 lbs. Deb: 4/10/13																							
1913	StL-A	23	53	8	9	0	1	0	5	6	11	.170	.302	.208	51	-3	3			.933	2	S-22/3-1	0.1
1914	StL-A	7	23	1	2	0	0	0	1	2	4	.087	.160	.087	-27	-4	1	1	-0	.919	-0	/S-7	-0.4
1915	StL-A	59	150	13	33	5	0	0	6	14	25	.220	.308	.253	71	-5	6	6	-2	.951	1	O-45/3-2,P-1,2-1,S	-0.8
Total	3	89	226	22	44	5	1	0	12	22	40	.195	.292	.226	56	-11	10	7		.924	3	/O-45,S-30,3-3,2P	-1.1
■ **JIMMY WALSH** Walsh, Michael Timothy "Runt" b: 3/25/1886, Lima, Ohio d: 1/21/47, Baltimore, Md. BR/TR, 5'9", 174 lbs. Deb: 4/25/10																							
1910	Phi-N	88	242	28	60	8	3	3	31	25	38	.248	.323	.343	91	-3	5			.947	-2	2-26,O-26/S-9,3-5	-0.6
1911	Phi-N	94	289	29	78	20	3	1	31	21	30	.270	.324	.370	93	-4	5			.962	-6	O-48,2-14/S-9,3CP1	-1.1
1912	Phi-N	51	150	16	40	6	3	2	19	8	20	.267	.304	.387	83	-4	3			.944	0	2-31,3-12/C-5	-0.4
1913	Phi-N	26	30	3	10	4	0	0	5	1	5	.333	.355	.467	128	1	1			1.000	-1	/2-6,S-3,3-1,O-1	0.0
1914	Bal-F	120	428	54	132	25	4	10	65	22	56	.308	.345	.456	113	0	18			.932	3	*3-113/2-1,S-1,O-1	0.7
1915	Bal-F	106	401	43	121	20	1	9	60	21	44	.302	.340	.424	111	-1	12			.936	-9	*3-106	-0.6
	StL-F	17	31	5	6	1	0	0	1	3	4	.194	.306	.226	48	-2	1			.913	-1	/3-9	-0.3
	Yr	123	432	48	127	21	1	9	61	24	48	.294	.337	.410	106	-4	13			.934	-10	*3-115	-0.9
Total	6	502	1571	178	447	84	14	25	212	101	197	.285	.332	.404	102	-13	45			.925	-14	3-253/2-78,OSC1P	-2.3
■ **TOM WALSH** Walsh, Thomas Joseph b: 2/28/1886, Davenport, Iowa d: 3/16/63, Naples, Fla. BR/TR, 5'11", 170 lbs. Deb: 8/15/06																							
1906	Chi-N	2	1	0	0	0	0	0	0	0		.000	.000	.000	-95	-0	0			1.000	0	/C-2	0.0
■ **WALT WALSH** Walsh, Walter William b: 4/30/1897, Newark, N.J. d: 1/15/66, Avon By The Sea, N.J. BR/TR, 5'11", 170 lbs. Deb: 5/4/20																							
1920	Phi-N	2	0	0	0	0	0	0	0	0	0	—	—	—	—	0	0	0	0	.000	0	R	0.0
■ **ROXY WALTERS** Walters, Alfred John b: 11/5/1892, San Francisco, Cal. d: 6/3/56, Alameda, Cal. BR/TR, 5'8.5", 160 lbs. Deb: 9/16/15																							
1915	NY-A	2	3	0	1	0	0	0	0	0	0	.333	.333	.333	100	-0	0			1.000	2	/C-2	0.2
1916	NY-A	66	203	13	54	9	3	0	23	14	42	.266	.320	.340	96	-1	2			.974	17	C-65	2.2
1917	NY-A	61	171	16	45	2	0	0	14	9	22	.263	.304	.275	76	-5	2			.968	11	C-57	1.1
1918	NY-A	64	191	18	38	5	1	0	12	9	18	.199	.239	.236	42	-14	3			.953	-5	C-50/O-9	-1.8
1919	Bos-A	48	135	7	26	2	0	0	9	7	15	.193	.259	.207	33	-12	1			.982	5	C-47	-0.4
1920	Bos-A	88	258	25	51	11	1	0	28	30	21	.198	.303	.248	49	-18	2	2	-1	.980	8	C-85/1-2	-0.5
1921	Bos-A	54	169	17	34	4	1	0	14	10	11	.201	.254	.237	27	-19	3	0	1	.990	15	C-54	0.0
1922	Bos-A	38	98	4	19	2	0	0	6	6	8	.194	.240	.214	19	-12	0	0	0	.967	6	C-36	-0.4
1923	Bos-A	40	104	9	26	4	0	0	5	2	6	.250	.264	.288	45	-8	0	2	-1	.974	7	C-36/2-1	-0.2
1924	Cle-A	32	74	10	19	2	0	0	5	10	6	.257	.345	.284	63	-4	0	1	-1	.979	6	C-25/2-7	0.2
1925	Cle-A	5	20	0	4	0	0	0	0	0	2	.200	.200	.200	2	-3	0	0	0	1.000	-0	/C-5	-0.3
Total	11	498	1426	119	317	41	6	0	116	97	151	.222	.281	.259	51	-96	13	5		.975	70	C-462/O-9,2-8,1-2	0.1
■ **DAN WALTERS** Walters, Daniel Gene b: 8/15/66, Brunswick, Maine BR/TR, 6'4", 225 lbs. Deb: 6/1/92																							
1992	SD-N	57	179	14	45	11	1	4	22	10	28	.251	.298	.391	92	-2	1	0	0	.992	7	C-55	0.8
1993	SD-N	27	94	6	19	3	0	1	10	7	13	.202	.257	.266	40	-8	0	0	0	.970	-3	C-26	-1.0
Total	2	84	273	20	64	14	1	5	32	17	41	.234	.284	.348	73	-10	1	0	0	.985	4	/C-81	-0.2
■ **FRED WALTERS** Walters, Fred James "Whale" b: 9/4/12, Laurel, Miss. d: 2/1/80, Laurel, Miss. BR/TR, 6'1", 210 lbs. Deb: 4/17/45																							
1945	Bos-A	40	93	2	16	2	0	0	5	10	9	.172	.252	.194	29	-8	1	1	-0	.993	6	C-38	-0.1
■ **KEN WALTERS** Walters, Kenneth Rogers b: 11/11/33, Fresno, Cal. BR/TR, 6'1", 180 lbs. Deb: 4/12/60																							
1960	Phi-N	124	426	42	102	10	0	8	37	16	50	.239	.269	.319	60	-24	4	3	-1	.988	6	*O-119	-2.5
1961	Phi-N	86	180	23	41	8	2	2	14	5	25	.228	.253	.328	53	-12	2	2	-1	.975	-6	O-56/1-5,3-1	-2.1
1963	Cin-N	49	75	6	14	2	0	1	7	4	14	.187	.237	.253	40	-6	0	2	-1	.889	-5	O-21/1-1	-1.3
Total	3	259	681	71	157	20	2	11	58	25	89	.231	.261	.314	56	-42	6	7	-2	.979	-5	O-196/1-6,3-1	-5.9
■ **BUCKY WALTERS** Walters, William Henry b: 4/19/09, Philadelphia, Pa. d: 4/20/91, Abington, Pa. BR/TR, 6'1", 180 lbs. Deb: 9/18/31 MC																							
1931	Bos-N	9	38	2	8	2	0	0	0	0	3	.211	.211	.263	28	-4	0			.947	0	/3-6,2-3	-0.3
1932	Bos-N	22	75	8	14	3	1	0	4	2	18	.187	.208	.253	24	-8	0			.910	2	3-22	-0.5
1933	Bos-A	52	195	27	50	8	3	4	28	19	24	.256	.326	.390	90	-3	1	1	-0	.940	1	3-43/2-7	0.1
1934	Bos-A	23	88	10	19	4	4	4	18	3	12	.216	.242	.489	79	-4	0	0	0	.906	6	3-23	0.3
	Phi-N	83	300	36	78	20	3	4	38	19	54	.260	.308	.387	75	-11	1			.950	-7	3-80/2-3,P-2	-1.4
1935	Phi-N	49	96	14	24	2	1	0	6	9	12	.250	.314	.292	58	-6	0			1.000	1	P-24/O-5,2-2,3-1	-0.2
1936	Phi-N	64	121	12	29	10	1	1	16	7	15	.240	.281	.364	66	-6	0			.974	9	P-40/2-1,3-1	0.0
1937	Phi-N★	56	137	15	38	6	0	1	16	5	16	.277	.303	.343	69	-6	1			.988	5	P-37/3-8	-0.1
1938	Phi-N	15	35	6	10	2	0	1	3	1	5	.286	.306	.429	103	-0	1			.955	0	P-12	0.0
	Cin-N	36	64	10	9	1	0	0	5	7	18	.141	.236	.156	10	-8	0			.981	2	P-27	0.0
	Yr	51	99	16	19	3	0	1	8	8	23	.192	.259	.253	42	-8	1			.973	3	P-39	0.0
1939	*Cin-N☆	40	120	16	39	8	1	1	16	5	12	.325	.357	.433	111	2	1			.979	4	P-39	0.0
1940	*Cin-N★	37	117	11	24	3	0	1	18	4	14	.205	.231	.256	34	-11	2			.945	-1	P-36	0.0
1941	Cin-N★	39	106	6	20	6	0	0	9	7	13	.189	.239	.245	36	-9	0			.977	2	P-37	0.0
1942	Cin-N★	40	99	13	24	6	1	2	13	3	13	.242	.265	.384	89	-2	0			.961	1	P-34/O-1	-0.1
1943	Cin-N	37	90	11	24	7	1	1	12	6	15	.267	.313	.400	107	0	1			.971	1	P-34	0.0
1944	Cin-N★	37	107	9	30	4	0	0	13	8	18	.280	.330	.318	86	-2	0			**1.000**	1	P-34	0.0
1945	Cin-N	24	61	11	14	3	0	3	8	3	14	.230	.266	.426	93	-1	2			.975	-0	P-22	0.0
1946	Cin-N	24	55	6	7	2	0	0	5	4	12	.127	.186	.164	-0	-7	2			.940	2	P-22	0.0
1947	Cin-N	20	45	3	12	2	0	0	4	2	13	.267	.298	.311	62	-2	0			.962	-1	P-20	0.0
1948	Cin-N	7	15	1	4	0	0	0	2	0	2	.267	.267	.267	46	-1	0			1.000	1	/P-7,M	0.0
1950	Bos-N	1	2	0	0	0	0	0	0	0	0	.000	.000	.000	-99	-1	0			1.000	-0	/P-1	0.0
Total	19	715	1966	227	477	99	16	23	234	114	303	.243	.286	.344	69	-90	12	1		.974	28	P-428,3-184/2-16,O	-2.2
■ **DANNY WALTON** Walton, Daniel James "Mickey" b: 7/14/47, Los Angeles, Cal. BR/TR, 6', 200 lbs. Deb: 4/20/68																							
1968	Hou-N	2	2	0	0	0	0	0	0	0	1	.000	.000	.000	-99	-0	0	0	0	.000	0	H	-0.1
1969	Sea-A	23	92	12	20	1	2	3	10	5	26	.217	.280	.370	82	-3	2	0	1	.976	-1	O-23	-0.4
1970	Mil-A	117	397	32	102	20	1	17	66	51	126	.257	.350	.441	116	9	2	3	-1	.965	-6	*O-114	-0.4
1971	Mil-A	30	69	5	14	3	0	2	9	7	22	.203	.286	.333	76	-2	0	0	0	.923	-4	O-19/3-1	-0.7
	NY-A	5	14	1	2	0	0	1	2	0	7	.143	.143	.357	40	-1	0	0	0	1.000	-1	/O-4	-0.2
	Yr	35	83	6	16	3	0	3	11	7	29	.193	.264	.337	71	-3	0	0	0	.933	-4	O-23/3-1	-0.9
1973	Min-A	37	96	13	17	1	1	4	8	17	28	.177	.301	.333	75	-3	0	0	0	1.000	-3	O-18,D-11/3-1	-0.7
1975	Min-A	42	63	4	11	2	0	1	8	4	18	.175	.224	.254	34	-6	0	0	0	.962	-1	/1-7,C-2,D-6	-0.7
1976	LA-N	18	15	0	2	0	0	0	2	1	2	.133	.188	.133	-8	-2	0	0	0	.000	0	H	-0.3
1977	Hou-N	13	21	0	4	0	0	0	1	0	5	.190	.190	.190	3	-3	0	0	0	.956	-0	/1-5	-0.3

YEAR	TM/L	G	AB	R	H	2B	3B	HR	RBI	BB	SO	AVG	OBP	SLG	PRO+	BR/A	SB	CS	SBR	FA	FR	G/POS	TPR
1980	Tex-A	10	10	2	2	0	0	0	1	3	5	.200	.385	.200	67	-0	0	0	0	.000	0	/D-1	0.0
Total	9	297	779	69	174	27	4	28	107	88	240	.223	.310	.376	90	-12	4	3	-1	.966	-15	O-178/D-18,1-12,C3	-3.8

■ JEROME WALTON

Walton, Jerome O'Terrell b: 7/8/65, Newnan, Ga. BR/TR, 6'1", 175 lbs. Deb: 4/4/89

YEAR	TM/L	G	AB	R	H	2B	3B	HR	RBI	BB	SO	AVG	OBP	SLG	PRO+	BR/A	SB	CS	SBR	FA	FR	G/POS	TPR
1989	*Chi-N	116	475	64	139	23	3	5	46	27	77	.293	.339	.385	99	-1	24	7	3	.990	4	*O-115	0.3
1990	Chi-N	101	392	63	103	16	2	2	21	50	70	.263	.352	.329	82	-8	14	7	0	.977	3	O-98	-0.8
1991	Chi-N	123	270	42	59	13	1	5	17	19	55	.219	.277	.330	67	-12	7	3	0	.983	-10	*O-101	-2.5
1992	Chi-N	30	55	7	7	0	1	0	1	9	13	.127	.273	.164	26	-5	1	2	-1	.944	-3	O-24	-1.0
1993	Cal-A	5	2	2	0	0	0	0	0	1	2	.000	.333	.000	-2	-0	1	0	0	1.000	0	/O-1,D-4	0.0
1994	Cin-N	46	68	10	21	4	0	1	9	4	12	.309	.347	.412	98	-0	1	3	-2	1.000	-6	O-26/1-7	-0.8
1995	*Cin-N	102	162	32	47	12	1	8	22	17	25	.290	.372	.525	134	8	10	7	-1	.982	-15	O-89/1-3	-1.0
1996	Atl-N	37	47	9	16	5	0	1	4	5	10	.340	.404	.511	132	2	0	0	0	1.000	-3	O-28	-0.1
1997	*Bal-A	26	68	8	20	1	0	3	9	4	10	.294	.333	.441	103	0	0	0	0	1.000	-3	O-19/1-5,D-2	-0.4
1998	TB-A	12	34	4	11	3	0	0	3	2	6	.324	.361	.412	96	-0	0	0	0	1.000	1	/O-8,D-3	0.1
Total	10	598	1573	241	423	77	8	25	132	138	280	.269	.335	.376	91	-16	58	29	0	.984	-33	O-509/1-15,D-9	-6.2

■ REGGIE WALTON

Walton, Reginald Sherard b: 10/24/52, Kansas City, Mo. BR/TR, 6'3", 205 lbs. Deb: 6/13/80

YEAR	TM/L	G	AB	R	H	2B	3B	HR	RBI	BB	SO	AVG	OBP	SLG	PRO+	BR/A	SB	CS	SBR	FA	FR	G/POS	TPR
1980	Sea-A	31	83	8	23	6	0	2	9	3	10	.277	.310	.422	98	-1	2	2	-1	.929	-2	O-17,D-11	-0.4
1981	Sea-A	12	6	1	0	0	0	0	0	1	2	.000	.143	.000	-54	-1	0	0	0	.000	-2	/O-4,D-1	-0.3
1982	Pit-N	13	15	1	3	1	0	0	0	1	1	.200	.294	.267	56	-1	0	0	0	.000	-1	/O-2	-0.2
Total	3	56	104	10	26	7	0	2	9	5	13	.250	.297	.375	83	-3	2	2	-1	.929	-5	/O-23,D-12	-0.9

■ BILL WAMBSGANSS

Wambsganss, William Adolph b: 3/19/1894, Cleveland, Ohio d: 12/8/85, Lakewood, Ohio BR/TR, 5'11", 175 lbs. Deb: 8/4/14

YEAR	TM/L	G	AB	R	H	2B	3B	HR	RBI	BB	SO	AVG	OBP	SLG	PRO+	BR/A	SB	CS	SBR	FA	FR	G/POS	TPR
1914	Cle-A	43	143	12	31	6	2	0	12	8	24	.217	.277	.287	67	-6	2	7	-4	.921	-1	S-36/2-4	-0.9
1915	Cle-A	121	375	30	73	4	4	0	21	36	50	.195	.272	.227	48	-23	8	9	-3	.938	7	2-78,3-35	-1.9
1916	Cle-A	136	475	57	117	14	4	0	45	41	40	.246	.313	.293	77	-13	13			.925	-8	*S-106,2-24/3-5	-1.6
1917	Cle-A	141	499	52	127	17	6	0	43	37	42	.255	.315	.313	85	-9	16			.951	15	*2-137/1-3	1.4
1918	Cle-A	87	315	34	93	15	2	0	40	21	21	.295	.345	.356	102	0	16			.952	-2	2-87	0.4
1919	Cle-A	139	526	60	146	17	6	2	60	32	24	.278	.323	.344	82	-13	18			.963	11	*2-139	0.5
1920	*Cle-A	153	565	83	138	16	11	1	55	54	26	.244	.316	.317	66	-28	9	18	-8	.960	8	*2-153	-2.1
1921	Cle-A	107	410	80	117	28	5	2	47	44	27	.285	.359	.393	90	-6	13	7	-0	.963	-18	*2-103/3-2	-2.0
1922	Cle-A	142	538	89	141	22	6	0	47	60	26	.262	.341	.325	74	-19	17	10	-1	.961	-9	*2-125,S-16	-2.4
1923	Cle-A	101	345	59	100	20	4	1	59	43	15	.290	.373	.380	99	0	10	9	-2	.963	5	2-88/3-4	0.4
1924	Bos-A	156	632	93	174	41	5	0	49	54	33	.275	.336	.356	79	-21	14	8	-1	.963	14	*2-156	-0.5
1925	Bos-A	111	360	50	83	12	4	1	41	52	21	.231	.329	.294	59	-22	3	5	-2	.957	4	*2-103/1-6	-1.7
1926	Phi-A	54	54	11	19	3	0	0	1	8	8	.352	.444	.407	116	2	1	1	-0	.923	0	S-17/2-8	0.2
Total	13	1491	5237	710	1359	215	59	7	520	490	357	.259	.328	.327	78	-157	140	74		.958	26	*2-1205,S-175/31	-10.2

■ LLOYD WANER

Waner, Lloyd James "Little Poison" b: 3/16/06, Harrah, Okla. d: 7/22/82, Oklahoma City, Okla. BL/TR, 5'9", 150 lbs. Deb: 4/12/27 FH

YEAR	TM/L	G	AB	R	H	2B	3B	HR	RBI	BB	SO	AVG	OBP	SLG	PRO+	BR/A	SB	CS	SBR	FA	FR	G/POS	TPR
1927	*Pit-N	150	629	**133**	223	17	6	2	27	37	23	.355	.396	.410	108	9	14			.976	-1	*O-150/2-1	-0.2
1928	Pit-N	152	659	121	221	22	14	5	61	40	13	.335	.377	.434	107	7	8			.980	7	*O-152	0.3
1929	Pit-N	151	662	134	234	28	**20**	5	74	37	20	.353	.395	.479	113	13	6			.987	16	*O-151	1.7
1930	Pit-N	68	260	32	94	8	3	1	36	5	5	.362	.376	.427	93	-2	3			.983	2	O-65	-0.5
1931	Pit-N	154	681	90	**214**	25	13	4	57	39	16	.314	.352	.407	104	4	7			.979	**18**	*O-153/2-1	1.2
1932	Pit-N	134	565	90	188	27	11	2	38	31	11	.333	.367	.430	116	12	6			.986	12	*O-131	1.6
1933	Pit-N	121	500	59	138	14	5	0	26	22	8	.276	.307	.324	80	-13	3			.982	1	*O-114	-1.9
1934	Pit-N	140	611	95	173	27	6	1	48	38	12	.283	.326	.352	80	-17	6			.979	12	*O-139	-1.1
1935	Pit-N	122	537	83	166	22	14	0	46	22	10	.309	.336	.402	95	-5	1			.989	6	*O-121	-0.3
1936	Pit-N	106	414	67	133	13	8	1	31	31	5	.321	.369	.399	104	3	1			.984	1	O-92	0.0
1937	Pit-N	129	537	80	177	23	4	1	45	34	12	.330	.370	.393	107	6	3			.988	6	*O-123	0.8
1938	Pit-N☆	147	619	79	194	25	7	5	57	28	11	.313	.343	.401	103	2	5			.986	2	*O-144	-0.1
1939	Pit-N	112	379	49	108	15	3	0	24	17	13	.285	.321	.340	79	-11	0			.992	6	O-92/3-1	-0.8
1940	Pit-N	72	166	30	43	3	0	0	3	5	5	.259	.285	.277	56	-10	2			.989	-1	O-42	-1.3
1941	Pit-N	3	4	2	1	0	0	0	1	2	0	.250	.500	.250	116	0	0			1.000	0	/O-1	0.1
	Bos-N	19	51	7	21	1	0	0	4	2	0	.412	.434	.431	151	3	1			.969	-1	O-15	0.2
	Cin-N	55	164	17	42	4	1	0	6	8	0	.256	.291	.293	64	-8	0			.986	-3	O-44	-1.4
	Yr	77	219	26	64	5	1	0	11	12	0	.292	.329	.324	85	-4	1			.981	-4	O-60	-1.1
1942	Phi-N	101	287	23	75	7	3	0	10	16	6	.261	.300	.307	82	-7	1			.967	-1	O-75	-1.2
1944	Bro-N	15	14	3	4	0	0	0	1	3	0	.286	.412	.286	101	0	0			1.000	-2	/O-4	-0.2
	Pit-N	19	14	2	5	0	0	0	2	2	0	.357	.438	.357	120	1	0			1.000	-2	/O-7	-0.2
	Yr	34	28	5	9	0	0	0	3	5	0	.321	.424	.321	110	1	0			1.000	-4	O-11	-0.4
1945	Pit-N	23	19	5	5	0	0	0	1	1	3	.263	.300	.263	55	-1	0			1.000	-0	/O-3	-0.1
Total	18	1993	7772	1201	2459	281	118	27	598	420	173	.316	.353	.393	99	-13	67			.983	76	*O-1818/2-2,3-1	-3.4

■ PAUL WANER

Waner, Paul Glee "Big Poison" b: 4/16/03, Harrah, Okla. d: 8/29/65, Sarasota, Fla. BL/TL, 5'8.5", 153 lbs. Deb: 4/13/26 FCH

YEAR	TM/L	G	AB	R	H	2B	3B	HR	RBI	BB	SO	AVG	OBP	SLG	PRO+	BR/A	SB	CS	SBR	FA	FR	G/POS	TPR
1926	Pit-N	144	536	101	180	35	**22**	8	79	66	19	.336	**.413**	.528	144	34	11			.976	8	*O-139	**3.1**
1927	*Pit-N	155	623	114	**237**	42	**18**	9	**131**	60	14	**.380**	.437	.549	152	46	5			.980	8	*O-143,1-14	4.2
1928	Pit-N	152	602	**142**	223	**50**	19	6	86	77	16	.370	.446	.547	152	48	6			.975	5	*O-131,1-24	4.0
1929	Pit-N	151	596	131	200	43	15	15	100	89	24	.336	.424	.534	133	32	15			.986	2	*O-143/1-7	2.1
1930	Pit-N	145	589	117	217	32	18	8	77	57	18	.368	.428	.525	128	29	18			.959	-3	*O-143	1.4
1931	Pit-N	150	559	88	180	35	10	6	70	73	21	.322	.404	.453	131	27	6			.976	15	*O-138,1-10	3.1
1932	Pit-N	154	630	107	215	**62**	10	8	82	56	24	.341	.397	.510	144	39	13			.974	3	*O-154	3.2
1933	Pit-N★	154	618	101	191	38	16	7	70	60	20	.309	.372	.456	136	29	3			.981	5	*O-154	2.7
1934	Pit-N★	146	599	**122**	**217**	32	16	14	90	68	24	**.362**	.429	.539	154	47	8			.985	7	*O-145	4.6
1935	Pit-N★	139	549	98	176	29	12	11	78	61	22	.321	.392	.477	128	23	2			.983	3	*O-136	2.0
1936	Pit-N	148	585	107	218	53	9	5	94	74	29	**.373**	.446	.520	156	48	7			.960	9	*O-145	4.9
1937	Pit-N★	154	619	94	219	30	9	2	74	63	34	.354	.413	.441	132	30	4			.970	1	*O-150/1-3	2.5
1938	Pit-N	148	625	77	175	31	6	6	69	47	28	.280	.331	.378	94	-5	2			.977	-3	*O-147	-1.3
1939	Pit-N	125	461	62	151	30	6	3	45	35	18	.328	.375	.438	120	13	0			.978	2	*O-106	1.1
1940	Pit-N	89	238	32	69	16	1	1	32	23	14	.290	.352	.378	102	1	0			.985	-5	O-45/1-8	-0.7
1941	Bro-N	11	35	5	6	0	0	0	4	8	0	.171	.326	.171	41	-2	0			.923	-2	/O-9	-0.5
	Bos-N	95	294	40	82	10	2	2	46	47	14	.279	.378	.347	110	6	1			.965	-4	O-77/1-7	-0.3
	Yr	106	329	45	88	10	2	2	50	55	14	.267	.372	.328	102	3	1			.961	-6	O-86/1-7	-0.8
1942	Bos-N	114	333	43	86	17	1	1	39	62	20	.258	.376	.324	108	6	2			.969	-8	O-94	-0.7
1943	Bro-N	82	225	29	70	16	0	1	26	35	9	.311	.406	.396	132	11	0			.960	-1	O-57	0.7
1944	Bro-N	83	136	16	39	4	1	0	16	27	7	.287	.405	.331	111	4	0			.983	-2	O-32	0.0
	NY-A	9	7	1	1	0	0	0	1	2	1	.143	.333	.143	37	-0	1	0	0	.000	0	H	0.0
1945	NY-A	1	0	0	0	0	0	0	0	1	0	—	1.000	—	191	0	0	0	0	.000	0	H	0.0
Total	20	2549	9459	1627	3152	605	191	113	1309	1091	376	.333	.404	.473	133	464	104	0		.975	40	*O-2288/1-73	36.1

■ JACK WANNER

Wanner, Clarence Curtis "Johnny" b: 11/29/1885, Geneseo, Ill. d: 5/28/19, Geneseo, Ill. BR/TR, 5'11.5", 190 lbs. Deb: 9/28/09

YEAR	TM/L	G	AB	R	H	2B	3B	HR	RBI	BB	SO	AVG	OBP	SLG	PRO+	BR/A	SB	CS	SBR	FA	FR	G/POS	TPR
1909	NY-A	3	8	0	1	0	0	0	0	2		.125	.300	.125	35	-0	1			.600	-2	/S-2	-0.3

■ PEE-WEE WANNINGER

Wanninger, Paul Louis b: 12/12/02, Birmingham, Ala. d: 3/7/81, N.Augusta, S.C. BL/TR, 5'7", 150 lbs. Deb: 4/22/25

YEAR	TM/L	G	AB	R	H	2B	3B	HR	RBI	BB	SO	AVG	OBP	SLG	PRO+	BR/A	SB	CS	SBR	FA	FR	G/POS	TPR
1925	NY-A	117	403	35	95	13	6	1	22	11	34	.236	.256	.305	43	-36	3	5	-2	.944	-6	*S-111/3-3,2-1	-3.1
1927	Bos-A	18	60	4	12	0	0	0	1	6	2	.200	.284	.200	28	-6	2	4	-2	.890	-1	S-15	-0.8
	Cin-N	28	93	14	23	2	2	0	8	6	7	.247	.293	.312	64	-5	0			.953	6	S-28	0.4
Total	2	163	556	53	130	15	8	1	31	23	43	.234	.266	.295	45	-47	5	9		.941	-1	S-154/3-3,2-1	-3.5

■ AARON WARD

Ward, Aaron Lee b: 8/28/1896, Booneville, Ark. d: 1/30/61, New Orleans, La. BR/TR, 5'10.5", 160 lbs. Deb: 8/14/17

YEAR	TM/L	G	AB	R	H	2B	3B	HR	RBI	BB	SO	AVG	OBP	SLG	PRO+	BR/A	SB	CS	SBR	FA	FR	G/POS	TPR
1917	NY-A	8	26	0	3	0	0	0	1	1	5	.115	.148	.115	-19	-4	0			.926	-2	/S-7	-0.7

YEAR	TM/L	G	AB	R	H	2B	3B	HR	RBI	BB	SO	AVG	OBP	SLG	PRO+	BR/A	SB	CS	SBR	FA	FR	G/POS	TPR
1918	NY-A	20	32	2	4	1	0	0	1	2	7	.125	.176	.156	0	-4	1			.941	4	S-12/O-4,2-3	0.0
1919	NY-A	27	34	5	7	2	0	0	2	5	6	.206	.308	.265	61	-2	0			1.000	2	/1-5,3-3,S-2,2-1	0.0
1920	NY-A	127	496	62	127	18	7	11	54	33	84	.256	.304	.387	79	-17	7	5	-1	.965	22	*3-114,S-12	1.1
1921	*NY-A	153	556	77	170	30	10	5	75	42	68	.306	.363	.423	98	-2	6	8	-3	.961	19	*2-124,3-33	1.8
1922	*NY-A	154	558	69	149	19	5	7	68	45	64	.267	.328	.357	77	-19	6	4	-1	.974	3	*2-152/3-2	-1.3
1923	*NY-A	152	567	79	161	26	11	10	82	56	65	.284	.351	.422	101	-0	8	8	-2	**.980**	13	*2-152	1.2
1924	NY-A	120	400	42	101	13	10	8	66	40	45	.253	.324	.395	85	-11	1	4	-2	.973	8	*2-120/S-1	-0.4
1925	NY-A	125	439	41	108	22	3	4	38	49	49	.246	.326	.337	70	-20	1	4	-2	.966	-11	*2-113,3-10	-2.9
1926	NY-A	22	31	5	10	2	0	0	3	2	6	.323	.364	.387	97	-0	0	0	0	1.000	-4	/2-4,3-1	-0.4
1927	Chi-A	145	463	75	125	25	8	5	56	63	56	.270	.360	.391	97	-1	6	5	-1	.963	-19	*2-139/3-6	-1.6
1928	Cle-A	6	9	0	1	0	0	0	0	1	2	.111	.200	.111	-16	-2	0	0	0	.818	2	/3-3,S-2,2-1	0.1
Total	12	1059	3611	457	966	158	54	50	446	339	457	.268	.335	.383	85	-81	36	38		.970	35	2-809,3-172/S10	-3.1

■ **CHUCK WARD** Ward, Charles William b: 7/30/1894, St.Louis, Mo. d: 4/4/69, Indian Rocks, Fla. BR/TR, 5′11.5″, 170 lbs. Deb: 4/11/17

YEAR	TM/L	G	AB	R	H	2B	3B	HR	RBI	BB	SO	AVG	OBP	SLG	PRO+	BR/A	SB	CS	SBR	FA	FR	G/POS	TPR
1917	Pit-N	125	423	25	100	12	3	0	43	32	43	.236	.302	.279	76	-11	5			.912	-27	*S-112/2-8,3-5	-3.7
1918	Bro-N	2	6	0	2	0	0	0	3	0	0	.333	.333	.333	104	0	0			1.000	-1	/3-2	-0.1
1919	Bro-N	45	150	7	35	1	2	0	8	7	11	.233	.277	.267	62	-7	0			.920	-6	3-45	-1.2
1920	Bro-N	19	71	7	11	1	0	0	4	3	3	.155	.200	.169	6	-8	1	0	0	.928	-9	S-19	-1.7
1921	Bro-N	12	28	1	2	1	0	0	0	4	2	.071	.188	.107	-19	-5	0	0	0	.937	4	S-12	0.0
1922	Bro-N	33	91	12	25	5	1	0	14	5	8	.275	.320	.352	74	-4	1	1	-0	.934	-3	S-31/3-2	-0.4
Total	6	236	769	52	175	20	6	0	72	51	67	.228	.286	.269	63	-34	7	1		.919	-41	S-174/3-54,2-8	-7.1

■ **CHRIS WARD** Ward, Chris Gilbert b: 5/18/49, Oakland, Cal. BL/TL, 6′, 180 lbs. Deb: 9/10/72

YEAR	TM/L	G	AB	R	H	2B	3B	HR	RBI	BB	SO	AVG	OBP	SLG	PRO+	BR/A	SB	CS	SBR	FA	FR	G/POS	TPR
1972	Chi-N	1	1	0	0	0	0	0	0	0	0	.000	.000	.000	-90	-0	0	0	0	.000	0	H	0.0
1974	Chi-N	92	137	8	28	4	0	1	15	18	13	.204	.297	.255	53	-8	0	2	-1	.977	1	O-22/1-6	-0.9
Total	2	93	138	8	28	4	0	1	15	18	13	.203	.295	.254	52	-8	0	2	-1	.977	1	/O-22,1-6	-0.9

■ **DARYLE WARD** Ward, Daryle Lamar b: 6/27/75, Lynwood, Cal. BL/TL, 6′2″, 240 lbs. Deb: 5/14/98 F

YEAR	TM/L	G	AB	R	H	2B	3B	HR	RBI	BB	SO	AVG	OBP	SLG	PRO+	BR/A	SB	CS	SBR	FA	FR	G/POS	TPR
1998	Hou-N	4	3	1	1	0	0	0	0	1	2	.333	.500	.333	126	0	0	0	0	.000	0	/H	0.0

■ **PIGGY WARD** Ward, Frank Gray b: 4/16/1867, Chambersburg, Pa. d: 10/24/12, Altoona, Pa. BB/TR, 5′9.5″, 196 lbs. Deb: 6/12/1883 F

YEAR	TM/L	G	AB	R	H	2B	3B	HR	RBI	BB	SO	AVG	OBP	SLG	PRO+	BR/A	SB	CS	SBR	FA	FR	G/POS	TPR
1883	Phi-N	1	5	0	0	0	0	0	0	0	2	.000	.000	.000	-99	-1				1.000	-1	/3-1	-0.2
1889	Phi-N	7	25	0	4	1	0	0	4	0	7	.160	.160	.200	0	-3	1			.848	-2	/2-6,O-1	-0.5
1891	Pit-N	6	18	3	6	0	0	0	2	3	3	.333	.455	.333	134	1	3			.833	-1	/O-5	0.0
1892	Bal-N	56	186	28	54	6	5	1	33	31	18	.290	.403	.392	137	10	10			.892	1	O-43/2-7,S-5,C-1	0.9
1893	Bal-N	11	49	11	12	1	3	0	5	5	2	.245	.327	.388	88	-1	4			.846	-1	/O-9,1-2	-0.2
	Cin-N	42	150	44	42	4	1	0	10	37	10	.280	.440	.320	101	3	27			.827	-2	O-40/1-1	-0.1
	Yr	53	199	55	54	5	4	0	15	42	12	.271	.415	.337	99	2	31			.832	-3	O-49/1-3	-0.3
1894	Was-N	98	347	86	105	11	7	0	36	80	31	.303	.447	.375	103	9	41			.900	-23	2-79,O-12/S-3,3-1	-0.9
Total	6	221	780	172	223	23	16	1	90	156	73	.286	.419	.360	106	17	86			.852	-29	O-110/2-92,S-8,13C	-1.0

■ **GARY WARD** Ward, Gary Lamell b: 12/6/53, Los Angeles, Cal. BR/TR, 6′2″, 202 lbs. Deb: 9/3/79

YEAR	TM/L	G	AB	R	H	2B	3B	HR	RBI	BB	SO	AVG	OBP	SLG	PRO+	BR/A	SB	CS	SBR	FA	FR	G/POS	TPR
1979	Min-A	10	14	2	4	0	0	0	1	3	3	.286	.412	.286	89	-0	0	1	-1	1.000	-1	/O-5,D-3	-0.1
1980	Min-A	13	41	11	19	6	2	1	10	3	6	.463	.500	.780	228	7	0	0	0	1.000	-2	O-12	0.4
1981	Min-A	85	295	42	78	7	6	3	29	28	48	.264	.328	.359	92	-3	5	2	0	.975	6	O-80/D-2	0.0
1982	Min-A	152	570	85	165	33	7	28	91	37	105	.289	.334	.519	127	19	13	1	3	.989	13	*O-150/D-2	3.0
1983	Min-A★	157	623	76	173	34	5	19	88	44	98	.278	.328	.440	105	4	8	1	2	.978	**26**	*O-152/D-2	2.6
1984	Tex-A	155	602	97	171	21	7	21	79	55	95	.284	.344	.447	113	10	7	5	-1	.987	12	*O-148/D-5	1.7
1985	Tex-A★	154	593	77	170	28	7	15	70	39	97	.287	.332	.433	106	4	26	7	4	.969	2	*O-153/D-1	0.5
1986	Tex-A	105	380	54	120	15	2	5	51	31	72	.316	.373	.405	109	6	12	8	-1	.996	13	*O-104/D-1	1.4
1987	NY-A	146	529	65	131	22	1	16	78	33	101	.248	.293	.384	78	-17	9	1	2	.985	-4	O-94,D-36,1-15	-2.3
1988	NY-A	91	231	26	52	8	0	4	24	24	41	.225	.304	.312	73	-8	0	1	-1	.992	-4	O-54,1-11/3-2,D-9	-1.5
1989	NY-A	8	17	3	5	1	0	0	1	3	5	.294	.400	.353	115	1	0	0	0	1.000	-1	/O-6,D-1	-0.1
	Det-A	105	275	24	69	10	2	9	29	21	54	.251	.304	.400	99	-1	1	3	-2	.990	0	O-51,1-26,D-26	-0.6
	Yr	113	292	27	74	11	2	9	30	24	59	.253	.310	.397	100	-1	1	3	-2	.991	-1	O-57,D-27,1-26	-0.7
1990	Det-A	106	309	32	79	11	2	9	46	30	50	.256	.324	.392	98	-1	2	0	1	.988	-4	O-85,D-13/1-2	-0.7
Total	12	1287	4479	594	1236	196	41	130	597	351	775	.276	.330	.425	104	20	83	30	7	.984	55	*O-1094,D-101/13	4.3

■ **JIM WARD** Ward, James H. H. b: 3/2/1855, Boston, Mass. d: 6/4/1886, Boston, Mass. Deb: 8/3/1876

YEAR	TM/L	G	AB	R	H	2B	3B	HR	RBI	BB	SO	AVG	OBP	SLG	PRO+	BR/A	SB	CS	SBR	FA	FR	G/POS	TPR
1876	Phi-N	1	4	1	2	0	0	0	1	0	1	.500	.500	.500	236	1				.750	-0	/C-1	0.0

■ **RUBE WARD** Ward, John Andrew b: 2/6/1879, New Lexington, Ohio d: 1/17/45, Akron, Ohio Deb: 4/28/02

YEAR	TM/L	G	AB	R	H	2B	3B	HR	RBI	BB	SO	AVG	OBP	SLG	PRO+	BR/A	SB	CS	SBR	FA	FR	G/POS	TPR
1902	Bro-N	13	31	4	9	1	0	0	2	2		.290	.333	.323	102	0	0			.850	-1	O-11	-0.2

■ **JOHN WARD** Ward, John E. b: Washington, D.C. Deb: 5/23/1884

YEAR	TM/L	G	AB	R	H	2B	3B	HR	RBI	BB	SO	AVG	OBP	SLG	PRO+	BR/A	SB	CS	SBR	FA	FR	G/POS	TPR
1884	Was-U	1	4	0	1	0	0	0		0		.250	.250	.250	54	-0				.000	-1	/O-1	-0.1

■ **JAY WARD** Ward, John Francis b: 9/9/38, Brookfield, Mo. BR/TR, 6′1″, 185 lbs. Deb: 5/6/63 C

YEAR	TM/L	G	AB	R	H	2B	3B	HR	RBI	BB	SO	AVG	OBP	SLG	PRO+	BR/A	SB	CS	SBR	FA	FR	G/POS	TPR
1963	Min-A	9	15	0	1	1	0	0	2	1	5	.067	.125	.133	-27	-3	0	0	0	1.000	-1	/3-4,O-1	-0.3
1964	Min-A	12	31	4	7	2	0	0	2	6	13	.226	.351	.290	80	-1	0	0	0	.977	0	/2-9,O-3	0.0
1970	Cin-N	6	3	0	0	0	0	0	0	2	1	.000	.400	.000	17	-0	0	0	0	1.000	-0	/3-2,1-1,2-1	0.0
Total	3	27	49	4	8	3	0	0	4	9	19	.163	.293	.224	46	-3	0	0	0	.977	-1	/2-10,3-6,O-4,1-1	-0.3

■ **JOHN WARD** Ward, John Montgomery b: 3/3/1860, Bellefonte, Pa. d: 3/4/25, Augusta, Ga. BL/TR, 5′9″, 165 lbs. Deb: 7/15/1878 MH

YEAR	TM/L	G	AB	R	H	2B	3B	HR	RBI	BB	SO	AVG	OBP	SLG	PRO+	BR/A	SB	CS	SBR	FA	FR	G/POS	TPR
1878	Pro-N	37	138	14	27	5	4	1	15	2	13	.196	.207	.312	69	-5				.866	2	P-37	0.0
1879	Pro-N	83	364	71	104	9	4	2	41	7	14	.286	.299	.349	115	6				.938	3	*P-70,3-16/O-8	0.1
1880	Pro-N	86	356	53	81	12	2	0	27	6	16	.228	.240	.272	76	-9				.983	14	*P-70,3-25/O-2,M	0.7
1881	Pro-N	85	357	56	87	18	6	0	53	5	10	.244	.254	.328	83	-7				.887	6	O-40,P-39,S-13	-0.3
1882	Pro-N	83	355	58	87	10	3	1	39	13	22	.245	.272	.299	83	-7				.824	10	O-50,P-33/S-4	0.1
1883	NY-N	88	380	76	97	18	7	7	54	8	25	.255	.271	.395	100	-0				.859	19	O-56,P-34/3-5,S2	1.3
1884	NY-N	113	482	98	122	11	8	2	51	28	47	.253	.294	.322	91	-5				.847	8	O-59,2-47/P-9,M	0.2
1885	NY-N	111	446	72	101	8	9	0	37	17	39	.226	.255	.285	75	-12				.904	6	*S-111	-0.4
1886	NY-N	122	491	82	134	17	5	2	81	19	46	.273	.300	.340	93	-5	36			.870	-3	*S-122	-0.6
1887	NY-N	129	545	114	184	16	5	1	53	29	12	.338	.375	.391	119	15	**111**			**.919**	30	*S-129	3.9
1888	*NY-N	122	510	70	128	14	5	2	49	9	13	.251	.265	.310	84	-10	38			.857	-3	*S-122	-1.0
1889	*NY-N	114	479	87	143	13	4	1	67	27	7	.299	.339	.349	92	-5	62			.890	6	*S-108/2-7	0.6
1890	Bro-P	128	561	134	188	15	12	4	60	51	22	.335	.393	.426	112	8	63			.878	21	*S-128,M	2.9
1891	Bro-N	105	441	85	122	13	5	0	39	36	10	.277	.335	.329	94	-3	57			.878	-0	S-87,2-18,M	0.3
1892	Bro-N	148	614	109	163	13	3	1	47	82	19	.265	.355	.301	103	6	**88**			.920	3	*2-148,M	1.1
1893	NY-N	135	588	129	193	27	9	2	77	47	5	.328	.379	.415	111	8	46			.918	7	*2-134,M	1.5
1894	*NY-N	136	540	100	143	12	5	0	77	34	6	.265	.310	.306	49	-45	39			.924	5	*2-136,M	-2.6
Total	17	1825	7647	1408	2104	231	96	26	867	420	326	.275	.314	.341	93	-69	540			.885	133	S-826,2-491,PO/3	7.8

■ **JOE WARD** Ward, Joseph A. b: 9/2/1884, Philadelphia, Pa. d: 8/11/34, Philadelphia, Pa. TR , Deb: 4/24/06

YEAR	TM/L	G	AB	R	H	2B	3B	HR	RBI	BB	SO	AVG	OBP	SLG	PRO+	BR/A	SB	CS	SBR	FA	FR	G/POS	TPR
1906	Phi-N	35	129	12	38	8	6	0	11	5		.295	.321	.450	140	5	2			.929	-6	3-27/2-3,S-1	0.0
1909	NY-A	9	28	3	5	0	0	0	0	1		.179	.233	.179	30	-2	2			.846	-5	/2-7,1-1	-0.9
	Phi-N	74	184	21	49	8	2	0	23	9		.266	.304	.332	96	-1	7			.944	-10	2-48/S-8,1-5,O-2	-1.3
1910	Phi-N	48	124	11	18	2	1	0	13	3	11	.145	.178	.177	4	-15	1			.975	2	1-32/S-1,3-1	-1.5
Total	3	166	465	47	110	18	9	0	47	18	11	.237	.271	.314	78	-14	12			.929	-20	/2-58,1-38,3-28,SO	-3.7

■ **HAP WARD** Ward, Joseph Nichols b: 11/15/1885, Leesburg, N.J. d: 9/13/79, Elmer, N.J. Deb: 5/18/12

YEAR	TM/L	G	AB	R	H	2B	3B	HR	RBI	BB	SO	AVG	OBP	SLG	PRO+	BR/A	SB	CS	SBR	FA	FR	G/POS	TPR
1912	Det-A	1	2	0	0	0	0	0	0	0		.000	.000	.000	-99	-1	0			1.000	0	/O-1	0.0

■ KEVIN WARD
Ward, Kevin Michael b: 9/28/61, Lansdale, Pa. BR/TR, 6'1", 195 lbs. Deb: 5/10/91

YEAR	TM/L	G	AB	R	H	2B	3B	HR	RBI	BB	SO	AVG	OBP	SLG	PRO+	BR/A	SB	CS	SBR	FA	FR	G/POS	TPR
1991	SD-N	44	107	13	26	7	2	2	8	9	27	.243	.308	.402	95	-1	1	4	-2	.982	-2	O-33	-0.6
1992	SD-N	81	147	12	29	5	0	3	12	14	38	.197	.276	.293	60	-8	2	3	-1	.946	-6	O-51	-1.7
Total	2	125	254	25	55	12	2	5	20	23	65	.217	.289	.339	75	-9	3	7	-3	.961	-9	/O-84	-2.3

■ PETE WARD
Ward, Peter Thomas b: 7/26/39, Montreal, Que., Can BL/TR, 6'1", 200 lbs. Deb: 9/21/62 C

YEAR	TM/L	G	AB	R	H	2B	3B	HR	RBI	BB	SO	AVG	OBP	SLG	PRO+	BR/A	SB	CS	SBR	FA	FR	G/POS	TPR
1962	Bal-A	8	21	1	3	2	0	0	2	4	5	.143	.280	.238	44	-2	0	0	0	1.000	-0	/O-6	-0.2
1963	Chi-A	157	600	80	177	34	6	22	84	52	77	.295	.356	.482	135	27	7	6	-2	.923	-5	*3-154/2-1,S-1	2.1
1964	Chi-A	144	539	61	152	28	3	23	94	56	76	.282	.352	.473	131	22	1	1	-0	.958	13	*3-138	3.4
1965	Chi-A	138	507	62	125	25	3	10	57	56	83	.247	.329	.367	104	2	2	4	-2	.952	9	*3-134/2-1	0.7
1966	Chi-A	84	251	22	55	7	1	3	28	24	49	.219	.295	.291	74	-8	3	1	0	.989	-2	O-59,3-16/1-5	-1.4
1967	Chi-A	146	467	49	109	16	2	18	62	61	109	.233	.336	.392	119	12	3	2	-0	.991	-17	O-89,1-39,3-22	-1.3
1968	Chi-A	125	399	43	86	15	0	15	50	76	85	.216	.355	.366	117	11	4	3	-1	.946	-9	3-77,1-31,O-22	-0.1
1969	Chi-A	105	199	22	49	7	0	6	32	33	38	.246	.362	.372	101	1	0	0	0	.994	-2	1-25,3-21/O-9	-0.3
1970	NY-A	66	77	5	20	2	2	1	18	9	17	.260	.337	.377	102	0	0	0	0	1.000	-1	1-13	-0.1
Total	9	973	3060	345	776	136	17	98	427	371	539	.254	.342	.405	116	65	20	17	-4	.945	-14	3-562,O-185,1/2S	2.8

■ PRESTON WARD
Ward, Preston Meyer b: 7/24/27, Columbia, Mo. BL/TR, 6'3", 198 lbs. Deb: 4/20/48

YEAR	TM/L	G	AB	R	H	2B	3B	HR	RBI	BB	SO	AVG	OBP	SLG	PRO+	BR/A	SB	CS	SBR	FA	FR	G/POS	TPR
1948	Bro-N	42	146	9	38	9	2	1	21	15	23	.260	.329	.370	86	-3	0			.990	-2	1-38	-0.5
1950	Chi-N	80	285	31	72	11	2	6	33	27	42	.253	.317	.368	81	-8	3			.995	10	1-76	0.0
1953	Chi-N	33	100	10	23	5	0	4	12	18	21	.230	.347	.400	92	-1	3	1	0	.961	-7	O-27/1-7	-0.8
	Pit-N	88	281	35	59	7	1	8	27	44	39	.210	.319	.327	69	-12	1	3	-2	.991	4	1-78	-1.2
	Yr	121	381	45	82	12	1	12	39	62	60	.215	.327	.346	76	-13	4	4	-1	.991	-2	1-85,O-27	-2.0
1954	Pit-N	117	360	37	97	16	2	7	48	39	61	.269	.341	.383	90	-5	0	0	0	.984	5	1-48,O-42,3-11	-0.4
1955	Pit-N	84	179	16	38	7	4	5	25	22	28	.212	.299	.380	80	-6	0	0	0	.998	2	1-48/O-1	-0.6
1956	Pit-N	16	30	3	10	0	1	1	11	6	4	.333	.444	.500	157	3	0	0	0	1.000	-5	/3-5,O-5	-0.2
	Cle-A	87	150	18	38	10	0	6	21	16	20	.253	.325	.440	98	-1	0	0	0	.988	2	1-60,O-17	-0.1
1957	Cle-A	10	11	2	2	1	0	0	0	0	2	.182	.182	.273	23	-1	0	0	0	1.000	-0	/1-1	-0.1
1958	Cle-A	48	148	22	50	3	1	4	21	10	27	.338	.384	.453	133	6	0	1	-1	.957	-3	3-24,1-21	0.2
	KC-A	81	268	28	68	10	1	6	24	27	36	.254	.322	.366	87	-5	0	1	-1	.989	-7	1-39,3-34/O-2	-1.5
	Yr	129	416	50	118	13	2	10	45	37	63	.284	.344	.397	103	2	0	2	-1	.992	-10	1-60,3-58/O-2	-1.3
1959	KC-A	58	109	8	27	4	1	2	19	7	12	.248	.293	.358	76	-4	0	0	0	.982	-3	1-22/O-1	-0.8
Total	9	744	2067	219	522	83	15	50	262	231	315	.253	.328	.380	88	-36	7	6		.992	-3	1-438/O-95,3-74	-6.0

■ TURNER WARD
Ward, Turner Max b: 4/11/65, Orlando, Fla. BB/TR, 6'2", 200 lbs. Deb: 9/10/90

YEAR	TM/L	G	AB	R	H	2B	3B	HR	RBI	BB	SO	AVG	OBP	SLG	PRO+	BR/A	SB	CS	SBR	FA	FR	G/POS	TPR
1990	Cle-A	14	46	10	16	2	1	1	10	3	8	.348	.388	.500	147	3	3	0	1	.957	0	O-13/D-1	0.4
1991	Cle-A	40	100	11	23	7	0	0	5	10	16	.230	.300	.300	66	-4	0	0	0	1.000	-2	O-38	-0.7
	Tor-A	8	13	1	4	0	0	0	2	1	2	.308	.357	.308	83	-0	0	0	0	1.000	-1	/O-6	-0.2
	Yr	48	113	12	27	7	0	0	7	11	18	.239	.306	.301	68	-5	0	0	0	1.000	-3	O-44	-0.9
1992	Tor-A	18	29	7	10	3	0	1	3	4	4	.345	.424	.552	164	3	0	1	-1	1.000	-1	O-12	0.1
1993	Tor-A	72	167	20	32	4	2	4	28	23	26	.192	.293	.311	62	-9	3	3	-1	.990	-7	O-65/1-1	-1.7
1994	Mil-A	102	367	55	85	15	2	9	45	52	68	.232	.332	.357	74	-14	6	2	1	.985	3	O-99/3-1	-1.2
1995	Mil-A	44	129	19	34	3	1	4	16	14	21	.264	.340	.395	86	-3	6	1	1	.989	-2	O-40/D-1	-0.4
1996	Mil-A	43	67	7	12	2	1	2	10	13	17	.179	.313	.328	60	-4	3	0	1	1.000	-4	O-32/D-1	-0.7
1997	Pit-N	71	167	33	59	16	1	7	33	18	17	.353	.422	.587	158	14	4	1	1	1.000	-10	O-54	0.4
1998	Pit-N	123	282	33	74	13	3	9	46	27	40	.262	.335	.426	94	-2	5	4	-1	.983	-5	O-97/D-1	-0.9
Total	9	535	1367	196	349	65	11	37	198	165	219	.255	.340	.400	91	-17	30	12	2	.989	-29	O-456/D-4,3-1,1-1	-4.9

■ BUZZY WARES
Wares, Clyde Ellsworth b: 3/23/1886, Vandalia, Mich. d: 5/26/64, South Bend, Ind. BR/TR, 5'10", 150 lbs. Deb: 9/15/13 C

YEAR	TM/L	G	AB	R	H	2B	3B	HR	RBI	BB	SO	AVG	OBP	SLG	PRO+	BR/A	SB	CS	SBR	FA	FR	G/POS	TPR
1913	StL-A	11	35	5	10	2	0	0	1	1	3	.286	.306	.343	92	-1	2			.973	-4	/2-9	-0.5
1914	StL-A	81	215	20	45	10	1	0	23	28	35	.209	.300	.265	73	-7	10	10	-3	.903	-2	S-68/2-8	-0.7
Total	2	92	250	25	55	12	1	0	24	29	38	.220	.301	.276	76	-7	12	10		.973	-6	/S-68,2-17	-1.2

■ FRED WARNER
Warner, Frederick John Rodney b: 1855, Philadelphia, Pa. d: 2/13/1886, Philadelphia, Pa. 5'7", 155 lbs. Deb: 4/30/1875

YEAR	TM/L	G	AB	R	H	2B	3B	HR	RBI	BB	SO	AVG	OBP	SLG	PRO+	BR/A	SB	CS	SBR	FA	FR	G/POS	TPR
1875	Cen-n	14	57	11	14	4	0	0	2	1	2	.246	.259	.316	107	1	0	0	0	.784	-0	O-14	0.1
1876	Phi-N	1	3	0	0	0	0	0	0	0	0	.000	.000	.000	-99	-1				.600	-0	/O-1	-0.1
1878	Ind-N	43	165	19	41	4	0	0	10	2	15	.248	.257	.273	86	-2				.907	-3	*S-41/O-2	-0.3
1879	Cle-N	76	316	32	77	11	4	0	22	2	20	.244	.248	.304	82	-6				.827	0	3-54,O-21/1-1	-0.5
1883	Phi-N	39	141	13	32	6	1	0	13	5	21	.227	.253	.284	69	-5				.775	-9	3-38/O-1	-1.2
1884	Bro-a	84	352	40	78	4	0	1		17		.222	.259	.241	64	-13				.824	-6	*3-84	-1.7
Total	5	243	977	104	228	25	5	1	45	26	56	.233	.254	.272	73	-27				.815	-18	3-176/S-41,O-25,1-1	-3.8

■ HOOKS WARNER
Warner, Hoke Hayden b: 5/22/1894, Del Rio, Tex. d: 2/19/47, San Francisco, Cal BL/TR, 5'10.5", 170 lbs. Deb: 8/21/16

YEAR	TM/L	G	AB	R	H	2B	3B	HR	RBI	BB	SO	AVG	OBP	SLG	PRO+	BR/A	SB	CS	SBR	FA	FR	G/POS	TPR
1916	Pit-N	44	168	12	40	1	1	2	14	6	19	.238	.264	.292	70	-6	6			.899	-11	3-42/2-1	-1.9
1917	Pit-N	3	5	0	1	0	0	0	0	0	1	.200	.200	.200	22	-0	0			1.000	1	/3-1	0.1
1919	Pit-N	6	8	0	1	0	0	0	2	3	1	.125	.364	.125	48	-0	0			.818	1	/3-3	0.0
1921	Chi-N	14	38	4	8	1	0	0	3	2	1	.211	.268	.237	35	-3	1	1	-0	.957	-1	3-10	-0.4
Total	4	67	219	16	50	2	1	2	19	11	22	.228	.268	.274	61	-10	7	1		.906	-10	/3-56,2-1	-2.2

■ JOHN WARNER
Warner, John Joseph b: 8/15/1872, New York, N.Y. d: 12/21/43, Far Rockaway, N.Y. BL/TR, 5'11", 165 lbs. Deb: 4/23/1895

YEAR	TM/L	G	AB	R	H	2B	3B	HR	RBI	BB	SO	AVG	OBP	SLG	PRO+	BR/A	SB	CS	SBR	FA	FR	G/POS	TPR
1895	Bos-N	3	7	2	1	0	0	0	1	1	0	.143	.333	.143	24	-1	0			.917	1	/C-3	0.0
	Lou-N	67	232	20	62	4	2	1	20	11	16	.267	.320	.315	68	-11	10			.931	-10	C-64/1-3,2-1	-1.2
	Yr	70	239	22	63	4	2	1	21	12	16	.264	.320	.310	67	-11	10			.930	-10	C-67/1-3,2-1	-1.2
1896	Lou-N	33	110	9	25	1	1	0	10	10	10	.227	.303	.255	50	-8	3			.939	9	C-32/1-1	0.4
	NY-N	19	54	9	14	1	0	0	3	3	7	.259	.310	.278	57	-3	1			.922	-1	C-19	-0.2
	Yr	52	164	18	39	2	1	0	13	13	17	.238	.306	.262	52	-11	4			.934	9	C-51/1-1	0.2
1897	NY-N	110	397	50	109	6	3	2	51	26		.275	.344	.320	78	-11	8			.952	16	*C-110	1.4
1898	NY-N	110	373	40	96	14	5	0	42	22		.257	.316	.322	86	-7	9			.968	15	*C-109/O-1	1.7
1899	NY-N	88	293	38	78	8	1	0	19	15		.266	.315	.300	72	-11	15			.952	12	C-82/1-3	0.7
1900	NY-N	34	108	15	27	4	0	0	13	8		.250	.319	.287	71	-4	1			.948	3	C-31	0.1
1901	NY-N	87	291	19	70	6	1	0	20	3		.241	.268	.268	58	-16	3			.967	-3	C-84	-1.1
1902	Bos-A	65	222	19	52	5	7	0	12	13		.234	.286	.320	66	-11	0			.979	4	C-64	0.0
1903	NY-N	89	285	38	81	8	5	0	34	7		.284	.322	.347	87	-5	5			**.986**	12	C-85	1.4
1904	NY-N	86	287	29	57	5	1	1	15	14		.199	.253	.233	48	-17	7			**.982**	2	C-86	-0.7
1905	StL-N	41	137	9	35	2	2	1	12	6		.255	.301	.321	88	-2	2			.958	3	C-41	0.5
	Det-A	36	119	12	24	2	3	0	7	8		.202	.252	.269	65	-5	2			.974	1	C-36	0.0
1906	Det-A	50	153	15	37	4	2	0	10	12		.242	.326	.294	92	-1	4			.978	9	C-49	1.3
	Was-A	32	103	5	21	4	1	1	9	2		.204	.226	.291	65	-5	3			.968	9	C-32	0.8
	Yr	82	256	20	58	8	3	1	19	14		.227	.288	.293	82	-5	7			.974	18	C-81	2.1
1907	Was-A	72	207	11	53	5	0	0	17	12		.256	.306	.280	95	-1	3			.971	-8	C-64	-0.5
1908	Was-A	51	116	8	28	2	1	0	8	8		.241	.313	.276	100	0	7			.982	1	C-41/1-1	0.5
Total	14	1073	3494	348	870	81	35	6	303	181	33	.249	.303	.297	74	-118	83			.966	73	*C-1032/1-8,O-1,2-1	5.1

■ JACKIE WARNER
Warner, John Joseph b: 8/1/43, Monrovia, Cal. BR/TR, 6', 180 lbs. Deb: 4/12/66

YEAR	TM/L	G	AB	R	H	2B	3B	HR	RBI	BB	SO	AVG	OBP	SLG	PRO+	BR/A	SB	CS	SBR	FA	FR	G/POS	TPR
1966	Cal-A	45	123	22	26	4	1	7	16	9	55	.211	.265	.431	99	-1	0	0	0	.984	-2	O-37	-0.4

■ JACK WARNER
Warner, John Ralph b: 8/29/03, Evansville, Ind. d: 3/13/86, Mt.Vernon, Ill. BR/TR, 5'9.5", 165 lbs. Deb: 9/24/25

YEAR	TM/L	G	AB	R	H	2B	3B	HR	RBI	BB	SO	AVG	OBP	SLG	PRO+	BR/A	SB	CS	SBR	FA	FR	G/POS	TPR
1925	Det-A	10	39	7	13	0	0	0	2	3	6	.333	.381	.333	84	-1	0	0	0	1.000	-2	3-10	-0.2
1926	Det-A	100	311	41	78	8	6	0	34	38	24	.251	.342	.315	71	-12	8	4	0	.956	-4	3-95/S-3	-1.0
1927	Det-A	139	559	78	149	22	9	1	45	47	45	.267	.330	.343	74	-21	14	4	2	.947	-5	*3-138	-1.7
1928	Det-A	75	206	33	44	4	4	0	13	16	15	.214	.274	.272	43	-17	4	4	-1	.944	6	3-52/S-7	-0.9

YEAR	TM/L	G	AB	R	H	2B	3B	HR	RBI	BB	SO	AVG	OBP	SLG	PRO+	BR/A	SB	CS	SBR	FA	FR	G/POS	TPR
1929	Bro-N	17	62	3	17	2	0	0	4	7	6	.274	.348	.306	65	-3	3			.945	-2	S-17	-0.3
1930	Bro-N	21	25	4	8	1	0	0	0	2	7	.320	.370	.360	79	-1	1			1.000	2	/3-8	0.1
1931	Bro-N	9	4	2	2	0	0	0	0	1	1	.500	.600	.500	200	1	0			1.000	2	/S-2,3-1	0.3
1933	Phi-N	107	340	31	76	15	1	0	22	28	33	.224	.285	.274	53	-20	1			.973	3	2-71,3-30/S-1	-1.2
Total	8	478	1546	199	387	52	20	1	120	142	137	.250	.319	.312	65	-75	31	12		.950	0	3-334/2-71,S-30	-4.9
■ HAL WARNOCK	Warnock, Harold Charles b: 1/6/12, New York, N.Y. d: 2/8/97, Tucson, Ariz. BL/TR, 6′2″, 180 lbs. Deb: 9/2/35																						
1935	StL-A	6	7	1	2	2	0	0	0	0	3	.286	.286	.571	112	0	0	0	0	1.000	-1	/O-2	-0.1
■ BENNIE WARREN	Warren, Bennie Louis b: 3/2/12, Elk City, Okla. d: 5/11/94, Oklahoma City, Okla. BR/TR, 6′1″, 184 lbs. Deb: 9/13/39																						
1939	Phi-N	18	56	4	13	0	0	1	7	7	7	.232	.317	.286	65	-3	0			.958	-4	C-17	-0.5
1940	Phi-N	106	289	33	71	6	1	12	34	40	46	.246	.339	.398	107	3	1			.975	-4	C-97/1-1	0.6
1941	Phi-N	121	345	34	74	13	2	9	35	44	66	.214	.309	.342	86	-6	0			.973	-4	*C-110	-0.2
1942	Phi-N	90	225	19	47	6	3	7	20	24	36	.209	.288	.356	92	-3	0			.972	-2	C-78/1-1	0.1
1946	NY-N	39	69	7	11	1	1	4	8	14	21	.159	.301	.377	91	-1	0			.965	1	C-30	0.2
1947	NY-N	3	5	0	1	0	0	0	0	0	1	.200	.200	.200	6	-1	0			1.000	-1	/C-3	-0.1
Total	6	377	989	97	217	26	7	33	104	129	177	.219	.313	.360	92	-11	1			.972	-13	C-335/1-2	0.1
■ BILL WARREN	Warren, William Hackney "Hack" b: 2/11/1883, Missouri d: 1/28/60, Whiteville, Tenn. BR/TR, 5′8″, 165 lbs. Deb: 4/30/14																						
1914	Ind-F	26	50	5	12	2	0	0	5	5	7	.240	.309	.280	55	-4	2			.931	-5	C-23	-0.8
1915	New-F	5	3	0	1	0	0	0	1	0	0	.333	.333	.333	93	-0	0			1.000	-0	/C-1,1-1	0.0
Total	2	31	53	5	13	2	0	0	6	5	7	.245	.310	.283	57	-4	2			.932	-5	/C-24,1-1	-0.8
■ RABBIT WARSTLER	Warstler, Harold Burton b: 9/13/03, N.Canton, Ohio d: 5/31/64, N.Canton, Ohio BR/TR, 5′7.5″, 150 lbs. Deb: 7/24/30																						
1930	Bos-A	54	162	16	30	2	3	1	13	20	21	.185	.275	.253	36	-16	0	2	-1	.947	-3	S-54	-1.3
1931	Bos-A	66	181	20	44	5	3	0	10	15	27	.243	.308	.304	65	-9	2	3	-1	.933	1	2-42,S-19/3-1	-0.5
1932	Bos-A	115	388	26	82	15	5	0	34	22	43	.211	.259	.276	40	-35	9	6	-1	.939	**28**	*S-107	0.1
1933	Bos-A	92	322	44	70	13	1	1	17	42	36	.217	.308	.273	55	-20	2	4	-2	.951	1	S-87	-1.4
1934	Phi-A	117	419	56	99	19	3	1	36	51	30	.236	.321	.303	64	-22	9	3	1	.969	16	*2-107/S-2	0.1
1935	Phi-A	138	496	62	124	20	7	3	59	56	53	.250	.326	.337	72	-20	8	4	0	.959	2	*2-136/3-2	-0.7
1936	Phi-A	66	236	27	59	8	6	1	24	36	16	.250	.354	.347	75	-9	0	0	0	.973	11	2-66	0.6
	Bos-N	74	304	27	64	6	0	0	17	22	33	.211	.266	.230	37	-27	2			.948	13	S-74	-0.9
1937	Bos-N	149	555	57	124	20	0	3	36	51	62	.223	.291	.276	60	-31	4			.942	-11	*S-149	-3.1
1938	Bos-N	142	467	37	108	10	4	0	40	48	38	.231	.303	.270	65	-22	3			.937	-7	*S-135/2-7	-1.9
1939	Bos-N	114	342	34	83	11	3	0	24	24	31	.243	.292	.292	62	-19	2			.953	1	S-49,2-43,3-21	-1.1
1940	Bos-N	33	57	6	12	0	0	0	4	10	5	.211	.328	.211	54	-3	0			.974	-1	2-24/3-2,S-1	-0.3
	Chi-N	45	159	19	36	4	1	1	18	8	19	.226	.263	.283	52	-11	1			.939	-1	S-28,2-17	-0.9
	Yr	78	216	25	48	4	1	1	22	18	24	.222	.282	.264	53	-14	1			.960	-2	2-41,S-29/3-2	-1.2
Total	11	1205	4088	431	935	133	36	11	332	405	414	.229	.300	.287	59	-243	42	22		.942	49	S-705,2-442/3-26	-11.3
■ CARL WARWICK	Warwick, Carl Wayne b: 2/27/37, Dallas, Tex. BR/TL, 5′10″, 170 lbs. Deb: 4/11/61																						
1961	LA-N	19	11	2	1	0	0	0	1	2	3	.091	.231	.091	-9	-2	0	0	0	1.000	-4	O-12	-0.6
	StL-N	55	152	27	38	6	2	4	16	18	33	.250	.329	.395	83	-4	3	0	1	.970	-5	O-48	-1.1
	Yr	74	163	29	39	6	2	4	17	20	36	.239	.322	.374	77	-5	3	0	1	.970	-10	O-60	-1.7
1962	StL-N	13	23	4	8	0	0	1	4	2	2	.348	.400	.478	123	1	2	0	1	1.000	-1	O-10	0.0
	Hou-N	130	477	63	124	17	1	16	60	38	77	.260	.315	.400	98	-3	2	3	-1	.986	1	*O-128	-1.1
	Yr	143	500	67	132	17	1	17	64	40	79	.264	.319	.404	98	-3	4	3	-1	.986	-0	*O-138	-1.1
1963	Hou-N	150	528	49	134	19	5	7	47	49	70	.254	.320	.348	98	-1	3	3	-1	.988	-2	*O-141/1-2	-1.3
1964	*StL-N	88	158	14	41	7	1	3	15	11	30	.259	.308	.373	83	-3	2	0	1	.933	-6	O-49	-1.1
1965	StL-N	50	77	3	12	2	1	0	6	4	18	.156	.198	.208	13	-9	1	0	0	.960	-3	O-21/1-4	-1.3
	Bal-A	9	14	3	0	0	0	0	0	3	2	.000	.176	.000	-44	-3	0	0	0	1.000	-1	/O-3	-0.4
1966	Chi-N	16	22	3	5	0	0	0	0	0	6	.227	.227	.227	27	-2	0	0	0	1.000	-2	O-10	-0.4
Total	6	530	1462	168	363	51	10	31	149	127	241	.248	.309	.360	87	-26	13	6	0	.980	-24	O-422/1-6	-7.3
■ BILL WARWICK	Warwick, Firmin Newton b: 11/26/1897, Philadelphia, Pa. d: 12/19/84, San Antonio, Tex. BR/TR, 6′0.5″, 180 lbs. Deb: 7/18/21																						
1921	Pit-N	1	1	0	0	0	0	0	0	0	0	.000	.000	.000	-97	-0	0	0	0	.500	-0	/C-1	0.0
1925	StL-N	13	41	8	12	1	2	1	6	5	5	.293	.370	.488	114	1	0	1	-1	1.000	-4	C-13	-0.3
1926	StL-N	9	14	0	5	0	0	0	2	0	2	.357	.357	.357	89	-0	0			.923	2	/C-9	0.2
Total	3	23	56	8	17	1	2	1	8	5	7	.304	.361	.446	105	0	0	1		.954	-2	/C-23	-0.1
■ JIMMY WASDELL	Wasdell, James Charles b: 5/15/14, Cleveland, Ohio d: 8/6/83, New Port Richey, Fla. BL/TL, 5′11″, 185 lbs. Deb: 9/3/37																						
1937	Was-A	32	110	13	28	4	4	2	12	7	13	.255	.299	.418	82	-4	0	1	-1	.995	-0	1-21/O-7	-0.7
1938	Was-A	53	140	19	33	2	1	2	16	12	12	.236	.296	.307	55	-10	5	2	0	.996	-1	1-26/O-6	-1.3
1939	Was-A	29	109	12	33	5	1	0	13	9	16	.303	.361	.367	94	-1	3	1	0	.964	-2	1-28	-0.6
1940	Was-A	10	35	3	3	1	0	0	0	2	7	.086	.135	.114	-37	-7	0	0	0	1.000	-1	/1-8	-0.9
	Bro-N	77	230	35	64	14	4	3	37	18	24	.278	.333	.413	99	-1	4			.947	-7	O-42,1-17	-1.1
1941	*Bro-N	94	265	39	79	14	3	4	48	16	15	.298	.345	.419	110	3	2			.956	-6	O-54,1-15	-0.8
1942	Pit-N	122	409	44	106	11	2	3	38	47	22	.259	.337	.318	90	-4	1			.957	-3	O-97/1-7	-1.4
1943	Pit-N	4	2	0	1	0	0	0	1	2	0	.500	.750	.500	256	1	0			.000	0	H	0.1
	Phi-N	141	522	54	136	19	6	4	67	46	22	.261	.323	.343	96	-3	6			.988	-8	1-82,O-56	-2.0
	Yr	145	524	54	137	19	6	4	68	48	22	.261	.326	.344	97	-2	6			.988	-8	1-82,O-56	-1.9
1944	Phi-N	133	451	47	125	20	3	3	40	45	17	.277	.344	.355	100	1	0			.980	-9	*O-121/1-4	-1.5
1945	Phi-N	134	500	65	150	19	8	7	60	32	11	.300	.346	.412	113	7	7			.967	-2	O-65,1-63	-0.2
1946	Phi-N	26	51	7	13	0	2	1	5	3	2	.255	.309	.392	101	-0	0			.923	-2	O-11/1-2	-0.3
	Cle-A	32	41	1	11	0	0	0	4	4	4	.268	.333	.268	74	-1	1	0	0	.939	-2	/1-4,O-3	-0.3
1947	Cle-A	1	1	0	0	0	0	0	0	0	0	.000	.000	.000	-99	-0	0	0	0	.000	0	H	0.0
Total	11	888	2866	339	782	109	34	29	341	243	165	.273	.332	.365	96	-20	29	4		.966	-45	O-462,1-277	-11.0
■ LINK WASEM	Wasem, Lincoln William b: 1/30/11, Birmingham, Ohio d: 3/6/79, S.Laguna, Cal. BR/TR, 5′9.5″, 180 lbs. Deb: 5/5/37																						
1937	Bos-N	2	1	0	0	0	0	0	0	0	0	.000	.000	.000	-99	-0	0			1.000	0	/C-2	0.0
■ LIBE WASHBURN	Washburn, Libeus b: 6/16/1874, Lyme, N.H. d: 3/22/40, Malone, N.Y. BB/TL, 5′10″, 180 lbs. Deb: 5/30/02																						
1902	NY-N	6	9	1	4	0	0	0	0	2		.444	.615	.444	229	2	1			1.000	-1	/O-3	0.1
1903	Phi-N	8	18	1	3	0	0	0	1	1		.167	.211	.167	8	-2	0			1.000	-1	/P-4,O-2	-0.1
Total	2	14	27	2	7	0	0	0	1	3		.259	.375	.259	89	-0	1			1.000	-1	/O-5,P-4	0.0
■ CLAUDELL WASHINGTON	Washington, Claudell b: 8/31/54, Los Angeles, Cal. BL/TL, 6′, 190 lbs. Deb: 7/5/74																						
1974	*Oak-A	73	221	16	63	10	5	0	19	13	44	.285	.328	.376	109	2	6	8	-3	.985	-1	D-38,O-32	-0.5
1975	*Oak-A★	148	590	86	182	24	7	10	77	32	80	.308	.349	.424	120	14	40	15	3	.978	-3	*O-148	0.8
1976	Oak-A	134	490	65	126	20	6	5	53	30	90	.257	.304	.353	96	-4	37	20	-1	.963	-2	*O-126/D-4	-1.3
1977	Tex-A	129	521	63	148	31	2	12	68	25	112	.284	.321	.420	99	-2	21	8	2	.978	-1	*O-127/D-1	-0.7
1978	Tex-A	12	42	1	7	0	0	0	2	1	12	.167	.186	.167	-0	-6	0	1	-1	.917	-1	/O-7,D-4	-0.8
	Chi-A	86	314	33	83	16	5	6	31	12	57	.264	.294	.404	94	-4	5	5	-2	.959	-2	O-82/D-1	-1.1
	Yr	98	356	34	90	16	5	6	33	13	69	.253	.281	.376	83	-9	5	6	-2	.957	-3	O-89/D-5	-1.9
1979	Chi-A	131	471	79	132	33	5	13	66	28	93	.280	.325	.454	108	4	19	11	-1	.974	4	*O-122/D-3	0.1
1980	Chi-A	32	90	15	26	4	2	1	12	5	19	.289	.333	.411	103	0	4	2	0	.933	-2	O-23/D-2	-0.2
	NY-N	79	284	38	78	16	4	10	42	20	63	.275	.325	.465	121	7	17	5	2	.978	2	O-70	0.8
1981	Atl-N	85	320	37	93	22	3	5	37	15	47	.291	.330	.425	110	3	12	6	0	.993	2	O-79	0.2
1982	*Atl-N	150	563	94	150	24	6	16	80	50	107	.266	.333	.416	104	3	33	10	4	.950	-4	*O-139	-0.2
1983	Atl-N	134	496	75	138	24	8	9	44	35	103	.278	.326	.413	96	-3	31	9	4	.974	2	*O-128	-0.1
1984	Atl-N★	120	416	62	119	21	2	17	61	59	77	.286	.376	.469	127	16	21	9	1	.967	-5	*O-107	0.8
1985	Atl-N	122	398	62	110	14	6	15	43	40	66	.276	.344	.455	115	7	14	4	2	.962	-14	O-99	-0.8

YEAR	TM/L	G	AB	R	H	2B	3B	HR	RBI	BB	SO	AVG	OBP	SLG	PRO+	BR/A	SB	CS	SBR	FA	FR	G/POS	TPR
1986	Atl-N	40	137	17	37	11	0	5	14	14	26	.270	.338	.460	112	2	4	7	-3	.957	-5	O-38	-0.8
	NY-A	54	135	19	32	5	0	6	16	7	33	.237	.285	.407	87	-3	6	1	1	.985	-6	O-39	-0.8
1987	NY-A	102	312	42	87	17	0	9	44	27	54	.279	.336	.420	100	-0	10	1	2	.988	0	O-72,D-13	0.0
1988	NY-A	126	455	62	140	22	3	11	64	24	74	.308	.345	.442	120	11	15	6	1	.984	2	*O-117	1.0
1989	Cal-A	110	418	53	114	18	4	13	42	27	84	.273	.320	.428	111	5	13	5	1	.975	-3	*O-100/D-7	0.1
1990	Cal-A	12	34	3	6	1	0	1	3	2	8	.176	.222	.294	44	-3	1	0	0	1.000	1	/O-9	-0.2
	NY-A	33	80	4	13	1	1	0	6	2	17	.162	.183	.200	7	-10	3	1	0	1.000	1	O-21/D-2	-1.0
	Yr	45	114	7	19	2	1	1	9	4	25	.167	.195	.228	18	-13	4	1	1	1.000	2	O-30/D-2	-1.2
Total	17	1912	6787	926	1884	334	69	164	824	468	1266	.278	.328	.420	106	40	312	134	13	.973	-37	*O-1685/D-75	-4.7

■ HERB WASHINGTON
Washington, Herbert Lee b: 11/16/51, Belzoni, Miss. BR/TR, 6′, 170 lbs. Deb: 4/4/74

YEAR	TM/L	G	AB	R	H	2B	3B	HR	RBI	BB	SO	AVG	OBP	SLG	PRO+	BR/A	SB	CS	SBR	FA	FR	G/POS	TPR
1974	*Oak-A	92	0	29	0	0	0	0	0	0	0	—	—	—	—	0	29	16	-1	.000	0	R	-0.3
1975	Oak-A	13	0	4	0	0	0	0	0	0	0	—	—	—	—	0	2	1	0	.000	0	R	0.0
Total	2	105	0	33	0	0	0	0	0	0	0	—	—	—	—	0	31	17	-1		0	-0,-0	-0.3

■ LA RUE WASHINGTON
Washington, La Rue b: 9/7/53, Long Beach, Cal. BR/TR, 6′, 170 lbs. Deb: 9/7/78

YEAR	TM/L	G	AB	R	H	2B	3B	HR	RBI	BB	SO	AVG	OBP	SLG	PRO+	BR/A	SB	CS	SBR	FA	FR	G/POS	TPR
1978	Tex-A	3	3	0	0	0	0	0	0	0	1	.000	.000	.000	-99	-1	0	0	0	1.000	2	/2-2,D-1	0.1
1979	Tex-A	25	18	5	5	0	0	0	2	4	0	.278	.409	.278	90	0	2	1	0	1.000	-3	O-13/3-1,D-1	-0.3
Total	2	28	21	5	5	0	0	0	2	4	1	.238	.360	.238	67	-1	2	1	0	1.000	-1	/O-13,D-2,2-2,3-1	-0.2

■ RON WASHINGTON
Washington, Ronald b: 4/29/52, New Orleans, La. BR/TR, 5′11″, 163 lbs. Deb: 9/10/77 C

YEAR	TM/L	G	AB	R	H	2B	3B	HR	RBI	BB	SO	AVG	OBP	SLG	PRO+	BR/A	SB	CS	SBR	FA	FR	G/POS	TPR
1977	LA-N	10	19	4	7	0	0	0	1	0	2	.368	.400	.368	108	0	1	1	-0	.857	-2	S-10	-0.1
1981	Min-A	28	84	8	19	3	1	0	5	4	14	.226	.270	.286	56	-5	4	1	1	.951	6	S-26/O-2	0.4
1982	Min-A	119	451	48	122	17	6	5	39	14	79	.271	.292	.368	78	-14	3	3	-1	.972	-44	S-91,2-37/3-1	-5.1
1983	Min-A	99	317	28	78	7	3	4	26	22	50	.246	.297	.325	69	-13	10	5	0	.962	-17	S-81,2-14/3-1,D-1	-2.2
1984	Min-A	88	197	25	58	11	5	3	23	4	31	.294	.312	.447	102	0	1	1	-0	.978	-16	S-71/2-9,3-2,D-4	-1.2
1985	Min-A	70	135	24	37	6	4	1	14	8	15	.274	.315	.400	89	-2	5	1	1	.951	-4	S-31,2-24/3-7,1D	-0.3
1986	Min-A	48	74	15	19	3	0	4	11	3	21	.257	.286	.459	96	-1	1	2	-1	.917	0	2-16,D-15/S-7,3-3	-0.2
1987	Bal-A	26	79	7	16	3	1	1	6	1	15	.203	.213	.304	36	-7	0	1	-1	1.000	2	3-20/2-3,O-2,S-1,D	-0.6
1988	Cle-A	69	223	30	57	14	2	2	21	9	35	.256	.300	.363	82	-5	3	3	-1	.933	-14	S-54/3-8,2-7,D-1	-1.6
1989	Hou-N	7	7	1	1	1	0	0	0	0	4	.143	.143	.286	20	-1	0	0	0	.000	-0	/2-1,3-1	-0.1
Total	10	564	1586	190	414	65	22	20	146	65	266	.261	.294	.368	79	-49	28	18	-2	.958	-88	S-372,2-111/3DO1	-11.0

■ GEORGE WASHINGTON
Washington, Sloan Vernon "Vern" b: 6/4/07, Linden, Tex. d: 2/17/85, Linden, Tex. BL/TR, 5′11.5″, 190 lbs. Deb: 4/17/35

YEAR	TM/L	G	AB	R	H	2B	3B	HR	RBI	BB	SO	AVG	OBP	SLG	PRO+	BR/A	SB	CS	SBR	FA	FR	G/POS	TPR
1935	Chi-A	108	339	40	96	22	3	8	47	10	18	.283	.310	.437	89	-7	1	0	0	.974	0	O-79	-0.9
1936	Chi-A	20	49	6	8	2	0	1	5	1	4	.163	.180	.265	8	-7	0	0	0	.938	-2	O-12	-0.8
Total	2	128	388	46	104	24	3	9	52	11	22	.268	.294	.415	78	-15	1	0	0	.970	-2	/O-91	-1.7

■ U L WASHINGTON
Washington, U L b: 10/27/53, Stringtown, Okla. BB/TR, 5′11″, 175 lbs. Deb: 9/6/77

YEAR	TM/L	G	AB	R	H	2B	3B	HR	RBI	BB	SO	AVG	OBP	SLG	PRO+	BR/A	SB	CS	SBR	FA	FR	G/POS	TPR
1977	KC-A	10	20	0	4	1	1	0	1	5	4	.200	.360	.350	94	-0	1	0	0	.872	0	/S-9	0.1
1978	KC-A	69	129	10	34	2	1	0	9	10	20	.264	.317	.295	71	-5	12	6	0	.927	-11	S-49,2-19/D-1	-1.2
1979	KC-A	101	268	32	68	12	5	2	25	20	44	.254	.306	.358	77	-9	10	7	-1	.970	3	S-50,2-46/3-1,D-3	0.0
1980	*KC-A	153	549	79	150	16	11	6	53	53	78	.273	.337	.375	94	-4	20	7	2	.957	-26	*S-152	-1.1
1981	*KC-A	98	339	40	77	19	1	2	29	41	43	.227	.311	.307	79	-8	10	10	-3	.973	-21	S-98	-2.4
1982	KC-A	119	437	64	125	19	3	10	60	38	48	.286	.343	.412	106	4	23	7	3	.961	-11	*S-117/D-1	0.7
1983	KC-A	144	547	76	129	19	6	5	41	48	78	.236	.299	.320	70	-22	40	7	8	.947	-10	*S-140/D-1	-1.0
1984	*KC-A	63	170	18	38	6	0	1	10	14	31	.224	.283	.276	55	-10	4	6	-2	.961	0	S-61	-0.7
1985	Mon-N	68	193	24	48	9	4	1	17	15	33	.249	.303	.352	88	-4	6	3	0	.978	-10	2-43/S-9,3-3	-1.2
1986	Pit-N	72	135	14	27	0	4	0	10	15	27	.200	.280	.259	49	-9	6	0	2	.947	-8	S-51/2-3	-1.2
1987	Pit-N	10	10	1	3	0	0	0	0	2	3	.300	.417	.300	93	0	0	0	0	.833	-0	/S-1,3-1	0.0
Total	11	907	2797	358	703	103	36	27	255	261	409	.251	.315	.343	82	-67	132	53	8	.956	-93	S-737,2-111/D-6,3-5	-8.0

■ MARK WASINGER
Wasinger, Mark Thomas b: 8/4/61, Monterey, Cal. BR/TR, 6′, 165 lbs. Deb: 5/27/86

YEAR	TM/L	G	AB	R	H	2B	3B	HR	RBI	BB	SO	AVG	OBP	SLG	PRO+	BR/A	SB	CS	SBR	FA	FR	G/POS	TPR
1986	SD-N	3	8	0	0	0	0	0	1	0	2	.000	.000	.000	-99	-2	0	0	0	.500	-1	/3-3,2-1	-0.4
1987	SF-N	44	80	16	22	3	0	1	3	8	14	.275	.341	.350	88	-1	2	0	1	.973	3	3-21,2-10/S-2	0.2
1988	SF-N	3	2	1	0	0	0	0	0	0	0	.000	.000	.000	-99	-1	0	0	0	.000	0	/3-1	-0.1
Total	3	50	90	17	22	3	0	1	4	8	16	.244	.306	.311	68	-4	2	0	1	.907	2	/3-25,2-11,S-2	-0.3

■ FRED WATERMAN
Waterman, Frederick A. b: 12/1845, New York, N.Y. d: 12/16/1899, Cincinnati, Ohio 5′7.5″, 148 lbs. Deb: 5/5/1871

YEAR	TM/L	G	AB	R	H	2B	3B	HR	RBI	BB	SO	AVG	OBP	SLG	PRO+	BR/A	SB	CS	SBR	FA	FR	G/POS	TPR
1871	Oly-n	32	158	46	50	7	4	0	17	10	0	.316	.357	.411	127	7	11	3	2	.695	2	*3-28/C-6	0.6
1872	Oly-n	9	45	13	17	1	2	0	6	0	0	.378	.378	.489	173	4	0	0	0	.843	3	/3-7,C-2,M	0.4
1873	Was-n	15	80	20	28	1	1	0	12	1	1	.350	.358	.387	125	3	0	0	0	.617	-6	/S-9,O-4,3-2	-0.3
1875	Chi-n	5	20	2	6	0	0	0	3	0	2	.300	.300	.300	108	0	0	1	-1	.545	-3	/3-5	-0.3
Total	4 n	61	303	81	101	9	7	0	38	11	3	.333	.357	.409	132	13	11	4	1	.713	-4	/3-42,S-9,C-8,O-4	0.4

■ JOHN WATHAN
Wathan, John David b: 10/4/49, Cedar Rapids, Iowa BR/TR, 6′2″, 205 lbs. Deb: 5/26/76 MC

YEAR	TM/L	G	AB	R	H	2B	3B	HR	RBI	BB	SO	AVG	OBP	SLG	PRO+	BR/A	SB	CS	SBR	FA	FR	G/POS	TPR
1976	*KC-A	27	42	5	12	1	0	0	5	2	5	.286	.333	.310	88	-1	0	2	-1	.984	-1	C-23/1-3	-0.2
1977	*KC-A	55	119	18	39	5	3	2	21	5	8	.328	.355	.471	122	3	2	0	1	.993	-2	C-35/1-5,D-2	0.2
1978	*KC-A	67	190	19	57	10	1	2	28	3	12	.300	.325	.395	99	-1	2	1	0	1.000	1	1-47,C-21	-0.2
1979	KC-A	90	199	26	41	7	3	2	28	7	24	.206	.233	.302	42	-16	2	1	0	.993	-2	1-49,C-23,D-11,/O-3	-2.0
1980	*KC-A	126	453	57	138	14	7	6	58	50	42	.305	.377	.406	114	10	17	3	3	.982	-11	C-77,O-35,1-12	0.4
1981	*KC-A	89	301	24	76	9	3	1	19	19	23	.252	.301	.312	78	-9	11	6	-0	.979	-11	C-73,O-16/1-1	-1.8
1982	KC-A	121	448	79	121	11	3	3	51	48	46	.270	.343	.328	85	-7	36	9	5	.980	-17	*C-120/1-3	-1.5
1983	KC-A	128	437	49	107	18	3	2	32	27	56	.245	.290	.314	66	-20	28	7	4	.985	-4	C-92,1-37/O-9	-1.8
1984	*KC-A	97	171	17	31	7	1	2	10	21	34	.181	.271	.269	50	-12	6	6	-2	.975	5	C-59,1-33/O-1,D-4	-0.7
1985	*KC-A	60	145	11	34	8	1	1	9	17	15	.234	.319	.324	76	-4	1	1	-0	.986	12	C-49/1-6,D-2	0.9
Total	10	860	2505	305	656	90	25	21	261	199	265	.262	.320	.343	83	-56	105	36	10	.982	-31	C-572,1-196/O-64,D	-6.7

■ DAVE WATKINS
Watkins, David Roger b: 3/15/44, Owensboro, Ky. BR/TR, 5′10″, 185 lbs. Deb: 4/9/69

YEAR	TM/L	G	AB	R	H	2B	3B	HR	RBI	BB	SO	AVG	OBP	SLG	PRO+	BR/A	SB	CS	SBR	FA	FR	G/POS	TPR
1969	Phi-N	69	148	17	26	2	1	4	12	22	53	.176	.291	.284	63	-7	2	3	-1	.981	-5	C-54/O-5,3-1	-1.2

■ GEORGE WATKINS
Watkins, George Archibald b: 6/4/1900, Freestone Co., Tex d: 6/1/70, Houston, Tex. BL/TR, 6′, 175 lbs. Deb: 4/15/30

YEAR	TM/L	G	AB	R	H	2B	3B	HR	RBI	BB	SO	AVG	OBP	SLG	PRO+	BR/A	SB	CS	SBR	FA	FR	G/POS	TPR
1930	*StL-N	119	391	85	146	32	7	17	87	24	49	.373	.415	.621	141	25	5			.956	-6	O-89,1-13/2-1	1.1
1931	*StL-N	131	503	93	145	30	13	13	51	31	66	.288	.336	.477	112	7	15			.958	-6	*O-129	-0.7
1932	StL-N	127	458	67	143	35	3	9	63	45	46	.312	.384	.461	122	15	18			.949	3	*O-120	1.0
1933	StL-N	138	525	66	146	24	5	5	62	39	62	.278	.342	.371	98	-0	11			.953	1	*O-135	-0.7
1934	NY-N	105	296	38	73	18	3	6	33	24	34	.247	.316	.389	90	-5	2			.944	-10	O-81	-1.7
1935	Phi-N	150	600	80	162	25	5	17	76	40	78	.270	.320	.413	87	-12	3			.958	5	*O-148	-1.2
1936	Phi-N	19	70	7	17	4	0	2	5	5	13	.243	.293	.386	74	-3	2			.889	-3	O-17	-0.6
	Bro-N	105	364	54	93	24	6	4	43	38	34	.255	.334	.387	93	-4	5			.969	-4	O-98	-1.1
	Yr	124	434	61	110	28	6	6	48	43	47	.253	.328	.387	90	-6	7			.959	-7	*O-115	-1.7
Total	7	894	3207	490	925	192	42	73	420	246	382	.288	.347	.443	105	24	61			.954	-20	O-817/1-13,2-1	-3.9

■ ED WATKINS
Watkins, James Edward b: 6/21/1877, Philadelphia, Pa. d: 3/29/33, Kelvin, Ariz. Deb: 9/6/02

YEAR	TM/L	G	AB	R	H	2B	3B	HR	RBI	BB	SO	AVG	OBP	SLG	PRO+	BR/A	SB	CS	SBR	FA	FR	G/POS	TPR
1902	Phi-N	1	3	0	0	0	0	0	0	1		.000	.250	.000	-22	-0	0			1.000	-0	/O-1	-0.1

■ BILL WATKINS
Watkins, William Henry b: 5/5/1858, Brantford, Ont., Can d: 6/9/37, Port Huron, Mich. 5′10″, 156 lbs. Deb: 8/1/1884 M

YEAR	TM/L	G	AB	R	H	2B	3B	HR	RBI	BB	SO	AVG	OBP	SLG	PRO+	BR/A	SB	CS	SBR	FA	FR	G/POS	TPR
1884	Ind-a	34	127	16	26	4	0	0		5		.205	.241	.236	58	-6				.845	-6	3-23/2-9,S-2,M	-1.0

■ PAT WATKINS
Watkins, William Patrick b: 9/2/72, Raleigh, N.C. BR/TR, 6′2″, 185 lbs. Deb: 9/9/97

YEAR	TM/L	G	AB	R	H	2B	3B	HR	RBI	BB	SO	AVG	OBP	SLG	PRO+	BR/A	SB	CS	SBR	FA	FR	G/POS	TPR
1997	Cin-N	17	29	2	6	2	0	0	0	0	5	.207	.207	.276	25	-3	1	0	0	1.000	-3	O-15	-0.6

YEAR	TM/L	G	AB	R	H	2B	3B	HR	RBI	BB	SO	AVG	OBP	SLG	PRO+	BR/A	SB	CS	SBR	FA	FR	G/POS	TPR
1998	Cin-N	83	147	11	39	8	1	2	15	8	26	.265	.308	.374	75	-6	1	3	-2	.971	-12	O-77	-1.9
Total	2	100	176	13	45	10	1	2	15	8	31	.256	.292	.358	67	-9	2	3	-1	.974	-15	/O-92	-2.5

■ NEAL WATLINGTON

Watlington, Julius Neal b: 12/25/22, Yanceyville, N.C. BL/TR, 6', 195 lbs. Deb: 7/10/53

YEAR	TM/L	G	AB	R	H	2B	3B	HR	RBI	BB	SO	AVG	OBP	SLG	PRO+	BR/A	SB	CS	SBR	FA	FR	G/POS	TPR
1953	Phi-A	21	44	4	7	1	0	0	3	3	8	.159	.213	.182	7	-6	0	1	-1	.978	0	/C-9	-0.6

■ ART WATSON

Watson, Arthur Stanhope "Watty" b: 1/11/1884, Jeffersonville, Ind. d: 5/9/50, Buffalo, N.Y. BL/TR, 5'10", 175 lbs. Deb: 5/19/14

YEAR	TM/L	G	AB	R	H	2B	3B	HR	RBI	BB	SO	AVG	OBP	SLG	PRO+	BR/A	SB	CS	SBR	FA	FR	G/POS	TPR
1914	Bro-F	22	46	7	13	4	1	1	3	1	6	.283	.298	.478	110	-0	0			.977	2	C-18	0.3
1915	Bro-F	9	19	4	5	0	3	0	1	3	4	.263	.364	.579	164	1	0			.957	-3	/C-7	-0.1
	Buf-F	22	30	6	14	1	0	1	13	0	4	.467	.467	.600	195	3	0			.778	-4	/C-6,O-1	-0.1
	Yr	31	49	10	19	1	3	1	14	3	8	.388	.423	.592	182	4	0			.878	-7	C-13/O-1	-0.2
Total	2	53	95	17	32	5	4	2	17	4	14	.337	.364	.537	147	4	0			.946	-5	/C-31,O-1	0.1

■ JOHNNY WATSON

Watson, John Thomas b: 1/16/08, Tazewell, Va. d: 4/29/65, Huntington, W.Va. BL/TR, 6', 175 lbs. Deb: 9/26/30

YEAR	TM/L	G	AB	R	H	2B	3B	HR	RBI	BB	SO	AVG	OBP	SLG	PRO+	BR/A	SB	CS	SBR	FA	FR	G/POS	TPR
1930	Det-A	4	12	1	3	2	0	0	3	1	2	.250	.308	.417	80	-0	0	0	0	.933	-1	/S-4	-0.1

■ BOB WATSON

Watson, Robert Jose "Bull" b: 4/10/46, Los Angeles, Cal. BR/TR, 6'2", 205 lbs. Deb: 9/9/66 C

YEAR	TM/L	G	AB	R	H	2B	3B	HR	RBI	BB	SO	AVG	OBP	SLG	PRO+	BR/A	SB	CS	SBR	FA	FR	G/POS	TPR
1966	Hou-N	1	1	0	0	0	0	0	0	0	0	.000	.000	.000	-99	-0	0	0	0	.000	0	H	0.0
1967	Hou-N	6	14	1	3	0	0	1	2	0	3	.214	.214	.429	82	-0	0	0	0	.958	0	/1-3	-0.1
1968	Hou-N	45	140	13	32	7	0	2	8	13	32	.229	.299	.321	88	-2	1	0	0	.885	-5	O-40	-1.0
1969	Hou-N	20	40	3	11	3	0	0	3	6	5	.275	.396	.350	113	1	0	0	0	1.000	-1	/O-6,1-5,C-1	0.0
1970	Hou-N	97	327	48	89	19	2	11	61	24	59	.272	.330	.443	110	3	1	1	-0	.992	-8	1-83/C-6,O-1	-1.2
1971	Hou-N	129	468	49	135	17	3	9	67	41	56	.288	.348	.395	113	8	0	3	-2	.985	-10	O-87,1-45	-1.3
1972	Hou-N	147	548	74	171	27	4	16	86	53	83	.312	.381	.464	142	30	1	1	-0	.978	-6	*O-143/1-2	1.8
1973	Hou-N★	158	573	97	179	24	3	16	94	85	73	.312	.405	.449	137	31	1	4	-2	.969	-1	*O-142,1-26/C-3	2.2
1974	Hou-N	150	524	69	156	19	4	11	67	60	61	.298	.373	.412	125	18	3	4	-2	.981	-10	*O-140,1-35	0.1
1975	Hou-N★	132	485	67	157	27	1	18	85	40	50	.324	.379	.495	152	32	3	5	-2	.993	-2	*1-118/O-9	2.1
1976	Hou-N	157	585	76	183	31	3	16	102	62	64	.313	.382	.458	151	38	3	3	-1	.990	-2	*1-155	2.6
1977	Hou-N	151	554	77	160	38	6	22	110	57	69	.289	.362	.498	141	30	5	0	2	.994	12	*1-146	3.5
1978	Hou-N	139	461	51	133	25	4	14	79	51	57	.289	.364	.451	137	22	3	1	0	.992	10	*1-128	2.6
1979	Hou-N	49	163	15	39	4	0	3	18	16	23	.239	.307	.319	75	-6	0	0	0	.993	3	1-44	-0.6
	Bos-A	84	312	48	105	19	4	13	53	29	33	.337	.402	.548	145	20	3	2	-0	.988	2	1-58,D-26	1.7
1980	*NY-A	130	469	62	144	25	3	13	68	48	56	.307	.373	.456	128	18	2	1	0	.990	-2	*1-104,D-21	1.0
1981	*NY-A	59	156	15	33	3	3	6	12	24	17	.212	.317	.385	103	1	0	0	0	.997	-1	1-50/D-6	-0.3
1982	NY-A	7	17	3	4	3	0	0	3	3	0	.235	.350	.412	110	0	0	0	0	1.000	-1	/1-6,D-1	-0.1
	Atl-N	57	114	16	28	3	1	5	22	14	20	.246	.328	.421	104	1	1	1	-0	1.000	-4	1-27/O-2	-0.5
1983	Atl-N	65	149	14	46	9	0	6	37	18	23	.309	.383	.490	131	6	0	2	-1	.984	-3	1-34	0.0
1984	Atl-N	49	85	4	18	4	0	2	12	9	12	.212	.287	.329	68	-4	0	0	0	.983	1	1-19	-0.4
Total	19	1832	6185	802	1826	307	41	184	989	653	796	.295	.367	.447	130	247	27	28	-9	.991	-27	*1-1088,O-570/DC	12.1

■ ALLIE WATT

Watt, Albert Bailey b: 12/12/1899, Philadelphia, Pa. d: 3/15/68, Norfolk, Va. BR/TR, 5'8", 154 lbs. Deb: 10/3/20 F

YEAR	TM/L	G	AB	R	H	2B	3B	HR	RBI	BB	SO	AVG	OBP	SLG	PRO+	BR/A	SB	CS	SBR	FA	FR	G/POS	TPR
1920	Was-A	1	1	0	1	1	0	0	1	0	0	1.000	1.000	2.000	700	1	0	0	0	1.000	0	/2-1	0.1

■ JOHNNY WATWOOD

Watwood, John Clifford "Lefty" b: 8/17/05, Alexander City, Ala. d: 3/1/80, Goodwater, Ala. BL/TL, 6'1", 186 lbs. Deb: 4/16/29

YEAR	TM/L	G	AB	R	H	2B	3B	HR	RBI	BB	SO	AVG	OBP	SLG	PRO+	BR/A	SB	CS	SBR	FA	FR	G/POS	TPR
1929	Chi-A	85	278	33	84	12	6	2	28	22	21	.302	.355	.410	98	-1	6	3	0	.942	-2	O-77	-0.7
1930	Chi-A	133	427	75	129	25	4	2	51	52	35	.302	.382	.393	100	2	5	7	-3	.989	3	1-62,O-52	-0.7
1931	Chi-A	128	367	51	104	16	6	1	47	56	30	.283	.380	.368	103	4	9	3	1	.944	3	*O-102/1-4	0.2
1932	Chi-A	13	49	5	15	2	0	0	0	1	3	.306	.333	.347	82	-1	0	0	0	.960	-2	O-13	-0.4
	Bos-A	95	266	26	66	11	0	0	30	20	11	.248	.301	.289	55	-17	7	4	-0	.945	-1	O-46,1-18	-2.2
	Yr	108	315	31	81	13	0	0	30	21	14	.257	.306	.298	59	-19	7	4	-0	.948	-4	O-59,1-18	-2.6
1933	Bos-A	13	30	2	4	0	0	0	2	3	3	.133	.212	.133	-7	-5	0	0	0	.950	-1	/O-9	-0.5
1939	Phi-N	2	6	0	1	0	0	0	0	0	0	.167	.167	.167	-11	-1	0			.933	-1	/1-2	-0.2
Total	6	469	1423	192	403	66	16	5	158	154	103	.283	.356	.363	89	-19	27	17		.948	-0	O-299/1-86	-4.5

■ BOB WAY

Way, Robert Clinton b: 4/2/06, Emlenton, Pa. d: 6/20/74, Pittsburgh, Pa. BR/TR, 5'10.5", 168 lbs. Deb: 4/12/27

YEAR	TM/L	G	AB	R	H	2B	3B	HR	RBI	BB	SO	AVG	OBP	SLG	PRO+	BR/A	SB	CS	SBR	FA	FR	G/POS	TPR
1927	Chi-A	5	3	3	1	0	0	0	1	0	0	.333	.333	.333	75	-0	0	0	0	1.000	0	/2-1	0.0

■ ROY WEATHERLY

Weatherly, Cyril Roy "Stormy" b: 2/25/15, Warren, Tex. d: 1/19/91, Woodville, Tex. BL/TR, 5'6.5", 170 lbs. Deb: 6/27/36

YEAR	TM/L	G	AB	R	H	2B	3B	HR	RBI	BB	SO	AVG	OBP	SLG	PRO+	BR/A	SB	CS	SBR	FA	FR	G/POS	TPR
1936	Cle-A	84	349	64	117	28	6	8	53	16	29	.335	.364	.519	115	6	3	8	-4	.973	4	O-84	0.3
1937	Cle-A	53	134	19	27	4	0	5	13	6	14	.201	.246	.343	47	-12	1	1	-0	.964	-3	O-38/3-1	-1.5
1938	Cle-A	83	210	32	55	14	3	2	18	14	14	.262	.308	.386	74	-9	8	5	-1	.975	-1	O-55	-1.1
1939	Cle-A	95	323	43	100	16	6	1	32	19	23	.310	.348	.406	95	-3	7	2	1	.961	-8	O-76	-1.1
1940	Cle-A	135	578	90	175	35	11	12	59	27	26	.303	.335	.464	108	4	9	8	-2	.969	6	*O-135	0.1
1941	Cle-A	102	363	59	105	21	5	3	37	32	20	.289	.350	.399	103	1	2	5	-2	.968	-8	O-88	-1.4
1942	Cle-A	128	473	61	122	23	7	5	39	35	25	.258	.310	.368	96	-5	8	13	-5	.991	2	*O-117	-1.4
1943	*NY-A	77	280	37	74	8	3	7	28	18	9	.264	.311	.389	104	0	4	7	-3	.983	-2	O-68	-0.9
1946	NY-A	2	2	0	1	0	0	0	0	0	0	.500	.500	.500	178	0	0	0	0	.000	0	H	0.0
1950	NY-N	52	69	10	18	3	3	0	11	13	10	.261	.378	.391	102	1	0			1.000	-1	O-15	-0.1
Total	10	811	2781	415	794	152	44	43	290	180	170	.286	.331	.418	99	-16	42	49		.975	-10	O-676/3-1	-7.1

■ ART WEAVER

Weaver, Arthur Coggshall "Six O'Clock" b: 4/7/1879, Wichita, Kan. d: 3/23/17, Denver, Colo. TR , 6'1", 160 lbs. Deb: 9/14/02

YEAR	TM/L	G	AB	R	H	2B	3B	HR	RBI	BB	SO	AVG	OBP	SLG	PRO+	BR/A	SB	CS	SBR	FA	FR	G/POS	TPR
1902	StL-N	11	33	2	6	2	0	0	3	1		.182	.206	.242	40	-2	0			.983	2	C-11	0.0
1903	StL-N	16	49	4	12	0	0	0	5	4		.245	.302	.245	58	-3	1			.969	3	C-16	0.2
	Pit-N	16	48	8	11	0	1	0	3	2		.229	.260	.271	50	-3	0			.978	-1	C-11/1-5	-0.3
	Yr	32	97	12	23	0	1	0	8	6		.237	.282	.258	54	-6	1			.972	2	C-27/1-5	-0.1
1905	StL-A	28	92	5	11	2	1	0	3	1		.120	.129	.163	-8	-11	0			.962	5	C-28	-0.4
1908	Chi-A	15	35	1	7	1	0	0	1	1		.200	.222	.229	47	-2	0			.953	-5	C-15	-0.7
Total	4	86	257	20	47	5	2	0	15	9		.183	.211	.218	31	-22	1			.967	4	/C-81,1-5	-1.2

■ BUCK WEAVER

Weaver, George Daniel b: 8/18/1890, Pottstown, Pa. d: 1/31/56, Chicago, Ill. BB/TR, 5'11", 170 lbs. Deb: 4/11/12

YEAR	TM/L	G	AB	R	H	2B	3B	HR	RBI	BB	SO	AVG	OBP	SLG	PRO+	BR/A	SB	CS	SBR	FA	FR	G/POS	TPR
1912	Chi-A	147	523	55	117	21	8	1	43	9		.224	.245	.300	58	-31	12			.915	-6	*S-147	-2.5
1913	Chi-A	151	533	51	145	17	8	4	52	15	60	.272	.302	.356	94	-7	20			.929	**34**	*S-151	4.2
1914	Chi-A	136	541	64	133	20	9	2	28	20	40	.246	.279	.327	83	-14	14	20	-8	.928	5	*S-134	-0.6
1915	Chi-A	148	563	83	151	18	11	3	49	32	58	.268	.316	.355	98	-4	24	20	-5	.939	1	*S-148	0.4
1916	Chi-A	151	582	78	132	27	6	3	38	30	48	.227	.280	.309	76	-19	22	13	-1	.941	7	3-85,S-66	-0.8
1917	*Chi-A	118	447	64	127	16	5	3	32	27	29	.284	.332	.362	110	4	19			**.949**	9	*3-107,S-10	1.7
1918	Chi-A	112	420	37	126	12	5	0	29	11	24	.300	.323	.352	103	-1	20			.941	-0	S-98,3-11/2-1	0.4
1919	*Chi-A	140	571	89	169	33	9	3	75	11	21	.296	.315	.401	100	-3	22			.963	0	3-97,S-43	0.4
1920	Chi-A	151	629	102	208	34	8	2	74	28	23	.331	.365	.420	107	6	19	17	-5	.933	-10	*3-127,S-25	-0.1
Total	9	1254	4809	623	1308	198	69	21	420	183	303	.272	.307	.355	92	-68	172	70		.935	39	S-822,3-427/2-1	3.1

■ JIM WEAVER

Weaver, James Francis b: 10/10/59, Kingston, N.Y. BL/TL, 6'3", 190 lbs. Deb: 4/10/85

YEAR	TM/L	G	AB	R	H	2B	3B	HR	RBI	BB	SO	AVG	OBP	SLG	PRO+	BR/A	SB	CS	SBR	FA	FR	G/POS	TPR
1985	Det-A	12	7	2	1	1	0	0	0	1	4	.143	.250	.286	47	-1	0	1	-1	1.000	-2	/O-4,D-4	-0.3
1987	Sea-A	7	4	2	0	0	0	0	0	2	3	.000	.333	.000	-1	-1	1	1	-0	1.000	-1	/O-4	-0.1
1989	SF-N	12	20	2	4	3	0	0	2	0	7	.200	.200	.350	56	-1	1	0	0	1.000	-2	/O-8	-0.3
Total	3	31	31	6	5	4	0	0	2	3	14	.161	.235	.290	47	-2	2	2	-1	1.000	-4	/O-16,D-4	-0.7

■ FARMER WEAVER

Weaver, William B. b: 3/23/1865, Parkersburg, W.Va. d: 1/23/43, Akron, Ohio BL , Deb: 9/16/1888

YEAR	TM/L	G	AB	R	H	2B	3B	HR	RBI	BB	SO	AVG	OBP	SLG	PRO+	BR/A	SB	CS	SBR	FA	FR	G/POS	TPR
1888	Lou-a	26	112	12	28	1	1	0	8	3		.250	.276	.277	79	-3	12			.878	-2	O-26	-0.5
1889	Lou-a	124	499	62	145	17	6	0	60	40	22	.291	.352	.349	102	2	21			.918	-1	*O-123/C-2,3-1,2-1	-0.1
1890	*Lou-a	130	557	101	161	27	9	3	67	29		.289	.333	.386	115	8	45			.933	-1	*O-127/S-2,3-1	0.2
1891	Lou-a	135	565	76	160	25	7	1	55	33	23	.283	.335	.358	99	-2	30			**.956**	17	*O-132/C-4	0.9

YEAR	TM/L	G	AB	R	H	2B	3B	HR	RBI	BB	SO	AVG	OBP	SLG	PRO+	BR/A	SB	CS	SBR	FA	FR	G/POS	TPR
1892	Lou-N	138	551	58	140	15	4	0	57	40	17	.254	.315	.296	92	-4	30			.902	-11	*O-122,C-15/1-1	-1.8
1893	Lou-N	106	439	79	128	17	7	2	49	27	12	.292	.348	.376	100	-0	17			.913	-1	O-85,C-21	-0.3
1894	Lou-N	64	244	19	54	5	2	3	24	7	11	.221	.249	.295	33	-27	3			.958	-0	O-35,C-17,1-10,/2-1	-2.2
	Pit-N	30	115	16	40	7	2	0	24	6	1	.348	.405	.443	105	1	4			.943	-10	C-14,S-12/3-5,O-1	-0.5
	Yr	94	359	35	94	12	4	3	48	13	12	.262	.301	.343	58	-25	7			.947	-10	O-36,C-31,S1/32	-2.7
Total	7	753	3082	423	856	114	38	9	344	185	86	.278	.330	.348	95	-25	162			.927	-9	O-651/C-73,S132	-4.3
■ **SKEETER WEBB**	Webb, James Laverne b: 11/4/09, Meridian, Miss. d: 7/8/86, Meridian, Miss. BR/TR, 5'9.5", 150 lbs. Deb: 7/20/32																						
1932	StL-N	1	0	0	0	0	0	0	0	0	0	—	—	—	—	0	0			.000	0	/S-1	0.0
1938	Cle-A	20	58	11	16	2	0	0	2	8	7	.276	.364	.310	72	-2	1	0	0	.964	-2	S-13/3-3,2-2	-0.3
1939	Cle-A	81	269	28	71	14	1	2	26	15	24	.264	.305	.346	68	-13	1	1	-0	.932	-9	S-81	-1.4
1940	Chi-A	84	334	33	79	11	2	1	29	30	33	.237	.299	.290	53	-23	3	6	-3	.969	-10	2-74/S-7,3-1	-2.8
1941	Chi-A	29	84	7	16	2	0	0	6	3	9	.190	.227	.214	18	-10	1	0	0	.940	6	2-18/S-5,3-3	-0.3
1942	Chi-A	32	94	5	16	2	1	0	4	4	13	.170	.204	.213	18	-10	1	2	-1	.961	2	2-29	-0.9
1943	Chi-A	58	213	15	50	5	2	0	22	6	19	.235	.256	.277	56	-12	5	4	-1	.953	-3	2-54	-1.4
1944	Chi-A	139	513	44	108	19	6	0	30	20	39	.211	.242	.271	47	-37	7	3	0	.944	-5	*S-135/2-5	-3.2
1945	*Det-A	118	407	43	81	12	2	0	21	30	35	.199	.254	.238	41	-31	8	7	-2	.957	23	*S-104,2-11	-0.2
1946	Det-A	64	169	12	37	1	1	0	17	9	18	.219	.258	.237	37	-14	3	3	-1	.972	15	2-50/S-8	0.3
1947	Det-A	50	79	13	16	3	0	0	6	7	9	.203	.267	.241	41	-6	3	0	1	.992	12	2-30/S-6	0.8
1948	Phi-A	23	54	5	8	2	0	0	3	0	9	.148	.148	.185	-12	-9	0	0	0	1.000	3	/2-9,S-8	-0.5
Total	12	699	2274	216	498	73	15	3	166	132	215	.219	.263	.268	46	-168	33	26		.946	32	S-368,2-282/3-7	-9.9
■ **EARL WEBB**	Webb, William Earl b: 9/17/1897, Bon Air, Tenn. d: 5/23/65, Jamestown, Tenn. BL/TR, 6'1", 185 lbs. Deb: 8/13/25																						
1925	NY-N	4	3	0	0	0	0	0	0	1	1	.000	.250	.000	-31	-1	0	0	0	.000	0	H	-0.1
1927	Chi-N	102	332	58	100	18	4	14	52	48	31	.301	.391	.506	138	18	3			.959	2	O-86	1.4
1928	Chi-N	62	140	22	35	7	3	3	23	14	17	.250	.318	.407	90	-3	0			.986	2	O-31	-0.3
1930	Bos-A	127	449	61	145	30	6	16	66	44	56	.323	.385	.523	133	22	2	1	0	.959	-5	*O-116	0.7
1931	Bos-A	151	589	96	196	**67**	3	14	103	70	51	.333	.404	.528	151	43	2	2	-1	.948	-2	*O-151	2.8
1932	Bos-A	52	192	23	54	9	1	5	27	25	15	.281	.364	.417	105	2	0	0	0	.964	-3	O-50/1-2	-0.4
	Det-A	88	338	49	97	19	8	3	51	39	18	.287	.361	.417	97	-1	1	1	-0	.955	0	O-85	-0.6
	Yr	140	530	72	151	28	9	8	78	64	33	.285	.362	.417	100	0	1	1	-0	.958	-2	*O-135/1-2	-1.0
1933	Det-A	6	11	1	3	0	0	0	3	3	0	.273	.429	.273	87	0	0	0	0	1.000	-1	/O-2	-0.1
	Chi-A	58	107	16	31	5	0	1	8	16	13	.290	.382	.364	103	1	0	0	0	1.000	-4	O-16,1-10	-0.4
	Yr	64	118	17	34	5	0	1	11	19	13	.288	.387	.356	101	1	0	0	0	1.000	-5	O-18,1-10	-0.5
Total	7	650	2161	326	661	155	25	56	333	260	202	.306	.381	.478	125	82	8	4		.958	-11	O-537/1-12	3.0
■ **BILL WEBB**	Webb, William Joseph b: 6/25/1895, Chicago, Ill. d: 1/12/43, Chicago, Ill. BR/TR, 5'10", 161 lbs. Deb: 9/17/17 C																						
1917	Pit-N	5	15	1	3	0	0	0	0	2	3	.200	.294	.200	51	-1	0			1.000	1	/2-4,S-1	0.0
■ **HARRY WEBER**	Weber, Harry b: Indianapolis, Ind. Deb: 7/22/1884																						
1884	Ind-a	3	8	0	0	0	0	0		0		.000	.111	.000	-62	-1				.794	1	/C-3	0.0
■ **JOE WEBER**	Weber, Joseph Edward b: 2/15/1862, Hamilton, Ont., Canada d: 12/15/21, Hamilton, Ont., Canada Deb: 5/30/1884																						
1884	Det-N	2	8	0	0	0	0	0	0	0	2	.000	.000	.000	-99	-2				.750	0	/O-2	-0.2
■ **LENNY WEBSTER**	Webster, Leonard Irell b: 2/10/65, New Orleans, La. BR/TR, 5'9", 191 lbs. Deb: 9/1/89																						
1989	Min-A	14	20	3	6	2	0	0	1	3	2	.300	.391	.400	116	1	0	0	0	1.000	-2	C-14	-0.1
1990	Min-A	2	6	1	2	1	0	0	0	1	1	.333	.429	.500	149	0	0	0	0	1.000	-1	/C-2	0.0
1991	Min-A	18	34	7	10	1	0	3	8	6	10	.294	.400	.588	162	3	0	0	0	.986	1	C-17	0.7
1992	Min-A	53	118	10	33	10	1	1	13	9	11	.280	.331	.407	102	0	0	2	-1	.995	1	C-49/D-1	0.2
1993	Min-A	49	106	14	21	2	0	1	8	11	8	.198	.274	.245	40	-9	1	0	0	1.000	3	C-45/D-1	-0.4
1994	Mon-N	57	143	13	39	10	0	5	23	16	24	.273	.370	.448	111	3	0	0	0	.996	-1	C-46	0.4
1995	Phi-N	49	150	18	40	9	0	4	14	16	27	.267	.337	.407	94	-1	0	0	0	.990	1	C-43	0.2
1996	Mon-N	78	174	18	40	10	0	2	17	25	21	.230	.333	.322	72	-6	0	0	0	.998	10	C-63	0.7
1997	*Bal-A	98	259	29	66	8	1	7	37	22	46	.255	.318	.375	82	-7	0	1	-1	.995	9	C-97/D-1	0.6
1998	Bal-A	108	309	37	88	16	0	10	46	15	38	.285	.318	.434	95	-3	0	0	0	.993	-6	*C-102/D-4	-0.3
Total	10	526	1319	150	345	69	2	33	167	124	188	.262	.330	.392	90	-20	1	3	-2	.995	19	C-478/D-7	2.0
■ **MITCH WEBSTER**	Webster, Mitchell Dean b: 5/16/59, Larned, Kan. BB/TL, 6'1", 185 lbs. Deb: 9/2/83																						
1983	Tor-A	11	11	2	2	0	0	0	0	1	1	.182	.250	.182	20	-1	0	0	0	1.000	-3	/O-7,D-2	-0.4
1984	Tor-A	26	22	9	5	2	1	0	4	1	7	.227	.261	.409	79	-1	0	1	-1	.875	-3	O-10/1-1,D-9	-0.3
1985	Tor-A	4	1	0	0	0	0	0	0	0	1	.000	.000	.000	-98	-0	0	1	-1	.000	-1	/O-2,D-2	-0.2
	Mon-N	74	212	32	58	8	2	11	30	20	33	.274	.336	.486	135	9	15	9	-1	.993	-5	O-64	0.1
1986	Mon-N	151	576	89	167	31	**13**	8	49	57	78	.290	.358	.431	117	14	36	15	2	.977	4	*O-146	1.5
1987	Mon-N	156	588	101	165	30	8	15	63	70	95	.281	.363	.435	107	7	33	10	4	.982	1	*O-153	0.6
1988	Mon-N	81	259	33	66	5	2	2	13	36	37	.255	.357	.313	90	-2	12	10	-2	.994	-3	O-71	-1.0
	Chi-N	70	264	36	70	11	6	4	26	19	50	.265	.322	.398	101	0	10	4	1	.971	2	O-65	0.1
	Yr	151	523	69	136	16	8	6	39	55	87	.260	.340	.356	95	-2	22	14	-2	.982	1	*O-136	-0.9
1989	*Chi-N	98	272	40	70	12	4	3	19	30	55	.257	.333	.364	92	-2	14	2	3	.965	-1	O-74	-0.3
1990	Cle-A	128	437	58	110	20	6	12	55	20	61	.252	.289	.407	93	-6	22	6	3	.991	9	*O-118/1-3,D-3	0.4
1991	Cle-A	13	32	2	4	0	0	0	0	3	9	.125	.200	.125	-8	-5	2	2	-1	1.000	-1	O-10	-0.6
	Pit-N	36	97	9	17	3	4	1	9	9	31	.175	.245	.320	59	-6	0	0	0	.963	-2	O-29	-0.8
	LA-N	58	74	12	21	5	1	1	10	9	21	.284	.361	.419	122	2	0	1	-1	1.000	-8	O-36/1-1	-0.8
	Yr	94	171	21	38	8	5	2	19	18	52	.222	.296	.363	86	-3	0	1	-1	.978	-10	O-65/1-1	-1.6
1992	LA-N	135	262	33	70	12	5	6	35	27	49	.267	.340	.420	116	5	11	5	0	.977	-12	O-90	-0.9
1993	LA-N	88	172	26	42	6	2	2	14	11	24	.244	.297	.337	74	-7	4	6	-2	.950	-9	O-56	-1.9
1994	LA-N	82	84	16	23	4	0	4	12	8	13	.274	.344	.464	116	2	1	2	-1	1.000	-12	O-48	-1.1
1995	*LA-N	54	56	6	10	1	1	1	3	4	14	.179	.246	.286	44	-5	0	0	0	1.000	-7	O-25	-1.2
Total	13	1265	3419	504	900	150	55	70	342	325	578	.263	.332	.401	101	5	160	73	4	.980	-50	*O-1004/D-16,1-5	-6.8
■ **RAY WEBSTER**	Webster, Ramon Alberto b: 8/31/42, Colon, Panama BL/TL, 6', 185 lbs. Deb: 4/11/67																						
1967	KC-A	122	360	41	92	15	4	11	51	32	44	.256	.320	.411	118	7	5	3	-0	.989	-3	1-83,O-15	-0.1
1968	Oak-A	66	196	17	42	11	1	3	23	12	24	.214	.260	.327	81	-5	3	0	1	.988	-1	1-55	-1.1
1969	Oak-A	64	77	5	20	0	1	1	13	12	8	.260	.367	.325	99	0	0	0	0	1.000	1	1-13	0.1
1970	SD-N	95	116	12	30	3	0	2	11	11	12	.259	.323	.336	80	-3	1	1	-0	.981	-1	1-15/O-1	-0.6
1971	SD-N	10	8	0	1	0	0	0	0	2	1	.125	.300	.125	26	-1	0	0	0	.000	0	H	-0.1
	Oak-A	7	5	0	0	0	0	0	0	0	2	.000	.000	.000	-99	-1	0	0	0	1.000	0	/1-1	-0.1
	Chi-N	16	16	1	5	2	0	0	0	1	3	.313	.353	.438	107	0	0	0	0	1.000	0	/1-1	0.0
Total	5	380	778	76	190	31	6	17	98	70	94	.244	.309	.365	99	-3	9	4	0	.989	-4	1-168/O-16	-1.9
■ **RAY WEBSTER**	Webster, Raymond George b: 11/15/37, Grass Valley, Cal. BR/TR, 6', 175 lbs. Deb: 4/17/59																						
1959	Cle-A	40	74	10	15	2	1	2	10	5	7	.203	.253	.338	63	-4	1	0	0	.929	0	2-24/3-4	-0.3
1960	Bos-A	7	3	1	0	0	0	0	1	1	0	.000	.250	.000	-25	-1	0	0	0	1.000	1	/2-1	0.0
Total	2	47	77	11	15	2	1	2	11	6	7	.195	.253	.325	59	-5	1	0	0	.931	1	/2-25,3-4	-0.3
■ **PETE WECKBECKER**	Weckbecker, Peter b: 8/30/1864, Butler, Pa. d: 5/16/35, Hampton, Va. 5'7", 150 lbs. Deb: 10/5/1889																						
1889	Ind-N	1	1	0	0	0	0	0	2	0	0	.000	.000	.000	-98	-0	0			1.000	0	/C-1	0.0
1890	*Lou-a	32	101	17	24	1	0	0	11	8		.238	.300	.248	63	-4	7			.941	1	C-32	-0.1
Total	2	33	102	17	24	1	0	0	13	8	0	.235	.297	.245	61	-5	7			.941	1	/C-33	-0.1
■ **ERIC WEDGE**	Wedge, Eric Michael b: 1/27/68, Fort Wayne, Ind. BR/TR, 6'3", 215 lbs. Deb: 10/5/91																						
1991	Bos-A	1	1	0	1	0	0	0	0	0	0	1.000	1.000	1.000	434	0	0	0	0	.000	0	/D-1	0.0

YEAR	TM/L	G	AB	R	H	2B	3B	HR	RBI	BB	SO	AVG	OBP	SLG	PRO+	BR/A	SB	CS	SBR	FA	FR	G/POS	TPR
1992	Bos-A	27	68	11	17	2	0	5	11	13	18	.250	.370	.500	133	3	0	0	0	1.000	-0	D-20/C-5	0.2
1993	Col-N	9	11	2	2	0	0	0	1	0	4	.182	.182	.182	-2	-2	0	0	0	1.000	1	/C-1	-0.1
1994	Bos-A	2	6	0	0	0	0	0	0	1	3	.000	.143	.000	-56	-1	0	0	0	.000	0	/D-2	-0.1
Total	4	39	86	13	20	2	0	5	12	14	25	.233	.340	.430	104	1	0	0	0	1.000	0	/D-23,C-6	0.0

■ **BERT WEEDEN** Weeden, Charles Albert b: 12/21/1882, Northwood, N.H. d: 1/7/39, Northwood, N.H. BL/TL, 6′, 200 lbs. Deb: 6/4/11

YEAR	TM/L	G	AB	R	H	2B	3B	HR	RBI	BB	SO	AVG	OBP	SLG	PRO+	BR/A	SB	CS	SBR	FA	FR	G/POS	TPR
1911	Bos-N	1	1	0	0	0	0	0	0	0	0	.000	.000	.000	-93	-0	0			.000	0	H	0.0

■ **JOHNNY WEEKLY** Weekly, Johnny b: 6/14/37, Waterproof, La. d: 11/24/74, Walnut Creek, Cal. BR/TR, 6′ ", 200 lbs. Deb: 4/13/62

YEAR	TM/L	G	AB	R	H	2B	3B	HR	RBI	BB	SO	AVG	OBP	SLG	PRO+	BR/A	SB	CS	SBR	FA	FR	G/POS	TPR
1962	Hou-N	13	26	3	5	1	0	2	2	7	4	.192	.364	.462	129	1	0	0	0	1.000	-1	/O-7	0.0
1963	Hou-N	34	80	4	18	3	0	3	14	7	14	.225	.295	.375	98	-0	0	0	0	1.000	1	O-23	-0.1
1964	Hou-N	6	15	0	2	0	0	0	3	1	3	.133	.188	.133	-8	-2	0	0	0	1.000	1	/O-5	-0.2
Total	3	53	121	7	25	4	0	5	19	15	21	.207	.299	.364	92	-1	0	0	0	1.000	1	/O-35	-0.3

■ **JOHN WEHNER** Wehner, John Paul b: 6/29/67, Pittsburgh, Pa. BR/TR, 6′3″, 205 lbs. Deb: 7/17/91

YEAR	TM/L	G	AB	R	H	2B	3B	HR	RBI	BB	SO	AVG	OBP	SLG	PRO+	BR/A	SB	CS	SBR	FA	FR	G/POS	TPR
1991	Pit-N	37	106	15	36	7	0	0	7	7	17	.340	.381	.406	123	3	3	0	1	.936	7	3-36	1.2
1992	*Pit-N	55	123	11	22	6	0	0	4	12	22	.179	.252	.228	37	-10	3	0	1	.961	5	3-34,1-13/2-5	-0.6
1993	Pit-N	29	35	3	5	0	0	0	0	6	10	.143	.268	.143	14	-4	0	0	0	1.000	-1	O-13/2-3,3-3	-0.5
1994	Pit-N	2	4	1	1	1	0	0	3	0	1	.250	.250	.500	88	-0	0	0	0	1.000	0	/3-1	0.0
1995	Pit-N	52	107	13	33	0	3	0	5	10	17	.308	.368	.364	92	-1	3	1	0	1.000	-4	O-23,3-19/C-1,S-1	-0.5
1996	Pit-N	86	139	19	36	9	1	2	13	8	22	.259	.299	.381	76	-5	1	5	-3	.971	-1	O-29,3-24,2-12,/C-1	-0.8
1997	*Fla-N	44	36	8	10	2	0	0	2	2	5	.278	.333	.333	79	-1	1	0	0	1.000	-8	O-27/3-6	-0.9
1998	Fla-N	53	88	10	20	2	0	0	5	7	12	.227	.284	.250	42	-7	1	0	0	1.000	-3	O-23/3-8	-1.0
Total	8	358	638	80	163	27	4	2	39	52	106	.255	.313	.320	71	-25	12	6	0	.965	-4	3-131,O-115/21CS	-3.1

■ **RALPH WEIGEL** Weigel, Ralph Richard "Wig" b: 10/2/21, Coldwater, Ohio d: 4/15/92, Memphis, Tenn. BR/TR, 6′1″, 180 lbs. Deb: 9/18/46

YEAR	TM/L	G	AB	R	H	2B	3B	HR	RBI	BB	SO	AVG	OBP	SLG	PRO+	BR/A	SB	CS	SBR	FA	FR	G/POS	TPR
1946	Cle-A	6	12	0	2	0	0	0	0	0	2	.167	.167	.167	-7	-2	1	0	0	1.000	-1	/C-6	-0.3
1948	Chi-A	66	163	8	38	7	3	0	26	13	18	.233	.294	.313	64	-9	1	2	-1	.969	-7	C-39/O-2	-1.4
1949	Was-A	34	60	4	14	2	0	0	4	8	6	.233	.324	.267	58	-3	0	1	-1	.985	1	C-21	-0.3
Total	3	106	235	12	54	9	3	0	30	21	26	.230	.296	.294	59	-14	2	3	-1	.976	-8	/C-66,O-2	-2.0

■ **PODGE WEIHE** Weihe, John Garibaldi b: 11/13/1862, Cincinnati, Ohio d: 4/15/14, Cincinnati, Ohio BR/TR, 5′11″, 175 lbs. Deb: 8/6/1883

YEAR	TM/L	G	AB	R	H	2B	3B	HR	RBI	BB	SO	AVG	OBP	SLG	PRO+	BR/A	SB	CS	SBR	FA	FR	G/POS	TPR
1883	Cin-a	1	4	1	1	0	0	0		0		.250	.250	.250	58	-0				1.000	0	/O-1	0.0
1884	Ind-a	63	256	29	65	13	2	4		9		.254	.279	.367	112	3				.860	-0	O-58/2-4,1-3	0.2
Total	2	64	260	30	66	13	2	4		9		.254	.279	.365	111	3				.864	0	/O-59,2-4,1-3	0.2

■ **DICK WEIK** Weik, Richard Henry "Legs" b: 11/17/27, Waterloo, Iowa d: 4/21/91, Harvey, Ill. BR/TR, 6′3.5″, 184 lbs. Deb: 9/8/48

YEAR	TM/L	G	AB	R	H	2B	3B	HR	RBI	BB	SO	AVG	OBP	SLG	PRO+	BR/A	SB	CS	SBR	FA	FR	G/POS	TPR
1948	Was-A	3	4	1	3	0	1	0	0	0	0	.750	.750	1.250	439	2	0	0	0	1.000	-0	/P-3	0.0
1949	Was-A	28	28	3	5	0	0	0	2	1	8	.179	.207	.179	2	-4	0	0	0	.964	1	P-27	0.0
1950	Was-A	14	13	0	2	0	0	0	0	0	3	.154	.154	.154	-22	-2	0	0	0	1.000	-1	P-14	0.0
	Cle-A	11	5	0	1	1	0	0	0	0	4	.200	.200	.400	52	-0	0	0	0	1.000	0	P-11	0.0
	Yr	25	18	0	3	1	0	0	0	0	7	.167	.167	.222	-1	-3	0	0	0	1.000	-1	P-25	0.0
1953	Cle-A	1	0	1	0	0	0	0	0	0	0	—	—	—	—	0	0	0	0	.000	0	R	0.0
	Det-A	12	2	1	1	1	0	0	1	0	1	.500	.500	1.000	300	1	0	0	0	1.000	0	P-12	0.0
	Yr	13	2	2	1	1	0	0	1	0	1	.500	.500	1.000	301	1	0	0	0	1.000	0	P-12	0.0
1954	Det-A	9	1	0	0	0	0	0	0	0	0	.000	.000	.000	-99	-0	0	0	0	.500	-1	/P-9	0.0
Total	5	78	53	6	12	2	1	0	3	1	16	.226	.241	.302	43	-5	0	0	0	.958	0	/P-76	0.0

■ **ELMER WEINGARTNER** Weingartner, Elmer William "Dutch" b: 8/13/18, Cleveland, Ohio BR/TR, 5′11″, 178 lbs. Deb: 4/19/45

YEAR	TM/L	G	AB	R	H	2B	3B	HR	RBI	BB	SO	AVG	OBP	SLG	PRO+	BR/A	SB	CS	SBR	FA	FR	G/POS	TPR
1945	Cle-A	20	39	5	9	1	0	0	1	4	11	.231	.302	.256	66	-2	0	0	0	.871	-3	S-20	-0.4

■ **PHIL WEINTRAUB** Weintraub, Philip "Mickey" b: 10/12/07, Chicago, Ill. d: 6/21/87, Palm Springs, Cal BL/TL, 6′1″, 195 lbs. Deb: 9/5/33

YEAR	TM/L	G	AB	R	H	2B	3B	HR	RBI	BB	SO	AVG	OBP	SLG	PRO+	BR/A	SB	CS	SBR	FA	FR	G/POS	TPR
1933	NY-N	8	15	3	3	0	0	1	1	3	2	.200	.333	.400	110	0	0			.667	-3	/O-6	-0.3
1934	NY-N	31	74	13	26	2	0	0	15	15	10	.351	.461	.378	130	4	0			.944	-4	O-20	0.0
1935	NY-N	64	112	18	27	3	3	1	6	17	13	.241	.341	.348	87	-2	0			.975	-3	1-19/O-7	-0.6
1937	Cin-N	49	177	27	48	10	4	3	20	19	25	.271	.345	.424	113	3	1			.976	-2	O-47	-0.1
	NY-N	6	9	3	3	2	0	0	1	1	1	.333	.400	.556	155	1	0			1.000	-0	/O-1	0.0
	Yr	55	186	30	51	12	4	3	21	20	26	.274	.348	.430	115	4	1			.976	-3	O-48	-0.1
1938	Phi-N	100	351	51	109	23	2	4	45	64	43	.311	.422	.422	137	21	1			.988	2	1-98	1.2
1944	NY-N	104	361	55	114	18	9	13	77	59	59	.316	.412	.524	162	31	0			.992	3	1-99	2.9
1945	NY-N	82	283	45	77	9	1	10	42	54	29	.272	.389	.417	122	10	2			.993	3	1-77	0.8
Total	7	444	1382	215	407	67	19	32	207	232	182	.295	.398	.440	133	69	4			.990	-4	1-293/O-81	3.9

■ **AL WEIS** Weis, Albert John b: 4/2/38, Franklin Square, N.Y BB/TR, 6′, 170 lbs. Deb: 9/15/62

YEAR	TM/L	G	AB	R	H	2B	3B	HR	RBI	BB	SO	AVG	OBP	SLG	PRO+	BR/A	SB	CS	SBR	FA	FR	G/POS	TPR
1962	Chi-A	7	12	2	1	0	0	0	0	2	3	.083	.267	.083	-1	-2	1	0	0	.882	-1	/S-4,2-1,3-1	-0.2
1963	Chi-A	99	210	41	57	9	0	0	18	18	37	.271	.335	.314	85	-4	15	1	4	.990	14	2-48,S-27/3-1	1.9
1964	Chi-A	133	328	36	81	4	4	2	23	22	41	.247	.300	.302	70	-13	22	7	2	.966	12	*2-116/S-9,O-2	0.9
1965	Chi-A	103	135	29	40	4	3	1	12	12	22	.296	.362	.393	122	4	4	1	1	.975	25	2-74/S-7,3-2,O-2	3.4
1966	Chi-A	129	187	20	29	4	1	0	9	17	50	.155	.233	.187	24	-18	3	5	-2	.987	**37**	2-96,S-18	2.2
1967	Chi-A	50	53	9	13	2	0	0	4	1	7	.245	.273	.283	67	-2	3	3	-1	.986	11	2-32,S-13	1.0
1968	NY-N	90	274	15	47	6	0	1	14	21	63	.172	.236	.204	33	-22	3	1	0	.958	7	S-59,2-29/3-2	-1.0
1969	*NY-N	103	247	20	53	9	2	2	23	15	51	.215	.260	.291	53	-16	3	3	-1	.960	13	S-52,2-43/3-1	0.3
1970	NY-N	75	121	20	25	7	1	1	11	7	21	.207	.256	.306	50	-9	1	1	-0	.952	2	2-44,S-15	-0.4
1971	NY-N	11	11	3	0	0	0	0	1	2	4	.000	.154	.000	-54	-2	0	0	0	1.000	1	/2-5,3-2	-0.2
Total	10	800	1578	195	346	45	11	7	115	117	299	.219	.279	.275	59	-84	55	22	3	.975	121	2-488,S-204/3-9,O-4	7.9

■ **BUTCH WEIS** Weis, Arthur John b: 3/2/01, St.Louis, Mo. d: 5/4/97, St.Louis, Mo. BL/TL, 5′11″, 180 lbs. Deb: 4/15/22

YEAR	TM/L	G	AB	R	H	2B	3B	HR	RBI	BB	SO	AVG	OBP	SLG	PRO+	BR/A	SB	CS	SBR	FA	FR	G/POS	TPR
1922	Chi-N	2	2	2	1	0	0	0	0	0	0	.500	.500	.500	156	0	0	0	0	.000	0	H	0.0
1923	Chi-N	22	26	2	6	1	0	0	2	5	8	.231	.355	.269	67	-1	0	1	-1	1.000	-1	/O-6	-0.3
1924	Chi-N	37	133	19	37	8	1	0	23	15	14	.278	.356	.353	90	-1	4	5	-2	.978	6	O-36	0.0
1925	Chi-N	67	180	16	48	5	3	2	25	23	22	.267	.350	.361	81	-5	2	4	-2	.964	-5	O-47	-1.3
Total	4	128	341	39	92	14	4	2	50	43	44	.270	.353	.352	84	-7	6	10	-4	.973	0	/O-89	-1.6

■ **BUD WEISER** Weiser, Harry Budson b: 1/8/1891, Shamokin, Pa. d: 7/31/61, Shamokin, Pa. BR/TR, 5′11″, 165 lbs. Deb: 4/29/15

YEAR	TM/L	G	AB	R	H	2B	3B	HR	RBI	BB	SO	AVG	OBP	SLG	PRO+	BR/A	SB	CS	SBR	FA	FR	G/POS	TPR
1915	Phi-N	37	64	6	9	2	0	0	8	7	12	.141	.236	.172	24	-6	2	2	-1	.897	-5	O-20	-1.4
1916	Phi-N	4	10	1	3	1	0	0	1	0	3	.300	.300	.400	110	0	0			1.000	-1	/O-4	-0.1
Total	2	41	74	7	12	3	0	0	9	7	15	.162	.244	.203	36	-6	2	2		.912	-6	/O-24	-1.5

■ **GARY WEISS** Weiss, Gary Lee b: 12/27/55, Brenham, Tex. BB/TR, 5′10″, 170 lbs. Deb: 9/13/80

YEAR	TM/L	G	AB	R	H	2B	3B	HR	RBI	BB	SO	AVG	OBP	SLG	PRO+	BR/A	SB	CS	SBR	FA	FR	G/POS	TPR
1980	LA-N	8	0	2	0	0	0	0	0	0	0	—	—	—	—	0	0	0	0	.000	0	/R	0.0
1981	LA-N	14	19	2	2	0	0	0	1	1	4	.105	.150	.105	-28	-3	0	0	0	.920	-1	S-13	-0.4
Total	2	22	19	4	2	0	0	0	1	1	4	.105	.150	.105	-28	-3	0	0	0	.920	-1	/S-13	-0.4

■ **JOE WEISS** Weiss, Joseph Harold b: 1/27/1894, Chicago, Ill. d: 7/7/67, Cedar Rapids, Iowa BR/TR, 6′, 165 lbs. Deb: 8/29/15

YEAR	TM/L	G	AB	R	H	2B	3B	HR	RBI	BB	SO	AVG	OBP	SLG	PRO+	BR/A	SB	CS	SBR	FA	FR	G/POS	TPR
1915	Chi-F	29	85	6	19	1	2	0	11	3	24	.224	.250	.282	53	-7	0			.992	-1	1-29	-1.0

■ **WALT WEISS** Weiss, Walter William b: 11/28/63, Tuxedo, N.Y. BB/TR, 6′, 175 lbs. Deb: 7/12/87

YEAR	TM/L	G	AB	R	H	2B	3B	HR	RBI	BB	SO	AVG	OBP	SLG	PRO+	BR/A	SB	CS	SBR	FA	FR	G/POS	TPR
1987	Oak-A	16	26	3	12	4	0	0	1	2	2	.462	.500	.615	208	4	1	2	-1	.974	5	S-11/D-2	0.8
1988	*Oak-A	147	452	44	113	17	3	3	39	35	56	.250	.317	.321	82	-10	4	4	-1	.979	10	*S-147	1.0
1989	*Oak-A	84	236	30	55	11	0	3	21	21	39	.233	.298	.318	76	-7	6	1	1	.953	-14	S-84	-1.5
1990	*Oak-A	138	445	50	118	17	1	2	35	46	53	.265	.339	.321	89	-5	9	3	1	.979	-26	*S-137	-2.0
1991	Oak-A	40	133	15	30	6	1	0	13	12	14	.226	.290	.286	63	-7	6	0	2	.970	-10	S-40	-1.2

YEAR	TM/L	G	AB	R	H	2B	3B	HR	RBI	BB	SO	AVG	OBP	SLG	PRO+	BR/A	SB	CS	SBR	FA	FR	G/POS	TPR
1992	*Oak-A	103	316	36	67	5	2	0	21	43	39	.212	.308	.241	59	-16	6	3	0	.956	-14	*S-103	-2.4
1993	Fla-N	158	500	50	133	14	2	1	39	79	73	.266	.369	.308	79	-11	7	3	0	.977	-18	*S-153	-1.7
1994	Col-N	110	423	58	106	11	4	1	32	56	58	.251	.338	.303	59	-25	12	7	-1	.973	3	*S-110	-1.3
1995	*Col-N	137	427	65	111	17	3	1	25	98	57	.260	.404	.321	73	-17	15	3	3	.974	12	*S-136	0.9
1996	Col-N	155	517	89	146	20	2	8	48	80	78	.282	.385	.375	82	-14	10	2	2	.957	-7	*S-155	-0.6
1997	Col-N	121	393	52	106	23	5	4	38	66	56	.270	.377	.384	81	-11	5	2	0	.983	20	*S-119	1.8
1998	*Atl-N★	96	347	64	97	18	2	0	27	59	53	.280	.389	.343	91	-2	7	1	2	.967	-7	S-96	0.2
Total	12	1305	4215	556	1094	163	25	23	339	597	578	.260	.356	.326	78	-122	88	31	8	.971	-47	*S-1291/D-2	-6.0

■ **JOHNNY WELAJ** Welaj, John Ludwig b: 5/27/14, Moss Creek, Pa. BR/TR, 6', 164 lbs. Deb: 5/2/39

YEAR	TM/L	G	AB	R	H	2B	3B	HR	RBI	BB	SO	AVG	OBP	SLG	PRO+	BR/A	SB	CS	SBR	FA	FR	G/POS	TPR
1939	Was-A	63	201	23	55	11	2	1	33	13	20	.274	.318	.363	80	-7	13	2	3	.975	-4	O-55	-0.9
1940	Was-A	88	215	31	55	9	0	3	21	19	20	.256	.322	.340	77	-7	8	7	-2	.978	-1	O-53	-1.2
1941	Was-A	49	96	16	20	4	0	0	5	6	16	.208	.255	.250	36	-9	3	1	0	.979	-0	O-19	-1.0
1943	Phi-A	93	281	45	68	16	1	0	15	15	17	.242	.280	.306	72	-11	12	5	1	.960	0	O-72	-1.5
Total	4	293	793	115	198	40	3	4	74	53	73	.250	.298	.323	71	-34	36	15	2	.970	-5	O-199	-4.6

■ **CURT WELCH** Welch, Curtis Benton b: 2/10/1862, Williamsport, O. d: 8/29/1896, E.Liverpool, Ohio BR/TR, 5'10", 175 lbs. Deb: 5/1/1884

YEAR	TM/L	G	AB	R	H	2B	3B	HR	RBI	BB	SO	AVG	OBP	SLG	PRO+	BR/A	SB	CS	SBR	FA	FR	G/POS	TPR
1884	Tol-a	109	425	61	95	24	5	0		10		.224	.248	.304	76	-12				.888	16	*O-107/2-2,C-2,1-1	0.2
1885	*StL-a	112	432	84	117	18	8	3	69	23		.271	.318	.370	112	5				**.946**	14	*O-112	1.4
1886	*StL-a	138	563	114	158	31	13	2	95	29		.281	.332	.393	121	11	59			**.952**	14	*O-138/2-2	1.9
1887	*StL-a	131	544	98	151	32	7	3	108	25		.278	.322	.379	86	-15	89			.941	19	*O-123/2-8,1-1	0.2
1888	Phi-a	136	549	125	155	22	8	1	61	33		.282	.355	.357	129	20	95			.952	4	*O-135/2-3	1.9
1889	Phi-a	125	516	134	140	**39**	6	0	39	67	30	.271	.375	.370	114	13	66			.923	8	*O-125	1.5
1890	Phi-a	103	396	100	106	21	4	2	40	49		.268	.392	.356	123	16	64			.919	14	*O-103/P-1	2.3
	Bal-a	19	68	16	9	4	0	0	5	9		.132	.253	.191	30	-6	8			.974	2	O-17/1-2	-0.4
	Yr	122	464	116	115	25	4	2	45	58		.248	.372	.332	109	9	72			.926	16	*O-120/1-2,P-1	1.9
1891	Bal-a	132	514	122	138	22	10	3	55	77	42	.268	.400	.368	119	17	50			.946	19	*O-113,2-21/S-2	2.8
1892	Bal-N	63	237	42	56	1	3	1	22	36	9	.236	.363	.278	92	-0	14			.905	-4	O-63	-0.6
	Cin-N	25	94	14	19	0	2	1	7	7	8	.202	.299	.277	75	-3	7			.925	-0	O-25	-0.4
	Yr	88	331	56	75	1	5	2	29	43	17	.227	.345	.278	88	-3	21			.911	-4	O-88	-1.0
1893	Lou-N	14	47	5	8	1	0	0	2	16	4	.170	.400	.191	64	-1	1			.912	-0	O-14	-0.1
Total	10	1107	4385	915	1152	215	66	16	503	381	93	.263	.345	.353	107	45	453			.933	107	*O-1075/2-36,1SCP	10.7

■ **FRANK WELCH** Welch, Frank Tiguer "Bugger" b: 8/10/1897, Birmingham, Ala. d: 7/25/57, Birmingham, Ala. BR/TR, 5'9", 175 lbs. Deb: 9/9/19

YEAR	TM/L	G	AB	R	H	2B	3B	HR	RBI	BB	SO	AVG	OBP	SLG	PRO+	BR/A	SB	CS	SBR	FA	FR	G/POS	TPR
1919	Phi-A	15	54	5	9	1	1	2	7	7	10	.167	.262	.333	66	-3	0			.909	0	O-15	-0.4
1920	Phi-A	100	360	43	93	17	5	4	40	26	41	.258	.312	.367	78	-12	2	9	-5	.937	-6	O-97	-2.9
1921	Phi-A	115	403	48	115	18	6	7	45	34	43	.285	.347	.412	92	-5	6	0	2	.943	3	*O-104	-0.8
1922	Phi-A	114	375	43	97	17	3	11	49	40	40	.259	.335	.408	90	-6	3	4	-2	.949	-0	*O-104	-1.5
1923	Phi-A	125	421	56	125	19	9	4	55	48	40	.297	.374	.413	106	4	1	4	-2	.967	3	*O-117	-0.2
1924	Phi-A	94	293	47	85	13	2	5	31	35	27	.290	.372	.399	98	-1	2	3	-1	.985	1	O-74	-0.5
1925	Phi-A	85	202	40	56	5	4	4	41	29	14	.277	.373	.401	90	-3	2	1	0	.968	-3	O-57	-0.8
1926	Phi-A	75	174	26	49	8	1	4	23	26	9	.282	.381	.408	100	0	2	5	-2	.975	-5	O-49	-1.0
1927	Bos-A	15	28	2	5	2	0	0	4	5	1	.179	.303	.250	46	-2	0	2	-1	1.000	2	/O-6	-0.2
Total	9	738	2310	310	634	100	31	41	295	250	225	.274	.350	.398	92	-27	18	28		.955	-5	O-623	-8.3

■ **HERB WELCH** Welch, Herbert M. "Dutch" b: 10/19/1898, RoEllen, Tenn. d: 4/13/67, Memphis, Tenn. BL/TR, 5'6", 154 lbs. Deb: 9/15/25

YEAR	TM/L	G	AB	R	H	2B	3B	HR	RBI	BB	SO	AVG	OBP	SLG	PRO+	BR/A	SB	CS	SBR	FA	FR	G/POS	TPR
1925	Bos-A	13	38	2	11	0	1	0	2	0	6	.289	.289	.342	60	-2	0	0	0	.893	5	S-13	0.4

■ **TUB WELCH** Welch, James T. b: 7/3/1866, St.Louis, Mo. TR, 5'11", 230 lbs. Deb: 6/12/1890

YEAR	TM/L	G	AB	R	H	2B	3B	HR	RBI	BB	SO	AVG	OBP	SLG	PRO+	BR/A	SB	CS	SBR	FA	FR	G/POS	TPR
1890	Tol-a	35	108	15	31	3	1	1	14	8		.287	.358	.361	109	1	7			.930	0	C-25,1-10	0.2
1895	Lou-N	47	153	18	37	4	1	1	8	13	7	.242	.310	.301	62	-8	2			.888	-1	C-28,1-20	-0.5
Total	2	82	261	33	68	7	2	2	22	21	7	.261	.330	.326	80	-7	9			.911	-1	/C-53,1-30	-0.3

■ **MILT WELCH** Welch, Milton Edward b: 7/26/24, Farmersville, Ill BR/TR, 5'10", 175 lbs. Deb: 6/5/45

YEAR	TM/L	G	AB	R	H	2B	3B	HR	RBI	BB	SO	AVG	OBP	SLG	PRO+	BR/A	SB	CS	SBR	FA	FR	G/POS	TPR
1945	Det-A	1	2	0	0	0	0	0	0	0	1	.000	.000	.000	-94	-0	0	0	0	1.000	1	/C-1	0.0

■ **HARRY WELCHONCE** Welchonce, Harry Monroe "Welch" b: 11/20/1883, North Point, Pa. d: 2/26/77, Arcadia, Cal. BL/TR, 6', 170 lbs. Deb: 4/17/11

YEAR	TM/L	G	AB	R	H	2B	3B	HR	RBI	BB	SO	AVG	OBP	SLG	PRO+	BR/A	SB	CS	SBR	FA	FR	G/POS	TPR
1911	Phi-N	26	66	9	14	4	0	0	6	7	8	.212	.288	.273	56	-4	0			.929	-3	O-17	-0.8

■ **MIKE WELDAY** Welday, Lyndon Earl b: 12/19/1879, Conway, Iowa d: 5/28/42, Leavenworth, Kan. BL/TL, Deb: 4/21/07

YEAR	TM/L	G	AB	R	H	2B	3B	HR	RBI	BB	SO	AVG	OBP	SLG	PRO+	BR/A	SB	CS	SBR	FA	FR	G/POS	TPR
1907	Chi-A	24	35	2	8	1	1	0	0	6		.229	.341	.314	113	1	0			.938	-3	O-15	-0.2
1909	Chi-A	29	74	3	14	0	0	0	5	4		.189	.231	.189	34	-5	2			.886	1	O-20	-0.6
Total	2	53	109	5	22	1	1	0	5	10		.202	.269	.229	60	-5	2			.900	-2	/O-35	-0.8

■ **OLLIE WELF** Welf, Oliver Henry b: 1/17/1889, Cleveland, Ohio d: 6/15/67, Cleveland, Ohio BR/TL, 5'9", 160 lbs. Deb: 8/30/16

YEAR	TM/L	G	AB	R	H	2B	3B	HR	RBI	BB	SO	AVG	OBP	SLG	PRO+	BR/A	SB	CS	SBR	FA	FR	G/POS	TPR
1916	Cle-A	1	0	0	0	0	0	0	0	0	0	—	—	—	—	0	0			.000	0	R	0.0

■ **BRAD WELLMAN** Wellman, Brad Eugene b: 8/17/59, Lodi, Cal. BR/TR, 6', 170 lbs. Deb: 9/4/82

YEAR	TM/L	G	AB	R	H	2B	3B	HR	RBI	BB	SO	AVG	OBP	SLG	PRO+	BR/A	SB	CS	SBR	FA	FR	G/POS	TPR
1982	SF-N	6	4	1	1	0	0	0	0	0	1	.250	.250	.250	40	-0	0	0	0	1.000	0	/2-2	0.0
1983	SF-N	82	182	15	39	3	0	1	16	22	39	.214	.299	.247	55	-11	5	3	-0	.965	2	2-74/S-2	-0.7
1984	SF-N	93	265	23	60	9	1	2	25	19	41	.226	.278	.291	62	-14	10	5	0	.977	16	2-54,S-34/3-9	0.7
1985	SF-N	71	174	16	41	11	1	0	16	4	33	.236	.269	.310	65	-9	5	2	0	.983	-2	2-36,3-25/S-3	-1.1
1986	SF-N	12	13	0	2	0	0	0	1	1	2	.154	.214	.154	3	-2	0	0	0	1.000	-0	/S-8,2-1,3-1	-0.2
1987	LA-N	3	4	1	1	0	0	0	1	0	1	.250	.250	.250	34	-0	0	0	0	1.000	1	/2-1,S-1,3-1	0.0
1988	KC-A	71	107	11	29	3	0	1	6	6	23	.271	.322	.327	81	-3	1	2	-1	.972	15	2-46,S-15/3-4,D-3	1.3
1989	KC-A	103	178	30	41	4	0	2	12	7	36	.230	.263	.287	55	-11	5	3	-0	.995	19	2-64,S-34/3-3,D-1	1.1
Total	8	441	927	97	214	30	2	6	77	59	176	.231	.282	.287	61	-48	26	15	-1	.978	50	2-278/S-97,3-43,D-4	1.1

■ **BOB WELLMAN** Wellman, Robert Joseph b: 7/15/25, Norwood, Ohio d: 12/20/94, Villa Hills, Ky. BR/TR, 6'4", 210 lbs. Deb: 9/23/48

YEAR	TM/L	G	AB	R	H	2B	3B	HR	RBI	BB	SO	AVG	OBP	SLG	PRO+	BR/A	SB	CS	SBR	FA	FR	G/POS	TPR
1948	Phi-A	4	10	1	2	0	1	0	0	3	2	.200	.385	.400	109	0	0	0	0	1.000	0	/1-2,O-1	0.0
1950	Phi-A	11	15	1	5	0	0	1	1	0	3	.333	.333	.533	121	0	0	0	0	1.000	-0	/O-2	0.0
Total	2	15	25	2	7	0	1	1	1	3	5	.280	.357	.480	117	1	0	0	0	.889	0	/O-3,1-2	0.0

■ **GREG WELLS** Wells, Gregory De Wayne b: 4/25/54, McIntosh, Ala. BR/TR, 6'5", 218 lbs. Deb: 8/10/81

YEAR	TM/L	G	AB	R	H	2B	3B	HR	RBI	BB	SO	AVG	OBP	SLG	PRO+	BR/A	SB	CS	SBR	FA	FR	G/POS	TPR
1981	Tor-A	32	73	7	18	5	0	0	5	5	12	.247	.295	.315	71	-3	0	2	-1	.994	-0	1-22/D-3	-0.5
1982	Min-A	15	54	5	11	1	2	0	3	1	8	.204	.218	.296	39	-5	0	0	0	.962	-2	1-10/D-5	-0.7
Total	2	47	127	12	29	6	2	0	8	6	20	.228	.263	.307	58	-7	0	2	-1	.983	-2	/1-32,D-8	-1.2

■ **JAKE WELLS** Wells, Jacob b: 8/9/1863, Memphis, Tenn. d: 3/16/27, Hendersonville, N.C. BR/TR, 5'11", 167 lbs. Deb: 8/10/1888

YEAR	TM/L	G	AB	R	H	2B	3B	HR	RBI	BB	SO	AVG	OBP	SLG	PRO+	BR/A	SB	CS	SBR	FA	FR	G/POS	TPR
1888	Det-N	16	57	5	9	1	0	0	2	0	5	.158	.158	.175	6	-6	0			.917	5	C-16	0.0
1890	StL-a	30	105	17	25	3	0	0	12	10		.238	.333	.267	67	-5	1			.941	2	C-28/O-3	-0.1
Total	2	46	162	22	34	4	0	0	14	10	5	.210	.277	.235	50	-11	1			.932	6	/C-44,O-3	-0.1

■ **LEO WELLS** Wells, Leo Donald b: 7/18/17, Kansas City, Kan. BR/TR, 5'9", 170 lbs. Deb: 4/16/42

YEAR	TM/L	G	AB	R	H	2B	3B	HR	RBI	BB	SO	AVG	OBP	SLG	PRO+	BR/A	SB	CS	SBR	FA	FR	G/POS	TPR
1942	Chi-A	35	62	8	12	2	0	1	4	4	5	.194	.242	.274	46	-5	1	0	0	1.000	11	S-12/3-6	0.7
1946	Chi-A	45	127	11	24	4	1	1	11	12	34	.189	.259	.260	47	-9	3	4	-2	.942	8	3-38/S-2	-0.3
Total	2	80	189	19	36	6	1	2	15	16	39	.190	.254	.265	47	-14	4	4	-1	.938	19	/3-44,S-14	0.4

■ **JIMMY WELSH** Welsh, James Daniel b: 10/9/02, Denver, Colo. d: 10/30/70, Oakland, Cal. BL/TR, 6'1", 174 lbs. Deb: 4/14/25

YEAR	TM/L	G	AB	R	H	2B	3B	HR	RBI	BB	SO	AVG	OBP	SLG	PRO+	BR/A	SB	CS	SBR	FA	FR	G/POS	TPR
1925	Bos-N	122	484	69	151	25	8	7	63	20	24	.312	.350	.440	110	5	7	4	-0	.960	6	*O-116/2-3	0.4
1926	Bos-N	134	490	69	136	18	11	3	57	33	28	.278	.333	.378	100	-1	6			.965	10	*O-129	0.0
1927	Bos-N	131	497	72	143	26	7	9	54	23	27	.288	.330	.423	109	4	11			.969	13	*O-129/1-1	0.9
1928	NY-N	124	476	77	146	22	5	9	54	29	30	.307	.357	.431	104	3	4			.981	-0	*O-117	-0.5

YEAR	TM/L	G	AB	R	H	2B	3B	HR	RBI	BB	SO	AVG	OBP	SLG	PRO+	BR/A	SB	CS	SBR	FA	FR	G/POS	TPR
1929	NY-N	38	129	25	32	7	0	2	8	9	3	.248	.331	.349	69	-6	3			.940	-6	O-35	-1.4
	Bos-N	53	186	24	54	8	7	2	16	13	9	.290	.350	.441	98	-1	1			.979	9	O-51	0.4
	Yr	91	315	49	86	15	7	4	24	22	12	.273	.342	.403	86	-7	4			.970	2	O-86	-1.0
1930	Bos-N	113	422	51	116	21	9	3	36	29	23	.275	.327	.389	75	-18	5			.980	11	*O-110	-1.3
Total	6	715	2684	387	778	127	47	35	288	156	144	.290	.340	.411	98	-14	37	4		.971	42	O-687/2-3,1-1	-1.5

■ **LEW WENDELL** Wendell, Lewis Charles b: 3/22/1892, New York, N.Y. d: 7/11/53, Brooklyn, N.Y. BR/TR, 5'11", 178 lbs. Deb: 6/10/15

YEAR	TM/L	G	AB	R	H	2B	3B	HR	RBI	BB	SO	AVG	OBP	SLG	PRO+	BR/A	SB	CS	SBR	FA	FR	G/POS	TPR
1915	NY-N	20	36	0	8	1	1	0	5	2	7	.222	.263	.306	76	-1	0			.920	-5	C-18	-0.6
1916	NY-N	2	2	0	0	0	0	0	0	0	2	.000	.000	.000	-99	-0	0			.000	0	H	-0.1
1924	Phi-N	21	32	3	8	1	0	0	2	3	5	.250	.314	.281	54	-2	0	0	0	1.000	-1	C-17	-0.3
1925	Phi-N	18	26	0	2	0	0	0	3	1	3	.077	.111	.077	-47	-6	0	0	0	.909	-1	/C-9	-0.6
1926	Phi-N	1	4	0	0	0	0	0	0	0	0	.000	.000	.000	-95	-1	0			.333	-1	/C-1	-0.2
Total	5	62	100	3	18	2	1	0	10	6	17	.180	.226	.220	23	-10	0	0		.925	-8	/C-45	-1.8

■ **JACK WENTZ** Wentz, John George (b: John George Wernz) b: 3/4/1863, Louisville, Ky. d: 9/14/07, Louisville, Ky. BR/TR, 5'10.5", 175 lbs. Deb: 4/15/1891

YEAR	TM/L	G	AB	R	H	2B	3B	HR	RBI	BB	SO	AVG	OBP	SLG	PRO+	BR/A	SB	CS	SBR	FA	FR	G/POS	TPR
1891	Lou-a	1	4	0	1	0	0	0	0	0	0	.250	.250	.250	44	-0	0			.667	-1	/2-1	-0.1

■ **STAN WENTZEL** Wentzel, Stanley Aaron b: 1/13/17, Lorane, Pa. d: 11/28/91, St.Lawrence, Pa. BR/TR, 6'1", 200 lbs. Deb: 9/23/45

YEAR	TM/L	G	AB	R	H	2B	3B	HR	RBI	BB	SO	AVG	OBP	SLG	PRO+	BR/A	SB	CS	SBR	FA	FR	G/POS	TPR
1945	Bos-N	4	19	3	4	0	1	0	6	0	3	.211	.211	.316	45	-1	1			1.000	-1	/O-4	-0.3

■ **JULIE WERA** Wera, Julian Valentine b: 2/9/02, Winona, Minn. d: 12/12/75, Rochester, Minn. BR/TR, 5'8", 164 lbs. Deb: 4/14/27

YEAR	TM/L	G	AB	R	H	2B	3B	HR	RBI	BB	SO	AVG	OBP	SLG	PRO+	BR/A	SB	CS	SBR	FA	FR	G/POS	TPR
1927	NY-A	38	42	7	10	3	0	1	8	1	5	.238	.273	.381	70	-2	0	0	0	1.000	3	3-19	0.1
1929	NY-A	5	12	1	5	0	0	0	2	1	1	.417	.462	.417	137	1	0	0	0	1.000	-1	/3-4	0.0
Total	2	43	54	8	15	3	0	1	10	2	6	.278	.316	.389	85	-1	0	0	0	1.000	2	/3-23	0.1

■ **BILLY WERBER** Werber, William Murray b: 6/20/08, Berwyn, Md. BR/TR, 5'10", 170 lbs. Deb: 6/25/30

YEAR	TM/L	G	AB	R	H	2B	3B	HR	RBI	BB	SO	AVG	OBP	SLG	PRO+	BR/A	SB	CS	SBR	FA	FR	G/POS	TPR
1930	NY-A	4	14	5	4	0	0	0	2	3	1	.286	.412	.286	84	-0	0	0	0	.955	1	/S-3,3-1	0.1
1933	NY-A	3	2	0	0	0	0	0	0	0	0	.000	.000	.000	-99	-1	0	0	0	.000	0	/3-1	-0.1
	Bos-A	108	425	64	110	30	6	3	39	33	39	.259	.312	.379	83	-11	15	5	2	.910	-17	S-71,3-38/2-2	-1.8
	Yr	111	427	64	110	30	6	3	39	33	39	.258	.311	.377	82	-12	15	5	2	.910	-17	S-71,3-39/2-2	-1.9
1934	Bos-A	152	623	129	200	41	10	11	67	77	37	.321	.397	.472	115	14	**40**	15	3	.941	20	*3-130,S-22	4.1
1935	Bos-A	124	462	84	118	30	3	14	61	69	41	.255	.357	.424	95	-4	**29**	7	5	.942	17	*3-123	2.1
1936	Bos-A	145	535	89	147	29	6	10	67	89	37	.275	.382	.407	90	-8	23	13	-1	.935	-12	*3-101,O-45/2-1	-1.7
1937	Phi-A	128	493	85	144	31	4	7	70	74	39	.292	.386	.414	103	4	**35**	13	3	.958	0	*3-125/O-3	1.0
1938	Phi-A	134	499	92	129	22	7	11	69	93	37	.259	.377	.397	96	-1	19	15	-3	.935	0	*3-134	-0.2
1939	*Cin-N	147	599	**115**	173	35	5	5	57	91	46	.289	.388	.389	109	11	15			.933	13	*3-147	2.5
1940	*Cin-N	143	584	105	162	35	5	12	48	68	40	.277	.361	.416	113	11	16			**.962**	3	*3-143	1.7
1941	Cin-N	109	418	56	100	9	2	4	46	53	24	.239	.328	.299	77	-11	14			.959	13	*3-107	0.4
1942	NY-N	98	370	51	76	9	2	1	13	51	22	.205	.308	.249	64	-15	9			.927	10	3-93	-0.4
Total	11	1295	5024	875	1363	271	50	78	539	701	363	.271	.364	.392	97	-10	215	68		.944	49	*3-1143/S-96,O-48,2	7.7

■ **PERRY WERDEN** Werden, Percival Wherritt b: 7/21/1865, St.Louis, Mo. d: 1/9/34, Minneapolis, Minn. BR/TR, 6'2", 220 lbs. Deb: 4/24/1884

YEAR	TM/L	G	AB	R	H	2B	3B	HR	RBI	BB	SO	AVG	OBP	SLG	PRO+	BR/A	SB	CS	SBR	FA	FR	G/POS	TPR
1884	StL-U	18	76	7	18	2	0	0		2		.237	.256	.263	56	-6				.893	-1	P-16/O-6	-0.2
1888	Was-N	3	10	0	3	0	0	0	2	1	4	.300	.364	.300	120	0	0			.857	-0	/O-3	0.0
1890	Tol-a	128	498	113	147	22	**20**	6	72	78		.295	.404	.456	149	32	59			.972	6	*1-124/O-5	2.7
1891	Bal-a	139	552	102	160	20	18	6	104	52	59	.290	.363	.424	124	15	46			.980	1	*1-139	0.7
1892	StL-N	149	598	73	154	22	6	8	84	59	52	.258	.328	.355	112	9	20			.982	12	*1-149	1.2
1893	StL-N	125	500	73	138	22	**29**	1	94	49	25	.276	.349	.442	109	4	11			.968	3	*1-124/O-1	0.3
1897	Lou-N	131	506	76	153	21	14	5	83	40		.302	.366	.429	113	9	14			.984	18	*1-131	2.4
Total	7	693	2740	444	773	109	87	26	439	281	140	.282	.359	.414	119	63	150			.978	38	1-667/P-16,O-15	7.1

■ **JOHNNY WERHAS** Werhas, John Charles "Peaches" b: 2/7/38, Highland Park, Mich. BR/TR, 6'2", 200 lbs. Deb: 4/14/64

YEAR	TM/L	G	AB	R	H	2B	3B	HR	RBI	BB	SO	AVG	OBP	SLG	PRO+	BR/A	SB	CS	SBR	FA	FR	G/POS	TPR
1964	LA-N	29	83	6	16	2	1	0	8	13	12	.193	.302	.241	59	-4	0	0	0	.952	4	3-28	-0.1
1965	LA-N	4	3	1	0	0	0	0	0	1	2	.000	.250	.000	-24	-0	0	0	0	1.000	-0	/1-1	-0.1
1967	LA-N	7	7	0	1	0	0	0	0	0	3	.143	.143	.143	-20	-1	0	0	0	.000	0	H	-0.1
	Cal-A	49	75	8	12	1	1	2	6	10	22	.160	.267	.280	64	-3	0	0	0	.963	1	3-30/1-4,O-1	-0.3
Total	3	89	168	15	29	3	2	2	14	24	39	.173	.280	.250	57	-9	0	0	0	.956	4	/3-58,1-5,O-1	-0.6

■ **DON WERNER** Werner, Donald Paul b: 3/8/53, Appleton, Wis. BR/TR, 6'1", 185 lbs. Deb: 9/2/75

YEAR	TM/L	G	AB	R	H	2B	3B	HR	RBI	BB	SO	AVG	OBP	SLG	PRO+	BR/A	SB	CS	SBR	FA	FR	G/POS	TPR
1975	Cin-N	7	8	0	1	0	0	0	0	0	0	.125	.222	.125	-2	-1	0	0	0	.923	0	/C-7	-0.1
1976	Cin-N	3	4	0	2	1	0	0	1	1	1	.500	.600	.750	275	1	0	0	0	1.000	1	/C-3	0.2
1977	Cin-N	10	23	3	4	0	0	2	4	2	3	.174	.240	.435	75	-1	0	1	-1	1.000	1	C-10	0.0
1978	Cin-N	50	113	7	17	2	1	0	11	14	30	.150	.250	.186	23	-11	1	0	0	.987	5	C-49	-0.6
1980	Cin-N	24	64	2	11	2	0	0	5	7	10	.172	.264	.203	32	-6	1	0	0	.962	1	C-24	-0.4
1981	Tex-A	2	8	1	2	0	0	0	0	0	2	.250	.250	.250	47	-1	0	1	-1	.000	0	/D-2	-0.1
1982	Tex-A	22	59	4	12	2	0	0	3	3	7	.203	.242	.237	34	-5	0	0	0	.980	1	C-22	-0.4
Total	7	118	279	17	49	7	1	2	24	27	53	.176	.256	.229	36	-24	2	2	-1	.979	9	C-115/D-2	-1.4

■ **JOE WERRICK** Werrick, Joseph Abraham b: 10/25/1861, St.Paul, Minn. d: 5/10/43, St.Peter, Minn. BR/TR, 5'9", 151 lbs. Deb: 9/27/1884

YEAR	TM/L	G	AB	R	H	2B	3B	HR	RBI	BB	SO	AVG	OBP	SLG	PRO+	BR/A	SB	CS	SBR	FA	FR	G/POS	TPR
1884	StP-U	9	27	3	2	0	0	0		1		.074	.107	.074	-81	-8				.756	-0	/S-9	-0.8
1886	Lou-a	136	561	75	140	20	14	3	62	33		.250	.294	.351	96	-6	19			.853	-1	*3-136	-0.3
1887	Lou-a	136	533	90	152	21	13	7	99	38		.285	.336	.413	106	2	49			.831	-0	*3-136	0.4
1888	Lou-a	111	413	49	89	12	7	0	51	30		.215	.274	.278	79	-9	15			.811	-13	3-89,S-11/2-8,O-3	-1.8
Total	4	392	1534	217	383	53	34	10	212	102		.250	.300	.348	94	-21	83			.834	-14	3-361/S-20,2-8,O-3	-2.5

■ **DON WERT** Wert, Donald Ralph b: 7/29/38, Strasburg, Pa. BR/TR, 5'9", 165 lbs. Deb: 5/11/63

YEAR	TM/L	G	AB	R	H	2B	3B	HR	RBI	BB	SO	AVG	OBP	SLG	PRO+	BR/A	SB	CS	SBR	FA	FR	G/POS	TPR
1963	Det-A	78	251	31	65	6	2	7	25	24	51	.259	.329	.382	95	-1	3	3	-1	.957	3	3-47,2-21/S-8	0.4
1964	Det-A	148	525	63	135	18	5	9	55	50	74	.257	.329	.362	91	-6	3	4	-2	.965	0	*3-142/S-4	-0.9
1965	Det-A	162	609	81	159	22	2	12	54	73	71	.261	.343	.363	100	1	5	6	-2	**.976**	5	*3-161/S-3,2-1	0.0
1966	Det-A	150	559	56	150	20	2	11	70	64	69	.268	.346	.370	103	4	6	3	0	.972	-18	*3-150	-1.9
1967	Det-A	142	534	60	137	23	2	6	40	44	59	.257	.321	.341	93	-4	1	1	-0	.978	-5	*3-140/S-1	-1.1
1968	*Det-A★	150	536	44	107	15	1	12	37	37	79	.200	.258	.299	66	-22	0	3	-2	.966	-6	*3-150/S-2	-3.5
1969	Det-A	132	423	46	95	11	1	14	50	49	60	.225	.307	.355	81	-11	3	1	0	.966	-0	*3-129	-1.1
1970	Det-A	128	363	34	79	13	0	6	33	44	56	.218	.309	.303	69	-15	1	3	-2	.953	-2	*3-117/2-2	-2.0
1971	Was-A	20	40	2	2	1	0	0	2	4	10	.050	.156	.075	-35	-7	0	0	0	1.000	-4	/S-7,3-7,2-1	-1.1
Total	9	1110	3840	417	929	129	15	77	366	389	529	.242	.317	.343	87	-61	22	24	-8	.968	-27	*3-1043/S-25,2-25	-11.2

■ **DENNIS WERTH** Werth, Dennis Dean b: 12/29/52, Lincoln, Ill. BR/TR, 6'1", 200 lbs. Deb: 9/17/79

YEAR	TM/L	G	AB	R	H	2B	3B	HR	RBI	BB	SO	AVG	OBP	SLG	PRO+	BR/A	SB	CS	SBR	FA	FR	G/POS	TPR
1979	NY-A	3	4	1	1	0	0	0	0	0	0	.250	.250	.250	36	-0	0	0	0	1.000	0	/1-1	0.0
1980	NY-A	39	65	15	20	3	0	3	12	12	19	.308	.416	.492	150	5	0	1	-1	1.000	-2	1-12/O-8,C-1,3-1,D	0.2
1981	NY-A	34	55	7	6	1	0	0	1	12	12	.109	.269	.127	18	-5	1	0	0	1.000	0	1-19/O-8,C-3,D-4	-0.6
1982	KC-A	41	15	5	2	0	0	0	2	4	2	.133	.316	.133	29	-1	0	0	0	.990	2	1-35/C-2	0.1
Total	4	117	139	28	29	4	0	3	15	28	33	.209	.341	.302	82	-2	1	1	-0	.996	1	/1-67,O-16,D-12,C3	-0.3

■ **DEL WERTZ** Wertz, Dwight Lyman Moody b: 10/11/1888, Canton, Ohio d: 5/26/58, Sarasota, Fla. BR/TR, 5'10", 160 lbs. Deb: 5/23/14

YEAR	TM/L	G	AB	R	H	2B	3B	HR	RBI	BB	SO	AVG	OBP	SLG	PRO+	BR/A	SB	CS	SBR	FA	FR	G/POS	TPR
1914	Buf-F	3	0	1	0	0	0	0	0	0	0	—	—	—	—	0	0			1.000	0	/S-1	0.0

■ **VIC WERTZ** Wertz, Victor Woodrow b: 2/9/25, York, Pa. d: 7/7/83, Detroit, Mich. BL/TR, 6', 186 lbs. Deb: 4/15/47

YEAR	TM/L	G	AB	R	H	2B	3B	HR	RBI	BB	SO	AVG	OBP	SLG	PRO+	BR/A	SB	CS	SBR	FA	FR	G/POS	TPR
1947	Det-A	102	333	60	96	22	4	6	44	47	66	.288	.376	.432	121	10	2	0	1	.965	-2	O-83	0.4
1948	Det-A	119	391	49	97	19	9	7	67	48	70	.248	.335	.396	92	-6	0	0	0	.954	1	O-98	-1.0
1949	Det-A★	155	608	96	185	26	6	20	133	80	61	.304	.385	.465	124	20	2	3	-1	.981	2	*O-155	1.3
1950	Det-A	149	559	99	172	37	4	27	123	91	55	.308	.408	.533	135	29	0	1	-1	.967	-8	*O-145	1.3

YEAR	TM/L	G	AB	R	H	2B	3B	HR	RBI	BB	SO	AVG	OBP	SLG	PRO+	BR/A	SB	CS	SBR	FA	FR	G/POS	TPR
1951	Det-A★	138	501	86	143	24	4	27	94	78	61	.285	.383	.511	139	27	0	3	-2	.989	3	*O-131	2.3
1952	Det-A☆	85	285	46	70	15	3	17	51	46	44	.246	.352	.498	134	12	1	0	0	.986	3	O-79	1.2
	StL-A	37	130	22	45	5	0	6	19	23	20	.346	.444	.523	164	12	0	0	0	.955	-3	O-36	0.8
	Yr	122	415	68	115	20	3	23	70	69	64	.277	.381	.506	143	24	1	0	0	.976	0	*O-115	2.0
1953	StL-A	128	440	61	118	18	6	19	70	72	44	.268	.376	.466	124	15	1	4	-2	.974	7	*O-121	1.6
1954	Bal-A	29	94	5	19	1	0	1	13	11	17	.202	.286	.245	50	-6	0	0	0	.963	2	O-27	-0.6
	*Cle-A	94	295	33	81	14	2	14	48	34	40	.275	.350	.478	123	8	0	2	-1	.989	2	1-83/O-5	0.5
	Yr	123	389	38	100	15	2	15	61	45	57	.257	.334	.422	106	2	0	2	-1	.989	4	1-83,O-32	-0.1
1955	Cle-A	74	257	30	65	11	2	14	55	32	33	.253	.338	.475	112	3	1	1	-0	.984	-3	1-63/O-9	-0.4
1956	Cle-A	136	481	65	127	22	0	32	106	75	87	.264	.369	.509	127	18	0	0	0	.991	1	*1-133	1.0
1957	Cle-A★	144	515	84	145	21	0	28	105	78	88	.282	.378	.485	136	26	2	3	-1	.988	-2	*1-139	1.5
1958	Cle-A	25	43	5	12	1	0	3	12	5	7	.279	.354	.512	139	2	0	0	0	.980	0	/1-8	0.2
1959	Bos-A	94	247	38	68	13	0	7	49	22	32	.275	.339	.413	101	0	0	0	0	.992	2	1-64	-0.2
1960	Bos-A	131	443	45	125	22	0	19	103	37	54	.282	.339	.460	110	5	0	2	-1	.987	3	*1-117	-0.1
1961	Bos-A	99	317	33	83	16	2	11	60	38	43	.262	.345	.429	103	1	0	0	0	.991	3	1-86	-0.2
	Det-A	8	6	0	1	0	0	0	1	0	1	.167	.167	.167	-10	-1	0	0	0	.000	0	H	-0.1
	Yr	107	323	33	84	16	2	11	61	38	44	.260	.342	.424	101	0	0	0	0	.991	3	1-86	-0.3
1962	Det-A	74	105	7	34	2	0	5	18	5	13	.324	.360	.486	121	3	0	0	0	.988	0	1-16	0.2
1963	Det-A	6	5	0	0	0	0	0	0	0	1	.000	.000	.000	-97	-1	0	0	0	.000	0	H	-0.1
	Min-A	35	44	3	6	0	0	3	7	6	5	.136	.240	.341	59	-3	0	0	0	1.000	1	/1-6	-0.2
	Yr	41	49	3	6	0	0	3	7	6	6	.122	.218	.306	44	-4	0	0	0	1.000	1	/1-6	-0.3
Total	17	1862	6099	867	1692	289	42	266	1178	828	842	.277	.366	.469	121	177	9	19	-9	.973	12	O-889,1-715	9.4

■ JIM WESSINGER Wessinger, James Michael b: 9/25/55, Utica, N.Y. BR/TR, 5′10″, 165 lbs. Deb: 8/4/79

YEAR	TM/L	G	AB	R	H	2B	3B	HR	RBI	BB	SO	AVG	OBP	SLG	PRO+	BR/A	SB	CS	SBR	FA	FR	G/POS	TPR
1979	Atl-N	10	7	2	0	0	0	0	0	1	4	.000	.125	.000	-59	-2	0	0	0	.833	1	/2-2	-0.1

■ MAX WEST West, Max Edward b: 11/28/16, Dexter, Mo. BL/TR, 6′1.5″, 182 lbs. Deb: 4/19/38

YEAR	TM/L	G	AB	R	H	2B	3B	HR	RBI	BB	SO	AVG	OBP	SLG	PRO+	BR/A	SB	CS	SBR	FA	FR	G/POS	TPR
1938	Bos-N	123	418	47	98	16	5	10	63	38	38	.234	.300	.368	92	-6	5			.986	-9	*O-109/1-7	-1.9
1939	Bos-N	130	449	67	128	26	6	19	82	51	55	.285	.364	.497	139	23	1			.974	-7	*O-124	1.2
1940	Bos-N★	139	524	72	137	27	5	7	72	65	54	.261	.344	.372	103	3	2			.975	1	*O-102,1-36	-0.5
1941	Bos-N	138	484	63	134	28	4	12	68	72	68	.277	.373	.426	130	20	5			.981	6	*O-132	1.9
1942	Bos-N	134	452	54	115	22	0	16	56	68	59	.254	.354	.409	126	15	4			.991	-1	1-85,O-50	0.7
1946	Bos-N	1	1	0	0	0	0	0	0	0	1	.000	.000	.000	-99	-0	0			1.000	-0	/1-1	0.0
	Cin-N	72	202	16	43	13	0	5	18	32	36	.213	.323	.351	95	-1	1			.952	-1	O-58	-0.5
	Yr	73	203	16	43	13	0	5	18	32	37	.212	.322	.350	94	-2	1			.952	-1	O-58/1-1	-0.5
1948	Pit-N	87	146	19	26	4	0	8	21	27	29	.178	.310	.370	82	-4	1			.991	-4	1-32,O-16	-0.8
Total	7	824	2676	338	681	136	20	77	380	353	340	.254	.344	.407	114	50	19			.975	-15	O-591,1-161	0.1

■ BUCK WEST West, Milton Douglas b: 8/29/1860, Spring Mill, Ohio d: 1/13/29, Mansfield, Ohio BL/TR, 5′10″, 200 lbs. Deb: 8/24/1884

YEAR	TM/L	G	AB	R	H	2B	3B	HR	RBI	BB	SO	AVG	OBP	SLG	PRO+	BR/A	SB	CS	SBR	FA	FR	G/POS	TPR
1884	Cin-a	33	131	20	32	2	8	1	15	2		.244	.256	.405	107	0				.825	-6	O-33	-0.5
1890	Cle-N	37	151	20	37	6	1	2	29	7	11	.245	.283	.338	82	-4	4			.831	-1	O-37	-0.6
Total	2	70	282	40	69	8	9	3	44	9	11	.245	.271	.369	94	-4	4			.828	-7	/O-70	-1.1

■ DICK WEST West, Richard Thomas b: 11/24/15, Louisville, Ky. d: 3/13/96, Fort Wayne, Ind. BR/TR, 6′2″, 180 lbs. Deb: 9/28/38

YEAR	TM/L	G	AB	R	H	2B	3B	HR	RBI	BB	SO	AVG	OBP	SLG	PRO+	BR/A	SB	CS	SBR	FA	FR	G/POS	TPR
1938	Cin-N	1	1	0	0	0	0	0	0	0	0	.000	.000	.000	-99	-0	0			.000	0	H	0.0
1939	Cin-N	8	19	1	4	0	0	0	4	1	4	.211	.250	.211	25	-2	0			1.000	-1	/O-5,C-1	-0.3
1940	Cin-N	7	28	4	11	2	0	1	6	0	2	.393	.393	.571	161	2	1			1.000	-3	/C-7	0.0
1941	Cin-N	67	172	15	37	5	2	1	17	6	23	.215	.246	.285	49	-12	4			.970	-3	C-64	-1.2
1942	Cin-N	33	79	9	14	3	0	1	8	5	13	.177	.226	.253	40	-6	1			.989	3	C-17/O-6	-0.3
1943	Cin-N	3	0	1	0	0	0	0	0	0	0	—	—	—	—	0	0			.000	0	R	0.0
Total	6	119	299	30	66	10	2	3	35	12	42	.221	.253	.298	55	-18	6			.977	-4	/C-89,O-11	-1.8

■ SAM WEST West, Samuel Filmore b: 10/5/04, Longview, Tex. d: 11/23/85, Lubbock, Tex. BL/TL, 5′11″, 165 lbs. Deb: 4/17/27 C

YEAR	TM/L	G	AB	R	H	2B	3B	HR	RBI	BB	SO	AVG	OBP	SLG	PRO+	BR/A	SB	CS	SBR	FA	FR	G/POS	TPR
1927	Was-A	38	67	9	16	4	1	0	6	8	8	.239	.320	.328	69	-3	1	0	0	.939	-1	O-18	-0.5
1928	Was-A	125	378	59	114	30	7	3	40	20	23	.302	.338	.442	104	1	5	6	-2	**.996**	-10	*O-116	-1.7
1929	Was-A	142	510	60	136	16	8	3	75	45	41	.267	.326	.347	73	-20	9	8	-2	.978	15	*O-139	-1.6
1930	Was-A	120	411	75	135	22	10	6	67	37	34	.328	.385	.474	116	10	5	5	-2	.972	3	*O-118	0.4
1931	Was-A	132	526	77	175	43	13	3	91	30	37	.333	.369	.481	121	14	6	8	-3	.990	21	*O-127	2.2
1932	Was-A	146	554	88	159	27	12	6	83	48	57	.287	.345	.412	96	-4	4	5	-2	.979	19	*O-143	0.5
1933	StL-A★	133	517	93	155	25	12	11	48	59	49	.300	.373	.458	112	8	10	8	-2	.988	8	*O-127	0.8
1934	StL-A★	122	482	90	157	22	10	9	55	62	55	.326	.403	.469	115	11	3	5	-2	.972	7	*O-120	1.0
1935	StL-A☆	138	527	93	158	37	4	10	70	75	46	.300	.388	.442	109	8	1	6	-3	**.989**	17	*O-135	1.5
1936	StL-A	152	533	78	148	26	4	7	70	94	70	.278	.386	.381	87	-8	2	0	1	.983	9	*O-148	-0.4
1937	StL-A★	122	457	68	150	37	4	7	58	46	28	.328	.390	.473	115	11	1	1	-0	.987	12	*O-105	1.7
1938	StL-A	44	165	17	51	8	2	1	27	14	9	.309	.363	.400	91	-2	1	0	0	.971	-3	O-41	-0.6
	Was-A	92	344	51	104	19	5	5	47	33	21	.302	.363	.430	105	2	1	1	-0	.983	-3	O-85	-0.3
	Yr	136	509	68	155	27	7	6	74	47	30	.305	.363	.420	100	-0	2	1	0	.979	-6	*O-126	-0.9
1939	Was-A	115	390	52	110	20	8	3	52	67	29	.282	.387	.397	109	7	1	1	-0	.992	3	O-89,1-17	0.5
1940	Was-A	57	99	7	25	6	1	1	18	16	13	.253	.357	.364	93	-1	0	2	-1	.990	-1	1-12/O-9	-0.4
1941	Was-A	26	37	3	10	0	0	0	6	11	2	.270	.438	.270	95	1	1	0	0	1.000	-0	/O-8	0.0
1942	Chi-A	49	151	14	35	5	0	0	25	31	18	.232	.363	.265	80	-2	2	0	1	.983	-3	O-45	-0.7
Total	16	1753	6148	934	1838	347	101	75	838	696	540	.299	.371	.425	103	34	53	56	-18	.983	93	*O-1573/1-29	2.4

■ MAX WEST West, Walter Maxwell b: 7/14/04, Sunset, Tex. d: 4/25/71, Houston, Tex. BR/TR, 5′11″, 165 lbs. Deb: 9/18/28

YEAR	TM/L	G	AB	R	H	2B	3B	HR	RBI	BB	SO	AVG	OBP	SLG	PRO+	BR/A	SB	CS	SBR	FA	FR	G/POS	TPR
1928	Bro-N	7	21	4	6	1	1	0	1	4	1	.286	.400	.429	118	1	0			.882	1	/O-6	0.2
1929	Bro-N	5	8	1	2	1	0	0	1	1	0	.250	.333	.375	77	-0	0			1.000	-1	/O-2	-0.1
Total	2	12	29	5	8	2	1	0	2	5	1	.276	.382	.414	107	0	0			.895	1	/O-8	0.1

■ BILLY WEST West, William Nelson b: 8/21/1840, Philadelphia, Pa. Deb: 5/22/1874

YEAR	TM/L	G	AB	R	H	2B	3B	HR	RBI	BB	SO	AVG	OBP	SLG	PRO+	BR/A	SB	CS	SBR	FA	FR	G/POS	TPR
1874	Atl-n	9	35	4	8	1	0	0	2	1	2	.229	.250	.257	71	-1	0	0	0	.707	-1	/2-9,C-1,S-1	-0.2
1876	NY-N	1	4	0	0	0	0	0	0	0	0	.000	.000	.000	-99	-1				1.000	-0	/2-1	-0.1

■ OSCAR WESTERBERG Westerberg, Oscar William b: 7/8/1882, Alameda, Cal. d: 4/17/09, Alameda, Cal. BB/TR, Deb: 9/5/07

YEAR	TM/L	G	AB	R	H	2B	3B	HR	RBI	BB	SO	AVG	OBP	SLG	PRO+	BR/A	SB	CS	SBR	FA	FR	G/POS	TPR
1907	Bos-N	2	6	0	2	0	0	0	1	1		.333	.429	.333	139	0	0			1.000	-1	/S-2	0.0

■ JIM WESTLAKE Westlake, James Patrick b: 7/3/30, Sacramento, Cal. BL/TL, 6′1″, 190 lbs. Deb: 4/16/55 F

YEAR	TM/L	G	AB	R	H	2B	3B	HR	RBI	BB	SO	AVG	OBP	SLG	PRO+	BR/A	SB	CS	SBR	FA	FR	G/POS	TPR
1955	Phi-N	1	1	0	0	0	0	0	0	0	1	.000	.000	.000	-99	-0	0	0	0	.000	0	H	0.0

■ WALLY WESTLAKE Westlake, Waldon Thomas b: 11/8/20, Gridley, Cal. BR/TR, 6′, 186 lbs. Deb: 4/15/47 F

YEAR	TM/L	G	AB	R	H	2B	3B	HR	RBI	BB	SO	AVG	OBP	SLG	PRO+	BR/A	SB	CS	SBR	FA	FR	G/POS	TPR
1947	Pit-N	112	407	59	111	17	4	17	69	27	63	.273	.324	.459	103	-0	5			.988	4	*O-109	-0.2
1948	Pit-N	132	428	78	122	10	6	17	65	46	40	.285	.360	.456	117	10	2			.976	-0	*O-125	0.3
1949	Pit-N	147	525	77	148	24	8	23	104	45	69	.282	.345	.490	118	12	6			.982	5	*O-143	1.0
1950	Pit-N	139	477	69	136	15	6	24	95	48	78	.285	.359	.493	118	11	1			**.991**	4	*O-123	1.0
1951	Pit-N	50	181	28	51	4	0	16	45	9	26	.282	.323	.569	131	7	0	1	-1	.908	5	3-34,O-11	1.0
	StL-N★	73	267	36	68	8	5	6	39	24	42	.255	.325	.390	91	-4	1	2	-1	.982	2	O-68	-0.5
	Yr	123	448	64	119	12	5	22	84	33	68	.266	.324	.462	107	3	1	3	-2	.984	7	O-79,3-34	0.5
1952	StL-N	21	74	7	16	3	0	0	10	8	11	.216	.293	.257	53	-5	1	1	-0	1.000	6	O-15	0.1
	Cin-N	59	183	29	37	4	0	3	14	31	29	.202	.324	.273	67	-7	0	2	-1	.992	-2	O-56	-1.2
	Yr	80	257	36	53	7	0	3	24	39	40	.206	.315	.268	63	-12	1	3	-2	.995	5	O-71	-1.1
	Cle-A	29	69	11	16	4	1	1	9	8	16	.232	.312	.362	93	-1	1	0	0	1.000	-3	O-28	-0.5
1953	Cle-A	82	218	42	72	7	1	9	46	35	29	.330	.427	.495	153	17	2	0	1	.963	-11	O-72	0.5
1954	*Cle-A	85	240	36	63	9	2	11	42	26	37	.262	.340	.454	114	4	0	1	-1	.964	-7	O-70	-0.6

YEAR	TM/L	G	AB	R	H	2B	3B	HR	RBI	BB	SO	AVG	OBP	SLG	PRO+	BR/A	SB	CS	SBR	FA	FR	G/POS	TPR
1955	Cle-A	16	20	2	5	1	0	0	1	3	5	.250	.348	.300	73	-1	0	0	0	1.000	-0	/O-7	-0.1
	Bal-A	8	24	0	3	1	0	0	0	6	5	.125	.300	.167	30	-2	0	0	0	1.000	-1	/O-7	-0.4
	Yr	24	44	2	8	2	0	0	1	9	10	.182	.321	.227	49	-3	0	0	0	1.000	-2	O-14	-0.5
1956	Phi-N	5	4	0	0	0	0	0	0	1	3	.000	.200	.000	-41	-1	0	0	0	.000	0	H	-0.1
Total	10	958	3117	474	848	107	33	127	539	317	453	.272	.346	.450	111	41	19	7		.983	1	O-834/3-34	0.3
■ AL WESTON	Weston, Alfred John b: 12/11/05, Lynn, Mass. d: 11/13/97, San Diego, Cal. BR/TR, 6', 195 lbs. Deb: 7/7/29																						
1929	Bos-N	3	3	0	0	0	0	0	0	0	2	.000	.000	.000	-99	-1	0			.000	0	H	-0.1
■ WES WESTRUM	Westrum, Wesley Noreen b: 11/28/22, Clearbrook, Minn. BR/TR, 5'11", 185 lbs. Deb: 9/17/47 MC																						
1947	NY-N	6	12	1	5	1	0	0	2	0	2	.417	.417	.500	142	1	0			1.000	0	/C-2	0.1
1948	NY-N	66	125	14	20	3	1	4	16	20	36	.160	.276	.296	54	-8	3			.981	8	C-63	0.3
1949	NY-N	64	169	23	41	4	1	7	28	37	39	.243	.385	.402	111	4	1			.980	-0	C-62	0.7
1950	NY-N	140	437	68	103	13	3	23	71	92	73	.236	.371	.437	111	9	2			**.999**	10	*C-139	2.5
1951	*NY-N	124	361	59	79	12	0	20	70	104	93	.219	.400	.418	119	14	1	0	0	.987	8	*C-122	2.8
1952	NY-N☆	114	322	47	71	11	0	14	43	76	68	.220	.374	.385	110	7	1	2	-1	.978	-4	*C-112	0.8
1953	NY-N☆	107	290	40	65	5	0	12	30	56	73	.224	.352	.366	86	-5	2	0	1	.982	4	*C-106/3-1	0.4
1954	*NY-N	98	246	25	46	3	1	8	27	45	60	.187	.320	.305	63	-13	0	1	-1	.985	12	C-98	0.3
1955	NY-N	69	137	11	29	1	0	4	18	24	18	.212	.333	.307	71	-5	0	1	-1	.987	10	C-68	0.6
1956	NY-N	68	132	10	29	5	2	3	8	25	28	.220	.348	.356	91	-1	0	0	0	.982	13	C-67	1.4
1957	NY-N	63	91	4	15	1	0	1	2	10	24	.165	.255	.209	27	-9	0	1	-1	.966	2	C-63	-0.7
Total	11	919	2322	302	503	59	8	96	315	489	514	.217	.357	.373	95	-6	10	5		.985	64	C-902/3-1	9.2
■ JEFF WETHERBY	Wetherby, Jeffrey Barrett b: 10/18/63, Granada Hills, Cal. BL/TL, 6'2", 195 lbs. Deb: 6/7/89																						
1989	Atl-N	52	48	5	10	2	1	1	7	4	6	.208	.269	.354	75	-2	1	0	0	1.000	-2	/O-9	-0.4
■ DUTCH WETZEL	Wetzel, Franklin Burton b: 7/7/1893, Columbus, Ind. d: 3/5/42, Hollywood, Cal. BR/TR, 5'9.5", 177 lbs. Deb: 9/15/20																						
1920	StL-A	7	21	5	9	1	1	0	5	4	1	.429	.520	.571	183	3	0	1	-1	.875	0	/O-6	0.2
1921	StL-A	61	119	16	25	2	0	2	10	9	20	.210	.271	.277	38	-11	0	0	0	.981	-2	O-27	-1.4
Total	2	68	140	21	34	3	1	2	15	13	21	.243	.312	.321	59	-8	0	1	-1	.957	-2	/O-33	-1.2
■ BILL WHALEY	Whaley, William Carl b: 2/10/1899, Indianapolis, Ind. d: 3/3/43, Indianapolis, Ind. BR/TR, 5'11", 178 lbs. Deb: 4/18/23																						
1923	StL-A	23	50	5	12	2	1	0	1	4	2	.240	.309	.320	62	-3	0	0	0	1.000	-0	O-13	-0.4
■ BERT WHALING	Whaling, Albert James b: 6/22/1888, Los Angeles, Cal. d: 1/21/65, Sawtelle, Cal. BR/TR, 6', 185 lbs. Deb: 4/22/13																						
1913	Bos-N	79	211	22	51	8	2	0	25	10	32	.242	.283	.299	65	-10	3			**.990**	1	C-77	-0.4
1914	Bos-N	60	172	18	36	7	0	0	12	21	28	.209	.303	.250	65	-7	2			.981	12	C-59	1.0
1915	Bos-N	72	190	10	42	6	2	0	13	8	38	.221	.264	.274	66	-8	0	1	-1	.986	1	C-69	-0.3
Total	3	211	573	50	129	21	4	0	50	39	98	.225	.283	.276	65	-25	5	1		.986	14	C-205	0.3
■ MACK WHEAT	Wheat, McKinley Davis b: 6/9/1893, Polo, Mo. d: 8/14/79, Los Banos, Cal. BR/TR, 5'11.5", 167 lbs. Deb: 4/14/15 F																						
1915	Bro-N	8	14	0	1	0	0	0	0	0	5	.071	.071	.071	-56	-3	0			.957	-0	/C-8	-0.3
1916	Bro-N	2	2	0	0	0	0	0	0	0	1	.000	.000	.000	-97	-0	0			1.000	0	/C-2	0.0
1917	Bro-N	29	60	2	8	1	0	0	0	1	12	.133	.161	.150	-4	-7	1			.968	1	C-18/O-9	-0.7
1918	Bro-N	57	157	11	34	7	1	1	3	8	24	.217	.255	.293	67	-6	2			.966	-1	C-38/O-7	-0.6
1919	Bro-N	41	112	5	23	3	0	0	8	2	22	.205	.246	.232	43	-8	1			.944	-4	C-38	-0.9
1920	Phi-N	78	230	15	52	10	3	3	20	8	35	.226	.261	.335	67	-10	3	1	0	.961	9	C-74	0.4
1921	Phi-N	10	27	1	5	2	1	0	4	0	3	.185	.241	.333	47	-2	0	0	0	.980	5	/C-9	0.3
Total	7	225	602	34	123	23	5	4	35	19	102	.204	.241	.279	52	-37	7	1		.961	9	C-187/O-16	-1.8
■ ZACK WHEAT	Wheat, Zachary Davis "Buck" b: 5/23/1888, Hamilton, Mo. d: 3/11/72, Sedalia, Mo. BL/TR, 5'10", 170 lbs. Deb: 9/11/09 FH																						
1909	Bro-N	26	102	15	31	7	3	0	4	6		.304	.343	.431	145	5	1			.952	2	O-26	0.6
1910	Bro-N	156	606	78	172	36	15	2	55	47	80	.284	.341	.403	120	13	16			.962	6	*O-156	1.2
1911	Bro-N	140	534	55	153	26	13	5	76	29	58	.287	.332	.412	112	6	21			.955	-3	*O-136	-0.4
1912	Bro-N	123	453	70	138	28	7	8	65	39	40	.305	.367	.450	128	16	16			.968	3	*O-120	1.2
1913	Bro-N	138	535	64	161	28	10	7	58	25	45	.301	.335	.430	114	8	19			.978	9	*O-135	1.1
1914	Bro-N	145	533	66	170	26	9	9	89	47	50	.319	.377	.452	143	27	20			.962	18	*O-144	4.1
1915	Bro-N	146	528	64	136	15	12	5	66	52	42	.258	.330	.360	107	5	21	14	-2	.953	10	*O-144	0.6
1916	*Bro-N	149	568	76	177	32	13	9	73	43	49	.312	.366	**.461**	149	32	19			.975	9	*O-149	3.7
1917	Bro-N	109	362	38	113	15	11	1	41	20	18	.312	.352	.423	133	13	5			.979	6	O-98	1.7
1918	Bro-N	105	409	39	137	15	3	0	51	16	17	**.335**	.369	.386	131	14	9			.979	4	*O-105	1.4
1919	Bro-N	137	536	70	159	23	11	5	62	33	27	.297	.344	.409	123	14	15			.971	-1	*O-137	0.4
1920	*Bro-N	148	583	89	191	26	13	9	73	48	21	.328	.385	.463	138	29	8	10	-4	.971	-4	*O-148	1.1
1921	Bro-N	148	568	91	182	31	10	14	85	44	19	.320	.372	.484	121	16	11	8	-2	.965	-4	*O-148	-0.1
1922	Bro-N	152	600	92	201	29	12	16	112	45	22	.335	.388	.503	129	25	9	6	-1	**.991**	2	*O-152	1.5
1923	Bro-N	98	349	63	131	13	5	8	65	23	12	.375	.417	.510	148	24	3	3	-1	.908	-11	O-87	0.6
1924	Bro-N	141	566	92	212	41	8	14	97	49	18	.375	.428	.549	165	52	3	4	-2	.965	5	*O-139	4.5
1925	Bro-N	150	616	125	221	42	14	14	103	45	22	.359	.403	.541	143	38	3	1	0	.962	0	*O-149	2.7
1926	Bro-N	111	411	68	119	31	2	5	35	21	14	.290	.326	.411	99	-2	4			.955	2	*O-102	-0.8
1927	Phi-A	88	247	34	80	12	1	1	38	18	5	.324	.379	.393	95	-1	2	3	-1	.983	-3	O-62	-0.8
Total	19	2410	9106	1289	2884	476	172	132	1248	650	559	.317	.367	.450	129	335	205	49		.966	50	*O-2337	24.3
■ WOODY WHEATON	Wheaton, Elwood Pierce b: 10/3/14, Philadelphia, Pa. d: 12/11/95, Lancaster, Pa. BL/TL, 5'8.5", 160 lbs. Deb: 9/28/43																						
1943	Phi-A	7	30	2	6	2	0	0	2	3	2	.200	.294	.267	65	-1	0	0	0	1.000	1	/O-7	-0.1
1944	Phi-A	30	59	1	11	2	0	0	5	5	3	.186	.250	.220	35	-5	1	2	-1	1.000	2	P-11/O-8	-0.2
Total	2	37	89	3	17	4	0	0	7	8	5	.191	.265	.236	45	-6	1	2	-1	.981	3	/O-15,P-11	-0.3
■ DON WHEELER	Wheeler, Donald Wesley "Scott" b: 9/29/22, Minneapolis, Minn BR/TR, 5'10", 175 lbs. Deb: 4/23/49																						
1949	Chi-A	67	192	17	46	9	2	1	22	27	19	.240	.333	.323	76	-6	2	0	1	.976	3	C-58	0.0
■ ED WHEELER	Wheeler, Edward b: 6/15/1878, Sherman, Mich. d: 8/15/60, Ft.Worth, Tex. BB/TR, 5'10", 160 lbs. Deb: 5/10/02																						
1902	Bro-N	30	96	4	12	0	0	0	5	3		.125	.152	.125	-15	-13	1			.863	-3	3-11,2-10/S-5	-1.6
■ ED WHEELER	Wheeler, Edward Raymond b: 5/24/15, Los Angeles, Cal. d: 8/4/83, Centralia, Wash. BR/TR, 5'9", 160 lbs. Deb: 4/19/45																						
1945	Cle-A	46	72	12	14	2	0	0	1	8	13	.194	.275	.222	47	-5	1	1	-0	.912	-6	3-14,S-11/2-3	-1.1
■ GEORGE WHEELER	Wheeler, George Harrison "Heavy" b: 11/10/1881, Shelburn, Ind. d: 6/14/18, Clinton, Ind. BL/TR, 5'9.5", 180 lbs. Deb: 7/27/10																						
1910	Cin-N	3	3	0	0	0	0	0	0	0	2	.000	.000	.000	-99	-1	0			.000	0	H	-0.1
■ HARRY WHEELER	Wheeler, Harry Eugene b: 3/3/1858, Versailles, Ind. d: 10/9/1900, Cincinnati, Ohio BR/TR, 5'11", 165 lbs. Deb: 6/19/1878 M																						
1878	Pro-N	7	27	7	4	0	0	0	1	2	15	.148	.207	.148	18	-2				.875	-2	/P-7	0.0
1879	Cin-N	1	3	0	0	0	0	0	0	0	2	.000	.000	.000	-99	-1				1.000	-0	/O-1,P-1	-0.1
1880	Cle-N	1	4	0	1	0	0	0	0	0	0	.250	.250	.250	72	-0				1.000	-0	/O-1	0.0
	Cin-N	17	65	1	6	2	0	0	2	0	15	.092	.092	.123	-28	-8				.750	1	O-17	-0.7
	Yr	18	69	1	7	2	0	0	2	0	15	.101	.101	.130	-22	-8				.759	1	O-18	-0.7
1882	Cin-a	76	344	59	86	11	11	1	29	7		.250	.265	.355	102	-1				.808	-5	*O-64,1-12/P-4	-0.7
1883	Col-a	82	371	42	84	6	7	0		6		.226	.239	.280	72	-10				.803	-2	*O-82/2-1,P-1	-1.2
1884	StL-a	5	19	0	5	2	0	0		1		.263	.300	.368	113	0				.600	-1	/O-5	-0.1
	KC-U	14	62	11	16	1	0	0		3		.258	.292	.274	83	-3				.769	0	O-13/P-1,M	-0.3
	CP-U	37	158	29	36	5	3	1		4		.228	.247	.316	70	-11				.774	-5	O-37	-1.4
	Bal-U	17	69	3	18	2	0	0		0		.261	.261	.290	60	-5				.815	-1	O-17	-0.6

YEAR	TM/L	G	AB	R	H	2B	3B	HR	RBI	BB	SO	AVG	OBP	SLG	PRO+	BR/A	SB	CS	SBR	FA	FR	G/POS	TPR
	Yr	68	289	43	70	8	3	1		7		.242	.260	.301	70	-19				.781	-5	O-67/P-1	-2.3
Total	6	257	1122	152	256	29	21	2	32	23	32	.228	.244	.297	74	-41				.791	-14	O-237/P-14,1-12,2-1	-5.1

■ DICK WHEELER

Wheeler, Richard (b: Richard Wheeler Maynard) b: 1/14/1898, Keene, N.H. d: 2/12/62, Lexington, Mass. BR/TR, 5'11", 185 lbs. Deb: 6/17/18

YEAR	TM/L	G	AB	R	H	2B	3B	HR	RBI	BB	SO	AVG	OBP	SLG	PRO+	BR/A	SB	CS	SBR	FA	FR	G/POS	TPR
1918	StL-N	3	6	0	0	0	0	0	0	0	3	.000	.000	.000	-99	-1	0			.000	-1	/O-2	-0.3

■ BOBBY WHEELOCK

Wheelock, Warren H. b: 8/6/1864, Charlestown, Mass. d: 3/13/28, Boston, Mass. BR/TR, 5'8", 160 lbs. Deb: 5/19/1887

YEAR	TM/L	G	AB	R	H	2B	3B	HR	RBI	BB	SO	AVG	OBP	SLG	PRO+	BR/A	SB	CS	SBR	FA	FR	G/POS	TPR
1887	Bos-N	48	166	32	42	4	2	2	15	15	15	.253	.315	.337	81	-4	20			.878	-7	O-28,S-20/2-4	-0.9
1890	Col-a	52	190	24	45	6	1	1	16	25		.237	.326	.295	89	-2	34			.885	-1	S-52	0.0
1891	Col-a	136	498	82	114	15	1	0	39	78	55	.229	.336	.263	76	-12	52			.899	19	*S-136	1.3
Total	3	236	854	138	201	25	4	3	70	118	70	.235	.330	.285	80	-18	106			.894	11	S-208/O-28,2-4	0.4

■ JIMMY WHELAN

Whelan, James Francis b: 5/11/1890, Kansas City, Mo. d: 11/29/29, Dayton, Ohio BR/TR, 5'8.5", 165 lbs. Deb: 4/24/13

YEAR	TM/L	G	AB	R	H	2B	3B	HR	RBI	BB	SO	AVG	OBP	SLG	PRO+	BR/A	SB	CS	SBR	FA	FR	G/POS	TPR
1913	StL-N	1	1	0	0	0	0	0	0	0	0	.000	.000	.000	-99	-0	0			.000	0	H	0.0

■ TOM WHELAN

Whelan, Thomas Joseph b: 1/3/1894, Lynn, Mass. d: 6/26/57, Boston, Mass. BR/TR, 5'11", 175 lbs. Deb: 8/13/20

YEAR	TM/L	G	AB	R	H	2B	3B	HR	RBI	BB	SO	AVG	OBP	SLG	PRO+	BR/A	SB	CS	SBR	FA	FR	G/POS	TPR
1920	Bos-N	1	1	0	0	0	0	0	0	1	1	.000	.500	.000	54	0	0	0	0	1.000	0	/1-1	0.0

■ PETE WHISENANT

Whisenant, Thomas Peter b: 12/14/29, Asheville, N.C. d: 3/22/96, Port Charlotte, Fla. BR/TR, 6'2", 200 lbs. Deb: 4/16/52 C

YEAR	TM/L	G	AB	R	H	2B	3B	HR	RBI	BB	SO	AVG	OBP	SLG	PRO+	BR/A	SB	CS	SBR	FA	FR	G/POS	TPR
1952	Bos-N	24	52	3	10	2	0	0	7	4	13	.192	.250	.231	35	-5	1	1	-0	.973	2	O-14	-0.3
1955	StL-N	58	115	10	22	5	1	2	9	5	29	.191	.225	.304	39	-10	2	0	1	.964	-1	O-40	-1.2
1956	Chi-N	103	314	37	75	16	3	11	46	24	53	.239	.295	.414	89	-5	8	2	1	.992	6	O-93	-0.3
1957	Cin-N	67	90	18	19	3	2	5	11	5	24	.211	.253	.456	80	-3	0	1	-1	.982	-9	O-43	-1.4
1958	Cin-N	85	203	33	48	9	2	11	40	18	37	.236	.299	.463	93	-3	3	0	1	1.000	-1	O-66/2-1	-0.6
1959	Cin-N	36	71	13	17	2	0	5	11	8	18	.239	.316	.479	105	0	0	0	0	.966	-2	O-21	-0.3
1960	Cin-N	1	1	0	0	0	0	0	0	0	0	.000	.000	.000	-98	-0	0	0	0	.000	0	H	0.0
	Cle-A	7	6	0	1	0	0	0	0	0	2	.167	.167	.167	-10	-1	0	0	0	1.000	-1	/O-2	-0.2
	Was-A	58	115	19	26	9	0	3	9	19	14	.226	.336	.383	95	-1	2	1	0	1.000	-9	O-47	-1.2
	Yr	65	121	19	27	9	0	3	9	19	16	.223	.329	.372	90	-2	2	1	0	1.000	-10	O-49	-1.4
1961	Min-A	10	6	1	0	0	0	0	0	1	2	.000	.143	.000	-55	-1	0	0	0	1.000	-2	/O-5	-0.3
	Cin-N	26	15	6	3	0	0	0	1	2	4	.200	.294	.200	34	-1	1	0	0	1.000	-4	O-12/C-1,3-1	-0.5
Total	8	475	988	140	221	46	8	37	134	86	196	.224	.287	.399	80	-30	17	5	2	.988	-20	O-343/3-1,C-1,2-1	-6.3

■ LARRY WHISENTON

Whisenton, Larry b: 7/3/56, St.Louis, Mo. BL/TL, 6'1", 190 lbs. Deb: 9/17/77

YEAR	TM/L	G	AB	R	H	2B	3B	HR	RBI	BB	SO	AVG	OBP	SLG	PRO+	BR/A	SB	CS	SBR	FA	FR	G/POS	TPR
1977	Atl-N	4	4	1	1	0	0	0	1	0	3	.250	.250	.250	31	-0	0	0	0	.000	0	H	-0.1
1978	Atl-N	6	16	1	3	1	0	0	2	1	2	.188	.235	.250	32	-1	0	0	0	1.000	-1	/O-4	-0.2
1979	Atl-N	13	37	3	9	2	1	0	1	3	3	.243	.300	.351	72	-1	1	0	0	1.000	3	O-13	0.1
1981	Atl-N	9	5	1	1	0	0	0	0	2	1	.200	.429	.200	81	0	0	0	0	.000	-1	/O-2	-0.1
1982	*Atl-N	84	143	21	34	7	2	4	17	23	33	.238	.343	.399	103	1	2	2	-1	.964	-2	O-34	-0.3
Total	5	116	205	27	48	10	3	4	21	29	42	.234	.329	.371	90	-2	3	2	-0	.968	-1	/O-53	-0.6

■ LEW WHISTLER

Whistler, Lewis W. (b: Lewis Wissler) b: 3/10/1868, St.Louis, Mo. d: 12/30/59, St.Louis, Mo. TR, 5'10.5", 178 lbs. Deb: 8/7/1890

YEAR	TM/L	G	AB	R	H	2B	3B	HR	RBI	BB	SO	AVG	OBP	SLG	PRO+	BR/A	SB	CS	SBR	FA	FR	G/POS	TPR
1890	NY-N	45	170	27	49	9	7	2	29	20	37	.288	.366	.459	140	8	8			.982	-2	1-45	0.4
1891	NY-N	72	265	39	65	8	7	3	38	24	45	.245	.315	.362	101	0	4			.852	-16	S-33,O-22/1-7,23	-1.3
1892	Bal-N	52	209	32	47	6	6	2	21	18	22	.225	.296	.340	90	-3	12			.973	-1	1-51/O-1	-0.7
	Lou-N	80	285	42	67	4	7	5	34	30	45	.235	.312	.351	109	3	14			.978	-2	1-72,2-10	-0.2
	Yr	132	494	74	114	10	13	7	55	48	67	.231	.305	.346	101	-0	26			.976	-3	*1-123,2-10/O-1	-0.9
1893	Lou-N	13	47	5	10	1	1	0	9	5	5	.213	.302	.277	59	-3	1			.946	-0	1-13	-0.3
	StL-N	10	38	5	9	1	0	0	2	3	2	.237	.293	.263	48	-3	0			.923	-1	/O-9,1-1	-0.4
	Yr	23	85	10	19	2	1	0	11	8	7	.224	.298	.271	54	-6	1			.949	-2	1-14/O-9	-0.7
Total	4	272	1014	150	247	29	28	12	133	100	156	.244	.318	.363	103	3	39			.976	-22	1-189/S-33,O-32,23	-2.5

■ LOU WHITAKER

Whitaker, Louis Rodman b: 5/12/57, Brooklyn, N.Y. BL/TR, 5'11", 160 lbs. Deb: 9/9/77

YEAR	TM/L	G	AB	R	H	2B	3B	HR	RBI	BB	SO	AVG	OBP	SLG	PRO+	BR/A	SB	CS	SBR	FA	FR	G/POS	TPR
1977	Det-A	11	32	5	8	1	0	0	2	4	6	.250	.333	.281	66	-1	2	2	-1	1.000	-3	/2-9	-0.5
1978	Det-A	139	484	71	138	12	7	3	58	61	65	.285	.366	.357	101	3	7	7	-2	.978	12	*2-136/D-2	2.3
1979	Det-A	127	423	75	121	14	8	3	42	78	66	.286	.398	.378	107	8	20	10	0	.986	1	*2-126	1.7
1980	Det-A	145	477	68	111	19	1	1	45	73	79	.233	.335	.283	69	-18	8	4	0	.985	-3	*2-143	-1.2
1981	Det-A	109	335	48	88	14	4	5	36	40	42	.263	.343	.373	103	2	5	3	-0	.985	6	*2-108	1.4
1982	Det-A	152	560	76	160	22	8	15	65	48	58	.286	.343	.434	111	8	11	3	2	**.988**	12	*2-149/D-1	3.0
1983	Det-A★	161	643	94	206	40	6	12	72	67	70	.320	.385	.457	134	31	17	10	-1	.983	-13	*2-160	2.4
1984	*Det-A★	143	558	90	161	25	1	13	56	62	63	.289	.360	.407	112	10	6	5	-1	.979	-11	*2-142	0.3
1985	Det-A★	152	609	102	170	29	8	21	73	80	56	.279	.365	.456	124	21	6	4	-1	.985	-16	*2-150	1.0
1986	Det-A★	144	584	95	157	26	6	20	73	63	70	.269	.340	.437	110	8	13	8	-1	.984	-1	*2-141	1.1
1987	*Det-A†	149	604	110	160	38	6	16	59	71	108	.265	.343	.427	107	7	13	5	1	.976	-14	*2-148	0.0
1988	Det-A	115	403	54	111	18	2	12	55	66	61	.275	.377	.419	128	17	2	0	1	.984	-23	*2-110	-0.1
1989	Det-A	148	509	77	128	21	1	28	85	89	59	.251	.366	.462	135	25	6	3	0	.985	-1	*2-146/D-2	2.9
1990	Det-A	132	472	75	112	22	2	18	60	74	71	.237	.341	.407	107	5	8	2	1	.991	12	*2-130/D-1	2.1
1991	Det-A	138	470	94	131	26	2	23	78	90	45	.279	.397	.489	142	29	4	2	0	**.994**	-11	*2-135/D-3	2.1
1992	Det-A	130	453	77	126	26	0	19	71	81	46	.278	.389	.461	137	24	6	4	-1	.984	-15	*2-119,D-10	1.2
1993	Det-A	119	383	72	111	32	1	9	67	78	46	.290	.415	.449	133	22	3	3	-1	.981	14	*2-110	3.6
1994	Det-A	92	322	67	97	21	2	12	43	41	47	.301	.382	.491	122	11	2	0	1	.970	-3	2-83/D-5	1.1
1995	Det-A	84	249	36	73	14	0	14	44	31	41	.293	.376	.518	130	11	4	0	1	.985	-11	2-63/D-8	0.4
Total	19	2390	8570	1386	2369	420	65	244	1084	1197	1099	.276	.366	.426	117	223	143	75	-2	.984	-69	*2-2308/D-32	24.8

■ STEVE WHITAKER

Whitaker, Stephen Edward b: 5/7/43, Tacoma, Wash. BL/TR, 6'1", 187 lbs. Deb: 8/23/66

YEAR	TM/L	G	AB	R	H	2B	3B	HR	RBI	BB	SO	AVG	OBP	SLG	PRO+	BR/A	SB	CS	SBR	FA	FR	G/POS	TPR
1966	NY-A	31	114	15	28	3	2	7	15	9	24	.246	.306	.491	130	4	0	0	0	.955	-0	O-31	0.3
1967	NY-A	122	441	37	107	12	3	11	50	23	89	.243	.285	.358	92	-6	2	5	-2	.982	6	*O-114	-0.9
1968	NY-A	28	60	3	7	2	0	0	3	8	18	.117	.221	.150	14	-6	0	1	-1	.917	-1	O-14	-1.0
1969	Sea-A	69	116	15	29	2	1	6	13	12	29	.250	.326	.440	114	2	2	0	1	.962	-2	O-39	-0.1
1970	SF-N	16	27	3	3	1	0	0	4	2	14	.111	.172	.148	-13	-4	0	0	0	.857	-2	/O-9	-0.7
Total	5	266	758	73	174	20	6	24	85	54	174	.230	.285	.367	92	-10	4	6	-2	.967	0	O-207	-2.4

■ FUZZ WHITE

White, Albert Eugene b: 6/27/18, Springfield, Mo. BL/TR, 6', 175 lbs. Deb: 9/17/40

YEAR	TM/L	G	AB	R	H	2B	3B	HR	RBI	BB	SO	AVG	OBP	SLG	PRO+	BR/A	SB	CS	SBR	FA	FR	G/POS	TPR
1940	StL-A	2	2	0	0	0	0	0	0	0	0	.000	.000	.000	-98	-1	0	0	0	.000	0	H	-0.1
1947	NY-N	7	13	3	3	0	0	0	0	0	0	.231	.231	.231	23	-1	0			1.000	0	/O-5	-0.2
Total	2	9	15	3	3	0	0	0	0	0	0	.200	.200	.200	6	-2	0	0		1.000	0	/O-5	-0.3

■ C. B. WHITE

White, C.B. b: Wakeman, Ohio Deb: 6/1/1883

YEAR	TM/L	G	AB	R	H	2B	3B	HR	RBI	BB	SO	AVG	OBP	SLG	PRO+	BR/A	SB	CS	SBR	FA	FR	G/POS	TPR
1883	Phi-N	1	1	0	0	0	0	0	0	0	0	.000	.000	.000	-99	-0				.667	0	/S-1,3-1	0.0

■ CHARLIE WHITE

White, Charles b: 8/12/28, Kinston, N.C. d: 5/26/98, Seattle, Wash. BL/TR, 5'11", 192 lbs. Deb: 4/18/54

YEAR	TM/L	G	AB	R	H	2B	3B	HR	RBI	BB	SO	AVG	OBP	SLG	PRO+	BR/A	SB	CS	SBR	FA	FR	G/POS	TPR
1954	Mil-N	50	93	14	22	4	0	1	8	9	8	.237	.304	.312	65	-5	0	0	0	.981	-2	C-28	-0.6
1955	Mil-N	12	30	3	7	1	0	0	4	5	7	.233	.361	.267	74	-1	0	0	0	1.000	-2	C-10	-0.2
Total	2	62	123	17	29	5	0	1	12	14	15	.236	.319	.301	67	-6	0	0	0	.986	-4	/C-38	-0.8

■ DERRICK WHITE

White, Derrick Ramon b: 10/12/69, San Rafael, Cal. BR/TR, 6'1", 220 lbs. Deb: 7/22/93

YEAR	TM/L	G	AB	R	H	2B	3B	HR	RBI	BB	SO	AVG	OBP	SLG	PRO+	BR/A	SB	CS	SBR	FA	FR	G/POS	TPR
1993	Mon-N	17	49	6	11	3	0	2	4	2	12	.224	.269	.408	75	-2	2	0	1	.993	-0	1-17	-0.3
1995	Det-A	39	48	3	9	2	0	0	2	0	7	.188	.188	.229	8	-6	1	0	0	.981	-1	1-16,D-11/O-9	-0.8
1998	Chi-N	11	10	1	1	0	0	1	2	0	5	.100	.100	.400	20	-1	0	0	0	.000	-1	/O-1	-0.2
	Col-N	9	9	0	0	0	0	0	0	0	4	.000	.000	.000	-84	-2	0	0	0	1.000	-1	/O-2,D-1	-0.3
	Yr	20	19	1	1	0	0	1	2	0	9	.053	.053	.211	-33	-4	0	0	0	1.000	-1	/O-3,D-1	-0.5
Total	3	76	116	10	21	5	0	3	8	2	28	.181	.202	.302	29	-12	3	0	1	.990	-3	/1-33,O-12,D-12	-1.6

■ DEVON WHITE White, Devon Markes b: 12/29/62, Kingston, Jamaica BB/TR, 6'2", 182 lbs. Deb: 9/2/85

YEAR	TM/L	G	AB	R	H	2B	3B	HR	RBI	BB	SO	AVG	OBP	SLG	PRO+	BR/A	SB	CS	SBR	FA	FR	G/POS	TPR
1985	Cal-A	21	7	7	1	0	0	0	0	1	3	.143	.333	.143	37	-1	3	1	0	1.000	-5	O-16	-0.5
1986	*Cal-A	29	51	8	12	1	1	1	3	6	8	.235	.316	.353	83	-1	6	0	2	.961	-3	O-28	-0.3
1987	Cal-A	159	639	103	168	33	5	24	87	39	135	.263	.307	.443	99	-3	32	11	3	.980	14	*O-159	0.8
1988	Cal-A	122	455	76	118	22	2	11	51	23	84	.259	.298	.389	93	-5	17	8	0	.976	15	*O-116	0.7
1989	Cal-A★	156	636	86	156	18	13	12	56	31	129	.245	.283	.371	84	-15	44	16	4	.989	15	*O-154/D-1	-0.1
1990	Cal-A	125	443	57	96	17	3	11	44	44	116	.217	.292	.343	79	-13	21	6	3	.972	8	*O-122	-0.5
1991	*Tor-A	156	642	110	181	40	10	17	60	55	135	.282	.345	.455	115	12	33	10	4	**.998**	17	*O-156	2.9
1992	*Tor-A	153	641	98	159	26	7	17	60	47	133	.248	.304	.390	89	-10	37	4	9	.985	15	*O-152/D-1	1.0
1993	*Tor-A★	146	598	116	163	42	6	15	52	57	127	.273	.343	.438	108	6	34	4	8	.993	13	*O-145	2.3
1994	Tor-A	100	403	67	109	24	6	13	49	21	80	.270	.315	.457	95	-4	11	3	2	.978	8	O-98	0.3
1995	Tor-A	101	427	61	121	23	5	10	53	29	97	.283	.336	.431	99	-2	11	2	2	.989	8	O-99	0.6
1996	Fla-N	146	552	77	151	37	6	17	84	38	99	.274	.329	.455	108	5	22	6	3	.987	2	*O-139	0.6
1997	*Fla-N	74	265	37	65	13	1	6	34	32	65	.245	.342	.370	90	-3	13	5	1	.987	4	O-71	0.1
1998	Ari-N	146	563	84	157	32	1	22	85	42	102	.279	.339	.456	103	2	22	8	2	.987	8	*O-144	1.1
Total	14	1634	6322	987	1657	328	66	176	718	465	1313	.262	.319	.418	98	-33	306	84	41	.985	121	*O-1599/D-2	9.0

■ DON WHITE White, Donald William b: 1/8/19, Everett, Wash. d: 6/15/87, Carlsbad, Cal. BR/TR, 6'1", 195 lbs. Deb: 4/19/48

YEAR	TM/L	G	AB	R	H	2B	3B	HR	RBI	BB	SO	AVG	OBP	SLG	PRO+	BR/A	SB	CS	SBR	FA	FR	G/POS	TPR
1948	Phi-A	86	253	29	62	14	2	1	28	19	16	.245	.303	.328	68	-12	0	1	-1	.957	-4	O-54,3-17	-1.9
1949	Phi-A	57	169	12	36	6	0	0	10	14	12	.213	.273	.249	40	-15	2	0	1	.989	-2	O-48/3-4	-1.8
Total	2	143	422	41	98	20	2	1	38	33	28	.232	.291	.296	57	-27	2	1	0	.971	-6	O-102/3-21	-3.7

■ ED WHITE White, Edward Perry b: 4/6/26, Anniston, Ala. d: 9/28/82, Lakeland, Fla. BR/TR, 6'2", 200 lbs. Deb: 9/16/55

YEAR	TM/L	G	AB	R	H	2B	3B	HR	RBI	BB	SO	AVG	OBP	SLG	PRO+	BR/A	SB	CS	SBR	FA	FR	G/POS	TPR
1955	Chi-A	3	4	0	2	0	0	0	0	1	1	.500	.600	.500	193	1	0	0	0	1.000	-0	/O-2	0.0

■ ELDER WHITE White, Elder Lafayette b: 12/23/34, Colerain, N.C. BR/TR, 5'11", 165 lbs. Deb: 4/10/62

YEAR	TM/L	G	AB	R	H	2B	3B	HR	RBI	BB	SO	AVG	OBP	SLG	PRO+	BR/A	SB	CS	SBR	FA	FR	G/POS	TPR
1962	Chi-N	23	53	4	8	2	0	0	1	8	11	.151	.274	.189	26	-5	3	0	1	.986	0	S-15/3-1	-0.3

■ ELMER WHITE White, Elmer b: 5/23/1850, Caton, N.Y. d: 3/17/1872, Caton, N.Y. Deb: 5/4/1871

YEAR	TM/L	G	AB	R	H	2B	3B	HR	RBI	BB	SO	AVG	OBP	SLG	PRO+	BR/A	SB	CS	SBR	FA	FR	G/POS	TPR
1871	Cle-n	15	70	13	18	2	0	0	9	1	6	.257	.268	.286	63	-3	0	1	-1	.783	-1	O-15/C-3	-0.2

■ FRANK WHITE White, Frank b: 9/4/50, Greenville, Miss. BR/TR, 5'11", 170 lbs. Deb: 6/12/73 C

YEAR	TM/L	G	AB	R	H	2B	3B	HR	RBI	BB	SO	AVG	OBP	SLG	PRO+	BR/A	SB	CS	SBR	FA	FR	G/POS	TPR
1973	KC-A	51	139	20	31	6	1	0	5	8	23	.223	.265	.281	50	-9	3	1	0	.937	7	S-37,2-11	0.2
1974	KC-A	99	204	19	45	6	3	1	18	5	33	.221	.239	.294	50	-13	3	4	-2	.962	25	2-50,S-29,3-16,/D-3	1.4
1975	KC-A	111	304	43	76	10	2	7	36	20	39	.250	.298	.365	84	-7	11	3	2	.987	15	2-67,S-42/3-4,CD	1.6
1976	*KC-A	152	446	39	102	17	6	2	46	19	42	.229	.265	.307	67	-19	20	11	-1	.973	**21**	*2-130,S-37	1.2
1977	*KC-A	152	474	59	116	21	5	5	50	25	67	.245	.285	.342	70	-20	23	5	4	**.989**	-3	*2-152/S-4	-0.9
1978	*KC-A★	143	461	66	127	24	6	7	50	26	59	.275	.318	.399	98	-2	13	10	-2	.978	-17	*2-140	-1.1
1979	KC-A★	127	467	73	124	26	4	10	48	25	54	.266	.304	.403	87	-9	28	8	4	.982	-23	*2-125	-2.0
1980	*KC-A	154	560	70	148	23	4	7	60	19	69	.264	.291	.357	76	-19	19	6	2	.988	-7	*2-153	-1.5
1981	*KC-A★	94	364	35	91	17	1	9	38	19	50	.250	.287	.376	91	-5	4	2	0	.988	-16	2-93	-1.7
1982	KC-A★	145	524	71	156	45	6	11	56	16	65	.298	.321	.469	114	8	10	7	-1	.978	-15	*2-144	0.0
1983	KC-A	146	549	52	143	35	6	11	77	20	51	.260	.286	.406	88	-11	13	5	1	**.990**	9	*2-145	0.6
1984	*KC-A	129	479	58	130	22	5	17	56	27	72	.271	.313	.445	106	3	5	5	-2	.985	13	*2-129	1.9
1985	*KC-A	149	563	62	140	25	1	22	69	28	86	.249	.285	.414	88	-11	10	4	1	.980	14	*2-149	1.0
1986	KC-A★	151	566	76	154	37	3	22	84	43	88	.272	.326	.465	110	6	4	4	-1	.987	-0	*2-151/S-1,3-1	1.1
1987	KC-A	154	563	67	138	32	2	17	78	51	86	.245	.310	.400	84	-13	1	3	-2	.987	8	*2-152/D-1	0.0
1988	KC-A	150	537	48	126	25	1	8	58	21	67	.235	.269	.330	66	-25	7	3	0	**.994**	7	*2-148/D-3	-1.2
1989	KC-A	135	418	34	107	22	1	2	36	30	52	.256	.309	.328	80	-11	3	2	-0	.985	7	*2-132/O-1	-0.1
1990	KC-A	82	241	20	52	14	1	2	21	10	32	.216	.256	.307	58	-14	1	0	0	.978	1	2-79/O-1	-1.2
Total	18	2324	7859	912	2006	407	58	160	886	412	1035	.255	.295	.383	85	-173	178	83	4	.984	45	*2-2150,S-150/3DOC	-0.7

■ DOC WHITE White, Guy Harris b: 4/9/1879, Washington, D.C. d: 2/19/69, Silver Spring, Md. BL/TL, 6'1", 150 lbs. Deb: 4/22/01

YEAR	TM/L	G	AB	R	H	2B	3B	HR	RBI	BB	SO	AVG	OBP	SLG	PRO+	BR/A	SB	CS	SBR	FA	FR	G/POS	TPR
1901	Phi-N	31	98	15	27	3	1	1	10	2		.276	.297	.357	87	-2	1			.951	2	P-31/O-1	0.0
1902	Phi-N	61	179	17	47	3	1	1	15	11		.263	.305	.307	89	-2	5			.931	-2	P-36,O-19	-0.6
1903	Chi-A	38	99	10	20	3	0	0	5	19		.202	.331	.232	74	-2	1			.969	3	P-37/O-1	0.0
1904	Chi-A	33	76	7	12	2	0	0	2	10		.158	.256	.184	42	-5	3			.951	1	P-30/O-2	-0.1
1905	Chi-A	37	90	7	15	4	1	0	7	4		.167	.202	.233	40	-6	3			.961	2	P-36/O-1	0.1
1906	*Chi-A	29	65	11	12	1	1	0	3	13		.185	.321	.231	75	-1	3			.922	2	P-28/O-1	0.0
1907	Chi-A	48	90	12	20	1	0	0	2	12		.222	.314	.233	77	-2	2			**.986**	4	P-46/O-2,2-1	-0.1
1908	Chi-A	51	109	12	25	1	0	0	10	12		.229	.306	.239	79	-2	4			**.986**	6	P-41/O-3	-0.1
1909	Chi-A	72	192	24	45	1	5	0	7	33		.234	.347	.292	106	3	7			.926	-4	O-40,P-24	-0.3
1910	Chi-A	56	126	14	25	1	2	0	8	14		.198	.279	.238	65	-5	2			.972	1	P-33,O-14	-0.3
1911	Chi-A	39	78	12	20	1	1	0	6	7		.256	.318	.295	74	-3	1			.919	-1	P-34/1-2,O-1	0.0
1912	Chi-A	32	56	5	7	1	1	0	0	7		.125	.222	.179	15	-6	0			**1.000**	-1	P-32	0.0
1913	Chi-A	20	25	1	3	0	0	0	0	3	1	.120	.214	.120	-2	-3	0			.959	2	P-19/1-1	0.0
Total	13	547	1283	147	278	22	13	2	75	147	1	.217	.298	.259	74	-36	32			.960	15	P-427/O-85,1-3,2-1	-1.4

■ DEACON WHITE White, James Laurie b: 12/7/1847, Caton, N.Y. d: 7/7/39, Aurora, Ill. BL/TR, 5'11", 175 lbs. Deb: 5/4/1871 FM

YEAR	TM/L	G	AB	R	H	2B	3B	HR	RBI	BB	SO	AVG	OBP	SLG	PRO+	BR/A	SB	CS	SBR	FA	FR	G/POS	TPR
1871	Cle-n	29	146	40	47	6	5	1	21	4	1	.322	.340	.452	132	7	2	2	-1	.821	-5	*C-29/S-2,2-1,3O	0.1
1872	Cle-n	22	109	21	37	2	2	0	22	4	1	.339	.363	.394	140	6	0	0	0	.882	1	C-14/2-7,O-5,M	0.4
1873	Bos-n	60	310	79	121	15	6	0	**66**	0	2	.390	.390	.477	144	14	6	2	1	.845	2	*C-56/O-9	1.1
1874	Bos-n	70	352	75	106	5	7	3	52	5	0	.301	.311	.381	114	4	1	1	-0	.839	-0	*C-58,O-21/1-1	0.4
1875	Bos-n	80	371	76	136	23	3	1	60	3	2	**.367**	.372	.453	178	27	2	3	-1	.880	15	*C-75,O-14/1-1	3.6
1876	Chi-N	66	303	66	104	18	1	1	**60**	7	3	.343	.358	.419	141	11				.844	7	*C-63/O-3,1-3,3P	1.7
1877	Bos-N	59	266	51	**103**	14	**11**	2	**49**	8	3	**.387**	.405	**.545**	**190**	**26**				.963	1	1-35,O-19/C-7	2.3
1878	Cin-N	61	258	41	81	4	1	0	29	10	5	.314	.340	.337	136	11				.909	-4	*C-48,O-16/3-1	0.7
1879	Cin-N	78	333	55	110	16	6	1	52	6	9	.330	.342	.423	159	21				.901	2	*C-59,O-21/1-2,M	2.2
1880	Cin-N	35	141	21	42	4	2	0	7	9	7	.298	.340	.355	137	6				.738	-3	O-33/1-3,2-1	0.1
1881	Buf-N	78	319	58	99	24	4	0	53	9	8	.310	.329	.411	133	12				.943	-9	1-26,2-25,O-17,/3C	0.2
1882	Buf-N	83	337	51	95	17	0	1	33	15	16	.282	.313	.341	108	3				.837	-10	*3-63,C-20	-0.4
1883	Buf-N	94	391	62	114	14	5	0	47	23	18	.292	.331	.353	106	3				.797	-10	*3-77,C-22	-0.6
1884	Buf-N	110	452	82	147	16	11	5	74	32	13	.325	.370	.442	149	25				.825	-7	*3-108/C-3	1.7
1885	Buf-N	98	404	54	118	6	6	0	57	12	11	.292	.313	.337	106	2				.888	1	*3-98	0.4
1886	Det-N	124	491	65	142	19	5	1	76	31	35	.289	.331	.354	106	3	9			.847	-9	*3-124	-0.2
1887	*Det-N	111	449	71	136	20	11	3	75	26	15	.303	.353	.416	109	5	20			.848	-0	*3-106/O-3,1-2	0.6
1888	Det-N	125	527	75	157	22	5	4	71	21	24	.298	.336	.381	128	16	12			.857	-3	*3-125	1.5
1889	Pit-N	55	225	35	57	10	1	0	26	16	18	.253	.314	.307	82	-5	2			.872	-10	3-52/1-3	-1.2
1890	Buf-P	122	439	62	114	13	4	0	47	67	30	.260	.381	.308	93	2	3			.905	19	3-64,1-57/S-1,P-1	1.6
Total	5 n	261	1288	291	447	51	23	5	221	16	6	.347	.355	.434	143	57	11	8	-2	.855	12	C-232/O-50,2-8,1S3	5.6
Total	15	1299	5335	849	1619	217	73	18	756	292	215	.303	.344	.382	123	138	46			.853	-33	3-826,C-226,1O/2PS	10.6

■ JERRY WHITE White, Jerome Cardell b: 8/23/52, Shirley, Mass. BB/TR, 5'11", 165 lbs. Deb: 9/16/74 C

YEAR	TM/L	G	AB	R	H	2B	3B	HR	RBI	BB	SO	AVG	OBP	SLG	PRO+	BR/A	SB	CS	SBR	FA	FR	G/POS	TPR
1974	Mon-N	9	10	0	4	1	1	0	2	0	0	.400	.400	.700	193	1	3	0	1	1.000	-2	/O-7	0.0
1975	Mon-N	39	97	14	29	4	1	2	7	10	7	.299	.364	.423	113	2	5	2	0	.976	2	O-30	0.3
1976	Mon-N	114	278	32	68	11	1	2	21	27	31	.245	.316	.313	76	-8	15	7	0	.982	-10	O-92	-2.2
1977	Mon-N	16	21	4	4	0	0	0	1	1	3	.190	.227	.190	14	-3	1	0	0	1.000	-2	/O-8	-0.4
1978	Mon-N	18	10	2	2	0	0	0	0	1	3	.200	.273	.200	34	-1	1	0	0	.000	-1	/O-3	-0.2
	Chi-N	59	136	22	37	6	0	1	10	23	16	.272	.377	.338	90	-1	4	3	-1	.981	-3	O-54	-0.6
	Yr	77	146	24	39	6	0	1	10	24	19	.267	.371	.329	89	-1	5	3	-0	.981	-4	O-57	-0.8
1979	Mon-N	88	138	30	41	7	1	3	18	21	23	.297	.394	.428	125	6	8	4	0	.983	-8	O-43	-0.3

YEAR	TM/L	G	AB	R	H	2B	3B	HR	RBI	BB	SO	AVG	OBP	SLG	PRO+	BR/A	SB	CS	SBR	FA	FR	G/POS	TPR
1980	Mon-N	110	214	22	56	9	3	7	23	30	37	.262	.355	.430	118	5	8	7	-2	.946	-12	O-84	-1.1
1981	*Mon-N	59	119	11	26	5	1	3	11	13	17	.218	.295	.353	82	-3	5	2	0	.952	-5	O-39	-0.9
1982	Mon-N	69	115	13	28	6	1	2	13	8	26	.243	.304	.365	85	-2	3	3	-1	1.000	-4	O-30	-0.8
1983	Mon-N	40	34	4	5	1	0	0	0	12	8	.147	.383	.176	60	-1	4	0	1	1.000	-3	O-13	-0.3
1986	StL-N	25	24	1	3	0	0	1	3	2	3	.125	.192	.250	21	-3	0	0	0	1.000	-1	/O-6	-0.4
Total	11	646	1196	155	303	50	9	21	109	148	174	.253	.339	.363	94	-8	57	28	0	.974	-48	O-409	-6.9

■ JACK WHITE

White, John Peter b: 8/31/05, New York, N.Y. d: 6/19/71, Flushing, N.Y. BB/TR, 5'7.5", 150 lbs. Deb: 6/22/27

YEAR	TM/L	G	AB	R	H	2B	3B	HR	RBI	BB	SO	AVG	OBP	SLG	PRO+	BR/A	SB	CS	SBR	FA	FR	G/POS	TPR
1927	Cin-N	5	4	1	0	0	0	0	0	0	0	.000	.000	.000	-99	-1	0			1.000	0	/2-3,S-2	-0.1
1928	Cin-N	1	3	0	0	0	0	0	0	0	1	.000	.000	.000	-99	-1	0			.833	-1	/2-1	-0.1
Total	2	6	7	1	0	0	0	0	0	0	1	.000	.000	.000	-99	-2	0			.929	-0	/2-4,S-2	-0.2

■ JACK WHITE

White, John Wallace b: 1/19/1878, Traders Point, Ind. d: 9/30/63, Indianapolis, Ind BR/TR, 5'6", Deb: 6/26/04

YEAR	TM/L	G	AB	R	H	2B	3B	HR	RBI	BB	SO	AVG	OBP	SLG	PRO+	BR/A	SB	CS	SBR	FA	FR	G/POS	TPR
1904	Bos-N	1	5	1	0	0	0	0	0	0		.000	.000	.000	-99	-1	0			1.000	1	/O-1	-0.1

■ JO-JO WHITE

White, Joyner Clifford b: 6/1/09, Red Oak, Ga. d: 10/9/86, Tacoma, Wash. BL/TR, 5'11", 165 lbs. Deb: 4/15/32 FMC

YEAR	TM/L	G	AB	R	H	2B	3B	HR	RBI	BB	SO	AVG	OBP	SLG	PRO+	BR/A	SB	CS	SBR	FA	FR	G/POS	TPR
1932	Det-A	80	208	25	54	6	3	2	21	22	19	.260	.330	.346	73	-8	6	8	-3	.962	-0	O-48	-1.3
1933	Det-A	91	234	43	59	9	5	2	34	27	26	.252	.337	.359	83	-6	5	5	-2	.977	0	O-54	-0.9
1934	*Det-A	115	384	97	120	18	5	0	44	69	39	.313	.419	.385	108	9	28	6	**5**	.959	-0	*O-100	0.8
1935	*Det-A	114	412	82	99	13	12	2	32	68	42	.240	.348	.345	83	-10	19	10	-0	.962	-2	O-98	-1.4
1936	Det-A	58	51	11	14	3	0	0	6	9	10	.275	.383	.333	78	-1	2	0	1	.938	-7	O-18	-0.7
1937	Det-A	94	305	50	75	5	7	0	21	50	40	.246	.354	.308	67	-14	12	7	-1	.973	-3	O-82	-1.9
1938	Det-A	78	206	40	54	6	1	0	15	30	15	.262	.359	.301	63	-11	3	4	-2	.967	0	O-55	-1.2
1943	Phi-A	139	500	69	124	17	7	1	30	61	51	.248	.335	.316	91	-4	12	4	1	.966	-4	*O-133	-1.5
1944	Phi-A	85	267	30	59	4	2	1	21	40	27	.221	.329	.262	71	-8	5	4	-1	.949	-1	O-74/S-1	-1.5
	Cin-N	24	85	9	20	2	0	0	5	10	7	.235	.316	.259	65	-4	0			1.000	1	O-23	-0.4
Total	9	878	2652	456	678	83	42	8	229	386	276	.256	.353	.328	82	-57	92	48		.965	-16	O-685/S-1	-10.0

■ MIKE WHITE

White, Joyner Michael b: 12/18/38, Detroit, Mich. BR/TR, 5'8", 160 lbs. Deb: 9/21/63 F

YEAR	TM/L	G	AB	R	H	2B	3B	HR	RBI	BB	SO	AVG	OBP	SLG	PRO+	BR/A	SB	CS	SBR	FA	FR	G/POS	TPR
1963	Hou-N	3	7	0	2	0	0	0	0	0	0	.286	.286	.286	69	-0	0	0	0	1.000	1	/2-2	0.1
1964	Hou-N	89	280	30	76	11	3	0	27	20	47	.271	.320	.332	89	-4	1	1	-0	.978	2	O-72,2-10/3-3	-0.5
1965	Hou-N	8	9	0	0	0	0	0	0	1	2	.000	.100	.000	-74	-2	0	0	0	1.000	-0	/3-1	-0.3
Total	3	100	296	30	78	11	3	0	27	21	49	.264	.312	.321	84	-7	1	1	-0	.985	3	/O-72,2-12,3-4	-0.7

■ MYRON WHITE

White, Myron Alan b: 8/1/57, Long Beach, Cal. BL/TL, 5'11", 180 lbs. Deb: 9/4/78

YEAR	TM/L	G	AB	R	H	2B	3B	HR	RBI	BB	SO	AVG	OBP	SLG	PRO+	BR/A	SB	CS	SBR	FA	FR	G/POS	TPR
1978	LA-N	7	4	1	2	0	0	0	1	0	1	.500	.500	.500	181	0	0	1	-1	1.000	-1	/O-4	-0.2

■ RONDELL WHITE

White, Rondell Bernard b: 2/23/72, Milledgeville, Ga. BR/TR, 6'1", 205 lbs. Deb: 9/1/93

YEAR	TM/L	G	AB	R	H	2B	3B	HR	RBI	BB	SO	AVG	OBP	SLG	PRO+	BR/A	SB	CS	SBR	FA	FR	G/POS	TPR
1993	Mon-N	23	73	9	19	3	1	2	15	7	16	.260	.325	.411	91	-1	1	2	-1	1.000	-3	O-21	-0.6
1994	Mon-N	40	97	16	27	10	1	2	13	9	18	.278	.358	.464	111	2	1	1	-0	.946	-3	O-29	-0.2
1995	Mon-N	130	474	87	140	33	4	13	57	41	87	.295	.359	.464	111	8	25	5	5	.986	6	*O-119	1.4
1996	Mon-N	88	334	35	98	19	4	6	41	22	53	.293	.341	.428	99	-1	14	6	1	.990	5	O-86	0.4
1997	Mon-N	151	592	84	160	29	5	28	82	31	111	.270	.318	.478	105	2	16	8	0	**.992**	17	*O-151	1.6
1998	Mon-N★	97	357	54	107	21	2	17	58	30	57	.300	.365	.513	129	15	16	7	1	.996	16	O-96/D-1	2.9
Total	6	529	1927	285	551	115	17	68	266	140	342	.286	.343	.469	110	24	73	29	5	.990	38	O-502/D-1	5.5

■ ROY WHITE

White, Roy Hilton b: 12/27/43, Los Angeles, Cal. BB/TR, 5'10", 172 lbs. Deb: 9/7/65 C

YEAR	TM/L	G	AB	R	H	2B	3B	HR	RBI	BB	SO	AVG	OBP	SLG	PRO+	BR/A	SB	CS	SBR	FA	FR	G/POS	TPR
1965	NY-A	14	42	7	14	2	0	0	3	4	7	.333	.404	.381	125	2	2	1	0	1.000	-1	O-10/2-1	0.1
1966	NY-A	115	316	39	71	13	2	7	20	37	43	.225	.308	.345	91	-4	14	7	0	.957	0	O-82/2-2	-0.7
1967	NY-A	70	214	22	48	8	0	2	18	19	25	.224	.291	.290	75	-7	10	4	1	.968	-6	O-36,3-17	-1.6
1968	NY-A	159	577	89	154	20	7	17	62	73	50	.267	.352	.414	136	25	20	11	-1	.997	10	*O-154	2.9
1969	NY-A★	130	448	55	130	30	5	7	74	81	51	.290	.400	.426	136	25	18	10	-1	.989	11	*O-126	2.9
1970	NY-A☆	162	609	109	180	30	6	22	94	95	66	.296	.391	.473	144	38	24	10	1	.994	7	*O-161	3.9
1971	NY-A	147	524	86	153	22	7	19	84	86	66	.292	.399	.469	154	40	14	7	0	**1.000**	10	*O-145	4.5
1972	NY-A	155	556	76	150	29	0	10	54	**99**	59	.270	.385	.376	131	26	23	7	3	.994	9	*O-155	3.4
1973	NY-A	162	639	88	157	22	3	18	60	78	81	.246	.330	.374	101	1	16	9	-1	.977	4	*O-162	-0.3
1974	NY-A	136	473	68	130	19	8	7	43	67	44	.275	.369	.393	121	15	15	6	1	.993	3	O-67,D-53	1.5
1975	NY-A	148	556	81	161	32	5	12	59	72	50	.290	.373	.430	129	22	16	15	-4	.984	11	*O-135/1-7,D-2	2.3
1976	*NY-A	156	626	**104**	179	29	3	14	65	83	52	.286	.370	.409	129	24	31	13	2	.987	6	*O-156	2.6
1977	*NY-A	143	519	72	139	25	2	14	52	75	58	.268	.360	.405	109	8	18	11	-1	.981	10	*O-135/D-4	1.1
1978	*NY-A	103	346	44	93	13	3	8	43	42	35	.269	.351	.393	112	6	10	4	1	.992	-4	O-74,D-23	-0.1
1979	NY-A	81	205	24	44	6	0	3	27	23	21	.215	.294	.288	59	-12	2	2	-1	1.000	0	D-29,O-27	-1.4
Total	15	1881	6650	964	1803	300	51	160	758	934	708	.271	.363	.404	122	211	233	117	-0	.988	71	*O-1625,D-111/312	21.1

■ SAMMY WHITE

White, Samuel Charles b: 7/7/27, Wenatchee, Wash. d: 8/5/91, Princeville, Hawaii BR/TR, 6'3", 195 lbs. Deb: 9/26/51

YEAR	TM/L	G	AB	R	H	2B	3B	HR	RBI	BB	SO	AVG	OBP	SLG	PRO+	BR/A	SB	CS	SBR	FA	FR	G/POS	TPR
1951	Bos-A	4	11	0	2	0	0	0	0	0	3	.182	.182	.182	-1	-2	0	0	0	1.000	1	/C-4	-0.1
1952	Bos-A	115	381	35	107	20	2	10	49	16	43	.281	.310	.423	95	-4	2	3	-1	.983	-2	*C-110	-0.2
1953	Bos-A☆	136	476	59	130	34	2	13	64	29	48	.273	.318	.435	96	-4	3	2	-0	.986	9	*C-131	1.0
1954	Bos-A	137	493	46	139	25	2	14	75	21	50	.282	.311	.426	90	-8	1	3	-2	.979	13	*C-133	0.9
1955	Bos-A	143	544	65	142	30	4	11	64	44	58	.261	.324	.392	84	-13	1	2	-1	.984	-0	*C-143	-0.9
1956	Bos-A	114	392	28	96	15	2	5	44	35	40	.245	.307	.332	61	-23	2	1	0	.984	7	*C-114	-1.0
1957	Bos-A	111	340	24	73	10	1	3	31	25	38	.215	.268	.276	46	-25	0	1	-1	.985	-4	*C-111	-2.7
1958	Bos-A	102	328	25	85	15	3	6	35	21	37	.259	.306	.378	81	-9	1	1	-0	.988	-2	*C-102	-0.6
1959	Bos-A	119	377	34	107	13	4	1	42	23	39	.284	.327	.347	81	-9	4	2	0	.990	0	*C-119	-0.3
1961	Mil-N	21	63	1	14	1	0	1	5	2	9	.222	.246	.286	43	-5	0	0	0	.974	4	C-20	0.0
1962	Phi-N	41	97	7	21	4	0	2	12	2	16	.216	.240	.320	50	-7	0	0	0	.975	5	C-40	-0.1
Total	11	1043	3502	324	916	167	20	66	421	218	381	.262	.307	.377	79	-109	14	15	-5	.984	30	*C-1027	-4.0

■ SAM WHITE

White, Samuel Lambeth b: 8/23/1892, Greater Preston, Yorkshire, England d: 11/11/29, Philadelphia, Pa. BL/TR, 6', 185 lbs. Deb: 9/8/19

YEAR	TM/L	G	AB	R	H	2B	3B	HR	RBI	BB	SO	AVG	OBP	SLG	PRO+	BR/A	SB	CS	SBR	FA	FR	G/POS	TPR
1919	Bos-N	1	1	0	0	0	0	0	0	0	0	.000	.000	.000	-99	-0	0			1.000	2	/C-1	0.1

■ BARNEY WHITE

White, William Barney "Bear" b: 6/25/23, Paris, Tex. BR/TR, 5'11", 186 lbs. Deb: 6/5/45

YEAR	TM/L	G	AB	R	H	2B	3B	HR	RBI	BB	SO	AVG	OBP	SLG	PRO+	BR/A	SB	CS	SBR	FA	FR	G/POS	TPR
1945	Bro-N	4	1	2	0	0	0	0	0	1	1	.000	.500	.000	46	0	0			1.000	0	/S-1,3-1	0.0

■ BILL WHITE

White, William De Kova b: 1/28/34, Lakewood, Fla. BL/TL, 6', 195 lbs. Deb: 5/7/56

YEAR	TM/L	G	AB	R	H	2B	3B	HR	RBI	BB	SO	AVG	OBP	SLG	PRO+	BR/A	SB	CS	SBR	FA	FR	G/POS	TPR
1956	NY-N	138	508	63	130	23	7	22	59	47	72	.256	.324	.459	108	5	15	8	-0	.989	2	*1-138/O-2	-0.3
1958	SF-N	26	29	5	7	1	0	1	4	7	5	.241	.389	.379	107	1	1	0	0	1.000	-1	/1-3,O-2	0.0
1959	StL-N☆	138	517	77	156	33	9	12	72	34	61	.302	.347	.470	108	5	15	10	-2	.962	-2	O-92,1-71	-0.6
1960	StL-N★	144	554	81	157	27	10	16	79	42	83	.283	.336	.455	105	3	12	6	0	.990	-6	*1-123,O-29	-1.4
1961	StL-N★	153	591	89	169	28	11	20	90	64	84	.286	.357	.472	107	6	8	11	-4	.989	-2	*1-151	-1.4
1962	StL-N	159	614	93	199	31	3	20	102	58	69	.324	.388	.482	120	18	9	7	-2	.993	1	*1-146,O-27	0.8
1963	StL-N★	162	658	106	200	26	8	27	109	59	100	.304	.361	.491	131	25	10	9	-2	.991	-2	*1-162	1.5
1964	*StL-N★	160	631	92	191	37	4	21	102	52	103	.303	.357	.474	121	17	7	6	-2	**.996**	-1	*1-160	0.8
1965	StL-N	148	543	82	157	26	3	24	73	63	86	.289	.367	.481	125	18	3	3	-1	.992	6	*1-144	1.6
1966	Phi-N	159	577	85	159	23	6	22	103	68	109	.276	.355	.451	122	18	16	6	1	**.994**	7	*1-158	1.6
1967	Phi-N	110	308	29	77	6	2	8	33	52	61	.250	.364	.360	107	5	6	1	1	.993	0	1-95	0.1
1968	Phi-N	127	385	34	92	16	2	9	40	39	79	.239	.312	.361	102	1	0	1	-1	.994	4	*1-111	-0.4
1969	StL-N	49	57	7	12	1	0	0	4	11	15	.211	.338	.228	61	-2	1	0	0	1.000	1	1-15	-0.2
Total	13	1673	5972	843	1706	278	65	202	870	596	927	.286	.353	.455	115	120	103	68	-10	.992	8	*1-1477,O-152	2.1

■ BILL WHITE

White, William Dighton b: 5/1/1860, Bridgeport, Ohio d: 12/29/24, Bellaire, Ohio TR , Deb: 5/3/1884

YEAR	TM/L	G	AB	R	H	2B	3B	HR	RBI	BB	SO	AVG	OBP	SLG	PRO+	BR/A	SB	CS	SBR	FA	FR	G/POS	TPR
1884	Pit-a	74	291	25	66	7	10	0		13		.227	.262	.320	87	-4				.807	-11	S-60,3-10/O-4	-1.4

YEAR	TM/L	G	AB	R	H	2B	3B	HR	RBI	BB	SO	AVG	OBP	SLG	PRO+	BR/A	SB	CS	SBR	FA	FR	G/POS	TPR
1886	Lou-a	135	557	96	143	17	10	1	66	37		.257	.304	.329	93	-7	14			.871	17	*S-135/P-1	1.0
1887	Lou-a	132	512	85	129	7	9	2	79	47		.252	.315	.313	74	-18	41			.869	22	*S-132	0.4
1888	Lou-a	49	198	35	55	6	5	1	30	7		.278	.313	.374	122	4	15			.816	-3	S-38,3-11	0.3
	*StL-a	76	275	31	48	2	3	2	30	21		.175	.238	.225	44	-18	6			.892	-3	S-74/2-2	-1.8
	Yr	125	473	66	103	8	8	3	60	28		.218	.269	.288	74	-15	21			.864	-6	*S-112,3-11/2-2	-1.5
Total	4	466	1833	272	441	39	37	6	205	125		.241	.292	.312	82	-43	76			.860	22	S-439/3-21,O-4,2P	-1.5
■ BILL WHITE	White, William Edward b: Milner, Ga. Deb: 6/21/1879																						
1879	Pro-N	1	4	1	1	0	0	0	0	0	1	.250	.250	.250	67	-0				1.000	0	/1-1	0.0
■ WARREN WHITE	White, William Warren (a.k.a. William Warren) 5'10.5", 170 lbs. Deb: 6/17/1871 M																						
1871	Oly-n	1	4	0	0	0	0	0	0	0	0	.000	.000	.000	-99	-1	0	0	0	1.000	-1	/2-1	-0.1
1872	Nat-n	10	45	7	13	0	0	0	4	0	0	.289	.289	.289	67	-3	0	0	0	.861	8	/3-9,S-1,M	0.3
1873	Was-n	39	160	29	43	3	4	0	21	0	1	.269	.269	.338	82	-3	1	1	-0	.717	5	*3-37/S-3	0.0
1874	Bal-n	45	211	21	57	1	0	0	17	2	2	.270	.277	.275	78	-5	1	0	0	.782	**25**	*3-45/C-3,M	1.6
1875	Chi-n	69	287	37	71	9	0	0	23	0	3	.247	.247	.279	82	-5	5	10	-5	.813	7	*3-59/S-5,O-5,2-2	-0.3
1884	Was-U	4	18	2	1	0	0	0		0		.056	.056	.056	-68	-4				.692	-1	/3-2,S-1,2-1	-0.5
Total	5 n	164	707	94	184	13	4	0	65	2	6	.260	.262	.290	78	-17	7	11	-5	.779	44	3-150/S-9,O-5,C2	1.5
■ ED WHITED	Whited, Edward Morris b: 2/9/64, Bristol, Pa. BR/TR, 6'3", 195 lbs. Deb: 7/5/89																						
1989	Atl-N	36	74	5	12	3	0	1	4	6	15	.162	.225	.243	33	-6	1	0	0	.914	-0	3-29/1-3	-0.7
■ BURGESS WHITEHEAD	Whitehead, Burgess Urquhart "Whitey" b: 6/29/10, Tarboro, N.C. d: 11/25/93, Windsor, N.C. BR/TR, 5'10.5", 160 lbs. Deb: 4/30/33																						
1933	StL-N	12	7	2	2	0	0	0	1	0	1	.286	.286	.286	60	-0	0			1.000	0	/S-9,2-3	0.0
1934	*StL-N	100	332	55	92	13	5	1	24	12	19	.277	.310	.355	73	-13	5			.962	-1	2-48,S-29,3-28	-0.9
1935	StL-N★	107	338	45	89	10	2	0	33	11	14	.263	.289	.305	57	-20	5			.980	5	2-80/3-8,S-6	-1.0
1936	*NY-N	154	632	99	176	31	3	4	47	29	32	.278	.317	.356	82	-16	14			.969	29	*2-153	2.3
1937	*NY-N★	152	574	64	164	15	6	5	52	28	20	.286	.323	.359	84	-13	7			**.974**	26	*2-152	2.3
1939	NY-N	95	335	31	80	6	3	2	24	24	19	.239	.299	.293	59	-19	1			.970	21	2-91/S-4,3-1	0.7
1940	NY-N	133	568	68	160	9	6	4	36	26	17	.282	.319	.340	81	-15	9			.947	13	3-74,2-57/S-4	0.3
1941	NY-N	116	403	41	92	15	4	1	23	14	10	.228	.258	.293	54	-25	7			.970	-0	*2-104/3-1	-1.9
1946	Pit-N	55	127	10	28	1	2	0	5	6	6	.220	.261	.260	47	-9	3			.963	-6	2-30/3-4,S-1	-1.4
Total	9	924	3316	415	883	100	31	17	245	150	138	.266	.304	.331	72	-130	51			.972	86	2-718,3-116/S-53	0.4
■ MILT WHITEHEAD	Whitehead, Milton P. b: 1862, Canada d: 8/15/01, Highland, Cal. BB, Deb: 4/20/1884																						
1884	StL-U	99	393	61	83	15	1	1		8		.211	.227	.262	46	-37				.803	-11	*S-94/O-2,P-1,23	-4.2
	KC-U	5	22	2	3	0	0	0		0		.136	.136	.136	-20	-4				.857	-1	/2-3,C-1,S-1,3-1	-0.4
	Yr	104	415	63	86	15	1	1		8		.207	.222	.255	43	-41				.804	-12	S-95/2-4,O-2,3PC	-4.6
■ GIL WHITEHOUSE	Whitehouse, Gilbert Arthur b: 10/15/1893, Somerville, Mass. d: 2/14/26, Brewer, Me. BB/TR, 5'10", 170 lbs. Deb: 6/20/12																						
1912	Bos-N	2	3	0	0	0	0	0	0	0	3	.000	.000	.000	-98	-1	0			.667	-1	/C-2	-0.2
1915	New-F	35	120	16	27	6	2	0	9	6	16	.225	.268	.308	66	-8	3			.949	-1	O-28/P-1,C-1	-1.1
Total	2	37	123	16	27	6	2	0	9	6	19	.220	.262	.301	61	-9	3			.846	-2	/O-28,C-3,P-1	-1.3
■ GURDON WHITELEY	Whiteley, Gurdon W. b: 10/5/1859, Ashaway, R.I. d: 11/24/24, Cranston, R.I. 5'11", 190 lbs. Deb: 8/7/1884																						
1884	Cle-N	8	34	4	5	0	0	0	0	1	8	.147	.171	.147	1	-4				.800	1	/O-8	-0.3
1885	Bos-N	33	135	14	25	2	2	1	7	1	25	.185	.191	.252	44	-8				.781	-2	O-32/C-1	-1.0
Total	2	41	169	18	30	2	2	1	7	2	33	.178	.187	.231	34	-12				.785	-1	/O-40,C-1	-1.3
■ GEORGE WHITEMAN	Whiteman, George "Lucky" b: 12/23/1882, Peoria, Ill. d: 2/10/47, Houston, Tex. BR/TR, 5'7", 160 lbs. Deb: 9/13/07																						
1907	Bos-A	4	12	0	2	0	0	0	1	0		.167	.167	.167	6	-1	0			1.000	-1	/O-2	-0.2
1913	NY-A	11	32	8	11	3	1	0	2	7	2	.344	.462	.500	181	4	2			.938	1	O-11	0.5
1918	*Bos-A	71	214	24	57	14	0	1	28	20	9	.266	.335	.346	107	2	9			.935	-11	O-69	-1.5
Total	3	86	258	32	70	17	1	1	31	27	11	.271	.345	.357	113	4	11			.936	-11	/O-82	-1.2
■ MARK WHITEN	Whiten, Mark Anthony b: 11/25/66, Pensacola, Fla. BB/TR, 6'3", 215 lbs. Deb: 7/12/90																						
1990	Tor-A	33	88	12	24	1	1	2	7	7	14	.273	.326	.375	94	-1	2	0	1	1.000	2	O-30/D-2	0.1
1991	Tor-A	46	149	12	33	4	3	2	19	11	35	.221	.280	.329	65	-7	0	1	-1	1.000	3	O-42	-0.6
	Cle-A	70	258	34	66	14	4	7	26	19	50	.256	.312	.422	100	-0	4	2	0	.962	11	O-67/D-3	0.9
	Yr	116	407	46	99	18	7	9	45	30	85	.243	.300	.388	87	-8	4	3	-1	.975	14	*O-109/D-3	0.3
1992	Cle-A	148	508	73	129	19	4	9	43	72	102	.254	.349	.360	101	2	16	12	-2	.980	13	*O-144/D-2	1.0
1993	StL-N	152	562	81	142	13	4	25	99	58	110	.253	.325	.423	100	-0	15	8	-0	.971	1	*O-148	-0.3
1994	StL-N	92	334	57	98	18	2	14	53	37	75	.293	.366	.485	122	10	10	5	0	.964	15	O-90	2.3
1995	Bos-A	32	108	13	20	3	0	1	10	8	23	.185	.241	.241	25	-12	1	0	0	1.000	2	O-31/D-1	-1.0
	Phi-N	60	212	38	57	10	1	11	37	31	63	.269	.365	.481	120	6	7	0	2	.965	2	O-55	0.8
1996	Phi-N	60	182	33	43	8	0	7	21	33	62	.236	.356	.396	97	-0	13	3	2	.945	3	O-51	0.4
	Atl-N	36	90	12	23	5	1	3	17	16	25	.256	.368	.433	105	1	2	5	-2	.933	-2	O-29	-0.4
	Yr	96	272	45	66	13	1	10	38	49	87	.243	.360	.408	99	1	15	8	-0	.942	1	O-80	0.0
	Sea-A	40	140	31	42	7	0	12	33	21	40	.300	.399	.607	149	11	2	1	0	.969	4	O-39	1.3
1997	NY-A	69	215	34	57	11	0	5	24	30	47	.265	.360	.386	96	-1	4	2	0	.954	-3	O-57/D-6	-0.4
1998	*Cle-A	88	226	31	64	14	0	6	29	29	60	.283	.372	.425	103	2	2	1	0	.970	-4	O-72/P-1,D-5	-0.3
Total	9	926	3072	461	798	127	20	104	418	372	706	.260	.343	.416	102	10	78	40	-1	.970	47	O-855/D-19,P-1	3.8
■ FRED WHITFIELD	Whitfield, Fred Dwight b: 1/7/38, Vandiver, Ala. BL/TL, 6'1", 190 lbs. Deb: 5/27/62																						
1962	StL-N	73	158	20	42	7	1	8	34	7	30	.266	.301	.475	95	-2	1	0	0	.987	1	1-38	-0.2
1963	Cle-A	109	346	44	87	17	3	21	54	24	61	.251	.307	.500	123	9	0	1	-1	.987	-3	1-92	0.1
1964	Cle-A	101	293	29	79	13	1	10	29	12	58	.270	.303	.423	100	-1	0	5	-3	.992	-2	1-79	-0.9
1965	Cle-A	132	468	49	137	23	1	26	90	16	42	.293	.319	.513	131	16	2	2	-1	.993	4	*1-122	1.4
1966	Cle-A	137	502	59	121	15	2	27	78	27	76	.241	.285	.440	105	1	1	2	-1	.991	-4	*1-132	-1.3
1967	Cle-A	100	257	24	56	10	0	9	31	25	45	.218	.290	.362	91	-3	3	3	-1	.993	4	1-66	-0.5
1968	Cin-N	87	171	15	44	8	0	6	32	9	29	.257	.302	.409	105	1	0	3	-2	.981	-1	1-41	-0.5
1969	Cin-N	74	74	2	11	0	0	1	8	18	27	.149	.315	.189	42	-5	0	0	0	.985	1	1-14	-0.5
1970	Mon-N	4	15	0	1	0	0	0	0	1	3	.067	.125	.067	-47	-3	0	0	0	.976	2	/1-4	-0.2
Total	9	817	2284	242	578	93	8	108	356	139	371	.253	.301	.443	107	14	7	16	-8	.990	3	1-588	-2.6
■ TERRY WHITFIELD	Whitfield, Terry Bertland b: 1/12/53, Blythe, Cal. BL/TR, 6'1", 197 lbs. Deb: 9/29/74																						
1974	NY-A	2	5	0	1	0	0	0	0	0	1	.200	.200	.200	16	-1	0	0	0	.000	-1	/O-1	-0.1
1975	NY-A	28	81	9	22	1	1	0	7	1	17	.272	.280	.309	67	-4	1	0	0	.978	0	O-25/D-1	-0.4
1976	NY-A	1	0	0	0	0	0	0	0	0	0	—	—	—	—	0	0	0	0	.000	-1	/O-1	-0.1
1977	SF-N	114	326	41	93	21	3	7	36	20	46	.285	.330	.433	103	1	2	3	-1	.972	-3	O-84	-0.6
1978	SF-N	149	488	70	141	20	2	10	32	33	69	.289	.337	.400	109	5	5	11	-5	.988	0	*O-140	-0.6
1979	SF-N	133	394	52	113	20	4	5	44	36	47	.287	.353	.396	111	6	5	4	-1	.957	2	*O-106	0.3
1980	SF-N	118	321	38	95	16	2	4	26	20	44	.296	.339	.396	107	3	4	2	0	.987	-0	O-95	-0.1
1984	LA-N	87	180	15	44	8	0	4	18	17	35	.244	.313	.356	88	-3	1	4	-2	.988	-5	O-58	-1.1
1985	*LA-N	79	104	8	27	7	0	3	16	6	27	.260	.300	.413	101	-0	0	0	0	.926	-5	O-28	-0.6
1986	LA-N	19	14	0	1	0	0	0	0	5	2	.071	.316	.071	14	-1	0	0	0	1.000	-0	/O-1	-0.2
Total	10	730	1913	233	537	93	12	33	179	138	288	.281	.332	.394	103	6	18	24	-9	.976	-12	O-539/D-1	-3.5
■ ED WHITING	Whiting, Edward C. (a.k.a. Harry Zieber) b: 1860, Philadelphia, Pa. BL/TR, 188 lbs. Deb: 5/2/1882																						
1882	Bal-a	74	308	43	80	14	5	0		7		.260	.276	.338	115	5				.834	-7	*C-72/1-3,O-2	0.0
1883	Lou-a	58	240	35	70	16	4	2		9		.292	.317	.417	145	12				.884	-8	C-50/O-6,2-2,3-1,1	0.6
1884	Lou-a	42	157	16	35	7	3	0	18	9		.223	.274	.306	93	-1				.891	-2	C-40/O-2,1-2	0.1

YEAR	TM/L	G	AB	R	H	2B	3B	HR	RBI	BB	SO	AVG	OBP	SLG	PRO+	BR/A	SB	CS	SBR	FA	FR	G/POS	TPR
1886	Was-N	6	21	0	0	0	0	0	0	1	12	.000	.045	.000	-90	-5	0			.919	-3	/C-6	-0.6
Total	4	180	726	94	185	37	12	2	18	26	12	.255	.282	.347	114	12	0			.866	-20	C-168/O-10,1-6,23	0.1

■ DICK WHITMAN
Whitman, Dick Corwin b: 11/9/20, Woodburn, Ore. BL/TR, 5'11", 170 lbs. Deb: 4/16/46

YEAR	TM/L	G	AB	R	H	2B	3B	HR	RBI	BB	SO	AVG	OBP	SLG	PRO+	BR/A	SB	CS	SBR	FA	FR	G/POS	TPR
1946	Bro-N	104	265	39	69	15	3	2	31	22	19	.260	.317	.362	92	-3	5			1.000	-2	O-85	-0.9
1947	Bro-N	4	10	1	4	0	0	0	2	1	0	.400	.455	.400	124	0	0			1.000	0	/O-3	0.0
1948	Bro-N	60	165	24	48	13	0	0	20	14	12	.291	.346	.370	91	-2	4			.990	-1	O-48	-0.5
1949	*Bro-N	23	49	8	9	2	0	0	2	4	4	.184	.245	.224	26	-5	0			.952	-1	O-11	-0.7
1950	*Phi-N	75	132	21	33	7	0	0	12	10	10	.250	.317	.303	65	-6	1			.983	-4	O-32	-1.1
1951	Phi-N	19	17	0	2	0	0	0	0	0	1	.118	.118	.118	-37	-3	0	0	0	.000	-3	/O-6	-0.6
Total	6	285	638	93	165	37	3	2	67	51	46	.259	.316	.335	78	-20	10	0		.992	-11	O-185	-3.8

■ FRANK WHITMAN
Whitman, Walter Franklin "Hooker" b: 8/15/24, Marengo, Ind. d: 2/6/94, Maryville, Ill. BR/TR, 6'2", 175 lbs. Deb: 6/30/46

YEAR	TM/L	G	AB	R	H	2B	3B	HR	RBI	BB	SO	AVG	OBP	SLG	PRO+	BR/A	SB	CS	SBR	FA	FR	G/POS	TPR
1946	Chi-A	17	16	7	1	0	0	0	1	2	6	.063	.211	.063	-22	-3	0	1	-1	1.000	4	/S-6,1-1,2-1	0.1
1948	Chi-A	3	6	0	0	0	0	0	0	0	3	.000	.000	.000	-99	-2	0	0	0	.500	-1	/S-1	-0.3
Total	2	20	22	7	1	0	0	0	1	2	9	.045	.160	.045	-43	-4	0	1	-1	.885	3	/S-7,2-1,1-1	-0.2

■ DAN WHITMER
Whitmer, Daniel Charles b: 11/23/55, Redlands, Cal. BR/TR, 6'3", 195 lbs. Deb: 7/20/80 C

YEAR	TM/L	G	AB	R	H	2B	3B	HR	RBI	BB	SO	AVG	OBP	SLG	PRO+	BR/A	SB	CS	SBR	FA	FR	G/POS	TPR
1980	Cal-A	48	87	8	21	3	0	0	7	4	21	.241	.275	.276	53	-6	1	0	0	1.000	4	C-48	0.0
1981	Tor-A	7	9	0	1	1	0	0	0	1	2	.111	.200	.222	20	-1	0	0	0	1.000	1	/C-7	0.0
Total	2	55	96	8	22	4	0	0	7	5	23	.229	.267	.271	49	-7	1	0	0	1.000	5	/C-55	0.0

■ DARRELL WHITMORE
Whitmore, Darrell Lamont b: 11/18/68, Front Royal, Va. BL/TR, 6'1", 210 lbs. Deb: 6/25/93

YEAR	TM/L	G	AB	R	H	2B	3B	HR	RBI	BB	SO	AVG	OBP	SLG	PRO+	BR/A	SB	CS	SBR	FA	FR	G/POS	TPR
1993	Fla-N	76	250	24	51	8	2	4	19	10	72	.204	.249	.300	44	-20	4	2	0	.979	2	O-69	-2.0
1994	Fla-N	9	22	1	5	1	0	0	0	3	5	.227	.320	.273	55	-1	0	1	-1	1.000	1	/O-6	-0.1
1995	Fla-N	27	58	6	11	2	0	1	2	5	15	.190	.254	.276	40	-5	0	0	0	.960	-3	O-16	-0.8
Total	3	112	330	31	67	11	2	5	21	18	92	.203	.255	.294	44	-27	4	3	-1	.978	-0	/O-91	-2.9

■ PINKY WHITNEY
Whitney, Arthur Carter b: 1/2/05, San Antonio, Tex. d: 9/1/87, Center, Tex. BR/TR, 5'10", 165 lbs. Deb: 4/11/28

YEAR	TM/L	G	AB	R	H	2B	3B	HR	RBI	BB	SO	AVG	OBP	SLG	PRO+	BR/A	SB	CS	SBR	FA	FR	G/POS	TPR
1928	Phi-N	151	585	73	176	35	4	10	103	36	30	.301	.342	.426	96	-4	3			.955	3	*3-149	0.7
1929	Phi-N	154	612	89	200	43	14	8	115	61	35	.327	.390	.482	108	7	7			.967	**21**	*3-154	3.1
1930	Phi-N	149	606	87	207	41	5	8	117	40	41	.342	.383	.465	97	-3	3			.965	20	*3-148	2.3
1931	Phi-N	130	501	64	144	36	5	9	74	30	38	.287	.331	.433	96	-4	6			.948	-6	*3-128	-0.2
1932	Phi-N	154	624	93	186	33	11	13	124	35	66	.298	.335	.449	97	-4	6			**.960**	5	*3-151/2-5	1.2
1933	Phi-N	31	121	12	32	4	0	3	19	8	8	.264	.310	.372	83	-3	1			.963	-4	3-30	-0.6
	Bos-N	100	382	42	94	17	2	8	49	25	23	.246	.296	.364	95	-4	2			.971	1	3-85,2-18	0.4
	Yr	131	503	54	126	21	2	11	68	33	31	.250	.299	.366	92	-6	3			.969	-4	*3-115,2-18	-0.2
1934	Bos-N	146	563	58	146	26	2	12	79	25	54	.259	.294	.377	85	-14	7			**.968**	3	*3-111,2-36/S-2	-0.5
1935	Bos-N	126	458	41	125	23	4	4	60	24	36	.273	.312	.367	89	-8	2			.958	6	3-74,2-49	0.4
1936	Bos-N	10	40	1	7	0	0	0	5	2	4	.175	.233	.175	12	-5	0			.971	1	3-10	-0.3
	Phi-N★	114	411	44	121	17	3	6	59	37	33	.294	.354	.394	92	-5	2			.955	10	*3-111/2-1	0.9
	Yr	124	451	45	128	17	3	6	64	39	37	.284	.343	.375	86	-9	2			.956	11	*3-121/2-1	0.6
1937	Phi-N	138	487	56	166	19	4	8	79	43	44	.341	.395	.446	118	13	6			**.982**	3	*3-130	1.9
1938	Phi-N	102	300	27	83	9	1	3	38	27	22	.277	.336	.343	90	-4	0			.934	-2	3-75/1-4,2-2	-0.5
1939	Phi-N	34	75	9	14	0	1	1	6	7	4	.187	.256	.253	38	-7	0			.991	1	1-12/2-8,3-2	-0.7
Total	12	1539	5765	696	1701	303	56	93	927	400	438	.295	.343	.415	96	-43	45			.961	62	*3-1358,2-119/1S	8.1

■ ART WHITNEY
Whitney, Arthur Wilson b: 1/16/1858, Brockton, Mass. d: 8/15/43, Lowell, Mass. BR/TR, 5'8", 155 lbs. Deb: 5/1/1880 F

YEAR	TM/L	G	AB	R	H	2B	3B	HR	RBI	BB	SO	AVG	OBP	SLG	PRO+	BR/A	SB	CS	SBR	FA	FR	G/POS	TPR
1880	Wor-N	76	302	38	67	13	5	1	36	9	15	.222	.244	.308	79	-7				.860	-1	*3-76	-0.6
1881	Det-N	58	214	23	39	7	5	0	9	7	15	.182	.208	.262	45	-13				.849	7	*3-58	-0.5
1882	Pro-N	11	40	2	3	0	0	0	1	2	11	.075	.119	.075	-36	-6				.784	-2	S-11	-0.7
	Det-N	31	115	10	21	0	0	0	4	1	12	.183	.190	.183	20	-10				.854	1	3-22/S-8,P-3	-0.6
	Yr	42	155	12	24	0	0	0	5	3	23	.155	.171	.155	5	-16				.854	-1	3-22,S-19/P-3	-1.3
1884	Pit-a	23	94	10	28	4	0	0		1		.298	.305	.340	109	1				.916	4	3-21/O-1,S-1	0.4
1885	Pit-a	90	373	53	87	10	4	0	28	16		.233	.267	.282	74	-11				**.918**	-14	*S-75/3-8,2-4,O-3	-2.1
1886	Pit-a	136	511	70	122	13	4	0	55	51		.239	.315	.280	87	-6	15			**.906**	11	*3-95,S-42/P-1	0.7
1887	Pit-N	119	431	57	112	11	4	0	51	55	18	.260	.346	.304	87	-4	10			**.924**	-4	*3-119	-0.5
1888	*NY-N	90	328	28	72	1	4	1	28	8	22	.220	.240	.256	59	-15	7			.887	7	3-90	-0.7
1889	*NY-N	129	473	71	103	12	2	1	59	56	39	.218	.303	.258	57	-26	19			.882	0	*3-129/P-1	-1.8
1890	NY-P	119	442	71	97	12	3	0	45	64	19	.219	.322	.260	52	-31	8			.865	-12	3-88,S-31	-3.1
1891	Cin-a	93	347	42	69	6	1	3	33	31	20	.199	.270	.248	44	-27	8			.903	-5	3-93	-2.4
	StL-a	3	11	0	0	0	0	0	0	1	2	.000	.083	.000	-66	-2	0			.867	2	/3-3	-0.1
	Yr	96	358	42	69	6	1	3	33	32	22	.193	.265	.240	41	-29	8			**.902**	-3	3-96	-2.5
Total	11	978	3681	475	820	89	32	6	349	302	173	.223	.285	.269	64	-158	67			.888	-6	3-802,S-168/P-5,2O	-12.0

■ FRANK WHITNEY
Whitney, Frank Thomas "Jumbo" b: 2/18/1856, Brockton, Mass. d: 10/30/43, Baltimore, Md. BR/TR, 5'7.5", 152 lbs. Deb: 5/17/1876 F

YEAR	TM/L	G	AB	R	H	2B	3B	HR	RBI	BB	SO	AVG	OBP	SLG	PRO+	BR/A	SB	CS	SBR	FA	FR	G/POS	TPR
1876	Bos-N	34	139	27	33	7	1	0	15	1	3	.237	.243	.302	79	-3				.818	3	O-34/2-1	-0.1

■ JIM WHITNEY
Whitney, James Evans "Grasshopper Jim" b: 11/10/1857, Conklin, N.Y. d: 5/21/1891, Binghamton, N.Y. BL/TR, 6'2", 172 lbs. Deb: 5/2/1881

YEAR	TM/L	G	AB	R	H	2B	3B	HR	RBI	BB	SO	AVG	OBP	SLG	PRO+	BR/A	SB	CS	SBR	FA	FR	G/POS	TPR
1881	Bos-N	75	282	37	72	17	3	0	32	19	18	.255	.302	.337	106	3				.808	-9	*P-66,O-15/1-2	-0.5
1882	Bos-N	61	251	49	81	18	7	5	48	24	13	.323	.382	.510	183	24				.886	-3	P-49/O-9,1-6	-0.1
1883	Bos-N	96	409	78	115	27	10	5	57	25	29	.281	.323	.433	124	11				.921	-4	P-62,O-40/1-2	0.0
1884	Bos-N	66	270	41	70	17	5	3	40	16	38	.259	.301	.393	117	5				**1.000**	-1	P-38,O-15,1-15,/3-1	-0.4
1885	Bos-N	72	290	35	68	8	4	0	36	17	24	.234	.277	.290	86	-4				.901	5	P-51,O-17/1-5	-0.3
1886	KC-N	67	247	25	59	13	3	2	23	29	39	.239	.319	.340	94	-2	5			.927	6	P-46,O-22/3-1	-0.1
1887	Was-N	54	201	29	53	9	6	2	22	18	24	.264	.324	.398	105	2	10			.905	2	P-47/O-7	-0.2
1888	Was-N	42	141	13	24	0	0	1	17	7	20	.170	.209	.191	30	-11	3			.882	-2	P-39/O-3,1-1	-0.2
1889	Ind-N	10	32	6	12	4	1	0	4	5	6	.375	.474	.563	185	4	2			1.000	-1	/P-9,O-1	0.0
1890	Phi-a	7	21	3	5	0	0	0	1	1		.238	.273	.238	52	-1	0			.900	-1	/P-6,O-1	0.0
Total	10	550	2144	316	559	113	39	18	280	161	211	.261	.313	.375	112	30	20			.900	-9	P-413,O-130/1-31,3	-1.8

■ ERNIE WHITT
Whitt, Leo Ernest b: 6/13/52, Detroit, Mich. BL/TR, 6'2", 200 lbs. Deb: 9/12/76

YEAR	TM/L	G	AB	R	H	2B	3B	HR	RBI	BB	SO	AVG	OBP	SLG	PRO+	BR/A	SB	CS	SBR	FA	FR	G/POS	TPR
1976	Bos-A	8	18	4	4	2	0	1	3	2	2	.222	.300	.500	117	0	0	0	0	1.000	-1	/C-8	0.0
1977	Tor-A	23	41	4	7	3	0	0	6	2	12	.171	.209	.244	23	-4	0	0	0	1.000	1	C-14	-0.3
1978	Tor-A	2	4	0	0	0	0	0	0	1	1	.000	.200	.000	-38	-1	0	0	0	1.000	0	/C-1	0.0
1980	Tor-A	106	295	23	70	12	2	6	34	22	30	.237	.290	.353	72	-12	1	3	-2	.986	6	*C-105	-0.4
1981	Tor-A	74	195	16	46	9	0	1	16	20	30	.236	.307	.297	70	-7	5	2	0	.991	9	C-72	0.5
1982	Tor-A	105	284	28	74	14	2	11	42	26	34	.261	.323	.440	98	-1	3	1	0	.982	1	C-98/D-1	0.3
1983	Tor-A	123	344	53	88	15	2	17	56	50	55	.256	.350	.459	114	7	1	1	-0	.992	6	*C-119	1.7
1984	Tor-A	124	315	35	75	12	1	15	46	43	49	.238	.331	.425	104	2	0	3	-2	.994	12	*C-118	1.7
1985	*Tor-A★	139	412	55	101	21	2	19	64	47	59	.245	.324	.444	105	2	3	6	-3	.988	6	*C-134	1.1
1986	Tor-A	131	395	48	106	19	2	16	56	35	39	.268	.328	.448	106	3	0	1	-1	.991	-4	*C-129	0.6
1987	Tor-A	135	446	57	120	24	1	19	75	44	50	.269	.336	.455	105	3	0	1	-1	.994	6	*C-131	1.6
1988	Tor-A	127	398	63	100	11	2	16	70	61	38	.251	.352	.410	112	8	4	2	0	.994	-6	*C-123	1.1
1989	*Tor-A	129	385	42	101	24	1	11	53	52	53	.262	.350	.416	117	9	5	4	-1	.992	-2	*C-115/D-8	1.3
1990	Atl-N	67	180	14	31	8	0	2	10	23	27	.172	.266	.250	40	-14	0	2	-1	.991	2	C-59	-1.1
1991	Bal-A	35	62	5	15	2	0	0	3	8	12	.242	.329	.274	71	-2	0	0	0	1.000	-1	C-20/D-2	-0.2
Total	15	1328	3774	447	938	176	15	134	534	436	491	.249	.327	.410	98	-9	22	26	-9	.991	36	*C-1246/D-11	7.9

■ POSSUM WHITTED
Whitted, George Bostic b: 2/4/1890, Durham, N.C. d: 10/16/62, Wilmington, N.C. BR/TR, 5'8.5", 168 lbs. Deb: 9/16/12

YEAR	TM/L	G	AB	R	H	2B	3B	HR	RBI	BB	SO	AVG	OBP	SLG	PRO+	BR/A	SB	CS	SBR	FA	FR	G/POS	TPR
1912	StL-N	12	46	7	12	3	0	0	7	3	5	.261	.306	.326	75	-2	1			.857	-3	3-12	-0.5
1913	StL-N	123	404	44	89	10	5	0	38	31	44	.220	.282	.270	59	-21	9			.989	5	O-41,S-38,3-22,/21	-1.5

YEAR	TM/L	G	AB	R	H	2B	3B	HR	RBI	BB	SO	AVG	OBP	SLG	PRO+	BR/A	SB	CS	SBR	FA	FR	G/POS	TPR
1914	StL-N	20	31	3	4	1	0	0	1	0	3	.129	.129	.161	-14	-4	1			.889	-3	/3-5,O-3,2-1	-0.8
	*Bos-N	66	218	36	57	11	4	2	31	18	18	.261	.326	.376	109	2	10			.967	4	O-38,2-15/1-4,3S	0.5
	Yr	86	249	39	61	12	4	2	32	18	21	.245	.304	.349	95	-2	11			.957	1	O-41,2-16/3-9,1S	-0.3
1915	*Phi-N	128	448	46	126	17	3	1	43	29	47	.281	.328	.339	101	0	24	15	-2	.978	4	*O-119/1-7	-0.4
1916	Phi-N	147	526	68	148	20	12	6	68	19	46	.281	.309	.399	113	6	29	17	-2	.964	5	*O-136,1-16	0.2
1917	Phi-N	149	553	69	155	24	9	3	70	30	56	.280	.317	.373	107	3	10			.977	4	*O-141,1-10/3-7,2-1	0.0
1918	Phi-N	24	86	7	21	4	0	0	3	4	10	.244	.278	.291	69	-3	4			.982	2	O-22/1-1	-0.2
1919	Phi-N	78	289	32	72	14	1	3	32	14	20	.249	.284	.336	80	-7	5			.955	0	O-47,2-26/1-2	-1.0
	Pit-N	35	131	15	51	7	7	0	21	6	4	.389	.420	.550	183	13	7			.988	3	1-33/3-2,O-1	1.5
	Yr	113	420	47	123	21	8	3	53	20	24	.293	.327	.402	112	5	12			.955	3	O-48,1-35,2-26,/3-2	0.5
1920	Pit-N	134	494	53	129	11	12	1	74	35	36	.261	.314	.338	85	-10	11	11	-3	.961	-3	*3-125,1-10/O-1	-1.1
1921	Pit-N	108	403	60	114	23	7	7	63	26	21	.283	.328	.427	96	-3	5	10	-5	.988	9	*O-102/1-7	-0.6
1922	Bro-N	1	1	0	0	0	0	0	0	0	0	.000	.000	.000	-99	-0	0	0	0	.000	0	H	0.0
Total	11	1025	3630	440	978	145	60	23	451	215	310	.269	.313	.361	95	-27	116	53		.975	27	O-651,3-177/12S	-3.9

■ FLOYD WICKER

Wicker, Floyd Euliss b: 9/12/43, Burlington, N.C. BL/TR, 6′2″, 175 lbs. Deb: 6/23/68

YEAR	TM/L	G	AB	R	H	2B	3B	HR	RBI	BB	SO	AVG	OBP	SLG	PRO+	BR/A	SB	CS	SBR	FA	FR	G/POS	TPR
1968	StL-N	5	4	2	2	0	0	0	0	0	0	.500	.500	.500	204	0	0	0	0	.000	0	H	0.1
1969	Mon-N	41	39	2	4	0	0	0	2	2	20	.103	.146	.103	-29	-7	0	0	0	1.000	-2	O-11	-1.0
1970	Mil-A	15	41	3	8	1	0	1	3	1	8	.195	.214	.293	38	-4	0	0	0	1.000	-1	O-12	-0.5
1971	Mil-A	11	8	0	1	0	0	0	0	2	0	.125	.300	.125	24	-1	0	0	0	.000	0	H	-0.1
	SF-N	9	21	3	3	0	0	0	1	2	5	.143	.250	.143	14	-2	0	0	0	1.000	1	/O-7	-0.2
Total	4	81	113	10	18	1	0	1	6	7	33	.159	.215	.195	15	-13	0	0	0	1.000	-3	/O-30	-1.7

■ AL WICKLAND

Wickland, Albert b: 1/27/1888, Chicago, Ill. d: 3/14/80, Port Washington, Wis. BL/TL, 5′7″, 155 lbs. Deb: 8/21/13

YEAR	TM/L	G	AB	R	H	2B	3B	HR	RBI	BB	SO	AVG	OBP	SLG	PRO+	BR/A	SB	CS	SBR	FA	FR	G/POS	TPR
1913	Cin-N	26	79	7	17	5	5	0	8	6	19	.215	.279	.405	94	-1	3			.983	1	O-24	-0.2
1914	Chi-F	157	536	74	148	31	10	6	68	**81**	58	.276	.375	.405	119	7	17			.962	-1	*O-157	-0.1
1915	Chi-F	30	86	11	21	2	2	1	5	13	11	.244	.343	.349	101	-1	3			.946	-2	O-24	-0.4
	Pit-F	110	389	63	117	12	8	1	30	52	47	.301	.386	.380	117	5	23			.968	4	*O-109	0.4
	Yr	140	475	74	138	14	10	2	35	65	58	.291	.378	.375	114	4	26			.966	2	*O-133	0.0
1918	Bos-N	95	332	55	87	7	13	4	32	53	39	.262	.367	.398	139	17	12			.975	3	O-95	1.6
1919	NY-A	26	46	2	7	1	0	0	1	2	10	.152	.188	.174	2	-6	0			1.000	-4	O-15	-1.1
Total	5	444	1468	212	397	58	38	12	144	207	184	.270	.364	.386	117	22	58			.968	-1	O-424	0.2

■ CHRIS WIDGER

Widger, Christopher Jon b: 5/21/71, Wilmington, Del. BR/TR, 6′3″, 195 lbs. Deb: 6/23/95

YEAR	TM/L	G	AB	R	H	2B	3B	HR	RBI	BB	SO	AVG	OBP	SLG	PRO+	BR/A	SB	CS	SBR	FA	FR	G/POS	TPR
1995	*Sea-A	23	45	2	9	0	0	1	2	3	11	.200	.250	.267	34	-4	0	0	0	1.000	-4	C-19/O-3,D-1	-0.8
1996	Sea-A	8	11	1	2	0	0	0	0	0	5	.182	.250	.182	12	-1	0	0	0	.905	-0	/C-7	-0.2
1997	Mon-N	91	278	30	65	20	3	7	37	22	59	.234	.292	.403	80	-9	2	0	1	.981	-7	C-85	-1.0
1998	Mon-N	125	417	36	97	18	1	15	53	29	85	.233	.283	.388	75	-17	6	1	1	.983	1	*C-123	-0.6
Total	4	247	751	69	173	38	4	23	92	54	160	.230	.284	.383	73	-32	8	1	2	.982	-11	C-234/O-3,D-1	-2.6

■ TOM WIEDENBAUER

Wiedenbauer, Thomas John b: 11/5/58, Menomonie, Wis. BR/TR, 6′1″, 180 lbs. Deb: 9/14/79

YEAR	TM/L	G	AB	R	H	2B	3B	HR	RBI	BB	SO	AVG	OBP	SLG	PRO+	BR/A	SB	CS	SBR	FA	FR	G/POS	TPR
1979	Hou-N	4	6	0	4	1	0	0	2	0	2	.667	.667	.833	326	2	0	0	0	1.000	-1	/O-3	0.1

■ STUMP WIEDMAN

Wiedman, George Edward b: 2/17/1861, Rochester, N.Y. d: 3/2/05, New York, N.Y. BR/TR, 5′7.5″, 165 lbs. Deb: 8/26/1880 U

YEAR	TM/L	G	AB	R	H	2B	3B	HR	RBI	BB	SO	AVG	OBP	SLG	PRO+	BR/A	SB	CS	SBR	FA	FR	G/POS	TPR
1880	Buf-N	23	78	8	8	1	0	0	3	2	11	.103	.125	.115	-18	-9				.893	-3	P-17,O-13	-0.5
1881	Det-N	13	47	8	12	1	0	0	5	2	2	.255	.286	.277	75	-1				**1.000**	-2	P-13	0.0
1882	Det-N	50	193	20	42	7	1	0	20	2	19	.218	.226	.264	57	-9				.906	0	P-46/O-6,S-1	0.0
1883	Det-N	79	313	34	58	6	1	1	24	4	38	.185	.196	.220	27	-26				.909	-2	P-52,O-35/2-4	-1.2
1884	Det-N	81	300	24	49	6	0	0	26	13	41	.163	.198	.183	22	-26				.846	-3	O-53,P-26/S-1,2-1	-1.9
1885	Det-N	44	153	7	24	2	1	1	14	8	32	.157	.199	.203	30	-12				.869	-5	P-38/O-7,2-1	-0.3
1886	KC-N	51	179	13	30	2	0	0	7	5	46	.168	.190	.179	12	-19	3			.936	3	P-51/O-3	-0.1
1887	Det-N	21	82	12	17	2	0	1	11	3	3	.207	.235	.268	38	-7	6			.837	-1	P-21/O-2	-0.1
	NY-a	14	46	5	7	1	1	0	1	4		.152	.220	.217	23	-5	2			.882	2	P-12/O-3	0.0
	NY-N	1	3	0	1	0	0	0	0	0	0	.333	.333	.333	90	-0	0			.500	-0	/P-1	0.0
1888	NY-N	2	7	1	0	0	0	0	1	2	1	.000	.222	.000	-24	-1	0			.714	-0	/P-2	0.0
Total	9	379	1401	132	248	28	4	3	112	45	193	.177	.203	.209	28	-114	11			.885	-10	P-279,O-122/2-6,S-2	-4.1

■ TOM WIEGHAUS

Wieghaus, Thomas Robert b: 2/1/57, Chicago Heights, Ill BR/TR, 6′, 195 lbs. Deb: 10/4/81

YEAR	TM/L	G	AB	R	H	2B	3B	HR	RBI	BB	SO	AVG	OBP	SLG	PRO+	BR/A	SB	CS	SBR	FA	FR	G/POS	TPR
1981	Mon-N	1	1	0	0	0	0	0	0	0	0	.000	.000	.000	-99	-0	0	0	0	1.000	1	/C-1	0.1
1983	Mon-N	1	0	0	0	0	0	0	0	0	0	—	—	—	—	0	0	0	0	1.000	-0	/C-1	0.0
1984	Hou-N	6	10	0	0	0	0	0	1	1	3	.000	.091	.000	-78	-2	0	0	0	1.000	2	/C-6	0.0
Total	3	8	11	0	0	0	0	0	1	1	3	.000	.083	.000	-80	-3	0	0	0	1.000	3	/C-8	0.1

■ WHITEY WIETELMANN

Wietelmann, William Frederick b: 3/15/19, Zanesville, Ohio BB/TR, 6′, 170 lbs. Deb: 9/6/39 C

YEAR	TM/L	G	AB	R	H	2B	3B	HR	RBI	BB	SO	AVG	OBP	SLG	PRO+	BR/A	SB	CS	SBR	FA	FR	G/POS	TPR
1939	Bos-N	23	69	2	14	1	0	0	5	2	9	.203	.225	.217	21	-8	1			.953	2	S-22/2-1	-0.5
1940	Bos-N	35	41	3	8	1	0	0	1	5	5	.195	.283	.220	43	-3	0			.962	3	2-15/3-9,S-3	0.0
1941	Bos-N	16	33	1	3	0	0	0	0	1	2	.091	.118	.091	-43	-6	0			1.000	3	2-10/S-5,3-2	-0.3
1942	Bos-N	13	34	4	7	2	0	0	0	4	5	.206	.289	.265	64	-1	0			.941	-1	S-11/2-1	-0.1
1943	Bos-N	153	534	33	115	14	1	0	39	46	40	.215	.281	.245	53	-31	9			.957	20	*S-153	0.0
1944	Bos-N	125	417	46	100	18	1	2	32	33	25	.240	.300	.302	67	-18	0			.954	-6	*S-103,2-23/3-1	-1.6
1945	Bos-N	123	428	53	116	15	3	4	33	39	27	.271	.335	.348	89	-6	4			.972	3	2-87,S-39/3-2,P-1	0.4
1946	Bos-N	44	78	7	16	0	0	0	5	14	8	.205	.326	.205	52	-4	0			.915	-6	S-16/3-8,2-4,P-3	-0.9
1947	Pit-N	48	128	21	30	4	1	1	7	12	10	.234	.300	.305	59	-7	0			.885	-13	S-22,2-14/3-6,1-1	-1.9
Total	9	580	1762	.170	409	55	6	7	122	156	131	.232	.298	.282	63	-85	14			.952	4	S-374,2-155/3P1	-4.9

■ ALAN WIGGINS

Wiggins, Alan Anthony b: 2/17/58, Los Angeles, Cal. d: 1/6/91, Los Angeles, Cal. BB/TR, 6′2″, 160 lbs. Deb: 9/4/81

YEAR	TM/L	G	AB	R	H	2B	3B	HR	RBI	BB	SO	AVG	OBP	SLG	PRO+	BR/A	SB	CS	SBR	FA	FR	G/POS	TPR
1981	SD-N	15	14	4	5	0	0	0	0	1	0	.357	.400	.357	125	0	2	0	1	.750	-1	/O-4	0.0
1982	SD-N	72	254	40	65	3	3	1	15	13	19	.256	.295	.303	71	-10	33	6	6	.967	1	O-68/2-1	-0.5
1983	SD-N	144	503	83	139	20	2	0	22	65	43	.276	.360	.324	94	-2	66	13	12	.992	-1	*O-105,1-45	0.4
1984	*SD-N	158	596	106	154	19	7	3	34	75	57	.258	.344	.329	90	-6	70	21	8	.962	-29	*2-157	-2.2
1985	SD-N	10	37	3	2	1	0	0	0	2	4	.054	.103	.081	-49	-7	0	1	-1	1.000	-3	/2-9	-1.2
	Bal-A	76	298	43	85	11	4	0	21	29	16	.285	.353	.349	96	-1	30	13	1	.960	-24	2-76	-2.1
1986	Bal-A	71	239	30	60	3	1	0	11	22	20	.251	.314	.272	62	-12	21	7	2	.978	-19	2-66/D-1	-2.6
1987	Bal-A	85	306	37	71	4	2	1	15	28	34	.232	.299	.268	53	-20	20	7	2	.983	-0	D-44,2-33/O-5	-1.7
Total	7	631	2247	346	581	61	19	5	118	235	193	.259	.331	.309	80	-57	242	68	32	.967	-76	2-342,O-182/D-45,1	-9.9

■ DEL WILBER

Wilber, Delbert Quentin "Babe" b: 2/24/19, Lincoln Park, Mich BR/TR, 6′3″, 200 lbs. Deb: 4/21/46 MC

YEAR	TM/L	G	AB	R	H	2B	3B	HR	RBI	BB	SO	AVG	OBP	SLG	PRO+	BR/A	SB	CS	SBR	FA	FR	G/POS	TPR
1946	StL-N	4	4	0	0	0	0	0	0	1	0	.000	.200	.000	-39	-1	0			1.000	1	/C-4	0.0
1947	StL-N	51	99	7	23	8	1	0	12	5	13	.232	.269	.333	57	-6	0			.983	1	C-34	-0.4
1948	StL-N	27	58	5	11	2	0	0	10	4	9	.190	.242	.224	25	-6	0			.949	-3	C-26	-0.8
1949	StL-N	2	4	0	1	0	0	0	0	0	0	.250	.250	.250	33	-0	0			1.000	0	/C-2	0.0
1951	Phi-N	84	245	30	68	7	3	8	34	17	26	.278	.324	.429	102	0	0	1	-1	.978	4	C-73	0.6
1952	Phi-N	2	2	0	0	0	0	0	0	0	1	.000	.000	.000	-99	-1	0	0	0	.000	0	H	-0.1
	Bos-A	47	135	7	36	10	1	3	23	7	20	.267	.308	.422	94	-2	1	0	0	.995	1	C-39	0.1
1953	Bos-A	58	112	16	27	6	1	7	29	6	21	.241	.286	.500	103	-0	0	0	0	.980	-3	C-28/1-2	-0.2
1954	Bos-A	24	61	2	8	2	1	1	7	4	6	.131	.185	.246	15	-7	0	0	0	.950	-5	C-18	-1.3
Total	8	299	720	67	174	35	7	19	115	44	96	.242	.287	.389	79	-23	1	1		.978	-4	C-224/1-2	-2.1

■ CLAUDE WILBORN

Wilborn, Claude Edward b: 9/1/12, Woodsdale, N.C. d: 11/13/92, Roxboro, N.C. BL/TR, 6′1″, 180 lbs. Deb: 9/8/40

YEAR	TM/L	G	AB	R	H	2B	3B	HR	RBI	BB	SO	AVG	OBP	SLG	PRO+	BR/A	SB	CS	SBR	FA	FR	G/POS	TPR
1940	Bos-N	5	7	0	0	0	0	0	0	0	1	.000	.000	.000	-99	-2	0			.500	-1	/O-3	-0.4

YEAR	TM/L	G	AB	R	H	2B	3B	HR	RBI	BB	SO	AVG	OBP	SLG	PRO+	BR/A	SB	CS	SBR	FA	FR	G/POS	TPR
■ TED WILBORN	Wilborn, Thaddeus Iglehart b: 12/16/58, Waco, Tex. BB/TR, 6', 165 lbs. Deb: 4/5/79																						
1979	Tor-A	22	12	3	0	0	0	0	0	1	7	.000	.077	.000	-76	-3	0	1	-1	.875	-2	/O-7,D-4	-0.5
1980	NY-A	8	8	2	2	0	0	0	1	0	1	.250	.250	.250	38	-1	0	0	0	1.000	1	/O-3	0.0
Total	2	30	20	5	2	0	0	0	1	1	8	.100	.143	.100	-33	-4	0	1	-1	.933	-1	/O-10,D-4	-0.5
■ JOHN WILEY	Wiley, John Deb: 6/23/1884																						
1884	Was-U	1	4	0	0	0	0	0		0		.000	.000	.000	-99	-1				.333	-1	/3-1	-0.2
■ ROB WILFONG	Wilfong, Robert Donald b: 9/1/53, Pasadena, Cal. BL/TR, 6'1", 185 lbs. Deb: 4/10/77																						
1977	Min-A	73	171	22	42	1	1	1	13	17	26	.246	.321	.281	67	-7	10	4	1	.959	4	2-66/D-1	0.0
1978	Min-A	92	199	23	53	8	0	1	11	19	27	.266	.336	.322	84	-4	8	4	0	.986	6	2-80/D-5	0.7
1979	Min-A	140	419	71	131	22	6	9	59	29	54	.313	.360	.458	115	8	11	4	1	.979	21	*2-133/O-3	3.6
1980	Min-A	131	416	55	103	16	5	8	45	34	61	.248	.309	.368	79	-12	10	6	-1	**.995**	-4	*2-120/O-6	-1.1
1981	Min-A	93	305	32	75	11	3	3	19	29	43	.246	.311	.331	80	-8	2	4	-2	.980	4	2-93	-0.1
1982	Min-A	25	81	7	13	1	0	0	5	7	13	.160	.236	.173	14	-9	0	2	-1	.980	-0	2-22	-1.0
	*Cal-A	55	102	17	25	4	2	1	11	7	17	.245	.294	.353	77	-3	4	0	1	.982	9	2-28/3-5,O-3,S-2,D	0.7
	Yr	80	183	24	38	5	2	1	16	14	30	.208	.268	.273	49	-13	4	2	0	.981	9	2-50/3-5,O-3,S-2,D	-0.3
1983	Cal-A	65	177	17	45	7	1	2	17	10	25	.254	.294	.339	74	-6	0	2	-1	.995	12	2-39,3-13/S-6,D-1	0.6
1984	Cal-A	108	307	31	76	13	2	6	33	20	53	.248	.298	.362	82	-8	3	2	-0	.975	3	2-97/S-4,D-1	-0.2
1985	Cal-A	83	217	16	41	3	0	4	13	16	32	.189	.245	.258	38	-19	4	1	1	.986	21	2-69/D-2	0.5
1986	*Cal-A	92	288	25	63	11	3	3	33	16	34	.219	.265	.309	56	-18	1	4	-2	.982	9	2-90	-0.8
1987	SF-N	2	8	2	1	0	0	1	2	1	2	.125	.222	.500	89	-0	1	0	0	.833	-2	/2-2	-0.2
Total	11	959	2690	318	668	97	23	39	261	205	387	.248	.305	.345	77	-86	54	33	-4	.982	80	2-839/3-18,S-12,OD	2.7
■ SPIDER WILHELM	Wilhelm, Charles Ernest b: 5/23/29, Baltimore, Md. d: 10/20/92, Venice, Fla. BR/TR, 5'9", 170 lbs. Deb: 9/6/53																						
1953	Phi-A	7	7	1	2	1	0	0	0	0	3	.286	.286	.429	87	-0	0	0	0	.875	-0	/S-6	0.0
■ JIM WILHELM	Wilhelm, James Webster b: 9/20/52, San Rafael, Cal. BR/TR, 6'3", 190 lbs. Deb: 9/4/78																						
1978	SD-N	10	19	2	7	2	0	0	4	0	2	.368	.400	.474	155	1	1	0	0	1.000	-3	O-10	-0.1
1979	SD-N	39	103	8	25	4	3	0	8	2	12	.243	.257	.340	65	-5	1	1	-0	.985	0	O-30	-0.6
Total	2	49	122	10	32	6	3	0	12	2	14	.262	.280	.361	79	-4	2	1	0	.987	-2	/O-40	-0.7
■ JOE WILHOIT	Wilhoit, Joseph William b: 12/20/1885, Hiawatha, Kan. d: 9/25/30, Santa Barbara, Cal. BL/TR, 6'2", 175 lbs. Deb: 4/12/16																						
1916	Bos-N	116	383	44	88	13	4	2	38	27	45	.230	.282	.300	82	-8	18			.979	2	*O-108	-1.4
1917	Bos-N	54	186	20	51	5	0	1	10	17	15	.274	.335	.317	107	2	5			.928	-3	O-52	-0.4
	Pit-N	9	10	0	2	0	0	0	0	1	1	.200	.273	.200	45	-1	0			1.000	-0	/O-3,1-1	-0.1
	*NY-N	34	50	9	17	2	2	0	8	8	5	.340	.431	.460	179	5	0			1.000	-2	O-11	0.3
	Yr	97	246	29	70	7	2	1	18	26	21	.285	.353	.341	118	6	5			.941	-5	O-66/1-1	-0.2
1918	NY-N	64	135	13	37	3	3	0	15	17	14	.274	.355	.341	115	3	4			.975	-8	O-55	-0.7
1919	Bos-A	6	18	7	6	0	0	0	2	5	2	.333	.478	.333	138	1	1			1.000	-1	/O-5	0.0
Total	4	283	782	93	201	23	9	3	73	75	82	.257	.323	.321	101	2	28			.969	-11	O-234/1-1	-2.3
■ DENNEY WILIE	Wilie, Dennis Ernest b: 9/22/1890, Mt.Calm, Tex. d: 6/20/66, Hayward, Cal. BL/TL, 5'8", 155 lbs. Deb: 7/27/11																						
1911	StL-N	28	51	10	12	3	1	0	3	8	11	.235	.361	.333	97	0	3			1.000	-3	O-15	-0.3
1912	StL-N	30	48	2	11	0	1	0	6	7	9	.229	.351	.271	73	-1	0			.917	-3	O-16	-0.5
1915	Cle-A	45	131	14	33	4	1	2	10	26	18	.252	.384	.344	115	4	2	6	-3	.910	-2	O-35	-0.4
Total	3	103	230	26	56	7	3	2	19	41	38	.243	.372	.326	102	2	5	6		.925	-8	/O-66	-1.2
■ HARRY WILKE	Wilke, Henry Joseph b: 12/14/1900, Cincinnati, Ohio d: 6/21/91, Hamilton, Ohio BR/TR, 5'10.5", 171 lbs. Deb: 5/12/27																						
1927	Chi-N	3	9	0	0	0	0	0	0	0	1	.000	.000	.000	-99	-3	0			1.000	0	/3-3	-0.2
■ CURTIS WILKERSON	Wilkerson, Curtis Vernon b: 4/26/61, Petersburg, Va. BB/TR, 5'9", 158 lbs. Deb: 9/10/83																						
1983	Tex-A	16	35	7	6	0	1	0	1	2	5	.171	.216	.229	23	-4	3	0	1	1.000	2	/S-9,2-2,3-2	0.0
1984	Tex-A	153	484	47	120	12	0	1	26	22	72	.248	.283	.279	55	-29	12	10	-2	.944	-28	*S-116,2-47	-4.9
1985	Tex-A	129	360	35	88	11	6	0	22	22	63	.244	.295	.308	65	-17	14	7	0	.957	3	*S-110,2-19/D-2	-0.4
1986	Tex-A	110	236	27	56	10	3	0	15	11	42	.237	.274	.305	56	-14	9	7	-2	.968	15	2-60,S-56/D-2	0.3
1987	Tex-A	85	138	28	37	5	3	2	14	6	16	.268	.308	.391	84	-3	6	3	0	.946	11	S-33,2-28,3-18,/D-4	0.9
1988	Tex-A	117	338	41	99	12	5	0	28	26	43	.293	.347	.358	95	-2	9	4	0	.970	10	2-87,S-24,3-11,/D-1	1.3
1989	*Chi-N	77	160	18	39	4	2	1	10	8	33	.244	.280	.313	64	-7	4	2	0	.881	4	3-26,2-15/S-7,O-1	-0.3
1990	Chi-N	77	186	21	41	5	1	0	16	7	36	.220	.249	.258	37	-16	2	2	-1	.888	-4	3-52,2-14/S-1,O-1	-2.1
1991	*Pit-N	85	191	20	36	9	1	2	18	15	40	.188	.248	.277	48	-13	2	1	0	.992	3	2-30,S-15,3-14	-0.9
1992	KC-A	111	296	27	74	10	1	2	29	18	47	.250	.295	.311	68	-13	18	7	1	.968	-4	S-69,2-39/3-5,D-1	-1.1
1993	KC-A	12	28	1	4	0	0	0	0	1	6	.143	.172	.143	-13	-4	2	0	1	1.000	-1	2-10/S-4	-0.4
Total	11	972	2452	272	600	78	23	8	179	138	403	.245	.288	.305	63	-123	81	43	-2	.957	11	S-444,2-351,3/DO	-7.6
■ RICK WILKINS	Wilkins, Richard David b: 6/4/67, Jacksonville, Fla. BL/TR, 6'2", 210 lbs. Deb: 6/6/91																						
1991	Chi-N	86	203	21	45	9	0	6	22	19	56	.222	.307	.355	82	-5	3	3	-1	.993	9	C-82	0.7
1992	Chi-N	83	244	20	66	9	1	8	22	28	53	.270	.346	.414	111	4	0	2	-1	.993	10	C-73	1.8
1993	Chi-N	136	446	78	135	23	1	30	73	50	99	.303	.377	.561	149	30	2	1	0	.996	5	*C-133	4.2
1994	Chi-N	100	313	44	71	25	2	7	39	40	86	.227	.318	.387	84	-8	4	3	-1	.993	-5	C-95/1-2	-0.7
1995	Chi-N	50	162	24	31	2	0	6	14	36	51	.191	.342	.315	76	-5	0	0	0	.988	-6	C-49/1-2	-0.8
	Hou-N	15	40	6	10	1	0	1	5	10	10	.250	.400	.350	107	1	0	0	0	1.000	-1	C-13	0.1
	Yr	65	202	30	41	3	0	7	19	46	61	.203	.353	.322	82	-4	0	0	0	.990	-7	C-62/1-2	-0.7
1996	Hou-N	84	254	34	54	8	2	6	23	46	81	.213	.336	.331	83	-5	0	1	-1	.990	-7	C-82	-0.8
	SF-N	52	157	19	46	10	0	8	36	21	40	.293	.376	.510	136	8	0	2	-1	.991	-7	C-42/1-7	0.1
	Yr	136	411	53	100	18	2	14	59	67	121	.243	.351	.399	104	3	0	3	-2	.990	-15	*C-124/1-7	-0.7
1997	SF-N	66	190	18	37	5	0	6	23	17	65	.195	.261	.316	51	-14	0	0	0	.986	1	C-57	-1.0
	*Sea-A	5	12	2	3	1	0	1	4	1	2	.250	.308	.583	127	0	0	0	0	1.000	-0	/C-3,D-2	0.0
1998	Sea-A	19	41	5	8	1	1	1	4	4	14	.195	.267	.341	57	-3	0	0	0	1.000	-1	/C-6,1-6,D-2	-0.3
	NY-N	5	15	3	2	0	0	0	1	2	2	.133	.235	.133	-1	-2	0	0	0	.957	-2	/C-4	-0.4
Total	8	701	2077	274	508	94	7	80	266	274	559	.245	.336	.412	101	2	9	12	-5	.992	-4	C-639/1-17,D-4	2.9
■ BOBBY WILKINS	Wilkins, Robert Linwood b: 8/11/22, Denton, N.C. BR/TR, 5'9", 165 lbs. Deb: 4/18/44																						
1944	Phi-A	24	25	7	6	0	0	0	3	1	4	.240	.296	.240	55	-1	0	0	0	.943	5	/S-9	0.4
1945	Phi-A	62	154	22	40	6	0	0	4	10	17	.260	.305	.299	76	-5	2	4	-2	.923	0	S-40/O-4	-0.4
Total	2	86	179	29	46	6	0	0	7	11	21	.257	.304	.291	73	-6	2	4	-2	.926	5	/S-49,O-4	0.0
■ ED WILKINSON	Wilkinson, Edward Henry b: 6/20/1890, Jacksonville, Ore d: 4/9/18, Tucson, Ariz. BR/TR, 6', 170 lbs. Deb: 7/4/11																						
1911	NY-A	10	13	2	3	0	0	0	1	0		.231	.231	.231	27	-1	0			.800	-1	/O-3,2-1	-0.2
■ BOB WILL	Will, Robert Lee "Butch" b: 7/15/31, Berwyn, Ill. BL/TL, 5'10.5", 175 lbs. Deb: 4/16/57																						
1957	Chi-N	70	112	13	25	3	0	1	10	5	21	.223	.256	.277	44	-9	1	0	0	.963	-5	O-30	-1.5
1958	Chi-N	6	4	1	1	0	0	0	0	2	0	.250	.500	.250	108	0	0	0	0	.000	0	/O-1	0.0
1960	Chi-N	138	475	58	121	20	9	6	53	47	54	.255	.323	.373	91	-6	1	5	-3	.992	2	*O-121	-1.3
1961	Chi-N	86	113	9	29	9	0	0	8	15	19	.257	.344	.336	80	-3	0	1	-1	1.000	-6	O-30/1-1	-1.0
1962	Chi-N	87	92	6	22	3	0	2	15	13	22	.239	.333	.337	78	-3	0	0	0	1.000	-1	/O-9	-0.4
1963	Chi-N	23	23	0	4	0	0	0	1	1	3	.174	.208	.174	11	-3	0	0	0	1.000	-0	/1-1	-0.3
Total	6	410	819	87	202	35	9	9	87	83	119	.247	.317	.344	80	-22	2	6	-3	.988	-10	O-191/1-2	-4.5
■ JERRY WILLARD	Willard, Gerald Duane b: 3/14/60, Oxnard, Cal. BL/TR, 6'2", 195 lbs. Deb: 4/11/84																						
1984	Cle-A	87	246	21	55	8	1	10	37	26	55	.224	.298	.386	86	-5	1	0	0	.981	-1	C-76/D-1	-0.2
1985	Cle-A	104	300	39	81	13	0	7	36	28	59	.270	.334	.383	97	-1	0	0	0	.990	0	C-96/D-1	0.4

YEAR	TM/L	G	AB	R	H	2B	3B	HR	RBI	BB	SO	AVG	OBP	SLG	PRO+	BR/A	SB	CS	SBR	FA	FR	G/POS	TPR
1986	Oak-A	75	161	17	43	7	0	4	26	22	28	.267	.362	.385	112	3	0	1	-1	.994	-11	C-71/D-1	-0.5
1987	Oak-A	7	6	1	1	0	0	0	0	2	1	.167	.375	.167	55	-0	0	0	0	1.000	-0	/1-1,3-1,D-3	-0.1
1990	Chi-A	3	3	0	0	0	0	0	0	0	2	.000	.000	.000	-99	-1	0	0	0	.000	0	/C-1	-0.1
1991	*Atl-N	17	14	1	3	0	0	1	4	2	5	.214	.313	.429	100	-0	0	0	0	1.000	0	/C-1	0.0
1992	Atl-N	26	23	2	8	1	0	2	7	1	3	.348	.375	.652	175	2	0	0	0	1.000	0	/C-1	0.3
	Mon-N	21	25	0	3	0	0	0	1	1	7	.120	.154	.120	-22	-4	0	0	0	.952	0	/1-5	-0.4
	Yr	47	48	2	11	1	0	2	8	2	10	.229	.260	.375	76	-2	0	0	0	.952	1	/1-5,C-1	-0.1
1994	Sea-A	6	5	1	1	0	0	1	3	1	1	.200	.333	.800	177	1	0	0	0	.000	-0	/C-1,D-1	0.0
Total	8	346	783	82	195	29	1	25	114	83	161	.249	.323	.384	95	-5	1	1	-0	.988	-11	C-247/D-7,1-6,3-1	-0.6

■ RIP WILLIAMS Williams, Alva Mitchel "Buff" b: 1/31/1882, Carthage, Ill. d: 7/23/33, Keokuk, Iowa BR/TR, 6'0.5", 187 lbs. Deb: 4/12/11

YEAR	TM/L	G	AB	R	H	2B	3B	HR	RBI	BB	SO	AVG	OBP	SLG	PRO+	BR/A	SB	CS	SBR	FA	FR	G/POS	TPR
1911	Bos-A	95	284	36	68	8	5	0	31	24		.239	.314	.303	73	-10	9			.975	1	1-57,C-38	-0.6
1912	Was-A	61	157	14	50	11	4	0	22	7		.318	.352	.439	125	4	2			.978	4	C-48	1.2
1913	Was-A	66	106	9	30	6	2	1	12	9	16	.283	.339	.406	115	2	3			.985	-4	C-18/1-9,O-5	-0.1
1914	Was-A	81	169	17	47	6	4	1	22	13	19	.278	.341	.379	112	2	2	2	-1	.975	-5	C-44/1-8,O-1	0.0
1915	Was-A	91	197	14	48	8	4	0	31	18	20	.244	.320	.325	91	-2	4	3	-1	.967	8	C-40,1-15/3-1	0.8
1916	Was-A	76	202	16	54	10	2	0	20	15	19	.267	.324	.337	100	-0	5			.982	-9	1-34,C-23/3-1	-0.9
1918	Cle-A	28	71	5	17	2	2	0	7	9	6	.239	.325	.324	87	-1	2			.980	-2	1-21/C-1	-0.4
Total	7	498	1186	111	314	51	23	2	145	95	80	.265	.328	.352	97	-6	27	5		.977	-6	C-212,1-144/O-6,3-2	-0.0

■ ART WILLIAMS Williams, Arthur Franklin b: 8/26/1877, Somerville, Mass. d: 5/16/41, Arlington, Va. TR , Deb: 5/7/02

YEAR	TM/L	G	AB	R	H	2B	3B	HR	RBI	BB	SO	AVG	OBP	SLG	PRO+	BR/A	SB	CS	SBR	FA	FR	G/POS	TPR
1902	Chi-N	47	160	17	37	3	0	0	14	15		.231	.309	.250	75	-4	9			.917	-3	O-24,1-19	-0.9

■ GUS WILLIAMS Williams, August Joseph "Gloomy Gus" b: 5/7/1888, Omaha, Neb. d: 4/16/64, Sterling, Ill. BL/TL, 6', 185 lbs. Deb: 4/12/11 F

YEAR	TM/L	G	AB	R	H	2B	3B	HR	RBI	BB	SO	AVG	OBP	SLG	PRO+	BR/A	SB	CS	SBR	FA	FR	G/POS	TPR
1911	StL-A	9	26	1	7	3	0	0	4	0		.269	.296	.385	93	-0	0			.867	-1	/O-7	-0.2
1912	StL-A	64	216	32	63	13	7	2	32	27		.292	.370	.444	138	10	18			.930	2	O-62	0.9
1913	StL-A	148	538	72	147	21	16	5	53	57	87	.273	.346	.400	121	13	31			.951	4	*O-143	1.1
1914	StL-A	144	499	51	126	19	6	4	47	36	120	.253	.308	.339	98	-3	35	20	-2	.933	2	*O-142	-0.9
1915	StL-A	45	119	15	24	2	2	1	11	6	16	.202	.246	.277	59	-7	11	1	3	.949	-5	O-35	-1.1
Total	5	410	1398	171	367	58	31	12	147	126	223	.263	.327	.374	110	14	95	21		.939	2	O-389	-0.2

■ BERNIE WILLIAMS Williams, Bernabe (Figueroa) b: 9/13/68, San Juan, P.R. BB/TR, 6'2", 205 lbs. Deb: 7/7/91

YEAR	TM/L	G	AB	R	H	2B	3B	HR	RBI	BB	SO	AVG	OBP	SLG	PRO+	BR/A	SB	CS	SBR	FA	FR	G/POS	TPR
1991	NY-A	85	320	43	76	19	4	3	34	48	57	.237	.339	.350	91	-3	10	5	0	.979	6	O-85	0.0
1992	NY-A	62	261	39	73	14	2	5	26	29	36	.280	.354	.406	113	5	7	6	-2	.995	8	O-62	1.1
1993	NY-A	139	567	67	152	31	4	12	68	53	106	.268	.335	.400	100	-0	9	9	-3	.989	6	*O-139	-0.1
1994	NY-A	108	408	80	118	29	1	12	57	61	54	.289	.386	.453	120	14	16	9	-1	.990	5	*O-107	1.4
1995	*NY-A	144	563	93	173	29	9	18	82	75	98	.307	.393	.487	129	25	8	6	-1	.982	16	*O-144	3.3
1996	*NY-A	143	551	108	168	26	7	29	102	82	72	.305	.395	.535	132	28	17	4	3	.986	9	*O-140/D-2	3.3
1997	*NY-A★	129	509	107	167	35	6	21	100	73	80	.328	.413	.544	148	38	15	8	-0	.993	-5	*O-128	2.8
1998	*NY-A†	128	499	101	169	30	5	26	97	74	81	**.339**	.425	.575	160	46	15	9	-1	.990	2	*O-123/D-5	4.1
Total	8	938	3678	638	1096	213	38	126	566	495	584	.298	.384	.479	127	152	97	56	-5	.987	46	O-928/D-7	15.9

■ BERNIE WILLIAMS Williams, Bernard b: 10/8/48, Alameda, Cal. BR/TR, 6'1", 175 lbs. Deb: 9/7/70

YEAR	TM/L	G	AB	R	H	2B	3B	HR	RBI	BB	SO	AVG	OBP	SLG	PRO+	BR/A	SB	CS	SBR	FA	FR	G/POS	TPR
1970	SF-N	7	16	2	5	2	0	0	1	2	1	.313	.389	.438	122	1	1	1	-0	1.000	1	/O-6	0.1
1971	SF-N	35	73	8	13	1	0	1	5	12	24	.178	.294	.233	52	-4	1	1	-0	.933	-5	O-27	-1.1
1972	SF-N	46	68	12	13	3	1	3	9	7	22	.191	.267	.397	85	-2	0	0	0	1.000	2	O-15	-0.1
1974	SD-N	14	15	1	2	0	0	0	0	0	6	.133	.133	.133	-26	-3	0	0	0	1.000	-1	/O-3	-0.4
Total	4	102	172	23	33	6	1	4	15	21	53	.192	.280	.308	66	-8	2	2	-1	.974	-3	/O-51	-1.5

■ BILLY WILLIAMS Williams, Billy Leo b: 6/15/38, Whistler, Ala. BL/TR, 6'1", 175 lbs. Deb: 8/6/59 CH

YEAR	TM/L	G	AB	R	H	2B	3B	HR	RBI	BB	SO	AVG	OBP	SLG	PRO+	BR/A	SB	CS	SBR	FA	FR	G/POS	TPR
1959	Chi-N	18	33	0	5	0	1	0	2	1	7	.152	.176	.212	3	-5	0	0	0	1.000	-0	O-10	-0.5
1960	Chi-N	12	47	4	13	0	2	2	7	5	12	.277	.346	.489	127	2	0	0	0	.962	0	O-12	0.1
1961	Chi-N	146	529	75	147	20	7	25	86	45	70	.278	.340	.484	114	10	6	0	2	.954	-2	*O-135	0.2
1962	Chi-N★	159	618	94	184	22	8	22	91	70	72	.298	.373	.466	119	17	9	9	-3	.967	16	*O-159	2.0
1963	Chi-N	161	612	87	175	36	9	25	95	68	78	.286	.359	.497	136	29	7	6	-2	.987	16	*O-160	3.7
1964	Chi-N★	162	645	100	201	39	2	33	98	59	84	.312	.371	.532	145	38	10	7	-1	.950	1	*O-162	3.0
1965	Chi-N★	164	645	115	203	39	6	34	108	65	76	.315	.380	.552	155	46	10	1	2	.968	0	*O-164	4.3
1966	Chi-N	162	648	100	179	23	5	29	91	69	61	.276	.350	.461	122	19	6	3	0	.976	8	*O-162	2.0
1967	Chi-N	162	634	92	176	21	12	28	84	68	67	.278	.349	.481	129	24	6	3	0	.989	-3	*O-162	1.3
1968	Chi-N★	163	642	91	185	30	8	30	98	48	53	.288	.340	.500	140	29	4	1	1	.967	-11	*O-163	1.1
1969	Chi-N	163	642	103	188	33	10	21	95	59	70	.293	.356	.474	116	12	3	2	-0	.957	2	*O-159	0.5
1970	Chi-N	161	636	**137**	**205**	34	4	42	129	72	65	.322	.393	.586	142	35	7	1	2	.989	8	*O-160	3.6
1971	Chi-N	157	594	86	179	27	5	28	93	77	44	.301	.384	.505	131	24	7	5	-1	.977	7	*O-154	2.4
1972	Chi-N★	150	574	95	191	34	6	37	122	62	59	**.333**	.403	**.606**	166	48	3	1	0	.984	-3	*O-144/1-5	4.1
1973	Chi-N★	156	576	72	166	22	2	20	86	76	72	.288	.372	.438	115	13	4	3	-1	.985	12	*O-138,1-19	1.7
1974	Chi-N	117	404	55	113	22	0	16	68	67	44	.280	.383	.453	128	16	4	5	-2	.986	2	1-65,O-43	1.1
1975	*Oak-A	155	520	68	127	20	1	23	81	76	68	.244	.343	.419	117	12	0	0	0	.971	-0	*D-145/1-7	0.8
1976	Oak-A	120	351	36	74	12	0	11	41	58	44	.211	.323	.339	98	0	4	2	0	.000	-0	*D-106/O-1	-0.3
Total	18	2488	9350	1410	2711	434	88	426	1475	1045	1046	.290	.364	.492	131	371	90	49	-2	.973	52	*O-2088,D-251/1-96	31.1

■ DALLAS WILLIAMS Williams, Dallas McKinley b: 2/28/58, Brooklyn, N.Y. BL/TL, 5'11", 165 lbs. Deb: 9/19/81

YEAR	TM/L	G	AB	R	H	2B	3B	HR	RBI	BB	SO	AVG	OBP	SLG	PRO+	BR/A	SB	CS	SBR	FA	FR	G/POS	TPR
1981	Bal-A	2	2	0	1	0	0	0	0	0	0	.500	.500	.500	189	0	0	0	0	1.000	-0	/O-1	0.0
1983	Cin-N	18	36	2	2	0	0	0	1	3	6	.056	.128	.056	-46	-7	0	0	0	1.000	-1	O-12	-0.9
Total	2	20	38	2	3	0	0	0	1	3	6	.079	.146	.079	-35	-7	0	0	0	1.000	-2	/O-13	-0.9

■ DANA WILLIAMS Williams, Dana Lamont b: 3/20/63, Weirton, W.Va. BR/TR, 5'10", 170 lbs. Deb: 6/21/89 C

YEAR	TM/L	G	AB	R	H	2B	3B	HR	RBI	BB	SO	AVG	OBP	SLG	PRO+	BR/A	SB	CS	SBR	FA	FR	G/POS	TPR
1989	Bos-A	8	5	1	1	1	0	0	0	0	1	.200	.333	.400	100	0	0	0	0	1.000	0	/O-1,D-2	0.0

■ DAVEY WILLIAMS Williams, David Carlous b: 11/2/27, Dallas, Tex. BR/TR, 5'10", 160 lbs. Deb: 9/16/49 C

YEAR	TM/L	G	AB	R	H	2B	3B	HR	RBI	BB	SO	AVG	OBP	SLG	PRO+	BR/A	SB	CS	SBR	FA	FR	G/POS	TPR
1949	NY-N	13	50	7	12	1	1	1	5	7	4	.240	.333	.360	86	-1	0			.953	-10	2-13	-1.1
1951	*NY-N	30	64	17	17	1	0	2	8	5	8	.266	.319	.375	85	-1	1	1	-0	1.000	2	2-22	0.1
1952	NY-N	138	540	70	137	26	3	13	55	48	63	.254	.324	.385	95	-4	2	3	-1	.973	-15	*2-138	-1.4
1953	NY-N★	112	340	51	101	11	2	3	34	44	19	.297	.382	.368	95	-1	2	5	-2	.982	0	2-95	0.2
1954	*NY-N	142	544	65	121	18	3	9	46	43	33	.222	.285	.316	56	-35	1	1	-0	**.982**	-7	*2-142	-3.3
1955	NY-N	82	247	25	62	4	1	4	15	17	17	.251	.305	.324	67	-12	0	2	-1	.968	-8	2-71	-1.6
Total	6	517	1785	235	450	61	10	32	163	164	144	.252	.321	.351	79	-54	6	12		.978	-38	2-481	-7.1

■ KEITH WILLIAMS Williams, David Keith b: 4/21/72, Bedford, Pa. BR/TR, 6', 190 lbs. Deb: 6/7/96

YEAR	TM/L	G	AB	R	H	2B	3B	HR	RBI	BB	SO	AVG	OBP	SLG	PRO+	BR/A	SB	CS	SBR	FA	FR	G/POS	TPR
1996	SF-N	9	20	0	5	0	0	0	0	0	6	.250	.250	.250	34	-2	0	0	0	1.000	0	/O-4	-0.2

■ DEWEY WILLIAMS Williams, Dewey Edgar "Dee" b: 2/5/16, Durham, N.C. BR/TR, 6', 160 lbs. Deb: 6/28/44

YEAR	TM/L	G	AB	R	H	2B	3B	HR	RBI	BB	SO	AVG	OBP	SLG	PRO+	BR/A	SB	CS	SBR	FA	FR	G/POS	TPR
1944	Chi-N	79	262	23	63	7	2	0	27	23	18	.240	.302	.282	65	-12	2			.981	4	C-77	-0.3
1945	*Chi-N	59	100	16	28	2	2	2	5	13	13	.280	.363	.400	114	2	0			.978	2	C-54	0.6
1946	Chi-N	4	5	0	1	0	0	0	0	0	2	.200	.200	.200	14	-1	0			1.000	0	/C-2	0.0
1947	Chi-N	3	2	0	0	0	0	0	0	0	1	.000	.000	.000	-99	-1	0			.000	0	/C-1	-0.1
1948	Cin-N	48	95	9	16	2	0	1	5	10	18	.168	.248	.221	29	-10	0			.961	-3	C-47	-1.1
Total	5	193	464	48	108	11	4	3	37	46	52	.233	.302	.293	67	-20	2			.976	3	C-181	-0.9

■ EARL WILLIAMS Williams, Earl Baxter b: 1/27/03, Cumberland Gap, Tenn. d: 3/10/58, Knoxville, Tenn. BR/TR, 6'0.5", 185 lbs. Deb: 5/27/28

YEAR	TM/L	G	AB	R	H	2B	3B	HR	RBI	BB	SO	AVG	OBP	SLG	PRO+	BR/A	SB	CS	SBR	FA	FR	G/POS	TPR
1928	Bos-N	3	2	0	0	0	0	0	0	0	1	.000	.000	.000	-99	-1	0			1.000	0	/C-1	-0.1

YEAR	TM/L	G	AB	R	H	2B	3B	HR	RBI	BB	SO	AVG	OBP	SLG	PRO+	BR/A	SB	CS	SBR	FA	FR	G/POS	TPR
■ **EARL WILLIAMS**	Williams, Earl Craig b: 7/14/48, Newark, N.J. BR/TR, 6'3", 220 lbs. Deb: 9/13/70																						
1970	Atl-N	10	19	4	7	4	0	0	5	3	4	.368	.455	.579	165	2	0	0	0	1.000	1	/1-4,3-3	0.3
1971	Atl-N	145	497	64	129	14	1	33	87	42	80	.260	.326	.491	121	12	0	1	-1	.981	-8	C-72,3-42,1-31	0.4
1972	Atl-N	151	565	72	146	24	2	28	87	62	118	.258	.338	.457	113	9	0	0	0	.980	-19	*C-116,3-21,1-20	-0.7
1973	*Bal-A	132	459	58	109	18	1	22	83	66	107	.237	.337	.425	114	9	0	2	-1	.987	-9	C-95,1-42/D-2	0.0
1974	*Bal-A	118	413	47	105	16	0	14	52	40	79	.254	.330	.395	111	6	0	2	-1	.983	-14	C-75,1-47/D-1	-0.9
1975	Atl-N	111	383	42	92	13	0	11	50	34	63	.240	.307	.360	82	-10	0	0	0	.989	-5	1-90,C-11	-2.1
1976	Atl-N	61	184	18	39	3	0	9	26	19	33	.212	.289	.375	82	-5	0	0	0	.995	-9	C-38,1-17	-1.4
	Mon-N	61	190	17	45	10	2	8	29	14	32	.237	.289	.437	100	-1	0	0	0	.981	6	1-47,C-13	0.3
	Yr	122	374	35	84	13	2	17	55	33	65	.225	.289	.406	91	-6	0	0	0	.986	-2	1-64,C-51	-1.1
1977	Oak-A	100	348	39	84	13	0	13	38	18	58	.241	.288	.391	84	-8	2	0	1	.989	-4	D-45,C-36,1-29	-1.3
Total	8	889	3058	361	756	115	6	138	457	298	574	.247	.321	.424	105	14	2	5	-2	.984	-60	C-456,1-327/3-66,D	-5.4
■ **EDDIE WILLIAMS**	Williams, Edward Laquan b: 11/1/64, Shreveport, La. BR/TR, 6', 185 lbs. Deb: 4/18/86																						
1986	Cle-A	5	7	2	1	0	0	0	1	0	3	.143	.143	.143	-22	-1	0	0	0	.000	-2	/O-4	-0.3
1987	Cle-A	22	64	9	11	4	0	1	4	9	19	.172	.284	.281	50	-5	0	0	0	.982	2	3-22	-0.3
1988	Cle-A	10	21	3	4	0	0	0	1	0	3	.190	.227	.190	18	-2	0	0	0	1.000	3	3-10	0.0
1989	Chi-A	66	201	25	55	8	0	3	10	18	31	.274	.345	.358	101	1	1	2	-1	.909	1	3-65	0.1
1990	SD-N	14	42	5	12	3	0	3	4	5	6	.286	.362	.571	151	3	0	1	-1	.897	-1	3-13	0.1
1994	SD-N	49	175	32	58	11	1	11	42	15	26	.331	.394	.594	158	14	0	1	-1	.988	-2	1-46/3-1	0.7
1995	SD-N	97	296	35	77	11	1	12	47	23	47	.260	.322	.426	99	-1	0	0	0	.989	-1	1-81	-0.9
1996	Det-A	77	215	22	43	5	0	6	26	18	50	.200	.268	.307	45	-18	0	2	-1	1.000	-0	D-52/1-7,3-3,O-2	-2.2
1997	LA-N	8	7	0	1	0	0	0	1	1	1	.143	.250	.143	7	-1	0	0	0	.000	0	/H	-0.1
	Pit-N	30	89	12	22	5	0	3	11	10	24	.247	.337	.404	91	-1	1	0	0	.991	-3	1-26	-0.6
	Yr	38	96	12	23	5	0	3	12	11	25	.240	.330	.385	87	-2	1	0	0	.991	-3	1-26	-0.7
1998	SD-N	17	28	1	4	0	0	0	3	2	6	.143	.200	.143	-10	-5	0	0	0	1.000	-0	/1-7	-0.5
Total	10	395	1145	146	288	47	2	39	150	101	216	.252	.321	.398	91	-17	2	6	-3	.989	-4	1-167,3-114/D-52,O	-4.0
■ **DIB WILLIAMS**	Williams, Edwin Dibrell b: 1/19/10, Greenbrier, Ark. d: 4/2/92, Searcy, Ark. BR/TR, 5'11.5", 175 lbs. Deb: 4/27/30																						
1930	Phi-A	67	191	24	50	10	3	3	22	15	19	.262	.322	.393	77	-7	2	1	0	.951	4	2-39,S-19/3-1	0.0
1931	*Phi-A	86	294	41	79	12	2	6	40	19	21	.269	.313	.384	78	-10	2	0	1	.931	7	S-72,2-10/O-1	0.5
1932	Phi-A	62	215	30	54	10	1	4	24	22	23	.251	.329	.363	76	-8	0	1	-1	.952	7	2-53/S-3	0.1
1933	Phi-A	115	408	52	118	20	5	11	73	32	35	.289	.342	.444	106	2	1	0	0	.921	-9	S-84,2-29/1-2	0.0
1934	Phi-A	66	205	25	56	10	1	2	17	21	18	.273	.341	.361	84	-5	0	1	-1	.956	-0	2-53/S-2	-0.2
1935	Phi-A	4	10	0	1	0	0	0	0	0	1	.100	.100	.100	-49	-2	0	0	0	1.000	-2	/2-2	-0.4
	Bos-A	75	251	26	63	12	0	3	25	24	23	.251	.319	.335	65	-13	2	0	1	.952	-5	3-30,2-29,S-15,/1-1	-1.4
	Yr	79	261	26	64	12	0	3	25	24	24	.245	.311	.326	61	-15	2	0	1	.973	-7	2-31,3-30,S-15,/1-1	-1.8
Total	6	475	1574	198	421	74	12	29	201	133	140	.267	.327	.385	82	-43	7	3	0	.955	1	2-215,S-195/310	-1.4
■ **DENNY WILLIAMS**	Williams, Evon Daniel b: 12/13/1899, Portland, Ore. d: 3/23/29, San Clemente, Cal. BL/TR, 5'8.5", 150 lbs. Deb: 4/15/21																						
1921	Cin-N	10	7	0	0	0	0	0	0	0	2	.000	.000	.000	-99	-2	0	1	-1	1.000	-0	/O-1	-0.3
1924	Bos-A	25	85	17	31	3	0	0	4	10	5	.365	.438	.400	117	3	3	3	-1	.972	-2	O-19	-0.1
1925	Bos-A	69	218	28	50	1	3	0	13	17	11	.229	.285	.261	39	-20	2	6	-3	.953	-2	O-52	-2.7
1928	Bos-A	16	18	1	4	0	0	0	1	1	1	.222	.263	.222	29	-2	0	0	0	1.000	-2	/O-6	-0.4
Total	4	120	328	46	85	4	3	0	18	28	19	.259	.319	.290	56	-21	5	10	-5	.959	-7	/O-78	-3.5
■ **CY WILLIAMS**	Williams, Fred b: 12/21/1887, Wadena, Ind. d: 4/23/74, Eagle River, Wis. BL/TL, 6'2", 180 lbs. Deb: 7/18/12																						
1912	Chi-N	28	62	3	15	1	1	0	1	6	14	.242	.309	.290	65	-3	2			1.000	-2	O-22	-0.6
1913	Chi-N	49	156	17	35	3	3	4	32	5	26	.224	.262	.359	76	-6	5			.976	-5	O-44	-1.3
1914	Chi-N	55	94	12	19	2	2	0	5	13	13	.202	.312	.266	73	-3	2			.941	-3	O-27	-0.7
1915	Chi-N	151	518	59	133	22	6	13	64	26	49	.257	.305	.398	112	5	15	10	-2	.968	4	*O-149	0.1
1916	Chi-N	118	405	55	113	19	9	**12**	66	51	64	.279	.372	.459	140	19	6			.989	-4	*O-116	1.1
1917	Chi-N	138	468	53	113	22	4	5	42	38	78	.241	.308	.338	91	-5	8			.960	12	*O-136	0.0
1918	Phi-N	94	351	49	97	14	1	6	39	27	30	.276	.337	.373	109	4	10			.968	0	O-91	-0.1
1919	Phi-N	109	435	54	121	21	1	9	39	30	43	.278	.335	.393	111	5	9			.970	4	*O-108	0.2
1920	Phi-N	148	590	88	192	36	10	**15**	72	32	45	.325	.364	.497	139	28	18	12	-2	.972	10	*O-147	2.6
1921	Phi-N	146	562	67	180	28	6	18	75	30	32	.320	.357	.488	112	9	5	15	-8	.979	16	*O-146	0.6
1922	Phi-N	151	584	98	180	30	6	26	92	74	49	.308	.392	.514	120	17	11	14	-5	.973	2	*O-150	0.3
1923	Phi-N	136	535	98	157	22	3	**41**	114	59	57	.293	.371	.576	131	21	11	10	-3	.981	-3	*O-135	0.6
1924	Phi-N	148	558	101	183	31	11	24	93	67	49	.328	.403	.552	137	28	7	12	-5	.962	-3	*O-145	1.1
1925	Phi-N	107	314	78	104	11	5	13	60	53	34	.331	.435	.522	132	17	4	9	-4	.989	-5	O-96	0.2
1926	Phi-N	107	336	63	116	13	4	18	53	38	35	.345	.418	**.568**	155	26	2			.963	-8	O-93	1.2
1927	Phi-N	131	492	86	135	18	2	**30**	98	61	57	.274	.365	.502	128	19	0			.970	1	*O-130	1.2
1928	Phi-N	99	238	31	61	9	0	12	37	54	34	.256	.400	.445	117	8	0			1.000	-2	O-69	0.1
1929	Phi-N	66	65	11	19	2	0	5	21	22	9	.292	.471	.554	144	5	0			.966	-0	O-11	0.4
1930	Phi-N	21	17	1	8	2	0	0	2	4	3	.471	.571	.588	169	2	0			1.000	-1	/O-3	0.1
Total	19	2002	6780	1024	1981	306	74	251	1005	690	721	.292	.365	.470	123	197	115	82		.973	16	*O-1818	7.1
■ **PAPA WILLIAMS**	Williams, Fred b: 7/17/13, Meridian, Miss. d: 11/2/93, Meridian, Miss. BR/TR, 6'1", 200 lbs. Deb: 4/19/45																						
1945	Cle-A	16	19	0	4	0	0	0	0	1	2	.211	.250	.211	36	-2	0	0	0	1.000	0	/1-3	-0.1
■ **GEORGE WILLIAMS**	Williams, George b: 10/23/39, Detroit, Mich. BR/TR, 5'11", 165 lbs. Deb: 7/16/61																						
1961	Phi-N	17	36	4	9	0	0	0	1	4	4	.250	.325	.250	56	-2	0	0	0	.967	2	2-15	0.1
1962	Hou-N	5	8	1	3	1	0	0	2	0	1	.375	.375	.500	143	0	0	0	0	1.000	0	/2-3	0.1
1964	KC-A	37	91	10	19	6	0	0	2	6	12	.209	.265	.275	49	-6	0	0	0	.970	-3	2-20/S-2,3-2,O-2	-0.8
Total	3	59	135	15	31	7	0	0	5	10	17	.230	.288	.281	56	-8	0	0	0	.970	-1	/2-38,O-2,3-2,S-2	-0.6
■ **GEORGE WILLIAMS**	Williams, George Erik b: 4/22/69, LaCrosse, Wis. BB/TR, 5'10", 190 lbs. Deb: 7/14/95																						
1995	Oak-A	29	79	13	23	5	1	3	14	11	21	.291	.391	.494	136	4	0	0	0	.956	-3	C-13,D-10	0.1
1996	Oak-A	56	132	17	20	5	0	3	10	28	32	.152	.313	.258	47	-10	0	0	0	.982	-3	C-43,D-11	-1.2
1997	Oak-A	76	201	30	58	9	1	3	22	35	46	.289	.399	.388	108	4	0	1	-1	.984	-11	C-67/D-1	-0.4
Total	3	161	412	60	101	19	2	9	46	74	99	.245	.369	.367	93	-2	0	1	-1	.980	-18	C-123/D-22	-1.5
■ **GERALD WILLIAMS**	Williams, Gerald Floyd b: 8/10/66, New Orleans, La. BR/TR, 6'2", 190 lbs. Deb: 9/15/92																						
1992	NY-A	15	27	7	8	2	0	3	6	0	3	.296	.296	.704	174	2	2	0	1	.913	-1	O-12	0.2
1993	NY-A	42	67	11	10	2	3	0	6	1	14	.149	.186	.269	21	-8	2	0	1	.956	-8	O-37/D-1	-1.6
1994	NY-A	57	86	19	25	8	0	4	13	4	17	.291	.322	.523	118	2	1	3	-2	.957	-11	O-43/D-2	-1.0
1995	*NY-A	100	182	33	45	18	2	6	28	22	34	.247	.332	.467	106	1	4	2	0	.993	-6	O-92/D-2	-0.6
1996	NY-A	99	233	37	63	15	4	5	30	15	39	.270	.325	.433	90	-4	7	8	-3	.978	-11	O-92/D-2	-1.8
	Mil-A	26	92	6	19	4	0	0	4	4	18	.207	.247	.250	25	-11	3	1	0	.987	4	O-26	-0.6
	Yr	125	325	43	82	19	4	5	34	19	57	.252	.304	.382	71	-15	10	9	-2	.981	-7	*O-118/D-2	-2.4
1997	Mil-A	155	566	73	143	32	2	10	41	19	90	.253	.284	.369	68	-27	23	9	2	.992	3	*O-154/D-1	-2.5
1998	*Atl-N	129	266	46	81	19	2	10	44	17	48	.305	.353	.504	116	6	11	5	0	.970	-12	*O-120	-0.6
Total	7	623	1519	232	394	100	13	38	172	82	263	.259	.305	.417	84	-38	53	28	-1	.981	-41	O-576/D-8	-8.5
■ **HARRY WILLIAMS**	Williams, Harry Peter b: 6/23/1890, Omaha, Neb. d: 12/21/63, Huntington Park, Cal. BR/TR, 6'1.5", 200 lbs. Deb: 8/7/13 F																						
1913	NY-A	27	82	18	21	3	1	1	12	15	10	.256	.378	.354	114	2	6			.981	-2	1-27	0.0
1914	NY-A	59	178	9	29	5	2	1	17	26	26	.163	.287	.230	56	-9	3	6	-3	.976	-5	1-58	-2.1
Total	2	86	260	27	50	8	3	2	29	41	36	.192	.316	.269	75	-7	9	6		.977	-7	/1-85	-2.1

■ **JIM WILLIAMS** Williams, James Alfred b: 4/29/47, Zachary, La. BR/TR, 6'2", 190 lbs. Deb: 9/8/69

YEAR	TM/L	G	AB	R	H	2B	3B	HR	RBI	BB	SO	AVG	OBP	SLG	PRO+	BR/A	SB	CS	SBR	FA	FR	G/POS	TPR
1969	SD-N	13	25	4	7	1	0	0	2	3	11	.280	.357	.320	95	-0	0	0	0	.900	-0	/O-6	-0.1
1970	SD-N	11	14	4	4	0	0	0	0	1	3	.286	.333	.286	70	-1	1	0	0	1.000	-1	/O-6	-0.1
Total	2	24	39	8	11	1	0	0	2	4	14	.282	.349	.308	86	-1	1	0	0	.938	-2	/O-12	-0.2

■ **JIMY WILLIAMS** Williams, James Francis b: 10/4/43, Santa Maria, Cal. BR/TR, 5'10", 170 lbs. Deb: 4/26/66 MC

YEAR	TM/L	G	AB	R	H	2B	3B	HR	RBI	BB	SO	AVG	OBP	SLG	PRO+	BR/A	SB	CS	SBR	FA	FR	G/POS	TPR
1966	StL-N	13	11	1	3	0	0	0	1	1	5	.273	.333	.273	71	-0	0	0	0	1.000	-2	/S-7,2-3	-0.2
1967	StL-N	1	2	0	0	0	0	0	0	0	1	.000	.000	.000	-99	-1	0	0	0	1.000	1	/S-1	0.0
Total	2	14	13	1	3	0	0	0	1	1	6	.231	.286	.231	46	-1	0	0	0	1.000	-1	/S-8,2-3	-0.2

■ **JIMMY WILLIAMS** Williams, James Thomas b: 12/20/1876, St.Louis, Mo. d: 1/16/65, St.Petersburg, Fla BR/TR, 5'9", 175 lbs. Deb: 4/15/1899

YEAR	TM/L	G	AB	R	H	2B	3B	HR	RBI	BB	SO	AVG	OBP	SLG	PRO+	BR/A	SB	CS	SBR	FA	FR	G/POS	TPR
1899	Pit-N	152	617	126	219	28	**27**	9	116	60		.355	.417	.532	160	50	26			.902	7	*3-152	5.2
1900	*Pit-N	106	416	73	110	15	11	5	68	32		.264	.323	.389	95	-4	18			.889	6	*3-103/S-4	0.3
1901	Bal-A	130	501	113	159	26	**21**	7	96	56		.317	.388	.495	138	25	21			.935	-2	*2-130	2.5
1902	Bal-A	125	498	83	156	27	**21**	8	83	36		.313	.361	.500	131	19	14			.945	4	*2-104,3-19/1-1	2.5
1903	NY-A	132	502	60	134	30	12	3	82	39		.267	.326	.392	108	5	9			**.957**	16	*2-132	2.6
1904	NY-A	146	559	62	147	31	7	2	74	38		.263	.314	.354	106	4	14			.951	17	*2-146	2.7
1905	NY-A	129	470	54	107	20	8	6	62	50		.228	.306	.343	95	-3	14			**.964**	6	*2-129	0.4
1906	NY-A	139	501	62	139	25	7	3	77	44		.277	.342	.373	112	7	8			.958	11	*2-139	2.0
1907	NY-A	139	504	53	136	17	11	2	63	35		.270	.319	.359	107	3	14			.966	-3	*2-139	-0.1
1908	StL-A	148	539	63	127	20	7	4	53	55		.236	.310	.321	104	3	7			.963	5	*2-148	0.8
1909	StL-A	110	374	32	73	3	6	0	22	29		.195	.257	.235	60	-17	6			.962	-6	*2-109	-2.9
Total	11	1456	5481	781	1507	242	138	49	796	474		.275	.337	.396	114	90	151			.955	61	*2-1176,3-274/S-4,1	16.0

■ **KEN WILLIAMS** Williams, Kenneth Roy b: 6/28/1890, Grants Pass, Ore. d: 1/22/59, Grants Pass, Ore. BL/TR, 6', 170 lbs. Deb: 7/14/15

YEAR	TM/L	G	AB	R	H	2B	3B	HR	RBI	BB	SO	AVG	OBP	SLG	PRO+	BR/A	SB	CS	SBR	FA	FR	G/POS	TPR
1915	Cin-N	71	219	22	53	10	4	0	16	15	20	.242	.297	.324	86	-4	4	3	-1	.948	2	O-62	-0.6
1916	Cin-N	10	27	1	3	0	0	0	1	2	5	.111	.172	.111	-12	-4	1			.955	1	O-10	-0.3
1918	StL-A	2	1	0	0	0	0	0	1	1	0	.000	.500	.000	53	0	0			.000	0	H	0.0
1919	StL-A	65	227	32	68	10	5	6	35	26	25	.300	.376	.467	133	10	7			.937	4	O-63	1.0
1920	StL-A	141	521	90	160	34	13	10	72	41	26	.307	.362	.480	118	12	18	8	1	.961	8	*O-138	1.0
1921	StL-A	146	547	115	190	31	7	24	117	74	42	.347	.429	.561	142	35	20	17	-4	.932	7	*O-145	2.5
1922	StL-A	153	585	128	194	34	11	**39**	**155**	74	31	.332	.413	.627	162	51	37	20	-1	.970	7	*O-153	4.4
1923	StL-A	147	555	106	198	37	12	29	91	79	32	.357	.439	.623	168	54	18	17	-5	.967	12	*O-145	4.8
1924	StL-A	114	398	78	129	21	4	18	84	69	17	.324	.425	.533	137	23	20	11	-1	.968	6	*O-109	1.9
1925	StL-A	102	411	83	136	31	5	25	105	37	14	.331	.390	**.613**	144	24	10	5	0	.955	5	*O-102	2.0
1926	StL-A	108	347	55	97	15	7	17	74	39	23	.280	.354	.510	118	7	5	4	-1	.948	1	O-92/2-1	0.1
1927	StL-A	131	423	70	136	23	6	17	74	57	30	.322	.403	.525	135	21	9	7	-2	.965	6	*O-113	1.8
1928	Bos-A	133	462	59	140	25	1	8	67	37	15	.303	.356	.413	104	2	4	9	-4	.971	-3	*O-127	-1.3
1929	Bos-A	74	139	21	48	14	2	3	21	15	7	.345	.409	.540	146	9	1	5	-3	.963	-5	O-39/1-2	0.0
Total	14	1397	4862	860	1552	285	77	196	913	566	287	.319	.393	.530	136	241	154	106		.958	49	*O-1298/1-2,2-1	17.3

■ **KENNY WILLIAMS** Williams, Kenneth Royal b: 4/6/64, Berkeley, Cal. BR/TR, 6'2", 187 lbs. Deb: 9/2/86

YEAR	TM/L	G	AB	R	H	2B	3B	HR	RBI	BB	SO	AVG	OBP	SLG	PRO+	BR/A	SB	CS	SBR	FA	FR	G/POS	TPR
1986	Chi-A	15	31	2	4	0	0	1	1	1	11	.129	.182	.226	10	-4	1	1	-0	1.000	0	O-10/D-1	-0.4
1987	Chi-A	116	391	48	110	18	2	11	50	10	83	.281	.315	.422	91	-6	21	10	0	.981	6	*O-115	-0.3
1988	Chi-A	73	220	18	35	4	2	8	28	10	64	.159	.223	.305	46	-16	6	5	-1	.959	-4	O-38,3-32/D-3	-2.3
1989	Det-A	94	258	29	53	5	1	6	23	18	63	.205	.270	.302	63	-13	9	4	0	.979	4	O-87/1-1,D-1	-1.1
1990	Det-A	57	83	10	11	2	0	0	5	3	24	.133	.172	.157	-7	-12	2	2	-1	1.000	-3	O-47/D-6	-1.7
	Tor-A	49	72	13	14	6	1	0	8	7	18	.194	.275	.306	61	-4	7	2	1	1.000	-7	O-30/D-9	-1.0
	Yr	106	155	23	25	8	1	0	13	10	42	.161	.222	.226	25	-16	9	4	0	1.000	-10	O-77,D-15	-2.7
1991	Tor-A	13	29	5	6	2	0	1	3	4	5	.207	.324	.379	90	-0	1	0	0	1.000	-0	/O-9,D-2	0.0
	Mon-N	34	70	11	19	5	2	0	1	3	22	.271	.311	.400	100	-0	2	1	0	.957	1	O-24	0.0
Total	6	451	1154	136	252	42	8	27	119	56	290	.218	.271	.339	66	-55	49	25	-0	.981	-3	O-360/3-32,D-22,1-1	-6.8

■ **MARK WILLIAMS** Williams, Mark Westley b: 7/28/53, Elmira, N.Y. BL/TL, 6', 180 lbs. Deb: 5/20/77

YEAR	TM/L	G	AB	R	H	2B	3B	HR	RBI	BB	SO	AVG	OBP	SLG	PRO+	BR/A	SB	CS	SBR	FA	FR	G/POS	TPR
1977	Oak-A	3	2	0	0	0	0	0	1	1	1	.000	.333	.000	0	-0	0	0	0	1.000	-0	/O-1	0.0

■ **MATT WILLIAMS** Williams, Matthew Derrick b: 11/28/65, Bishop, Cal. BR/TR, 6'2", 210 lbs. Deb: 4/11/87

YEAR	TM/L	G	AB	R	H	2B	3B	HR	RBI	BB	SO	AVG	OBP	SLG	PRO+	BR/A	SB	CS	SBR	FA	FR	G/POS	TPR
1987	SF-N	84	245	28	46	9	2	8	21	16	68	.188	.240	.339	54	-17	4	3	-1	.975	20	S-70,3-17	0.7
1988	SF-N	52	156	17	32	6	1	8	19	8	41	.205	.253	.410	91	-3	0	1	-1	.967	10	3-43,S-14	0.7
1989	*SF-N	84	292	31	59	18	1	18	50	14	72	.202	.244	.455	98	-3	1	2	-1	.961	6	3-73,S-30	0.4
1990	SF-N★	159	617	87	171	27	2	33	**122**	33	138	.277	.321	.488	124	17	7	4	-0	.959	4	*3-159	2.2
1991	SF-N	157	589	72	158	24	5	34	98	33	128	.268	.314	.499	129	19	5	5	-2	.964	9	*3-155/S-4	2.8
1992	SF-N	146	529	58	120	13	5	20	66	39	109	.227	.287	.384	94	-7	7	7	-2	.945	7	*3-144	-0.2
1993	SF-N	145	579	105	170	33	4	38	110	27	80	.294	.330	.561	137	27	1	3	-2	.970	3	*3-144	2.8
1994	SF-N★	112	445	74	119	16	3	**43**	96	33	87	.267	.321	.607	141	23	1	0	0	.963	9	*3-110	3.2
1995	SF-N†	76	283	53	95	17	1	23	65	30	58	.336	.403	.647	177	30	2	0	1	.958	6	3-74	3.5
1996	SF-N†	105	404	69	122	16	1	22	85	39	91	.302	.372	.510	135	20	1	2	-1	.951	2	3-92,1-13/S-1	1.9
1997	*Cle-A	151	596	86	157	32	3	32	105	34	108	.263	.308	.488	100	-3	12	4	1	.970	7	*3-151	0.6
1998	Ari-N	135	510	72	136	26	1	20	71	43	102	.267	.327	.439	96	-4	5	1	1	.972	7	*3-134	0.7
Total	12	1406	5245	752	1385	237	29	299	908	349	1082	.264	.315	.491	117	100	46	32	-5	.962	91	*3-1296,S-119/1-13	19.3

■ **OTTO WILLIAMS** Williams, Otto George b: 11/2/1877, Newark, N.J. d: 3/19/37, Omaha, Neb. BR/TR, 5'8", 165 lbs. Deb: 10/5/02 C

YEAR	TM/L	G	AB	R	H	2B	3B	HR	RBI	BB	SO	AVG	OBP	SLG	PRO+	BR/A	SB	CS	SBR	FA	FR	G/POS	TPR
1902	StL-N	2	5	0	2	0	0	0	2	1		.400	.500	.400	185	1	1			.813	1	/S-2	0.2
1903	StL-N	53	187	10	38	4	2	0	9	9		.203	.240	.246	40	-15	6			.885	-5	S-52/2-1	-1.7
	Chi-N	38	130	14	29	5	0	0	13	4		.223	.246	.262	46	-9	8			.937	5	S-26/2-7,1-3,3-1	-0.3
	Yr	91	317	24	67	9	2	0	22	13		.211	.242	.252	42	-24	14			.904	0	S-78/2-8,1-3,3-1	-2.0
1904	Chi-N	57	185	21	37	4	1	0	8	13		.200	.256	.232	51	-10	9			.973	-0	O-21,1-11,S-10,/23	-1.2
1906	Was-A	20	51	3	7	0	0	0	2	2		.137	.185	.137	1	-6	0			.897	1	/S-8,2-6,1-2,3-1	-0.6
Total	4	170	558	48	113	13	3	0	34	29		.203	.244	.237	43	-40	24			.905	1	/S-98,O-21,2-20,13	-3.6

■ **REGGIE WILLIAMS** Williams, Reginald Bernard b: 5/5/66, Laurens, S.C. BB/TR, 6'1", 180 lbs. Deb: 9/8/92

YEAR	TM/L	G	AB	R	H	2B	3B	HR	RBI	BB	SO	AVG	OBP	SLG	PRO+	BR/A	SB	CS	SBR	FA	FR	G/POS	TPR
1992	Cal-A	14	26	5	6	1	1	0	2	1	10	.231	.259	.346	68	-1	0	2	-1	1.000	-1	O-12/D-2	-0.4
1995	LA-N	15	11	2	1	0	0	0	1	2	3	.091	.231	.091	-12	-2	0	0	0	1.000	-4	O-14	-0.6
1998	Ana-A	29	38	7	13	1	0	1	5	7	12	.342	.457	.447	135	2	3	3	-1	1.000	-6	O-24/D-2	-0.4
Total	3	58	75	14	20	2	1	1	8	10	25	.267	.360	.360	94	-0	3	5	-2	1.000	-11	/O-50,D-4	-1.4

■ **REGGIE WILLIAMS** Williams, Reginald Dewayne b: 8/29/60, Memphis, Tenn. BR/TR, 5'11", 185 lbs. Deb: 9/2/85

YEAR	TM/L	G	AB	R	H	2B	3B	HR	RBI	BB	SO	AVG	OBP	SLG	PRO+	BR/A	SB	CS	SBR	FA	FR	G/POS	TPR
1985	LA-N	22	9	4	3	0	0	0	0	0	4	.333	.333	.333	90	-0	1	0	0	.900	-3	O-15	-0.3
1986	LA-N	128	303	35	84	14	2	4	32	23	57	.277	.332	.376	102	0	9	3	1	.984	-16	*O-124	-1.8
1987	LA-N	39	36	6	4	0	0	0	4	5	9	.111	.220	.111	-9	-6	1	1	-0	.913	-8	O-30	-1.4
1988	Cle-A	11	31	7	7	2	0	1	3	0	6	.226	.226	.387	66	-1	0	0	0	1.000	-2	O-11	-0.4
Total	4	200	379	52	98	16	2	5	39	28	76	.259	.313	.351	87	-7	11	4	1	.974	-29	O-180	-3.9

■ **DICK WILLIAMS** Williams, Richard Hirschfeld b: 5/7/29, St.Louis, Mo. BR/TR, 6', 190 lbs. Deb: 6/10/51 MC

YEAR	TM/L	G	AB	R	H	2B	3B	HR	RBI	BB	SO	AVG	OBP	SLG	PRO+	BR/A	SB	CS	SBR	FA	FR	G/POS	TPR
1951	Bro-N	23	60	5	12	3	1	1	5	4	10	.200	.250	.333	54	-4	0	0	0	1.000	-2	O-15	-0.6
1952	Bro-N	36	68	13	21	4	1	0	11	2	10	.309	.329	.397	99	-0	0	0	0	1.000	-2	O-25/1-1,3-1	-0.2
1953	*Bro-N	30	55	4	12	2	0	2	5	3	10	.218	.271	.364	62	-3	0	0	0	.923	-7	O-24	-1.1
1954	Bro-N	16	34	5	5	0	0	1	2	2	7	.147	.194	.235	11	-5	0	0	0	1.000	-4	O-14	-0.9
1956	Bro-N	7	7	0	2	0	0	0	0	0	1	.286	.286	.286	50	-0	0	0	0	.000	0	H	0.0
	Bal-A	87	353	45	101	18	4	11	37	30	40	.286	.342	.453	117	7	5	5	-2	.990	-3	O-81,1-10,2-10,/3-4	-0.2
1957	Bal-A	47	167	16	39	10	2	1	17	14	21	.234	.293	.335	76	-6	0	1	-1	1.000	0	O-26,3-15,1-12	-0.8

YEAR	TM/L	G	AB	R	H	2B	3B	HR	RBI	BB	SO	AVG	OBP	SLG	PRO+	BR/A	SB	CS	SBR	FA	FR	G/POS	TPR
	Cle-A	67	205	33	58	7	0	6	17	12	19	.283	.326	.405	99	-1	3	4	-2	.973	-3	O-37,3-19	-0.7
	Yr	114	372	49	97	17	2	7	34	26	40	.261	.311	.374	89	-7	3	5	-2	.984	-2	O-63,3-34,1-12	-1.5
1958	Bal-A	128	409	36	113	17	0	4	32	37	47	.276	.339	.347	94	-3	0	6	-4	1.000	-9	O-70,3-45,1-26,/2-7	-2.0
1959	KC-A	130	488	72	130	33	1	16	75	28	60	.266	.313	.436	102	-0	4	1	1	.957	-8	3-80,1-32,O-23,/2-3	-1.1
1960	KC-A	127	420	47	121	31	0	12	65	39	68	.288	.350	.448	113	7	0	0	0	.951	5	3-57,1-34,O-25	0.9
1961	Bal-A	103	310	37	64	15	2	8	24	20	38	.206	.255	.345	61	-19	0	4	-2	.968	-10	O-75,1-20/3-2	-3.6
1962	Bal-A	82	178	20	44	7	1	1	18	14	26	.247	.306	.315	72	-7	0	0	0	1.000	-2	O-29,1-21/3-4	-1.2
1963	Bos-A	79	136	15	35	8	0	2	12	15	25	.257	.331	.360	91	-1	0	0	0	.976	-6	3-17,1-11/O-7	-0.9
1964	Bos-A	61	69	10	11	2	0	5	11	7	10	.159	.247	.406	74	-3	0	0	0	1.000	5	1-21,3-13/O-5	0.2
Total	13	1023	2959	358	768	157	12	70	331	227	392	.260	.315	.392	92	-38	12	21	-9	.989	-46	O-456,3-257,1/2	-12.2

■ RINALDO WILLIAMS
Williams, Rinaldo Lewis b: 12/18/1893, Santa Cruz, Cal. d: 4/24/66, Cottonwood, Ariz. BL/TR, Deb: 10/8/14

YEAR	TM/L	G	AB	R	H	2B	3B	HR	RBI	BB	SO	AVG	OBP	SLG	PRO+	BR/A	SB	CS	SBR	FA	FR	G/POS	TPR
1914	Bro-F	4	15	1	4	2	0	0	0	0	0	.267	.267	.400	81	-1	0			.923	-0	/3-4	-0.1

■ BOB WILLIAMS
Williams, Robert Elias b: 4/27/1884, Monday, Ohio d: 8/6/62, Nelsonville, Ohio BR/TR, 6′, 190 lbs. Deb: 7/3/11

YEAR	TM/L	G	AB	R	H	2B	3B	HR	RBI	BB	SO	AVG	OBP	SLG	PRO+	BR/A	SB	CS	SBR	FA	FR	G/POS	TPR
1911	NY-A	20	47	3	9	2	0	0	8	5		.191	.269	.234	38	-4	1			.942	-1	C-20	-0.3
1912	NY-A	20	44	7	6	1	0	0	3	9		.136	.283	.159	26	-4	0			.930	-2	C-20	-0.5
1913	NY-A	6	19	0	3	0	0	0	0	1	3	.158	.200	.158	5	-2	0			.971	0	/C-6	-0.2
Total	3	46	110	10	18	3	0	0	11	15	3	.164	.264	.191	28	-10	1			.941	-2	/C-46	-1.0

■ TED WILLIAMS
Williams, Theodore Samuel "The Kid', "The Thumper" or "The Splendid Splinter"
b: 8/30/18, San Diego, Cal. BL/TR, 6′3″, 205 lbs. Deb: 4/20/39 MH

YEAR	TM/L	G	AB	R	H	2B	3B	HR	RBI	BB	SO	AVG	OBP	SLG	PRO+	BR/A	SB	CS	SBR	FA	FR	G/POS	TPR
1939	Bos-A	149	565	131	185	44	11	31	**145**	107	64	.327	.436	.609	158	51	2	1	0	.945	2	*O-149	4.3
1940	Bos-A★	144	561	**134**	193	43	14	23	113	96	54	.344	**.442**	.594	159	52	4	4	-1	.960	1	*O-143/P-1	4.0
1941	Bos-A★	143	456	**135**	185	33	3	**37**	120	**145**	27	**.406**	**.551**	**.735**	**232**	**98**	2	4	-2	.961	-5	*O-133	**7.9**
1942	Bos-A★	150	522	**141**	186	34	5	**36**	**137**	**145**	51	**.356**	**.499**	**.648**	**214**	**87**	3	2	-0	.988	3	*O-150	**8.1**
1946	*Bos-A★	150	514	**142**	176	37	8	38	123	**156**	44	.342	**.497**	**.667**	**211**	**85**	0	0	0	.971	-0	*O-150	**7.9**
1947	Bos-A★	156	528	**125**	181	40	9	**32**	**114**	**162**	47	**.343**	**.499**	**.634**	**199**	**79**	0	1	-1	.975	1	*O-156	**7.2**
1948	Bos-A★	137	509	124	188	**44**	3	25	127	**126**	41	**.369**	**.497**	**.615**	**185**	**68**	4	0	1	.983	0	*O-134	5.8
1949	Bos-A★	155	566	**150**	194	**39**	3	**43**	**159**	**162**	48	.343	**.490**	**.650**	**187**	**77**	1	1	-0	.983	3	*O-155	**6.7**
1950	Bos-A★	89	334	82	106	24	1	28	97	82	21	.317	.452	.647	163	32	3	0	1	.956	-4	O-86	2.4
1951	Bos-A★	148	531	109	169	28	4	30	126	**144**	45	.318	**.464**	**.556**	159	**49**	1	1	-0	.988	3	*O-147	**4.5**
1952	Bos-A	6	10	2	4	0	1	1	3	2	2	.400	.500	.900	264	2	0	0	0	1.000	-0	/O-2	0.2
1953	Bos-A†	37	91	17	37	6	0	13	34	19	10	.407	.509	.901	261	20	0	1	-1	.970	-4	O-26	1.5
1954	Bos-A★	117	386	93	133	23	1	29	89	**136**	32	.345	**.516**	.635	**193**	**58**	0	0	0	.982	-3	*O-115	**5.0**
1955	Bos-A★	98	320	77	114	21	3	28	83	91	24	.356	.501	.703	203	50	2	0	1	.989	-1	O-93	4.4
1956	Bos-A★	136	400	71	138	28	2	24	82	102	39	.345	**.479**	.605	164	41	0	0	0	.973	-4	*O-110	3.0
1957	Bos-A★	132	420	96	163	28	1	38	87	119	43	**.388**	**.528**	**.731**	**227**	82	0	1	-1	.995	-3	*O-125	7.1
1958	Bos-A★	129	411	81	135	23	2	26	85	98	49	**.328**	**.462**	.584	174	46	1	0	0	.957	-12	*O-114	2.9
1959	Bos-A★	103	272	32	69	15	0	10	43	52	27	.254	.377	.419	113	6	0	0	0	.970	-8	O-76	-0.5
1960	Bos-A★	113	310	56	98	15	0	29	72	75	41	.316	.454	.645	187	40	1	1	-0	.993	-2	O-87	3.3
Total	19	2292	7706	1798	2654	525	71	521	1839	2019	709	.344	.483	.634	186	1024	24	17	-3	.974	-34	*O-2151/P-1	85.7

■ WALT WILLIAMS
Williams, Walter Allen "No-Neck" b: 12/19/43, Brownwood, Tex. BR/TR, 5′6″, 185 lbs. Deb: 4/21/64 C

YEAR	TM/L	G	AB	R	H	2B	3B	HR	RBI	BB	SO	AVG	OBP	SLG	PRO+	BR/A	SB	CS	SBR	FA	FR	G/POS	TPR
1964	Hou-N	10	9	1	0	0	0	0	0	0	2	.000	.000	.000	-99	-2	1	0	0	1.000	-1	/O-5	-0.3
1967	Chi-A	104	275	35	66	16	3	3	15	17	20	.240	.289	.353	92	-3	3	2	-0	.983	-2	O-73	-1.0
1968	Chi-A	63	133	6	32	6	0	1	8	4	17	.241	.273	.308	75	-4	0	1	-1	1.000	-2	O-34	-1.0
1969	Chi-A	135	471	59	143	22	1	3	32	26	33	.304	.344	.374	96	-3	6	2	1	.985	2	*O-111	-0.6
1970	Chi-A	110	315	43	79	18	1	3	15	19	30	.251	.298	.343	73	-12	3	3	-1	.949	2	O-79	-1.5
1971	Chi-A	114	361	43	106	17	3	8	35	24	27	.294	.346	.424	114	6	5	5	-2	1.000	-2	O-90/3-1	-0.2
1972	Chi-A	77	221	22	55	7	1	2	11	13	20	.249	.291	.317	79	-6	6	1	1	.990	1	O-57/3-1	-0.7
1973	Cle-A	104	350	43	101	15	1	8	38	14	29	.289	.318	.406	101	-1	9	4	0	.970	5	O-61,D-26	0.1
1974	NY-A	43	53	5	6	0	0	0	3	1	10	.113	.130	.113	-30	-9	1	0	0	.955	-6	O-24/D-3	-1.6
1975	NY-A	82	185	27	52	5	1	5	16	8	23	.281	.321	.400	105	1	0	1	-1	.982	-3	O-31,D-17/2-6	-0.5
Total	10	842	2373	284	640	106	11	33	173	126	211	.270	.311	.365	91	-33	34	19	-1	.981	-6	O-565/D-46,2-6,3-2	-7.3

■ WASH WILLIAMS
Williams, Washington J. b: Philadelphia, Pa. d: 1/1890, Philadelphia, Pa. 5′11″, 180 lbs. Deb: 8/5/1884

YEAR	TM/L	G	AB	R	H	2B	3B	HR	RBI	BB	SO	AVG	OBP	SLG	PRO+	BR/A	SB	CS	SBR	FA	FR	G/POS	TPR
1884	Ric-a	2	8	0	2	0	0	0		0		.250	.250	.250	64	-0				.500	-1	/O-2	-0.1
1885	Chi-N	1	4	0	1	0	0	0	0	0	0	.250	.250	.250	54	-0				.500	-0	/O-1,P-1	-0.1
Total	2	3	12	0	3	0	0	0	0	0	0	.250	.250	.250	61	-1				.500	-1	/O-3,P-1	-0.2

■ BILLY WILLIAMS
Williams, William b: 6/13/33, Newberry, S.C. BL/TR, 6′3″, 195 lbs. Deb: 8/15/69

YEAR	TM/L	G	AB	R	H	2B	3B	HR	RBI	BB	SO	AVG	OBP	SLG	PRO+	BR/A	SB	CS	SBR	FA	FR	G/POS	TPR
1969	Sea-A	4	10	1	0	0	0	0	0	1	3	.000	.167	.000	-51	-2	0	0	0	1.000	1	/O-3	-0.2

■ WOODY WILLIAMS
Williams, Woodrow Wilson b: 8/21/12, Pamplin, Va. d: 2/24/95, Appomattox, Va. BR/TR, 5′11″, 175 lbs. Deb: 9/5/38

YEAR	TM/L	G	AB	R	H	2B	3B	HR	RBI	BB	SO	AVG	OBP	SLG	PRO+	BR/A	SB	CS	SBR	FA	FR	G/POS	TPR
1938	Bro-N	20	51	6	17	1	1	0	6	4	1	.333	.382	.392	111	1	1			.931	-7	S-18/3-1	-0.5
1943	Cin-N	30	69	8	26	2	1	0	11	1	3	.377	.386	.435	139	3	0			.986	1	2-12/3-7,S-5	0.5
1944	Cin-N	155	653	73	157	23	3	1	35	44	24	.240	.290	.289	66	-30	7			**.971**	15	*2-155	-0.6
1945	Cin-N	133	482	46	114	14	0	0	27	39	24	.237	.296	.266	58	-27	6			.969	-10	*2-133	-2.9
Total	4	338	1255	133	314	40	5	1	79	88	52	.250	.301	.292	69	-52	14			.971	-1	2-300/S-23,3-8	-3.5

■ ANTONE WILLIAMSON
Williamson, Anthony Joseph b: 7/18/73, Harbor City, Cal. BL/TR, 6′1″, 195 lbs. Deb: 5/31/97

YEAR	TM/L	G	AB	R	H	2B	3B	HR	RBI	BB	SO	AVG	OBP	SLG	PRO+	BR/A	SB	CS	SBR	FA	FR	G/POS	TPR
1997	Mil-A	24	54	2	11	3	0	0	6	4	8	.204	.259	.259	35	-5	0	1	-1	.977	-1	1-14/D-4	-0.7

■ NED WILLIAMSON
Williamson, Edward Nagle b: 10/24/1857, Philadelphia, Pa. d: 3/3/1894, Mountain Valley Springs, Ark BR/TR, 5′11″, 210 lbs. Deb: 5/1/1878

YEAR	TM/L	G	AB	R	H	2B	3B	HR	RBI	BB	SO	AVG	OBP	SLG	PRO+	BR/A	SB	CS	SBR	FA	FR	G/POS	TPR
1878	Ind-N	63	250	31	58	10	2	1	19	5	15	.232	.247	.300	91	-2				.867	-4	*3-63	-0.3
1879	Chi-N	80	320	66	94	20	13	1	36	24	31	.294	.343	.447	149	16				**.871**	17	*3-70/1-6,C-4	3.2
1880	Chi-N	75	311	65	78	20	2	0	31	15	26	.251	.285	.328	101	-0				**.893**	12	*3-63,C-11/2-3	1.4
1881	Chi-N	82	343	56	92	12	6	1	48	19	19	.268	.307	.347	100	-0				**.909**	22	*3-76/2-4,P-3,SC	2.2
1882	Chi-N	83	348	66	98	27	4	3	60	27	21	.282	.333	.408	130	11				**.881**	16	*3-83/P-1	2.6
1883	Chi-N	98	402	83	111	**49**	5	2	59	22	48	.276	.314	.438	118	8				.807	18	*3-97/C-3,P-1	2.1
1884	Chi-N	107	417	84	116	18	8	**27**	84	42	56	.278	.344	.554	164	28				.861	24	*3-99,C-10/P-2	4.7
1885	*Chi-N	113	407	87	97	16	5	3	65	**75**	60	.238	.357	.324	107	3				**.892**	12	*3-113/P-2,C-1	1.5
1886	*Chi-N	121	430	69	93	17	8	6	58	80	71	.216	.339	.335	92	-5	13			.869	-2	*S-121/C-4,P-2	-0.6
1887	Chi-N	127	439	77	117	20	14	9	78	73	57	.267	.377	.437	111	5	45			.890	-31	*S-127/P-1	-2.1
1888	Chi-N	132	452	75	113	9	14	8	73	65	71	.250	.352	.385	126	14	25			.884	-12	*S-132	0.5
1889	Chi-N	47	173	16	41	3	1	1	30	23	22	.237	.340	.283	71	-6	2			.844	-24	S-47	-2.4
1890	Chi-P	73	261	34	51	7	3	2	26	36	35	.195	.311	.268	53	-17	3			.809	-20	3-52,S-21	-2.8
Total	13	1201	4553	809	1159	228	85	64	667	506	532	.255	.332	.384	112	55	88			.866	28	3-716,S-450/CP21	10.0

■ HOWIE WILLIAMSON
Williamson, Nathaniel Howard b: 12/23/04, Little Rock, Ark. d: 8/15/69, Texarkana, Ark. BL/TL, 6′, 170 lbs. Deb: 7/7/28

YEAR	TM/L	G	AB	R	H	2B	3B	HR	RBI	BB	SO	AVG	OBP	SLG	PRO+	BR/A	SB	CS	SBR	FA	FR	G/POS	TPR
1928	StL-N	10	9	0	2	0	0	0	0	1	4	.222	.300	.222	38	-1	0			.000	0	H	-0.1

■ JULIUS WILLIGROD
Willigrod, Julius b: Iowa d: 11/27/06, San Francisco, Cal BL, Deb: 7/15/1882

YEAR	TM/L	G	AB	R	H	2B	3B	HR	RBI	BB	SO	AVG	OBP	SLG	PRO+	BR/A	SB	CS	SBR	FA	FR	G/POS	TPR
1882	Det-N	1	3	0	1	0	0	0	1	0	1	.333	.333	.333	115	0				1.000	-1	/S-1	0.0
	Cle-N	9	36	5	5	1	1	0	2	3	7	.139	.205	.222	38	-2				.813	-3	/O-9	-0.5
	Yr	10	39	5	6	1	1	0	3	3	8	.154	.214	.231	44	-2				.813	-3	/O-9,S-1	-0.5

■ HUGH WILLINGHAM
Willingham, Thomas Hugh b: 5/30/06, Dalhart, Tex. d: 6/15/88, ElReno, Okla. BR/TR, 6′, 180 lbs. Deb: 9/13/30

YEAR	TM/L	G	AB	R	H	2B	3B	HR	RBI	BB	SO	AVG	OBP	SLG	PRO+	BR/A	SB	CS	SBR	FA	FR	G/POS	TPR
1930	Chi-A	3	4	2	1	0	0	0	0	2	1	.250	.500	.250	100	0	0	0	0	1.000	-0	/2-1	0.0
1931	Phi-N	23	35	5	9	2	1	1	3	2	9	.257	.297	.457	93	-1	0			.875	0	/S-8,3-2,O-1	0.0
1932	Phi-N	4	2	0	0	0	0	0	0	0	0	.000	.000	.000	-89	-1	0			.000	0	H	-0.1

YEAR	TM/L	G	AB	R	H	2B	3B	HR	RBI	BB	SO	AVG	OBP	SLG	PRO+	BR/A	SB	CS	SBR	FA	FR	G/POS	TPR
1933	Phi-N	1	1	0	0	0	0	0	0	0	0	.000	.000	.000	-89	-0	0			.000	0	H	0.0
Total	4	31	42	7	10	2	1	1	3	4	10	.238	.304	.405	82	-1	0	0		.875	-0	/S-8,3-2,O-1,2-1	-0.1
■ WILLS Wills Deb: 5/14/1884																							
1884	Was-a	4	15	1	2	2	0	0		0		.133	.133	.267	31	-1				.889	2	/O-4	0.1
	KC-U	5	21	2	3	1	0	0		0		.143	.143	.190	0	-3				1.000	1	/O-5	-0.3
Total	1	9	36	3	5	3	0	0		0		.139	.139	.222	13	-4				.938	2	/O-9	-0.2
■ DAVE WILLS Wills, Davis Bowles b: 1/26/1877, Charlottesville, Va. d: 10/12/59, Washington, D.C. BL/TL, Deb: 6/8/1899																							
1899	Lou-N	24	94	15	21	3	1	0	12	2		.223	.240	.277	41	-8	1			.957	-3	1-24	-1.0
■ BUMP WILLS Wills, Elliott Taylor b: 7/27/52, Washington, D.C. BB/TR, 5'9", 177 lbs. Deb: 4/7/77 F																							
1977	Tex-A	152	541	87	155	28	6	9	62	65	96	.287	.363	.410	109	8	28	12	1	.982	3	*2-150/S-2,1-1,D-1	2.3
1978	Tex-A	157	539	78	135	17	4	9	57	63	91	.250	.333	.347	91	-5	52	14	7	.981	21	*2-156	3.5
1979	Tex-A	146	543	90	148	21	3	5	46	53	58	.273	.342	.350	88	-8	35	11	4	.976	8	*2-146	1.3
1980	Tex-A	146	578	102	152	31	5	5	58	51	71	.263	.326	.360	90	-7	34	9	5	.984	19	*2-144	2.5
1981	Tex-A	102	410	51	103	13	2	2	41	32	49	.251	.307	.307	82	-10	12	9	-2	.983	9	*2-101/D-1	0.4
1982	Chi-N	128	419	64	114	18	4	6	38	46	76	.272	.351	.377	101	2	35	10	5	.963	-18	*2-103	-0.7
Total	6	831	3030	472	807	128	24	36	302	310	441	.266	.338	.360	94	-20	196	65	20	.979	41	2-800/D-2,S-2,1-1	9.3
■ MAURY WILLS Wills, Maurice Morning b: 10/2/32, Washington, D.C. BB/TR, 5'11", 170 lbs. Deb: 6/6/59 FM																							
1959	*LA-N	83	242	27	63	5	2	0	7	13	27	.260	.298	.298	55	-15	7	3	0	.966	2	S-82	-0.7
1960	LA-N	148	516	75	152	15	2	0	27	35	47	.295	.343	.331	80	-13	**50**	12	**8**	.945	21	*S-145	2.7
1961	LA-N★	148	613	105	173	12	10	1	31	59	50	.282	.346	.339	76	-19	**35**	15	2	.959	12	*S-148	0.6
1962	LA-N★	165	695	130	208	13	**10**	6	48	51	57	.299	.349	.373	100	-0	**104**	13	**23**	.956	-5	*S-165	3.3
1963	*LA-N☆	134	527	83	159	19	3	0	34	44	48	.302	.357	.349	112	8	**40**	19	1	.959	-5	*S-109,3-33	1.3
1964	LA-N	158	630	81	173	15	5	2	34	41	73	.275	.319	.324	88	-11	**53**	17	**6**	.963	-8	*S-149/3-6	-0.2
1965	*LA-N★	158	650	92	186	14	7	0	33	40	64	.286	.331	.329	93	-6	**94**	31	10	.970	21	*S-155	3.7
1966	*LA-N★	143	594	60	162	14	2	1	39	34	60	.273	.314	.308	80	-16	38	24	-3	.967	9	*S-139/3-4	0.3
1967	Pit-N	149	616	92	186	12	9	3	45	31	44	.302	.336	.365	100	0	29	10	3	.948	9	*3-144/S-2	1.2
1968	Pit-N	153	627	76	174	12	6	0	31	45	57	.278	.327	.316	95	-3	52	21	3	.957	-9	*3-141,S-10	-0.9
1969	Mon-N	47	189	23	42	3	0	0	8	20	21	.222	.297	.238	51	-12	15	6	1	.950	-3	S-46/2-1	-0.9
	LA-N	104	434	57	129	7	8	4	39	39	40	.297	.357	.378	114	8	25	15	-1	.969	7	*S-104	2.6
	Yr	151	623	80	171	10	8	4	47	59	61	.274	.338	.335	94	-5	40	21	-1	.963	4	*S-150/2-1	1.7
1970	LA-N	132	522	77	141	19	3	0	34	50	34	.270	.334	.318	79	-15	28	13	1	.959	-19	*S-126/3-4	-1.9
1971	LA-N	149	601	73	169	14	3	3	44	40	44	.281	.326	.329	92	-7	15	8	-0	.978	1	*S-144/3-4	1.3
1972	LA-N	71	132	16	17	3	1	0	4	10	18	.129	.190	.167	2	-17	1	1	-0	.984	-4	S-31,3-26	-1.9
Total	14	1942	7588	1067	2134	177	71	20	458	552	684	.281	.331	.331	88	-118	586	208	51	.963	30	*S-1555,3-362/2-1	10.5
■ KID WILLSON Wilson, Frank Hoxie b: 11/3/1895, Bloomington, Neb. d: 4/17/64, Union Gap, Wash. BL/TL, 6'1", 190 lbs. Deb: 7/2/18																							
1918	Chi-A	4	1	2	0	0	0	0	0	1	1	.000	.500	.000	50	0	0			.000	0	H	0.0
1927	Chi-A	7	10	1	1	0	0	0	1	0	2	.100	.100	.100	-49	-2	0	0	0	1.000	0	/O-2	-0.2
Total	2	11	11	3	1	0	0	0	1	1	3	.091	.167	.091	-31	-2	0	0		1.000	0	/O-2	-0.2
■ WALT WILMOT Wilmot, Walter Robert b: 10/18/1863, Plover, Wis. d: 2/1/29, Chicago, Ill. BB/TR, Deb: 4/20/1888																							
1888	Was-N	119	473	61	106	16	9	4	43	23	55	.224	.263	.321	91	-5	46			.872	11	*O-119	0.3
1889	Was-N	108	432	88	125	19	**19**	9	57	51	32	.289	.367	.484	146	26	40			.927	15	*O-108	3.2
1890	Chi-N	139	571	114	159	15	13	**13**	99	64	44	.278	.353	.419	120	12	76			.938	13	*O-139	1.8
1891	Chi-N	121	498	102	137	14	10	11	71	55	21	.275	.353	.410	122	13	42			.922	-5	*O-121	0.4
1892	Chi-N	92	380	47	82	7	7	2	35	40	20	.216	.297	.287	76	-11	31			.903	2	O-92	-1.2
1893	Chi-N	94	392	69	118	14	14	3	61	40	8	.301	.367	.431	114	7	39			.873	-0	*O-93	0.1
1894	Chi-N	133	597	134	197	45	12	5	130	35	23	.330	.368	.471	96	-8	74			.872	-7	*O-133	-1.8
1895	Chi-N	108	466	86	132	16	6	8	72	30	19	.283	.327	.395	80	-16	28			.914	4	*O-108	-1.7
1897	NY-N	11	34	8	9	2	0	1	4	2		.265	.306	.412	91	-1	1			.938	0	/O-9	-0.1
1898	NY-N	35	138	16	33	4	2	2	22	9		.239	.286	.341	82	-4	4			.886	-5	O-34	-1.1
Total	10	960	3981	725	1098	152	92	58	594	349	222	.276	.337	.404	105	14	381			.903	28	O-956	-0.1
■ ARCHIE WILSON Wilson, Archie Clifton b: 11/25/23, Los Angeles, Cal. BR/TR, 6', 175 lbs. Deb: 9/18/51																							
1951	NY-A	4	4	0	0	0	0	0	0	1	0	.000	.200	.000	-44	-1	0	0	0	1.000	-0	/O-2	-0.1
1952	NY-A	3	2	0	1	0	0	0	1	0	0	.500	.500	.500	190	0	0	0	0	.000	0	H	0.0
	Was-A	26	96	8	20	2	3	0	14	5	11	.208	.255	.292	54	-6	0	0	0	.971	1	O-24	-0.7
	Bos-A	18	38	1	10	3	0	0	2	2	3	.263	.300	.342	73	-1	0	0	0	.944	-2	O-13	-0.4
	Yr	47	136	9	31	5	3	0	17	7	14	.228	.271	.309	61	-8	0	0	0	.966	-1	O-37	-1.1
Total	2	51	140	9	31	5	3	0	17	7	14	.221	.268	.300	58	-8	0	0	0	.967	-1	/O-39	-1.2
■ ART WILSON Wilson, Arthur Earl "Dutch" b: 12/11/1885, Macon, Ill. d: 6/12/60, Chicago, Ill. BR/TR, 5'8", 170 lbs. Deb: 9/29/08																							
1908	NY-N	1	0	0	0	0	0	0	0	0		—	—	—	—	0	0			.000	0	R	0.0
1909	NY-N	19	42	4	10	2	1	0	5	4		.238	.304	.333	96	-0	0			.985	-4	C-19	-0.4
1910	NY-N	26	52	10	14	4	1	0	5	9	6	.269	.387	.385	125	2	2			.975	-1	C-25/1-1	0.3
1911	*NY-N	66	109	17	33	9	1	1	17	19	12	.303	.411	.431	132	5	6			.963	-6	C-64	0.3
1912	*NY-N	65	121	17	35	6	0	3	19	13	14	.289	.358	.413	107	1	2			.960	1	C-61	0.5
1913	*NY-N	54	79	5	15	0	1	0	8	11	11	.190	.289	.215	45	-5	1			.965	6	C-49	0.3
1914	Chi-F	137	440	78	128	31	8	10	64	70	80	.291	.394	.466	142	20	13			.974	14	*C-132	**4.6**
1915	Chi-F	96	269	44	82	11	2	7	31	65	38	.305	.442	.439	157	21	8			.980	-8	C-87	2.0
1916	Pit-N	53	128	11	33	5	2	1	12	13	27	.258	.331	.352	109	2	4			.981	-9	C-39	-0.5
	Chi-N	36	114	5	22	3	1	0	5	6	14	.193	.233	.237	40	-8	1			.953	-4	C-34	-1.1
	Yr	89	242	16	55	8	3	1	17	19	41	.227	.286	.298	76	-7	5			.967	-13	C-73	-1.6
1917	Chi-N	81	211	17	45	9	2	2	25	32	36	.213	.322	.303	85	-3	6			.968	7	C-75	1.2
1918	Bos-N	89	280	15	69	8	2	0	19	24	31	.246	.310	.289	87	-4	5			.977	-10	C-85	-0.8
1919	Bos-N	71	191	14	49	8	1	0	16	25	19	.257	.346	.309	102	1	2			.977	-2	C-64/1-1	0.5
1920	Bos-N	16	19	0	1	0	0	0	0	1	1	.053	.143	.053	-44	-4	0	0	0	1.000	-2	/3-6,C-2	-0.5
1921	Cle-A	2	1	0	0	0	0	0	0	0	0	.000	.000	.000	-99	-0	0	0	0	1.000	0	/C-2	0.0
Total	14	812	2056	237	536	96	22	24	226	292	289	.261	.357	.364	110	28	50	0		.972	-18	C-738/3-6,1-2	6.4
■ ARTIE WILSON Wilson, Arthur Lee b: 10/28/20, Springfield, Ala. BL/TR, 5'10", 162 lbs. Deb: 4/18/51																							
1951	NY-N	19	22	2	4	0	0	0	1	2	1	.182	.250	.182	18	-2	2	0	1	1.000	3	/2-3,S-3,1-2	0.1
■ CHARLIE WILSON Wilson, Charles Woodrow "Swamp Baby" b: 1/13/05, Clinton, S.C. d: 12/19/70, Rochester, N.Y. BB/TR, 5'10.5", 178 lbs. Deb: 4/14/31																							
1931	Bos-N	16	58	7	11	4	0	1	11	3	5	.190	.230	.310	45	-5	0			.917	-2	3-14	-0.6
1932	StL-N	24	96	7	19	3	3	1	2	3	8	.198	.222	.323	43	-8	0			.935	-7	S-24	-1.2
1933	StL-N	1	1	0	0	0	0	0	0	0	1	.000	.000	.000	-95	-0	0			.000	0	/S-1	0.0
1935	StL-N	16	31	1	10	0	0	0	1	2	2	.323	.364	.323	83	-1	0			.933	-1	/3-8	-0.1
Total	4	57	186	15	40	7	3	2	14	8	16	.215	.247	.317	50	-13	0			.935	-10	/S-25,3-22	-1.9
■ CRAIG WILSON Wilson, Craig b: 11/28/64, Annapolis, Md. BR/TR, 5'11", 175 lbs. Deb: 9/6/89																							
1989	StL-N	6	4	1	1	0	0	0	1	1	2	.250	.400	.250	87	-0	0	0	0	.500	-0	/3-2	0.0
1990	StL-N	55	121	13	30	2	0	0	7	8	14	.248	.295	.264	55	-7	0	2	-1	.971	-0	3-13,O-13/2-9,1-1	-0.9
1991	StL-N	60	82	5	14	2	0	0	13	6	10	.171	.227	.195	20	-9	0	0	0	.905	-1	3-12/O-5,1-4,2-3	-1.1
1992	StL-N	61	106	6	33	6	0	0	13	10	18	.311	.371	.368	113	2	1	2	-1	.970	-3	3-18,2-11/O-3	-0.2
1993	KC-A	21	49	6	13	1	0	1	3	7	6	.265	.357	.347	85	-1	1	1	-0	1.000	-3	3-15/2-1,O-1	-0.4
Total	5	203	362	31	91	11	0	1	37	32	50	.251	.312	.290	68	-15	2	5	-2	.957	-8	/3-60,2-24,O-22,1-5	-2.6

YEAR	TM/L	G	AB	R	H	2B	3B	HR	RBI	BB	SO	AVG	OBP	SLG	PRO+	BR/A	SB	CS	SBR	FA	FR	G/POS	TPR

■ CRAIG WILSON   Wilson, Craig Franklin   b: 9/3/70, Chicago, Ill.   BR/TR, 6', 185 lbs.   Deb: 9/5/98

| 1998 | Chi-A | 13 | 47 | 14 | 22 | 5 | 0 | 3 | 10 | 3 | 6 | .468 | .500 | .766 | 229 | 9 | 1 | 0 | 0 | 1.000 | -3 | /S-8,2-4,3-2 | 0.6 |

■ DAN WILSON   Wilson, Daniel Allen   b: 3/25/69, Arlington Heights, Ill.   BR/TR, 6'3", 190 lbs.   Deb: 9/7/92

1992	Cin-N	12	25	2	9	1	0	0	3	3	8	.360	.429	.400	132	1	0	0	0	1.000	0	/C-9	0.2
1993	Cin-N	36	76	6	17	3	0	0	8	9	16	.224	.306	.263	54	-5	0	0	0	.994	-0	C-35	-0.4
1994	Sea-A	91	282	24	61	14	2	3	27	10	57	.216	.246	.312	42	-25	1	2	-1	.986	6	C-91	-1.4
1995	*Sea-A	119	399	40	111	22	3	9	51	33	63	.278	.336	.416	94	-4	2	1	0	.995	12	*C-119	1.4
1996	Sea-A★	138	491	51	140	24	0	18	83	32	88	.285	.333	.444	94	-5	1	2	-1	.996	-2	*C-135	-0.1
1997	*Sea-A	146	508	66	137	31	1	15	74	39	72	.270	.328	.423	95	-4	7	2	1	.995	1	*C-144	0.6
1998	Sea-A	96	325	39	82	17	1	9	44	24	56	.252	.314	.394	82	-9	2	1	0	.994	-9	C-94	-1.0
Total	7	638	2106	228	557	112	7	54	290	150	360	.264	.318	.401	84	-51	13	8	-1	.994	6	C-627	-0.7

■ DESI WILSON   Wilson, Desi Bernard   b: 5/9/69, Glen Cove, N.Y.   BL/TL, 6'7", 230 lbs.   Deb: 8/7/96

| 1996 | SF-N | 41 | 118 | 10 | 32 | 2 | 0 | 2 | 12 | 12 | 27 | .271 | .338 | .339 | 83 | -3 | 0 | 2 | -1 | .984 | -1 | 1-33 | -0.8 |

■ EDDIE WILSON   Wilson, Edward Francis   b: 9/7/09, Hamden, Conn.   d: 4/11/79, Hamden, Conn.   BL/TL, 5'11", 165 lbs.   Deb: 6/21/36

1936	Bro-N	52	173	28	60	8	1	3	25	14	25	.347	.402	.457	129	7	3			.926	-5	O-47	0.0
1937	Bro-N	36	54	11	12	4	1	1	8	17	14	.222	.408	.389	116	2	1			.966	-3	O-21	-0.2
Total	2	88	227	39	72	12	2	4	33	31	39	.317	.404	.441	126	10	4			.936	-9	/O-68	-0.2

■ ENRIQUE WILSON   Wilson, Enrique (Martes)   b: 7/27/75, Santo Domingo, D.R.   BB/TR, 5'11", 160 lbs.   Deb: 9/24/97

1997	Cle-A	5	15	2	5	0	0	0	2	0	2	.333	.333	.333	72	-1	0	0	0	.941	2	/S-4,2-1	0.1
1998	*Cle-A	32	90	13	29	6	0	2	12	4	8	.322	.358	.456	106	1	2	4	-2	.989	1	2-22,S-10/3-2	0.1
Total	2	37	105	15	34	6	0	2	14	4	10	.324	.355	.438	101	0	2	4	-2	.989	3	/2-23,S-14,3-2	0.2

■ FRANK WILSON   Wilson, Francis Edward "Squash"   b: 4/20/01, Malden, Mass.   d: 11/25/74, Leicester, Mass.   BL/TR, 6', 185 lbs.   Deb: 6/20/24

1924	Bos-N	61	215	20	51	7	0	1	15	23	22	.237	.311	.284	63	-11	3	4	-2	.973	3	O-55	-1.3
1925	Bos-N	12	31	3	13	1	1	0	4	1		.419	.486	.516	171	4	2	1	0	1.000	1	O-10	0.3
1926	Bos-N	87	236	22	56	11	3	0	23	20	21	.237	.300	.309	70	-10	3			.934	1	O-56	-1.3
1928	Cle-A	2	1	0	0	0	0	0	0	1	0	.000	.500	.000	41	0	0	0	0	.000	0	H	0.0
	StL-A	6	5	1	0	0	0	0	0	0	0	.000	.000	.000	-97	-1	0	0	0	.000	-0	/O-1	-0.2
	Yr	8	6	1	0	0	0	0	0	1	0	.000	.143	.000	-58	-1	0	0	0	.000	-0	/O-1	-0.2
Total	4	168	488	46	120	19	4	1	38	48	44	.246	.315	.307	72	-19	8	5		.958	4	O-122	-2.5

■ TUG WILSON   Wilson, George Archer   b: 1860, Brooklyn, N.Y.   d: 11/28/14, New York, N.Y.   5'8", 175 lbs.   Deb: 5/9/1884

| 1884 | Bro-a | 24 | 82 | 13 | 19 | 4 | 0 | 0 | | 5 | | .232 | .276 | .280 | 81 | -2 | | | | .826 | -3 | O-12,C-10/1-3,2-1 | -0.4 |

■ SQUANTO WILSON   Wilson, George Francis   b: 3/29/1889, Old Town, Me.   d: 3/26/67, Winthrop, Maine   BB/TR, 5'9.5", 170 lbs.   Deb: 10/2/11

1911	Det-A	5	16	2	3	0	0	0	2	0		.188	.278	.188	29	-1	0			.900	-1	/C-5	-0.2
1914	Bos-A	1	0	0	0	0	0	0	0	0		—	—	—	—	0	0			.000	0	/1-1	0.0
Total	2	6	16	2	3	0	0	0	2	0	0	.188	.278	.188	29	-1	0			.900	-1	/C-5,1-1	-0.2

■ ICEHOUSE WILSON   Wilson, George Peacock   b: 9/14/12, Maricopa, Cal.   d: 10/13/73, Moraga, Cal.   BR/TR, 6', 186 lbs.   Deb: 5/31/34

| 1934 | Det-A | 1 | 1 | 0 | 0 | 0 | 0 | 0 | 0 | 0 | 0 | .000 | .000 | .000 | -99 | -0 | 0 | | | .000 | 0 | H | 0.0 |

■ GEORGE WILSON   Wilson, George Washington "Teddy"   b: 8/30/25, Cherryville, N.C.   d: 10/29/74, Gastonia, N.C.   BL/TR, 6'1.5", 185 lbs.   Deb: 4/15/52

1952	Chi-A	8	9	0	1	0	0	0	1	1	2	.111	.200	.111	-12	-1	0	0	0	1.000	0	/O-1	-0.1
	NY-N	62	112	9	27	7	0	2	16	3	14	.241	.261	.357	69	-5	0	0	0	.923	-3	O-21/1-2	-0.9
1953	NY-N	11	8	0	1	0	0	0	2	2		.125	.364	.125	34	-1	0	0	0	.000	0	H	-0.1
1956	NY-N	53	68	5	9	1	0	1	2	5	14	.132	.192	.191	3	-9	0	0	0	1.000	0	/O-8	-1.0
	*NY-A	11	12	1	2	0	0	0	3	0		.167	.333	.167	37	-1	0	0	0	.750	-2	/O-6	-0.3
Total	3	145	209	15	40	8	0	4	24	14	32	.191	.246	.273	44	-17	0	0	0	.932	-5	/O-36,1-2	-2.4

■ GLENN WILSON   Wilson, Glenn Dwight   b: 12/22/58, Baytown, Tex.   BR/TR, 6'1", 190 lbs.   Deb: 4/15/82

1982	Det-A	84	322	39	94	15	1	12	34	14	51	.292	.323	.457	111	4	2	3	-1	.987	7	O-80/D-4	0.8
1983	Det-A	144	503	55	135	25	6	11	65	25	79	.268	.307	.408	97	-3	1	1	-0	.988	-7	*O-143	-1.5
1984	Phi-N	132	341	28	82	21	3	6	31	17	56	.240	.279	.372	80	-10	7	1	2	.968	-12	*O-109/3-4	-2.4
1985	Phi-N★	161	608	73	167	39	5	14	102	35	117	.275	.314	.424	102	-0	7	4	-0	.968	20	*O-158	1.6
1986	Phi-N	155	584	70	158	30	4	15	84	42	91	.271	.324	.413	98	-2	5	1	1	.989	21	*O-154	1.5
1987	Phi-N	154	569	55	150	21	2	14	54	38	82	.264	.311	.381	80	-17	3	6	-3	.968	15	*O-154/P-1	-0.9
1988	Sea-A	78	284	28	71	10	1	3	17	15	52	.250	.288	.324	68	-12	1	1	-0	.980	1	O-75/D-2	-1.5
	Pit-N	37	126	11	34	8	0	2	15	3	18	.270	.292	.381	93	-2	0	0	0	.985	1	O-35	-0.4
1989	Pit-N	100	330	42	93	20	4	9	49	32	39	.282	.347	.448	130	12	1	4	-2	.977	1	O-85,1-10	0.9
	Hou-N	28	102	8	22	6	0	2	15	5	14	.216	.252	.333	68	-5	0	1	-1	.966	5	O-25	-0.1
	Yr	128	432	50	115	26	4	11	64	37	53	.266	.326	.421	116	8	1	5	-3	.974	6	*O-110,1-10	0.8
1990	Hou-N	118	368	42	90	14	0	10	55	26	64	.245	.296	.364	83	-9	0	3	-2	.975	7	*O-108/1-1	-0.6
1993	Pit-N	10	14	0	2	0	0	0	0	0	6	.143	.143	.143	-23	-2	0	0	0	.875	0	/O-5	-0.2
Total	10	1201	4151	451	1098	209	26	98	521	253	672	.265	.309	.398	93	-46	27	25	-7	.977	57	*O-1131/1-11,D3P	-2.8

■ GRADY WILSON   Wilson, Grady Herbert   b: 11/23/22, Columbus, Ga.   BR/TR, 6'0.5", 170 lbs.   Deb: 5/15/48

| 1948 | Pit-N | 12 | 10 | 1 | 1 | 1 | 0 | 0 | 1 | 0 | 3 | .100 | .100 | .200 | -20 | -2 | 0 | | | .846 | 1 | /S-7 | -0.1 |

■ HENRY WILSON   Wilson, Henry C.   b: 4/8/1877, Baltimore, Md.   Deb: 10/12/1898

| 1898 | Bal-N | 1 | 2 | 0 | 0 | 0 | 0 | 0 | 0 | 1 | | .000 | .333 | .000 | -2 | -0 | 0 | | | 1.000 | 0 | /C-1 | 0.0 |

■ JIMMIE WILSON   Wilson, James "Ace"   b: 7/23/1900, Philadelphia, Pa.   d: 5/31/47, Bradenton, Fla.   BR/TR, 6'1.5", 200 lbs.   Deb: 4/17/23   MC

1923	Phi-N	85	252	27	66	9	0	1	25	4	17	.262	.276	.310	49	-19	4	2	0	.960	-3	C-69/O-2	-1.9
1924	Phi-N	95	280	32	78	16	3	6	39	17	12	.279	.322	.421	87	-6	5	4	-1	.968	5	C-82/1-2,O-1	0.3
1925	Phi-N	108	335	42	110	19	3	3	54	32	25	.328	.390	.430	100	1	5	3	-0	.982	-9	C-89/O-1	-0.3
1926	Phi-N	90	279	40	85	10	2	4	32	25	20	.305	.362	.398	99	-0	3			.950	0	C-79	0.5
1927	Phi-N	128	443	50	122	15	2	2	45	34	15	.275	.330	.332	77	-14	13			.975	-19	*C-124	-2.4
1928	Phi-N	21	70	11	21	4	1	0	13	9	8	.300	.380	.386	97	-0	3			.990	2	C-20	0.3
	*StL-N	120	411	45	106	26	2	2	50	45	24	.258	.333	.345	76	-14	9			.983	1	*C-120	-0.3
	Yr	141	481	56	127	30	3	2	63	54	32	.264	.340	.351	79	-14	12			.985	2	*C-140	0.0
1929	StL-N	120	394	59	128	27	8	4	71	43	19	.325	.394	.464	111	7	4			.972	5	*C-119	2.0
1930	*StL-N	107	362	54	115	25	7	1	58	28	17	.318	.384	.434	90	-6	8			.987	10	*C-99	1.2
1931	*StL-N	115	383	45	105	20	2	0	51	28	15	.274	.332	.337	77	-12	5			.985	11	*C-110	0.6
1932	StL-N	92	274	36	68	16	2	2	28	15	18	.248	.290	.343	67	-13	9			.982	2	C-75/1-3,2-1	-0.7
1933	StL-N★	113	369	34	94	17	0	1	45	23	33	.255	.300	.309	71	-14	6			.982	2	*C-107	-0.6
1934	Phi-N	91	277	25	81	11	0	3	35	14	10	.292	.326	.365	75	-10	1			.987	6	C-77/1-1,2-1,M	-0.4
1935	Phi-N★	93	290	38	81	20	0	1	37	19	19	.279	.326	.359	76	-10	4			.982	8	C-78/2-1,M	0.2
1936	Phi-N	85	230	25	64	12	0	1	27	12	21	.278	.314	.343	70	-10	5			.960	-6	C-63/1-1,M	-1.3
1937	Phi-N	39	87	15	24	3	0	0	8	6	4	.276	.323	.345	75	-3	1			.978	-1	C-22/1-2,M	-0.4
1938	Phi-N	3	2	0	0	0	0	0	0	0	0	.000	.000	.000	-99	-1	0			1.000	0	/C-1,M	0.0
1939	Cin-N	3	3	0	1	0	0	0	0	0	0	.333	.333	.333	79	-0	0			.000	0	/C-1	0.0
1940	*Cin-N	16	37	2	9	2	0	0	3	2	1	.243	.282	.297	59	-2	1			.982	3	C-16	0.2
Total	18	1525	4778	580	1358	252	32	32	621	356	280	.284	.336	.370	82	-123	86	9		.977	11	*C-1351/1-9,O-4,2-3	-3.0

■ GARY WILSON   Wilson, James Garrett   b: 1/12/1877, Baltimore, Md.   d: 5/1/69, Randallstown, Md.   BR/TR, 5'7", 168 lbs.   Deb: 9/27/02

| 1902 | Bos-A | 2 | 8 | 0 | 1 | 0 | 0 | 0 | 0 | 1 | 0 | .125 | .125 | .125 | -30 | -1 | 0 | | | .800 | 0 | /2-2 | -0.1 |

YEAR	TM/L	G	AB	R	H	2B	3B	HR	RBI	BB	SO	AVG	OBP	SLG	PRO+	BR/A	SB	CS	SBR	FA	FR	G/POS	TPR

■ JIM WILSON   Wilson, James George b: 12/29/60, Corvallis, Ore. BR/TR, 6'3", 230 lbs. Deb: 9/13/85

1985	Cle-A	4	14	2	5	0	0	0	4	1	3	.357	.400	.357	110	0	0	0	0	1.000	-1	/1-2,D-2	-0.1
1989	Sea-A	5	8	0	0	0	0	0	0	0	3	.000	.000	.000	-97	-2	0	0	0	.000	0	/D-5	-0.2
Total	2	9	22	2	5	0	0	0	4	1	6	.227	.261	.227	36	-2	0	0	0	1.000	-1	/D-7,1-2	-0.3

■ CHIEF WILSON   Wilson, John Owen b: 8/21/1883, Austin, Tex. d: 2/22/54, Bertram, Tex. BL/TR, 6'2", 185 lbs. Deb: 4/15/08

1908	Pit-N	144	529	47	120	8	7	3	43	22		.227	.260	.285	74	-16	12			.955	1	*O-144	-2.5
1909	*Pit-N	154	569	64	155	22	12	4	59	19		.272	.303	.374	102	-2	17			.957	6	*O-154	-0.2
1910	Pit-N	146	536	59	148	14	13	4	50	21	68	.276	.312	.373	94	-6	8			.972	3	*O-146	-1.1
1911	Pit-N	148	544	72	163	34	12	12	107	41	55	.300	.353	.472	125	15	10			.977	7	*O-146	1.5
1912	Pit-N	152	583	80	175	19	36	11	95	35	67	.300	.342	.513	134	22	16			.961	1	*O-152	1.6
1913	Pit-N	155	580	71	154	12	14	10	73	32	62	.266	.307	.386	102	-1	9			.969	6	*O-155	-0.3
1914	StL-N	154	580	64	150	27	12	9	73	32	66	.259	.302	.393	107	2	14			.983	17	*O-154	1.3
1915	StL-N	107	348	33	96	13	6	3	39	19	43	.276	.321	.374	110	3	8	15	-7	.984	12	*O-105	0.5
1916	StL-N	120	355	30	85	8	2	3	32	20	46	.239	.289	.299	81	-8	4			.955	-11	*O-113	-2.7
Total	9	1280	4624	520	1246	157	114	59	571	241	407	.269	.311	.391	105	-3	99	15		.968	42	*O-1269	-1.9

■ LES WILSON   Wilson, Lester Wilbur "Tug" b: 7/17/1885, St.Louis, Mich. d: 4/4/69, Edmonds, Wash. BL/TR, 5'11", 170 lbs. Deb: 7/15/11

| 1911 | Bos-A | 5 | 7 | 0 | 0 | 0 | 0 | 0 | 0 | 0 | 2 | .000 | .222 | .000 | -36 | -1 | 0 | | | 1.000 | -1 | /O-3 | -0.2 |

■ HACK WILSON   Wilson, Lewis Robert b: 4/26/1900, Ellwood City, Pa. d: 11/23/48, Baltimore, Md. BR/TR, 5'6", 190 lbs. Deb: 9/29/23 H

1923	NY-N	3	10	0	2	0	0	0	0	0	1	.200	.200	.200	6	-1	0	0	0	.857	-1	/O-3	-0.2
1924	*NY-N	107	383	62	113	19	12	10	57	44	46	.295	.369	.486	131	16	4	3	-1	.967	-7	*O-103	0.2
1925	NY-N	62	180	28	43	7	4	6	30	21	33	.239	.322	.422	92	-3	5	2	0	.975	-11	O-50	-1.5
1926	Chi-N	142	529	97	170	36	8	21	109	69	61	.321	.406	.539	150	38	10			.973	2	*O-140	3.0
1927	Chi-N	146	551	119	175	30	12	30	129	71	70	.318	.401	.579	160	45	13			.967	-1	*O-146	3.5
1928	Chi-N	145	520	89	163	32	9	31	120	77	94	.313	.404	.588	159	44	4			.960	-10	*O-143	2.3
1929	*Chi-N	150	574	135	198	30	5	39	159	78	83	.345	.425	.618	155	49	3			.970	-3	*O-150	3.2
1930	Chi-N	155	585	146	208	35	6	56	190	105	84	.356	.454	.723	177	74	3			.951	-7	*O-155	4.8
1931	Chi-N	112	395	66	103	22	4	13	61	63	69	.261	.362	.435	112	7	1			.978	-5	*O-103	-0.5
1932	Bro-N	135	481	77	143	37	5	23	123	51	85	.297	.366	.538	142	28	2			.955	-9	*O-125	1.1
1933	Bro-N	117	360	41	96	13	2	9	54	52	50	.267	.359	.389	119	10	7			.963	-7	O-90/2-5	-0.1
1934	Bro-N	67	172	24	45	5	0	6	27	40	33	.262	.401	.395	120	7	0			.974	-3	O-43	0.2
	Phi-N	7	20	0	2	0	0	0	3	3	4	.100	.217	.100	-11	-3	0			1.000	-1	/O-6	-0.4
	Yr	74	192	24	47	5	0	6	30	43	37	.245	.383	.365	105	3	0			.977	-4	O-49	-0.2
Total	12	1348	4760	884	1461	266	67	244	1062	674	713	.307	.395	.545	145	311	52	5		.965	-62	*O-1257/2-5	15.6

■ TACK WILSON   Wilson, Michael b: 5/16/55, Shreveport, La. BR/TR, 5'10", 185 lbs. Deb: 4/9/83

1983	Min-A	5	4	4	1	1	0	0	1	0	0	.250	.250	.500	97	-0	0	0	0	1.000	-0	/O-1,D-2	0.0
1987	Cal-A	7	2	5	1	0	0	0	0	1	0	.500	.667	.500	224	1	0	0	0	1.000	-1	/O-4,D-2	-0.1
Total	2	12	6	9	2	1	0	0	1	1	0	.333	.429	.500	150	0	0	0	0	1.000	-2	/O-5,D-4	-0.1

■ NIGEL WILSON   Wilson, Nigel Edward b: 1/12/70, Oshawa, Ont., Can. BL/TL, 6'1", 185 lbs. Deb: 9/8/93

1993	Fla-N	7	16	0	0	0	0	0	0	0	11	.000	.000	.000	-95	-4	0	0	0	1.000	-0	/O-3	-0.5
1995	Cin-N	5	7	0	0	0	0	0	0	0	4	.000	.000	.000	-99	-2	0	0	0	1.000	-0	/O-2	-0.2
1996	*Cle-A	10	12	2	3	0	0	2	5	1	6	.250	.308	.750	157	1	0	0	0	.000	-0	/O-1,D-3	0.0
Total	3	22	35	2	3	0	0	2	5	1	21	.086	.111	.257	-7	-5	0	0	0	1.000	-1	/O-6,D-3	-0.7

■ PARKE WILSON   Wilson, Parke Asel b: 10/26/1867, Keithsburg, Ill. d: 12/20/34, Hermosa Beach, Cal BR/TR, 5'11", 166 lbs. Deb: 7/19/1893

1893	NY-N	31	114	16	28	4	1	2	21	7	9	.246	.289	.351	70	-6	5			.969	-7	C-31	-0.8
1894	NY-N	49	175	35	58	5	5	1	32	14	5	.331	.387	.434	99	-0	8			.841	-9	C-34,1-15	-0.5
1895	NY-N	67	238	32	56	9	0	0	30	14	16	.235	.281	.273	44	-20	11			.938	3	C-53,1-11/3-3	-1.0
1896	NY-N	75	253	33	60	2	0	0	23	13	14	.237	.277	.245	39	-22	9			.936	-4	C-71/1-2	-1.5
1897	NY-N	46	154	29	46	9	3	0	22	15		.299	.365	.396	104	1	5			.929	-2	C-30,1-10/O-4,2-1	0.2
1898	NY-N	1	4	0	0	0	0	0	0	0	0	.000	.000	.000	-99	-1	0			1.000	0	/O-1	-0.1
1899	NY-N	97	328	49	88	8	6	0	42	43		.268	.360	.329	93	-1	16			.925	-8	C-31,1-29,S-19,3/O	-0.5
Total	7	366	1266	194	336	37	15	3	170	106	44	.265	.327	.325	73	-49	54			.926	-27	C-250/1-67,S3O2	-4.2

■ PRESTON WILSON   Wilson, Preston James Richard b: 7/19/74, Bamberg, S.C. BR/TR, 6'2", 193 lbs. Deb: 5/7/98 F

1998	NY-N	8	20	3	6	2	0	0	2	2	8	.300	.364	.400	99	0	1	1	-0	.909	-1	/O-7	-0.1
	Fla-N	14	31	4	2	0	0	1	1	4	13	.065	.194	.161	-6	-5	0	0	0	1.000	-2	O-11	-0.7
	Yr	22	51	7	8	2	0	1	3	6	21	.157	.259	.255	35	-5	1	1	-0	.958	-3	O-18	-0.8

■ BOB WILSON   Wilson, Robert b: 2/22/25, Dallas, Tex. d: 4/23/85, Dallas, Tex. BR/TR, 5'11", 197 lbs. Deb: 5/17/58

| 1958 | LA-N | 3 | 5 | 0 | 1 | 0 | 0 | 0 | 0 | 0 | 1 | .200 | .200 | .200 | 6 | -1 | 0 | 0 | 0 | 1.000 | -0 | /O-1 | -0.1 |

■ RED WILSON   Wilson, Robert James b: 3/7/29, Milwaukee, Wis. BR/TR, 6', 200 lbs. Deb: 9/22/51

1951	Chi-A	4	11	1	3	1	0	0	0	1	2	.273	.333	.364	90	-0	0	0	0	1.000	-1	/C-4	-0.1
1952	Chi-A	2	3	0	0	0	0	0	0	0	1	.000	.000	.000	-99	-1	0	0	0	1.000	1	/C-2	0.0
1953	Chi-A	71	164	21	41	6	1	0	10	26	12	.250	.353	.299	75	-5	2	3	-1	.981	10	C-63	0.6
1954	Chi-A	8	20	2	4	0	0	1	1	1	2	.200	.238	.350	58	-1	0	0	0	1.000	4	C-8	0.3
	Det-A	54	170	22	48	11	1	2	22	27	12	.282	.381	.394	115	4	3	1	0	.996	4	C-53	0.9
	Yr	62	190	24	52	11	1	3	23	28	14	.274	.367	.389	108	3	3	1	0	.997	6	C-61	1.2
1955	Det-A	78	241	26	53	9	0	2	17	26	23	.220	.296	.282	57	-14	1	2	-1	.984	-6	C-72	-1.9
1956	Det-A	78	228	32	66	12	2	7	38	42	18	.289	.400	.452	124	9	2	1	0	.991	3	C-78	1.5
1957	Det-A	60	180	21	43	8	1	3	25	19	25	.239	.344	.344	86	-3	2	3	-1	1.000	-1	C-60	-0.1
1958	Det-A	103	298	31	89	13	1	9	29	35	30	.299	.376	.379	101	2	10	0	3	.992	7	*C-101	1.8
1959	Det-A	67	228	28	60	17	2	4	35	10	23	.263	.300	.408	88	-4	2	2	-1	.988	2	C-64	0.0
1960	Det-A	45	134	17	29	4	0	1	14	16	14	.216	.300	.276	54	-8	3	0	1	.980	-0	C-45	-0.5
	Cle-A	32	88	5	19	3	0	1	10	6	7	.216	.274	.284	53	-6	0	0	0	.989	7	C-30	0.3
	Yr	77	222	22	48	7	0	2	24	22	21	.216	.290	.275	53	-14	3	0	1	.984	7	C-75	-0.2
Total	10	602	1765	206	455	84	8	24	189	215	163	.258	.341	.355	87	-28	25	12	0	.990	31	C-580	2.8

■ MIKE WILSON   Wilson, Samuel Marshall b: 12/2/1896, Edge Hill, Pa. d: 5/16/78, Boynton Beach, Fla BR/TR, 5'10.5", 160 lbs. Deb: 6/4/21

| 1921 | Pit-N | 5 | 4 | 0 | 0 | 0 | 0 | 0 | 0 | 0 | 0 | .000 | .000 | .000 | -97 | -1 | 0 | 0 | 0 | .833 | -1 | /C-5 | -0.1 |

■ NEIL WILSON   Wilson, Samuel O'Neil b: 6/14/35, Lexington, Tenn. BL/TR, 6'1", 175 lbs. Deb: 4/17/60

| 1960 | SF-N | 6 | 10 | 0 | 0 | 0 | 0 | 0 | 0 | 0 | 1 | .000 | .091 | .000 | -77 | -2 | 0 | 0 | 0 | .958 | -0 | /C-6 | -0.2 |

■ TOM WILSON   Wilson, Thomas G. "Slats" b: 6/3/1890, Fleming, Kan. d: 3/7/53, San Pedro, Cal. BB/TR, 6'1.5", 160 lbs. Deb: 9/8/14

| 1914 | Was-A | 1 | 1 | 0 | 0 | 0 | 0 | 0 | 0 | 0 | 0 | .000 | .000 | .000 | -96 | -0 | 0 | | | .000 | 0 | /C-1 | 0.0 |

■ BILL WILSON   Wilson, William Donald b: 11/6/28, Central City, Neb. BR/TR, 6'2", 200 lbs. Deb: 9/24/50

1950	Chi-A	3	6	0	0	0	0	0	0	2	2	.000	.250	.000	-33	-1	0	0	0	1.000	-1	/O-2	-0.2
1953	Chi-A	9	17	1	1	0	0	0	0	1	5	.059	.111	.059	-51	-4	0	0	0	1.000	-0	/O-3	-0.4
1954	Chi-A	20	35	4	6	1	0	2	5	7	5	.171	.310	.371	83	-1	0	0	-1	.943	-2	O-19	-0.4
	Phi-A	94	323	43	77	10	1	15	33	39	59	.238	.335	.415	104	1	1	2	-1	.989	8	O-91	0.5
	Yr	114	358	47	83	11	1	17	38	46	64	.232	.333	.411	102	0	1	2	-1	.984	6	*O-110	0.1
1955	KC-A	98	273	39	61	12	0	15	38	24	63	.223	.289	.432	91	-5	1	2	-1	.969	-3	O-82/P-1	-1.2
Total	4	224	654	87	145	23	1	32	77	72	136	.222	.308	.407	92	-10	2	4	-2	.979	3	O-197/P-1	-1.7

■ BILL WILSON
Wilson, William G. b: 10/28/1867, Hannibal, Mo. d: 5/9/24, St.Paul, Minn. TR , Deb: 4/30/1890

YEAR	TM/L	G	AB	R	H	2B	3B	HR	RBI	BB	SO	AVG	OBP	SLG	PRO+	BR/A	SB	CS	SBR	FA	FR	G/POS	TPR
1890	Pit-N	83	304	30	65	11	3	0	21	22	50	.214	.271	.270	65	-13	5			.874	2	C-38,O-25,1-18,/S-1	-0.8
1897	Lou-N	105	381	43	81	12	4	1	41	18		.213	.257	.273	41	-33	9			.940	-1	*C-103/3-1	-1.9
1898	Lou-N	29	102	5	17	1	2	1	13	5		.167	.213	.245	32	-9	3			.895	-4	C-28/1-1	-1.0
Total	3	217	787	78	163	24	9	2	75	45	50	.207	.257	.268	49	-56	17			.912	-3	C-169/O-25,1-19,3S	-3.7

■ MOOKIE WILSON
Wilson, William Hayward b: 2/9/56, Bamberg, S.C. BB/TR, 5'10", 170 lbs. Deb: 9/2/80 CF

YEAR	TM/L	G	AB	R	H	2B	3B	HR	RBI	BB	SO	AVG	OBP	SLG	PRO+	BR/A	SB	CS	SBR	FA	FR	G/POS	TPR
1980	NY-N	27	105	16	26	5	3	0	4	12	19	.248	.325	.352	91	-1	7	7	-2	.973	2	O-26	-0.3
1981	NY-N	92	328	49	89	8	8	3	14	20	59	.271	.317	.372	96	-2	24	12	0	.983	6	O-80	0.1
1982	NY-N	159	639	90	178	25	9	5	55	32	102	.279	.315	.369	91	-8	58	16	8	.988	17	*O-156	1.3
1983	NY-N	152	638	91	176	25	6	7	51	18	103	.276	.300	.367	85	-15	54	16	7	.984	13	*O-148	0.0
1984	NY-N	154	587	88	162	28	10	10	54	26	90	.276	.309	.409	102	-1	46	9	8	.990	17	*O-146	2.1
1985	NY-N	93	337	56	93	16	8	6	26	28	52	.276	.332	.424	113	5	24	9	2	.964	2	O-83	0.7
1986	*NY-N	123	381	61	110	17	5	9	45	32	72	.289	.345	.430	116	8	25	7	3	.979	-6	*O-114	0.2
1987	NY-N	124	385	58	115	19	7	9	34	35	85	.299	.360	.455	120	11	21	6	3	.963	-8	*O-109	0.3
1988	*NY-N	112	378	61	112	17	5	8	41	27	63	.296	.346	.431	128	13	15	4	2	.976	-7	*O-104	0.6
1989	NY-N	80	249	22	51	10	1	3	18	10	47	.205	.238	.289	53	-16	7	4	-0	.975	-3	O-71	-2.2
	*Tor-A	54	238	32	71	9	1	2	17	3	37	.298	.313	.370	93	-3	12	1	3	.991	-3	O-54	-0.5
1990	Tor-A	147	588	81	156	36	4	3	51	31	102	.265	.302	.355	82	-15	23	4	5	.992	8	*O-141/D-6	-0.6
1991	*Tor-A	86	241	26	58	12	4	2	28	8	35	.241	.280	.349	70	-10	11	3	2	.973	-1	O-41,D-34	-1.2
Total	12	1403	5094	731	1397	227	71	67	438	282	866	.274	.315	.386	96	-35	327	98	39	.982	38	*O-1273/D-40	0.5

■ WILLIE WILSON
Wilson, Willie James b: 7/9/55, Montgomery, Ala. BB/TR, 6'3", 195 lbs. Deb: 9/4/76

YEAR	TM/L	G	AB	R	H	2B	3B	HR	RBI	BB	SO	AVG	OBP	SLG	PRO+	BR/A	SB	CS	SBR	FA	FR	G/POS	TPR
1976	KC-A	12	6	0	1	0	0	0	0	0	2	.167	.167	.167	-2	-1	2	1	0	.875	-2	/O-6	-0.2
1977	KC-A	13	34	10	11	2	0	0	1	1	8	.324	.343	.382	97	-0	6	3	0	.960	0	/O-9,D-2	0.0
1978	*KC-A	127	198	43	43	8	2	0	16	16	33	.217	.282	.278	57	-11	46	12	7	.978	-14	*O-112/D-6	-2.1
1979	KC-A	154	588	113	185	18	13	6	49	28	92	.315	.353	.420	106	4	**83**	12	**18**	.985	15	*O-152/D-2	2.9
1980	*KC-A	161	705	**133**	**230**	28	**15**	3	49	28	81	.326	.357	.421	112	11	79	10	**18**	.988	22	*O-159	4.3
1981	*KC-A	102	439	54	133	10	7	1	32	18	42	.303	.336	.364	103	1	34	8	5	.987	22	*O-101	2.6
1982	KC-A★	136	585	87	194	19	**15**	3	46	26	81	**.332**	.366	.431	118	14	37	11	5	.987	15	*O-135	2.9
1983	KC-A★	137	576	90	159	22	8	2	33	33	75	.276	.316	.352	84	-13	59	8	13	.975	1	*O-136	-0.3
1984	*KC-A	128	541	81	163	24	9	2	44	39	56	.301	.352	.390	104	3	47	5	**11**	.990	10	*O-128	2.1
1985	*KC-A	141	605	87	168	25	**21**	4	43	29	94	.278	.316	.408	96	-4	43	11	6	.995	3	*O-140	0.0
1986	KC-A	156	631	77	170	20	7	9	44	31	97	.269	.313	.366	82	-16	34	8	5	.993	5	*O-155	-1.0
1987	KC-A	146	610	97	170	18	**15**	4	30	32	88	.279	.321	.377	82	-16	59	11	**11**	**.997**	3	*O-143/D-2	-0.6
1988	KC-A	147	591	81	155	17	**11**	1	37	22	106	.262	.291	.333	74	-21	35	7	6	.989	-0	*O-142	-2.0
1989	KC-A	112	383	58	97	17	7	3	43	27	78	.253	.304	.358	86	-7	24	6	4	.977	-3	*O-108/D-1	-1.0
1990	KC-A	115	307	49	89	13	3	2	42	30	57	.290	.357	.371	106	3	24	6	4	1.000	-6	*O-106/D-1	-0.1
1991	Oak-A	113	294	38	70	14	4	0	28	18	43	.238	.291	.313	71	-12	20	5	3	.983	-4	O-87/D-9	-1.4
1992	*Oak-A	132	396	38	107	15	5	0	37	35	65	.270	.331	.333	91	-4	28	8	4	.981	7	*O-120/D-5	0.4
1993	Chi-N	105	221	29	57	11	3	1	11	11	40	.258	.302	.348	75	-8	7	2	1	.991	-18	O-82	-2.7
1994	Chi-N	17	21	4	5	0	2	0	0	1	6	.238	.273	.429	80	-1	1	0	0	1.000	-3	O-10	-0.4
Total	19	2154	7731	1169	2207	281	147	41	585	425	1144	.285	.328	.376	93	-77	668	134	120	.987	53	*O-2031/D-28	3.4

■ ED WINCENIAK
Winceniak, Edward Joseph b: 4/16/29, Chicago, Ill. BR/TR, 5'9", 165 lbs. Deb: 4/25/56

YEAR	TM/L	G	AB	R	H	2B	3B	HR	RBI	BB	SO	AVG	OBP	SLG	PRO+	BR/A	SB	CS	SBR	FA	FR	G/POS	TPR
1956	Chi-N	15	17	1	2	0	0	0	0	1	3	.118	.167	.118	-22	-3	0	0	0	.889	-0	/3-4,2-1	-0.3
1957	Chi-N	17	50	5	12	3	0	1	8	2	9	.240	.269	.360	68	-2	0	0	0	1.000	-3	/S-5,3-4,2-3	-0.5
Total	2	32	67	6	14	3	0	1	8	3	12	.209	.243	.299	45	-5	0	0	0	.955	-3	/3-8,S-5,2-4	-0.8

■ GORDIE WINDHORN
Windhorn, Gordon Ray b: 12/19/33, Watseka, Ill. BR/TR, 6'1", 185 lbs. Deb: 9/10/59

YEAR	TM/L	G	AB	R	H	2B	3B	HR	RBI	BB	SO	AVG	OBP	SLG	PRO+	BR/A	SB	CS	SBR	FA	FR	G/POS	TPR
1959	NY-A	7	11	0	0	0	0	0	0	0	3	.000	.000	.000	-99	-3	0	0	0	1.000	-1	/O-4	-0.4
1961	LA-N	34	33	10	8	2	1	2	6	4	3	.242	.324	.545	115	1	0	1	-1	.944	-2	O-17	-0.3
1962	KC-A	14	19	1	3	1	0	0	1	0	3	.158	.158	.211	-2	-3	0	0	0	1.000	-2	O/-7	-0.4
	LA-A	40	45	9	8	6	0	0	1	7	10	.178	.288	.311	63	-2	1	1	-0	1.000	-7	O-27	-1.0
	Yr	54	64	10	11	7	0	0	2	7	13	.172	.254	.281	44	-5	1	1	-0	1.000	-9	O-34	-1.4
Total	3	95	108	20	19	9	1	2	8	11	19	.176	.252	.333	55	-7	1	2	-1	.981	-12	O/-55	-2.1

■ BILL WINDLE
Windle, Willis Brewer b: 12/13/04, Galena, Kan. d: 12/8/81, Corpus Christi, Tex BL/TL, 5'11.5", 170 lbs. Deb: 9/27/28

YEAR	TM/L	G	AB	R	H	2B	3B	HR	RBI	BB	SO	AVG	OBP	SLG	PRO+	BR/A	SB	CS	SBR	FA	FR	G/POS	TPR
1928	Pit-N	1	1	1	1	1	0	0	0	0	0	1.000	1.000	2.000	641	1	0			1.000	0	/1-1	0.1
1929	Pit-N	2	1	0	0	0	0	0	0	0	1	.000	.000	.000	-98	-0	0			1.000	-0	/1-2	0.0
Total	2	3	2	1	1	1	0	0	0	0	1	.500	.500	1.000	264	0	0			1.000	-0	/1-3	0.1

■ ROBBIE WINE
Wine, Robert Paul Jr. b: 7/13/62, Norristown, Pa. BR/TR, 6'2", 190 lbs. Deb: 9/2/86 F

YEAR	TM/L	G	AB	R	H	2B	3B	HR	RBI	BB	SO	AVG	OBP	SLG	PRO+	BR/A	SB	CS	SBR	FA	FR	G/POS	TPR
1986	Hou-N	9	12	2	3	1	0	0	0	1	4	.250	.308	.333	79	-0	0	0	0	1.000	3	/C-8	0.3
1987	Hou-N	14	29	1	3	1	0	0	0	1	10	.103	.133	.138	-29	-5	0	0	0	.979	-1	C-12	-0.6
Total	2	23	41	3	6	2	0	0	0	2	14	.146	.186	.195	2	-6	0	0	0	.988	2	/C-20	-0.3

■ BOBBY WINE
Wine, Robert Paul Sr. b: 9/17/38, New York, N.Y. BR/TR, 6'1", 187 lbs. Deb: 9/20/60 FMC

YEAR	TM/L	G	AB	R	H	2B	3B	HR	RBI	BB	SO	AVG	OBP	SLG	PRO+	BR/A	SB	CS	SBR	FA	FR	G/POS	TPR
1960	Phi-N	4	14	1	2	0	0	0	0	0	2	.143	.143	.143	-22	-2	0	0	0	1.000	0	/S-4	-0.2
1962	Phi-N	112	311	30	76	15	0	4	25	11	49	.244	.270	.331	62	-17	2	0	1	.979	7	S-89,3-20	-0.3
1963	Phi-N	142	418	29	90	14	3	6	44	14	83	.215	.242	.306	58	-23	1	3	-2	.971	15	*S-132/3-8	-0.2
1964	Phi-N	126	283	28	60	8	3	4	34	25	37	.212	.276	.304	64	-13	1	0	0	.965	7	*S-108,3-16	0.0
1965	Phi-N	139	394	31	90	8	1	5	33	31	69	.228	.285	.292	64	-19	0	0	0	.967	22	*S-135/1-4	1.2
1966	Phi-N	46	89	8	21	5	0	0	5	6	13	.236	.292	.292	63	-4	0	1	-1	.974	12	S-40/O-2	0.9
1967	Phi-N	135	363	27	69	12	5	2	28	29	77	.190	.250	.267	48	-25	3	2	-0	**.980**	29	*S-134/1-2	1.6
1968	Phi-N	27	71	5	12	3	0	2	7	6	17	.169	.234	.296	58	-4	0	0	0	.972	3	S-25/3-1	0.2
1969	Mon-N	121	370	23	74	8	1	3	25	28	49	.200	.256	.251	43	-28	0	0	0	.949	17	*S-118/1-1,3-1	0.1
1970	Mon-N	159	501	40	116	21	3	3	51	39	94	.232	.288	.303	59	-29	0	1	-1	.976	20	*S-159	0.7
1971	Mon-N	119	340	25	68	9	0	1	16	25	46	.200	.255	.235	39	-27	0	0	0	.982	2	*S-119	-1.2
1972	Mon-N	34	18	2	4	1	0	0	0	0	2	.222	.222	.278	41	-1	0	0	0	1.000	5	3-21/S-4,2-1	0.4
Total	12	1164	3172	249	682	104	16	30	268	214	538	.215	.265	.286	54	-194	7	7	-2	.971	137	*S-1067/3-67,1O2	3.2

■ RALPH WINEGARNER
Winegarner, Ralph Lee b: 10/29/09, Benton, Kan. d: 4/14/88, Wichita, Kan. BR/TR, 6', 182 lbs. Deb: 9/20/30 C

YEAR	TM/L	G	AB	R	H	2B	3B	HR	RBI	BB	SO	AVG	OBP	SLG	PRO+	BR/A	SB	CS	SBR	FA	FR	G/POS	TPR
1930	Cle-A	5	22	5	10	1	0	0	2	1	7	.455	.478	.500	143	2	0	0	0	.857	1	/3-5	0.2
1932	Cle-A	7	7	1	1	0	0	0	0	0	5	.143	.143	.143	-24	-1	0	0	0	.750	-0	/P-5	0.0
1934	Cle-A	32	51	9	10	2	0	1	5	3	11	.196	.241	.294	37	-5	0	0	0	1.000	1	P-22/O-1	0.0
1935	Cle-A	65	84	11	26	4	1	3	17	9	12	.310	.376	.488	120	2	1	1	-0	.944	2	P-25/O-4,3-3,1-1	0.2
1936	Cle-A	18	16	0	2	0	0	0	2	1	6	.125	.176	.125	-24	-3	0	0	0	1.000	-0	/P-9	0.0
1949	StL-A	9	5	2	2	0	0	1	2	1	2	.400	.500	1.000	280	1	0	0	0	1.000	-0	/P-9	0.0
Total	6	136	185	28	51	7	1	5	28	15	43	.276	.330	.405	86	-4	1	1	-0	.952	2	/P-70,3-8,O-5,1-1	0.4

■ DAVE WINFIELD
Winfield, David Mark b: 10/3/51, St.Paul, Minn. BR/TR, 6'6", 220 lbs. Deb: 6/19/73

YEAR	TM/L	G	AB	R	H	2B	3B	HR	RBI	BB	SO	AVG	OBP	SLG	PRO+	BR/A	SB	CS	SBR	FA	FR	G/POS	TPR
1973	SD-N	56	141	9	39	4	1	3	12	12	19	.277	.333	.383	107	1	0	0	0	.956	-1	O-36/1-1	-0.2
1974	SD-N	145	498	57	132	18	4	20	75	40	96	.265	.321	.438	116	8	9	7	-2	.960	7	*O-131	0.8
1975	SD-N	143	509	74	136	20	2	15	76	69	82	.267	.358	.403	118	13	23	4	5	.972	10	*O-138	2.2
1976	SD-N	137	492	81	139	26	4	13	69	65	78	.283	.370	.431	138	24	26	7	4	.982	12	*O-134	3.6
1977	SD-N★	157	615	104	169	29	7	25	92	58	75	.275	.337	.467	126	19	16	7	1	.972	20	*O-156	3.4
1978	SD-N★	158	587	88	181	30	5	24	97	55	81	.308	.370	.499	153	39	21	9	1	.979	-19	*O-154/1-2	1.5
1979	SD-N★	159	597	97	184	27	10	34	**118**	85	71	.308	.396	.558	**167**	**55**	15	9	-1	.986	11	*O-157	**5.9**
1980	SD-N★	162	558	89	154	25	6	20	87	79	83	.276	.368	.450	135	27	23	7	3	.987	-4	*O-159	2.0
1981	*NY-A★	105	388	52	114	25	1	13	68	43	41	.294	.366	.464	140	20	11	1	3	.985	-6	*O-102/D-1	1.4

YEAR	TM/L	G	AB	R	H	2B	3B	HR	RBI	BB	SO	AVG	OBP	SLG	PRO+	BR/A	SB	CS	SBR	FA	FR	G/POS	TPR
1982	NY-A★	140	539	84	151	24	8	37	106	45	64	.280	.336	.560	143	29	5	3	-0	.974	12	*O-135/D-4	3.7
1983	NY-A★	152	598	99	169	26	8	32	116	58	77	.283	.348	.513	139	30	15	6	1	.978	-11	*O-151	1.5
1984	NY-A★	141	567	106	193	34	4	19	100	53	71	.340	.397	.515	156	43	6	4	-1	.994	2	*O-140	4.0
1985	NY-A★	155	633	105	174	34	6	26	114	52	96	.275	.330	.471	119	15	19	7	2	.991	12	*O-152/D-2	2.2
1986	NY-A★	154	565	90	148	31	5	24	104	77	106	.262	.352	.462	121	17	6	5	-1	.984	5	*O-145/3-2,D-6	1.5
1987	NY-A★	156	575	83	158	22	1	27	97	76	96	.275	.359	.457	116	14	5	6	-2	.989	-4	*O-145/D-8	0.2
1988	NY-A★	149	559	96	180	37	2	25	107	69	88	.322	.398	.530	159	44	9	4	0	.989	-3	*O-141/D-4	3.7
1990	NY-A	20	61	7	13	3	0	2	6	4	13	.213	.273	.361	75	-2	0	0	0	1.000	-3	O-12/D-7	-0.5
	Cal-A	112	414	63	114	18	2	19	72	48	68	.275	.352	.466	130	16	0	1	-1	.989	-6	*O-108/D-3	0.7
	Yr	132	475	70	127	21	2	21	78	52	81	.267	.342	.453	122	14	0	1	-1	.989	-8	*O-120,D-10	0.2
1991	Cal-A	150	568	75	149	27	4	28	86	56	109	.262	.330	.472	119	13	7	2	1	.990	-1	*O-115,D-34	0.9
1992	*Tor-A	156	583	92	169	33	3	26	108	82	89	.290	.378	.491	136	28	2	3	-1	1.000	1	*D-130,O-26	2.3
1993	Min-A	143	547	72	148	27	2	21	76	45	106	.271	.326	.442	104	2	2	3	-1	1.000	0	*D-105,O-31/1-5	-0.4
1994	Min-A	77	294	35	74	15	3	10	43	31	51	.252	.323	.425	91	-5	2	1	0	1.000	0	D-76/O-1	-0.8
1995	Cle-A	46	115	11	22	5	0	2	4	14	26	.191	.285	.287	49	-9	1	0	0	.000	0	D-39	-1.0
Total	22	2973	11003	1669	3110	540	88	465	1833	1216	1686	.283	.355	.475	130	440	223	96	9	.982	34	*O-2469,D-419/1-8,3	38.6

■ AL WINGO
Wingo, Absalom Holbrook "Red" b: 5/6/1898, Norcross, Ga. d: 10/9/64, Detroit, Mich. BL/TR, 5'11", 180 lbs. Deb: 9/9/19 F

YEAR	TM/L	G	AB	R	H	2B	3B	HR	RBI	BB	SO	AVG	OBP	SLG	PRO+	BR/A	SB	CS	SBR	FA	FR	G/POS	TPR
1919	Phi-A	15	59	9	18	1	3	0	2	4	12	.305	.349	.424	115	1	0			.815	-3	O-15	-0.3
1924	Det-A	78	150	21	43	12	2	1	26	21	13	.287	.374	.413	105	1	2	5	-2	.925	-8	O-43	-1.1
1925	Det-A	130	440	104	163	34	10	5	68	69	31	.370	.456	.527	151	37	14	13	-4	.971	8	*O-122	3.1
1926	Det-A	108	298	45	84	19	0	1	45	52	32	.282	.389	.356	94	-1	4	2	0	.923	4	O-74/3-2	-0.2
1927	Det-A	75	137	15	32	8	2	0	20	25	14	.234	.352	.321	74	-5	1	0	0	.891	-3	O-34	-0.9
1928	Det-A	87	242	30	69	13	2	2	30	40	17	.285	.389	.380	101	2	2	2	-1	.968	-3	O-71	-0.6
Total	6	493	1326	224	409	87	19	9	191	211	119	.308	.404	.423	114	36	23	22		.944	-6	O-359/3-2	-0.0

■ ED WINGO
Wingo, Edmond Armand (b: Edmond Armand La Riviere)
b: 10/8/1895, St.Anne De Bellevue, Que., Canada d: 12/5/64, Lachine, Que., Can. BR/TR, 5'6", 145 lbs. Deb: 10/2/20

YEAR	TM/L	G	AB	R	H	2B	3B	HR	RBI	BB	SO	AVG	OBP	SLG	PRO+	BR/A	SB	CS	SBR	FA	FR	G/POS	TPR
1920	Phi-A	1	4	0	1	0	0	0	1	0	0	.250	.250	.250	32	-0	0	0	0	1.000	1	/C-1	0.0

■ IVEY WINGO
Wingo, Ivey Brown b: 7/8/1890, Gainesville, Ga. d: 3/1/41, Waycross, Ga. BL/TR, 5'10", 160 lbs. Deb: 4/20/11 FMC

YEAR	TM/L	G	AB	R	H	2B	3B	HR	RBI	BB	SO	AVG	OBP	SLG	PRO+	BR/A	SB	CS	SBR	FA	FR	G/POS	TPR
1911	StL-N	25	57	4	12	2	0	0	3	3	7	.211	.250	.246	40	-5	0			.916	0	C-18	-0.3
1912	StL-N	100	310	38	82	18	8	2	44	23	45	.265	.317	.394	96	-3	8			.957	4	C-92	0.9
1913	StL-N	112	307	25	78	5	8	2	35	17	41	.254	.295	.342	83	-8	18			.945	-4	C-98/1-5,O-1	-0.4
1914	StL-N	80	237	24	71	8	5	4	26	18	17	.300	.352	.426	132	9	15			.958	-3	C-70/O-4	1.2
1915	Cin-N	119	339	26	75	11	6	3	29	13	33	.221	.250	.316	69	-14	10	11	-4	.966	3	C-98/O-1	-0.8
1916	Cin-N	119	347	30	85	8	11	2	40	25	27	.245	.298	.349	100	-0	4			.958	7	*C-107,M	1.6
1917	Cin-N	121	399	37	106	16	11	2	39	25	13	.266	.311	.376	115	6	9			.967	-5	*C-120	1.2
1918	Cin-N	100	323	35	82	15	6	0	31	19	18	.254	.297	.337	95	-3	6			.973	-6	C-93/O-5	-0.1
1919	*Cin-N	76	245	30	67	12	6	0	27	23	19	.273	.336	.371	115	5	4			.969	3	C-75	1.6
1920	Cin-N	108	364	32	96	11	5	2	38	19	13	.264	.300	.338	84	-8	6	4	-1	.958	-10	*C-107/2-2	-1.2
1921	Cin-N	97	295	20	79	7	6	3	38	21	14	.268	.319	.363	84	-7	3	2	-0	.959	5	C-92/O-1	0.3
1922	Cin-N	80	260	24	74	13	3	3	45	23	11	.285	.343	.392	91	-4	1	4	-2	.964	4	C-78	0.2
1923	Cin-N	61	171	10	45	9	2	1	24	9	11	.263	.304	.357	75	-6	1	1	-0	.969	3	C-57	-0.1
1924	Cin-N	66	192	21	55	5	4	1	23	14	8	.286	.338	.370	91	-2	1	1	-0	.989	5	C-65/1-1	0.5
1925	Cin-N	55	146	6	30	7	0	0	12	11	8	.205	.261	.253	33	-15	1	2	-1	.965	3	C-55	-0.9
1926	Cin-N	7	10	0	2	0	0	0	1	1	0	.200	.333	.200	48	-1	0			1.000	-0	/C-7	-0.1
1929	Cin-N	1	1	0	0	0	0	0	0	0	0	.000	.000	.000	-99	-0	0			.000	0	/C-1	0.0
Total	17	1327	4003	362	1039	147	81	25	455	264	285	.260	.307	.355	91	-56	87	25		.962	11	*C-1233/O-12,1-6,2	3.6

■ GEORGE WINKELMAN
Winkelman, George Edward b: 2/18/1865, Washington, D.C. d: 5/19/60, Washington, D.C. BL/TL, Deb: 8/4/1883

YEAR	TM/L	G	AB	R	H	2B	3B	HR	RBI	BB	SO	AVG	OBP	SLG	PRO+	BR/A	SB	CS	SBR	FA	FR	G/POS	TPR
1883	Lou-a	4	13	2	0	0	0	0		1		.000	.071	.000	-81	-3				.625	0	/O-4	-0.2
1886	Was-N	1	5	0	1	0	0	0	0	0	1	.200	.200	.200	23	-0	0			.000	-1	/O-1,P-1	0.0
Total	2	5	18	2	1	0	0	0	0	1	1	.056	.105	.056	-51	-3	0			.625	-0	/O-5,P-1	-0.2

■ RANDY WINN
Winn, Dwight Randolph b: 6/9/74, Los Angeles, Cal. BB/TR, 6'2", 175 lbs. Deb: 5/11/98

YEAR	TM/L	G	AB	R	H	2B	3B	HR	RBI	BB	SO	AVG	OBP	SLG	PRO+	BR/A	SB	CS	SBR	FA	FR	G/POS	TPR
1998	TB-A	109	338	51	94	9	9	1	17	29	69	.278	.337	.367	80	-10	26	12	1	.980	-3	O-96/D-4	-1.3

■ HERM WINNINGHAM
Winningham, Herman Son b: 12/1/61, Orangeburg, S.C. BL/TR, 5'11", 185 lbs. Deb: 9/1/84

YEAR	TM/L	G	AB	R	H	2B	3B	HR	RBI	BB	SO	AVG	OBP	SLG	PRO+	BR/A	SB	CS	SBR	FA	FR	G/POS	TPR
1984	NY-N	14	27	5	11	1	1	0	5	1	7	.407	.429	.519	167	2	2	1	0	1.000	-4	O-10	-0.2
1985	Mon-N	125	312	30	74	6	5	3	21	28	72	.237	.300	.317	77	-10	20	9	1	.983	-4	*O-116	-1.7
1986	Mon-N	90	185	23	40	6	3	4	11	18	51	.216	.286	.346	74	-7	12	7	-1	.980	-7	O-66/S-1	-1.7
1987	Mon-N	137	347	34	83	20	3	4	41	34	68	.239	.307	.349	71	-14	29	10	3	.975	-8	*O-131	-2.2
1988	Mon-N	47	90	10	21	2	1	0	6	12	18	.233	.324	.278	71	-3	4	5	-2	.982	-3	O-30	-0.9
	Cin-N	53	113	6	26	1	3	0	15	5	27	.230	.263	.292	57	-6	8	3	1	1.000	-3	O-42	-1.1
	Yr	100	203	16	47	3	4	0	21	17	45	.232	.291	.286	63	-9	12	8	-1	.992	-7	O-72	-2.0
1989	Cin-N	115	251	40	63	11	3	3	13	24	50	.251	.316	.355	88	-4	14	5	1	.980	-7	O-85	-1.1
1990	*Cin-N	84	160	20	41	8	5	3	17	14	31	.256	.316	.425	98	-1	6	4	-1	1.000	-9	O-64	-1.2
1991	Cin-N	98	169	17	38	6	1	1	4	11	40	.225	.272	.290	56	-10	4	4	-1	.953	-8	O-66	-2.1
1992	Bos-A	105	234	27	55	8	1	1	14	10	53	.235	.266	.291	52	-15	6	5	-1	.975	-4	O-67/D-6	-2.2
Total	9	868	1888	212	452	69	26	19	147	157	417	.239	.298	.334	74	-67	105	53	-0	.980	-58	O-677/D-6,S-1	-14.4

■ TOM WINSETT
Winsett, John Thomas "Long Tom" b: 11/24/09, McKenzie, Tenn. d: 7/20/87, Memphis, Tenn. BL/TR, 6'2", 190 lbs. Deb: 4/20/30

YEAR	TM/L	G	AB	R	H	2B	3B	HR	RBI	BB	SO	AVG	OBP	SLG	PRO+	BR/A	SB	CS	SBR	FA	FR	G/POS	TPR
1930	Bos-A	1	1	0	0	0	0	0	0	0	1	.000	.000	.000	-99	-0	0	0	0	.000	0	H	0.0
1931	Bos-A	64	76	6	15	1	0	1	7	4	21	.197	.247	.250	33	-8	0	0	0	1.000	-0	/O-8	-0.8
1933	Bos-A	6	12	1	1	0	0	0	0	1	6	.083	.154	.083	-36	-2	0	0	0	1.000	-2	/O-4	-0.4
1935	StL-N	7	12	2	6	1	0	0	2	2	3	.500	.571	.583	203	2	0			.000	-1	/O-2	0.1
1936	Bro-N	22	85	13	20	7	0	1	18	11	14	.235	.330	.353	83	-2	0			1.000	1	O-21	-0.1
1937	Bro-N	118	350	32	83	15	5	5	42	45	64	.237	.329	.351	84	-7	3			.960	1	*O-101/P-1	-0.9
1938	Bro-N	12	30	6	9	1	0	1	7	6	4	.300	.417	.433	131	2	0			.882	-2	/O-9	0.0
Total	7	230	566	60	134	25	5	8	76	69	113	.237	.325	.341	79	-16	3	0		.963	-2	O-145/P-1	-2.1

■ MATT WINTERS
Winters, Matthew Littleton b: 3/18/60, Buffalo, N.Y. BL/TR, 6'3", 215 lbs. Deb: 5/30/89

YEAR	TM/L	G	AB	R	H	2B	3B	HR	RBI	BB	SO	AVG	OBP	SLG	PRO+	BR/A	SB	CS	SBR	FA	FR	G/POS	TPR
1989	KC-A	42	107	14	25	6	0	2	9	14	23	.234	.322	.346	89	-1	0	0	0	.939	-4	O-31/D-3	-0.6

■ KETTLE WIRTS
Wirts, Elwood Vernon b: 10/31/1897, Consumne, Cal. d: 7/12/68, Sacramento, Cal. BR/TR, 5'11", 170 lbs. Deb: 7/20/21

YEAR	TM/L	G	AB	R	H	2B	3B	HR	RBI	BB	SO	AVG	OBP	SLG	PRO+	BR/A	SB	CS	SBR	FA	FR	G/POS	TPR
1921	Chi-N	7	11	0	2	0	0	0	1	0	3	.182	.182	.182	-3	-2	0	0	0	1.000	1	/C-5	-0.1
1922	Chi-N	31	58	7	10	2	0	1	6	12	15	.172	.314	.259	48	-4	0	0	0	.968	-5	C-27	-0.8
1923	Chi-N	5	5	2	1	0	0	0	1	2	0	.200	.429	.200	71	-0	0	0	0	1.000	1	/C-3	0.1
1924	Chi-A	6	12	0	1	0	0	0	0	2	2	.083	.214	.083	-22	-2	1	0	0	1.000	1	/C-5	-0.1
Total	4	49	86	9	14	2	0	1	8	16	20	.163	.294	.221	35	-8	1	0	0	.981	-3	/C-40	-0.9

■ HUGHIE WISE
Wise, Hugh Edward b: 3/9/06, Campbellsville, Ky. d: 7/21/87, Plantation, Fla. BB/TR, 6', 178 lbs. Deb: 9/26/30

YEAR	TM/L	G	AB	R	H	2B	3B	HR	RBI	BB	SO	AVG	OBP	SLG	PRO+	BR/A	SB	CS	SBR	FA	FR	G/POS	TPR
1930	Det-A	2	6	0	2	0	0	0	0	0	0	.333	.333	.333	68	-0	0	0	0	1.000	1	/C-2	0.1

■ CASEY WISE
Wise, Kendall Cole b: 9/8/32, Lafayette, Ind. BB/TR, 6', 170 lbs. Deb: 4/16/57

YEAR	TM/L	G	AB	R	H	2B	3B	HR	RBI	BB	SO	AVG	OBP	SLG	PRO+	BR/A	SB	CS	SBR	FA	FR	G/POS	TPR
1957	Chi-N	43	106	12	19	3	1	0	7	11	14	.179	.256	.226	32	-10	0	0	0	.940	3	2-31/S-5	-0.5
1958	*Mil-N	31	71	8	14	1	0	0	0	4	8	.197	.240	.211	23	-8	1	1	-0	1.000	0	2-10/S-7,3-1	-0.7
1959	Mil-N	22	76	11	13	2	0	1	5	10	5	.171	.267	.237	39	-7	0	0	0	.989	-7	2-20/S-5	-1.3
1960	Det-A	30	68	6	10	0	2	2	5	4	9	.147	.194	.294	29	-7	1	0	0	.983	3	2-17,S-10/3-1	-0.3
Total	4	126	321	37	56	6	3	3	17	29	36	.174	.243	.240	31	-32	2	1	0	.968	-2	/2-78,S-27,3-2	-2.8

YEAR	TM/L	G	AB	R	H	2B	3B	HR	RBI	BB	SO	AVG	OBP	SLG	PRO+	BR/A	SB	CS	SBR	FA	FR	G/POS	TPR

■ NICK WISE Wise, Nicholas Joseph b: 6/15/1866, Boston, Mass. d: 1/15/23, Boston, Mass. BR/TR, 5'11", 194 lbs. Deb: 6/20/1888

| 1888 | Bos-N | 1 | 3 | 0 | 0 | 0 | 0 | 0 | 0 | 0 | 0 | .000 | .000 | .000 | -98 | -1 | | 0 | | .000 | -0 | /O-1,C-1 | -0.1 |

■ SAM WISE Wise, Samuel Washington "Modoc" b: 8/18/1857, Akron, Ohio d: 1/22/10, Akron, Ohio BL/TR, 5'10.5", 170 lbs. Deb: 7/30/1881

1881	Det-N	1	4	0	2	0	0	0	0	0	0	.500	.500	.500	207	0				.571	-0	/3-1	0.0
1882	Bos-N	78	298	44	66	11	4	4	34	5	45	.221	.234	.326	77	-8				.852	-13	*S-72/3-6	-1.5
1883	Bos-N	96	406	73	110	25	7	4	58	13	74	.271	.294	.397	105	2				.823	-2	*S-96	0.1
1884	Bos-N	114	426	60	91	15	9	4	41	25	104	.214	.257	.319	81	-9				.884	6	*S-107/2-7	-0.2
1885	Bos-N	107	424	71	120	20	10	4	46	25	61	.283	.323	.406	139	18				.858	13	*S-79,2-22/O-6	3.1
1886	Bos-N	96	387	71	112	19	12	4	72	33	61	.289	.345	.432	140	19	31			.956	-24	1-57,2-20,S-18/O-1	-1.0
1887	Bos-N	113	467	103	156	27	17	9	92	36	44	.334	.390	.522	151	32	43			.869	-6	S-72,O-27,2-16	2.2
1888	Bos-N	105	417	66	100	19	12	4	40	34	66	.240	.306	.372	113	6	33			.888	10	S-89/3-6,1-5,O-4,2	1.7
1889	Was-N	121	472	79	118	15	8	4	62	61	62	.250	.341	.341	97	-0	24			.916	-23	2-72,S-26,3-13,O-10	-1.6
1890	Buf-P	119	505	95	148	29	11	5	102	46	45	.293	.359	.424	119	13	19			.906	5	*2-119	2.0
1891	Bal-a	103	388	70	96	14	5	1	48	62	52	.247	.364	.317	94	-1	33			.888	-13	*2-99/S-4	-0.8
1893	Was-N	122	521	102	162	27	17	5	77	49	27	.311	.375	.457	124	16	20			.924	14	*2-91,3-31	2.7
Total	12	1175	4715	834	1281	221	112	48	672	389	643	.272	.332	.397	115	89	203			.859	-33	S-563,2-448/130	6.7

■ PHIL WISNER Wisner, Philip N. b: 7/1869, Washington, D.C. d: 7/5/36, Washington, D.C. TR , Deb: 8/30/1895

| 1895 | Was-N | 1 | 0 | 0 | 0 | 0 | 0 | 0 | 0 | 0 | 0 | — | — | — | — | 0 | | 0 | | .250 | -1 | /S-1 | 0.0 |

■ DAVE WISSMAN Wissman, David Alvin b: 2/17/41, Greenfield, Mass. BL/TR, 6'2", 178 lbs. Deb: 9/15/64

| 1964 | Pit-N | 16 | 27 | 2 | 4 | 0 | 0 | 0 | 1 | 4 | 9 | .148 | .179 | .148 | -7 | -4 | 0 | 0 | 0 | 1.000 | -1 | O-10 | -0.6 |

■ TEX WISTERZIL Wisterzil, George John b: 3/7/1891, Detroit, Mich. d: 6/27/64, San Antonio, Tex. BR/TR, 5'9.5", 150 lbs. Deb: 4/14/14

1914	Bro-F	149	534	54	137	18	10	0	66	34	47	.257	.314	.328	76	-27	17			.956	16	*3-149	-0.6
1915	Bro-F	36	106	13	33	3	3	0	21	21	7	.311	.438	.396	137	5	8			.949	3	3-31	1.0
	Chi-F	7	20	3	4	1	0	0	0	3	2	.200	.304	.250	60	-1	0			.955	0	/3-6	-0.1
	StL-F	8	24	1	5	1	0	0	4	2	2	.208	.296	.250	52	-2	2			.939	2	/3-8	0.1
	Chi-F	42	144	12	36	3	1	0	14	5	10	.250	.280	.285	63	-10	2			.968	8	3-42	0.0
	Yr	93	294	29	78	8	4	0	39	31	21	.265	.345	.320	90	-7	12			.958	14	3-87	1.0
Total	2	242	828	83	215	26	14	0	105	65	68	.260	.326	.325	81	-34	29			.957	29	3-236	0.4

■ MICKEY WITEK Witek, Nicholas Joseph b: 12/19/15, Luzerne, Pa. d: 8/24/90, Kingston, Pa. BR/TR, 5'10", 170 lbs. Deb: 4/16/40

1940	NY-N	119	433	34	111	7	0	3	31	24	17	.256	.295	.293	62	-22	2			.958	19	S-89,2-32	0.7
1941	NY-N	26	94	11	34	5	0	1	16	4	2	.362	.388	.447	132	4	0			.933	2	2-23	0.7
1942	NY-N	148	553	72	144	19	6	5	48	36	20	.260	.306	.344	89	-9	2			.978	-1	*2-147	0.0
1943	NY-N	153	622	68	195	17	0	6	55	41	23	.314	.356	.370	109	7	1			.967	16	*2-153	3.3
1946	NY-N	82	284	32	75	13	2	4	29	28	10	.264	.330	.366	97	-1	1			.962	-12	2-42,3-35	-1.1
1947	NY-N	51	160	22	35	4	1	3	17	15	12	.219	.286	.313	58	-10	1			.983	11	2-40/3-3	0.4
1949	NY-A	1	1	0	1	0	0	0	0	0	0	1.000	1.000	1.000	430	0	0	0	0	.000	0	H	0.0
Total	7	580	2147	239	595	65	9	22	196	148	84	.277	.324	.347	90	-30	7	0		.969	34	2-437/S-89,3-38	4.0

■ FRANK WITHROW Withrow, Frank Blaine "Kid" b: 6/14/1891, Greenwood, Mo. d: 9/5/66, Omaha, Neb. BR/TR, 5'11.5", 187 lbs. Deb: 4/15/20

1920	Phi-N	48	132	8	24	7	0	0	12	6	26	.182	.239	.227	33	-11	0	0	0	.973	6	C-48	-0.5
1922	Phi-N	10	21	3	7	2	0	0	3	5	5	.333	.417	.429	108	0	0	0	0	.909	1	/C-8	0.2
Total	2	58	153	11	31	6	0	0	15	11	31	.203	.265	.255	45	-11	0	0	0	.965	4	/C-56	-0.3

■ CORKY WITHROW Withrow, Raymond Wallace b: 11/28/37, High Coal, W.Va. BR/TR, 6'3.5", 197 lbs. Deb: 9/6/63

| 1963 | StL-N | 6 | 9 | 0 | 0 | 0 | 0 | 0 | 0 | 0 | 2 | .000 | .000 | .000 | -91 | -2 | 0 | 0 | 0 | 1.000 | -0 | /O-2 | -0.3 |

■ RON WITMEYER Witmeyer, Ronald Herman b: 6/28/67, West Islip, N.Y. BL/TL, 6'3", 215 lbs. Deb: 8/25/91

| 1991 | Oak-A | 11 | 19 | 0 | 1 | 0 | 0 | 0 | 0 | 0 | 5 | .053 | .053 | .053 | -75 | -4 | 0 | 0 | 0 | 1.000 | 0 | /1-8 | -0.5 |

■ KEVIN WITT Witt, Kevin Joseph b: 1/5/76, High Point, N.C. BL/TR, 6'4", 195 lbs. Deb: 9/15/98

| 1998 | Tor-A | 5 | 7 | 0 | 1 | 0 | 0 | 0 | 0 | 0 | 3 | .143 | .143 | .143 | -25 | -1 | 0 | 0 | 0 | 1.000 | 0 | /1-1 | -0.1 |

■ WHITEY WITT Witt, Lawton Walter (b: Ladislaw Waldemar Wittkowski) b: 9/28/1895, Orange, Mass. d: 7/14/88, Salem Co., N.J. BL/TR, 5'7", 150 lbs. Deb: 4/12/16

1916	Phi-A	143	563	64	138	16	15	2	36	55	71	.245	.315	.337	101	-1	19			.902	-1	*S-142	0.6
1917	Phi-A	128	452	62	114	13	4	0	28	65	45	.252	.346	.299	98	-1	12			.935	5	*S-111/O-7,3-6	1.2
1919	Phi-A	122	460	56	123	15	6	0	33	46	26	.267	.334	.326	85	-9	11			.972	0	O-59,2-56/3-2	-1.3
1920	Phi-A	65	218	29	70	11	3	1	25	27	16	.321	.396	.413	113	5	2	3	-1	.960	-8	O-50,2-10/S-2	-0.8
1921	Phi-A	154	629	100	198	31	11	4	45	77	52	.315	.390	.418	106	7	16	15	-4	.959	-2	*O-154	-1.0
1922	*NY-A	140	528	98	157	11	6	4	40	89	29	.297	.400	.364	98	3	5	8	-3	.976	-5	*O-139	-1.5
1923	*NY-A	146	596	113	187	18	10	6	56	67	42	.314	.386	.408	107	8	2	7	-4	.979	2	*O-144	-0.3
1924	NY-A	147	600	88	178	26	5	1	36	46	20	.297	.346	.362	83	-15	9	7	-2	.976	-1	*O-144	-2.6
1925	NY-A	31	40	9	8	2	1	0	0	6	2	.200	.304	.300	55	-3	1	1	0	1.000	-1	O-10	-0.4
1926	Bro-N	63	85	13	22	1	0	0	3	12	6	.259	.351	.294	76	-2	1	0		.920	-1	O-22	-0.5
Total	10	1139	4171	632	1195	144	62	18	302	489	309	.287	.362	.364	97	-6	78	41		.971	-16	O-729,S-255/2-66,3	-6.6

■ JERRY WITTE Witte, Jerome Charles b: 7/30/15, St.Louis, Mo. BR/TR, 6'1", 190 lbs. Deb: 9/10/46

1946	StL-A	18	73	7	14	2	0	4	9	0	18	.192	.192	.301	35	-7	0	0	0	.967	-2	1-18	-1.1
1947	StL-A	34	99	4	14	2	1	2	12	11	22	.141	.227	.242	30	-10	0	0	0	.983	-1	1-27	-1.3
Total	2	52	172	11	28	4	1	6	21	11	40	.163	.213	.267	32	-16	0	0	0	.977	-4	/1-45	-2.4

■ JOHN WOCKENFUSS Wockenfuss, Johnny Bilton b: 2/27/49, Welch, W.Va. BR/TR, 6', 190 lbs. Deb: 8/11/74

1974	Det-A	13	29	1	4	1	0	0	2	3	2	.138	.219	.172	13	-3	0	0	0	.932	-1	C-13	-0.4
1975	Det-A	35	118	15	27	6	3	1	13	10	15	.229	.289	.432	97	-1	0	0	0	.982	4	C-34	0.4
1976	Det-A	60	144	18	32	7	2	3	10	17	14	.222	.309	.361	92	-1	0	3	-2	.941	-7	C-59	-1.0
1977	Det-A	53	164	26	45	8	1	9	25	14	18	.274	.340	.500	117	3	0	0	0	.985	-7	C-37/O-9,D-3	-0.2
1978	Det-A	71	187	23	53	5	0	7	22	21	14	.283	.359	.422	116	4	0	0	1	.978	-8	O-60/D-2	-0.7
1979	Det-A	87	231	27	61	9	1	15	46	18	40	.264	.323	.506	116	4	2	2	-1	.996	0	1-31,C-20,D-18/O-6	0.2
1980	Det-A	126	372	56	102	13	2	16	65	68	64	.274	.391	.449	126	16	1	4	0	.983	0	1-52,D-28,C-25,O-23	1.1
1981	Det-A	70	172	20	37	4	0	9	25	28	22	.215	.325	.395	103	1	0	0	0	.984	-3	D-39,1-25/C-5,O-1	-0.5
1982	Det-A	70	193	28	58	9	0	8	32	29	21	.301	.392	.472	135	10	0	1	0	.981	-6	C-24,1-17,D-17,O/3	0.6
1983	Det-A	92	245	32	66	8	1	9	44	31	37	.269	.351	.420	114	5	1	1	-0	1.000	4	D-39,C-29,1-13/3O	0.8
1984	Phi-N	86	180	20	52	3	1	6	24	30	24	.289	.390	.417	125	7	1	0	0	.996	-7	1-39,C-21/3-2	0.0
1985	Phi-N	32	37	1	6	0	0	0	2	8	7	.162	.311	.162	35	-1	0	0	0	1.000	1	/1-7,C-2	-0.4
Total	12	795	2072	267	543	73	11	86	310	277	278	.262	.351	.432	114	42	5	11	-5	.972	-27	C-269,1-184,DO/3	-0.1

■ ANDY WOEHR Woehr, Andrew Emil b: 2/4/1896, Fort Wayne, Ind. d: 7/24/90, Fort Wayne, Ind. BR/TR, 5'11", 165 lbs. Deb: 9/15/23

1923	Phi-N	13	41	3	14	2	0	1	3	1	1	.341	.357	.390	87	-1	0	0	0	.975	3	3-13	0.3
1924	Phi-N	50	152	11	33	4	5	0	17	5	8	.217	.252	.309	44	-12	2	2	-1	.920	-5	3-44/2-1	-1.5
Total	2	63	193	14	47	6	5	1	20	6	9	.244	.274	.330	53	-13	2	2	-1	.935	-2	/3-57,2-1	-1.2

■ JOE WOERLIN Woerlin, Joseph b: 10/9/1864, France d: 6/22/19, St.Louis, Mo. Deb: 7/21/1895

| 1895 | Was-N | 1 | 3 | 1 | 1 | 0 | 0 | 0 | 0 | 0 | 0 | .333 | .333 | .333 | 73 | -0 | 0 | | | 1.000 | -1 | /S-1 | 0.0 |

■ JIM WOHLFORD Wohlford, James Eugene b: 2/28/51, Visalia, Cal. BR/TR, 5'11", 175 lbs. Deb: 9/1/72

| 1972 | KC-A | 15 | 25 | 3 | 6 | 1 | 0 | 0 | 2 | 3 | 3 | .240 | .321 | .280 | 80 | -1 | 0 | 0 | 0 | .950 | -2 | /2-8 | -0.3 |
| 1973 | KC-A | 45 | 109 | 21 | 29 | 1 | 3 | 2 | 10 | 11 | 12 | .266 | .333 | .385 | 95 | -1 | 1 | 1 | -0 | 1.000 | 3 | D-19,O-13 | 0.1 |

YEAR	TM/L	G	AB	R	H	2B	3B	HR	RBI	BB	SO	AVG	OBP	SLG	PRO+	BR/A	SB	CS	SBR	FA	FR	G/POS	TPR
1974	KC-A	143	501	55	136	16	7	2	44	39	74	.271	.328	.343	88	-7	16	13	-3	.982	1	*O-138/D-1	-1.6
1975	KC-A	116	353	45	90	10	5	0	30	34	37	.255	.322	.312	78	-10	12	7	-1	.953	-6	*O-102/D-4	-2.0
1976	*KC-A	107	293	47	73	10	2	1	24	29	24	.249	.319	.307	83	-6	22	16	-3	.975	-1	O-93/2-1,D-3	-1.3
1977	Mil-A	129	391	41	97	16	3	2	36	21	49	.248	.288	.320	65	-19	17	16	-5	.981	-2	*O-125/2-1,D-1	-2.9
1978	Mil-A	46	118	16	35	7	2	1	19	6	10	.297	.331	.415	108	1	3	2	-0	.982	-5	O-35/D-4	-0.5
1979	Mil-A	63	175	19	46	13	1	1	17	8	28	.263	.295	.366	77	-6	6	2	1	.969	-2	O-55/D-5	-0.9
1980	SF-N	91	193	17	54	6	4	1	24	13	23	.280	.329	.368	96	-1	1	4	-2	.989	-2	O-49/3-1	-0.7
1981	SF-N	50	68	4	11	3	0	1	7	4	9	.162	.208	.250	30	-6	0	0	0	1.000	-3	O-10	-1.0
1982	SF-N	97	250	37	64	12	1	2	25	30	36	.256	.336	.336	89	-3	8	3	1	.992	-2	O-72	-0.6
1983	Mon-N	83	141	7	39	8	0	1	14	5	14	.277	.301	.355	82	-4	0	0	0	.988	-11	O-61	-1.6
1984	Mon-N	95	213	20	64	13	2	5	29	14	19	.300	.344	.451	127	7	3	0	1	.989	-2	O-59/3-2	0.4
1985	Mon-N	70	125	7	24	5	1	1	15	16	18	.192	.284	.272	60	-7	0	2	-1	1.000	-5	O-43	-1.4
1986	Mon-N	70	94	10	25	4	2	1	11	9	17	.266	.330	.383	97	-0	0	2	-1	1.000	-3	O-22/3-6	-0.5
Total	15	1220	3049	349	793	125	33	21	305	241	376	.260	.316	.343	85	-62	89	68	-14	.980	-41	O-877/D-37,2-10,3-9	-14.8

■ JOHN WOJCIK

Wojcik, John Joseph b: 4/6/42, Olean, N.Y. BL/TR, 6′ ", 175 lbs. Deb: 9/9/62

YEAR	TM/L	G	AB	R	H	2B	3B	HR	RBI	BB	SO	AVG	OBP	SLG	PRO+	BR/A	SB	CS	SBR	FA	FR	G/POS	TPR
1962	KC-A	16	43	8	13	4	0	0	9	13	4	.302	.474	.395	131	3	3	0	1	1.000	-1	O-12	0.2
1963	KC-A	19	59	7	11	0	0	0	2	8	8	.186	.284	.186	33	-5	2	0	1	1.000	0	O-17	-0.5
1964	KC-A	6	22	1	3	0	0	0	0	2	8	.136	.208	.136	-2	-3	0	0	0	1.000	0	/O-6	-0.4
Total	3	41	124	16	27	4	0	0	11	23	20	.218	.345	.250	64	-5	5	0	2	1.000	-1	/O-35	-0.7

■ RAY WOLF

Wolf, Raymond Bernard "Grandpa" b: 7/15/04, Chicago, Ill. d: 10/6/79, Fort Worth, Tex. BR/TR, 5′11", 175 lbs. Deb: 7/27/27

YEAR	TM/L	G	AB	R	H	2B	3B	HR	RBI	BB	SO	AVG	OBP	SLG	PRO+	BR/A	SB	CS	SBR	FA	FR	G/POS	TPR
1927	Cin-N	1	1	0	0	0	0	0	0	0	0	.000	.000	.000	-99	-0	0			1.000	-0	/1-1	0.0

■ JIMMY WOLF

Wolf, William Van Winkle "Chicken" b: 5/12/1862, Louisville, Ky. d: 5/16/03, Louisville, Ky. BR/TR, 5′9", 190 lbs. Deb: 5/2/1882 M

YEAR	TM/L	G	AB	R	H	2B	3B	HR	RBI	BB	SO	AVG	OBP	SLG	PRO+	BR/A	SB	CS	SBR	FA	FR	G/POS	TPR
1882	Lou-a	78	318	46	95	11	8	0		9		.299	.318	.384	144	14				.902	-2	*O-70/S-9,1-1,P-1	1.1
1883	Lou-a	98	389	59	102	17	9	1		5		.262	.272	.360	110	4				.890	17	*O-78,C-20/S-5,2-1	1.9
1884	Lou-a	110	486	79	146	24	11	3	73	4		.300	.310	.414	140	20				.884	0	*O-101,C-11/S-1,31	1.7
1885	Lou-a	112	483	79	141	23	17	1	52	11		.292	.309	.416	128	13				.917	-0	*O-111/C-2,3-1,P-1	0.9
1886	Lou-a	130	545	93	148	17	12	3	61	27		.272	.310	.363	105	-0	23			.934	9	*O-122/1-8,C-3,2P	0.5
1887	Lou-a	137	569	103	160	27	13	2	102	34		.281	.331	.385	97	-4	45			.940	8	*O-128,1-11	0.1
1888	Lou-a	128	538	80	154	28	11	0	67	25		.286	.320	.379	126	15	41			.886	7	O-85,S-39/3-4,C1	1.8
1889	Lou-a	130	546	72	159	20	9	3	57	29	34	.291	.333	.377	104	2	18			.946	-1	O-88,1-16,2S/3M	-0.1
1890	*Lou-a	134	543	100	**197**	29	11	4	98	43		**.363**	.421	.479	169	46	46			.939	-2	*O-123,3-12	3.6
1891	Lou-a	138	537	67	136	17	8	1	82	42	36	.253	.317	.320	83	-12	13			.918	5	*O-133/1-5,3-1	-1.0
1892	StL-N	3	14	1	2	0	0	0	1	0	1	.143	.143	.143	-14	-2	0			1.000	-1	/O-3	-0.3
Total	11	1198	4968	779	1440	213	109	18	593	229	71	.290	.327	.387	118	97	186			.918	41	*O-1042/S-64,1C32P	10.2

■ HARRY WOLFE

Wolfe, Harold "Whitey" b: 11/24/1890, Massachusetts d: 7/28/71, Fort Wayne, Ind. BR/TR, 5′8", 160 lbs. Deb: 4/15/17

YEAR	TM/L	G	AB	R	H	2B	3B	HR	RBI	BB	SO	AVG	OBP	SLG	PRO+	BR/A	SB	CS	SBR	FA	FR	G/POS	TPR
1917	Chi-N	9	5	1	2	0	0	0	1	1	1	.400	.500	.400	164	0	0			1.000	0	/O-2,S-1	0.1
	Pit-N	3	5	0	0	0	0	0	0	1	4	.000	.167	.000	-45	-1	0			.875	1	/2-1,S-1	0.0
	Yr	12	10	1	2	0	0	0	1	2	5	.200	.333	.200	61	-0	0			1.000	1	/O-2,S-2,2-1	0.1

■ LARRY WOLFE

Wolfe, Laurence Marcy b: 3/2/53, Melbourne, Fla. BR/TR, 5′11", 170 lbs. Deb: 9/16/77

YEAR	TM/L	G	AB	R	H	2B	3B	HR	RBI	BB	SO	AVG	OBP	SLG	PRO+	BR/A	SB	CS	SBR	FA	FR	G/POS	TPR
1977	Min-A	8	25	3	6	1	0	0	6	1	0	.240	.269	.280	51	-2	0	0	0	1.000	0	/3-8	-0.2
1978	Min-A	88	235	25	55	10	1	3	25	36	27	.234	.336	.323	85	-4	0	1	-1	.953	6	3-81/S-7	0.1
1979	Bos-A	47	78	12	19	4	0	3	15	17	21	.244	.385	.410	109	1	0	0	0	.963	6	2-27/3-9,S-2,C1D	0.8
1980	Bos-A	18	23	3	3	1	0	1	4	0	5	.130	.130	.304	15	-3	0	0	0	1.000	1	3-14/D-4	-0.2
Total	4	161	361	43	83	16	1	7	50	54	53	.230	.332	.338	84	-7	0	1	-1	.957	13	3-112/2-27,S-9,D1C	0.5

■ POLLY WOLFE

Wolfe, Roy Chamberlain b: 9/1/1888, Knoxville, Ill. d: 11/21/38, Morris, Ill. BL/TR, 5′10", 170 lbs. Deb: 9/22/12

YEAR	TM/L	G	AB	R	H	2B	3B	HR	RBI	BB	SO	AVG	OBP	SLG	PRO+	BR/A	SB	CS	SBR	FA	FR	G/POS	TPR
1912	Chi-A	1	1	0	0	0	0	0	0	0		.000	.000	.000	-99	-0	0			.000	0	H	0.0
1914	Chi-A	8	28	0	6	0	0	0	0	3	6	.214	.290	.214	53	-2	1	1	-0	.875	-1	/O-7	-0.4
Total	2	9	29	0	6	0	0	0	0	3	6	.207	.281	.207	47	-2	1	1		.875	-1	/O-7	-0.4

■ ABE WOLSTENHOLME

Wolstenholme, Abraham Lincoln b: 3/4/1861, Philadelphia, Pa. d: 3/4/16, Philadelphia, Pa. Deb: 6/4/1883

YEAR	TM/L	G	AB	R	H	2B	3B	HR	RBI	BB	SO	AVG	OBP	SLG	PRO+	BR/A	SB	CS	SBR	FA	FR	G/POS	TPR
1883	Phi-N	3	11	0	1	1	0	0	0	0	0	.091	.091	.182	-22	-2				.727	-3	/C-2,O-1	-0.4

■ HARRY WOLTER

Wolter, Harry Meigs b: 7/11/1884, Monterey, Cal. d: 7/7/70, Palo Alto, Cal. BL/TL, 5′10", 175 lbs. Deb: 5/14/07

YEAR	TM/L	G	AB	R	H	2B	3B	HR	RBI	BB	SO	AVG	OBP	SLG	PRO+	BR/A	SB	CS	SBR	FA	FR	G/POS	TPR
1907	Cin-N	4	15	1	2	0	0	0	1	0		.133	.133	.133	-16	-2	0			1.000	-0	/O-4	-0.3
	Pit-N	1	1	0	0	0	0	0	0	0		.000	.000	.000	-99	-0	0			.000	-0	/P-1	0.0
	StL-N	16	47	4	16	0	0	0	6	3		.340	.380	.340	130	2	1			.962	3	O-12/P-3	0.5
	Yr	21	63	5	18	0	0	0	7	3		.286	.318	.286	91	-1	1			.969	3	O-16/P-4	0.2
1909	Bos-A	54	121	14	29	2	4	2	10	9		.240	.292	.372	107	1	2			.978	-1	1-17,P-11/O-9	0.0
1910	NY-A	135	479	84	128	15	9	4	42	66		.267	.364	.361	120	13	39			.940	-3	*O-129/1-2	0.4
1911	NY-A	122	434	78	132	17	15	4	36	62		.304	.396	.440	125	15	28			.951	4	*O-113/1-2	1.3
1912	NY-A	12	32	8	11	2	1	0	1	10		.344	.512	.469	171	4	5			.923	-1	/O-9	0.2
1913	NY-A	127	425	53	108	18	6	2	43	80	50	.254	.377	.339	109	9	13			.946	-7	*O-121	-0.5
1917	Chi-N	117	353	44	88	15	7	0	28	38	40	.249	.324	.331	94	-2	7			.942	-4	O-97/1-1	-1.2
Total	7	588	1907	286	514	69	42	12	167	268	90	.270	.365	.369	114	39	95			.941	-10	O-494/1-22,P-15	0.4

■ HARRY WOLVERTON

Wolverton, Harry Sterling "Fighting Harry"
b: 12/6/1873, Mt.Vernon, Ohio d: 2/4/37, Oakland, Cal. BL/TR, 5′11", 205 lbs. Deb: 9/25/1898 M

YEAR	TM/L	G	AB	R	H	2B	3B	HR	RBI	BB	SO	AVG	OBP	SLG	PRO+	BR/A	SB	CS	SBR	FA	FR	G/POS	TPR
1898	Chi-N	13	49	4	16	1	0	0	2	1		.327	.353	.347	101	0	1			.848	3	3-13	0.3
1899	Chi-N	99	389	50	111	14	11	1	49	30		.285	.350	.386	105	2	14			.860	-6	3-98/S-1	-0.2
1900	Chi-N	3	11	2	2	0	0	0	0	2		.182	.308	.182	38	-1	1			.875	-2	/3-3	-0.2
	Phi-N	101	383	42	108	10	8	3	58	20		.282	.323	.373	92	-5	4			.881	-9	*3-101	-1.3
	Yr	104	394	44	110	10	8	3	58	22		.279	.322	.368	91	-6	5			.881	-11	*3-104	-1.5
1901	Phi-N	93	379	42	117	15	4	0	43	22		.309	.356	.369	108	4	13			**.921**	3	3-93	0.8
1902	Was-A	59	249	35	62	8	3	1	23	13		.249	.292	.317	68	-11	8			.904	3	3-59	-0.7
	Phi-N	34	136	12	40	3	2	0	16	9		.294	.347	.346	114	2	3			.931	9	3-34	1.2
1903	Phi-N	123	494	72	152	13	12	0	53	18		.308	.342	.383	110	5	10			**.941**	1	*3-123	0.7
1904	Phi-N	102	398	43	106	15	5	0	49	26		.266	.321	.329	105	2	18			.925	1	*3-102	0.7
1905	Bos-N	122	463	38	104	15	7	2	55	23		.225	.276	.300	73	-16	10			.934	4	*3-122	-0.8
1912	NY-A	34	50	6	15	1	1	0	4	2		.300	.340	.360	94	-0	1			.821	-1	/3-8,M	-0.1
Total	9	783	3001	346	833	95	53	7	352	166		.278	.326	.352	96	-17	83			.909	6	3-756/S-1	0.4

■ TONY WOMACK

Womack, Anthony Darrell b: 9/25/69, Chatham, Va. BL/TR, 5′9", 160 lbs. Deb: 9/10/93

YEAR	TM/L	G	AB	R	H	2B	3B	HR	RBI	BB	SO	AVG	OBP	SLG	PRO+	BR/A	SB	CS	SBR	FA	FR	G/POS	TPR
1993	Pit-N	15	24	5	2	0	0	0	0	3	3	.083	.185	.083	-25	-4	2	0	1	.971	5	/S-6	0.2
1994	Pit-N	5	12	4	4	0	0	0	1	2	3	.333	.429	.333	101	0	0	0	0	.750	-3	/2-3,S-2	-0.3
1996	Pit-N	17	30	11	10	3	1	0	7	6	1	.333	.459	.500	149	3	2	0	1	1.000	-4	/O-6,2-4	-0.1
1997	Pit-N★	155	641	85	178	26	9	6	50	43	109	.278	.326	.374	81	-17	**60**	7	**14**	.974	3	*2-152/S-4	0.8
1998	Pit-N	159	655	85	185	26	7	3	45	38	94	.282	.322	.357	75	-24	**58**	8	**13**	.978	7	*2-152/O-5,S-2	0.7
Total	5	351	1362	190	379	55	17	9	103	92	210	.278	.326	.363	78	-43	122	15	28	.974	8	2-311/S-14,O-11	1.3

■ SID WOMACK

Womack, Sidney Kirk "Tex" b: 10/2/1896, Greensburg, La. d: 8/28/58, Jackson, Miss. BR/TR, 5′10.5", 185 lbs. Deb: 8/15/26

YEAR	TM/L	G	AB	R	H	2B	3B	HR	RBI	BB	SO	AVG	OBP	SLG	PRO+	BR/A	SB	CS	SBR	FA	FR	G/POS	TPR
1926	Bos-N	1	3	0	0	0	0	0	1	0	0	.000	.000	.000	-99	-1	0			1.000	0	/C-1	-0.1

■ WOOD

Wood Deb: 9/30/1874

YEAR	TM/L	G	AB	R	H	2B	3B	HR	RBI	BB	SO	AVG	OBP	SLG	PRO+	BR/A	SB	CS	SBR	FA	FR	G/POS	TPR
1874	Bal-n	1	5	0	0	0	0	0	0	0	1	.000	.000	.000	-99	-1	0	0	0	.000	-2	/2-1	-0.3

YEAR	TM/L	G	AB	R	H	2B	3B	HR	RBI	BB	SO	AVG	OBP	SLG	PRO+	BR/A	SB	CS	SBR	FA	FR	G/POS	TPR
■ DOC WOOD	Wood, Charles Spencer b: 2/28/1900, Batesville, Miss. d: 11/3/74, New Orleans, La. BR/TR, 5'10", 150 lbs. Deb: 7/21/23																						
1923	Phi-A	3	3	0	1	0	0	0	0	0	0	.333	.333	.333	75	-0	0	0	0	.833	1	/S-3	0.1
■ TED WOOD	Wood, Edward Robert b: 1/4/67, Mansfield, Ohio BL/TL, 6'2", 178 lbs. Deb: 9/4/91																						
1991	SF-N	10	25	0	3	0	0	0	1	2	11	.120	.185	.120	-13	-4	0	0	0	.909	-1	/O-8	-0.6
1992	SF-N	24	58	5	12	2	0	1	3	6	15	.207	.292	.293	70	-2	0	0	0	.972	1	O-16	-0.2
1993	Mon-N	13	26	4	5	1	0	0	3	3	3	.192	.276	.231	36	-2	0	0	0	1.000	-0	/O-8	-0.3
Total	3	47	109	9	20	3	0	1	7	11	29	.183	.264	.239	42	-8	0	0	0	.968	-1	/O-32	-1.1
■ FRED WOOD	Wood, Fred S. b: 1863, Hamilton, Ont., Canada d: 8/23/33, New York, N.Y. 5'5", 150 lbs. Deb: 5/14/1884 F																						
1884	Det-N	12	42	4	2	0	0	0	1	3	18	.048	.111	.048	-51	-7				.889	-1	/C-7,O-6,S-1	-0.7
1885	Buf-N	1	4	0	1	0	0	0	0	0	0	.250	.250	.250	60	-0				.833	-0	/C-1	0.0
Total	2	13	46	4	3	0	0	0	1	3	18	.065	.122	.065	-41	-7				.883	-1	/C-8,O-6,S-1	-0.7
■ GEORGE WOOD	Wood, George A. "Dandy" b: 11/9/1858, Boston, Mass. d: 4/4/24, Harrisburg, Pa. BL/TR, 5'10.5", 175 lbs. Deb: 5/1/1880 MU																						
1880	Wor-N	81	327	37	80	16	5	0	28	10	37	.245	.267	.324	91	-4				.887	-7	*O-80/3-2,1-1	-1.2
1881	Det-N	80	337	54	100	18	9	2	32	19	32	.297	.334	.421	131	11				.862	-2	*O-80	0.7
1882	Det-N	84	375	69	101	12	12	**7**	29	14	30	.269	.296	.421	127	11				.884	2	*O-84	1.2
1883	Det-N	99	441	81	133	26	11	5	47	25	37	.302	.339	.444	142	23				.876	9	*O-99/P-1	2.6
1884	Det-N	114	473	79	119	16	10	8	29	39	75	.252	.309	.378	122	13				.896	3	*O-114/3-1	1.3
1885	Det-N	82	362	62	105	19	8	5	28	13	19	.290	.315	.428	138	14				.885	0	O-70,3-12/S-1,P-1	1.2
1886	Phi-N	106	450	81	123	18	15	4	50	23	75	.273	.309	.407	115	7	9			.904	-5	*O-97/S-6,3-3	0.0
1887	Phi-N	113	491	118	142	22	19	14	66	40	51	.289	.350	.497	125	14	19			.873	-10	*O-104/S-3,3-3,2-3	0.3
1888	Phi-N	106	433	67	99	19	6	6	51	39	44	.229	.303	.342	100	0	20			.905	0	*O-104/3-2,P-2	-0.3
1889	Phi-N	97	422	77	106	21	4	5	53	53	33	.251	.336	.355	86	-9	17			.915	-4	O-92/S-6,P-1	-1.3
	Bal-a	3	10	1	2	0	0	0	1	0	2	.200	.200	.200	14	-1	1			1.000	-0	/O-3	-0.1
1890	Phi-P	132	539	115	156	20	14	9	102	51	35	.289	.360	.429	108	4	20			.895	14	*O-132/3-1	1.1
1891	Phi-a	132	528	105	163	18	14	3	61	72	52	.309	.399	.413	128	20	22			.939	7	*O-122/3-6,S-5,M	2.1
1892	Bal-N	21	76	9	17	1	1	0	10	10	8	.224	.330	.263	78	-2	1			.911	2	O-21	0.0
	Cin-N	30	107	10	21	2	4	0	14	10	17	.196	.271	.290	71	-4	4			.863	-2	O-30	-0.6
	Yr	51	183	19	38	3	5	0	24	20	25	.208	.296	.279	74	-6	5			.885	1	O-51	-0.6
Total	13	1280	5371	965	1467	228	132	68	601	418	547	.273	.329	.403	116	98	113			.895	10	*O-1232/3-30,SP21	7.0
■ HARRY WOOD	Wood, Harold Austin b: 2/10/1881, Waterville, Maine d: 5/18/55, Bethesda, Md. BL/TR, 5'10", 155 lbs. Deb: 4/19/03																						
1903	Cin-N	2	3	0	0	0	0	0	0	1		.000	.250	.000	-24	-0	0			.000	-1	/O-2	-0.1
■ JAKE WOOD	Wood, Jacob b: 6/22/37, Elizabeth, N.J. BR/TR, 6'1", 170 lbs. Deb: 4/11/61																						
1961	Det-A	162	663	96	171	17	**14**	11	69	58	141	.258	.321	.376	83	-16	30	9	4	.969	-27	*2-162	-2.1
1962	Det-A	111	367	68	83	10	5	8	30	33	59	.226	.292	.346	68	-17	24	3	**5**	.950	-31	2-90	-3.3
1963	Det-A	85	351	50	95	11	2	11	27	24	61	.271	.330	.407	102	1	18	5	2	.958	-11	2-81/3-1	0.0
1964	Det-A	64	125	11	29	2	2	1	7	4	24	.232	.256	.304	54	-8	0	0	0	.989	-1	1-11,2-10/3-6,O-1	-1.0
1965	Det-A	58	104	12	30	3	0	2	7	10	19	.288	.357	.375	107	1	3	3	-1	.977	-2	2-20/1-1,S-1,3-1	0.0
1966	Det-A	98	230	39	58	9	3	2	27	28	48	.252	.336	.343	94	-1	4	3	-1	.968	-13	2-52/3-4,1-2	-1.2
1967	Det-A	14	20	2	1	1	0	0	0	1	7	.050	.095	.100	-41	-3	0	0	0	1.000	-0	/1-2,2-2	-0.4
	Cin-N	16	17	1	2	0	0	0	1	1	3	.118	.167	.118	-15	-3	0	0	0	1.000	-0	/O-2	-0.3
Total	7	608	1877	279	469	53	26	35	168	159	362	.250	.313	.362	82	-46	79	23	10	.963	-85	2-417/1-16,3-12,OS	-8.3
■ JIMMY WOOD	Wood, James Leon b: 12/1/1844, Brooklyn, N.Y. d: 11/30/1886, TR , 5'8.5", 150 lbs. Deb: 5/8/1871 M																						
1871	Chi-n	28	135	45	51	10	6	1	29	11	3	.378	.425	.563	163	9	18	2	**4**	**.887**	9	*2-28,M	1.2
1872	Tro-n	25	113	40	38	11	4	2	27	2	1	.336	.348	.558	172	9	3	0	1	.886	-0	2-25,M	0.5
	Eck-n	7	30	10	6	1	1	0	0	4	1	.200	.294	.300	98	1	1	0	0	.840	-1	/2-7,M	0.0
	Yr	32	143	50	44	12	5	2	27	6	2	.308	.336	.503	158	10	4	0	1	.875	-1	2-32	0.5
1873	Phi-n	42	209	67	67	11	1	0	27	8	1	.321	.346	.383	112	3	8	3	1	.850	4	*2-42,M	0.2
Total	3 n	102	487	162	162	33	12	3	83	25	6	.333	.365	.468	140	21	30	5	6	.868	12	2-102	1.9
■ JASON WOOD	Wood, Jason William b: 12/16/69, San Bernardino, Cal. BR/TR, 6'1", 170 lbs. Deb: 4/1/98																						
1998	Oak-A	3	1	1	0	0	0	0	0	0	1	.000	.000	.000	-99	-0	0	0	0	1.000	1	/S-2,3-1	0.1
	Det-A	10	23	5	8	2	0	1	1	3	4	.348	.423	.565	153	2	0	1	-1	1.000	-1	/1-6,S-1,D-3	0.0
	Yr	13	24	6	8	2	0	1	1	3	5	.333	.407	.542	144	2	0	1	-1	1.000	0	/1-6,S-3,D-3,3-1	0.1
■ JOE WOOD	Wood, Joe "Smokey Joe" (b: Howard Ellsworth Wood) b: 10/25/1889, Kansas City, Mo. d: 7/27/85, West Haven, Conn BR/TR, 5'11", 180 lbs. Deb: 8/24/08 F																						
1908	Bos-A	6	7	1	0	0	0	0	0	0		.000	.000	.000	-97	-1	0			.889	-0	/P-6	0.0
1909	Bos-A	24	55	4	9	0	1	0	3	2		.164	.207	.200	28	-5	0			.971	-4	P-24	0.0
1910	Bos-A	35	69	9	18	2	1	1	5	5		.261	.311	.362	108	0	0			.975	2	P-35	0.0
1911	Bos-A	44	88	15	23	4	2	2	11	10		.261	.343	.420	114	1	1			.947	2	P-44	0.0
1912	*Bos-A	43	124	16	36	13	1	1	13	11		.290	.348	.435	118	2	0			.974	8	P-43	0.0
1913	Bos-A	24	56	10	15	5	0	0	10	4	7	.268	.317	.357	95	-1	1			.955	4	P-23	0.0
1914	Bos-A	21	43	2	6	1	0	0	1	3	14	.140	.213	.163	13	-5	1			1.000	1	P-18	0.0
1915	Bos-A	29	54	6	14	1	1	1	7	5	10	.259	.322	.370	111	0	1	1	-0	.982	1	P-25	0.0
1917	Cle-A	10	6	1	0	0	0	0	0	0	3	.000	.000	.000	-93	-1	0			1.000	0	/P-5	0.0
1918	Cle-A	119	422	41	125	22	4	5	66	36	38	.296	.356	.403	118	8	8			.962	0	O-95,2-19/1-4	0.5
1919	Cle-A	72	192	30	49	10	6	0	27	32	21	.255	.367	.370	101	1	3			.932	-8	O-64/P-1	-1.1
1920	*Cle-A	61	137	25	37	11	2	1	30	25	16	.270	.390	.401	107	2	1	1	-0	.987	-6	O-55/P-1	-0.7
1921	Cle-A	66	194	32	71	16	5	4	60	25	17	.366	.438	.562	151	15	2	0	1	.973	-13	O-64	-0.1
1922	Cle-A	142	505	74	150	33	8	8	92	50	63	.297	.367	.442	109	7	5	1	1	.960	2	*O-141	0.0
Total	14	696	1952	266	553	118	31	23	325	208	189	.283	.357	.411	110	25	23	3	1	.962	-11	O-419,P-225/2-19,1	-1.4
■ JOE WOOD	Wood, Joseph Perry "J.P." or "Little Joe" b: 10/3/19, Houston, Tex. d: 3/25/85, Houston, Tex. BR/TR, 5'9.5", 160 lbs. Deb: 5/2/43																						
1943	Det-A	60	164	22	53	4	4	1	17	6	13	.323	.347	.415	114	2	2	2	-1	.896	-16	2-22,3-18	-1.4
■ KEN WOOD	Wood, Kenneth Lanier b: 7/1/24, Lincolnton, N.C. BR/TR, 6', 200 lbs. Deb: 4/28/48																						
1948	StL-A	10	24	2	2	0	1	0	2	1	4	.083	.120	.167	-24	-4	0	0	0	1.000	1	/O-5	-0.4
1949	StL-A	7	6	0	0	0	0	0	0	1	2	.000	.143	.000	-58	-1	0	0	0	.000	-1	/O-3	-0.3
1950	StL-A	128	369	42	83	24	0	13	62	38	58	.225	.299	.396	74	-17	0	4	-2	.952	-2	O-94	-2.3
1951	StL-A	109	333	40	79	19	0	15	44	27	49	.237	.296	.429	92	-6	1	2	-1	.959	-4	*O-100	-1.4
1952	Bos-A	15	20	0	2	0	0	0	0	3	4	.100	.217	.100	-9	-3	0	0	0	.889	-4	O-13	-0.7
	Was-A	61	210	26	50	8	6	6	32	30	21	.238	.333	.419	112	3	0	1	-1	.954	8	O-56	0.9
	Yr	76	230	26	52	8	6	6	32	33	25	.226	.323	.391	99	-1	0	1	-1	.951	5	O-69	0.2
1953	Was-A	12	33	0	7	1	0	0	3	2	3	.212	.257	.242	36	-3	0	0	0	1.000	1	/O-7	-0.3
Total	6	342	995	110	223	52	7	34	143	102	141	.224	.298	.393	81	-31	1	7	-4	.956	-1	O-278	-4.5
■ BOB WOOD	Wood, Robert Lynn b: 7/28/1865, Thorn Hill, Ohio d: 5/22/43, Churchill, Ohio BR/TR, 5'8.5", 153 lbs. Deb: 5/2/1898																						
1898	Cin-N	39	109	14	30	6	0	0	16	9		.275	.331	.330	84	-2	1			.943	1	C-29/O-1,1-1	0.1
1899	Cin-N	62	194	34	61	11	7	0	24	25		.314	.406	.443	131	9	3			.937	-10	C-53/O-2,3-2,1-1	0.3
1900	Cin-N	45	139	17	37	8	1	0	22	10		.266	.320	.338	84	-3	3			.967	-6	C-18,3-15/O-1	-0.7
1901	Cle-A	98	346	45	101	23	3	1	49	12		.292	.327	.384	101	-0	6			.952	-1	C-84/3-4,O-3,12S	0.7
1902	Cle-A	81	258	23	76	18	2	0	40	27		.295	.375	.380	114	6	1			.941	-7	C-52,1-16/O-2,23	0.4
1904	Det-A	49	175	15	43	6	2	1	17	5		.246	.271	.320	89	-3	1			.974	10	C-47	1.3
1905	Det-A	8	24	1	2	1	0	0	0	1		.083	.120	.125	-22	-3	0			.886	-0	/C-7	-0.3
Total	7	382	1245	149	350	73	15	2	168	89		.281	.339	.369	102	3	15			.951	-14	C-290/3-22,1O2S	1.8

YEAR	TM/L	G	AB	R	H	2B	3B	HR	RBI	BB	SO	AVG	OBP	SLG	PRO+	BR/A	SB	CS	SBR	FA	FR	G/POS	TPR
■ ROY WOOD Wood, Roy Winton "Woody" b: 8/29/1892, Monticello, Ark. d: 4/6/74, Fayetteville, Ark. BR/TR, 6', 175 lbs. Deb: 6/16/13																							
1913	Pit-N	14	35	4	10	4	0	0	2	1	8	.286	.306	.400	105	0	0			.895	1	/O-8,1-1	0.1
1914	Cle-A	72	220	24	52	6	3	1	15	13	26	.236	.300	.305	79	-6	6	9	-4	.946	-1	O-40,1-20	-1.4
1915	Cle-A	33	78	5	15	2	1	0	3	2	13	.192	.232	.244	41	-6	1	2	-1	.990	-2	1-21/O-2	-0.9
Total	3	119	333	33	77	12	4	1	20	16	47	.231	.285	.300	73	-12	7	11		.936	-1	/O-50,1-42	-2.2
■ LARRY WOODALL Woodall, Charles Lawrence b: 7/26/1894, Staunton, Va. d: 5/16/63, Cambridge, Mass. BR/TR, 5'9", 165 lbs. Deb: 5/20/20 C																							
1920	Det-A	18	49	4	12	1	0	0	5	2	6	.245	.275	.265	45	-4	0	0	0	.988	2	C-15	-0.1
1921	Det-A	46	80	10	29	4	1	0	14	6	7	.363	.407	.438	117	2	1	0	0	.966	-7	C-25	-0.4
1922	Det-A	50	125	19	43	2	2	0	18	8	11	.344	.388	.392	107	2	0	1	-1	.977	-10	C-40	-0.7
1923	Det-A	71	148	20	41	12	2	1	19	22	9	.277	.371	.405	106	2	2	1	0	.983	-5	C-60	-0.1
1924	Det-A	67	165	23	51	9	2	0	25	21	5	.309	.387	.388	102	1	0	0	0	.986	0	C-62	0.4
1925	Det-A	75	171	20	35	4	1	0	13	24	8	.205	.303	.240	39	-15	1	0	0	.967	-7	C-75	-1.8
1926	Det-A	67	146	18	34	5	0	0	15	15	2	.233	.304	.267	49	-11	0	0	0	.979	-4	C-59	-1.1
1927	Det-A	88	246	28	69	8	6	0	39	37	9	.280	.375	.362	90	-2	9	1	2	**.997**	4	C-86	0.8
1928	Det-A	65	186	19	39	7	1	0	13	24	10	.210	.300	.258	47	-14	3	1	0	.992	4	C-62	-0.4
1929	Det-A	1	1	0	0	0	0	0	0	0	0	.000	.000	.000	-99	-0	0	0	0	.000	0	H	0.0
Total	10	548	1317	161	353	52	15	1	161	159	67	.268	.347	.333	77	-40	16	4	2	.984	-22	C-484	-3.4
■ DARRELL WOODARD Woodard, Darrell Lee b: 12/10/56, Wilmar, Ark. BR/TR, 5'11", 160 lbs. Deb: 8/6/78																							
1978	Oak-A	33	9	10	0	0	0	0	0	1	1	.000	.100	.000	-73	-2	3	4	-2	.964	9	2-14/3-1,D-1	0.5
■ MIKE WOODARD Woodard, Michael Cary b: 3/2/60, Melrose Park, Ill. BL/TR, 5'9", 155 lbs. Deb: 9/11/85																							
1985	SF-N	24	82	12	20	1	0	0	9	5	3	.244	.287	.256	56	-5	6	1	1	.990	-5	2-23	-0.9
1986	SF-N	48	79	14	20	2	1	1	5	10	9	.253	.337	.342	92	-1	7	2	1	.986	-2	2-23/S-2,3-2	-0.1
1987	SF-N	10	19	0	4	1	0	0	1	0	1	.211	.211	.263	26	-2	0	0	0	1.000	2	/2-8	0.0
1988	Chi-A	18	45	3	6	0	1	0	4	1	5	.133	.170	.178	-2	-6	1	1	-0	.975	4	2-14/D-2	-0.2
Total	4	100	225	29	50	4	2	1	19	16	18	.222	.277	.271	55	-14	14	4	2	.985	-1	/2-68,D-2,3-2,S-2	-1.2
■ RED WOODHEAD Woodhead, James b: 7/9/1851, Chelsea, Mass. d: 9/7/1881, Boston, Mass. 5'6", 160 lbs. Deb: 4/15/1873																							
1873	Mar-n	1	5	1	0	0	0	0	0	0	0	.000	.000	.000	-99	-1	0	0	0	.900	2	/S-1	0.0
1879	Syr-N	34	131	4	21	1	0	0	2	0	23	.160	.160	.168	9	-12				.792	-7	3-34	-1.7
■ GENE WOODLING Woodling, Eugene Richard b: 8/16/22, Akron, Ohio BL/TR, 5'9.5", 195 lbs. Deb: 9/23/43 C																							
1943	Cle-A	8	25	5	8	2	1	1	5	1	5	.320	.346	.600	186	2	0	0	0	1.000	-1	/O-6	0.2
1946	Cle-A	61	133	8	25	1	4	0	9	16	13	.188	.280	.256	54	-8	1	2	-1	1.000	-3	O-37	-1.4
1947	Pit-N	22	79	7	21	2	2	0	10	7	5	.266	.326	.342	75	-3	0			.968	1	O-21	-0.2
1949	*NY-A	112	296	60	80	13	7	5	44	52	21	.270	.381	.412	110	5	2	2	-1	.982	-10	O-98	-1.0
1950	*NY-A	122	449	81	127	20	10	6	60	70	31	.283	.381	.412	106	5	5	3	-0	.993	10	*O-118	1.0
1951	*NY-A	120	420	65	118	15	8	15	71	62	37	.281	.373	.462	130	17	0	4	-2	.993	1	*O-116	1.1
1952	*NY-A	122	408	58	126	19	6	12	63	59	31	.309	.397	.473	151	28	1	4	-2	**.996**	6	*O-118	2.8
1953	*NY-A	125	395	64	121	26	4	10	58	82	29	.306	**.429**	.468	147	30	2	7	-4	**.996**	4	*O-119	2.6
1954	NY-A	97	304	33	76	12	5	3	40	53	35	.250	.361	.352	99	1	3	4	-2	.983	-1	O-89	-0.5
1955	Bal-A	47	145	22	32	6	2	3	18	24	18	.221	.335	.352	91	-2	1	1	-0	1.000	-8	O-44	-1.2
	Cle-A	79	259	33	72	15	1	5	35	36	15	.278	.372	.402	104	2	2	4	-2	.993	-3	O-70	-0.5
	Yr	126	404	55	104	21	3	8	53	60	33	.257	.359	.384	100	1	3	5	-2	.995	-11	*O-114	-1.7
1956	Cle-A	100	317	56	83	17	0	8	38	69	29	.262	.398	.391	107	6	2	6	-3	.981	-0	O-85	-0.2
1957	Cle-A	133	430	74	138	25	2	19	78	64	35	.321	.412	.521	155	34	0	5	-3	.992	11	*O-113	3.5
1958	Bal-A	133	413	57	114	16	1	15	65	66	49	.276	.378	.429	128	18	4	2	0	.974	-10	*O-116	0.1
1959	Bal-A★	140	440	63	132	22	2	14	77	78	35	.300	.405	.455	139	26	1	1	-0	.981	-13	*O-124	0.8
1960	Bal-A	140	435	68	123	18	3	11	62	84	40	.283	.403	.414	123	18	3	0	1	.995	-3	*O-124	1.0
1961	Was-A	110	342	39	107	16	4	10	57	50	24	.313	.404	.471	135	18	1	0	0	.988	-3	O-90	1.1
1962	Was-A	44	107	19	30	4	0	5	16	24	5	.280	.421	.458	138	7	1	0	0	.953	-4	O-30	0.1
	NY-N	81	190	18	52	8	1	5	24	24	22	.274	.358	.405	103	1	0	0	0	.986	-4	O-48	-0.5
Total	17	1796	5587	830	1585	257	63	147	830	921	479	.284	.388	.431	123	206	29	45		.989	-29	*O-1566	8.8
■ SAM WOODRUFF Woodruff, Orville Francis b: 12/27/1876, Chilo, Ohio d: 7/22/37, Cincinnati, Ohio BR/TR, 5'9", 160 lbs. Deb: 4/14/04																							
1904	Cin-N	87	306	20	58	14	3	0	20	19		.190	.244	.255	50	-19	9			.932	-4	3-61,2-17/S-8,O-1	-2.1
1910	Cin-N	21	61	6	9	1	0	0	2	7	8	.148	.235	.164	18	-6	2			.933	-1	3-17/2-4	-0.7
Total	2	108	367	26	67	15	3	0	22	26	8	.183	.242	.240	45	-25	11			.932	-5	/3-78,2-21,S-8,O-1	-2.8
■ PETE WOODRUFF Woodruff, Peter Frank b: 6/1873, New York BR/TR, Deb: 9/19/1899																							
1899	NY-N	20	61	11	15	1	1	2	7	9		.246	.343	.393	105	0	3			1.000	-1	O-19/1-1	-0.2
■ AL WOODS Woods, Alvis b: 8/8/53, Oakland, Cal. BL/TL, 6'3", 195 lbs. Deb: 4/7/77																							
1977	Tor-A	122	440	58	125	17	4	6	35	36	38	.284	.338	.382	94	-3	8	7	-2	.969	-2	*O-115/D-4	-1.2
1978	Tor-A	62	220	19	53	12	3	3	25	11	23	.241	.280	.364	78	-7	1	2	-1	.978	3	O-60	-0.7
1979	Tor-A	132	436	57	121	24	4	5	36	40	28	.278	.340	.385	94	-3	6	4	-1	.967	3	*O-127/D-2	-0.5
1980	Tor-A	109	373	54	112	18	2	15	47	37	35	.300	.365	.480	124	12	4	4	-1	.991	6	O-88,D-13	1.3
1981	Tor-A	85	288	20	71	15	0	1	21	19	31	.247	.293	.309	69	-11	3	4	-2	.973	3	O-77/D-2	-1.4
1982	Tor-A	85	201	20	47	11	1	3	24	21	20	.234	.306	.343	71	-8	1	3	-2	.970	-7	O-64,D-10	-1.8
1986	Min-A	23	28	5	9	1	0	2	8	3	5	.321	.387	.571	153	2	0	0	0	.000	0	/D-7	0.2
Total	7	618	1986	233	538	98	14	35	196	167	180	.271	.328	.387	93	-19	23	24	-8	.974	6	O-531/D-38	-4.1
■ GARY WOODS Woods, Gary Lee b: 7/20/54, Santa Barbara, Cal BR/TR, 6'2", 190 lbs. Deb: 9/14/76																							
1976	Oak-A	6	8	0	1	0	0	0	0	0	3	.125	.125	.125	-28	-1	0	0	0	1.000	-1	/O-4,D-1	-0.2
1977	Tor-A	60	227	21	49	9	1	0	17	7	38	.216	.246	.264	38	-19	5	4	-1	.994	3	O-60	-2.0
1978	Tor-A	8	19	1	3	1	0	0	0	1	1	.158	.200	.211	15	-2	1	0	0	1.000	-0	/O-6	-0.2
1980	*Hou-N	19	53	8	20	5	0	2	15	2	9	.377	.400	.585	186	6	1	0	0	1.000	-2	O-14	0.4
1981	*Hou-N	54	110	10	23	4	1	0	12	11	22	.209	.281	.264	58	-6	2	1	0	.984	-3	O-40	-1.0
1982	Chi-N	117	245	28	66	15	1	4	30	21	48	.269	.327	.388	97	-1	3	3	-1	1.000	-14	*O-103	-1.9
1983	Chi-N	93	190	25	46	9	0	4	22	15	27	.242	.298	.353	76	-6	5	3	-0	.971	-11	O-73/2-1	-2.0
1984	*Chi-N	87	98	13	23	4	1	3	10	15	21	.235	.336	.388	94	-1	2	1	0	1.000	-13	O-62/2-3	-1.5
1985	Chi-N	81	82	11	20	3	0	0	4	14	18	.244	.354	.280	72	-3	0	1	-1	1.000	-13	O-56	-1.8
Total	9	525	1032	117	251	50	4	13	110	86	187	.243	.303	.337	76	-34	19	13	-2	.992	-54	O-418/2-4,D-1	-10.2
■ JIM WOODS Woods, James Jerome "Woody" b: 9/17/39, Chicago, Ill. BR/TR, 6', 175 lbs. Deb: 9/27/57																							
1957	Chi-N	2	0	1	0	0	0	0	0	0	0	—	—	—	—	0	0	0	0	.000	0	R	0.0
1960	Phi-N	11	34	4	6	0	0	1	3	3	13	.176	.243	.265	39	-3	0	0	0	.939	2	3-11	-0.1
1961	Phi-N	23	48	6	11	3	0	2	9	4	15	.229	.302	.417	89	-1	0	0	0	.968	-1	3-15	-0.1
Total	3	36	82	11	17	3	0	3	12	7	28	.207	.278	.354	69	-4	0	0	0	.953	1	/3-26	-0.2
■ RON WOODS Woods, Ronald Lawrence b: 2/1/43, Hamilton, Ohio BR/TR, 5'10", 173 lbs. Deb: 4/22/69																							
1969	Det-A	17	15	3	4	0	0	1	3	2	3	.267	.353	.467	122	0	0	0	0	1.000	-2	/O-7	-0.2
	NY-A	72	171	18	30	5	2	1	7	22	29	.175	.273	.246	48	-12	2	0	1	1.000	-3	O-67	-1.8
	Yr	89	186	21	34	5	2	2	10	24	32	.183	.280	.263	54	-11	2	0	1	1.000	-5	O-74	-2.0
1970	NY-A	95	225	30	51	5	3	8	27	33	35	.227	.326	.382	100	-0	4	2	0	.974	-6	O-78	-1.0
1971	NY-A	25	32	4	8	1	0	1	2	4	2	.250	.333	.375	107	0	0	0	0	.929	-1	/O-9	-0.1
	Mon-N	51	138	26	41	7	3	1	17	19	18	.297	.382	.413	125	5	0	2	-1	.989	-1	O-45	0.1
1972	Mon-N	97	221	21	57	5	1	10	31	22	33	.258	.325	.425	110	2	3	3	-1	.991	-11	O-73	-1.3
1973	Mon-N	135	318	45	73	11	3	3	31	56	34	.230	.345	.311	80	-7	12	6	0	.977	-9	*O-114	-2.0

YEAR	TM/L	G	AB	R	H	2B	3B	HR	RBI	BB	SO	AVG	OBP	SLG	PRO+	BR/A	SB	CS	SBR	FA	FR	G/POS	TPR
1974	Mon-N	90	127	15	26	0	0	1	12	17	17	.205	.303	.228	48	-8	6	5	-1	.987	-12	O-61	-2.4
Total	6	582	1247	162	290	34	12	26	130	175	171	.233	.328	.342	87	-19	27	18	-3	.984	-45	O-454	-8.7
■ TRACY WOODSON Woodson, Tracy Michael b: 10/5/62, Richmond, Va. BR/TR, 6'3", 215 lbs. Deb: 4/7/87																							
1987	LA-N	53	136	14	31	8	1	1	11	9	21	.228	.286	.324	63	-7	1	1	-0	.958	-1	3-45/1-7	-1.0
1988	*LA-N	65	173	15	43	4	1	3	15	7	32	.249	.282	.335	79	-5	1	2	-1	.938	-5	3-41,1-25	-1.3
1989	LA-N	4	6	0	0	0	0	0	0	0	1	.000	.000	.000	-99	-2	0	0	0	1.000	0	/3-1	-0.2
1992	StL-N	31	114	9	35	8	0	1	22	3	10	.307	.331	.404	110	1	0	0	0	.945	-6	3-26/1-3	-0.6
1993	StL-N	62	77	4	16	2	0	0	2	1	14	.208	.218	.234	21	-9	0	0	0	.909	2	3-28,1-11	-0.7
Total	5	215	506	42	125	22	2	5	50	20	78	.247	.281	.328	70	-22	2	3	-1	.943	-10	3-141/1-46	-3.8
■ WOODY WOODWARD Woodward, William Frederick b: 9/23/42, Miami, Fla. BR/TR, 6'2", 185 lbs. Deb: 9/9/63																							
1963	Mil-N	10	2	1	0	0	0	0	0	0	0	.000	.000	.000	-99	-1	0	0	0	1.000	3	/S-5	0.2
1964	Mil-N	77	115	18	24	2	1	0	11	6	28	.209	.260	.243	43	-9	0	1	-1	.958	13	2-40,S-18/3-7,1-1	0.6
1965	Mil-N	112	265	17	55	7	4	0	11	10	50	.208	.236	.264	41	-21	2	2	-1	.977	11	*S-107/2-8	-0.6
1966	Atl-N	144	455	46	120	23	3	0	43	37	54	.264	.325	.327	81	-11	2	2	-1	.973	-6	2-79,S-73	-0.7
1967	Atl-N	136	429	30	97	15	2	0	25	37	51	.226	.289	.270	62	-21	0	6	-4	**.982**	9	*2-120,S-16	-0.7
1968	Atl-N	12	24	2	4	1	0	0	1	1	6	.167	.200	.208	23	-2	1	0	0	.973	3	/S-6,3-2,2-1	0.2
	Cin-N	56	119	13	29	2	0	0	10	7	23	.244	.297	.261	64	-5	1	0	0	.968	-3	S-41/2-9,1-1	-0.5
	Yr	68	143	15	33	3	0	0	11	8	29	.231	.281	.252	58	-7	2	0	1	.969	-1	S-47,2-10/3-2,1-1	-0.3
1969	Cin-N	97	241	36	63	12	0	0	15	24	40	.261	.333	.311	77	-7	3	2	-0	.966	-2	S-93/2-2	0.0
1970	*Cin-N	100	264	23	59	8	3	1	14	20	21	.223	.283	.288	53	-17	1	2	-1	.973	2	S-77,3-20,2-10,/1-2	-0.8
1971	Cin-N	136	273	22	66	9	1	0	18	27	28	.242	.310	.282	70	-10	4	0	1	.987	-5	S-85,3-63/2-9	-0.6
Total	9	880	2187	208	517	79	14	1	148	169	301	.236	.295	.287	64	-103	14	15	-5	.974	23	S-521,2-278/3-92,1	-2.9
■ JUNIOR WOOTEN Wooten, Earl Hazwell b: 1/16/24, Pelzer, S.C. BR/TL, 5'11", 160 lbs. Deb: 9/16/47																							
1947	Was-A	6	24	0	2	0	0	0	1	0	4	.083	.083	.083	-55	-5	1	0	0	.905	-1	/O-6	-0.6
1948	Was-A	88	258	34	66	8	3	1	23	24	21	.256	.324	.322	74	-10	2	1	0	.979	1	O-73/1-6,P-1	-1.2
Total	2	94	282	34	68	8	3	1	24	24	25	.241	.305	.301	64	-15	3	1	0	.972	1	/O-79,1-6,P-1	-1.8
■ FAVEL WORDSWORTH Wordsworth, Favel Perry b: 12/22/1850, New York, N.Y. d: 8/12/1888, New York, N.Y. Deb: 4/28/1873																							
1873	Res-n	12	42	5	10	0	0	0	3	2	1	.238	.273	.238	58	-2	0	0	0	.643	-3	S-11/O-1	-0.4
■ CHUCK WORKMAN Workman, Charles Thomas b: 1/6/15, Leeton, Mo. d: 1/3/53, Kansas City, Mo. BL/TR, 6', 175 lbs. Deb: 9/18/38																							
1938	Cle-A	2	5	1	2	0	0	0	0	0	0	.400	.400	.400	103	0	0	0	0	.500	-0	/O-1	0.0
1941	Cle-A	9	4	2	0	0	0	0	0	1	1	.000	.200	.000	-45	-1	0	0	0	.000	0	H	-0.1
1943	Bos-N	153	615	71	153	17	1	10	67	53	72	.249	.311	.328	86	-11	12			.988	6	*O-149/1-3,3-1	-1.5
1944	Bos-N	140	418	46	87	18	3	11	53	42	41	.208	.287	.344	74	-15	1			.983	-3	*O-103,3-19	-2.3
1945	Bos-N	139	514	77	141	16	2	25	87	51	58	.274	.347	.459	122	14	9			.910	-17	*3-107,O-24	-0.1
1946	Bos-N	25	48	5	8	2	0	2	7	3	11	.167	.231	.333	58	-3	0			.920	-1	O-12	-0.5
	Pit-N	58	145	11	32	4	1	2	16	11	19	.221	.280	.303	64	-7	2			1.000	6	O-40/3-1	-0.3
	Yr	83	193	16	40	6	1	4	23	14	30	.207	.268	.311	63	-10	2			.986	5	O-52/3-1	-0.8
Total	6	526	1749	213	423	57	7	50	230	161	202	.242	.311	.368	91	-24	24	0		.985	-8	O-329,3-128/1-3	-4.8
■ HANK WORKMAN Workman, Henry Kilgariff b: 2/5/26, Los Angeles, Cal. BL/TR, 6'1", 185 lbs. Deb: 9/4/50																							
1950	NY-A	2	5	1	1	0	0	0	0	0	1	.200	.200	.200	3	-1	0	0	0	1.000	-0	/1-1	-0.1
■ HERB WORTH Worth, Herbert b: 5/2/1847, Brooklyn, N.Y. d: 4/27/14, Brooklyn, N.Y. Deb: 7/29/1872																							
1872	Atl-n	1	5	1	1	1	0	0	1	0	0	.200	.200	.400	68	-0	0	0	0	1.000	0	/O-1	0.0
■ CRAIG WORTHINGTON Worthington, Craig Richard b: 4/17/65, Los Angeles, Cal. BR/TR, 6', 200 lbs. Deb: 4/26/88																							
1988	Bal-A	26	81	5	15	2	0	2	4	9	24	.185	.267	.284	56	-5	1	0	0	.961	1	3-26	-0.4
1989	Bal-A	145	497	57	123	23	0	15	70	61	114	.247	.335	.384	105	4	1	2	-1	.951	-10	*3-145	-0.6
1990	Bal-A	133	425	46	96	17	0	8	44	63	96	.226	.330	.322	86	-7	1	2	-1	.945	-12	*3-131/D-2	-1.9
1991	Bal-A	31	102	11	23	3	0	4	12	12	14	.225	.313	.373	93	-1	0	1	-1	.975	-3	3-30	-0.4
1992	Cle-A	9	24	0	4	0	0	0	2	2	4	.167	.231	.167	13	-3	0	1	-1	.857	2	/3-9	-0.2
1995	Cin-N	10	18	1	5	1	0	1	2	2	1	.278	.350	.500	122	1	0	0	0	1.000	0	/1-4,3-2	0.0
	Tex-A	26	68	4	15	4	0	2	6	7	8	.221	.293	.368	69	-3	0	0	0	.980	-0	3-26	-0.3
1996	Tex-A	13	19	2	3	0	0	1	4	6	3	.158	.360	.316	69	-1	0	0	0	.917	1	/3-7,1-6	0.0
Total	7	393	1234	126	284	50	0	33	144	162	264	.230	.323	.351	90	-15	3	6	-3	.950	-21	3-376/1-10,D-2	-3.8
■ RED WORTHINGTON Worthington, Robert Lee b: 4/24/06, Alhambra, Cal. d: 12/8/63, Sepulveda, Cal. BR/TR, 5'11", 170 lbs. Deb: 4/14/31																							
1931	Bos-N	128	491	47	143	25	10	4	44	26	38	.291	.328	.407	100	-1	1			**.988**	-3	*O-124	-1.3
1932	Bos-N	105	435	62	132	35	8	8	61	15	24	.303	.330	.476	118	9	1			.987	-1	*O-104	0.1
1933	Bos-N	17	45	3	7	4	0	0	0	1	3	.156	.174	.244	20	-5	0			.900	-1	O-10	-0.7
1934	Bos-N	41	65	6	16	5	0	0	6	6	5	.246	.319	.323	78	-2	0			.920	-1	O-11	-0.3
	StL-N	1	1	0	0	0	0	0	0	0	1	.000	.000	.000	-94	-0	0			.000	0	H	0.0
	Yr	42	66	6	16	5	0	0	6	6	6	.242	.315	.318	75	-2	0			.920	-1	O-11	-0.3
Total	4	292	1037	118	298	69	18	12	111	48	71	.287	.321	.423	103	1	2			.981	-7	O-249	-2.2
■ CHUCK WORTMAN Wortman, William Lewis b: 1/5/1892, Baltimore, Md. d: 8/19/77, Las Vegas, Nev. BR/TR, 5'7", 150 lbs. Deb: 7/20/16																							
1916	Chi-N	69	234	17	47	4	2	2	16	18	22	.201	.258	.261	54	-13	4			.908	-21	S-69	-3.5
1917	Chi-N	75	190	24	33	4	1	0	9	18	23	.174	.245	.205	36	-14	6			.918	-8	S-65/2-1,3-1	-2.2
1918	*Chi-N	17	17	4	2	0	0	1	3	1	2	.118	.167	.294	39	-1	3			.864	2	/2-8,S-4	0.1
Total	3	161	441	45	82	8	3	3	28	37	47	.186	.249	.238	46	-28	13			.913	-27	S-138/2-9,3-1	-5.6
■ RON WOTUS Wotus, Ronald Allan b: 3/3/61, Colchester, Conn. BR/TR, 6'1", 164 lbs. Deb: 9/3/83 C																							
1983	Pit-N	5	3	0	0	0	0	0	0	0	1	.000	.000	.000	-98	-1	0	0	0	1.000	1	/S-2,2-1	0.0
1984	Pit-N	27	55	4	12	6	0	0	2	6	8	.218	.295	.327	75	-2	0	0	0	.976	9	S-17/2-7	0.9
Total	2	32	58	4	12	6	0	0	2	6	9	.207	.281	.310	66	-3	0	0	0	.976	10	/S-19,2-8	0.9
■ JIMMY WOULFE Woulfe, James Joseph b: 11/25/1859, New Orleans, La. d: 12/20/24, New Orleans, La. TR , 5'11", Deb: 5/16/1884																							
1884	Cin-a	8	34	3	5	0	1	0	2	1		.147	.171	.206	22	-3				.625	-3	/O-7,3-1	-0.6
	Pit-a	15	53	7	6	1	0	0	1	0		.113	.113	.132	-20	-7				.893	1	O-15	-0.6
	Yr	23	87	10	11	1	1	0	3	1		.126	.136	.161	-3	-10				.795	-2	O-22/3-1	-1.2
■ AL WRIGHT Wright, Albert Edgar "A-1" b: 11/11/12, San Francisco, Cal BR/TR, 6'1.5", 170 lbs. Deb: 4/25/33																							
1933	Bos-N	4	1	0	1	0	0	0	0	0	0	1.000	1.000	1.000	515	1	0			.500	-0	/2-3	0.0
■ AB WRIGHT Wright, Albert Owen b: 11/16/05, Terlton, Okla. d: 5/23/95, Muskogee, Okla. BR/TR, 6'3", 200 lbs. Deb: 4/20/35																							
1935	Cle-A	67	160	17	38	11	1	2	18	10	17	.237	.291	.356	65	-9	2	1	0	.984	-8	O-47	-1.7
1944	Bos-N	71	195	20	50	9	0	7	35	18	31	.256	.326	.410	102	0	0			.968	-4	O-47	-0.6
Total	2	138	355	37	88	20	1	9	53	28	48	.248	.310	.386	85	-9	2	1		.974	-11	/O-94	-2.3
■ CY WRIGHT Wright, Ceylon b: 8/16/1893, Minneapolis, Minn. d: 11/7/47, Hines, Ill. BL/TR, 5'9", 150 lbs. Deb: 6/30/16																							
1916	Chi-A	8	18	0	0	0	0	0	0	1	7	.000	.053	.000	-83	-4	0			.844	-1	/S-8	-0.5
■ GLENN WRIGHT Wright, Forest Glenn "Buckshot" b: 2/6/01, Archie, Mo. d: 4/6/84, Olathe, Kan. BR/TR, 5'11", 170 lbs. Deb: 4/15/24																							
1924	Pit-N	153	616	80	177	28	18	7	111	27	52	.287	.318	.425	96	-5	14	6	1	.946	11	*S-153	2.3
1925	*Pit-N	153	614	97	189	32	10	18	121	31	32	.308	.341	.480	100	-2	3	7	-3	.939	0	*S-153/3-1	1.1
1926	Pit-N	119	458	73	141	15	15	8	77	19	26	.308	.335	.459	106	2	6			.927	-13	*S-116	0.2
1927	*Pit-N	143	570	78	160	26	4	9	105	39	46	.281	.328	.388	85	-13	4			.942	-17	*S-143	-1.5
1928	Pit-N	108	407	63	126	20	8	8	66	21	53	.310	.343	.457	103	1	3			.927	-24	*S-101/1-1,O-1	-1.1

YEAR	TM/L	G	AB	R	H	2B	3B	HR	RBI	BB	SO	AVG	OBP	SLG	PRO+	BR/A	SB	CS	SBR	FA	FR	G/POS	TPR
1929	Bro-N	24	25	4	5	0	0	1	6	3	6	.200	.286	.320	51	-2	0			.667	-3	/S-3	-0.4
1930	Bro-N	135	532	83	171	28	12	22	126	32	70	.321	.360	.543	116	11	2			.964	-2	*S-134	2.2
1931	Bro-N	77	268	36	76	9	4	9	32	14	35	.284	.324	.448	106	1	1			.942	6	S-75	1.4
1932	Bro-N	127	446	50	122	31	5	11	60	12	57	.274	.293	.439	96	-4	4			.939	8	*S-122/1-2	1.3
1933	Bro-N	71	192	19	49	13	0	1	18	11	24	.255	.299	.339	85	-4	1			.936	-4	S-51/1-9,3-2	-0.6
1935	Chi-A	9	25	1	3	1	0	0	1	0	6	.120	.120	.160	-27	-5	0	0	0	.943	0	/2-7	-0.4
Total	11	1119	4153	584	1219	203	76	94	723	209	407	.294	.328	.447	99	-19	38	13		.941	-37	*S-1051/1-12,230	4.5
■ GEORGE WRIGHT	Wright, George b: 1/28/1847, Yonkers, N.Y. d: 8/21/37, Boston, Mass. BR/TR, 5'9.5", 150 lbs. Deb: 5/5/1871 FMH																						
1871	Bos-n	16	80	33	33	7	5	0	11	6	1	.412	.453	.625	200	10	9	1	2	.816	5	S-15/1-1	1.1
1872	Bos-n	48	255	87	86	16	6	2	32	3	1	.337	.345	.471	141	10	14	4	2	.838	22	*S-48	2.3
1873	Bos-n	59	325	99	126	19	8	3	50	8	2	.388	.402	.523	160	20	3	5	-2	**.808**	15	*S-59	2.2
1874	Bos-n	60	313	76	103	10	**15**	2	44	5	6	.329	.340	.476	150	15	2	0	1	.821	4	*S-60/3-1	1.4
1875	Bos-n	79	408	106	136	20	7	2	61	2	6	.333	.337	.431	159	22	13	6	0	.861	4	*S-79/P-2	2.0
1876	Bos-N	70	335	72	100	18	6	1	34	8	9	.299	.315	.397	134	11				.888	13	*S-68/2-2,P-1	2.1
1877	Bos-N	61	290	58	80	15	1	0	35	9	15	.276	.298	.334	95	-2				.878	9	*2-58/S-3	0.8
1878	Bos-N	59	267	35	60	5	1	0	12	6	22	.225	.242	.251	58	-13				**.947**	11	*S-59	0.1
1879	Pro-N	85	388	79	107	15	10	1	42	13	20	.276	.299	.374	122	9				.924	21	*S-85,M	3.2
1880	Bos-N	1	4	2	1	0	0	0	0	0	0	.250	.250	.250	72	-0				1.000	-0	/S-1	0.0
1881	Bos-N	7	25	4	5	0	0	0	0	3	1	.200	.286	.200	58	-1				.963	-3	/S-7	-0.3
1882	Pro-N	46	185	14	30	1	2	0	9	4	36	.162	.180	.189	19	-16				.873	-7	S-46	-2.0
Total	5 n	262	1381	401	484	72	41	9	198	24	16	.350	.362	.482	156	78	41	16	3	.831	50	S-261/P-2,3-1,1-1	9.0
Total	7	329	1494	264	383	54	20	2	132	43	103	.256	.277	.323	93	-11				.911	42	S-269/2-60,P-1	3.9
■ GEORGE WRIGHT	Wright, George De Witt b: 12/22/58, Oklahoma City, Okla BB/TR, 5'11", 180 lbs. Deb: 4/10/82																						
1982	Tex-A	150	557	69	147	20	5	11	50	30	78	.264	.305	.377	91	-8	3	7	-3	.981	11	*O-149	-0.5
1983	Tex-A	162	634	79	175	28	6	18	80	41	82	.276	.322	.424	106	3	8	7	-2	.985	10	*O-161	0.7
1984	Tex-A	101	383	40	93	19	4	9	48	15	54	.243	.275	.384	78	-13	0	2	-1	.983	-3	O-80,D-18	-2.0
1985	Tex-A	109	363	21	69	13	0	2	18	25	49	.190	.242	.242	33	-33	4	7	-3	.991	-1	*O-102/D-4	-4.1
1986	Tex-A	49	106	10	23	3	1	2	7	4	23	.217	.252	.321	53	-7	3	5	-2	.969	-5	O-42	-1.5
	Mon-N	56	117	12	22	5	2	0	5	11	28	.188	.264	.265	47	-9	1	1	-0	1.000	-2	O-32	-1.3
Total	5	627	2160	231	529	88	18	42	208	126	314	.245	.289	.361	78	-66	19	29	-12	.984	10	O-566/D-22	-8.7
■ JOE WRIGHT	Wright, Joseph S. b: 1873, Pittsburgh, Pa. BL/TL, 5'8", 175 lbs. Deb: 7/14/1895																						
1895	Lou-N	60	228	30	63	10	4	1	30	12	28	.276	.315	.368	81	-7	7			.963	-2	O-60	-1.1
1896	Lou-N	2	7	0	2	0	0	0	0	0	1	.286	.286	.286	53	-0	0			1.000	-0	/O-2	-0.1
	Pit-N	15	52	5	16	2	1	0	6	1	2	.308	.321	.385	89	-1	1			.958	-2	O-12/3-1	-0.3
	Yr	17	59	5	18	2	1	0	6	1	3	.305	.317	.373	85	-1	1			.962	-2	O-14/3-1	-0.4
Total	2	77	287	35	81	12	5	1	36	13	31	.282	.316	.369	82	-8	8			.963	-5	/O-74,3-1	-1.5
■ PAT WRIGHT	Wright, Patrick Francis b: 7/5/1865, Pottsville, Pa. d: 5/29/43, Springfield, Ill. BB/TR, 6'2", 190 lbs. Deb: 7/11/1890																						
1890	Chi-N	1	2	0	0	0	0	0	0	1	0	.000	.333	.000	-1	-0	0			1.000	0	/2-1	0.0
■ SAM WRIGHT	Wright, Samuel b: 11/25/1848, New York, N.Y. d: 5/6/28, Boston, Mass. BR/TR, 5'7.5", 146 lbs. Deb: 4/21/1875 F																						
1875	NH-n	33	127	10	24	4	0	0	5	1	1	.189	.195	.220	51	-5	1	0	0	.807	12	S-33	0.5
1876	Bos-N	2	8	0	1	0	0	0	0	0	0	.125	.125	.125	-16	-1				.778	-0	/S-2	-0.1
1880	Cin-N	9	34	0	3	0	0	0	0	0	5	.088	.088	.088	-40	-5				.889	-2	/S-9	-0.6
1881	Bos-N	1	4	0	1	0	0	0	0	0	0	.250	.250	.250	60	-0				.667	-1	/S-1	-0.1
Total	3	12	46	0	5	0	0	0	0	0	5	.109	.109	.109	-27	-6				.843	-3	/S-12	-0.8
■ TAFFY WRIGHT	Wright, Taft Shedron b: 8/10/11, Tabor City, N.C. d: 10/22/81, Orlando, Fla. BL/TR, 5'10", 180 lbs. Deb: 4/18/38																						
1938	Was-A	100	263	37	92	18	10	2	36	13	17	.350	.389	.517	134	13	1	2	-1	.982	-4	O-60	0.5
1939	Was-A	129	499	77	154	29	11	4	93	38	19	.309	.359	.435	110	6	1	2	-1	.950	-3	*O-123	-0.2
1940	Chi-A	147	581	79	196	31	9	5	88	43	25	.337	.385	.448	114	12	4	7	-3	.963	-4	*O-144	-0.2
1941	Chi-A	136	513	71	165	35	5	10	97	60	27	.322	.399	.468	130	23	5	4	-1	.973	-2	*O-134	1.1
1942	Chi-A	85	300	43	100	13	5	0	47	48	9	.333	.432	.410	141	19	1	8	-5	.968	-1	O-81	1.0
1946	Chi-A	115	422	46	116	19	4	7	52	42	17	.275	.342	.389	108	4	10	3	1	.991	-3	*O-107	-0.3
1947	Chi-A	124	401	48	130	13	0	4	54	48	17	.324	.398	.387	123	14	8	6	-1	.971	-4	*O-100	0.4
1948	Chi-A	134	455	50	127	15	6	4	61	38	18	.279	.341	.365	91	-7	2	1	0	.987	1	*O-114	-1.2
1949	Phi-A	59	149	14	35	2	5	2	25	16	6	.235	.321	.356	82	-4	0	0	0	.970	-0	O-35	-0.6
Total	9	1029	3583	465	1115	175	55	38	553	346	155	.311	.376	.423	116	80	32	33	-10	.972	-21	O-898	0.5
■ TOM WRIGHT	Wright, Thomas Everette b: 9/22/23, Shelby, N.C. BL/TR, 5'11.5", 180 lbs. Deb: 9/15/48																						
1948	Bos-A	3	2	1	1	0	1	0	0	0	0	.500	.500	1.500	400	1	0	0	0	.000	0	H	0.1
1949	Bos-A	5	4	1	1	1	0	0	1	1	1	.250	.400	.500	128	0	0	0	0	.000	0	H	0.0
1950	Bos-A	54	107	17	34	7	0	0	20	6	18	.318	.360	.383	82	-3	0	0	0	.953	-2	O-24	-0.6
1951	Bos-A	28	63	8	14	1	1	1	9	11	8	.222	.347	.317	73	-2	0	0	0	.950	-4	O-18	-0.6
1952	StL-A	29	66	6	16	0	0	1	6	12	20	.242	.359	.288	79	-1	1	1	-0	.976	1	O-18	-0.2
	Chi-A	60	132	15	34	10	2	1	21	16	16	.258	.342	.386	102	0	1	0	0	.969	-2	O-34	-0.2
	Yr	89	198	21	50	10	2	2	27	28	36	.253	.348	.354	94	-1	2	1	0	.971	-1	O-52	-0.4
1953	Chi-A	77	132	14	33	5	3	2	25	12	21	.250	.322	.379	86	-3	0	0	0	.978	-5	O-33	-0.9
1954	Was-A	76	171	13	42	4	4	1	17	18	38	.246	.325	.333	85	-4	0	0	0	1.000	-2	O-43	-0.7
1955	Was-A	7	7	0	0	0	0	0	0	0	1	.000	.000	.000	-99	-2	0	0	0	.000	0	H	-0.2
1956	Was-A	2	1	0	0	0	0	0	0	0	0	.000	.000	.000	-99	-0	0	0	0	.000	0	H	0.0
Total	9	341	685	75	175	28	11	6	99	76	123	.255	.336	.355	85	-14	2	1	0	.977	-13	O-170	-3.3
■ DICK WRIGHT	Wright, Willard James b: 5/5/1890, Worcester, N.Y. d: 1/24/52, Bethlehem, Pa. BR/TR, 5'10", 170 lbs. Deb: 6/30/15																						
1915	Bro-F	4	5	0	0	0	0	0	0	0	0	.000	.000	.000	-99	-1	0			.833	-1	/C-3	-0.2
■ HARRY WRIGHT	Wright, William Henry b: 1/10/1835, Sheffield, England d: 10/3/1895, Atlantic City, N.J. BR/TR, 5'9.5", 157 lbs. Deb: 5/5/1871 FMH																						
1871	Bos-n	31	147	42	44	5	2	0	26	13	2	.299	.356	.361	103	1	7	1	2	.855	-0	*O-30/P-9,S-1,M	0.2
1872	Bos-n	48	208	39	52	5	1	0	23	9	2	.250	.281	.284	70	-8	0	0	0	.866	-4	*O-48/P-7,M	-0.7
1873	Bos-n	58	266	57	67	10	4	2	35	10	3	.252	.279	.342	77	-10	1	1	-0	.837	-4	*O-58,P-13,M	-0.8
1874	Bos-n	40	184	44	58	4	2	2	27	4	3	.315	.330	.391	123	4	1	0	0	.827	-2	*O-40/P-6,M	0.2
1875	Bos-n	1	4	1	1	0	0	0	0	0	1	.250	.250	.250	72	-0	0	0	0	1.000	-0	/O-1,M	0.0
1876	Bos-N	1	3	0	0	0	0	0	0	0	1	.000	.000	.000	-98	-1				.000	-0	/O-1,M	-0.1
1877	Bos-N	1	4	0	0	0	0	0	0	0	1	.000	.000	.000	-97	-1				.667	1	/O-1,M	0.0
Total	5 n	178	809	183	222	24	9	4	111	36	11	.274	.305	.341	90	-13	9	2	2	.846	-11	O-177/P-35,S-1	-1.1
Total	2	2	7	0	0	0	0	0	0	0	2	.000	.000	.000	-97	-1				.667	0	/O-2	-0.1
■ BILL WRIGHT	Wright, William Hiram Deb: 9/16/1887																						
1887	Was-N	1	3	0	2	0	0	0	0	0	0	.667	.667	.667	286	1	0			.778	-0	/C-1	0.0
■ RASTY WRIGHT	Wright, William Smith b: 1/31/1863, Birmingham, Mich. d: 10/14/22, Duluth, Minn. BL, 6'1", 185 lbs. Deb: 4/17/1890																						
1890	Syr-a	88	348	82	106	10	6	0	27	69		.305	.428	.368	150	29	30			.907	4	O-88	2.5
	Cle-N	13	45	7	5	1	0	0	2	12	4	.111	.298	.133	27	-4	3			.917	-1	O-13	-0.4
Total	1	101	393	89	111	11	6	0	29	81	4	.282	.412	.341	135	25	33			.908	3	O-101	2.1
■ RUSS WRIGHTSTONE	Wrightstone, Russell Guy b: 3/18/1893, Bowmansdale, Pa. d: 2/25/69, Harrisburg, Pa. BL/TR, 5'10.5", 176 lbs. Deb: 4/19/20																						
1920	Phi-N	76	206	23	54	6	1	3	17	10	25	.262	.303	.345	82	-5	3	2	-0	.934	6	3-56/S-2,2-1	0.3
1921	Phi-N	109	372	59	110	13	4	9	51	18	20	.296	.332	.425	92	-5	4	4	-1	.922	4	3-54,O-37/2-4	-0.1
1922	Phi-N	99	331	56	101	18	6	5	33	28	17	.305	.365	.441	98	-2	4	5	-2	.973	13	3-40,S-35/1-2	1.4

YEAR	TM/L	G	AB	R	H	2B	3B	HR	RBI	BB	SO	AVG	OBP	SLG	PRO+	BR/A	SB	CS	SBR	FA	FR	G/POS	TPR
1923	Phi-N	119	392	59	107	21	7	7	57	21	19	.273	.315	.416	82	-12	5	2	0	.942	-4	3-72,S-21/2-9	-0.7
1924	Phi-N	118	388	55	119	24	4	7	58	27	15	.307	.363	.443	102	1	5	4	-1	.944	-8	3-97/2-9,S-5,O-1	-0.1
1925	Phi-N	92	286	48	99	18	5	14	61	19	18	.346	.389	.591	135	14	0	3	-2	.937	-19	O-45,S-12,3-11,2/1	-0.8
1926	Phi-N	112	368	55	113	23	1	7	57	27	11	.307	.356	.432	106	3	5			.977	-0	1-53,3-37,2-13,/O-5	0.2
1927	Phi-N	141	533	62	163	24	5	6	75	48	20	.306	.365	.403	104	4	9			.989	1	*1-136/2-1,3-1	-0.4
1928	Phi-N	33	91	7	19	5	1	1	11	14	5	.209	.321	.319	65	-4	0			.936	-4	O-26/1-4	-1.0
	NY-N	30	25	3	4	0	0	1	5	3	2	.160	.250	.280	38	-2	0			1.000	-0	/1-2	-0.2
	Yr	63	116	10	23	5	1	2	16	17	7	.198	.306	.310	60	-7	0			.936	-4	O-26/1-6	-1.2
Total	9	929	2992	427	889	152	34	60	425	215	152	.297	.349	.431	99	-9	35	20		.942	-12	3-368,1-203,O/S2	-1.4

■ ZEKE WRIGLEY

Wrigley, George Watson b: 1/18/1874, Philadelphia, Pa. d: 9/28/52, Philadelphia, Pa. 5′8.5″, 150 lbs. Deb: 8/31/1896

YEAR	TM/L	G	AB	R	H	2B	3B	HR	RBI	BB	SO	AVG	OBP	SLG	PRO+	BR/A	SB	CS	SBR	FA	FR	G/POS	TPR
1896	Was-N	5	9	1	1	0	0	0	2	1	1	.111	.200	.111	-17	-2	0			.909	3	/2-3,S-1	0.1
1897	Was-N	104	388	65	110	14	8	3	64	21		.284	.320	.384	86	-9	5			.885	-2	O-36,S-33,3-30,/2-9	-1.0
1898	Was-N	111	400	50	98	9	10	2	39	20		.245	.283	.333	76	-14	10			.895	11	S-97,2-11/O-3,3-1	0.2
1899	NY-N	4	15	1	3	0	0	0	1	1		.200	.250	.200	25	-2	1			.818	-1	/3-5	-0.3
	Bro-N	15	49	4	10	2	2	0	11	3		.204	.250	.327	56	-3	2			.870	-4	S-14/3-1	-0.5
	Yr	19	64	5	13	2	2	0	12	4		.203	.250	.297	49	-5	3			.870	-5	S-14/3-6	-0.8
Total	4	239	861	121	222	25	20	5	117	46	1	.258	.296	.351	78	-29	18			.892	7	S-145/O-39,3-37,2	-1.5

■ RICK WRONA

Wrona, Richard James b: 12/10/63, Tulsa, Okla. BR/TR, 6′1″, 185 lbs. Deb: 9/3/88

YEAR	TM/L	G	AB	R	H	2B	3B	HR	RBI	BB	SO	AVG	OBP	SLG	PRO+	BR/A	SB	CS	SBR	FA	FR	G/POS	TPR
1988	Chi-N	4	6	0	0	0	0	0	0	0	1	.000	.000	.000	-96	-1	0	0	0	1.000	1	/C-2	0.0
1989	*Chi-N	38	92	11	26	2	1	2	14	2	21	.283	.305	.391	91	-1	0	0	0	.983	2	C-37	0.2
1990	Chi-N	16	29	3	5	0	0	0	0	2	11	.172	.226	.172	10	-3	1	0	0	.970	3	C-16	0.0
1992	Cin-N	11	23	0	4	0	0	0	0	0	3	.174	.174	.174	-1	-3	0	0	0	.965	3	C-10/1-1	0.0
1993	Chi-A	4	8	0	1	0	0	0	1	0	4	.125	.125	.125	-33	-1	0	0	0	1.000	-1	/C-4	-0.2
1994	Mil-A	6	10	2	5	4	0	1	3	1	1	.500	.545	1.200	319	3	0	0	0	.923	-1	/C-5,1-1	0.2
Total	6	79	168	16	41	6	1	3	18	5	41	.244	.270	.345	68	-8	1	0	0	.976	8	/C-74,1-2	0.2

■ YATS WUESTLING

Wuestling, George b: 10/18/03, St.Louis, Mo. d: 4/26/70, St.Louis, Mo. BR/TR, 5′11″, 167 lbs. Deb: 6/15/29

YEAR	TM/L	G	AB	R	H	2B	3B	HR	RBI	BB	SO	AVG	OBP	SLG	PRO+	BR/A	SB	CS	SBR	FA	FR	G/POS	TPR
1929	Det-A	54	150	13	30	4	1	0	16	9	24	.200	.250	.240	27	-16	1	3	-2	.943	-2	S-52/2-1,3-1	-1.4
1930	Det-A	4	9	0	0	0	0	0	0	2	3	.000	.182	.000	-48	-2	0	0	0	.842	1	/S-4	-0.1
	NY-A	25	58	5	11	0	1	0	3	4	14	.190	.242	.224	20	-7	0	1	-1	.918	4	S-21/3-3	-0.2
	Yr	29	67	5	11	0	1	0	3	6	17	.164	.233	.194	10	-9	0	1	-1	.904	5	S-25/3-3	-0.3
Total	2	83	217	18	41	4	2	0	19	15	41	.189	.245	.226	21	-26	1	4	-2	.931	2	/S-77,3-4,2-1	-1.7

■ JOE WYATT

Wyatt, Loral John b: 4/6/1900, Petersburg, Ind. d: 12/5/70, Oblong, Ill. BR/TR, 6′1″, 175 lbs. Deb: 9/11/24

YEAR	TM/L	G	AB	R	H	2B	3B	HR	RBI	BB	SO	AVG	OBP	SLG	PRO+	BR/A	SB	CS	SBR	FA	FR	G/POS	TPR
1924	Cle-A	4	12	1	2	0	0	0	1	2	1	.167	.286	.167	18	-1	0	0	0	.833	-1	/O-4	-0.3

■ REN WYLIE

Wylie, James Renwick b: 12/14/1861, Elizabeth, Pa. d: 8/17/51, Wilkinsburg, Pa. BR/TR, 5′11″, 155 lbs. Deb: 8/11/1882

YEAR	TM/L	G	AB	R	H	2B	3B	HR	RBI	BB	SO	AVG	OBP	SLG	PRO+	BR/A	SB	CS	SBR	FA	FR	G/POS	TPR
1882	Pit-a	1	3	0	0	0	0	0		0		.000	.000	.000	-99	-1				1.000	0	/O-1	0.0

■ FRANK WYMAN

Wyman, Frank H. b: 5/10/1862, Haverhill, Mass. d: 2/4/16, Everett, Mass. Deb: 6/10/1884

YEAR	TM/L	G	AB	R	H	2B	3B	HR	RBI	BB	SO	AVG	OBP	SLG	PRO+	BR/A	SB	CS	SBR	FA	FR	G/POS	TPR
1884	KC-U	30	124	16	27	4	0	0		3		.218	.236	.250	55	-11				.743	5	O-25/P-3,1-3,3-3	-0.5
	CP-U	2	8	1	3	0	0	0		0		.375	.375	.375	129	0				.846	-0	/1-2	-0.1
	Yr	32	132	17	30	4	0	0		3		.227	.244	.258	60	-10				.743	4	O-25/1-5,P-3,3-3	-0.6

■ BUTCH WYNEGAR

Wynegar, Harold Delano b: 3/14/56, York, Pa. BB/TR, 6′, 194 lbs. Deb: 4/9/76

YEAR	TM/L	G	AB	R	H	2B	3B	HR	RBI	BB	SO	AVG	OBP	SLG	PRO+	BR/A	SB	CS	SBR	FA	FR	G/POS	TPR
1976	Min-A★	149	534	58	139	21	2	10	69	79	63	.260	.358	.363	109	9	0	0	0	.978	-10	*C-137,D-15	0.3
1977	Min-A★	144	532	76	139	22	3	10	79	68	61	.261	.347	.370	97	-1	2	3	-1	.993	-11	*C-142/3-1	-0.9
1978	Min-A	135	454	36	104	22	1	4	45	47	42	.229	.310	.308	73	-15	1	0	0	.988	-3	*C-131/3-1	-1.5
1979	Min-A	149	504	74	136	20	0	7	57	74	36	.270	.366	.351	91	-4	2	2	-1	.992	-4	*C-146/D-2	-0.4
1980	Min-A	146	486	61	124	18	3	5	57	63	36	.255	.343	.335	81	-11	3	1	0	.988	4	*C-142/D-1	-0.2
1981	Min-A	47	150	11	37	5	0	0	10	17	9	.247	.327	.280	72	-5	0	1	-1	.995	-1	C-37/D-9	-0.5
1982	Min-A	24	86	9	18	4	0	1	8	10	12	.209	.292	.291	59	-5	0	0	0	.986	-2	C-24	-0.5
	NY-A	63	191	27	56	8	1	3	20	40	21	.293	.418	.393	126	9	0	1	-1	.993	-1	C-62	1.1
	Yr	87	277	36	74	12	1	4	28	50	33	.267	.381	.361	106	4	0	1	-1	.991	-2	C-86	0.6
1983	NY-A	94	301	40	89	18	2	6	42	52	29	.296	.401	.429	133	16	1	1	-0	.985	-13	C-93	0.7
1984	NY-A	129	442	48	118	13	1	6	45	65	35	.267	.361	.342	99	2	1	4	-2	.993	-4	*C-126	0.3
1985	NY-A	102	309	27	69	15	0	5	32	64	43	.223	.357	.320	89	-2	0	0	0	.990	2	C-96	0.4
1986	NY-A	61	194	19	40	4	1	7	29	30	21	.206	.313	.345	80	-5	0	0	0	.994	-2	C-57	-0.3
1987	Cal-A	31	92	4	19	2	0	0	5	9	13	.207	.277	.228	37	-8	0	0	0	.994	3	C-28/D-1	-0.4
1988	Cal-A	27	55	8	14	4	1	1	8	8	7	.255	.349	.418	117	1	0	0	0	.981	-0	C-26	0.2
Total	13	1301	4330	498	1102	176	15	65	506	626	428	.255	.351	.347	93	-19	10	13	-5	.989	-43	*C-1247/D-28,3-2	-1.7

■ EARLY WYNN

Wynn, Early "Gus" b: 1/6/20, Hartford, Ala. BB/TR, 6′, 200 lbs. Deb: 9/13/39 CH

YEAR	TM/L	G	AB	R	H	2B	3B	HR	RBI	BB	SO	AVG	OBP	SLG	PRO+	BR/A	SB	CS	SBR	FA	FR	G/POS	TPR
1939	Was-A	3	6	0	1	0	0	0	1	1	1	.167	.286	.167	20	-1	0	0	0	1.000	-1	/P-3	0.0
1941	Was-A	5	15	1	2	1	0	0	0	0	5	.133	.133	.200	-14	-2	0	0	0	.917	0	/P-5	0.0
1942	Was-A	30	69	4	15	2	0	0	7	3	13	.217	.250	.246	40	-6	0	0	0	.953	-1	P-30	0.0
1943	Was-A	38	98	6	29	3	1	1	11	1	11	.296	.303	.378	102	-0	0	0	0	.947	-2	P-37	0.0
1944	Was-A	43	92	4	19	2	0	1	6	3	21	.207	.232	.261	42	-7	0	0	0	.972	-2	P-33	0.0
1946	Was-A	25	47	4	15	2	0	1	9	5	7	.319	.385	.426	134	2	0	0	0	.962	-0	P-17	0.0
1947	Was-A☆	54	120	6	33	6	0	2	13	1	19	.275	.281	.375	84	-3	0	0	0	.980	-1	P-33	0.0
1948	Was-A	73	106	9	23	3	1	0	16	14	22	.217	.308	.264	55	-7	0	0	0	.950	-1	P-33	0.0
1949	Cle-A	35	70	3	10	1	0	1	7	4	10	.143	.189	.200	3	-10	0	0	0	**1.000**	1	P-26	0.0
1950	Cle-A	39	77	12	18	5	1	2	10	10	12	.234	.322	.403	87	-2	0	0	0	.932	0	P-32	0.0
1951	Cle-A	41	108	8	20	8	1	1	13	7	9	.185	.235	.306	48	-9	0	0	0	.982	-1	P-37	0.0
1952	Cle-A	44	99	5	22	2	0	0	10	9	15	.222	.287	.242	52	-6	0	0	0	.943	-1	P-42	0.0
1953	Cle-A	37	91	11	25	2	0	3	10	7	17	.275	.327	.396	97	-1	0	0	0	**1.000**	-1	P-36	0.0
1954	*Cle-A	40	93	10	17	3	0	0	4	7	13	.183	.240	.215	25	-10	0	0	0	.957	-3	P-40	0.0
1955	Cle-A★	34	84	8	15	3	0	1	7	6	17	.179	.233	.250	29	-9	0	0	0	.944	-3	P-32	0.0
1956	Cle-A★	38	101	5	23	5	0	1	15	7	22	.228	.278	.307	53	-7	1	0	0	.955	1	P-38	0.0
1957	Cle-A★	40	86	4	10	0	0	0	4	11	23	.116	.216	.116	-7	-13	0	0	0	**1.000**	-1	P-40	0.0
1958	Chi-A★	40	75	7	15	1	0	0	11	10	25	.200	.294	.213	43	-6	0	0	0	**1.000**	-2	P-40	0.0
1959	*Chi-A★	37	90	11	22	7	0	2	8	9	18	.244	.320	.389	95	-1	0	0	0	.957	-1	P-37	0.0
1960	Chi-A★	36	75	8	15	2	1	1	7	14	17	.200	.333	.293	72	-3	0	0	0	.972	-2	P-36	0.0
1961	Chi-A	17	37	4	6	0	0	0	2	3	11	.162	.225	.162	5	-5	0	0	0	1.000	-2	P-17	0.0
1962	Chi-A	27	54	5	7	1	0	0	2	7	17	.130	.230	.148	4	-7	0	0	0	**1.000**	-2	P-27	0.0
1963	Cle-A	20	11	1	3	0	0	0	0	2	5	.273	.385	.273	89	-0	0	0	0	1.000	-0	P-20	0.0
Total	23	796	1704	136	365	59	5	17	173	141	330	.214	.275	.285	54	-111	1	0	0	.967	-25	P-691	0.0

■ JIMMY WYNN

Wynn, James Sherman "The Toy Cannon" b: 3/12/42, Hamilton, Ohio BR/TR, 5′9″, 170 lbs. Deb: 7/10/63

YEAR	TM/L	G	AB	R	H	2B	3B	HR	RBI	BB	SO	AVG	OBP	SLG	PRO+	BR/A	SB	CS	SBR	FA	FR	G/POS	TPR
1963	Hou-N	70	250	31	61	10	5	4	27	30	53	.244	.325	.372	107	2	4	2	0	.963	-2	O-53,S-21/3-2	-0.2
1964	Hou-N	67	219	19	49	7	0	5	18	24	58	.224	.303	.324	81	-5	5	5	-2	.958	5	O-64	-0.5
1965	Hou-N	157	564	90	155	30	7	22	73	84	126	.275	.374	.470	146	36	43	4	**11**	.978	20	*O-155	6.1
1966	Hou-N	105	418	62	107	21	1	18	62	41	81	.256	.324	.440	118	9	13	10	-2	.978	11	*O-104	1.3
1967	Hou-N★	158	594	102	148	29	3	37	107	74	137	.249	.334	.495	139	29	16	4	2	.968	9	*O-157	3.4
1968	Hou-N	156	542	85	146	23	5	26	67	90	131	.269	.378	.474	158	40	11	17	-7	.988	15	*O-153	4.5
1969	Hou-N	149	495	113	133	17	1	33	87	**148**	142	.269	.440	.507	168	53	23	7	3	.985	11	*O-149	6.0
1970	Hou-N	157	554	82	156	32	2	27	88	106	96	.282	.398	.493	143	36	24	5	4	.987	10	*O-151	4.2
1971	Hou-N	123	404	38	82	16	0	7	45	56	63	.203	.303	.295	72	-14	10	5	0	.988	2	*O-116	-2.0
1972	Hou-N	145	542	117	148	29	3	24	90	103	99	.273	.391	.470	147	36	17	7	1	.983	6	*O-144	3.9

YEAR	TM/L	G	AB	R	H	2B	3B	HR	RBI	BB	SO	AVG	OBP	SLG	PRO+	BR/A	SB	CS	SBR	FA	FR	G/POS	TPR
1973	Hou-N	139	481	90	106	14	5	20	55	91	102	.220	.349	.395	106	6	14	11	-2	.986	3	*O-133	0.0
1974	*LA-N★	150	535	104	145	17	4	32	108	108	104	.271	.393	.497	154	41	18	15	-4	.992	11	*O-148	4.3
1975	LA-N★	130	412	80	102	16	0	18	58	110	77	.248	.407	.417	135	25	7	3	0	.983	-1	*O-120	2.0
1976	Atl-N	148	449	75	93	19	1	17	66	**127**	111	.207	.382	.367	107	9	16	6	1	.971	11	*O-138	1.6
1977	NY-A	30	77	7	11	2	1	1	3	15	16	.143	.283	.234	43	-6	1	0	0	1.000	2	D-15/O-8	-0.5
	Mil-A	36	117	10	23	3	1	0	10	17	31	.197	.299	.239	49	-8	3	0	1	.967	-1	O-17,D-15	-0.9
	Yr	66	194	17	34	5	2	1	13	32	47	.175	.292	.237	46	-14	4	0	1	.981	1	D-30,O-25	-1.4
Total	15	1920	6653	1105	1665	285	39	291	964	1224	1427	.250	.369	.436	129	289	225	101	7	.981	110	*O-1810/D-30,S-21,3	33.2

■ MARVELL WYNNE

Wynne, Marvell b: 12/17/59, Chicago, Ill. BL/TL, 5'11", 185 lbs. Deb: 6/15/83

YEAR	TM/L	G	AB	R	H	2B	3B	HR	RBI	BB	SO	AVG	OBP	SLG	PRO+	BR/A	SB	CS	SBR	FA	FR	G/POS	TPR
1983	Pit-N	103	366	66	89	16	2	7	26	38	52	.243	.319	.355	85	-7	12	10	-2	.983	-0	*O-102	-1.4
1984	Pit-N	154	653	77	174	24	11	0	39	42	81	.266	.311	.337	82	-16	24	19	-4	.990	5	*O-154	-2.1
1985	Pit-N	103	337	21	69	6	3	2	18	18	48	.205	.247	.258	42	-26	10	5	0	.987	6	O-99	-2.5
1986	SD-N	137	288	34	76	19	2	7	37	15	45	.264	.303	.417	98	-2	11	11	-3	.986	-11	*O-125	-1.9
1987	SD-N	98	188	17	47	8	2	2	24	20	37	.250	.322	.346	80	-5	11	6	-0	.981	-10	O-71	-1.7
1988	SD-N	128	333	37	88	13	4	11	42	31	62	.264	.327	.426	117	7	3	4	-2	.987	-11	*O-113	-1.0
1989	SD-N	105	294	19	74	11	1	6	35	12	41	.252	.283	.357	82	-8	4	1	1	.971	-7	O-96	-1.7
	*Chi-N	20	48	8	9	2	1	1	4	1	7	.188	.220	.333	52	-3	2	0	1	.944	-2	O-13	-0.6
	Yr	125	342	27	83	13	2	7	39	13	48	.243	.275	.354	77	-11	6	1	1	.968	-10	*O-109	-2.3
1990	Chi-N	92	186	21	38	8	2	4	19	14	25	.204	.264	.333	59	-11	3	2	-0	.991	-9	O-66	-2.2
Total	8	940	2693	300	664	107	28	40	244	191	398	.247	.298	.352	81	-72	80	58	-11	.985	-41	O-839	-15.1

■ JOHNNY WYROSTEK

Wyrostek, John Barney b: 7/12/19, Fairmont City, Ill. d: 12/12/86, St.Louis, Mo. BL/TR, 6'2", 180 lbs. Deb: 9/10/42

YEAR	TM/L	G	AB	R	H	2B	3B	HR	RBI	BB	SO	AVG	OBP	SLG	PRO+	BR/A	SB	CS	SBR	FA	FR	G/POS	TPR
1942	Pit-N	9	35	0	4	0	1	0	3	3	2	.114	.184	.171	4	-4	0			1.000	1	/O-8	-0.4
1943	Pit-N	51	79	7	12	3	0	0	1	3	15	.152	.183	.190	7	-9	0			.919	-5	O-20/3-2,1-1,2-1	-1.6
1946	Phi-N	145	545	73	153	30	4	6	45	70	42	.281	.366	.383	116	12	7			.981	17	*O-142	2.4
1947	Phi-N	128	454	68	124	24	7	5	51	61	45	.273	.364	.390	104	4	7			.971	1	*O-126	-0.2
1948	Cin-N	136	512	74	140	24	9	17	76	52	63	.273	.344	.455	119	12	7			.977	4	*O-130	0.8
1949	Cin-N	134	474	54	118	20	4	9	46	58	63	.249	.333	.365	86	-9	7			.971	1	*O-129	-1.4
1950	Cin-N★	131	509	70	145	34	5	8	76	52	38	.285	.357	.418	103	2	1			.980	-2	*O-129/1-4	-0.5
1951	Cin-N★	142	537	52	167	31	3	2	61	54	54	.311	.376	.391	105	5	2	1	0	.970	-7	*O-139	-0.7
1952	Cin-N	30	106	12	25	1	3	1	10	18	7	.236	.347	.330	89	-1	1	2	-1	1.000	2	O-29/1-1	-0.1
	Phi-N	98	321	45	88	16	3	1	37	44	26	.274	.363	.352	100	2	1	7	-4	.972	8	O-88	0.2
	Yr	128	427	57	113	17	6	2	47	62	33	.265	.359	.347	97	0	2	9	-5	.980	10	*O-117/1-1	0.1
1953	Phi-N	125	409	42	111	14	2	6	47	38	43	.271	.339	.359	83	-10	0	3	-2	.962	2	*O-110	-1.3
1954	Phi-N	92	259	28	62	12	4	3	28	29	39	.239	.318	.351	74	-10	0	0	0	.990	-5	O-55,1-22	-1.7
Total	11	1221	4240	525	1149	209	45	58	481	482	437	.271	.349	.383	98	-5	33	13		.975	16	*O-1105/1-28,3-2,2	-4.5

■ HENRY YAIK

Yaik, Henry b: 3/1/1864, Detroit, Mich. d: 9/21/35, Detroit, Mich. BL , 5'11", 185 lbs. Deb: 10/3/1888

YEAR	TM/L	G	AB	R	H	2B	3B	HR	RBI	BB	SO	AVG	OBP	SLG	PRO+	BR/A	SB	CS	SBR	FA	FR	G/POS	TPR
1888	Pit-N	2	6	0	2	0	0	0	1	1	0	.333	.429	.333	158	0	0			.625	2	/O-1,C-1	0.2

■ AD YALE

Yale, William M. b: 4/17/1870, Bristol, Conn. d: 4/27/48, Bridgeport, Conn. Deb: 9/18/05

YEAR	TM/L	G	AB	R	H	2B	3B	HR	RBI	BB	SO	AVG	OBP	SLG	PRO+	BR/A	SB	CS	SBR	FA	FR	G/POS	TPR
1905	Bro-N	4	13	1	1	0	0	0	1	1		.077	.143	.077	-37	-2	0			1.000	-0	/1-4	-0.3

■ HUGH YANCY

Yancy, Hugh b: 10/16/49, Sarasota, Fla. BR/TR, 5'11", 170 lbs. Deb: 7/5/72

YEAR	TM/L	G	AB	R	H	2B	3B	HR	RBI	BB	SO	AVG	OBP	SLG	PRO+	BR/A	SB	CS	SBR	FA	FR	G/POS	TPR
1972	Chi-A	3	9	0	1	0	0	0	0	0	0	.111	.111	.111	-33	-1	0	1	-1	1.000	0	/3-3	-0.2
1974	Chi-A	1	0	0	0	0	0	0	0	0	0	—	—	—	—	-0	0	0	0	.000	0	/D-1	0.0
1976	Chi-A	3	10	0	1	1	0	0	0	0	3	.100	.100	.200	-14	-1	0	0	0	1.000	-1	/2-3	-0.2
Total	3	7	19	0	2	1	0	0	0	0	3	.105	.105	.158	-23	-3	0	1	-1	1.000	-0	/2-3,3-3,D-1	-0.4

■ GEORGE YANKOWSKI

Yankowski, George Edward b: 11/19/22, Cambridge, Mass. BR/TR, 6', 180 lbs. Deb: 8/17/42

YEAR	TM/L	G	AB	R	H	2B	3B	HR	RBI	BB	SO	AVG	OBP	SLG	PRO+	BR/A	SB	CS	SBR	FA	FR	G/POS	TPR
1942	Phi-A	6	13	0	2	1	0	0	2	0	2	.154	.154	.231	7	-2	0	0	0	1.000	0	/C-6	-0.1
1949	Chi-A	12	18	0	3	1	0	0	2	0	2	.167	.167	.222	3	-3	0	0	0	1.000	1	/C-6	-0.1
Total	2	18	31	0	5	2	0	0	4	0	4	.161	.161	.226	5	-4	0	0	0	1.000	1	/C-12	-0.2

■ GEORGE YANTZ

Yantz, George Webb b: 7/27/1886, Louisville, Ky. d: 2/26/67, Louisville, Ky. BR/TR, 5'6.5", 168 lbs. Deb: 9/30/12

YEAR	TM/L	G	AB	R	H	2B	3B	HR	RBI	BB	SO	AVG	OBP	SLG	PRO+	BR/A	SB	CS	SBR	FA	FR	G/POS	TPR
1912	Chi-N	1	1	0	1	0	0	0	0	0	0	1.000	1.000	1.000	450	0	0			.000	0	/C-1	0.0

■ YAM YARYAN

Yaryan, Clarence Everett b: 11/5/1892, Knowlton, Iowa d: 11/16/64, Birmingham, Ala. BR/TR, 5'10.5", 180 lbs. Deb: 4/23/21

YEAR	TM/L	G	AB	R	H	2B	3B	HR	RBI	BB	SO	AVG	OBP	SLG	PRO+	BR/A	SB	CS	SBR	FA	FR	G/POS	TPR
1921	Chi-A	45	102	11	31	8	2	0	15	9	16	.304	.366	.422	102	0	0	0	0	.933	-6	C-34	-0.4
1922	Chi-A	36	71	9	14	2	0	2	9	6	10	.197	.269	.310	51	-5	1	0	0	.966	-1	C-26	-0.5
Total	2	81	173	20	45	10	2	2	24	15	26	.260	.326	.376	81	-5	1	0	0	.948	-8	/C-60	-0.9

■ CARL YASTRZEMSKI

Yastrzemski, Carl Michael "Yaz" b: 8/22/39, Southampton, N.Y. BL/TR, 5'11", 182 lbs. Deb: 4/11/61 H

YEAR	TM/L	G	AB	R	H	2B	3B	HR	RBI	BB	SO	AVG	OBP	SLG	PRO+	BR/A	SB	CS	SBR	FA	FR	G/POS	TPR
1961	Bos-A	148	583	71	155	31	6	11	80	50	96	.266	.327	.396	90	-9	6	5	-1	.963	1	*O-147	-1.8
1962	Bos-A	160	646	99	191	43	6	19	94	66	82	.296	.364	.469	118	17	7	4	-0	.969	16	*O-160	2.2
1963	Bos-A★	151	570	91	**183**	**40**	3	14	68	**95**	72	**.321**	**.419**	.475	145	**38**	8	5	-1	.980	13	*O-151	**4.4**
1964	Bos-A	151	567	77	164	29	9	15	67	75	90	.289	.374	.451	122	19	6	5	-1	.973	28	*O-148/3-2	3.9
1965	Bos-A†	133	494	78	154	**45**	3	20	72	70	58	.312	**.398**	**.536**	**154**	**36**	7	6	-2	.987	6	*O-130	**3.6**
1966	Bos-A☆	160	594	81	165	**39**	2	16	80	84	60	.278	.368	.431	117	14	8	9	-3	.985	17	*O-158	2.2
1967	*Bos-A★	161	579	**112**	**189**	31	4	**44**	**121**	91	69	**.326**	**.421**	**.622**	**189**	**65**	10	8	-2	.978	13	*O-161	**7.3**
1968	Bos-A★	157	539	90	162	32	2	23	74	**119**	90	**.301**	**.429**	.495	168	**50**	13	6	0	.991	17	*O-155/1-3	**6.6**
1969	Bos-A★	162	603	96	154	28	2	40	111	101	91	.255	.363	.507	134	27	15	7	0	.985	10	*O-143,1-22	2.9
1970	Bos-A★	161	566	**125**	186	29	0	40	102	128	66	.329	**.453**	**.592**	**174**	**62**	23	13	-1	.990	2	1-94,O-69	**5.2**
1971	Bos-A★	148	508	75	129	21	2	15	70	106	60	.254	.384	.392	112	12	8	7	-2	.993	14	*O-146	1.8
1972	Bos-A★	125	455	70	120	18	2	12	68	67	44	.264	.363	.391	118	12	5	4	-1	.974	8	O-83,1-42	1.4
1973	Bos-A†	152	540	82	160	25	4	19	95	105	58	.296	.411	.463	138	30	9	7	-2	.994	-5	*1-107,3-31,O-14	1.5
1974	Bos-A★	148	515	**93**	155	25	2	15	79	104	48	.301	.421	.445	139	31	12	7	-1	.997	-7	1-84,O-63/D-4	1.6
1975	*Bos-A★	149	543	91	146	30	1	14	60	87	67	.269	.372	.405	110	9	8	4	0	.996	-1	*1-140/O-8,D-2	-0.1
1976	Bos-A★	155	546	71	146	23	2	21	102	80	67	.267	.362	.432	118	12	5	6	-2	.998	-8	1-94,O-51,D-10	-0.7
1977	Bos-A★	150	558	99	165	27	3	28	102	73	40	.296	.378	.505	124	18	11	1	3	**1.000**	14	*O-140/1-7,D-6	2.8
1978	Bos-A†	144	523	70	145	21	2	17	81	76	44	.277	.372	.423	111	9	4	5	-2	.986	6	O-71,1-50,D-27	0.6
1979	Bos-A★	147	518	69	140	28	1	21	87	62	46	.270	.351	.450	108	6	3	3	-1	.996	6	D-56,1-51,O-36	0.4
1980	Bos-A	105	364	49	100	21	1	15	50	44	38	.275	.353	.462	115	8	0	2	-1	1.000	-3	D-49,O-39,1-16	0.0
1981	Bos-A	91	338	36	83	14	1	7	53	49	28	.246	.341	.355	95	-1	0	1	-1	.992	3	D-48,1-39	-0.3
1982	Bos-A★	131	459	53	126	22	1	16	72	59	50	.275	.360	.431	110	7	0	1	-1	1.000	0	*D-102,1-14/O-2	0.2
1983	Bos-A★	119	380	38	101	24	0	10	56	54	29	.266	.360	.408	103	3	0	0	0	1.000	-1	*D-107/1-2,O-1	-0.2
Total	23	3308	11988	1816	3419	646	59	452	1844	1845	1393	.285	.382	.462	128	474	168	116	-19	.981	149	*O-2076,1-765,D/3	45.5

■ AL YATES

Yates, Albert Arthur b: 5/26/45, Jersey City, N.J. BR/TR, 6'2", 210 lbs. Deb: 5/13/71

YEAR	TM/L	G	AB	R	H	2B	3B	HR	RBI	BB	SO	AVG	OBP	SLG	PRO+	BR/A	SB	CS	SBR	FA	FR	G/POS	TPR
1971	Mil-A	24	47	5	13	2	0	1	4	3	7	.277	.320	.383	100	-0	1	0	0	1.000	1	O-12	0.0

■ BERT YEABSLEY

Yeabsley, Robert Watkins b: 12/17/1893, Philadelphia, Pa. d: 2/8/61, Philadelphia, Pa. BR/TR, 5'9.5", 175 lbs. Deb: 5/28/19

YEAR	TM/L	G	AB	R	H	2B	3B	HR	RBI	BB	SO	AVG	OBP	SLG	PRO+	BR/A	SB	CS	SBR	FA	FR	G/POS	TPR
1919	Phi-N	3	0	0	0	0	0	0	0	1	0	—	1.000	—	200	0	0			.000	0	H	0.0

■ GEORGE YEAGER

Yeager, George J. "Doc" b: 6/5/1874, Cincinnati, Ohio d: 7/5/40, Cincinnati, Ohio BR/TR, 5'10", 190 lbs. Deb: 9/25/1896

YEAR	TM/L	G	AB	R	H	2B	3B	HR	RBI	BB	SO	AVG	OBP	SLG	PRO+	BR/A	SB	CS	SBR	FA	FR	G/POS	TPR
1896	Bos-N	2	5	1	1	0	0	0	0	0	1	.200	.200	.200	5	-1	0			1.000	-0	/1-2	-0.1
1897	*Bos-N	30	95	20	23	2	3	2	15	7		.242	.294	.389	75	-4	2			.970	1	C-13,O-10/2-4,3-1	-0.2
1898	Bos-N	68	221	37	59	13	1	3	24	16		.267	.328	.376	96	-2	1			.951	-3	C-37,1-17/O-9,S-2	-0.2
1899	Bos-N	3	8	1	1	0	0	0	0	1		.125	.222	.125	-3	-1	0			1.000	0	/O-2,C-1	-0.1
1901	Cle-A	39	139	13	31	5	0	0	14	4		.223	.250	.259	43	-11	2			.964	3	C-25/1-5,O-3,2-2	-0.5
	Pit-N	26	91	9	24	2	1	0	10	4		.264	.302	.308	75	-3	1			.971	-2	C-20/3-4,1-1	-0.2

YEAR	TM/L	G	AB	R	H	2B	3B	HR	RBI	BB	SO	AVG	OBP	SLG	PRO+	BR/A	SB	CS	SBR	FA	FR	G/POS	TPR
1902	NY-N	38	108	6	22	2	1	0	9	11		.204	.277	.241	60	-5	1			.946	-1	C-27/1-3,O-1	-0.3
	Bal-A	11	38	3	7	1	0	0	1	2		.184	.225	.211	20	-4	0			.930	1	C-11	-0.2
Total	6	217	705	90	168	25	6	5	73	45	1	.238	.290	.312	69	-30	7			.953	-1	C-134/1-28,O23S	-1.8

■ JOE YEAGER

Yeager, Joseph F. "Little Joe" b: 8/28/1875, Philadelphia, Pa. d: 7/2/37, Detroit, Mich. BR/TR, 5'10", 160 lbs. Deb: 4/22/1898

YEAR	TM/L	G	AB	R	H	2B	3B	HR	RBI	BB	SO	AVG	OBP	SLG	PRO+	BR/A	SB	CS	SBR	FA	FR	G/POS	TPR
1898	Bro-N	43	134	12	23	5	1	0	15	7		.172	.218	.224	27	-13	1			.908	6	P-36/O-4,S-2,2-1	-0.1
1899	Bro-N	23	47	12	9	0	1	0	4	6		.191	.333	.234	55	-3	0			.914	3	S-11,P-10/O-1,3-1	0.1
1900	Bro-N	3	9	0	3	0	0	0	0	0		.333	.333	.333	79	-0	0			1.000	-1	/P-2,3-1	0.0
1901	Det-A	41	125	18	37	7	1	2	17	4		.296	.343	.416	105	1	3			.919	5	P-26,S-12/2-1	0.3
1902	Det-A	50	161	17	39	6	5	1	23	5		.242	.282	.360	76	-6	0			.957	-1	P-19,O-13,2-12,/S3	-0.8
1903	Det-A	109	402	36	103	15	6	0	43	18		.256	.303	.323	91	-4	9			.921	-9	*3-107/P-1,S-1	-1.2
1905	NY-A	115	401	54	107	16	7	0	42	25		.267	.330	.342	102	1	8			.923	0	3-91,S-21	0.5
1906	NY-A	57	123	20	37	6	1	0	12	13		.301	.407	.366	129	5	3			.905	-1	S-22,2-13/3-3	0.5
1907	StL-A	123	436	32	104	21	7	1	44	31		.239	.294	.326	98	-2	11			.938	7	3-91,2-17,S-10	1.0
1908	StL-A	10	15	3	5	1	0	0	1	1		.333	.474	.400	183	2	2			1.000	0	/2-4,S-1	0.2
Total	10	574	1853	204	467	77	29	4	201	110		.252	.312	.331	92	-20	37			.927	10	3-295/P-94,S-83,2O	0.5

■ STEVE YEAGER

Yeager, Stephen Wayne b: 11/24/48, Huntington, W.Va. BR/TR, 6', 190 lbs. Deb: 8/2/72

YEAR	TM/L	G	AB	R	H	2B	3B	HR	RBI	BB	SO	AVG	OBP	SLG	PRO+	BR/A	SB	CS	SBR	FA	FR	G/POS	TPR
1972	LA-N	35	106	18	29	0	1	4	15	16	26	.274	.374	.406	124	4	0	0	0	.984	9	C-35	1.4
1973	LA-N	54	134	18	34	5	0	2	10	15	33	.254	.342	.336	93	-1	1	0	0	.981	5	C-50	0.6
1974	*LA-N	94	316	41	84	16	1	12	41	32	77	.266	.337	.437	120	7	2	2	-1	.992	13	C-93	2.4
1975	LA-N	135	452	34	103	16	1	12	54	40	75	.228	.302	.347	83	-11	2	5	-2	.992	12	*C-135	0.4
1976	LA-N	117	359	42	77	11	3	11	35	30	84	.214	.288	.354	83	-9	3	1	0	.985	9	*C-115	0.4
1977	*LA-N	125	387	53	99	21	2	16	55	43	84	.256	.336	.444	108	4	1	3	-2	.977	12	*C-123	1.8
1978	*LA-N	94	228	19	44	7	0	4	23	36	41	.193	.303	.276	63	-11	0	0	0	.988	11	C-91	0.3
1979	LA-N	105	310	33	67	9	2	13	41	29	68	.216	.283	.384	81	-9	1	0	0	.984	11	*C-103	0.6
1980	LA-N	96	227	20	48	8	0	2	20	20	54	.211	.275	.273	55	-14	2	3	-1	.984	4	C-95	-0.9
1981	*LA-N	42	86	5	18	2	0	3	7	6	14	.209	.261	.337	71	-4	0	0	0	.994	1	C-40	-0.2
1982	LA-N	82	196	13	48	5	2	2	18	13	28	.245	.295	.321	74	-7	0	0	0	.990	7	C-76	0.2
1983	*LA-N	113	335	31	68	8	3	15	41	23	57	.203	.256	.379	74	-13	1	1	-0	.985	-6	*C-112	-1.5
1984	LA-N	74	197	16	45	4	0	4	29	20	38	.228	.300	.310	72	-7	1	2	-1	.994	-6	C-65	-1.2
1985	*LA-N	53	121	4	25	4	1	0	9	7	24	.207	.250	.256	43	-9	0	1	-1	.992	9	C-48	0.0
1986	Sea-A	50	130	10	27	2	0	2	12	12	23	.208	.275	.269	48	-9	0	0	0	1.000	-0	C-49	-0.7
Total	15	1269	3584	357	816	118	16	102	410	342	726	.228	.300	.355	83	-88	14	18	-7	.987	90	*C-1230	3.6

■ BILL YEATMAN

Yeatman, William Suter b: 3/1839, Alexandria, Va. d: 4/20/01, York, Pa. Deb: 4/20/1872

YEAR	TM/L	G	AB	R	H	2B	3B	HR	RBI	BB	SO	AVG	OBP	SLG	PRO+	BR/A	SB	CS	SBR	FA	FR	G/POS	TPR
1872	Nat-n	1	4	0	0	0	0	0	0	0	1	.000	.000	.000	-86	-1	0	0	0	.000	-0	/O-1	-0.1

■ ERIC YELDING

Yelding, Eric Girard b: 2/22/65, Montrose, Ala. BR/TR, 5'11", 165 lbs. Deb: 4/9/89

YEAR	TM/L	G	AB	R	H	2B	3B	HR	RBI	BB	SO	AVG	OBP	SLG	PRO+	BR/A	SB	CS	SBR	FA	FR	G/POS	TPR
1989	Hou-N	70	90	19	21	2	0	0	9	7	19	.233	.296	.256	61	-4	11	5	0	1.000	6	S-15,2-13/O-8	0.3
1990	Hou-N	142	511	69	130	9	5	1	28	39	87	.254	.307	.297	69	-21	64	25	4	.971	-6	O-94,S-40,2-10,/3-3	-2.2
1991	Hou-N	78	276	19	67	11	1	1	20	13	46	.243	.277	.301	66	-13	11	9	-2	.939	-14	S-72/O-4	-2.5
1992	Hou-N	9	8	1	2	0	0	0	0	0	3	.250	.250	.250	44	-1	0	0	0	.000	-1	/S-2,O-2	-0.2
1993	Chi-N	69	108	14	22	5	1	1	10	11	22	.204	.277	.296	54	-7	3	2	-0	.984	12	2-32/3-7,S-1,O-1	0.6
Total	5	368	993	122	242	27	7	3	67	70	177	.244	.294	.294	66	-46	89	41	2	.948	-3	S-130,O-109/2-55,3	-4.0

■ ARCHIE YELLE

Yelle, Archie Joseph b: 6/11/1892, Saginaw, Mich. d: 5/2/83, Woodland, Cal. BR/TR, 5'10.5", 170 lbs. Deb: 5/12/17

YEAR	TM/L	G	AB	R	H	2B	3B	HR	RBI	BB	SO	AVG	OBP	SLG	PRO+	BR/A	SB	CS	SBR	FA	FR	G/POS	TPR
1917	Det-A	25	51	4	7	1	0	0	0	5	4	.137	.214	.157	13	-5	2			.975	-1	C-24	-0.6
1918	Det-A	56	144	7	25	3	0	0	7	9	15	.174	.227	.194	28	-13	0			.948	7	C-52	-0.2
1919	Det-A	6	4	1	0	0	0	0	0	1	0	.000	.200	.000	-42	-1	0			.833	-1	/C-6	-0.1
Total	3	87	199	12	32	4	0	0	7	15	19	.161	.223	.181	23	-19	2			.952	5	/C-82	-0.9

■ STEVE YERKES

Yerkes, Stephen Douglas b: 5/15/1888, Hatboro, Pa. d: 1/31/71, Lansdale, Pa. BR/TR, 5'9", 165 lbs. Deb: 9/29/09

YEAR	TM/L	G	AB	R	H	2B	3B	HR	RBI	BB	SO	AVG	OBP	SLG	PRO+	BR/A	SB	CS	SBR	FA	FR	G/POS	TPR
1909	Bos-A	5	7	0	2	0	0	0	0	0		.286	.286	.286	79	-0	0			1.000	-1	/S-2	-0.1
1911	Bos-A	142	502	70	140	24	3	1	57	52		.279	.354	.345	96	-2	14			.927	-20	*S-116,2-14,3-11	-1.4
1912	*Bos-A	131	523	73	132	22	6	0	42	41		.252	.312	.317	76	-17	4			.943	-15	*2-131	-3.5
1913	Bos-A	137	483	67	129	29	6	1	48	50	32	.267	.338	.358	101	1	11			.957	-19	*2-129	-2.2
1914	Bos-A	92	293	23	64	17	2	1	23	14	23	.218	.259	.300	68	-13	5	6	-2	.972	4	2-91	-1.3
	Pit-F	39	142	18	48	9	5	1	25	11	13	.338	.386	.493	139	5	2			.974	8	S-39	1.6
1915	Pit-F	121	434	44	125	17	8	1	49	30	27	.288	.337	.371	100	-7	17			**.967**	-3	*2-114/S-8	-0.9
1916	Chi-N	44	137	12	36	6	2	1	10	9	7	.263	.308	.358	94	-1	1			.919	1	2-41	0.1
Total	7	711	2521	307	676	124	32	6	254	207	102	.268	.328	.350	93	-33	54	6		.956	-45	2-520,S-165/3-11	-7.7

■ TOM YEWCIC

Yewcic, Thomas "Kibby" b: 5/9/32, Conemaugh, Pa. BR/TR, 5'11", 180 lbs. Deb: 6/27/57

YEAR	TM/L	G	AB	R	H	2B	3B	HR	RBI	BB	SO	AVG	OBP	SLG	PRO+	BR/A	SB	CS	SBR	FA	FR	G/POS	TPR
1957	Det-A	1	1	0	0	0	0	0	0	0	0	.000	.000	.000	-97	-0	0	0	0	.833	1	/C-1	0.0

■ ED YEWELL

Yewell, Edwin Leonard b: 8/22/1862, Washington, D.C. d: 9/15/40, Washington, D.C. Deb: 5/12/1884

YEAR	TM/L	G	AB	R	H	2B	3B	HR	RBI	BB	SO	AVG	OBP	SLG	PRO+	BR/A	SB	CS	SBR	FA	FR	G/POS	TPR
1884	Was-a	27	93	14	23	3	1	0		1		.247	.263	.301	95	-0				.885	-3	2-11/O-8,3-7,S-2	-0.2
	Was-U	1	4	0	0	0	0	0		0		.000	.000	.000	-99	-1				.571	-0	/3-1	-0.1
Total	1	28	97	14	23	3	1	0		1		.237	.253	.289	85	-2				.773	-3	/2-11,3-8,O-8,S-2	-0.3

■ JOE YINGLING

Yingling, Joseph Granville b: 7/23/1866, Westminster, Md. d: 10/24/46, Manchester, Md. BR/TL, 5'7.5", 145 lbs. Deb: 5/28/1886

YEAR	TM/L	G	AB	R	H	2B	3B	HR	RBI	BB	SO	AVG	OBP	SLG	PRO+	BR/A	SB	CS	SBR	FA	FR	G/POS	TPR
1886	Was-N	1	2	0	0	0	0	0	0	0	1	.000	.000	.000	-99	-0	0			.500	0	/P-1	0.0
1894	Phi-N	1	4	0	1	0	0	0	0	0	1	.250	.250	.250	21	-1	0			1.000	-1	/S-1	-0.1
Total	2	2	6	0	1	0	0	0	0	0	2	.167	.167	.167	-14	-1	0			1.000	-1	/S-1,P-1	-0.1

■ BILL YOHE

Yohe, William Clyde b: 9/2/1878, Mt.Erie, Ill. d: 12/24/38, Bremerton, Wash. TR, 5'8", 180 lbs. Deb: 8/30/09

YEAR	TM/L	G	AB	R	H	2B	3B	HR	RBI	BB	SO	AVG	OBP	SLG	PRO+	BR/A	SB	CS	SBR	FA	FR	G/POS	TPR
1909	Was-A	21	72	6	15	2	0	0	4	3		.208	.240	.236	53	-4	2			.921	3	3-19	-0.1

■ TONY YORK

York, Anthony Batton b: 11/27/12, Irene, Tex. d: 4/18/70, Hillsboro, Tex. BR/TR, 5'10", 165 lbs. Deb: 4/18/44

YEAR	TM/L	G	AB	R	H	2B	3B	HR	RBI	BB	SO	AVG	OBP	SLG	PRO+	BR/A	SB	CS	SBR	FA	FR	G/POS	TPR
1944	Chi-N	28	85	4	20	1	0	0	7	4	11	.235	.270	.247	46	-6	0			.940	10	S-15,3-12	0.5

■ RUDY YORK

York, Preston Rudolph b: 8/17/13, Ragland, Ala. d: 2/5/70, Rome, Ga. BR/TR, 6'1", 209 lbs. Deb: 8/22/34 MC

YEAR	TM/L	G	AB	R	H	2B	3B	HR	RBI	BB	SO	AVG	OBP	SLG	PRO+	BR/A	SB	CS	SBR	FA	FR	G/POS	TPR
1934	Det-A	3	6	0	1	0	0	0	0	1	3	.167	.286	.167	19	-1	0	0	0	1.000	-0	/C-2	-0.1
1937	Det-A	104	375	72	115	18	3	35	103	41	52	.307	.375	.651	150	25	3	2	-0	.960	-19	C-54,3-41/1-2	0.9
1938	Det-A★	135	463	85	138	27	2	33	127	92	74	.298	.417	.579	139	28	1	2	-1	.990	-1	*C-116,O-14/1-1	2.8
1939	Det-A	102	329	66	101	16	1	20	68	41	50	.307	.387	.544	126	12	5	0	2	.985	-8	C-67,1-19	0.7
1940	*Det-A	155	588	105	186	46	6	33	134	89	88	.316	.410	.583	141	35	3	2	-0	.990	5	*1-155	2.3
1941	Det-A★	155	590	91	153	29	3	27	111	92	88	.259	.360	.456	104	3	3	1	0	.986	-1	*1-155	-1.0
1942	Det-A★	153	577	81	150	26	4	21	90	73	71	.260	.343	.428	107	5	3	3	-1	.988	15	*1-152	1.0
1943	Det-A★	155	571	90	155	22	11	**34**	**118**	84	88	.271	.366	**.527**	148	33	5	5	-2	.990	18	*1-155	4.3
1944	Det-A☆	151	583	77	161	27	7	18	98	68	73	.276	.353	.439	119	14	5	3	-0	.989	5	*1-151	1.1
1945	*Det-A	155	595	71	157	25	5	18	87	60	85	.264	.331	.413	109	5	6	6	-2	.988	-2	*1-155	-1.0
1946	*Bos-A★	154	579	78	160	30	6	17	119	86	93	.276	.371	.437	118	15	3	2	-0	.994	6	*1-154	1.2
1947	Bos-A	48	184	16	39	7	0	6	27	22	32	.212	.296	.348	73	-7	0	0	0	.995	1	1-48	-0.8
	Chi-A☆	102	400	40	97	18	4	15	64	36	55	.243	.305	.420	104	-0	1	0	0	.995	-1	*1-102	-0.5
	Yr	150	584	56	136	25	4	21	91	58	87	.233	.302	.397	94	-8	1	0	0	**.995**	0	*1-150	-1.3
1948	Phi-A	31	51	4	8	0	0	0	6	7	15	.157	.259	.157	12	-6	0	0	0	.988	-1	1-14	-0.7
Total	13	1603	5891	876	1621	291	52	277	1152	792	867	.275	.362	.483	121	160	38	26	-4	.990	16	*1-1263,C-239/3O	10.2

■ TOM YORK

York, Thomas Jefferson b: 7/13/1851, Brooklyn, N.Y. d: 2/17/36, New York, N.Y. BL, 5'9", 165 lbs. Deb: 5/9/1871 MU

YEAR	TM/L	G	AB	R	H	2B	3B	HR	RBI	BB	SO	AVG	OBP	SLG	PRO+	BR/A	SB	CS	SBR	FA	FR	G/POS	TPR
1871	Tro-n	29	145	36	37	5	7	2	23	9	1	.255	.299	.428	104	0	2	2	-1	.855	3	*O-29	0.3

YEAR	TM/L	G	AB	R	H	2B	3B	HR	RBI	BB	SO	AVG	OBP	SLG	PRO+	BR/A	SB	CS	SBR	FA	FR	G/POS	TPR
1872	Bal-n	51	248	66	66	10	4	1	41	4	1	.266	.278	.351	88	-5	2	1	0	.916	11	*O-51	0.5
1873	Bal-n	57	277	70	84	10	7	2	49	3	3	.303	.311	.412	113	4	3	1	0	**.872**	11	*O-57	1.2
1874	Phi-n	50	224	36	56	4	7	0	37	5	4	.250	.266	.330	87	-4	1	0	0	.861	8	*O-50	0.5
1875	Har-n	86	375	68	111	14	7	0	37	3	6	.296	.302	.371	126	8	7	3	0	.868	4	*O-86	1.1
1876	Har-N	67	263	47	68	12	7	1	39	10	4	.259	.286	.369	108	1				.899	2	*O-67	0.2
1877	Har-N	56	237	43	67	16	7	1	37	3	11	.283	.292	.422	137	10				.865	0	*O-56	0.7
1878	Pro-N	62	269	56	83	19	**10**	1	26	8	19	.309	.329	.465	159	16				.873	4	*O-62,M	1.6
1879	Pro-N	81	342	69	106	25	5	1	50	19	28	.310	.346	.421	154	20				.898	-4	*O-81	1.0
1880	Pro-N	53	203	21	43	9	2	0	18	8	29	.212	.242	.276	77	-4				.934	-3	O-53	-0.8
1881	Pro-N	85	316	57	96	23	5	2	47	29	26	.304	.362	.427	150	19				.859	-2	*O-85,M	1.4
1882	Pro-N	81	321	48	86	23	7	1	40	19	14	.268	.309	.393	123	8				.873	-3	*O-81	0.5
1883	Cle-N	100	381	56	99	29	5	2	46	**37**	55	.260	.325	.378	114	8				.864	0	*O-100	0.6
1884	Bal-a	83	314	64	70	14	7	1		34		.223	.318	.322	105	3				.843	-5	*O-83	-0.4
1885	Bal-a	22	87	6	23	4	2	0	12	8		.264	.326	.356	117	2				.938	1	O-22	0.2
Total	5 n	273	1269	276	354	43	32	5	187	24	15	.279	.292	.375	106	4	15	7	0	.875	37	O-273	3.6
Total	10	690	2733	467	741	174	57	10	315	175	186	.271	.317	.387	126	83				.878	-8	O-690	5.0

■ NED YOST Yost, Edgar Frederick b: 8/19/55, Eureka, Cal. BR/TR, 6'1", 190 lbs. Deb: 4/12/80 C

YEAR	TM/L	G	AB	R	H	2B	3B	HR	RBI	BB	SO	AVG	OBP	SLG	PRO+	BR/A	SB	CS	SBR	FA	FR	G/POS	TPR
1980	Mil-A	15	31	0	5	0	0	0	0	0	6	.161	.161	.161	-12	-5	0	0	0	1.000	2	C-15	-0.2
1981	Mil-A	18	27	4	6	0	0	3	3	3	6	.222	.300	.556	150	1	0	0	0	.956	2	C-16	0.4
1982	*Mil-A	40	98	13	27	6	3	1	8	7	20	.276	.324	.429	111	1	3	1	0	.977	-2	C-39/D-1	0.1
1983	Mil-A	61	196	21	44	5	1	6	28	5	36	.224	.244	.352	67	-10	1	0	0	.971	-6	C-61	-1.3
1984	Tex-A	80	242	15	44	4	0	6	25	6	47	.182	.202	.273	29	-23	1	2	-1	.995	-5	C-78	-2.7
1985	Mon-N	5	11	1	2	0	0	0	0	0	2	.182	.182	.182	2	-1	0	0	0	.962	1	/C-5	-0.1
Total	6	219	605	54	128	15	4	16	64	21	117	.212	.238	.329	56	-37	5	3	-0	.982	-8	C-214/D-1	-3.8

■ EDDIE YOST Yost, Edward Frederick Joseph "The Walking Man" b: 10/13/26, Brooklyn, N.Y. BR/TR, 5'10", 170 lbs. Deb: 8/16/44 MC

YEAR	TM/L	G	AB	R	H	2B	3B	HR	RBI	BB	SO	AVG	OBP	SLG	PRO+	BR/A	SB	CS	SBR	FA	FR	G/POS	TPR
1944	Was-A	7	14	3	2	0	0	0	0	1	2	.143	.200	.143	-1	-2	0	0	0	.917	-1	/3-3,S-2	-0.2
1946	Was-A	8	25	2	2	1	0	0	1	5	5	.080	.233	.120	1	-3	2	1	0	1.000	1	/3-7	-0.3
1947	Was-A	115	428	52	102	17	3	0	14	45	57	.238	.314	.292	71	-16	3	5	-2	.958	-9	*3-114	-2.8
1948	Was-A	145	555	74	138	32	11	2	50	82	51	.249	.349	.357	91	-7	4	3	-1	.966	-13	*3-145	-2.1
1949	Was-A	124	435	57	110	19	7	9	45	91	41	.253	.383	.391	107	7	3	3	-1	.954	-2	*3-122	0.1
1950	Was-A	155	573	114	169	26	2	11	58	**141**	63	.295	.440	.405	123	30	6	6	-2	.945	-2	*3-155	2.2
1951	Was-A	154	568	109	161	**36**	4	12	65	126	55	.283	.423	.424	132	32	6	4	-1	.954	-27	*3-152/O-3	0.3
1952	Was-A☆	157	587	92	137	32	3	12	49	**129**	73	.233	.378	.359	110	13	4	3	-1	.962	-35	*3-157	-2.7
1953	Was-A	152	577	107	157	30	7	9	45	**123**	59	.272	.403	.395	119	21	7	4	-0	.965	-13	*3-152	0.5
1954	Was-A	155	539	101	138	26	4	11	47	131	71	.256	.406	.380	123	24	7	3	0	.968	3	*3-155	2.5
1955	Was-A	122	375	64	91	17	5	7	48	95	54	.243	.410	.371	117	15	4	3	-1	.943	-6	*3-107	0.8
1956	Was-A	152	515	94	119	17	2	11	53	**151**	82	.231	.412	.336	100	9	8	5	-1	.963	11	*3-135/O-8	2.0
1957	Was-A	110	414	47	104	13	5	9	38	73	49	.251	.370	.372	104	5	1	11	-6	.952	-11	*3-107	-1.0
1958	Was-A	134	406	55	91	16	0	8	37	81	43	.224	.365	.323	93	-0	3	6	-3	**.964**	-15	*3-114/O-4,1-2	-1.8
1959	Det-A	148	521	**115**	145	19	0	21	61	**135**	77	.278	**.437**	.436	133	32	9	2	2	**.962**	-11	*3-146/2-1	2.3
1960	Det-A	143	497	78	129	23	2	14	47	**125**	69	.260	**.416**	.398	118	19	5	4	-1	.933	-27	*3-142	-1.0
1961	LA-A	76	213	29	43	4	0	3	15	50	48	.202	.358	.263	62	-10	0	1	-1	.964	-10	3-67	-2.0
1962	LA-A	52	104	22	25	9	1	0	10	30	21	.240	.415	.346	111	3	0	2	-1	.950	-3	3-28/1-7	0.0
Total	18	2109	7346	1215	1863	337	56	139	683	1614	920	.254	.395	.371	109	172	72	66	-18	.957	-169	*3-2008/O-15,1S2	-3.2

■ ELMER YOTER Yoter, Elmer Elsworth b: 6/26/1900, Plainfield, Pa. d: 7/26/66, Camp Hill, Pa. BR/TR, 5'7", 155 lbs. Deb: 9/9/21

YEAR	TM/L	G	AB	R	H	2B	3B	HR	RBI	BB	SO	AVG	OBP	SLG	PRO+	BR/A	SB	CS	SBR	FA	FR	G/POS	TPR
1921	Phi-A	3	3	0	0	0	0	0	0	0	0	.000	.000	.000	-99	-1	0	0	0	.000	0	H	-0.1
1924	Cle-A	19	66	3	18	1	1	0	7	5	8	.273	.324	.318	65	-3	0	0	0	.905	-2	3-19	-0.4
1927	Chi-N	13	27	2	6	1	1	0	5	4	4	.222	.323	.333	76	-1	0			.947	-0	3-11	-0.1
1928	Chi-N	1	0	0	0	0	0	0	0	0	0	—	—	—	—	0	0			.000	0	/3-1	0.0
Total	4	36	96	5	24	2	2	0	12	9	12	.250	.314	.313	63	-5	0	0		.915	-2	/3-31	-0.6

■ DEL YOUNG Young, Delmer Edward b: 5/11/12, Cleveland, Ohio d: 12/8/79, San Francisco, Cal. BB/TR, 5'11", 168 lbs. Deb: 4/19/37 F

YEAR	TM/L	G	AB	R	H	2B	3B	HR	RBI	BB	SO	AVG	OBP	SLG	PRO+	BR/A	SB	CS	SBR	FA	FR	G/POS	TPR
1937	Phi-N	109	360	36	70	9	2	0	24	18	55	.194	.235	.231	25	-37	6			.950	10	*2-108	-2.1
1938	Phi-N	108	340	27	78	13	2	0	31	20	35	.229	.276	.279	55	-21	0			.933	-2	S-87,2-17	-1.6
1939	Phi-N	77	217	22	57	9	2	3	20	8	24	.263	.289	.364	77	-8	1			.946	-18	S-55,2-17	-2.1
1940	Phi-N	15	33	2	8	0	1	0	1	2	1	.242	.286	.303	65	-2	0			.962	-0	/S-6,2-5	-0.1
Total	4	309	950	87	213	31	7	3	76	48	115	.224	.264	.281	48	-68	7			.938	-10	S-148,2-147	-5.9

■ DEL YOUNG Young, Delmer John b: 10/24/1885, Macon, Mo. d: 12/17/59, Cleveland, Ohio BL/TR, 5'11", 195 lbs. Deb: 9/24/09 F

YEAR	TM/L	G	AB	R	H	2B	3B	HR	RBI	BB	SO	AVG	OBP	SLG	PRO+	BR/A	SB	CS	SBR	FA	FR	G/POS	TPR
1909	Cin-N	2	7	0	2	0	0	0	1	1		.286	.375	.286	106	0	0			1.000	0	/O-2	0.0
1914	Buf-F	80	174	17	48	5	5	4	22	3	13	.276	.288	.431	92	-6				.944	-6	O-41	-1.4
1915	Buf-F	12	15	0	2	0	0	0	0	1	0	.133	.188	.133	-9	-2	1			.667	-1	/O-3	-0.4
Total	3	94	196	17	52	5	5	4	23	5	13	.265	.284	.403	85	-8	1			.933	-7	/O-46	-1.8

■ DMITRI YOUNG Young, Dmitri Dell b: 10/11/73, Vicksburg, Miss. BB/TR, 6'2", 215 lbs. Deb: 8/29/96

YEAR	TM/L	G	AB	R	H	2B	3B	HR	RBI	BB	SO	AVG	OBP	SLG	PRO+	BR/A	SB	CS	SBR	FA	FR	G/POS	TPR
1996	StL-N	16	29	3	7	0	0	0	2	4	5	.241	.353	.241	61	-1	0	1	-1	.976	-2	1-10	-0.4
1997	StL-N	110	333	38	86	14	3	5	34	38	63	.258	.338	.363	85	-7	6	5	-1	.985	-0	1-74,O-17/D-1	-1.5
1998	Cin-N	144	536	81	166	48	1	14	83	47	94	.310	.368	.481	116	13	2	4	-2	.940	-6	*O-105,1-44	0.1
Total	3	270	898	122	259	62	4	19	119	89	162	.288	.356	.430	103	4	8	10	-4	.987	-8	1-128,O-122/D-1	-1.8

■ DON YOUNG Young, Donald Wayne b: 10/18/45, Houston, Tex. BR/TR, 6'2", 185 lbs. Deb: 9/9/65

YEAR	TM/L	G	AB	R	H	2B	3B	HR	RBI	BB	SO	AVG	OBP	SLG	PRO+	BR/A	SB	CS	SBR	FA	FR	G/POS	TPR
1965	Chi-N	11	35	1	2	0	0	1	2	0	11	.057	.057	.143	-45	-7	0	0	0	.933	-2	O-11	-1.0
1969	Chi-N	101	272	36	65	12	3	6	27	38	74	.239	.343	.371	89	-4	1	5	-3	.975	-4	*O-100	-1.6
Total	2	112	307	37	67	12	3	7	29	38	85	.218	.314	.345	76	-10	1	5	-3	.972	-6	O-111	-2.6

■ ERIC YOUNG Young, Eric Orlando b: 5/18/67, New Brunswick, N.J. BR/TR, 5'9", 180 lbs. Deb: 7/30/92

YEAR	TM/L	G	AB	R	H	2B	3B	HR	RBI	BB	SO	AVG	OBP	SLG	PRO+	BR/A	SB	CS	SBR	FA	FR	G/POS	TPR
1992	LA-N	49	132	9	34	1	0	1	11	8	9	.258	.300	.288	68	-5	6	1	1	.957	10	2-43	0.7
1993	Col-N	144	490	82	132	16	8	3	42	63	41	.269	.357	.353	78	-15	42	19	1	.962	-10	2-79,O-52	-2.2
1994	Col-N	90	228	37	62	13	1	7	30	38	17	.272	.381	.430	95	-1	18	7	1	.981	1	O-60/2-1	0.0
1995	*Col-N	120	366	68	116	21	**9**	6	36	49	29	.317	.405	.473	101	-1	35	12	3	.973	-6	2-77,O-19	0.1
1996	Col-N★	141	568	113	184	23	4	8	74	47	31	.324	.396	.421	94	-6	**53**	19	5	.985	**28**	*2-139	3.4
1997	Col-N	118	468	78	132	29	6	6	45	57	37	.282	.366	.408	83	-13	32	12	2	.978	21	*2-117	1.8
	LA-N	37	154	28	42	4	2	2	16	14	17	.273	.349	.364	94	-1	13	2	3	.979	-14	2-37	-1.1
	Yr	155	622	106	174	33	8	8	61	71	54	.280	.362	.397	85	-13	45	14	5	.978	7	*2-154	0.7
1998	LA-N	117	452	78	129	24	1	8	43	45	32	.285	.357	.396	103	2	42	13	5	.976	-10	*2-114/D-1	0.5
Total	7	816	2858	493	831	131	31	41	297	321	213	.291	.371	.401	91	-40	241	85	21	.975	20	2-607,O-131/D-1	3.2

■ ERNIE YOUNG Young, Ernest Wesley b: 7/8/69, Chicago, Ill. BR/TR, 6'1", 190 lbs. Deb: 5/17/94

YEAR	TM/L	G	AB	R	H	2B	3B	HR	RBI	BB	SO	AVG	OBP	SLG	PRO+	BR/A	SB	CS	SBR	FA	FR	G/POS	TPR
1994	Oak-A	11	30	2	2	1	0	0	3	1	8	.067	.097	.100	-54	-7	0	0	0	.958	0	O-10/D-1	-0.6
1995	Oak-A	26	50	9	10	3	0	2	5	8	12	.200	.310	.380	83	-1	0	0	0	.946	-3	O-24	-0.5
1996	Oak-A	141	462	72	112	19	4	19	64	52	118	.242	.328	.424	90	-8	7	5	-1	.997	-1	*O-140	-1.1
1997	Oak-A	71	175	22	39	7	0	5	15	19	57	.223	.306	.349	72	-7	1	3	-2	.980	-4	O-66/D-1	-1.3
1998	KC-A	25	53	2	10	3	0	1	3	2	9	.189	.232	.302	36	-5	2	1	0	1.000	-1	O-24	-0.6
Total	5	274	770	107	173	33	4	27	90	82	204	.225	.307	.383	77	-28	10	9	-2	.989	-8	O-264/D-2	-4.1

■ GEORGE YOUNG Young, George Joseph b: 4/1/1890, Brooklyn, N.Y. d: 3/13/50, Brightwaters, N.Y. BL/TR, 6', 185 lbs. Deb: 8/10/13

YEAR	TM/L	G	AB	R	H	2B	3B	HR	RBI	BB	SO	AVG	OBP	SLG	PRO+	BR/A	SB	CS	SBR	FA	FR	G/POS	TPR
1913	Cle-A	2	2	0	0	0	0	0	0	0	0	.000	.000	.000	-97	-0	0			.000	0	H	-0.1

■ GERALD YOUNG
Young, Gerald Anthony b: 10/22/64, Tela, Honduras BB/TR, 6'2", 185 lbs. Deb: 7/8/87

YEAR	TM/L	G	AB	R	H	2B	3B	HR	RBI	BB	SO	AVG	OBP	SLG	PRO+	BR/A	SB	CS	SBR	FA	FR	G/POS	TPR
1987	Hou-N	71	274	44	88	9	2	1	15	26	27	.321	.382	.380	107	4	26	9	2	.980	5	O-67	0.8
1988	Hou-N	149	576	79	148	21	9	0	37	66	66	.257	.336	.325	94	-3	65	27	3	.992	13	*O-145	0.9
1989	Hou-N	146	533	71	124	17	3	0	38	74	60	.233	.328	.276	77	-13	34	25	-5	**.998**	26	*O-143	0.5
1990	Hou-N	57	154	15	27	4	1	1	4	20	23	.175	.270	.234	41	-12	6	3	0	.990	-2	O-50	-1.5
1991	Hou-N	108	142	26	31	3	1	1	11	24	17	.218	.331	.275	77	-4	16	5	2	1.000	-14	O-84	-1.8
1992	Hou-N	74	76	14	14	1	1	0	4	10	11	.184	.279	.224	46	-5	6	2	1	.964	-15	O-57	-2.2
1993	Col-N	19	19	5	1	0	0	0	1	4	1	.053	.217	.053	-20	-3	0	1	-1	.882	-3	O-11	-0.7
1994	StL-N	16	41	5	13	3	2	0	3	3	8	.317	.364	.488	122	1	2	1	0	1.000	-1	O-11	0.0
Total	8	640	1815	259	446	58	19	3	113	227	213	.246	.332	.304	82	-36	155	73	3	.990	9	O-568	-4.0

■ HERMAN YOUNG
Young, Herman John b: 4/14/1886, Boston, Mass. d: 12/13/66, Ipswich, Mass. BR/TR, 5'8", 155 lbs. Deb: 6/11/11

YEAR	TM/L	G	AB	R	H	2B	3B	HR	RBI	BB	SO	AVG	OBP	SLG	PRO+	BR/A	SB	CS	SBR	FA	FR	G/POS	TPR
1911	Bos-N	9	25	2	6	0	0	0	0	0	3	.240	.269	.240	40	-2	0			.905	4	/3-5,S-3	0.2

■ JOHN YOUNG
Young, John Thomas b: 2/9/49, Los Angeles, Cal. BL/TL, 6'3", 210 lbs. Deb: 9/9/71

YEAR	TM/L	G	AB	R	H	2B	3B	HR	RBI	BB	SO	AVG	OBP	SLG	PRO+	BR/A	SB	CS	SBR	FA	FR	G/POS	TPR
1971	Det-A	2	4	1	2	1	0	0	1	0	0	.500	.500	.750	241	1	0	0	0	1.000	-0	/1-1	0.0

■ KEVIN YOUNG
Young, Kevin Stacey b: 6/16/69, Alpena, Mich. BR/TR, 6'2", 219 lbs. Deb: 7/12/92

YEAR	TM/L	G	AB	R	H	2B	3B	HR	RBI	BB	SO	AVG	OBP	SLG	PRO+	BR/A	SB	CS	SBR	FA	FR	G/POS	TPR
1992	Pit-N	10	7	2	4	0	0	0	4	2	0	.571	.667	.571	256	2	1	0	0	.750	-1	/3-7,1-1	0.1
1993	Pit-N	141	449	38	106	24	3	6	47	36	82	.236	.306	.343	73	-17	2	2	-1	**.998**	7	*1-135/3-6	-2.1
1994	Pit-N	59	122	15	25	7	2	1	11	8	34	.205	.260	.320	49	-9	0	2	-1	1.000	1	1-37,3-17/O-1	-1.1
1995	Pit-N	56	181	13	42	9	0	6	22	8	53	.232	.272	.381	69	-9	1	3	-2	.919	6	3-48/1-6	-0.4
1996	KC-A	55	132	20	32	6	0	8	23	11	32	.242	.301	.470	91	-2	3	3	-1	1.000	-3	1-27,O-17/3-7,D-3	-0.8
1997	Pit-N	97	333	59	100	18	3	18	74	16	89	.300	.340	.535	123	9	11	2	2	.997	1	1-77,3-12,O-11	0.5
1998	Pit-N	159	592	88	160	40	2	27	108	44	127	.270	.332	.481	106	4	15	7	0	.994	-12	*1-157	-2.1
Total	7	577	1816	235	469	104	10	66	289	125	417	.258	.316	.436	93	-22	33	19	-2	.997	-2	1-440/3-97,O-29,D-3	-5.9

■ PEP YOUNG
Young, Lemuel Floyd b: 8/29/07, Jamestown, N.C. d: 1/14/62, Jamestown, N.C. BR/TR, 5'9", 162 lbs. Deb: 4/25/33

YEAR	TM/L	G	AB	R	H	2B	3B	HR	RBI	BB	SO	AVG	OBP	SLG	PRO+	BR/A	SB	CS	SBR	FA	FR	G/POS	TPR
1933	Pit-N	25	20	3	6	1	1	0	0	0	5	.300	.300	.450	112	0	0			1.000	0	/2-1,S-1	0.1
1934	Pit-N	19	17	3	4	0	0	0	2	0	6	.235	.235	.235	26	-2	0			1.000	2	/2-2,S-2	0.1
1935	Pit-N	128	494	60	131	25	10	7	82	21	59	.265	.298	.399	83	-13	2			.952	-12	*2-107/3-6,O-6,S-4	-1.6
1936	Pit-N	125	475	47	118	23	10	6	77	29	52	.248	.293	.377	77	-16	3			.966	-24	*2-123	-3.1
1937	Pit-N	113	408	43	106	20	3	9	54	26	63	.260	.306	.390	88	-8	4			.942	18	S-45,3-39,2-30	1.6
1938	Pit-N	149	562	58	156	36	5	4	79	40	64	.278	.329	.381	94	-5	7			.973	**32**	*2-149	3.5
1939	Pit-N	84	293	34	81	14	3	3	29	23	29	.276	.333	.375	92	-4	1			.967	3	2-84	0.4
1940	Pit-N	54	136	19	34	8	2	2	20	12	23	.250	.320	.382	94	-1	1			.909	-5	2-33/S-7,3-5	-0.4
1941	Cin-N	4	12	2	2	0	0	0	0	0	1	.167	.231	.167	13	-1	0			.923	1	/3-3	-0.1
	StL-N	2	2	0	0	0	0	0	0	0	2	.000	.000	.000	-94	-1	0			.000	0	H	-0.1
	Yr	6	14	2	2	0	0	0	0	0	3	.143	.200	.143	-2	-2	0			.923	1	/3-3	-0.2
1945	StL-N	27	47	5	7	1	0	1	4	1	8	.149	.167	.234	10	-6	0			.978	1	S-11/3-9,2-3	-0.5
Total	10	730	2466	274	645	128	34	32	347	152	312	.262	.308	.380	85	-56	18			.964	17	2-532/S-70,3-62,O-6	-0.1

■ MIKE YOUNG
Young, Michael Darren b: 3/20/60, Oakland, Cal. BB/TR, 6'2", 195 lbs. Deb: 9/14/82

YEAR	TM/L	G	AB	R	H	2B	3B	HR	RBI	BB	SO	AVG	OBP	SLG	PRO+	BR/A	SB	CS	SBR	FA	FR	G/POS	TPR
1982	Bal-A	6	2	2	0	0	0	0	0	0	1	.000	.000	.000	-99	-1	0	0	0	1.000	-0	/O-1,D-2	-0.1
1983	Bal-A	25	36	5	6	2	1	0	2	2	8	.167	.231	.278	40	-3	1	0	0	.929	-4	O-22/D-3	-0.7
1984	Bal-A	123	401	59	101	17	2	17	52	58	110	.252	.356	.431	119	12	6	2	1	.982	-9	*O-115/D-1	-0.1
1985	Bal-A	139	450	72	123	22	1	28	81	48	104	.273	.349	.513	136	21	1	5	-3	.975	-0	O-90,D-37	1.5
1986	Bal-A	117	369	43	93	15	1	9	42	49	90	.252	.344	.371	96	-1	3	1	0	.962	2	O-69,D-38	-0.1
1987	Bal-A	110	363	46	87	10	1	16	39	46	91	.240	.328	.405	96	-2	10	7	-1	.975	-3	O-60,D-47	-0.9
1988	Phi-N	75	146	13	33	14	0	1	14	26	43	.226	.347	.342	96	0	0	0	0	.938	-2	O-42	-0.3
	Mil-A	8	14	2	0	0	0	0	0	2	5	.000	.176	.000	-46	-3	0	0	0	.000	-1	/O-2,D-5	-0.4
1989	Cle-A	32	59	2	11	0	0	1	5	6	13	.186	.273	.237	44	-4	1	2	-1	1.000	-0	D-15/O-1	-0.6
Total	8	635	1840	244	454	80	6	72	235	237	465	.247	.339	.414	107	20	22	17	-4	.969	-18	O-402,D-148	-1.7

■ BABE YOUNG
Young, Norman Robert b: 7/1/15, Astoria, N.Y. d: 12/25/83, Everett, Mass. BL/TL, 6'2.5", 185 lbs. Deb: 9/26/36

YEAR	TM/L	G	AB	R	H	2B	3B	HR	RBI	BB	SO	AVG	OBP	SLG	PRO+	BR/A	SB	CS	SBR	FA	FR	G/POS	TPR
1936	NY-N	1	1	0	0	0	0	0	0	0	0	.000	.000	.000	-99	-0	0			.000	0	H	0.0
1939	NY-N	22	75	8	23	4	0	3	14	5	6	.307	.373	.480	127	3	0			.982	-2	1-22	-0.1
1940	NY-N	149	556	75	159	27	4	17	101	69	28	.286	.367	.441	121	16	4			.992	-2	*1-147	0.0
1941	NY-N	152	574	90	152	28	5	25	104	66	39	.265	.346	.462	124	17	1			.986	-4	*1-150	0.2
1942	NY-N	101	287	37	80	17	1	11	59	34	22	.279	.365	.460	140	14	1			.972	-4	O-54,1-18	0.7
1946	NY-N	104	291	30	81	11	0	7	33	30	21	.278	.346	.388	107	3	3			.988	-8	1-49,O-24	-0.9
1947	NY-N	14	14	0	1	1	0	0	0	0	1	.071	.071	.143	-44	-3	0			.000	0	H	-0.3
	Cin-N	95	364	55	103	21	3	14	79	35	26	.283	.349	.473	117	8	0			.990	-2	1-93	0.3
	Yr	109	378	55	104	22	3	14	79	35	27	.275	.340	.460	111	5	0			.990	-2	1-93	0.0
1948	Cin-N	49	130	11	30	7	2	1	12	19	12	.231	.329	.338	84	-3	0			.993	0	1-31/O-1	-0.3
	StL-N	41	111	14	27	5	2	1	13	16	6	.243	.339	.351	82	-3	0			.996	-4	1-35	-0.7
	Yr	90	241	25	57	12	4	2	25	35	18	.237	.333	.344	83	-5	0			.995	-4	1-66/O-1	-1.0
Total	8	728	2403	320	656	121	17	79	415	274	161	.273	.352	.436	117	52	9			.989	-25	1-545/O-79	-1.1

■ RALPH YOUNG
Young, Ralph Stuart b: 9/19/1889, Philadelphia, Pa. d: 1/24/65, Philadelphia, Pa. BB/TR, 5'5", 165 lbs. Deb: 4/10/13

YEAR	TM/L	G	AB	R	H	2B	3B	HR	RBI	BB	SO	AVG	OBP	SLG	PRO+	BR/A	SB	CS	SBR	FA	FR	G/POS	TPR
1913	NY-A	7	15	2	1	0	0	0	0	3	3	.067	.222	.067	-15	-2	2			.857	1	/S-7	0.0
1915	Det-A	123	378	44	92	6	5	0	31	53	31	.243	.339	.286	83	-7	12	11	-3	.950	8	*2-119	-0.1
1916	Det-A	153	528	60	139	16	6	1	45	62	43	.263	.342	.322	96	-2	20	20	-6	.966	-1	*2-146/S-6,3-1	-0.4
1917	Det-A	141	503	64	116	18	2	1	35	61	35	.231	.317	.280	83	-9	8			.958	8	*2-141	0.7
1918	Det-A	91	298	31	56	7	1	0	21	54	17	.188	.313	.218	63	-11	15			.939	-12	2-91	-1.9
1919	Det-A	125	456	63	96	13	5	1	25	53	32	.211	.294	.268	60	-24	8			.970	17	*2-120/S-5	-0.1
1920	Det-A	150	594	84	173	21	6	0	33	85	30	.291	.382	.347	96	1	8	13	-5	.969	-11	*2-150	-1.0
1921	Det-A	107	401	70	120	8	3	0	29	69	23	.299	.406	.334	91	-1	11	9	-2	.947	-23	*2-106	-2.2
1922	Phi-A	125	470	62	105	19	2	1	35	55	21	.223	.309	.279	53	-32	8	6	-1	.960	-15	*2-120	-4.4
Total	9	1022	3643	480	898	108	30	4	254	495	235	.247	.339	.296	79	-86	92	59		.959	-28	2-993/S-18,3-1	-9.4

■ DICK YOUNG
Young, Richard Ennis b: 6/3/28, Seattle, Wash. BL/TR, 5'11", 175 lbs. Deb: 9/11/51

YEAR	TM/L	G	AB	R	H	2B	3B	HR	RBI	BB	SO	AVG	OBP	SLG	PRO+	BR/A	SB	CS	SBR	FA	FR	G/POS	TPR
1951	Phi-N	15	68	7	16	5	0	0	2	3	6	.235	.268	.309	55	-4	0	1	-1	.922	-9	2-15	-1.4
1952	Phi-N	5	9	3	2	1	0	0	0	1	3	.222	.300	.333	76	-0	1	0	0	.900	-0	/2-2	0.0
Total	2	20	77	10	18	6	0	0	2	4	9	.234	.272	.312	58	-5	1	1	-0	.919	-9	/2-17	-1.4

■ BOBBY YOUNG
Young, Robert George b: 1/22/25, Granite, Md. d: 1/28/85, Baltimore, Md. BL/TR, 6'1", 175 lbs. Deb: 7/28/48

YEAR	TM/L	G	AB	R	H	2B	3B	HR	RBI	BB	SO	AVG	OBP	SLG	PRO+	BR/A	SB	CS	SBR	FA	FR	G/POS	TPR
1948	StL-N	3	1	0	0	0	0	0	0	0	1	.000	.000	.000	-95	-0	0			1.000	0	/3-1	0.0
1951	StL-A	147	611	75	159	13	9	1	31	44	51	.260	.310	.316	67	-28	8	7	-2	.980	1	*2-147	-2.2
1952	StL-A	149	575	59	142	15	9	4	39	56	48	.247	.314	.325	76	-19	3	3	-1	.984	-9	*2-149	-2.2
1953	StL-A	148	537	48	137	22	2	4	25	41	40	.255	.309	.326	70	-22	2	1	0	.977	-17	*2-148	-3.1
1954	Bal-A	130	432	43	106	13	6	4	24	54	42	.245	.331	.331	88	-7	4	4	-1	.976	-14	*2-127	-1.5
1955	Bal-A	59	186	5	37	3	0	1	8	11	23	.199	.244	.231	30	-19	1	4	-2	.985	3	2-58	-1.5
	Cle-A	18	45	7	14	1	1	0	6	1	2	.311	.326	.378	86	-1	0	0	0	.983	7	2-11/3-1	0.6
	Yr	77	231	12	51	4	1	1	14	12	25	.221	.259	.260	42	-19	1	4	-2	.985	9	2-69/3-1	-0.9
1956	Cle-A	1	0	0	0	0	0	0	0	0	0	—	—	—	—	0	0	0	0	.000	0	R	0.0
1958	Phi-N	32	60	7	14	1	1	1	4	1	5	.233	.246	.333	52	-4	0	0	0	.968	-2	2-21	-0.6
Total	8	687	2447	244	609	68	28	15	137	208	212	.249	.308	.318	71	-100	18	19		.980	-32	2-661/3-2	-10.5

■ RUSS YOUNG
Young, Russell Charles b: 9/15/02, Bryan, Ohio d: 5/13/84, Roseville, Cal. BB/TR, 6', 175 lbs. Deb: 4/16/31

YEAR	TM/L	G	AB	R	H	2B	3B	HR	RBI	BB	SO	AVG	OBP	SLG	PRO+	BR/A	SB	CS	SBR	FA	FR	G/POS	TPR
1931	StL-A	16	34	2	4	0	0	1	2	2	4	.118	.167	.206	-3	-5	0	0	0	1.000	2	C-16	-0.2

YEAR	TM/L	G	AB	R	H	2B	3B	HR	RBI	BB	SO	AVG	OBP	SLG	PRO+	BR/A	SB	CS	SBR	FA	FR	G/POS	TPR
■ **JOEL YOUNGBLOOD**	Youngblood, Joel Randolph b: 8/28/51, Houston, Tex. BR/TR, 6', 180 lbs. Deb: 4/13/76 C																						
1976	Cin-N	55	57	8	11	1	1	0	1	2	8	.193	.233	.246	35	-5	1	0	0	.938	-1	/O-9,3-6,C-1,2-1	-0.6
1977	StL-N	25	27	1	5	2	0	0	1	3	5	.185	.267	.259	43	-2	0	2	-1	1.000	-3	O-11/3-6	-0.7
	NY-N	70	182	16	46	11	1	0	11	13	40	.253	.303	.324	72	-7	1	3	-2	.954	2	2-33,O-22,3-10	-0.6
	Yr	95	209	17	51	13	1	0	12	16	45	.244	.298	.316	67	-10	1	5	-3	1.000	-1	O-33,2-33,3-16	-1.3
1978	NY-N	113	266	40	67	12	8	7	30	16	39	.252	.297	.436	106	1	4	0	1	.989	2	O-50,2-39/3-9,S-1	0.4
1979	NY-N	158	590	90	162	37	5	16	60	60	84	.275	.349	.436	117	13	18	13	-2	.985	4	*O-147,2-13,3-12	1.0
1980	NY-N	146	514	58	142	26	2	8	69	52	69	.276	.345	.381	105	4	14	11	-2	.984	15	*O-121,3-21/2-6	1.2
1981	NY-N★	43	143	16	50	10	2	4	25	12	19	.350	.408	.531	167	12	2	5	-2	.962	2	O-41	1.1
1982	NY-N	80	202	21	52	12	0	3	21	8	37	.257	.302	.361	85	-4	0	4	-2	.969	-9	O-63/2-8,S-1,3-1	-1.7
	Mon-N	40	90	16	18	2	0	0	8	9	21	.200	.294	.222	45	-6	2	1	0	1.000	-3	O-35	-1.0
	Yr	120	292	37	70	14	0	3	29	17	58	.240	.300	.318	73	-10	2	5	-2	.979	-12	O-98/2-8,S-1,3-1	-2.7
1983	SF-N	124	373	59	109	20	3	17	53	33	59	.292	.358	.499	139	19	7	4	-0	.948	-30	2-64,3-28,O-22	-1.1
1984	SF-N	134	469	50	119	17	1	10	51	48	86	.254	.328	.358	96	-2	5	6	-2	.887	-26	*3-117,O-11/2-5	-3.4
1985	SF-N	95	230	24	62	6	0	4	24	30	37	.270	.356	.348	103	2	3	2	-0	.955	-0	O-56/3-1	-0.1
1986	SF-N	97	184	20	47	12	0	5	28	18	34	.255	.325	.402	105	1	1	1	-0	1.000	-6	O-45/1-7,3-5,2-4,S	-0.7
1987	SF-N	69	91	9	23	3	0	3	11	5	13	.253	.299	.385	83	-2	1	1	-0	1.000	-3	O-22/3-2	-0.6
1988	SF-N	83	123	12	31	4	0	0	16	10	17	.252	.313	.285	76	-4	1	1	-0	.980	-11	O-45	-1.7
1989	Cin-N	76	118	13	25	5	0	3	13	13	21	.212	.301	.331	78	-3	0	1	-1	.970	-10	O-45	-1.6
Total	14	1408	3659	453	969	180	23	80	422	332	589	.265	.332	.392	103	15	60	55	-15	.981	-78	O-745,3-218,2/1SC	-10.1
■ **HENRY YOUNGMAN**	Youngman, Henry b: 1865, Indiana, Pa. d: 1/24/36, Pittsburgh, Pa. TR , Deb: 4/19/1890																						
1890	Pit-N	13	47	6	6	1	1	0	4	6	9	.128	.226	.191	25	-4	1			.750	-2	/3-7,2-6	-0.5
■ **ROSS YOUNGS**	Youngs, Ross Middlebrook "Pep" (b: Royce Middlebrook Youngs) b: 4/10/1897, Shiner, Tex. d: 10/22/27, San Antonio, Tex. BL/TR, 5'8", 162 lbs. Deb: 9/25/17 H																						
1917	NY-N	7	26	5	9	2	3	0	1	1	5	.346	.370	.654	218	3	1			1.000	1	/O-7	0.4
1918	NY-N	121	474	70	143	16	8	1	25	44	49	.302	.368	.376	129	18	10			.950	-6	*O-120/2-7	0.5
1919	NY-N	130	489	73	152	**31**	7	2	43	51	47	.311	.384	.415	142	26	24			.942	2	*O-130	2.1
1920	NY-N	153	581	92	204	27	14	6	78	75	55	.351	.427	.477	161	48	18	18	-5	.935	3	*O-153	3.6
1921	*NY-N	141	504	90	165	24	16	3	102	71	47	.327	.411	.456	129	24	21	17	-4	.978	-4	*O-137	0.6
1922	*NY-N	149	559	105	185	34	10	7	86	55	50	.331	.398	.465	121	18	17	9	-0	.942	4	*O-147	1.1
1923	*NY-N	152	596	**121**	200	33	12	3	87	73	36	.336	.412	.446	128	27	13	19	-8	.959	1	*O-152	1.0
1924	*NY-N	133	526	112	187	33	12	10	74	77	31	.356	.441	.521	161	49	11	9	-2	.955	-1	*O-132/2-2	3.6
1925	NY-N	130	500	82	132	24	6	6	53	66	51	.264	.354	.372	89	-7	17	11	-2	.952	-6	*O-127/2-3	-2.1
1926	NY-N	95	372	62	114	12	5	4	43	37	19	.306	.372	.398	109	5	21			.974	2	O-94	0.0
Total	10	1211	4627	812	1491	236	93	42	592	550	390	.322	.399	.441	131	212	153	83		.953	-4	*O-1199/2-12	10.8
■ **EDDIE YOUNT**	Yount, Floyd Edwin b: 12/19/16, Newton, N.C. d: 10/26/73, Newton, N.C. BR/TR, 6'1", 185 lbs. Deb: 9/9/37																						
1937	Phi-A	4	7	1	2	0	0	0	1	0	1	.286	.286	.286	45	-1	0	0	0	1.000	-0	/O-2	-0.1
1939	Pit-N	2	2	0	0	0	0	0	0	0	2	.000	.000	.000	-99	-1	0			.000	-0	H	-0.1
Total	2	6	9	1	2	0	0	0	1	0	3	.222	.222	.222	14	-1	0	0		1.000	-0	/O-2	-0.2
■ **ROBIN YOUNT**	Yount, Robin R b: 9/16/55, Danville, Ill. BR/TR, 6', 170 lbs. Deb: 4/5/74 F																						
1974	Mil-A	107	344	48	86	14	5	3	26	12	46	.250	.277	.346	79	-10	7	7	-2	.962	-11	*S-107	-1.1
1975	Mil-A	147	558	67	149	28	2	8	52	33	69	.267	.309	.367	90	-8	12	4	1	.939	-23	*S-145	-1.5
1976	Mil-A	161	638	59	161	19	3	2	54	38	69	.252	.294	.301	76	-20	16	11	-2	.963	-5	*S-161/O-1	-0.7
1977	Mil-A	154	605	66	174	34	4	4	49	41	80	.288	.335	.377	94	-5	16	7	1	.964	-9	*S-153	0.4
1978	Mil-A	127	502	66	147	23	9	9	71	24	43	.293	.326	.428	110	5	16	5	2	.959	22	*S-125	4.5
1979	Mil-A	149	577	72	154	26	5	8	51	35	52	.267	.310	.371	83	-15	11	8	-2	.969	5	*S-149	0.6
1980	Mil-A★	143	611	121	179	**49**	10	23	87	26	67	.293	.323	.519	131	22	20	5	3	.961	0	*S-133/D-9	4.0
1981	*Mil-A	96	377	50	103	15	5	10	49	22	37	.273	.317	.419	116	6	4	1	1	**.985**	28	S-93/D-3	4.5
1982	*Mil-A★	156	635	129	**210**	**46**	12	29	114	54	63	.331	.384	**.578**	**171**	**59**	14	3	2	.969	-4	*S-154/D-1	**7.0**
1983	Mil-A★	149	578	102	178	42	**10**	17	80	72	58	.308	.367	.503	155	44	12	5	1	.973	-5	*S-139/D-8	5.2
1984	Mil-A	160	624	105	186	27	7	16	80	67	67	.298	.367	.441	127	24	14	4	2	.971	15	*S-120,D-39	5.0
1985	Mil-A	122	466	76	129	26	3	15	68	49	56	.277	.348	.442	115	10	10	4	1	.970	4	*O-108,D-12/1-2	1.0
1986	Mil-A	140	522	82	163	31	7	9	46	62	73	.312	.389	.450	124	19	14	5	1	**.997**	12	*O-131/1-3,D-6	2.6
1987	Mil-A	158	635	99	198	25	9	21	103	76	94	.312	.386	.479	124	23	19	9	0	.987	8	*O-150/D-8	2.5
1988	Mil-A	162	621	92	190	38	**11**	13	91	63	63	.306	.373	.465	132	27	22	4	4	.996	15	*O-158/D-4	4.1
1989	Mil-A	160	614	101	195	38	9	21	103	63	71	.318	.387	.511	153	42	19	3	4	.981	4	*O-143,D-17	4.6
1990	Mil-A	158	587	98	145	17	5	17	77	78	89	.247	.341	.380	102	3	15	8	-0	.991	6	*O-157/D-1	0.5
1991	Mil-A	130	503	66	131	20	4	10	77	54	79	.260	.337	.376	99	0	6	4	-1	.994	4	*O-117,D-13	0.0
1992	Mil-A	150	557	71	147	40	3	8	77	53	81	.264	.331	.390	103	2	15	6	1	.995	2	*O-139,D-11	0.2
1993	Mil-A	127	454	62	117	25	3	8	51	44	93	.258	.330	.379	91	-5	9	2	2	.997	4	*O-114/1-7,D-6	-0.3
Total	20	2856	11008	1632	3142	583	126	251	1406	966	1350	.285	.346	.430	115	223	271	105	18	.964	71	*S-1479,O-1218,D/1	43.1
■ **JEFF YURAK**	Yurak, Jeffrey Lynn b: 2/26/54, Pasadena, Cal. BB/TR, 6'3", 195 lbs. Deb: 9/15/78																						
1978	Mil-A	5	5	0	0	0	0	0	0	1	0	.000	.167	.000	-49	-1	0	0	0	1.000	0	/O-1	-0.1
■ **SAL YVARS**	Yvars, Salvador Anthony b: 2/20/24, New York, N.Y. BR/TR, 5'10", 187 lbs. Deb: 9/27/47																						
1947	NY-N	1	5	0	1	0	0	0	0	0	2	.200	.200	.200	6	-1	0			1.000	-0	/C-1	-0.1
1948	NY-N	15	38	4	8	1	0	1	6	3	1	.211	.286	.316	62	-2	0			1.000	3	C-15	0.1
1949	NY-N	3	8	0	0	0	0	0	0	1	1	.000	.111	.000	-68	-2	0			1.000	1	/C-2	-0.1
1950	NY-N	9	14	0	2	0	0	0	0	1	2	.143	.200	.143	-8	-2	0			.963	2	/C-9	0.0
1951	*NY-N	25	41	9	13	2	0	2	3	5	7	.317	.417	.512	147	3	0	0	0	.942	-3	C-23	0.0
1952	NY-N	66	151	15	37	3	0	4	18	10	16	.245	.296	.344	77	-5	0	0	0	.988	7	C-59	0.4
1953	NY-N	23	47	1	13	0	0	0	1	7	1	.277	.370	.277	71	-2	0	0	0	1.000	1	C-20	0.0
	StL-N	30	57	4	14	2	0	1	6	4	6	.246	.306	.333	67	-3	0	1	-1	.989	2	C-26	-0.1
	Yr	53	104	5	27	2	0	1	7	11	7	.260	.336	.308	69	-4	0	1	-1	.994	3	C-46	-0.1
1954	StL-N	38	57	8	14	4	0	2	8	6	5	.246	.328	.421	93	-1	1	0	0	1.000	-2	C-21	-0.2
Total	8	210	418	41	102	12	0	10	42	37	41	.244	.315	.344	76	-14	1	1		.987	10	C-176	0.0
■ **ELMER ZACHER**	Zacher, Elmer Henry "Silver" b: 9/17/1883, Buffalo, N.Y. d: 12/20/44, Buffalo, N.Y. BR/TR, 5'9", 190 lbs. Deb: 4/30/10																						
1910	NY-N	1	0	0	0	0	0	0	0	0	0	—	—	—	—	0	0			1.000	-0	/O-1	0.0
	StL-N	47	132	7	28	5	1	0	10	10	19	.212	.278	.265	61	-7	3			.966	3	O-36/2-1	-0.6
	Yr	48	132	7	28	5	1	0	10	10	19	.212	.278	.265	61	-7	3			.966	2	O-37/2-1	-0.6
■ **FRED ZAHNER**	Zahner, Frederick Joseph b: 6/5/1870, Louisville, Ky. d: 7/24/1900, Louisville, Ky. Deb: 7/23/1894																						
1894	Lou-N	13	45	7	9	0	1	0	3	3	5	.200	.250	.244	21	-6	2			.778	-5	C-10/O-2,1-1	-0.8
1895	Lou-N	21	49	7	11	1	1	0	6	6	4	.224	.321	.286	61	-3	0			.824	-6	C-21	-0.6
Total	2	34	94	14	20	1	2	0	9	9	9	.213	.288	.266	42	-8	2			.805	-11	/C-31,O-2,1-1	-1.4
■ **FRANKIE ZAK**	Zak, Frank Thomas b: 2/22/22, Passaic, N.J. d: 2/6/72, Passaic, N.J. BR/TR, 5'10", 150 lbs. Deb: 4/21/44																						
1944	Pit-N☆	87	160	33	48	3	1	0	11	22	18	.300	.385	.331	99	1	6			.948	6	S-67	1.1
1945	Pit-N	15	28	2	4	2	0	0	3	3	5	.143	.226	.214	22	-3	0			.971	1	S-10/2-1	-0.2
1946	Pit-N	21	20	8	4	0	0	0	0	1	0	.200	.238	.200	24	-2	0			.929	9	S-10	0.7
Total	3	123	208	43	56	5	1	0	14	26	23	.269	.350	.303	82	-4	6			.948	15	/S-87,2-1	1.5
■ **JACK ZALUSKY**	Zalusky, John Francis b: 6/22/1879, Minneapolis, Minn d: 8/11/35, Minneapolis, Minn. BR/TR, 5'11.5", 172 lbs. Deb: 9/4/03																						
1903	NY-A	7	16	2	5	0	0	0	1	1		.313	.353	.313	95	-0				1.000	-1	/C-6,1-1	-0.1

■ EDUARDO ZAMBRANO
Zambrano, Eduardo Jose (Guerra) b: 2/1/66, Maracaibo, Venez. BR/TR, 6'2", 175 lbs. Deb: 9/19/93

YEAR	TM/L	G	AB	R	H	2B	3B	HR	RBI	BB	SO	AVG	OBP	SLG	PRO+	BR/A	SB	CS	SBR	FA	FR	G/POS	TPR
1993	Chi-N	8	17	1	5	0	0	0	2	1	3	.294	.333	.294	71	-1	0	0	0	1.000	-2	/O-4,1-2	-0.3
1994	Chi-N	67	116	17	30	7	0	6	18	16	29	.259	.353	.474	115	3	2	1	0	.944	-4	O-27/1-9,3-4	-0.2
Total	2	75	133	18	35	7	0	6	20	17	32	.263	.351	.451	109	2	2	1	0	.946	-6	/O-31,1-11,3-4	-0.5

■ JOE ZAPUSTAS
Zapustas, Joseph John b: 7/25/07, Boston, Mass. BR/TR, 6'1", 185 lbs. Deb: 9/28/33

YEAR	TM/L	G	AB	R	H	2B	3B	HR	RBI	BB	SO	AVG	OBP	SLG	PRO+	BR/A	SB	CS	SBR	FA	FR	G/POS	TPR
1933	Phi-A	2	5	0	1	0	0	0	0	0	0	.200	.200	.200	6	-1	0	0	0	1.000	-1	/O-2	-0.1

■ JOSE ZARDON
Zardon, Jose Antonio (Sanchez) "Guineo" b: 5/20/23, Havana, Cuba BR/TR, 6', 150 lbs. Deb: 4/18/45

YEAR	TM/L	G	AB	R	H	2B	3B	HR	RBI	BB	SO	AVG	OBP	SLG	PRO+	BR/A	SB	CS	SBR	FA	FR	G/POS	TPR
1945	Was-A	54	131	13	38	5	3	0	13	7	11	.290	.326	.374	112	1	3	1	0	.972	-1	O-43	-0.1

■ AL ZARILLA
Zarilla, Allen Lee "Zeke" b: 5/1/19, Los Angeles, Cal. d: 9/4/96, Honolulu, Hawaii BL/TR, 5'11", 180 lbs. Deb: 6/30/43 C

YEAR	TM/L	G	AB	R	H	2B	3B	HR	RBI	BB	SO	AVG	OBP	SLG	PRO+	BR/A	SB	CS	SBR	FA	FR	G/POS	TPR
1943	StL-A	70	228	27	58	7	1	2	17	17	20	.254	.309	.320	82	-5	1	1	-0	.962	-2	O-60	-1.1
1944	*StL-A	100	288	43	86	13	6	6	45	29	33	.299	.375	.448	127	10	1	1	-0	.977	-2	O-79	0.4
1946	StL-A	125	371	46	96	14	9	4	43	27	37	.259	.311	.377	87	-7	3	5	-2	.973	3	*O-107	-1.1
1947	StL-A	127	380	34	85	15	6	3	38	40	45	.224	.303	.318	71	-15	3	6	-3	.986	-10	*O-110	-3.5
1948	StL-A★	144	529	77	174	39	3	12	74	48	48	.329	.389	.482	128	19	11	6	-0	.962	-9	*O-136	0.3
1949	StL-A	15	56	10	14	1	0	1	6	8	2	.250	.354	.321	76	-2	1	1	-0	1.000	-5	O-15	-0.8
	Bos-A	124	474	68	133	32	4	9	71	48	51	.281	.352	.422	97	-3	4	4	-1	.984	-2	*O-122	-1.2
	Yr	139	530	78	147	33	4	10	77	56	53	.277	.352	.411	95	-5	5	5	-2	.985	-7	*O-137	-2.0
1950	Bos-A	130	471	92	153	32	10	9	74	76	47	.325	.423	.493	122	17	2	3	-1	.976	-4	*O-128	0.6
1951	Chi-A	120	382	56	98	21	2	10	60	60	57	.257	.363	.401	109	5	2	4	-2	.983	-12	*O-117	-1.2
1952	Chi-A	39	99	14	23	4	1	2	7	14	6	.232	.333	.354	90	-1	1	0	0	.974	-6	O-32	-0.8
	StL-A	48	130	20	31	6	0	1	9	27	15	.238	.373	.308	88	-1	2	1	0	.976	0	O-35	-0.2
	Bos-A	21	60	9	11	0	1	2	8	7	8	.183	.269	.317	58	-4	2	0	1	.941	-1	O-19	-0.5
	Yr	108	289	43	65	10	2	5	24	48	29	.225	.339	.325	83	-6	5	1	1	.968	-7	O-86	-1.5
1953	Bos-A	57	67	11	13	2	0	0	4	14	13	.194	.333	.224	50	-4	0	1	-1	.947	-5	O-18	-1.0
Total	10	1120	3535	507	975	186	43	61	456	415	382	.276	.357	.405	102	10	33	33	-10	.974	-53	O-978	-10.1

■ NORM ZAUCHIN
Zauchin, Norbert Henry b: 11/17/29, Royal Oak, Mich. BR/TR, 6'4.5", 220 lbs. Deb: 9/23/51

YEAR	TM/L	G	AB	R	H	2B	3B	HR	RBI	BB	SO	AVG	OBP	SLG	PRO+	BR/A	SB	CS	SBR	FA	FR	G/POS	TPR
1951	Bos-A	5	12	0	2	1	0	0	0	0	4	.167	.167	.250	11	-2	0	1	-1	.957	-0	/1-4	-0.2
1955	Bos-A	130	477	65	114	10	0	27	93	69	105	.239	.339	.430	97	-3	3	0	1	**.995**	1	*1-126	-0.8
1956	Bos-A	44	84	12	18	2	0	2	11	14	22	.214	.333	.310	63	-4	0	0	0	.990	-1	1-31	-0.6
1957	Bos-A	52	91	11	24	3	0	3	14	9	13	.264	.343	.396	96	-0	0	0	0	.972	0	1-36	-0.2
1958	Was-A	96	303	35	69	8	2	15	37	38	68	.228	.316	.416	101	0	0	0	0	.995	2	1-91	-0.4
1959	Was-A	19	71	11	15	4	0	3	4	7	14	.211	.291	.394	87	-1	2	0	1	.995	-2	1-19	-0.5
Total	6	346	1038	134	242	28	2	50	159	137	226	.233	.327	.408	93	-11	5	1	1	.993	0	1-307	-2.7

■ GREG ZAUN
Zaun, Gregory Owen b: 4/14/71, Glendale, Cal. BB/TR, 5'10", 170 lbs. Deb: 6/24/95

YEAR	TM/L	G	AB	R	H	2B	3B	HR	RBI	BB	SO	AVG	OBP	SLG	PRO+	BR/A	SB	CS	SBR	FA	FR	G/POS	TPR
1995	Bal-A	40	104	18	27	5	0	3	14	16	14	.260	.358	.394	94	-1	1	1	-0	.987	4	C-39/D-1	0.5
1996	Bal-A	50	108	16	25	8	1	1	13	11	15	.231	.314	.352	68	-5	0	0	0	.987	1	C-49	-0.2
	Fla-N	10	31	4	9	1	0	1	2	3	5	.290	.353	.419	106	0	1	0	0	1.000	0	C-10	0.2
1997	*Fla-N	58	143	21	43	10	2	2	20	26	18	.301	.415	.441	130	8	1	0	0	.978	4	C-50/1-1	1.4
1998	Fla-N	106	298	19	56	12	2	5	29	35	52	.188	.275	.292	50	-23	5	2	0	.986	-6	C-88/2-1	-2.1
Total	4	264	684	78	160	36	5	12	78	91	104	.234	.328	.354	79	-21	8	3	1	.985	4	C-236/2-1,1-1,D-1	-0.2

■ ZAY
Zay Deb: 10/7/1886

YEAR	TM/L	G	AB	R	H	2B	3B	HR	RBI	BB	SO	AVG	OBP	SLG	PRO+	BR/A	SB	CS	SBR	FA	FR	G/POS	TPR
1886	Bal-a	1	1	0	0	0	0	0	0	0		.000	.000	.000	-99	-0	0			.000	-0	/O-1,P-1	0.0

■ JOE ZDEB
Zdeb, Joseph Edmund b: 6/27/53, Compton, Ill. BR/TR, 5'11", 185 lbs. Deb: 4/7/77

YEAR	TM/L	G	AB	R	H	2B	3B	HR	RBI	BB	SO	AVG	OBP	SLG	PRO+	BR/A	SB	CS	SBR	FA	FR	G/POS	TPR
1977	*KC-A	105	195	26	58	5	2	2	23	16	23	.297	.351	.374	97	-1	6	5	-1	.970	-18	O-93/3-1,D-4	-2.2
1978	KC-A	60	127	18	32	2	3	0	11	7	18	.252	.291	.315	69	-5	3	0	1	.957	-9	O-52/2-1,3-1,D-1	-1.6
1979	KC-A	15	23	3	4	1	1	0	0	2	4	.174	.240	.304	45	-2	1	0	0	1.000	-1	/O-9	-0.3
Total	3	180	345	47	94	8	6	2	34	25	45	.272	.322	.348	83	-8	10	5	0	.967	-29	O-154/D-5,3-2,2-1	-4.1

■ DAVE ZEARFOSS
Zearfoss, David William Tilden b: 1/1/1868, Schenectady, N.Y. d: 9/12/45, Wilmington, Del. TR , 5'9", Deb: 4/17/1896

YEAR	TM/L	G	AB	R	H	2B	3B	HR	RBI	BB	SO	AVG	OBP	SLG	PRO+	BR/A	SB	CS	SBR	FA	FR	G/POS	TPR
1896	NY-N	19	60	5	13	1	1	0	6	5	5	.217	.288	.267	48	-4	2			.893	-4	C-19	-0.5
1897	NY-N	5	10	1	3	0	1	0	0	0		.300	.300	.500	112	0	0			.880	2	/C-5	0.2
1898	NY-N	1	1	0	1	0	0	0	0	0		1.000	1.000	1.000	489	0	0			1.000	1	/C-1	0.1
1904	StL-N	27	80	7	17	2	0	0	9	10		.213	.300	.237	70	-2	0			.966	-2	C-25	-0.2
1905	StL-N	20	51	2	8	0	1	0	2	4		.157	.218	.196	24	-5	0			.966	-0	C-19	-0.4
Total	5	72	202	15	42	3	3	0	17	19	5	.208	.279	.252	56	-11	2			.943	-3	/C-69	-0.8

■ GEORGE ZEBER
Zeber, George William b: 8/29/50, Ellwood City, Pa. BB/TR, 5'11", 170 lbs. Deb: 5/7/77

YEAR	TM/L	G	AB	R	H	2B	3B	HR	RBI	BB	SO	AVG	OBP	SLG	PRO+	BR/A	SB	CS	SBR	FA	FR	G/POS	TPR
1977	*NY-A	25	65	8	21	3	0	3	10	9	11	.323	.405	.508	149	5	0	0	0	.961	1	2-21/S-2,3-2,D-1	0.7
1978	NY-A	3	6	0	0	0	0	0	0	0	0	.000	.000	.000	-99	-2	0	0	0	.750	-1	/2-1	-0.3
Total	2	28	71	8	21	3	0	3	10	9	11	.296	.375	.465	129	3	0	0	0	.953	-0	/2-22,3-2,S-2,D-1	0.4

■ ROLLIE ZEIDER
Zeider, Rollie Hubert "Bunions" b: 11/16/1883, Auburn, Ind. d: 9/12/67, Garrett, Ind. BR/TR, 5'10", 162 lbs. Deb: 4/14/10

YEAR	TM/L	G	AB	R	H	2B	3B	HR	RBI	BB	SO	AVG	OBP	SLG	PRO+	BR/A	SB	CS	SBR	FA	FR	G/POS	TPR
1910	Chi-A	136	498	57	108	9	2	0	31	62		.217	.305	.243	75	-12	49			.931	-2	2-87,S-45/3-4	-1.6
1911	Chi-A	73	217	39	55	3	0	2	21	29		.253	.347	.295	82	-4	28			.997	-5	1-29,S-17,3-10,/2-9	-0.8
1912	Chi-A	130	420	57	103	12	10	1	42	50		.245	.330	.329	91	-4	47			.979	6	1-66,3-56/S-1	0.1
1913	Chi-A	16	20	4	7	0	0	0	2	4	1	.350	.458	.350	139	1	3			1.000	2	/3-6,1-3,2-1	0.4
	NY-A	50	159	15	37	2	0	0	12	25	9	.233	.341	.245	72	-4	3			.901	-14	S-24,2-19/1-4,3-2	-1.8
	Yr	66	179	19	44	2	0	0	14	29	10	.246	.354	.257	79	-3	6			.901	-11	S-24,2-20/3-8,1-7	-1.4
1914	Chi-F	119	452	60	124	13	2	1	36	44	28	.274	.344	.319	86	-15	35			.936	-0	*3-117/S-1	-1.2
1915	Chi-F	129	494	65	112	22	2	0	34	43	24	.227	.297	.279	66	-30	16			.941	1	2-83,3-30,S-21	-2.8
1916	Chi-N	98	345	29	81	11	2	1	22	26	26	.235	.294	.287	71	-11	9			.928	-8	3-55,2-33/O-7,S1	-2.0
1917	Chi-N	108	354	36	86	14	2	0	27	28	30	.243	.302	.294	77	-9	17			.901	-21	S-48,3-26,2-24,/1O	-3.0
1918	*Chi-N	82	251	31	56	3	2	0	26	23	20	.223	.288	.251	63	-10	16			.956	-11	2-79/1-1,3-1	-1.9
Total	9	941	3210	393	769	89	22	5	253	334	138	.240	.315	.286	77	-99	223			.945	-52	2-335,3-307,S1/O	-14.6

■ TODD ZEILE
Zeile, Todd Edward b: 9/9/65, Van Nuys, Cal. BR/TR, 6'1", 190 lbs. Deb: 8/18/89

YEAR	TM/L	G	AB	R	H	2B	3B	HR	RBI	BB	SO	AVG	OBP	SLG	PRO+	BR/A	SB	CS	SBR	FA	FR	G/POS	TPR
1989	StL-N	28	82	7	21	3	1	1	8	9	14	.256	.330	.354	92	-1	0	0	0	.971	-2	C-23	-0.1
1990	StL-N	144	495	62	121	25	3	15	57	67	77	.244	.337	.398	101	1	2	4	-2	.988	-11	*C-105,3-24,1-11,/O	-0.6
1991	StL-N	155	565	76	158	36	3	11	81	62	94	.280	.356	.412	115	12	17	11	-2	.943	-7	*3-154	0.4
1992	StL-N	126	439	51	113	18	4	7	48	68	70	.257	.357	.364	108	6	7	10	-4	.960	-7	*3-124	-0.5
1993	StL-N	157	571	82	158	36	1	17	103	70	76	.277	.356	.433	112	10	5	4	-1	.923	-5	*3-153	0.5
1994	StL-N	113	415	62	111	25	1	19	75	52	56	.267	.353	.470	114	9	1	3	-2	.960	3	*3-112	1.0
1995	StL-N	34	127	16	37	6	0	5	22	18	23	.291	.384	.457	121	4	1	0	0	.980	1	1-34	0.2
	Chi-N	79	299	34	68	16	0	9	30	16	53	.227	.274	.371	69	-14	0	0	0	.939	-10	3-75/O-2,1-1	-2.5
	Yr	113	426	50	105	22	0	14	52	34	76	.246	.308	.397	85	-10	1	0	0	.939	-9	3-75,1-35/O-2	-2.3
1996	Phi-N	134	500	61	134	24	0	20	80	67	88	.268	.356	.436	106	5	1	1	-0	.962	-14	*3-106,1-28	-1.2
	*Bal-A	29	117	17	28	8	0	5	19	15	16	.239	.326	.436	91	-2	0	0	0	.964	3	3-29	0.1
1997	LA-N	160	575	89	154	17	0	31	90	85	112	.268	.368	.459	124	21	8	7	-2	.931	-22	*3-160	-0.2
1998	LA-N	40	158	22	40	6	1	7	27	10	24	.253	.302	.437	95	-2	1	1	-0	.929	-12	3-40/1-1	-1.4
	Fla-N	66	234	37	68	12	1	6	39	31	34	.291	.378	.427	113	5	2	3	-1	.971	-3	3-65	0.2
	Yr	106	392	59	108	18	2	13	66	41	58	.276	.349	.431	107	4	3	4	-2	.957	-15	*3-105/1-1	-1.2
	*Tex-A	52	180	26	47	14	1	6	28	28	32	.261	.364	.450	106	2	1	0	0	.915	-2	3-52	0.0
Total	10	1317	4757	642	1258	246	16	159	707	598	769	.264	.350	.423	108	57	46	44	-13	.943	-88	*3-1094,C-128/1O	-4.1

YEAR	TM/L	G	AB	R	H	2B	3B	HR	RBI	BB	SO	AVG	OBP	SLG	PRO+	BR/A	SB	CS	SBR	FA	FR	G/POS	TPR
■ BART ZELLER	Zeller, Barton Wallace b: 7/22/41, Chicago Heights, Ill. BR/TR, 6'1", 185 lbs. Deb: 5/21/70 C																						
1970	StL-N	1	0	0	0	0	0	0	0	0	0	—	—	—	—	0	0	0	0	1.000	-0	/C-1	0.0
■ GUS ZERNIAL	Zernial, Gus Edward "Ozark Ike" b: 6/27/23, Beaumont, Tex. BR/TR, 6'2.5", 210 lbs. Deb: 4/19/49																						
1949	Chi-A	73	198	29	63	17	2	5	38	15	26	.318	.366	.500	132	8	0	1	-1	1.000	-5	O-46	0.0
1950	Chi-A	143	543	75	152	16	4	29	93	38	110	.280	.330	.484	110	3	0	2	-1	.969	2	*O-137	-0.2
1951	Chi-A	4	19	2	2	0	0	0	4	2	2	.105	.190	.105	-19	-3	0	0	0	.933	1	/O-4	-0.2
	Phi-A	139	552	90	151	30	5	33	125	61	99	.274	.350	.525	132	21	2	2	-1	.974	10	*O-138	2.4
	Yr	143	571	92	153	30	5	**33**	**129**	63	101	.268	.345	.511	127	18	2	2	-1	.972	11	*O-142	2.2
1952	Phi-A	145	549	76	144	15	1	29	100	70	87	.262	.347	.452	114	9	5	1	1	.972	-1	*O-141	0.4
1953	Phi-A★	147	556	85	158	21	3	42	108	57	79	.284	.355	.559	138	27	4	0	1	.972	13	*O-141	3.5
1954	Phi-A	97	336	42	84	8	2	14	62	30	60	.250	.319	.411	98	-2	0	0	0	.953	-1	O-90/1-2	-0.7
1955	KC-A	120	413	62	105	9	3	30	84	30	90	.254	.309	.508	116	6	1	0	0	.964	8	*O-103	0.9
1956	KC-A	109	272	36	61	12	0	16	44	33	66	.224	.317	.445	99	-2	2	0	1	.984	2	O-69	-0.3
1957	KC-A	131	437	56	103	20	1	27	69	34	84	.236	.292	.471	104	-0	1	1	-0	.952	0	*O-113/1-1	-0.8
1958	Det-A	66	124	8	40	7	1	5	23	6	25	.323	.354	.516	127	4	0	0	0	.939	-2	O-24	0.1
1959	Det-A	60	132	11	30	4	0	7	26	7	27	.227	.266	.417	80	-4	0	0	0	.972	-3	1-32/O-1	-0.9
Total	11	1234	4131	572	1093	159	22	237	776	383	755	.265	.331	.486	115	66	15	7	0	.968	24	*O-1007/1-35	4.2
■ CHARLIE ZIEGLER	Ziegler, Charles Wallace b: 1/13/1875, Canton, Ohio d: 4/18/04, Canton, Ohio Deb: 9/23/1899																						
1899	Cle-N	2	8	2	2	0	0	0	0	0		.250	.250	.250	40	-1	0			.750	-1	/S-1,2-1	-0.2
1900	Phi-N	3	11	0	3	0	0	0	1	0		.273	.273	.273	51	-1	0			.889	-1	/3-3	-0.2
Total	2	5	19	2	5	0	0	0	1	0		.263	.263	.263	47	-1	0			.889	-2	/3-3,2-1,S-1	-0.4
■ BENNY ZIENTARA	Zientara, Benedict Joseph b: 2/14/20, Chicago, Ill. d: 4/16/85, Lake Elsinore, Cal. BR/TR, 5'9", 165 lbs. Deb: 9/11/41																						
1941	Cin-N	9	21	3	6	0	0	0	2	1	3	.286	.318	.286	71	-1	0			.914	1	/2-6	0.1
1946	Cin-N	78	280	26	81	10	2	0	16	14	11	.289	.323	.339	91	-4	3			.970	24	2-39,3-36	2.4
1947	Cin-N	117	418	60	108	18	1	2	24	23	23	.258	.297	.321	64	-22	2			.976	-17	*2-100,3-13	-3.2
1948	Cin-N	74	187	17	35	1	2	0	7	12	11	.187	.236	.214	23	-20	0			.990	12	2-60/3-3,S-2	-0.5
Total	4	278	906	106	230	29	5	2	49	50	48	.254	.293	.304	64	-46	5			.976	20	2-205/3-52,S-2	-1.2
■ BILL ZIES	Zies, William BL , Deb: 8/9/1891																						
1891	StL-a	2	3	0	1	0	0	0	0	0	0	.333	.333	.333	79	-0	0			1.000	0	/C-2	0.0
■ CHIEF ZIMMER	Zimmer, Charles Louis b: 11/23/1860, Marietta, Ohio d: 8/22/49, Cleveland, Ohio BR/TR, 6', 190 lbs. Deb: 7/18/1884 MU																						
1884	Det-N	8	29	0	2	1	0	0	0	1	14	.069	.100	.103	-38	-4				.830	-1	/C-6,O-2	-0.5
1886	NY-a	6	19	1	3	0	0	0	1	1		.158	.238	.158	26	-2	0			.893	3	/C-6	0.2
1887	Cle-a	14	52	9	12	5	0	0	4	4		.231	.298	.327	76	-2	1			.923	-4	C-12/1-2	-0.4
1888	Cle-a	65	212	27	51	11	4	0	22	18		.241	.312	.330	109	3	15			.917	7	C-59/O-3,1-3,S-1	1.3
1889	Cle-N	84	259	47	67	9	9	1	21	44	35	.259	.368	.375	110	5	14			.931	7	C-81/1-3	1.6
1890	Cle-N	125	444	54	95	16	6	2	57	46	54	.214	.303	.291	75	-14	15			.937	12	*C-125	0.9
1891	Cle-N	116	440	55	112	21	4	3	69	33	49	.255	.312	.341	87	-9	15			.936	18	*C-116/3-1	1.8
1892	*Cle-N	111	413	63	108	29	13	1	64	32	47	.262	.325	.402	115	6	18			.938	11	*C-111	2.3
1893	Cle-N	57	227	27	70	13	7	2	41	16	15	.308	.357	.454	108	1	4			.968	8	C-56/3-1	1.1
1894	Cle-N	90	341	55	97	20	5	4	65	17	31	.284	.328	.408	74	-17	14			**.963**	10	*C-89	0.2
1895	*Cle-N	88	315	60	107	21	2	5	56	33	30	.340	.417	.467	121	10	14			.975	9	C-84/1-3	2.1
1896	*Cle-N	91	336	46	93	18	3	3	46	31	48	.277	.354	.375	87	-7	4			**.972**	9	*C-91/3-1	1.0
1897	Cle-N	80	294	50	93	22	3	0	40	25		.316	.378	.412	103	1	8			.976	7	C-80	1.4
1898	Cle-N	20	63	5	15	2	0	0	4	5		.238	.304	.270	66	-3	2			.970	4	C-19	0.3
1899	Cle-N	20	73	9	25	2	1	2	14	5		.342	.407	.479	154	5	1			.957	-1	C-20	0.5
	Lou-N	75	262	43	78	11	3	2	29	22		.298	.370	.385	107	3	9			.985	1	C-62,1-11	0.9
	Yr	95	335	52	103	13	4	4	43	27		.307	.378	.406	117	8	10			**.978**	0	C-82,1-11	1.4
1900	*Pit-N	82	271	27	80	7	10	0	35	17		.295	.361	.395	108	3	4			.961	5	C-78/1-2	1.4
1901	Pit-N	69	236	17	52	7	3	0	21	20		.220	.292	.275	63	-11	6			.975	-7	C-68	-1.0
1902	Pit-N	42	142	13	38	4	2	0	17	11		.268	.338	.324	101	0	4			.969	-1	C-41/1-1	0.4
1903	Phi-N	37	118	9	26	3	1	1	19	9		.220	.292	.288	68	-5	3			.968	4	C-35,M	0.3
Total	19	1280	4546	617	1224	222	76	26	625	390	323	.269	.339	.369	95	-35	151			.952	102	*C-1239/1-25,O3S	15.8
■ DON ZIMMER	Zimmer, Donald William b: 1/17/31, Cincinnati, Ohio BR/TR, 5'9", 177 lbs. Deb: 7/2/54 MC																						
1954	Bro-N	24	33	3	6	0	1	0	0	3	8	.182	.270	.242	34	-3	2	0	1	.939	3	S-13	0.1
1955	*Bro-N	88	280	38	67	10	1	15	50	19	66	.239	.292	.443	89	-5	5	3	-0	.976	9	2-62,S-21/3-8	0.9
1956	Bro-N	17	20	4	6	1	0	0	2	0	7	.300	.333	.350	78	-1	0	1	-1	.944	2	/S-8,3-3,2-1	0.1
1957	Bro-N	84	269	23	59	9	1	6	19	16	63	.219	.263	.327	52	-18	1	3	-2	.957	9	3-39,S-37/2-5	-0.6
1958	LA-N	127	455	52	119	15	2	17	60	28	92	.262	.306	.415	86	-10	14	2	3	.965	**33**	*S-114,3-12/2-1,O-1	3.5
1959	*LA-N	97	249	21	41	7	1	4	28	37	56	.165	.275	.249	38	-22	3	1	0	.972	2	S-88/3-5,2-1	-1.3
1960	Chi-N	132	368	37	95	16	7	6	35	27	56	.258	.309	.389	90	-5	8	6	-1	.980	6	2-75,3-45/S-5,O-2	0.6
1961	Chi-N★	128	477	57	120	25	4	13	40	25	70	.252	.292	.403	81	-14	5	1	1	.973	0	*2-116/3-5,O-1	-0.1
1962	NY-N	14	52	3	4	1	0	0	1	3	10	.077	.127	.096	-38	-10	0	1	-1	.961	5	3-14	-0.6
	Cin-N	63	192	16	48	11	2	2	16	14	30	.250	.304	.359	75	-7	1	2	-1	.949	-1	3-43,2-17/S-1	-0.7
	Yr	77	244	19	52	12	2	2	17	17	40	.213	.267	.303	51	-17	1	3	-2	.952	4	3-57,2-17/S-1	-1.3
1963	LA-N	22	23	4	5	1	0	1	2	3	10	.217	.308	.391	107	0	0	0	0	.933	2	3-10/2-1,S-1	0.2
	Was-A	83	298	37	74	12	1	13	44	18	57	.248	.296	.426	100	-1	3	2	-0	.935	3	3-78/2-2	0.2
1964	Was-A	121	341	38	84	16	2	12	38	27	94	.246	.302	.411	96	-2	1	3	-2	.955	-13	3-87/O-4,C-2,2-1	-1.9
1965	Was-A	95	226	20	45	6	0	2	17	26	59	.199	.287	.252	56	-13	2	0	1	.966	-7	C-33,3-26,2-12	-1.9
Total	12	1095	3283	353	773	130	22	91	352	246	678	.235	.291	.372	76	-112	45	25	-2	.941	53	3-375,2-294,S/CO	-1.5
■ EDDIE ZIMMERMAN	Zimmerman, Edward Desmond b: 1/4/1883, Oceanic, N.J. d: 5/6/45, Emmaus, Pa. BR/TR, 5'9", 160 lbs. Deb: 9/29/06																						
1906	StL-N	5	14	0	3	0	0	0	1	0		.214	.214	.214	35	-1	0			.929	-0	/3-5	-0.1
1911	Bro-N	122	417	31	77	10	7	3	36	34	37	.185	.249	.264	46	-32	9			**.961**	3	*3-122	-2.7
Total	2	127	431	31	80	10	7	3	37	34	37	.186	.248	.262	45	-33	9			.960	3	3-127	-2.8
■ JERRY ZIMMERMAN	Zimmerman, Gerald Robert b: 9/21/34, Omaha, Neb. d: 9/9/98, Neskowin, Ore. BR/TR, 6'2", 185 lbs. Deb: 4/14/61 C																						
1961	*Cin-N	76	204	8	42	5	0	0	10	11	21	.206	.253	.230	29	-20	1	1	-0	.975	3	C-76	-1.5
1962	Min-A	34	62	8	17	4	0	0	7	3	5	.274	.318	.339	74	-2	0	0	0	.992	2	C-34	0.1
1963	Min-A	39	56	3	13	1	0	0	3	2	8	.232	.259	.250	43	-4	0	0	0	1.000	6	C-39	0.2
1964	Min-A	63	120	6	24	3	0	0	12	10	15	.200	.278	.225	42	-9	0	0	0	.993	6	C-63	-0.2
1965	*Min-A	83	154	8	33	1	1	1	11	12	23	.214	.275	.253	49	-10	0	0	0	**.997**	12	C-82	0.5
1966	Min-A	60	119	11	30	4	1	1	15	15	23	.252	.341	.328	88	-1	0	0	0	.996	9	C-59	1.0
1967	Min-A	104	234	13	39	3	0	1	12	22	49	.167	.244	.192	28	-20	0	1	-1	.992	15	*C-104	-0.2
1968	Min-A	24	45	3	5	1	0	0	2	3	10	.111	.184	.133	-3	-5	0	0	0	.991	5	C-24	0.1
Total	8	483	994	60	203	22	2	3	72	78	154	.204	.270	.239	43	-73	1	2	-1	.991	58	C-481	0.0
■ HEINIE ZIMMERMAN	Zimmerman, Henry b: 2/9/1887, New York, N.Y. d: 3/14/69, New York, N.Y. BR/TR, 5'11.5", 176 lbs. Deb: 9/8/07																						
1907	*Chi-N	5	9	0	2	1	0	0	1	0		.222	.222	.333	70	-0	0			.789	1	/2-4,S-1,O-1	0.1
1908	Chi-N	46	113	17	33	4	1	0	9	1		.292	.298	.345	101	-0	2			.923	-10	2-20/O-8,S-1,3-1	-1.2
1909	Chi-N	65	183	23	50	9	2	0	21	3		.273	.285	.344	93	-3	7			.945	-7	2-31,S-12/3-4	-1.1
1910	*Chi-N	99	335	35	95	16	6	3	38	20	36	.284	.326	.394	111	3	7			.948	-10	2-32,S-26,3-23,/O1	-0.7
1911	Chi-N	143	535	80	164	22	17	9	85	25	50	.307	.343	.462	124	14	23			.946	-1	*2-108,3-20,1-11	1.1
1912	Chi-N	145	557	95	**207**	**41**	14	**14**	99	38	60	**.372**	.418	**.571**	**170**	**50**	23			.916	2	*3-121,1-22	5.1
1913	Chi-N	127	447	69	140	28	12	9	95	41	40	.313	.379	.490	147	26	18			.912	5	*3-125	3.4
1914	Chi-N	146	564	75	167	36	12	4	87	20	46	.296	.326	.424	123	12	17			.897	-21	*3-118,S-15,2-12	-0.4

YEAR	TM/L	G	AB	R	H	2B	3B	HR	RBI	BB	SO	AVG	OBP	SLG	PRO+	BR/A	SB	CS	SBR	FA	FR	G/POS	TPR
1915	Chi-N	139	520	65	138	28	11	3	62	21	33	.265	.300	.379	105	1	19	13	-2	.943	-9	*2-100,3-36/S-4	-0.8
1916	Chi-N	107	398	54	116	25	5	6	64	16	33	.291	.324	.425	116	6	15	12	-3	.932	7	3-85,2-14/S-4	1.9
	NY-N	40	151	22	41	4	0	0	19	7	10	.272	.304	.298	90	-2	9	8	-2	.943	-3	3-40/2-1	-0.5
	Yr	147	549	76	157	29	5	6	**83**	23	43	.286	.318	.390	110	5	24	20	-5	.935	4	*3-125,2-15/S-4	1.4
1917	*NY-N	150	585	61	174	22	9	5	**102**	16	43	.297	.317	.391	121	11	13			.947	13	*3-149/2-5	3.0
1918	NY-N	121	463	43	126	19	10	1	56	13	23	.272	.294	.363	102	-1	14			.955	-4	*3-100,1-19	-0.5
1919	NY-N	123	444	56	113	20	6	4	58	21	30	.255	.296	.354	96	-3	8			.940	-1	*3-123	0.1
Total	13	1456	5304	695	1566	275	105	58	796	242	404	.295	.331	.419	121	114	175	33		.928	-38	3-945,2-327/S10	9.5

■ ROY ZIMMERMAN Zimmerman, Roy Franklin b: 9/13/16, Pine Grove, Pa. d: 11/22/91, Pine Grove, Pa. BL/TL, 6′2″, 187 lbs. Deb: 9/2/45

YEAR	TM/L	G	AB	R	H	2B	3B	HR	RBI	BB	SO	AVG	OBP	SLG	PRO+	BR/A	SB	CS	SBR	FA	FR	G/POS	TPR
1945	NY-N	27	98	14	27	1	0	5	15	5	16	.276	.330	.439	111	1	1			.988	-2	1-25/O-1	-0.3

■ BILL ZIMMERMAN Zimmerman, William H. b: 1/20/1889, Kengen, Germany d: 10/4/52, Newark, N.J. BR/TR, 5′8.5″, 172 lbs. Deb: 4/14/15

YEAR	TM/L	G	AB	R	H	2B	3B	HR	RBI	BB	SO	AVG	OBP	SLG	PRO+	BR/A	SB	CS	SBR	FA	FR	G/POS	TPR
1915	Bro-N	22	57	3	16	2	0	0	7	4	8	.281	.328	.316	93	-0	1			.864	-4	O-18	-0.6

■ FRANK ZINN Zinn, Frank b: 12/21/1865, Phoenixville, Pa. d: 5/12/36, Manayunk, Pa. 5′8″, 150 lbs. Deb: 4/18/1888

YEAR	TM/L	G	AB	R	H	2B	3B	HR	RBI	BB	SO	AVG	OBP	SLG	PRO+	BR/A	SB	CS	SBR	FA	FR	G/POS	TPR
1888	Phi-a	2	7	0	0	0	0	0	0	1		.000	.125	.000	-59	-1	0			.938	-1	/C-2	-0.1

■ GUY ZINN Zinn, Guy b: 2/13/1887, Holbrook, W.Va. d: 10/6/49, Clarksburg, W.Va. BL/TR, 5′10.5″, 170 lbs. Deb: 9/11/11

YEAR	TM/L	G	AB	R	H	2B	3B	HR	RBI	BB	SO	AVG	OBP	SLG	PRO+	BR/A	SB	CS	SBR	FA	FR	G/POS	TPR
1911	NY-A	9	27	5	4	0	2	0	1	4		.148	.281	.296	57	-2	0			.923	-0	/O-8	-0.2
1912	NY-A	106	401	56	105	15	10	6	55	50		.262	.345	.394	105	2	17			.893	-12	*O-106	-1.5
1913	Bos-N	36	138	15	41	8	2	1	15	4	23	.297	.322	.406	105	0	3			.948	4	O-35	0.3
1914	Bal-F	61	225	30	63	10	6	3	25	16	26	.280	.336	.418	101	-3	6			.935	-5	O-57	-1.1
1915	Bal-F	102	312	30	84	18	3	5	43	35	28	.269	.343	.394	104	-3	2			.949	-5	O-88	-1.2
Total	5	314	1103	136	297	51	23	15	139	109	77	.269	.338	.398	103	-6	28			.927	-17	O-294	-3.7

■ BUD ZIPFEL Zipfel, Marion Sylvester b: 11/18/38, Belleville, Ill. BL/TR, 6′3″, 200 lbs. Deb: 7/26/61

YEAR	TM/L	G	AB	R	H	2B	3B	HR	RBI	BB	SO	AVG	OBP	SLG	PRO+	BR/A	SB	CS	SBR	FA	FR	G/POS	TPR
1961	Was-A	50	170	17	34	7	5	4	18	15	49	.200	.265	.371	69	-8	1	1	-0	.983	-4	1-44	-1.7
1962	Was-A	68	184	21	44	4	1	6	21	17	43	.239	.307	.370	82	-5	1	2	-1	.976	-2	1-26,O-23	-1.1
Total	2	118	354	38	78	11	6	10	39	32	92	.220	.287	.370	76	-13	2	3	-1	.981	-7	/1-70,O-23	-2.8

■ RICHIE ZISK Zisk, Richard Walter b: 2/6/49, Brooklyn, N.Y. BR/TR, 6′1″, 208 lbs. Deb: 9/8/71

YEAR	TM/L	G	AB	R	H	2B	3B	HR	RBI	BB	SO	AVG	OBP	SLG	PRO+	BR/A	SB	CS	SBR	FA	FR	G/POS	TPR
1971	Pit-N	7	15	2	3	1	0	1	2	4	7	.200	.368	.467	136	1	0	0	0	1.000	-1	/O-6	0.0
1972	Pit-N	17	37	4	7	3	0	0	4	7	10	.189	.318	.270	70	-1	0	0	0	.938	-2	O-12	-0.4
1973	Pit-N	103	333	44	108	23	7	10	54	21	63	.324	.364	.526	148	20	0	0	0	.987	2	O-84	1.9
1974	*Pit-N	149	536	75	168	30	3	17	100	65	91	.313	.388	.476	146	33	1	1	-0	.985	9	*O-141	3.6
1975	*Pit-N	147	504	69	146	27	3	20	75	68	109	.290	.376	.474	136	25	0	1	-1	.975	1	*O-140	2.0
1976	Pit-N	155	581	91	168	35	2	21	89	52	96	.289	.348	.465	128	20	1	0	0	.987	9	*O-152	2.4
1977	Chi-A★	141	531	78	154	17	6	30	101	55	98	.290	.360	.514	135	25	0	4	-2	.982	6	*O-109,D-28	2.3
1978	Tex-A★	140	511	68	134	19	1	22	85	58	76	.262	.341	.432	116	11	3	3	-1	.988	-2	O-90,D-49	0.2
1979	Tex-A	144	503	69	132	21	1	18	64	57	75	.262	.338	.416	103	2	1	1	-0	.972	-4	*O-134/D-3	-0.8
1980	Tex-A	135	448	48	130	17	1	19	77	39	72	.290	.347	.460	123	13	0	2	-1	.980	-3	D-86,O-37	0.5
1981	Sea-A	94	357	42	111	12	1	16	43	28	63	.311	.366	.485	138	17	0	2	-1	.000	0	D-93	1.3
1982	Sea-A	131	503	61	147	28	1	21	62	49	89	.292	.356	.477	123	15	2	1	0	.000	0	*D-130	1.1
1983	Sea-A	90	285	30	69	12	0	12	36	30	61	.242	.314	.411	94	-3	0	0	0	.000	0	D-84	-0.6
Total	13	1453	5144	681	1477	245	26	207	792	533	910	.287	.355	.466	126	176	8	15	-7	.981	14	O-905,D-473	13.5

■ BILLY ZITZMANN Zitzmann, William Arthur b: 11/19/1895, Long Island City, N.Y. d: 5/29/85, Passaic, N.J. BR/TR, 5′10.5″, 175 lbs. Deb: 4/17/19

YEAR	TM/L	G	AB	R	H	2B	3B	HR	RBI	BB	SO	AVG	OBP	SLG	PRO+	BR/A	SB	CS	SBR	FA	FR	G/POS	TPR
1919	Pit-N	11	26	5	5	1	0	0	2	0	6	.192	.192	.231	26	-2	2			.917	-2	/O-8	-0.5
	Cin-N	2	1	0	0	0	0	0	0	0	0	.000	.000	.000	-99	-0	0			.000	-1	/O-1	-0.1
	Yr	13	27	5	5	1	0	0	2	0	6	.185	.185	.222	22	-3	2			.917	-2	/O-9	-0.6
1925	Cin-N	104	301	53	76	13	3	0	21	35	22	.252	.342	.316	71	-12	11	11	-3	.959	-14	O-89/S-1	-3.3
1926	Cin-N	53	94	21	23	2	1	0	3	6	7	.245	.304	.287	61	-5	3			.965	-3	O-31	-1.0
1927	Cin-N	88	232	47	66	10	4	0	24	20	18	.284	.352	.362	94	-1	9			.958	-9	O-60/S-8,3-3	-1.3
1928	Cin-N	101	266	53	79	9	3	3	33	13	22	.297	.337	.387	90	-4	13			.958	-6	O-78/3-1	-1.5
1929	Cin-N	47	84	18	19	3	0	0	6	9	10	.226	.309	.262	45	-7	4			.940	-3	O-22/1-5	-1.0
Total	6	406	1004	197	268	38	11	3	89	83	85	.267	.333	.336	77	-32	42	11		.956	-37	O-289/S-9,1-5,3-4	-8.7

■ EDDIE ZOSKY Zosky, Edward James b: 2/10/68, Whittier, Cal. BR/TR, 6′, 175 lbs. Deb: 9/2/91

YEAR	TM/L	G	AB	R	H	2B	3B	HR	RBI	BB	SO	AVG	OBP	SLG	PRO+	BR/A	SB	CS	SBR	FA	FR	G/POS	TPR
1991	Tor-A	18	27	2	4	1	1	0	2	0	8	.148	.148	.259	10	-3	0	0	0	1.000	1	S-18	-0.1
1992	Tor-A	8	7	1	2	0	1	0	1	0	2	.286	.286	.571	129	0	0	0	0	.923	1	/S-8	0.1
1995	Fla-N	6	5	0	1	0	0	0	0	0	0	.200	.200	.200	6	-1	0	0	0	.667	-0	/S-4,2-1	-0.1
Total	3	32	39	3	7	1	2	0	3	0	10	.179	.179	.308	31	-4	0	0	0	.963	2	/S-30,2-1	-0.1

■ JON ZUBER Zuber, Jon Edward b: 12/10/69, Encino, Cal. BL/TL, 6′, 190 lbs. Deb: 4/19/96

YEAR	TM/L	G	AB	R	H	2B	3B	HR	RBI	BB	SO	AVG	OBP	SLG	PRO+	BR/A	SB	CS	SBR	FA	FR	G/POS	TPR
1996	Phi-N	30	91	7	23	4	0	1	10	6	11	.253	.299	.330	65	-5	1	0	0	.987	-2	1-22	-0.8
1998	Phi-N	38	45	6	11	3	1	2	6	6	9	.244	.346	.489	111	1	0	0	0	1.000	-0	/O-5,1-4	0.1
Total	2	68	136	13	34	7	1	3	16	12	20	.250	.315	.382	81	-4	1	0	0	.989	-2	/1-26,O-5	-0.7

■ BOB ZUPCIC Zupcic, Robert b: 8/18/66, Pittsburgh, Pa. BR/TR, 6′4″, 220 lbs. Deb: 9/7/91

YEAR	TM/L	G	AB	R	H	2B	3B	HR	RBI	BB	SO	AVG	OBP	SLG	PRO+	BR/A	SB	CS	SBR	FA	FR	G/POS	TPR
1991	Bos-A	18	25	3	4	0	0	1	3	1	6	.160	.192	.280	28	-3	0	0	0	.875	-5	O-16	-0.7
1992	Bos-A	124	392	46	108	19	1	3	43	25	60	.276	.325	.352	84	-8	2	2	-1	.977	-2	*O-114/D-5	-1.3
1993	Bos-A	141	286	40	69	24	2	2	26	27	54	.241	.311	.360	75	-10	5	2	0	.979	-19	*O-122/D-5	-3.0
1994	Bos-A	4	4	0	0	0	0	0	0	0	1	.000	.000	.000	-96	-1	0	1	-1	1.000	-0	/O-2,D-1	-0.2
	Chi-A	32	88	10	18	4	1	1	8	4	16	.205	.239	.307	40	-8	0	0	0	1.000	-1	O-28/3-2,1-1	-0.9
	Yr	36	92	10	18	4	1	1	8	4	17	.196	.229	.293	34	-9	0	1	-1	1.000	-1	O-30/3-2,D-1,1-1	-1.1
Total	4	319	795	99	199	47	4	7	80	57	137	.250	.305	.346	73	-30	7	5	-1	.977	-27	O-282/D-11,3-2,1-1	-6.1

■ FRANK ZUPO Zupo, Frank Joseph "Noodles" b: 8/29/39, San Francisco, Cal BL/TR, 5′11″, 182 lbs. Deb: 7/1/57

YEAR	TM/L	G	AB	R	H	2B	3B	HR	RBI	BB	SO	AVG	OBP	SLG	PRO+	BR/A	SB	CS	SBR	FA	FR	G/POS	TPR
1957	Bal-A	10	12	2	1	0	0	0	0	1	4	.083	.154	.083	-36	-2	0	0	0	.913	0	/C-8	-0.2
1958	Bal-A	1	2	0	0	0	0	0	0	0	1	.000	.000	.000	-99	-1	0	0	0	1.000	0	/C-1	0.0
1961	Bal-A	5	4	1	2	1	0	0	0	1	1	.500	.600	.750	268	1	0	0	0	1.000	0	/C-4	0.1
Total	3	16	18	3	3	1	0	0	0	2	6	.167	.250	.222	31	-2	0	0	0	.941	1	/C-13	-0.1

■ PAUL ZUVELLA Zuvella, Paul b: 10/31/58, San Mateo, Cal. BR/TR, 6′, 178 lbs. Deb: 9/4/82 C

YEAR	TM/L	G	AB	R	H	2B	3B	HR	RBI	BB	SO	AVG	OBP	SLG	PRO+	BR/A	SB	CS	SBR	FA	FR	G/POS	TPR
1982	Atl-N	2	1	0	0	0	0	0	0	0	0	.000	.000	.000	-96	-0	0	0	0	.800	1	/S-1	0.1
1983	Atl-N	3	5	0	0	0	0	0	0	2	1	.000	.375	.000	11	-0	0	0	0	.750	-2	/S-2	-0.2
1984	Atl-N	11	25	2	5	1	0	0	1	2	3	.200	.259	.240	38	-2	0	0	0	1.000	1	/2-6,S-6	-0.1
1985	Atl-N	81	190	16	48	8	1	0	4	16	14	.253	.311	.305	69	-8	2	0	1	.986	9	2-42,S-33/3-5	0.5
1986	NY-A	21	48	2	4	1	0	0	2	5	4	.083	.170	.104	-24	-8	0	0	0	.966	4	S-21	-0.3
1987	NY-A	14	34	2	6	0	0	0	0	0	4	.176	.176	.176	-6	-5	0	0	0	1.000	-1	/2-7,S-6,3-1	-0.6
1988	Cle-A	51	130	9	30	5	1	0	7	8	13	.231	.275	.285	56	-8	0	0	0	.959	-3	S-49	-0.8
1989	Cle-A	24	58	10	16	2	0	2	6	1	11	.276	.300	.414	98	-0	0	0	0	.963	-3	S-15/3-5,D-3	-0.3
1991	KC-A	2	0	0	0	0	0	0	0	0	0	—	—	—	—	0	0	0	0	.000	0	/3-2	0.0
Total	9	209	491	41	109	17	2	2	20	34	50	.222	.275	.277	52	-32	2	0	1	.959	5	S-133/2-55,3-13,D-3	-1.7

■ DUTCH ZWILLING Zwilling, Edward Harrison b: 11/2/1888, St.Louis, Mo. d: 3/27/78, LaCrescenta, Cal. BL/TL, 5′6.5″, 160 lbs. Deb: 8/14/10 C

YEAR	TM/L	G	AB	R	H	2B	3B	HR	RBI	BB	SO	AVG	OBP	SLG	PRO+	BR/A	SB	CS	SBR	FA	FR	G/POS	TPR
1910	Chi-A	27	87	7	16	5	0	0	5	11		.184	.283	.241	67	-3	1			.940	-2	O-27	-0.7
1914	Chi-F	154	592	91	185	38	8	**16**	95	46	68	.313	.363	.485	138	18	21			.962	2	*O-154	1.4
1915	Chi-F	150	548	65	157	32	7	13	**94**	67	65	.286	.366	.442	135	16	24			.979	8	*O-148/1-3	1.8
1916	Chi-N	35	53	4	6	1	0	1	8	4	6	.113	.175	.189	11	-6	0			1.000	-2	O-10	-0.9
Total	4	366	1280	167	364	76	15	30	202	128	139	.284	.351	.438	127	26	46			.969	6	O-339/1-3	1.6

The Pitcher Register

The Pitcher Register consists of the central pitching statistics of every man who has pitched in major league play since 1871, *without exception*. Pitcher batting is expressed in Batting Runs in the Pitcher Batting column, and in the newly added columns for base hits and batting average. Pitcher defense is expressed in Fielding Runs in the Pitcher Defense column.

The pitchers are listed alphabetically by surname and, when more than one pitcher bears the name, alphabetically by *given* name—not by "use name," by which we mean the name he may have had applied to him during his playing career. This is the standard method of alphabetizing used in other biographical reference works, and in the case of baseball it makes it easier to find a lesser-known player with a common surname like Smith or Johnson. This method also jibes with that employed in the Team Roster and Annual Record where, for example, Charles "Old Hoss" Radbourn is shown not as the puzzling O. Radbourn or H. Radbourn, as some reference books have it, but as C. Radbourn. On the whole, we have been conservative in ascribing nicknames, doing so only when the player was in fact known by that name during his playing days.

Each person in the Pitcher Register can be found by finding the Pitcher Register list in the Contents and selecting the title whose names alphabetically surround the surname of pitcher you desire. Pitcher batting and pitcher defense, because the win-denominated numbers they produce are so small, are not sorted for single-season leaders (although the all-time leaders in these categories, single season and lifetime, will be found in the separate section called "All-Time Leaders"). Symbols denoting All-Star Game selection and/or play appear to the right of the team/league column. An additional finding aid is an asterisk alongside the team for which a player appeared in postseason competition, thus making for easy cross-reference to the earlier sections on postseason play.

The record of a man who pitched in more than one season is given in one line for each season, plus a career total line. If he pitched for more than one team in a given year, his totals for each team are given on separate lines; and if the teams for which he pitched in his "traded year" are in the same league, then his full record is stated in both separate and combined fashion. (In the odd case of a man playing for three or more clubs in one year, with some of these clubs being in the same league, the combined total line will reflect only his play in that one league.) A man who pitched in only one year has no additional career total line since it would be identical to his seasonal listing.

In *Total Baseball 1*, fractional innings were calculated for teams in the Annual Record but were rounded off to the nearest whole inning for individuals, in accordance with baseball scoring practice.

Pitching records for the National Association are included in the Pitcher Register because the editors, like most baseball historians, regard it as a major league, inasmuch as it was the only professional league of its day and supplied the National League of 1876 with most of its personnel. Unless Major League Baseball reverses the position it adopted in 1969 and restores the NA to official major league status, we will continue the practice of carrying separate totals for the National Association rather than integrating them into the career marks of those pitchers whose major league tenures began before 1876 and concluded in that year or after it.

Gaps remain elsewhere in the official record of baseball and in the ongoing process of sabermetric reconstruction. The reader will note occasional blank elements in biographical lines; these are not typographical lapses but signs that the information does not exist or has not yet been found. However, unlike the case of batting records, there are no incomplete statistical columns for pitchers. Where official statistics did not exist or the raw data have not survived, as with batters facing pitchers before 1908 in the American League and before 1903 in the National, we have constructed figures from the available raw data. For example, to obtain a pitcher's BFP—Batters Facing Pitchers—for calculating Opponents' On Base Percentage or Batting Average, we have subtracted league base hits from league at-bats, divided by league innings pitched, multiplied by the pitcher's innings and added his hits and walks allowed and hit-by-pitch, if available.

For a key to the team and league abbreviations used in the Pitcher Register go to the last page of the book. For a guide to the other procedures and abbreviations employed in the Pitcher Register, review the comments on the prodigiously extended pitching record on the next page.

Looking at the biographical line for any pitcher, we see first his use name in full capitals, then his given name and nickname (and any other name he may have used or been born with, such as the matronymic of a Latin American player). His date and place of birth follow "b" and his date and place of death follow "d"; years through 1900 are expressed fully, in four digits, and years after 1900 are expressed in only their last two digits. Then come his manner of batting and throwing, abbreviated for a left-handed batter who throws right as BL/TR (a switch-hitter would be shown as BB for "bats both" and a switch thrower as TB for "throws both"). Next, and for most pitchers last, is the pitcher's debut date.

Some pitchers continue in major league baseball after their pitching days are through, as managers, coaches, or even umpires. A pitcher whose biographical line concludes with an M can also be located in the Manager

Roster; one whose line bears a C will be listed in the Coach Roster; and one with a U occupies a place in the Umpire Roster. (In the last case we have placed a U on the biographical line only for those pitchers who umpired in at least six games in a year, for in the 19th century—and especially in the years of the National Association—there were literally hundreds of players who were pressed into service as umpires for a game or two; it would be mislead-

ing to accord such pitchers the same code we give to Bob Emslie or Bill Dinneen.) The select few who have been enshrined in the Baseball Hall of Fame are noted with an H. They are also listed in the Hall of Fame Roster found toward the end of "Awards and Honors." An F in this line denotes family connection—father-son-grandfather-grandson or brother.

YEAR TM/L	W	L	PCT	G	GS	CG	SH	SV	IP	H	HR	BB	SO	RAT	ERA	ERA+	OAV	OOB	BH	AVG	PB	PR	/A	PD	TPI
● **RIP VAN WINKLE**					Van Winkle, Rip "Half Moon" (Also Played in 1874 as Geoffrey Crayon)																				
					b: 4/30/1820, Plattekill, N.Y.			d: 12/12/80, Hudson, N.Y.			BL/TL, 5'5", 145 lbs.				Deb: 5/7/1874 MUCHF ♦										
1874 Bos-n	27	30	.474	57	57	56	1	0	498	502	5	18	20	9.4	3.90	104	.258	.270	40	.167	-3	5	3	-1	-0.1
1875 Wes-n	29	22	.569	52	51	50	2	1	450	491	4	25	16	10.3	4.02	106	.260	.272	50	.200	1	7	7	0	0.5
1883 Bal-a	5	18	.217	27	23	19	0	1	196	207	7	76	77	13.0	3.44	101	.274	.340	18	.180	-0	-3	1	0	-0.1
1884 Was-U	0	1	.000	1	1	1	0	0	8	10	0	2	3	13.5	4.50	110	.309	.349	0	.000	1	-0	-0	0	0.0
KC-U	5	2	.714	8	6	5	0	0	52	66	0	9	14	13.0	4.33	104	.312	.340	9	.250	2	3	1	0	0.1
Yr	5	3	.625	7	7	6	0	0	60	76	0	11	17	13.0	4.35	104	.311	.341	9	.225	2	3	1	0	0.1
1890 Cin-P	0	0	—	1	1	1	0	0	0	5	2	2	0	∞	∞	-97	1.000	1.000	1	.250	0	-2	-2	0	-0.2
1907 NY-N	16	13	.552	35	34	18	0	2	251	224	19	78	170	10.8	2.76	126	.236	.293	30	.250	1	17	20	2	2.2
1908 NY-N	16	12	.571	36	35	14	1	5	278	224	15	48	205	8.8	2.20	130	.215	.250	25	.200	1	24	20	-3	2.2
1909 NY-N	25	7	.781	36	35	18	0	5	273	202	24	82	208	9.4	2.21	164	.201	.261	20	.147	-1	42	43	1	4.2
1910 NY-N	18	12	.600	37	36	19	0	2	291	230	21	83	283	9.4	2.81	135	.211	.267	38	.277	4	40	32	1	3.6
1911 NY-N	20	10	.667	36	35	21	0	4	286	210	18	61	289	8.6	1.76	188	.202	.246	40	.296	4	54	49	-1	5.5
1912 NY-N	21	12	.636	35	35	13	0	3	262	215	23	77	249	10.0	2.92	116	.219	.275	34	.281	3	18	14	1	1.7
1913 NY-N	19	10	.655	36	36	18	0	3	290	219	23	64	251	8.8	2.08	184	.202	.247	31	.263	3	51	56	2	5.9
1914 Ind-F	11	11	.500	32	32	12	0	5	236	199	19	75	201	10.4	3.20	126	.226	.287	22	.227	-1	11	22	1	2.2
1915 NY-N	22	9	.710	36	36	15	0	5	280	217	11	88	243	9.8	2.38	155	.211	.274	33	.311	3	39	41	1	4.2
1936 NY-N☆	7	3	.700	13	13	5	0	3	96	79	7	28	72	10.0	3.00	140	.218	.274	11	.196	1	10	13	3	1.5
Bos-A	5	7	.417	16	16	1	0	0	104	114	8	29	72	12.4	3.81	112	.271	.317	20	.189	0	4	5	-2	0.7
1967 *Bos-A★	0	1	.000	1	1	0	0	0	⅓	5	2	1	1	180.0	108.00	1200	.833	.857	0	.000	0	-2	-2	0	-0.2
Total 2 n	56	52	.519	109	108	106	3	1	948	993	9	43	36	9.8	3.96	105	.259	.271	90	.184	-2	12	7	7	0.4
Total 14	190	128	.597	384	375	180	1	38	2903	2486	199	803	2338	10.2	2.76	134	.226	.285	294	.224	23	304	313	6	33.6

A black diamond appears at the end of the biographical line for pitchers who also appear in the Player Register by virtue of their having played in 100 or more games at another position, including pinch hitter, or having played more than half of their total major league games at another position, or having played more games at a position other than pitcher in at least one year.

The explanations for the statistical column heads follow; for more technical information about formulas and calculations, see the Glossary. The vertical rules in the column-header line separate the stats into six logical groupings: year, team, league; wins and losses; game-related counting stats; inning-related counting stats; basic calculated averages; pitcher batting; sabermetric figures of more complex calculation; and run-denominated Linear Weights stats for pitching, fielding, and Total Pitcher Index.

Note that the TPI (Total Pitcher Index) in this edition differs from those in earlier volumes, because for players who were both batters and pitchers, the method of allocating Wins between TPI and TPR (Total Player Rating) was improved. Previously, if a pitcher pitched in over half his games, all his batting was included with his pitcher rating (TPI); if he pitched in less than half his games, his Batting Wins were thrown over to his batter rating (TPR), with his TPI including only his Pitching Wins and Pitcher Defense. The new method prorates batting proportionally with the number of games pitched. In addition, fielding ratings at nonpitching positions for players who pitched in over half their games, previously omitted, are now part of the Total Baseball Ranking. In any case, the TPR values of batter-pitchers should remain about the same. Thus in 1918, Babe Ruth now has a batter rating of 2.6 Wins and a pitcher rating of 2.9 (total 5.5). Prior to the fourth edition his marks used to be 4.1 and 1.0, respectively, or 5.1 overall, with none of his batting counted in with his

pitching record even though he pitched 20 of 95 games. The large jump in his pitcher rating is because now his pitcher batting is compared against average batting for pitchers.

Also—and this is a key difference—the formula for Total Pitcher Index has been revised to employ the Relief Ranking formula (see Glossary) for all pitchers, not just relievers. The principal effect will be to calculate Pitcher Wins for relievers instead of Adjusted Pitcher Runs, as was formerly the case. The TPI will still be the sum of pitching, batting, fielding, and baserunning runs, but the Pitcher Runs will be expressed as Ranking Runs rather than Adjusted Pitching Runs. Check the Glossary for the specifics, but the net effect will be to raise the TPIs of relief closers and, to a lesser extent, starters who average a high number of innings per start, and to lower somewhat the TPIs of mopup relievers (few saves, few decisions) and starters with many no-decision games.

Taken out from the Pitcher Register of earlier editions are the following statistics: Hits Per Game and Bases on Balls Per Game (still available in the Annual Record and Leaders sections, and now stated in combined fashion as Ratio); Strikeouts Per Game (still available in the Annual Record and Leaders sections and, in any event, fairly evident from a glance at the SO and IP columns); Park Factor for pitchers (still available from the Annual Record); Clutch Pitching Index, newly developed for Total Baseball but which we have judged to be of lesser interest and value than the more established sabermetric measures (still, it is present in the Annual Record and Leaders sections); and Wins Above Team, a stat that has so many cautions associated with it that we judged it to be of little value when applied to all pitchers.

Finally, we have made an upward adjustment to overall league performance in the Federal League of 1914-15 and the Union Association of 1884 (thus lowering individual

ratings), because while both leagues are regarded as major leagues, there can be no doubt that their caliber of play was not equivalent to that in the rival leagues of those years. Suffice it to say here that league earned run averages were reduced by 20 percent for the UA and 10 percent for the FL. A full explanantion of the adjustment procedure may be found in the Glossary, under "League Performance."

YEAR Year in which a man pitched (When a space in the column is blank, this indicates that the man pitched for two or more clubs in the last year stated in the column; if those clubs were in the same league, then the man will also have a combined total line, beginning with the abbreviation "Yr" placed in the TM/L column.)

* Denotes postseason play, World Series or League Championship Series.

Yr Year's totals for pitching with two or more clubs in same league (see comments for YEAR)

★ Named to All-Star Game, played

☆ Named to All-Star Game, did not play

† Named to All-Star Game, replaced because of injury

TM/L Team and League (see comments for YEAR)

W Wins

L Losses

PCT Win Percentage (Wins divided by decisions)

G Games pitched

GS Games Started

CG Complete Games

SH Shutouts (Complete-game shutouts only)

SV Saves (Employing definition in force at the time, and 1969 definition for years prior to 1969)

IP Innings Pitched (Fractional innings included, as discussed above)

H Hits allowed

HR Home Runs allowed

BB Bases on Balls allowed

SO Strikeouts

RAT Ratio (Hits allowed plus walks allowed per nine innings)

ERA Earned Run Average (In a handful of cases, a pitcher will have faced one or more batters for his full season's work yet failed to retire any of them [thus having an innings pitched figure of zero]; if any of the men he put on base came around to score earned runs, these runs produced an infinite ERA, expressed in the pitcher's record as ∞. (see Van Winkle's 1890 season)

ERA+ Adjusted Earned Run Average normalized to league average and adjusted for home-park factor. (See comments for /A.)

OAV Opponents' Batting Average

OOB Opponents' On Base Percentage

BH Base Hits (as a batter)

AVG Batting Average

PB Pitcher Batting (Expressed in Batting Runs. Pitcher Batting is park-adjusted and weighted, for those who played primarily at other positions, by the ratio of games pitched to games played. For more technical data about Runs Per Win and Batting Run formulas, see Glossary.)

PR Pitching Runs (Linear Weights measure of runs saved *beyond* what a league-average pitcher might have saved, defined as zero. New to this edition, the formula used to calculate Relief Ranking is now employed for all pitchers; this creates small differences for starters but large differences for relievers, especially closers [see Glossary for further detail]. Occasionally the curious figure of − 0 will appear in this column, or in the columns of other Linear Weights measures of batting, fielding, and the TPI. This "negative zero" figure signifies a run contribution that falls below the league average, but to so small a degree that it cannot be said to have cost the team a run.

/A Adjusted (This signifies that the stat to the immediate left, in this instance Pitching Runs, is here normalized to league average and adjusted for home-park factor. A mark of 100 is a league-average performance, and superior marks exceed 100. An innovation for this edition is to use three-year averages for pitching park factors. If a team moved, or the park changed dramatically, then two-year averages are employed; if the park was used for only one year, then of course only that run-scoring data is used.)

PD Pitcher Defense (Expressed in Fielding Runs. See comment above on PB and see Glossary.)

TPI Total Pitcher Index (The sum, expressed in wins beyond league average, of a pitcher's Pitching Runs, [now expressed as Ranking Runs—see Glossary] Batting Runs—in the AL since 1973—and Fielding Runs, all divided by the Runs Per Win factor for that year—which is generally around 10, historically in the 9–11 range; see Glossary.)

Total For players whose careers include play in the National Association as well as other major leagues, two totals are given, as described above and as illustrated in Rip Van Winkle's record, where the record of his years in the National Association is shown alongside the notation "Total 2 n," where *2* stands for the number of years totaled and *n* stands for National Association. For players whose careers began in 1876 or later, the lifetime record is shown alongside the notation "Total x," where *x* stands for the number of post-1875 years totaled.

YEAR	TM/L	W	L	PCT	G	GS	CG	SH	SV	IP	H	HR	BB	SO	RAT	ERA	ERA+	OAV	OOB	BH	AVG	PB	PR	/A	PD	TPI
● **DON AASE**	Aase, Donald William b: 9/8/54, Orange, Cal. BR/TR, 6'3", 210 lbs. Deb: 7/26/77																									
1977	Bos-A	6	2	.750	13	13	4	2	0	92^1	85	6	19	49	10.2	3.12	144	.244	.285	0	—	0	10	14	-0	1.0
1978	Cal-A	11	8	.579	29	29	6	1	0	178^2	185	14	80	93	13.4	4.03	90	.270	.348	0	—	0	-5	-8	0	-0.7
1979	*Cal-A	9	10	.474	37	28	7	1	2	185^1	200	19	77	96	13.5	4.81	85	.277	.347	0	—	0	-12	-15	-2	-1.4
1980	Cal-A	8	13	.381	40	21	5	1	2	175	193	13	66	74	13.4	4.06	97	.287	.351	0	—	0	-1	-3	-1	-0.3
1981	Cal-A	4	4	.500	39	0	0	0	11	65^1	56	4	24	38	11.0	2.34	156	.234	.304	0	—	0	10	9	-0	1.5
1982	Cal-A	3	3	.500	24	0	0	0	4	52	45	5	23	40	11.8	3.46	117	.243	.327	0	—	0	4	3	-0	0.4
1984	Cal-A	4	1	.800	23	0	0	0	8	39	30	1	19	28	11.3	1.62	246	.221	.316	0	—	0	10	10	-0	1.7
1985	Bal-A	10	6	.625	54	0	0	0	14	88	83	6	35	67	12.2	3.78	106	.258	.332	0	—	0	4	2	0	0.5
1986	Bal-A★	6	7	.462	66	0	0	0	34	81^2	71	6	28	67	10.9	2.98	139	.234	.298	0	—	0	11	11	0	2.4
1987	Bal-A	1	0	1.000	7	0	0	0	2	8	8	1	4	3	13.5	2.25	195	.276	.364	0	—	0	2	2	-0	0.5
1988	Bal-A	0	0	—	35	0	0	0	0	46^2	40	4	37	28	14.9	4.05	96	.240	.377	0	—	0	-0	-1	-1	0.0
1989	NY-N	1	5	.167	49	0	0	0	2	59^1	56	5	26	34	12.6	3.94	83	.245	.324	0	.000	-1	-3	-4	0	-0.5
1990	LA-N	3	1	.750	32	0	0	0	3	38	33	5	19	24	12.3	4.97	74	.232	.323	0	—	0	-5	-6	-1	-0.7
Total	13	66	60	.524	448	91	22	5	82	1109^1	1085	89	457	641	12.6	3.80	103	.259	.333	0	.000	-1	23	15	-5	4.4
● **BERT ABBEY**	Abbey, Bert Wood b: 11/29/1869, Essex, Vt. d: 6/11/62, Essex Junction, Vt. BR/TR, 5'11", 175 lbs. Deb: 6/14/1892																									
1892	Was-N	5	18	.217	27	22	19	0	1	195^2	207	7	76	77	13.3	3.45	94	.261	.330	9	.120	-3	-4	-4	2	-0.5
1893	Chi-N	2	4	.333	7	7	5	0	0	56	74	1	20	6	15.8	5.46	85	.308	.371	6	.231	-0	-5	-5	0	-0.4
1894	Chi-N	2	7	.222	11	11	10	0	0	92	119	3	37	24	15.6	5.18	108	.310	.375	5	.128	-5	1	4	-1	-0.2
1895	Chi-N	0	1	.000	1	1	1	0	0	8	10	0	2	3	14.6	4.50	113	.303	.361	1	.333	-0	0	1	0	0.1
	Bro-N	5	2	.714	8	6	5	0	0	52	66	0	9	14	13.5	4.33	102	.304	.341	5	.263	1	3	0	1	0.2
	Yr	5	3	.625	9	7	6	0	0	60	76	0	11	17	13.5	4.35	103	.303	.340	6	.273	1	3	1	1	0.3
1896	Bro-N	8	8	.500	25	18	12	0	0	164^1	210	7	48	37	14.6	5.15	80	.308	.361	12	.190	-0	-14	-19	-2	-1.5
Total	5	22	40	.355	79	65	52	0	1	568	686	18	192	161	14.3	4.52	92	.292	.352	38	.169	-8	-19	-23	0	-2.3
● **CHARLIE ABBEY**	Abbey, Charles S. b: 10/14/1866, Falls City, Neb. d: 4/27/26, San Francisco, Cal. BL/TL, 5'8.5", 169 lbs. Deb: 8/16/1893 ♦																									
1896	Was-N	0	0	—	1	0	0	0	0	2	6	0	0	0	27.0	4.50	98	.500	.500	79	.262	0	-0	-0	-0	0.0
● **JIM ABBOTT**	Abbott, James Anthony b: 9/19/67, Flint, Mich. BL/TL, 6'3", 210 lbs. Deb: 4/8/89																									
1989	Cal-A	12	12	.500	29	29	4	2	0	181^1	190	13	74	115	13.3	3.92	97	.274	.347	0	—	0	-1	-2	-1	-0.2
1990	Cal-A	10	14	.417	33	33	4	1	0	211^2	246	16	72	105	13.7	4.51	85	.295	.355	0	—	0	-14	-16	1	-1.5
1991	Cal-A	18	11	.621	34	34	5	1	0	243	222	14	73	158	11.1	2.89	142	.244	.304	0	—	0	33	33	3	4.1
1992	Cal-A	7	15	.318	29	29	7	0	0	211	208	12	68	130	11.9	2.77	144	.263	.325	0	—	0	27	28	2	3.0
1993	NY-A	11	14	.440	32	32	4	1	0	214	221	22	73	95	12.5	4.37	95	.271	.334	0	—	0	-1	-5	1	-0.1
1994	NY-A	9	8	.529	24	24	2	0	0	160^1	167	24	64	90	13.1	4.55	101	.273	.344	0	—	0	5	0	0	0.3
1995	Chi-A	6	4	.600	17	17	3	0	0	112^1	116	10	35	45	12.2	3.36	132	.269	.325	0	—	0	17	14	-0	1.1
	Cal-A	5	4	.556	13	13	1	1	0	84^2	93	4	29	41	13.1	4.15	113	.280	.340	0	—	0	5	5	1	0.5
	Yr	11	8	.579	30	30	4	1	0	197	209	14	64	86	12.5	3.70	123	.273	.330	0	—	0	22	19	0	1.6
1996	Cal-A	2	18	.100	27	23	1	0	0	142	171	23	78	58	16.0	7.48	67	.306	.395	0	—	0	-39	-39	1	-4.1
1998	Chi-A	5	0	1.000	5	5	0	0	0	31^2	35	2	12	14	13.6	4.55	100	.292	.361	0	—	0	0	0	1	0.2
Total	9	85	100	.459	243	239	31	6	0	1592	1669	140	578	851	12.9	4.12	102	.274	.340	0	—	0	31	18	8	3.3
● **KYLE ABBOTT**	Abbott, Lawrence Kyle b: 2/18/68, Newburyport, Mass. BL/TL, 6'4", 200 lbs. Deb: 9/10/91																									
1991	Cal-A	1	2	.333	5	3	0	0	0	19^2	22	2	13	12	16.5	4.58	90	.301	.414	0	—	0	-1	-1	0	-0.1
1992	Phi-N	1	14	.067	31	19	0	0	0	133^1	147	20	45	88	13.0	5.13	68	.283	.341	2	.069	-1	-24	-24	-1	-2.8
1995	Phi-N	2	0	1.000	18	0	0	0	0	28^1	28	3	16	21	14.0	3.81	111	.267	.364	1	.500	0	1	1	0	0.1
1996	Cal-A	0	1	.000	3	0	0	0	0	4	10	1	5	3	33.8	20.25	25	.500	.600	0	—	0	-7	-7	0	-1.1
Total	4	4	17	.190	57	22	0	0	0	185^1	207	26	79	124	14.0	5.20	71	.288	.360	3	.097	-1	-31	-31	-1	-3.9
● **DAN ABBOTT**	Abbott, Leander Franklin "Big Dan" b: 3/16/1862, Portage, Ohio d: 2/13/30, Ottawa Lake, Mich. BR/TR, 5'11", 190 lbs. Deb: 4/19/1890																									
1890	Tol-a	0	2	.000	3	1	1	0	1	13	19	0	8	1	19.4	6.23	63	.328	.418	1	.143	0	-3	-3	1	-0.4
● **PAUL ABBOTT**	Abbott, Paul David b: 9/15/67, Van Nuys, Cal. BR/TR, 6'3", 185 lbs. Deb: 8/21/90																									
1990	Min-A	0	5	.000	7	7	0	0	0	34^2	37	0	28	25	17.1	5.97	70	.282	.412	0	—	0	-8	-7	-1	-1.1
1991	Min-A	3	1	.750	15	3	0	0	0	47^1	38	5	36	43	14.1	4.75	90	.232	.370	0	—	0	-3	-3	-0	-0.5
1992	Min-A	0	0	—	6	0	0	0	0	11	12	1	5	13	14.7	3.27	124	.279	.367	0	—	0	1	1	1	-0.1
1993	Cle-A	0	1	.000	5	5	0	0	0	18^1	19	5	11	7	14.7	6.38	68	.260	.357	0	—	0	-4	-4	0	-0.2
1998	Sea-A	3	1	.750	4	4	0	0	0	24^2	24	2	10	22	12.4	4.01	115	.255	.327	0	—	0	2	2	-0	0.2
Total	5	6	8	.429	37	19	0	0	0	136	130	13	90	110	14.7	5.03	85	.257	.372	0	—	0	-13	-11	-0	-1.7
● **GLENN ABBOTT**	Abbott, William Glenn b: 2/16/51, Little Rock, Ark. BR/TR, 6'6", 200 lbs. Deb: 7/29/73																									
1973	Oak-A	1	0	1.000	5	3	1	0	0	18^2	16	3	7	6	11.1	3.86	92	.225	.295	0	—	0	-0	-1	-0	0.0
1974	Oak-A	5	7	.417	19	17	3	0	0	96	89	4	34	38	11.8	3.00	111	.247	.317	0	—	0	7	3	-0	0.4
1975	*Oak-A	5	5	.500	30	15	3	1	0	114^1	109	12	50	51	12.7	4.25	85	.253	.333	0	—	0	-6	-8	-1	-0.5
1976	Oak-A	2	4	.333	19	10	0	0	0	62^1	87	6	16	27	15.0	5.49	61	.333	.374	0	—	0	-14	-15	0	-1.1
1977	Sea-A	12	13	.480	36	34	7	0	0	204^1	212	32	56	100	12.3	4.45	92	.270	.328	0	—	0	-9	-8	-0	-0.9
1978	Sea-A	7	15	.318	29	28	8	1	0	155^1	191	22	44	67	13.7	5.27	72	.303	.350	0	—	0	-26	-25	0	-3.1
1979	Sea-A	4	10	.286	23	19	3	0	0	116^2	138	19	38	25	13.8	5.17	84	.301	.358	0	—	0	-12	-11	-0	-1.2
1980	Sea-A	12	12	.500	31	31	7	2	0	215	228	27	49	78	11.7	4.10	101	.272	.315	0	—	0	-2	1	2	0.3
1981	Sea-A	4	9	.308	22	20	1	0	0	130^1	127	14	28	35	10.7	3.94	98	.258	.298	0	—	0	-4	-1	-0	-0.4
1983	Sea-A	5	3	.625	14	14	2	0	0	82^1	103	9	15	38	13.3	4.59	93	.311	.349	0	—	0	-5	-3	-1	-0.5
	Det-A	2	1	.667	7	7	1	1	0	46^2	43	5	7	11	9.6	1.93	203	.244	.273	0	—	0	11	10	-1	0.7
	Yr	7	4	.636	21	21	3	1	0	129	146	14	22	49	11.7	3.63	114	.285	.314	0	—	0	6	7	-1	0.2
1984	Det-A	3	4	.429	13	8	1	0	0	44	62	9	8	8	14.7	5.93	66	.326	.360	0	—	0	-9	-10	0	-1.3
Total	11	62	83	.428	248	206	37	5	0	1286	1405	162	352	484	12.5	4.39	89	.280	.331	0	—	0	-69	-67	-0	-7.6
● **AL ABER**	Aber, Albert Julius "Lefty" b: 7/31/27, Cleveland, Ohio d: 5/20/93, Garfield Heights, Ohio BL/TL, 6'2", 195 lbs. Deb: 9/15/50																									
1950	Cle-A	1	0	1.000	1	1	1	0	0	9	5	0	4	4	9.0	2.00	217	.167	.265	0	.000	0	3	2	-0	0.2
1953	Cle-A	1	1	.500	6	0	0	0	0	6	6	0	9	4	22.5	7.50	50	.240	.441	0	—	1	-2	-2	0	-0.6
	Det-A	4	3	.571	17	10	2	0	0	66^2	63	3	41	34	14.0	4.45	91	.260	.367	3	.130	-1	-3	-3	1	-0.3
	Yr	5	4	.556	23	10	2	0	0	72^2	69	3	50	38	14.7	4.71	86	.258	.375	3	.130	-1	-6	-5	1	-0.9
1954	Det-A	5	11	.313	32	18	4	0	3	124^2	121	8	40	54	11.8	3.97	93	.257	.320	5	.128	-1	-3	-4	1	-0.6
1955	Det-A	6	3	.667	39	1	0	0	3	80	86	9	28	37	12.8	3.37	114	.275	.334	1	.059	-2	5	4	1	0.3
1956	Det-A	4	4	.500	42	0	0	0	7	63	65	1	25	21	13.1	3.43	120	.270	.343	3	.300	1	5	5	0	0.7
1957	Det-A	3	3	.500	28	0	0	0	1	37	46	6	11	15	14.1	6.81	57	.315	.367	1	.125	-0	-12	-12	1	-1.8
	KC-A	0	0	—	3	0	0	0	0	3	6	2	2	0	24.0	12.00	33	.400	.471	1	1.000	0	-3	-3	0	0.1
	Yr	3	3	.500	31	0	0	0	1	40	52	8	13	15	14.6	7.20	54	.317	.367	2	.222	0	-15	-15	1	-1.7
Total	6	24	25	.490	168	30	7	0	14	389^1	398	29	160	169	13.0	4.18	93	.269	.342	14	.140	-3	-11	-13	3	-2.0
● **BILL ABERNATHIE**	Abernathie, William Edward b: 1/30/29, Torrance, Cal. BR/TR, 5'10", 190 lbs. Deb: 9/27/52																									
1952	Cle-A	0	0	—	1	0	0	0	1	2	4	1	1	0	22.5	13.50	25	.444	.500	0	.000	-0	-2	-2	-0	-0.2
● **TED ABERNATHY**	Abernathy, Talmadge Lafayette b: 10/30/21, Mebane, N.C. BR/TL, 6'2", 210 lbs. Deb: 9/19/42																									
1942	Phi-A	0	0	—	1	0	0	0	0	2^2	2	0	3	1	16.9	10.13	37	.222	.417	0	—	0	-2	-2	0	0.0
1943	Phi-A	0	3	.000	5	2	1	0	0	14^2	24	0	13	10	22.7	12.89	26	.353	.457	1	.250	0	-16	-15	0	-2.3
1944	Phi-A	0	0	—	1	0	0	0	0	3	5	0	1	2	18.0	3.00	116	.417	.462	0	.000	-0	0	0	-0	0.0
Total	3	0	3	.000	7	2	1	0	0	20^1	31	0	17	13	21.2	11.07	31	.348	.453	1	.200	0	-17	-17	0	-2.3
● **TED ABERNATHY**	Abernathy, Theodore Wade b: 3/6/33, Stanley, N.C. BR/TR, 6'4", 215 lbs. Deb: 4/13/55																									
1955	Was-A	5	9	.357	40	14	3	2	0	119^1	136	9	67	79	15.8	5.96	64	.294	.392	4	.154	-1	-26	-28	1	-2.9

YEAR	TM/L	W	L	PCT	G	GS	CG	SH	SV	IP	H	HR	BB	SO	RAT	ERA	ERA+	OAV	OOB	BH	AVG	PB	PR	/A	PD	TPI
1956	Was-A	1	3	.250	5	4	2	0	0	30^1	35	2	10	18	13.6	4.15	104	.292	.351	2	.182	-0	0	1	2	0.2
1957	Was-A	2	10	.167	26	16	2	0	0	85	100	9	65	50	17.9	6.78	57	.314	.437	4	.167	0	-28	-27	1	-3.2
1960	Was-A	0	0	—	2	0	0	0	0	3	4	0	4	1	24.0	12.00	32	.308	.471	1	1.000	0	-3	-3	0	0.1
1963	Cle-A	7	2	.778	43	0	0	0	12	59^1	54	3	29	47	12.6	2.88	126	.251	.340	2	.400	1	5	5	2	1.3
1964	Cle-A	2	6	.250	53	0	0	0	11	72^2	66	5	46	57	14.1	4.33	83	.247	.362	0	.000	-1	-6	-6	3	-0.6
1965	Chi-N	4	6	.400	**84**	0	0	0	**31**	136^1	113	7	56	104	11.5	2.57	143	.227	.311	3	.167	0	15	17	4	2.6
1966	Chi-N	1	3	.250	20	0	0	0	4	27^2	26	4	17	18	14.6	6.18	60	.255	.372	0	.000	-0	-8	-8	2	-1.2
	Atl-N	4	4	.500	38	0	0	0	4	65^1	58	5	36	42	12.9	3.86	94	.247	.347	2	.250	1	-2	-2	1	-0.1
	Yr	5	7	.417	58	0	0	0	8	93	84	9	53	60	13.3	4.55	80	.248	.349	2	.167	0	-10	-9	2	-1.3
1967	Cin-N	6	3	.667	**70**	0	0	0	**28**	106^1	63	1	41	88	9.2	1.27	295	.170	.261	1	.059	-1	**25**	**29**	2	**4.5**
1968	Cin-N	10	7	.588	**78**	0	0	0	13	134^2	111	9	55	64	11.4	2.47	128	.228	.312	0	.000	-1	8	10	3	1.9
1969	Chi-N	4	3	.571	56	0	0	0	3	85^1	75	8	42	55	12.4	3.16	127	.234	.325	2	.250	0	4	8	2	1.0
1970	Chi-N	0	0	—	11	0	0	0	1	9	9	0	5	2	15.0	2.00	225	.281	.395	0	—	0	2	3	0	0.1
	StL-N	1	0	1.000	11	0	0	0	1	18^1	15	0	12	8	14.7	2.95	140	.246	.395	0	.000	-0	2	2	1	0.2
	Yr	1	0	1.000	22	0	0	0	2	27^1	24	0	17	10	14.5	2.63	161	.255	.386	0	.000	-0	4	5	1	0.3
	KC-A	9	3	.750	36	0	0	0	12	55^2	41	3	38	49	12.9	2.59	144	.209	.340	3	.214	0	7	7	0	1.8
1971	KC-A	4	6	.400	63	0	0	0	23	81	60	3	50	55	12.9	2.56	134	.210	.339	1	.077	-1	8	8	2	1.6
1972	KC-A	3	4	.429	45	0	0	0	5	58^1	44	2	19	28	10.2	1.70	179	.210	.284	0	.000	-1	9	9	1	1.3
Total	14	63	69	.477	681	34	7	2	148	1147^2	1010	70	592	765	12.9	3.46	106	.241	.341	25	.138	-4	12	26	27	8.6

● WOODY ABERNATHY
Abernathy, Virgil Woodrow b: 2/1/15, Forest City, N.C. d: 12/5/94, Louisville, Ky. BL/TL, 6', 170 lbs. Deb: 7/28/46

YEAR	TM/L	W	L	PCT	G	GS	CG	SH	SV	IP	H	HR	BB	SO	RAT	ERA	ERA+	OAV	OOB	BH	AVG	PB	PR	/A	PD	TPI
1946	NY-N	1	1	.500	15	1	0	0	1	40	32	5	10	6	9.4	3.37	102	.232	.284	0	.000	-1	0	0	-1	-0.2
1947	NY-N	0	0	—	1	0	0	0	0	2	4	0	1	0	22.5	9.00	45	.400	.455	0	—	0	-1	-1	-0	0.0
Total	2	1	1	.500	16	1	0	0	1	42	36	5	11	6	10.1	3.64	95	.243	.296	0	.000	-1	-1	-1	-1	-0.2

● HARRY ABLES
Ables, Harry Terrell "Hans" b: 10/4/1884, Terrell, Tex. d: 2/8/51, San Antonio, Tex. BR/TL, 6'2.5", 200 lbs. Deb: 9/4/05

YEAR	TM/L	W	L	PCT	G	GS	CG	SH	SV	IP	H	HR	BB	SO	RAT	ERA	ERA+	OAV	OOB	BH	AVG	PB	PR	/A	PD	TPI
1905	StL-A	0	3	.000	6	3	1	0	0	30^2	37	0	13	11	14.7	3.82	67	.301	.368	0	.000	-1	-4	-4	-1	-0.6
1909	Cle-A	1	1	.500	5	3	3	0	0	29^2	26	1	10	24	11.2	2.12	120	.226	.294	0	.000	-1	1	1	-1	-0.2
1911	NY-A	0	1	.000	3	2	0	0	0	11	16	0	7	6	18.8	9.82	37	.333	.418	0	.000	-1	-8	-8	-0	-0.6
Total	3	1	5	.167	14	8	4	0	0	71^1	79	1	30	41	13.9	4.04	67	.276	.347	0	.000	-4	-11	-11	-2	-1.4

● GEORGE ABRAMS
Abrams, George Allen b: 11/9/1899, Seattle, Wash. d: 12/5/86, Clearwater, Fla. BR/TR, 5'9", 170 lbs. Deb: 4/19/23

YEAR	TM/L	W	L	PCT	G	GS	CG	SH	SV	IP	H	HR	BB	SO	RAT	ERA	ERA+	OAV	OOB	BH	AVG	PB	PR	/A	PD	TPI
1923	Cin-N	0	0	—	3	0	0	0	0	4^2	10	0	3	1	27.0	9.64	40	.500	.583	1	1.000	0	-3	-3	-0	0.0

● JOHNNY ABREGO
Abrego, Johnny Ray b: 7/4/62, Corpus Christi, Tex BR/TR, 6', 185 lbs. Deb: 9/4/85

YEAR	TM/L	W	L	PCT	G	GS	CG	SH	SV	IP	H	HR	BB	SO	RAT	ERA	ERA+	OAV	OOB	BH	AVG	PB	PR	/A	PD	TPI
1985	Chi-N	1	1	.500	6	5	0	0	0	24	32	3	12	13	16.5	6.38	63	.352	.427	0	.000	-1	-7	-6	0	-0.5

● JUAN ACEVEDO
Acevedo, Juan Carlos b: 5/5/70, Juarez, Mexico BR/TR, 6'2", 195 lbs. Deb: 4/30/95

YEAR	TM/L	W	L	PCT	G	GS	CG	SH	SV	IP	H	HR	BB	SO	RAT	ERA	ERA+	OAV	OOB	BH	AVG	PB	PR	/A	PD	TPI
1995	Col-N	4	6	.400	17	11	0	0	0	65^2	82	15	20	40	14.8	6.44	84	.317	.379	1	.056	-2	-17	-8	-1	-1.2
1997	NY-N	3	1	.750	25	2	0	0	0	47^2	52	6	22	33	14.7	3.59	112	.286	.375	0	.000	-1	3	2	0	0.1
1998	StL-N	8	3	.727	50	9	0	0	15	98^1	83	7	29	56	10.6	2.56	163	.236	.301	3	.176	0	18	18	0	2.4
Total	3	15	10	.600	92	22	0	0	15	211^2	217	28	71	129	12.8	4.00	113	.274	.344	4	.098	-2	5	12	0	1.3

● JIM ACKER
Acker, James Justin b: 9/24/58, Freer, Tex. BR/TR, 6'2", 212 lbs. Deb: 4/7/83

YEAR	TM/L	W	L	PCT	G	GS	CG	SH	SV	IP	H	HR	BB	SO	RAT	ERA	ERA+	OAV	OOB	BH	AVG	PB	PR	/A	PD	TPI
1983	Tor-A	5	1	.833	38	5	0	0	1	97^2	103	7	38	44	13.7	4.33	99	.273	.352	0	—	0	-3	-0	1	-0.1
1984	Tor-A	3	5	.375	32	3	0	0	1	72	79	3	25	33	13.8	4.38	94	.286	.358	0	—	0	-3	-2	-0	-0.5
1985	*Tor-A	7	2	.778	61	0	0	0	10	86^1	86	7	43	42	13.8	3.23	130	.268	.360	0	—	0	9	9	1	1.2
1986	Tor-A	2	4	.333	23	5	0	0	0	60	63	6	22	32	13.1	4.35	97	.281	.351	0	—	0	-1	-1	1	0.0
	Atl-N	3	8	.273	21	14	0	0	0	95	100	7	26	37	12.0	3.79	105	.274	.324	3	.107	-1	1	2	1	0.2
1987	Atl-N	4	9	.308	68	0	0	0	14	114^2	109	11	51	68	12.9	4.16	104	.253	.338	3	.214	0	-1	2	1	0.5
1988	Atl-N	0	4	.000	21	1	0	0	0	42	45	6	14	25	12.9	4.71	78	.280	.341	2	.400	1	-6	-5	0	-0.3
1989	Atl-N	0	6	.000	59	0	0	0	2	97^2	84	5	20	68	9.7	2.67	137	.237	.280	1	.143	-0	9	11	1	0.7
	*Tor-A	2	1	.667	14	0	0	0	0	28^1	24	1	12	24	11.8	1.59	237	.235	.322	0	—	0	7	7	1	0.9
1990	Tor-A	4	4	.500	59	0	0	0	1	91^2	103	9	30	54	13.4	3.83	103	.281	.341	0	—	0	1	1	0	0.2
1991	*Tor-A	3	5	.375	54	4	0	0	1	88^1	77	16	36	44	11.7	5.20	81	.238	.318	0	—	0	-11	-10	0	-0.8
1992	Sea-A	0	0	—	17	0	0	0	0	30^2	45	4	12	11	16.7	5.28	75	.338	.393	0	—	0	-5	-4	-0	0.0
Total	10	33	49	.402	467	32	0	0	30	904^1	918	82	329	482	12.7	3.97	102	.267	.337	9	.167	0	-5	10	8	2.0

● TOM ACKER
Acker, Thomas James b: 3/7/30, Paterson, N.J. BR/TR, 6'4", 215 lbs. Deb: 4/20/56

YEAR	TM/L	W	L	PCT	G	GS	CG	SH	SV	IP	H	HR	BB	SO	RAT	ERA	ERA+	OAV	OOB	BH	AVG	PB	PR	/A	PD	TPI
1956	Cin-N	4	3	.571	29	7	1	1	1	83^2	60	7	29	54	9.8	2.37	168	.201	.277	1	.053	-1	13	15	1	1.2
1957	Cin-N	10	5	.667	49	6	1	0	4	108^2	122	16	41	67	14.2	4.97	83	.293	.368	1	.053	-1	-13	-10	-0	-1.5
1958	Cin-N	4	3	.571	38	10	3	0	1	124^2	126	10	43	90	12.4	4.55	91	.266	.331	2	.067	-1	-8	-6	-2	-0.6
1959	Cin-N	1	2	.333	37	0	0	0	2	63^1	57	10	37	45	13.9	4.12	98	.246	.359	1	.111	-0	-1	-0	-1	-0.2
Total	4	19	13	.594	153	23	5	1	8	380^1	365	43	150	256	12.6	4.12	99	.257	.335	5	.065	-3	-10	-1	-2	-1.1

● FRITZ ACKLEY
Ackley, Florian Frederick b: 4/10/37, Hayward, Wis. BL/TR, 6'1.5", 202 lbs. Deb: 9/21/63

YEAR	TM/L	W	L	PCT	G	GS	CG	SH	SV	IP	H	HR	BB	SO	RAT	ERA	ERA+	OAV	OOB	BH	AVG	PB	PR	/A	PD	TPI
1963	Chi-A	1	0	1.000	2	2	0	0	0	13	7	2	7	11	9.7	2.08	169	.167	.286	1	.200	0	2	2	0	0.2
1964	Chi-A	0	0	—	3	2	0	0	0	6^1	10	2	4	6	19.9	8.53	41	.345	.424	1	1.000	1	-3	-4	0	0.1
Total	2	1	0	1.000	5	4	0	0	0	19^1	17	4	11	17	13.0	4.19	83	.239	.341	2	.333	1	-1	-2	1	0.3

● CY ACOSTA
Acosta, Cecilio (Miranda) b: 11/22/46, Sabino, Mexico BR/TR, 5'10", 165 lbs. Deb: 6/4/72

YEAR	TM/L	W	L	PCT	G	GS	CG	SH	SV	IP	H	HR	BB	SO	RAT	ERA	ERA+	OAV	OOB	BH	AVG	PB	PR	/A	PD	TPI
1972	Chi-A	3	0	1.000	26	0	0	0	5	34^2	25	2	17	28	10.9	1.56	201	.210	.309	0	.000	-0	6	6	-1	0.7
1973	Chi-A	10	6	.625	48	0	0	0	18	97	66	8	39	60	10.4	2.23	178	.193	.289	0	.000	-0	17	19	-1	3.6
1974	Chi-A	0	3	.000	27	0	0	0	3	45^2	43	3	18	19	13.0	3.74	100	.256	.346	0	.000	-0	-1	-0	0	0.0
1975	Phi-N	0	0	—	6	0	0	0	1	8^2	9	2	3	2	12.5	6.23	60	.273	.333	0	—	0	-3	-2	-0	-0.1
Total	4	13	9	.591	107	0	0	0	27	186	143	15	77	109	11.2	2.66	140	.216	.309	0	.000	-1	20	22	-2	4.2

● ED ACOSTA
Acosta, Eduardo Elixbet b: 3/9/44, Boquete, Panama BB/TR, 6'5", 215 lbs. Deb: 9/7/70

YEAR	TM/L	W	L	PCT	G	GS	CG	SH	SV	IP	H	HR	BB	SO	RAT	ERA	ERA+	OAV	OOB	BH	AVG	PB	PR	/A	PD	TPI
1970	Pit-N	0	0	—	3	0	0	0	1	2^2	5	1	2	1	27.0	13.50	29	.417	.533	0	—	0	-3	-3	-0	-0.2
1971	SD-N	3	3	.500	8	6	3	1	0	46	43	4	7	16	9.8	2.74	120	.246	.275	0	.000	-2	4	3	-1	0.1
1972	SD-N	3	6	.333	46	2	0	0	0	89	105	7	30	53	14.0	4.45	74	.302	.362	1	.083	-0	-10	-11	-1	-1.2
Total	3	6	9	.400	57	8	3	1	1	137^2	153	12	39	70	12.8	4.05	81	.286	.339	1	.034	-2	-9	-11	-1	-1.3

● JOSE ACOSTA
Acosta, Jose "Acostica" b: 3/4/1891, Havana, Cuba d: 11/16/77, Havana, Cuba BR/TR, 5'6", 134 lbs. Deb: 7/28/20 F

YEAR	TM/L	W	L	PCT	G	GS	CG	SH	SV	IP	H	HR	BB	SO	RAT	ERA	ERA+	OAV	OOB	BH	AVG	PB	PR	/A	PD	TPI
1920	Was-A	5	4	.556	17	5	4	1	1	82^2	92	1	26	9	12.8	4.03	93	.290	.344	6	.240	1	-2	-3	-3	-0.4
1921	Was-A	5	4	.556	33	7	2	0	3	115^2	148	4	36	30	14.3	4.36	94	.317	.366	2	.067	-2	-1	-3	-1	-0.5
1922	Chi-A	0	2	.000	5	1	0	0	0	15	25	4	6	6	18.6	8.40	48	.417	.470	1	.200	0	-7	-7	-0	-0.8
Total	3	10	10	.500	55	13	6	1	4	213^1	265	9	68	45	14.0	4.51	88	.314	.365	9	.150	-1	-10	-13	-4	-1.7

● MARK ACRE
Acre, Mark Robert b: 9/16/68, Concord, Cal. BR/TR, 6'8", 235 lbs. Deb: 5/13/94

YEAR	TM/L	W	L	PCT	G	GS	CG	SH	SV	IP	H	HR	BB	SO	RAT	ERA	ERA+	OAV	OOB	BH	AVG	PB	PR	/A	PD	TPI
1994	Oak-A	5	1	.833	34	0	0	0	0	34^1	24	4	23	21	12.6	3.41	130	.202	.336	0	—	0	5	4	-1	1.0
1995	Oak-A	1	2	.333	43	0	0	0	0	52	52	7	28	47	14.2	5.71	78	.256	.352	0	—	0	-6	-7	-1	-0.3
1996	Oak-A	1	3	.250	22	0	0	0	2	25	38	4	9	18	17.6	6.12	80	.339	.398	0	—	0	-3	-3	-0	-0.5
1997	Oak-A	2	0	1.000	15	0	0	0	0	15^2	21	1	8	12	16.7	5.74	79	.318	.392	0	—	0	-2	-2	-0	-0.2
Total	4	9	6	.600	114	0	0	0	2	127	135	16	68	98	14.7	5.17	88	.270	.363	0	—	0	-6	-9	-2	-0.0

● ACE ADAMS
Adams, Ace Townsend b: 3/2/12, Willows, Cal. BR/TR, 5'10.5", 182 lbs. Deb: 4/15/41

YEAR	TM/L	W	L	PCT	G	GS	CG	SH	SV	IP	H	HR	BB	SO	RAT	ERA	ERA+	OAV	OOB	BH	AVG	PB	PR	/A	PD	TPI
1941	NY-N	4	1	.800	38	0	0	0	1	71	84	3	35	18	15.2	4.82	77	.304	.385	1	.083	-1	-9	-9	-1	-0.8
1942	NY-N	7	4	.636	**61**	0	0	0	11	88	69	1	31	33	10.2	1.84	183	.223	.293	1	.100	-1	**14**	**15**	0	2.3
1943	NY-N☆	11	7	.611	**70**	3	1	0	9	140^1	121	5	55	46	11.4	2.82	122	.236	.311	4	.125	-1	9	10	-1	1.1
1944	NY-N	8	11	.421	**65**	4	1	0	**13**	137^2	149	8	58	32	13.8	4.25	86	.279	.354	3	.103	-2	-10	-9	-2	-1.6
1945	NY-N	11	9	.550	**65**	0	0	0	**15**	113	109	7	44	39	12.3	3.42	114	.252	.324	3	.188	0	5	6	1	1.3

YEAR TM/L	W	L	PCT	G	GS	CG	SH	SV	IP	H	HR	BB	SO	RAT	ERA	ERA+	OAV	OOB	BH	AVG	PB	PR	/A	PD	TPI
1946 NY-N	0	1	.000	3	0	0	0	0	2^2	9	2	1	3	33.8	16.88	20	.500	.526	0	—	0	-4	-4	0	-1.1
Total 6	41	33	.554	302	7	2	0	49	552^2	541	26	224	171	12.6	3.47	104	.260	.334	12	.121	-4	5	9	-2	1.2

● BABE ADAMS

Adams, Charles Benjamin b: 5/18/1882, Tipton, Ind. d: 7/27/68, Silver Spring, Md BL/TR, 5'11.5", 185 lbs. Deb: 4/18/06

YEAR TM/L	W	L	PCT	G	GS	CG	SH	SV	IP	H	HR	BB	SO	RAT	ERA	ERA+	OAV	OOB	BH	AVG	PB	PR	/A	PD	TPI
1906 StL-N	0	1	.000	1	1	0	0	0	4	9	0	2	0	24.8	13.50	19	.474	.524	0	.000	-0	-5	-5	0	-0.8
1907 Pit-N	0	2	.000	4	3	1	0	0	22	40	1	3	11	18.8	6.95	35	.408	.442	2	.286	0	-11	-11	0	-0.8
1909 *Pit-N	12	3	.800	25	12	7	3	2	130	88	0	23	65	7.9	1.11	246	.196	.240	2	.051	-3	22	23	-1	2.5
1910 Pit-N	18	9	.667	34	30	16	3	0	245	217	4	60	101	10.4	2.24	138	.240	.291	16	.193	1	22	23	-5	2.0
1911 Pit-N	22	12	.647	40	37	24	6	0	293^1	253	5	42	133	**9.3**	2.33	147	.237	**.271**	26	.252	4	35	36	-8	3.5
1912 Pit-N	11	8	.579	28	20	11	2	0	170^1	169	4	35	63	10.9	2.91	112	.262	.303	12	.226	4	10	7	-2	0.8
1913 Pit-N	21	10	.677	43	37	24	4	0	313^2	271	8	49	144	9.2	2.15	140	.235	.267	33	.289	9	37	30	-1	3.7
1914 Pit-N	13	16	.448	40	35	19	3	1	283	253	5	39	91	9.5	2.51	105	.244	**.276**	16	.165	1	9	4	-2	0.3
1915 Pit-N	14	14	.500	40	30	17	2	2	245	229	6	34	62	9.7	2.87	95	.252	.280	12	.141	-2	-3	-4	-0	-0.7
1916 Pit-N	2	9	.182	16	10	4	1	0	72^1	91	2	12	22	13.2	5.72	47	.320	.355	6	.273	2	-25	-24	0	-3.2
1918 Pit-N	1	1	.500	3	3	2	0	0	22^2	15	0	4	6	7.5	1.19	241	.197	.237	3	.333	1	4	4	-1	0.5
1919 Pit-N	17	10	.630	34	29	23	6	1	263^1	213	1	23	92	**8.2**	1.98	152	.220	**.241**	17	.185	-0	27	30	-4	2.7
1920 Pit-N	17	13	.567	35	33	19	**8**	2	263	240	6	18	84	**8.9**	2.16	149	.244	**.259**	13	.146	-5	29	31	-2	2.8
1921 Pit-N	14	5	.737	25	20	11	2	0	160	155	4	18	55	**9.7**	2.64	**145**	.251	**.272**	16	.254	3	20	21	-2	2.5
1922 Pit-N	8	11	.421	27	19	12	4	0	171^1	191	1	15	39	11.0	3.57	114	.287	.307	16	.286	4	10	10	1	1.4
1923 Pit-N	13	7	.650	26	22	11	0	1	158^2	196	8	25	38	12.6	4.42	91	.309	.336	15	.273	5	-7	-7	-2	-0.7
1924 Pit-N	3	1	.750	9	3	2	0	0	39^2	31	1	3	5	7.7	1.13	338	.209	.225	2	.182	-0	12	12	-1	1.0
1925 *Pit-N	6	5	.545	33	10	3	0	3	101^1	129	7	17	18	13.2	5.42	82	.306	.338	7	.226	0	-13	-11	-2	-1.2
1926 Pit-N	2	3	.400	19	0	0	0	3	36^2	51	5	8	7	14.5	6.14	64	.347	.381	2	.222	-0	-9	-9	-1	-1.3
Total 19	194	140	.581	482	354	206	44	15	2995^1	2841	68	430	1036	10.0	2.76	118	.253	.284	216	.212	24	161	161	-32	15.0

● RED ADAMS

Adams, Charles Dwight b: 10/7/21, Parlier, Cal. BR/TR, 6', 185 lbs. Deb: 5/5/46 C

YEAR TM/L	W	L	PCT	G	GS	CG	SH	SV	IP	H	HR	BB	SO	RAT	ERA	ERA+	OAV	OOB	BH	AVG	PB	PR	/A	PD	TPI
1946 Chi-N	0	1	.000	8	0	0	0	0	12	18	1	7	8	18.8	8.25	40	.353	.431	0	.000	-0	-6	-7	1	-0.5

● DAN ADAMS

Adams, Daniel Leslie "Rube" b: 6/19/1887, St.Louis, Mo. d: 10/6/64, St.Louis, Mo. BR/TR, 5'11.5", 165 lbs. Deb: 5/22/14

YEAR TM/L	W	L	PCT	G	GS	CG	SH	SV	IP	H	HR	BB	SO	RAT	ERA	ERA+	OAV	OOB	BH	AVG	PB	PR	/A	PD	TPI
1914 KC-F	4	9	.308	36	14	6	0	3	136	141	3	52	38	13.2	3.51	79	.273	.347	7	.152	-2	-9	-11	-1	-1.3
1915 KC-F	0	2	.000	11	2	0	0	0	35	41	2	13	16	14.1	4.63	57	.301	.367	1	.111	-1	-7	-8	0	-0.5
Total 2	4	11	.267	47	16	6	0	3	171	182	5	65	54	13.4	3.74	74	.279	.351	8	.145	-2	-17	-19	-1	-1.8

● WILLIE ADAMS

Adams, James Irvin b: 9/27/1890, Clearfield, Pa. d: 6/18/37, Albany, N.Y. BR/TR, 6'4", 180 lbs. Deb: 6/30/12

YEAR TM/L	W	L	PCT	G	GS	CG	SH	SV	IP	H	HR	BB	SO	RAT	ERA	ERA+	OAV	OOB	BH	AVG	PB	PR	/A	PD	TPI
1912 StL-A	2	3	.400	13	5	0	0	0	46^1	50	0	19	16	13.8	3.88	85	.284	.360	0	.000	-2	-3	-3	-1	-0.6
1913 StL-A	0	0	—	4	0	0	0	0	9	12	1	4	5	19.0	10.00	29	.286	.388	0	.000	0	-7	-7	-0	0.0
1914 Pit-F	1	1	.500	15	2	1	0	2	55^1	70	4	22	14	15.1	3.74	77	.326	.391	1	.067	-1	-5	-5	-1	-0.5
1918 Phi-A	5	12	.294	32	14	7	0	0	169	164	2	97	39	14.5	4.42	66	.272	.383	8	.140	-3	-31	-28	1	-2.9
1919 Phi-A	0	0	—	1	0	0	0	0	4^2	7	1	2	0	19.3	3.86	89	.389	.476	0	.000	-0	-0	-0	-0	0.0
Total 5	8	16	.333	65	21	8	0	2	284^1	303	8	144	74	14.8	4.37	69	.287	.383	9	.102	-6	-46	-43	-2	-4.0

● JOE ADAMS

Adams, Joseph Edward b: 10/28/1877, Cowden, Ill. d: 10/8/52, Montgomery City, Mo BR/TL, 6', 190 lbs. Deb: 4/26/02

YEAR TM/L	W	L	PCT	G	GS	CG	SH	SV	IP	H	HR	BB	SO	RAT	ERA	ERA+	OAV	OOB	BH	AVG	PB	PR	/A	PD	TPI
1902 StL-N	0	0	—	1	0	0	0	0	4	9	0	2	0	27.0	9.00	30	.450	.522	0	.000	-0	-3	-3	1	0.0

● KARL ADAMS

Adams, Karl Tutwiler "Rebel" b: 8/11/1891, Columbus, Ga. d: 9/17/67, Everett, Wash. BR/TR, 6'2", 170 lbs. Deb: 4/19/14

YEAR TM/L	W	L	PCT	G	GS	CG	SH	SV	IP	H	HR	BB	SO	RAT	ERA	ERA+	OAV	OOB	BH	AVG	PB	PR	/A	PD	TPI
1914 Cin-N	0	0	—	4	0	0	0	0	8	14	0	5	5	21.4	9.00	33	.424	.500	1	.500	0	-6	-5	0	0.1
1915 Chi-N	1	9	.100	26	12	3	0	0	107	105	5	43	57	12.6	4.71	59	.267	.342	0	.000	-4	-23	-23	0	-2.4
Total 2	1	9	.100	30	12	3	0	0	115	119	5	48	62	13.2	5.01	56	.279	.355	1	.031	-4	-29	-28	0	-2.3

● RICK ADAMS

Adams, Reuben Alexander b: 12/23/1878, Paris, Tex. d: 3/10/55, Paris, Tex. BL/TL, 6', 165 lbs. Deb: 7/13/05

YEAR TM/L	W	L	PCT	G	GS	CG	SH	SV	IP	H	HR	BB	SO	RAT	ERA	ERA+	OAV	OOB	BH	AVG	PB	PR	/A	PD	TPI
1905 Was-A	2	5	.286	11	6	3	1	0	62^2	63	1	24	25	13.6	3.59	74	.264	.351	4	.174	0	-7	-7	0	-0.6

● BOB ADAMS

Adams, Robert Andrew b: 1/20/07, Birmingham, Ala. d: 3/6/70, Jacksonville, Fla. BR/TR, 6'0.5", 165 lbs. Deb: 9/27/31

YEAR TM/L	W	L	PCT	G	GS	CG	SH	SV	IP	H	HR	BB	SO	RAT	ERA	ERA+	OAV	OOB	BH	AVG	PB	PR	/A	PD	TPI
1931 Phi-N	0	1	.000	1	1	0	0	0	6	14	0	1	3	22.5	9.00	47	.424	.441	0	.000	-0	-3	-3	-0	-0.4
1932 Phi-N	0	0	—	4	0	0	0	0	6	7	0	2	2	13.5	1.50	294	.318	.375	0	—	0	2	2	0	0.0
Total 2	0	1	.000	5	1	0	0	0	12	21	0	3	5	18.0	5.25	82	.382	.414	0	.000	-0	-2	-1	0	-0.4

● BOB ADAMS

Adams, Robert Burdette b: 7/24/01, Holyoke, Mass. d: 10/17/96, Lemoyne, Pa. BR/TR, 5'11", 168 lbs. Deb: 9/22/25

YEAR TM/L	W	L	PCT	G	GS	CG	SH	SV	IP	H	HR	BB	SO	RAT	ERA	ERA+	OAV	OOB	BH	AVG	PB	PR	/A	PD	TPI
1925 Bos-A	0	0	—	2	0	0	0	0	5^2	10	1	3	1	20.6	7.94	57	.417	.481	1	.333	0	-2	-2	1	0.1

● TERRY ADAMS

Adams, Terry Wayne b: 3/6/73, Mobile, Ala. BR/TR, 6'3", 205 lbs. Deb: 8/10/95

YEAR TM/L	W	L	PCT	G	GS	CG	SH	SV	IP	H	HR	BB	SO	RAT	ERA	ERA+	OAV	OOB	BH	AVG	PB	PR	/A	PD	TPI
1995 Chi-N	1	1	.500	18	0	0	0	1	18	22	0	10	15	16.0	6.50	63	.289	.372	0	—	0	-5	-5	-0	-0.5
1996 Chi-N	3	6	.333	69	0	0	0	4	101	84	6	49	78	11.9	2.94	147	.231	.324	0	.000	-0	14	16	-0	1.3
1997 Chi-N	2	9	.182	74	0	0	0	18	74	91	3	40	64	16.1	4.62	93	.306	.391	0	.000	-0	-3	-3	-0	-0.5
1998 Chi-N	7	7	.500	63	0	0	0	1	72^2	72	7	41	73	14.1	4.33	101	.255	.352	0	.000	-0	-1	0	0	0.1
Total 4	13	23	.361	224	0	0	0	24	265^2	269	16	140	230	14.0	4.03	107	.264	.355	0	.000	-1	5	8	-0	0.4

● WILLIE ADAMS

Adams, William Edward b: 10/8/72, Gallup, N.Mex. BR/TR, 6'7", 215 lbs. Deb: 6/11/96

YEAR TM/L	W	L	PCT	G	GS	CG	SH	SV	IP	H	HR	BB	SO	RAT	ERA	ERA+	OAV	OOB	BH	AVG	PB	PR	/A	PD	TPI
1996 Oak-A	3	4	.429	12	12	1	1	0	76^1	76	11	23	68	12.3	4.01	123	.257	.321	0	—	0	8	8	-1	0.6
1997 Oak-A	3	5	.375	13	12	0	0	0	58^1	73	9	32	37	16.8	8.18	55	.307	.398	0	—	0	-23	-24	0	-2.5
Total 2	6	9	.400	25	24	1	1	0	134^2	149	20	55	105	14.2	5.81	82	.279	.356	0	—	0	-15	-16	-0	-1.9

● JOEL ADAMSON

Adamson, Joel Lee b: 7/2/71, Lakewood, Cal. BL/TL, 6'4", 185 lbs. Deb: 4/10/96

YEAR TM/L	W	L	PCT	G	GS	CG	SH	SV	IP	H	HR	BB	SO	RAT	ERA	ERA+	OAV	OOB	BH	AVG	PB	PR	/A	PD	TPI
1996 Fla-N	0	0	—	9	0	0	0	0	11	18	1	7	7	21.3	7.36	55	.400	.491	0	—	0	-4	-4	0	0.0
1997 Mil-A	5	3	.625	30	6	0	0	0	76^1	78	13	19	56	12.0	3.54	130	.265	.321	0	.000	-0	9	9	-0	0.8
1998 Ari-N	0	3	.000	5	5	0	0	0	23	25	5	11	14	15.3	8.22	52	.284	.382	3	.429	1	-10	-10	-0	-0.9
Total 3	5	6	.455	44	11	0	0	0	110^1	121	19	37	77	13.6	4.89	92	.283	.353	3	.300	1	-5	-5	0	-0.1

● MIKE ADAMSON

Adamson, John Michael b: 9/13/47, San Diego, Cal. BR/TR, 6'2", 185 lbs. Deb: 7/1/67

YEAR TM/L	W	L	PCT	G	GS	CG	SH	SV	IP	H	HR	BB	SO	RAT	ERA	ERA+	OAV	OOB	BH	AVG	PB	PR	/A	PD	TPI
1967 Bal-A	0	1	.000	3	2	0	0	0	9^2	9	1	12	8	19.6	8.38	38	.257	.447	1	.500	0	-6	-6	-0	-0.5
1968 Bal-A	0	2	.000	2	2	0	0	0	7^2	9	2	4	4	15.3	9.39	31	.281	.361	1	.333	1	-5	-6	-0	-1.1
1969 Bal-A	0	1	.000	6	0	0	0	0	8	10	0	6	2	18.0	4.50	79	.357	.471	0	.000	-0	-1	-1	1	-0.1
Total 3	0	4	.000	11	4	0	0	0	25^1	28	3	22	14	17.8	7.46	43	.295	.427	2	.333	1	-12	-12	-0	-1.7

● GRADY ADKINS

Adkins, Grady Emmett "Butcher Boy" b: 6/29/1897, Jacksonville, Ark d: 3/31/66, Little Rock, Ark. BR/TR, 5'11", 175 lbs. Deb: 4/13/28

YEAR TM/L	W	L	PCT	G	GS	CG	SH	SV	IP	H	HR	BB	SO	RAT	ERA	ERA+	OAV	OOB	BH	AVG	PB	PR	/A	PD	TPI
1928 Chi-A	10	16	.385	36	27	14	0	1	224^2	235	12	89	54	13.2	3.73	109	.278	.351	10	.143	-3	8	8	-1	0.4
1929 Chi-A	2	11	.154	31	15	5	0	0	138^1	168	12	67	24	15.4	5.33	80	.303	.379	11	.239	3	-17	-16	2	-0.8
Total 2	12	27	.308	67	42	19	0	1	363	403	24	156	78	14.0	4.34	95	.288	.363	21	.181	-1	-9	-8	1	-0.4

● DEWEY ADKINS

Adkins, John Dewey b: 5/11/18, Norcatur, Kan. BR/TR, 6'2", 195 lbs. Deb: 9/19/42

YEAR TM/L	W	L	PCT	G	GS	CG	SH	SV	IP	H	HR	BB	SO	RAT	ERA	ERA+	OAV	OOB	BH	AVG	PB	PR	/A	PD	TPI
1942 Was-A	0	0	—	1	1	0	0	0	6^1	7	0	6	3	18.5	9.95	37	.259	.394	1	.500	0	-4	-4	-0	0.0
1943 Was-A	0	0	—	7	0	0	0	0	10^1	9	0	5	1	12.2	2.61	123	.250	.341	0	—	0	1	1	-1	-0.1
1949 Chi-N	2	4	.333	30	5	1	0	0	82^1	98	10	39	43	15.0	5.68	71	.298	.372	4	.200	1	-15	-15	1	-0.7
Total 3	2	4	.333	38	6	1	0	0	99	114	10	50	47	14.9	5.64	70	.291	.371	5	.227	1	-19	-19	0	-0.8

● DOC ADKINS

Adkins, Merle Theron b: 8/5/1872, Troy, Wis. d: 2/21/34, Durham, N.C. BR/TR, 5'10.5", 220 lbs. Deb: 6/24/02

YEAR TM/L	W	L	PCT	G	GS	CG	SH	SV	IP	H	HR	BB	SO	RAT	ERA	ERA+	OAV	OOB	BH	AVG	PB	PR	/A	PD	TPI
1902 Bos-A	1	1	.500	4	2	1	0	0	20	30	2	7	3	16.6	4.05	88	.345	.394	2	.222	-0	-1	-1	0	-0.1
1903 NY-A	0	0	—	2	1	0	0	1	7	10	0	5	0	20.6	7.71	40	.333	.444	0	.000	-0	-4	-4	-1	-0.2
Total 2	1	1	.500	6	3	1	0	1	27	40	2	12	3	17.7	5.00	69	.342	.408	2	.167	-1	-5	-5	-0	-0.3

● STEVE ADKINS

Adkins, Steven Thomas b: 10/26/64, Chicago, Ill. BR/TL, 6'6", 210 lbs. Deb: 9/12/90

YEAR TM/L	W	L	PCT	G	GS	CG	SH	SV	IP	H	HR	BB	SO	RAT	ERA	ERA+	OAV	OOB	BH	AVG	PB	PR	/A	PD	TPI
1990 NY-A	1	2	.333	5	5	0	0	0	24	19	4	29	14	18.0	6.38	62	.226	.425	0	—	0	-7	-6	-0	-0.7

● JUAN AGOSTO Agosto, Juan Roberto (Gonzalez) b: 2/23/58, Rio Piedras, P.R. BL/TL, 6'2", 190 lbs. Deb: 9/7/81

YEAR	TM/L	W	L	PCT	G	GS	CG	SH	SV	IP	H	HR	BB	SO	RAT	ERA	ERA+	OAV	OOB	BH	AVG	PB	PR	/A	PD	TPI
1981	Chi-A	0	0	—	2	0	0	0	0	5^2	5	1	0	3	9.5	4.76	75	.238	.273	0	—	0	-1	-1	0	0.1
1982	Chi-A	0	0	—	1	0	0	0	0	2	7	0	0	1	31.5	18.00	22	.538	.538	0	—	0	-3	-3	0	0.0
1983	*Chi-A	2	2	.500	39	0	0	0	7	41^2	41	2	11	29	11.4	4.10	102	.283	.338	0	—	0	-0	0	0	0.0
1984	Chi-A	2	1	.667	49	0	0	0	7	55^1	54	2	34	26	14.8	3.09	135	.270	.384	0	—	0	6	7	2	0.4
1985	Chi-A	4	3	.571	54	0	0	0	1	60^1	45	3	23	39	10.6	3.58	121	.210	.296	0	—	0	4	5	2	0.7
1986	Chi-A	0	2	.000	9	0	0	0	0	4^2	6	0	4	3	19.3	7.71	56	.300	.417	0	—	0	-2	-2	-0	-0.7
	Min-A	1	2	.333	17	1	0	0	1	20^1	43	1	14	9	26.1	8.85	49	.443	.522	0	—	0	-11	-10	0	-1.4
	Yr	1	4	.200	26	1	0	0	1	25	49	1	18	12	24.8	8.64	50	.419	.504	0	—	0	-12	-12	0	-2.1
1987	Hou-N	1	1	.500	27	0	0	0	2	27^1	26	1	10	6	11.9	2.63	149	.248	.313	0	.000	-0	4	4	1	0.4
1988	Hou-N	10	2	.833	75	0	0	0	4	91^2	74	6	30	33	10.2	2.26	147	.226	.291	0	.000	-0	12	11	4	1.9
1989	Hou-N	4	5	.444	71	0	0	0	1	83	81	3	32	46	12.5	2.93	116	.256	.329	1	.200	0	5	4	1	0.6
1990	Hou-N	9	8	.529	**82**	0	0	0	4	92^1	91	4	39	50	13.4	4.29	87	.261	.347	0	.000	-0	-5	-6	2	-0.9
1991	StL-N	5	3	.625	72	0	0	0	2	86	92	4	39	34	14.5	4.81	77	.291	.383	1	.333	1	-11	-10	1	-0.8
1992	StL-N	2	4	.333	22	0	0	0	0	31^2	39	2	9	13	14.5	6.25	54	.312	.372	0	.000	-0	-10	-10	1	-1.7
	Sea-A	0	0	—	17	1	0	0	0	18^1	27	0	3	12	14.7	5.89	67	.346	.370	0	—	0	-4	-4	0	0.0
1993	Hou-N	0	0	—	6	0	0	0	0	6	8	1	0	3	12.0	6.00	65	.308	.308	0	—	0	-1	-1	-0	0.0
Total	13	40	33	.548	543	2	0	0	29	626^1	639	30	248	307	13.2	4.01	94	.272	.349	2	.100	-1	-16	-17	14	-1.4

● RICK AGUILERA Aguilera, Richard Warren b: 12/31/61, San Gabriel, Cal. BR/TR, 6'5", 205 lbs. Deb: 6/12/85

YEAR	TM/L	W	L	PCT	G	GS	CG	SH	SV	IP	H	HR	BB	SO	RAT	ERA	ERA+	OAV	OOB	BH	AVG	PB	PR	/A	PD	TPI
1985	NY-N	10	7	.588	21	19	2	0	0	122^1	118	8	37	74	11.6	3.24	107	.258	.317	10	.278	3	5	3	-0	0.7
1986	*NY-N	10	7	.588	28	20	2	0	0	141^2	145	15	36	104	11.9	3.88	91	.263	.316	8	.157	2	-2	-5	2	-0.2
1987	NY-N	11	3	.786	18	17	1	0	0	115	124	12	33	77	12.5	3.60	105	.276	.330	9	.225	3	6	2	2	0.8
1988	*NY-N	0	4	.000	11	3	0	0	0	24^2	29	2	10	16	14.6	6.93	46	.296	.367	1	.250	0	-10	-10	0	-1.4
1989	NY-N	6	6	.500	36	0	0	0	7	69^1	59	3	21	80	10.6	2.34	140	.231	.295	0	.000	-0	9	7	-0	1.3
	Min-A	3	5	.375	11	11	3	0	0	75^2	71	5	17	57	10.6	3.21	129	.245	.289	0	—	0	6	8	1	0.8
1990	Min-A	5	3	.625	56	0	0	0	32	65^1	55	5	19	61	10.7	2.76	151	.224	.291	0	—	0	8	10	-1	1.9
1991	*Min-A★	4	5	.444	63	0	0	0	42	69	44	3	30	61	9.8	2.35	182	.183	.277	0	—	0	13	15	-0	3.3
1992	Min-A★	2	6	.250	64	0	0	0	41	66^2	60	7	17	52	10.5	2.84	143	.238	.289	0	—	0	8	9	-1	1.8
1993	Min-A★	4	3	.571	65	0	0	0	34	72^1	60	9	14	59	9.3	3.11	140	.223	.264	0	—	0	10	10	1	1.7
1994	Min-A	1	4	.200	44	0	0	0	23	44^2	57	7	10	46	13.5	3.63	134	.306	.342	0	—	0	6	6	1	1.3
1995	Min-A	1	1	.500	22	0	0	0	12	25	20	2	6	29	9.7	2.52	189	.222	.278	0	—	0	6	6	-0	1.0
	*Bos-A	2	2	.500	30	0	0	0	20	30^1	26	4	7	23	9.8	2.67	182	.228	.273	0	—	0	7	7	0	1.7
	Yr	3	3	.500	52	0	0	0	32	55^1	46	6	13	52	9.6	2.60	185	.222	.268	0	—	0	13	14	0	2.7
1996	Min-A	8	6	.571	19	19	2	0	0	111^1	124	20	27	83	12.4	5.42	94	.276	.321	0	—	0	-5	-4	-2	-0.5
1997	Min-A	5	4	.556	61	0	0	0	26	68^1	65	9	22	68	11.7	3.82	122	.257	.321	0	—	0	6	6	1	1.3
1998	Min-A	4	9	.308	68	0	0	0	38	74^1	75	8	15	57	11.0	4.24	111	.262	.301	0	—	0	3	4	-0	0.9
Total	14	76	75	.503	617	89	10	0	275	1176	1132	119	321	947	11.3	3.55	116	.252	.307	28	.203	8	76	73	4	16.4

● HANK AGUIRRE Aguirre, Henry John b: 1/31/31, Azusa, Cal. d: 9/5/94, Bloomfield Hills, Mich. BR/TL, 6'4", 205 lbs. Deb: 9/10/55 C

YEAR	TM/L	W	L	PCT	G	GS	CG	SH	SV	IP	H	HR	BB	SO	RAT	ERA	ERA+	OAV	OOB	BH	AVG	PB	PR	/A	PD	TPI
1955	Cle-A	2	0	1.000	4	1	1	1	0	12^2	6	0	12	6	12.8	1.42	281	.143	.333	0	.000	-1	4	4	-0	0.4
1956	Cle-A	3	5	.375	16	9	2	1	1	65^1	63	7	27	31	12.5	3.72	113	.253	.329	2	.111	-2	3	4	-1	0.2
1957	Cle-A	1	1	.500	10	1	0	0	0	20^1	26	0	13	9	17.3	5.75	65	.317	.411	0	.000	-1	-4	-5	-0	-0.5
1958	Det-A	3	4	.429	44	3	0	0	5	69^2	67	5	27	38	12.3	3.75	108	.255	.326	3	.214	0	0	2	1	0.3
1959	Det-A	0	0	—	3	0	0	0	0	2^2	4	0	3	3	23.6	3.38	120	.364	.500	0	—	0	0	0	0	0.0
1960	Det-A	5	3	.625	37	6	1	0	10	94^2	75	7	30	80	10.3	2.85	139	.217	.286	1	.036	-3	11	12	-2	0.7
1961	Det-A	4	4	.500	45	0	0	0	8	55^1	44	5	38	32	13.7	3.25	126	.224	.356	0	.000	-1	5	5	-1	0.7
1962	Det-A★	16	8	.667	42	22	11	2	3	216	162	14	65	156	9.7	**2.21**	**184**	**.205**	**.269**	2	.027	-8	**42**	**45**	-3	3.7
1963	Det-A	14	15	.483	38	33	14	3	0	225^2	222	25	68	134	11.9	3.67	102	.256	.316	10	.132	-2	-1	2	-3	-0.3
1964	Det-A	5	10	.333	32	27	3	0	1	161^2	134	15	59	88	11.2	3.79	97	.223	.301	3	.057	-4	-3	-2	-3	-0.9
1965	Det-A	14	10	.583	32	32	10	2	0	208^1	185	24	60	141	11.0	3.59	97	.236	.298	6	.086	-2	-3	-3	-1	-0.7
1966	Det-A	3	9	.250	30	14	2	0	0	103^2	104	14	26	50	11.5	3.82	91	.260	.310	3	.120	0	-4	-4	-2	-0.6
1967	Det-A	0	1	.000	31	1	0	0	0	41^1	34	2	17	33	11.1	2.40	136	.219	.297	1	.500	1	4	4	0	0.2
1968	LA-N	1	2	.333	25	0	0	0	3	39^1	32	0	13	25	11.0	0.69	403	.227	.306	0	.000	-0	10	9	-1	0.8
1969	Chi-N	1	0	1.000	41	0	0	0	1	45	45	2	12	19	11.8	2.60	155	.269	.326	2	.400	0	5	7	1	0.3
1970	Chi-N	3	0	1.000	17	0	0	0	1	14	13	3	9	11	14.8	4.50	100	.250	.371	0	.000	-0	-1	0	-0	-0.1
Total	16	75	72	.510	447	149	44	9	33	1375^2	1216	123	479	856	11.4	3.24	116	.236	.307	33	.085	-21	67	79	-16	4.2

● PAT AHEARNE Ahearne, Patrick Howard b: 12/10/69, San Francisco, Cal. BR/TR, 6'3", 195 lbs. Deb: 6/14/95

YEAR	TM/L	W	L	PCT	G	GS	CG	SH	SV	IP	H	HR	BB	SO	RAT	ERA	ERA+	OAV	OOB	BH	AVG	PB	PR	/A	PD	TPI
1995	Det-A	0	2	.000	4	3	0	0	0	10	20	2	5	4	22.5	11.70	41	.400	.455	0	—	0	-8	-8	0	-1.1

● EDDIE AINSMITH Ainsmith, Edward Wilbur "Dorf" b: 2/4/1892, Cambridge, Mass. d: 9/6/81, Ft.Lauderdale, Fla BR/TR, 5'11", 180 lbs. Deb: 8/9/10 ♦

YEAR	TM/L	W	L	PCT	G	GS	CG	SH	SV	IP	H	HR	BB	SO	RAT	ERA	ERA+	OAV	OOB	BH	AVG	PB	PR	/A	PD	TPI
1913	Was-A	0	0	—	1	0	0	0	0	0^1	2	0	0	0	54.0	54.00	5	.667	.667	49	.214	0	-2	-2	0	0.0

● RALEIGH AITCHISON Aitchison, Raleigh Leonidas b: 12/5/1887, Tyndall, S.D. d: 9/26/58, Columbus, Kan. BR/TL, 5'11.5", 175 lbs. Deb: 4/19/11

YEAR	TM/L	W	L	PCT	G	GS	CG	SH	SV	IP	H	HR	BB	SO	RAT	ERA	ERA+	OAV	OOB	BH	AVG	PB	PR	/A	PD	TPI
1911	Bro-N	0	1	.000	1	0	0	0	0	1^1	1	0	1	0	13.5	0.00	—	.200	.333	0	—	0	1	0	-0	0.4
1914	Bro-N	12	7	.632	26	17	8	3	0	172^1	156	4	60	87	11.4	2.66	107	.244	.312	10	.196	1	2	4	-3	0.2
1915	Bro-N	0	4	.000	7	5	2	0	0	32^2	36	3	6	14	12.1	4.96	56	.267	.308	0	.000	-0	-8	-8	0	-0.9
Total	3	12	12	.500	34	22	10	3	0	206^1	193	7	67	101	11.6	3.01	95	.247	.311	10	.169	1	-5	-4	-3	-0.3

● JACK AKER Aker, Jackie Delane b: 7/13/40, Tulare, Cal. BR/TR, 6'2", 190 lbs. Deb: 5/3/64 C

YEAR	TM/L	W	L	PCT	G	GS	CG	SH	SV	IP	H	HR	BB	SO	RAT	ERA	ERA+	OAV	OOB	BH	AVG	PB	PR	/A	PD	TPI
1964	KC-A	0	1	.000	9	0	0	0	0	16^1	17	6	10	7	18.2	8.82	43	.266	.412	0	.000	-0	-9	-9	1	-0.5
1965	KC-A	4	3	.571	34	0	0	0	3	51^1	45	3	18	26	11.6	3.16	111	.242	.319	0	.000	-1	2	2	1	0.3
1966	KC-A	8	4	.667	66	0	0	0	**32**	113	81	7	28	68	8.9	1.99	171	.201	.258	2	.095	-1	**18**	**18**	3	3.2
1967	KC-A	3	8	.273	57	0	0	0	12	88	87	9	32	65	12.5	4.30	74	.264	.334	1	.125	-0	-10	-11	2	-1.5
1968	Oak-A	4	4	.500	54	0	0	0	11	74^2	72	6	33	44	13.4	4.10	69	.258	.349	1	.143	-0	-9	-11	0	-1.5
1969	Sea-A	0	2	.000	15	0	0	0	3	16^2	25	4	13	7	21.1	7.56	48	.357	.464	0	.000	0	-7	-7	1	-1.0
	NY-A	8	4	.667	38	0	0	0	11	65^2	51	4	22	40	10.6	2.06	169	.217	.295	1	.111	-0	11	10	2	2.4
	Yr	8	6	.571	53	0	0	0	14	82^1	76	8	35	47	12.6	3.17	111	.248	.333	1	.100	-0	4	3	2	1.4
1970	NY-A	4	2	.667	41	0	0	0	16	70	57	3	20	36	10.4	2.06	171	.226	.293	1	.063	-1	13	11	-0	1.3
1971	NY-A	4	4	.500	41	0	0	0	4	55^2	48	3	26	24	12.0	2.59	125	.238	.325	0	.000	-0	5	4	1	0.7
1972	NY-A	0	0	—	4	0	0	0	0	6	5	0	3	1	13.5	3.00	98	.238	.360	0	—	0	0	-0	1	0.1
	Chi-N	6	6	.500	48	0	0	0	17	67	65	4	23	36	12.5	2.96	129	.259	.333	0	.000	-0	4	6	2	1.7
1973	Chi-N	4	5	.444	47	0	0	0	12	63^2	76	8	23	25	14.3	4.10	96	.308	.371	0	.000	-1	-3	-1	2	-0.1
1974	Atl-N	0	1	.000	17	0	0	0	0	16^2	17	3	9	7	14.0	3.78	100	.298	.394	0	.000	-0	-0	-0	0	0.0
	NY-N	2	1	.667	24	0	0	0	2	41^1	33	4	14	18	10.7	3.48	102	.213	.287	1	.500	1	1	0	-1	0.0
	Yr	2	2	.500	41	0	0	0	2	58	50	7	23	25	11.6	3.57	102	.234	.314	1	.333	1	0	0	-1	0.0
Total	11	47	45	.511	495	0	0	0	123	746	679	64	274	404	12.0	3.28	105	.247	.324	7	.076	-5	14	13	13	5.1

● DARREL AKERFELDS Akerfelds, Darrel Wayne b: 6/12/62, Denver, Colo. BR/TR, 6'2", 210 lbs. Deb: 8/1/86

YEAR	TM/L	W	L	PCT	G	GS	CG	SH	SV	IP	H	HR	BB	SO	RAT	ERA	ERA+	OAV	OOB	BH	AVG	PB	PR	/A	PD	TPI
1986	Oak-A	0	0	—	2	0	0	0	0	5^1	7	2	3	5	16.9	6.75	57	.304	.385	0	—	0	-2	-2	0	0.0
1987	Cle-A	2	6	.250	16	13	1	0	0	74^2	84	18	38	42	15.5	6.75	67	.284	.378	0	—	0	-19	-18	-0	-1.7
1989	Tex-A	0	1	.000	6	0	0	0	0	11	11	1	5	9	13.1	3.27	121	.250	.327	0	—	0	1	1	0	0.1
1990	Phi-N	5	2	.714	71	0	0	0	3	93	65	10	54	42	11.8	3.77	101	.201	.320	1	.167	-0	0	0	-1	0.0
1991	Phi-N	2	1	.667	30	0	0	0	0	49^2	49	5	27	31	14.3	5.26	70	.257	.357	0	.000	-0	-9	-9	1	-0.5
Total	5	9	10	.474	125	13	1	0	3	233^2	216	36	127	129	13.7	5.08	79	.246	.350	1	.111	-0	-28	-28	0	-2.1

● JERRY AKERS Akers, Albert Earl b: 11/1/1887, Shelbyville, Ind. d: 5/15/79, Bay Pines, Fla. BR/TR, 5'11", 175 lbs. Deb: 5/4/12

YEAR	TM/L	W	L	PCT	G	GS	CG	SH	SV	IP	H	HR	BB	SO	RAT	ERA	ERA+	OAV	OOB	BH	AVG	PB	PR	/A	PD	TPI
1912	Was-A	1	1	.500	5	1	0	0	0	20^1	24	1	15	11	18.1	4.87	68	.300	.423	2	.333	0	-4	-3	-1	-0.4

● GIBSON ALBA Alba, Gibson Alberto (Rosado) b: 1/18/60, Santiago, D.R. BL/TL, 6′2″, 160 lbs. Deb: 5/3/88

YEAR	TM/L	W	L	PCT	G	GS	CG	SH	SV	IP	H	HR	BB	SO	RAT	ERA	ERA+	OAV	OOB	BH	AVG	PB	PR	/A	PD	TPI
1988	StL-N	0	0	—	3	0	0	0	0	3^{1}	1	0	2	3	8.1	2.70	129	.091	.231	0	—	0	0	0	-0	0.0

● JOE ALBANESE Albanese, Joseph Peter b: 6/26/33, New York, N.Y. BR/TR, 6′3″, 215 lbs. Deb: 7/18/58

YEAR	TM/L	W	L	PCT	G	GS	CG	SH	SV	IP	H	HR	BB	SO	RAT	ERA	ERA+	OAV	OOB	BH	AVG	PB	PR	/A	PD	TPI
1958	Was-A	0	0	—	6	0	0	0	0	6	8	1	2	3	15.0	4.50	85	.348	.400	0	—	0	-0	-0	0	0.0

● JOSE ALBERRO Alberro, Jose Edgardo b: 6/29/69, San Juan, P.R. BR/TR, 6′2″, 190 lbs. Deb: 4/27/95

YEAR	TM/L	W	L	PCT	G	GS	CG	SH	SV	IP	H	HR	BB	SO	RAT	ERA	ERA+	OAV	OOB	BH	AVG	PB	PR	/A	PD	TPI
1995	Tex-A	0	0	—	12	0	0	0	0	20^{2}	26	2	12	10	17.0	7.40	65	.299	.390	0	—	0	-6	-6	0	0.0
1996	Tex-A	0	1	.000	5	1	0	0	0	9^{1}	14	1	7	2	20.3	5.79	91	.368	.467	0	—	0	-1	-1	0	-0.1
1997	Tex-A	0	3	.000	10	4	0	0	0	28^{1}	37	4	17	11	17.5	7.94	60	.303	.393	0	—	0	-11	-10	0	-0.8
Total	3	0	4	.000	27	5	0	0	0	58^{1}	77	7	36	23	17.7	7.41	66	.312	.404	0	—	0	-18	-16	1	-0.9

● CY ALBERTS Alberts, Frederick Joseph b: 1/14/1882, Grand Rapids, Mich d: 8/27/17, Fort Wayne, Ind. BR/TR, 6′, 230 lbs. Deb: 9/17/10

YEAR	TM/L	W	L	PCT	G	GS	CG	SH	SV	IP	H	HR	BB	SO	RAT	ERA	ERA+	OAV	OOB	BH	AVG	PB	PR	/A	PD	TPI
1910	StL-N	1	2	.333	4	3	2	0	0	27^{2}	35	1	20	10	17.9	6.18	48	.330	.437	0	.000	-0	-10	-10	-1	-1.0

● ED ALBOSTA Albosta, Edward John "Rube" b: 10/27/18, Saginaw, Mich. BR/TR, 6′1″, 175 lbs. Deb: 9/3/41

YEAR	TM/L	W	L	PCT	G	GS	CG	SH	SV	IP	H	HR	BB	SO	RAT	ERA	ERA+	OAV	OOB	BH	AVG	PB	PR	/A	PD	TPI
1941	Bro-N	0	2	.000	2	2	0	0	0	13	11	1	8	5	13.2	6.23	59	.239	.352	0	.000	-1	-4	-4	0	-0.5
1946	Pit-N	0	6	.000	17	6	0	0	0	39^{2}	41	3	35	19	17.5	6.13	58	.266	.405	1	.125	-0	-12	-11	0	-1.6
Total	2	0	8	.000	19	8	0	0	0	52^{2}	52	4	43	24	16.4	6.15	58	.260	.393	1	.083	-1	-16	-15	0	-2.1

● ED ALBRECHT Albrecht, Edward Arthur b: 2/28/29, Affton, Mo. d: 12/29/79, Cahokia, Ill. BR/TR, 5′10.5″, 165 lbs. Deb: 10/2/49

YEAR	TM/L	W	L	PCT	G	GS	CG	SH	SV	IP	H	HR	BB	SO	RAT	ERA	ERA+	OAV	OOB	BH	AVG	PB	PR	/A	PD	TPI
1949	StL-A	1	0	1.000	1	1	1	0	0	5	1	0	4	1	9.0	5.40	84	.063	.250	0	.000	-0	-1	-0	0	-0.1
1950	StL-A	0	1	.000	2	1	0	0	0	6^{2}	6	0	7	1	17.6	5.40	92	.250	.419	0	.000	-0	-1	-0	-0	-0.1
Total	2	1	1	.500	3	2	1	0	0	11^{2}	7	0	11	2	13.9	5.40	88	.175	.353	0	.000	-0	-1	-1	-0	-0.2

● VIC ALBURY Albury, Victor b: 5/12/47, Key West, Fla. BL/TL, 6′, 190 lbs. Deb: 8/7/73

YEAR	TM/L	W	L	PCT	G	GS	CG	SH	SV	IP	H	HR	BB	SO	RAT	ERA	ERA+	OAV	OOB	BH	AVG	PB	PR	/A	PD	TPI
1973	Min-A	1	0	1.000	14	0	0	0	0	23^{1}	13	1	19	13	12.3	2.70	147	.169	.333	0	—	0	3	3	-1	0.0
1974	Min-A	8	9	.471	32	22	4	1	0	164	159	19	80	85	13.4	4.12	91	.259	.350	0	—	0	-9	-7	-1	-0.8
1975	Min-A	6	7	.462	32	15	2	0	1	135	115	16	97	72	14.4	4.53	84	.237	.368	0	.000	-0	-11	-11	1	-0.9
1976	Min-A	3	1	.750	23	0	0	0	0	50^{1}	51	0	24	23	13.8	3.58	100	.271	.360	0	—	0	-0	-0	-0	-0.1
Total	4	18	17	.514	101	37	6	1	1	372^{2}	338	36	220	193	13.8	4.11	91	.247	.357	0	.000	-0	-18	-14	-1	-1.8

● SANTO ALCALA Alcala, Santo (b: Santo Anibal (Alcala)) b: 12/23/52, San Pedro De Macoris, D.R. BR/TR, 6′5″, 195 lbs. Deb: 4/10/76

YEAR	TM/L	W	L	PCT	G	GS	CG	SH	SV	IP	H	HR	BB	SO	RAT	ERA	ERA+	OAV	OOB	BH	AVG	PB	PR	/A	PD	TPI
1976	Cin-N	11	4	.733	30	21	3	1	0	132	131	12	67	67	13.7	4.70	74	.261	.352	6	.140	-0	-18	-18	-1	-2.0
1977	Cin-N	1	1	.500	7	2	0	0	0	15^{2}	22	1	7	9	17.2	5.74	68	.349	.423	0	.000	-0	-3	-3	0	-0.4
	Mon-N	2	6	.250	31	10	0	0	2	101^{2}	104	12	47	64	13.5	4.69	81	.263	.344	2	.080	-1	-9	-10	-1	-1.0
	Yr	3	7	.300	38	12	0	0	2	117^{1}	126	13	54	73	14.0	4.83	79	.273	.352	2	.071	-1	-12	-13	-1	-1.4
Total	2	14	11	.560	68	33	3	1	2	249^{1}	257	25	121	140	13.9	4.76	77	.268	.353	8	.113	-2	-30	-31	-2	-3.4

● DALE ALDERSON Alderson, Dale Leonard b: 3/9/18, Belden, Neb. d: 2/12/82, Garden Grove, Cal. BR/TR, 5′10″, 190 lbs. Deb: 9/18/43

YEAR	TM/L	W	L	PCT	G	GS	CG	SH	SV	IP	H	HR	BB	SO	RAT	ERA	ERA+	OAV	OOB	BH	AVG	PB	PR	/A	PD	TPI
1943	Chi-N	0	1	.000	4	2	0	0	0	14	21	2	3	4	15.4	6.43	52	.356	.387	0	.000	-0	-5	-5	0	-0.3
1944	Chi-N	0	0	—	12	1	0	0	0	21^{2}	31	2	9	7	16.6	6.65	53	.344	.404	0	.000	-1	-7	-7	1	0.0
Total	2	0	1	.000	16	3	0	0	0	35^{2}	52	4	12	11	16.1	6.56	53	.349	.398	0	.000	-1	-12	-12	1	-0.3

● SCOTT ALDRED Aldred, Scott Phillip b: 6/12/68, Flint, Mich. BL/TL, 6′4″, 195 lbs. Deb: 9/9/90

YEAR	TM/L	W	L	PCT	G	GS	CG	SH	SV	IP	H	HR	BB	SO	RAT	ERA	ERA+	OAV	OOB	BH	AVG	PB	PR	/A	PD	TPI
1990	Det-A	1	2	.333	4	3	0	0	0	14^{1}	13	0	10	7	15.1	3.77	105	.265	.400	0	—	0	0	0	-0	0.0
1991	Det-A	2	4	.333	11	11	1	0	0	57^{1}	58	9	30	35	13.8	5.18	80	.266	.355	0	—	0	-7	-7	0	-0.6
1992	Det-A	3	8	.273	16	13	0	0	0	65	80	12	33	34	16.1	6.78	58	.307	.391	0	—	0	-21	-20	1	-2.8
1993	Col-N	0	0	—	5	0	0	0	0	6^{2}	10	1	9	5	27.0	10.80	44	.357	.526	0	—	0	-5	-4	0	0.0
	Mon-N	1	0	1.000	3	0	0	0	0	5^{1}	9	1	1	4	16.9	6.75	62	.375	.400	0	—	0	-2	-2	0	-0.2
	Yr	1	0	1.000	8	0	0	0	0	12	19	2	10	9	21.8	9.00	50	.358	.460	0	—	0	-7	-6	0	-0.2
1996	Det-A	0	4	.000	11	8	0	0	0	43^{1}	60	9	26	36	18.5	9.35	54	.328	.420	0	—	0	-21	-21	-1	-1.5
	Min-A	6	5	.545	25	17	0	0	0	122	134	20	42	75	13.2	5.09	100	.281	.343	0	—	0	-1	0	-1	-0.1
	Yr	6	9	.400	36	25	0	0	0	165^{1}	194	29	68	111	14.4	6.21	82	.292	.360	0	—	0	-22	-20	-2	-1.6
1997	Min-A	2	10	.167	17	15	0	0	0	77^{1}	102	20	28	33	15.5	7.68	61	.323	.383	0	—	0	-27	-26	-1	-3.2
1998	TB-A	0	0	—	48	0	0	0	0	31^{1}	33	1	12	21	13.5	3.73	131	.280	.356	0	—	0	3	4	1	0.0
Total	7	15	33	.313	140	67	1	0	0	422^{2}	499	73	191	250	15.0	6.24	74	.298	.375	0	—	0	-80	-75	-1	-8.4

● MIKE ALDRETE Aldrete, Michael Peter b: 1/29/61, Carmel, Cal. BL/TL, 5′11″, 185 lbs. Deb: 5/28/86 ♦

YEAR	TM/L	W	L	PCT	G	GS	CG	SH	SV	IP	H	HR	BB	SO	RAT	ERA	ERA+	OAV	OOB	BH	AVG	PB	PR	/A	PD	TPI
1996	*NY-A	0	0	—	1	0	0	0	0	1	1	0	0	0	9.0	0.00	—	.333	.333	17	.250	0	1	1	0	0.0

● JAY ALDRICH Aldrich, Jay Robert b: 4/14/61, Alexandria, La. BR/TR, 6′3″, 210 lbs. Deb: 6/5/87

YEAR	TM/L	W	L	PCT	G	GS	CG	SH	SV	IP	H	HR	BB	SO	RAT	ERA	ERA+	OAV	OOB	BH	AVG	PB	PR	/A	PD	TPI
1987	Mil-A	3	1	.750	31	0	0	0	0	58^{1}	71	8	13	22	13.3	4.94	93	.306	.348	0	—	0	-3	-2	-1	-0.4
1989	Mil-A	1	0	1.000	16	0	0	0	1	26	24	3	13	12	13.2	3.81	101	.253	.349	0	—	0	0	0	0	0.1
	Atl-N	1	2	.333	8	0	0	0	0	12^{1}	7	0	6	7	9.5	2.19	167	.167	.271	0	.000	-0	2	2	-0	0.4
1990	Bal-A	1	2	.333	7	0	0	0	1	12	17	1	7	5	18.0	8.25	46	.327	.407	0	—	0	-6	-6	0	-1.3
Total	3	6	5	.545	62	0	0	0	2	108^{2}	119	12	39	46	13.3	4.72	89	.283	.348	0	.000	-0	-7	-6	-1	-1.2

● VIC ALDRIDGE Aldridge, Victor Eddington b: 10/25/1893, Indian Springs, Ind. d: 4/17/73, Terre Haute, Ind. BR/TR, 5′9.5″, 175 lbs. Deb: 4/15/17

YEAR	TM/L	W	L	PCT	G	GS	CG	SH	SV	IP	H	HR	BB	SO	RAT	ERA	ERA+	OAV	OOB	BH	AVG	PB	PR	/A	PD	TPI
1917	Chi-N	6	6	.500	30	6	1	1	2	106^{2}	100	1	37	44	11.7	3.12	93	.252	.319	4	.138	-2	-5	-3	3	-0.2
1918	Chi-N	0	1	.000	3	0	0	0	0	12^{1}	11	0	6	10	12.4	1.46	191	.275	.370	1	.333	0	2	2	-0	0.2
1922	Chi-N	16	15	.516	36	34	20	2	0	258^{1}	287	14	56	66	12.4	3.52	119	.286	.332	26	.260	3	17	20	1	2.5
1923	Chi-N	16	9	.640	30	30	15	2	0	217	209	17	67	64	11.5	3.48	115	.251	.307	19	.268	3	12	12	-1	1.5
1924	Chi-N	15	12	.556	32	32	20	0	0	244^{1}	261	10	80	74	12.8	3.50	112	.279	.341	15	.176	-3	10	11	-0	0.7
1925	*Pit-N	15	7	.682	30	26	14	1	0	213^{1}	218	15	74	88	12.5	3.63	123	.269	.334	20	.233	-1	15	20	-3	1.3
1926	Pit-N	10	13	.435	30	26	12	1	1	190	204	7	73	61	13.3	4.07	97	.279	.348	16	.225	-1	-5	-3	-2	-0.6
1927	*Pit-N	15	10	.600	35	34	17	1	1	239^{1}	248	16	74	86	12.3	4.25	97	.270	.328	21	.219	-0	-9	-4	-3	-0.7
1928	NY-N	4	7	.364	22	16	3	0	2	119^{1}	133	7	45	33	13.7	4.83	81	.285	.352	11	.275	2	-11	-12	-1	-0.9
Total	9	97	80	.548	248	204	102	8	6	1600^{2}	1671	87	512	526	12.5	3.76	107	.273	.333	133	.229	2	26	44	-7	3.8

● DOYLE ALEXANDER Alexander, Doyle Lafayette b: 9/4/50, Cordova, Ala. BR/TR, 6′3″, 205 lbs. Deb: 6/26/71

YEAR	TM/L	W	L	PCT	G	GS	CG	SH	SV	IP	H	HR	BB	SO	RAT	ERA	ERA+	OAV	OOB	BH	AVG	PB	PR	/A	PD	TPI
1971	LA-N	6	6	.500	17	12	4	0	0	92^{1}	105	6	18	30	12.1	3.80	85	.282	.317	9	.273	3	-3	-6	-1	-0.5
1972	Bal-A	6	8	.429	35	9	2	2	2	106^{1}	78	5	30	49	9.2	2.45	125	.203	.262	2	.080	-1	7	7	2	1.1
1973	*Bal-A	12	8	.600	29	26	10	0	0	174^{2}	169	19	52	63	11.7	3.86	97	.258	.319	0	—	0	-1	-3	1	-0.1
1974	Bal-A	6	9	.400	30	12	2	0	0	114^{1}	127	7	43	40	13.7	4.01	86	.290	.359	0	—	0	-5	-7	3	-0.5
1975	Bal-A	8	8	.500	32	11	3	1	1	133^{1}	127	7	47	46	11.8	3.04	116	.251	.316	0	—	0	11	7	2	1.0
1976	Bal-A	3	4	.429	11	6	2	1	0	64^{1}	58	3	24	17	11.5	3.50	94	.247	.317	0	—	0	0	-2	1	0.2
	*NY-A	10	5	.667	19	19	5	2	0	136^{2}	114	9	39	41	10.3	3.29	104	.229	.289	0	—	0	3	2	-2	0.0
	Yr	13	9	.591	30	25	7	3	0	201	172	12	63	58	10.7	3.36	100	.234	.297	0	—	0	4	0	-1	0.2
1977	Tex-A	17	11	.607	34	34	12	1	0	237	221	24	82	82	11.6	3.65	112	.246	.311	0	—	0	11	11	1	1.4
1978	Tex-A	9	10	.474	31	28	7	1	0	191	198	18	71	81	12.7	3.86	97	.270	.336	0	—	0	-2	-3	2	-0.1
1979	Tex-A	5	7	.417	23	18	0	0	0	113^{1}	114	3	69	50	14.6	4.45	93	.268	.371	0	—	0	-3	-4	2	-0.1
1980	Atl-N	14	11	.560	35	35	7	1	0	231^{2}	227	20	74	114	11.8	4.20	89	.256	.316	15	.181	0	-15	-12	3	-0.8
1981	SF-N	11	7	.611	24	24	1	1	0	152^{1}	156	11	44	77	11.9	2.89	118	.263	.316	9	.176	1	10	9	-2	1.0
1982	NY-A	1	7	.125	16	11	0	0	0	66^{2}	81	14	14	26	12.8	6.08	66	.298	.332	0	—	0	-15	-15	-0	-1.5
1983	NY-A	0	2	.000	8	5	0	0	0	28^{1}	31	6	7	17	12.1	6.35	61	.277	.319	0	—	0	-7	-8	-0	-0.3
	Tor-A	7	6	.538	17	15	5	0	0	116^{2}	126	14	26	46	11.8	3.93	109	.279	.319	0	—	0	2	5	0	0.2
	Yr	7	8	.467	25	20	5	0	0	145	157	20	33	63	11.9	4.41	96	.278	.319	0	—	0	-6	-3	0	-0.1
1984	Tor-A	17	6	**.739**	36	35	11	2	0	261^{2}	238	21	59	139	10.3	3.13	131	.242	.287	0	—	0	25	28	-0	2.2
1985	*Tor-A	17	10	.630	36	36	6	1	0	260^{2}	268	28	67	142	11.8	3.45	122	.266	.315	0	—	0	20	22	0	2.1
1986	Tor-A	5	4	.556	17	17	3	0	0	111	120	18	20	65	11.7	4.46	95	.273	.310	0	—	0	-3	-3	-1	-0.3
	Atl-N	6	6	.500	17	17	2	0	0	117^{1}	135	9	17	74	11.7	3.84	104	.287	.312	8	.211	1	-2	2	-1	0.2

YEAR	TM/L	W	L	PCT	G	GS	CG	SH	SV	IP	H	HR	BB	SO	RAT	ERA	ERA+	OAV	OOB	BH	AVG	PB	PR	/A	PD	TPI
1987	Atl-N	5	10	.333	16	16	3	0	0	117^{2}	115	21	27	64	11.0	4.13	105	.257	.302	1	.029	-3	-1	3	-2	-0.1
	*Det-A	9	0	1.000	11	11	3	3	0	88^{1}	63	3	26	44	9.1	1.53	276	.201	.263	0	—	0	29	26	0	3.0
1988	Det-A☆	14	11	.560	34	34	5	1	0	229	260	30	46	126	12.2	4.32	88	.282	.320	0	—	0	-9	-13	-3	-1.5
1989	Det-A	6	18	.250	33	33	5	1	0	223	245	28	76	95	13.2	4.44	86	.280	.341	0	—	0	-14	-15	0	-1.4
Total	19	194	174	.527	561	464	98	18	3	3367^{2}	3376	324	978	1528	11.8	3.76	102	.261	.316	44	.166	1	38	32	7	5.2

● GERALD ALEXANDER Alexander, Gerald Paul b: 3/26/68, Baton Rouge, La. BR/TR, 5′11″, 190 lbs. Deb: 9/9/90

YEAR	TM/L	W	L	PCT	G	GS	CG	SH	SV	IP	H	HR	BB	SO	RAT	ERA	ERA+	OAV	OOB	BH	AVG	PB	PR	/A	PD	TPI
1990	Tex-A	0	0	—	3	2	0	0	0	7	14	0	5	8	25.7	7.71	51	.438	.526	0	—	0	-3	-3	0	0.0
1991	Tex-A	5	3	.625	30	9	0	0	0	89^{1}	93	11	48	50	14.5	5.24	77	.272	.366	0	—	0	-11	-12	0	-0.9
1992	Tex-A	1	0	1.000	3	0	0	0	0	1^{2}	5	1	1	1	32.4	27.00	14	.500	.545	0	—	0	-4	-4	0	-1.7
Total	3	6	3	.667	36	11	0	0	0	98	112	12	54	59	15.6	5.79	69	.292	.385	0	—	0	-19	-19	0	-2.6

● PETE ALEXANDER Alexander, Grover Cleveland b: 2/26/1887, Elba, Neb. d: 11/4/50, St.Paul, Neb. BR/TR, 6′1″, 185 lbs. Deb: 4/15/11 H

YEAR	TM/L	W	L	PCT	G	GS	CG	SH	SV	IP	H	HR	BB	SO	RAT	ERA	ERA+	OAV	OOB	BH	AVG	PB	PR	/A	PD	TPI
1911	Phi-N	**28**	13	.683	48	37	**31**	**7**	3	**367**	285	5	129	227	10.3	2.57	134	**.219**	.293	24	.174	-2	34	35	1	3.6
1912	Phi-N	19	17	.528	46	34	25	3	3	**310^{1}**	289	11	105	**195**	11.6	2.81	129	.251	.317	19	.186	0	21	28	1	3.1
1913	Phi-N	22	8	.733	47	36	23	**9**	2	306^{1}	288	9	75	159	10.8	2.79	120	.254	.302	13	.126	-4	14	19	2	1.4
1914	Phi-N	**27**	15	.643	46	39	**32**	6	1	**355**	327	8	76	**214**	10.5	2.38	123	.244	.290	32	.234	2	16	22	4	3.3
1915	*Phi-N	**31**	10	**.756**	49	42	**36**	**12**	3	**376^{1}**	253	3	64	**241**	**7.8**	**1.22**	**225**	**.191**	**.234**	22	.169	0	**64**	**64**	7	**8.6**
1916	Phi-N	**33**	12	.733	48	45	**38**	**16**	3	**389**	323	6	50	**167**	8.9	**1.55**	**171**	.230	.262	33	.239	8	**46**	**48**	1	**7.3**
1917	Phi-N	**30**	13	.698	45	44	**34**	**8**	0	**388**	336	4	56	**200**	9.2	**1.83**	153	.234	.266	30	.216	4	**38**	**42**	2	**5.9**
1918	Chi-N	2	1	.667	3	3	3	0	0	26	19	0	3	15	8.0	1.73	161	.207	.240	1	.100	-1	3	3	0	0.3
1919	Chi-N	16	11	.593	30	27	20	**9**	1	235	180	3	38	121	8.3	**1.72**	**167**	**.211**	.245	12	.171	1	31	30	5	**4.4**
1920	Chi-N	**27**	14	.659	46	40	**33**	7	5	**363^{1}**	335	8	69	**173**	10.0	**1.91**	**168**	.248	.285	27	.229	4	**50**	**52**	2	**7.1**
1921	Chi-N	15	13	.536	31	30	21	**3**	1	252	286	10	33	77	11.4	3.39	113	.296	.320	29	.305	6	11	12	-1	1.8
1922	Chi-N	16	13	.552	33	31	20	1	1	245^{2}	283	8	34	48	11.7	3.63	116	.295	.321	15	.176	-2	13	16	3	1.7
1923	Chi-N	22	12	.647	39	36	26	3	2	305	308	17	30	72	**10.0**	3.19	126	.259	**.277**	24	.216	0	28	28	4	3.2
1924	Chi-N	12	5	.706	21	20	12	0	0	169^{1}	183	9	25	33	11.1	3.03	129	.272	.299	15	.231	1	16	16	2	1.7
1925	Chi-N	15	11	.577	32	30	20	1	0	236	270	14	29	63	11.5	3.39	127	.288	.312	19	.241	3	23	24	-2	2.3
1926	Chi-N	3	3	.500	7	7	4	0	0	52	55	0	7	12	10.7	3.46	111	.270	.294	7	.467	3	2	2	1	0.6
	*StL-N	9	7	.563	23	16	11	2	2	148^{1}	136	8	24	35	9.8	2.91	134	.242	.276	6	.120	-4	15	16	-0	1.3
	Yr	12	10	.545	30	23	15	2	2	200^{1}	191	8	31	47	**10.1**	3.05	127	.250	**.281**	13	.200	-1	17	19	1	1.9
1927	StL-N	21	10	.677	37	30	22	2	3	268	261	11	38	48	**10.1**	2.52	157	.258	**.286**	23	.245	3	**42**	**43**	1	**5.2**
1928	*StL-N	16	9	.640	34	31	18	1	2	243^{2}	262	15	37	59	11.1	3.36	119	.277	.306	25	.291	6	17	17	-1	2.1
1929	StL-N	9	8	.529	22	19	8	0	0	132	149	10	23	33	11.8	3.89	120	.285	.317	2	.049	-4	12	11	2	1.0
1930	Phi-N	0	3	.000	9	3	0	0	0	21^{2}	40	5	6	6	19.1	9.14	60	.396	.430	0	.000	-0	-10	-9	-1	-1.0
Total	20	373	208	.642	696	600	437	90	32	5190	4868	164	951	2198	10.2	2.56	135	.250	.288	378	.209	24	484	522	31	64.9

● MANNY ALEXANDER Alexander, Manuel De Jesus (b: Manuel De Jesus (Alexander))
b: 3/20/71, San Pedro De Macoris, D.R. BR/TR, 5′10″, 165 lbs. Deb: 9/18/92 ♦

YEAR	TM/L	W	L	PCT	G	GS	CG	SH	SV	IP	H	HR	BB	SO	RAT	ERA	ERA+	OAV	OOB	BH	AVG	PB	PR	/A	PD	TPI
1996	*Bal-A	0	0	—	1	0	0	0	0	0^{2}	1	1	4	0	67.5	67.50	7	.500	.833	7	.103	-0	-5	-5	0	0.0

● BOB ALEXANDER Alexander, Robert Somerville b: 8/7/22, Vancouver, B.C., Can d: 4/7/93, Oceanside, Cal. BR/TR, 6′2.5″, 205 lbs. Deb: 4/11/55

YEAR	TM/L	W	L	PCT	G	GS	CG	SH	SV	IP	H	HR	BB	SO	RAT	ERA	ERA+	OAV	OOB	BH	AVG	PB	PR	/A	PD	TPI
1955	Bal-A	1	0	1.000	4	0	0	0	0	4	8	0	2	1	24.8	13.50	28	.444	.524	0	—	0	-4	-4	-0	-0.9
1957	Cle-A	0	1	.000	5	0	0	0	0	7	10	0	5	1	20.6	9.00	41	.357	.471	0	.000	-0	-4	-4	-0	-0.6
Total	2	1	1	.500	9	0	0	0	0	11	18	0	7	2	22.1	10.64	35	.391	.491	0	.000	-0	-8	-8	-1	-1.5

● ANTONIO ALFONSECA Alfonseca, Antonio b: 4/16/72, LaRomana, D.R. BR/TR, 6′5″, 235 lbs. Deb: 6/17/97

YEAR	TM/L	W	L	PCT	G	GS	CG	SH	SV	IP	H	HR	BB	SO	RAT	ERA	ERA+	OAV	OOB	BH	AVG	PB	PR	/A	PD	TPI
1997	*Fla-N	1	3	.250	17	0	0	0	0	25^{2}	36	3	10	19	16.5	4.91	82	.324	.385	0	.000	-0	-2	-3	-0	-0.4
1998	Fla-N	4	6	.400	58	0	0	0	8	70^{2}	75	10	33	46	14.1	4.08	100	.281	.366	0	.000	-0	1	0	-1	-0.1
Total	2	5	9	.357	75	0	0	0	8	96^{1}	111	13	43	65	14.8	4.30	95	.294	.372	0	.000	-1	-1	-2	-1	-0.5

● BRIAN ALLARD Allard, Brian Marshall b: 1/3/58, Spring Valley, Ill. BR/TR, 6′1″, 175 lbs. Deb: 8/8/79

YEAR	TM/L	W	L	PCT	G	GS	CG	SH	SV	IP	H	HR	BB	SO	RAT	ERA	ERA+	OAV	OOB	BH	AVG	PB	PR	/A	PD	TPI
1979	Tex-A	1	3	.250	7	4	2	0	0	33^{1}	36	4	13	14	13.2	4.32	96	.283	.350	0	—	0	-0	-1	0	0.0
1980	Tex-A	0	1	.000	5	2	0	0	0	14^{1}	13	0	10	10	15.1	5.65	69	.236	.364	0	—	0	-3	-3	-0	-0.1
1981	Sea-A	3	2	.600	7	7	1	0	0	48	48	5	8	20	10.5	3.75	103	.265	.296	0	—	0	-0	1	-0	-0.1
Total	3	4	6	.400	19	13	3	0	0	95^{2}	97	9	31	44	12.1	4.23	94	.267	.327	0	—	0	-3	-3	-1	-0.2

● FRANK ALLEN Allen, Frank Leon b: 8/26/1889, Newbern, Ala. d: 7/30/33, Gainesville, Ala. BR/TL, 5′9″, 175 lbs. Deb: 4/24/12

YEAR	TM/L	W	L	PCT	G	GS	CG	SH	SV	IP	H	HR	BB	SO	RAT	ERA	ERA+	OAV	OOB	BH	AVG	PB	PR	/A	PD	TPI
1912	Bro-N	3	9	.250	20	15	5	1	0	109	119	1	57	58	14.6	3.63	92	.285	.373	6	.167	2	-3	-3	0	-0.1
1913	Bro-N	4	18	.182	34	25	11	0	2	174^{2}	144	6	81	82	12.1	2.83	116	.231	.329	7	.137	-1	7	9	-3	0.7
1914	Bro-N	8	14	.364	36	21	10	1	0	171^{1}	165	6	57	68	11.8	3.10	92	.265	.330	6	.128	0	-6	-5	-1	-0.7
	Pit-F	1	0	1.000	1	1	1	0	0	7	9	0	0	3	11.6	5.14	56	.321	.321	1	.500	1	-2	-2	-0	-0.1
1915	Pit-F	23	13	.639	41	37	24	6	0	283^{1}	230	9	100	127	10.8	2.51	108	.227	.304	7	.079	-6	7	6	-1	0.1
1916	Bos-N	8	2	.800	19	14	7	2	1	113	102	1	31	63	10.9	2.07	120	.244	.302	7	.206	3	7	5	-1	0.7
1917	Bos-N	3	11	.214	29	14	2	0	0	112	124	3	47	56	14.2	3.94	65	.297	.376	5	.172	2	-15	-17	-2	-2.1
Total	6	50	67	.427	180	127	60	10	3	970^{1}	893	26	373	457	12.1	2.93	98	.252	.330	39	.135	1	-5	-7	-8	-1.5

● JOHN ALLEN Allen, John Marshall b: 10/27/1890, Berkeley Springs, W.Va. d: 9/24/67, Hagerstown, Md. BR/TR, 6′1″, 170 lbs. Deb: 6/2/14

YEAR	TM/L	W	L	PCT	G	GS	CG	SH	SV	IP	H	HR	BB	SO	RAT	ERA	ERA+	OAV	OOB	BH	AVG	PB	PR	/A	PD	TPI
1914	Bal-F	0	0	—	1	0	0	0	0	2	2	0	2	2	22.5	18.00	17	.286	.500	0	—	0	-3	-3	0	0.0

● JOHNNY ALLEN Allen, John Thomas b: 9/30/05, Lenoir, N.C. d: 3/29/59, St.Petersburg, Fla BR/TR, 6′, 180 lbs. Deb: 4/19/32

YEAR	TM/L	W	L	PCT	G	GS	CG	SH	SV	IP	H	HR	BB	SO	RAT	ERA	ERA+	OAV	OOB	BH	AVG	PB	PR	/A	PD	TPI
1932	*NY-A	17	4	**.810**	33	21	13	3	4	192	162	10	76	109	11.4	3.70	110	.228	.306	9	.123	-2	17	8	-1	0.5
1933	NY-A	15	7	.682	25	24	10	1	1	184^{2}	171	9	87	119	12.8	4.39	89	.242	.328	13	.181	0	-2	-10	-1	-1.1
1934	NY-A	5	2	.714	13	10	4	0	0	71^{2}	62	3	32	54	12.1	2.89	141	.227	.313	5	.192	1	13	9	0	0.9
1935	NY-A	13	6	.684	23	23	12	2	0	167	149	11	58	113	11.4	3.61	112	**.238**	.307	15	.224	1	16	8	1	1.0
1936	Cle-A	20	10	.667	36	31	19	4	1	243	234	5	97	165	12.3	3.44	146	.256	.328	14	.161	-3	43	43	2	4.5
1937	Cle-A	15	1	**.938**	24	20	14	0	0	173	157	4	60	87	11.5	2.55	181	.244	.313	6	.090	-7	40	40	1	2.7
1938	Cle-A★	14	8	.636	30	27	13	0	0	200	189	15	81	112	12.3	4.18	111	.246	.321	20	.253	4	13	10	2	1.5
1939	Cle-A	9	7	.563	28	26	9	2	0	175	199	9	56	79	13.3	4.58	96	.291	.347	16	.225	1	1	-3	3	0.1
1940	Cle-A	9	8	.529	32	17	5	3	5	138^{2}	126	3	48	62	11.5	3.44	123	.243	.311	10	.208	0	15	12	-0	1.4
1941	StL-A	2	5	.286	20	9	2	0	1	67	89	4	29	27	16.1	6.58	65	.319	.387	3	.136	0	-18	-17	-0	-1.6
	*Bro-N	3	0	1.000	11	4	1	0	0	57^{1}	38	6	12	21	7.8	2.51	146	.188	.234	1	.050	-2	7	7	-0	0.1
1942	Bro-N	10	6	.625	27	15	5	1	3	118	106	11	39	50	11.2	3.20	102	.238	.302	7	.179	-0	1	1	0	0.0
1943	Bro-N	5	1	.833	17	1	0	0	1	38	42	3	25	15	16.3	4.26	79	.280	.390	3	.429	2	-4	-4	-0	-0.4
	NY-N	1	3	.250	15	0	0	0	2	41	37	4	14	24	11.2	3.07	112	.245	.309	0	.000	-2	1	2	1	0.1
	Yr	6	4	.600	32	1	0	0	3	79	79	7	39	39	13.4	3.65	93	.261	.345	3	.143	-0	-2	-2	1	-0.3
1944	NY-N	4	7	.364	18	13	2	1	0	84	88	7	24	33	12.2	4.07	90	.260	.313	2	.083	-2	-4	-4	-1	-0.8
Total	13	142	75	.654	352	241	109	17	18	1950^{1}	1849	104	738	1070	12.1	3.75	113	.249	.321	124	.173	-8	138	102	6	8.9

● LLOYD ALLEN Allen, Lloyd Cecil b: 5/8/50, Merced, Cal. BR/TR, 6′1″, 185 lbs. Deb: 9/1/69

YEAR	TM/L	W	L	PCT	G	GS	CG	SH	SV	IP	H	HR	BB	SO	RAT	ERA	ERA+	OAV	OOB	BH	AVG	PB	PR	/A	PD	TPI
1969	Cal-A	0	1	.000	4	1	0	0	0	10	5	1	10	5	13.5	5.40	65	.147	.341	1	.500	1	-2	-2	1	-0.1
1970	Cal-A	1	1	.500	8	2	0	0	0	24	23	0	11	12	13.1	2.63	138	.261	.350	0	.000	-0	3	3	-0	0.1
1971	Cal-A	4	6	.400	54	1	0	0	15	94	75	4	40	72	11.0	2.49	130	.221	.303	5	.294	2	10	8	0	1.4
1972	Cal-A	3	7	.300	42	6	0	0	5	85^{1}	76	7	55	53	14.1	3.48	84	.240	.357	2	.118	-1	-4	-5	-1	-0.9
1973	Cal-A	0	0	—	5	0	0	0	1	8^{2}	15	0	5	4	20.8	10.38	34	.417	.488	0	—	0	-6	-7	-0	-0.2
	Tex-A	0	6	.000	23	5	0	0	1	41	58	3	39	25	22.4	9.22	40	.326	.459	0	—	0	-25	-25	1	-3.2
	Yr	0	6	.000	28	5	0	0	2	49^{2}	73	3	44	29	22.1	9.42	39	.338	.460	0	—	0	-31	-32	1	-3.4
1974	Tex-A	0	1	.000	14	0	0	0	0	22	24	2	18	18	17.6	6.55	54	.276	.406	0	—	0	-7	-7	-1	-0.4
	Chi-A	0	1	.000	6	2	0	0	0	7	7	0	12	3	25.7	10.29	36	.259	.500	0	—	0	-5	-5	-0	-0.7
	Yr	0	2	.000	20	2	0	0	0	29	31	2	30	21	19.2	7.45	48	.265	.419	0	—	0	-12	-12	-1	-1.1
1975	Chi-A	0	2	.000	3	2	0	0	0	5^{1}	8	2	6	2	23.6	11.81	33	.348	.483	0	—	0	-5	-5	0	-1.3
Total	7	8	25	.242	159	19	0	0	22	297^{1}	291	19	196	194	15.1	4.69	70	.258	.373	8	.200	2	-41	-46	0	-5.3

YEAR TM/L	W	L	PCT	G	GS	CG	SH	SV	IP	H	HR	BB	SO	RAT	ERA	ERA+	OAV	OOB	BH	AVG	PB	PR	/A	PD	TPI
● **MYRON ALLEN** Allen, Myron Smith "Zeke" b: 3/22/1854, Kingston, N.Y. d: 3/8/24, Kingston, N.Y. BR/TR, 5'8", 150 lbs. Deb: 7/19/1883 ♦																									
1883 NY-N	0	1	.000	1	1	1	0	0	8	8	0	3	0	12.4	1.13	275	.276	.344	0	.000	-1	2	2	-0	0.1
1887 Cle-a	1	0	1.000	2	0	0	0	0	9^2	9	0	3	1	12.1	0.93	466	.243	.317	128	.276	0	4	4	-0	0.3
1888 KC-a	0	2	.000	2	2	2	0	0	18	17	0	1	2	10.0	2.50	137	.239	.270	29	.213	0	1	2	1	0.3
Total 3	1	3	.250	5	3	3	0	0	35^2	34	0	7	3	11.1	1.77	205	.248	.299	157	.259	-0	7	7	0	0.7
● **NEIL ALLEN** Allen, Neil Patrick b: 1/24/58, Kansas City, Kan. BR/TR, 6'2", 190 lbs. Deb: 4/15/79																									
1979 NY-N	6	10	.375	50	5	0	0	8	99	100	4	47	65	13.4	3.55	103	.268	.350	0	.000	-2	2	1	0	0.0
1980 NY-N	7	10	.412	59	0	0	0	22	97^1	87	7	40	79	11.7	3.70	96	.244	.320	2	.143	-0	-1	-2	-1	-0.4
1981 NY-N	7	6	.538	43	0	0	0	18	66^2	64	4	26	50	12.2	2.97	117	.259	.330	1	.200	1	4	4	1	1.1
1982 NY-N	3	7	.300	50	0	0	0	19	64^2	65	5	30	59	13.4	3.06	119	.266	.349	1	.167	1	4	4	-0	0.9
1983 NY-N	2	7	.222	21	4	1	1	2	54	57	6	36	32	15.5	4.50	81	.278	.386	0	.000	-1	-5	-5	-0	-1.0
StL-N	10	6	.625	25	18	4	2	0	121^2	122	6	48	74	12.6	3.70	98	.265	.335	5	.128	-1	-1	-1	-0	-0.2
Yr	12	13	.480	46	22	5	3	2	175^2	179	12	84	106	13.5	3.94	92	.268	.351	5	.102	-2	-6	-6	-1	-1.2
1984 StL-N	9	6	.600	57	1	0	0	3	119	105	6	49	66	11.6	3.55	98	.239	.315	6	.240	2	0	-1	1	0.1
1985 StL-N	1	4	.200	23	1	0	0	2	29	32	3	17	10	15.5	5.59	63	.283	.382	0	.000	-0	-6	-7	0	-1.2
NY-A	1	0	1.000	17	0	0	0	1	29^1	26	1	13	16	12.0	2.76	145	.234	.315	0	—	0	5	4	-0	0.1
1986 Chi-A	7	2	.778	22	17	2	2	0	113	101	8	38	57	11.2	3.82	113	.244	.311	0	—	-0	4	6	-0	0.3
1987 Chi-A	0	7	.000	15	10	0	0	0	49^2	74	6	26	26	18.5	7.07	65	.365	.442	0	—	0	-14	-14	-0	-1.6
NY-A	0	1	.000	8	1	0	0	0	24^2	23	2	10	16	12.0	3.65	120	.242	.314	0	—	0	2	2	-0	0.1
Yr	0	8	.000	23	11	0	0	0	74^1	97	8	36	42	16.1	5.93	76	.321	.393	0	—	0	-12	-12	-1	-1.5
1988 NY-A	5	3	.625	41	2	0	1	0	117^1	121	14	37	61	12.3	3.84	103	.268	.326	0	—	0	2	1	-2	-0.1
1989 Cle-A	0	1	.000	3	0	0	0	0	3	8	1	0	0	24.0	15.00	26	.500	.500	0	—	0	-4	-4	0	-1.0
Total 11	58	70	.453	434	59	7	6	75	988^1	985	73	417	611	12.8	3.88	97	.264	.339	15	.130	-1	-9	-11	-3	-2.9
● **BOB ALLEN** Allen, Robert Earl "Thin Man" b: 7/2/14, Smithville, Tenn. BR/TR, 6'1", 165 lbs. Deb: 9/19/37																									
1937 Phi-N	0	1	.000	3	1	0	0	0	12	18	2	8	8	19.5	6.75	64	.321	.406	1	.333	0	-4	-3	-1	-0.3
● **BOB ALLEN** Allen, Robert Gray b: 10/23/37, Tatum, Tex. BL/TL, 6'2", 185 lbs. Deb: 4/14/61																									
1961 Cle-A	3	2	.600	48	0	0	0	3	81^2	96	7	40	42	15.1	3.75	105	.294	.373	2	.167	0	3	2	-0	0.1
1962 Cle-A	1	1	.500	30	0	0	0	4	30^2	29	5	25	23	15.8	5.87	66	.250	.383	0	.000	-1	-6	-7	0	-0.6
1963 Cle-A	1	2	.333	43	0	0	0	2	56	58	5	29	51	14.1	4.66	78	.266	.355	1	.200	-0	-6	-6	0	-0.4
1966 Cle-A	2	2	.500	36	0	0	0	5	51^1	56	2	13	33	12.4	4.21	82	.273	.323	1	.111	-0	-4	-4	1	-0.4
1967 Cle-A	0	5	.000	47	0	0	0	5	54^1	49	4	25	50	12.4	2.98	110	.243	.329	0	—	0	2	2	1	0.3
Total 5	7	12	.368	204	0	0	0	19	274	288	23	132	199	14.0	4.11	89	.270	.353	4	.129	-1	-13	-14	2	-1.0
● **DANA ALLISON** Allison, Dana Eric b: 8/14/66, Front Royal, Va. BR/TL, 6'3", 215 lbs. Deb: 4/9/91																									
1991 Oak-A	1	1	.500	11	0	0	0	0	11	16	0	5	4	17.2	7.36	52	.381	.447	0	—	0	-4	-4	-0	-0.6
● **DOUG ALLISON** Allison, Douglas L. b: 7/1845, Philadelphia, Pa. d: 12/19/16, Washington, D.C. BR/TR, 5'10.5", 160 lbs. Deb: 5/5/1871 F♦																									
1878 Pro-N	0	0	—	1	0	0	0	0	5	11	0	1	0	21.6	1.80	123	.440	.462	22	.289	0	0	0	-0	0.0
● **MACK ALLISON** Allison, Mack Pendleton b: 1/23/1887, Owensboro, Ky. d: 3/13/64, Mount Vernon, Mo. BR/TR, 6'1", 185 lbs. Deb: 9/13/11																									
1911 StL-A	2	1	.667	3	3	3	0	0	26^1	24	0	5	2	10.6	2.05	165	.253	.304	2	.200	-0	4	4	-1	0.3
1912 StL-A	6	17	.261	31	20	11	1	1	169	171	4	49	43	12.0	3.62	92	.269	.327	7	.135	-3	-6	-6	-1	-1.1
1913 StL-A	1	3	.250	11	4	3	0	0	51^1	52	0	13	12	11.9	2.28	129	.287	.345	0	.000	-2	4	4	-2	-0.1
Total 3	9	21	.300	45	27	17	1	1	246^2	247	4	67	57	11.9	3.17	102	.271	.328	9	.118	-6	2	2	-4	-0.9
● **CARLOS ALMANZAR** Almanzar, Carlos Manuel (Giron) b: 11/6/73, Santiago, D.R. BR/TR, 6'2", 166 lbs. Deb: 9/4/97																									
1997 Tor-A	0	1	.000	4	0	0	0	0	3^1	1	1	1	4	5.4	2.70	170	.091	.167	0	—	0	1	1	-0	0.1
1998 Tor-A	2	2	.500	25	0	0	0	0	28^2	34	4	8	20	13.5	5.34	87	.286	.336	0	—	0	-2	-2	-0	-0.3
Total 2	2	3	.400	29	0	0	0	0	32	35	5	9	24	12.7	5.06	92	.269	.321	0	—	0	-2	-2	-0	-0.2
● **LUIS ALOMA** Aloma, Luis (Barba) "Witto" b: 7/23/23, Havana, Cuba d: 4/7/97, Park Ridge, Ill. BR/TR, 6'2", 195 lbs. Deb: 4/19/50																									
1950 Chi-A	7	2	.778	42	0	0	0	4	87^2	77	6	53	49	13.4	3.80	118	.234	.342	1	.067	-2	8	7	-0	0.4
1951 Chi-A	6	0	1.000	25	1	1	1	3	69^1	52	3	24	25	10.1	1.82	222	.215	.291	7	.350	2	18	17	-2	1.5
1952 Chi-A	3	1	.750	25	0	0	0	6	40	42	5	11	18	12.1	4.27	85	.278	.331	0	.000	-1	-3	-3	-0	-0.5
1953 Chi-A	2	0	1.000	24	0	0	0	2	38^1	41	7	23	23	15.0	4.70	86	.283	.381	0	.000	-1	-3	-3	0	-0.2
Total 4	18	3	.857	116	1	1	1	15	235^1	212	21	111	115	12.5	3.44	120	.245	.333	8	.167	-2	20	18	-2	1.2
● **MATTY ALOU** Alou, Mateo Rojas (b: Mateo Rojas (Alou)) b: 12/22/38, Haina, D.R. BL/TL, 5'9", 160 lbs. Deb: 9/26/60 F♦																									
1965 SF-N	0	0	—	1	0	0	0	0	2	3	0	1	3	18.0	0.00	—	.333	.400	75	.231	0	1	1	-0	0.0
● **GARVIN ALSTON** Alston, Garvin James b: 12/8/71, Mt.Vernon, N.Y. BR/TR, 6'2", 185 lbs. Deb: 6/6/96																									
1996 Col-N	1	0	1.000	6	0	0	0	0	6	9	1	3	5	19.5	9.00	58	.375	.464	0	.000	-0	-3	-3	0	-0.4
● **PORFI ALTAMIRANO** Altamirano, Porfirio (Ramirez) b: 5/17/52, Darillo, Nic. BR/TR, 6', 175 lbs. Deb: 5/9/82																									
1982 Phi-N	5	1	.833	29	0	0	0	2	39	41	2	14	26	12.9	4.15	88	.281	.348	1	.250	0	-2	-2	0	-0.3
1983 Phi-N	2	3	.400	31	0	0	0	0	41^1	38	9	15	24	12.0	3.70	96	.255	.331	0	.000	-0	-0	-1	0	-0.1
1984 Chi-N	0	0	—	5	0	0	0	0	11^1	8	2	1	7	7.1	4.76	82	.195	.214	0	.000	-0	-1	-1	0	0.0
Total 3	7	4	.636	65	0	0	0	2	91^2	87	13	30	57	11.8	4.03	91	.259	.325	1	.125	-0	-4	-4	1	-0.4
● **ERNIE ALTEN** Alten, Ernest Matthias "Lefty" b: 12/1/1894, Avon, Ohio d: 9/9/81, Napa, Cal. BL/TL, 6', 175 lbs. Deb: 4/17/20																									
1920 Det-A	0	1	.000	14	1	0	0	0	23	40	2	9	4	19.6	9.00	41	.392	.446	0	.000	-1	-13	-13	0	-0.5
● **NICK ALTROCK** Altrock, Nicholas b: 9/15/1876, Cincinnati, Ohio d: 1/20/65, Washington, D.C. BB/TL, 5'10", 197 lbs. Deb: 7/14/1898 C♦																									
1898 Lou-N	3	3	.500	11	7	6	0	0	70	89	2	21	13	14.5	4.50	79	.307	.360	7	.241	0	-7	-7	2	-0.3
1902 Bos-A	0	2	.000	3	2	1	0	1	18	19	0	7	5	13.5	2.00	179	.271	.346	0	.000	-1	3	3	1	0.3
1903 Bos-A	0	1	.000	1	1	1	0	0	8	13	0	4	3	19.1	9.00	34	.361	.425	2	.667	1	-5	-5	1	-0.3
Chi-A	4	3	.571	12	8	6	1	0	71	59	3	19	19	10.3	2.15	130	.226	.286	9	.300	2	6	5	3	1.1
Yr	4	4	.500	13	9	7	1	0	79	72	3	23	22	11.2	2.85	99	.242	.303	11	.333	4	1	-0	4	0.8
1904 Chi-A	19	14	.576	38	36	31	6	1	307	274	2	48	87	9.5	2.96	83	.240	.272	22	.198	1	-12	-17	4	-1.3
1905 Chi-A	23	12	.657	38	34	31	3	0	315^2	274	3	63	97	9.7	1.88	131	.236	.276	14	.125	-3	27	21	8	2.8
1906 *Chi-A	20	13	.606	38	30	25	4	0	287^2	269	0	42	99	9.8	2.06	123	.250	.281	16	.160	-1	20	15	4	2.1
1907 Chi-A	7	13	.350	30	21	15	1	2	213^2	210	3	31	61	10.2	2.57	93	.259	.288	13	.181	1	-1	-4	5	0.2
1908 Chi-A	5	7	.417	23	13	8	1	2	136	127	2	18	21	9.7	2.71	85	.248	.276	10	.204	1	-5	-6	5	0.1
1909 Chi-A	0	1	.000	1	1	1	0	0	9	16	0	1	2	17.0	5.00	47	.485	.500	0	.000	-0	-3	-3	0	-0.3
Was-A	1	3	.250	9	5	2	0	0	38	55	0	5	9	14.4	5.45	45	.333	.357	1	.053	-1	-13	-13	0	-1.3
Yr	1	4	.200	10	6	3	0	0	47	71	0	6	11	14.9	5.36	45	.359	.380	1	.045	-1	-15	-15	1	-1.6
1912 Was-A	0	1	.000	1	0	0	0	0	1	1	0	2	0	27.0	18.00	19	.200	.429	0	.000	-0	-2	-2	-0	-0.9
1913 Was-A	0	0	—	4	0	0	0	0	9	7	0	4	2	12.0	5.00	59	.184	.279	0	.000	-0	-2	-2	0	0.0
1914 Was-A	0	0	—	1	0	0	0	0	1	3	0	0	0	27.0	0.00	—	.750	.750	0	—	0	0	0	-0	0.0
1915 Was-A	0	0	—	1	0	0	0	1	3	7	0	1	2	24.0	9.00	33	.438	.471	0	.000	-0	-2	-2	-0	-0.2
1918 Was-A	1	2	.333	5	3	1	0	0	24	24	1	6	5	11.6	3.00	91	.279	.333	1	.125	0	-1	-1	0	0.0
1919 Was-A	0	0	—	1	0	0	0	0	0	4	0	0	0	—	∞	—	1.000	1.000	0	—	0	-4	-4	0	-0.3
1924 Was-A	0	0	—	1	0	0	0	0	2	4	0	0	0	18.0	0.00	—	.500	.500	1	1.000	1	1	1	0	0.1
Total 16	83	75	.525	218	161	128	16	7	1514	1455	16	272	425	10.4	2.67	95	.254	.291	97	.176	1	2	-21	34	1.8
● **TAVO ALVAREZ** Alvarez, Cesar Octavio b: 11/25/71, Ciudad Obregon, Mexico BR/TR, 6'3", 245 lbs. Deb: 8/21/95																									
1995 Mon-N	1	5	.167	8	8	0	0	0	37^1	46	2	14	17	15.2	6.75	64	.297	.366	0	.000	-1	-11	-10	-0	-1.5
1996 Mon-N	2	1	.667	11	5	0	0	0	21	19	0	12	9	13.7	3.00	144	.235	.340	2	.500	1	3	3	0	0.5
Total 2	3	6	.333	19	13	0	0	0	58^1	65	2	26	26	14.7	5.40	80	.275	.357	2	.125	-1	-8	-7	-0	-1.0

YEAR	TM/L	W	L	PCT	G	GS	CG	SH	SV	IP	H	HR	BB	SO	RAT	ERA	ERA+	OAV	OOB	BH	AVG	PB	PR	/A	PD	TPI
● **JOSE ALVAREZ**	Alvarez, Jose Lino b: 4/12/56, Tampa, Fla. BR/TR, 5'10", 170 lbs. Deb: 10/1/81																									
1981	Atl-N	0	0	—	1	0	0	0	0	2	0	0	0	2	0.0	0.00	—	.000	.000	0	—	0	1	1	-0	0.0
1982	Atl-N	0	0	—	7	0	0	0	0	7^2	8	1	2	6	11.7	4.70	79	.308	.357	0	—	0	-1	-1	0	0.0
1988	Atl-N	5	6	.455	60	0	0	0	3	102^1	88	7	53	81	12.9	2.99	123	.240	.346	3	.375	1	5	8	1	1.1
1989	Atl-N	3	3	.500	30	0	0	0	2	50^1	44	4	24	45	12.3	2.86	128	.237	.327	0	.000	-0	4	4	1	0.6
Total	4	8	9	.471	98	0	0	0	5	162^1	140	12	79	134	12.5	2.99	123	.240	.337	3	.273	1	9	12	2	1.7
● **WILSON ALVAREZ**	Alvarez, Wilson Eduardo (Fuenmayor) b: 3/24/70, Maracaibo, Venez. BL/TL, 6'1", 235 lbs. Deb: 7/24/89																									
1989	Tex-A	0	1	.000	1	1	0	0	0	0	3	2	2	0	—	∞	—	1.000	1.000	0	—	0	-3	-3	0	-0.3
1991	Chi-A	3	2	.600	10	9	2	1	0	56^1	47	9	29	32	12.1	3.51	113	.230	.326	0	—	0	4	3	-0	0.3
1992	Chi-A	5	3	.625	34	9	0	0	1	100^1	103	12	65	66	15.4	5.20	74	.272	.384	0	—	0	-14	-15	-0	-1.1
1993	*Chi-A	15	8	.652	31	31	1	1	0	207^2	168	14	122	155	12.9	2.95	142	.230	.346	0	—	0	32	28	-0	2.9
1994	Chi-A★	12	8	.600	24	24	2	1	0	161^2	147	16	62	108	11.6	3.45	135	.241	.311	0	—	0	24	22	-2	2.2
1995	Chi-A	8	11	.421	29	29	3	0	0	175	171	21	93	118	13.7	4.32	103	.258	.351	0	—	0	8	3	1	0.5
1996	Chi-A	15	10	.600	35	35	0	0	0	217^1	216	21	97	181	13.1	4.22	112	.258	.338	0	—	0	19	13	0	1.5
1997	Chi-A	9	8	.529	22	22	2	1	0	145^2	126	9	55	110	11.4	3.03	145	.232	.306	0	.000	-0	25	22	-1	2.2
	*SF-N	4	3	.571	11	11	0	0	0	66^1	54	9	36	69	12.3	4.48	92	.224	.327	3	.130	-0	-2	-3	-1	-0.3
1998	TB-A	6	14	.300	25	25	0	0	0	142^2	130	18	68	107	13.1	4.73	104	.239	.333	0	—	0	-1	3	-3	-0.1
Total	9	77	68	.531	222	196	10	4	1	1273	1165	131	629	946	12.9	3.93	113	.245	.337	3	.115	-0	90	72	-5	7.8
● **RED AMES**	Ames, Leon Kessling b: 8/2/1882, Warren, Ohio d: 10/8/36, Warren, Ohio BB/TR, 5'10.5", 185 lbs. Deb: 9/14/03																									
1903	NY-N	2	0	1.000	2	2	2	1	0	14	5	0	8	14	8.4	1.29	260	.114	.250	0	.000	-1	3	3	-1	0.3
1904	NY-N	4	6	.400	16	13	11	1	3	115	94	2	38	93	10.6	2.27	120	.222	.291	5	.125	-1	6	6	-0	0.3
1905	*NY-N	22	8	.733	34	31	21	2	0	262^2	220	2	105	198	11.2	2.74	107	.230	.308	14	.144	-1	8	6	1	0.5
1906	NY-N	12	10	.545	31	25	15	1	1	203^1	166	1	93	156	11.6	2.66	98	.223	.312	4	.066	-3	-0	-1	3	-0.1
1907	NY-N	10	12	.455	39	26	17	2	1	233^1	184	4	108	146	11.6	2.16	115	.219	.315	12	.174	2	8	8	3	1.3
1908	NY-N	7	4	.636	18	15	5	0	1	114^1	96	0	27	81	9.8	1.81	133	.232	.281	7	.194	-0	7	8	1	0.9
1909	NY-N	15	10	.600	34	26	20	2	1	244	217	2	81	156	11.1	2.69	95	.241	.306	6	.074	-5	-3	-4	7	-0.2
1910	NY-N	12	11	.522	33	23	13	3	0	190^1	161	3	63	94	10.9	2.22	133	.237	.308	11	.177	-1	17	16	4	2.1
1911	*NY-N	11	10	.524	34	23	13	1	2	205	170	0	54	118	10.0	2.68	126	.223	.277	6	.094	-3	16	16	3	1.4
1912	*NY-N	11	5	.688	33	22	9	2	2	179	194	3	35	83	11.7	2.46	137	.281	.320	13	.224	1	19	18	2	1.8
1913	NY-N	2	1	.667	8	5	2	0	1	41^2	35	0	8	30	9.5	2.16	144	.241	.286	2	.154	-1	5	4	2	0.5
	Cin-N	11	13	.458	31	24	12	1	2	187^1	185	7	70	80	12.5	2.88	113	.265	.336	6	.102	-4	7	8	0	0.5
	Yr	13	14	.481	39	29	14	1	3	229	220	7	78	110	11.9	2.75	117	.261	.327	8	.111	-5	12	12	2	1.0
1914	Cin-N	15	23	.395	47	37	18	4	**6**	297	274	8	94	128	11.3	2.64	111	.248	.311	12	.128	-4	5	10	4	1.3
1915	Cin-N	2	4	.333	17	7	4	1	1	68	82	2	24	26	14.0	4.50	64	.311	.368	1	.050	-1	-13	-12	1	-1.1
	StL-N	9	3	.750	15	14	8	2	1	113^1	93	1	32	48	9.9	2.46	113	.226	.282	4	.114	-2	4	4	2	0.4
	Yr	11	7	.611	32	21	12	3	2	181^1	175	3	56	74	11.5	3.23	87	.259	.316	5	.091	-3	-10	-8	2	-0.7
1916	StL-N	11	16	.407	45	25	10	2	**8**	228	225	3	57	98	11.3	2.64	100	.263	.313	12	.176	-0	-1	0	-2	-0.2
1917	StL-N	15	10	.600	43	19	10	2	3	209	189	2	57	62	10.7	2.71	99	.249	.304	12	.188	2	-0	-0	4	0.7
1918	StL-N	9	14	.391	27	25	17	0	1	206^2	192	1	52	68	10.8	2.31	117	.252	.304	10	.156	-1	10	9	-1	0.9
1919	StL-N	3	5	.375	23	6	1	0	1	70	88	1	25	19	14.7	4.89	57	.314	.373	4	.222	-0	-15	-16	-2	-2.0
	Phi-N	0	2	.000	3	2	1	0	1	16	26	0	3	4	16.3	6.19	52	.400	.426	2	.400	1	-6	-5	0	-0.6
	Yr	3	7	.300	26	8	2	0	2	86	114	1	28	23	14.9	5.13	56	.329	.380	6	.261	1	-21	-22	-2	-2.6
Total	17	183	167	.523	533	370	209	27	36	3198	2896	42	1034	1702	11.2	2.63	108	.245	.310	143	.141	-21	77	77	32	8.7
● **DOC AMOLE**	Amole, Morris George b: 7/5/1878, Coatesville, Pa. d: 3/7/12, Wilmington, Del. BR/TL, 5'9", 165 lbs. Deb: 8/19/1897																									
1897	Bal-N	4	4	.500	11	7	6	0	0	70	67	0	17	19	11.6	2.57	162	.250	.309	3	.107	-3	14	12	0	0.9
1898	Was-N	0	6	.000	7	5	4	0	0	49^1	83	0	22	11	20.3	7.84	47	.369	.439	2	.100	-2	-23	-23	1	-2.1
Total	2	4	10	.286	18	12	10	0	0	119^1	150	0	39	30	15.2	4.75	84	.304	.369	5	.104	-4	-10	-10	1	-1.2
● **VICENTE AMOR**	Amor, Vicente (Alvarez) b: 8/8/32, Havana, Cuba BR/TR, 6'3", 182 lbs. Deb: 4/16/55																									
1955	Chi-N	0	1	.000	4	0	0	0	0	6	11	0	3	3	21.0	4.50	91	.407	.467	0	—	0	-0	-0	1	0.0
1957	Cin-N	1	2	.333	9	4	1	0	0	27^1	39	2	10	9	16.8	5.93	69	.345	.408	1	.167	-0	-6	-6	-0	-0.6
Total	2	1	3	.250	13	4	1	0	0	33^1	50	2	13	12	17.6	5.67	72	.357	.419	1	.167	-0	-7	-6	0	-0.6
● **WALTER ANCKER**	Ancker, Walter b: 4/10/1894, New York, N.Y. d: 2/13/54, Englewood, N.J. BR/TR, 6'1", 190 lbs. Deb: 9/3/15																									
1915	Phi-A	0	0	—	4	1	0	0	0	17^2	19	1	17	4	19.9	3.57	82	.279	.443	0	.000	-1	-1	-1	0	-0.1
● **LARRY ANDERSEN**	Andersen, Larry Eugene b: 5/6/53, Portland, Ore. BR/TR, 6'3", 205 lbs. Deb: 9/5/75																									
1975	Cle-A	0	0	—	3	0	0	0	0	5^2	4	0	2	4	9.5	4.76	79	.200	.273	0	—	0	-1	-1	0	0.0
1977	Cle-A	0	1	.000	11	0	0	0	0	14^1	10	1	9	8	11.9	3.14	126	.200	.322	0	—	0	1	1	1	0.2
1979	Cle-A	0	0	—	8	0	0	0	0	16^2	25	3	4	7	15.7	7.56	56	.357	.392	0	—	0	-6	-6	0	0.0
1981	Sea-A	3	3	.500	41	0	0	0	5	67^2	57	4	18	40	10.2	2.66	145	.228	.285	0	—	0	7	9	-0	0.7
1982	Sea-A	0	0	—	40	1	0	0	1	79^2	100	16	23	32	14.3	5.99	71	.311	.364	0	—	0	-17	-15	1	-0.1
1983	*Phi-N	1	0	1.000	17	0	0	0	0	26^1	19	0	9	14	9.6	2.39	149	.200	.269	0	.000	-0	4	3	0	0.1
1984	Phi-N	3	7	.300	64	0	0	0	4	90^2	85	5	25	54	10.9	2.38	152	.248	.299	0	.000	-0	12	13	0	1.4
1985	Phi-N	3	3	.500	57	0	0	0	3	73	78	5	26	50	13.2	4.32	85	.274	.341	0	.000	-0	-6	-5	2	-0.3
1986	Phi-N	0	0	—	10	0	0	0	0	12^2	19	0	3	9	15.6	4.26	90	.388	.423	0	—	0	-1	-1	0	0.0
	*Hou-N	2	1	.667	38	0	0	0	1	64^2	64	2	23	33	12.2	2.78	129	.276	.344	0	.000	-1	7	6	0	0.2
	Yr	2	1	.667	48	0	0	0	1	77^1	83	2	26	42	12.8	3.03	120	.294	.356	0	.000	-1	6	5	0	0.2
1987	Hou-N	9	5	.643	67	0	0	0	5	101^2	95	7	41	94	12.2	3.45	113	.246	.322	1	.167	0	7	5	-0	0.7
1988	Hou-N	2	4	.333	53	0	0	0	5	82^2	82	3	20	66	11.2	2.94	113	.254	.299	2	.333	1	5	3	-0	0.3
1989	Hou-N	4	4	.500	60	0	0	0	3	87^2	63	2	24	85	8.9	1.54	220	.198	.254	1	.333	0	**19**	18	1	1.8
1990	Hou-N	5	2	.714	50	0	0	0	6	73^2	61	2	24	68	10.5	1.95	190	.229	.296	0	.000	-0	15	14	1	1.6
	*Bos-A	0	0	—	15	0	0	0	1	22	18	0	3	25	9.0	1.23	332	.220	.256	0	—	0	7	7	-1	-0.2
1991	SD-N	3	4	.429	38	0	0	0	13	47	39	0	13	40	10.0	2.30	165	.231	.286	0	.000	-0	7	8	0	1.5
1992	SD-N	1	1	.500	34	0	0	0	2	35	26	2	8	35	9.0	3.34	107	.202	.254	0	.000	0	1	1	0	0.1
1993	*Phi-N	3	2	.600	64	0	0	0	0	61^2	54	4	21	67	11.1	2.92	136	.233	.299	1	1.000	0	8	7	-1	0.5
1994	Phi-N	1	2	.333	29	0	0	0	0	32^2	33	2	15	27	13.2	4.41	97	.256	.333	0	—	0	-1	-0	-0	0.0
Total	17	40	39	.506	699	1	0	0	49	995^1	932	58	311	758	11.4	3.15	119	.249	.309	5	.132	-0	68	68	5	8.5
● **ALLAN ANDERSON**	Anderson, Allan Lee b: 1/7/64, Lancaster, Ohio BL/TL, 6', 186 lbs. Deb: 6/11/86																									
1986	Min-A	3	6	.333	21	10	1	0	0	84^1	106	11	30	51	14.6	5.55	78	.316	.374	0	—	0	-13	-12	0	-1.0
1987	Min-A	1	0	1.000	4	2	0	0	0	12^1	20	3	10	3	21.9	10.95	42	.392	.492	0	—	0	-9	-9	-0	-0.7
1988	Min-A	16	9	.640	30	30	3	1	0	202^1	199	14	37	83	10.8	**2.45**	**166**	.261	.301	0	—	0	34	36	1	4.5
1989	Min-A	17	10	.630	33	33	4	1	0	196^2	214	15	53	69	12.5	3.80	109	.275	.327	0	.000	-0	2	7	-1	0.9
1990	Min-A	7	18	.280	31	31	5	1	0	188^2	214	20	39	82	12.3	4.53	92	.289	.329	0	—	0	-13	-8	2	-1.1
1991	Min-A	5	11	.313	29	22	2	0	0	134^1	148	24	42	51	13.1	4.96	86	.281	.340	0	—	0	-13	-10	-0	-1.1
Total	6	49	54	.476	148	128	15	3	0	818^2	901	87	211	339	12.5	4.11	101	.282	.331	0	.000	-0	-12	5	2	1.5
● **RED ANDERSON**	Anderson, Arnold Revola b: 6/19/12, Lawton, Iowa d: 8/7/72, Sioux City, Iowa BR/TR, 6'3", 210 lbs. Deb: 9/19/37																									
1937	Was-A	0	1	.000	2	1	0	0	0	10^2	11	0	11	3	19.4	6.75	66	.282	.451	0	.000	-0	-3	-3	0	-0.2
1940	Was-A	1	1	.500	2	2	2	0	0	14	12	0	5	3	10.9	3.86	108	.245	.315	3	.600	1	1	0	0	0.2
1941	Was-A	4	6	.400	32	6	1	0	0	112	127	7	53	34	14.7	4.18	97	.296	.377	8	.258	2	-0	-2	-1	0.0
Total	3	5	8	.385	36	9	3	0	0	136^2	150	7	69	40	14.7	4.35	94	.290	.378	11	.282	3	-2	-4	-1	0.0
● **BRIAN ANDERSON**	Anderson, Brian James b: 4/26/72, Portsmouth, Va. BL/TL, 6'1", 190 lbs. Deb: 9/10/93																									
1993	Cal-A	0	0	—	4	1	0	0	0	11^1	11	1	2	4	10.3	3.97	113	.256	.289	0	—	0	0	1	-0	-0.3
1994	Cal-A	7	5	.583	18	18	0	0	0	101^2	120	13	27	47	13.5	5.22	94	.300	.352	0	—	0	-5	-4	-1	-0.6
1995	Cal-A	6	8	.429	18	17	1	0	0	99^2	110	24	30	45	12.9	5.87	80	.282	.338	0	—	0	-13	-13	-0	-1.4

YEAR	TM/L	W	L	PCT	G	GS	CG	SH	SV	IP	H	HR	BB	SO	RAT	ERA	ERA+	OAV	OOB	BH	AVG	PB	PR	/A	PD	TPI
1996	Cle-A	3	1	.750	10	9	0	0	0	51^{1}	58	9	14	21	12.6	4.91	100	.296	.343	0	—	0	0	-0	1	0.1
1997	*Cle-A	4	2	.667	8	8	0	0	0	48	55	7	11	22	12.4	4.69	100	.301	.340	0	—	0	-1	-0	1	-0.2
1998	Ari-N	12	13	.480	32	32	2	1	0	208	221	39	24	95	10.8	4.33	100	.274	.299	7	.106	-3	-2	-0	3	0.0
Total	6	32	29	.525	90	85	3	1	0	520	575	93	108	234	12.0	4.88	94	.285	.325	7	.106	-3	-20	-17	2	-2.4
● DAVE ANDERSON	Anderson, David S. b: 10/10/1868, Chester, Pa. d: 3/22/1897, Chester, Pa. TL , Deb: 8/24/1889																									
1889	Phi-N	0	1	.000	5	2	1	0	0	23	30	2	14	8	17.2	7.43	59	.306	.393	2	.182	-0	-9	-8	0	-0.3
1890	Phi-N	1	1	.500	3	2	1	0	0	19^{1}	31	0	11	7	20.0	7.45	49	.352	.430	1	.111	-1	-8	-8	0	-0.7
	Pit-N	2	11	.154	13	13	13	0	0	108	116	2	49	41	14.3	4.67	71	.266	.350	3	.071	-5	-13	-16	4	-1.6
	Yr	3	12	.200	16	15	14	0	0	127^{1}	147	2	60	48	15.1	5.09	66	.280	.361	4	.078	-6	-21	-25	4	-2.3
Total	2	3	13	.188	21	17	15	0	0	150^{1}	177	4	74	56	15.5	5.45	64	.285	.368	6	.097	-6	-30	-33	4	-2.6
● JOHN ANDERSON	Anderson, John Charles b: 11/23/32, St.Paul, Minn. BR/TR, 6'1", 190 lbs. Deb: 8/17/58																									
1958	Phi-N	0	0	—	5	1	0	0	0	16	26	5	4	9	17.4	7.88	50	.361	.403	0	.000	-0	-7	-7	-0	0.0
1960	Bal-A	0	0	—	4	0	0	0	0	4^{2}	8	0	4	1	23.1	13.50	28	.444	.545	0	—	0	-5	-5	0	0.0
1962	StL-N	0	0	—	5	0	0	0	1	6^{1}	4	0	3	3	9.9	1.42	300	.182	.280	0	—	0	2	2	-0	0.0
	Hou-N	0	0	—	10	0	0	0	0	17^{2}	26	1	3	6	14.8	5.09	73	.338	.363	0	.000	-0	-2	-3	1	0.0
	Yr	0	0	—	15	0	0	0	1	24	30	1	6	9	13.5	4.13	94	.300	.340	0	.000	-0	-0	-1	0	0.0
Total	3	0	0	—	24	1	0	0	1	44^{2}	64	6	14	19	15.9	6.45	60	.339	.387	0	.000	-0	-12	-13	0	0.0
● FRED ANDERSON	Anderson, John Frederick b: 12/11/1885, Calahaln, N.C. d: 11/8/57, Winston-Salem, N.C. BR/TR, 6'2", 180 lbs. Deb: 9/25/09																									
1909	Bos-A	0	0	—	1	1	0	0	0	8	3	0	1	5	4.5	1.13	222	.115	.148	0	.000	-0	1	1	0	0.0
1913	Bos-A	0	6	.000	10	8	4	0	0	57^{1}	84	0	21	32	16.6	5.97	49	.350	.405	1	.050	-2	-19	-19	-0	-2.0
1914	Buf-F	13	15	.464	37	28	21	2	0	260^{1}	243	8	64	144	10.7	3.08	96	.249	.297	17	.189	-3	-6	-3	-1	-0.7
1915	Buf-F	19	13	.594	36	28	14	5	0	240	192	5	72	142	10.0	2.51	111	.222	.285	12	.150	-5	6	8	-1	0.4
1916	NY-N	9	13	.409	38	27	13	2	2	188	206	7	38	98	11.9	3.40	72	.277	.316	8	.138	-0	-16	-20	-2	-2.7
1917	*NY-N	8	8	.500	38	18	8	1	3	162	122	1	34	69	**8.8**	1.44	**177**	.209	**.255**	3	.071	-3	23	20	-1	1.7
1918	NY-N	4	2	.667	18	4	2	1	**3**	70^{2}	62	1	17	24	10.3	2.67	98	.246	.299	0	.000	-3	1	-0	3	0.0
Total	7	53	57	.482	178	114	62	11	8	986^{1}	912	22	247	514	10.7	2.86	95	.248	.298	41	.131	-16	-11	-15	-2	-3.3
● BUD ANDERSON	Anderson, Karl Adam b: 5/27/56, Westbury, N.Y. BR/TR, 6'3", 210 lbs. Deb: 6/11/82																									
1982	Cle-A	3	4	.429	25	5	1	0	0	80^{2}	84	4	30	44	12.8	3.35	122	.268	.334	0	—	0	7	7	-0	0.5
1983	Cle-A	1	6	.143	39	1	0	0	7	68^{1}	64	8	32	32	12.6	4.08	104	.255	.339	0	—	0	-0	1	-1	0.0
Total	2	4	10	.286	64	6	1	0	7	149	148	12	62	76	12.7	3.68	113	.262	.337	0	—	0	6	8	-1	0.5
● LARRY ANDERSON	Anderson, Lawrence Dennis b: 12/3/52, Maywood, Cal. BR/TR, 6'3", 190 lbs. Deb: 9/25/74																									
1974	Mil-A	0	0	—	2	0	0	0	0	2^{1}	2	0	1	3	11.6	0.00	—	.250	.333	0	—	0	1	1	0	0.0
1975	Mil-A	1	0	1.000	8	1	1	1	0	30^{1}	36	3	6	13	12.5	5.04	76	.298	.331	0	—	0	-4	-4	0	-0.1
1977	Chi-A	1	3	.250	6	0	0	0	0	8^{2}	10	1	15	7	26.0	9.35	44	.286	.500	0	—	0	-5	-5	-0	-1.8
Total	3	2	3	.400	16	1	1	1	0	41^{1}	48	4	22	23	15.2	5.66	68	.293	.376	0	—	0	-8	-8	0	-1.9
● MATT ANDERSON	Anderson, Matthew Jason b: 8/17/76, Louisville, Ky. BR/TR, 6'4", 200 lbs. Deb: 6/25/98																									
1998	Det-A	5	1	.833	42	0	0	0	0	44	38	3	31	44	14.5	3.27	144	.250	.384	0	—	0	7	7	0	0.8
● MIKE ANDERSON	Anderson, Michael Allen b: 6/22/51, Florence, S.C. BR/TR, 6'2", 200 lbs. Deb: 9/2/71 F♦																									
1979	Phi-N	0	0	—	1	0	0	0	0	1	2	0	0	2	18.0	0.00	—	.400	.400	18	.231	0	0	0	0	0.0
● MIKE ANDERSON	Anderson, Michael James b: 7/30/66, Austin, Tex. BR/TR, 6'3", 200 lbs. Deb: 9/7/93																									
1993	Cin-N	0	0	—	3	0	0	0	0	5^{1}	12	3	3	4	25.3	18.56	22	.444	.500	0	.000	-0	-9	-9	0	0.0
● CRAIG ANDERSON	Anderson, Norman Craig b: 7/1/38, Washington, D.C. BR/TR, 6'2", 205 lbs. Deb: 6/23/61																									
1961	StL-N	4	3	.571	25	0	0	0	1	38^{2}	38	3	12	21	11.9	3.26	135	.255	.315	3	.333	1	3	5	0	0.9
1962	NY-N	3	17	.150	50	14	2	0	4	131^{1}	150	18	63	62	14.9	5.35	78	.278	.359	3	.094	-2	-20	-17	3	-2.3
1963	NY-N	0	2	.000	3	2	0	0	0	9^{1}	17	0	3	6	19.3	8.68	40	.362	.400	1	.333	0	-6	-5	0	-0.9
1964	NY-N	0	1	.000	4	1	0	0	0	13	21	0	3	5	16.6	5.54	65	.382	.414	0	.000	-0	-3	-3	0	-0.2
Total	4	7	23	.233	82	17	2	0	5	192^{1}	226	21	81	94	14.6	5.10	81	.286	.357	7	.149	-1	-26	-20	3	-2.5
● RICK ANDERSON	Anderson, Richard Arlen b: 11/29/56, Everett, Wash. BR/TR, 6', 175 lbs. Deb: 6/9/86																									
1986	NY-N	2	1	.667	15	5	0	0	1	49^{2}	45	3	11	21	10.1	2.72	130	.245	.287	1	.091	-1	6	5	-1	0.2
1987	KC-A	0	2	.000	6	2	0	0	0	13	26	3	9	12	25.6	13.85	33	.394	.481	0	—	0	-14	-13	0	-1.6
1988	KC-A	2	1	.667	7	3	0	0	0	34	41	3	9	9	13.5	4.24	94	.308	.357	0	—	0	-1	-1	-1	-0.2
Total	3	4	4	.500	28	10	0	0	1	96^{2}	112	9	29	42	13.4	4.75	81	.292	.347	1	.091	-1	-9	-10	-1	-1.6
● RICK ANDERSON	Anderson, Richard Lee b: 12/25/53, Inglewood, Cal. d: 6/23/89, Wilmington, Cal. BR/TR, 6'2", 210 lbs. Deb: 9/18/79																									
1979	NY-A	0	0	—	1	0	0	0	0	2^{1}	1	0	4	0	19.3	3.86	106	.167	.500	0	—	0	0	0	1	0.1
1980	Sea-A	0	0	—	5	2	0	0	0	9^{2}	8	1	10	7	16.8	3.72	111	.229	.400	0	—	0	0	0	-0	-0.1
Total	2	0	0	—	6	2	0	0	0	12	9	1	14	7	17.3	3.75	110	.220	.418	0	—	0	0	0	0	0.0
● BOB ANDERSON	Anderson, Robert Carl b: 9/29/35, E.Chicago, Ind. BR/TR, 6'4.5", 210 lbs. Deb: 7/31/57																									
1957	Chi-N	0	1	.000	8	0	0	0	0	16^{1}	20	2	8	7	16.0	7.71	50	.317	.403	0	.000	-1	-7	-7	0	-0.4
1958	Chi-N	3	3	.500	17	8	2	0	0	65^{2}	61	3	29	51	12.5	3.97	99	.255	.338	2	.118	-1	-0	-0	0	-0.1
1959	Chi-N	12	13	.480	37	36	7	1	0	235^{1}	245	21	77	113	12.5	4.13	96	.272	.333	6	.075	-4	-5	-5	1	-0.8
1960	Chi-N	9	11	.450	38	30	5	0	1	203^{2}	201	26	68	115	12.2	4.11	92	.255	.320	12	.169	0	-8	-8	1	-0.6
1961	Chi-N	7	10	.412	57	12	1	0	8	152	162	14	56	96	13.0	4.26	98	.275	.340	6	.143	0	-4	-1	4	0.2
1962	Chi-N	2	7	.222	57	4	0	0	4	107^{2}	111	9	60	82	14.7	5.02	83	.266	.364	3	.130	0	-13	-10	-0	-0.9
1963	Det-A	3	1	.750	32	3	0	0	0	60	58	5	21	38	12.8	3.30	113	.258	.337	4	.444	2	2	3	-0	0.3
Total	7	36	46	.439	246	93	15	1	13	840^{2}	858	80	319	502	12.9	4.26	93	.266	.337	33	.134	-4	-34	-29	5	-2.3
● SCOTT ANDERSON	Anderson, Scott Richard b: 8/1/62, Corvallis, Ore. BR/TR, 6'6", 190 lbs. Deb: 4/8/87																									
1987	Tex-A	0	1	.000	8	0	0	0	0	11^{1}	17	0	8	6	20.6	9.53	47	.347	.448	0	—	0	-6	-6	1	-0.4
1990	Mon-N	0	1	.000	4	3	0	0	0	18	12	1	5	16	8.5	3.00	122	.188	.246	0	.000	-0	2	1	-0	0.0
1995	KC-A	1	0	1.000	6	4	0	0	0	25^{1}	29	3	8	6	13.5	5.33	90	.290	.349	0	—	0	-2	-2	-0	-0.1
Total	3	1	2	.333	18	7	0	0	0	54^{2}	58	4	21	28	13.3	5.43	80	.272	.343	0	.000	-0	-7	-7	0	-0.5
● VARNEY ANDERSON	Anderson, Varney Samuel "Varn" b: 6/18/1866, Geneva, Ill. d: 11/5/41, Rockford, Ill. BR/TR, 5'10", 165 lbs. Deb: 8/1/1889																									
1889	Ind-N	0	1	.000	2	1	1	0	0	12	13	0	9	3	18.8	4.50	93	.265	.410	0	.000	-1	-1	-0	0	-0.1
1894	Was-N	0	2	.000	2	2	2	0	0	14	15	0	6	3	14.1	7.07	74	.273	.355	3	.429	0	-3	-3	-0	-0.2
1895	Was-N	9	16	.360	29	25	18	0	0	204^{2}	288	13	97	35	17.4	5.89	81	.327	.400	28	.289	3	-25	-25	1	-1.8
1896	Was-N	0	1	.000	2	2	1	0	0	9	23	0	3	0	26.0	13.00	34	.469	.500	3	.600	1	-9	-9	-1	-0.6
Total	4	9	20	.310	35	30	22	0	0	239^{2}	339	13	115	41	17.6	6.16	78	.328	.402	34	.298	4	-37	-37	0	-2.7
● WALTER ANDERSON	Anderson, Walter Carl "Lefty" b: 9/25/1897, Grand Rapids, Mich. d: 1/6/90, Battle Creek, Mich. BL/TL, 6'2", 160 lbs. Deb: 5/14/17																									
1917	Phi-A	0	0	—	14	2	0	0	0	38^{2}	32	0	21	10	12.6	3.03	91	.246	.355	3	.429	1	-2	-1	-0	0.1
1919	Phi-A	1	0	1.000	3	0	0	0	0	14	13	0	8	10	14.1	3.86	89	.245	.355	0	.000	-1	-1	-1	0	-0.1
Total	2	1	0	1.000	17	2	0	0	0	52^{2}	45	0	29	20	13.0	3.25	90	.246	.355	3	.273	0	-3	-2	-0	0.0
● BILL ANDERSON	Anderson, William Edward "Lefty" b: 11/28/1895, Boston, Mass. d: 3/13/83, Medford, Mass. BR/TL, 6'1", 165 lbs. Deb: 9/10/25																									
1925	Bos-N	0	0	—	2	0	0	0	0	2^{2}	5	0	2	1	23.6	10.13	40	.500	.583	0	.000	-0	-2	-2	-0	0.0
● WINGO ANDERSON	Anderson, Wingo Charlie b: 8/13/1886, Alvarado, Tex. d: 12/19/50, Fort Worth, Tex. BL/TL, 5'10.5", 150 lbs. Deb: 4/16/10																									
1910	Cin-N	0	0	—	7	2	0	0	0	17^{1}	16	0	17	11	17.7	4.67	62	.258	.425	1	.200	-0	-3	-3	-1	-0.1

YEAR	TM/L	W	L	PCT	G	GS	CG	SH	SV	IP	H	HR	BB	SO	RAT	ERA	ERA+	OAV	OOB	BH	AVG	PB	PR	/A	PD	TPI
● JOHN ANDRE	Andre, John Edward b: 1/3/23, Brockton, Mass. d: 11/25/76, Centerville, Mass. BL/TR, 6'4", 200 lbs. Deb: 4/16/55																									
1955	Chi-N	0	1	.000	22	3	0	0	1	45	45	7	28	19	14.8	5.80	70	.259	.365	1	.111	-1	-9	-9	-0	-0.3
● ELBERT ANDREWS	Andrews, Elbert De Vore b: 12/11/01, Greenwood, S.C. d: 11/25/79, Greenwood, S.C. BL/TR, 6', 175 lbs. Deb: 5/1/25																									
1925	Phi-A	0	0	—	6	0	0	0	0	8	12	0	11	0	25.9	10.13	46	.375	.535	0	—	0	-5	-5	-0	0.0
● HUB ANDREWS	Andrews, Herbert Carl b: 8/31/22, Burbank, Okla. BR/TR, 6', 170 lbs. Deb: 4/20/47																									
1947	NY-N	0	0	—	7	0	0	0	0	8^2	14	1	4	2	18.7	6.23	65	.368	.429	0	—	0	-2	-2	0	0.0
1948	NY-N	0	0	—	1	0	0	0	0	3	3	0	0	0	9.0	0.00	—	.300	.300	0	—	0	1	1	0	0.0
Total	2	0	0	—	8	0	0	0	0	11^2	17	1	4	2	16.2	4.63	87	.354	.404	0	—	0	-1	-1	0	0.0
● IVY ANDREWS	Andrews, Ivy Paul "Poison" b: 5/6/07, Dora, Ala. d: 11/24/70, Birmingham, Ala. BR/TR, 6'1", 200 lbs. Deb: 8/15/31																									
1931	NY-A	2	0	1.000	7	3	1	0	0	34^1	36	3	8	10	11.5	4.19	95	.273	.314	2	.182	0	1	-1	-0	0.0
1932	NY-A	2	1	.667	4	1	1	0	0	24^2	20	0	9	7	10.6	1.82	223	.215	.284	2	.222	1	7	6	0	0.8
	Bos-A	8	6	.571	25	19	8	0	0	141^2	144	4	53	30	12.6	3.81	118	.262	.329	7	.137	-3	11	11	-1	0.5
	Yr	10	7	.588	29	20	9	0	0	166^1	164	4	62	37	12.3	3.52	126	.255	.322	9	.150	-2	18	17	-0	1.3
1933	Bos-A	7	13	.350	34	17	5	0	1	140	157	8	61	37	14.1	4.95	88	.279	.350	9	.214	-0	-10	-9	-1	-1.2
1934	StL-A	4	11	.267	43	13	2	0	3	139	166	7	65	51	15.0	4.66	107	.301	.375	14	.350	3	-3	5	-2	0.6
1935	StL-A	13	7	.650	50	20	10	0	1	213^1	231	10	53	43	12.0	3.54	135	.273	.317	9	.132	-5	22	30	-2	1.7
1936	StL-A	7	12	.368	36	25	11	0	1	191^1	221	19	50	33	12.7	4.84	111	.286	.330	10	.169	-1	4	11	-2	0.7
1937	Cle-A	3	4	.429	20	4	1	1	0	59^2	76	3	9	16	12.8	4.37	105	.311	.336	3	.250	1	2	2	-1	0.1
	*NY-A	3	2	.600	11	5	3	1	1	49	49	2	17	17	12.1	3.12	142	.259	.320	1	.067	-1	8	7	0	0.6
	Yr	6	6	.500	31	9	4	2	1	108^2	125	5	26	33	12.5	3.81	119	.289	.329	4	.148	-1	10	9	-0	0.7
1938	NY-A	1	3	.250	19	1	1	0	1	48	51	3	17	13	12.8	3.00	151	.268	.329	2	.167	-0	10	8	0	0.6
Total	8	50	59	.459	249	108	43	2	8	1041	1151	59	342	257	12.9	4.14	115	.279	.335	59	.185	-6	51	70	-9	4.4
● JOHN ANDREWS	Andrews, John Richard b: 2/9/49, Monterey Park, Cal. BL/TL, 5'10", 175 lbs. Deb: 4/8/73																									
1973	StL-N	1	1	.500	16	0	0	0	0	18^1	16	3	11	5	13.3	4.42	82	.235	.342	1	.500	0	-2	-2	-0	-0.2
● NATE ANDREWS	Andrews, Nathan Hardy b: 9/30/13, Pembroke, N.C. d: 4/26/91, Winston-Salem, N.C. BR/TR, 6', 195 lbs. Deb: 5/1/37																									
1937	StL-N	0	0	—	4	0	0	0	0	9	12	1	3	6	15.0	4.00	100	.324	.375	0	—	0	-0	-0	0	0.1
1939	StL-N	1	2	.333	11	1	0	0	0	16	24	0	12	6	20.3	6.75	61	.343	.439	0	.000	-0	-5	-5	0	-0.8
1940	Cle-A	0	1	.000	6	0	0	0	0	12	16	1	6	3	16.5	6.00	70	.327	.400	0	—	0	-2	-2	1	-0.1
1941	Cle-A	0	0	—	2	0	0	0	0	2^1	3	0	2	1	19.3	11.57	34	.300	.417	0	.000	-0	-2	-2	-0	0.0
1943	Bos-N	14	20	.412	36	34	23	3	0	283^2	253	11	75	80	10.6	2.57	133	.238	.291	14	.156	-0	26	27	2	3.4
1944	Bos-N☆	16	15	.516	37	34	16	2	2	257^1	263	14	74	76	11.9	3.22	119	.261	.312	10	.114	-4	11	17	1	1.8
1945	Bos-N	7	12	.368	21	19	8	0	0	137^2	160	9	52	26	13.9	4.58	84	.295	.356	9	.209	0	-12	-11	-0	-1.4
1946	Cin-N	2	4	.333	7	7	3	0	0	43^1	50	2	8	13	12.3	3.95	85	.281	.316	1	.071	-1	-3	-3	-0	-0.5
	NY-N	1	0	1.000	3	2	0	0	0	12	17	2	4	5	15.8	6.00	57	.362	.412	1	.500	1	-3	-3	-0	-0.2
	Yr	3	4	.429	10	9	3	0	0	55^1	67	4	12	18	12.8	4.39	77	.296	.332	2	.125	-0	-6	-6	-0	-0.7
Total	8	41	54	.432	127	97	50	5	2	773^1	798	40	236	216	12.1	3.46	106	.265	.321	35	.146	-4	10	17	4	2.3
● FRED ANDRUS	Andrus, Frederick Hotham b: 8/23/1850, Washington, Mich. d: 11/10/37, Detroit, Mich. BR/TR, 6'2", 185 lbs. Deb: 7/25/1876 ♦																									
1884	Chi-N	1	0	1.000	1	1	1	0	0	9	11	1	2	2	13.0	2.00	157	.297	.333	1	.200	0	1	1	0	0.1
● JOAQUIN ANDUJAR	Andujar, Joaquin b: 12/21/52, San Pedro De Macoris, D.R. BB/TR, 6', 180 lbs. Deb: 4/8/76																									
1976	Hou-N	9	10	.474	28	25	9	4	0	172^1	163	8	75	59	12.5	3.60	89	.255	.334	8	.140	-0	-2	-8	-1	-0.9
1977	Hou-N☆	11	8	.579	26	25	4	1	0	158^2	149	11	64	69	12.3	3.69	97	.251	.328	10	.189	2	4	-2	2	0.2
1978	Hou-N	5	7	.417	35	13	2	0	1	110^2	88	3	58	55	12.2	3.42	97	.224	.330	3	.130	-0	2	-1	2	0.1
1979	Hou-N★	12	12	.500	46	23	8	0	4	194	168	7	88	77	12.0	3.43	102	.233	.319	5	.088	-0	6	2	4	0.6
1980	*Hou-N	3	8	.273	35	14	0	0	2	122	132	8	43	75	12.9	3.91	84	.277	.337	5	.172	2	-4	-8	1	-0.3
1981	Hou-N	2	3	.400	9	3	0	0	0	23^2	29	2	12	18	15.6	4.94	67	.296	.373	0	.000	-0	-4	-4	-1	-0.9
	StL-N	6	1	.857	11	8	1	0	0	55^1	56	4	11	19	10.9	3.74	95	.265	.302	0	.000	-2	-2	-1	0	-0.3
	Yr	8	4	.667	20	11	1	0	0	79	85	6	23	37	12.3	4.10	85	.273	.323	0	.000	-2	-5	-5	-0	-1.2
1982	*StL-N	15	10	.600	38	37	9	5	0	265^2	237	11	50	137	10.0	2.47	146	.240	.282	15	.158	-1	33	34	2	3.2
1983	StL-N	6	16	.273	39	34	5	2	1	225	215	23	75	125	11.7	4.16	87	.253	.316	6	.082	-3	-13	-14	5	-1.0
1984	StL-N†	**20**	14	.588	36	36	12	**4**	0	**261^1**	218	20	70	147	10.2	3.34	104	.229	.286	11	.131	3	7	4	3	1.0
1985	*StL-N†	21	12	.636	38	38	10	2	0	269^2	265	15	82	112	11.9	3.40	104	.260	.322	10	.106	-2	6	4	-1	0.2
1986	Oak-A	12	7	.632	28	26	7	1	1	155^1	139	23	56	72	11.5	3.82	101	.239	.310	0	—	0	6	1	0	0.1
1987	Oak-A	3	5	.375	13	13	1	0	0	60^2	63	11	26	32	13.6	6.08	68	.269	.350	0	—	0	-11	-13	0	-1.3
1988	Hou-N	2	5	.286	23	10	0	0	0	78^2	94	9	21	35	13.7	4.00	83	.297	.350	4	.211	2	-5	-6	0	-0.3
Total	13	127	118	.518	405	305	68	19	9	2153	2016	155	731	1032	11.7	3.58	98	.250	.316	77	.127	-1	24	-13	18	0.4
● LUIS ANDUJAR	Andujar, Luis (Sanchez) b: 11/22/72, Bani, D.R. BR/TR, 6'2", 175 lbs. Deb: 9/8/95																									
1995	Chi-A	2	1	.667	5	5	0	0	0	30^1	26	4	14	9	12.2	3.26	136	.230	.320	0	—	0	5	4	-1	0.5
1996	Chi-A	0	2	.000	5	5	0	0	0	23	32	4	15	6	18.4	8.22	58	.337	.427	0	—	0	-8	-9	-0	-0.3
	Tor-A	1	1	.500	3	2	0	0	0	14^1	14	4	1	5	10.0	5.02	100	.264	.291	0	—	0	-0	-0	-1	0.0
	Yr	1	3	.250	8	7	0	0	0	37^1	46	8	16	11	15.2	6.99	69	.307	.377	0	—	0	-8	-9	-1	-0.3
1997	Tor-A	0	6	.000	17	8	0	0	0	50	76	9	21	28	17.5	6.48	71	.352	.409	0	—	0	-11	-11	-0	-1.1
1998	Tor-A	0	0	—	5	0	0	0	0	5^2	12	0	2	1	22.2	9.53	49	.429	.467	0	—	0	-3	-3	-0	0.0
Total	4	3	10	.231	35	20	0	0	0	123^1	160	21	53	49	15.7	5.98	77	.317	.384	0	—	0	-17	-18	-2	-0.9
● NORM ANGELINI	Angelini, Norman Stanley b: 9/24/47, San Francisco, Cal. BL/TL, 5'11", 175 lbs. Deb: 7/22/72																									
1972	KC-A	2	1	.667	21	0	0	0	2	16	13	1	12	16	14.6	2.25	135	.228	.371	0	.000	-0	1	1	-0	0.3
1973	KC-A	0	0	—	7	0	0	0	1	3^2	2	0	7	3	22.1	4.91	84	.200	.529	0	—	0	-0	-0	-0	-0.1
Total	2	2	1	.667	28	0	0	0	3	19^2	15	1	19	19	16.0	2.75	117	.224	.402	0	.000	-0	1	1	-0	0.2
● CAP ANSON	Anson, Adrian Constantine b: 4/11/1852, Marshalltown, Iowa d: 4/14/22, Chicago, Ill. BR/TR, 6', 227 lbs. Deb: 5/6/1871 MH♦																									
1883	Chi-N	0	0	—	2	0	0	0	1	3	1	0	1	0	6.0	0.00	—	.091	.167	127	.308	1	1	1	0	0.1
1884	Chi-N	0	1	.000	1	0	0	0	0	1	3	2	1	1	36.0	18.00	17	.375	.444	159	.335	0	-2	-2	0	-0.9
Total	2	0	1	.000	3	0	0	0	1	4	4	2	2	1	13.5	4.50	71	.211	.286	2995	.329	1	-1	-1	0	-0.8
● JOHNNY ANTONELLI	Antonelli, John August b: 4/12/30, Rochester, N.Y. BL/TL, 6', 190 lbs. Deb: 7/4/48																									
1948	Bos-N	0	0	—	4	0	0	0	1	4	2	0	3	0	11.3	2.25	170	.143	.294	0	—	0	1	1	0	0.1
1949	Bos-N	3	7	.300	22	10	3	1	0	96	99	6	42	48	13.4	3.56	106	.273	.351	3	.120	-1	5	2	-1	0.0
1950	Bos-N	2	3	.400	20	6	2	1	0	57^2	81	2	22	33	16.7	5.93	65	.335	.399	2	.125	-1	-11	-13	0	-1.0
1953	Mil-N	12	12	.500	31	26	11	2	1	175^1	167	15	71	131	12.3	3.18	123	.242	.314	11	.177	0	22	14	1	1.9
1954	*NY-N★	21	7	**.750**	39	37	18	**6**	2	258^2	209	22	94	152	10.7	**2.30**	**176**	**.219**	.293	16	.163	0	**51**	**50**	2	**5.5**
1955	NY-N	14	16	.467	38	34	14	2	1	235^1	206	24	82	143	11.4	3.33	121	.234	.307	17	.207	3	19	18	1	2.6
1956	NY-N★	20	13	.606	41	36	15	5	1	258^1	225	20	75	145	10.6	2.86	132	.234	.292	14	.157	1	26	27	1	3.6
1957	NY-N☆	12	18	.400	40	30	8	3	0	212^1	228	19	67	114	12.6	3.77	104	.276	.333	11	.153	3	3	4	-2	0.6
1958	SF-N☆	16	13	.552	41	34	13	0	3	241^2	216	31	87	143	11.4	3.28	116	.239	.308	19	.226	4	18	14	-3	1.7
1959	SF-N★	19	10	.655	40	38	17	**4**	1	282	247	29	76	165	10.4	3.10	123	.233	.286	16	.158	1	27	22	-1	2.2
1960	SF-N	6	7	.462	41	10	1	1	11	112^1	106	7	47	57	12.4	3.77	92	.253	.331	8	.235	2	-0	-4	-1	-0.3
1961	Cle-A	0	4	.000	11	7	0	0	0	48	68	8	18	23	16.3	6.56	60	.338	.395	4	.267	1	-14	-14	1	-0.8
	Mil-N	1	0	1.000	9	0	0	0	0	10^2	16	2	3	8	16.0	7.59	49	.340	.380	0	.000	-0	-4	-5	-0	-0.4
Total	12	126	110	.534	377	268	102	25	21	1992^1	1870	185	687	1162	11.7	3.34	116	.247	.313	121	.178	15	141	118	-1	15.7
● BOB APODACA	Apodaca, Robert John b: 1/31/50, Los Angeles, Cal. BR/TR, 5'11", 170 lbs. Deb: 9/18/73 C																									
1973	NY-N	0	0	—	1	0	0	0	0	0	0	0	2	0	—	∞	—	—	1.000	0	—	0	-1	-1	0	-0.1
1974	NY-N	6	6	.500	35	8	1	0	3	103	92	7	42	54	11.9	3.50	102	.241	.319	3	.120	0	1	1	-1	0.1
1975	NY-N	3	4	.429	46	0	0	0	13	84^2	66	4	28	45	10.0	1.49	232	.222	.289	4	.364	2	20	18	2	2.6

YEAR	TM/L	W	L	PCT	G	GS	CG	SH	SV	IP	H	HR	BB	SO	RAT	ERA	ERA+	OAV	OOB	BH	AVG	PB	PR	/A	PD	TPI
1976	NY-N	3	7	.300	43	3	0	0	5	89^{2}	71	4	29	45	10.3	2.81	117	.223	.293	2	.125	0	7	5	1	0.7
1977	NY-N	4	8	.333	59	0	0	0	5	84	83	7	30	53	12.2	3.43	109	.255	.319	1	.167	-0	4	3	1	0.5
Total	5	16	25	.390	184	11	1	0	26	361^{1}	312	22	131	197	11.2	2.86	123	.236	.307	10	.172	2	32	26	4	3.8

● LUIS APONTE
Aponte, Luis Eduardo (Yuripe) b: 6/14/53, ElTigre, Venez. BR/TR, 6', 185 lbs. Deb: 9/4/80

YEAR	TM/L	W	L	PCT	G	GS	CG	SH	SV	IP	H	HR	BB	SO	RAT	ERA	ERA+	OAV	OOB	BH	AVG	PB	PR	/A	PD	TPI
1980	Bos-A	0	0	—	4	0	0	0	0	7	6	0	2	1	10.3	1.29	328	.250	.308	0	—	0	2	2	0	-0.2
1981	Bos-A	1	0	1.000	7	0	0	0	1	15^{2}	11	0	3	11	8.0	0.57	674	.208	.250	0	—	0	5	6	1	0.4
1982	Bos-A	2	2	.500	40	0	0	0	3	85	78	5	25	44	10.9	3.18	136	.246	.301	0	—	0	8	11	2	0.5
1983	Bos-A	5	4	.556	34	0	0	0	3	62	74	7	23	32	14.4	3.63	120	.301	.365	0	—	0	3	5	1	0.7
1984	Cle-A	1	0	1.000	25	0	0	0	0	50^{1}	53	5	15	25	12.3	4.11	99	.269	.324	0	—	0	-1	-0	-1	-0.1
Total	5	9	6	.600	110	0	0	0	7	220	222	17	68	113	12.0	3.27	129	.265	.323	0	—	0	18	23	3	1.3

● KEVIN APPIER
Appier, Robert Kevin b: 12/6/67, Lancaster, Cal. BR/TR, 6'2", 195 lbs. Deb: 6/14/89

YEAR	TM/L	W	L	PCT	G	GS	CG	SH	SV	IP	H	HR	BB	SO	RAT	ERA	ERA+	OAV	OOB	BH	AVG	PB	PR	/A	PD	TPI
1989	KC-A	1	4	.200	6	5	0	0	0	21^{2}	34	3	12	10	19.1	9.14	42	.374	.447	0	—	0	-13	-13	-1	-2.2
1990	KC-A	12	8	.600	32	24	3	3	0	185^{2}	179	13	54	127	11.6	2.76	139	.252	.310	0	—	0	24	22	-0	2.3
1991	KC-A	13	10	.565	34	31	6	3	0	207^{2}	205	13	61	158	11.6	3.42	120	.255	.309	0	—	0	15	16	0	1.7
1992	KC-A	15	8	.652	30	30	3	0	0	208^{1}	167	10	68	150	10.2	2.46	165	.217	.282	0	—	0	34	37	0	3.8
1993	KC-A	18	8	.692	34	34	5	1	0	238^{2}	183	8	81	186	10.0	**2.56**	**179**	.212	.280	0	—	0	**47**	**53**	-2	**4.8**
1994	KC-A	7	6	.538	23	23	1	0	0	155	137	11	63	145	11.8	3.83	131	.240	.320	0	—	0	17	20	-1	1.2
1995	KC-A★	15	10	.600	31	31	4	1	0	201^{1}	163	14	80	185	11.2	3.89	123	.221	.304	0	—	0	18	20	-0	2.1
1996	KC-A	14	11	.560	32	32	5	1	0	211^{1}	192	17	75	207	11.6	3.62	138	.245	.315	0	—	0	32	33	-1	3.2
1997	KC-A	9	13	.409	34	34	4	1	0	235^{2}	215	24	74	196	11.2	3.40	139	.243	.304	0	.000	-1	30	34	-1	2.7
1998	KC-A	1	2	.333	3	3	0	0	0	15	21	3	5	9	16.2	7.80	63	.339	.397	0	—	0	-5	-5	-0	-1.0
Total	10	105	80	.568	259	247	31	10	0	1680^{1}	1496	116	573	1373	11.3	3.34	135	.238	.305	0	.000	-1	200	218	-5	18.6

● FRED APPLEGATE
Applegate, Frederick Romaine b: 5/9/1879, Williamsport, Pa. d: 4/21/68, Williamsport, Pa. BR/TR, 6'2", 180 lbs. Deb: 9/30/04

YEAR	TM/L	W	L	PCT	G	GS	CG	SH	SV	IP	H	HR	BB	SO	RAT	ERA	ERA+	OAV	OOB	BH	AVG	PB	PR	/A	PD	TPI
1904	Phi-A	1	2	.333	3	3	3	0	0	21	29	0	8	12	16.3	6.43	42	.330	.392	2	.286	0	-9	-9	0	-1.0

● ED APPLETON
Appleton, Edward Samuel "Whitey" b: 2/29/1892, Arlington, Tex. d: 1/27/32, Arlington, Tex. BR/TR, 6'0.5", 173 lbs. Deb: 4/16/15

YEAR	TM/L	W	L	PCT	G	GS	CG	SH	SV	IP	H	HR	BB	SO	RAT	ERA	ERA+	OAV	OOB	BH	AVG	PB	PR	/A	PD	TPI
1915	Bro-N	4	10	.286	34	10	5	0	0	138^{1}	133	3	66	50	13.5	3.32	84	.263	.357	7	.159	-0	-9	-8	-1	-0.9
1916	Bro-N	1	2	.333	14	3	1	0	1	47	49	1	18	14	13.0	3.06	88	.278	.349	2	.167	-0	-2	-2	-1	-0.3
Total	2	5	12	.294	48	13	6	0	1	185^{1}	182	4	84	64	13.4	3.25	85	.267	.355	9	.161	-1	-11	-10	-2	-1.2

● PETE APPLETON
Appleton, Peter William "Jake" (a.k.a. Jablonowski In 1927-33)
b: 5/20/04, Terryville, Conn. d: 1/18/74, Trenton, N.J. BR/TR, 5'11", 180 lbs. Deb: 9/14/27

YEAR	TM/L	W	L	PCT	G	GS	CG	SH	SV	IP	H	HR	BB	SO	RAT	ERA	ERA+	OAV	OOB	BH	AVG	PB	PR	/A	PD	TPI
1927	Cin-N	2	1	.667	6	2	2	1	0	29^{2}	29	0	17	3	14.0	1.82	208	.261	.359	6	.545	2	7	6	1	0.9
1928	Cin-N	3	4	.429	31	3	0	0	0	82^{2}	101	7	22	20	13.6	4.68	85	.311	.358	10	.323	3	-6	-7	2	0.0
1930	Cle-A	8	7	.533	39	7	2	0	1	118^{2}	122	8	53	45	13.7	4.02	120	.274	.357	8	.200	-1	8	11	2	1.2
1931	Cle-A	4	4	.500	29	4	3	0	0	79^{2}	100	2	29	25	14.7	4.63	100	.293	.350	5	.208	0	-2	-0	-0	0.0
1932	Cle-A	0	0	—	4	0	0	0	0	5	11	1	3	1	25.2	16.20	29	.407	.467	0	—	0	-7	-6	0	0.0
	Bos-A	0	3	.000	11	3	0	0	0	46	49	2	26	15	15.1	4.11	109	.265	.362	3	.176	-0	2	2	2	0.3
	Yr	0	3	.000	15	3	0	0	0	51	60	3	29	16	16.1	5.29	85	.283	.374	3	.176	-0	-5	-4	2	0.3
1933	NY-A	0	0	—	1	0	0	0	0	2	3	0	1	0	18.0	0.00	—	.375	.444	0	—	0	1	1	0	0.0
1936	Was-A	14	9	.609	38	20	12	1	3	201^{2}	199	7	77	77	12.5	3.53	135	.254	.324	19	.250	2	34	28	1	3.0
1937	Was-A	8	15	.348	35	18	7	4	2	168	167	16	72	62	13.1	4.39	101	.260	.339	11	.186	-2	4	1	3	0.2
1938	Was-A	7	9	.438	43	10	5	0	5	164^{1}	175	12	61	62	13.0	4.60	98	.270	.333	15	.254	3	3	-2	-0	0.1
1939	Was-A	5	10	.333	40	4	2	0	6	102^{2}	104	7	48	50	13.7	4.56	95	.265	.351	4	.160	-1	1	-2	0	-0.4
1940	Chi-A	4	0	1.000	25	0	0	0	5	57^{2}	54	8	28	21	13.0	5.62	79	.248	.336	3	.176	-0	-8	-8	-0	-0.7
1941	Chi-A	0	3	.000	13	0	0	0	1	27^{1}	27	4	17	12	15.1	5.27	78	.257	.371	1	.250	0	-3	-4	0	-0.3
1942	Chi-A	0	0	—	4	0	0	0	0	4^{2}	2	0	3	2	9.6	3.86	93	.133	.278	0	—	0	-0	-0	0	0.0
	StL-A	1	1	.500	14	0	0	0	2	27^{1}	25	1	11	12	11.9	2.96	125	.243	.316	1	.167	1	2	2	1	0.4
	Yr	1	1	.500	18	0	0	0	2	32	27	1	14	14	11.5	3.09	119	.229	.311	1	.167	1	2	2	1	0.4
1945	StL-A	0	0	—	2	0	0	0	0	2^{1}	3	0	7	1	38.6	15.43	23	.273	.556	0	—	0	-3	-3	0	0.0
	Was-A	1	0	1.000	6	2	1	0	1	21^{1}	16	1	11	12	11.4	3.38	92	.211	.310	1	.200	-0	-0	-1	-0	-0.1
	Yr	1	0	1.000	8	2	1	0	1	23^{2}	19	1	18	13	14.1	4.56	69	.218	.352	1	.200	-0	-3	-4	0	-0.1
Total	14	57	66	.463	341	73	34	6	26	1141	1187	76	486	420	13.4	4.30	104	.268	.343	87	.233	7	33	19	12	4.6

● LUIS AQUINO
Aquino, Luis Antonio (Colon) b: 5/19/64, Santurce, P.R. BR/TR, 6'1", 195 lbs. Deb: 8/8/86

YEAR	TM/L	W	L	PCT	G	GS	CG	SH	SV	IP	H	HR	BB	SO	RAT	ERA	ERA+	OAV	OOB	BH	AVG	PB	PR	/A	PD	TPI
1986	Tor-A	1	1	.500	7	0	0	0	0	11^{1}	14	2	3	5	13.5	6.35	66	.304	.347	0	—	0	-3	-3	-0	-0.4
1988	KC-A	1	0	1.000	7	5	1	1	0	29	33	1	17	11	15.8	2.79	143	.282	.378	0	—	0	4	4	-0	0.1
1989	KC-A	6	8	.429	34	16	2	1	0	141^{1}	148	6	35	68	11.9	3.50	110	.271	.320	0	—	0	6	5	1	0.6
1990	KC-A	4	1	.800	20	3	1	0	0	68^{1}	59	6	27	28	11.9	3.16	121	.237	.321	0	—	0	6	5	0	0.4
1991	KC-A	8	4	.667	38	18	1	1	3	157	152	10	47	80	11.6	3.44	120	.253	.311	0	—	0	11	12	0	0.9
1992	KC-A	3	6	.333	15	13	0	0	0	67^{2}	81	5	20	11	13.6	4.52	90	.303	.354	0	—	0	-4	-4	1	-0.5
1993	Fla-N	6	8	.429	38	13	0	0	0	110^{2}	115	6	40	67	13.0	3.42	126	.276	.346	2	.080	-2	8	11	4	1.5
1994	Fla-N	2	1	.667	29	1	0	0	0	50^{2}	39	3	22	22	11.4	3.73	117	.210	.303	1	.167	-0	3	4	1	0.3
1995	Mon-N	0	2	.000	29	0	0	0	2	37^{1}	47	4	11	22	14.7	3.86	111	.301	.359	1	.333	1	1	2	-0	0.1
	SF-N	0	1	.000	5	0	0	0	0	5	10	2	2	4	21.6	14.40	28	.400	.444	0	.000	-0	-6	-6	0	-0.9
	Yr	0	3	.000	34	0	0	0	2	42^{1}	57	6	13	26	14.9	5.10	84	.308	.354	1	.250	0	-4	-4	-0	-0.8
Total	9	31	32	.492	222	69	5	3	5	678^{1}	698	45	224	318	12.6	3.68	111	.267	.331	4	.114	-1	26	31	6	2.1

● FRED ARCHER
Archer, Frederick Marvin "Lefty" b: 3/7/10, Johnson City, Tenn. d: 10/31/81, Charlotte, N.C. BL/TL, 6', 193 lbs. Deb: 9/5/36

YEAR	TM/L	W	L	PCT	G	GS	CG	SH	SV	IP	H	HR	BB	SO	RAT	ERA	ERA+	OAV	OOB	BH	AVG	PB	PR	/A	PD	TPI
1936	Phi-A	2	3	.400	6	5	2	0	0	36^{2}	41	3	15	9	14.5	6.38	80	.289	.369	4	.267	0	-5	-5	-0	-0.5
1937	Phi-A	0	0	—	1	0	0	0	0	3	4	0	0	2	12.0	6.00	79	.333	.333	0	—	0	-0	-0	0	0.0
Total	2	2	3	.400	7	5	2	0	0	39^{2}	45	3	15	11	14.3	6.35	80	.292	.366	4	.267	1	-6	-6	0	-0.5

● JIM ARCHER
Archer, James William b: 5/25/32, Max Meadows, Va. BR/TL, 6', 190 lbs. Deb: 4/30/61

YEAR	TM/L	W	L	PCT	G	GS	CG	SH	SV	IP	H	HR	BB	SO	RAT	ERA	ERA+	OAV	OOB	BH	AVG	PB	PR	/A	PD	TPI
1961	KC-A	9	15	.375	39	27	9	2	5	205^{1}	204	11	60	110	11.8	3.20	131	.257	.313	4	.063	-5	19	22	-0	2.0
1962	KC-A	0	1	.000	18	1	0	0	0	27^{2}	40	8	10	12	16.3	9.43	45	.342	.394	1	1.000	0	-17	-16	-0	-0.5
Total	2	9	16	.360	57	28	9	2	5	233	244	19	70	122	12.3	3.94	106	.268	.323	5	.078	-4	2	6	-1	1.5

● RUGGER ARDIZOIA
Ardizoia, Rinaldo Joseph b: 11/20/19, Oleggio, Italy BR/TR, 5'11", 180 lbs. Deb: 4/30/47

YEAR	TM/L	W	L	PCT	G	GS	CG	SH	SV	IP	H	HR	BB	SO	RAT	ERA	ERA+	OAV	OOB	BH	AVG	PB	PR	/A	PD	TPI
1947	NY-A	0	0	—	1	0	0	0	0	2	4	1	1	0	22.5	9.00	39	.500	.556	0	—	0	-1	-1	0	0.0

● FRANK ARELLANES
Arellanes, Frank Julian b: 1/28/1882, Santa Cruz, Cal. d: 12/13/18, San Jose, Cal. BR/TR, 6', 180 lbs. Deb: 7/28/08

YEAR	TM/L	W	L	PCT	G	GS	CG	SH	SV	IP	H	HR	BB	SO	RAT	ERA	ERA+	OAV	OOB	BH	AVG	PB	PR	/A	PD	TPI
1908	Bos-A	4	3	.571	11	8	6	1	0	79	60	1	18	33	9.2	1.82	135	.205	.259	5	.167	0	5	6	-1	0.4
1909	Bos-A	16	12	.571	45	28	17	1	**8**	230^{2}	192	3	43	82	9.4	2.18	114	.229	.270	13	.167	-1	8	8	0	0.9
1910	Bos-A	4	7	.364	18	13	2	0	0	100	106	1	24	33	12.0	2.88	89	.283	.332	6	.176	0	-4	-4	0	-0.4
Total	3	24	22	.522	74	49	25	2	8	409^{2}	358	5	85	148	10.0	2.28	110	.238	.283	24	.169	-1	9	10	-1	0.9

● RUDY ARIAS
Arias, Rodolfo (Martinez) b: 6/6/31, Las Villas, Cuba BL/TL, 5'10", 165 lbs. Deb: 4/10/59

YEAR	TM/L	W	L	PCT	G	GS	CG	SH	SV	IP	H	HR	BB	SO	RAT	ERA	ERA+	OAV	OOB	BH	AVG	PB	PR	/A	PD	TPI
1959	Chi-A	2	0	1.000	34	0	0	0	2	44	49	7	20	28	14.3	4.09	92	.277	.354	0	.000	-1	-1	-2	1	-0.1

● DON ARLICH
Arlich, Donald Louis b: 2/15/43, Wayne, Mich. BL/TL, 6'2", 185 lbs. Deb: 10/2/65

YEAR	TM/L	W	L	PCT	G	GS	CG	SH	SV	IP	H	HR	BB	SO	RAT	ERA	ERA+	OAV	OOB	BH	AVG	PB	PR	/A	PD	TPI
1965	Hou-N	0	0	—	1	1	0	0	0	6	5	0	1	0	9.0	3.00	112	.227	.261	0	.000	-0	0	0	-0	0.0
1966	Hou-N	0	1	.000	7	0	0	0	0	4	11	0	4	1	36.0	15.75	22	.478	.571	0	.000	-0	-5	-5	-0	-1.2
Total	2	0	1	.000	8	1	0	0	0	10	16	0	5	1	19.8	8.10	42	.356	.431	0	.000	-0	-5	-5	-0	-1.2

● STEVE ARLIN
Arlin, Stephen Ralph b: 9/25/45, Seattle, Wash. BR/TR, 6'3.5", 195 lbs. Deb: 6/17/69

YEAR	TM/L	W	L	PCT	G	GS	CG	SH	SV	IP	H	HR	BB	SO	RAT	ERA	ERA+	OAV	OOB	BH	AVG	PB	PR	/A	PD	TPI
1969	SD-N	0	1	.000	4	1	0	0	0	10^{2}	13	2	9	9	18.6	9.28	38	.289	.407	0	.000	-0	-7	-7	-0	-0.6
1970	SD-N	1	0	1.000	2	2	1	1	0	12^{2}	11	0	8	3	13.5	2.84	140	.244	.358	0	.000	-1	2	2	0	0.1
1971	SD-N	9	19	.321	36	34	10	4	0	227^{2}	211	8	103	156	12.7	3.48	95	.244	.329	9	.123	-1	-0	-5	-1	-0.8

YEAR	TM/L	W	L	PCT	G	GS	CG	SH	SV	IP	H	HR	BB	SO	RAT	ERA	ERA+	OAV	OOB	BH	AVG	PB	PR	/A	PD	TPI
1972	SD-N	10	21	.323	38	37	12	3	0	250	217	19	122	159	12.5	3.60	91	.237	.332	11	.153	3	-4	-9	-0	-0.8
1973	SD-N	11	14	.440	34	27	7	3	0	180	196	26	72	98	13.4	5.10	68	.278	.346	10	.167	1	-29	-33	-1	-3.9
1974	SD-N	1	7	.125	16	12	1	0	1	64	85	5	37	18	17.4	5.91	60	.326	.413	2	.111	-1	-16	-17	-0	-2.0
	Cle-A	2	5	.286	11	10	1	0	0	43^2	59	1	22	20	16.7	6.60	55	.333	.407	0	—	0	-14	-14	-1	-2.0
Total	6	34	67	.337	141	123	32	11	1	788^2	792	61	373	463	13.5	4.33	78	.263	.348	32	.139	1	-69	-82	-3	-10.0

● ORVILLE ARMBRUST

Armbrust, Orville Martin b: 3/2/10, Beirne, Ark. d: 10/2/67, Mobile, Ala. BR/TR, 5′10″, 195 lbs. Deb: 9/18/34

YEAR	TM/L	W	L	PCT	G	GS	CG	SH	SV	IP	H	HR	BB	SO	RAT	ERA	ERA+	OAV	OOB	BH	AVG	PB	PR	/A	PD	TPI
1934	Was-A	1	0	1.000	3	2	0	0	0	12^2	10	1	3	3	9.2	2.13	203	.208	.255	0	.000	-1	3	3	1	0.2

● HOWARD ARMSTRONG

Armstrong, Howard Elmer b: 12/2/1889, E.Claridon, Ohio d: 3/8/26, Canisteo, N.Y. BR/TR, 5′9″, 165 lbs. Deb: 9/30/11

YEAR	TM/L	W	L	PCT	G	GS	CG	SH	SV	IP	H	HR	BB	SO	RAT	ERA	ERA+	OAV	OOB	BH	AVG	PB	PR	/A	PD	TPI
1911	Phi-A	0	1	.000	1	0	0	0	0	3	3	0	1	0	12.0	0.00	—	.273	.333	0	.000	-0	1	1	0	0.4

● JACK ARMSTRONG

Armstrong, Jack William b: 3/7/65, Englewood, N.J. BR/TR, 6′5″, 215 lbs. Deb: 6/21/88

YEAR	TM/L	W	L	PCT	G	GS	CG	SH	SV	IP	H	HR	BB	SO	RAT	ERA	ERA+	OAV	OOB	BH	AVG	PB	PR	/A	PD	TPI
1988	Cin-N	4	7	.364	14	13	0	0	0	65^1	63	8	38	45	13.9	5.79	62	.256	.356	2	.095	-1	-17	-16	1	-2.4
1989	Cin-N	2	3	.400	9	8	0	0	0	42^2	40	5	21	23	12.9	4.64	78	.245	.332	0	.000	-1	-5	-5	0	-0.6
1990	*Cin-N★	12	9	.571	29	27	2	1	0	166	151	9	59	110	11.7	3.42	115	.241	.313	5	.106	-2	7	10	0	1.0
1991	Cin-N	7	13	.350	27	24	1	0	0	139^2	158	25	54	93	13.8	5.48	69	.293	.359	4	.093	-2	-28	-26	-0	-3.4
1992	Cle-A	6	15	.286	35	23	1	0	0	166^2	176	23	67	114	13.3	4.64	84	.269	.340	0	—	0	-13	-14	1	-1.3
1993	Fla-N	9	17	.346	36	33	0	0	0	196^1	210	29	78	118	13.5	4.49	96	.271	.343	10	.152	-2	-10	-4	-0	-0.6
1994	Tex-A	0	1	.000	2	2	0	0	0	10	9	3	2	7	9.9	3.60	134	.231	.268	0	—	0	1	1	-0	0.1
Total	7	40	65	.381	152	130	4	1	0	786^2	807	102	319	510	13.1	4.58	87	.265	.338	21	.114	-6	-65	-53	2	-7.2

● MIKE ARMSTRONG

Armstrong, Michael Dennis b: 3/7/54, Glen Cove, N.Y. BR/TR, 6′3″, 206 lbs. Deb: 8/12/80

YEAR	TM/L	W	L	PCT	G	GS	CG	SH	SV	IP	H	HR	BB	SO	RAT	ERA	ERA+	OAV	OOB	BH	AVG	PB	PR	/A	PD	TPI
1980	SD-N	0	0	—	11	0	0	0	0	14^1	16	3	13	14	18.2	5.65	61	.296	.433	0	.000	-0	-3	-4	-0	-0.1
1981	SD-N	0	2	.000	10	0	0	0	0	12	14	1	11	9	18.8	6.00	54	.311	.446	0	—	0	-3	-4	-0	-0.6
1982	KC-A	5	5	.500	52	0	0	0	6	112^2	88	9	43	75	10.7	3.20	128	.215	.295	0	—	0	11	11	-1	0.9
1983	KC-A	10	7	.588	58	0	0	0	3	102^2	86	11	45	52	11.7	3.86	106	.228	.315	0	—	0	2	2	-0	0.4
1984	NY-A	3	2	.600	36	0	0	0	1	54^1	47	6	26	43	12.1	3.48	109	.239	.327	0	—	0	3	2	-0	0.5
1985	NY-A	0	0	—	9	0	0	0	0	14^2	9	4	2	11	6.8	3.07	130	.173	.204	0	—	0	2	2	-0	0.1
1986	NY-A	0	1	.000	7	1	0	0	0	8^2	13	4	5	8	18.7	9.35	44	.351	.429	0	—	0	-5	-5	-0	-0.4
1987	Cle-A	1	0	1.000	14	0	0	0	1	18^2	27	4	10	9	17.8	8.68	52	.333	.407	0	—	0	-9	-9	-0	-0.5
Total	8	19	17	.528	197	1	0	0	11	338	300	42	155	221	12.3	4.10	97	.240	.326	0	.000	-0	-2	-4	-3	0.3

● SCOTT ARNOLD

Arnold, Scott Gentry b: 8/18/62, Lexington, Ky. BR/TR, 6′2″, 210 lbs. Deb: 4/7/88

YEAR	TM/L	W	L	PCT	G	GS	CG	SH	SV	IP	H	HR	BB	SO	RAT	ERA	ERA+	OAV	OOB	BH	AVG	PB	PR	/A	PD	TPI
1988	StL-N	0	0	—	6	0	0	0	0	6^2	9	0	4	8	17.6	5.40	64	.321	.406	0	—	0	-1	-1	0	0.0

● TONY ARNOLD

Arnold, Tony Dale b: 5/3/59, ElPaso, Tex. BR/TR, 5′11″, 170 lbs. Deb: 8/9/86

YEAR	TM/L	W	L	PCT	G	GS	CG	SH	SV	IP	H	HR	BB	SO	RAT	ERA	ERA+	OAV	OOB	BH	AVG	PB	PR	/A	PD	TPI
1986	Bal-A	0	2	.000	11	0	0	0	0	25^1	25	0	11	7	12.8	3.55	116	.278	.356	0	—	0	2	2	1	0.3
1987	Bal-A	0	0	—	27	0	0	0	0	53	71	8	17	18	15.3	5.77	76	.330	.385	0	—	0	-8	-8	2	0.2
Total	2	0	2	.000	38	0	0	0	0	78^1	96	8	28	25	14.5	5.06	85	.315	.376	0	—	0	-6	-6	3	0.5

● BRAD ARNSBERG

Arnsberg, Bradley James b: 8/20/63, Seattle, Wash. BR/TR, 6′4″, 215 lbs. Deb: 9/6/86

YEAR	TM/L	W	L	PCT	G	GS	CG	SH	SV	IP	H	HR	BB	SO	RAT	ERA	ERA+	OAV	OOB	BH	AVG	PB	PR	/A	PD	TPI
1986	NY-A	0	0	—	2	1	0	0	0	8	13	1	1	3	15.8	3.38	121	.342	.359	0	—	0	1	1	-0	0.0
1987	NY-A	1	3	.250	6	2	0	0	0	19^1	22	5	13	14	16.3	5.59	78	.289	.393	0	—	0	-2	-3	1	-0.4
1989	Tex-A	2	1	.667	16	1	0	0	1	48	45	6	22	26	13.1	4.13	96	.247	.338	0	—	0	-1	-1	1	0.0
1990	Tex-A	6	1	.857	53	0	0	0	5	62^2	56	4	33	44	13.1	2.15	182	.235	.333	0	—	0	12	12	1	1.5
1991	Tex-A	0	1	.000	9	0	0	0	0	9^2	10	5	5	8	14.0	8.38	48	.256	.341	0	—	0	-5	-5	-0	-0.4
1992	Cle-A	0	0	—	8	0	0	0	0	10^2	13	6	11	5	21.9	11.81	33	.317	.481	0	—	0	-9	-9	-0	0.1
Total	6	9	6	.600	94	4	0	0	6	158^1	159	27	85	100	14.3	4.26	94	.259	.356	0	—	0	-5	-5	2	0.8

● ORIE ARNTZEN

Arntzen, Orie Edgar "Old Folks" b: 10/18/09, Beverly, Ill. d: 1/28/70, Cedar Rapids, Iowa BR/TR, 6′1″, 200 lbs. Deb: 4/20/43

YEAR	TM/L	W	L	PCT	G	GS	CG	SH	SV	IP	H	HR	BB	SO	RAT	ERA	ERA+	OAV	OOB	BH	AVG	PB	PR	/A	PD	TPI
1943	Phi-A	4	13	.235	32	20	9	0	0	164^1	172	5	69	66	13.5	4.22	81	.277	.354	8	.160	-1	-17	-15	-3	-1.9

● RENE AROCHA

Arocha, Rene (Magaly) b: 2/24/66, Havana, Cuba BR/TR, 6′, 180 lbs. Deb: 4/9/93

YEAR	TM/L	W	L	PCT	G	GS	CG	SH	SV	IP	H	HR	BB	SO	RAT	ERA	ERA+	OAV	OOB	BH	AVG	PB	PR	/A	PD	TPI
1993	StL-N	11	8	.579	32	29	1	0	0	188	197	20	31	96	11.1	3.78	105	.271	.304	6	.103	-2	5	4	-1	0.1
1994	StL-N	4	4	.500	45	7	1	1	11	83	94	9	21	62	12.9	4.01	104	.286	.336	1	.111	0	2	1	-0	0.1
1995	StL-N	3	5	.375	41	0	0	0	0	49^2	55	6	18	25	13.8	3.99	105	.297	.369	0	.000	-0	1	1	0	0.2
1997	SF-N	0	0	—	6	0	0	0	0	10^1	17	2	5	7	20.0	11.32	36	.370	.442	0	.000	-0	-8	-8	1	0.0
Total	4	18	17	.514	124	36	2	1	11	331	363	37	75	190	12.2	4.11	99	.282	.327	7	.101	-2	0	-2	-0	0.4

● GERRY ARRIGO

Arrigo, Gerald William b: 6/12/41, Chicago, Ill. BL/TL, 6′1″, 195 lbs. Deb: 6/12/61

YEAR	TM/L	W	L	PCT	G	GS	CG	SH	SV	IP	H	HR	BB	SO	RAT	ERA	ERA+	OAV	OOB	BH	AVG	PB	PR	/A	PD	TPI
1961	Min-A	0	1	.000	7	2	0	0	0	9^2	9	0	10	6	19.6	10.24	41	.265	.457	1	.500	0	-7	-6	0	-0.5
1962	Min-A	0	0	—	1	0	0	0	0	1	3	0	1	1	36.0	18.00	23	.600	.667	0	—	0	-2	-2	0	0.0
1963	Min-A	1	2	.333	5	1	0	0	0	15^2	12	2	4	13	9.2	2.87	127	.211	.262	0	.000	-0	1	1	0	0.2
1964	Min-A	7	4	.636	41	12	2	1	1	105^1	97	11	45	96	12.3	3.84	93	.244	.324	5	.172	1	-3	-3	0	-0.2
1965	Cin-N	2	4	.333	27	5	0	0	2	54	75	4	30	43	17.8	6.17	61	.342	.426	2	.167	1	-16	-15	-1	-1.7
1966	Cin-N	0	0	—	3	0	0	0	0	7^1	7	2	3	3	12.3	4.91	79	.250	.323	0	.000	-0	-1	-1	-0	0.0
	NY-N	3	3	.500	17	5	0	0	0	43^1	47	5	16	28	13.1	3.74	97	.276	.339	5	.500	3	-1	-0	1	0.3
	Yr	3	3	.500	20	5	0	0	0	50^2	54	7	19	31	13.0	3.91	94	.273	.336	5	.455	3	-2	-1	0	0.3
1967	Cin-N	6	6	.500	32	5	1	1	1	74	61	6	35	56	12.2	3.16	119	.232	.331	4	.211	1	2	5	-2	0.7
1968	Cin-N	12	10	.545	36	31	5	1	0	205^1	181	13	77	140	11.5	3.33	95	.237	.310	5	.075	-2	-8	-4	1	-0.5
1969	Cin-N	4	7	.364	20	16	1	0	0	91	89	9	61	35	15.6	4.15	91	.256	.379	5	.161	-0	-6	-4	-2	-0.7
1970	Chi-A	0	3	.000	5	3	0	0	0	13^1	24	4	9	12	22.3	12.83	30	.393	.471	0	.000	-0	-13	-13	-0	-2.2
Total	10	35	40	.467	194	80	9	3	4	620	605	56	291	433	13.3	4.14	85	.258	.345	27	.151	2	-52	-42	-3	-4.6

● ROLANDO ARROJO

Arrojo, Luis Rolando b: 7/18/68, Santa Clara, Cuba BR/TR, 6′4″, 215 lbs. Deb: 4/1/98

YEAR	TM/L	W	L	PCT	G	GS	CG	SH	SV	IP	H	HR	BB	SO	RAT	ERA	ERA+	OAV	OOB	BH	AVG	PB	PR	/A	PD	TPI
1998	TB-A★	14	12	.538	32	32	2	2	0	202	195	21	65	152	12.4	3.56	137	.256	.330	0	.000	-0	24	30	3	3.8

● FERNANDO ARROYO

Arroyo, Fernando b: 3/21/52, Sacramento, Cal. BR/TR, 6′3″, 195 lbs. Deb: 6/28/75

YEAR	TM/L	W	L	PCT	G	GS	CG	SH	SV	IP	H	HR	BB	SO	RAT	ERA	ERA+	OAV	OOB	BH	AVG	PB	PR	/A	PD	TPI
1975	Det-A	2	1	.667	14	2	1	0	0	53^1	56	5	22	25	13.3	4.56	88	.272	.345	0	—	0	-5	-3	1	-0.1
1977	Det-A	8	18	.308	38	28	8	1	0	209^1	227	23	52	60	12.0	4.17	103	.278	.321	0	—	0	-3	3	6	0.6
1978	Det-A	0	0	—	2	0	0	0	0	4^1	8	1	0	1	18.7	8.31	47	.400	.429	0	—	0	-2	-2	0	-0.1
1979	Det-A	1	1	.500	6	0	0	0	0	12	17	3	4	7	15.8	8.25	52	.340	.389	0	—	0	-5	-5	0	-0.8
1980	Min-A	6	6	.500	21	11	1	1	0	92^1	97	7	32	27	12.8	4.68	93	.273	.337	0	—	0	-7	-3	-1	-1.0
1981	Min-A	7	10	.412	23	19	2	0	0	128^1	144	11	34	39	12.8	3.93	100	.290	.342	0	—	0	-4	0	0	-0.3
1982	Min-A	0	1	.000	6	0	0	0	0	13^2	17	2	6	4	15.1	5.27	81	.321	.390	0	—	0	-2	-2	1	-0.2
	Oak-A	0	0	—	10	0	0	0	0	22^1	23	4	7	9	12.5	5.24	75	.271	.333	0	—	0	-3	-3	0	0.3
	Yr	0	1	.000	16	0	0	0	0	36	40	6	13	13	13.5	5.25	77	.288	.353	0	—	0	-5	-5	1	0.1
1986	Oak-A	0	0	—	1	0	0	0	0	0	0	0	3	0	—	—	—	—	1.000	0	—	0	0	0	0	0.5
Total	8	24	37	.393	121	60	12	2	0	535^2	589	56	160	172	12.8	4.44	94	.283	.337	0	—	0	-30	-16	7	-1.1

● LUIS ARROYO

Arroyo, Luis Enrique b: 2/18/27, Penuelas, P.R. BL/TL, 5′8″, 190 lbs. Deb: 4/20/55

YEAR	TM/L	W	L	PCT	G	GS	CG	SH	SV	IP	H	HR	BB	SO	RAT	ERA	ERA+	OAV	OOB	BH	AVG	PB	PR	/A	PD	TPI
1955	StL-N☆	11	8	.579	35	24	9	1	0	159	162	22	63	68	12.8	4.19	97	.261	.331	13	.232	1	-3	-2	-2	-0.4
1956	Pit-N	3	3	.500	18	2	1	0	0	28^2	36	5	12	17	15.1	4.71	80	.298	.361	2	.500	1	-3	-3	0	-0.5
1957	Pit-N	3	11	.214	54	10	0	0	1	130^2	151	19	31	101	13.0	4.68	81	.282	.329	5	.156	-1	-12	-13	-2	-1.5
1959	Cin-N	1	0	1.000	10	0	0	0	0	13^2	17	0	11	8	18.4	3.95	103	.321	.438	0	.000	-0	-0	0	0	0.0
1960	*NY-A	5	1	.833	29	0	0	0	7	40^2	30	2	22	29	11.5	2.88	125	.207	.311	0	.000	-0	5	3	0	0.5
1961	*NY-A☆	15	5	.750	**65**	0	0	0	**29**	119	83	5	49	87	10.2	2.19	169	.199	.288	7	.280	2	**24**	20	-1	**4.3**
1962	NY-A	1	3	.250	27	0	0	0	7	33^2	33	5	17	21	13.6	4.81	78	.262	.354	2	.500	1	-3	-4	-1	-0.6
1963	NY-A	1	1	.500	6	0	0	0	0	6	12	0	3	5	22.5	13.50	26	.444	.500	0	—	0	-7	-7	-0	-1.8
Total	8	40	32	.556	244	36	10	1	44	531^1	524	58	208	336	12.6	3.93	98	.256	.329	29	.227	3	2	-5	-5	0.0

YEAR	TM/L	W	L	PCT	G	GS	CG	SH	SV	IP	H	HR	BB	SO	RAT	ERA	ERA+	OAV	OOB	BH	AVG	PB	PR	/A	PD	TPI
● **RUDY ARROYO**	Arroyo, Rudolph b: 6/19/50, New York, N.Y. BL/TL, 6'2", 195 lbs. Deb: 6/1/71																									
1971	StL-N	0	1	.000	9	0	0	0	0	11^2	18	2	5	5	17.7	5.40	67	.375	.434	0	.000	-0	-3	-2	-0	-0.2
● **HARRY ARUNDEL**	Arundel, Harry b: 2/1855, Philadelphia, Pa. d: 3/25/04, Cleveland, Ohio TR, 5'6", 145 lbs. Deb: 7/19/1875																									
1875	Atl-n	0	1	.000	1	1	0	0	0	2^1	6	0	0	0	23.1	7.71	27	.400	.400	0	.000	-1	-1	-1		-0.4
1882	Pit-a	4	10	.286	14	14	13	0	0	120	155	3	23	47	13.4	4.65	56	.294	.323	10	.189	0	-26	-27	5	-2.0
1884	Pro-N	1	0	1.000	1	1	1	0	0	9	8	0	4	4	12.0	1.00	285	.250	.333	1	.333	0	2	2	-0	0.2
Total	2	5	10	.333	15	15	14	0	0	129	163	3	27	51	13.3	4.40	60	.291	.324	11	.196	0	-24	-25	5	-1.8
● **KEN ASH**	Ash, Kenneth Lowther b: 9/16/01, Anmoore, W.Va. d: 11/15/79, Clarksburg, W.Va. BR/TR, 5'11", 165 lbs. Deb: 4/17/25																									
1925	Chi-A	0	0	—	2	0	0	0	0	4	7	2	0	0	15.8	9.00	46	.389	.389	0	—	0	-2	-2	-0	0.0
1928	Cin-N	3	3	.500	8	5	2	0	0	36	43	1	13	6	14.3	6.50	61	.314	.377	1	.071	-1	-10	-10	0	-1.4
1929	Cin-N	1	5	.167	29	7	2	0	2	82	91	2	30	26	13.8	4.83	95	.292	.363	3	.143	-1	-1	-2	-0	-0.3
1930	Cin-N	2	0	1.000	16	1	1	0	0	39^1	37	1	16	15	12.1	3.43	141	.268	.344	2	.182	-1	7	6	1	0.3
Total	4	6	8	.429	55	13	5	0	2	161^1	178	6	59	47	13.6	4.96	90	.294	.363	6	.130	-3	-6	-9	1	-1.4
● **ANDY ASHBY**	Ashby, Andrew Jason b: 7/11/67, Kansas City, Mo. BR/TR, 6'5", 190 lbs. Deb: 6/10/91																									
1991	Phi-N	1	5	.167	8	8	0	0	0	42	41	5	19	26	13.5	6.00	61	.256	.346	1	.083	-1	-11	-11	0	-1.4
1992	Phi-N	1	3	.250	10	8	0	0	0	37	42	6	21	24	15.6	7.54	46	.290	.383	1	.091	-0	-17	-17	0	-1.6
1993	Col-N	0	4	.000	20	9	0	0	1	54	89	5	32	33	20.7	8.50	56	.377	.458	4	.267	0	-27	-22	1	-1.4
	SD-N	3	6	.333	12	12	0	0	0	69	79	14	24	44	13.6	5.48	75	.295	.355	1	.048	-1	-11	-10	0	-1.2
	Yr	3	10	.231	32	21	0	0	1	123	168	19	56	77	16.5	6.80	65	.329	.397	5	.139	-1	-38	-33	1	-2.6
1994	SD-N	6	11	.353	24	24	4	0	0	164^1	145	16	43	121	10.5	3.40	121	.233	.286	8	.163	-0	15	13	0	1.2
1995	SD-N	12	10	.545	31	31	2	2	0	192^2	180	17	62	150	11.8	2.94	137	.252	.322	8	.163	-0	26	23	-2	2.3
1996	*SD-N	9	5	.643	24	24	1	0	0	150^2	147	17	34	85	11.0	3.23	123	.259	.305	11	.244	3	17	12	1	1.5
1997	SD-N	9	11	.450	30	30	2	0	0	200^2	207	17	49	144	11.7	4.13	94	.266	.314	4	.067	-3	2	-6	1	-0.6
1998	*SD-N★	17	9	.654	33	33	5	1	0	226^2	223	23	58	151	11.4	3.34	115	.259	.311	8	.111	-2	23	12	1	1.2
Total	8	58	64	.475	192	179	14	3	1	1137	1153	120	342	778	12.1	4.01	99	.265	.324	46	.138	-3	17	-4	3	-0.0
● **PAUL ASSENMACHER**	Assenmacher, Paul Andre b: 12/10/60, Detroit, Mich. BL/TL, 6'3", 200 lbs. Deb: 4/12/86																									
1986	Atl-N	7	3	.700	61	0	0	0	7	68^1	61	5	26	56	11.5	2.50	159	.241	.312	0	.000	-0	9	11	1	1.9
1987	Atl-N	1	1	.500	52	0	0	0	2	54^2	58	8	24	39	13.7	5.10	85	.260	.335	0	.000	-0	-6	-5	-1	-0.3
1988	Atl-N	8	7	.533	64	0	0	0	5	79^1	72	4	32	71	11.9	3.06	120	.251	.328	1	.333	1	3	5	0	1.2
1989	Atl-N	1	3	.250	49	0	0	0	0	57^2	55	2	16	64	11.2	3.59	102	.249	.303	0	.000	-0	-1	0	0	0.0
	*Chi-N	2	1	.667	14	0	0	0	0	19	19	1	12	15	14.7	5.21	72	.275	.383	0	.000	-0	-4	-3	0	-0.5
	Yr	3	4	.429	63	0	0	0	0	76^2	74	3	28	79	12.0	3.99	92	.253	.318	0	.000	-1	-4	-3	1	-0.5
1990	Chi-N	7	2	.778	74	1	0	0	10	103	90	10	36	95	11.1	2.80	146	.239	.308	0	.000	-1	11	15	1	1.5
1991	Chi-N	7	8	.467	75	0	0	0	15	102^2	85	10	31	117	10.4	3.24	120	.223	.287	1	.250	0	5	7	-1	1.2
1992	Chi-N	4	4	.500	70	0	0	0	8	68	72	6	26	67	13.4	4.10	88	.271	.342	0	.000	-0	-5	-4	-1	-0.6
1993	Chi-N	2	1	.667	46	0	0	0	0	38^2	44	5	13	34	13.3	3.49	114	.288	.343	1	.500	0	2	2	-0	0.1
	NY-A	2	2	.500	26	0	0	0	0	17^1	10	0	9	11	10.4	3.12	133	.175	.299	0	—	0	2	2	-0	0.4
1994	Chi-A	1	2	.333	44	0	0	0	1	33	26	2	13	29	10.9	3.55	132	.224	.308	0	—	0	5	4	0	0.4
1995	*Cle-A	6	2	.750	47	0	0	0	0	38^1	32	3	12	40	11.0	2.82	167	.225	.299	0	—	0	8	8	0	1.4
1996	*Cle-A	4	2	.667	63	0	0	0	1	46^2	46	1	14	44	12.3	3.09	158	.260	.328	0	—	0	10	9	-0	1.0
1997	*Cle-A	5	0	1.000	75	0	0	0	4	49	43	5	15	53	10.8	2.94	159	.231	.292	0	—	0	9	10	0	1.0
1998	*Cle-A	2	5	.286	69	0	0	0	3	47	54	5	19	43	14.2	3.26	147	.286	.354	0	—	0	7	8	-0	1.0
Total	13	59	43	.578	829	1	0	0	56	822^2	767	67	298	778	11.9	3.35	123	.248	.318	3	.083	-0	57	72	0	9.7
● **PEDRO ASTACIO**	Astacio, Pedro Julio (Pura) b: 11/28/69, Hato Mayor, D.R. BR/TR, 6'2", 190 lbs. Deb: 7/3/92																									
1992	LA-N	5	5	.500	11	11	4	4	0	82	80	1	20	43	11.2	1.98	174	.255	.304	3	.125	-1	14	13	-0	1.6
1993	LA-N	14	9	.609	31	31	3	2	0	186^1	165	14	68	122	11.5	3.57	107	.239	.312	10	.161	-1	10	5	-1	0.3
1994	LA-N	6	8	.429	23	23	3	1	0	149	142	18	47	108	11.7	4.29	91	.252	.314	3	.064	-3	-1	-6	-1	-0.9
1995	*LA-N	7	8	.467	48	11	1	1	0	104	103	12	29	80	11.8	4.24	89	.261	.318	3	.125	-0	-1	-5	0	-0.7
1996	*LA-N	9	8	.529	35	32	0	0	0	211^2	207	18	67	130	12.0	3.44	112	.261	.326	6	.088	-4	18	10	1	0.4
1997	LA-N	7	9	.438	26	24	2	1	0	153^2	151	15	47	115	11.8	4.10	94	.256	.316	6	.146	-0	2	-4	2	-0.2
	Col-N	5	1	.833	7	7	0	0	0	48^2	49	9	14	51	12.6	4.25	122	.262	.330	1	.077	-1	-0	5	1	0.6
	Yr	12	10	.545	33	31	2	1	0	202^1	200	24	61	166	11.8	4.14	101	.255	.313	7	.130	-1	1	1	3	0.4
1998	Col-N	13	14	.481	35	34	0	0	0	209^1	245	39	74	170	14.4	6.23	81	.294	.364	8	.129	-2	-47	-27	2	-3.1
Total	7	66	62	.516	216	173	13	9	0	1144^2	1142	126	366	819	12.2	4.18	98	.262	.326	40	.117	-12	-5	-10	4	-2.0
● **KEITH ATHERTON**	Atherton, Keith Rowe b: 2/19/59, Newport News, Va. BR/TR, 6'4", 200 lbs. Deb: 7/14/83																									
1983	Oak-A	2	5	.286	29	0	0	0	4	68^1	53	7	23	40	10.1	2.77	139	.215	.285	0	.000	-0	10	8	-1	0.8
1984	Oak-A	7	6	.538	57	0	0	0	2	104	110	13	39	58	13.1	4.33	86	.274	.341	0	—	0	-4	-7	-2	-1.0
1985	Oak-A	4	7	.364	56	0	0	0	3	104^2	89	17	42	77	11.3	4.30	90	.231	.306	0	—	0	-2	-5	-2	-0.3
1986	Oak-A	1	2	.333	13	0	0	0	0	15^1	18	2	11	8	17.0	5.87	66	.295	.403	0	—	0	-3	-3	-0	-0.2
	Min-A	5	8	.385	47	0	0	0	10	81^2	82	9	35	59	13.0	3.75	115	.264	.340	0	—	0	4	5	-0	0.7
	Yr	6	10	.375	60	0	0	0	10	97	100	11	46	67	13.6	4.08	104	.267	.349	0	—	0	1	2	-0	0.5
1987	*Min-A	7	5	.583	59	0	0	0	2	79^1	81	10	30	51	13.0	4.54	102	.262	.335	0	—	0	-1	1	-0	0.1
1988	Min-A	7	5	.583	49	0	0	0	3	74	65	10	22	43	10.8	3.41	119	.235	.296	0	—	0	5	5	-0	0.7
1989	Cle-A	0	3	.000	32	0	0	0	2	39	48	7	13	13	14.1	4.15	95	.293	.345	0	—	0	-1	-1	-1	-0.2
Total	7	33	41	.446	342	0	0	0	26	566^1	546	75	215	349	12.3	3.99	101	.253	.324	0	.000	-0	8	3	-6	0.6
● **TOMMY ATKINS**	Atkins, Francis Montgomery b: 12/9/1887, Ponca, Neb. d: 5/7/56, Cleveland, Ohio BL/TL, 5'10.5", 165 lbs. Deb: 10/2/09																									
1909	Phi-A	0	0	—	1	1	0	0	0	6	6	0	5	4	16.5	4.50	53	.261	.393	0	.000	-0	-1	-1	0	0.0
1910	Phi-A	3	2	.600	15	3	2	0	2	57	53	0	23	29	12.2	2.68	88	.254	.330	2	.118	-1	-1	-2	0	-0.3
Total	2	3	2	.600	16	4	2	0	2	63	59	0	28	33	12.6	2.86	83	.254	.337	2	.105	-1	-2	-3	0	-0.3
● **JAMES ATKINS**	Atkins, James Curtis b: 3/10/21, Birmingham, Ala. BL/TR, 6'3", 205 lbs. Deb: 9/29/50																									
1950	Bos-A	0	0	—	1	0	0	0	0	4^2	4	1	4	0	17.4	3.86	127	.235	.409	0	.000	-0	0	1	-0	0.0
1952	Bos-A	0	1	.000	3	1	0	0	0	10^1	11	0	7	2	15.7	3.48	113	.275	.383	2	.667	1	0	1	0	0.1
Total	2	0	1	.000	4	1	0	0	0	15	15	1	11	2	16.2	3.60	118	.263	.391	2	.400	0	1	1	0	0.1
● **AL ATKINSON**	Atkinson, Albert Wright b: 3/9/1861, Clinton, Ill. d: 6/17/52, Elkhorn Township, Mo. BR/TR, 5'11.5", 165 lbs. Deb: 5/1/1884																									
1884	Phi-a	11	11	.500	22	22	20	1	0	184	186	3	21	93	10.6	4.21	80	.244	.274	16	.193	-1	-20	-17	0	-1.7
	CP-U	6	10	.375	16	16	16	1	0	140	127	1	21	104	9.5	2.76	88	.226	.253	14	.206	-5	-5	-5	1	-0.9
	Bal-U	3	5	.375	8	8	8	0	0	69^2	60	4	12	50	9.3	2.33	115	.217	.249	4	.138	-4	1	3	0	-0.1
	Yr	9	15	.375	24	24	24	1	0	209^2	187	5	33	154	9.4	2.62	96	.223	.252	18	.186	-9	-4	-2	1	-1.0
1886	Phi-a	25	17	.595	45	45	44	1	0	396^2	414	11	101	154	12.2	3.95	89	.256	.308	18	.122	-6	-22	-20	-2	-2.4
1887	Phi-a	6	8	.429	15	15	11	0	0	124^2	156	2	54	34	15.6	5.92	72	.292	.364	12	.203	-1	-22	-23	1	-1.8
Total	3	51	51	.500	106	106	99	3	0	915	943	21	209	435	11.7	3.96	85	.251	.297	64	.165	-16	-68	-61	-1	-6.9
● **BILL ATKINSON**	Atkinson, William Cecil Glenn b: 10/4/54, Chatham, Ont., Can. BL/TR, 5'7", 165 lbs. Deb: 9/18/76																									
1976	Mon-N	0	0	—	4	0	0	0	0	5	3	0	1	4	7.2	0.00	—	.176	.222	0	—	0	2	2	0	0.0
1977	Mon-N	7	2	.778	55	0	0	0	7	83^1	72	12	29	56	10.9	3.35	114	.234	.300	1	.200	-0	5	4	1	0.6
1978	Mon-N	2	2	.500	29	0	0	0	3	45^1	45	5	28	32	14.7	4.37	81	.268	.376	2	.500	1	-4	-4	0	-0.3
1979	Mon-N	2	0	1.000	10	0	0	0	1	13^2	9	0	4	7	8.6	1.98	186	.170	.228	0	.000	-0	3	3	-0	0.3
Total	4	11	4	.733	98	0	0	0	11	147^1	129	17	62	99	11.7	3.42	108	.236	.315	3	.300	1	6	5	1	0.6
● **DEREK AUCOIN**	Aucoin, Derek Alfred b: 3/27/70, Lachine, Que., Can. BR/TR, 6'7", 235 lbs. Deb: 5/21/96																									
1996	Mon-N	0	1	.000	2	0	0	0	0	2^2	3	0	1	1	13.5	3.38	128	.300	.364	0	—	0	0	0	0	0.1

YEAR	TM/L	W	L	PCT	G	GS	CG	SH	SV	IP	H	HR	BB	SO	RAT	ERA	ERA+	OAV	OOB	BH	AVG	PB	PR	/A	PD	TPI
● DON AUGUST August, Donald Glenn b: 7/3/63, Inglewood, Cal. BR/TR, 6'3", 190 lbs. Deb: 6/2/88																										
1988	Mil-A	13	7	.650	24	22	6	1	0	148^1	137	12	48	66	11.2	3.09	129	.245	.305	0	—	0	14	15	2	2.1
1989	Mil-A	12	12	.500	31	25	2	1	0	142^1	175	17	58	51	14.9	5.31	72	.302	.368	0	—	0	-23	-23	1	-3.3
1990	Mil-A	0	3	.000	5	0	0	0	0	11	13	0	5	2	14.7	6.55	59	.295	.367	0	—	0	-3	-3	0	-0.7
1991	Mil-A	9	8	.529	28	23	1	1	0	138^1	166	18	47	62	14.1	5.47	73	.301	.359	0	—	0	-21	-23	0	-2.3
Total	4	34	30	.531	88	70	9	3	0	440	491	47	158	181	13.4	4.64	85	.283	.345	0	—	0	-33	-35	4	-4.2
● JERRY AUGUSTINE Augustine, Gerald Lee b: 7/24/52, Kewaunee, Wis. BL/TL, 6', 185 lbs. Deb: 9/9/75																										
1975	Mil-A	2	0	1.000	5	3	1	0	0	26^2	26	2	12	8	13.2	3.04	126	.274	.361	0	—	0	2	2	-0	0.1
1976	Mil-A	9	12	.429	39	24	5	3	0	171^2	167	9	56	59	11.9	3.30	106	.261	.324	0	—	0	4	4	-2	0.3
1977	Mil-A	12	18	.400	33	33	10	1	0	209	222	23	72	68	12.8	4.48	91	.277	.339	0	—	0	-10	-10	0	-1.2
1978	Mil-A	13	12	.520	35	30	9	2	0	188^1	204	14	61	59	12.9	4.54	83	.280	.339	0	—	0	-16	-16	2	-1.7
1979	Mil-A	9	6	.600	43	2	0	0	5	85^2	95	6	30	41	13.2	3.47	120	.284	.344	0	—	0	7	7	-2	1.0
1980	Mil-A	4	3	.571	39	1	0	0	2	69^2	83	5	36	22	15.6	4.52	86	.301	.385	0	—	0	-4	-5	0	-0.4
1981	Mil-A	2	2	.500	27	2	0	0	2	61^1	75	4	18	26	13.8	4.26	80	.300	.349	0	—	0	-4	-6	0	-0.3
1982	Mil-A	1	3	.250	20	2	1	0	0	62	63	13	26	22	13.2	5.08	74	.267	.345	0	—	0	-7	-9	-1	-0.2
1983	Mil-A	3	3	.500	34	7	1	0	2	64^1	89	11	25	40	16.1	5.74	65	.328	.387	0	—	0	-12	-14	-0	-1.3
1984	Mil-A	0	0	—	4	0	0	0	0	5^1	4	0	4	3	15.2	0.00	—	.211	.375	0	—	0	2	2	0	0.0
Total	10	55	59	.482	279	104	27	6	11	944	1028	87	340	348	13.2	4.23	90	.281	.346	0	—	0	-37	-45	-3	-3.7
● ELDEN AUKER Auker, Elden Le Roy "Submarine" b: 9/21/10, Norcatur, Kan. BR/TR, 6'2", 194 lbs. Deb: 8/10/33																										
1933	Det-A	3	3	.500	15	6	2	1	0	55	63	3	25	17	14.7	5.24	82	.285	.363	2	.118	-1	-6	-6	-1	-0.7
1934	*Det-A	15	7	.682	43	18	10	2	1	205	234	9	56	86	12.9	3.42	128	.288	.336	11	.149	-2	24	22	3	2.1
1935	*Det-A	18	7	**.720**	36	25	13	2	0	195	213	13	61	63	13.1	3.83	109	.279	.340	16	.216	1	14	7	1	1.0
1936	Det-A	13	16	.448	35	31	14	2	0	215^1	263	11	83	66	14.6	4.89	101	.302	.365	24	.308	7	4	1	5	1.2
1937	Det-A	17	9	.654	39	32	19	1	1	252^2	250	13	97	73	12.6	3.88	120	.260	.331	18	.198	4	21	22	5	2.9
1938	Det-A	11	10	.524	27	24	12	1	0	160^2	184	14	56	46	13.7	5.27	95	.284	.346	5	.088	-4	-9	-5	3	-0.6
1939	Bos-A	9	10	.474	31	25	6	1	0	151	183	13	61	43	14.6	5.36	88	.294	.358	12	.226	2	-12	-11	2	-0.8
1940	StL-A	16	11	.593	38	35	20	2	0	263^2	299	17	96	78	13.6	3.96	116	.281	.342	19	.213	3	12	18	2	2.1
1941	StL-A	14	15	.483	34	31	13	0	0	216	268	20	85	60	14.8	5.50	78	.303	.365	10	.125	-3	-32	-29	1	-3.3
1942	StL-A	14	13	.519	35	34	17	2	0	249	273	16	86	62	13.1	4.08	91	.277	.337	14	.161	-1	-12	-11	1	-1.1
Total	10	130	101	.563	333	261	126	14	2	1963^1	2230	129	706	594	13.6	4.42	101	.285	.347	131	.187	6	3	11	21	2.8
● JOE AUSANIO Ausanio, Joseph John b: 12/9/65, Kingston, N.Y. BR/TR, 6'1", 205 lbs. Deb: 7/14/94																										
1994	NY-A	2	1	.667	13	0	0	0	0	15^2	16	3	6	15	12.6	5.17	88	.254	.319	0	—	0	-1	-1	0	0.0
1995	NY-A	2	0	1.000	28	0	0	0	1	37^2	42	9	23	36	15.5	5.73	80	.286	.382	0	—	0	-4	-5	-0	-0.2
Total	2	4	1	.800	41	0	0	0	1	53^1	58	12	29	51	14.7	5.57	83	.276	.364	0	—	0	-5	-6	-0	-0.2
● DENNIS AUST Aust, Dennis Kay b: 11/25/40, Tecumseh, Neb. BR/TR, 5'11", 180 lbs. Deb: 9/6/65																										
1965	StL-N	0	0	—	6	0	0	0	1	7^1	6	0	2	7	9.8	4.91	78	.214	.267	0	.000	-0	-1	-1	0	0.0
1966	StL-N	0	1	.000	9	0	0	0	1	9^2	12	1	6	7	16.8	6.52	55	.308	.400	0	.000	-0	-3	-3	-0	-0.4
Total	2	0	1	.000	15	0	0	0	2	17	18	1	8	14	13.8	5.82	64	.269	.347	0	.000	-0	-4	-4	0	-0.4
● JIM AUSTIN Austin, James Parker b: 12/7/63, Farmville, Va. BR/TR, 6'2", 200 lbs. Deb: 7/4/91																										
1991	Mil-A	0	0	—	5	0	0	0	0	8^2	8	1	11	3	22.8	8.31	48	.276	.512	0	—	0	-4	-4	0	0.1
1992	Mil-A	5	2	.714	47	0	0	0	0	58^1	38	2	32	30	11.1	1.85	207	.191	.309	0	—	0	14	13	-1	1.5
1993	Mil-A	1	2	.333	31	0	0	0	0	33	28	3	13	15	11.5	3.82	111	.230	.309	0	—	0	2	2	-0	0.1
Total	3	6	4	.600	83	0	0	0	0	100	74	6	56	48	12.2	3.06	130	.211	.330	0	—	0	11	10	-1	1.7
● RICK AUSTIN Austin, Rick Gerald b: 10/27/46, Seattle, Wash. BR/TL, 6'4", 190 lbs. Deb: 6/21/70																										
1970	Cle-A	2	5	.286	31	8	1	1	3	67^2	74	10	26	53	13.7	4.79	83	.281	.353	2	.111	0	-8	-6	1	-0.5
1971	Cle-A	0	0	—	23	0	0	0	1	23	25	3	20	20	18.8	5.09	75	.291	.440	0	.000	-0	-4	-3	0	0.0
1975	Mil-A	2	3	.400	32	0	0	0	2	40	32	3	32	30	14.6	4.05	95	.222	.367	0	—	0	-1	-1	-1	-0.2
1976	Mil-A	0	0	—	3	0	0	0	0	5^1	10	1	0	3	18.6	5.06	69	.435	.458	0	—	0	-1	-1	0	0.0
Total	4	4	8	.333	89	8	1	1	6	136	141	17	78	106	15.0	4.63	84	.273	.377	2	.105	0	-14	-11	1	-0.7
● AL AUTRY Autry, Albert b: 2/29/52, Modesto, Cal. BR/TR, 6'5", 225 lbs. Deb: 9/14/76																										
1976	Atl-N	1	0	1.000	1	1	0	0	0	5	4	2	3	3	12.6	5.40	70	.222	.333	0	.000	-0	-1	-1	-0	-0.2
● STEVE AVERY Avery, Steven Thomas b: 4/14/70, Trenton, Mich. BL/TL, 6'4", 190 lbs. Deb: 6/13/90																										
1990	Atl-N	3	11	.214	21	20	1	1	0	99	121	7	45	75	15.3	5.64	72	.302	.375	4	.133	-1	-20	-18	2	-2.1
1991	*Atl-N	18	8	.692	35	35	3	1	0	210^1	189	21	65	137	11.0	3.38	115	.240	.300	17	.215	3	7	12	-0	1.8
1992	*Atl-N	11	11	.500	35	35	2	2	0	233^2	216	14	71	129	11.1	3.20	114	.246	.302	13	.171	2	8	12	-0	1.2
1993	*Atl-N★	18	6	.750	35	35	3	1	0	223^1	216	14	43	125	10.4	2.94	136	.261	.297	12	.160	1	27	27	2	2.9
1994	Atl-N	8	3	.727	24	24	1	0	0	151^2	127	15	55	122	11.0	4.04	105	.227	.301	5	.102	-2	3	3	0	0.1
1995	*Atl-N	7	13	.350	29	29	3	1	0	173^1	165	22	52	141	11.6	4.67	91	.252	.312	11	.208	3	-10	-8	2	-0.3
1996	*Atl-N	7	10	.412	24	23	1	0	0	131	146	10	40	86	13.1	4.47	99	.285	.341	11	.239	5	-4	-1	1	0.5
1997	Bos-A	6	7	.462	22	18	0	0	0	96^2	127	15	49	51	16.6	6.42	72	.320	.397	0	.000	-0	-20	-19	1	-2.1
1998	Bos-A	10	7	.588	34	23	0	0	0	123^2	128	14	64	57	14.3	5.02	92	.269	.361	0	.000	-0	-5	-6	4	-0.2
Total	9	88	76	.537	259	242	14	6	0	1442^2	1435	132	484	923	12.1	4.10	101	.261	.324	73	.178	10	-13	4	12	1.8
● JAY AVREA Avrea, James Epherium b: 7/6/20, Cleburne, Tex. d: 6/26/87, Dallas, Tex. BR/TR, 6'1.5", 175 lbs. Deb: 4/22/50																										
1950	Cin-N	0	0	—	2	0	0	0	0	5^1	6	0	3	2	15.2	3.38	125	.273	.360	0	.000	-0	0	1	-0	0.0
● BOBBY AYALA Ayala, Robert Joseph b: 7/8/69, Ventura, Cal. BR/TR, 6'3", 200 lbs. Deb: 9/5/92																										
1992	Cin-N	2	1	.667	5	5	0	0	0	29	33	1	13	23	14.6	4.34	83	.297	.376	0	.000	-1	-3	-2	1	-0.2
1993	Cin-N	7	10	.412	43	9	0	0	3	98	106	16	45	65	14.5	5.60	72	.274	.360	2	.095	-1	-17	-17	-1	-2.9
1994	Sea-A	4	3	.571	46	0	0	0	18	56^2	42	2	26	76	10.8	2.86	171	.203	.292	0	—	0	12	13	-0	2.0
1995	*Sea-A	6	5	.545	63	0	0	0	19	71	73	9	30	77	13.8	4.44	107	.262	.346	0	—	0	2	2	-0	0.4
1996	Sea-A	6	3	.667	50	0	0	0	3	67^1	65	10	25	61	12.3	5.88	84	.256	.327	0	—	0	-7	-7	0	-0.8
1997	*Sea-A	10	5	.667	71	0	0	0	8	96^2	91	14	41	92	12.6	3.82	118	.260	.343	0	—	0	8	7	-0	1.1
1998	Sea-A	1	10	.091	62	0	0	0	8	75^1	100	9	26	68	15.2	7.29	64	.323	.377	0	—	0	-22	-22	-0	-3.1
Total	7	36	37	.493	340	14	0	0	59	494	510	61	206	462	13.4	4.99	90	.269	.347	2	.067	-2	-26	-26	-0	-3.5
● MANUEL AYBAR Aybar, Manuel Antonio b: 10/5/74, Bani, D.R. BR/TR, 6'1", 165 lbs. Deb: 8/4/97																										
1997	StL-N	2	4	.333	12	12	0	0	0	68	66	8	29	41	13.1	4.24	98	.263	.349	3	.143	-0	-0	-1	-0	-0.1
1998	StL-N	6	6	.500	20	14	0	0	0	81^1	90	6	42	57	14.8	5.98	70	.281	.368	6	.222	1	-16	-16	-0	-1.9
Total	2	8	10	.444	32	26	0	0	0	149^1	156	14	71	98	14.0	5.18	80	.273	.360	9	.188	1	-16	-17	-1	-2.0
● JAKE AYDELOTT Aydelott, Jacob Stuart b: 7/6/1861, N.Manchester, Ind. d: 10/22/26, Detroit, Mich. 6', 180 lbs. Deb: 5/15/1884																										
1884	Ind-a	5	7	.417	12	12	11	0	0	106	129	0	29	30	13.4	4.92	67	.282	.324	5	.114	-3	-20	-19	-2	-2.0
1886	Phi-a	0	2	.000	2	2	2	0	0	18	21	0	12	5	16.5	4.00	88	.304	.407	0	.000	-1	-1	-1	-0	-0.2
Total	2	5	9	.357	14	14	13	0	0	124	150	0	41	35	13.9	4.79	69	.285	.336	5	.100	-4	-21	-20	-2	-2.2
● BILL AYERS Ayers, William Oscar b: 9/27/19, Newnan, Ga. d: 9/24/80, Newnan, Ga. BR/TR, 6'3", 185 lbs. Deb: 4/17/47																										
1947	NY-N	0	3	.000	13	4	0	0	1	35^1	46	7	14	22	15.5	8.15	50	.322	.386	2	.250	0	-16	-16	1	-1.2
● DOC AYERS Ayers, Yancy Wyatt b: 5/20/1890, Fancy Gap, Va. d: 5/26/68, Pulaski, Va. BR/TR, 6'1", 185 lbs. Deb: 9/9/13																										
1913	Was-A	1	1	.500	4	2	1	1	1	17^2	12	0	4	17	8.7	1.53	193	.182	.239	0	.000	-1	3	3	1	0.3
1914	Was-A	11	15	.423	49	32	8	3	3	265^1	221	5	54	148	9.6	2.54	111	.238	.286	14	.169	-0	6	8	-2	0.5
1915	Was-A	14	9	.609	40	16	8	2	3	211^1	178	1	38	96	9.5	2.21	134	.234	.276	12	.190	-1	17	18	-4	1.2
1916	Was-A	5	8	.385	43	17	7	0	2	157	173	4	52	69	13.1	3.78	74	.285	.346	6	.140	-2	-17	-17	-4	-2.1

YEAR	TM/L	W	L	PCT	G	GS	CG	SH	SV	IP	H	HR	BB	SO	RAT	ERA	ERA+	OAV	OOB	BH	AVG	PB	PR	/A	PD	TPI
1917	Was-A	11	10	.524	40	15	12	3	1	207^2	192	3	59	78	11.2	2.17	121	.256	.317	13	.206	-0	11	11	-1	1.0
1918	Was-A	10	12	.455	40	24	11	4	3	219^2	215	2	63	67	11.7	2.83	96	.261	.319	10	.152	-2	-1	-2	-0	-0.5
1919	Was-A	0	6	.000	11	5	0	0	1	43^2	52	0	17	12	15.0	2.89	111	.317	.395	5	.417	2	2	2	1	0.4
	Det-A	5	3	.625	24	5	3	1	0	93^2	88	2	31	32	11.7	2.69	119	.254	.320	3	.125	-1	6	5	-0	0.3
	Yr	5	9	.357	35	10	3	1	1	137^1	140	2	48	44	12.5	2.75	116	.272	.337	8	.222	0	7	7	0	0.7
1920	Det-A	7	14	.333	46	23	8	3	1	208^2	217	6	62	103	12.4	3.88	96	.280	.340	9	.153	-2	-2	-4	-0	-0.6
1921	Det-A	0	0	—	2	1	0	0	0	4	9	0	2	0	24.8	9.00	47	.450	.500	0	—	0	-2	-2	-0	0.0
Total	9	64	78	.451	299	140	58	17	15	1428^2	1357	23	382	622	11.3	2.84	105	.259	.315	72	.171	-8	22	21	-10	0.5

● BOB AYRAULT Ayrault, Robert Cunningham b: 4/27/66, South Lake Tahoe, Cal. BR/TR, 6′4″, 230 lbs. Deb: 6/7/92

YEAR	TM/L	W	L	PCT	G	GS	CG	SH	SV	IP	H	HR	BB	SO	RAT	ERA	ERA+	OAV	OOB	BH	AVG	PB	PR	/A	PD	TPI
1992	Phi-N	2	2	.500	30	0	0	0	0	43^1	32	0	17	27	10.4	3.12	112	.209	.292	0	—	0	2	2	0	0.2
1993	Phi-N	2	0	1.000	10	0	0	0	0	10^1	18	1	10	8	25.3	9.58	41	.375	.492	0	.000	-0	-6	-6	-0	-1.1
	Sea-A	1	1	.500	14	0	0	0	0	19^2	18	1	6	7	11.0	3.20	137	.254	.312	0	—	0	2	3	-0	0.2
Total	2	5	3	.625	54	0	0	0	0	73^1	68	2	33	42	12.6	4.05	94	.250	.336	0	.000	-0	-2	-2	-0	-0.7

● BOB BABCOCK Babcock, Robert Ernest b: 8/25/49, New Castle, Pa. BR/TR, 6′5″, 210 lbs. Deb: 7/22/79

YEAR	TM/L	W	L	PCT	G	GS	CG	SH	SV	IP	H	HR	BB	SO	RAT	ERA	ERA+	OAV	OOB	BH	AVG	PB	PR	/A	PD	TPI
1979	Tex-A	0	0	—	4	0	0	0	0	5^1	7	1	7	6	23.6	10.13	41	.318	.483	0	—	0	-4	-4	0	0.0
1980	Tex-A	1	2	.333	19	0	0	0	0	23^1	20	3	8	15	11.6	4.63	84	.238	.319	0	—	0	-2	-2	-0	-0.2
1981	Tex-A	1	1	.500	16	0	0	0	0	28^2	21	2	16	18	11.9	2.20	158	.219	.336	0	—	0	5	4	-0	0.3
Total	3	2	3	.400	39	0	0	0	0	57^1	48	6	31	39	12.9	3.92	94	.238	.347	0	—	0	-0	-1	-0	0.1

● JOHNNY BABICH Babich, John Charles b: 5/14/13, Albion, Cal. BR/TR, 6′1.5″, 185 lbs. Deb: 6/19/34

YEAR	TM/L	W	L	PCT	G	GS	CG	SH	SV	IP	H	HR	BB	SO	RAT	ERA	ERA+	OAV	OOB	BH	AVG	PB	PR	/A	PD	TPI
1934	Bro-N	7	11	.389	25	19	7	0	1	135	148	5	51	62	13.4	4.20	93	.281	.347	7	.140	-3	-2	-4	2	-0.6
1935	Bro-N	7	14	.333	37	24	7	2	0	143^1	191	7	52	55	15.4	6.66	60	.317	.373	9	.184	-0	-42	-43	0	-5.1
1936	Bos-N	0	0	—	3	0	0	0	0	6	11	1	6	1	27.0	10.50	37	.440	.563	0	.000	-0	-4	-4	0	0.0
1940	Phi-A	14	13	.519	31	30	16	1	0	229^1	222	16	80	94	11.9	3.73	119	.248	.310	10	.116	-6	17	18	0	1.4
1941	Phi-A	2	7	.222	16	14	4	0	0	78^1	85	9	31	19	13.7	6.09	69	.281	.353	10	.400	4	-17	-17	1	-1.1
Total	5	30	45	.400	112	87	34	3	1	592	657	38	220	231	13.5	4.93	85	.279	.343	36	.171	-5	-49	-50	3	-5.4

● LES BACKMAN Backman, Lester John b: 3/20/1888, Cleves, Ohio d: 11/8/75, Cincinnati, Ohio BR/TR, 6′0.5″, 195 lbs. Deb: 7/3/09

YEAR	TM/L	W	L	PCT	G	GS	CG	SH	SV	IP	H	HR	BB	SO	RAT	ERA	ERA+	OAV	OOB	BH	AVG	PB	PR	/A	PD	TPI
1909	StL-N	3	11	.214	21	15	8	0	0	128^1	146	1	39	35	13.2	4.14	61	.302	.357	4	.103	-1	-22	-23	-0	-2.5
1910	StL-N	6	7	.462	26	11	4	0	2	116	117	4	53	41	13.3	3.03	98	.265	.346	4	.114	0	0	-1	-0	-0.1
Total	2	9	18	.333	47	26	12	0	2	244^1	263	5	92	76	13.3	3.61	76	.284	.352	8	.108	-1	-22	-24	-1	-2.6

● EDDIE BACON Bacon, Edgar Suter b: 4/8/1895, Franklin Co., Ky. d: 10/2/63, Louisville, Ky. Deb: 8/13/17 ♦

YEAR	TM/L	W	L	PCT	G	GS	CG	SH	SV	IP	H	HR	BB	SO	RAT	ERA	ERA+	OAV	OOB	BH	AVG	PB	PR	/A	PD	TPI
1917	Phi-A	0	0	—	1	0	0	0	0	6	5	0	7	0	18.0	6.00	46	.238	.429	3	.500	1	-2	-2	1	0.3

● MIKE BACSIK Bacsik, Michael James b: 4/1/52, Dallas, Tex. BR/TR, 6′1″, 185 lbs. Deb: 6/15/75

YEAR	TM/L	W	L	PCT	G	GS	CG	SH	SV	IP	H	HR	BB	SO	RAT	ERA	ERA+	OAV	OOB	BH	AVG	PB	PR	/A	PD	TPI
1975	Tex-A	1	2	.333	7	3	0	0	0	26^2	28	1	9	13	12.8	3.71	101	.275	.339	0	—	0	0	0	-0	0.0
1976	Tex-A	3	2	.600	23	0	0	0	0	55	66	3	26	21	15.4	4.25	84	.308	.388	0	—	0	-4	-4	-1	-0.4
1977	Tex-A	0	0	—	2	0	0	0	0	2^1	9	1	0	1	34.7	19.29	21	.563	.563	0	—	0	-4	-4	0	0.0
1979	Min-A	4	2	.667	31	0	0	0	0	65^2	61	6	29	33	12.3	4.39	100	.249	.328	0	—	0	-1	-0	-0	-0.1
1980	Min-A	0	0	—	10	0	0	0	0	23	26	1	11	9	14.5	4.30	101	.286	.363	0	—	0	-1	0	0	-0.1
Total	5	8	6	.571	73	3	0	0	0	172^2	190	12	75	77	14.0	4.43	91	.284	.359	0	—	0	-10	-8	-1	-0.6

● FRED BACZEWSKI Baczewski, Frederic John "Lefty" b: 5/15/26, St.Paul, Minn. d: 11/14/76, Culver City, Cal. BL/TL, 6′2.5″, 185 lbs. Deb: 4/26/53

YEAR	TM/L	W	L	PCT	G	GS	CG	SH	SV	IP	H	HR	BB	SO	RAT	ERA	ERA+	OAV	OOB	BH	AVG	PB	PR	/A	PD	TPI
1953	Chi-N	0	0	—	9	0	0	0	0	10	20	1	6	3	24.3	6.30	71	.435	.509	1	.500	0	-2	-2	-0	0.0
	Cin-N	11	4	.733	24	18	10	1	1	138^1	125	13	52	58	11.6	3.45	126	.244	.315	8	.178	-0	13	14	-3	1.1
	Yr	11	4	.733	33	18	10	1	1	148^1	145	14	58	61	12.4	3.64	120	.259	.330	9	.191	0	11	12	-3	1.1
1954	Cin-N	6	6	.500	29	22	4	1	0	130	159	22	53	43	14.7	5.26	80	.305	.370	3	.071	-3	-17	-15	-1	-1.7
1955	Cin-N	0	0	—	1	0	0	0	0	1	2	2	0	0	18.0	18.00	24	.400	.400	0	—	0	-2	-2	-0	0.0
Total	3	17	10	.630	63	40	14	2	1	279^1	306	38	111	104	13.5	4.45	96	.282	.351	12	.135	-3	-8	-5	-4	-0.6

● LORE BADER Bader, Lore Verne "King" b: 4/27/1888, Bader, Ill. d: 6/2/73, LeRoy, Kan. BL/TR, 6′, 175 lbs. Deb: 9/30/12 C

YEAR	TM/L	W	L	PCT	G	GS	CG	SH	SV	IP	H	HR	BB	SO	RAT	ERA	ERA+	OAV	OOB	BH	AVG	PB	PR	/A	PD	TPI
1912	NY-N	2	0	1.000	2	1	1	0	0	10	9	0	6	3	14.4	0.90	376	.250	.372	0	.000	-0	3	3	0	0.5
1917	Bos-A	2	0	1.000	15	1	0	0	1	38^1	48	1	18	14	15.7	2.35	110	.306	.381	3	.300	1	1	1	1	0.2
1918	Bos-A	1	3	.250	5	4	2	1	0	27	26	1	12	10	13.7	3.33	81	.271	.369	1	.111	-1	-2	-2	-1	-0.5
Total	3	5	3	.625	22	6	3	1	1	75^1	83	2	36	27	14.8	2.51	109	.287	.376	4	.182	-0	2	2	-0	0.2

● ED BAECHT Baecht, Edward Joseph b: 5/15/07, Paden, Okla. d: 8/15/57, Grafton, Ill. BR/TR, 6′3″, 195 lbs. Deb: 4/24/26

YEAR	TM/L	W	L	PCT	G	GS	CG	SH	SV	IP	H	HR	BB	SO	RAT	ERA	ERA+	OAV	OOB	BH	AVG	PB	PR	/A	PD	TPI
1926	Phi-N	2	0	1.000	28	1	1	0	0	56	73	4	28	14	16.4	6.11	68	.324	.402	2	.143	-1	-14	-12	2	-0.3
1927	Phi-N	0	1	.000	1	1	0	0	0	6	12	0	2	0	21.0	12.00	34	.429	.467	0	.000	-0	-5	-5	0	-0.6
1928	Phi-N	1	1	.500	9	1	0	0	0	24	37	1	9	10	17.3	6.00	71	.385	.438	1	.143	-0	-5	-5	0	-0.3
1931	Chi-N	2	4	.333	22	6	2	0	0	67	64	1	32	34	14.0	3.76	103	.250	.351	5	.278	1	1	1	1	0.2
1932	Chi-N	0	0	—	1	0	0	0	0	1	1	0	1	0	18.0	0.00	—	.333	.500	0	—	0	0	0	-0	0.0
1937	StL-A	0	0	—	3	0	0	0	0	6^1	13	3	6	3	29.8	12.79	38	.419	.538	0	.000	-0	-6	-6	0	0.0
Total	6	5	6	.455	64	9	3	0	0	160^1	200	9	78	61	16.2	5.56	73	.313	.397	8	.190	-1	-29	-27	3	-1.0

● JIM BAGBY Bagby, James Charles Jacob Jr. b: 9/8/16, Cleveland, Ohio d: 9/2/88, Marietta, Ga. BR/TR, 6′2″, 170 lbs. Deb: 4/18/38 F

YEAR	TM/L	W	L	PCT	G	GS	CG	SH	SV	IP	H	HR	BB	SO	RAT	ERA	ERA+	OAV	OOB	BH	AVG	PB	PR	/A	PD	TPI
1938	Bos-A	15	11	.577	43	25	10	1	2	198^2	218	9	90	73	14.1	4.21	117	.283	.360	13	.191	-1	13	16	2	1.9
1939	Bos-A	5	5	.500	21	11	3	0	0	80	119	7	36	35	17.7	7.09	67	.347	.412	10	.294	3	-22	-21	-0	-1.9
1940	Bos-A	10	16	.385	36	21	6	1	2	182^2	217	15	83	57	14.8	4.73	95	.296	.368	15	.203	-0	-7	-5	0	-0.6
1941	Cle-A	9	15	.375	33	27	12	0	2	200^2	214	10	76	53	13.3	4.04	98	.273	.341	18	.243	2	2	-2	2	0.1
1942	Cle-A☆	17	9	.654	38	35	16	4	1	270^2	267	19	64	54	11.0	2.96	117	.258	.302	18	.189	1	21	15	0	1.5
1943	Cle-A☆	17	14	.548	36	33	16	3	1	**273**	248	15	80	70	10.9	3.10	100	.240	.296	30	.268	4	6	0	2	0.9
1944	Cle-A	4	5	.444	13	10	2	0	0	79	101	2	34	12	15.8	4.33	76	.312	.384	7	.226	1	-8	-9	0	-0.8
1945	Cle-A	8	11	.421	25	19	11	3	1	159^1	171	3	59	38	13.1	3.73	87	.279	.344	17	.293	3	-6	-8	3	-0.3
1946	*Bos-A	7	6	.538	21	11	6	1	0	106^2	117	4	49	16	14.1	3.71	99	.279	.356	5	.119	-2	-2	-1	-0	-0.3
1947	Pit-N	5	4	.556	37	6	2	0	0	115^2	143	14	37	23	14.4	4.67	90	.304	.361	7	.219	1	-8	-6	1	-0.2
Total	10	97	96	.503	303	198	84	13	9	1666^1	1815	98	608	431	13.2	3.96	97	.278	.342	140	.226	12	-11	-23	10	0.3

● JIM BAGBY Bagby, James Charles Jacob Sr. "Sarge" b: 10/5/1889, Barnett, Ga. d: 7/28/54, Marietta, Ga. BB/TR, 6′, 170 lbs. Deb: 4/22/12 F

YEAR	TM/L	W	L	PCT	G	GS	CG	SH	SV	IP	H	HR	BB	SO	RAT	ERA	ERA+	OAV	OOB	BH	AVG	PB	PR	/A	PD	TPI
1912	Cin-N	2	1	.667	5	1	0	0	0	17^1	17	2	9	10	13.5	3.12	108	.270	.361	0	.000	-1	1	0	0	0.0
1917	Cle-A	23	13	.639	49	37	26	8	7	320^2	277	6	73	83	10.0	1.96	144	.235	.283	25	.231	2	25	31	-3	3.8
1918	Cle-A	17	16	.515	**45**	31	23	2	6	271^1	274	0	78	57	11.7	2.69	112	.276	.330	21	.212	-0	3	10	-2	1.0
1919	Cle-A	17	11	.607	35	32	21	0	3	241^1	258	3	44	61	11.4	2.80	120	.275	.310	23	.258	5	12	15	-0	2.1
1920	*Cle-A	**31**	12	**.721**	**48**	38	**30**	3	0	**339^2**	338	9	79	73	11.2	2.89	132	.266	.311	33	.252	6	34	34	-7	3.8
1921	Cle-A	14	12	.538	40	26	13	0	4	191^2	238	14	44	37	13.4	4.70	91	.308	.348	15	.197	-1	-9	9	-2	-1.4
1922	Cle-A	4	5	.444	25	10	4	0	1	98^1	134	5	39	25	16.1	6.32	63	.340	.404	11	.262	3	-25	-25	1	-1.7
1923	Pit-N	3	2	.600	21	6	2	0	3	68^2	95	6	25	16	15.9	5.24	76	.336	.392	1	.050	-2	-9	-9	-1	-0.9
Total	8	111	72	.607	268	181	119	13	24	1549	1631	45	391	362	11.9	3.20	109	.277	.324	129	.226	12	31	50	-13	6.7

● STAN BAHNSEN Bahnsen, Stanley Raymond b: 12/15/44, Council Bluffs, Ia. BR/TR, 6′2″, 203 lbs. Deb: 9/9/66

YEAR	TM/L	W	L	PCT	G	GS	CG	SH	SV	IP	H	HR	BB	SO	RAT	ERA	ERA+	OAV	OOB	BH	AVG	PB	PR	/A	PD	TPI
1966	NY-A	1	1	.500	4	3	1	0	1	23	15	3	7	16	8.6	3.52	94	.181	.244	1	.143	-0	-0	-1	-0	-0.1
1968	NY-A	17	12	.586	37	34	10	1	0	267^1	216	14	68	162	9.6	2.05	141	.221	.273	4	.049	-4	27	25	-2	2.2
1969	NY-A	9	16	.360	40	33	5	2	1	220^2	222	28	90	130	12.7	3.83	91	.260	.331	5	.083	-3	-5	-9	1	-1.2
1970	NY-A	14	11	.560	36	35	6	2	0	232^2	227	23	75	116	11.8	3.33	106	.256	.316	11	.149	-0	10	5	1	0.5
1971	NY-A	14	12	.538	36	34	14	3	0	242	221	20	72	110	11.1	3.35	97	.248	.308	12	.152	0	3	-3	3	0.0
1972	Chi-A	21	16	.568	43	41	5	1	0	252^1	263	22	73	157	12.2	3.60	87	.268	.323	14	.152	-1	-15	-13	2	-1.8
1973	Chi-A	18	21	.462	42	42	14	4	0	282^1	290	20	117	120	13.1	3.57	111	.269	.343	0	—	0	8	12	2	1.8
1974	Chi-A	12	15	.444	38	35	10	1	0	216^1	230	17	110	102	14.3	4.70	79	.277	.364	0	—	0	-26	-23	1	-2.6
1975	Chi-A	4	6	.400	12	12	2	0	0	67^1	78	9	40	31	16.2	6.01	64	.291	.389	0	—	0	-17	-16	-0	-2.0

YEAR	TM/L	W	L	PCT	G	GS	CG	SH	SV	IP	H	HR	BB	SO	RAT	ERA	ERA+	OAV	OOB	BH	AVG	PB	PR	/A	PD	TPI
	Oak-A	6	7	.462	21	16	2	0	0	100	88	2	37	49	11.5	3.24	112	.238	.313	0	.000	-0	6	4	0	0.5
	Yr	10	13	.435	33	28	4	0	0	167^1	166	11	77	80	13.2	4.36	85	.259	.342	0	.000	-0	-11	-12	0	-1.5
1976	Oak-A	8	7	.533	35	14	1	1	0	143	124	13	43	82	10.6	3.34	101	.232	.292	0	—	0	3	0	1	0.1
1977	Oak-A	1	2	.333	11	2	0	0	1	22	24	5	13	21	15.5	6.14	66	.286	.388	0	—	0	-5	-5	-1	-0.7
	Mon-N	8	9	.471	23	22	3	1	0	127^1	142	14	38	58	12.7	4.81	79	.283	.333	5	.119	-1	-13	-14	-0	-1.7
1978	Mon-N	1	5	.167	44	1	0	0	7	75	74	9	31	44	12.6	3.84	92	.261	.334	1	.091	-1	-2	-3	-0	-0.4
1979	Mon-N	3	1	.750	55	0	0	0	5	94^1	80	10	42	71	11.6	3.15	116	.236	.320	1	.071	-0	6	5	-0	0.2
1980	Mon-N	7	6	.538	57	0	0	0	4	91^1	80	7	33	48	11.1	3.05	117	.235	.302	1	.111	1	6	5	-0	0.8
1981	*Mon-N	2	1	.667	25	3	0	0	1	49	45	7	24	28	12.9	4.96	70	.247	.338	1	.111	-0	-8	-8	-1	-0.7
1982	Cal-A	0	1	.000	7	0	0	0	0	9^2	13	0	8	5	19.6	4.66	87	.310	.420	0	—	0	-1	-1	-0	-0.1
	Phi-N	0	0	—	8	0	0	0	0	13^1	8	0	3	9	7.4	1.35	271	.182	.234	0	—	0	3	3	-0	0.0
Total	16	146	149	.495	574	327	73	16	20	2529	2440	223	924	1359	12.1	3.60	97	.255	.323	56	.117	-9	-20	-35	4	-5.2

● **ED BAHR** Bahr, Edson Garfield b: 10/16/19, Rouleau, Sask., Canada BR/TR, 6'1.5", 172 lbs. Deb: 5/1/46

YEAR	TM/L	W	L	PCT	G	GS	CG	SH	SV	IP	H	HR	BB	SO	RAT	ERA	ERA+	OAV	OOB	BH	AVG	PB	PR	/A	PD	TPI
1946	Pit-N	8	6	.571	27	14	7	0	0	136^2	128	8	52	44	12.2	2.63	134	.254	.330	8	.178	-1	12	14	-0	1.3
1947	Pit-N	3	5	.375	19	11	1	0	0	82^1	82	5	43	25	14.0	4.59	92	.263	.358	2	.087	-2	-5	-3	-1	-0.6
Total	2	11	11	.500	46	25	8	0	0	219	210	13	95	69	12.9	3.37	112	.257	.341	10	.147	-3	7	10	-1	0.7

● **GROVER BAICHLEY** Baichley, Grover Cleveland b: 1/7/1890, Toledo, Ill. d: 6/30/46, San Jose, Cal. BR/TR, 5'9", 165 lbs. Deb: 8/24/14

YEAR	TM/L	W	L	PCT	G	GS	CG	SH	SV	IP	H	HR	BB	SO	RAT	ERA	ERA+	OAV	OOB	BH	AVG	PB	PR	/A	PD	TPI
1914	StL-A	0	0	—	4	0	0	0	0	7	9	0	3	3	15.4	5.14	53	.346	.414	0	.000	-0	-2	-2	0	0.0

● **SCOTT BAILES** Bailes, Scott Alan b: 12/18/61, Chillicothe, Ohio BL/TL, 6'2", 184 lbs. Deb: 4/9/86

YEAR	TM/L	W	L	PCT	G	GS	CG	SH	SV	IP	H	HR	BB	SO	RAT	ERA	ERA+	OAV	OOB	BH	AVG	PB	PR	/A	PD	TPI
1986	Cle-A	10	10	.500	62	10	0	0	7	112^2	123	12	43	60	13.3	4.95	84	.276	.342	0	—	0	-10	-10	-1	-1.7
1987	Cle-A	7	8	.467	39	17	0	0	6	120^1	145	21	47	65	14.7	4.64	98	.296	.362	0	—	0	-2	-2	0	-0.2
1988	Cle-A	9	14	.391	37	21	5	2	0	145	149	22	46	53	12.2	4.90	84	.266	.324	0	—	0	-15	-13	-0	-1.9
1989	Cle-A	5	9	.357	34	11	0	0	0	113^2	116	7	29	47	11.7	4.28	93	.269	.320	0	—	0	-5	-4	0	-0.5
1990	Cal-A	2	0	1.000	27	0	0	0	0	35^1	46	8	20	16	17.1	6.37	60	.315	.401	0	—	0	-10	-10	1	-0.3
1991	Cal-A	1	2	.333	42	0	0	0	0	51^2	41	5	22	41	11.7	4.18	98	.218	.313	0	—	0	-0	-0	0	0.0
1992	Cal-A	3	1	.750	32	0	0	0	0	38^2	59	7	28	25	20.5	7.45	53	.351	.447	0	—	0	-15	-15	-0	-1.4
1997	Tex-A	1	0	1.000	24	0	0	0	0	22	18	2	10	14	11.5	2.86	167	.231	.318	0	—	0	4	5	1	0.3
1998	Tex-A	1	0	1.000	46	0	0	0	0	40^1	61	5	11	30	16.1	6.47	75	.351	.389	0	—	0	-8	-7	-1	-0.2
Total	9	39	44	.470	343	59	5	2	13	679^2	758	89	256	351	13.6	4.95	85	.283	.349	0	—	0	-61	-56	0	-5.9

● **SWEETBREADS BAILEY** Bailey, Abraham Lincoln b: 2/12/1895, Joliet, Ill. d: 9/27/39, Joliet, Ill. BR/TR, 6', 184 lbs. Deb: 5/23/19

YEAR	TM/L	W	L	PCT	G	GS	CG	SH	SV	IP	H	HR	BB	SO	RAT	ERA	ERA+	OAV	OOB	BH	AVG	PB	PR	/A	PD	TPI
1919	Chi-N	3	5	.375	21	5	0	0	0	71^1	75	2	20	19	12.4	3.15	91	.288	.346	7	.389	3	-2	-2	2	0.3
1920	Chi-N	1	2	.333	21	1	0	0	0	36^2	55	1	11	8	16.7	7.12	45	.359	.410	1	.143	-0	-16	-16	1	-1.2
1921	Chi-N	0	0	—	3	0	0	0	0	5	6	0	2	2	16.2	3.60	106	.300	.391	0	—	0	0	0	0	0.0
	Bro-N	0	0	—	7	0	0	0	0	24^1	35	1	7	6	15.9	5.18	75	.368	.417	0	.000	-0	-4	-3	-0	-0.1
	Yr	0	0	—	10	0	0	0	0	29^1	41	1	9	8	15.6	4.91	79	.353	.405	0	.000	-0	-4	-3	-0	-0.1
Total	3	4	7	.364	52	6	0	0	0	137^1	171	4	40	35	14.3	4.59	69	.324	.379	8	.267	2	-22	-22	2	-1.0

● **ROGER BAILEY** Bailey, Charles Roger b: 10/3/70, Chattahoochee, Fla. BR/TR, 6'1", 180 lbs. Deb: 4/27/95

YEAR	TM/L	W	L	PCT	G	GS	CG	SH	SV	IP	H	HR	BB	SO	RAT	ERA	ERA+	OAV	OOB	BH	AVG	PB	PR	/A	PD	TPI
1995	Col-N	7	6	.538	39	6	0	0	0	81^1	88	9	39	33	14.2	4.98	108	.283	.365	2	.125	-1	-7	4	-0	0.4
1996	Col-N	2	3	.400	24	11	0	0	1	83^2	94	7	52	45	15.8	6.24	84	.288	.388	5	.263	2	-19	-10	3	0.0
1997	Col-N	9	10	.474	29	29	5	2	0	191	210	27	70	84	13.8	4.29	121	.283	.356	13	.210	-0	-2	19	5	2.2
Total	3	18	19	.486	92	46	5	2	1	356	392	43	161	162	14.4	4.90	107	.284	.366	20	.206	1	-28	13	8	2.6

● **HARVEY BAILEY** Bailey, Harvey Francis b: 11/24/1876, Adrian, Mich. d: 7/10/22, Toledo, Ohio TL, 6', 160 lbs. Deb: 6/30/1899

YEAR	TM/L	W	L	PCT	G	GS	CG	SH	SV	IP	H	HR	BB	SO	RAT	ERA	ERA+	OAV	OOB	BH	AVG	PB	PR	/A	PD	TPI
1899	Bos-N	6	4	.600	12	11	8	0	0	86^2	83	7	35	26	12.9	3.95	105	.252	.334	8	.235	0	-1	2	-1	0.1
1900	Bos-N	0	0	—	4	1	0	0	0	20	24	0	11	9	16.6	4.95	83	.296	.394	2	.222	0	-3	-2	1	0.1
Total	2	6	4	.600	16	12	8	0	0	106^2	107	7	46	35	13.6	4.13	100	.260	.346	10	.233	0	-4	0	-0	0.2

● **HOWARD BAILEY** Bailey, Howard L b: 7/31/57, Grand Haven, Mich. BR/TL, 6', 195 lbs. Deb: 4/12/81

YEAR	TM/L	W	L	PCT	G	GS	CG	SH	SV	IP	H	HR	BB	SO	RAT	ERA	ERA+	OAV	OOB	BH	AVG	PB	PR	/A	PD	TPI
1981	Det-A	1	4	.200	9	5	0	0	0	36^2	45	4	13	17	15.0	7.36	51	.308	.377	0	—	0	-15	-15	1	-1.7
1982	Det-A	0	0	—	8	0	0	0	1	10	6	0	2	3	7.2	0.00	—	.182	.229	0	—	0	5	5	0	0.1
1983	Det-A	5	5	.500	33	3	0	0	0	72	69	11	25	21	12.0	4.88	80	.255	.322	0	—	0	-7	-8	0	-0.9
Total	3	6	9	.400	50	8	0	0	1	118^2	120	15	40	41	12.5	5.23	74	.267	.333	0	—	0	-17	-18	1	-2.5

● **JIM BAILEY** Bailey, James Hopkins b: 12/16/34, Strawberry Plains, Tenn. BB/TL, 6'2.5", 210 lbs. Deb: 9/10/59 F

YEAR	TM/L	W	L	PCT	G	GS	CG	SH	SV	IP	H	HR	BB	SO	RAT	ERA	ERA+	OAV	OOB	BH	AVG	PB	PR	/A	PD	TPI
1959	Cin-N	0	1	.000	3	1	0	0	0	11^2	17	1	6	7	18.5	6.17	66	.333	.414	0	.000	-0	-3	-3	-0	-0.3

● **KING BAILEY** Bailey, Linwood C. b: 11/1870, Virginia d: 11/19/17, Macon, Ga. BL/TL, 6' ", 185 lbs. Deb: 9/21/1895

YEAR	TM/L	W	L	PCT	G	GS	CG	SH	SV	IP	H	HR	BB	SO	RAT	ERA	ERA+	OAV	OOB	BH	AVG	PB	PR	/A	PD	TPI
1895	Cin-N	1	0	1.000	1	1	1	0	0	8	13	0	0	0	15.8	5.63	88	.361	.378	2	.500	1	-1	-1	0	0.0

● **CORY BAILEY** Bailey, Phillip Cory b: 1/24/71, Marion, Ill. BR/TR, 6'1", 202 lbs. Deb: 9/1/93

YEAR	TM/L	W	L	PCT	G	GS	CG	SH	SV	IP	H	HR	BB	SO	RAT	ERA	ERA+	OAV	OOB	BH	AVG	PB	PR	/A	PD	TPI
1993	Bos-A	0	1	.000	11	0	0	0	0	15^2	12	0	12	11	13.8	3.45	134	.231	.375	0	—	0	2	2	1	-0.3
1994	Bos-A	0	1	.000	5	0	0	0	0	4^1	10	2	3	4	27.0	12.46	40	.476	.542	0	—	0	-4	-4	-0	-0.9
1995	StL-N	0	0	—	3	0	0	0	0	3^2	2	0	2	5	9.8	7.36	57	.154	.267	0	—	0	-1	-1	0	0.0
1996	StL-N	5	2	.714	51	0	0	0	0	57	57	1	30	38	13.9	3.00	139	.263	.355	0	.000	1	8	7	-0	0.8
1997	SF-N	0	1	.000	7	0	0	0	0	9^2	15	1	4	5	17.7	8.38	49	.375	.432	1	1.000	0	-4	-5	-0	-0.4
1998	SF-N	0	0	—	5	0	0	0	0	3^1	2	1	1	2	8.1	2.70	150	.167	.231	0	—	0	1	1	-0	0.0
Total	6	5	5	.500	82	0	0	0	0	93^2	98	5	52	65	14.5	4.23	101	.276	.370	1	.500	1	0	1	-0	-0.8

● **STEVE BAILEY** Bailey, Steven John b: 2/12/42, Bronx, N.Y. BR/TR, 6'1", 194 lbs. Deb: 4/14/67

YEAR	TM/L	W	L	PCT	G	GS	CG	SH	SV	IP	H	HR	BB	SO	RAT	ERA	ERA+	OAV	OOB	BH	AVG	PB	PR	/A	PD	TPI
1967	Cle-A	2	5	.286	32	1	0	0	2	64^2	62	5	42	46	14.9	3.90	84	.259	.377	0	.000	-1	-5	-5	0	-0.6
1968	Cle-A	0	1	.000	2	1	0	0	0	5	4	1	2	1	10.8	3.60	82	.235	.316	0	—	0	-0	-0	-0	-0.1
Total	2	2	6	.250	34	2	0	0	2	69^2	66	6	44	47	14.6	3.88	84	.258	.373	0	.000	-1	-5	-5	-0	-0.7

● **BILL BAILEY** Bailey, William F. b: 4/12/1889, Ft.Smith, Ark. d: 11/2/26, Houston, Tex. BL/TL, 5'11", 165 lbs. Deb: 9/17/07

YEAR	TM/L	W	L	PCT	G	GS	CG	SH	SV	IP	H	HR	BB	SO	RAT	ERA	ERA+	OAV	OOB	BH	AVG	PB	PR	/A	PD	TPI
1907	StL-A	4	1	.800	6	5	3	0	0	48^1	39	0	15	17	10.8	2.42	104	.223	.299	3	.150	-1	1	0	-1	-0.2
1908	StL-A	3	5	.375	22	12	7	0	0	106^2	85	2	50	42	11.6	3.04	79	.220	.314	3	.088	-2	-8	-8	-2	-1.1
1909	StL-A	9	10	.474	32	20	17	1	0	199	174	2	75	114	11.5	2.44	99	.248	.325	22	.286	5	-0	-1	-1	0.5
1910	StL-A	3	18	.143	34	20	13	0	0	192^1	186	2	97	90	13.7	3.32	74	.262	.359	13	.206	0	-17	-18	-1	-2.0
1911	StL-A	0	3	.000	7	2	2	0	0	31^2	42	1	16	8	17.1	4.55	74	.339	.423	0	.000	-2	-4	-4	0	-0.5
1912	StL-A	0	1	.000	3	2	0	0	0	10^2	15	0	10	2	21.1	9.28	36	.341	.463	1	.500	1	-7	-7	-1	-0.5
1914	Bal-F	7	9	.438	19	18	10	1	0	128^2	106	2	68	131	12.7	3.08	99	.230	.338	7	.163	-1	-3	-1	3	0.1
1915	Bal-F	6	19	.240	36	23	11	2	0	190^1	179	8	115	98	14.3	4.63	62	.255	.366	15	.231	-0	-40	-37	-1	-4.6
	Chi-F	3	1	.750	5	5	3	3	0	33^1	23	1	10	24	8.9	2.16	116	.202	.266	2	.222	0	2	1	1	0.2
	Yr	9	20	.310	41	28	14	5	0	223^2	202	9	125	122	13.2	4.27	66	.245	.344	17	.230	-0	-38	-36	-1	-4.4
1918	Det-A	1	2	.333	8	4	1	0	0	37^2	53	0	26	13	19.1	5.97	45	.368	.468	1	.077	-1	-13	-14	-1	-1.1
1921	StL-N	2	5	.286	19	6	3	1	0	74	95	1	22	20	14.5	4.26	86	.330	.381	2	.091	-2	-4	-5	1	-0.5
1922	StL-N	0	2	.000	12	0	0	0	0	31^2	38	1	23	11	17.3	5.40	72	.325	.436	2	.286	0	-5	-5	1	-0.2
Total	11	38	76	.333	203	117	70	8	0	1084^1	1035	20	527	570	13.3	3.57	77	.261	.354	71	.194	-3	-97	-98	-1	-9.9

● **BOB BAILOR** Bailor, Robert Michael b: 7/10/51, Connellsville, Pa. BR/TR, 5'11", 170 lbs. Deb: 9/6/75 C♦

YEAR	TM/L	W	L	PCT	G	GS	CG	SH	SV	IP	H	HR	BB	SO	RAT	ERA	ERA+	OAV	OOB	BH	AVG	PB	PR	/A	PD	TPI
1980	Tor-A	0	0	—	3	0	0	0	0	2^1	4	0	1	0	19.3	7.71	56	.364	.417	82	.236	1	-1	-1	-0	0.0

● **LOREN BAIN** Bain, Herbert Loren b: 7/4/22, Staples, Minn. d: 11/24/96, Chetek, Wis. BR/TR, 6', 190 lbs. Deb: 6/23/45

YEAR	TM/L	W	L	PCT	G	GS	CG	SH	SV	IP	H	HR	BB	SO	RAT	ERA	ERA+	OAV	OOB	BH	AVG	PB	PR	/A	PD	TPI
1945	NY-N	0	0	—	3	0	0	0	0	8	10	1	4	1	16.9	7.88	50	.323	.417	1	.333	0	-4	-4	-0	0.0

● **DOUG BAIR** Bair, Charles Douglas b: 8/22/49, Defiance, Ohio BR/TR, 6', 180 lbs. Deb: 9/13/76

YEAR	TM/L	W	L	PCT	G	GS	CG	SH	SV	IP	H	HR	BB	SO	RAT	ERA	ERA+	OAV	OOB	BH	AVG	PB	PR	/A	PD	TPI
1976	Pit-N	0	0	—	4	0	0	0	0	6^1	4	0	5	4	12.8	5.68	61	.174	.321	0	—	0	-2	-2	-0	0.0
1977	Oak-A	4	6	.400	45	0	0	0	8	83^1	78	11	57	68	14.6	3.46	116	.253	.370	0	—	0	6	5	1	0.9

YEAR	TM/L	W	L	PCT	G	GS	CG	SH	SV	IP	H	HR	BB	SO	RAT	ERA	ERA+	OAV	OOB	BH	AVG	PB	PR	/A	PD	TPI
1978	Cin-N	7	6	.538	70	0	0	0	28	100^1	87	6	38	91	11.2	1.97	180	.236	.307	2	.143	-0	18	18	-1	3.2
1979	*Cin-N	11	7	.611	65	0	0	0	16	94^1	93	7	51	86	14.0	4.29	87	.256	.353	0	.000	-1	-6	-6	-1	-1.4
1980	Cin-N	3	6	.333	61	0	0	0	6	85	91	7	39	62	13.9	4.24	84	.277	.355	0	.000	-0	-6	-6	2	-0.6
1981	Cin-N	2	2	.500	24	0	0	0	0	39	42	5	17	16	13.6	5.77	62	.271	.343	1	.333	1	-10	-10	-1	-0.9
	StL-N	2	0	1.000	11	0	0	0	1	15^2	13	0	2	14	8.6	3.45	103	.224	.250	0	.000	-0	0	0	-0	0.0
	Yr	4	2	.667	35	0	0	0	1	54^2	55	5	19	30	12.2	5.10	70	.258	.319	1	.167	1	-10	-9	-1	-0.9
1982	*StL-N	5	3	.625	63	0	0	0	8	91^2	69	7	36	68	10.4	2.55	142	.211	.291	1	.077	-1	11	11	0	1.0
1983	StL-N	1	1	.500	26	0	0	0	1	29^2	24	4	13	21	11.2	3.03	119	.224	.308	0	.000	-0	2	2	-0	0.1
	Det-A	7	3	.700	27	1	0	0	4	55^2	51	8	19	39	11.5	3.88	101	.242	.307	0	—	0	1	0	-0	0.2
1984	*Det-A	5	3	.625	47	1	0	0	4	93^2	82	10	36	57	11.3	3.75	105	.238	.310	0	—	0	3	2	1	0.3
1985	Det-A	2	0	1.000	21	3	0	0	0	49	54	3	25	30	14.7	6.24	65	.281	.367	0	—	0	-11	-12	1	-0.3
	StL-N	0	0	—	2	0	0	0	0	2	1	0	2	0	13.5	0.00	—	.167	.375	0	—	0	1	1	-0	0.0
1986	Oak-A	2	3	.400	31	0	0	0	4	45	37	5	18	40	11.0	3.00	129	.224	.301	0	—	0	6	4	0	1.1
1987	Phi-N	2	0	1.000	11	0	0	0	0	13^2	17	4	5	10	14.5	5.93	72	.309	.367	0	.000	-0	-3	-3	-0	-0.4
1988	Tor-A	0	0	—	10	0	0	0	0	13^1	14	2	3	8	11.5	4.05	97	.280	.321	0	—	0	-0	-0	0	0.0
1989	Pit-N	2	3	.400	44	0	0	0	1	67^1	52	4	28	56	10.7	2.27	148	.211	.292	1	.200	0	9	8	1	0.7
1990	Pit-N	0	0	—	22	0	0	0	0	24^1	30	3	11	19	15.2	4.81	75	.306	.376	0	.000	-0	-3	-3	0	0.0
Total	15	55	43	.561	584	5	0	0	81	909^1	839	86	405	689	12.4	3.63	103	.246	.328	5	.096	-2	15	10	2	3.9

● BOB BAIRD Baird, Robert Allen b: 1/16/40, Knoxville, Tenn. d: 4/11/74, Chattanooga, Tenn. BL/TL, 6'4", 195 lbs. Deb: 9/3/62

YEAR	TM/L	W	L	PCT	G	GS	CG	SH	SV	IP	H	HR	BB	SO	RAT	ERA	ERA+	OAV	OOB	BH	AVG	PB	PR	/A	PD	TPI
1962	Was-A	0	1	.000	3	3	0	0	0	10^2	13	0	8	3	17.7	6.75	60	.310	.420	0	.000	-0	-3	-3	-0	-0.3
1963	Was-A	0	3	.000	5	3	0	0	0	11^2	12	1	7	7	15.4	7.71	48	.261	.370	1	.333	0	-5	-5	-0	-1.1
Total	2	0	4	.000	8	6	0	0	0	22^1	25	1	15	10	16.5	7.25	53	.284	.394	1	.167	-0	-9	-8	-1	-1.4

● JERSEY BAKELY Bakely, Edward Enoch (b: Edward Enoch Bakley) b: 4/17/1864, Blackwood, N.J. d: 2/17/15, Philadelphia, Pa. BR/TR, Deb: 5/11/1883

YEAR	TM/L	W	L	PCT	G	GS	CG	SH	SV	IP	H	HR	BB	SO	RAT	ERA	ERA+	OAV	OOB	BH	AVG	PB	PR	/A	PD	TPI
1883	Phi-a	5	3	.625	8	8	7	0	0	61^1	65	0	12	14	11.3	3.23	108	.255	.288	5	.192	1	1	2	-0	0.2
1884	Phi-U	14	25	.359	39	38	38	1	0	344^2	390	0	76	204	12.2	4.47	52	.267	.303	22	.132	-16	-77	-82	-3	-8.2
	Wil-U	0	2	.000	2	2	2	0	0	17	24	0	1	9	13.2	4.24	63	.312	.321	0	.000	-1	-3	-3	0	-0.3
	KC-U	2	3	.400	5	5	3	0	0	33	29	0	4	13	9.0	2.45	91	.220	.243	3	.150	-2	-0	-1	-1	-0.3
	Yr	16	30	.348	46	45	43	1	0	394^2	443	0	81	226	11.9	4.29	54	.265	.299	25	.130	-18	-81	-86	-4	-8.8
1888	Cle-a	25	33	.431	61	61	60	4	0	532^2	518	14	128	212	11.2	2.97	104	.246	.294	26	.134	-6	5	7	-1	0.1
1889	Cle-N	12	22	.353	36	34	33	2	0	304^1	296	9	106	105	12.1	2.96	136	.247	.313	15	.135	-1	36	36	2	3.4
1890	Cle-P	12	25	.324	43	38	32	0	0	326^1	412	13	147	67	15.6	4.47	89	.295	.365	28	.203	-2	-9	-18	-3	-1.8
1891	Was-a	2	10	.167	13	12	11	0	0	104^1	127	6	60	32	16.6	5.35	70	.291	.384	10	.222	-0	-19	-19	-2	-1.7
	Bal-a	4	2	.667	8	6	5	0	0	59	48	1	30	13	12.1	2.29	163	.214	.310	2	.095	0	9	10	-1	0.8
	Yr	6	12	.333	21	18	16	0	0	163^1	175	7	90	45	14.7	4.24	88	.262	.351	12	.182	-0	-9	-9	-3	-0.9
Total	6	76	125	.378	215	204	191	7	0	1782^2	1909	43	564	669	12.7	3.66	91	.262	.318	111	.153	-26	-57	-68	-9	-7.8

● DAVE BAKENHASTER Bakenhaster, David Lee b: 3/5/45, Columbus, O. BR/TR, 5'10", 168 lbs. Deb: 6/20/64

YEAR	TM/L	W	L	PCT	G	GS	CG	SH	SV	IP	H	HR	BB	SO	RAT	ERA	ERA+	OAV	OOB	BH	AVG	PB	PR	/A	PD	TPI
1964	StL-N	0	0	—	2	0	0	0	0	3	9	1	1	0	30.0	6.00	63	.474	.500	0	—	0	-1	-1	0	0.0

● AL BAKER Baker, Albert Jones b: 2/28/06, Batesville, Miss. d: 11/6/82, Kenedy, Tex. BR/TR, 5'11", 170 lbs. Deb: 8/20/38

YEAR	TM/L	W	L	PCT	G	GS	CG	SH	SV	IP	H	HR	BB	SO	RAT	ERA	ERA+	OAV	OOB	BH	AVG	PB	PR	/A	PD	TPI
1938	Bos-A	0	0	—	3	0	0	0	0	7^2	13	2	2	2	18.8	9.39	53	.371	.421	0	.000	-1	-4	-4	-0	-0.1

● BOCK BAKER Baker, Charles "Smiling Bock" b: 7/17/1878, Troy, N.Y. d: 8/17/40, New York, N.Y. TL, 5'9", 181 lbs. Deb: 4/28/01

YEAR	TM/L	W	L	PCT	G	GS	CG	SH	SV	IP	H	HR	BB	SO	RAT	ERA	ERA+	OAV	OOB	BH	AVG	PB	PR	/A	PD	TPI
1901	Cle-A	0	1	.000	1	1	1	0	0	8	23	0	6	0	33.8	5.63	63	.500	.566	0	.000	-1	-2	-2	0	-0.2
	Phi-A	0	1	.000	1	1	0	0	0	6	6	0	6	1	18.0	10.50	36	.261	.414	1	.333	0	-5	-4	-0	-0.5
	Yr	0	2	.000	2	2	1	0	0	14	29	0	12	1	26.4	7.71	47	.414	.500	1	.143	-1	-6	-6	-0	-0.7

● ERNIE BAKER Baker, Earnest Gould b: 8/8/1875, Concord, Mich. d: 10/25/45, Homer, Mich. BR/TR, 5'10", 160 lbs. Deb: 8/18/05

YEAR	TM/L	W	L	PCT	G	GS	CG	SH	SV	IP	H	HR	BB	SO	RAT	ERA	ERA+	OAV	OOB	BH	AVG	PB	PR	/A	PD	TPI
1905	Cin-N	0	0	—	1	0	0	0	0	4	7	1	0	1	18.0	4.50	73	.412	.444	0	.000	-0	-1	-1	-0	-0.1

● JESSE BAKER Baker, Jesse Ormond b: 6/3/1888, Anderson Island, Wash. d: 9/26/72, Tacoma, Wash. BL/TL, 5'11", 188 lbs. Deb: 4/23/11

YEAR	TM/L	W	L	PCT	G	GS	CG	SH	SV	IP	H	HR	BB	SO	RAT	ERA	ERA+	OAV	OOB	BH	AVG	PB	PR	/A	PD	TPI
1911	Chi-A	2	7	.222	22	8	3	0	1	94	101	3	30	51	12.9	3.93	82	.288	.351	3	.103	-2	-6	-7	1	-0.7

● KIRTLEY BAKER Baker, Kirtley "Whitey" b: 6/24/1869, Aurora, Ind. d: 4/15/27, Covington, Ky. BR/TR, 5'9", 160 lbs. Deb: 5/7/1890 ♦

YEAR	TM/L	W	L	PCT	G	GS	CG	SH	SV	IP	H	HR	BB	SO	RAT	ERA	ERA+	OAV	OOB	BH	AVG	PB	PR	/A	PD	TPI
1890	Pit-N	3	19	.136	25	21	19	2	0	178^1	209	11	86	76	15.9	5.60	59	.284	.374	10	.147	-1	-40	-46	-0	-4.3
1893	Bal-N	3	8	.273	15	12	8	0	0	91^2	138	5	58	26	19.7	8.44	56	.337	.426	17	.298	2	-38	-38	3	-2.7
1894	Bal-N	0	1	.000	1	0	0	0	0	0	1	0	2	0	—	∞	—	1.000	1.000	0	.000	-0	-5	-5	-0	-0.3
1898	Was-N	2	3	.400	6	5	4	0	0	47	56	1	18	7	14.2	3.06	120	.293	.354	5	.278	2	3	3	-1	0.4
1899	Was-N	1	7	.125	11	6	3	0	0	54	79	3	22	6	17.8	6.83	57	.339	.410	3	.158	-1	-18	-18	2	-1.9
Total	5	9	38	.191	58	44	34	2	0	371	483	20	186	115	17.0	6.28	60	.307	.391	35	.211	1	-99	-103	4	-8.8

● NEAL BAKER Baker, Neal Vernon b: 4/30/04, Harlingen, Tex. d: 1/5/82, Houston, Tex. BR/TR, 6'1", 175 lbs. Deb: 6/26/27

YEAR	TM/L	W	L	PCT	G	GS	CG	SH	SV	IP	H	HR	BB	SO	RAT	ERA	ERA+	OAV	OOB	BH	AVG	PB	PR	/A	PD	TPI
1927	Phi-A	0	0	—	5	2	0	0	0	17^1	27	2	7	3	17.7	5.71	75	.365	.420	1	.167	-0	-3	-3	0	0.0

● NORM BAKER Baker, Norman Leslie b: 10/14/1863, Philadelphia, Pa. d: 2/20/49, Hurffville, N.J. Deb: 5/21/1883

YEAR	TM/L	W	L	PCT	G	GS	CG	SH	SV	IP	H	HR	BB	SO	RAT	ERA	ERA+	OAV	OOB	BH	AVG	PB	PR	/A	PD	TPI
1883	Pit-a	0	2	.000	3	3	2	0	0	19	24	0	11	5	16.6	3.32	97	.289	.372	0	.000	-2	-0	-0	-1	-0.2
1885	Lou-a	13	12	.520	25	24	24	1	0	217	210	3	69	79	12.0	3.40	95	.241	.304	18	.207	-1	-4	-4	-2	-0.6
1890	Bal-a	1	1	.500	2	2	2	0	0	17	16	0	6	10	11.6	3.71	109	.242	.306	0	.000	-1	0	1	0	0.0
Total	3	14	15	.483	30	29	28	1	0	253	250	3	86	94	12.3	3.42	96	.245	.309	18	.170	-3	-3	-4	-2	-0.8

● SCOTT BAKER Baker, Scott b: 5/18/70, San Jose, Cal. BL/TL, 6'2", 175 lbs. Deb: 7/17/95

YEAR	TM/L	W	L	PCT	G	GS	CG	SH	SV	IP	H	HR	BB	SO	RAT	ERA	ERA+	OAV	OOB	BH	AVG	PB	PR	/A	PD	TPI
1995	Oak-A	0	0	—	1	0	0	0	0	3^2	5	0	5	3	27.0	9.82	46	.333	.524	0	—	0	-2	-2	-0	0.4

● STEVE BAKER Baker, Steven Byrne b: 8/30/56, Eugene, Ore. BR/TR, 6', 185 lbs. Deb: 5/25/78

YEAR	TM/L	W	L	PCT	G	GS	CG	SH	SV	IP	H	HR	BB	SO	RAT	ERA	ERA+	OAV	OOB	BH	AVG	PB	PR	/A	PD	TPI
1978	Det-A	2	4	.333	15	10	0	0	0	63^1	66	6	42	39	15.3	4.55	85	.276	.384	0	—	0	-6	-5	-1	-0.7
1979	Det-A	1	7	.125	21	12	0	0	1	84	97	13	51	54	16.5	6.64	65	.296	.400	0	—	0	-23	-22	-1	-2.0
1982	Oak-A	1	1	.500	5	3	0	0	0	25^2	30	3	4	14	11.9	4.56	86	.288	.315	0	—	0	-1	-2	-0	-0.2
1983	Oak-A	3	3	.500	35	1	0	0	5	54	59	4	26	23	14.5	4.33	89	.282	.367	0	—	0	-2	-3	-1	0.0
	StL-N	0	1	.000	8	0	0	0	0	10	10	0	4	1	13.5	1.80	201	.286	.375	0	—	0	2	2	0	0.2
Total	4	7	16	.304	84	26	0	0	6	237	262	26	127	131	15.1	5.13	78	.286	.379	0	—	0	-29	-29	-3	-2.7

● TOM BAKER Baker, Thomas Calvin "Rattlesnake" b: 6/11/13, Nursery, Tex. d: 1/3/91, Fort Worth, Tex. BR/TR, 6'1.5", 180 lbs. Deb: 8/15/35

YEAR	TM/L	W	L	PCT	G	GS	CG	SH	SV	IP	H	HR	BB	SO	RAT	ERA	ERA+	OAV	OOB	BH	AVG	PB	PR	/A	PD	TPI
1935	Bro-N	1	0	1.000	11	1	1	0	0	42	48	2	20	10	14.6	4.29	93	.277	.352	9	.474	4	-1	-1	-1	0.2
1936	Bro-N	1	8	.111	35	8	2	0	2	87^2	98	3	48	35	15.2	4.72	88	.288	.379	7	.233	1	-7	-6	0	-0.4
1937	Bro-N	0	1	.000	7	0	0	0	0	8^1	14	1	5	2	21.6	8.64	47	.378	.465	0	—	0	-4	-4	0	-0.4
	NY-N	1	0	1.000	13	0	0	0	0	31	30	0	16	11	13.4	4.06	96	.268	.359	2	.222	-0	-1	-1	-0	-0.1
	Yr	1	1	.500	20	0	0	0	0	39^1	44	1	21	13	14.9	5.03	78	.293	.380	2	.222	-0	-5	-5	-0	-0.5
1938	NY-N	0	0	—	2	0	0	0	0	4	5	0	3	0	18.0	6.75	56	.313	.421	0	—	0	-1	-1	0	0.0
Total	4	3	9	.250	68	9	3	0	2	173	195	6	92	58	15.1	4.73	85	.288	.375	18	.310	5	-14	-13	-1	-0.7

● TOM BAKER Baker, Thomas Henry b: 5/6/34, Port Townsend, Wash. d: 3/9/80, Port Townsend, Wash BL/TL, 6', 195 lbs. Deb: 8/2/63

YEAR	TM/L	W	L	PCT	G	GS	CG	SH	SV	IP	H	HR	BB	SO	RAT	ERA	ERA+	OAV	OOB	BH	AVG	PB	PR	/A	PD	TPI
1963	Chi-N	0	1	.000	10	1	0	0	0	18	20	2	7	14	14.0	3.00	117	.282	.354	0	.000	-0	1	1	0	0.0

● MIKE BALAS Balas, Mitchell Francis (b: Mitchell Francis Balaski) b: 5/17/10, Lowell, Mass. BR/TR, 6', 195 lbs. Deb: 4/27/38

YEAR	TM/L	W	L	PCT	G	GS	CG	SH	SV	IP	H	HR	BB	SO	RAT	ERA	ERA+	OAV	OOB	BH	AVG	PB	PR	/A	PD	TPI
1938	Bos-N	0	0	—	1	0	0	0	0	1^1	3	0	0	0	20.3	6.75	51	.375	.375	0	—	0	-0	-0	-0	0.0

● JACK BALDSCHUN Baldschun, Jack Edward b: 10/16/36, Greenville, O. BR/TR, 6', 190 lbs. Deb: 4/28/61

YEAR	TM/L	W	L	PCT	G	GS	CG	SH	SV	IP	H	HR	BB	SO	RAT	ERA	ERA+	OAV	OOB	BH	AVG	PB	PR	/A	PD	TPI
1961	Phi-N	5	3	.625	**65**	0	0	0	3	99^2	90	7	49	59	13.0	3.88	105	.243	.339	0	.000	-1	2	2	0	0.1
1962	Phi-N	12	7	.632	67	0	0	0	13	112^2	95	6	58	95	12.4	2.96	131	.231	.328	1	.063	-1	12	11	1	2.1
1963	Phi-N	11	7	.611	65	0	0	0	16	113^2	99	7	42	89	11.4	2.30	141	.232	.306	0	.000	-2	13	12	1	2.2
1964	Phi-N	6	9	.400	71	0	0	0	21	118^1	111	8	40	96	11.7	3.12	111	.246	.312	4	.250	1	6	5	1	1.1

YEAR	TM/L	W	L	PCT	G	GS	CG	SH	SV	IP	H	HR	BB	SO	RAT	ERA	ERA+	OAV	OOB	BH	AVG	PB	PR	/A	PD	TPI
1965	Phi-N	5	8	.385	65	0	0	0	6	99	102	4	42	81	13.5	3.82	91	.273	.352	0	.000	-1	-3	-4	1	-0.6
1966	Cin-N	1	5	.167	42	0	0	0	0	57^{1}	71	4	25	44	15.7	5.49	71	.318	.397	1	.333	0	-12	-10	0	-0.9
1967	Cin-N	0	0	—	9	0	0	0	0	13	15	0	9	12	16.6	4.15	90	.283	.387	0	.000	-0	-1	-1	-0	0.0
1969	SD-N	7	2	.778	61	0	0	0	1	77	80	7	29	67	13.0	4.79	74	.264	.332	1	.250	0	-10	-11	-0	-1.2
1970	SD-N	1	0	1.000	12	0	0	0	0	13^{1}	24	2	4	12	18.9	10.13	39	.375	.412	0	—	0	-9	-9	-0	-0.6
Total	9	48	41	.539	457	0	0	0	60	704	687	45	298	555	12.9	3.69	98	.257	.336	7	.090	-3	-3	-5	4	2.2
● LADY BALDWIN	Baldwin, Charles Busted b: 4/8/1859, Oramel, N.Y. d: 3/7/37, Hastings, Mich. BL/TL, 5'11", 160 lbs. Deb: 9/30/1884 ♦																									
1884	Mil-U	1	1	.500	2	2	2	0	0	17	7	0	1	21	4.2	2.65	50	.117	.131	6	.222	-0	-0	-2	-0	-0.2
1885	Det-N	11	9	.550	21	20	19	1	1	179^{1}	137	2	28	135	**8.3**	1.86	153	**.197**	**.228**	30	.242	3	19	20	2	2.4
1886	Det-N	**42**	13	.764	56	56	55	**7**	0	487	371	11	100	**323**	**8.7**	2.24	148	**.202**	**.243**	41	.201	3	58	58	4	6.1
1887	*Det-N	13	10	.565	24	24	24	1	0	211	225	8	61	60	12.4	3.84	105	.269	.323	23	.271	3	6	5	1	0.6
1888	Det-N	3	3	.500	6	6	5	0	0	53	76	5	15	26	15.6	5.43	51	.322	.365	6	.261	2	-15	-16	-1	-1.3
1890	Bro-N	1	0	1.000	2	1	0	0	0	7^{2}	15	0	4	4	22.3	7.04	49	.395	.452	0	.000	-0	-3	-3	0	-0.3
	Buf-P	2	5	.286	7	7	7	0	0	62	90	5	24	13	17.0	4.50	91	.325	.385	8	.286	1	-2	-3	-0	-0.1
Total	6	73	41	.640	118	116	112	9	1	1017	921	31	233	582	10.3	2.85	118	.232	.276	114	.231	12	63	58	5	7.2
● KID BALDWIN	Baldwin, Clarence Geoghan b: 11/1/1864, Newport, Ky. d: 7/10/1897, Cincinnati, Ohio BR/TR, 5'6", 147 lbs. Deb: 7/27/1884 ♦																									
1885	Cin-a	0	0	—	2	1	0	0	0	4	5	0	6	1	24.8	9.00	36	.294	.478	17	.135	-0	-3	-3	0	0.0
● DAVE BALDWIN	Baldwin, David George b: 3/30/38, Tucson, Ariz. BR/TR, 6'2", 200 lbs. Deb: 9/6/66																									
1966	Was-A	0	0	—	4	0	0	0	0	7	8	0	1	4	11.6	3.86	90	.267	.290	0	—	0	-0	-0	-0	0.0
1967	Was-A	2	4	.333	58	0	0	0	12	68^{2}	53	2	20	52	10.1	1.70	186	.215	.285	0	.000	-0	12	11	1	1.5
1968	Was-A	0	2	.000	40	0	0	0	5	42	40	7	12	30	11.1	4.07	72	.260	.313	0	.000	0	-5	-5	1	-0.4
1969	Was-A	2	4	.333	43	0	0	0	4	66^{2}	57	4	34	51	13.0	4.05	86	.236	.342	0	.000	-1	-3	-4	-0	-0.6
1970	Mil-A	2	1	.667	28	0	0	0	1	35^{1}	25	4	18	26	11.0	2.55	149	.205	.307	1	.500	0	5	5	2	0.7
1973	Chi-A	0	0	—	3	0	0	0	0	5	7	0	4	1	19.8	3.60	110	.368	.478	0	—	0	0	0	0	0.0
Total	6	6	11	.353	176	0	0	0	22	224^{2}	190	17	89	164	11.5	3.08	108	.234	.316	1	.067	-1	8	6	4	1.2
● HARRY BALDWIN	Baldwin, Howard Edward b: 6/3/1900, Baltimore, Md. d: 1/23/58, Baltimore, Md. BR/TR, 5'11", 160 lbs. Deb: 5/4/24																									
1924	*NY-N	3	1	.750	10	2	1	0	0	33^{2}	42	5	11	5	14.2	4.28	86	.309	.361	4	.364	1	-2	-2	-0	-0.2
1925	NY-N	0	0	—	1	0	0	0	0	1	3	0	1	0	36.0	9.00	45	.500	.571	0	—	0	-1	-1	-0	0.0
Total	2	3	1	.750	11	2	1	0	0	34^{2}	45	5	12	5	14.8	4.41	83	.317	.370	4	.364	1	-2	-3	-0	-0.2
● JAMES BALDWIN	Baldwin, James J. b: 7/15/71, Southern Pines, N.C. BR/TR, 6'3", 210 lbs. Deb: 4/30/95																									
1995	Chi-A	0	1	.000	6	4	0	0	0	14^{2}	32	6	9	10	25.2	12.89	35	.444	.506	0	—	0	-13	-14	0	-0.5
1996	Chi-A	11	6	.647	28	28	0	0	0	169	168	24	57	127	12.2	4.42	107	.257	.320	0	—	0	11	6	-1	0.7
1997	Chi-A	12	15	.444	32	32	1	0	0	200	205	19	83	140	13.2	5.27	83	.262	.337	0	.000	-0	-16	-20	-1	-2.3
1998	Chi-A	13	6	.684	37	24	1	0	0	159	176	18	60	108	13.9	5.32	86	.278	.349	0	.000	-0	-12	-14	-2	-1.6
Total	4	36	28	.563	103	88	2	0	0	542^{2}	581	67	209	385	13.4	5.22	87	.271	.341	0	.000	-0	-30	-41	-4	-3.7
● MARK BALDWIN	Baldwin, Marcus Elmore "Fido" b: 10/29/1863, Pittsburgh, Pa. d: 11/10/29, Pittsburgh, Pa. BR/TR, 6', 190 lbs. Deb: 5/2/1887																									
1887	Chi-N	18	17	.514	40	39	35	1	**1**	334	329	23	122	164	12.6	3.40	132	.248	.319	26	.187	-4	25	41	-3	2.6
1888	Chi-N	13	15	.464	30	30	27	2	0	251	241	13	99	157	12.7	2.76	110	.249	.327	16	.151	-1	2	7	2	0.8
1889	Col-a	27	34	.443	**63**	59	54	6	1	**513^{2}**	458	9	274	**368**	13.2	3.61	100	.231	.331	39	.188	1	14	1	1	0.2
1890	Chi-P	**33**	24	.579	**58**	56	**53**	1	0	**492**	494	10	249	**206**	13.9	3.35	130	.250	.339	45	.212	-1	48	54	3	4.8
1891	Pit-N	21	28	.429	53	51	48	2	1	437^{2}	385	10	227	197	13.1	2.76	119	.227	.327	27	.153	-3	29	26	1	2.1
1892	Pit-N	26	27	.491	56	53	45	0	0	440^{1}	447	11	194	157	13.6	3.47	95	.253	.334	18	.101	-12	-9	-9	-2	-2.1
1893	Pit-N	0	0	—	1	1	0	0	0	2^{1}	6	0	1	0	27.0	11.57	39	.462	.500	0	.000	-0	-2	-2	0	0.0
	NY-N	16	20	.444	45	39	33	2	2	331^{1}	335	6	141	100	13.3	4.10	114	.255	.332	17	.127	-11	21	20	-3	0.5
	Yr	16	20	.444	46	40	33	2	**2**	333^{2}	341	6	142	100	13.4	4.15	112	.257	.334	17	.126	-11	19	19	-3	0.5
Total	7	154	165	.483	346	328	295	14	5	2802^{1}	2695	82	1307	1349	13.2	3.37	113	.244	.331	188	.163	-31	128	139	-1	8.9
● O. F. BALDWIN	Baldwin, Orson F. b: 11/3/1881, Carson City, Mich. d: 2/16/42, Los Angeles, Cal. TR, 185 lbs. Deb: 9/6/08																									
1908	StL-N	1	3	.250	4	4	0	0	0	14^{2}	16	0	11	5	18.4	6.14	38	.302	.448	0	.000	-1	-6	-6	-0	-1.5
● RICK BALDWIN	Baldwin, Rickey Alan b: 6/1/53, Fresno, Cal. BL/TR, 6'3", 180 lbs. Deb: 4/10/75																									
1975	NY-N	3	5	.375	54	0	0	0	6	97^{1}	97	4	34	54	12.5	3.33	104	.263	.332	3	.200	0	3	1	1	0.2
1976	NY-N	0	0	—	11	0	0	0	0	22^{2}	14	0	10	9	10.3	2.38	138	.189	.302	1	.333	0	3	2	0	0.0
1977	NY-N	1	2	.333	40	0	0	0	1	62^{2}	62	6	31	23	14.1	4.45	84	.265	.363	2	.500	1	-4	-5	1	-0.1
Total	3	4	7	.364	105	0	0	0	7	182^{2}	173	10	75	86	12.8	3.60	98	.256	.339	6	.273	1	2	-1	1	0.1
● JEFF BALLARD	Ballard, Jeffrey Scott b: 8/13/63, Billings, Mont. BL/TL, 6'2", 198 lbs. Deb: 5/9/87																									
1987	Bal-A	2	8	.200	14	14	0	0	0	69^{2}	100	15	35	27	17.4	6.59	67	.344	.414	0	—	0	-17	-17	0	-1.8
1988	Bal-A	8	12	.400	25	25	6	1	0	153^{1}	167	15	42	41	12.6	4.40	89	.278	.332	0	—	0	-7	-9	-2	-1.0
1989	Bal-A	18	8	.692	35	35	4	1	0	215^{1}	240	16	57	62	12.6	3.43	111	.287	.336	0	—	0	11	9	4	1.6
1990	Bal-A	2	11	.154	44	17	0	0	0	133^{1}	152	22	42	50	13.3	4.93	77	.289	.345	0	—	0	-15	-17	0	-1.3
1991	Bal-A	6	12	.333	26	22	0	0	0	123^{2}	153	16	28	37	13.3	5.60	71	.302	.341	0	—	0	-21	-23	-1	-2.7
1993	Pit-N	4	1	.800	25	5	0	0	0	53^{2}	70	3	15	16	14.6	4.86	83	.332	.382	4	.364	1	-5	-5	1	-0.2
1994	Pit-N	1	1	.500	28	0	0	0	2	24^{1}	32	5	10	11	15.9	6.66	65	.323	.391	1	.500	0	-7	-6	-0	-0.5
Total	7	41	53	.436	197	118	10	2	2	773^{1}	914	92	229	244	13.5	4.71	83	.298	.350	5	.385	2	-60	-67	2	-5.9
● JAY BALLER	Baller, Jay Scot b: 10/6/60, Stayton, Ore. BR/TR, 6'7", 225 lbs. Deb: 9/19/82																									
1982	Phi-N	0	0	—	4	1	0	0	0	8	7	1	2	7	11.3	3.38	109	.226	.294	0	—	0	0	0	-0	0.0
1985	Chi-N	2	3	.400	20	4	0	0	1	52	52	8	17	31	12.1	3.46	115	.260	.321	0	.000	-1	1	3	-0	0.2
1986	Chi-N	2	4	.333	36	0	0	0	5	53^{2}	58	7	28	42	14.8	5.37	75	.275	.365	0	.000	-1	-10	-8	-1	-1.1
1987	Chi-N	0	1	.000	23	0	0	0	0	29^{1}	38	4	20	27	17.8	6.75	63	.325	.423	1	1.000	0	-9	-8	-0	-0.2
1990	KC-A	0	1	.000	3	0	0	0	0	2^{1}	4	1	2	1	27.0	15.43	25	.364	.500	0	—	0	-3	-3	-0	-0.9
1992	Phi-N	0	0	—	8	0	0	0	0	11	10	5	10	9	16.4	8.18	43	.250	.400	0	—	0	-6	-6	-0	0.0
Total	6	4	9	.308	94	5	0	0	6	156^{1}	169	26	79	117	14.6	5.24	77	.277	.365	1	.071	-1	-26	-21	-2	-2.0
● MARK BALLINGER	Ballinger, Mark Alan b: 1/31/49, Glendale, Cal. BR/TR, 6'6", 205 lbs. Deb: 8/6/71																									
1971	Cle-A	1	2	.333	18	0	0	0	0	34^{2}	30	3	13	25	11.4	4.67	82	.233	.308	1	.200	-0	-5	-3	-0	-0.3
● WIN BALLOU	Ballou, Noble Winfield b: 11/30/1897, Mount Morgan, Ky. d: 1/30/63, San Francisco, Cal BR/TL, 5'10.5", 170 lbs. Deb: 8/24/25																									
1925	*Was-A	1	1	.500	10	1	1	0	0	27^{2}	38	1	13	13	16.6	4.55	93	.342	.411	1	.143	-0	-0	-1	0	-0.1
1926	StL-A	11	10	.524	43	14	5	0	2	154	186	12	71	59	15.3	4.79	90	.311	.387	2	.048	-3	-13	-9	3	-1.0
1927	StL-A	5	6	.455	21	11	4	0	0	90^{1}	105	4	46	17	15.1	4.78	91	.309	.393	1	.036	-4	-6	-4	-0	-0.8
1929	Bro-N	2	3	.400	25	1	0	0	0	57^{2}	69	5	38	20	16.7	6.71	69	.304	.404	1	.063	-2	-13	-13	2	-0.9
Total	4	19	20	.487	99	27	10	0	2	329^{2}	398	22	168	109	15.6	5.11	86	.312	.394	5	.054	-9	-33	-27	5	-2.8
● TONY BALSAMO	Balsamo, Anthony Fred b: 11/21/37, Brooklyn, N.Y. BR/TR, 6'2", 185 lbs. Deb: 4/14/62																									
1962	Chi-N	0	1	.000	18	0	0	0	0	29^{1}	34	1	20	27	16.9	6.44	64	.293	.401	1	.200	0	-8	-7	1	-0.1
● GEORGE BAMBERGER	Bamberger, George Irvin b: 8/1/25, Staton Island, N.Y. BR/TR, 6', 175 lbs. Deb: 4/19/51 MC																									
1951	NY-N	0	0	—	2	0	0	0	0	2	4	2	2	1	27.0	18.00	22	.444	.545	0	—	0	-3	-3	0	0.0
1952	NY-N	0	0	—	5	0	0	0	0	4	6	1	6	0	27.0	9.00	41	.353	.522	0	—	0	-2	-2	0	0.0
1959	Bal-A	0	0	—	3	1	0	0	1	8^{1}	15	1	2	2	18.4	7.56	50	.405	.436	0	.000	-0	-3	-3	0	-0.1
Total	3	0	0	—	10	1	0	0	1	14^{1}	25	4	10	3	22.0	9.42	40	.397	.479	0	.000	-0	-9	-9	0	-0.1
● SAL BANDO	Bando, Salvatore Leonard b: 2/13/44, Cleveland, O. BR/TR, 6', 205 lbs. Deb: 9/3/66 FC♦																									
1979	Mil-A	0	0	—	1	0	0	0	0	3	3	0	0	0	9.0	6.00	69	.231	.231	117	.246	0	-1	-1	-0	0.0

YEAR	TM/L	W	L	PCT	G	GS	CG	SH	SV	IP	H	HR	BB	SO	RAT	ERA	ERA+	OAV	OOB	BH	AVG	PB	PR	/A	PD	TPI
● **EDDIE BANE**	Bane, Edward Norman b: 3/22/52, Chicago, Ill. BR/TL, 5'9", 160 lbs. Deb: 7/4/73																									
1973	Min-A	0	5	.000	23	6	0	0	2	60^1	62	5	30	42	14.0	4.92	80	.270	.359	0	—	0	-7	-6	1	-0.7
1975	Min-A	3	1	.750	4	4	0	0	0	28^1	28	2	15	14	14.0	2.86	134	.262	.358	0	—	0	3	3	-1	0.2
1976	Min-A	4	7	.364	17	15	1	0	0	79^1	92	6	39	24	14.9	5.11	70	.290	.368	0	—	0	-14	-13	-2	-2.0
Total	3	7	13	.350	44	25	1	0	2	168	182	13	84	80	14.4	4.66	81	.278	.363	0	—	0	-19	-17	-1	-2.5
● **DICK BANEY**	Baney, Richard Lee b: 11/1/46, Fullerton, Cal. BR/TR, 6', 185 lbs. Deb: 7/11/69																									
1969	Sea-A	1	0	1.000	9	1	0	0	0	18^2	21	2	7	9	13.5	3.86	94	.292	.354	0	.000	-0	-0	-0	-0	-0.1
1973	Cin-N	2	1	.667	11	1	0	0	2	30^2	26	1	6	17	10.6	2.93	116	.234	.298	2	.222	1	2	2	-1	0.1
1974	Cin-N	1	0	1.000	22	1	0	0	1	41	51	4	17	12	14.9	5.49	64	.305	.370	0	.000	-1	-9	-9	-1	-0.4
Total	3	4	1	.800	42	3	0	0	3	90^1	98	7	30	38	13.2	4.28	81	.280	.344	2	.125	-0	-7	-8	-3	-0.4
● **DAN BANKHEAD**	Bankhead, Daniel Robert b: 5/3/20, Empire, Ala. d: 5/2/76, Houston, Tex. BR/TR, 6'1", 184 lbs. Deb: 8/26/47																									
1947	*Bro-N	0	0	—	4	0	0	0	1	10	15	1	8	6	21.6	7.20	57	.341	.453	1	.250	1	-3	-3	-0	0.0
1950	Bro-N	9	4	.692	41	12	2	1	3	129^1	119	16	88	96	14.5	5.50	75	.252	.371	9	.231	1	-19	-20	-1	-1.8
1951	Bro-N	0	1	.000	7	1	0	0	0	14	27	5	14	9	26.4	15.43	25	.422	.526	0	.000	-0	-18	-18	0	-1.1
Total	3	9	5	.643	52	13	2	1	4	153^1	161	22	110	111	16.1	6.52	63	.277	.395	10	.222	2	-41	-41	-1	-2.9
● **SCOTT BANKHEAD**	Bankhead, Michael Scott b: 7/31/63, Raleigh, N.C. BR/TR, 5'10", 185 lbs. Deb: 5/25/86																									
1986	KC-A	8	9	.471	24	17	0	0	0	121	121	14	37	94	12.0	4.61	92	.259	.318	0	—	0	-6	-5	-0	-0.7
1987	Sea-A	9	8	.529	27	25	2	0	0	149^1	168	35	37	95	12.5	5.42	87	.283	.329	0	—	0	-16	-12	-2	-1.5
1988	Sea-A	7	9	.438	21	21	2	1	0	135	115	8	38	102	10.3	3.07	136	.224	.278	0	—	0	13	16	-1	1.7
1989	Sea-A	14	6	.700	33	33	3	2	0	210^1	187	19	63	140	10.8	3.34	121	.239	.298	0	—	0	13	16	-2	1.3
1990	Sea-A	0	2	.000	4	4	0	0	0	13	18	2	7	10	17.3	11.08	36	.333	.410	0	—	0	-10	-10	-0	-1.3
1991	Sea-A	3	6	.333	17	9	0	0	0	60^2	73	8	21	28	14.2	4.90	84	.297	.357	0	—	0	-5	-5	-0	-0.7
1992	Cin-N	10	4	.714	54	0	0	0	1	70^2	57	4	29	53	11.3	2.93	123	.218	.304	2	.222	0	5	5	-2	0.9
1993	Bos-A	2	1	.667	40	0	0	0	0	64^1	59	7	29	47	12.3	3.50	132	.250	.332	0	—	0	6	8	-1	0.2
1994	Bos-A	3	2	.600	27	0	0	0	0	37^2	34	5	12	25	11.0	4.54	111	.239	.299	0	—	0	1	2	-1	-0.1
1995	NY-A	1	1	.500	20	1	0	0	0	39	44	9	16	20	13.8	6.00	77	.278	.345	0	—	0	-6	-6	-1	-0.3
Total	10	57	48	.543	267	110	7	3	1	901	876	111	289	614	11.8	4.18	102	.254	.314	2	.222	0	-6	10	-11	-0.5
● **BILL BANKS**	Banks, William John (b: William John Yerrick) b: 2/26/1874, Danville, Pa. d: 9/8/36, Danville, Pa. BR/TR, 5'11", 150 lbs. Deb: 9/27/1895																									
1895	Bos-N	1	0	1.000	1	1	1	0	0	7	7	0	4	4	14.1	0.00	—	.259	.355	0	.000	-1	4	4	0	0.5
1896	Bos-N	0	3	.000	4	3	2	0	0	23	42	2	13	6	22.3	10.57	43	.389	.463	3	.273	0	-16	-15	-1	-1.4
Total	2	1	3	.250	5	4	3	0	0	30	49	2	17	10	20.4	8.10	58	.363	.442	3	.214	-1	-12	-11	-1	-0.9
● **WILLIE BANKS**	Banks, Willie Anthony b: 2/27/69, Jersey City, N.J. BR/TR, 6'1", 202 lbs. Deb: 7/31/91																									
1991	Min-A	1	1	.500	5	3	0	0	0	17^1	21	1	12	16	17.1	5.71	75	.288	.388	0	—	0	-3	-3	-1	-0.6
1992	Min-A	4	4	.500	16	12	0	0	0	71	80	6	37	37	15.1	5.70	71	.288	.375	0	—	0	-14	-13	-0	-1.5
1993	Min-A	11	12	.478	31	30	0	0	0	171^1	186	17	78	138	14.0	4.04	108	.280	.358	0	—	0	5	6	-1	0.6
1994	Chi-N	8	12	.400	23	23	1	1	0	138^1	139	16	56	91	12.8	5.40	77	.261	.333	5	.122	-1	-18	-19	-2	-2.6
1995	Chi-N	0	1	.000	10	0	0	0	0	11^2	27	5	12	9	30.1	15.43	27	.458	.549	0	.000	-0	-15	-15	0	-1.0
	LA-N	0	2	.000	6	6	0	0	0	29	36	2	16	23	16.4	4.03	94	.303	.390	1	.125	0	0	-1	0	0.0
	Fla-N	2	3	.400	9	9	0	0	0	50	43	7	30	30	13.3	4.32	98	.235	.346	6	.353	2	-1	-1	-0	0.1
	Yr	2	6	.250	25	15	0	0	0	90^2	106	14	58	62	16.4	5.66	72	.291	.390	7	.269	2	-15	-16	0	-0.9
1997	NY-A	3	0	1.000	5	1	0	0	0	14	9	0	6	8	10.3	1.93	230	.188	.291	0	—	0	4	4	0	0.8
1998	NY-A	1	1	.500	9	0	0	0	0	14^1	20	4	12	8	20.7	10.05	44	.323	.440	0	—	0	-9	-9	1	-0.9
	Ari-N	1	2	.333	33	0	0	0	1	43^2	34	2	25	32	12.4	3.09	139	.217	.328	0	.000	-0	6	6	0	0.4
Total	7	31	38	.449	147	84	1	1	1	560^2	595	60	284	392	14.3	4.93	86	.273	.360	12	.176	1	-44	-44	-2	-4.7
● **FLOYD BANNISTER**	Bannister, Floyd Franklin b: 6/10/55, Pierre, S.D. BL/TL, 6'1", 195 lbs. Deb: 4/19/77																									
1977	Hou-N	8	9	.471	24	23	4	1	0	142^2	138	11	68	112	13.2	4.04	88	.254	.341	9	.188	0	-2	-7	-1	-0.9
1978	Hou-N	3	9	.250	28	16	2	2	0	110^1	120	13	63	94	15.0	4.81	69	.280	.374	5	.161	0	-15	-18	-2	-2.0
1979	Sea-A	10	15	.400	30	30	6	2	0	182^1	185	25	68	115	12.7	4.05	108	.260	.328	0	—	0	3	6	-2	0.4
1980	Sea-A	9	13	.409	32	32	8	0	0	217^2	200	24	66	155	11.1	3.47	119	.239	.296	0	—	0	14	16	-1	1.4
1981	Sea-A	9	9	.500	21	20	5	2	0	121^1	128	14	39	85	12.6	4.45	87	.268	.327	0	—	0	-11	-8	-1	-1.3
1982	Sea-A★	12	13	.480	35	35	5	3	0	247	225	32	77	**209**	11.1	3.43	124	.243	.303	0	—	0	18	22	-1	1.9
1983	*Chi-A	16	10	.615	34	34	5	2	0	217^1	191	19	71	193	10.9	3.35	125	.233	.295	0	—	0	17	20	-1	1.9
1984	Chi-A	14	11	.560	34	33	4	0	0	218	211	30	80	152	12.3	4.83	86	.252	.322	0	.000	-0	-20	-16	-2	-1.8
1985	Chi-A	10	14	.417	34	34	4	1	0	210^2	211	30	100	198	13.5	4.87	89	.261	.346	0	—	0	-17	-13	-1	-1.5
1986	Chi-A	10	14	.417	28	27	6	1	0	165^1	162	17	48	92	11.5	3.54	122	.259	.314	0	—	0	12	14	-1	1.7
1987	Chi-A	16	11	.593	34	34	11	2	0	228^2	216	38	49	124	10.4	3.58	128	.246	.286	0	—	0	22	25	-3	2.3
1988	KC-A	12	13	.480	31	31	2	0	0	189^1	182	22	68	113	12.1	4.33	92	.248	.316	0	—	0	-8	-7	-0	-0.9
1989	KC-A	4	1	.800	14	14	0	0	0	75^1	87	8	18	35	12.7	4.66	83	.290	.332	0	—	0	-7	-7	1	-0.3
1991	Cal-A	0	0	—	16	0	0	0	0	25	25	5	10	16	12.6	3.96	104	.266	.337	0	—	0	0	0	-1	0.0
1992	Tex-A	1	1	.500	36	0	0	0	0	37	39	3	21	30	15.3	6.32	60	.281	.387	0	—	0	-10	-10	0	-0.3
Total	15	134	143	.484	431	363	62	16	0	2388	2320	291	846	1723	12.1	4.06	101	.253	.319	14	.175	0	-3	16	-15	0.6
● **JIMMY BANNON**	Bannon, James Henry "Foxy Grandpa" b: 5/5/1871, Amesbury, Mass. d: 3/24/48, Glen Rock, N.J. BR/TR, 5'5", 160 lbs. Deb: 6/15/1893 F♦																									
1893	StL-N	0	1	.000	1	1	0	0	0	4	10	1	5	1	38.3	22.50	21	.455	.586	36	.336	0	-8	-8	-0	-1.0
1894	Bos-N	0	0	—	1	0	0	0	0	2	4	1	1	0	22.5	0.00	—	.400	.455	166	.336	0	1	1	0	0.0
1895	Bos-N	0	0	—	1	0	0	0	0	3	4	0	2	1	18.0	6.00	85	.308	.400	171	.350	0	-0	-0	0	0.0
Total	3	0	1	.000	3	1	0	0	0	9	18	2	8	2	28.0	12.00	42	.400	.509	460	.321	1	-7	-7	-0	-1.0
● **JACK BANTA**	Banta, Jackie Kay b: 6/24/25, Hutchinson, Kan. BL/TR, 6'2.5", 175 lbs. Deb: 9/18/47																									
1947	Bro-N	0	1	.000	3	1	0	0	0	7^2	7	1	4	3	14.1	7.04	59	.226	.333	0	.000	-0	-3	-2	1	-0.2
1948	Bro-N	0	1	.000	2	1	0	0	0	3^1	5	0	5	1	27.0	8.10	49	.385	.556	0	.000	-0	-2	-2	-0	-0.4
1949	*Bro-N	10	6	.625	48	12	2	1	3	152^1	125	12	68	97	11.8	3.37	122	.223	.314	5	.109	-2	11	12	1	1.1
1950	Bro-N	4	4	.500	16	5	1	0	2	41^1	39	2	36	15	17.0	4.35	94	.252	.402	2	.167	-0	-1	-1	-1	-0.3
Total	4	14	12	.538	69	19	3	1	5	204^2	176	15	113	116	13.1	3.78	108	.232	.339	7	.115	-2	6	7	0	0.2
● **TRAVIS BAPTIST**	Baptist, Travis Steven b: 12/30/71, Forest Grove, Ore. BL/TL, 6', 195 lbs. Deb: 8/1/98																									
1998	Min-A	0	1	.000	13	0	0	0	0	27	34	5	11	11	15.0	5.67	83	.321	.385	0	—	0	-3	-3	0	-0.1
● **BRIAN BARBER**	Barber, Brian Scott b: 3/4/73, Hamilton, Ohio BR/TR, 6'1", 170 lbs. Deb: 8/12/95																									
1995	StL-N	2	1	.667	9	4	0	0	0	29^1	31	4	16	27	14.4	5.22	80	.279	.370	1	.125	-0	-3	-3	-1	-0.4
1996	StL-N	0	0	—	1	1	0	0	0	3	4	0	6	1	33.0	15.00	28	.364	.611	0	—	0	-4	-4	-0	0.0
1998	KC-A	2	4	.333	8	8	0	0	0	42	45	5	13	24	12.6	6.00	82	.276	.333	0	—	0	-6	-5	-1	-0.7
Total	3	4	5	.444	18	13	0	0	0	74^1	80	9	35	52	14.2	6.05	76	.281	.363	1	.125	-0	-13	-12	-2	-1.1
● **STEVE BARBER**	Barber, Stephen David b: 2/22/39, Takoma Park, Md. BL/TL, 6', 200 lbs. Deb: 4/21/60																									
1960	Bal-A	10	7	.588	36	27	6	1	2	181^2	148	10	113	112	13.1	3.22	118	.226	.343	3	.056	-4	13	12	0	0.7
1961	Bal-A	18	12	.600	37	34	14	**8**	1	248^1	194	13	130	150	11.8	3.33	115	.218	.319	13	.162	2	19	14	4	2.2
1962	Bal-A	9	6	.600	28	19	5	2	0	140^1	145	9	61	89	13.3	3.46	107	.262	.337	3	.071	-2	8	4	1	0.3
1963	Bal-A†	20	13	.606	39	36	11	2	0	258^2	253	12	92	180	12.1	2.75	126	.258	.324	12	.138	-0	25	21	2	2.8
1964	Bal-A	9	13	.409	36	26	4	0	1	157	144	15	81	118	13.3	3.84	93	.248	.347	7	.149	1	-4	-5	3	-0.3
1965	Bal-A	15	10	.600	37	32	7	2	0	220^2	177	16	81	130	10.6	2.69	129	.224	.297	5	.077	-2	19	19	1	2.1
1966	Bal-A☆	10	5	.667	25	22	5	3	0	133^1	104	6	49	91	10.5	2.30	145	.218	.294	3	.068	-3	17	15	1	1.5
1967	Bal-A	4	9	.308	15	15	1	1	0	74^2	47	5	61	48	13.6	4.10	77	.185	.353	2	.091	-1	-7	-8	0	-1.3
	NY-A	6	9	.400	17	17	3	1	0	97^2	103	4	54	70	14.7	4.05	77	.278	.375	5	.172	1	-9	-10	-1	-1.4
	Yr	10	18	.357	32	32	4	2	0	172^1	150	9	115	118	14.0	4.07	77	.238	.358	7	.137	1	-16	-18	-1	-2.7

YEAR	TM/L	W	L	PCT	G	GS	CG	SH	SV	IP	H	HR	BB	SO	RAT	ERA	ERA+	OAV	OOB	BH	AVG	PB	PR	/A	PD	TPI
1968	NY-A	6	5	.545	20	19	3	1	0	128^1	127	7	64	87	13.6	3.23	90	.256	.345	2	.051	-1	-4	-5	0	-0.5
1969	Sea-A	4	7	.364	25	16	0	0	0	86^1	99	9	48	69	15.4	4.80	76	.292	.381	5	.200	1	-11	-11	0	-1.2
1970	Chi-N	0	1	.000	5	0	0	0	0	5^2	10	0	6	3	25.4	9.53	47	.417	.533	0	—	0	-3	-3	-0	-0.5
	Atl-N	0	1	.000	5	2	0	0	0	14^2	17	3	5	11	14.1	4.91	87	.288	.354	1	.250	0	-1	-1	-0	-0.1
	Yr	0	2	.000	10	2	0	0	0	20^1	27	3	11	14	17.3	6.20	70	.325	.411	1	.250	0	-5	-4	-0	-0.6
1971	Atl-N	3	1	.750	39	3	0	0	2	75	92	6	25	40	14.3	4.80	77	.301	.357	2	.154	-0	-11	-9	0	-0.5
1972	Atl-N	0	0	—	5	0	0	0	0	15^2	18	1	6	6	14.4	5.74	66	.290	.362	1	.200	-0	-4	-3	1	0.1
	Cal-A	4	4	.500	34	3	0	0	2	58	37	4	30	34	10.6	2.02	144	.188	.298	1	.143	1	7	6	-1	0.9
1973	Cal-A	3	2	.600	50	1	0	0	4	89^1	90	5	32	58	12.6	3.53	101	.265	.333	0	—	0	3	0	-1	0.5
1974	SF-N	0	1	.000	13	0	0	0	1	13^2	13	0	12	13	16.5	5.27	72	.255	.397	0	—	0	-3	-2	-1	-0.2
Total	15	121	106	.533	466	272	59	21	13	1999	1818	125	950	1309	12.7	3.36	105	.245	.334	65	.115	-6	54	34	10	5.1

● STEVE BARBER Barber, Steven Lee b: 3/13/48, Grand Rapids, Mich. BR/TR, 6'1", 190 lbs. Deb: 4/9/70

YEAR	TM/L	W	L	PCT	G	GS	CG	SH	SV	IP	H	HR	BB	SO	RAT	ERA	ERA+	OAV	OOB	BH	AVG	PB	PR	/A	PD	TPI
1970	Min-A	0	0	—	18	0	0	0	2	27^1	26	1	18	14	15.1	4.61	81	.263	.387	0	.000	-0	-3	-3	-0	-0.1
1971	Min-A	1	0	1.000	4	2	0	0	0	11^2	8	2	13	4	16.2	6.17	58	.190	.382	0	.000	-1	-4	-3	-0	-0.3
Total	2	1	0	1.000	22	2	0	0	2	39	34	3	31	18	15.5	5.08	72	.241	.385	0	.000	-1	-6	-6	-1	-0.4

● FRANK BARBERICH Barberich, Frank Frederick b: 2/3/1882, Newtown, N.Y. d: 5/1/65, Ocala, Fla. BB/TR, 5'10.5", 175 lbs. Deb: 9/17/07

YEAR	TM/L	W	L	PCT	G	GS	CG	SH	SV	IP	H	HR	BB	SO	RAT	ERA	ERA+	OAV	OOB	BH	AVG	PB	PR	/A	PD	TPI
1907	Bos-N	1	1	.500	2	2	1	0	0	12^1	19	0	5	1	17.5	5.84	44	.358	.414	0	.000	-0	-5	-5	0	-0.7
1910	Bos-A	0	0	—	2	0	0	0	0	5	7	0	2	0	16.2	7.20	35	.350	.409	0	.000	-0	-3	-3	0	0.0
Total	2	1	1	.500	4	2	1	0	0	17^1	26	0	7	1	17.1	6.23	41	.356	.412	0	.000	-1	-7	-7	0	-0.7

● CURT BARCLAY Barclay, Curtis Cordell b: 8/22/31, Chicago, Ill. d: 3/25/85, Missoula, Montana BR/TR, 6'3", 210 lbs. Deb: 4/21/57

YEAR	TM/L	W	L	PCT	G	GS	CG	SH	SV	IP	H	HR	BB	SO	RAT	ERA	ERA+	OAV	OOB	BH	AVG	PB	PR	/A	PD	TPI
1957	NY-N	9	9	.500	37	28	5	2	0	183	196	21	48	67	12.1	3.44	114	.274	.321	11	.190	0	9	10	3	1.2
1958	SF-N	1	0	1.000	6	1	0	0	0	16	16	3	5	6	13.5	2.81	136	.258	.343	4	.667	2	2	2	0	0.3
1959	SF-N	0	0	—	1	0	0	0	0	0^1	2	0	2	0	108.0	54.00	7	.500	.667	0	—	0	-2	-2	-0	0.0
Total	3	10	9	.526	44	29	5	2	0	199^1	214	24	55	73	12.4	3.48	113	.274	.325	15	.234	2	9	10	3	1.5

● RAY BARE Bare, Raymond Douglas b: 4/15/49, Miami, Fla. d: 3/29/94, Miami, Fla. BR/TR, 6'2", 195 lbs. Deb: 7/30/72

YEAR	TM/L	W	L	PCT	G	GS	CG	SH	SV	IP	H	HR	BB	SO	RAT	ERA	ERA+	OAV	OOB	BH	AVG	PB	PR	/A	PD	TPI
1972	StL-N	0	1	.000	14	0	0	0	1	16^2	18	0	6	5	13.0	0.54	630	.281	.343	0	—	0	5	5	-0	0.4
1974	StL-N	1	2	.333	10	3	0	0	0	24^1	25	2	9	6	12.6	5.92	60	.281	.347	1	.200	-0	-6	-6	1	-0.6
1975	Det-A	8	13	.381	29	21	6	1	0	150^2	174	10	47	71	13.3	4.48	90	.293	.346	0	—	0	-12	-8	2	-1.1
1976	Det-A	7	8	.467	30	21	3	2	0	134	157	13	51	59	14.0	4.63	80	.293	.354	0	—	0	-17	-14	1	-1.4
1977	Det-A	0	2	.000	5	4	0	0	0	14^1	24	3	7	4	19.5	12.56	34	.381	.443	0	—	0	-14	-13	1	-1.6
Total	5	16	26	.381	88	49	9	3	1	340	398	28	120	145	13.7	4.79	80	.296	.354	1	.200	-0	-43	-36	4	-4.3

● JOHN BARFIELD Barfield, John David b: 10/15/64, Pine Bluff, Ark. BL/TL, 6'1", 185 lbs. Deb: 9/7/89

YEAR	TM/L	W	L	PCT	G	GS	CG	SH	SV	IP	H	HR	BB	SO	RAT	ERA	ERA+	OAV	OOB	BH	AVG	PB	PR	/A	PD	TPI
1989	Tex-A	0	1	.000	4	2	0	0	0	11^2	15	0	4	9	14.7	6.17	64	.319	.373	0	—	0	-3	-3	-0	-0.3
1990	Tex-A	4	3	.571	33	0	0	0	1	44^1	42	2	13	17	11.4	4.67	84	.268	.327	0	—	0	-4	-4	0	-0.5
1991	Tex-A	4	4	.500	28	9	0	0	1	83^1	96	11	22	27	12.7	4.54	89	.289	.333	0	—	0	-4	-5	-0	-0.4
Total	3	8	8	.500	65	11	0	0	2	139^1	153	13	39	53	12.5	4.72	85	.285	.335	0	—	0	-11	-11	-0	-1.2

● CLYDE BARFOOT Barfoot, Clyde Raymond "Foots" b: 7/8/1891, Richmond, Va. d: 3/11/71, Highland Park, Cal BR/TR, 6', 170 lbs. Deb: 4/13/22

YEAR	TM/L	W	L	PCT	G	GS	CG	SH	SV	IP	H	HR	BB	SO	RAT	ERA	ERA+	OAV	OOB	BH	AVG	PB	PR	/A	PD	TPI
1922	StL-N	4	5	.444	42	2	1	0	2	117^2	139	2	30	19	13.7	4.21	92	.307	.363	12	.353	5	-1	-4	1	0.2
1923	StL-N	3	3	.500	33	2	1	1	1	101^1	112	7	27	23	12.4	3.73	105	.289	.337	7	.189	-1	3	2	0	0.0
1926	Det-A	1	2	.333	11	1	0	0	2	31^1	42	4	9	7	14.6	4.88	83	.318	.362	1	.200	0	-3	-3	1	-0.2
Total	3	8	10	.444	86	5	2	1	5	250^1	293	13	66	49	13.3	4.10	95	.301	.353	20	.263	4	-1	-5	1	0.0

● GREG BARGAR Bargar, Greg Robert b: 1/27/59, Inglewood, Cal. BR/TR, 6'2", 185 lbs. Deb: 7/17/83

YEAR	TM/L	W	L	PCT	G	GS	CG	SH	SV	IP	H	HR	BB	SO	RAT	ERA	ERA+	OAV	OOB	BH	AVG	PB	PR	/A	PD	TPI
1983	Mon-N	2	0	1.000	8	3	0	0	0	20	23	6	8	9	14.4	6.75	53	.271	.340	1	.167	-0	-7	-7	-1	-0.7
1984	Mon-N	0	1	.000	3	1	0	0	0	8	8	1	7	2	16.9	7.88	43	.286	.429	0	.000	-0	-4	-4	0	-0.4
1986	StL-N	0	2	.000	22	0	0	0	0	27^1	36	3	10	12	16.1	5.60	65	.330	.402	0	.000	-0	-6	-6	1	-0.4
Total	3	2	3	.400	33	4	0	0	0	55^1	67	10	25	23	15.6	6.34	57	.302	.382	1	.111	-0	-16	-17	0	-1.5

● CY BARGER Barger, Eros Bolivar b: 5/18/1885, Jamestown, Ky. d: 9/23/64, Columbia, Ky. BL/TR, 6', 160 lbs. Deb: 8/30/06

YEAR	TM/L	W	L	PCT	G	GS	CG	SH	SV	IP	H	HR	BB	SO	RAT	ERA	ERA+	OAV	OOB	BH	AVG	PB	PR	/A	PD	TPI
1906	NY-A	0	0	—	2	1	0	0	1	5^1	7	0	3	3	16.9	10.13	29	.318	.400	1	.333	0	-4	-4	-0	-0.2
1907	NY-A	0	0	—	1	0	0	0	0	6	10	0	1	0	18.0	3.00	93	.370	.414	0	.000	-0	-0	-0	-1	-0.1
1910	Bro-N	15	15	.500	35	30	25	2	1	271^2	267	2	107	87	12.6	2.88	105	.275	.351	24	.231	3	5	5	2	1.0
1911	Bro-N	11	15	.423	30	30	21	1	0	217^1	224	4	71	60	12.5	3.52	95	.279	.342	33	.228	1	-3	-4	1	-0.2
1912	Bro-N	1	9	.100	16	11	6	1	0	94	120	4	42	30	15.9	5.46	61	.326	.401	7	.189	-0	-21	-22	1	-1.9
1914	Pit-F	10	16	.385	33	26	18	1	1	228^1	252	7	63	70	12.7	4.34	66	.290	.342	17	.205	-1	-37	-37	-2	-4.0
1915	Pit-F	9	8	.529	34	13	8	1	6	153	130	1	47	47	10.6	2.29	118	.238	.303	15	.278	2	7	7	-1	0.9
Total	7	46	63	.422	151	111	78	5	9	975^2	1010	18	334	297	12.7	3.56	85	.280	.346	97	.227	5	-54	-56	-0	-4.5

● BRIAN BARK Bark, Brian Stuart b: 8/26/68, Baltimore, Md. BL/TL, 5'9", 170 lbs. Deb: 7/6/95

YEAR	TM/L	W	L	PCT	G	GS	CG	SH	SV	IP	H	HR	BB	SO	RAT	ERA	ERA+	OAV	OOB	BH	AVG	PB	PR	/A	PD	TPI
1995	Bos-A	0	0	—	3	0	0	0	0	2^1	2	0	1	0	11.6	0.00	—	.286	.375	0	—	0	1	1	-0	-0.1

● LEN BARKER Barker, Leonard Harold b: 7/7/55, Fort Knox, Ky. BR/TR, 6'5", 225 lbs. Deb: 9/14/76

YEAR	TM/L	W	L	PCT	G	GS	CG	SH	SV	IP	H	HR	BB	SO	RAT	ERA	ERA+	OAV	OOB	BH	AVG	PB	PR	/A	PD	TPI
1976	Tex-A	1	0	1.000	2	2	1	1	0	15	7	0	6	7	9.0	2.40	149	.149	.273	0	—	0	2	2	-0	0.1
1977	Tex-A	4	1	.800	15	3	0	0	1	47^1	36	1	24	51	11.6	2.66	153	.217	.319	0	—	0	7	7	1	0.8
1978	Tex-A	1	5	.167	29	0	0	0	4	52^1	63	6	29	33	16.2	4.82	78	.304	.395	0	—	0	-6	-6	0	-0.7
1979	Cle-A	6	6	.500	29	19	2	0	0	137^1	146	6	70	93	14.3	4.92	87	.277	.364	0	—	0	-11	-10	-1	-0.9
1980	Cle-A	19	12	.613	36	36	8	1	0	246^1	237	17	92	**187**	12.1	4.17	98	.252	.320	0	—	0	-4	-3	-2	-0.5
1981	Cle-A★	8	7	.533	22	22	9	3	0	154^1	150	7	46	**127**	11.5	3.91	93	.249	.303	0	—	0	-4	-5	-0	-0.4
1982	Cle-A	15	11	.577	33	33	10	1	0	244^2	211	17	88	187	11.1	3.90	105	.232	.301	0	—	0	5	5	-0	0.5
1983	Cle-A	8	13	.381	24	24	4	1	0	149^2	150	16	52	105	12.3	5.11	83	.266	.330	0	—	0	-17	-15	-1	-2.0
	Atl-N	1	3	.250	6	6	0	0	0	33	31	0	14	21	12.3	3.82	102	.248	.324	1	.125	-0	-1	0	1	0.1
1984	Atl-N	7	8	.467	21	20	1	0	0	126^1	120	10	38	95	11.4	3.85	100	.254	.312	2	.053	-1	-4	0	3	0.2
1985	Atl-N	2	9	.182	20	18	0	0	0	73^2	84	10	37	47	14.9	6.35	61	.288	.370	0	.000	-2	-23	-21	-1	-3.0
1987	Mil-A	2	1	.667	11	11	0	0	0	43^2	54	6	17	22	15.0	5.36	85	.303	.371	0	—	0	-4	-4	-0	-0.4
Total	11	74	76	.493	248	194	35	7	5	1323^2	1289	96	513	975	12.4	4.34	93	.256	.327	3	.048	-3	-59	-48	-1	-6.2

● BRIAN BARKLEY Barkley, Brian Edward b: 12/8/75, Conroe, Tex. BL/TL, 6'2", 180 lbs. Deb: 5/28/98 F

YEAR	TM/L	W	L	PCT	G	GS	CG	SH	SV	IP	H	HR	BB	SO	RAT	ERA	ERA+	OAV	OOB	BH	AVG	PB	PR	/A	PD	TPI
1998	Bos-A	0	0	—	6	0	0	0	0	11	16	2	9	2	21.3	9.82	47	.340	.456	0	—	0	-6	-6	-0	0.0

● JEFF BARKLEY Barkley, Jeffrey Carver b: 11/21/59, Hickory, N.C. BB/TR, 6'3", 185 lbs. Deb: 9/16/84 F

YEAR	TM/L	W	L	PCT	G	GS	CG	SH	SV	IP	H	HR	BB	SO	RAT	ERA	ERA+	OAV	OOB	BH	AVG	PB	PR	/A	PD	TPI
1984	Cle-A	0	0	—	3	0	0	0	0	4	6	0	1	4	15.8	6.75	61	.353	.389	0	—	0	-1	-1	0	-0.1
1985	Cle-A	0	3	.000	21	0	0	0	1	41	37	5	15	30	11.4	5.27	78	.243	.311	0	—	0	-5	-5	0	-0.3
Total	2	0	3	.000	24	0	0	0	1	45	43	5	16	34	11.8	5.40	76	.254	.319	0	—	0	-6	-6	0	-0.4

● MIKE BARLOW Barlow, Michael Roswell b: 4/30/48, Stamford, N.Y. BL/TR, 6'6", 215 lbs. Deb: 6/18/75

YEAR	TM/L	W	L	PCT	G	GS	CG	SH	SV	IP	H	HR	BB	SO	RAT	ERA	ERA+	OAV	OOB	BH	AVG	PB	PR	/A	PD	TPI
1975	StL-N	0	0	—	9	0	0	0	0	7^2	11	0	3	2	17.6	4.70	80	.355	.429	0	—	0	-1	-1	-0	0.0
1976	Hou-N	2	2	.500	16	0	0	0	0	22	27	0	17	11	18.0	4.50	71	.318	.431	0	.000	-0	-2	-3	1	-0.5
1977	Cal-A	4	2	.667	20	1	0	0	1	59	53	3	27	25	12.8	4.58	86	.249	.344	0	—	0	-3	-4	0	-0.1
1978	Cal-A	0	0	—	1	0	0	0	0	2	3	0	0	1	13.5	4.50	80	.375	.375	0	—	0	-0	-0	-0	0.0
1979	*Cal-A	1	1	.500	35	0	0	0	0	86	106	8	30	33	14.7	5.13	79	.314	.376	0	—	0	-9	-10	-0	0.0
1980	Tor-A	3	1	.750	40	1	0	0	5	55	57	4	21	19	13.1	4.09	105	.273	.345	0	—	0	-0	1	-0	-0.1
1981	Tor-A	0	0	—	12	0	0	0	0	15	22	1	6	5	19.2	4.20	94	.338	.427	0	—	0	-1	-0	0	0.0
Total	7	10	6	.625	133	2	0	0	6	246^2	279	16	104	96	14.5	4.63	86	.294	.373	0	.000	-0	-17	-18	0	-0.7

● CHARLIE BARNABE Barnabe, Charles Edward b: 6/12/1900, Russell Gulch, Colo. d: 8/16/77, Waco, Tex. BL/TL, 5'11.5", 164 lbs. Deb: 4/14/27

YEAR	TM/L	W	L	PCT	G	GS	CG	SH	SV	IP	H	HR	BB	SO	RAT	ERA	ERA+	OAV	OOB	BH	AVG	PB	PR	/A	PD	TPI
1927	Chi-A	0	5	.000	17	4	1	0	0	61	86	2	20	5	16.4	5.31	76	.351	.411	3	.158	1	-8	-9	1	-0.4

YEAR	TM/L	W	L	PCT	G	GS	CG	SH	SV	IP	H	HR	BB	SO	RAT	ERA	ERA+	OAV	OOB	BH	AVG	PB	PR	/A	PD	TPI
1928	Chi-A	0	2	.000	7	2	0	0	0	9^{2}	17	0	0	3	16.8	6.52	62	.395	.409	4	.500	2	-3	-3	1	-0.2
Total	2	0	7	.000	24	6	1	0	0	70^{2}	103	2	20	8	16.4	5.48	74	.358	.411	7	.259	3	-11	-11	1	-0.6
● BRIAN BARNES	Barnes, Brian Keith b: 3/25/67, Roanoke Rapids, N.C. BL/TL, 5'9", 170 lbs. Deb: 9/14/90																									
1990	Mon-N	1	1	.500	4	4	1	0	0	28	25	2	7	23	10.3	2.89	126	.236	.283	0	.000	-1	3	2	0	0.1
1991	Mon-N	5	8	.385	28	27	1	0	0	160	135	16	84	117	12.7	4.22	86	.233	.336	4	.082	-1	-10	-11	1	-0.7
1992	Mon-N	6	6	.500	21	17	0	0	0	100	77	9	46	65	11.3	2.97	117	.213	.307	8	.276	2	6	6	0	0.9
1993	Mon-N	2	6	.250	52	8	0	0	3	100	105	9	48	60	13.8	4.41	95	.274	.355	3	.150	-0	-4	-3	-0	-0.2
1994	Cle-A	0	1	.000	6	0	0	0	0	13^{1}	12	2	15	5	18.2	5.40	87	.235	.409	0	—	0	-1	-1	-0	-0.1
	LA-N	0	0	—	5	0	0	0	0	5	10	1	4	5	25.2	7.20	54	.400	.483	0	—	0	-2	-2	-0	0.0
Total	5	14	22	.389	116	56	2	0	3	406^{1}	364	39	204	275	12.8	3.94	95	.242	.335	15	.140	1	-7	-8	1	0.0
● FRANK BARNES	Barnes, Frank b: 8/26/26, Longwood, Miss. BR/TR, 6', 170 lbs. Deb: 9/22/57																									
1957	StL-N	0	1	.000	3	1	0	0	0	10	13	0	9	5	19.8	4.50	88	.317	.440	0	.000	-0	-1	-1	-0	-0.1
1958	StL-N	1	1	.500	8	1	0	0	0	19	19	3	16	17	17.5	7.58	54	.260	.407	1	.167	-0	-8	-7	-0	-0.7
1960	StL-N	0	1	.000	4	1	0	0	1	7^{2}	8	1	9	8	21.1	3.52	116	.267	.450	0	.000	-0	0	0	-0	0.0
Total	3	1	3	.250	15	3	0	0	1	36^{2}	40	4	34	30	18.9	5.89	69	.278	.425	1	.100	-1	-8	-7	-1	-0.8
● FRANK BARNES	Barnes, Frank Samuel "Lefty" b: 1/9/1900, Dallas, Tex. d: 9/27/67, Houston, Tex. BL/TL, 6'2.5", 195 lbs. Deb: 4/18/29																									
1929	Det-A	0	1	.000	4	1	0	0	0	5	10	0	3	0	25.2	7.20	60	.400	.483	0	.000	-0	-2	-2	0	-0.3
1930	NY-A	0	1	.000	2	2	0	0	0	12^{1}	13	0	13	2	19.7	8.03	54	.283	.450	2	.333	1	-5	-5	1	-0.1
Total	2	0	2	.000	6	3	0	0	0	17^{1}	23	0	16	2	21.3	7.79	55	.324	.461	2	.286	1	-6	-7	2	-0.4
● JESSE BARNES	Barnes, Jesse Lawrence "Nubby" b: 8/26/1892, Perkins, Okla. d: 9/9/61, Santa Rosa, N.Mex. BL/TR, 6', 170 lbs. Deb: 7/30/15 F																									
1915	Bos-N	3	0	1.000	9	3	2	0	0	45^{1}	41	1	10	16	10.9	1.39	186	.244	.302	3	.176	0	7	6	-1	0.3
1916	Bos-N	6	15	.286	33	18	9	3	1	163	154	3	37	55	10.8	2.37	105	.254	.302	9	.188	0	4	2	4	0.7
1917	Bos-N	13	21	.382	50	33	27	2	1	295	261	3	50	107	9.6	2.68	95	.241	.277	24	.238	4	1	-4	3	0.3
1918	NY-N	6	1	.857	9	9	4	2	0	54^{2}	53	0	13	12	10.9	1.81	145	.255	.299	4	.222	-0	6	5	2	0.9
1919	NY-N	**25**	9	.735	38	34	23	4	1	295^{2}	263	8	35	92	9.1	2.40	117	.236	.260	32	.267	5	17	13	3	2.4
1920	NY-N	20	15	.571	43	34	23	2	0	292^{2}	271	9	56	63	10.1	2.64	113	.250	.288	22	.204	-2	16	11	3	1.3
1921	*NY-N	15	9	.625	42	31	15	1	6	258^{2}	298	13	44	56	12.0	3.10	118	.299	.331	19	.207	-1	20	16	1	1.4
1922	*NY-N	13	8	.619	37	29	14	2	0	212^{2}	236	10	38	52	11.7	3.51	114	.278	.311	14	.182	-1	14	12	3	1.2
1923	NY-N	3	1	.750	12	4	1	0	1	36	48	1	13	12	15.3	6.25	61	.329	.384	3	.273	0	-9	-10	1	-0.8
	Bos-N	10	14	.417	31	23	12	5	2	195^{1}	204	8	43	41	11.4	2.76	144	.270	.310	10	.147	-4	27	27	3	2.9
	Yr	13	15	.464	43	27	13	5	3	231^{1}	252	9	56	53	12.0	3.31	120	.280	.322	13	.165	-4	18	17	4	2.1
1924	Bos-N	15	20	.429	37	32	21	**4**	0	267^{2}	292	7	53	49	11.6	3.23	118	.284	.319	20	.222	-1	19	18	1	2.1
1925	Bos-N	11	16	.407	32	28	17	0	0	216^{1}	255	14	63	55	13.3	4.53	88	.297	.346	16	.198	-1	-6	-13	-2	-1.5
1926	Bro-N	10	11	.476	31	24	10	1	1	158	204	6	35	29	13.7	5.24	73	.321	.358	14	.237	-0	-25	-25	-1	-2.9
1927	Bro-N	2	10	.167	18	10	2	0	0	78^{2}	106	5	25	14	15.0	5.72	69	.331	.380	5	.217	-0	-16	-15	-0	-2.0
Total	13	152	150	.503	422	312	180	26	13	2569^{2}	2686	88	515	653	11.3	3.22	104	.273	.310	195	.214	1	74	41	20	6.3
● JUNIE BARNES	Barnes, Junie Shoaf "Lefty" b: 12/1/11, Linwood, N.C. d: 12/31/63, Jacksonville, N.C. BL/TL, 5'11.5", 170 lbs. Deb: 9/12/34																									
1934	Cin-N	0	0	—	2	0	0	0	0	0^{1}	0	0	1	0	27.0	0.00	—	.000	.500	0	—	0	0	0	0	0.0
● RICH BARNES	Barnes, Richard Monroe b: 7/21/59, Palm Beach, Fla. BR/TL, 6'4", 186 lbs. Deb: 7/18/82																									
1982	Chi-A	0	2	.000	6	2	0	0	1	17	21	1	4	6	14.3	4.76	85	.292	.346	0	—	0	-1	-1	0	-0.1
1983	Cle-A	1	1	.500	4	2	0	0	0	11^{2}	18	0	10	2	21.6	6.94	61	.375	.483	0	—	0	-4	-4	-0	-0.7
Total	2	1	3	.250	10	4	0	0	1	28^{2}	39	1	14	8	17.3	5.65	73	.325	.404	0	—	0	-5	-5	0	-0.8
● BOB BARNES	Barnes, Robert Avery "Lefty" b: 1/6/02, Washburn, Ill. d: 12/8/93, Peoria, Ill. BL/TL, 5'11.5", 150 lbs. Deb: 7/8/24																									
1924	Chi-A	0	0	—	2	0	0	0	0	4^{2}	14	1	0	1	27.0	19.29	21	.519	.519	0	.000	-0	-8	-8	0	0.0
● ROSS BARNES	Barnes, Roscoe Charles b: 5/8/1850, Mount Morris, N.Y. d: 2/5/15, Chicago, Ill. BR/TR, 5'8.5", 145 lbs. Deb: 5/5/1871 U♦																									
1876	Chi-N	0	0	—	1	0	0	0	0	1^{1}	7	0	0	0	47.3	20.25	12	.538	.538	138	.429	1	-3	-3	0	0.0
● VIRGIL BARNES	Barnes, Virgil Jennings "Zeke" b: 3/5/1897, Ontario, Kan. d: 7/24/58, Wichita, Kan. BR/TR, 6', 165 lbs. Deb: 9/25/19 F																									
1919	NY-N	0	0	—	1	0	0	0	0	2	6	0	1	1	31.5	18.00	16	.545	.583	0	—	0	-3	-3	-0	0.0
1920	NY-N	0	1	.000	1	1	0	0	0	7	9	0	1	2	12.9	3.86	78	.310	.333	0	.000	-0	-1	-1	0	-0.1
1922	NY-N	1	0	1.000	22	2	1	0	2	51^{2}	46	1	11	16	9.9	3.48	115	.243	.285	2	.167	-1	4	3	0	0.1
1923	*NY-N	2	3	.400	22	2	0	0	1	53	59	2	19	6	13.2	3.91	98	.285	.345	0	.000	-2	1	-0	0	-0.2
1924	*NY-N	16	10	.615	35	29	15	1	3	229^{1}	239	10	57	59	11.6	3.06	120	.270	.314	14	.182	-2	21	15	2	1.6
1925	NY-N	15	11	.577	32	27	17	1	2	221^{2}	242	9	53	53	12.0	3.53	114	.281	.323	9	.101	-9	18	12	0	0.4
1926	NY-N	8	13	.381	31	25	9	2	1	185	183	4	56	54	11.8	2.87	131	.261	.318	3	.054	-7	20	18	-1	1.1
1927	NY-N	14	11	.560	35	29	12	2	2	228^{2}	251	14	51	66	12.0	3.98	97	.283	.325	9	.108	-7	-1	-3	-1	-1.1
1928	NY-N	3	3	.500	10	9	3	1	0	55^{1}	71	3	18	11	14.5	5.04	78	.330	.382	2	.091	-2	-6	-7	-1	-0.9
	Bos-N	2	7	.222	16	10	1	0	0	60^{1}	86	3	26	7	16.7	5.82	67	.344	.406	1	.059	-2	-12	-13	-1	-1.8
	Yr	5	10	.333	26	19	4	1	0	115^{2}	157	6	44	18	15.6	5.45	72	.338	.395	3	.077	-3	-19	-20	-1	-2.7
Total	9	61	59	.508	205	134	58	7	11	1094	1192	46	293	275	12.3	3.66	105	.282	.329	40	.108	-31	38	22	1	-0.9
● REX BARNEY	Barney, Rex Edward b: 12/19/24, Omaha, Neb. d: 8/12/97, Baltimore, Md. BR/TR, 6'3", 185 lbs. Deb: 8/18/43																									
1943	Bro-N	2	2	.500	9	8	1	0	0	45^{1}	36	4	41	23	15.7	6.35	53	.217	.378	1	.056	-2	-15	-15	-0	-1.4
1946	Bro-N	2	5	.286	16	9	1	0	0	53^{2}	46	2	51	36	16.3	5.87	58	.240	.399	4	.235	1	-15	-15	-0	-1.7
1947	*Bro-N	5	2	.714	28	9	0	0	0	77^{2}	66	4	59	36	14.7	4.75	87	.240	.378	3	.111	-1	-6	-5	-1	-0.6
1948	Bro-N	15	13	.536	44	34	12	4	0	246^{2}	193	17	122	138	11.7	3.10	129	.217	.315	14	.167	-2	23	25	-4	1.9
1949	*Bro-N	9	8	.529	38	20	6	2	1	140^{2}	108	15	89	80	12.8	4.41	93	.216	.338	10	.213	0	-6	-5	-3	-0.8
1950	Bro-N	2	1	.667	20	1	0	0	0	33^{2}	25	6	48	23	20.0	6.42	64	.214	.449	1	.125	0	-9	-9	-1	-0.7
Total	6	35	31	.530	155	81	20	6	1	597^{2}	474	48	410	336	13.5	4.31	91	.221	.350	33	.164	-4	-26	-24	-9	-3.3
● EDGAR BARNHART	Barnhart, Edgar Vernon b: 9/16/04, Providence, Mo. d: 9/14/84, Columbia, Mo. BL/TR, 5'10", 160 lbs. Deb: 9/23/24																									
1924	StL-A	0	0	—	1	0	0	0	0	1	0	0	2	0	18.0	0.00	—	.000	.400	0	—	0	0	1	0	0.0
● LES BARNHART	Barnhart, Leslie Earl "Barney" b: 2/23/05, Hoxie, Kan. d: 10/7/71, Scottsdale, Ariz. BR/TR, 6', 180 lbs. Deb: 9/22/28																									
1928	Cle-A	0	1	.000	2	1	0	0	0	9	13	1	4	1	17.0	7.00	59	.325	.386	1	.500	0	-3	-3	-1	-0.3
1930	Cle-A	1	0	1.000	1	1	0	0	0	8^{1}	12	0	4	1	17.3	6.48	74	.364	.432	0	.000	-1	-2	-2	0	-0.2
Total	2	1	1	.500	3	2	0	0	0	17^{1}	25	1	8	2	17.1	6.75	66	.342	.407	1	.200	-0	-5	-4	-0	-0.5
● GEORGE BARNICLE	Barnicle, George Bernard "Barney" b: 8/26/17, Fitchburg, Mass. d: 10/10/90, Largo, Fla. BR/TR, 6'2", 175 lbs. Deb: 9/6/39																									
1939	Bos-N	2	2	.500	6	1	0	0	0	18^{1}	16	1	8	15	11.8	4.91	75	.235	.316	0	.000	-1	-2	-2	0	-0.5
1940	Bos-N	1	0	1.000	13	2	1	0	0	32^{2}	28	1	31	11	17.9	7.44	50	.233	.414	0	.000	-1	-13	-14	1	-0.5
1941	Bos-N	0	1	.000	1	1	0	0	0	6^{2}	5	0	4	2	13.5	6.75	53	.238	.385	0	.000	-0	-2	-2	0	-0.3
Total	3	3	3	.500	20	4	1	0	0	57^{2}	49	2	43	28	15.5	6.55	56	.234	.382	0	.000	-2	-17	-18	1	-1.3
● ED BARNOWSKI	Barnowski, Edward Anthony b: 8/23/43, Scranton, Pa. BR/TR, 6'2", 195 lbs. Deb: 9/8/65																									
1965	Bal-A	0	0	—	4	0	0	0	0	4^{1}	3	0	7	6	20.8	2.08	167	.200	.455	0	—	0	1	1	-0	0.0
1966	Bal-A	0	0	—	2	0	0	0	0	3	4	0	1	2	15.0	3.00	111	.364	.417	0	—	0	0	0	0	0.0
Total	2	0	0	—	6	0	0	0	0	7^{1}	7	0	8	8	18.4	2.45	139	.269	.441	0	—	0	1	1	0	0.0
● SALOME BAROJAS	Barojas, Salome (Romero) b: 6/16/57, Cordoba, Mex. BR/TR, 5'9", 188 lbs. Deb: 4/11/82																									
1982	Chi-A	6	6	.500	61	0	0	0	21	106^{2}	96	9	46	56	12.1	3.54	114	.244	.324	0	—	0	6	6	3	1.2
1983	*Chi-A	3	3	.500	52	0	0	0	12	87^{1}	70	2	32	38	11.0	2.47	169	.224	.306	0	—	0	15	17	0	1.3
1984	Chi-A	3	2	.600	24	0	0	0	1	39^{1}	48	3	19	18	15.3	4.58	91	.310	.385	0	—	0	-3	-2	1	-0.3
	Sea-A	6	5	.545	19	14	0	0	1	95^{1}	88	12	41	37	12.5	3.97	101	.249	.332	0	—	0	0	0	1	0.1
	Yr	9	7	.563	43	14	0	0	2	134^{2}	136	15	60	55	13.3	4.14	97	.268	.349	0	—	0	-2	-2	2	-0.2

YEAR	TM/L	W	L	PCT	G	GS	CG	SH	SV	IP	H	HR	BB	SO	RAT	ERA	ERA+	OAV	OOB	BH	AVG	PB	PR	/A	PD	TPI
1985	Sea-A	0	5	.000	17	4	0	0	0	52^{2}	65	6	33	27	16.7	5.98	70	.305	.398	0	—	0	-11	-10	0	-0.9
1988	Phi-N	0	0	—	6	0	0	0	0	8^{2}	7	1	8	1	15.6	8.31	43	.250	.417	0	—	0	-5	-5	-0	0.0
Total	5	18	21	.462	179	18	0	0	35	390	374	33	179	177	13.0	3.95	103	.257	.342	0	—	0	4	6	5	1.4

● JIM BARR Barr, James Leland b: 2/10/48, Lynwood, Cal. BR/TR, 6'3", 205 lbs. Deb: 7/31/71

YEAR	TM/L	W	L	PCT	G	GS	CG	SH	SV	IP	H	HR	BB	SO	RAT	ERA	ERA+	OAV	OOB	BH	AVG	PB	PR	/A	PD	TPI
1971	*SF-N	1	1	.500	17	0	0	0	0	35^{1}	33	3	5	16	9.9	3.57	95	.254	.287	0	.000	-0	-0	-1	1	0.0
1972	SF-N	8	10	.444	44	18	8	2	2	179	166	16	41	86	10.6	2.87	122	.246	.292	9	.184	1	12	12	1	1.4
1973	SF-N	11	17	.393	41	33	8	3	2	231^{1}	240	24	49	88	11.4	3.81	100	.268	.310	10	.152	-1	-4	0	-1	-0.1
1974	SF-N	13	9	.591	44	27	11	5	2	239^{2}	223	17	47	84	10.2	2.74	139	.251	.290	18	.254	4	23	28	1	3.1
1975	SF-N	13	14	.481	35	33	12	2	0	244	244	17	58	77	11.3	3.06	124	.265	.310	9	.118	-3	15	20	3	2.2
1976	SF-N	15	12	.556	37	37	8	3	0	252^{1}	260	9	60	75	11.5	2.89	126	.266	.310	12	.162	2	17	21	3	2.8
1977	SF-N	12	16	.429	38	38	6	2	0	234^{1}	286	18	56	97	13.3	4.76	82	.306	.347	10	.132	-2	-22	-22	3	-2.3
1978	SF-N	8	11	.421	32	25	5	2	1	163	180	7	35	44	11.9	3.53	98	.281	.319	5	.100	-3	1	-2	1	-0.4
1979	Cal-A	10	12	.455	36	25	5	0	0	197	217	22	55	69	12.6	4.20	97	.287	.338	0	—	0	0	-3	2	0.1
1980	Cal-A	1	4	.200	24	7	0	0	1	68	90	12	23	22	15.4	5.56	71	.323	.380	0	—	0	-12	-12	-1	-0.8
1982	SF-N	4	3	.571	53	9	1	1	2	128^{2}	125	9	20	36	10.4	3.29	109	.262	.297	8	.250	1	4	4	0	0.4
1983	SF-N	5	3	.625	53	0	0	0	2	92^{2}	106	7	20	47	12.3	3.98	89	.294	.332	2	.133	-0	-4	-5	0	-0.4
Total	12	101	112	.474	454	252	64	20	12	2065^{1}	2170	161	469	741	11.6	3.56	105	.273	.316	83	.162	-0	31	42	12	6.0

● BOB BARR Barr, Robert Alexander b: 3/12/08, Newton, Mass. BR/TR, 6', 175 lbs. Deb: 9/11/35

YEAR	TM/L	W	L	PCT	G	GS	CG	SH	SV	IP	H	HR	BB	SO	RAT	ERA	ERA+	OAV	OOB	BH	AVG	PB	PR	/A	PD	TPI
1935	Bro-N	0	0	—	2	0	0	0	0	2^{1}	5	0	2	0	27.0	3.86	103	.385	.467	0	—	0	0	0	-0	0.0

● BOB BARR Barr, Robert McClelland b: 12/1856, Washington, D.C. d: 3/11/30, Washington, D.C. BR/TR, 6'1", 192 lbs. Deb: 6/23/1883

YEAR	TM/L	W	L	PCT	G	GS	CG	SH	SV	IP	H	HR	BB	SO	RAT	ERA	ERA+	OAV	OOB	BH	AVG	PB	PR	/A	PD	TPI
1883	Pit-a	6	18	.250	26	23	19	0	**1**	203^{1}	263	5	28	81	12.9	4.38	73	.294	.316	35	.246	3	-24	-26	1	-2.1
1884	Was-a	9	23	.281	32	32	32	2	0	281	311	9	31	138	11.4	3.46	88	.258	.284	20	.148	-2	-7	-13	-1	-1.5
	Ind-a	3	11	.214	16	16	15	0	0	132	160	2	19	69	12.5	4.98	66	.275	.304	12	.185	0	-25	-25	-1	-2.1
	Yr	12	34	.261	48	48	47	2	0	413	471	11	50	207	11.5	3.94	79	.262	.284	32	.160	-2	-32	-38	-2	-3.6
1886	Was-N	3	18	.143	23	23	21	1	0	191^{2}	221	7	54	80	12.9	4.41	74	.280	.326	13	.165	-2	-23	-24	-1	-2.4
1890	Roc-a	28	24	.538	57	54	52	3	0	493^{1}	458	7	219	209	12.6	3.25	110	.239	.321	36	.179	-1	34	17	3	1.6
1891	NY-N	0	4	.000	5	4	2	0	0	27	47	1	12	11	20.7	5.33	60	.367	.434	1	.091	-0	-6	-6	0	-0.7
Total	5	49	98	.333	159	152	141	6	1	1328^{1}	1460	31	363	588	12.6	3.85	87	.265	.314	117	.185	-3	-52	-77	1	-7.2

● STEVE BARR Barr, Steven Charles b: 9/8/51, St.Louis, Mo. BL/TL, 6'4", 200 lbs. Deb: 10/1/74

YEAR	TM/L	W	L	PCT	G	GS	CG	SH	SV	IP	H	HR	BB	SO	RAT	ERA	ERA+	OAV	OOB	BH	AVG	PB	PR	/A	PD	TPI
1974	Bos-A	1	0	1.000	1	1	1	0	0	9	7	0	6	3	13.0	4.00	96	.212	.333	0	—	0	-0	-0	0	-0.4
1975	Bos-A	0	1	.000	3	2	0	0	0	7	11	1	7	2	23.1	2.57	158	.367	.486	0	—	0	1	1	-0	-0.5
1976	Tex-A	2	6	.250	20	10	3	0	0	67^{2}	70	10	44	27	15.2	5.59	64	.269	.375	0	—	0	-16	-15	0	-1.6
Total	3	3	7	.300	24	13	4	0	0	83^{2}	88	11	57	32	15.6	5.16	71	.272	.382	0	—	0	-15	-14	0	-2.5

● RED BARRETT Barrett, Charles Henry b: 2/14/15, Santa Barbara, Cal d: 7/28/90, Wilson, N.C. BR/TR, 5'11", 183 lbs. Deb: 9/15/37

YEAR	TM/L	W	L	PCT	G	GS	CG	SH	SV	IP	H	HR	BB	SO	RAT	ERA	ERA+	OAV	OOB	BH	AVG	PB	PR	/A	PD	TPI
1937	Cin-N	0	0	—	1	0	0	0	0	6^{1}	5	0	2	1	9.9	1.42	263	.227	.292	0	.000	-0	2	2	-0	-0.1
1938	Cin-N	2	0	1.000	6	2	2	0	0	28^{2}	28	2	15	5	13.5	3.14	116	.257	.347	1	.143	-0	2	2	-0	0.0
1939	Cin-N	0	0	—	2	0	0	0	0	5^{1}	5	0	1	1	10.1	1.69	227	.263	.300	0	.000	-0	1	1	0	0.0
1940	Cin-N	1	0	1.000	3	0	0	0	0	2^{2}	5	0	1	0	20.3	6.75	56	.455	.500	0	—	0	-1	-1	0	-0.3
1943	Bos-N	12	18	.400	38	31	14	3	0	255	240	11	63	64	10.8	3.18	107	.250	.298	11	.136	-4	6	7	1	0.4
1944	Bos-N	9	16	.360	42	30	11	1	2	230^{1}	257	13	63	54	12.6	4.06	94	.279	.327	13	.173	-1	-12	-6	2	-0.6
1945	Bos-N	2	3	.400	9	5	2	0	2	38	43	6	16	13	14.2	4.74	81	.281	.353	2	.222	-0	-4	-4	1	-0.4
	StL-N†	21	9	.700	36	29	22	3	0	246^{2}	244	12	38	63	10.3	2.74	137	.256	.285	10	.112	-5	29	28	-1	2.5
	Yr	**23**	12	.657	45	34	**24**	3	2	**284**^{2}	287	18	54	76	10.8	3.00	125	.259	.294	12	.122	-5	25	24	0	2.1
1946	StL-N	3	2	.600	23	9	1	1	2	67	75	5	24	22	13.6	4.03	86	.282	.346	1	.059	-1	-5	-4	-0	-0.4
1947	Bos-N	11	12	.478	36	30	12	3	1	210^{2}	200	16	53	53	10.9	3.55	110	.244	.292	8	.111	-2	12	8	-0	0.5
1948	*Bos-N	7	8	.467	34	13	3	0	0	128^{1}	132	9	26	40	11.1	3.65	105	.268	.305	7	.179	-1	4	3	1	0.3
1949	Bos-N	1	1	.500	23	0	0	0	0	44^{1}	58	4	10	17	14.2	5.68	66	.326	.368	1	.200	-0	-8	-9	1	-0.3
Total	11	69	69	.500	253	149	67	11	7	1263^{1}	1292	78	312	333	11.5	3.53	105	.264	.309	54	.136	-16	28	26	5	1.6

● FRANK BARRETT Barrett, Francis Joseph "Red" b: 7/1/13, Ft.Lauderdale, Fla d: 3/6/98, Leesburg, Fla. BR/TR, 6'2", 173 lbs. Deb: 10/1/39

YEAR	TM/L	W	L	PCT	G	GS	CG	SH	SV	IP	H	HR	BB	SO	RAT	ERA	ERA+	OAV	OOB	BH	AVG	PB	PR	/A	PD	TPI
1939	StL-N	0	1	.000	1	0	0	0	0	1^{2}	1	0	1	3	10.8	5.40	76	.167	.286	0	—	0	-0	-0	0	-0.1
1944	Bos-A	8	7	.533	38	2	0	0	8	90^{1}	93	5	42	40	13.5	3.69	92	.271	.352	4	.143	-1	-3	-3	-0	-0.6
1945	Bos-A	4	3	.571	37	0	0	0	3	86	77	0	29	35	11.1	2.62	130	.249	.314	5	.250	1	7	8	-1	0.7
1946	Bos-N	2	4	.333	23	0	0	0	1	35^{1}	35	2	17	12	13.5	5.09	67	.252	.338	0	.000	-1	-7	-7	1	-1.0
1950	Pit-N	1	2	.333	5	0	0	0	0	4^{1}	5	1	1	0	12.5	4.15	106	.357	.400	0	—	0	-0	0	0	0.1
Total	5	15	17	.469	104	2	0	0	12	217^{2}	211	8	90	90	12.5	3.51	98	.260	.336	9	.167	-1	-2	-2	1	-0.9

● TIM BARRETT Barrett, Timothy Wayne b: 1/24/61, Huntingburg, Ind. BL/TR, 6'1", 185 lbs. Deb: 7/18/88

YEAR	TM/L	W	L	PCT	G	GS	CG	SH	SV	IP	H	HR	BB	SO	RAT	ERA	ERA+	OAV	OOB	BH	AVG	PB	PR	/A	PD	TPI
1988	Mon-N	0	0	—	4	0	0	0	1	9^{1}	10	2	2	5	11.6	5.79	62	.270	.308	0	.000	-0	-2	-2	-0	-0.1

● DICK BARRETT Barrett, Tracy Souter "Kewpie Dick" (a.k.a. Richard Oliver 1933 And Richard Oliver Barrett 1934-43)
b: 9/28/06, Montoursville, Pa d: 10/30/66, Seattle, Wash. BR/TR, 5'9", 175 lbs. Deb: 6/27/33

YEAR	TM/L	W	L	PCT	G	GS	CG	SH	SV	IP	H	HR	BB	SO	RAT	ERA	ERA+	OAV	OOB	BH	AVG	PB	PR	/A	PD	TPI
1933	Phi-A	4	4	.500	15	7	3	0	0	70^{1}	74	2	49	26	15.9	5.76	74	.272	.385	6	.286	2	-12	-12	0	-0.9
1934	Bos-N	1	3	.250	15	3	0	0	0	32^{1}	50	2	12	14	17.3	6.68	57	.365	.416	1	.143	-0	-9	-10	1	-1.0
1943	Chi-N	0	4	.000	15	4	0	0	0	45	52	2	28	20	16.2	4.80	70	.291	.389	1	.111	-1	-7	-7	-0	-0.7
	Phi-N	10	9	.526	23	20	10	2	1	169^{1}	137	5	51	65	10.1	2.39	141	.221	.282	7	.143	-0	19	18	0	2.2
	Yr	10	13	.435	38	24	10	2	1	214^{1}	189	7	79	85	11.3	2.90	116	.236	.306	8	.138	-1	12	11	0	1.5
1944	Phi-N	12	18	.400	37	27	11	1	0	221^{1}	223	7	88	74	12.8	3.86	94	.262	.333	16	.216	2	-6	-6	2	-0.3
1945	Phi-N	8	20	.286	36	30	8	0	1	190^{2}	217	11	92	72	14.9	5.38	71	.281	.363	9	.145	-1	-33	-33	1	-4.2
Total	5	35	58	.376	141	91	32	3	2	729	753	29	320	271	13.4	4.28	86	.266	.343	40	.180	1	-49	-50	4	-4.9

● BILL BARRETT Barrett, William Joseph "Whispering Bill" b: 5/28/1900, Cambridge, Mass. d: 1/26/51, Cambridge, Mass. BR/TR, 6', 175 lbs. Deb: 5/13/21 ♦

YEAR	TM/L	W	L	PCT	G	GS	CG	SH	SV	IP	H	HR	BB	SO	RAT	ERA	ERA+	OAV	OOB	BH	AVG	PB	PR	/A	PD	TPI
1921	Phi-A	1	0	1.000	4	0	0	0	0	5	2	0	9	2	19.8	7.20	62	.133	.458	7	.233	0	-2	-2	0	-0.2

● FRANCISCO BARRIOS Barrios, Francisco Javier (Jimenez)
b: 6/10/53, Hermosillo, Mex. d: 4/9/82, Hermosillo, Mexico BR/TR, 6'3", 195 lbs. Deb: 8/18/74

YEAR	TM/L	W	L	PCT	G	GS	CG	SH	SV	IP	H	HR	BB	SO	RAT	ERA	ERA+	OAV	OOB	BH	AVG	PB	PR	/A	PD	TPI
1974	Chi-A	0	0	—	2	0	0	0	0	2	7	0	2	2	40.5	27.00	14	.538	.600	0	—	0	-5	-5	-0	-0.2
1976	Chi-A	5	9	.357	35	14	6	0	3	141^{2}	136	13	46	81	11.8	4.32	83	.255	.318	0	—	0	-13	-12	-1	-1.3
1977	Chi-A	14	7	.667	33	31	9	0	0	231^{1}	241	22	58	119	11.8	4.12	99	.267	.315	0	—	0	-2	-1	-1	-0.1
1978	Chi-A	9	15	.375	33	32	9	2	0	195^{2}	180	13	85	79	12.5	4.05	94	.246	.330	0	—	0	-6	-5	2	-0.4
1979	Chi-A	8	3	.727	15	15	2	0	0	94^{2}	88	9	33	28	12.0	3.61	118	.242	.314	0	—	0	6	7	-1	0.6
1980	Chi-A	1	1	.500	3	3	0	0	0	16^{1}	21	4	8	2	16.5	4.96	81	.323	.405	0	—	0	-2	-2	-0	-0.2
1981	Chi-A	1	3	.250	8	7	1	0	0	36^{1}	45	3	14	12	14.9	3.96	90	.292	.355	0	—	0	-1	-2	-0	-0.2
Total	7	38	38	.500	129	102	27	2	3	718	718	64	246	323	12.4	4.15	94	.260	.326	0	—	0	-22	-20	-1	-1.8

● MANUEL BARRIOS Barrios, Manuel Antonio b: 9/21/74, Cabecera, Panama BR/TR, 6', 170 lbs. Deb: 9/16/97

YEAR	TM/L	W	L	PCT	G	GS	CG	SH	SV	IP	H	HR	BB	SO	RAT	ERA	ERA+	OAV	OOB	BH	AVG	PB	PR	/A	PD	TPI
1997	Hou-N	0	0	—	2	0	0	0	0	3	6	0	3	3	27.0	12.00	33	.400	.500	0	—	0	-3	-3	-0	0.0
1998	Fla-N	0	0	—	2	0	0	0	0	2^{2}	4	1	2	1	20.3	3.38	121	.364	.462	0	—	0	0	0	-0	0.0
	LA-N	0	0	—	1	0	0	0	0	1	0	0	2	0	18.0	0.00	—	.000	.500	0	—	0	1	1	-0	0.0
	Yr	0	0	—	3	0	0	0	0	3^{2}	4	1	4	1	19.6	2.45	164	.308	.471	0	—	0	1	1	-0	0.0
Total	2	0	0	—	5	0	0	0	0	6^{2}	10	1	7	4	23.0	6.75	60	.357	.486	0	—	0	-2	-2	-0	0.0

● FRANK BARRON Barron, Frank John b: 8/6/1890, St.Marys, W.Va. d: 9/18/64, St.Marys, W.Va. BL/TL, 6'1", 175 lbs. Deb: 8/19/14

YEAR	TM/L	W	L	PCT	G	GS	CG	SH	SV	IP	H	HR	BB	SO	RAT	ERA	ERA+	OAV	OOB	BH	AVG	PB	PR	/A	PD	TPI
1914	Was-A	0	0	—	1	0	0	0	0	1	1	0	0	1	9.0	0.00	—	.333	.333	0	—	0	0	0	0	0.0

● ED BARRY Barry, Edward "Jumbo" b: 10/2/1882, Madison, Wis. d: 6/19/20, Montague, Mass. TL, 6'3", 185 lbs. Deb: 8/21/05

YEAR	TM/L	W	L	PCT	G	GS	CG	SH	SV	IP	H	HR	BB	SO	RAT	ERA	ERA+	OAV	OOB	BH	AVG	PB	PR	/A	PD	TPI
1905	Bos-A	1	2	.333	7	5	2	0	0	40^{2}	38	2	15	18	12.6	2.88	94	.248	.331	1	.091	-0	-1	-1	-2	-0.3

YEAR TM/L	W	L	PCT	G	GS	CG	SH	SV	IP	H	HR	BB	SO	RAT	ERA	ERA+	OAV	OOB	BH	AVG	PB	PR	/A	PD	TPI
1906 Bos-A	0	3	.000	3	3	3	0	0	21	23	2	5	10	13.3	6.00	46	.280	.344	1	.111	-0	-8	-8	0	-0.9
1907 Bos-A	0	1	.000	2	2	1	0	0	17^{1}	13	1	5	6	9.9	2.08	124	.210	.279	0	.000	-0	1	1	-0	0.0
Total 3	1	6	.143	12	10	6	0	0	79	74	5	25	34	12.2	3.53	76	.249	.324	2	.087	-1	-8	-7	-2	-1.2
● **HARDIN BARRY**	Barry, Hardin "Finn" b: 3/26/1891, Susanville, Cal. d: 11/5/69, Carson City, Nev. BR/TR, 6', 185 lbs. Deb: 6/21/12																								
1912 Phi-A	0	0	—	3	0	0	0	0	13	18	0	4	3	15.9	7.62	40	.360	.418	0	.000	-0	-6	-7	-0	-0.1
● **TOM BARRY**	Barry, Thomas Arthur b: 4/10/1879, St.Louis, Mo. d: 6/4/46, St.Louis, Mo. TR, 5'9", 155 lbs. Deb: 4/15/04																								
1904 Phi-N	0	1	.000	1	1	0	0	0	0^{2}	6	0	1	1	94.5	40.50	7	.667	.700	0	—	0	-3	-3	0	-1.7
● **BOB BARTHELSON**	Barthelson, Robert Edward b: 7/15/24, New Haven, Conn. BR/TR, 6', 185 lbs. Deb: 7/4/44																								
1944 NY-N	1	1	.500	7	1	0	0	0	9^{2}	13	2	5	4	16.8	4.66	79	.310	.383	0	—	0	-1	-1	-0	-0.2
● **JOHN BARTHOLD**	Barthold, John Francis "Hans" b: 4/14/1882, Philadelphia, Pa. d: 11/4/46, Fairview Village, Pa. BB/TR, 5'11", 180 lbs. Deb: 5/17/04																								
1904 Phi-A	0	0	—	4	0	0	0	0	10^{2}	12	0	8	5	17.7	5.06	53	.286	.412	1	.333	1	-3	-3	0	0.1
● **LES BARTHOLOMEW**	Bartholomew, Lester Justin b: 4/4/03, Madison, Wis. d: 9/19/72, Barrington, Ill. BR/TL, 5'11.5", 195 lbs. Deb: 4/11/28																								
1928 Pit-N	0	0	—	6	0	0	0	0	22^{2}	31	2	9	6	15.9	7.15	57	.356	.417	1	.143	-0	-8	-8	-0	0.0
1932 Chi-A	0	0	—	3	0	0	0	0	5^{1}	5	0	6	1	18.6	5.06	85	.250	.423	0	.000	-0	-0	-0	0	0.0
Total 2	0	0	—	9	0	0	0	0	28	36	2	15	7	16.4	6.75	61	.336	.418	1	.125	-0	-8	-8	-0	0.0
● **BILL BARTLEY**	Bartley, William Jackson b: 1/8/1885, Cincinnati, Ohio d: 5/17/65, Cincinnati, Ohio BR/TR, 5'11.5", 190 lbs. Deb: 9/15/03																								
1903 NY-N	0	0	—	1	0	0	0	0	3	3	0	4	2	21.0	0.00	—	.273	.467	0	.000	-0	1	1	0	0.0
1906 Phi-A	0	0	—	3	0	0	0	1	8^{2}	10	0	6	6	16.6	9.35	29	.294	.400	1	.333	1	-6	-6	1	0.0
1907 Phi-A	0	1	.000	15	3	2	0	0	56^{1}	44	0	19	16	10.1	2.24	116	.218	.285	2	.095	-2	2	2	-0	-0.1
Total 3	0	1	.000	19	3	2	0	1	68	57	0	29	24	11.4	3.04	87	.231	.312	3	.120	-1	-3	-3	0	-0.1
● **SHAWN BARTON**	Barton, Shawn Edward b: 5/14/63, Los Angeles, Cal. BR/TL, 6'3", 195 lbs. Deb: 8/6/92																								
1992 Sea-A	0	1	.000	14	0	0	0	0	12^{1}	10	1	7	4	12.4	2.92	136	.238	.347	0	—	0	1	1	0	0.1
1995 SF-N	4	1	.800	52	0	0	0	1	44^{1}	37	3	19	22	11.8	4.26	96	.237	.328	0	—	0	-0	-1	1	0.0
1996 SF-N	0	0	—	7	0	0	0	0	8^{1}	19	2	1	3	21.6	9.72	42	.442	.455	0	—	0	-5	-5	0	0.0
Total 3	4	2	.667	73	0	0	0	1	65	66	6	27	29	13.2	4.71	86	.274	.352	0	—	0	-4	-5	1	0.1
● **CHARLIE BARTSON**	Bartson, Charles Franklin b: 3/13/1865, Peoria, Ill. d: 6/9/36, Peoria, Ill. 6', 170 lbs. Deb: 5/14/1890																								
1890 Chi-P	9	10	.474	26	20	17	0	1	197	226	8	66	52	13.9	4.11	106	.276	.339	13	.167	-3	3	5	5	0.6
● **JIM BASKETTE**	Baskette, James Blaine "Big Jim" b: 12/10/1887, Athens, Tenn. d: 7/30/42, Athens, Tenn. BR/TR, 6'2", 185 lbs. Deb: 9/22/11																								
1911 Cle-A	1	2	.333	4	2	2	0	0	21^{1}	21	0	9	8	13.1	3.38	101	.273	.356	2	.333	1	-0	0	-0	0.0
1912 Cle-A	8	4	.667	29	11	7	1	1	116	109	2	46	51	12.6	3.18	107	.252	.334	5	.125	-1	2	3	-3	-0.1
1913 Cle-A	0	0	—	2	1	0	0	0	4^{2}	8	1	2	0	19.3	5.79	52	.400	.455	1	1.000	1	-1	-1	0	0.1
Total 3	9	6	.600	35	14	9	1	1	142	138	3	57	59	12.9	3.30	103	.261	.342	8	.170	1	0	2	-3	0.0
● **NORM BASS**	Bass, Norman Delaney b: 1/21/39, Laurel, Miss. BR/TR, 6'3", 205 lbs. Deb: 4/23/61																								
1961 KC-A	11	11	.500	40	23	6	2	0	170^{2}	164	17	82	74	13.2	4.69	89	.255	.343	7	.119	-2	-13	-10	-3	-1.6
1962 KC-A	2	6	.250	22	10	0	0	0	75^{1}	96	7	46	33	17.0	6.09	69	.317	.407	1	.045	-2	-18	-16	1	-1.5
1963 KC-A	0	0	—	3	1	0	0	0	7^{2}	11	2	9	4	23.5	11.74	33	.333	.476	0	.000	-0	-7	-7	-0	0.0
Total 3	13	17	.433	65	34	6	2	0	253^{2}	271	26	137	111	14.6	5.32	79	.277	.368	8	.098	-4	-37	-32	-2	-3.1
● **DICK BASS**	Bass, Richard William b: 7/7/06, Rogersville, Tenn. d: 2/3/89, Graceville, Fla. BR/TR, 6'2", 175 lbs. Deb: 9/21/39																								
1939 Was-A	0	1	.000	1	1	0	0	0	8	7	0	6	1	15.8	6.75	64	.241	.389	0	.000	-0	-2	-2	-0	-0.2
● **CHARLIE BASTIAN**	Bastian, Charles J. b: 7/4/1860, Philadelphia, Pa. d: 1/18/32, Pennsauken, N.J. BR/TR, 5'6.5", 145 lbs. Deb: 8/18/1884 ♦																								
1884 Wil-U	0	0	—	1	0	0	0	0	6	6	0	0	2	9.0	3.00	89	.240	.240	12	.200	-0	-0	-0	-0	0.0
● **JOE BATCHELDER**	Batchelder, Joseph Edmund "Win" b: 7/11/1898, Wenham, Mass. d: 5/5/89, Beverly, Mass. BR/TL, 5'7", 165 lbs. Deb: 9/29/23																								
1923 Bos-N	1	0	1.000	4	1	1	0	0	9	12	2	1	2	14.0	7.00	57	.353	.389	0	.000	0	-3	-3	-0	-0.3
1924 Bos-N	0	0	—	3	0	0	0	0	4^{2}	4	0	2	2	11.6	3.86	99	.235	.316	0	.000	-0	0	-0	0	0.0
1925 Bos-N	0	0	—	4	0	0	0	0	7	10	0	1	2	14.1	5.14	78	.357	.379	0	.000	-0	-1	-1	0	0.0
Total 3	1	0	1.000	11	1	1	0	0	20^{2}	26	2	4	6	13.5	5.66	70	.329	.369	0	.000	-0	-4	-4	0	-0.3
● **RICH BATCHELOR**	Batchelor, Richard Anthony b: 4/8/67, Florence, S.C. BR/TR, 6'1", 195 lbs. Deb: 9/3/93																								
1993 StL-N	0	0	—	9	0	0	0	0	10	14	1	3	4	15.3	8.10	49	.359	.405	0	.000	-0	-5	-5	-0	0.0
1996 StL-N	2	0	1.000	11	0	0	0	0	15	9	0	1	11	6.0	1.20	348	.173	.189	0	.000	-0	5	5	-0	0.6
1997 StL-N	1	1	.500	10	0	0	0	0	16	21	0	7	8	16.9	4.50	92	.323	.405	0	—	0	-1	-1	-1	-0.1
SD-N	2	0	1.000	13	0	0	0	0	12^{2}	19	2	7	10	19.2	7.82	50	.358	.443	0	—	0	-5	-6	0	-0.8
Yr	3	1	.750	23	0	0	0	0	28^{2}	40	2	14	18	17.3	5.97	68	.333	.407	0	—	0	-6	-6	-1	-0.9
Total 3	5	1	.833	43	0	0	0	0	53^{2}	63	3	18	33	14.1	5.03	81	.301	.365	0	.000	-0	-5	-6	-1	-0.3
● **DICK BATES**	Bates, Charles Richard b: 10/7/45, McArthur, Ohio BL/TR, 6', 190 lbs. Deb: 4/27/69																								
1969 Sea-A	0	0	—	1	0	0	0	0	1^{2}	3	1	3	3	32.4	27.00	13	.375	.545	0	—	0	-4	-4	0	0.0
● **FRANK BATES**	Bates, Creed Frank b: Chattanooga, Tenn. Deb: 10/7/1898																								
1898 Cle-N	2	1	.667	4	4	4	0	0	29	30	0	11	5	13.0	3.10	117	.265	.336	1	.111	0	2	2	-0	0.1
1899 StL-N	0	0	—	2	0	0	0	0	8^{2}	7	0	5	0	12.5	1.04	383	.219	.324	1	.333	1	3	3	-0	0.0
Cle-N	1	18	.053	20	19	17	0	0	153	239	6	105	13	21.6	7.24	51	.355	.458	14	.215	1	-57	-60	0	-5.3
Yr	1	18	.053	22	19	17	0	0	161^{2}	246	6	110	13	21.1	6.90	54	.348	.452	15	.221	2	-55	-58	-0	-5.3
Total 2	3	19	.136	26	23	21	0	0	190^{2}	276	6	121	18	19.9	6.33	58	.337	.437	16	.208	2	-53	-56	-0	-5.2
● **JOHN BATES**	Bates, John William b: 5/28/1868, Ohio d: 3/24/19, Oakland, Cal. Deb: 8/25/1889																								
1889 KC-a	0	1	.000	1	1	1	0	0	8	15	0	5	3	22.5	13.50	31	.385	.455	0	.000	-1	-9	-8	-0	-0.7
● **MIGUEL BATISTA**	Batista, Miguel Jerez (Decartes) b: 2/19/71, Santo Domingo, D.R. BR/TR, 6', 160 lbs. Deb: 4/11/92																								
1992 Pit-N	0	0	—	1	0	0	0	0	2	4	1	3	1	31.5	9.00	38	.400	.538	0	—	0	-1	-1	-0	0.0
1996 Fla-N	0	0	—	9	0	0	0	0	11^{1}	9	0	7	6	12.7	5.56	73	.231	.348	0	—	0	-2	-2	-0	0.0
1997 Chi-N	0	5	.000	11	6	0	0	0	36^{1}	36	4	24	27	15.1	5.70	75	.267	.381	0	.000	-1	-6	-6	0	-0.7
1998 Mon-N	3	5	.375	56	13	0	0	0	135	141	12	65	92	14.1	3.80	108	.274	.362	0	.000	-4	6	5	1	-0.1
Total 4	3	10	.231	77	19	0	0	0	184^{2}	190	17	99	126	14.4	4.34	95	.272	.368	0	.000	-4	-3	-4	0	-0.8
● **JOE BATTIN**	Battin, Joseph V. b: 11/11/1851, Philadelphia, Pa. d: 12/10/37, Akron, Ohio BR/TR, Deb: 8/11/1871 MU♦																								
1877 StL-N	0	0	—	1	0	0	0	0	3^{2}	3	0	1	1	9.8	4.91	53	.200	.250	45	.199	0	-1	-1	-0	0.0
1883 Pit-a	0	0	—	2	0	0	0	0	4	9	0	1	0	22.5	2.25	143	.429	.455	83	.214	0	0	0	-0	0.0
Total 2	0	0	—	3	0	0	0	0	7^{2}	12	0	2	1	16.4	3.52	83	.333	.368	313	.218	0	-0	-1	-0	0.0
● **CHRIS BATTON**	Batton, Christopher Sean b: 8/24/54, Los Angeles, Cal. BR/TR, 6'4", 195 lbs. Deb: 9/19/76																								
1976 Oak-A	0	0	—	2	1	0	0	0	4	5	1	3	4	18.0	9.00	37	.313	.421	0	—	0	-2	-3	-0	0.1
● **LOU BAUER**	Bauer, Louis Walter b: 11/30/1898, Egg Harbor City, N.J. d: 2/4/79, Pomona, N.J. BR/TR, 6', 175 lbs. Deb: 8/13/18																								
1918 Phi-A	0	0	—	1	0	0	0	0	0	0	0	2	0	—	∞	—	—	1.000	0	—	0	-1	-1	0	-0.1
● **AL BAUERS**	Bauers, Albert J. b: 1850, Columbus, Ohio d: 9/6/13, Wilkes-Barre, Pa. TL, Deb: 9/22/1884 U																								
1884 Col-a	1	2	.333	3	3	3	0	0	25	22	1	14	13	13.0	4.68	65	.224	.321	3	.273	0	-4	-5	0	-0.4
1886 StL-N	0	4	.000	4	4	3	0	0	28^{2}	31	1	27	13	18.2	5.97	54	.267	.406	2	.167	-1	-8	-9	-1	-1.0
Total 2	1	6	.143	7	7	6	0	0	53^{2}	53	2	41	26	15.8	5.37	58	.248	.369	5	.217	-0	-12	-13	-1	-1.4

● RUSS BAUERS Bauers, Russell Lee b: 5/10/14, Townsend, Wis. d: 1/1/95, Hines, Ill. BL/TR, 6'3", 195 lbs. Deb: 8/20/36

YEAR	TM/L	W	L	PCT	G	GS	CG	SH	SV	IP	H	HR	BB	SO	RAT	ERA	ERA+	OAV	OOB	BH	AVG	PB	PR	/A	PD	TPI
1936	Pit-N	0	0	—	1	1	0	0	0	1^1	2	0	4	0	47.3	33.75	12	.500	.778	0	—	0	-4	-4	-0	0.0
1937	Pit-N	13	6	.684	34	19	11	2	1	187^2	174	2	80	118	12.4	2.88	134	.245	.325	15	.217	1	22	21	3	2.3
1938	Pit-N	13	14	.481	40	34	12	2	3	243	207	7	99	117	11.6	3.07	124	.233	.314	21	.239	4	19	20	-3	2.1
1939	Pit-N	2	4	.333	15	8	1	0	1	53^2	46	4	25	12	12.1	3.35	114	.240	.330	4	.211	-0	3	3	-1	0.2
1940	Pit-N	0	2	.000	15	2	0	0	0	30^2	42	2	18	11	18.2	7.63	50	.323	.413	2	.286	0	-13	-13	0	-0.7
1941	Pit-N	1	3	.250	8	5	1	0	1	37^1	40	1	25	20	15.7	5.54	65	.267	.371	5	.357	1	-8	-8	-1	-0.8
1946	Chi-N	2	1	.667	15	2	2	0	1	43^1	45	1	19	22	13.5	3.53	94	.273	.351	3	.300	1	-1	-1	-0	0.1
1950	StL-A	0	0	—	1	0	0	0	0	2	6	0	1	0	31.5	4.50	110	.600	.636	0	—	0	0	0	0	0.0
Total	8	31	30	.508	129	71	27	4	6	599	562	17	271	300	12.7	3.53	107	.250	.334	50	.242	7	19	17	-2	3.2

● FRANK BAUMANN Baumann, Frank Matt "The Beau" b: 7/1/33, St.Louis, Mo. BL/TL, 6'1", 210 lbs. Deb: 7/31/55

YEAR	TM/L	W	L	PCT	G	GS	CG	SH	SV	IP	H	HR	BB	SO	RAT	ERA	ERA+	OAV	OOB	BH	AVG	PB	PR	/A	PD	TPI
1955	Bos-A	2	1	.667	7	5	0	0	0	34	38	2	17	27	14.8	5.82	74	.281	.366	3	.231	-0	-7	-6	0	-0.4
1956	Bos-A	2	1	.667	7	1	0	0	0	24^2	22	3	14	18	13.1	3.28	141	.234	.333	3	.333	1	2	4	-1	0.4
1957	Bos-A	1	0	1.000	4	1	0	0	0	12	13	1	3	7	12.8	3.75	106	.277	.333	1	.500	0	0	0	-0	0.0
1958	Bos-A	2	2	.500	10	7	2	0	0	52^1	56	4	27	31	15.0	4.47	90	.276	.372	3	.214	1	-4	-3	-1	-0.2
1959	Bos-A	6	4	.600	26	10	2	0	1	95^2	96	11	55	48	14.3	4.05	100	.259	.357	6	.207	1	-2	0	1	0.1
1960	Chi-A	13	6	.684	47	20	7	2	3	185^1	169	11	53	71	10.8	**2.67**	142	.247	.302	8	.154	1	25	23	-2	2.1
1961	Chi-A	10	13	.435	53	23	5	1	3	187^2	249	22	59	75	14.9	5.61	70	.318	.368	16	.262	6	-33	-35	1	-3.1
1962	Chi-A	7	6	.538	40	10	3	1	4	119^2	117	10	36	55	11.7	3.38	115	.258	.316	8	.267	4	8	7	0	1.2
1963	Chi-A	2	1	.667	24	1	0	0	1	50^1	52	2	17	31	12.3	3.04	115	.265	.324	1	.091	-0	3	3	0	0.1
1964	Chi-A	0	3	.000	22	0	0	0	1	32	40	4	16	19	15.8	6.19	56	.320	.397	0	.000	-0	-9	-10	-0	-1.0
1965	Chi-N	0	1	.000	4	0	0	0	0	3^2	4	0	3	2	17.2	7.36	50	.286	.412	0	—	0	-2	-1	0	-0.4
Total	11	45	38	.542	244	78	19	4	13	797^1	856	70	300	384	13.2	4.11	95	.276	.342	49	.218	14	-19	-19	-2	-1.2

● GEORGE BAUMGARDNER Baumgardner, George Washington b: 7/22/1891, Barboursville, W.Va. d: 12/13/70, Barboursville, W.Va. BL/TR, 5'11", 178 lbs. Deb: 4/14/12

YEAR	TM/L	W	L	PCT	G	GS	CG	SH	SV	IP	H	HR	BB	SO	RAT	ERA	ERA+	OAV	OOB	BH	AVG	PB	PR	/A	PD	TPI
1912	StL-A	11	13	.458	30	27	18	2	0	218^1	222	1	79	102	12.9	3.38	98	.274	.346	11	.145	-0	-2	-2	-0	-0.1
1913	StL-A	10	20	.333	38	31	23	2	1	253^1	267	6	84	78	12.8	3.13	94	.283	.348	13	.167	2	-5	-5	-2	-0.5
1914	StL-A	16	14	.533	45	18	9	3	1	183^2	152	3	84	93	12.0	2.79	97	.229	.323	7	.132	-1	-1	-2	-1	-0.6
1915	StL-A	0	2	.000	7	1	1	0	0	22^1	29	0	11	6	16.1	4.43	65	.358	.435	0	.000	-1	-4	-4	1	-0.4
1916	StL-A	1	0	1.000	4	2	0	0	0	8	12	0	5	4	19.1	7.88	35	.364	.447	0	.000	0	-4	-5	-1	-0.6
Total	5	38	49	.437	124	79	51	7	2	685^2	682	10	263	283	12.8	3.22	93	.269	.345	31	.144	-0	-16	-17	-2	-2.2

● ROSS BAUMGARTEN Baumgarten, Ross b: 5/27/55, Highland Park, Ill. BL/TL, 6'1", 180 lbs. Deb: 8/16/78

YEAR	TM/L	W	L	PCT	G	GS	CG	SH	SV	IP	H	HR	BB	SO	RAT	ERA	ERA+	OAV	OOB	BH	AVG	PB	PR	/A	PD	TPI
1978	Chi-A	2	2	.500	7	4	1	1	0	23	29	3	9	15	15.3	5.87	65	.315	.382	0	—	0	-5	-5	-0	-0.8
1979	Chi-A	13	8	.619	28	28	4	3	0	190^2	175	18	83	72	12.2	3.54	120	.243	.322	0	—	0	14	15	-0	1.5
1980	Chi-A	2	12	.143	24	23	3	1	0	136	127	10	52	66	11.9	3.44	117	.256	.327	0	—	0	9	9	2	1.1
1981	Chi-A	5	9	.357	19	19	2	1	0	101^2	101	9	40	52	12.6	4.07	88	.260	.331	0	—	0	-5	-6	0	-0.7
1982	Pit-N	0	5	.000	12	10	0	0	0	44	60	3	27	17	17.8	6.55	57	.347	.435	1	.083	-1	-14	-14	0	-1.5
Total	5	22	36	.379	90	84	10	6	0	495^1	492	43	211	222	12.8	4.00	100	.263	.339	1	.083	-1	-1	-1	2	-0.4

● HARRY BAUMGARTNER Baumgartner, Harry E. b: 10/8/1892, S.Pittsburg, Tenn. d: 12/3/30, Augusta, Ga. BR/TR, 5'11", 175 lbs. Deb: 9/6/20

YEAR	TM/L	W	L	PCT	G	GS	CG	SH	SV	IP	H	HR	BB	SO	RAT	ERA	ERA+	OAV	OOB	BH	AVG	PB	PR	/A	PD	TPI
1920	Det-A	0	1	.000	9	0	0	0	0	18	18	1	6	7	12.0	4.00	93	.273	.333	1	.250	0	-0	-1	0	0.0

● STAN BAUMGARTNER Baumgartner, Stanwood Fulton b: 12/14/1894, Houston, Tex. d: 10/4/55, Philadelphia, Pa. BL/TL, 6', 175 lbs. Deb: 6/26/14

YEAR	TM/L	W	L	PCT	G	GS	CG	SH	SV	IP	H	HR	BB	SO	RAT	ERA	ERA+	OAV	OOB	BH	AVG	PB	PR	/A	PD	TPI
1914	Phi-N	2	2	.500	15	4	2	1	0	60^1	60	0	16	24	11.6	3.28	90	.270	.325	1	.053	-1	-3	-2	-1	-0.4
1915	Phi-N	0	2	.000	16	1	0	0	0	48^1	38	2	23	27	11.5	2.42	113	.226	.323	1	.083	-1	2	2	1	0.1
1916	Phi-N	0	0	—	1	0	0	0	0	4	5	0	1	0	13.5	2.25	118	.333	.375	0	.000	-0	0	0	-0	0.0
1921	Phi-N	3	6	.333	22	7	2	0	0	66^2	103	8	22	13	17.1	7.02	60	.355	.404	6	.200	0	-24	-21	-1	-2.4
1922	Phi-N	1	1	.500	6	1	0	0	0	9^2	18	1	5	2	21.4	6.52	72	.409	.469	1	.333	0	-3	-2	0	-0.3
1924	Phi-A	13	6	.684	36	16	12	1	4	181	181	6	73	45	12.8	2.88	**149**	.271	.347	13	.217	-0	27	28	-2	2.5
1925	Phi-A	6	3	.667	37	12	2	1	3	113^1	120	2	35	18	12.9	3.57	130	.275	.338	7	.233	-0	10	14	-1	0.9
1926	Phi-A	1	1	.500	10	1	0	0	0	22^1	28	0	10	0	15.3	4.03	103	.326	.396	1	.333	0	-0	0	1	0.1
Total	8	26	21	.553	143	42	18	3	7	505^2	553	19	185	129	13.4	3.70	109	.287	.354	30	.190	-2	9	19	-3	0.5

● GEORGE BAUSEWINE Bausewine, George W. b: 3/22/1869, Philadelphia, Pa. d: 7/29/47, Norristown, Pa. 6'2", 207 lbs. Deb: 9/14/1889 U

YEAR	TM/L	W	L	PCT	G	GS	CG	SH	SV	IP	H	HR	BB	SO	RAT	ERA	ERA+	OAV	OOB	BH	AVG	PB	PR	/A	PD	TPI
1889	Phi-a	1	4	.200	7	6	6	0	0	55^1	64	1	33	18	17.2	3.90	97	.281	.393	1	.048	-2	-0	-1	0	-0.2

● ED BAUTA Bauta, Eduardo (Galvez) b: 1/6/35, Florida, Cuba BR/TR, 6'3", 200 lbs. Deb: 7/6/60

YEAR	TM/L	W	L	PCT	G	GS	CG	SH	SV	IP	H	HR	BB	SO	RAT	ERA	ERA+	OAV	OOB	BH	AVG	PB	PR	/A	PD	TPI
1960	StL-N	0	0	—	9	0	0	0	1	15^2	14	4	11	6	14.9	6.32	65	.237	.366	0	.000	-0	-4	-4	-0	-0.1
1961	StL-N	2	0	1.000	13	0	0	0	5	19^1	12	2	5	12	7.9	1.40	315	.171	.227	2	.500	1	6	6	-0	1.1
1962	StL-N	1	0	1.000	20	0	0	0	1	32^1	28	5	21	25	13.9	5.01	85	.239	.360	1	.250	0	-4	-3	0	-0.1
1963	StL-N	3	4	.429	38	0	0	0	3	52^2	55	2	21	30	13.3	3.93	90	.279	.355	0	.000	-1	-4	-2	-1	-0.5
	NY-N	0	0	—	9	0	0	0	0	19	22	0	9	13	14.7	5.21	67	.289	.365	0	.000	-0	-4	-4	-0	0.0
	Yr	3	4	.429	47	0	0	0	3	71^2	77	2	30	43	13.4	4.27	83	.278	.349	0	.000	-1	-8	-6	-1	-0.5
1964	NY-N	0	2	.000	8	0	0	0	1	10	17	1	3	3	18.0	5.40	66	.395	.435	0	—	0	-2	-2	0	-0.4
Total	5	6	6	.500	97	0	0	0	11	149	148	14	70	89	13.4	4.35	89	.263	.349	3	.176	-0	-13	-8	-1	-0.0

● JOSE BAUTISTA Bautista, Jose Joaquin (Arias) b: 7/25/64, Bani, D.R. BR/TR, 6'2", 205 lbs. Deb: 4/9/88

YEAR	TM/L	W	L	PCT	G	GS	CG	SH	SV	IP	H	HR	BB	SO	RAT	ERA	ERA+	OAV	OOB	BH	AVG	PB	PR	/A	PD	TPI
1988	Bal-A	6	15	.286	33	25	3	0	0	171^2	171	21	45	76	11.7	4.30	91	.258	.311	0	—	0	-6	-8	-1	-0.7
1989	Bal-A	3	4	.429	15	10	0	0	0	78	84	17	15	30	11.5	5.31	71	.274	.310	0	—	0	-12	-13	-1	-1.1
1990	Bal-A	1	0	1.000	22	0	0	0	0	26^2	28	4	7	15	11.8	4.05	94	.272	.318	0	—	0	-0	-1	-0	-0.1
1991	Bal-A	0	1	.000	5	0	0	0	0	5^1	13	1	5	3	32.1	16.88	23	.464	.559	0	—	0	-8	-8	0	-1.1
1993	Chi-N	10	3	.769	58	7	1	0	2	111^2	105	11	27	63	11.0	2.82	141	.250	.303	4	.190	0	15	14	1	1.7
1994	Chi-N	4	5	.444	58	0	0	0	1	69^1	75	10	17	45	12.3	3.89	107	.284	.335	0	.000	-0	2	2	-0	0.2
1995	SF-N	3	8	.273	52	6	0	0	0	100^2	120	24	26	45	13.5	6.44	63	.295	.345	0	.000	-2	-25	-26	-1	-2.8
1996	SF-N	3	4	.429	37	1	0	0	0	69^2	66	10	15	28	10.7	3.36	122	.249	.294	1	.111	-0	7	6	0	0.5
1997	Det-A	2	2	.500	21	0	0	0	0	40^1	55	6	12	19	15.4	6.69	68	.324	.375	0	—	0	-10	-9	-0	-0.8
	StL-N	0	0	—	11	0	0	0	0	12^1	15	2	2	4	13.1	6.57	63	.300	.340	0	—	0	-3	-3	-0	0.0
Total	9	32	42	.432	312	49	4	0	3	685^2	732	106	171	328	12.2	4.62	87	.273	.323	5	.100	-2	-41	-46	-3	-4.2

● BILL BAYNE Bayne, William Lear "Beverly" b: 4/18/1899, Pittsburgh, Pa. d: 5/22/81, St.Louis, Mo. BL/TL, 5'9", 160 lbs. Deb: 9/20/19

YEAR	TM/L	W	L	PCT	G	GS	CG	SH	SV	IP	H	HR	BB	SO	RAT	ERA	ERA+	OAV	OOB	BH	AVG	PB	PR	/A	PD	TPI
1919	StL-A	1	1	.500	2	2	1	0	0	12	16	0	6	0	16.5	5.25	63	.320	.393	2	.400	0	-3	-3	0	-0.3
1920	StL-A	5	6	.455	18	13	6	1	0	99^2	102	3	41	38	13.5	3.70	106	.279	.363	6	.171	-2	1	2	-2	-0.2
1921	StL-A	11	5	.688	47	14	6	1	3	164	167	8	80	82	13.8	4.72	95	.270	.358	18	.300	5	-8	-4	-1	0.0
1922	StL-A	4	5	.444	26	9	3	0	2	92^2	86	5	37	38	12.8	4.56	91	.249	.338	7	.233	-1	-5	-4	-2	-0.6
1923	StL-A	2	2	.500	19	2	0	0	0	46	49	4	31	15	16.2	4.50	93	.287	.405	3	.231	-0	-3	-2	-1	-0.2
1924	StL-A	1	3	.250	22	3	0	0	0	50^2	47	4	29	20	14.9	4.44	102	.250	.373	6	.429	2	-1	0	-1	0.2
1928	Cle-A	2	5	.286	37	6	3	0	3	108^2	128	3	43	39	15.0	5.13	81	.309	.388	11	.367	3	-13	-12	2	-0.4
1929	Bos-A	5	5	.500	27	6	2	0	0	84^1	111	9	29	26	15.8	6.72	64	.326	.392	8	.320	2	-23	-23	1	-1.9
1930	Bos-A	0	0	—	1	0	0	0	0	4	5	1	1	1	13.5	4.50	102	.294	.333	1	.500	0	0	0	0	0.0
Total	9	31	32	.492	199	55	21	2	8	662	711	37	297	259	14.4	4.84	87	.283	.370	62	.290	10	-55	-45	-3	-3.4

● WALTER BEALL Beall, Walter Esau b: 7/29/1899, Washington, D.C. d: 1/28/59, Suitland, Md. BR/TR, 5'10", 178 lbs. Deb: 9/3/24

YEAR	TM/L	W	L	PCT	G	GS	CG	SH	SV	IP	H	HR	BB	SO	RAT	ERA	ERA+	OAV	OOB	BH	AVG	PB	PR	/A	PD	TPI
1924	NY-A	2	0	1.000	4	2	0	0	0	23	19	2	17	18	14.1	3.52	118	.237	.371	1	.143	-1	2	2	-1	0.0
1925	NY-A	0	1	.000	8	1	0	0	0	11^1	11	0	19	8	26.2	12.71	34	.282	.541	0	.000	-1	-10	-11	0	-0.8
1926	NY-A	2	4	.333	20	9	1	0	1	81^2	71	2	68	56	16.0	3.53	109	.240	.392	3	.136	0	4	3	1	0.3
1927	NY-A	0	0	—	1	0	0	0	0	1	1	0	0	0	9.0	9.00	43	.333	.333	0	—	0	-1	-1	-0	0.0
1929	Was-A	1	0	1.000	3	0	0	0	0	7	8	0	7	3	19.3	3.86	110	.348	.500	0	.000	-1	0	0	0	0.0
Total	5	5	5	.500	36	12	1	0	1	124	110	4	111	85	16.7	4.43	90	.249	.410	4	.114	-1	-4	-6	0	-0.5

YEAR	TM/L	W	L	PCT	G	GS	CG	SH	SV	IP	H	HR	BB	SO	RAT	ERA	ERA+	OAV	OOB	BH	AVG	PB	PR	/A	PD	TPI
● **ALEX BEAM**	Beam, Alexander Rodger b: 11/21/1870, Johnstown, Pa. d: 4/17/38, Nogales, Ariz. Deb: 5/25/1889																									
1889	Pit-N	1	1	.500	2	2	2	0	0	18	11	0	15	1	13.0	6.50	58	.172	.329	1	.167	0	-5	-6	-0	-0.4
● **ERNIE BEAM**	Beam, Ernest Joseph b: 3/17/1867, Mansfield, Ohio d: 9/12/18, Mansfield, Ohio TR , 6'0.5", 185 lbs. Deb: 5/2/1895																									
1895	Phi-N	0	2	.000	9	1	1	0	**3**	24^2	33	1	25	3	21.5	11.31	42	.314	.450	2	.182	-1	-18	-18	-0	-1.4
● **CHARLIE BEAMON**	Beamon, Charles Alfonzo Sr. b: 12/25/34, Oakland, Cal. BR/TR, 5'11", 195 lbs. Deb: 9/26/56 F																									
1956	Bal-A	2	0	1.000	2	1	1	1	0	13	9	0	8	14	11.8	1.38	283	.191	.309	0	.000	-1	4	4	0	0.5
1957	Bal-A	0	0	—	4	1	0	0	0	8^2	8	1	7	5	16.6	5.19	69	.229	.372	0	.000	-0	-1	-2	-0	0.0
1958	Bal-A	1	3	.250	21	3	0	0	0	49^2	47	3	21	26	13.4	4.35	83	.266	.363	0	.000	-1	-3	-4	2	-0.2
Total	3	3	3	.500	27	5	1	1	0	71^1	64	4	36	45	13.5	3.91	93	.247	.354	0	.000	-2	-1	-2	2	0.3
● **BELVE BEAN**	Bean, Beveric Benton "Bill" b: 4/23/05, Mullin, Tex. d: 6/1/88, Comanche, Tex. BR/TR, 6'1.5", 197 lbs. Deb: 5/30/30																									
1930	Cle-A	3	3	.500	23	3	1	0	2	74^1	99	7	32	19	15.9	5.45	89	.331	.396	9	.346	2	-7	-5	0	-0.2
1931	Cle-A	0	1	.000	4	0	0	0	0	7	11	0	4	3	20.6	6.43	72	.379	.471	0	.000	-0	-2	-1	0	-0.2
1933	Cle-A	1	2	.333	27	2	0	0	0	70^1	80	6	20	41	12.9	5.25	85	.300	.351	4	.182	-1	-8	-6	1	-0.2
1934	Cle-A	5	1	.833	21	1	0	0	0	51^1	53	2	21	20	13.5	3.86	118	.265	.344	3	.200	0	4	4	1	0.5
1935	Cle-A	0	0	—	1	0	0	0	0	1	2	1	0	0	18.0	9.00	50	.400	.400	0	—	0	-1	-0	-0	0.0
	Was-A	2	0	1.000	10	2	0	0	0	31	43	5	19	6	18.0	7.26	60	.339	.425	3	.375	3	-10	-10	-1	-0.4
	Yr	2	0	1.000	11	2	0	0	0	32	45	6	19	6	18.0	7.31	59	.341	.424	3	.375	3	-10	-11	-1	-0.4
Total	5	11	7	.611	86	8	1	0	2	235	288	21	96	89	14.9	5.32	86	.311	.378	19	.264	4	-22	-19	1	-0.5
● **DAVE BEARD**	Beard, Charles David b: 10/2/59, Atlanta, Ga. BL/TR, 6'5", 215 lbs. Deb: 7/16/80																									
1980	Oak-A	0	1	.000	13	0	0	0	1	16	12	0	7	12	11.3	3.38	112	.218	.317	0	—	0	1	1	-0	0.4
1981	*Oak-A	1	1	.500	8	0	0	0	3	13	9	1	4	15	9.7	2.77	126	.191	.269	0	—	0	1	1	0	0.2
1982	Oak-A	10	9	.526	54	2	0	0	11	91^2	85	9	35	73	11.9	3.44	114	.244	.315	0	—	0	6	5	-0	1.3
1983	Oak-A	5	5	.500	43	0	0	0	10	61	55	8	36	40	13.7	5.61	69	.246	.355	0	—	0	-10	-12	-1	-1.8
1984	Sea-A	3	2	.600	43	0	0	0	5	76	88	15	33	40	14.8	5.80	69	.291	.369	0	—	0	-15	-15	-0	-1.0
1985	Chi-N	0	0	—	9	0	0	0	0	12^2	16	2	7	4	16.3	6.39	62	.314	.397	0	—	0	-4	-3	-0	0.0
1989	Det-A	0	2	.000	2	1	0	0	0	5^1	9	2	2	1	20.3	5.06	75	.375	.444	0	—	0	-1	-1	0	-0.2
Total	7	19	20	.487	172	3	0	0	30	275^2	274	37	124	185	13.3	4.70	83	.261	.344	0	—	0	-21	-25	-2	-1.1
● **MIKE BEARD**	Beard, Michael Richard b: 6/21/50, Little Rock, Ark. BL/TL, 6'1", 185 lbs. Deb: 9/7/74																									
1974	Atl-N	0	0	—	6	0	0	0	0	9^1	5	1	1	7	6.8	2.89	131	.156	.206	0	—	0	1	1	0	0.0
1975	Atl-N	4	0	1.000	34	2	0	0	0	70^1	71	4	28	27	12.9	3.20	118	.265	.339	1	.111	-0	3	4	0	0.2
1976	Atl-N	0	2	.000	30	0	0	0	1	33^2	38	1	14	8	13.9	4.28	89	.299	.369	0	.000	-0	-3	-2	1	0.0
1977	Atl-N	0	0	—	4	0	0	0	0	4^2	14	3	2	1	30.9	9.64	46	.452	.485	0	—	0	-3	-3	0	0.0
Total	4	4	2	.667	74	2	0	0	1	118	128	9	45	43	13.4	3.74	102	.279	.348	1	.100	-0	-2	1	1	0.2
● **RALPH BEARD**	Beard, Ralph William b: 2/11/29, Cincinnati, Ohio BR/TR, 6'5", 200 lbs. Deb: 6/29/54																									
1954	StL-N	0	4	.000	13	10	0	0	0	58	62	2	28	17	14.3	3.72	110	.278	.364	1	.059	-1	2	2	-1	-0.1
● **GENE BEARDEN**	Bearden, Henry Eugene b: 9/5/20, Lexa, Ark. BL/TL, 6'3", 204 lbs. Deb: 5/10/47																									
1947	Cle-A	0	0	—	1	0	0	0	0	0^1	2	0	1	0	81.0	81.00	4	.667	.750	0	—	0	-3	-3	0	0.0
1948	*Cle-A	20	7	.741	37	29	15	6	1	229^2	187	9	106	80	11.6	**2.43**	**167**	.229	.320	23	.256	5	47	**42**	3	5.5
1949	Cle-A	8	8	.500	32	19	5	0	0	127	140	6	92	41	16.6	5.10	78	.286	.401	5	.111	-3	-13	-16	4	-1.6
1950	Cle-A	1	3	.250	14	3	0	0	0	45^1	57	5	32	10	17.7	6.15	70	.328	.432	2	.154	1	-8	-9	-1	-0.7
	Was-A	3	5	.375	12	9	4	0	0	68^1	81	1	33	20	15.3	4.21	107	.297	.377	5	.227	1	3	2	0	0.3
	Yr	4	8	.333	26	12	4	0	0	113^2	138	6	65	30	16.2	4.99	89	.309	.399	7	.200	2	-5	-7	-0	-0.4
1951	Was-A	0	0	—	1	1	0	0	0	2^2	6	0	2	1	27.0	16.88	24	.429	.500	0	—	0	-4	-4	-0	0.0
	Det-A	3	4	.429	37	4	2	1	0	106	112	6	58	38	14.5	4.33	96	.275	.366	6	.188	1	-2	-2	0	0.0
	Yr	3	4	.429	38	5	2	1	0	108^2	118	6	60	39	14.8	4.64	90	.280	.371	6	.188	1	-6	-6	-0	0.0
1952	StL-A	7	8	.467	34	16	3	0	0	150^2	158	13	78	45	14.2	4.30	91	.270	.357	23	.354	6	-10	-6	1	0.1
1953	Chi-A	3	3	.500	25	3	0	0	0	58^1	48	8	33	24	12.5	2.93	137	.223	.327	4	.190	-1	7	7	-0	0.6
Total	7	45	38	.542	193	84	29	7	1	788^1	791	48	435	259	14.1	3.96	103	.266	.361	68	.236	10	17	12	7	4.2
● **GARY BEARE**	Beare, Gary Ray b: 8/22/52, San Diego, Cal. BR/TR, 6'4", 205 lbs. Deb: 9/7/76																									
1976	Mil-A	2	3	.400	6	5	2	0	0	41	43	4	15	32	12.7	3.29	106	.274	.337	0	—	0	1	1	-0	0.2
1977	Mil-A	3	3	.500	17	6	0	0	0	58^2	63	6	38	32	15.6	6.44	63	.276	.382	0	—	0	-16	-15	2	-1.2
Total	2	5	6	.455	23	11	2	0	0	99^2	106	10	53	64	14.4	5.15	74	.275	.364	0	—	0	-15	-15	1	-1.0
● **LARRY BEARNARTH**	Bearnarth, Lawrence Donald b: 9/11/41, New York, N.Y. BR/TR, 6'2", 203 lbs. Deb: 4/16/63 C																									
1963	NY-N	3	8	.273	58	2	0	0	4	126^1	127	7	47	48	12.8	3.42	102	.268	.340	6	.200	1	-2	1	2	0.5
1964	NY-N	5	5	.500	44	1	0	0	3	78	79	6	38	31	13.7	4.15	86	.271	.360	2	.143	-0	-5	-5	3	-0.4
1965	NY-N	3	5	.375	40	3	0	0	1	60^2	75	6	28	16	15.9	4.60	77	.304	.384	1	.111	0	-7	-7	0	-0.8
1966	NY-N	2	3	.400	29	1	0	0	0	54^2	59	11	20	27	13.2	4.45	82	.281	.346	1	.111	-0	-5	-5	1	-0.3
1971	Mil-A	0	0	—	2	0	0	0	0	3	10	1	2	2	36.0	18.00	19	.556	.600	0	—	0	-5	-5	0	0.0
Total	5	13	21	.382	173	7	0	0	8	322^2	350	31	135	124	13.9	4.13	86	.282	.358	10	.161	1	-24	-21	7	-1.0
● **KEVIN BEARSE**	Bearse, Kevin Gerard b: 11/7/65, Jersey City, N.J. BL/TL, 6'2", 195 lbs. Deb: 4/15/90																									
1990	Cle-A	0	2	.000	3	3	0	0	0	7^2	16	2	5	2	27.0	12.91	30	.421	.511	0	—	0	-8	-8	-0	-1.4
● **CHRIS BEASLEY**	Beasley, Christopher Charles b: 6/23/62, Jackson, Tenn. BR/TR, 6'2", 190 lbs. Deb: 7/20/91																									
1991	Cal-A	0	1	.000	22	0	0	0	0	26^2	26	2	10	14	12.5	3.38	122	.257	.330	0	—	0	2	2	0	0.1
● **ED BEATIN**	Beatin, Ebenezer Ambrose b: 8/10/1866, Baltimore, Md. d: 5/9/25, Baltimore, Md. BR/TL, 5'9", 162 lbs. Deb: 8/2/1887																									
1887	Det-N	1	1	.500	2	2	2	0	0	18	13	2	8	6	11.0	4.00	101	.203	.301	0	.000	-1	0	0	-0	-0.1
1888	Det-N	5	7	.417	12	12	12	1	0	107	111	6	16	44	10.9	2.86	97	.251	.280	14	.250	5	-0	-1	0	0.4
1889	Cle-N	20	15	.571	36	36	35	3	0	317^2	316	12	141	126	13.1	3.57	113	.251	.330	14	.116	-5	16	16	-1	0.9
1890	Cle-N	22	30	.423	54	54	53	1	0	474^1	518	11	186	155	13.6	3.83	93	.269	.339	27	.141	-9	-14	-13	3	-1.7
1891	Cle-N	0	3	.000	5	4	2	0	0	29	39	1	21	4	20.5	5.28	66	.310	.431	1	.077	-1	-6	-6	-0	-0.6
Total	5	48	56	.462	109	108	104	5	0	946	997	32	372	335	13.3	3.68	99	.261	.332	56	.144	-12	-4	-4	1	-1.1
● **JIM BEATTIE**	Beattie, James Louis b: 7/4/54, Hampton, Va. BR/TR, 6'6", 220 lbs. Deb: 4/25/78																									
1978	*NY-A	6	9	.400	25	22	0	0	0	128	123	8	51	65	12.8	3.73	97	.255	.336	0	—	0	1	-2	1	-0.1
1979	NY-A	3	6	.333	15	13	1	1	0	76	85	5	41	32	14.9	5.21	78	.294	.382	0	—	0	-8	-10	1	-0.8
1980	Sea-A	5	15	.250	33	29	3	0	0	187^1	205	19	98	67	14.7	4.85	85	.286	.375	0	—	0	-17	-15	0	-1.4
1981	Sea-A	3	2	.600	13	9	0	0	1	66^2	59	2	18	36	10.7	2.97	130	.232	.288	0	—	0	5	7	0	0.5
1982	Sea-A	8	12	.400	28	26	6	1	0	172^1	149	13	65	140	11.2	3.34	127	.233	.305	0	—	0	14	17	1	1.7
1983	Sea-A	10	15	.400	30	29	8	2	0	196^2	197	12	66	132	12.2	3.84	111	.259	.321	0	—	0	5	9	3	1.1
1984	Sea-A	12	16	.429	32	32	12	2	0	211	206	13	75	119	12.2	3.41	117	.260	.328	0	—	0	14	13	1	1.9
1985	Sea-A	5	6	.455	18	15	1	1	0	70^1	93	9	33	45	16.5	7.29	58	.316	.391	0	—	0	-25	-24	-1	-3.2
1986	Sea-A	0	6	.000	9	7	0	0	0	40^1	57	7	14	24	16.5	6.02	70	.341	.402	0	—	0	-8	-8	1	-1.0
Total	9	52	87	.374	203	182	31	7	1	1148^2	1174	88	461	660	13.0	4.17	98	.267	.341	0	—	0	-20	-12	7	-1.3
● **BLAINE BEATTY**	Beatty, Gordon Blaine b: 4/25/64, Victoria, Tex. BL/TL, 6'2", 185 lbs. Deb: 9/16/89																									
1989	NY-N	0	0	—	2	1	0	0	0	6	5	1	2	3	10.5	1.50	218	.217	.280	1	.500	0	1	1	0	0.0
1991	NY-N	0	0	—	5	0	0	0	0	9^2	9	0	4	7	12.1	2.79	130	.250	.325	0	—	0	1	1	0	0.0
Total	2	0	0	—	7	1	0	0	0	15^2	14	1	6	10	11.5	2.30	152	.237	.308	1	.500	0	2	2	0	0.0
● **JOHNNY BEAZLEY**	Beazley, John Andrew "Nig" b: 5/25/18, Nashville, Tenn. d: 4/21/90, Nashville, Tenn. BR/TR, 6'1.5", 190 lbs. Deb: 9/28/41																									
1941	StL-N	1	0	1.000	1	1	1	0	0	9	10	0	3	4	13.0	1.00	376	.294	.351	0	.000	-0	3	3	-0	0.3

YEAR	TM/L	W	L	PCT	G	GS	CG	SH	SV	IP	H	HR	BB	SO	RAT	ERA	ERA+	OAV	OOB	BH	AVG	PB	PR	/A	PD	TPI
1942	*StL-N	21	6	.778	43	23	13	3	3	215^1	181	4	73	91	10.7	2.13	161	.226	.293	10	.137	-1	28	31	0	4.0
1946	*StL-N	7	5	.583	19	18	5	0	0	103	109	6	55	36	14.7	4.46	77	.275	.368	8	.242	1	-12	-11	-1	-1.2
1947	Bos-N	2	0	1.000	9	2	2	0	0	28^2	30	1	19	12	15.4	4.40	89	.273	.380	0	.000	-1	-1	-2	-0	-0.2
1948	Bos-N	0	1	.000	3	2	0	0	0	16	19	2	7	4	14.6	4.50	85	.284	.351	0	.000	-1	-1	-1	-0	-0.1
1949	Bos-N	0	0	—	1	0	0	0	0	2	0	0	0	0	0.0	0.00	—	.000	.000	0	—	0	1	1	-0	0.0
Total	6	31	12	.721	76	46	21	3	3	374	349	13	157	147	12.3	3.01	116	.247	.325	18	.150	-1	18	20	-1	2.8

● BUCK BECANNON

Becannon, James Melvin b: 8/22/1859, New York, N.Y. d: 11/5/23, New York, N.Y. 5'10", 165 lbs. Deb: 10/15/1884 ♦

YEAR	TM/L	W	L	PCT	G	GS	CG	SH	SV	IP	H	HR	BB	SO	RAT	ERA	ERA+	OAV	OOB	BH	AVG	PB	PR	/A	PD	TPI
1884	*NY-a	1	0	1.000	1	1	1	0	0	6	2	0	2	2	6.0	1.50	208	.091	.167	0	.000	-0	1	1	0	0.1
1885	NY-a	2	8	.200	10	10	10	0	0	85	108	5	24	13	14.5	6.25	47	.296	.348	10	.303	2	-28	-31	0	-2.4
Total	2	3	8	.273	11	11	11	0	0	91	110	5	26	15	13.9	5.93	50	.284	.337	10	.244	2	-27	-30	0	-2.3

● GEORGE BECHTEL

Bechtel, George A. b: 1848, Philadelphia, Pa. 5'11", 165 lbs. Deb: 5/20/1871 ♦

YEAR	TM/L	W	L	PCT	G	GS	CG	SH	SV	IP	H	HR	BB	SO	RAT	ERA	ERA+	OAV	OOB	BH	AVG	PB	PR	/A	PD	TPI
1871	Ath-n	1	2	.333	3	3	2	0	0	26	43	0	11	1	18.7	7.96	51	.319	.370	33	.351	1	-11	-11		-0.6
1873	Phi-n	0	2	.000	3	2	1	0	0	16	27	0	2	0	16.3	4.50	73	.318	.333	63	.244	0	-2	-2		-0.2
1874	Phi-n	1	3	.250	6	4	4	0	0	39	57	0	1	0	13.4	1.62	137	.297	.301	42	.278	1	2	3		0.2
1875	Cen-n	2	12	.143	14	14	14	0	0	126	169	0	5	6	12.4	2.71	80	.274	.280	17	.279	3	-7	-8		-0.4
	Ath-n	3	1	.750	4	4	4	0	0	36	41	0	3	3	11.0	2.50	96	.279	.293	46	.280	0	-1	-0		0.0
	Yr	5	13	.278	18	18	18	0	0	162	210	0	8	9	12.1	2.67	83	.275	.283	63	.280	4	-8	-8		-0.4
Total	4 n	7	20	.259	30	27	25	0	0	243	337	0	22	10	13.3	3.19	70	.287	.300	275	.282	6	-26	-26		-1.0

● GEORGE BECK

Beck, Ernest George B. b: 2/21/1890, South Bend, Ind. d: 10/29/73, South Bend, Ind. BR/TR, 5'11", 165 lbs. Deb: 5/15/14

YEAR	TM/L	W	L	PCT	G	GS	CG	SH	SV	IP	H	HR	BB	SO	RAT	ERA	ERA+	OAV	OOB	BH	AVG	PB	PR	/A	PD	TPI
1914	Cle-A	0	0	—	1	0	0	0	0	1	1	0	0	0	18.0	0.00	—	.250	.400	0	—	0	0	0	-0	0.0

● FRANK BECK

Beck, Frank J. (b: Frank J. Hengstebeck) b: 4/29/1860, Poughkeepsie, N.Y. d: 2/8/41, Detroit, Mich. TR, 5'9", 141 lbs. Deb: 5/2/1884 ♦

YEAR	TM/L	W	L	PCT	G	GS	CG	SH	SV	IP	H	HR	BB	SO	RAT	ERA	ERA+	OAV	OOB	BH	AVG	PB	PR	/A	PD	TPI
1884	Pit-a	0	3	.000	3	3	3	0	0	25	33	0	6	11	15.8	6.12	55	.306	.370	4	.333	1	-8	-8	0	-0.6
	Bal-U	0	2	.000	2	2	1	0	0	9	17	0	4	7	21.0	8.00	34	.378	.429	2	.100	-1	-6	-5	0	-0.8
Total	1	0	5	.000	5	5	4	0	0	34	50	0	10	18	17.2	6.62	48	.327	.387	6	.188	-0	-14	-13	0	-1.4

● RICH BECK

Beck, Richard Henry b: 1/21/41, Pasco, Wash. BB/TR, 6'3", 190 lbs. Deb: 9/14/65

YEAR	TM/L	W	L	PCT	G	GS	CG	SH	SV	IP	H	HR	BB	SO	RAT	ERA	ERA+	OAV	OOB	BH	AVG	PB	PR	/A	PD	TPI
1965	NY-A	2	1	.667	3	3	1	1	0	21	22	1	7	10	12.4	2.14	159	.275	.333	0	.000	-0	3	3	0	0.4

● ROD BECK

Beck, Rodney Roy b: 8/3/68, Burbank, Cal. BR/TR, 6'1", 236 lbs. Deb: 5/6/91

YEAR	TM/L	W	L	PCT	G	GS	CG	SH	SV	IP	H	HR	BB	SO	RAT	ERA	ERA+	OAV	OOB	BH	AVG	PB	PR	/A	PD	TPI
1991	SF-N	1	1	.500	31	0	0	0	1	52^1	53	4	13	38	11.5	3.78	95	.273	.322	1	.500	0	-1	-1	0	0.0
1992	SF-N	3	3	.500	65	0	0	0	17	92	62	4	15	87	7.7	1.76	188	.190	.230	1	.500	0	18	16	-0	1.6
1993	SF-N★	3	1	.750	76	0	0	0	48	79^1	57	11	13	86	8.3	2.16	181	.201	.243	0	.000	-0	17	15	-1	2.2
1994	SF-N★	2	4	.333	48	0	0	0	28	48^2	49	10	13	39	11.5	2.77	144	.261	.308	0	.000	-0	8	7	-0	1.3
1995	SF-N	5	6	.455	60	0	0	0	33	58^2	60	7	21	42	12.7	4.45	92	.267	.335	1	.333	0	-2	-2	-0	-0.6
1996	SF-N	0	9	.000	63	0	0	0	35	62	56	9	10	48	9.7	3.34	122	.238	.272	1	.333	0	6	5	-1	1.1
1997	*SF-N☆	7	4	.636	73	0	0	0	37	70	67	7	8	53	9.9	3.47	119	.248	.275	0	—	0	6	5	-1	1.1
1998	*Chi-N	3	4	.429	**81**	0	0	0	51	80^1	86	11	20	81	12.1	3.02	144	.269	.316	0	.000	-0	11	12	1	2.3
Total	8	24	32	.429	497	0	0	0	250	543^1	490	63	113	474	10.2	2.98	131	.240	.284	4	.222	0	62	56	-2	9.0

● BOOM-BOOM BECK

Beck, Walter William b: 10/16/04, Decatur, Ill. d: 5/7/87, Champaign, Ill. BR/TR, 6'2", 200 lbs. Deb: 9/22/24 C

YEAR	TM/L	W	L	PCT	G	GS	CG	SH	SV	IP	H	HR	BB	SO	RAT	ERA	ERA+	OAV	OOB	BH	AVG	PB	PR	/A	PD	TPI
1924	StL-A	0	0	—	1	0	0	0	0	1	2	0	1	0	27.0	0.00	—	.667	.750	0	—	0	0	1	0	0.0
1927	StL-A	1	0	1.000	3	1	1	0	0	11^1	15	0	5	6	16.7	5.56	78	.333	.412	1	.250	-0	-2	-2	-0	-0.1
1928	StL-A	2	3	.400	16	4	2	0	0	49	52	4	20	17	14.0	4.41	95	.289	.373	6	.429	1	-2	-1	-0	0.0
1933	Bro-N	12	20	.375	43	35	15	3	1	257	270	9	69	89	12.3	3.54	91	.267	.321	18	.189	0	-6	-9	-0	-1.1
1934	Bro-N	2	6	.250	22	9	2	0	0	57	72	6	32	24	17.2	7.42	53	.301	.395	4	.235	1	-21	-22	1	-2.4
1939	Phi-N	7	14	.333	34	16	12	0	3	182^2	203	11	64	77	13.3	4.73	85	.284	.345	9	.132	-3	-16	-15	-0	-1.8
1940	Phi-N	4	9	.308	29	15	4	0	0	129^1	147	13	41	38	13.7	4.31	90	.286	.349	2	.056	-3	-7	-6	1	-0.7
1941	Phi-N	1	9	.100	34	7	2	0	0	95^1	104	8	35	34	13.3	4.63	80	.276	.341	3	.120	-2	-11	-10	-3	-1.4
1942	Phi-N	0	1	.000	26	1	0	0	0	53	69	4	17	10	14.8	4.75	70	.325	.378	4	.333	1	-8	-9	-1	-0.1
1943	Phi-N	0	0	—	4	0	0	0	0	13^2	24	1	5	3	20.4	9.88	34	.393	.456	2	.500	1	-10	-10	-0	0.0
1944	Det-A	1	2	.333	28	2	0	0	1	74	67	5	27	25	11.8	3.89	92	.243	.317	7	.318	2	-4	-3	-2	-0.1
1945	Cin-N	2	4	.333	11	5	2	0	1	47^2	42	0	12	9	10.4	3.40	111	.236	.288	3	.214	-0	2	2	0	0.2
	Pit-N	6	1	.857	14	5	4	0	0	63	54	2	14	20	9.7	2.14	184	.234	.278	2	.125	-1	12	13	-0	1.2
	Yr	8	5	.615	25	10	6	0	1	110^2	96	2	26	29	9.9	2.68	144	.234	.280	5	.167	-1	14	15	-0	1.4
Total	12	38	69	.355	265	100	44	3	6	1034	1121	63	342	352	13.1	4.30	86	.277	.340	61	.187	-2	-72	-71	-5	-6.3

● CHARLIE BECKER

Becker, Charles S. "Buck" b: 10/14/1888, Washington, D.C. d: 7/30/28, Washington, D.C. BL/TL, 6'2", 180 lbs. Deb: 8/2/11

YEAR	TM/L	W	L	PCT	G	GS	CG	SH	SV	IP	H	HR	BB	SO	RAT	ERA	ERA+	OAV	OOB	BH	AVG	PB	PR	/A	PD	TPI
1911	Was-A	3	5	.375	11	5	5	1	0	71^1	80	2	23	31	13.9	4.04	81	.268	.335	5	.227	-0	-5	-6	-1	-0.6
1912	Was-A	0	0	—	4	0	0	0	0	9	8	0	6	5	14.0	3.00	111	.258	.378	1	.500	0	0	0	-0	0.0
Total	2	3	5	.375	15	5	5	1	0	80^1	88	2	29	36	13.9	3.92	84	.267	.340	6	.250	0	-5	-6	-1	-0.6

● BOB BECKER

Becker, Robert Charles b: 8/15/1875, Syracuse, N.Y. d: 10/11/51, Syracuse, N.Y. TL , Deb: 9/6/1897

YEAR	TM/L	W	L	PCT	G	GS	CG	SH	SV	IP	H	HR	BB	SO	RAT	ERA	ERA+	OAV	OOB	BH	AVG	PB	PR	/A	PD	TPI
1897	Phi-N	0	2	.000	5	2	2	0	0	24	32	0	7	10	15.0	5.63	75	.317	.367	1	.111	-0	-3	-4	-0	-0.3
1898	Phi-N	0	0	—	1	0	0	0	0	5	6	0	5	0	19.8	10.80	32	.300	.440	0	.000	0	-4	-4	0	0.0
Total	2	0	2	.000	6	2	2	0	0	29	38	0	12	10	15.8	6.52	62	.314	.381	1	.100	-0	-7	-8	-0	-0.3

● ROBBIE BECKETT

Beckett, Robert Joseph b: 7/16/72, Austin, Tex. BR/TL, 6'5", 235 lbs. Deb: 9/12/96

YEAR	TM/L	W	L	PCT	G	GS	CG	SH	SV	IP	H	HR	BB	SO	RAT	ERA	ERA+	OAV	OOB	BH	AVG	PB	PR	/A	PD	TPI
1996	Col-N	0	0	—	5	0	0	0	0	5^1	6	3	9	6	25.3	13.50	39	.286	.500	0	—	0	-6	-5	-0	0.0
1997	Col-N	0	0	—	2	0	0	0	0	1^2	1	0	1	2	10.8	5.40	96	.167	.286	0	—	0	0	0	0	0.0
Total	2	0	0	—	7	0	0	0	0	7	7	3	10	8	21.9	11.57	45	.259	.459	0	—	0	-6	-5	-0	0.0

● JAKE BECKLEY

Beckley, Jacob Peter "Eagle Eye" b: 8/4/1867, Hannibal, Mo. d: 6/25/18, Kansas City, Mo. BL/TL, 5'10", 200 lbs. Deb: 6/20/1888 H♦

YEAR	TM/L	W	L	PCT	G	GS	CG	SH	SV	IP	H	HR	BB	SO	RAT	ERA	ERA+	OAV	OOB	BH	AVG	PB	PR	/A	PD	TPI
1902	Cin-N	0	1	.000	1	1	0	0	0	4	9	0	1	2	22.5	6.75	44	.450	.476	175	.330	0	-2	-2	1	-0.2

● JIM BECKMAN

Beckman, James Joseph (b: Reinhardt Boeckman) b: 3/1/05, Cincinnati, Ohio d: 12/5/74, Montgomery, Ohio BR/TR, 5'10", 172 lbs. Deb: 7/27/27

YEAR	TM/L	W	L	PCT	G	GS	CG	SH	SV	IP	H	HR	BB	SO	RAT	ERA	ERA+	OAV	OOB	BH	AVG	PB	PR	/A	PD	TPI
1927	Cin-N	0	1	.000	4	1	0	0	0	12^1	18	2	6	0	18.2	5.84	65	.340	.417	0	.000	-0	-3	-3	-1	-0.3
1928	Cin-N	0	1	.000	6	0	0	0	0	15^1	19	1	9	4	16.4	5.87	67	.306	.394	0	.000	-0	-3	-3	-0	-0.3
Total	2	0	2	.000	10	1	0	0	0	27^2	37	3	15	4	17.2	5.86	66	.322	.405	0	.000	-0	-6	-6	-1	-0.6

● BILL BECKMANN

Beckmann, William Aloysius b: 12/8/07, Clayton, Mo. d: 1/2/90, Florissant, Mo. BR/TR, 6', 175 lbs. Deb: 5/2/39

YEAR	TM/L	W	L	PCT	G	GS	CG	SH	SV	IP	H	HR	BB	SO	RAT	ERA	ERA+	OAV	OOB	BH	AVG	PB	PR	/A	PD	TPI
1939	Phi-A	7	11	.389	27	19	7	2	0	155^1	198	15	41	20	13.9	5.39	87	.312	.355	13	.250	0	-13	-12	-2	-1.2
1940	Phi-A	8	4	.667	34	9	6	2	1	127^1	132	11	35	47	11.9	4.17	107	.265	.314	8	.205	-1	3	4	-2	0.1
1941	Phi-A	5	9	.357	22	15	4	0	1	130	141	11	33	28	12.2	4.57	92	.270	.315	9	.191	0	-6	-6	-3	-0.8
1942	Phi-A	0	1	.000	5	1	0	0	0	20^1	24	1	9	10	14.6	7.08	53	.289	.359	2	.500	1	-8	-7	-1	-0.2
	StL-N	1	0	1.000	2	0	0	0	0	7	4	0	1	3	6.4	0.00	—	.200	.238	0	.000	-0	3	3	0	0.4
Total	4	21	25	.457	90	44	17	4	2	440	499	38	119	108	12.7	4.79	92	.284	.330	32	.224	1	-22	-18	-7	-1.7

● JOE BECKWITH

Beckwith, Thomas Joseph b: 1/28/55, Opelika, Ala. BL/TR, 6'3", 200 lbs. Deb: 7/21/79

YEAR	TM/L	W	L	PCT	G	GS	CG	SH	SV	IP	H	HR	BB	SO	RAT	ERA	ERA+	OAV	OOB	BH	AVG	PB	PR	/A	PD	TPI
1979	LA-N	1	2	.333	17	0	0	0	2	37^1	42	4	15	28	13.7	4.34	84	.284	.350	0	.000	-1	-3	-3	0	-0.3
1980	LA-N	3	3	.500	38	0	0	0	0	59^2	60	1	23	40	12.7	1.96	178	.263	.333	0	.000	0	11	10	-1	0.9
1982	LA-N	2	1	.667	19	1	0	0	1	40	38	2	14	33	11.7	2.70	128	.252	.315	0	.000	-1	4	3	-1	0.1
1983	*LA-N	3	4	.429	42	3	0	0	1	71	73	5	35	50	13.8	3.55	101	.264	.348	1	.200	1	1	0	1	0.1
1984	KC-A	8	4	.667	49	1	0	0	2	100^2	92	13	25	75	10.6	3.40	119	.247	.298	0	—	0	7	7	0	0.8
1985	*KC-A	1	5	.167	49	0	0	0	1	95	99	9	32	80	12.7	4.07	102	.269	.333	0	—	0	1	1	0	0.0
1986	LA-N	0	0	—	15	0	0	0	0	18^1	28	5	6	13	16.7	6.87	50	.350	.395	0	—	0	-6	-7	-1	-0.1
Total	7	18	19	.486	229	5	0	0	7	422	432	39	150	319	12.6	3.54	107	.266	.331	1	.053	-1	14	12	-0	1.5

● JULIO BECQUER

Becquer, Julio (Villegas) b: 12/20/31, Havana, Cuba BL/TL, 5'11.5", 178 lbs. Deb: 9/13/55 ♦

YEAR	TM/L	W	L	PCT	G	GS	CG	SH	SV	IP	H	HR	BB	SO	RAT	ERA	ERA+	OAV	OOB	BH	AVG	PB	PR	/A	PD	TPI
1960	Was-A	0	0	—	1	0	0	0	0	1	1	1	0	0	9.0	9.00	43	.250	.250	75	.252	0	-1	-1	-0	0.0

YEAR TM/L	W	L	PCT	G	GS	CG	SH	SV	IP	H	HR	BB	SO	RAT	ERA	ERA+	OAV	OOB	BH	AVG	PB	PR	/A	PD	TPI
1961 Min-A	0	0	—	1	0	0	0	0	1^1	4	0	1	0	33.8	20.25	21	.500	.556	20	.238	0	-2	-2	-0	0.0
Total 2	0	0	—	2	0	0	0	0	2^1	5	1	1	0	23.1	15.43	26	.417	.462	238	.244	0	-3	-3	-0	0.0

● PHIL BEDGOOD

Bedgood, Phillip Burlette b: 3/8/1898, Harrison, Ga. d: 11/8/27, Fort Pierce, Fla. BR/TR, 6'3", 218 lbs. Deb: 9/20/22

YEAR TM/L	W	L	PCT	G	GS	CG	SH	SV	IP	H	HR	BB	SO	RAT	ERA	ERA+	OAV	OOB	BH	AVG	PB	PR	/A	PD	TPI
1922 Cle-A	1	0	1.000	1	1	1	0	0	9	7	0	4	5	14.0	4.00	100	.233	.378	0	.000	-0	0	0	-0	0.0
1923 Cle-A	0	2	.000	9	2	0	0	0	18^2	16	0	14	7	15.4	5.30	75	.246	.395	1	.250	0	-3	-3	-0	-0.2
Total 2	1	2	.333	10	3	1	0	0	27^2	23	0	18	12	15.0	4.88	82	.242	.390	1	.167	0	-3	-3	-0	-0.2

● HUGH BEDIENT

Bedient, Hugh Carpenter b: 10/23/1889, Gerry, N.Y. d: 7/21/65, Jamestown, N.Y. BR/TR, 6', 185 lbs. Deb: 4/26/12

YEAR TM/L	W	L	PCT	G	GS	CG	SH	SV	IP	H	HR	BB	SO	RAT	ERA	ERA+	OAV	OOB	BH	AVG	PB	PR	/A	PD	TPI
1912 *Bos-A	20	9	.690	41	28	19	0	2	231	206	6	55	122	10.3	2.92	116	.240	.288	14	.192	1	10	12	1	1.6
1913 Bos-A	15	14	.517	43	28	15	1	5	259	255	0	67	122	11.4	2.78	106	.261	.312	10	.125	-3	4	5	-4	-0.3
1914 Bos-A	8	12	.400	42	16	7	1	2	177^1	187	4	45	70	12.0	3.60	75	.281	.331	5	.100	-2	-17	-18	-1	-2.3
1915 Buf-F	16	18	.471	53	30	16	2	**10**	269^1	284	5	69	106	11.9	3.17	88	.274	.321	9	.108	-5	-13	-11	-2	-2.2
Total 4	59	53	.527	179	102	57	4	19	936^2	932	15	236	420	11.4	3.08	96	.263	.312	38	.133	-9	-16	-12	-7	-3.2

● ANDY BEDNAR

Bednar, Andrew Jackson b: 8/16/08, Streator, Ill. d: 11/26/37, Graham, Tex. BR/TR, 5'10.5", 180 lbs. Deb: 9/6/30

YEAR TM/L	W	L	PCT	G	GS	CG	SH	SV	IP	H	HR	BB	SO	RAT	ERA	ERA+	OAV	OOB	BH	AVG	PB	PR	/A	PD	TPI
1930 Pit-N	0	0	—	2	0	0	0	0	1^1	4	0	1	1	33.8	27.00	18	.500	.556	0	—	0	-3	-3	0	0.0
1931 Pit-N	0	0	—	3	0	0	0	0	4	10	1	0	2	22.5	11.25	34	.476	.476	0	—	0	-3	-3	0	0.0
Total 2	0	0	—	5	0	0	0	0	5^1	14	1	1	3	25.3	15.19	27	.483	.500	0	—	0	-7	-7	0	0.0

● STEVE BEDROSIAN

Bedrosian, Stephen Wayne b: 12/6/57, Methuen, Mass. BR/TR, 6'3", 200 lbs. Deb: 8/14/81

YEAR TM/L	W	L	PCT	G	GS	CG	SH	SV	IP	H	HR	BB	SO	RAT	ERA	ERA+	OAV	OOB	BH	AVG	PB	PR	/A	PD	TPI
1981 Atl-N	1	2	.333	15	1	0	0	0	24^1	15	2	15	9	11.5	4.44	81	.169	.295	0	.000	-0	-3	-2	-0	-0.3
1982 *Atl-N	8	6	.571	64	3	0	0	11	137^2	102	7	57	123	10.7	2.42	154	.206	.293	1	.038	-2	18	20	-0	2.0
1983 Atl-N	9	10	.474	70	1	0	0	19	120	100	11	51	114	11.6	3.60	108	.229	.315	2	.105	-1	0	4	0	0.6
1984 Atl-N	9	6	.600	40	4	0	0	11	83^2	65	5	33	81	10.6	2.37	163	.210	.289	2	.118	-1	11	14	-1	2.6
1985 Atl-N	7	15	.318	37	37	0	0	0	206^2	198	17	111	134	13.7	3.83	100	.254	.351	5	.078	-4	-6	0	-2	-0.5
1986 Phi-N	8	6	.571	68	0	0	0	29	90^1	79	12	34	82	11.3	3.39	114	.232	.301	1	.200	0	3	5	-1	0.9
1987 Phi-N★	5	3	.625	65	0	0	0	**40**	89	79	11	28	74	10.9	2.83	150	.237	.298	0	.000	-0	12	14	-1	2.1
1988 Phi-N	6	6	.500	57	0	0	0	28	74^1	75	6	27	61	12.3	3.75	95	.257	.320	0	.000	-0	-3	-2	-0	-0.4
1989 Phi-N	2	3	.400	28	0	0	0	6	33^2	21	7	17	24	10.4	3.21	110	.183	.293	0	—	0	1	1	-0	0.2
*SF-N	1	4	.200	40	0	0	0	17	51	35	5	22	34	10.1	2.65	127	.192	.279	1	.167	-0	5	4	-1	0.5
Yr	3	7	.300	68	0	0	0	23	84^2	56	12	39	58	10.1	2.87	120	.187	.280	1	.167	-0	6	5	-2	0.7
1990 SF-N	9	9	.500	68	0	0	0	17	79^1	72	6	44	43	13.4	4.20	87	.241	.342	2	.500	1	-4	-5	0	-1.1
1991 *Min-A	5	3	.625	56	0	0	0	6	77^1	70	11	35	44	12.6	4.42	96	.243	.331	0	—	0	-3	-1	-1	-0.3
1993 Atl-N	5	2	.714	49	0	0	0	0	49^2	34	4	14	33	9.1	1.63	246	.194	.262	0	.000	-0	13	13	-0	1.6
1994 Atl-N	0	2	.000	46	0	0	0	0	46	41	4	18	43	11.9	3.33	128	.243	.323	1	.500	0	5	5	-0	0.2
1995 Atl-N	1	2	.333	29	0	0	0	0	28	40	6	12	22	17.0	6.11	70	.354	.421	0	—	0	-6	-6	-0	-0.6
Total 14	76	79	.490	732	46	0	0	184	1191	1026	114	518	921	11.9	3.38	114	.232	.317	15	.098	-7	46	64	-9	7.5

● FRED BEEBE

Beebe, Frederick Leonard b: 12/31/1880, Lincoln, Neb. d: 10/30/57, Elgin, Ill. BR/TR, 6'1", 190 lbs. Deb: 4/17/06

YEAR TM/L	W	L	PCT	G	GS	CG	SH	SV	IP	H	HR	BB	SO	RAT	ERA	ERA+	OAV	OOB	BH	AVG	PB	PR	/A	PD	TPI
1906 Chi-N	6	1	.857	14	6	4	0	1	70	56	1	32	55	12.0	2.70	98	.210	.306	3	.103	-1	-1	-0	-1	-0.3
StL-N	9	9	.500	20	19	16	1	0	160^2	115	1	68	116	10.8	3.02	87	.208	.305	10	.172	0	-7	-7	-0	-0.8
Yr	15	10	.600	34	25	20	1	1	230^2	171	2	100	**171**	10.9	2.93	90	.207	.300	13	.149	-1	-7	-8	-1	-1.1
1907 StL-N	7	19	.269	31	29	24	4	0	238^1	192	1	109	141	11.7	2.72	92	.230	.326	11	.128	-3	-7	-6	1	-0.8
1908 StL-N	5	13	.278	29	19	12	0	0	174^1	134	3	66	72	10.5	2.63	90	**.193**	.267	7	.125	-2	-5	-5	2	-0.6
1909 StL-N	15	21	.417	44	34	18	1	1	287^2	256	5	104	105	11.5	2.82	90	.229	.299	18	.167	-2	-7	-9	1	-1.3
1910 Cin-N	12	14	.462	35	26	11	2	0	214^1	193	3	94	93	12.3	3.07	95	.246	.333	12	.164	-2	-1	-4	3	-0.3
1911 Phi-N	3	3	.500	9	8	3	0	0	48^1	52	2	24	20	14.7	4.47	77	.297	.391	5	.263	2	-6	-6	1	-0.3
1916 Cle-A	5	3	.625	20	12	5	1	2	100^2	92	1	37	32	11.6	2.41	125	.251	.321	6	.214	1	5	7	-0	0.6
Total 7	62	83	.428	202	153	93	9	4	1294^1	1090	17	534	634	11.6	2.86	93	.227	.311	72	.158	-8	-28	-30	6	-3.8

● MATT BEECH

Beech, Lucas Matthew b: 1/20/72, Oakland, Cal. BL/TL, 6'2", 190 lbs. Deb: 8/8/96

YEAR TM/L	W	L	PCT	G	GS	CG	SH	SV	IP	H	HR	BB	SO	RAT	ERA	ERA+	OAV	OOB	BH	AVG	PB	PR	/A	PD	TPI
1996 Phi-N	1	4	.200	8	8	0	0	0	41^1	49	8	11	33	13.7	6.97	62	.306	.362	1	.071	-1	-13	-12	-0	-1.3
1997 Phi-N	4	9	.308	24	24	0	0	0	136^2	147	25	57	120	13.8	5.07	84	.279	.355	5	.167	-0	-13	-13	0	-1.0
1998 Phi-N	3	9	.250	21	21	0	0	0	117	126	19	63	113	14.8	5.15	85	.275	.368	5	.152	-1	-12	-10	-1	-1.1
Total 3	8	22	.267	53	53	0	0	0	295	322	52	131	266	14.2	5.37	80	.281	.361	11	.143	-2	-38	-35	-1	-3.4

● ED BEECHER

Beecher, Edward Harry b: 7/2/1860, Guilford, Conn. d: 9/12/35, Hartford, Conn. BL/TL, 5'10", 185 lbs. Deb: 6/28/1887 ♦

YEAR TM/L	W	L	PCT	G	GS	CG	SH	SV	IP	H	HR	BB	SO	RAT	ERA	ERA+	OAV	OOB	BH	AVG	PB	PR	/A	PD	TPI
1890 Buf-P	0	0	—	1	0	0	0	0	6	10	0	3	0	19.5	12.00	34	.357	.419	159	.297	0	-5	-5	-0	0.0

● ROY BEECHER

Beecher, Leroy "Colonel" b: 5/10/1884, Swanton, Ohio d: 10/11/52, Toledo, Ohio BL/TR, 6'2", 180 lbs. Deb: 9/29/07

YEAR TM/L	W	L	PCT	G	GS	CG	SH	SV	IP	H	HR	BB	SO	RAT	ERA	ERA+	OAV	OOB	BH	AVG	PB	PR	/A	PD	TPI
1907 NY-N	0	2	.000	2	2	2	0	0	14	17	0	6	5	14.8	2.57	96	.293	.359	0	.000	-1	-0	-0	-0	-0.1
1908 NY-N	0	0	—	2	0	0	0	1	5^2	11	0	3	0	22.2	7.94	30	.440	.500	1	.333	1	-4	-3	0	-0.1
Total 2	0	2	.000	4	2	2	0	1	19^2	28	0	9	5	16.9	4.12	60	.337	.402	1	.125	-0	-4	-4	0	-0.2

● FRED BEENE

Beene, Freddy Ray b: 11/24/42, Angleton, Tex. BB/TR, 5'9", 160 lbs. Deb: 9/18/68

YEAR TM/L	W	L	PCT	G	GS	CG	SH	SV	IP	H	HR	BB	SO	RAT	ERA	ERA+	OAV	OOB	BH	AVG	PB	PR	/A	PD	TPI
1968 Bal-A	0	0	—	1	0	0	0	0	1	2	0	1	1	27.0	9.00	33	.500	.600	0	—	0	-1	-1	0	0.0
1969 Bal-A	0	0	—	2	0	0	0	0	2^2	2	0	1	0	10.1	0.00	—	.200	.273	0	—	0	1	1	0	0.0
1970 Bal-A	0	0	—	4	0	0	0	0	6	8	1	5	4	19.5	6.00	61	.320	.433	0	—	0	-2	-2	-0	0.0
1972 NY-A	1	3	.250	29	1	0	0	3	57^2	55	3	24	37	12.5	2.34	126	.256	.333	0	.000	-1	5	4	0	0.2
1973 NY-A	6	0	1.000	19	4	0	0	1	91	67	5	27	49	9.4	1.68	218	.209	.273	0	—	0	22	20	-1	1.6
1974 NY-A	0	0	—	6	0	0	0	1	10	9	1	2	10	10.8	2.70	131	.231	.286	0	—	0	1	1	0	0.2
Cle-A	4	4	.500	32	0	0	0	2	73	68	7	26	35	11.7	4.93	73	.246	.314	0	—	0	-11	-11	1	-1.0
Yr	4	4	.500	38	0	0	0	3	83	77	8	28	45	11.5	4.66	77	.244	.307	0	—	0	-10	-10	1	-0.8
1975 Cle-A	1	0	1.000	19	1	0	0	1	46^2	63	4	25	20	17.6	6.94	54	.323	.408	0	—	0	-16	-16	0	-0.4
Total 7	12	7	.632	112	6	0	0	8	288	274	21	111	156	12.3	3.63	97	.253	.326	0	.000	-1	-1	-3	2	0.6

● ANDY BEENE

Beene, Ramon Andrew b: 10/13/56, Freeport, Tex. BR/TR, 6'3", 205 lbs. Deb: 9/22/83

YEAR TM/L	W	L	PCT	G	GS	CG	SH	SV	IP	H	HR	BB	SO	RAT	ERA	ERA+	OAV	OOB	BH	AVG	PB	PR	/A	PD	TPI
1983 Mil-A	0	0	—	1	0	0	0	0	2	3	0	1	0	18.0	4.50	83	.333	.400	0	—	0	-0	-0	-0	0.8
1984 Mil-A	0	2	.000	5	3	0	0	0	18^2	28	1	9	11	18.8	11.09	35	.350	.429	0	—	0	-15	-15	0	-1.0
Total 2	0	2	.000	6	3	0	0	0	20^2	31	1	10	11	18.7	10.45	37	.348	.426	0	—	0	-15	-15	0	-0.2

● CLARENCE BEERS

Beers, Clarence Scott b: 12/9/18, ElDorado, Kan. BR/TR, 6', 175 lbs. Deb: 5/2/48

YEAR TM/L	W	L	PCT	G	GS	CG	SH	SV	IP	H	HR	BB	SO	RAT	ERA	ERA+	OAV	OOB	BH	AVG	PB	PR	/A	PD	TPI
1948 StL-N	0	0	—	1	0	0	0	0	0^2	3	0	1	0	54.0	13.50	30	.500	.571	0	—	0	-1	-1	-0	0.0

● JOE BEGGS

Beggs, Joseph Stanley "Fireman" b: 11/4/10, Rankin, Pa. d: 7/19/83, Indianapolis, Ind BR/TR, 6'1", 182 lbs. Deb: 4/19/38

YEAR TM/L	W	L	PCT	G	GS	CG	SH	SV	IP	H	HR	BB	SO	RAT	ERA	ERA+	OAV	OOB	BH	AVG	PB	PR	/A	PD	TPI
1938 NY-A	3	2	.600	14	9	4	0	0	58^1	69	7	20	8	13.7	5.40	84	.299	.355	5	.250	1	-4	-6	2	-0.2
1940 *Cin-N	12	3	.800	37	1	0	0	**7**	76^2	68	1	21	25	10.6	2.00	190	.243	.298	4	.190	-0	**16**	**15**	1	3.3
1941 Cin-N	4	3	.571	37	0	0	0	5	57	57	2	27	19	13.3	3.79	95	.313	.402	3	.300	1	-1	-1	0	-0.1
1942 Cin-N	6	5	.545	38	0	0	0	8	88^2	65	4	33	24	10.0	2.13	154	.206	.283	0	.000	-3	12	11	3	1.6
1943 Cin-N	7	6	.538	39	4	4	2	6	115^1	121	0	25	28	11.4	2.34	142	.276	.315	5	.143	-1	**13**	**12**	1	1.5
1944 Cin-N	1	0	1.000	1	1	1	0	0	9	8	0	0	2	8.0	2.00	174	.222	.222	0	.000	-1	2	1	0	0.1
1946 Cin-N	12	10	.545	28	22	14	2	1	190	175	15	39	38	10.2	2.32	144	.247	.287	14	.222	2	23	22	1	2.9
1947 Cin-N	0	3	.000	11	4	0	0	0	32^1	42	4	6	11	13.4	5.29	78	.316	.345	1	.091	-1	-4	-4	1	-0.4
NY-N	3	3	.500	32	0	0	0	2	66	81	6	18	23	13.6	4.23	96	.300	.346	1	.077	-1	-1	-1	-0	-0.2
Yr	3	6	.333	43	4	0	0	2	98^1	123	10	24	34	13.5	4.58	89	.305	.346	2	.083	-2	-6	-5	0	-0.6
1948 NY-N	0	0	—	1	0	0	0	0	0^1	2	0	0	0	54.0	0.00	—	.667	.667	0	—	0	0	0	0	0.0
Total 9	48	35	.578	238	41	23	4	29	693^2	688	39	189	178	11.4	2.96	122	.265	.316	33	.167	-3	55	50	8	8.5

● ED BEGLEY

Begley, Edward N. (b: Edward N. Bagley) b: 1863, New York, N.Y. d: 7/24/19, Waterbury, Conn. Deb: 5/3/1884

YEAR TM/L	W	L	PCT	G	GS	CG	SH	SV	IP	H	HR	BB	SO	RAT	ERA	ERA+	OAV	OOB	BH	AVG	PB	PR	/A	PD	TPI
1884 NY-N	12	18	.400	31	30	30	0	0	266	296	9	99	104	13.4	4.16	72	.263	.323	22	.182	-3	-35	-35	-2	-3.4

YEAR	TM/L	W	L	PCT	G	GS	CG	SH	SV	IP	H	HR	BB	SO	RAT	ERA	ERA+	OAV	OOB	BH	AVG	PB	PR	/A	PD	TPI
1885	NY-a	4	9	.308	15	14	10	0	0	115	131	5	48	44	14.6	4.93	60	.278	.355	9	.173	-0	-21	-25	1	-2.1
Total	2	16	27	.372	46	44	40	0	0	381	427	14	147	148	13.7	4.39	68	.268	.333	31	.179	-3	-56	-60	-1	-5.5

● PETIE BEHAN Behan, Charles Frederick b: 12/11/1887, Dallas City, Pa. d: 1/22/57, Bradford, Pa. BR/TR, 5'10", 160 lbs. Deb: 9/16/21

YEAR	TM/L	W	L	PCT	G	GS	CG	SH	SV	IP	H	HR	BB	SO	RAT	ERA	ERA+	OAV	OOB	BH	AVG	PB	PR	/A	PD	TPI
1921	Phi-N	0	1	.000	2	2	1	0	0	10^2	17	0	1	3	15.2	5.91	72	.354	.367	0	.000	-1	-3	-2	-0	-0.2
1922	Phi-N	4	2	.667	7	5	3	1	0	47^1	49	3	14	13	12.2	2.47	189	.259	.314	5	.250	-0	9	12	-1	1.3
1923	Phi-N	3	12	.200	31	17	5	0	2	131	182	11	57	27	16.5	5.50	84	.336	.401	8	.186	-2	-22	-13	-1	-1.5
Total	3	7	15	.318	40	24	9	1	2	189	248	14	72	43	15.3	4.76	97	.319	.378	13	.194	-3	-16	-3	-2	-0.4

● RICK BEHENNA Behenna, Richard Kipp b: 3/6/60, Miami, Fla. BR/TR, 6'2", 170 lbs. Deb: 4/12/83

YEAR	TM/L	W	L	PCT	G	GS	CG	SH	SV	IP	H	HR	BB	SO	RAT	ERA	ERA+	OAV	OOB	BH	AVG	PB	PR	/A	PD	TPI
1983	Atl-N	3	3	.500	14	6	0	0	0	37^1	37	7	12	17	12.1	4.58	85	.255	.316	4	.333	2	-4	-3	-0	-0.3
	Cle-A	0	2	.000	5	4	0	0	0	26	22	0	14	9	12.8	4.15	102	.232	.336	0	—	0	-0	0	0	-0.2
1984	Cle-A	0	3	.000	3	3	0	0	0	9^2	17	5	8	6	24.2	13.97	29	.386	.491	0	—	0	-11	-11	0	-2.1
1985	Cle-A	0	2	.000	4	4	0	0	0	19^2	29	3	8	4	16.9	7.78	53	.354	.411	0	—	0	-8	-8	-1	-0.7
Total	3	3	10	.231	26	17	0	0	0	92^2	105	15	42	36	14.6	6.12	66	.287	.365	4	.333	2	-23	-21	-1	-3.3

● MEL BEHNEY Behney, Melvin Brian b: 9/2/47, Newark, N.J. BL/TL, 6'2", 180 lbs. Deb: 8/14/70

YEAR	TM/L	W	L	PCT	G	GS	CG	SH	SV	IP	H	HR	BB	SO	RAT	ERA	ERA+	OAV	OOB	BH	AVG	PB	PR	/A	PD	TPI
1970	Cin-N	0	2	.000	5	1	0	0	0	10	15	1	8	2	20.7	4.50	90	.341	.442	0	.000	-0	-1	-1	-0	-0.1

● HANK BEHRMAN Behrman, Henry Bernard b: 6/27/21, Brooklyn, N.Y. d: 1/20/87, New York, N.Y. BR/TR, 5'11", 174 lbs. Deb: 4/17/46

YEAR	TM/L	W	L	PCT	G	GS	CG	SH	SV	IP	H	HR	BB	SO	RAT	ERA	ERA+	OAV	OOB	BH	AVG	PB	PR	/A	PD	TPI
1946	Bro-N	11	5	.688	47	11	2	0	4	150^2	138	3	69	78	12.5	2.93	115	.241	.325	4	.095	-3	8	8	-2	0.3
1947	*Bro-N	0	0	—	2	0	0	0	0	3^2	3	1	4	2	17.2	9.82	42	.231	.412	0	—	0	-2	-2	0	0.0
	Pit-N	0	2	.000	10	2	0	0	0	24^2	33	6	17	11	19.0	9.12	46	.347	.456	0	.000	-1	-14	-13	-1	-1.1
	*Bro-N	5	3	.625	38	6	0	0	8	88^1	94	9	44	31	14.1	5.30	78	.274	.357	6	.231	1	-12	-11	-1	-1.2
	Yr	5	5	.500	50	8	0	0	8	116^2	130	16	65	44	15.0	6.25	66	.287	.376	6	.188	-0	-28	-27	-2	-2.3
1948	Bro-N	5	4	.556	34	4	2	1	7	91	95	7	42	42	13.8	4.05	99	.268	.350	3	.107	-2	-1	-1	-0	-0.3
1949	NY-N	3	3	.500	43	4	1	1	0	71^1	64	5	52	25	14.6	4.92	81	.239	.363	1	.077	-1	-7	-7	-0	-0.6
Total	4	24	17	.585	174	27	5	2	19	429^2	427	31	228	189	13.9	4.40	87	.259	.352	14	.122	-5	-28	-28	-5	-2.9

● TIM BELCHER Belcher, Timothy Wayne b: 10/19/61, Mount Gilead, Ohio BR/TR, 6'3", 220 lbs. Deb: 9/6/87

YEAR	TM/L	W	L	PCT	G	GS	CG	SH	SV	IP	H	HR	BB	SO	RAT	ERA	ERA+	OAV	OOB	BH	AVG	PB	PR	/A	PD	TPI
1987	LA-N	4	2	.667	6	5	0	0	0	34	30	2	7	23	9.8	2.38	166	.240	.280	2	.200	0	6	6	-0	1.0
1988	*LA-N	12	6	.667	36	27	4	1	4	179^2	143	8	51	152	9.8	2.91	115	.217	.275	4	.071	-2	11	8	-1	0.6
1989	LA-N	15	12	.556	39	30	**10**	**8**	1	230	182	20	80	200	10.5	2.82	121	.217	.291	7	.100	-2	17	15	-2	1.4
1990	LA-N	9	9	.500	24	24	5	2	0	153	136	17	48	102	10.9	4.00	91	.240	.302	7	.163	1	-4	-6	-2	-0.7
1991	LA-N	10	9	.526	33	33	2	1	0	209^1	189	10	75	156	11.4	2.62	137	.240	.307	8	.119	-2	25	23	-2	1.6
1992	Cin-N	15	14	.517	35	34	2	1	0	227^2	201	17	80	149	11.2	3.91	92	.238	.307	8	.105	-2	-10	-8	-0	-1.2
1993	Cin-N	9	6	.600	22	22	4	2	0	137	134	11	47	101	12.4	4.47	90	.254	.324	10	.200	1	-6	-7	-1	-0.7
	*Chi-A	3	5	.375	12	11	1	1	0	71^2	64	8	27	34	11.6	4.40	95	.242	.314	0	—	0	-1	-2	-1	-0.2
1994	Det-A	7	15	.318	25	25	3	0	0	162	192	21	78	76	15.2	5.89	82	.290	.368	0	—	0	-20	-19	1	-1.9
1995	*Sea-A	10	12	.455	28	28	1	0	0	179^1	188	19	88	96	14.1	4.52	105	.269	.354	0	—	0	4	4	-1	0.4
1996	KC-A	15	11	.577	35	35	4	1	0	238^2	262	28	68	113	12.7	3.92	128	.281	.334	0	—	0	28	29	-0	2.7
1997	KC-A	13	12	.520	32	32	3	1	0	213^1	242	31	70	113	13.4	5.02	94	.288	.346	0	.000	-1	-11	-7	-1	-0.8
1998	KC-A	14	14	.500	34	34	2	0	0	234	247	37	73	130	12.6	4.27	115	.272	.331	1	.200	0	10	17	-3	1.4
Total	12	136	127	.517	361	340	41	18	5	2269^2	2210	229	792	1445	12.1	3.97	105	.255	.321	47	.123	-6	50	51	-11	3.6

● STAN BELINDA Belinda, Stanley Peter b: 8/6/66, Huntingdon, Pa. BR/TR, 6'3", 187 lbs. Deb: 9/8/89

YEAR	TM/L	W	L	PCT	G	GS	CG	SH	SV	IP	H	HR	BB	SO	RAT	ERA	ERA+	OAV	OOB	BH	AVG	PB	PR	/A	PD	TPI
1989	Pit-N	0	1	.000	8	0	0	0	0	10^1	13	0	2	10	13.1	6.10	55	.295	.326	0	—	0	-3	-3	-0	-0.3
1990	*Pit-N	3	4	.429	55	0	0	0	8	58^1	48	4	29	55	12.0	3.55	102	.227	.324	0	.000	-1	2	0	-1	-0.1
1991	*Pit-N	7	5	.583	60	0	0	0	16	78^1	50	10	35	71	10.2	3.45	104	.184	.286	0	.000	-0	2	1	-1	0.1
1992	*Pit-N	6	4	.600	59	0	0	0	18	71^1	58	8	29	57	11.0	3.15	109	.223	.301	2	.667	1	3	2	-1	0.4
1993	Pit-N	3	1	.750	40	0	0	0	19	42^1	35	4	11	30	10.0	3.61	112	.224	.280	0	.000	-0	2	2	-0	0.3
	KC-A	1	1	.500	23	0	0	0	0	27^1	30	2	6	25	12.2	4.28	107	.280	.325	0	—	0	0	1	-1	0.0
1994	KC-A	2	2	.500	37	0	0	0	1	49	47	6	24	37	14.0	5.14	97	.250	.350	0	—	0	-2	-1	-1	-0.2
1995	*Bos-A	8	1	.889	63	0	0	0	10	69^2	51	5	28	57	10.7	3.10	157	.205	.295	0	—	0	12	14	-1	1.6
1996	Bos-A	2	1	.667	31	0	0	0	2	28^2	31	3	20	18	17.3	6.59	77	.272	.399	0	—	0	-5	-5	-0	-0.6
1997	Cin-N	1	5	.167	84	0	0	0	1	99^1	84	11	33	114	11.4	3.71	115	.229	.308	1	.333	0	5	6	-2	0.2
1998	Cin-N	4	8	.333	40	0	0	0	1	61^1	46	7	28	57	11.0	3.23	134	.212	.305	0	.000	-0	7	7	0	1.4
Total	10	37	33	.529	500	0	0	0	76	596	493	60	245	531	11.6	3.79	110	.226	.312	3	.150	1	23	24	-7	2.8

● BO BELINSKY Belinsky, Robert b: 12/7/36, New York, N.Y. BL/TL, 6'2", 191 lbs. Deb: 4/18/62

YEAR	TM/L	W	L	PCT	G	GS	CG	SH	SV	IP	H	HR	BB	SO	RAT	ERA	ERA+	OAV	OOB	BH	AVG	PB	PR	/A	PD	TPI
1962	LA-A	10	11	.476	33	31	5	3	1	187^1	149	12	122	145	13.6	3.56	109	.216	.344	10	.167	1	9	6	-0	0.7
1963	LA-A	2	9	.182	13	13	2	0	0	76^2	78	12	35	60	13.7	5.75	60	.262	.347	2	.074	-2	-18	-20	1	-2.5
1964	LA-A	9	8	.529	23	22	4	1	0	135^1	120	8	49	91	11.6	2.86	115	.240	.315	4	.095	-1	11	6	-1	0.5
1965	Phi-N	4	9	.308	30	14	3	0	1	109^2	103	13	48	71	12.9	4.84	71	.248	.334	6	.188	1	-16	-17	-1	-2.0
1966	Phi-N	0	2	.000	9	1	0	0	0	15^1	14	3	5	8	12.9	2.93	123	.250	.344	1	.333	0	1	1	0	0.2
1967	Hou-N	3	9	.250	27	18	0	0	0	115^1	112	12	54	80	13.6	4.68	71	.255	.347	3	.077	-2	-17	-18	-2	-2.1
1969	Pit-N	0	3	.000	8	3	0	0	0	17^2	17	1	14	15	16.8	4.58	76	.266	.412	0	.000	-0	-2	-2	0	-0.4
1970	Cin-N	0	0	—	3	0	0	0	0	8	10	0	6	6	18.0	4.50	90	.294	.400	1	1.000	1	-0	-0	-0	0.1
Total	8	28	51	.354	146	102	14	4	2	665^1	603	61	333	476	13.2	4.10	86	.241	.340	27	.131	-2	-32	-43	-4	-5.5

● CHARLIE BELL Bell, Charles C. b: 8/12/1868, Cincinnati, Ohio d: 2/7/37, Cincinnati, Ohio TR , Deb: 10/13/1889 F♦

YEAR	TM/L	W	L	PCT	G	GS	CG	SH	SV	IP	H	HR	BB	SO	RAT	ERA	ERA+	OAV	OOB	BH	AVG	PB	PR	/A	PD	TPI
1889	KC-a	1	0	1.000	1	1	1	0	0	9	4	0	3	3	8.0	1.00	418	.129	.229	1	.167	0	3	3	1	0.4
1891	Lou-a	2	6	.250	10	9	8	0	0	77	93	4	20	16	14.1	4.68	78	.289	.346	1	.036	-2	-8	-9	-2	-1.0
	Cin-a	1	0	1.000	1	1	1	0	0	9	2	0	3	1	6.0	0.00	—	.069	.182	2	.500	0	4	4	0	0.5
	Yr	3	6	.333	11	10	9	0	0	86	95	4	23	17	12.5	4.19	88	.265	.311	3	.094	-2	-4	-5	-1	-0.5
Total	2	4	6	.400	12	11	10	0	0	95	99	4	26	20	12.8	3.88	97	.259	.323	4	.105	-2	-2	-1	-1	-0.1

● ERIC BELL Bell, Eric Alvin b: 10/27/63, Modesto, Cal. BL/TL, 6'3", 195 lbs. Deb: 9/24/85

YEAR	TM/L	W	L	PCT	G	GS	CG	SH	SV	IP	H	HR	BB	SO	RAT	ERA	ERA+	OAV	OOB	BH	AVG	PB	PR	/A	PD	TPI
1985	Bal-A	0	0	—	4	0	0	0	0	5^2	4	1	4	4	12.7	4.76	85	.200	.333	0	—	0	-0	-0	0	0.1
1986	Bal-A	1	2	.333	4	4	0	0	0	23^1	23	4	14	18	14.3	5.01	82	.258	.359	0	—	0	-2	-2	-1	-0.3
1987	Bal-A	10	13	.435	33	29	2	0	0	165	174	32	78	111	13.9	5.45	81	.271	.351	0	—	0	-18	-19	-1	-2.3
1991	Cle-A	4	0	1.000	10	0	0	0	0	18	5	0	5	7	5.5	0.50	830	.091	.180	0	—	0	7	7	-0	1.6
1992	Cle-A	0	2	.000	7	1	0	0	0	15^1	22	1	9	10	18.8	7.63	51	.349	.438	0	—	0	-6	-6	1	-0.6
1993	Hou-N	0	1	.000	10	0	0	0	0	7^1	10	0	2	2	14.7	6.14	63	.313	.353	0	—	0	-2	-2	-0	-0.3
Total	6	15	18	.455	68	34	2	0	0	234^2	238	38	112	152	13.6	5.18	83	.264	.348	0	—	0	-22	-23	-2	-1.8

● GARY BELL Bell, Gary b: 11/17/36, San Antonio, Tex. BR/TR, 6'1", 198 lbs. Deb: 6/1/58

YEAR	TM/L	W	L	PCT	G	GS	CG	SH	SV	IP	H	HR	BB	SO	RAT	ERA	ERA+	OAV	OOB	BH	AVG	PB	PR	/A	PD	TPI
1958	Cle-A	12	10	.545	33	23	10	0	1	182	141	17	73	110	10.8	3.31	110	.213	.296	11	.196	2	9	7	-2	0.7
1959	Cle-A	16	11	.593	44	28	12	1	5	234	208	28	105	136	12.2	4.04	91	.238	.323	18	.240	3	-5	-9	-2	-0.9
1960	Cle-A★	9	10	.474	28	23	6	2	1	154^2	139	15	82	109	13.3	4.13	90	.242	.344	7	.149	-0	-4	-7	1	-0.7
1961	Cle-A	12	16	.429	34	34	11	2	0	228^1	214	32	100	163	12.6	4.10	96	.245	.326	16	.198	1	-2	-4	-1	-0.4
1962	Cle-A	10	9	.526	57	6	1	0	12	107^2	104	14	52	80	13.3	4.26	91	.264	.354	5	.208	1	-4	-5	-1	-0.8
1963	Cle-A	8	5	.615	58	7	0	0	5	119	91	13	52	98	11.1	2.95	123	.208	.298	3	.115	-1	9	9	1	1.0
1964	Cle-A	8	6	.571	56	2	0	0	4	106	106	15	53	89	13.8	4.33	83	.260	.351	6	.375	2	-8	-9	-1	-1.0
1965	Cle-A	6	5	.545	60	0	0	0	17	103^2	86	7	50	86	12.0	3.04	115	.226	.319	1	.063	-0	5	5	-1	0.6
1966	Cle-A☆	14	15	.483	40	37	12	0	0	254^1	211	19	79	194	10.4	3.22	107	.228	.291	10	.132	-1	6	6	2	0.8
1967	Cle-A	1	5	.167	9	9	1	0	0	60^2	50	7	24	39	11.1	3.71	88	.234	.314	0	.000	-2	-3	-3	1	-0.4
	*Bos-A	12	8	.600	29	24	8	0	3	165^1	143	16	47	115	10.6	3.16	110	.231	.290	12	.203	1	1	6	-1	0.8
	Yr	13	13	.500	38	33	9	0	3	226	193	23	71	154	10.7	3.31	104	.231	.295	12	.162	-1	-2	3	0	0.4
1968	Bos-A☆	11	11	.500	35	27	9	3	1	199^1	177	7	68	103	11.3	3.12	101	.239	.308	13	.220	2	-3	1	0	0.3
1969	Sea-A	2	6	.250	13	11	1	1	2	61^1	76	8	34	30	16.4	4.70	77	.305	.393	3	.214	1	-7	-7	0	-0.7
	Chi-A	0	0	—	23	2	0	0	0	38^2	48	8	23	26	17.0	6.28	61	.308	.403	0	.000	-0	-11	-10	0	0.0

YEAR	TM/L	W	L	PCT	G	GS	CG	SH	SV	IP	H	HR	BB	SO	RAT	ERA	ERA+	OAV	OOB	BH	AVG	PB	PR	/A	PD	TPI
	Yr	2	6	.250	36	13	1	1	2	100	124	16	57	56	16.5	5.31	70	.302	.390	3	.158	1	-19	-18	0	-0.7
Total	12	121	117	.508	519	233	71	9	51	2015	1794	206	842	1378	12.0	3.68	98	.239	.320	105	.185	9	-17	-18	-3	-0.7

● GEORGE BELL Bell, George Glenn "Farmer" b: 11/2/1874, Greenwood, N.Y. d: 12/25/41, New York, N.Y. BR/TR, 6′, 195 lbs. Deb: 4/17/07

YEAR	TM/L	W	L	PCT	G	GS	CG	SH	SV	IP	H	HR	BB	SO	RAT	ERA	ERA+	OAV	OOB	BH	AVG	PB	PR	/A	PD	TPI
1907	Bro-N	8	16	.333	35	27	20	3	1	263^{2}	222	1	77	88	10.4	2.25	104	.238	.300	8	.095	-2	6	3	2	0.3
1908	Bro-N	4	15	.211	29	19	12	2	1	155^{1}	162	3	45	63	12.1	3.59	65	.270	.324	8	.170	1	-21	-22	1	-2.4
1909	Bro-N	16	15	.516	33	30	29	6	1	256	236	5	73	95	11.0	2.71	96	.251	.307	15	.167	1	-3	-3	2	-0.1
1910	Bro-N	10	27	.270	44	36	25	4	1	310	267	4	82	102	10.2	2.64	115	.241	.296	13	.134	-4	13	13	-3	0.7
1911	Bro-N	5	6	.455	19	12	6	2	0	101	123	2	28	28	13.6	4.28	78	.315	.364	4	.121	-1	-10	-11	2	-1.0
Total	5	43	79	.352	160	124	92	17	4	1086	1010	15	305	376	11.0	2.85	94	.254	.310	48	.137	-6	-14	-20	4	-2.5

● HI BELL Bell, Herman S b: 7/16/1897, Mt.Sherman, Ky. d: 6/7/49, Glendale, Cal. BR/TR, 6′, 185 lbs. Deb: 4/16/24

YEAR	TM/L	W	L	PCT	G	GS	CG	SH	SV	IP	H	HR	BB	SO	RAT	ERA	ERA+	OAV	OOB	BH	AVG	PB	PR	/A	PD	TPI
1924	StL-N	3	8	.273	28	10	5	0	1	113^{1}	124	5	29	29	12.5	4.92	77	.292	.344	2	.065	-2	-13	-14	0	-1.5
1926	*StL-N	6	6	.500	27	8	3	0	2	85	82	1	17	27	10.7	3.18	123	.255	.296	3	.120	-1	6	7	-1	0.6
1927	StL-N	1	3	.250	25	1	0	0	0	57^{1}	71	5	22	31	14.8	3.92	101	.317	.381	1	.091	-1	-0	0	0	-0.1
1929	StL-N	0	2	.000	7	0	0	0	0	13	19	1	4	4	15.9	6.92	67	.339	.383	0	.000	-0	-3	-3	-0	-0.5
1930	*StL-N	4	3	.571	39	9	2	0	**8**	115^{1}	143	4	23	42	13.1	3.90	129	.299	.334	2	.077	-3	**14**	**14**	1	0.7
1932	NY-N	8	4	.667	35	10	3	0	2	120	132	12	16	25	11.3	3.68	101	.280	.307	3	.088	-2	3	0	-1	-0.3
1933	*NY-N	6	5	.545	38	7	1	1	5	105^{1}	100	4	20	24	10.4	2.05	157	.246	.285	4	.138	-1	**15**	**14**	-1	1.3
1934	NY-N	4	3	.571	22	2	0	0	6	54	72	2	12	9	14.3	3.67	105	.319	.358	2	.105	-1	2	1	-1	0.0
Total	8	32	34	.485	221	47	14	1	24	663^{1}	743	34	143	191	12.2	3.69	107	.285	.326	17	.096	-12	23	19	-4	0.2

● JERRY BELL Bell, Jerry Houston b: 10/6/47, Madison, Tenn. BB/TR, 6′4″, 190 lbs. Deb: 9/6/71

YEAR	TM/L	W	L	PCT	G	GS	CG	SH	SV	IP	H	HR	BB	SO	RAT	ERA	ERA+	OAV	OOB	BH	AVG	PB	PR	/A	PD	TPI
1971	Mil-A	2	1	.667	8	0	0	0	0	14^{2}	10	0	6	8	9.8	3.07	113	.200	.286	0	—	0	1	1	-0	0.1
1972	Mil-A	5	1	.833	25	3	0	0	0	70^{2}	50	1	33	20	11.0	1.66	183	.209	.313	1	.071	-1	11	11	1	0.9
1973	Mil-A	9	9	.500	31	25	8	0	1	183^{2}	185	14	70	57	12.7	3.97	95	.263	.334	0	—	0	-3	-4	1	-0.1
1974	Mil-A	1	0	1.000	5	0	0	0	0	14	17	2	5	4	14.1	2.57	141	.315	.373	0	—	0	2	2	-0	0.1
Total	4	17	11	.607	69	28	8	0	1	283	262	17	114	89	12.2	3.28	109	.250	.329	1	.071	-1	10	9	1	1.0

● RALPH BELL Bell, Ralph Albert "Lefty" b: 11/6/1890, Kahoka, Mo. d: 10/18/59, Burlington, Iowa BL/TL, 5′11.5″, 170 lbs. Deb: 7/16/12

YEAR	TM/L	W	L	PCT	G	GS	CG	SH	SV	IP	H	HR	BB	SO	RAT	ERA	ERA+	OAV	OOB	BH	AVG	PB	PR	/A	PD	TPI
1912	Chi-A	0	0	—	3	0	0	0	0	6	8	1	8	5	24.0	9.00	36	.333	.500	0	.000	-0	-4	-4	0	0.0

● BILL BELL Bell, William Samuel "Ding Dong" b: 10/24/33, Goldsboro, N.C. d: 10/11/62, Durham, N.C. BR/TR, 6′3″, 200 lbs. Deb: 9/5/52

YEAR	TM/L	W	L	PCT	G	GS	CG	SH	SV	IP	H	HR	BB	SO	RAT	ERA	ERA+	OAV	OOB	BH	AVG	PB	PR	/A	PD	TPI
1952	Pit-N	0	1	.000	4	1	0	0	0	15^{2}	16	3	13	4	16.7	4.60	87	.254	.382	0	.000	-0	-2	-1	0	-0.1
1955	Pit-N	0	0	—	1	0	0	0	0	1	0	0	1	0	9.0	0.00	—	.000	.250	0	—	0	0	0	-0	0.0
Total	2	0	1	.000	5	1	0	0	0	16^{2}	16	3	14	4	16.2	4.32	93	.242	.375	0	.000	-0	-1	-1	0	-0.1

● RIGO BELTRAN Beltran, Rigoberto b: 11/13/69, Tijuana, Mex. BL/TL, 5′11″, 185 lbs. Deb: 6/2/97

YEAR	TM/L	W	L	PCT	G	GS	CG	SH	SV	IP	H	HR	BB	SO	RAT	ERA	ERA+	OAV	OOB	BH	AVG	PB	PR	/A	PD	TPI
1997	StL-N	1	2	.333	35	4	0	0	1	54^{1}	47	3	17	50	10.6	3.48	119	.237	.298	1	.143	0	4	4	1	0.3
1998	NY-N	0	0	—	7	0	0	0	0	8	6	1	4	5	11.3	3.38	123	.214	.313	0	.000	-0	1	1	-0	0.0
Total	2	1	2	.333	42	4	0	0	1	62^{1}	53	4	21	55	10.7	3.47	120	.235	.300	1	.125	0	5	5	1	0.3

● CHIEF BENDER Bender, Charles Albert b: 5/5/1884, Crow Wing Co., Minn d: 5/22/54, Philadelphia, Pa. BR/TR, 6′2″, 185 lbs. Deb: 4/20/03 CH

YEAR	TM/L	W	L	PCT	G	GS	CG	SH	SV	IP	H	HR	BB	SO	RAT	ERA	ERA+	OAV	OOB	BH	AVG	PB	PR	/A	PD	TPI
1903	Phi-A	17	14	.548	36	33	29	2	0	270	239	6	65	127	11.0	3.07	100	.237	.299	22	.183	-1	-3	-0	-1	-0.2
1904	Phi-A	10	11	.476	29	20	18	4	0	203^{2}	167	1	59	149	10.2	2.87	93	.225	.285	18	.228	3	-6	-4	-2	-0.4
1905	*Phi-A	18	11	.621	35	23	18	4	0	229	193	5	90	142	11.6	2.83	94	.230	.313	20	.217	2	-4	-4	3	-0.1
1906	Phi-A	15	10	.600	36	27	24	0	**3**	238^{1}	208	5	48	159	10.0	2.53	108	.238	.284	25	.253	7	4	5	-1	1.3
1907	Phi-A	16	8	.667	33	24	20	4	3	219^{1}	185	1	34	112	9.1	2.05	127	.231	.265	23	.230	3	12	13	-2	1.7
1908	Phi-A	8	9	.471	18	17	14	2	1	138^{2}	121	1	21	85	9.4	1.75	146	.236	.270	11	.220	2	10	12	-2	1.8
1909	Phi-A	18	8	.692	34	29	24	5	1	250	196	1	45	161	8.9	1.66	145	.214	.254	20	.215	4	23	21	2	2.9
1910	*Phi-A	23	5	**.821**	30	28	25	3	0	250	182	1	47	155	8.6	1.58	150	.207	.255	25	.269	8	26	22	2	3.8
1911	*Phi-A	17	5	**.773**	31	24	16	2	3	216^{1}	198	2	58	114	10.8	2.16	146	.252	.307	13	.165	-3	28	24	1	2.0
1912	Phi-A	13	8	.619	27	19	12	1	2	171	169	1	33	90	10.7	2.74	113	.277	.315	9	.150	-1	11	7	-2	0.4
1913	*Phi-A	21	10	.677	48	21	14	2	**13**	236^{2}	208	2	59	135	10.3	2.21	125	.228	.277	12	.154	0	19	15	-2	1.9
1914	*Phi-A	17	3	**.850**	28	23	14	7	2	179	159	4	55	107	10.8	2.26	115	.240	.299	9	.145	0	10	7	-0	0.8
1915	Bal-F	4	16	.200	26	23	15	0	1	178^{1}	198	5	37	89	12.2	3.99	72	.298	.342	16	.267	3	-25	-22	-1	-2.1
1916	Phi-N	7	7	.500	27	13	4	0	3	122^{2}	137	3	34	43	13.3	3.74	71	.287	.347	12	.279	4	-15	-15	2	-1.3
1917	Phi-N	8	2	.800	20	10	8	4	2	113	84	1	26	43	9.3	1.67	168	.215	.277	8	.205	1	13	14	-2	1.3
1925	Chi-A	0	0	—	1	0	0	0	0	1	1	1	1	0	18.0	18.00	23	.333	.500	0	—	0	-2	-2	-0	0.0
Total	16	212	127	.625	459	334	255	40	34	3017	2645	40	712	1711	10.3	2.46	111	.239	.291	243	.212	33	101	94	-5	13.8

● ALAN BENES Benes, Alan Paul b: 1/21/72, Evansville, Ind. BR/TR, 6′5″, 215 lbs. Deb: 9/19/95 F

YEAR	TM/L	W	L	PCT	G	GS	CG	SH	SV	IP	H	HR	BB	SO	RAT	ERA	ERA+	OAV	OOB	BH	AVG	PB	PR	/A	PD	TPI
1995	StL-N	1	2	.333	3	3	0	0	0	16	24	2	4	20	16.3	8.44	50	.343	.387	0	.000	-1	-8	-8	-0	-1.1
1996	*StL-N	13	10	.565	34	32	3	1	0	191	192	27	87	131	13.5	4.90	85	.266	.350	9	.148	-0	-15	-15	-2	-1.8
1997	StL-N	9	9	.500	23	23	2	0	0	161^{2}	128	13	68	160	11.1	2.89	143	.219	.304	9	.173	0	23	22	-1	2.3
Total	3	23	21	.523	60	58	5	1	0	368^{2}	344	42	159	311	12.6	4.17	100	.250	.333	18	.151	-0	1	-0	-3	-0.6

● ANDY BENES Benes, Andrew Charles b: 8/20/67, Evansville, Ind. BR/TR, 6′6″, 240 lbs. Deb: 8/11/89 F

YEAR	TM/L	W	L	PCT	G	GS	CG	SH	SV	IP	H	HR	BB	SO	RAT	ERA	ERA+	OAV	OOB	BH	AVG	PB	PR	/A	PD	TPI
1989	SD-N	6	3	.667	10	10	0	0	0	66^{2}	51	7	31	66	11.2	3.51	100	.213	.305	6	.250	2	-0	-0	0	0.2
1990	SD-N	10	11	.476	32	31	2	0	0	192^{1}	177	18	69	140	11.6	3.60	106	.242	.309	6	.100	-2	4	5	-3	0.0
1991	SD-N	15	11	.577	33	33	4	1	0	223	194	23	59	167	10.4	3.03	125	.232	.286	2	.032	-2	16	19	-1	1.9
1992	SD-N	13	14	.481	34	34	2	2	0	231^{1}	230	14	61	169	11.5	3.35	107	.264	.316	10	.149	2	4	6	0	0.9
1993	SD-N★	15	15	.500	34	34	4	2	0	230^{2}	200	23	86	179	11.3	3.78	109	.232	.305	9	.125	-0	7	9	-3	0.7
1994	SD-N	6	14	.300	25	25	2	2	0	172^{1}	155	20	51	**189**	10.8	3.86	106	.237	.294	8	.163	-0	7	5	1	0.6
1995	SD-N	4	7	.364	19	19	1	1	0	118^{2}	121	10	45	126	12.9	4.17	97	.262	.333	6	.150	-0	0	-2	-1	-0.3
	*Sea-A	7	2	.778	12	12	0	0	0	63	72	8	33	45	15.3	5.86	81	.287	.374	0	—	0	-8	-8	-0	-1.0
1996	*StL-N	18	10	.643	36	34	3	1	1	230^{1}	215	28	77	160	11.6	3.83	109	.247	.312	11	.151	-0	10	9	-3	0.7
1997	StL-N	10	7	.588	26	26	0	0	0	177	149	9	61	175	10.9	3.10	134	.230	.301	12	.218	2	22	21	-2	1.9
1998	Ari-N	14	13	.519	34	34	1	0	0	231^{1}	221	25	74	164	11.7	3.97	109	.251	.314	11	.169	3	7	9	-1	1.2
Total	10	118	107	.524	295	292	19	9	1	1936^{2}	1785	185	647	1580	11.5	3.68	109	.244	.309	81	.143	4	68	72	-12	6.8

● RAY BENGE Benge, Raymond Adelphia b: 4/22/02, Jacksonville, Tex. d: 6/27/97, Centerville, Tex. BR/TR, 5′9.5″, 160 lbs. Deb: 9/26/25

YEAR	TM/L	W	L	PCT	G	GS	CG	SH	SV	IP	H	HR	BB	SO	RAT	ERA	ERA+	OAV	OOB	BH	AVG	PB	PR	/A	PD	TPI
1925	Cle-A	1	0	1.000	2	2	1	1	0	11^{2}	9	0	3	3	9.3	1.54	286	.205	.255	2	.400	0	4	4	-1	0.3
1926	Cle-A	1	0	1.000	8	0	0	0	0	11^{2}	15	0	4	3	14.7	3.86	105	.313	.365	1	.333	0	0	0	0	0.1
1928	Phi-N	8	18	.308	40	28	12	1	1	201^{2}	219	15	88	68	13.9	4.55	94	.286	.363	12	.207	-0	-13	-6	-2	-0.8
1929	Phi-N	11	15	.423	38	27	9	2	4	199	255	24	77	78	15.2	6.29	83	.322	.385	15	.203	-3	-35	-24	-3	-3.0
1930	Phi-N	11	15	.423	38	29	14	0	1	225^{2}	305	22	81	70	15.4	5.70	96	.328	.382	18	.205	-3	-18	-6	-1	-0.9
1931	Phi-N	14	18	.438	38	31	16	2	2	247	251	12	61	117	11.6	3.17	134	.262	.310	18	.205	-2	19	30	-2	3.3
1932	Phi-N	13	12	.520	41	28	13	2	6	222^{1}	247	15	58	89	12.5	4.05	109	.281	.329	13	.173	-3	-4	9	-1	0.6
1933	Bro-N	10	17	.370	37	30	16	2	1	228^{2}	238	11	55	74	11.8	3.42	94	.268	.315	14	.184	0	-2	-5	-3	-0.9
1934	Bro-N	14	12	.538	36	32	14	1	0	227	252	11	61	64	12.5	4.32	90	.272	.319	15	.169	-2	-7	-11	-1	-1.3
1935	Bro-N	9	9	.500	23	17	5	1	1	124^{2}	142	12	47	39	13.7	4.48	89	.289	.353	9	.191	-1	-6	-7	-2	-1.1
1936	Bos-N	7	9	.438	21	19	2	0	0	115	161	6	38	32	15.7	5.79	66	.333	.382	6	.140	-3	-23	-25	-2	-3.2
	Phi-N	1	4	.200	15	6	0	0	1	45^{2}	70	3	19	13	17.5	4.73	96	.350	.406	0	.000	-1	-4	-1	-2	-0.4
	Yr	8	13	.381	36	25	2	0	1	160^{2}	231	9	57	45	16.1	5.49	73	.337	.388	6	.113	-4	-26	-26	-4	-3.6
1938	Cin-N	1	1	.500	9	0	0	0	2	15^{1}	13	1	6	5	11.2	4.11	89	.228	.302	1	.333	0	-1	-1	-0	-0.1
Total	12	101	130	.437	346	249	102	12	19	1875^{1}	2177	132	598	655	13.5	4.52	95	.292	.347	124	.188	-17	-89	-46	-18	-7.4

● ARMANDO BENITEZ Benitez, Armando German b: 11/3/72, Ramon Santana, D.R. BR/TR, 6′4″, 180 lbs. Deb: 7/28/94

YEAR	TM/L	W	L	PCT	G	GS	CG	SH	SV	IP	H	HR	BB	SO	RAT	ERA	ERA+	OAV	OOB	BH	AVG	PB	PR	/A	PD	TPI
1994	Bal-A	0	0	—	3	0	0	0	0	10	8	0	4	14	11.7	0.90	556	.216	.310	0	—	0	4	5	0	-0.1
1995	Bal-A	1	5	.167	44	0	0	0	2	47^{2}	37	8	37	56	14.9	5.66	84	.213	.366	0	—	0	-5	-5	-1	-0.7
1996	*Bal-A	1	0	1.000	18	0	0	0	4	14^{1}	7	2	6	20	8.2	3.77	131	.143	.236	0	—	0	2	2	-0	0.2

YEAR TM/L	W	L	PCT	G	GS	CG	SH	SV	IP	H	HR	BB	SO	RAT	ERA	ERA+	OAV	OOB	BH	AVG	PB	PR	/A	PD	TPI
1997 *Bal-A	4	5	.444	71	0	0	0	9	73^1	49	7	43	106	11.4	2.45	179	.191	.309	0	—	0	17	16	-1	2.0
1998 Bal-A	5	6	.455	71	0	0	0	22	68^1	48	10	39	87	12.0	3.82	118	.199	.320	0	—	0	6	5	-0	1.0
Total 5	11	16	.407	207	0	0	0	37	213^2	149	27	129	283	12.2	3.62	126	.197	.322	0	—	0	25	23	-3	2.4

● MIKE BENJAMIN Benjamin, Michael Paul b: 11/22/65, Euclid, Ohio BR/TR, 6', 169 lbs. Deb: 7/7/89 ♦

YEAR TM/L	W	L	PCT	G	GS	CG	SH	SV	IP	H	HR	BB	SO	RAT	ERA	ERA+	OAV	OOB	BH	AVG	PB	PR	/A	PD	TPI
1997 Bos-A	0	0	—	1	0	0	0	0	1	0	0	0	0	0.0	0.00	—	.000	.000	27	.233	0	1	1	0	0.0

● HENRY BENN Benn, Henry Omer b: 1/25/1890, Viola, Wis. d: 6/4/67, Madison, Wis. BR/TR, 6', 190 lbs. Deb: 9/24/14

YEAR TM/L	W	L	PCT	G	GS	CG	SH	SV	IP	H	HR	BB	SO	RAT	ERA	ERA+	OAV	OOB	BH	AVG	PB	PR	/A	PD	TPI
1914 Cle-A	0	0	—	1	0	0	0	0	1	0	0	0	1	0.0	0.00	—	.000	.000	0	—	0	0	0	-0	0.0

● DAVE BENNETT Bennett, David Hans b: 11/7/45, Berkeley, Cal. BR/TR, 6'5", 195 lbs. Deb: 6/12/64 F

YEAR TM/L	W	L	PCT	G	GS	CG	SH	SV	IP	H	HR	BB	SO	RAT	ERA	ERA+	OAV	OOB	BH	AVG	PB	PR	/A	PD	TPI
1964 Phi-N	0	0	—	1	0	0	0	0	1	2	0	0	1	18.0	9.00	39	.400	.400	0	—	0	-1	-1	0	0.0

● DENNIS BENNETT Bennett, Dennis John b: 10/5/39, Oakland, Cal. BL/TL, 6'5", 205 lbs. Deb: 5/12/62 F

YEAR TM/L	W	L	PCT	G	GS	CG	SH	SV	IP	H	HR	BB	SO	RAT	ERA	ERA+	OAV	OOB	BH	AVG	PB	PR	/A	PD	TPI
1962 Phi-N	9	9	.500	31	24	7	2	3	174^2	144	17	68	149	11.2	3.81	102	.224	.304	8	.127	-1	3	1	-1	0.0
1963 Phi-N	9	5	.643	23	16	6	1	1	119^1	102	12	33	82	10.5	2.64	122	.231	.290	9	.225	3	9	8	0	1.3
1964 Phi-N	12	14	.462	41	32	7	2	1	208	222	23	58	125	12.3	3.68	94	.280	.333	13	.197	3	-3	-5	-1	-0.3
1965 Bos-A	5	7	.417	34	18	3	0	0	141^2	152	15	53	85	13.4	4.38	85	.279	.350	7	.179	2	-15	-10	-1	-0.7
1966 Bos-A	3	3	.500	16	13	0	0	0	75	75	9	23	47	11.9	3.24	117	.261	.318	3	.130	1	2	5	-1	0.3
1967 Bos-A	4	3	.571	13	11	4	1	0	69^2	72	12	22	34	12.4	3.88	90	.268	.328	3	.120	-0	-5	-3	-0	-0.4
NY-N	1	1	.500	8	6	0	0	0	26^1	37	4	7	14	15.4	5.13	66	.336	.381	2	.250	0	-5	-5	0	-0.3
1968 Cal-A	0	5	.000	16	7	1	0	1	48^1	46	6	17	36	12.5	3.54	82	.250	.327	1	.077	-1	-3	-3	1	-0.4
Total 7	43	47	.478	182	127	28	6	6	863	850	98	281	572	12.1	3.69	96	.260	.324	46	.166	7	-18	-13	-2	-0.5

● ERIK BENNETT Bennett, Erik Hans b: 9/13/68, Yreka, Cal. BR/TR, 6'2", 205 lbs. Deb: 5/15/95

YEAR TM/L	W	L	PCT	G	GS	CG	SH	SV	IP	H	HR	BB	SO	RAT	ERA	ERA+	OAV	OOB	BH	AVG	PB	PR	/A	PD	TPI
1995 Cal-A	0	0	—	1	0	0	0	0	0^1	0	0	0	0	0.0	0.00	—	.000	.000	0	—	0	0	0	0	0.0
1996 Min-A	2	0	1.000	24	0	0	0	1	27^1	33	7	16	13	16.8	7.90	65	.306	.405	0	—	0	-9	-8	0	-0.5
Total 2	2	0	1.000	25	0	0	0	1	27^2	33	7	16	13	16.6	7.81	65	.303	.402	0	—	0	-9	-8	0	-0.5

● FRANK BENNETT Bennett, Francis Allen "Chip" b: 10/27/04, Mardela Springs, Md. d: 3/18/66, Wilmington, Del. BR/TR, 5'10.5", 163 lbs. Deb: 9/17/27

YEAR TM/L	W	L	PCT	G	GS	CG	SH	SV	IP	H	HR	BB	SO	RAT	ERA	ERA+	OAV	OOB	BH	AVG	PB	PR	/A	PD	TPI
1927 Bos-A	0	1	.000	4	1	0	0	0	12^1	15	0	6	1	15.3	2.92	145	.333	.412	0	.000	-1	2	2	0	0.1
1928 Bos-A	0	0	—	1	0	0	0	0	1	1	0	0	0	9.0	0.00	—	.250	.250	0	—	0	0	0	0	0.0
Total 2	0	1	.000	5	1	0	0	0	13^1	16	0	6	1	14.9	2.70	156	.327	.400	0	.000	-1	2	2	0	0.1

● JOEL BENNETT Bennett, Joel Todd b: 1/31/70, Binghamton, N.Y. BR/TR, 6'1", 160 lbs. Deb: 7/15/98

YEAR TM/L	W	L	PCT	G	GS	CG	SH	SV	IP	H	HR	BB	SO	RAT	ERA	ERA+	OAV	OOB	BH	AVG	PB	PR	/A	PD	TPI
1998 Bal-A	0	0	—	2	0	0	0	0	2	2	0	3	0	22.5	4.50	100	.250	.455	0	—	0	0	0	-0	0.1

● SHAYNE BENNETT Bennett, Shayne Anthony b: 4/10/72, Adelaide, South Australia BR/TR, 6'5", 200 lbs. Deb: 8/22/97

YEAR TM/L	W	L	PCT	G	GS	CG	SH	SV	IP	H	HR	BB	SO	RAT	ERA	ERA+	OAV	OOB	BH	AVG	PB	PR	/A	PD	TPI
1997 Mon-N	0	1	.000	16	0	0	0	0	22^2	21	2	9	8	11.9	3.18	132	.247	.319	0	.000	0	3	3	-1	0.1
1998 Mon-N	5	5	.500	62	0	0	0	1	91^2	97	8	45	59	14.5	5.50	75	.276	.368	0	.000	-0	-13	-14	0	-1.4
Total 2	5	6	.455	78	0	0	0	1	114^1	118	10	54	67	14.0	5.04	82	.271	.359	0	.000	-0	-10	-12	-1	-1.3

● ALLEN BENSON Benson, Allen Wilbert "Bullet Ben" b: 7/12/08, Hurley, S.Dak. BR/TR, 6'1", 185 lbs. Deb: 8/19/34

YEAR TM/L	W	L	PCT	G	GS	CG	SH	SV	IP	H	HR	BB	SO	RAT	ERA	ERA+	OAV	OOB	BH	AVG	PB	PR	/A	PD	TPI
1934 Was-A	0	1	.000	2	2	0	0	0	9^2	19	0	5	4	24.2	12.10	36	.413	.491	0	.000	-0	-8	-8	-0	-0.7

● CY BENTLEY Bentley, Clytus G. b: 11/23/1850, East Haven, Conn. d: 2/26/1873, Middletown, Conn. Deb: 4/26/1872

YEAR TM/L	W	L	PCT	G	GS	CG	SH	SV	IP	H	HR	BB	SO	RAT	ERA	ERA+	OAV	OOB	BH	AVG	PB	PR	/A	PD	TPI
1872 Man-n	2	15	.118	18	17	15	0	0	149	272	4	12	5	17.2	6.10	59	.338	.348	27	.235	-2	-41	-42		-2.7

● JACK BENTLEY Bentley, John Needles b: 3/8/1895, Sandy Spring, Md. d: 10/24/69, Olney, Md. BL/TL, 5'11.5", 200 lbs. Deb: 9/6/13 ♦

YEAR TM/L	W	L	PCT	G	GS	CG	SH	SV	IP	H	HR	BB	SO	RAT	ERA	ERA+	OAV	OOB	BH	AVG	PB	PR	/A	PD	TPI
1913 Was-A	1	0	1.000	3	1	0	0	1	11	5	0	2	5	5.7	0.00	—	.147	.194	0	.000	-0	4	4	0	0.4
1914 Was-A	5	7	.417	30	11	3	2	**4**	125^1	110	3	53	55	11.9	2.37	119	.249	.334	11	.275	2	5	6	-1	0.8
1915 Was-A	0	2	.000	4	2	0	0	0	11^1	8	0	3	0	8.7	0.79	374	.200	.256	0	.000	-0	3	3	-0	0.4
1916 Was-A	0	0	—	2	0	0	0	0	1^1	0	0	1	1	6.8	0.00	—	.000	.250	0	—	0	0	0	-0	0.0
1923 *NY-N	13	8	.619	31	26	12	1	3	183	198	10	67	80	13.3	4.48	85	.277	.343	38	.427	16	-10	-13	-1	0.0
1924 *NY-N	16	5	.762	28	24	13	1	1	188	196	11	56	60	12.3	3.78	97	.273	.329	26	.265	4	2	-2	-1	0.0
1925 NY-N	11	9	.550	28	22	11	0	0	157	200	10	59	47	14.9	5.04	80	.323	.383	30	.303	6	-14	-18	-1	-0.9
1926 Phi-N	0	2	.000	7	3	0	0	0	25^1	37	2	10	7	16.7	8.17	51	.327	.382	62	.258	1	-12	-11	-0	-0.7
NY-N	0	0	—	1	0	0	0	0	2	0	0	2	1	9.0	0.00	—	.000	.250	1	.250	-0	1	1	-0	0.0
Yr	0	2	.000	8	3	0	0	0	27^1	37	2	12	8	16.1	7.57	54	.311	.374	63	.258	1	-11	-11	-0	-0.7
1927 NY-N	0	0	—	4	0	0	0	0	9^2	7	1	10	3	16.8	2.79	138	.206	.400	2	.222	1	1	1	-0	0.1
Total 9	46	33	.582	138	89	39	4	9	714	761	37	263	259	13.1	4.01	91	.280	.346	170	.291	28	-20	-28	-3	0.1

● AL BENTON Benton, John Alton b: 3/18/11, Noble, Okla. d: 4/14/68, Lynwood, Cal. BR/TR, 6'4", 215 lbs. Deb: 4/18/34

YEAR TM/L	W	L	PCT	G	GS	CG	SH	SV	IP	H	HR	BB	SO	RAT	ERA	ERA+	OAV	OOB	BH	AVG	PB	PR	/A	PD	TPI
1934 Phi-A	7	9	.438	32	21	7	0	1	155	145	7	88	58	13.6	4.88	90	.249	.349	6	.109	-4	-7	-9	0	-1.1
1935 Phi-A	3	4	.429	27	9	0	0	0	78^1	110	7	47	42	18.2	7.70	59	.328	.413	1	.040	-3	-28	-27	-1	-2.3
1938 Det-A	5	3	.625	19	10	6	0	0	95^1	93	10	39	33	12.6	3.30	151	.259	.333	4	.121	-3	16	18	1	1.1
1939 Det-A	6	8	.429	37	16	3	0	5	150	182	11	58	67	14.5	4.56	107	.294	.355	4	.091	-4	1	5	0	0.1
1940 Det-A	6	10	.375	42	0	0	0	**17**	79^1	93	5	36	50	14.6	4.42	107	.294	.366	0	.000	-3	-0	3	-0	0.4
1941 Det-A☆	15	6	.714	38	14	7	1	7	157^2	130	11	65	63	11.3	2.97	153	**.221**	.302	3	.060	-5	21	28	-0	3.1
1942 Det-A★	7	13	.350	35	30	9	1	2	226^2	210	9	84	110	11.7	2.90	136	.246	.314	5	.075	-5	19	26	-1	1.6
1945 *Det-A	13	8	.619	31	27	12	5	3	191^2	175	7	63	76	11.3	2.02	174	.241	.303	4	.063	-6	29	32	2	3.2
1946 Det-A	11	7	.611	28	15	6	1	1	140^2	132	9	58	60	12.2	3.65	100	.245	.319	9	.184	-1	-2	0	1	0.0
1947 Det-A	6	7	.462	36	14	4	0	7	133	147	11	61	33	14.1	4.40	86	.288	.365	6	.154	-2	-10	-9	-0	-1.1
1948 Det-A	2	2	.500	30	0	0	0	3	44^1	45	4	36	18	16.6	5.68	77	.273	.406	2	.182	-0	-7	-6	0	-0.6
1949 Cle-A	9	6	.600	40	11	4	2	10	135^2	116	7	51	41	11.1	2.12	188	.238	.312	5	.132	-2	31	28	-2	2.9
1950 Cle-A	4	2	.667	36	0	0	0	4	63	57	7	30	26	12.6	3.57	121	.243	.331	1	.083	-1	7	5	-1	0.4
1952 Bos-A	4	3	.571	24	0	0	0	6	37^2	37	1	17	20	12.9	2.39	165	.268	.348	0	.000	-1	5	6	-0	1.2
Total 14	98	88	.527	455	167	58	10	66	1688^1	1672	106	733	697	12.9	3.66	115	.259	.336	50	.098	-39	74	102	-1	8.9

● RUBE BENTON Benton, John Clebon b: 6/27/1887, Clinton, N.C. d: 12/12/37, Dothan, Ala. BL/TL, 6'1", 190 lbs. Deb: 6/28/10

YEAR TM/L	W	L	PCT	G	GS	CG	SH	SV	IP	H	HR	BB	SO	RAT	ERA	ERA+	OAV	OOB	BH	AVG	PB	PR	/A	PD	TPI
1910 Cin-N	0	1	.000	12	2	0	0	0	38	44	1	23	15	16.1	4.74	62	.282	.378	1	.091	-1	-7	-8	1	-0.2
1911 Cin-N	3	3	.500	6	6	5	0	0	44^2	44	0	23	28	14.1	2.01	164	.270	.370	2	.143	-0	7	6	-1	0.7
1912 Cin-N	18	20	.474	**50**	39	22	2	2	302	316	2	118	162	13.5	3.10	108	.278	.356	14	.135	-6	10	9	2	0.5
1913 Cin-N	11	7	.611	23	22	9	1	0	144^1	140	4	60	68	13.0	3.49	93	.265	.350	10	.208	1	-5	-4	-1	-0.4
1914 Cin-N	16	18	.471	41	35	16	4	2	271	223	3	95	121	10.9	2.96	99	.228	.303	13	.143	-3	-5	-1	0	-0.4
1915 Cin-N	6	13	.316	35	21	6	2	4	176^1	165	2	67	83	12.6	3.32	86	.257	.340	11	.208	-0	-11	-9	2	-0.8
NY-N	3	5	.375	10	6	3	0	1	60^2	57	0	9	26	10.5	2.82	91	.253	.297	5	.217	1	-0	-2	-0	-0.1
Yr	9	18	.333	45	27	9	2	5	237	222	2	76	109	11.5	3.19	87	.252	.315	16	.211	1	-12	-11	2	-0.9
1916 NY-N	16	8	.667	38	29	15	3	2	238^2	210	5	58	115	10.5	2.87	85	.241	.296	7	.090	-4	-7	-11	-1	-1.8
1917 *NY-N	15	9	.625	35	25	14	3	3	215	190	5	41	70	10.0	2.72	94	.238	.281	12	.167	-1	-0	-4	-2	-0.8
1918 NY-N	1	2	.333	3	3	2	0	0	24	17	0	3	9	7.5	1.88	140	.202	.230	1	.143	1	2	2	0	0.4
1919 NY-N	17	11	.607	35	28	11	1	2	209	181	5	52	53	10.2	2.63	107	.237	.289	13	.194	-1	7	4	-1	0.4
1920 NY-N	9	16	.360	33	25	12	4	2	193^1	222	8	31	52	11.9	3.03	99	.291	.321	6	.092	-7	2	-1	4	-0.3
1921 NY-N	5	2	.714	18	9	3	1	0	72	72	2	17	11	11.1	2.88	128	.266	.309	3	.143	-1	7	6	-1	0.4
1923 Cin-N	14	10	.583	33	26	15	0	1	219	243	10	57	59	12.5	3.66	106	.284	.333	23	.287	4	8	5	1	0.9
1924 Cin-N	7	9	.438	32	19	6	1	1	162^2	166	2	24	42	10.7	2.77	136	.266	.297	12	.261	2	20	18	1	2.0
1925 Cin-N	9	10	.474	33	16	6	1	1	146^2	182	3	34	36	13.3	4.05	102	.301	.340	9	.200	1	4	1	-1	0.1
Total 15	150	144	.510	437	311	145	23	21	2517^1	2472	52	712	950	11.7	3.09	102	.261	.319	142	.172	-14	33	13	4	0.6

● LARRY BENTON Benton, Lawrence James b: 11/20/1897, St.Louis, Mo. d: 4/3/53, Amberley, Ohio BR/TR, 5'11", 165 lbs. Deb: 4/25/23

YEAR TM/L	W	L	PCT	G	GS	CG	SH	SV	IP	H	HR	BB	SO	RAT	ERA	ERA+	OAV	OOB	BH	AVG	PB	PR	/A	PD	TPI
1923 Bos-N	5	9	.357	35	9	1	0	0	128	141	4	57	42	14.2	4.99	80	.293	.373	5	.161	-1	-14	-14	1	-1.3
1924 Bos-N	5	7	.417	30	13	4	0	1	128	129	4	64	41	13.8	4.15	92	.274	.365	3	.091	-3	-4	-5	-0	-0.7

YEAR	TM/L	W	L	PCT	G	GS	CG	SH	SV	IP	H	HR	BB	SO	RAT	ERA	ERA+	OAV	OOB	BH	AVG	PB	PR	/A	PD	TPI
1925	Bos-N	14	7	.667	31	21	16	2	1	183^1	170	6	70	49	11.9	3.09	130	.249	.320	14	.241	2	24	19	-1	2.0
1926	Bos-N	14	14	.500	43	27	12	1	1	231^2	244	10	81	103	12.9	3.85	92	.280	.346	12	.154	-4	-1	-8	-3	-1.4
1927	Bos-N	4	2	.667	11	10	3	0	0	60^1	72	3	27	25	15.1	4.48	83	.310	.387	4	.222	1	-4	-5	-1	-0.4
	NY-N	13	5	.722	29	23	8	1	2	173	183	9	54	65	12.4	3.95	98	.275	.331	8	.160	-2	-1	-2	-0	-0.4
	Yr	17	7	**.708**	40	33	11	1	2	233^1	255	12	81	90	13.0	4.09	93	.284	.344	12	.176	-1	-4	-7	-1	-0.8
1928	NY-N	**25**	9	**.735**	42	36	**28**	2	4	310^1	299	14	71	90	10.7	2.73	144	.258	.300	16	.143	-3	44	41	-0	3.9
1929	NY-N	11	17	.393	39	30	14	3	3	237	276	16	61	63	12.8	4.14	111	.297	.340	9	.105	-6	15	12	1	0.7
1930	NY-N	1	3	.250	8	4	1	0	1	30	42	8	14	16	16.8	7.80	61	.323	.389	3	.300	2	-9	-10	-0	-1.0
	Cin-N	7	12	.368	35	22	9	0	1	177^2	246	7	45	47	14.7	5.12	94	.337	.375	11	.177	-2	-3	-6	-3	-0.9
	Yr	8	15	.348	43	26	10	0	2	207^2	288	15	59	63	15.0	5.50	87	.334	.377	14	.194	-0	-12	-16	-3	-1.9
1931	Cin-N	10	15	.400	38	23	12	2	2	204^1	240	6	53	35	12.9	3.35	112	.299	.343	11	.167	-1	12	9	1	1.0
1932	Cin-N	6	13	.316	35	21	7	0	2	179^2	201	10	27	35	11.4	4.31	90	.285	.311	11	.204	0	-9	-9	-1	-0.9
1933	Cin-N	10	11	.476	34	19	7	2	2	152^2	160	5	36	33	11.7	3.71	91	.271	.316	9	.170	-1	-6	-5	-2	-1.0
1934	Cin-N	0	1	.000	16	1	0	0	2	29	53	1	7	5	18.6	6.52	63	.393	.423	2	.286	0	-8	-8	-0	-0.3
1935	Bos-N	2	3	.400	29	0	0	0	0	72	103	6	24	21	16.0	6.88	55	.338	.388	4	.200	0	-23	-25	-1	-1.5
Total	13	127	128	.498	455	259	122	13	22	2297	2559	109	691	670	12.8	4.03	98	.288	.341	122	.165	-17	14	-16	-8	-2.2

● SID BENTON Benton, Sidney Wright b: 8/4/1895, Buckner, Ark. d: 3/8/77, Fayetteville, Ark. BR/TR, 6′1″, 170 lbs. Deb: 4/18/22

YEAR	TM/L	W	L	PCT	G	GS	CG	SH	SV	IP	H	HR	BB	SO	RAT	ERA	ERA+	OAV	OOB	BH	AVG	PB	PR	/A	PD	TPI
1922	StL-N	0	0	—	1	0	0	0	0	0	0	0	2	0	—	—	—	—	1.000	0	—	0	0	0	0	0.0

● JOE BENZ Benz, Joseph Louis "Blitzen" or "Butcher Boy" b: 1/21/1886, New Alsace, Ind. d: 4/22/57, Chicago, Ill. BR/TR, 6′1.5″, 196 lbs. Deb: 8/16/11

YEAR	TM/L	W	L	PCT	G	GS	CG	SH	SV	IP	H	HR	BB	SO	RAT	ERA	ERA+	OAV	OOB	BH	AVG	PB	PR	/A	PD	TPI
1911	Chi-A	3	2	.600	12	6	1	0	0	55^2	52	0	13	28	10.8	2.26	142	.251	.302	1	.059	-2	7	6	1	0.4
1912	Chi-A	13	17	.433	42	31	12	3	0	238^2	231	5	70	97	11.7	2.90	110	.259	.319	10	.132	-5	11	8	1	0.5
1913	Chi-A	7	10	.412	33	17	6	1	1	151	146	1	59	79	12.3	2.74	107	.254	.325	9	.180	-1	3	3	4	0.7
1914	Chi-A	15	19	.441	48	35	16	4	2	283^1	245	4	66	142	9.9	2.26	119	.236	.282	12	.130	-3	15	14	6	2.0
1915	Chi-A	15	11	.577	39	28	17	2	0	238^1	209	4	43	81	9.6	2.11	141	.238	.276	10	.127	-5	22	23	3	2.2
1916	Chi-A	9	5	.643	28	16	6	4	0	142	108	0	32	57	9.1	2.03	136	.214	.265	3	.065	-4	13	12	1	0.8
1917	Chi-A	7	3	.700	19	13	7	2	0	94^2	76	1	23	25	9.6	2.47	108	.220	.272	5	.167	-1	2	2	0	0.1
1918	Chi-A	8	8	.500	29	17	10	1	0	154	156	1	28	30	10.9	2.63	104	.269	.304	11	.216	-1	3	2	3	0.5
1919	Chi-A	0	0	—	1	0	0	0	0	2	2	0	0	0	9.0	0.00	—	.250	.250	0	—	0	1	1	0	0.0
Total	9	77	75	.507	251	163	75	17	3	1359^2	1225	16	334	539	10.5	2.43	119	.243	.294	61	.138	-21	76	70	19	7.2

● JASON BERE Bere, Jason Phillip b: 5/26/71, Cambridge, Mass. BR/TR, 6′3″, 185 lbs. Deb: 5/27/93

YEAR	TM/L	W	L	PCT	G	GS	CG	SH	SV	IP	H	HR	BB	SO	RAT	ERA	ERA+	OAV	OOB	BH	AVG	PB	PR	/A	PD	TPI
1993	*Chi-A	12	5	.706	24	24	1	0	0	142^2	109	12	81	129	12.3	3.47	120	.210	.323	0	—	0	13	11	-0	1.4
1994	Chi-A★	12	2	**.857**	24	24	0	0	0	141^2	119	17	80	127	12.7	3.81	122	.229	.333	0	—	0	16	13	-1	1.1
1995	Chi-A	8	15	.348	27	27	1	0	0	137^2	151	21	106	110	17.2	7.19	62	.277	.400	0	—	0	-38	-42	1	-5.2
1996	Chi-A	0	1	.000	5	5	0	0	0	16^2	26	3	18	19	23.8	10.26	46	.356	.484	0	—	0	-10	-10	0	-0.4
1997	Chi-A	4	2	.667	6	6	0	0	0	28^2	20	4	17	21	12.6	4.71	93	.198	.331	0	—	0	-0	-1	-0	-0.2
1998	Chi-A	3	7	.300	18	15	0	0	0	83^2	98	14	58	53	17.0	6.45	71	.293	.400	0	—	0	-17	-18	-1	-1.7
	Cin-N	3	2	.600	9	7	0	0	0	43^2	39	3	20	31	12.4	4.12	105	.242	.330	0	.000	-1	1	1	-0	-0.1
Total	6	42	34	.553	113	108	2	0	0	594^2	562	74	380	490	14.5	5.13	87	.250	.362	0	.000	-1	-35	-45	-2	-5.1

● JUAN BERENGUER Berenguer, Juan Bautista b: 11/30/54, Aguadulce, Pan. BR/TR, 5′11″, 215 lbs. Deb: 8/17/78

YEAR	TM/L	W	L	PCT	G	GS	CG	SH	SV	IP	H	HR	BB	SO	RAT	ERA	ERA+	OAV	OOB	BH	AVG	PB	PR	/A	PD	TPI
1978	NY-N	0	2	.000	5	3	0	0	0	13	17	1	11	8	20.1	8.31	42	.327	.453	0	.000	-0	-7	-7	-0	-1.0
1979	NY-N	1	1	.500	5	5	0	0	0	30^2	28	2	12	25	12.0	2.93	124	.252	.331	1	.143	0	3	2	-1	0.1
1980	NY-N	0	1	.000	6	0	0	0	0	9^1	9	1	10	7	18.3	5.79	61	.250	.413	0	—	0	-2	-2	0	-0.2
1981	KC-A	0	4	.000	8	3	0	0	0	19^2	22	4	16	20	18.3	8.69	41	.289	.426	0	—	0	-11	-11	-1	-1.9
	Tor-A	2	9	.182	12	11	1	0	0	71	62	7	35	29	12.7	4.31	91	.235	.331	0	—	0	-5	-3	-1	-0.6
	Yr	2	13	.133	20	14	1	0	0	90^2	84	11	51	49	13.7	5.26	73	.243	.346	0	—	0	-16	-14	-2	-2.5
1982	Det-A	0	0	—	2	1	0	0	0	6^2	5	0	9	8	18.9	6.75	60	.200	.412	0	—	0	-2	-2	-0	0.0
1983	Det-A	9	5	.643	37	19	2	1	1	157^2	110	19	71	129	10.7	3.14	124	.193	.289	0	—	0	16	13	-2	1.0
1984	Det-A	11	10	.524	31	27	2	1	0	168^1	146	14	79	118	12.3	3.48	113	.232	.323	0	—	0	10	8	-1	0.8
1985	Det-A	5	6	.455	31	13	0	0	0	95	96	12	48	82	13.7	5.59	73	.259	.346	0	—	0	-15	-16	1	-1.6
1986	SF-N	2	3	.400	46	4	0	0	4	73^1	64	4	44	72	13.5	2.70	130	.242	.354	1	.143	-0	8	7	-1	0.4
1987	*Min-A	8	1	.889	47	6	0	0	4	112	100	10	47	110	11.8	3.94	117	.238	.315	0	—	0	6	8	-1	0.4
1988	Min-A	8	4	.667	57	1	0	0	2	100	74	7	61	99	12.2	3.96	103	.207	.325	0	—	0	0	1	0	0.0
1989	Min-A	9	3	.750	56	0	0	0	3	106	96	11	47	93	12.3	3.48	119	.246	.330	0	—	0	5	8	-1	0.6
1990	Min-A	8	5	.615	51	0	0	0	0	100^1	85	9	58	77	13.0	3.41	122	.232	.340	0	—	0	6	8	-2	0.8
1991	Atl-N	0	3	.000	49	0	0	0	17	64^1	43	5	20	53	9.2	2.24	174	.189	.263	0	.000	-1	10	12	-0	1.0
1992	Atl-N	3	1	.750	28	0	0	0	1	33^1	35	7	16	19	14.0	5.13	71	.269	.354	0	.000	-0	-6	-5	-0	-0.7
	KC-A	1	4	.200	19	2	0	0	0	44^2	42	3	20	26	12.7	5.64	72	.247	.330	0	—	0	-8	-8	-0	-0.8
Total	15	67	62	.519	490	95	5	2	32	1205^1	1034	116	604	975	12.5	3.90	103	.232	.328	2	.083	-1	7	14	-11	-1.7

● BRUCE BERENYI Berenyi, Bruce Michael b: 8/21/54, Bryan, Ohio BR/TR, 6′3″, 215 lbs. Deb: 7/5/80

YEAR	TM/L	W	L	PCT	G	GS	CG	SH	SV	IP	H	HR	BB	SO	RAT	ERA	ERA+	OAV	OOB	BH	AVG	PB	PR	/A	PD	TPI
1980	Cin-N	2	2	.500	6	6	0	0	0	27^2	34	1	23	19	18.5	7.81	46	.318	.438	0	.000	-1	-13	-13	-0	-1.6
1981	Cin-N	9	6	.600	21	20	5	3	0	126	97	3	77	106	12.4	3.50	101	.211	.324	8	.190	1	-0	1	-1	0.1
1982	Cin-N	9	18	.333	34	34	4	1	0	222^1	208	8	96	157	12.4	3.36	110	.255	.335	15	.242	3	6	8	2	1.5
1983	Cin-N	9	14	.391	32	31	4	1	0	186^1	173	9	102	151	13.4	3.86	98	.247	.345	12	.218	2	-5	-1	3	0.3
1984	Cin-N	3	7	.300	13	11	0	0	0	51	63	0	42	53	18.5	6.00	63	.306	.423	1	.063	-1	-14	-13	0	-2.2
	NY-N	9	6	.600	19	19	0	0	0	115	100	6	53	81	12.1	3.76	94	.238	.325	9	.243	2	-2	-3	-1	-0.3
	Yr	12	13	.480	32	30	0	0	0	166	163	6	95	134	14.0	4.45	81	.260	.358	10	.189	0	-16	-15	-1	-2.5
1985	NY-N	1	0	1.000	3	3	0	0	0	13^2	8	0	10	10	12.5	2.63	131	.170	.328	1	.250	0	1	1	1	0.2
1986	NY-N	2	2	.500	14	7	0	0	0	39^2	47	5	22	30	15.9	6.35	56	.299	.389	0	.000	-1	-12	-12	-0	-1.2
Total	7	44	55	.444	142	131	13	5	0	781^2	730	32	425	607	13.4	4.03	91	.251	.347	46	.197	4	-38	-32	3	-3.2

● HEINIE BERGER Berger, Charles b: 1/7/1882, LaSalle, Ill. d: 2/10/54, Lakewood, Ohio TR , 5′9″, Deb: 5/6/07

YEAR	TM/L	W	L	PCT	G	GS	CG	SH	SV	IP	H	HR	BB	SO	RAT	ERA	ERA+	OAV	OOB	BH	AVG	PB	PR	/A	PD	TPI
1907	Cle-A	3	3	.500	14	7	5	1	0	87^1	74	0	20	50	9.8	2.99	84	.232	.279	5	.179	0	-4	-5	-1	-0.5
1908	Cle-A	13	8	.619	29	24	16	0	0	199^1	152	1	66	101	10.0	2.12	113	.219	.290	8	.108	-4	6	6	-0	0.1
1909	Cle-A	13	14	.481	34	29	19	4	1	247	221	2	58	162	10.6	2.73	94	.256	.312	11	.133	-1	-7	-5	0	-0.7
1910	Cle-A	3	4	.429	13	8	2	0	0	65^1	57	0	32	24	12.7	3.03	85	.243	.341	3	.143	-1	-4	-3	-1	-0.5
Total	4	32	29	.525	90	68	42	5	1	599	504	3	176	337	10.5	2.60	96	.239	.303	27	.131	-6	-9	-7	-2	-1.6

● SEAN BERGMAN Bergman, Sean Frederick b: 4/11/70, Joliet, Ill. BR/TR, 6′4″, 205 lbs. Deb: 7/7/93

YEAR	TM/L	W	L	PCT	G	GS	CG	SH	SV	IP	H	HR	BB	SO	RAT	ERA	ERA+	OAV	OOB	BH	AVG	PB	PR	/A	PD	TPI
1993	Det-A	1	4	.200	9	6	1	0	0	39^2	47	6	23	19	16.1	5.67	76	.294	.386	0	—	0	-6	-6	0	-0.6
1994	Det-A	2	1	.667	3	3	0	0	0	17^2	22	2	7	12	15.3	5.60	86	.301	.370	0	—	0	-2	-1	-0	-0.2
1995	Det-A	7	10	.412	28	28	1	1	0	135^1	169	19	67	86	16.0	5.12	93	.307	.386	0	—	0	-6	-5	-1	-0.7
1996	SD-N	6	8	.429	41	14	0	0	0	113^1	119	14	33	85	12.2	4.37	91	.274	.328	3	.100	-1	-2	-5	1	-0.5
1997	SD-N	2	4	.333	44	9	0	0	0	99	126	11	38	74	15.2	6.09	64	.316	.380	3	.231	1	-21	-24	1	-1.1
1998	Hou-N	12	9	.571	31	27	1	0	0	172	183	20	42	100	12.0	3.72	109	.268	.316	5	.083	-3	10	7	-2	0.2
Total	6	30	36	.455	156	87	3	1	0	577	666	72	210	376	13.9	4.77	88	.290	.353	11	.107	-3	-27	-36	-1	-2.9

● JACK BERLY Berly, John Chambers b: 5/24/03, Natchitoches, La. d: 6/26/77, Houston, Tex. BR/TR, 5′11.5″, 190 lbs. Deb: 4/22/24

YEAR	TM/L	W	L	PCT	G	GS	CG	SH	SV	IP	H	HR	BB	SO	RAT	ERA	ERA+	OAV	OOB	BH	AVG	PB	PR	/A	PD	TPI
1924	StL-N	0	0	—	4	0	0	0	0	8	8	2	4	2	13.5	5.63	67	.267	.353	0	.000	-0	-2	-2	0	0.0
1931	NY-N	7	8	.467	27	11	4	1	0	111^1	114	6	51	45	13.7	3.88	95	.270	.354	6	.171	-1	-0	-2	1	-0.2
1932	Phi-N	1	2	.333	21	1	1	0	2	46	61	4	21	15	16.2	7.63	58	.333	.405	0	.000	-1	-19	-16	1	-1.1
1933	Phi-N	2	3	.400	13	6	1	1	0	50	62	5	22	4	15.5	5.04	76	.307	.381	4	.308	0	-9	-7	1	-0.5
Total	4	10	13	.435	65	18	6	2	2	215^1	245	17	98	66	14.6	5.02	78	.292	.371	10	.167	-2	-30	-27	3	-1.8

● VICTOR BERNAL Bernal, Victor Hugo b: 10/6/53, Los Angeles, Cal. BR/TR, 6′1″, 175 lbs. Deb: 4/6/77

YEAR	TM/L	W	L	PCT	G	GS	CG	SH	SV	IP	H	HR	BB	SO	RAT	ERA	ERA+	OAV	OOB	BH	AVG	PB	PR	/A	PD	TPI
1977	SD-N	1	1	.500	15	0	0	0	0	20^1	23	4	9	6	14.2	5.31	67	.287	.360	0	.000	-0	-3	-4	-0	-0.4

YEAR	TM/L	W	L	PCT	G	GS	CG	SH	SV	IP	H	HR	BB	SO	RAT	ERA	ERA+	OAV	OOB	BH	AVG	PB	PR	/A	PD	TPI
● DWIGHT BERNARD Bernard, Dwight Vern b: 5/31/52, Mt.Vernon, Ill. BR/TR, 6'2", 170 lbs. Deb: 6/29/78																										
1978	NY-N	1	4	.200	30	1	0	0	0	48	54	4	27	26	15.2	4.31	81	.297	.388	1	.200	0	-4	-4	0	-0.4
1979	NY-N	0	3	.000	32	1	0	0	0	44	59	2	26	20	17.4	4.70	77	.331	.417	0	—	0	-5	-5	0	-0.3
1981	*Mil-A	0	0	—	6	0	0	0	0	5	5	0	6	1	19.8	3.60	95	.263	.440	0	—	0	0	-0	-0	0.1
1982	*Mil-A	3	1	.750	47	0	0	0	6	79	78	4	27	45	12.1	3.76	101	.263	.326	0	—	0	3	0	-1	0.1
Total	4	4	8	.333	115	2	0	0	6	176	196	10	86	92	14.5	4.14	88	.290	.371	1	.200	1	-6	-9	-1	-0.5
● JOE BERNARD Bernard, Joseph Carl "J.C." b: 3/24/1882, Brighton, Ill. d: 9/22/60, Springfield, Ill BR/TR, 6'1", 175 lbs. Deb: 9/23/09																										
1909	StL-N	0	0	—	1	0	0	0	0	1	1	0	2	2	27.0	0.00	—	.250	.500	0	—	0	0	0	0	0.0
● BILL BERNHARD Bernhard, William Henry "Strawberry Bill" b: 3/16/1871, Clarence, N.Y. d: 3/30/49, San Diego, Cal. BB/TR, 6'1", 205 lbs. Deb: 4/24/1899																										
1899	Phi-N	6	6	.500	21	12	10	1	0	132^1	120	3	36	23	11.0	2.65	139	.242	.301	13	.241	0	18	15	-0	1.2
1900	Phi-N	15	10	.600	32	27	20	0	2	218^2	284	3	74	49	14.9	4.77	76	.313	.368	14	.154	-5	-26	-28	1	-2.9
1901	Phi-A	17	10	.630	31	27	26	1	0	257	328	6	50	58	13.3	4.52	84	.307	.339	20	.187	-1	-24	-21	4	-1.6
1902	Phi-A	1	0	1.000	1	1	1	0	0	9	7	0	3	1	10.0	1.00	367	.212	.278	0	.000	-1	3	3	-1	0.1
	Cle-A	17	5	.773	27	24	22	3	1	217	169	4	34	57	8.6	2.20	157	.216	.253	18	.200	-1	33	30	1	2.8
	Yr	18	5	**.783**	28	25	23	3	1	226	176	4	37	58	**8.7**	2.15	161	**.215**	**.254**	18	.191	-2	36	33	1	2.9
1903	Cle-A	14	5	.737	20	19	18	3	0	165^2	151	1	21	60	9.3	2.12	135	.242	.267	12	.185	-1	16	14	1	1.5
1904	Cle-A	23	13	.639	38	37	35	4	0	320^2	323	3	55	137	10.7	2.13	119	.263	.296	22	.177	-1	17	14	-1	1.4
1905	Cle-A	7	13	.350	22	19	17	0	0	174^1	185	5	34	56	11.4	3.36	78	.274	.309	6	.087	-6	-14	-14	0	-2.1
1906	Cle-A	16	15	.516	31	30	23	2	0	255^1	235	1	47	85	10.1	2.54	103	.248	.287	21	.212	2	4	2	2	0.7
1907	Cle-A	0	4	.000	8	4	3	0	0	42	58	0	11	19	14.8	3.21	78	.330	.369	3	.200	0	-3	-3	0	-0.3
Total	9	116	81	.589	231	200	175	14	3	1792	1860	26	365	545	11.3	3.04	102	.268	.307	129	.180	-13	23	11	7	0.8
● WALTER BERNHARDT Bernhardt, Walter Jacob b: 5/20/1893, Pleasant Village, Pa. d: 7/26/58, Watertown, N.Y. BR/TR, 6'2", 175 lbs. Deb: 7/16/18																										
1918	NY-A	0	0	—	1	0	0	0	0	0^2	0	0	0	1	0.0	0.00	—	.000	.000	0	—	0	0	0	0	0.0
● JOE BERRY Berry, Jonas Arthur "Jittery Joe" b: 12/16/04, Huntsville, Ark. d: 9/27/58, Anaheim, Cal. BL/TR, 5'10.5", 145 lbs. Deb: 9/6/42																										
1942	Chi-N	0	0	—	2	0	0	0	0	2	7	0	2	1	40.5	18.00	18	.538	.600	0	—	0	-3	-3	0	0.0
1944	Phi-A	10	8	.556	53	0	0	0	**12**	111^1	78	4	23	44	8.3	1.94	179	.192	.238	3	.120	-1	18	**19**	2	3.6
1945	Phi-A	8	7	.533	**52**	0	0	0	5	130^1	114	5	38	51	10.5	2.35	146	.232	.287	5	.143	-1	**15**	**16**	1	2.0
1946	Phi-A	0	1	.000	5	0	0	0	0	13	15	1	3	5	13.2	2.77	128	.288	.339	1	.333	0	1	1	0	0.1
	Cle-A	3	6	.333	21	0	0	0	1	37^1	32	4	21	16	12.8	3.38	98	.235	.338	2	.286	0	1	-0	-1	-0.1
	Yr	3	7	.300	26	0	0	0	1	50^1	47	5	24	21	12.7	3.22	105	.249	.333	3	.300	1	2	1	-0	0.0
Total	4	21	22	.488	133	0	0	0	18	294	246	14	87	117	10.3	2.45	140	.224	.282	11	.157	-2	31	32	3	5.6
● FRANK BERTAINA Bertaina, Frank Louis b: 4/14/44, San Francisco, Cal. BL/TL, 5'11", 180 lbs. Deb: 8/1/64																										
1964	Bal-A	1	0	1.000	6	4	1	1	0	26	18	3	13	18	10.7	2.77	129	.198	.298	0	.000	-1	2	2	0	0.1
1965	Bal-A	0	0	—	2	1	0	0	0	6	9	0	4	5	19.5	6.00	58	.360	.448	0	.000	-0	-2	-2	0	0.0
1966	Bal-A	2	5	.286	16	9	0	0	0	63^1	52	3	36	46	13.1	3.13	107	.226	.341	2	.105	-1	2	1	-2	-0.1
1967	Bal-A	1	1	.500	5	2	0	0	0	21^2	17	4	14	19	12.9	3.32	95	.224	.344	1	.111	-0	-0	-0	-0	-0.1
	Was-A	6	5	.545	18	17	4	4	0	95^2	90	8	37	67	11.9	2.92	108	.251	.322	2	.057	-3	3	3	-1	0.0
	Yr	7	6	.538	23	19	4	4	0	117^1	107	12	51	86	12.1	2.99	106	.246	.325	3	.068	-3	3	2	-1	-0.1
1968	Was-A	7	13	.350	27	23	1	0	0	127^1	133	15	69	81	14.7	4.66	63	.273	.369	5	.132	-0	-24	-25	-0	-3.7
1969	Was-A	1	3	.250	14	5	0	0	0	35^2	43	8	23	25	16.7	6.56	53	.291	.386	4	.364	2	-12	-12	0	-1.0
	Bal-A	0	0	—	3	0	0	0	0	6	1	0	3	5	6.0	0.00	—	.063	.211	1	1.000	1	2	2	-0	0.1
	Yr	1	3	.250	17	5	0	0	0	41^2	44	8	26	30	15.1	5.62	62	.267	.366	5	.417	3	-9	-10	0	-0.9
1970	StL-N	1	2	.333	8	5	0	0	0	31^1	36	1	15	14	14.6	3.16	130	.293	.370	1	.143	0	3	3	-0	0.3
Total	7	19	29	.396	99	66	6	5	0	413	399	42	214	280	13.6	3.84	85	.257	.350	16	.127	-1	-24	-27	-2	-4.4
● MIKE BERTOTTI Bertotti, Michael David b: 1/18/70, Jersey City, N.J. BL/TL, 6'1", 185 lbs. Deb: 7/29/95																										
1995	Chi-A	1	1	.500	4	4	0	0	0	14^1	23	6	11	15	23.2	12.56	35	.365	.481	0	—	0	-12	-13	-0	-1.1
1996	Chi-A	2	0	1.000	15	2	0	0	0	28	28	5	20	19	15.4	5.14	92	.257	.372	0	—	0	-0	-1	0	0.3
1997	Chi-A	0	0	—	9	0	0	0	0	3^2	9	0	2	4	27.0	7.36	59	.450	.500	0	—	0	-1	-1	-0	0.2
Total	3	3	1	.750	28	6	0	0	0	46	60	11	33	38	18.8	7.63	61	.313	.421	0	—	0	-14	-15	-0	-0.6
● LEFTY BERTRAND Bertrand, Roman Mathias b: 2/28/09, Cobden, Minn. BR/TL, 6', 180 lbs. Deb: 4/15/36																										
1936	Phi-N	0	0	—	1	0	0	0	0	2	3	1	2	1	22.5	9.00	50	.333	.455	0	—	0	-1	-1	-0	0.0
● ANDRES BERUMEN Berumen, Andres b: 4/5/71, Tijuana, Mexico BR/TR, 6'2", 210 lbs. Deb: 4/27/95																										
1995	SD-N	2	3	.400	37	0	0	0	1	44^1	37	3	36	42	15.4	5.68	71	.226	.374	0	.000	-0	-7	-8	-1	-0.9
1996	SD-N	0	0	—	3	0	0	0	0	3^1	3	1	2	4	16.2	5.40	73	.231	.375	0	—	0	-0	-1	-0	0.0
Total	2	2	3	.400	40	0	0	0	1	47^2	40	4	38	46	15.5	5.66	71	.226	.374	0	.000	-0	-8	-9	-1	-0.9
● FRED BESANA Besana, Frederick Cyril b: 4/5/31, Lincoln, Cal. BR/TL, 6'3.5", 200 lbs. Deb: 4/18/56																										
1956	Bal-A	1	0	1.000	7	2	0	0	0	17^2	22	0	14	7	19.4	5.60	70	.310	.437	0	.000	-0	-3	-3	1	-0.1
● HERMAN BESSE Besse, Herman A. b: 8/16/11, St.Louis, Mo. d: 8/13/72, Los Angeles, Cal. BL/TL, 6'2", 190 lbs. Deb: 4/19/40																										
1940	Phi-A	0	3	.000	17	5	0	0	0	53	70	10	34	19	18.2	8.83	50	.315	.413	5	.263	2	-26	-26	-1	-1.1
1941	Phi-A	2	0	1.000	6	2	1	0	0	19^2	28	4	12	8	18.3	10.07	42	.329	.412	1	.200	-0	-13	-13	0	-1.0
1942	Phi-A	2	9	.182	30	14	4	0	1	133	163	7	69	78	16.0	6.16	61	.300	.383	12	.226	2	-37	-35	-2	-2.6
1943	Phi-A	1	1	.500	5	1	0	0	0	16^1	18	2	4	3	12.7	3.31	103	.295	.348	0	.000	-1	-0	0	0	-0.1
1946	Phi-A	0	2	.000	7	3	0	0	1	20^2	19	1	9	10	12.2	5.23	68	.247	.326	0	.000	-0	-4	-4	-0	-0.4
Total	5	5	15	.250	65	25	5	0	2	242^2	298	24	128	118	16.1	6.79	58	.302	.386	18	.200	2	-80	-77	-3	-5.2
● DON BESSENT Bessent, Fred Donald b: 3/13/31, Jacksonville, Fla. d: 7/7/90, Jacksonville, Fla. BR/TR, 6', 175 lbs. Deb: 7/17/55																										
1955	*Bro-N	8	1	.889	24	2	1	0	3	63^1	51	7	21	29	10.2	2.70	150	.220	.285	2	.100	-2	9	10	-0	1.2
1956	*Bro-N	4	3	.571	38	0	0	0	9	79^1	63	5	31	52	10.7	2.50	159	.221	.297	2	.111	-1	11	13	-1	1.2
1957	Bro-N	1	3	.250	27	0	0	0	0	44	58	5	19	24	15.8	5.73	73	.328	.393	1	.250	0	-9	-8	-0	-0.7
1958	LA-N	1	0	1.000	19	0	0	0	0	24^1	24	3	17	13	15.5	3.33	123	.270	.393	0	.000	-0	2	2	1	0.1
Total	4	14	7	.667	108	2	1	0	12	211	196	20	88	118	12.2	3.33	122	.250	.327	5	.114	-3	13	17	-1	1.8
● KARL BEST Best, Karl Jon b: 3/6/59, Aberdeen, Wash. BR/TR, 6'4", 210 lbs. Deb: 8/19/83																										
1983	Sea-A	0	1	.000	4	0	0	0	0	5^1	14	2	5	3	35.4	13.50	32	.483	.583	0	—	0	-6	-5	-0	-1.0
1984	Sea-A	1	1	.500	5	0	0	0	0	6	7	0	0	6	10.5	3.00	133	.292	.292	0	—	0	1	1	-0	0.3
1985	Sea-A	2	1	.667	15	0	0	0	4	32^1	25	1	6	32	8.9	1.95	216	.207	.250	0	—	0	8	8	-0	0.8
1986	Sea-A	2	3	.400	26	0	0	0	1	35^2	35	3	21	23	14.4	4.04	105	.255	.358	0	—	0	1	1	-1	0.0
1988	Min-A	0	0	—	11	0	0	0	0	12	15	1	7	9	16.5	6.00	68	.306	.393	0	—	0	-3	-3	-0	-0.1
Total	5	5	6	.455	61	0	0	0	5	91^1	96	7	39	73	13.7	4.04	104	.267	.345	0	—	0	1	2	-2	0.0
● JIM BETHKE Bethke, James Charles b: 11/5/46, Falls City, Neb. BR/TR, 6'3", 185 lbs. Deb: 4/12/65																										
1965	NY-N	2	0	1.000	25	0	0	0	0	40	41	3	22	19	15.5	4.27	83	.266	.379	0	.000	-0	-3	-3	1	-0.1
● JEFF BETTENDORF Bettendorf, Jeffrey Allen b: 12/10/60, Lompoc, Cal. BR/TR, 6'3", 180 lbs. Deb: 4/8/84																										
1984	Oak-A	0	0	—	3	0	0	0	1	9^2	9	3	5	5	13.0	4.66	80	.243	.333	0	—	0	-1	-1	-0	0.4
● HARRY BETTS Betts, Harold Matthew "Chubby" or "Ginger" b: 6/19/1881, Alliance, Ohio d: 5/22/46, San Antonio, Tex. BR/TR, 5'10", 200 lbs. Deb: 9/22/03																										
1903	StL-N	0	1	.000	1	1	1	0	0	9	11	0	5	2	18.0	10.00	33	.297	.409	0	.000	-0	-7	-7	-0	-0.5
1913	Cin-N	0	0	—	1	0	0	0	0	3^1	1	0	3	0	13.5	2.70	120	.143	.455	0	.000	-0	0	0	-0	0.0
Total	2	0	1	.000	2	1	1	0	0	12^1	12	0	8	2	16.8	8.03	41	.273	.418	0	.000	-1	-7	-7	-0	-0.5

● HUCK BETTS Betts, Walter Martin b: 2/18/1897, Millsboro, Del. d: 6/13/87, Millsboro, Del. BR/TR, 5'11", 170 lbs. Deb: 4/26/20

YEAR	TM/L	W	L	PCT	G	GS	CG	SH	SV	IP	H	HR	BB	SO	RAT	ERA	ERA+	OAV	OOB	BH	AVG	PB	PR	/A	PD	TPI
1920	Phi-N	1	1	.500	27	4	1	0	0	88^{1}	86	3	33	18	12.3	3.57	96	.261	.332	2	.080	-2	-4	-1	-1	-0.3
1921	Phi-N	3	7	.300	32	2	1	0	4	100^{2}	141	8	14	28	14.2	4.47	95	.337	.365	8	.267	0	-8	-3	0	-0.2
1922	Phi-N	1	0	1.000	7	0	0	0	0	15	23	3	8	4	18.6	9.60	49	.348	.419	0	.000	-0	-9	-8	-0	-0.5
1923	Phi-N	2	4	.333	19	4	3	0	1	84^{1}	100	7	14	18	12.6	3.09	149	.314	.351	3	.097	-3	9	14	0	0.6
1924	Phi-N	7	10	.412	37	9	2	0	2	144^{1}	160	8	42	46	12.9	4.30	104	.286	.341	7	.156	-2	-7	3	-2	-0.1
1925	Phi-N	4	5	.444	35	7	1	0	1	97^{1}	146	10	38	28	17.3	5.55	86	.342	.400	10	.294	2	-14	-8	1	-0.4
1932	Bos-N	13	11	.542	31	27	16	3	1	221^{2}	229	9	35	32	10.7	2.80	134	.267	.295	19	.241	2	27	24	-2	2.4
1933	Bos-N	11	11	.500	35	26	17	2	4	242	225	9	55	40	10.4	2.79	110	.248	.290	17	.224	2	15	7	4	1.4
1934	Bos-N	17	10	.630	40	27	10	2	3	213	258	17	42	69	12.8	4.06	94	.296	.330	13	.188	1	0	-6	-2	-0.7
1935	Bos-N	2	9	.182	44	19	2	1	0	159^{2}	213	9	40	40	14.4	5.47	69	.321	.362	7	.159	-0	-26	-30	1	-1.7
Total	10	61	68	.473	307	125	53	8	16	1366^{1}	1581	83	321	323	12.7	3.93	98	.292	.334	86	.197	-2	-18	-9	-0	0.5

● BILL BEVENS Bevens, Floyd Clifford b: 10/21/16, Hubbard, Ore. d: 10/26/91, Salem, Ore. BR/TR, 6'3.5", 210 lbs. Deb: 5/12/44

YEAR	TM/L	W	L	PCT	G	GS	CG	SH	SV	IP	H	HR	BB	SO	RAT	ERA	ERA+	OAV	OOB	BH	AVG	PB	PR	/A	PD	TPI
1944	NY-A	4	1	.800	8	5	3	0	0	43^{2}	44	4	13	16	12.0	2.68	130	.273	.331	1	.063	-2	4	4	-0	0.2
1945	NY-A	13	9	.591	29	25	14	2	0	184	174	12	68	76	11.9	3.67	94	.254	.322	7	.111	-4	-6	-4	1	-0.9
1946	NY-A	16	13	.552	31	31	18	3	0	249^{2}	213	11	78	120	10.5	2.23	154	.232	.293	7	.083	-4	35	34	-4	3.0
1947	*NY-A	7	13	.350	28	23	11	1	0	165	167	13	77	77	13.4	3.82	93	.264	.345	7	.121	-3	-2	-5	-0	-0.9
Total	4	40	36	.526	96	84	46	6	0	642^{1}	598	40	236	289	11.7	3.08	113	.250	.318	22	.100	-13	31	29	-4	1.4

● BRIAN BEVIL Bevil, Brian Scott b: 9/5/71, Houston, Tex. BR/TR, 6'3", 190 lbs. Deb: 6/17/96

YEAR	TM/L	W	L	PCT	G	GS	CG	SH	SV	IP	H	HR	BB	SO	RAT	ERA	ERA+	OAV	OOB	BH	AVG	PB	PR	/A	PD	TPI
1996	KC-A	1	0	1.000	3	1	0	0	0	11^{1}	9	2	5	7	11.5	5.73	87	.237	.326	0	—	0	-1	-1	0	0.0
1997	KC-A	1	2	.333	18	0	0	0	1	16^{1}	16	1	9	13	14.3	6.61	71	.267	.371	0	—	0	-4	-3	-0	-0.7
1998	KC-A	3	1	.750	39	0	0	0	0	40	47	4	22	47	16.2	6.30	78	.283	.377	0	—	0	-7	-6	-1	-0.7
Total	3	5	3	.625	60	1	0	0	1	67^{1}	72	7	36	67	15.0	6.28	78	.273	.368	0	—	0	-12	-11	-1	-1.4

● LOU BEVIL Bevil, Louis Eugene (b: Louis Eugene Bevilacqua) b: 11/27/22, Nelson, Ill. d: 2/1/73, Dixon, Ill. BB/TR, 5'11.5", 190 lbs. Deb: 9/2/42

YEAR	TM/L	W	L	PCT	G	GS	CG	SH	SV	IP	H	HR	BB	SO	RAT	ERA	ERA+	OAV	OOB	BH	AVG	PB	PR	/A	PD	TPI
1942	Was-A	0	1	.000	4	1	0	0	0	9^{2}	9	0	11	2	19.6	6.52	56	.265	.457	0	.000	-0	-3	-3	-0	-0.3

● BEN BEVILLE Beville, Clarence Benjamin b: 8/28/1877, Colusa, Cal. d: 1/5/37, Yountville, Cal. BR/TR, 5'9", 190 lbs. Deb: 5/24/01

YEAR	TM/L	W	L	PCT	G	GS	CG	SH	SV	IP	H	HR	BB	SO	RAT	ERA	ERA+	OAV	OOB	BH	AVG	PB	PR	/A	PD	TPI
1901	Bos-A	0	2	.000	2	2	1	0	0	9	8	0	9	1	18.0	4.00	88	.235	.409	2	.286	0	-0	-0	-0	-0.1

● JIM BIBBY Bibby, James Blair b: 10/29/44, Franklinton, N.C. BR/TR, 6'5", 235 lbs. Deb: 9/4/72

YEAR	TM/L	W	L	PCT	G	GS	CG	SH	SV	IP	H	HR	BB	SO	RAT	ERA	ERA+	OAV	OOB	BH	AVG	PB	PR	/A	PD	TPI
1972	StL-N	1	3	.250	6	6	0	0	0	40^{1}	29	4	19	28	10.9	3.35	102	.206	.304	1	.125	0	0	0	0	0.1
1973	StL-N	0	2	.000	6	3	0	0	0	16	19	2	17	12	21.4	9.56	38	.306	.469	0	.000	0	-10	-11	0	-1.1
	Tex-A	9	10	.474	26	23	11	2	1	180^{1}	121	14	106	155	11.6	3.24	115	**.192**	.314	0	—	0	11	10	-2	0.8
1974	Tex-A	19	19	.500	41	41	11	5	0	264	255	25	113	149	12.9	4.74	75	.255	.336	0	—	0	-33	-34	1	-4.3
1975	Tex-A	2	6	.250	12	12	4	1	0	68^{1}	73	2	28	31	13.6	5.00	75	.274	.348	0	—	0	-9	-9	-1	-1.0
	Cle-A	5	9	.357	24	12	2	0	1	112^{2}	99	7	50	62	11.9	3.20	118	.235	.316	0	—	0	7	7	1	0.9
	Yr	7	15	.318	36	24	6	1	1	181	172	9	78	93	12.4	3.88	97	.248	.324	0	—	0	-2	-2	0	-0.1
1976	Cle-A	13	7	.650	34	21	4	3	1	163^{1}	162	6	56	84	12.1	3.20	109	.266	.329	0	—	0	6	5	-1	0.5
1977	Cle-A	12	13	.480	37	30	9	2	2	206^{2}	197	17	73	141	11.9	3.57	110	.250	.317	0	—	0	11	9	-2	0.8
1978	Pit-N	8	7	.533	34	14	3	2	1	107	100	10	39	72	11.9	3.53	105	.246	.315	4	.129	1	1	2	0	0.4
1979	*Pit-N	12	4	.750	34	17	4	1	0	137^{2}	110	9	47	103	10.5	2.81	138	.218	.290	8	.178	2	14	16	-2	1.8
1980	Pit-N★	19	6	**.760**	35	34	6	1	0	238^{1}	210	20	88	144	11.5	3.32	110	.238	.312	12	.156	2	7	8	-2	0.8
1981	Pit-N	6	3	.667	14	14	2	2	0	93^{2}	79	4	26	48	10.3	2.50	144	.225	.282	4	.143	1	10	11	-1	1.1
1983	Pit-N	5	12	.294	29	12	0	0	2	78	92	10	51	44	16.6	6.69	55	.297	.398	2	.111	-1	-27	-26	-0	-5.0
1984	Tex-A	0	0	—	8	0	0	0	0	16^{1}	19	1	10	6	16.0	4.41	94	.297	.392	0	—	0	-1	-0	-0	-0.1
Total	12	111	101	.524	340	239	56	19	8	1722^{2}	1565	131	723	1079	12.2	3.76	98	.243	.323	31	.148	5	-11	-11	-8	-4.3

● VERN BICKFORD Bickford, Vernon Edgell b: 8/17/20, Hellier, Ky. d: 5/6/60, Concord, Va. BR/TR, 6', 185 lbs. Deb: 4/24/48

YEAR	TM/L	W	L	PCT	G	GS	CG	SH	SV	IP	H	HR	BB	SO	RAT	ERA	ERA+	OAV	OOB	BH	AVG	PB	PR	/A	PD	TPI
1948	*Bos-N	11	5	.688	33	22	10	1	1	146	125	9	63	60	11.8	3.27	117	.226	.309	10	.204	1	11	9	-1	0.9
1949	Bos-N★	16	11	.593	37	36	15	2	0	230^{2}	246	20	106	101	14.0	4.25	89	.273	.354	15	.185	1	-5	-12	2	-1.1
1950	Bos-N	19	14	.576	40	39	**27**	2	0	**311^{2}**	293	25	122	126	12.2	3.47	111	.248	.321	16	.138	-4	23	13	-1	0.7
1951	Bos-N	11	9	.550	25	20	12	3	0	164^{2}	146	7	76	76	12.5	3.12	118	.240	.330	6	.115	-2	15	10	3	1.2
1952	Bos-N	7	12	.368	26	22	7	1	0	161^{1}	165	7	64	62	12.9	3.74	97	.269	.340	9	.176	0	-0	-2	-0	-0.2
1953	Mil-N	2	5	.286	20	9	2	0	0	58	60	8	35	25	15.1	5.28	74	.279	.385	1	.067	-1	-6	-9	1	-0.9
1954	Bal-A	0	1	.000	1	1	0	0	0	4	5	0	1	0	13.5	9.00	40	.333	.375	0	.000	-0	-2	-2	0	-0.4
Total	7	66	57	.537	182	149	73	9	2	1076^{1}	1040	76	467	450	12.8	3.71	102	.254	.335	57	.156	-7	36	7	3	0.2

● DAN BICKHAM Bickham, Daniel Denison b: 10/31/1864, Dayton, Ohio d: 3/3/51, Dayton, Ohio BR/TR, 5'10", 160 lbs. Deb: 8/13/1886

YEAR	TM/L	W	L	PCT	G	GS	CG	SH	SV	IP	H	HR	BB	SO	RAT	ERA	ERA+	OAV	OOB	BH	AVG	PB	PR	/A	PD	TPI
1886	Cin-a	1	0	1.000	1	1	1	0	0	9	13	0	3	6	16.0	3.00	117	.351	.400	1	.333	0	0	1	0	0.1

● CHARLIE BICKNELL Bicknell, Charles Stephen "Bud" b: 7/27/28, Plainfield, N.J. BR/TR, 5'11", 170 lbs. Deb: 4/22/48

YEAR	TM/L	W	L	PCT	G	GS	CG	SH	SV	IP	H	HR	BB	SO	RAT	ERA	ERA+	OAV	OOB	BH	AVG	PB	PR	/A	PD	TPI
1948	Phi-N	0	1	.000	17	1	0	0	0	25^{2}	29	5	17	5	16.1	5.96	66	.287	.390	0	.000	-1	-6	-6	-1	-0.3
1949	Phi-N	0	0	—	13	0	0	0	0	28^{1}	32	3	17	4	16.2	7.62	52	.291	.395	0	.000	1	-11	-12	0	0.0
Total	2	0	1	.000	30	1	0	0	0	54	61	8	34	9	16.2	6.83	58	.289	.393	0	.000	-0	-17	-17	-1	-0.3

● MIKE BIELECKI Bielecki, Michael Joseph b: 7/31/59, Baltimore, Md. BR/TR, 6'3", 195 lbs. Deb: 9/14/84

YEAR	TM/L	W	L	PCT	G	GS	CG	SH	SV	IP	H	HR	BB	SO	RAT	ERA	ERA+	OAV	OOB	BH	AVG	PB	PR	/A	PD	TPI
1984	Pit-N	0	0	—	4	0	0	0	0	4^{1}	4	0	0	1	8.3	0.00	—	.250	.250	0	—	0	2	2	0	0.0
1985	Pit-N	2	3	.400	12	7	0	0	0	45^{2}	45	5	31	22	15.2	4.53	79	.257	.372	0	.000	-1	-5	-5	1	-0.5
1986	Pit-N	6	11	.353	31	27	0	0	0	148^{2}	149	10	83	83	14.2	4.66	82	.262	.358	3	.063	-3	-16	-14	-1	-1.8
1987	Pit-N	2	3	.400	8	8	2	0	0	45^{2}	43	6	12	25	11.0	4.73	87	.250	.303	1	.063	-1	-3	-3	-0	-0.4
1988	Chi-N	2	2	.500	19	5	0	0	0	48^{1}	55	4	16	33	13.2	3.35	108	.284	.338	1	.100	-0	1	1	-0	0.0
1989	*Chi-N	18	7	**.720**	33	33	4	3	0	212^{1}	187	16	81	147	11.4	3.14	120	.237	.308	3	.043	-5	8	15	-1	1.0
1990	Chi-N	8	11	.421	36	29	0	0	1	168	188	13	70	103	14.1	4.93	83	.287	.361	7	.163	-0	-21	-16	3	-1.4
1991	Chi-N	13	11	.542	39	25	0	0	0	172	169	18	54	72	11.8	4.50	86	.262	.321	3	.065	-2	-16	-12	1	-1.7
	Atl-N	0	0	—	2	0	0	0	0	1^{2}	2	0	2	3	21.6	0.00	—	.286	.444	0	—	0	1	1	0	0.0
	Yr	13	11	.542	41	25	0	0	0	173^{2}	171	18	56	75	11.8	4.46	87	.259	.317	3	.065	-2	-15	-11	1	-1.7
1992	Atl-N	2	4	.333	19	14	1	1	0	80^{2}	77	2	27	62	11.7	2.57	143	.254	.317	3	.125	-1	8	10	1	0.7
1993	Cle-A	4	5	.444	13	13	0	0	0	68^{2}	90	8	23	38	15.1	5.90	73	.310	.365	0	—	0	-12	-12	0	-1.2
1994	Atl-N	2	0	1.000	19	1	0	0	0	27	28	2	12	18	13.7	4.00	106	.277	.360	0	.000	-0	1	1	0	0.0
1995	Cal-A	4	6	.400	22	11	0	0	0	75^{1}	80	15	31	45	13.6	5.97	79	.273	.349	0	—	0	-11	-11	0	-1.1
1996	*Atl-N	4	3	.571	40	5	0	0	2	75^{1}	63	8	33	71	11.5	2.63	167	.224	.306	1	.100	0	13	15	1	1.4
1997	Atl-N	3	7	.300	50	0	0	0	2	57^{1}	56	9	21	60	12.2	4.08	102	.250	.317	0	.000	-0	1	1	0	0.1
Total	14	70	73	.490	347	178	7	4	5	1231	1236	116	496	783	12.8	4.18	95	.262	.335	22	.078	-14	-49	-27	3	-4.9

● HARRY BIEMILLER Biemiller, Harry Lee b: 10/9/1897, Baltimore, Md. d: 5/25/65, Orlando, Fla. BR/TR, 6'1", 171 lbs. Deb: 8/26/20

YEAR	TM/L	W	L	PCT	G	GS	CG	SH	SV	IP	H	HR	BB	SO	RAT	ERA	ERA+	OAV	OOB	BH	AVG	PB	PR	/A	PD	TPI
1920	Was-A	1	0	1.000	5	2	1	0	0	17	21	1	13	10	18.0	4.76	78	.318	.430	0	.000	-1	-2	-2	-1	-0.1
1925	Cin-N	0	1	.000	23	1	0	0	2	47	45	2	21	9	14.0	4.02	102	.280	.386	0	.000	-0	1	0	2	0.1
Total	2	1	1	.500	28	3	1	0	2	64	66	3	34	19	15.0	4.22	95	.291	.399	0	.000	-1	-1	-1	2	0.1

● LOU BIERBAUER Bierbauer, Louis W. b: 9/28/1865, Erie, Pa. d: 1/31/26, Erie, Pa. BL/TR, 5'8", 140 lbs. Deb: 4/17/1886 ♦

YEAR	TM/L	W	L	PCT	G	GS	CG	SH	SV	IP	H	HR	BB	SO	RAT	ERA	ERA+	OAV	OOB	BH	AVG	PB	PR	/A	PD	TPI
1886	Phi-a	0	0	—	2	0	0	0	0	10^{2}	8	0	5	1	11.0	4.22	83	.178	.260	118	.226	-0	-1	-1	-0	0.0
1887	Phi-a	0	0	—	1	0	0	0	1	1^{2}	0	0	0	0	0.0	0.00	—	.000	.000	144	.272	0	0	0	0	0.1
1888	Phi-a	0	0	—	1	0	0	0	0	3	5	0	0	3	15.0	0.00	—	.357	.357	143	.267	0	1	1	0	0.0
Total	3	0	0	—	4	0	0	0	1	14^{2}	13	0	5	5	11.0	3.07	112	.210	.269	1521	.267	0	1	1	-1	0.1

● LYLE BIGBEE Bigbee, Lyle Randolph "Al" b: 8/22/1893, Sweet Home, Ore. d: 8/5/42, Portland, Ore. BL/TR, 6', 180 lbs. Deb: 4/15/20 F♦

YEAR	TM/L	W	L	PCT	G	GS	CG	SH	SV	IP	H	HR	BB	SO	RAT	ERA	ERA+	OAV	OOB	BH	AVG	PB	PR	/A	PD	TPI
1920	Phi-A	0	3	.000	12	2	0	0	0	45	66	5	25	12	18.2	8.00	50	.369	.446	14	.187	0	-21	-20	0	-1.1
1921	Pit-N	0	0	—	5	0	0	0	0	8	4	0	4	1	9.0	1.13	341	.154	.267	0	.000	-0	2	2	-0	0.0
Total	2	0	3	.000	17	2	0	0	0	53	70	5	29	13	16.8	6.96	57	.341	.423	14	.182	-0	-19	-17	0	-1.1

● CHARLIE BIGGS
Biggs, Charles Orval b: 9/15/06, French Lick, Ind. d: 5/24/54, French Lick, Ind. BR/TR, 6'1", 185 lbs. Deb: 9/3/32

YEAR	TM/L	W	L	PCT	G	GS	CG	SH	SV	IP	H	HR	BB	SO	RAT	ERA	ERA+	OAV	OOB	BH	AVG	PB	PR	/A	PD	TPI
1932	Chi-A	1	1	.500	6	4	0	0	0	24^2	32	2	12	1	17.1	6.93	62	.314	.402	1	.111	-0	-7	-7	-0	-0.5

● LARRY BIITTNER
Biittner, Lawrence David b: 7/27/45, Pocahontas, Ia. BL/TL, 6'2", 205 lbs. Deb: 7/17/70 ◆

YEAR	TM/L	W	L	PCT	G	GS	CG	SH	SV	IP	H	HR	BB	SO	RAT	ERA	ERA+	OAV	OOB	BH	AVG	PB	PR	/A	PD	TPI
1977	Chi-N	0	0	—	1	0	0	0	0	1^1	5	3	1	3	40.5	40.50	11	.556	.600	147	.298	0	-5	-5	0	0.0

● JIM BILBREY
Bilbrey, James Melvin b: 4/20/24, Rickman, Tenn. d: 12/26/85, Toledo, Ohio BR/TR, 6'2.5", 205 lbs. Deb: 5/17/49

YEAR	TM/L	W	L	PCT	G	GS	CG	SH	SV	IP	H	HR	BB	SO	RAT	ERA	ERA+	OAV	OOB	BH	AVG	PB	PR	/A	PD	TPI
1949	StL-A	0	0	—	1	0	0	0	0	1	1	0	3	0	36.0	18.00	25	.250	.571	0	—	0	-2	-1	0	0.0

● EMIL BILDILLI
Bildilli, Emil "Hill Billy" b: 9/16/12, Diamond, Ind. d: 9/16/46, Hartford City, Ind. BR/TL, 5'10", 170 lbs. Deb: 8/24/37

YEAR	TM/L	W	L	PCT	G	GS	CG	SH	SV	IP	H	HR	BB	SO	RAT	ERA	ERA+	OAV	OOB	BH	AVG	PB	PR	/A	PD	TPI
1937	StL-A	0	1	.000	4	1	0	0	0	8	12	1	3	2	16.9	10.13	48	.353	.405	0	.000	-0	-5	-5	1	-0.4
1938	StL-A	1	2	.333	5	3	2	0	0	21^2	33	3	11	11	18.3	7.06	70	.359	.427	2	.250	-0	-5	-5	-0	-0.5
1939	StL-A	1	1	.500	2	2	2	0	0	19	21	0	6	8	12.8	3.32	147	.266	.318	0	.000	-0	3	3	0	0.3
1940	StL-A	2	4	.333	28	11	3	0	1	97	113	12	52	32	15.5	5.57	82	.298	.386	6	.200	-1	-13	-11	3	-0.4
1941	StL-A	0	0	—	2	0	0	0	0	2^1	5	0	3	2	30.9	11.57	37	.417	.533	0	—	0	-2	-2	0	0.0
Total	5	4	8	.333	41	17	7	0	1	148	184	16	75	55	15.9	5.84	80	.309	.388	8	.178	-2	-22	-19	4	-1.0

● HARRY BILLIARD
Billiard, Harry Pree "Pree" b: 11/11/1883, Monroe, Ind. d: 6/3/23, Wooster, Ohio BR/TR, 6', 190 lbs. Deb: 7/31/08

YEAR	TM/L	W	L	PCT	G	GS	CG	SH	SV	IP	H	HR	BB	SO	RAT	ERA	ERA+	OAV	OOB	BH	AVG	PB	PR	/A	PD	TPI
1908	NY-A	0	0	—	6	0	0	0	0	17	15	1	14	10	18.0	2.65	94	.234	.410	1	.167	-0	-0	-0	-1	-0.1
1914	Ind-F	8	7	.533	32	16	5	0	2	125^2	117	4	63	45	13.4	3.72	84	.257	.356	7	.184	-1	-12	-8	-2	-1.3
1915	New-F	0	1	.000	14	2	0	0	1	28^1	32	0	28	7	20.0	5.72	45	.291	.447	2	.333	0	-9	-10	1	-0.3
Total	3	8	8	.500	52	18	5	0	3	171	164	5	105	62	14.9	3.95	75	.260	.379	10	.200	-1	-22	-19	-2	-1.7

● JACK BILLINGHAM
Billingham, John Eugene b: 2/21/43, Orlando, Fla. BR/TR, 6'4", 215 lbs. Deb: 4/11/68

YEAR	TM/L	W	L	PCT	G	GS	CG	SH	SV	IP	H	HR	BB	SO	RAT	ERA	ERA+	OAV	OOB	BH	AVG	PB	PR	/A	PD	TPI
1968	LA-N	3	0	1.000	50	1	0	0	8	70^2	54	0	30	46	11.0	2.17	128	.215	.304	0	.000	0	6	5	1	0.4
1969	Hou-N	6	7	.462	52	4	1	0	2	82^2	92	12	29	71	13.7	4.25	83	.290	.359	1	.071	0	-6	-6	-0	-1.0
1970	Hou-N	13	9	.591	46	24	8	2	0	187^2	190	10	63	134	12.6	3.98	97	.259	.326	6	.103	-2	1	-2	1	-0.3
1971	Hou-N	10	16	.385	33	33	8	3	0	228^1	205	9	68	139	11.4	3.39	99	.243	.311	9	.123	-3	2	-1	0	-0.4
1972	*Cin-N	12	12	.500	36	31	8	4	1	217^2	197	18	64	137	11.1	3.18	101	.241	.301	5	.070	-4	7	1	-1	-0.4
1973	*Cin-N☆	19	10	.655	40	40	16	**7**	0	**293^1**	257	20	95	155	11.1	3.04	112	.236	.303	6	.065	-5	20	12	2	0.8
1974	Cin-N	19	11	.633	36	35	8	3	0	212^1	233	16	64	103	12.8	3.94	88	.288	.345	5	.075	-5	-8	-11	1	-1.9
1975	*Cin-N	15	10	.600	33	32	5	0	0	208	222	22	76	79	13.3	4.11	87	.279	.348	7	.108	-1	-11	-12	-2	-1.6
1976	*Cin-N	12	10	.545	34	29	5	2	1	177	190	17	62	76	13.0	4.32	81	.279	.343	14	.237	3	-16	-16	-1	-1.6
1977	Cin-N	10	10	.500	36	23	3	2	0	161^2	195	16	56	76	14.5	5.23	75	.306	.371	9	.161	-1	-24	-23	2	-2.4
1978	Det-A	15	8	.652	30	30	10	4	0	201^2	218	16	65	59	13.0	3.88	100	.284	.346	0	—	0	-3	-0	-1	-0.2
1979	Det-A	10	7	.588	35	19	2	0	3	158	163	13	60	59	13.1	3.30	131	.275	.348	0	—	0	16	18	-1	1.7
1980	Det-A	0	0	—	8	0	0	0	0	7^1	11	1	6	3	20.9	7.36	56	.355	.459	0	—	0	-3	-3	0	-0.1
	Bos-A	1	3	.250	7	4	0	0	0	24^1	45	6	12	4	22.6	11.10	38	.413	.488	0	—	0	-19	-19	-0	-2.4
	Yr	1	3	.250	15	4	0	0	0	31^2	56	7	18	7	22.2	10.23	41	.397	.479	0	—	0	-22	-21	-0	-2.5
Total	13	145	113	.562	476	305	74	27	15	2230^2	2272	176	750	1141	12.6	3.83	94	.268	.335	62	.111	-17	-37	-59	0	-9.4

● JOSH BILLINGS
Billings, Haskell Clark b: 9/27/07, New York, N.Y. d: 12/26/83, Greenbrae, Cal. BR/TR, 5'11", 180 lbs. Deb: 8/17/27

YEAR	TM/L	W	L	PCT	G	GS	CG	SH	SV	IP	H	HR	BB	SO	RAT	ERA	ERA+	OAV	OOB	BH	AVG	PB	PR	/A	PD	TPI
1927	Det-A	5	4	.556	10	9	5	0	0	67	64	3	39	18	14.6	4.84	87	.259	.373	7	.259	0	-5	-5	-1	-0.5
1928	Det-A	5	10	.333	21	16	3	1	0	110^2	118	4	59	48	14.8	5.12	80	.276	.371	10	.286	3	-13	-12	-0	-1.2
1929	Det-A	0	1	.000	8	0	0	0	0	19^1	27	0	9	1	17.2	5.12	84	.365	.440	0	.000	-1	-2	-2	1	-0.1
Total	3	10	15	.400	39	25	8	1	0	197	209	7	107	67	15.0	5.03	83	.279	.378	17	.250	2	-20	-19	0	-1.8

● DOUG BIRD
Bird, James Douglas b: 3/5/50, Corona, Cal. BR/TR, 6'4", 180 lbs. Deb: 4/29/73

YEAR	TM/L	W	L	PCT	G	GS	CG	SH	SV	IP	H	HR	BB	SO	RAT	ERA	ERA+	OAV	OOB	BH	AVG	PB	PR	/A	PD	TPI
1973	KC-A	4	4	.500	54	0	0	0	20	102^1	81	10	30	83	9.9	2.99	137	.217	.279	0	—	0	9	13	-2	1.0
1974	KC-A	7	6	.538	55	1	1	0	10	92^1	100	6	27	62	12.5	2.73	140	.286	.339	0	—	0	9	11	1	1.8
1975	KC-A	9	6	.600	51	4	0	0	11	105^1	100	7	40	81	12.1	3.25	119	.258	.331	0	—	0	6	7	-1	1.0
1976	*KC-A	12	10	.545	39	27	2	1	2	197^2	191	17	31	107	10.2	3.37	104	.251	.283	0	—	0	3	3	-2	0.1
1977	*KC-A	11	4	.733	53	5	0	0	14	118^1	120	14	29	83	11.6	3.88	104	.270	.319	0	—	0	2	2	-1	0.2
1978	*KC-A	6	6	.500	40	6	0	0	1	98^2	110	8	31	48	13.0	5.29	72	.284	.340	0	—	0	-17	-16	-0	-1.9
1979	Phi-N	2	0	1.000	32	1	1	0	0	61	73	7	16	33	13.4	5.16	74	.305	.354	1	.167	0	-10	-9	-1	-0.4
1980	NY-A	3	0	1.000	22	1	0	0	1	50^2	47	3	14	17	11.0	2.66	147	.257	.313	0	—	0	8	7	1	0.5
1981	NY-A	5	1	.833	17	4	0	0	0	53^1	58	5	16	28	12.5	2.70	132	.280	.332	0	—	0	6	5	0	0.6
	Chi-N	4	5	.444	12	12	2	1	0	75^1	72	5	16	34	10.6	3.58	103	.254	.297	2	.100	-1	-1	1	-1	-0.1
1982	Chi-N	9	14	.391	35	33	2	1	0	191	230	26	30	71	12.4	5.14	73	.297	.325	8	.143	-2	-33	-30	-2	-3.5
1983	Bos-A	1	4	.200	22	6	0	0	1	67^2	91	14	16	33	14.5	6.65	65	.324	.365	0	—	0	-19	-17	-0	-1.3
Total	11	73	60	.549	432	100	8	3	60	1213^2	1273	122	296	680	11.8	3.99	96	.272	.319	11	.134	-2	-36	-23	-8	-2.0

● RED BIRD
Bird, James Edward b: 4/25/1890, Stephenville, Tex. d: 3/23/72, Murfreesboro, Ark. BL/TL, 5'11", 170 lbs. Deb: 9/17/21

YEAR	TM/L	W	L	PCT	G	GS	CG	SH	SV	IP	H	HR	BB	SO	RAT	ERA	ERA+	OAV	OOB	BH	AVG	PB	PR	/A	PD	TPI
1921	Was-A	0	0	—	1	0	0	0	0	5	5	0	1	2	12.6	5.40	76	.294	.368	0	.000	-0	-1	-1	0	0.0

● MIKE BIRKBECK
Birkbeck, Michael Lawrence b: 3/10/61, Orrville, Ohio BR/TR, 6'1", 190 lbs. Deb: 8/17/86

YEAR	TM/L	W	L	PCT	G	GS	CG	SH	SV	IP	H	HR	BB	SO	RAT	ERA	ERA+	OAV	OOB	BH	AVG	PB	PR	/A	PD	TPI
1986	Mil-A	1	1	.500	7	4	0	0	0	22	24	0	12	13	14.7	4.50	96	.282	.371	0	—	0	-1	-0	-0	-0.1
1987	Mil-A	1	4	.200	10	10	1	0	0	45	63	8	19	25	16.4	6.20	74	.335	.396	0	—	0	-9	-8	1	-0.7
1988	Mil-A	10	8	.556	23	23	0	0	0	124	141	10	37	64	13.0	4.72	84	.285	.336	0	—	0	-10	-10	2	-1.1
1989	Mil-A	0	4	.000	9	9	1	0	0	44^2	57	4	22	31	16.5	5.44	71	.310	.392	0	—	0	-8	-8	0	-0.7
1992	NY-N	0	1	.000	1	1	0	0	0	7	12	3	1	2	16.7	9.00	39	.387	.406	0	.000	-0	-4	-4	0	-0.5
1995	NY-N	0	1	.000	4	4	0	0	0	27^2	22	2	2	14	7.8	1.63	249	.220	.235	2	.333	1	8	7	-0	0.4
Total	6	12	19	.387	54	51	2	0	0	270^1	319	27	93	149	13.8	4.86	84	.295	.353	2	.250	1	-24	-24	2	-2.7

● RALPH BIRKOFER
Birkofer, Ralph Joseph "Lefty" b: 11/5/08, Cincinnati, Ohio d: 3/16/71, Cincinnati, Ohio BL/TL, 5'11", 213 lbs. Deb: 4/25/33

YEAR	TM/L	W	L	PCT	G	GS	CG	SH	SV	IP	H	HR	BB	SO	RAT	ERA	ERA+	OAV	OOB	BH	AVG	PB	PR	/A	PD	TPI
1933	Pit-N	4	2	.667	9	8	3	1	0	50^2	43	1	17	20	10.8	2.31	144	.229	.296	7	.318	1	6	6	-0	0.8
1934	Pit-N	11	12	.478	41	24	11	0	1	204	227	11	66	71	13.1	4.10	100	.277	.335	17	.227	1	-1	0	-2	-0.1
1935	Pit-N	9	7	.563	37	18	8	1	1	150^1	173	5	42	80	13.2	4.07	101	.283	.335	14	.241	2	-1	1	-3	0.0
1936	Pit-N	7	5	.583	34	13	2	0	0	109^1	130	4	41	44	14.5	4.69	86	.295	.362	9	.220	-0	-8	-8	-3	-1.0
1937	Bro-N	0	2	.000	11	1	0	0	0	29^2	45	3	9	9	16.4	6.67	60	.341	.383	3	.273	1	-9	-9	-1	-0.5
Total	5	31	28	.525	132	64	24	2	2	544	618	24	175	224	13.4	4.19	96	.282	.340	50	.242	5	-13	-10	-8	-0.8

● BABE BIRRER
Birrer, Werner Joseph b: 7/4/29, Buffalo, N.Y. BR/TR, 6', 195 lbs. Deb: 6/5/55

YEAR	TM/L	W	L	PCT	G	GS	CG	SH	SV	IP	H	HR	BB	SO	RAT	ERA	ERA+	OAV	OOB	BH	AVG	PB	PR	/A	PD	TPI
1955	Det-A	4	3	.571	36	3	1	0	3	80^1	77	9	29	28	11.9	4.15	93	.248	.313	3	.158	2	-2	-3	-1	-0.1
1956	Bal-A	0	0	—	4	0	0	0	0	5^1	9	0	1	1	16.9	6.75	58	.360	.385	0	.000	-0	-2	-2	-0	0.0
1958	LA-N	0	0	—	16	0	0	0	1	34	43	4	7	16	13.5	4.50	91	.309	.347	4	.571	2	-2	-2	-1	0.1
Total	3	4	3	.571	56	3	1	0	4	119^2	129	13	37	45	12.6	4.36	90	.272	.326	7	.259	4	-5	-6	-2	0.0

● TIM BIRTSAS
Birtsas, Timothy Dean b: 9/5/60, Pontiac, Mich. BL/TL, 6'7", 240 lbs. Deb: 5/3/85

YEAR	TM/L	W	L	PCT	G	GS	CG	SH	SV	IP	H	HR	BB	SO	RAT	ERA	ERA+	OAV	OOB	BH	AVG	PB	PR	/A	PD	TPI
1985	Oak-A	10	6	.625	29	25	2	0	0	141^1	124	18	91	94	13.9	4.01	96	.238	.354	0	—	0	2	-2	-3	-0.3
1986	Oak-A	0	0	—	2	0	0	0	0	2	2	1	4	1	27.0	22.50	17	.286	.545	0	—	0	-4	-4	-0	0.2
1988	Cin-N	1	3	.250	36	4	0	0	0	64^1	61	6	24	38	12.3	4.20	85	.250	.325	0	.000	-1	-5	-4	-1	-0.5
1989	Cin-N	2	2	.500	42	1	0	0	1	69^2	68	5	27	57	12.7	3.75	96	.261	.337	1	.250	1	-2	-1	-1	0.0
1990	Cin-N	1	3	.250	29	0	0	0	0	51^1	69	7	24	41	16.5	3.86	102	.325	.397	0	.000	-0	-0	0	0	0.0
Total	5	14	14	.500	138	30	2	0	1	328^2	324	37	170	231	13.8	4.08	93	.260	.354	1	.056	-0	-10	-11	-4	-0.6

● FRANK BISCAN
Biscan, Frank Stephen "Porky" b: 3/13/20, Mt.Olive, Ill. d: 5/22/59, St.Louis, Mo. BL/TL, 5'11", 190 lbs. Deb: 5/3/42

YEAR	TM/L	W	L	PCT	G	GS	CG	SH	SV	IP	H	HR	BB	SO	RAT	ERA	ERA+	OAV	OOB	BH	AVG	PB	PR	/A	PD	TPI
1942	StL-A	0	1	.000	11	0	0	0	1	27	13	1	11	10	8.0	2.33	159	.143	.235	0	.000	-0	4	4	0	0.1
1946	StL-A	1	1	.500	16	0	0	0	1	22^2	28	0	22	9	19.9	5.16	72	.318	.455	0	.000	-0	-4	-4	-0	-0.4
1948	StL-A	6	7	.462	47	4	1	0	2	98^2	129	3	71	45	19.1	6.11	75	.322	.435	5	.192	1	-20	-17	0	-1.9
Total	3	7	9	.438	74	4	1	0	4	148^1	170	4	104	64	17.2	5.28	81	.294	.409	5	.143	-0	-20	-17	0	-2.2

YEAR TM/L	W	L	PCT	G	GS	CG	SH	SV	IP	H	HR	BB	SO	RAT	ERA	ERA+	OAV	OOB	BH	AVG	PB	PR	/A	PD	TPI
● **CHARLIE BISHOP** Bishop, Charles Tuller b: 1/1/24, Atlanta, Ga. d: 7/5/93, Lawrenceville, Ga. BR/TR, 6'2", 195 lbs. Deb: 8/22/52																									
1952 Phi-A	2	2	.500	6	5	1	0	0	30^2	29	2	24	17	15.6	6.46	61	.238	.363	1	.111	-0	-9	-9	0	-0.9
1953 Phi-A	3	14	.176	39	20	1	1	2	160^2	174	15	86	66	14.8	5.66	76	.282	.375	5	.089	-4	-30	-24	2	-2.5
1954 Phi-A	4	6	.400	20	12	4	0	1	96	98	10	50	34	14.3	4.41	89	.275	.372	4	.121	-2	-7	-5	-2	-0.8
1955 KC-A	1	0	1.000	4	0	0	0	0	6^2	6	1	8	4	23.0	5.40	77	.261	.500	1	.500	0	-1	-1	-0	-0.1
Total 4	10	22	.313	69	37	6	1	3	294	307	28	168	121	14.9	5.33	77	.275	.376	11	.110	-6	-47	-39	1	-4.3
● **JIM BISHOP** Bishop, James Morton b: 1/28/1898, Montgomery City, Mo. d: 9/20/73, Montgomery City, Mo. BR/TR, 6', 195 lbs. Deb: 4/26/23																									
1923 Phi-N	0	3	.000	15	0	0	0	1	32^2	48	2	11	5	17.1	6.34	73	.353	.413	0	.000	-2	-8	-6	1	-0.6
1924 Phi-N	0	1	.000	7	1	0	0	0	16^2	24	3	7	3	16.7	6.48	69	.348	.408	1	.200	-0	-5	-4	0	-0.2
Total 2	0	4	.000	22	1	0	0	1	49^1	72	5	18	8	17.0	6.39	71	.351	.412	1	.067	-2	-13	-10	1	-0.8
● **LLOYD BISHOP** Bishop, Lloyd Clifton b: 4/25/1890, Conway Springs, Kan. d: 6/18/68, Wichita, Kan. BR/TR, 6', 180 lbs. Deb: 9/5/14																									
1914 Cle-A	0	1	.000	3	1	0	0	0	8	14	0	3	1	19.1	5.63	51	.389	.436	0	.000	-0	-3	-2	-0	-0.3
● **BILL BISHOP** Bishop, William Henry "Lefty" b: 10/22/1900, Houtzdale, Pa. d: 2/14/56, St.Joseph, Mo. BL/TL, 5'8", 170 lbs. Deb: 9/15/21																									
1921 Phi-A	0	0	—	2	0	0	0	0	7	8	0	10	4	23.1	9.00	50	.267	.450	0	.000	-1	-4	-4	0	0.0
● **BILL BISHOP** Bishop, William Robinson b: 12/27/1869, Adamsburg, Pa. d: 12/15/32, Pittsburgh, Pa. Deb: 9/13/1886																									
1886 Pit-a	0	1	.000	2	2	2	0	0	17	17	0	11	4	15.4	3.18	107	.221	.326	1	.143	-1	1	0	-1	-0.1
1887 Pit-N	0	3	.000	3	3	3	0	0	27	45	2	22	4	23.0	13.33	29	.354	.457	0	.000	-1	-28	-28	-0	-1.9
1889 Chi-N	0	0	—	2	0	0	0	2	3	6	0	6	1	36.0	18.00	23	.400	.571	0	.000	0	-5	-5	-0	-0.5
Total 3	0	4	.000	7	5	5	0	2	47	68	2	39	9	21.1	9.96	37	.311	.421	1	.059	-2	-32	-33	-1	-2.5
● **HI BITHORN** Bithorn, Hiram Gabriel (Sosa) b: 3/18/16, Santurce, P.R. d: 1/1/52, ElMante, Mex. BR/TR, 6'1", 200 lbs. Deb: 4/15/42																									
1942 Chi-N	9	14	.391	38	16	9	0	2	171^1	191	8	81	65	14.3	3.68	87	.296	.374	7	.123	-1	-7	-9	-1	-1.4
1943 Chi-N	18	12	.600	39	30	19	**7**	2	249^2	227	8	65	86	10.6	2.60	129	.244	.294	16	.174	-0	22	21	1	2.6
1946 Chi-N	6	5	.545	26	7	2	1	1	86^2	97	5	25	34	12.7	3.84	86	.283	.332	5	.179	-0	-4	-5	-0	-0.7
1947 Chi-A	1	0	1.000	2	0	0	0	0	2	2	0	0	0	9.0	0.00	—	.286	.286	0	—	0	1	1	-0	0.4
Total 4	34	31	.523	105	53	30	8	5	509^2	517	21	171	185	12.2	3.16	104	.268	.328	28	.158	-2	12	7	-0	0.9
● **JOE BITKER** Bitker, Joseph Anthony b: 2/12/64, Glendale, Cal. BR/TR, 6'1", 175 lbs. Deb: 7/31/90																									
1990 Oak-A	0	0	—	1	0	0	0	0	3	1	0	1	2	6.0	0.00	—	.111	.200	0	—	0	1	1	0	0.2
Tex-A	0	0	—	5	0	0	0	0	9	7	0	3	6	11.0	3.00	131	.212	.297	0	—	0	1	1	0	0.0
Yr	0	0	—	6	0	0	0	0	12	8	0	4	8	9.8	2.25	172	.190	.277	0	—	0	2	2	0	0.2
1991 Tex-A	1	0	1.000	9	0	0	0	0	14^2	17	4	8	16	15.3	6.75	60	.274	.357	0	—	0	-4	-4	-0	-0.2
Total 2	1	0	1.000	15	0	0	0	0	26^2	25	4	12	24	12.8	4.73	84	.240	.325	0	—	0	-2	-2	0	0.0
● **JEFF BITTIGER** Bittiger, Jeffrey Scott b: 4/13/62, Jersey City, N.J. BR/TR, 5'10", 175 lbs. Deb: 9/2/86																									
1986 Phi-N	1	1	.500	3	3	0	0	0	14^2	16	2	7	8	14.7	5.52	70	.271	.358	1	.333	1	-3	-3	0	-0.2
1987 Min-A	1	0	1.000	3	1	0	0	0	8^1	11	2	0	5	13.0	5.40	85	.314	.333	0	—	0	-1	-1	0	-0.1
1988 Chi-A	2	4	.333	25	7	0	0	0	61^2	59	11	29	33	12.8	4.23	94	.255	.338	0	—	0	-2	-2	-1	-0.2
1989 Chi-A	0	1	.000	2	1	0	0	0	9^2	9	2	6	7	14.0	6.52	58	.257	.366	0	—	0	-3	-3	-0	-0.3
Total 4	4	6	.400	33	12	0	0	0	94^1	95	17	42	53	13.3	4.77	84	.264	.344	1	.333	1	-8	-8	-1	-0.8
● **JIM BIVIN** Bivin, James Nathaniel b: 12/11/09, Jackson, Miss. d: 11/7/82, Pueblo, Colo. BR/TR, 6', 155 lbs. Deb: 4/16/35																									
1935 Phi-N	2	9	.182	47	14	0	0	1	161^2	220	20	65	54	16.0	5.79	78	.316	.377	7	.146	-1	-32	-23	-1	-1.5
● **DAVE BLACK** Black, David b: 4/19/1892, Chicago, Ill. d: 10/27/36, Pittsburgh, Pa. BL/TR, 6'2", 175 lbs. Deb: 5/2/14																									
1914 Chi-F	1	0	1.000	8	1	1	0	0	25	28	1	4	19	11.5	6.12	43	.311	.340	2	.286	1	-9	-10	0	-0.3
1915 Chi-F	6	7	.462	25	10	2	0	0	121^1	104	3	33	43	10.6	2.45	103	.241	.304	4	.108	-3	4	1	2	-0.1
Bal-F	1	3	.250	8	4	1	0	0	34	32	2	15	10	13.0	3.71	77	.260	.350	3	.250	0	-4	-3	1	-0.3
Yr	7	10	.412	33	14	3	0	0	155^1	136	5	48	53	10.8	2.72	95	.243	.305	7	.143	-3	0	-2	2	-0.4
1923 Bos-A	0	0	—	2	0	0	0	0	1	2	0	0	0	18.0	0.00	—	.500	.500	0	—	0	0	0	-0	0.0
Total 3	8	10	.444	43	15	4	0	0	181^1	166	6	52	72	11.2	3.18	82	.256	.319	9	.161	-2	-8	-11	2	-0.7
● **DON BLACK** Black, Donald Paul b: 7/20/16, Salix, Iowa d: 4/21/59, Cuyahoga Falls, O. BR/TR, 6', 185 lbs. Deb: 4/24/43																									
1943 Phi-A	6	16	.273	33	26	12	1	1	208	193	8	110	65	13.4	4.20	81	.247	.344	13	.188	-1	-21	-19	0	-1.9
1944 Phi-A	10	12	.455	29	27	8	0	0	177^1	177	6	75	78	13.0	4.06	86	.259	.336	11	.186	-1	-12	-11	-0	-1.4
1945 Phi-A	5	11	.313	26	18	8	0	0	125^1	154	5	69	47	16.0	5.17	66	.307	.391	6	.162	-2	-25	-24	-1	-3.1
1946 Cle-A	1	2	.333	18	4	0	0	0	43^2	45	5	21	15	13.8	4.53	73	.273	.358	2	.200	0	-5	-6	1	-0.3
1947 Cle-A	10	12	.455	30	28	8	3	0	190^2	177	17	85	72	12.4	3.92	89	.249	.330	12	.182	-1	-5	-9	1	-1.0
1948 Cle-A	2	2	.500	18	10	1	0	0	52	57	5	40	16	17.0	5.37	76	.282	.403	3	.200	-0	-6	-8	0	-0.5
Total 6	34	55	.382	154	113	37	4	1	797	803	46	400	293	13.7	4.35	80	.264	.352	47	.184	-4	-74	-76	0	-8.2
● **BUD BLACK** Black, Harry Ralston b: 6/30/57, San Mateo, Cal. BL/TL, 6'2", 180 lbs. Deb: 9/5/81																									
1981 Sea-A	0	0	—	2	0	0	0	0	1	2	0	3	0	45.0	0.00	—	.500	.714	0	—	0	0	0	0	-0.2
1982 KC-A	4	6	.400	22	14	0	0	0	88^1	92	10	34	40	13.1	4.58	89	.269	.340	0	—	0	-5	-5	-0	-0.5
1983 KC-A	10	7	.588	24	24	3	0	0	161^1	159	19	43	58	11.4	3.79	107	.257	.308	0	—	0	5	5	2	0.7
1984 *KC-A	17	12	.586	35	35	8	1	0	257	226	22	64	140	**10.3**	3.12	129	.233	**.283**	0	—	0	25	26	3	3.1
1985 *KC-A	10	15	.400	33	33	5	2	0	205^2	216	17	59	122	12.4	4.33	96	.268	.324	0	—	0	-4	-4	-1	-0.5
1986 KC-A	5	10	.333	56	4	0	0	9	121	100	14	43	68	11.2	3.20	133	.225	.303	0	—	0	13	14	1	1.8
1987 KC-A	8	6	.571	29	18	0	0	1	122^1	126	16	35	61	12.2	3.60	126	.265	.322	0	—	0	12	13	-0	1.3
1988 KC-A	2	1	.667	17	0	0	0	0	22	23	2	11	19	13.9	4.91	81	.267	.351	0	—	0	-2	-2	-0	-0.3
Cle-A	2	3	.400	16	7	0	0	1	59	59	6	23	44	13.1	5.03	82	.262	.341	0	—	0	-7	-6	1	-0.4
Yr	4	4	.500	33	7	0	0	1	81	82	8	34	63	13.3	5.00	82	.264	.344	0	—	0	-9	-8	0	-0.7
1989 Cle-A	12	11	.522	33	32	6	3	0	222^1	213	14	52	88	10.8	3.36	118	.252	.296	0	—	0	13	15	-1	1.4
1990 Cle-A	11	10	.524	29	29	5	2	0	191	171	17	58	103	11.0	3.53	111	.236	.296	0	—	0	8	8	-0	0.8
Tor-A	2	1	.667	3	2	0	0	0	15^2	10	2	3	3	8.0	4.02	98	.189	.246	0	—	0	-0	-0	1	0.0
Yr	13	11	.542	32	31	5	2	0	206^2	181	19	61	106	10.6	3.57	110	.230	.286	0	—	0	8	8	0	0.8
1991 SF-N	12	16	.429	34	34	3	3	0	214^1	201	25	71	104	11.6	3.99	90	.251	.315	13	.183	1	-7	-10	2	-0.9
1992 SF-N	10	12	.455	28	28	2	1	0	177	178	23	59	82	12.1	3.97	83	.263	.323	3	.056	-3	-9	-13	1	-1.6
1993 SF-N	8	2	.800	16	16	0	0	0	93^2	89	13	33	45	11.9	3.56	110	.256	.325	9	.243	2	5	4	1	0.7
1994 SF-N	4	2	.667	10	10	0	0	0	54^1	50	9	16	28	11.4	4.47	90	.245	.309	1	.059	-1	-2	-3	-0	-0.4
1995 Cle-A	4	2	.667	11	10	0	0	0	47^1	63	8	16	34	15.0	6.85	69	.317	.367	0	—	0	-11	-11	0	-1.2
Total 15	121	116	.511	398	296	32	12	11	2053^1	1978	217	623	1039	11.6	3.84	103	.253	.312	26	.145	-1	33	30	9	3.8
● **JOE BLACK** Black, Joseph b: 2/8/24, Plainfield, N.J. BR/TR, 6'2", 220 lbs. Deb: 5/1/52																									
1952 *Bro-N	15	4	.789	56	2	1	0	15	142^1	102	9	41	85	9.1	2.15	169	.201	.262	5	.139	-1	**25**	**24**	-2	3.3
1953 *Bro-N	6	3	.667	34	3	0	0	5	72^2	74	12	27	42	12.6	5.33	80	.259	.325	4	.235	0	-8	-9	-0	-1.1
1954 Bro-N	0	0	—	5	0	0	0	0	7	11	3	5	3	20.6	11.57	35	.355	.444	0	—	0	-6	-6	-0	0.0
1955 Bro-N	1	0	1.000	6	0	0	0	0	15^1	15	1	5	9	11.7	2.93	138	.273	.333	1	.333	0	2	2	-0	0.1
Cin-N	5	2	.714	32	11	1	0	3	102^1	106	13	25	54	11.5	4.22	100	.263	.306	3	.100	-2	-2	0	-0	-0.3
Yr	6	2	.750	38	11	1	0	3	117^2	121	14	30	63	11.5	4.05	104	.264	.309	4	.121	-2	-0	2	-1	-0.2
1956 Cin-N	3	2	.600	32	0	0	0	2	61^2	61	11	25	27	12.6	4.52	88	.256	.327	0	.000	-1	-5	-4	-1	-0.5
1957 Was-A	0	1	.000	7	0	0	0	0	12^2	22	4	1	2	16.3	7.11	55	.393	.404	0	—	0	-5	-5	0	-0.3
Total 6	30	12	.714	172	16	2	0	25	414	391	53	129	222	11.3	3.91	102	.248	.306	13	.135	-5	1	3	-3	1.2
● **BOB BLACK** Black, Robert Benjamin b: 12/10/1862, Cincinnati, Ohio d: 3/21/33, Sioux City, Iowa 5'5.5", 155 lbs. Deb: 8/19/1884 ♦																									
1884 KC-U	4	9	.308	16	15	13	0	0	123	127	1	17	93	10.5	3.22	69	.249	.273	36	.247	1	-11	-13	2	-0.8

● BUD BLACK
Black, William Carroll b: 7/9/32, St.Louis, Mo. BR/TR, 6'3", 197 lbs. Deb: 9/13/52

YEAR	TM/L	W	L	PCT	G	GS	CG	SH	SV	IP	H	HR	BB	SO	RAT	ERA	ERA+	OAV	OOB	BH	AVG	PB	PR	/A	PD	TPI
1952	Det-A	0	1	.000	2	2	0	0	0	8	14	0	5	0	21.4	10.13	38	.389	.463	0	.000	-0	-6	-6	-0	-0.6
1955	Det-A	1	1	.500	3	2	1	1	0	14	12	0	8	7	14.1	1.29	299	.231	.355	1	.250	0	4	4	0	0.6
1956	Det-A	1	1	.500	5	1	0	0	0	10	10	2	5	7	13.5	3.60	114	.256	.341	0	.000	-0	1	1	0	0.1
Total	3	2	3	.400	10	5	1	1	0	32	36	2	18	14	15.8	4.22	93	.283	.381	1	.111	-1	-1	-1	0	0.1

● CHARLIE BLACKBURN
Blackburn, Foster Edwin b: 1/6/1895, Chicago, Ill. d: 3/9/84, New Port Richey, Fla. BR/TR, 6'1", 165 lbs. Deb: 4/17/15

YEAR	TM/L	W	L	PCT	G	GS	CG	SH	SV	IP	H	HR	BB	SO	RAT	ERA	ERA+	OAV	OOB	BH	AVG	PB	PR	/A	PD	TPI
1915	KC-F	0	1	.000	7	2	0	0	0	15^2	19	2	13	7	18.4	8.62	31	.306	.427	0	.000	-1	-10	-10	0	-0.6
1921	Chi-A	0	0	—	1	0	0	0	0	1	0	0	1	0	9.0	0.00	—	.000	.333	0	—	0	0	0	-0	0.0
Total	2	0	1	.000	8	2	0	0	0	16^2	19	2	14	7	17.8	8.10	34	.297	.423	0	.000	-1	-10	-10	0	-0.6

● GEORGE BLACKBURN
Blackburn, George W. "Smiling George" b: 9/21/1871, Ozark, Mo. TR, 5'11", 184 lbs. Deb: 7/6/1897

YEAR	TM/L	W	L	PCT	G	GS	CG	SH	SV	IP	H	HR	BB	SO	RAT	ERA	ERA+	OAV	OOB	BH	AVG	PB	PR	/A	PD	TPI
1897	Bal-N	2	2	.500	5	4	3	0	0	33	34	2	12	1	12.8	6.82	61	.264	.331	1	.077	-2	-9	-10	-0	-1.0

● JIM BLACKBURN
Blackburn, James Ray "Bones" b: 6/19/24, Warsaw, Ky. d: 10/26/69, Cincinnati, Ohio BR/TR, 6'4", 175 lbs. Deb: 7/24/48

YEAR	TM/L	W	L	PCT	G	GS	CG	SH	SV	IP	H	HR	BB	SO	RAT	ERA	ERA+	OAV	OOB	BH	AVG	PB	PR	/A	PD	TPI
1948	Cin-N	0	2	.000	16	0	0	0	0	32^1	38	1	14	10	14.5	4.18	94	.302	.371	0	.000	-0	-1	-1	-0	-0.1
1951	Cin-N	0	0	—	2	0	0	0	0	3^2	8	3	2	1	29.5	17.18	24	.444	.545	0	—	0	-5	-5	0	0.0
Total	2	0	2	.000	18	0	0	0	0	36	46	4	16	11	16.0	5.50	71	.319	.395	0	.000	-0	-6	-6	-0	-0.1

● RON BLACKBURN
Blackburn, Ronald Hamilton b: 4/23/35, Mt.Airy, N.C. d: 4/29/98, Morganton, N.C. BR/TR, 6'0.5", 160 lbs. Deb: 4/15/58

YEAR	TM/L	W	L	PCT	G	GS	CG	SH	SV	IP	H	HR	BB	SO	RAT	ERA	ERA+	OAV	OOB	BH	AVG	PB	PR	/A	PD	TPI
1958	Pit-N	2	1	.667	38	2	0	0	3	63^2	61	7	27	31	12.9	3.39	114	.261	.345	2	.286	1	4	3	1	0.4
1959	Pit-N	1	1	.500	26	0	0	0	1	44^1	50	5	15	19	13.6	3.65	106	.286	.349	1	.200	1	1	1	-1	0.1
Total	2	3	2	.600	64	2	0	0	4	108	111	12	42	50	13.2	3.50	110	.271	.346	3	.250	2	5	4	0	0.5

● LENA BLACKBURNE
Blackburne, Russell Aubrey "Slats"
b: 10/23/1886, Clifton Heights, Pa. d: 2/29/68, Riverside, N.J. BR/TR, 5'11", 160 lbs. Deb: 4/14/10 MC♦

YEAR	TM/L	W	L	PCT	G	GS	CG	SH	SV	IP	H	HR	BB	SO	RAT	ERA	ERA+	OAV	OOB	BH	AVG	PB	PR	/A	PD	TPI
1929	Chi-A	0	0	—	1	0	0	0	0	0^1	1	0	0	0	27.0	0.00	—	1.000	1.000	0	—	0	0	0	0	0.0

● EWELL BLACKWELL
Blackwell, Ewell "The Whip" b: 10/23/22, Fresno, Cal. d: 10/29/96, Hendersonville, N.C. BR/TR, 6'6", 195 lbs. Deb: 4/21/42

YEAR	TM/L	W	L	PCT	G	GS	CG	SH	SV	IP	H	HR	BB	SO	RAT	ERA	ERA+	OAV	OOB	BH	AVG	PB	PR	/A	PD	TPI
1942	Cin-N	0	0	—	2	0	0	0	0	3	3	0	3	1	18.0	6.00	55	.231	.375	0	.000	-0	-1	-1	0	0.0
1946	Cin-N★	9	13	.409	33	25	10	**5**	0	194^1	160	1	79	100	11.3	2.45	136	.226	.307	6	.107	-3	21	19	4	2.3
1947	Cin-N★	**22**	8	.733	33	33	**23**	6	0	273	227	10	95	**193**	10.7	2.47	166	.234	.304	13	.123	-5	48	49	5	**5.2**
1948	Cin-N★	7	9	.438	22	20	4	1	1	138^2	134	12	52	114	12.3	4.54	86	.251	.323	11	.229	1	-9	-10	4	-0.5
1949	Cin-N★	5	5	.500	30	4	0	0	1	76^2	80	7	34	55	13.7	4.23	99	.271	.352	4	.211	-0	-2	-0	1	0.1
1950	Cin-N★	17	15	.531	40	32	18	1	4	261	203	12	112	188	11.3	2.97	143	**.210**	.301	13	.146	-2	34	**37**	2	**4.3**
1951	Cin-N★	16	15	.516	38	32	11	2	2	232^2	204	16	97	120	12.0	3.44	118	.233	.315	24	.293	7	13	16	0	2.9
1952	Cin-N	3	12	.200	23	17	3	0	0	102	107	6	60	48	15.2	5.38	70	.275	.379	5	.156	-0	-19	-18	-0	-2.4
	*NY-A	1	0	1.000	5	2	0	0	1	16	12	0	12	7	13.5	0.56	591	.203	.338	1	.200	-0	6	5	-0	0.4
1953	NY-A	2	0	1.000	8	4	0	0	1	19^2	17	2	13	11	14.2	3.66	101	.233	.356	0	.000	-1	1	0	-0	-0.1
1955	KC-A	0	1	.000	2	0	0	0	0	4	3	1	5	2	20.3	6.75	62	.250	.500	0	—	0	-1	-1	-0	-0.3
Total	10	82	78	.512	236	169	69	15	10	1321	1150	67	562	839	12.0	3.30	120	.235	.319	77	.174	-3	91	96	16	11.9

● GEORGE BLAEHOLDER
Blaeholder, George Franklin b: 1/26/04, Orange, Cal. d: 12/29/47, Garden Grove, Cal. BR/TR, 5'11", 175 lbs. Deb: 4/20/25

YEAR	TM/L	W	L	PCT	G	GS	CG	SH	SV	IP	H	HR	BB	SO	RAT	ERA	ERA+	OAV	OOB	BH	AVG	PB	PR	/A	PD	TPI
1925	StL-A	0	0	—	2	0	0	0	0	2	6	3	1	1	36.0	31.50	15	.600	.667	0	—	0	-6	-6	-0	0.0
1927	StL-A	0	1	.000	1	1	1	0	0	9	8	1	4	2	13.0	5.00	87	.258	.361	1	.333	0	-1	-1	0	0.0
1928	StL-A	10	15	.400	38	26	9	1	3	214^1	235	23	52	87	12.1	4.37	96	.280	.324	15	.211	2	-8	-4	5	0.2
1929	StL-A	14	15	.483	42	24	13	**4**	2	222	237	18	61	72	12.1	4.18	106	.275	.323	9	.122	-4	2	6	6	0.9
1930	StL-A	11	13	.458	37	23	10	1	4	191^1	235	20	46	70	13.3	4.61	106	.303	.343	12	.185	-1	1	6	-1	0.4
1931	StL-A	11	15	.423	35	32	13	1	0	226^1	280	15	56	79	13.4	4.53	102	.295	.335	11	.143	-3	-4	3	3	0.3
1932	StL-A	14	14	.500	42	36	16	1	0	258^1	304	19	76	80	13.3	4.70	103	.290	.340	12	.136	-4	-6	4	0	0.1
1933	StL-A	15	19	.441	38	36	14	3	0	255^2	283	24	69	63	12.4	4.72	99	.280	.326	14	.182	-1	-12	-2	3	0.0
1934	StL-A	14	18	.438	39	33	14	1	3	234^1	276	16	68	66	13.2	4.22	118	.296	.343	7	.093	-5	7	20	0	1.9
1935	StL-A	1	1	.500	6	2	0	0	0	17^2	25	3	6	0	15.8	7.13	67	.342	.392	0	.000	-1	-5	-5	1	-0.4
	Phi-A	6	10	.375	23	22	10	1	0	149	173	10	49	22	13.4	3.99	114	.289	.343	2	.043	-6	8	9	2	0.4
	Yr	7	11	.389	29	24	10	1	0	166^2	198	13	55	22	13.7	4.32	106	.295	.348	2	.040	-7	3	5	2	0.0
1936	Cle-A	8	4	.667	35	16	6	1	0	134^1	158	21	47	30	13.9	5.09	99	.295	.356	6	.130	-3	-1	-1	2	-0.2
Total	11	104	125	.454	338	251	106	14	12	1914^1	2220	173	535	572	13.0	4.54	103	.290	.337	89	.142	-25	-26	30	20	3.6

● DENNIS BLAIR
Blair, Dennis Herman b: 6/5/54, Middletown, Ohio BR/TR, 6'5", 182 lbs. Deb: 5/26/74

YEAR	TM/L	W	L	PCT	G	GS	CG	SH	SV	IP	H	HR	BB	SO	RAT	ERA	ERA+	OAV	OOB	BH	AVG	PB	PR	/A	PD	TPI
1974	Mon-N	11	7	.611	22	22	4	1	0	146	113	7	72	76	11.7	3.27	117	.210	.308	6	.118	-2	6	9	3	1.2
1975	Mon-N	8	15	.348	30	27	1	0	0	163^1	150	14	106	82	14.3	3.80	101	.251	.366	7	.143	-1	-3	0	-1	-0.2
1976	Mon-N	0	2	.000	5	4	1	0	0	15^2	21	1	11	9	19.5	4.02	92	.300	.410	0	.000	-0	-1	-1	-0	-0.1
1980	SD-N	0	1	.000	5	1	0	0	0	14	18	3	3	11	13.5	6.43	53	.310	.344	1	.200	0	-4	-5	-1	-0.3
Total	4	19	25	.432	62	54	6	1	0	339	302	25	192	178	13.4	3.69	103	.239	.344	14	.128	-4	-3	4	1	0.6

● WILLIE BLAIR
Blair, William Allen b: 12/18/65, Paintsville, Ky. BR/TR, 6'1", 185 lbs. Deb: 4/11/90

YEAR	TM/L	W	L	PCT	G	GS	CG	SH	SV	IP	H	HR	BB	SO	RAT	ERA	ERA+	OAV	OOB	BH	AVG	PB	PR	/A	PD	TPI
1990	Tor-A	3	5	.375	27	6	0	0	0	68^2	66	4	28	43	12.5	4.06	97	.250	.324	0	—	0	-1	-1	-1	-0.3
1991	Cle-A	2	3	.400	11	5	0	0	0	36	58	7	10	13	17.3	6.75	62	.377	.418	0	—	0	-11	-10	0	-1.3
1992	Hou-N	5	7	.417	29	8	0	0	0	78^2	74	5	25	48	11.6	4.00	84	.249	.312	1	.059	-1	-4	-6	-1	-1.0
1993	Col-N	6	10	.375	46	18	1	0	0	146	184	20	42	84	14.1	4.75	100	.306	.354	4	.111	-2	-11	0	-1	-0.2
1994	Col-N	0	5	.000	47	1	0	0	3	77^2	98	9	39	68	16.3	5.79	86	.308	.391	0	.000	-1	-14	-7	-1	-0.6
1995	SD-N	7	5	.583	40	12	0	0	0	114	112	11	45	83	12.6	4.34	93	.262	.335	0	.000	-2	-2	-4	-1	-0.7
1996	*SD-N	2	6	.250	60	0	0	0	1	88	80	13	29	67	11.9	4.60	86	.240	.314	0	.000	-0	-4	-6	-2	-0.7
1997	Det-A	16	8	.667	29	27	2	0	0	175	186	18	46	90	12.1	4.17	110	.273	.322	0	.000	-0	8	8	-2	0.7
1998	Ari-N	4	15	.211	23	23	0	0	0	146^2	165	27	51	71	13.4	5.34	81	.292	.353	4	.083	-3	-18	-17	1	-2.0
	NY-N	1	1	.500	11	2	0	0	0	28^2	23	4	10	21	10.7	3.14	133	.228	.304	1	.250	1	3	3	0	0.3
	Yr	5	16	.238	34	25	0	0	0	175^1	188	31	61	92	12.8	4.98	86	.279	.340	5	.096	-2	-15	-14	2	-1.7
Total	9	46	65	.414	323	102	3	0	4	959^1	1046	118	325	588	13.1	4.67	92	.279	.341	10	.070	-8	-54	-39	-7	-5.8

● BILL BLAIR
Blair, William Ellsworth b: 9/17/1863, Pittsburgh, Pa. d: 2/22/1890, Pittsburgh, Pa. BL/TL, 5'8.5", 172 lbs. Deb: 7/19/1888

YEAR	TM/L	W	L	PCT	G	GS	CG	SH	SV	IP	H	HR	BB	SO	RAT	ERA	ERA+	OAV	OOB	BH	AVG	PB	PR	/A	PD	TPI
1888	Phi-a	1	3	.250	4	4	3	0	0	31	29	0	8	16	11.0	2.61	114	.238	.290	4	.308	1	2	1	1	0.3

● DICK BLAISDELL
Blaisdell, Howard Carleton b: 6/18/1862, Bradford, Mass. d: 8/20/1886, Malden, Mass. Deb: 7/9/1884

YEAR	TM/L	W	L	PCT	G	GS	CG	SH	SV	IP	H	HR	BB	SO	RAT	ERA	ERA+	OAV	OOB	BH	AVG	PB	PR	/A	PD	TPI
1884	KC-U	0	3	.000	3	3	3	0	0	26	49	0	4	8	18.3	8.65	26	.377	.396	5	.313	0	-18	-19	-1	-1.4

● ED BLAKE
Blake, Edward James b: 12/23/25, E.St.Louis, Ill. BR/TR, 5'11", 175 lbs. Deb: 5/1/51

YEAR	TM/L	W	L	PCT	G	GS	CG	SH	SV	IP	H	HR	BB	SO	RAT	ERA	ERA+	OAV	OOB	BH	AVG	PB	PR	/A	PD	TPI
1951	Cin-N	0	0	—	3	0	0	0	0	4	10	3	1	1	24.8	11.25	36	.476	.500	0	—	0	-3	-3	0	0.0
1952	Cin-N	0	0	—	2	0	0	0	0	3	3	0	0	0	9.0	0.00	—	.250	.250	0	—	0	1	1	0	0.0
1953	Cin-N	0	0	—	1	0	0	0	0	0	1	0	1	0	—	∞	—	1.000	1.000	0	—	0	-2	-2	0	-0.2
1957	KC-A	0	0	—	2	0	0	0	0	1^2	1	1	2	0	16.2	5.40	73	.167	.375	0	—	0	-0	-0	-0	0.0
Total	4	0	0	—	8	0	0	0	0	8^2	15	4	4	1	19.7	8.31	48	.375	.432	0	—	0	-4	-4	1	-0.2

● SHERIFF BLAKE
Blake, John Frederick b: 9/17/1899, Ansted, W.Va. d: 10/31/82, Beckley, W.Va. BB/TR, 6', 180 lbs. Deb: 6/29/20

YEAR	TM/L	W	L	PCT	G	GS	CG	SH	SV	IP	H	HR	BB	SO	RAT	ERA	ERA+	OAV	OOB	BH	AVG	PB	PR	/A	PD	TPI
1920	Pit-N	0	0	—	6	0	0	0	0	13^1	21	0	6	7	18.9	8.10	40	.368	.438	1	.250	-0	-7	-7	0	0.0
1924	Chi-N	6	6	.500	29	11	4	0	1	106^1	123	3	44	42	14.3	4.57	85	.299	.370	9	.290	1	-8	-8	1	-0.6
1925	Chi-N	10	18	.357	36	31	14	0	2	231^1	260	17	114	93	14.7	4.86	89	.287	.370	12	.152	-4	-15	-14	0	-1.8
1926	Chi-N	11	12	.478	39	27	11	4	1	197^2	204	7	92	95	13.8	3.60	107	.280	.366	14	.215	-1	5	5	2	0.7
1927	Chi-N	13	14	.481	32	27	13	2	0	224^1	238	3	82	64	13.0	3.29	117	.282	.348	16	.193	-2	16	14	3	1.6
1928	Chi-N	17	11	.607	34	29	16	**4**	1	240^2	209	4	101	78	11.7	2.47	156	.240	.321	19	.216	0	41	37	-2	3.8
1929	*Chi-N	14	13	.519	35	30	13	1	1	218^1	244	8	103	70	14.4	4.29	108	.291	.370	14	.173	-2	10	8	-2	0.5
1930	Chi-N	10	14	.417	34	24	7	0	0	186^2	213	14	99	80	15.2	4.82	101	.291	.378	15	.227	-1	3	1	3	0.3
1931	Chi-N	0	4	.000	16	5	0	0	0	50	64	4	26	29	16.4	5.22	74	.312	.392	8	.500	3	-8	-8	1	-0.2

YEAR	TM/L	W	L	PCT	G	GS	CG	SH	SV	IP	H	HR	BB	SO	RAT	ERA	ERA+	OAV	OOB	BH	AVG	PB	PR	/A	PD	TPI
	Phi-N	4	5	.444	14	9	1	0	1	71	90	2	35	31	16.2	5.58	76	.305	.384	6	.240	0	-13	-11	2	-0.9
	Yr	4	9	.308	30	14	1	0	1	121	154	6	61	60	16.2	5.43	75	.307	.386	14	.341	3	-21	-18	3	-1.1
1937	StL-A	2	2	.500	15	1	0	0	1	36^2	55	5	20	12	18.4	7.61	63	.350	.424	1	.100	-1	-12	-11	0	-1.1
	StL-N	0	3	.000	14	2	2	0	0	43^2	45	1	18	20	13.0	3.71	107	.271	.342	3	.300	0	1	1	0	0.2
Total	10	87	102	.460	304	196	81	11	8	1620	1766	68	740	621	14.1	4.13	101	.284	.363	118	.211	-6	12	9	9	2.5

● AL BLANCHE Blanche, Prosper Albert (b: Prosper Bilangio) b: 9/21/09, Somerville, Mass. d: 4/2/97, Melrose, Mass. BR/TR, 6', 178 lbs. Deb: 8/23/35

YEAR	TM/L	W	L	PCT	G	GS	CG	SH	SV	IP	H	HR	BB	SO	RAT	ERA	ERA+	OAV	OOB	BH	AVG	PB	PR	/A	PD	TPI
1935	Bos-N	0	0	—	6	0	0	0	0	17^1	14	0	5	4	9.9	1.56	243	.230	.288	1	.167	-0	5	4	0	0.0
1936	Bos-N	0	1	.000	11	0	0	0	1	16	20	1	8	4	16.3	6.19	62	.303	.387	1	.250	0	-4	-4	1	-0.2
Total	2	0	1	.000	17	0	0	0	1	33^1	34	1	13	8	13.0	3.78	101	.268	.340	2	.200	-0	1	0	1	-0.2

● GIL BLANCO Blanco, Gilbert Henry b: 12/15/45, Phoenix, Ariz. BL/TL, 6'5", 205 lbs. Deb: 4/24/65

YEAR	TM/L	W	L	PCT	G	GS	CG	SH	SV	IP	H	HR	BB	SO	RAT	ERA	ERA+	OAV	OOB	BH	AVG	PB	PR	/A	PD	TPI
1965	NY-A	1	1	.500	17	1	0	0	0	20^1	16	1	12	14	12.8	3.98	85	.232	.354	0	—	0	-1	-1	-1	-0.2
1966	KC-A	2	4	.333	11	8	0	0	0	38^1	31	3	36	21	16.7	4.70	72	.237	.415	2	.167	-0	-5	-6	0	-0.8
Total	2	3	5	.375	28	9	0	0	0	58^2	47	4	48	35	15.3	4.45	76	.235	.395	2	.167	-0	-7	-7	-0	-1.0

● FRED BLANDING Blanding, Frederick James "Fritz" b: 2/8/1886, Redlands, Cal. d: 7/16/50, Salem, Va. BR/TR, 5'11", 185 lbs. Deb: 9/15/10

YEAR	TM/L	W	L	PCT	G	GS	CG	SH	SV	IP	H	HR	BB	SO	RAT	ERA	ERA+	OAV	OOB	BH	AVG	PB	PR	/A	PD	TPI
1910	Cle-A	2	2	.500	6	5	4	1	0	45^1	43	0	12	25	11.7	2.78	93	.254	.319	2	.111	-1	-1	-1	-1	-0.3
1911	Cle-A	7	11	.389	29	16	11	0	2	176	190	5	60	80	13.1	3.68	93	.283	.347	17	.262	2	-7	-5	0	-0.3
1912	Cle-A	18	14	.563	39	31	23	1	1	262	259	4	79	75	11.7	2.92	117	.267	.324	21	.226	1	12	14	0	1.8
1913	Cle-A	15	10	.600	41	22	14	3	0	215	234	6	72	63	12.9	2.55	119	.282	.341	21	.244	4	9	12	-2	1.5
1914	Cle-A	4	9	.308	29	12	5	0	0	116	133	0	54	35	14.6	3.96	73	.301	.378	4	.103	-2	-16	-14	1	-1.6
Total	5	46	46	.500	144	86	57	5	3	814^1	859	15	277	278	12.7	3.13	102	.279	.341	65	.216	4	-3	6	-2	1.1

● FRED BLANK Blank, Frederick August b: 6/18/1874, DeSoto, Mo. d: 2/5/36, St.Louis, Mo. BL/TL, 6'0.5", 175 lbs. Deb: 6/20/1894

YEAR	TM/L	W	L	PCT	G	GS	CG	SH	SV	IP	H	HR	BB	SO	RAT	ERA	ERA+	OAV	OOB	BH	AVG	PB	PR	/A	PD	TPI
1894	Cin-N	0	1	.000	1	1	1	0	0	8	5	0	9	1	15.8	4.50	124	.179	.378	0	.000	-1	1	1	1	0.1

● HOMER BLANKENSHIP Blankenship, Homer "Si" b: 8/4/02, Bonham, Tex. d: 6/22/74, Longview, Tex. BR/TR, 6', 185 lbs. Deb: 9/6/22 F

YEAR	TM/L	W	L	PCT	G	GS	CG	SH	SV	IP	H	HR	BB	SO	RAT	ERA	ERA+	OAV	OOB	BH	AVG	PB	PR	/A	PD	TPI
1922	Chi-A	0	0	—	4	0	0	0	0	13	21	1	5	3	18.0	4.85	84	.389	.441	0	.000	-1	-1	-1	-0	-0.1
1923	Chi-A	1	1	.500	4	0	0	0	1	5	9	0	1	1	18.0	3.60	110	.429	.455	0	—	0	0	0	0	0.1
1928	Pit-N	0	2	.000	5	2	1	0	0	21^2	27	1	9	6	15.0	5.82	70	.321	.387	3	.375	1	-4	-4	1	-0.2
Total	3	1	3	.250	13	2	1	0	1	39^2	57	2	15	10	16.3	5.22	78	.358	.414	3	.250	0	-5	-5	1	-0.2

● KEVIN BLANKENSHIP Blankenship, Kevin De Wayne b: 1/26/63, Anaheim, Cal. BR/TR, 6', 180 lbs. Deb: 9/20/88

YEAR	TM/L	W	L	PCT	G	GS	CG	SH	SV	IP	H	HR	BB	SO	RAT	ERA	ERA+	OAV	OOB	BH	AVG	PB	PR	/A	PD	TPI
1988	Atl-N	0	1	.000	2	2	0	0	0	10^2	7	0	7	5	12.7	3.38	109	.194	.341	0	.000	-0	0	0	-0	0.0
	Chi-N	1	0	1.000	1	1	0	0	0	5	7	2	1	4	14.4	7.20	50	.318	.348	0	.000	-0	-2	-2	-0	-0.4
	Yr	1	1	.500	3	3	0	0	0	15^2	14	2	8	9	12.6	4.60	79	.237	.328	0	.000	-1	-2	-2	-1	-0.4
1989	Chi-N	0	0	—	2	0	0	0	0	5^1	4	0	2	2	10.1	1.69	223	.200	.273	0	.000	-0	1	1	-0	0.0
1990	Chi-N	0	2	.000	3	2	0	0	0	12^1	13	1	6	5	13.9	5.84	70	.265	.345	0	.000	-0	-3	-2	0	-0.4
Total	3	1	3	.250	8	5	0	0	0	33^1	31	3	16	16	13.0	4.59	83	.244	.333	0	.000	-1	-4	-3	-1	-0.8

● TED BLANKENSHIP Blankenship, Theodore b: 5/10/01, Bonham, Tex. d: 1/14/45, Atoka, Okla. BR/TR, 6'1", 170 lbs. Deb: 7/2/22 F

YEAR	TM/L	W	L	PCT	G	GS	CG	SH	SV	IP	H	HR	BB	SO	RAT	ERA	ERA+	OAV	OOB	BH	AVG	PB	PR	/A	PD	TPI
1922	Chi-A	8	10	.444	24	15	7	0	1	127^2	124	4	47	42	12.2	3.81	107	.266	.335	7	.171	-1	3	4	0	0.4
1923	Chi-A	9	14	.391	44	23	9	1	0	204^2	219	8	100	57	14.2	4.35	91	.287	.372	16	.211	2	-8	-9	-1	-0.8
1924	Chi-A	7	6	.538	25	11	7	0	1	129^1	167	1	38	36	14.3	5.01	82	.317	.364	15	.326	6	-11	-13	-2	-0.8
1925	Chi-A	17	8	.680	40	23	16	3	1	232	218	11	69	81	11.1	3.03	137	.253	.308	18	.205	2	35	29	-4	2.5
1926	Chi-A	13	10	.565	29	26	15	1	1	209^1	217	13	65	66	12.2	3.61	107	.273	.328	10	.132	-2	10	6	-2	0.1
1927	Chi-A	12	17	.414	37	34	11	3	0	236^2	280	14	74	51	13.5	5.06	80	.299	.352	15	.188	3	-24	-27	-3	-2.6
1928	Chi-A	9	11	.450	27	22	8	0	0	158	186	9	80	36	15.3	4.61	88	.306	.388	10	.169	-2	-10	-10	-2	-1.4
1929	Chi-A	0	2	.000	8	1	0	0	0	18^1	28	3	9	7	18.2	8.84	48	.359	.425	1	.250	-0	-9	-9	-1	-0.9
1930	Chi-A	2	1	.667	7	1	0	0	0	14^2	23	0	7	2	19.0	9.20	50	.371	.443	1	.200	-0	-7	-7	-1	-1.2
Total	9	77	79	.494	241	156	73	8	4	1330^2	1462	63	489	378	13.3	4.29	94	.287	.351	93	.196	7	-22	-36	-15	-4.7

● CY BLANTON Blanton, Darrell Elijah b: 7/6/08, Waurika, Okla. d: 9/13/45, Norman, Okla. BL/TR, 5'11.5", 180 lbs. Deb: 9/23/34

YEAR	TM/L	W	L	PCT	G	GS	CG	SH	SV	IP	H	HR	BB	SO	RAT	ERA	ERA+	OAV	OOB	BH	AVG	PB	PR	/A	PD	TPI
1934	Pit-N	0	1	.000	1	1	0	0	0	8	5	1	4	5	11.3	3.38	122	.161	.278	0	.000	0	1	1	0	0.1
1935	Pit-N	18	13	.581	35	31	23	**4**	1	254^1	220	3	55	142	**9.8**	**2.58**	**159**	**.229**	**.272**	13	.134	-4	**41**	**43**	2	**4.7**
1936	Pit-N	13	15	.464	44	32	15	**4**	3	235^2	235	9	55	127	11.2	3.51	115	.257	.301	13	.155	-3	13	14	1	1.3
1937	Pit-N★	14	12	.538	36	34	14	4	0	242^2	250	13	76	143	12.3	3.30	117	.266	.324	14	.165	-0	17	15	-0	1.4
1938	Pit-N	11	7	.611	29	26	10	1	0	172^2	190	13	46	80	12.4	3.70	103	.281	.329	13	.203	-1	2	2	2	0.3
1939	Pit-N	2	3	.400	10	6	1	0	0	42	45	4	10	11	11.8	4.29	90	.266	.307	4	.286	1	-2	-2	-0	-0.2
1940	Phi-N	4	3	.571	13	10	5	0	0	77	82	7	21	24	12.2	4.32	90	.272	.322	2	.083	-1	-4	-4	0	-0.4
1941	Phi-N☆	6	13	.316	28	25	7	1	0	163^2	186	11	57	64	13.5	4.51	82	.284	.344	6	.118	-2	-16	-15	-3	-2.0
1942	Phi-N	0	4	.000	6	3	0	0	0	22^1	30	3	13	15	17.7	5.64	59	.345	.436	1	.125	-0	-6	-6	0	-1.0
Total	9	68	71	.489	202	168	75	14	4	1218^1	1243	64	337	611	11.8	3.55	110	.262	.314	66	.154	-11	45	49	2	4.2

● WADE BLASINGAME Blasingame, Wade Allen b: 11/22/43, Deming, N.Mex. BL/TL, 6'1", 185 lbs. Deb: 9/17/63

YEAR	TM/L	W	L	PCT	G	GS	CG	SH	SV	IP	H	HR	BB	SO	RAT	ERA	ERA+	OAV	OOB	BH	AVG	PB	PR	/A	PD	TPI
1963	Mil-N	0	0	—	2	0	0	0	0	3	7	0	2	6	27.0	12.00	27	.467	.529	0	—	0	-3	-3	0	0.0
1964	Mil-N	9	5	.643	28	13	3	1	2	116^2	113	15	51	70	12.7	4.24	83	.257	.334	7	.175	3	-9	-9	0	-0.7
1965	Mil-N	16	10	.615	38	36	10	1	1	224^2	200	17	116	117	12.9	3.77	94	.244	.341	15	.185	3	-6	-6	1	-0.2
1966	Atl-N	3	7	.300	16	12	0	0	0	67^2	71	5	25	34	13.0	5.32	68	.272	.340	5	.217	1	-13	-13	-0	-1.6
1967	Atl-N	1	0	1.000	10	4	0	0	0	25^1	27	1	21	20	17.4	4.62	72	.287	.422	1	.143	0	-4	-4	0	0.0
	Hou-N	4	7	.364	15	14	0	0	0	77	91	9	27	46	14.0	5.96	56	.298	.359	4	.182	2	-22	-23	-0	-2.7
	Yr	5	7	.417	25	18	0	0	0	102^1	118	10	48	66	14.8	5.63	59	.295	.373	5	.172	2	-26	-26	0	-2.7
1968	Hou-N	1	2	.333	22	2	0	0	1	36	45	3	10	22	13.8	4.75	62	.308	.353	0	.000	0	-7	-7	1	-0.5
1969	Hou-N	0	5	.000	26	5	0	0	1	52	66	4	33	33	17.5	5.37	66	.306	.402	0	.000	-1	-10	-11	0	-1.1
1970	Hou-N	3	3	.500	13	13	1	0	0	77^2	76	4	23	55	11.7	3.48	112	.261	.320	2	.083	-0	5	3	0	0.3
1971	Hou-N	9	11	.450	30	28	2	0	0	158^1	177	11	45	93	13.4	4.60	73	.285	.346	10	.204	4	-20	-22	1	-2.0
1972	Hou-N	0	0	—	10	0	0	0	0	8^1	4	1	8	9	15.1	8.64	39	.148	.378	0	—	0	-5	-5	0	0.0
	NY-A	0	1	.000	12	1	0	0	0	17	14	5	11	7	13.8	4.24	70	.250	.382	0	.000	0	-2	-2	1	0.0
Total	10	46	51	.474	222	128	16	2	5	863^2	891	75	372	512	13.5	4.52	77	.271	.350	44	.166	14	-96	-101	4	-8.5

● STEVE BLASS Blass, Stephen Robert b: 4/18/42, Canaan, Conn. BR/TR, 6', 165 lbs. Deb: 5/10/64

YEAR	TM/L	W	L	PCT	G	GS	CG	SH	SV	IP	H	HR	BB	SO	RAT	ERA	ERA+	OAV	OOB	BH	AVG	PB	PR	/A	PD	TPI
1964	Pit-N	5	8	.385	24	13	3	1	0	104^2	107	9	45	67	13.2	4.04	87	.266	.341	2	.067	-1	-6	-6	0	-0.8
1966	Pit-N	11	7	.611	34	25	1	0	0	155^2	173	12	46	76	12.8	3.87	92	.284	.336	12	.231	1	-5	-5	-3	-0.7
1967	Pit-N	6	8	.429	32	16	2	0	0	126^2	126	12	47	72	12.4	3.55	95	.261	.329	5	.128	-1	-3	-3	0	-0.3
1968	Pit-N	18	6	**.750**	33	31	12	7	0	220^1	191	13	57	132	10.3	2.12	138	.234	.288	11	.138	-1	21	20	-1	2.1
1969	Pit-N	16	10	.615	38	32	9	0	2	210	207	21	86	147	12.8	4.46	78	.258	.335	21	.250	6	-20	-23	-3	-1.8
1970	Pit-N	10	12	.455	31	31	6	1	0	196^2	187	14	73	120	12.1	3.52	111	.254	.326	8	.114	-2	11	8	0	0.6
1971	*Pit-N	15	8	.652	33	33	12	**5**	0	240	226	16	68	136	11.1	2.85	119	.249	.303	10	.120	-3	16	14	1	1.1
1972	*Pit-N★	19	8	.704	33	32	11	2	0	249^2	227	18	84	117	11.4	2.49	134	.246	.311	15	.183	1	27	23	2	2.9
1973	Pit-N	3	9	.250	23	18	1	0	0	88^2	109	11	84	27	20.8	9.85	36	.313	.462	10	.417	4	-61	-62	1	-6.3
1974	Pit-N	0	0	—	1	0	0	0	0	5	5	2	7	2	21.6	9.00	38	.238	.429	0	.000	-0	-3	-3	0	0.0
Total	10	103	76	.575	282	231	57	16	2	1597^1	1558	128	597	896	12.4	3.63	94	.258	.328	94	.172	4	-21	-37	3	-3.2

● STEVE BLATERIC Blateric, Stephen Lawrence b: 3/20/44, Denver, Colo. BR/TR, 6'3", 200 lbs. Deb: 9/17/71

YEAR	TM/L	W	L	PCT	G	GS	CG	SH	SV	IP	H	HR	BB	SO	RAT	ERA	ERA+	OAV	OOB	BH	AVG	PB	PR	/A	PD	TPI
1971	Cin-N	0	0	—	2	0	0	0	0	2^2	5	2	0	4	20.3	13.50	25	.385	.429	0	—	0	-3	-3	0	0.0
1972	NY-A	0	0	—	1	0	0	0	0	4	2	0	0	4	4.5	0.00	—	.143	.143	0	.000	-0	1	1	0	0.0
1975	Cal-A	0	0	—	2	0	0	0	0	4^1	9	0	1	5	20.8	6.23	57	.429	.455	0	—	0	-1	-1	-0	0.4
Total	3	0	0	—	5	0	0	0	0	11	16	2	1	13	14.7	5.73	57	.333	.360	0	.000	-0	-3	-3	0	0.4

● HENRY BLAUVELT Blauvelt, Henry Russell b: 4/8/1873, Nyack, N.Y. d: 12/28/26, Portland, Ore. Deb: 6/22/1890

YEAR	TM/L	W	L	PCT	G	GS	CG	SH	SV	IP	H	HR	BB	SO	RAT	ERA	ERA+	OAV	OOB	BH	AVG	PB	PR	/A	PD	TPI
1890	Roc-a	0	0	—	2	0	0	0	0	12^1	19	0	8	5	19.7	10.22	35	.339	.422	3	.500	1	-9	-9	0	0.1

YEAR	TM/L	W	L	PCT	G	GS	CG	SH	SV	IP	H	HR	BB	SO	RAT	ERA	ERA+	OAV	OOB	BH	AVG	PB	PR	/A	PD	TPI
● **GARY BLAYLOCK** Blaylock, Gary Nelson b: 10/11/31, Clarkton, Mo. BR/TR, 6′, 196 lbs. Deb: 4/10/59 C																										
1959	StL-N	4	5	.444	26	12	3	0	0	100	117	14	43	61	14.6	5.13	83	.298	.371	4	.118	0	-13	-10	1	-0.7
	NY-A	0	1	.000	15	1	0	0	0	25^2	30	0	15	20	16.1	3.51	104	.306	.404	1	.500	1	1	0	-0	0.0
Total	1	4	6	.400	41	13	3	0	0	125^2	147	14	58	81	14.9	4.80	86	.300	.377	5	.139	1	-12	-10	0	-0.7
● **BOB BLAYLOCK** Blaylock, Robert Edward b: 6/28/35, Chattanooga, Okla BR/TR, 6′1″, 185 lbs. Deb: 7/22/56																										
1956	StL-N	1	6	.143	14	6	0	0	0	41	45	7	24	39	15.1	6.37	59	.276	.369	1	.091	-1	-12	-12	0	-1.8
1959	StL-N	0	1	.000	3	1	0	0	0	9	8	1	3	3	11.0	4.00	106	.229	.289	0	.000	-0	-0	0	0	0.0
Total	2	1	7	.125	17	7	0	0	0	50	53	8	27	42	14.4	5.94	65	.268	.356	1	.083	-1	-12	-12	0	-1.8
● **RON BLAZIER** Blazier, Ronald Patrick b: 7/30/71, Altoona, Pa. BR/TR, 6′6″, 215 lbs. Deb: 5/31/96																										
1996	Phi-N	3	1	.750	27	0	0	0	0	38^1	49	6	10	25	13.9	5.87	73	.310	.351	1	1.000	0	-7	-7	-1	-0.6
1997	Phi-N	1	1	.500	36	0	0	0	0	53^2	62	8	21	42	13.9	5.03	84	.290	.353	2	.400	1	-5	-5	-1	-0.2
Total	2	4	2	.667	63	0	0	0	0	92	111	14	31	67	13.9	5.38	79	.298	.352	3	.500	1	-12	-11	-2	-0.8
● **RAY BLEMKER** Blemker, Raymond b: 8/9/37, Huntingburg, Ind. d: 2/15/94, Evansville, Ind BR/TL, 5′11″, 190 lbs. Deb: 7/3/60																										
1960	KC-A	0	0	—	1	0	0	0	0	1^2	3	1	2	0	32.4	27.00	15	.375	.545	0	—	0	-4	-4	-0	0.0
● **CLARENCE BLETHEN** Blethen, Clarence Waldo "Climax" b: 7/11/1893, Dover-Foxcroft, Maine d: 4/11/73, Frederick, Md. BL/TR, 5′11″, 165 lbs. Deb: 9/17/23																										
1923	Bos-A	0	0	—	5	0	0	0	0	17^2	29	0	7	2	18.3	7.13	58	.382	.434	0	.000	-1	-6	-6	-1	-0.2
1929	Bro-N	0	0	—	2	0	0	0	0	2	4	0	3	0	31.5	9.00	51	.444	.583	0	—	0	-1	-1	0	0.0
Total	2	0	0	—	7	0	0	0	0	19^2	33	0	10	2	19.7	7.32	57	.388	.453	0	.000	-1	-7	-7	-1	-0.2
● **BOB BLEWETT** Blewett, Robert Lawrence b: 6/28/1877, Fond Du Lac, Wis. d: 3/17/58, Sedro Woolley, Wash. BL/TL, 5′11″, 170 lbs. Deb: 6/17/02																										
1902	NY-N	0	2	.000	5	3	2	0	0	28	39	0	7	8	15.1	4.82	58	.328	.370	0	.000	-1	-6	-6	-1	-0.6
● **ELMER BLISS** Bliss, Elmer Ward b: 3/9/1875, Penfield, Pa. d: 3/18/62, Bradford, Pa. BL/TR, 6′, 180 lbs. Deb: 9/28/03 ♦																										
1903	NY-A	1	0	1.000	1	0	0	0	0	7	4	0	0	3	5.1	0.00	—	.167	.167	0	.000	-0	2	2	-0	0.3
● **TERRY BLOCKER** Blocker, Terry Fennell b: 8/18/59, Columbia, S.C. BL/TL, 6′2″, 195 lbs. Deb: 4/11/85 ♦																										
1989	Atl-N	0	0	—	1	0	0	0	0	1	0	0	2	0	18.0	0.00	—	.000	.500	7	.226	0	0	0	0	0.0
● **BEN BLOMDAHL** Blomdahl, Benjamin Earl b: 12/30/70, Long Beach, Cal. BR/TR, 6′2″, 185 lbs. Deb: 4/28/95																										
1995	Det-A	0	0	—	14	0	0	0	1	24^1	36	5	13	15	18.1	7.77	61	.356	.430	0	—	0	-8	-8	1	0.0
● **JOE BLONG** Blong, Joseph Myles b: 9/17/1853, St.Louis, Mo. d: 9/16/1892, St.Louis, Mo. BR/TR, Deb: 5/4/1875 ♦																										
1875	RS-n	3	12	.200	15	15	12	1	0	129	169	0	2	14	11.9	3.07	71	.284	.286	10	.147	-4	-12	-13		-1.1
1876	StL-N	0	0	—	1	0	0	0	0	4	2	0	1	0	6.8	0.00	—	.154	.214	62	.235	-0	1	1	0	0.0
1877	StL-N	10	9	.526	25	21	17	0	0	187^1	203	0	38	51	11.6	2.74	95	.262	.296	47	.216	0	1	-3	-2	-0.4
Total	2	10	9	.526	26	21	17	0	0	191^1	205	0	39	51	11.5	2.68	97	.260	.295	109	.226	0	2	-2	-1	-0.4
● **VIDA BLUE** Blue, Vida Rochelle b: 7/28/49, Mansfield, La. BB/TL, 6′, 189 lbs. Deb: 7/20/69																										
1969	Oak-A	1	1	.500	12	4	0	0	1	42	49	13	18	24	14.4	6.64	52	.290	.358	0	.000	-0	-14	-15	-1	-0.8
1970	Oak-A	2	0	1.000	6	6	2	2	0	38^2	20	0	12	35	7.7	2.09	169	.152	.228	3	.200	2	7	6	0	0.5
1971	*Oak-A★	24	8	.750	39	39	24	**8**	0	312	209	19	88	301	**8.7**	**1.82**	183	**.189**	**.252**	12	.118	-2	57	53	-4	4.9
1972	*Oak-A	6	10	.375	25	23	5	4	0	151	117	11	48	111	9.9	2.80	101	.215	.280	2	.044	-2	4	1	-2	-0.4
1973	*Oak-A	20	9	.690	37	37	13	4	0	263^2	214	26	105	158	11.0	3.28	108	.224	.303	0	.000	-0	16	8	-2	0.5
1974	*Oak-A	17	15	.531	40	40	12	1	0	282^1	246	17	98	174	11.0	3.25	102	.236	.303	0	—	0	11	2	-5	-0.1
1975	*Oak-A★	22	11	.667	39	38	13	2	1	278	243	21	99	189	11.2	3.01	120	.236	.307	0	—	0	24	19	-2	2.0
1976	Oak-A	18	13	.581	37	37	20	6	0	298^1	268	9	63	166	10.0	2.35	143	.239	.280	0	—	0	**39**	33	-3	3.1
1977	Oak-A†	14	19	.424	38	38	16	1	0	279^2	284	23	86	157	11.9	3.83	105	.264	.319	0	.000	-0	7	6	-1	0.5
1978	SF-N★	18	10	.643	35	35	9	4	0	258	233	12	70	171	10.6	2.79	124	.246	.298	6	.076	2	23	19	-2	2.0
1979	SF-N	14	14	.500	34	34	10	0	0	237	246	23	111	138	13.6	5.01	70	.272	.352	10	.120	0	-34	-40	2	-3.9
1980	SF-N†	14	10	.583	31	31	10	3	0	224	202	14	61	129	10.6	2.97	119	.242	.294	5	.074	-4	16	14	2	1.3
1981	SF-N★	8	6	.571	18	18	1	0	0	124^2	97	7	54	63	11.0	2.45	140	.217	.303	7	.200	2	14	14	2	2.0
1982	KC-A	13	12	.520	31	31	6	2	0	181	163	20	80	103	12.1	3.78	108	.238	.318	0	—	0	6	6	-0	0.7
1983	KC-A	0	5	.000	19	14	1	0	0	85^1	96	12	35	53	14.0	6.01	68	.286	.357	0	—	0	-18	-18	-0	-1.0
1985	SF-N	8	8	.500	33	20	1	0	0	131	115	17	80	103	13.5	4.47	77	.240	.350	4	.133	1	-13	-15	0	-1.6
1986	SF-N	10	10	.500	28	28	0	0	0	156^2	137	19	77	100	12.3	3.27	107	.239	.329	4	.093	1	8	4	-1	0.5
Total	17	209	161	.565	502	473	143	37	2	3343^1	2939	263	1185	2175	11.2	3.27	108	.237	.305	53	.104	-2	152	95	-17	10.2
● **JIM BLUEJACKET** Bluejacket, James (b: James Smith) b: 7/8/1887, Adair, Okla. d: 3/26/47, Pekin, Ill. BR/TR, 6′2.5″, 200 lbs. Deb: 8/6/14 F																										
1914	Bro-F	4	5	.444	17	7	3	1	1	67	77	2	19	29	12.9	3.76	76	.302	.350	3	.136	-1	-7	-7	1	-0.8
1915	Bro-F	10	11	.476	24	21	10	2	0	162^2	155	2	75	48	12.7	3.15	86	.258	.340	8	.131	-5	-8	-8	-4	-1.8
1916	Cin-N	0	1	.000	3	2	0	0	0	7	12	0	3	1	19.3	7.71	34	.400	.455	0	.000	-0	-4	-4	-0	-0.6
Total	3	14	17	.452	44	30	13	3	1	236^2	244	4	97	78	13.0	3.46	80	.275	.347	11	.129	-6	-18	-18	-3	-3.2
● **JAIME BLUMA** Bluma, James Andrew b: 5/18/72, Beaufort, S.C. BR/TR, 5′11″, 195 lbs. Deb: 8/9/96																										
1996	KC-A	0	0	—	17	0	0	0	5	20	18	2	4	14	10.8	3.60	139	.247	.304	0	—	0	3	3	1	0.2
● **CLINT BLUME** Blume, Clinton Willis b: 10/17/1898, Brooklyn, N.Y. d: 6/12/73, Islip, N.Y. BR/TR, 5′11″, 175 lbs. Deb: 9/30/22																										
1922	NY-N	1	0	1.000	1	1	1	0	0	9	7	0	1	2	8.0	1.00	400	.212	.235	1	1.000	1	3	3	-1	0.4
1923	NY-N	2	0	1.000	12	1	0	0	0	24	22	0	20	2	16.5	3.75	102	.265	.419	0	.000	-0	1	0	-1	-0.1
Total	2	3	0	1.000	13	2	1	0	0	33	29	0	21	4	14.2	3.00	129	.250	.374	1	.167	1	4	3	-1	0.3
● **BERT BLYLEVEN** Blyleven, Rik Aalbert b: 4/6/51, Zeist, Holland BR/TR, 6′3″, 207 lbs. Deb: 6/5/70																										
1970	*Min-A	10	9	.526	27	25	5	1	0	164	143	17	47	135	10.5	3.18	117	.232	.289	7	.140	-1	10	10	-2	0.8
1971	Min-A	16	15	.516	38	38	17	5	0	278^1	267	21	59	224	10.7	2.81	126	.255	.298	12	.132	-3	20	23	-0	2.2
1972	Min-A	17	17	.500	39	38	11	3	0	287^1	247	22	69	228	10.2	2.73	118	.233	.286	15	.160	-1	11	15	1	2.0
1973	Min-A★	20	17	.541	40	40	25	**9**	0	325	296	16	67	258	10.3	2.52	**157**	.242	.287	0	—	0	**47**	**52**	-2	5.7
1974	Min-A	17	17	.500	37	37	19	3	0	281	244	14	77	249	10.6	2.66	140	.233	.292	0	—	0	30	33	0	4.0
1975	Min-A	15	10	.600	35	35	20	3	0	275^2	219	24	84	233	10.0	3.00	127	.219	.283	0	—	0	24	25	3	2.4
1976	Min-A	4	5	.444	12	12	4	0	0	95^1	101	3	35	75	13.2	3.12	115	.283	.354	0	—	0	4	5	0	0.5
	Tex-A	9	11	.450	24	24	14	6	0	202^1	182	11	46	144	10.5	2.76	130	.242	.293	0	—	0	17	19	2	2.0
	Yr	13	16	.448	36	36	18	6	0	297^2	283	14	81	219	11.2	2.87	125	.254	.309	0	—	0	21	23	2	2.5
1977	Tex-A	14	12	.538	30	30	15	5	0	234^2	181	20	69	182	**9.9**	2.72	150	.214	.279	0	—	0	35	35	0	3.8
1978	Pit-N	14	10	.583	34	34	11	4	0	243^2	217	17	66	182	10.7	3.03	122	.235	.290	11	.129	-2	15	18	1	1.6
1979	*Pit-N	12	5	.706	37	37	4	0	0	237^1	238	21	92	172	12.7	3.60	108	.265	.338	9	.129	-3	3	7	-2	0.0
1980	Pit-N	8	13	.381	34	32	5	2	0	216^2	219	20	59	168	11.5	3.82	95	.262	.311	5	.082	-4	-5	-4	-0	-0.8
1981	Cle-A	11	7	.611	20	20	9	1	0	159^1	145	9	40	107	10.7	2.88	126	.245	.298	0	—	0	14	13	-2	1.4
1982	Cle-A	2	2	.500	4	4	0	0	0	20^1	16	2	11	19	12.0	4.87	84	.211	.310	0	—	0	-2	-2	0	-0.3
1983	Cle-A	7	10	.412	24	24	5	0	0	156^1	160	8	44	123	12.3	3.91	108	.267	.328	0	—	0	3	6	1	0.6
1984	Cle-A	19	7	.731	33	32	12	4	0	245	204	19	74	170	10.4	2.87	143	.224	.287	0	—	0	31	33	0	3.4
1985	Cle-A★	9	11	.450	23	23	15	4	0	179^2	163	14	49	129	11.0	3.26	127	.240	.298	0	—	0	18	18	-1	1.7
	Min-A	8	5	.615	14	14	9	1	0	114	101	9	26	77	10.2	3.00	147	.237	.284	0	—	0	15	18	-0	1.8
	Yr	17	16	.515	37	37	**24**	**5**	0	**293^2**	264	23	75	**206**	10.5	3.16	134	.236	.286	0	—	0	32	35	-1	3.5
1986	Min-A	17	14	.548	36	36	16	3	0	**271^2**	262	50	58	215	10.9	4.01	107	.250	.295	0	—	0	5	9	-1	0.8
1987	*Min-A	15	12	.556	37	37	8	1	0	267	249	46	101	196	12.1	4.01	115	.249	.323	0	—	0	13	18	2	1.7
1988	Min-A	10	17	.370	33	33	7	0	0	207^1	240	21	51	145	13.3	5.43	75	.294	.348	0	—	0	-34	-31	-1	-3.6
1989	Cal-A	17	5	.773	33	33	8	**5**	0	241	225	14	44	131	10.3	2.73	140	.248	.289	0	—	0	31	29	1	2.7
1990	Cal-A	8	7	.533	23	23	2	0	0	134	163	15	25	69	13.1	5.24	73	.303	.342	0	—	0	-20	-21	0	-2.0

YEAR	TM/L	W	L	PCT	G	GS	CG	SH	SV	IP	H	HR	BB	SO	RAT	ERA	ERA+	OAV	OOB	BH	AVG	PB	PR	/A	PD	TPI
1992	Cal-A	8	12	.400	25	24	1	0	0	133	150	17	29	70	12.5	4.74	84	.285	.329	0	—	0	-12	-11	-1	-1.6
Total	22	287	250	.534	692	685	242	60	0	4970	4632	430	1322	3701	11.1	3.31	117	.247	.303	59	.131	-13	271	317	1	30.8
● **MIKE BLYZKA**	Blyzka, Michael John (b: Michael John Bliska) b: 12/25/28, Hamtramck, Mich. BR/TR, 5'11.5", 190 lbs. Deb: 4/21/53																									
1953	StL-A	2	6	.250	33	9	2	0	0	94^1	110	6	56	23	15.8	6.39	66	.292	.383	0	.000	-3	-25	-23	-1	-2.0
1954	Bal-A	1	5	.167	37	0	0	0	1	86^1	83	2	51	35	14.0	4.69	76	.254	.354	2	.133	-1	-9	-11	0	-0.8
Total	2	3	11	.214	70	9	2	0	1	180^2	193	8	107	58	14.9	5.58	70	.274	.370	2	.053	-4	-34	-34	-0	-2.8
● **CHARLIE BOARDMAN**	Boardman, Charles Louis b: 4/27/1893, Seneca Falls, N.Y. d: 8/10/68, Sacramento, Cal. BL/TL, 6'2.5", 194 lbs. Deb: 9/26/13																									
1913	Phi-A	0	2	.000	2	2	1	0	0	9	10	0	6	4	16.0	2.00	138	.294	.400	0	.000	-0	1	1	-0	0.1
1914	Phi-A	0	0	—	2	0	0	0	0	7^1	10	0	4	2	17.2	4.91	53	.357	.438	0	.000	-0	-2	-2	-0	0.0
1915	StL-N	1	0	1.000	3	1	1	0	0	19	12	0	15	7	12.8	2.84	98	.188	.342	2	.286	0	-0	-0	-0	0.0
Total	3	1	2	.333	7	3	2	0	0	35^1	32	0	25	13	14.5	3.06	90	.254	.377	2	.167	-0	-1	-1	-1	0.1
● **DOUG BOCHTLER**	Bochtler, Douglas Eugene b: 7/5/70, W.Palm Beach, Fla. BR/TR, 6'3", 205 lbs. Deb: 5/5/95																									
1995	SD-N	4	4	.500	34	0	0	0	1	45^1	38	5	19	45	11.3	3.57	113	.239	.320	0	.000	-0	3	2	0	0.4
1996	*SD-N	2	4	.333	63	0	0	0	3	65^2	45	6	39	68	11.6	3.02	132	.195	.314	0	—	0	9	7	-1	0.5
1997	SD-N	3	6	.333	54	0	0	0	2	60^1	51	3	50	46	15.2	4.77	81	.229	.372	0	—	0	-4	-6	-1	-0.9
1998	Det-A	0	2	.000	51	0	0	0	0	67^1	73	17	42	45	15.8	6.15	77	.279	.384	0	—	0	-11	-11	-1	-0.4
Total	4	9	16	.360	202	0	0	0	6	238^2	207	31	150	204	13.7	4.45	93	.237	.351	0	.000	-0	-3	-8	-3	-0.4
● **RANDY BOCKUS**	Bockus, Randy Walter b: 10/5/60, Canton, Ohio BL/TR, 6'2", 190 lbs. Deb: 9/10/86																									
1986	SF-N	0	0	—	5	0	0	0	0	7	7	1	6	4	16.7	2.57	137	.241	.371	0	.000	-0	1	1	1	0.0
1987	SF-N	1	0	1.000	12	0	0	0	0	17^1	17	2	4	9	10.9	3.63	106	.266	.309	0	.000	-0	1	0	-0	0.0
1988	SF-N	1	1	.500	20	0	0	0	0	32	35	2	13	18	13.8	4.78	68	.297	.371	1	.167	0	-5	-5	0	-0.3
1989	Det-A	0	0	—	2	0	0	0	0	5^1	7	0	2	2	15.2	5.06	75	.333	.391	0	—	0	-1	-1	-0	0.0
Total	4	2	1	.667	39	0	0	0	0	61^2	66	5	25	33	13.4	4.23	83	.284	.357	1	.125	-0	-4	-5	1	-0.3
● **MIKE BODDICKER**	Boddicker, Michael James b: 8/23/57, Cedar Rapids, Iowa BR/TR, 5'11", 172 lbs. Deb: 10/4/80																									
1980	Bal-A	0	1	.000	1	1	0	0	0	7^1	6	1	5	4	13.5	6.14	64	.207	.324	0	—	0	-2	-2	-0	-0.2
1981	Bal-A	0	0	—	2	0	0	0	0	5^2	6	1	2	2	12.7	4.76	76	.261	.320	0	—	0	-1	-1	-0	0.0
1982	Bal-A	1	0	1.000	7	0	0	0	0	25^2	25	2	12	20	13.0	3.51	115	.258	.339	0	—	0	2	2	0	0.1
1983	*Bal-A	16	8	.667	27	26	10	**5**	0	179	141	13	52	120	9.7	2.77	143	**.216**	.274	0	—	0	26	24	3	3.4
1984	Bal-A☆	**20**	11	.645	34	34	16	4	0	261^1	218	23	81	128	10.5	**2.79**	139	.228	.292	0	—	0	**35**	31	6	**4.2**
1985	Bal-A	12	17	.414	32	32	9	2	0	203^1	227	13	89	135	14.2	4.07	99	.286	.361	0	—	0	2	-1	6	0.4
1986	Bal-A	14	12	.538	33	33	7	0	0	218^1	214	30	74	175	12.3	4.70	88	.255	.323	0	—	0	-13	-14	3	-1.0
1987	Bal-A	10	12	.455	33	33	7	2	0	226	212	29	78	152	11.8	4.18	105	.248	.316	0	—	0	7	5	4	0.8
1988	Bal-A	6	12	.333	21	21	4	0	0	147	149	14	51	100	12.9	3.86	101	.265	.338	0	—	0	2	1	-1	0.0
	*Bos-A	7	3	.700	15	14	1	1	0	89	85	3	26	56	11.5	2.63	156	.257	.317	0	—	0	13	15	2	1.8
	Yr	13	15	.464	36	35	5	1	0	236	234	17	77	156	12.0	3.39	117	.256	.316	0	—	0	15	15	1	1.8
1989	Bos-A	15	11	.577	34	34	3	2	0	211^2	217	19	71	145	12.7	4.00	103	.267	.333	0	—	0	-3	2	1	0.4
1990	*Bos-A	17	8	.680	34	34	4	0	0	228	225	16	69	143	12.0	3.36	121	.258	.319	0	—	0	14	18	1	1.9
1991	KC-A	12	12	.500	30	29	1	0	0	180^2	188	13	59	79	13.0	4.08	101	.272	.340	0	—	0	0	1	2	0.3
1992	KC-A	1	4	.200	29	8	0	0	3	86^2	92	5	37	47	14.2	4.98	81	.269	.354	0	—	0	-10	-9	1	-0.4
1993	Mil-A	3	5	.375	10	10	1	0	0	54	77	6	15	24	16.0	5.67	75	.338	.389	0	—	0	-8	-9	0	-1.0
Total	14	134	116	.536	342	309	63	16	3	2123^2	2082	188	721	1330	12.2	3.80	107	.257	.325	0	—	0	64	65	28	10.7
● **GEORGE BOEHLER**	Boehler, George Henry b: 1/2/1892, Lawrenceburg, Ind. d: 6/23/58, Lawrenceburg, Ind BR/TR, 6'2", 180 lbs. Deb: 9/13/12																									
1912	Det-A	0	2	.000	5	4	2	0	0	32	50	0	14	15	18.6	6.47	50	.365	.431	1	.100	-1	-11	-11	1	-0.6
1913	Det-A	0	1	.000	1	1	1	0	0	8	11	0	6	2	21.4	6.75	43	.355	.487	1	.333	1	-3	-3	1	-0.3
1914	Det-A	2	3	.400	18	6	2	0	0	63	54	1	48	37	15.7	3.57	79	.242	.394	3	.176	1	-6	-5	-0	-0.4
1915	Det-A	1	1	.500	8	0	0	0	0	15	19	0	4	7	14.4	1.80	168	.328	.381	3	.750	2	2	2	-0	0.4
1916	Det-A	1	1	.500	5	2	1	0	0	13^1	12	0	9	8	15.5	4.73	61	.261	.404	0	.000	0	-3	-3	1	-0.3
1920	StL-A	0	1	.000	3	1	0	0	0	7	10	1	4	2	18.0	7.71	51	.303	.378	0	.000	0	-3	-3	0	-0.3
1921	StL-A	0	0	—	1	0	0	0	0	1	1	0	0	0	9.0	0.00	—	.500	.500	0	—	0	0	0	-0	0.0
1923	Pit-N	1	3	.250	10	3	1	0	0	28^1	33	1	26	12	19.1	6.04	66	.314	.455	3	.300	1	-6	-6	-0	-0.7
1926	Bro-N	1	0	1.000	10	1	0	0	0	34^2	42	1	23	10	17.7	4.41	87	.302	.412	3	.250	0	-2	-2	-1	-0.1
Total	9	6	12	.333	61	18	7	0	0	202^1	232	4	134	93	17.1	4.71	70	.300	.415	14	.233	3	-33	-32	1	-2.3
● **JOE BOEHLING**	Boehling, John Joseph b: 3/20/1891, Richmond, Va. d: 9/8/41, Richmond, Va. BL/TL, 5'11", 168 lbs. Deb: 6/20/12																									
1912	Was-A	0	0	—	3	0	0	0	0	5	4	0	6	2	21.6	7.20	46	.235	.480	0	—	0	-2	-2	0	0.0
1913	Was-A	17	7	.708	38	25	18	3	4	235^1	197	3	82	110	11.0	2.14	138	.229	.303	19	.221	1	21	21	2	2.6
1914	Was-A	13	8	.619	27	24	14	2	0	196	180	3	76	91	12.2	3.03	93	.258	.339	17	.239	4	-6	-5	2	0.1
1915	Was-A	14	13	.519	40	32	14	2	0	229^1	217	5	119	108	13.5	3.22	92	.255	.352	13	.173	0	-7	-6	2	-0.4
1916	Was-A	9	11	.450	27	19	7	2	0	139^2	134	1	54	52	12.3	3.09	90	.260	.333	7	.171	1	-4	-5	4	-0.2
	Cle-A	2	4	.333	12	9	3	0	0	60^2	63	0	23	18	13.1	2.67	113	.281	.353	5	.263	1	1	2	1	0.4
	Yr	11	15	.423	39	28	10	2	0	200^1	197	1	77	70	12.4	2.97	96	.265	.336	12	.200	1	-3	-2	4	0.2
1917	Cle-A	1	6	.143	12	7	1	0	0	46^1	50	1	16	11	13.4	4.66	61	.291	.361	3	.188	-0	-10	-9	-0	-1.4
1920	Cle-A	0	1	.000	3	2	0	0	0	13	16	0	10	4	18.0	4.85	78	.333	.448	2	.500	1	-2	-2	0	0.0
Total	7	56	50	.528	162	118	57	9	4	925^1	861	13	386	396	12.5	2.97	98	.254	.337	66	.212	7	-10	-5	11	1.1
● **BRIAN BOEHRINGER**	Boehringer, Brian Edward b: 1/8/69, St.Louis, Mo. BB/TR, 6'2", 180 lbs. Deb: 4/30/95																									
1995	NY-A	0	3	.000	7	3	0	0	0	17^2	24	5	22	10	23.9	13.75	34	.320	.480	0	—	0	-18	-18	-1	-2.2
1996	*NY-A	2	4	.333	15	3	0	0	0	46^1	46	6	21	37	13.2	5.44	91	.260	.342	0	—	0	-2	-3	-0	-0.3
1997	*NY-A	3	2	.600	34	0	0	0	0	48	39	4	32	53	13.3	2.63	169	.225	.346	0	—	0	10	10	0	0.9
1998	*SD-N	5	2	.714	56	1	0	0	0	76^1	75	10	45	67	14.6	4.36	88	.257	.364	0	.000	-0	-1	-5	-0	-0.4
Total	4	10	11	.476	112	7	0	0	0	188^1	184	25	120	167	14.8	5.07	85	.257	.368	0	.000	-0	-11	-16	-1	-2.0
● **LARRY BOERNER**	Boerner, Lawrence Hyer b: 1/21/05, Staunton, Va. d: 10/16/69, Staunton, Va. BR/TR, 6'4.5", 175 lbs. Deb: 6/30/32																									
1932	Bos-A	0	4	.000	21	5	0	0	0	61	71	2	37	19	16.4	5.02	90	.302	.404	0	.000	-3	-4	-4	0	-0.4
● **JOE BOEVER**	Boever, Joseph Martin b: 10/4/60, Kirkwood, Mo. BR/TR, 6'1", 200 lbs. Deb: 7/19/85																									
1985	StL-N	0	0	—	13	0	0	0	0	16^1	17	3	4	20	11.6	4.41	80	.270	.313	0	—	0	-1	-2	-0	0.0
1986	StL-N	0	1	.000	11	0	0	0	0	21^2	19	2	11	8	12.5	1.66	219	.232	.323	1	.500	0	5	5	-0	0.2
1987	Atl-N	1	0	1.000	14	0	0	0	0	18^1	29	4	12	18	20.1	7.36	59	.367	.451	0	—	0	-7	-6	-0	-0.3
1988	Atl-N	0	2	.000	16	0	0	0	1	20^1	12	1	1	7	6.2	1.77	208	.182	.206	0	—	0	4	4	0	0.5
1989	Atl-N	4	11	.267	66	0	0	0	21	82^1	78	6	34	68	12.4	3.94	93	.252	.328	0	.000	-0	-4	-3	1	-0.5
1990	Atl-N	1	3	.250	33	0	0	0	8	42^1	40	6	35	35	15.9	4.68	86	.252	.387	0	.000	-0	-4	-3	-1	-0.5
	Phi-N	2	3	.400	34	0	0	0	6	46	37	0	16	40	10.4	2.15	178	.215	.282	0	.000	-0	8	9	0	1.1
	Yr	3	6	.333	67	0	0	0	14	88^1	77	6	51	75	13.0	3.36	117	.231	.333	0	.000	-0	4	6	-1	0.6
1991	Phi-N	3	5	.375	68	0	0	0	0	98^1	90	10	54	89	13.2	3.84	95	.245	.341	1	.333	0	-2	-2	-1	-0.2
1992	Hou-N	3	6	.333	**81**	0	0	0	2	111^1	103	3	45	67	12.3	2.51	134	.248	.327	0	.000	-1	12	11	0	0.8
1993	Oak-A	4	2	.667	42	0	0	0	0	79^1	87	8	33	49	14.1	3.86	106	.280	.356	0	—	0	4	2	0	0.5
	Det-A	2	1	.667	19	0	0	0	3	23	14	1	11	14	9.8	2.74	156	.179	.281	0	—	0	4	4	-0	0.6
	Yr	6	3	.667	61	0	0	0	3	102^1	101	9	44	63	12.8	3.61	114	.255	.330	0	—	0	8	6	-0	1.1
1994	Det-A	9	2	.818	46	0	0	0	3	81^1	80	12	37	49	13.2	3.98	122	.263	.347	0	—	0	7	8	1	1.0
1995	Det-A	5	7	.417	60	0	0	0	3	98^2	128	17	44	71	16.0	6.39	74	.319	.391	0	—	0	-18	-18	-1	-1.9
1996	Pit-N	0	2	.000	13	0	0	0	2	15	17	2	6	6	14.4	5.40	81	.288	.364	0	.000	-0	-2	-2	-0	-0.3
Total	12	34	45	.430	516	0	0	0	49	754^1	751	75	343	541	13.2	3.93	102	.262	.344	2	.118	-1	7	7	-2	1.0
● **JOHN BOGART**	Bogart, John Renzie "Big John" b: 9/21/1900, Bloomsburg, Pa. d: 12/7/86, Clarence, N.Y. BR/TR, 6'2", 195 lbs. Deb: 9/17/20																									
1920	Det-A	2	1	.667	4	2	0	0	0	23^2	16	0	18	5	12.9	3.04	122	.195	.340	2	.250	-0	2	2	-1	0.1

YEAR	TM/L	W	L	PCT	G	GS	CG	SH	SV	IP	H	HR	BB	SO	RAT	ERA	ERA+	OAV	OOB	BH	AVG	PB	PR	/A	PD	TPI
● RAY BOGGS	Boggs, Raymond Joseph "Lefty" b: 12/12/04, Reamsville, Kan. d: 11/27/89, Grand Junction, Colo. BL/TL, 6'0.5", 170 lbs. Deb: 9/1/28																									
1928	Bos-N	0	0	—	4	0	0	0	0	5	2	0	7	0	21.6	5.40	72	.167	.545	0	—	0	-1	-1	-0	0.0
● TOMMY BOGGS	Boggs, Thomas Winton b: 10/25/55, Poughkeepsie, N.Y. BR/TR, 6'2", 200 lbs. Deb: 7/19/76																									
1976	Tex-A	1	7	.125	13	13	3	0	0	90^1	87	7	34	36	12.2	3.49	103	.257	.326	0	—	0	0	1	-1	-0.1
1977	Tex-A	0	3	.000	6	6	0	0	0	27^1	40	1	12	15	17.5	5.93	69	.351	.417	0	—	0	-6	-6	-0	-0.6
1978	Atl-N	2	8	.200	16	12	1	1	0	59	80	8	26	21	16.3	6.71	60	.323	.389	3	.167	0	-21	-17	-2	-2.7
1979	Atl-N	0	2	.000	3	3	0	0	0	12^2	21	0	4	1	18.5	6.39	63	.362	.413	1	.250	0	-4	-3	0	-0.4
1980	Atl-N	12	9	.571	32	26	4	3	0	192^1	180	14	46	84	10.8	3.42	109	.249	.298	10	.159	-2	4	7	-2	0.3
1981	Atl-N	3	13	.188	25	24	2	0	0	142^2	140	11	54	81	12.4	4.10	87	.265	.336	7	.152	-1	-10	-8	-1	-1.0
1982	Atl-N	2	2	.500	10	10	0	0	0	46^1	43	2	22	29	13.0	3.30	113	.253	.345	4	.235	0	2	2	-0	0.2
1983	Atl-N	0	0	—	5	0	0	0	0	6^1	8	1	1	5	12.8	5.68	68	.320	.346	0	—	0	-1	-1	-0	0.0
1985	Tex-A	0	0	—	4	0	0	0	0	7	13	3	2	6	19.3	11.57	37	.382	.417	0	—	0	-6	-6	0	0.0
Total	9	20	44	.313	114	94	10	4	0	584	612	47	201	278	12.7	4.22	89	.273	.337	25	.169	-2	-41	-31	-5	-4.3
● WADE BOGGS	Boggs, Wade Anthony b: 6/15/58, Omaha, Neb. BL/TR, 6'2", 197 lbs. Deb: 4/10/82 ◆																									
1997	*NY-A	0	0	—	1	0	0	0	0	1	0	0	1	1	9.0	0.00	—	.000	.250	103	.292	1	1	0	0	0.0
● WARREN BOGLE	Bogle, Warren Frederick b: 10/19/46, Passaic, N.J. BL/TL, 6'4", 220 lbs. Deb: 7/31/68																									
1968	Oak-A	0	0	—	16	1	0	0	0	23	26	3	8	26	13.3	4.30	65	.283	.340	0	.000	-1	-3	-4	1	0.0
● BRIAN BOHANON	Bohanon, Brian Edward b: 8/1/68, Denton, Tex. BL/TL, 6'2", 220 lbs. Deb: 4/10/90																									
1990	Tex-A	0	3	.000	11	6	0	0	0	34	40	6	18	15	15.9	6.62	59	.296	.387	0	—	0	-10	-10	1	-0.7
1991	Tex-A	4	3	.571	11	11	1	0	0	61^1	66	4	23	34	13.4	4.84	83	.274	.342	0	—	0	-5	-6	-1	-0.5
1992	Tex-A	1	1	.500	18	7	0	0	0	45^2	57	7	25	29	16.4	6.31	60	.297	.381	0	—	0	-12	-13	-0	-0.3
1993	Tex-A	4	4	.500	36	8	0	0	0	92^2	107	8	46	45	15.2	4.76	87	.296	.382	0	—	0	-5	-6	1	-0.1
1994	Tex-A	2	2	.500	11	5	0	0	0	37^1	51	7	8	26	14.5	7.23	67	.321	.357	0	—	0	-10	-10	0	-0.8
1995	Det-A	1	1	.500	52	10	0	0	1	105^2	121	10	41	63	14.1	5.54	86	.285	.354	0	—	0	-10	-9	-0	-0.1
1996	Tor-A	0	1	.000	20	0	0	0	1	22	27	4	19	17	19.6	7.77	64	.303	.436	0	—	0	-7	-7	-0	-0.3
1997	NY-N	6	4	.600	19	14	0	0	0	94^1	95	9	34	66	12.7	3.82	106	.258	.328	6	.182	0	4	2	-1	0.2
1998	NY-N	2	4	.333	25	4	0	0	0	54^1	47	4	21	39	12.3	3.15	132	.234	.325	6	.429	2	7	6	2	1.0
	LA-N	5	7	.417	14	14	2	0	0	97^1	74	9	36	72	10.6	2.40	162	.213	.296	6	.207	2	20	16	2	2.3
	Yr	7	11	.389	39	18	2	0	0	151^2	121	13	57	111	10.9	2.67	150	.218	.297	12	.279	4	26	22	3	3.3
Total	9	25	30	.455	217	79	3	0	2	644^2	685	68	271	406	13.8	4.72	89	.272	.350	18	.237	5	-28	-36	4	0.7
● PAT BOHEN	Bohen, Leo Ignatius b: 9/30/1891, Oakland, Iowa d: 4/8/42, Napa, Cal. BR/TR, 5'10.5", 155 lbs. Deb: 10/1/13																									
1913	Phi-A	0	1	.000	1	1	1	0	0	8	3	0	2	5	5.6	1.13	246	.115	.179	0	.000	-0	2	1	-0	0.1
1914	Pit-N	0	0	—	1	0	0	0	0	1	2	0	2	0	45.0	18.00	15	.500	.714	0	.000	-0	-2	-2	-0	0.0
Total	2	0	1	.000	2	1	1	0	0	9	5	0	4	5	10.0	3.00	92	.167	.286	0	.000	-1	-0	-0	-0	0.1
● CHARLIE BOHN	Bohn, Charles b: 1857, Cleveland, Ohio d: 8/1/03, Cleveland, Ohio BR/TR, 5'9", 165 lbs. Deb: 6/20/1882 ◆																									
1882	Lou-a	1	1	.500	2	2	2	0	0	18	21	0	3	1	12.0	3.00	83	.273	.300	2	.154	-0	-1	-1	0	-0.1
● JOHN BOHNET	Bohnet, John Kelly b: 1/18/61, Pasadena, Cal. BB/TL, 6', 175 lbs. Deb: 5/10/82																									
1982	Cle-A	0	0	—	3	3	0	0	0	11^2	11	4	7	4	14.7	6.94	59	.250	.365	0	—	0	-4	-4	0	0.0
● DAN BOITANO	Boitano, Danny Jon b: 3/22/53, Sacramento, Cal. BR/TR, 6', 185 lbs. Deb: 10/1/78																									
1978	Phi-N	0	0	—	1	0	0	0	0	1	0	0	1	0	9.0	0.00	—	.000	.250	0	—	0	0	0	0	0.0
1979	Mil-A	0	0	—	5	0	0	0	0	6	6	1	3	5	13.5	1.50	278	.273	.360	0	—	0	2	2	0	0.0
1980	Mil-A	0	1	.000	11	0	0	0	0	17^2	26	7	6	11	16.8	8.15	47	.342	.398	0	—	0	-8	-8	0	-0.2
1981	NY-N	2	1	.667	15	0	0	0	0	16^1	21	2	5	8	15.4	5.51	63	.309	.373	0	—	0	-4	-4	0	-0.6
1982	Tex-A	0	0	—	19	0	0	0	0	30^1	33	5	13	28	14.2	5.34	72	.280	.361	0	—	0	-4	-5	-0	0.2
Total	5	2	2	.500	51	0	0	0	0	71^1	86	15	28	52	15.0	5.68	67	.300	.372	0	—	0	-14	-15	-0	-0.6
● DICK BOKELMANN	Bokelmann, Richard Werner b: 10/26/26, Arlington Heights, Ill. BR/TR, 6'0.5", 180 lbs. Deb: 8/3/51																									
1951	StL-N	3	3	.500	20	1	0	0	3	52^1	49	2	31	22	13.9	3.78	105	.245	.349	0	.000	-2	1	1	-1	-0.1
1952	StL-N	0	1	.000	11	0	0	0	0	12^2	20	0	7	5	19.2	9.24	40	.357	.429	0	—	0	-8	-8	1	-0.5
1953	StL-N	0	0	—	3	0	0	0	0	3	4	0	0	0	12.0	6.00	71	.308	.308	0	—	0	-1	-1	0	0.0
Total	3	3	4	.429	34	1	0	0	3	68	73	2	38	27	14.8	4.90	80	.271	.364	0	.000	-2	-7	-7	0	-0.6
● JOE BOKINA	Bokina, Joseph b: 4/4/10, Northampton, Mass. d: 10/25/91, Chattanooga, Tenn. BR/TR, 6', 184 lbs. Deb: 4/16/36																									
1936	Was-A	0	2	.000	5	1	0	0	0	8^1	15	0	6	5	22.7	8.64	55	.395	.477	0	.000	-0	-3	-4	-0	-0.7
● BERNIE BOLAND	Boland, Bernard Anthony b: 1/21/1892, Rochester, N.Y. d: 9/12/73, Detroit, Mich. BR/TR, 5'8.5", 168 lbs. Deb: 4/14/15																									
1915	Det-A	13	7	.650	45	18	8	1	3	202^2	167	2	75	72	11.0	3.11	98	.230	.307	11	.175	-1	-4	-2	0	-0.2
1916	Det-A	10	3	.769	46	9	5	1	3	130^1	111	1	73	59	13.0	3.94	73	.240	.349	8	.250	2	-16	-15	-3	-1.7
1917	Det-A	16	11	.593	43	28	13	3	6	238	192	0	95	89	11.1	2.68	99	.226	.308	4	.056	-5	-1	-1	0	-0.7
1918	Det-A	14	10	.583	29	25	14	4	0	204	176	1	67	63	11.0	2.65	101	.236	.304	12	.174	0	3	0	-1	-0.1
1919	Det-A	14	16	.467	35	30	18	1	1	242^2	222	7	80	71	11.3	3.04	105	.253	.318	8	.108	-3	5	4	-2	0.0
1920	Det-A	0	2	.000	4	3	1	0	0	17^1	23	0	14	4	20.3	7.79	48	.348	.476	1	.143	-0	-8	-8	0	-0.7
1921	StL-A	1	4	.200	7	6	0	0	0	27	34	2	28	6	21.0	9.33	48	.309	.453	1	.100	-1	-15	-15	-0	-2.0
Total	7	68	53	.562	209	119	59	10	13	1062	925	13	432	364	11.7	3.25	91	.241	.322	45	.138	-8	-35	-36	-5	-5.4
● BILL BOLDEN	Bolden, William Horace "Big Bill" b: 5/9/1893, Dandridge, Tenn. d: 12/8/66, Jefferson City, Tenn. BR/TR, 6'4", 200 lbs. Deb: 6/27/19																									
1919	StL-N	0	1	.000	3	1	0	0	0	12	17	0	4	4	16.5	5.25	53	.340	.400	1	.333	0	-3	-3	0	-0.2
● STEW BOLEN	Bolen, Stewart O'Neal b: 10/12/02, Jackson, Ala. d: 8/30/69, Mobile, Ala. BL/TL, 5'11", 180 lbs. Deb: 4/15/26																									
1926	StL-A	0	0	—	5	0	0	0	0	14^2	21	2	6	7	16.6	6.14	70	.356	.415	2	.500	1	-3	-3	-0	0.0
1927	StL-A	0	1	.000	3	1	1	0	0	9^2	14	0	5	7	17.7	8.38	52	.368	.442	1	.333	0	-5	-4	0	-0.3
1931	Phi-N	3	12	.200	28	16	2	0	0	98^2	117	5	63	55	16.8	6.39	66	.297	.399	5	.156	-1	-28	-23	0	-3.1
1932	Phi-N	0	0	—	5	0	0	0	0	16	18	0	10	3	16.9	2.81	157	.281	.395	1	.143	-0	2	3	-0	-0.1
Total	4	3	13	.188	41	17	3	0	0	139	170	7	84	72	16.8	6.09	70	.306	.403	9	.196	-0	-34	-28	-0	-3.5
● BOBBY BOLIN	Bolin, Bobby Donald b: 1/29/39, Hickory Grove, S.C. BR/TR, 6'4", 200 lbs. Deb: 4/18/61																									
1961	SF-N	2	2	.500	37	1	0	0	5	48	37	6	37	48	14.4	3.19	120	.210	.356	2	.286	0	5	3	-1	0.3
1962	*SF-N	7	3	.700	41	5	2	0	5	92	84	10	35	74	12.1	3.62	105	.243	.321	6	.261	2	3	2	-1	0.3
1963	SF-N	10	6	.625	47	12	2	0	7	137^1	128	13	57	134	12.6	3.28	98	.242	.324	5	.143	2	0	-1	-2	-0.2
1964	SF-N	6	9	.400	38	23	5	3	1	174^2	143	16	77	146	11.9	3.25	110	.220	.313	5	.100	0	6	6	-1	0.5
1965	SF-N	14	6	.700	45	13	2	0	2	163	125	17	56	135	10.2	2.76	130	.214	.288	9	.167	1	14	15	-2	1.8
1966	SF-N	11	10	.524	36	34	10	4	1	224^1	174	25	70	143	10.2	2.89	127	.211	.281	13	.171	3	18	19	-2	1.9
1967	SF-N	6	8	.429	37	15	0	0	0	120	120	16	50	69	13.0	4.88	67	.258	.333	8	.242	2	-20	-21	-1	-2.2
1968	SF-N	10	5	.667	34	19	6	3	0	176^2	128	9	46	126	9.1	1.99	148	.200	.258	5	.091	-1	20	19	-1	1.5
1969	SF-N	7	7	.500	30	22	2	0	0	146^1	149	17	49	102	12.6	4.43	79	.260	.326	6	.154	3	-14	-15	-1	-1.1
1970	Mil-A	5	11	.313	32	20	3	0	1	132	131	20	67	81	13.8	4.91	77	.256	.346	7	.194	2	-18	-16	-1	-1.7
	Bos-A	2	0	1.000	6	0	0	0	2	8	2	0	5	8	9.0	0.00	—	.080	.258	0	.000	-0	3	4	0	1.1
	Yr	7	11	.389	38	20	3	0	3	140	133	20	72	89	13.2	4.63	82	.243	.332	7	.189	2	-14	-13	-1	-0.6
1971	Bos-A	5	3	.625	52	0	0	0	6	69^2	74	7	24	51	12.7	4.26	87	.273	.332	3	.250	0	-6	-4	-1	-0.6
1972	Bos-A	0	1	.000	21	0	0	0	5	30^2	24	3	11	27	10.6	2.93	109	.209	.283	0	.000	-0	0	1	-0	0.0
1973	Bos-A	3	4	.429	39	0	0	0	15	53^1	45	5	13	31	10.0	2.70	149	.232	.284	0	—	0	7	8	1	1.6
Total	13	88	75	.540	495	164	32	10	50	1576	1364	164	597	1175	11.5	3.40	103	.231	.308	69	.163	15	18	19	-13	3.2

● GREG BOLLO Bollo, Gregory Gene b: 11/16/43, Detroit, Mich. BR/TR, 6'4", 183 lbs. Deb: 5/9/65

YEAR	TM/L	W	L	PCT	G	GS	CG	SH	SV	IP	H	HR	BB	SO	RAT	ERA	ERA+	OAV	OOB	BH	AVG	PB	PR	/A	PD	TPI
1965	Chi-A	0	0	—	15	0	0	0	0	22^2	12	5	9	16	9.1	3.57	89	.152	.256	0	—	0	-0	-1	0	0.0
1966	Chi-A	0	1	.000	3	1	0	0	0	7	7	0	3	4	14.1	2.57	123	.269	.367	0	.000	-0	1	0	-0	0.0
Total	2	0	1	.000	18	1	0	0	0	29^2	19	5	12	20	10.3	3.34	96	.181	.283	0	.000	-0	0	-0	0	0.0

● RODNEY BOLTON Bolton, Rodney Earl b: 9/23/68, Chattanooga, Tenn. BR/TR, 6'2", 190 lbs. Deb: 4/10/93

YEAR	TM/L	W	L	PCT	G	GS	CG	SH	SV	IP	H	HR	BB	SO	RAT	ERA	ERA+	OAV	OOB	BH	AVG	PB	PR	/A	PD	TPI
1993	Chi-A	2	6	.250	9	8	0	0	0	42^1	55	4	16	17	15.3	7.44	56	.314	.375	0	—	0	-15	-15	1	-2.0
1995	Chi-A	0	2	.000	8	3	0	0	0	22	33	4	14	10	19.2	8.18	54	.351	.435	0	—	0	-8	-9	0	-0.4
Total	2	2	8	.200	17	11	0	0	0	64^1	88	8	30	27	16.6	7.69	56	.327	.397	0	—	0	-23	-24	1	-2.4

● TOM BOLTON Bolton, Thomas Edward b: 5/6/62, Nashville, Tenn. BL/TL, 6'3", 175 lbs. Deb: 5/17/87

YEAR	TM/L	W	L	PCT	G	GS	CG	SH	SV	IP	H	HR	BB	SO	RAT	ERA	ERA+	OAV	OOB	BH	AVG	PB	PR	/A	PD	TPI
1987	Bos-A	1	0	1.000	29	0	0	0	0	61^2	83	5	27	49	16.3	4.38	104	.329	.399	0	—	0	1	1	0	-0.2
1988	Bos-A	1	3	.250	28	0	0	0	1	30^1	35	1	14	21	14.5	4.75	87	.285	.358	0	—	0	-3	-2	1	-0.5
1989	Bos-A	0	4	.000	4	4	0	0	0	17^1	21	1	10	9	16.1	8.31	49	.292	.378	0	—	0	-9	-8	-0	-1.8
1990	*Bos-A	10	5	.667	21	16	3	0	0	119^2	111	6	47	65	12.1	3.38	120	.251	.327	0	—	0	7	9	1	0.7
1991	Bos-A	8	9	.471	25	19	0	0	0	110	136	16	51	64	15.4	5.24	82	.308	.381	0	—	0	-14	-11	-1	-1.9
1992	Bos-A	1	2	.333	21	1	0	0	0	29	34	0	14	23	15.5	3.41	123	.286	.370	0	—	0	2	3	0	-0.2
	Cin-N	3	3	.500	16	8	0	0	0	46^1	52	9	23	27	15.0	5.24	69	.284	.370	0	.000	-1	-9	-8	0	-1.1
1993	Det-A	6	6	.500	43	8	0	0	0	102^2	113	5	45	66	14.5	4.47	96	.282	.364	0	—	0	-2	-2	0	-0.1
1994	Bal-A	1	2	.333	22	0	0	0	0	23^1	29	3	13	12	16.2	5.40	93	.309	.393	0	—	0	-2	-1	0	-0.4
Total	8	31	34	.477	209	56	3	0	1	540^1	614	46	244	336	14.6	4.56	93	.289	.366	0	.000	-1	-28	-20	2	-5.5

● MARK BOMBACK Bomback, Mark Vincent b: 4/14/53, Portsmouth, Va. BR/TR, 5'11", 170 lbs. Deb: 9/12/78

YEAR	TM/L	W	L	PCT	G	GS	CG	SH	SV	IP	H	HR	BB	SO	RAT	ERA	ERA+	OAV	OOB	BH	AVG	PB	PR	/A	PD	TPI
1978	Mil-A	0	0	—	2	1	0	0	0	1^2	5	1	1	1	32.4	16.20	23	.500	.545	0	—	0	-2	-2	-0	0.0
1980	NY-N	10	8	.556	36	25	2	1	0	162^2	191	17	49	68	13.5	4.09	87	.297	.350	10	.233	3	-9	-10	2	-0.4
1981	Tor-A	5	5	.500	20	11	0	0	0	90^1	84	6	35	33	12.0	3.89	101	.251	.323	0	—	0	-2	1	0	0.1
1982	Tor-A	1	5	.167	16	8	0	0	0	59^2	87	10	25	22	17.3	6.03	74	.343	.408	0	—	0	-13	-10	0	-1.3
Total	4	16	18	.471	74	45	2	1	0	314^1	367	34	110	124	13.9	4.47	86	.295	.356	10	.233	3	-27	-22	3	-1.6

● TOMMY BOND Bond, Thomas Henry b: 4/2/1856, Granard, Ireland d: 1/24/41, Boston, Mass. BR/TR, 5'7.5", 160 lbs. Deb: 5/5/1874 MU♦

YEAR	TM/L	W	L	PCT	G	GS	CG	SH	SV	IP	H	HR	BB	SO	RAT	ERA	ERA+	OAV	OOB	BH	AVG	PB	PR	/A	PD	TPI
1874	Atl-n	22	32	.407	55	55	55	1	0	497	606	15	8	42	11.1	2.03	101	.266	.268	54	.220	-0	8	1		.9
1875	Har-n	19	16	.543	40	39	37	6	0	352	302	3	7	70	7.9	1.41	167	.216	.219	77	.266	3	32	**37**		3.7
1876	Har-N	31	13	.705	45	45	45	6	0	408	355	2	13	88	8.1	1.68	141	.220	.227	50	.275	1	29	32	5	3.2
1877	Bos-N	**40**	17	**.702**	58	58	58	**6**	0	521	530	5	36	**170**	**9.8**	**2.11**	133	.249	**.261**	59	.228	-4	**41**	41	3	3.5
1878	Bos-N	**40**	19	**.678**	**59**	59	**57**	**9**	0	**532**^{2}	571	5	33	**182**	10.2	2.06	115	.269	.280	50	.212	-4	15	18	2	1.3
1879	Bos-N	43	19	.694	64	64	59	**11**	0	555^1	543	8	24	155	**9.2**	**1.96**	**126**	.251	.259	62	.241	2	33	**32**	7	**3.8**
1880	Bos-N	26	29	.473	63	57	49	3	0	493	559	1	45	118	11.0	2.67	85	.274	.290	62	.220	-2	-16	-22	10	-1.4
1881	Bos-N	0	3	.000	3	3	2	0	0	25^1	40	3	2	2	14.9	4.26	62	.360	.372	2	.200	-0	-4	-5	1	-0.4
1882	Wor-N	0	1	.000	2	2	0	0	0	12^1	12	0	7	2	13.9	4.38	71	.218	.306	4	.133	-1	-2	-2	-0	-0.2
1884	Bos-U	13	9	.591	23	21	19	0	0	189	185	3	14	128	9.5	3.00	79	.239	.253	48	.296	-0	-12	-13	3	-1.0
	Ind-a	0	5	.000	5	5	5	0	0	43	62	5	4	15	14.2	5.65	58	.310	.330	3	.130	-1	-11	-11	-1	-1.1
Total	2 n	41	48	.461	95	94	92	7	0	849	908	18	15	112	9.8	1.77	123	.247	.250	131	.245	2	41	38		4.6
Total	8	193	115	.627	322	314	294	35	0	2779^2	2857	32	178	860	9.8	2.25	110	.255	.267	340	.236	-9	71	70	30	7.7

● RICKY BONES Bones, Ricardo Ricky b: 4/7/69, Salinas, P.R. BR/TR, 6', 190 lbs. Deb: 8/11/91

YEAR	TM/L	W	L	PCT	G	GS	CG	SH	SV	IP	H	HR	BB	SO	RAT	ERA	ERA+	OAV	OOB	BH	AVG	PB	PR	/A	PD	TPI
1991	SD-N	4	6	.400	11	11	0	0	0	54	57	3	18	31	12.5	4.83	79	.269	.326	1	.077	-0	-7	-6	-1	-1.2
1992	Mil-A	9	10	.474	31	28	0	0	0	163^1	169	27	48	65	12.5	4.57	84	.264	.324	0	—	0	-12	-13	-1	-1.4
1993	Mil-A	11	11	.500	32	31	3	0	0	203^2	222	28	63	63	12.9	4.86	87	.278	.336	0	—	0	-12	-14	-1	-1.2
1994	Mil-A☆	10	9	.526	24	24	4	1	0	170^2	166	17	45	57	11.3	3.43	147	.255	.306	0	—	0	26	30	-3	2.5
1995	Mil-A	10	12	.455	32	31	3	0	0	200^1	218	26	83	77	13.7	4.63	108	.281	.353	0	—	0	2	8	2	0.5
1996	Mil-A	7	14	.333	32	23	0	0	0	145	170	28	62	59	15.0	5.83	89	.294	.371	0	—	0	-14	-10	-2	-1.6
	NY-A	0	0	—	4	1	0	0	0	7	14	2	6	4	27.0	14.14	35	.438	.538	0	—	0	-7	-7	0	0.0
	Yr	7	14	.333	36	24	0	0	0	152	184	30	68	63	15.0	6.22	83	.295	.365	0	—	0	-21	-18	-2	-1.6
1997	Cin-N	0	1	.000	9	2	0	0	0	17^2	31	2	11	8	22.4	10.19	42	.378	.463	0	.000	-0	-12	-12	0	-0.6
	KC-A	4	7	.364	21	11	1	0	0	78^1	102	10	25	36	15.2	5.97	79	.325	.384	0	—	0	-12	-11	0	-1.3
1998	KC-A	2	2	.500	32	0	0	0	1	53^1	49	4	24	38	12.5	3.04	162	.244	.327	0	.000	-0	10	11	2	0.9
Total	8	57	72	.442	228	162	11	1	1	1093^1	1198	147	385	438	13.4	4.82	96	.279	.345	1	.063	-1	-38	-25	-4	-3.4

● JULIO BONETTI Bonetti, Julio Giacomo b: 7/14/11, Genoa, Italy d: 6/17/52, Belmont, Cal. BR/TR, 6', 180 lbs. Deb: 4/22/37

YEAR	TM/L	W	L	PCT	G	GS	CG	SH	SV	IP	H	HR	BB	SO	RAT	ERA	ERA+	OAV	OOB	BH	AVG	PB	PR	/A	PD	TPI
1937	StL-A	4	11	.267	28	16	7	0	1	143^1	190	13	60	43	15.8	5.84	83	.321	.385	7	.149	-2	-19	-16	2	-1.3
1938	StL-A	2	3	.400	17	0	0	0	0	28^1	41	1	13	7	17.2	6.35	78	.350	.415	0	.000	-1	-5	-4	0	-0.7
1940	Chi-N	0	0	—	1	0	0	0	0	1^1	3	0	4	0	47.3	20.25	19	.429	.636	0	—	0	-2	-2	-0	0.0
Total	3	6	14	.300	46	16	7	0	1	173	234	14	77	50	16.3	6.03	80	.327	.394	7	.127	-3	-27	-23	2	-2.0

● HANK BONEY Boney, Henry Tate "Haney" b: 10/28/03, Wallace, N.C. BR/TR, 5'11", 176 lbs. Deb: 6/28/27

YEAR	TM/L	W	L	PCT	G	GS	CG	SH	SV	IP	H	HR	BB	SO	RAT	ERA	ERA+	OAV	OOB	BH	AVG	PB	PR	/A	PD	TPI
1927	NY-N	0	0	—	3	0	0	0	0	4	4	0	2	0	13.5	2.25	171	.267	.353	0	—	0	1	1	-0	0.0

● TINY BONHAM Bonham, Ernest Edward b: 8/16/13, Ione, Cal. d: 9/15/49, Pittsburgh, Pa. BR/TR, 6'2", 215 lbs. Deb: 8/5/40

YEAR	TM/L	W	L	PCT	G	GS	CG	SH	SV	IP	H	HR	BB	SO	RAT	ERA	ERA+	OAV	OOB	BH	AVG	PB	PR	/A	PD	TPI
1940	NY-A	9	3	.750	12	12	10	3	0	99^1	83	4	13	37	8.7	1.90	212	.224	.250	7	.189	0	27	24	-2	2.5
1941	*NY-A	9	6	.600	23	14	7	1	2	126^2	118	12	31	43	10.7	2.98	132	.246	.294	8	.160	-1	16	13	-3	1.1
1942	*NY-A☆	21	5	**.808**	28	27	**22**	**6**	0	226	199	11	24	71	**8.9**	2.27	152	.237	**.259**	9	.122	-2	**35**	29	-4	2.6
1943	*NY-A☆	15	8	.652	28	26	17	4	1	225^2	197	13	52	71	10.0	2.27	142	.236	.282	15	.197	0	26	24	-5	2.0
1944	NY-A	12	9	.571	26	25	17	1	0	213^2	228	14	41	54	11.3	2.99	116	.273	.307	10	.133	-3	10	12	-3	0.5
1945	NY-A	8	11	.421	23	23	12	0	0	180^2	186	11	22	42	10.4	3.29	105	.265	.288	15	.238	3	2	4	-3	0.3
1946	NY-A	5	8	.385	18	14	6	2	3	104^2	97	6	23	30	10.3	3.70	93	.243	.284	4	.129	-0	-2	-3	-2	-0.6
1947	Pit-N	11	8	.579	33	18	7	3	3	149^2	167	17	35	63	12.3	3.85	110	.277	.319	7	.156	-0	3	6	-3	0.4
1948	Pit-N	6	10	.375	22	20	7	0	0	135^2	145	18	23	42	11.3	4.31	94	.276	.310	8	.163	-2	-5	-4	-4	-0.9
1949	Pit-N	7	4	.636	18	14	5	1	0	89	81	11	23	25	10.5	4.25	99	.246	.295	1	.045	-1	-2	-0	-2	-0.3
Total	10	103	72	.589	231	193	110	21	9	1551	1501	117	287	478	10.4	3.06	120	.254	.289	84	.161	-7	110	105	-29	7.6

● BILL BONHAM Bonham, William Gordon b: 10/1/48, Glendale, Cal. BR/TR, 6'3", 195 lbs. Deb: 4/7/71

YEAR	TM/L	W	L	PCT	G	GS	CG	SH	SV	IP	H	HR	BB	SO	RAT	ERA	ERA+	OAV	OOB	BH	AVG	PB	PR	/A	PD	TPI
1971	Chi-N	2	1	.667	33	2	0	0	0	60	63	6	36	41	15.6	4.65	85	.281	.392	2	.167	-0	-8	-5	1	-0.1
1972	Chi-N	1	1	.500	19	4	0	0	4	57^2	56	4	25	49	12.8	3.12	122	.260	.340	4	.286	1	2	4	0	0.4
1973	Chi-N	7	5	.583	44	15	3	0	6	152	126	10	64	121	11.5	3.02	131	.230	.315	4	.093	-3	11	16	4	1.4
1974	Chi-N	11	22	.333	44	36	10	2	1	242^2	246	13	109	191	13.4	3.86	99	.263	.343	12	.143	-3	-6	-1	5	0.1
1975	Chi-N	13	15	.464	38	36	7	2	0	229^1	254	15	109	165	14.4	4.71	82	.281	.361	15	.183	-0	-28	-22	1	-2.3
1976	Chi-N	9	13	.409	32	31	3	0	0	196	215	11	96	110	14.4	4.27	90	.283	.365	13	.200	1	-17	9	0	-0.8
1977	Chi-N	10	13	.435	34	34	1	0	0	214^2	207	15	82	134	12.2	4.36	101	.254	.324	15	.231	1	-11	1	3	0.5
1978	Cin-N	11	5	.688	23	23	1	0	0	140^1	151	9	50	83	13.0	3.53	101	.276	.337	8	.186	2	1	0	3	0.6
1979	Cin-N	9	7	.563	29	29	2	0	0	175^2	173	14	60	78	12.3	3.79	98	.261	.330	8	.140	-1	-1	-1	0	-0.2
1980	Cin-N	2	1	.667	4	4	0	0	0	19	21	1	5	13	12.3	4.74	75	.276	.321	0	.000	-0	-2	-2	-0	-0.4
Total	10	75	83	.475	300	214	27	4	11	1487^1	1512	98	636	985	13.2	4.01	97	.266	.343	81	.172	-2	-59	-20	18	-0.8

● JOE BONIKOWSKI Bonikowski, Joseph Peter b: 1/16/41, Philadelphia, Pa. BR/TR, 6', 175 lbs. Deb: 4/12/62

YEAR	TM/L	W	L	PCT	G	GS	CG	SH	SV	IP	H	HR	BB	SO	RAT	ERA	ERA+	OAV	OOB	BH	AVG	PB	PR	/A	PD	TPI
1962	Min-A	5	7	.417	30	13	3	0	2	99^2	95	6	38	45	12.1	3.88	105	.255	.325	4	.148	-1	1	2	1	0.3

● BILL BONNESS Bonness, William John "Lefty" b: 12/15/23, Cleveland, Ohio d: 12/3/77, Detroit, Mich. BR/TL, 6'4", 200 lbs. Deb: 9/26/44

YEAR	TM/L	W	L	PCT	G	GS	CG	SH	SV	IP	H	HR	BB	SO	RAT	ERA	ERA+	OAV	OOB	BH	AVG	PB	PR	/A	PD	TPI
1944	Cle-A	0	1	.000	2	1	0	0	0	7	11	0	5	1	23.1	7.71	43	.367	.486	0	.000	-0	-3	-3	0	-0.4

● GUS BONO Bono, Adlai Wendell b: 8/29/1894, Doe Run, Mo. d: 12/3/48, Dearborn, Mich. BR/TR, 5'11", 175 lbs. Deb: 9/13/20

YEAR	TM/L	W	L	PCT	G	GS	CG	SH	SV	IP	H	HR	BB	SO	RAT	ERA	ERA+	OAV	OOB	BH	AVG	PB	PR	/A	PD	TPI
1920	Was-A	0	2	.000	4	1	0	0	0	12^1	17	0	6	4	16.8	8.76	43	.315	.383	0	.000	-0	-7	-7	0	-0.9

YEAR	TM/L	W	L	PCT	G	GS	CG	SH	SV	IP	H	HR	BB	SO	RAT	ERA	ERA+	OAV	OOB	BH	AVG	PB	PR	/A	PD	TPI
● **GREG BOOKER**	Booker, Gregory Scott b: 6/22/60, Lynchburg, Va. BR/TR, 6'6", 233 lbs. Deb: 9/11/83 C																									
1983	SD-N	0	1	.000	6	1	0	0	0	11^2	18	2	9	5	20.8	7.71	45	.375	.474	0	.000	-0	-5	-5	0	-0.4
1984	*SD-N	1	1	.500	32	1	0	0	0	57^1	67	4	27	28	14.8	3.30	108	.295	.370	2	.286	1	2	2	0	0.1
1985	SD-N	0	1	.000	17	0	0	0	0	22^1	20	3	17	7	15.3	6.85	52	.247	.384	0	.000	-0	-8	-8	-0	-0.4
1986	SD-N	1	0	1.000	9	0	0	0	0	11	10	0	4	7	11.5	1.64	223	.233	.298	0	—	0	3	2	-0	0.2
1987	SD-N	1	1	.500	44	0	0	0	1	68^1	62	5	30	17	12.5	3.16	125	.246	.333	0	.000	-1	7	6	-0	0.1
1988	SD-N	2	2	.500	34	2	0	0	0	63^2	68	5	19	43	12.4	3.39	100	.278	.332	2	.250	1	0	0	1	0.1
1989	SD-N	0	1	.000	11	0	0	0	0	19	15	2	10	8	11.8	4.26	82	.224	.325	0	—	0	-2	-2	-0	-0.1
	Min-A	0	0	—	6	0	0	0	0	8^2	11	1	2	3	13.5	4.15	100	.306	.342	0	—	0	-0	-0	1	-0.5
1990	SF-N	0	0	—	2	0	0	0	0	2	7	0	0	1	31.5	13.50	27	.538	.538	0	—	0	-2	-2	-0	0.0
Total	8	5	7	.417	161	4	0	0	1	264	278	22	118	119	13.7	3.89	94	.275	.353	4	.174	1	-6	-7	1	-0.9
● **RED BOOLES**	Booles, Seabron Jesse b: 7/14/1880, Bernice, La. d: 3/16/55, Monroe, La. BL/TL, 5'10", 150 lbs. Deb: 7/30/09																									
1909	Cle-A	0	1	.000	4	1	0	0	0	22^2	20	0	8	6	11.5	1.99	129	.235	.309	1	.167	0	1	1	-0	0.1
● **DANNY BOONE**	Boone, Daniel Hugh b: 1/14/54, Long Beach, Cal. BL/TL, 5'8", 150 lbs. Deb: 4/11/81 F																									
1981	SD-N	1	0	1.000	37	0	0	0	2	63^1	63	2	21	43	12.1	2.84	115	.267	.329	2	.500	1	5	3	1	0.3
1982	SD-N	1	0	1.000	10	0	0	0	1	16	21	2	3	8	13.5	5.63	61	.323	.353	1	.200	0	-4	-4	0	-0.2
	Hou-N	0	1	.000	10	0	0	0	1	12^2	7	1	4	4	7.8	3.55	93	.171	.244	0	.000	-0	0	-0	0	0.0
	Yr	1	1	.500	20	0	0	0	2	28^2	28	3	7	12	11.0	4.71	72	.264	.310	1	.167	0	-4	-4	0	-0.2
1990	Bal-A	0	0	—	4	1	0	0	0	9^2	12	1	3	2	14.9	2.79	136	.308	.372	0	—	0	1	1	0	0.3
Total	3	2	1	.667	61	1	0	0	4	101^2	103	6	31	57	12.0	3.36	99	.270	.329	3	.300	1	2	-0	1	0.4
● **GEORGE BOONE**	Boone, George Morris b: 3/1/1871, Louisville, Ky. d: 9/24/10, Louisville, Ky. Deb: 4/23/1891																									
1891	Lou-a	0	0	—	4	1	0	0	1	15	15	0	9	4	14.4	7.80	47	.250	.348	2	.333	0	-7	-7	-0	-0.1
● **DAN BOONE**	Boone, James Albert b: 1/19/1895, Samantha, Ala. d: 5/11/68, Tuscaloosa, Ala. BR/TR, 6'2", 190 lbs. Deb: 9/10/19																									
1919	Phi-A	0	1	.000	3	2	0	0	0	14^2	24	0	10	1	20.9	6.75	51	.375	.459	0	.000	-1	-6	-5	1	-0.3
1921	Det-A	0	0	—	1	0	0	0	0	2	1	0	2	0	13.5	0.00	—	.200	.429	0	.000	-0	1	1	0	0.0
1922	Cle-A	4	6	.400	11	10	4	2	0	75^1	87	3	19	9	12.8	4.06	99	.298	.343	5	.192	-1	-0	-1	0	-0.1
1923	Cle-A	4	6	.400	27	4	2	0	0	70^1	93	3	31	15	16.3	6.01	66	.322	.393	4	.211	0	-16	-16	3	-1.6
Total	4	8	13	.381	42	16	6	2	0	162^1	205	6	62	25	15.0	5.10	77	.315	.378	9	.180	-1	-21	-21	4	-2.0
● **AMOS BOOTH**	Booth, Amos Smith "Darling" b: 9/14/1853, Cincinnati, O. d: 7/1/21, Miamisburg, Ohio BR/TR, 5'9", 159 lbs. Deb: 4/25/1876 ♦																									
1876	Cin-N	0	1	.000	3	1	0	0	0	9^2	22	0	0	0	20.5	9.31	24	.431	.431	71	.261	0	-8	-8	-0	-0.6
1877	Cin-N	1	7	.125	12	8	6	0	0	86	114	1	13	18	13.3	3.56	74	.296	.319	27	.172	-1	-7	-9	-1	-0.8
Total	2	1	8	.111	15	9	6	0	0	95^2	136	1	13	18	14.0	4.14	63	.312	.332	98	.224	-1	-15	-16	-1	-1.4
● **EDDIE BOOTH**	Booth, Edward H. b: Brooklyn, N.Y. Deb: 4/26/1872 ♦																									
1876	NY-N	0	0	—	1	0	0	0	0	5	16	0	0	0	28.8	10.80	20	.471	.471	49	.215	-0	-5	-5	-0	0.0
● **JOHN BOOZER**	Boozer, John Morgan b: 7/6/38, Columbia, S.C. d: 1/24/86, Lexington, S.C. BR/TR, 6'3", 205 lbs. Deb: 7/22/62																									
1962	Phi-N	0	0	—	9	0	0	0	0	20^1	22	3	10	13	14.2	5.75	67	.282	.364	0	.000	-0	-4	-4	-0	0.0
1963	Phi-N	3	4	.429	26	8	2	0	1	83	67	11	33	69	11.0	2.93	110	.227	.307	3	.143	-0	3	3	-2	0.0
1964	Phi-N	3	4	.429	22	3	0	0	2	60^1	64	6	18	51	12.5	5.07	68	.271	.328	1	.077	-1	-10	-11	1	-1.2
1966	Phi-N	0	0	—	2	2	0	0	0	5^1	8	1	3	5	18.6	6.75	53	.348	.423	0	.000	-0	-2	-2	0	0.0
1967	Phi-N	5	4	.556	28	7	1	0	1	74^2	86	6	24	48	13.4	4.10	83	.292	.347	4	.211	1	-6	-6	0	-0.6
1968	Phi-N	2	2	.500	38	0	0	0	5	68^2	76	3	15	49	12.2	3.67	82	.279	.322	1	.111	-0	-5	-5	0	-0.4
1969	Phi-N	1	2	.333	46	2	0	0	6	82	91	12	36	47	13.9	4.28	83	.283	.356	3	.333	1	-6	-7	-1	-0.3
Total	7	14	16	.467	171	22	3	0	15	394^1	414	42	139	282	12.8	4.09	82	.272	.336	12	.162	-0	-30	-31	-2	-2.5
● **PEDRO BORBON**	Borbon, Pedro (Rodriguez) b: 12/2/46, Valverde, Mao, D.R. BR/TR, 6'2", 185 lbs. Deb: 4/9/69 F																									
1969	Cal-A	2	3	.400	22	0	0	0	0	41	55	5	11	20	15.4	6.15	57	.324	.378	0	.000	-0	-12	-12	-0	-1.4
1970	Cin-N	0	2	.000	12	1	0	0	0	17^1	21	2	6	6	15.6	6.75	60	.309	.390	0	.000	-0	-5	-5	2	-0.4
1971	Cin-N	0	0	—	3	0	0	0	0	4^1	3	1	1	4	8.3	4.15	81	.200	.250	0	—	0	-0	-0	-0	0.0
1972	*Cin-N	8	3	.727	62	2	0	0	11	122	115	5	32	48	11.1	3.17	101	.254	.307	1	.048	-1	4	1	-1	-0.1
1973	*Cin-N	11	4	.733	80	0	0	0	14	121	137	4	35	60	12.9	2.16	158	.298	.349	5	.333	1	**20**	17	-0	2.6
1974	Cin-N	10	7	.588	73	0	0	0	14	139	133	11	32	53	10.9	3.24	108	.255	.303	5	.192	-0	6	4	-1	0.4
1975	*Cin-N	9	5	.643	67	0	0	0	5	125	145	6	21	29	12.2	2.95	122	.301	.334	7	.292	2	9	9	-1	1.1
1976	*Cin-N	4	3	.571	69	1	0	0	8	121	135	4	31	53	12.6	3.35	105	.292	.342	4	.222	0	2	2	-0	0.1
1977	Cin-N	10	5	.667	73	0	0	0	18	127	131	7	24	48	11.2	3.19	123	.268	.307	4	.182	-0	10	10	-2	1.3
1978	Cin-N	8	2	.800	62	0	0	0	4	99^1	102	6	27	35	12.0	4.98	71	.274	.328	2	.182	-0	-16	-16	-0	-1.7
1979	Cin-N	2	2	.500	30	0	0	0	2	44^2	48	2	8	23	11.3	3.43	109	.277	.309	2	.333	0	2	2	0	0.2
	SF-N	4	3	.571	30	0	0	0	3	46	56	7	13	26	13.5	4.89	71	.303	.348	1	.333	0	-6	-7	-1	-1.1
	Yr	6	5	.545	60	0	0	0	5	90^2	104	9	21	49	12.4	4.17	87	.287	.326	3	.333	1	-4	-5	-1	-0.9
1980	StL-N	1	0	1.000	10	0	0	0	1	19	17	3	10	4	12.8	3.79	97	.250	.346	1	—	0	-0	-0	-0	-0.1
Total	12	69	39	.639	593	4	0	0	80	1026^2	1098	63	251	409	12.1	3.52	101	.280	.328	32	.205	2	14	3	-4	1.0
● **PEDRO BORBON**	Borbon, Pedro Felix (Marte) b: 11/15/67, Mao, D.R. BR/TL, 6'1", 205 lbs. Deb: 10/2/92 F																									
1992	Atl-N	0	1	.000	2	0	0	0	0	1^1	2	0	1	1	20.3	6.75	54	.333	.429	0	—	0	-0	-0	0	-0.3
1993	Atl-N	0	0	—	3	0	0	0	0	1^2	3	0	3	2	32.4	21.60	19	.429	.600	0	—	0	-3	-3	-0	0.0
1995	*Atl-N	2	2	.500	41	0	0	0	2	32	29	2	17	33	13.2	3.09	138	.240	.338	0	.000	-0	4	4	0	0.5
1996	Atl-N	3	0	1.000	43	0	0	0	1	36	26	1	7	31	8.5	2.75	160	.203	.250	1	1.000	0	6	7	0	0.6
Total	4	5	3	.625	89	0	0	0	3	71	60	3	28	67	11.4	3.42	126	.229	.308	1	.500	0	6	7	1	0.8
● **GEORGE BORCHERS**	Borchers, George Benard "Chief" b: 4/18/1869, Sacramento, Cal. d: 10/24/38, Sacramento, Cal. BB/TR, 5'10", 180 lbs. Deb: 5/18/1888																									
1888	Chi-N	4	4	.500	10	10	7	1	0	67	67	2	29	26	13.7	3.49	87	.251	.338	2	.061	-2	-5	-3	0	-0.5
1895	Lou-N	0	1	.000	1	1	0	0	0	0^2	1	0	3	0	54.0	27.00	17	.333	.667	0	—	0	-2	-2	-0	-1.1
Total	2	4	5	.444	11	11	7	1	0	67^2	68	2	32	26	14.1	3.72	82	.252	.344	2	.061	-2	-6	-5	-0	-1.6
● **JOE BORDEN**	Borden, Joseph Emley (a.k.a. Joseph Emley Josephs In 1875) b: 5/9/1854, Jacobstown, N.J. d: 10/14/29, Yeadon, Pa. BR/TR, 5'9", 140 lbs. Deb: 7/24/1875																									
1875	Phi-n	2	4	.333	7	7	7	2	0	66	47	0	7	9	**7.4**	1.50	152	**.181**	**.203**	3	.107	-3	5	6		0.1
1876	Bos-N	11	12	.478	29	24	16	2	1	218^1	257	4	51	34	12.7	2.89	78	.276	.313	25	.207	-3	-14	-15	-2	-1.7
● **RICH BORDI**	Bordi, Richard Albert b: 4/18/59, San Francisco, Cal. BR/TR, 6'7", 220 lbs. Deb: 7/16/80																									
1980	Oak-A	0	0	—	1	0	0	0	0	2	4	0	0	0	18.0	4.50	84	.400	.400	0	—	0	-0	-0	-0	0.0
1981	Oak-A	0	0	—	2	0	0	0	0	2	1	0	1	0	9.0	0.00	—	.143	.250	0	—	0	1	1	-0	0.0
1982	Sea-A	0	2	.000	7	2	0	0	0	13	18	4	1	10	13.8	8.31	51	.310	.333	0	—	0	-6	-6	-0	-0.9
1983	Chi-N	0	2	.000	11	1	0	0	1	25^1	34	2	12	20	16.3	4.97	76	.321	.390	0	.000	-0	-4	-3	0	-0.3
1984	Chi-N	5	2	.714	31	7	0	0	4	83^1	78	11	20	41	10.6	3.46	113	.242	.287	1	.053	-1	1	4	-1	0.1
1985	NY-A	6	8	.429	51	3	0	0	2	98	95	5	29	64	11.5	3.21	124	.253	.308	0	—	0	10	9	-1	1.2
1986	Bal-A	6	4	.600	52	1	0	0	3	107	105	13	41	83	12.6	4.46	93	.254	.327	0	—	0	-3	-4	1	-0.2
1987	NY-A	3	1	.750	16	1	0	0	0	33	42	7	12	23	14.7	7.64	57	.309	.365	0	—	0	-12	-12	-1	-1.2
1988	Oak-A	0	1	.000	2	2	0	0	0	7^2	6	0	5	6	12.9	4.70	80	.214	.333	0	—	0	-1	-1	-0	-0.1
Total	9	20	20	.500	173	17	0	0	10	371^1	383	42	121	247	12.4	4.34	93	.263	.322	1	.043	-2	-13	-12	-2	-1.4
● **BILL BORDLEY**	Bordley, William Clarke b: 1/9/58, Los Angeles, Cal. BR/TL, 6'3", 185 lbs. Deb: 6/30/80																									
1980	SF-N	2	3	.400	8	6	0	0	0	30^2	34	3	21	11	16.1	4.70	75	.288	.396	1	.167	0	-4	-4	1	-0.5
● **PAUL BORIS**	Boris, Paul Stanley b: 12/13/55, Irvington, N.J. BR/TR, 6'2", 200 lbs. Deb: 5/21/82																									
1982	Min-A	1	2	.333	23	0	0	0	0	49^2	46	8	19	30	12.1	3.99	106	.246	.322	0	—	0	0	1	-1	-0.2

YEAR	TM/L	W	L	PCT	G	GS	CG	SH	SV	IP	H	HR	BB	SO	RAT	ERA	ERA+	OAV	OOB	BH	AVG	PB	PR	/A	PD	TPI
● FRANK BORK Bork, Frank Bernard b: 7/13/40, Buffalo, N.Y. BR/TL, 6'2", 175 lbs. Deb: 4/15/64																										
1964	Pit-N	2	2	.500	33	2	0	0	2	42	51	6	11	31	13.5	4.07	86	.295	.341	1	.200	0	-2	-3	0	-0.2
● TOM BORLAND Borland, Thomas Bruce "Spike" b: 2/14/33, ElDorado, Kan. BL/TL, 6'3", 172 lbs. Deb: 5/15/60																										
1960	Bos-A	0	4	.000	26	4	0	0	3	51	67	4	23	32	15.9	6.53	62	.322	.390	0	.000	-2	-15	-14	0	-1.3
1961	Bos-A	0	0	—	1	0	0	0	0	1	3	0	0	0	27.0	18.00	23	.500	.500	0	—	0	-2	-2	-0	0.0
Total	2	0	4	.000	27	4	0	0	3	52	70	4	23	32	16.1	6.75	60	.327	.392	0	.000	-2	-17	-16	0	-1.3
● TOBY BORLAND Borland, Toby Shawn b: 5/29/69, Ruston, La. BR/TR, 6'6", 186 lbs. Deb: 5/27/94																										
1994	Phi-N	1	0	1.000	24	0	0	0	1	34^1	31	1	14	26	12.8	2.36	182	.248	.343	0	.000	-0	7	7	-0	0.2
1995	Phi-N	1	3	.250	50	0	0	0	6	74	81	3	37	59	15.0	3.77	112	.277	.368	1	.200	0	3	4	-1	0.2
1996	Phi-N	7	3	.700	69	0	0	0	0	90^2	83	9	43	76	12.8	4.07	106	.239	.327	0	.000	-0	1	2	-1	0.1
1997	NY-N	0	1	.000	13	0	0	0	1	13^1	11	1	14	7	17.6	6.08	66	.220	.400	0	—	0	-3	-3	-0	-0.3
	Bos-A	0	0	—	3	0	0	0	0	3^1	6	1	7	1	40.5	13.50	34	.400	.625	0	—	0	-3	-3	-0	-0.1
1998	Phi-N	0	0	—	6	0	0	0	0	9	8	1	5	9	13.0	5.00	87	.242	.342	0	—	0	-1	-1	-0	0.0
Total	5	9	7	.563	165	0	0	0	8	224^2	220	16	120	178	14.2	4.01	107	.255	.356	1	.083	-1	5	7	-2	0.1
● JOE BOROWSKI Borowski, Joseph Thomas b: 5/4/71, Bayonne, N.J. BR/TR, 6'2", 225 lbs. Deb: 7/9/95																										
1995	Bal-A	0	0	—	6	0	0	0	0	7^1	5	0	4	3	11.0	1.23	387	.192	.300	0	—	0	3	3	0	-0.1
1996	Atl-N	2	4	.333	22	0	0	0	0	26	33	4	13	15	16.3	4.85	91	.324	.405	0	.000	-0	-2	-1	2	-0.1
1997	Atl-N	2	2	.500	20	0	0	0	0	24	27	2	16	6	16.1	3.75	111	.287	.391	0	—	0	1	1	0	0.2
	NY-A	0	1	.000	1	0	0	0	0	2	2	0	4	2	27.0	9.00	49	.250	.500	0	—	0	-1	-1	-0	-0.3
1998	NY-A	1	0	1.000	8	0	0	0	0	9^2	11	0	4	7	14.0	6.52	68	.289	.357	0	—	0	-2	-2	0	-0.1
Total	4	5	7	.417	57	0	0	0	0	69	78	6	41	33	15.7	4.43	99	.291	.387	0	.000	-0	-1	-0	2	-0.4
● HANK BOROWY Borowy, Henry Ludwig b: 5/12/16, Bloomfield, N.J. BR/TR, 6', 175 lbs. Deb: 4/18/42																										
1942	*NY-A	15	4	.789	25	21	13	4	1	178^1	157	6	66	85	11.3	2.52	136	.233	.301	11	.157	-1	22	18	1	1.9
1943	*NY-A	14	9	.609	29	27	14	3	0	217^1	195	11	72	113	11.1	2.82	114	.241	.305	15	.203	3	12	10	1	1.4
1944	NY-A★	17	12	.586	35	30	19	3	2	252^2	224	15	88	107	11.1	2.64	132	.236	.301	12	.133	-3	22	24	1	2.5
1945	NY-A†	10	5	.667	18	18	7	1	0	132^1	107	6	58	35	11.3	3.13	111	.221	.305	11	.220	1	3	5	1	0.8
	*Chi-N	11	2	.846	15	14	11	1	1	122^1	105	2	47	47	11.2	**2.13**	171	.231	.303	7	.171	0	23	21	-1	2.1
1946	Chi-N	12	10	.545	32	28	8	1	0	201	220	9	61	95	12.6	3.76	88	.274	.326	13	.181	1	-8	-10	0	-0.9
1947	Chi-N	8	12	.400	40	25	7	1	2	183	190	19	63	75	12.5	4.38	90	.267	.328	7	.125	-1	-6	-9	0	-0.9
1948	Chi-N	5	10	.333	39	17	2	1	1	127	156	9	49	50	14.5	4.89	80	.308	.369	8	.222	2	-13	-14	2	-1.1
1949	Phi-N	12	12	.500	28	28	12	1	0	193^1	188	19	63	43	11.7	4.19	94	.259	.319	13	.213	3	-3	-5	-2	-0.4
1950	Phi-N	0	0	—	3	0	0	0	0	6^1	5	0	4	3	12.8	5.68	71	.250	.375	0	—	0	-1	-1	-0	0.0
	Pit-N	1	3	.250	11	3	0	0	0	25^1	32	6	9	9	14.9	6.39	69	.311	.372	1	.167	-0	-6	-6	0	-0.8
	Yr	1	3	.250	14	3	0	0	0	31^2	37	6	13	12	14.5	6.25	69	.301	.372	1	.167	-0	-7	-7	0	-0.8
	Det-A	1	1	.500	13	2	1	0	0	32^2	23	3	16	12	10.7	3.31	142	.205	.305	1	.143	-0	5	5	-0	0.2
1951	Det-A	2	2	.500	26	1	0	0	0	45^1	58	3	27	16	17.1	6.95	60	.314	.404	0	.000	-1	-14	-14	1	-1.1
Total	10	108	82	.568	314	214	94	16	7	1717	1660	108	623	690	12.0	3.50	104	.254	.320	99	.173	3	35	24	5	3.7
● CHRIS BOSIO Bosio, Christopher Louis b: 4/3/63, Carmichael, Cal. BR/TR, 6'3", 225 lbs. Deb: 8/3/86																										
1986	Mil-A	0	4	.000	10	4	0	0	0	34^2	41	9	13	29	14.0	7.01	62	.293	.353	0	—	0	-11	-10	0	-1.1
1987	Mil-A	11	8	.579	46	19	2	1	2	170	187	18	50	150	12.6	5.24	87	.276	.327	0	—	0	-15	-13	1	-1.3
1988	Mil-A	7	15	.318	38	22	9	1	6	182	190	13	38	84	11.4	3.36	118	.268	.307	0	—	0	12	12	3	1.8
1989	Mil-A	15	10	.600	33	33	8	2	0	234^2	225	16	48	173	10.7	2.95	130	.249	.291	0	—	0	24	23	1	2.5
1990	Mil-A	4	9	.308	20	20	4	1	0	132^2	131	15	38	76	11.7	4.00	97	.258	.313	0	—	0	-1	-2	2	0.0
1991	Mil-A	14	10	.583	32	32	5	1	0	204^2	187	15	58	117	11.1	3.25	122	.244	.304	0	—	0	19	16	-1	1.8
1992	Mil-A	16	6	.727	33	33	4	2	0	231^1	223	21	44	120	10.5	3.62	106	.254	.293	0	—	0	8	6	0	0.7
1993	Sea-A	9	9	.500	29	24	3	1	1	164^1	138	14	59	119	11.1	3.45	128	.229	.304	0	—	0	16	17	0	1.7
1994	Sea-A	4	10	.286	19	19	4	0	0	125	137	15	40	67	12.9	4.32	113	.277	.333	0	—	0	7	8	2	0.8
1995	*Sea-A	10	8	.556	31	31	0	0	0	170	211	18	69	85	15.1	4.92	96	.312	.380	0	—	0	-4	-4	0	-0.4
1996	Sea-A	4	4	.500	18	9	0	0	0	60^2	72	8	24	39	14.8	5.93	83	.299	.372	0	—	0	-6	-7	0	-0.7
Total	11	94	93	.503	309	246	39	9	9	1710	1742	162	481	1059	11.9	3.96	106	.264	.318	0	—	0	49	47	9	5.8
● SHAWN BOSKIE Boskie, Shawn Kealoha b: 3/28/67, Hawthorne, Nev. BR/TR, 6'3", 200 lbs. Deb: 5/20/90																										
1990	Chi-N	5	6	.455	15	15	1	0	0	97^2	99	8	31	49	12.1	3.69	111	.265	.323	8	.222	1	1	4	0	0.6
1991	Chi-N	4	9	.308	28	20	0	0	0	129	150	14	52	62	14.4	5.23	74	.294	.364	7	.171	2	-22	-19	1	-1.5
1992	Chi-N	5	11	.313	23	18	0	0	0	91^2	96	14	36	39	13.4	5.01	72	.284	.360	5	.185	1	-15	-14	1	-2.1
1993	Chi-N	5	3	.625	39	2	0	0	0	65^2	63	7	21	39	12.5	3.43	116	.258	.335	3	.273	1	4	4	-1	0.4
1994	Chi-N	0	0	—	2	0	0	0	0	3^2	3	0	0	2	7.4	0.00	—	.214	.214	0	—	0	2	2	0	0.0
	Phi-N	4	6	.400	18	14	1	0	0	84^1	85	14	29	59	12.5	5.23	82	.258	.323	3	.115	1	-10	-9	0	-0.8
	Yr	4	6	.400	20	14	1	0	0	88	88	14	29	61	12.3	5.01	85	.256	.319	3	.115	1	-8	-7	-1	-0.8
	Sea-A	0	1	.000	2	1	0	0	0	2^2	4	1	1	0	16.9	6.75	72	.333	.385	0	—	0	-1	-1	0	-0.3
1995	Cal-A	7	7	.500	20	20	1	0	0	111^2	127	16	25	51	12.8	5.64	83	.281	.329	0	—	0	-12	-12	0	-1.1
1996	Cal-A	12	11	.522	37	28	1	0	0	189^1	226	40	67	133	14.5	5.32	94	.294	.360	0	—	0	-7	-7	0	-0.7
1997	Bal-A	6	6	.500	28	9	0	0	1	77	95	14	26	50	14.4	6.43	68	.304	.362	0	—	0	-16	-17	0	-2.2
1998	Mon-N	1	3	.250	5	5	0	0	0	17^2	34	5	4	10	20.4	9.17	45	.415	.455	0	.000	-0	-10	-10	0	-1.7
Total	9	49	63	.438	217	132	4	0	1	870^1	982	133	292	494	13.6	5.14	84	.286	.349	26	.179	5	-84	-78	3	-9.4
● DICK BOSMAN Bosman, Richard Allen b: 2/17/44, Kenosha, Wis. BR/TR, 6'3", 208 lbs. Deb: 6/1/66 C																										
1966	Was-A	2	6	.250	13	7	0	0	0	39	60	4	12	20	16.6	7.62	45	.361	.404	3	.250	0	-18	-18	-1	-3.1
1967	Was-A	3	1	.750	7	7	2	1	0	51^1	38	3	10	25	8.4	1.75	180	.204	.245	3	.200	0	8	8	-1	0.7
1968	Was-A	2	9	.182	46	10	0	0	1	139	139	9	35	63	11.5	3.69	79	.262	.312	6	.200	1	-11	-12	-0	-0.9
1969	Was-A	14	5	.737	31	26	5	2	1	193	156	11	39	99	9.2	**2.19**	**158**	.220	.262	6	.094	-1	31	27	1	2.7
1970	Was-A	16	12	.571	36	34	7	3	0	230^2	212	16	71	134	11.1	3.00	118	.245	.304	11	.138	-2	18	14	0	1.4
1971	Was-A	12	16	.429	35	35	7	1	0	236^2	245	29	71	113	12.2	3.73	89	.272	.329	7	.093	-1	-7	-11	-2	-1.6
1972	Tex-A	8	10	.444	29	29	1	1	0	173^1	183	11	48	105	12.3	3.63	83	.273	.327	5	.094	-2	-11	-12	1	-1.3
1973	Tex-A	2	5	.286	7	7	1	1	0	40^1	42	6	17	14	13.4	4.24	88	.268	.343	0	—	0	-2	-2	-0	-0.4
	Cle-A	1	8	.111	22	17	2	0	0	97	130	19	29	41	15.3	6.22	63	.320	.374	0	—	0	-26	-25	-1	-2.1
	Yr	3	13	.188	29	24	3	1	0	137^1	172	25	46	55	14.7	5.64	69	.304	.363	0	—	0	-28	-27	-1	-2.5
1974	Cle-A	7	5	.583	25	18	2	1	0	127^1	126	13	29	56	11.0	4.10	88	.255	.298	0	—	0	-7	-7	-2	-0.8
1975	Cle-A	0	2	.000	6	3	0	0	0	28^2	33	3	8	11	13.8	4.08	93	.292	.355	0	—	0	-1	-1	-0	-0.1
	*Oak-A	11	4	.733	22	21	2	0	0	122^2	112	12	24	42	10.2	3.52	103	.240	.281	0	—	0	3	1	-1	0.2
	Yr	11	6	.647	28	24	2	0	0	151^1	145	15	32	53	10.7	3.63	101	.248	.290	0	—	0	3	0	-1	0.1
1976	Oak-A	4	2	.667	27	15	0	0	0	112	118	13	19	34	11.1	4.10	82	.274	.306	0	—	0	-7	-9	0	-0.4
Total	11	82	85	.491	306	229	29	10	2	1591	1594	149	412	757	11.5	3.67	93	.261	.312	41	.125	-5	-29	-46	-5	-5.7
● MEL BOSSER Bosser, Melvin Edward b: 2/8/14, Johnstown, Pa. d: 3/26/86, Crossville, Tenn. BR/TR, 6', 173 lbs. Deb: 4/29/45																										
1945	Cin-N	2	0	1.000	7	2	0	0	0	16	9	0	17	3	14.6	3.38	111	.158	.351	0	.000	-1	1	1	-0	0.0
● ANDY BOSWELL Boswell, Andrew Cottrell b: 9/5/1874, New Gretna, N.J. d: 2/3/36, Ocean City, N.J. TR, 6'1", 165 lbs. Deb: 5/10/1895																										
1895	NY-N	2	2	.500	5	4	3	0	0	34	41	1	22	18	17.5	5.82	80	.293	.400	3	.188	-1	-4	-4	-1	-0.5
	Was-N	1	2	.333	6	3	3	0	0	30	44	1	19	12	19.5	6.00	80	.336	.428	4	.286	0	-4	-4	-0	-0.3
	Yr	3	4	.429	11	7	6	0	0	64	85	2	41	30	18.0	5.91	80	.310	.404	7	.233	-1	-8	-8	-1	-0.8
● DAVE BOSWELL Boswell, David Wilson b: 1/20/45, Baltimore, Md. BR/TR, 6'3", 185 lbs. Deb: 9/18/64																										
1964	Min-A	2	0	1.000	4	4	0	0	0	23^1	21	4	12	25	12.7	4.24	84	.236	.327	2	.222	0	-2	-2	1	-0.1
1965	*Min-A	6	5	.545	27	12	1	0	0	106	77	20	46	85	10.9	3.40	105	.204	.298	12	.316	4	1	2	-1	0.5
1966	Min-A	12	5	.706	28	21	8	1	0	169^1	120	19	65	173	10.1	3.14	115	.197	.280	9	.143	-1	6	9	1	0.8

YEAR	TM/L	W	L	PCT	G	GS	CG	SH	SV	IP	H	HR	BB	SO	RAT	ERA	ERA+	OAV	OOB	BH	AVG	PB	PR	/A	PD	TPI
1967	Min-A	14	12	.538	37	32	11	3	0	222^2	162	14	107	204	11.2	3.27	106	.202	.302	16	.219	4	-1	5	-1	0.8
1968	Min-A	10	13	.435	34	28	7	2	0	190	148	19	87	143	11.5	3.32	93	.213	.307	14	.233	5	-7	-5	-2	-0.3
1969	*Min-A	20	12	.625	39	38	10	0	0	256^1	215	18	99	190	11.3	3.23	113	.226	.304	16	.170	3	11	12	-2	1.5
1970	Min-A	3	7	.300	18	15	0	0	0	68^2	80	12	44	45	16.5	6.42	58	.292	.394	4	.160	-0	-21	-21	-1	-2.7
1971	Det-A	0	0	—	3	0	0	0	0	4^1	3	0	6	3	18.7	6.23	58	.200	.429	0	—	0	-1	-1	0	0.0
	Bal-A	1	2	.333	15	1	0	0	0	24^2	32	4	15	14	17.1	4.38	77	.305	.392	1	.200	0	-3	-3	0	-0.3
	Yr	1	2	.333	18	1	0	0	0	29	35	4	21	17	17.4	4.66	73	.289	.394	1	.200	0	-4	-4	0	-0.3
Total	8	68	56	.548	205	151	37	6	0	1065^1	858	110	481	882	11.6	3.52	99	.219	.310	74	.202	13	-17	-4	-4	0.2

● DEREK BOTELHO Botelho, Derek Wayne b: 8/2/56, Long Beach, Cal. BR/TR, 6'2", 180 lbs. Deb: 7/18/82

YEAR	TM/L	W	L	PCT	G	GS	CG	SH	SV	IP	H	HR	BB	SO	RAT	ERA	ERA+	OAV	OOB	BH	AVG	PB	PR	/A	PD	TPI
1982	KC-A	2	1	.667	8	4	0	0	0	24	25	4	8	12	12.4	4.13	99	.275	.333	0	—	0	-0	-0	-0	0.0
1985	Chi-N	1	3	.250	11	7	1	0	0	44	52	8	23	23	15.8	5.32	75	.299	.387	2	.143	-0	-8	-6	-0	-0.6
Total	2	3	4	.429	19	11	1	0	0	68	77	12	31	35	14.6	4.90	82	.291	.369	2	.143	-0	-9	-7	-1	-0.6

● RICKY BOTTALICO Bottalico, Ricky Paul b: 8/26/69, New Britain, Conn. BL/TR, 6'1", 200 lbs. Deb: 7/29/94

YEAR	TM/L	W	L	PCT	G	GS	CG	SH	SV	IP	H	HR	BB	SO	RAT	ERA	ERA+	OAV	OOB	BH	AVG	PB	PR	/A	PD	TPI
1994	Phi-N	0	0	—	3	0	0	0	0	3	3	0	1	3	12.0	0.00	—	.250	.308	0	—	0	1	1	-0	0.0
1995	Phi-N	5	3	.625	62	0	0	0	1	87^2	50	7	42	87	9.9	2.46	171	.167	.277	0	.000	-1	17	17	-1	1.3
1996	Phi-N★	4	5	.444	61	0	0	0	34	67^2	47	6	23	74	9.6	3.19	135	.197	.274	1	.333	1	8	8	-1	1.7
1997	Phi-N	2	5	.286	69	0	0	0	34	74	68	7	42	89	13.6	3.65	116	.245	.349	0	.000	-0	5	5	-1	0.8
1998	Phi-N	1	5	.167	39	0	0	0	6	43^1	54	7	25	27	16.6	6.44	68	.305	.394	0	—	0	-11	-10	0	-1.4
Total	5	12	18	.400	234	0	0	0	75	275^2	222	27	133	280	11.9	3.56	120	.221	.318	1	.111	-0	20	22	-2	2.4

● KENT BOTTENFIELD Bottenfield, Kent Dennis b: 11/14/68, Portland, Ore. BB/TR, 6'3", 237 lbs. Deb: 7/6/92

YEAR	TM/L	W	L	PCT	G	GS	CG	SH	SV	IP	H	HR	BB	SO	RAT	ERA	ERA+	OAV	OOB	BH	AVG	PB	PR	/A	PD	TPI
1992	Mon-N	1	2	.333	10	4	0	0	1	32^1	26	1	11	14	10.6	2.23	156	.217	.288	3	.375	1	5	4	-1	0.5
1993	Mon-N	2	5	.286	23	11	0	0	0	83	93	11	33	33	14.2	4.12	101	.288	.363	4	.167	-0	-1	0	-0	0.0
	Col-N	3	5	.375	14	14	1	0	0	76^2	86	13	38	30	14.7	6.10	78	.302	.386	7	.269	1	-18	-11	2	-0.8
	Yr	5	10	.333	37	25	1	0	0	159^2	179	24	71	63	14.1	5.07	88	.292	.366	11	.220	1	-18	-11	2	-0.8
1994	Col-N	3	1	.750	15	1	0	0	1	24^2	28	1	10	15	14.6	5.84	85	.283	.360	0	.000	-0	-4	-2	-1	-0.4
	SF-N	0	0	—	1	0	0	0	0	1^2	5	1	0	0	27.0	10.80	37	.556	.556	0	—	0	-1	-1	-0	0.0
	Yr	3	1	.750	16	1	0	0	1	26^1	33	2	10	15	14.7	6.15	80	.300	.358	0	.000	-0	-6	-4	-1	-0.4
1996	Chi-N	3	5	.375	48	0	0	0	1	61^2	59	3	19	33	11.8	2.63	165	.255	.320	1	.500	0	11	12	1	1.5
1997	Chi-N	2	3	.400	64	0	0	0	2	84	82	13	35	74	12.8	3.86	112	.259	.337	0	.000	-0	3	4	-1	0.1
1998	StL-N	4	6	.400	44	17	0	0	4	133^2	128	13	57	98	12.7	4.44	94	.254	.335	3	.088	-2	-3	-4	1	-0.4
Total	6	18	27	.400	219	47	1	0	9	497^2	507	56	203	297	13.2	4.27	101	.269	.346	18	.182	-1	-8	2	1	0.5

● RALPH BOTTING Botting, Ralph Wayne b: 5/12/55, Houlton, Maine BL/TL, 6', 195 lbs. Deb: 6/28/79

YEAR	TM/L	W	L	PCT	G	GS	CG	SH	SV	IP	H	HR	BB	SO	RAT	ERA	ERA+	OAV	OOB	BH	AVG	PB	PR	/A	PD	TPI
1979	Cal-A	2	0	1.000	12	1	0	0	0	29^2	46	6	15	22	18.8	8.80	46	.362	.434	0	—	0	-15	-16	-0	-0.9
1980	Cal-A	0	3	.000	6	6	0	0	0	26^1	40	1	13	12	18.1	5.81	68	.348	.414	0	—	0	-5	-6	-0	-0.5
Total	2	2	3	.400	18	7	0	0	0	56	86	7	28	34	18.5	7.39	54	.355	.424	0	—	0	-20	-21	-0	-1.4

● BOB BOTZ Botz, Robert Allen b: 4/28/35, Milwaukee, Wis. BR/TR, 5'11", 170 lbs. Deb: 5/8/62

YEAR	TM/L	W	L	PCT	G	GS	CG	SH	SV	IP	H	HR	BB	SO	RAT	ERA	ERA+	OAV	OOB	BH	AVG	PB	PR	/A	PD	TPI
1962	LA-A	2	1	.667	35	0	0	0	2	63	71	7	11	24	12.0	3.43	113	.285	.321	0	.000	-1	4	3	-1	-0.1

● DENIS BOUCHER Boucher, Denis b: 3/7/68, Montreal, Que., Can. BR/TL, 6'1", 195 lbs. Deb: 4/12/91

YEAR	TM/L	W	L	PCT	G	GS	CG	SH	SV	IP	H	HR	BB	SO	RAT	ERA	ERA+	OAV	OOB	BH	AVG	PB	PR	/A	PD	TPI
1991	Tor-A	0	3	.000	7	7	0	0	0	35^1	39	6	16	16	14.5	4.58	92	.279	.361	0	—	0	-2	-1	1	-0.2
	Cle-A	1	4	.200	5	5	0	0	0	22^2	35	6	8	13	17.1	8.34	50	.350	.398	0	—	0	-11	-11	0	-1.7
	Yr	1	7	.125	12	12	0	0	0	58	74	12	24	29	15.2	6.05	69	.305	.367	0	—	0	-13	-12	1	-1.9
1992	Cle-A	2	2	.500	8	7	0	0	0	41	48	9	20	17	15.1	6.37	61	.302	.383	0	—	0	-11	-11	-1	-0.9
1993	Mon-N	3	1	.750	5	5	0	0	0	28^1	24	1	3	14	8.6	1.91	219	.229	.250	1	.167	0	7	7	-0	1.0
1994	Mon-N	0	1	.000	10	2	0	0	0	18^2	24	6	7	17	14.9	6.75	63	.324	.383	1	.333	1	-5	-5	0	-0.2
Total	4	6	11	.353	35	26	0	0	0	146	170	28	54	77	14.0	5.42	76	.294	.357	2	.222	1	-22	-21	0	-2.0

● CARL BOULDIN Bouldin, Carl Edward b: 9/17/39, Germantown, Ky. BB/TR, 6'2", 180 lbs. Deb: 9/2/61

YEAR	TM/L	W	L	PCT	G	GS	CG	SH	SV	IP	H	HR	BB	SO	RAT	ERA	ERA+	OAV	OOB	BH	AVG	PB	PR	/A	PD	TPI
1961	Was-A	0	1	.000	2	1	0	0	0	3^1	9	0	2	2	29.7	16.20	25	.500	.550	0	.000	-0	-5	-5	0	-0.9
1962	Was-A	1	2	.333	6	3	1	0	0	20	26	0	9	12	16.2	5.85	69	.321	.396	0	.000	-1	-4	-4	-0	-0.6
1963	Was-A	2	2	.500	10	3	0	0	0	23^1	31	3	8	10	15.0	5.79	64	.307	.358	0	.000	-1	-6	-5	0	-0.9
1964	Was-A	0	3	.000	9	3	0	0	0	25	30	2	11	12	15.5	5.40	69	.294	.374	0	.000	-0	-5	-5	-0	-0.6
Total	4	3	8	.273	27	10	1	0	0	71^2	96	5	30	36	16.2	6.15	62	.318	.385	0	.000	-2	-19	-19	0	-3.0

● JAKE BOULTES Boultes, Jacob John b: 8/6/1884, St.Louis, Mo. d: 12/24/55, St.Louis, Mo. TR, 6'3", Deb: 4/18/07

YEAR	TM/L	W	L	PCT	G	GS	CG	SH	SV	IP	H	HR	BB	SO	RAT	ERA	ERA+	OAV	OOB	BH	AVG	PB	PR	/A	PD	TPI
1907	Bos-N	5	9	.357	24	12	11	0	0	139^2	140	1	50	49	12.8	2.71	94	.266	.338	9	.132	-2	-4	-2	4	0.0
1908	Bos-N	3	5	.375	17	5	1	0	0	74^2	80	7	8	28	10.7	3.01	80	.274	.296	3	.143	-0	-5	-5	-0	-0.7
1909	Bos-N	0	0	—	1	0	0	0	0	8	9	2	0	1	11.3	6.75	42	.290	.313	1	.333	0	-4	-3	-0	0.0
Total	3	8	14	.364	42	17	12	0	0	222^1	229	10	58	78	12.0	2.96	85	.269	.324	13	.141	-2	-13	-11	4	-0.7

● STEVE BOURGEOIS Bourgeois, Steven James b: 8/4/72, Lutcher, La. BR/TR, 6'1", 220 lbs. Deb: 4/3/96

YEAR	TM/L	W	L	PCT	G	GS	CG	SH	SV	IP	H	HR	BB	SO	RAT	ERA	ERA+	OAV	OOB	BH	AVG	PB	PR	/A	PD	TPI
1996	SF-N	1	3	.250	15	5	0	0	0	40	60	4	21	17	19.1	6.30	65	.355	.438	3	.273	2	-9	-10	0	-0.6

● JIM BOUTON Bouton, James Alan b: 3/8/39, Newark, N.J. BR/TR, 6', 185 lbs. Deb: 4/22/62

YEAR	TM/L	W	L	PCT	G	GS	CG	SH	SV	IP	H	HR	BB	SO	RAT	ERA	ERA+	OAV	OOB	BH	AVG	PB	PR	/A	PD	TPI
1962	NY-A	7	7	.500	36	16	3	1	2	133	124	9	59	71	12.4	3.99	94	.254	.334	2	.063	-2	-0	-4	0	-0.5
1963	*NY-A★	21	7	.750	40	30	12	6	1	249^1	191	18	87	148	10.1	2.53	139	.212	.284	6	.072	-6	31	27	-1	2.3
1964	*NY-A	18	13	.581	38	37	11	4	0	271^1	227	32	60	125	9.7	3.02	120	.225	.273	13	.130	-3	18	18	-3	1.3
1965	NY-A	4	15	.211	30	25	2	0	0	151^1	158	23	60	97	13.3	4.82	71	.269	.342	4	.093	-0	-23	-24	-0	-2.8
1966	NY-A	3	8	.273	24	19	3	0	1	120^1	117	13	38	65	11.7	2.69	123	.257	.315	4	.105	-2	10	8	1	0.7
1967	NY-A	1	0	1.000	17	1	0	0	0	44^1	47	5	18	31	13.4	4.67	67	.275	.347	0	.000	-0	-7	-8	0	-0.2
1968	NY-A	1	1	.500	12	3	1	0	0	44	49	5	9	24	12.3	3.68	79	.287	.330	0	.000	-0	-3	-4	1	-0.1
1969	Sea-A	2	1	.667	57	1	0	0	1	92	77	12	38	68	11.4	3.91	93	.219	.299	0	.000	-1	-3	-3	1	-0.1
	Hou-N	0	2	.000	16	1	1	0	1	30^2	32	1	12	32	13.5	4.11	86	.267	.343	0	.000	-0	-2	-2	0	-0.2
1970	Hou-N	4	6	.400	29	6	1	0	0	73^1	84	5	33	49	14.5	5.40	72	.285	.359	6	.353	2	-11	-12	-0	-1.3
1978	Atl-N	1	3	.250	5	5	0	0	0	29	25	4	21	10	14.3	4.97	82	.234	.359	0	.000	-1	-4	-3	-0	-0.5
Total	10	62	63	.496	304	144	34	11	6	1238^2	1131	127	435	720	11.5	3.57	99	.243	.311	35	.101	-13	5	-5	-1	-1.4

● MIKE BOVEE Bovee, Michael Craig b: 8/21/73, San Diego, Cal. BR/TR, 5'10", 200 lbs. Deb: 9/13/97

YEAR	TM/L	W	L	PCT	G	GS	CG	SH	SV	IP	H	HR	BB	SO	RAT	ERA	ERA+	OAV	OOB	BH	AVG	PB	PR	/A	PD	TPI
1997	Ana-A	0	0	—	3	0	0	0	0	3^1	3	1	1	5	10.8	5.40	85	.231	.286	0	—	0	-0	-0	-0	0.0

● RYAN BOWEN Bowen, Ryan Eugene b: 2/10/68, Hanford, Cal. BR/TR, 6', 185 lbs. Deb: 7/22/91

YEAR	TM/L	W	L	PCT	G	GS	CG	SH	SV	IP	H	HR	BB	SO	RAT	ERA	ERA+	OAV	OOB	BH	AVG	PB	PR	/A	PD	TPI
1991	Hou-N	6	4	.600	14	13	0	0	0	71^2	73	4	36	49	14.1	5.15	68	.268	.360	4	.182	1	-12	-13	-2	-1.6
1992	Hou-N	0	7	.000	11	9	0	0	0	33^2	48	8	30	22	21.4	10.96	31	.333	.455	1	.111	-0	-28	-28	-1	-4.6
1993	Fla-N	8	12	.400	27	27	2	1	0	156^2	156	11	87	98	14.1	4.42	98	.263	.360	6	.118	-1	-7	-2	-0	-0.3
1994	Fla-N	1	5	.167	8	8	1	0	0	47^1	50	9	19	32	13.5	4.94	88	.273	.348	5	.357	2	-4	-3	-1	-0.2
1995	Fla-N	2	0	1.000	4	3	0	0	0	16^2	23	3	12	15	18.9	3.78	111	.329	.427	2	.333	0	1	1	-0	0.1
Total	5	17	28	.378	64	60	3	1	0	326	350	35	184	216	15.0	5.30	76	.277	.373	18	.176	2	-49	-46	-4	-6.6

● CY BOWEN Bowen, Sutherland McCoy b: 2/17/1871, Kingston, Ind. d: 1/25/25, Greensburg, Ind. BR/TR, 6', 175 lbs. Deb: 4/28/1896

YEAR	TM/L	W	L	PCT	G	GS	CG	SH	SV	IP	H	HR	BB	SO	RAT	ERA	ERA+	OAV	OOB	BH	AVG	PB	PR	/A	PD	TPI
1896	NY-N	0	1	.000	2	1	1	0	0	12	12	0	9	3	18.0	6.00	70	.261	.414	1	.333	0	-2	-2	0	-0.1

● FRANK BOWERMAN Bowerman, Frank Eugene "Mike" b: 12/5/1868, Romeo, Mich. d: 11/30/48, Romeo, Mich. BR/TR, 6'2", 190 lbs. Deb: 8/24/1895 M◆

YEAR	TM/L	W	L	PCT	G	GS	CG	SH	SV	IP	H	HR	BB	SO	RAT	ERA	ERA+	OAV	OOB	BH	AVG	PB	PR	/A	PD	TPI
1904	NY-N	0	0	—	1	0	0	0	0	1	3	0	1	0	36.0	9.00	30	.429	.500	67	.232	0	-1	-1	-0	0.0

● SHANE BOWERS Bowers, Shane Patrick b: 7/27/71, Glendora, Cal. BR/TR, 6'4", 215 lbs. Deb: 7/26/97

YEAR	TM/L	W	L	PCT	G	GS	CG	SH	SV	IP	H	HR	BB	SO	RAT	ERA	ERA+	OAV	OOB	BH	AVG	PB	PR	/A	PD	TPI
1997	Min-A	0	3	.000	5	5	0	0	0	19	27	2	8	7	17.1	8.05	58	.329	.396	0	—	0	-7	-7	-0	-0.9

YEAR	TM/L	W	L	PCT	G	GS	CG	SH	SV	IP	H	HR	BB	SO	RAT	ERA	ERA+	OAV	OOB	BH	AVG	PB	PR	/A	PD	TPI
● **STEW BOWERS**	Bowers, Stewart Cole "Doc" b: 2/26/15, New Freedom, Pa. BB/TR, 6′, 170 lbs. Deb: 8/5/35 ♦																									
1935	Bos-A	2	1	.667	10	2	1	0	0	23^2	26	1	17	5	16.4	3.42	139	.283	.394	1	.200	0	3	3	0	0.4
1936	Bos-A	0	0	—	5	0	0	0	0	5^2	10	1	2	0	19.1	9.53	56	.370	.414	0	—	0	-3	-3	-0	0.0
Total	2	2	1	.667	15	2	1	0	0	29^1	36	2	19	5	16.9	4.60	106	.303	.399	1	.200	0	-0	1	-0	0.4
● **GRANT BOWLER**	Bowler, Grant Tierney "Moose" b: 10/24/07, Denver, Col. d: 6/25/68, Denver, Colo. BR/TR, 6′, 190 lbs. Deb: 8/21/31																									
1931	Chi-A	0	1	.000	13	3	1	0	0	35^1	40	1	24	15	16.3	5.35	80	.288	.393	1	.100	-0	-4	-4	-1	-0.2
1932	Chi-A	0	0	—	4	0	0	0	0	6^1	15	1	3	2	25.6	15.63	28	.484	.529	0	.000	-0	-8	-8	0	0.0
Total	2	0	1	.000	17	3	1	0	0	41^2	55	2	27	17	17.7	6.91	62	.324	.416	1	.083	-1	-12	-12	-1	-0.2
● **CHARLIE BOWLES**	Bowles, Charles James b: 3/15/17, Norwood, Mass. BR/TR, 6′3″, 180 lbs. Deb: 9/25/43																									
1943	Phi-A	1	1	.500	2	2	2	0	0	18	17	0	4	6	10.5	3.00	113	.258	.300	1	.125	-1	1	1	0	0.0
1945	Phi-A	0	3	.000	8	4	1	0	0	33^1	35	3	23	11	15.7	5.13	67	.273	.384	5	.238	0	-7	-6	0	-0.5
Total	2	1	4	.200	10	6	3	0	0	51^1	52	3	27	17	13.9	4.38	78	.268	.357	6	.207	-0	-6	-5	0	-0.5
● **EMMETT BOWLES**	Bowles, Emmett Jerome "Chief" b: 8/2/1898, Wanette, Okla. d: 9/3/59, Flagstaff, Ariz. BR/TR, 6′, 180 lbs. Deb: 9/12/22																									
1922	Chi-A	0	0	—	1	0	0	0	0	1	2	0	1	0	27.0	27.00	15	.500	.600	0	—	0	-3	-3	-0	0.0
● **ABE BOWMAN**	Bowman, Alvah Edson b: 1/25/1893, Greenup, Ill. d: 10/11/79, Longview, Tex. BR/TR, 6′1″, 190 lbs. Deb: 5/19/14																									
1914	Cle-A	2	7	.222	22	10	2	1	0	72^2	74	0	45	27	15.2	4.46	65	.277	.389	1	.048	-2	-14	-13	-0	-1.7
1915	Cle-A	0	1	.000	2	1	0	0	0	1^1	1	0	3	0	27.0	20.25	15	.250	.571	0	—	0	-3	-3	1	-1.2
Total	2	2	8	.200	24	11	2	1	0	74	75	0	48	27	15.4	4.74	61	.277	.393	1	.048	-2	-16	-15	0	-2.9
● **JOE BOWMAN**	Bowman, Joseph Emil b: 6/17/10, Kansas City, Kan. d: 11/22/90, Kansas City, Mo. BL/TR, 6′2″, 190 lbs. Deb: 4/18/32 ♦																									
1932	Phi-A	0	1	.000	7	0	0	0	0	11	14	2	6	4	18.8	8.18	55	.318	.434	1	1.000	0	-5	-4	1	-0.2
1934	NY-N	5	4	.556	30	10	3	0	3	107^1	119	9	36	36	13.2	3.61	107	.279	.338	5	.172	0	5	3	-0	0.2
1935	Phi-N	7	10	.412	33	17	6	1	1	148^1	157	13	56	58	13.2	4.25	107	.269	.337	13	.194	0	-4	5	-0	0.5
1936	Phi-N	9	20	.310	40	28	12	0	1	203^2	243	14	53	80	13.4	5.04	90	.289	.336	15	.195	-1	-23	-11	-2	-1.7
1937	Pit-N	8	8	.500	30	19	7	0	1	128	161	11	35	38	13.9	4.57	85	.306	.351	10	.213	2	-9	-10	0	-1.0
1938	Pit-N	3	4	.429	17	1	0	0	1	60	68	2	20	25	13.2	4.65	82	.285	.340	7	.333	2	-6	-6	-1	-0.5
1939	Pit-N	10	14	.417	37	27	10	1	1	184^2	217	15	43	58	13.0	4.48	86	.292	.336	33	.344	12	-12	-13	0	-0.3
1940	Pit-N	9	10	.474	32	24	10	0	2	187^2	209	10	66	57	13.5	4.46	85	.274	.337	22	.244	9	-13	-14	0	-0.3
1941	Pit-N	3	2	.600	18	7	1	1	1	69^1	77	3	28	22	13.8	2.99	121	.278	.346	8	.258	1	5	5	-0	0.5
1944	Bos-A	12	8	.600	26	24	10	1	0	168^1	175	14	64	53	12.9	4.81	71	.269	.336	20	.200	3	-26	-26	-2	-2.7
1945	Bos-A	0	2	.000	3	3	0	0	0	11^2	18	1	9	0	20.8	9.26	37	.360	.458	2	.222	0	-8	-8	-0	-1.0
	Cin-N	11	13	.458	25	24	15	1	0	185^2	198	8	68	71	13.2	3.59	105	.270	.338	5	.070	-5	4	4	-2	-0.2
Total	11	77	96	.445	298	184	74	5	11	1465^2	1656	102	484	502	13.4	4.40	89	.282	.341	141	.221	24	-89	-77	-7	-6.7
● **BOB BOWMAN**	Bowman, Robert James b: 10/3/10, Keystone, W.Va. d: 9/4/72, Bluefield, W.Va. BR/TR, 5′10.5″, 160 lbs. Deb: 4/21/39																									
1939	StL-N	13	5	.722	51	15	4	2	**9**	169^1	141	8	60	78	10.7	2.60	158	.232	.302	4	.085	-3	25	28	-1	2.7
1940	StL-N	7	5	.583	28	17	7	0	0	114^1	118	9	43	43	13.0	4.33	92	.267	.337	2	.061	-2	-6	-4	-0	-0.7
1941	NY-N	6	7	.462	29	6	2	0	1	80^1	100	10	36	25	15.3	5.71	65	.302	.372	1	.048	-1	-19	-18	1	-2.6
1942	Chi-N	0	0	—	1	0	0	0	0	1	1	0	0	0	9.0	0.00	—	.250	.250	0	—	0	0	0	-0	0.0
Total	4	26	17	.605	109	38	13	2	10	365	360	27	139	146	12.5	3.82	104	.260	.330	7	.069	-5	0	6	-1	-0.6
● **BOB BOWMAN**	Bowman, Robert Leroy b: 5/10/31, Laytonville, Cal. BR/TR, 6′1″, 195 lbs. Deb: 4/16/55 ♦																									
1959	Phi-N	0	1	.000	5	0	0	0	0	6	5	1	5	0	15.0	6.00	68	.227	.370	10	.127	-0	-1	-1	0	-0.2
● **ROGER BOWMAN**	Bowman, Roger Clinton b: 8/18/27, Amsterdam, N.Y. d: 7/21/97, Los Angeles, Cal. BR/TL, 6′, 175 lbs. Deb: 9/22/49																									
1949	NY-N	0	0	—	2	2	0	0	0	6^1	6	1	7	4	18.5	4.26	93	.261	.433	0	.000	-0	-0	-0	1	0.0
1951	NY-N	2	4	.333	9	5	0	0	0	26^1	35	2	22	24	19.8	6.15	64	.297	.411	0	.000	-0	-6	-7	-1	-1.3
1952	NY-N	0	0	—	2	1	0	0	0	3	6	0	3	3	30.0	12.00	31	.429	.556	0	.000	-0	-3	-3	-0	0.0
1953	Pit-N	0	4	.000	30	2	0	0	0	65^1	65	9	29	36	13.1	4.82	93	.261	.341	2	.286	0	-4	-3	0	-0.1
1955	Pit-N	0	3	.000	7	2	0	0	0	16^2	25	2	10	8	19.4	8.64	48	.347	.434	1	.500	0	-9	-8	0	-1.2
Total	5	2	11	.154	50	12	0	0	0	117^2	137	14	71	75	16.2	5.81	73	.288	.385	3	.167	-0	-22	-20	1	-2.6
● **SUMNER BOWMAN**	Bowman, Sumner Sallade b: 2/9/1867, Millersburg, Pa. d: 1/11/54, Millersburg, Pa. BL/TL, 6′, 160 lbs. Deb: 6/11/1890																									
1890	Phi-N	0	0	—	1	1	0	0	0	8	11	0	2	2	15.8	7.88	46	.314	.368	2	.500	1	-4	-4	-0	0.0
	Pit-N	2	5	.286	9	7	6	0	0	70^2	100	1	50	22	20.5	6.62	50	.324	.435	10	.278	2	-24	-26	-0	-1.7
	Yr	2	5	.286	10	8	6	0	0	78^2	111	1	52	24	19.9	6.75	49	.322	.426	12	.300	2	-28	-30	-0	-1.7
1891	Phi-a	2	5	.286	8	8	8	0	0	68	73	0	37	22	15.2	3.44	111	.265	.363	13	.241	0	2	3	-1	0.2
Total	2	4	10	.286	18	16	14	0	0	146^2	184	1	89	46	17.8	5.22	68	.297	.400	25	.266	3	-26	-27	-1	-1.5
● **TED BOWSFIELD**	Bowsfield, Edward Oliver b: 1/10/35, Vernon, B.C., Canada BR/TL, 6′1″, 190 lbs. Deb: 7/20/58																									
1958	Bos-A	4	2	.667	16	10	2	0	0	65^2	58	3	36	38	13.0	3.84	104	.233	.332	4	.154	-1	-1	1	1	0.1
1959	Bos-A	0	1	.000	5	2	0	0	0	9	16	2	9	4	25.0	15.00	27	.390	.500	0	.000	-0	-11	-11	-0	-1.0
1960	Bos-A	1	2	.333	17	2	0	0	2	21	20	1	13	18	14.6	5.14	79	.260	.374	1	.250	0	-3	-3	1	-0.3
	Cle-A	3	4	.429	11	6	1	1	0	40^2	47	1	20	14	14.8	5.09	73	.296	.374	1	.100	-0	-5	-6	1	-0.9
	Yr	4	6	.400	28	8	1	1	2	61^2	67	2	33	32	14.6	5.11	75	.280	.368	2	.143	-0	-8	-9	1	-1.2
1961	LA-A	11	8	.579	41	21	4	1	0	157	154	18	63	88	12.5	3.73	121	.255	.327	7	.137	-1	5	14	-1	1.3
1962	LA-A	9	8	.529	34	25	1	0	1	139	154	12	40	52	12.7	4.40	88	.277	.328	6	.162	1	-7	-8	-3	-1.1
1963	KC-A	5	7	.417	41	11	2	1	3	111^1	115	14	47	67	13.3	4.45	88	.269	.345	1	.043	-1	-10	-7	2	-0.6
1964	KC-A	4	7	.364	50	9	2	1	0	118^2	135	12	31	45	12.9	4.10	93	.285	.334	2	.095	-1	-6	-4	0	-0.4
Total	7	37	39	.487	215	86	12	4	6	662^1	699	63	259	326	13.2	4.35	93	.270	.339	22	.127	-3	-38	-24	1	-2.9
● **OIL CAN BOYD**	Boyd, Dennis Ray b: 10/6/59, Meridian, Miss. BR/TR, 6′1″, 155 lbs. Deb: 9/13/82																									
1982	Bos-A	0	1	.000	3	1	0	0	0	8^1	11	2	2	2	14.0	5.40	80	.314	.351	0	—	0	-1	-1	-0	-0.1
1983	Bos-A	4	8	.333	15	13	5	0	0	98^2	103	9	23	43	11.6	3.28	132	.269	.312	0	—	0	9	12	-1	0.8
1984	Bos-A	12	12	.500	29	26	10	3	0	197^2	207	18	53	134	11.9	4.37	95	.269	.317	0	—	0	-8	-5	2	-0.3
1985	Bos-A	15	13	.536	35	35	13	3	0	272^1	273	26	67	154	11.4	3.70	116	.261	.308	0	—	0	13	18	3	1.9
1986	*Bos-A	16	10	.615	30	30	10	0	0	214^1	222	32	45	129	11.3	3.78	110	.265	.304	0	—	0	9	9	1	1.1
1987	Bos-A	1	3	.250	7	7	0	0	0	36^2	47	6	9	12	14.2	5.89	77	.315	.363	0	—	0	-6	-6	1	-0.5
1988	Bos-A	9	7	.563	23	23	1	0	0	129^2	147	25	41	71	13.2	5.34	77	.289	.344	0	—	0	-20	-18	-1	-2.1
1989	Bos-A	3	2	.600	10	10	0	0	0	59	57	8	19	26	11.6	4.42	93	.253	.311	0	—	0	-4	-2	1	-0.3
1990	Mon-N	10	6	.625	31	31	3	3	0	190^2	164	19	52	113	10.3	2.93	125	.233	.289	3	.051	-4	18	15	-1	0.6
1991	Mon-N	6	8	.429	19	19	1	1	0	120^1	115	9	40	82	11.6	3.52	103	.256	.316	3	.083	-1	2	1	-1	-0.1
	Tex-A	2	7	.222	12	12	0	0	0	62	81	12	17	33	14.2	6.68	60	.314	.356	0	—	0	-18	-18	-1	-2.2
Total	10	78	77	.503	214	207	43	10	0	1389^2	1427	166	368	799	11.7	4.04	101	.266	.315	6	.063	-5	-5	5	3	-1.2
● **GARY BOYD**	Boyd, Gary Lee b: 8/22/46, Pasadena, Cal. BR/TR, 6′4″, 200 lbs. Deb: 8/1/69																									
1969	Cle-A	0	2	.000	8	3	0	0	0	11	8	1	14	9	18.0	9.00	42	.205	.415	0	.000	-0	-7	-6	-0	-1.0
● **JAKE BOYD**	Boyd, Jacob Henry b: 1/19/1874, Martinsburg, W.Va. d: 8/12/32, Gettysburg, Pa. TL , 160 lbs. Deb: 9/20/1894 ♦																									
1894	Was-N	0	3	.000	3	3	3	0	0	19	37	1	14	3	24.6	8.53	62	.402	.486	3	.143	-1	-7	-7	0	-0.7
1895	Was-N	2	11	.154	14	12	8	0	0	85^1	126	1	35	16	18.0	7.07	68	.338	.409	42	.268	2	-22	-21	1	-2.1
1896	Was-N	1	2	.333	4	2	2	0	0	32	45	0	15	6	18.6	6.75	65	.328	.418	1	.077	-1	-8	-8	0	-0.6
Total	3	3	16	.158	21	17	13	0	0	136^1	208	2	64	25	19.1	7.20	66	.346	.423	46	.241	-1	-37	-37	2	-3.4
● **RAY BOYD**	Boyd, Raymond C. b: 2/11/1887, Hortonville, Ind. d: 2/11/20, Hortonville, Ind. BR/TR, 5′10″, 160 lbs. Deb: 9/24/10																									
1910	StL-A	0	2	.000	3	2	1	0	0	14^1	16	0	5	6	13.8	4.40	56	.286	.355	1	.200	-0	-3	-3	-1	-0.5
1911	Cin-N	2	2	.500	7	4	3	0	1	44	34	0	19	20	11.3	2.66	124	.206	.296	1	.083	-0	4	3	-0	0.2
Total	2	2	4	.333	10	6	4	0	1	58^1	50	0	24	26	11.9	3.09	101	.226	.310	2	.118	-0	1	0	-1	-0.3

YEAR TM/L	W	L	PCT	G	GS	CG	SH	SV	IP	H	HR	BB	SO	RAT	ERA	ERA+	OAV	OOB	BH	AVG	PB	PR	/A	PD	TPI
● **BILL BOYD**	Boyd, William J. b: 12/22/1852, New York, N.Y. d: 9/30/12, Jamaica, N.Y. Deb: 4/22/1872 MU ♦																								
1875 Atl-n	0	0	—	1	0	0	0	0	1^{2}	4	0	0	0	21.6	0.00	—	.444	.444	44	.291	0	0	0		0.0
● **CLOYD BOYER**	Boyer, Cloyd Victor "Junior" b: 9/1/27, Alba, Mo. BR/TR, 6'1", 188 lbs. Deb: 4/23/49 FC																								
1949 StL-N	0	0	—	4	1	0	0	0	3^{1}	5	0	7	0	32.4	10.80	39	.357	.571	0	—	0	-3	-2	0	0.0
1950 StL-N	7	7	.500	36	14	6	1	1	120^{1}	105	15	49	82	11.7	3.52	122	.233	.312	6	.182	0	8	10	0	1.1
1951 StL-N	2	5	.286	19	8	1	0	1	63^{1}	68	9	46	40	16.6	5.26	75	.286	.408	4	.200	0	-9	-9	-2	-1.1
1952 StL-N	6	6	.500	23	14	4	2	0	110^{1}	108	11	47	44	13.0	4.24	88	.258	.338	8	.211	2	-6	-6	-2	-0.6
1955 KC-A	5	5	.500	30	11	2	0	0	98^{1}	107	21	69	32	16.7	6.22	67	.282	.402	2	.069	-2	-25	-22	-1	-2.2
Total 5	20	23	.465	112	48	13	3	2	395^{2}	393	56	218	198	14.3	4.73	86	.262	.362	20	.167	1	-34	-30	-4	-2.8
● **HENRY BOYLE**	Boyle, Henry J. "Handsome Henry" b: 9/20/1860, Philadelphia, Pa. d: 5/25/32, Philadelphia, Pa. TR , Deb: 7/9/1884 ♦																								
1884 StL-U	15	3	.833	19	16	16	2	1	150	118	3	10	88	7.7	1.74	138	.202	.215	68	.260	-1	12	11	-1	0.8
1885 StL-N	16	24	.400	42	39	39	1	0	366^{2}	346	2	100	133	10.9	2.75	100	.239	.288	52	.202	1	3	-0	-1	0.0
1886 StL-N	9	15	.375	25	24	23	2	0	210	183	5	46	101	9.8	**1.76**	**184**	.220	.261	27	.250	4	36	34	1	3.9
1887 Ind-N	13	24	.351	38	38	37	0	0	328	356	11	69	85	12.0	3.65	114	.265	.307	27	.191	-1	15	18	-4	1.2
1888 Ind-N	15	22	.405	37	37	36	3	0	323	315	11	58	98	10.7	3.26	91	.245	.283	18	.144	-3	-15	-11	3	-1.1
1889 Ind-N	21	23	.477	46	45	38	2	0	378^{2}	422	14	95	97	12.6	3.92	106	.273	.321	38	.245	5	4	11	-5	1.1
Total 6	89	111	.445	207	199	189	10	1	1756^{1}	1740	46	378	602	11.0	3.06	110	.247	.289	230	.219	5	56	61	-7	5.9
● **HARRY BOYLES**	Boyles, Harry "Stretch" b: 11/29/13, Granite City, Ill. BR/TR, 6'5", 185 lbs. Deb: 8/3/38																								
1938 Chi-A	0	4	.000	9	2	1	0	1	29^{1}	31	2	25	18	17.8	5.22	94	.263	.400	1	.125	-1	-1	-1	1	-0.1
1939 Chi-A	0	0	—	2	0	0	0	0	3^{1}	4	0	6	1	27.0	10.80	44	.308	.526	0	.000	-0	-2	-2	-0	0.0
Total 2	0	4	.000	11	2	1	0	1	32^{2}	35	2	31	19	18.7	5.79	84	.267	.415	1	.111	-1	-4	-3	1	-0.1
● **MARSHALL BOZE**	Boze, Marshall Wayne b: 5/23/71, San Manuel, Ariz. BR/TR, 6'1", 214 lbs. Deb: 4/28/96																								
1996 Mil-A	0	2	.000	25	0	0	0	1	32^{1}	47	5	25	19	21.7	7.79	67	.362	.484	0	—	0	-10	-9	1	-0.5
● **GENE BRABENDER**	Brabender, Eugene Mathew b: 8/16/41, Madison, Wis. d: 12/27/96, Madison, Wis. BR/TR, 6'5.5", 225 lbs. Deb: 5/11/66																								
1966 Bal-A	4	3	.571	31	1	0	0	2	71	57	4	29	62	11.0	3.55	94	.229	.312	1	.077	-1	-1	-2	0	-0.2
1967 Bal-A	6	4	.600	14	14	3	1	0	94	77	6	23	71	9.7	3.35	94	.220	.270	2	.071	-1	-1	-2	-0	-0.3
1968 Bal-A	6	7	.462	37	15	3	2	3	125	116	9	48	92	12.0	3.31	88	.248	.322	3	.086	-0	-5	-5	-1	-0.7
1969 Sea-A	13	14	.481	40	29	7	1	0	202^{1}	193	26	103	139	13.7	4.36	83	.254	.353	9	.129	-1	-17	-16	-3	-2.4
1970 Mil-A	6	15	.286	29	21	2	0	1	128^{2}	127	8	79	76	14.5	6.02	63	.255	.359	4	.098	-2	-33	-32	-0	-4.7
Total 5	35	43	.449	151	80	15	4	6	621	570	53	282	440	12.6	4.25	80	.245	.332	19	.102	-5	-56	-58	-3	-8.3
● **JACK BRACKEN**	Bracken, John James b: 4/14/1881, Cleveland, Ohio d: 7/16/54, Highland Park, Mich. BR/TR, 5'11", 175 lbs. Deb: 8/7/01																								
1901 Cle-A	4	8	.333	12	12	12	0	0	100	137	4	31	18	16.0	6.21	57	.322	.381	10	.227	0	-28	-30	-1	-2.6
● **JOHN BRACKENRIDGE**	Brackenridge, John Givler b: 12/24/1880, Harrisburg, Pa. d: 3/20/53, Harrisburg, Pa. BR/TR, 6', Deb: 4/15/04																								
1904 Phi-N	0	1	.000	7	1	0	0	0	34	37	4	16	11	15.1	5.56	48	.298	.396	2	.154	-0	-11	-11	2	-0.1
● **DON BRADEY**	Bradey, Donald Eugene b: 10/4/34, Charlotte, N.C. BR/TR, 5'9", 180 lbs. Deb: 9/25/64																								
1964 Hou-N	0	2	.000	3	1	0	0	0	2^{1}	6	0	3	2	34.7	19.29	18	.429	.529	0	—	0	-4	-4	-0	-2.2
● **CHAD BRADFORD**	Bradford, Chadwick L. b: 9/14/74, Jackson, Miss. BR/TR, 6'5", 205 lbs. Deb: 8/1/98																								
1998 Chi-A	2	1	.667	29	0	0	0	1	30^{2}	27	0	7	11	10.0	3.23	141	.229	.272	0	—	0	5	5	0	0.5
● **LARRY BRADFORD**	Bradford, Larry b: 12/21/49, Chicago, Ill. d: 9/11/98, Atlanta, Ga. BR/TL, 6'1", 200 lbs. Deb: 9/24/77																								
1977 Atl-N	0	0	—	2	0	0	0	0	2^{2}	3	1	0	1	10.1	3.38	132	.273	.273	0	—	0	0	0	0	0.0
1979 Atl-N	1	0	1.000	21	0	0	0	2	19	11	0	10	11	10.4	0.95	427	.172	.293	0	.000	-0	6	7	0	0.5
1980 Atl-N	3	4	.429	56	0	0	0	4	55^{1}	49	3	22	32	11.7	2.44	153	.243	.320	0	.000	-0	7	8	-0	1.1
1981 Atl-N	2	0	1.000	25	0	0	0	1	26^{2}	26	1	12	14	12.8	3.71	96	.268	.349	1	1.000	0	-1	-0	0	0.0
Total 4	6	4	.600	104	0	0	0	7	103^{2}	89	5	44	58	11.7	2.52	150	.238	.321	1	.200	-0	13	14	1	1.6
● **BILL BRADFORD**	Bradford, William D b: 8/28/21, Choctaw, Ark. BR/TR, 6'2", 180 lbs. Deb: 4/24/56																								
1956 KC-A	0	0	—	1	0	0	0	0	2	2	2	1	0	13.5	9.00	48	.250	.333	0	—	0	-1	-1	0	0.0
● **FRED BRADLEY**	Bradley, Fred Langdon b: 7/31/20, Parsons, Kan. BR/TR, 6'1", 180 lbs. Deb: 5/1/48																								
1948 Chi-A	0	0	—	8	0	0	0	0	15^{2}	11	2	4	2	9.2	4.60	93	.190	.254	0	.000	-0	-1	-1	0	0.0
1949 Chi-A	0	0	—	1	1	0	0	0	2	4	0	3	0	31.5	13.50	31	.444	.583	0	.000	-0	-2	-2	0	0.0
Total 2	0	0	—	9	1	0	0	0	17^{2}	15	2	7	2	11.7	5.60	76	.224	.307	0	.000	-0	-3	-3	0	0.0
● **FOGHORN BRADLEY**	Bradley, George H. b: 7/1/1855, Milford, Mass. d: 4/3/1900, Philadelphia, Pa. BR/TR, Deb: 8/23/1876 U																								
1876 Bos-N	9	10	.474	22	21	16	1	1	173^{1}	201	1	16	16	11.3	2.49	91	.263	.279	19	.232	-1	-4	-5	-1	-0.5
● **GEORGE BRADLEY**	Bradley, George Washington "Grin" b: 7/13/1852, Reading, Pa. d: 10/2/31, Philadelphia, Pa. BR/TR, 5'10.5", 175 lbs. Deb: 5/4/1875 ♦																								
1875 StL-n	33	26	.559	60	60	57	5	0	535^{2}	540	3	17	60	9.4	2.13	94	.241	.247	62	.244	7	5	-7		0.1
1876 StL-N	45	19	.703	64	64	63	**16**	0	573	470	3	38	103	**8.0**	**1.23**	**174**	**.211**	**.224**	66	.249	4	**69**	58	1	5.8
1877 Chi-N	18	23	.439	50	44	35	2	0	394	452	4	39	59	11.2	3.31	90	.269	.286	52	.243	0	-22	-15	1	-1.3
1879 Tro-N	13	40	.245	54	54	53	3	0	487	590	12	26	133	11.4	2.85	88	.275	.284	62	.247	4	-19	-19	4	-0.7
1880 Pro-N	13	8	.619	28	20	16	4	2	196	158	2	6	54	7.5	1.38	160	.210	.217	70	.227	1	22	18	1	1.9
1881 Cle-N	2	4	.333	6	6	5	0	0	51	70	2	3	6	12.9	3.88	67	.320	.329	60	.249	0	-6	-7	-1	-0.7
1882 Cle-N	6	9	.400	18	16	15	0	0	147	164	5	22	32	11.4	3.73	75	.264	.289	21	.183	-3	-14	-15	3	-1.2
1883 Phi-a	16	7	.696	26	23	22	0	0	214^{1}	215	7	22	56	10.0	3.15	110	.244	.263	73	.234	0	4	8	-1	0.5
1884 Cin-U	25	15	.625	41	38	36	3	0	342	350	7	23	168	9.8	2.71	95	.248	.260	43	.190	-12	-10	-6	2	-1.4
Total 8	138	125	.525	287	265	245	28	2	2404^{1}	2469	42	179	611	9.9	2.50	103	.248	.262	456	.228	-5	23	19	11	2.9
● **HERB BRADLEY**	Bradley, Herbert Theodore b: 1/3/03, Agenda, Kan. d: 10/16/59, Clay Center, Kan. BR/TR, 6', 170 lbs. Deb: 5/9/27																								
1927 Bos-A	1	1	.500	6	2	2	0	0	23	16	0	7	6	9.8	3.13	135	.198	.278	3	.429	1	3	3	-0	0.3
1928 Bos-A	0	3	.000	15	5	1	1	0	47^{1}	64	2	16	14	15.6	7.23	57	.339	.396	2	.154	-1	-17	-16	1	-0.8
1929 Bos-A	0	0	—	3	0	0	0	0	4	7	1	2	0	20.3	6.75	63	.438	.500	0	.000	-0	-1	-1	0	0.0
Total 3	1	4	.200	24	7	3	1	0	74^{1}	87	3	25	20	14.0	5.93	70	.304	.368	5	.238	-0	-15	-15	1	-0.5
● **RYAN BRADLEY**	Bradley, Ryan J. b: 10/26/75, Covina, Cal. BR/TR, 6'4", 220 lbs. Deb: 8/22/98																								
1998 NY-A	2	1	.667	5	1	0	0	0	12^{2}	12	2	9	13	15.6	5.68	78	.250	.379	0	—	0	-1	-2	-0	-0.3
● **BERT BRADLEY**	Bradley, Steven Bert b: 12/23/56, Athens, Ga. BB/TR, 6'1", 190 lbs. Deb: 9/3/83																								
1983 Oak-A	0	0	—	6	0	0	0	0	8^{1}	14	1	4	3	19.4	6.48	59	.400	.462	0	—	0	-2	-2	1	0.1
● **TOM BRADLEY**	Bradley, Thomas William b: 3/16/47, Asheville, N.C. BR/TR, 6'3", 185 lbs. Deb: 9/9/69																								
1969 Cal-A	0	1	.000	3	0	0	0	0	2	9	1	0	2	40.5	27.00	13	.600	.600	0	—	0	-5	-5	0	-1.8
1970 Cal-A	2	5	.286	17	11	1	1	0	69^{2}	71	3	33	53	13.6	4.13	87	.270	.354	3	.167	0	-3	-4	-0	-0.3
1971 Chi-A	15	15	.500	45	39	7	6	2	285^{2}	273	16	74	206	11.0	2.96	121	.248	.297	15	.156	-1	16	20	-2	1.8
1972 Chi-A	15	14	.517	40	40	11	2	0	260	225	19	65	209	10.1	2.98	105	.231	.280	12	.132	-2	2	4	-0	0.2
1973 SF-N	13	12	.520	35	34	6	1	0	224	212	26	69	136	11.4	3.90	98	.246	.304	15	.195	1	-6	-2	-2	-0.3
1974 SF-N	8	11	.421	30	21	2	0	0	134^{1}	152	15	52	72	13.7	5.16	74	.282	.346	3	.075	-2	-23	-20	-1	-2.9
1975 SF-N	2	3	.400	13	6	0	0	0	42	57	6	18	13	16.3	6.21	61	.326	.392	0	.000	-1	-12	-11	0	-1.2
Total 7	55	61	.474	183	151	27	10	2	1017^{2}	999	86	311	691	11.7	3.72	96	.254	.311	48	.145	-5	-31	-19	-5	-4.5
● **BILL BRADLEY**	Bradley, William Joseph b: 2/13/1878, Cleveland, Ohio d: 3/11/54, Cleveland, Ohio BR/TR, 6', 185 lbs. Deb: 8/26/1899 M ♦																								
1901 Cle-A	0	0	—	1	0	0	0	0	1	4	0	0	0	36.0	0.00	—	.571	.571	151	.293	0	0	0	-0	0.0

YEAR	TM/L	W	L	PCT	G	GS	CG	SH	SV	IP	H	HR	BB	SO	RAT	ERA	ERA+	OAV	OOB	BH	AVG	PB	PR	/A	PD	TPI
● **JOE BRADSHAW** Bradshaw, Joe Siah b: 8/17/1897, RoEllen, Tenn. d: 1/30/85, Tavares, Fla. BR/TR, 6′2.5″, 200 lbs. Deb: 5/9/29																										
1929	Bro-N	0	0	—	2	0	0	0	0	4	3	0	4	1	20.3	4.50	103	.231	.474	0	—	0	0	0	0	0.0
● **NEAL BRADY** Brady, Cornelius Joseph b: 3/4/1897, Covington, Ky. d: 6/19/47, Fort Mitchell, Ky BR/TR, 6′0.5″, 197 lbs. Deb: 9/25/15																										
1915	NY-A	0	0	—	2	1	0	0	0	8^2	9	0	7	6	16.6	3.12	94	.281	.410	0	.000	-1	-0	-0	-0	-0.1
1917	NY-A	1	0	1.000	2	1	0	0	0	9	6	0	5	4	11.0	2.00	134	.188	.297	1	.500	0	1	1	0	0.2
1925	Cin-N	1	3	.250	20	3	2	0	1	63^2	73	4	20	12	13.7	4.66	88	.289	.350	6	.240	1	-3	-4	0	-0.1
Total	3	2	3	.400	24	5	2	0	1	81^1	88	4	32	22	13.7	4.20	91	.278	.351	7	.226	1	-2	-3	1	0.0
● **JIM BRADY** Brady, James Joseph "Diamond Jim" b: 3/2/36, Jersey City, N.J. BL/TL, 6′2″, 185 lbs. Deb: 5/12/56																										
1956	Det-A	0	0	—	6	0	0	0	0	6^1	15	3	11	3	36.9	28.42	14	.484	.619	0	—	0	-17	-17	0	0.0
● **KING BRADY** Brady, James Ward b: 5/28/1881, Elmer, N.J. d: 8/21/47, Albany, N.Y. BR/TR, 6′, 190 lbs. Deb: 9/21/05																										
1905	Phi-N	1	1	.500	2	2	2	0	0	13	19	0	2	3	14.5	3.46	84	.333	.356	1	.200	-0	-1	-1	-0	-0.1
1906	Pit-N	1	1	.500	3	2	1	0	0	23	30	0	4	14	13.3	2.35	114	.313	.340	1	.100	-1	1	1	-1	-0.1
1907	Pit-N	0	0	—	1	0	0	0	0	2	2	0	1	0	13.5	0.00	—	.286	.375	0	—	0	1	1	-0	0.0
1908	Bos-A	1	0	1.000	1	1	1	1	0	9	8	0	0	3	8.0	0.00	—	.242	.242	0	.000	-0	2	2	-0	0.2
1912	Bos-N	0	0	—	1	0	0	0	0	2^2	5	0	3	0	27.0	20.25	18	.313	.421	0	.000	-0	-5	-5	0	0.0
Total	5	3	2	.600	8	5	4	1	0	49^2	64	0	10	20	13.4	3.08	89	.306	.338	2	.111	-1	-2	-2	-1	0.0
● **BILL BRADY** Brady, William Aloysius "King" b: 8/18/1889, New York, N.Y. TR , 6′2″, Deb: 7/9/12																										
1912	Bos-N	0	0	—	1	0	0	0	0	1	2	0	0	0	18.0	0.00	—	.500	.500	0	—	0	0	0	-0	0.0
● **DICK BRAGGINS** Braggins, Richard Realf b: 12/25/1879, Mercer, Pa. d: 8/16/63, Lake Wales, Fla. BR/TR, 5′11″, 170 lbs. Deb: 5/16/01																										
1901	Cle-A	1	2	.333	4	3	2	0	0	32	44	1	15	1	16.9	4.78	74	.324	.395	2	.154	-1	-4	-4	0	-0.4
● **ASA BRAINARD** Brainard, Asa "Count" b: 1841, Albany, N.Y. d: 12/29/1888, Denver, Colo. TR , 5′8.5″, 150 lbs. Deb: 5/5/1871 ♦																										
1871	Oly-n	12	15	.444	30	30	30	0	0	264	361	4	37	13	13.6	4.50	93	.288	.308	30	.224	-6	-8	-10		-1.0
1872	Oly-n	2	7	.222	9	9	9	0	0	79	148	0	5	1	17.4	6.38	56	.333	.341	16	.372	4	-24	-24		-1.5
	Man-n	0	2	.000	2	2	1	0	0	8	13	0	0	0	14.6	5.63	64	.260	.260	5	.200	-0	-2	-2		-0.3
	Yr	2	9	.182	11	11	10	0	0	87	161	0	5	1	17.2	6.31	57	.326	.333	21	.309	3	-26	-26		-1.8
1873	Bal-n	5	7	.417	14	14	12	0	0	108^2	182	0	9	3	15.8	4.14	79	.323	.334	18	.261	0	-11	-11		-0.8
1874	Bal-n	5	22	.185	30	27	25	0	0	240	405	1	27	8	16.2	3.71	60	.327	.341	47	.240	-1	-41	-40		-3.3
Total	4 n	24	53	.312	85	82	77	0	0	699^2	1109	5	78	25	15.3	4.40	50	.312	.327	116	.248	-4	-172	-170		-6.9
● **AL BRAITHWOOD** Braithwood, Alfred b: 2/15/1892, Braceville, Ill. d: 11/24/60, Rowlesburg, W.Va. BR/TL, 6′1.5″, 145 lbs. Deb: 9/1/15																										
1915	Pit-F	0	0	—	2	0	0	0	0	3	0	0	0	2	0.0	0.00	—	.000	.000	0	—	0	1	1	-0	0.0
● **ERV BRAME** Brame, Ervin Beckham b: 10/12/01, Big Rock, Tenn. d: 11/22/49, Hopkinsville, Ky. BL/TR, 6′2″, 190 lbs. Deb: 4/14/28																										
1928	Pit-N	7	4	.636	24	11	6	0	0	95^2	110	5	44	22	14.6	5.08	80	.291	.366	13	.265	4	-12	-11	-1	-0.8
1929	Pit-N	16	11	.593	37	28	19	1	0	229^2	250	17	71	68	12.6	4.55	105	.278	.331	36	.310	12	4	6	-4	1.2
1930	Pit-N	17	8	.680	32	29	**22**	0	1	235^2	291	21	56	55	13.4	4.70	106	.305	.346	41	.353	11	7	7	-3	1.3
1931	Pit-N	9	13	.409	26	21	15	2	0	179^2	211	14	45	33	12.8	4.21	91	.295	.336	26	.274	6	-7	-7	-2	-0.4
1932	Pit-N	3	1	.750	23	3	0	0	0	51	84	6	16	10	17.6	7.41	51	.365	.407	5	.250	1	-20	-20	-1	-1.4
Total	5	52	37	.584	142	92	62	3	1	791^2	946	63	232	188	13.5	4.76	94	.298	.347	121	.306	33	-27	-25	-11	-0.1
● **RALPH BRANCA** Branca, Ralph Theodore Joseph "Hawk" b: 1/6/26, Mt.Vernon, N.Y. BR/TR, 6′3″, 220 lbs. Deb: 6/12/44																										
1944	Bro-N	0	2	.000	21	1	0	0	1	44^2	46	2	32	16	16.7	7.05	50	.274	.405	0	.000	-1	-17	-17	-0	-0.9
1945	Bro-N	5	6	.455	16	15	7	0	1	109^2	73	4	79	69	12.5	3.04	124	.189	.327	4	.100	-3	9	9	0	0.6
1946	Bro-N	3	1	.750	24	10	2	2	3	67^1	62	4	41	42	13.8	3.88	87	.246	.352	2	.111	0	-3	-4	-1	-0.3
1947	*Bro-N☆	21	12	.636	43	36	15	4	1	280	251	22	98	148	11.4	2.67	155	.240	.309	12	.124	-3	43	46	-4	4.4
1948	Bro-N★	14	9	.609	36	28	11	1	1	215^2	189	24	80	122	11.4	3.51	114	.232	.304	15	.203	1	11	12	-4	0.8
1949	*Bro-N☆	13	5	.722	34	27	9	2	1	186^2	181	21	91	109	13.2	4.39	93	.253	.339	5	.081	-2	-7	-6	-4	-1.1
1950	Bro-N	7	9	.438	43	15	5	0	7	142	152	24	55	100	13.1	4.69	87	.271	.336	4	.118	1	-9	-9	-1	-1.0
1951	Bro-N	13	12	.520	42	27	13	3	3	204	180	19	85	118	11.8	3.26	120	.237	.316	11	.175	-1	16	15	-3	1.4
1952	Bro-N	4	2	.667	16	7	2	0	0	61	52	8	21	26	11.4	3.84	95	.232	.309	3	.158	-0	-1	-1	-1	-0.2
1953	Bro-N	0	0	—	7	0	0	0	0	11	15	4	5	5	18.0	9.82	43	.341	.431	0	—	0	-7	-7	0	0.0
	Det-A	4	7	.364	17	14	7	0	1	102	98	7	31	50	11.6	4.15	98	.253	.311	4	.118	-1	-2	-1	-1	-0.3
1954	Det-A	3	3	.500	17	5	0	0	0	45^1	63	10	30	15	18.9	5.76	64	.330	.426	4	.308	2	-10	-10	-0	-1.1
	NY-A	1	0	1.000	5	3	0	0	0	12^2	9	0	13	7	16.3	2.84	121	.209	.404	2	.500	1	1	1	0	0.1
	Yr	4	3	.571	22	8	0	0	0	58	72	10	43	22	18.0	5.12	71	.304	.413	6	.353	2	-9	-10	-0	-1.0
1956	Bro-N	0	0	—	1	0	0	0	0	2	1	0	2	2	13.5	0.00	—	.143	.333	0	—	0	1	1	0	0.0
Total	12	88	68	.564	322	188	71	12	19	1484	1372	149	663	829	12.5	3.79	104	.245	.328	66	.142	-6	25	27	-18	2.4
● **HARVEY BRANCH** Branch, Harvey Alfred b: 2/8/39, Memphis, Tenn. BR/TL, 6′, 175 lbs. Deb: 9/18/62																										
1962	StL-N	0	1	.000	1	1	0	0	0	5	5	1	5	2	18.0	5.40	79	.263	.417	0	.000	-0	-1	-1	0	-0.1
● **NORM BRANCH** Branch, Norman Downs "Red" b: 3/22/15, Spokane, Wash. d: 11/21/71, Navasota, Tex. BR/TR, 6′3″, 200 lbs. Deb: 5/5/41																										
1941	NY-A	5	1	.833	27	0	0	0	2	47	37	2	26	28	12.1	2.87	137	.224	.330	0	.000	-1	7	6	1	0.6
1942	NY-A	0	1	.000	10	0	0	0	2	15^2	18	3	16	13	19.5	6.32	54	.290	.436	1	.333	0	-5	-5	0	-0.4
Total	2	5	2	.714	37	0	0	0	4	62^2	55	5	42	41	13.9	3.73	102	.242	.361	1	.077	-1	2	1	1	0.2
● **ROY BRANCH** Branch, Roy b: 7/12/53, St.Louis, Mo. BR/TR, 6′, 175 lbs. Deb: 9/11/79																										
1979	Sea-A	0	1	.000	2	2	0	0	0	11^1	12	2	7	6	15.1	7.94	55	.273	.373	0	—	0	-5	-5	-0	-0.4
● **MARK BRANDENBURG** Brandenburg, Mark Clay b: 7/14/70, Houston, Tex. BR/TR, 6′, 180 lbs. Deb: 7/20/95																										
1995	Tex-A	0	1	.000	11	0	0	0	0	27^1	36	5	7	21	14.5	5.93	81	.316	.361	0	—	0	-4	-3	-0	-0.2
1996	Tex-A	1	3	.250	26	0	0	0	0	47^2	48	3	25	37	14.2	3.21	163	.262	.357	0	—	0	9	11	-1	0.5
	Bos-A	4	2	.667	29	0	0	0	0	28^1	28	5	8	29	11.8	3.81	133	.250	.306	0	—	0	4	4	0	0.7
	Yr	5	5	.500	55	0	0	0	0	76	76	8	33	66	13.0	3.43	151	.254	.330	0	—	0	13	15	-1	1.2
1997	Bos-A	0	2	.000	31	0	0	0	0	41	49	3	16	34	14.7	5.49	84	.299	.368	0	—	0	-4	-4	0	-0.3
Total	3	5	8	.385	97	0	0	0	0	144^1	161	16	56	121	13.9	4.49	110	.281	.351	0	—	0	5	7	-1	0.7
● **CHICK BRANDOM** Brandom, Chester Milton b: 3/31/1887, Coldwater, Kan. d: 10/7/58, Santa Ana, Cal. BR/TR, 5′8″, 161 lbs. Deb: 9/3/08																										
1908	Pit-N	1	0	1.000	3	1	1	0	1	17	13	0	4	8	9.5	0.53	435	.228	.290	1	.143	-0	3	3	0	0.3
1909	Pit-N	1	0	1.000	13	2	0	0	2	40^2	33	0	10	21	9.7	1.11	246	.239	.295	1	.100	-1	7	7	1	0.3
1915	New-F	1	1	.500	16	1	1	0	0	50^1	55	0	15	15	12.7	3.40	75	.293	.348	2	.200	1	-4	-5	1	-0.1
Total	3	3	1	.750	32	4	2	0	3	108	101	0	29	44	11.1	2.08	124	.264	.320	4	.148	-0	6	6	2	0.5
● **BUCKY BRANDON** Brandon, Darrell G b: 7/8/40, Nacogdoches, Tex. BR/TR, 6′2″, 200 lbs. Deb: 4/19/66																										
1966	Bos-A	8	8	.500	40	17	5	2	2	157^2	129	13	70	101	11.6	3.31	115	.222	.310	8	.182	1	2	9	0	1.1
1967	Bos-A	5	11	.313	39	19	2	0	3	157^2	147	21	59	96	12.2	4.17	84	.245	.320	8	.186	1	-16	-12	-0	-1.2
1968	Bos-A	0	0	—	8	0	0	0	0	12^2	19	1	9	10	20.6	6.39	49	.333	.433	0	.000	-0	-5	-5	0	0.0
1969	Sea-A	0	1	.000	8	1	0	0	0	15	15	4	16	10	19.8	8.40	43	.250	.423	0	—	0	-8	-8	0	-0.5
	Min-A	0	0	—	3	0	0	0	0	3^1	5	1	3	1	21.6	2.70	135	.357	.471	0	.000	0	0	0	-0	0.0
	Yr	0	1	.000	11	1	0	0	0	18^1	20	5	19	11	19.1	7.36	49	.263	.411	0	.000	0	-8	-8	-0	-0.5
1971	Phi-N	6	6	.500	52	0	0	0	4	83	81	5	47	44	13.9	3.90	90	.264	.362	2	.154	-0	-4	-4	-1	-0.6
1972	Phi-N	7	7	.500	42	6	0	0	2	104^1	106	9	46	67	13.6	3.45	104	.268	.353	1	.067	-1	0	2	-2	-0.1
1973	Phi-N	2	4	.333	36	0	0	0	2	56^1	54	5	25	25	13.1	5.43	70	.261	.349	1	.200	0	-11	-10	0	-1.1
Total	7	28	37	.431	228	43	7	2	13	590	556	59	275	354	13.0	4.04	90	.250	.339	20	.164	1	-42	-27	-2	-2.4
● **ED BRANDT** Brandt, Edward Arthur "Big Ed" b: 2/17/05, Spokane, Wash. d: 11/1/44, Spokane, Wash. BL/TL, 6′1″, 190 lbs. Deb: 4/26/28																										
1928	Bos-N	9	21	.300	38	32	12	1	0	225^1	234	22	109	84	14.0	5.07	77	.273	.359	17	.243	5	-27	-29	2	-2.6

YEAR	TM/L	W	L	PCT	G	GS	CG	SH	SV	IP	H	HR	BB	SO	RAT	ERA	ERA+	OAV	OOB	BH	AVG	PB	PR	/A	PD	TPI
1929	Bos-N	8	13	.381	26	21	13	0	0	167^2	196	12	83	50	15.2	5.53	85	.302	.385	15	.234	2	-15	-16	2	-1.2
1930	Bos-N	4	11	.267	41	13	4	1	1	147^1	168	15	59	65	13.9	5.01	99	.291	.356	12	.240	1	-1	-1	2	0.1
1931	Bos-N	18	11	.621	33	29	23	3	2	250	228	11	77	112	11.1	2.92	130	.244	.304	21	.256	5	26	24	3	3.6
1932	Bos-N	16	16	.500	35	31	19	2	1	254	271	11	57	79	11.8	3.97	95	.275	.318	19	.207	-0	-3	-6	1	-0.5
1933	Bos-N	18	14	.563	41	32	23	4	4	287^2	256	10	77	104	10.5	2.60	118	.245	.298	30	.309	9	24	15	-0	2.7
1934	Bos-N	16	14	.533	40	28	20	3	5	255	249	13	83	106	11.9	3.53	108	.254	.315	23	.240	4	15	8	-3	1.1
1935	Bos-N	5	19	.208	29	25	12	0	0	174^2	224	12	66	61	15.0	5.00	76	.319	.378	13	.210	-0	-19	-24	1	-2.6
1936	Bro-N	11	13	.458	38	29	12	1	2	234	246	14	65	104	12.1	3.50	118	.268	.319	16	.190	0	14	16	-2	1.3
1937	Pit-N	11	10	.524	33	25	7	2	2	176^1	177	11	67	74	12.6	3.11	124	.263	.332	10	.169	1	16	15	1	1.8
1938	Pit-N	5	4	.556	24	13	5	1	0	96^1	93	3	35	38	12.0	3.46	110	.250	.314	11	.297	2	4	4	-1	0.5
Total	11	121	146	.453	378	278	150	18	17	2268^1	2342	134	778	877	12.5	3.86	101	.269	.332	187	.236	30	34	5	6	4.2

● BILL BRANDT Brandt, William George b: 3/21/15, Aurora, Ind. d: 5/16/68, Fort Wayne, Ind. BR/TR, 5'8.5", 170 lbs. Deb: 9/20/41

YEAR	TM/L	W	L	PCT	G	GS	CG	SH	SV	IP	H	HR	BB	SO	RAT	ERA	ERA+	OAV	OOB	BH	AVG	PB	PR	/A	PD	TPI
1941	Pit-N	0	1	.000	2	1	0	0	0	7	5	0	3	0	10.3	3.86	94	.200	.286	0	.000	-0	-0	-0	-0	-0.1
1942	Pit-N	1	1	.500	3	3	1	0	0	16^1	23	1	5	4	15.4	4.96	68	.343	.389	1	.143	-0	-3	-3	-0	-0.4
1943	Pit-N	4	1	.800	29	3	0	0	0	57^1	57	3	19	17	12.1	3.14	111	.248	.308	1	.143	-0	2	2	-0	0.1
Total	3	5	3	.625	34	7	1	0	0	80^2	85	4	27	21	12.6	3.57	97	.264	.323	2	.133	-1	-2	-1	-1	-0.4

● CLIFF BRANTLEY Brantley, Clifford b: 4/12/68, Staten Island, N.Y. BR/TR, 6'1", 190 lbs. Deb: 9/3/91

YEAR	TM/L	W	L	PCT	G	GS	CG	SH	SV	IP	H	HR	BB	SO	RAT	ERA	ERA+	OAV	OOB	BH	AVG	PB	PR	/A	PD	TPI
1991	Phi-N	2	2	.500	6	5	0	0	0	31^2	26	0	19	25	13.4	3.41	107	.228	.348	0	.000	-1	1	1	0	0.0
1992	Phi-N	2	6	.250	28	9	0	0	0	76^1	71	6	58	32	15.7	4.60	76	.251	.386	3	.214	1	-9	-9	0	-0.8
Total	2	4	8	.333	34	14	0	0	0	108	97	6	77	57	15.0	4.25	83	.244	.375	3	.136	0	-8	-9	0	-0.8

● JEFF BRANTLEY Brantley, Jeffrey Hoke b: 9/5/63, Florence, Ala. BR/TR, 5'11", 190 lbs. Deb: 8/5/88

YEAR	TM/L	W	L	PCT	G	GS	CG	SH	SV	IP	H	HR	BB	SO	RAT	ERA	ERA+	OAV	OOB	BH	AVG	PB	PR	/A	PD	TPI
1988	SF-N	0	1	.000	9	1	0	0	1	20^2	22	2	6	11	12.6	5.66	58	.275	.333	1	.500	0	-5	-6	1	-0.2
1989	*SF-N	7	1	.875	59	1	0	0	0	97^1	101	10	37	69	12.9	4.07	83	.271	.340	1	.083	-1	-6	-8	0	-0.6
1990	SF-N★	5	3	.625	55	0	0	0	19	86^2	77	3	33	61	11.7	1.56	234	.240	.317	2	.286	1	22	20	0	2.7
1991	SF-N	5	2	.714	67	0	0	0	15	95^1	78	8	52	81	12.7	2.45	146	.225	.335	0	.000	-0	13	12	-1	1.1
1992	SF-N	7	7	.500	56	4	0	0	7	91^2	67	8	45	86	11.3	2.95	112	.207	.310	1	.111	0	6	4	-1	0.5
1993	SF-N	5	6	.455	53	12	0	0	0	113^2	112	19	46	76	13.1	4.28	91	.259	.340	3	.107	-1	-3	-5	-2	-0.7
1994	Cin-N	6	6	.500	50	0	0	0	15	65^1	46	6	28	63	10.2	2.48	167	.202	.289	0	.000	-0	13	12	0	2.5
1995	*Cin-N	3	2	.600	56	0	0	0	28	70^1	53	11	20	62	9.5	2.82	146	.206	.266	0	.000	-0	11	10	-1	1.3
1996	Cin-N	1	2	.333	66	0	0	0	**44**	71	54	7	28	76	10.4	2.41	176	.215	.294	0	.000	-0	14	14	-1	2.0
1997	Cin-N	1	1	.500	13	0	0	0	1	11^2	9	2	7	16	13.9	3.86	111	.205	.340	0	—	0	0	1	-0	0.1
1998	StL-N	0	5	.000	48	0	0	0	14	50^2	40	12	18	48	10.5	4.44	94	.220	.294	0	—	0	-1	-1	-1	-0.3
Total	11	40	36	.526	532	18	0	0	144	774^1	659	88	320	649	11.7	3.15	120	.232	.315	8	.118	-2	63	53	-5	8.4

● KITTY BRASHEAR Brashear, Norman C. b: 8/27/1877, Mansfield, Ohio d: 12/22/34, Los Angeles, Cal. BR/TR, Deb: 6/25/1899 F

YEAR	TM/L	W	L	PCT	G	GS	CG	SH	SV	IP	H	HR	BB	SO	RAT	ERA	ERA+	OAV	OOB	BH	AVG	PB	PR	/A	PD	TPI
1899	Lou-N	1	0	1.000	3	0	0	0	0	8	8	0	2	5	12.4	4.50	86	.258	.324	1	.500	0	-1	-1	0	0.0

● JOHN BRAUN Braun, John Paul b: 12/26/39, Madison, Wis. BR/TR, 6'5", 218 lbs. Deb: 10/2/64

YEAR	TM/L	W	L	PCT	G	GS	CG	SH	SV	IP	H	HR	BB	SO	RAT	ERA	ERA+	OAV	OOB	BH	AVG	PB	PR	/A	PD	TPI
1964	Mil-N	0	0	—	1	0	0	0	0	2	2	0	1	1	13.5	0.00	—	.286	.375	0	—	0	1	1	-0	0.0

● GARLAND BRAXTON Braxton, Edgar Garland b: 6/10/1900, Snow Camp, N.C. d: 2/25/66, Norfolk, Va. BB/TL, 5'11", 152 lbs. Deb: 5/27/21

YEAR	TM/L	W	L	PCT	G	GS	CG	SH	SV	IP	H	HR	BB	SO	RAT	ERA	ERA+	OAV	OOB	BH	AVG	PB	PR	/A	PD	TPI
1921	Bos-N	1	3	.250	17	2	0	0	0	37^1	44	0	17	16	15.2	4.82	76	.310	.391	0	.000	-1	-4	-5	1	-0.5
1922	Bos-N	1	2	.333	25	5	2	0	0	66^2	75	3	24	15	13.9	3.38	118	.286	.355	1	.063	-2	5	5	-1	0.0
1925	NY-A	1	1	.500	3	2	0	0	0	19^1	26	1	5	11	14.9	6.52	65	.338	.386	2	.333	0	-5	-5	0	-0.4
1926	NY-A	5	1	.833	37	1	0	0	2	67^1	71	1	19	30	12.0	2.67	144	.275	.325	6	.300	1	10	9	0	0.9
1927	Was-A	10	9	.526	**58**	2	0	0	**13**	155^1	144	5	33	96	10.4	2.95	138	.246	.289	9	.231	0	**20**	**19**	-2	2.2
1928	Was-A	13	11	.542	38	24	15	2	6	218^1	177	7	44	94	**9.3**	**2.51**	**160**	**.222**	**.267**	9	.125	-4	37	36	0	3.5
1929	Was-A	12	10	.545	37	20	9	0	4	182	219	6	51	59	13.5	4.85	88	.299	.346	8	.148	-1	-12	-12	-1	-1.5
1930	Was-A	3	2	.600	15	0	0	0	5	27^1	22	3	9	7	10.2	3.29	140	.222	.287	0	.000	-1	4	4	-1	0.6
	Chi-A	4	10	.286	19	10	2	0	1	90^2	127	9	33	44	16.0	6.45	72	.333	.388	2	.087	-2	-18	-18	-1	-2.5
	Yr	7	12	.368	34	10	2	0	6	118	149	12	42	51	14.6	5.72	81	.310	.367	2	.071	-2	-14	-14	-2	-1.9
1931	Chi-A	0	3	.000	17	3	0	0	1	47^1	71	1	23	28	18.3	6.85	62	.338	.409	1	.091	-1	-13	-14	1	-0.8
	StL-A	0	0	—	11	1	0	0	0	18	27	2	10	7	19.0	10.50	44	.370	.452	2	.667	1	-12	-12	-0	0.1
	Yr	0	3	.000	28	4	0	0	1	65^1	98	3	33	35	18.2	7.85	56	.344	.414	3	.214	0	-25	-25	0	-0.7
1933	StL-A	0	1	.000	5	1	0	0	0	8^1	11	0	8	5	21.6	9.72	48	.289	.426	0	.000	-0	-5	-5	-0	-0.5
Total	10	50	53	.485	282	71	28	2	32	938	1014	38	276	412	12.6	4.13	101	.278	.332	40	.156	-8	8	2	-5	1.1

● AL BRAZLE Brazle, Alpha Eugene "Cotton" b: 10/19/13, Loyal, Okla. d: 10/24/73, Grand Junction, Colo. BL/TL, 6'2", 185 lbs. Deb: 7/25/43

YEAR	TM/L	W	L	PCT	G	GS	CG	SH	SV	IP	H	HR	BB	SO	RAT	ERA	ERA+	OAV	OOB	BH	AVG	PB	PR	/A	PD	TPI
1943	*StL-N	8	2	.800	13	9	8	1	0	88	74	0	29	26	10.5	1.53	219	.231	.295	9	.281	2	18	18	0	2.4
1946	*StL-N	11	10	.524	37	15	6	2	0	153^1	152	1	55	58	12.3	3.29	105	.261	.327	11	.212	-0	2	3	0	0.3
1947	StL-N	14	8	.636	44	19	7	0	4	168	186	7	48	85	12.6	2.84	146	.284	.335	14	.219	1	23	24	3	3.4
1948	StL-N	10	6	.625	42	23	6	2	1	156^1	171	8	50	55	12.7	3.80	108	.281	.335	8	.145	-2	3	5	3	0.6
1949	StL-N	14	8	.636	39	25	9	1	0	206^1	208	18	61	75	12.0	3.18	131	.263	.321	11	.134	-4	20	22	-0	1.7
1950	StL-N	11	9	.550	46	12	3	0	6	164^2	188	12	80	47	14.9	4.10	105	.296	.378	13	.213	-1	1	4	-1	0.3
1951	StL-N	6	5	.545	56	8	5	0	7	154^1	139	13	60	66	11.9	3.09	128	.245	.322	5	.109	-3	**15**	**15**	-2	0.6
1952	StL-N	12	5	.706	46	6	3	1	**16**	109^1	75	7	42	55	9.7	2.72	137	.198	.280	4	.125	-1	12	12	-2	1.9
1953	StL-N	6	7	.462	60	0	0	0	**18**	92	101	8	43	57	14.3	4.21	101	.280	.360	5	.333	1	1	1	2	0.4
1954	StL-N	5	4	.556	58	0	0	0	8	84^1	93	10	24	30	12.8	4.16	99	.288	.343	0	.000	-2	-1	-0	-1	-0.3
Total	10	97	64	.602	441	117	47	7	60	1376^2	1387	84	492	554	12.4	3.31	120	.266	.332	80	.177	-9	93	103	3	11.3

● HARRY BRECHEEN Brecheen, Harry David "Harry The Cat" b: 10/14/14, Broken Bow, Okla. BL/TL, 5'10", 160 lbs. Deb: 4/22/40 C

YEAR	TM/L	W	L	PCT	G	GS	CG	SH	SV	IP	H	HR	BB	SO	RAT	ERA	ERA+	OAV	OOB	BH	AVG	PB	PR	/A	PD	TPI
1940	StL-N	0	0	—	3	0	0	0	0	3^1	2	0	2	4	10.8	0.00	—	.167	.286	0	—	0	1	1	0	0.0
1943	*StL-N	9	6	.600	29	13	8	1	4	135^1	98	4	39	68	9.3	2.26	149	.206	.270	8	.190	1	17	17	1	2.1
1944	*StL-N	16	5	.762	30	22	13	3	0	189^1	174	8	46	88	10.6	2.85	124	.242	.290	11	.162	1	16	14	-0	1.5
1945	StL-N	15	4	**.789**	24	18	13	3	2	157^1	136	5	44	63	10.6	2.52	149	.238	.298	7	.123	-1	22	21	-1	2.3
1946	*StL-N	15	15	.500	36	30	14	**5**	3	231^1	212	8	67	117	11.0	2.49	139	.244	.301	11	.133	-3	24	25	2	3.1
1947	StL-N★	16	11	.593	29	28	18	1	1	223^1	220	20	66	89	11.6	3.30	125	.260	.316	20	.241	5	19	21	1	2.9
1948	StL-N☆	20	7	**.741**	33	30	21	**7**	1	233^1	193	6	49	**149**	**9.4**	**2.24**	**183**	.222	**.265**	12	.146	-1	45	**48**	1	**5.5**
1949	StL-N	14	11	.560	32	31	14	2	1	214^2	207	18	65	88	11.7	3.35	124	.252	.312	21	.273	5	16	19	-1	2.5
1950	StL-N	8	11	.421	27	23	12	2	1	163^1	151	18	45	80	11.0	3.80	113	.244	.298	14	.241	3	6	9	-0	1.2
1951	StL-N	8	4	.667	24	16	5	0	2	138^2	134	11	54	57	12.3	3.25	122	.256	.327	12	.218	2	11	11	-0	1.1
1952	StL-N	7	5	.583	25	13	4	1	2	100^1	82	12	28	54	10.1	3.32	112	.223	.283	6	.207	1	5	4	2	0.9
1953	StL-A	5	13	.278	26	16	3	0	1	117^1	122	7	31	44	12.0	3.07	137	.269	.320	7	.179	-1	12	15	2	2.3
Total	12	133	92	.591	318	240	125	25	18	1907^2	1731	117	536	901	10.9	2.92	133	.242	.298	129	.192	11	194	205	6	25.4

● BILL BRECKINRIDGE Breckinridge, William Robertson b: 10/16/07, Tulsa, Okla. d: 8/23/58, Tulsa, Okla. BR/TR, 5'11", 175 lbs. Deb: 6/30/29

YEAR	TM/L	W	L	PCT	G	GS	CG	SH	SV	IP	H	HR	BB	SO	RAT	ERA	ERA+	OAV	OOB	BH	AVG	PB	PR	/A	PD	TPI
1929	Phi-A	0	0	—	3	1	0	0	0	10	10	0	16	2	23.4	8.10	52	.270	.491	0	.000	-1	-4	-4	-1	-0.1

● FRED BREINING Breining, Fred Lawrence b: 11/15/55, San Francisco, Cal. BR/TR, 6'4", 185 lbs. Deb: 9/4/80

YEAR	TM/L	W	L	PCT	G	GS	CG	SH	SV	IP	H	HR	BB	SO	RAT	ERA	ERA+	OAV	OOB	BH	AVG	PB	PR	/A	PD	TPI
1980	SF-N	0	0	—	5	0	0	0	0	6^2	8	0	4	3	17.6	5.40	65	.333	.448	0	—	0	-1	-1	-0	0.0
1981	SF-N	5	2	.714	45	1	0	0	1	77^2	66	4	38	37	12.3	2.55	135	.243	.340	0	.000	-1	8	8	-0	0.5
1982	SF-N	11	6	.647	54	9	2	0	0	143^1	146	6	52	98	12.5	3.08	117	.269	.334	6	.207	1	8	8	1	1.2
1983	SF-N	11	12	.478	32	32	6	0	0	202^2	202	15	60	117	11.9	3.82	93	.259	.316	10	.149	1	-4	-6	-1	-0.6
1984	Mon-N	0	0	—	4	0	0	0	0	6^2	4	0	5	5	12.2	1.35	254	.190	.346	0	.000	-0	2	2	-0	0.0
Total	5	27	20	.574	140	42	8	0	1	437	426	25	159	260	12.2	3.34	106	.260	.329	16	.148	1	12	10	-0	1.1

● ALONZO BREITENSTEIN Breitenstein, Alonzo b: 11/9/1857, Utica, N.Y. d: 6/19/32, Utica, N.Y. Deb: 7/7/1883

YEAR	TM/L	W	L	PCT	G	GS	CG	SH	SV	IP	H	HR	BB	SO	RAT	ERA	ERA+	OAV	OOB	BH	AVG	PB	PR	/A	PD	TPI
1883	Phi-N	0	1	.000	1	1	0	0	0	5	8	0	2	0	18.0	9.00	34	.320	.370	0	.000	-0	-3	-3	-0	-0.5

YEAR	TM/L	W	L	PCT	G	GS	CG	SH	SV	IP	H	HR	BB	SO	RAT	ERA	ERA+	OAV	OOB	BH	AVG	PB	PR	/A	PD	TPI
● **TED BREITENSTEIN**	Breitenstein, Theodore P. "Theo" b: 6/1/1869, St.Louis, Mo. d: 5/3/35, St.Louis, Mo. BL/TL, 5'9", 167 lbs. Deb: 4/28/1891																									
1891	StL-a	2	0	1.000	6	1	1	1	1	28^2	15	2	14	13	9.1	2.20	191	.150	.254	0	.000	-2	5	6	-1	0.2
1892	StL-N	9	19	.321	39	32	28	1	0	282^1	280	8	148	126	13.8	4.69	68	.248	.339	16	.122	-3	-44	-47	3	-3.7
1893	StL-N	19	24	.442	48	42	38	1	1	382^2	359	8	156	102	12.3	**3.18**	**149**	.241	.316	29	.181	-5	63	66	2	5.5
1894	StL-N	27	23	.540	**56**	50	**46**	1	0	**447^1**	497	21	191	140	14.1	4.79	113	.278	.352	40	.220	-1	27	31	3	2.6
1895	StL-N	19	30	.388	54	50	**46**	1	1	429^2	458	16	178	127	13.6	4.44	109	.269	.343	42	.193	-7	16	19	3	1.3
1896	StL-N	18	26	.409	44	43	37	1	0	339^2	376	12	138	114	13.8	4.48	97	.278	.347	42	.259	3	-4	-5	4	0.2
1897	Cin-N	23	12	.657	40	39	32	2	0	320^1	345	3	91	98	12.5	3.62	126	.273	.326	33	.266	3	25	33	-0	3.1
1898	Cin-N	20	14	.588	39	37	32	3	0	315^2	313	2	123	68	12.7	3.42	112	.257	.330	26	.215	1	7	15	3	1.7
1899	Cin-N	13	9	.591	26	24	21	0	0	210^2	219	2	71	59	12.8	3.59	109	.268	.333	37	.352	9	6	8	-0	1.5
1900	Cin-N	10	10	.500	24	20	18	1	0	192^1	205	4	79	39	13.9	3.65	101	.272	.352	24	.190	-0	1	0	2	0.2
1901	StL-N	0	3	.000	3	3	1	0	0	15	24	1	14	3	22.8	6.60	48	.358	.469	2	.333	0	-5	-6	1	-0.8
Total	11	160	170	.485	379	341	300	12	3	2964^1	3091	79	1203	889	13.3	4.04	109	.265	.338	291	.216	-3	96	121	20	11.8
● **AD BRENNAN**	Brennan, Addison Foster b: 7/18/1881, LaHarpe, Kan. d: 1/7/62, Kansas City, Mo. BL/TL, 5'11", 170 lbs. Deb: 5/19/10																									
1910	Phi-N	2	0	1.000	19	5	2	0	0	73^1	72	2	28	28	12.6	2.33	134	.264	.339	7	.280	1	6	6	-2	0.1
1911	Phi-N	2	1	.667	5	3	1	0	0	22^2	22	0	12	12	13.9	3.57	96	.259	.357	2	.222	-0	-0	-0	0	0.0
1912	Phi-N	11	9	.550	27	19	13	1	2	174	185	4	49	78	12.3	3.57	102	.274	.326	15	.254	4	-3	1	2	0.7
1913	Phi-N	14	12	.538	40	24	12	1	1	207	204	5	46	94	11.1	2.39	139	.268	.314	11	.164	-2	19	22	0	2.5
1914	Chi-F	5	5	.500	16	11	5	1	0	85^2	84	6	21	31	11.2	3.57	74	.256	.305	8	.250	1	-7	-9	-1	-0.9
1915	Chi-F	3	9	.250	19	13	7	2	0	106	117	4	30	40	13.1	3.74	67	.287	.346	5	.185	0	-12	-14	-2	-1.7
1918	Was-A	0	0	—	2	1	0	0	0	5^1	7	0	5	0	21.9	5.06	54	.241	.371	0	.000	-0	-1	-1	0	0.0
	Cle-A	0	0	—	1	0	0	0	0	3	3	0	3	0	18.0	3.00	100	.333	.500	0	—	0	-0	0	-0	0.0
	Yr	0	0	—	3	1	0	0	0	8^1	10	0	8	0	19.4	4.32	65	.256	.383	0	.000	-0	-1	-1	-0	0.0
Total	7	37	36	.507	129	76	40	5	3	677	694	21	194	283	12.1	3.11	102	.270	.327	48	.218	4	1	4	-2	0.7
● **DON BRENNAN**	Brennan, James Donald b: 12/2/03, Augusta, Maine d: 4/26/53, Boston, Mass. BR/TR, 6', 210 lbs. Deb: 4/16/33																									
1933	NY-A	5	1	.833	18	10	3	0	3	85	92	4	47	46	14.7	4.98	78	.275	.365	7	.259	2	-7	-10	1	-0.4
1934	Cin-N	4	3	.571	28	7	2	0	2	78	89	3	35	31	14.4	3.81	107	.290	.364	5	.227	0	2	2	-1	0.2
1935	Cin-N	5	5	.500	38	5	2	1	5	114^1	101	4	44	48	11.7	3.15	126	.242	.320	3	.100	-1	11	11	-2	0.6
1936	Cin-N	5	2	.714	41	4	0	0	9	94^1	117	2	35	40	14.6	4.39	87	.305	.364	2	.080	-3	-4	-6	-0	-0.8
1937	Cin-N	1	1	.500	10	0	0	0	0	16	25	1	10	6	19.7	6.75	55	.347	.427	0	.000	-1	-5	-5	0	-0.6
	*NY-N	1	0	1.000	6	0	0	0	0	9^1	12	0	9	1	21.2	6.75	58	.316	.458	0	.000	0	-3	-3	-0	-0.3
	Yr	2	1	.667	16	0	0	0	0	25^1	37	1	19	7	20.3	6.75	56	.336	.438	0	.000	-1	-8	-8	-0	-0.9
Total	5	21	12	.636	141	26	7	1	19	397	436	14	180	172	14.1	4.19	94	.281	.358	17	.155	-2	-5	-12	-2	-1.3
● **TOM BRENNAN**	Brennan, Thomas Martin b: 10/30/52, Chicago, Ill. BR/TR, 6'1", 180 lbs. Deb: 9/5/81																									
1981	Cle-A	2	2	.500	7	6	1	0	0	48^1	49	5	14	15	11.7	3.17	114	.259	.310	0	—	0	3	2	1	0.3
1982	Cle-A	4	2	.667	30	4	0	0	2	92^2	112	9	10	46	12.0	4.27	95	.300	.322	0	—	0	-2	-2	0	-0.1
1983	Cle-A	2	2	.500	11	5	1	1	0	39^2	45	3	8	21	12.3	3.86	110	.288	.327	0	—	0	1	2	-0	0.1
1984	Chi-A	0	1	.000	4	1	0	0	0	6^2	8	1	3	3	14.9	4.05	103	.308	.379	0	—	0	-0	0	0	0.0
1985	LA-N	1	3	.250	12	4	0	0	0	31^2	41	2	11	17	14.8	7.39	47	.333	.388	1	.125	-0	-13	-14	1	-1.4
Total	5	9	10	.474	64	20	2	1	2	219	255	20	46	102	12.5	4.40	89	.294	.332	1	.125	-0	-12	-12	3	-1.1
● **WILLIAM BRENNAN**	Brennan, William Raymond b: 1/15/63, Tampa, Fla. BR/TR, 6'3", 200 lbs. Deb: 7/19/88																									
1988	LA-N	0	1	.000	4	2	0	0	0	9^1	13	0	6	7	18.3	6.75	49	.342	.432	0	.000	-0	-3	-4	0	-0.3
1993	Chi-N	2	1	.667	8	1	0	0	0	15	16	2	8	11	15.0	4.20	95	.291	.391	0	.000	0	-0	-0	0	0.0
Total	2	2	2	.500	12	3	0	0	0	24^1	29	2	14	18	16.3	5.18	72	.312	.407	0	.000	0	-4	-4	0	-0.3
● **JIM BRENNEMAN**	Brenneman, James Leroy b: 2/13/41, San Diego, Cal. BR/TR, 6'2", 180 lbs. Deb: 7/9/65																									
1965	NY-A	0	0	—	3	0	0	0	0	2	5	1	3	2	36.0	18.00	19	.455	.571	0	—	0	-3	-3	-0	0.0
● **BERT BRENNER**	Brenner, Delbert Henry "Dutch" b: 7/18/1887, Minneapolis, Minn d: 4/11/71, St.Louis Park, Minn. BR/TR, 6', 175 lbs. Deb: 9/21/12																									
1912	Cle-A	1	0	1.000	2	1	1	0	0	13	14	0	4	3	12.5	2.77	123	.286	.340	0	.000	-1	1	1	0	0.0
● **LYNN BRENTON**	Brenton, Lynn Davis "Buck" or "Herb" b: 10/7/1890, Peoria, Ill. d: 10/14/68, Los Angeles, Cal. BR/TR, 5'10", 165 lbs. Deb: 8/10/13																									
1913	Cle-A	0	0	—	1	0	0	0	0	2	4	0	0	2	18.0	9.00	34	.400	.400	0	—	0	-1	-1	-0	0.0
1915	Cle-A	2	3	.400	11	5	1	1	0	51	60	1	20	18	14.5	3.35	91	.308	.378	2	.118	-1	-2	-2	-1	-0.4
1920	Cin-N	2	1	.667	5	1	1	0	1	18^1	17	0	4	13	10.3	4.91	62	.236	.276	2	.250	0	-4	-4	2	-0.5
1921	Cin-N	1	8	.111	17	8	2	0	1	60	80	0	17	19	14.7	4.05	88	.342	.389	2	.133	-0	-2	-3	2	-0.2
Total	4	5	12	.294	34	14	4	1	2	131^1	161	1	41	52	14.0	3.97	83	.315	.369	6	.150	-1	-9	-10	3	-1.1
● **ROGER BRESNAHAN**	Bresnahan, Roger Philip "The Duke Of Tralee" b: 6/11/1879, Toledo, Ohio d: 12/4/44, Toledo, Ohio BR/TR, 5'9", 200 lbs. Deb: 8/27/1897 MCH♦																									
1897	Was-N	4	0	1.000	6	5	3	1	0	41	52	1	10	12	14.3	3.95	110	.306	.355	6	.375	1	2	2	-0	0.2
1901	Bal-A	0	1	.000	2	1	0	0	0	6	10	0	4	3	21.0	6.00	64	.370	.452	79	.268	0	-2	-1	0	-0.2
1910	StL-N	0	0	—	1	0	0	0	0	3^1	6	0	1	0	18.9	0.00	—	.400	.438	65	.278	0	1	1	1	0.1
Total	3	4	1	.800	9	6	3	1	0	50^1	68	1	15	15	15.4	3.93	107	.321	.374	1252	.279	2	1	1	0	0.1
● **RUBE BRESSLER**	Bressler, Raymond Bloom b: 10/23/1894, Coder, Pa. d: 11/7/66, Cincinnati, Ohio BR/TL, 6', 187 lbs. Deb: 4/24/14 ♦																									
1914	Phi-A	10	4	.714	29	10	8	1	2	147^2	112	1	56	96	10.5	1.77	148	.220	.302	11	.216	4	16	14	-2	1.5
1915	Phi-A	4	17	.190	32	20	7	1	2	178^1	183	3	118	69	15.5	5.20	56	.283	.399	8	.145	1	-45	-45	0	-4.5
1916	Phi-A	0	2	.000	4	2	0	0	0	15	16	0	14	8	19.2	6.60	43	.296	.457	1	.200	1	-6	-6	-0	-0.7
1917	Cin-N	0	0	—	2	1	0	0	0	9	15	0	5	2	20.0	6.00	44	.429	.500	1	.200	-0	-3	-3	-0	0.0
1918	Cin-N	8	5	.615	17	13	10	0	0	128	124	3	39	37	11.5	2.46	108	.261	.318	17	.274	4	4	3	3	1.1
1919	Cin-N	2	4	.333	13	4	1	0	0	41^2	37	1	8	13	9.7	3.46	80	.248	.287	34	.206	2	-3	-3	1	-0.3
1920	Cin-N	2	0	1.000	10	2	1	1	0	20^1	24	0	2	4	11.5	1.77	172	.300	.317	8	.267	0	3	3	0	0.3
Total	7	26	32	.448	107	52	27	3	2	540	511	8	242	229	12.8	3.40	81	.262	.348	1170	.301	12	-34	-38	1	-2.6
● **HERB BRETT**	Brett, Herbert James "Duke" b: 5/23/1900, Lawrenceville, Va. d: 11/25/74, St.Petersburg, Fla BR/TR, 6', 175 lbs. Deb: 8/8/24																									
1924	Chi-N	0	0	—	1	1	0	0	0	5^1	6	0	7	1	21.9	5.06	77	.300	.481	0	.000	-0	-1	-1	-0	-0.1
1925	Chi-N	1	1	.500	10	1	0	0	0	17^1	12	0	3	6	8.3	3.63	119	.194	.242	0	.000	-0	1	1	1	0.2
Total	2	1	1	.500	11	2	0	0	0	22^2	18	0	10	7	11.5	3.97	106	.220	.312	0	.000	-0	1	1	0	0.1
● **KEN BRETT**	Brett, Kenneth Alven b: 9/18/48, Brooklyn, N.Y. BL/TL, 5'11", 195 lbs. Deb: 9/27/67 F																									
1967	*Bos-A	0	0	—	1	0	0	0	0	2	3	0	0	2	13.5	4.50	77	.375	.375	0	—	0	-0	-0	-0	0.0
1969	Bos-A	2	3	.400	8	8	0	0	0	39^1	41	6	22	23	15.1	5.26	72	.275	.379	3	.300	2	-7	-6	0	-0.5
1970	Bos-A	8	9	.471	41	14	1	0	2	139^1	118	17	79	155	12.9	4.07	97	.223	.327	13	.317	6	-6	-2	1	0.5
1971	Bos-A	0	3	.000	29	2	0	0	1	59	57	7	35	57	14.2	5.34	69	.253	.356	2	.200	-0	-12	-11	-0	-0.6
1972	Mil-A	7	12	.368	26	22	2	1	0	133	121	13	49	74	11.6	4.53	67	.242	.311	10	.227	2	-22	-22	-2	-3.0
1973	Phi-N	13	9	.591	31	25	10	1	0	211^2	206	19	74	111	11.9	3.44	110	.259	.322	20	.250	8	5	8	2	1.9
1974	*Pit-N★	13	9	.591	27	27	10	3	0	191	192	9	52	96	11.6	3.30	104	.257	.308	27	.310	11	7	3	-0	1.5
1975	*Pit-N	9	5	.643	23	16	4	1	0	118	110	10	43	47	11.8	3.36	106	.250	.320	12	.231	4	3	2	0	0.7
1976	NY-A	0	0	—	2	0	0	0	1	2^1	2	0	0	1	7.7	0.00	—	.222	.222	0	—	0	1	1	-0	0.1
	Chi-A	10	12	.455	27	26	16	1	1	200^2	171	5	76	91	11.2	3.32	107	.234	.308	1	.083	-1	4	5	1	0.6
	Yr	10	12	.455	29	26	16	1	2	203	173	5	76	92	11.2	3.28	109	.233	.307	1	.083	-1	5	6	0	0.7
1977	Chi-A	6	4	.600	13	13	2	0	0	82^2	101	10	15	39	12.7	5.01	82	.305	.337	0	—	0	-9	-8	-0	-0.9
	Cal-A	7	10	.412	21	21	5	0	0	142	157	15	38	41	12.5	4.25	92	.287	.337	0	—	0	-3	-5	2	0.0
	Yr	13	14	.481	34	34	7	0	0	224^2	258	25	53	80	12.6	4.53	88	.293	.335	0	—	0	-12	-14	2	-0.9
1978	Cal-A	3	5	.375	31	10	1	1	1	100	100	12	42	43	12.9	4.95	73	.262	.336	0	—	0	-13	-15	2	-0.7
1979	Min-A	0	0	—	9	0	0	0	0	12^2	16	1	6	3	15.6	4.97	88	.320	.393	0	—	0	-1	-1	0	-0.3
	LA-N	4	3	.571	30	0	0	0	2	47	52	1	12	13	12.4	3.45	105	.277	.323	3	.273	1	1	1	2	0.4

YEAR	TM/L	W	L	PCT	G	GS	CG	SH	SV	IP	H	HR	BB	SO	RAT	ERA	ERA+	OAV	OOB	BH	AVG	PB	PR	/A	PD	TPI
1980	KC-A	0	0	—	8	0	0	0	1	13^1	8	0	5	4	9.5	0.00	—	.174	.269	0	—	0	6	6	0	0.1
1981	KC-A	1	1	.500	22	0	0	0	2	32^1	35	2	14	7	13.9	4.18	86	.282	.360	0	—	0	-2	-2	0	-0.1
Total	14	83	85	.494	349	184	51	8	11	1526^1	1490	127	562	807	12.2	3.93	93	.257	.325	91	.262	33	-47	-46	8	-0.3

● MARV BREUER Breuer, Marvin Howard "Baby Face" b: 4/29/14, Rolla, Mo. d: 1/17/91, Rolla, Mo. BR/TR, 6'2", 185 lbs. Deb: 5/4/39

YEAR	TM/L	W	L	PCT	G	GS	CG	SH	SV	IP	H	HR	BB	SO	RAT	ERA	ERA+	OAV	OOB	BH	AVG	PB	PR	/A	PD	TPI
1939	NY-A	0	0	—	1	0	0	0	0	1	2	0	1	0	27.0	9.00	48	.667	.750	0	—	0	-0	-1	0	0.0
1940	NY-A	8	9	.471	27	22	10	0	0	164	175	20	61	71	13.0	4.55	89	.267	.329	2	.037	-5	-3	-10	-1	-1.3
1941	*NY-A	9	7	.563	26	18	7	1	2	141	131	10	49	77	11.6	4.09	96	.243	.308	4	.087	-3	1	-2	-1	-0.6
1942	*NY-A	8	9	.471	27	19	6	0	1	164^1	157	11	37	72	10.7	3.07	112	.252	.295	3	.056	-3	11	7	-2	0.1
1943	NY-A	0	1	.000	5	1	0	0	0	14	22	0	6	6	18.0	8.36	39	.349	.406	1	.333	0	-8	-8	0	-0.5
Total	5	25	26	.490	86	60	23	1	3	484^1	487	41	154	226	12.0	4.03	94	.258	.315	10	.064	-11	0	-13	-3	-2.3

● JIM BREWER Brewer, James Thomas b: 11/17/37, Merced, Cal. d: 11/16/87, Tyler, Tex. BL/TL, 6'2", 195 lbs. Deb: 7/17/60 C

YEAR	TM/L	W	L	PCT	G	GS	CG	SH	SV	IP	H	HR	BB	SO	RAT	ERA	ERA+	OAV	OOB	BH	AVG	PB	PR	/A	PD	TPI
1960	Chi-N	0	3	.000	5	4	0	0	0	21^2	25	2	6	7	13.3	5.82	65	.272	.323	1	.167	0	-5	-5	0	-0.6
1961	Chi-N	1	7	.125	36	11	0	0	0	86^2	116	17	21	57	14.3	5.82	72	.321	.360	4	.182	0	-17	-16	-2	-1.4
1962	Chi-N	0	1	.000	6	1	0	0	0	5^2	10	2	3	1	20.6	9.53	44	.435	.500	0	—	0	-4	-3	0	-0.5
1963	Chi-N	3	2	.600	29	1	0	0	0	49^2	59	10	15	35	13.4	4.89	72	.294	.343	0	.000	0	-9	-8	-1	-0.8
1964	LA-N	4	3	.571	34	5	1	1	1	93	79	5	25	63	10.1	3.00	108	.232	.284	6	.273	2	6	2	-1	0.2
1965	*LA-N	3	2	.600	19	2	0	0	2	49^1	33	1	28	31	11.1	1.82	179	.196	.311	0	.000	-1	9	8	0	0.8
1966	*LA-N	0	2	.000	13	0	0	0	2	22	17	0	11	8	11.5	3.68	90	.221	.318	0	—	0	-0	-1	0	-0.1
1967	LA-N	5	4	.556	30	11	0	0	1	100^2	78	8	31	74	9.8	2.68	116	.218	.283	1	.045	-1	8	5	-1	0.2
1968	LA-N	8	3	.727	54	0	0	0	14	76^1	59	5	33	75	10.8	2.48	112	.219	.304	2	.222	0	4	2	0	0.5
1969	LA-N	7	6	.538	59	0	0	0	20	88^1	71	5	41	92	11.8	2.55	131	.221	.317	1	.091	0	10	8	0	1.5
1970	LA-N	7	6	.538	58	0	0	0	24	89	66	10	33	91	10.0	3.13	122	.207	.281	1	.083	-0	9	7	0	1.3
1971	LA-N	6	5	.545	55	0	0	0	22	81^1	55	4	24	66	8.7	1.88	172	.194	.257	3	.333	1	14	12	1	2.6
1972	LA-N	8	7	.533	51	0	0	0	17	78^1	41	6	25	69	7.8	1.26	264	.157	.236	0	.000	0	19	18	-0	4.5
1973	LA-N★	6	8	.429	56	0	0	0	20	71^2	58	8	25	56	10.4	3.01	114	.229	.299	2	.400	1	5	3	0	0.9
1974	*LA-N	4	4	.500	24	0	0	0	0	39^1	29	5	10	26	8.9	2.52	135	.207	.260	0	.000	-0	5	4	-1	0.7
1975	LA-N	3	1	.750	21	0	0	0	2	33	44	2	12	21	15.5	5.18	66	.333	.393	0	.000	-0	-6	-7	0	-0.8
	Cal-A	1	0	1.000	21	0	0	0	5	34^2	38	2	11	22	12.7	1.82	195	.279	.333	0	—	0	8	7	-1	0.9
1976	Cal-A	3	1	.750	13	0	0	0	2	20	20	0	6	16	11.7	2.70	123	.256	.310	0	—	0	2	1	0	0.3
Total	17	69	65	.515	584	35	1	1	132	1040^2	898	92	360	810	11.0	3.07	111	.236	.303	21	.150	1	59	38	-4	10.2

● JACK BREWER Brewer, John Herndon "Buddy" b: 7/21/19, Los Angeles, Cal. BR/TR, 6'2", 170 lbs. Deb: 7/15/44

YEAR	TM/L	W	L	PCT	G	GS	CG	SH	SV	IP	H	HR	BB	SO	RAT	ERA	ERA+	OAV	OOB	BH	AVG	PB	PR	/A	PD	TPI
1944	NY-N	1	4	.200	14	7	2	0	0	55	66	8	16	21	13.9	5.56	66	.288	.343	4	.211	0	-12	-12	-1	-1.0
1945	NY-N	8	6	.571	28	21	8	0	0	159^2	162	14	58	49	12.6	3.83	102	.260	.326	10	.179	-1	-1	1	-3	-0.3
1946	NY-N	0	0	—	1	0	0	0	0	2	3	0	2	3	22.5	13.50	25	.333	.455	0	—	0	-2	-2	-0	0.0
Total	3	9	10	.474	43	28	10	0	0	216^2	231	22	76	73	13.0	4.36	88	.268	.332	14	.187	-1	-15	-12	-3	-1.3

● ROD BREWER Brewer, Rodney Lee b: 2/24/66, Eustis, Fla. BL/TL, 6'3", 210 lbs. Deb: 9/5/90 ♦

YEAR	TM/L	W	L	PCT	G	GS	CG	SH	SV	IP	H	HR	BB	SO	RAT	ERA	ERA+	OAV	OOB	BH	AVG	PB	PR	/A	PD	TPI
1993	StL-N	0	0	—	1	0	0	0	0	1	3	1	2	1	45.0	45.00	9	.500	.625	42	.286	0	-5	-5	0	0.0

● TOM BREWER Brewer, Thomas Austin b: 9/3/31, Wadesboro, N.C. BR/TR, 6'1", 175 lbs. Deb: 4/18/54

YEAR	TM/L	W	L	PCT	G	GS	CG	SH	SV	IP	H	HR	BB	SO	RAT	ERA	ERA+	OAV	OOB	BH	AVG	PB	PR	/A	PD	TPI
1954	Bos-A	10	9	.526	33	23	7	0	0	162^2	152	15	95	69	14.1	4.65	88	.249	.356	16	.267	3	-17	-10	-2	-1.0
1955	Bos-A	11	10	.524	31	28	9	2	0	192^2	198	21	87	91	13.7	4.20	102	.263	.346	11	.151	-2	-5	2	3	0.3
1956	Bos-A★	19	9	.679	32	32	15	4	0	244^1	200	14	112	127	11.7	3.50	132	.220	.309	28	.298	4	18	30	4	4.1
1957	Bos-A	16	13	.552	32	32	15	2	0	238^1	225	24	93	128	12.3	3.85	103	.250	.325	19	.202	-1	-2	4	6	0.9
1958	Bos-A	12	12	.500	33	32	10	1	0	227^1	227	21	93	124	13.0	3.72	108	.259	.335	16	.195	-0	1	7	4	1.1
1959	Bos-A	10	12	.455	36	32	11	3	2	215^1	219	14	88	121	12.9	3.76	108	.265	.338	8	.111	-4	2	7	4	0.7
1960	Bos-A	10	15	.400	34	29	8	1	1	186^2	220	13	72	60	14.4	4.82	84	.301	.368	12	.194	0	-20	-16	3	-1.7
1961	Bos-A	3	2	.600	10	9	0	0	0	42	37	4	29	13	14.1	3.43	122	.242	.363	4	.286	1	3	3	1	0.6
Total	8	91	82	.526	241	217	75	13	3	1509^1	1478	126	669	733	13.1	4.00	104	.257	.338	114	.207	1	-19	27	22	5.0

● BILLY BREWER Brewer, William Robert b: 4/15/68, Fort Worth, Tex. BL/TL, 6'1", 175 lbs. Deb: 4/8/93

YEAR	TM/L	W	L	PCT	G	GS	CG	SH	SV	IP	H	HR	BB	SO	RAT	ERA	ERA+	OAV	OOB	BH	AVG	PB	PR	/A	PD	TPI
1993	KC-A	2	2	.500	46	0	0	0	0	39	31	6	20	28	11.8	3.46	132	.230	.329	0	—	0	4	5	-1	0.0
1994	KC-A	4	1	.800	50	0	0	0	3	38^2	28	4	16	25	10.7	2.56	195	.207	.301	0	—	0	10	10	0	1.3
1995	KC-A	2	4	.333	48	0	0	0	0	45^1	54	9	20	31	15.1	5.56	86	.290	.365	0	—	0	-4	-4	-0	-0.5
1996	NY-A	1	0	1.000	4	0	0	0	0	5^2	7	0	8	8	23.8	9.53	52	.292	.469	0	—	0	-3	-3	0	-0.4
1997	Oak-A	0	0	—	3	0	0	0	0	2	4	1	2	1	27.0	13.50	33	.444	.545	0	—	0	-2	-2	-0	0.0
	Phi-N	1	2	.333	25	0	0	0	0	22	15	2	11	16	10.6	3.27	130	.188	.286	0	.000	-0	2	2	0	0.3
1998	Phi-N	0	1	.000	2	0	0	0	0	0^1	3	0	2	0	135.0	108.00	4	.750	.833	0	—	0	-4	-4	0	-4.0
Total	6	10	10	.500	178	0	0	0	3	153	142	22	79	109	13.2	4.41	107	.248	.343	0	.000	-0	3	5	-0	-3.3

● JAMIE BREWINGTON Brewington, Jamie Chancellor b: 9/28/71, Greenville, N.C. BR/TR, 6'4", 180 lbs. Deb: 7/24/95

YEAR	TM/L	W	L	PCT	G	GS	CG	SH	SV	IP	H	HR	BB	SO	RAT	ERA	ERA+	OAV	OOB	BH	AVG	PB	PR	/A	PD	TPI
1995	SF-N	6	4	.600	13	13	0	0	0	75^1	68	8	45	45	14.0	4.54	90	.245	.359	5	.217	0	-3	-4	-0	-0.4

● ALAN BRICE Brice, Alan Healey b: 10/1/37, New York, N.Y. BR/TR, 6'5", 215 lbs. Deb: 9/22/61

YEAR	TM/L	W	L	PCT	G	GS	CG	SH	SV	IP	H	HR	BB	SO	RAT	ERA	ERA+	OAV	OOB	BH	AVG	PB	PR	/A	PD	TPI
1961	Chi-A	0	1	.000	3	0	0	0	0	3^1	4	0	3	3	18.9	0.00	—	.308	.438	0	—	0	1	1	-0	0.4

● RALPH BRICKNER Brickner, Ralph Harold "Brick" b: 5/2/25, Cincinnati, Ohio d: 5/9/94, Port Jefferson, N.Y. BR/TR, 6'3.5", 215 lbs. Deb: 5/4/52

YEAR	TM/L	W	L	PCT	G	GS	CG	SH	SV	IP	H	HR	BB	SO	RAT	ERA	ERA+	OAV	OOB	BH	AVG	PB	PR	/A	PD	TPI
1952	Bos-A	3	1	.750	14	1	0	0	1	33	32	1	11	9	11.7	2.18	181	.264	.326	2	.250	0	5	6	-1	0.8

● MARSHALL BRIDGES Bridges, Marshall "Sheriff" b: 6/2/31, Jackson, Miss. d: 9/3/90, Jackson, Miss. BB/TL, 6'1", 180 lbs. Deb: 6/17/59

YEAR	TM/L	W	L	PCT	G	GS	CG	SH	SV	IP	H	HR	BB	SO	RAT	ERA	ERA+	OAV	OOB	BH	AVG	PB	PR	/A	PD	TPI
1959	StL-N	6	3	.667	27	4	1	0	1	76	67	10	37	76	12.3	4.26	99	.240	.329	5	.217	2	-3	-0	-2	0.0
1960	StL-N	2	2	.500	20	1	0	0	1	31^1	33	2	16	27	14.4	3.45	119	.266	.355	0	.000	-0	1	2	-0	0.2
	Cin-N	4	0	1.000	14	0	0	0	2	25^1	14	1	7	26	7.5	1.07	359	.161	.223	1	.250	0	8	8	-0	1.4
	Yr	6	2	.750	34	1	0	0	3	56^2	47	3	23	53	11.1	2.38	167	.220	.295	1	.100	-0	9	10	-1	1.6
1961	Cin-N	0	1	.000	13	0	0	0	0	20^2	26	4	11	17	16.5	7.84	52	.317	.404	0	.000	-0	-9	-9	-0	-0.4
1962	*NY-A	8	4	.667	52	0	0	0	18	71^2	49	4	48	66	12.2	3.14	119	.194	.323	0	.000	-2	7	5	2	1.0
1963	NY-A	2	0	1.000	23	0	0	0	1	33	27	2	30	35	15.8	3.82	92	.237	.400	0	—	0	-1	-1	2	0.1
1964	Was-A	0	3	.000	17	0	0	0	2	30	37	3	17	16	16.2	5.70	65	.303	.388	0	.000	-0	-7	-7	-0	-0.7
1965	Was-A	1	2	.333	40	0	0	0	0	57^1	62	3	25	39	13.7	2.67	130	.268	.340	1	.143	0	5	5	-0	0.3
Total	7	23	15	.605	206	5	1	0	25	345^1	315	29	191	302	13.3	3.75	102	.244	.343	7	.119	-0	1	3	1	1.9

● TOMMY BRIDGES Bridges, Thomas Jefferson Davis b: 12/28/06, Gordonsville, Tenn d: 4/19/68, Nashville, Tenn. BR/TR, 5'10.5", 155 lbs. Deb: 8/13/30 C

YEAR	TM/L	W	L	PCT	G	GS	CG	SH	SV	IP	H	HR	BB	SO	RAT	ERA	ERA+	OAV	OOB	BH	AVG	PB	PR	/A	PD	TPI
1930	Det-A	3	2	.600	8	5	2	0	0	37^2	28	4	23	17	12.2	4.06	118	.215	.333	3	.300	1	2	3	-0	0.4
1931	Det-A	8	16	.333	35	23	8	2	0	173	182	13	108	105	15.1	4.99	92	.263	.363	8	.148	-2	-12	-8	-1	-1.2
1932	Det-A	14	12	.538	34	26	10	**4**	1	201	174	14	119	108	13.2	3.36	140	.233	.339	11	.164	-1	25	30	-1	3.2
1933	Det-A	14	12	.538	33	28	17	2	2	233	192	8	110	120	11.9	3.09	140	**.226**	.319	16	.205	2	31	32	1	3.5
1934	*Det-A☆	22	11	.667	36	35	23	3	1	275	249	16	104	151	11.7	3.67	120	.241	.312	12	.122	-4	25	22	-2	1.7
1935	*Det-A☆	21	10	.677	36	34	23	4	1	274^1	277	22	113	**163**	12.9	3.51	119	.259	.332	26	.239	3	29	20	-1	2.1
1936	Det-A†	**23**	11	.676	39	38	26	5	0	294^2	289	21	115	**175**	12.5	3.60	137	.255	.326	25	.212	0	47	44	2	4.4
1937	Det-A★	15	12	.556	34	31	18	3	0	245^1	267	15	91	138	13.2	4.07	115	.274	.338	23	.240	2	15	16	1	1.8
1938	Det-A	13	9	.591	25	20	13	0	1	151	171	14	58	101	13.8	4.59	109	.287	.353	7	.130	-1	3	7	-1	0.6
1939	Det-A★	17	7	.708	29	26	16	2	2	198	186	11	61	129	11.5	3.50	140	.243	.304	14	.197	0	25	31	-0	3.3
1940	*Det-A☆	12	9	.571	29	28	12	2	0	197^2	171	11	88	133	11.8	3.37	141	.229	.311	12	.176	-2	22	30	-1	2.6
1941	Det-A	9	12	.429	25	22	10	1	0	147^2	128	10	70	90	12.1	3.41	133	.233	.320	4	.085	-3	12	19	2	2.3
1942	Det-A	9	7	.563	23	22	11	2	1	174	164	6	61	97	11.8	2.74	144	.246	.313	6	.095	-2	18	23	1	1.9
1943	Det-A	12	7	.632	25	22	11	3	0	191^2	159	9	61	124	10.3	2.39	147	.226	.287	14	.219	2	19	24	-1	2.6
1945	*Det-A	1	0	1.000	4	1	0	0	0	11	14	2	2	6	13.1	3.27	107	.311	.340	0	.000	-0	0	0	1	0.0
1946	Det-A	1	1	.500	9	1	0	0	1	21^1	24	5	8	17	13.9	5.91	62	.279	.347	0	.000	0	-6	-5	0	-0.5
Total	16	194	138	.584	424	362	200	33	10	2826^1	2675	181	1192	1674	12.4	3.57	126	.248	.325	181	.180	-5	256	291	-3	28.7

YEAR TM/L	W	L	PCT	G	GS	CG	SH	SV	IP	H	HR	BB	SO	RAT	ERA	ERA+	OAV	OOB	BH	AVG	PB	PR	/A	PD	TPI
● BUTTONS BRIGGS Briggs, Herbert Theodore b: 7/8/1875, Poughkeepsie, N.Y. d: 2/18/11, Cleveland, Ohio BR/TR, 6'1", 180 lbs. Deb: 4/23/1896																									
1896 Chi-N	12	8	.600	26	21	19	0	1	194	202	6	108	84	15.1	4.31	105	.266	.368	10	.128	-6	1	5	-3	-0.4
1897 Chi-N	4	17	.190	22	22	21	0	0	186^2	246	6	85	60	16.4	5.26	85	.315	.388	13	.160	-6	-20	-16	-1	-2.0
1898 Chi-N	1	3	.250	4	4	3	0	0	30	38	0	10	14	14.7	5.70	63	.306	.363	6	.429	2	-7	-7	-0	-0.6
1904 Chi-N	19	11	.633	34	30	28	3	3	277	252	3	77	112	10.9	2.05	130	.246	.304	16	.170	-0	21	19	-4	1.6
1905 Chi-N	8	8	.500	20	20	13	5	0	168	141	1	52	68	10.7	2.14	139	.237	.304	3	.053	-4	16	16	-2	0.7
Total 5	44	47	.484	106	97	84	8	4	855^2	879	16	332	338	13.1	3.41	104	.268	.342	48	.148	-15	12	14	-10	-0.7
● JOHN BRIGGS Briggs, Jonathan Tift b: 1/24/34, Natoma, Cal. BR/TR, 5'10", 175 lbs. Deb: 4/17/56																									
1956 Chi-N	0	0	—	3	0	0	0	0	5^1	5	1	4	1	20.3	1.69	223	.238	.429	0	—	0	1	1	0	0.0
1957 Chi-N	0	1	.000	3	0	0	0	0	4^1	7	2	3	1	20.8	12.46	31	.368	.455	0	—	0	-4	-4	-0	-0.8
1958 Chi-N	5	5	.500	20	17	3	1	0	95^2	99	12	45	46	13.6	4.52	87	.270	.352	9	.257	2	-6	-6	-1	-0.5
1959 Cle-A	0	1	.000	4	1	0	0	0	12^2	12	1	3	5	10.7	2.13	173	.245	.288	0	.000	-0	2	2	-0	0.1
1960 Cle-A	4	2	.667	21	2	0	0	1	36^1	32	4	15	19	11.9	4.46	84	.250	.333	1	.125	-0	-2	-3	-1	-0.6
KC-A	0	2	.000	8	1	0	0	0	11^1	19	3	12	8	24.6	12.71	31	.380	.500	0	.000	-0	-11	-11	-0	-1.6
Yr	4	4	.500	29	3	0	0	1	47^2	51	7	27	27	14.7	6.42	59	.282	.375	1	.091	-1	-13	-14	-1	-2.2
Total 5	9	11	.450	59	21	3	1	1	165^2	174	23	82	80	14.2	5.00	77	.275	.363	10	.208	1	-20	-21	-2	-3.4
● NELSON BRILES Briles, Nelson Kelley b: 8/5/43, Dorris, Cal. BR/TR, 5'11", 200 lbs. Deb: 4/19/65																									
1965 StL-N	3	3	.500	37	2	0	0	4	82^1	79	4	26	52	12.1	3.50	110	.258	.328	2	.133	-0	0	3	-1	0.1
1966 StL-N	4	15	.211	49	17	0	0	6	154	162	14	54	100	13.0	3.21	112	.279	.348	3	.079	-2	7	6	1	0.7
1967 *StL-N	14	5	.737	49	14	4	2	6	155^1	139	8	40	94	10.7	2.43	135	.236	.290	6	.150	0	16	15	-2	1.8
1968 *StL-N	19	11	.633	33	33	13	4	0	243^2	251	18	55	141	11.6	2.81	103	.266	.311	11	.138	1	5	2	-2	0.1
1969 StL-N	15	13	.536	36	33	10	3	0	227^2	218	17	63	126	11.2	3.52	102	.251	.303	8	.105	-1	2	1	-1	-0.1
1970 StL-N	6	7	.462	30	19	1	1	0	106^2	129	14	36	59	14.1	6.24	66	.297	.353	7	.179	1	-26	-25	-2	-2.7
1971 *Pit-N	8	4	.667	37	14	4	2	1	136	131	12	35	76	11.2	3.04	111	.250	.301	10	.256	4	6	5	-1	0.7
1972 *Pit-N	14	11	.560	28	27	9	2	0	195^2	185	14	43	120	10.5	3.08	108	.249	.291	11	.157	-0	8	5	-1	0.6
1973 Pit-N	14	13	.519	33	33	7	1	0	218^2	201	19	51	94	10.4	2.84	124	.244	.288	14	.194	3	20	16	0	2.3
1974 KC-A	5	7	.417	18	17	3	0	0	103	118	9	21	41	12.3	4.02	95	.293	.331	0	—	0	-5	-2	-1	-0.7
1975 KC-A	6	6	.500	24	16	3	0	2	112	127	19	25	73	12.6	4.26	90	.285	.330	0	—	0	-6	-5	0	-0.6
1976 Tex-A	11	9	.550	32	31	7	1	1	210	224	17	47	98	11.7	3.26	110	.273	.314	0	—	0	6	8	-3	0.3
1977 Tex-A	6	4	.600	28	15	2	1	1	108^1	114	13	30	57	12.5	4.24	96	.275	.333	0	—	0	-2	-2	-1	-0.3
Bal-A	0	0	—	2	0	0	0	1	4	5	2	0	2	11.3	6.75	56	.294	.294	0	—	0	-1	-1	-0	0.0
Yr	6	4	.600	30	15	2	1	2	112^1	119	15	30	59	11.9	4.33	94	.271	.318	0	—	0	-3	-3	-1	-0.3
1978 Bal-A	4	4	.500	16	8	1	0	0	54^1	58	6	21	30	13.4	4.64	75	.279	.351	0	—	-0	-5	-7	-1	-1.0
Total 14	129	112	.535	452	279	64	17	22	2111^2	2141	186	547	1163	11.7	3.44	102	.264	.314	72	.154	5	25	19	-14	1.2
● FRANK BRILL Brill, Francis Hasbrouck (b: Francis Hasbrouck Briell) b: 3/30/1864, Astoria, N.Y. d: 11/19/44, Flushing, N.Y. BR/TR, 5'8", 155 lbs. Deb: 6/23/1884																									
1884 Det-N	2	10	.167	12	12	12	1	0	103	148	7	26	18	15.2	5.50	53	.312	.348	6	.136	-3	-29	-30	-2	-2.9
● JIM BRILLHEART Brillheart, James Benson b: 9/28/03, Dublin, Va. d: 9/2/72, Radford, Va. BR/TL, 5'11", 170 lbs. Deb: 4/17/22																									
1922 Was-A	4	6	.400	31	10	3	0	1	119^2	120	3	72	47	15.0	3.61	107	.275	.388	3	.083	-4	6	3	-2	-0.3
1923 Was-A	0	1	.000	12	0	0	0	0	18	27	1	12	8	20.0	7.00	54	.360	.455	0	.000	-0	-6	-6	0	-0.3
1927 Chi-N	4	2	.667	32	12	4	0	0	128^2	140	4	38	36	12.7	4.13	94	.286	.343	1	.023	-5	-3	-4	-1	-0.8
1931 Bos-A	0	0	—	11	1	0	0	0	19^2	27	2	15	7	19.2	5.49	78	.325	.429	2	.500	2	-2	-3	1	0.2
Total 4	8	9	.471	86	23	7	0	1	286	314	10	137	98	14.6	4.19	93	.290	.376	6	.070	-8	-6	-9	-2	-1.2
● BRAD BRINK Brink, Bradford Albert b: 1/20/65, Roseville, Cal. BR/TR, 6'2", 195 lbs. Deb: 5/17/92																									
1992 Phi-N	0	4	.000	8	7	0	0	0	41^1	53	2	13	16	14.6	4.14	84	.308	.360	1	.083	-0	-3	-3	-0	-0.3
1993 Phi-N	0	0	—	2	0	0	0	0	6	3	1	3	8	9.0	3.00	132	.143	.250	0	.000	-0	1	1	-0	0.0
1994 SF-N	0	0	—	4	0	0	0	0	8^1	4	1	4	3	8.6	1.08	371	.143	.250	0	.000	-0	3	3	0	0.0
Total 3	0	4	.000	14	7	0	0	0	55^2	60	4	20	27	13.1	3.56	102	.271	.335	1	.071	-1	1	0	-0	-0.3
● JOHN BRISCOE Briscoe, John Eric b: 9/22/67, LaGrange, Ill. BR/TR, 6'3", 185 lbs. Deb: 4/18/91																									
1991 Oak-A	0	0	—	11	0	0	0	0	14	12	3	10	9	14.1	7.07	54	.235	.361	0	—	0	-5	-5	-0	0.3
1992 Oak-A	0	1	.000	2	2	0	0	0	7	12	0	9	4	27.0	6.43	58	.400	.538	0	—	0	-2	-2	-0	-0.2
1993 Oak-A	1	0	1.000	17	0	0	0	0	24^2	26	2	26	24	19.0	8.03	51	.277	.433	0	—	0	-10	-11	0	0.1
1994 Oak-A	4	2	.667	37	0	0	0	1	49^1	31	7	39	45	13.0	4.01	110	.185	.341	0	—	0	4	2	-1	0.2
1995 Oak-A	0	1	.000	16	0	0	0	0	18^1	25	4	21	19	23.6	8.35	54	.347	.505	0	—	0	-7	-8	0	-0.2
1996 Oak-A	0	1	.000	17	0	0	0	1	26^1	18	2	24	14	14.4	3.76	131	.205	.375	0	—	0	4	3	-0	0.1
Total 6	5	5	.500	100	2	0	0	2	139^2	124	18	129	115	16.5	5.67	77	.247	.403	0	—	0	-16	-20	-1	0.3
● LOU BRISSIE Brissie, Leland Victor b: 6/5/24, Anderson, S.C. BL/TL, 6'4", 215 lbs. Deb: 9/28/47																									
1947 Phi-A	0	1	.000	1	1	0	0	0	7	9	1	5	4	18.0	6.43	59	.310	.412	0	.000	-0	-2	-2	0	-0.3
1948 Phi-A	14	10	.583	39	25	11	0	5	194	202	6	95	127	13.9	4.13	104	.269	.352	18	.237	0	3	3	-2	0.2
1949 Phi-A★	16	11	.593	34	29	18	0	3	229^1	220	20	118	118	13.5	4.28	96	.251	.344	24	.267	3	-2	-4	-4	-0.5
1950 Phi-A	7	19	.269	46	31	15	2	8	246	237	22	117	101	13.1	4.02	113	.253	.338	15	.172	-3	15	14	-0	1.1
1951 Phi-A	0	2	.000	2	2	0	0	0	13^1	20	0	8	3	18.9	6.75	63	.357	.438	1	.200	-0	-4	-4	-0	-0.5
Cle-A	4	3	.571	54	4	1	0	9	112^1	90	5	61	50	12.3	3.20	118	.223	.329	6	.261	0	11	7	-2	0.4
Yr	4	5	.444	56	6	1	0	9	125^2	110	5	69	53	13.0	3.58	107	.239	.342	7	.250	0	8	4	-2	-0.1
1952 Cle-A	3	2	.600	42	1	0	0	2	82^2	68	5	34	28	11.1	3.48	96	.221	.299	3	.250	1	2	-1	1	0.1
1953 Cle-A	0	0	—	16	0	0	0	2	13	21	2	13	5	23.5	7.62	49	.389	.507	0	—	0	-5	-6	-0	-0.2
Total 7	44	48	.478	234	93	45	2	29	897^2	867	61	451	436	13.4	4.07	102	.254	.343	67	.227	1	19	8	-7	0.3
● JIM BRITT Britt, James Edward b: 2/25/1856, Brooklyn, N.Y. d: 2/28/23, San Francisco, Cal Deb: 5/2/1872																									
1872 Atl-n	9	28	.243	37	37	37	0	0	336	570	6	19	13	15.8	4.34	104	.328	.335	40	.256	-8	-26	6		-0.1
1873 Atl-n	17	36	.321	54	54	**51**	1	0	480^2	696	6	40	15	13.8	3.89	78	.300	.312	47	.196	-3	-34	-46		-3.5
Total 2 n	26	64	.289	91	91	88	1	0	816^2	1266	12	59	28	14.6	4.08	74	.312	.322	87	.220	-11	-75	-94		-3.6
● JACK BRITTIN Brittin, John Albert b: 3/4/24, Athens, Ill. d: 1/5/94, Springfield, Ill. BR/TR, 5'11", 175 lbs. Deb: 9/15/50																									
1950 Phi-N	0	0	—	3	0	0	0	0	4	2	0	3	3	11.3	4.50	90	.143	.294	0	—	0	-0	-0	0	0.0
1951 Phi-N	0	0	—	3	0	0	0	0	4	5	0	6	3	24.8	9.00	43	.294	.478	0	—	0	-2	-2	0	0.0
Total 2	0	0	—	6	0	0	0	0	8	7	0	9	6	18.0	6.75	58	.226	.400	0	—	0	-2	-2	0	0.0
● JIM BRITTON Britton, James Allan b: 3/25/44, N.Tonawanda, N.Y. BR/TR, 6'5", 225 lbs. Deb: 9/20/67																									
1967 Atl-N	0	2	.000	2	2	0	0	0	13^1	15	2	2	4	11.5	6.08	55	.278	.304	0	.000	-0	-4	-4	-0	-0.6
1968 Atl-N	4	6	.400	34	9	2	2	3	90	81	1	34	61	11.7	3.10	97	.245	.320	3	.143	-0	-1	-1	-0	-0.2
1969 *Atl-N	7	5	.583	24	13	2	1	1	88	69	10	49	60	12.1	3.78	95	.218	.323	4	.190	0	-2	-2	-1	-0.3
1971 Mon-N	2	3	.400	16	6	0	0	0	45^2	49	10	27	23	15.4	5.72	62	.274	.375	0	.000	-1	-11	-11	-1	-1.3
Total 4	13	16	.448	76	30	4	3	4	237	214	23	112	148	12.5	4.03	83	.243	.332	7	.127	-2	-18	-18	-2	-2.4
● TONY BRIZZOLARA Brizzolara, Anthony John b: 1/14/57, Santa Monica, Cal. BR/TR, 6'5", 215 lbs. Deb: 5/19/79																									
1979 Atl-N	6	9	.400	20	19	2	0	0	107^1	133	6	33	64	14.2	5.28	77	.303	.356	1	.029	-3	-18	-15	0	-2.1
1983 Atl-N	1	0	1.000	14	0	0	0	1	20^1	22	2	6	17	12.4	3.54	109	.278	.329	0	—	0	0	1	-0	0.0
1984 Atl-N	1	2	.333	10	4	0	0	0	29	33	4	13	17	14.3	5.28	73	.284	.357	0	.000	-1	-5	-5	0	-0.5
Total 3	8	11	.421	44	23	2	0	1	156^2	188	12	52	98	14.0	5.06	79	.297	.353	1	.024	-4	-24	-19	-0	-2.6
● JOHNNY BROACA Broaca, John Joseph b: 10/3/09, Lawrence, Mass. d: 5/16/85, Lawrence, Mass. BR/TR, 5'11", 190 lbs. Deb: 6/2/34																									
1934 NY-A	12	9	.571	26	24	13	1	0	177^1	203	9	65	74	13.7	4.16	98	.284	.344	2	.030	-7	7	-2	-2	-1.0
1935 NY-A	15	7	.682	29	27	14	2	0	201	199	16	79	78	12.4	3.58	113	.254	.323	12	.150	-4	19	10	-3	0.3
1936 NY-A	12	7	.632	37	27	12	1	3	206	235	16	66	84	13.2	4.24	110	.284	.337	9	.110	-6	18	10	-2	-0.1

YEAR	TM/L	W	L	PCT	G	GS	CG	SH	SV	IP	H	HR	BB	SO	RAT	ERA	ERA+	OAV	OOB	BH	AVG	PB	PR	/A	PD	TPI
1937	NY-A	1	4	.200	7	6	3	0	0	44	58	5	17	9	15.3	4.70	94	.324	.383	0	.000	-2	-0	-1	-1	-0.4
1939	Cle-A	4	2	.667	22	2	0	0	0	46	53	5	28	13	15.8	4.70	94	.288	.382	0	.000	-2	-0	-1	-0	-0.3
Total	5	44	29	.603	121	86	42	4	3	674^1	748	51	255	258	13.4	4.08	105	.278	.341	23	.091	-21	44	15	-8	-1.5
● **PETE BROBERG**	Broberg, Peter Sven b: 3/2/50, W.Palm Beach, Fla. BR/TR, 6′3″, 205 lbs. Deb: 6/20/71																									
1971	Was-A	5	9	.357	18	18	7	1	0	124^2	104	10	53	89	12.1	3.47	95	.228	.322	5	.114	0	-0	-2	-1	-0.3
1972	Tex-A	5	12	.294	39	25	3	2	1	176^1	153	14	85	133	12.8	4.29	70	.237	.338	4	.078	-2	-24	-25	1	-2.5
1973	Tex-A	5	9	.357	22	20	6	1	0	118^2	130	8	66	57	15.2	5.61	66	.283	.379	0	—	0	-24	-25	-0	-2.6
1974	Tex-A	0	4	.000	12	2	0	0	0	29	29	7	13	15	13.3	8.07	44	.264	.347	0	—	0	-14	-15	-0	-1.6
1975	Mil-A	14	16	.467	38	32	7	2	0	220^1	219	17	106	100	13.9	4.13	93	.263	.357	0	—	0	-9	-7	-0	-0.9
1976	Mil-A	1	7	.125	20	11	1	0	0	92^1	99	5	72	28	17.1	4.97	70	.281	.409	0	—	0	-15	-15	-1	-1.3
1977	Chi-N	1	2	.333	22	0	0	0	0	36	34	8	18	20	13.0	4.75	92	.256	.344	0	.000	-1	-3	-1	0	-0.2
1978	Oak-A	10	12	.455	35	26	2	0	0	165^2	174	16	65	94	13.1	4.62	79	.269	.338	0	—	0	-16	-18	1	-2.0
Total	8	41	71	.366	206	134	26	6	1	963	942	85	478	536	13.8	4.56	78	.259	.353	9	.089	-3	-105	-109	-0	-11.4
● **DOUG BROCAIL**	Brocail, Douglas Keith b: 5/16/67, Clearfield, Pa. BL/TR, 6′5″, 235 lbs. Deb: 9/8/92																									
1992	SD-N	0	0	—	3	3	0	0	0	14	17	2	5	15	14.1	6.43	56	.298	.355	1	.200	0	-5	-4	-0	0.0
1993	SD-N	4	13	.235	24	24	0	0	0	128^1	143	16	42	70	13.3	4.56	91	.282	.342	6	.182	-0	-7	-6	0	-0.7
1994	SD-N	0	0	—	12	0	0	0	0	17	21	1	5	11	14.8	5.82	71	.304	.368	0	.000	-0	-3	-3	-0	0.0
1995	Hou-N	6	4	.600	36	7	0	0	1	77^1	87	10	22	39	13.2	4.19	92	.280	.335	4	.250	1	-0	-3	-0	-0.2
1996	Hou-N	1	5	.167	23	4	0	0	0	53	58	7	23	34	14.1	4.58	84	.289	.367	0	.000	-1	-2	-4	-0	-0.6
1997	Det-A	3	4	.429	61	4	0	0	2	78	74	10	36	60	13.0	3.23	142	.256	.345	0	—	0	12	12	1	1.0
1998	Det-A	5	2	.714	60	0	0	0	0	62^2	47	2	18	55	9.5	2.73	173	.211	.273	0	—	0	13	14	0	1.4
Total	7	19	28	.404	219	42	0	0	3	430^1	447	48	151	284	12.8	4.10	102	.270	.337	11	.164	-0	8	5	0	0.9
● **CHRIS BROCK**	Brock, Terence Christopher b: 2/5/70, Orlando, Fla. BR/TR, 6′, 175 lbs. Deb: 6/11/97																									
1997	Atl-N	0	0	—	7	6	0	0	0	30^2	34	2	19	16	15.6	5.58	75	.288	.387	1	.100	-0	-5	-5	1	0.1
1998	SF-N	0	0	—	13	0	0	0	0	27^2	31	3	7	19	12.4	3.90	104	.279	.322	1	.250	0	1	0	-1	0.0
Total	2	0	0	—	20	6	0	0	0	58^1	65	5	26	35	14.0	4.78	86	.284	.357	2	.143	-0	-4	-4	1	0.1
● **LEW BROCKETT**	Brockett, Lewis Albert "King" b: 7/23/1880, Brownsville, Ill. d: 9/19/60, Norris City, Ill. BR/TR, 5′10.5″, 168 lbs. Deb: 4/25/07																									
1907	NY-A	1	2	.333	8	4	1	0	0	46^1	58	1	26	13	16.7	6.22	45	.309	.398	4	.182	-0	-19	-18	-1	-1.2
1909	NY-A	10	8	.556	26	18	10	3	1	170	148	3	59	70	11.3	2.12	119	.245	.318	17	.283	3	7	8	4	1.7
1911	NY-A	2	4	.333	16	8	2	0	0	75^1	73	3	39	25	14.0	4.66	77	.256	.356	12	.308	2	-11	-9	1	-0.4
Total	3	13	14	.481	50	30	13	3	1	291^2	279	7	124	108	12.8	3.43	83	.259	.343	33	.273	5	-23	-19	3	0.1
● **DICK BRODOWSKI**	Brodowski, Richard Stanley b: 7/26/32, Bayonne, N.J. BR/TR, 6′2″, 190 lbs. Deb: 6/15/52																									
1952	Bos-A	5	5	.500	20	12	4	0	0	114^2	111	12	50	42	12.9	4.40	90	.252	.333	8	.205	1	-9	-6	0	-0.4
1955	Bos-A	1	0	1.000	16	0	0	0	0	32	36	5	25	10	17.4	5.63	76	.295	.419	5	.500	3	-6	-5	1	0.2
1956	Was-A	0	3	.000	7	3	1	0	0	17^2	31	5	12	8	21.9	9.17	47	.397	.478	0	.000	-1	-10	-10	0	-1.3
1957	Was-A	0	1	.000	6	0	0	0	0	11^1	12	2	10	4	18.3	11.12	35	.261	.404	0	.000	-0	-9	-9	0	-0.7
1958	Cle-A	1	0	1.000	5	0	0	0	0	10	3	0	6	12	8.1	0.00	—	.100	.250	0	.000	-0	4	4	-0	0.4
1959	Cle-A	2	2	.500	18	0	0	0	5	30	19	3	21	9	12.9	1.80	205	.181	.333	2	.333	0	7	6	-1	1.0
Total	6	9	11	.450	72	15	5	0	5	215^2	212	27	124	85	14.4	4.76	84	.258	.361	15	.242	3	-23	-19	0	-0.8
● **ERNIE BROGLIO**	Broglio, Ernest Gilbert b: 8/27/35, Berkeley, Cal. BR/TR, 6′2″, 200 lbs. Deb: 4/11/59																									
1959	StL-N	7	12	.368	35	25	6	3	0	181^1	174	20	89	133	13.1	4.72	90	.250	.335	6	.098	-3	-15	-10	1	-1.1
1960	StL-N	**21**	9	**.700**	52	24	9	3	0	226^1	172	18	100	188	10.9	2.74	**149**	.213	.301	14	.206	2	26	**34**	1	4.8
1961	StL-N	9	12	.429	29	26	7	2	0	174^2	166	19	75	113	12.5	4.12	107	.248	.325	9	.145	-2	-2	5	-1	0.3
1962	StL-N	12	9	.571	34	30	11	4	0	222^1	193	22	93	132	11.7	3.00	143	.237	.316	10	.139	-2	23	31	1	2.6
1963	StL-N	18	8	.692	39	35	11	5	0	250	202	24	90	145	10.7	2.99	119	.216	.287	10	.112	-3	8	16	0	1.3
1964	StL-N	3	5	.375	11	11	3	1	0	69^1	65	7	26	36	11.9	3.50	109	.247	.317	2	.095	-0	0	2	-0	0.2
	Chi-N	4	7	.364	18	16	3	0	1	100^1	111	12	30	46	12.6	4.04	92	.281	.332	10	.286	3	-6	-4	-1	-0.2
	Yr	7	12	.368	29	27	6	1	1	169^2	176	19	56	82	12.3	3.82	98	.267	.324	12	.214	2	-5	-1	-2	0.0
1965	Chi-N	1	6	.143	26	6	0	0	0	50^2	63	7	46	22	19.4	6.93	53	.313	.441	0	.000	-0	-19	-18	-1	-2.4
1966	Chi-N	2	6	.250	15	11	2	0	1	62^1	70	14	38	34	15.6	6.35	58	.290	.387	7	.368	3	-19	-19	2	-1.7
Total	8	77	74	.510	259	184	52	18	2	1337^1	1216	143	587	849	12.2	3.74	107	.242	.322	68	.158	-2	-3	39	1	3.8
● **KEN BRONDELL**	Brondell, Kenneth Leroy b: 10/17/21, Bradshaw, Neb. BR/TR, 6′1″, 195 lbs. Deb: 5/3/44																									
1944	NY-N	0	1	.000	7	2	1	0	0	19^1	27	3	8	1	16.3	8.38	44	.329	.389	0	.000	-1	-10	-10	-1	-0.6
● **JEFF BRONKEY**	Bronkey, Jacob Jeffrey b: 9/18/65, Kabul, Afghanistan BR/TR, 6′3″, 215 lbs. Deb: 5/2/93																									
1993	Tex-A	1	1	.500	21	0	0	0	1	36	39	4	11	18	12.8	4.00	104	.285	.342	0	.000	-0	1	1	1	0.1
1994	Mil-A	1	1	.500	16	0	0	0	1	20^2	20	3	12	13	13.9	4.35	116	.247	.344	0	—	0	1	2	0	0.1
1995	Mil-A	0	0	—	8	0	0	0	0	12^1	15	0	6	5	15.3	3.65	137	.313	.389	0	—	0	1	2	-0	0.0
Total	3	2	2	.500	45	0	0	0	2	69	74	7	29	36	13.6	4.04	113	.278	.351	0	.000	-0	4	4	1	0.2
● **JIM BRONSTAD**	Bronstad, James Warren b: 6/22/36, Ft.Worth, Tex. BR/TR, 6′3″, 196 lbs. Deb: 6/7/59																									
1959	NY-A	0	3	.000	16	3	0	0	2	29^1	34	2	13	14	14.7	5.22	70	.288	.364	0	.000	-0	-4	-5	0	-0.6
1963	Was-A	1	3	.250	25	0	0	0	1	57^1	66	9	22	22	14.0	5.65	66	.297	.363	0	.000	-1	-13	-12	1	-0.9
1964	Was-A	0	1	.000	4	0	0	0	0	7	10	0	2	9	15.4	5.14	72	.345	.387	0	—	0	-1	-1	-0	-0.2
Total	3	1	7	.125	45	3	0	0	3	93^2	110	11	37	45	14.3	5.48	67	.298	.365	0	.000	-2	-18	-19	2	-1.7
● **IKE BROOKENS**	Brookens, Edward Dwain b: 1/3/49, Chambersburg, Pa. BR/TR, 6′5″, 170 lbs. Deb: 6/17/75																									
1975	Det-A	0	0	—	3	0	0	0	0	10^1	11	3	5	8	14.8	5.23	77	.282	.378	0	—	0	-2	-1	0	-0.1
● **HARRY BROOKS**	Brooks, Harry Frank b: 11/30/1865, Philadelphia, Pa. d: 12/5/45, Philadelphia, Pa. Deb: 7/24/1886 ♦																									
1886	NY-a	0	1	.000	1	1	0	0	0	2	9	0	2	0	49.5	36.00	9	.429	.478	0	.000	-0	-7	-7	-0	-1.5
● **JIM BROSNAN**	Brosnan, James Patrick b: 10/24/29, Cincinnati, O. BR/TR, 6′4″, 210 lbs. Deb: 4/15/54																									
1954	Chi-N	1	0	1.000	18	0	0	0	0	33^1	44	9	18	17	17.0	9.45	44	.331	.414	1	.125	-0	-20	-19	1	-0.4
1956	Chi-N	5	9	.357	30	10	1	1	1	95	95	9	45	51	13.3	3.79	100	.270	.353	4	.182	-0	-0	-0	-1	-0.1
1957	Chi-N	5	5	.500	41	5	1	0	0	98^2	79	11	46	73	11.5	3.38	115	.219	.310	5	.250	2	6	5	1	0.8
1958	Chi-N	3	4	.429	8	8	2	0	0	51^2	41	3	29	24	12.2	3.14	125	.225	.332	2	.105	-1	5	4	1	0.6
	StL-N	8	4	.667	33	12	2	0	7	115	107	10	50	65	12.4	3.44	120	.250	.330	3	.097	-1	6	9	0	0.9
	Yr	11	8	.579	41	20	4	0	7	166^2	148	13	79	89	12.3	3.35	121	.241	.329	5	.100	-2	11	13	1	1.5
1959	StL-N	1	3	.250	20	1	0	0	2	33	34	5	15	18	13.6	4.91	86	.276	.360	2	.286	1	-4	-2	1	-0.1
	Cin-N	8	3	.727	26	9	1	1	2	83^1	79	7	26	56	11.9	3.35	121	.248	.314	1	.043	-2	6	7	1	0.7
	Yr	9	6	.600	46	10	1	1	4	116^1	113	12	41	74	12.3	3.79	108	.255	.324	3	.100	-1	2	4	1	0.6
1960	Cin-N	7	2	.778	57	2	0	0	12	99	79	4	22	62	9.2	2.36	162	.225	.271	3	.200	2	15	16	-0	2.0
1961	*Cin-N	10	4	.714	53	0	0	0	16	80	77	7	18	40	10.7	3.04	134	.249	.291	2	.154	-0	9	9	1	1.9
1962	Cin-N	4	4	.500	48	0	0	0	13	64^2	76	6	18	51	13.1	3.34	120	.292	.338	0	.000	-1	4	5	-1	0.7
1963	Cin-N	0	1	.000	6	0	0	0	0	4^2	8	2	3	4	21.2	7.71	43	.421	.500	0	—	0	-2	-2	0	-0.4
	Chi-A	3	8	.273	45	0	0	0	14	73	71	7	22	46	11.5	2.84	124	.263	.318	4	.308	1	6	5	-0	1.1
Total	9	55	47	.539	385	47	7	2	67	831^1	790	80	312	507	12.0	3.54	111	.254	.324	27	.153	1	31	36	3	7.7
● **TERRY BROSS**	Bross, Terrence Paul b: 3/30/66, ElPaso, Tex. BR/TR, 6′9″, 234 lbs. Deb: 9/4/91																									
1991	NY-N	0	0	—	8	0	0	0	0	10	7	1	3	5	9.0	1.80	202	.200	.263	0	—	0	2	2	-0	0.0
1993	SF-N	0	0	—	2	0	0	0	0	2	3	1	1	1	18.0	9.00	43	.333	.400	0	—	0	-1	-1	-0	0.0
Total	2	0	0	—	10	0	0	0	0	12	10	2	4	6	10.5	3.00	123	.227	.292	0	—	0	1	1	-1	0.0

YEAR	TM/L	W	L	PCT	G	GS	CG	SH	SV	IP	H	HR	BB	SO	RAT	ERA	ERA+	OAV	OOB	BH	AVG	PB	PR	/A	PD	TPI
● **FRANK BROSSEAU**	Brosseau, Franklin Lee b: 7/31/44, Drayton, N.D. BR/TR, 6'1", 180 lbs. Deb: 9/10/69																									
1969	Pit-N	0	0	—	2	0	0	0	0	1^2	2	0	2	2	21.6	10.80	32	.286	.444	0	—	0	-1	-1	-0	0.0
1971	Pit-N	0	0	—	1	0	0	0	0	2	1	0	0	0	4.5	0.00	—	.200	.200	0	—	0	1	1	0	0.0
Total	2	0	0	—	3	0	0	0	0	3^2	3	0	2	2	12.3	4.91	70	.250	.357	0	—	0	-1	-1	0	0.0
● **DAN BROUTHERS**	Brouthers, Dennis Joseph "Big Dan" b: 5/8/1858, Sylvan Lake, N.Y. d: 8/2/32, E.Orange, N.J. BL/TL, 6'2", 207 lbs. Deb: 6/23/1879 H♦																									
1879	Tro-N	0	2	.000	3	2	2	0	0	21	35	0	8	6	18.4	5.57	45	.343	.391	46	.274	1	-7	-7	-1	-0.5
1883	Buf-N	0	0	—	1	0	0	0	0	2	9	0	3	2	54.0	31.50	10	.643	.706	159	.374	1	-6	-6	-0	0.0
Total	2	0	2	.000	4	2	2	0	0	23	44	0	11	8	21.5	7.83	33	.379	.433	2296	.342	1	-13	-13	-1	-0.5
● **SCOTT BROW**	Brow, Scott John b: 3/17/69, Butte, Mont. BR/TR, 6'3", 200 lbs. Deb: 4/28/93																									
1993	Tor-A	1	1	.500	6	3	0	0	0	18	19	2	10	7	15.0	6.00	72	.275	.375	0	—	0	-3	-3	1	-0.2
1994	Tor-A	0	3	.000	18	0	0	0	2	29	34	4	19	15	16.8	5.90	82	.288	.391	0	—	0	-4	-3	0	-0.4
1996	Tor-A	1	0	1.000	18	1	0	0	0	38^2	45	5	25	23	16.3	5.59	90	.294	.393	0	—	0	-3	-3	-0	0.0
1998	Ari-N	1	0	1.000	17	0	0	0	0	21^1	22	2	14	13	15.2	7.17	60	.272	.379	0	.000	-0	-7	-7	-0	-0.3
Total	4	3	4	.429	59	4	0	0	2	107	120	13	68	58	16.0	6.06	78	.285	.387	0	.000	-0	-16	-16	1	-0.9
● **FRANK BROWER**	Brower, Frank Willard "Turkeyfoot" b: 3/26/1893, Gainesville, Va. d: 11/20/60, Baltimore, Md. BL/TR, 6'2", 180 lbs. Deb: 8/14/20 ♦																									
1924	Cle-A	0	0	—	4	0	0	0	0	9^2	7	0	4	0	11.2	0.93	459	.212	.316	30	.280	1	4	4	-0	0.0
● **ALTON BROWN**	Brown, Alton Leo "Deacon" b: 4/16/25, Norfolk, Va. BR/TR, 6'2", 195 lbs. Deb: 4/21/51																									
1951	Was-A	0	0	—	7	0	0	0	0	11^2	14	1	12	7	20.8	9.26	44	.298	.450	0	.000	-0	-7	-7	-0	0.0
● **BOARDWALK BROWN**	Brown, Carroll William b: 2/20/1887, Woodbury, N.J. d: 2/8/77, Burlington, N.J. BR/TR, 6'1.5", 178 lbs. Deb: 9/27/11																									
1911	Phi-A	0	1	.000	2	1	1	0	0	12	12	0	2	6	10.5	4.50	70	.267	.298	0	.000	-1	-2	-2	0	-0.2
1912	Phi-A	13	11	.542	34	24	15	3	0	199	204	2	87	64	13.6	3.66	84	.283	.367	11	.145	-3	-8	-13	3	-1.4
1913	Phi-A	17	11	.607	43	35	11	3	1	235^1	200	6	87	70	11.4	2.94	94	.219	.294	13	.159	-1	-0	-5	-2	-0.9
1914	Phi-A	1	5	.167	15	7	2	0	0	66	64	1	26	20	12.3	4.09	64	.268	.340	0	.000	-2	-10	-11	0	-1.1
	NY-A	6	5	.545	20	14	8	0	0	122^1	123	2	42	57	12.2	3.24	85	.271	.334	8	.182	1	-7	-6	3	-0.1
	Yr	7	10	.412	35	21	10	0	0	188^1	187	3	68	77	12.2	3.54	77	.270	.336	8	.125	-0	-17	-17	3	-1.2
1915	NY-A	3	6	.333	19	11	5	0	0	96^2	95	4	47	34	13.7	4.10	72	.275	.370	6	.188	-1	-12	-12	-0	-1.2
Total	5	40	39	.506	133	92	42	6	1	731^1	698	15	291	251	12.5	3.47	83	.257	.334	38	.147	-6	-39	-49	4	-4.9
● **CHARLIE BROWN**	Brown, Charles E. b: 1878, Baltimore, Md. TL, 6', 180 lbs. Deb: 8/4/1897																									
1897	Cle-N	1	2	.333	4	4	2	0	0	24^1	30	2	17	8	19.2	7.77	58	.300	.426	3	.273	0	-9	-9	-0	-0.8
● **BUSTER BROWN**	Brown, Charles Edward "Yank" b: 8/31/1881, Boone, Iowa d: 2/9/14, Sioux City, Iowa BR/TR, 6', 180 lbs. Deb: 6/22/05																									
1905	StL-N	8	11	.421	23	21	17	3	0	178^2	172	5	62	57	12.3	2.97	100	.260	.332	6	.092	-3	1	0	3	0.0
1906	StL-N	8	16	.333	32	27	21	0	0	238^1	208	2	112	109	12.5	2.64	99	.234	.327	14	.165	0	-0	-0	2	0.2
1907	StL-N	1	6	.143	9	8	6	0	0	63^2	57	2	45	17	15.1	3.39	74	.263	.401	7	.269	2	-7	-6	2	-0.3
	Phi-N	9	6	.600	21	16	13	4	0	130	118	3	56	38	12.5	2.42	100	.246	.333	10	.189	2	1	-0	-1	0.1
	Yr	10	12	.455	30	24	19	4	0	193^2	175	5	101	55	13.1	2.74	89	.250	.349	17	.215	3	-6	-6	1	-0.2
1908	Phi-N	0	0	—	3	0	0	0	0	7	9	0	5	3	19.3	2.57	94	.346	.469	1	.200	-0	-0	-0	1	0.1
1909	Phi-N	0	0	—	7	1	0	0	0	25	22	1	16	10	14.0	3.24	80	.259	.382	0	.000	-1	-2	-2	0	-0.1
	Bos-N	4	8	.333	18	17	8	2	0	123^1	108	1	56	32	12.5	3.14	90	.244	.339	7	.146	-2	-7	-4	1	-0.5
	Yr	4	8	.333	25	18	8	2	0	148^1	130	2	72	42	12.7	3.16	88	.246	.344	7	.123	-3	-9	-6	1	-0.6
1910	Bos-N	9	23	.281	46	29	16	1	2	263	251	4	94	88	11.9	2.67	125	.268	.337	16	.198	0	11	19	1	2.5
1911	Bos-N	8	18	.308	42	25	13	0	2	241	258	11	116	76	14.3	4.29	89	.284	.371	21	.250	3	-24	-13	0	-0.9
1912	Bos-N	4	15	.211	31	21	12	0	0	168^1	146	7	66	68	11.4	4.01	89	.239	.315	13	.213	1	-11	-8	0	-0.7
1913	Bos-N	0	0	—	2	0	0	0	0	13^1	19	0	3	3	16.2	4.73	70	.396	.453	0	.000	-0	-2	-2	-0	0.0
Total	9	51	103	.331	234	165	106	10	4	1451^2	1368	36	631	501	12.8	3.21	96	.258	.343	95	.182	3	-42	-18	8	0.4
● **CURLY BROWN**	Brown, Charles Roy "Lefty" b: 12/9/1888, Spring Hill, Kan. d: 6/10/68, Spring Hill, Kan. BL/TL, 5'10.5", 165 lbs. Deb: 9/8/11																									
1911	StL-A	1	2	.333	3	2	2	0	0	23	22	0	5	8	11.0	2.74	123	.247	.295	0	.000	-1	2	2	0	0.0
1912	StL-A	1	3	.250	16	4	2	1	0	64^2	69	0	35	28	14.9	4.87	68	.277	.373	5	.208	-0	-11	-11	-3	-0.9
1913	StL-A	1	1	.500	2	2	2	0	0	14	12	0	4	3	10.3	2.57	114	.245	.302	2	.400	1	1	1	-0	0.1
1915	Cin-N	0	2	.000	7	3	0	0	0	27	26	2	6	13	11.3	4.67	61	.245	.298	4	.364	1	-6	-5	-1	-0.4
Total	4	3	8	.273	28	11	6	1	0	128^2	129	2	50	52	12.9	4.20	76	.262	.337	11	.224	0	-15	-14	-4	-1.2
● **CLINT BROWN**	Brown, Clinton Harold b: 7/8/03, Blackash, Pa. d: 12/31/55, Rocky River, Ohio BL/TR, 6'1", 190 lbs. Deb: 9/27/28																									
1928	Cle-A	0	1	.000	2	1	1	0	0	11	14	0	2	2	13.1	4.91	84	.304	.333	1	.200	-0	-1	-1	0	-0.1
1929	Cle-A	0	2	.000	3	1	1	0	0	16^1	18	0	6	1	13.2	3.31	134	.286	.348	0	.000	-1	2	2	1	0.2
1930	Cle-A	11	13	.458	35	31	16	**3**	1	213^2	271	14	51	54	13.7	4.97	97	.314	.356	18	.247	2	-8	-3	2	0.0
1931	Cle-A	11	15	.423	39	33	12	2	0	233^1	284	10	55	50	13.1	4.71	98	.295	.333	15	.172	-2	-8	-2	4	0.0
1932	Cle-A	15	12	.556	37	32	21	1	1	262^2	298	14	50	59	12.1	4.08	116	.279	.314	25	.250	6	12	19	2	2.4
1933	Cle-A	11	12	.478	33	23	10	2	1	185	202	10	34	47	11.6	3.41	130	.276	.310	9	.145	-3	18	21	3	2.4
1934	Cle-A	4	3	.571	17	2	0	0	1	50^1	83	3	14	15	17.3	5.90	77	.359	.396	5	.294	1	-8	-8	-0	-0.8
1935	Cle-A	4	3	.571	23	5	1	0	2	49	61	3	14	20	14.0	5.14	88	.300	.349	2	.200	0	-4	-3	1	-0.4
1936	Chi-A	6	2	.750	38	2	0	0	5	83	106	5	24	19	14.4	4.99	104	.315	.366	4	.160	-0	0	2	0	0.2
1937	Chi-A	7	7	.500	**53**	0	0	0	**18**	100	92	7	36	51	11.6	3.42	135	.242	.309	4	.222	1	**13**	**13**	1	2.3
1938	Chi-A	1	3	.250	8	0	0	0	2	13^2	16	0	9	2	16.5	4.61	106	.333	.439	1	.500	1	0	0	1	0.3
1939	Chi-A	11	10	.524	**61**	0	0	0	18	118^1	127	8	27	41	11.7	3.88	122	.281	.322	4	.211	1	10	11	2	2.3
1940	Chi-A	4	6	.400	37	0	0	0	10	66	75	5	16	23	12.7	3.68	120	.284	.330	1	.071	-1	5	5	0	0.8
1941	Cle-A	3	3	.500	41	0	0	0	5	74^1	77	3	28	22	12.8	3.27	120	.279	.348	2	.118	0	7	6	3	0.8
1942	Cle-A	1	1	.500	7	0	0	0	0	9	16	2	2	4	19.0	6.00	57	.356	.396	0	.000	0	-2	-3	-0	-0.6
Total	15	89	93	.489	434	130	62	8	64	1485^2	1740	84	368	410	12.9	4.26	109	.291	.335	91	.199	5	37	60	19	9.8
● **CURT BROWN**	Brown, Curtis Steven b: 1/15/60, Ft.Lauderdale, Fla. BR/TR, 6'5", 200 lbs. Deb: 6/10/83																									
1983	Cal-A	1	1	.500	10	0	0	0	0	16	25	1	4	7	16.3	7.31	55	.368	.403	0	—	0	-6	-6	-0	-0.6
1984	NY-A	1	1	.500	13	0	0	0	0	16^2	18	1	4	10	11.9	2.70	140	.281	.324	0	—	0	2	2	0	0.3
1986	Mon-N	0	1	.000	6	0	0	0	0	12	15	0	2	4	12.8	3.00	123	.319	.347	0	.000	-0	1	1	0	0.1
1987	Mon-N	0	1	.000	5	0	0	0	0	7	10	2	4	6	18.0	7.71	54	.333	.412	0	—	0	-3	-3	0	-0.3
Total	4	2	4	.333	34	0	0	0	0	51^2	68	4	14	27	14.3	4.88	80	.325	.368	0	.000	-0	-5	-6	-0	-0.5
● **ED BROWN**	Brown, Edward P. b: Chicago, Ill. TR, 178 lbs. Deb: 8/19/1882 ♦																									
1882	StL-a	0	0	—	1	0	0	0	0	2	2	0	0	1	9.0	0.00	—	.250	.250	11	.183	-0	1	1	-0	0.0
1884	Tol-a	0	1	.000	1	1	1	0	0	9	19	0	4	1	24.0	9.00	38	.396	.453	27	.176	-0	-6	-6	-0	-0.4
Total	2	0	1	.000	2	1	1	0	0	11	21	0	4	2	21.3	7.36	45	.375	.426	38	.178	-0	-5	-5	-0	-0.4
● **ELMER BROWN**	Brown, Elmer Young "Shook" b: 3/25/1883, Southport, Ind. d: 1/23/55, Indianapolis, Ind. BL/TR, 5'11.5", 172 lbs. Deb: 9/16/11																									
1911	StL-A	1	1	.500	5	3	1	1	0	16^2	16	0	14	5	16.2	6.48	52	.242	.375	1	.125	-1	-6	-6	1	-0.6
1912	StL-A	5	8	.385	23	13	2	1	0	120^1	122	2	42	45	13.2	2.99	111	.280	.359	6	.167	-1	4	4	-1	0.3
1913	Bro-N	0	0	—	3	1	0	0	0	13	6	0	10	6	11.8	2.08	159	.158	.347	0	.000	-1	2	2	-0	-0.1
1914	Bro-N	1	2	.333	11	5	1	0	0	36^2	33	2	23	22	15.5	3.93	73	.402	.563	1	.083	-1	-5	-4	1	-0.4
1915	Bro-N	0	0	—	1	0	0	0	0	2	4	0	3	1	31.5	9.00	31	.500	.636	0	—	0	-1	-1	0	0.0
Total	5	7	11	.389	43	22	4	2	0	188^2	181	4	92	79	14.0	3.48	93	.287	.395	8	.133	-3	-6	-5	0	-0.8
● **HAL BROWN**	Brown, Hector Harold "Skinny" b: 12/11/24, Greensboro, N.C. BR/TR, 6'2", 182 lbs. Deb: 4/19/51 C																									
1951	Chi-A	0	0	—	3	0	0	0	1	8^2	15	3	4	4	19.7	9.35	43	.385	.442	2	1.000	1	-5	-5	0	0.0
1952	Chi-A	2	3	.400	24	8	1	0	0	72^1	82	8	21	31	12.8	4.23	86	.284	.332	3	.158	1	-4	-5	-0	-0.2
1953	Bos-A	11	6	.647	30	25	6	1	0	166^1	177	16	57	62	12.7	4.65	90	.269	.327	17	.293	5	-12	-8	-0	-0.4
1954	Bos-A	1	8	.111	40	5	1	0	0	118	126	6	41	66	13.0	4.12	100	.269	.331	3	.125	-0	-5	-0	1	0.0

YEAR	TM/L	W	L	PCT	G	GS	CG	SH	SV	IP	H	HR	BB	SO	RAT	ERA	ERA+	OAV	OOB	BH	AVG	PB	PR	/A	PD	TPI
1955	Bos-A	1	0	1.000	2	0	0	0	0	4	2	0	2	2	9.0	2.25	191	.143	.250	1	1.000	0	1	1	-0	0.2
	Bal-A	0	4	.000	15	5	1	0	0	57	51	5	26	26	12.2	4.11	93	.241	.324	0	.000	-1	-1	-2	-1	-0.3
	Yr	1	4	.200	17	5	1	0	0	61	53	5	28	28	12.0	3.98	97	.235	.319	1	.059	-1	-0	-1	-1	-0.1
1956	Bal-A	9	7	.563	35	14	4	1	2	151^{2}	142	18	37	57	10.7	4.04	97	.247	.294	8	.190	1	2	-2	0	0.0
1957	Bal-A	7	8	.467	25	20	7	2	1	150	132	17	37	62	10.3	3.90	92	.236	.285	10	.208	2	-2	-5	-1	-0.4
1958	Bal-A	7	5	.583	19	17	4	2	1	96^{2}	96	9	20	44	10.8	3.07	117	.259	.297	4	.148	-0	7	6	-0	0.6
1959	Bal-A	11	9	.550	31	21	2	0	3	164	158	16	32	81	10.5	3.79	100	.252	.290	2	.048	-3	1	-0	-1	-0.3
1960	Bal-A	12	5	.706	30	20	6	1	0	159	155	14	22	66	**10.1**	3.06	125	.258	**.286**	8	.182	3	14	13	-1	1.5
1961	Bal-A	10	6	.625	27	23	6	3	1	166^{2}	153	14	33	61	10.1	3.19	121	.247	.286	7	.140	-0	16	12	-0	1.0
1962	Bal-A	6	4	.600	22	11	0	0	1	85^{2}	88	12	21	25	11.8	4.10	90	.268	.318	8	.286	2	-1	-4	-1	-0.4
	NY-A	0	1	.000	2	1	0	0	0	6^{2}	9	3	2	2	14.9	6.75	56	.333	.379	0	.000	-0	-2	-2	-0	-0.3
	Yr	6	5	.545	24	12	0	0	1	92^{1}	97	15	23	27	11.7	4.29	86	.270	.314	8	.276	1	-3	-6	-1	-0.7
1963	Hou-N	5	11	.313	26	20	6	3	0	141^{1}	137	14	8	68	9.2	3.31	95	.255	.266	4	.093	-2	-0	-2	-3	-0.7
1964	Hou-N	3	15	.167	27	21	3	0	1	132	154	18	26	53	12.4	3.95	86	.292	.327	5	.128	-1	-6	-8	-2	-1.2
Total	14	85	92	.480	358	211	47	13	11	1680	1677	173	389	710	11.1	3.81	98	.260	.303	82	.169	8	2	-11	-10	-0.9

● JACKIE BROWN Brown, Jackie Gene b: 5/31/43, Holdenville, Okla. BR/TR, 6'1", 195 lbs. Deb: 7/2/70 FC

YEAR	TM/L	W	L	PCT	G	GS	CG	SH	SV	IP	H	HR	BB	SO	RAT	ERA	ERA+	OAV	OOB	BH	AVG	PB	PR	/A	PD	TPI
1970	Was-A	2	2	.500	24	5	1	0	0	57	49	8	37	47	13.6	3.95	90	.231	.345	2	.154	-0	-1	-2	-1	-0.3
1971	Was-A	3	4	.429	14	9	0	0	0	47	60	9	27	21	16.9	5.94	56	.316	.404	2	.133	-0	-13	-14	1	-1.8
1973	Tex-A	5	5	.500	25	3	2	1	2	66^{2}	82	7	25	45	14.7	3.92	95	.309	.373	0	—	0	-1	-1	-1	-0.3
1974	Tex-A	13	12	.520	35	26	9	2	0	216^{2}	219	13	74	134	12.3	3.57	100	.265	.329	0	—	0	1	-0	-1	-0.1
1975	Tex-A	5	5	.500	17	7	2	1	0	70^{1}	70	7	35	35	13.7	4.22	89	.266	.357	0	—	0	-3	-4	-2	-0.6
	Cle-A	1	2	.333	25	3	1	0	1	69^{1}	72	9	29	41	13.1	4.28	88	.276	.348	0	—	0	-4	-4	-0	-0.2
	Yr	6	7	.462	42	10	3	1	1	139^{2}	142	16	64	76	13.3	4.25	89	.269	.349	0	—	0	-7	-8	-2	-0.8
1976	Cle-A	9	11	.450	32	27	5	2	0	180	193	14	55	104	12.8	4.25	82	.276	.335	0	—	0	-15	-15	-1	-1.6
1977	Mon-N	9	12	.429	42	25	6	2	0	185^{2}	189	15	71	89	12.8	4.51	84	.264	.334	7	.125	-2	-12	-14	-2	-1.9
Total	7	47	53	.470	214	105	26	8	3	892^{2}	934	82	353	516	13.2	4.18	87	.272	.343	11	.131	-3	-48	-55	-7	-6.8

● KEVIN BROWN Brown, James Kevin b: 3/14/65, Milledgeville, Ga. BR/TR, 6'4", 195 lbs. Deb: 9/30/86

YEAR	TM/L	W	L	PCT	G	GS	CG	SH	SV	IP	H	HR	BB	SO	RAT	ERA	ERA+	OAV	OOB	BH	AVG	PB	PR	/A	PD	TPI
1986	Tex-A	1	0	1.000	1	1	0	0	0	5	6	0	0	4	10.8	3.60	119	.316	.316	0	—	0	0	0	0	0.1
1988	Tex-A	1	1	.500	4	4	1	0	0	23^{1}	33	2	8	12	16.2	4.24	96	.330	.385	0	—	0	-1	-0	-0	-0.1
1989	Tex-A	12	9	.571	28	28	7	0	0	191	167	10	70	104	11.4	3.35	118	.234	.305	0	—	0	11	13	3	1.7
1990	Tex-A	12	10	.545	26	26	6	2	0	180	175	13	60	88	11.9	3.60	109	.255	.318	0	.000	-0	6	6	-0	0.7
1991	Tex-A	9	12	.429	33	33	0	0	0	210^{2}	233	17	90	96	14.4	4.40	92	.284	.364	0	—	0	-7	-9	1	-0.7
1992	Tex-A★	**21**	11	.656	35	35	11	1	0	**265^{2}**	262	11	76	173	11.8	3.32	114	.260	.318	0	—	0	18	14	2	1.9
1993	Tex-A	15	12	.556	34	34	12	3	0	233	228	14	74	142	12.2	3.59	115	.252	.319	0	—	0	19	14	4	2.0
1994	Tex-A	7	9	.438	26	25	3	0	0	170	218	18	50	123	14.5	4.82	100	.314	.365	0	—	0	-0	0	3	0.3
1995	Bal-A	10	9	.526	26	26	3	1	0	172^{1}	155	10	48	117	11.1	3.60	132	.241	.303	0	—	0	21	22	7	2.7
1996	Fla-N★	17	11	.607	32	32	5	**3**	0	233	187	8	33	159	9.1	**1.89**	**215**	.220	.263	9	.120	-1	**60**	**56**	6	**7.3**
1997	*Fla-N★	16	8	.667	33	33	6	2	0	237^{1}	214	10	66	205	11.1	2.69	150	.240	.303	9	.125	-0	40	35	5	3.9
1998	*SD-N★	18	7	.720	36	35	7	3	0	257	225	8	49	257	9.9	2.38	161	.235	.280	17	.207	4	53	41	3	4.6
Total	12	139	99	.584	314	312	61	15	0	2178^{1}	2103	121	624	1480	11.7	3.30	124	.254	.314	35	.152	3	221	194	33	24.4

● JIM BROWN Brown, James W. H. b: 12/12/1860, Clinton Co., Pa. d: 4/6/08, Williamsport, Pa. Deb: 4/17/1884 ◆

YEAR	TM/L	W	L	PCT	G	GS	CG	SH	SV	IP	H	HR	BB	SO	RAT	ERA	ERA+	OAV	OOB	BH	AVG	PB	PR	/A	PD	TPI
1884	Alt-U	1	9	.100	11	11	7	0	0	74	99	0	36	39	16.4	5.35	50	.301	.370	22	.250	-2	-24	-22	0	-2.2
	NY-N	0	1	.000	1	1	1	0	0	9	10	0	8	2	18.0	5.00	60	.263	.391	0	.000	-1	-2	-2	-0	-0.2
	StP-U	1	4	.200	6	6	4	1	0	36	43	1	14	20	14.3	3.75	35	.277	.337	5	.313	4	-5	-10	0	-0.8
1886	Phi-a	0	1	.000	1	1	1	0	0	8^{1}	9	0	3	4	13.0	3.24	108	.265	.324	0	.000	-1	0	0	-0	0.0
Total	2	2	15	.118	19	19	13	1	0	127^{1}	161	1	61	65	15.7	4.74	50	.290	.360	27	.245	1	-31	-34	0	-3.2

● JOHN BROWN Brown, John J. "Ad" b: Trenton, N.J. Deb: 8/11/1897

YEAR	TM/L	W	L	PCT	G	GS	CG	SH	SV	IP	H	HR	BB	SO	RAT	ERA	ERA+	OAV	OOB	BH	AVG	PB	PR	/A	PD	TPI
1897	Bro-N	0	1	.000	1	1	0	0	0	5	7	0	4	0	25.2	7.20	57	.333	.500	1	.500	0	-2	-2	0	-0.2

● JOPHERY BROWN Brown, Jophery Clifford b: 1/22/45, Grambling, La. BL/TR, 6'2", 190 lbs. Deb: 9/21/68

YEAR	TM/L	W	L	PCT	G	GS	CG	SH	SV	IP	H	HR	BB	SO	RAT	ERA	ERA+	OAV	OOB	BH	AVG	PB	PR	/A	PD	TPI
1968	Chi-N	0	0	—	1	0	0	0	0	2	2	0	1	0	13.5	4.50	70	.286	.375	0	—	0	-0	-0	0	0.0

● JOE BROWN Brown, Joseph E. b: 4/4/1859, Warren, Pa. d: 6/28/1888, Warren, Pa. 5'10", 162 lbs. Deb: 8/16/1884 ◆

YEAR	TM/L	W	L	PCT	G	GS	CG	SH	SV	IP	H	HR	BB	SO	RAT	ERA	ERA+	OAV	OOB	BH	AVG	PB	PR	/A	PD	TPI
1884	Chi-N	4	2	.667	7	6	5	0	0	50	56	4	7	27	11.3	4.68	67	.258	.281	13	.213	-1	-9	-9	-0	-0.9
1885	Bal-a	0	4	.000	4	4	4	0	0	38	52	0	4	9	13.3	5.68	57	.306	.322	3	.158	-1	-10	-10	-0	-0.9
Total	2	4	6	.400	11	10	9	0	0	88	108	4	11	36	12.2	5.11	62	.279	.299	16	.200	-2	-20	-19	-1	-1.8

● JOE BROWN Brown, Joseph Henry b: 7/3/1900, Little Rock, Ark. d: 3/7/50, Los Angeles, Cal. BR/TR, 6', 176 lbs. Deb: 5/17/27

YEAR	TM/L	W	L	PCT	G	GS	CG	SH	SV	IP	H	HR	BB	SO	RAT	ERA	ERA+	OAV	OOB	BH	AVG	PB	PR	/A	PD	TPI
1927	Chi-A	0	0	—	1	1	0	0	0	0	2	0	1	0	—	∞	—	1.000	1.000	0	—	0	-3	-3	0	-0.2

● KEITH BROWN Brown, Keith Edward b: 2/14/64, Flagstaff, Ariz. BB/TR, 6'4", 215 lbs. Deb: 8/25/88

YEAR	TM/L	W	L	PCT	G	GS	CG	SH	SV	IP	H	HR	BB	SO	RAT	ERA	ERA+	OAV	OOB	BH	AVG	PB	PR	/A	PD	TPI
1988	Cin-N	2	1	.667	4	3	0	0	0	16^{1}	14	1	4	6	9.9	2.76	130	.237	.286	0	.000	-0	1	1	-0	0.2
1990	Cin-N	0	0	—	8	0	0	0	0	11^{1}	12	2	3	8	11.9	4.76	83	.286	.333	0	—	0	-1	-1	0	0.0
1991	Cin-N	0	0	—	11	0	0	0	0	12	15	0	6	4	15.8	2.25	169	.306	.382	0	—	0	2	2	0	0.0
1992	Cin-N	0	1	.000	2	2	0	0	0	8	10	2	5	5	16.9	4.50	80	.313	.405	0	.000	-0	-1	-1	-0	-0.1
Total	4	2	2	.500	25	5	0	0	0	47^{2}	51	5	18	23	13.0	3.40	110	.280	.345	0	.000	-1	1	2	-0	0.1

● KEVIN BROWN Brown, Kevin Dewayne b: 3/5/66, Oroville, Cal. BL/TL, 6'1", 185 lbs. Deb: 7/27/90

YEAR	TM/L	W	L	PCT	G	GS	CG	SH	SV	IP	H	HR	BB	SO	RAT	ERA	ERA+	OAV	OOB	BH	AVG	PB	PR	/A	PD	TPI
1990	NY-N	0	0	—	2	0	0	0	0	2	2	0	1	0	13.5	0.00	—	.250	.333	0	—	0	1	1	0	0.0
	Mil-A	1	1	.500	5	3	0	0	0	21	14	1	7	12	9.4	2.57	151	.182	.259	0	—	0	3	3	1	0.3
1991	Mil-A	2	4	.333	15	10	0	0	0	63^{2}	66	6	34	30	14.3	5.51	72	.270	.362	0	—	0	-10	-11	0	-0.8
1992	Sea-A	0	0	—	2	0	0	0	0	3	4	1	3	2	21.0	9.00	44	.333	.467	0	—	0	-2	-2	0	0.0
Total	3	3	5	.375	24	13	0	0	0	89^{2}	86	8	45	44	13.3	4.82	82	.252	.343	0	—	0	-8	-9	1	-0.5

● LEW BROWN Brown, Lewis J. "Blower" b: 2/1/1858, Leominster, Mass. d: 1/15/1889, Boston, Mass. BR/TR, 5'10.5", 185 lbs. Deb: 6/17/1876 ◆

YEAR	TM/L	W	L	PCT	G	GS	CG	SH	SV	IP	H	HR	BB	SO	RAT	ERA	ERA+	OAV	OOB	BH	AVG	PB	PR	/A	PD	TPI
1878	Pro-N	0	0	—	1	0	0	0	0	1	0	0	4	0	36.0	18.00	12	.000	.500	74	.305	0	-2	-2	0	0.0
1884	Bos-U	0	0	—	1	0	0	0	1	1	6	0	1	0	63.0	36.00	7	.667	.700	75	.231	-0	-4	-4	-0	-0.6
Total	2	0	0	—	2	0	0	0	1	2	6	0	5	0	49.5	27.00	8	.462	.611	379	.248	0	-5	-5	0	-0.6

● LLOYD BROWN Brown, Lloyd Andrew "Gimpy" b: 12/25/04, Beeville, Tex. d: 1/14/74, Opa-Locka, Fla. BL/TL, 5'9", 170 lbs. Deb: 7/17/25

YEAR	TM/L	W	L	PCT	G	GS	CG	SH	SV	IP	H	HR	BB	SO	RAT	ERA	ERA+	OAV	OOB	BH	AVG	PB	PR	/A	PD	TPI
1925	Bro-N	0	3	.000	17	5	1	0	0	63^{1}	79	1	25	23	15.1	4.12	101	.319	.385	2	.087	-2	1	0	0	-0.2
1928	Was-A	4	4	.500	27	10	2	0	1	107	112	7	40	38	13.0	4.04	99	.273	.341	5	.161	0	0	-0	3	0.3
1929	Was-A	8	7	.533	40	15	7	1	0	168	186	7	69	48	13.7	4.18	101	.297	.368	11	.220	3	1	1	2	0.5
1930	Was-A	16	12	.571	38	22	10	1	1	197	220	6	65	59	13.2	4.25	108	.293	.354	14	.215	2	9	8	3	1.4
1931	Was-A	15	14	.517	42	32	15	1	0	258^{2}	256	13	79	79	11.7	3.20	134	.257	.311	22	.229	3	34	31	1	3.4
1932	Was-A	15	12	.556	46	24	10	2	5	202^{2}	239	11	55	53	13.1	4.44	97	.296	.342	7	.100	-5	1	-3	1	-0.7
1933	StL-A	1	6	.143	8	6	0	0	0	39	57	1	17	7	17.1	7.15	65	.350	.411	3	.273	1	-12	-11	1	-1.4
	Bos-A	8	11	.421	33	21	9	2	1	163^{1}	180	4	64	37	13.4	4.02	109	.281	.347	16	.281	6	5	6	4	1.7
	Yr	9	17	.346	41	27	9	2	1	202^{1}	237	5	81	44	14.1	4.63	96	.295	.360	19	.279	7	-8	-4	5	0.3
1934	Cle-A	5	10	.333	38	15	5	0	6	117	116	7	51	39	13.1	3.85	118	.263	.342	7	.233	1	8	9	0	1.2
1935	Cle-A	8	7	.533	42	8	4	2	4	122	123	6	37	45	12.0	3.61	125	.265	.323	4	.108	-2	**11**	**12**	1	1.2
1936	Cle-A	8	10	.444	24	16	12	1	1	140^{1}	166	13	45	34	13.7	4.17	121	.294	.349	10	.222	2	14	14	1	1.7
1937	Cle-A	2	6	.250	31	5	2	0	0	77	107	4	27	32	16.0	6.55	70	.329	.386	4	.167	-1	-16	-17	1	-1.4
1940	Phi-N	1	3	.250	18	2	0	0	3	37^{2}	58	3	16	16	17.7	6.21	63	.354	.411	1	.077	-1	-10	-10	0	-1.2
Total	12	91	105	.464	404	181	77	10	21	1693	1899	83	590	510	13.3	4.20	105	.288	.348	106	.192	6	45	42	19	6.5

● MACE BROWN Brown, Mace Stanley b: 5/21/09, North English, Ia. BR/TR, 6'1", 190 lbs. Deb: 5/21/35 C

YEAR	TM/L	W	L	PCT	G	GS	CG	SH	SV	IP	H	HR	BB	SO	RAT	ERA	ERA+	OAV	OOB	BH	AVG	PB	PR	/A	PD	TPI
1935	Pit-N	4	1	.800	18	5	2	0	0	72^{2}	84	5	22	28	13.1	3.59	114	.287	.337	4	.167	-0	3	4	2	0.4

YEAR	TM/L	W	L	PCT	G	GS	CG	SH	SV	IP	H	HR	BB	SO	RAT	ERA	ERA+	OAV	OOB	BH	AVG	PB	PR	/A	PD	TPI
1936	Pit-N	10	11	.476	47	10	3	0	3	165	178	8	55	56	12.8	3.87	105	.275	.332	10	.167	-2	3	3	1	0.3
1937	Pit-N	7	2	.778	50	2	0	0	**7**	107^{2}	109	2	45	60	13.0	4.18	92	.261	.334	9	.300	2	-3	-4	-1	-0.2
1938	Pit-N★	15	9	.625	**51**	2	0	0	5	132^{2}	155	5	44	55	13.5	3.80	100	.294	.349	5	.132	-2	-0	-0	-0	-0.2
1939	Pit-N	9	13	.409	47	19	8	1	7	200^{1}	232	8	52	71	12.8	3.37	114	.293	.338	7	.109	-4	12	10	1	0.8
1940	Pit-N	10	9	.526	48	17	5	1	**7**	173	181	5	49	73	12.1	3.49	109	.267	.318	6	.115	-1	7	6	1	0.7
1941	Pit-N	0	0	—	1	0	0	0	0	1^{1}	2	0	0	0	13.5	0.00	—	.333	.333	0	—	0	1	1	0	0.0
	Bro-N	3	2	.600	24	0	0	0	3	42^{2}	31	3	26	22	12.2	3.16	116	.208	.330	0	.000	-1	2	2	1	0.3
	Yr	3	2	.600	25	0	0	0	3	44	33	3	26	22	12.3	3.07	119	.213	.330	0	.000	-1	3	3	1	0.3
1942	Bos-A	9	3	.750	34	0	0	0	6	60^{1}	56	4	28	20	12.5	3.43	109	.255	.339	1	.067	-1	2	2	1	0.4
1943	Bos-A	6	6	.500	**49**	0	0	0	9	93^{1}	71	2	51	40	11.8	2.12	156	.222	.329	1	.059	-1	**12**	**12**	0	1.7
1946	*Bos-A	3	1	.750	18	0	0	0	1	26^{1}	26	2	16	10	14.4	2.05	179	.268	.372	0	.000	-1	4	5	1	0.7
Total	10	76	57	.571	387	55	18	2	48	1075^{1}	1125	44	388	435	12.7	3.46	110	.271	.335	43	.137	-11	43	43	6	4.9

● MARK BROWN

Brown, Mark Anthony b: 7/13/59, Bellows Falls, Vt. BB/TR, 6'2", 190 lbs. Deb: 8/9/84

YEAR	TM/L	W	L	PCT	G	GS	CG	SH	SV	IP	H	HR	BB	SO	RAT	ERA	ERA+	OAV	OOB	BH	AVG	PB	PR	/A	PD	TPI
1984	Bal-A	1	2	.333	9	0	0	0	0	23	22	2	7	10	11.7	3.91	99	.256	.319	0	—	0	0	-0	-0	0.0
1985	Min-A	0	0	—	6	0	0	0	0	15^{2}	21	1	7	5	16.1	6.89	64	.333	.400	0	—	0	-5	-4	-0	-0.1
Total	2	1	2	.333	15	0	0	0	0	38^{2}	43	3	14	15	13.5	5.12	80	.289	.354	0	—	0	-5	-4	-1	-0.1

● MIKE BROWN

Brown, Michael Gary b: 3/4/59, Camden County, N.J. BR/TR, 6'2", 195 lbs. Deb: 9/16/82

YEAR	TM/L	W	L	PCT	G	GS	CG	SH	SV	IP	H	HR	BB	SO	RAT	ERA	ERA+	OAV	OOB	BH	AVG	PB	PR	/A	PD	TPI
1982	Bos-A	1	0	1.000	3	0	0	0	0	6	7	0	1	4	12.0	0.00	—	.304	.333	0	—	0	3	3	-0	0.4
1983	Bos-A	6	6	.500	19	18	3	1	0	104	110	12	43	35	13.4	4.67	93	.276	.350	0	—	0	-7	-4	-1	-0.5
1984	Bos-A	1	8	.111	15	11	0	0	0	67	104	9	19	32	16.9	6.85	61	.347	.391	0	—	0	-21	-20	0	-2.3
1985	Bos-A	0	0	—	2	1	0	0	0	3^{1}	9	0	3	3	32.4	21.60	20	.500	.571	0	—	0	-6	-6	-0	-0.1
1986	Bos-A	4	4	.500	15	10	0	0	0	57^{1}	72	10	25	32	15.4	5.34	78	.316	.386	0	—	0	-7	-7	0	-0.9
	Sea-A	0	2	.000	6	2	0	0	0	15^{2}	19	4	11	9	17.2	7.47	57	.302	.405	0	—	0	-6	-6	0	-0.6
	Yr	4	6	.400	21	12	0	0	0	73	91	14	36	41	15.7	5.79	72	.308	.384	0	—	0	-13	-13	1	-1.5
1987	Sea-A	0	0	—	1	0	0	0	0	0^{1}	3	0	0	0	81.0	54.00	9	.750	.750	0	—	0	-2	-2	0	-0.2
Total	6	12	20	.375	61	42	3	1	0	253^{2}	324	35	102	115	15.3	5.75	74	.313	.378	0	—	0	-47	-42	0	-4.2

● MORDECAI BROWN

Brown, Mordecai Peter Centennial "Three Finger" or "Miner"
b: 10/19/1876, Nyesville, Ind. d: 2/14/48, Terre Haute, Ind. BB/TR, 5'10", 175 lbs. Deb: 4/19/03 MH

YEAR	TM/L	W	L	PCT	G	GS	CG	SH	SV	IP	H	HR	BB	SO	RAT	ERA	ERA+	OAV	OOB	BH	AVG	PB	PR	/A	PD	TPI
1903	StL-N	9	13	.409	26	24	19	1	0	201	231	7	59	83	13.3	2.60	126	.293	.347	15	.195	-0	15	15	2	1.6
1904	Chi-N	15	10	.600	26	23	21	4	1	212^{1}	155	1	50	81	**8.9**	1.86	143	**.199**	**.253**	19	.213	1	21	19	-1	2.3
1905	Chi-N	18	12	.600	30	24	24	4	0	249	219	3	44	89	9.5	2.17	138	.235	.271	13	.140	-1	23	23	-0	2.4
1906	*Chi-N	26	6	.813	36	32	27	**9**	3	277^{1}	198	1	61	144	**8.5**	**1.04**	**254**	.202	**.252**	20	.204	1	**49**	**49**	2	**6.8**
1907	*Chi-N	20	6	.769	34	27	20	6	3	233	180	2	40	107	8.7	1.39	179	.221	.262	13	.153	-0	28	29	4	**4.0**
1908	*Chi-N	29	9	.763	44	31	27	9	**5**	312^{1}	214	1	49	123	7.7	1.47	160	.195	.232	25	.207	1	31	31	-1	4.1
1909	Chi-N	**27**	9	.750	**50**	34	**32**	8	**7**	**342^{2}**	246	1	53	172	8.0	1.31	193	.202	.239	22	.176	1	**49**	**47**	-1	5.4
1910	*Chi-N	25	14	.641	46	31	**27**	**6**	**7**	295^{1}	256	3	64	143	**9.9**	1.86	155	.232	**.277**	18	.175	-0	39	34	3	4.9
1911	Chi-N	21	11	.656	**53**	27	21	0	**13**	270	267	5	55	129	10.9	2.80	118	.262	.303	23	.253	5	18	15	-4	1.9
1912	Chi-N	5	6	.455	15	8	5	2	0	88^{2}	92	2	20	34	11.5	2.64	126	.274	.317	9	.290	2	8	7	-2	0.8
1913	Cin-N	11	12	.478	39	16	11	1	6	173^{1}	174	7	44	41	11.4	2.91	112	.277	.325	11	.204	-0	6	7	-1	0.7
1914	StL-F	12	6	.667	26	18	13	2	0	175	172	7	43	81	11.2	3.29	92	.254	.302	15	.254	1	-8	-5	-2	-0.6
	Bro-F	2	5	.286	9	8	5	0	0	57^{2}	63	1	18	32	12.6	4.21	68	.276	.329	4	.211	-1	-9	-9	-0	-1.0
	Yr	14	11	.560	35	26	18	2	0	232^{2}	235	8	61	113	11.4	3.52	85	.259	.306	19	.244	0	-16	-13	-3	-1.6
1915	Chi-F	17	8	.680	35	25	17	3	4	236^{1}	189	2	64	95	9.9	2.09	120	.220	.279	24	.293	5	17	11	3	2.0
1916	Chi-N	2	3	.400	12	4	2	0	0	48^{1}	52	0	9	21	12.1	3.91	74	.289	.337	4	.250	0	-7	-5	-0	-0.5
Total	14	239	130	.648	481	332	271	55	49	3172^{1}	2708	43	673	1375	9.8	2.06	137	.233	.278	235	.206	15	279	266	1	34.8

● MYRL BROWN

Brown, Myrl Lincoln b: 10/10/1894, Waynesboro, Pa. d: 2/23/81, Harrisburg, Pa. BR/TR, 5'11", 172 lbs. Deb: 8/19/22

YEAR	TM/L	W	L	PCT	G	GS	CG	SH	SV	IP	H	HR	BB	SO	RAT	ERA	ERA+	OAV	OOB	BH	AVG	PB	PR	/A	PD	TPI
1922	Pit-N	3	1	.750	7	5	2	0	0	34^{2}	42	2	13	9	14.3	5.97	68	.296	.355	3	.273	1	-7	-7	0	-0.6

● NORM BROWN

Brown, Norman Ladelle b: 2/1/19, Evergreen, N.C. d: 5/31/95, Bennettsville, S.C. BB/TR, 6'3", 180 lbs. Deb: 10/3/43

YEAR	TM/L	W	L	PCT	G	GS	CG	SH	SV	IP	H	HR	BB	SO	RAT	ERA	ERA+	OAV	OOB	BH	AVG	PB	PR	/A	PD	TPI
1943	Phi-A	0	0	—	1	1	0	0	0	7	5	0	0	1	6.4	0.00	—	.185	.185	0	.000	-0	3	3	0	0.0
1946	Phi-A	0	1	.000	4	0	0	0	0	7^{1}	8	2	6	3	17.2	6.14	58	.267	.389	0	—	0	-2	-2	-0	-0.3
Total	2	0	1	.000	5	1	0	0	0	14^{1}	13	2	6	4	11.9	3.14	111	.228	.302	0	.000	-0	0	1	0	-0.3

● PAUL BROWN

Brown, Paul Dwayne b: 6/18/41, Ft.Smith, Ark. BR/TR, 6'1", 190 lbs. Deb: 7/23/61 F

YEAR	TM/L	W	L	PCT	G	GS	CG	SH	SV	IP	H	HR	BB	SO	RAT	ERA	ERA+	OAV	OOB	BH	AVG	PB	PR	/A	PD	TPI
1961	Phi-N	0	1	.000	5	1	0	0	0	10	13	3	8	1	19.8	8.10	50	.325	.449	1	.500	0	-5	-4	-0	-0.4
1962	Phi-N	0	6	.000	23	9	0	0	1	63^{2}	74	9	33	29	15.5	5.94	65	.298	.387	2	.154	0	-14	-15	-1	-1.3
1963	Phi-N	0	1	.000	6	2	0	0	0	15^{1}	15	2	5	11	12.9	4.11	79	.238	.314	1	.500	0	-1	-1	0	0.0
1968	Phi-N	0	0	—	2	0	0	0	0	4	6	0	1	4	15.8	9.00	33	.353	.389	0	—	0	-3	-3	-0	0.0
Total	4	0	8	.000	36	12	0	0	1	93	108	14	47	45	15.6	6.00	63	.293	.382	4	.235	1	-23	-23	-0	-1.7

● RAY BROWN

Brown, Paul Percival b: 1/31/1889, Chicago, Ill. d: 5/29/55, Los Angeles, Cal. BR/TR, 6'1", 172 lbs. Deb: 9/29/09

YEAR	TM/L	W	L	PCT	G	GS	CG	SH	SV	IP	H	HR	BB	SO	RAT	ERA	ERA+	OAV	OOB	BH	AVG	PB	PR	/A	PD	TPI
1909	Chi-N	1	0	1.000	1	1	1	0	0	9	5	0	4	2	9.0	2.00	127	.172	.273	0	.000	-0	1	1	-0	0.0

● STUB BROWN

Brown, Richard P. b: 8/3/1870, Baltimore, Md. d: 3/11/48, Baltimore, Md. TL, 6'2", 220 lbs. Deb: 8/15/1893

YEAR	TM/L	W	L	PCT	G	GS	CG	SH	SV	IP	H	HR	BB	SO	RAT	ERA	ERA+	OAV	OOB	BH	AVG	PB	PR	/A	PD	TPI
1893	Bal-N	0	0	—	2	0	0	0	0	9	13	0	5	0	19.0	6.00	79	.325	.413	1	.200	-0	-1	-1	-0	-0.1
1894	Bal-N	4	0	1.000	9	6	3	0	0	49^{2}	59	3	24	8	15.2	4.89	112	.292	.370	2	.087	-4	2	3	-1	-0.2
1897	Cin-N	0	1	.000	2	1	1	0	0	13	17	1	8	2	17.3	4.15	110	.315	.403	0	.000	-1	0	1	0	-0.1
Total	3	4	1	.800	13	7	4	0	0	71^{2}	89	4	37	10	16.1	4.90	106	.301	.382	3	.091	-5	1	2	-1	-0.4

● BOB BROWN

Brown, Robert Murray b: 4/1/11, Dorchester, Mass. d: 8/3/90, Pembroke, Mass. BR/TR, 6'0.5", 190 lbs. Deb: 4/21/30

YEAR	TM/L	W	L	PCT	G	GS	CG	SH	SV	IP	H	HR	BB	SO	RAT	ERA	ERA+	OAV	OOB	BH	AVG	PB	PR	/A	PD	TPI
1930	Bos-N	0	0	—	3	0	0	0	0	6	10	0	8	1	27.0	10.50	47	.417	.563	0	.000	-0	-4	-4	0	0.0
1931	Bos-N	0	1	.000	3	1	0	0	0	6^{1}	9	0	3	2	17.1	8.53	44	.375	.444	1	.500	0	-3	-3	0	-0.4
1932	Bos-N	14	7	.667	35	28	9	0	1	213	187	6	104	110	12.4	3.30	114	.238	.329	13	.194	-0	14	11	-1	0.9
1933	Bos-N	0	0	—	5	0	0	0	0	6^{2}	6	0	3	3	12.2	2.70	114	.250	.333	0	.000	-0	0	0	-0	0.0
1934	Bos-N	1	3	.250	16	8	2	1	0	58^{1}	59	2	36	21	15.1	5.71	67	.262	.371	5	.238	0	-11	-12	-1	-0.8
1935	Bos-N	1	8	.111	15	10	2	1	0	65	79	2	36	17	15.9	6.37	59	.302	.386	2	.105	-1	-17	-19	-1	-2.3
1936	Bos-N	0	2	.000	2	2	0	0	0	8^{1}	10	1	3	5	14.0	5.40	71	.278	.333	0	.000	-0	-1	-1	0	-0.3
Total	7	16	21	.432	79	49	13	2	1	363^{2}	360	11	193	159	13.8	4.48	84	.261	.354	21	.183	-2	-22	-28	-3	-2.9

● SCOTT BROWN

Brown, Scott Edward b: 8/30/56, DeQuincy, La. BR/TR, 6'2", 220 lbs. Deb: 8/11/81

YEAR	TM/L	W	L	PCT	G	GS	CG	SH	SV	IP	H	HR	BB	SO	RAT	ERA	ERA+	OAV	OOB	BH	AVG	PB	PR	/A	PD	TPI
1981	Cin-N	1	0	1.000	10	0	0	0	0	13	16	0	1	7	11.8	2.77	128	.314	.327	0	.000	-0	1	1	-0	0.1

● STEVE BROWN

Brown, Steven Elbert b: 2/12/57, San Francisco, Cal. BR/TR, 6'5", 200 lbs. Deb: 8/1/83

YEAR	TM/L	W	L	PCT	G	GS	CG	SH	SV	IP	H	HR	BB	SO	RAT	ERA	ERA+	OAV	OOB	BH	AVG	PB	PR	/A	PD	TPI
1983	Cal-A	2	3	.400	12	4	2	1	0	46	45	4	16	23	11.9	3.52	114	.256	.318	0	—	0	3	3	-0	0.2
1984	Cal-A	0	1	.000	3	3	0	0	0	11	16	0	9	5	20.5	9.00	44	.340	.446	0	—	0	-6	-6	-0	-0.5
Total	2	2	4	.333	15	7	2	1	0	57	61	4	25	28	13.6	4.58	87	.274	.347	0	—	0	-3	-4	-0	-0.3

● TOM BROWN

Brown, Thomas Dale b: 8/10/49, Lafayette, La. BR/TR, 6'1", 170 lbs. Deb: 9/14/78

YEAR	TM/L	W	L	PCT	G	GS	CG	SH	SV	IP	H	HR	BB	SO	RAT	ERA	ERA+	OAV	OOB	BH	AVG	PB	PR	/A	PD	TPI
1978	Sea-A	0	0	—	6	0	0	0	0	13	14	2	4	8	12.5	4.15	92	.286	.340	0	—	0	-1	-1	0	0.0

● TOM BROWN

Brown, Thomas Tarlton b: 9/21/1860, Liverpool, England d: 10/25/27, Washington, D.C. BL/TR, 5'10", 168 lbs. Deb: 7/6/1882 MU♦

YEAR	TM/L	W	L	PCT	G	GS	CG	SH	SV	IP	H	HR	BB	SO	RAT	ERA	ERA+	OAV	OOB	BH	AVG	PB	PR	/A	PD	TPI
1882	Bal-a	0	0	—	2	0	0	0	0	8^{1}	13	0	6	2	20.5	1.08	255	.333	.422	55	.304	1	1	2	-1	0.0
1883	Col-a	0	1	.000	3	1	1	0	0	14	14	0	10	6	15.4	5.79	53	.246	.358	115	.274	1	-4	-4	-1	-0.2
1884	Col-a	2	1	.667	4	0	0	0	0	19	27	0	7	5	16.1	7.11	43	.281	.330	123	.273	1	-8	-9	-1	-1.0
1885	Pit-a	0	0	—	2	0	0	0	0	6	0	0	3	2	9.0	3.00	107	.000	.207	134	.307	1	0	0	-0	0.0
1886	Pit-a	0	0	—	1	0	0	0	0	2	2	0	5	1	31.5	9.00	38	.125	.333	131	.285	0	-1	-1	0	0.0
Total	5	2	2	.500	12	1	1	0	0	49^{1}	56	0	31	16	16.4	5.29	57	.242	.340	1951	.265	4	-12	-12	-2	-1.2

YEAR	TM/L	W	L	PCT	G	GS	CG	SH	SV	IP	H	HR	BB	SO	RAT	ERA	ERA+	OAV	OOB	BH	AVG	PB	PR	/A	PD	TPI
● **JUMBO BROWN** Brown, Walter George b: 4/30/07, Greene, R.I. d: 10/2/66, Freeport, N.Y. BR/TR, 6'4", 295 lbs. Deb: 8/26/25																										
1925	Chi-N	0	0	—	2	0	0	0	0	6	5	0	4	0	13.5	3.00	144	.217	.333	0	.000	-0	1	1	0	0.0
1927	Cle-A	0	2	.000	8	0	0	0	0	18^{2}	19	3	26	8	22.2	6.27	67	.284	.489	2	.667	1	-4	-4	0	-0.2
1928	Cle-A	0	1	.000	5	0	0	0	0	14^{2}	19	0	15	12	20.9	6.75	61	.365	.507	2	.667	1	-4	-4	-0	-0.1
1932	NY-A	5	2	.714	19	3	3	1	1	55^{2}	58	1	30	31	14.6	4.53	90	.270	.364	4	.174	-1	-0	-3	1	-0.2
1933	NY-A	7	5	.583	21	8	1	0	0	74	78	3	52	55	15.8	5.23	74	.269	.380	5	.179	-1	-8	-11	-0	-1.5
1935	NY-A	6	5	.545	20	8	3	1	0	87^{1}	94	2	37	41	13.5	3.61	112	.279	.350	10	.313	3	8	4	0	0.8
1936	NY-A	1	4	.200	20	3	0	0	1	64	93	4	29	19	17.2	5.91	79	.352	.416	0	.000	-3	-6	-9	1	-0.8
1937	Cin-N	1	0	1.000	4	1	0	0	0	9^{2}	16	0	3	4	17.7	8.38	45	.390	.432	0	.000	0	-5	-5	-0	-0.5
	NY-N	1	0	1.000	4	0	0	0	0	8^{2}	5	0	5	4	10.4	1.04	374	.172	.294	0	—	0	3	3	1	0.4
	Yr	2	0	1.000	8	1	0	0	0	18^{1}	21	0	8	8	14.2	4.91	78	.300	.372	0	.000	0	-2	-2	0	-0.1
1938	NY-N	5	3	.625	43	0	0	0	5	90	65	5	28	42	9.4	1.80	209	.204	.271	3	.188	1	**20**	**20**	-1	1.8
1939	NY-N	4	0	1.000	31	0	0	0	7	56^{1}	69	1	25	24	15.2	4.15	95	.304	.375	4	.364	1	-1	-1	0	0.0
1940	NY-N	2	4	.333	41	0	0	0	**7**	55^{1}	49	5	25	31	12.0	3.42	114	.232	.314	1	.100	-1	3	3	-1	0.2
1941	NY-N	1	5	.167	31	0	0	0	**8**	57	49	2	21	30	11.1	3.32	111	.238	.308	1	.111	-1	2	2	-1	0.2
Total	12	33	31	.516	249	23	7	2	29	597^{1}	619	26	300	301	13.9	4.07	99	.271	.357	32	.204	2	7	-4	-0	0.1
● **WALTER BROWN** Brown, Walter Irving b: 4/23/15, Jamestown, N.Y. d: 2/3/91, Westfield, N.Y. BR/TR, 5'11", 175 lbs. Deb: 5/16/47																										
1947	StL-A	1	0	1.000	19	0	0	0	0	46	50	3	28	10	15.3	4.89	79	.294	.394	0	.000	-1	-6	-5	0	-0.2
● **CAL BROWNING** Browning, Calvin Duane b: 3/16/38, Burns Flat, Okla. BL/TL, 5'11", 190 lbs. Deb: 6/12/60																										
1960	StL-N	0	0	—	1	0	0	0	0	0^{2}	5	1	1	0	81.0	40.50	10	.714	.750	0	—	0	-3	-3	-0	0.0
● **FRANK BROWNING** Browning, Frank "Dutch" b: 10/29/1882, Falmouth, Ky. d: 5/20/48, San Antonio, Tex. BR/TR, 5'6", 155 lbs. Deb: 4/16/10																										
1910	Det-A	2	2	.500	11	6	2	0	3	49	51	0	10	16	11.2	2.57	102	.262	.298	0	.000	-2	-0	0	1	0.0
● **PETE BROWNING** Browning, Louis Rogers "The Gladiator" b: 6/17/1861, Louisville, Ky. d: 9/10/05, Louisville, Ky. BR/TR, 6', 180 lbs. Deb: 5/2/1882 ♦																										
1884	Lou-a	0	1	.000	1	1	0	0	0	0^{1}	2	0	2	0	135.0	54.00	6	1.000	1.000	150	.336	1	-2	-2	0	-1.9
● **TOM BROWNING** Browning, Thomas Leo b: 4/28/60, Casper, Wyoming BL/TL, 6'1", 190 lbs. Deb: 9/9/84																										
1984	Cin-N	1	0	1.000	3	3	0	0	0	23^{1}	27	0	5	14	12.3	1.54	245	.303	.340	1	.143	-0	5	6	-0	0.2
1985	Cin-N	20	9	.690	38	38	6	4	0	261^{1}	242	29	73	155	11.0	3.55	107	.245	.299	17	.193	2	1	7	-2	0.8
1986	Cin-N	14	13	.519	39	39	4	2	0	243^{1}	225	26	70	147	10.9	3.81	102	.245	.299	14	.163	-1	-3	2	-3	-0.2
1987	Cin-N	10	13	.435	32	31	2	0	0	183	201	27	61	117	13.1	5.02	85	.284	.345	8	.154	0	-19	-16	-2	-1.8
1988	Cin-N	18	5	.783	36	36	5	2	0	250^{2}	205	36	64	124	9.9	3.41	105	.224	.280	12	.145	0	1	5	-3	0.2
1989	Cin-N	15	12	.556	37	37	9	2	0	249^{2}	241	31	64	118	11.1	3.39	106	.255	.304	7	.090	-3	3	6	-1	0.1
1990	*Cin-N	15	9	.625	35	35	2	1	0	227^{2}	235	24	52	99	11.5	3.80	104	.266	.311	7	.093	-3	-0	4	-2	-0.2
1991	Cin-N☆	14	14	.500	36	36	1	0	0	230^{1}	241	32	56	115	11.8	4.18	91	.266	.312	12	.171	2	-13	-10	-3	-1.3
1992	Cin-N	6	5	.545	16	16	0	0	0	87	108	6	28	33	14.3	5.07	71	.311	.366	7	.226	1	-15	-14	0	-1.5
1993	Cin-N	7	7	.500	21	20	0	0	0	114	159	15	20	53	14.2	4.74	85	.333	.361	8	.216	2	-9	-9	1	-0.6
1994	Cin-N	3	1	.750	7	7	2	1	0	40^{2}	34	8	13	22	10.6	4.20	98	.222	.287	2	.143	-0	0	-0	-0	-0.1
1995	KC-A	0	2	.000	2	2	0	0	0	10	13	2	5	3	16.2	8.10	59	.302	.375	0	—	0	-4	-4	0	-0.5
Total	12	123	90	.577	302	300	31	12	0	1921	1931	236	511	1000	11.6	3.94	97	.262	.312	95	.153	2	-51	-24	-15	-4.9
● **MARK BROWNSON** Brownson, Mark Phillip b: 6/17/75, Lake Worth, Fla. BL/TR, 6'2", 185 lbs. Deb: 7/21/98																										
1998	Col-N	1	0	1.000	2	2	1	1	0	13^{1}	16	2	2	8	12.8	4.73	107	.296	.333	0	.000	-1	-1	0	-0	-0.1
● **BRUCE BRUBAKER** Brubaker, Bruce Ellsworth b: 12/29/41, Harrisburg, Pa. BR/TR, 6'1", 198 lbs. Deb: 4/15/67																										
1967	LA-N	0	0	—	1	0	0	0	0	1^{1}	3	1	0	2	20.3	20.25	15	.429	.429	0	—	0	-3	-3	0	0.0
1970	Mil-A	0	0	—	1	0	0	0	0	2	2	1	1	0	13.5	9.00	42	.250	.333	0	—	0	-1	-1	-0	0.0
Total	2	0	0	—	2	0	0	0	0	3^{1}	5	2	1	2	16.2	13.50	26	.333	.375	0	—	0	-4	-4	0	0.0
● **LOU BRUCE** Bruce, Louis R. b: 1/16/1877, St.Regis, N.Y. d: 2/9/68, Ilion, N.Y. BL/TR, 5'5", 145 lbs. Deb: 6/22/04 ♦																										
1904	Phi-A	0	0	—	2	0	0	0	0	11	11	1	2	2	10.6	4.91	55	.262	.295	27	.267	0	-3	-3	0	0.1
● **BOB BRUCE** Bruce, Robert James b: 5/16/33, Detroit, Mich. BR/TR, 6'3", 210 lbs. Deb: 9/14/59																										
1959	Det-A	0	1	.000	2	1	0	0	0	2	2	1	3	1	22.5	9.00	45	.250	.455	0	—	0	-1	-1	-0	-0.4
1960	Det-A	4	7	.364	34	15	1	0	0	130	127	16	56	76	13.0	3.74	106	.250	.331	7	.179	0	2	3	1	0.3
1961	Det-A	1	2	.333	14	6	0	0	0	44^{2}	57	6	24	25	16.7	4.43	92	.320	.407	1	.111	0	-2	-2	-1	-0.2
1962	Hou-N	10	9	.526	32	27	6	0	0	175	164	16	82	135	13.3	4.06	92	.248	.342	11	.200	5	-2	-6	0	-0.1
1963	Hou-N	5	9	.357	30	25	1	1	0	170^{1}	162	7	60	123	12.2	3.59	88	.250	.321	7	.127	2	-6	-8	-1	-0.6
1964	Hou-N	15	9	.625	35	29	9	4	0	202^{1}	191	8	33	135	10.1	2.76	124	.246	.279	12	.190	2	18	15	-0	2.0
1965	Hou-N	9	18	.333	35	34	7	1	0	229^{2}	241	22	38	145	11.3	3.72	90	.270	.307	9	.122	-1	-5	-9	0	-1.1
1966	Hou-N	3	13	.188	25	23	1	0	0	129^{2}	160	16	29	71	13.7	5.34	64	.301	.346	3	.077	-2	-25	-28	0	-3.2
1967	Atl-N	2	3	.400	12	7	1	0	1	38^{2}	42	3	15	22	13.5	4.89	68	.269	.337	2	.167	0	-7	-7	-1	-0.9
Total	9	49	71	.408	219	167	26	6	1	1122^{1}	1146	95	340	733	12.3	3.85	91	.263	.323	52	.150	6	-28	-43	-2	-4.2
● **FRED BRUCKBAUER** Bruckbauer, Frederick John b: 5/27/38, New Ulm, Minn. BR/TR, 6'1", 185 lbs. Deb: 4/25/61																										
1961	Min-A	0	0	—	1	0	0	0	0	0	3	0	1	0	—	∞	—	1.000	1.000	0	—	0	-3	-3	0	-0.3
● **ANDY BRUCKMILLER** Bruckmiller, Andrew b: 1/1/1882, McKeesport, Pa. d: 1/12/70, McKeesport, Pa. BR/TR, 5'11", 175 lbs. Deb: 6/26/05																										
1905	Det-A	0	0	—	1	0	0	0	0	1	4	0	1	1	45.0	27.00	10	.571	.625	0	.000	-0	-3	-3	-0	0.0
● **MIKE BRUHERT** Bruhert, Michael Edwin b: 6/24/51, Jamaica, N.Y. BR/TR, 6'6", 220 lbs. Deb: 4/9/78																										
1978	NY-N	4	11	.267	27	22	1	1	0	133^{2}	171	6	34	56	13.9	4.78	73	.317	.359	3	.075	-3	-18	-19	-0	-2.2
● **DUFF BRUMLEY** Brumley, Duff Lechaun b: 8/25/70, Cleveland, Tenn. BR/TR, 6'4", 195 lbs. Deb: 6/1/94																										
1994	Tex-A	0	0	—	2	0	0	0	0	3^{1}	6	1	5	4	29.7	16.20	30	.400	.550	0	—	0	-4	-4	-0	0.0
● **GREG BRUMMETT** Brummett, Gregory Scott b: 4/20/67, Wichita, Kan. BR/TR, 6', 180 lbs. Deb: 5/29/93																										
1993	SF-N	2	3	.400	8	8	0	0	0	46	53	9	13	20	12.9	4.70	83	.294	.342	0	.000	-1	-3	-4	-0	-0.5
	Min-A	2	1	.667	5	5	0	0	0	26^{2}	29	3	15	10	14.9	5.74	76	.299	.393	0	—	0	-4	-4	-1	-0.4
Total	1	4	4	.500	13	13	0	0	0	72^{2}	82	12	28	30	13.6	5.08	80	.296	.361	0	.000	-1	-8	-8	-1	-0.9
● **JACK BRUNER** Bruner, Jack Raymond b: 7/1/24, Waterloo, Iowa BL/TL, 6'1", 185 lbs. Deb: 9/16/49																										
1949	Chi-A	1	2	.333	4	2	0	0	0	7^{2}	10	0	8	4	21.1	8.22	51	.357	.500	0	.000	-0	-3	-3	-0	-1.1
1950	Chi-A	0	0	—	9	0	0	0	0	12^{1}	7	0	14	8	16.1	3.65	123	.184	.415	0	—	0	1	1	-0	0.0
	StL-A	1	2	.333	13	1	0	0	1	35	36	4	23	16	15.7	4.63	107	.267	.381	0	.000	-1	-0	1	-1	-0.1
	Yr	1	2	.333	22	1	0	0	1	47^{1}	43	4	37	24	15.6	4.37	110	.247	.385	0	.000	-1	1	2	-1	-0.1
Total	2	2	4	.333	26	3	0	0	1	55	53	4	45	28	16.5	4.91	96	.264	.406	0	.000	-1	-2	-1	-1	-1.2
● **ROY BRUNER** Bruner, Walter Roy b: 2/10/17, Cecilia, Ky. d: 11/30/86, St.Matthews, Ky. BR/TR, 6', 165 lbs. Deb: 9/14/39																										
1939	Phi-N	0	4	.000	4	4	2	0	0	27	38	3	13	11	17.0	6.67	60	.339	.408	1	.111	-1	-8	-8	-1	-1.0
1940	Phi-N	0	0	—	2	0	0	0	0	6^{1}	5	2	6	4	15.6	5.68	69	.227	.393	1	.500	0	-1	-1	0	0.1
1941	Phi-N	0	3	.000	13	1	0	0	0	29^{1}	37	1	25	13	19.0	4.91	75	.336	.459	0	.000	-0	-5	-4	-0	-0.5
Total	3	0	7	.000	19	5	2	0	0	62^{2}	80	6	44	28	17.8	5.74	67	.328	.431	2	.118	-1	-14	-13	-1	-1.4
● **GEORGE BRUNET** Brunet, George Stuart "Lefty" b: 6/8/35, Houghton, Mich. d: 10/25/91, Poza Rica, Mex. BR/TL, 6'1", 210 lbs. Deb: 9/14/56																										
1956	KC-A	0	0	—	6	1	0	0	0	9	10	1	11	5	21.0	7.00	62	.286	.457	0	.000	-0	-3	-3	0	0.0
1957	KC-A	0	1	.000	4	2	0	0	0	11^{1}	13	2	4	3	13.5	5.56	71	.277	.333	0	.000	-0	-2	-2	-0	-0.2
1959	KC-A	0	0	—	2	0	0	0	0	4^{2}	10	2	7	7	34.7	11.57	35	.435	.581	0	—	0	-4	-4	1	0.1
1960	KC-A	0	2	.000	3	2	0	0	0	10^{1}	12	0	10	4	20.0	4.35	91	.308	.460	0	.000	-0	-1	-0	1	0.0
	Mil-N	2	0	1.000	17	6	0	0	0	49^{2}	53	6	22	39	13.8	5.07	68	.275	.352	1	.091	-1	-7	-9	0	-0.4

YEAR	TM/L	W	L	PCT	G	GS	CG	SH	SV	IP	H	HR	BB	SO	RAT	ERA	ERA+	OAV	OOB	BH	AVG	PB	PR	/A	PD	TPI
1961	Mil-N	0	0	—	5	0	0	0	0	5	7	1	2	0	16.2	5.40	69	.412	.474	0	—	0	-1	-1	0	0.0
1962	Hou-N	2	4	.333	17	11	2	0	0	54	62	2	21	36	13.8	4.50	83	.291	.355	1	.059	-1	-3	-5	1	-0.5
1963	Hou-N	0	3	.000	5	2	0	0	0	12^2	24	2	6	11	21.3	7.11	44	.393	.448	0	.000	-0	-5	-6	0	-1.1
	Bal-A	0	1	.000	16	0	0	0	1	20	25	3	9	13	15.7	5.40	64	.301	.376	0	.000	-0	-4	-4	0	-0.2
1964	LA-A	2	2	.500	10	7	0	0	0	42^1	38	2	25	36	13.4	3.61	91	.237	.341	2	.182	0	0	-2	-0	-0.1
1965	Cal-A	9	11	.450	41	26	8	3	2	197	149	9	69	141	10.1	2.56	133	.209	.282	3	.054	-2	20	18	-1	1.4
1966	Cal-A	13	13	.500	41	32	8	2	0	212	183	21	106	148	12.5	3.31	101	.234	.329	7	.103	-2	3	1	-0	0.0
1967	Cal-A	11	19	.367	40	37	7	2	1	250	203	19	90	165	10.7	3.31	95	.223	.295	6	.077	-4	-2	-5	-2	-1.2
1968	Cal-A	13	17	.433	39	36	8	5	0	245^1	191	23	68	132	9.6	2.86	102	.215	.273	6	.081	-3	3	1	-2	-0.5
1969	Cal-A	6	7	.462	23	19	2	2	0	100^2	98	15	39	56	12.3	3.84	91	.255	.325	1	.037	-1	-2	-4	-1	-0.7
	Sea-A	2	5	.286	12	11	2	0	0	63^2	70	11	28	37	13.9	5.37	68	.280	.353	3	.150	1	-12	-12	1	-1.1
	Yr	8	12	.400	35	30	4	2	0	164^1	168	26	67	93	12.9	4.44	80	.264	.334	4	.085	-0	-15	-16	-0	-1.8
1970	Was-A	8	6	.571	24	20	2	1	0	118	124	10	48	67	13.2	4.42	80	.275	.346	6	.158	1	-9	-11	-1	-1.2
	Pit-N	1	1	.500	12	1	0	0	0	16^2	19	1	9	17	15.7	2.70	144	.311	.408	0	.000	-0	2	2	0	0.2
1971	StL-N	0	1	.000	7	0	0	0	0	9^1	12	3	7	4	18.3	5.79	62	.316	.422	1	.333	0	-2	-2	-0	-0.2
Total	15	69	93	.426	324	213	39	15	4	1431^2	1303	133	581	921	12.0	3.62	92	.244	.320	37	.089	-14	-31	-46	-4	-5.7
● TOM BRUNO	Bruno, Thomas Michael b: 1/26/53, Chicago, Ill. BR/TR, 6'5", 210 lbs. Deb: 8/1/76																									
1976	KC-A	1	0	1.000	12	0	0	0	0	17^1	20	3	9	11	15.1	6.75	52	.290	.372	0	—	0	-6	-6	-0	-0.4
1977	Tor-A	0	1	.000	12	0	0	0	0	18^1	30	4	13	9	21.6	7.85	53	.366	.458	0	—	0	-8	-7	0	-0.4
1978	StL-N	4	3	.571	18	3	0	0	1	49^2	38	3	17	33	10.0	1.99	176	.209	.276	1	.083	-1	9	8	-1	1.1
1979	StL-N	2	3	.400	27	1	0	0	0	38^1	37	1	22	27	14.3	4.23	89	.253	.359	1	.200	0	-2	-2	-0	-0.2
Total	4	7	7	.500	69	4	0	0	1	123^2	125	11	61	80	13.8	4.22	87	.261	.348	2	.118	-1	-7	-7	-1	0.1
● WILL BRUNSON	Brunson, William Donald b: 3/20/70, Irving, Tex. BL/TL, 6'4", 185 lbs. Deb: 6/21/98																									
1998	LA-N	0	1	.000	2	0	0	0	0	2^1	3	0	2	1	19.3	11.57	34	.333	.455	0	—	0	-2	-2	-0	-0.6
	Det-A	0	0	—	8	0	0	0	0	3	2	0	1	1	9.0	0.00	—	.200	.273	0	—	0	2	2	0	0.0
Total	1	0	1	.000	10	0	0	0	0	5^1	5	0	3	2	13.5	5.06	86	.263	.364	0	—	0	-0	-0	0	-0.6
● JIM BRUSKE	Bruske, James Scott b: 10/7/64, E.St.Louis, Ill. BR/TR, 6'1", 185 lbs. Deb: 8/25/95																									
1995	LA-N	0	0	—	9	0	0	0	1	10	12	0	4	5	15.3	4.50	84	.300	.378	0	—	0	-0	-1	-0	0.0
1996	LA-N	0	0	—	11	0	0	0	0	12^2	17	2	3	12	14.9	5.68	68	.315	.362	0	—	0	-2	-3	0	0.0
1997	SD-N	4	1	.800	28	0	0	0	0	44^2	37	4	25	32	12.7	3.63	107	.228	.335	1	.167	0	3	1	-1	0.1
1998	LA-N	3	0	1.000	35	0	0	0	1	44	47	2	19	31	14.1	3.48	112	.272	.354	0	.000	-0	4	2	-1	0.0
	SD-N	0	0	—	4	0	0	0	0	7	10	1	4	4	18.0	3.86	99	.333	.412	0	—	0	0	-0	-0	0.0
	Yr	3	0	1.000	39	0	0	0	1	51	57	3	23	35	14.1	3.53	110	.277	.349	0	.000	-0	4	2	-1	0.0
	NY-A	1	0	1.000	3	1	0	0	0	9	9	2	1	3	10.0	3.00	148	.257	.278	0	—	0	2	1	-0	0.2
Total	4	8	1	.889	90	1	0	0	2	127^1	132	11	56	87	13.7	3.82	102	.267	.349	1	.111	-0	6	1	-2	0.3
● WARREN BRUSSTAR	Brusstar, Warren Scott b: 2/2/52, Oakland, Cal. BR/TR, 6'3", 200 lbs. Deb: 5/6/77																									
1977	*Phi-N	7	2	.778	46	0	0	0	3	71^1	64	7	24	46	11.2	2.65	151	.250	.317	0	.000	-1	10	11	1	1.4
1978	*Phi-N	6	3	.667	58	0	0	0	0	88^2	74	0	30	60	10.9	2.33	153	.239	.312	1	.143	0	12	12	2	1.4
1979	Phi-N	1	0	1.000	13	0	0	0	1	14^1	23	1	4	3	17.0	6.91	55	.383	.422	0	—	0	-5	-5	0	-0.4
1980	*Phi-N	2	2	.500	26	0	0	0	0	38^2	42	3	13	21	12.8	3.72	102	.286	.344	0	.000	-0	-1	0	0	0.0
1981	*Phi-N	0	1	.000	14	0	0	0	0	12^1	12	0	10	8	16.8	4.38	83	.250	.390	0	—	0	-1	-1	0	-0.1
1982	Phi-N	2	3	.400	22	0	0	0	2	22^2	31	2	5	11	14.7	4.76	77	.348	.389	0	.000	-0	-3	-3	0	-0.6
	Chi-A	2	0	1.000	10	0	0	0	0	18^1	19	2	3	8	11.3	3.44	117	.257	.295	0	—	0	1	1	1	0.2
1983	Chi-N	3	1	.750	59	0	0	0	1	80^1	67	1	37	46	11.9	2.35	161	.234	.326	0	.000	-0	11	13	0	0.6
1984	*Chi-N	1	1	.500	41	0	0	0	3	63^2	57	4	21	36	11.2	3.11	126	.247	.312	1	.200	1	3	6	-0	0.3
1985	Chi-N	4	3	.571	51	0	0	0	4	74^1	87	8	36	34	15.3	6.05	66	.292	.374	1	.143	0	-20	-17	-2	-1.9
Total	9	28	16	.636	340	0	0	0	14	484^2	476	28	183	273	12.5	3.51	109	.265	.337	3	.094	-1	8	17	2	0.9
● CLAY BRYANT	Bryant, Claiborne Henry b: 11/16/11, Madison Heights, Va. BR/TR, 6'2.5", 195 lbs. Deb: 4/19/35 C																									
1935	Chi-N	1	2	.333	9	1	0	0	2	22^2	34	1	7	13	16.3	5.16	76	.358	.402	2	.333	2	-3	-3	-0	-0.2
1936	Chi-N	1	2	.333	26	0	0	0	0	57^1	57	0	24	35	13.0	3.30	121	.259	.337	5	.417	1	**5**	**4**	1	0.4
1937	Chi-N	9	3	.750	38	9	4	1	3	135^1	117	1	78	75	13.0	4.26	94	.232	.336	14	.311	5	-5	-4	-3	-0.2
1938	*Chi-N	19	11	.633	44	30	17	3	2	270^1	235	6	125	**135**	12.0	3.10	124	.235	.321	24	.226	4	21	22	-3	2.4
1939	Chi-N	2	1	.667	4	4	2	0	0	31^1	42	3	14	9	16.4	5.74	69	.307	.375	3	.214	0	-6	-6	-1	-0.5
1940	Chi-N	0	1	.000	8	0	0	0	0	26^1	26	2	14	5	13.7	4.78	78	.265	.357	3	.333	1	-3	-3	0	0.0
Total	6	32	20	.615	129	44	23	4	7	543^1	511	13	262	272	12.9	3.73	104	.249	.335	51	.266	13	8	10	-6	1.9
● RON BRYANT	Bryant, Ronald Raymond b: 11/12/47, Redlands, Cal. BB/TL, 6', 190 lbs. Deb: 9/29/67																									
1967	SF-N	0	0	—	1	0	0	0	0	4	3	0	0	2	9.0	4.50	73	.200	.250	0	.000	-0	-1	-1	-0	0.0
1969	SF-N	4	3	.571	16	8	0	0	1	57^2	60	8	25	30	13.6	4.37	80	.271	.351	3	.188	1	-5	-6	-0	-0.6
1970	SF-N	5	8	.385	34	11	1	0	0	96	103	7	38	66	13.4	4.78	83	.274	.344	3	.111	-1	-8	-9	1	-1.0
1971	*SF-N	7	10	.412	27	22	3	2	0	140	146	9	49	79	12.7	3.79	90	.272	.336	10	.200	1	-5	-6	0	-0.6
1972	SF-N	14	7	.667	35	28	11	4	0	214	176	20	77	107	10.7	2.90	120	.224	.295	12	.171	1	13	14	-4	0.9
1973	SF-N	**24**	12	.667	41	39	8	0	0	270	240	23	115	143	12.1	3.53	108	.234	.316	16	.168	1	4	9	0	1.2
1974	SF-N	3	15	.167	41	23	0	0	0	126^2	142	11	68	75	15.2	5.61	68	.286	.376	4	.129	-1	-28	-26	-0	-3.4
1975	StL-N	0	1	.000	10	1	0	0	0	8^2	20	2	7	7	28.0	16.62	23	.444	.519	0	.000	-0	-13	-12	0	-1.2
Total	8	57	56	.504	205	132	23	6	1	917	890	80	379	509	12.7	4.02	91	.254	.331	48	.165	0	-42	-36	-4	-4.7
● T.R. BRYDEN	Bryden, Thomas Ray b: 1/17/59, Moses Lake, Wash. BR/TR, 6'4", 190 lbs. Deb: 4/10/86																									
1986	Cal-A	2	1	.667	16	0	0	0	0	34^1	38	4	21	25	16.0	6.55	63	.290	.396	0	—	0	-9	-9	0	-0.6
● TOD BRYNAN	Brynan, Charles Ruley b: 7/1863, Philadelphia, Pa. d: 5/10/25, Philadelphia, Pa. BR/TR, Deb: 6/22/1888																									
1888	Chi-N	2	1	.667	3	3	2	0	0	25	29	2	7	11	13.7	6.48	47	.271	.328	2	.182	0	-10	-10	-1	-0.9
1891	Bos-N	0	1	.000	1	1	0	0	0	1	4	0	3	0	63.0	54.00	7	.571	.700	0	—	0	-6	-6	-0	-1.9
Total	2	2	2	.500	4	4	2	0	0	26	33	2	10	11	15.6	8.31	37	.289	.357	2	.182	0	-16	-15	-1	-2.8
● JIM BUCHANAN	Buchanan, James Forrest b: 7/1/1876, Chatham Hill, Va. d: 6/15/49, Norfolk, Neb. BL/TR, 5'10", 165 lbs. Deb: 4/16/05																									
1905	StL-A	5	9	.357	22	15	12	1	**2**	141^1	149	2	27	54	11.3	3.50	73	.272	.309	7	.152	-0	-13	-15	0	-1.5
● BOB BUCHANAN	Buchanan, Robert Gordon b: 5/3/61, Ridley Park, Pa. BL/TL, 6'1", 185 lbs. Deb: 7/13/85																									
1985	Cin-N	1	0	1.000	14	0	0	0	0	16	25	4	9	3	19.1	8.44	45	.368	.442	0	.000	-0	-9	-8	0	-0.5
1989	KC-A	0	0	—	2	0	0	0	0	3^1	5	1	3	3	21.6	16.20	24	.333	.444	0	—	0	-5	-5	-0	0.0
Total	2	1	0	1.000	16	0	0	0	0	19^1	30	5	12	6	19.6	9.78	39	.361	.442	0	.000	-0	-13	-13	-0	-0.5
● GARY BUCKELS	Buckels, Gary Scott b: 7/22/65, LaMirada, Cal. BR/TR, 6', 185 lbs. Deb: 7/23/94																									
1994	StL-N	0	1	.000	10	0	0	0	0	12	8	2	7	9	11.3	2.25	185	.186	.300	0	.000	-0	3	3	0	0.2
● GARLAND BUCKEYE	Buckeye, Garland Maiers "Gob" b: 10/16/1897, Heron Lake, Minn. d: 11/14/75, Stone Lake, Wis. BB/TL, 6', 260 lbs. Deb: 6/19/18																									
1918	Was-A	0	0	—	1	0	0	0	0	2	3	0	6	2	40.5	18.00	15	.333	.600	0	—	0	-3	-3	0	0.0
1925	Cle-A	13	8	.619	30	18	11	1	0	153	161	3	58	49	13.2	3.65	121	.267	.338	14	.226	2	13	13	-1	1.7
1926	Cle-A	6	9	.400	32	18	5	1	0	165^2	160	3	69	36	12.8	3.10	131	.264	.345	12	.200	2	17	18	-2	1.4
1927	Cle-A	10	17	.370	35	25	13	2	1	204^2	231	6	74	38	13.6	3.96	106	.296	.360	19	.268	3	4	6	-1	0.8
1928	Cle-A	1	5	.167	9	6	0	0	0	35	58	2	5	6	16.7	6.69	62	.389	.417	1	.111	-1	-10	-10	-0	-1.4
	NY-N	0	0	—	1	0	0	0	0	3^2	9	1	2	3	27.0	14.73	27	.409	.458	1	.500	1	-4	-4	0	0.1
Total	5	30	39	.435	108	67	29	4	1	564	622	15	214	134	13.6	3.91	108	.287	.356	47	.230	7	16	19	-3	2.6
● ED BUCKINGHAM	Buckingham, Edward Taylor b: 5/12/1874, Metuchen, N.J. d: 7/30/42, Bridgeport, Conn. Deb: 8/30/1895																									
1895	Was-N	0	0	—	1	1	0	0	0	3	6	0	2	1	24.0	6.00	80	.400	.471	0	.000	-0	-0	-0	0	0.0

YEAR	TM/L	W	L	PCT	G	GS	CG	SH	SV	IP	H	HR	BB	SO	RAT	ERA	ERA+	OAV	OOB	BH	AVG	PB	PR	/A	PD	TPI
● **JESS BUCKLES** Buckles, Jesse Robert "Jim" b: 5/20/1890, LaVerne, Cal. d: 8/2/75, Westminster, Cal. BL/TL, 6'2.5", 205 lbs. Deb: 9/17/16																										
1916	NY-A	0	0	—	2	0	0	0	0	4	3	0	1	2	9.0	2.25	128	.188	.235	0	.000	-0	0	0	-0	0.0
● **JOHN BUCKLEY** Buckley, John Edward b: 3/20/1869, Marlborough, Mass. d: 5/3/42, Westborough, Mass. BL/TR, 6'1", 200 lbs. Deb: 7/15/1890																										
1890	Buf-P	1	3	.250	4	4	4	0	0	34	49	5	16	4	17.2	7.68	53	.325	.389	0	.000	-2	-13	-14	0	-1.1
● **MIKE BUDDIE** Buddie, Michael J. b: 12/12/70, Berea, Ohio BR/TR, 6'3", 210 lbs. Deb: 4/6/98																										
1998	NY-A	4	1	.800	24	2	0	0	0	41^2	46	5	13	20	13.4	5.62	79	.284	.348	0	—	0	-4	-5	-1	-0.6
● **MIKE BUDNICK** Budnick, Michael Joe b: 9/15/19, Astoria, Ore. BR/TR, 6'1", 200 lbs. Deb: 4/18/46																										
1946	NY-N	2	3	.400	35	7	1	1	3	88^1	75	13	48	36	12.5	3.16	109	.231	.330	6	.300	3	2	3	1	0.5
1947	NY-N	0	0	—	7	1	0	0	0	12	16	0	10	6	19.5	10.50	39	.314	.426	1	.250	0	-9	-9	0	0.0
Total	2	2	3	.400	42	8	1	1	3	100^1	91	13	58	42	13.4	4.04	87	.242	.343	7	.292	3	-6	-6	1	0.5
● **CHARLIE BUFFINTON** Buffinton, Charles G. b: 6/14/1861, Fall River, Mass. d: 9/23/07, Fall River, Mass. BR/TR, 6'1", 180 lbs. Deb: 5/17/1882 M♦																										
1882	Bos-N	2	3	.400	5	5	4	1	0	42	53	2	14	17	14.4	4.07	70	.296	.347	13	.260	0	-5	-6	1	-0.5
1883	Bos-N	25	14	.641	43	41	34	4	1	333	346	4	51	188	10.7	3.03	102	.254	.281	81	.238	0	4	3	-1	0.1
1884	Bos-N	48	16	.750	67	67	63	8	0	587	506	15	76	417	8.9	2.15	135	.219	.244	94	.267	12	54	48	3	5.7
1885	Bos-N	22	27	.449	51	50	49	6	0	434^1	425	10	112	242	11.1	2.88	93	.246	.292	81	.240	5	-3	-9	6	0.0
1886	Bos-N	7	10	.412	18	17	16	0	0	151	203	4	39	47	14.4	4.59	70	.308	.346	51	.290	4	-21	-23	-1	-1.8
1887	Phi-N	21	17	.553	40	38	35	1	0	332^1	352	16	92	160	12.1	3.66	116	.264	.313	72	.268	2	15	21	7	2.6
1888	Phi-N	28	17	.622	46	46	43	6	0	400^1	324	6	59	199	8.7	1.91	155	.213	.244	29	.181	-1	42	47	10	**5.8**
1889	Phi-N	28	16	.636	47	43	37	2	0	380	390	10	121	153	12.2	3.24	134	.257	.315	32	.208	-3	33	47	2	4.3
1890	Phi-P	19	15	.559	36	33	28	0	1	283^1	312	8	126	89	14.1	3.81	112	.268	.343	41	.273	4	13	15	1	1.6
1891	Bos-a	29	9	**.763**	48	43	33	2	1	363^2	303	8	120	158	**10.6**	2.55	137	.219	**.284**	34	.188	-0	47	38	6	3.6
1892	Bal-N	4	8	.333	13	13	9	0	0	97	130	4	46	30	16.6	4.92	70	.309	.381	15	.349	4	-18	-16	2	-1.1
Total	11	233	152	.605	414	396	351	30	3	3404	3344	87	856	1700	11.2	2.96	114	.246	.292	543	.245	27	162	161	35	20.3
● **BOB BUHL** Buhl, Robert Ray b: 8/12/28, Saginaw, Mich. BR/TR, 6'2", 190 lbs. Deb: 4/17/53																										
1953	Mil-N	13	8	.619	30	18	8	3	0	154^1	133	9	73	83	12.2	2.97	132	.235	.326	6	.113	-3	23	16	1	1.8
1954	Mil-N	2	7	.222	31	14	2	1	3	110^1	117	5	65	57	15.0	4.00	93	.277	.376	1	.032	-3	1	-3	-0	-0.6
1955	Mil-N	13	11	.542	38	27	11	1	1	201^2	168	13	109	117	12.4	3.21	117	.227	.327	6	.105	-4	18	12	-1	0.9
1956	Mil-N	18	8	.692	38	33	13	2	0	216^2	190	18	105	86	12.3	3.32	104	.236	.326	7	.096	-4	11	3	0	0.0
1957	*Mil-N	18	7	**.720**	34	31	14	2	0	216^2	191	15	121	117	13.0	2.74	128	.241	.341	6	.082	-3	27	18	-2	1.4
1958	Mil-N	5	2	.714	11	10	3	0	1	73	74	5	30	27	12.9	3.45	102	.260	.332	5	.200	0	4	1	1	0.2
1959	Mil-N	15	9	.625	31	25	12	**4**	0	198	181	19	74	105	11.7	2.86	124	.243	.313	4	.057	-5	24	15	3	1.5
1960	Mil-N★	16	9	.640	36	33	11	2	0	238^2	202	23	103	121	11.6	3.09	111	.229	.312	14	.157	-2	18	9	3	1.0
1961	Mil-N	9	10	.474	32	28	9	1	0	188^1	180	23	98	77	13.5	4.11	91	.256	.351	4	.067	-4	-2	-8	1	-1.0
1962	Mil-N	0	1	.000	1	1	0	0	0	2	6	0	4	1	45.0	22.50	17	.545	.667	0	.000	-0	-4	-4	-0	-1.1
	Chi-N	12	13	.480	34	30	8	1	0	212	204	23	94	109	12.9	3.69	112	.255	.338	0	.000	-6	6	11	-2	0.4
	Yr	12	14	.462	35	31	8	1	0	214	210	23	98	110	13.2	3.87	107	.259	.343	0	.000	-6	2	7	-2	-0.7
1963	Chi-N	11	14	.440	37	34	6	0	0	226	219	24	62	108	11.3	3.38	104	.259	.312	8	.108	-3	-2	3	1	0.1
1964	Chi-N	15	14	.517	36	35	11	3	0	227^2	208	22	68	107	11.1	3.83	97	.244	.303	7	.096	-2	-8	-3	2	-0.3
1965	Chi-N	13	11	.542	32	31	2	0	0	184^1	207	26	57	92	12.9	4.39	84	.284	.335	4	.060	-4	-17	-15	0	-2.2
1966	Chi-N	0	0	—	1	1	0	0	0	2^1	4	1	1	1	19.3	15.43	24	.400	.455	0	.000	-0	-3	-3	0	0.0
	Phi-N	6	8	.429	32	18	1	0	1	132	156	10	39	59	13.6	4.77	75	.298	.351	4	.098	-2	-17	-17	1	-1.8
	Yr	6	8	.429	33	19	1	0	1	134^1	160	11	40	60	13.7	4.96	73	.299	.352	4	.095	-2	-20	-20	1	-1.8
1967	Phi-N	0	0	—	3	0	0	0	0	3	6	2	2	1	24.0	12.00	28	.462	.533	0	—	0	-3	-3	0	0.0
Total	15	166	132	.557	457	369	111	20	6	2587	2446	238	1105	1268	12.5	3.55	103	.251	.330	76	.089	-43	75	36	8	0.3
● **DE WAYNE BUICE** Buice, De Wayne Allison b: 8/20/57, Lynwood, Cal. BR/TR, 6', 170 lbs. Deb: 4/25/87																										
1987	Cal-A	6	7	.462	57	0	0	0	17	114	87	12	40	109	10.2	3.39	127	.213	.287	0	—	0	13	11	0	1.5
1988	Cal-A	2	4	.333	32	0	0	0	3	41^1	45	5	19	38	13.9	5.88	66	.287	.364	0	—	0	-9	-9	0	-1.2
1989	Tor-A	1	0	1.000	7	0	0	0	0	17	13	2	13	10	13.8	5.82	65	.220	.361	0	—	0	-4	-4	0	-0.2
Total	3	9	11	.450	96	0	0	0	20	172^1	145	19	72	157	11.4	4.23	98	.232	.314	0	—	0	1	-2	0	0.1
● **CY BUKER** Buker, Cyril Owen b: 2/5/19, Greenwood, Wis. BL/TR, 5'11", 190 lbs. Deb: 5/17/45																										
1945	Bro-N	7	2	.778	42	4	0	0	5	87^1	90	2	45	48	14.0	3.30	114	.268	.356	3	.188	-0	5	4	-1	0.4
● **JIM BULLINGER** Bullinger, James Eric b: 8/21/65, New Orleans, La. BR/TR, 6'2", 185 lbs. Deb: 5/27/92 F																										
1992	Chi-N	2	8	.200	39	9	1	0	7	85	72	9	54	36	13.8	4.66	77	.233	.354	5	.250	2	-11	-10	2	-0.8
1993	Chi-N	1	0	1.000	15	0	0	0	1	16^2	18	1	9	10	14.6	4.32	92	.277	.365	0	.000	-0	-1	-1	-0	-0.1
1994	Chi-N	6	2	.750	33	10	1	0	2	100	87	6	34	72	11.0	3.60	115	.235	.300	3	.136	1	7	6	-1	0.4
1995	Chi-N	12	8	.600	24	24	1	1	0	150	152	14	65	93	13.6	4.14	99	.265	.349	6	.128	1	1	-1	1	0.1
1996	Chi-N	6	10	.375	37	20	1	1	1	129^1	144	15	68	90	15.3	6.54	66	.283	.376	8	.250	5	-33	-32	1	-2.8
1997	Mon-N	7	12	.368	36	25	2	2	0	155^1	165	17	74	87	14.5	5.56	75	.276	.367	9	.209	2	-24	-24	2	-2.2
1998	Sea-A	0	1	.000	2	1	0	0	0	5^2	13	3	2	4	23.8	15.88	29	.433	.469	0	—	0	-7	-7	-0	-0.9
Total	7	34	41	.453	186	89	6	4	11	642	651	65	306	392	13.9	5.06	81	.265	.355	31	.188	10	-68	-67	4	-6.3
● **KIRK BULLINGER** Bullinger, Kirk Matthew b: 10/28/69, New Orleans, La. BR/TR, 6'2", 170 lbs. Deb: 8/30/98 F																										
1998	Mon-N	1	0	1.000	8	0	0	0	0	7	14	1	0	2	18.0	9.00	46	.400	.400	0	.000	-0	-4	-4	0	-0.4
● **RED BULLOCK** Bullock, Malton Joseph b: 10/12/11, Biloxi, Miss. d: 6/27/88, Pascagoula, Miss. BL/TL, 6'1", 192 lbs. Deb: 5/19/36																										
1936	Phi-A	0	2	.000	12	2	0	0	0	16^2	19	0	37	7	30.2	14.04	36	.271	.523	0	.000	-1	-17	-17	0	-1.5
● **MELVIN BUNCH** Bunch, Melvin Lynn b: 11/4/71, Texarkana, Tex. BR/TR, 6'1", 165 lbs. Deb: 5/6/95																										
1995	KC-A	1	3	.250	13	5	0	0	0	40	42	11	14	19	12.6	5.62	85	.261	.320	0	—	0	-4	-4	-1	-0.5
● **WALLY BUNKER** Bunker, Wallace Edward b: 1/25/45, Seattle, Wash. BR/TR, 6'2", 197 lbs. Deb: 9/29/63																										
1963	Bal-A	0	1	.000	1	1	0	0	0	4	10	1	3	1	29.3	13.50	26	.476	.542	1	.500	0	-4	-4	-0	-0.7
1964	Bal-A	19	5	**.792**	29	29	12	1	0	214	161	17	62	96	9.5	2.69	133	.207	.269	5	.069	-2	22	21	1	2.2
1965	Bal-A	10	8	.556	34	27	4	1	2	189	170	16	58	84	11.0	3.38	103	.242	.303	4	.073	-1	2	2	-1	-0.1
1966	*Bal-A	10	6	.625	29	24	3	0	0	142^2	151	16	48	89	12.7	4.29	78	.269	.329	5	.104	-0	-14	-15	-1	-1.7
1967	Bal-A	3	7	.300	29	9	1	0	1	88	83	7	31	51	11.9	4.09	77	.254	.322	2	.077	-2	-8	-9	1	-1.1
1968	Bal-A	2	0	1.000	18	10	2	1	0	71	59	4	14	44	9.4	2.41	121	.225	.267	2	.111	-0	5	4	-0	0.1
1969	KC-A	12	11	.522	35	31	10	1	2	222^2	198	29	62	130	10.7	3.23	114	.238	.294	10	.143	0	10	11	3	1.5
1970	KC-A	2	11	.154	24	15	2	1	0	121^2	109	16	50	59	11.8	4.22	89	.238	.313	2	.065	-0	-7	-6	-1	-0.8
1971	KC-A	2	3	.400	7	6	0	0	0	32^1	35	7	6	15	11.4	5.01	68	.271	.304	0	.000	-1	-6	-6	-0	-0.9
Total	9	60	52	.536	206	152	34	5	5	1085^1	976	113	334	569	11.0	3.51	99	.240	.300	31	.094	-5	-1	-3	1	-1.5
● **JIM BUNNING** Bunning, James Paul David b: 10/23/31, Southgate, Ky. BR/TR, 6'3", 195 lbs. Deb: 7/20/55 H																										
1955	Det-A	3	5	.375	15	8	0	0	1	51	59	8	32	37	16.6	6.35	60	.291	.395	3	.200	-0	-14	-14	0	-1.9
1956	Det-A	5	1	.833	15	3	0	0	1	53^1	55	6	28	34	14.0	3.71	111	.257	.343	6	.333	2	3	2	-1	0.4
1957	Det-A★	**20**	8	.714	45	30	14	1	1	**267**^{1}	214	33	72	182	10.0	2.69	143	.218	.279	20	.213	3	**33**	**35**	-5	3.3
1958	Det-A	14	12	.538	35	34	10	3	0	219^2	188	28	79	177	11.3	3.52	115	.228	.304	14	.187	-1	6	12	-3	1.0
1959	Det-A★	17	13	.567	40	35	14	1	1	249^2	220	37	75	**201**	11.0	3.89	104	.234	.298	17	.191	1	-1	5	-5	0.1
1960	Det-A	11	14	.440	36	34	10	3	0	252	217	20	64	**201**	10.4	2.79	**142**	.236	.293	13	.160	-2	**30**	**33**	-1	2.6
1961	Det-A★	17	11	.607	38	37	12	4	1	268	232	25	71	194	10.5	3.19	128	.229	.285	13	.130	-4	25	27	-2	2.0
1962	Det-A★	19	10	.655	41	35	12	2	6	258	262	28	74	184	12.2	3.59	113	.261	.320	23	.242	4	11	14	-5	1.4
1963	Det-A★	12	13	.480	39	35	6	2	1	248^1	245	38	69	196	11.6	3.88	97	.254	.307	13	.155	-1	-7	-4	-2	-0.6
1964	Phi-N★	19	8	.704	41	39	13	5	2	284^1	248	23	46	219	9.7	2.63	132	.233	.274	12	.121	-2	29	27	-4	1.8
1965	Phi-N	19	9	.679	39	39	15	7	0	291	253	23	62	268	10.1	2.60	133	.232	.281	22	.214	4	30	28	0	3.1

YEAR	TM/L	W	L	PCT	G	GS	CG	SH	SV	IP	H	HR	BB	SO	RAT	ERA	ERA+	OAV	OOB	BH	AVG	PB	PR	/A	PD	TPI
1966	Phi-N★	19	14	.576	43	41	16	**5**	1	314	260	26	55	252	9.6	2.41	149	.223	.270	19	.179	1	42	41	-3	4.1
1967	Phi-N	17	15	.531	40	40	16	**6**	0	**302**^{1}	241	18	73	**253**	9.7	2.29	149	.217	.273	17	.163	2	**36**	**38**	-3	4.1
1968	Pit-N	4	14	.222	27	26	3	1	0	160	168	14	48	95	12.6	3.88	75	.272	.333	5	.098	-2	-16	-17	-3	-2.3
1969	Pit-N	10	9	.526	25	25	4	0	0	156	147	10	49	124	11.7	3.81	92	.249	.313	2	.043	-3	-4	-6	-3	-1.3
	LA-N	3	1	.750	9	9	1	0	0	56^1	65	5	10	33	12.1	3.36	99	.288	.321	2	.111	-1	1	-0	-1	-0.2
	Yr	13	10	.565	34	34	5	0	0	212^1	212	15	59	157	11.5	3.69	93	.257	.307	4	.062	-4	-2	-6	-4	-1.5
1970	Phi-N	10	15	.400	34	33	4	0	0	219	233	19	56	147	12.2	4.11	97	.274	.325	9	.127	-2	-2	-3	-1	-0.6
1971	Phi-N	5	12	.294	29	16	1	0	1	110	126	11	37	58	13.8	5.48	64	.297	.362	3	.120	0	-25	-24	-0	-3.4
Total	17	224	184	.549	591	519	151	40	16	3760^1	3433	372	1000	2855	11.0	3.27	114	.242	.299	213	.167	-1	179	192	-41	13.6

● **DAVE BURBA** Burba, David Allen b: 7/7/66, Dayton, Ohio BR/TR, 6′4″, 240 lbs. Deb: 9/8/90

YEAR	TM/L	W	L	PCT	G	GS	CG	SH	SV	IP	H	HR	BB	SO	RAT	ERA	ERA+	OAV	OOB	BH	AVG	PB	PR	/A	PD	TPI
1990	Sea-A	0	0	—	6	0	0	0	0	8	8	0	2	4	12.4	4.50	88	.267	.333	0	—	0	-1	-0	0	0.0
1991	Sea-A	2	2	.500	22	2	0	0	1	36^2	34	6	14	16	11.8	3.68	112	.245	.314	0	—	0	2	2	-0	0.1
1992	SF-N	2	7	.222	23	11	0	0	0	70^2	80	4	31	47	14.4	4.97	67	.287	.362	1	.067	-1	-11	-13	-1	-1.7
1993	SF-N	10	3	.769	54	5	0	0	0	95^1	95	14	37	88	12.7	4.25	92	.265	.338	5	.294	2	-2	-4	0	-0.3
1994	SF-N	3	6	.333	57	0	0	0	0	74	59	5	45	84	13.4	4.38	91	.221	.346	0	.000	-0	-1	-3	-1	-0.4
1995	SF-N	4	2	.667	37	0	0	0	0	43^1	38	5	25	46	13.1	4.98	82	.235	.337	0	—	0	-4	-4	-0	-0.6
	*Cin-N	6	2	.750	15	9	1	1	0	63^1	52	4	26	50	11.1	3.27	126	.223	.301	1	.067	-0	6	6	-1	0.6
	Yr	10	4	.714	52	9	1	1	0	106^2	90	9	51	96	11.9	3.97	103	.227	.315	1	.067	-0	3	2	-1	0.0
1996	Cin-N	11	13	.458	34	33	0	0	0	195	179	18	97	148	12.8	3.83	110	.244	.334	7	.104	-1	8	9	-2	0.6
1997	Cin-N	11	10	.524	30	27	2	0	0	160	157	22	73	131	13.4	4.72	90	.255	.343	9	.196	1	-9	-8	1	-0.8
1998	*Cle-A	15	10	.600	32	31	0	0	0	203^2	210	30	69	132	12.6	4.11	116	.269	.334	1	.167	1	12	15	-0	1.7
Total	9	64	55	.538	310	118	3	1	1	950	912	108	419	746	12.9	4.23	100	.253	.336	24	.142	2	-0	-2	-4	-0.8

● **BILL BURBACH** Burbach, William David b: 8/22/47, Dickeyville, Wis. BR/TR, 6′4″, 215 lbs. Deb: 4/11/69

YEAR	TM/L	W	L	PCT	G	GS	CG	SH	SV	IP	H	HR	BB	SO	RAT	ERA	ERA+	OAV	OOB	BH	AVG	PB	PR	/A	PD	TPI
1969	NY-A	6	8	.429	31	24	2	1	0	140^2	112	15	102	82	13.8	3.65	95	.219	.351	4	.100	-1	-0	-3	-1	-0.4
1970	NY-A	0	2	.000	4	4	0	0	0	16^2	23	2	9	10	17.8	10.26	34	.324	.407	0	.000	-1	-12	-12	-0	-1.2
1971	NY-A	0	1	.000	2	0	0	0	0	3^1	6	0	5	3	29.7	10.80	30	.400	.550	0	.000	-0	-3	-3	-0	-0.7
Total	3	6	11	.353	37	28	2	1	0	160^2	141	17	116	95	14.6	4.48	78	.236	.363	4	.085	-2	-15	-18	-1	-2.3

● **LARRY BURCHART** Burchart, Larry Wayne b: 2/8/46, Tulsa, Okla. BR/TR, 6′3″, 205 lbs. Deb: 4/10/69

YEAR	TM/L	W	L	PCT	G	GS	CG	SH	SV	IP	H	HR	BB	SO	RAT	ERA	ERA+	OAV	OOB	BH	AVG	PB	PR	/A	PD	TPI
1969	Cle-A	0	2	.000	29	0	0	0	0	42^1	42	2	24	26	14.2	4.25	89	.266	.366	0	—	0	-3	-2	-1	-0.2

● **FRED BURCHELL** Burchell, Frederick Duff b: 7/14/1879, Perth Amboy, N.J. d: 11/20/51, Jordan, N.Y. BL/TL, 5′11″, 175 lbs. Deb: 4/17/03

YEAR	TM/L	W	L	PCT	G	GS	CG	SH	SV	IP	H	HR	BB	SO	RAT	ERA	ERA+	OAV	OOB	BH	AVG	PB	PR	/A	PD	TPI
1903	Phi-N	0	3	.000	6	3	2	0	0	44	48	0	14	12	13.1	2.86	114	.293	.356	3	.188	-1	2	2	-0	0.0
1907	Bos-A	0	1	.000	2	1	0	0	0	10	8	0	2	6	9.9	2.70	95	.222	.282	1	.200	-0	-0	-0	-0	0.0
1908	Bos-A	10	8	.556	31	19	9	0	0	179^2	161	2	65	94	11.9	2.96	83	.247	.326	17	.246	1	-11	-10	-2	-1.1
1909	Bos-A	3	3	.500	10	5	1	0	0	52	51	1	11	12	11.1	2.94	85	.271	.318	3	.158	-0	-3	-3	1	-0.3
Total	4	13	15	.464	49	28	12	0	0	285^2	268	3	92	124	11.8	2.93	89	.258	.328	24	.220	-0	-12	-10	-2	-1.4

● **FREDDIE BURDETTE** Burdette, Freddie Thomason b: 9/15/36, Moultrie, Ga. BR/TR, 6′1″, 170 lbs. Deb: 9/5/62

YEAR	TM/L	W	L	PCT	G	GS	CG	SH	SV	IP	H	HR	BB	SO	RAT	ERA	ERA+	OAV	OOB	BH	AVG	PB	PR	/A	PD	TPI
1962	Chi-N	0	0	—	8	0	0	0	1	9^2	5	2	8	5	12.1	3.72	111	.161	.333	0	.000	-0	0	0	-0	0.0
1963	Chi-N	0	0	—	4	0	0	0	0	4^2	5	1	2	1	13.5	3.86	91	.313	.389	0	—	0	-0	-0	0	0.0
1964	Chi-N	1	0	1.000	18	0	0	0	0	20	17	2	10	4	12.6	3.15	118	.243	.346	1	1.000	0	1	1	-0	0.1
Total	3	1	0	1.000	30	0	0	0	1	34^1	27	5	20	10	12.6	3.41	112	.231	.348	1	.500	0	1	2	-0	0.1

● **LEW BURDETTE** Burdette, Selva Lewis b: 11/22/26, Nitro, W.Va. BR/TR, 6′2″, 190 lbs. Deb: 9/26/50 C

YEAR	TM/L	W	L	PCT	G	GS	CG	SH	SV	IP	H	HR	BB	SO	RAT	ERA	ERA+	OAV	OOB	BH	AVG	PB	PR	/A	PD	TPI
1950	NY-A	0	0	—	2	0	0	0	0	1^1	3	0	0	0	20.3	6.75	64	.500	.500	0	—	0	-0	-0	0	0.0
1951	Bos-N	0	0	—	3	0	0	0	0	4^1	6	0	5	1	24.9	6.23	59	.375	.545	0	.000	-0	-1	-1	0	0.0
1952	Bos-N	6	11	.353	45	9	5	0	7	137	138	8	47	47	12.3	3.61	100	.265	.328	4	.114	-0	2	-0	1	0.0
1953	Mil-N	15	5	.750	46	13	6	1	8	175	177	7	56	58	12.2	3.24	121	.264	.326	9	.170	-1	20	13	2	1.5
1954	Mil-N	15	14	.517	38	32	13	4	0	238	224	17	62	79	11.0	2.76	135	.251	.302	7	.089	-5	35	26	1	2.5
1955	Mil-N	13	8	.619	42	33	11	2	0	230	253	25	73	70	13.0	4.03	93	.280	.337	20	.233	3	0	-7	2	-0.1
1956	Mil-N	19	10	.655	39	35	16	**6**	1	256^1	234	22	52	110	10.1	**2.70**	128	.241	.282	16	.186	1	30	22	1	2.6
1957	*Mil-N★	17	9	.654	37	33	14	1	0	256^2	260	25	59	78	11.3	3.72	94	.264	.307	13	.148	1	5	-6	2	-0.3
1958	*Mil-N	20	10	**.667**	40	36	19	3	0	275^1	279	18	50	113	10.9	2.91	121	.264	.301	24	.242	9	**32**	19	3	3.1
1959	Mil-N★	**21**	15	.583	41	39	20	**4**	1	289^2	312	38	38	105	10.9	4.07	87	.273	.297	21	.202	6	-4	-17	0	-1.3
1960	Mil-N	19	13	.594	45	32	**18**	4	4	275^2	277	19	35	83	10.3	3.36	102	.260	.287	16	.176	5	12	2	5	1.2
1961	Mil-N	18	11	.621	40	36	14	3	0	**272**^{1}	295	31	33	92	10.9	4.00	94	.273	.296	21	.204	5	1	-8	2	0.0
1962	Mil-N	10	9	.526	37	19	6	1	2	143^2	172	26	23	59	12.3	4.89	78	.298	.327	9	.176	0	-15	-17	1	-1.9
1963	Mil-N	6	5	.545	15	13	4	1	0	84	71	15	24	28	10.3	3.64	88	.228	.285	1	.038	-0	-3	-4	-0	-0.6
	StL-N	3	8	.273	21	14	3	0	2	98	106	6	16	45	11.8	3.77	94	.278	.319	3	.097	-1	-5	-2	-2	-0.5
	Yr	9	13	.409	36	27	7	1	2	182	177	21	40	73	11.1	3.71	92	.255	.302	4	.070	-2	-9	-6	-2	-1.1
1964	StL-N	1	0	1.000	8	0	0	0	0	10	10	1	3	3	11.7	1.80	211	.256	.310	0	.000	-0	2	2	-0	0.2
	Chi-N	9	9	.500	28	17	8	2	0	131	152	15	19	40	11.8	4.88	76	.292	.319	12	.279	6	-20	-17	2	-1.4
	Yr	10	9	.526	36	17	8	2	0	141	162	16	22	43	11.8	4.66	80	.289	.317	12	.273	6	-18	-15	2	-1.2
1965	Chi-N	0	2	.000	7	3	0	0	0	20^1	26	3	4	5	13.7	5.31	69	.299	.337	2	.333	1	-4	-4	-0	-0.2
	Phi-N	3	3	.500	19	9	1	1	0	70^2	95	5	17	23	14.9	5.48	63	.329	.376	6	.300	1	-15	-16	0	-1.1
	Yr	3	5	.375	26	12	1	1	0	91	121	8	21	28	14.5	5.44	65	.321	.365	8	.308	2	-19	-20	0	-1.3
1966	Cal-A	7	2	.778	54	0	0	0	5	79^2	80	4	12	27	10.5	3.39	99	.268	.298	1	.125	-0	0	-0	-1	-0.1
1967	Cal-A	1	0	1.000	19	0	0	0	1	18^1	16	4	0	8	8.3	4.91	64	.232	.243	0	—	0	-3	-4	0	-0.2
Total	18	203	144	.585	626	373	158	33	31	3067^1	3186	289	628	1074	11.4	3.66	99	.268	.308	185	.183	30	68	-18	19	3.4

● **BILL BURDICK** Burdick, William Byron b: 10/11/1859, Austin, Minn. d: 10/23/49, Spokane, Wash. BR/TR, Deb: 7/23/1888

YEAR	TM/L	W	L	PCT	G	GS	CG	SH	SV	IP	H	HR	BB	SO	RAT	ERA	ERA+	OAV	OOB	BH	AVG	PB	PR	/A	PD	TPI
1888	Ind-N	10	10	.500	20	20	20	0	0	176	168	12	43	55	11.1	2.81	105	.242	.292	10	.147	-2	1	3	-0	0.0
1889	Ind-N	2	4	.333	10	4	2	0	1	45^2	58	7	13	16	14.0	4.53	92	.301	.345	2	.118	-0	-3	-2	-0	-0.2
Total	2	12	14	.462	30	24	22	0	1	221^2	226	19	56	71	11.7	3.17	101	.255	.304	12	.141	-3	-2	1	-0	-0.2

● **TOM BURGMEIER** Burgmeier, Thomas Henry b: 8/2/43, St.Paul, Minn. BL/TL, 5′11″, 185 lbs. Deb: 4/10/68 C

YEAR	TM/L	W	L	PCT	G	GS	CG	SH	SV	IP	H	HR	BB	SO	RAT	ERA	ERA+	OAV	OOB	BH	AVG	PB	PR	/A	PD	TPI
1968	Cal-A	1	4	.200	56	2	0	0	5	72^2	65	5	24	33	11.0	4.33	67	.250	.313	0	.000	0	-11	-12	4	-0.6
1969	KC-A	3	1	.750	31	0	0	0	0	54	67	5	21	23	14.8	4.17	88	.316	.380	3	.167	-0	-3	-3	2	0.0
1970	KC-A	6	6	.500	41	0	0	0	1	68^1	59	6	23	43	10.8	3.16	118	.236	.300	2	.143	-0	4	4	2	0.9
1971	KC-A	9	7	.563	67	0	0	0	17	88^1	71	3	30	44	11.0	1.73	198	.223	.303	5	.250	2	17	17	3	4.4
1972	KC-A	6	2	.750	51	0	0	0	9	55^1	67	0	33	18	16.4	4.23	72	.313	.407	4	.333	1	-7	-7	1	-1.2
1973	KC-A	0	0	—	6	0	0	0	1	10	13	2	4	4	16.2	5.40	76	.310	.383	0	—	0	-2	-1	-0	-0.4
1974	Min-A	5	3	.625	50	0	0	0	4	91^2	92	7	26	34	11.8	4.52	83	.270	.325	0	—	0	-9	-8	3	-0.6
1975	Min-A	5	8	.385	46	0	0	0	11	75^2	76	7	23	41	11.9	3.09	124	.264	.321	0	—	0	6	6	0	1.2
1976	Min-A	8	1	.889	57	0	0	0	1	115^1	95	11	29	45	9.8	2.50	143	.226	.279	0	—	0	13	14	2	1.2
1977	Min-A	6	4	.600	61	0	0	0	7	97^1	113	15	33	35	13.7	5.09	78	.299	.358	0	—	0	-11	-12	1	-1.1
1978	Bos-A	2	1	.667	35	1	0	0	4	61^1	74	7	23	24	14.7	4.40	93	.302	.369	0	—	0	-4	-2	1	-0.2
1979	Bos-A	3	2	.600	44	0	0	0	4	88^2	89	8	16	60	11.1	2.74	161	.263	.304	0	—	0	15	16	1	0.6
1980	Bos-A☆	5	4	.556	62	0	0	0	24	99	87	3	20	54	9.9	2.00	211	.241	.285	0	—	0	22	24	3	3.7
1981	Bos-A	4	5	.444	32	0	0	0	6	59^2	61	5	17	35	12.4	2.87	135	.268	.329	0	—	0	5	7	1	1.0
1982	Bos-A	7	0	1.000	40	0	0	0	2	102^1	98	6	22	44	10.7	2.29	188	.259	.303	0	—	0	20	23	2	1.4
1983	Oak-A	6	7	.462	49	0	0	0	4	96	89	2	32	39	11.3	2.81	137	.244	.305	0	—	0	13	11	2	1.7
1984	Oak-A	3	0	1.000	17	0	0	0	2	23	15	2	8	8	9.0	2.35	159	.190	.264	0	—	0	4	4	0	0.8
Total	17	79	55	.590	745	3	0	0	102	1258^2	1231	94	384	584	11.8	3.23	118	.261	.321	14	.212	2	72	81	27	12.8

● **ENRIQUE BURGOS** Burgos, Enrique (Calles) b: 10/7/65, Chorrera, Panama BL/TL, 6′4″, 195 lbs. Deb: 7/15/93

YEAR	TM/L	W	L	PCT	G	GS	CG	SH	SV	IP	H	HR	BB	SO	RAT	ERA	ERA+	OAV	OOB	BH	AVG	PB	PR	/A	PD	TPI
1993	KC-A	0	1	.000	5	0	0	0	0	5	5	0	6	6	21.6	9.00	51	.238	.429	0	—	0	-3	-2	0	-0.8

YEAR TM/L	W	L	PCT	G	GS	CG	SH	SV	IP	H	HR	BB	SO	RAT	ERA	ERA+	OAV	OOB	BH	AVG	PB	PR	/A	PD	TPI
1995 SF-N	0	0	—	5	0	0	0	0	8^1	14	1	6	12	22.7	8.64	47	.378	.477	0	—	0	-4	-4	-0	0.0
Total 2	0	1	.000	10	0	0	0	0	13^1	19	1	12	18	22.3	8.78	49	.328	.458	0	—	0	-7	-7	-0	-0.8

● SANDY BURK Burk, Charles Sanford b: 4/22/1887, Columbus, Ohio d: 10/11/34, Brooklyn, N.Y. BR/TR, 5'8", 155 lbs. Deb: 9/12/10

YEAR TM/L	W	L	PCT	G	GS	CG	SH	SV	IP	H	HR	BB	SO	RAT	ERA	ERA+	OAV	OOB	BH	AVG	PB	PR	/A	PD	TPI
1910 Bro-N	0	3	.000	4	3	1	0	0	19^1	17	0	27	14	21.4	6.05	50	.258	.484	0	.000	-1	-6	-6	0	-0.9
1911 Bro-N	1	3	.250	13	7	1	0	0	58	54	1	47	15	16.1	5.12	65	.261	.405	2	.105	-1	-11	-12	0	-0.8
1912 Bro-N	0	0	—	2	0	0	0	0	8^1	9	0	3	2	13.0	3.24	103	.273	.333	1	.250	0	0	0	0	0.0
StL-N	1	3	.250	12	4	2	0	1	44^2	37	0	12	17	10.1	2.42	142	.236	.294	0	.000	-2	5	5	-1	0.2
Yr	1	3	.250	14	4	2	0	1	53	46	0	15	19	10.5	2.55	134	.242	.301	1	.067	-1	5	5	-1	0.2
1913 StL-N	0	2	.000	19	7	0	0	1	70	81	1	33	29	15.4	5.14	63	.290	.377	2	.091	-2	-15	-15	-0	-0.6
1915 Pit-F	2	0	1.000	2	2	1	0	0	18	8	0	11	9	9.5	1.00	271	.140	.279	1	.167	-0	3	3	-1	0.3
Total 5	4	11	.267	52	23	5	0	2	218^1	206	2	133	86	14.5	4.25	76	.258	.372	6	.090	-6	-24	-24	-2	-1.8

● ELMER BURKART Burkart, Elmer Robert "Swede" b: 2/1/17, Torresdale, Pa. d: 2/6/95, Baltimore, Md. BR/TR, 6'2", 190 lbs. Deb: 9/14/36

YEAR TM/L	W	L	PCT	G	GS	CG	SH	SV	IP	H	HR	BB	SO	RAT	ERA	ERA+	OAV	OOB	BH	AVG	PB	PR	/A	PD	TPI
1936 Phi-N	0	0	—	2	2	0	0	0	7^2	4	0	12	2	18.8	3.52	129	.160	.432	0	.000	-0	0	1	0	0.0
1937 Phi-N	0	0	—	7	0	0	0	0	16	20	0	9	4	16.3	6.19	70	.323	.408	0	.000	-1	-4	-3	0	-0.1
1938 Phi-N	0	1	.000	2	1	1	0	0	10	12	0	3	1	14.4	4.50	86	.286	.348	0	.000	-0	-1	-1	-0	-0.1
1939 Phi-N	1	0	1.000	5	0	0	0	0	8^1	11	0	2	2	14.0	4.32	93	.344	.382	1	1.000	1	-0	-0	-0	0.0
Total 4	1	1	.500	16	3	1	0	0	42	47	0	26	9	15.9	4.93	85	.292	.394	1	.083	-1	-5	-3	-0	-0.2

● JAMES BURKE Burke, James b: Attleboro, Mass. Deb: 6/10/1882

YEAR TM/L	W	L	PCT	G	GS	CG	SH	SV	IP	H	HR	BB	SO	RAT	ERA	ERA+	OAV	OOB	BH	AVG	PB	PR	/A	PD	TPI
1882 Buf-N	0	1	.000	1	1	0	0	0	4	10	0	0	0	22.5	11.25	26	.435	.435	0	.000	-1	-4	-4	1	-0.6
1883 Buf-N	0	0	—	1	1	0	0	0	8	9	0	3	1	13.5	5.63	56	.243	.300	1	.200	-0	-2	-2	-0	0.0
1884 Bos-U	19	15	.559	38	36	34	0	0	322	326	10	31	255	10.0	2.85	84	.245	.263	41	.223	-7	-15	-17	-4	-2.3
Total 3	19	16	.543	40	38	34	0	0	334	345	10	34	256	10.2	3.02	80	.249	.267	42	.218	-8	-21	-23	-4	-2.9

● JOHN BURKE Burke, John C. b: 2/9/70, Durango, Colo. BB/TR, 6'4", 220 lbs. Deb: 8/13/96

YEAR TM/L	W	L	PCT	G	GS	CG	SH	SV	IP	H	HR	BB	SO	RAT	ERA	ERA+	OAV	OOB	BH	AVG	PB	PR	/A	PD	TPI
1996 Col-N	2	1	.667	11	0	0	0	0	15^2	21	3	7	19	16.7	7.47	70	.318	.392	1	.500	0	-6	-4	0	-0.6
1997 Col-N	2	5	.286	17	9	0	0	0	59	83	13	26	39	17.5	6.56	79	.329	.405	3	.158	-1	-15	-9	-1	-1.1
Total 2	4	6	.400	28	9	0	0	0	74^2	104	16	33	58	17.4	6.75	77	.327	.402	4	.190	-1	-21	-13	-1	-1.7

● JOHN BURKE Burke, John Patrick b: 1/27/1877, Hazleton, Pa. d: 8/4/50, Jersey City, N.J. BR/TR, Deb: 6/27/02 ♦

YEAR TM/L	W	L	PCT	G	GS	CG	SH	SV	IP	H	HR	BB	SO	RAT	ERA	ERA+	OAV	OOB	BH	AVG	PB	PR	/A	PD	TPI
1902 NY-N	0	1	.000	2	1	1	0	0	14	21	0	3	3	15.4	5.79	48	.344	.375	2	.154	-0	-5	-5	0	-0.3

● BOBBY BURKE Burke, Robert James "Lefty" b: 1/23/07, Joliet, Ill. d: 2/8/71, Joliet, Ill. BL/TL, 6'0.5", 150 lbs. Deb: 4/16/27

YEAR TM/L	W	L	PCT	G	GS	CG	SH	SV	IP	H	HR	BB	SO	RAT	ERA	ERA+	OAV	OOB	BH	AVG	PB	PR	/A	PD	TPI
1927 Was-A	3	2	.600	36	6	1	0	0	100	91	6	32	20	11.7	3.96	103	.245	.316	3	.125	-2	2	1	0	-0.2
1928 Was-A	2	4	.333	26	7	2	1	0	85^1	87	1	18	27	11.3	3.90	103	.277	.320	5	.250	1	1	1	0	0.2
1929 Was-A	6	8	.429	37	17	4	0	0	141	154	6	55	51	13.6	4.79	89	.279	.349	6	.140	-3	-8	-9	-2	-1.2
1930 Was-A	3	4	.429	24	4	2	0	3	74^1	62	2	29	35	11.4	3.63	127	.229	.310	4	.174	-1	8	8	-1	0.5
1931 Was-A	8	3	.727	30	13	3	1	2	128^2	124	6	50	38	12.3	4.27	101	.255	.327	10	.213	-0	2	0	0	0.0
1932 Was-A	3	6	.333	22	10	2	0	0	91	98	4	44	32	14.1	5.14	84	.272	.353	5	.200	0	-7	-8	-1	-0.8
1933 Was-A	4	3	.571	25	6	4	1	0	64	64	1	31	28	13.6	3.23	129	.256	.343	4	.235	0	7	7	0	0.7
1934 Was-A	8	8	.500	37	15	7	1	0	168	155	2	72	52	12.2	3.21	134	.245	.323	13	.228	2	24	21	0	1.9
1935 Was-A	1	8	.111	15	10	2	0	0	66^1	90	7	27	16	16.1	7.46	58	.327	.391	4	.182	-0	-22	-23	1	-2.4
1937 Phi-N	0	0	—	2	0	0	0	0	0	1	0	2	0	—	∞	—	.500	.750	0	—	0	-1	-1	0	-0.1
Total 10	38	46	.452	254	88	27	4	5	918^2	926	35	360	299	12.8	4.29	99	.263	.336	54	.194	-3	6	-3	-3	-1.4

● STEVE BURKE Burke, Steven Michael b: 3/5/55, Stockton, Cal. BB/TR, 6'2", 200 lbs. Deb: 9/10/77

YEAR TM/L	W	L	PCT	G	GS	CG	SH	SV	IP	H	HR	BB	SO	RAT	ERA	ERA+	OAV	OOB	BH	AVG	PB	PR	/A	PD	TPI
1977 Sea-A	0	1	.000	6	0	0	0	0	15^2	12	0	7	6	10.9	2.87	143	.226	.317	0	—	0	2	2	0	0.2
1978 Sea-A	0	1	.000	18	0	0	0	0	49	46	2	24	16	13.0	3.49	109	.258	.350	0	—	0	1	2	0	0.1
Total 2	0	2	.000	24	0	0	0	0	64^2	58	2	31	22	12.5	3.34	116	.251	.342	0	—	0	4	4	0	0.3

● TIM BURKE Burke, Timothy Philip b: 2/19/59, Omaha, Neb. BR/TR, 6'3", 205 lbs. Deb: 4/8/85

YEAR TM/L	W	L	PCT	G	GS	CG	SH	SV	IP	H	HR	BB	SO	RAT	ERA	ERA+	OAV	OOB	BH	AVG	PB	PR	/A	PD	TPI
1985 Mon-N	9	4	.692	**78**	0	0	0	8	120^1	86	9	44	87	10.2	2.39	142	.204	.290	1	.100	-0	**16**	13	1	1.6
1986 Mon-N	9	7	.563	68	2	0	0	4	101^1	103	7	46	82	13.6	2.93	126	.262	.345	0	.000	-0	9	9	1	1.4
1987 Mon-N	7	0	1.000	55	0	0	0	18	91	64	3	17	58	8.0	1.19	354	.196	.235	0	.000	-1	**29**	**30**	1	3.2
1988 Mon-N	3	5	.375	61	0	0	0	18	82	84	7	25	42	12.3	3.40	106	.272	.332	0	.000	-0	0	2	0	0.3
1989 Mon-N★	9	3	.750	68	0	0	0	28	84^2	68	6	22	54	9.6	2.55	138	.225	.278	0	.000	-0	9	9	1	1.9
1990 Mon-N	3	3	.500	58	0	0	0	20	75	71	6	21	47	11.3	2.52	145	.247	.303	1	.167	0	11	9	2	1.4
1991 Mon-N	3	4	.429	37	0	0	0	5	46	41	3	14	25	11.5	4.11	88	.243	.316	0	.000	-0	-2	-3	0	-0.4
NY-N	3	3	.500	35	0	0	0	1	55^2	55	5	12	34	10.8	2.75	132	.255	.294	0	.000	-1	6	6	1	0.6
Yr	6	7	.462	72	0	0	0	6	101^2	96	8	26	59	10.8	3.36	108	.246	.293	0	.000	-1	4	3	1	0.2
1992 NY-N	1	2	.333	15	0	0	0	0	15^2	26	1	3	7	16.7	5.74	60	.366	.392	0	—	0	-4	-4	0	-0.7
NY-A	2	2	.500	23	0	0	0	0	27^2	26	2	15	8	13.7	3.25	120	.250	.350	0	—	0	2	2	1	0.4
Total 8	49	33	.598	498	2	0	0	102	699^1	624	49	219	444	11.1	2.72	135	.240	.304	2	.045	-2	76	74	7	9.7

● BILLY BURKE Burke, William Ignatius b: 7/11/1889, Clinton, Mass. d: 2/9/67, Worcester, Mass. BL/TL, 5'10", 165 lbs. Deb: 4/30/10

YEAR TM/L	W	L	PCT	G	GS	CG	SH	SV	IP	H	HR	BB	SO	RAT	ERA	ERA+	OAV	OOB	BH	AVG	PB	PR	/A	PD	TPI
1910 Bos-N	1	0	1.000	19	1	1	0	0	64	68	1	29	22	13.9	4.08	82	.302	.387	4	.190	-1	-7	-5	-1	-0.2
1911 Bos-N	0	1	.000	2	1	0	0	0	3^1	6	0	5	1	29.7	18.90	20	.429	.579	1	1.000	0	-6	-6	-0	-1.1
Total 2	1	1	.500	21	2	1	0	0	67^1	74	1	34	23	14.7	4.81	70	.310	.400	5	.227	-0	-13	-11	-2	-1.3

● BILL BURKE Burke, William R. b: 11/1865, Cincinnati, Ohio d: 3/17/39, Atchison, Kan. 6', 200 lbs. Deb: 7/20/1887

YEAR TM/L	W	L	PCT	G	GS	CG	SH	SV	IP	H	HR	BB	SO	RAT	ERA	ERA+	OAV	OOB	BH	AVG	PB	PR	/A	PD	TPI
1887 Det-N	0	1	.000	2	2	1	0	0	15	21	0	5	3	16.8	6.00	67	.318	.384	2	.250	-0	-3	-3	-0	-0.2

● JESSE BURKETT Burkett, Jesse Cail "Crab" b: 12/4/1868, Wheeling, W.Va. d: 5/27/53, Worcester, Mass. BL/TL, 5'8", 155 lbs. Deb: 4/22/1890 CH♦

YEAR TM/L	W	L	PCT	G	GS	CG	SH	SV	IP	H	HR	BB	SO	RAT	ERA	ERA+	OAV	OOB	BH	AVG	PB	PR	/A	PD	TPI
1890 NY-N	3	10	.231	21	14	6	0	0	118	134	3	92	82	18.3	5.57	63	.277	.407	124	.309	8	-26	-27	2	-1.7
1894 Cle-N	0	0	—	1	0	0	0	0	4	6	0	1	0	15.8	4.50	121	.333	.368	187	.358	0	0	0	-0	0.0
1902 StL-A	0	1	.000	1	0	0	0	0	1	4	0	1	2	45.0	9.00	39	.571	.625	169	.306	0	-1	-1	0	-0.4
Total 3	3	11	.214	23	14	6	0	0	123	144	3	94	84	18.4	5.56	64	.283	.408	2850	.338	9	-26	-27	2	-2.1

● JOHN BURKETT Burkett, John David b: 11/28/64, New Brighton, Pa. BR/TR, 6'2", 211 lbs. Deb: 9/15/87

YEAR TM/L	W	L	PCT	G	GS	CG	SH	SV	IP	H	HR	BB	SO	RAT	ERA	ERA+	OAV	OOB	BH	AVG	PB	PR	/A	PD	TPI
1987 SF-N	0	0	—	3	0	0	0	0	6	7	2	3	5	16.5	4.50	85	.304	.407	0	.000	-0	-0	-0	0	0.0
1990 SF-N	14	7	.667	33	32	2	0	1	204	201	18	61	118	11.7	3.79	96	.257	.314	3	.048	-3	-0	-3	-1	-0.7
1991 SF-N	12	11	.522	36	34	3	1	0	206^2	223	19	60	131	12.8	4.18	86	.277	.335	5	.091	-1	-11	-14	-1	-1.6
1992 SF-N	13	9	.591	32	32	3	1	0	189^2	194	13	45	107	11.5	3.84	86	.264	.310	1	.018	-3	-7	-11	-3	-1.8
1993 SF-N★	**22**	7	.759	34	34	2	1	0	231^2	224	18	40	145	10.7	3.65	107	.255	.296	9	.118	-1	10	7	1	0.8
1994 SF-N	6	8	.429	25	25	0	0	0	159^1	176	14	36	85	12.4	3.62	111	.286	.332	3	.059	-4	11	7	0	0.2
1995 Fla-N	14	14	.500	30	30	4	0	0	188^1	208	22	57	126	13.0	4.30	98	.282	.339	7	.106	-2	-3	-2	0	-0.4
1996 Fla-N	6	10	.375	24	24	1	0	0	154	154	15	42	108	11.6	4.32	94	.263	.316	9	.173	0	-2	-4	0	-0.4
*Tex-A	5	2	.714	10	10	1	1	0	68^2	75	4	16	47	12.2	4.06	129	.280	.325	0	—	0	7	9	-1	0.3
1997 Tex-A	9	12	.429	30	30	2	0	0	189^1	240	20	30	139	13.0	4.56	105	.307	.335	1	.200	0	-0	5	1	0.5
1998 Tex-A	9	13	.409	32	32	0	0	0	195	230	19	46	131	13.1	5.68	85	.292	.337	0	.000	-0	-22	-18	-2	-1.9
Total 10	110	93	.542	289	283	18	4	1	1792^2	1932	164	436	1142	12.2	4.21	97	.276	.324	38	.089	-15	-18	-29	-4	-5.0

● KEN BURKHART Burkhart, Kenneth William (b: Kenneth William Burkhardt) b: 11/18/16, Knoxville, Tenn. BR/TR, 6'1", 190 lbs. Deb: 4/21/45 U

YEAR TM/L	W	L	PCT	G	GS	CG	SH	SV	IP	H	HR	BB	SO	RAT	ERA	ERA+	OAV	OOB	BH	AVG	PB	PR	/A	PD	TPI
1945 StL-N	18	8	.692	42	22	12	4	2	217^1	206	9	66	67	11.4	2.90	129	.251	.309	13	.181	1	22	20	-1	2.2
1946 StL-N	6	3	.667	25	13	5	2	2	100	111	4	36	32	13.4	2.88	120	.282	.346	5	.147	-0	6	6	-2	0.4
1947 StL-N	3	6	.333	34	6	1	0	1	95	108	13	23	44	12.8	5.21	79	.292	.340	3	.125	-1	-12	-11	1	-1.0
1948 StL-N	0	0	—	20	0	0	0	1	37^1	50	4	14	16	15.9	5.54	74	.331	.395	1	.250	0	-7	-6	1	0.0
Cin-N	0	3	.000	16	0	0	0	0	41^2	42	3	16	14	12.7	6.91	57	.255	.324	3	.333	2	-14	-14	-0	-0.7
Yr	0	3	.000	36	0	0	0	1	79	92	7	30	30	14.0	6.27	64	.289	.352	4	.308	2	-20	-20	0	-0.7

YEAR	TM/L	W	L	PCT	G	GS	CG	SH	SV	IP	H	HR	BB	SO	RAT	ERA	ERA+	OAV	OOB	BH	AVG	PB	PR	/A	PD	TPI
1949	Cin-N	0	0	—	11	0	0	0	1	28^1	29	2	10	8	12.4	3.18	132	.282	.345	2	.286	0	3	3	0	0.1
Total	5	27	20	.574	148	41	18	6	7	519^2	546	35	165	181	12.5	3.84	99	.273	.332	27	.180	2	-2	-1	-2	1.0

● WALLY BURNETTE

Burnette, Wallace Harper b: 6/20/29, Blairs, Va. BR/TR, 6'0.5", 178 lbs. Deb: 7/15/56

YEAR	TM/L	W	L	PCT	G	GS	CG	SH	SV	IP	H	HR	BB	SO	RAT	ERA	ERA+	OAV	OOB	BH	AVG	PB	PR	/A	PD	TPI
1956	KC-A	6	8	.429	18	14	4	1	0	121^1	115	13	39	54	11.6	2.89	150	.252	.314	2	.051	-4	17	19	-1	1.5
1957	KC-A	7	12	.368	38	9	1	0	1	113	115	8	44	57	12.7	4.30	92	.268	.338	8	.250	1	-6	-4	2	-0.4
1958	KC-A	1	1	.500	12	4	0	0	0	28^1	29	2	14	11	13.7	3.49	112	.264	.347	1	.167	0	1	1	-1	0.0
Total	3	14	21	.400	68	27	5	1	1	262^2	259	23	97	122	12.3	3.56	116	.260	.328	11	.143	-4	11	16	1	1.1

● DENNIS BURNS

Burns, Dennis b: 5/24/1898, Tiff City, Mo. d: 5/21/69, Tulsa, Okla. BR/TR, 5'10", 180 lbs. Deb: 9/22/23

YEAR	TM/L	W	L	PCT	G	GS	CG	SH	SV	IP	H	HR	BB	SO	RAT	ERA	ERA+	OAV	OOB	BH	AVG	PB	PR	/A	PD	TPI
1923	Phi-A	2	1	.667	4	3	2	0	0	27	21	1	7	8	9.3	2.00	205	.210	.262	1	.111	-1	6	6	-0	0.6
1924	Phi-A	6	8	.429	37	17	7	0	1	154	191	3	68	26	15.2	5.08	84	.314	.384	6	.143	-2	-15	-14	-0	-1.3
Total	2	8	9	.471	41	20	9	0	1	181	212	4	75	34	14.3	4.62	92	.299	.367	7	.137	-3	-9	-7	-0	-0.7

● FARMER BURNS

Burns, James "Slab" b: Ashtabula, Ohio TR, 5'7", 168 lbs. Deb: 7/6/01

YEAR	TM/L	W	L	PCT	G	GS	CG	SH	SV	IP	H	HR	BB	SO	RAT	ERA	ERA+	OAV	OOB	BH	AVG	PB	PR	/A	PD	TPI
1901	StL-N	0	0	—	1	0	0	0	0	1	2	0	1	0	36.0	9.00	35	.400	.571	0	—	0	-1	-1	-0	0.0

● DICK BURNS

Burns, Richard Simon b: 12/26/1863, Holyoke, Mass. d: 11/16/37, Holyoke, Mass. BL/TL, 5'7", 140 lbs. Deb: 5/3/1883 ♦

YEAR	TM/L	W	L	PCT	G	GS	CG	SH	SV	IP	H	HR	BB	SO	RAT	ERA	ERA+	OAV	OOB	BH	AVG	PB	PR	/A	PD	TPI
1883	Det-N	2	12	.143	17	13	13	0	0	127^2	172	8	33	30	14.5	4.51	69	.301	.339	26	.186	-2	-19	-20	-0	-1.8
1884	Cin-U	23	15	.605	40	40	34	1	0	329^2	298	7	47	167	9.4	2.46	104	.225	.252	107	.306	3	-1	4	0	0.6
1885	StL-N	0	0	—	1	0	0	0	0	3	3	0	0	2	9.0	9.00	31	.250	.250	12	.222	0	-2	-2	1	0.1
Total	3	25	27	.481	58	53	47	1	0	460^1	473	15	80	199	10.8	3.07	89	.248	.278	145	.267	2	-22	-18	1	-1.1

● BRITT BURNS

Burns, Robert Britt b: 6/8/59, Houston, Tex. BL/TL, 6'5", 218 lbs. Deb: 8/5/78

YEAR	TM/L	W	L	PCT	G	GS	CG	SH	SV	IP	H	HR	BB	SO	RAT	ERA	ERA+	OAV	OOB	BH	AVG	PB	PR	/A	PD	TPI
1978	Chi-A	0	2	.000	2	2	0	0	0	7^2	14	2	3	3	20.0	12.91	29	.378	.425	0	—	0	-8	-8	0	-1.3
1979	Chi-A	0	0	—	6	0	0	0	0	5	10	1	1	2	19.8	5.40	79	.435	.458	0	—	0	-1	-1	-0	0.0
1980	Chi-A	15	13	.536	34	32	11	1	0	238	213	17	63	133	10.6	2.84	142	.241	.295	0	—	0	32	31	-1	3.5
1981	Chi-A☆	10	6	.625	24	23	5	1	0	156^2	139	14	49	108	11.1	2.64	135	.238	.303	0	—	0	18	16	-4	1.3
1982	Chi-A	13	5	.722	28	28	5	1	0	169^1	168	12	67	116	12.6	4.04	100	.257	.329	0	—	0	1	-0	-3	-0.3
1983	*Chi-A	10	11	.476	29	26	8	4	0	173^2	165	14	55	115	11.7	3.58	117	.249	.311	0	—	0	9	12	-2	1.0
1984	Chi-A	4	12	.250	34	16	2	0	3	117	130	7	45	85	13.8	5.00	83	.280	.349	0	—	0	-13	-11	-0	-1.4
1985	Chi-A	18	11	.621	36	34	8	4	0	227	206	26	79	172	11.4	3.96	109	.242	.308	0	—	0	5	9	-1	0.8
Total	8	70	60	.538	193	161	39	11	3	1094^1	1045	93	362	734	11.8	3.66	111	.251	.315	0	—	0	42	49	-11	3.6

● TOM BURNS

Burns, Thomas Everett b: 3/30/1857, Honesdale, Pa. d: 3/19/02, Jersey City, N.J. BR/TR, 5'7", 152 lbs. Deb: 5/1/1880 MU♦

YEAR	TM/L	W	L	PCT	G	GS	CG	SH	SV	IP	H	HR	BB	SO	RAT	ERA	ERA+	OAV	OOB	BH	AVG	PB	PR	/A	PD	TPI
1880	Chi-N	0	0	—	1	0	0	0	0	1^1	2	0	2	1	27.0	0.00	—	.250	.400	103	.309	0	0	0	0	0.0

● OYSTER BURNS

Burns, Thomas P. b: 9/6/1864, Philadelphia, Pa. d: 11/11/28, Brooklyn, N.Y. BR/TR, 5'8", 183 lbs. Deb: 8/18/1884 ♦

YEAR	TM/L	W	L	PCT	G	GS	CG	SH	SV	IP	H	HR	BB	SO	RAT	ERA	ERA+	OAV	OOB	BH	AVG	PB	PR	/A	PD	TPI
1884	Bal-a	0	0	—	2	0	0	0	**1**	9	12	0	2	6	14.0	3.00	116	.343	.378	39	.298	1	0	0	-0	0.0
1885	Bal-a	7	4	.636	15	11	10	1	**3**	105^2	112	2	21	30	12.4	3.58	91	.266	.321	74	.231	3	-4	-4	-1	-0.2
1887	Bal-a	1	0	1.000	3	0	0	0	0	11^1	16	0	4	2	18.3	9.53	43	.291	.371	188	.341	2	-7	-7	-1	-0.4
1888	Bal-a	0	1	.000	5	0	0	0	0	12^2	12	0	3	2	10.7	4.26	70	.240	.283	97	.298	2	-2	-2	-0	-0.1
Total	4	8	5	.615	25	11	10	1	4	138^2	152	2	30	40	12.9	4.09	81	.271	.326	1389	.300	7	-12	-12	-2	-0.7

● TODD BURNS

Burns, Todd Edward b: 7/6/63, Maywood, Cal. BR/TR, 6'2", 190 lbs. Deb: 5/31/88

YEAR	TM/L	W	L	PCT	G	GS	CG	SH	SV	IP	H	HR	BB	SO	RAT	ERA	ERA+	OAV	OOB	BH	AVG	PB	PR	/A	PD	TPI
1988	*Oak-A	8	2	.800	17	14	2	0	1	102^2	93	8	34	57	11.2	3.16	120	.241	.304	0	—	0	9	7	-1	0.8
1989	*Oak-A	6	5	.545	50	2	0	0	8	96^1	66	3	28	49	8.9	2.24	164	.196	.260	0	—	0	18	15	-1	2.0
1990	*Oak-A	3	3	.500	43	2	0	0	3	78^2	78	8	32	43	12.6	2.97	125	.263	.334	0	—	0	8	6	-1	0.7
1991	Oak-A	1	0	1.000	9	0	0	0	0	13^1	10	2	8	3	12.2	3.38	114	.217	.333	0	—	0	1	1	0	0.4
1992	Tex-A	3	5	.375	35	10	0	0	1	103	97	8	32	55	11.6	3.84	99	.248	.311	0	—	0	1	-1	-1	-0.1
1993	Tex-A	0	4	.000	25	5	0	0	0	65	63	6	32	35	13.4	4.57	91	.253	.343	0	—	0	-2	-3	-1	0.0
	StL-N	0	4	.000	24	0	0	0	0	30^2	32	8	9	10	12.0	6.16	64	.274	.325	0	.000	-0	-7	-7	-1	-1.0
Total	6	21	23	.477	203	33	2	0	13	489^2	439	43	175	252	11.4	3.47	110	.241	.310	0	.000	-0	28	19	-6	2.8

● BILL BURNS

Burns, William Thomas "Sleepy Bill" b: 1/29/1880, San Saba, Tex. d: 6/6/53, Ramona, Cal. BB/TL, 6'2", 195 lbs. Deb: 4/18/08

YEAR	TM/L	W	L	PCT	G	GS	CG	SH	SV	IP	H	HR	BB	SO	RAT	ERA	ERA+	OAV	OOB	BH	AVG	PB	PR	/A	PD	TPI
1908	Was-A	6	11	.353	23	19	11	2	0	164	135	3	18	55	8.6	1.70	134	.229	.257	8	.148	-1	13	11	3	1.4
1909	Was-A	1	1	.500	6	4	1	0	0	29^1	25	0	7	13	10.7	1.23	198	.229	.294	3	.273	0	4	4	0	0.4
	Chi-A	7	13	.350	23	19	10	3	0	168	161	2	34	50	10.9	2.04	115	.264	.312	9	.153	1	8	6	1	0.9
	Yr	8	14	.364	29	23	11	3	0	197^1	186	2	41	63	10.7	1.92	123	.258	.305	12	.171	1	12	10	1	1.3
1910	Chi-A	0	0	—	1	0	0	0	0	0^1	0	0	1	0	27.0	0.00	—	.000	.500	0	—	0	0	0	0	0.0
	Cin-N	8	13	.381	31	21	13	2	0	178^2	183	3	49	57	12.3	3.48	84	.273	.333	16	.262	2	-9	-11	1	-0.9
1911	Cin-N	1	0	1.000	6	3	0	0	1	17^2	17	1	3	5	11.7	3.06	108	.254	.315	3	.429	2	1	0	1	0.3
	Phi-N	6	10	.375	21	14	8	3	1	121	132	5	26	47	12.2	3.42	101	.287	.333	6	.150	-1	-0	0	2	0.0
	Yr	7	10	.412	27	17	8	3	2	138^2	149	6	29	52	11.9	3.38	102	.281	.326	9	.191	0	0	1	3	0.3
1912	Det-A	1	4	.200	6	5	2	0	0	38^2	52	0	9	6	14.7	5.35	61	.338	.382	3	.231	1	-9	-9	-0	-0.8
Total	5	30	52	.366	117	85	45	10	2	717^2	705	14	147	233	11.2	2.72	100	.265	.313	48	.196	4	8	0	7	1.3

● PETE BURNSIDE

Burnside, Peter Willits b: 7/2/30, Evanston, Ill. BR/TL, 6'2", 190 lbs. Deb: 9/20/55

YEAR	TM/L	W	L	PCT	G	GS	CG	SH	SV	IP	H	HR	BB	SO	RAT	ERA	ERA+	OAV	OOB	BH	AVG	PB	PR	/A	PD	TPI
1955	NY-N	1	0	1.000	2	2	1	0	0	12^2	10	1	9	2	13.5	2.84	142	.204	.328	1	.200	0	2	2	-0	0.1
1957	NY-N	1	4	.200	10	9	1	1	0	30^2	47	5	13	18	17.9	8.80	45	.356	.418	0	.000	-1	-17	-17	-0	-2.3
1958	SF-N	0	0	—	6	1	0	0	0	10^2	20	3	5	4	21.1	6.75	56	.400	.455	0	—	0	-3	-3	-0	0.0
1959	Det-A	1	3	.250	30	0	0	0	1	62	55	7	25	49	11.9	3.77	108	.237	.317	0	.000	-1	1	2	0	0.1
1960	Det-A	7	7	.500	31	15	2	0	2	113^2	122	14	50	71	13.9	4.28	93	.277	.356	4	.148	-1	-5	-4	-1	-0.6
1961	Was-A	4	9	.308	33	16	4	2	2	113^1	106	11	51	56	12.7	4.53	89	.251	.335	2	.059	-3	-6	-6	-1	-1.0
1962	Was-A	5	11	.313	40	20	6	0	2	149^2	152	20	51	74	12.3	4.45	91	.263	.325	2	.057	-3	-8	-7	-2	-1.1
1963	Bal-A	0	1	.000	6	0	0	0	0	7^1	11	0	2	6	17.2	4.91	71	.344	.400	0	.000	-0	-1	-1	-0	-0.2
	Was-A	0	1	.000	38	1	0	0	0	67^1	84	12	24	23	14.4	6.15	60	.308	.364	1	.091	-0	-19	-18	-1	-0.4
	Yr	0	2	.000	44	1	0	0	0	74^2	95	12	26	29	14.6	6.03	61	.310	.364	1	.083	-1	-20	-19	-2	-0.6
Total	8	19	36	.345	196	64	14	3	7	567^1	607	73	230	303	13.5	4.81	82	.275	.347	10	.076	-8	-57	-53	-6	-5.4

● SHELDON BURNSIDE

Burnside, Sheldon John b: 12/22/54, South Bend, Ind. BR/TL, 6'5", 200 lbs. Deb: 9/4/78

YEAR	TM/L	W	L	PCT	G	GS	CG	SH	SV	IP	H	HR	BB	SO	RAT	ERA	ERA+	OAV	OOB	BH	AVG	PB	PR	/A	PD	TPI
1978	Det-A	0	0	—	2	0	0	0	0	4	4	0	2	3	13.5	9.00	43	.250	.333	0	—	0	-2	-2	-0	-0.2
1979	Det-A	1	1	.500	10	0	0	0	0	21^1	28	2	8	13	15.6	6.33	68	.333	.398	0	—	0	-5	-5	0	-0.6
1980	Cin-N	1	0	1.000	7	0	0	0	0	4^2	6	1	1	2	13.5	1.93	185	.333	.368	0	.000	-0	1	1	1	0.2
Total	3	2	1	.667	19	0	0	0	0	30	38	3	11	18	15.0	6.00	69	.322	.385	0	.000	-0	-6	-6	1	-0.6

● GEORGE BURPO

Burpo, George Harvie b: 6/19/22, Jenkins, Ky. BR/TL, 6', 195 lbs. Deb: 6/9/46

YEAR	TM/L	W	L	PCT	G	GS	CG	SH	SV	IP	H	HR	BB	SO	RAT	ERA	ERA+	OAV	OOB	BH	AVG	PB	PR	/A	PD	TPI
1946	Cin-N	0	0	—	2	0	0	0	0	2^1	4	0	5	1	34.7	15.43	22	.400	.600	0	—	0	-3	-3	-0	0.0

● HARRY BURRELL

Burrell, Harry J. b: 5/26/1869, Bethel, Vt. d: 12/11/14, Omaha, Neb. BR/TL, Deb: 9/13/1891

YEAR	TM/L	W	L	PCT	G	GS	CG	SH	SV	IP	H	HR	BB	SO	RAT	ERA	ERA+	OAV	OOB	BH	AVG	PB	PR	/A	PD	TPI
1891	StL-a	4	2	.667	7	4	3	0	0	43	51	4	21	19	15.5	4.81	87	.285	.366	5	.227	-0	-5	-3	-0	-0.4

● AL BURRIS

Burris, Alva Burton b: 1/28/1874, Warwick, Md. d: 3/24/38, Salisbury, Md. BR/TR, Deb: 6/22/1894

YEAR	TM/L	W	L	PCT	G	GS	CG	SH	SV	IP	H	HR	BB	SO	RAT	ERA	ERA+	OAV	OOB	BH	AVG	PB	PR	/A	PD	TPI
1894	Phi-N	0	0	—	1	0	0	0	0	5	14	0	2	0	28.8	18.00	28	.500	.533	2	.500	1	-7	-7	0	0.0

● RAY BURRIS

Burris, Bertram Ray b: 8/22/50, Idabel, Okla. BR/TR, 6'5", 200 lbs. Deb: 4/8/73 C

YEAR	TM/L	W	L	PCT	G	GS	CG	SH	SV	IP	H	HR	BB	SO	RAT	ERA	ERA+	OAV	OOB	BH	AVG	PB	PR	/A	PD	TPI
1973	Chi-N	1	1	.500	31	1	0	0	0	64^2	65	2	27	57	12.8	2.92	135	.261	.333	1	.143	0	5	7	1	0.3
1974	Chi-N	3	5	.375	40	5	0	0	1	75	91	8	26	40	14.5	6.60	58	.300	.363	1	.077	-1	-25	-23	-1	-2.5
1975	Chi-N	15	10	.600	36	35	8	2	0	238^1	259	25	73	108	12.7	4.12	93	.281	.337	15	.183	1	-13	-7	-4	-1.0
1976	Chi-N	15	13	.536	37	36	10	4	0	249	251	22	70	112	11.8	3.11	124	.263	.317	9	.111	-4	11	21	0	1.9
1977	Chi-N	14	16	.467	39	39	5	1	0	221	270	29	67	105	13.8	4.72	93	.305	.356	12	.174	1	-20	-8	3	-0.7
1978	Chi-N	7	13	.350	40	32	4	1	1	198^2	210	15	79	94	13.5	4.76	85	.274	.349	7	.115	-1	-26	-16	2	-1.5
1979	Chi-N	0	0	—	14	0	0	0	0	21^2	23	0	15	14	16.2	6.23	66	.284	.402	0	.000	0	-6	-5	0	0.1

YEAR	TM/L	W	L	PCT	G	GS	CG	SH	SV	IP	H	HR	BB	SO	RAT	ERA	ERA+	OAV	OOB	BH	AVG	PB	PR	/A	PD	TPI
	NY-A	1	3	.250	15	0	0	0	0	27^2	40	5	10	19	16.3	6.18	66	.342	.394	0	—	0	-6	-6	-0	-0.6
	NY-N	0	2	.000	4	4	0	0	0	21^2	21	2	6	10	11.6	3.32	109	.247	.304	1	.167	-0	1	1	0	0.1
1980	NY-N	7	13	.350	29	29	1	0	0	170^1	181	20	54	83	12.6	4.02	88	.277	.336	5	.098	-2	-8	-9	-1	-1.3
1981	*Mon-N	9	7	.563	22	21	4	0	0	135^2	117	9	41	52	10.7	3.05	114	.235	.297	7	.189	1	7	7	-1	0.7
1982	Mon-N	4	14	.222	37	15	2	0	2	123^2	143	14	53	55	14.4	4.73	77	.297	.369	5	.179	1	-16	-15	-1	-2.0
1983	Mon-N	4	7	.364	40	17	2	1	0	154	139	13	56	100	11.5	3.68	97	.244	.314	9	.231	3	-1	-2	0	0.2
1984	Oak-A	13	10	.565	34	28	5	1	0	211^2	193	15	90	93	12.4	3.15	119	.244	.327	0	—	0	20	14	-3	1.1
1985	Mil-A	9	13	.409	29	28	6	0	0	170^1	182	25	53	81	12.6	4.81	87	.272	.328	0	—	0	-13	-12	-1	-1.4
1986	StL-N	4	5	.444	23	10	0	0	0	82	92	13	32	34	14.0	5.60	65	.287	.359	4	.148	0	-17	-18	-1	-1.8
1987	Mil-A	2	2	.500	10	2	0	0	0	23	33	4	12	8	17.6	5.87	78	.351	.425	0	—	0	-4	-3	0	-0.6
Total	15	108	134	.446	480	302	47	10	4	2188^1	2310	221	764	1065	12.9	4.17	93	.274	.338	76	.151	-1	-110	-75	-6	-9.0

● JOHN BURROWS Burrows, John b: 10/30/13, Winnfield, La. d: 4/27/87, Coal Run, Ohio BR/TL, 5'10", 200 lbs. Deb: 4/25/43

YEAR	TM/L	W	L	PCT	G	GS	CG	SH	SV	IP	H	HR	BB	SO	RAT	ERA	ERA+	OAV	OOB	BH	AVG	PB	PR	/A	PD	TPI
1943	Phi-A	0	1	.000	4	1	0	0	0	7^2	8	0	9	3	21.1	8.22	41	.276	.462	0	.000	-0	-4	-4	-0	-0.5
	Chi-N	0	2	.000	23	1	0	0	2	32^2	25	0	16	18	11.8	3.86	87	.205	.307	2	.667	1	-2	-2	0	0.0
1944	Chi-N	0	0	—	3	0	0	0	0	3	7	0	3	1	30.0	18.00	20	.467	.556	0	—	0	-5	-5	0	0.0
Total	2	0	3	.000	30	2	0	0	2	43^1	40	0	28	22	14.7	5.61	60	.241	.360	2	.500	1	-11	-11	0	-0.5

● TERRY BURROWS Burrows, Terry Dale b: 11/28/68, Lake Charles, La. BL/TL, 6'1", 185 lbs. Deb: 6/12/94

YEAR	TM/L	W	L	PCT	G	GS	CG	SH	SV	IP	H	HR	BB	SO	RAT	ERA	ERA+	OAV	OOB	BH	AVG	PB	PR	/A	PD	TPI
1994	Tex-A	0	0	—	1	0	0	0	0	1	1	1	1	0	18.0	9.00	54	.250	.400	0	—	0	-0	-0	0	0.0
1995	Tex-A	2	2	.500	28	3	0	0	1	44^2	60	11	19	22	16.3	6.45	75	.323	.391	0	—	0	-9	-8	-1	-0.7
1996	Mil-A	2	0	1.000	8	0	0	0	0	12^2	12	2	10	5	16.3	2.84	182	.261	.404	0	—	0	3	3	-0	0.4
1997	SD-N	0	2	.000	13	0	0	0	0	10^1	12	1	8	8	18.3	10.45	37	.286	.412	0	—	0	-7	-8	0	-1.2
Total	4	4	4	.500	50	3	0	0	1	68^2	85	15	38	35	16.6	6.42	74	.306	.397	0	—	0	-13	-13	-1	-1.5

● JIM BURTON Burton, Jim Scott b: 10/27/49, Royal Oak, Mich. BR/TL, 6'3", 195 lbs. Deb: 6/10/75

YEAR	TM/L	W	L	PCT	G	GS	CG	SH	SV	IP	H	HR	BB	SO	RAT	ERA	ERA+	OAV	OOB	BH	AVG	PB	PR	/A	PD	TPI
1975	*Bos-A	1	2	.333	29	4	0	0	1	53	58	6	19	39	13.1	2.89	141	.276	.336	0	—	0	5	7	0	-0.3
1977	Bos-A	0	0	—	1	0	0	0	0	2^2	2	0	1	3	10.1	0.00	—	.200	.273	0	—	0	1	1	-0	-0.7
Total	2	1	2	.333	30	4	0	0	1	55^2	60	6	20	42	12.9	2.75	149	.273	.333	0	—	0	6	8	-0	-1.0

● MOE BURTSCHY Burtschy, Edward Frank b: 4/18/22, Cincinnati, Ohio BR/TR, 6'3", 208 lbs. Deb: 6/17/50

YEAR	TM/L	W	L	PCT	G	GS	CG	SH	SV	IP	H	HR	BB	SO	RAT	ERA	ERA+	OAV	OOB	BH	AVG	PB	PR	/A	PD	TPI
1950	Phi-A	0	1	.000	9	1	0	0	0	19	22	2	21	12	20.8	7.11	64	.289	.449	0	.000	-0	-5	-5	0	-0.2
1951	Phi-A	0	0	—	7	0	0	0	0	17	18	0	12	4	16.4	5.29	81	.277	.397	1	.333	0	-2	-2	0	0.0
1954	Phi-A	5	4	.556	46	0	0	0	4	94^2	80	7	53	54	13.4	3.80	103	.234	.350	2	.118	-1	-1	1	0	0.0
1955	KC-A	2	0	1.000	7	0	0	0	0	11^1	17	0	10	9	22.2	10.32	40	.354	.475	1	.333	0	-8	-8	-0	-1.1
1956	KC-A	3	1	.750	21	0	0	0	0	43^1	41	6	30	18	15.4	3.95	110	.263	.392	1	.125	-1	1	2	2	0.3
Total	5	10	6	.625	90	1	0	0	4	185^1	178	15	126	97	15.4	4.71	88	.259	.385	5	.139	-1	-15	-12	1	-1.0

● DENNIS BURTT Burtt, Dennis Allen b: 11/29/57, San Diego, Cal. BB/TR, 6', 180 lbs. Deb: 9/4/85

YEAR	TM/L	W	L	PCT	G	GS	CG	SH	SV	IP	H	HR	BB	SO	RAT	ERA	ERA+	OAV	OOB	BH	AVG	PB	PR	/A	PD	TPI
1985	Min-A	2	2	.500	5	2	0	0	0	28^1	20	2	7	9	8.6	3.81	116	.200	.252	0	—	0	1	2	0	0.1
1986	Min-A	0	0	—	3	0	0	0	0	2	7	1	3	1	45.0	31.50	14	.538	.625	0	—	0	-6	-6	-0	-0.1
Total	2	2	2	.500	8	2	0	0	0	30^1	27	3	10	10	11.0	5.64	78	.239	.301	0	—	0	-5	-4	0	0.0

● DICK BURWELL Burwell, Richard Matthew b: 1/23/40, Alton, Ill. BR/TR, 6'1", 190 lbs. Deb: 9/13/60

YEAR	TM/L	W	L	PCT	G	GS	CG	SH	SV	IP	H	HR	BB	SO	RAT	ERA	ERA+	OAV	OOB	BH	AVG	PB	PR	/A	PD	TPI
1960	Chi-N	0	0	—	3	1	0	0	0	9^2	11	2	7	1	17.7	5.59	68	.306	.432	1	.333	0	-2	-2	-0	0.0
1961	Chi-N	0	0	—	2	0	0	0	0	4	6	0	4	0	22.5	9.00	46	.375	.500	0	.000	-0	-2	-2	0	0.0
Total	2	0	0	—	5	1	0	0	0	13^2	17	2	11	1	19.1	6.59	59	.327	.453	1	.250	0	-4	-4	0	0.0

● BILL BURWELL Burwell, William Edwin b: 3/27/1895, Jarbalo, Kan. d: 6/11/73, Ormond Beach, Fla BL/TR, 5'11", 175 lbs. Deb: 5/1/20 MC

YEAR	TM/L	W	L	PCT	G	GS	CG	SH	SV	IP	H	HR	BB	SO	RAT	ERA	ERA+	OAV	OOB	BH	AVG	PB	PR	/A	PD	TPI
1920	StL-A	6	4	.600	33	2	0	0	4	113^1	133	5	42	30	14.2	3.65	107	.303	.369	7	.167	-2	2	3	-0	0.1
1921	StL-A	2	4	.333	33	3	1	0	2	84^1	102	2	29	17	14.2	5.12	87	.309	.368	6	.240	-0	-8	-6	-1	-0.5
1928	Pit-N	1	0	1.000	4	1	0	0	0	20^2	18	2	8	2	11.3	5.23	78	.234	.306	2	.222	-0	-3	-3	1	-0.1
Total	3	9	8	.529	70	6	1	0	6	218^1	253	9	79	49	13.9	4.37	95	.299	.363	15	.197	-2	-9	-5	-1	-0.5

● MIKE BUSBY Busby, Michael James b: 12/27/72, Lomita, Cal. BR/TR, 6'4", 210 lbs. Deb: 4/7/96

YEAR	TM/L	W	L	PCT	G	GS	CG	SH	SV	IP	H	HR	BB	SO	RAT	ERA	ERA+	OAV	OOB	BH	AVG	PB	PR	/A	PD	TPI
1996	StL-N	0	1	.000	1	1	0	0	0	4	9	4	4	4	31.5	18.00	23	.409	.519	1	.500	0	-6	-6	0	-0.8
1997	StL-N	0	2	.000	3	3	0	0	0	14^1	24	2	4	6	17.6	8.79	47	.393	.431	2	.500	1	-7	-7	-0	-0.7
1998	StL-N	5	2	.714	26	2	0	0	0	46	45	3	15	33	12.7	4.50	93	.254	.330	0	.000	-0	-1	-2	-0	-0.3
Total	3	5	5	.500	30	6	0	0	0	64^1	78	9	23	43	15.0	6.30	66	.300	.370	3	.333	1	-15	-15	-1	-1.8

● STEVE BUSBY Busby, Steven Lee b: 9/29/49, Burbank, Cal. BR/TR, 6'2", 205 lbs. Deb: 9/8/72

YEAR	TM/L	W	L	PCT	G	GS	CG	SH	SV	IP	H	HR	BB	SO	RAT	ERA	ERA+	OAV	OOB	BH	AVG	PB	PR	/A	PD	TPI
1972	KC-A	3	1	.750	5	5	3	0	0	40	28	1	8	31	8.1	1.57	192	.200	.243	3	.200	0	7	6	-1	0.7
1973	KC-A	16	15	.516	37	37	7	1	0	238^1	246	18	105	174	13.5	4.23	97	.271	.350	0	—	0	-11	-3	2	-0.7
1974	KC-A☆	22	14	.611	38	38	20	3	0	292^1	284	14	92	198	11.9	3.39	113	.258	.320	0	—	0	8	14	3	1.5
1975	KC-A★	18	12	.600	34	34	18	3	0	260^1	233	18	81	160	11.0	3.08	125	.242	.303	0	—	0	20	22	4	2.6
1976	KC-A	3	3	.500	13	13	1	0	0	71^2	58	7	49	29	13.8	4.40	80	.218	.346	0	—	0	-7	-7	-0	-0.6
1978	KC-A	1	0	1.000	7	5	0	0	0	21^1	24	2	15	10	17.3	7.59	50	.282	.402	0	—	0	-9	-9	0	-0.6
1979	KC-A	6	6	.500	22	12	4	0	0	94^1	71	10	64	45	12.9	3.63	118	.220	.349	0	—	0	6	7	2	0.8
1980	KC-A	1	3	.250	11	6	0	0	0	42^1	59	3	19	12	17.0	6.17	66	.335	.406	0	—	0	-10	-10	-0	-0.9
Total	8	70	54	.565	167	150	53	7	0	1060^2	1003	73	433	659	12.4	3.72	105	.253	.330	3	.200	0	4	20	10	2.8

● DON BUSCHHORN Buschhorn, Donald Lee b: 4/29/46, Independence, Mo. BR/TR, 6', 170 lbs. Deb: 5/15/65

YEAR	TM/L	W	L	PCT	G	GS	CG	SH	SV	IP	H	HR	BB	SO	RAT	ERA	ERA+	OAV	OOB	BH	AVG	PB	PR	/A	PD	TPI
1965	KC-A	0	1	.000	12	3	0	0	0	31	36	7	8	9	13.1	4.35	80	.295	.344	2	.500	1	-3	-3	-0	0.0

● GUY BUSH Bush, Guy Terrell "The Mississippi Mudcat" b: 8/23/01, Aberdeen, Miss. d: 7/2/85, Shannon, Miss. BR/TR, 6', 175 lbs. Deb: 9/17/23

YEAR	TM/L	W	L	PCT	G	GS	CG	SH	SV	IP	H	HR	BB	SO	RAT	ERA	ERA+	OAV	OOB	BH	AVG	PB	PR	/A	PD	TPI
1923	Chi-N	0	0	—	1	0	0	0	0	1	1	0	0	2	9.0	0.00	—	.250	.250	0	—	0	0	0	0	0.0
1924	Chi-N	2	5	.286	16	8	4	0	0	80^2	91	7	24	36	13.1	4.02	97	.285	.339	4	.154	-1	-1	-1	-2	-0.4
1925	Chi-N	6	13	.316	42	15	5	0	**4**	182	213	15	52	76	13.3	4.30	101	.300	.350	11	.193	-2	-1	0	4	0.2
1926	Chi-N	13	9	.591	35	15	7	2	2	157^1	149	3	42	32	11.1	2.86	134	.258	.311	8	.167	-2	17	17	-1	1.9
1927	Chi-N	10	10	.500	36	22	9	1	2	193^1	177	3	79	62	12.2	3.03	128	.250	.330	8	.123	-4	19	18	0	1.3
1928	Chi-N	15	6	.714	42	24	9	2	2	204^1	229	10	86	61	14.1	3.83	100	.293	.367	6	.082	-6	4	0	-1	-0.6
1929	*Chi-N	18	7	.720	**50**	29	18	2	**8**	270^2	277	16	107	82	12.9	3.66	126	.265	.335	15	.165	-4	32	29	0	2.0
1930	Chi-N	15	10	.600	46	25	11	0	3	225	291	22	86	75	15.2	6.20	79	.316	.376	22	.282	3	-31	-33	1	-2.5
1931	Chi-N	16	8	.667	39	24	14	1	2	180^1	190	9	66	54	12.9	4.49	86	.268	.332	7	.123	-2	-13	-13	4	-1.3
1932	*Chi-N	19	11	.633	40	30	15	1	0	238^2	262	13	70	73	12.8	3.21	118	.278	.332	15	.179	0	18	15	1	1.8
1933	Chi-N	20	12	.625	41	32	20	4	2	259	261	9	68	84	11.5	2.75	119	.257	.304	11	.125	-1	17	15	4	2.1
1934	Chi-N	18	10	.643	40	27	15	1	2	209^1	213	15	54	75	11.5	3.83	101	.262	.309	16	.229	1	5	1	1	0.3
1935	Pit-N	11	11	.500	41	25	8	1	2	204^1	237	16	40	42	12.4	4.32	95	.285	.321	8	.127	-1	-7	-5	-1	-0.6
1936	Pit-N	1	3	.250	16	0	0	0	2	34^2	49	3	11	10	15.6	5.97	68	.336	.382	3	.333	0	-8	-7	1	-0.7
	Bos-N	4	5	.444	15	11	5	0	0	90^1	98	2	20	28	11.8	3.39	113	.281	.320	3	.120	-1	6	4	1	0.4
	Yr	5	8	.385	31	11	5	0	2	125	147	5	31	38	12.8	4.10	95	.297	.338	6	.176	-0	-1	-3	1	-0.3
1937	Bos-N	8	15	.348	32	20	11	1	1	180^2	201	8	48	56	12.4	3.54	101	.282	.328	6	.111	-2	8	1	1	0.0
1938	StL-N	0	1	.000	6	0	0	0	1	6	6	1	3	1	13.5	4.50	88	.286	.375	0	—	0	-0	-0	-0	-0.1
1945	Cin-N	0	0	—	4	0	0	0	1	4^1	5	0	3	1	16.6	8.31	45	.278	.381	0	—	0	-2	-2	-0	-0.1
Total	17	176	136	.564	542	307	151	16	34	2722	2950	152	859	850	12.7	3.86	103	.277	.334	143	.161	-22	64	41	12	3.7

● JOE BUSH Bush, Leslie Ambrose "Bullet Joe" b: 11/27/1892, Brainerd, Minn. d: 11/1/74, Ft.Lauderdale, Fla. BR/TR, 5'9", 173 lbs. Deb: 9/30/12

YEAR	TM/L	W	L	PCT	G	GS	CG	SH	SV	IP	H	HR	BB	SO	RAT	ERA	ERA+	OAV	OOB	BH	AVG	PB	PR	/A	PD	TPI
1912	Phi-A	0	0	—	1	1	0	0	0	8	14	0	4	3	20.3	7.88	39	.368	.429	2	.500	1	-4	-4	-0	0.1
1913	*Phi-A	15	6	.714	39	16	6	1	3	200^1	199	3	66	81	12.1	3.82	72	.248	.310	11	.157	-0	-20	-23	4	-2.0
1914	*Phi-A	17	13	.567	38	23	14	2	2	206	184	2	81	109	11.9	3.06	85	.242	.322	14	.189	2	-7	-10	-0	-1.3
1915	Phi-A	5	15	.250	25	18	8	0	0	145^2	137	3	89	89	14.2	4.14	71	.263	.375	7	.143	-3	-19	-20	0	-2.7
1916	Phi-A	15	24	.385	40	33	25	8	0	286^2	222	3	130	157	11.1	2.57	111	.219	.310	14	.140	-4	8	9	5	1.4

YEAR	TM/L	W	L	PCT	G	GS	CG	SH	SV	IP	H	HR	BB	SO	RAT	ERA	ERA+	OAV	OOB	BH	AVG	PB	PR	/A	PD	TPI
1917	Phi-A	11	17	.393	37	31	17	4	2	233^1	207	3	111	121	12.3	2.47	111	.241	.328	16	.200	1	5	7	0	1.1
1918	*Bos-A	15	15	.500	36	31	26	7	2	272^2	241	3	91	125	11.1	2.11	127	.242	.307	27	.276	6	20	17	3	3.1
1919	Bos-A	0	0	—	3	2	0	0	0	9	11	0	4	3	15.0	5.00	60	.324	.395	2	.400	1	-2	-2	0	0.1
1920	Bos-A	15	15	.500	35	32	18	0	1	243^2	287	3	94	88	14.4	4.25	86	.300	.369	25	.245	2	-12	-16	3	-1.4
1921	Bos-A	16	9	.640	37	32	21	3	1	254^1	244	10	93	96	12.1	3.50	121	.260	.330	39	.325	6	22	20	1	2.7
1922	*NY-A	26	7	**.788**	39	30	20	0	3	255^1	240	16	85	92	11.5	3.31	121	.252	.314	31	.326	8	21	20	1	3.1
1923	*NY-A	19	15	.559	37	30	22	3	0	275^2	263	7	117	125	12.6	3.43	115	.260	.340	31	.274	7	17	16	1	2.6
1924	NY-A	17	16	.515	39	31	19	3	1	252	262	9	109	80	13.5	3.57	116	.273	.352	42	.339	14	18	16	2	3.4
1925	StL-A	14	14	.500	33	30	15	2	0	208^2	230	18	91	63	13.9	5.09	92	.284	.357	26	.255	3	-16	-10	2	-0.4
1926	Was-A	1	8	.111	12	11	3	0	0	71^1	83	6	35	27	15.5	6.69	58	.292	.380	7	.233	1	-21	-22	0	-2.2
	Pit-N	6	6	.500	19	12	9	2	3	110^2	97	7	35	38	10.9	3.01	131	.236	.299	13	.265	2	10	11	-1	1.3
1927	Pit-N	1	2	.333	5	3	0	0	0	6^2	14	1	5	1	25.7	13.50	30	.412	.487	3	.600	1	-7	-7	0	-2.1
	NY-N	1	1	.500	3	2	1	0	0	12	18	1	5	6	17.3	7.50	51	.340	.397	2	.500	1	-5	-5	-0	-0.6
	Yr	2	3	.400	8	5	1	0	0	18^2	32	2	10	7	20.3	9.64	41	.368	.433	5	.556	2	-12	-12	0	-2.7
1928	Phi-A	2	1	.667	11	2	1	0	1	35^1	39	1	18	15	14.8	5.09	79	.300	.389	1	.067	-1	-4	-4	1	-0.4
Total	17	196	184	.516	489	370	225	35	19	3087^1	2992	96	1263	1319	12.6	3.51	99	.259	.335	313	.253	49	4	-8	21	5.8

● **JACK BUSHELMAN** Bushelman, John Francis b: 8/29/1885, Cincinnati, Ohio d: 10/26/55, Roanoke, Va. BR/TR, 6'2", 175 lbs. Deb: 10/5/09

YEAR	TM/L	W	L	PCT	G	GS	CG	SH	SV	IP	H	HR	BB	SO	RAT	ERA	ERA+	OAV	OOB	BH	AVG	PB	PR	/A	PD	TPI
1909	Cin-N	0	1	.000	1	1	1	0	0	7	7	1	4	3	14.1	2.57	101	.241	.333	0	.000	-0	0	0	-0	-0.1
1911	Bos-A	0	1	.000	3	1	1	0	0	12	8	0	10	5	14.3	3.00	109	.186	.352	0	.000	-0	0	0	-0	0.0
1912	Bos-A	1	0	1.000	3	0	0	0	0	7^2	9	0	5	5	16.4	4.70	72	.310	.412	0	.000	-0	-1	-1	0	-0.1
Total	3	1	2	.333	7	2	2	0	0	26^2	24	1	19	13	14.9	3.38	93	.238	.364	0	.000	-1	-1	-1	-0	-0.2

● **FRANK BUSHEY** Bushey, Francis Clyde b: 8/1/06, Wheaton, Kan. d: 3/18/72, Topeka, Kan. BR/TR, 6', 180 lbs. Deb: 9/17/27

YEAR	TM/L	W	L	PCT	G	GS	CG	SH	SV	IP	H	HR	BB	SO	RAT	ERA	ERA+	OAV	OOB	BH	AVG	PB	PR	/A	PD	TPI
1927	Bos-A	0	0	—	1	0	0	0	0	1^1	2	0	2	0	27.0	6.75	63	.500	.667	0	—	0	-0	-0	-0	0.0
1930	Bos-A	0	1	.000	11	0	0	0	0	30	34	1	15	4	15.3	6.30	73	.306	.398	1	.111	-1	-6	-6	0	-0.2
Total	2	0	1	.000	12	0	0	0	0	31^1	36	1	17	4	15.8	6.32	73	.313	.410	1	.111	-1	-6	-6	0	-0.2

● **CHRIS BUSHING** Bushing, Christopher Shaun b: 11/4/67, Rockville Centre, N.Y. BR/TR, 6', 190 lbs. Deb: 9/3/93

YEAR	TM/L	W	L	PCT	G	GS	CG	SH	SV	IP	H	HR	BB	SO	RAT	ERA	ERA+	OAV	OOB	BH	AVG	PB	PR	/A	PD	TPI
1993	Cin-N	0	0	—	6	0	0	0	0	4^1	9	1	4	3	27.0	12.46	32	.450	.542	0	—	0	-4	-4	-0	0.0

● **TOM BUSKEY** Buskey, Thomas William b: 2/20/47, Harrisburg, Pa. BR/TR, 6'3", 220 lbs. Deb: 8/5/73

YEAR	TM/L	W	L	PCT	G	GS	CG	SH	SV	IP	H	HR	BB	SO	RAT	ERA	ERA+	OAV	OOB	BH	AVG	PB	PR	/A	PD	TPI
1973	NY-A	0	1	.000	8	0	0	0	1	16^2	18	2	4	8	12.4	5.40	68	.286	.338	0	—	0	-3	-3	-0	0.0
1974	NY-A	0	1	.000	4	0	0	0	1	5^2	10	1	3	3	22.2	6.35	55	.400	.483	0	—	0	-2	-2	-0	-0.3
	Cle-A	2	6	.250	51	0	0	0	17	93	93	10	33	40	12.3	3.19	113	.263	.327	0	—	0	4	4	1	0.7
	Yr	2	7	.222	55	0	0	0	18	98^2	103	11	36	43	12.8	3.38	107	.271	.336	0	—	0	3	3	1	0.4
1975	Cle-A	5	3	.625	50	0	0	0	7	77	69	7	29	29	11.6	2.57	147	.252	.326	0	—	0	10	10	2	1.4
1976	Cle-A	5	4	.556	39	0	0	0	1	94^1	88	9	34	32	11.9	3.63	96	.256	.328	0	—	0	-1	-1	1	0.0
1977	Cle-A	0	0	—	21	0	0	0	0	34	45	6	8	15	14.3	5.29	74	.313	.353	0	—	0	-5	-5	-0	0.2
1978	Tor-A	0	1	.000	8	0	0	0	0	13^1	14	1	5	7	12.8	3.38	116	.275	.339	0	—	0	1	1	1	0.0
1979	Tor-A	6	10	.375	44	0	0	0	7	78^2	74	10	25	44	11.4	3.43	126	.249	.310	0	—	0	7	8	2	1.7
1980	Tor-A	3	1	.750	33	0	0	0	0	66^2	68	11	26	34	12.7	4.45	97	.278	.347	0	—	0	-3	-1	0	-0.4
Total	8	21	27	.438	258	0	0	0	34	479^1	479	57	167	212	12.3	3.66	105	.267	.332	0	—	0	9	11	5	3.3

● **MAX BUTCHER** Butcher, Albert Maxwell b: 9/21/10, Holden, W.Va. d: 9/15/57, Man, W.Va. BR/TR, 6'2", 220 lbs. Deb: 4/20/36

YEAR	TM/L	W	L	PCT	G	GS	CG	SH	SV	IP	H	HR	BB	SO	RAT	ERA	ERA+	OAV	OOB	BH	AVG	PB	PR	/A	PD	TPI
1936	Bro-N	6	6	.500	38	15	5	0	2	147^2	154	11	59	55	13.0	3.96	104	.268	.337	6	.125	-3	1	3	-2	-0.2
1937	Bro-N	11	15	.423	39	24	8	1	0	191^2	203	12	75	57	13.4	4.27	94	.280	.354	10	.161	-1	-8	-5	3	-0.4
1938	Bro-N	5	4	.556	24	8	3	0	2	72^2	104	9	39	21	17.8	6.56	59	.334	.410	4	.160	0	-22	-21	1	-2.3
	Phi-N	4	8	.333	12	12	11	0	0	98^1	94	6	31	29	11.6	2.93	133	.253	.314	9	.257	1	9	10	0	1.3
	Yr	9	12	.429	36	20	14	0	2	171	198	15	70	50	14.2	4.47	87	.290	.358	13	.217	1	-13	-11	2	-1.0
1939	Phi-N	2	13	.133	19	16	3	0	0	104^1	131	10	51	27	15.8	5.61	71	.308	.383	7	.184	-1	-20	-19	-2	-2.5
	Pit-N	4	4	.500	14	12	5	2	0	86^2	104	2	23	21	13.2	3.43	112	.297	.340	3	.097	-2	5	4	2	0.3
	Yr	6	17	.261	33	28	8	2	0	191	235	12	74	48	14.6	4.62	85	.302	.363	10	.145	-3	-15	-15	-0	-2.2
1940	Pit-N	8	9	.471	35	24	6	2	2	136^1	161	13	46	40	13.7	6.01	63	.290	.346	15	.300	4	-33	-33	1	-3.2
1941	Pit-N	17	12	.586	33	32	19	0	0	236	249	11	66	61	12.1	3.05	118	.265	.314	15	.183	-1	15	15	0	1.7
1942	Pit-N	5	8	.385	24	18	9	0	1	150^2	144	7	44	49	11.3	2.93	116	.247	.303	7	.143	-2	6	8	0	0.5
1943	Pit-N	10	8	.556	33	21	10	2	1	193^2	191	4	57	45	11.6	2.60	134	.262	.317	10	.164	-1	17	19	0	1.6
1944	Pit-N	13	11	.542	35	27	13	5	1	199	216	8	46	43	11.9	3.12	119	.273	.314	12	.190	-0	11	13	3	1.7
1945	Pit-N	10	8	.556	28	20	12	2	0	169^1	184	7	46	37	12.4	3.03	130	.277	.328	12	.222	0	15	17	1	1.8
Total	10	95	106	.473	334	229	104	14	9	1786^1	1935	100	583	485	12.8	3.73	101	.276	.333	110	.184	-6	-3	11	8	0.3

● **JOHN BUTCHER** Butcher, John Daniel b: 3/8/57, Glendale, Cal. BR/TR, 6'4", 190 lbs. Deb: 9/8/80

YEAR	TM/L	W	L	PCT	G	GS	CG	SH	SV	IP	H	HR	BB	SO	RAT	ERA	ERA+	OAV	OOB	BH	AVG	PB	PR	/A	PD	TPI
1980	Tex-A	3	3	.500	6	6	1	0	0	35^1	34	2	13	27	12.0	4.08	96	.248	.313	0	—	0	-0	-1	0	0.2
1981	Tex-A	1	2	.333	5	3	1	1	0	27^2	18	0	8	19	8.5	1.63	213	.186	.248	0	—	0	6	6	0	0.9
1982	Tex-A	1	5	.167	18	13	2	0	1	94^1	102	10	34	39	13.2	4.87	80	.280	.345	0	—	0	-8	-10	2	-0.4
1983	Tex-A	6	6	.500	38	6	1	1	5	123	128	8	41	58	12.4	3.51	114	.270	.329	0	—	0	8	7	0	0.8
1984	Min-A	13	11	.542	34	34	8	1	0	225	242	18	53	83	12.0	3.44	122	.276	.320	0	—	0	14	19	-1	1.6
1985	Min-A	11	14	.440	34	33	8	2	0	207^2	239	24	43	92	12.5	4.98	88	.289	.328	0	—	0	-19	-13	0	-1.5
1986	Min-A	0	3	.000	16	10	1	0	0	70	82	11	24	29	13.8	6.30	68	.294	.352	0	—	0	-17	-16	0	-0.7
	Cle-A	1	5	.167	13	8	1	1	0	50^2	86	6	13	16	18.1	6.93	60	.381	.421	0	—	0	-15	-16	-1	-1.5
	Yr	1	8	.111	29	18	2	1	0	120^2	168	17	37	45	15.5	6.56	65	.330	.379	0	—	0	-32	-31	-1	-2.2
Total	7	36	49	.424	164	113	23	6	6	833^2	931	79	229	363	12.7	4.42	94	.284	.334	0	—	0	-32	-24	1	-0.6

● **MIKE BUTCHER** Butcher, Michael Dana b: 5/10/65, Davenport, Iowa BR/TR, 6'1", 200 lbs. Deb: 7/6/92

YEAR	TM/L	W	L	PCT	G	GS	CG	SH	SV	IP	H	HR	BB	SO	RAT	ERA	ERA+	OAV	OOB	BH	AVG	PB	PR	/A	PD	TPI
1992	Cal-A	2	2	.500	19	0	0	0	0	27^2	29	3	13	24	14.3	3.25	122	.264	.352	0	—	0	2	2	-0	0.3
1993	Cal-A	1	0	1.000	23	0	0	0	8	28^1	21	2	15	24	12.1	2.86	158	.204	.317	0	—	0	5	5	-1	0.3
1994	Cal-A	2	1	.667	33	0	0	0	1	29^2	31	2	23	19	17.0	6.67	73	.274	.406	0	—	0	-6	-6	1	-0.5
1995	Cal-A	6	1	.857	40	0	0	0	0	51^1	49	7	31	29	14.2	4.73	99	.257	.363	0	—	0	-0	-0	-1	-0.1
Total	4	11	4	.733	115	0	0	0	9	137	130	14	82	96	14.4	4.47	102	.251	.361	0	—	0	0	1	-0	0.0

● **SAL BUTERA** Butera, Salvatore Philip b: 9/25/52, Richmond Hill, N.Y BR/TR, 6', 190 lbs. Deb: 4/10/80 C◆

YEAR	TM/L	W	L	PCT	G	GS	CG	SH	SV	IP	H	HR	BB	SO	RAT	ERA	ERA+	OAV	OOB	BH	AVG	PB	PR	/A	PD	TPI
1985	Mon-N	0	0	—	1	0	0	0	0	1	0	0	0	0	0.0	0.00	—	.000	.000	24	.200	0	0	0	-0	0.0
1986	Cin-N	0	0	—	1	0	0	0	0	1	0	0	1	1	9.0	0.00	—	.000	.250	27	.239	0	0	0	-0	0.0
Total	2	0	0	—	2	0	0	0	0	2	0	0	1	1	4.5	0.00	—	.000	.143	182	.227	0	1	1	-0	0.0

● **BILL BUTLAND** Butland, Wilburn Rue b: 3/22/18, Terre Haute, Ind. d: 9/19/97, Terre Haute, Ind. BR/TL, 6'5", 185 lbs. Deb: 5/29/40

YEAR	TM/L	W	L	PCT	G	GS	CG	SH	SV	IP	H	HR	BB	SO	RAT	ERA	ERA+	OAV	OOB	BH	AVG	PB	PR	/A	PD	TPI
1940	Bos-A	1	2	.333	3	3	1	0	0	21	27	0	10	5	15.9	5.57	81	.307	.378	0	.000	-1	-3	-3	1	-0.3
1942	Bos-A	7	1	.875	23	10	6	2	1	111^1	85	8	33	46	9.8	2.51	149	.206	.270	1	.036	-1	14	15	0	1.0
1946	Bos-A	1	0	1.000	5	2	0	0	0	16^1	23	3	13	10	19.8	11.02	33	.343	.450	1	.250	0	-14	-13	0	-0.7
1947	Bos-A	0	0	—	1	0	0	0	0	2	3	0	0	1	13.5	4.50	86	.333	.333	0	—	0	-0	-0	-0	0.0
Total	4	9	3	.750	32	15	7	2	1	150^2	138	11	56	62	11.8	3.88	99	.240	.310	2	.051	-2	-2	-1	1	0.0

● **ADAM BUTLER** Butler, Adam Christopher b: 8/17/73, Fairfax, Va. BL/TL, 6'2", 225 lbs. Deb: 3/31/98

YEAR	TM/L	W	L	PCT	G	GS	CG	SH	SV	IP	H	HR	BB	SO	RAT	ERA	ERA+	OAV	OOB	BH	AVG	PB	PR	/A	PD	TPI
1998	Atl-N	0	1	.000	8	0	0	0	0	5	5	1	6	7	21.6	10.80	39	.278	.480	0	—	0	-4	-4	-0	-0.6

● **CECIL BUTLER** Butler, Cecil Dean "Slewfoot" b: 10/23/37, Dallas, Ga. BR/TR, 6'4", 195 lbs. Deb: 4/23/62

YEAR	TM/L	W	L	PCT	G	GS	CG	SH	SV	IP	H	HR	BB	SO	RAT	ERA	ERA+	OAV	OOB	BH	AVG	PB	PR	/A	PD	TPI
1962	Mil-N	2	0	1.000	9	2	1	0	0	31	26	4	9	22	10.2	2.61	145	.217	.271	0	.000	-1	5	4	0	0.2
1964	Mil-N	0	0	—	2	0	0	0	0	4^1	7	2	0	2	14.5	8.31	42	.368	.368	0	—	0	-2	-2	0	0.0
Total	2	2	0	1.000	11	2	1	0	0	35^1	33	6	9	24	10.7	3.31	114	.237	.284	0	.000	-1	2	2	0	0.2

● **CHARLIE BUTLER** Butler, Charles Thomas b: 5/12/06, Green Cove Springs, Fla. d: 5/10/64, Brunswick, Ga. BR/TL, 6'1.5", 210 lbs. Deb: 5/1/33

YEAR	TM/L	W	L	PCT	G	GS	CG	SH	SV	IP	H	HR	BB	SO	RAT	ERA	ERA+	OAV	OOB	BH	AVG	PB	PR	/A	PD	TPI
1933	Phi-N	0	0	—	1	0	0	0	0	1	1	0	2	0	27.0	9.00	42	.250	.500	0	—	0	-1	-1	-0	0.0

YEAR	TM/L	W	L	PCT	G	GS	CG	SH	SV	IP	H	HR	BB	SO	RAT	ERA	ERA+	OAV	OOB	BH	AVG	PB	PR	/A	PD	TPI
● IKE BUTLER Butler, Isaac Burr b: 8/22/1873, Langston, Mich. d: 3/17/48, Oakland, Cal. TR , 6′, 175 lbs. Deb: 8/5/02																										
1902	Bal-A	1	10	.091	16	14	12	0	0	116^1	168	1	45	13	16.6	5.34	71	.337	.394	6	.113	-3	-23	-20	-1	-1.9
● BILL BUTLER Butler, William Franklin b: 3/12/47, Hyattsville, Md. BL/TL, 6′2″, 210 lbs. Deb: 4/9/69																										
1969	KC-A	9	10	.474	34	29	5	4	0	193^2	174	15	91	156	12.5	3.90	94	.240	.328	3	.050	-4	-6	-5	-3	-1.1
1970	KC-A	4	12	.250	25	25	2	1	0	140^2	117	17	87	75	13.1	3.77	99	.229	.342	2	.045	-3	-1	-1	-2	-0.6
1971	KC-A	1	2	.333	14	6	0	0	0	44^1	45	6	18	32	12.8	3.45	99	.268	.339	1	.083	-1	0	-0	-0	-0.1
1972	Cle-A	0	0	—	6	2	0	0	0	11^2	9	1	10	6	14.7	1.54	208	.220	.373	0	.000	-0	2	2	-0	0.0
1974	Min-A	4	6	.400	26	12	2	0	1	98^2	91	9	56	79	13.5	4.10	91	.251	.353	0	—	0	-5	-4	-2	-0.8
1975	Min-A	5	4	.556	23	8	1	0	0	81^2	100	12	35	55	14.9	5.95	64	.301	.368	0	—	0	-20	-19	-0	-2.0
1977	Min-A	0	1	.000	6	4	0	0	0	21	19	5	15	5	15.0	6.86	58	.244	.372	0	—	0	-7	-7	-1	-0.2
Total	7	23	35	.397	134	86	10	5	1	591^2	555	65	312	408	13.3	4.21	88	.250	.345	6	.051	-7	-37	-33	-9	-4.8
● TOM BUTTERS Butters, Thomas Arden b: 4/8/38, Delaware, O. BR/TR, 6′2″, 195 lbs. Deb: 9/8/62																										
1962	Pit-N	0	0	—	4	0	0	0	0	6	5	0	6	10	18.0	1.50	262	.238	.429	0	—	0	2	2	0	0.0
1963	Pit-N	0	0	—	6	1	0	0	0	16^1	15	1	8	11	13.8	4.41	75	.259	.368	1	.333	0	-2	-2	-0	0.0
1964	Pit-N	2	2	.500	28	4	0	0	0	64^1	52	3	37	58	12.5	2.38	148	.221	.327	2	.182	0	8	8	-1	0.4
1965	Pit-N	0	1	.000	5	0	0	0	0	9	9	2	5	6	14.0	7.00	50	.250	.341	0	.000	-0	-3	-3	0	-0.4
Total	4	2	3	.400	43	5	0	0	0	95^2	81	6	56	85	13.2	3.10	113	.231	.342	3	.200	0	4	4	-1	0.0
● FRANK BUTTERY Buttery, Frank b: 5/13/1851, Silvermine, Conn. d: 12/16/02, Silvermine, Conn. Deb: 4/26/1872 ♦																										
1872	Man-n	3	2	.600	7	5	5	0	0	54	88	1	2	0	15.0	4.50	80	.326	.331	24	.258	-1	-5	-5		-0.4
● RALPH BUXTON Buxton, Ralph Stanley "Buck" b: 6/7/14, Rainton, Sask., Canada d: 1/6/88, San Leandro, Cal. BR/TR, 5′11.5″, 163 lbs. Deb: 9/11/38																										
1938	Phi-A	0	1	.000	5	0	0	0	0	9^1	12	1	5	9	16.4	4.82	100	.324	.405	0	.000	-0	-0	0	-0	0.0
1949	NY-A	0	1	.000	14	0	0	0	2	26^2	22	3	16	14	12.8	4.05	100	.229	.339	0	.000	-0	0	-0	-0	-0.1
Total	2	0	2	.000	19	0	0	0	2	36	34	4	21	23	13.8	4.25	100	.256	.357	0	.000	-1	0	-0	-0	-0.1
● JOHN BUZHARDT Buzhardt, John William b: 8/17/36, Prosperity, S.C. BR/TR, 6′2″, 198 lbs. Deb: 9/10/58																										
1958	Chi-N	3	0	1.000	6	2	1	0	0	24^1	16	2	7	9	8.5	1.85	212	.184	.245	1	.125	-0	6	6	1	0.7
1959	Chi-N	4	5	.444	31	10	1	1	0	101^1	107	12	29	33	12.2	4.97	79	.271	.322	2	.069	-1	-12	-12	1	-1.0
1960	Phi-N	5	16	.238	30	29	5	0	0	200^1	198	14	68	73	12.0	3.86	100	.259	.321	10	.161	-1	-2	0	-1	-0.1
1961	Phi-N	6	18	.250	41	27	6	1	0	202^1	200	28	65	92	12.1	4.49	91	.263	.326	6	.105	-2	-10	-9	0	-1.2
1962	Chi-A	8	12	.400	28	25	8	2	0	152^1	156	16	59	64	12.9	4.19	93	.264	.335	6	.118	-2	-4	-5	2	-0.6
1963	Chi-A	9	4	.692	19	18	6	3	0	126^1	100	8	31	59	9.7	2.42	145	.216	.273	4	.083	-3	17	15	1	1.4
1964	Chi-A	10	8	.556	31	25	8	3	0	160	150	13	35	97	10.6	2.98	116	.250	.295	11	.204	2	11	8	0	1.2
1965	Chi-A	13	8	.619	32	30	4	1	1	188^2	167	12	56	108	11.0	3.01	106	.242	.305	7	.125	0	10	4	-1	0.3
1966	Chi-A	6	11	.353	33	22	5	4	1	150^1	144	13	30	66	10.7	3.83	83	.248	.289	5	.116	-1	-7	-11	3	-1.0
1967	Chi-A	3	9	.250	28	7	0	0	0	88^2	100	11	37	33	14.5	3.96	78	.294	.373	4	.200	0	-7	-8	0	-1.1
	Bal-A	0	1	.000	7	1	0	0	0	11^2	14	1	5	7	14.7	4.63	68	.298	.365	0	.000	-0	-2	-2	0	-0.1
	Yr	3	10	.231	35	8	0	0	0	100^1	114	12	42	40	14.0	4.04	77	.288	.356	4	.190	0	-9	-10	1	-1.2
	Hou-N	0	0	—	1	0	0	0	0	0^2	0	0	0	0	0.0	0.00	—	.000	.000	0	—	0	0	0	0	0.0
1968	Hou-N	4	4	.500	39	4	0	0	5	83^2	73	0	35	37	12.0	3.12	95	.239	.325	4	.250	1	-1	-2	1	0.0
Total	11	71	96	.425	326	200	44	15	7	1490^2	1425	130	457	678	11.6	3.66	97	.253	.314	60	.135	-7	-1	-16	7	-1.5
● BUD BYERLY Byerly, Eldred William b: 10/26/20, Webster Groves, Mo BR/TR, 6′2.5″, 185 lbs. Deb: 9/26/43																										
1943	StL-N	1	0	1.000	2	2	0	0	0	13	14	0	5	6	13.2	3.46	97	.280	.345	0	.000	-0	-0	-0	-0	-0.1
1944	*StL-N	2	2	.500	9	4	2	0	0	42^1	37	2	20	13	12.1	3.40	104	.228	.313	2	.167	-0	1	1	1	0.1
1945	StL-N	4	5	.444	33	8	2	0	0	95	111	3	41	39	14.5	4.74	79	.288	.358	5	.217	1	-10	-10	2	-0.6
1950	Cin-N	0	1	.000	4	1	0	0	0	14^2	12	1	4	5	9.8	2.45	173	.218	.271	0	.000	-0	3	3	-0	0.1
1951	Cin-N	2	1	.667	40	0	0	0	0	66	69	6	25	28	13.1	3.27	125	.267	.337	0	.000	-0	5	6	1	0.3
1952	Cin-N	0	1	.000	12	2	0	0	1	24^2	29	0	7	14	13.1	5.11	74	.309	.356	1	.200	0	-4	-4	0	-0.2
1956	Was-A	2	4	.333	25	0	0	0	4	51^2	45	6	14	19	10.6	2.96	146	.243	.303	1	.091	-1	7	8	0	0.9
1957	Was-A	6	6	.500	47	0	0	0	6	95	94	6	22	39	11.1	3.13	125	.264	.309	1	.067	-1	7	8	1	1.1
1958	Was-A	2	0	1.000	17	0	0	0	1	24	34	4	11	13	17.3	6.75	56	.347	.418	0	.000	-0	-8	-8	-0	-0.7
	Bos-A	1	2	.333	18	0	0	0	0	30^1	31	1	7	16	11.6	1.78	225	.272	.320	0	.000	-1	7	7	-0	0.6
	Yr	3	2	.600	35	0	0	0	1	54^1	65	5	18	29	13.9	3.98	99	.302	.359	0	.000	-1	-1	-0	-0	-0.1
1959	SF-N	1	0	1.000	11	0	0	0	0	13	11	2	5	4	11.1	1.38	275	.234	.308	0	—	0	4	4	1	0.3
1960	SF-N	1	0	1.000	19	0	0	0	2	22	32	3	6	13	16.0	5.32	65	.340	.386	0	.000	-0	-4	-4	-0	-0.3
Total	11	22	22	.500	237	17	4	0	14	491^2	519	34	167	209	12.7	3.70	105	.273	.335	10	.118	-4	8	10	4	1.5
● HARRY BYRD Byrd, Harry Gladwin b: 2/3/25, Darlington, S.C. d: 5/14/85, Darlington, S.C. BR/TR, 6′1″, 188 lbs. Deb: 4/21/50																										
1950	Phi-A	0	0	—	6	0	0	0	0	10^2	25	3	9	2	30.4	16.88	27	.481	.571	0	.000	-0	-15	-15	-0	0.0
1952	Phi-A	15	15	.500	37	28	15	3	2	228^1	244	12	98	116	13.8	3.31	120	.274	.351	10	.133	-3	9	16	0	1.8
1953	Phi-A	11	20	.355	40	37	11	2	0	236^2	279	23	115	122	15.5	5.51	78	.294	.379	18	.222	-1	-40	-32	-1	-3.8
1954	NY-A	9	7	.563	25	21	5	1	0	132^1	131	10	43	52	12.3	2.99	115	.258	.324	9	.196	1	11	7	-1	0.7
1955	Bal-A	3	2	.600	14	8	1	1	1	65^1	64	7	28	25	13.6	4.55	84	.261	.354	3	.158	-0	-4	-5	-1	-0.4
	Chi-A	4	6	.400	25	12	1	1	1	91	85	10	30	44	11.6	4.65	85	.251	.315	2	.067	-3	-7	-7	0	-1.0
	Yr	7	8	.467	39	20	2	2	2	156^1	149	17	58	69	12.0	4.61	85	.251	.320	5	.102	-3	-11	-12	-1	-1.4
1956	Chi-A	0	1	.000	3	1	0	0	0	4^1	9	0	4	0	27.0	10.38	39	.474	.565	0	.000	-0	-3	-3	0	-0.6
1957	Det-A	4	3	.571	37	1	0	0	5	59	53	6	28	20	12.7	3.36	115	.249	.342	0	.000	-1	3	3	-1	0.3
Total	7	46	54	.460	187	108	33	8	9	827^2	890	71	355	381	14.0	4.35	91	.277	.356	42	.160	-8	-46	-36	-3	-3.0
● JEFF BYRD Byrd, Jeffrey Alan b: 11/11/56, LaMesa, Cal. BR/TR, 6′3″, 195 lbs. Deb: 6/20/77																										
1977	Tor-A	2	13	.133	17	17	1	0	0	87^1	98	5	68	40	17.1	6.18	68	.286	.404	0	—	0	-21	-19	1	-2.8
● PAUL BYRD Byrd, Paul Gregory b: 12/3/70, Louisville, Ky. BR/TR, 6′1″, 185 lbs. Deb: 7/28/95																										
1995	NY-N	2	0	1.000	17	0	0	0	0	22	18	1	7	26	10.6	2.05	198	.222	.292	1	1.000	0	5	5	0	0.4
1996	NY-N	1	2	.333	38	0	0	0	0	46^2	48	7	21	31	13.3	4.24	94	.265	.342	0	.000	-0	-0	-1	-0	-0.1
1997	Atl-N	4	4	.500	31	4	0	0	0	53	47	6	28	37	13.4	5.26	79	.235	.341	1	.143	-0	-6	-6	-1	-0.9
1998	Atl-N	0	0	—	1	0	0	0	0	2	4	0	1	1	22.5	13.50	31	.400	.455	0	—	0	-2	-2	-0	0.0
	Phi-N	5	2	.714	8	8	2	1	0	55	41	6	17	38	9.5	2.29	190	.203	.265	3	.167	0	12	13	-0	1.6
	Yr	5	2	.714	9	8	2	1	0	57	45	6	18	39	9.9	2.68	162	.212	.274	3	.167	0	10	11	-0	1.6
Total	4	12	8	.600	95	12	2	1	0	178^2	158	20	74	133	11.9	3.78	110	.234	.315	5	.179	0	9	8	-1	1.0
● TIM BYRDAK Byrdak, Timothy Christopher b: 10/31/73, Oak Lawn, Ill. BL/TL, 5′11″, 170 lbs. Deb: 8/7/98																										
1998	KC-A	0	0	—	3	0	0	0	0	1^2	5	1	0	1	27.0	5.40	91	.556	.556	0	—	0	-0	-0	-0	-0.1
● JERRY BYRNE Byrne, Gerald Wilfred b: 2/2/07, Parnell, Mich. d: 8/11/55, Lansing, Mich. BR/TR, 6′, 170 lbs. Deb: 8/31/29																										
1929	Chi-A	0	1	.000	3	1	0	0	0	7^1	11	0	6	1	20.9	7.36	58	.379	.486	0	.000	-0	-3	-3	-0	-0.3
● TOMMY BYRNE Byrne, Thomas Joseph b: 12/31/19, Baltimore, Md. BL/TL, 6′1″, 182 lbs. Deb: 4/27/43																										
1943	NY-A	2	1	.667	11	2	0	0	0	31^2	28	1	35	22	18.8	6.54	49	.248	.437	1	.091	-0	-11	-12	0	-1.0
1946	NY-A	0	1	.000	4	1	0	0	0	9^1	7	1	8	5	15.4	5.79	60	.194	.356	2	.222	0	-2	-2	0	-0.2
1947	NY-A	0	0	—	4	1	0	0	0	4^1	5	0	6	2	22.8	4.15	85	.294	.478	0	—	0	-0	-0	0	0.0
1948	NY-A	8	5	.615	31	11	5	1	2	133^2	79	8	101	93	12.7	3.30	124	.172	.332	15	.326	6	15	12	-1	1.5
1949	*NY-A	15	7	.682	32	30	12	3	0	196	125	11	179	129	14.6	3.72	109	**.183**	.362	16	.193	1	10	7	-3	0.5
1950	NY-A☆	15	9	.625	31	31	10	2	0	203^1	188	23	160	118	16.2	4.74	91	.245	.387	22	.272	7	-4	-10	-2	-0.5
1951	NY-A	2	1	.667	9	3	0	0	0	21	16	0	36	14	23.6	6.86	56	.213	.482	2	.222	1	-6	-7	-0	-0.8
	StL-A	4	10	.286	19	17	7	2	0	122^2	104	5	114	57	16.9	3.82	115	.235	.404	16	.281	3	4	8	-1	1.1
	Yr	6	11	.353	28	20	7	2	0	143^2	120	5	150	71	17.7	4.26	101	.230	.413	18	.273	4	-2	1	-1	0.3
1952	StL-A	7	14	.333	29	24	14	0	0	196	182	16	112	91	14.0	4.68	84	.247	.354	21	.250	5	-22	-17	-4	-1.5

YEAR	TM/L	W	L	PCT	G	GS	CG	SH	SV	IP	H	HR	BB	SO	RAT	ERA	ERA+	OAV	OOB	BH	AVG	PB	PR	/A	PD	TPI
1953	Chi-A	2	0	1.000	6	6	0	0	0	16	18	0	26	4	24.8	10.13	40	.295	.506	3	.167	1	-11	-11	0	-1.0
	Was-A	0	5	.000	6	5	2	0	0	33^2	35	3	22	22	15.5	4.28	91	.276	.387	1	.059	-1	-1	-1	0	-0.2
	Yr	2	5	.286	12	11	2	0	0	49^2	53	3	48	26	18.5	6.16	64	.282	.430	4	.114	-0	-12	-12	1	-1.2
1954	NY-A	3	2	.600	5	5	4	1	0	40	36	1	19	24	12.4	2.70	127	.240	.325	7	.368	4	5	3	0	0.9
1955	*NY-A	16	5	**.762**	27	22	9	3	2	160	137	12	87	76	13.0	3.15	119	.237	.344	16	.205	4	14	11	-1	1.6
1956	*NY-A	7	3	.700	37	8	1	0	6	109^2	108	9	72	52	14.9	3.36	115	.262	.374	14	.269	6	10	6	1	1.2
1957	*NY-A	4	6	.400	30	4	1	0	2	84^2	70	8	60	57	14.6	4.36	82	.227	.364	7	.189	4	-5	-7	-1	-0.5
Total	13	85	69	.552	281	170	65	12	12	1362	1138	98	1037	766	14.9	4.11	97	.229	.371	143	.238	41	-5	-20	-11	1.1

● **MARTY BYSTROM** Bystrom, Martin Eugene b: 7/26/58, Coral Gables, Fla. BR/TR, 6'5", 200 lbs. Deb: 9/7/80

YEAR	TM/L	W	L	PCT	G	GS	CG	SH	SV	IP	H	HR	BB	SO	RAT	ERA	ERA+	OAV	OOB	BH	AVG	PB	PR	/A	PD	TPI
1980	*Phi-N	5	0	1.000	6	5	1	1	0	36	26	1	9	21	8.8	1.50	252	.195	.246	1	.071	-1	8	9	1	1.4
1981	Phi-N	4	3	.571	9	9	1	0	0	53^2	55	3	16	24	12.1	3.35	108	.264	.320	2	.118	-1	1	2	1	0.1
1982	Phi-N	5	6	.455	19	16	1	0	0	89	93	2	35	50	13.4	4.85	76	.277	.354	3	.125	-0	-12	-12	-1	-1.5
1983	*Phi-N	6	9	.400	24	23	1	1	0	119^1	136	6	44	87	14.1	4.60	77	.285	.353	9	.237	2	-13	-14	-1	-1.5
1984	Phi-N	4	4	.500	11	11	0	0	0	56^2	66	5	22	36	14.0	5.08	71	.283	.345	3	.158	-0	-9	-9	-0	-1.2
	NY-A	2	2	.500	7	7	0	0	0	39^1	34	3	13	24	11.0	2.97	127	.230	.296	0	—	0	4	4	-1	0.6
1985	NY-A	3	2	.600	8	8	0	0	0	41	44	8	19	16	14.0	5.71	70	.280	.362	0	—	0	-7	-8	0	-0.6
Total	6	29	26	.527	84	79	4	2	0	435	454	28	158	258	13.0	4.26	86	.268	.336	18	.161	0	-28	-28	-1	-2.7

● **JOSE CABRERA** Cabrera, Jose Alberto b: 3/24/72, Santiago, D.R. BR/TR, 6', 200 lbs. Deb: 7/15/97

YEAR	TM/L	W	L	PCT	G	GS	CG	SH	SV	IP	H	HR	BB	SO	RAT	ERA	ERA+	OAV	OOB	BH	AVG	PB	PR	/A	PD	TPI
1997	Hou-N	0	0	—	12	0	0	0	0	15^1	6	1	6	18	7.0	1.17	340	.125	.222	0	.000	-0	5	5	0	0.0
1998	Hou-N	0	0	—	3	0	0	0	0	4^1	7	0	1	1	16.6	8.31	49	.389	.421	0	—	0	-2	-2	0	0.0
Total	2	0	0	—	15	0	0	0	0	19^2	13	1	7	19	9.2	2.75	146	.197	.274	0	.000	-0	3	3	0	0.0

● **GREG CADARET** Cadaret, Gregory James b: 2/27/62, Detroit, Mich. BL/TL, 6'3", 214 lbs. Deb: 7/5/87

YEAR	TM/L	W	L	PCT	G	GS	CG	SH	SV	IP	H	HR	BB	SO	RAT	ERA	ERA+	OAV	OOB	BH	AVG	PB	PR	/A	PD	TPI
1987	Oak-A	6	2	.750	29	0	0	0	0	39^2	37	6	24	30	14.1	4.54	91	.252	.360	0	—	0	-0	-2	1	0.3
1988	*Oak-A	5	2	.714	58	0	0	0	3	71^2	60	2	36	64	12.2	2.89	131	.226	.320	0	—	0	9	7	0	0.7
1989	Oak-A	0	0	—	26	0	0	0	0	27^2	21	0	19	14	13.0	2.28	162	.214	.342	0	—	0	5	4	1	0.1
	NY-A	5	5	.500	20	13	3	1	0	92^1	109	7	38	66	14.5	4.58	84	.298	.367	0	—	0	-7	-7	0	-0.7
	Yr	5	5	.500	46	13	3	1	0	120	130	7	57	80	14.2	4.05	94	.279	.360	0	—	0	-2	-3	1	-0.6
1990	NY-A	5	4	.556	54	6	0	0	3	121^1	120	8	64	80	13.7	4.15	96	.268	.361	0	—	0	-3	-2	2	0.0
1991	NY-A	8	6	.571	68	5	0	0	3	121^2	110	8	59	105	12.6	3.62	114	.246	.337	0	—	0	6	7	1	0.8
1992	NY-A	4	8	.333	46	11	1	1	1	103^2	104	12	74	73	15.6	4.25	92	.267	.387	0	—	0	-4	-4	1	-0.3
1993	Cin-N	2	1	.667	34	0	0	0	1	32^2	40	3	23	23	17.6	4.96	81	.305	.413	0	.000	-0	-3	-3	-0	-0.3
	KC-A	1	1	.500	13	0	0	0	0	15^1	14	0	7	2	12.9	2.93	156	.264	.361	0	—	0	2	3	0	0.3
1994	Tor-A	0	1	.000	21	0	0	0	0	20	24	4	17	15	18.4	5.85	82	.289	.410	0	—	0	-2	-2	-0	-0.1
	Det-A	1	0	1.000	17	0	0	0	2	20	17	0	16	14	14.8	3.60	135	.227	.363	0	—	0	3	3	1	0.2
	Yr	1	1	.500	38	0	0	0	2	40	41	4	33	29	16.6	4.72	102	.259	.387	0	—	0	0	0	1	0.1
1997	Ana-A	0	0	—	15	0	0	0	0	13^2	11	1	8	11	13.8	3.29	139	.220	.350	0	—	0	2	2	-0	0.0
1998	Ana-A	1	2	.333	39	0	0	0	1	37	38	6	15	37	13.6	4.14	113	.257	.337	0	—	0	2	2	-0	0.1
	Tex-A	0	0	—	11	0	0	0	0	7^2	11	1	3	5	16.4	4.70	103	.355	.412	0	—	0	-0	0	-0	0.0
	Yr	1	2	.333	50	0	0	0	1	44^2	49	7	18	42	13.5	4.23	111	.269	.335	0	—	0	2	2	-0	0.1
Total	10	38	32	.543	451	35	4	2	14	724^1	716	58	403	539	14.1	3.99	102	.262	.360	0	.000	-0	9	7	6	1.1

● **LEON CADORE** Cadore, Leon Joseph "Caddy" b: 11/20/1890, Chicago, Ill. d: 3/16/58, Spokane, Wash. BR/TR, 6'1", 190 lbs. Deb: 4/28/15

YEAR	TM/L	W	L	PCT	G	GS	CG	SH	SV	IP	H	HR	BB	SO	RAT	ERA	ERA+	OAV	OOB	BH	AVG	PB	PR	/A	PD	TPI
1915	Bro-N	0	2	.000	7	2	1	0	0	21	28	0	8	12	16.3	5.57	50	.337	.409	0	.000	-1	-7	-7	0	-0.7
1916	Bro-N	0	0	—	1	0	0	0	0	6	10	0	0	2	15.0	4.50	60	.370	.370	0	.000	-0	-1	-1	0	0.0
1917	Bro-N	13	13	.500	37	30	21	1	3	264	231	3	63	115	10.3	2.45	114	.241	.292	24	.261	5	8	10	-2	1.4
1918	Bro-N	1	0	1.000	2	2	1	1	0	17	6	0	2	5	4.8	0.53	526	.115	.164	0	.000	-0	4	4	0	0.2
1919	Bro-N	14	12	.538	35	27	16	3	0	250^2	228	5	39	94	9.8	2.37	125	.245	.280	14	.161	-3	15	17	-3	1.0
1920	*Bro-N	15	14	.517	35	30	16	4	0	254^1	256	4	56	79	11.1	2.62	122	.270	.313	20	.220	2	15	17	1	2.3
1921	Bro-N	13	14	.481	35	30	12	1	0	211^2	243	17	46	79	12.5	4.17	93	.292	.334	14	.187	-1	-9	-7	-1	-1.0
1922	Bro-N	8	15	.348	29	21	13	0	0	190^1	224	13	57	49	13.3	4.35	94	.299	.349	19	.268	4	-5	-6	-3	-0.5
1923	Bro-N	4	1	.800	8	4	3	0	0	36	39	2	13	5	13.0	3.25	119	.291	.354	1	.077	-1	3	3	-1	0.1
	Chi-A	0	1	.000	1	1	0	0	0	2^1	6	0	2	3	30.9	23.14	17	.500	.571	0	—	0	-5	-5	-0	-1.1
1924	NY-N	0	0	—	2	0	0	0	0	4	2	0	3	2	11.3	0.00	—	.154	.313	0	—	0	2	2	0	0.0
Total	10	68	72	.486	192	147	83	10	3	1257^1	1273	44	289	445	11.4	3.14	106	.269	.314	92	.208	5	19	27	-8	1.7

● **CHARLIE CADY** Cady, Charles B. b: 12/1865, Chicago, Ill. d: 6/7/09, Kankakee, Ill. 5'11", 180 lbs. Deb: 9/5/1883 ♦

YEAR	TM/L	W	L	PCT	G	GS	CG	SH	SV	IP	H	HR	BB	SO	RAT	ERA	ERA+	OAV	OOB	BH	AVG	PB	PR	/A	PD	TPI
1883	Cle-N	0	1	.000	1	1	1	0	0	8	13	0	4	5	19.1	7.88	40	.361	.425	0	.000	-1	-4	-4	-0	-0.4
1884	CP-U	3	1	.750	4	4	4	0	0	35	37	0	13	15	12.9	2.83	86	.253	.314	2	.100	-1	-2	-2	-0	-0.3
Total	2	3	2	.600	5	5	5	0	0	43	50	0	17	20	14.0	3.77	68	.275	.337	2	.059	-2	-6	-6	-0	-0.7

● **JOHN CAHILL** Cahill, John Patrick Parnell "Patsy"
b: 4/30/1865, San Francisco, Cal d: 10/31/01, Pleasanton, Cal. BR/TR, 5'7.5", 168 lbs. Deb: 5/31/1884 ♦

YEAR	TM/L	W	L	PCT	G	GS	CG	SH	SV	IP	H	HR	BB	SO	RAT	ERA	ERA+	OAV	OOB	BH	AVG	PB	PR	/A	PD	TPI
1884	Col-a	1	0	1.000	2	1	1	0	0	16	15	0	4	1	12.4	5.06	60	.211	.282	46	.219	0	-3	-4	-0	-0.2
1886	StL-N	1	0	1.000	2	0	0	0	0	12	11	0	3	2	10.5	3.00	108	.268	.318	92	.199	-0	0	0	0	0.0
1887	Ind-N	0	2	.000	6	1	1	0	0	22	40	2	19	5	25.0	14.32	29	.430	.535	54	.205	-1	-25	-25	-1	-1.6
Total	3	2	2	.500	10	2	2	0	0	50	66	2	26	8	17.5	8.64	41	.322	.411	192	.205	-1	-28	-28	-1	-1.8

● **LES CAIN** Cain, Leslie b: 1/13/48, San Luis Obispo, Cal. BL/TL, 6'1", 200 lbs. Deb: 4/28/68

YEAR	TM/L	W	L	PCT	G	GS	CG	SH	SV	IP	H	HR	BB	SO	RAT	ERA	ERA+	OAV	OOB	BH	AVG	PB	PR	/A	PD	TPI
1968	Det-A	1	0	1.000	8	4	0	0	0	24	25	1	20	13	16.9	3.00	100	.269	.398	1	.143	0	-0	0	0	0.1
1970	Det-A	12	7	.632	29	29	5	0	0	180^2	167	15	98	156	13.5	3.84	97	.247	.349	11	.162	0	-2	-2	-0	-0.2
1971	Det-A	10	9	.526	26	26	3	1	0	144^2	121	14	91	118	13.6	4.35	82	.228	.348	8	.145	-0	-14	-12	-1	-1.6
1972	Det-A	0	3	.000	5	5	0	0	0	23^2	18	2	16	16	12.9	3.80	83	.209	.333	1	.143	-0	-2	-2	-0	-0.3
Total	4	23	19	.548	68	64	8	1	0	373	331	32	225	303	13.7	3.98	90	.239	.351	21	.153	-0	-19	-16	-1	-2.0

● **SUGAR CAIN** Cain, Merritt Patrick b: 4/5/07, Macon, Ga. d: 4/3/75, Atlanta, Ga. BL/TR, 5'11", 190 lbs. Deb: 4/15/32

YEAR	TM/L	W	L	PCT	G	GS	CG	SH	SV	IP	H	HR	BB	SO	RAT	ERA	ERA+	OAV	OOB	BH	AVG	PB	PR	/A	PD	TPI
1932	Phi-A	3	4	.429	10	6	3	0	0	45	42	1	28	24	14.0	5.00	90	.256	.365	3	.250	1	-3	-2	-0	-0.3
1933	Phi-A	13	12	.520	38	32	16	1	1	218	244	18	137	43	15.9	4.25	101	.280	.379	16	.200	-1	1	1	-1	-0.1
1934	Phi-A	9	17	.346	36	32	15	0	0	230^2	235	15	128	66	14.3	4.41	99	.266	.360	13	.159	-3	2	-1	-1	-0.4
1935	Phi-A	0	5	.000	6	5	0	0	0	26	39	1	19	5	20.1	6.58	69	.382	.479	0	.000	-1	-6	-6	0	-1.0
	StL-A	9	8	.529	31	24	8	0	0	167^2	197	7	104	68	16.4	5.26	91	.290	.388	11	.193	-2	-15	-9	-3	-1.2
	Yr	9	13	.409	37	29	8	0	0	193^2	236	8	123	73	16.9	5.44	88	.302	.400	11	.169	-4	-21	-15	-3	-2.2
1936	StL-A	1	1	.500	4	3	1	0	0	16^1	20	0	9	8	16.0	6.61	81	.286	.367	2	.286	0	-3	-2	-0	-0.2
	Chi-A	14	10	.583	30	26	14	1	0	195^1	228	18	75	42	14.2	4.75	110	.293	.359	7	.103	-4	6	10	-3	0.4
	Yr	15	11	.577	34	29	15	1	0	211^2	248	18	84	50	14.3	4.89	107	.292	.360	9	.120	-4	3	8	-3	0.2
1937	Chi-A	4	2	.667	18	6	1	0	0	68^2	88	7	51	17	18.2	6.16	75	.325	.432	4	.182	-1	-12	-12	-0	-0.9
1938	Chi-A	0	1	.000	5	3	0	0	0	19^2	26	0	18	6	20.1	4.58	107	.321	.444	0	.000	-1	0	1	-1	-0.2
Total	7	53	60	.469	178	137	58	2	1	987^1	1119	67	569	279	15.5	4.83	96	.287	.380	56	.163	-13	-29	-21	-9	-3.9

● **BOB CAIN** Cain, Robert Max "Sugar" b: 10/16/24, Longford, Kan. d: 4/8/97, Cleveland, Ohio BL/TL, 6', 165 lbs. Deb: 9/18/49 ♦

YEAR	TM/L	W	L	PCT	G	GS	CG	SH	SV	IP	H	HR	BB	SO	RAT	ERA	ERA+	OAV	OOB	BH	AVG	PB	PR	/A	PD	TPI
1949	Chi-A	0	0	—	6	0	0	0	1	11	7	0	5	5	9.8	2.45	170	.179	.273	0	.000	-0	2	2	-0	0.0
1950	Chi-A	9	12	.429	34	23	11	1	2	171^2	153	12	109	77	14.0	3.93	114	.244	.361	12	.197	-0	12	11	0	1.1
1951	Chi-A	1	2	.333	4	4	1	0	0	26^1	25	3	13	3	14.0	3.76	107	.248	.350	3	.333	1	1	1	-0	0.1
	Det-A	11	10	.524	35	22	6	1	2	149^1	135	12	82	58	13.7	4.70	89	.239	.347	13	.245	2	-10	-9	0	-0.9
	Yr	12	12	.500	39	26	7	1	2	175^2	160	15	95	61	13.6	4.56	91	.240	.344	16	.258	3	-9	-8	-0	-0.8
1952	StL-A	12	10	.545	29	27	8	1	2	170	169	15	62	70	12.3	4.13	95	.264	.331	8	.138	-1	-9	-4	-2	-0.8
1953	StL-A	4	10	.286	32	13	1	0	1	99^2	129	8	45	36	15.8	6.23	67	.310	.379	6	.200	0	-25	-22	-2	-2.9
Total	5	37	44	.457	140	89	27	3	8	628	618	50	316	249	13.7	4.50	93	.259	.351	42	.196	0	-27	-21	-4	-3.4

YEAR	TM/L	W	L	PCT	G	GS	CG	SH	SV	IP	H	HR	BB	SO	RAT	ERA	ERA+	OAV	OOB	BH	AVG	PB	PR	/A	PD	TPI
● CHARLIE CALDWELL Caldwell, Charles William "Chuck" b: 8/2/01, Bristol, Va. d: 11/1/57, Princeton, N.J. BR/TR, 5'10", 180 lbs. Deb: 7/7/25																										
1925	NY-A	0	0	—	3	0	0	0	0	2^2	7	0	3	1	33.8	16.88	25	.467	.556	0	.000	-0	-4	-4	-0	0.0
● EARL CALDWELL Caldwell, Earl Welton "Teach" b: 4/9/05, Sparks, Tex. d: 9/15/81, Mission, Tex. BR/TR, 6'1", 178 lbs. Deb: 9/8/28																										
1928	Phi-N	1	4	.200	5	5	1	1	0	34^2	46	5	17	6	16.4	5.71	75	.348	.423	1	.111	-0	-7	-6	0	-0.7
1935	StL-A	3	2	.600	6	5	2	1	0	36^2	34	2	17	5	12.5	3.68	130	.245	.327	2	.182	-0	3	5	1	0.6
1936	StL-A	7	16	.304	41	25	10	2	2	189	252	15	83	59	16.7	6.00	90	.319	.394	11	.190	-1	-20	-13	-1	-1.4
1937	StL-A	0	0	—	9	2	0	0	0	29	39	3	13	8	16.8	6.83	71	.317	.391	2	.222	0	-7	-6	0	0.0
1945	Chi-A	6	7	.462	27	11	5	1	4	105^1	108	8	37	45	12.6	3.59	92	.265	.331	8	.216	-0	-3	-3	3	-0.1
1946	Chi-A	13	4	.765	39	0	0	0	8	90^2	60	2	29	42	8.9	2.08	164	.186	.255	3	.167	1	**14**	**13**	1	3.0
1947	Chi-A	1	4	.200	40	0	0	0	8	54^1	53	4	30	22	13.9	3.64	100	.261	.359	0	.000	-1	0	0	-1	-0.2
1948	Chi-A	1	5	.167	25	1	0	0	3	39	53	3	22	10	17.8	5.31	80	.335	.423	0	.000	-0	-4	-5	-0	-0.7
	Bos-A	1	1	.500	8	0	0	0	0	9	11	2	11	5	23.0	13.00	34	.333	.511	1	.333	0	-9	-9	-0	-1.5
	Yr	2	6	.250	33	1	0	0	3	48	64	5	33	15	18.4	6.75	63	.332	.432	1	.125	-0	-13	-13	-1	-2.2
Total	8	33	43	.434	200	49	18	5	25	587^2	656	44	259	202	14.4	4.69	92	.284	.363	28	.178	-2	-32	-25	3	-1.0
● RALPH CALDWELL Caldwell, Ralph Grant "Lefty" b: 1/18/1884, Philadelphia, Pa. d: 8/5/69, W.Trenton, N.J. BL/TL, 5'9", 155 lbs. Deb: 9/10/04																										
1904	Phi-N	2	2	.500	6	5	5	0	0	41	40	1	15	30	12.5	4.17	64	.242	.313	8	.444	3	-7	-7	0	-0.3
1905	Phi-N	1	3	.250	7	2	1	0	1	34	44	1	7	29	14.3	4.24	69	.321	.367	0	.000	-2	-5	-5	-1	-0.8
Total	2	3	5	.375	13	7	6	0	1	75	84	2	22	59	13.3	4.20	66	.278	.337	8	.242	1	-11	-12	-1	-1.1
● MIKE CALDWELL Caldwell, Ralph Michael b: 1/22/49, Tarboro, N.C. BR/TL, 6', 185 lbs. Deb: 9/4/71																										
1971	SD-N	1	0	1.000	6	0	0	0	0	6^2	4	0	3	5	9.5	0.00	—	.174	.269	1	1.000	1	3	2	0	0.5
1972	SD-N	7	11	.389	42	20	4	2	2	163^2	183	10	49	102	13.0	4.01	82	.282	.337	7	.140	-1	-10	-13	5	-1.1
1973	SD-N	5	14	.263	55	13	3	1	10	149	146	8	53	86	12.1	3.74	93	.260	.326	5	.143	-1	-1	-5	2	-0.5
1974	SF-N	14	5	.737	31	27	6	2	0	189^1	176	17	63	83	11.6	2.95	129	.249	.314	9	.143	-2	14	18	4	2.0
1975	SF-N	7	13	.350	38	21	4	0	1	163^1	194	16	48	57	13.6	4.79	79	.296	.348	7	.159	-0	-21	-18	2	-1.9
1976	SF-N	1	7	.125	50	9	0	0	2	107^1	145	5	20	55	14.0	4.86	75	.324	.356	3	.158	-0	-16	-15	1	-1.0
1977	Cin-N	0	0	—	14	0	0	0	1	24^2	25	1	8	11	12.0	4.01	98	.260	.317	2	.500	2	-0	-0	-0	0.1
	Mil-A	5	8	.385	21	12	2	0	0	94^1	101	6	36	38	13.3	4.58	89	.271	.338	0	—	0	-5	-5	3	-0.4
1978	Mil-A	22	9	.710	37	34	**23**	6	1	293^1	258	14	54	131	9.8	2.36	159	.234	.274	0	—	0	46	45	1	5.0
1979	Mil-A	16	6	**.727**	30	30	16	4	0	235	252	18	39	89	11.3	3.29	126	.278	.311	0	—	0	24	23	5	2.4
1980	Mil-A	13	11	.542	34	33	11	2	1	225^1	248	29	56	74	12.2	4.03	96	.285	.330	0	—	0	0	-4	0	-0.4
1981	*Mil-A	11	9	.550	24	23	3	0	0	144^1	151	18	38	41	11.8	3.93	87	.272	.319	0	—	0	-4	-8	-0	-1.0
1982	*Mil-A	17	13	.567	35	34	12	3	0	258	269	30	58	75	11.4	3.91	97	.271	.311	0	—	0	5	-4	2	0.1
1983	Mil-A	12	11	.522	32	32	10	2	0	228^1	269	35	51	58	12.7	4.53	82	.296	.334	0	—	0	-12	-20	-0	-1.5
1984	Mil-A	6	13	.316	26	19	4	1	0	126	160	11	21	34	13.0	4.64	83	.314	.343	0	—	0	-9	-11	1	-1.4
Total	14	137	130	.513	475	307	98	23	18	2408^2	2581	218	597	939	12.0	3.81	99	.276	.322	34	.157	-2	11	-14	24	0.9
● RAY CALDWELL Caldwell, Raymond Benjamin "Rube" or "Sum" b: 4/26/1888, Corydon, Pa. d: 8/17/67, Salamanca, N.Y. BL/TR, 6'2", 190 lbs. Deb: 9/9/10 ◆																										
1910	NY-A	1	0	1.000	6	2	1	0	1	19^1	19	1	9	17	13.0	3.72	71	.260	.341	0	.000	-1	-3	-2	-0	-0.3
1911	NY-A	14	14	.500	41	26	19	1	1	255	240	7	79	145	11.7	3.35	107	.260	.327	40	.272	3	-0	7	-3	0.8
1912	NY-A	8	16	.333	30	26	13	3	0	183^1	196	1	67	95	13.2	4.47	80	.277	.344	18	.237	1	-23	-18	1	-1.7
1913	NY-A	9	8	.529	27	16	15	2	1	164^1	131	5	60	87	11.0	2.41	124	.219	.299	28	.289	3	10	11	-1	1.7
1914	NY-A	18	9	.667	31	23	22	5	0	213	153	5	51	92	8.8	1.94	142	.205	.260	22	.195	1	19	19	-2	2.5
1915	NY-A	19	16	.543	36	35	31	3	0	305	266	6	107	130	11.2	2.89	101	.244	.315	35	.243	8	2	1	-3	0.6
1916	NY-A	5	12	.294	21	18	14	1	0	165^2	142	6	65	76	11.7	2.99	97	.243	.327	19	.204	-0	-3	-2	-1	-0.3
1917	NY-A	13	16	.448	32	29	21	1	0	236	199	8	76	102	10.7	2.86	94	.234	.302	32	.258	6	-5	-5	-1	0.3
1918	NY-A	9	8	.529	24	21	14	1	1	176^2	173	2	62	59	12.0	3.06	93	.261	.325	44	.291	4	-5	-4	-3	-0.1
1919	Bos-A	7	4	.636	18	12	6	1	0	86^1	92	1	31	23	13.1	3.96	76	.279	.346	13	.271	1	-7	-9	-2	-1.0
	Cle-A	5	1	.833	6	6	4	1	0	52^2	33	1	19	24	9.2	1.71	196	.181	.266	8	.348	2	9	10	-1	1.3
	Yr	12	5	.706	24	18	10	2	0	139	125	2	50	47	11.5	3.11	101	.243	.312	21	.296	4	2	1	-3	0.3
1920	*Cle-A	20	10	.667	34	33	20	1	0	237^2	286	9	63	80	13.4	3.86	98	.303	.350	19	.213	1	-2	-2	-3	-0.5
1921	Cle-A	6	6	.500	37	12	4	1	4	147	159	7	49	76	12.9	4.90	87	.275	.333	11	.208	0	-10	-10	-0	-0.8
Total	12	134	120	.528	343	259	184	21	8	2242	2089	59	738	1006	11.6	3.22	99	.253	.319	289	.248	31	-20	-4	-19	2.5
● JEFF CALHOUN Calhoun, Jeffrey Wilton b: 4/11/58, LaGrange, Ga. BL/TL, 6'2", 190 lbs. Deb: 9/2/84																										
1984	Hou-N	0	1	.000	9	0	0	0	0	15^1	5	0	2	11	4.1	1.17	283	.100	.135	0	—	0	4	4	-0	0.2
1985	Hou-N	2	5	.286	44	0	0	0	4	63^2	56	2	24	47	11.3	2.54	136	.243	.315	0	.000	-0	7	6	0	0.8
1986	*Hou-N	1	0	1.000	20	0	0	0	0	26^2	28	3	12	14	13.5	3.71	97	.264	.339	0	—	0	0	-0	-1	-0.1
1987	Phi-N	3	1	.750	42	0	0	0	1	42^2	25	1	26	31	11.0	1.48	287	.168	.295	0	.000	-0	12	13	1	1.2
1988	Phi-N	0	0	—	3	0	0	0	0	2^1	6	2	1	1	27.0	15.43	23	.462	.500	0	—	0	-3	-3	-0	0.0
Total	5	6	7	.462	118	0	0	0	5	150^2	120	8	65	104	11.1	2.51	147	.219	.303	0	.000	-0	21	20	-0	2.1
● FRED CALIGIURI Caligiuri, Frederick John b: 10/22/18, W.Hickory, Pa. BR/TR, 6', 190 lbs. Deb: 9/3/41																										
1941	Phi-A	2	2	.500	5	5	4	0	0	43	45	2	14	7	12.3	2.93	143	.257	.312	4	.200	1	6	6	-1	0.5
1942	Phi-A	0	3	.000	13	2	0	0	1	36^2	45	2	18	20	16.0	6.38	59	.300	.382	1	.083	-0	-11	-11	-0	-0.9
Total	2	2	5	.286	18	7	4	0	1	79^2	90	4	32	27	14.0	4.52	89	.277	.345	5	.156	1	-5	-5	-1	-0.4
● WILL CALIHAN Calihan, William T. (b: William T. Callahan) b: 1869, Oswego, N.Y. d: 12/20/17, Rochester, N.Y. 5'8", 150 lbs. Deb: 4/17/1890																										
1890	Roc-a	18	15	.545	37	36	31	0	0	296^1	276	4	125	127	12.7	3.28	109	.239	.322	23	.145	-3	19	9	3	0.8
1891	Phi-a	6	6	.500	13	11	11	0	0	112	151	7	47	28	16.9	6.43	59	.312	.387	11	.196	-1	-34	-32	2	-2.4
Total	2	24	21	.533	50	47	42	0	0	408^1	427	11	172	155	13.8	4.14	88	.261	.341	34	.158	-5	-14	-23	4	-1.6
● BEN CALLAHAN Callahan, Benjamin Franklin b: 5/19/57, Mt.Airy, N.C. BR/TR, 6'7", 230 lbs. Deb: 6/22/83																										
1983	Oak-A	1	2	.333	4	2	0	0	0	9^1	18	0	5	2	22.2	12.54	31	.400	.460	0	—	0	-9	-9	0	-1.8
● NIXEY CALLAHAN Callahan, James Joseph b: 3/18/1874, Fitchburg, Mass. d: 10/4/34, Boston, Mass. BR/TR, 5'10.5", 180 lbs. Deb: 5/12/1894 M◆																										
1894	Phi-N	1	2	.333	9	2	1	0	2	33^2	64	3	17	9	23.0	9.89	52	.398	.470	5	.238	-1	-17	-18	1	-1.3
1897	Chi-N	12	9	.571	23	22	21	1	0	189^2	221	6	55	52	13.5	4.03	111	.289	.343	105	.292	3	6	9	1	1.2
1898	Chi-N	20	10	.667	31	31	30	2	0	274^1	267	2	71	73	11.4	2.46	146	.253	.307	43	.262	4	35	34	1	3.9
1899	Chi-N	21	12	.636	35	34	33	3	0	294^1	327	5	76	77	13.1	3.06	123	.281	.338	39	.260	4	26	23	5	3.0
1900	Chi-N	13	16	.448	32	32	32	2	0	285^1	347	5	74	77	14.0	3.82	94	.299	.353	27	.235	2	-4	-7	6	0.2
1901	Chi-A	15	8	.652	27	22	20	1	0	215^1	195	4	50	70	10.6	2.42	144	.239	.290	39	.331	8	30	25	6	3.9
1902	Chi-A	16	14	.533	35	31	29	2	0	282^1	287	8	89	75	12.3	3.60	94	.264	.326	51	.234	3	-1	-7	6	0.2
1903	Chi-A	1	2	.333	3	3	3	0	0	28	40	0	5	12	14.8	4.50	62	.333	.365	128	.292	1	-5	-5	1	-0.3
Total	8	99	73	.576	195	177	169	11	2	1603	1748	33	437	445	12.8	3.39	109	.276	.332	901	.273	25	70	54	26	10.8
● JOHN CALLAHAN Callahan, John W. b: Moberly, Mo. Deb: 9/3/1898																										
1898	StL-N	0	2	.000	2	2	1	0	0	8^1	18	2	7	2	29.2	16.20	23	.429	.529	0	.000	-1	-12	-11	0	-1.6
● JOE CALLAHAN Callahan, Joseph Thomas b: 10/8/16, E.Boston, Mass. d: 5/24/49, S.Boston, Mass. BR/TR, 6'2", 170 lbs. Deb: 9/13/39																										
1939	Bos-N	1	0	1.000	4	1	1	0	0	17^1	17	0	3	8	10.9	3.12	119	.250	.292	0	.000	-0	2	1	0	0.1
1940	Bos-N	0	2	.000	6	2	0	0	0	15	20	1	13	3	19.8	10.20	36	.351	.471	0	.000	-1	-11	-11	1	-1.2
Total	2	1	2	.333	10	3	1	0	0	32^1	37	1	16	11	15.0	6.40	58	.296	.380	0	.000	-1	-9	-10	1	-1.1
● RAY CALLAHAN Callahan, Raymond James "Pat" b: 8/29/1891, Ashland, Wis. d: 1/23/73, Olympia, Wash. BL/TL, 5'10.5", 170 lbs. Deb: 9/12/15																										
1915	Cin-N	0	0	—	3	0	0	0	0	6^1	12	1	1	4	18.5	8.53	34	.364	.382	1	.333	0	-4	-4	-0	0.0
● DICK CALMUS Calmus, Richard Lee b: 1/7/44, Los Angeles, Cal. BR/TR, 6'4", 187 lbs. Deb: 4/22/63																										
1963	LA-N	3	1	.750	21	1	0	0	0	44	32	3	16	25	9.8	2.66	114	.204	.277	0	.000	-1	3	2	-1	0.0

YEAR	TM/L	W	L	PCT	G	GS	CG	SH	SV	IP	H	HR	BB	SO	RAT	ERA	ERA+	OAV	OOB	BH	AVG	PB	PR	/A	PD	TPI
1967	Chi-N	0	0	—	1	1	0	0	0	4^1	5	2	0	1	10.4	8.31	43	.278	.278	1	.500	0	-2	-2	0	0.0
Total	2	3	1	.750	22	2	0	0	0	48^1	37	5	16	26	9.9	3.17	97	.211	.277	1	.125	-0	1	-1	-1	0.0
● MARK CALVERT	Calvert, Mark b: 9/29/56, Tulsa, Okla. BR/TR, 6'1", 195 lbs. Deb: 4/17/83																									
1983	SF-N	1	4	.200	18	4	0	0	0	37^1	46	2	34	14	20.0	6.27	56	.307	.444	0	.000	-1	-11	-11	1	-1.4
1984	SF-N	2	4	.333	10	5	1	0	0	32	40	4	9	5	14.1	5.06	69	.303	.352	0	.000	-1	-5	-6	0	-1.0
Total	2	3	8	.273	28	9	1	0	0	69^1	86	6	43	19	17.3	5.71	62	.305	.404	0	.000	-1	-16	-17	1	-2.4
● PAUL CALVERT	Calvert, Paul Leo Emile b: 10/6/17, Montreal, Que., Can. BR/TR, 6', 185 lbs. Deb: 9/24/42																									
1942	Cle-A	0	0	—	1	0	0	0	0	2	0	0	2	2	9.0	0.00	—	.000	.286	0	—	0	1	1	-0	0.0
1943	Cle-A	0	0	—	5	0	0	0	0	8^1	6	0	6	2	14.0	4.32	72	.200	.351	0	.000	-0	-1	-1	0	0.0
1944	Cle-A	1	3	.250	35	4	0	0	0	77	89	4	38	31	14.8	4.56	72	.289	.367	4	.267	1	-10	-11	2	-0.2
1945	Cle-A	0	0	—	1	0	0	0	0	1^1	3	0	1	1	27.0	13.50	24	.429	.500	0	—	0	-2	-2	0	0.0
1949	Was-A	6	17	.261	34	23	5	0	1	160^2	175	11	86	52	14.7	5.43	78	.279	.368	7	.137	-2	-22	-21	3	-2.5
1950	Det-A	2	2	.500	32	0	0	0	4	51^1	71	7	25	14	17.2	6.31	74	.324	.398	0	.000	-1	-10	-9	1	-0.7
1951	Det-A	0	0	—	1	0	0	0	0	1	1	0	0	0	9.0	0.00	—	.250	.250	0	—	0	0	0	0	0.0
Total	7	9	22	.290	109	27	5	0	5	301^2	345	22	158	102	15.2	5.31	76	.287	.373	11	.149	-2	-43	-43	5	-3.4
● ERNIE CAMACHO	Camacho, Ernest Carlos b: 2/1/55, Salinas, Cal. BR/TR, 6'1", 180 lbs. Deb: 5/22/80																									
1980	Oak-A	0	0	—	5	0	0	0	0	11^2	20	2	5	9	20.1	6.94	54	.364	.426	0	—	0	-4	-4	-0	0.0
1981	Pit-N	0	1	.000	7	3	0	0	0	21^2	23	0	15	11	15.8	4.98	72	.295	.409	0	.000	-0	-4	-3	-0	-0.2
1983	Cle-A	0	1	.000	4	0	0	0	0	5^1	5	1	2	2	13.5	5.06	84	.250	.348	0	—	0	-1	-0	-0	-0.3
1984	Cle-A	5	9	.357	69	0	0	0	23	100	83	6	37	48	10.9	2.43	168	.229	.303	0	—	0	17	18	-0	3.2
1985	Cle-A	0	1	.000	2	0	0	0	0	3^1	4	0	1	2	13.5	8.10	51	.333	.385	0	—	0	-1	-1	0	-0.3
1986	Cle-A	2	4	.333	51	0	0	0	20	57^1	60	1	31	36	14.6	4.08	101	.269	.363	0	—	0	1	0	1	0.1
1987	Cle-A	0	1	.000	15	0	0	0	1	13^2	21	1	5	9	19.1	9.22	49	.350	.426	0	—	0	-7	-7	1	-0.5
1988	Hou-N	0	3	.000	13	0	0	0	1	17^2	25	1	12	13	18.8	7.64	43	.352	.446	0	.000	-0	-8	-8	0	-1.4
1989	SF-N	3	0	1.000	13	0	0	0	0	16^1	10	1	11	14	11.6	2.76	122	.175	.309	0	.000	-0	1	1	1	0.3
1990	SF-N	0	0	—	8	0	0	0	0	10	10	1	3	8	11.7	3.60	101	.256	.310	0	—	0	0	0	-0	0.0
	StL-N	0	0	—	6	0	0	0	0	5^2	7	2	6	7	20.6	7.94	48	.318	.464	0	—	0	-3	-3	0	0.0
	Yr	0	0	—	14	0	0	0	0	15^2	17	3	9	15	14.9	5.17	72	.279	.371	0	—	0	-2	-3	-0	0.0
Total	10	10	20	.333	193	3	0	0	45	262^2	268	16	128	159	13.8	4.21	94	.268	.356	0	.000	-1	-8	-8	1	0.9
● FRED CAMBRIA	Cambria, Frederick Dennis b: 1/22/48, Cambria Heights, N.Y. BR/TR, 6'2", 195 lbs. Deb: 8/26/70																									
1970	Pit-N	1	2	.333	6	5	0	0	0	33^1	37	2	12	14	13.5	3.51	111	.272	.336	2	.200	1	2	1	0	0.2
● JACK CAMERON	Cameron, John William "Happy Jack" b: 9/1884, Nova Scotia, Can. d: 8/17/51, Boston, Mass. Deb: 9/13/06 ♦																									
1906	Bos-N	0	0	—	2	1	0	0	0	6	4	0	6	2	15.0	0.00	—	.211	.400	11	.180	-0	2	2	0	0.0
● HARRY CAMNITZ	Camnitz, Henry Richardson b: 10/26/1884, McKinney, Ky. d: 1/6/51, Louisville, Ky. BR/TR, 6'1", 168 lbs. Deb: 4/14/09 F																									
1909	Pit-N	0	0	—	1	0	0	0	0	4	6	0	1	1	15.8	4.50	60	.353	.389	0	.000	-0	-1	-1	0	0.0
1911	StL-N	1	0	1.000	2	0	0	0	0	2	0	0	1	2	4.5	0.00	—	.000	.143	0	—	0	1	1	-0	0.4
Total	2	1	0	1.000	3	0	0	0	0	6	6	0	2	3	12.0	3.00	98	.261	.320	0	.000	-0	-0	-0	0	0.4
● HOWIE CAMNITZ	Camnitz, Samuel Howard "Red" b: 8/22/1881, Covington, Ky. d: 3/2/60, Louisville, Ky. BR/TR, 5'9", 169 lbs. Deb: 4/22/04 F																									
1904	Pit-N	1	4	.200	10	2	2	0	0	49	48	0	20	21	13.0	4.22	65	.259	.341	1	.063	-1	-8	-8	-1	-1.0
1906	Pit-N	1	0	1.000	2	1	1	1	0	9	6	0	5	5	11.0	2.00	134	.188	.297	0	.000	-0	1	1	-0	0.0
1907	Pit-N	13	8	.619	31	19	15	4	1	180	135	0	59	85	9.9	2.15	113	.211	.281	3	.050	-5	6	6	-0	0.0
1908	Pit-N	16	9	.640	38	26	17	3	2	236^2	182	6	69	118	9.7	1.56	148	.210	.272	6	.083	-3	21	20	-1	1.7
1909	*Pit-N	25	6	**.806**	41	30	20	6	3	283	207	1	68	133	9.0	1.62	168	.211	.267	12	.138	-0	31	35	-3	3.7
1910	Pit-N	12	13	.480	38	31	16	1	2	260	246	1	61	120	11.0	3.22	96	.256	.308	11	.125	-3	-5	-3	-2	-0.9
1911	Pit-N	20	15	.571	40	33	18	1	1	267^2	245	8	84	139	11.2	3.13	110	.248	.309	12	.143	-3	8	9	-3	0.4
1912	Pit-N	22	12	.647	41	32	22	2	2	276^2	256	8	82	121	11.4	2.83	115	.251	.315	23	.235	1	18	13	-3	1.2
1913	Pit-N	6	17	.261	36	22	5	1	2	192^1	203	7	84	64	13.8	3.74	81	.282	.363	9	.153	-1	-12	-16	1	-1.8
	Phi-N	3	3	.500	9	5	1	0	1	49	49	1	23	21	13.6	3.67	91	.268	.356	1	.063	-1	-3	-2	-1	-0.5
	Yr	9	20	.310	45	27	6	1	3	241^1	252	8	107	85	13.5	3.73	83	.277	.354	10	.133	-3	-14	-17	-0	-2.3
1914	Pit-F	14	19	.424	36	34	20	1	1	262	256	8	90	82	12.2	3.23	89	.258	.324	14	.161	-5	-10	-11	-5	-2.1
1915	Pit-F	0	0	—	4	2	0	0	0	20	19	1	11	6	13.5	4.50	60	.257	.353	0	.000	-1	-4	-4	-1	-0.2
Total	11	133	106	.556	326	237	137	20	15	2085^1	1852	41	656	915	11.1	2.75	106	.242	.307	92	.136	-24	43	40	-18	0.5
● RICK CAMP	Camp, Rick Lamar b: 6/10/53, Trion, Ga. BR/TR, 6', 198 lbs. Deb: 9/15/76																									
1976	Atl-N	0	1	.000	5	1	0	0	0	11^1	13	0	2	6	11.9	6.35	60	.302	.333	0	.000	-0	-4	-3	1	-0.2
1977	Atl-N	6	3	.667	54	0	0	0	10	78^2	89	6	47	51	15.7	4.00	111	.283	.377	0	.000	-1	-1	4	-0	0.4
1978	Atl-N	2	4	.333	42	4	0	0	0	74^1	99	5	32	23	16.2	3.75	108	.329	.399	0	.000	-1	-1	2	-0	0.1
1980	Atl-N	6	4	.600	77	0	0	0	22	108^1	92	3	29	33	10.4	1.91	196	.235	.294	1	.111	-0	20	22	4	3.3
1981	Atl-N	9	3	.750	48	0	0	0	17	76	68	5	12	47	9.6	1.78	202	.239	.272	0	.000	-1	14	**15**	0	3.0
1982	*Atl-N	11	13	.458	51	21	3	0	5	177^1	199	18	52	68	12.8	3.65	102	.291	.342	1	.024	-3	-1	1	1	-0.1
1983	Atl-N	10	9	.526	40	16	1	0	0	140	146	16	38	61	12.1	3.79	102	.270	.323	3	.077	-2	-3	1	0	0.0
1984	Atl-N	8	6	.571	31	21	1	0	0	148^2	134	11	63	69	12.0	3.27	118	.245	.325	5	.111	-2	5	10	0	0.7
1985	Atl-N	4	6	.400	66	2	0	0	3	127^2	130	8	61	49	13.8	3.95	97	.263	.349	3	.231	1	-5	-1	-2	-0.2
Total	9	56	49	.533	414	65	5	0	57	942^1	970	72	336	407	12.7	3.37	114	.269	.335	13	.074	-8	25	51	3	7.0
● KID CAMP	Camp, Winfield Scott b: 1870, Columbus, Ohio d: 3/2/1895, Omaha, Neb. TR, 6', 160 lbs. Deb: 5/3/1892 F																									
1892	Pit-N	0	1	.000	4	1	1	0	0	23	31	4	9	6	16.0	6.26	53	.310	.373	1	.091	-1	-8	-8	-1	-0.5
1894	Chi-N	0	1	.000	3	2	2	0	0	22	34	0	12	6	19.2	6.55	86	.351	.427	0	.000	-3	-3	-2	0	-0.2
Total	2	0	2	.000	7	3	3	0	0	45	65	4	21	12	17.6	6.40	69	.330	.400	1	.045	-4	-11	-10	-1	-0.7
● BERT CAMPANERIS	Campaneris, Dagoberto (Blanco) "Campy" (b: Dagoberto Campaneria (Blanco)) b: 3/9/42, Pueblo Nuevo, Cuba BR/TR, 5'10", 160 lbs. Deb: 7/23/64 ♦																									
1965	KC-A	0	0	—	1	0	0	0	0	1	1	0	2	1	27.0	9.00	39	.333	.600	156	.270	0	-1	-1	0	0.0
● ARCHIE CAMPBELL	Campbell, Archibald Stewart "Iron Man" b: 10/20/03, Maplewood, N.J. d: 12/22/89, Sparks, Nevada BR/TR, 6', 180 lbs. Deb: 4/21/28																									
1928	NY-A	0	1	.000	13	1	0	0	2	24	30	0	11	9	15.4	5.25	72	.288	.357	1	.250	0	-3	-4	-1	-0.3
1929	Was-A	0	1	.000	4	0	0	0	0	4	10	1	5	1	33.8	15.75	27	.500	.600	0	—	0	-5	-5	0	-0.9
1930	Cin-N	2	4	.333	23	3	1	0	4	58	71	2	31	19	16.0	5.43	89	.311	.396	4	.267	0	-3	-4	2	-0.2
Total	3	2	6	.250	40	4	1	0	6	86	111	3	47	29	16.6	5.86	77	.315	.398	5	.263	0	-11	-13	2	-1.4
● DAVE CAMPBELL	Campbell, David Alan b: 9/3/51, Princeton, Ind. BR/TR, 6'3", 210 lbs. Deb: 5/6/77																									
1977	Atl-N	0	6	.000	65	0	0	0	13	88^2	78	7	33	42	11.6	3.05	146	.239	.315	1	.083	-1	9	14	-2	1.0
1978	Atl-N	4	4	.500	53	0	0	0	1	69^1	67	10	49	45	15.7	4.80	84	.258	.385	0	—	0	-9	-6	0	-0.7
Total	2	4	10	.286	118	0	0	0	14	158	145	17	82	87	13.4	3.82	112	.247	.348	1	.083	-1	-1	8	-2	0.3
● HUGH CAMPBELL	Campbell, Hugh F. b: 1846, Ireland d: 3/1/1881, Elizabeth, N.J. Deb: 4/28/1873 F																									
1873	Res-n	2	16	.111	19	18	18	0	0	165	250	6	7	5	14.0	2.84	118	.296	.302	13	.149	-5	8	9		0.5
● JIM CAMPBELL	Campbell, James Marcus b: 5/19/66, Santa Maria, Cal. BL/TL, 5'11", 175 lbs. Deb: 8/21/90																									
1990	KC-A	1	0	1.000	2	2	0	0	0	9^2	15	1	1	2	14.9	8.38	46	.349	.364	0	—	0	-5	-5	-0	-0.3
● JOHN CAMPBELL	Campbell, John Millard b: 9/13/07, Washington, D.C. d: 4/24/95, Daytona Beach, Fla. BR/TR, 6'1.5", 184 lbs. Deb: 7/23/33																									
1933	Was-A	0	0	—	1	0	0	0	0	1	1	0	1	0	18.0	0.00	—	.200	.333	0	—	0	0	0	-0	0.0
● KEVIN CAMPBELL	Campbell, Kevin Wade b: 12/6/64, Marianna, Ark. BR/TR, 6'2", 225 lbs. Deb: 7/19/91																									
1991	Oak-A	1	0	1.000	14	0	0	0	0	23	13	4	14	16	11.0	2.74	140	.167	.301	0	—	0	3	3	0	0.2

YEAR	TM/L	W	L	PCT	G	GS	CG	SH	SV	IP	H	HR	BB	SO	RAT	ERA	ERA+	OAV	OOB	BH	AVG	PB	PR	/A	PD	TPI
1992	Oak-A	2	3	.400	32	5	0	0	1	65	66	4	45	38	15.4	5.12	73	.267	.380	0	—	0	-9	-10	-1	-0.7
1993	Oak-A	0	0	—	11	0	0	0	0	16	20	1	11	9	18.0	7.31	56	.313	.421	0	—	0	-5	-6	-0	0.0
1994	Min-A	1	0	1.000	14	0	0	0	0	24^2	20	2	5	15	9.5	2.92	167	.233	.283	0	—	0	5	5	1	0.2
1995	Min-A	0	0	—	6	0	0	0	0	9^2	8	0	5	5	12.1	4.66	102	.235	.333	0	—	0	0	0	-0	0.0
Total	5	4	3	.571	77	5	0	0	1	138^1	127	11	80	83	13.7	4.55	89	.250	.355	0	—	0	-5	-8	-1	-0.3

● MIKE CAMPBELL Campbell, Michael Thomas b: 2/17/64, Seattle, Wash. BR/TR, 6′3″, 210 lbs. Deb: 7/4/87

YEAR	TM/L	W	L	PCT	G	GS	CG	SH	SV	IP	H	HR	BB	SO	RAT	ERA	ERA+	OAV	OOB	BH	AVG	PB	PR	/A	PD	TPI
1987	Sea-A	1	4	.200	9	9	1	0	0	49^1	41	9	25	35	12.4	4.74	99	.224	.324	0	—	0	-2	-0	0	-0.4
1988	Sea-A	6	10	.375	20	20	2	0	0	114^2	128	18	43	63	13.4	5.89	71	.280	.342	0	—	0	-24	-22	-1	-2.8
1989	Sea-A	1	2	.333	5	5	0	0	0	21	28	4	10	6	16.3	7.29	55	.301	.369	0	—	0	-8	-8	-0	-1.1
1992	Tex-A	0	1	.000	1	0	0	0	0	3^2	3	1	2	2	12.3	9.82	39	.231	.333	0	—	0	-2	-2	-0	-0.4
1994	SD-N	1	1	.500	3	2	0	0	0	8^1	13	5	5	10	19.4	12.96	32	.351	.429	1	.333	0	-8	-8	-0	-1.4
1996	Chi-N	3	1	.750	13	5	0	0	0	36^1	29	7	10	19	9.7	4.46	97	.216	.271	4	.364	2	-1	-1	-1	0.0
Total	6	12	19	.387	51	41	3	0	0	233^1	242	44	95	135	13.1	5.86	73	.264	.334	5	.357	2	-45	-41	-2	-6.1

● BILLY CAMPBELL Campbell, William James b: 11/5/1873, Pittsburgh, Pa. d: 10/6/57, Cincinnati, Ohio BL/TL, 5′10″, 165 lbs. Deb: 4/17/05

YEAR	TM/L	W	L	PCT	G	GS	CG	SH	SV	IP	H	HR	BB	SO	RAT	ERA	ERA+	OAV	OOB	BH	AVG	PB	PR	/A	PD	TPI
1905	StL-N	1	1	.500	2	2	2	0	0	17	27	0	7	2	18.0	7.41	40	.365	.420	1	.143	-0	-8	-8	1	-0.7
1907	Cin-N	3	0	1.000	3	3	3	0	0	21	19	0	3	4	9.4	2.14	121	.244	.272	2	.250	0	1	1	1	0.2
1908	Cin-N	12	13	.480	35	24	19	2	2	221^1	203	3	44	73	10.5	2.60	89	.252	.299	6	.083	-3	-6	-7	4	-0.8
1909	Cin-N	7	11	.389	30	15	7	0	2	148^1	162	0	39	37	12.7	2.67	97	.288	.344	6	.140	-1	-1	-1	2	0.0
Total	4	23	25	.479	70	44	31	2	4	407^2	411	3	93	116	11.5	2.80	88	.270	.320	15	.115	-4	-15	-16	8	-1.3

● BILL CAMPBELL Campbell, William Richard b: 8/9/48, Highland Park, Mich. BR/TR, 6′3″, 190 lbs. Deb: 7/14/73

YEAR	TM/L	W	L	PCT	G	GS	CG	SH	SV	IP	H	HR	BB	SO	RAT	ERA	ERA+	OAV	OOB	BH	AVG	PB	PR	/A	PD	TPI
1973	Min-A	3	3	.500	28	2	0	0	7	51^2	44	5	20	42	11.3	3.14	126	.226	.301	0	—	0	4	5	0	0.4
1974	Min-A	8	7	.533	63	0	0	0	19	120^1	109	4	55	89	12.4	2.62	142	.242	.327	0	—	0	13	15	1	2.2
1975	Min-A	4	6	.400	47	7	2	1	5	121	119	13	46	76	12.4	3.79	101	.262	.333	0	.000	-0	-0	0	1	0.1
1976	Min-A	17	5	**.773**	**78**	0	0	0	20	167^2	145	9	62	115	11.4	3.01	119	.234	.309	0	—	0	10	11	-0	1.5
1977	Bos-A★	13	9	.591	69	0	0	0	**31**	140	112	13	60	114	11.4	2.96	152	.224	.313	0	—	0	17	24	2	3.9
1978	Bos-A	7	5	.583	29	0	0	0	4	50^2	62	3	17	47	14.0	3.91	105	.308	.362	0	—	0	-1	1	1	-0.1
1979	Bos-A	3	4	.429	41	0	0	0	9	54^2	55	5	23	25	13.0	4.28	103	.262	.338	0	—	0	-0	1	1	0.1
1980	Bos-A	4	0	1.000	23	0	0	0	0	41^1	44	1	22	17	14.4	4.79	88	.284	.373	0	—	0	-3	-3	-1	-0.4
1981	Bos-A	1	1	.500	30	0	0	0	7	48^1	45	5	20	37	12.1	3.17	122	.245	.319	0	—	0	3	4	0	0.2
1982	Chi-N	3	6	.333	62	0	0	0	8	100	89	6	40	71	11.6	3.69	101	.245	.319	1	.143	-0	-1	0	2	0.3
1983	Chi-N	6	8	.429	**82**	0	0	0	8	122^1	128	4	49	97	13.1	4.49	84	.275	.346	1	.100	-1	-12	-9	2	-1.0
1984	Phi-N	6	5	.545	57	0	0	0	1	81^1	68	2	35	52	11.4	3.43	106	.222	.302	0	.000	-0	1	2	-1	0.1
1985	*StL-N	5	3	.625	50	0	0	0	4	64^1	55	5	21	41	10.9	3.50	101	.230	.298	2	.333	1	1	0	-1	0.0
1986	Det-A	3	6	.333	34	0	0	0	3	55^2	46	5	21	37	11.0	3.88	106	.230	.306	0	—	0	2	1	-1	0.2
1987	Mon-N	0	0	—	7	0	0	0	0	10	18	2	4	4	19.8	8.10	52	.360	.407	0	.000	0	-4	-4	0	0.0
Total	15	83	68	.550	700	9	2	1	126	1229^1	1139	82	495	864	12.1	3.54	110	.248	.324	4	.154	1	28	47	5	7.5

● CARDELL CAMPER Camper, Cardell b: 7/6/52, Boley, Okla. BR/TR, 6′3″, 208 lbs. Deb: 9/11/77

YEAR	TM/L	W	L	PCT	G	GS	CG	SH	SV	IP	H	HR	BB	SO	RAT	ERA	ERA+	OAV	OOB	BH	AVG	PB	PR	/A	PD	TPI
1977	Cle-A	1	0	1.000	3	1	0	0	0	9^1	7	0	4	9	10.6	3.86	102	.200	.282	0	—	0	0	0	-0	0.2

● SAL CAMPFIELD Campfield, William Holton b: 2/19/1868, Meadville, Pa. d: 5/16/52, Meadville, Pa. BR/TR, 6′0.5″, Deb: 5/15/1896

YEAR	TM/L	W	L	PCT	G	GS	CG	SH	SV	IP	H	HR	BB	SO	RAT	ERA	ERA+	OAV	OOB	BH	AVG	PB	PR	/A	PD	TPI
1896	NY-N	1	1	.500	6	2	2	0	0	27	31	1	6	6	13.0	4.00	105	.284	.333	2	.167	-0	1	1	-1	0.0

● SAL CAMPISI Campisi, Salvatore John b: 8/11/42, Brooklyn, N.Y. BR/TR, 6′2″, 210 lbs. Deb: 8/15/69

YEAR	TM/L	W	L	PCT	G	GS	CG	SH	SV	IP	H	HR	BB	SO	RAT	ERA	ERA+	OAV	OOB	BH	AVG	PB	PR	/A	PD	TPI
1969	StL-N	1	0	1.000	7	0	0	0	0	9^2	4	0	6	7	9.3	0.93	384	.121	.256	0	—	0	3	3	0	0.3
1970	StL-N	2	2	.500	37	0	0	0	4	49^1	53	2	37	26	17.0	2.92	141	.282	.408	0	.000	-0	6	7	-0	0.6
1971	Min-A	0	0	—	6	0	0	0	0	4^1	5	1	4	2	18.7	4.15	86	.294	.429	0	—	0	-0	-0	0	0.0
Total	3	3	2	.600	50	0	0	0	4	63^1	62	3	47	35	15.9	2.70	148	.261	.389	0	.000	-0	9	9	0	0.9

● HUGH CANAVAN Canavan, Hugh Edward "Hugo" b: 5/13/1897, Worcester, Mass. d: 9/4/67, Boston, Mass. BL/TL, 5′8″, 160 lbs. Deb: 4/23/18

YEAR	TM/L	W	L	PCT	G	GS	CG	SH	SV	IP	H	HR	BB	SO	RAT	ERA	ERA+	OAV	OOB	BH	AVG	PB	PR	/A	PD	TPI
1918	Bos-N	0	4	.000	11	3	3	0	0	46^2	70	0	15	18	17.4	6.36	42	.366	.427	2	.095	-0	-19	-19	1	-1.4

● JOHN CANDELARIA Candelaria, John Robert "Candy Man" b: 11/6/53, New York, N.Y. BL/TL, 6′7″, 232 lbs. Deb: 6/8/75

YEAR	TM/L	W	L	PCT	G	GS	CG	SH	SV	IP	H	HR	BB	SO	RAT	ERA	ERA+	OAV	OOB	BH	AVG	PB	PR	/A	PD	TPI
1975	*Pit-N	8	6	.571	18	18	4	1	0	120^2	95	8	36	95	9.9	2.76	128	.212	.273	6	.140	-0	12	10	-1	1.0
1976	Pit-N	16	7	.696	32	31	11	4	1	220	173	22	60	138	9.6	3.15	111	.216	.273	14	.184	3	9	8	-1	1.1
1977	Pit-N☆	20	5	**.800**	33	33	6	1	0	230^2	197	29	50	133	9.7	**2.34**	**170**	.232	.276	18	.225	4	**40**	42	-2	4.7
1978	Pit-N	12	11	.522	30	29	3	1	1	189	191	15	49	94	11.7	3.24	114	.261	.312	9	.173	3	7	10	-2	1.3
1979	*Pit-N	14	9	.609	33	30	8	0	0	207	201	25	41	101	10.7	3.22	121	.253	.292	9	.132	-1	12	15	0	1.5
1980	Pit-N	11	14	.440	35	34	7	0	1	233^1	246	14	50	97	11.5	4.01	91	.276	.317	15	.195	2	-11	-10	-1	-0.8
1981	Pit-N	2	2	.500	6	6	0	0	0	40^2	42	3	11	14	11.7	3.54	101	.271	.319	3	.231	0	-0	0	-0	0.0
1982	Pit-N	12	7	.632	31	30	1	1	1	174^2	166	13	37	133	10.7	2.94	126	.255	.299	12	.222	3	13	15	-1	1.8
1983	Pit-N	15	8	.652	33	32	2	0	0	197^2	191	15	45	157	10.8	3.23	115	.257	.302	9	.138	-0	9	10	-2	0.9
1984	Pit-N	12	11	.522	33	28	3	1	2	185^1	179	19	34	133	10.4	2.72	132	.256	.291	8	.129	1	18	18	-2	2.1
1985	Pit-N	2	4	.333	37	0	0	0	9	54^1	57	7	14	47	11.9	3.64	98	.275	.324	0	.000	-0	-0	-0	-0	-0.1
	Cal-A	7	3	.700	13	13	1	1	0	71	70	7	24	53	12.3	3.80	108	.262	.330	0	—	0	3	2	-1	0.3
1986	*Cal-A	10	2	.833	16	16	1	1	0	91^2	68	4	26	81	9.5	2.55	161	.206	.270	0	—	0	17	16	-1	1.9
1987	Cal-A	8	6	.571	20	20	0	0	0	116^2	127	17	20	74	11.4	4.71	91	.279	.311	0	—	0	-3	-5	1	-0.2
	NY-N	2	0	1.000	3	3	0	0	0	12^1	17	1	3	10	14.6	5.84	65	.333	.370	1	.200	0	-2	-3	0	-0.4
1988	NY-A	13	7	.650	25	24	6	2	1	157	150	18	23	121	10.0	3.38	116	.248	.278	0	—	0	10	10	0	1.2
1989	NY-A	3	3	.500	10	6	1	0	0	49	49	8	12	37	11.2	5.14	75	.258	.302	0	—	0	-7	-7	-0	-0.8
	Mon-N	0	2	.000	12	0	0	0	0	16^1	17	3	4	14	11.6	3.31	107	.283	.328	0	—	0	0	0	-0	0.0
1990	Min-A	7	3	.700	34	1	0	0	4	58^1	55	9	9	44	9.9	3.39	122	.244	.274	0	—	0	3	5	-1	0.7
	Tor-A	0	3	.000	13	2	0	0	1	21^1	32	2	11	19	19.0	5.48	72	.356	.437	0	—	0	-4	-4	1	-0.4
	Yr	7	6	.538	47	3	0	0	5	79^2	87	11	20	63	12.3	3.95	104	.274	.321	0	—	0	-0	1	-0	0.3
1991	LA-N	1	1	.500	59	0	0	0	2	33^2	31	3	11	38	11.2	3.74	96	.252	.313	0	—	0	-0	-1	-1	-0.1
1992	LA-N	2	5	.286	50	0	0	0	5	25^1	20	1	13	23	11.7	2.84	121	.220	.317	0	—	0	2	2	0	0.6
1993	Pit-N	0	3	.000	24	0	0	0	1	19^2	25	2	9	17	16.0	8.24	49	.313	.389	0	—	0	-9	-9	-1	-1.4
Total	19	177	122	.592	600	356	54	13	29	2525^2	2399	245	592	1673	10.8	3.33	114	.251	.298	104	.174	15	117	126	-13	14.9

● MILO CANDINI Candini, Mario Cain b: 8/3/17, Manteca, Cal. d: 3/17/98, Manteca, Cal. BR/TR, 6′, 187 lbs. Deb: 5/1/43

YEAR	TM/L	W	L	PCT	G	GS	CG	SH	SV	IP	H	HR	BB	SO	RAT	ERA	ERA+	OAV	OOB	BH	AVG	PB	PR	/A	PD	TPI
1943	Was-A	11	7	.611	28	21	8	3	1	166	144	3	65	67	11.4	2.49	128	.238	.313	9	.161	-1	15	13	1	1.4
1944	Was-A	6	7	.462	28	10	4	2	1	103	110	3	49	31	14.0	4.11	79	.276	.357	10	.313	3	-8	-10	-0	-0.9
1946	Was-A	2	0	1.000	9	0	0	0	1	21^2	15	1	4	6	7.9	2.08	161	.192	.232	2	.333	1	3	3	-0	0.4
1947	Was-A	3	4	.429	38	2	0	0	1	87	96	5	35	31	13.6	5.17	72	.273	.339	3	.167	-0	-14	-14	0	-1.0
1948	Was-A	2	3	.400	35	4	1	0	3	94^1	96	1	63	23	15.3	5.15	84	.267	.378	8	.364	3	-9	-8	0	-0.2
1949	Was-A	0	0	—	3	0	0	0	1	5^2	4	0	1	1	7.9	4.76	89	.200	.238	1	1.000	0	-0	-0	-0	0.0
1950	Phi-N	1	0	1.000	18	0	0	0	0	30	32	2	15	10	14.1	2.70	150	.281	.364	1	.167	-0	5	4	1	0.2
1951	Phi-N	1	0	1.000	15	0	0	0	0	30	33	3	18	14	15.3	6.00	64	.275	.370	1	.333	1	-7	-7	0	-0.1
Total	8	26	21	.553	174	37	13	5	8	537^2	530	18	250	183	13.1	3.92	92	.259	.341	35	.243	7	-15	-19	1	-0.2

● TOM CANDIOTTI Candiotti, Thomas Caesar b: 8/31/57, Walnut Creek, Cal. BR/TR, 6′2″, 200 lbs. Deb: 8/8/83

YEAR	TM/L	W	L	PCT	G	GS	CG	SH	SV	IP	H	HR	BB	SO	RAT	ERA	ERA+	OAV	OOB	BH	AVG	PB	PR	/A	PD	TPI
1983	Mil-A	4	4	.500	10	8	2	1	0	55^2	62	4	16	21	12.9	3.23	116	.291	.346	0	—	0	5	3	-1	0.5
1984	Mil-A	2	2	.500	8	6	0	0	0	32^1	38	5	10	23	13.4	5.29	73	.277	.327	0	—	0	-5	-5	-1	-0.6
1986	Cle-A	16	12	.571	36	34	**17**	3	0	252^1	234	18	106	167	12.4	3.57	116	.246	.326	0	—	0	17	16	3	1.9
1987	Cle-A	7	18	.280	32	32	7	2	0	201^2	193	28	93	111	12.9	4.78	95	.250	.333	0	—	0	-7	-6	0	-0.6
1988	Cle-A	14	8	.636	31	31	11	1	0	216^2	225	15	53	137	11.8	3.28	125	.272	.321	0	—	0	16	20	2	2.1
1989	Cle-A	13	10	.565	31	31	4	0	0	206	188	10	55	124	10.8	3.10	128	.242	.295	0	—	0	18	20	4	2.5
1990	Cle-A	15	11	.577	31	29	3	1	0	202	207	23	55	128	11.9	3.65	107	.263	.316	0	—	0	6	6	3	1.0
1991	Cle-A	7	6	.538	15	15	3	0	0	108^1	88	6	28	86	9.8	2.24	185	.218	.272	0	—	0	22	23	-0	2.7

YEAR	TM/L	W	L	PCT	G	GS	CG	SH	SV	IP	H	HR	BB	SO	RAT	ERA	ERA+	OAV	OOB	BH	AVG	PB	PR	/A	PD	TPI
	*Tor-A	6	7	.462	19	19	3	0	0	129^2	114	6	45	81	11.3	2.98	141	.236	.306	0	—	0	16	18	0	1.7
	Yr	13	13	.500	34	34	6	0	0	238	202	12	73	167	10.6	2.65	158	.225	.287	0	—	0	38	41	-0	4.4
1992	LA-N	11	15	.423	32	30	6	2	0	203^2	177	13	63	152	10.7	3.00	115	.237	.299	6	.107	-1	11	10	1	1.2
1993	LA-N	8	10	.444	33	32	2	0	0	213^2	192	12	71	155	11.3	3.12	122	.241	.308	8	.133	-1	22	17	-0	1.2
1994	LA-N	7	7	.500	23	22	5	0	0	153	149	9	54	102	12.2	4.12	95	.259	.328	7	.140	-1	2	-3	1	-0.3
1995	LA-N	7	14	.333	30	30	1	1	0	190^1	187	18	58	141	12.0	3.50	108	.255	.318	6	.109	-1	14	6	-0	0.4
1996	*LA-N	9	11	.450	28	27	1	0	0	152^1	172	18	43	79	12.9	4.49	86	.288	.339	4	.089	-2	-5	-11	3	-1.1
1997	LA-N	10	7	.588	41	18	0	0	0	135	128	21	40	89	11.9	3.60	107	.248	.315	3	.094	-1	9	4	1	0.4
1998	Oak-A	11	16	.407	33	33	3	0	0	201	222	30	63	98	13.2	4.84	94	.281	.341	1	1.000	1	-4	-6	2	-0.4
Total	15	147	158	.482	433	397	68	11	0	2653^2	2576	236	853	1694	11.9	3.64	110	.255	.318	35	.117	-7	138	111	19	12.6

● JOHN CANEIRA Caneira, John Cascaes b: 10/7/52, Waterbury, Conn. BR/TR, 6'3", 180 lbs. Deb: 9/10/77

YEAR	TM/L	W	L	PCT	G	GS	CG	SH	SV	IP	H	HR	BB	SO	RAT	ERA	ERA+	OAV	OOB	BH	AVG	PB	PR	/A	PD	TPI
1977	Cal-A	2	2	.500	6	4	0	0	0	28^2	27	5	16	17	13.5	4.08	96	.252	.350	0	—	0	-0	-1	-1	0.2
1978	Cal-A	0	0	—	2	2	0	0	0	7^2	8	2	3	0	12.9	7.04	51	.286	.355	0	—	0	-3	-3	-0	0.1
Total	2	2	2	.500	8	6	0	0	0	36^1	35	7	19	17	13.4	4.71	82	.259	.351	0	—	0	-3	-3	-1	0.3

● JOHN CANGELOSI Cangelosi, John Anthony b: 3/10/63, Brooklyn, N.Y. BB/TL, 5'8", 160 lbs. Deb: 6/3/85 ♦

YEAR	TM/L	W	L	PCT	G	GS	CG	SH	SV	IP	H	HR	BB	SO	RAT	ERA	ERA+	OAV	OOB	BH	AVG	PB	PR	/A	PD	TPI
1988	Pit-N	0	0	—	1	0	0	0	0	2	1	0	0	0	4.5	0.00	—	.143	.143	30	.254	0	1	1	-0	0.0
1995	Hou-N	0	0	—	1	0	0	0	0	1	0	0	1	0	9.0	0.00	—	.000	.250	64	.318	0	0	0	0	0.0
1997	*Fla-N	0	0	—	1	0	0	0	0	1	0	0	1	0	9.0	0.00	—	.000	.250	47	.245	0	0	0	-0	0.0
Total	3	0	0	—	3	0	0	0	0	4	1	0	2	0	6.8	0.00	—	.077	.200	500	.250	1	2	2	0	0.0

● JOSE CANO Cano, Joselito (Soriano) b: 3/7/62, Boca De Soco, D.R. BR/TR, 6'3", 175 lbs. Deb: 8/28/89

YEAR	TM/L	W	L	PCT	G	GS	CG	SH	SV	IP	H	HR	BB	SO	RAT	ERA	ERA+	OAV	OOB	BH	AVG	PB	PR	/A	PD	TPI
1989	Hou-N	1	1	.500	6	3	1	0	0	23	24	2	7	8	12.1	5.09	67	.267	.320	0	.000	-1	-4	-4	-0	-0.4

● JOSE CANSECO Canseco, Jose (Capas) b: 7/2/64, Havana, Cuba BR/TR, 6'4", 240 lbs. Deb: 9/2/85 F♦

YEAR	TM/L	W	L	PCT	G	GS	CG	SH	SV	IP	H	HR	BB	SO	RAT	ERA	ERA+	OAV	OOB	BH	AVG	PB	PR	/A	PD	TPI
1993	Tex-A	0	0	—	1	0	0	0	0	1	2	0	3	0	45.0	27.00	15	.500	.714	59	.255	1	-3	-3	0	0.0

● GUY CANTRELL Cantrell, Guy Dewey "Gunner" b: 4/9/04, Clarita, Okla. d: 1/31/61, McAlester, Okla. BR/TR, 6', 190 lbs. Deb: 8/18/25

YEAR	TM/L	W	L	PCT	G	GS	CG	SH	SV	IP	H	HR	BB	SO	RAT	ERA	ERA+	OAV	OOB	BH	AVG	PB	PR	/A	PD	TPI
1925	Bro-N	1	0	1.000	14	3	1	0	0	36	42	0	14	13	14.3	3.00	139	.294	.361	0	.000	-1	5	5	1	0.1
1927	Bro-N	0	0	—	6	0	0	0	0	10	10	0	6	5	14.4	2.70	147	.250	.348	1	.333	0	1	1	0	0.0
	Phi-A	0	2	.000	2	2	2	0	0	18	25	0	7	7	16.0	5.00	85	.338	.395	1	.167	-0	-2	-1	0	-0.2
1930	Det-A	1	5	.167	16	2	1	0	0	35	38	5	20	20	15.2	5.66	85	.271	.366	0	.000	-2	-4	-3	1	-0.5
Total	3	2	7	.222	38	7	4	0	0	99	115	5	47	45	14.9	4.27	103	.290	.368	2	.074	-3	1	1	2	-0.6

● BEN CANTWELL Cantwell, Benjamin Caldwell b: 4/13/02, Milan, Tenn. d: 12/4/62, Salem, Mo. BR/TR, 6'1", 168 lbs. Deb: 8/19/27

YEAR	TM/L	W	L	PCT	G	GS	CG	SH	SV	IP	H	HR	BB	SO	RAT	ERA	ERA+	OAV	OOB	BH	AVG	PB	PR	/A	PD	TPI
1927	NY-N	1	1	.500	5	2	1	0	0	19^2	26	1	2	6	13.3	4.12	94	.313	.337	2	.250	0	-0	-1	-0	-0.1
1928	NY-N	1	0	1.000	7	1	0	0	1	18^1	20	1	4	0	12.3	4.42	89	.282	.329	2	.500	1	-1	-1	1	0.1
	Bos-N	3	3	.500	22	10	3	0	0	90	112	7	36	18	15.0	5.10	77	.304	.369	5	.172	-1	-11	-12	1	-0.7
	Yr	4	3	.571	29	11	3	0	1	108^1	132	8	40	18	14.5	4.98	79	.300	.361	7	.212	-0	-12	-13	2	-0.6
1929	Bos-N	4	13	.235	27	20	8	0	2	157	171	11	52	25	12.9	4.47	105	.280	.338	9	.180	0	4	4	4	0.7
1930	Bos-N	9	15	.375	31	21	10	0	2	173^1	213	15	45	43	13.4	4.88	101	.312	.355	19	.302	2	2	1	4	0.7
1931	Bos-N	7	9	.438	33	16	9	2	2	156^1	160	4	34	32	11.2	3.63	104	.262	.301	13	.228	0	4	3	3	0.6
1932	Bos-N	13	11	.542	37	9	3	1	5	146	133	6	33	33	10.5	2.96	127	.247	.296	14	.280	2	15	13	3	2.6
1933	Bos-N	20	10	**.667**	40	29	18	2	2	254^2	242	12	54	57	10.6	2.62	117	.249	.291	12	.141	-1	20	13	4	1.8
1934	Bos-N	5	11	.313	27	19	6	1	5	143^1	163	8	34	45	12.5	4.33	88	.285	.327	12	.279	1	-4	-8	2	-0.5
1935	Bos-N	4	25	.138	39	24	13	0	0	210^2	235	15	44	34	12.0	4.61	82	.282	.320	19	.284	4	-14	-19	2	-1.7
1936	Bos-N	9	9	.500	34	12	4	0	2	133^1	127	8	35	42	11.2	3.04	126	.252	.306	8	.195	1	15	12	3	1.7
1937	NY-N	0	1	.000	1	1	0	0	0	4	6	1	1	1	15.8	9.00	43	.375	.412	0	—	0	-2	-2	0	-0.4
	Bro-N	0	0	—	13	0	0	0	0	27^1	32	1	8	12	13.2	4.61	88	.288	.336	1	.167	-0	-2	-2	2	0.2
	Yr	0	1	.000	14	1	0	0	0	31^1	38	2	9	13	13.5	5.17	78	.299	.346	1	.167	0	-4	-4	2	-0.2
Total	11	76	108	.413	316	164	75	6	21	1534	1640	90	382	348	12.0	3.91	100	.275	.321	116	.231	8	25	-2	28	5.0

● MIKE CANTWELL Cantwell, Michael Joseph b: 1/15/1896, Washington, D.C. d: 1/5/53, Oteen, N.C. BL/TL, 5'10", 155 lbs. Deb: 8/17/16 F

YEAR	TM/L	W	L	PCT	G	GS	CG	SH	SV	IP	H	HR	BB	SO	RAT	ERA	ERA+	OAV	OOB	BH	AVG	PB	PR	/A	PD	TPI
1916	NY-A	0	0	—	1	0	0	0	0	2	0	0	2	0	9.0	0.00	—	.000	.333	0	—	0	1	1	-0	0.0
1919	Phi-N	1	3	.250	5	3	2	0	0	27^1	36	1	9	6	15.5	5.60	58	.343	.405	2	.222	-0	-8	-7	-1	-1.0
1920	Phi-N	0	3	.000	5	1	0	0	0	23^1	25	1	15	8	16.6	3.86	89	.284	.406	1	.143	-1	-2	-1	0	-0.2
Total	3	1	6	.143	11	4	2	0	0	52^2	61	2	26	14	15.7	4.61	71	.310	.404	3	.188	-1	-9	-8	-1	-1.2

● TOM CANTWELL Cantwell, Thomas Aloysius b: 12/23/1888, Washington, D.C. d: 4/1/68, Washington, D.C. BR/TR, 6', 170 lbs. Deb: 5/19/09 F

YEAR	TM/L	W	L	PCT	G	GS	CG	SH	SV	IP	H	HR	BB	SO	RAT	ERA	ERA+	OAV	OOB	BH	AVG	PB	PR	/A	PD	TPI
1909	Cin-N	1	0	1.000	6	1	1	0	0	21^2	16	0	7	7	10.0	1.66	156	.205	.279	3	.600	1	2	2	-0	0.3
1910	Cin-N	0	0	—	2	0	0	0	0	1^1	2	0	3	0	33.8	13.50	22	.400	.625	0	—	0	-2	-2	-0	0.0
Total	2	1	0	1.000	8	1	1	0	0	23	18	0	10	7	11.3	2.35	111	.217	.309	3	.600	1	0	1	-0	0.3

● MIKE CAPEL Capel, Michael Lee b: 10/13/61, Marshall, Tex. BR/TR, 6'1", 175 lbs. Deb: 5/7/88

YEAR	TM/L	W	L	PCT	G	GS	CG	SH	SV	IP	H	HR	BB	SO	RAT	ERA	ERA+	OAV	OOB	BH	AVG	PB	PR	/A	PD	TPI
1988	Chi-N	2	1	.667	22	0	0	0	0	29^1	34	5	13	19	15.3	4.91	73	.293	.379	0	.000	-0	-5	-4	-0	-0.5
1990	Mil-A	0	0	—	2	0	0	0	0	0^1	6	0	1	1	216.0	135.00	3	.857	.889	0	—	0	-5	-5	0	0.0
1991	Hou-N	1	3	.250	25	0	0	0	3	32^2	33	3	15	23	13.2	3.03	116	.266	.345	0	—	0	2	2	0	0.2
Total	3	3	4	.429	49	0	0	0	3	62^1	73	8	29	43	15.3	4.62	77	.296	.379	0	.000	-0	-7	-7	-0	-0.3

● DOUG CAPILLA Capilla, Douglas Edmund b: 1/7/52, Honolulu, Hawaii BL/TL, 5'8", 175 lbs. Deb: 9/12/76

YEAR	TM/L	W	L	PCT	G	GS	CG	SH	SV	IP	H	HR	BB	SO	RAT	ERA	ERA+	OAV	OOB	BH	AVG	PB	PR	/A	PD	TPI
1976	StL-N	1	0	1.000	7	0	0	0	0	8^1	8	0	4	5	13.0	5.40	65	.242	.324	0	—	0	-2	-2	0	-0.2
1977	StL-N	0	0	—	2	0	0	0	0	2^1	2	0	2	1	15.4	15.43	25	.222	.364	0	—	0	-3	-3	0	0.0
	Cin-N	7	8	.467	22	16	1	0	0	106^1	94	10	59	74	13.1	4.23	93	.237	.338	2	.059	-3	-4	-4	-1	-0.8
	Yr	7	8	.467	24	16	1	0	0	108^2	96	10	61	75	13.2	4.47	88	.236	.339	2	.059	-3	-7	-7	-1	-0.8
1978	Cin-N	0	1	.000	6	3	0	0	0	11	14	1	11	9	20.5	9.82	36	.318	.455	0	.000	-0	-8	-8	-0	-0.7
1979	Cin-N	1	0	1.000	5	0	0	0	0	6^1	7	1	5	0	18.5	8.53	44	.269	.406	1	1.000	0	-3	-3	0	-0.4
	Chi-N	0	1	.000	13	1	0	0	0	17^1	14	1	7	10	10.9	2.60	159	.206	.280	0	—	0	2	3	0	0.2
	Yr	1	1	.500	18	1	0	0	0	23^2	21	2	12	10	12.5	4.18	96	.221	.308	1	1.000	0	-1	-0	1	-0.2
1980	Chi-N	2	8	.200	39	11	0	0	0	89^2	82	7	51	51	13.7	4.12	95	.253	.360	4	.190	0	-5	-2	1	-0.1
1981	Chi-N	1	0	1.000	42	0	0	0	0	51	52	1	34	28	15.5	3.18	116	.284	.402	0	.000	-0	2	3	0	0.0
Total	6	12	18	.400	136	31	1	0	0	292^1	273	21	173	178	14.0	4.34	89	.252	.359	7	.115	-3	-21	-15	0	-2.0

● GEORGE CAPPUZZELLO Cappuzzello, George Angelo b: 1/15/54, Youngstown, Ohio BR/TL, 6', 175 lbs. Deb: 5/31/81

YEAR	TM/L	W	L	PCT	G	GS	CG	SH	SV	IP	H	HR	BB	SO	RAT	ERA	ERA+	OAV	OOB	BH	AVG	PB	PR	/A	PD	TPI
1981	Det-A	1	1	.500	18	3	0	0	1	33^2	28	2	18	19	12.8	3.48	108	.222	.329	0	—	0	1	1	-0	0.0
1982	Hou-N	0	1	.000	17	0	0	0	0	19^1	16	2	7	13	12.1	2.79	119	.232	.329	0	.000	-0	2	1	0	0.1
Total	2	1	2	.333	35	3	0	0	1	53	44	4	25	32	12.6	3.23	112	.226	.329	0	.000	-0	2	2	0	0.1

● BUZZ CAPRA Capra, Lee William b: 10/1/47, Chicago, Ill. BR/TR, 5'10", 168 lbs. Deb: 9/15/71

YEAR	TM/L	W	L	PCT	G	GS	CG	SH	SV	IP	H	HR	BB	SO	RAT	ERA	ERA+	OAV	OOB	BH	AVG	PB	PR	/A	PD	TPI
1971	NY-N	0	1	.000	3	0	0	0	0	5^1	3	0	5	6	13.5	8.44	40	.167	.348	0	.000	-0	-3	-3	0	-0.5
1972	NY-N	3	2	.600	14	6	0	0	0	53	50	7	27	45	13.1	4.58	73	.253	.342	3	.250	1	-7	-7	1	-0.4
1973	NY-N	2	7	.222	24	0	0	0	4	42	35	4	28	35	13.9	3.86	94	.233	.361	0	.000	0	-1	-1	0	-0.2
1974	Atl-N☆	16	8	.667	39	27	11	5	1	217	163	13	84	137	10.4	**2.28**	**166**	**.208**	.287	11	.164	0	32	36	-3	3.7
1975	Atl-N	4	7	.364	12	12	5	0	0	78^1	77	8	28	35	12.2	4.25	89	.257	.322	1	.043	-2	-5	-4	1	-0.7
1976	Atl-N	0	1	.000	5	0	0	0	0	9^1	9	0	6	4	14.5	8.68	44	.265	.375	0	—	0	-5	-5	0	-0.5
1977	Atl-N	6	11	.353	45	16	0	0	0	139^1	142	28	80	100	14.6	5.36	83	.263	.362	4	.111	-2	-22	-14	-1	-1.7
Total	7	31	37	.456	142	61	16	5	5	544^1	479	60	258	362	12.4	3.87	100	.237	.326	19	.135	-2	-12	1	-1	-0.3

● PAT CARAWAY Caraway, Cecil Bradford Patrick b: 9/26/05, Erath Co., Tex. d: 6/9/74, ElPaso, Tex. BL/TL, 6'4", 175 lbs. Deb: 4/19/30

YEAR	TM/L	W	L	PCT	G	GS	CG	SH	SV	IP	H	HR	BB	SO	RAT	ERA	ERA+	OAV	OOB	BH	AVG	PB	PR	/A	PD	TPI
1930	Chi-A	10	10	.500	38	21	9	1	1	193^1	194	11	57	83	11.8	3.86	120	.267	.323	11	.172	-1	17	16	3	1.6
1931	Chi-A	10	24	.294	51	32	11	1	2	220	268	17	101	55	15.4	6.22	68	.295	.370	14	.194	-1	-45	-48	-1	-6.1

YEAR	TM/L	W	L	PCT	G	GS	CG	SH	SV	IP	H	HR	BB	SO	RAT	ERA	ERA+	OAV	OOB	BH	AVG	PB	PR	/A	PD	TPI
1932	Chi-A	2	6	.250	19	9	1	0	0	64^2	80	6	37	13	16.7	6.82	63	.304	.396	3	.143	-1	-17	-18	0	-1.8
Total	3	22	40	.355	108	62	21	2	3	478	542	34	195	151	14.1	5.35	83	.286	.356	28	.178	-3	-45	-50	2	-6.3

● JOHN CARDEN

Carden, John Bruton b: 5/19/21, Killeen, Tex. d: 2/8/49, Mexia, Tex. BR/TR, 6′5″, 210 lbs. Deb: 5/18/46

YEAR	TM/L	W	L	PCT	G	GS	CG	SH	SV	IP	H	HR	BB	SO	RAT	ERA	ERA+	OAV	OOB	BH	AVG	PB	PR	/A	PD	TPI
1946	NY-N	0	0	—	1	0	0	0	0	2	4	0	4	1	40.5	22.50	15	.400	.600	0	—	0	-4	-4	-0	0.0

● CONRAD CARDINAL

Cardinal, Conrad Seth b: 3/30/42, Brooklyn, N.Y. BR/TR, 6′1″, 190 lbs. Deb: 4/11/63

YEAR	TM/L	W	L	PCT	G	GS	CG	SH	SV	IP	H	HR	BB	SO	RAT	ERA	ERA+	OAV	OOB	BH	AVG	PB	PR	/A	PD	TPI
1963	Hou-N	0	1	.000	6	1	0	0	0	13^1	15	0	7	7	14.9	6.08	52	.283	.367	0	.000	-0	-4	-4	0	-0.3

● BEN CARDONI

Cardoni, Armand Joseph "Big Ben" b: 8/21/20, Jessup, Pa. d: 4/2/69, Jessup, Pa. BR/TR, 6′3″, 195 lbs. Deb: 8/22/43

YEAR	TM/L	W	L	PCT	G	GS	CG	SH	SV	IP	H	HR	BB	SO	RAT	ERA	ERA+	OAV	OOB	BH	AVG	PB	PR	/A	PD	TPI
1943	Bos-N	0	0	—	11	0	0	0	1	28	38	1	14	5	17.0	6.43	53	.336	.414	0	.000	-1	-9	-9	0	-0.2
1944	Bos-N	0	6	.000	22	5	1	0	0	75^2	83	5	37	24	14.4	3.93	97	.284	.367	4	.235	-0	-3	-1	-1	-0.1
1945	Bos-N	0	0	—	3	0	0	0	0	4	6	0	3	5	22.5	9.00	43	.300	.417	0	—	0	-2	-2	-0	0.0
Total	3	0	6	.000	36	5	1	0	1	107^2	127	6	54	34	15.4	4.76	78	.299	.382	4	.167	-1	-14	-13	-1	-0.3

● DON CARDWELL

Cardwell, Donald Eugene b: 12/7/35, Winston-Salem, N.C. BR/TR, 6′4″, 210 lbs. Deb: 4/21/57

YEAR	TM/L	W	L	PCT	G	GS	CG	SH	SV	IP	H	HR	BB	SO	RAT	ERA	ERA+	OAV	OOB	BH	AVG	PB	PR	/A	PD	TPI
1957	Phi-N	4	8	.333	30	19	5	1	1	128^1	122	17	42	92	11.8	4.91	78	.251	.316	7	.200	1	-15	-16	-0	-1.2
1958	Phi-N	3	6	.333	16	14	3	0	0	107^2	99	16	37	77	11.5	4.51	88	.241	.307	8	.211	1	-7	-7	0	-0.4
1959	Phi-N	9	10	.474	25	22	5	1	0	153	135	22	65	106	12.0	4.06	101	.238	.320	3	.055	-3	-2	1	-3	-0.5
1960	Phi-N	1	2	.333	5	4	0	0	0	28^1	28	4	11	21	12.7	4.45	87	.262	.336	2	.250	2	-2	-2	-0	0.0
	Chi-N	8	14	.364	31	26	6	1	0	177	166	19	68	129	12.2	4.37	86	.249	.323	14	.203	3	-12	-12	-2	-1.1
	Yr	9	16	.360	36	30	6	1	0	205^1	194	23	79	150	12.2	4.38	87	.250	.324	16	.208	5	-14	-13	-2	-1.1
1961	Chi-N	15	14	.517	39	38	13	3	0	259^1	243	22	88	156	11.8	3.82	110	.246	.314	10	.105	-1	6	10	2	1.2
1962	Chi-N	7	16	.304	41	29	6	1	4	195^2	205	27	60	104	12.6	4.92	84	.267	.327	9	.148	-0	-21	-17	1	-1.7
1963	Pit-N	13	15	.464	33	32	7	2	0	213^2	195	21	52	112	11.1	3.07	107	.245	.305	6	.085	-2	5	5	-1	0.4
1964	Pit-N	1	2	.333	4	4	1	1	0	19^1	15	1	7	10	11.6	2.79	126	.217	.316	1	.143	-0	2	2	0	0.3
1965	Pit-N	13	10	.565	37	34	12	2	0	240^1	214	21	59	107	10.7	3.18	110	.239	.295	12	.162	3	10	9	2	1.3
1966	Pit-N	6	6	.500	32	14	1	0	1	101^2	112	15	27	60	12.8	4.60	78	.282	.337	3	.103	-1	-11	-12	2	-1.1
1967	NY-N	5	9	.357	26	16	3	3	0	118^1	112	8	39	71	12.0	3.57	95	.249	.319	6	.158	2	-3	-2	2	0.2
1968	NY-N	7	13	.350	29	25	5	1	1	179^2	156	9	50	82	10.8	2.96	102	.233	.296	3	.049	-3	1	1	2	0.0
1969	*NY-N	8	10	.444	30	21	4	0	0	152^1	145	15	47	60	11.6	3.01	121	.252	.314	8	.170	1	10	11	2	1.6
1970	NY-N	0	2	.000	16	1	0	0	0	25	31	3	6	8	14.4	6.48	62	.316	.374	0	.000	-1	-7	-7	0	-0.5
	Atl-N	2	1	.667	16	2	1	1	0	23	31	5	13	16	17.6	9.00	48	.326	.413	2	.400	1	-13	-12	1	-1.2
	Yr	2	3	.400	32	3	1	1	0	48	62	8	19	24	15.4	7.69	54	.312	.374	2	.200	-0	-19	-19	1	-1.7
Total	14	102	138	.425	410	301	72	17	7	2122^2	2009	225	671	1211	11.8	3.92	95	.250	.315	94	.135	2	-59	-47	10	-2.7

● TEX CARLETON

Carleton, James Otto b: 8/19/06, Comanche, Tex. d: 1/11/77, Fort Worth, Tex. BB/TR, 6′1.5″, 180 lbs. Deb: 4/17/32

YEAR	TM/L	W	L	PCT	G	GS	CG	SH	SV	IP	H	HR	BB	SO	RAT	ERA	ERA+	OAV	OOB	BH	AVG	PB	PR	/A	PD	TPI
1932	StL-N	10	13	.435	44	22	9	3	0	196^1	198	12	70	113	12.4	4.08	96	.261	.326	9	.150	-2	-4	-3	2	-0.3
1933	StL-N	17	11	.607	44	33	15	4	3	277	263	15	97	147	11.8	3.38	103	.249	.315	17	.187	1	-1	3	-1	0.3
1934	*StL-N	16	11	.593	40	31	16	0	2	240^2	260	14	52	103	11.9	4.26	99	.271	.314	17	.193	1	-5	-1	0	-0.1
1935	*Chi-N	11	8	.579	31	22	8	0	1	171	169	17	60	84	12.2	3.89	101	.257	.322	8	.129	-3	2	1	2	0.0
1936	Chi-N	14	10	.583	35	26	12	**4**	1	197^1	204	14	67	88	12.6	3.65	109	.268	.332	14	.233	6	8	7	2	1.6
1937	Chi-N	16	8	.667	32	27	18	4	0	208^1	183	10	94	105	12.1	3.15	126	.236	.321	12	.169	1	18	19	1	2.2
1938	*Chi-N	10	9	.526	33	24	9	0	0	167^2	213	11	74	80	15.8	5.42	71	.307	.381	15	.231	3	-30	-30	-0	-2.7
1940	Bro-N	6	6	.500	34	17	4	1	2	149	140	12	47	88	11.5	3.81	105	.245	.305	8	.186	-0	1	3	-1	0.1
Total	8	100	76	.568	293	202	91	16	9	1607^1	1630	105	561	808	12.5	3.91	100	.261	.326	100	.185	6	-13	-0	6	1.1

● CISCO CARLOS

Carlos, Francisco Manuel b: 9/17/40, Monrovia, Cal. BR/TR, 6′3″, 205 lbs. Deb: 8/25/67

YEAR	TM/L	W	L	PCT	G	GS	CG	SH	SV	IP	H	HR	BB	SO	RAT	ERA	ERA+	OAV	OOB	BH	AVG	PB	PR	/A	PD	TPI
1967	Chi-A	2	0	1.000	8	7	1	1	0	41^2	23	0	9	27	7.1	0.86	359	.161	.216	1	.063	-1	11	10	0	0.4
1968	Chi-A	4	14	.222	29	21	0	0	0	122^1	121	13	37	57	12.4	3.90	78	.258	.326	2	.065	-1	-13	-12	2	-1.7
1969	Chi-A	4	3	.571	25	4	0	0	0	49^1	52	4	23	28	14.6	5.66	68	.274	.367	0	.000	-1	-11	-10	1	-1.3
	Was-A	1	1	.500	6	4	0	0	0	17^2	23	2	6	5	14.8	4.58	76	.348	.403	1	.200	1	-2	-2	0	-0.1
	Yr	5	4	.556	31	8	0	0	0	67	75	6	29	33	14.0	5.37	70	.287	.359	1	.067	-0	-13	-12	1	-1.4
1970	Was-A	0	0	—	5	0	0	0	0	6	3	0	4	2	10.5	1.50	237	.150	.292	0	—	0	1	1	0	0.0
Total	4	11	18	.379	73	36	1	1	0	237	222	19	79	119	12.0	3.72	88	.250	.322	4	.065	-3	-13	-12	3	-2.7

● DON CARLSEN

Carlsen, Donald Herbert b: 10/15/26, Chicago, Ill. BR/TR, 6′1″, 175 lbs. Deb: 4/28/48

YEAR	TM/L	W	L	PCT	G	GS	CG	SH	SV	IP	H	HR	BB	SO	RAT	ERA	ERA+	OAV	OOB	BH	AVG	PB	PR	/A	PD	TPI
1948	Chi-N	0	0	—	1	0	0	0	0	1	5	0	2	1	63.0	36.00	11	.625	.700	0	—	0	-4	-4	0	0.0
1951	Pit-N	2	3	.400	7	6	2	0	0	43	50	4	14	20	13.6	4.19	101	.292	.349	4	.250	0	-1	0	-1	0.0
1952	Pit-N	0	1	.000	5	1	0	0	0	10	20	1	5	2	22.5	10.80	37	.417	.472	1	.333	0	-8	-8	1	-0.6
Total	3	2	4	.333	13	7	2	0	0	54	75	5	21	23	16.2	6.00	70	.330	.390	5	.263	0	-12	-11	0	-0.6

● DAN CARLSON

Carlson, Daniel Steven b: 1/26/70, Portland, Ore. BR/TR, 6′1″, 185 lbs. Deb: 9/15/96

YEAR	TM/L	W	L	PCT	G	GS	CG	SH	SV	IP	H	HR	BB	SO	RAT	ERA	ERA+	OAV	OOB	BH	AVG	PB	PR	/A	PD	TPI
1996	SF-N	1	0	1.000	5	0	0	0	0	10	13	2	2	4	13.5	2.70	151	.310	.341	0	.000	-0	2	2	-0	0.1
1997	SF-N	0	0	—	6	0	0	0	0	15^1	20	5	8	14	16.4	7.63	54	.317	.394	0	.000	-0	-6	-6	-0	0.0
1998	TB-A	0	0	—	10	0	0	0	0	17^2	25	3	8	16	18.3	7.64	64	.347	.434	0	—	0	-6	-5	-0	-0.4
Total	3	1	0	1.000	21	0	0	0	0	43	58	10	18	34	16.5	6.49	68	.328	.399	0	.000	-0	-10	-10	-1	-0.3

● HAL CARLSON

Carlson, Harold Gust b: 5/17/1892, Rockford, Ill. d: 5/28/30, Chicago, Ill. BR/TR, 6′, 180 lbs. Deb: 4/13/17

YEAR	TM/L	W	L	PCT	G	GS	CG	SH	SV	IP	H	HR	BB	SO	RAT	ERA	ERA+	OAV	OOB	BH	AVG	PB	PR	/A	PD	TPI
1917	Pit-N	7	11	.389	34	17	9	1	1	161^1	140	0	49	68	10.8	2.90	98	.241	.304	6	.122	-2	-3	-1	2	-0.2
1918	Pit-N	0	1	.000	3	2	0	0	0	12	12	1	5	5	12.8	3.75	77	.286	.362	1	.200	-0	-1	-1	-0	-0.1
1919	Pit-N	8	10	.444	22	14	7	1	0	141	114	0	39	49	9.9	2.23	135	.243	.303	7	.163	-1	11	12	1	1.7
1920	Pit-N	14	13	.519	39	31	16	3	3	246^2	262	4	63	62	12.1	3.36	96	.281	.331	23	.271	3	-6	-4	-5	-0.6
1921	Pit-N	4	8	.333	31	10	3	0	4	109^2	121	6	23	37	12.0	4.27	90	.290	.330	10	.294	1	-6	-5	1	-0.4
1922	Pit-N	9	12	.429	39	18	6	0	2	145^1	193	10	58	64	15.8	5.70	72	.323	.386	15	.268	3	-26	-26	2	-2.7
1923	Pit-N	0	0	—	4	0	0	0	0	13^1	19	2	2	4	14.9	4.73	85	.358	.393	0	.000	-0	-1	-1	0	0.0
1924	Phi-N	8	17	.320	38	23	12	1	2	203^2	267	9	55	66	14.4	4.86	92	.329	.374	21	.276	2	-22	-9	1	-0.8
1925	Phi-N	13	14	.481	35	32	18	**4**	0	234	281	19	52	80	13.0	4.23	113	.298	.338	17	.183	-2	1	14	-1	1.1
1926	Phi-N	17	12	.586	35	34	20	3	0	267^1	293	9	47	55	11.5	3.23	128	.281	.313	23	.240	2	18	27	-4	2.6
1927	Phi-N	4	5	.444	11	9	4	0	1	63^2	80	7	18	13	13.9	5.23	79	.316	.362	6	.240	0	-9	-8	-1	-1.0
	Chi-N	12	8	.600	27	22	15	2	0	184^1	201	9	27	27	11.2	3.17	122	.280	.307	11	.164	-3	15	14	-0	1.0
	Yr	16	13	.552	38	31	19	2	1	248	281	16	45	40	11.9	3.70	106	.289	.322	17	.185	-3	6	6	-1	0.0
1928	Chi-N	3	2	.600	20	4	2	0	4	56^1	74	4	15	11	14.2	5.91	65	.329	.371	5	.263	0	-12	-13	0	-1.1
1929	*Chi-N	11	5	.688	31	14	6	2	2	111^2	131	8	31	35	13.1	5.16	90	.292	.340	9	.231	1	-5	-7	2	-0.6
1930	Chi-N	4	2	.667	8	6	3	0	0	51^2	68	5	14	14	14.5	5.05	97	.313	.358	5	.250	0	-0	-1	1	0.0
Total	14	114	120	.487	377	236	121	17	19	2002	2256	93	498	590	12.5	3.97	99	.291	.337	159	.223	4	-49	-9	-0	-1.1

● LEON CARLSON

Carlson, Leon Alton "Swede" b: 2/17/1895, Jamestown, N.Y. d: 9/15/61, Jamestown, N.Y. BR/TR, 6′3″, 195 lbs. Deb: 5/31/20

YEAR	TM/L	W	L	PCT	G	GS	CG	SH	SV	IP	H	HR	BB	SO	RAT	ERA	ERA+	OAV	OOB	BH	AVG	PB	PR	/A	PD	TPI
1920	Was-A	0	0	—	3	0	0	0	0	12^1	14	1	2	3	11.7	3.65	102	.292	.320	1	.167	-0	0	0	-0	-0.1

● STEVE CARLTON

Carlton, Steven Norman "Lefty" b: 12/22/44, Miami, Fla. BL/TL, 6′4″, 210 lbs. Deb: 4/12/65 H

YEAR	TM/L	W	L	PCT	G	GS	CG	SH	SV	IP	H	HR	BB	SO	RAT	ERA	ERA+	OAV	OOB	BH	AVG	PB	PR	/A	PD	TPI
1965	StL-N	0	0	—	15	2	0	0	0	25	27	3	8	21	13.0	2.52	153	.287	.350	0	.000	-0	3	4	1	0.0
1966	StL-N	3	3	.500	9	9	2	1	0	52	56	2	18	25	12.8	3.12	115	.280	.339	4	.267	1	3	3	0	0.4
1967	*StL-N	14	9	.609	30	28	11	2	1	193	173	10	62	168	11.1	2.98	110	.238	.300	11	.153	1	8	6	0	0.8
1968	*StL-N★	13	11	.542	34	33	10	5	0	231^2	214	11	61	162	10.8	2.99	97	.246	.298	12	.164	2	-0	-2	-1	-0.1
1969	StL-N★	17	11	.607	31	31	12	2	0	236^1	185	15	93	210	10.7	2.17	165	.216	.295	17	.213	5	37	37	-1	4.9
1970	StL-N	10	19	.345	34	33	13	2	0	253^2	239	25	109	193	12.4	3.73	110	.251	.329	16	.200	2	9	11	-1	1.2
1971	StL-N☆	20	9	.690	37	36	18	4	0	273^1	275	23	98	172	12.4	3.56	101	.262	.328	17	.177	1	-3	1	-0	0.2
1972	Phi-N★	**27**	10	.730	41	41	**30**	8	0	**346^1**	257	17	87	**310**	9.0	**1.97**	**182**	.206	.259	23	.197	4	**57**	**62**	-2	**7.4**
1973	Phi-N	13	20	.394	40	40	**18**	3	0	**293^1**	293	29	113	223	12.5	3.90	97	.260	.329	16	.160	0	-8	-3	-1	-0.4
1974	Phi-N☆	16	13	.552	39	39	17	1	0	291	249	21	136	**240**	12.1	3.22	117	.234	.323	25	.245	2	13	18	-1	1.9
1975	Phi-N	15	14	.517	37	37	14	3	0	255^1	217	24	104	192	11.4	3.56	105	.233	.312	14	.156	-0	2	5	-1	0.4

YEAR TM/L	W	L	PCT	G	GS	CG	SH	SV	IP	H	HR	BB	SO	RAT	ERA	ERA+	OAV	OOB	BH	AVG	PB	PR	/A	PD	TPI
1976 *Phi-N	20	7	**.741**	35	35	13	2	0	252^{2}	224	19	72	195	10.6	3.13	113	.237	.291	20	.217	2	10	12	-4	1.0
1977 *Phi-N☆	**23**	10	.697	36	36	17	2	0	283	229	25	89	198	10.2	2.64	151	.223	.287	26	.268	8	40	43	1	6.0
1978 *Phi-N	16	13	.552	34	34	12	3	0	247^{1}	228	30	63	161	10.7	2.84	126	.246	.297	25	.291	7	20	20	1	3.3
1979 Phi-N★	18	11	.621	35	35	13	4	0	251	202	25	89	213	10.6	3.62	106	.219	.292	21	.223	3	3	6	-1	0.9
1980 *Phi-N☆	**24**	9	.727	38	38	13	3	0	**304**	243	15	90	**286**	9.9	2.34	**162**	.218	.278	19	.188	-1	**43**	**49**	-1	**5.3**
1981 *Phi-N☆	13	4	.765	24	24	10	1	0	190	152	9	62	179	10.2	2.42	150	.222	.288	9	.134	-0	23	26	-1	2.2
1982 Phi-N★	**23**	11	.676	38	38	**19**	**6**	0	**295^{2}**	253	17	86	**286**	10.3	3.10	118	.232	.289	22	.218	4	16	18	-1	2.4
1983 *Phi-N	15	16	.484	37	37	8	3	0	**283^{2}**	277	20	84	**275**	11.5	3.11	115	.258	.314	19	.196	3	16	14	-1	1.7
1984 Phi-N	13	7	.650	33	33	1	0	0	229	214	14	79	163	11.5	3.58	102	.246	.309	16	.190	2	0	1	-3	0.0
1985 Phi-N	1	8	.111	16	16	0	0	0	92	84	6	53	48	13.4	3.33	111	.249	.350	5	.179	0	3	4	1	0.4
1986 Phi-N	4	8	.333	16	16	0	0	0	83	102	15	45	62	15.9	6.18	62	.297	.379	7	.206	1	-23	-21	-1	-2.7
SF-N	1	3	.250	6	6	0	0	0	30	36	4	16	18	15.9	5.10	69	.303	.390	2	.182	1	-5	-5	1	-0.5
Yr	5	11	.313	22	22	0	0	0	113	138	19	61	80	15.9	5.89	64	.297	.380	9	.200	2	-27	-27	-0	-3.2
Chi-A	4	3	.571	10	10	0	0	0	63^{1}	58	6	25	40	11.8	3.69	117	.252	.325	0	—	0	3	4	-1	0.1
1987 Cle-A	5	9	.357	23	14	3	0	1	109	111	17	63	71	14.5	5.37	84	.266	.364	0	—	0	-11	-10	-0	-1.2
Min-A	1	5	.167	9	7	0	0	0	43	54	7	23	20	16.5	6.70	69	.310	.397	0	—	0	-11	-10	0	-1.3
Yr	6	14	.300	32	21	3	0	1	152	165	24	86	91	15.0	5.74	79	.276	.369	0	—	0	-22	-20	-0	-2.5
1988 Min-A	0	1	.000	4	1	0	0	0	9^{2}	20	5	5	5	23.3	16.76	24	.408	.463	0	—	0	-14	-14	-0	-1.1
Total 24	329	244	.574	741	709	254	55	2	5217^{1}	4672	414	1833	4136	11.3	3.22	115	.240	.308	346	.201	49	236	277	-18	33.2

● DON CARMAN

Carman, Donald Wayne b: 8/14/59, Oklahoma City, Okla BL/TL, 6'3", 195 lbs. Deb: 10/1/83

YEAR TM/L	W	L	PCT	G	GS	CG	SH	SV	IP	H	HR	BB	SO	RAT	ERA	ERA+	OAV	OOB	BH	AVG	PB	PR	/A	PD	TPI
1983 Phi-N	0	0	—	1	0	0	0	1	1	0	0	0	0	0.0	0.00	—	.000	.000	0	—	0	0	0	0	0.1
1984 Phi-N	0	1	.000	11	0	0	0	0	13^{1}	14	2	6	16	13.5	5.40	67	.255	.328	0	.000	-0	-3	-3	-0	-0.2
1985 Phi-N	9	4	.692	71	0	0	0	7	86^{1}	52	6	38	87	9.6	2.08	177	.178	.277	0	.000	-0	14	15	0	2.5
1986 Phi-N	10	5	.667	50	14	2	1	1	134^{1}	113	11	52	98	11.3	3.22	120	.234	.313	0	.000	-3	7	9	2	0.9
1987 Phi-N	13	11	.542	35	35	3	2	0	211	194	34	69	125	11.4	4.22	100	.244	.308	5	.082	-3	-3	0	-3	-0.6
1988 Phi-N	10	14	.417	36	32	2	0	0	201^{1}	211	20	70	116	12.7	4.29	83	.270	.333	3	.048	-5	-19	-16	-3	-2.6
1989 Phi-N	5	15	.250	49	20	0	0	0	149^{1}	152	21	86	81	14.5	5.24	68	.260	.358	1	.029	-3	-29	-28	-1	-3.9
1990 Phi-N	6	2	.750	59	1	0	0	1	86^{2}	69	13	38	58	11.5	4.15	92	.218	.310	3	.273	1	-3	-3	0	-0.2
1991 Cin-N	0	2	.000	28	0	0	0	1	36	40	8	19	15	15.0	5.25	72	.286	.375	0	.000	-1	-6	-6	0	-0.3
1992 Tex-A	0	0	—	2	0	0	0	0	2^{1}	4	0	0	2	15.4	7.71	49	.364	.364	0	—	0	-1	-1	-0	0.0
Total 10	53	54	.495	342	102	7	3	11	921^{2}	849	115	378	598	12.2	4.11	92	.245	.323	12	.057	-14	-42	-32	-5	-4.3

● CHET CARMICHAEL

Carmichael, Chester Keller b: 1/9/1888, Muncie, Ind. d: 8/22/60, Rochester, N.Y. BR/TR, 5'11.5", 200 lbs. Deb: 9/5/09

YEAR TM/L	W	L	PCT	G	GS	CG	SH	SV	IP	H	HR	BB	SO	RAT	ERA	ERA+	OAV	OOB	BH	AVG	PB	PR	/A	PD	TPI
1909 Cin-N	0	0	—	2	0	0	0	0	7	9	0	3	2	18.0	0.00	—	.321	.424	0	.000	-0	2	2	-0	-0.1

● RAFAEL CARMONA

Carmona, Rafael b: 10/2/72, Rio Piedras, P.R. BL/TR, 6'2", 185 lbs. Deb: 5/18/95

YEAR TM/L	W	L	PCT	G	GS	CG	SH	SV	IP	H	HR	BB	SO	RAT	ERA	ERA+	OAV	OOB	BH	AVG	PB	PR	/A	PD	TPI
1995 Sea-A	2	4	.333	15	3	0	0	1	47^{2}	55	9	34	28	17.2	5.66	84	.293	.406	0	—	0	-5	-5	0	-0.6
1996 Sea-A	8	3	.727	53	1	0	0	1	90^{1}	95	11	55	62	15.2	4.28	115	.273	.377	0	—	0	7	7	-0	0.7
1997 Sea-A	0	0	—	4	0	0	0	0	5^{2}	3	1	2	6	7.9	3.18	141	.150	.227	0	—	0	1	1	-0	0.0
Total 3	10	7	.588	72	4	0	0	2	143^{2}	153	21	91	96	15.6	4.70	103	.275	.382	0	—	0	3	3	0	0.1

● EDDIE CARNETT

Carnett, Edwin Elliott "Lefty" b: 10/21/16, Springfield, Mo. BL/TL, 6', 185 lbs. Deb: 4/19/41 ♦

YEAR TM/L	W	L	PCT	G	GS	CG	SH	SV	IP	H	HR	BB	SO	RAT	ERA	ERA+	OAV	OOB	BH	AVG	PB	PR	/A	PD	TPI
1941 Bos-N	0	0	—	2	0	0	0	0	1^{1}	4	0	3	2	47.3	20.25	18	.500	.636	0	—	0	-2	-2	0	0.0
1944 Chi-A	0	0	—	2	0	0	0	0	2	3	1	0	1	13.5	9.00	38	.333	.333	126	.276	1	-1	-1	0	0.0
1945 Cle-A	0	0	—	2	0	0	0	0	2	0	0	0	1	0.0	0.00	—	.000	.000	16	.219	0	1	1	-0	0.0
Total 3	0	0	—	6	0	0	0	0	5^{1}	7	1	3	4	16.9	8.44	40	.304	.385	142	.268	1	-3	-3	0	0.0

● PAT CARNEY

Carney, Patrick Joseph "Doc" b: 8/7/1876, Holyoke, Mass. d: 1/9/53, Worcester, Mass. BL/TL, 6', 200 lbs. Deb: 9/20/01 ♦

YEAR TM/L	W	L	PCT	G	GS	CG	SH	SV	IP	H	HR	BB	SO	RAT	ERA	ERA+	OAV	OOB	BH	AVG	PB	PR	/A	PD	TPI
1902 Bos-N	0	1	.000	2	1	0	0	0	5	6	1	3	3	18.0	9.00	31	.300	.417	141	.270	0	-3	-3	-0	-0.6
1903 Bos-N	4	5	.444	10	9	9	0	0	78	93	2	31	29	14.5	4.04	79	.284	.349	94	.240	2	-7	-7	-0	-0.6
1904 Bos-N	0	4	.000	4	3	1	0	0	26^{1}	40	1	12	5	18.1	5.81	47	.364	.431	57	.204	0	-9	-9	-0	-1.1
Total 3	4	10	.286	16	13	10	0	0	109^{1}	139	4	46	37	15.6	4.69	66	.303	.372	308	.247	2	-19	-20	-1	-2.3

● CHRIS CARPENTER

Carpenter, Christopher John b: 4/27/75, Exeter, N.H. BR/TR, 6'6", 215 lbs. Deb: 5/12/97

YEAR TM/L	W	L	PCT	G	GS	CG	SH	SV	IP	H	HR	BB	SO	RAT	ERA	ERA+	OAV	OOB	BH	AVG	PB	PR	/A	PD	TPI
1997 Tor-A	3	7	.300	14	13	1	1	0	81^{1}	108	7	37	55	16.3	5.09	90	.325	.396	0	—	0	-5	-5	-1	-0.6
1998 Tor-A	12	7	.632	33	24	1	1	0	175	177	18	61	136	12.5	4.37	106	.265	.332	0	.000	-0	5	5	-1	0.4
Total 2	15	14	.517	47	37	2	2	0	256^{1}	285	25	98	191	13.7	4.60	101	.285	.353	0	.000	-0	1	1	-2	-0.2

● CRIS CARPENTER

Carpenter, Cris Howell b: 4/5/65, St.Augustine, Fla. BR/TR, 6'1", 185 lbs. Deb: 5/14/88

YEAR TM/L	W	L	PCT	G	GS	CG	SH	SV	IP	H	HR	BB	SO	RAT	ERA	ERA+	OAV	OOB	BH	AVG	PB	PR	/A	PD	TPI
1988 StL-N	2	3	.400	8	8	1	0	0	47^{2}	56	3	9	24	12.5	4.72	74	.298	.333	2	.143	-0	-7	-7	-0	-0.7
1989 StL-N	4	4	.500	36	5	0	0	0	68	70	4	26	35	13.0	3.18	114	.262	.332	4	.444	1	2	3	-0	0.5
1990 StL-N	0	0	—	4	0	0	0	0	8	5	2	2	6	7.9	4.50	85	.167	.219	0	.000	-0	-1	-1	-0	0.0
1991 StL-N	10	4	.714	59	0	0	0	0	66	53	6	20	47	10.0	4.23	88	.220	.280	1	.333	0	-4	-4	-0	-0.7
1992 StL-N	5	4	.556	73	0	0	0	1	88	69	10	27	46	10.2	2.97	114	.220	.291	1	.333	0	5	4	-1	0.4
1993 Fla-N	0	1	.000	29	0	0	0	0	37^{1}	29	1	13	26	10.6	2.89	149	.212	.289	0	—	0	5	6	-0	0.2
Tex-A	4	1	.800	27	0	0	0	1	32	35	4	12	27	13.8	4.22	98	.289	.363	0	—	0	0	-0	-0	0.0
1994 Tex-A	2	5	.286	47	0	0	0	5	59	69	7	20	39	13.6	5.03	96	.291	.346	0	—	0	-2	-1	-0	-0.2
1996 Mil-A	0	0	—	8	0	0	0	0	8^{1}	12	1	2	2	15.1	7.56	69	.333	.368	0	—	0	-2	-2	-0	-0.2
Total 8	27	22	.551	291	13	1	0	7	414^{1}	398	38	131	252	11.7	3.91	99	.254	.315	8	.267	1	-2	-1	-1	-0.7

● LEW CARPENTER

Carpenter, Lewis Emmett b: 8/16/13, Woodstock, Ga. d: 4/25/79, Marietta, Ga. BR/TR, 6'2", 195 lbs. Deb: 5/1/43

YEAR TM/L	W	L	PCT	G	GS	CG	SH	SV	IP	H	HR	BB	SO	RAT	ERA	ERA+	OAV	OOB	BH	AVG	PB	PR	/A	PD	TPI
1943 Was-A	0	0	—	4	0	0	0	0	3^{1}	1	0	4	1	16.2	0.00	—	.125	.462	0	—	0	1	1	-0	0.0

● PAUL CARPENTER

Carpenter, Paul Calvin b: 8/12/1894, Granville, Ohio d: 3/14/68, Newark, Ohio BR/TR, 5'11", 165 lbs. Deb: 7/26/16

YEAR TM/L	W	L	PCT	G	GS	CG	SH	SV	IP	H	HR	BB	SO	RAT	ERA	ERA+	OAV	OOB	BH	AVG	PB	PR	/A	PD	TPI
1916 Pit-N	0	0	—	5	0	0	0	0	7^{2}	8	0	4	5	14.1	1.17	229	.258	.343	0	.000	-0	1	1	0	0.0

● BOB CARPENTER

Carpenter, Robert Louis b: 12/12/17, Chicago, Ill. BR/TR, 6'3", 195 lbs. Deb: 9/12/40

YEAR TM/L	W	L	PCT	G	GS	CG	SH	SV	IP	H	HR	BB	SO	RAT	ERA	ERA+	OAV	OOB	BH	AVG	PB	PR	/A	PD	TPI
1940 NY-N	2	0	1.000	5	3	2	0	0	33	29	2	14	25	11.7	2.73	142	.238	.316	1	.100	-0	4	4	-0	0.2
1941 NY-N	11	6	.647	29	19	8	1	2	131^{2}	138	15	42	42	12.4	3.83	97	.265	.323	7	.156	-0	-3	-2	-3	-0.5
1942 NY-N	11	10	.524	28	25	12	2	0	185^{2}	192	13	51	53	11.8	3.15	107	.263	.312	12	.185	-1	3	4	-3	0.1
1946 NY-N	1	3	.250	12	6	1	1	0	39	37	7	18	13	12.7	4.85	71	.245	.325	1	.100	-0	-6	-6	-1	-0.7
1947 NY-N	0	0	—	2	0	0	0	0	3	5	0	3	0	24.0	12.00	34	.385	.500	0	—	0	-3	-3	0	0.0
Chi-N	0	1	.000	4	1	0	0	0	7^{1}	10	1	4	1	17.2	4.91	80	.323	.400	1	1.000	0	-1	-1	0	0.0
Yr	0	1	.000	6	1	0	0	0	10^{1}	15	1	7	1	19.2	6.97	57	.341	.431	1	1.000	0	-3	-3	0	0.0
Total 5	25	20	.556	80	54	23	4	2	399^{2}	411	38	132	134	12.3	3.60	98	.262	.321	22	.168	-1	-5	-3	-6	-0.9

● FRANK CARPIN

Carpin, Frank Dominic b: 9/14/38, Brooklyn, N.Y. BL/TL, 5'10", 172 lbs. Deb: 5/25/65

YEAR TM/L	W	L	PCT	G	GS	CG	SH	SV	IP	H	HR	BB	SO	RAT	ERA	ERA+	OAV	OOB	BH	AVG	PB	PR	/A	PD	TPI
1965 Pit-N	3	1	.750	39	0	0	0	4	39^{2}	35	0	24	27	14.1	3.18	111	.243	.363	0	.000	-0	2	1	1	0.3
1966 Hou-N	1	0	1.000	10	0	0	0	0	6	9	0	6	2	22.5	7.50	46	.346	.469	0	—	0	-3	-3	-0	-0.5
Total 2	4	1	.800	49	0	0	0	4	45^{2}	44	0	30	29	15.2	3.74	93	.259	.379	0	.000	-0	-1	-1	1	-0.2

● GIOVANNI CARRARA

Carrara, Giovanni (Jimenez) b: 3/4/68, Edo Anzoategui, Venez. BR/TR, 6'2", 210 lbs. Deb: 7/29/95

YEAR TM/L	W	L	PCT	G	GS	CG	SH	SV	IP	H	HR	BB	SO	RAT	ERA	ERA+	OAV	OOB	BH	AVG	PB	PR	/A	PD	TPI
1995 Tor-A	2	4	.333	12	7	1	0	0	48^{2}	64	10	25	27	16.6	7.21	65	.320	.398	0	—	0	-14	-14	-1	-1.4
1996 Tor-A	0	1	.000	11	0	0	0	0	15	23	5	12	10	21.0	11.40	44	.359	.461	0	—	0	-11	-11	-0	-0.6
Cin-N	1	0	1.000	8	5	0	0	0	23	31	6	13	13	18.0	5.87	72	.323	.414	0	.000	-1	-4	-4	-0	-0.2
1997 Cin-N	0	1	.000	2	2	0	0	0	10^{1}	14	4	6	5	17.4	7.84	54	.333	.417	0	.000	-0	-4	-4	0	-0.3
Total 3	3	6	.333	33	14	1	0	0	97	132	25	56	55	17.7	7.61	60	.328	.414	0	.000	-1	-33	-32	-1	-2.5

● HECTOR CARRASCO

Carrasco, Hector (Pacheco) b: 10/22/69, San Pedro De Macoris, D.R. BR/TR, 6'2", 175 lbs. Deb: 4/4/94

YEAR TM/L	W	L	PCT	G	GS	CG	SH	SV	IP	H	HR	BB	SO	RAT	ERA	ERA+	OAV	OOB	BH	AVG	PB	PR	/A	PD	TPI
1994 Cin-N	5	6	.455	45	0	0	0	6	56^{1}	42	3	30	41	11.8	2.24	185	.210	.319	0	.000	-1	12	12	-0	2.2
1995 *Cin-N	2	7	.222	64	0	0	0	5	87^{1}	86	1	46	64	13.8	4.12	100	.257	.350	0	.000	-1	1	-0	-1	-0.2

YEAR	TM/L	W	L	PCT	G	GS	CG	SH	SV	IP	H	HR	BB	SO	RAT	ERA	ERA+	OAV	OOB	BH	AVG	PB	PR	/A	PD	TPI
1996	Cin-N	4	3	.571	56	0	0	0	0	74^1	58	6	45	59	12.6	3.75	113	.214	.328	1	.200	0	4	4	0	0.3
1997	Cin-N	1	2	.333	38	0	0	0	0	51^1	51	3	25	46	14.0	3.68	116	.250	.343	0	—	0	3	3	-1	0.1
	KC-A	1	6	.143	28	0	0	0	0	34^2	29	4	16	30	12.7	5.45	86	.227	.331	0	—	0	-3	-3	0	-0.5
1998	Min-A	4	2	.667	63	0	0	0	1	61^2	75	4	31	46	15.6	4.38	107	.304	.384	0	—	0	2	2	0	0.2
Total	5	17	26	.395	294	0	0	0	12	365^2	341	21	193	286	13.5	3.86	112	.246	.344	1	.056	-1	18	18	-1	2.1
● ALEX CARRASQUEL	Carrasquel, Alejandro Eloy (Aparicio) b: 7/24/12, Caracas, Venez. d: 8/19/69, Caracas, Venez. BR/TR, 6'1", 182 lbs. Deb: 4/23/39																									
1939	Was-A	5	9	.357	40	17	7	0	2	159^1	165	7	68	41	13.2	4.69	93	.266	.340	7	.167	1	-1	-6	0	-0.3
1940	Was-A	6	2	.750	28	0	0	0	0	48	42	4	29	19	13.3	4.88	86	.240	.348	0	.000	-1	-3	-4	0	-0.6
1941	Was-A	6	2	.750	35	5	4	0	2	96^2	103	7	49	30	14.2	3.44	117	.278	.364	2	.095	0	8	6	4	0.9
1942	Was-A	7	7	.500	35	15	7	1	4	152^1	161	7	53	40	12.7	3.43	107	.267	.327	6	.136	-0	4	4	1	0.5
1943	Was-A	11	7	.611	39	13	4	1	5	144^1	160	3	54	48	13.4	3.68	87	.279	.342	8	.186	1	-6	-8	1	-0.8
1944	Was-A	8	7	.533	43	7	3	0	2	134	143	8	50	35	13.1	3.43	95	.273	.339	7	.194	1	0	-3	1	0.0
1945	Was-A	7	5	.583	35	7	5	2	1	122^2	105	5	40	38	10.6	2.71	114	.228	.289	3	.083	-2	9	5	-0	0.3
1949	Chi-A	0	0	—	3	0	0	0	0	3^2	8	1	4	1	29.5	14.73	28	.421	.522	0	—	0	-4	-4	0	0.0
Total	8	50	39	.562	258	64	30	4	16	861	887	42	347	252	13.0	3.73	98	.265	.335	33	.144	0	6	-9	8	-0.0
● AMALIO CARRENO	Carreno, Amalio Rafael (Adrian) b: 4/11/64, Chacachacare, Ven. BR/TR, 6', 170 lbs. Deb: 7/7/91																									
1991	Phi-N	0	0	—	3	0	0	0	0	3^1	5	1	3	2	27.0	16.20	23	.333	.500	0	.000	-0	-5	-5	-0	0.0
● BILL CARRICK	Carrick, William Martin "Doughnut Bill" b: 9/5/1873, Erie, Pa. d: 3/7/32, Philadelphia, Pa. TR , Deb: 7/30/1898																									
1898	NY-N	3	1	.750	5	4	4	0	0	39^2	39	0	21	10	14.7	3.40	102	.255	.363	3	.167	-1	1	0	1	0.0
1899	NY-N	16	27	.372	44	43	**40**	3	0	361^2	485	4	122	60	15.6	4.65	81	.320	.378	18	.138	-6	-32	-36	2	-3.7
1900	NY-N	19	22	.463	**45**	41	32	1	0	341^2	415	7	92	63	13.7	3.53	102	.299	.348	20	.174	-3	6	3	-0	0.0
1901	Was-A	14	22	.389	42	37	34	0	0	324	367	12	93	70	13.3	3.75	98	.282	.339	20	.159	-5	-3	-3	0	-0.7
1902	Was-A	11	17	.393	31	30	28	0	0	257^2	344	10	72	36	14.8	4.86	76	.320	.368	20	.185	-2	-37	-33	-3	-3.3
Total	5	63	89	.414	167	155	138	4	0	1324^2	1650	33	400	239	14.4	4.14	89	.304	.359	81	.163	-16	-64	-68	-0	-7.7
● DON CARRITHERS	Carrithers, Donald George b: 9/15/49, Lynwood, Cal. BR/TR, 6'2", 180 lbs. Deb: 8/1/70																									
1970	SF-N	2	1	.667	11	2	0	0	0	22	31	5	14	14	18.4	7.36	54	.333	.421	0	.000	-0	-8	-8	-0	-1.0
1971	*SF-N	5	3	.625	22	12	2	1	1	80^1	77	6	37	41	13.0	4.03	84	.254	.339	3	.176	0	-5	-6	-1	-0.5
1972	SF-N	4	8	.333	25	14	2	0	1	90	108	10	42	42	15.5	5.80	60	.296	.376	6	.207	1	-23	-23	0	-2.8
1973	SF-N	1	2	.333	25	3	0	0	0	58	64	2	35	36	16.0	4.81	79	.278	.383	4	.250	0	-7	-6	1	-0.1
1974	Mon-N	5	2	.714	22	3	0	0	1	60	56	6	17	31	11.4	3.00	128	.249	.310	4	.286	0	4	6	1	0.8
1975	Mon-N	5	3	.625	19	14	5	2	0	101	90	7	38	37	11.8	3.30	116	.240	.317	6	.176	0	4	6	2	0.7
1976	Mon-N	6	12	.333	34	19	2	0	0	140^1	153	9	78	71	15.3	4.43	84	.286	.384	4	.108	-1	-14	-11	1	-1.3
1977	Min-A	0	1	.000	7	0	0	0	0	14^1	16	2	6	3	14.4	6.91	58	.271	.348	0	—	0	-5	-5	0	-0.2
Total	8	28	32	.467	165	67	11	3	3	566	595	47	267	275	14.1	4.45	83	.272	.358	27	.176	0	-55	-48	5	-4.4
● CLAY CARROLL	Carroll, Clay Palmer "Hawk" b: 5/2/41, Clanton, Ala. BR/TR, 6'1", 200 lbs. Deb: 9/2/64																									
1964	Mil-N	2	0	1.000	11	1	0	0	1	20^1	15	1	3	17	8.0	1.77	199	.200	.231	0	.000	-0	4	4	1	0.5
1965	Mil-N	0	1	.000	19	1	0	0	1	34^2	35	3	13	16	12.7	4.41	80	.269	.340	0	.000	-1	-3	-3	-0	-0.2
1966	Atl-N	8	7	.533	**73**	3	0	0	11	144^1	127	8	29	67	10.0	2.37	154	.236	.280	3	.100	-2	20	20	1	2.3
1967	Atl-N	6	12	.333	42	7	1	0	0	93	111	6	29	35	13.8	5.52	60	.304	.360	1	.063	-1	-22	-23	1	-4.0
1968	Atl-N	0	1	.000	10	0	0	0	0	22^1	26	1	6	10	12.9	4.84	62	.310	.356	0	.000	-0	-5	-5	0	-0.2
	Cin-N	7	7	.500	58	1	0	0	17	121^2	102	3	32	61	10.4	2.29	138	.230	.290	6	.250	1	9	12	1	2.2
	Yr	7	8	.467	68	1	0	0	17	144	128	4	38	71	10.8	2.69	117	.242	.300	6	.207	1	5	7	2	2.0
1969	Cin-N	12	6	.667	71	4	0	0	7	150^2	149	9	78	90	14.0	3.52	107	.262	.358	6	.207	2	1	4	3	1.0
1970	*Cin-N	9	4	.692	65	0	0	0	16	104^1	104	4	27	63	11.5	2.59	156	.259	.309	1	.071	-1	17	17	1	2.5
1971	Cin-N☆	10	4	.714	61	0	0	0	15	93^2	78	5	42	64	11.7	2.50	134	.234	.324	1	.100	-1	10	9	4	2.0
1972	*Cin-N☆	6	4	.600	**65**	0	0	0	**37**	96	89	5	32	51	11.4	2.25	143	.256	.321	2	.182	0	13	10	1	2.2
1973	*Cin-N	8	8	.500	53	5	0	0	14	92^2	111	5	34	41	14.6	3.69	92	.307	.374	3	.214	0	-0	-3	1	-0.5
1974	Cin-N	12	5	.706	57	3	0	0	6	100^2	96	3	30	46	11.3	2.15	163	.256	.311	3	.167	-0	16	15	2	2.8
1975	*Cin-N	7	5	.583	56	2	0	0	7	96^1	93	2	32	44	12.0	2.62	137	.255	.320	0	.000	-2	11	10	-1	1.1
1976	Chi-A	4	4	.500	29	0	0	0	6	77^1	67	1	24	38	10.8	2.56	139	.242	.307	0	—	0	8	9	0	1.0
1977	StL-N	4	2	.667	51	1	0	0	4	90	77	8	24	34	10.2	2.50	154	.238	.293	1	.091	-1	14	13	1	1.0
	Chi-A	1	3	.250	8	0	0	0	1	11^1	14	3	4	4	14.3	4.76	86	.311	.367	0	—	0	-1	-1	0	-0.3
1978	Pit-N	0	0	—	2	0	0	0	0	4	2	0	3	0	11.3	2.25	164	.143	.294	0	—	0	1	1	0	0.0
Total	15	96	73	.568	731	28	1	0	143	1353^1	1296	67	442	681	11.8	2.94	120	.257	.321	27	.130	-5	93	90	17	13.4
● ED CARROLL	Carroll, Edgar Fleischer b: 7/27/07, Baltimore, Md. d: 10/13/84, Rossville, Md. BR/TR, 6'3", 185 lbs. Deb: 5/1/29																									
1929	Bos-A	1	0	1.000	24	3	0	0	0	67^1	77	6	20	13	13.5	5.61	76	.291	.349	1	.063	-2	-10	-10	0	-0.3
● OWNIE CARROLL	Carroll, Owen Thomas b: 11/11/02, Kearny, N.J. d: 6/8/75, Orange, N.J. BR/TR, 5'10.5", 165 lbs. Deb: 6/20/25																									
1925	Det-A	2	2	.500	10	4	1	0	0	40^2	46	1	28	12	16.8	3.76	114	.293	.406	6	.375	1	3	2	-2	0.2
1927	Det-A	10	6	.625	31	15	8	0	0	172	186	5	73	41	13.9	3.98	106	.281	.358	12	.174	-2	3	4	2	0.3
1928	Det-A	16	12	.571	34	28	19	2	2	231	219	6	87	51	12.2	3.27	126	.262	.337	19	.194	-0	20	21	1	2.4
1929	Det-A	9	17	.346	34	26	12	0	1	202	249	10	86	54	15.3	4.63	93	.310	.383	17	.230	2	-9	-8	2	-0.5
1930	Det-A	0	5	.000	6	3	0	0	0	20^1	30	3	9	4	17.3	10.62	45	.333	.394	1	.143	-1	-13	-13	0	-2.2
	NY-A	0	1	.000	10	1	0	0	0	32^2	49	2	18	8	19.6	6.61	65	.374	.464	2	.200	0	-7	-8	1	-0.1
	Yr	0	6	.000	16	4	0	0	0	53	79	5	27	12	18.7	8.15	55	.357	.437	3	.176	-0	-21	-22	1	-2.3
	Cin-N	0	1	.000	3	2	1	0	0	14	17	3	3	0	12.9	4.50	107	.309	.345	1	.200	-0	1	1	0	0.0
1931	Cin-N	3	9	.250	29	12	4	0	0	107^1	135	6	51	24	15.9	5.53	67	.314	.392	7	.206	0	-20	-21	1	-1.9
1932	Cin-N	10	19	.345	32	26	15	0	1	210	245	7	44	55	12.8	4.50	86	.286	.328	16	.208	2	-14	-15	-1	-1.7
1933	Bro-N	13	15	.464	33	31	11	0	0	226^1	248	9	54	45	12.3	3.78	85	.281	.327	11	.149	-1	-11	-14	3	-1.4
1934	Bro-N	1	3	.250	26	5	0	0	1	74^1	108	9	33	17	17.2	6.42	61	.342	.406	6	.240	1	-19	-21	3	-0.6
Total	9	64	90	.416	248	153	71	2	5	1330^2	1532	61	486	311	14.0	4.43	89	.294	.359	98	.200	2	-68	-72	11	-5.5
● DICK CARROLL	Carroll, Richard Thomas "Shadow" b: 7/21/1884, Cleveland, Ohio d: 11/22/45, Cleveland, Ohio BR/TR, 6'2", Deb: 9/25/09																									
1909	NY-A	0	0	—	2	1	0	0	0	5	7	1	1	1	14.4	3.60	70	.292	.320	1	.500	0	-1	-1	-0	0.0
● TOM CARROLL	Carroll, Thomas Michael b: 11/5/52, Utica, N.Y. BL/TR, 6'3", 190 lbs. Deb: 7/7/74																									
1974	Cin-N	4	3	.571	16	13	0	0	0	78^1	68	11	44	37	12.9	3.68	95	.231	.331	4	.154	-1	-1	-2	-1	-0.3
1975	Cin-N	4	1	.800	12	7	0	0	0	47	52	1	26	14	15.3	4.98	72	.284	.379	0	.000	-2	-7	-7	-1	-0.9
Total	2	8	4	.667	28	20	0	0	0	125^1	120	12	70	51	13.8	4.16	85	.252	.350	4	.100	-2	-8	-9	-2	-1.2
● KID CARSEY	Carsey, Wilfred b: 10/22/1870, New York, N.Y. d: 3/29/60, Miami, Fla. BL/TR, 5'7", 168 lbs. Deb: 4/8/1891 ♦																									
1891	Was-a	14	37	.275	54	53	46	1	0	415	513	17	161	174	15.2	4.99	75	.293	.362	28	.150	-5	-58	-57	6	-5.1
1892	Phi-N	19	16	.543	43	36	30	1	1	317^2	320	6	104	76	12.4	3.12	104	.251	.314	20	.153	-3	6	5	2	0.3
1893	Phi-N	20	15	.571	39	35	30	1	0	318^1	375	7	124	50	14.6	4.81	95	.285	.355	27	.186	-7	-5	-8	2	-1.2
1894	Phi-N	18	12	.600	35	31	26	0	0	277	349	22	102	41	15.2	5.56	92	.304	.370	34	.272	3	-7	-14	2	-0.7
1895	Phi-N	24	16	.600	44	40	35	0	1	342^1	460	14	118	64	15.7	4.92	97	.317	.376	41	.291	3	-5	-5	-1	-0.3
1896	Phi-N	11	11	.500	27	21	18	1	1	187^1	273	4	72	36	17.0	5.62	77	.337	.397	18	.222	1	-26	-27	1	-2.2
1897	Phi-N	2	1	.667	4	4	2	0	0	28	35	0	16	1	16.7	5.14	82	.304	.394	3	.231	-1	-3	-3	-0	-0.3
	StL-N	3	8	.273	12	11	11	0	0	99	133	5	31	14	15.3	6.00	73	.319	.372	13	.302	2	-19	-18	1	-1.2
	Yr	5	9	.357	16	15	13	0	0	127	168	5	47	15	15.5	5.81	75	.315	.375	16	.286	2	-21	-20	1	-1.5
1898	StL-N	2	12	.143	20	13	10	0	0	123^2	177	2	37	10	16.3	6.33	60	.333	.387	21	.200	-0	-37	-35	2	-3.0
1899	Cle-N	1	8	.111	10	9	8	0	0	77^2	109	2	24	11	15.6	5.68	65	.330	.379	10	.278	1	-16	-17	1	-1.3
	Was-N	1	2	.333	4	3	2	0	0	29	27	0	4	3	9.9	3.72	105	.248	.281	0	.000	-2	0	1	1	-0.1
	Yr	2	10	.167	14	12	10	0	0	106^2	136	2	28	14	13.9	5.15	73	.308	.351	10	.213	-1	-15	-17	2	-1.4
1901	Bro-N	1	0	1.000	2	0	0	0	0	7	9	1	3	4	16.7	10.29	33	.310	.394	0	.000	-0	-5	-5	-0	-0.6
Total	10	116	138	.457	294	256	218	4	3	2222	2780	80	796	484	15.0	4.95	85	.300	.363	221	.213	-8	-175	-183	14	-15.7

YEAR	TM/L	W	L	PCT	G	GS	CG	SH	SV	IP	H	HR	BB	SO	RAT	ERA	ERA+	OAV	OOB	BH	AVG	PB	PR	/A	PD	TPI
● **AL CARSON**	Carson, Albert James "Soldier" b: 8/22/1882, Chicago, Ill. d: 11/26/62, San Diego, Cal. TR , Deb: 5/6/10																									
1910	Chi-N	0	0	—	2	0	0	0	0	6^2	6	0	1	2	9.5	4.05	71	.240	.269	0	.000	0	-1	-1	0	0.0
● **ANDY CARTER**	Carter, Andrew Godfrey b: 11/9/68, Philadelphia, Pa. BL/TL, 6'5", 200 lbs. Deb: 5/3/94																									
1994	Phi-N	0	2	.000	20	0	0	0	0	34^1	34	5	12	18	13.6	4.46	96	.268	.359	0	.000	-1	-1	-1	-1	-0.2
1995	Phi-N	0	0	—	4	0	0	0	0	7^1	4	3	2	6	8.6	6.14	69	.167	.259	1	1.000	0	-2	-2	-0	0.0
Total	2	0	2	.000	24	0	0	0	0	41^2	38	8	14	24	12.7	4.75	90	.252	.343	1	.143	-0	-3	-2	-1	-0.2
● **ARNOLD CARTER**	Carter, Arnold Lee "Hook" or "Lefty" b: 3/14/18, Rainelle, W.Va. d: 4/12/89, Louisville, Ky. BL/TL, 5'10", 170 lbs. Deb: 4/29/44																									
1944	Cin-N	11	7	.611	33	18	9	3	3	148^2	143	1	40	33	11.3	2.60	134	.256	.309	12	.250	5	17	15	1	2.4
1945	Cin-N	2	4	.333	13	6	2	1	0	46^2	54	2	13	4	13.3	3.09	122	.286	.338	3	.176	0	4	3	0	0.5
Total	2	13	11	.542	46	24	11	4	3	195^1	197	3	53	37	11.7	2.72	131	.264	.317	15	.231	5	20	18	1	2.9
● **NICK CARTER**	Carter, Conrad Powell b: 5/19/1879, Oatlands, Va. d: 11/23/61, Grasonville, Md. BR/TR, 5'8", 140 lbs. Deb: 4/14/08																									
1908	Phi-A	2	5	.286	14	4	2	0	0	60^2	58	1	17	17	11.4	2.97	86	.270	.329	2	.100	-2	-4	-3	1	-0.4
● **JEFF CARTER**	Carter, Jeffrey Allen b: 12/3/64, Tampa, Fla. BR/TR, 6'3", 195 lbs. Deb: 7/31/91																									
1991	Chi-A	0	1	.000	5	2	0	0	0	12	8	1	5	2	9.8	5.25	76	.182	.265	0	—	0	-2	-2	-0	-0.2
● **LARRY CARTER**	Carter, Larry Gene b: 5/22/65, Charleston, W.Va. BR/TR, 6'5", 195 lbs. Deb: 9/6/92																									
1992	SF-N	1	5	.167	6	6	0	0	0	33	34	6	18	21	14.2	4.64	71	.270	.361	2	.200	1	-4	-5	-1	-0.8
● **PAUL CARTER**	Carter, Paul Warren "Nick" b: 5/1/1894, Lake Park, Ga. d: 9/11/84, Lake Park, Ga. BL/TR, 6'3", 175 lbs. Deb: 9/15/14																									
1914	Cle-A	1	3	.250	5	4	1	0	0	24^2	35	0	5	9	14.6	2.92	99	.340	.370	0	.000	-1	-0	-0	-0	-0.1
1915	Cle-A	1	1	.500	11	2	2	0	0	42	44	1	18	14	13.3	3.21	95	.272	.344	3	.214	1	-1	-1	1	0.1
1916	Chi-N	2	2	.500	8	5	2	0	0	36	26	1	17	14	10.8	2.75	106	.203	.297	2	.167	-0	-1	1	1	0.2
1917	Chi-N	5	8	.385	23	13	6	0	2	113^1	115	2	19	34	10.9	3.26	89	.276	.313	6	.171	-0	-7	-4	-1	-0.7
1918	Chi-N	3	2	.600	21	4	1	0	2	73	78	2	19	13	12.1	2.71	103	.290	.339	6	.240	0	0	1	2	0.2
1919	Chi-N	5	4	.556	28	7	2	0	1	85	81	1	28	17	11.8	2.65	109	.252	.316	7	.269	1	3	2	-0	0.3
1920	Chi-N	3	6	.333	31	8	2	0	2	106	131	3	36	14	14.6	4.67	69	.324	.387	6	.171	-1	-18	-17	-2	-1.7
Total	7	20	26	.435	127	43	16	0	7	480	510	10	142	115	12.4	3.32	89	.283	.339	30	.195	-1	-24	-19	1	-1.7
● **SOL CARTER**	Carter, Solomon Mobley "Buck" b: 12/23/08, Picayune, Miss. BR/TR, 6', 178 lbs. Deb: 4/15/31																									
1931	Phi-A	0	0	—	2	0	0	0	0	2^1	1	0	4	1	19.3	19.29	23	.143	.455	0	—	0	-4	-4	1	0.0
● **BOB CARUTHERS**	Caruthers, Robert Lee "Parisian Bob" b: 1/5/1864, Memphis, Tenn. d: 8/5/11, Peoria, Ill. BL/TR, 5'7", 138 lbs. Deb: 9/7/1884 MU ♦																									
1884	StL-a	7	2	.778	13	7	7	0	0	82^2	61	1	15	58	8.6	2.61	125	.189	.232	22	.268	2	6	6	-1	0.6
1885	*StL-a	**40**	13	**.755**	53	53	53	6	0	482^1	430	3	57	190	9.4	**2.07**	**158**	.230	.260	50	.225	6	**63**	**64**	0	6.6
1886	*StL-a	30	14	.682	44	43	42	2	0	387^1	323	3	86	166	9.7	2.32	148	.217	.263	106	.334	26	48	48	-2	6.8
1887	*StL-a	29	9	**.763**	39	39	39	2	0	341	337	6	61	74	10.9	3.30	138	.247	.287	130	.357	20	38	47	7	6.2
1888	Bro-a	29	15	.659	44	43	42	4	0	391^2	337	4	53	140	9.2	2.39	125	.224	.255	77	.230	10	29	26	1	3.5
1889	*Bro-a	**40**	11	**.784**	56	50	46	**7**	1	445	444	16	104	118	11.3	3.13	119	.252	.298	43	.250	17	35	29	2	4.2
1890	*Bro-N	23	11	.676	37	33	30	1	0	300	292	9	87	64	11.7	3.09	111	.247	.305	63	.265	11	16	12	3	2.2
1891	Bro-N	18	14	.563	38	32	29	2	1	297	323	7	107	69	13.4	3.12	106	.267	.333	48	.281	11	7	6	1	1.7
1892	StL-N	2	10	.167	16	10	10	0	1	101^2	131	10	27	21	14.5	5.84	55	.300	.350	142	.277	6	-29	-30	0	-2.4
Total	9	218	99	.688	340	310	298	24	3	2828^2	2678	59	597	900	10.7	2.83	123	.240	.285	695	.282	111	214	206	11	29.4
● **CHUCK CARY**	Cary, Charles Douglas b: 3/3/60, Whittier, Cal. BL/TL, 6'4", 210 lbs. Deb: 8/22/85																									
1985	Det-A	0	1	.000	16	0	0	0	2	23^2	16	2	8	22	9.9	3.42	119	.190	.277	0	—	0	2	2	-0	0.1
1986	Det-A	1	2	.333	22	0	0	0	0	31^2	33	3	15	21	13.6	3.41	121	.273	.353	0	—	0	3	3	-0	0.2
1987	Atl-N	1	1	.500	13	0	0	0	1	16^2	17	3	4	15	11.9	3.78	115	.266	.319	0	.000	-0	1	1	0	0.1
1988	Atl-N	0	0	—	7	0	0	0	0	8^1	8	1	4	7	14.0	6.48	57	.250	.351	0	—	0	-3	-3	-0	0.0
1989	NY-A	4	4	.500	22	11	2	0	0	99^1	78	13	29	79	9.7	3.26	119	.209	.266	0	—	0	7	7	-2	0.4
1990	NY-A	6	12	.333	28	27	2	0	0	156^2	155	21	55	134	12.1	4.19	95	.260	.323	0	—	0	-5	-4	-1	-0.5
1991	NY-A	1	6	.143	10	9	0	0	0	53^1	61	6	32	34	15.7	5.91	70	.285	.378	0	—	0	-11	-10	-0	-1.2
1993	Chi-A	1	0	1.000	16	0	0	0	0	20^2	22	1	11	10	15.7	5.23	80	.286	.396	0	—	0	-2	-2	0	0.1
Total	8	14	26	.350	134	47	4	0	3	410^1	390	50	158	322	12.2	4.17	96	.250	.322	0	.000	-0	-9	-7	-4	-0.8
● **SCOTT CARY**	Cary, Scott Russell "Red" b: 4/11/23, Kendallville, Ind. BL/TL, 5'11.5", 168 lbs. Deb: 5/1/47																									
1947	Was-A	3	1	.750	23	3	1	0	0	54^2	73	5	20	25	15.5	5.93	63	.312	.369	1	.077	-1	-13	-13	-1	-1.0
● **JERRY CASALE**	Casale, Jerry Joseph b: 9/27/33, Brooklyn, N.Y. BR/TR, 6'2", 200 lbs. Deb: 9/14/58																									
1958	Bos-A	0	0	—	2	0	0	0	0	3	1	0	2	3	9.0	0.00	—	.111	.273	0	—	0	1	1	0	0.0
1959	Bos-A	13	8	.619	31	26	9	3	0	179^2	162	20	89	93	12.8	4.31	94	.238	.331	10	.169	3	-9	-5	-4	-0.7
1960	Bos-A	2	9	.182	29	14	1	0	0	96^1	113	14	67	54	16.9	6.17	66	.294	.400	9	.273	3	-25	-23	-0	-2.0
1961	LA-A	1	5	.167	13	7	0	0	1	42^2	52	9	25	35	16.5	6.54	69	.297	.388	6	.462	3	-12	-10	-0	-0.9
	Det-A	0	0	—	3	1	0	0	0	12	15	3	3	6	13.5	5.25	78	.313	.353	0	.000	-0	-2	-2	0	0.0
	Yr	1	5	.167	16	8	0	0	1	54^2	67	12	28	41	15.6	6.26	71	.298	.375	6	.375	3	-14	-11	-0	-0.9
1962	Det-A	1	2	.333	18	1	0	0	0	36^2	33	5	18	16	12.5	4.66	87	.236	.323	0	.000	-1	-3	-2	0	-0.2
Total	5	17	24	.415	96	49	10	3	1	370^1	376	51	204	207	14.3	5.08	81	.262	.356	25	.216	7	-49	-40	-5	-3.8
● **JOE CASCARELLA**	Cascarella, Joseph Thomas "Crooning Joe" b: 6/28/07, Philadelphia, Pa. BR/TR, 5'10.5", 175 lbs. Deb: 4/17/34																									
1934	Phi-A	12	15	.444	42	22	9	2	1	194^1	214	8	104	71	14.9	4.68	94	.288	.377	6	.094	-4	-4	-6	2	-0.9
1935	Phi-A	1	6	.143	9	3	1	0	0	32^1	29	1	22	15	14.2	5.29	86	.252	.372	1	.125	-1	-3	-3	2	-0.4
	Bos-A	0	3	.000	6	4	0	0	0	17	25	3	11	9	19.1	6.88	69	.329	.414	0	.000	-0	-5	-4	0	-0.6
	Yr	1	9	.100	15	7	1	0	0	49^1	54	4	33	24	15.9	5.84	79	.283	.388	1	.100	-1	-8	-7	2	-1.0
1936	Bos-A	0	2	.000	10	1	0	0	0	20^2	27	0	9	7	15.7	6.97	76	.329	.396	0	.000	-1	-4	-4	0	-0.3
	Was-A	9	8	.529	22	16	7	1	1	139^1	147	7	54	34	13.4	4.07	117	.276	.349	7	.143	-2	15	11	-2	0.7
	Yr	9	10	.474	32	17	7	1	1	160	174	7	63	41	13.7	4.44	109	.283	.355	7	.132	-3	11	7	-2	0.4
1937	Was-A	0	5	.000	10	4	1	0	1	32^1	50	3	23	10	20.6	8.07	55	.347	.440	2	.222	-0	-12	-13	0	-1.6
	Cin-N	1	2	.333	11	3	2	0	1	43^2	44	1	22	16	13.6	3.92	95	.263	.349	1	.091	-1	-0	-1	-0	-0.1
1938	Cin-N	4	7	.364	33	1	0	0	4	61	66	2	22	30	13.0	4.57	80	.275	.336	3	.167	-1	-5	-6	-0	-1.2
Total	5	27	48	.360	143	54	20	3	8	540^2	602	25	267	192	14.6	4.84	91	.287	.370	20	.121	-9	-19	-26	1	-4.4
● **CHARLIE CASE**	Case, Charles Emmett b: 9/7/1879, Smith Landing, O. d: 4/16/64, Batavia, Ohio BR/TR, 6', 170 lbs. Deb: 7/5/01																									
1901	Cin-N	1	2	.333	3	3	3	0	0	27	34	0	6	5	13.3	4.67	69	.306	.342	1	.100	-1	-4	-4	-0	-0.5
1904	Pit-N	10	5	.667	18	17	14	3	0	141	129	0	31	49	10.5	2.94	93	.243	.290	9	.170	1	-3	-3	1	-0.2
1905	Pit-N	11	11	.500	31	24	18	3	1	217	202	2	66	57	11.7	2.57	117	.251	.319	7	.103	-2	10	10	-3	0.5
1906	Pit-N	1	1	.500	2	2	1	0	0	11	8	0	5	3	11.5	5.73	47	.190	.292	1	.500	1	-4	-4	0	-0.5
Total	4	23	19	.548	54	46	36	6	1	396	373	2	108	114	11.4	2.93	99	.251	.310	18	.135	-1	-0	-1	-3	-0.7
● **DAN CASEY**	Casey, Daniel Maurice b: 11/20/1862, Binghamton, N.Y. d: 2/8/43, Washington, D.C. BR/TL, 6', 180 lbs. Deb: 8/18/1884 F																									
1884	Wil-U	1	1	.500	2	2	2	0	0	18	23	0	4	10	13.5	1.00	266	.291	.325	1	.167	-1	3	3	-0	0.2
1885	Det-N	4	8	.333	12	12	12	1	0	104	105	1	35	79	12.1	3.29	86	.256	.315	5	.116	-3	-5	-5	1	-0.7
1886	Phi-N	24	18	.571	44	44	39	4	0	369	326	8	104	193	10.5	2.41	137	.223	.275	23	.152	-5	37	36	-1	2.9
1887	Phi-N	28	13	.683	45	45	43	**4**	0	390^1	377	15	115	119	11.7	**2.86**	**148**	.246	.305	27	.165	-11	53	60	-2	3.7
1888	Phi-N	14	18	.438	33	33	31	2	0	285^2	298	6	48	108	11.1	3.15	94	.259	.291	18	.153	-4	-10	-6	1	-0.9
1889	Phi-N	6	10	.375	20	20	15	1	0	152^2	170	4	72	65	14.7	3.77	115	.273	.356	15	.221	-2	4	10	0	0.7
1890	Syr-a	19	22	.463	45	42	40	2	0	360^2	365	8	165	169	13.6	4.14	85	.255	.337	26	.162	-4	-11	-24	2	-2.3
Total	7	96	90	.516	201	198	182	14	0	1680^1	1664	42	543	743	12.0	3.18	113	.249	.309	115	.162	-27	71	75	1	3.6

YEAR	TM/L	W	L	PCT	G	GS	CG	SH	SV	IP	H	HR	BB	SO	RAT	ERA	ERA+	OAV	OOB	BH	AVG	PB	PR	/A	PD	TPI
● **HUGH CASEY** Casey, Hugh Thomas b: 10/14/13, Atlanta, Ga. d: 7/3/51, Atlanta, Ga. BR/TR, 6′1″, 207 lbs. Deb: 4/29/35																										
1935	Chi-N	0	0	—	13	0	0	0	0	25^2	29	2	14	10	15.1	3.86	102	.279	.364	1	.167	-0	0	0	0	0.0
1939	Bro-N	15	10	.600	40	25	15	0	1	227^1	228	13	54	79	11.6	2.93	137	.260	.311	15	.203	0	25	28	2	3.1
1940	Bro-N	11	8	.579	44	10	5	2	2	154	136	13	51	53	11.3	3.62	110	.237	.306	9	.250	2	4	6	1	1.0
1941	*Bro-N	14	11	.560	45	18	4	1	7	162	155	8	57	61	11.8	3.89	94	.251	.316	6	.120	-1	-5	-4	2	-0.6
1942	Bro-N	6	3	.667	50	2	0	0	**13**	112	91	3	44	54	11.0	2.25	145	.221	.300	4	.148	-0	13	13	-1	1.2
1946	Bro-N	11	5	.688	46	1	0	0	5	99^2	101	2	33	31	12.3	1.99	170	.267	.329	3	.136	-1	**16**	**15**	3	2.9
1947	*Bro-N	10	4	.714	46	0	0	0	**18**	76^2	75	7	29	40	12.4	3.99	104	.260	.331	1	.056	-1	1	1	0	0.1
1948	Bro-N	3	0	1.000	22	0	0	0	4	36	59	6	17	7	19.5	8.00	50	.391	.459	0	.000	-1	-16	-16	-0	-1.6
1949	Pit-N	4	1	.800	33	0	0	0	5	38^2	50	4	14	9	15.1	4.66	90	.314	.374	1	.333	0	-3	-2	-2	-0.4
	NY-A	1	0	1.000	4	0	0	0	0	7^2	11	0	8	5	22.3	8.22	49	.324	.452	0	.000	-0	-3	-4	-0	-0.4
Total	9	75	42	.641	343	56	24	3	55	939^2	935	58	321	349	12.3	3.45	110	.260	.325	40	.164	-2	32	38	6	5.3
● **BILL CASEY** Casey, William B. b: St.Louis, Mo. Deb: 8/17/1887																										
1887	Phi-a	0	0	—	1	0	0	0	0	1	4	0	1	0	45.0	18.00	24	.667	.714	0	—	0	-2	-2	-0	0.0
● **CARL CASHION** Cashion, Jay Carl b: 6/6/1891, Mecklenburg Co, N.C. d: 11/17/35, Lake Millicent, Wis. BL/TR, 6′2″, 200 lbs. Deb: 8/4/11																										
1911	Was-A	1	5	.167	11	9	5	0	0	71^1	67	4	47	26	15.3	4.16	79	.220	.338	12	.324	2	-6	-7	1	-0.2
1912	Was-A	10	6	.625	26	17	13	1	1	170^1	150	4	103	84	13.6	3.17	105	.250	.365	22	.214	2	3	3	-1	0.5
1913	Was-A	1	1	.500	4	3	0	0	0	9	7	0	14	3	24.0	6.00	49	.269	.558	3	.250	0	-3	-3	0	-0.5
1914	Was-A	0	1	.000	2	1	0	0	0	5	4	0	6	1	19.8	10.80	26	.250	.478	0	.000	-0	-4	-4	0	-0.7
Total	4	12	13	.480	43	30	18	1	1	255^2	228	8	170	114	14.6	3.70	89	.241	.366	37	.242	5	-11	-11	1	-0.9
● **LARRY CASIAN** Casian, Lawrence Paul b: 10/28/65, Lynwood, Cal. BR/TL, 6′, 170 lbs. Deb: 9/9/90																										
1990	Min-A	2	1	.667	5	3	0	0	0	22^1	26	2	4	11	12.1	3.22	129	.306	.337	0	—	0	2	2	-0	0.3
1991	Min-A	0	0	—	15	0	0	0	0	18^1	28	4	7	6	17.7	7.36	58	.354	.414	0	—	0	-7	-6	0	-0.3
1992	Min-A	1	0	1.000	6	0	0	0	0	6^2	7	0	1	2	10.8	2.70	150	.259	.286	0	—	0	1	1	0	-0.1
1993	Min-A	5	3	.625	54	0	0	0	1	56^2	59	1	14	31	11.8	3.02	144	.268	.315	0	—	0	8	8	-1	1.0
1994	Min-A	1	3	.250	33	0	0	0	1	40^2	57	11	12	18	15.7	7.08	69	.343	.394	0	—	0	-10	-10	1	-0.8
	Cle-A	0	2	.000	7	0	0	0	0	8^1	16	1	4	2	21.6	8.64	55	.421	.476	0	—	0	-4	-4	0	-0.7
	Yr	1	5	.167	40	0	0	0	1	49	73	12	16	20	16.3	7.35	66	.351	.397	0	—	0	-14	-14	1	-1.5
1995	Chi-N	1	0	1.000	42	0	0	0	0	23^1	23	1	15	11	14.7	1.93	213	.258	.365	0	.000	-0	6	6	0	0.2
1996	Chi-N	1	1	.500	35	0	0	0	0	24	14	2	11	15	9.8	1.88	231	.187	.299	0	—	0	6	7	0	0.5
1997	Chi-N	0	1	.000	12	0	0	0	0	9^2	16	3	2	7	17.7	7.45	58	.364	.404	0	.000	-0	-3	-3	-0	-0.3
	KC-A	0	2	.000	32	0	0	0	0	26^2	32	5	6	16	12.8	5.06	93	.299	.336	0	—	0	-1	-1	0	-0.1
1998	Chi-A	0	0	—	4	0	0	0	0	4	8	0	1	6	24.8	11.25	40	.400	.478	0	—	0	-3	-3	0	0.0
Total	9	11	13	.458	245	3	0	0	2	240^2	286	30	77	125	13.9	4.56	97	.301	.358	0	.000	-0	-6	-3	2	-0.3
● **CRAIG CASKEY** Caskey, Craig Douglas b: 12/11/49, Visalia, Cal. BB/TL, 5′11″, 185 lbs. Deb: 7/19/73																										
1973	Mon-N	0	0	—	9	1	0	0	0	14^1	15	3	4	6	12.6	5.65	67	.278	.339	0	.000	-0	-3	-3	0	0.0
● **ED CASSIAN** Cassian, Edward T. b: 11/8/1867, Wilbraham, Mass. d: 9/10/18, Meriden, Conn. TR, 5′8″, 160 lbs. Deb: 6/26/1891																										
1891	Phi-N	1	3	.250	6	4	3	0	0	38	40	0	16	10	14.0	2.84	120	.260	.341	2	.118	-1	2	2	1	0.1
	Was-a	2	4	.333	7	5	5	0	0	53	73	4	35	14	19.2	5.60	67	.316	.417	9	.346	2	-11	-11	0	-0.7
Total	1	3	7	.300	13	9	8	0	0	91	113	4	51	24	17.0	4.45	81	.294	.387	11	.256	1	-9	-9	1	-0.6
● **JOHN CASSIDY** Cassidy, John P. b: 1857, Brooklyn, N.Y. d: 7/2/1891, Brooklyn, N.Y. BR/TL, 5′8″, 168 lbs. Deb: 4/24/1875 ♦																										
1875	Atl-n	1	21	.045	30	22	18	0	0	213^2	284	3	11	9	12.4	3.03	69	.277	.285	29	.175	-3	-19	-23		-1.9
1877	Har-N	1	1	.500	2	2	2	0	0	18	24	0	1	2	12.5	5.00	49	.320	.329	95	.378	1	-4	-5	-0	-0.4
● **GEORGE CASTER** Caster, George Jasper "Ug" b: 8/4/07, Colton, Cal. d: 12/18/55, Lakewood, Cal. BR/TR, 6′1.5″, 180 lbs. Deb: 9/10/34																										
1934	Phi-A	3	2	.600	5	3	2	0	0	37	32	3	14	15	11.9	3.41	129	.235	.320	4	.267	0	4	4	1	0.6
1935	Phi-A	1	4	.200	25	1	0	0	1	63^1	86	8	37	24	17.8	6.25	73	.322	.408	5	.227	0	-13	-12	2	-0.7
1937	Phi-A	12	19	.387	34	33	19	3	0	231^2	227	23	107	100	13.1	4.43	106	.258	.339	19	.211	-1	5	7	0	0.8
1938	Phi-A	16	20	.444	42	40	20	2	1	281^1	310	25	117	112	13.8	4.35	111	.277	.347	20	.198	1	14	15	-2	1.6
1939	Phi-A	9	9	.500	28	17	7	1	0	136	144	16	45	59	12.7	4.90	96	.276	.337	9	.209	-1	-4	-3	0	-0.4
1940	Phi-A	4	19	.174	36	24	11	0	2	178^1	234	18	69	75	15.4	6.56	68	.312	.372	8	.129	-3	-43	-42	-1	-4.7
1941	StL-A	3	7	.300	32	9	3	0	3	104^1	105	12	37	36	12.4	5.00	86	.259	.324	3	.103	-2	-10	-8	1	-0.8
1942	StL-A	8	2	.800	39	0	0	0	5	80	62	3	39	34	11.7	2.81	132	.217	.317	1	.067	-1	8	8	1	1.0
1943	StL-A	6	8	.429	35	0	0	0	8	76^1	69	4	41	43	13.1	2.12	157	.246	.345	3	.136	-1	10	10	0	2.1
1944	StL-A	6	6	.500	42	0	0	0	**12**	81	91	5	33	46	13.8	2.44	147	.284	.351	5	.250	0	9	10	-0	1.9
1945	StL-A	1	2	.333	10	0	0	0	1	15^2	20	0	7	9	15.5	6.89	51	.308	.375	1	.333	0	-6	-6	-0	-1.1
	*Det-A	5	1	.833	22	0	0	0	2	51^1	47	3	27	23	13.3	3.86	91	.250	.350	2	.182	0	-3	-2	-0	-0.2
	Yr	6	3	.667	32	0	0	0	3	67	67	3	34	32	13.8	4.57	77	.265	.356	3	.214	0	-9	-8	-0	-1.3
1946	Det-A	2	1	.667	26	0	0	0	4	41^1	42	1	24	19	14.6	5.66	65	.264	.364	1	.143	-0	-10	-9	1	-0.8
Total	12	76	100	.432	376	127	62	6	39	1377^2	1469	121	597	595	13.7	4.54	96	.273	.349	81	.184	-7	-39	-27	2	-0.7
● **TONY CASTILLO** Castillo, Antonio Jose (Jimenez) b: 3/1/63, Quibor, Venez. BL/TL, 5′10″, 188 lbs. Deb: 8/14/88																										
1988	Tor-A	1	0	1.000	14	0	0	0	0	15	10	2	2	14	7.2	3.00	131	.200	.231	0	—	0	2	2	0	0.1
1989	Tor-A	1	1	.500	17	0	0	0	1	17^2	23	0	10	10	17.3	6.11	62	.333	.425	0	—	0	-4	-5	-0	-0.4
	Atl-N	0	1	.000	12	0	0	0	0	9^1	8	0	4	5	11.6	4.82	76	.222	.300	0	.000	-0	-1	-1	0	-0.1
1990	Atl-N	5	1	.833	52	3	0	0	1	76^2	93	5	20	64	13.4	4.23	95	.302	.347	1	.143	0	-4	-2	1	0.0
1991	Atl-N	1	1	.500	7	0	0	0	0	8^2	13	3	5	8	18.7	7.27	53	.342	.419	0	—	0	-3	-3	-0	-0.7
	NY-N	1	0	1.000	10	3	0	0	0	23^2	27	1	6	10	12.5	1.90	191	.281	.324	0	.000	-0	5	5	1	0.2
	Yr	2	1	.667	17	3	0	0	0	32^1	40	4	11	18	14.2	3.34	111	.299	.352	0	.000	-0	1	1	0	-0.5
1993	*Tor-A	3	2	.600	51	0	0	0	0	50^2	44	4	22	28	11.7	3.38	128	.242	.324	0	—	0	5	5	0	0.5
1994	Tor-A	5	2	.714	41	0	0	0	1	68	66	7	28	43	12.8	2.51	192	.260	.340	0	—	0	17	17	1	1.7
1995	Tor-A	1	5	.167	55	0	0	0	13	72^2	64	7	24	38	11.3	3.22	146	.243	.314	0	—	0	12	12	-0	1.2
1996	Tor-A	2	3	.400	40	0	0	0	1	72^1	72	9	20	48	11.7	4.23	118	.260	.314	0	—	0	6	6	1	0.5
	Chi-A	3	1	.750	15	0	0	0	1	22^2	23	1	4	9	11.1	1.59	299	.267	.308	0	—	0	9	8	-0	1.3
	Yr	5	4	.556	55	0	0	0	2	95	95	10	24	57	11.4	3.60	137	.259	.306	0	—	0	15	14	1	1.8
1997	Chi-A	4	4	.500	64	0	0	0	4	62^1	74	6	23	42	14.1	4.91	89	.296	.358	0	.000	-0	-2	-4	2	-0.3
1998	Chi-A	1	2	.333	25	0	0	0	0	27	38	7	11	14	17.0	8.00	57	.328	.395	0	—	0	-10	-10	1	-0.8
Total	10	28	23	.549	403	6	0	0	22	526^2	555	52	179	333	12.8	3.93	113	.274	.337	1	.077	-1	30	31	6	3.2
● **CARLOS CASTILLO** Castillo, Carlos b: 4/21/75, Boston, Mass. BR/TR, 6′2″, 240 lbs. Deb: 4/2/97																										
1997	Chi-A	2	1	.667	37	2	0	0	1	66^1	68	9	33	43	13.8	4.48	98	.265	.351	1	1.000	0	1	-1	-1	-0.1
1998	Chi-A	6	4	.600	54	2	0	0	0	100^1	94	17	35	64	12.0	5.11	89	.246	.318	0	.000	-0	-5	-6	0	-0.5
Total	2	8	5	.615	91	4	0	0	1	166^2	162	26	68	107	12.7	4.86	92	.254	.331	1	.500	0	-5	-7	-1	-0.6
● **MANNY CASTILLO** Castillo, Esteban Manuel Antonio (Cabrera) b: 4/1/57, Santo Domingo, D.R. BB/TR, 5′9″, 160 lbs. Deb: 9/1/80 ♦																										
1983	Sea-A	0	0	—	1	0	0	0	0	2^2	8	3	3	2	40.5	23.63	18	.533	.632	42	.207	0	-6	-6	-0	0.0
● **FRANK CASTILLO** Castillo, Frank Anthony b: 4/1/69, ElPaso, Tex. BR/TR, 6′1″, 190 lbs. Deb: 6/27/91																										
1991	Chi-N	6	7	.462	18	18	4	0	0	111^2	107	5	33	73	11.3	4.35	89	.252	.306	5	.143	-0	-8	-6	-0	-0.7
1992	Chi-N	10	11	.476	33	33	0	0	0	205^1	179	19	63	135	10.9	3.46	104	.232	.295	6	.092	-2	1	3	-1	0.0
1993	Chi-N	5	8	.385	29	25	2	0	0	141^1	162	20	39	84	13.4	4.84	82	.293	.349	7	.163	-0	-13	-13	3	-0.9
1994	Chi-N	2	1	.667	4	4	1	0	0	23	25	3	5	19	11.7	4.30	96	.278	.316	0	.000	-1	-0	-0	-0	-0.1
1995	Chi-N	11	10	.524	29	29	2	2	0	188	179	22	52	135	11.3	3.21	128	.248	.303	6	.102	-2	20	19	-1	1.6
1996	Chi-N	7	16	.304	33	33	1	1	0	182^1	209	28	46	139	13.0	5.28	82	.288	.337	5	.088	-3	-22	-19	0	-2.3
1997	Chi-N	6	9	.400	20	19	0	0	0	98	113	9	44	67	14.8	5.42	79	.292	.370	5	.152	-1	-13	-12	-0	-1.7

YEAR TM/L	W	L	PCT	G	GS	CG	SH	SV	IP	H	HR	BB	SO	RAT	ERA	ERA+	OAV	OOB	BH	AVG	PB	PR	/A	PD	TPI
Col-N	6	3	.667	14	14	0	0	0	86^1	107	16	25	59	14.2	5.42	95	.308	.362	2	.080	-2	-12	-2	-1	-0.5
Yr	12	12	.500	34	33	0	0	0	184^1	220	25	69	126	14.3	5.42	87	.298	.361	7	.121	-2	-25	-15	-1	-2.2
1998 Det-A	3	9	.250	27	19	0	0	1	116	150	17	44	81	15.4	6.83	69	.316	.380	0	.000	-0	-28	-27	-0	-2.4
Total 8	56	74	.431	207	194	10	3	1	1152	1231	139	351	792	12.7	4.63	90	.274	.332	36	.110	-11	-75	-59	-1	-7.0

● JUAN CASTILLO

Castillo, Juan Francisco (Azdura) b: 6/23/70, Caracas, Venez. BR/TR, 6'5", 205 lbs. Deb: 7/26/94

YEAR TM/L	W	L	PCT	G	GS	CG	SH	SV	IP	H	HR	BB	SO	RAT	ERA	ERA+	OAV	OOB	BH	AVG	PB	PR	/A	PD	TPI
1994 NY-N	0	0	—	2	2	0	0	0	11^2	17	2	5	1	17.0	6.94	60	.362	.423	1	.200	0	-4	-4	1	0.1

● BOBBY CASTILLO

Castillo, Robert Ernie b: 4/18/55, Los Angeles, Cal. BR/TR, 5'10", 170 lbs. Deb: 9/10/77

YEAR TM/L	W	L	PCT	G	GS	CG	SH	SV	IP	H	HR	BB	SO	RAT	ERA	ERA+	OAV	OOB	BH	AVG	PB	PR	/A	PD	TPI
1977 LA-N	1	0	1.000	6	1	0	0	0	11^1	12	2	2	7	11.1	3.97	96	.279	.311	0	.000	-0	-0	-0	0	0.0
1978 LA-N	0	4	.000	18	0	0	0	1	34	28	2	33	30	16.1	3.97	88	.239	.407	0	.000	-1	-1	-2	0	-0.3
1979 LA-N	2	0	1.000	19	0	0	0	7	24^1	26	0	13	25	14.8	1.11	328	.277	.370	0	.000	-0	7	7	0	0.9
1980 LA-N	8	6	.571	61	0	0	0	5	98^1	70	4	45	60	10.6	2.75	127	.206	.301	1	.111	-0	9	8	1	1.2
1981 *LA-N	2	4	.333	34	1	0	0	5	50^2	50	5	24	35	13.1	5.33	62	.262	.344	4	.444	2	-10	-11	-1	-1.3
1982 Min-A	13	11	.542	40	25	6	1	0	218^2	194	26	85	123	11.5	3.66	116	.241	.313	0	—	0	10	14	-2	1.2
1983 Min-A	8	12	.400	27	25	3	0	0	158^1	170	17	65	90	13.4	4.77	89	.278	.348	0	—	0	-13	-9	1	-1.0
1984 Min-A	2	1	.667	10	2	0	0	0	25^1	14	2	19	7	11.7	1.78	237	.177	.337	0	—	0	6	7	-0	0.6
1985 *LA-N	2	2	.500	35	5	0	0	0	68	59	9	41	57	13.4	5.43	64	.230	.339	1	.100	-0	-14	-15	0	-0.8
Total 9	38	40	.487	250	59	9	1	18	689	623	67	327	434	12.5	3.94	99	.246	.333	6	.154	0	-6	-2	-1	0.5

● SLICK CASTLEMAN

Castleman, Clydell b: 9/8/13, Donelson, Tenn. d: 3/2/98, Nashville, Tenn. BR/TR, 6', 185 lbs. Deb: 5/9/34

YEAR TM/L	W	L	PCT	G	GS	CG	SH	SV	IP	H	HR	BB	SO	RAT	ERA	ERA+	OAV	OOB	BH	AVG	PB	PR	/A	PD	TPI
1934 NY-N	1	0	1.000	7	0	0	0	0	16^2	18	1	10	5	15.1	5.40	72	.277	.373	1	.250	1	-2	-3	1	0.0
1935 NY-N	15	6	.714	29	25	9	1	0	173^2	186	14	64	64	13.0	4.09	94	.268	.330	12	.179	-0	-1	-5	1	-0.4
1936 *NY-N	4	7	.364	29	12	2	1	1	111^2	148	6	56	54	16.8	5.64	69	.323	.403	5	.128	-1	-20	-22	1	-1.9
1937 NY-N	11	6	.647	23	23	10	2	0	160^1	148	19	33	78	10.2	3.31	117	.247	.287	4	.070	-5	11	10	-3	0.3
1938 NY-N	4	5	.444	21	14	4	0	0	90^2	108	4	37	18	14.7	4.17	90	.296	.365	3	.097	-2	-4	-4	-1	-0.6
1939 NY-N	1	2	.333	12	4	0	0	0	33^2	36	1	23	6	15.8	4.54	86	.286	.396	3	.333	1	-2	-2	-1	-0.2
Total 6	36	26	.581	121	78	25	4	1	586^2	644	45	223	225	13.4	4.25	91	.279	.345	28	.135	-6	-19	-25	-2	-2.8

● ROY CASTLETON

Castleton, Royal Eugene b: 7/26/1885, Salt Lake City, Utah d: 6/24/67, Los Angeles, Cal. BR/TL, 5'11", 167 lbs. Deb: 4/16/07

YEAR TM/L	W	L	PCT	G	GS	CG	SH	SV	IP	H	HR	BB	SO	RAT	ERA	ERA+	OAV	OOB	BH	AVG	PB	PR	/A	PD	TPI
1907 NY-A	1	1	.500	3	2	1	0	0	16	11	1	3	3	7.9	2.81	99	.196	.237	0	.000	-1	-0	-0	-0	-0.1
1909 Cin-N	1	1	.500	4	1	1	0	0	14	14	0	6	5	14.1	1.93	135	.275	.373	2	.667	1	1	1	0	0.3
1910 Cin-N	1	2	.333	4	2	1	0	0	13^2	15	0	6	5	14.5	3.29	89	.288	.373	0	.000	-1	-0	-1	0	-0.2
Total 3	3	4	.429	11	5	3	0	0	43^2	40	1	15	13	12.0	2.68	104	.252	.328	2	.154	-0	0	0	0	0.0

● PAUL CASTNER

Castner, Paul Henry "Lefty" b: 2/16/1897, St.Paul, Minn. d: 3/3/86, St.Paul, Minn. BL/TL, 5'11", 187 lbs. Deb: 8/6/23

YEAR TM/L	W	L	PCT	G	GS	CG	SH	SV	IP	H	HR	BB	SO	RAT	ERA	ERA+	OAV	OOB	BH	AVG	PB	PR	/A	PD	TPI
1923 Chi-A	0	0	—	6	0	0	0	0	10	14	0	5	0	17.1	6.30	63	.326	.396	0	.000	-0	-3	-3	0	0.0

● BILL CASTRO

Castro, William Radhames (Checo) b: 12/13/53, Santiago, D.R. BR/TR, 5'11", 170 lbs. Deb: 8/20/74 C

YEAR TM/L	W	L	PCT	G	GS	CG	SH	SV	IP	H	HR	BB	SO	RAT	ERA	ERA+	OAV	OOB	BH	AVG	PB	PR	/A	PD	TPI
1974 Mil-A	0	0	—	8	0	0	0	0	18	19	2	5	10	12.0	4.50	80	.264	.312	0	—	0	-2	-2	0	0.0
1975 Mil-A	3	2	.600	18	5	0	0	1	75	78	3	17	25	11.6	2.52	152	.271	.316	0	—	0	10	11	0	0.7
1976 Mil-A	4	6	.400	39	0	0	0	8	70^1	70	4	19	23	11.8	3.45	101	.265	.322	0	—	0	1	0	-0	0.2
1977 Mil-A	8	6	.571	51	0	0	0	13	69^1	76	7	23	28	13.1	4.15	98	.293	.356	0	—	0	-1	-1	1	0.0
1978 Mil-A	5	4	.556	42	0	0	0	8	49^2	43	2	14	17	11.4	1.81	207	.234	.309	0	—	0	11	11	0	2.3
1979 Mil-A	3	1	.750	39	0	0	0	6	44^1	40	2	13	10	10.8	2.03	205	.244	.299	0	—	0	11	11	-0	1.1
1980 Mil-A	2	4	.333	56	0	0	0	8	84^1	89	2	17	32	11.5	2.77	139	.274	.314	0	—	0	12	10	1	1.2
1981 NY-A	1	1	.500	11	0	0	0	0	19	26	2	5	4	14.7	3.79	94	.329	.369	0	—	0	-0	-0	-0	0.0
1982 KC-A	3	2	.600	21	4	0	0	1	75^2	72	8	20	37	11.2	3.45	118	.243	.296	0	—	0	5	5	-1	0.2
1983 KC-A	2	0	1.000	18	0	0	0	0	40^2	51	4	12	17	15.0	6.64	61	.300	.364	0	—	0	-12	-12	0	-0.5
Total 10	31	26	.544	303	9	0	0	45	546^1	564	36	145	203	12.0	3.33	117	.268	.322	0	—	0	35	34	0	5.2

● ELI CATES

Cates, Eli Eldo b: 1/26/1877, Greens Fork, Ind. d: 5/29/64, Anderson, Ind. BR/TR, 5'9.5", 175 lbs. Deb: 4/20/08 ◆

YEAR TM/L	W	L	PCT	G	GS	CG	SH	SV	IP	H	HR	BB	SO	RAT	ERA	ERA+	OAV	OOB	BH	AVG	PB	PR	/A	PD	TPI
1908 Was-A	4	8	.333	19	10	7	0	0	113^2	112	3	32	33	11.5	2.53	90	.261	.314	11	.186	1	-2	-3	1	0.0

● MIKE CATHER

Cather, Michael Peter b: 12/17/70, San Diego, Cal. BR/TR, 6'2", 195 lbs. Deb: 7/13/97

YEAR TM/L	W	L	PCT	G	GS	CG	SH	SV	IP	H	HR	BB	SO	RAT	ERA	ERA+	OAV	OOB	BH	AVG	PB	PR	/A	PD	TPI
1997 *Atl-N	2	4	.333	35	0	0	0	0	37^2	23	1	19	29	10.5	2.39	175	.174	.288	0	.000	-0	8	7	0	1.1
1998 Atl-N	2	2	.500	36	0	0	0	0	41^1	39	7	12	33	11.5	3.92	108	.255	.317	0	—	0	1	1	-0	0.1
Total 2	4	6	.400	71	0	0	0	0	79	62	8	31	62	11.1	3.19	132	.218	.303	0	.000	-0	9	9	0	1.2

● TED CATHER

Cather, Theodore Physick b: 5/20/1889, Chester, Pa. d: 4/9/45, Elkton, Md. BR/TR, 5'10.5", 178 lbs. Deb: 9/23/12 ◆

YEAR TM/L	W	L	PCT	G	GS	CG	SH	SV	IP	H	HR	BB	SO	RAT	ERA	ERA+	OAV	OOB	BH	AVG	PB	PR	/A	PD	TPI
1913 StL-N	0	0	—	1	0	0	0	0	0^1	1	0	2	0	108.0	54.00	6	.500	.800	39	.213	0	-2	-2	0	0.0

● HARDIN CATHEY

Cathey, Hardin Abner "Lil Abner" b: 7/6/19, Burns, Tenn. d: 7/27/97, Nashville, Tenn. BR/TR, 6'4", 190 lbs. Deb: 4/16/42

YEAR TM/L	W	L	PCT	G	GS	CG	SH	SV	IP	H	HR	BB	SO	RAT	ERA	ERA+	OAV	OOB	BH	AVG	PB	PR	/A	PD	TPI
1942 Was-A	1	1	.500	12	2	0	0	0	30^1	44	1	16	8	17.8	7.42	49	.341	.414	3	.375	1	-13	-13	-0	-0.7

● KEEFE CATO

Cato, John Keefe b: 5/6/58, Yonkers, N.Y. BR/TR, 6'1", 185 lbs. Deb: 6/13/83

YEAR TM/L	W	L	PCT	G	GS	CG	SH	SV	IP	H	HR	BB	SO	RAT	ERA	ERA+	OAV	OOB	BH	AVG	PB	PR	/A	PD	TPI
1983 Cin-N	1	0	1.000	4	0	0	0	0	3^2	2	0	1	3	7.4	2.45	155	.154	.214	0	—	0	0	1	-0	0.1
1984 Cin-N	0	1	.000	8	0	0	0	1	15^2	22	5	4	12	14.9	8.04	47	.344	.382	2	.500	1	-8	-7	0	-0.4
Total 2	1	1	.500	12	0	0	0	1	19^1	24	5	5	15	13.5	6.98	54	.312	.354	2	.500	1	-7	-7	0	-0.3

● JOHN CATTANACH

Cattanach, John Leckie b: 5/10/1863, Providence, R.I. d: 11/10/26, Providence, R.I. 5'10", 190 lbs. Deb: 6/5/1884

YEAR TM/L	W	L	PCT	G	GS	CG	SH	SV	IP	H	HR	BB	SO	RAT	ERA	ERA+	OAV	OOB	BH	AVG	PB	PR	/A	PD	TPI
1884 Pro-N	0	0	—	1	1	0	0	0	5	2	0	4	2	10.8	9.00	32	.100	.250	0	.000	-1	-3	-3	-0	-0.1
StL-U	1	1	.500	2	2	2	0	0	17	12	0	4	13	8.5	2.12	113	.185	.232	0	.000	-2	1	1	0	-0.1
Total 1	1	1	.500	3	3	2	0	0	22	14	0	8	15	9.0	3.68	68	.165	.237	0	.000	-2	-3	-3	-0	-0.2

● BILL CAUDILL

Caudill, William Holland b: 7/13/56, Santa Monica, Cal. BR/TR, 6'1", 210 lbs. Deb: 5/12/79

YEAR TM/L	W	L	PCT	G	GS	CG	SH	SV	IP	H	HR	BB	SO	RAT	ERA	ERA+	OAV	OOB	BH	AVG	PB	PR	/A	PD	TPI
1979 Chi-N	1	7	.125	29	12	0	0	0	90	89	16	41	104	13.4	4.80	86	.255	.340	1	.059	-1	-11	-7	1	-0.7
1980 Chi-N	4	6	.400	72	2	0	0	1	127^2	100	10	59	112	11.3	2.19	179	.223	.314	2	.222	0	20	**25**	-1	1.8
1981 Chi-N	1	5	.167	30	10	0	0	0	71	87	9	31	45	15.2	5.83	63	.301	.373	2	.143	0	-18	-17	-1	-1.4
1982 Sea-A	12	9	.571	70	0	0	0	26	95^2	65	9	35	111	9.5	2.35	180	.192	.270	0	—	0	18	20	-1	**5.1**
1983 Sea-A	2	8	.200	63	0	0	0	26	72^2	70	10	38	73	13.6	4.71	90	.257	.353	0	—	0	-5	-4	-1	-1.1
1984 Oak-A★	9	7	.563	68	0	0	0	36	96^1	77	9	31	89	10.1	2.71	138	.218	.281	0	.000	-0	14	11	-2	2.4
1985 Tor-A	4	6	.400	67	0	0	0	14	69^1	53	9	35	46	11.7	2.99	141	.209	.310	0	—	0	9	9	-1	1.4
1986 Tor-A	2	4	.333	40	0	0	0	2	36^1	36	6	17	32	13.6	6.19	68	.254	.342	0	—	0	-8	-8	-1	-1.3
1987 Oak-A	0	0	—	6	0	0	0	1	8	10	3	1	8	12.4	9.00	46	.294	.314	0	—	0	-4	-4	-0	0.1
Total 9	35	52	.402	445	24	0	0	106	667	587	81	288	620	12.0	3.68	110	.237	.320	5	.122	-1	14	26	-7	6.3

● RED CAUSEY

Causey, Cecil Algernon b: 8/11/1893, Georgetown, Fla. d: 11/11/60, Avon Park, Fla. BR/TR, 6'1", 160 lbs. Deb: 4/26/18

YEAR TM/L	W	L	PCT	G	GS	CG	SH	SV	IP	H	HR	BB	SO	RAT	ERA	ERA+	OAV	OOB	BH	AVG	PB	PR	/A	PD	TPI
1918 NY-N	11	6	.647	29	18	10	2	2	158^1	143	2	42	48	10.9	2.79	94	.245	.304	6	.125	-3	-0	-3	-1	-0.7
1919 NY-N	9	3	.750	19	16	6	0	0	105	99	5	38	25	11.9	3.69	76	.251	.320	5	.132	-1	-9	-10	-1	-1.3
Bos-N	4	5	.444	10	10	3	0	0	69	81	1	20	14	13.3	4.57	63	.308	.359	2	.095	-2	-13	-13	0	-1.7
Yr	13	8	.619	29	26	9	0	0	174	180	6	58	39	12.4	4.03	70	.273	.333	7	.119	-3	-22	-23	-1	-3.0
1920 Phi-N	7	14	.333	35	26	11	1	3	181^1	203	4	79	30	14.5	4.32	79	.299	.376	11	.186	-2	-24	-18	-2	-2.4
1921 Phi-N	3	3	.500	7	7	4	0	0	50^2	58	4	11	8	12.4	2.84	149	.294	.335	3	.150	-1	5	8	-0	0.8
NY-N	1	1	.500	7	1	0	0	0	14^2	13	0	6	1	11.7	2.45	149	.228	.302	1	.333	0	2	2	-0	0.2
Yr	4	4	.500	14	8	4	0	0	65^1	71	4	17	9	12.1	2.76	149	.278	.324	4	.174	-1	7	10	-0	1.0
1922 NY-N	4	3	.571	24	2	1	0	1	70^2	69	2	34	13	13.1	3.18	126	.262	.347	5	.238	-0	7	6	1	0.6
Total 5	39	35	.527	131	80	35	3	6	649^2	666	18	230	139	12.6	3.59	89	.273	.340	33	.157	-9	-31	-29	-3	-4.5

● PUG CAVET

Cavet, Tiller H. b: 12/26/1889, McGregor, Tex. d: 8/4/66, San Luis Obispo, Cal. BL/TL, 6'3", 176 lbs. Deb: 4/25/11

YEAR TM/L	W	L	PCT	G	GS	CG	SH	SV	IP	H	HR	BB	SO	RAT	ERA	ERA+	OAV	OOB	BH	AVG	PB	PR	/A	PD	TPI
1911 Det-A	0	0	—	1	1	0	0	0	4	6	0	1	1	15.8	4.50	77	.316	.350	0	.000	-0	-1	-0	-0	0.0
1914 Det-A	7	7	.500	31	14	6	1	2	151^1	129	2	44	51	10.8	2.44	115	.238	.306	5	.106	-2	5	6	1	0.5

YEAR	TM/L	W	L	PCT	G	GS	CG	SH	SV	IP	H	HR	BB	SO	RAT	ERA	ERA+	OAV	OOB	BH	AVG	PB	PR	/A	PD	TPI
1915	Det-A	4	2	.667	17	7	2	0	1	71	83	1	22	26	13.6	4.06	75	.300	.355	6	.250	1	-9	-8	-0	-0.5
Total	3	11	9	.550	49	22	8	1	3	226^{1}	218	3	67	78	11.8	2.98	97	.260	.323	11	.153	-0	-4	-2	1	0.0
● ART CECCARELLI	Ceccarelli, Arthur Edward "Chic" b: 4/2/30, New Haven, Conn. BR/TL, 6', 190 lbs. Deb: 5/3/55																									
1955	KC-A	4	7	.364	31	16	3	1	0	123^{2}	123	20	71	68	14.1	5.31	79	.258	.354	3	.079	-3	-19	-16	-2	-1.7
1956	KC-A	0	1	.000	3	2	0	0	0	10	13	3	4	2	16.2	7.20	60	.317	.391	0	.000	-0	-3	-3	1	-0.2
1957	Bal-A	0	5	.000	20	8	1	0	0	58	62	3	31	30	14.7	4.50	80	.278	.371	0	.000	-2	-5	-6	-1	-0.7
1959	Chi-N	5	5	.500	18	15	4	2	0	102	95	19	37	56	11.7	4.76	83	.245	.312	3	.091	-1	-9	-9	-1	-1.0
1960	Chi-N	0	0	—	7	1	0	0	0	13	16	1	4	10	13.8	5.54	68	.296	.345	0	—	0	-3	-3	-0	0.0
Total	5	9	18	.333	79	42	8	3	0	306^{2}	309	46	147	166	13.5	5.05	79	.261	.345	6	.068	-6	-38	-37	-3	-3.6
● JOSE CECENA	Cecena, Jose Isabel (Lugo) b: 8/20/63, Ciudad Obregon, Mexico BR/TR, 5'11", 180 lbs. Deb: 4/6/88																									
1988	Tex-A	0	0	—	22	0	0	0	1	26^{1}	20	2	23	27	15.4	4.78	85	.213	.378	0	—	0	-2	-2	-0	-0.1
● REX CECIL	Cecil, Rex Rolston b: 10/8/16, Lindsay, Okla. d: 10/30/66, Long Beach, Cal. BL/TR, 6'3", 195 lbs. Deb: 8/13/44																									
1944	Bos-A	4	5	.444	11	9	4	0	0	61	72	5	33	33	15.6	5.16	66	.286	.371	5	.278	2	-12	-12	-0	-1.4
1945	Bos-A	2	5	.286	7	7	1	0	0	45	46	4	27	30	14.6	5.20	66	.261	.360	6	.300	1	-9	-9	1	-1.1
Total	2	6	10	.375	18	16	5	0	0	106	118	9	60	63	15.2	5.18	66	.276	.366	11	.289	2	-21	-21	1	-2.5
● PETE CENTER	Center, Marvin Earl b: 4/22/12, Hazel Green, Ky. BR/TR, 6'4", 190 lbs. Deb: 9/11/42																									
1942	Cle-A	0	0	—	1	0	0	0	0	3^{1}	7	0	4	0	32.4	16.20	21	.438	.571	0	.000	-0	-5	-5	-0	0.0
1943	Cle-A	1	2	.333	24	1	0	0	1	42^{1}	29	3	18	10	10.0	2.76	112	.201	.290	0	.000	-1	3	2	-1	0.0
1945	Cle-A	6	3	.667	31	8	2	0	1	85^{2}	89	2	28	34	12.4	3.99	81	.270	.329	2	.091	-2	-6	-7	-2	-1.1
1946	Cle-A	0	2	.000	21	0	0	0	1	29	29	2	20	6	15.5	4.97	67	.269	.388	0	.000	-0	-5	-5	-0	-0.4
Total	4	7	7	.500	77	9	2	0	3	160^{1}	154	7	70	50	12.7	4.10	79	.258	.338	2	.065	-3	-13	-16	-3	-1.5
● RICK CERONE	Cerone, Richard Aldo b: 5/19/54, Newark, N.J. BR/TR, 5'11", 192 lbs. Deb: 8/17/75 ♦																									
1987	NY-A	0	0	—	2	0	0	0	0	2	0	0	1	1	4.5	0.00	—	.000	.143	69	.243	1	1	1	-0	0.0
● JOHN CERUTTI	Cerutti, John Joseph b: 4/28/60, Albany, N.Y. BL/TL, 6'2", 200 lbs. Deb: 9/1/85																									
1985	Tor-A	0	2	.000	4	1	0	0	0	6^{2}	10	1	4	5	20.3	5.40	78	.323	.417	0	—	0	-1	-1	0	-0.3
1986	Tor-A	9	4	.692	34	20	2	1	1	145^{1}	150	25	47	89	12.3	4.15	102	.268	.326	0	—	0	0	1	0	0.0
1987	Tor-A	11	4	.733	44	21	2	0	0	151^{1}	144	30	59	92	12.1	4.40	102	.251	.322	0	—	0	1	2	-2	-0.1
1988	Tor-A	6	7	.462	46	12	0	0	1	123^{2}	120	12	42	65	12.0	3.13	126	.256	.322	0	—	0	11	11	3	1.4
1989	*Tor-A	11	11	.500	33	31	3	1	0	205^{1}	214	19	53	69	12.0	3.07	123	.273	.323	0	—	0	19	16	3	2.0
1990	Tor-A	9	9	.500	30	23	0	0	0	140	162	23	49	49	13.8	4.76	83	.297	.359	0	—	0	-13	-13	-0	-1.5
1991	Det-A	3	6	.333	38	8	1	0	2	88^{2}	94	9	37	29	13.5	4.57	91	.276	.351	0	—	0	-5	-4	1	-0.3
Total	7	49	43	.533	229	116	8	2	4	861	894	119	291	398	12.6	3.94	103	.271	.333	0	—	0	13	12	4	1.2
● RAY CHADWICK	Chadwick, Ray Charles b: 11/17/62, Durham, N.C. BB/TR, 6'2", 180 lbs. Deb: 7/29/86																									
1986	Cal-A	0	5	.000	7	7	0	0	0	27^{1}	39	5	15	9	18.1	7.24	57	.336	.417	0	—	0	-9	-10	0	-1.3
● LEON CHAGNON	Chagnon, Leon Wilbur "Shag" b: 9/28/02, Pittsfield, N.H. d: 7/30/53, Amesbury, Mass. BR/TR, 6', 182 lbs. Deb: 10/5/29																									
1929	Pit-N	0	0	—	1	1	0	0	0	7	11	1	1	4	15.4	9.00	53	.333	.353	0	.000	-0	-3	-3	0	0.0
1930	Pit-N	0	3	.000	18	4	3	0	0	62	92	9	23	27	17.4	6.82	73	.355	.418	4	.200	-1	-13	-13	0	-0.5
1932	Pit-N	9	6	.600	30	10	4	1	0	128	140	10	34	52	12.4	3.94	97	.276	.324	9	.225	2	-1	-2	-2	-0.2
1933	Pit-N	6	4	.600	39	5	1	0	1	100	100	2	17	35	10.8	3.69	90	.259	.296	1	.048	-2	-4	-4	-1	-0.7
1934	Pit-N	4	1	.800	33	1	0	0	1	58	68	5	24	19	14.4	4.81	86	.288	.356	3	.231	0	-5	-4	1	-0.2
1935	NY-N	0	2	.000	14	1	0	0	1	38^{1}	32	7	5	16	8.7	3.52	109	.232	.259	0	.000	-1	2	1	0	0.0
Total	6	19	16	.543	135	22	8	1	3	393^{1}	443	34	104	153	12.8	4.51	87	.284	.333	17	.162	-2	-24	-25	-1	-1.6
● BOB CHAKALES	Chakales, Robert Edward "Chick" b: 8/10/27, Asheville, N.C. BR/TR, 6'1", 185 lbs. Deb: 4/21/51																									
1951	Cle-A	3	4	.429	17	10	2	1	0	68^{1}	80	3	43	32	16.2	4.74	80	.292	.388	7	.350	2	-5	-7	-0	-0.5
1952	Cle-A	1	2	.333	5	1	0	0	0	12	19	2	8	7	20.3	9.75	34	.388	.474	2	.500	1	-8	-9	-1	-1.6
1953	Cle-A	0	2	.000	7	3	1	0	0	27	28	2	10	6	13.0	2.67	141	.283	.355	2	.286	0	4	3	0	0.3
1954	Cle-A	2	0	1.000	3	0	0	0	0	10^{1}	4	0	12	3	13.9	0.87	422	.114	.340	1	.333	1	3	3	-0	0.7
	Bal-A	3	7	.300	38	6	0	0	3	89^{1}	81	8	43	44	12.6	3.73	96	.245	.333	8	.364	2	-0	-1	0	0.1
	Yr	5	7	.417	41	6	0	0	3	99^{2}	85	8	55	47	12.7	3.43	105	.232	.334	9	.360	3	3	2	-0	0.8
1955	Chi-A	0	0	—	7	0	0	0	0	12^{1}	11	2	6	6	12.4	1.46	271	.256	.347	0	.000	-0	3	3	0	0.0
	Was-A	2	3	.400	29	0	0	0	0	54^{2}	55	4	25	28	13.3	5.27	73	.263	.345	0	.000	-1	-8	-9	-1	-0.8
	Yr	2	3	.400	36	0	0	0	0	67	66	6	31	34	13.2	4.57	84	.262	.345	0	.000	-1	-5	-5	1	-0.8
1956	Was-A	4	4	.500	43	1	0	0	4	96	94	3	57	33	14.4	4.03	107	.268	.375	3	.150	-1	1	3	1	0.3
1957	Was-A	0	1	.000	4	2	0	0	0	18^{1}	20	2	10	12	14.7	5.40	72	.274	.361	1	.143	0	-3	-3	0	-0.1
	Bos-A	0	2	.000	18	0	0	0	3	32	53	5	11	16	18.3	8.16	49	.379	.428	2	.667	1	-16	-15	-1	-1.1
	Yr	0	3	.000	22	2	0	0	3	50^{1}	73	7	21	28	17.0	7.15	55	.341	.403	3	.300	1	-19	-18	-0	-1.2
Total	7	15	25	.375	171	23	3	1	10	420^{1}	445	31	225	187	14.5	4.54	85	.277	.369	26	.271	5	-28	-31	1	-2.7
● GEORGE CHALMERS	Chalmers, George W. "Dut" b: 6/7/1888, Edinburgh, Scot. d: 8/5/60, Bronx, N.Y. BR/TR, 6'1", 189 lbs. Deb: 9/21/10																									
1910	Phi-N	1	1	.500	4	3	2	0	0	22	21	0	11	12	13.5	5.32	59	.280	.379	1	.143	-0	-6	-5	1	-0.3
1911	Phi-N	13	10	.565	38	22	11	3	4	208^{2}	196	5	101	101	13.0	3.11	111	.256	.346	13	.178	-1	7	8	-1	0.6
1912	Phi-N	3	4	.429	12	8	3	0	0	57^{2}	64	4	37	22	16.1	3.28	111	.296	.404	3	.188	-0	1	2	-2	0.0
1913	Phi-N	3	10	.231	26	15	4	0	1	116	133	3	51	46	14.7	4.81	69	.296	.374	7	.212	-1	-21	-19	1	-1.9
1914	Phi-N	0	3	.000	3	2	1	0	0	18	23	0	15	6	19.5	5.50	53	.324	.448	0	.000	-1	-5	-5	0	-0.8
1915	*Phi-N	8	9	.471	26	20	13	1	1	170^{1}	159	3	45	82	10.8	2.48	110	.255	.305	10	.169	-0	5	5	1	0.4
1916	Phi-N	1	4	.200	12	8	2	0	0	53^{2}	49	2	19	21	11.7	3.19	83	.244	.315	0	.000	-2	-3	-3	0	-0.5
Total	7	29	41	.414	121	78	36	4	6	646^{1}	645	17	279	290	13.1	3.41	93	.269	.348	34	.163	-5	-22	-18	1	-2.5
● CRAIG CHAMBERLAIN	Chamberlain, Craig Philip b: 2/2/57, Hollywood, Cal. BR/TR, 6'1", 190 lbs. Deb: 8/12/79																									
1979	KC-A	4	4	.500	10	10	4	0	0	69^{2}	68	7	18	30	11.2	3.75	114	.261	.311	0	—	0	4	4	-2	0.2
1980	KC-A	0	1	.000	5	0	0	0	0	9^{1}	10	3	5	3	14.5	6.75	60	.270	.357	0	—	0	-3	-3	0	-0.3
Total	2	4	5	.444	15	10	4	0	0	79	78	10	23	33	11.6	4.10	103	.262	.317	0	—	0	1	1	-2	-0.1
● ELTON CHAMBERLAIN	Chamberlain, Elton P. "Icebox" b: 11/5/1867, Buffalo, N.Y. d: 9/22/29, Baltimore, Md. BR/TR, 5'9", 168 lbs. Deb: 9/13/1886																									
1886	Lou-a	0	3	.000	4	4	4	0	0	31^{1}	39	0	17	18	16.1	6.61	55	.287	.366	3	.158	-0	-11	-10	-0	-0.7
1887	Lou-a	18	16	.529	36	36	35	1	0	309	340	8	117	118	13.7	3.79	116	.274	.343	26	.198	-3	17	21	1	1.5
1888	Lou-a	14	9	.609	24	24	21	1	0	196	177	2	59	119	11.3	2.53	122	.232	.297	18	.191	0	12	12	1	1.4
	*StL-a	11	2	.846	14	14	13	1	0	112	61	1	27	57	7.6	1.61	203	.154	.220	5	.100	-3	18	21	-1	1.7
	Yr	25	11	.694	38	38	34	2	0	308	238	3	86	176	9.6	2.19	143	.204	.262	23	.160	-3	30	33	0	3.1
1889	StL-a	32	15	.681	53	51	44	3	1	421^{2}	376	18	165	202	11.9	2.97	142	.231	.309	34	.199	-2	41	59	-3	4.7
1890	StL-a	3	1	.750	5	5	3	0	0	35	47	1	26	14	18.8	5.91	73	.311	.412	2	.133	-1	-8	-6	0	-0.6
	Col-a	12	6	.667	25	21	19	6	0	175	128	2	70	114	10.6	2.21	162	.198	.285	15	.231	3	32	27	-2	2.4
	Yr	15	7	.682	30	26	22	**6**	0	210	175	3	96	128	12.0	2.83	131	.220	.310	17	.213	1	24	21	-2	1.8
1891	Phi-a	22	23	.489	49	46	44	0	0	405^{2}	397	10	206	204	13.6	4.22	91	.248	.338	33	.188	2	-22	-18	0	-1.4
1892	Cin-N	19	23	.452	52	49	43	2	0	406^{1}	391	8	170	169	12.8	3.39	96	.243	.322	36	.225	3	-5	-5	-4	-0.6
1893	Cin-N	16	12	.571	34	27	19	1	0	241	248	3	112	59	14.0	3.73	128	.258	.345	19	.196	-3	25	28	-2	2.0
1894	Cin-N	10	9	.526	23	22	18	1	0	177^{2}	220	10	91	57	16.4	5.77	96	.301	.387	22	.314	4	-9	-4	-1	-0.1
1896	Cle-N	0	1	.000	2	2	1	0	0	11	21	0	5	2	22.1	7.36	62	.396	.458	0	.000	-0	-4	-3	-0	-0.3
Total	10	157	120	.567	321	301	264	16	1	2521^{2}	2445	63	1065	1133	12.9	3.57	112	.246	.326	213	.203	-2	88	119	-11	10.0
● BILL CHAMBERLAIN	Chamberlain, William Vincent b: 4/21/09, Stoughton, Mass. d: 2/6/94, Brockton, Mass. BR/TL, 5'10.5", 173 lbs. Deb: 8/2/32																									
1932	Chi-A	0	5	.000	12	5	0	0	0	41^{1}	39	3	25	11	13.9	4.57	95	.250	.354	1	.100	-1	-0	-1	-1	-0.2

YEAR	TM/L	W	L	PCT	G	GS	CG	SH	SV	IP	H	HR	BB	SO	RAT	ERA	ERA+	OAV	OOB	BH	AVG	PB	PR	/A	PD	TPI
● CLIFF CHAMBERS Chambers, Clifford Day "Lefty" b: 1/10/22, Portland, Ore. BL/TL, 6'3", 208 lbs. Deb: 4/24/48																										
1948	Chi-N	2	9	.182	29	12	3	1	0	103^2	100	4	48	51	13.1	4.43	88	.254	.339	4	.133	-1	-5	-6	0	-0.6
1949	Pit-N	13	7	.650	34	21	10	1	0	177^1	186	15	58	93	12.6	3.96	106	.268	.329	13	.236	3	2	5	1	0.9
1950	Pit-N	12	15	.444	37	33	11	2	0	249^1	262	18	92	93	13.0	4.30	102	.265	.332	26	.289	7	-4	2	-2	0.7
1951	Pit-N	3	6	.333	10	10	2	1	0	59^2	64	5	31	19	14.9	5.58	76	.276	.371	7	.333	2	-11	-9	-2	-1.1
	StL-N	11	6	.647	21	16	9	1	0	129^1	120	13	56	45	12.2	3.83	104	.251	.329	8	.163	0	2	2	-2	0.1
	Yr	14	12	.538	31	26	11	2	0	189	184	18	87	64	12.9	4.38	92	.257	.338	15	.214	2	-9	-7	-3	-1.0
1952	StL-N	4	4	.500	26	13	2	1	1	98^1	110	8	33	47	13.3	4.12	90	.285	.344	9	.281	3	-4	-4	0	0.0
1953	StL-N	3	6	.333	32	8	0	0	0	79^2	82	7	43	26	14.2	4.86	88	.266	.358	2	.118	-1	-5	-5	0	-0.6
Total	6	48	53	.475	189	113	37	7	1	897^1	924	70	361	374	13.1	4.29	96	.266	.338	69	.235	13	-26	-16	-4	-0.6
● JOHNNIE CHAMBERS Chambers, Johnnie Monroe b: 9/10/11, Copperhill, Tenn d: 5/11/77, Palatka, Fla. BL/TR, 6', 185 lbs. Deb: 5/4/37																										
1937	StL-N	0	0	—	2	0	0	0	0	2	5	0	2	1	31.5	18.00	22	.455	.538	0	—	0	-3	-3	-0	0.0
● ROME CHAMBERS Chambers, Richard Jerome b: 8/31/1875, Weaverville, N.C. d: 8/30/02, Weaverville, N.C. BL/TL, 6'2", 173 lbs. Deb: 5/7/00																										
1900	Bos-N	0	0	—	1	0	0	0	1	4	5	0	5	2	22.5	11.25	37	.313	.476	0	.000	-0	-3	-3	-0	-0.2
● BILL CHAMBERS Chambers, William Christopher b: 9/13/1889, Cameron, W.Va. d: 3/27/62, Fort Wayne, Ind. BR/TR, 5'9", 185 lbs. Deb: 7/11/10																										
1910	StL-N	0	0	—	1	0	0	0	0	1	1	0	0	0	9.0	0.00	—	.250	.250	0	—	0	0	0	-0	0.0
● BILL CHAMPION Champion, Buford Billy b: 9/18/47, Shelby, N.C. BR/TR, 6'4", 188 lbs. Deb: 6/4/69																										
1969	Phi-N	5	10	.333	23	20	4	2	1	116^2	130	7	63	70	15.1	5.01	71	.286	.376	6	.171	0	-18	-19	1	-2.1
1970	Phi-N	0	2	.000	7	1	0	0	0	14	21	3	10	12	20.6	9.00	44	.375	.478	0	.000	-0	-8	-8	0	-0.9
1971	Phi-N	3	5	.375	37	9	0	0	0	108^2	100	10	48	49	12.5	4.39	80	.249	.334	3	.111	-1	-11	-10	1	-0.8
1972	Phi-N	4	14	.222	30	22	2	0	0	132^2	155	11	54	54	14.2	5.09	71	.301	.368	5	.147	0	-24	-22	1	-2.7
1973	Mil-A	5	8	.385	37	11	2	0	1	136^1	139	10	62	67	13.5	3.70	102	.267	.350	0	—	0	2	1	2	0.5
1974	Mil-A	11	4	.733	31	23	2	0	0	161^2	168	12	49	60	12.1	3.62	100	.270	.323	0	—	0	-0	-0	-1	-0.1
1975	Mil-A	6	6	.500	27	13	3	1	0	110	125	11	55	40	14.7	5.89	65	.290	.370	0	—	0	-26	-25	1	-2.4
1976	Mil-A	0	1	.000	10	3	0	0	0	24^1	35	0	13	8	18.1	7.03	50	.361	.441	0	—	0	-9	-10	1	-0.2
Total	8	34	50	.405	202	102	13	3	2	804^1	873	64	354	360	13.9	4.69	78	.282	.358	14	.141	-1	-95	-93	4	-8.7
● DEAN CHANCE Chance, Wilmer Dean b: 6/1/41, Plain Twsp., Ohio BR/TR, 6'3", 200 lbs. Deb: 9/11/61																										
1961	LA-A	0	2	.000	5	4	0	0	0	18^1	33	0	5	11	19.1	6.87	66	.412	.453	0	.000	-1	-6	-5	1	-0.4
1962	LA-A	14	10	.583	50	24	6	2	8	206^2	195	14	66	127	11.6	2.96	130	.250	.313	4	.062	-5	23	21	1	2.0
1963	LA-A	13	18	.419	45	35	6	2	3	248	229	10	90	168	11.9	3.19	107	.243	.316	12	.150	-1	12	6	1	0.8
1964	LA-A★	**20**	9	.690	46	35	**15**	**11**	4	**278^1**	194	7	86	207	9.1	**1.65**	**199**	.195	.261	7	.079	-5	**61**	**51**	-2	4.7
1965	Cal-A	15	10	.600	36	33	10	4	0	225^2	197	12	101	164	12.2	3.15	108	.238	.328	7	.093	-2	8	6	3	0.8
1966	Cal-A	12	17	.414	41	37	11	2	1	259^2	206	18	114	180	11.3	3.08	109	.222	.312	2	.026	-6	10	8	2	0.4
1967	Min-A★	20	14	.588	41	39	**18**	5	1	**283^2**	244	17	68	220	10.1	2.73	127	.229	.279	3	.033	-6	16	23	2	2.4
1968	Min-A	16	16	.500	43	39	15	6	1	292	224	15	63	234	9.2	2.53	122	.211	.261	5	.054	-6	15	18	3	1.8
1969	*Min-A	5	4	.556	20	15	1	0	0	88^1	76	6	35	50	11.7	2.95	124	.233	.315	1	.042	-1	7	7	-1	0.4
1970	Cle-A	9	8	.529	45	19	1	1	4	155	172	18	59	109	13.8	4.24	93	.287	.357	3	.071	-3	-9	-5	-1	-0.9
	NY-N	0	1	.000	3	0	0	0	1	2	3	0	2	0	22.5	13.50	30	.500	.625	0	—	0	-2	-2	0	-1.0
1971	Det-A	4	6	.400	31	14	0	0	0	89^2	91	5	50	64	14.6	3.51	102	.265	.364	0	.000	-2	-1	1	-0	-0.2
Total	11	128	115	.527	406	294	83	33	23	2147^1	1864	122	739	1534	11.2	2.92	119	.234	.305	44	.066	-37	134	131	8	10.8
● ED CHANDLER Chandler, Edward Oliver b: 2/17/22, Pinson, Ala. BR/TR, 6'2", 190 lbs. Deb: 4/18/47																										
1947	Bro-N	0	1	.000	15	1	0	0	1	29^2	31	7	12	8	13.0	6.37	65	.263	.331	0	.000	0	-8	-7	0	-0.3
● SPUD CHANDLER Chandler, Spurgeon Ferdinand b: 9/12/07, Commerce, Ga. d: 1/9/90, S.Pasadena, Fla. BR/TR, 6', 181 lbs. Deb: 5/6/37 C																										
1937	NY-A	7	4	.636	12	10	6	2	0	82^1	79	8	20	31	10.9	2.84	156	.253	.300	4	.133	-2	16	15	2	1.7
1938	NY-A	14	5	.737	23	23	14	2	0	172	183	7	47	36	12.1	4.03	113	.271	.320	14	.203	2	15	10	4	1.5
1939	NY-A	3	0	1.000	11	0	0	0	0	19	26	0	9	4	16.6	2.84	153	.329	.398	2	.400	1	4	3	1	0.6
1940	NY-A	8	7	.533	27	24	6	1	0	172	184	12	60	56	13.1	4.60	88	.275	.341	9	.150	1	-4	-11	3	-0.4
1941	*NY-A	10	4	.714	28	20	11	4	4	163^2	146	5	60	60	11.3	3.19	123	.239	.307	11	.183	-1	17	13	3	1.3
1942	*NY-A★	16	5	.762	24	24	17	3	0	200^2	176	13	74	74	11.4	2.38	145	.237	.309	15	.211	4	29	24	3	3.2
1943	*NY-A☆	**20**	4	**.833**	30	30	**20**	**5**	0	253	197	5	54	134	**9.1**	**1.64**	**197**	.215	**.261**	25	.258	7	**47**	**44**	3	**5.7**
1944	NY-A	0	0	—	1	1	0	0	0	6	6	1	1	1	12.0	4.50	77	.300	.364	0	.000	-0	-1	-1	0	0.0
1945	NY-A	2	1	.667	4	4	2	1	0	31	30	2	7	12	10.7	4.65	75	.250	.291	4	.333	1	-4	-4	0	-0.3
1946	NY-A☆	20	8	.714	34	32	20	6	2	257^1	200	7	90	138	10.2	2.10	164	.218	.288	14	.149	-0	40	39	4	4.8
1947	*NY-A☆	9	5	.643	17	16	13	2	0	128	100	4	41	68	9.9	2.46	144	.214	.277	12	.245	4	18	15	3	2.5
Total	11	109	43	.717	211	184	109	26	6	1485	1327	64	463	614	11.0	2.84	132	.240	.301	110	.201	17	176	149	27	20.6
● ESTY CHANEY Chaney, Esty Clyon b: 1/29/1891, Hadley, Pa. d: 2/5/52, Cleveland, Ohio BR/TR, 5'11", 170 lbs. Deb: 8/2/13																										
1913	Bos-A	0	0	—	1	0	0	0	0	1	1	0	2	0	27.0	9.00	33	.200	.429	0	—	0	-1	-1	-0	0.0
1914	Bro-F	0	0	—	1	0	0	0	0	4	7	0	2	1	20.3	6.75	43	.389	.450	0	.000	-0	-2	-2	-0	0.0
Total	2	0	0	—	2	0	0	0	0	5	8	0	4	1	21.6	7.20	40	.348	.444	0	.000	-0	-2	-2	-0	0.0
● DARRIN CHAPIN Chapin, Darrin John b: 2/1/66, Warren, Ohio BR/TR, 6', 170 lbs. Deb: 9/21/91																										
1991	NY-A	0	1	.000	3	0	0	0	0	5^1	3	0	6	5	15.2	5.06	82	.158	.360	0	—	0	-1	-1	0	-0.1
1992	Phi-N	0	0	—	1	0	0	0	0	2	2	1	0	1	9.0	9.00	39	.250	.250	0	—	0	-1	-1	-0	0.0
Total	2	0	1	.000	4	0	0	0	0	7^1	5	1	6	6	13.5	6.14	65	.185	.333	0	—	0	-2	-2	0	-0.1
● TINY CHAPLIN Chaplin, James Bailey b: 7/13/05, Los Angeles, Cal. d: 3/25/39, National City, Cal BR/TR, 6'1", 195 lbs. Deb: 4/13/28																										
1928	NY-N	0	2	.000	12	1	0	0	0	24	27	0	8	5	13.1	4.50	87	.284	.340	0	.000	-1	-1	-2	-1	-0.2
1930	NY-N	2	6	.250	19	8	3	0	1	73	89	8	16	20	13.4	5.18	91	.305	.349	2	.105	-0	-2	-4	0	-0.3
1931	NY-N	3	0	1.000	16	3	1	0	1	42^1	39	2	16	7	12.1	3.19	116	.242	.318	2	.182	0	3	2	-1	0.1
1936	Bos-N	10	15	.400	40	31	14	0	2	231^2	273	21	62	86	13.1	4.12	93	.294	.340	17	.202	-0	-3	-7	2	-0.6
Total	4	15	23	.395	87	43	18	0	4	371	428	31	102	118	13.1	4.25	94	.290	.340	21	.176	-1	-2	-10	1	-1.0
● ED CHAPMAN Chapman, Edwin Volney b: 11/28/05, Courtland, Miss. BB/TR, 6'1", 185 lbs. Deb: 8/6/33																										
1933	Was-A	0	0	—	6	1	0	0	0	9	10	2	2	4	12.0	8.00	52	.270	.308	0	.000	-0	-4	-4	-0	-0.1
● FRED CHAPMAN Chapman, Frederick Joseph b: 11/24/1872, Little Cooley, Pa. d: 12/14/57, Union City, Pa. BR/TR, 5'8", 165 lbs. Deb: 7/22/1887																										
1887	Phi-a	0	0	—	1	1	1	0	0	5	8	0	2	4	18.0	7.20	60	.364	.417	0	.000	-0	-2	-2	-0	0.0
● BEN CHAPMAN Chapman, William Benjamin b: 12/25/08, Nashville, Tenn. d: 7/7/93, Hoover, Ala. BR/TR, 6', 190 lbs. Deb: 4/15/30 MC♦																										
1944	Bro-N	5	3	.625	11	9	6	0	0	79^1	75	4	33	37	12.6	3.40	104	.242	.321	14	.368	6	2	1	-2	0.6
1945	Bro-N	3	3	.500	10	7	2	0	0	53^2	64	3	32	23	16.6	5.53	68	.296	.394	3	.136	-1	-10	-11	1	-1.0
	Phi-N	0	0	—	3	0	0	0	0	7	7	0	6	4	16.7	7.71	50	.259	.394	16	.314	0	-3	-3	-0	0.0
	Yr	3	3	.500	13	7	2	0	0	60^2	71	3	38	27	16.2	5.79	65	.289	.384	19	.260	-0	-13	-14	0	-1.0
1946	Phi-N	0	0	—	1	0	0	0	0	1	1	0	0	1	9.0	0.00	—	.200	.200	0	.000	-0	0	0	0	0.0
Total	3	8	6	.571	25	16	8	0	0	141	147	7	71	65	14.3	4.40	83	.263	.353	1958	.302	6	-11	-12	-1	-0.4
● BILL CHAPPELLE Chappelle, William Hogan "Big Bill" b: 3/22/1884, Waterloo, N.Y. d: 12/31/44, Mineola, N.Y. BR/TR, 6'2", 206 lbs. Deb: 8/20/08																										
1908	Bos-N	2	4	.333	13	6	3	1	0	70^1	60	0	17	23	10.4	1.79	135	.233	.290	1	.048	-1	4	5	1	0.4
1909	Bos-N	1	1	.500	5	3	2	0	0	29	31	0	11	8	13.3	1.86	151	.279	.350	4	.364	2	2	3	1	0.6
	Cin-N	0	0	—	1	0	0	0	1	4	5	0	2	0	18.0	2.25	115	.278	.381	0	.000	-0	0	0	-0	0.0
	Yr	1	1	.500	6	3	2	0	1	33	36	0	13	8	13.6	1.91	146	.277	.347	4	.333	2	3	3	1	0.6
1914	Bro-F	4	2	.667	16	6	4	0	0	74^1	71	1	29	31	12.5	3.15	91	.255	.332	0	.000	-4	-2	-2	-1	-0.7
Total	3	7	7	.500	35	15	9	1	1	177^2	167	1	59	62	11.9	2.38	113	.251	.321	5	.089	-3	5	6	1	0.3

YEAR	TM/L	W	L	PCT	G	GS	CG	SH	SV	IP	H	HR	BB	SO	RAT	ERA	ERA+	OAV	OOB	BH	AVG	PB	PR	/A	PD	TPI
● **NORM CHARLTON** Charlton, Norman Wood b: 1/6/63, Fort Polk, La. BB/TL, 6′3″, 205 lbs. Deb: 8/19/88																										
1988	Cin-N	4	5	.444	10	10	0	0	0	61^1	60	6	20	39	12.0	3.96	90	.256	.320	0	.000	-1	-4	-3	-0	-0.5
1989	Cin-N	8	3	.727	69	0	0	0	0	95^1	67	5	40	98	10.3	2.93	123	.197	.285	0	.000	-1	6	7	-0	0.7
1990	*Cin-N	12	9	.571	56	16	1	1	2	154^1	131	10	70	117	12.0	2.74	144	.231	.320	5	.135	0	18	21	1	2.8
1991	Cin-N	3	5	.375	39	11	0	0	1	108^1	92	6	34	77	11.0	2.91	131	.236	.307	1	.043	-2	9	11	1	0.7
1992	Cin-N★	4	2	.667	64	0	0	0	26	81^1	79	7	26	90	12.0	2.99	120	.262	.326	1	.200	0	5	6	-1	0.7
1993	Sea-A	1	3	.250	34	0	0	0	18	34^2	22	4	17	48	10.1	2.34	188	.179	.279	0	—	0	8	8	-0	1.5
1995	Phi-N	2	5	.286	25	0	0	0	0	22	23	2	15	12	16.8	7.36	57	.280	.410	1	1.000	1	-8	-8	-1	-2.1
	*Sea-A	2	1	.667	30	0	0	0	14	47^2	23	2	16	58	7.6	1.51	314	.143	.225	0	—	0	17	17	0	1.8
1996	Sea-A	4	7	.364	70	0	0	0	20	75^2	68	7	38	73	12.7	4.04	122	.244	.336	0	—	0	8	8	0	1.3
1997	*Sea-A	3	8	.273	71	0	0	0	14	69^1	89	7	47	55	18.2	7.27	62	.312	.417	0	—	0	-21	-21	1	-3.4
1998	Bal-A	2	1	.667	36	0	0	0	0	35	46	5	25	41	18.3	6.94	65	.305	.403	0	—	0	-9	-9	1	-0.6
	Atl-N	0	0	—	13	0	0	0	1	13	7	0	8	6	11.1	1.38	306	.167	.314	0	.000	-0	4	4	0	0.1
Total	10	45	49	.479	517	37	1	1	96	798	707	61	356	714	12.3	3.62	113	.239	.326	8	.092	-2	34	41	1	3.0
● **PETE CHARTON** Charton, Frank Lane b: 12/21/42, Jackson, Tenn. BL/TR, 6′2″, 190 lbs. Deb: 4/19/64																										
1964	Bos-A	0	2	.000	25	5	0	0	0	65	67	12	24	37	12.7	5.26	73	.275	.342	1	.100	-0	-12	-10	2	-0.2
● **HAL CHASE** Chase, Harold Homer "Prince Hal" b: 2/13/1883, Los Gatos, Cal. d: 5/18/47, Colusa, Cal. BR/TL, 6′, 175 lbs. Deb: 4/14/05 M♦																										
1908	NY-A	0	0	—	1	0	0	0	0	0^1	0	0	0	0	0.0	0.00	—	.000	.000	104	.257	0	0	0	0	0.0
● **KEN CHASE** Chase, Kendall Fay "Lefty" b: 10/6/13, Oneonta, N.Y. d: 1/16/85, Oneonta, N.Y. BL/TL, 6′2″, 210 lbs. Deb: 4/23/36																										
1936	Was-A	0	0	—	1	0	0	0	0	2^1	2	0	4	1	23.1	11.57	41	.250	.500	1	1.000	1	-2	-2	-0	0.0
1937	Was-A	4	3	.571	14	9	4	0	0	76^1	74	4	60	43	15.8	4.13	107	.257	.385	1	.034	-4	4	3	-0	-0.2
1938	Was-A	9	10	.474	32	21	7	0	1	150	151	4	113	64	16.1	5.58	81	.268	.394	10	.208	1	-13	-18	1	-1.7
1939	Was-A	10	19	.345	32	31	15	1	0	232	215	10	114	118	12.8	3.80	114	.243	.330	15	.169	-3	21	14	0	1.3
1940	Was-A	15	17	.469	35	34	20	1	0	261^2	260	14	143	129	14.0	3.23	129	.261	.357	15	.163	-1	33	27	-1	2.8
1941	Was-A	6	18	.250	33	30	8	1	0	205^2	228	11	115	98	15.1	5.08	80	.280	.371	11	.149	-2	-21	-24	-1	-2.4
1942	Bos-A	5	1	.833	13	10	4	0	0	80^1	82	5	41	34	13.8	3.81	98	.263	.348	6	.182	1	-1	-1	-1	-0.1
1943	Bos-A	0	4	.000	7	5	0	0	0	27^1	36	0	30	9	21.7	6.91	48	.316	.458	1	.091	-1	-11	-11	0	-1.4
	NY-N	4	12	.250	21	20	4	1	0	129^1	140	7	74	86	15.0	4.11	84	.275	.369	9	.214	0	-10	-9	-1	-1.2
Total	8	53	84	.387	188	160	62	4	1	1165	1188	55	694	582	14.7	4.27	97	.265	.365	69	.165	-8	-0	-19	-0	-2.9
● **JIM CHATTERTON** Chatterton, James M. b: 10/14/1864, Brooklyn, N.Y. d: 12/15/44, Tewksbury, Mass. Deb: 6/7/1884 ♦																										
1884	KC-U	0	1	.000	1	1	0	0	0	5	11	0	2	2	23.4	3.60	62	.407	.448	2	.133	-0	-1	-1	0	-0.1
● **ANTHONY CHAVEZ** Chavez, Anthony Francisco b: 10/22/70, Turlock, Cal. BR/TR, 5′11″, 180 lbs. Deb: 9/2/97																										
1997	Ana-A	0	0	—	7	0	0	0	0	9^2	7	1	5	10	11.2	0.93	491	.206	.308	0	—	0	4	4	1	0.1
● **NESTOR CHAVEZ** Chavez, Nestor Isais (Silva) b: 7/6/47, Chacao, Venez. d: 3/16/69, Maracaibo, Venez. BR/TR, 6′, 170 lbs. Deb: 9/9/67																										
1967	SF-N	1	0	1.000	2	0	0	0	0	5	4	0	3	3	12.6	0.00	—	.211	.318	0	.000	-0	2	2	0	0.4
● **DAVE CHEADLE** Cheadle, David Baird b: 2/19/52, Greensboro, N.C. BL/TL, 6′2″, 203 lbs. Deb: 9/16/73																										
1973	Atl-N	0	1	.000	2	0	0	0	0	2	2	1	3	2	22.5	18.00	22	.250	.455	0	—	0	-3	-3	-0	-1.1
● **CHARLIE CHECH** Chech, Charles William b: 4/27/1878, Madison, Wis. d: 1/31/38, Los Angeles, Cal. BR/TR, 5′11.5″, 190 lbs. Deb: 4/14/05																										
1905	Cin-N	14	14	.500	39	25	20	1	0	267^2	300	4	77	79	13.0	2.89	114	.288	.344	17	.191	1	3	12	-0	1.2
1906	Cin-N	1	4	.200	11	5	5	0	3	66	59	1	24	17	12.1	2.32	119	.243	.326	5	.200	1	2	3	0	0.4
1908	Cle-A	11	7	.611	27	20	14	4	0	165^2	136	2	34	51	9.6	1.74	137	.229	.279	5	.104	-1	12	12	1	1.4
1909	Bos-A	7	5	.583	17	13	6	1	0	106^2	107	3	27	40	11.7	2.95	85	.260	.314	3	.083	-2	-6	-5	-0	-0.9
Total	4	33	30	.524	94	63	45	6	3	606	602	10	162	187	11.8	2.52	113	.263	.320	30	.152	-1	12	21	1	2.1
● **ROBINSON CHECO** Checo, Robinson (Perez) b: 9/9/71, Santo Domingo, D.R. BR/TR, 6′1″, 185 lbs. Deb: 9/16/97																										
1997	Bos-A	1	1	.500	5	2	0	0	0	13^1	12	0	3	14	10.1	3.38	137	.235	.278	0	—	0	2	2	-0	0.1
1998	Bos-A	0	2	.000	2	2	0	0	0	7^2	11	3	5	5	18.8	9.39	49	.379	.471	0	—	0	-4	-4	-0	-0.8
Total	2	1	3	.250	7	4	0	0	0	21	23	3	8	19	13.3	5.57	83	.287	.352	0	—	0	-2	-2	-1	-0.7
● **VIRGIL CHEEVES** Cheeves, Virgil Earl "Chief" b: 2/12/01, Oklahoma City, Okla. d: 5/5/79, Dallas, Tex. BR/TR, 6′, 195 lbs. Deb: 9/7/20																										
1920	Chi-N	0	0	—	5	2	0	0	0	18	16	0	7	3	11.5	3.50	92	.250	.324	0	.000	-0	-1	-1	-1	-0.1
1921	Chi-N	11	12	.478	37	22	9	1	0	163	192	8	47	39	13.7	4.64	82	.309	.366	8	.167	-2	-15	-15	-3	-2.2
1922	Chi-N	12	11	.522	39	22	9	1	2	182^2	195	9	76	40	13.8	4.09	103	.281	.360	13	.210	1	0	2	-1	0.2
1923	Chi-N	3	4	.429	19	8	0	0	0	71^1	89	8	37	13	16.3	6.18	65	.314	.399	4	.174	-1	-17	-17	-1	-1.6
1924	Cle-A	0	0	—	8	1	0	0	0	17^1	26	2	17	2	22.8	7.79	55	.388	.518	1	.250	0	-7	-7	0	0.0
1927	NY-N	0	0	—	3	0	0	0	0	6^1	8	1	4	1	17.1	4.26	90	.333	.429	0	—	0	-0	-0	0	0.0
Total	6	26	27	.491	111	55	18	2	2	458^2	526	28	188	98	14.5	4.73	84	.300	.375	26	.184	-1	-40	-38	-5	-3.7
● **ITALO CHELINI** Chelini, Italo Vincent "Chilly" or "Lefty" b: 10/10/14, San Francisco, Cal d: 8/25/72, San Francisco, Cal BL/TL, 5′10.5″, 175 lbs. Deb: 9/12/35																										
1935	Chi-A	0	0	—	2	0	0	0	0	5	7	1	4	1	21.6	12.60	37	.350	.480	1	.500	0	-5	-4	0	0.0
1936	Chi-A	4	3	.571	18	6	5	0	0	83^2	100	8	30	16	14.0	4.95	105	.291	.348	5	.156	-1	1	2	-1	-0.1
1937	Chi-A	0	1	.000	4	0	0	0	0	8^2	15	2	0	3	16.6	10.38	44	.405	.421	0	.000	0	-6	-6	-0	-0.5
Total	3	4	4	.500	24	6	5	0	0	97^1	122	11	34	20	14.6	5.83	88	.304	.362	6	.171	-1	-9	-8	-1	-0.6
● **BRUCE CHEN** Chen, Bruce Kastulo b: 6/19/77, Panama City, Panama BB/TL, 6′1″, 150 lbs. Deb: 9/7/98																										
1998	Atl-N	2	0	1.000	4	4	0	0	0	20^1	23	3	9	17	14.6	3.98	106	.287	.367	1	.143	-0	1	1	-1	0.0
● **LARRY CHENEY** Cheney, Laurance Russell b: 5/2/1886, Belleville, Kan. d: 1/6/69, Daytona Beach, Fla. BR/TR, 6′1.5″, 185 lbs. Deb: 9/9/11																										
1911	Chi-N	1	0	1.000	3	1	0	0	0	10	8	0	3	11	9.9	0.00	—	.229	.289	1	.250	0	4	4	1	0.5
1912	Chi-N	**26**	10	.722	42	37	**28**	4	0	303^1	262	5	111	140	11.3	2.85	117	.234	.307	24	.226	5	19	16	-2	1.9
1913	Chi-N	21	14	.600	**54**	36	25	2	**11**	305	271	7	98	136	11.1	2.57	124	.241	.306	20	.192	2	22	21	-0	2.6
1914	Chi-N	20	18	.526	**50**	40	21	6	5	311^1	239	9	140	157	11.2	2.54	109	.215	.308	18	.180	3	9	8	1	1.4
1915	Chi-N	8	9	.471	25	18	6	2	0	131^1	120	1	55	68	12.3	3.56	78	.246	.327	6	.150	-1	-12	-11	2	-1.4
	Bro-N	0	2	.000	5	4	1	0	0	27	16	0	17	11	11.7	1.67	167	.174	.315	1	.143	0	3	3	0	0.3
	Yr	8	11	.421	30	22	7	2	0	158^1	136	1	72	79	11.9	3.24	86	.233	.319	7	.149	-1	-9	-8	2	-1.1
1916	*Bro-N	18	12	.600	41	32	15	5	0	253	178	5	105	166	10.4	1.92	140	**.198**	.289	9	.114	-3	20	21	-1	2.3
1917	Bro-N	8	12	.400	35	24	14	1	2	210^1	185	4	73	102	11.3	2.35	119	.239	.309	14	.206	2	8	10	-1	1.2
1918	Bro-N	11	13	.458	32	21	15	0	1	200^2	177	2	74	83	11.7	3.00	93	.241	.319	16	.242	2	-5	-5	1	-0.2
1919	Bro-N	1	3	.250	9	4	2	0	0	39	45	1	14	14	14.1	4.15	72	.300	.367	2	.182	-0	-5	-5	-0	-0.6
	Bos-N	0	2	.000	8	2	0	0	0	33	35	0	15	13	13.6	3.55	81	.294	.373	2	.182	0	-2	-3	0	-0.1
	Phi-N	2	5	.286	9	6	5	0	0	57^1	69	2	28	25	15.4	4.55	71	.315	.395	2	.095	-2	-10	-8	-1	-1.2
	Yr	3	10	.231	26	12	7	0	0	129^1	149	3	57	52	14.4	4.18	73	.304	.378	6	.140	-2	-18	-16	-1	-1.9
Total	9	116	100	.537	313	225	132	20	19	1881^1	1605	36	733	926	11.5	2.70	109	.234	.313	115	.186	9	49	52	0	6.7
● **TOM CHENEY** Cheney, Thomas Edgar b: 10/14/34, Morgan, Ga. BR/TR, 6′, 180 lbs. Deb: 4/21/57																										
1957	StL-N	0	1	.000	4	3	0	0	0	9	6	0	15	10	21.0	5.00	79	.207	.477	0	.000	-0	-1	-1	0	-0.1
1959	StL-N	0	1	.000	11	2	0	0	0	11^2	17	2	11	8	23.1	6.94	61	.354	.492	0	—	0	-4	-4	0	-0.3
1960	*Pit-N	2	2	.500	11	8	1	1	0	52	44	5	33	35	13.3	3.98	94	.238	.353	3	.176	0	-1	-1	-2	-0.2
1961	Pit-N	0	0	—	1	0	0	0	0	0	1	1	4	0	—	∞	—	.500	.833	0	—	0	-4	-4	0	-0.3
	Was-A	1	3	.250	10	7	0	0	0	29^2	32	8	26	20	17.6	8.80	46	.283	.417	4	.500	2	-16	-16	-1	-1.6
1962	Was-A	7	9	.438	37	23	4	3	1	173^1	134	12	97	147	12.1	3.17	127	.213	.320	3	.063	-3	15	17	0	1.1
1963	Was-A	8	9	.471	23	21	7	4	0	136^1	99	14	40	97	9.2	2.71	137	.202	.264	5	.109	-3	14	15	-2	1.3
1964	Was-A	1	3	.250	15	6	1	0	1	48^2	45	10	13	25	10.7	3.70	100	.245	.294	3	.250	0	-0	0	-0	0.0

YEAR	TM/L	W	L	PCT	G	GS	CG	SH	SV	IP	H	HR	BB	SO	RAT	ERA	ERA+	OAV	OOB	BH	AVG	PB	PR	/A	PD	TPI
1966	Was-A	0	1	.000	3	1	0	0	0	5^1	4	1	6	3	18.6	5.06	68	.222	.440	0	—	0	-1	-1	0	-0.1
Total	8	19	29	.396	115	71	13	8	2	466	382	53	245	345	12.2	3.77	103	.225	.325	18	.135	-3	2	5	-4	-0.2
● JACK CHESBRO	Chesbro, John Dwight "Happy Jack" b: 6/5/1874, N.Adams, Mass. d: 11/6/31, Conway, Mass. BR/TR, 5'9", 180 lbs. Deb: 7/12/1899 CH																									
1899	Pit-N	6	9	.400	19	17	15	0	0	149	165	3	59	28	14.2	4.11	93	.280	.357	9	.155	-3	-4	-5	-3	-0.9
1900	Pit-N	15	13	.536	32	26	20	3	1	215^2	220	4	79	56	13.0	3.67	99	.264	.336	15	.176	-1	1	-1	-2	-0.4
1901	Pit-N	21	10	**.677**	36	28	26	**6**	1	287^2	261	4	52	129	10.2	2.38	137	.240	.284	25	.216	3	30	28	-3	2.7
1902	Pit-N	**28**	6	**.824**	35	33	31	**8**	1	286^1	242	1	62	136	10.2	2.17	126	.229	.285	20	.179	-2	19	18	-2	1.6
1903	NY-A	21	15	.583	40	36	33	1	0	324^2	300	7	74	147	10.6	2.77	113	.245	.293	23	.185	-1	7	13	2	1.4
1904	NY-A	**41**	12	**.774**	**55**	51	**48**	6	0	**454^2**	338	4	88	239	8.6	1.82	149	**.208**	.252	41	.236	6	39	**45**	5	**6.9**
1905	NY-A	19	15	.559	41	38	24	3	0	303^1	262	5	71	156	10.1	2.20	134	.235	.284	21	.188	0	15	25	1	3.0
1906	NY-A	23	17	.575	**49**	42	24	4	1	325	314	2	75	152	11.0	2.96	100	.257	.305	26	.208	-1	-10	0	-0	-0.1
1907	NY-A	10	10	.500	30	25	17	1	0	206	192	0	46	78	10.7	2.53	110	.249	.297	15	.197	-1	0	6	1	0.6
1908	NY-A	14	20	.412	45	31	20	3	1	288^2	276	6	67	124	11.1	2.93	85	.256	.307	18	.176	-2	-17	-15	1	-1.8
1909	NY-A	0	4	.000	9	4	2	0	0	49^2	70	2	13	17	15.6	6.34	40	.347	.394	3	.176	-0	-21	-21	1	-1.5
	Bos-A	0	1	.000	1	1	0	0	0	6	7	1	4	3	16.5	4.50	56	.318	.423	1	.500	0	-1	-1	-0	-0.2
	Yr	0	5	.000	10	5	2	0	0	55^2	77	3	17	20	15.2	6.14	41	.339	.385	4	.211	0	-23	-22	1	-1.7
Total	11	198	132	.600	392	332	260	35	5	2896^2	2647	39	690	1265	10.7	2.68	111	.244	.297	217	.197	-2	58	96	-1	11.3
● BOB CHESNES	Chesnes, Robert Vincent b: 5/6/21, Oakland, Cal. d: 5/23/79, Everett, Wash. BB/TR, 6', 180 lbs. Deb: 5/6/48																									
1948	Pit-N	14	6	.700	25	23	15	0	0	194^1	180	13	90	69	12.7	3.57	114	.247	.333	25	.275	7	8	11	3	2.1
1949	Pit-N	7	13	.350	27	25	8	1	1	145^1	153	15	82	49	14.9	5.88	71	.276	.374	17	.250	6	-30	-27	3	-2.4
1950	Pit-N	3	3	.500	9	7	2	0	0	39	44	7	17	12	14.8	5.54	79	.293	.376	2	.154	-0	-6	-5	2	-0.5
Total	3	24	22	.522	61	55	25	1	1	378^2	377	35	189	130	13.7	4.66	89	.263	.354	44	.256	12	-27	-21	8	-0.8
● MITCH CHETKOVICH	Chetkovich, Mitchell b: 7/21/17, Fairpoint, Ohio d: 8/24/71, Grass Valley, Cal. BR/TR, 6'3.5", 208 lbs. Deb: 4/19/45																									
1945	Phi-N	0	0	—	4	0	0	0	0	3	2	0	3	0	15.0	0.00	—	.182	.357	0	—	0	1	1	-0	0.0
● TONY CHEVEZ	Chevez, Silvio Antonio (b: Silvio Antonio Aguilera (Chevez)) b: 6/20/54, Telica, Nicaragua BR/TR, 5'11", 177 lbs. Deb: 5/31/77																									
1977	Bal-A	0	0	—	4	0	0	0	0	8	10	3	8	7	22.5	12.38	31	.294	.455	0	—	0	-7	-8	-0	0.5
● SCOTT CHIAMPARINO	Chiamparino, Scott Michael b: 8/22/66, San Mateo, Cal. BR/TR, 6'2", 190 lbs. Deb: 9/5/90																									
1990	Tex-A	1	2	.333	6	6	0	0	0	37^2	36	1	12	19	11.9	2.63	149	.250	.316	0	—	0	5	5	-1	0.3
1991	Tex-A	1	0	1.000	5	5	0	0	0	22^1	26	1	12	8	15.3	4.03	100	.295	.380	0	—	0	0	-0	-1	-0.1
1992	Tex-A	0	4	.000	4	4	0	0	0	25^1	25	2	5	13	10.7	3.55	107	.260	.297	0	—	0	1	1	-1	0.3
Total	3	2	6	.250	15	15	0	0	0	85^1	87	4	29	40	12.4	3.27	120	.265	.329	0	—	0	7	6	-2	0.5
● FLOYD CHIFFER	Chiffer, Floyd John b: 4/20/56, Glen Cove, N.Y. BR/TR, 6'2", 185 lbs. Deb: 4/7/82																									
1982	SD-N	4	3	.571	51	0	0	0	4	79^1	73	9	34	48	12.6	2.95	116	.247	.333	0	.000	-1	6	4	-0	0.3
1983	SD-N	0	2	.000	15	0	0	0	1	22^2	17	0	10	15	10.7	3.18	110	.210	.297	0	.000	-0	1	1	0	0.1
1984	SD-N	1	0	1.000	15	1	0	0	0	28	42	1	16	20	18.6	7.71	46	.347	.423	0	.000	-0	-13	-13	-1	-0.5
Total	3	5	5	.500	81	1	0	0	5	130	132	10	60	83	13.6	4.02	86	.266	.349	0	.000	-1	-6	-8	-1	-0.1
● HARRY CHILD	Child, Harry Stephen Patrick (b: Harry Stephen Patrick Chesley) b: 5/23/05, Baltimore, Md. d: 11/8/72, Alexandria, Va. BB/TR, 5'11", 187 lbs. Deb: 7/16/30																									
1930	Was-A	0	0	—	5	0	0	0	0	10	10	1	5	5	13.5	6.30	73	.263	.349	1	.250	-0	-2	-2	0	0.0
● BILL CHILDERS	Childers, William b: St.Louis, Mo. Deb: 7/27/1895																									
1895	Lou-N	0	0	—	1	0	0	0	0	0	2	0	6	0	—	∞	—	1.000	1.000	0	—	0	-6	-6	0	-0.4
● ROCKY CHILDRESS	Childress, Rodney Osborne b: 2/18/62, Santa Rosa, Cal. BR/TR, 6'2", 195 lbs. Deb: 5/17/85																									
1985	Phi-N	0	1	.000	16	1	0	0	0	33^1	45	3	9	14	14.6	6.21	59	.326	.367	1	.167	-0	-10	-9	-0	-0.3
1986	Phi-N	0	0	—	2	0	0	0	0	2^2	4	0	1	1	16.9	6.75	57	.364	.417	0	—	0	-1	-1	-0	0.0
1987	Hou-N	1	2	.333	32	0	0	0	0	48^1	46	4	18	26	11.9	2.98	131	.260	.328	0	.000	-0	6	5	-0	0.2
1988	Hou-N	1	0	1.000	11	0	0	0	0	23^1	26	3	9	24	13.9	6.17	54	.280	.350	1	.250	0	-7	-7	-1	-0.3
Total	4	2	3	.400	61	1	0	0	0	107^2	121	10	37	65	13.3	4.76	78	.289	.348	2	.167	-0	-12	-13	-1	-0.4
● BOB CHIPMAN	Chipman, Robert Howard "Mr. Chips" b: 10/11/18, Brooklyn, N.Y. d: 11/8/73, Huntington, N.Y. BL/TL, 6'2", 190 lbs. Deb: 9/28/41																									
1941	Bro-N	1	0	1.000	1	0	0	0	0	5	3	0	1	3	7.2	0.00	—	.150	.190	0	.000	-0	2	2	-0	0.4
1942	Bro-N	0	0	—	2	0	0	0	0	1^1	1	0	2	1	20.3	0.00	—	.250	.500	0	—	0	0	0	0	0.0
1943	Bro-N	0	0	—	1	0	0	0	0	1^2	2	0	2	0	21.6	0.00	—	.400	.571	0	—	0	1	1	-0	0.0
1944	Bro-N	3	1	.750	11	3	1	0	0	36^1	38	1	24	20	15.4	4.21	84	.270	.376	2	.182	-0	-2	-3	0	-0.3
	Chi-N	9	9	.500	26	21	8	1	2	129	147	9	40	41	13.0	3.49	101	.288	.340	5	.104	-3	2	1	-0	-0.2
	Yr	12	10	.545	37	24	9	1	2	165^1	185	10	64	61	13.6	3.65	97	.284	.348	7	.119	-3	-1	-2	-0	-0.5
1945	*Chi-N	4	5	.444	25	10	3	1	0	72	63	4	34	29	12.3	3.50	104	.230	.317	3	.176	1	2	1	1	0.2
1946	Chi-N	6	5	.545	34	10	5	3	2	109^1	103	8	54	42	13.0	3.13	106	.255	.344	2	.061	-3	3	2	-1	-0.2
1947	Chi-N	7	6	.538	32	17	5	1	0	134^2	135	6	66	51	13.4	3.68	107	.264	.348	4	.091	-3	6	4	1	0.2
1948	Chi-N	2	1	.667	34	3	0	0	4	60^1	73	5	24	16	14.5	3.58	109	.293	.355	4	.250	1	3	2	1	0.4
1949	Chi-N	7	8	.467	38	11	3	1	1	113^1	110	7	63	46	13.9	3.97	102	.248	.344	3	.125	-0	1	1	-1	-0.1
1950	Bos-N	7	7	.500	27	12	4	0	1	124	127	10	37	40	12.2	4.43	87	.262	.319	6	.154	-1	-4	-8	-3	-1.1
1951	Bos-N	4	3	.571	33	0	0	0	4	52	59	5	19	17	13.8	4.85	76	.284	.349	1	.100	-1	-5	-7	-0	-1.0
1952	Bos-N	1	1	.500	29	0	0	0	0	41^2	28	5	20	16	10.4	2.81	129	.188	.284	2	.400	1	4	4	0	0.3
Total	12	51	46	.526	293	87	29	7	14	880^2	889	60	386	322	13.1	3.72	100	.261	.338	32	.128	-8	13	1	-2	-1.4
● STEVE CHITREN	Chitren, Stephen Vincent b: 6/8/67, Tokyo, Japan BR/TR, 6', 180 lbs. Deb: 9/15/90																									
1990	Oak-A	1	0	1.000	8	0	0	0	0	17^2	7	0	4	19	5.6	1.02	365	.117	.172	0	—	0	6	5	0	0.4
1991	Oak-A	1	4	.200	56	0	0	0	4	60^1	59	8	32	47	14.2	4.33	89	.258	.358	0	—	0	-2	-3	-0	-0.3
Total	2	2	4	.333	64	0	0	0	4	78	66	8	36	66	12.2	3.58	106	.228	.322	0	—	0	4	2	-0	0.1
● NELSON CHITTUM	Chittum, Nelson Boyd b: 3/25/33, Harrisonburg, Va. BR/TR, 6'1", 180 lbs. Deb: 8/17/58																									
1958	StL-N	0	1	.000	13	2	0	0	0	29^1	31	5	7	13	12.0	6.44	64	.265	.312	1	.250	0	-8	-8	0	-0.2
1959	Bos-A	3	0	1.000	21	0	0	0	0	30^1	29	0	11	12	11.9	1.19	342	.266	.333	1	.200	0	9	10	1	1.0
1960	Bos-A	0	0	—	6	0	0	0	0	8^1	8	0	6	5	15.1	4.32	94	.242	.359	0	.000	-0	-0	-0	0	0.0
Total	3	3	1	.750	40	2	0	0	0	68	68	5	24	30	12.3	3.84	106	.263	.327	2	.200	0	0	2	1	0.8
● BOB CHLUPSA	Chlupsa, Robert Joseph b: 9/16/45, New York, N.Y. BR/TR, 6'7", 215 lbs. Deb: 7/16/70																									
1970	StL-N	0	2	.000	14	0	0	0	0	16^1	26	2	9	10	19.3	8.82	47	.366	.438	0	—	0	-9	-9	1	-0.8
1971	StL-N	0	0	—	1	0	0	0	0	2	3	0	0	1	13.5	9.00	40	.333	.333	0	—	0	-1	-1	0	0.0
Total	2	0	2	.000	15	0	0	0	0	18^1	29	2	9	11	18.7	8.84	46	.363	.427	0	—	0	-10	-10	1	-0.8
● JIN HO CHO	Cho, Jin Ho b: 8/16/75, Jun Ju City, S.Korea BR/TR, 6', 175 lbs. Deb: 7/4/98																									
1998	Bos-A	0	3	.000	4	4	0	0	0	18^2	28	4	3	15	15.4	8.20	56	.341	.372	0	—	0	-7	-7	-0	-0.9
● DON CHOATE	Choate, Donald Leon b: 7/2/38, Potosi, Mo. BR/TR, 6', 185 lbs. Deb: 9/12/60																									
1960	SF-N	0	0	—	4	0	0	0	0	8	7	0	4	7	12.4	2.25	155	.233	.324	0	—	0	1	1	0	0.0
● BOBBY CHOUINARD	Chouinard, Robert William b: 5/1/72, Manila, Philippines BR/TR, 6'1", 188 lbs. Deb: 5/26/96																									
1996	Oak-A	4	2	.667	13	11	0	0	0	59	75	10	32	32	16.8	6.10	81	.316	.404	0	—	0	-7	-8	1	-0.5
1998	Mil-N	0	0	—	1	0	0	0	0	3	5	0	0	1	15.0	3.00	143	.455	.455	0	—	0	0	0	0	0.0
	Ari-N	0	2	.000	26	2	0	0	0	38^1	41	5	11	26	12.2	4.23	102	.268	.317	0	.000	-0	0	0	-0	0.0
	Yr	0	2	.000	27	2	0	0	0	41^1	46	5	11	27	12.4	4.14	104	.279	.324	0	.000	-0	0	1	-0	0.0
Total	2	4	4	.500	40	13	0	0	0	100^1	121	15	43	59	15.0	5.29	88	.302	.374	0	.000	-0	-7	-7	1	-0.5

YEAR TM/L	W	L	PCT	G	GS	CG	SH	SV	IP	H	HR	BB	SO	RAT	ERA	ERA+	OAV	OOB	BH	AVG	PB	PR	/A	PD	TPI
● **CHIEF CHOUNEAU**	Chouneau, William (b: William Cadreau) b: 9/17/1889, Cloquet, Minn. d: 9/17/48, Cloquet, Minn. BR/TR, 5'9", 150 lbs. Deb: 10/9/10																								
1910 Chi-A	0	1	.000	1	1	0	0	0	5^1	7	0	0	1	11.8	3.38	71	.292	.292	0	.000	1	-1	-1	-0	-0.1
● **MIKE CHRIS**	Chris, Michael b: 10/8/57, Santa Monica, Cal. BL/TL, 6'3", 180 lbs. Deb: 7/31/79																								
1979 Det-A	3	3	.500	13	8	0	0	0	39	46	3	21	31	15.5	6.92	62	.297	.381	0	—	0	-12	-11	1	-1.4
1982 SF-N	0	2	.000	9	6	0	0	0	26	23	2	26	10	17.3	4.85	74	.245	.413	1	.143	-0	-4	-4	1	-0.2
1983 SF-N	0	0	—	7	0	0	0	0	13^1	16	1	16	5	23.0	8.10	44	.308	.486	0	.000	-0	-7	-7	-0	-0.1
Total 3	3	5	.375	29	14	0	0	0	78^1	85	6	63	46	17.3	6.43	61	.282	.411	1	.111	-0	-22	-22	1	-1.7
● **GARY CHRISTENSON**	Christenson, Gary Richard b: 5/5/53, Mineola, N.Y. BL/TL, 6'5", 200 lbs. Deb: 9/1/79																								
1979 KC-A	0	0	—	6	0	0	0	0	10^2	10	1	2	4	10.1	3.38	126	.250	.286	0	—	0	1	1	0	0.0
1980 KC-A	3	0	1.000	24	0	0	0	1	31^1	35	4	18	16	15.8	5.17	78	.278	.377	0	—	0	-4	-4	1	-0.4
Total 2	3	0	1.000	30	0	0	0	1	42	45	5	20	20	14.4	4.71	87	.271	.356	0	—	0	-3	-3	1	-0.4
● **LARRY CHRISTENSON**	Christenson, Larry Richard b: 11/10/53, Everett, Wash. BR/TR, 6'4", 215 lbs. Deb: 4/13/73																								
1973 Phi-N	1	4	.200	10	9	1	0	0	34^1	53	3	20	11	19.4	6.55	58	.366	.446	0	.000	-1	-11	-11	-0	-1.4
1974 Phi-N	1	1	.500	10	1	0	0	2	23	20	2	15	18	13.7	4.30	88	.241	.357	0	.000	-1	-2	-1	-0	-0.2
1975 Phi-N	11	6	.647	29	26	5	2	1	171^2	149	12	45	88	10.2	3.67	102	.236	.288	14	.246	5	-1	1	-3	0.4
1976 Phi-N	13	8	.619	32	29	2	0	0	168^2	199	8	42	54	12.9	3.68	96	.297	.339	10	.196	4	-3	-3	-3	-0.2
1977 *Phi-N	19	6	.760	34	34	5	1	0	219^1	229	21	69	118	12.5	4.06	98	.268	.327	10	.135	1	-4	-2	-2	-0.3
1978 *Phi-N	13	14	.481	33	33	9	3	0	228	209	16	47	131	10.1	3.24	110	.244	.284	5	.075	-2	9	8	-0	0.7
1979 Phi-N	5	10	.333	19	17	2	0	0	106	118	9	30	53	12.7	4.50	85	.291	.342	9	.290	5	-9	-8	-0	-0.6
1980 *Phi-N	5	1	.833	14	14	0	0	0	73^2	62	4	27	49	11.2	4.03	94	.227	.304	7	.368	3	-4	-2	1	0.3
1981 *Phi-N	4	7	.364	20	15	0	0	1	106^2	108	8	30	70	11.7	3.54	102	.267	.319	3	.100	-1	-1	1	-1	-0.1
1982 Phi-N	9	10	.474	33	33	3	0	0	223	212	15	53	145	10.8	3.47	106	.253	.300	5	.075	-3	3	5	-1	0.0
1983 Phi-N	2	4	.333	9	9	0	0	0	48^1	42	2	17	44	11.2	3.91	91	.233	.303	1	.059	-1	-2	-2	1	-0.2
Total 11	83	71	.539	243	220	27	6	4	1402^2	1401	100	395	781	11.7	3.79	98	.262	.315	64	.150	10	-24	-12	-8	-1.6
● **CLAY CHRISTIANSEN**	Christiansen, Clay C. b: 6/28/58, Wichita, Kan. BR/TR, 6'5", 205 lbs. Deb: 5/10/84																								
1984 NY-A	2	4	.333	24	1	0	0	2	38^2	50	4	12	27	14.7	6.05	63	.309	.360	0	—	0	-9	-10	-0	-1.4
● **JASON CHRISTIANSEN**	Christiansen, Jason Samuel b: 9/21/69, Omaha, Neb. BR/TL, 6'5", 230 lbs. Deb: 4/26/95																								
1995 Pit-N	1	3	.250	63	0	0	0	0	56^1	49	5	34	53	13.7	4.15	104	.234	.350	0	.000	-0	0	1	-0	0.0
1996 Pit-N	3	3	.500	33	0	0	0	0	44^1	56	7	19	38	15.4	6.70	65	.311	.380	0	.000	-0	-12	-12	0	-1.4
1997 Pit-N	3	0	1.000	39	0	0	0	0	33^2	37	2	17	37	15.0	2.94	146	.274	.364	0	—	0	5	5	-0	0.4
1998 Pit-N	3	3	.500	60	0	0	0	6	64^2	51	2	27	71	10.9	2.51	173	.216	.297	1	.250	0	12	13	-1	1.2
Total 4	10	9	.526	195	0	0	0	6	199	193	16	97	199	13.4	3.98	108	.254	.343	1	.111	-0	5	7	-1	0.2
● **MIKE CHRISTOPHER**	Christopher, Michael Wayne b: 11/3/63, Petersburg, Va. BR/TR, 6'5", 206 lbs. Deb: 9/10/91																								
1991 LA-N	0	0	—	3	0	0	0	0	4	2	0	3	2	11.3	0.00	—	.167	.333	0	—	0	2	2	0	0.0
1992 Cle-A	0	0	—	10	0	0	0	0	18	17	2	10	13	13.5	3.00	130	.254	.351	0	—	0	2	2	0	0.1
1993 Cle-A	0	0	—	9	0	0	0	0	11^2	14	3	2	8	12.3	3.86	112	.286	.314	0	—	0	1	1	-0	0.0
1995 Det-A	4	0	1.000	36	0	0	0	1	61^1	71	8	14	34	12.8	3.82	125	.292	.336	0	—	0	6	6	-0	0.4
1996 Det-A	1	1	.500	13	0	0	0	0	30	47	12	11	19	17.4	9.30	54	.351	.400	0	—	0	-14	-14	-0	-0.8
Total 5	5	1	.833	71	0	0	0	1	125	151	25	40	76	13.9	4.90	94	.299	.353	0	—	0	-4	-4	-1	-0.3
● **RUSS CHRISTOPHER**	Christopher, Russell Ormand b: 9/12/17, Richmond, Cal. d: 12/5/54, Richmond, Cal. BR/TR, 6'3", 180 lbs. Deb: 4/14/42 F																								
1942 Phi-A	4	13	.235	30	18	10	0	1	165	154	8	99	58	14.0	3.82	99	.254	.362	5	.089	-3	-3	-1	6	0.2
1943 Phi-A	5	8	.385	24	15	5	0	2	133	120	3	58	56	12.2	3.45	98	.242	.325	7	.156	-1	-2	-1	8	0.6
1944 Phi-A	14	14	.500	35	24	13	1	1	215^1	200	6	63	84	11.4	2.97	117	.245	.306	18	.222	3	11	12	5	2.6
1945 Phi-A†	13	13	.500	33	27	17	2	2	227^1	213	9	75	100	11.8	3.17	108	.251	.319	13	.171	-1	5	7	7	1.5
1946 Phi-A	5	7	.417	30	13	1	0	0	119^1	119	5	44	79	12.5	4.30	82	.254	.322	5	.139	-0	-11	-10	4	-0.5
1947 Phi-A	10	7	.588	44	0	0	0	12	80^2	70	4	33	33	11.5	2.90	131	.236	.313	2	.125	-0	7	8	1	2.0
1948 *Cle-A	3	2	.600	45	0	0	0	**17**	59	55	3	27	14	12.5	2.90	140	.247	.328	0	.000	-0	9	8	0	1.0
Total 7	54	64	.458	241	97	46	3	35	999^2	931	38	399	424	12.2	3.37	106	.248	.325	50	.158	-3	17	24	31	7.4
● **BUBBA CHURCH**	Church, Emory Nicholas b: 9/12/24, Birmingham, Ala. BR/TR, 6', 180 lbs. Deb: 4/30/50																								
1950 Phi-N	8	6	.571	31	18	8	2	1	142	113	12	56	50	10.7	2.73	149	.225	.303	8	.182	0	22	21	-0	1.9
1951 Phi-N	15	11	.577	38	33	15	4	1	247	246	17	90	104	12.3	3.53	109	.261	.326	22	.256	5	12	9	-2	1.1
1952 Phi-N	0	0	—	2	1	0	0	0	5	11	0	1	3	23.4	10.80	34	.440	.481	0	.000	-0	-4	-4	0	0.0
Cin-N	5	9	.357	29	22	5	1	0	153^1	173	21	48	47	13.1	4.34	87	.301	.358	12	.240	3	-10	-10	-1	-0.6
Yr	5	9	.357	31	23	5	1	0	158^1	184	21	49	50	13.4	4.55	83	.306	.361	12	.235	3	-14	-14	-1	-0.6
1953 Cin-N	3	3	.500	11	7	2	0	0	43^2	55	9	19	12	15.7	5.98	73	.318	.392	4	.267	1	-8	-8	-0	-0.8
Chi-N	4	5	.444	27	11	1	0	1	104^1	115	16	49	47	14.3	5.00	89	.276	.355	7	.212	1	-8	-6	-1	-0.5
Yr	7	8	.467	38	18	3	0	1	148	170	25	68	59	14.6	5.29	84	.288	.363	11	.229	2	-17	-14	-1	-1.3
1954 Chi-N	1	3	.250	7	3	1	0	0	14^2	21	8	13	8	20.9	9.82	43	.350	.466	0	.000	-1	-9	-9	0	-2.0
1955 Chi-N	0	0	—	2	0	0	0	0	3^1	4	1	1	3	13.5	5.40	76	.286	.333	0	.000	-0	-1	-0	-0	-0.1
Total 6	36	37	.493	147	95	32	7	4	713^1	738	84	277	274	12.9	4.10	97	.272	.342	53	.226	9	-7	-8	-4	-1.0
● **LEN CHURCH**	Church, Leonard b: 3/21/42, Chicago, Ill. d: 4/22/88, Richardson, Tex. BB/TR, 6', 190 lbs. Deb: 8/27/66																								
1966 Chi-N	0	1	.000	4	0	0	0	0	6	10	1	7	3	25.5	7.50	49	.400	.531	0	.000	-0	-3	-3	0	-0.4
● **CHUCK CHURN**	Churn, Clarence Nottingham b: 2/1/30, Bridgetown, Va. BR/TR, 6'3", 205 lbs. Deb: 4/18/57																								
1957 Pit-N	0	0	—	5	0	0	0	0	8^1	9	1	4	4	14.0	4.32	88	.333	.419	0	.000	-0	-0	-0	1	0.1
1958 Cle-A	0	0	—	6	0	0	0	0	8^2	12	1	5	4	17.7	6.23	59	.343	.425	0	—	0	-2	-2	-0	0.0
1959 *LA-N	3	2	.600	14	0	0	0	1	30^2	28	2	10	24	11.4	4.99	85	.255	.322	1	.167	0	-4	-3	0	-0.3
Total 3	3	2	.600	25	0	0	0	1	47^2	49	4	19	32	13.0	5.10	79	.285	.359	1	.143	0	-6	-6	1	-0.2
● **MARK CIARDI**	Ciardi, Mark Thomas b: 8/19/61, New Brunswick, N.J. BR/TR, 6' ", 180 lbs. Deb: 4/9/87																								
1987 Mil-A	1	1	.500	4	3	0	0	0	16^1	26	5	9	8	19.3	9.37	49	.361	.432	0	—	0	-9	-9	0	-0.9
● **AL CICOTTE**	Cicotte, Alva Warren "Bozo" b: 12/23/29, Melvindale, Mich. d: 11/29/82, Westland, Mich. BR/TR, 6'3", 185 lbs. Deb: 4/22/57																								
1957 NY-A	2	2	.500	20	2	0	0	2	65^1	57	5	30	36	12.1	3.03	118	.237	.325	3	.150	-0	6	4	0	0.2
1958 Was-A	0	3	.000	8	4	0	0	0	28	36	3	14	14	16.1	4.82	79	.316	.391	2	.200	-0	-3	-3	-1	-0.4
Det-A	3	1	.750	14	2	0	0	0	43	50	1	15	21	13.6	3.56	113	.307	.365	3	.176	-1	1	2	1	0.3
Yr	3	4	.429	22	6	0	0	0	71	86	4	29	35	14.6	4.06	97	.309	.375	5	.185	-1	-2	-1	1	-0.1
1959 Cle-A	3	1	.750	26	1	0	0	1	44	46	4	25	23	14.9	5.32	69	.299	.403	1	.333	1	-7	-8	0	-0.6
1961 StL-N	2	6	.250	29	7	0	0	1	75	83	16	34	51	14.3	5.28	83	.283	.362	6	.286	1	-10	-7	0	-0.6
1962 Hou-N	0	0	—	5	0	0	0	0	4^2	8	1	1	4	17.4	3.86	97	.381	.409	0	—	0	0	-0	-0	0.0
Total 5	10	13	.435	102	16	0	0	4	260	280	30	119	149	14.0	4.36	90	.284	.364	15	.211	0	-14	-12	1	-1.1
● **EDDIE CICOTTE**	Cicotte, Edward Victor "Knuckles" b: 6/19/1884, Springwells, Mich. d: 5/5/69, Detroit, Mich. BB/TR, 5'9", 175 lbs. Deb: 9/3/05																								
1905 Det-A	1	1	.500	3	1	1	0	0	18	25	0	5	6	15.0	3.50	78	.329	.370	3	.429	1	-2	-2	-1	-0.2
1908 Bos-A	11	12	.478	39	24	17	2	2	207^1	198	0	59	95	11.6	2.43	101	.256	.318	17	.236	2	-1	1	0	0.4
1909 Bos-A	14	5	.737	27	17	10	1	1	162^1	117	3	56	82	9.6	1.94	129	.207	.280	12	.235	3	10	10	-0	1.5
1910 Bos-A	15	11	.577	36	30	20	3	0	250	213	4	86	104	11.2	2.74	93	.233	.308	12	.141	-1	-6	-5	3	-0.4
1911 Bos-A	11	15	.423	35	25	16	1	0	220	236	2	73	106	12.8	2.82	116	.282	.342	10	.141	-2	13	11	1	1.0
1912 Bos-A	1	3	.250	9	6	2	0	0	46	58	0	15	20	14.5	5.67	60	.319	.374	2	.154	0	-12	-12	1	-0.8
Chi-A	9	7	.563	20	18	13	1	0	152	159	3	37	70	11.6	2.84	113	.277	.320	13	.245	1	8	6	2	1.0
Yr	10	10	.500	29	24	15	1	0	198	217	3	52	90	12.2	3.50	93	.286	.332	15	.227	1	-4	-6	3	0.2
1913 Chi-A	18	11	.621	41	30	18	3	1	268	224	2	73	121	10.1	1.58	185	.226	.281	13	.143	-3	40	40	7	5.0
1914 Chi-A	11	16	.407	45	30	15	4	3	269^1	220	0	72	122	9.9	2.04	132	.232	.288	14	.163	-1	21	19	7	2.7

YEAR	TM/L	W	L	PCT	G	GS	CG	SH	SV	IP	H	HR	BB	SO	RAT	ERA	ERA+	OAV	OOB	BH	AVG	PB	PR	/A	PD	TPI
1915	Chi-A	13	12	.520	39	26	15	1	3	223^{1}	216	2	48	106	10.9	3.02	99	.261	.306	14	.209	1	-2	-1	0	0.0
1916	Chi-A	15	7	**.682**	44	19	11	2	5	187	138	1	70	91	10.1	1.78	155	.218	.296	12	.211	2	22	20	1	2.9
1917	*Chi-A	**28**	12	.700	49	35	29	7	4	**346^{2}**	246	2	70	150	**8.3**	**1.53**	**174**	.203	**.248**	20	.179	1	**44**	**43**	-1	**5.4**
1918	Chi-A	12	19	.387	38	30	24	1	2	266	275	2	40	104	10.7	2.77	99	.271	.300	14	.163	2	0	-1	-0	0.0
1919	*Chi-A	**29**	7	**.806**	40	35	**30**	5	1	**306^{2}**	256	5	49	110	**9.0**	1.82	175	.228	.261	20	.202	1	48	46	-4	5.2
1920	Chi-A	21	10	.677	37	35	28	4	2	303^{1}	316	6	74	87	11.6	3.26	115	.275	.320	22	.196	-3	18	17	0	1.4
Total	14	209	148	.585	502	361	249	35	24	3226	2897	32	827	1374	10.5	2.38	123	.245	.297	198	.186	4	201	195	15	25.1

● PETE CIMINO Cimino, Peter William b: 10/17/42, Philadelphia, Pa. BR/TR, 6'2", 195 lbs. Deb: 9/22/65

YEAR	TM/L	W	L	PCT	G	GS	CG	SH	SV	IP	H	HR	BB	SO	RAT	ERA	ERA+	OAV	OOB	BH	AVG	PB	PR	/A	PD	TPI
1965	Min-A	0	0	—	1	0	0	0	0	1	0	0	0	0	0.0	0.00	—	.000	.000	0	—	0	0	0	-0	0.0
1966	Min-A	2	5	.286	35	0	0	0	4	64^{2}	53	4	30	57	11.7	2.92	123	.222	.311	0	.000	-0	4	5	-1	0.5
1967	Cal-A	3	3	.500	46	1	0	0	1	88^{1}	73	12	31	80	10.8	3.26	96	.229	.301	5	.417	2	-0	-1	-1	-0.1
1968	Cal-A	0	0	—	4	0	0	0	0	7	7	0	4	2	14.1	2.57	113	.259	.355	0	—	0	0	0	-0	0.0
Total	4	5	8	.385	86	1	0	0	5	161	133	16	65	139	11.2	3.07	108	.226	.306	5	.278	1	4	4	-2	0.4

● FRANK CIMORELLI Cimorelli, Frank Thomas b: 8/2/68, Poughkeepsie, N.Y. BR/TR, 6', 175 lbs. Deb: 4/30/94

YEAR	TM/L	W	L	PCT	G	GS	CG	SH	SV	IP	H	HR	BB	SO	RAT	ERA	ERA+	OAV	OOB	BH	AVG	PB	PR	/A	PD	TPI
1994	StL-N	0	0	—	11	0	0	0	1	13^{1}	20	0	10	1	21.6	8.78	47	.345	.457	0	.000	-0	-7	-7	-1	-0.2

● LOU CIOLA Ciola, Louis Alexander b: 9/6/22, Norfolk, Va. d: 10/18/81, Austin, Minn. BR/TR, 5'9", 165 lbs. Deb: 7/25/43

YEAR	TM/L	W	L	PCT	G	GS	CG	SH	SV	IP	H	HR	BB	SO	RAT	ERA	ERA+	OAV	OOB	BH	AVG	PB	PR	/A	PD	TPI
1943	Phi-A	1	3	.250	12	3	2	0	0	43^{2}	48	2	22	7	14.6	5.56	61	.273	.357	3	.167	-1	-11	-11	-0	-1.0

● GALEN CISCO Cisco, Galen Bernard b: 3/7/36, St.Marys, Ohio BR/TR, 5'11", 215 lbs. Deb: 6/11/61 C

YEAR	TM/L	W	L	PCT	G	GS	CG	SH	SV	IP	H	HR	BB	SO	RAT	ERA	ERA+	OAV	OOB	BH	AVG	PB	PR	/A	PD	TPI
1961	Bos-A	2	4	.333	17	8	0	0	0	52^{1}	67	5	28	26	16.3	6.71	62	.325	.406	1	.100	-0	-16	-15	-0	-1.5
1962	Bos-A	4	7	.364	23	9	1	0	0	83	95	11	50	43	16.0	6.72	61	.292	.392	2	.080	-1	-25	-24	1	-2.6
	NY-N	1	1	.500	4	2	1	0	0	19^{1}	15	0	11	13	13.5	3.26	128	.208	.337	0	.000	-1	1	2	-0	0.1
1963	NY-N	7	15	.318	51	17	1	0	0	155^{2}	165	15	64	81	13.6	4.34	80	.273	.349	5	.132	0	-18	-15	-0	-2.0
1964	NY-N	6	19	.240	36	25	5	2	0	191^{2}	182	17	54	78	11.4	3.62	99	.256	.313	6	.111	-0	-2	-1	2	0.1
1965	NY-N	4	8	.333	35	17	1	1	0	112^{1}	119	12	51	58	13.7	4.49	79	.272	.349	7	.259	2	-12	-12	-2	-1.1
1967	Bos-A	0	1	.000	11	0	0	0	1	22^{1}	21	4	8	8	11.7	3.63	96	.266	.333	0	.000	-0	-1	-0	0	-0.1
1969	KC-A	1	1	.500	15	0	0	0	1	22^{1}	17	4	15	18	12.9	3.63	102	.215	.340	0	—	0	-0	0	0	0.1
Total	7	25	56	.309	192	78	9	3	2	659	681	68	281	325	13.4	4.56	81	.271	.349	21	.128	0	-72	-64	1	-7.0

● RALPH CITARELLA Citarella, Ralph Alexander b: 2/7/58, East Orange, N.J. BR/TR, 6', 180 lbs. Deb: 9/13/83

YEAR	TM/L	W	L	PCT	G	GS	CG	SH	SV	IP	H	HR	BB	SO	RAT	ERA	ERA+	OAV	OOB	BH	AVG	PB	PR	/A	PD	TPI
1983	StL-N	0	0	—	6	0	0	0	0	11	8	0	3	4	9.0	1.64	221	.205	.262	0	.000	-0	2	2	-0	0.0
1984	StL-N	0	1	.000	10	2	0	0	0	22^{1}	20	0	7	15	12.1	3.63	96	.238	.319	1	.250	0	-0	-0	0	0.0
1987	Chi-A	0	0	—	5	0	0	0	0	11	13	4	4	9	15.5	7.36	62	.302	.388	0	—	0	-4	-3	-0	-0.1
Total	3	0	1	.000	21	2	0	0	0	44^{1}	41	4	14	28	12.2	4.06	93	.247	.324	1	.200	0	-1	-1	0	-0.1

● BOBBY CLACK Clack, Robert S. "Gentlemanly Bob" (b: Robert S. Clark)
b: 6/1850, England d: 10/22/33, Danvers, Mass. BR/TR, 5'9", 153 lbs. Deb: 5/13/1874 ♦

YEAR	TM/L	W	L	PCT	G	GS	CG	SH	SV	IP	H	HR	BB	SO	RAT	ERA	ERA+	OAV	OOB	BH	AVG	PB	PR	/A	PD	TPI
1876	Cin-N	0	0	—	1	0	0	0	0	2	2	0	0	0	9.0	4.50	49	.250	.250	19	.161	-0	-0	-1	0	0.0

● JIM CLANCY Clancy, James b: 12/18/55, Chicago, Ill. BR/TR, 6'4", 220 lbs. Deb: 7/26/77

YEAR	TM/L	W	L	PCT	G	GS	CG	SH	SV	IP	H	HR	BB	SO	RAT	ERA	ERA+	OAV	OOB	BH	AVG	PB	PR	/A	PD	TPI
1977	Tor-A	4	9	.308	13	13	4	1	0	76^{2}	80	7	47	44	14.9	5.05	83	.280	.381	0	—	0	-8	-7	-1	-1.0
1978	Tor-A	10	12	.455	31	30	7	0	0	193^{2}	199	10	91	106	13.5	4.09	96	.270	.351	0	—	0	-7	-4	1	-0.4
1979	Tor-A	2	7	.222	12	11	2	0	0	63^{2}	65	8	31	33	13.6	5.51	79	.272	.356	0	—	0	-9	-8	0	-1.0
1980	Tor-A	13	16	.448	34	34	15	2	0	250^{2}	217	19	128	152	12.5	3.30	130	.233	.327	0	—	0	20	28	-0	2.7
1981	Tor-A	6	12	.333	22	22	2	0	0	125	126	12	64	56	14.0	4.90	80	.262	.355	0	—	0	-17	-13	-3	-2.1
1982	Tor-A★	16	14	.533	40	40	11	3	0	266^{2}	251	26	77	139	11.1	3.71	121	.248	.302	0	—	0	11	23	-2	2.1
1983	Tor-A	15	11	.577	34	34	11	1	0	223	238	23	61	99	12.1	3.91	110	.271	.319	0	—	0	4	10	-2	0.8
1984	Tor-A	13	15	.464	36	36	5	0	0	219^{2}	249	25	88	118	13.9	5.12	80	.287	.355	0	—	0	-28	-25	0	-2.7
1985	*Tor-A	9	6	.600	23	23	1	0	0	128^{2}	117	15	37	66	10.8	3.78	111	.241	.295	0	—	0	5	6	-1	0.6
1986	Tor-A	14	14	.500	34	34	6	3	0	219^{1}	202	24	63	126	11.0	3.94	107	.243	.299	0	—	0	6	7	1	0.8
1987	Tor-A	15	11	.577	37	37	5	1	0	241^{1}	234	24	80	180	11.7	3.54	127	.255	.315	0	—	0	24	25	2	2.6
1988	Tor-A	11	13	.458	36	31	4	0	1	196^{1}	207	26	47	118	12.1	4.49	87	.272	.322	0	—	0	-11	-12	-1	-1.4
1989	Hou-N	7	14	.333	33	26	1	0	0	147	155	13	66	91	13.5	5.08	67	.269	.344	6	.146	-0	-26	-28	-3	-3.8
1990	Hou-N	2	8	.200	33	10	0	0	1	76	100	4	33	44	16.1	6.51	57	.322	.392	3	.214	0	-23	-24	1	-2.7
1991	Hou-N	0	3	.000	30	0	0	0	5	55	37	5	20	33	9.3	2.78	126	.193	.269	0	.000	-0	6	4	-1	0.1
	*Atl-N	3	2	.600	24	0	0	0	3	34^{2}	36	3	14	17	13.2	5.71	68	.267	.340	0	.000	-0	-8	-7	0	-1.1
	Yr	3	5	.375	54	0	0	0	8	89^{2}	73	8	34	50	10.8	3.91	93	.222	.297	0	.000	-1	-2	-3	-1	-1.0
Total	15	140	167	.456	472	381	74	11	10	2517^{1}	2513	244	947	1422	12.5	4.23	98	.261	.329	9	.148	-0	-62	-26	-8	-6.5

● BRYAN CLARK Clark, Bryan Donald b: 7/12/56, Madera, Cal. BL/TL, 6'2", 185 lbs. Deb: 4/11/81

YEAR	TM/L	W	L	PCT	G	GS	CG	SH	SV	IP	H	HR	BB	SO	RAT	ERA	ERA+	OAV	OOB	BH	AVG	PB	PR	/A	PD	TPI
1981	Sea-A	2	5	.286	29	9	1	0	2	93^{1}	92	3	55	52	14.3	4.34	89	.261	.363	0	—	0	-7	-5	1	-0.3
1982	Sea-A	5	2	.714	37	5	1	1	0	114^{2}	104	6	58	70	12.7	2.75	154	.241	.331	0	—	0	17	19	1	1.2
1983	Sea-A	7	10	.412	41	17	2	0	0	162^{1}	160	14	72	76	13.0	3.94	108	.261	.342	0	—	0	2	6	3	0.8
1984	Tor-A	1	2	.333	20	3	0	0	0	45^{2}	66	6	22	21	17.5	5.91	69	.342	.412	0	—	0	-10	-9	1	-0.4
1985	Cle-A	3	4	.429	31	3	0	0	2	62^{2}	78	8	34	24	16.1	6.32	65	.311	.393	0	—	0	-15	-15	1	-1.5
1986	Chi-A	0	0	—	5	0	0	0	0	8	8	0	2	5	11.3	4.50	96	.276	.323	0	—	0	-0	-0	-0	-0.1
1987	Chi-A	0	0	—	11	0	0	0	0	18^{2}	19	1	8	8	13.0	2.41	190	.297	.375	0	—	0	4	4	-1	-0.1
1990	Sea-A	2	0	1.000	12	0	0	0	0	11	9	0	10	3	15.5	3.27	121	.237	.396	0	—	0	1	1	0	0.2
Total	8	20	23	.465	186	37	4	1	4	516^{1}	536	38	261	259	14.0	4.15	100	.272	.359	0	—	0	-8	1	7	-0.2

● ED CLARK Clark, Edward C. b: Cincinnati, Ohio Deb: 7/4/1886

YEAR	TM/L	W	L	PCT	G	GS	CG	SH	SV	IP	H	HR	BB	SO	RAT	ERA	ERA+	OAV	OOB	BH	AVG	PB	PR	/A	PD	TPI
1886	Phi-a	0	1	.000	1	1	1	0	0	8	10	2	2	2	15.8	6.75	52	.294	.368	0	.000	-0	-3	-3	-0	-0.3
1891	Col-a	0	0	—	1	0	0	0	0	2	2	0	0	1	9.0	0.00	—	.250	.250	0	.000	-0	1	1	0	0.0
Total	2	0	1	.000	2	1	1	0	0	10	12	2	2	3	14.4	5.40	65	.286	.348	0	.000	-0	-2	-2	-0	-0.3

● GEORGE CLARK Clark, George Myron b: 5/19/1891, Smithland, Iowa d: 11/14/40, Sioux City, Iowa BR/TL, 6', 190 lbs. Deb: 5/16/13

YEAR	TM/L	W	L	PCT	G	GS	CG	SH	SV	IP	H	HR	BB	SO	RAT	ERA	ERA+	OAV	OOB	BH	AVG	PB	PR	/A	PD	TPI
1913	NY-A	0	1	.000	11	1	0	0	0	19	22	1	19	5	20.8	9.00	33	.272	.427	2	.500	1	-13	-13	-0	-0.5

● GINGER CLARK Clark, Harvey Daniel b: 3/7/1879, Wooster, Ohio d: 5/10/43, Lake Charles, La. BR/TR, 5'11", 165 lbs. Deb: 8/11/02

YEAR	TM/L	W	L	PCT	G	GS	CG	SH	SV	IP	H	HR	BB	SO	RAT	ERA	ERA+	OAV	OOB	BH	AVG	PB	PR	/A	PD	TPI
1902	Cle-A	1	0	1.000	1	0	0	0	0	6	10	0	3	1	21.0	6.00	57	.370	.452	2	.500	1	-2	-2	0	-0.1

● MARK CLARK Clark, Mark Willard b: 5/12/68, Bath, Ill. BR/TR, 6'5", 225 lbs. Deb: 9/6/91

YEAR	TM/L	W	L	PCT	G	GS	CG	SH	SV	IP	H	HR	BB	SO	RAT	ERA	ERA+	OAV	OOB	BH	AVG	PB	PR	/A	PD	TPI
1991	StL-N	1	1	.500	7	2	0	0	0	22^{1}	17	3	11	13	11.3	4.03	92	.215	.311	0	.000	-1	-1	-1	-0	-0.2
1992	StL-N	3	10	.231	20	20	1	1	0	113^{1}	117	12	36	44	12.2	4.45	76	.265	.321	5	.139	-1	-12	-13	-2	-1.7
1993	Cle-A	7	5	.583	26	15	1	0	0	109^{1}	119	18	25	57	11.9	4.28	101	.279	.321	0	—	0	0	1	-2	-0.1
1994	Cle-A	11	3	.786	20	20	4	1	0	127^{1}	133	14	40	60	12.5	3.82	124	.273	.333	0	—	0	14	13	1	1.3
1995	Cle-A	9	7	.563	22	21	2	0	0	124^{2}	143	13	42	68	13.6	5.27	89	.288	.348	0	—	0	-8	-8	-0	-0.9
1996	NY-N	14	11	.560	32	32	2	0	0	212^{1}	217	20	48	142	11.4	3.43	117	.265	.308	3	.043	-5	18	14	-2	0.8
1997	NY-N	8	7	.533	23	22	1	0	0	142	158	18	47	72	13.2	4.25	95	.289	.348	2	.047	-2	-1	-3	-1	-0.5
	Chi-N	6	1	.857	9	9	2	0	0	63	55	6	12	51	9.7	2.86	151	.226	.266	0	.000	-2	9	10	0	0.9
	Yr	14	8	.636	32	31	3	0	0	205	213	24	59	123	12.0	3.82	108	.268	.319	2	.030	-4	9	7	-0	0.4
1998	*Chi-N	9	14	.391	33	33	2	1	0	213^{2}	236	23	48	161	12.1	4.84	90	.278	.320	4	.065	-3	-15	-12	-2	-1.5
Total	8	68	59	.535	192	174	15	3	0	1128	1195	127	309	668	12.2	4.21	100	.272	.323	14	.058	-14	6	-0	-6	-1.9

● MIKE CLARK Clark, Michael John b: 2/12/22, Camden, N.J. d: 1/25/96, Camden, N.J. BR/TR, 6'4", 190 lbs. Deb: 7/27/52

YEAR	TM/L	W	L	PCT	G	GS	CG	SH	SV	IP	H	HR	BB	SO	RAT	ERA	ERA+	OAV	OOB	BH	AVG	PB	PR	/A	PD	TPI
1952	StL-N	2	0	1.000	12	4	0	0	0	25^{1}	32	2	14	10	16.3	6.04	61	.311	.393	0	.000	-1	-6	-7	0	-0.5
1953	StL-N	1	0	1.000	23	2	0	0	1	35^{2}	46	2	21	17	17.4	4.79	89	.315	.408	0	.000	-1	-2	-2	1	-0.1
Total	2	3	0	1.000	35	6	0	0	1	61	78	4	35	27	17.0	5.31	76	.313	.402	0	.000	-1	-9	-9	1	-0.6

YEAR	TM/L	W	L	PCT	G	GS	CG	SH	SV	IP	H	HR	BB	SO	RAT	ERA	ERA+	OAV	OOB	BH	AVG	PB	PR	/A	PD	TPI
● SPIDER CLARK	Clark, Owen F. b: 9/16/1867, Brooklyn, N.Y. d: 2/8/1892, Brooklyn, N.Y. TR, 5'10", 150 lbs. Deb: 5/2/1889 ♦																									
1890	Buf-P	0	0	—	1	0	0	0	0	4	8	0	2	2	22.5	6.75	61	.400	.455	69	.265	0	-1	-1	-0	0.0
● PHIL CLARK	Clark, Philip James b: 10/3/32, Albany, Ga. BR/TR, 6'3", 210 lbs. Deb: 4/15/58																									
1958	StL-N	0	1	.000	7	0	0	0	1	7^2	11	2	3	1	16.4	3.52	117	.355	.412	0	.000	-0	0	1	-0	0.0
1959	StL-N	0	1	.000	7	0	0	0	0	7	8	0	8	5	20.6	12.86	33	.286	.444	0	—	0	-7	-7	0	-0.8
Total	2	0	2	.000	14	0	0	0	1	14^2	19	2	11	6	18.4	7.98	52	.322	.429	0	.000	-0	-7	-6	-0	-0.8
● RICKEY CLARK	Clark, Rickey Charles b: 3/21/46, Mt.Clemens, Mich. BR/TR, 6'2", 170 lbs. Deb: 4/22/67																									
1967	Cal-A	12	11	.522	32	30	1	1	0	174	144	15	69	81	11.3	2.59	121	.224	.305	2	.040	-4	12	11	1	1.1
1968	Cal-A	1	11	.083	21	17	0	0	0	94^1	74	4	54	60	12.3	3.53	82	.217	.326	3	.107	-1	-6	-6	1	-0.9
1969	Cal-A	0	0	—	6	1	0	0	0	9^2	12	2	7	6	17.7	5.59	62	.300	.404	1	.500	0	-2	-2	-1	0.0
1971	Cal-A	2	1	.667	11	7	1	1	1	44	36	6	28	28	13.5	2.86	113	.220	.340	4	.267	1	3	2	-1	0.2
1972	Cal-A	4	9	.308	26	15	2	0	1	109^2	105	10	55	61	13.3	4.51	64	.261	.352	3	.097	-1	-18	-20	1	-2.3
Total	5	19	32	.373	96	70	4	2	2	431^2	371	37	213	236	12.4	3.38	90	.233	.328	13	.103	-5	-10	-16	1	-1.9
● BOB CLARK	Clark, Robert William b: 8/22/1897, Newport, Pa. d: 5/18/44, Carlsbad, N.Mex. BR/TR, 6'3", 188 lbs. Deb: 5/26/20																									
1920	Cle-A	1	2	.333	11	2	2	1	0	42	59	0	13	8	15.6	3.43	111	.383	.435	2	.200	-0	2	2	-0	0.0
1921	Cle-A	0	0	—	5	0	0	0	0	9^1	23	2	6	2	28.9	14.46	29	.511	.577	0	.000	-1	-11	-11	-0	-0.1
Total	2	1	2	.333	16	2	2	1	0	51^1	82	2	19	10	18.1	5.44	71	.412	.468	2	.154	-1	-9	-9	-1	-0.1
● TERRY CLARK	Clark, Terry Lee b: 10/18/60, Los Angeles, Cal. BR/TR, 6'2", 196 lbs. Deb: 7/7/88																									
1988	Cal-A	6	6	.500	15	15	2	1	0	94	120	8	31	39	14.5	5.07	76	.323	.375	0	—	0	-12	-13	0	-1.2
1989	Cal-A	0	2	.000	4	2	0	0	0	11	13	0	3	7	13.1	4.91	78	.310	.356	0	—	0	-1	-1	0	-0.2
1990	Hou-N	0	0	—	1	1	0	0	0	4	9	0	3	2	27.0	13.50	27	.429	.500	1	.500	0	-4	-4	-0	0.0
1995	Atl-N	0	0	—	3	0	0	0	0	3^2	3	0	5	2	19.6	4.91	87	.231	.444	0	—	0	-0	-0	0	0.0
	Bal-A	2	5	.286	38	0	0	0	1	39	40	3	15	18	12.9	3.46	137	.276	.348	0	—	0	5	6	-1	0.8
1996	KC-A	1	1	.500	12	0	0	0	0	17^1	28	3	7	12	18.2	7.79	64	.350	.402	0	—	0	-5	-5	-0	-0.5
	Hou-N	0	2	.000	5	0	0	0	0	6^1	16	1	2	5	27.0	11.37	34	.471	.514	0	—	0	-5	-5	1	-1.2
1997	Cle-A	0	3	.000	4	4	0	0	0	26^1	29	3	13	13	14.4	6.15	76	.284	.365	0	—	0	-5	-4	0	-0.4
	Tex-A	1	4	.200	9	5	0	0	0	30^2	41	3	10	11	15.6	5.87	82	.325	.384	1	1.000	0	-4	-4	1	-0.4
	Yr	1	7	.125	13	9	0	0	0	57	70	6	23	24	15.0	6.00	79	.304	.373	1	1.000	0	-9	-8	1	-0.8
Total	6	10	23	.303	91	27	2	1	1	232^1	299	21	89	109	15.2	5.54	78	.320	.381	2	.667	1	-32	-32	1	-3.1
● OTIE CLARK	Clark, William Otis b: 5/22/18, Boscobel, Wis. BR/TR, 6'1.5", 190 lbs. Deb: 4/17/45																									
1945	Bos-A	4	4	.500	12	9	4	1	0	82	86	6	19	20	11.6	3.07	111	.268	.311	5	.208	0	3	3	-2	0.1
● WATTY CLARK	Clark, William Watson "Lefty" b: 5/16/02, St.Joseph, La. d: 3/4/72, Clearwater, Fla. BL/TL, 6'0.5", 175 lbs. Deb: 5/28/24																									
1924	Cle-A	1	3	.250	12	1	0	0	0	25^2	38	0	14	6	18.9	7.01	61	.345	.429	2	.222	1	-8	-8	-0	-1.0
1927	Bro-N	7	2	.778	27	3	1	0	2	73^2	74	2	19	32	11.4	2.32	171	.265	.312	3	.143	-1	**13**	**13**	0	1.5
1928	Bro-N	12	9	.571	40	19	10	2	3	194^2	193	4	50	85	11.3	2.68	148	.259	.306	10	.152	-2	28	28	1	2.7
1929	Bro-N	16	19	.457	41	36	19	3	1	**279**	295	14	71	140	11.9	3.74	123	.270	.316	16	.165	-3	30	27	-0	2.5
1930	Bro-N	13	13	.500	44	24	9	1	6	200	209	20	38	81	11.1	4.18	117	.271	.306	14	.206	0	17	16	0	1.9
1931	Bro-N	14	10	.583	34	28	16	3	1	233^1	243	4	52	96	11.4	3.20	119	.267	.308	21	.250	4	17	16	-3	1.6
1932	Bro-N	20	12	.625	40	36	19	2	0	273	282	10	49	99	11.0	3.49	109	.264	.299	21	.216	1	12	10	1	1.3
1933	Bro-N	2	4	.333	11	8	4	1	1	50^2	61	2	6	14	12.4	4.80	67	.303	.333	2	.154	-0	-8	-9	-0	-1.0
	NY-N	3	4	.429	16	5	0	0	0	44	58	3	11	11	14.3	4.70	68	.317	.359	3	.273	1	-7	-7	1	-0.9
	Yr	5	8	.385	27	13	4	1	1	94^2	119	5	17	25	13.0	4.75	68	.307	.338	5	.208	1	-15	-16	0	-1.9
1934	NY-N	1	2	.333	5	4	1	0	0	18^2	23	5	5	6	13.5	6.75	57	.295	.337	1	.167	0	-6	-6	0	-0.7
	Bro-N	2	0	1.000	17	1	0	0	0	25^1	40	0	9	10	17.8	5.33	73	.345	.397	1	.125	-1	-4	-4	-0	-0.4
	Yr	3	2	.600	22	5	1	0	0	44	63	5	14	16	16.0	5.93	66	.325	.373	2	.143	-0	-9	-10	-0	-1.1
1935	Bro-N	13	8	.619	33	25	11	1	0	207	215	11	28	35	10.6	3.30	120	.264	.289	14	.177	-0	16	15	2	1.6
1936	Bro-N	7	11	.389	33	16	1	1	2	120	162	11	28	28	14.3	4.43	93	.316	.351	9	.231	0	-5	-4	0	-0.5
1937	Bro-N	0	0	—	2	0	0	0	0	2^1	4	0	3	0	27.0	7.71	52	.308	.438	0	—	0	-1	-1	0	0.0
Total	12	111	97	.534	355	206	91	14	16	1747^1	1897	86	383	643	11.8	3.66	112	.275	.315	117	.196	1	96	87	1	8.6
● LEFTY CLARKE	Clarke, Alan Thomas b: 3/8/1896, Clarksville, Md. d: 3/11/75, Cheverly, Md. BB/TL, 5'11", 180 lbs. Deb: 10/2/21																									
1921	Cin-N	0	1	.000	1	1	1	0	0	5	7	0	2	1	16.2	5.40	66	.304	.360	0	.000	-0	-1	-1	-0	-0.2
● HENRY CLARKE	Clarke, Henry Tefft b: 8/28/1875, Bellevue, Neb. d: 3/28/50, Colorado Springs, Colo. BR/TR, Deb: 6/26/1897 ♦																									
1897	Cle-N	0	4	.000	5	4	3	0	0	30^2	32	4	12	3	13.8	6.16	73	.267	.348	7	.280	0	-6	-6	-1	-0.6
1898	Chi-N	1	0	1.000	1	1	1	0	0	9	8	0	5	1	14.0	2.00	179	.235	.350	1	.250	0	2	2	-0	0.2
Total	2	1	4	.200	6	5	4	0	0	39^2	40	4	17	4	13.8	5.22	82	.260	.349	8	.276	0	-5	-4	-1	-0.4
● RUFE CLARKE	Clarke, Rufus Rivers b: 4/13/1900, Estill, S.C. d: 2/8/83, Columbia, S.C. BR/TR, 6'1", 203 lbs. Deb: 9/3/23 F																									
1923	Det-A	1	1	.500	5	0	0	0	0	6	6	0	6	2	19.5	4.50	86	.300	.481	0	—	0	-0	-0	0	-0.1
1924	Det-A	0	0	—	2	0	0	0	0	5^1	3	0	5	1	15.2	3.38	122	.158	.360	0	.000	-0	1	0	-0	0.0
Total	2	1	1	.500	7	0	0	0	0	11^1	9	0	11	3	17.5	3.97	100	.231	.423	0	.000	-0	0	0	0	-0.1
● STAN CLARKE	Clarke, Stanley Martin b: 8/9/60, Toledo, Ohio BL/TL, 6'1", 180 lbs. Deb: 6/7/83																									
1983	Tor-A	1	1	.500	10	0	0	0	0	11	10	2	5	7	12.3	3.27	131	.256	.341	0	—	0	1	1	0	0.0
1985	Tor-A	0	0	—	4	0	0	0	0	4	3	1	2	2	11.3	4.50	94	.214	.313	0	—	0	-0	-0	0	0.0
1986	Tor-A	0	1	.000	10	0	0	0	0	12^2	18	4	10	9	19.9	9.24	46	.375	.483	0	—	0	-7	-7	0	-0.5
1987	Sea-A	2	2	.500	22	0	0	0	0	23	31	7	10	13	16.0	5.48	86	.333	.398	0	—	0	-3	-2	-0	-0.4
1989	KC-A	0	2	.000	2	2	0	0	0	7	14	2	4	2	23.1	15.43	25	.438	.500	0	—	0	-9	-9	-0	-1.5
1990	StL-N	0	0	—	2	0	0	0	0	3^1	2	0	0	3	5.4	2.70	141	.167	.167	0	—	0	0	0	-0	0.0
Total	6	3	6	.333	50	2	0	0	0	61	78	16	31	36	16.1	6.79	64	.328	.405	0	—	0	-18	-17	-0	-2.4
● WEBBO CLARKE	Clarke, Vibert Ernesto b: 6/8/28, Colon, Panama d: 6/14/70, Cristobal, C.Z. BL/TL, 6', 165 lbs. Deb: 9/4/55																									
1955	Was-A	0	0	—	7	2	0	0	0	21^1	17	2	14	9	13.1	4.64	83	.221	.341	1	.167	-0	-2	-2	0	0.0
● DAD CLARKE	Clarke, William H. b: 1/7/1865, Oswego, N.Y. d: 6/3/11, Lorain, Ohio BB/TR, Deb: 4/23/1888																									
1888	Chi-N	1	0	1.000	2	2	1	0	0	16	23	2	6	6	17.4	5.06	60	.315	.383	2	.286	2	-4	-4	0	0.0
1891	Col-a	1	2	.333	4	3	2	0	0	21	30	0	16	2	20.1	6.86	50	.326	.431	1	.111	0	-7	-8	-0	-0.8
1894	NY-N	3	4	.429	15	6	5	0	1	84	114	3	26	15	15.3	4.93	106	.320	.371	8	.216	-0	4	3	0	0.1
1895	NY-N	18	15	.545	37	30	27	1	1	281^2	336	5	60	67	13.0	3.39	137	.291	.333	29	.240	-2	44	39	-3	3.1
1896	NY-N	17	24	.415	48	40	33	1	1	351	431	9	60	66	12.9	4.26	99	.300	.332	30	.204	-4	4	-2	-3	-0.8
1897	NY-N	2	1	.667	6	4	2	0	0	31	43	1	11	10	16.3	6.10	68	.326	.386	3	.167	-1	-6	-7	-0	-0.6
	Lou-N	2	4	.333	7	6	6	0	0	54^2	74	3	10	7	14.2	3.95	108	.320	.354	5	.227	-1	2	2	-0	0.1
	Yr	4	5	.444	13	10	8	0	0	85^2	117	4	21	17	14.7	4.73	89	.321	.361	8	.200	-2	-4	-5	-0	-0.5
1898	Lou-N	0	1	.000	1	1	1	0	0	9	10	1	2	1	14.0	5.00	72	.278	.350	0	.000	-1	-1	-1	-0	-0.2
Total	7	44	51	.463	120	92	77	2	3	848^1	1061	24	191	174	13.6	4.17	106	.302	.344	78	.214	-6	35	23	-6	0.9
● DAD CLARKSON	Clarkson, Arthur Hamilton b: 8/31/1866, Cambridge, Mass. d: 2/5/11, Somerville, Mass. BR/TR, 5'10", 165 lbs. Deb: 8/20/1891 F																									
1891	NY-N	1	2	.333	5	2	1	0	0	28	24	0	18	11	14.5	2.89	111	.222	.349	4	.444	2	1	1	0	0.3
1892	Bos-N	1	0	1.000	1	1	1	0	0	7	5	0	3	0	10.3	1.29	273	.192	.276	0	.000	-0	2	2	-0	0.2
1893	StL-N	12	9	.571	24	21	17	1	0	186^1	194	4	79	37	13.9	3.48	136	.260	.342	10	.133	-5	25	26	1	1.8
1894	StL-N	8	17	.320	32	32	24	1	0	233^1	318	9	117	46	17.2	6.36	85	.321	.399	16	.182	-4	-27	-25	1	-2.0
1895	StL-N	1	6	.143	7	7	7	0	0	61	91	7	26	9	17.6	7.38	66	.340	.402	1	.043	-3	-18	-17	-1	-1.6
	Bal-N	12	3	.800	20	14	10	0	0	142	169	5	64	23	15.0	3.87	123	.291	.365	8	.140	-4	14	14	2	0.9
	Yr	13	9	.591	27	21	17	0	0	203	260	12	90	32	15.7	4.92	97	.306	.375	9	.112	-7	-3	-3	1	-0.7

YEAR	TM/L	W	L	PCT	G	GS	CG	SH	SV	IP	H	HR	BB	SO	RAT	ERA	ERA+	OAV	OOB	BH	AVG	PB	PR	/A	PD	TPI
1896	Bal-N	4	2	.667	7	4	3	0	0	47	72	1	18	7	17.6	4.98	86	.348	.405	5	.278	0	-3	-4	-0	-0.4
Total	6	39	39	.500	96	81	63	2	0	704^2	873	26	325	133	15.8	4.90	99	.298	.376	44	.161	-14	-6	-3	2	-0.8

● JOHN CLARKSON Clarkson, John Gibson b: 7/1/1861, Cambridge, Mass. d: 2/4/09, Belmont, Mass. BR/TR, 5'10", 155 lbs. Deb: 5/2/1882 FH

YEAR	TM/L	W	L	PCT	G	GS	CG	SH	SV	IP	H	HR	BB	SO	RAT	ERA	ERA+	OAV	OOB	BH	AVG	PB	PR	/A	PD	TPI
1882	Wor-N	1	2	.333	3	3	2	0	0	24	49	0	2	3	19.1	4.50	69	.392	.402	4	.364	1	-4	-4	0	-0.3
1884	Chi-N	10	3	.769	14	13	12	0	0	118	94	10	25	102	9.1	2.14	147	.208	.249	22	.262	4	11	13	3	1.8
1885	*Chi-N	**53**	16	.768	**70**	70	**68**	**10**	0	**623**	497	21	97	**308**	8.6	1.85	163	.208	.239	61	.216	2	**67**	**80**	8	**8.7**
1886	*Chi-N	36	17	.679	55	55	50	3	0	466^2	419	20	86	313	9.7	2.41	150	.229	.264	49	.233	1	47	**63**	4	6.4
1887	Chi-N	**38**	21	.644	**60**	59	**56**	2	0	**523**	513	20	92	**237**	10.5	3.08	146	.246	.281	52	.242	2	**58**	**82**	9	**8.3**
1888	Bos-N	33	20	.623	54	54	53	3	0	**483^1**	448	17	119	223	10.7	2.76	103	.236	.284	40	.195	2	5	5	3	0.9
1889	Bos-N	**49**	19	**.721**	**73**	72	**68**	**8**	1	**620**	589	16	203	**284**	**11.7**	**2.73**	**153**	.243	**.306**	54	.206	0	**89**	**99**	11	**10.1**
1890	Bos-N	26	18	.591	44	44	43	2	0	383	370	14	140	138	12.4	3.27	115	.246	.317	43	.249	3	13	21	-1	2.0
1891	Bos-N	33	19	.635	55	51	47	3	**3**	460^2	435	18	154	141	11.8	2.79	131	.240	.305	42	.225	3	28	44	4	4.8
1892	Bos-N	8	6	.571	16	16	15	4	0	145^2	115	4	60	48	11.1	2.35	150	.208	.292	13	.228	1	15	19	0	1.7
	*Cle-N	17	10	.630	29	28	27	1	1	243^1	235	4	72	91	11.5	2.55	133	.244	.299	14	.139	-5	20	23	-1	1.5
	Yr	25	16	.610	45	44	42	5	1	389	350	8	132	139	11.2	2.48	139	.230	.293	27	.171	-4	35	41	-1	3.2
1893	Cle-N	16	17	.485	36	35	31	0	1	295	358	11	95	62	14.0	4.45	110	.291	.344	27	.206	-4	7	14	3	1.1
1894	Cle-N	8	10	.444	22	18	13	1	0	150^2	173	6	46	28	13.1	4.42	124	.285	.335	11	.200	-2	15	17	2	1.4
Total	12	328	178	.648	531	518	485	37	5	4536^1	4295	161	1191	1978	11.0	2.81	134	.240	.291	432	.219	9	371	476	46	48.4

● WALTER CLARKSON Clarkson, Walter Hamilton b: 11/3/1878, Cambridge, Mass. d: 10/10/46, Cambridge, Mass. BR/TR, 5'10", 150 lbs. Deb: 7/2/04 F

YEAR	TM/L	W	L	PCT	G	GS	CG	SH	SV	IP	H	HR	BB	SO	RAT	ERA	ERA+	OAV	OOB	BH	AVG	PB	PR	/A	PD	TPI
1904	NY-A	1	2	.333	13	4	2	0	1	66^1	63	3	25	43	13.3	5.02	54	.251	.343	7	.269	2	-18	-17	-1	-0.8
1905	NY-A	3	3	.500	9	4	3	0	0	46	40	1	13	35	10.8	3.91	75	.235	.297	1	.053	-2	-6	-5	-1	-0.9
1906	NY-A	9	4	.692	32	16	9	3	0	151	135	6	55	64	11.6	2.32	128	.242	.316	8	.157	-1	6	11	-1	0.7
1907	NY-A	1	1	.500	5	2	0	0	1	17^1	19	1	8	3	15.1	6.23	45	.279	.372	2	.286	0	-7	-7	0	-0.7
	Cle-A	4	6	.400	17	10	9	1	0	90^2	77	1	29	32	10.8	1.99	126	.232	.299	1	.036	-3	6	5	-0	0.1
	Yr	5	7	.417	22	12	9	1	1	108	96	2	37	35	11.3	2.67	96	.239	.308	3	.086	-3	-1	-1	-0	-0.6
1908	Cle-A	0	0	—	2	1	0	0	0	3^1	6	0	2	1	27.0	10.80	22	.400	.526	1	1.000	0	-3	-3	-0	0.0
Total	5	18	16	.529	78	37	23	4	2	374^2	340	12	132	178	11.9	3.17	88	.244	.320	20	.152	-4	-23	-16	-4	-1.6

● BILL CLARKSON Clarkson, William Henry "Blackie" b: 9/27/1898, Portsmouth, Va. d: 8/27/71, Raleigh, N.C. BR/TR, 5'11", 160 lbs. Deb: 5/2/27

YEAR	TM/L	W	L	PCT	G	GS	CG	SH	SV	IP	H	HR	BB	SO	RAT	ERA	ERA+	OAV	OOB	BH	AVG	PB	PR	/A	PD	TPI
1927	NY-N	3	9	.250	26	7	2	0	2	86^2	92	3	52	28	15.1	4.36	88	.280	.380	1	.050	-1	-4	-5	0	-0.7
1928	NY-N	0	0	—	4	0	0	0	0	5^2	10	0	1	3	17.5	7.94	49	.455	.478	0	—	0	-2	-3	-0	0.0
	Bos-N	0	2	.000	19	2	0	0	0	34^2	53	2	22	8	19.7	6.75	58	.349	.434	0	.000	-0	-11	-11	1	-0.5
	Yr	0	2	.000	23	2	0	0	0	40^1	63	2	23	11	19.4	6.92	57	.362	.439	0	.000	-0	-13	-13	1	-0.5
1929	Bos-N	0	1	.000	2	1	0	0	0	7	16	0	4	0	25.7	10.29	45	.485	.541	1	.500	0	-4	-4	0	-0.4
Total	3	3	12	.200	51	10	2	0	2	134	171	5	79	39	16.9	5.44	72	.319	.408	2	.080	-1	-22	-23	1	-1.6

● MARTY CLARY Clary, Martin Keith b: 4/3/62, Detroit, Mich. BR/TR, 6'4", 190 lbs. Deb: 9/5/87

YEAR	TM/L	W	L	PCT	G	GS	CG	SH	SV	IP	H	HR	BB	SO	RAT	ERA	ERA+	OAV	OOB	BH	AVG	PB	PR	/A	PD	TPI
1987	Atl-N	0	1	.000	7	1	0	0	0	14^2	20	2	4	7	15.3	6.14	71	.328	.379	0	.000	-0	-3	-3	-0	-0.2
1989	Atl-N	4	3	.571	18	17	2	1	0	108^2	103	6	31	30	11.2	3.15	116	.249	.303	5	.161	0	4	6	0	0.5
1990	Atl-N	1	10	.091	33	14	0	0	0	101^2	128	9	39	44	14.9	5.67	71	.308	.368	0	.000	-3	-21	-18	1	-2.0
Total	3	5	14	.263	58	32	2	1	0	225	251	17	74	81	13.1	4.48	86	.282	.339	5	.083	-2	-20	-15	1	-1.7

● GOWELL CLASET Claset, Gowell Sylvester "Lefty" b: 11/26/07, Battle Creek, Mich d: 3/8/81, St.Petersburg, Fla. BB/TL, 6'3.5", 210 lbs. Deb: 4/12/33

YEAR	TM/L	W	L	PCT	G	GS	CG	SH	SV	IP	H	HR	BB	SO	RAT	ERA	ERA+	OAV	OOB	BH	AVG	PB	PR	/A	PD	TPI
1933	Phi-A	2	0	1.000	8	1	0	0	0	11^1	23	1	11	6	27.0	9.53	45	.426	.523	1	.500	1	-7	-7	0	-0.8

● FRITZ CLAUSEN Clausen, Frederick William b: 4/26/1869, New York, N.Y. d: 2/11/60, Memphis, Tenn. BR/TL, 5'11", 190 lbs. Deb: 7/23/1892

YEAR	TM/L	W	L	PCT	G	GS	CG	SH	SV	IP	H	HR	BB	SO	RAT	ERA	ERA+	OAV	OOB	BH	AVG	PB	PR	/A	PD	TPI
1892	Lou-N	9	13	.409	24	24	24	2	0	200	181	3	87	94	12.2	3.06	100	.232	.311	13	.155	-3	5	0	-1	-0.3
1893	Lou-N	1	4	.200	5	5	3	0	0	33	41	2	22	4	17.5	6.00	73	.295	.395	3	.214	-1	-5	-6	0	-0.7
	Chi-N	6	2	.750	10	9	8	0	1	76	71	1	39	31	13.6	3.08	150	.240	.338	4	.121	-3	13	13	0	0.8
	Yr	7	6	.538	15	14	11	0	1	109	112	3	61	35	14.7	3.96	115	.257	.355	7	.149	-4	8	7	0	0.1
1894	Chi-N	0	1	.000	1	1	0	0	0	4^1	5	0	3	1	16.6	10.38	54	.294	.400	0	.000	-0	-2	-2	0	-0.3
1896	Lou-N	0	2	.000	2	2	1	0	0	11	17	1	6	4	21.3	6.55	66	.347	.448	0	.000	-1	-3	-3	0	-0.4
Total	4	16	22	.421	42	41	36	2	1	324^1	315	7	157	134	13.4	3.58	101	.246	.334	20	.147	-8	8	2	-0	-0.9

● AL CLAUSS Clauss, Albert Stanley "Lefty" b: 6/24/1891, New Haven, Conn. d: 9/13/52, New Haven, Conn. BR/TL, 5'10.5", 178 lbs. Deb: 4/22/13

YEAR	TM/L	W	L	PCT	G	GS	CG	SH	SV	IP	H	HR	BB	SO	RAT	ERA	ERA+	OAV	OOB	BH	AVG	PB	PR	/A	PD	TPI
1913	Det-A	0	1	.000	5	1	0	0	0	13^1	11	0	12	1	16.9	4.73	62	.220	.391	0	.000	-1	-3	-3	-0	-0.3

● DANNY CLAY Clay, Danny Bruce b: 10/24/61, Sun Valley, Cal. BR/TR, 6'1", 190 lbs. Deb: 5/1/88

YEAR	TM/L	W	L	PCT	G	GS	CG	SH	SV	IP	H	HR	BB	SO	RAT	ERA	ERA+	OAV	OOB	BH	AVG	PB	PR	/A	PD	TPI
1988	Phi-N	0	1	.000	17	0	0	0	0	24	27	5	21	12	18.0	6.00	59	.303	.436	0	.000	-0	-7	-7	-1	-0.3

● KEN CLAY Clay, Kenneth Earl b: 4/6/54, Lynchburg, Va. BR/TR, 6'3", 195 lbs. Deb: 6/7/77

YEAR	TM/L	W	L	PCT	G	GS	CG	SH	SV	IP	H	HR	BB	SO	RAT	ERA	ERA+	OAV	OOB	BH	AVG	PB	PR	/A	PD	TPI
1977	*NY-A	2	3	.400	21	3	0	0	1	55^2	53	6	24	20	12.6	4.37	90	.251	.331	0	—	0	-2	-3	0	-0.2
1978	*NY-A	3	4	.429	28	6	0	0	0	75^2	89	3	21	32	13.3	4.28	85	.291	.340	0	—	0	-4	-6	-1	-0.5
1979	NY-A	1	7	.125	32	5	0	0	2	78^1	88	12	25	28	13.2	5.40	75	.291	.350	0	—	0	-10	-12	0	-1.1
1980	Tex-A	2	3	.400	8	8	0	0	0	43	43	4	29	17	15.7	4.60	85	.256	.375	0	—	0	-3	-3	-1	-0.3
1981	Sea-A	2	7	.222	22	14	0	0	0	101	116	10	42	32	14.3	4.63	83	.294	.366	0	—	0	-11	-9	-2	-0.9
Total	5	10	24	.294	111	36	0	0	3	353^2	389	35	141	129	13.8	4.68	83	.281	.353	0	—	0	-30	-32	-3	-3.0

● MARK CLEAR Clear, Mark Alan b: 5/27/56, Los Angeles, Cal. BR/TR, 6'4", 215 lbs. Deb: 4/4/79

YEAR	TM/L	W	L	PCT	G	GS	CG	SH	SV	IP	H	HR	BB	SO	RAT	ERA	ERA+	OAV	OOB	BH	AVG	PB	PR	/A	PD	TPI
1979	*Cal-A★	11	5	.688	52	0	0	0	14	109	87	6	68	98	13.0	3.63	112	.219	.337	0	—	0	7	5	-1	0.8
1980	Cal-A	11	11	.500	58	0	0	0	9	106^1	82	2	65	105	12.9	3.30	119	.216	.338	0	—	0	9	7	-1	1.6
1981	Bos-A	8	3	.727	34	0	0	0	9	76^2	69	11	51	82	14.3	4.11	94	.239	.357	0	—	0	-4	-2	-1	-0.5
1982	Bos-A☆	14	9	.609	55	0	0	0	14	105	92	11	61	109	13.7	3.00	144	.238	.352	0	—	0	13	15	-0	3.5
1983	Bos-A	4	5	.444	48	0	0	0	4	96	101	10	68	81	16.1	6.28	69	.273	.390	0	—	0	-24	-21	-1	-2.2
1984	Bos-A	8	3	.727	47	0	0	0	8	67	47	2	70	76	16.0	4.03	103	.198	.385	0	—	0	-0	1	0	0.1
1985	Bos-A	1	3	.250	41	0	0	0	3	55^2	45	1	50	55	16.2	3.72	115	.225	.392	0	—	0	3	3	1	0.3
1986	Mil-A	5	5	.500	59	0	0	0	16	73^2	53	4	36	85	11.0	2.20	197	.201	.299	0	—	0	16	17	-0	2.8
1987	Mil-A	8	5	.615	58	1	0	0	6	78^1	70	9	55	81	14.9	4.48	102	.239	.368	0	—	0	-0	1	1	0.2
1988	Mil-A	1	0	1.000	25	0	0	0	0	29	23	4	21	26	13.7	2.79	142	.215	.344	0	—	0	4	4	-0	0.0
1990	Cal-A	0	0	—	4	0	0	0	0	7^2	5	0	9	6	18.8	5.87	65	.200	.444	0	—	0	-2	-2	-0	0.0
Total	11	71	49	.592	481	1	0	0	83	804^1	674	60	554	804	14.1	3.85	109	.228	.357	0	—	0	21	30	-3	6.6

● JOE CLEARY Cleary, Joseph Christopher "Fire" b: 12/3/18, Cork, Ireland BR/TR, 5'9", 150 lbs. Deb: 8/4/45

YEAR	TM/L	W	L	PCT	G	GS	CG	SH	SV	IP	H	HR	BB	SO	RAT	ERA	ERA+	OAV	OOB	BH	AVG	PB	PR	/A	PD	TPI
1945	Was-A	0	0	—	1	0	0	0	0	0^1	5	0	3	1	216.0	189.00	2	.833	.889	0	—	0	-7	-7	0	0.0

● ROGER CLEMENS Clemens, William Roger b: 8/4/62, Dayton, Ohio BR/TR, 6'4", 220 lbs. Deb: 5/15/84

YEAR	TM/L	W	L	PCT	G	GS	CG	SH	SV	IP	H	HR	BB	SO	RAT	ERA	ERA+	OAV	OOB	BH	AVG	PB	PR	/A	PD	TPI
1984	Bos-A	9	4	.692	21	20	5	1	0	133^1	146	13	29	126	11.9	4.32	96	.271	.311	0	—	0	-5	-2	0	-0.3
1985	Bos-A	7	5	.583	15	15	3	1	0	98^1	83	5	37	74	11.3	3.29	130	.228	.304	0	—	0	9	11	0	1.2
1986	*Bos-A★	**24**	4	**.857**	33	33	10	1	0	254	179	21	67	238	**8.9**	**2.48**	**168**	**.195**	**.253**	0	—	0	**48**	**48**	-1	4.9
1987	Bos-A	**20**	9	**.690**	36	36	**18**	**7**	0	281^2	248	19	83	256	10.9	2.97	153	.235	.296	0	—	0	46	49	-2	4.4
1988	*Bos-A★	18	12	.600	35	35	**14**	**8**	0	264	217	17	62	**291**	9.7	2.93	140	.220	.270	0	—	0	30	35	-2	3.3
1989	Bos-A	17	11	.607	35	35	8	3	0	253^1	215	20	93	230	11.2	3.13	131	.231	.307	0	—	0	21	27	-1	2.6
1990	*Bos-A☆	21	6	.778	31	31	7	**4**	0	228^1	193	7	54	209	10.0	**1.93**	**211**	.228	.280	0	—	0	**50**	**54**	1	**6.7**
1991	Bos-A★	18	10	.643	35	35	13	**4**	0	**271^1**	219	15	65	**241**	9.6	**2.62**	**164**	.221	.272	0	—	0	**44**	**51**	1	**4.8**
1992	Bos-A★	18	11	.621	32	32	11	**5**	0	246^2	203	11	62	208	10.0	**2.41**	**175**	.224	.280	0	—	0	**42**	**49**	-0	**5.8**
1993	Bos-A	11	14	.440	29	29	2	1	0	191^2	175	17	67	160	11.9	4.46	103	.244	.318	0	—	0	-3	3	-1	0.3
1994	Bos-A	9	7	.563	24	24	3	1	0	170^2	124	15	71	168	10.5	2.85	**177**	**.203**	.291	0	—	0	**37**	**41**	-0	3.1
1995	*Bos-A	10	5	.667	23	23	0	0	0	140	141	15	60	132	13.8	4.18	117	.259	.348	0	—	0	8	11	1	0.9
1996	Bos-A	10	13	.435	34	34	6	2	0	242^2	216	19	106	**257**	12.1	3.63	140	.237	.319	1	1.000	0	37	39	-1	3.1
1997	Tor-A★	**21**	7	.750	34	34	**9**	**3**	0	**264**	204	9	68	**292**	**9.7**	**2.05**	**224**	.213	**.274**	1	.500	1	**74**	**75**	2	**8.0**

YEAR	TM/L	W	L	PCT	G	GS	CG	SH	SV	IP	H	HR	BB	SO	RAT	ERA	ERA+	OAV	OOB	BH	AVG	PB	PR	/A	PD	TPI
1998	Tor-A★	**20**	6	.769	33	33	5	3	0	234^2	169	11	88	**271**	10.1	**2.65**	**175**	**.197**	.278	0	.000	-0	**52**	**52**	-0	**5.3**
Total	15	233	124	.653	450	449	114	44	0	3274^2	2732	214	1012	3153	10.6	2.95	151	.225	.290	2	.286	1	492	544	-2	54.1
● **BILL CLEMENSEN** Clemensen, William Melville b: 6/20/19, New Brunswick, N.J. d: 2/18/94, Alta, Cal. BR/TR, 6′1″, 193 lbs. Deb: 5/22/39																										
1939	Pit-N	0	1	.000	12	1	0	0	0	27	32	0	20	13	18.3	7.33	52	.311	.437	2	.333	1	-10	-10	1	-0.1
1941	Pit-N	1	0	1.000	2	1	1	0	0	13	7	0	7	4	9.7	2.77	130	.159	.275	0	.000	-1	1	1	-0	0.0
1946	Pit-N	0	0	—	1	0	0	0	0	2	0	0	0	2	0.0	0.00	—	.000	.000	0	—	0	1	1	-0	0.0
Total	3	1	1	.500	15	2	1	0	0	42	39	0	27	19	14.8	5.57	67	.255	.377	2	.200	0	-8	-8	1	-0.1
● **MATT CLEMENT** Clement, Matthew Paul b: 8/12/74, McCandless Twsp., Pa. BR/TR, 6′3″, 190 lbs. Deb: 9/6/98																										
1998	SD-N	2	0	1.000	4	2	0	0	0	13^2	15	0	7	13	14.5	4.61	83	.283	.367	0	.000	-0	-1	-1	-0	-0.2
● **PAT CLEMENTS** Clements, Patrick Brian b: 2/2/62, McCloud, Cal. BR/TL, 6′, 180 lbs. Deb: 4/9/85																										
1985	Cal-A	5	0	1.000	41	0	0	0	1	62	47	4	25	19	10.7	3.34	123	.218	.305	0	—	0	6	5	1	0.5
	Pit-N	0	2	.000	27	0	0	0	2	34^1	39	2	15	17	14.2	3.67	97	.289	.360	1	.333	0	-0	-0	-1	-0.1
1986	Pit-N	0	4	.000	65	0	0	0	2	61	53	1	32	31	12.8	2.80	137	.251	.355	0	.000	-1	6	7	1	0.5
1987	NY-A	3	3	.500	55	0	0	0	7	80	91	4	30	36	13.9	4.95	89	.299	.368	0	—	0	-4	-5	1	-0.3
1988	NY-A	0	0	—	6	1	0	0	0	8^1	12	1	4	3	17.3	6.48	61	.343	.410	0	—	0	-2	-2	0	0.1
1989	SD-N	4	1	.800	23	1	0	0	0	39	39	4	15	18	12.5	3.92	89	.267	.335	0	.000	-1	-2	-2	0	-0.3
1990	SD-N	0	0	—	9	0	0	0	0	13	20	1	7	6	18.7	4.15	92	.357	.429	0	—	0	-1	-0	0	0.0
1991	SD-N	1	0	1.000	12	0	0	0	0	14^1	13	0	9	8	13.8	3.77	101	.255	.367	0	.000	-0	-0	0	0	0.0
1992	SD-N	2	1	.667	27	0	0	0	0	23^2	25	0	12	11	14.8	2.66	134	.281	.379	0	.000	-0	2	2	1	0.3
	Bal-A	2	0	1.000	23	0	0	0	0	24^2	23	0	11	9	13.1	3.28	122	.258	.353	0	—	0	2	2	1	0.2
Total	8	17	11	.607	288	2	0	0	12	360^1	362	17	160	158	13.3	3.77	105	.272	.355	1	.059	-1	6	7	4	0.9
● **CHRIS CLEMONS** Clemons, Christopher Hale b: 10/31/72, Baytown, Tex. BR/TR, 6′4″, 220 lbs. Deb: 7/23/97																										
1997	Chi-A	0	2	.000	5	2	0	0	0	12^2	19	4	11	8	22.0	8.53	51	.345	.463	0	—	0	-6	-6	-0	-0.7
● **LANCE CLEMONS** Clemons, Lance Levis b: 7/6/47, Philadelphia, Pa. BL/TL, 6′2″, 205 lbs. Deb: 8/12/71																										
1971	KC-A	1	0	1.000	10	3	0	0	0	24	26	2	12	20	14.6	4.13	83	.263	.348	2	.286	2	-2	-2	0	0.2
1972	StL-N	0	1	.000	3	1	0	0	0	5^1	8	1	5	2	23.6	10.13	34	.364	.500	0	.000	-0	-4	-4	0	-0.6
1974	Bos-A	1	0	1.000	6	0	0	0	0	6^1	8	1	4	1	18.5	9.95	39	.296	.406	0	—	0	-4	-4	0	-0.6
Total	3	2	1	.667	19	4	0	0	0	35^2	42	4	21	23	16.7	6.06	58	.284	.384	2	.250	2	-10	-10	0	-1.0
● **REGGIE CLEVELAND** Cleveland, Reginald Leslie b: 5/23/48, Swift Current, Sask., Canada BR/TR, 6′1″, 195 lbs. Deb: 10/1/69																										
1969	StL-N	0	0	—	1	1	0	0	0	4	7	0	1	3	18.0	9.00	40	.368	.400	0	.000	-0	-2	-2	-0	0.0
1970	StL-N	0	4	.000	16	1	0	0	0	26	31	3	18	22	17.0	7.62	54	.298	.402	1	.250	0	-10	-10	-1	-1.4
1971	StL-N	12	12	.500	34	34	10	2	0	222	238	20	53	148	12.0	4.01	90	.271	.317	14	.171	-1	-14	-10	-0	-1.1
1972	StL-N	14	15	.483	33	33	11	3	0	230^2	229	21	60	153	11.5	3.94	86	.258	.308	17	.239	3	-13	-14	-1	-1.5
1973	StL-N	14	10	.583	32	32	6	3	0	224	211	13	61	122	11.1	3.01	121	.246	.300	17	.230	4	16	16	-2	1.8
1974	Bos-A	12	14	.462	41	27	10	0	0	221^1	234	25	69	103	12.7	4.31	89	.271	.332	0	—	0	-17	-12	1	-1.2
1975	*Bos-A	13	9	.591	31	20	3	1	0	170^2	173	19	52	78	12.0	4.43	92	.263	.320	0	—	0	-12	-7	-0	-0.8
1976	Bos-A	10	9	.526	41	14	3	0	2	170	159	3	61	76	11.9	3.07	127	.246	.315	0	—	0	8	16	-0	0.8
1977	Bos-A	11	8	.579	36	27	9	1	2	190^1	211	20	43	85	12.2	4.26	105	.281	.323	0	—	0	-4	5	-1	-0.1
1978	Bos-A	0	1	.000	1	0	0	0	0	0^1	1	0	0	0	27.0	0.00	—	.333	.333	0	—	0	0	0	0	0.2
	Tex-A	5	7	.417	53	0	0	0	12	75^2	65	5	23	46	10.8	3.09	121	.236	.301	0	—	0	6	5	0	1.0
	Yr	5	8	.385	54	0	0	0	12	76	66	5	23	46	10.9	3.08	122	.237	.302	0	—	0	6	6	0	1.2
1979	Mil-A	1	5	.167	29	1	0	0	4	55	77	9	23	22	16.4	6.71	62	.344	.405	0	—	0	-15	-16	-1	-1.8
1980	Mil-A	11	9	.550	45	13	5	2	4	154^1	150	9	49	54	11.9	3.73	104	.254	.317	0	—	0	5	2	-1	0.3
1981	Mil-A	2	3	.400	35	0	0	0	1	64^2	57	5	30	18	12.2	5.15	66	.239	.327	0	—	0	-11	-12	-1	-1.0
Total	13	105	106	.498	428	203	57	12	25	1809	1843	152	543	930	12.1	4.01	95	.264	.321	49	.211	6	-63	-38	-9	-4.8
● **TEX CLEVENGER** Clevenger, Truman Eugene b: 7/9/32, Visalia, Cal. BR/TR, 6′1″, 180 lbs. Deb: 4/18/54																										
1954	Bos-A	2	4	.333	23	8	1	0	0	67^2	67	9	29	43	13.0	4.79	86	.262	.341	3	.214	0	-8	-5	0	-0.4
1956	Was-A	0	0	—	20	1	0	0	0	31^2	33	4	21	17	15.3	5.40	80	.264	.370	0	.000	-0	-4	-4	-0	0.0
1957	Was-A	7	6	.538	52	9	2	0	8	139^2	139	11	47	75	12.2	4.19	93	.261	.326	7	.212	1	-6	-5	1	-0.2
1958	Was-A	9	9	.500	**55**	4	0	0	6	124	119	12	50	70	12.3	4.35	88	.251	.324	3	.136	0	-8	-7	3	-0.8
1959	Was-A	8	5	.615	50	7	2	2	8	117^1	114	9	51	71	12.8	3.91	100	.256	.335	4	.174	1	-1	0	4	0.5
1960	Was-A	5	11	.313	53	11	1	0	7	128^2	150	10	49	49	14.1	4.20	93	.298	.363	2	.091	-1	-5	-4	-1	-0.7
1961	LA-A	2	1	.667	12	0	0	0	1	16	13	1	13	11	14.6	1.69	267	.220	.361	0	.000	-0	4	5	1	1.0
	NY-A	1	1	.500	21	0	0	0	0	31^2	35	3	21	14	16.2	4.83	77	.287	.396	1	.250	0	-3	-4	1	-0.1
	Yr	3	2	.600	33	0	0	0	1	47^2	48	4	34	25	15.7	3.78	105	.265	.384	1	.143	0	1	1	1	0.9
1962	NY-A	2	0	1.000	21	0	0	0	0	38	36	3	17	11	12.8	2.84	132	.248	.331	0	.000	-0	5	4	0	0.1
Total	8	36	37	.493	307	40	6	2	30	694^2	706	62	298	361	13.2	4.18	94	.265	.342	20	.157	1	-26	-20	8	-0.6
● **STEW CLIBURN** Cliburn, Stewart Walker b: 12/19/56, Jackson, Miss. BR/TR, 6′, 195 lbs. Deb: 9/17/84 F																										
1984	Cal-A	0	0	—	1	0	0	0	0	2	3	0	1	1	18.0	13.50	29	.333	.400	0	—	0	-2	-2	0	0.0
1985	Cal-A	9	3	.750	44	0	0	0	6	99	87	5	26	48	10.4	2.09	197	.241	.294	0	—	0	23	22	1	2.9
1988	Cal-A	4	2	.667	40	1	0	0	0	84	83	11	32	42	13.0	4.07	95	.266	.346	0	—	0	-1	-2	0	0.1
Total	3	13	5	.722	85	1	0	0	6	185	173	16	59	91	11.6	3.11	128	.254	.320	0	—	0	20	18	2	3.0
● **JIM CLINTON** Clinton, James Lawrence "Big Jim" b: 8/10/1850, New York, N.Y. d: 9/3/21, Brooklyn, N.Y. BR/TR, 5′8.5″, 174 lbs. Deb: 5/18/1872 MU♦																										
1875	Atl-n	1	13	.071	17	14	9	0	0	123	141	0	5	7	10.7	2.41	86	.262	.268	10	.123	-5	-3	-5		-0.7
1876	Lou-N	0	1	.000	1	1	1	0	0	9	12	0	0	1	12.0	6.00	45	.279	.279	22	.338	0	-4	-3	0	-0.2
● **TONY CLONINGER** Cloninger, Tony Lee b: 8/13/40, Lincoln Co., N.C. BR/TR, 6′, 210 lbs. Deb: 6/15/61 C																										
1961	Mil-N	7	2	.778	19	10	3	0	0	84	84	16	33	51	12.6	5.25	71	.258	.328	5	.167	-0	-11	-14	1	-1.3
1962	Mil-N	8	3	.727	24	15	4	1	0	111	113	10	46	69	13.0	4.30	88	.264	.337	4	.103	-2	-4	-6	0	-0.7
1963	Mil-N	9	11	.450	41	18	4	2	1	145^1	131	17	63	100	12.1	3.78	85	.239	.320	5	.135	-0	-8	-9	-2	-1.4
1964	Mil-N	19	14	.576	38	34	15	3	2	242^2	206	20	82	163	10.8	3.56	99	.231	.298	21	.241	3	-1	-1	-0	0.2
1965	Mil-N	24	11	.686	40	38	16	1	1	279	247	20	119	211	11.9	3.29	107	.236	.316	17	.162	2	8	7	-1	0.9
1966	Atl-N	14	11	.560	39	38	11	1	1	257^2	253	29	116	178	13.1	4.12	88	.258	.340	26	.234	10	-15	-14	-0	-0.3
1967	Atl-N	4	7	.364	16	16	1	0	0	76^2	85	13	31	55	13.6	5.17	64	.285	.353	5	.200	1	-15	-16	-0	-2.0
1968	Atl-N	1	3	.250	8	1	0	0	0	19	15	0	11	7	12.3	4.26	70	.227	.338	0	.000	-0	-3	-3	0	-0.6
	Cin-N	4	3	.571	17	17	2	2	0	91^1	81	7	48	65	13.0	4.04	78	.233	.331	7	.206	3	-11	-9	-0	-0.4
	Yr	5	6	.455	25	18	2	2	0	110^1	96	7	59	72	12.9	4.08	77	.231	.331	7	.184	3	-13	-12	-0	-1.0
1969	Cin-N	11	17	.393	35	34	6	2	0	189^2	184	24	103	103	13.9	5.03	75	.250	.346	12	.167	1	-30	-27	-2	-3.6
1970	*Cin-N	9	7	.563	30	18	0	0	1	148	136	10	78	56	13.3	3.83	105	.249	.347	10	.213	3	4	3	2	0.8
1971	Cin-N	3	6	.333	28	8	1	1	0	97^1	79	12	49	51	12.2	3.88	86	.230	.332	7	.259	1	-5	-6	0	-0.3
1972	StL-N	0	2	.000	17	0	0	0	0	26	29	2	19	11	17.0	5.19	66	.293	.412	0	.000	-0	-5	-5	1	-0.3
Total	12	113	97	.538	352	247	63	13	6	1767^2	1643	180	798	1120	12.6	4.07	88	.247	.330	119	.192	21	-96	-98	-2	-9.0
● **BRAD CLONTZ** Clontz, John Bradley b: 4/25/71, Stuart, Va. BR/TR, 6′1″, 180 lbs. Deb: 4/26/95																										
1995	*Atl-N	8	1	.889	59	0	0	0	4	69	71	5	22	55	12.7	3.65	117	.269	.334	0	.000	-0	4	5	0	0.6
1996	*Atl-N	6	3	.667	**81**	0	0	0	1	80^2	78	11	33	49	12.6	5.69	77	.255	.331	0	.000	0	-13	-12	1	-1.1
1997	Atl-N	5	1	.833	51	0	0	0	1	48	52	3	18	42	13.3	3.75	111	.286	.353	0	.000	-0	2	2	-1	0.2
1998	LA-N	2	0	1.000	18	0	0	0	0	20^2	15	3	10	14	11.8	5.66	69	.200	.310	0	.000	-0	-3	-4	-1	-0.4
	NY-N	0	0	—	2	0	0	0	0	3	4	1	2	2	18.0	9.00	46	.333	.429	0	—	0	-2	-2	0	0.0
	Yr	2	0	1.000	20	0	0	0	0	23^2	19	4	12	16	11.8	6.08	65	.213	.307	0	.000	-0	-5	-6	-1	-0.4
Total	4	21	5	.808	211	0	0	0	6	221^1	220	23	85	162	12.8	4.68	91	.262	.337	0	.000	-0	-12	-10	-1	-0.7

YEAR	TM/L	W	L	PCT	G	GS	CG	SH	SV	IP	H	HR	BB	SO	RAT	ERA	ERA+	OAV	OOB	BH	AVG	PB	PR	/A	PD	TPI
● AL CLOSTER	Closter, Alan Edward b: 6/15/43, Creighton, Neb. BL/TL, 6'2", 190 lbs. Deb: 4/19/66																									
1966	Was-A	0	0	—	1	0	0	0	0	0^1	1	0	2	0	81.0	0.00	—	.500	.750	0	—	0	0	0	0	0.0
1971	NY-A	2	2	.500	14	1	0	0	0	28^1	33	4	13	22	15.2	5.08	64	.289	.372	0	.000	-1	-5	-6	1	-0.8
1972	NY-A	0	0	—	2	0	0	0	0	2^1	2	1	4	2	23.1	11.57	25	.250	.500	0	.000	-0	-2	-2	0	0.0
1973	Atl-N	0	0	—	4	0	0	0	0	4^1	7	1	4	2	22.8	14.54	27	.389	.500	0	—	0	-5	-5	0	0.0
Total	4	2	2	.500	21	1	0	0	0	35^1	43	6	23	26	17.3	6.62	50	.303	.407	0	.000	-1	-12	-13	1	-0.8
● KEN CLOUDE	Cloude, Kenneth Brian b: 1/9/75, Baltimore, Md. BR/TR, 6'1", 200 lbs. Deb: 8/9/97																									
1997	Sea-A	4	2	.667	10	9	0	0	0	51	41	8	26	46	12.4	5.12	88	.218	.323	0	.000	-0	-3	-4	-0	-0.4
1998	Sea-A	8	10	.444	30	30	0	0	0	155^1	187	29	80	114	15.6	6.37	73	.296	.378	0	.000	-0	-30	-30	-1	-2.9
Total	2	12	12	.500	40	39	0	0	0	206^1	228	37	106	160	14.8	6.06	76	.278	.365	0	.000	-0	-33	-34	-1	-3.3
● ED CLOUGH	Clough, Edgar George "Big Ed" or "Spec" b: 10/28/06, Wiconisco, Pa. d: 1/30/44, Harrisburg, Pa. BL/TL, 6', 188 lbs. Deb: 8/28/24 ♦																									
1925	StL-N	0	1	.000	3	1	0	0	0	10	11	1	5	3	15.3	8.10	53	.289	.386	1	.250	-0	-4	-4	-0	-0.4
1926	StL-N	0	0	—	1	0	0	0	0	2	5	0	3	0	40.5	22.50	17	.556	.692	0	.000	-0	-4	-4	-0	0.0
Total	2	0	1	.000	4	1	0	0	0	12	16	1	8	3	19.5	10.50	40	.340	.456	2	.105	-0	-8	-8	-0	-0.4
● BILL CLOWERS	Clowers, William Perry b: 8/14/1898, San Marcos, Tex. d: 1/13/78, Sweeny, Tex. BL/TL, 5'11", 175 lbs. Deb: 7/20/26																									
1926	Bos-A	0	0	—	2	0	0	0	0	1^2	2	0	0	0	10.8	0.00	—	.333	.333	0	—	0	1	1	0	0.0
● BRYAN CLUTTERBUCK	Clutterbuck, Bryan Richard b: 12/17/59, Detroit, Mich. BR/TR, 6'4", 223 lbs. Deb: 7/18/86																									
1986	Mil-A	0	1	.000	20	0	0	0	0	56^2	68	8	16	38	13.7	4.29	101	.296	.347	0	—	0	-1	0	-0	0.0
1989	Mil-A	2	5	.286	14	11	1	0	0	67^1	73	11	16	29	11.9	4.14	93	.269	.310	0	—	0	-2	-2	-2	-0.4
Total	2	2	6	.250	34	11	1	0	0	124	141	19	32	67	12.7	4.21	96	.281	.327	0	—	0	-3	-2	-2	-0.4
● DAVID CLYDE	Clyde, David Eugene b: 4/22/55, Kansas City, Kan. BL/TL, 6'1", 185 lbs. Deb: 6/27/73																									
1973	Tex-A	4	8	.333	18	18	0	0	0	93^1	106	8	54	74	15.8	5.01	74	.293	.390	0	—	0	-12	-13	-0	-1.3
1974	Tex-A	3	9	.250	28	21	4	0	0	117	129	14	47	52	13.8	4.38	81	.286	.359	0	—	0	-10	-11	-2	-1.2
1975	Tex-A	0	1	.000	1	1	0	0	0	7	6	0	6	2	15.4	2.57	146	.273	.429	0	—	0	1	1	-0	0.1
1978	Cle-A	8	11	.421	28	25	5	0	0	153^1	166	4	60	83	13.4	4.28	87	.280	.350	0	—	0	-9	-9	-1	-1.1
1979	Cle-A	3	4	.429	9	8	1	0	0	45^2	50	7	13	17	12.6	5.91	72	.279	.332	0	—	0	-9	-8	-0	-1.1
Total	5	18	33	.353	84	73	10	0	0	416^1	457	33	180	228	14.0	4.63	81	.285	.361	0	—	0	-39	-41	-4	-4.6
● TOM CLYDE	Clyde, Thomas Knox b: 8/17/23, Wachapreague, Va. BR/TR, 6'3", 195 lbs. Deb: 5/31/43																									
1943	Phi-A	0	0	—	4	0	0	0	0	6	7	1	4	0	18.0	9.00	38	.304	.429	0	.000	-0	-4	-4	-0	-0.1
● ANDY COAKLEY	Coakley, Andrew James (a.k.a. Jack McAllister In 1902) b: 11/20/1882, Providence, R.I. d: 9/27/63, New York, N.Y. BL/TR, 6', 165 lbs. Deb: 9/17/02																									
1902	Phi-A	2	1	.667	3	3	3	0	0	27	25	0	9	9	12.0	2.67	138	.245	.319	3	.375	1	3	3	0	0.5
1903	Phi-A	0	3	.000	6	3	2	0	0	37^2	48	2	11	20	14.6	5.50	56	.310	.363	3	.200	-0	-11	-10	-0	-0.8
1904	Phi-A	4	3	.571	8	8	7	2	0	62	48	1	23	33	10.6	1.89	142	.215	.294	2	.087	-2	5	5	-0	0.3
1905	*Phi-A	18	8	.692	35	31	21	3	0	255	227	2	73	145	10.8	1.84	145	.240	.299	13	.138	-3	23	23	-1	1.9
1906	Phi-A	7	8	.467	22	16	10	0	0	149	144	0	44	59	11.5	3.14	87	.257	.314	7	.143	-2	-7	-7	-3	-1.1
1907	Cin-N	17	16	.515	37	30	21	1	1	265^1	269	1	79	89	12.0	2.34	111	.274	.332	6	.071	-6	4	8	-3	0.0
1908	Cin-N	8	18	.308	32	28	20	4	2	242^1	219	3	64	61	10.7	1.86	124	.249	.303	7	.092	-4	14	12	-4	0.4
	Chi-N	2	0	1.000	4	3	2	1	0	20^1	14	0	6	7	8.9	0.89	266	.192	.253	0	.000	-1	3	3	-0	0.2
	Yr	10	18	.357	36	31	22	5	2	262^2	233	3	70	68	10.4	1.78	130	.244	.295	7	.085	-5	17	15	-5	0.6
1909	Chi-N	0	1	.000	1	1	0	0	0	2	7	0	3	1	45.0	18.00	14	.583	.667	0	—	0	-3	-3	0	-1.0
1911	NY-A	0	1	.000	2	1	1	0	0	11^2	20	0	2	4	17.0	5.40	67	.377	.400	1	.250	0	-3	-2	0	-0.2
Total	9	58	59	.496	150	124	87	11	3	1072^1	1021	9	314	428	11.4	2.35	111	.256	.315	42	.117	-16	28	32	-12	0.2
● JIM COATES	Coates, James Alton b: 8/4/32, Farnham, Va. BR/TR, 6'4", 192 lbs. Deb: 9/21/56																									
1956	NY-A	0	0	—	2	0	0	0	0	2	1	0	4	0	27.0	13.50	29	.167	.545	0	—	0	-2	-2	0	0.0
1959	NY-A	6	1	.857	37	4	2	0	0	100^1	89	10	36	64	11.5	2.87	127	.234	.305	2	.095	-1	11	9	0	0.4
1960	*NY-A★	13	3	.813	35	18	6	2	1	149^1	139	16	66	73	12.5	4.28	84	.248	.330	12	.250	4	-7	-12	-2	-1.0
1961	*NY-A	11	5	.688	43	11	4	1	5	141^1	128	15	53	80	12.0	3.44	108	.243	.321	1	.029	-3	9	4	-0	0.1
1962	*NY-A	7	6	.538	50	6	0	0	6	117^2	119	9	50	67	13.3	4.44	84	.263	.343	4	.125	-1	-6	-9	-2	-1.3
1963	Was-A	2	4	.333	20	2	0	0	0	44^1	51	4	21	31	15.2	5.28	70	.297	.383	0	.000	-1	-8	-8	0	-1.0
	Cin-N	0	0	—	9	0	0	0	0	16^1	21	2	7	11	15.4	5.51	61	.313	.378	0	.000	-0	-4	-4	0	0.0
1965	Cal-A	2	0	1.000	17	0	0	0	3	28	23	1	16	15	12.5	3.54	96	.228	.333	0	.000	-0	-0	-0	-0	-0.1
1966	Cal-A	1	1	.500	9	4	1	1	0	31^2	32	3	10	16	11.9	3.98	84	.258	.313	1	.091	-1	-2	-2	-0	-0.2
1967	Cal-A	1	2	.333	25	1	0	0	0	52^1	47	5	23	39	12.7	4.30	73	.244	.336	1	.333	1	-6	-7	0	-0.3
Total	9	43	22	.662	247	46	13	4	15	683^1	650	65	286	396	12.7	4.00	90	.252	.332	21	.131	-3	-15	-30	-4	-3.4
● GEORGE COBB	Cobb, George Woodworth b: 9/25/1865, Independence, Ia. d: 8/19/26, Pomona, Cal. 6', 168 lbs. Deb: 4/15/1892																									
1892	Bal-N	10	37	.213	53	47	42	0	0	394^1	495	21	140	159	14.9	4.86	71	.295	.356	36	.209	5	-69	-63	2	-5.3
● HERB COBB	Cobb, Herbert Edward b: 8/6/04, Pinetops, N.C. d: 1/8/80, Tarboro, N.C. BR/TR, 5'11", 150 lbs. Deb: 4/21/29																									
1929	StL-A	0	0	—	1	0	0	0	0	1	3	1	1	0	36.0	36.00	12	.600	.667	0	—	0	-4	-4	-0	0.0
● TY COBB	Cobb, Tyrus Raymond "The Georgia Peach" b: 12/18/1886, Narrows, Ga. d: 7/17/61, Atlanta, Ga. BL/TR, 6'1", 175 lbs. Deb: 8/30/05 MH♦																									
1918	Det-A	0	0	—	2	0	0	0	0	4	6	0	2	0	18.0	4.50	59	.400	.471	161	.382	1	-1	-1	-0	0.0
1925	Det-A	0	0	—	1	0	0	0	1	1	0	0	0	0	0.0	0.00	—	.000	.000	157	.378	1	0	0	0	0.1
Total	2	0	0	—	3	0	0	0	1	5	6	0	2	0	14.4	3.60	83	.333	.400	4189	.366	2	-0	-0	0	0.1
● JAIME COCANOWER	Cocanower, James Stanley b: 2/14/57, San Juan, P.R. BR/TR, 6'4", 200 lbs. Deb: 9/7/83																									
1983	Mil-A	2	0	1.000	5	3	1	0	0	30	21	1	12	8	10.2	1.80	208	.200	.288	0	—	0	8	6	0	0.7
1984	Mil-A	8	16	.333	33	27	1	0	0	174^2	188	13	78	65	14.2	4.02	96	.279	.362	0	—	0	-1	-3	1	-0.2
1985	Mil-A	6	8	.429	24	15	3	1	0	116^1	122	6	73	44	15.7	4.33	96	.274	.386	0	—	0	-2	-2	0	-0.2
1986	Mil-A	0	1	.000	17	2	0	0	0	44^2	40	1	38	22	16.1	4.43	98	.248	.398	0	—	0	-1	-1	1	0.1
Total	4	16	25	.390	79	47	5	1	0	365^2	371	21	201	139	14.6	3.99	100	.268	.369	0	—	0	3	0	3	0.4
● GOAT COCHRAN	Cochran, Alvah Jackson "Al" or "Goat" b: 1/31/1891, Concord, Ga. d: 5/23/47, Atlanta, Ga. BR/TR, 5'10", 175 lbs. Deb: 8/25/15																									
1915	Cin-N	0	0	—	1	0	0	0	0	2	5	0	0	1	22.5	9.00	32	.455	.455	0	—	0	-1	-1	-0	0.0
● GENE COCREHAM	Cocreham, Eugene b: 11/14/1884, Luling, Tex. d: 12/27/45, Luling, Tex. BR/TR, 6'3.5", 192 lbs. Deb: 9/25/13																									
1913	Bos-N	0	1	.000	1	1	0	0	0	8^1	13	0	4	3	19.4	7.56	43	.371	.450	0	.000	-1	-4	-4	0	-0.4
1914	Bos-N	3	4	.429	15	3	1	0	0	44^2	48	2	27	15	15.1	4.84	57	.296	.397	1	.100	-0	-10	-10	-1	-1.7
1915	Bos-N	0	0	—	1	0	0	0	0	1^2	3	0	0	0	16.2	5.40	48	.429	.429	0	—	0	-0	-1	-0	0.0
Total	3	3	5	.375	17	4	1	0	0	54^2	64	2	31	18	15.8	5.27	54	.314	.407	1	.071	-1	-15	-15	-2	-2.1
● CHRIS CODIROLI	Codiroli, Christopher Allen b: 3/26/58, Oxnard, Cal. BR/TR, 6'1", 160 lbs. Deb: 9/11/82																									
1982	Oak-A	1	2	.333	3	3	0	0	0	16^2	16	1	4	5	10.8	4.32	90	.246	.290	0	—	0	-0	-1	0	0.0
1983	Oak-A	12	12	.500	37	31	7	2	1	205^2	208	17	72	85	12.6	4.46	86	.264	.331	0	—	0	-9	-14	-2	-1.5
1984	Oak-A	6	4	.600	28	14	1	0	1	89^1	111	16	34	44	14.9	5.84	64	.304	.368	0	—	0	-18	-21	-0	-2.0
1985	Oak-A	14	14	.500	37	37	4	0	0	226	228	23	78	111	12.3	4.46	86	.259	.321	0	—	0	-8	-15	-1	-1.7
1986	Oak-A	5	8	.385	16	16	1	0	0	91^2	91	15	38	43	12.9	4.03	96	.250	.324	0	—	0	2	-2	1	-0.1
1987	Oak-A	0	2	.000	3	3	0	0	0	11^1	12	1	8	4	16.7	8.74	47	.273	.396	0	—	0	-5	-6	-0	-0.7
1988	Cle-A	0	4	.000	14	2	0	0	1	19^1	32	2	10	12	20.9	9.31	44	.372	.455	0	—	0	-11	-11	0	-2.2
1990	KC-A	0	1	.000	6	2	0	0	0	10^1	13	1	17	8	29.6	9.58	40	.325	.557	0	—	0	-7	-7	-0	-0.6
Total	8	38	47	.447	144	108	13	2	3	670^1	711	76	261	312	13.4	4.87	79	.270	.341	0	—	0	-58	-76	-2	-8.8

● SLICK COFFMAN Coffman, George David b: 12/11/10, Veto, Ala. BR/TR, 6′, 155 lbs. Deb: 5/21/37 F

YEAR	TM/L	W	L	PCT	G	GS	CG	SH	SV	IP	H	HR	BB	SO	RAT	ERA	ERA+	OAV	OOB	BH	AVG	PB	PR	/A	PD	TPI
1937	Det-A	7	5	.583	28	5	1	0	0	101	121	8	39	22	14.5	4.37	107	.295	.361	5	.172	0	3	3	-1	0.3
1938	Det-A	4	4	.500	39	6	1	0	2	95^2	120	6	48	31	15.8	6.02	83	.310	.386	4	.167	-0	-13	-11	-1	-0.9
1939	Det-A	2	1	.667	23	1	0	0	0	42^1	51	4	22	10	15.7	6.38	77	.295	.378	0	.000	-0	-8	-7	0	-0.5
1940	StL-A	2	2	.500	31	4	1	0	1	74^2	108	5	23	26	15.8	6.27	73	.334	.379	3	.200	-0	-16	-14	1	-0.6
Total	4	15	12	.556	121	16	3	0	3	313^2	400	23	132	89	15.4	5.60	85	.309	.375	12	.164	-0	-34	-28	-1	-1.7

● KEVIN COFFMAN Coffman, Kevin Reese b: 1/19/65, Austin, Tex. BR/TR, 6′2″, 175 lbs. Deb: 9/5/87

YEAR	TM/L	W	L	PCT	G	GS	CG	SH	SV	IP	H	HR	BB	SO	RAT	ERA	ERA+	OAV	OOB	BH	AVG	PB	PR	/A	PD	TPI
1987	Atl-N	2	3	.400	5	5	0	0	0	25^1	31	2	22	14	19.9	4.62	94	.313	.452	1	.100	-0	-2	-1	1	-0.1
1988	Atl-N	2	6	.250	18	11	0	0	0	67	62	3	54	24	16.1	5.78	64	.251	.393	5	.227	2	-17	-16	0	-1.5
1990	Chi-N	0	2	.000	8	2	0	0	0	18^1	26	0	19	9	22.1	11.29	36	.333	.464	1	.200	0	-15	-15	1	-1.3
Total	3	4	11	.267	31	18	0	0	0	110^2	119	5	95	47	18.0	6.42	61	.281	.420	7	.189	1	-34	-31	2	-2.9

● DICK COFFMAN Coffman, Samuel Richard b: 12/18/06, Veto, Ala. d: 3/24/72, Athens, Ala. BR/TR, 6′2″, 195 lbs. Deb: 4/28/27 F

YEAR	TM/L	W	L	PCT	G	GS	CG	SH	SV	IP	H	HR	BB	SO	RAT	ERA	ERA+	OAV	OOB	BH	AVG	PB	PR	/A	PD	TPI
1927	Was-A	0	1	.000	5	2	0	0	0	16	20	0	2	5	13.5	3.38	120	.313	.353	1	.333	0	1	1	0	0.1
1928	StL-A	4	5	.444	29	7	3	0	1	85^2	122	7	37	25	16.8	6.09	69	.359	.423	1	.043	-3	-20	-18	0	-1.9
1929	StL-A	1	1	.500	27	3	1	1	1	52^2	61	3	14	11	13.3	5.98	74	.295	.348	0	.000	-1	-10	-9	0	-0.4
1930	StL-A	8	18	.308	38	30	12	1	1	196	250	14	69	54	14.9	5.14	95	.311	.369	9	.136	-5	-11	-6	0	-1.1
1931	StL-A	9	13	.409	32	17	11	2	1	169^1	159	10	51	39	11.3	3.88	119	.241	.298	4	.078	-5	9	14	-2	1.0
1932	StL-A	5	3	.625	9	6	3	0	0	61	66	3	21	14	13.1	3.10	157	.277	.341	1	.045	-2	9	12	-1	1.1
	Was-A	1	6	.143	22	9	2	1	0	76^1	92	2	31	17	14.6	4.83	89	.307	.373	2	.091	-1	-3	-4	-1	-0.5
	Yr	6	9	.400	31	15	5	1	0	137^1	158	5	52	31	13.8	4.06	112	.293	.356	3	.068	-3	6	7	-2	0.6
1933	StL-A	3	7	.300	21	13	3	1	1	81	114	9	39	19	17.2	5.89	79	.329	.399	1	.037	-3	-14	-11	0	-1.4
1934	StL-A	9	10	.474	40	21	6	1	3	173	212	11	59	55	14.2	4.53	110	.303	.358	11	.216	-1	-1	9	0	0.8
1935	StL-A	5	11	.313	41	18	5	0	2	143^2	206	14	46	34	15.9	6.14	78	.335	.383	6	.146	-1	-27	-21	-1	-2.2
1936	*NY-N	7	5	.583	42	2	0	0	7	101^2	119	7	23	26	12.7	3.90	100	.296	.337	4	.200	-0	1	0	1	0.1
1937	*NY-N	8	3	.727	42	1	0	0	3	80	93	4	31	30	14.4	3.04	128	.289	.359	7	.368	2	**8**	**8**	0	1.3
1938	NY-N	8	4	.667	**51**	3	1	1	**12**	111^1	116	3	21	21	11.3	3.48	108	.268	.306	2	.071	-3	4	4	-2	0.0
1939	NY-N	1	2	.333	28	0	0	0	3	38	50	1	6	9	14.0	3.08	128	.316	.353	0	.000	-1	4	4	-0	0.2
1940	Bos-N	1	5	.167	31	0	0	0	3	48^1	63	4	11	11	14.2	5.40	69	.323	.365	1	.083	-1	-8	-9	-1	-1.2
1945	Phi-N	2	1	.667	14	0	0	0	0	26^1	39	0	2	2	14.0	5.13	75	.351	.363	1	.250	0	-4	-4	1	-0.2
Total	15	72	95	.431	472	132	47	8	38	1460^1	1782	92	463	372	14.1	4.65	96	.302	.357	51	.127	-22	-61	-33	-2	-4.3

● DICK COGAN Cogan, Richard Henry b: 12/5/1871, Paterson, N.J. d: 5/2/48, Paterson, N.J. BR/TR, 5′7″, 150 lbs. Deb: 5/10/1897

YEAR	TM/L	W	L	PCT	G	GS	CG	SH	SV	IP	H	HR	BB	SO	RAT	ERA	ERA+	OAV	OOB	BH	AVG	PB	PR	/A	PD	TPI
1897	Bal-N	0	0	—	1	0	0	0	0	2	4	0	2	0	31.5	13.50	31	.400	.538	0	.000	-0	-2	-2	-0	0.0
1899	Chi-N	2	3	.400	5	5	5	0	0	44	54	1	24	9	16.8	4.30	87	.302	.396	5	.200	1	-2	-3	-1	-0.2
1900	NY-N	0	0	—	2	0	0	0	0	8	10	0	6	1	18.0	6.75	54	.303	.410	1	.125	-0	-3	-3	-0	0.0
Total	3	2	3	.400	8	5	5	0	0	54	68	1	32	10	17.5	5.00	75	.306	.405	6	.176	0	-7	-8	-1	-0.2

● HY COHEN Cohen, Hyman b: 1/29/31, Brooklyn, N.Y. BR/TR, 6′5″, 220 lbs. Deb: 4/17/55

YEAR	TM/L	W	L	PCT	G	GS	CG	SH	SV	IP	H	HR	BB	SO	RAT	ERA	ERA+	OAV	OOB	BH	AVG	PB	PR	/A	PD	TPI
1955	Chi-N	0	0	—	7	1	0	0	0	17	28	2	10	4	20.6	7.94	51	.378	.459	0	.000	-0	-7	-7	-0	0.0

● SYD COHEN Cohen, Sydney Harry b: 5/7/06, Baltimore, Md. d: 4/9/88, ElPaso, Tex. BB/TL, 5′11″, 180 lbs. Deb: 9/18/34 F

YEAR	TM/L	W	L	PCT	G	GS	CG	SH	SV	IP	H	HR	BB	SO	RAT	ERA	ERA+	OAV	OOB	BH	AVG	PB	PR	/A	PD	TPI
1934	Was-A	1	1	.500	3	2	2	0	0	18	25	2	6	6	15.5	7.50	58	.333	.383	3	.273	0	-6	-6	1	-0.4
1936	Was-A	0	2	.000	19	1	0	0	1	36	44	4	14	21	15.3	5.25	91	.303	.377	0	.000	-1	-1	-2	2	0.0
1937	Was-A	2	4	.333	33	0	0	0	4	55	64	1	17	22	13.3	3.11	142	.299	.351	2	.143	-1	9	8	2	0.9
Total	3	3	7	.300	55	3	2	0	5	109	133	7	37	49	14.3	4.54	100	.306	.365	5	.152	-2	2	-0	5	0.5

● ROCKY COLAVITO Colavito, Rocco Domenico b: 8/10/33, New York, N.Y. BR/TR, 6′3″, 190 lbs. Deb: 9/10/55 C♦

YEAR	TM/L	W	L	PCT	G	GS	CG	SH	SV	IP	H	HR	BB	SO	RAT	ERA	ERA+	OAV	OOB	BH	AVG	PB	PR	/A	PD	TPI
1958	Cle-A	0	0	—	1	0	0	0	0	3	0	0	3	1	9.0	0.00	—	.000	.273	148	.303	1	1	1	0	0.0
1968	NY-A	1	0	1.000	1	0	0	0	0	2^2	1	0	2	1	10.1	0.00	—	.111	.273	20	.220	0	1	1	-0	0.4
Total	2	1	0	1.000	2	0	0	0	0	5^2	1	0	5	2	9.5	0.00	—	.059	.273	1730	.266	1	2	2	0	0.4

● VINCE COLBERT Colbert, Vincent Norman b: 12/20/45, Washington, D.C. BR/TR, 6′4″, 200 lbs. Deb: 5/19/70

YEAR	TM/L	W	L	PCT	G	GS	CG	SH	SV	IP	H	HR	BB	SO	RAT	ERA	ERA+	OAV	OOB	BH	AVG	PB	PR	/A	PD	TPI
1970	Cle-A	1	1	.500	23	0	0	0	2	31	37	4	16	17	15.7	7.26	55	.298	.383	0	.000	-0	-12	-11	0	-0.8
1971	Cle-A	7	6	.538	50	10	2	0	2	142^2	140	11	71	74	13.7	3.97	96	.265	.358	4	.138	-0	-8	-2	0	-0.2
1972	Cle-A	1	7	.125	22	11	1	1	0	74^2	74	8	38	36	14.3	4.58	70	.267	.370	4	.200	1	-13	-11	0	-1.1
Total	3	9	14	.391	95	21	3	1	4	248^1	251	23	125	127	14.1	4.57	80	.270	.365	8	.157	0	-33	-25	1	-2.1

● JIM COLBORN Colborn, James William b: 5/22/46, Santa Paula, Cal. BR/TR, 6′, 191 lbs. Deb: 7/13/69

YEAR	TM/L	W	L	PCT	G	GS	CG	SH	SV	IP	H	HR	BB	SO	RAT	ERA	ERA+	OAV	OOB	BH	AVG	PB	PR	/A	PD	TPI
1969	Chi-N	1	0	1.000	6	2	0	0	0	14^2	15	2	9	4	15.3	3.07	131	.283	.397	0	.000	-0	1	2	0	0.1
1970	Chi-N	3	1	.750	34	5	0	0	4	72^2	88	3	23	50	13.9	3.59	125	.298	.351	1	.067	-1	4	7	1	0.4
1971	Chi-N	0	1	.000	14	0	0	0	0	10^1	18	1	3	2	18.3	6.97	56	.383	.420	0	—	0	-4	-3	0	-0.3
1972	Mil-A	7	7	.500	39	12	4	1	0	147^2	135	14	43	97	11.0	3.11	97	.245	.302	3	.081	-1	-1	-1	-1	-0.4
1973	Mil-A☆	20	12	.625	43	36	22	4	1	314^1	297	21	87	135	11.1	3.18	118	.251	.304	0	—	0	22	20	2	2.2
1974	Mil-A	10	13	.435	33	31	10	1	0	224	230	27	60	83	11.9	4.06	89	.268	.320	0	—	0	-11	-11	0	-1.0
1975	Mil-A	11	13	.458	36	29	8	1	2	206^1	215	18	65	79	12.4	4.27	90	.270	.329	0	—	0	-11	-10	1	-1.0
1976	Mil-A	9	15	.375	32	32	7	0	0	225^2	232	20	54	101	11.5	3.71	94	.268	.312	0	—	0	-5	-5	-0	-0.6
1977	KC-A	18	14	.563	36	35	6	1	0	239	233	22	81	103	12.3	3.62	112	.255	.324	0	—	0	12	11	1	1.4
1978	KC-A	1	2	.333	8	3	0	0	0	28^1	31	4	12	8	14.3	4.76	80	.282	.363	0	—	0	-3	-3	1	-0.3
	Sea-A	3	10	.231	20	19	3	0	0	114^1	125	21	38	26	13.3	5.35	71	.279	.343	0	—	0	-20	-20	3	-1.7
	Yr	4	12	.250	28	22	3	0	0	142^2	156	25	50	34	13.4	5.24	73	.279	.344	0	—	0	-23	-23	3	-2.0
Total	10	83	88	.485	301	204	60	8	7	1597^1	1619	153	475	688	12.0	3.80	98	.265	.322	4	.073	-3	-17	-14	7	-1.2

● TOM COLCOLOUGH Colcolough, Thomas Bernard b: 10/8/1870, Charleston, S.C. d: 12/10/19, Charleston, S.C. BR/TR, 5′10.5″, 180 lbs. Deb: 8/1/1893

YEAR	TM/L	W	L	PCT	G	GS	CG	SH	SV	IP	H	HR	BB	SO	RAT	ERA	ERA+	OAV	OOB	BH	AVG	PB	PR	/A	PD	TPI
1893	Pit-N	1	0	1.000	8	3	1	0	**2**	43^2	45	1	32	7	15.9	4.12	110	.259	.374	2	.143	0	3	2	-1	0.0
1894	Pit-N	8	5	.615	22	14	11	0	0	148^2	207	5	70	29	17.1	7.08	74	.326	.397	14	.200	-3	-29	-30	0	-1.9
1895	Pit-N	1	1	.500	6	5	2	0	0	35^1	38	1	21	15	16.3	5.60	81	.271	.386	5	.333	3	-3	-4	-1	0.0
1899	NY-N	4	5	.444	11	8	7	0	0	81^2	85	1	41	14	14.2	3.97	95	.268	.357	10	.270	1	-1	-2	1	0.0
Total	4	14	11	.560	47	30	21	0	2	309^1	375	8	164	65	16.1	5.67	82	.296	.383	31	.228	1	-31	-35	0	-1.9

● BERT COLE Cole, Albert George b: 7/1/1896, San Francisco, Cal. d: 5/30/75, San Mateo, Cal. BL/TL, 6′1″, 180 lbs. Deb: 4/19/21

YEAR	TM/L	W	L	PCT	G	GS	CG	SH	SV	IP	H	HR	BB	SO	RAT	ERA	ERA+	OAV	OOB	BH	AVG	PB	PR	/A	PD	TPI
1921	Det-A	7	4	.636	20	11	7	1	1	109^2	134	3	36	22	14.3	4.27	100	.305	.363	13	.283	3	0	0	-1	0.2
1922	Det-A	1	6	.143	23	5	2	1	0	79^1	105	4	39	21	16.4	4.88	80	.313	.387	4	.160	-1	-7	-9	0	-0.7
1923	Det-A	13	5	.722	52	13	6	1	5	163	183	9	61	32	13.7	4.14	93	.284	.351	14	.255	2	-3	-5	-1	-0.4
1924	Det-A	3	9	.250	28	12	2	1	2	109^1	135	4	35	16	14.3	4.69	88	.314	.371	10	.270	1	-6	-7	1	-0.5
1925	Det-A	2	3	.400	14	2	1	0	1	33^2	44	2	15	7	16.0	5.88	73	.336	.408	3	.273	0	-6	-6	1	-0.7
	Cle-A	1	1	.500	13	2	0	0	1	44	55	1	25	9	16.6	6.14	72	.322	.411	2	.154	-0	-9	-8	-0	-0.4
	Yr	3	4	.429	27	4	1	0	2	77^2	99	3	40	16	16.2	6.03	73	.327	.407	5	.208	0	-14	-14	0	-1.1
1927	Chi-A	1	4	.200	27	2	0	0	0	66^2	79	3	19	12	13.6	4.72	86	.309	.363	3	.167	-1	-4	-5	2	-0.3
Total	6	28	32	.467	177	47	18	4	10	605^2	735	26	230	119	14.6	4.67	87	.305	.370	49	.239	5	-34	-40	2	-2.8

● DAVE COLE Cole, David Bruce b: 8/29/30, Williamsport, Md. BR/TR, 6′2″, 175 lbs. Deb: 9/9/50

YEAR	TM/L	W	L	PCT	G	GS	CG	SH	SV	IP	H	HR	BB	SO	RAT	ERA	ERA+	OAV	OOB	BH	AVG	PB	PR	/A	PD	TPI
1950	Bos-N	0	1	.000	4	0	0	0	0	8	7	0	3	8	12.4	1.13	342	.259	.355	0	.000	-0	3	2	-0	0.2
1951	Bos-N	2	4	.333	23	7	1	0	0	67^2	64	3	64	33	17.3	4.26	86	.254	.409	6	.353	4	-2	-4	0	0.0
1952	Bos-N	1	1	.500	22	3	0	0	0	44^2	38	2	42	22	16.7	4.03	90	.241	.409	0	.000	-1	-1	-2	0	-0.2
1953	Mil-N	0	1	.000	10	0	0	0	0	14^2	17	1	14	13	19.0	8.59	46	.279	.413	1	.500	1	-7	-8	0	-0.3
1954	Chi-N	3	8	.273	18	14	2	1	0	84	74	7	62	37	14.7	5.36	78	.241	.370	6	.214	1	-12	-11	-0	-1.1
1955	Phi-N	0	3	.000	7	3	0	0	0	18^1	21	3	14	6	17.2	6.38	62	.304	.422	1	.200	-0	-5	-5	0	-0.7
Total	6	6	18	.250	84	27	3	1	0	237^1	221	16	199	119	16.2	4.93	79	.253	.395	14	.230	5	-25	-27	1	-2.1

● ED COLE
Cole, Edward William (b: Edward William Kisleauskas) b: 3/22/09, Wilkes-Barre, Pa. BR/TR, 5'11", 170 lbs. Deb: 4/22/38

YEAR	TM/L	W	L	PCT	G	GS	CG	SH	SV	IP	H	HR	BB	SO	RAT	ERA	ERA+	OAV	OOB	BH	AVG	PB	PR	/A	PD	TPI
1938	StL-A	1	5	.167	36	6	1	0	3	88^2	116	8	48	26	17.2	5.18	96	.313	.399	3	.143	-1	-4	-2	-1	-0.3
1939	StL-A	0	2	.000	6	0	0	0	0	6^1	8	1	6	5	19.9	7.11	68	.308	.438	0	.000	-0	-2	-2	0	-0.4
Total	2	1	7	.125	42	6	1	0	3	95	124	9	54	31	17.3	5.31	94	.312	.401	3	.136	-2	-6	-4	-1	-0.7

● KING COLE
Cole, Leonard Leslie b: 4/15/1886, Toledo, Iowa d: 1/6/16, Bay City, Mich. BR/TR, 6'1", 170 lbs. Deb: 10/6/09

YEAR	TM/L	W	L	PCT	G	GS	CG	SH	SV	IP	H	HR	BB	SO	RAT	ERA	ERA+	OAV	OOB	BH	AVG	PB	PR	/A	PD	TPI
1909	Chi-N	1	0	1.000	1	1	1	1	0	9	6	0	3	1	9.0	0.00	—	.194	.265	3	.750	2	3	3	-0	0.7
1910	*Chi-N	20	4	**.833**	33	29	21	4	1	239^2	174	2	130	114	11.8	1.80	**160**	**.211**	.325	21	.231	2	33	29	-1	3.0
1911	Chi-N	18	7	.720	32	27	13	2	0	221^1	188	3	99	101	12.0	3.13	106	.236	.328	12	.152	-2	7	4	-2	0.0
1912	Chi-N	1	2	.333	8	3	0	0	0	19	36	2	8	9	21.8	10.89	31	.409	.469	2	.400	1	-16	-16	0	-1.9
	Pit-N	2	2	.500	12	5	2	0	0	49	61	1	18	11	14.9	6.43	51	.330	.395	2	.133	-1	-16	-17	-0	-1.3
	Yr	3	4	.429	20	8	2	0	0	68	97	3	26	20	16.5	7.68	43	.353	.413	4	.200	0	-32	-33	0	-3.2
1914	NY-A	10	9	.526	33	15	8	2	0	141^2	151	3	51	43	12.9	3.30	84	.288	.352	2	.048	-3	-9	-9	-3	-1.8
1915	NY-A	2	3	.400	10	6	2	0	1	51	41	2	22	19	11.6	3.18	92	.224	.317	1	.077	-1	-1	-1	-0	-0.3
Total	6	54	27	.667	129	86	47	9	2	730^2	657	13	331	298	12.5	3.12	97	.250	.340	43	.173	-2	-0	-7	-6	-1.6

● VICTOR COLE
Cole, Victor Alexander b: 1/23/68, Leningrad, Russia BB/TR, 5'10", 160 lbs. Deb: 6/6/92

YEAR	TM/L	W	L	PCT	G	GS	CG	SH	SV	IP	H	HR	BB	SO	RAT	ERA	ERA+	OAV	OOB	BH	AVG	PB	PR	/A	PD	TPI
1992	Pit-N	0	2	.000	8	4	0	0	0	23	23	1	14	12	14.5	5.48	63	.261	.363	0	.000	-0	-5	-5	0	-0.5

● JOHN COLEMAN
Coleman, John b: Bristol, Pa. TR , Deb: 6/23/1890

YEAR	TM/L	W	L	PCT	G	GS	CG	SH	SV	IP	H	HR	BB	SO	RAT	ERA	ERA+	OAV	OOB	BH	AVG	PB	PR	/A	PD	TPI
1890	Phi-N	0	1	.000	1	1	0	0	0	1^2	4	0	3	2	37.8	21.60	17	.444	.583	0	—	0	-3	-3	-0	-1.0

● JOHN COLEMAN
Coleman, John b: 1874, Lees Summit, Mo. TL , 5'10", 174 lbs. Deb: 9/25/1895

YEAR	TM/L	W	L	PCT	G	GS	CG	SH	SV	IP	H	HR	BB	SO	RAT	ERA	ERA+	OAV	OOB	BH	AVG	PB	PR	/A	PD	TPI
1895	StL-N	0	1	.000	1	1	1	0	0	8	12	1	8	5	23.6	13.50	36	.343	.477	1	.200	-0	-8	-8	0	-0.6

● JOHN COLEMAN
Coleman, John Francis b: 3/6/1863, Saratoga Springs, N.Y d: 5/31/22, Detroit, Mich. BL/TR, 5'9.5", 170 lbs. Deb: 5/1/1883 ♦

YEAR	TM/L	W	L	PCT	G	GS	CG	SH	SV	IP	H	HR	BB	SO	RAT	ERA	ERA+	OAV	OOB	BH	AVG	PB	PR	/A	PD	TPI
1883	Phi-N	12	48	.200	65	61	59	3	0	538^1	772	17	48	159	13.7	4.87	63	.309	.322	83	.234	4	-103	-106	1	-8.1
1884	Phi-N	5	15	.250	21	19	14	1	0	154^1	216	9	22	37	13.9	4.90	61	.308	.329	42	.246	2	-33	-33	1	-2.9
	Phi-a	0	2	.000	3	2	2	0	0	21	28	0	2	5	14.6	3.43	99	.304	.347	22	.206	0	-0	-0	0	0.0
1885	Phi-a	2	2	.500	8	3	3	0	0	60^1	82	0	5	12	13.0	3.43	100	.366	.380	119	.299	2	-1	0	-0	0.2
1886	Phi-a	1	1	.500	3	1	1	0	0	20^2	18	1	5	2	10.5	2.61	134	.225	.279	121	.246	0	2	2	-0	0.2
1889	Phi-a	3	2	.600	5	5	4	0	0	34	38	2	14	6	14.0	2.91	130	.273	.344	1	.053	-2	4	3	1	0.2
1890	Pit-N	0	2	.000	2	2	1	0	0	14	28	1	6	3	21.9	9.64	34	.406	.453	2	.182	0	-9	-10	-0	-0.9
Total	6	23	72	.242	107	93	84	4	0	842^2	1182	30	102	224	13.8	4.68	67	.311	.330	645	.257	7	-142	-144	3	-11.3

● JOE COLEMAN
Coleman, Joseph Howard b: 2/3/47, Boston, Mass. BR/TR, 6'3", 195 lbs. Deb: 9/28/65 FC

YEAR	TM/L	W	L	PCT	G	GS	CG	SH	SV	IP	H	HR	BB	SO	RAT	ERA	ERA+	OAV	OOB	BH	AVG	PB	PR	/A	PD	TPI
1965	Was-A	2	0	1.000	2	2	2	0	0	18	9	0	8	7	8.5	1.50	232	.153	.254	0	.000	-1	4	4	1	0.5
1966	Was-A	1	0	1.000	1	1	1	0	0	9	6	0	2	4	8.0	2.00	173	.188	.235	0	.000	-0	1	1	0	0.2
1967	Was-A	8	9	.471	28	22	3	0	0	134	154	6	47	77	14.1	4.63	68	.291	.359	2	.056	-1	-21	-22	-2	-2.9
1968	Was-A	12	16	.429	33	33	12	2	0	223	212	19	51	139	11.1	3.27	89	.250	.302	9	.129	-1	-7	-9	-1	-1.3
1969	Was-A	12	13	.480	40	36	12	4	1	247^2	222	26	100	182	11.9	3.27	106	.243	.322	9	.107	-2	10	5	1	0.3
1970	Was-A	8	12	.400	39	29	6	1	0	218^2	190	25	89	152	11.6	3.58	99	.233	.311	8	.119	2	3	-1	0	0.2
1971	Det-A	20	9	.690	39	38	16	3	0	286	241	17	96	236	10.8	3.15	114	.229	.298	9	.094	-3	10	14	-2	0.8
1972	*Det-A†	19	14	.576	40	39	9	3	0	280	216	23	110	222	10.8	2.80	112	.214	.297	9	.110	-2	8	11	-1	0.9
1973	Det-A	23	15	.605	40	40	13	2	0	288^1	283	32	93	202	12.0	3.53	116	.258	.322	0	—	0	9	18	-0	1.9
1974	Det-A	14	12	.538	41	41	11	2	0	285^2	272	30	158	177	13.9	4.32	88	.254	.356	0	—	0	-22	-16	2	-1.3
1975	Det-A	10	18	.357	31	31	6	1	0	201	234	27	85	125	14.7	5.55	72	.291	.366	0	—	0	-40	-34	0	-4.1
1976	Det-A	2	5	.286	12	12	1	0	0	66^2	80	1	34	38	16.1	4.86	76	.308	.398	0	—	0	-10	-9	2	-0.7
	Chi-N	2	8	.200	39	4	0	0	4	79	72	9	35	66	12.4	4.10	94	.246	.330	2	.154	-0	-5	-2	0	-0.3
1977	Oak-A	4	4	.500	43	12	2	0	2	127^2	114	11	49	55	11.6	2.96	136	.241	.314	0	—	0	16	15	-0	0.9
1978	Oak-A	3	0	1.000	10	0	0	0	0	19^2	12	1	5	4	7.8	1.37	265	.185	.243	0	—	0	5	5	0	0.8
	Tor-A	2	0	1.000	31	0	0	0	0	60^2	67	6	30	28	14.5	4.60	85	.286	.370	0	—	0	-6	-5	-1	-0.3
	Yr	5	0	1.000	41	0	0	0	0	80^1	79	7	35	32	12.9	3.81	101	.263	.342	0	—	0	-0	0	-1	0.5
1979	SF-N	0	0	—	5	0	0	0	0	3^2	3	0	2	0	14.7	0.00	—	.231	.375	0	—	0	2	1	-0	0.0
	Pit-N	0	0	—	10	0	0	0	0	20^2	29	1	9	14	17.0	6.10	64	.326	.394	1	.200	0	-5	-5	-1	0.0
	Yr	0	0	—	15	0	0	0	0	24^1	32	1	11	14	16.3	5.18	74	.308	.379	1	.200	0	-4	-4	-1	0.0
Total	15	142	135	.513	484	340	94	18	7	2569^1	2416	234	1003	1728	12.3	3.70	97	.250	.327	49	.106	-10	-48	-28	-2	-4.4

● JOE COLEMAN
Coleman, Joseph Patrick b: 7/30/22, Medford, Mass. d: 4/9/97, Ft.Myers, Fla. BR/TR, 6'2.5", 200 lbs. Deb: 9/19/42 F

YEAR	TM/L	W	L	PCT	G	GS	CG	SH	SV	IP	H	HR	BB	SO	RAT	ERA	ERA+	OAV	OOB	BH	AVG	PB	PR	/A	PD	TPI
1942	Phi-A	0	1	.000	1	0	0	0	0	6	8	0	1	0	13.5	3.00	126	.308	.333	0	.000	-1	0	1	-0	0.0
1946	Phi-A	0	2	.000	4	2	0	0	0	13	19	1	8	8	18.7	5.54	64	.345	.429	2	.400	1	-3	-3	-0	-0.4
1947	Phi-A	6	12	.333	32	21	9	2	1	160^1	171	17	62	65	13.1	4.32	88	.275	.341	7	.146	-1	-11	-9	-2	-1.3
1948	Phi-A★	14	13	.519	33	29	13	3	0	215^2	224	11	90	86	13.1	4.09	105	.269	.341	9	.122	-4	5	5	-1	0.0
1949	Phi-A	13	14	.481	33	30	18	1	1	240^1	249	12	127	109	14.2	3.86	107	.271	.361	14	.177	0	9	7	-5	0.3
1950	Phi-A	0	5	.000	15	6	2	0	0	54	74	9	50	12	20.7	8.50	54	.332	.454	1	.059	-1	-24	-24	-2	-1.9
1951	Phi-A	1	6	.143	28	9	1	0	1	96^1	117	12	59	34	16.7	5.98	72	.305	.402	7	.259	1	-20	-18	-1	-1.2
1953	Phi-A	3	4	.429	21	9	2	1	0	90	85	8	49	18	13.5	4.00	107	.254	.352	8	.286	1	-0	3	-2	0.2
1954	Bal-A	13	17	.433	33	32	15	4	0	221^1	184	16	96	103	11.5	3.50	102	.232	.317	13	.176	2	6	2	1	0.7
1955	Bal-A	0	1	.000	6	2	0	0	0	11^2	19	5	10	4	23.1	10.80	35	.373	.484	2	.667	1	-9	-9	-0	-0.6
	Det-A	2	1	.667	17	0	0	0	3	25^1	22	1	14	5	13.1	3.20	120	.239	.346	3	.750	1	2	2	0	0.4
	Yr	2	2	.500	23	2	0	0	3	37	41	6	24	9	16.1	5.59	69	.281	.386	5	.714	3	-7	-7	0	-0.2
Total	10	52	76	.406	223	140	60	11	6	1134	1172	92	566	444	13.9	4.38	92	.271	.357	66	.182	2	-44	-44	-12	-3.8

● PERCY COLEMAN
Coleman, Pierce D. b: 10/15/1876, Mason, Ohio d: 2/16/48, Van Nuys, Cal. TR , Deb: 7/2/1897

YEAR	TM/L	W	L	PCT	G	GS	CG	SH	SV	IP	H	HR	BB	SO	RAT	ERA	ERA+	OAV	OOB	BH	AVG	PB	PR	/A	PD	TPI
1897	StL-N	1	2	.333	12	4	2	0	0	57^1	99	0	32	10	21.7	8.16	54	.375	.455	6	.214	-1	-25	-24	1	-0.9
1898	Cin-N	0	1	.000	1	1	1	0	0	9	13	0	3	2	17.0	3.00	128	.333	.395	0	.000	-1	1	1	-0	0.0
Total	2	1	3	.250	13	5	3	0	0	66^1	112	0	35	12	21.0	7.46	58	.370	.448	6	.194	-1	-24	-23	0	-0.9

● RIP COLEMAN
Coleman, Walter Gary b: 7/31/31, Troy, N.Y. BL/TL, 6'2", 185 lbs. Deb: 8/15/55

YEAR	TM/L	W	L	PCT	G	GS	CG	SH	SV	IP	H	HR	BB	SO	RAT	ERA	ERA+	OAV	OOB	BH	AVG	PB	PR	/A	PD	TPI
1955	*NY-A	2	1	.667	10	6	0	0	1	29	40	2	16	15	17.7	5.28	71	.331	.413	2	.200	1	-4	-5	0	-0.4
1956	NY-A	3	5	.375	29	9	0	0	2	88^1	97	6	42	42	14.3	3.67	105	.285	.366	1	.042	-3	5	2	0	-0.1
1957	KC-A	0	7	.000	19	6	1	1	0	41	53	5	25	15	17.1	5.93	67	.325	.415	0	.000	-1	-10	-9	0	-1.4
1959	KC-A	2	10	.167	29	11	2	0	2	81	85	8	34	54	13.3	4.56	88	.273	.347	2	.080	-2	-6	-5	-0	-0.9
	Bal-A	0	0	—	3	0	0	0	0	4	4	0	2	4	13.5	0.00	—	.267	.353	0	—	0	2	2	1	0.1
	Yr	2	10	.167	32	11	2	0	2	85	89	8	36	58	13.2	4.34	92	.271	.342	2	.080	-2	-5	-3	1	-0.8
1960	Bal-A	0	2	.000	5	1	0	0	0	4	8	0	5	0	31.5	11.25	34	.444	.583	0	.000	-0	-3	-3	0	-1.3
Total	5	7	25	.219	95	33	3	1	5	247^1	287	21	124	130	15.1	4.58	85	.296	.379	5	.072	-5	-17	-18	2	-4.0

● ALLAN COLLAMORE
Collamore, Allan Edward b: 6/5/1887, Worcester, Mass. d: 8/8/80, Battle Creek, Mich. BR/TR, 6', 170 lbs. Deb: 4/15/11

YEAR	TM/L	W	L	PCT	G	GS	CG	SH	SV	IP	H	HR	BB	SO	RAT	ERA	ERA+	OAV	OOB	BH	AVG	PB	PR	/A	PD	TPI
1911	Phi-A	0	1	.000	2	0	0	0	0	2	6	0	3	1	49.5	36.00	9	.600	.733	0	—	0	-7	-7	-0	-1.9
1914	Cle-A	3	7	.300	27	8	3	0	0	105^1	100	3	49	32	13.2	3.25	89	.264	.357	3	.094	-2	-6	-4	-1	-0.7
1915	Cle-A	2	5	.286	11	6	5	2	0	64^1	52	1	22	15	10.4	2.38	128	.235	.305	4	.174	0	4	5	1	0.6
Total	3	5	13	.278	40	14	8	2	0	171^2	158	4	74	48	12.6	3.30	89	.259	.347	7	.127	-2	-9	-7	-0	-2.0

● HAP COLLARD
Collard, Earl Clinton b: 8/29/1898, Williams, Ariz. d: 7/9/68, Jamestown, Cal. BR/TR, 6', 170 lbs. Deb: 4/23/27

YEAR	TM/L	W	L	PCT	G	GS	CG	SH	SV	IP	H	HR	BB	SO	RAT	ERA	ERA+	OAV	OOB	BH	AVG	PB	PR	/A	PD	TPI
1927	Cle-A	0	0	—	4	0	0	0	0	5^1	8	0	3	2	18.6	5.06	83	.333	.407	0	—	0	-1	-1	0	0.0
1928	Cle-A	0	0	—	1	0	0	0	0	4	4	0	4	1	18.0	2.25	184	.250	.400	1	1.000	0	1	1	-0	0.0
1930	Phi-N	6	12	.333	30	15	4	0	0	127	188	15	39	25	16.3	6.80	80	.350	.397	9	.205	-2	-26	-19	1	-2.1
Total	3	6	12	.333	35	15	4	0	0	136^1	200	15	46	28	16.4	6.60	81	.347	.398	10	.222	-1	-26	-19	1	-2.1

● ORLIN COLLIER
Collier, Orlin Edward b: 2/17/07, E.Prairie, Mo. d: 9/9/44, Memphis, Tenn. BR/TR, 5'11.5", 180 lbs. Deb: 9/11/31

YEAR	TM/L	W	L	PCT	G	GS	CG	SH	SV	IP	H	HR	BB	SO	RAT	ERA	ERA+	OAV	OOB	BH	AVG	PB	PR	/A	PD	TPI
1931	Det-A	0	1	.000	2	2	0	0	0	10^1	17	0	7	3	20.9	7.84	59	.362	.444	0	.000	-0	-4	-4	-0	-0.3

YEAR	TM/L	W	L	PCT	G	GS	CG	SH	SV	IP	H	HR	BB	SO	RAT	ERA	ERA+	OAV	OOB	BH	AVG	PB	PR	/A	PD	TPI
● HARRY COLLIFLOWER — Colliflower, James Harry "Collie" b: 3/11/1869, Petersville, Md. d: 8/12/61, Washington, D.C. BL/TL, 5′11.5″, 175 lbs. Deb: 7/21/1899 U																										
1899	Cle-N	1	11	.083	14	12	11	0	0	98	152	6	41	8	18.7	8.17	45	.353	.422	23	.303	2	-47	-49	0	-4.0
● DAN COLLINS — Collins, Daniel Thomas b: 7/12/1854, St.Louis, Mo. d: 9/21/1883, New Orleans, La. Deb: 6/8/1874 ♦																										
1874	Chi-n	1	1	.500	2	2	1	0	0	11	22	0	2	0	19.6	4.91	45	.386	.407	1	.083	-1	-3	-3		-0.4
● DON COLLINS — Collins, Donald Edward b: 9/15/52, Lyons, Ga. BR/TL, 6′2″, 195 lbs. Deb: 5/4/77																										
1977	Atl-N	3	9	.250	40	6	0	0	2	70^{2}	82	8	41	27	15.8	5.09	87	.299	.392	0	.000	-1	-9	-5	-1	-1.1
1980	Cle-A	0	0	—	4	0	0	0	0	6	9	0	7	0	24.0	7.50	54	.346	.485	0	—	0	-2	-2	-0	0.0
Total	2	3	9	.250	44	6	0	0	2	76^{2}	91	8	48	27	16.4	5.28	84	.303	.401	0	.000	-1	-12	-7	-1	-1.1
● RIP COLLINS — Collins, Harry Warren b: 2/26/1896, Weatherford, Tex. d: 5/27/68, Bryan, Tex. BR/TR, 6′1″, 205 lbs. Deb: 4/19/20																										
1920	NY-A	14	8	.636	36	18	10	2	1	187^{1}	171	6	79	66	12.7	3.22	119	.247	.337	8	.129	-4	12	13	-1	0.8
1921	*NY-A	11	5	.688	28	16	7	2	0	137^{1}	158	6	78	64	16.1	5.44	78	.293	.392	11	.196	-1	-18	-18	-1	-2.0
1922	Bos-A	14	11	.560	32	29	15	3	0	210^{2}	219	4	103	69	14.2	3.76	109	.274	.364	12	.158	-3	7	8	-1	0.5
1923	Det-A	3	7	.300	17	14	3	1	0	92^{1}	104	3	22	25	13.3	4.87	79	.284	.342	3	.111	-2	-9	-10	0	-1.1
1924	Det-A	14	7	.667	34	30	11	1	0	216	199	6	63	75	11.1	3.21	128	.249	.307	11	.145	-5	25	22	0	1.4
1925	Det-A	6	11	.353	26	20	5	0	0	140	149	7	52	33	13.3	4.56	94	.281	.352	5	.119	-4	-3	-4	4	-0.4
1926	Det-A	8	8	.500	30	13	5	3	1	122	128	4	44	44	13.2	2.73	149	.278	.350	6	.154	-1	17	18	1	2.2
1927	Det-A	13	7	.650	30	25	10	1	0	172^{2}	207	5	59	37	14.3	4.69	90	.312	.375	11	.204	0	-11	-9	5	-0.5
1929	StL-A	11	6	.647	26	20	10	1	1	155^{1}	162	16	73	47	14.0	4.00	111	.270	.355	17	.274	4	4	7	0	1.1
1930	StL-A	9	7	.563	35	20	6	1	2	171^{2}	168	11	63	75	12.4	4.35	112	.259	.330	7	.130	-2	6	10	-0	0.6
1931	StL-A	5	5	.500	17	14	2	0	0	107	130	5	38	34	14.2	3.79	122	.307	.366	5	.147	-1	7	10	1	0.9
Total	11	108	82	.568	311	219	84	15	5	1712^{1}	1795	73	674	569	13.4	3.99	106	.275	.351	96	.165	-18	38	45	9	3.5
● ORTH COLLINS — Collins, Orth Stein "Buck" b: 4/27/1880, Lafayette, Ind. d: 12/13/49, Ft.Lauderdale, Fla BL/TR, 6′, 150 lbs. Deb: 6/1/04 ♦																										
1909	Was-A	0	0	—	1	0	0	0	0	1	0	0	0	1	0.0	0.00	—	.000	.000	0	.000	-0	0	0	-0	0.0
● PHIL COLLINS — Collins, Philip Eugene "Fidgety Phil" b: 8/27/01, Chicago, Ill. d: 8/14/48, Chicago, Ill. BR/TR, 5′11″, 175 lbs. Deb: 10/7/23																										
1923	Chi-N	1	0	1.000	1	1	0	0	0	5	8	0	1	2	16.2	3.60	111	.400	.429	0	.000	-0	0	0	1	0.1
1929	Phi-N	9	7	.563	43	11	3	0	5	153^{1}	172	18	83	61	15.2	5.75	90	.284	.374	11	.190	-0	-18	-10	-1	-1.0
1930	Phi-N	16	11	.593	47	25	17	1	3	239	287	22	86	87	14.4	4.78	114	.299	.363	22	.253	3	5	18	-2	1.8
1931	Phi-N	12	16	.429	42	27	16	2	4	240^{1}	268	14	83	73	13.3	3.86	110	.283	.344	16	.168	-4	0	10	1	0.8
1932	Phi-N	14	12	.538	43	21	6	0	3	184^{1}	231	21	65	66	14.7	5.27	84	.314	.375	18	.265	2	-29	-18	-0	-2.0
1933	Phi-N	8	13	.381	42	13	5	1	**6**	151	178	9	57	40	14.4	4.11	93	.293	.360	7	.132	-2	-13	-5	-1	-1.1
1934	Phi-N	13	18	.419	45	32	15	0	1	254	277	30	87	72	13.0	4.18	113	.273	.333	15	.170	-5	-3	15	-3	0.9
1935	Phi-N	0	2	.000	3	3	0	0	0	14^{2}	24	5	9	4	20.3	11.66	39	.348	.423	0	.000	-1	-12	-12	0	-1.2
	StL-N	7	6	.538	26	8	2	0	2	82^{2}	96	6	26	18	13.6	4.57	90	.290	.347	4	.160	-1	-5	-4	-1	-0.8
	Yr	7	8	.467	29	11	2	0	2	97^{1}	120	11	35	22	14.6	5.64	74	.300	.361	4	.129	-2	-18	-16	-1	-2.0
Total	8	80	85	.485	292	141	64	4	24	1324^{1}	1541	125	497	423	14.1	4.66	100	.291	.356	93	.193	-8	-75	-3	-7	-2.5
● RAY COLLINS — Collins, Raymond Williston b: 2/11/1887, Colchester, Vt. d: 1/9/70, Burlington, Vt. BL/TL, 6′1″, 185 lbs. Deb: 7/19/09																										
1909	Bos-A	4	3	.571	12	8	4	2	0	73^{2}	70	2	18	31	10.8	2.81	89	.269	.317	3	.130	-0	-3	-3	1	-0.2
1910	Bos-A	13	11	.542	35	26	18	4	1	244^{2}	205	1	41	109	9.1	1.62	158	.229	.264	15	.179	-1	25	25	-4	2.1
1911	Bos-A	11	12	.478	31	24	14	0	1	194^{2}	184	1	44	86	10.7	2.40	136	.256	.302	9	.150	0	20	19	-3	1.7
1912	*Bos-A	13	8	.619	27	24	17	4	0	199^{1}	192	4	42	82	10.7	2.53	135	.256	.297	11	.169	0	17	19	-3	1.6
1913	Bos-A	19	8	.704	30	30	19	3	0	246^{2}	242	3	37	88	10.3	2.63	112	.263	.293	12	.150	2	8	9	-4	0.7
1914	Bos-A	20	13	.606	39	30	16	6	0	272^{1}	252	3	56	72	10.2	2.51	107	.258	.298	11	.139	-0	7	5	-6	0.0
1915	Bos-A	4	7	.364	25	9	2	0	2	104^{2}	101	1	31	43	11.4	4.30	65	.261	.317	8	.286	5	-16	-18	-3	-1.7
Total	7	84	62	.575	199	151	90	19	4	1336	1246	15	269	511	10.3	2.51	115	.254	.294	69	.165	6	59	58	-22	4.2
● JACKIE COLLUM — Collum, Jack Dean b: 6/21/27, Victor, Ia. BL/TL, 5′7″, 163 lbs. Deb: 9/21/51																										
1951	StL-N	2	1	.667	3	2	1	1	0	17	11	0	10	5	11.1	1.59	250	.204	.328	3	.429	1	4	4	0	1.0
1952	StL-N	0	0	—	2	0	0	0	0	3	2	0	1	0	9.0	0.00	—	.200	.273	0	—	0	1	1	0	0.0
1953	StL-N	0	0	—	7	0	0	0	0	11^{1}	15	1	4	5	15.1	6.35	67	.326	.380	0	.000	-0	-3	-3	1	0.1
	Cin-N	7	11	.389	30	12	4	1	3	124^{2}	123	8	39	51	12.1	3.75	116	.263	.328	10	.278	3	7	8	1	1.4
	Yr	7	11	.389	37	12	4	1	3	136	138	9	43	56	12.4	3.97	109	.269	.333	10	.256	2	5	6	2	1.5
1954	Cin-N	7	3	.700	36	2	1	0	0	79	86	8	32	28	14.0	3.76	112	.283	.361	3	.231	2	3	4	3	0.9
1955	Cin-N	9	8	.529	32	17	5	0	1	134	128	17	37	49	11.2	3.63	117	.254	.308	10	.250	2	6	9	-0	1.3
1956	StL-N	6	2	.750	38	1	0	0	7	60	63	6	27	17	13.8	4.20	90	.281	.364	3	.214	1	-3	-3	1	-0.3
1957	Chi-N	1	1	.500	9	0	0	0	1	10^{2}	8	0	9	7	15.2	6.75	57	.211	.375	0	—	0	-3	-3	0	-0.6
	Bro-N	0	0	—	3	0	0	0	0	4^{1}	7	1	1	3	16.6	8.31	50	.368	.400	0	—	0	-2	-2	-0	0.0
	Yr	1	1	.500	12	0	0	0	1	15	15	1	10	10	15.0	7.20	55	.254	.362	0	—	0	-6	-5	-0	-0.6
1958	LA-N	0	0	—	2	0	0	0	0	3^{1}	4	2	2	0	16.2	8.10	51	.308	.400	0	.000	-0	-2	-1	0	0.0
1962	Min-A	0	2	.000	8	3	0	0	0	15^{1}	29	1	11	5	23.5	11.15	37	.414	.494	0	.000	-0	-12	-12	0	-1.3
	Cle-A	0	0	—	1	0	0	0	0	1^{1}	4	0	0	1	27.0	13.50	29	.571	.571	0	—	0	-1	-1	0	0.0
	Yr	0	2	.000	9	3	0	0	0	16^{2}	33	1	11	6	23.8	11.34	36	.418	.489	0	.000	-0	-14	-13	0	-1.3
Total	9	32	28	.533	171	37	11	2	12	464	480	44	173	171	13.0	4.15	101	.273	.344	29	.246	8	-4	1	6	2.5
● BARTOLO COLON — Colon, Bartolo b: 5/24/75, Altamira, D.R. BR/TR, 6′, 185 lbs. Deb: 4/4/97																										
1997	Cle-A	4	7	.364	19	17	1	0	0	94	107	12	45	66	14.8	5.65	83	.286	.367	0	.000	-0	-11	-10	1	-0.9
1998	*Cle-A★	14	9	.609	31	31	6	2	0	204	205	15	79	158	12.7	3.71	129	.260	.330	1	.500	0	21	24	2	2.6
Total	2	18	16	.529	50	48	7	2	0	298	312	27	124	224	13.3	4.32	110	.268	.342	1	.333	0	10	14	2	1.7
● DICK COLPAERT — Colpaert, Richard Charles b: 1/3/44, Fraser, Mich. BR/TR, 5′10″, 182 lbs. Deb: 7/21/70																										
1970	Pit-N	1	0	1.000	8	0	0	0	0	10^{2}	9	3	8	6	14.3	5.91	66	.237	.370	0	—	0	-2	-2	-0	-0.2
● LOYD COLSON — Colson, Loyd Albert b: 11/4/47, Wellington, Tex. BR/TR, 6′1″, 190 lbs. Deb: 9/25/70																										
1970	NY-A	0	0	—	1	0	0	0	0	2	3	0	0	3	13.5	4.50	78	.333	.333	0	—	0	-0	-0	0	0.0
● LARRY COLTON — Colton, Lawrence Robert b: 6/8/42, Los Angeles, Cal. BL/TR, 6′3″, 200 lbs. Deb: 5/6/68																										
1968	Phi-N	0	0	—	1	0	0	0	0	2	3	0	0	2	13.5	4.50	67	.333	.333	0	—	0	-0	-0	-0	0.0
● GEOFF COMBE — Combe, Geoffrey Wade b: 2/1/56, Melrose, Mass. BR/TR, 6′2″, 185 lbs. Deb: 9/2/80																										
1980	Cin-N	0	0	—	4	0	0	0	0	6^{2}	9	0	4	10	17.6	10.80	33	.346	.433	0	—	0	-5	-5	0	0.0
1981	Cin-N	1	0	1.000	14	0	0	0	0	17^{2}	27	3	10	9	18.8	7.64	46	.370	.446	0	—	0	-8	-8	-0	-0.5
Total	2	1	0	1.000	18	0	0	0	0	24^{1}	36	3	14	19	18.5	8.51	42	.364	.442	0	—	0	-13	-13	-0	-0.5
● PAT COMBS — Combs, Patrick Dennis b: 10/29/66, Newport, R.I. BL/TL, 6′3″, 200 lbs. Deb: 9/5/89																										
1989	Phi-N	4	0	1.000	6	6	1	1	0	38^{2}	36	2	6	30	9.8	2.09	169	.248	.278	2	.167	0	6	6	-1	0.7
1990	Phi-N	10	10	.500	32	31	3	2	0	183^{1}	179	12	86	108	13.2	4.07	94	.257	.342	9	.150	0	-6	-5	-0	-0.5
1991	Phi-N	2	6	.250	14	13	1	0	0	64^{1}	64	7	43	41	15.2	4.90	75	.254	.367	2	.133	1	-9	-9	-0	-1.0
1992	Phi-N	1	1	.500	4	4	0	0	0	18^{2}	20	0	12	11	15.4	7.71	45	.278	.381	1	.125	0	-9	-9	1	-0.7
Total	4	17	17	.500	56	54	5	3	0	305	299	21	147	190	13.3	4.22	88	.257	.343	14	.147	2	-17	-16	-1	-1.5
● JORGE COMELLAS — Comellas, Jorge (Pous) "Pancho" b: 12/7/16, Havana, Cuba BR/TR, 6′, 190 lbs. Deb: 4/19/45																										
1945	Chi-N	0	2	.000	7	1	0	0	0	12	11	1	6	6	12.8	4.50	81	.244	.333	0	.000	-0	-1	-1	1	-0.1
● STEVE COMER — Comer, Steven Michael b: 1/13/54, Minneapolis, Minn. BB/TR, 6′3″, 205 lbs. Deb: 4/15/78 C																										
1978	Tex-A	11	5	.688	30	11	3	2	1	117^{1}	107	5	37	65	11.1	2.30	163	.249	.310	0	—	0	19	19	1	2.6
1979	Tex-A	17	12	.586	36	36	6	1	0	242^{1}	230	24	84	86	12.0	3.68	113	.252	.320	0	—	0	14	13	-0	1.4

YEAR	TM/L	W	L	PCT	G	GS	CG	SH	SV	IP	H	HR	BB	SO	RAT	ERA	ERA+	OAV	OOB	BH	AVG	PB	PR	/A	PD	TPI
1980	Tex-A	2	4	.333	12	11	0	0	0	41^{2}	65	5	22	9	19.2	7.99	49	.367	.443	0	—	0	-18	-19	-0	-2.2
1981	Tex-A	8	2	.800	36	1	0	0	6	77^{1}	70	1	31	22	11.9	2.56	135	.241	.317	0	—	0	9	8	1	1.3
1982	Tex-A	1	6	.143	37	3	1	0	6	97	133	11	36	23	15.9	5.10	76	.342	.400	0	—	0	-11	-13	-0	-0.8
1983	Phi-N	1	0	1.000	3	1	0	0	0	8^{2}	11	0	3	1	14.5	5.19	69	.314	.368	0	.000	-0	-2	-2	-0	-0.2
1984	Cle-A	4	8	.333	22	20	1	0	0	117^{1}	146	11	39	39	14.5	5.68	72	.309	.366	0	—	0	-22	-21	0	-1.9
Total	7	44	37	.543	176	83	11	3	13	701^{2}	762	57	252	245	13.2	4.13	95	.281	.347	0	.000	-0	-10	-15	1	0.2
● **CHARLIE COMISKEY**	Comiskey, Charles Albert "Commy" or "The Old Roman" b: 8/15/1859, Chicago, Ill. d: 10/26/31, Eagle River, Wis. BR/TR, 6′, 180 lbs. Deb: 5/2/1882 MH ♦																									
1882	StL-a	0	1	.000	2	1	1	0	0	8	12	0	3	2	16.9	0.00	—	.324	.375	80	.243	0	2	2	0	0.3
1884	StL-a	0	0	—	1	0	0	0	0	4	1	0	0	4	2.3	2.25	145	.059	.059	109	.237	0	0	0	-0	0.0
1889	StL-a	0	0	—	1	0	0	0	0	0^{1}	0	0	0	0	0.0	0.00	—	.000	.000	168	.286	0	0	0	0	0.0
Total	3	0	1	.000	4	1	1	0	0	12^{1}	13	0	3	6	11.7	0.73	410	.236	.276	1530	.264	0	3	3	-0	0.3
● **JACK COMPTON**	Compton, Harry Leroy b: 3/9/1882, Lancaster, Ohio d: 7/4/74, Lancaster, Ohio BR/TR, 5′9″, 157 lbs. Deb: 9/7/11																									
1911	Cin-N	0	1	.000	8	3	0	0	1	25^{1}	19	0	15	6	12.4	3.91	85	.204	.321	2	.333	0	-1	-2	-0	-0.1
● **CLINT COMPTON**	Compton, Robert Clinton b: 11/1/50, Montgomery, Ala. BL/TL, 5′11″, 185 lbs. Deb: 10/3/72																									
1972	Chi-N	0	0	—	1	0	0	0	0	2	2	0	2	0	18.0	9.00	42	.286	.444	0	—	0	-1	-1	-0	0.0
● **KEITH COMSTOCK**	Comstock, Keith Martin b: 12/23/55, San Francisco, Cal. BL/TL, 6′, 175 lbs. Deb: 4/3/84																									
1984	Min-A	0	0	—	4	0	0	0	0	6^{1}	6	2	4	2	14.2	8.53	49	.261	.370	0	—	0	-3	-3	0	-0.2
1987	SF-N	2	0	1.000	15	0	0	0	1	20^{2}	19	1	10	21	12.6	3.05	126	.253	.341	0	.000	-0	2	2	0	0.2
	SD-N	0	1	.000	26	0	0	0	0	36	33	4	21	38	13.5	5.50	72	.252	.355	0	.000	-0	-6	-6	-1	-0.2
	Yr	2	1	.667	41	0	0	0	1	56^{2}	52	5	31	59	13.2	4.61	85	.251	.349	0	.000	-0	-3	-4	-1	0.0
1988	SD-N	0	0	—	7	0	0	0	0	8	8	1	3	9	12.4	6.75	50	.250	.314	0	—	0	-3	-3	0	0.0
1989	Sea-A	1	2	.333	31	0	0	0	0	25^{2}	26	2	10	22	12.6	2.81	144	.268	.336	0	—	0	3	3	-0	0.2
1990	Sea-A	7	4	.636	60	0	0	0	2	56	40	4	26	50	10.6	2.89	137	.206	.300	0	—	0	6	7	1	1.3
1991	Sea-A	0	0	—	1	0	0	0	0	0^{1}	2	0	1	0	81.0	54.00	8	.667	.750	0	—	0	-2	-2	0	0.0
Total	6	10	7	.588	144	0	0	0	3	153	134	14	75	142	12.3	4.06	97	.241	.332	0	.000	-0	-2	-2	0	1.3
● **RALPH COMSTOCK**	Comstock, Ralph Remick "Commy" b: 11/24/1890, Sylvania, Ohio d: 9/13/66, Toledo, Ohio BR/TR, 5′10″, 168 lbs. Deb: 8/26/13																									
1913	Det-A	2	5	.286	10	7	1	0	1	60^{1}	90	0	16	37	16.0	5.37	54	.344	.384	5	.227	1	-16	-16	0	-1.6
1915	Bos-A	1	0	1.000	3	0	0	0	0	9	10	2	2	1	12.0	2.00	139	.294	.333	0	.000	0	1	1	0	0.1
	Pit-F	3	3	.500	12	7	3	0	2	52^{2}	44	3	7	18	8.9	3.25	83	.237	.268	0	.000	-2	-3	-3	-0	-0.6
1918	Pit-N	5	6	.455	15	8	6	0	1	81	78	0	14	44	10.4	3.00	96	.259	.297	5	.192	-0	-2	-1	0	-0.2
Total	3	11	14	.440	40	22	10	0	4	203	222	5	39	100	11.7	3.72	76	.284	.321	10	.152	-2	-21	-20	-0	-2.3
● **DAVE CONCEPCION**	Concepcion, David Ismael (Benitez) b: 6/17/48, Aragua, Venez. BR/TR, 6′1″, 180 lbs. Deb: 4/6/70 ♦																									
1988	Cin-N	0	0	—	1	0	0	0	0	1^{1}	2	0	0	1	13.5	0.00	—	.333	.333	39	.198	0	1	1	0	0.0
● **DAVID CONE**	Cone, David Brian b: 1/2/63, Kansas City, Mo. BL/TR, 6′1″, 190 lbs. Deb: 6/8/86																									
1986	KC-A	0	0	—	11	0	0	0	0	22^{2}	29	2	13	21	17.1	5.56	76	.309	.398	0	—	0	-3	-3	-0	-0.1
1987	NY-N	5	6	.455	21	13	1	0	1	99^{1}	87	11	44	68	12.3	3.71	102	.239	.329	2	.065	-1	4	1	-0	-0.1
1988	*NY-N★	20	3	**.870**	35	28	8	4	0	231^{1}	178	10	80	213	10.2	2.22	145	.213	.285	12	.150	1	32	26	-1	2.5
1989	NY-N	14	8	.636	34	33	7	2	0	219^{2}	183	20	74	190	10.7	3.52	93	.223	.290	18	.234	4	-1	-6	-2	-0.4
1990	NY-N	14	10	.583	31	30	6	2	0	211^{2}	177	21	65	**233**	10.3	3.23	116	.226	.286	14	.200	3	13	12	-0	1.6
1991	NY-N	14	14	.500	34	34	5	2	0	232^{2}	204	13	73	**241**	10.9	3.29	111	.235	.298	9	.125	-1	10	9	0	1.0
1992	NY-N★	13	7	.650	27	27	7	**5**	0	196^{2}	162	12	82	214	11.6	2.88	120	.223	.309	6	.092	-2	14	13	-0	1.1
	*Tor-A	4	3	.571	8	7	0	0	0	53	39	3	29	47	12.1	2.55	160	.206	.321	0	—	0	8	9	-1	1.1
1993	KC-A	11	14	.440	34	34	6	1	0	254	205	20	114	191	11.7	3.33	137	.223	.315	0	—	0	28	35	-1	3.0
1994	KC-A★	16	5	.762	23	23	4	3	0	171^{2}	130	15	54	132	10.0	2.94	170	.209	.279	0	—	0	36	39	0	**4.4**
1995	Tor-A	9	6	.600	17	17	5	2	0	130^{1}	113	12	41	102	11.0	3.38	139	.232	.298	0	—	0	19	19	0	2.0
	*NY-A	9	2	.818	13	13	1	0	0	99	82	12	47	89	11.8	3.82	121	.223	.313	0	—	0	10	9	-1	0.8
	Yr	18	8	.692	30	30	6	2	0	**229**^{1}	195	24	88	191	11.1	3.57	131	.226	.299	0	—	0	29	28	-1	2.8
1996	*NY-A	7	2	.778	11	11	1	0	0	72	50	3	34	71	10.8	2.88	172	.198	.298	0	—	0	17	16	-1	1.8
1997	*NY-A★	12	6	.667	29	29	1	0	0	195	155	17	86	222	11.3	2.82	158	.218	.306	0	.000	-0	38	35	-2	2.7
1998	*NY-A	**20**	7	.741	31	31	3	0	0	207^{2}	186	20	59	209	11.3	3.55	125	.237	.303	0	.000	-0	25	21	0	2.4
Total	13	168	93	.644	359	330	55	21	1	2396^{2}	1980	191	895	2243	11.1	3.17	128	.224	.301	61	.152	4	249	233	-8	23.8
● **BOB CONE**	Cone, Robert Earl b: 2/27/1894, Galveston, Tex. d: 5/24/55, Galveston, Tex. BR/TR, 6′2″, 172 lbs. Deb: 7/25/15																									
1915	Phi-A	0	0	—	1	1	0	0	0	0^{2}	5	0	0	0	67.5	40.50	7	.714	.714	0	—	0	-3	-3	-0	0.0
● **DICK CONGER**	Conger, Richard b: 4/3/21, Los Angeles, Cal. d: 2/16/70, Los Angeles, Cal. BR/TR, 6′, 185 lbs. Deb: 4/22/40																									
1940	Det-A	1	0	1.000	2	0	0	0	0	3	2	0	3	1	15.0	3.00	159	.200	.385	0	—	0	0	1	-0	0.2
1941	Pit-N	0	0	—	2	1	0	0	0	4	3	0	3	2	13.5	0.00	—	.214	.353	0	—	0	2	2	-0	0.0
1942	Pit-N	0	0	—	2	1	0	0	0	8^{1}	9	0	5	3	15.1	2.16	157	.290	.389	0	.000	-0	1	1	1	0.0
1943	Phi-N	2	7	.222	13	10	2	0	0	54^{2}	72	3	24	18	16.6	6.09	55	.327	.406	1	.063	-1	-16	-17	-0	-2.4
Total	4	3	7	.300	19	12	2	0	0	70	86	3	35	24	16.2	5.14	67	.313	.400	1	.053	-1	-13	-13	0	-2.2
● **ALLEN CONKWRIGHT**	Conkwright, Allen Howard "Red" b: 12/4/1896, Sedalia, Mo. d: 7/30/91, LaMesa, Cal. BR/TR, 5′10″, 170 lbs. Deb: 9/16/20																									
1920	Det-A	2	1	.667	5	3	0	0	1	19^{1}	29	0	16	4	20.9	6.98	53	.397	.506	1	.200	1	-7	-7	0	-0.9
● **GENE CONLEY**	Conley, Donald Eugene b: 11/10/30, Muskogee, Okla. BR/TR, 6′8″, 225 lbs. Deb: 4/17/52																									
1952	Bos-N	0	3	.000	4	3	0	0	0	12^{2}	23	4	9	6	24.2	7.82	46	.397	.493	2	.400	1	-6	-6	-0	-1.1
1954	Mil-N★	14	9	.609	28	27	12	2	0	194^{1}	171	17	79	113	11.9	2.96	126	.240	.322	12	.156	-2	24	16	-1	1.5
1955	Mil-N★	11	7	.611	22	21	10	0	0	158	152	23	52	107	11.7	4.16	90	.254	.315	11	.204	-1	-2	-7	-0	-0.8
1956	Mil-N	8	9	.471	31	19	5	1	3	158^{1}	169	13	52	68	12.7	3.13	111	.276	.335	7	.156	-1	11	6	-1	0.5
1957	*Mil-N	9	9	.500	35	18	6	1	1	148	133	9	64	61	12.1	3.16	111	.244	.325	9	.196	1	12	6	-0	0.7
1958	Mil-N	0	6	.000	26	7	0	0	2	72	89	8	17	53	13.8	4.88	72	.309	.356	3	.188	1	-7	-11	0	-0.8
1959	Phi-N★	12	7	.632	25	22	12	3	1	180	159	13	42	102	10.1	3.00	**137**	.235	.281	16	.239	2	19	22	-0	2.5
1960	Phi-N	8	14	.364	29	25	9	2	0	183^{1}	192	10	42	117	11.6	3.68	105	.272	.314	8	.127	-1	2	4	-2	0.2
1961	Bos-A	11	14	.440	33	30	6	2	1	199^{2}	229	33	65	113	13.4	4.91	85	.287	.343	16	.219	4	-20	-17	-1	-1.5
1962	Bos-A	15	14	.517	34	33	9	2	1	241^{2}	238	28	68	134	11.6	3.95	105	.256	.310	18	.207	3	1	5	-1	0.8
1963	Bos-A	3	4	.429	9	9	0	0	0	40^{2}	51	4	21	14	16.2	6.64	57	.305	.386	3	.200	0	-14	-13	-1	-1.9
Total	11	91	96	.487	276	214	69	13	9	1588^{2}	1606	162	511	888	12.2	3.82	101	.264	.324	105	.192	8	20	6	-6	0.1
● **ED CONLEY**	Conley, Edward J. b: 7/10/1864, Sandwich, Mass. d: 10/16/1894, Cumberland, R.I. 5′8″, 142 lbs. Deb: 7/20/1884																									
1884	Pro-N	4	4	.500	8	8	8	1	0	71	63	4	22	33	10.8	2.15	132	.223	.280	4	.143	-2	7	5	-1	0.2
● **SNIPE CONLEY**	Conley, James Patrick b: 4/25/1894, Cressona, Pa. d: 1/7/78, DeSoto, Tex. BR/TR, 5′11.5″, 179 lbs. Deb: 5/20/14																									
1914	Bal-F	4	6	.400	35	11	4	2	1	125	112	2	47	86	11.9	2.52	120	.259	.340	4	.114	-3	5	7	-1	0.1
1915	Bal-F	1	4	.200	25	6	4	0	0	86	97	5	32	40	13.9	4.29	67	.314	.386	6	.250	1	-15	-14	-1	-0.7
1918	Cin-N	2	0	1.000	5	0	0	0	1	13^{2}	17	2	5	2	14.5	5.27	51	.321	.379	1	.250	0	-4	-4	0	-0.6
Total	3	7	10	.412	65	17	8	2	2	224^{2}	226	9	84	128	12.8	3.36	88	.284	.360	11	.175	-1	-14	-10	-1	-1.2
● **BOB CONLEY**	Conley, Robert Burns b: 2/1/34, Mousie, Ky. BR/TR, 6′1″, 188 lbs. Deb: 9/11/58																									
1958	Phi-N	0	0	—	2	2	0	0	0	8^{1}	9	0	1	0	10.8	7.56	52	.273	.294	0	.000	-0	-3	-3	-0	0.0
● **BERT CONN**	Conn, Albert Thomas b: 9/22/1879, Philadelphia, Pa. d: 11/2/44, Philadelphia, Pa. TR, Deb: 9/16/1898 ♦																									
1898	Phi-N	0	1	.000	1	1	0	0	0	7	13	1	2	3	19.3	6.43	53	.394	.429	1	.333	1	-2	-2	-0	-0.2
1900	Phi-N	0	2	.000	4	1	1	0	0	17^{1}	29	0	16	2	26.5	8.31	44	.372	.510	3	.333	1	-9	-9	-1	-0.8
Total	2	0	3	.000	5	2	1	0	0	24^{1}	42	1	18	5	24.4	7.77	46	.378	.489	8	.267	2	-11	-11	-1	-1.0

● SARGE CONNALLY Connally, George Walter b: 8/31/1898, McGregor, Tex. d: 1/27/78, Temple, Tex. BR/TR, 5'11", 170 lbs. Deb: 9/10/21

YEAR	TM/L	W	L	PCT	G	GS	CG	SH	SV	IP	H	HR	BB	SO	RAT	ERA	ERA+	OAV	OOB	BH	AVG	PB	PR	/A	PD	TPI
1921	Chi-A	0	1	.000	5	2	0	0	0	22^1	29	0	10	6	16.1	6.45	66	.330	.404	4	.500	2	-5	-5	0	0.0
1923	Chi-A	0	0	—	3	0	0	0	0	8^2	7	0	12	3	20.8	6.23	64	.241	.476	1	.333	0	-2	-2	-0	0.0
1924	Chi-A	7	13	.350	44	13	6	0	6	160	177	4	68	55	14.3	4.05	102	.290	.369	11	.220	-1	3	1	3	0.3
1925	Chi-A	6	7	.462	40	2	0	0	8	104^2	122	2	58	45	15.6	4.64	89	.310	.402	7	.250	1	-3	-6	3	-0.3
1926	Chi-A	6	5	.545	31	8	5	0	3	108^1	128	0	35	47	13.7	3.16	122	.300	.356	5	.156	-1	10	9	2	0.9
1927	Chi-A	10	15	.400	43	18	11	1	5	198^1	217	8	83	58	14.0	4.08	99	.292	.370	22	.328	4	1	-1	1	0.4
1928	Chi-A	2	5	.286	28	5	1	0	2	74^1	89	1	29	28	14.8	4.84	84	.313	.385	2	.105	-1	-7	-7	-0	-0.7
1929	Chi-A	0	0	—	11	0	0	0	1	11^1	13	0	8	3	16.7	4.76	90	.317	.429	0	—	0	-1	-1	-0	0.0
1931	Cle-A	5	5	.500	17	9	5	0	1	85^2	87	7	50	37	15.0	4.20	110	.256	.361	5	.185	0	2	4	-0	0.4
1932	Cle-A	8	6	.571	35	7	4	1	3	112^1	119	6	42	32	13.1	4.33	110	.266	.333	7	.175	-0	2	5	0	0.6
1933	Cle-A	5	3	.625	41	3	1	0	1	103	112	4	49	30	14.3	4.89	91	.271	.353	6	.231	1	-7	-5	-2	-0.5
1934	Cle-A	0	0	—	5	0	0	0	1	5^1	4	0	5	1	15.2	5.06	90	.222	.391	0	.000	-0	-0	-0	0	0.0
Total	12	49	60	.450	303	67	33	2	31	994^1	1104	32	449	345	14.4	4.30	98	.288	.368	70	.233	5	-7	-8	5	1.1

● STEVE CONNELLY Connelly, Steven Lee b: 4/27/74, Long Beach, Cal. BR/TR, 6'4", 210 lbs. Deb: 6/28/98

YEAR	TM/L	W	L	PCT	G	GS	CG	SH	SV	IP	H	HR	BB	SO	RAT	ERA	ERA+	OAV	OOB	BH	AVG	PB	PR	/A	PD	TPI
1998	Oak-A	0	0	—	3	0	0	0	0	4^2	10	0	4	1	28.9	1.93	236	.435	.536	0	—	0	1	1	0	0.1

● BILL CONNELLY Connelly, William Wirt "Wild Bill" b: 6/29/25, Alberta, Va. d: 11/27/80, Richmond, Va. BL/TR, 6', 175 lbs. Deb: 8/22/45

YEAR	TM/L	W	L	PCT	G	GS	CG	SH	SV	IP	H	HR	BB	SO	RAT	ERA	ERA+	OAV	OOB	BH	AVG	PB	PR	/A	PD	TPI
1945	Phi-A	1	1	.500	2	1	0	0	0	8	7	0	8	0	16.9	4.50	76	.259	.429	0	.000	0	-1	-1	-0	-0.2
1950	Chi-A	0	0	—	2	0	0	0	0	2^1	5	1	1	0	23.1	11.57	39	.455	.500	0	—	0	-2	-2	-0	0.0
	Det-A	0	0	—	2	0	0	0	0	4	4	1	2	1	13.5	6.75	69	.250	.333	0	.000	0	-1	-1	0	0.0
	Yr	0	0	—	4	0	0	0	0	6^1	9	2	3	1	17.1	8.53	54	.333	.400	0	.000	0	-3	-3	0	0.0
1952	NY-N	5	0	1.000	11	4	0	0	0	31^2	22	4	25	22	13.4	4.55	81	.208	.359	4	.364	3	-3	-3	1	-0.1
1953	NY-N	0	1	.000	8	2	0	0	0	20^1	33	4	17	11	22.1	11.07	39	.371	.472	0	.000	-1	-15	-15	-0	-0.7
Total	4	6	2	.750	25	7	0	0	0	66^1	71	10	53	34	16.8	6.92	57	.285	.411	4	.211	3	-22	-22	-0	-1.0

● ED CONNOLLY Connolly, Edward Joseph Jr. b: 12/3/39, Brooklyn, N.Y. d: 7/1/98, New Canaan, Conn. BL/TL, 6'1", 190 lbs. Deb: 4/19/64 F

YEAR	TM/L	W	L	PCT	G	GS	CG	SH	SV	IP	H	HR	BB	SO	RAT	ERA	ERA+	OAV	OOB	BH	AVG	PB	PR	/A	PD	TPI
1964	Bos-A	4	11	.267	27	15	1	1	0	80^2	80	3	64	73	16.7	4.91	79	.261	.398	3	.167	0	-12	-9	-1	-1.7
1967	Cle-A	2	1	.667	15	4	0	0	0	49^1	63	6	34	45	17.9	7.48	44	.315	.417	2	.182	0	-23	-23	-0	-1.3
Total	2	6	12	.333	42	19	1	1	0	130	143	9	98	118	17.2	5.88	62	.282	.405	5	.172	0	-35	-33	-2	-3.0

● JOHN CONNOR Connor, John b: 8/1854, Glasgow, Scotland d: 10/13/32, Boston, Mass. Deb: 7/26/1884

YEAR	TM/L	W	L	PCT	G	GS	CG	SH	SV	IP	H	HR	BB	SO	RAT	ERA	ERA+	OAV	OOB	BH	AVG	PB	PR	/A	PD	TPI
1884	Bos-N	1	4	.200	7	7	7	0	0	60	70	1	18	29	13.2	3.15	92	.275	.322	2	.080	-3	-1	-2	0	-0.3
1885	Buf-N	0	1	.000	1	1	1	0	0	9	14	0	2	0	16.0	4.00	75	.378	.410	0	.000	-0	-1	-1	-1	-0.2
	Lou-a	1	3	.250	4	4	4	0	0	35	43	0	12	19	14.7	4.89	66	.295	.356	2	.143	-1	-6	-6	-1	-0.7
Total	2	2	8	.200	12	12	12	0	0	104	127	1	32	48	13.9	3.81	79	.290	.341	4	.095	-4	-9	-9	-1	-1.2

● JOE CONNORS Connors, Joseph P. b: Paterson, N.J. Deb: 5/3/1884 ♦

YEAR	TM/L	W	L	PCT	G	GS	CG	SH	SV	IP	H	HR	BB	SO	RAT	ERA	ERA+	OAV	OOB	BH	AVG	PB	PR	/A	PD	TPI
1884	Alt-U	0	1	.000	1	1	1	0	0	9	18	0	5	0	23.0	7.00	38	.391	.451	1	.091	-1	-5	-4	0	-0.4
	KC-U	0	1	.000	2	1	1	0	0	12	24	1	0	1	18.0	4.50	50	.393	.393	1	.091	-1	-3	-3	-1	-0.3
	Yr	0	2	.000	3	2	2	0	0	21	42	1	5	1	20.1	5.57	43	.393	.420	2	.091	-2	-7	-7	-0	-0.7

● BILL CONNORS Connors, William Joseph b: 11/2/41, Schenectady, N.Y. BR/TR, 6'1", 180 lbs. Deb: 5/3/66 C

YEAR	TM/L	W	L	PCT	G	GS	CG	SH	SV	IP	H	HR	BB	SO	RAT	ERA	ERA+	OAV	OOB	BH	AVG	PB	PR	/A	PD	TPI
1966	Chi-N	0	1	.000	11	0	0	0	0	16	20	4	7	3	15.2	7.31	50	.308	.375	0	—	0	-7	-6	-0	-0.4
1967	NY-N	0	0	—	6	1	0	0	0	13	8	3	5	13	9.7	6.23	54	.170	.264	0	.000	-0	-4	-4	-0	-0.1
1968	NY-N	0	1	.000	9	0	0	0	0	14	21	0	7	8	18.6	9.00	34	.339	.414	1	1.000	1	-9	-9	0	-0.6
Total	3	0	2	.000	26	1	0	0	0	43	49	7	19	24	14.7	7.53	45	.282	.359	1	.500	1	-20	-20	-0	-1.1

● TED CONOVAR Conovar, Theodore "Huck" b: 3/10/1868, Lexington, Ky. d: 7/27/10, Paris, Ky. BR/TR, 5'10.5", 165 lbs. Deb: 5/26/1889

YEAR	TM/L	W	L	PCT	G	GS	CG	SH	SV	IP	H	HR	BB	SO	RAT	ERA	ERA+	OAV	OOB	BH	AVG	PB	PR	/A	PD	TPI
1889	Cin-a	0	0	—	1	0	0	0	1	2	4	0	2	1	27.0	13.50	29	.400	.500	0	—	0	-2	-2	-0	-0.2

● TIM CONROY Conroy, Timothy James b: 4/3/60, McKeesport, Pa. BL/TL, 5'11", 185 lbs. Deb: 6/23/78

YEAR	TM/L	W	L	PCT	G	GS	CG	SH	SV	IP	H	HR	BB	SO	RAT	ERA	ERA+	OAV	OOB	BH	AVG	PB	PR	/A	PD	TPI
1978	Oak-A	0	0	—	2	2	0	0	0	4^2	3	0	9	0	25.1	7.71	47	.188	.500	0	—	0	-2	-2	-0	0.1
1982	Oak-A	2	2	.500	5	5	1	0	0	25^1	20	1	18	17	13.5	3.55	110	.222	.352	0	—	0	1	1	-0	0.2
1983	Oak-A	7	10	.412	39	18	3	1	0	162^1	141	17	98	112	13.4	3.94	98	.232	.340	0	—	0	2	-1	-2	-0.2
1984	Oak-A	1	6	.143	38	14	0	0	0	93	82	11	63	69	14.2	5.23	72	.236	.356	0	—	0	-13	-15	-1	-0.9
1985	Oak-A	0	1	.000	16	2	0	0	0	25^1	22	3	15	8	13.5	4.26	90	.237	.349	0	—	0	-0	-1	-0	0.0
1986	StL-N	5	11	.313	25	21	1	0	0	115^1	122	15	56	79	14.1	5.23	70	.275	.360	4	.138	1	-19	-20	-1	-2.5
1987	StL-N	3	2	.600	10	9	0	0	0	40^2	48	0	25	22	16.4	5.53	75	.306	.404	0	.000	-2	-7	-6	-1	-0.8
Total	7	18	32	.360	135	71	5	1	0	466^2	438	47	284	307	14.1	4.69	81	.249	.357	4	.091	-1	-37	-46	-6	-4.1

● JIM CONSTABLE Constable, Jimmy Lee "Sheriff" b: 6/14/33, Jonesborough, Tenn. BB/TL, 6'1", 185 lbs. Deb: 6/24/56

YEAR	TM/L	W	L	PCT	G	GS	CG	SH	SV	IP	H	HR	BB	SO	RAT	ERA	ERA+	OAV	OOB	BH	AVG	PB	PR	/A	PD	TPI
1956	NY-N	0	0	—	3	0	0	0	0	4^1	9	0	7	1	35.3	14.54	26	.429	.586	0	—	0	-5	-5	-0	0.0
1957	NY-N	1	1	.500	16	0	0	0	0	28^1	27	2	7	13	12.1	2.86	138	.262	.333	0	.000	-0	3	3	-0	0.1
1958	SF-N	1	0	1.000	9	0	0	0	1	8	10	1	3	4	14.6	5.63	68	.323	.382	1	1.000	1	-1	-2	1	-0.1
	Cle-A	0	1	.000	6	2	0	0	0	9^1	17	1	4	3	21.2	11.57	32	.415	.478	2	1.000	1	-8	-8	-0	-0.7
	Was-A	0	1	.000	15	2	0	0	0	27^2	29	3	15	25	14.6	4.88	78	.271	.366	1	.250	0	-3	-3	-0	-0.1
	Yr	0	2	.000	21	4	0	0	0	37	46	4	19	28	16.1	6.57	57	.309	.391	3	.500	1	-12	-11	-1	-0.8
1962	Mil-N	1	1	.500	3	2	1	1	1	18	14	1	4	12	9.0	2.00	190	.222	.269	0	.000	-0	4	4	-1	0.4
1963	SF-N	0	0	—	4	0	0	0	0	2^1	3	0	1	1	15.4	3.86	83	.333	.400	0	—	0	-0	-0	0	0.0
Total	5	3	4	.429	56	6	1	1	2	98	109	8	41	59	14.4	4.87	78	.291	.371	4	.235	2	-11	-11	-1	-0.4

● SANDY CONSUEGRA Consuegra, Sandalio Simeon (Castello) b: 9/3/20, Potrerillos, Cuba BR/TR, 5'10", 165 lbs. Deb: 6/10/50

YEAR	TM/L	W	L	PCT	G	GS	CG	SH	SV	IP	H	HR	BB	SO	RAT	ERA	ERA+	OAV	OOB	BH	AVG	PB	PR	/A	PD	TPI
1950	Was-A	7	8	.467	21	18	8	2	2	124^2	132	6	57	38	13.7	4.40	102	.270	.347	7	.175	-1	2	1	0	0.1
1951	Was-A	7	8	.467	40	12	5	0	3	146	140	10	63	31	12.5	4.01	102	.251	.327	10	.233	-0	2	1	1	0.2
1952	Was-A	6	0	1.000	30	2	0	0	5	73^2	80	2	27	19	13.1	3.05	116	.276	.338	3	.176	-0	5	4	-1	0.3
1953	Was-A	0	0	—	4	0	0	0	0	5	9	0	4	0	23.4	10.80	36	.391	.481	0	—	0	-4	-4	0	0.0
	Chi-A	7	5	.583	29	13	5	1	3	124	122	9	28	30	11.0	2.54	158	.258	.302	2	.057	-4	20	20	3	1.9
	Yr	7	5	.583	33	13	5	1	3	129	131	9	32	30	11.5	2.86	141	.264	.311	2	.057	-4	16	17	3	1.9
1954	Chi-A★	16	3	**.842**	39	17	3	2	3	154	142	9	35	31	10.3	2.69	139	.248	.292	11	.229	1	18	18	1	2.4
1955	Chi-A	6	5	.545	44	7	3	0	7	126^1	120	4	18	35	10.0	2.64	150	.256	.286	3	.103	-2	**19**	**18**	-0	1.5
1956	Chi-A	1	2	.333	28	1	0	0	3	38^1	45	0	11	7	13.4	5.17	79	.296	.348	0	.000	-1	-4	-5	0	-0.5
	Bal-A	1	1	.500	4	1	0	0	0	8^2	10	2	2	1	12.5	4.15	94	.294	.333	1	.500	0	0	-0	-0	0.0
	Yr	2	3	.400	32	2	0	0	3	47	55	2	13	8	13.0	4.98	82	.293	.338	1	.167	-0	-4	-5	-0	-0.5
1957	Bal-A	0	0	—	5	0	0	0	0	5	4	0	0	0	7.2	1.80	200	.211	.211	0	—	0	1	1	0	0.0
	NY-N	0	0	—	4	0	0	0	0	3^2	7	1	1	1	19.6	2.45	160	.389	.421	0	—	0	1	1	0	0.0
Total	8	51	32	.614	248	71	24	5	26	809^1	811	43	246	193	11.8	3.37	119	.262	.318	37	.170	-5	59	57	4	5.9

● NARDI CONTRERAS Contreras, Arnaldo Juan b: 9/19/51, Tampa, Fla. BB/TR, 6'2", 193 lbs. Deb: 5/23/80 C

YEAR	TM/L	W	L	PCT	G	GS	CG	SH	SV	IP	H	HR	BB	SO	RAT	ERA	ERA+	OAV	OOB	BH	AVG	PB	PR	/A	PD	TPI
1980	Chi-A	0	0	—	8	0	0	0	0	13^2	18	1	7	8	17.8	5.93	68	.333	.429	0	—	0	-3	-3	0	0.0

● JIM CONVERSE Converse, James Daniel b: 8/17/71, San Francisco, Cal. BL/TR, 5'9", 180 lbs. Deb: 5/22/93

YEAR	TM/L	W	L	PCT	G	GS	CG	SH	SV	IP	H	HR	BB	SO	RAT	ERA	ERA+	OAV	OOB	BH	AVG	PB	PR	/A	PD	TPI
1993	Sea-A	1	3	.250	4	4	0	0	0	20^1	23	0	14	10	16.4	5.31	83	.295	.402	0	—	0	-2	-2	1	-0.3
1994	Sea-A	0	5	.000	13	8	0	0	0	48^2	73	5	40	39	21.1	8.69	56	.353	.460	0	—	0	-21	-21	-0	-1.7
1995	Sea-A	0	3	.000	6	1	0	0	1	11	16	2	8	9	19.6	7.36	64	.348	.444	0	—	0	-3	-3	-0	-0.8
	KC-A	1	0	1.000	9	0	0	0	0	12^1	12	0	8	5	14.6	5.84	82	.267	.377	0	—	0	-2	-1	0	-0.1
	Yr	1	3	.250	15	1	0	0	1	23^1	28	2	16	14	17.0	6.56	73	.308	.411	0	—	0	-5	-5	0	-0.9
1997	KC-A	0	0	—	3	0	0	0	0	5	4	2	5	3	16.2	3.60	131	.222	.391	0	—	0	1	1	-0	0.0
Total	4	2	11	.154	35	13	0	0	1	97^1	128	9	75	66	18.9	7.21	66	.325	.434	0	—	0	-28	-27	1	-2.9

YEAR	TM/L	W	L	PCT	G	GS	CG	SH	SV	IP	H	HR	BB	SO	RAT	ERA	ERA+	OAV	OOB	BH	AVG	PB	PR	/A	PD	TPI
● **JIM CONWAY**	Conway, James P. b: 10/8/1858, Clifton, Pa. TR , Deb: 5/5/1884 F																									
1884	Bro-a	3	9	.250	13	13	10	0	0	105^1	132	4	15	25	12.8	4.44	75	.289	.316	6	.128	-4	-14	-13	-2	-1.6
1885	Phi-a	0	1	.000	2	2	1	0	0	12^1	19	0	2	0	15.3	7.30	47	.358	.382	0	.000	-0	-6	-5	-0	-0.4
1889	KC-a	19	19	.500	41	37	33	0	0	335	334	12	90	115	11.8	3.25	129	.252	.306	31	.208	-6	22	35	1	2.7
Total	3	22	29	.431	56	52	44	0	0	452^2	485	16	107	140	12.1	3.64	109	.264	.311	37	.183	-10	3	16	-1	0.7
● **JERRY CONWAY**	Conway, Jerome Patrick b: 6/7/01, Holyoke, Mass. d: 4/16/80, Holyoke, Mass. BL/TL, 6'2", 190 lbs. Deb: 8/31/20																									
1920	Was-A	0	0	—	1	0	0	0	0	2	1	0	1	0	9.0	0.00	—	.167	.286	0	—	0	1	1	-0	0.0
● **PETE CONWAY**	Conway, Peter J. b: 10/30/1866, Burmont, Pa. d: 1/13/03, Clifton Heights, Pa. BR/TR, 5'10.5", 162 lbs. Deb: 8/10/1885 F♦																									
1885	Buf-N	10	17	.370	27	27	26	1	0	210	256	10	44	94	12.9	4.67	64	.287	.320	10	.111	-4	-43	-39	1	-4.2
1886	KC-N	5	15	.250	23	20	19	0	0	180	236	6	61	81	14.9	5.75	66	.294	.343	47	.242	0	-49	-39	-2	-3.4
	Det-N	6	5	.545	11	11	11	0	0	91	93	1	25	35	11.7	3.36	99	.255	.303	8	.186	1	-0	-1	-0	-0.1
	Yr	11	20	.355	34	31	30	0	0	271	329	7	86	116	13.8	4.95	73	.282	.331	55	.232	1	-49	-40	-2	-3.5
1887	*Det-N	8	9	.471	17	17	16	0	0	146	132	3	47	40	11.3	2.90	140	.235	.300	22	.232	0	19	19	3	1.9
1888	Det-N	30	14	.682	45	45	43	4	0	391	315	11	57	176	8.9	2.26	123	.208	**.243**	46	.275	15	26	22	3	3.9
1889	Pit-N	2	1	.667	3	3	2	0	0	22	26	1	16	2	17.2	4.91	76	.286	.393	1	.100	0	-2	-3	0	-0.2
Total	5	61	61	.500	126	123	117	5	0	1040	1058	32	250	428	11.5	3.59	90	.250	.295	134	.224	12	-50	-42	4	-2.1
● **DICK CONWAY**	Conway, Richard Butler b: 4/25/1865, Lowell, Mass. d: 9/9/26, Lowell, Mass. BL/TR, 5'7.5", 140 lbs. Deb: 7/22/1886 F																									
1886	Bal-a	2	7	.222	9	9	8	0	0	76^2	106	6	43	64	17.8	6.81	50	.312	.394	7	.206	0	-29	-29	2	-2.2
1887	Bos-N	9	15	.375	26	26	25	0	0	222^1	249	10	86	45	13.8	4.66	87	.276	.343	36	.248	2	-14	-15	1	-1.0
1888	Bos-N	4	2	.667	6	6	6	0	0	53	49	2	8	12	10.4	2.38	120	.240	.282	4	.160	-1	3	3	-0	0.2
Total	3	15	24	.385	41	41	39	0	0	352	404	18	137	121	14.2	4.78	78	.279	.347	47	.230	1	-40	-41	2	-3.0
● **JOE CONZELMAN**	Conzelman, Joseph Harrison b: 7/14/1885, Bristol, Conn. d: 4/17/79, Mountain Brook, Ala. BR/TR, 6', 170 lbs. Deb: 5/1/13																									
1913	Pit-N	0	1	.000	3	2	1	0	0	15	13	0	5	9	11.4	1.20	252	.245	.322	0	.000	-1	3	3	0	0.1
1914	Pit-N	5	6	.455	33	9	4	1	2	101	88	2	40	39	11.7	2.94	90	.254	.337	3	.111	-2	-2	-3	2	-0.4
1915	Pit-N	1	1	.500	18	1	0	0	0	47^1	41	0	20	22	12.2	3.42	80	.248	.340	1	.091	-1	-4	-4	1	-0.2
Total	3	6	8	.429	54	12	5	1	2	163^1	142	2	65	70	11.8	2.92	93	.252	.336	4	.095	-3	-2	-4	2	-0.5
● **ANDY COOK**	Cook, Andrew Bernard b: 8/30/67, Memphis, Tenn. BR/TR, 6'5", 215 lbs. Deb: 5/9/93																									
1993	NY-A	0	1	.000	4	0	0	0	0	5^1	4	1	7	4	18.6	5.06	82	.200	.407	0	—	0	-0	-1	0	0.0
● **DENNIS COOK**	Cook, Dennis Bryan b: 10/4/62, LaMarque, Tex. BL/TL, 6'3", 185 lbs. Deb: 9/12/88																									
1988	SF-N	2	1	.667	4	4	1	1	0	22	9	1	11	13	8.2	2.86	114	.125	.241	0	.000	1	1	1	-1	0.1
1989	SF-N	1	0	1.000	2	2	1	0	0	15	13	1	5	9	10.8	1.80	187	.245	.310	1	.167	1	3	3	0	0.3
	Phi-N	6	8	.429	21	16	1	1	0	106	97	17	33	58	11.2	3.99	89	.243	.304	8	.222	1	-6	-5	-1	-0.7
	Yr	7	8	.467	23	18	2	1	0	121	110	18	38	67	11.2	3.72	95	.243	.305	9	.214	2	-3	-3	-1	-0.4
1990	Phi-N	8	3	.727	42	13	2	1	1	141^2	132	13	54	58	11.9	3.56	107	.250	.322	13	.310	4	4	4	-0	0.7
	LA-N	1	1	.500	5	3	0	0	0	14^1	23	7	2	6	15.7	7.53	49	.365	.385	2	.286	1	-6	-6	0	-0.6
	Yr	9	4	.692	47	16	2	1	1	156	155	20	56	64	12.2	3.92	97	.259	.323	15	.306	5	-2	-2	-0	0.1
1991	LA-N	1	0	1.000	20	1	0	0	0	17^2	12	0	7	8	9.7	0.51	705	.203	.288	0	.000	-0	6	6	0	0.3
1992	Cle-A	5	7	.417	32	25	1	0	0	158	156	29	50	96	11.8	3.82	102	.255	.314	0	—	0	2	2	-2	-0.1
1993	Cle-A	5	5	.500	25	6	0	0	0	54	62	9	16	34	13.3	5.67	76	.295	.351	0	—	0	-8	-8	-1	-1.3
1994	Chi-A	3	1	.750	38	0	0	0	0	33	29	4	14	26	11.7	3.55	132	.230	.307	0	—	0	5	4	-0	0.4
1995	Cle-A	0	0	—	11	0	0	0	0	12^2	16	3	10	13	19.2	6.39	73	.320	.443	0	—	0	-2	-2	0	0.0
	Tex-A	0	2	.000	35	1	0	0	2	45	47	6	16	40	12.8	4.00	121	.280	.346	0	—	0	4	4	-1	0.1
	Yr	0	2	.000	46	1	0	0	2	57^2	63	9	26	53	14.0	4.53	106	.288	.366	0	—	0	1	2	-1	0.1
1996	*Tex-A	5	2	.714	60	0	0	0	0	70^1	53	2	35	64	12.2	4.09	128	.214	.328	0	—	0	7	9	-1	0.6
1997	*Fla-N	1	2	.333	59	0	0	0	0	62^1	64	4	28	63	13.6	3.90	103	.267	.348	5	.556	3	2	1	0	0.4
1998	NY-N	8	4	.667	73	0	0	0	1	68	60	5	27	79	11.9	2.38	175	.240	.321	0	.000	-0	14	13	0	2.2
Total	11	46	36	.561	427	71	6	3	4	820	773	101	308	567	12.1	3.80	107	.251	.324	29	.269	10	25	25	-5	2.4
● **EARL COOK**	Cook, Earl Davis b: 12/10/08, Stouffville, Ont., Canada d: 11/21/96, Markham, Ont., Canada BR/TR, 6', 195 lbs. Deb: 9/12/41																									
1941	Det-A	0	0	—	1	0	0	0	0	2	4	0	0	1	18.0	4.50	101	.400	.400	0	—	0	-0	0	0	0.0
● **GLEN COOK**	Cook, Glen Patrick b: 9/8/59, Buffalo, N.Y. BR/TR, 5'11", 180 lbs. Deb: 6/23/85																									
1985	Tex-A	2	3	.400	9	7	0	0	0	40	53	12	18	19	16.6	9.45	45	.327	.404	0	—	0	-24	-23	-1	-2.3
● **MIKE COOK**	Cook, Michael Horace b: 8/14/63, Charleston, S.C. BR/TR, 6'3", 200 lbs. Deb: 7/1/86																									
1986	Cal-A	0	2	.000	5	1	0	0	0	9	13	3	7	6	20.0	9.00	46	.333	.435	0	—	0	-5	-5	0	-0.8
1987	Cal-A	1	2	.333	16	1	0	0	0	34^1	34	7	18	27	13.6	5.50	78	.264	.354	0	—	0	-4	-5	0	-0.2
1988	Cal-A	0	1	.000	3	0	0	0	0	3^2	4	0	1	2	14.7	4.91	79	.308	.400	0	—	0	-0	-0	-0	-0.1
1989	Min-A	0	1	.000	15	0	0	0	0	21^1	22	1	17	15	16.9	5.06	82	.268	.400	0	—	0	-3	-2	-1	-0.6
1993	Bal-A	0	0	—	2	0	0	0	0	3	1	0	2	3	9.0	0.00	—	.091	.231	0	—	0	1	1	-0	-0.1
Total	5	1	6	.143	41	2	0	0	0	71^1	74	11	45	53	15.3	5.55	76	.270	.377	0	—	0	-11	-11	0	-1.8
● **ROLLIN COOK**	Cook, Rollin Edward b: 10/5/1890, Toledo, Ohio d: 8/11/75, Toledo, Ohio BR/TR, 5'9", 152 lbs. Deb: 7/6/15																									
1915	StL-A	0	0	—	5	0	0	0	0	13^2	16	0	9	7	17.1	7.24	40	.276	.382	1	.250	0	-7	-7	0	0.0
● **RON COOK**	Cook, Ronald Wayne b: 7/11/47, Jefferson, Tex. BL/TL, 6'1", 175 lbs. Deb: 4/10/70																									
1970	Hou-N	4	4	.500	41	7	0	0	2	82^1	80	4	42	50	13.7	3.72	104	.274	.371	4	.235	2	3	1	-0	0.3
1971	Hou-N	0	4	.000	5	4	0	0	0	25^2	23	2	8	10	11.2	4.91	69	.237	.302	2	.250	0	-4	-4	0	-0.6
Total	2	4	8	.333	46	11	0	0	2	108	103	6	50	60	13.1	4.00	94	.265	.354	6	.240	2	-1	-3	-0	-0.3
● **STEVE COOKE**	Cooke, Steven Montague b: 1/14/70, Lihue, Hawaii BR/TL, 6'6", 229 lbs. Deb: 7/28/92																									
1992	Pit-N	2	0	1.000	11	0	0	0	1	23	22	2	4	10	10.2	3.52	98	.253	.286	1	.333	0	-0	-0	-0	0.0
1993	Pit-N	10	10	.500	32	32	3	1	0	210^2	207	22	59	132	11.5	3.89	104	.258	.312	11	.155	-1	4	4	-2	0.0
1994	Pit-N	4	11	.267	25	23	2	0	0	134^1	157	21	46	74	13.9	5.02	86	.298	.360	8	.190	0	-12	-11	-1	-1.1
1996	Pit-N	0	0	—	3	0	0	0	0	8^1	11	1	5	7	17.3	7.56	58	.314	.400	0	.000	-0	-3	-3	-0	0.0
1997	Pit-N	9	15	.375	32	32	0	0	0	167^1	184	15	77	109	14.5	4.30	100	.284	.368	3	.058	-4	-2	-0	1	-0.3
1998	Cin-N	1	0	1.000	1	1	0	0	0	6	4	0	0	3	7.5	1.50	288	.182	.217	1	.500	0	2	2	0	0.4
Total	6	26	36	.419	104	88	5	1	1	549^2	585	61	191	335	13.0	4.31	97	.276	.341	24	.140	-3	-12	-9	-4	-1.0
● **DANNY COOMBS**	Coombs, Daniel Bernard b: 3/23/42, Lincoln, Me. BR/TL, 6'5", 210 lbs. Deb: 9/27/63																									
1963	Hou-N	0	0	—	1	0	0	0	0	0^1	3	0	0	0	81.0	27.00	12	.750	.750	0	—	0	-1	-1	0	0.0
1964	Hou-N	1	1	.500	7	1	0	0	0	18	21	1	10	14	16.0	5.00	68	.300	.395	0	.000	-0	-3	-3	0	-0.4
1965	Hou-N	0	2	.000	26	3	0	0	0	47	54	3	23	35	15.3	4.79	70	.292	.379	1	.111	0	-7	-7	1	-0.2
1966	Hou-N	0	0	—	2	0	0	0	0	2^2	4	0	0	3	13.5	3.38	101	.333	.333	0	.000	-0	0	0	-0	0.0
1967	Hou-N	3	0	1.000	6	2	0	0	0	24^1	21	0	9	23	11.1	3.33	99	.233	.303	1	.125	0	-0	0	0	0.0
1968	Hou-N	4	3	.571	40	2	0	0	2	46^2	52	0	17	29	13.5	3.28	90	.286	.350	4	.400	1	-2	-2	1	-0.1
1969	Hou-N	0	1	.000	8	0	0	0	0	8	12	0	2	3	16.9	6.75	52	.364	.417	0	.000	-0	-3	-3	-0	-0.4
1970	SD-N	10	14	.417	35	27	5	1	0	188^1	185	12	76	105	12.6	3.30	121	.256	.329	5	.096	-2	16	14	-2	1.3
1971	SD-N	1	6	.143	19	7	0	0	0	57^2	81	10	25	37	16.5	6.24	53	.327	.388	3	.214	1	-18	-19	1	-1.9
Total	9	19	27	.413	144	42	5	1	2	393	433	26	162	249	13.8	4.08	88	.280	.351	14	.140	-0	-17	-21	0	-1.7
● **JACK COOMBS**	Coombs, John Wesley "Colby Jack" b: 11/18/1882, LeGrand, Iowa d: 4/15/57, Palestine, Tex. BB/TR, 6', 185 lbs. Deb: 7/5/06 MC♦																									
1906	Phi-A	10	10	.500	23	18	13	1	0	173	144	0	68	90	11.4	2.50	109	.229	.312	16	.239	1	4	4	-0	0.6
1907	Phi-A	6	9	.400	23	17	10	2	2	132^2	109	2	64	73	12.3	3.12	83	.227	.329	8	.167	-1	-8	-8	0	-1.0
1908	Phi-A	7	5	.583	26	18	10	4	0	153	130	1	64	80	11.6	2.00	128	.233	.316	56	.255	4	7	10	0	1.1
1909	Phi-A	12	11	.522	30	24	18	6	1	205^2	156	1	73	97	10.3	2.32	104	.213	.289	14	.169	1	4	2	-0	0.3

YEAR	TM/L	W	L	PCT	G	GS	CG	SH	SV	IP	H	HR	BB	SO	RAT	ERA	ERA+	OAV	OOB	BH	AVG	PB	PR	/A	PD	TPI
1910	*Phi-A	**31**	9	.775	**45**	38	35	**13**	1	353	248	0	115	224	9.4	1.30	183	.201	.273	29	.220	4	48	42	-5	4.8
1911	*Phi-A	**28**	12	.700	47	40	26	1	2	336^2	360	8	119	185	13.2	3.53	89	.280	.348	45	.319	14	-7	-14	-3	-0.5
1912	Phi-A	21	10	.677	40	32	23	1	2	262^1	227	5	94	120	11.4	3.29	93	.241	.316	28	.255	6	1	-6	-1	-0.1
1913	Phi-A	0	0	—	2	2	0	0	0	5^1	5	0	6	0	20.3	10.13	27	.250	.444	1	.333	1	-4	-4	-0	0.0
1914	Phi-A	0	1	.000	2	2	0	0	0	8	8	0	3	1	13.5	4.50	58	.267	.353	3	.273	0	-2	-2	-0	-0.2
1915	Bro-N	15	10	.600	29	24	17	2	0	195^2	166	1	91	56	12.6	2.58	108	.236	.337	21	.280	4	4	4	-4	0.5
1916	*Bro-N	13	8	.619	27	20	10	3	0	159	136	3	44	47	10.3	2.66	101	.239	.296	11	.180	-0	-1	0	-6	-0.6
1917	Bro-N	7	11	.389	31	14	9	0	0	141	147	7	49	34	13.0	3.96	71	.284	.355	10	.227	2	-20	-18	-3	-2.4
1918	Bro-N	8	14	.364	27	20	16	2	0	189	191	10	49	44	11.5	3.81	73	.266	.315	19	.168	-0	-22	-22	-3	-2.7
1920	Det-A	0	0	—	2	0	0	0	0	5^2	7	0	2	1	14.3	3.18	117	.318	.375	0	.000	-0	0	0	-0	0.0
Total	14	158	110	.590	354	269	187	35	8	2320	2034	38	841	1052	11.5	2.78	99	.241	.316	261	.235	36	3	-8	-25	-0.2

● BOBBY COOMBS
Coombs, Raymond Franklin b: 2/2/08, Goodwins Mills, Me. d: 10/21/91, Ogunquit, Me. BR/TR, 5'9.5", 160 lbs. Deb: 6/8/33

YEAR	TM/L	W	L	PCT	G	GS	CG	SH	SV	IP	H	HR	BB	SO	RAT	ERA	ERA+	OAV	OOB	BH	AVG	PB	PR	/A	PD	TPI
1933	Phi-A	0	1	.000	21	0	0	0	2	31^1	47	4	20	8	19.2	7.47	57	.348	.432	2	.400	1	-11	-11	-0	-0.4
1943	NY-N	0	1	.000	9	0	0	0	0	16	33	1	8	5	23.1	12.94	27	.423	.477	0	.000	0	-17	-17	0	-0.9
Total	2	0	2	.000	30	0	0	0	2	47^1	80	5	28	13	20.5	9.32	43	.376	.448	2	.286	1	-28	-28	-0	-1.3

● WILLIAM COON
Coon, William K. b: 3/21/1855, Pennsylvania d: 8/30/15, Burlington, N.J. Deb: 9/4/1875 ♦

YEAR	TM/L	W	L	PCT	G	GS	CG	SH	SV	IP	H	HR	BB	SO	RAT	ERA	ERA+	OAV	OOB	BH	AVG	PB	PR	/A	PD	TPI
1876	Phi-N	0	0	—	2	0	0	0	0	7	9	0	0	0	11.6	5.14	47	.257	.257	50	.227	-0	-2	-2	-0	0.0

● JOHNNY COONEY
Cooney, John Walter b: 3/18/01, Cranston, R.I. d: 7/8/86, Sarasota, Fla. BR/TL, 5'10", 165 lbs. Deb: 4/19/21 FMC♦

YEAR	TM/L	W	L	PCT	G	GS	CG	SH	SV	IP	H	HR	BB	SO	RAT	ERA	ERA+	OAV	OOB	BH	AVG	PB	PR	/A	PD	TPI
1921	Bos-N	0	1	.000	8	1	0	0	0	20^2	19	3	10	9	12.6	3.92	93	.241	.326	1	.200	-0	-0	-1	0	0.0
1922	Bos-N	1	2	.333	4	3	1	0	0	25	19	0	6	7	9.4	2.16	185	.224	.283	0	.000	-1	5	5	0	0.4
1923	Bos-N	3	5	.375	23	8	5	2	0	98	92	3	22	23	10.7	3.31	121	.246	.293	25	.379	4	8	7	-2	0.7
1924	Bos-N	8	9	.471	34	19	12	2	2	181	176	4	50	67	11.4	3.18	120	.260	.314	33	.254	2	14	13	-1	1.1
1925	Bos-N	14	14	.500	31	29	20	2	0	245^2	267	18	50	65	11.7	3.48	115	.274	.312	33	.320	5	22	14	1	2.4
1926	Bos-N	3	3	.500	19	8	3	1	0	83^1	106	0	29	23	15.3	4.00	89	.320	.387	38	.302	3	-2	-4	0	0.1
1928	Bos-N	3	7	.300	24	5	2	0	1	89^2	106	7	31	18	13.8	4.32	91	.303	.360	7	.171	-0	-3	-4	3	-0.1
1929	Bos-N	2	3	.400	14	2	1	0	3	45	57	4	22	11	15.8	5.00	94	.315	.389	23	.319	2	-1	-2	1	0.1
1930	Bos-N	0	0	—	2	0	0	0	0	7	16	2	3	1	25.7	18.00	27	.471	.526	0	.000	-1	-10	-10	1	0.0
Total	9	34	44	.436	159	75	44	7	6	795^1	858	41	223	224	12.4	3.72	106	.278	.331	965	.286	15	32	19	4	4.7

● BOB COONEY
Cooney, Robert Daniel b: 7/12/07, Glens Falls, N.Y. d: 5/4/76, Glens Falls, N.Y. BR/TR, 5'11", 160 lbs. Deb: 9/6/31

YEAR	TM/L	W	L	PCT	G	GS	CG	SH	SV	IP	H	HR	BB	SO	RAT	ERA	ERA+	OAV	OOB	BH	AVG	PB	PR	/A	PD	TPI
1931	StL-A	0	3	.000	5	4	1	0	0	39^1	46	1	20	13	15.3	4.12	113	.291	.374	5	.385	1	1	2	-0	0.2
1932	StL-A	1	2	.333	23	3	1	0	1	71	94	8	36	23	16.7	6.97	70	.324	.402	0	.000	-3	-20	-17	-2	-1.0
Total	2	1	5	.167	28	7	2	0	1	110^1	140	9	56	36	16.2	5.95	80	.313	.393	5	.143	-2	-19	-14	-2	-0.8

● BILL COONEY
Cooney, William A. "Cush" b: 4/7/1883, Boston, Mass. d: 11/6/28, Roxbury, Mass. TR , Deb: 9/22/09 ♦

YEAR	TM/L	W	L	PCT	G	GS	CG	SH	SV	IP	H	HR	BB	SO	RAT	ERA	ERA+	OAV	OOB	BH	AVG	PB	PR	/A	PD	TPI
1909	Bos-N	0	0	—	3	0	0	0	0	6^1	4	0	2	3	8.5	1.42	198	.182	.250	3	.300	0	1	1	-0	0.0

● WILBUR COOPER
Cooper, Arley Wilbur b: 2/24/1892, Bearsville, W.Va. d: 8/7/73, Encino, Cal. BR/TL, 5'11", 175 lbs. Deb: 8/29/12

YEAR	TM/L	W	L	PCT	G	GS	CG	SH	SV	IP	H	HR	BB	SO	RAT	ERA	ERA+	OAV	OOB	BH	AVG	PB	PR	/A	PD	TPI
1912	Pit-N	3	0	1.000	6	4	3	2	0	38	32	1	15	30	11.1	1.66	197	.227	.301	2	.154	-0	7	7	-0	0.4
1913	Pit-N	5	3	.625	30	9	3	1	0	93	98	0	45	39	14.0	3.29	92	.276	.361	2	.077	-1	-1	-3	-2	-0.5
1914	Pit-N	16	15	.516	40	34	19	0	0	266^2	246	4	79	102	11.1	2.13	125	.254	.313	19	.207	1	20	16	0	2.0
1915	Pit-N	5	16	.238	38	20	11	1	4	185^2	180	4	52	71	11.7	3.30	83	.262	.323	7	.117	-3	-11	-12	1	-1.5
1916	Pit-N	12	11	.522	42	23	16	2	2	246	189	4	74	111	9.8	1.87	144	.215	.279	17	.215	0	21	22	-1	2.2
1917	Pit-N	17	11	.607	40	34	23	7	1	297^2	276	4	54	99	10.1	2.36	120	.258	.297	21	.204	2	12	16	-3	1.5
1918	Pit-N	19	14	.576	38	29	26	2	**3**	273^1	219	2	65	117	9.7	2.11	136	.223	.279	23	.242	3	20	23	-2	3.1
1919	Pit-N	19	13	.594	35	32	**27**	4	1	286^2	229	10	74	106	10.0	2.67	113	.225	.287	29	.287	6	8	11	-5	1.4
1920	Pit-N	24	15	.615	44	37	28	3	2	327	307	4	52	114	10.2	2.39	134	.253	.290	25	.221	1	27	30	-3	3.2
1921	Pit-N	**22**	14	.611	38	38	29	2	0	**327**	341	9	80	134	11.9	3.25	118	.272	.320	31	.254	4	19	21	-3	2.2
1922	Pit-N	23	14	.622	41	36	**27**	4	0	294^2	330	13	61	129	12.2	3.18	128	.286	.326	29	.269	9	**30**	**29**	-2	**4.0**
1923	Pit-N	17	19	.472	39	38	26	1	0	294^2	331	11	71	77	12.6	3.57	112	.288	.335	28	.262	4	14	14	-1	1.7
1924	Pit-N	20	14	.588	38	35	25	**4**	1	268^2	296	13	40	62	11.4	3.28	117	.283	.313	36	.346	10	17	17	-4	2.5
1925	Chi-N	12	14	.462	32	26	13	0	0	212^1	249	18	61	41	13.3	4.28	101	.291	.341	17	.207	1	-0	1	-2	-0.1
1926	Chi-N	2	1	.667	8	8	3	2	0	55	65	6	21	18	14.1	4.42	87	.311	.374	7	.389	3	-4	-4	-1	0.0
	Det-A	0	4	.000	8	3	0	0	0	13^2	27	0	9	2	25.7	11.20	36	.443	.534	0	.000	-1	-11	-11	0	-2.4
Total	15	216	178	.548	517	406	279	35	14	3480	3415	103	853	1252	11.3	2.89	116	.262	.312	293	.239	39	168	180	-27	19.7

● CAL COOPER
Cooper, Calvin Asa b: 8/11/22, Great Falls, S.C. d: 7/4/94, Clinton, S.C. BR/TR, 6'2.5", 180 lbs. Deb: 9/14/48

YEAR	TM/L	W	L	PCT	G	GS	CG	SH	SV	IP	H	HR	BB	SO	RAT	ERA	ERA+	OAV	OOB	BH	AVG	PB	PR	/A	PD	TPI
1948	Was-A	0	0	—	1	0	0	0	0	1	5	1	1	0	54.0	45.00	10	.625	.667	0	—	0	-5	-5	-0	0.0

● DON COOPER
Cooper, Donald James b: 1/15/57, New York, N.Y. BR/TR, 6'1", 185 lbs. Deb: 4/9/81

YEAR	TM/L	W	L	PCT	G	GS	CG	SH	SV	IP	H	HR	BB	SO	RAT	ERA	ERA+	OAV	OOB	BH	AVG	PB	PR	/A	PD	TPI
1981	Min-A	1	5	.167	27	2	0	0	0	58^2	61	9	32	33	14.4	4.30	92	.274	.367	0	—	0	-4	-2	-1	-0.6
1982	Min-A	0	1	.000	6	1	0	0	0	11^1	14	0	11	5	19.9	9.53	45	.311	.446	0	—	0	-7	-7	-0	-0.7
1983	Tor-A	0	0	—	4	0	0	0	0	5^1	8	3	0	5	13.5	6.75	64	.348	.348	0	—	0	-2	-1	-0	-0.5
1985	NY-A	0	0	—	7	0	0	0	0	10	12	2	3	4	13.5	5.40	74	.300	.349	0	—	0	-1	-2	-0	0.2
Total	4	1	6	.143	44	3	0	0	0	85^1	95	14	46	47	15.0	5.27	76	.287	.376	0	—	0	-14	-12	-2	-1.6

● GUY COOPER
Cooper, Guy Evans "Rebel" b: 1/28/1893, Rome, Ga. d: 8/2/51, Santa Monica, Cal. BB/TR, 6'1", 185 lbs. Deb: 5/2/14

YEAR	TM/L	W	L	PCT	G	GS	CG	SH	SV	IP	H	HR	BB	SO	RAT	ERA	ERA+	OAV	OOB	BH	AVG	PB	PR	/A	PD	TPI
1914	NY-A	0	0	—	1	0	0	0	0	3	3	0	2	3	15.0	9.00	31	.273	.385	0	.000	-0	-2	-2	0	0.0
	Bos-A	1	0	1.000	9	1	0	0	0	22	23	1	9	5	14.3	5.32	51	.299	.393	0	.000	-1	-6	-6	-1	-0.5
	Yr	1	0	1.000	10	1	0	0	0	25	26	1	11	8	14.4	5.76	47	.295	.392	0	.000	-1	-8	-8	-1	-0.5
1915	Bos-A	0	0	—	1	0	0	0	0	2	0	0	2	0	9.0	0.00	—	.000	.286	0	—	0	1	1	-0	0.0
Total	2	1	0	1.000	11	1	0	0	0	27	26	1	13	8	14.0	5.33	51	.280	.385	0	.000	-1	-8	-8	-1	-0.5

● MORT COOPER
Cooper, Morton Cecil b: 3/2/13, Atherton, Mo. d: 11/17/58, Little Rock, Ark. BR/TR, 6'2", 210 lbs. Deb: 9/14/38 F

YEAR	TM/L	W	L	PCT	G	GS	CG	SH	SV	IP	H	HR	BB	SO	RAT	ERA	ERA+	OAV	OOB	BH	AVG	PB	PR	/A	PD	TPI
1938	StL-N	2	1	.667	4	3	1	0	1	23^2	17	1	12	11	11.4	3.04	130	.195	.300	2	.222	0	2	2	1	0.4
1939	StL-N	12	6	.667	45	26	7	2	4	210^2	208	6	97	130	13.1	3.25	127	.260	.342	16	.232	3	16	20	-3	1.6
1940	StL-N	11	12	.478	38	29	16	3	3	230^2	225	12	86	95	12.3	3.63	110	.253	.321	13	.157	-2	6	9	-2	0.4
1941	StL-N	13	9	.591	29	25	12	0	0	186^2	175	15	69	118	11.9	3.91	96	.244	.313	13	.186	-0	-6	-3	-1	-0.5
1942	*StL-N★	**22**	7	.759	37	35	22	**10**	0	278^2	207	9	68	152	**9.0**	**1.78**	**193**	**.204**	**.258**	19	.184	-1	**48**	**51**	-3	**5.0**
1943	*StL-N★	**21**	8	**.724**	37	32	24	6	3	274	228	5	79	141	10.2	2.30	146	.226	.286	17	.170	-1	33	32	-2	3.2
1944	*StL-N	22	7	.759	34	33	22	**7**	1	252^1	227	6	60	97	10.4	2.46	143	.239	.288	19	.202	2	32	30	-5	3.0
1945	StL-N	2	0	1.000	4	3	1	0	0	23^2	20	1	7	14	10.6	1.52	246	.227	.292	2	.333	1	6	6	-1	0.5
	Bos-N†	7	4	.636	20	11	4	1	1	78	77	4	27	45	12.1	3.35	115	.257	.320	6	.231	1	4	4	0	0.7
	Yr	9	4	.692	24	14	5	1	1	101^2	97	5	34	59	11.7	2.92	130	.249	.311	8	.250	2	10	10	-0	1.2
1946	Bos-N☆	13	11	.542	28	27	15	4	1	199	181	16	39	83	**9.9**	3.12	110	.239	**.276**	14	.209	1	6	7	-3	0.6
1947	Bos-N	2	5	.286	10	7	2	0	0	46^2	48	2	13	15	12.2	4.05	96	.271	.328	0	.000	-1	0	-1	-1	-0.3
	NY-N	1	5	.167	8	8	2	0	0	36^2	51	7	13	12	15.7	7.12	57	.323	.374	6	.429	4	-12	-12	-1	-1.4
	Yr	3	10	.231	18	15	4	0	0	83^1	99	9	26	27	13.5	5.40	74	.294	.344	6	.222	2	-12	-13	-2	-1.7
1949	Chi-N	0	0	—	1	0	0	0	0	0	2	1	1	0	—	∞	—	1.000	1.000	0	—	0	-3	-3	0	-0.3
Total	11	128	75	.631	295	239	128	33	14	1840^2	1666	85	571	913	11.1	2.97	123	.240	.300	127	.194	6	132	143	-20	12.9

● PAT COOPER
Cooper, Orge Patterson b: 11/26/17, Albemarle, N.C. d: 3/15/93, Charlotte, N.C. BR/TR, 6'3", 180 lbs. Deb: 5/11/46 ♦

YEAR	TM/L	W	L	PCT	G	GS	CG	SH	SV	IP	H	HR	BB	SO	RAT	ERA	ERA+	OAV	OOB	BH	AVG	PB	PR	/A	PD	TPI
1946	Phi-A	0	0	—	1	0	0	0	0	1	1	0	1	0	18.0	0.00	—	.250	.400	0	—	0	0	0	-0	0.0

● MAYS COPELAND
Copeland, Mays b: 8/31/13, Mountain View, Ark d: 11/29/82, Indio, Cal. BR/TR, 6', 180 lbs. Deb: 4/27/35

YEAR	TM/L	W	L	PCT	G	GS	CG	SH	SV	IP	H	HR	BB	SO	RAT	ERA	ERA+	OAV	OOB	BH	AVG	PB	PR	/A	PD	TPI
1935	StL-N	0	0	—	1	0	0	0	0	0^2	2	0	0	0	27.0	13.50	30	.667	.667	0	—	0	-1	-1	0	0.0

● ROCKY COPPINGER
Coppinger, John Thomas b: 3/19/74, ElPaso, Tex. BR/TR, 6'5", 245 lbs. Deb: 6/11/96

YEAR	TM/L	W	L	PCT	G	GS	CG	SH	SV	IP	H	HR	BB	SO	RAT	ERA	ERA+	OAV	OOB	BH	AVG	PB	PR	/A	PD	TPI
1996	Bal-A†	10	6	.625	23	22	0	0	0	125	126	25	60	104	13.5	5.18	95	.263	.348	0	—	0	-3	-4	-2	-0.5

YEAR	TM/L	W	L	PCT	G	GS	CG	SH	SV	IP	H	HR	BB	SO	RAT	ERA	ERA+	OAV	OOB	BH	AVG	PB	PR	/A	PD	TPI
1997	Bal-A	1	1	.500	5	4	0	0	0	20	21	2	16	22	17.1	6.30	70	.273	.404	0	—	0	-4	-4	-0	-0.3
1998	Bal-A	0	0	—	6	1	0	0	0	15^2	16	3	7	13	13.2	5.17	87	.246	.319	0	—	0	-1	-1	-0	0.1
Total	3	11	7	.611	34	27	0	0	0	160^2	163	30	83	139	13.9	5.32	91	.262	.352	0	—	0	-7	-9	-2	-0.7
● **HENRY COPPOLA**	Coppola, Henry Peter b: 8/6/12, E.Douglas, Mass. d: 7/10/90, Norfolk, Mass. BR/TR, 5'11", 175 lbs. Deb: 4/19/35																									
1935	Was-A	3	4	.429	19	5	2	1	0	59^1	72	6	29	19	15.5	5.92	73	.300	.378	1	.071	-0	-10	-11	-0	-1.1
1936	Was-A	0	0	—	6	0	0	0	1	14	17	1	12	2	18.6	4.50	106	.315	.439	1	.333	1	1	0	0	0.1
Total	2	3	4	.429	25	5	2	1	1	73^1	89	7	41	21	16.1	5.65	78	.303	.390	2	.118	0	-9	-10	0	-1.0
● **DOUG CORBETT**	Corbett, Douglas Mitchell b: 11/4/52, Sarasota, Fla. BR/TR, 6'1", 185 lbs. Deb: 4/10/80																									
1980	Min-A	8	6	.571	73	0	0	0	23	136^1	102	7	42	89	9.6	1.98	220	.213	.278	0	—	0	**31**	**36**	3	4.5
1981	Min-A☆	2	6	.250	**54**	0	0	0	17	87^2	80	5	34	60	11.7	2.57	154	.239	.309	0	—	0	11	13	2	1.6
1982	Min-A	0	2	.000	10	0	0	0	3	22	27	3	10	15	15.1	5.32	80	.300	.370	0	—	0	-3	-3	1	-0.4
	Cal-A	1	7	.125	33	0	0	0	8	57	46	8	25	37	11.2	5.05	80	.223	.307	0	—	0	-6	-6	0	-0.9
	Yr	1	9	.100	43	0	0	0	11	79	73	11	35	52	12.3	5.13	80	.247	.326	0	—	0	-9	-9	1	-1.3
1983	Cal-A	1	1	.500	11	0	0	0	0	17^1	26	1	4	18	16.1	3.63	110	.351	.392	0	—	0	1	1	-0	0.1
1984	Cal-A	5	1	.833	45	1	0	0	4	85	76	2	30	48	11.4	2.12	187	.244	.314	0	—	0	18	17	0	1.4
1985	Cal-A	3	3	.500	30	0	0	0	0	46	49	7	20	24	13.7	4.89	84	.274	.350	0	—	0	-4	-4	0	-0.4
1986	*Cal-A	4	2	.667	46	0	0	0	10	78^2	66	11	22	36	10.2	3.66	112	.231	.288	0	—	0	5	4	1	0.6
1987	Bal-A	0	2	.000	11	0	0	0	1	23	25	5	13	16	14.9	7.83	56	.281	.373	0	—	0	-9	-9	1	-0.6
Total	8	24	30	.444	313	1	0	0	66	553	497	49	200	343	11.4	3.32	125	.242	.312	0	—	0	43	50	8	5.9
● **JOE CORBETT**	Corbett, Joseph A. b: 12/4/1875, San Francisco, Cal. d: 5/2/45, San Francisco, Cal. BR/TR, 5'10", Deb: 8/23/1895																									
1895	Was-N	0	2	.000	3	3	3	0	0	19	26	3	9	3	17.5	5.68	84	.321	.402	2	.133	-1	-2	-2	0	-0.2
1896	*Bal-N	3	0	1.000	8	3	3	0	1	41	31	0	17	28	11.6	2.20	195	.208	.310	6	.273	1	10	9	-1	0.6
1897	*Bal-N	24	8	.750	37	37	34	1	0	313	330	2	115	149	13.4	3.11	134	.269	.341	37	.247	-0	42	37	2	3.1
1904	StL-N	5	8	.385	14	14	12	0	0	108^2	110	2	51	68	14.0	4.39	61	.240	.327	9	.209	1	-20	-20	0	-2.0
Total	4	32	18	.640	62	57	52	1	1	481^2	497	7	192	248	13.5	3.42	113	.259	.338	54	.235	1	30	24	2	1.5
● **SHERMAN CORBETT**	Corbett, Sherman Stanley b: 11/3/62, New Braunfels, Tex. BL/TL, 6'4", 205 lbs. Deb: 5/29/88																									
1988	Cal-A	2	1	.667	34	0	0	0	1	45^2	47	2	23	28	13.8	4.14	93	.273	.359	0	—	0	-1	-1	-0	0.0
1989	Cal-A	0	0	—	4	0	0	0	0	5^1	3	1	1	3	6.8	3.38	113	.158	.200	0	—	0	0	0	-0	0.0
1990	Cal-A	0	0	—	4	0	0	0	0	5	8	0	3	2	19.8	9.00	42	.364	.440	0	—	0	-3	-3	-0	0.0
Total	3	2	1	.667	42	0	0	0	1	56	58	3	27	33	13.7	4.50	86	.272	.354	0	—	0	-3	-4	-1	0.0
● **RAY CORBIN**	Corbin, Alton Ray b: 2/12/49, Live Oak, Fla. BR/TR, 6'2", 200 lbs. Deb: 4/6/71																									
1971	Min-A	8	11	.421	52	11	2	0	3	140^1	141	19	70	83	13.7	4.10	87	.265	.353	7	.206	1	-10	-9	1	-1.0
1972	Min-A	8	9	.471	31	19	5	3	0	161^2	135	12	53	83	10.8	2.62	123	.230	.300	4	.082	-2	8	11	-2	0.7
1973	Min-A	8	5	.615	51	7	1	0	14	148^1	124	7	60	83	11.5	3.03	130	.229	.311	0	—	0	13	15	-1	1.4
1974	Min-A	7	6	.538	29	15	1	0	0	112^1	133	8	40	50	14.1	5.29	70	.294	.356	0	—	0	-21	-19	1	-2.1
1975	Min-A	5	7	.417	18	11	3	0	0	89^2	105	13	38	49	14.6	5.12	75	.295	.366	0	—	0	-13	-13	1	-1.5
Total	5	36	38	.486	181	63	12	3	17	652^1	638	59	261	348	12.7	3.84	95	.258	.334	11	.133	-2	-23	-15	-0	-2.5
● **ARCHIE CORBIN**	Corbin, Archie Ray b: 12/30/67, Beaumont, Tex. BR/TR, 6'4", 190 lbs. Deb: 9/10/91																									
1991	KC-A	0	0	—	2	0	0	0	0	2^1	3	0	2	1	19.3	3.86	107	.300	.417	0	—	0	0	0	-0	0.0
1996	Bal-A	2	0	1.000	18	0	0	0	0	27^1	22	2	22	20	14.8	2.30	214	.222	.369	0	—	0	8	8	-1	0.5
Total	2	2	0	1.000	20	0	0	0	0	29^2	25	2	24	21	15.2	2.43	200	.229	.373	0	—	0	8	8	-1	0.5
● **JACK CORCORAN**	Corcoran, John H. b: 1860, Lowell, Mass. Deb: 5/1/1884 ♦																									
1884	Bro-a	0	0	—	1	0	0	0	0	1	0	0	1	0	9.0	0.00	—	.000	.091	39	.211	0	0	0	-0	0.0
● **LARRY CORCORAN**	Corcoran, Lawrence J. b: 8/10/1859, Brooklyn, N.Y. d: 10/14/1891, Newark, N.J. BL/TR, 120 lbs. Deb: 5/1/1880 F♦																									
1880	Chi-N	43	14	.754	63	60	57	4	2	536^1	404	6	99	**268**	8.4	1.95	124	.199	.236	66	.231	-0	25	28	6	3.1
1881	Chi-N	**31**	14	.689	45	44	43	4	0	396^2	380	10	78	150	10.4	2.31	118	.242	.278	42	.222	-1	20	19	-2	1.4
1882	Chi-N	27	12	**.692**	39	39	38	3	0	355^2	281	5	63	170	**8.7**	**1.95**	**147**	**.200**	**.234**	35	.207	-2	38	36	1	3.1
1883	Chi-N	34	20	.630	56	53	51	3	0	473^2	483	7	82	216	10.7	2.49	128	.247	.277	55	.209	-1	34	37	1	3.3
1884	Chi-N	35	23	.603	60	59	57	7	0	516^2	473	35	116	272	10.3	2.40	130	.229	.270	61	.243	2	33	42	7	4.6
1885	Chi-N	5	2	.714	7	7	6	1	0	59^1	63	2	24	10	13.2	3.64	83	.259	.326	6	.273	2	-5	-4	0	-0.3
	NY-N	2	1	.667	3	3	2	0	0	25	24	1	11	10	12.6	2.88	93	.245	.321	5	.357	1	-0	-1	1	0.1
	Yr	7	3	.700	10	10	8	1	0	84^1	87	3	35	20	13.0	3.42	85	.255	.324	11	.306	3	-6	-5	1	-0.2
1886	Was-N	0	1	.000	2	1	1	0	0	14	16	0	4	3	12.9	5.79	57	.271	.317	15	.185	0	-4	-4	-0	-0.2
1887	Ind-N	0	2	.000	2	2	1	0	0	15	23	3	19	4	26.4	12.60	33	.338	.494	2	.200	-0	-14	-14	0	-1.1
Total	8	177	89	.665	277	268	256	22	2	2392^1	2147	69	496	1103	10.0	2.36	122	.226	.264	287	.223	1	127	139	14	14.0
● **MIKE CORCORAN**	Corcoran, Michael b: Brooklyn, N.Y. Deb: 7/15/1884 F																									
1884	Chi-N	0	1	.000	1	1	1	0	0	9	16	1	7	2	23.0	4.00	78	.372	.460	0	.000	-0	-1	-1	-0	-0.1
● **FRANCISCO CORDOVA**	Cordova, Francisco b: 4/26/72, Veracruz, Mex. BR/TR, 5'11", 165 lbs. Deb: 4/2/96																									
1996	Pit-N	4	7	.364	59	6	0	0	12	99	103	11	20	95	11.4	4.09	107	.263	.303	2	.125	-1	1	3	1	0.3
1997	Pit-N	11	8	.579	29	29	2	2	0	178^2	175	14	49	121	11.7	3.63	118	.259	.317	5	.089	-2	11	13	2	1.2
1998	Pit-N	13	14	.481	33	33	3	2	0	220^1	204	22	69	157	11.3	3.31	131	.245	.305	9	.120	-2	23	25	-1	2.6
Total	3	28	29	.491	121	68	5	4	12	498	482	47	138	373	11.5	3.58	121	.254	.309	16	.109	-5	35	41	2	4.1
● **BRYAN COREY**	Corey, Bryan Scott b: 10/21/73, Thousand Oaks, Cal. BR/TR, 6'1", 170 lbs. Deb: 5/13/98																									
1998	Ari-N	0	0	—	3	0	0	0	0	4	6	1	2	1	20.3	9.00	48	.375	.474	0	—	0	-2	-2	0	0.0
● **ED COREY**	Corey, Edward Norman "Ike" (b: Abraham Simon Cohen) b: 7/13/1899, Chicago, Ill. d: 9/17/70, Kenosha, Wis. BR/TR, 6', 170 lbs. Deb: 7/2/18																									
1918	Chi-A	0	0	—	1	0	0	0	0	2	2	0	1	0	13.5	4.50	61	.333	.429	0	.000	-0	-0	-0	0	0.0
● **FRED COREY**	Corey, Frederick Harrison b: 1857, S.Kingston, R.I. d: 11/27/12, Providence, R.I. BR/TR, Deb: 5/1/1878 ♦																									
1878	Pro-N	1	2	.333	5	5	2	0	0	23	22	0	7	7	11.3	2.35	94	.250	.305	3	.143	-1	-0	-0	-1	-0.1
1880	Wor-N	8	9	.471	25	17	9	2	2	148^1	131	6	16	47	8.9	2.43	107	.219	.239	24	.174	-3	-1	3	-3	-0.2
1881	Wor-N	6	15	.286	23	21	20	1	0	188^2	231	3	31	33	12.5	3.72	81	.299	.326	45	.222	-1	-20	-15	-1	-1.5
1882	Wor-N	1	13	.071	21	14	12	0	0	139	180	5	19	36	12.9	3.56	87	.286	.307	63	.247	0	-10	-7	1	-0.4
1883	Phi-a	10	7	.588	18	16	15	0	0	148^1	182	3	24	42	12.5	3.40	102	.283	.309	77	.258	2	-2	1	1	0.3
1885	Phi-a	1	0	1.000	1	1	1	0	0	9	18	2	1	3	19.0	7.00	49	.419	.432	94	.245	0	-4	-4	0	-0.3
Total	6	27	46	.370	93	74	59	3	2	656^1	764	19	98	168	11.8	3.32	91	.276	.300	427	.246	-3	-36	-21	-2	-2.2
● **POP CORKHILL**	Corkhill, John Stewart b: 4/11/1858, Parkesburg, Pa. d: 4/4/21, Pennsauken, N.J. BL/TR, 5'10", 180 lbs. Deb: 5/1/1883 ♦																									
1884	Cin-a	1	0	1.000	1	0	0	0	0	5	1	0	2	4	5.4	1.80	185	.063	.167	124	.274	0	1	1	-0	0.1
1885	Cin-a	1	4	.200	8	1	0	0	1	37	36	2	10	12	11.4	3.65	89	.243	.296	111	.252	1	-2	-2	0	-0.1
1886	Cin-a	0	0	—	1	0	0	0	0	0^2	1	0	0	1	13.5	13.50	26	.125	.125	143	.265	0	-1	-1	0	0.0
1887	Cin-a	1	0	1.000	5	0	0	0	0	14^2	22	0	5	3	16.6	5.52	79	.324	.370	168	.311	1	-2	-2	-0	-0.1
1888	Cin-a	0	0	—	2	0	0	0	1	5	8	1	0	1	14.4	10.80	29	.348	.348	133	.271	0	-4	-4	-0	-0.2
Total	5	3	4	.429	17	1	0	0	2	62^1	68	3	17	21	12.4	4.62	76	.259	.306	1120	.254	3	-8	-8	-1	-0.3
● **MIKE CORKINS**	Corkins, Michael Patrick b: 5/25/46, Riverside, Cal. BR/TR, 6'1", 200 lbs. Deb: 9/8/69																									
1969	SD-N	1	3	.250	6	4	0	0	0	17	27	3	8	13	18.5	8.47	42	.370	.432	0	.000	0	-9	-9	0	-1.7
1970	SD-N	5	6	.455	24	18	1	0	0	111	109	11	79	75	15.6	4.62	86	.258	.379	8	.216	2	-7	-8	-1	-0.6
1971	SD-N	0	0	—	8	0	0	0	0	13	14	1	6	16	13.8	3.46	95	.280	.357	0	—	0	0	-0	-0	0.0
1972	SD-N	6	9	.400	47	9	2	1	6	140	125	14	62	108	12.3	3.54	93	.240	.325	9	.237	3	-1	-4	0	-0.1
1973	SD-N	5	8	.385	47	11	2	0	3	122	130	12	61	82	14.9	4.50	77	.274	.370	7	.212	4	-11	-14	-2	-1.2

YEAR TM/L	W	L	PCT	G	GS	CG	SH	SV	IP	H	HR	BB	SO	RAT	ERA	ERA+	OAV	OOB	BH	AVG	PB	PR	/A	PD	TPI
1974 SD-N	2	2	.500	25	2	0	0	0	56^1	53	5	32	41	13.7	4.79	74	.255	.357	0	.000	-0	-7	-8	-1	-0.6
Total 6	19	28	.404	157	44	5	1	9	459^1	458	46	248	335	14.2	4.39	81	.262	.360	24	.202	10	-36	-43	-4	-4.2
● RHEAL CORMIER Cormier, Rheal Paul b: 4/23/67, Moncton, N.B., Can. BL/TL, 5'10", 185 lbs. Deb: 8/15/91																									
1991 StL-N	4	5	.444	11	10	2	0	0	67^2	74	5	8	38	11.2	4.12	90	.277	.303	5	.238	1	-3	-3	-1	-0.4
1992 StL-N	10	10	.500	31	30	3	0	0	186	194	15	33	117	11.2	3.68	92	.269	.306	6	.102	-2	-4	-6	1	-0.7
1993 StL-N	7	6	.538	38	21	1	0	0	145^1	163	18	27	75	12.0	4.33	91	.284	.321	11	.234	2	-5	-6	1	-0.2
1994 StL-N	3	2	.600	7	7	0	0	0	39^2	40	6	7	26	11.3	5.45	76	.256	.301	4	.286	1	-5	-6	-1	-0.5
1995 *Bos-A	7	5	.583	48	12	0	0	0	115	131	12	31	69	12.9	4.07	120	.294	.344	0	—	0	8	10	1	0.8
1996 Mon-N	7	10	.412	33	27	1	1	0	159^2	165	16	41	100	12.1	4.17	103	.270	.325	8	.186	1	1	3	3	0.6
1997 Mon-N	0	1	.000	1	1	0	0	0	1^1	4	1	1	0	33.8	33.75	12	.500	.556	0	—	0	-4	-4	-0	-1.4
Total 7	38	39	.494	169	108	7	1	0	714^2	771	73	148	425	11.9	4.18	96	.277	.320	34	.185	3	-12	-13	4	-1.8
● MARDIE CORNEJO Cornejo, Nieves Mardie b: 8/5/51, Wellington, Kan. BR/TR, 6'3", 200 lbs. Deb: 4/8/78																									
1978 NY-N	4	2	.667	25	0	0	0	3	36^2	37	1	14	17	13.3	2.45	142	.285	.367	0	—	0	5	4	-0	0.7
● REID CORNELIUS Cornelius, Jonathan Reid b: 6/2/70, Thomasville, Ala. BR/TR, 6', 200 lbs. Deb: 4/29/95																									
1995 Mon-N	0	0	—	8	0	0	0	0	9	11	3	5	4	18.0	8.00	54	.306	.419	0	—	0	-4	-4	-0	0.0
NY-N	3	7	.300	10	10	0	0	0	57^2	64	8	25	35	14.0	5.15	79	.284	.359	2	.100	-1	-6	-7	1	-1.1
Yr	3	7	.300	18	10	0	0	0	66^2	75	11	30	39	14.3	5.54	74	.285	.361	2	.100	-1	-10	-11	1	-1.1
● JEFF CORNELL Cornell, Jeffery Ray b: 2/10/57, Kansas City, Mo. BB/TR, 5'11", 170 lbs. Deb: 6/2/84																									
1984 SF-N	1	3	.250	23	0	0	0	0	38^1	51	4	22	19	17.4	6.10	57	.340	.428	0	.000	-0	-11	-11	-1	-1.2
● BRAD CORNETT Cornett, Brad Byron b: 2/4/69, Lamesa, Tex. BR/TR, 6'3", 190 lbs. Deb: 6/8/94																									
1994 Tor-A	1	3	.250	9	4	0	0	0	31	40	1	11	22	15.7	6.68	72	.331	.400	0	—	0	-6	-6	0	-0.7
1995 Tor-A	0	0	—	5	0	0	0	0	5	9	1	3	4	23.4	9.00	52	.429	.520	0	—	0	-2	-2	0	0.1
Total 2	1	3	.250	14	4	0	0	0	36	49	2	14	26	16.8	7.00	69	.345	.419	0	—	0	-9	-9	0	-0.6
● TERRY CORNUTT Cornutt, Terry Stanton b: 10/2/52, Roseburg, Ore. BR/TR, 6'2", 195 lbs. Deb: 4/9/77																									
1977 SF-N	1	2	.333	28	1	0	0	0	44^1	38	4	22	23	12.2	3.86	101	.229	.319	0	.000	-0	0	0	-1	-0.1
1978 SF-N	0	0	—	1	0	0	0	0	3	1	0	0	0	3.0	0.00	—	.100	.100	0	—	0	1	1	-0	0.0
Total 2	1	2	.333	29	1	0	0	0	47^1	39	4	22	23	11.6	3.61	107	.222	.308	0	.000	-0	1	1	-1	-0.1
● ED CORREA Correa, Edwin Josue (Andino) b: 4/29/66, Hato Rey, P.R. BR/TR, 6'2", 192 lbs. Deb: 9/18/85																									
1985 Chi-A	1	0	1.000	5	1	0	0	0	10^1	11	2	11	10	19.2	6.97	62	.275	.431	0	—	0	-3	-3	-0	-0.6
1986 Tex-A	12	14	.462	32	32	4	2	0	202^1	167	15	126	189	13.2	4.23	102	.223	.337	0	—	0	-1	2	3	0.3
1987 Tex-A	3	5	.375	15	15	0	0	0	70	83	17	52	61	17.9	7.59	59	.296	.414	0	—	0	-24	-24	-0	-2.2
Total 3	16	19	.457	52	48	4	2	0	282^2	261	34	189	260	14.6	5.16	84	.244	.361	0	—	0	-29	-26	2	-2.5
● FRANK CORRIDON Corridon, Frank J. "Fiddler" b: 11/25/1880, Newport, R.I. d: 2/21/41, Syracuse, N.Y. BR/TR, 6', 170 lbs. Deb: 4/15/04																									
1904 Chi-N	5	5	.500	12	10	9	0	0	100^1	88	2	37	34	11.8	3.05	87	.240	.321	13	.224	0	-3	-4	3	-0.1
Phi-N	6	5	.545	12	11	11	1	0	94^1	88	2	28	44	11.8	2.19	122	.250	.320	6	.171	-0	6	5	3	0.8
Yr	11	10	.524	24	21	20	1	0	194^2	176	4	65	78	11.5	2.64	101	.242	.312	19	.204	0	2	1	6	0.7
1905 Phi-N	10	12	.455	35	26	18	1	1	212	203	2	57	79	11.7	3.48	84	.257	.319	15	.208	4	-11	-13	2	-0.6
1907 Phi-N	18	14	.563	37	32	23	3	2	274	228	0	89	131	10.7	2.46	98	.230	.299	16	.165	0	0	-1	5	0.4
1908 Phi-N	14	10	.583	27	24	18	2	1	208^1	178	0	48	50	10.0	2.51	97	.239	.290	9	.123	-2	-3	-2	3	-0.1
1909 Phi-N	11	7	.611	27	19	11	3	0	171	147	0	61	69	11.3	2.11	123	.242	.318	11	.186	0	9	9	5	1.6
1910 StL-N	6	14	.300	30	18	9	0	3	156	168	1	55	51	13.4	3.81	78	.283	.353	10	.196	-0	-13	-14	3	-1.5
Total 6	70	67	.511	180	140	99	10	7	1216	1100	7	375	458	11.4	2.80	95	.247	.315	80	.180	3	-16	-20	24	0.5
● JIM CORSI Corsi, James Bernard b: 9/9/61, Newton, Mass. BR/TR, 6'1", 220 lbs. Deb: 6/28/88																									
1988 Oak-A	0	1	.000	11	1	0	0	0	21^1	20	1	6	10	11.0	3.80	100	.260	.313	0	—	0	0	-0	-0	0.1
1989 Oak-A	1	2	.333	22	0	0	0	0	38^1	26	2	10	21	8.7	1.88	196	.194	.255	0	—	0	9	8	-0	0.6
1991 Hou-N	0	5	.000	47	0	0	0	0	77^2	76	6	23	53	11.5	3.71	95	.259	.312	0	.000	-0	-0	-2	1	0.0
1992 *Oak-A	4	2	.667	32	0	0	0	0	44	44	2	18	19	12.7	1.43	261	.273	.346	0	—	0	12	11	1	1.7
1993 Fla-N	0	2	.000	15	0	0	0	0	20^1	28	1	10	7	16.8	6.64	65	.337	.409	0	—	0	-6	-5	0	-0.4
1995 Oak-A	2	4	.333	38	0	0	0	2	45	31	2	26	26	11.8	2.20	203	.203	.326	0	—	0	13	11	1	1.5
1996 Oak-A	6	0	1.000	56	0	0	0	3	73^2	71	6	34	43	13.2	4.03	122	.269	.359	0	—	0	8	7	2	0.9
1997 Bos-A	5	3	.625	52	0	0	0	2	57^2	56	1	21	40	12.6	3.43	135	.255	.331	0	—	0	7	8	0	0.9
1998 *Bos-A	3	2	.600	59	0	0	0	0	66	58	6	23	49	11.2	2.59	178	.235	.303	0	.000	-0	15	15	1	1.1
Total 9	21	21	.500	332	1	0	0	7	444	410	27	171	268	12.0	3.16	134	.251	.326	0	.000	-0	58	53	7	6.4
● BARRY CORT Cort, Barry Lee b: 4/15/56, Toronto, Ont., Can. BR/TR, 6'5", 210 lbs. Deb: 4/22/77																									
1977 Mil-A	1	1	.500	7	3	1	0	0	24^1	25	1	9	17	12.9	3.33	122	.281	.354	0	—	0	2	2	0	0.2
● AL CORWIN Corwin, Elmer Nathan b: 12/3/26, Newburgh, N.Y. BR/TR, 6'1", 170 lbs. Deb: 7/25/51																									
1951 *NY-N	5	1	.833	15	8	3	1	1	59	49	7	21	30	10.7	3.66	107	.222	.289	1	.050	-2	2	2	-2	-0.2
1952 NY-N	6	1	.857	21	7	1	0	2	67^2	58	5	36	36	12.5	2.66	139	.237	.335	2	.095	-1	8	8	-1	0.6
1953 NY-N	6	4	.600	48	7	2	1	2	106^2	122	17	68	49	16.3	4.98	86	.290	.393	9	.281	4	-8	-8	-1	-0.4
1954 NY-N	1	3	.250	20	0	0	0	0	31^1	35	4	14	14	14.1	4.02	100	.297	.371	0	.000	-0	0	0	-1	-0.1
1955 NY-N	0	1	.000	13	0	0	0	0	24^2	25	3	17	13	15.3	4.01	100	.263	.375	0	.000	-0	0	0	-0	-0.1
Total 5	18	10	.643	117	22	6	2	5	289^1	289	36	156	142	13.9	3.98	101	.263	.356	12	.152	0	2	1	-6	-0.2
● MIKE COSGROVE Cosgrove, Michael John b: 2/17/51, Phoenix, Ariz. BL/TL, 6'1", 180 lbs. Deb: 9/10/72																									
1972 Hou-N	0	1	.000	7	1	0	0	1	13^2	16	2	3	7	12.5	4.61	73	.286	.322	0	.000	-0	-2	-2	-1	-0.2
1973 Hou-N	1	1	.500	13	0	0	0	0	10	11	1	8	2	17.1	1.80	202	.282	.404	0	—	0	2	2	-0	0.3
1974 Hou-N	7	3	.700	45	0	0	0	2	90	76	2	39	47	11.6	3.50	99	.232	.316	1	.056	-1	1	-0	-1	-0.2
1975 Hou-N	1	2	.333	32	3	1	0	5	71^1	62	2	37	32	12.5	3.03	111	.245	.341	2	.154	0	5	3	0	0.2
1976 Hou-N	3	4	.429	22	16	1	1	0	89^2	106	6	58	34	16.7	5.52	58	.303	.405	2	.087	-1	-20	-23	-0	-1.7
Total 5	12	11	.522	119	20	2	1	8	274^2	271	13	145	122	13.7	4.03	83	.264	.357	5	.089	-2	-14	-21	-2	-1.6
● JIM COSMAN Cosman, James Henry b: 2/19/43, Brockport, N.Y. BR/TR, 6'4.5", 211 lbs. Deb: 10/2/66																									
1966 StL-N	1	0	1.000	1	1	1	1	0	9	2	0	2	5	5.0	0.00	—	.074	.167	0	.000	-0	4	4	-0	0.4
1967 StL-N	1	0	1.000	10	5	0	0	0	31^1	21	2	24	11	14.4	3.16	104	.198	.370	1	.125	-0	1	0	-1	-0.1
1970 Chi-N	0	0	—	1	0	0	0	0	1	3	1	1	0	36.0	27.00	17	.600	.667	0	—	0	-3	-2	0	0.0
Total 3	2	0	1.000	12	6	1	1	0	41^1	26	3	27	16	12.8	3.05	111	.188	.345	1	.091	-1	2	2	-1	0.3
● JOHN COSTELLO Costello, John Reilly b: 12/24/60, Bronx, N.Y. BR/TR, 6'1", 190 lbs. Deb: 6/2/88																									
1988 StL-N	5	2	.714	36	0	0	0	1	49^2	44	3	25	38	12.5	1.81	192	.235	.325	0	.000	-0	9	9	-1	1.2
1989 StL-N	5	4	.556	48	0	0	0	3	62^1	48	5	20	40	10.1	3.32	109	.213	.283	0	.000	-1	1	2	-1	0.1
1990 StL-N	0	0	—	4	0	0	0	0	4^1	7	1	1	1	18.7	6.23	61	.368	.429	0	—	0	-1	-1	-0	0.0
Mon-N	0	0	—	4	0	0	0	0	6^1	5	2	1	1	8.5	5.68	64	.208	.240	0	—	0	-1	-1	-0	0.0
Yr	0	0	—	8	0	0	0	0	10^2	12	3	2	2	11.8	5.91	63	.273	.304	0	—	0	-3	-3	-0	0.0
1991 SD-N	1	0	1.000	27	0	0	0	0	35	37	2	17	24	13.9	3.09	123	.276	.358	0	.000	-0	2	3	-0	0.0
Total 4	11	6	.647	119	0	0	0	4	157^2	141	13	64	104	11.9	2.97	122	.239	.317	0	.000	-1	10	11	-3	1.3
● DAN COTTER Cotter, Daniel Joseph b: 4/14/1867, Boston, Mass. d: 9/4/35, Boston, Mass. BR/TR, Deb: 7/16/1890																									
1890 Buf-P	0	1	.000	1	1	1	0	0	9	18	1	7	0	25.0	14.00	29	.400	.481	0	.000	-1	-10	-10	-0	-0.7
● ENSIGN COTTRELL Cottrell, Ensign Stover b: 8/29/1888, Hoosick Falls, N.Y d: 2/27/47, Syracuse, N.Y. BL/TL, 5'9.5", 173 lbs. Deb: 6/21/11																									
1911 Pit-N	0	0	—	1	0	0	0	0	1	4	0	1	0	45.0	9.00	38	.667	.714	0	—	0	-1	-1	-0	0.0
1912 Chi-N	0	0	—	1	0	0	0	0	4	8	0	1	1	20.3	9.00	37	.444	.474	0	.000	-0	-2	-3	-0	0.0

YEAR	TM/L	W	L	PCT	G	GS	CG	SH	SV	IP	H	HR	BB	SO	RAT	ERA	ERA+	OAV	OOB	BH	AVG	PB	PR	/A	PD	TPI
1913	Phi-A	1	0	1.000	2	1	1	0	0	10	15	0	2	3	15.3	5.40	51	.326	.354	1	.250	1	-3	-3	-0	-0.2
1914	Bos-N	0	1	.000	1	1	0	0	0	1	2	0	3	1	45.0	9.00	31	.333	.556	0	—	0	-1	-1	0	-0.5
1915	NY-A	0	1	.000	7	0	0	0	0	21^{1}	29	2	7	7	15.6	3.38	87	.330	.385	0	.000	-1	-1	-1	0	-0.1
Total	5	1	2	.333	12	2	1	0	0	37^{1}	58	2	14	12	17.6	4.82	61	.354	.408	1	.083	-0	-8	-8	-0	-0.8

● JOHNNY COUCH Couch, John Daniel b: 3/31/1891, Vaughn, Mont. d: 12/8/75, San Mateo, Cal. BL/TR, 6', 180 lbs. Deb: 4/11/17

YEAR	TM/L	W	L	PCT	G	GS	CG	SH	SV	IP	H	HR	BB	SO	RAT	ERA	ERA+	OAV	OOB	BH	AVG	PB	PR	/A	PD	TPI
1917	Det-A	0	0	—	3	0	0	0	0	13^{1}	13	0	1	1	9.5	2.70	98	.255	.269	0	.000	-0	-0	-0	0	0.0
1922	Cin-N	16	9	.640	43	33	18	2	1	264	301	13	56	45	12.3	3.89	103	.289	.328	12	.132	-3	6	3	1	0.0
1923	Cin-N	2	7	.222	19	8	1	0	0	69^{1}	98	2	15	14	14.7	5.97	65	.344	.377	4	.174	-1	-15	-16	-1	-1.9
	Phi-N	2	4	.333	11	7	2	0	0	65	91	4	21	18	15.9	5.26	87	.335	.389	6	.250	0	-9	-5	-0	-0.5
	Yr	4	11	.267	30	15	3	0	0	134^{1}	189	6	36	32	15.3	5.63	75	.339	.383	10	.213	-1	-24	-21	-1	-2.4
1924	Phi-N	4	8	.333	37	7	3	0	3	137	170	13	39	23	13.8	4.73	94	.306	.352	10	.204	-1	-13	-4	1	-0.3
1925	Phi-N	5	6	.455	34	7	2	1	2	94^{1}	112	9	39	11	14.5	5.44	88	.298	.365	5	.161	-1	-12	-7	1	-0.7
Total	5	29	34	.460	147	62	26	3	6	643	785	41	171	112	13.5	4.63	91	.304	.350	37	.167	-6	-43	-29	2	-3.4

● MIKE COUCHEE Couchee, Michael Eugene b: 12/4/57, San Jose, Cal. BR/TR, 6', 190 lbs. Deb: 4/5/83 C

YEAR	TM/L	W	L	PCT	G	GS	CG	SH	SV	IP	H	HR	BB	SO	RAT	ERA	ERA+	OAV	OOB	BH	AVG	PB	PR	/A	PD	TPI
1983	SD-N	0	1	.000	8	0	0	0	0	14	12	1	6	5	11.6	5.14	68	.214	.290	1	.500	0	-2	-3	-0	-0.2

● ED COUGHLIN Coughlin, Edward E. b: 8/5/1861, Hartford, Conn. d: 12/25/52, Hartford, Conn. Deb: 5/15/1884 ♦

YEAR	TM/L	W	L	PCT	G	GS	CG	SH	SV	IP	H	HR	BB	SO	RAT	ERA	ERA+	OAV	OOB	BH	AVG	PB	PR	/A	PD	TPI
1884	Buf-N	0	0	—	1	0	0	0	0	0	3	0	0	0	—	∞	—	.600	.600	1	.250	-0	-3	-3	0	-0.2

● ROSCOE COUGHLIN Coughlin, William Edward b: 3/15/1868, Walpole, Mass. d: 3/20/51, Chelsea, Mass. TR, 5'10", 160 lbs. Deb: 4/22/1890

YEAR	TM/L	W	L	PCT	G	GS	CG	SH	SV	IP	H	HR	BB	SO	RAT	ERA	ERA+	OAV	OOB	BH	AVG	PB	PR	/A	PD	TPI
1890	Chi-N	4	6	.400	11	10	10	0	0	95	102	3	40	29	13.8	4.26	86	.266	.342	10	.256	1	-7	-6	1	-0.4
1891	NY-N	3	4	.429	8	7	6	0	0	61	74	5	23	22	14.8	3.84	83	.289	.355	3	.130	1	-3	-4	1	-0.2
Total	2	7	10	.412	19	17	16	0	0	156	176	8	63	51	14.2	4.10	85	.275	.347	13	.210	2	-11	-11	2	-0.6

● FRITZ COUMBE Coumbe, Frederick Nicholas b: 12/13/1889, Antrim, Pa. d: 3/21/78, Paradise, Cal. BL/TL, 6', 152 lbs. Deb: 4/22/14

YEAR	TM/L	W	L	PCT	G	GS	CG	SH	SV	IP	H	HR	BB	SO	RAT	ERA	ERA+	OAV	OOB	BH	AVG	PB	PR	/A	PD	TPI
1914	Bos-A	1	2	.333	17	5	1	0	1	62^{1}	49	0	16	17	9.4	1.44	186	.222	.274	2	.111	-1	9	9	0	0.4
	Cle-A	1	5	.167	14	5	2	0	0	55^{1}	59	0	16	22	12.8	3.25	89	.288	.351	6	.261	1	-3	-2	1	-0.1
	Yr	2	7	.222	31	10	3	0	1	117^{2}	108	0	32	39	11.0	2.29	121	.254	.312	8	.195	0	6	6	1	0.3
1915	Cle-A	4	7	.364	30	12	4	1	2	114	123	1	37	37	12.9	3.47	88	.294	.355	10	.270	1	-7	-5	3	-0.2
1916	Cle-A	7	5	.583	29	13	7	2	0	120^{1}	121	1	27	39	11.1	2.02	149	.279	.323	2	.057	-3	11	13	5	1.5
1917	Cle-A	8	6	.571	34	10	4	1	5	134^{1}	119	0	35	30	10.5	2.14	132	.251	.307	6	.154	-1	8	10	3	1.3
1918	Cle-A	13	7	.650	30	17	9	0	3	150	164	4	52	41	13.0	3.06	98	.286	.347	12	.214	-1	-5	-1	5	0.3
1919	Cle-A	1	1	.500	8	2	0	0	1	23^{2}	32	2	9	7	15.6	5.32	63	.348	.406	3	.500	1	-6	-5	0	-0.3
1920	Cin-N	0	1	.000	3	0	0	0	0	14^{2}	17	0	4	7	12.9	4.91	62	.304	.350	3	.231	1	-3	-3	0	-0.1
1921	Cin-N	3	4	.429	28	6	3	0	1	86^{2}	89	2	21	12	11.5	3.22	111	.280	.326	8	.320	1	5	3	2	0.7
Total	8	38	38	.500	193	70	30	4	13	761^{1}	773	10	217	212	11.9	2.80	108	.277	.332	52	.206	-1	10	20	20	3.5

● HARRY COURTNEY Courtney, Henry Seymour b: 11/19/1898, Asheville, N.C. d: 12/11/54, Lyme, Conn. BL/TL, 6'4", 185 lbs. Deb: 9/13/19

YEAR	TM/L	W	L	PCT	G	GS	CG	SH	SV	IP	H	HR	BB	SO	RAT	ERA	ERA+	OAV	OOB	BH	AVG	PB	PR	/A	PD	TPI
1919	Was-A	3	0	1.000	4	3	2	1	0	26^{1}	25	0	19	6	15.0	2.73	117	.269	.393	2	.200	-0	1	1	-1	0.0
1920	Was-A	8	11	.421	37	24	10	1	0	188	223	6	77	48	14.8	4.74	79	.298	.371	16	.232	4	-20	-21	-3	-1.8
1921	Was-A	6	9	.400	30	15	3	0	1	132^{2}	159	7	71	26	16.1	5.63	73	.305	.397	14	.298	2	-20	-22	-0	-1.9
1922	Was-A	0	1	.000	5	0	0	0	0	10	11	0	9	4	18.0	3.60	107	.306	.444	0	.000	-1	0	0	-0	0.0
	Chi-A	5	6	.455	18	11	5	0	0	86^{2}	100	5	37	28	14.3	4.98	82	.299	.371	9	.273	3	-9	-9	-1	-0.7
	Yr	5	7	.417	23	11	5	0	0	96^{2}	111	5	46	32	14.7	4.84	84	.300	.379	9	.243	2	-9	-8	-1	-0.7
Total	4	22	27	.449	94	53	20	2	1	443^{2}	518	18	213	112	15.2	4.91	79	.299	.382	41	.252	7	-47	-50	-5	-4.4

● JOHN COURTRIGHT Courtright, John Charles b: 5/30/70, Marion, Ohio BL/TL, 6'2", 185 lbs. Deb: 5/6/95

YEAR	TM/L	W	L	PCT	G	GS	CG	SH	SV	IP	H	HR	BB	SO	RAT	ERA	ERA+	OAV	OOB	BH	AVG	PB	PR	/A	PD	TPI
1995	Cin-N	0	0	—	1	0	0	0	0	1	2	0	0	0	18.0	9.00	46	.500	.500	0	—	0	-1	-1	-0	0.0

● HARRY COVELESKI Coveleski, Harry Frank "The Giant Killer" (b: Harry Frank Kowalewski) b: 4/23/1886, Shamokin, Pa. d: 8/4/50, Shamokin, Pa. BB/TL, 6', 180 lbs. Deb: 9/10/07 F

YEAR	TM/L	W	L	PCT	G	GS	CG	SH	SV	IP	H	HR	BB	SO	RAT	ERA	ERA+	OAV	OOB	BH	AVG	PB	PR	/A	PD	TPI
1907	Phi-N	1	0	1.000	4	0	0	0	0	20	10	0	3	6	6.3	0.00	—	.147	.194	0	.000	-0	5	5	-0	0.2
1908	Phi-N	4	1	.800	6	5	5	2	0	43^{2}	29	0	12	22	8.9	1.24	196	.196	.265	2	.133	-0	5	6	1	0.8
1909	Phi-N	6	10	.375	24	17	8	2	1	121^{2}	109	0	49	56	12.1	2.74	95	.247	.329	4	.108	-2	-2	-2	1	-0.4
1910	Cin-N	1	1	.500	7	4	2	0	0	39^{1}	35	1	42	27	18.5	5.26	55	.246	.431	1	.063	-1	-10	-10	1	-0.5
1914	Det-A	22	12	.647	44	36	23	5	2	303^{1}	251	4	100	124	10.8	2.49	113	.227	.298	23	.242	5	8	11	7	2.3
1915	Det-A	22	13	.629	**50**	38	20	1	4	312^{2}	271	2	87	150	10.9	2.45	124	.233	.298	18	.175	-2	17	20	4	2.4
1916	Det-A	21	11	.656	44	39	22	3	2	324^{1}	278	6	63	108	9.8	1.97	145	.237	.282	25	.212	1	31	32	4	3.9
1917	Det-A	4	6	.400	16	11	2	0	0	69	70	0	14	15	11.2	2.61	101	.265	.307	5	.227	-0	0	0	2	0.2
1918	Det-A	0	1	.000	3	1	1	0	0	14	17	0	6	3	14.8	3.86	69	.315	.383	1	.250	0	-2	-2	1	-0.1
Total	9	81	55	.596	198	151	83	13	9	1248	1070	13	376	511	10.8	2.39	118	.235	.301	79	.189	-0	54	61	20	8.8

● STAN COVELESKI Coveleski, Stanley Anthony (b: Stanislaus Kowalewski) b: 7/13/1889, Shamokin, Pa. d: 3/20/84, South Bend, Ind. BR/TR, 5'11", 166 lbs. Deb: 9/10/12 FH

YEAR	TM/L	W	L	PCT	G	GS	CG	SH	SV	IP	H	HR	BB	SO	RAT	ERA	ERA+	OAV	OOB	BH	AVG	PB	PR	/A	PD	TPI
1912	Phi-A	2	1	.667	5	2	2	1	0	21	18	0	4	9	9.9	3.43	90	.231	.277	1	.143	-0	-0	-1	-1	-0.2
1916	Cle-A	15	13	.536	45	27	11	1	3	232	247	6	58	76	11.9	3.41	88	.278	.323	13	.173	-0	-15	-10	2	-1.1
1917	Cle-A	19	14	.576	45	36	24	**9**	4	298^{1}	202	3	94	133	9.0	1.81	157	**.194**	.261	13	.134	-4	28	34	-4	3.1
1918	Cle-A	22	13	.629	38	33	25	2	1	311	261	2	76	87	9.9	1.82	165	.229	.279	21	.191	-3	33	41	-0	4.6
1919	Cle-A	24	12	.667	43	34	24	4	4	286	286	2	60	118	11.0	2.61	128	.267	.308	20	.213	4	20	23	3	3.6
1920	*Cle-A	24	14	.632	41	38	26	3	2	315	284	6	65	**133**	**10.1**	2.49	153	**.243**	**.285**	25	.225	3	**46**	**46**	3	**5.9**
1921	Cle-A	23	13	.639	43	40	28	2	2	315	341	6	84	99	12.3	3.37	126	.280	.329	18	.155	-6	32	31	7	3.2
1922	Cle-A	17	14	.548	35	33	21	3	2	276^{2}	292	14	64	98	11.6	3.32	121	.274	.316	10	.101	-7	22	21	1	1.5
1923	Cle-A	13	14	.481	33	31	17	**5**	2	228	251	8	42	54	11.6	**2.76**	**143**	.282	.316	7	.089	-8	**31**	30	3	2.9
1924	Cle-A	15	16	.484	37	33	18	2	0	240^{1}	286	6	73	58	13.6	4.04	106	.294	.346	11	.134	-5	5	6	-0	0.2
1925	*Was-A	20	5	**.800**	32	32	15	3	0	241	230	7	73	58	11.4	**2.84**	**149**	.255	.312	9	.111	-8	42	37	0	2.6
1926	Was-A	14	11	.560	36	34	11	3	1	245^{1}	272	1	81	50	12.9	3.12	124	.286	.342	17	.207	1	25	20	1	2.1
1927	Was-A	2	1	.667	5	4	0	0	0	14^{1}	13	0	8	3	13.2	3.14	129	.250	.350	2	.333	0	2	1	-0	0.3
1928	NY-A	5	1	.833	12	8	2	0	0	58	72	5	20	5	14.3	5.74	66	.323	.379	1	.053	-2	-11	-13	1	-1.2
Total	14	215	142	.602	450	385	224	38	21	3082	3055	66	802	981	11.4	2.89	128	.262	.311	168	.159	-34	259	276	16	27.5

● CHET COVINGTON Covington, Chester Rogers "Chesty" b: 11/6/10, Cairo, Ill. d: 6/11/76, Pembroke Park, Fla. BB/TL, 6'2", 195 lbs. Deb: 4/23/44

YEAR	TM/L	W	L	PCT	G	GS	CG	SH	SV	IP	H	HR	BB	SO	RAT	ERA	ERA+	OAV	OOB	BH	AVG	PB	PR	/A	PD	TPI
1944	Phi-N	1	1	.500	19	0	0	0	0	38^{2}	46	2	8	13	12.6	4.66	78	.297	.331	0	.000	-1	-4	-4	-0	-0.3

● TEX COVINGTON Covington, William Wilkes b: 3/19/1887, Henryville, Tenn. d: 12/10/31, Denison, Tex. BL/TR, 6'1", 175 lbs. Deb: 4/25/11 F

YEAR	TM/L	W	L	PCT	G	GS	CG	SH	SV	IP	H	HR	BB	SO	RAT	ERA	ERA+	OAV	OOB	BH	AVG	PB	PR	/A	PD	TPI
1911	Det-A	7	1	.875	17	6	5	0	0	83^{2}	94	2	33	29	14.7	4.09	85	.297	.381	6	.188	-1	-7	-6	-1	-0.7
1912	Det-A	3	4	.429	14	9	2	1	0	63^{1}	58	0	30	19	12.9	4.12	79	.253	.347	2	.133	0	-6	-6	-1	-0.6
Total	2	10	5	.667	31	15	7	1	0	147	152	2	63	48	14.0	4.10	82	.278	.367	8	.170	-1	-13	-12	-2	-1.3

● JOE COWLEY Cowley, Joseph Alan b: 8/15/58, Lexington, Ky. BR/TR, 6'5", 210 lbs. Deb: 4/13/82

YEAR	TM/L	W	L	PCT	G	GS	CG	SH	SV	IP	H	HR	BB	SO	RAT	ERA	ERA+	OAV	OOB	BH	AVG	PB	PR	/A	PD	TPI
1982	Atl-N	1	2	.333	17	8	0	0	0	52^{1}	53	6	16	27	12.0	4.47	83	.265	.323	3	.200	-0	-5	-4	-0	-0.2
1984	NY-A	9	2	.818	16	11	3	1	0	83^{1}	75	12	31	71	11.7	3.56	106	.234	.305	0	—	0	4	2	0	0.6
1985	NY-A	12	6	.667	30	26	1	0	0	159^{2}	132	29	85	97	12.6	3.95	101	.224	.328	0	—	0	4	1	-0	0.2
1986	Chi-A	11	11	.500	27	27	4	0	0	162^{1}	133	20	83	132	12.1	3.88	111	.223	.321	0	—	0	5	8	-1	0.9
1987	Phi-N	0	4	.000	5	4	0	0	0	11^{2}	21	2	17	5	30.9	15.43	27	.389	.548	1	.333	1	-15	-15	-1	-3.2
Total	5	33	25	.569	95	76	8	1	0	469^{1}	414	69	232	332	12.7	4.20	96	.235	.329	4	.222	1	-7	-8	-1	-1.7

● DANNY COX Cox, Danny Bradford b: 9/21/59, Northampton, England BR/TR, 6'4", 235 lbs. Deb: 8/6/83

YEAR	TM/L	W	L	PCT	G	GS	CG	SH	SV	IP	H	HR	BB	SO	RAT	ERA	ERA+	OAV	OOB	BH	AVG	PB	PR	/A	PD	TPI
1983	StL-N	3	6	.333	12	12	0	0	0	83	92	6	23	36	12.5	3.25	111	.286	.333	2	.074	-2	3	3	1	0.2
1984	StL-N	9	11	.450	29	27	1	1	0	156^{1}	171	9	54	70	13.4	4.03	86	.289	.355	7	.132	0	-8	-10	1	-1.1
1985	*StL-N	18	9	.667	35	35	10	4	0	241	226	19	64	131	10.9	2.88	123	.251	.303	12	.152	1	19	18	-1	1.9

YEAR TM/L	W	L	PCT	G	GS	CG	SH	SV	IP	H	HR	BB	SO	RAT	ERA	ERA+	OAV	OOB	BH	AVG	PB	PR	/A	PD	TPI
1986 StL-N	12	13	.480	32	32	8	0	0	220	189	14	60	108	10.3	2.90	125	.234	.289	5	.077	-3	20	18	-5	1.1
1987 *StL-N	11	9	.550	31	31	2	0	0	199^1	224	17	71	101	13.5	3.88	107	.290	.352	8	.116	-2	4	6	-1	0.3
1988 StL-N	3	8	.273	13	13	0	0	0	86	89	6	25	47	12.0	3.98	87	.272	.326	1	.043	-2	-5	-5	0	-0.7
1991 Phi-N	4	6	.400	23	17	0	0	0	102^1	98	14	39	46	12.1	4.57	80	.258	.329	3	.103	-1	-10	-10	-1	-1.0
1992 Phi-N	2	2	.500	9	7	0	0	0	38^1	46	3	19	30	15.3	5.40	65	.299	.376	1	.091	-1	-8	-8	1	-0.8
*Pit-N	3	1	.750	16	0	0	0	3	24^1	20	2	8	18	10.4	3.33	103	.225	.289	0	.000	0	0	0	-0	0.0
Yr	5	3	.625	25	7	0	0	3	62^2	66	5	27	48	13.4	4.60	76	.269	.342	1	.071	-1	-8	-8	0	-0.8
1993 *Tor-A	7	6	.538	44	0	0	0	2	83^2	73	8	29	84	11.0	3.12	138	.230	.294	0	—	0	11	11	-1	1.5
1994 Tor-A	1	1	.500	10	0	0	0	3	18^2	7	0	7	14	7.2	1.45	333	.113	.214	0	—	0	7	7	-0	0.8
1995 Tor-A	1	3	.250	24	0	0	0	0	45	57	4	33	38	18.2	7.40	64	.317	.425	0	—	0	-13	-13	-0	-1.0
Total 11	74	75	.497	278	174	21	5	8	1298	1292	102	432	723	12.1	3.64	103	.263	.325	39	.109	-9	21	17	-6	1.2
● ERNIE COX	Cox, Ernest Thompson b: 2/19/1894, Birmingham, Ala. d: 4/29/74, Birmingham, Ala. BL/TR, 6'1", 180 lbs. Deb: 5/5/22																								
1922 Chi-A	0	0	—	1	0	0	0	0	1	1	0	2	0	27.0	18.00	23	.250	.500	0	—	0	-2	-2	-0	0.0
● GEORGE COX	Cox, George Melvin b: 11/15/04, Sherman, Tex. d: 12/17/95, Bedford, Tex. BR/TR, 6'1", 170 lbs. Deb: 4/12/28																								
1928 Chi-A	1	2	.333	26	2	0	0	0	89	110	6	39	22	15.3	5.26	77	.313	.385	2	.077	-2	-12	-12	2	-0.4
● GLENN COX	Cox, Glenn Melvin b: 2/3/31, Montebello, Cal. BR/TR, 6'2", 210 lbs. Deb: 9/20/55																								
1955 KC-A	0	2	.000	2	2	0	0	0	2^1	11	0	1	2	46.3	30.86	14	.611	.632	0	.000	-0	-7	-7	0	-2.7
1956 KC-A	0	2	.000	3	3	1	0	0	23^1	15	2	22	6	14.3	4.24	102	.203	.385	0	.000	-1	-0	0	-1	-0.2
1957 KC-A	1	0	1.000	10	0	0	0	0	14^1	18	1	9	8	17.0	5.02	79	.321	.415	0	.000	0	-2	-2	0	-0.1
1958 KC-A	0	0	—	2	0	0	0	0	3^2	6	1	3	1	22.1	9.82	40	.400	.500	0	—	0	-2	-2	0	0.0
Total 4	1	4	.200	17	5	1	0	0	43^2	50	4	35	17	17.5	6.39	65	.307	.429	0	.000	-1	-12	-11	-1	-3.0
● CASEY COX	Cox, Joseph Casey b: 7/3/41, Long Beach, Cal. BR/TR, 6'5", 200 lbs. Deb: 4/15/66																								
1966 Was-A	4	5	.444	66	0	0	0	7	113	104	6	35	46	11.4	3.50	99	.250	.314	0	.000	-1	-1	-1	0	-0.1
1967 Was-A	7	4	.636	54	0	0	0	1	73	67	2	21	32	11.3	2.96	107	.250	.314	0	.000	-0	2	2	0	0.2
1968 Was-A	0	1	.000	4	0	0	0	0	7^2	7	0	0	4	8.2	2.35	124	.250	.250	0	—	0	1	0	-0	0.0
1969 Was-A	12	7	.632	52	13	4	0	0	171^2	161	15	64	73	11.8	2.78	125	.251	.320	5	.106	-2	16	13	-1	1.1
1970 Was-A	8	12	.400	37	30	1	0	1	192^1	211	27	44	68	12.1	4.45	80	.285	.329	7	.121	-2	-16	-19	-2	-2.2
1971 Was-A	5	7	.417	54	11	0	0	7	124^1	131	9	40	43	12.9	3.98	83	.273	.338	2	.077	-1	-7	-9	-1	-1.2
1972 Tex-A	3	5	.375	35	4	0	0	4	65^1	73	7	26	27	13.8	4.41	68	.277	.344	1	.111	1	-10	-10	-0	-1.3
NY-A	0	1	.000	5	1	0	0	0	11^2	13	0	3	4	13.9	4.63	64	.289	.360	0	—	0	-2	-2	-0	-0.2
Yr	3	6	.333	40	5	0	0	4	77	86	7	29	31	13.7	4.44	68	.276	.341	1	.111	1	-12	-12	-0	-1.5
1973 NY-A	0	0	—	1	0	0	0	0	3	5	0	1	0	24.0	6.00	61	.357	.471	0	—	0	-1	-1	0	0.1
Total 8	39	42	.481	308	59	5	0	20	762	772	66	234	297	12.2	3.70	91	.266	.327	15	.099	-6	-17	-27	-3	-3.6
● LES COX	Cox, Leslie Warren b: 8/14/05, Junction, Tex. d: 10/14/34, San Angelo, Tex. BR/TR, 6', 164 lbs. Deb: 9/11/26																								
1926 Chi-A	0	1	.000	2	0	0	0	0	5	6	2	5	3	19.8	5.40	72	.261	.393	1	.500	0	-1	-1	0	-0.2
● RED COX	Cox, Plateau Rex b: 2/16/1895, Laurel Springs, N.C. d: 10/15/84, Roanoke, Va. BL/TR, 6'2", 190 lbs. Deb: 4/17/20																								
1920 Det-A	0	0	—	3	0	0	0	0	5	9	0	3	1	21.6	5.40	69	.375	.444	0	.000	-0	-1	-1	-0	0.0
● TERRY COX	Cox, Terry Lee b: 3/30/49, Odessa, Tex. BR/TR, 6'5", 215 lbs. Deb: 9/7/70																								
1970 Cal-A	0	0	—	3	0	0	0	0	2^1	4	0	0	3	15.4	3.86	94	.400	.400	0	—	0	-0	-0	0	0.0
● BILL COX	Cox, William Donald b: 6/23/13, Ashmore, Ill. d: 2/16/88, Charleston, Ill. BR/TR, 6'1", 185 lbs. Deb: 6/6/36																								
1936 StL-N	0	0	—	2	0	0	0	0	2^2	4	0	1	1	16.9	6.75	58	.333	.385	0	—	0	-1	-1	-0	0.0
1937 Chi-A	1	0	1.000	3	2	1	1	0	12^2	9	0	5	8	9.9	0.71	648	.200	.280	1	.250	0	6	5	-0	0.4
1938 Chi-A	0	2	.000	7	1	0	0	0	11^2	11	0	13	5	18.5	6.94	70	.244	.414	0	.000	-0	-3	-3	-0	-0.4
StL-A	1	4	.200	22	7	1	0	0	63	81	8	35	16	16.6	7.00	71	.315	.397	1	.059	-1	-15	-14	0	-1.0
Yr	1	6	.143	29	8	1	0	0	74^2	92	8	48	21	16.9	6.99	71	.305	.400	1	.053	-2	-18	-17	0	-1.4
1939 StL-A	0	2	.000	4	2	1	0	0	9^1	10	0	8	8	17.4	9.64	50	.256	.383	0	.000	-0	-5	-5	1	-0.8
1940 StL-A	0	1	.000	12	0	0	0	0	17^1	23	3	12	7	18.2	7.27	63	.333	.432	0	.000	-0	-6	-5	0	-0.2
Total 5	2	9	.182	50	12	3	1	0	116^2	138	11	74	45	16.4	6.56	74	.296	.392	2	.080	-2	-24	-22	1	-2.0
● BILL COYLE	Coyle, William Claude b: Pittsburgh, Pa. TR, Deb: 7/7/1893																								
1893 Bos-N	0	1	.000	2	1	0	0	0	8	14	1	3	2	19.1	9.00	55	.368	.415	0	.000	-1	-4	-4	0	-0.4
● CHARLIE COZART	Cozart, Charles Rhubin b: 10/17/19, Lenoir, N.C. BR/TL, 6', 190 lbs. Deb: 4/17/45																								
1945 Bos-N	1	0	1.000	5	0	0	0	0	8	10	2	15	4	28.1	10.13	38	.303	.521	0	.000	-0	-6	-6	1	-0.5
● ROY CRABB	Crabb, James Roy b: 8/23/1890, Monticello, Iowa d: 3/30/40, Lewistown, Mont. BR/TR, 5'11", 160 lbs. Deb: 8/10/12																								
1912 Chi-A	0	1	.000	2	1	0	0	0	8^2	6	0	4	3	10.4	1.04	308	.214	.313	0	.000	-0	2	2	0	0.2
Phi-A	2	4	.333	7	7	3	0	0	43^1	48	0	17	12	14.3	3.74	82	.287	.367	0	.000	-3	-2	-3	0	-0.6
Yr	2	5	.286	9	8	3	0	0	52	54	0	21	15	13.7	3.29	94	.277	.359	0	.000	-3	0	-1	0	-0.4
● GEORGE CRABLE	Crable, George E. b: 12/1885, Nebraska BL/TL, 6'1", 190 lbs. Deb: 8/3/10																								
1910 Bro-N	0	0	—	2	1	1	0	0	7^1	5	0	5	3	14.7	4.91	62	.217	.400	0	.000	0	-2	-2	0	0.0
● TIM CRABTREE	Crabtree, Timothy Lyle b: 10/13/69, Jackson, Mich. BR/TR, 6'4", 205 lbs. Deb: 6/23/95																								
1995 Tor-A	0	2	.000	31	0	0	0	0	32	30	1	13	21	12.7	3.09	152	.240	.321	0	—	0	6	6	1	0.4
1996 Tor-A	5	3	.625	53	0	0	0	1	67^1	59	4	22	57	11.2	2.54	107	.231	.300	0	—	0	18	18	0	1.9
1997 Tor-A	3	3	.500	37	0	0	0	2	40^2	65	7	17	26	18.6	7.08	65	.374	.435	0	—	0	-11	-11	1	-1.4
1998 *Tex-A	6	1	.857	64	0	0	0	0	85^1	86	3	35	60	13.1	3.59	135	.264	.341	0	.000	-0	10	12	-1	0.7
Total 4	14	9	.609	185	0	0	0	3	225^1	240	15	87	164	13.5	3.83	126	.273	.345	0	.000	-0	23	25	1	1.6
● WALT CRADDOCK	Craddock, Walter Anderson b: 3/25/32, Pax, W.Va. d: 7/6/80, Parma Heights, O. BR/TL, 5'11.5", 176 lbs. Deb: 9/3/55																								
1955 KC-A	0	2	.000	4	2	0	0	0	15	18	3	10	9	16.8	7.80	54	.300	.400	0	.000	-1	-6	-6	-0	-0.7
1956 KC-A	0	2	.000	2	2	0	0	0	9^1	9	1	10	8	18.3	6.75	64	.265	.432	0	.000	-0	-3	-3	-0	-0.5
1958 KC-A	0	3	.000	23	1	0	0	0	36^2	41	4	20	22	15.2	5.89	66	.289	.380	0	.000	-0	-9	-8	0	-0.6
Total 3	0	7	.000	29	5	0	0	0	61	68	8	40	39	16.1	6.49	62	.288	.394	0	.000	-1	-18	-17	0	-1.8
● MOLLY CRAFT	Craft, Maurice Montague b: 11/28/1895, Portsmouth, Va. d: 10/25/78, Los Angeles, Cal. BR/TR, 6'2", 165 lbs. Deb: 8/8/16																								
1916 Was-A	0	1	.000	2	1	1	0	0	11	12	0	6	9	14.7	3.27	85	.316	.409	0	.000	-0	-1	-1	0	0.0
1917 Was-A	0	0	—	8	0	0	0	1	14	17	0	8	2	16.1	3.86	68	.315	.403	1	.500	0	-2	-2	0	0.0
1918 Was-A	0	0	—	3	0	0	0	0	7	5	0	1	5	7.7	1.29	212	.208	.240	0	.000	-0	1	1	0	0.0
1919 Was-A	0	3	.000	16	2	0	0	1	48^2	59	2	18	17	14.6	3.88	83	.309	.374	2	.111	-2	-4	-4	0	-0.4
Total 4	0	4	.000	29	3	1	0	2	80^2	93	2	33	33	14.3	3.57	84	.303	.374	3	.115	-2	-5	-5	1	-0.4
● HOWARD CRAGHEAD	Craghead, Howard Oliver "Judge" b: 5/25/08, Selma, Cal. d: 7/15/62, San Diego, Cal. BR/TR, 6'2", 200 lbs. Deb: 4/30/31																								
1931 Cle-A	0	0	—	4	0	0	0	0	5^2	8	0	2	2	15.9	6.35	73	.320	.370	0	—	0	-1	-1	0	0.0
1933 Cle-A	0	0	—	11	0	0	0	0	17^1	19	1	10	2	15.6	6.23	71	.292	.395	0	.000	-0	-4	-3	0	0.0
Total 2	0	0	—	15	0	0	0	0	23	27	1	12	4	15.7	6.26	72	.300	.388	0	.000	-0	-5	-5	0	0.0
● GEORGE CRAIG	Craig, George McCarthy "Lefty" b: 11/15/1887, Philadelphia, Pa. d: 4/23/11, Indianapolis, Ind. TL, Deb: 7/19/07																								
1907 Phi-A	0	0	—	2	0	0	0	0	1^2	2	0	3	0	37.8	10.80	24	.286	.583	0	.000	-0	-2	-2	-0	0.0
● PETE CRAIG	Craig, Peter Joel b: 7/10/40, LaSalle, Ontario, Canada BL/TR, 6'5", 220 lbs. Deb: 9/6/64																								
1964 Was-A	0	0	—	2	1	0	0	0	1^2	8	1	4	0	64.8	48.60	8	.667	.750	0	—	0	-8	-8	-0	0.0
1965 Was-A	0	3	.000	3	3	0	0	0	14^1	18	1	8	2	16.3	8.16	43	.321	.406	2	.667	1	-7	-7	1	-1.1

YEAR TM/L	W	L	PCT	G	GS	CG	SH	SV	IP	H	HR	BB	SO	RAT	ERA	ERA+	OAV	OOB	BH	AVG	PB	PR	/A	PD	TPI
1966 Was-A	0	0	—	1	0	0	0	0	2	2	0	1	1	13.5	4.50	77	.250	.333	0	—	0	-0	-0	-0	0.0
Total 3	0	3	.000	6	4	0	0	0	18	28	2	13	3	20.5	11.50	30	.368	.461	2	.667	1	-16	-16	0	-1.1

● ROGER CRAIG Craig, Roger Lee b: 2/17/30, Durham, N.C. BR/TR, 6'4", 191 lbs. Deb: 7/17/55 MC

YEAR TM/L	W	L	PCT	G	GS	CG	SH	SV	IP	H	HR	BB	SO	RAT	ERA	ERA+	OAV	OOB	BH	AVG	PB	PR	/A	PD	TPI
1955 *Bro-N	5	3	.625	21	10	3	0	2	90^2	81	8	43	48	12.4	2.78	146	.238	.325	2	.077	-2	13	13	-1	0.8
1956 *Bro-N	12	11	.522	35	32	8	2	1	199	169	25	87	109	11.8	3.71	107	.231	.316	1	.016	-5	1	6	-2	-0.2
1957 Bro-N	6	9	.400	32	13	1	0	0	111^1	102	18	47	69	12.2	4.61	90	.249	.329	4	.138	-1	-9	-5	1	-0.7
1958 LA-N	2	1	.667	9	2	1	0	0	32	30	3	12	16	11.8	4.50	91	.242	.309	0	.000	-1	-2	-1	-1	-0.3
1959 *LA-N	11	5	.688	29	17	7	**4**	0	152^2	122	13	45	76	9.9	2.06	205	.217	.276	3	.058	-4	32	**37**	-1	3.2
1960 LA-N	8	3	.727	21	15	6	1	0	115^2	99	8	43	69	11.3	3.27	121	.230	.305	2	.056	-2	6	9	-0	0.5
1961 LA-N	5	6	.455	40	14	2	0	2	112^2	130	22	52	63	14.9	6.15	71	.288	.367	4	.148	-0	-27	-23	-1	-2.2
1962 NY-N	10	24	.294	42	33	13	0	3	233^1	261	35	70	118	13.0	4.51	93	.288	.343	4	.053	-5	-15	-9	4	-1.3
1963 NY-N	5	22	.185	46	31	14	0	2	236	249	28	58	108	11.9	3.78	92	.267	.314	6	.087	-2	-13	-8	3	-0.8
1964 *StL-N	7	9	.438	39	19	3	0	5	166	180	16	35	84	11.9	3.25	117	.276	.317	10	.208	2	5	10	2	1.4
1965 Cin-N	1	4	.200	40	0	0	0	3	64^1	74	6	25	30	14.3	3.64	103	.289	.359	2	.182	-0	-1	1	-0	0.1
1966 Phi-N	2	1	.667	14	0	0	0	1	22^2	31	4	5	13	14.3	5.56	65	.326	.360	0	.000	-0	-5	-5	1	-0.6
Total 12	74	98	.430	368	186	58	7	19	1536^1	1528	186	522	803	12.2	3.83	104	.259	.323	38	.085	-22	-13	25	4	-0.1

● JERRY CRAM Cram, Gerald Allen b: 12/9/47, Los Angeles, Cal. BR/TR, 6', 180 lbs. Deb: 9/3/69

YEAR TM/L	W	L	PCT	G	GS	CG	SH	SV	IP	H	HR	BB	SO	RAT	ERA	ERA+	OAV	OOB	BH	AVG	PB	PR	/A	PD	TPI
1969 KC-A	0	1	.000	5	2	0	0	0	16^2	15	0	6	10	11.3	3.24	114	.231	.296	0	.000	-0	1	1	-0	0.0
1974 NY-N	0	1	.000	10	0	0	0	0	22^1	22	1	4	8	10.5	1.61	221	.275	.310	1	.333	0	5	5	0	0.2
1975 NY-N	0	1	.000	4	0	0	0	0	5	7	2	2	2	16.2	5.40	64	.333	.391	0	—	0	-1	-1	0	-0.2
1976 KC-A	0	0	—	4	0	0	0	0	4^1	8	0	1	2	18.7	6.23	56	.421	.450	0	—	0	-1	-1	0	0.0
Total 4	0	3	.000	23	2	0	0	0	48^1	52	3	13	22	12.1	2.98	120	.281	.328	1	.167	-0	3	3	0	0.0

● DOC CRAMER Cramer, Roger Maxwell "Flit" b: 7/22/05, Beach Haven, N.J. d: 9/9/90, Manahawkin, N.J. BL/TR, 6'2", 185 lbs. Deb: 9/18/29 C♦

YEAR TM/L	W	L	PCT	G	GS	CG	SH	SV	IP	H	HR	BB	SO	RAT	ERA	ERA+	OAV	OOB	BH	AVG	PB	PR	/A	PD	TPI
1938 Bos-A★	0	0	—	1	0	0	0	0	4	3	0	3	1	13.5	4.50	110	.214	.353	198	.301	0	0	0	0	0.0

● BILL CRAMER Cramer, William Wendell b: 5/21/1891, Bedford, Ind. d: 9/11/66, Fort Wayne, Ind. BR/TR, 6', 175 lbs. Deb: 6/25/12

YEAR TM/L	W	L	PCT	G	GS	CG	SH	SV	IP	H	HR	BB	SO	RAT	ERA	ERA+	OAV	OOB	BH	AVG	PB	PR	/A	PD	TPI
1912 Cin-N	0	0	—	1	0	0	0	0	2^1	6	0	0	2	23.1	0.00	—	.500	.500	0	.000	-0	1	1	-0	0.0

● DOC CRANDALL Crandall, James Otis b: 10/8/1887, Wadena, Ind. d: 8/17/51, Bell, Cal. BR/TR, 5'10.5", 180 lbs. Deb: 4/24/08 ♦

YEAR TM/L	W	L	PCT	G	GS	CG	SH	SV	IP	H	HR	BB	SO	RAT	ERA	ERA+	OAV	OOB	BH	AVG	PB	PR	/A	PD	TPI
1908 NY-N	12	12	.500	32	24	13	0	0	214^2	198	3	59	77	11.2	2.93	82	.248	.307	16	.222	5	-14	-12	-1	-1.1
1909 NY-N	6	4	.600	30	8	4	0	6	122	117	5	33	55	11.3	2.88	89	.252	.305	10	.244	3	-4	-4	2	0.1
1910 NY-N	17	4	.810	42	18	13	2	5	207^2	194	10	43	73	10.4	2.56	116	.246	.289	25	.342	10	11	9	-1	1.9
1911 *NY-N	15	5	.750	41	15	9	2	5	198^2	199	10	51	94	11.6	2.63	128	.256	.307	27	.239	5	17	16	2	2.3
1912 *NY-N	13	7	.650	37	10	7	0	2	162	181	7	35	60	12.1	3.61	94	.286	.326	25	.313	6	-4	-4	-0	0.2
1913 *NY-N	2	4	.333	24	1	1	0	5	55^1	61	2	13	28	12.2	3.09	101	.293	.338	7	.280	2	1	0	1	0.3
*NY-N	2	0	1.000	11	1	1	0	1	42^1	41	1	11	14	11.1	2.55	122	.248	.295	8	.364	3	3	3	1	0.5
Yr	4	4	.500	35	2	2	0	6	97^2	102	3	24	42	11.6	2.86	109	.273	.317	15	.319	5	**4**	**3**	1	0.8
1914 StL-F	13	9	.591	27	21	18	1	0	196	194	8	52	84	11.4	3.54	86	.256	.305	86	.309	7	-14	-11	-1	-0.4
1915 StL-F	21	15	.583	51	33	22	4	1	312^2	307	5	77	117	11.3	2.59	111	.263	.314	40	.284	12	5	10	1	2.6
1916 StL-A	0	0	—	2	0	0	0	0	1^1	7	0	1	0	60.8	27.00	10	.636	.692	1	.083	-0	-4	-4	-0	-0.1
1918 Bos-N	1	2	.333	5	3	3	0	0	34	39	1	4	4	11.6	2.38	113	.307	.333	8	.286	1	1	1	0	0.3
Total 10	102	62	.622	302	134	91	9	25	1546^2	1538	52	379	606	11.4	2.92	101	.261	.310	253	.285	54	-1	5	1	6.6

● ED CRANE Crane, Edward Nicholas "Cannon-Ball" b: 5/27/1862, Boston, Mass. d: 9/20/1896, Rochester, N.Y. BR/TR, 5'10.5", 204 lbs. Deb: 4/17/1884 ♦

YEAR TM/L	W	L	PCT	G	GS	CG	SH	SV	IP	H	HR	BB	SO	RAT	ERA	ERA+	OAV	OOB	BH	AVG	PB	PR	/A	PD	TPI
1884 Bos-U	0	2	.000	4	2	1	0	0	18	17	1	6	13	11.5	4.00	60	.233	.291	122	.285	0	-3	-3	1	-0.2
1886 Was-N	1	7	.125	10	8	7	1	0	70	91	5	53	39	18.5	7.20	46	.313	.419	50	.171	-1	-30	-30	0	-2.5
1888 *NY-N	5	6	.455	12	11	11	2	1	92^2	70	3	40	58	10.9	2.43	113	.193	.277	6	.162	1	4	3	1	0.5
1889 *NY-N	14	10	.583	29	25	23	0	0	230	221	10	136	130	14.4	3.68	107	.245	.350	21	.204	3	9	7	-4	0.4
1890 NY-P	16	19	.457	43	35	28	0	0	330^1	323	12	208	116	14.7	4.63	98	.245	.352	46	.315	8	-15	-3	-3	0.0
1891 Cin-a	14	14	.500	32	31	25	1	0	250	216	3	139	122	13.3	**2.45**	**168**	.225	.332	17	.155	-6	35	46	-2	3.5
Cin-N	4	8	.333	15	13	11	1	0	116^2	134	3	64	51	15.5	4.09	83	.277	.365	5	.109	-3	-10	-9	0	-1.0
1892 NY-N	16	24	.400	47	42	35	2	1	364^1	350	10	189	174	13.6	3.80	85	.243	.335	40	.245	4	-21	-24	-0	-1.8
1893 NY-N	2	4	.333	10	7	4	0	0	68^1	84	2	41	11	17.3	5.93	79	.294	.393	12	.462	4	-10	-10	-1	-0.3
Bro-N	0	2	.000	2	2	1	0	0	10	19	2	9	5	26.1	13.50	33	.388	.492	2	.400	0	-10	-10	-0	-1.1
Yr	2	6	.250	12	9	5	0	0	78^1	103	4	50	16	17.7	6.89	67	.302	.393	14	.452	5	-19	-20	-1	-1.4
Total 8	72	96	.429	204	176	146	7	2	1550^1	1525	51	885	719	14.3	3.99	95	.247	.347	335	.238	11	-49	-35	-9	-2.5

● CARLOS CRAWFORD Crawford, Carlos Lamonte b: 10/4/71, Charlotte, N.C. BR/TR, 6'1", 185 lbs. Deb: 6/7/96

YEAR TM/L	W	L	PCT	G	GS	CG	SH	SV	IP	H	HR	BB	SO	RAT	ERA	ERA+	OAV	OOB	BH	AVG	PB	PR	/A	PD	TPI
1996 Phi-N	0	1	.000	1	1	0	0	0	3^2	7	1	2	4	24.5	4.91	88	.389	.476	0	.000	-0	-0	-0	-0	-0.1

● LARRY CRAWFORD Crawford, Charles Lowrie b: 4/27/14, Swissvale, Pa. d: 12/20/94, Hanover, Pa. BL/TL, 6'1", 165 lbs. Deb: 7/21/37

YEAR TM/L	W	L	PCT	G	GS	CG	SH	SV	IP	H	HR	BB	SO	RAT	ERA	ERA+	OAV	OOB	BH	AVG	PB	PR	/A	PD	TPI
1937 Phi-N	0	0	—	6	0	0	0	0	6	12	2	1	2	19.5	15.00	29	.387	.406	0	—	0	-7	-7	-0	0.0

● JIM CRAWFORD Crawford, James Frederick "Catfish" b: 9/29/50, Chicago, Ill. BL/TL, 6'3", 200 lbs. Deb: 4/6/73

YEAR TM/L	W	L	PCT	G	GS	CG	SH	SV	IP	H	HR	BB	SO	RAT	ERA	ERA+	OAV	OOB	BH	AVG	PB	PR	/A	PD	TPI
1973 Hou-N	2	4	.333	48	0	0	0	6	70	69	7	33	56	13.4	4.50	81	.256	.341	3	.231	1	-7	-7	1	-0.5
1975 Hou-N	3	5	.375	44	2	0	0	4	86^2	92	0	37	37	13.6	3.63	93	.280	.356	5	.294	2	-0	-3	0	0.0
1976 Det-A	1	8	.111	32	5	1	0	2	109^1	115	4	43	68	13.0	4.53	82	.275	.343	0	—	0	-12	-10	5	-0.6
1977 Det-A	7	8	.467	37	7	0	0	1	126	156	13	50	91	14.8	4.79	90	.310	.373	0	—	0	-10	-7	1	-0.7
1978 Det-A	2	3	.400	20	0	0	0	0	39^1	45	3	19	24	15.1	4.35	89	.292	.377	0	—	0	-3	-2	-0	-0.4
Total 5	15	28	.349	181	14	1	0	13	431^1	477	27	182	276	13.9	4.40	86	.285	.357	8	.267	3	-32	-29	6	-2.2

● JOE CRAWFORD Crawford, Joseph Randal b: 5/2/70, Gainesville, Fla. BL/TL, 6'3", 225 lbs. Deb: 4/7/97

YEAR TM/L	W	L	PCT	G	GS	CG	SH	SV	IP	H	HR	BB	SO	RAT	ERA	ERA+	OAV	OOB	BH	AVG	PB	PR	/A	PD	TPI
1997 NY-N	4	3	.571	19	2	0	0	0	46^1	36	7	13	25	9.5	3.30	122	.216	.272	0	.000	-1	5	4	0	0.4

● STEVE CRAWFORD Crawford, Steven Ray b: 4/29/58, Pryor, Okla. BR/TR, 6'5", 225 lbs. Deb: 9/2/80

YEAR TM/L	W	L	PCT	G	GS	CG	SH	SV	IP	H	HR	BB	SO	RAT	ERA	ERA+	OAV	OOB	BH	AVG	PB	PR	/A	PD	TPI
1980 Bos-A	2	0	1.000	6	4	2	0	0	32^1	41	3	8	10	13.6	3.62	117	.306	.345	0	—	0	1	2	-0	-0.1
1981 Bos-A	0	5	.000	14	11	0	0	0	57^2	69	10	18	29	14.0	4.99	77	.301	.360	0	—	0	-9	-7	0	-0.6
1982 Bos-A	1	0	1.000	5	0	0	0	0	9	14	0	0	2	14.0	2.00	215	.341	.341	0	—	0	2	2	-0	0.2
1984 Bos-A	5	0	1.000	35	0	0	0	1	62	69	6	21	21	13.2	3.34	125	.286	.346	0	—	0	4	6	-0	0.1
1985 Bos-A	6	5	.545	44	1	0	0	12	91	103	5	28	58	13.0	3.76	114	.289	.340	0	—	0	4	5	1	0.5
1986 *Bos-A	0	2	.000	40	0	0	0	4	57^1	69	5	19	32	13.8	3.92	106	.308	.362	0	—	0	2	2	0	0.1
1987 Bos-A	5	4	.556	29	0	0	0	0	72^2	91	13	32	43	15.5	5.33	85	.314	.386	0	—	0	-7	-6	1	-0.7
1989 KC-A	3	1	.750	25	0	0	0	0	54	48	2	19	33	11.7	2.83	136	.242	.318	0	—	0	6	6	2	0.6
1990 KC-A	5	4	.556	46	0	0	0	1	80	79	7	23	54	11.8	4.16	92	.254	.312	0	—	0	-2	-3	1	-0.1
1991 KC-A	3	2	.600	33	0	0	0	1	46^2	60	3	18	38	15.2	5.98	69	.311	.373	0	—	0	-10	-10	-0	-1.0
Total 10	30	23	.566	277	16	2	0	19	562^2	643	54	186	320	13.5	4.17	99	.290	.348	0	—	0	-8	-3	3	-1.0

● DOUG CREEK Creek, Paul Douglas b: 3/1/69, Winchester, Va. BL/TL, 5'10", 205 lbs. Deb: 9/17/95

YEAR TM/L	W	L	PCT	G	GS	CG	SH	SV	IP	H	HR	BB	SO	RAT	ERA	ERA+	OAV	OOB	BH	AVG	PB	PR	/A	PD	TPI
1995 StL-N	0	0	—	6	0	0	0	0	6^2	2	0	3	10	6.8	0.00	—	.095	.208	0	—	0	3	3	-0	0.0
1996 SF-N	0	2	.000	63	0	0	0	0	48^1	45	11	32	38	14.7	6.52	63	.243	.361	0	.000	-0	-12	-13	-1	-0.6
1997 SF-N	1	2	.333	3	3	0	0	0	13^1	12	1	14	14	17.6	6.75	61	.240	.406	1	.333	0	-4	-4	0	-0.7
Total 3	1	4	.200	72	3	0	0	0	68^1	59	12	49	62	14.5	5.93	69	.230	.358	1	.250	0	-13	-14	-1	-1.3

● JACK CREEL Creel, Jack Dalton "Tex" b: 4/23/16, Kyle, Tex. BR/TR, 6', 165 lbs. Deb: 4/22/45

YEAR TM/L	W	L	PCT	G	GS	CG	SH	SV	IP	H	HR	BB	SO	RAT	ERA	ERA+	OAV	OOB	BH	AVG	PB	PR	/A	PD	TPI
1945 StL-N	5	4	.556	26	8	2	0	2	87	78	5	45	34	13.3	4.14	90	.245	.349	2	.077	-2	-3	-4	0	-0.5

● KEITH CREEL Creel, Steven Keith b: 2/4/59, Dallas, Tex. BR/TR, 6'2", 180 lbs. Deb: 5/25/82

YEAR TM/L	W	L	PCT	G	GS	CG	SH	SV	IP	H	HR	BB	SO	RAT	ERA	ERA+	OAV	OOB	BH	AVG	PB	PR	/A	PD	TPI
1982 KC-A	1	4	.200	9	6	0	0	0	41^2	43	8	25	13	14.7	5.40	76	.267	.366	0	—	0	-6	-6	0	-0.6
1983 KC-A	2	5	.286	25	10	1	0	0	89^1	116	17	35	31	15.4	6.35	64	.320	.382	0	—	0	-23	-23	-1	-1.6

YEAR	TM/L	W	L	PCT	G	GS	CG	SH	SV	IP	H	HR	BB	SO	RAT	ERA	ERA+	OAV	OOB	BH	AVG	PB	PR	/A	PD	TPI
1985	Cle-A	2	5	.286	15	8	0	0	0	62	73	7	23	31	14.2	4.79	86	.296	.360	0	—	0	-4	-5	-1	-0.5
1987	Tex-A	0	0	—	6	0	0	0	0	9^{2}	12	2	5	5	15.8	4.66	96	.293	.370	0	—	0	-0	-0	0	0.0
Total	4	5	14	.263	55	24	1	0	0	202^{2}	244	34	88	80	14.9	5.60	74	.300	.372	0	—	0	-33	-33	-2	-2.7
● BOB CREMINS Cremins, Robert Anthony "Lefty" or "Crooked Arm" b: 2/15/06, Pelham Manor, N.Y. BL/TL, 5'11", 178 lbs. Deb: 8/17/27																										
1927	Bos-A	0	0	—	4	0	0	0	0	5^{1}	5	0	3	0	13.5	5.06	83	.250	.348	0	—	0	-1	-0	0	0.0
● WALKER CRESS Cress, Walker James "Foots" b: 3/6/17, Ben Hur, Va. d: 4/21/96, Baton Rouge, La. BR/TR, 6'5", 205 lbs. Deb: 4/27/48																										
1948	Cin-N	0	1	.000	30	2	1	0	0	60	60	2	42	33	15.5	4.50	87	.271	.390	4	.500	2	-4	-4	-1	0.0
1949	Cin-N	0	0	—	3	0	0	0	0	2	2	0	3	0	22.5	0.00	—	.286	.500	0	—	0	1	1	-0	0.0
Total	2	0	1	.000	33	2	1	0	0	62	62	2	45	33	15.7	4.35	90	.272	.394	4	.500	2	-3	-3	-1	0.0
● TIM CREWS Crews, Stanley Timothy b: 4/3/61, Tampa, Fla. d: 3/23/93, Orlando, Fla. BR/TR, 6', 192 lbs. Deb: 7/27/87																										
1987	LA-N	1	1	.500	20	0	0	0	3	29	30	2	8	20	12.4	2.48	160	.268	.328	0	.000	-0	5	5	0	0.4
1988	LA-N	4	0	1.000	42	0	0	0	0	71^{2}	77	3	16	45	11.7	3.14	106	.278	.317	1	.200	0	2	2	-1	0.0
1989	LA-N	0	1	.000	44	0	0	0	1	61^{2}	69	7	23	56	13.7	3.21	106	.284	.351	0	—	0	2	1	-0	0.0
1990	LA-N	4	5	.444	66	2	0	0	5	107^{1}	98	9	24	76	10.3	2.77	132	.238	.282	0	.000	-1	12	11	-1	0.7
1991	LA-N	2	3	.400	60	0	0	0	6	76	75	7	19	53	11.1	3.43	105	.256	.301	0	.000	0	2	1	0	0.1
1992	LA-N	0	3	.000	49	2	0	0	0	78	95	6	20	43	13.5	5.19	66	.310	.357	2	.286	0	-15	-15	-1	-0.6
Total	6	11	13	.458	281	4	0	0	15	423^{2}	444	34	110	293	11.9	3.44	103	.270	.319	3	.136	-0	9	5	-3	0.6
● JERRY CRIDER Crider, Jerry Stephen b: 9/2/41, Sioux Falls, S.D. BR/TR, 6'2", 200 lbs. Deb: 5/21/69																										
1969	Min-A	1	0	1.000	21	1	0	0	1	28^{2}	31	3	15	16	15.1	4.71	78	.284	.381	4	.444	2	-3	-3	0	0.1
1970	Chi-A	4	7	.364	32	8	0	0	4	91	101	13	34	40	13.5	4.45	88	.288	.354	2	.083	-1	-7	-6	-2	-1.0
Total	2	5	7	.417	53	9	0	0	5	119^{2}	132	16	49	56	13.9	4.51	85	.287	.361	6	.182	1	-11	-9	-2	-0.9
● CHUCK CRIM Crim, Charles Robert b: 7/23/61, Van Nuys, Cal. BR/TR, 6', 185 lbs. Deb: 4/8/87																										
1987	Mil-A	6	8	.429	53	5	0	0	12	130	133	15	39	56	12.1	3.67	125	.266	.323	0	—	0	11	13	-0	1.4
1988	Mil-A	7	6	.538	**70**	0	0	0	9	105	95	11	28	58	10.7	2.91	136	.247	.302	0	—	0	12	12	0	1.6
1989	Mil-A	9	7	.563	**76**	0	0	0	7	117^{2}	114	7	36	59	11.6	2.83	136	.259	.318	0	—	0	14	13	-1	1.7
1990	Mil-A	3	5	.375	67	0	0	0	11	85^{2}	88	7	23	39	11.9	3.47	112	.261	.312	0	—	0	4	4	0	0.5
1991	Mil-A	8	5	.615	66	0	0	0	3	91^{1}	115	9	25	39	14.0	4.63	86	.305	.351	0	—	0	-5	-7	0	-0.8
1992	Cal-A	7	6	.538	57	0	0	0	1	87	100	11	29	30	14.0	5.17	77	.293	.359	0	—	0	-12	-12	0	-1.6
1993	Cal-A	2	2	.500	11	0	0	0	0	15^{1}	17	2	5	10	14.1	5.87	77	.298	.375	0	—	0	-3	-2	1	-0.5
1994	Chi-N	5	4	.556	49	1	0	0	2	64^{1}	69	9	24	43	13.2	4.48	93	.271	.336	0	.000	-0	-2	-2	0	-0.3
Total	8	47	43	.522	449	6	0	0	45	696^{1}	731	71	209	334	12.4	3.83	107	.272	.329	0	.000	-0	20	19	-0	2.0
● JACK CRIMIAN Crimian, John Melvin b: 2/17/26, Philadelphia, Pa. BR/TR, 5'10", 180 lbs. Deb: 7/3/51																										
1951	StL-N	1	0	1.000	11	0	0	0	1	17	24	3	8	5	16.9	9.00	44	.338	.405	1	.333	0	-10	-10	-0	-0.6
1952	StL-N	0	0	—	5	0	0	0	0	8^{1}	15	4	4	4	20.5	9.72	38	.417	.475	0	.000	0	-6	-6	-0	0.0
1956	KC-A	4	8	.333	54	7	0	0	3	129	129	19	49	59	12.8	5.51	79	.265	.339	5	.227	1	-19	-17	-0	-1.4
1957	Det-A	0	1	.000	4	0	0	0	0	5^{2}	9	1	4	1	20.6	12.71	30	.375	.464	0	—	0	-6	-6	-0	-0.8
Total	4	5	9	.357	74	7	0	0	4	160	177	27	65	69	13.9	6.36	67	.287	.360	6	.231	1	-40	-38	-1	-2.8
● DODE CRISS Criss, Dode b: 3/12/1885, Sherman, Miss. d: 9/8/55, Sherman, Miss. BL/TR, 6'2", 200 lbs. Deb: 4/20/08 ♦																										
1908	StL-A	0	1	.000	9	1	0	0	0	18	15	1	13	9	15.5	6.50	37	.250	.408	28	.341	1	-8	-8	-1	-0.4
1909	StL-A	1	5	.167	11	6	3	0	0	55^{1}	53	0	32	43	14.2	3.42	71	.262	.369	14	.292	5	-6	-6	-1	-0.1
1910	StL-A	2	1	.667	6	0	0	0	0	19^{1}	12	0	9	9	11.6	1.40	177	.176	.309	21	.231	1	2	2	-0	0.5
1911	StL-A	0	2	.000	4	2	0	0	0	18^{1}	24	0	10	9	17.7	8.35	40	.333	.429	21	.253	0	-10	-10	0	-0.8
Total	4	3	9	.250	30	9	3	0	0	111	104	1	64	70	14.5	4.38	59	.259	.375	84	.276	8	-22	-22	-2	-0.8
● BILL CRISTALL Cristall, William Arthur "Lefty" b: 9/12/1878, Odessa, Russia d: 1/28/39, Buffalo, N.Y. BL/TL, 5'7", 145 lbs. Deb: 9/3/01																										
1901	Cle-A	1	5	.167	6	6	5	1	0	48^{1}	54	1	30	12	16.4	4.84	73	.280	.388	7	.350	2	-6	-7	2	-0.3
● LEO CRISTANTE Cristante, Dante Leo b: 12/10/26, Detroit, Mich. d: 8/24/77, Dearborn, Mich. BR/TR, 6'1", 195 lbs. Deb: 4/21/51																										
1951	Phi-N	1	1	.500	10	1	0	0	0	22	28	3	9	6	15.5	4.91	78	.318	.388	1	.167	-0	-2	-3	0	-0.2
1955	Det-A	0	1	.000	20	1	0	0	0	36^{2}	37	1	14	9	12.5	3.19	120	.261	.327	0	.000	-1	3	3	-1	-0.2
Total	2	1	2	.333	30	2	0	0	0	58^{2}	65	4	23	15	13.7	3.84	100	.283	.350	1	.077	-1	1	0	-1	-0.4
● MORRIE CRITCHLEY Critchley, Morris Arthur b: 3/26/1850, New London, Conn. d: 3/6/10, Pittsburgh, Pa. 6'1", 190 lbs. Deb: 5/8/1882																										
1882	Pit-a	1	0	1.000	1	1	1	1	0	9	7	0	1	3	8.0	0.00	—	.200	.222	0	.000	-1	3	3	0	0.2
	StL-a	0	4	.000	4	4	4	0	0	34	43	3	7	2	13.2	4.24	66	.289	.321	3	.214	-0	-6	-5	-1	-0.6
	Yr	1	4	.200	5	5	5	1	0	43	50	3	8	5	12.1	3.35	83	.272	.302	3	.158	-1	-3	-3	-1	-0.4
● CLAUDE CROCKER Crocker, Claude Arthur b: 7/20/24, Caroleen, N.C. BR/TR, 6'2", 185 lbs. Deb: 8/1/44																										
1944	Bro-N	0	0	—	2	0	0	0	0	3^{1}	6	0	5	1	29.7	10.80	33	.400	.550	1	1.000	0	-3	-3	0	0.1
1945	Bro-N	0	0	—	1	0	0	0	1	2	2	0	1	1	13.5	0.00	—	.286	.375	0	—	0	1	1	-0	0.1
Total	2	0	0	—	3	0	0	0	1	5^{1}	8	0	6	2	23.6	6.75	54	.364	.500	1	1.000	0	-2	-2	0	0.2
● RAY CRONE Crone, Raymond Hayes b: 8/7/31, Memphis, Tenn. BR/TR, 6'2", 185 lbs. Deb: 4/13/54																										
1954	Mil-N	1	0	1.000	19	2	1	0	1	49	44	6	19	33	11.8	2.02	184	.247	.323	2	.200	-0	11	9	-0	0.2
1955	Mil-N	10	9	.526	33	15	6	1	0	140^{1}	117	11	42	76	10.2	3.46	108	.227	.285	7	.159	-1	9	5	0	0.4
1956	Mil-N	11	10	.524	35	21	6	0	2	169^{2}	173	19	44	73	11.6	3.87	89	.263	.311	6	.122	1	-2	-8	-1	-0.9
1957	Mil-N	3	1	.750	11	5	2	0	0	42^{1}	54	8	15	15	14.7	4.46	78	.312	.367	2	.182	1	-3	-5	1	-0.2
	NY-N	4	8	.333	25	17	2	0	1	120^{2}	131	11	40	56	13.0	4.33	91	.272	.331	1	.025	-4	-6	-5	2	-0.6
	Yr	7	9	.438	36	22	4	0	1	163	185	19	55	71	13.4	4.36	88	.282	.340	3	.059	-3	-9	-10	3	-0.8
1958	SF-N	1	2	.333	14	1	0	0	0	24	35	5	13	7	18.0	6.75	56	.354	.429	0	.000	-0	-7	-8	-0	-0.9
Total	5	30	30	.500	137	61	17	1	4	546	554	60	173	260	12.1	3.87	95	.263	.321	18	.115	-3	2	-12	2	-2.0
● JACK CRONIN Cronin, John J. b: 5/26/1874, Staten Island, N.Y d: 7/12/29, Middletown, N.Y. BR/TR, 6' ", 200 lbs. Deb: 8/24/1895																										
1895	Bro-N	0	0	—	2	0	0	0	2	5	10	0	3	1	23.4	10.80	41	.417	.481	1	.500	1	-3	-4	-0	-0.2
1898	Pit-N	2	2	.500	4	4	2	1	0	28	35	0	8	9	13.8	3.54	101	.304	.350	1	.100	-0	0	0	0	0.0
1899	Cin-N	2	2	.500	5	5	5	0	0	41	56	2	16	9	16.9	5.49	71	.324	.397	2	.118	-1	-7	-7	-1	-0.7
1901	Det-A	13	16	.448	30	28	21	1	0	219^{2}	261	6	42	62	12.9	3.89	99	.292	.331	21	.247	2	-6	-1	-3	-0.2
1902	Det-A	0	0	—	4	0	0	0	0	17^{1}	26	1	8	5	19.2	9.35	39	.347	.430	0	.000	-1	-11	-11	0	-0.1
	Bal-A	3	5	.375	10	8	8	0	0	75^{2}	66	1	24	20	10.7	2.62	144	.236	.296	4	.148	-1	8	10	2	1.1
	Yr	3	5	.375	14	8	8	0	0	93	92	2	32	25	12.0	3.87	97	.257	.318	4	.118	-2	-3	-1	3	1.0
	NY-N	5	6	.455	13	12	11	0	0	114	105	3	18	52	9.7	2.45	115	.245	.275	11	.169	-1	4	5	0	0.3
1903	NY-N	6	4	.600	20	11	8	0	1	115^{2}	130	5	37	50	13.5	3.81	88	.284	.345	9	.196	0	-7	-6	0	-0.5
1904	Bro-N	12	23	.343	40	34	33	4	0	307	284	10	79	110	11.0	2.70	102	.245	.300	17	.157	-3	1	2	0	-0.1
Total	7	43	58	.426	128	102	88	6	3	923^{1}	973	28	235	318	12.1	3.40	96	.270	.321	66	.180	-5	-20	-13	-1	-0.4
● GEORGE CROSBY Crosby, George Washington b: 1860, Iowa d: 1/9/13, San Francisco, Cal. Deb: 5/22/1884																										
1884	Chi-N	1	2	.333	3	3	3	0	0	28	27	3	12	11	12.5	3.54	89	.227	.298	4	.308	1	-2	-1	1	0.0
● KEN CROSBY Crosby, Kenneth Stewart b: 12/15/47, New Denver, B.C., Canada BR/TR, 6'2", 179 lbs. Deb: 8/5/75																										
1975	Chi-N	1	0	1.000	9	0	0	0	0	8^{1}	10	0	7	6	18.4	3.24	119	.294	.415	0	—	0	0	1	0	0.1
1976	Chi-N	0	0	—	7	1	0	0	0	12	20	3	8	5	21.0	12.00	32	.377	.459	1	.500	0	-11	-11	0	0.0
Total	2	1	0	1.000	16	1	0	0	0	20^{1}	30	3	15	11	19.9	8.41	46	.345	.441	1	.500	1	-11	-10	0	0.1
● LEM CROSS Cross, George Lewis b: 1/9/1872, Sanbornton, N.H. d: 10/9/30, Manchester, N.H. TR, 5'9", 155 lbs. Deb: 8/6/1893																										
1893	Cin-N	0	2	.000	3	3	2	0	0	21	24	3	9	7	14.1	5.57	86	.279	.347	2	.333	1	-2	-2	0	0.0

YEAR	TM/L	W	L	PCT	G	GS	CG	SH	SV	IP	H	HR	BB	SO	RAT	ERA	ERA+	OAV	OOB	BH	AVG	PB	PR	/A	PD	TPI
1894	Cin-N	3	4	.429	8	7	3	0	0	53	94	8	21	11	20.4	8.49	65	.381	.440	6	.231	-1	-19	-17	-1	-1.5
Total	2	3	6	.333	11	10	5	0	0	74	118	11	30	18	18.6	7.66	70	.354	.416	8	.250	-0	-21	-19	-0	-1.5
● **DOUG CROTHERS**	Crothers, Douglas b: 11/16/1859, Natchez, Miss. d: 3/29/07, St.Louis, Mo. BR/TR, Deb: 8/3/1884																									
1884	KC-U	1	2	.333	3	3	3	0	0	25	26	0	6	11	11.5	1.80	124	.250	.291	2	.133	-2	2	1	-1	-0.1
1885	NY-a	7	11	.389	18	18	18	1	0	154	192	4	49	40	14.2	5.08	58	.293	.344	8	.157	0	-31	-36	0	-3.1
Total	2	8	13	.381	21	21	21	1	0	179	218	4	55	51	13.8	4.63	62	.287	.337	10	.152	-1	-30	-35	-0	-3.2
● **BILL CROUCH**	Crouch, William Henry "Skip" b: 12/3/1886, Marshallton, Del. d: 12/22/45, Highland Park, Mich. BL/TL, 6'1", 210 lbs. Deb: 7/12/10 F																									
1910	StL-A	0	0	—	1	1	1	0	0	8	6	0	7	2	14.6	3.38	73	.231	.394	0	.000	-0	-1	-1	-0	-0.1
● **BILL CROUCH**	Crouch, Wilmer Elmer b: 8/20/10, Wilmington, Del. d: 12/26/80, Howell, Mich. BB/TR, 6'1", 180 lbs. Deb: 5/9/39 F																									
1939	Bro-N	4	0	1.000	6	3	3	0	0	38^1	37	3	14	10	12.0	2.58	156	.255	.321	2	.133	-1	6	6	-1	0.5
1941	Phi-N	2	3	.400	20	5	1	0	1	59	65	4	17	26	12.5	4.42	84	.286	.336	1	.091	-0	-5	-5	2	-0.3
	StL-N	1	2	.333	18	4	0	0	6	45	45	2	14	15	11.8	3.00	125	.271	.328	0	.000	-1	3	4	-1	0.1
	Yr	3	5	.375	38	9	1	0	7	104	110	6	31	41	12.2	3.81	98	.280	.333	1	.042	-2	-2	-1	1	-0.2
1945	StL-N	1	0	1.000	6	0	0	0	0	13^1	12	1	7	4	13.5	3.38	111	.255	.364	0	.000	-0	1	1	0	0.0
Total	3	8	5	.615	50	12	4	0	7	155^2	159	10	52	55	12.3	3.47	110	.272	.332	3	.073	-3	4	6	0	0.3
● **ZACH CROUCH**	Crouch, Zachary Quinn b: 10/26/65, Folsom, Cal. BL/TL, 6'3", 180 lbs. Deb: 6/4/88																									
1988	Bos-A	0	0	—	3	0	0	0	0	1^1	4	0	2	0	40.5	6.75	61	.571	.667	0	—	0	-0	-0	0	-0.2
● **RICH CROUSHORE**	Croushore, Richard Steven b: 8/7/70, Lakehurst, N.J. BR/TR, 6'4", 210 lbs. Deb: 5/18/98																									
1998	StL-N	0	3	.000	41	0	0	0	8	54^1	44	6	29	47	12.8	4.97	84	.213	.321	0	—	0	-4	-5	1	-0.3
● **DEAN CROW**	Crow, Paul Dean b: 8/21/72, Garland, Tex. BL/TR, 6'4", 215 lbs. Deb: 5/29/98																									
1998	Det-A	2	2	.500	32	0	0	0	0	45^2	55	6	16	18	14.4	3.94	119	.313	.376	0	—	0	4	4	-0	0.3
● **ALVIN CROWDER**	Crowder, Alvin Floyd "General" b: 1/11/1899, Winston-Salem, N.C d: 4/3/72, Winston-Salem, N.C. BL/TR, 5'10", 170 lbs. Deb: 7/24/26																									
1926	Was-A	7	4	.636	19	12	6	0	1	100	97	3	60	26	14.3	3.96	98	.261	.367	9	.237	1	1	-1	1	0.1
1927	Was-A	4	7	.364	15	11	4	2	0	67^1	58	3	42	22	13.6	4.54	89	.232	.347	3	.136	-1	-3	-4	-1	-0.7
	StL-A	3	5	.375	21	8	2	1	3	73^2	71	3	42	30	13.9	5.01	87	.260	.361	6	.261	0	-7	-5	-1	-0.6
	Yr	7	12	.368	36	19	6	3	3	141	129	6	84	52	13.7	4.79	88	.246	.351	9	.200	-1	-10	-9	-2	-1.3
1928	StL-A	21	5	**.808**	41	31	19	1	2	244	238	11	91	99	12.2	3.69	114	.258	.325	15	.188	-2	10	14	-5	0.7
1929	StL-A	17	15	.531	40	34	19	**4**	4	266^2	272	22	93	79	12.3	3.92	113	.271	.332	18	.188	-3	10	15	-2	1.1
1930	StL-A	3	7	.300	13	10	5	1	1	77^1	85	11	27	42	13.2	4.66	105	.283	.345	4	.160	-2	-0	2	1	0.1
	Was-A	15	9	.625	27	25	20	0	1	202^1	191	6	69	65	11.6	3.60	128	.249	.312	13	.171	-2	24	22	-4	1.7
	Yr	18	16	.529	40	35	25	1	2	279^2	276	17	96	107	12.0	3.89	120	.259	.320	17	.168	-4	23	24	-3	1.8
1931	Was-A	18	11	.621	44	26	13	1	2	234^1	255	13	72	85	12.6	3.88	111	.275	.328	19	.216	-1	13	11	-3	0.7
1932	Was-A	**26**	13	.667	50	39	21	3	1	**327**	319	17	77	103	10.9	3.33	130	.252	.295	27	.221	2	42	36	-2	3.5
1933	*Was-A★	**24**	15	.615	**52**	35	17	0	4	299^1	311	14	81	110	11.9	3.97	105	.267	.316	19	.186	1	10	7	-3	0.5
1934	Was-A	4	10	.286	29	13	4	0	3	100^2	142	9	38	39	16.1	6.79	64	.326	.380	7	.219	1	-26	-28	-1	-3.2
	*Det-A	5	1	.833	9	9	3	1	0	66^2	81	3	20	30	13.6	4.18	105	.295	.342	4	.133	-2	2	2	-1	-0.2
	Yr	9	11	.450	38	22	7	1	3	167^1	223	12	58	69	15.1	5.75	76	.314	.365	11	.177	-1	-23	-26	-2	-3.4
1935	*Det-A	16	10	.615	33	32	16	2	0	241	269	16	67	59	12.7	4.26	98	.285	.335	17	.183	-2	5	-2	-3	-0.7
1936	Det-A	4	3	.571	9	7	1	0	0	44	64	5	21	10	17.4	8.39	59	.342	.409	3	.150	-1	-16	-17	-0	-2.0
Total	11	167	115	.592	402	292	150	16	22	2344^1	2453	136	800	799	12.5	4.12	105	.270	.330	164	.194	-12	64	52	-24	1.0
● **JIM CROWELL**	Crowell, James Everette b: 5/14/74, Minneapolis, Minn. BL/TL, 6'4", 220 lbs. Deb: 9/12/97																									
1997	Cin-N	0	1	.000	2	1	0	0	0	6^1	12	2	5	3	24.2	9.95	43	.414	.500	0	.000	-0	-4	-4	0	-0.5
● **CAP CROWELL**	Crowell, Minot Joy b: 9/5/1892, Roxbury, Mass. d: 9/30/62, Central Falls, R.I. BR/TR, 6'1", 178 lbs. Deb: 6/23/15																									
1915	Phi-A	2	6	.250	10	8	4	0	0	54^1	56	1	47	15	17.9	5.47	54	.292	.443	5	.227	-0	-15	-15	-0	-2.0
1916	Phi-A	0	5	.000	9	6	1	0	0	39^2	43	0	34	15	17.9	4.99	57	.289	.427	0	.000	-2	-10	-9	-1	-1.3
Total	2	2	11	.154	19	14	5	0	0	94	99	1	81	30	17.9	5.27	55	.290	.436	5	.147	-2	-25	-25	-1	-3.3
● **BILLY CROWELL**	Crowell, William Theodore b: 11/6/1865, Cincinnati, Ohio d: 7/24/35, Ft.Worth, Tex. BR/TR, 5'8.5", 160 lbs. Deb: 4/20/1887																									
1887	Cle-a	14	31	.311	45	45	45	1	0	389^1	541	9	138	72	16.2	4.88	89	.327	.386	22	.141	-13	-25	-23	-3	-3.1
1888	Cle-a	5	13	.278	18	18	16	0	0	150^2	212	8	61	61	16.8	5.79	53	.320	.385	5	.086	-5	-46	-45	-1	-4.4
	Lou-a	0	1	.000	1	1	1	0	0	9	12	1	6	5	19.0	6.00	51	.308	.413	0	.000	-0	-3	-3	0	-0.2
	Yr	5	14	.263	19	19	17	0	0	159^2	224	9	67	66	16.5	5.81	53	.315	.375	5	.082	-5	-49	-48	-0	-4.6
Total	2	19	45	.297	64	64	62	1	0	549	765	18	205	138	16.4	5.15	77	.325	.386	27	.124	-18	-74	-71	-4	-7.7
● **WOODY CROWSON**	Crowson, Thomas Woodrow b: 9/9/18, Fuquay Sprgs., N.C d: 8/14/47, Mayodan, N.C. BR/TR, 6'2", 185 lbs. Deb: 4/17/45																									
1945	Phi-A	0	0	—	1	0	0	0	0	3	2	0	3	2	15.0	6.00	57	.200	.385	0	.000	-0	-1	-1	0	0.0
● **CAL CRUM**	Crum, Calvin N. b: 7/27/1890, Cooks Mills, Ill. d: 12/7/45, Tulsa, Okla. BR/TR, 6'1", 175 lbs. Deb: 4/17/17																									
1917	Bos-N	0	0	—	1	0	0	0	0	1	1	0	1	0	18.0	0.00	—	.250	.400	0	—	0	0	0	0	0.0
1918	Bos-N	0	1	.000	1	1	0	0	0	2^1	6	0	3	0	38.6	15.43	17	.600	.714	0	.000	-0	-3	-3	0	-0.9
Total	2	0	1	.000	2	1	0	0	0	3^1	7	0	4	0	32.4	10.80	24	.500	.632	0	.000	-0	-3	-3	1	-0.9
● **ROY CRUMPLER**	Crumpler, Roy Maxton b: 7/8/1896, Clinton, N.C. d: 10/6/69, Fayetteville, N.C. BL/TL, 6'1", 195 lbs. Deb: 9/16/20																									
1920	Det-A	1	0	1.000	2	2	1	0	0	13	17	2	11	2	20.1	5.54	67	.315	.439	3	.333	1	-3	-3	-0	-0.1
1925	Phi-N	0	0	—	3	1	0	0	0	4^2	8	0	2	1	19.3	7.71	62	.381	.435	0	.000	-0	-2	-2	0	0.0
Total	2	1	0	1.000	5	3	1	0	0	17^2	25	2	13	3	19.9	6.11	65	.333	.438	3	.273	1	-4	-4	-0	-0.1
● **DICK CRUTCHER**	Crutcher, Richard Louis b: 11/25/1889, Frankfort, Ky. d: 6/19/52, Frankfort, Ky. BR/TR, 5'9", 148 lbs. Deb: 4/14/14																									
1914	Bos-N	5	7	.417	33	15	5	1	0	158^2	169	4	66	48	13.7	3.46	80	.293	.371	8	.148	-1	-12	-12	1	-0.9
1915	Bos-N	2	2	.500	14	4	1	0	2	43^2	50	1	16	17	14.0	4.33	60	.309	.378	3	.231	1	-8	-8	0	-0.7
Total	2	7	9	.438	47	19	6	1	2	202^1	219	5	82	65	13.7	3.65	75	.296	.373	11	.164	-0	-19	-21	1	-1.6
● **NELSON CRUZ**	Cruz, Nelson b: 9/13/72, Puerto Plaza, D.R. BR/TR, 6'1", 160 lbs. Deb: 8/1/97																									
1997	Chi-A	0	2	.000	19	0	0	0	0	26^1	29	6	9	23	13.0	6.49	67	.274	.330	0	—	0	-6	-6	-0	-0.4
● **TODD CRUZ**	Cruz, Todd Ruben b: 11/23/55, Highland Park, Mich BR/TR, 6', 175 lbs. Deb: 9/4/78 ♦																									
1984	Bal-A	0	0	—	1	0	0	0	0	1	0	0	0	0	0.0	0.00	—	.000	.000	31	.218	0	0	0	0	0.0
● **VICTOR CRUZ**	Cruz, Victor Manuel (b: Victor Manuel De La Cruz (Gil)) b: 12/24/57, Rancho Viejo La Vega, D.R. BR/TR, 5'9", 200 lbs. Deb: 6/24/78																									
1978	Tor-A	7	3	.700	32	0	0	0	9	47^1	28	0	35	51	12.2	1.71	229	.179	.333	0	—	0	11	12	-0	2.8
1979	Cle-A	3	9	.250	61	0	0	0	10	78^2	70	10	44	63	13.2	4.23	100	.244	.346	0	—	0	-0	0	-2	-0.2
1980	Cle-A	6	7	.462	55	0	0	0	12	86	71	10	27	88	10.6	3.45	118	.229	.297	0	—	0	6	6	-1	0.8
1981	Pit-N	1	1	.500	22	0	0	0	1	34	33	6	15	28	13.0	2.65	136	.264	.348	0	.000	-0	3	4	0	0.2
1983	Tex-A	1	3	.250	17	0	0	0	5	25	16	2	10	18	9.7	1.44	278	.184	.276	0	—	0	7	7	-0	1.4
Total	5	18	23	.439	187	0	0	0	37	271	218	28	131	248	11.8	3.09	131	.226	.323	0	.000	-0	27	28	-4	5.0
● **COOKIE CUCCURULLO**	Cuccurullo, Arthur Joseph b: 2/8/18, Asbury Park, N.J. d: 1/23/83, W.Orange, N.J. BL/TL, 5'10", 168 lbs. Deb: 10/3/43																									
1943	Pit-N	0	1	.000	1	1	0	0	0	7	10	0	3	3	16.7	6.43	54	.357	.419	0	—	1	-2	-2	0	-0.2
1944	Pit-N	2	1	.667	32	4	0	0	4	106^1	110	5	44	31	13.3	4.06	91	.270	.346	14	.368	5	-5	-4	1	0.4
1945	Pit-N	1	3	.250	29	4	0	0	1	56^2	68	2	34	17	16.4	5.24	75	.305	.399	3	.214	-0	-9	-8	0	-0.6
Total	3	3	5	.375	62	9	0	0	5	170	188	7	81	51	14.5	4.55	83	.286	.367	17	.327	5	-17	-15	1	-0.4
● **JIM CUDWORTH**	Cudworth, James Alaric "Cuddy" b: 8/22/1858, Fairhaven, Mass. d: 12/21/43, Middleboro, Mass. BR/TR, 6', 165 lbs. Deb: 7/27/1884 ♦																									
1884	KC-U	0	0	—	2	1	1	0	0	17	19	1	3	6	11.6	4.24	53	.264	.293	17	.147	-1	-3	-4	-1	-0.1

YEAR	TM/L	W	L	PCT	G	GS	CG	SH	SV	IP	H	HR	BB	SO	RAT	ERA	ERA+	OAV	OOB	BH	AVG	PB	PR	/A	PD	TPI
● **CHARLIE CUELLAR** Cuellar, Jesus Patracis b: 8/23/17, Ybor City, Fla. d: 10/11/94, Tampa, Fla. BR/TR, 5'11", 183 lbs. Deb: 7/2/50																										
1950	Chi-A	0	0	—	2	0	0	0	0	1^1	6	0	3	1	60.8	33.75	13	.600	.692	0	—	0	-4	-4	0	0.0
● **MIKE CUELLAR** Cuellar, Miguel Angel (Santana) b: 5/8/37, Santa Clara, Cuba BL/TL, 5'11", 175 lbs. Deb: 4/18/59																										
1959	Cin-N	0	0	—	2	0	0	0	0	4	7	1	4	5	24.8	15.75	26	.368	.478	0	.000	-0	-5	-5	-0	0.0
1964	StL-N	5	5	.500	32	7	1	0	4	72	80	8	33	56	14.3	4.50	85	.288	.365	0	.000	-2	-8	-6	1	-0.9
1965	Hou-N	1	4	.200	25	4	0	0	2	56	55	3	21	46	12.4	3.54	95	.262	.332	0	.000	-1	0	-1	0	-0.2
1966	Hou-N	12	10	.545	38	28	11	1	2	227^1	193	10	52	175	9.7	2.22	154	.229	.274	8	.113	-1	35	30	0	2.9
1967	Hou-N★	16	11	.593	36	32	16	3	1	246^1	233	16	63	203	10.9	3.03	109	.248	.296	13	.140	1	9	8	-0	0.9
1968	Hou-N	8	11	.421	28	24	11	2	1	170^2	152	8	45	133	10.4	2.74	108	.237	.289	11	.193	2	5	4	-0	0.7
1969	*Bal-A	23	11	.676	39	39	18	5	0	290^2	213	18	79	182	9.1	2.38	149	.204	**.261**	12	.117	-3	**40**	**38**	-0	4.1
1970	*Bal-A☆	**24**	8	**.750**	40	40	**21**	4	0	297^2	273	34	69	190	10.4	3.48	105	.242	.286	10	.089	-4	8	6	-3	-0.2
1971	*Bal-A★	20	9	.690	38	38	21	4	0	292^1	250	30	78	124	10.1	3.08	109	.234	.287	11	.103	-4	12	9	1	0.5
1972	Bal-A	18	12	.600	35	35	17	4	0	248^1	197	21	71	132	9.7	2.57	119	.220	.277	11	.126	-1	13	14	0	1.6
1973	*Bal-A	18	13	.581	38	38	17	2	0	267	265	29	84	140	11.8	3.27	114	.258	.314	0	—	0	16	14	0	1.6
1974	*Bal-A☆	22	10	**.688**	38	38	20	5	0	269^1	253	17	86	106	11.4	3.11	111	.252	.312	0	—	0	15	10	-3	0.9
1975	Bal-A	14	12	.538	36	36	17	5	0	256	229	17	84	105	11.0	3.66	96	.249	.313	0	—	0	3	-4	2	-0.1
1976	Bal-A	4	13	.235	26	19	2	1	1	107	129	8	50	32	15.2	4.96	66	.307	.383	0	—	0	-17	-20	-0	-2.7
1977	Cal-A	0	1	.000	2	1	0	0	0	3^1	9	2	3	3	32.4	18.90	21	.500	.571	0	—	0	-5	-6	-0	-1.0
Total	15	185	130	.587	453	379	172	36	11	2808	2538	222	822	1632	10.8	3.14	109	.243	.299	76	.115	-13	122	92	-2	8.1
● **BOBBY CUELLAR** Cuellar, Robert b: 8/20/52, Alice, Tex. BR/TR, 5'11", 188 lbs. Deb: 9/9/77																										
1977	Tex-A	0	0	—	4	0	0	0	0	6^2	4	1	2	3	8.1	1.35	302	.182	.250	0	—	0	2	2	-0	-0.1
● **BERT CUETO** Cueto, Dagoberto (Concepcion) b: 8/14/37, San Luis, Cuba BR/TR, 6'4", 170 lbs. Deb: 6/18/61																										
1961	Min-A	1	3	.250	7	5	0	0	0	21^1	27	7	10	5	16.0	7.17	59	.300	.376	0	.000	-0	-7	-7	0	-1.1
● **JACK CULLEN** Cullen, John Patrick b: 10/6/39, Newark, N.J. BR/TR, 5'11", 170 lbs. Deb: 9/9/62																										
1962	NY-A	0	0	—	2	0	0	0	1	3	2	0	2	2	12.0	0.00	—	.182	.308	0	—	0	1	1	-0	0.1
1965	NY-A	3	4	.429	12	9	2	1	0	59	59	2	21	25	12.2	3.05	112	.262	.325	3	.150	-0	3	2	1	0.3
1966	NY-A	1	0	1.000	5	0	0	0	0	11^1	11	0	5	7	12.7	3.97	84	.256	.333	0	.000	-0	-1	-1	-0	-0.1
Total	3	4	4	.500	19	9	2	1	1	73^1	72	2	28	34	12.3	3.07	111	.258	.326	3	.130	-1	3	3	0	0.3
● **NICK CULLOP** Cullop, Henry Nicholas "Tomato Face" (b: Heinrich Nicholas Kolop) b: 10/16/1900, St.Louis, Mo. d: 12/8/78, Westerville, Ohio BR/TR, 6', 200 lbs. Deb: 4/14/26 ♦																										
1927	Cle-A	0	0	—	1	0	0	0	0	1	3	0	0	0	27.0	9.00	47	.600	.600	16	.235	0	-1	-1	-0	0.0
● **NICK CULLOP** Cullop, Norman Andrew b: 9/17/1887, Chilhowie, Va. d: 4/15/61, Tazewell, Va. BL/TL, 5'11.5", 172 lbs. Deb: 5/20/13																										
1913	Cle-A	3	6	.333	23	8	4	0	0	97^2	105	3	35	30	13.2	4.42	69	.291	.358	4	.129	-1	-16	-15	1	-1.4
1914	Cle-A	0	1	.000	1	0	0	0	0	3^1	4	0	1	3	13.5	2.70	107	.364	.417	0	.000	-0	0	0	-0	0.0
	KC-F	14	19	.424	44	36	22	4	1	295^2	256	6	87	149	10.8	2.34	119	.235	.299	14	.141	-5	18	14	1	1.1
1915	KC-F	22	11	.667	44	36	22	3	2	302^1	278	8	67	111	10.5	2.44	108	.249	.297	18	.188	-1	10	6	6	1.2
1916	NY-A	13	6	.684	28	22	9	0	1	167	151	4	32	77	10.0	2.05	141	.243	.284	6	.109	-3	14	16	-5	1.0
1917	NY-A	5	9	.357	30	18	5	2	1	146^1	161	2	31	27	11.9	3.32	81	.307	.348	7	.159	-1	-11	-10	-0	-1.1
1921	StL-A	0	2	.000	4	1	0	0	0	11^2	18	1	6	3	18.5	8.49	53	.340	.407	0	.000	-1	-5	-5	0	-0.7
Total	6	57	54	.514	174	121	62	9	5	1024	973	24	259	400	11.1	2.73	102	.258	.310	49	.149	-12	10	6	3	0.1
● **BUD CULLOTON** Culloton, Bernard Aloysius b: 5/19/1897, Kingston, N.Y. d: 11/9/76, Kingston, N.Y. BR/TR, 5'11", 180 lbs. Deb: 4/16/25																										
1925	Pit-N	0	1	.000	9	1	0	0	0	21	19	1	1	3	8.6	2.57	173	.241	.250	0	.000	-0	4	4	-0	0.1
1926	Pit-N	0	0	—	4	0	0	0	0	3^2	3	0	6	1	22.1	7.36	53	.214	.450	0	—	0	-1	-1	0	0.0
Total	2	0	1	.000	13	1	0	0	0	24^2	22	1	7	4	10.6	3.28	133	.237	.290	0	.000	-0	3	3	-0	0.1
● **RAY CULP** Culp, Raymond Leonard b: 8/6/41, Elgin, Tex. BR/TR, 6', 200 lbs. Deb: 4/10/63																										
1963	Phi-N★	14	11	.560	34	30	10	5	0	203^1	148	15	102	176	11.3	2.97	109	.206	.309	9	.136	-0	7	6	-0	0.7
1964	Phi-N	8	7	.533	30	19	3	1	0	135	139	15	56	96	13.3	4.13	84	.263	.340	5	.114	-1	-9	-10	-1	-1.2
1965	Phi-N	14	10	.583	33	30	11	2	0	204^1	188	14	78	134	12.2	3.22	108	.243	.322	6	.088	-2	7	6	-1	0.3
1966	Phi-N	7	4	.636	34	12	1	0	1	110^2	106	19	53	100	13.5	5.04	71	.246	.338	2	.077	-2	-18	-18	-1	-1.9
1967	Chi-N	8	11	.421	30	22	4	1	0	152^2	138	22	59	111	11.7	3.89	91	.239	.311	5	.098	-1	-9	-6	-1	-0.9
1968	Bos-A	16	6	.727	35	30	11	6	0	216^1	166	18	82	190	10.7	2.91	108	.210	.292	8	.114	-1	2	6	-1	0.4
1969	Bos-A★	17	8	.680	32	32	9	2	0	227	195	25	79	172	11.1	3.81	100	.231	.302	12	.152	1	-5	-0	-0	0.0
1970	Bos-A	17	14	.548	33	33	15	1	0	251^1	211	22	91	197	11.2	3.04	130	.224	.300	12	.124	-3	19	26	-1	2.6
1971	Bos-A	14	16	.467	35	35	12	3	0	242^1	236	21	67	151	11.4	3.60	103	.253	.307	8	.118	-2	-4	2	-2	-0.1
1972	Bos-A	5	8	.385	16	16	4	1	0	105	104	8	53	52	13.7	4.46	72	.260	.351	7	.212	1	-16	-15	0	-1.7
1973	Bos-A	2	6	.250	10	9	0	0	0	50^1	46	9	32	32	14.7	4.47	90	.247	.369	0	—	0	-4	-3	0	-0.4
Total	11	122	101	.547	322	268	80	22	1	1898^1	1677	188	752	1411	11.8	3.58	99	.235	.314	74	.123	-11	-29	-5	-8	-2.2
● **BILL CULP** Culp, William Edward b: 6/11/1887, Bellaire, Ohio d: 9/3/69, Arnold, Pa. BB/TR, 6'1.5", 165 lbs. Deb: 9/8/10																										
1910	Phi-N	0	0	—	4	0	0	0	1	6^2	8	0	4	4	16.2	8.10	39	.333	.429	0	.000	-0	-4	-4	1	-0.1
● **GEORGE CULVER** Culver, George Raymond b: 7/8/43, Salinas, Cal. BR/TR, 6'2", 185 lbs. Deb: 9/7/66																										
1966	Cle-A	0	2	.000	5	1	0	0	0	9^2	15	1	7	6	21.4	8.38	41	.357	.460	0	.000	-0	-5	-5	0	-0.9
1967	Cle-A	7	3	.700	53	1	0	0	3	75	71	2	31	41	13.0	3.96	82	.258	.346	1	.250	0	-6	-6	1	-0.7
1968	Cin-N	11	16	.407	42	35	5	2	2	226^1	229	8	84	114	13.0	3.22	98	.264	.339	8	.121	-1	-6	-2	2	-0.1
1969	Cin-N	5	7	.417	32	13	0	0	4	101^1	117	8	52	58	15.8	4.26	88	.291	.384	3	.097	-2	-8	-6	2	-0.7
1970	StL-N	3	3	.500	11	7	2	0	0	56^2	64	6	24	23	14.1	4.61	89	.284	.356	3	.176	0	-4	-3	2	-0.1
	Hou-N	3	3	.500	32	0	0	0	3	45	44	1	21	31	13.6	3.20	121	.254	.345	1	.250	0	4	3	-1	0.4
	Yr	6	6	.500	43	7	2	0	3	101^2	108	7	45	54	13.8	3.98	101	.270	.348	4	.190	0	1	0	1	0.3
1971	Hou-N	5	8	.385	59	0	0	0	7	95^1	89	4	38	57	12.2	2.64	127	.257	.334	1	.091	-1	9	8	1	1.2
1972	Hou-N	6	2	.750	45	0	0	0	2	97^1	73	7	43	82	11.2	3.05	110	.212	.309	3	.158	0	4	3	-0	0.3
1973	LA-N	4	4	.500	28	0	0	0	2	42	45	4	21	23	14.4	3.00	115	.292	.381	0	.000	-0	3	2	1	0.5
	Phi-N	3	1	.750	14	0	0	0	0	18^2	26	0	15	7	19.8	4.82	79	.342	.451	0	—	0	-2	-2	1	-0.4
	Yr	7	5	.583	42	0	0	0	2	60^2	71	4	36	30	15.9	3.56	100	.305	.398	0	.000	-0	1	-0	2	0.1
1974	Phi-N	1	0	1.000	14	0	0	0	0	21^2	20	1	16	9	15.4	6.65	57	.267	.402	0	.000	-0	-7	-7	-0	-0.4
Total	9	48	49	.495	335	57	7	2	23	789	793	42	352	451	13.6	3.62	96	.266	.352	20	.124	-4	-18	-13	8	-0.9
● **JOHN CUMBERLAND** Cumberland, John Sheldon b: 5/10/47, Westbrook, Me. BR/TL, 6', 190 lbs. Deb: 9/27/68 C																										
1968	NY-A	0	0	—	1	0	0	0	0	2	3	1	1	1	18.0	9.00	32	.333	.400	0	—	0	-1	-1	0	0.0
1969	NY-A	0	0	—	2	0	0	0	0	4	3	0	4	0	15.8	4.50	77	.231	.412	0	—	0	-0	-0	0	0.0
1970	NY-A	3	4	.429	15	8	1	0	0	64	62	9	15	38	10.8	3.94	89	.252	.295	1	.059	-1	-2	-3	-1	-0.5
	SF-N	2	0	1.000	7	0	0	0	0	11	6	0	4	6	8.2	0.82	486	.158	.238	0	.000	-0	4	4	0	0.6
1971	*SF-N	9	6	.600	45	21	5	2	2	185	153	22	55	65	10.1	2.92	116	.223	.281	7	.119	-2	11	10	-3	0.2
1972	SF-N	0	4	.000	9	6	0	0	0	25	38	6	7	8	16.2	8.64	40	.336	.375	1	.111	-0	-14	-14	-1	-2.1
	StL-N	1	1	.500	14	1	0	0	0	21^2	23	6	7	7	12.5	6.65	51	.291	.349	0	.000	-1	-8	-8	-1	-0.8
	Yr	1	5	.167	23	7	0	0	0	46^2	61	12	14	15	14.5	7.71	45	.316	.362	1	.071	-1	-22	-22	-2	-2.9
1974	Cal-A	0	1	.000	17	0	0	0	0	21^2	24	2	10	12	14.1	3.74	92	.289	.366	0	—	0	-0	-1	-0	-0.1
Total	6	15	16	.484	110	36	6	2	2	334^1	312	46	103	137	11.2	3.82	90	.246	.303	9	.099	-5	-11	-14	-6	-2.7
● **JOHN CUMMINGS** Cummings, John Russell b: 5/10/69, Torrance, Cal. BL/TL, 6'3", 200 lbs. Deb: 4/10/93																										
1993	Sea-A	0	6	.000	10	8	1	0	0	46^1	59	6	16	19	15.0	6.02	73	.316	.376	0	—	0	-9	-8	-0	-0.9
1994	Sea-A	2	4	.333	17	8	0	0	0	64	66	7	37	33	14.5	5.63	87	.270	.367	0	—	0	-6	-5	-1	-0.5
1995	Sea-A	0	0	—	4	0	0	0	0	5^1	8	0	7	4	25.3	11.81	40	.400	.556	0	—	0	-4	-4	0	0.0
	*LA-N	3	1	.750	35	0	0	0	0	39	38	3	10	21	11.1	3.00	126	.250	.296	0	.000	-0	5	3	-0	0.2

YEAR	TM/L	W	L	PCT	G	GS	CG	SH	SV	IP	H	HR	BB	SO	RAT	ERA	ERA+	OAV	OOB	BH	AVG	PB	PR	/A	PD	TPI
1996	LA-N	0	1	.000	4	0	0	0	0	5^1	12	1	2	5	23.6	6.75	57	.462	.500	0	—	0	-2	-2	0	-0.3
	Det-A	3	3	.500	21	0	0	0	0	31^2	36	3	20	24	16.5	5.12	99	.283	.389	0	—	0	-0	-0	-0	-0.1
1997	Det-A	2	0	1.000	19	0	0	0	0	24^2	32	3	14	8	16.8	5.47	84	.311	.393	0	—	0	-2	-2	0	-0.2
Total	5	10	15	.400	110	16	1	0	0	216^1	251	23	106	114	15.0	5.33	85	.292	.373	0	.000	-0	-18	-19	-1	-1.8
● STEVE CUMMINGS	Cummings, Steven Brent b: 7/15/64, Houston, Tex. BB/TR, 6'2", 200 lbs. Deb: 6/24/89																									
1989	Tor-A	2	0	1.000	5	2	0	0	0	21	18	1	11	8	12.9	3.00	126	.231	.333	0	—	0	2	2	-0	0.1
1990	Tor-A	0	0	—	6	2	0	0	0	12^1	22	4	5	4	20.4	5.11	77	.431	.491	0	—	0	-2	-2	-0	-0.1
Total	2	2	0	1.000	11	4	0	0	0	33^1	40	5	16	12	15.7	3.78	101	.310	.395	0	—	0	0	0	-0	0.0
● CANDY CUMMINGS	Cummings, William Arthur b: 10/18/1848, Ware, Mass. d: 5/16/24, Toledo, Ohio BR/TR, 5'9", 120 lbs. Deb: 4/22/1872 H																									
1872	Mut-n	33	20	.623	**55**	55	**53**	**3**	0	**497**	605	2	30	43	11.5	2.97	113	.273	.283	52	.208	-4	37	22		0.9
1873	Bal-n	28	14	.667	42	42	42	1	0	382	475	4	33	34	12.0	2.66	122	.274	.287	48	.250	2	25	25		1.7
1874	Phi-n	28	26	.519	54	54	52	3	0	483	616	4	18	61	11.8	1.96	113	.276	.282	52	.225	-4	12	14		0.4
1875	Har-n	35	12	.745	48	47	46	**7**	0	416	397	0	4	**82**	8.7	1.60	146	.235	.236	44	.199	-5	29	34		2.8
1876	Har-N	16	8	.667	24	24	24	5	0	216	215	0	14	26	9.5	1.67	142	.239	.251	17	.162	-8	15	17	-2	0.6
1877	Cin-N	5	14	.263	19	19	16	0	0	155^2	219	2	13	11	13.4	4.34	61	.315	.327	14	.200	0	-26	-29	0	-2.6
Total	4 n	124	72	.633	199	198	193	14	0	1778	2093	10	85	220	11.0	2.31	122	.266	.274	196	.219	-10	103	100		5.8
Total	2	21	22	.488	43	43	40	5	0	371^2	434	2	27	37	11.2	2.78	90	.272	.284	31	.177	-7	-11	-12	-2	-2.0
● WILL CUNNANE	Cunnane, William Joseph b: 4/24/74, Suffern, N.Y. BR/TR, 6'2", 175 lbs. Deb: 4/3/97																									
1997	SD-N	6	3	.667	54	8	0	0	0	91^1	114	11	49	79	16.6	5.81	67	.305	.393	5	.357	3	-16	-20	-1	-1.5
1998	SD-N	0	0	—	3	0	0	0	0	3	4	1	1	1	15.0	6.00	64	.308	.357	0	—	0	-1	-1	0	0.0
Total	2	6	3	.667	57	8	0	0	0	94^1	118	12	50	80	16.5	5.82	67	.305	.391	5	.357	3	-17	-20	-1	-1.5
● BRUCE CUNNINGHAM	Cunningham, Bruce Lee b: 9/29/05, San Francisco, Cal. d: 3/8/84, Hayward, Cal. BR/TR, 5'10.5", 165 lbs. Deb: 5/7/29																									
1929	Bos-N	4	6	.400	17	8	4	0	1	91^2	100	7	32	22	13.2	4.52	104	.282	.344	4	.148	-0	2	2	1	0.2
1930	Bos-N	5	6	.455	36	6	2	0	0	106^2	121	7	41	28	13.7	5.48	90	.289	.352	6	.194	0	-6	-6	3	-0.2
1931	Bos-N	3	12	.200	33	16	6	1	1	136^2	157	7	54	32	14.0	4.48	85	.296	.363	3	.071	-4	-9	-10	4	-1.0
1932	Bos-N	1	0	1.000	18	3	0	0	0	47	50	1	19	21	14.0	3.45	109	.281	.363	2	.222	2	2	2	1	0.3
Total	4	13	24	.351	104	33	12	1	2	382	428	22	146	103	13.7	4.64	93	.289	.356	15	.138	-2	-11	-14	9	-0.7
● BERT CUNNINGHAM	Cunningham, Ellsworth Elmer b: 11/25/1865, Wilmington, Del. d: 5/14/52, Cragmere, Del. BR/TR, 187 lbs. Deb: 9/15/1887 U																									
1887	Bro-a	0	2	.000	3	3	3	0	0	23	26	0	13	8	16.8	5.09	85	.263	.371	0	.000	-1	-2	-2	-0	-0.2
1888	Bal-a	22	29	.431	51	51	50	0	0	453^1	412	8	157	186	11.9	3.39	88	.233	.307	33	.186	-2	-17	-21	0	-2.1
1889	Bal-a	16	19	.457	39	33	29	0	1	279^1	306	11	141	140	14.9	4.87	81	.270	.358	27	.206	-3	-32	-29	-0	-2.9
1890	Phi-P	3	9	.250	14	11	11	0	0	108^2	133	0	67	33	17.1	5.22	82	.289	.387	6	.115	-4	-12	-11	1	-1.1
	Buf-P	9	15	.375	25	25	24	2	0	211	251	8	134	78	16.7	5.84	70	.283	.381	23	.228	1	-38	-41	-1	-3.1
	Yr	12	24	.333	39	36	35	2	0	319^2	384	8	201	111	16.6	5.63	74	.283	.378	29	.190	-4	-50	-52	0	-4.2
1891	Bal-a	11	14	.440	30	25	21	0	0	237^2	241	8	138	59	14.8	4.01	93	.254	.356	15	.150	-2	-8	-7	2	-0.6
1895	Lou-N	11	16	.407	31	28	24	1	0	231	299	6	104	49	15.9	4.75	97	.309	.378	30	.300	6	1	-3	2	0.4
1896	Lou-N	7	14	.333	27	20	17	0	1	189^1	242	6	74	37	15.8	5.09	85	.308	.380	22	.250	3	-15	-16	2	-0.9
1897	Lou-N	14	13	.519	29	27	25	0	0	234^2	286	2	72	49	14.2	4.14	103	.298	.355	22	.237	-0	4	3	2	0.5
1898	Lou-N	28	15	.651	44	42	41	0	0	362	387	8	65	34	11.7	3.16	113	.272	.313	32	.229	2	18	17	-1	1.8
1899	Lou-N	17	17	.500	39	37	33	1	0	323^2	385	4	75	36	13.2	3.84	101	.295	.340	40	.260	3	1	1	6	0.8
1900	Chi-N	4	3	.571	8	7	7	0	0	64	84	0	21	7	15.3	4.36	83	.316	.375	4	.148	-1	-5	-5	-1	-0.6
1901	Chi-N	0	1	.000	1	1	1	0	0	9	11	0	3	2	14.0	5.00	65	.297	.350	0	.000	0	-2	-2	1	-0.1
Total	12	142	167	.460	341	310	286	4	2	2726^2	3063	61	1064	718	14.1	4.22	91	.277	.349	254	.217	1	-105	-117	12	-8.1
● GEORGE CUNNINGHAM	Cunningham, George Harold b: 7/13/1894, Sturgeon Lake, Minn. d: 3/10/72, Chattanooga, Tenn. BR/TR, 5'11", 185 lbs. Deb: 4/14/16 ◆																									
1916	Det-A	7	10	.412	35	14	5	0	2	150^1	146	0	74	68	13.4	2.75	104	.269	.360	11	.268	5	1	2	1	0.9
1917	Det-A	2	7	.222	44	8	4	0	4	139	113	2	51	49	10.9	2.91	91	.227	.304	6	.176	1	-4	-4	0	-0.2
1918	Det-A	6	7	.462	27	14	10	0	1	140	131	0	38	39	11.2	3.15	84	.255	.312	25	.223	3	-6	-8	0	-0.3
1919	Det-A	1	1	.500	17	0	0	0	1	47^2	54	0	15	11	14.0	4.91	65	.292	.361	5	.217	2	-9	-9	0	-0.1
Total	4	16	25	.390	123	36	19	0	8	477	444	2	178	167	12.1	3.13	89	.255	.330	47	.224	11	-17	-19	2	0.3
● MIKE CUNNINGHAM	Cunningham, Mody b: 6/14/1882, Lancaster, S.C. d: 12/10/69, Lancaster, S.C. BR/TR, 5'10.5", 175 lbs. Deb: 8/31/06																									
1906	Phi-A	1	0	1.000	5	1	1	0	0	28	29	1	9	15	12.5	3.21	85	.271	.333	4	.333	1	-2	-2	-0	0.0
● NIG CUPPY	Cuppy, George Joseph (b: George Koppe) b: 7/3/1869, Logansport, Ind. d: 7/27/22, Elkhart, Ind. BR/TR, 5'7", 160 lbs. Deb: 4/16/1892																									
1892	*Cle-N	28	13	.683	47	42	38	1	1	376	333	9	121	103	11.1	2.51	135	.228	.291	36	.214	0	32	37	3	3.8
1893	Cle-N	17	10	.630	31	30	24	0	0	243^2	316	6	75	39	14.8	4.47	109	.305	.357	27	.248	1	5	11	-1	0.8
1894	Cle-N	24	15	.615	43	33	29	**3**	0	316	381	11	128	65	14.8	4.56	120	.295	.363	35	.259	1	27	32	1	2.9
1895	*Cle-N	26	14	.650	47	40	36	1	2	353	384	9	95	91	12.4	3.54	141	.273	.323	40	.286	7	49	57	4	5.8
1896	*Cle-N	25	14	.641	46	40	35	1	1	358	388	8	75	86	11.8	3.12	146	.274	.314	38	.270	6	50	56	4	5.9
1897	Cle-N	10	6	.625	19	17	13	1	0	138	150	3	26	23	11.8	3.20	141	.275	.314	8	.145	-4	17	20	-1	1.5
1898	Cle-N	9	8	.529	18	15	13	1	0	128	147	4	25	27	12.5	3.30	110	.286	.327	5	.104	-4	4	4	-2	0.0
1899	StL-N	11	8	.579	21	21	18	1	0	171^2	203	3	26	25	12.3	3.15	127	.294	.324	13	.186	-3	14	16	0	1.3
1900	Bos-N	8	4	.667	17	13	9	0	1	105^1	107	8	24	23	11.7	3.08	134	.263	.314	11	.262	1	7	12	-1	1.2
1901	Bos-A	4	6	.400	13	11	9	0	0	93^1	111	1	14	22	12.2	4.15	85	.292	.321	10	.204	0	-5	-6	-2	-0.7
Total	10	162	98	.623	302	262	224	9	5	2283	2520	62	609	504	12.6	3.48	127	.275	.325	223	.233	6	200	239	6	22.5
● SAMMY CURRAN	Curran, Simon Francis b: 10/30/1874, Dorchester, Mass. d: 5/19/36, Dorchester, Mass. TL, Deb: 8/1/02																									
1902	Bos-N	0	0	—	1	0	0	0	0	6^2	6	0	0	3	8.1	1.35	209	.240	.240	0	.000	-0	1	1	-0	-0.1
● LAFAYETTE CURRENCE	Currence, Delancy Lafayette b: 12/3/51, Rock Hill, S.C. BB/TL, 5'11", 175 lbs. Deb: 7/24/75																									
1975	Mil-A	0	2	.000	8	1	0	0	0	18^2	25	5	14	7	18.8	7.71	50	.316	.419	0	—	0	-8	-8	-1	-0.8
● MURPHY CURRIE	Currie, Archibald Murphy b: 8/31/1893, Fayetteville, N.C. d: 6/22/39, Asheboro, N.C. BR/TR, 5'11.5", 185 lbs. Deb: 8/31/16																									
1916	StL-N	0	0	—	6	0	0	0	0	14^1	7	1	9	8	10.0	1.88	140	.149	.286	0	.000	-0	1	1	-1	-0.1
● CLARENCE CURRIE	Currie, Clarence Franklin b: 12/30/1878, Glencoe, Ont., Can. d: 7/15/41, Little Chute, Wis BR/TR, Deb: 4/25/02																									
1902	Cin-N	3	4	.429	10	7	6	1	0	65^1	70	1	17	20	12.3	3.72	81	.273	.324	2	.083	-2	-7	-5	1	-0.7
	StL-N	7	5	.583	15	12	10	2	0	124^2	125	0	35	30	12.0	2.60	105	.261	.319	9	.196	-0	3	2	2	0.4
	Yr	10	9	.526	25	19	16	3	0	190	195	1	52	50	12.0	2.98	95	.265	.318	11	.157	-2	-4	-3	3	-0.3
1903	StL-N	4	12	.250	22	16	13	1	1	148	155	7	60	52	13.7	4.01	81	.281	.362	4	.085	-3	-12	-12	4	-1.1
	Chi-N	1	2	.333	6	3	2	0	1	33^1	35	1	9	9	12.7	2.97	106	.254	.313	5	.417	2	1	1	1	0.3
	Yr	5	14	.263	28	19	15	1	2	181^1	190	8	69	61	13.0	3.82	85	.271	.339	9	.153	-1	-11	-12	5	-0.8
Total	2	15	23	.395	53	38	31	4	2	371^1	385	9	121	111	12.8	3.39	89	.270	.336	20	.155	-4	-15	-15	8	-1.1
● BILL CURRIE	Currie, William Cleveland b: 11/29/28, Leary, Ga. BR/TR, 6', 175 lbs. Deb: 4/13/55																									
1955	Was-A	0	0	—	3	0	0	0	0	4^1	7	3	2	2	20.8	12.46	31	.350	.435	0	—	0	-4	-4	0	0.0
● GEORGE CURRY	Curry, George James "Soldier Boy" b: 12/21/1888, Bridgeport, Conn. d: 10/5/63, West Haven, Conn. BR/TR, 6', 185 lbs. Deb: 7/16/11																									
1911	StL-A	0	3	.000	3	3	0	0	0	15^2	19	0	24	2	24.7	7.47	45	.339	.538	0	.000	-1	-7	-7	-0	-1.1
● STEVE CURRY	Curry, Stephen Thomas b: 9/13/65, Winter Park, Fla. BR/TR, 6'6", 217 lbs. Deb: 7/10/88																									
1988	Bos-A	0	1	.000	3	3	0	0	0	11	15	0	14	4	23.7	8.18	50	.357	.518	0	—	0	-5	-5	0	-0.4
● WES CURRY	Curry, Wesley b: 4/1/1860, Wilmington, Del. d: 5/19/33, Philadelphia, Pa. Deb: 8/6/1884 U																									
1884	Ric-a	0	2	.000	2	2	2	0	0	16	15	2	3	1	10.7	5.06	66	.221	.264	2	.250	-0	-3	-3	-0	-0.3

YEAR	TM/L	W	L	PCT	G	GS	CG	SH	SV	IP	H	HR	BB	SO	RAT	ERA	ERA+	OAV	OOB	BH	AVG	PB	PR	/A	PD	TPI
● CLIFF CURTIS	Curtis, Clifton Garfield b: 7/3/1883, Delaware, Ohio d: 4/23/43, Utica, Ohio BR/TR, 6'2", 180 lbs. Deb: 8/23/09																									
1909	Bos-N	4	5	.444	10	9	8	2	0	83	53	1	30	22	9.2	1.41	200	.191	.275	1	.034	-3	11	13	1	1.3
1910	Bos-N	6	24	.200	43	37	12	2	2	251	251	9	124	75	13.9	3.55	94	.277	.371	12	.146	-4	-14	-6	6	-0.6
1911	Bos-N	1	8	.111	12	9	5	0	1	77	79	4	34	23	13.4	4.44	86	.265	.344	7	.250	-0	-9	-5	1	-0.5
	Chi-N	1	2	.333	4	1	0	0	0	7	7	0	5	4	19.3	3.86	86	.241	.405	1	.500	0	-0	-0	0	-0.1
	Phi-N	2	1	.667	8	5	3	1	0	45	45	0	15	13	12.2	2.60	132	.260	.323	4	.267	0	4	4	-0	0.2
	Yr	4	11	.267	24	15	8	1	1	129	131	4	54	40	13.0	3.77	97	.259	.332	12	.267	0	-5	-1	0	-0.4
1912	Phi-N	2	5	.286	10	8	2	0	0	50	55	3	17	20	13.7	3.24	112	.286	.357	0	.000	-2	1	2	1	0.2
	Bro-N	4	7	.364	19	9	3	0	1	80	72	4	37	22	12.9	3.94	85	.250	.347	8	.308	1	-5	-5	-0	-0.5
	Yr	6	12	.333	29	17	5	0	1	130	127	7	54	42	12.9	3.67	94	.262	.344	8	.195	-1	-4	-3	1	-0.3
1913	Bro-N	8	9	.471	30	16	6	0	2	151^2	145	1	55	57	12.3	3.26	101	.255	.328	6	.122	-3	-1	1	2	-0.1
Total	5	28	61	.315	136	94	39	5	6	744^2	707	22	317	236	12.8	3.31	101	.259	.344	39	.159	-10	-13	3	9	-0.1
● JACK CURTIS	Curtis, Jack Patrick b: 1/11/37, Rhodhiss, N.C. BL/TL, 5'10", 175 lbs. Deb: 4/22/61																									
1961	Chi-N	10	13	.435	31	27	6	0	0	180^1	220	23	51	57	13.6	4.89	85	.303	.350	10	.167	3	-17	-14	0	-1.2
1962	Chi-N	0	2	.000	4	3	0	0	0	18	18	2	6	8	12.0	3.50	118	.277	.338	1	.250	0	1	1	-0	0.1
	Mil-N	4	4	.500	30	5	0	0	1	75^2	82	8	27	40	13.2	4.16	91	.282	.347	4	.222	2	-2	-3	-1	-0.2
	Yr	4	6	.400	34	8	0	0	1	93^2	100	10	33	48	13.0	4.04	96	.280	.344	5	.227	2	-1	-2	-1	-0.1
1963	Cle-A	0	0	—	4	0	0	0	0	5	8	0	5	3	25.2	18.00	20	.348	.483	0	—	0	-8	-8	0	0.0
Total	3	14	19	.424	69	35	6	0	1	279	328	33	89	108	13.6	4.84	84	.297	.352	15	.183	5	-26	-24	-1	-1.3
● JOHN CURTIS	Curtis, John Duffield b: 3/9/48, Newton, Mass. BL/TL, 6'2", 185 lbs. Deb: 8/13/70																									
1970	Bos-A	0	0	—	1	0	0	0	0	2^1	4	1	1	1	19.3	11.57	34	.333	.385	0	—	0	-2	-2	0	0.0
1971	Bos-A	2	2	.500	5	3	1	0	0	26	30	3	6	19	12.5	3.12	119	.291	.330	1	.111	-0	1	2	-1	0.1
1972	Bos-A	11	8	.579	26	21	8	3	0	154^1	161	8	50	106	12.3	3.73	86	.271	.328	5	.094	-2	-12	-9	-0	-1.4
1973	Bos-A	13	13	.500	35	30	10	4	0	221^1	225	24	83	101	12.6	3.58	112	.264	.331	0	—	0	6	11	-1	1.0
1974	StL-N	10	14	.417	33	29	5	2	1	195	199	15	83	89	13.1	3.78	94	.267	.342	10	.159	-0	-4	-5	0	-0.6
1975	StL-N	8	9	.471	39	18	4	0	1	146^2	151	13	65	67	13.4	3.44	109	.268	.346	8	.211	2	3	5	2	0.9
1976	StL-N	6	11	.353	37	15	3	1	1	134	139	11	65	52	13.7	4.50	79	.276	.359	7	.200	2	-15	-14	0	-1.5
1977	SF-N	3	3	.500	43	9	1	1	1	77	95	5	48	47	16.8	5.49	71	.314	.409	3	.231	1	-14	-14	1	-0.7
1978	SF-N	4	3	.571	46	0	0	0	1	63	60	1	29	38	12.7	3.71	93	.262	.345	0	.000	-0	-1	-2	0	-0.2
1979	SF-N	10	9	.526	27	18	3	2	0	120^2	121	15	42	85	12.2	4.18	84	.257	.318	5	.147	1	-6	-9	-1	-1.3
1980	SD-N	10	8	.556	30	27	6	0	0	187	184	9	67	71	12.2	3.51	98	.262	.329	12	.194	1	2	-2	1	0.0
1981	SD-N	2	6	.250	28	8	0	0	0	66^2	70	11	30	31	13.6	5.13	63	.275	.353	1	.077	-1	-12	-14	-0	-1.7
1982	SD-N	8	6	.571	26	18	1	1	0	116^1	121	15	46	54	13.0	4.10	83	.271	.341	11	.297	3	-6	-9	-1	-0.8
	Cal-A	0	1	.000	8	0	0	0	1	12	16	0	3	10	14.3	6.00	68	.320	.358	0	—	0	-3	-3	-0	-0.3
1983	Cal-A	1	2	.333	37	3	0	0	5	90	89	5	40	36	13.1	3.80	106	.258	.339	0	—	0	3	2	-1	0.0
1984	Cal-A	1	2	.333	17	0	0	0	0	28^2	30	4	11	18	12.9	4.40	90	.263	.328	0	—	0	-1	-1	0	-0.1
Total	15	89	97	.478	438	199	42	14	11	1641	1695	140	669	825	13.0	3.96	91	.270	.341	63	.175	5	-61	-63	-1	-6.6
● VERN CURTIS	Curtis, Vernon Eugene "Turk" b: 5/24/20, Cairo, Ill. d: 6/24/92, Cairo, Ill. BR/TR, 6', 170 lbs. Deb: 9/6/43																									
1943	Was-A	0	0	—	2	0	0	0	0	4	3	0	6	1	20.3	6.75	47	.200	.429	0	—	0	-2	-2	-0	0.0
1944	Was-A	0	1	.000	3	1	0	0	0	9^2	8	0	3	2	10.2	2.79	117	.235	.297	0	.000	-0	1	0	-0	0.0
1946	Was-A	0	0	—	11	0	0	0	0	16^1	19	1	10	7	16.0	7.16	47	.297	.392	0	.000	-0	-7	-7	0	0.0
Total	3	0	1	.000	16	1	0	0	0	30	30	1	19	10	14.7	5.70	58	.265	.371	0	.000	-1	-7	-8	-0	0.0
● ED CUSHMAN	Cushman, Edgar Leander b: 3/27/1852, Eagleville, Ohio d: 9/26/15, Erie, Pa. BR/TL, 6', 177 lbs. Deb: 7/6/1883																									
1883	Buf-N	3	3	.500	7	7	5	0	0	50^1	61	0	17	34	13.9	3.93	81	.285	.338	5	.217	-0	-4	-4	-0	-0.4
1884	Mil-U	4	0	1.000	4	4	4	2	0	36	10	0	3	47	3.3	1.00	132	.082	.104	1	.091	-2	6	1	-1	-0.1
1885	Phi-a	3	7	.300	10	10	10	0	0	87	101	1	17	37	12.5	3.52	98	.269	.306	7	.189	-1	-3	-1	-1	-0.3
	NY-a	8	14	.364	22	22	22	0	0	191	158	2	33	133	9.1	2.78	106	.210	.246	10	.145	-1	10	4	-2	0.1
	Yr	11	21	.344	32	32	32	0	0	278	259	3	50	170	10.1	3.01	103	.229	.263	17	.160	-2	7	3	-3	-0.2
1886	NY-a	17	21	.447	38	38	37	2	0	325^2	278	6	99	167	10.4	3.12	109	.220	.277	19	.151	-7	12	10	0	0.4
1887	NY-a	10	15	.400	26	26	25	0	0	220	310	9	83	64	16.4	5.97	71	.325	.384	23	.247	3	-41	-42	-1	-3.1
1890	Tol-a	17	21	.447	40	38	34	0	1	315^2	346	5	107	125	13.2	4.19	94	.270	.331	13	.100	-9	-11	-8	-5	-2.0
Total	6	62	81	.434	147	145	137	4	1	1225^2	1264	23	359	607	12.1	3.86	92	.254	.308	78	.160	-17	-32	-43	-10	-5.4
● HARVEY CUSHMAN	Cushman, Harvey Barnes b: 7/10/1877, Rockland, Me. d: 12/27/20, Emsworth, Pa. Deb: 8/24/02																									
1902	Pit-N	0	4	.000	4	4	3	0	0	25^2	30	0	31	12	22.1	7.36	37	.291	.463	2	.200	-0	-13	-13	-1	-1.6
● MIKE CVENGROS	Cvengros, Michael John b: 12/1/01, Pana, Ill. d: 8/2/70, Hot Springs, Ark. BL/TL, 5'8", 159 lbs. Deb: 9/30/22																									
1922	NY-N	0	1	.000	1	1	1	0	0	9	6	1	3	3	10.0	4.00	100	.194	.286	0	.000	-0	0	0	0	0.0
1923	Chi-A	12	13	.480	40	26	14	0	3	214^1	216	6	107	86	14.1	4.41	90	.269	.364	15	.203	-1	-10	-11	0	-1.2
1924	Chi-A	3	12	.200	26	15	2	0	0	105^2	119	5	67	36	16.1	5.88	70	.300	.405	6	.200	2	-19	-21	0	-2.2
1925	Chi-A	3	9	.250	22	11	4	0	0	104^2	109	7	55	32	14.4	4.30	97	.278	.371	5	.152	-1	1	-2	-0	-0.3
1927	*Pit-N	2	1	.667	23	4	0	0	1	53^2	55	3	24	21	13.4	3.35	123	.271	.351	3	.158	-0	3	5	1	0.3
1929	Chi-N	5	4	.556	32	2	0	0	2	64	82	2	29	23	15.8	4.64	99	.319	.390	6	.400	2	1	-0	0	0.2
Total	6	25	40	.385	144	59	21	0	6	551^1	587	24	285	201	14.6	4.59	90	.282	.374	35	.201	1	-24	-28	1	-3.2
● JIM CZAJKOWSKI	Czajkowski, James Mark b: 12/18/63, Parma, Ohio BB/TR, 6'4", 215 lbs. Deb: 7/29/94																									
1994	Col-N	0	0	—	5	0	0	0	0	8^2	9	2	6	2	18.7	4.15	120	.281	.439	0	—	0	0	1	0	0.0
● OMAR DAAL	Daal, Omar Jesus (Cordero) b: 3/1/72, Maracaibo, Venez. BL/TL, 6'3", 175 lbs. Deb: 4/24/93																									
1993	LA-N	2	3	.400	47	0	0	0	0	35^1	36	5	21	19	14.5	5.09	75	.277	.377	0	—	0	-4	-5	0	-0.6
1994	LA-N	0	0	—	24	0	0	0	0	13^2	12	1	5	9	11.2	3.29	119	.245	.315	0	—	0	1	1	-0	0.0
1995	LA-N	4	0	1.000	28	0	0	0	0	20	29	1	15	11	20.2	7.20	53	.354	.459	0	—	0	-7	-8	-0	-1.3
1996	Mon-N	4	5	.444	64	6	0	0	0	87^1	74	10	37	82	11.5	4.02	107	.228	.309	0	.000	-1	2	3	1	0.2
1997	Mon-N	1	2	.333	33	0	0	0	1	30^1	48	4	15	16	19.3	9.79	43	.378	.451	1	.200	0	-19	-19	1	-1.6
	Tor-A	1	1	.500	9	3	0	0	0	27	34	3	6	28	13.3	4.00	115	.304	.339	0	—	0	2	2	0	0.1
1998	Ari-N	8	12	.400	33	23	3	1	0	162^2	146	12	51	132	11.1	2.88	150	.245	.308	5	.109	-1	24	26	2	3.1
Total	6	20	23	.465	238	32	3	1	1	376^1	379	36	150	297	12.8	4.23	100	.267	.340	6	.097	-2	-0	-0	4	-0.1
● JOHN D'ACQUISTO	D'Acquisto, John Francis b: 12/24/51, San Diego, Cal. BR/TR, 6'2", 205 lbs. Deb: 9/2/73																									
1973	SF-N	1	1	.500	7	3	1	0	0	27^2	23	4	19	29	13.7	3.58	107	.219	.339	0	.000	-1	0	1	-0	-0.1
1974	SF-N	12	14	.462	38	36	5	1	0	215	182	13	124	167	13.1	3.77	101	.227	.334	8	.113	-1	-4	1	-4	-0.4
1975	SF-N	2	4	.333	10	6	0	0	0	28	29	5	34	22	20.9	10.29	37	.264	.445	0	.000	-0	-21	-20	-1	-3.4
1976	SF-N	3	8	.273	28	19	0	0	0	106	93	5	102	53	16.8	5.35	68	.243	.406	7	.269	2	-22	-20	-0	-1.8
1977	StL-N	0	0	—	3	2	0	0	0	8^1	5	0	10	9	17.3	4.32	89	.185	.421	0	.000	-0	-0	-0	-0	0.0
	SD-N	1	2	.333	17	12	0	0	0	44	49	3	47	45	19.8	6.95	51	.297	.455	0	.000	-0	-15	-17	0	-1.0
	Yr	1	2	.333	20	14	0	0	0	52^1	54	3	57	54	19.3	6.54	55	.278	.444	0	.000	-1	-15	-17	0	-1.0
1978	SD-N	4	3	.571	45	3	0	0	10	93	60	2	56	104	11.3	2.13	156	.185	.307	4	.190	1	15	12	-1	1.2
1979	SD-N	9	13	.409	51	11	1	1	2	133^2	140	15	86	97	15.4	4.92	72	.275	.383	4	.129	1	-18	-21	-2	-3.2
1980	SD-N	2	3	.400	39	0	0	0	1	67	67	2	36	44	14.0	3.76	91	.270	.365	0	.000	-1	-1	-2	-0	-0.3
	Mon-N	0	2	.000	11	0	0	0	2	20^2	14	0	9	15	10.0	2.18	164	.206	.299	0	—	0	3	3	0	0.4
	Yr	2	5	.286	50	0	0	0	3	87^2	81	2	45	59	12.9	3.39	102	.252	.343	0	.000	-1	2	1	-0	0.1
1981	Cal-A	0	0	—	6	0	0	0	0	19^1	26	2	12	8	18.2	10.71	34	.338	.433	0	—	0	-15	-15	-0	0.0
1982	Oak-A	0	1	.000	11	0	0	0	0	17	20	1	9	7	15.4	5.29	74	.290	.372	0	—	0	-2	-3	0	0.1
Total	10	34	51	.400	266	92	7	2	15	779^2	708	52	544	600	14.7	4.56	79	.245	.368	23	.127	0	-79	-81	-9	-8.5
● JOHN DAGENHARD	Dagenhard, John Douglas b: 4/25/17, Magnolia, Ohio BR/TR, 6'2", 195 lbs. Deb: 9/28/43																									
1943	Bos-N	1	0	1.000	2	1	1	0	0	11	9	0	4	2	12.3	0.00	—	.225	.326	0	.000	-0	4	4	1	0.5

● PETE DAGLIA
Daglia, Peter George b: 2/28/07, Napa, Cal. d: 3/11/52, Willits, Cal. BR/TR, 6'3", 210 lbs. Deb: 6/8/32

YEAR	TM/L	W	L	PCT	G	GS	CG	SH	SV	IP	H	HR	BB	SO	RAT	ERA	ERA+	OAV	OOB	BH	AVG	PB	PR	/A	PD	TPI
1932	Chi-A	2	4	.333	12	5	2	0	0	50	67	4	20	16	16.4	5.76	75	.324	.394	1	.077	-1	-7	-8	-1	-0.9

● JAY DAHL
Dahl, Jay Steven b: 12/6/45, San Bernardino, Cal. d: 6/20/65, Salisbury, N.C. BB/TL, 5'10", 183 lbs. Deb: 9/27/63

YEAR	TM/L	W	L	PCT	G	GS	CG	SH	SV	IP	H	HR	BB	SO	RAT	ERA	ERA+	OAV	OOB	BH	AVG	PB	PR	/A	PD	TPI
1963	Hou-N	0	1	.000	1	1	0	0	0	2^{2}	7	0	0	0	23.6	16.88	19	.438	.438	0	—	0	-4	-4	-0	-0.9

● JERRY DAHLKE
Dahlke, Jerome Alexander "Joe" b: 6/8/30, Marathon, Wis. BR/TR, 6', 180 lbs. Deb: 5/6/56

YEAR	TM/L	W	L	PCT	G	GS	CG	SH	SV	IP	H	HR	BB	SO	RAT	ERA	ERA+	OAV	OOB	BH	AVG	PB	PR	/A	PD	TPI
1956	Chi-A	0	0	—	5	0	0	0	0	2^{1}	5	0	6	1	42.4	19.29	21	.455	.647	0	—	0	-4	-4	0	0.0

● SAM DAILEY
Dailey, Samuel Laurence b: 3/31/04, Oakford, Ill. d: 12/2/79, Columbia, Mo. BL/TR, 5'11", 168 lbs. Deb: 7/4/29

YEAR	TM/L	W	L	PCT	G	GS	CG	SH	SV	IP	H	HR	BB	SO	RAT	ERA	ERA+	OAV	OOB	BH	AVG	PB	PR	/A	PD	TPI
1929	Phi-N	2	2	.500	20	5	0	0	0	51^{1}	74	5	23	18	17.2	7.54	69	.349	.415	1	.059	-2	-16	-13	-1	-1.1

● VINCE DAILEY
Dailey, Vincent Perry b: 12/25/1864, Osceola, Pa. d: 11/14/19, Hornell, N.Y. 6', 200 lbs. Deb: 4/21/1890 ♦

YEAR	TM/L	W	L	PCT	G	GS	CG	SH	SV	IP	H	HR	BB	SO	RAT	ERA	ERA+	OAV	OOB	BH	AVG	PB	PR	/A	PD	TPI
1890	Cle-N	0	1	.000	2	1	0	0	0	7	12	0	7	0	24.4	7.71	46	.364	.475	71	.289	1	-3	-3	0	-0.3

● BILL DAILEY
Dailey, William Garland b: 5/13/35, Arlington, Va. BR/TR, 6'3", 185 lbs. Deb: 8/17/61

YEAR	TM/L	W	L	PCT	G	GS	CG	SH	SV	IP	H	HR	BB	SO	RAT	ERA	ERA+	OAV	OOB	BH	AVG	PB	PR	/A	PD	TPI
1961	Cle-A	1	0	1.000	12	0	0	0	0	19	16	0	6	7	10.4	0.95	415	.232	.293	0	.000	-0	6	6	0	0.3
1962	Cle-A	2	2	.500	27	0	0	0	1	42^{2}	43	0	17	24	13.1	3.59	108	.270	.348	0	.000	-0	2	1	-0	0.1
1963	Min-A	6	3	.667	66	0	0	0	21	108^{2}	80	9	19	72	8.2	1.99	183	.208	.246	5	.238	2	20	20	2	3.0
1964	Min-A	1	2	.333	14	0	0	0	0	15^{1}	23	3	17	6	25.8	8.22	44	.377	.537	0	—	0	-8	-8	0	-1.4
Total	4	10	7	.588	119	0	0	0	22	185^{2}	162	12	59	109	11.0	2.76	135	.241	.308	5	.192	1	20	20	3	2.0

● ED DAILY
Daily, Edward M. b: 9/7/1862, Providence, R.I. d: 10/21/1891, Washington, D.C. BR/TR, 5'10.5", 174 lbs. Deb: 5/4/1885 F♦

YEAR	TM/L	W	L	PCT	G	GS	CG	SH	SV	IP	H	HR	BB	SO	RAT	ERA	ERA+	OAV	OOB	BH	AVG	PB	PR	/A	PD	TPI
1885	Phi-N	26	23	.531	50	50	49	4	0	440	370	12	90	140	9.4	2.21	126	.217	.256	38	.207	-0	30	28	-4	2.4
1886	Phi-N	16	9	.640	27	23	22	1	0	218	211	7	59	95	11.1	3.06	108	.242	.290	70	.227	3	6	6	2	0.8
1887	Phi-N	0	4	.000	6	5	4	0	0	41^{1}	52	2	25	7	16.8	7.19	59	.289	.376	30	.283	1	-14	-14	1	-0.8
	Was-N	0	1	.000	1	1	1	0	0	7	5	0	6	3	14.1	7.71	53	.208	.367	78	.251	0	-3	-3	0	-0.3
	Yr	0	5	.000	7	6	5	0	0	48^{1}	57	2	31	10	16.4	7.26	58	.279	.374	108	.259	1	-17	-16	1	-1.1
1888	Was-N	2	7	.222	9	8	8	0	0	73^{2}	88	7	19	20	13.4	4.89	57	.278	.325	102	.225	1	-17	-17	0	-1.5
1889	Col-a	0	0	—	2	0	0	0	1	1^{2}	1	0	4	2	27.0	21.60	17	.167	.500	148	.256	0	-3	-3	-0	-0.4
1890	Bro-a	10	15	.400	27	27	27	0	0	235^{2}	252	3	93	82	13.9	4.05	96	.265	.342	94	.239	3	-5	-4	2	0.1
	NY-N	2	0	1.000	2	1	1	0	0	16	6	0	6	0	9.0	2.25	156	.113	.254	2	.133	-1	2	2	1	0.2
	*Lou-a	6	3	.667	12	10	9	1	0	93	83	2	30	31	11.3	1.94	199	.232	.298	20	.250	2	20	20	2	2.1
1891	Lou-a	4	8	.333	15	14	11	0	0	111^{1}	149	6	48	27	16.6	5.74	64	.310	.382	16	.250	2	-25	-26	0	-1.9
Total	7	66	70	.485	151	139	132	6	1	1237^{2}	1217	39	380	407	11.9	3.39	98	.246	.305	616	.239	12	-8	-11	5	0.7

● HUGH DAILY
Daily, Hugh Ignatius "One Arm" (b: Harry Criss) b: 1857, Baltimore, Md. BR/TR, 6'2", 180 lbs. Deb: 5/1/1882

YEAR	TM/L	W	L	PCT	G	GS	CG	SH	SV	IP	H	HR	BB	SO	RAT	ERA	ERA+	OAV	OOB	BH	AVG	PB	PR	/A	PD	TPI
1882	Buf-N	15	14	.517	29	29	29	0	0	255^{2}	246	6	70	116	11.1	2.99	98	.234	.282	18	.164	-6	-3	-2	-5	-1.1
1883	Cle-N	23	19	.548	45	43	40	4	1	378^{2}	360	5	99	171	10.9	2.42	130	.243	.291	18	.127	-10	30	31	-1	1.8
1884	CP-U	27	27	.500	56	56	54	5	0	484^{2}	430	11	71	469	9.3	2.43	100	.222	.249	43	.219	-11	1	1	1	-0.8
	Was-U	1	1	.500	2	2	2	0	0	16	16	0	1	14	9.6	2.25	107	.242	.254	0	.000	-1	0	0	-0	-0.1
	Yr	28	28	.500	58	58	56	5	0	500^{2}	446	11	72	**483**	9.3	2.43	101	.223	.250	43	.214	-12	1	1	1	-0.9
1885	StL-N	3	8	.273	11	11	10	1	0	91^{1}	92	5	44	31	13.4	3.94	70	.252	.333	3	.086	-3	-11	-12	-0	-1.4
1886	Was-N	0	6	.000	6	6	6	0	0	49	69	2	40	15	20.0	7.35	45	.332	.440	2	.125	-1	-22	-22	-0	-1.9
1887	Cle-a	4	12	.250	16	16	16	0	0	139^{2}	181	1	44	30	14.7	3.67	118	.311	.362	4	.069	-8	10	10	-1	0.1
Total	6	73	87	.456	165	163	157	10	1	1415	1394	30	369	846	11.2	2.92	101	.245	.291	88	.157	-39	5	6	-6	-3.4

● BRUCE DalCANTON
DalCanton, John Bruce b: 6/15/42, California, Pa. BR/TR, 6'2", 205 lbs. Deb: 9/3/67 C

YEAR	TM/L	W	L	PCT	G	GS	CG	SH	SV	IP	H	HR	BB	SO	RAT	ERA	ERA+	OAV	OOB	BH	AVG	PB	PR	/A	PD	TPI
1967	Pit-N	2	1	.667	8	2	1	0	0	24	19	1	10	13	11.3	1.88	179	.211	.297	2	.333	1	4	4	-1	0.5
1968	Pit-N	1	1	.500	7	0	0	0	2	17	7	0	6	8	7.9	2.12	138	.127	.238	0	.000	-0	2	2	-1	0.1
1969	Pit-N	8	2	.800	57	0	0	0	5	86^{1}	79	3	49	56	13.3	3.34	105	.252	.353	3	.300	2	2	1	-0	0.4
1970	Pit-N	9	4	.692	41	6	1	0	1	84^{2}	94	7	39	53	14.2	4.57	85	.282	.359	0	.000	-1	-5	-6	-1	-1.0
1971	KC-A	8	6	.571	25	22	2	0	0	141^{1}	144	8	44	58	12.0	3.44	100	.262	.317	4	.087	-3	0	-0	-2	-0.4
1972	KC-A	6	6	.500	35	16	1	0	2	132^{1}	135	7	29	75	11.2	3.40	89	.265	.306	4	.098	-2	-5	-5	-2	-0.9
1973	KC-A	4	3	.571	32	3	1	0	3	97^{1}	108	8	46	38	14.6	4.81	85	.284	.367	0	—	0	-11	-8	0	-0.7
1974	KC-A	8	10	.444	31	22	9	2	0	175^{1}	135	5	82	96	11.4	3.13	122	.211	.306	0	—	0	9	13	0	1.4
1975	KC-A	0	2	.000	4	2	0	0	0	8^{2}	23	0	7	5	32.2	15.58	25	.479	.554	0	—	0	-11	-11	0	-1.8
	Atl-N	2	7	.222	26	9	0	0	3	67	63	2	24	38	12.5	3.36	112	.248	.327	2	.105	-1	2	3	1	0.4
1976	Atl-N	3	5	.375	42	1	0	0	1	73^{1}	67	6	42	36	13.6	3.56	106	.244	.348	2	.222	0	-0	2	1	0.3
1977	Chi-A	0	2	.000	8	0	0	0	2	24	20	1	13	9	12.4	3.75	109	.230	.330	0	—	0	1	1	-1	0.0
Total	11	51	49	.510	316	83	15	2	19	931^{1}	894	48	391	485	12.6	3.67	99	.253	.331	17	.113	-3	-12	-5	-3	-1.7

● GENE DALE
Dale, Emmett Eugene b: 6/16/1889, St.Louis, Mo. d: 3/20/58, St.Louis, Mo. BR/TR, 6'3", 179 lbs. Deb: 9/19/11

YEAR	TM/L	W	L	PCT	G	GS	CG	SH	SV	IP	H	HR	BB	SO	RAT	ERA	ERA+	OAV	OOB	BH	AVG	PB	PR	/A	PD	TPI
1911	StL-N	0	2	.000	5	2	0	0	0	14^{2}	13	0	16	13	19.0	6.75	50	.250	.443	2	.400	1	-5	-5	0	-0.6
1912	StL-N	0	5	.000	19	3	1	0	0	61^{2}	76	4	51	37	19.0	6.57	52	.311	.436	6	.273	1	-22	-22	-1	-1.5
1915	Cin-N	18	17	.514	49	35	20	4	3	296^{2}	256	6	107	104	11.2	2.46	116	.243	.316	20	.220	2	10	13	-1	1.7
1916	Cin-N	3	4	.429	17	5	2	0	0	69^{2}	80	3	33	23	14.9	5.17	50	.304	.386	3	.143	-0	-20	-20	1	-1.8
Total	4	21	28	.429	90	45	23	4	3	442^{2}	425	13	207	177	13.1	3.60	81	.263	.352	31	.223	3	-37	-34	-1	-2.2

● BUD DALEY
Daley, Leavitt Leo b: 10/7/32, Orange, Cal. BL/TL, 6'1", 185 lbs. Deb: 9/10/55

YEAR	TM/L	W	L	PCT	G	GS	CG	SH	SV	IP	H	HR	BB	SO	RAT	ERA	ERA+	OAV	OOB	BH	AVG	PB	PR	/A	PD	TPI
1955	Cle-A	0	1	.000	2	1	0	0	0	7	10	1	1	2	14.1	6.43	62	.333	.355	0	.000	-0	-2	-2	0	-0.2
1956	Cle-A	1	0	1.000	14	0	0	0	0	20^{1}	21	2	14	13	17.7	6.20	68	.273	.417	0	.000	-0	-5	-5	1	-0.1
1957	Cle-A	2	8	.200	34	10	1	0	2	87^{1}	99	7	40	54	15.4	4.43	84	.279	.368	4	.200	0	-6	-7	1	-0.6
1958	KC-A	3	2	.600	26	5	1	0	0	70^{2}	67	5	19	39	11.7	3.31	118	.249	.313	2	.125	-1	4	5	1	0.3
1959	KC-A★	16	13	.552	39	29	12	2	1	216^{1}	212	24	62	125	11.9	3.16	127	.257	.317	23	.295	4	17	20	-0	3.1
1960	KC-A★	16	16	.500	37	35	13	1	0	231	234	27	96	126	13.2	4.56	87	.263	.341	12	.160	1	-18	-15	1	-1.6
1961	KC-A	4	8	.333	16	10	2	0	1	63^{2}	84	6	22	36	15.7	4.95	84	.319	.383	2	.111	-1	-7	-5	1	-0.9
	*NY-A	8	9	.471	23	17	7	0	0	129^{2}	127	17	51	83	12.6	3.96	94	.257	.331	6	.133	-1	1	-3	-1	-0.6
	Yr	12	17	.414	39	27	9	0	1	193^{1}	211	23	73	119	13.4	4.28	90	.275	.341	8	.127	-2	-6	-9	-0	-1.5
1962	*NY-A	7	5	.583	43	6	0	0	4	105^{1}	105	8	21	55	11.2	3.59	104	.258	.303	5	.185	-0	4	2	-0	0.2
1963	NY-A	0	0	—	1	0	0	0	1	1	2	0	0	0	18.0	0.00	—	.667	.667	0	—	0	0	0	-0	0.1
1964	NY-A	3	2	.600	13	3	0	0	1	35	37	3	25	16	17.0	4.63	78	.274	.402	2	.250	1	-4	-4	1	-0.4
Total	10	60	64	.484	248	116	36	3	10	967^{1}	998	100	351	549	13.1	4.03	97	.266	.339	56	.192	3	-15	-14	4	-0.7

● BILL DALEY
Daley, William b: 6/27/1868, Poughkeepsie, N.Y d: 5/4/22, Poughkeepsie, N.Y. TL , Deb: 7/17/1889

YEAR	TM/L	W	L	PCT	G	GS	CG	SH	SV	IP	H	HR	BB	SO	RAT	ERA	ERA+	OAV	OOB	BH	AVG	PB	PR	/A	PD	TPI
1889	Bos-N	3	3	.500	9	7	4	0	0	48	34	1	43	40	14.8	4.31	97	.193	.357	3	.150	-1	-2	-1	3	0.1
1890	Bos-P	18	7	**.720**	34	25	19	2	2	235	246	7	167	110	16.2	3.60	122	.258	.373	17	.155	-5	17	21	-1	1.1
1891	Bos-a	8	6	.571	19	11	10	0	**2**	126^{2}	119	6	81	68	14.7	2.98	117	.240	.354	10	.169	-3	10	7	1	0.4
Total	3	29	16	.644	62	43	33	2	4	409^{2}	399	14	291	218	15.6	3.49	117	.245	.366	30	.159	-8	25	27	3	1.6

● MIKE DALTON
Dalton, Michael Edward b: 3/27/63, Palo Alto, Cal. BR/TL, 6', 215 lbs. Deb: 5/31/91

YEAR	TM/L	W	L	PCT	G	GS	CG	SH	SV	IP	H	HR	BB	SO	RAT	ERA	ERA+	OAV	OOB	BH	AVG	PB	PR	/A	PD	TPI
1991	Det-A	0	0	—	4	0	0	0	0	8	12	2	2	4	15.8	3.38	123	.333	.368	0	—	0	1	1	0	-0.1

● GEORGE DALY
Daly, George Josephs "Pecks" b: 7/28/1887, Buffalo, N.Y. d: 12/12/57, Buffalo, N.Y. BR/TR, 5'10.5", 175 lbs. Deb: 9/26/09

YEAR	TM/L	W	L	PCT	G	GS	CG	SH	SV	IP	H	HR	BB	SO	RAT	ERA	ERA+	OAV	OOB	BH	AVG	PB	PR	/A	PD	TPI
1909	NY-N	0	3	.000	3	3	3	0	0	21	31	0	8	8	17.1	6.00	43	.341	.400	1	.111	-1	-8	-8	-1	-1.1

● JEFF D'AMICO
D'Amico, Jeffrey Charles b: 12/27/75, St.Petersburg, Fla. BR/TR, 6'7", 250 lbs. Deb: 6/28/96

YEAR	TM/L	W	L	PCT	G	GS	CG	SH	SV	IP	H	HR	BB	SO	RAT	ERA	ERA+	OAV	OOB	BH	AVG	PB	PR	/A	PD	TPI
1996	Mil-A	6	6	.500	17	17	0	0	0	86	88	21	31	53	12.5	5.44	95	.267	.330	0	—	0	-4	-2	-1	-0.4
1997	Mil-A	9	7	.563	23	23	1	1	0	135^{2}	139	25	43	94	12.6	4.71	98	.264	.329	0	.000	-0	-2	-1	-1	-0.3
Total	2	15	13	.536	40	40	1	1	0	221^{2}	227	46	74	147	12.5	4.99	97	.265	.329	0	.000	-0	-7	-4	-2	-0.7

YEAR	TM/L	W	L	PCT	G	GS	CG	SH	SV	IP	H	HR	BB	SO	RAT	ERA	ERA+	OAV	OOB	BH	AVG	PB	PR	/A	PD	TPI
● **BILL DAMMANN**	Dammann, William Henry "Wee Willie" b: 8/9/1872, Chicago, Ill. d: 12/6/48, Lynnhaven, Va. BL/TL, 5'7", 155 lbs. Deb: 4/24/1897																									
1897	Cin-N	6	4	.600	16	11	7	1	0	95	122	2	37	21	15.5	4.74	96	.309	.375	5	.161	-1	-4	-2	1	-0.1
1898	Cin-N	16	10	.615	35	22	16	2	2	224^{2}	277	3	67	51	14.1	3.61	106	.301	.353	16	.195	1	0	6	-3	0.4
1899	Cin-N	2	1	.667	9	5	3	1	1	48	74	0	11	2	16.1	4.88	80	.351	.386	1	.056	-2	-5	-5	0	-0.4
Total	3	24	15	.615	60	38	26	4	3	367^{2}	473	5	115	74	14.7	4.06	99	.310	.363	22	.168	-1	-10	-1	-2	-0.1
● **ART DANEY**	Daney, Arthur Lee b: 7/9/04, Talihina, Okla. d: 3/11/88, Phoenix, Ariz. BR/TR, 5'11", 165 lbs. Deb: 5/25/28																									
1928	Phi-A	0	0	—	1	0	0	0	0	1	1	0	0	0	9.0	0.00	—	.250	.250	0	—	0	0	0	0	0.0
● **DAVE DANFORTH**	Danforth, David Charles "Dauntless Dave" b: 3/7/1890, Granger, Tex. d: 9/19/70, Baltimore, Md. BL/TL, 6', 167 lbs. Deb: 8/1/11																									
1911	Phi-A	4	1	.800	14	2	1	0	1	33^{2}	29	1	17	21	13.1	3.74	84	.240	.348	1	.167	0	-1	-2	-0	-0.3
1912	Phi-A	0	0	—	3	0	0	0	0	20^{1}	26	0	12	8	16.8	3.98	77	.338	.427	2	.250	0	-2	-2	0	0.0
1916	Chi-A	6	5	.545	28	8	1	0	2	93^{2}	87	1	37	49	12.2	3.27	85	.259	.338	2	.087	-1	-5	-5	1	-0.6
1917	*Chi-A	11	6	.647	**50**	9	1	1	**9**	173	155	1	74	79	12.1	2.65	100	.244	.325	6	.130	0	0	0	-3	-0.3
1918	Chi-A	6	15	.286	39	11	5	0	2	139	148	1	40	48	12.5	3.43	80	.288	.345	6	.143	-2	-10	-11	0	-1.8
1919	Chi-A	1	2	.333	15	1	0	0	1	41^{2}	58	1	20	17	17.1	7.78	41	.333	.405	1	.111	0	-21	-21	-0	-1.5
1922	StL-A	5	2	.714	20	10	3	0	1	79^{2}	93	1	38	48	14.9	3.28	127	.304	.383	2	.087	-2	7	8	-1	0.3
1923	StL-A	16	14	.533	38	29	16	0	1	226^{1}	221	4	87	96	12.7	3.94	106	.262	.340	15	.211	2	1	6	-0	0.9
1924	StL-A	15	12	.556	41	27	11	1	4	219^{2}	246	16	69	65	13.0	4.51	100	.292	.348	13	.171	-2	-7	0	-3	-0.4
1925	StL-A	7	9	.438	38	15	5	0	2	159	172	19	61	53	13.4	4.36	107	.284	.353	8	.174	-2	1	6	-4	-0.1
Total	10	71	66	.518	286	112	43	2	23	1186	1235	45	455	484	13.1	3.89	95	.277	.349	56	.160	-6	-37	-25	-10	-3.8
● **CHUCK DANIEL**	Daniel, Charles Edward b: 9/17/33, Bluffton, Ark. BR/TR, 6'2", 195 lbs. Deb: 9/21/57																									
1957	Det-A	0	0	—	1	0	0	0	0	2^{1}	3	1	0	2	11.6	7.71	50	.333	.333	0	—	0	-1	-1	-0	0.0
● **BENNIE DANIELS**	Daniels, Bennie b: 6/17/32, Tuscaloosa, Ala. BL/TR, 6'1.5", 193 lbs. Deb: 9/24/57																									
1957	Pit-N	0	1	.000	1	1	0	0	0	7	5	0	3	2	10.3	1.29	295	.208	.296	0	.000	-0	2	2	1	0.3
1958	Pit-N	0	3	.000	8	5	1	0	0	27^{2}	31	3	15	7	15.3	5.53	70	.290	.382	1	.125	-0	-5	-5	1	-0.4
1959	Pit-N	7	9	.438	34	12	0	0	1	100^{2}	115	9	39	67	13.9	5.45	71	.287	.353	9	.310	6	-17	-18	-1	-2.0
1960	Pit-N	1	3	.250	10	6	0	0	0	40^{1}	52	4	17	16	15.4	7.81	48	.311	.375	3	.188	-0	-18	-18	1	-1.5
1961	Was-A	12	11	.522	32	28	12	1	0	212	184	14	80	110	11.3	3.44	117	.237	.311	15	.197	3	14	14	1	1.8
1962	Was-A	7	16	.304	44	21	3	1	2	161^{1}	172	14	68	66	13.5	4.85	83	.280	.354	6	.130	-1	-16	-15	5	-1.5
1963	Was-A	5	10	.333	35	24	6	1	1	168^{2}	163	19	58	88	11.8	4.38	85	.250	.312	7	.152	1	-14	-12	3	-0.6
1964	Was-A	8	10	.444	33	24	3	2	0	163	147	20	64	73	11.7	3.70	100	.245	.317	6	.128	0	-1	0	3	0.3
1965	Was-A	5	13	.278	33	18	1	0	1	116^{1}	135	16	39	42	13.5	4.72	74	.290	.345	4	.133	0	-16	-16	-0	-2.3
Total	9	45	76	.372	230	139	26	5	5	997	1004	99	383	471	12.6	4.44	86	.264	.332	51	.170	9	-72	-69	12	-5.9
● **CHARLIE DANIELS**	Daniels, Charles L. b: 7/1/1861, Roxbury, Mass. d: 2/9/38, Boston, Mass. Deb: 4/18/1884																									
1884	Bos-U	0	2	.000	2	2	2	0	0	16^{2}	20	0	2	12	11.9	4.32	55	.278	.297	3	.273	0	-3	-4	-0	-0.3
● **PETE DANIELS**	Daniels, Peter J. "Smiling Pete" b: 4/8/1864, County Cavan, Ireland d: 2/13/28, Indianapolis, Ind. BL/TL, Deb: 4/19/1890																									
1890	Pit-N	1	2	.333	4	4	3	0	0	28	40	1	12	8	17.7	7.07	47	.325	.399	4	.333	1	-11	-12	-0	-0.8
1898	StL-N	1	6	.143	10	6	3	0	0	54^{2}	62	0	14	13	13.0	3.62	105	.283	.335	3	.176	0	-0	1	-0	0.1
Total	2	2	8	.200	14	10	6	0	0	82^{2}	102	1	26	21	14.6	4.79	76	.298	.358	7	.241	1	-11	-11	-0	-0.7
● **GEORGE DARBY**	Darby, George William "Deacon" b: 2/6/1869, Kansas City, Mo. d: 2/25/37, Sacramento, Cal. BR/TR, 5'10.5", 160 lbs. Deb: 4/28/1893																									
1893	Cin-N	1	1	.500	4	3	2	0	0	29	41	2	18	6	19.2	7.76	62	.323	.419	3	.300	0	-10	-10	1	-0.4
● **PAT DARCY**	Darcy, Patrick Leonard b: 5/12/50, Troy, Ohio BL/TR, 6'3", 175 lbs. Deb: 9/12/74																									
1974	Cin-N	1	0	1.000	6	2	0	0	0	17	17	2	8	14	13.2	3.71	94	.262	.342	1	.333	0	-0	-0	-0	0.0
1975	*Cin-N	11	5	.688	27	22	1	0	1	130^{2}	134	4	59	46	13.3	3.58	100	.269	.346	4	.085	-3	1	0	-0	-0.3
1976	Cin-N	2	3	.400	11	4	0	0	2	39	41	2	22	15	14.5	6.23	56	.279	.373	2	.182	1	-12	-12	-1	-1.5
Total	3	14	8	.636	44	28	1	0	3	186^{2}	192	8	89	75	13.5	4.15	86	.270	.352	7	.115	-2	-11	-12	-1	-1.8
● **VIC DARENSBOURG**	Darensbourg, Victor Anthony b: 11/13/70, Los Angeles, Cal. BL/TL, 5'10", 165 lbs. Deb: 4/1/98																									
1998	Fla-N	0	7	.000	59	0	0	0	1	71	52	5	30	74	10.4	3.68	111	.207	.292	0	.000	-1	4	3	-1	0.2
● **ALVIN DARK**	Dark, Alvin Ralph "Blackie" b: 1/7/22, Comanche, Okla. BR/TR, 5'11", 185 lbs. Deb: 7/14/46 MC ◆																									
1953	NY-N	0	0	—	1	1	0	0	0	1	1	1	1	0	18.0	18.00	24	.250	.400	194	.300	0	-2	-2	-0	0.0
● **RON DARLING**	Darling, Ronald Maurice b: 8/19/60, Honolulu, Hawaii BR/TR, 6'3", 195 lbs. Deb: 9/6/83																									
1983	NY-N	1	3	.250	5	5	1	0	0	35^{1}	31	0	17	23	13.0	2.80	129	.248	.352	1	.100	-1	3	3	0	0.3
1984	NY-N	12	9	.571	33	33	2	2	0	205^{2}	179	17	104	136	12.6	3.81	93	.235	.331	10	.149	-1	-5	-6	2	-0.5
1985	NY-N☆	16	6	.727	36	35	4	2	0	248	214	21	114	167	12.0	2.90	119	.235	.323	13	.171	2	19	15	3	1.9
1986	*NY-N	15	6	.714	34	34	4	2	0	237	203	21	81	184	10.9	2.81	126	.234	.302	8	.099	-2	24	19	3	1.8
1987	NY-N	12	8	.600	32	32	2	0	0	207^{2}	183	24	96	167	12.2	4.29	88	.233	.319	8	.123	1	-5	-12	4	-0.6
1988	*NY-N	17	9	.654	34	34	7	4	0	240^{2}	218	24	60	161	10.6	3.25	99	.245	.297	18	.220	6	5	-1	0	0.5
1989	NY-N	14	14	.500	33	33	4	0	0	217^{1}	214	19	70	153	11.9	3.52	93	.258	.318	9	.123	1	-1	-6	2	-0.5
1990	NY-N	7	9	.438	33	18	1	0	0	126	135	20	44	99	13.1	4.50	83	.273	.338	4	.129	0	-10	-11	1	-1.1
1991	NY-N	5	6	.455	17	17	0	0	0	102^{1}	96	9	28	58	11.4	3.87	94	.251	.313	4	.118	-0	-2	-3	-0	-0.3
	Mon-N	0	2	.000	3	3	0	0	0	17	25	6	5	11	16.4	7.41	49	.333	.383	1	.167	0	-7	-7	-0	-0.7
	Yr	5	8	.385	20	20	0	0	0	119^{1}	121	15	33	69	11.7	4.37	83	.259	.309	5	.125	-0	-9	-10	-0	-1.0
	Oak-A	3	7	.300	12	12	0	0	0	75	64	7	38	60	12.5	4.08	94	.237	.335	0	—	0	0	-2	0	0.2
1992	*Oak-A	15	10	.600	33	33	4	3	0	206^{1}	198	15	72	99	12.0	3.66	102	.253	.319	0	—	0	6	2	-1	0.3
1993	Oak-A	5	9	.357	31	29	3	0	0	178	198	22	72	95	13.9	5.16	79	.281	.352	0	—	0	-17	-21	-2	-1.4
1994	Oak-A	10	11	.476	25	25	4	0	0	160	162	18	59	108	12.8	4.50	98	.267	.339	0	.000	-0	5	-1	0	-0.1
1995	Oak-A	4	7	.364	21	21	1	0	0	104	124	16	46	69	15.1	6.23	72	.296	.371	0	—	0	-18	-20	2	-1.6
Total	13	136	116	.540	382	364	37	13	0	2360^{1}	2244	239	906	1590	12.2	3.87	95	.252	.325	76	.144	6	-1	-51	15	-1.8
● **BOB DARNELL**	Darnell, Robert Jack b: 11/6/30, Wewoka, Okla. d: 1/1/95, Fredersburg, Tex. BR/TR, 5'10", 175 lbs. Deb: 8/10/54																									
1954	Bro-N	0	0	—	6	1	0	0	0	14^{1}	15	2	7	5	13.8	3.14	130	.278	.361	0	.000	-0	1	2	0	0.0
1956	Bro-N	0	0	—	1	0	0	0	0	1^{1}	1	0	0	0	6.8	0.00	—	.200	.200	0	—	0	1	1	-0	0.0
Total	2	0	0	—	7	1	0	0	0	15^{2}	16	2	7	5	13.2	2.87	142	.271	.348	0	.000	-0	2	2	0	0.0
● **MIKE DARR**	Darr, Michael Edward b: 3/23/56, Pomona, Cal. BR/TR, 6'4", 190 lbs. Deb: 9/6/77																									
1977	Tor-A	0	1	.000	1	1	0	0	0	1^{1}	3	1	4	1	54.0	33.75	12	.429	.667	0	—	0	-4	-4	0	-1.5
● **GEORGE DARROW**	Darrow, George Oliver b: 7/12/03, Beloit, Kan. d: 3/24/83, Sun City, Ariz. BL/TL, 6', 180 lbs. Deb: 4/22/34																									
1934	Phi-N	2	6	.250	17	8	2	0	1	49	57	4	28	14	16.3	5.51	86	.302	.403	2	.133	0	-8	-4	0	-0.6
● **BOBBY DARWIN**	Darwin, Arthur Bobby Lee b: 2/16/43, Los Angeles, Cal. BR/TR, 6'2", 200 lbs. Deb: 9/30/62 ◆																									
1962	LA-A	0	1	.000	1	1	0	0	0	3^{1}	8	0	4	6	32.4	10.80	36	.421	.522	0	.000	-0	-3	-3	-0	-0.5
1969	LA-N	0	0	—	3	0	0	0	0	3^{2}	4	0	5	0	27.0	9.82	34	.333	.579	0	—	0	-3	-3	-0	0.0
Total	2	0	1	.000	4	1	0	0	0	7	12	0	9	6	29.6	10.29	35	.387	.548	559	.251	-0	-5	-5	-0	-0.5
● **DANNY DARWIN**	Darwin, Daniel Wayne b: 10/25/55, Bonham, Tex. BR/TR, 6'3", 190 lbs. Deb: 9/8/78 F																									
1978	Tex-A	1	0	1.000	3	1	0	0	0	8^{2}	11	0	1	8	12.5	4.15	90	.324	.343	0	—	0	-0	-0	-0	-0.1
1979	Tex-A	4	4	.500	20	6	1	0	0	78	50	5	30	58	9.8	4.04	103	.186	.280	0	—	0	2	1	-1	0.0
1980	Tex-A	13	4	.765	53	2	0	0	8	109^{2}	98	4	50	104	12.3	2.63	148	.243	.329	0	—	0	17	15	-0	2.6
1981	Tex-A	9	9	.500	22	22	6	2	0	146	115	12	57	98	11.0	3.64	95	.218	.302	0	—	0	0	-3	-1	-0.2
1982	Tex-A	10	8	.556	56	1	0	0	7	89	95	6	37	61	13.6	3.44	113	.279	.354	0	—	0	6	4	2	1.3
1983	Tex-A	8	13	.381	28	26	9	2	0	183	175	9	62	92	11.8	3.49	115	.250	.313	0	—	0	12	10	-1	1.0
1984	Tex-A	8	12	.400	35	32	5	1	0	223^{2}	249	19	54	123	12.4	3.94	105	.279	.323	0	—	0	1	5	-2	0.1

YEAR	TM/L	W	L	PCT	G	GS	CG	SH	SV	IP	H	HR	BB	SO	RAT	ERA	ERA+	OAV	OOB	BH	AVG	PB	PR	/A	PD	TPI
1985	Mil-A	8	18	.308	39	29	11	1	2	217^2	212	34	65	125	11.6	3.80	109	.254	.311	0	—	0	8	9	-3	0.7
1986	Mil-A	6	8	.429	27	14	5	1	0	130^1	120	13	35	80	10.9	3.52	123	.246	.300	0	—	0	9	12	1	1.1
	Hou-N	5	2	.714	12	8	1	0	0	54^1	50	3	9	40	9.8	2.32	155	.239	.271	1	.063	-1	8	8	-1	0.8
1987	Hou-N	9	10	.474	33	30	3	1	0	195^2	184	17	69	134	11.9	3.59	109	.246	.314	12	.182	2	11	7	-2	0.7
1988	Hou-N	8	13	.381	44	20	3	0	3	192	189	20	48	129	11.4	3.84	86	.259	.311	4	.071	-1	-8	-11	2	-1.1
1989	Hou-N	11	4	.733	68	0	0	0	7	122	92	8	33	104	9.4	2.36	143	.212	.271	2	.118	-1	15	14	-1	1.6
1990	Hou-N	11	4	.733	48	17	3	0	2	162^2	136	11	31	109	**9.5**	**2.21**	**168**	.225	**.267**	5	.132	1	29	27	-1	2.4
1991	Bos-A	3	6	.333	12	12	0	0	0	68	71	15	15	42	11.9	5.16	83	.263	.311	0	—	0	-8	-7	0	-1.0
1992	Bos-A	9	9	.500	51	15	2	0	3	161^1	159	11	53	124	12.1	3.96	106	.257	.321	0	—	0	-0	4	-1	0.1
1993	Bos-A	15	11	.577	34	34	2	1	0	229^1	196	31	49	130	**9.7**	3.26	142	.230	**.274**	0	—	0	27	35	-0	3.4
1994	Bos-A	7	5	.583	13	13	0	0	0	75^2	101	13	24	54	15.0	6.30	80	.317	.366	0	—	0	-13	-11	-0	-1.4
1995	Tor-A	1	8	.111	13	11	1	0	0	65	91	13	24	36	16.3	7.62	62	.340	.400	0	—	0	-21	-21	-1	-2.4
	Tex-A	2	2	.500	7	4	0	0	0	34	40	12	7	22	12.7	7.15	68	.292	.331	0	—	0	-9	-9	-0	-0.9
	Yr	3	10	.231	20	15	1	0	0	99	131	25	31	58	14.8	7.45	64	.317	.366	0	—	0	-30	-30	-2	-3.3
1996	Pit-N	7	9	.438	19	19	0	0	0	122^1	117	9	16	69	10.2	3.02	144	.253	.287	8	.205	2	16	18	1	2.6
	Hou-N	3	2	.600	15	6	0	0	0	42^1	43	7	11	27	12.8	5.95	65	.267	.337	1	.100	-0	-8	-10	-1	-1.1
	Yr	10	11	.476	34	25	0	0	0	164^2	160	16	27	96	10.5	3.77	112	.253	.290	9	.184	2	8	8	0	1.5
1997	Chi-A	4	8	.333	21	17	1	0	0	113^1	130	21	31	62	12.9	4.13	106	.286	.333	0	.000	-0	5	3	1	0.3
	SF-N	1	3	.250	10	7	0	0	0	44	51	5	14	30	13.5	4.91	84	.288	.344	2	.133	-0	-3	-4	0	-0.3
1998	SF-N	8	10	.444	33	25	0	0	0	148^2	176	23	49	81	13.8	5.51	74	.297	.353	4	.089	-2	-21	-24	0	-2.6
Total	21	171	182	.484	716	371	53	9	32	3016^2	2951	321	874	1942	11.7	3.84	106	.256	.313	39	.128	-0	75	72	-11	7.6

● JEFF DARWIN Darwin, Jeffrey Scott b: 7/6/69, Sherman, Tex. BR/TR, 6'3", 180 lbs. Deb: 6/13/94 F

YEAR	TM/L	W	L	PCT	G	GS	CG	SH	SV	IP	H	HR	BB	SO	RAT	ERA	ERA+	OAV	OOB	BH	AVG	PB	PR	/A	PD	TPI
1994	Sea-A	0	0	—	2	0	0	0	0	4	7	1	3		24.8	13.50	36	.389	.500	0	—	0	-4	-4	-0	0.0
1996	Chi-A	0	1	.000	22	0	0	0	0	30^2	26	5	9	15	10.9	2.93	162	.232	.301	0	—	0	7	6	-0	0.5
1997	Chi-A	0	1	.000	14	0	0	0	0	13^2	17	1	7	9	15.8	5.27	83	.298	.375	0	—	0	-1	-1	-0	-0.1
Total	3	0	2	.000	38	0	0	0	0	48^1	50	7	19	25	13.4	4.47	104	.267	.344	0	—	0	2	1	-1	0.4

● DOUG DASCENZO Dascenzo, Douglas Craig b: 6/30/64, Cleveland, Ohio BB/TL, 5'8", 160 lbs. Deb: 9/2/88 ♦

YEAR	TM/L	W	L	PCT	G	GS	CG	SH	SV	IP	H	HR	BB	SO	RAT	ERA	ERA+	OAV	OOB	BH	AVG	PB	PR	/A	PD	TPI
1990	Chi-N	0	0	—	1	0	0	0	0	1	1	0	0	0	9.0	0.00	—	.333	.333	61	.253	0	0	0	0	0.0
1991	Chi-N	0	0	—	3	0	0	0	0	4	2	0	2	2	9.0	0.00	—	.154	.267	61	.255	1	2	2	-0	0.0
Total	2	0	0	—	4	0	0	0	0	5	3	0	2	2	9.0	0.00	—	.188	.278	287	.234	1	2	2	-0	0.0

● LEE DASHNER Dashner, Lee Claire "Lefty" b: 4/25/1887, Renault, Ill. d: 12/16/59, ElDorado, Kan. BB/TL, 5'11.5", 192 lbs. Deb: 8/4/13

YEAR	TM/L	W	L	PCT	G	GS	CG	SH	SV	IP	H	HR	BB	SO	RAT	ERA	ERA+	OAV	OOB	BH	AVG	PB	PR	/A	PD	TPI
1913	Cle-A	0	0	—	1	0	0	0	0	1^2	0	0	0	2	0.0	5.40	56	.000	.000	0	—	0	-0	-0	-0	0.0

● FRANK DASSO Dasso, Francis Joseph Nicholas b: 8/31/17, Chicago, Ill. BR/TR, 5'11.5", 185 lbs. Deb: 4/22/45

YEAR	TM/L	W	L	PCT	G	GS	CG	SH	SV	IP	H	HR	BB	SO	RAT	ERA	ERA+	OAV	OOB	BH	AVG	PB	PR	/A	PD	TPI
1945	Cin-N	4	5	.444	16	12	6	0	0	95^2	89	9	53	39	13.4	3.67	102	.253	.351	5	.161	-1	1	1	0	0.1
1946	Cin-N	0	0	—	2	0	0	0	0	1	2	0	2	1	36.0	27.00	12	.400	.571	0	—	0	-3	-3	0	0.0
Total	2	4	5	.444	18	12	6	0	0	96^2	91	9	55	40	13.6	3.91	96	.255	.354	5	.161	-1	-1	-2	0	0.1

● DAN DAUB Daub, Daniel William "Mickey" b: 1/12/1868, Middletown, Ohio d: 3/25/51, Bradenton, Fla. BR/TR, 5'10", 160 lbs. Deb: 8/31/1892

YEAR	TM/L	W	L	PCT	G	GS	CG	SH	SV	IP	H	HR	BB	SO	RAT	ERA	ERA+	OAV	OOB	BH	AVG	PB	PR	/A	PD	TPI
1892	Cin-N	1	2	.333	4	3	2	0	0	25	23	0	13	7	13.7	2.88	113	.235	.336	0	.000	-1	1	1	0	0.0
1893	Bro-N	6	6	.500	12	12	12	0	0	103	104	3	61	25	14.9	3.84	115	.254	.358	8	.190	-2	9	7	3	0.7
1894	Bro-N	10	12	.455	34	27	15	0	0	224	291	7	91	45	16.1	6.11	81	.311	.383	18	.189	-6	-19	-29	-1	-2.4
1895	Bro-N	10	10	.500	25	21	16	0	0	184^2	212	4	51	36	13.4	4.29	102	.284	.339	14	.197	-2	10	2	2	0.2
1896	Bro-N	12	11	.522	32	24	18	0	0	225	255	4	63	53	13.0	3.60	115	.283	.335	19	.226	2	19	13	4	1.5
1897	Bro-N	6	11	.353	19	16	11	0	0	137^2	180	8	48	19	15.6	6.08	67	.313	.376	11	.224	2	-27	-30	-0	-2.5
Total	6	45	52	.464	126	103	74	0	0	899^1	1065	26	327	185	14.5	4.75	93	.291	.357	70	.201	-6	-7	-36	8	-2.5

● HOOKS DAUSS Dauss, George August (b: George August Daus)
b: 9/22/1889, Indianapolis, Ind d: 7/27/63, St.Louis, Mo. BR/TR, 5'10.5", 168 lbs. Deb: 9/28/12

YEAR	TM/L	W	L	PCT	G	GS	CG	SH	SV	IP	H	HR	BB	SO	RAT	ERA	ERA+	OAV	OOB	BH	AVG	PB	PR	/A	PD	TPI
1912	Det-A	1	1	.500	2	2	2	0	0	17	11	0	9	7	12.2	3.18	103	.186	.324	1	.250	1	0	0	1	0.2
1913	Det-A	13	12	.520	33	29	22	2	1	225	188	4	82	107	11.3	2.48	118	.228	.308	14	.177	3	11	11	-1	1.5
1914	Det-A	19	15	.559	45	35	22	3	3	302	286	3	87	150	11.7	2.86	98	.257	.321	21	.216	6	-4	-2	1	0.4
1915	Det-A	24	13	.649	46	35	27	1	2	309^2	261	1	115	132	11.2	2.50	121	.235	.313	15	.146	0	15	18	9	3.2
1916	Det-A	19	12	.613	39	29	18	1	4	238^2	220	2	90	95	12.3	3.21	89	.257	.339	16	.222	8	-10	-9	2	-0.1
1917	Det-A	17	14	.548	37	31	22	6	2	270^2	243	3	87	102	11.2	2.43	109	.245	.311	11	.126	-1	7	7	4	1.1
1918	Det-A	12	16	.429	33	26	21	1	3	249^2	243	3	58	73	11.2	2.99	89	.263	.313	14	.182	3	-6	-9	2	-0.5
1919	Det-A	21	9	.700	34	32	22	2	0	256^1	262	9	63	73	11.6	3.55	90	.267	.315	14	.144	-3	-9	-10	6	-0.8
1920	Det-A	13	21	.382	38	32	18	0	0	270^1	308	11	84	82	13.3	3.56	105	.289	.345	14	.169	1	7	5	8	1.5
1921	Det-A	10	15	.400	32	28	16	0	1	233	275	11	81	68	14.3	4.33	99	.297	.362	23	.261	2	-1	-1	5	0.6
1922	Det-A	13	13	.500	39	25	12	1	4	218^2	251	7	59	78	13.0	4.20	92	.289	.339	15	.208	3	-4	-8	1	-0.5
1923	Det-A	21	13	.618	50	39	22	4	3	316	331	10	78	105	11.8	3.62	107	.272	.319	24	.231	5	13	9	2	1.4
1924	Det-A	12	11	.522	40	10	5	0	6	131^1	155	6	40	44	13.4	4.59	90	.302	.354	5	.132	-2	-5	-7	0	-1.2
1925	Det-A	16	11	.593	35	30	16	1	1	228	238	11	85	58	12.9	3.16	136	.272	.339	15	.185	1	31	29	-1	3.0
1926	Det-A	12	6	.667	35	5	0	0	9	124^1	135	6	49	27	13.3	4.20	97	.287	.354	10	.238	4	2	-2	-0	0.1
Total	15	223	182	.551	538	388	245	22	39	3390^2	3407	87	1067	1201	12.2	3.30	103	.266	.329	212	.189	32	44	33	38	9.9

● VIC DAVALILLO Davalillo, Victor Jose (Romero) b: 7/31/36, Cabimas, Venez. BL/TL, 5'7", 155 lbs. Deb: 4/9/63 F♦

YEAR	TM/L	W	L	PCT	G	GS	CG	SH	SV	IP	H	HR	BB	SO	RAT	ERA	ERA+	OAV	OOB	BH	AVG	PB	PR	/A	PD	TPI
1969	StL-N	0	0	—	2	0	0	0	0	0	2	0	2	0	—	∞	—	1.000	1.000	26	.265	0	-1	-1	0	-0.1

● CLAUDE DAVENPORT Davenport, Claude Edwin "Big Dave"
b: 5/28/1898, Runge, Tex. d: 6/13/76, Corpus Christi, Tex. BR/TR, 6'6", 193 lbs. Deb: 10/2/20 F

YEAR	TM/L	W	L	PCT	G	GS	CG	SH	SV	IP	H	HR	BB	SO	RAT	ERA	ERA+	OAV	OOB	BH	AVG	PB	PR	/A	PD	TPI
1920	NY-N	0	0	—	1	0	0	0	0	2	2	1	1	0	13.5	4.50	67	.250	.333	0	.000	-0	-0	-0	-0	0.0

● DAVE DAVENPORT Davenport, David W. b: 2/20/1890, DeRidder, La. d: 10/16/54, ElDorado, Ark. BR/TR, 6'6", 220 lbs. Deb: 4/17/14 F

YEAR	TM/L	W	L	PCT	G	GS	CG	SH	SV	IP	H	HR	BB	SO	RAT	ERA	ERA+	OAV	OOB	BH	AVG	PB	PR	/A	PD	TPI
1914	Cin-N	2	2	.500	10	6	3	1	2	54	38	1	30	22	11.8	2.50	117	.202	.321	2	.111	-1	2	3	-0	0.1
	StL-F	8	13	.381	33	26	13	2	4	215^2	204	3	80	142	12.1	3.46	88	.251	.324	6	.088	-6	-14	-10	1	-1.4
1915	StL-F	22	18	.550	**55**	46	**30**	**10**	1	**392^2**	300	5	96	**229**	9.2	2.20	131	**.215**	.268	12	.092	-11	23	**30**	-8	0.9
1916	StL-A	12	11	.522	**59**	31	13	1	2	290^2	267	4	100	129	11.6	2.85	96	.256	.326	10	.137	3	-1	-3	-3	-0.3
1917	StL-A	17	17	.500	47	39	20	2	2	280^2	273	5	105	100	12.4	3.08	84	.260	.331	9	.098	-6	-13	-15	-1	-2.5
1918	StL-A	10	11	.476	31	22	12	2	1	180	182	0	69	60	12.9	3.25	84	.273	.347	7	.135	1	-9	-10	2	-0.9
1919	StL-A	2	11	.154	24	16	5	0	0	123^1	135	4	41	37	13.0	3.94	84	.280	.339	3	.077	-4	-10	-9	1	-1.1
Total	6	73	83	.468	259	186	96	18	12	1537	1399	22	521	719	11.5	2.93	97	.248	.316	49	.104	-24	-22	-15	-9	-5.2

● LUM DAVENPORT Davenport, Joubert Lum b: 6/27/1900, Tucson, Ariz. d: 4/21/61, Dallas, Tex. BL/TL, 6'1", 165 lbs. Deb: 5/2/21

YEAR	TM/L	W	L	PCT	G	GS	CG	SH	SV	IP	H	HR	BB	SO	RAT	ERA	ERA+	OAV	OOB	BH	AVG	PB	PR	/A	PD	TPI
1921	Chi-A	0	3	.000	13	2	0	0	0	35^1	41	1	32	9	18.8	6.88	62	.318	.457	7	.412	2	-10	-10	-0	-0.6
1922	Chi-A	1	1	.500	9	1	0	0	0	16^2	14	2	13	9	14.6	10.80	38	.233	.370	0	.000	-0	-13	-12	0	-1.2
1923	Chi-A	0	0	—	2	0	0	0	0	4^1	7	0	4	1	22.8	6.23	64	.438	.550	1	1.000	0	-1	-1	0	0.0
1924	Chi-A	0	0	—	1	0	0	0	0	2	1	0	2	1	13.5	0.00	—	.125	.300	0	—	0	1	1	-0	0.0
Total	4	1	4	.200	25	3	0	0	0	58^1	63	3	51	20	17.7	7.71	54	.296	.434	8	.381	2	-23	-23	-0	-1.8

● MIKE DAVEY Davey, Michael Gerard b: 6/2/52, Spokane, Wash. BR/TL, 6'2", 190 lbs. Deb: 8/13/77

YEAR	TM/L	W	L	PCT	G	GS	CG	SH	SV	IP	H	HR	BB	SO	RAT	ERA	ERA+	OAV	OOB	BH	AVG	PB	PR	/A	PD	TPI
1977	Atl-N	0	0	—	16	0	0	0	2	16	19	1	9	7	15.8	5.06	88	.302	.389	0	.000	-0	-2	-1	-0	-0.1
1978	Atl-N	0	0	—	3	0	0	0	0	2^2	1	0	1	0	6.8	0.00	—	.125	.222	0	—	0	1	1	-0	0.0
Total	2	0	0	—	19	0	0	0	2	18^2	20	1	10	7	14.5	4.34	101	.282	.370	0	.000	-0	-1	0	-0	-0.1

● RAY DAVIAULT Daviault, Raymond Joseph Robert b: 5/27/34, Montreal, Que., Can BR/TR, 6'1", 170 lbs. Deb: 4/13/62

YEAR	TM/L	W	L	PCT	G	GS	CG	SH	SV	IP	H	HR	BB	SO	RAT	ERA	ERA+	OAV	OOB	BH	AVG	PB	PR	/A	PD	TPI
1962	NY-N	1	5	.167	36	3	0	0	0	81	92	14	48	51	16.0	6.22	67	.288	.388	1	.067	-1	-21	-18	-1	-1.4

YEAR	TM/L	W	L	PCT	G	GS	CG	SH	SV	IP	H	HR	BB	SO	RAT	ERA	ERA+	OAV	OOB	BH	AVG	PB	PR	/A	PD	TPI
● BOB DAVIDSON	Davidson, Robert Banks b: 1/6/63, Bad Kurznach, W.Ger. BR/TR, 6', 185 lbs. Deb: 7/15/89																									
1989	NY-A	0	0	—	1	0	0	0	0	1	1	1	1	0	18.0	18.00	21	.250	.400	0	—	0	-2	-2	0	0.0
● TED DAVIDSON	Davidson, Thomas Eugene b: 10/4/39, Las Vegas, Nev. BR/TL, 6', 192 lbs. Deb: 7/24/65																									
1965	Cin-N	4	3	.571	24	1	0	0	1	68^2	57	5	17	54	10.0	2.23	168	.233	.288	0	.000	-2	10	12	0	1.0
1966	Cin-N	5	4	.556	54	0	0	0	4	85^1	82	11	23	54	11.2	3.90	100	.253	.305	0	.000	-1	-3	-0	-0	-0.2
1967	Cin-N	1	0	1.000	9	0	0	0	0	13	13	0	3	6	11.1	4.15	90	.250	.291	0	—	0	-1	-1	0	0.0
1968	Cin-N	1	0	1.000	23	0	0	0	0	21^2	27	3	7	7	14.1	6.23	51	.307	.358	0	.000	-0	-8	-7	0	-0.4
	Atl-N	0	0	—	4	0	0	0	0	6^2	10	2	4	3	18.9	6.75	44	.345	.424	0	—	0	-3	-3	0	0.0
	Yr	1	0	1.000	27	0	0	0	0	28^1	37	5	11	10	15.2	6.35	49	.316	.375	0	.000	0	-11	-10	0	-0.4
Total	4	11	7	.611	114	1	0	0	5	195^1	189	21	54	124	11.3	3.69	101	.256	.309	0	.000	-3	-5	1	1	0.4
● JERRY DAVIE	Davie, Gerald Lee b: 2/10/33, Detroit, Mich. BR/TR, 6', 180 lbs. Deb: 4/14/59																									
1959	Det-A	2	2	.500	11	5	1	0	0	36^2	40	8	17	20	15.0	4.17	97	.265	.355	4	.400	2	-1	-0	1	0.2
● GEORGE DAVIES	Davies, George Washington b: 2/22/1868, Portage, Wis. d: 9/22/06, Waterloo, Wis. 180 lbs. Deb: 8/18/1891																									
1891	Mil-a	7	5	.583	12	12	12	1	0	102	94	2	35	61	11.6	2.65	166	.237	.303	9	.243	1	12	20	-1	1.9
1892	Cle-N	10	16	.385	26	26	23	0	0	215^2	201	4	69	95	11.5	2.59	131	.237	.299	12	.138	-5	17	19	3	1.7
1893	Cle-N	0	2	.000	3	3	1	0	0	15	28	1	10	3	22.8	11.40	43	.389	.463	2	.333	0	-11	-11	0	-0.9
	NY-N	1	1	.500	5	1	1	0	0	36^1	41	1	13	7	13.4	6.19	75	.275	.333	4	.333	2	-6	-6	0	0.0
	Yr	1	3	.250	8	4	2	0	0	51^1	69	2	23	10	16.1	7.71	61	.312	.377	6	.333	2	-17	-17	1	-0.9
Total	3	18	24	.429	46	42	37	1	0	369	364	8	127	166	12.2	3.32	116	.248	.312	27	.190	-3	12	22	2	2.7
● CHICK DAVIES	Davies, Lloyd Garrison b: 3/6/1892, Peabody, Mass. d: 9/5/73, Middletown, Conn. BL/TL, 5'8", 145 lbs. Deb: 7/11/14 ♦																									
1914	Phi-A	1	0	1.000	1	1	1	0	0	9	8	0	3	4	11.0	1.00	261	.258	.324	11	.239	0	2	2	0	0.3
1915	Phi-A	1	2	.333	4	2	0	0	0	15^1	20	0	12	2	19.4	8.80	33	.339	.458	24	.182	0	-10	-10	1	-1.5
1925	NY-N	0	0	—	2	1	0	0	0	7^1	13	0	4	5	20.9	6.14	66	.361	.425	0	.000	-0	-2	-2	0	0.0
1926	NY-N	2	4	.333	38	1	0	0	**6**	89	96	3	35	27	13.2	3.94	95	.277	.344	4	.222	1	-1	-2	1	0.0
Total	4	4	6	.400	45	5	1	0	6	120^2	137	3	54	38	14.3	4.48	80	.290	.364	39	.193	1	-11	-12	2	-1.2
● CHILI DAVIS	Davis, Charles Theodore b: 1/17/60, Kingston, Jamaica BB/TR, 6'3", 210 lbs. Deb: 4/10/81 ♦																									
1993	Cal-A	0	0	—	1	0	0	0	0	2	0	0	0	0	4.5	0.00	—	.000	.143	139	.243	0	1	1	-0	0.0
● CURT DAVIS	Davis, Curtis Benton "Coonskin" b: 9/7/03, Greenfield, Mo. d: 10/13/65, Covina, Cal. BR/TR, 6'2", 185 lbs. Deb: 4/21/34																									
1934	Phi-N	19	17	.528	**51**	31	18	3	5	274^1	283	14	60	99	11.5	2.95	160	.269	.313	20	.211	-2	34	54	9	**7.8**
1935	Phi-N	16	14	.533	44	27	19	3	2	231	264	14	47	74	12.4	3.66	124	.285	.324	13	.173	-1	9	22	2	2.8
1936	Phi-N	2	4	.333	10	8	3	0	0	60^1	71	6	19	18	13.6	4.62	98	.291	.345	4	.154	-1	-4	-1	0	-0.2
	Chi-N★	11	9	.550	24	20	10	0	1	153	146	11	31	52	10.5	3.00	133	.251	.290	8	.151	-2	17	17	3	2.1
	Yr	13	13	.500	34	28	13	0	1	213^1	217	17	50	70	11.3	3.46	120	.263	.306	12	.152	-3	13	16	3	1.9
1937	Chi-N	10	5	.667	28	14	8	0	1	123^2	138	7	30	32	12.6	4.08	98	.286	.334	12	.300	4	-2	-1	2	0.4
1938	StL-N	12	8	.600	40	21	8	2	3	173^1	187	9	27	36	11.2	3.63	109	.272	.301	13	.228	2	3	6	1	1.0
1939	StL-N☆	22	16	.579	49	31	13	3	7	248	279	18	48	70	12.0	3.63	113	.280	.315	40	.381	12	8	13	1	3.3
1940	StL-N	0	4	.000	14	7	0	0	1	54	73	4	19	12	15.5	5.17	77	.327	.383	0	.000	-2	-8	-7	1	-0.6
	Bro-N	8	7	.533	22	18	9	0	2	137	135	13	19	46	10.2	3.81	105	.256	.283	6	.128	-1	1	3	1	0.3
	Yr	8	11	.421	36	25	9	0	3	191	208	17	38	58	11.6	4.19	95	.277	.312	6	.091	-3	-7	-4	2	-0.3
1941	*Bro-N	13	7	.650	28	16	10	5	2	154^1	141	6	27	50	9.9	2.97	123	.244	.280	11	.186	2	11	12	4	2.1
1942	Bro-N	15	6	.714	32	26	13	5	2	206	179	10	51	60	10.4	2.36	138	.233	.287	12	.176	-0	22	21	3	2.5
1943	Bro-N	10	13	.435	31	21	8	2	3	164^1	182	8	39	47	12.2	3.78	89	.281	.324	9	.164	-1	-7	-8	2	-0.9
1944	Bro-N	10	11	.476	31	23	12	1	4	194	207	12	39	49	11.6	3.34	106	.270	.310	10	.159	-2	6	5	2	0.5
1945	Bro-N	10	10	.500	24	18	10	0	0	149^2	171	9	21	39	11.7	3.25	116	.280	.308	7	.137	-1	9	8	0	1.0
1946	Bro-N	0	0	—	1	0	0	0	0	2	3	1	2	0	27.0	13.50	25	.375	.545	0	—	0	-2	-2	0	0.0
Total	13	158	131	.547	429	281	141	24	33	2325	2459	142	479	684	11.6	3.42	116	.270	.310	165	.203	7	96	139	31	22.1
● DIXIE DAVIS	Davis, Frank Talmadge b: 10/12/1890, Wilsons Mills, N.C. d: 2/4/44, Raleigh, N.C. BR/TR, 5'11", 155 lbs. Deb: 7/12/12																									
1912	Cin-N	0	1	.000	7	0	0	0	0	26^2	25	0	16	12	14.2	2.70	124	.258	.368	2	.200	-0	2	2	-1	0.0
1915	Chi-A	0	0	—	2	0	0	0	0	3	2	0	2	2	15.0	0.00	—	.250	.455	0	—	0	1	1	0	0.0
1918	Phi-N	0	2	.000	17	2	1	0	0	47	43	1	30	18	14.0	3.06	98	.247	.358	0	.000	-0	-2	-0	-1	-0.2
1920	StL-A	18	12	.600	38	31	22	0	0	269^1	250	10	149	85	13.6	3.17	123	.256	.359	25	.266	3	19	22	-4	2.0
1921	StL-A	16	16	.500	40	36	20	2	0	265^1	279	12	123	100	14.0	4.44	101	.281	.366	20	.211	-3	-5	1	-1	-0.3
1922	StL-A	11	6	.647	25	25	7	2	0	174^1	162	10	87	65	13.3	4.08	102	**.250**	.345	8	.136	-3	-1	1	-0	-0.3
1923	StL-A	4	6	.400	19	17	5	1	0	109^1	106	4	63	36	14.3	3.62	115	.259	.365	10	.250	0	4	7	-2	0.3
1924	StL-A	11	13	.458	29	24	11	5	0	160^1	159	9	72	45	13.3	4.10	110	.263	.347	7	.152	-2	2	7	-1	0.7
1925	StL-A	12	7	.632	35	22	9	0	1	180^1	192	10	106	58	15.2	4.59	102	.279	.380	11	.172	-4	-4	2	1	-0.1
1926	StL-A	3	8	.273	27	7	2	0	1	83	93	7	40	39	14.5	4.66	92	.292	.372	4	.167	-0	-6	-3	-0	-0.5
Total	10	75	71	.514	239	164	77	10	2	1318^2	1311	63	688	460	14.0	3.97	107	.267	.362	87	.197	-10	12	39	-10	1.6
● GEORGE DAVIS	Davis, George Allen "Iron" b: 3/9/1890, Lancaster, N.Y. d: 6/4/61, Buffalo, N.Y. BB/TR, 5'10.5", 175 lbs. Deb: 7/16/12																									
1912	NY-A	1	4	.200	10	7	5	0	0	54	61	3	28	22	15.3	6.50	55	.293	.385	2	.111	-1	-19	-17	-2	-1.6
1913	Bos-N	0	0	—	2	0	0	0	0	8	7	1	5	3	13.5	4.50	73	.241	.353	0	.000	-0	-1	-1	-0	-0.1
1914	Bos-N	3	3	.500	9	6	4	1	0	55^2	42	1	26	26	11.5	3.40	81	.215	.317	3	.167	0	-4	-4	-2	-0.6
1915	Bos-N	3	3	.500	15	9	4	0	0	73^1	85	2	19	26	13.3	3.80	68	.304	.356	6	.261	1	-9	-10	0	-0.6
Total	4	7	10	.412	36	22	13	1	0	191	195	7	78	77	13.3	4.48	66	.274	.354	11	.180	-0	-33	-33	-3	-2.9
● STORM DAVIS	Davis, George Earl b: 12/26/61, Dallas, Tex. BR/TR, 6'4", 207 lbs. Deb: 4/29/82																									
1982	Bal-A	8	4	.667	29	8	1	0	0	100^2	96	8	28	67	11.1	3.49	116	.257	.308	0	—	0	7	6	-0	0.7
1983	*Bal-A	13	7	.650	34	29	6	1	0	200^1	180	14	64	125	11.1	3.59	110	.238	.299	0	—	0	10	8	-2	0.7
1984	Bal-A	14	9	.609	35	31	10	2	1	225	205	7	71	105	11.2	3.12	124	.247	.310	0	—	0	22	19	-3	1.7
1985	Bal-A	10	8	.556	31	28	8	1	0	175	172	11	70	93	12.5	4.53	89	.256	.327	0	—	0	-7	-10	-1	-0.7
1986	Bal-A	9	12	.429	25	25	2	0	0	154	166	16	49	96	12.6	3.62	114	.275	.330	0	—	0	9	9	2	1.3
1987	SD-N	2	7	.222	21	10	0	0	0	62^2	70	5	36	37	15.5	6.18	64	.280	.375	1	.063	-1	-15	-15	0	-2.0
	Oak-A	1	1	.500	5	5	0	0	0	30^1	28	3	11	28	11.6	3.26	126	.241	.307	0	—	0	4	3	-1	0.7
1988	*Oak-A	16	7	.696	33	33	1	0	0	201^2	211	16	91	127	13.5	3.70	102	.274	.352	0	—	0	6	2	-2	0.0
1989	*Oak-A	19	7	.731	31	31	1	0	0	169^1	187	19	68	91	13.7	4.36	84	.288	.358	0	—	0	-9	-13	-2	-1.7
1990	KC-A	7	10	.412	21	20	0	0	0	112	129	9	35	62	13.2	4.74	81	.281	.332	0	—	0	-10	-11	-1	-1.5
1991	KC-A	3	9	.250	51	9	1	1	2	114^1	140	11	46	53	14.7	4.96	83	.306	.370	0	—	0	-11	-11	-1	-1.2
1992	Bal-A	7	3	.700	48	2	0	0	4	89^1	79	5	36	53	11.8	3.43	117	.244	.323	0	—	0	5	6	1	0.7
1993	Oak-A	2	6	.250	19	8	0	0	0	62^2	68	5	33	37	14.8	6.18	66	.276	.367	0	—	0	-13	-15	0	-1.5
	Det-A	0	2	.000	24	0	0	0	4	35^1	25	4	15	36	10.4	3.06	140	.198	.289	0	—	0	5	5	-0	0.3
	Yr	2	8	.200	43	8	0	0	4	98	93	9	48	73	13.0	5.05	82	.247	.334	0	—	0	-8	-10	1	-1.2
1994	Det-A	2	4	.333	35	0	0	0	0	48	36	3	34	38	13.1	3.56	136	.207	.337	0	—	0	7	7	1	0.8
Total	13	113	96	.541	442	239	30	5	11	1780^2	1792	136	687	1048	12.6	4.02	99	.263	.332	1	.063	-1	10	-11	-8	-1.7
● GEORGE DAVIS	Davis, George Stacey b: 8/23/1870, Cohoes, N.Y. d: 10/17/40, Philadelphia, Pa. BB/TR, 5'9", 180 lbs. Deb: 4/19/1890 MH♦																									
1891	Cle-N	0	1	.000	3	0	0	0	1	4	8	0	3	4	24.8	15.75	22	.400	.478	165	.289	1	-6	-5	-0	-1.1
● JIM DAVIS	Davis, James Bennett b: 9/15/24, Red Bluff, Cal. d: 12/6/95, San Mateo, Cal. BB/TL, 6', 180 lbs. Deb: 4/18/54																									
1954	Chi-N	11	7	.611	46	12	2	0	4	127^2	114	12	51	58	11.8	3.52	119	.247	.326	2	.063	-1	8	10	1	1.3
1955	Chi-N	7	11	.389	42	16	0	0	3	133^2	122	16	58	62	12.3	4.44	92	.246	.327	1	.027	-4	-6	-5	-1	-1.1
1956	Chi-N	5	7	.417	46	11	2	1	2	120^1	116	11	59	66	13.5	3.66	103	.256	.349	5	.179	-0	1	1	1	0.2
1957	StL-N	0	1	.000	10	0	0	0	1	13^2	18	1	6	5	15.8	5.27	75	.340	.407	0	.000	-0	-2	-2	0	-0.2
	NY-N	1	0	1.000	10	0	0	0	0	11	13	2	5	6	14.7	6.55	60	.283	.353	1	1.000	0	-3	-3	0	-0.2

YEAR	TM/L	W	L	PCT	G	GS	CG	SH	SV	IP	H	HR	BB	SO	RAT	ERA	ERA+	OAV	OOB	BH	AVG	PB	PR	/A	PD	TPI
	Yr	1	1	.500	20	0	0	0	1	24^2	31	3	11	11	15.3	5.84	68	.310	.378	1	.500	0	-5	-5	0	-0.4
Total	4	24	26	.480	154	39	4	1	10	406^1	383	42	179	197	12.7	4.01	100	.253	.337	9	.091	-5	-2	0	1	-0.0
● **JOEL DAVIS**	Davis, Joel Clark b: 1/30/65, Jacksonville, Fla. BL/TR, 6′5″, 205 lbs. Deb: 8/11/85																									
1985	Chi-A	3	3	.500	12	11	1	0	0	71^1	71	6	26	37	12.4	4.16	104	.256	.322	0	—	0	-0	1	-2	-0.4
1986	Chi-A	4	5	.444	19	19	1	0	0	105^1	115	9	51	54	14.3	4.70	92	.280	.361	0	—	0	-6	-5	1	-0.5
1987	Chi-A	1	5	.167	13	9	1	0	0	55	56	7	29	25	13.9	5.73	80	.264	.353	0	—	0	-8	-7	-1	-0.9
1988	Chi-A	0	1	.000	5	2	0	0	0	16	21	4	5	10	14.6	6.75	59	.328	.377	0	—	0	-5	-5	-0	-0.3
Total	4	8	14	.364	49	41	3	0	0	247^2	263	26	111	126	13.7	4.91	89	.273	.349	0	—	0	-19	-15	-3	-2.1
● **DAISY DAVIS**	Davis, John Henry Albert b: 11/28/1858, Boston, Mass. d: 11/5/02, Lynn, Mass. TR , Deb: 5/6/1884																									
1884	StL-a	10	12	.455	25	24	20	1	0	198^1	196	1	35	143	11.1	2.90	112	.249	.293	15	.172	-2	8	8	-1	0.4
	Bos-N	1	3	.250	4	4	3	0	0	31	50	2	8	13	16.8	7.84	37	.355	.389	0	.000	-3	-17	-17	0	-1.6
1885	Bos-N	5	6	.455	11	11	10	1	0	94^1	110	2	28	30	13.2	4.29	63	.280	.328	7	.189	-0	-15	-17	-1	-1.7
Total	2	16	21	.432	40	39	33	2	0	323^2	356	5	71	186	12.3	3.78	81	.269	.313	22	.157	-5	-25	-26	-2	-2.9
● **JOHN DAVIS**	Davis, John Kirk b: 1/5/63, Chicago, Ill. BR/TR, 6′7″, 215 lbs. Deb: 7/24/87																									
1987	KC-A	5	2	.714	27	0	0	0	2	43^2	29	0	26	24	11.7	2.27	201	.195	.322	0	—	0	11	11	0	1.5
1988	Chi-A	2	5	.286	34	1	0	0	1	63^2	77	5	50	37	18.5	6.64	60	.297	.419	0	—	0	-19	-19	-0	-1.9
1989	Chi-A	0	1	.000	4	0	0	0	1	6	5	2	2	5	10.5	4.50	85	.217	.280	0	—	0	-0	-0	0	0.1
1990	SD-N	0	1	.000	6	0	0	0	0	9^1	9	1	4	7	12.5	5.79	66	.257	.333	0	.000	-0	-2	-2	-0	-0.2
Total	4	7	9	.438	71	1	0	0	4	122^2	120	8	82	73	15.3	4.92	85	.258	.375	0	.000	-0	-11	-10	0	-0.5
● **BUD DAVIS**	Davis, John Wilbur "Country" b: 12/7/1896, Merry Point, Va. d: 5/26/67, Williamsburg, Va. BL/TR, 6′, 207 lbs. Deb: 4/19/15																									
1915	Phi-A	0	2	.000	18	2	2	0	0	66^2	65	1	59	18	17.6	4.05	72	.273	.429	8	.308	2	-8	-8	-1	0.0
● **MARK DAVIS**	Davis, Mark William b: 10/19/60, Livermore, Cal. BL/TL, 6′4″, 205 lbs. Deb: 9/12/80																									
1980	Phi-N	0	0	—	2	1	0	0	0	7	4	0	5	5	11.6	2.57	147	.160	.300	1	.500	0	1	1	-0	0.0
1981	Phi-N	1	4	.200	9	9	0	0	0	43	49	7	24	29	15.3	7.74	47	.299	.388	1	.091	-0	-20	-20	-0	-2.0
1983	SF-N	6	4	.600	20	20	2	2	0	111	93	14	50	83	11.8	3.49	101	.227	.315	4	.133	0	2	1	-1	0.0
1984	SF-N	5	17	.227	46	27	1	0	0	174^2	201	25	54	124	13.4	5.36	65	.293	.349	6	.130	0	-34	-36	-2	-4.2
1985	SF-N	5	12	.294	77	1	0	0	7	114^1	89	13	41	131	10.5	3.54	97	.219	.295	3	.250	1	1	-1	-1	-0.2
1986	SF-N	5	7	.417	67	2	0	0	4	84^1	63	6	34	90	10.5	2.99	118	.212	.295	1	.125	0	7	5	-0	0.7
1987	SF-N	4	5	.444	20	11	1	0	0	70^2	72	9	28	51	13.2	4.71	82	.273	.351	5	.217	2	-5	-7	-1	-0.7
	SD-N	5	3	.625	43	0	0	0	2	62^1	51	5	31	47	12.1	3.18	124	.224	.322	2	.286	0	6	5	0	0.7
	Yr	9	8	.529	63	11	1	0	2	133	123	14	59	98	12.5	3.99	98	.247	.329	7	.233	2	1	-1	-0	0.0
1988	SD-N★	5	10	.333	62	0	0	0	28	98^1	70	2	42	102	10.3	2.01	169	.199	.284	2	.200	1	16	15	2	3.6
1989	SD-N★	4	3	.571	70	0	0	0	**44**	92^2	66	6	31	92	9.6	1.85	189	.200	.273	0	.000	-1	17	17	-1	2.6
1990	KC-A	2	7	.222	53	3	0	0	6	68^2	71	9	52	73	16.6	5.11	75	.259	.385	0	—	0	-9	-10	-1	-1.3
1991	KC-A	6	3	.667	29	5	0	0	1	62^2	55	6	39	47	13.6	4.45	93	.240	.353	0	—	0	-2	-2	-0	-0.3
1992	KC-A	1	3	.250	13	6	0	0	0	36^1	42	6	28	19	17.3	7.18	56	.294	.409	0	—	0	-13	-13	0	-1.3
	Atl-N	1	0	1.000	14	0	0	0	0	16^2	22	3	13	15	19.4	7.02	52	.314	.429	0	.000	-0	-7	-6	-1	-0.4
1993	Phi-N	1	2	.333	25	0	0	0	0	31^1	35	4	24	28	17.2	5.17	77	.273	.392	1	.333	0	-4	-4	-0	-0.4
	SD-N	0	3	.000	35	0	0	0	4	38^1	44	6	20	42	15.0	3.52	117	.295	.379	0	.000	-0	2	3	0	0.2
	Yr	1	5	.167	60	0	0	0	4	69^2	79	10	44	70	15.9	4.26	95	.284	.382	1	.250	0	-2	-2	-0	-0.2
1994	SD-N	0	1	.000	20	0	0	0	0	16^1	20	4	13	15	18.2	8.82	47	.299	.412	0	—	0	-8	-9	0	-0.4
1997	Mil-A	0	0	—	19	0	0	0	0	16^1	21	4	5	14	14.9	5.51	84	.323	.380	0	—	0	-2	-2	1	0.1
Total	15	51	84	.378	624	85	4	2	96	1145	1068	129	534	1007	12.8	4.17	88	.249	.336	26	.156	5	-54	-62	-4	-3.3
● **BOB DAVIS**	Davis, Robert Edward b: 9/11/33, New York, N.Y. BR/TR, 6′, 170 lbs. Deb: 7/26/58																									
1958	KC-A	0	4	.000	8	4	0	0	0	31	45	5	12	22	17.1	7.84	50	.346	.410	1	.167	-0	-14	-14	0	-1.5
1960	KC-A	0	0	—	21	0	0	0	1	32	31	1	22	28	15.2	3.66	109	.263	.383	1	.250	0	1	1	1	0.1
Total	2	0	4	.000	29	4	0	0	1	63	76	6	34	50	16.1	5.71	69	.306	.396	2	.200	-0	-13	-12	2	-1.4
● **RON DAVIS**	Davis, Ronald Gene b: 8/6/55, Houston, Tex. BR/TR, 6′4″, 207 lbs. Deb: 7/29/78																									
1978	NY-A	0	0	—	4	0	0	0	0	2^1	3	0	3	0	23.1	11.57	31	.333	.500	0	—	0	-2	-2	0	0.1
1979	NY-A	14	2	.875	44	0	0	0	9	85^1	84	5	28	43	11.9	2.85	143	.262	.323	0	.000	-0	13	12	1	2.3
1980	*NY-A	9	3	.750	53	0	0	0	7	131	121	9	32	65	10.9	2.95	133	.246	.299	0	.000	-0	16	14	0	1.4
1981	*NY-A★	4	5	.444	43	0	0	0	6	73	47	6	25	83	8.9	2.71	132	.186	.259	0	—	0	8	7	-1	0.9
1982	Min-A	3	9	.250	63	0	0	0	22	106	106	16	47	89	13.1	4.42	96	.261	.339	0	—	0	-4	-2	-0	-0.3
1983	Min-A	5	8	.385	66	0	0	0	30	89	89	6	33	84	12.6	3.34	127	.266	.338	0	—	0	7	9	-2	1.4
1984	Min-A	7	11	.389	64	0	0	0	29	83	79	11	41	74	13.2	4.55	92	.253	.344	0	—	0	-5	-3	-0	-1.1
1985	Min-A	2	6	.250	57	0	0	0	25	64^2	55	7	35	72	13.1	3.48	127	.230	.338	0	—	0	5	7	-0	0.8
1986	Min-A	2	6	.250	36	0	0	0	2	38^2	55	7	29	30	20.5	9.08	47	.340	.451	0	—	0	-21	-21	0	-3.8
	Chi-N	0	2	.000	17	0	0	0	0	20	31	3	3	10	15.3	7.65	53	.356	.378	0	.000	-0	-9	-8	-1	-0.8
1987	Chi-N	0	0	—	21	0	0	0	0	32^1	43	8	12	31	15.3	5.85	73	.328	.385	0	—	0	-6	-6	-1	-0.1
	LA-N	0	0	—	4	0	0	0	0	4	7	0	6	1	31.5	6.75	59	.412	.583	0	—	0	-1	-1	0	0.0
	Yr	0	0	—	25	0	0	0	0	36^1	50	8	18	32	17.1	5.94	71	.336	.411	0	—	0	-8	-7	-0	-0.1
1988	SF-N	1	1	.500	9	0	0	0	0	17^1	15	4	6	15	11.4	4.67	70	.234	.310	0	.000	-0	-2	-3	0	-0.3
Total	11	47	53	.470	481	0	0	0	130	746^2	735	82	300	597	12.7	4.05	101	.260	.336	0	.000	-1	-3	3	-3	0.5
● **PEACHES DAVIS**	Davis, Roy Thomas b: 5/31/05, Glen Rose, Tex. d: 4/28/95, Duncan, Okla. BL/TR, 6′3.5″, 190 lbs. Deb: 7/11/36																									
1936	Cin-N	8	8	.500	26	15	5	0	5	125^2	139	7	36	32	12.7	3.58	107	.280	.331	7	.163	-1	6	3	0	0.3
1937	Cin-N	11	13	.458	42	24	11	1	3	218	252	5	51	59	12.6	3.59	104	.295	.337	10	.128	-4	8	3	-3	-0.3
1938	Cin-N	7	12	.368	29	19	11	1	1	167^2	193	9	40	28	12.6	3.97	92	.290	.331	15	.246	1	-3	-6	-3	-0.8
1939	Cin-N	1	0	1.000	20	0	0	0	2	30^2	43	5	11	4	16.1	6.46	59	.341	.399	1	.333	0	-9	-9	0	-0.3
Total	4	27	33	.450	117	58	27	2	11	542	627	26	138	123	12.8	3.87	96	.293	.337	33	.178	-4	2	-8	-6	-1.1
● **STEVE DAVIS**	Davis, Steven Kennon b: 8/4/60, San Antonio, Tex. BL/TL, 6′1″, 195 lbs. Deb: 8/25/85																									
1985	Tor-A	2	1	.667	10	5	0	0	0	28	23	5	13	22	11.6	3.54	119	.223	.310	0	—	0	2	2	-0	0.0
1986	Tor-A	0	0	—	3	0	0	0	0	3^2	8	2	5	5	31.9	17.18	25	.471	.591	0	—	0	-5	-5	-0	-0.2
1989	Cle-A	1	1	.500	12	2	0	0	0	25^2	34	2	14	12	16.8	8.06	49	.318	.397	0	—	0	-12	-12	-0	-0.9
Total	3	3	2	.600	25	7	0	0	0	57^1	65	9	32	39	15.2	6.44	64	.286	.375	0	—	0	-15	-15	-1	-1.1
● **TIM DAVIS**	Davis, Timothy Howard b: 7/14/70, Marianna, Fla. BL/TL, 5′11″, 165 lbs. Deb: 4/4/94																									
1994	Sea-A	2	2	.500	42	1	0	0	2	49^1	57	4	25	28	15.1	4.01	122	.295	.379	0	—	0	4	5	0	0.4
1995	Sea-A	2	1	.667	5	5	0	0	0	24	30	2	18	19	18.0	6.38	74	.306	.414	0	—	0	-4	-4	1	-0.4
1996	Sca-A	2	2	.500	40	0	0	0	0	42^2	43	4	17	34	13.1	4.01	123	.259	.335	0	—	0	5	4	-0	0.3
1997	Sea-A	0	0	—	2	0	0	0	0	6^2	6	1	4	10	14.9	6.75	67	.231	.355	0	—	0	-2	-2	0	0.1
Total	4	6	5	.545	89	6	0	0	2	122^2	136	11	64	91	15.0	4.62	105	.282	.370	0	—	0	3	3	1	0.4
● **WILEY DAVIS**	Davis, Wiley Anderson b: 8/1/1875, Seymour, Tenn. d: 9/22/42, Detroit, Mich. BR/TR, 5′10″, 165 lbs. Deb: 4/18/1896																									
1896	Cin-N	1	1	.500	2	0	0	0	0	4^1	8	0	2	1	20.8	8.31	55	.400	.455	0	.000	0	-2	-2	1	-0.5
● **WOODY DAVIS**	Davis, Woodrow Wilson "Babe" b: 4/25/13, Nicholls, Ga. BL/TR, 6′1″, 200 lbs. Deb: 5/2/38																									
1938	Det-A	0	0	—	2	0	0	0	0	6	3	0	4	1	10.5	1.50	333	.158	.304	0	.000	-0	2	2	-0	0.0
● **MIKE DAVISON**	Davison, Michael Lynn b: 8/4/45, Galesburg, Ill. BL/TL, 6′1″, 170 lbs. Deb: 10/1/69																									
1969	SF-N	0	0	—	1	0	0	0	0	2	2	0	0	2	9.0	4.50	78	.250	.250	0	—	0	-0	-0	-0	0.0
1970	SF-N	3	5	.375	31	0	0	0	1	36	46	4	22	21	17.0	6.50	61	.324	.415	0	.000	0	-10	-10	1	-1.9
Total	2	3	5	.375	32	0	0	0	1	38	48	4	22	23	16.6	6.39	62	.320	.407	0	.000	0	-10	-10	1	-1.9

YEAR	TM/L	W	L	PCT	G	GS	CG	SH	SV	IP	H	HR	BB	SO	RAT	ERA	ERA+	OAV	OOB	BH	AVG	PB	PR	/A	PD	TPI
● SCOTT DAVISON	Davison, Scotty Ray b: 10/16/70, Inglewood, Cal. BR/TR, 6′, 190 lbs. Deb: 9/4/95																									
1995	Sea-A	0	0	—	3	0	0	0	0	4^1	7	1	1	3	16.6	6.23	76	.350	.381	0	—	0	-1	-1	0	0.0
1996	Sea-A	0	0	—	5	0	0	0	0	9	11	6	3	9	14.0	9.00	55	.297	.350	0	—	0	-4	-4	0	0.0
Total	2	0	0	—	8	0	0	0	0	13^1	18	7	4	12	14.9	8.10	60	.316	.361	0	—	0	-5	-5	0	0.0
● BILL DAWLEY	Dawley, William Chester b: 2/6/58, Norwich, Conn. BR/TR, 6′4″, 240 lbs. Deb: 4/15/83																									
1983	Hou-N★	6	6	.500	48	0	0	0	14	79^2	51	9	22	60	8.4	2.82	120	.185	.247	2	.222	0	7	5	-1	0.8
1984	Hou-N	11	4	.733	60	0	0	0	5	98	82	5	35	47	10.7	1.93	172	.234	.303	3	.333	2	18	15	-1	2.5
1985	Hou-N	5	3	.625	49	0	0	0	2	81	76	7	37	48	12.6	3.56	97	.259	.341	2	.200	0	0	-1	0	0.0
1986	Chi-A	0	7	.000	46	0	0	0	2	97^2	91	10	28	66	11.1	3.32	130	.247	.302	0	.000	-0	9	11	-1	0.6
1987	StL-N	5	8	.385	60	0	0	0	2	96^2	93	15	38	65	12.3	4.47	93	.259	.332	2	.167	0	-4	-3	1	-0.3
1988	Phi-N	0	2	.000	8	0	0	0	0	8^2	16	3	4	3	20.8	13.50	26	.381	.435	0	—	0	-10	-10	-0	-1.9
1989	Oak-A	0	0	—	4	0	0	0	0	9	11	0	2	3	14.0	4.00	92	.297	.350	0	—	0	-0	-0	-0	0.0
Total	7	27	30	.474	275	0	0	0	25	470^2	420	49	166	292	11.3	3.42	109	.243	.311	9	.214	3	21	16	-2	1.7
● JOE DAWSON	Dawson, Ralph Fenton b: 3/9/1897, Bow, Wash. d: 1/4/78, Longview, Tex. BR/TR, 5′11″, 182 lbs. Deb: 7/4/24																									
1924	Cle-A	1	2	.333	4	4	0	0	0	20^1	24	0	21	7	20.4	6.64	64	.300	.451	2	.286	0	-5	-5	1	-0.6
1927	*Pit-N	3	7	.300	20	7	4	0	0	80^2	80	2	32	17	12.5	4.46	92	.268	.338	5	.200	-1	-5	-3	-1	-0.5
1928	Pit-N	7	7	.500	31	7	1	0	3	128^2	116	6	56	36	12.1	3.29	124	.242	.322	12	.279	3	10	11	-3	1.2
1929	Pit-N	0	1	.000	4	0	0	0	0	8^2	13	2	3	2	16.6	8.31	57	.342	.390	1	.500	1	-3	-3	-0	-0.3
Total	4	11	17	.393	59	18	5	0	3	238^1	233	10	112	62	13.1	4.15	99	.260	.343	20	.260	3	-4	-1	-3	-0.2
● REX DAWSON	Dawson, Rexford Paul b: 2/10/1889, Skagit Co., Wash. d: 10/20/58, Indianapolis, Ind. BL/TR, 6′, 185 lbs. Deb: 10/3/13																									
1913	Was-A	0	0	—	1	0	0	0	0	1	1	0	0	1	9.0	0.00	—	.250	.250	0	—	0	0	0	-0	0.0
● PEA RIDGE DAY	Day, Clyde Henry b: 8/26/1899, Pea Ridge, Ark. d: 3/21/34, Kansas City, Mo. BR/TR, 6′, 190 lbs. Deb: 9/19/24																									
1924	StL-N	1	1	.500	3	3	1	0	0	17^2	22	0	6	3	14.3	4.58	82	.306	.359	1	.125	-1	-1	-2	-0	-0.3
1925	StL-N	2	4	.333	17	4	1	0	1	40	53	5	7	13	14.2	6.30	69	.325	.364	2	.154	-1	-9	-9	-1	-1.3
1926	Cin-N	0	0	—	4	0	0	0	0	7^1	13	1	2	2	18.4	7.36	50	.406	.441	0	.000	-0	-3	-3	-0	-0.1
1931	Bro-N	2	2	.500	22	2	1	0	1	57^1	75	5	13	30	13.8	4.55	84	.315	.351	4	.222	0	-4	-5	-1	-0.4
Total	4	5	7	.417	46	9	3	0	2	122^1	163	11	28	48	14.3	5.30	75	.323	.362	7	.171	-2	-18	-18	-2	-2.1
● BILL DAY	Day, William M. b: 7/28/1867, Wilmington, Del. d: 8/16/23, Wilmington, Del. TR , 5′8″, 150 lbs. Deb: 8/20/1889																									
1889	Phi-N	0	3	.000	4	3	2	0	0	19	16	0	23	20	18.5	5.21	83	.222	.411	0	.000	-2	-3	-2	-0	-0.4
1890	Phi-N	1	1	.500	4	2	2	0	0	23^2	26	0	12	9	14.5	3.04	120	.271	.352	1	.100	-1	1	2	-1	-0.1
	Pit-N	0	6	.000	6	6	6	0	0	50	66	1	24	10	16.4	5.22	63	.308	.381	1	.043	-4	-9	-11	1	-1.1
	Yr	1	7	.125	10	8	8	0	0	73^2	92	1	36	19	15.8	4.52	75	.297	.372	2	.061	-5	-8	-9	1	-1.2
Total	2	1	10	.091	14	11	10	0	0	92^2	108	1	59	39	16.3	4.66	77	.283	.380	2	.047	-6	-10	-11	0	-1.6
● KEN DAYLEY	Dayley, Kenneth Grant b: 2/25/59, Jerome, Idaho BL/TL, 6′, 175 lbs. Deb: 5/13/82																									
1982	Atl-N	5	6	.455	20	11	0	0	0	71^1	79	9	25	34	13.1	4.54	82	.286	.346	5	.250	1	-7	-6	-2	-1.0
1983	Atl-N	5	8	.385	24	16	0	0	0	104^2	100	12	39	70	12.1	4.30	90	.257	.328	7	.219	1	-8	-5	-2	-0.7
1984	Atl-N	0	3	.000	4	4	0	0	0	18^2	28	5	6	10	16.9	5.30	73	.341	.393	2	.500	1	-4	-3	0	-0.4
	StL-N	0	2	.000	3	2	0	0	0	5	16	1	5	0	37.8	18.00	19	.615	.677	0	—	0	-8	-8	-0	-2.1
	Yr	0	5	.000	7	6	0	0	0	23^2	44	6	11	10	20.9	7.99	47	.404	.458	2	.500	1	-12	-11	0	-2.5
1985	*StL-N	4	4	.500	57	0	0	0	11	65^1	65	2	18	62	11.4	2.76	128	.263	.313	2	.400	1	6	6	2	1.1
1986	StL-N	0	3	.000	31	0	0	0	5	38^2	42	1	11	33	12.6	3.26	112	.275	.327	1	.200	0	2	2	0	0.2
1987	*StL-N	9	5	.643	53	0	0	0	4	61	52	2	33	63	12.8	2.66	156	.234	.339	0	—	0	10	10	-1	2.2
1988	StL-N	2	7	.222	54	0	0	0	5	55^1	48	2	19	38	11.1	2.77	126	.239	.308	0	.000	-0	4	4	-0	0.7
1989	StL-N	4	3	.571	71	0	0	0	12	75^1	63	3	30	40	11.1	2.87	127	.228	.304	0	.000	-1	5	6	-2	0.5
1990	StL-N	4	4	.500	58	0	0	0	2	73^1	63	5	30	51	11.4	3.56	107	.233	.310	0	.000	-1	2	2	-0	0.1
1991	Tor-A	0	0	—	8	0	0	0	0	4^1	7	0	5	3	27.0	6.23	67	.368	.520	0	—	0	-1	-1	0	0.0
1993	Tor-A	0	0	—	2	0	0	0	0	0^2	1	0	4	2	67.5	0.00	—	.333	.714	0	—	0	0	0	0	0.0
Total	11	33	45	.423	385	33	0	0	39	573^2	564	42	225	406	12.5	3.64	103	.261	.332	17	.210	3	1	7	-5	0.6
● REN DEAGLE	Deagle, Lorenzo Burroughs b: 6/26/1858, New York, N.Y. d: 12/24/36, Kansas City, Mo. BR/TR, 5′9″, 190 lbs. Deb: 5/17/1883																									
1883	Cin-a	10	8	.556	18	18	17	1	0	148	136	0	34	48	10.3	2.31	141	.229	.270	9	.129	-5	16	15	-1	0.9
1884	Cin-a	3	1	.750	4	4	4	1	0	34	39	0	9	12	13.0	5.03	66	.322	.374	0	.000	-2	-7	-6	-0	-0.7
	Lou-a	4	6	.400	12	12	8	0	0	87^1	80	0	13	23	10.3	2.58	120	.238	.281	6	.133	-3	7	5	1	0.3
	Yr	7	7	.500	16	16	12	1	0	121^1	119	0	22	35	11.0	3.26	97	.260	.304	6	.103	-5	-0	-1	1	-0.4
Total	2	17	15	.531	34	34	29	2	0	269^1	255	0	56	83	10.7	2.74	117	.242	.286	15	.117	-9	16	14	-1	0.5
● COT DEAL	Deal, Ellis Fergason b: 1/23/23, Arapaho, Okla. BB/TR, 5′10.5″, 185 lbs. Deb: 9/11/47 C																									
1947	Bos-A	0	1	.000	5	2	0	0	0	12^2	20	0	7	6	19.2	9.24	42	.364	.435	2	.500	1	-8	-8	0	-0.5
1948	Bos-A	1	0	1.000	4	0	0	0	0	4	3	0	3	2	13.5	0.00	—	.200	.333	0	—	0	2	2	0	0.5
1950	StL-N	0	0	—	3	0	0	0	0	1	3	0	2	1	45.0	18.00	24	.500	.625	0	—	0	-2	-2	-0	0.0
1954	StL-N	2	3	.400	33	0	0	0	1	71^2	85	14	36	25	15.7	6.28	65	.297	.383	2	.100	0	-18	-17	-0	-1.1
Total	4	3	4	.429	45	2	0	0	1	89^1	111	14	48	34	16.4	6.55	63	.307	.394	4	.167	1	-25	-24	-0	-1.1
● CHUBBY DEAN	Dean, Alfred Lovill b: 8/24/16, Mt.Airy, N.C. d: 12/21/70, Riverside, Cal. BL/TL, 5′11″, 181 lbs. Deb: 4/14/36 ♦																									
1937	Phi-A	1	0	1.000	2	1	0	0	0	9	7	0	6	4	13.0	4.00	118	.219	.342	81	.262	0	1	1	0	0.1
1938	Phi-A	2	1	.667	6	1	0	0	0	23	22	3	15	3	14.5	3.52	137	.250	.359	6	.300	2	3	3	1	0.6
1939	Phi-A	5	8	.385	54	1	0	0	7	116^2	132	8	80	39	16.4	5.25	90	.289	.395	27	.351	8	-8	-7	1	0.2
1940	Phi-A	6	13	.316	30	19	8	1	1	159^1	220	21	63	38	16.0	6.61	67	.324	.381	26	.289	4	-39	-38	1	-2.9
1941	Phi-A	2	4	.333	18	7	2	0	0	75^2	90	9	35	22	14.9	6.19	68	.294	.367	9	.243	2	-17	-17	0	-0.9
	Cle-A	1	4	.200	8	8	2	0	0	53^1	57	3	24	14	13.7	4.39	90	.282	.358	4	.160	0	-1	-3	1	-0.1
	Yr	3	8	.273	26	15	4	0	0	129	147	12	59	36	14.4	5.44	75	.289	.363	13	.210	2	-19	-19	1	-1.0
1942	Cle-A	8	11	.421	27	22	8	0	1	172^2	170	7	66	46	12.3	3.81	91	.261	.329	27	.267	8	-3	-7	-3	-0.2
1943	Cle-A	5	5	.500	17	9	3	0	0	76	83	1	34	29	14.0	4.50	69	.281	.358	9	.196	1	-10	-12	-1	-1.4
Total	7	30	46	.395	162	68	23	1	9	685^2	781	52	323	195	14.5	5.08	79	.288	.364	287	.274	25	-75	-80	-1	-4.6
● DORY DEAN	Dean, Charles Wilson b: 11/6/1852, Cincinnati, Ohio d: 5/4/35, Nashville, Tenn. BR/TR, Deb: 6/22/1876																									
1876	Cin-N	4	26	.133	30	30	26	0	0	262^2	397	1	24	22	14.4	3.73	59	.322	.335	36	.261	1	-42	-45	-1	-3.7
● HARRY DEAN	Dean, James Harry b: 5/12/15, Rockmart, Ga. d: 6/1/60, Rockmart, Ga. BR/TR, 6′4″, 185 lbs. Deb: 4/16/41																									
1941	Was-A	0	0	—	2	0	0	0	0	2	2	0	3	0	27.0	4.50	90	.250	.500	0	—	0	-0	-0	-0	0.0
● DIZZY DEAN	Dean, Jay Hanna b: 1/16/10, Lucas, Ark. d: 7/17/74, Reno, Nevada BR/TR, 6′2″, 182 lbs. Deb: 9/28/30 FCH																									
1930	StL-N	1	0	1.000	1	1	1	0	0	9	3	0	3	5	6.0	1.00	502	.103	.188	1	.333	0	4	4	1	0.5
1932	StL-N	18	15	.545	46	33	16	**4**	2	**286**	280	14	102	**191**	12.2	3.30	119	.260	.327	25	.258	5	18	20	-1	2.5
1933	StL-N	20	18	.526	**48**	34	**26**	3	4	293	279	11	64	**199**	10.7	3.04	114	.250	.293	19	.181	1	10	14	-5	1.4
1934	*StL-N★	**30**	7	**.811**	50	33	24	**7**	7	311^2	288	14	75	**195**	10.7	2.66	159	.241	.289	29	.246	4	49	54	-2	6.4
1935	StL-N★	**28**	12	.700	50	36	**29**	3	5	**325^1**	324	16	77	**190**	11.2	3.04	135	.256	.300	30	.234	4	35	38	-5	4.3
1936	StL-N★	24	13	.649	**51**	34	**28**	2	**11**	**315**	310	21	53	195	10.5	3.17	124	.253	.285	27	.223	1	30	27	-4	2.8
1937	StL-N★	13	10	.565	27	25	17	4	1	197^1	200	9	33	120	10.7	2.69	148	.259	.291	15	.227	2	27	28	-3	3.0
1938	*Chi-N	7	1	.875	13	10	3	1	0	74^2	63	2	8	22	8.7	1.81	212	.226	.250	5	.192	-0	16	17	-1	1.6
1939	Chi-N	6	4	.600	19	13	7	2	0	96^1	98	4	17	27	10.8	3.36	117	.261	.294	5	.147	-1	6	6	-1	0.4
1940	Chi-N	3	3	.500	10	9	3	0	0	54	68	4	20	18	14.7	5.17	73	.306	.364	4	.222	0	-8	-9	1	-0.7
1941	Chi-N	0	0	—	1	1	0	0	0	1	3	0	0	1	27.0	18.00	19	.429	.429	0	—	0	-2	-2	0	0.0
1947	StL-A	0	0	—	1	1	0	0	0	4	3	0	1	0	9.0	0.00	—	.231	.286	1	1.000	0	2	2	-0	0.0
Total	12	150	83	.644	317	230	154	26	30	1967^1	1919	95	453	1163	11.0	3.02	130	.253	.298	161	.225	15	187	201	-20	22.2

YEAR	TM/L	W	L	PCT	G	GS	CG	SH	SV	IP	H	HR	BB	SO	RAT	ERA	ERA+	OAV	OOB	BH	AVG	PB	PR	/A	PD	TPI
● **PAUL DEAN** Dean, Paul Dee "Daffy" b: 8/14/13, Lucas, Ark. d: 3/17/81, Springdale, Ark. BR/TR, 6', 175 lbs. Deb: 4/18/34 F																										
1934	*StL-N	19	11	.633	39	26	16	5	2	233^{1}	225	19	52	150	10.9	3.43	123	.248	.292	20	.241	1	16	21	-6	1.9
1935	StL-N	19	12	.613	46	33	19	2	5	269^{2}	261	16	55	143	10.8	3.37	122	.249	.292	12	.133	-5	19	22	-6	1.2
1936	StL-N	5	5	.500	17	14	5	0	1	92	113	3	20	28	13.1	4.60	86	.300	.337	2	.059	-4	-6	-7	-3	-1.3
1937	StL-N	0	0	—	1	0	0	0	0	0	1	0	2	0	—	∞	—	1.000	1.000	0	—	0	-3	-3	0	-0.3
1938	StL-N	3	1	.750	5	4	2	1	0	31	37	3	5	14	12.2	2.61	151	.298	.326	2	.182	-0	4	5	-1	0.5
1939	StL-N	0	1	.000	16	2	0	0	0	43	54	4	10	16	13.6	6.07	68	.310	.351	1	.111	-1	-10	-9	-0	-0.3
1940	NY-N	4	4	.500	27	7	2	0	0	99^{1}	110	8	29	32	12.6	3.90	100	.281	.330	3	.115	-2	-1	-0	-1	-0.3
1941	NY-N	0	0	—	5	0	0	0	0	5^{2}	8	0	3	3	17.5	3.18	116	.320	.393	0	—	0	0	0	-0	0.0
1943	StL-A	0	0	—	3	1	0	0	0	13^{1}	16	0	3	1	13.5	3.38	99	.296	.345	0	.000	-0	-0	-0	-0	-0.1
Total	9	50	34	.595	159	87	44	8	8	787^{1}	825	53	179	387	11.7	3.75	109	.266	.309	40	.156	-10	20	28	-18	1.3
● **WAYLAND DEAN** Dean, Wayland Ogden b: 6/20/02, Richwood, W.Va. d: 4/10/30, Huntington, W.Va. BB/TR, 6'1", 178 lbs. Deb: 4/17/24																										
1924	*NY-N	6	12	.333	26	20	6	0	0	125^{2}	139	9	45	39	13.5	5.01	73	.280	.346	8	.200	1	-16	-19	3	-2.0
1925	NY-N	10	7	.588	33	14	6	1	1	151^{1}	169	13	50	53	13.3	4.64	87	.282	.342	12	.235	3	-6	-10	0	-0.7
1926	Phi-N	8	16	.333	33	26	15	1	0	203^{2}	245	9	89	52	14.9	4.91	84	.307	.379	27	.265	5	-24	-17	-1	-1.4
1927	Phi-N	0	1	.000	2	0	0	0	0	3	6	0	2	1	24.0	12.00	34	.500	.571	2	.667	1	-3	-3	0	-0.5
	Chi-N	0	0	—	2	0	0	0	0	2	0	0	2	2	13.5	0.00	—	.000	.429	0	—	0	1	1	0	0.0
	Yr	0	1	.000	4	0	0	0	0	5	6	0	4	3	19.8	7.20	56	.375	.524	2	.667	1	-2	-2	0	-0.5
Total	4	24	36	.400	96	60	27	2	1	485^{2}	559	31	188	147	14.1	4.87	82	.293	.360	49	.250	10	-48	-47	2	-4.6
● **DENNIS DeBARR** DeBarr, Dennis Lee b: 1/16/53, Cheyenne, Wyo. BL/TL, 6'2", 190 lbs. Deb: 5/14/77																										
1977	Tor-A	0	1	.000	14	0	0	0	0	21^{1}	29	1	8	10	15.6	5.91	71	.337	.394	0	—	0	-4	-4	-0	-0.2
● **JOE DeBERRY** DeBerry, Joseph Gaddy b: 11/29/1896, Mt.Gilead, N.C. d: 10/9/44, Southern Pines, N.C BL/TR, 6'1", 175 lbs. Deb: 8/24/20																										
1920	StL-A	2	4	.333	10	7	3	1	0	54^{2}	65	2	20	12	14.3	4.94	79	.307	.372	3	.167	-1	-7	-6	0	-0.6
1921	StL-A	0	1	.000	10	1	0	0	0	12^{1}	15	0	10	1	18.2	6.57	68	.300	.417	0	.000	-0	-3	-3	0	-0.2
Total	2	2	5	.286	20	8	3	1	0	67	80	2	30	13	15.0	5.24	77	.305	.381	3	.150	-1	-10	-9	0	-0.8
● **DAVE DeBUSSCHERE** DeBusschere, David Albert b: 10/16/40, Detroit, Mich. BR/TR, 6'6", 225 lbs. Deb: 4/22/62																										
1962	Chi-A	0	0	—	12	0	0	0	0	18	5	1	23	8	14.5	2.00	195	.089	.363	0	—	0	4	4	0	0.0
1963	Chi-A	3	4	.429	24	10	1	1	0	84^{1}	80	9	34	53	12.6	3.09	113	.249	.329	1	.045	-2	5	4	0	0.2
Total	2	3	4	.429	36	10	1	1	0	102^{1}	85	10	57	61	12.9	2.90	123	.225	.335	1	.045	-2	9	8	0	0.2
● **ART DECATUR** Decatur, Arthur Rue b: 1/14/1894, Cleveland, Ohio d: 4/25/66, Talladega, Ala. BR/TR, 6'1", 190 lbs. Deb: 4/15/22																										
1922	Bro-N	3	4	.429	29	3	1	0	1	87^{2}	87	3	29	31	12.0	2.77	147	.265	.327	2	.080	-2	13	13	-2	0.6
1923	Bro-N	3	3	.500	36	5	2	0	3	97^{2}	101	3	32	25	12.4	2.58	150	.264	.325	0	.000	-3	**15**	**14**	-2	0.4
1924	Bro-N	10	9	.526	31	10	3	0	1	126^{1}	156	12	27	38	13.3	4.13	91	.308	.348	5	.114	-4	-4	-5	-2	-1.3
1925	Bro-N	0	0	—	1	0	0	0	0	1	3	0	0	0	27.0	18.00	23	.600	.600	0	—	0	-2	-2	-0	0.0
	Phi-N	4	13	.235	25	15	4	0	2	128	170	13	35	31	14.6	5.27	91	.316	.360	2	.049	-5	-14	-7	-2	-1.4
	Yr	4	13	.235	26	15	4	0	2	129	173	13	35	31	14.7	5.37	89	.319	.362	2	.049	-5	-16	-9	-2	-1.4
1926	Phi-N	0	0	—	2	1	0	0	0	3	6	0	2	0	24.0	6.00	69	.375	.444	0	.000	-0	-1	-1	-0	0.0
1927	Phi-N	3	5	.375	29	3	0	0	0	94^{2}	130	11	20	27	14.6	7.42	56	.334	.373	6	.222	0	-37	-35	-2	-2.7
Total	6	23	34	.404	153	37	10	0	7	538^{1}	653	42	145	152	13.6	4.51	92	.302	.349	15	.094	-14	-29	-23	-10	-4.4
● **MARTY DECKER** Decker, Dee Martin b: 6/7/57, Upland, Cal. BR/TR, 5'10", 168 lbs. Deb: 9/20/83																										
1983	SD-N	0	0	—	4	0	0	0	0	8^{2}	5	1	3	9	9.3	2.08	168	.167	.265	0	—	0	1	1	0	0.0
● **JOE DECKER** Decker, George Henry b: 6/16/47, Storm Lake, Ia. BR/TR, 6', 180 lbs. Deb: 9/18/69																										
1969	Chi-N	1	0	1.000	4	1	0	0	0	12^{1}	10	0	6	13	11.7	2.92	138	.222	.314	0	.000	-0	1	2	-0	0.1
1970	Chi-N	2	7	.222	24	17	1	0	0	108^{2}	108	12	56	79	13.9	4.64	97	.263	.357	6	.176	1	-7	-2	-1	-0.1
1971	Chi-N	3	2	.600	21	4	0	0	0	45^{2}	62	2	25	37	17.1	4.73	83	.343	.422	2	.250	1	-6	-4	1	-0.3
1972	Chi-N	1	0	1.000	5	1	0	0	0	12^{2}	9	1	4	7	9.2	2.13	179	.188	.250	0	.000	-0	2	2	-0	0.1
1973	Min-A	10	10	.500	29	24	6	3	0	170^{1}	167	12	88	109	13.7	4.17	95	.260	.352	0	—	0	-7	-4	0	-0.4
1974	Min-A	16	14	.533	37	37	11	1	0	248^{2}	234	24	97	158	12.1	3.29	113	.252	.324	0	—	0	9	12	-2	1.1
1975	Min-A	1	3	.250	10	7	1	0	0	26^{1}	25	2	36	8	20.8	8.54	45	.260	.462	0	—	0	-14	-14	-0	-1.8
1976	Min-A	2	7	.222	13	12	0	0	0	58	60	3	51	35	17.4	5.28	68	.273	.412	0	—	0	-11	-11	1	-1.5
1979	Sea-A	0	1	.000	9	2	0	0	0	27^{1}	27	2	14	12	13.5	4.28	102	.255	.342	0	—	0	-0	0	1	0.0
Total	9	36	44	.450	152	105	19	4	0	710	702	58	377	458	13.8	4.17	94	.262	.355	8	.174	1	-34	-19	-1	-2.8
● **JEFF DEDMON** Dedmon, Jeffrey Linden b: 3/4/60, Torrance, Cal. BL/TR, 6'2", 200 lbs. Deb: 9/2/83																										
1983	Atl-N	0	0	—	5	0	0	0	0	4	10	1	0	3	22.5	13.50	29	.455	.455	0	—	0	-4	-4	0	0.0
1984	Atl-N	4	3	.571	54	0	0	0	4	81	86	5	35	51	13.7	3.78	102	.277	.354	0	.000	-1	-2	1	2	0.2
1985	Atl-N	6	3	.667	60	0	0	0	0	86	84	5	49	41	14.0	4.08	94	.264	.364	1	.111	-0	-5	-2	3	0.1
1986	Atl-N	6	6	.500	57	0	0	0	3	99^{2}	90	8	39	58	12.0	2.98	133	.242	.320	2	.125	-1	8	11	2	1.4
1987	Atl-N	3	4	.429	53	3	0	0	4	89^{2}	82	8	42	40	12.5	3.91	111	.246	.332	4	.250	1	2	4	1	0.5
1988	Cle-A	1	0	1.000	21	0	0	0	1	33^{2}	35	3	21	17	15.8	4.54	90	.276	.391	0	—	0	-2	-2	1	0.1
Total	6	20	16	.556	250	3	0	0	12	394	387	30	186	210	13.3	3.84	105	.261	.348	7	.149	-0	-3	8	9	2.3
● **JIM DEDRICK** Dedrick, James Michael b: 4/4/68, Los Angeles, Cal. BB/TR, 6', 185 lbs. Deb: 8/12/95																										
1995	Bal-A	0	0	—	6	0	0	0	0	7^{2}	8	1	6	3	17.6	2.35	202	.308	.455	0	—	0	2	2	0	0.0
● **DUMMY DEEGAN** Deegan, William John b: 11/16/1874, Bronx, N.Y. d: 5/17/57, Bronx, N.Y. Deb: 8/3/01																										
1901	NY-N	0	1	.000	2	1	1	0	0	17	27	0	6	8	17.5	6.35	52	.355	.402	0	.000	-1	-6	-6	0	-0.3
● **JOHN DEERING** Deering, John Thomas b: 6/25/1879, Lynn, Mass. d: 2/15/43, Beverly, Mass. BR/TR, 6', 180 lbs. Deb: 5/12/03																										
1903	Det-A	3	4	.429	10	8	5	0	0	60^{2}	77	3	24	14	15.1	3.86	75	.308	.371	8	.333	2	-6	-6	-1	-0.5
	NY-A	4	3	.571	9	7	6	1	0	60	59	0	18	14	11.7	3.75	83	.257	.313	1	.043	-3	-5	-4	-1	-0.8
	Yr	7	7	.500	19	15	11	1	0	120^{2}	136	3	42	28	13.4	3.80	79	.283	.342	9	.191	-0	-11	-11	-2	-1.3
● **MIKE DEGERICK** Degerick, Michael Arthur b: 4/1/43, New York, N.Y. BR/TR, 6'2", 178 lbs. Deb: 9/4/61																										
1961	Chi-A	0	0	—	1	0	0	0	0	1^{2}	2	0	1	0	16.2	5.40	72	.400	.500	0	—	0	-0	-0	0	0.0
1962	Chi-A	0	0	—	1	0	0	0	0	1	1	0	1	0	18.0	0.00	—	.250	.400	0	—	0	0	0	0	0.0
Total	2	0	0	—	2	0	0	0	0	2^{2}	3	0	2	0	16.9	3.38	116	.333	.455	0	—	0	0	0	0	0.0
● **RICK DeHART** DeHart, Rick Allen b: 3/21/70, Topeka, Kan. BL/TL, 6'1", 180 lbs. Deb: 7/16/97																										
1997	Mon-N	2	1	.667	23	0	0	0	0	29^{1}	33	7	14	29	14.4	5.52	76	.292	.370	0	.000	-0	-4	-4	0	-0.4
1998	Mon-N	0	0	—	26	0	0	0	1	28	34	3	13	14	15.1	4.82	85	.291	.362	0	—	0	-2	-2	1	0.1
Total	2	2	1	.667	49	0	0	0	1	57^{1}	67	10	27	43	14.8	5.18	80	.291	.366	0	.000	-0	-6	-7	1	-0.3
● **PEP DEININGER** Deininger, Otto Charles b: 10/10/1877, Wasseralfingen, Germany d: 9/25/50, Boston, Mass. BL/TL, 5'8.5", 180 lbs. Deb: 4/26/02 ♦																										
1902	Bos-A	0	0	—	2	1	0	0	0	12	19	3	9	2	22.5	9.75	37	.358	.469	2	.333	1	-8	-8	-1	0.1
● **MIKE DeJEAN** DeJean, Michel Dwain b: 9/28/70, Baton Rouge, La. BR/TR, 6'2", 205 lbs. Deb: 5/2/97																										
1997	Col-N	5	0	1.000	55	0	0	0	2	67^{2}	74	4	24	38	13.4	3.99	130	.280	.347	1	.333	0	2	9	0	0.7
1998	Col-N	3	1	.750	59	1	0	0	2	74^{1}	78	4	24	27	12.5	3.03	167	.285	.344	0	.000	-1	10	17	-1	0.7
Total	2	8	1	.889	114	1	0	0	4	142	152	8	48	65	12.9	3.49	147	.283	.346	1	.125	-0	12	26	-1	1.4
● **JOSE DeJESUS** DeJesus, Jose Luis b: 1/6/65, Brooklyn, N.Y. BR/TR, 6'5", 195 lbs. Deb: 9/9/88																										
1988	KC-A	0	1	.000	2	1	0	0	0	2^{2}	6	0	5	2	37.1	27.00	15	.429	.579	0	—	0	-7	-7	-0	-1.5
1989	KC-A	0	0	—	3	1	0	0	0	8	7	1	8	2	16.9	4.50	85	.241	.405	0	—	0	-1	-1	-0	0.0
1990	Phi-N	7	8	.467	22	22	3	1	0	130	97	10	73	87	11.9	3.74	102	.210	.321	3	.079	-1	1	1	-1	0.0
1991	Phi-N	10	9	.526	31	29	3	0	1	181^{2}	147	7	128	118	13.8	3.42	107	.224	.355	8	.129	-1	5	5	-3	0.1

YEAR	TM/L	W	L	PCT	G	GS	CG	SH	SV	IP	H	HR	BB	SO	RAT	ERA	ERA+	OAV	OOB	BH	AVG	PB	PR	/A	PD	TPI
1994	KC-A	3	1	.750	5	4	0	0	0	26^2	27	2	13	12	13.5	4.73	106	.276	.360	0	—	0	0	1	-1	-0.1
Total	5	20	19	.513	63	57	6	1	1	349	284	20	227	221	13.3	3.84	100	.226	.347	11	.110	-2	-1	-1	-4	-1.5
● TOMMY de la CRUZ	DeLa Cruz, Tomas (Rivero) b: 9/18/11, Marianao, Cuba d: 9/6/58, Havana, Cuba BR/TR, 6'2", 168 lbs. Deb: 4/20/44																									
1944	Cin-N	9	9	.500	34	20	9	0	1	191^1	170	9	45	65	10.2	3.25	108	.238	.284	9	.155	-0	8	5	-0	0.4
● ROLAND de la MAZA	DeLa Maza, Roland Robert b: 11/11/71, Granada Hills, Cal. BR/TR, 6'2", 195 lbs. Deb: 9/26/97																									
1997	KC-A	0	0	—	1	0	0	0	0	2	1	1	1	1	9.0	4.50	105	.125	.222	0	—	0	0	0	-0	-0.1
● JIM DELAHANTY	Delahanty, James Christopher b: 6/20/1879, Cleveland, Ohio d: 10/17/53, Cleveland, Ohio BR/TR, 5'10.5", 170 lbs. Deb: 4/19/01 F♦																									
1904	Bos-N	0	0	—	1	0	0	0	0	3^1	5	0	1	0	16.2	0.00	—	.357	.400	142	.285	0	1	1	0	0.0
1905	Bos-N	0	0	—	1	1	0	0	0	2	5	1	0	0	22.5	4.50	69	.500	.500	119	.258	0	-0	-0	0	0.0
Total	2	0	0	—	2	1	0	0	0	5^1	10	1	1	0	18.6	1.69	171	.417	.440	1159	.283	1	1	1	0	0.0
● ART DELANEY	Delaney, Arthur Dewey "Swede" (b: Arthur Dewey Helenius) b: 1/5/1895, Chicago, Ill. d: 5/2/70, Hayward, Cal. BR/TR, 5'10.5", 178 lbs. Deb: 4/16/24																									
1924	StL-N	1	0	1.000	8	1	1	0	0	20	19	0	6	2	11.2	1.80	210	.250	.305	2	.286	0	5	4	0	0.3
1928	Bos-N	9	17	.346	39	22	8	0	2	192^1	197	11	56	45	11.9	3.79	103	.267	.319	9	.143	-3	4	3	1	0.1
1929	Bos-N	3	5	.375	20	8	3	1	0	75	103	6	35	17	16.7	6.12	76	.336	.405	3	.143	0	-12	-12	-1	-1.0
Total	3	13	22	.371	67	31	12	1	2	287^1	319	17	97	64	13.1	4.26	96	.285	.343	14	.154	-2	-3	-5	0	-0.6
● FRANCISCO de la ROSA	DeLa Rosa, Francisco (Jimenez) b: 3/3/66, LaRomana, D.R. BB/TR, 5'11", 185 lbs. Deb: 9/7/91																									
1991	Bal-A	0	0	—	2	0	0	0	0	4	6	0	2	1	18.0	4.50	88	.353	.421	0	—	0	-0	-0	-0	0.3
● JOSE DeLEON	DeLeon, Jose (Chestaro) b: 12/20/60, Rancho Viejo, D.R. BR/TR, 6'3", 215 lbs. Deb: 7/23/83																									
1983	Pit-N	7	3	.700	15	15	3	2	0	108	75	5	47	118	10.3	2.83	131	.196	.285	2	.059	-1	10	10	-1	0.8
1984	Pit-N	7	13	.350	30	28	5	1	0	192^1	147	10	92	153	11.3	3.74	96	.214	.310	5	.085	-4	-3	-3	-3	-0.9
1985	Pit-N	2	19	.095	31	25	1	0	3	162^2	138	15	89	149	12.7	4.70	76	.231	.334	2	.056	-2	-20	-20	-1	-2.7
1986	Pit-N	1	3	.250	9	1	0	0	1	16^1	17	2	17	11	19.3	8.27	46	.266	.427	0	.000	0	-8	-8	0	-1.7
	Chi-A	4	5	.444	13	13	1	0	0	79	49	7	42	68	10.8	2.96	145	.179	.297	0	—	0	11	12	0	1.3
1987	Chi-A	11	12	.478	33	31	2	0	0	206	177	24	97	153	12.4	4.02	114	.230	.324	0	—	0	10	13	-3	0.8
1988	StL-N	13	10	.565	34	34	3	1	0	225^1	198	13	86	208	11.4	3.67	95	.237	.310	10	.139	-0	-6	-5	-2	-0.8
1989	StL-N	16	12	.571	36	36	5	3	0	244^2	173	16	80	**201**	9.5	3.05	119	**.197**	.269	8	.096	-4	12	16	-4	0.9
1990	StL-N	7	19	.269	32	32	0	0	0	182^2	168	15	86	164	12.8	4.43	86	.246	.335	6	.107	-1	-13	-13	-2	-1.9
1991	StL-N	5	9	.357	28	28	1	0	0	162^2	144	15	61	118	11.7	2.71	137	.239	.315	2	.043	-4	18	18	-2	0.9
1992	StL-N	2	7	.222	29	15	0	0	0	102^1	95	7	43	72	12.3	4.57	74	.245	.324	1	.048	-1	-12	-13	-1	-1.3
	Phi-N	0	1	.000	3	3	0	0	0	15	16	0	5	7	12.6	3.00	116	.281	.339	2	.400	1	1	1	-0	0.1
	Yr	2	8	.200	32	18	0	0	0	117^1	111	7	48	79	12.2	4.37	78	.246	.318	3	.115	-0	-11	-13	-2	-1.2
1993	Phi-N	3	0	1.000	24	3	0	0	0	47	39	5	27	34	13.6	3.26	122	.229	.351	0	.000	-1	4	4	-1	0.1
	*Chi-A	0	0	—	11	0	0	0	0	10^1	5	2	3	6	7.8	1.74	240	.152	.243	0	—	0	3	3	-0	0.0
1994	Chi-A	3	2	.600	42	0	0	0	2	67	48	5	31	67	11.4	3.36	139	.200	.307	0	—	0	11	10	-1	0.7
1995	Chi-A	5	3	.625	38	0	0	0	0	67^2	60	10	28	53	12.5	5.19	86	.238	.329	0	—	0	-4	-6	-1	-0.6
	Mon-N	0	1	.000	7	0	0	0	0	8^1	7	2	7	12	16.2	7.56	57	.233	.395	0	—	0	-3	-3	-0	-0.3
Total	13	86	119	.420	415	264	21	7	6	1897^1	1556	153	841	1594	11.7	3.76	102	.224	.313	38	.091	-16	9	15	-22	-4.6
● LUIS DeLEON	DeLeon, Luis Antonio (Tricoche) b: 8/19/58, Ponce, P.R. BR/TR, 6'1", 153 lbs. Deb: 9/6/81																									
1981	StL-N	0	1	.000	10	0	0	0	0	15^1	11	1	3	8	8.2	2.35	151	.200	.241	0	.000	-0	2	2	-0	0.1
1982	SD-N	9	5	.643	61	0	0	0	15	102	77	10	16	60	8.3	2.03	169	.212	.247	1	.091	0	18	16	1	2.7
1983	SD-N	6	6	.500	63	0	0	0	13	111	89	8	27	90	9.5	2.68	130	.224	.275	2	.143	0	12	10	-2	1.1
1984	SD-N	2	2	.500	32	0	0	0	0	42^2	44	12	12	44	12.7	5.48	65	.256	.319	0	.000	-0	-9	-9	-0	-0.8
1985	SD-N	0	3	.000	29	0	0	0	3	38^2	39	6	10	31	12.1	4.19	84	.267	.327	1	.200	0	-3	-3	-0	-0.3
1987	Bal-A	0	2	.000	11	0	0	0	1	20^2	19	1	8	13	12.6	4.79	92	.253	.341	0	—	0	-1	-1	-1	0.1
1989	Sea-A	0	0	—	1	1	0	0	0	4	5	1	1	2	15.8	2.25	179	.313	.389	0	—	0	1	1	-0	-0.2
Total	7	17	19	.472	207	1	0	0	32	334^1	284	39	77	248	10.0	3.12	114	.232	.284	4	.114	-0	20	16	-2	2.7
● FLAME DELHI	Delhi, Lee William b: 11/5/1892, Harqua Hala, Ariz. d: 5/9/66, San Rafael, Cal. BR/TR, 6'2.5", 198 lbs. Deb: 4/16/12																									
1912	Chi-A	0	0	—	1	0	0	0	0	3	7	0	3	2	30.0	9.00	36	.412	.500	0	—	0	-2	-2	0	0.0
● WHEEZER DELL	Dell, William George b: 6/11/1887, Tuscarora, Nev. d: 8/24/66, Independence, Cal. BR/TR, 6'4", 210 lbs. Deb: 4/22/12																									
1912	StL-N	0	0	—	3	0	0	0	0	2^1	3	0	3	0	23.1	11.57	30	.188	.316	0	—	0	-2	-2	-0	0.0
1915	Bro-N	11	10	.524	40	24	12	4	1	215	166	5	100	94	11.5	2.34	119	.218	.315	10	.152	-1	10	10	0	1.0
1916	*Bro-N	8	9	.471	32	16	9	2	1	155	143	2	43	76	11.0	2.26	118	.256	.314	4	.091	-2	6	7	-1	0.4
1917	Bro-N	0	4	.000	17	4	0	0	1	58	55	3	25	28	12.7	3.72	75	.263	.347	1	.063	-2	-7	-6	-1	-0.7
Total	4	19	23	.452	92	44	21	6	3	430^1	367	10	171	198	11.5	2.55	108	.237	.319	15	.119	-5	7	9	-2	0.7
● IKE DELOCK	Delock, Ivan Martin b: 11/11/29, Highland Park, Mich BR/TR, 5'11", 175 lbs. Deb: 4/17/52																									
1952	Bos-A	4	9	.308	39	7	1	1	5	95	88	9	50	46	13.3	4.26	92	.245	.341	1	.045	-1	-6	-3	-0	-0.6
1953	Bos-A	3	1	.750	23	1	0	0	1	48^2	60	2	20	22	15.2	4.44	95	.308	.378	1	.100	-1	-2	-1	-1	-0.2
1955	Bos-A	9	7	.563	29	18	6	0	3	143^2	136	16	61	88	12.6	3.76	114	.247	.326	7	.143	-1	3	8	-1	0.7
1956	Bos-A	13	7	.650	48	8	1	0	9	128^1	122	12	80	105	14.5	4.21	110	.252	.363	3	.103	-2	-1	6	0	0.7
1957	Bos-A	9	8	.529	49	2	0	0	11	94	80	11	45	62	12.3	3.83	104	.230	.323	1	.048	-1	-0	2	-1	0.1
1958	Bos-A	14	8	.636	31	19	9	1	2	160	155	13	56	82	11.9	3.37	119	.252	.315	3	.063	-4	7	11	-1	1.0
1959	Bos-A	11	6	.647	28	17	4	0	0	134^1	120	12	62	55	12.3	2.95	138	.236	.322	3	.064	-3	14	17	-2	1.5
1960	Bos-A	9	10	.474	24	23	3	1	0	129^1	145	21	52	49	14.0	4.73	85	.283	.354	5	.116	-3	-12	-10	-1	-1.6
1961	Bos-A	6	9	.400	28	28	3	1	0	156	185	24	52	80	13.8	4.90	85	.293	.349	5	.104	-2	-15	-13	-2	-1.4
1962	Bos-A	4	5	.444	17	13	4	2	0	86^1	89	10	24	49	11.8	3.75	110	.268	.317	2	.087	-1	2	4	-1	0.1
1963	Bos-A	1	2	.333	6	6	1	0	0	32	31	4	12	23	12.1	4.50	84	.246	.312	0	.000	-1	-3	-3	-0	-0.4
	Bal-A	1	3	.250	7	5	0	0	0	30^1	25	7	16	11	12.2	5.04	69	.236	.336	0	.000	-1	-5	-5	-0	-0.7
	Yr	2	5	.286	13	11	1	0	0	62^1	56	11	28	34	12.1	4.76	76	.240	.322	0	.000	-3	-8	-8	-0	-1.1
Total	11	84	75	.528	329	147	32	6	31	1238	1236	141	530	672	13.0	4.03	102	.259	.336	31	.086	-20	-19	12	-9	-0.8
● VALERIO de los SANTOS	DeLos Santos, Valerio Lorenzo b: 10/6/75, Las Matas De Farfan, D.R. BL/TL, 6'4", 185 lbs. Deb: 7/31/98																									
1998	Mil-N	0	0	—	13	0	0	0	0	21^2	11	4	2	18	5.4	2.91	148	.151	.173	0	—	0	3	3	-0	0.0
● RAMON de los SANTOS	DeLos Santos, Ramon (Genero) b: 1/19/49, Santo Domingo, D.R. BL/TL, 6'1", 175 lbs. Deb: 8/21/74																									
1974	Hou-N	1	1	.500	12	0	0	0	0	12^1	11	0	9	7	14.6	2.19	158	.234	.357	0	—	0	2	2	0	0.3
● RICH DeLUCIA	DeLucia, Richard Anthony b: 10/7/64, Reading, Pa. BR/TR, 6', 185 lbs. Deb: 9/8/90																									
1990	Sea-A	1	2	.333	5	5	1	0	0	36	30	2	9	20	9.8	2.00	198	.226	.275	0	—	0	8	8	-1	0.5
1991	Sea-A	12	13	.480	32	31	0	0	0	182	176	31	78	98	12.8	5.09	81	.260	.339	0	—	0	-20	-20	-2	-2.5
1992	Sea-A	3	6	.333	30	11	0	0	1	83^2	100	13	35	66	14.7	5.49	72	.293	.362	0	—	0	-14	-14	-1	-1.5
1993	Sea-A	3	6	.333	30	1	0	0	0	42^2	46	5	23	48	14.8	4.64	95	.272	.363	0	—	0	-2	-1	1	-0.2
1994	Cin-N	0	0	—	8	0	0	0	0	10^2	9	4	5	15	11.8	4.22	98	.214	.298	0	—	0	-0	-0	-0	0.0
1995	StL-N	8	7	.533	56	1	0	0	0	82^1	63	9	36	76	11.1	3.39	124	.213	.304	2	.200	0	7	7	0	1.3
1996	SF-N	3	6	.333	56	0	0	0	0	61^2	62	8	31	55	14.0	5.84	70	.259	.352	1	.250	0	-11	-12	1	-1.4
1997	SF-N	0	0	—	3	0	0	0	0	1^2	6	0	0	2	32.4	10.80	38	.500	.500	0	—	0	-1	-1	0	0.0
	Ana-A	6	4	.600	33	0	0	0	3	42^1	29	5	27	42	12.1	3.61	126	.204	.335	0	—	0	4	4	0	1.0
1998	Ana-A	2	6	.250	61	0	0	0	3	71^2	56	10	46	73	13.2	4.27	110	.221	.348	0	—	0	3	3	-1	0.2
Total	9	38	50	.432	314	49	1	0	7	614^2	577	87	290	495	12.9	4.58	92	.250	.338	3	.214	1	-26	-25	-2	-2.6
● FRED DEMARAIS	Demarais, Frederick b: 11/1/1866, Canada d: 3/6/19, Stamford, Conn. TR, 5'9", 168 lbs. Deb: 7/26/1890																									
1890	Chi-N	0	0	—	1	0	0	0	0	2	1	0	1	1	9.0	0.00	—	.143	.250	0	.000	-0	1	1	0	0.0

● **AL DEMAREE** Demaree, Albert Wentworth b: 9/8/1884, Quincy, Ill. d: 4/30/62, Los Angeles, Cal. BL/TR, 6′, 170 lbs. Deb: 9/26/12

YEAR	TM/L	W	L	PCT	G	GS	CG	SH	SV	IP	H	HR	BB	SO	RAT	ERA	ERA+	OAV	OOB	BH	AVG	PB	PR	/A	PD	TPI
1912	NY-N	1	0	1.000	2	2	1	1	0	16	17	0	2	11	10.7	1.69	200	.288	.311	0	.000	-1	3	3	0	0.1
1913	*NY-N	13	4	.765	31	25	11	2	2	199^{2}	176	4	38	76	9.9	2.21	141	.243	.286	7	.106	-3	22	20	-3	0.9
1914	NY-N	10	17	.370	38	29	13	2	0	224	219	3	77	89	12.2	3.09	86	.263	.331	9	.132	-2	-8	-11	-1	-1.6
1915	Phi-N	14	11	.560	32	26	13	3	1	209^{2}	201	4	58	69	11.2	3.05	90	.260	.314	12	.176	0	-7	-7	-5	-1.3
1916	Phi-N	19	14	.576	39	35	25	4	1	285	252	4	48	130	9.7	2.62	101	.242	.281	11	.109	-4	-0	1	-6	-1.1
1917	Chi-N	5	9	.357	24	18	6	1	1	141^{1}	125	5	37	43	10.4	2.55	114	.244	.297	5	.122	-1	3	6	1	0.4
	NY-N	4	5	.444	15	11	1	0	0	78^{1}	70	1	17	23	10.1	2.64	97	.239	.283	2	.111	-1	1	-1	0	-0.2
	Yr	9	14	.391	39	29	7	1	1	219^{2}	195	6	54	66	10.2	2.58	108	.241	.290	7	.119	-2	3	5	1	0.2
1918	NY-N	8	6	.571	26	14	8	2	1	142	143	5	25	39	10.8	2.47	106	.262	.297	6	.128	-3	5	2	-0	-0.1
1919	Bos-N	6	6	.500	25	13	6	0	3	128	147	8	35	34	12.9	3.80	75	.300	.348	2	.048	-5	-13	-13	-2	-2.0
Total	8	80	72	.526	232	173	84	15	9	1424	1350	34	337	514	10.9	2.77	100	.256	.304	54	.118	-20	6	0	-16	-4.9

● **LARRY DEMERY** Demery, Lawrence Calvin b: 6/4/53, Bakersfield, Cal. BR/TR, 6′, 170 lbs. Deb: 6/2/74

YEAR	TM/L	W	L	PCT	G	GS	CG	SH	SV	IP	H	HR	BB	SO	RAT	ERA	ERA+	OAV	OOB	BH	AVG	PB	PR	/A	PD	TPI
1974	*Pit-N	6	6	.500	19	15	2	0	0	95^{1}	95	12	51	51	13.8	4.25	81	.262	.354	5	.152	1	-7	-9	-1	-1.0
1975	*Pit-N	7	5	.583	45	8	1	0	4	114^{2}	95	7	43	59	11.1	2.90	122	.230	.307	3	.125	1	9	8	-1	0.9
1976	Pit-N	10	7	.588	36	15	4	1	2	145	123	8	58	72	11.4	3.17	110	.234	.313	5	.125	-1	5	5	-0	0.5
1977	Pit-N	6	5	.545	39	8	0	0	1	90^{1}	100	13	47	35	14.6	5.08	78	.279	.363	3	.150	-0	-12	-11	-0	-1.3
Total	4	29	23	.558	139	46	7	1	7	445^{1}	413	40	199	217	12.5	3.72	97	.249	.331	16	.137	0	-4	-6	-2	-0.9

● **HARRY DeMILLER** DeMiller, Harry b: 11/12/1867, Wooster, Ohio d: 10/19/28, Santa Ana, Cal. BR/TL, Deb: 8/20/1892

YEAR	TM/L	W	L	PCT	G	GS	CG	SH	SV	IP	H	HR	BB	SO	RAT	ERA	ERA+	OAV	OOB	BH	AVG	PB	PR	/A	PD	TPI
1892	Chi-N	1	1	.500	4	2	2	0	0	24	29	1	16	15	17.3	6.38	52	.287	.390	3	.300	1	-8	-8	0	-0.4

● **DON DeMOLA** DeMola, Donald John b: 7/5/52, Glen Cove, N.Y. BR/TR, 6′2″, 185 lbs. Deb: 4/13/74

YEAR	TM/L	W	L	PCT	G	GS	CG	SH	SV	IP	H	HR	BB	SO	RAT	ERA	ERA+	OAV	OOB	BH	AVG	PB	PR	/A	PD	TPI
1974	Mon-N	1	0	1.000	25	1	0	0	0	57^{2}	46	7	21	47	10.5	3.12	123	.223	.295	0	.000	-1	3	5	-1	0.0
1975	Mon-N	4	7	.364	60	0	0	0	1	97^{2}	92	8	42	63	12.7	4.15	92	.251	.335	0	.000	-1	-6	-4	-3	-0.8
Total	2	5	7	.417	85	1	0	0	1	155^{1}	138	15	63	110	11.9	3.77	102	.241	.321	0	.000	-1	-3	1	-3	-0.8

● **BEN DeMOTT** DeMott, Benyew Harrison b: 4/2/1889, Green Village, N.J. d: 7/5/63, Somerville, N.J. BR/TR, 6′, 192 lbs. Deb: 8/12/10

YEAR	TM/L	W	L	PCT	G	GS	CG	SH	SV	IP	H	HR	BB	SO	RAT	ERA	ERA+	OAV	OOB	BH	AVG	PB	PR	/A	PD	TPI
1910	Cle-A	0	3	.000	6	4	1	0	0	28^{1}	45	0	8	13	17.2	5.40	48	.388	.432	3	.167	-0	-9	-9	0	-0.9
1911	Cle-A	0	1	.000	1	1	0	0	0	3^{2}	10	0	2	2	29.5	12.27	28	.588	.632	0	.000	-0	-4	-4	0	-0.6
Total	2	0	4	.000	7	5	1	0	0	32	55	0	10	15	18.6	6.19	43	.414	.458	3	.136	-0	-13	-12	1	-1.5

● **CON DEMPSEY** Dempsey, Cornelius Francis b: 9/16/23, San Francisco, Cal. BR/TR, 6′4″, 190 lbs. Deb: 4/28/51

YEAR	TM/L	W	L	PCT	G	GS	CG	SH	SV	IP	H	HR	BB	SO	RAT	ERA	ERA+	OAV	OOB	BH	AVG	PB	PR	/A	PD	TPI
1951	Pit-N	0	2	.000	3	2	0	0	0	7	11	2	4	3	19.3	9.00	47	.393	.469	0	.000	-0	-4	-4	0	-0.8

● **RICK DEMPSEY** Dempsey, John Rikard b: 9/13/49, Fayetteville, Tenn. BR/TR, 6′, 190 lbs. Deb: 9/23/69 ♦

YEAR	TM/L	W	L	PCT	G	GS	CG	SH	SV	IP	H	HR	BB	SO	RAT	ERA	ERA+	OAV	OOB	BH	AVG	PB	PR	/A	PD	TPI
1991	Mil-A	0	0	—	2	0	0	0	0	2	3	0	1	0	18.0	4.50	88	.333	.400	34	.231	1	-0	-0	-0	0.0

● **MARK DEMPSEY** Dempsey, Mark Steven b: 12/17/57, Dayton, Ohio BR/TR, 6′6″, 220 lbs. Deb: 9/4/82

YEAR	TM/L	W	L	PCT	G	GS	CG	SH	SV	IP	H	HR	BB	SO	RAT	ERA	ERA+	OAV	OOB	BH	AVG	PB	PR	/A	PD	TPI
1982	SF-N	0	0	—	3	1	0	0	0	5^{2}	11	1	2	4	20.6	7.94	45	.440	.481	0	.000	-0	-3	-3	0	0.0

● **RYAN DEMPSTER** Dempster, Ryan Scott b: 5/3/77, Sechelt, B.C., Canada BR/TR, 6′2″, 195 lbs. Deb: 5/23/98

YEAR	TM/L	W	L	PCT	G	GS	CG	SH	SV	IP	H	HR	BB	SO	RAT	ERA	ERA+	OAV	OOB	BH	AVG	PB	PR	/A	PD	TPI
1998	Fla-N	1	5	.167	14	11	0	0	0	54^{2}	72	6	38	35	19.6	7.08	58	.336	.456	0	.000	-1	-17	-18	1	-1.7

● **BILL DENEHY** Denehy, William Francis b: 3/31/46, Middletown, Conn. BB/TR, 6′3″, 200 lbs. Deb: 4/16/67

YEAR	TM/L	W	L	PCT	G	GS	CG	SH	SV	IP	H	HR	BB	SO	RAT	ERA	ERA+	OAV	OOB	BH	AVG	PB	PR	/A	PD	TPI
1967	NY-N	1	7	.125	15	8	0	0	0	53^{2}	51	8	29	35	13.4	4.70	72	.248	.340	0	.000	-1	-8	-8	-1	-1.2
1968	Was-A	0	0	—	3	0	0	0	0	2	4	0	4	1	36.0	9.00	32	.444	.615	0	—	0	-1	-1	0	0.0
1971	Det-A	0	3	.000	31	1	0	0	1	49	47	4	28	27	14.5	4.22	85	.250	.359	0	.000	1	-4	-3	-0	-0.2
Total	3	1	10	.091	49	9	0	0	1	104^{2}	102	12	61	63	14.4	4.56	76	.253	.357	0	.000	0	-13	-13	-1	-1.4

● **BRIAN DENMAN** Denman, Brian John b: 2/12/56, Minneapolis, Minn. BR/TR, 6′4″, 205 lbs. Deb: 8/22/82

YEAR	TM/L	W	L	PCT	G	GS	CG	SH	SV	IP	H	HR	BB	SO	RAT	ERA	ERA+	OAV	OOB	BH	AVG	PB	PR	/A	PD	TPI
1982	Bos-A	3	4	.429	9	9	2	1	0	49	55	6	9	9	11.8	4.78	90	.282	.314	0	—	0	-4	-3	-0	-0.6

● **DON DENNIS** Dennis, Donald Ray b: 3/3/42, Uniontown, Kan. BR/TR, 6′2″, 190 lbs. Deb: 6/18/65

YEAR	TM/L	W	L	PCT	G	GS	CG	SH	SV	IP	H	HR	BB	SO	RAT	ERA	ERA+	OAV	OOB	BH	AVG	PB	PR	/A	PD	TPI
1965	StL-N	2	3	.400	41	0	0	0	6	55	47	3	16	29	10.5	2.29	168	.236	.296	2	.400	1	8	9	2	1.3
1966	StL-N	4	2	.667	38	1	0	0	2	59^{2}	73	8	17	25	13.7	4.98	72	.302	.350	1	.083	-1	-9	-9	3	-0.7
Total	2	6	5	.545	79	1	0	0	8	114^{2}	120	11	33	54	12.2	3.69	101	.272	.326	3	.176	-0	-1	0	4	0.6

● **JERRY DENNY** Denny, Jeremiah Dennis (b: Jeremiah Dennis Eldridge)
b: 3/16/1859, New York, N.Y. d: 8/16/27, Houston, Tex. BR/TR, 5′11.5″, 180 lbs. Deb: 5/2/1881 ♦

YEAR	TM/L	W	L	PCT	G	GS	CG	SH	SV	IP	H	HR	BB	SO	RAT	ERA	ERA+	OAV	OOB	BH	AVG	PB	PR	/A	PD	TPI
1888	Ind-N	0	0	—	1	0	0	0	0	4	5	1	4	1	20.3	9.00	33	.278	.409	137	.261	0	-3	-3	0	0.0

● **JOHN DENNY** Denny, John Allen b: 11/8/52, Prescott, Ariz. BR/TR, 6′3″, 190 lbs. Deb: 9/12/74

YEAR	TM/L	W	L	PCT	G	GS	CG	SH	SV	IP	H	HR	BB	SO	RAT	ERA	ERA+	OAV	OOB	BH	AVG	PB	PR	/A	PD	TPI
1974	StL-N	0	0	—	2	0	0	0	0	2	3	0	0	1	13.5	0.00	—	.273	.273	0	—	0	1	1	-0	0.0
1975	StL-N	10	7	.588	25	24	3	2	0	136	149	5	51	72	13.4	3.97	95	.280	.346	10	.227	1	-5	-3	2	-0.1
1976	StL-N	11	9	.550	30	30	8	3	0	207	189	11	74	74	11.8	**2.52**	**140**	.246	.318	15	.224	2	23	**23**	1	2.7
1977	StL-N	8	8	.500	26	26	3	1	0	149^{2}	165	9	62	60	14.0	4.51	85	.281	.355	5	.098	-3	-10	-11	3	-1.0
1978	StL-N	14	11	.560	33	33	11	2	0	234	200	13	74	103	10.8	2.96	119	.238	.304	13	.178	2	16	14	8	2.7
1979	StL-N	8	11	.421	31	31	5	2	0	206	206	24	100	99	13.5	4.85	78	.264	.350	9	.129	-1	-26	-25	2	-2.1
1980	Cle-A	8	6	.571	16	16	4	1	0	108^{2}	116	4	47	59	13.9	4.39	93	.284	.365	0	—	0	-4	-4	1	-0.4
1981	Cle-A	10	6	.625	19	19	6	3	0	145^{2}	139	9	66	94	12.9	3.15	115	.254	.338	0	—	0	8	8	5	1.4
1982	Cle-A	6	11	.353	21	21	5	0	0	138^{1}	126	11	73	94	13.3	5.01	81	.240	.340	0	—	0	-14	-14	1	-1.4
	Phi-N	0	2	.000	4	4	0	0	0	22^{1}	18	1	10	19	11.3	4.03	91	.217	.301	1	.167	0	-1	-1	1	0.1
1983	*Phi-N	**19**	6	**.760**	36	36	7	1	0	242^{2}	229	9	53	139	10.6	2.37	150	.250	.294	13	.169	0	**34**	32	1	3.5
1984	Phi-N	7	7	.500	22	22	2	0	0	154^{1}	122	11	29	94	9.0	2.45	148	.214	.257	9	.191	0	20	20	4	2.3
1985	Phi-N	11	14	.440	33	33	6	2	0	230^{2}	252	15	83	123	13.2	3.82	96	.282	.345	10	.123	-2	-6	-4	1	-0.4
1986	Cin-N	11	10	.524	27	27	2	1	0	171^{1}	179	15	56	115	12.6	4.20	92	.272	.333	12	.222	2	-9	-6	3	-0.3
Total	13	123	108	.532	325	322	62	18	0	2148^{2}	2093	137	778	1146	12.3	3.59	104	.258	.327	97	.170	2	25	30	31	7.0

● **EDDIE DENT** Dent, Elliott Estill b: 12/8/1887, Baltimore, Md. d: 11/25/74, Birmingham, Ala. BR/TR, 6′1″, 190 lbs. Deb: 8/31/09

YEAR	TM/L	W	L	PCT	G	GS	CG	SH	SV	IP	H	HR	BB	SO	RAT	ERA	ERA+	OAV	OOB	BH	AVG	PB	PR	/A	PD	TPI
1909	Bro-N	2	4	.333	6	5	4	0	0	42	47	2	15	17	13.3	4.29	60	.307	.369	1	.067	-1	-8	-8	-1	-1.2
1911	Bro-N	2	1	.667	5	3	1	0	0	31^{2}	30	0	10	3	11.9	3.69	90	.256	.326	1	.100	-0	-1	-1	0	-0.1
1912	Bro-N	0	0	—	1	0	0	0	0	1	4	0	1	1	45.0	36.00	9	.571	.625	0	.000	-0	-4	-4	0	0.0
Total	3	4	5	.444	12	8	5	0	0	74^{2}	81	2	26	21	13.1	4.46	65	.292	.357	2	.077	-2	-13	-13	-0	-1.3

● **ROGER DENZER** Denzer, Roger "Peaceful Valley" b: 10/5/1871, LeSeur, Minn. d: 9/18/49, LeSeur, Minn. BL/TR, 6′, 180 lbs. Deb: 4/24/1897

YEAR	TM/L	W	L	PCT	G	GS	CG	SH	SV	IP	H	HR	BB	SO	RAT	ERA	ERA+	OAV	OOB	BH	AVG	PB	PR	/A	PD	TPI
1897	Chi-N	2	8	.200	12	10	8	0	0	94^{2}	125	4	34	17	15.3	5.13	87	.315	.372	6	.154	-3	-9	-7	-1	-0.9
1901	NY-N	2	6	.250	11	9	3	1	0	61^{2}	69	2	5	22	11.1	3.36	99	.280	.300	2	.091	-1	-0	-0	-2	-0.3
Total	2	4	14	.222	23	19	11	1	0	156^{1}	194	6	39	39	13.6	4.43	90	.302	.345	8	.131	-4	-9	-8	-2	-1.2

● **GEORGE DERBY** Derby, George H. "Jonah" b: 7/6/1857, Webster, Mass. d: 7/4/25, Philadelphia, Pa. BL/TR, 6′, 175 lbs. Deb: 5/2/1881

YEAR	TM/L	W	L	PCT	G	GS	CG	SH	SV	IP	H	HR	BB	SO	RAT	ERA	ERA+	OAV	OOB	BH	AVG	PB	PR	/A	PD	TPI
1881	Det-N	29	26	.527	56	55	55	**9**	0	494^{2}	505	3	86	**212**	10.8	2.20	132	.251	.281	44	.186	-10	**32**	**39**	2	**3.0**
1882	Det-N	17	20	.459	40	39	38	3	0	362	386	8	81	182	11.6	3.26	90	.256	.294	29	.195	-6	-14	-13	1	-1.5
1883	Buf-N	2	10	.167	14	13	12	0	1	107^{2}	173	3	15	34	15.7	5.85	54	.334	.353	14	.237	-1	-32	-32	1	-2.6
Total	3	48	56	.462	110	107	105	12	1	964^{1}	1064	14	182	428	11.6	3.01	98	.263	.295	87	.196	-17	-15	-5	4	-1.1

● **PAUL DERRINGER** Derringer, Samuel Paul "Duke" b: 10/17/06, Springfield, Ky. d: 11/17/87, Sarasota, Fla. BR/TR, 6′3.5″, 205 lbs. Deb: 4/16/31

YEAR	TM/L	W	L	PCT	G	GS	CG	SH	SV	IP	H	HR	BB	SO	RAT	ERA	ERA+	OAV	OOB	BH	AVG	PB	PR	/A	PD	TPI
1931	*StL-N	18	8	**.692**	35	23	15	4	2	211^{2}	225	9	65	134	12.5	3.36	117	.274	.330	7	.097	-6	12	14	-0	0.9
1932	StL-N	11	14	.440	39	30	14	1	0	233^{1}	296	6	67	78	14.1	4.05	97	.310	.356	13	.178	-0	-4	-3	-2	-0.5
1933	StL-N	0	2	.000	3	2	1	0	0	17	24	0	9	3	18.0	4.24	82	.353	.436	0	.000	-1	-2	-1	0	-0.2
	Cin-N	7	25	.219	33	31	16	2	1	231	240	4	51	86	11.5	3.23	105	.271	.315	14	.184	-1	3	4	1	0.5
	Yr	7	27	.206	36	33	17	2	1	248	264	4	60	89	11.9	3.30	103	.277	.323	14	.173	-2	1	3	1	0.3

YEAR	TM/L	W	L	PCT	G	GS	CG	SH	SV	IP	H	HR	BB	SO	RAT	ERA	ERA+	OAV	OOB	BH	AVG	PB	PR	/A	PD	TPI
1934	Cin-N	15	21	.417	47	31	18	1	4	261	297	8	59	122	12.4	3.59	114	.283	.323	18	.196	0	14	14	-2	1.7
1935	Cin-N★	22	13	.629	45	33	20	3	2	276^2	295	13	49	120	11.3	3.51	113	.271	.305	13	.140	-5	16	14	3	1.4
1936	Cin-N	19	19	.500	**51**	37	13	2	5	282^1	331	11	42	121	12.0	4.02	95	.289	.316	18	.200	-1	0	-6	0	-0.8
1937	Cin-N	10	14	.417	43	26	12	1	1	222^2	240	7	55	94	11.9	4.04	92	.271	.313	16	.200	1	-3	-8	1	-0.6
1938	Cin-N☆	21	14	.600	41	37	**26**	4	3	**307**	315	20	49	132	10.7	2.93	124	.262	.291	21	.176	-0	29	24	-2	2.4
1939	*Cin-N★	25	7	**.781**	38	35	28	5	0	301	321	15	35	128	10.7	2.93	131	.272	.295	23	.209	0	33	30	-3	2.7
1940	*Cin-N★	20	12	.625	37	37	26	3	0	296^2	280	17	48	115	**10.0**	3.06	124	.246	**.276**	18	.167	-2	26	24	-4	1.8
1941	Cin-N★	12	14	.462	29	28	17	2	1	228^1	233	16	54	76	11.3	3.31	109	.266	.309	13	.155	-3	8	7	-1	0.4
1942	Cin-N†	10	11	.476	29	27	13	1	0	208^2	203	4	49	68	11.0	3.06	107	.250	.296	9	.132	-2	6	5	-4	-0.1
1943	Chi-N	10	14	.417	32	22	10	2	3	174	184	7	39	75	11.5	3.57	93	.264	.303	13	.224	1	-4	-4	-4	-0.9
1944	Chi-N	7	13	.350	42	16	7	0	3	180	205	13	39	69	12.2	4.15	85	.284	.321	9	.158	-2	-11	-12	-1	-1.5
1945	*Chi-N	16	11	.593	35	30	15	1	4	213^2	223	8	51	86	11.6	3.45	106	.265	.308	15	.200	0	8	5	-2	0.4
Total	15	223	212	.513	579	445	251	32	29	3645	3912	158	761	1507	11.6	3.46	108	.272	.310	220	.175	-20	131	108	-17	7.6
● **JIM DERRINGTON**	Derrington, Charles James "Blackie" b: 11/29/39, Compton, Cal. BL/TL, 6'3", 190 lbs. Deb: 9/30/56																									
1956	Chi-A	0	1	.000	1	1	0	0	0	6	9	2	6	3	22.5	7.50	55	.375	.500	1	.500	0	-2	-2	-0	-0.3
1957	Chi-A	0	1	.000	20	5	0	0	0	37	29	4	29	14	14.4	4.86	77	.216	.360	0	.000	-0	-4	-5	-1	-0.3
Total	2	0	2	.000	21	6	0	0	0	43	38	6	35	17	15.5	5.23	72	.241	.381	1	.167	0	-7	-7	-1	-0.6
● **JIM DESHAIES**	Deshaies, James Joseph b: 6/23/60, Massena, N.Y. BL/TL, 6'4", 220 lbs. Deb: 8/7/84																									
1984	NY-A	0	1	.000	2	2	0	0	0	7	14	1	7	5	27.0	11.57	33	.438	.538	0	—	0	-6	-6	0	-0.7
1985	Hou-N	0	0	—	2	0	0	0	0	3	1	0	0	2	3.0	0.00	—	.100	.100	0	—	0	1	1	-0	0.0
1986	Hou-N	12	5	.706	26	26	1	1	0	144	124	16	59	128	11.6	3.25	111	.234	.313	2	.047	-1	7	6	-2	0.3
1987	Hou-N	11	6	.647	26	25	1	0	0	152	149	22	57	104	12.2	4.62	85	.257	.324	5	.094	-0	-9	-12	-1	-1.2
1988	Hou-N	11	14	.440	31	31	3	2	0	207	164	20	72	127	10.3	3.00	111	.218	.288	3	.048	-4	10	7	-2	0.2
1989	Hou-N	15	10	.600	34	34	6	3	0	225^2	180	15	79	153	10.5	2.91	116	.217	.288	9	.120	-2	15	12	-1	0.9
1990	Hou-N	7	12	.368	34	34	2	0	0	209^1	186	21	84	119	12.0	3.78	98	.245	.326	4	.063	-3	0	-2	-1	-0.6
1991	Hou-N	5	12	.294	28	28	1	0	0	161	156	19	72	98	12.8	4.98	70	.259	.339	4	.098	-1	-23	-26	-2	-2.7
1992	SD-N	4	7	.364	15	15	0	0	0	96	92	6	33	46	11.8	3.28	109	.258	.323	6	.207	1	2	3	1	0.5
1993	Min-A	11	13	.458	27	27	1	0	0	167^1	159	24	51	80	11.6	4.41	99	.254	.317	0	—	0	-2	-1	-1	-0.2
	SF-N	2	2	.500	5	4	0	0	0	17	24	2	6	5	16.4	4.24	92	.348	.408	0	.000	-1	-0	-1	-0	-0.2
1994	Min-A	6	12	.333	25	25	0	0	0	130^1	170	30	54	78	15.6	7.39	66	.321	.386	0	—	0	-37	-37	-1	-3.9
1995	Phi-N	0	1	.000	2	2	0	0	0	5^1	15	3	1	6	27.0	20.25	21	.484	.500	0	.000	-0	-10	-9	-0	-1.2
Total	12	84	95	.469	257	253	15	6	0	1525	1434	179	575	951	12.0	4.14	91	.251	.323	33	.088	-12	-51	-65	-9	-8.8
● **JIMMIE DeSHONG**	DeShong, James Brooklyn b: 11/30/09, Harrisburg, Pa. d: 10/16/93, Lower Paxton Township, Pa. BR/TR, 5'11", 165 lbs. Deb: 4/12/32																									
1932	Phi-A	0	0	—	6	0	0	0	0	10	17	3	9	5	24.3	11.70	39	.378	.491	0	.000	-0	-8	-8	0	0.0
1934	NY-A	6	7	.462	31	12	6	0	3	133^2	126	6	56	40	12.4	4.11	99	.243	.319	8	.190	2	6	-1	-0	0.1
1935	NY-A	4	1	.800	29	3	0	0	3	69	64	6	33	30	12.9	3.26	124	.242	.331	1	.071	-1	9	6	2	0.5
1936	Was-A	18	10	.643	34	31	16	2	2	223^2	255	11	96	59	14.2	4.63	103	.285	.356	15	.190	2	10	4	-2	0.4
1937	Was-A	14	15	.483	37	34	20	0	1	264^1	290	15	124	86	14.2	4.90	90	.280	.359	19	.202	2	-8	-14	1	-1.0
1938	Was-A	5	8	.385	31	14	1	0	0	131^1	160	11	83	41	16.7	6.58	69	.310	.407	12	.261	3	-26	-30	0	-2.1
1939	Was-A	0	3	.000	7	6	1	0	0	40^2	56	7	31	12	19.3	8.63	50	.337	.442	3	.200	0	-18	-19	1	-1.0
Total	7	47	44	.516	175	100	44	2	9	872^2	968	59	432	273	14.6	5.08	87	.281	.363	58	.198	7	-35	-63	3	-3.1
● **JOHN DeSILVA**	DeSilva, John Reed b: 9/30/67, Fort Bragg, Cal. BR/TR, 6', 193 lbs. Deb: 8/15/93																									
1993	Det-A	0	0	—	1	0	0	0	0	1	2	0	0	0	18.0	9.00	48	.667	.667	0	—	0	-1	-1	0	0.0
	LA-N	0	0	—	3	0	0	0	0	5^1	6	0	1	6	11.8	6.75	57	.273	.304	0	—	0	-2	-2	-0	0.0
1995	Bal-A	1	0	1.000	2	2	0	0	0	8^2	8	3	7	1	16.6	7.27	65	.258	.410	0	—	0	-2	-2	0	-0.2
Total	2	1	0	1.000	6	2	0	0	0	15	16	3	8	7	15.0	7.20	61	.286	.385	0	—	0	-5	-5	0	-0.2
● **SHORTY DesJARDIEN**	DesJardien, Paul Raymond b: 8/24/1893, Coffeyville, Kan. d: 3/7/56, Monrovia, Cal. BR/TR, 6'4.5", 205 lbs. Deb: 5/20/16																									
1916	Cle-A	0	0	—	1	0	0	0	0	1	1	0	1	0	18.0	18.00	17	.200	.333	0	—	0	-2	-2	-0	0.0
● **RUBE DESSAU**	Dessau, Frank Rolland b: 3/29/1883, New Galilee, Pa. d: 5/6/52, York, Pa. BB/TR, 5'11", 175 lbs. Deb: 9/22/07																									
1907	Bos-N	0	1	.000	2	2	1	0	0	9^1	13	0	10	1	23.1	10.61	24	.394	.545	0	.000	-0	-8	-8	-0	-0.8
1910	Bro-N	2	3	.400	19	0	0	0	1	51^1	67	0	29	24	17.7	5.79	52	.328	.424	1	.067	-1	-16	-16	-1	-1.7
Total	2	2	4	.333	21	2	1	0	1	60^2	80	0	39	25	18.5	6.53	45	.338	.443	1	.053	-1	-24	-24	-2	-2.5
● **ELMER DESSENS**	Dessens, Elmer b: 1/13/72, Hermosillo, Mex. BR/TR, 6', 190 lbs. Deb: 6/24/96																									
1996	Pit-N	0	2	.000	15	3	0	0	0	25	40	2	4	13	15.8	8.28	53	.385	.407	2	.400	1	-11	-11	-0	-0.7
1997	Pit-N	0	0	—	3	0	0	0	0	3^1	2	0	0	2	8.1	0.00	—	.167	.231	0	—	0	2	2	0	0.0
1998	Pit-N	2	6	.250	43	5	0	0	0	74^2	90	10	25	43	13.9	5.67	76	.300	.354	0	.000	-1	-12	-11	-1	-1.2
Total	3	2	8	.200	61	8	0	0	0	103	132	12	29	58	14.2	6.12	71	.317	.363	2	.154	-0	-22	-20	-1	-1.9
● **JOHN DETTMER**	Dettmer, John Franklin b: 3/4/70, Centreville, Ill. BR/TR, 6', 185 lbs. Deb: 6/16/94																									
1994	Tex-A	0	6	.000	11	9	0	0	0	54	63	10	20	27	14.3	4.33	111	.286	.354	0	—	0	3	3	-0	0.3
1995	Tex-A	0	0	—	1	0	0	0	0	0^1	2	0	0	0	54.0	27.00	18	.667	.667	0	—	0	-1	-1	0	0.0
Total	2	0	6	.000	12	9	0	0	0	54^1	65	10	20	27	14.6	4.47	108	.291	.358	0	—	0	2	2	-0	0.3
● **TOM DETTORE**	Dettore, Thomas Anthony b: 11/17/47, Canonsburg, Pa. BL/TR, 6'4", 200 lbs. Deb: 6/11/73																									
1973	Pit-N	0	1	.000	12	1	0	0	0	22^2	33	1	14	13	19.9	5.96	59	.340	.439	0	.000	-0	-6	-6	-0	-0.3
1974	Chi-N	3	5	.375	16	9	0	0	0	64^2	64	4	31	43	14.1	4.18	91	.255	.351	5	.250	1	-4	-3	0	-0.1
1975	Chi-N	5	4	.556	36	5	0	0	0	85^1	88	8	31	46	13.5	5.38	71	.270	.350	6	.250	1	-17	-15	0	-1.3
1976	Chi-N	0	1	.000	4	0	0	0	0	7	11	3	2	4	16.7	10.29	38	.355	.394	0	—	0	-5	-5	-0	-0.6
Total	4	8	11	.421	68	15	0	0	0	179^2	196	16	78	106	14.6	5.21	73	.278	.365	11	.229	2	-32	-28	0	-2.3
● **MEL DEUTSCH**	Deutsch, Melvin Elliott b: 7/26/15, Caldwell, Tex. BR/TR, 6'4", 215 lbs. Deb: 4/21/46																									
1946	Bos-A	0	0	—	3	0	0	0	0	6^1	7	1	3	2	14.2	5.68	64	.280	.357	0	.000	-0	-2	-1	-0	0.0
● **CHARLIE DEVENS**	Devens, Charles b: 1/1/10, Milton, Mass. BR/TR, 6'1", 180 lbs. Deb: 9/24/32																									
1932	NY-A	1	0	1.000	1	1	1	0	0	9	6	0	7	4	13.0	2.00	204	.200	.351	0	.000	0	2	2	-0	0.2
1933	NY-A	3	3	.500	14	8	2	0	0	62	59	1	50	23	15.8	4.35	89	.250	.381	2	.095	-1	-1	-3	-1	-0.4
1934	NY-A	1	0	1.000	1	1	1	0	0	11	9	0	5	4	11.5	1.64	248	.225	.311	1	.500	1	3	3	0	0.5
Total	3	5	3	.625	16	10	4	0	0	82	74	1	62	31	14.9	3.73	105	.242	.370	3	.120	0	5	2	-1	0.3
● **ADRIAN DEVINE**	Devine, Paul Adrian b: 12/2/51, Galveston, Tex. BR/TR, 6'4", 205 lbs. Deb: 6/27/73																									
1973	Atl-N	2	3	.400	24	1	0	0	4	32^1	45	6	12	15	16.4	6.40	61	.338	.401	1	.250	0	-10	-9	-1	-1.5
1975	Atl-N	1	0	1.000	5	2	0	0	0	16^1	19	2	7	8	14.9	4.41	86	.284	.360	0	.000	-1	-1	-1	-0	-0.2
1976	Atl-N	5	6	.455	48	1	0	0	9	73	72	3	26	48	12.2	3.21	118	.255	.320	0	.000	-2	2	5	-1	0.6
1977	Tex-A	11	6	.647	56	2	0	0	15	105^2	102	8	31	67	11.7	3.58	114	.259	.319	0	—	0	6	6	2	1.2
1978	Atl-N	5	4	.556	31	6	0	0	3	65^1	84	3	25	26	15.0	5.92	68	.323	.382	1	.091	-1	-17	-14	0	-1.9
1979	Atl-N	1	2	.333	40	0	0	0	0	66^2	84	8	25	22	15.0	3.24	125	.311	.374	0	.000	-1	4	6	-0	0.1
1980	Tex-A	1	1	.500	13	0	0	0	0	28	49	4	9	8	19.0	4.82	81	.377	.421	0	—	0	-2	-3	-0	-0.2
Total	7	26	22	.542	217	12	0	0	31	387^1	455	34	135	194	14.0	4.21	95	.296	.357	2	.049	-3	-19	-9	0	-1.9
● **JIM DEVINE**	Devine, Walter James b: 10/5/1858, Brooklyn, N.Y. d: 1/11/05, Syracuse, N.Y. TL , Deb: 5/9/1883 ♦																									
1883	Bal-a	1	1	.500	2	2	1	0	0	11	15	0	1	3	13.1	7.36	47	.306	.320	2	.222	-0	-5	-5	-1	-0.6
● **HAL DEVINEY**	Deviney, Harold John b: 4/11/1893, Newton, Mass. d: 1/4/33, Westwood, Mass. BR/TR, Deb: 7/30/20																									
1920	Bos-A	0	0	—	1	0	0	0	0	3	7	0	2	0	27.0	15.00	24	.500	.563	2	1.000	2	-4	-4	-0	0.2

YEAR TM/L	W	L	PCT	G	GS	CG	SH	SV	IP	H	HR	BB	SO	RAT	ERA	ERA+	OAV	OOB	BH	AVG	PB	PR	/A	PD	TPI
● JIM DEVLIN Devlin, James Alexander b: 1849, Philadelphia, Pa. d: 10/10/1883, Philadelphia, Pa. BR/TR, 5'11", 175 lbs. Deb: 4/21/1873 ♦																									
1875 Chi-n	7	16	.304	28	24	24	0	0	224	254	0	12	23	10.7	1.93	118	.256	.265	92	.289	7	7	8		1.3
1876 Lou-N	30	35	.462	**68**	68	**66**	5	0	**622**	566	3	37	**122**	8.7	1.56	174	.224	.235	94	.315	2	51	**80**	1	**7.3**
1877 Lou-N	35	25	.583	**61**	61	**61**	4	0	**559**	617	4	41	141	10.6	2.25	**147**	.270	.283	72	.269	-2	34	**65**	2	**5.9**
Total 2	65	60	.520	129	129	127	9	0	1181	1183	7	78	263	9.6	1.89	159	.246	.258	166	.293	1	86	145	3	13.2
● JIM DEVLIN Devlin, James H. b: 4/16/1866, Troy, N.Y. d: 12/14/1900, Troy, N.Y. TL, 5'7", 135 lbs. Deb: 6/28/1886																									
1886 NY-N	0	0	—	1	0	0	0	1	2	3	0	4	2	31.5	18.00	18	.250	.438	0	.000	-0	-3	-3	0	-0.3
1887 Phi-N	0	2	.000	2	2	2	0	0	18	20	0	10	6	16.5	6.00	71	.267	.375	2	.333	0	-4	-4	0	-0.2
1888 *StL-a	6	5	.545	11	11	10	0	0	90^1	82	3	20	45	11.0	3.19	102	.233	.289	11	.297	2	-1	1	0	0.2
1889 StL-a	5	3	.625	9	8	5	0	0	60	56	0	24	37	13.1	2.40	176	.239	.328	5	.192	-2	10	12	1	1.3
Total 4	11	10	.524	23	21	17	0	1	170^1	161	3	58	90	12.5	3.38	109	.239	.316	18	.257	1	1	6	2	1.0
● CHARLIE DEWALD Dewald, Charles H. b: 9/1867, Newark, N.J. d: 8/22/04, Cleveland, Ohio TL, Deb: 9/2/1890																									
1890 Cle-P	2	0	1.000	2	2	2	0	0	14	13	0	5	6	11.6	0.64	618	.236	.300	3	.375	1	6	5	-0	0.6
● MARK DEWEY Dewey, Mark Alan b: 1/3/65, Grand Rapids, Mich. BR/TR, 6', 207 lbs. Deb: 8/24/90																									
1990 SF-N	1	1	.500	14	0	0	0	0	22^2	22	1	5	11	10.7	2.78	131	.259	.300	0	.000	0	3	2	-0	0.2
1992 NY-N	1	0	1.000	20	0	0	0	0	33^1	37	2	10	24	12.7	4.32	80	.280	.331	0	.000	-0	-3	-3	0	-0.1
1993 Pit-N	1	2	.333	21	0	0	0	7	26^2	14	0	10	14	9.1	2.36	171	.157	.265	0	—	0	5	5	0	0.8
1994 Pit-N	2	1	.667	45	0	0	0	1	51^1	61	4	19	30	14.6	3.68	117	.303	.372	1	1.000	0	3	4	-1	0.2
1995 SF-N	1	0	1.000	27	0	0	0	0	31^2	30	2	17	32	13.4	3.13	131	.254	.348	0	.000	-0	4	3	-0	0.1
1996 SF-N	6	3	.667	78	0	0	0	0	83^1	79	9	41	57	13.5	4.21	97	.257	.354	0	.000	-0	0	-1	2	0.0
Total 6	12	7	.632	205	0	0	0	8	249	243	18	102	168	12.9	3.65	110	.261	.341	1	.091	0	11	10	1	1.2
● CARLOS DIAZ Diaz, Carlos Antonio b: 1/7/58, Kaneohe, Hawaii BR/TL, 6', 170 lbs. Deb: 6/30/82																									
1982 Atl-N	3	2	.600	19	0	0	0	1	25^1	31	3	9	16	14.2	4.62	81	.307	.364	0	.000	-0	-3	-3	0	-0.5
NY-N	0	0	—	4	0	0	0	0	3^2	6	0	4	0	24.5	0.00	—	.353	.476	0	—	0	1	1	0	0.0
Yr	3	2	.600	23	0	0	0	1	29	37	3	13	16	15.5	4.03	92	.311	.379	0	.000	-0	-1	-1	0	-0.5
1983 NY-N	3	1	.750	54	0	0	0	2	83^1	62	1	35	64	10.6	2.05	177	.211	.297	0	.000	-0	15	15	1	0.8
1984 LA-N	1	0	1.000	37	0	0	0	1	41	47	4	24	36	15.6	5.49	64	.285	.376	0	.000	-0	-9	-9	-1	-0.3
1985 *LA-N	6	3	.667	46	0	0	0	0	79^1	70	7	18	73	10.0	2.61	133	.230	.273	0	.000	-0	9	8	-1	0.7
1986 LA-N	0	0	—	19	0	0	0	0	25^1	33	2	7	18	14.2	4.26	81	.317	.360	0	.000	-0	-2	-2	0	0.0
Total 5	13	6	.684	179	0	0	0	4	258	249	17	97	207	12.1	3.21	111	.253	.320	0	.000	-1	12	10	-0	0.7
● ROB DIBBLE Dibble, Robert Keith b: 1/24/64, Bridgeport, Conn. BL/TR, 6'4", 230 lbs. Deb: 6/29/88																									
1988 Cin-N	1	1	.500	37	0	0	0	0	59^1	43	2	21	59	9.9	1.82	197	.207	.283	0	.000	-0	11	12	-1	0.2
1989 Cin-N	10	5	.667	74	0	0	0	2	99	62	4	39	141	9.5	2.09	172	.176	.264	0	.000	-1	15	17	-1	2.3
1990 *Cin-N★	8	3	.727	68	0	0	0	11	98	62	3	34	136	8.9	1.74	226	.183	.259	0	.000	-1	**22**	**24**	-0	3.0
1991 Cin-N★	3	5	.375	67	0	0	0	31	82^1	67	5	25	124	10.1	3.17	120	.223	.282	0	.000	-0	5	6	-0	0.9
1992 Cin-N	3	5	.375	63	0	0	0	25	70^1	48	3	31	110	10.4	3.07	117	.193	.287	2	.400	1	3	4	-1	0.7
1993 Cin-N	1	4	.200	45	0	0	0	19	41^2	34	8	42	49	16.8	6.48	62	.225	.400	1	1.000	0	-11	-11	0	-2.0
1995 Chi-A	0	1	.000	16	0	0	0	1	14^1	7	1	27	16	23.2	6.28	71	.156	.493	0	—	0	-2	-3	0	0.0
Mil-A	1	1	.500	15	0	0	0	0	12	9	1	19	10	21.0	8.25	60	.225	.475	0	—	0	-5	-4	-0	-0.8
Yr	1	2	.333	31	0	0	0	1	26^1	16	2	46	26	21.2	7.18	65	.178	.456	0	—	0	-7	-7	-0	-0.8
Total 7	27	25	.519	385	0	0	0	89	477	332	27	238	645	11.0	2.98	128	.197	.301	3	.120	-1	38	44	-3	4.3
● PEDRO DIBUT Dibut, Pedro (Villafana) b: 11/18/1892, Cienfuegos, Cuba d: 12/4/79, Hialeah, Fla. BR/TR, 5'8", 190 lbs. Deb: 5/1/24																									
1924 Cin-N	3	0	1.000	7	2	2	0	0	36^2	24	1	12	15	8.8	2.21	170	.188	.257	3	.273	1	7	6	1	0.7
1925 Cin-N	0	0	—	1	0	0	0	0	0	3	0	0	0	—	∞	—	1.000	1.000	0	—	0	-2	-2	0	-0.2
Total 2	3	0	1.000	8	2	2	0	0	36^2	27	1	12	15	9.6	2.70	139	.206	.273	3	.273	1	5	4	1	0.5
● LEO DICKERMAN Dickerman, Leo Louis b: 10/31/1896, DeSoto, Mo. d: 4/30/82, Atkins, Ark. BR/TR, 6'4", 192 lbs. Deb: 4/21/23																									
1923 Bro-N	8	12	.400	35	20	7	1	0	159^2	180	4	72	58	14.3	3.72	104	.283	.357	13	.250	3	5	3	2	0.8
1924 Bro-N	0	0	—	7	2	0	0	0	19^2	20	0	16	9	17.4	5.49	68	.263	.404	1	.167	-0	-4	-4	0	0.0
StL-N	7	4	.636	18	13	8	1	0	119^2	108	6	51	28	12.0	2.41	157	.249	.328	9	.231	1	19	18	0	1.7
Yr	7	4	.636	25	15	8	1	0	139^1	128	6	67	37	12.6	2.84	133	.250	.337	10	.222	1	16	14	1	1.7
1925 StL-N	4	11	.267	29	18	7	2	1	130^2	135	10	79	40	14.9	5.58	77	.273	.376	5	.114	-3	-19	-18	4	-1.7
Total 3	19	27	.413	89	53	22	4	1	429^2	443	20	218	135	14.0	4.00	99	.270	.358	28	.199	1	2	-1	6	0.8
● GEORGE DICKERSON Dickerson, George Clark b: 12/1/1892, Renner, Tex. d: 7/9/38, Los Angeles, Cal. BR/TR, 6'1", 170 lbs. Deb: 8/2/17																									
1917 Cle-A	0	0	—	1	0	0	0	0	1	0	0	0	0	0.0	0.00	—	.000	.000	0	—	0	0	0	-0	0.0
● EMERSON DICKMAN Dickman, George Emerson b: 11/12/14, Buffalo, N.Y. d: 4/27/81, New York, N.Y. BR/TR, 6'2", 175 lbs. Deb: 6/27/36																									
1936 Bos-A	0	0	—	1	0	0	0	0	1	2	0	1	2	27.0	9.00	59	.400	.500	0	—	0	-0	-0	0	0.0
1938 Bos-A	5	5	.500	32	11	3	1	0	104	117	9	54	22	15.1	5.28	93	.288	.377	10	.286	4	-6	-4	-0	0.0
1939 Bos-A	8	3	.727	48	1	0	0	5	113^2	126	10	43	46	13.6	4.43	107	.282	.349	2	.056	-4	2	4	3	0.2
1940 Bos-A	8	6	.571	35	9	2	0	3	100	121	15	38	40	14.7	6.03	75	.291	.356	3	.107	-2	-18	-17	2	-2.1
1941 Bos-A	1	1	.500	9	3	1	0	0	31	37	4	17	16	15.7	6.39	65	.301	.386	1	.091	-1	-8	-8	-1	-0.6
Total 5	22	15	.595	125	24	6	1	8	349^2	403	38	153	126	14.6	5.33	88	.288	.363	16	.145	-2	-30	-25	4	-2.5
● JIM DICKSON Dickson, James Edward b: 4/20/38, Portland, Ore. BL/TR, 6'1", 185 lbs. Deb: 7/2/63																									
1963 Hou-N	0	1	.000	13	0	0	0	2	14^2	22	0	2	6	14.7	6.14	51	.344	.364	0	.000	-0	-5	-5	-0	-0.5
1964 Cin-N	1	0	1.000	4	0	0	0	0	5	8	0	5	6	23.4	7.20	50	.444	.565	0	—	0	-2	-2	0	-0.4
1965 KC-A	3	2	.600	68	0	0	0	0	85^2	68	6	47	54	12.3	3.47	101	.220	.327	0	.000	-0	-0	0	-1	-0.1
1966 KC-A	1	0	1.000	24	1	0	0	1	37	37	4	23	20	14.6	5.35	63	.264	.368	1	.250	0	-8	-8	-0	-0.3
Total 4	5	3	.625	109	1	0	0	3	142^1	135	10	77	86	13.5	4.36	79	.254	.351	1	.143	-0	-15	-15	-1	-1.3
● JASON DICKSON Dickson, Jason Royce b: 3/30/73, London, Ont., Can. BL/TR, 6', 190 lbs. Deb: 8/21/96																									
1996 Cal-A	1	4	.200	7	7	0	0	0	43^1	52	6	18	20	14.7	4.57	109	.306	.376	0	—	0	2	2	0	0.2
1997 Ana-A☆	13	9	.591	33	32	2	1	0	203^2	236	32	56	115	13.2	4.29	107	.289	.340	0	.000	-0	6	6	-2	0.4
1998 Ana-A	10	10	.500	27	18	0	0	0	122	147	17	41	61	14.3	6.05	78	.303	.365	0	.000	-0	-19	-18	-2	-2.6
Total 3	24	23	.511	67	57	2	1	0	369	435	55	115	196	13.8	4.90	95	.296	.352	0	.000	-0	-11	-10	-4	-2.0
● LANCE DICKSON Dickson, Lance Michael b: 10/19/69, Fullerton, Cal. BR/TL, 6', 185 lbs. Deb: 8/9/90																									
1990 Chi-N	0	3	.000	3	3	0	0	0	13^2	20	2	4	4	15.8	7.24	56	.370	.414	0	.000	-0	-5	-5	1	-0.8
● MURRY DICKSON Dickson, Murry Monroe b: 8/21/16, Tracy, Mo. d: 9/21/89, Kansas City, Kan. BR/TR, 5'10.5", 157 lbs. Deb: 9/30/39																									
1939 StL-N	0	0	—	1	0	0	0	0	3^2	1	0	1	2	4.9	0.00	—	.091	.167	0	.000	-0	2	2	0	0.0
1940 StL-N	0	0	—	1	1	0	0	0	1^2	5	0	1	0	32.4	16.20	25	.500	.545	0	—	0	-2	-2	-0	0.0
1942 StL-N	6	3	.667	36	7	2	0	2	120^2	91	1	61	66	11.4	2.91	118	.216	.316	8	.190	-0	5	7	1	0.6
1943 *StL-N	8	2	.800	31	7	2	0	0	115^2	119	4	49	44	13.1	3.58	94	.269	.343	9	.265	1	-3	-3	-0	-0.2
1946 *StL-N	15	6	**.714**	47	19	12	2	1	184^1	160	8	56	82	10.7	2.88	120	.234	.295	18	.277	4	11	12	4	2.2
1947 StL-N	13	16	.448	47	25	11	4	3	231^2	211	16	88	111	11.7	3.07	135	.243	.315	17	.213	1	25	27	1	3.4
1948 StL-N	12	16	.429	42	29	11	1	1	252^1	257	39	85	113	12.2	4.14	99	.265	.325	27	.281	4	-5	-1	1	0.3
1949 Pit-N	12	14	.462	44	20	11	2	0	224^1	216	17	80	89	12.1	3.29	128	.255	.324	17	.202	0	19	23	5	3.0
1950 Pit-N	10	15	.400	51	22	8	0	3	225	227	20	83	76	12.5	3.80	115	.260	.326	21	.256	3	9	15	2	2.0
1951 Pit-N	20	16	.556	45	35	19	3	2	288^2	294	32	101	112	12.5	4.02	105	.262	.327	30	.273	5	-2	7	4	1.7
1952 Pit-N	14	21	.400	43	34	21	2	2	277^2	278	26	76	112	11.5	3.57	112	.261	.311	24	.224	2	5	13	4	2.3
1953 Pit-N★	10	19	.345	45	26	10	1	4	200^2	240	27	58	88	13.5	4.53	99	.298	.348	7	.115	-4	-5	-1	-0	-0.5
1954 Phi-N	10	20	.333	40	31	12	4	3	226^1	256	31	73	64	13.2	3.78	107	.286	.342	15	.190	0	7	7	3	1.0
1955 Phi-N	12	11	.522	36	28	12	4	0	216	190	27	82	92	11.5	3.50	113	.238	.312	18	.220	1	13	11	1	1.3

YEAR	TM/L	W	L	PCT	G	GS	CG	SH	SV	IP	H	HR	BB	SO	RAT	ERA	ERA+	OAV	OOB	BH	AVG	PB	PR	/A	PD	TPI
1956	Phi-N	0	3	.000	3	3	0	0	0	23	20	1	12	1	12.5	5.09	73	.241	.337	3	.333	1	-3	-3	0	-0.3
	StL-N	13	8	.619	28	27	12	3	0	196^1	175	20	57	109	10.7	3.07	123	.240	.296	19	.247	4	15	16	4	2.5
	Yr	13	11	.542	31	30	12	3	0	219^1	195	21	69	110	10.9	3.28	115	.240	.301	22	.256	4	12	12	4	2.2
1957	StL-N	5	3	.625	14	13	3	1	0	74	87	8	25	29	13.7	4.14	96	.296	.353	6	.222	1	-2	-1	2	0.1
1958	KC-A	9	5	.643	27	9	3	0	1	99	99	12	31	46	12.0	3.27	119	.258	.317	9	.257	2	5	7	2	1.4
	*NY-A	1	2	.333	6	2	0	0	1	20^1	18	4	12	9	13.7	5.75	61	.237	.348	2	.286	0	-4	-5	-0	-0.7
	Yr	10	7	.588	33	11	3	0	2	119^1	117	16	43	55	12.1	3.70	104	.253	.318	11	.262	2	1	2	2	0.7
1959	KC-A	2	1	.667	38	0	0	0	0	71	85	9	27	36	14.2	4.94	81	.290	.350	3	.176	-1	-9	-7	-0	-0.4
Total	18	172	181	.487	625	338	149	27	23	3052^1	3029	302	1058	1281	12.2	3.66	110	.260	.323	253	.231	25	81	120	32	19.7

● WALT DICKSON Dickson, Walter R. "Hickory" b: 12/3/1878, New Summerfield, Tex. d: 12/9/18, Ardmore, Okla. BR/TR, 5′11.5″, 175 lbs. Deb: 4/26/10

YEAR	TM/L	W	L	PCT	G	GS	CG	SH	SV	IP	H	HR	BB	SO	RAT	ERA	ERA+	OAV	OOB	BH	AVG	PB	PR	/A	PD	TPI
1910	NY-N	1	0	1.000	12	1	0	0	0	29^2	31	1	9	9	12.1	5.46	54	.272	.325	1	.250	0	-8	-8	-1	-0.3
1912	Bos-N	3	19	.136	36	20	9	1	1	189	233	2	61	47	14.1	3.86	93	.320	.375	10	.167	-1	-9	-6	2	-0.6
1913	Bos-N	6	7	.462	19	15	8	0	0	128	118	4	45	47	11.5	3.23	102	.249	.316	8	.178	-1	-0	1	-1	-0.2
1914	Pit-F	9	19	.321	40	32	19	3	1	256^2	262	5	74	63	11.9	3.16	91	.273	.327	7	.084	-9	-8	-8	-0	-1.8
1915	Pit-F	7	5	.583	27	11	4	0	0	96^2	115	5	33	36	14.0	4.19	65	.316	.376	4	.129	-1	-16	-16	0	-1.9
Total	5	26	50	.342	134	79	40	4	2	700	759	17	222	202	12.7	3.60	86	.288	.345	30	.135	-12	-41	-38	0	-4.8

● GEORGE DIEHL Diehl, George Krause b: 2/25/18, Emmaus, Pa. d: 8/24/86, Kingsport, Tenn. BR/TR, 6′2″, 196 lbs. Deb: 4/19/42

YEAR	TM/L	W	L	PCT	G	GS	CG	SH	SV	IP	H	HR	BB	SO	RAT	ERA	ERA+	OAV	OOB	BH	AVG	PB	PR	/A	PD	TPI
1942	Bos-N	0	0	—	1	0	0	0	0	3^2	2	0	2	0	12.3	2.45	136	.167	.333	0	.000	-0	0	0	0	0.0
1943	Bos-N	0	0	—	1	0	0	0	0	4	4	0	3	1	15.8	4.50	76	.267	.389	0	.000	-0	-0	-0	1	0.1
Total	2	0	0	—	2	0	0	0	0	7^2	6	0	5	1	14.1	3.52	96	.222	.364	0	.000	-0	-0	-0	1	0.1

● LARRY DIERKER Dierker, Lawrence Edward b: 9/22/46, Hollywood, Cal BR/TR, 6′4″, 215 lbs. Deb: 9/22/64 M

YEAR	TM/L	W	L	PCT	G	GS	CG	SH	SV	IP	H	HR	BB	SO	RAT	ERA	ERA+	OAV	OOB	BH	AVG	PB	PR	/A	PD	TPI
1964	Hou-N	0	1	.000	3	1	0	0	0	9	7	1	3	5	10.0	2.00	171	.219	.286	0	.000	-0	2	1	-1	0.1
1965	Hou-N	7	8	.467	26	19	1	0	0	146^2	135	16	37	109	10.7	3.50	96	.240	.290	5	.100	-1	1	-2	-2	-0.5
1966	Hou-N	10	8	.556	29	28	8	2	0	187	173	17	45	108	10.5	3.18	108	.240	.285	10	.149	1	9	5	-1	0.5
1967	Hou-N	6	5	.545	15	15	4	0	0	99	95	4	25	68	11.0	3.36	98	.252	.300	7	.226	2	0	-1	-1	0.0
1968	Hou-N	12	15	.444	32	32	10	1	0	233^2	206	14	89	161	11.7	3.31	89	.240	.317	5	.068	-3	-9	-9	-2	-1.7
1969	Hou-N★	20	13	.606	39	37	20	4	0	305^1	240	18	72	232	9.2	2.33	152	.214	**.262**	17	.144	-1	43	41	-1	4.3
1970	Hou-N	16	12	.571	37	36	17	2	1	269^2	263	31	82	191	11.7	3.87	100	.254	.313	16	.174	-0	5	0	-1	-0.1
1971	Hou-N†	12	6	.667	24	23	6	2	0	159	150	8	33	91	10.5	2.72	124	.248	.289	4	.074	-3	13	11	0	1.0
1972	Hou-N	15	8	.652	31	31	12	5	0	214^2	209	14	51	115	11.1	3.40	99	.256	.304	13	.167	-0	1	-1	-2	-0.3
1973	Hou-N	1	1	.500	14	3	0	0	0	27	27	3	13	18	14.0	4.33	84	.265	.359	0	.000	-0	-2	-2	-0	-0.2
1974	Hou-N	11	10	.524	33	33	7	3	0	223^2	189	18	82	150	11.1	2.90	120	.232	.307	14	.197	1	18	14	0	1.4
1975	Hou-N	14	16	.467	34	34	14	2	0	232	225	24	91	127	12.5	4.00	84	.260	.335	7	.092	-4	-10	-16	-1	-2.4
1976	Hou-N	13	14	.481	28	28	7	4	0	187^2	171	9	72	112	11.9	3.69	86	.243	.319	9	.141	-1	-4	-10	-1	-1.6
1977	StL-N	2	6	.250	11	9	0	0	0	39^1	40	7	16	6	13.3	4.58	84	.267	.345	0	.000	-1	-3	-3	-0	-0.7
Total	14	139	123	.531	356	329	106	25	1	2333^2	2130	184	711	1493	11.1	3.31	103	.243	.303	107	.136	-12	65	29	-12	-0.2

● BILL DIETRICH Dietrich, William John "Bullfrog" b: 3/29/10, Philadelphia, Pa. d: 6/20/78, Philadelphia, Pa. BR/TR, 6′, 185 lbs. Deb: 4/13/33

YEAR	TM/L	W	L	PCT	G	GS	CG	SH	SV	IP	H	HR	BB	SO	RAT	ERA	ERA+	OAV	OOB	BH	AVG	PB	PR	/A	PD	TPI
1933	Phi-A	0	1	.000	8	1	0	0	0	17	13	1	19	4	16.9	5.82	74	.236	.432	1	.333	1	-3	-3	0	0.0
1934	Phi-A	11	12	.478	39	23	14	4	3	207^2	201	12	114	88	13.8	4.68	94	.255	.351	15	.208	3	-4	-7	-2	-0.5
1935	Phi-A	7	13	.350	43	15	8	1	3	185^1	203	7	101	59	14.8	5.39	84	.276	.364	5	.083	-6	-19	-17	-1	-2.2
1936	Phi-A	4	6	.400	21	4	0	0	3	71^2	91	4	40	34	16.5	6.53	78	.305	.388	3	.111	-2	-12	-11	1	-1.3
	Was-A	0	1	.000	5	0	0	0	0	8^1	13	0	6	4	20.5	9.72	49	.351	.442	0	—	0	-4	-5	0	-0.4
	Chi-A	4	4	.500	14	11	6	1	0	82^2	93	8	36	39	14.2	4.68	111	.284	.356	8	.267	1	3	5	-0	0.4
	Yr	8	11	.421	40	15	6	1	3	162^2	197	12	82	77	15.5	5.75	89	.297	.375	11	.193	-1	-13	-11	1	-1.3
1937	Chi-A	8	10	.444	29	20	7	1	1	143^1	162	15	72	62	14.7	4.90	94	.285	.366	8	.182	1	-4	-5	1	-0.3
1938	Chi-A	2	4	.333	8	7	1	0	0	48	49	7	31	11	15.0	5.44	90	.259	.364	1	.063	-1	-3	-3	-0	-0.4
1939	Chi-A	7	8	.467	25	19	2	0	0	127^2	134	14	56	43	13.5	5.22	91	.272	.349	8	.216	2	-8	-7	-1	-0.5
1940	Chi-A	10	6	.625	23	17	6	1	0	149^2	154	10	65	43	13.2	4.03	110	.266	.340	12	.240	3	6	7	-2	0.8
1941	Chi-A	5	8	.385	19	15	4	1	0	109^1	114	7	50	26	13.8	5.35	77	.263	.345	3	.088	0	-15	-15	-2	-1.6
1942	Chi-A	6	11	.353	26	23	6	0	0	160	173	16	70	39	13.9	4.89	74	.277	.355	5	.104	-1	-22	-23	-0	-2.3
1943	Chi-A	12	10	.545	26	26	12	2	0	186^2	180	4	53	52	11.3	2.80	119	.253	.307	8	.143	0	10	11	1	1.5
1944	Chi-A	16	17	.485	36	36	15	2	0	246	269	15	68	70	12.4	3.62	95	.279	.328	9	.117	-3	-5	-5	-1	-1.0
1945	Chi-A	7	10	.412	18	16	6	3	0	122^1	136	4	36	43	12.7	4.19	79	.279	.329	6	.167	0	-11	-12	0	-1.4
1946	Chi-A	3	3	.500	11	9	3	0	1	62	63	4	24	20	12.6	2.61	131	.267	.335	1	.053	-2	6	6	1	0.5
1947	Phi-A	5	2	.714	11	9	2	1	0	60^2	48	0	40	18	13.4	3.12	122	.223	.350	1	.063	-2	4	5	-1	0.3
1948	Phi-A	1	2	.333	4	2	0	0	0	15^1	21	0	9	5	17.6	5.87	73	.356	.441	0	.000	-0	-3	-3	0	-0.4
Total	16	108	128	.458	366	253	92	17	11	2003^2	2117	128	890	660	13.6	4.48	92	.271	.348	94	.150	-5	-85	-84	-3	-8.8

● DUTCH DIETZ Dietz, Lloyd Arthur b: 2/9/12, Cincinnati, Ohio d: 10/29/72, Beaumont, Tex. BR/TR, 5′11.5″, 180 lbs. Deb: 4/26/40

YEAR	TM/L	W	L	PCT	G	GS	CG	SH	SV	IP	H	HR	BB	SO	RAT	ERA	ERA+	OAV	OOB	BH	AVG	PB	PR	/A	PD	TPI
1940	Pit-N	0	1	.000	4	2	0	0	0	15^1	22	2	4	8	15.3	5.87	65	.355	.394	1	.143	-0	-3	-4	-0	-0.3
1941	Pit-N	7	2	.778	33	6	4	1	1	100^1	88	6	33	22	11.0	2.33	155	.233	.298	4	.160	-1	15	14	0	1.2
1942	Pit-N	6	9	.400	40	13	3	0	3	134^1	139	8	57	35	13.2	3.95	86	.268	.342	7	.200	1	-10	-8	-2	-1.1
1943	Pit-N	0	3	.000	8	0	0	0	0	9	12	0	4	4	17.0	6.00	58	.324	.405	0	—	0	-3	-3	1	-0.7
	Phi-N	1	1	.500	21	0	0	0	2	36	42	2	15	10	14.3	6.50	52	.292	.358	1	.167	0	-12	-13	-0	-0.8
	Yr	1	4	.200	29	0	0	0	2	45	54	2	19	14	14.6	6.40	53	.297	.363	1	.167	0	-15	-15	0	-1.5
Total	4	14	16	.467	106	21	7	1	6	295	303	18	113	79	12.8	3.87	90	.266	.334	13	.178	-0	-14	-13	-1	-1.7

● REESE DIGGS Diggs, Reese Wilson "Diggsy" b: 9/22/15, Mathews, Va. d: 10/30/78, Baltimore, Md. BB/TR, 6′2″, 180 lbs. Deb: 9/15/34

YEAR	TM/L	W	L	PCT	G	GS	CG	SH	SV	IP	H	HR	BB	SO	RAT	ERA	ERA+	OAV	OOB	BH	AVG	PB	PR	/A	PD	TPI
1934	Was-A	1	2	.333	4	3	2	0	0	21^1	26	3	15	2	17.3	6.75	64	.313	.418	2	.250	0	-5	-6	-0	-0.6

● JACK DiLAURO DiLauro, Jack Edward b: 5/3/43, Akron, Ohio BB/TL, 6′2″, 185 lbs. Deb: 5/15/69

YEAR	TM/L	W	L	PCT	G	GS	CG	SH	SV	IP	H	HR	BB	SO	RAT	ERA	ERA+	OAV	OOB	BH	AVG	PB	PR	/A	PD	TPI
1969	NY-N	1	4	.200	23	4	0	0	1	63^2	50	4	18	27	9.6	2.40	152	.216	.272	0	.000	-1	8	9	-0	0.5
1970	Hou-N	1	3	.250	42	0	0	0	3	33^2	34	4	17	23	13.6	4.28	91	.262	.347	0	.000	-0	-1	-1	-0	-0.2
Total	2	2	7	.222	65	4	0	0	4	97^1	84	8	35	50	11.0	3.05	122	.232	.300	0	.000	-2	8	7	-1	0.3

● GORDON DILLARD Dillard, Gordon Lee b: 5/20/64, Salinas, Cal. BL/TL, 6′1″, 190 lbs. Deb: 8/12/88

YEAR	TM/L	W	L	PCT	G	GS	CG	SH	SV	IP	H	HR	BB	SO	RAT	ERA	ERA+	OAV	OOB	BH	AVG	PB	PR	/A	PD	TPI
1988	Bal-A	0	0	—	2	1	0	0	0	3	3	1	4	2	21.0	6.00	65	.273	.467	0	—	0	-1	-1	0	0.1
1989	Phi-N	0	0	—	5	0	0	0	0	4	7	0	0	2	15.8	6.75	53	.368	.368	0	—	0	-1	-1	0	0.0
Total	2	0	0	—	7	1	0	0	0	7	10	1	4	4	18.0	6.43	58	.333	.412	0	—	0	-2	-2	0	0.1

● HARLEY DILLINGER Dillinger, Harley Hugh "Hoke" or "Lefty"
b: 10/30/1894, Pomeroy, Ohio d: 1/8/59, Cleveland, Ohio BR/TL, 5′11″, 175 lbs. Deb: 8/16/14

YEAR	TM/L	W	L	PCT	G	GS	CG	SH	SV	IP	H	HR	BB	SO	RAT	ERA	ERA+	OAV	OOB	BH	AVG	PB	PR	/A	PD	TPI
1914	Cle-A	0	1	.000	11	2	1	0	0	33^2	41	0	25	11	17.9	4.54	64	.325	.441	0	.000	-1	-7	-6	-1	-0.4

● BILL DILLMAN Dillman, William Howard b: 5/25/45, Trenton, N.J. BR/TR, 6′2″, 180 lbs. Deb: 4/14/67

YEAR	TM/L	W	L	PCT	G	GS	CG	SH	SV	IP	H	HR	BB	SO	RAT	ERA	ERA+	OAV	OOB	BH	AVG	PB	PR	/A	PD	TPI
1967	Bal-A	5	9	.357	32	15	2	1	3	124	115	13	33	69	11.0	4.35	72	.249	.303	5	.161	-0	-15	-17	-1	-2.0
1970	Mon-N	2	3	.400	18	0	0	0	0	30^2	28	4	18	17	13.8	5.28	78	.255	.364	0	.000	-0	-4	-4	0	-0.6
Total	2	7	12	.368	50	15	2	1	3	154^2	143	17	51	86	11.5	4.54	74	.250	.316	5	.152	-1	-20	-21	-1	-2.6

● STEVE DILLON Dillon, Stephen Edward b: 3/20/43, Yonkers, N.Y. BL/TL, 5′10″, 160 lbs. Deb: 9/5/63

YEAR	TM/L	W	L	PCT	G	GS	CG	SH	SV	IP	H	HR	BB	SO	RAT	ERA	ERA+	OAV	OOB	BH	AVG	PB	PR	/A	PD	TPI
1963	NY-N	0	0	—	1	0	0	0	0	1^2	3	0	0	1	16.2	10.80	32	.429	.429	0	—	0	-1	-1	0	0.0
1964	NY-N	0	0	—	2	0	0	0	0	3	4	1	2	2	18.0	9.00	40	.333	.429	0	—	0	-2	-2	-0	0.0
Total	2	0	0	—	3	0	0	0	0	4^2	7	1	2	3	17.4	9.64	37	.368	.429	0	—	0	-3	-3	-0	0.0

● FRANK DiMICHELE DiMichele, Frank Lawrence b: 2/16/65, Philadelphia, Pa. BR/TL, 6′3″, 205 lbs. Deb: 4/8/88

YEAR	TM/L	W	L	PCT	G	GS	CG	SH	SV	IP	H	HR	BB	SO	RAT	ERA	ERA+	OAV	OOB	BH	AVG	PB	PR	/A	PD	TPI
1988	Cal-A	0	0	—	4	0	0	0	0	4^2	5	2	2	1	13.5	9.64	40	.263	.333	0	—	0	-3	-3	-0	0.0

YEAR	TM/L	W	L	PCT	G	GS	CG	SH	SV	IP	H	HR	BB	SO	RAT	ERA	ERA+	OAV	OOB	BH	AVG	PB	PR	/A	PD	TPI
● **BILL DINNEEN**	Dinneen, William Henry "Big Bill" b: 4/5/1876, Syracuse, N.Y. d: 1/13/55, Syracuse, N.Y. BR/TR, 6'1", 190 lbs. Deb: 4/22/1898 U																									
1898	Was-N	9	16	.360	29	27	22	0	0	218^{1}	238	6	88	83	14.1	4.00	92	.275	.353	8	.100	-4	-9	-8	0	-1.2
1899	Was-N	14	20	.412	37	35	30	0	0	291	350	6	106	91	14.4	3.93	100	.297	.361	36	.303	5	-2	-0	4	0.8
1900	Bos-N	20	14	.588	40	37	33	1	0	320^{2}	304	11	105	107	11.7	3.12	133	.250	.314	35	.280	2	21	**36**	2	**3.6**
1901	Bos-N	15	18	.455	37	34	31	0	0	309^{1}	295	8	77	141	11.0	2.94	123	.250	.299	31	.211	0	13	23	-1	2.1
1902	Bos-A	21	21	.500	42	42	39	2	0	371^{1}	348	9	99	136	11.0	2.93	122	.248	.302	18	.128	-6	27	27	-6	1.3
1903	*Bos-A	21	13	.618	37	34	32	6	**2**	299	255	6	66	148	9.8	2.26	134	.230	.276	17	.160	-1	23	26	-1	2.6
1904	Bos-A	23	14	.622	37	37	37	5	0	335^{2}	283	8	63	153	9.3	2.20	122	.230	.268	25	.208	-0	15	18	-2	1.7
1905	Bos-A	12	14	.462	31	29	23	2	1	243^{2}	235	7	50	97	10.8	3.73	72	.255	.299	13	.148	-3	-29	-28	0	-3.2
1906	Bos-A	8	19	.296	28	27	22	1	0	218^{2}	209	4	52	60	10.8	2.92	94	.255	.300	7	.111	-1	-6	-4	-3	-0.9
1907	Bos-A	0	4	.000	5	5	3	0	0	32^{2}	42	5	8	8	14.3	5.23	49	.313	.361	0	.000	-1	-10	-10	-1	-1.2
	StL-A	7	10	.412	24	16	15	2	4	155^{1}	153	3	33	38	11.1	2.43	103	.260	.305	10	.204	2	2	1	-3	0.0
	Yr	7	14	.333	29	21	18	2	**4**	188	195	8	41	46	11.5	2.92	86	.269	.313	10	.169	1	-8	-8	-4	-1.2
1908	StL-A	14	7	.667	27	16	11	2	0	167	133	2	53	39	10.2	2.10	114	.231	.300	12	.203	0	5	5	-3	0.4
1909	StL-A	6	7	.462	17	13	8	3	0	112	112	3	29	26	11.4	3.46	70	.267	.316	7	.194	2	-12	-13	-0	-1.3
Total	12	170	177	.490	391	352	306	24	7	3074^{2}	2957	78	829	1127	11.3	3.01	107	.254	.308	219	.192	-6	38	70	-15	4.7
● **RON DIORIO**	Diorio, Ronald Michael b: 7/15/46, Waterbury, Conn. BR/TR, 6'6", 212 lbs. Deb: 8/9/73																									
1973	Phi-N	0	0	—	23	0	0	0	1	19^{1}	18	1	6	11	11.2	2.33	163	.257	.316	0	—	0	3	3	-0	0.0
1974	Phi-N	0	0	—	2	0	0	0	0	1	2	1	1	0	27.0	18.00	21	.400	.500	0	—	0	-2	-2	0	0.0
Total	2	0	0	—	25	0	0	0	1	20^{1}	20	2	7	11	12.0	3.10	122	.267	.329	0	—	0	1	2	0	0.0
● **FRANK DiPINO**	DiPino, Frank Michael b: 10/22/56, Syracuse, N.Y. BL/TL, 6', 180 lbs. Deb: 9/14/81																									
1981	Mil-A	0	0	—	2	0	0	0	0	2^{1}	0	0	3	3	11.6	0.00	—	.000	.300	0	—	0	1	1	-0	0.2
1982	Hou-N	2	2	.500	6	6	0	0	0	28^{1}	32	1	11	25	13.7	6.04	55	.302	.368	0	.000	-1	-8	-9	-1	-1.2
1983	Hou-N	3	4	.429	53	0	0	0	20	71^{1}	52	2	20	67	9.2	2.65	128	.205	.265	1	.167	1	8	6	1	1.0
1984	Hou-N	4	9	.308	57	0	0	0	14	75^{1}	74	3	36	65	13.3	3.35	99	.260	.345	0	.000	-1	2	-0	0	-0.1
1985	Hou-N	3	7	.300	54	0	0	0	6	76	69	7	43	49	13.5	4.03	86	.248	.353	2	.167	-0	-4	-5	-2	-0.8
1986	Hou-N	1	3	.250	31	0	0	0	3	40^{1}	27	5	16	27	10.0	3.57	101	.189	.280	1	.200	0	1	0	0	0.1
	Chi-N	2	4	.333	30	0	0	0	0	40	47	6	14	43	13.7	5.17	78	.297	.355	0	.000	-0	-6	-5	1	-0.6
	Yr	3	7	.300	61	0	0	0	3	80^{1}	74	11	30	70	11.7	4.37	87	.243	.311	1	.167	-0	-6	-5	2	-0.5
1987	Chi-N	3	3	.500	69	0	0	0	4	80	75	7	34	61	12.4	3.15	136	.252	.330	1	.500	0	8	10	1	0.9
1988	Chi-N	2	3	.400	63	0	0	0	6	90^{1}	102	6	32	69	13.4	4.98	72	.285	.344	1	.100	-0	-15	-14	-0	-1.0
1989	StL-N	9	0	1.000	67	0	0	0	0	88^{1}	73	6	20	44	9.5	2.45	148	.227	.273	1	.077	-1	10	12	0	1.1
1990	StL-N	5	2	.714	62	0	0	0	3	81	92	8	31	49	13.8	4.56	84	.294	.359	1	.250	0	-7	-7	1	-0.5
1992	StL-N	0	0	—	9	0	0	0	0	11	9	0	3	8	9.8	1.64	207	.220	.273	1	1.000	0	2	2	0	0.1
1993	KC-A	1	1	.500	11	0	0	0	0	15^{2}	21	2	6	5	16.7	6.89	66	.328	.403	0	—	0	-4	-4	0	-0.6
Total	12	35	38	.479	514	6	0	0	56	700	673	53	269	515	12.2	3.83	96	.256	.328	9	.125	-1	-12	-13	2	-1.4
● **JERRY DIPOTO**	Dipoto, Gerard Peter b: 5/24/68, Jersey City, N.J. BR/TR, 6'2", 200 lbs. Deb: 5/11/93																									
1993	Cle-A	4	4	.500	46	0	0	0	11	56^{1}	57	0	30	41	14.1	2.40	180	.270	.364	0	—	0	12	12	1	2.0
1994	Cle-A	0	0	—	7	0	0	0	0	15^{2}	26	1	10	9	21.3	8.04	59	.406	.493	0	—	0	-6	-6	-0	0.0
1995	NY-N	4	6	.400	58	0	0	0	2	78^{2}	77	2	29	49	12.6	3.78	107	.267	.343	0	.000	-1	4	2	0	0.3
1996	NY-N	7	2	.778	57	0	0	0	0	77^{1}	91	5	45	52	16.2	4.19	96	.298	.394	0	.000	-0	0	-2	0	-0.2
1997	Col-N	5	3	.625	74	0	0	0	16	95^{2}	108	6	33	74	13.6	4.70	110	.288	.352	1	.111	-1	-5	5	-0	0.4
1998	Col-N	3	4	.429	68	0	0	0	19	71^{1}	61	8	25	49	11.2	3.53	143	.232	.306	0	.000	0	6	12	-1	1.6
Total	6	23	19	.548	310	0	0	0	48	395	420	22	172	274	13.9	4.01	114	.279	.359	1	.063	-1	10	24	0	4.1
● **GEORGE DISCH**	Disch, George Charles b: 3/15/1879, Lincoln, Mo. d: 8/25/50, Rapid City, S.D. 5'11", Deb: 8/8/05																									
1905	Det-A	0	2	.000	8	3	1	0	0	47^{2}	43	1	8	14	10.0	2.64	103	.243	.283	2	.105	-1	0	0	0	-0.1
● **GLENN DISHMAN**	Dishman, Glenelg Edward b: 11/5/70, Baltimore, Md. BR/TL, 6'1", 195 lbs. Deb: 6/22/95																									
1995	SD-N	4	8	.333	19	16	0	0	0	97	104	11	34	43	13.2	5.01	80	.278	.345	6	.200	1	-9	-11	-1	-1.1
1996	SD-N	0	0	—	3	0	0	0	0	2^{1}	3	0	1	0	15.4	7.71	51	.300	.364	0	—	0	-1	-1	-0	0.0
	Phi-N	0	0	—	4	1	0	0	0	7	9	2	2	3	14.1	7.71	56	.321	.367	0	—	0	-3	-3	-0	0.0
	Yr	0	0	—	7	1	0	0	0	9^{1}	12	2	3	3	14.5	7.71	55	.316	.366	0	—	0	-4	-4	-0	0.0
1997	Det-A	1	2	.333	7	4	0	0	0	29	30	4	8	20	12.4	5.28	87	.268	.328	0	—	0	-2	-2	1	-0.1
Total	3	5	10	.333	33	21	0	0	0	135^{1}	146	17	45	66	13.1	5.25	79	.279	.343	6	.200	1	-15	-16	-0	-1.2
● **ALEC DISTASO**	Distaso, Alec John b: 12/23/48, Los Angeles, Cal. BR/TR, 6'2", 200 lbs. Deb: 4/20/69																									
1969	Chi-N	0	0	—	2	0	0	0	0	4^{2}	6	0	1	1	13.5	3.86	104	.316	.350	0	—	0	-0	0	0	0.0
● **ART DITMAR**	Ditmar, Arthur John b: 4/3/29, Winthrop, Mass. BR/TR, 6'2", 196 lbs. Deb: 4/19/54																									
1954	Phi-A	1	4	.200	14	5	0	0	0	39^{1}	50	4	36	14	19.9	6.41	61	.314	.444	1	.125	0	-12	-11	-0	-1.2
1955	KC-A	12	12	.500	35	22	7	1	1	175^{1}	180	23	86	79	14.0	5.03	83	.270	.360	13	.210	-0	-21	-17	1	-2.0
1956	KC-A	12	22	.353	44	34	14	2	1	254^{1}	254	30	108	126	13.1	4.42	98	.262	.340	13	.143	-4	-7	-3	-1	-0.8
1957	*NY-A	8	3	.727	46	11	0	0	6	127^{1}	128	9	35	64	11.7	3.25	110	.261	.313	7	.200	-0	8	5	-1	0.3
1958	*NY-A	9	8	.529	38	13	4	0	4	139^{2}	124	14	38	52	10.8	3.42	103	.237	.295	11	.250	2	5	2	-2	0.2
1959	NY-A	13	9	.591	38	25	7	1	1	202	156	17	52	96	**9.6**	2.90	126	.211	**.270**	15	.197	2	22	17	-1	1.8
1960	*NY-A	15	9	.625	34	28	8	1	0	200	195	25	56	65	11.3	3.06	117	.256	.308	11	.159	0	18	12	-2	1.1
1961	NY-A	2	3	.400	12	8	1	0	0	54^{1}	59	9	14	24	12.4	4.64	80	.285	.336	1	.053	-2	-4	-6	1	-0.6
	KC-A	0	5	.000	20	5	0	0	1	54	60	6	23	19	14.2	5.67	74	.286	.362	2	.167	-0	-10	-9	-0	-0.8
	Yr	2	8	.200	32	13	1	0	1	108^{1}	119	15	37	43	13.1	5.15	77	.281	.341	3	.097	-2	-14	-14	0	-1.4
1962	KC-A	0	2	.000	6	5	0	0	0	21^{2}	31	1	13	13	19.1	6.65	64	.323	.414	1	.167	-0	-6	-6	-0	-0.5
Total	9	72	77	.483	287	156	41	5	14	1268	1237	138	461	552	12.3	3.98	97	.256	.326	75	.178	-3	-7	-16	-6	-2.5
● **SONNY DIXON**	Dixon, John Craig b: 11/5/24, Charlotte, N.C. BB/TR, 6'2.5", 205 lbs. Deb: 4/20/53																									
1953	Was-A	5	8	.385	43	6	3	0	3	120	123	13	31	40	11.7	3.75	104	.267	.316	4	.154	0	3	2	2	0.4
1954	Was-A	1	2	.333	16	0	0	0	1	29^{2}	26	3	12	7	11.5	3.03	117	.236	.311	0	.000	-1	2	2	1	0.2
	Phi-A	5	7	.417	38	6	1	0	4	107^{1}	136	8	27	42	13.9	4.86	80	.308	.352	7	.250	2	-14	-11	3	-0.8
	Yr	6	9	.400	**54**	6	1	0	5	137	162	11	39	49	13.4	4.47	86	.293	.343	7	.206	1	-11	-10	3	-0.6
1955	KC-A	0	0	—	2	0	0	0	0	1^{2}	6	1	0	0	32.4	16.20	26	.545	.545	0	—	0	-2	-2	0	0.0
1956	NY-A	0	1	.000	3	0	0	0	1	4^{1}	5	0	5	1	20.8	2.08	186	.294	.455	0	.000	-0	1	1	0	0.2
Total	4	11	18	.379	102	12	4	0	9	263	296	25	75	90	12.9	4.17	93	.284	.335	11	.180	1	-9	-9	6	0.0
● **KEN DIXON**	Dixon, Kenneth John b: 10/17/60, Monroe, Va. BB/TR, 5'11", 166 lbs. Deb: 9/22/84																									
1984	Bal-A	0	1	.000	2	2	0	0	0	13	14	1	4	8	12.5	4.15	93	.269	.321	0	—	0	-0	-0	0	0.0
1985	Bal-A	8	4	.667	34	18	3	1	1	162	144	20	64	108	11.7	3.67	110	.237	.312	0	—	0	9	7	-1	0.3
1986	Bal-A	11	13	.458	35	33	2	0	0	202^{1}	194	33	83	170	12.4	4.58	90	.249	.322	0	—	0	-9	-10	-1	-1.1
1987	Bal-A	7	10	.412	34	15	0	0	5	105	128	31	27	91	13.4	6.43	68	.292	.334	0	—	0	-23	-24	-0	-3.3
Total	4	26	28	.481	105	68	5	1	6	482^{1}	480	85	178	377	12.4	4.66	89	.256	.322	0	—	0	-24	-28	-2	-4.1
● **STEVE DIXON**	Dixon, Steven Ross b: 8/3/69, Cincinnati, Ohio BL/TL, 6', 190 lbs. Deb: 9/7/93																									
1993	StL-N	0	0	—	4	0	0	0	0	2^{2}	7	1	5	2	40.5	33.75	12	.538	.667	0	—	0	-9	-9	0	0.0
1994	StL-N	0	0	—	2	0	0	0	0	2^{1}	3	0	8	1	42.4	23.14	18	.333	.647	0	—	0	-5	-5	-0	0.0
Total	2	0	0	—	6	0	0	0	0	5	10	1	13	3	41.4	28.80	14	.455	.657	0	—	0	-14	-14	0	0.0
● **TOM DIXON**	Dixon, Thomas Earl b: 4/23/55, Orlando, Fla. BR/TR, 5'11", 175 lbs. Deb: 7/30/77																									
1977	Hou-N	1	0	1.000	9	4	1	0	0	30^{1}	40	0	7	15	14.2	3.26	109	.320	.361	0	.000	-1	2	1	0	0.0
1978	Hou-N	7	11	.389	30	19	3	2	1	140	140	8	40	66	11.6	3.99	83	.265	.318	4	.100	-2	-6	-11	-1	-1.5
1979	Hou-N	1	2	.333	19	1	0	0	0	25^{2}	39	2	15	9	18.9	6.66	53	.348	.425	1	1.000	1	-8	-9	1	-0.8

YEAR	TM/L	W	L	PCT	G	GS	CG	SH	SV	IP	H	HR	BB	SO	RAT	ERA	ERA+	OAV	OOB	BH	AVG	PB	PR	/A	PD	TPI
1983	Mon-N	0	1	.000	4	0	0	0	0	3^2	6	1	1	4	19.6	9.82	37	.375	.444	0	—	0	-3	-3	-0	-0.6
Total	4	9	14	.391	62	24	4	2	1	199^2	225	11	63	94	13.1	4.33	78	.288	.343	5	.104	-2	-15	-21	-0	-2.9

● BILL DOAK
Doak, William Leopold "Spittin' Bill" b: 1/28/1891, Pittsburgh, Pa. d: 11/26/54, Bradenton, Fla. BR/TR, 6'0.5", 165 lbs. Deb: 9/1/12

YEAR	TM/L	W	L	PCT	G	GS	CG	SH	SV	IP	H	HR	BB	SO	RAT	ERA	ERA+	OAV	OOB	BH	AVG	PB	PR	/A	PD	TPI
1912	Cin-N	0	0	—	1	1	0	0	0	2	4	0	1	0	22.5	4.50	75	.444	.500	0	—	0	-0	-0	-0	0.0
1913	StL-N	2	8	.200	15	12	5	1	1	93	79	4	39	51	11.9	3.10	104	.236	.325	1	.032	-3	1	1	1	-0.1
1914	StL-N	19	6	.760	36	33	16	7	1	256	193	2	87	118	10.1	**1.72**	**162**	.216	.290	10	.118	-3	30	31	5	3.2
1915	StL-N	16	18	.471	38	36	19	3	1	276	263	4	85	124	11.6	2.64	106	.261	.323	15	.174	1	3	5	7	1.5
1916	StL-N	12	8	.600	29	26	11	2	0	192	177	5	55	82	11.0	2.63	101	.251	.308	8	.129	-2	-0	0	3	0.1
1917	StL-N	16	20	.444	44	37	16	3	2	281^1	257	6	85	111	11.2	3.10	87	.250	.312	12	.126	-4	-12	-13	5	-1.6
1918	StL-N	9	15	.375	31	23	16	1	1	211	191	3	60	74	10.9	2.43	111	.249	.306	12	.182	1	8	7	5	1.5
1919	StL-N	13	14	.481	31	29	13	3	0	202^2	182	5	55	69	10.6	3.11	90	.246	.299	7	.109	-4	-4	-7	5	-0.9
1920	StL-N	20	12	.625	39	37	20	5	1	270	256	7	80	90	11.4	2.53	118	.253	.312	10	.114	-6	18	14	0	0.9
1921	StL-N	15	6	**.714**	32	29	13	1	1	208^2	224	3	37	83	11.4	**2.59**	142	.278	.313	10	.143	-3	28	25	2	2.2
1922	StL-N	11	13	.458	37	29	8	2	2	180^1	222	12	69	73	14.7	5.54	70	.311	.374	7	.130	-3	-29	-34	0	-3.9
1923	StL-N	8	13	.381	30	26	7	2	0	185	199	4	69	53	13.2	3.26	120	.279	.346	3	.045	-9	15	13	3	0.8
1924	StL-N	2	1	.667	11	1	0	0	3	22	25	0	14	7	16.0	3.27	116	.313	.415	1	.200	-0	1	1	1	0.2
	Bro-N	11	5	.688	21	16	8	2	0	149^1	130	8	35	32	10.1	3.07	122	.239	.289	10	.179	-0	13	11	3	1.3
	Yr	13	6	.684	32	17	8	2	3	171^1	155	8	49	39	10.9	3.10	121	.249	.307	11	.180	-1	15	12	3	1.5
1927	Bro-N	11	8	.579	27	20	6	1	0	145	153	6	40	32	12.2	3.48	114	.271	.322	6	.128	-3	7	8	1	0.8
1928	Bro-N	3	8	.273	28	12	4	1	3	99^1	104	1	35	12	13.0	3.26	122	.271	.340	3	.111	-2	8	8	3	0.9
1929	StL-N	1	2	.333	3	2	0	0	0	9	17	1	5	3	22.0	12.00	39	.415	.478	0	.000	0	-7	-7	-0	-1.6
Total	16	169	157	.518	453	369	162	34	16	2782^2	2676	71	851	1014	11.6	2.98	107	.259	.319	115	.127	-42	80	64	43	5.3

● WALT DOANE
Doane, Walter Rudolph b: 3/12/1887, Bellevue, Idaho d: 10/19/35, W.Brandywine Township, Pa. BL/TR, 6', 165 lbs. Deb: 9/20/09 ♦

YEAR	TM/L	W	L	PCT	G	GS	CG	SH	SV	IP	H	HR	BB	SO	RAT	ERA	ERA+	OAV	OOB	BH	AVG	PB	PR	/A	PD	TPI
1909	Cle-A	0	1	.000	1	1	0	0	0	5	10	0	1	2	19.8	5.40	47	.400	.423	1	.111	-0	-2	-2	-0	-0.3
1910	Cle-A	0	0	—	6	0	0	0	0	17^2	31	1	8	7	20.4	5.60	46	.413	.476	2	.286	1	-6	-6	-1	0.0
Total	2	0	1	.000	7	1	0	0	0	22^2	41	1	9	9	20.3	5.56	46	.410	.464	3	.188	1	-8	-8	-1	-0.3

● JOHN DOBB
Dobb, John Kenneth "Lefty" b: 11/15/01, Muskegon, Mich. d: 7/31/91, Muskegon, Mich. BR/TL, 6'2", 180 lbs. Deb: 8/13/24

YEAR	TM/L	W	L	PCT	G	GS	CG	SH	SV	IP	H	HR	BB	SO	RAT	ERA	ERA+	OAV	OOB	BH	AVG	PB	PR	/A	PD	TPI
1924	Chi-A	0	0	—	2	0	0	0	0	2	4	0	1	2	22.5	9.00	46	.400	.455	0	—	0	-1	-1	-0	0.0

● RAY DOBENS
Dobens, Raymond Joseph "Lefty" b: 7/28/06, Nashua, N.H. d: 4/21/80, Stuart, Fla. BL/TL, 5'8", 175 lbs. Deb: 7/7/29

YEAR	TM/L	W	L	PCT	G	GS	CG	SH	SV	IP	H	HR	BB	SO	RAT	ERA	ERA+	OAV	OOB	BH	AVG	PB	PR	/A	PD	TPI
1929	Bos-A	0	0	—	11	2	0	0	0	28^1	32	0	9	4	13.3	3.81	112	.302	.362	3	.375	1	1	1	-1	0.0

● JESS DOBERNIC
Dobernic, Andrew Joseph b: 11/20/17, Mt.Olive, Ill. d: 7/16/98, St.Louis, Mo. BR/TR, 5'10", 170 lbs. Deb: 7/2/39

YEAR	TM/L	W	L	PCT	G	GS	CG	SH	SV	IP	H	HR	BB	SO	RAT	ERA	ERA+	OAV	OOB	BH	AVG	PB	PR	/A	PD	TPI
1939	Chi-A	0	1	.000	4	0	0	0	0	3^1	3	0	6	1	27.0	13.50	35	.231	.500	0	.000	-0	-3	-3	0	-0.7
1948	Chi-N	7	2	.778	54	0	0	0	1	85^2	67	8	40	48	11.3	3.15	124	.213	.303	2	.200	-0	8	7	-2	0.5
1949	Chi-N	0	0	—	4	0	0	0	0	4	9	2	4	0	29.3	20.25	20	.450	.542	0	—	0	-7	-7	-0	0.0
	Cin-N	0	0	—	14	0	0	0	0	19^1	28	7	16	6	20.5	9.78	43	.329	.436	0	.000	0	-12	-12	0	0.0
	Yr	0	0	—	18	0	0	0	0	23^1	37	9	20	6	22.0	11.57	36	.352	.456	0	.000	0	-20	-19	-0	0.0
Total	3	7	3	.700	76	0	0	0	1	112^1	107	17	66	55	14.0	5.21	76	.247	.349	2	.154	-0	-15	-15	-2	-0.2

● CHUCK DOBSON
Dobson, Charles Thomas b: 1/10/44, Kansas City, Mo. BR/TR, 6'4", 200 lbs. Deb: 4/19/66

YEAR	TM/L	W	L	PCT	G	GS	CG	SH	SV	IP	H	HR	BB	SO	RAT	ERA	ERA+	OAV	OOB	BH	AVG	PB	PR	/A	PD	TPI
1966	KC-A	4	6	.400	14	14	1	0	0	83^2	71	7	50	61	13.2	4.09	83	.234	.346	3	.115	-1	-6	-6	1	-0.7
1967	KC-A	10	10	.500	32	29	4	1	0	197^2	172	17	75	110	11.4	3.69	86	.233	.306	13	.181	0	-10	-11	-0	-1.1
1968	Oak-A	12	14	.462	35	34	11	3	0	225^1	197	20	80	168	11.2	3.00	94	.234	.303	15	.200	2	-0	-4	2	-0.2
1969	Oak-A	15	13	.536	35	35	11	1	0	235^1	244	16	80	137	12.4	3.86	89	.270	.330	8	.101	-3	-6	-11	-2	-1.7
1970	Oak-A	16	15	.516	41	40	13	**5**	0	267	230	32	92	149	11.0	3.74	95	.229	.297	11	.118	-3	-1	-6	-2	-1.2
1971	Oak-A	15	5	.750	30	30	7	1	0	189	185	24	71	100	12.2	3.81	88	.259	.327	13	.197	3	-7	-10	0	-0.7
1973	Oak-A	0	1	.000	1	1	0	0	0	2^1	6	1	2	3	30.9	7.71	46	.429	.500	0	—	0	-1	-1	0	-0.3
1974	Cal-A	2	3	.400	5	5	2	0	0	30	39	3	13	16	15.6	5.70	60	.315	.380	0	—	0	-5	-8	-0	-1.0
1975	Cal-A	0	2	.000	9	2	0	0	0	28	30	5	13	14	14.5	6.75	53	.275	.363	0	—	0	-9	-10	-1	-0.7
Total	9	74	69	.517	202	190	49	11	0	1258^1	1174	125	476	758	11.9	3.78	87	.247	.318	63	.153	-2	-48	-68	-1	-7.6

● JOE DOBSON
Dobson, Joseph Gordon "Burrhead" b: 1/20/17, Durant, Okla. d: 6/23/94, Jacksonville, Fla. BR/TR, 6'2", 197 lbs. Deb: 4/26/39

YEAR	TM/L	W	L	PCT	G	GS	CG	SH	SV	IP	H	HR	BB	SO	RAT	ERA	ERA+	OAV	OOB	BH	AVG	PB	PR	/A	PD	TPI
1939	Cle-A	2	3	.400	35	3	0	0	1	78	87	3	51	27	16.0	5.88	75	.290	.395	1	.056	-2	-11	-13	1	-0.8
1940	Cle-A	3	7	.300	40	7	2	1	3	100	101	8	48	57	13.4	4.95	85	.268	.351	3	.125	-1	-6	-8	-0	-0.8
1941	Bos-A	12	5	.706	27	18	7	1	0	134^1	136	8	67	69	13.7	4.49	93	.262	.349	7	.149	0	-5	-5	-2	-0.7
1942	Bos-A	11	9	.550	30	23	10	3	0	182^2	155	9	68	72	11.1	3.30	113	.231	.303	10	.145	-1	7	9	2	0.9
1943	Bos-A	7	11	.389	25	20	9	3	0	164^1	144	4	57	63	11.0	3.12	106	.239	.305	5	.096	-3	3	4	-2	-0.2
1946	*Bos-A	13	7	.650	32	24	9	1	0	166^2	148	11	68	91	11.7	3.24	113	.234	.309	5	.100	-2	5	8	2	0.9
1947	Bos-A	18	8	.692	33	31	15	1	1	228^2	203	15	73	110	10.9	2.95	132	.238	**.299**	16	.208	1	19	24	-2	2.5
1948	Bos-A☆	16	10	.615	38	32	16	5	2	245^1	237	14	92	116	12.1	3.56	123	.253	.320	17	.202	1	20	23	-1	2.2
1949	Bos-A	14	12	.538	33	27	12	2	2	212^2	219	12	97	87	13.5	3.85	113	.269	.348	10	.147	-1	8	12	-1	1.1
1950	Bos-A	15	10	.600	39	27	12	1	4	206^2	217	15	81	81	13.0	4.18	117	.275	.343	15	.214	1	9	16	1	2.0
1951	Chi-A	7	6	.538	28	21	6	0	3	146^2	136	17	51	67	11.5	3.62	111	.248	.312	3	.065	-6	8	7	0	0.0
1952	Chi-A	14	10	.583	29	25	11	3	1	200^2	164	11	60	101	10.0	2.51	145	.222	.280	12	.190	0	26	25	-2	2.8
1953	Chi-A	5	5	.500	23	15	3	1	1	100^2	96	10	37	50	11.9	3.67	110	.249	.314	2	.069	-2	4	4	-1	0.1
1954	Bos-A	0	0	—	2	0	0	0	0	2^2	5	0	1	1	20.3	6.75	61	.385	.429	0	—	0	-1	-1	0	0.0
Total	14	137	103	.571	414	273	112	22	18	2170	2048	137	851	992	12.1	3.62	112	.250	.322	106	.152	-15	86	105	-5	10.0

● PAT DOBSON
Dobson, Patrick Edward b: 2/12/42, Depew, N.Y. BR/TR, 6'3", 190 lbs. Deb: 5/31/67 C

YEAR	TM/L	W	L	PCT	G	GS	CG	SH	SV	IP	H	HR	BB	SO	RAT	ERA	ERA+	OAV	OOB	BH	AVG	PB	PR	/A	PD	TPI
1967	Det-A	1	2	.333	28	1	0	0	0	49^1	38	6	27	34	12.2	2.92	112	.216	.327	0	.000	-1	2	2	-1	0.0
1968	*Det-A	5	8	.385	47	10	2	1	7	125	89	13	48	93	10.0	2.66	113	.200	.281	4	.143	0	4	5	1	0.7
1969	Det-A	5	10	.333	49	9	1	0	9	105	100	10	39	64	12.0	3.60	104	.253	.322	2	.091	-1	0	2	0	0.1
1970	SD-N	14	15	.483	40	34	8	1	1	251	257	28	78	185	12.2	3.76	106	.265	.322	10	.141	-0	8	6	-0	0.5
1971	*Bal-A	20	8	.714	38	37	18	4	1	282^1	248	24	63	187	10.0	2.90	116	.235	.279	10	.110	-3	18	14	-1	0.9
1972	Bal-A☆	16	18	.471	38	36	13	3	0	268^1	220	13	69	161	9.8	2.65	116	.224	.278	12	.141	-2	12	13	-2	1.3
1973	Atl-N	3	7	.300	12	10	1	1	0	57^2	73	1	19	23	14.5	4.99	79	.315	.369	1	.067	-1	-9	-7	0	-1.2
	NY-A	9	8	.529	22	21	6	1	0	142^1	150	22	34	70	11.8	4.17	88	.266	.311	0	—	0	-6	-8	0	-0.8
1974	NY-A	19	15	.559	39	39	12	2	0	281	282	23	75	157	11.6	3.07	115	.262	.312	0	—	0	17	14	-1	1.5
1975	NY-A	11	14	.440	33	30	7	1	0	207^2	205	21	83	129	12.5	4.07	90	.261	.333	0	—	0	-7	-9	-0	-1.0
1976	Cle-A	16	12	.571	35	35	6	0	0	217^1	226	13	65	117	12.1	3.48	100	.272	.327	0	—	0	1	0	-1	0.0
1977	Cle-A	3	12	.200	33	17	0	0	1	133^1	155	23	65	81	14.9	6.14	64	.299	.378	0	—	0	-31	-33	0	-3.1
Total	11	122	129	.486	414	279	74	14	19	2120^1	2043	197	665	1301	11.6	3.54	100	.255	.314	39	.123	-8	10	-1	-3	-1.1

● GEORGE DOCKINS
Dockins, George Woodrow "Lefty" b: 5/5/17, Clyde, Kan. d: 1/22/97, Clyde, Kan. BL/TL, 6', 175 lbs. Deb: 5/5/45

YEAR	TM/L	W	L	PCT	G	GS	CG	SH	SV	IP	H	HR	BB	SO	RAT	ERA	ERA+	OAV	OOB	BH	AVG	PB	PR	/A	PD	TPI
1945	StL-N	8	6	.571	31	12	5	2	0	126^1	132	4	38	33	12.1	3.21	117	.269	.321	6	.176	1	8	8	-1	0.8
1947	Bro-N	0	0	—	4	0	0	0	0	5^1	10	2	2	1	20.3	11.81	35	.400	.444	0	.000	-0	-5	-5	0	0.0
Total	2	8	6	.571	35	12	5	2	0	131^2	142	6	40	34	12.4	3.55	106	.275	.327	6	.171	1	4	3	-0	0.8

● ROBERT DODD
Dodd, Robert Wayne b: 3/14/73, Kansas City, Kan. BL/TL, 6'3", 195 lbs. Deb: 5/28/98

YEAR	TM/L	W	L	PCT	G	GS	CG	SH	SV	IP	H	HR	BB	SO	RAT	ERA	ERA+	OAV	OOB	BH	AVG	PB	PR	/A	PD	TPI
1998	Phi-N	1	0	1.000	4	0	0	0	0	5	7	1	1	4	16.2	7.20	61	.333	.391	0	—	0	-2	-2	-0	-0.3

● SAM DODGE
Dodge, Samuel Edward b: 12/9/1889, Neath, Pa. d: 4/5/66, Utica, N.Y. BR/TR, 6'1", 170 lbs. Deb: 9/24/21

YEAR	TM/L	W	L	PCT	G	GS	CG	SH	SV	IP	H	HR	BB	SO	RAT	ERA	ERA+	OAV	OOB	BH	AVG	PB	PR	/A	PD	TPI
1921	Bos-A	0	0	—	1	0	0	0	0	1	1	0	1	0	18.0	9.00	47	.500	.667	0	—	0	-1	-1	-0	0.0
1922	Bos-A	0	0	—	3	0	0	0	0	6	11	0	3	3	21.0	4.50	91	.379	.438	0	.000	-0	-0	-0	0	0.0
Total	2	0	0	—	4	0	0	0	0	7	12	0	4	3	20.6	5.14	80	.387	.457	0	.000	-0	-1	-1	0	0.0

● FRED DOE
Doe, Alfred George "Count" b: 4/18/1864, Rockport, Mass. d: 10/4/38, Quincy, Mass. BR/TR, 5'10", 165 lbs. Deb: 8/23/1890

YEAR	TM/L	W	L	PCT	G	GS	CG	SH	SV	IP	H	HR	BB	SO	RAT	ERA	ERA+	OAV	OOB	BH	AVG	PB	PR	/A	PD	TPI
1890	Buf-P	0	1	.000	1	1	1	0	0	6	10	0	7	2	25.5	12.00	34	.357	.486	0	.000	-0	-5	-5	0	-0.5

YEAR	TM/L	W	L	PCT	G	GS	CG	SH	SV	IP	H	HR	BB	SO	RAT	ERA	ERA+	OAV	OOB	BH	AVG	PB	PR	/A	PD	TPI
	Pit-P	0	0	—	1	0	0	0	0	4	4	0	2	2	13.5	4.50	87	.250	.333	1	.500	0	-0	-0	-0	0.0
	Yr	0	1	.000	2	1	1	0	0	10	14	0	9	4	20.7	9.00	45	.318	.434	1	.250	-0	-5	-6	-0	-0.5

● ED DOHENY

Doheny, Edwin Richard b: 11/24/1873, Northfield, Vt. d: 12/29/16, Medfield, Mass. BL/TL, 5'10.5", 165 lbs. Deb: 9/16/1895

YEAR	TM/L	W	L	PCT	G	GS	CG	SH	SV	IP	H	HR	BB	SO	RAT	ERA	ERA+	OAV	OOB	BH	AVG	PB	PR	/A	PD	TPI
1895	NY-N	0	3	.000	3	3	3	0	0	25^{2}	37	2	19	9	20.7	6.66	70	.333	.444	1	.100	-1	-5	-6	-0	-0.5
1896	NY-N	6	7	.462	17	15	9	0	0	108^{1}	112	3	59	39	14.7	4.49	94	.265	.363	6	.150	-2	-1	-3	-0	-0.5
1897	NY-N	4	4	.500	10	10	10	0	0	85	69	0	45	37	12.9	2.12	196	.220	.333	7	.200	-1	21	19	3	1.6
1898	NY-N	7	19	.269	28	27	23	0	0	213	238	1	101	96	15.2	3.68	95	.280	.370	14	.163	-1	-2	-5	3	-0.3
1899	NY-N	14	17	.452	35	33	30	1	0	265^{1}	282	2	156	115	16.1	4.51	83	.272	.386	27	.241	0	-19	-22	5	-1.6
1900	NY-N	4	14	.222	20	18	12	0	0	133^{2}	148	2	96	44	17.9	5.45	66	.280	.411	12	.222	-0	-26	-27	2	-2.7
1901	NY-N	2	5	.286	10	6	6	0	0	74	88	1	17	36	13.5	4.50	73	.293	.344	10	.345	3	-10	-10	0	-0.5
	Pit-N	6	2	.750	11	10	6	1	0	76^{2}	68	1	22	28	11.2	2.00	164	.236	.302	3	.115	0	11	11	-2	0.9
	Yr	8	7	.533	21	16	12	1	0	150^{2}	156	2	39	64	11.9	3.23	102	.263	.313	13	.236	4	2	1	-1	0.4
1902	Pit-N	16	4	.800	22	21	19	2	0	188^{1}	161	0	61	88	11.3	2.53	108	.231	.307	12	.156	-2	5	4	-1	0.1
1903	Pit-N	16	8	.667	27	25	22	2	2	222^{2}	209	1	89	75	12.8	3.19	101	.252	.338	19	.209	-0	2	1	5	0.5
Total	9	75	83	.475	183	168	140	6	2	1392^{2}	1412	13	665	567	14.3	3.75	94	.263	.359	111	.198	-3	-24	-37	15	-3.0

● JOHN DOHERTY

Doherty, John Harold b: 6/11/67, New York, N.Y. BR/TR, 6'4", 210 lbs. Deb: 4/8/92

YEAR	TM/L	W	L	PCT	G	GS	CG	SH	SV	IP	H	HR	BB	SO	RAT	ERA	ERA+	OAV	OOB	BH	AVG	PB	PR	/A	PD	TPI
1992	Det-A	7	4	.636	47	11	0	0	3	116	131	4	25	37	12.4	3.88	102	.287	.329	0	—	0	1	1	1	0.2
1993	Det-A	14	11	.560	32	31	3	2	0	184^{2}	205	19	48	63	12.6	4.44	97	.286	.335	0	—	0	-2	-3	-2	-0.5
1994	Det-A	6	7	.462	18	17	2	0	0	101^{1}	139	13	26	28	14.9	6.48	75	.337	.380	0	—	0	-19	-18	2	-1.7
1995	Det-A	5	9	.357	48	2	0	0	6	113	130	10	37	46	13.8	5.10	93	.288	.350	0	—	0	-5	-4	1	-0.4
1996	Bos-A	0	0	—	3	0	0	0	0	6^{1}	8	1	4	3	18.5	5.68	89	.276	.382	0	—	0	-0	-0	1	-0.1
Total	5	32	31	.508	148	61	5	2	9	521^{1}	613	47	140	177	13.3	4.87	91	.296	.347	0	—	0	-26	-25	3	-2.5

● JOHN DOLAN

Dolan, John b: 9/12/1867, Newport, Ky. d: 5/8/48, Springfield, Ohio TR, 5'10", 170 lbs. Deb: 9/5/1890

YEAR	TM/L	W	L	PCT	G	GS	CG	SH	SV	IP	H	HR	BB	SO	RAT	ERA	ERA+	OAV	OOB	BH	AVG	PB	PR	/A	PD	TPI
1890	Cin-N	1	1	.500	2	2	2	0	0	18	17	3	10	9	14.0	4.50	79	.243	.346	1	.125	-1	-2	-2	-0	-0.2
1891	Col-a	12	11	.522	27	24	19	0	0	203^{1}	216	8	84	68	13.3	4.16	83	.263	.331	7	.090	-4	-10	-16	-2	-1.9
1892	Was-N	2	2	.500	5	4	3	0	0	37	39	0	15	8	13.4	4.38	74	.260	.331	3	.231	0	-4	-5	-1	-0.4
1893	StL-N	0	1	.000	3	1	1	0	1	17^{1}	26	1	7	1	17.7	4.15	114	.338	.400	1	.143	0	1	1	-0	0.0
1895	Chi-N	0	1	.000	2	2	1	0	0	11	16	0	6	1	18.8	6.55	78	.333	.418	0	.000	-0	-2	-2	0	-0.1
Total	5	15	16	.484	39	33	26	0	1	286^{2}	314	12	122	87	13.8	4.30	83	.269	.341	12	.110	-5	-17	-23	-3	-2.6

● COZY DOLAN

Dolan, Patrick Henry b: 12/3/1872, Cambridge, Mass. d: 3/29/07, Louisville, Ky. BL/TL, 5'10", 160 lbs. Deb: 4/26/1895 ♦

YEAR	TM/L	W	L	PCT	G	GS	CG	SH	SV	IP	H	HR	BB	SO	RAT	ERA	ERA+	OAV	OOB	BH	AVG	PB	PR	/A	PD	TPI
1895	Bos-N	11	7	.611	25	21	18	3	1	198^{1}	215	11	67	47	13.4	4.27	120	.272	.340	20	.241	-1	11	18	4	1.5
1896	Bos-N	1	4	.200	6	5	3	0	0	41	55	1	27	14	18.7	4.83	94	.318	.419	2	.143	-1	-2	-1	-0	-0.3
1905	Bos-N	0	1	.000	2	0	0	0	0	4	7	2	1	1	18.0	9.00	34	.368	.400	119	.275	1	-3	-3	-0	-0.5
1906	Bos-N	0	1	.000	2	0	0	0	0	12	12	1	6	7	13.5	4.50	60	.300	.391	136	.248	0	-2	-2	-1	-0.2
Total	4	12	13	.480	35	26	21	3	1	255^{1}	289	15	101	69	14.3	4.44	109	.283	.357	855	.269	-2	4	12	3	0.5

● TOM DOLAN

Dolan, Thomas J. b: 1/10/1859, New York, N.Y. d: 1/16/13, St.Louis, Mo. BR/TR, Deb: 9/30/1879 ♦

YEAR	TM/L	W	L	PCT	G	GS	CG	SH	SV	IP	H	HR	BB	SO	RAT	ERA	ERA+	OAV	OOB	BH	AVG	PB	PR	/A	PD	TPI
1883	StL-a	0	0	—	1	0	0	0	0	4	4	0	0	0	9.0	4.50	77	.250	.250	63	.214	-0	-1	-0	0	0.0

● ART DOLL

Doll, Arthur James "Moose" b: 5/7/13, Chicago, Ill. d: 4/28/78, Calumet City, Ill. BR/TR, 6'1", 190 lbs. Deb: 9/21/35 ♦

YEAR	TM/L	W	L	PCT	G	GS	CG	SH	SV	IP	H	HR	BB	SO	RAT	ERA	ERA+	OAV	OOB	BH	AVG	PB	PR	/A	PD	TPI
1936	Bos-N	0	1	.000	1	1	0	0	0	8	11	1	2	2	15.8	3.38	114	.355	.412	0	.000	-0	1	0	-0	0.0
1938	Bos-N	0	0	—	3	0	0	0	0	4	4	0	3	1	15.8	2.25	153	.286	.412	1	1.000	1	1	1	0	0.1
Total	2	0	1	.000	4	1	0	0	0	12	15	1	5	3	15.8	3.00	123	.333	.412	2	.154	0	1	1	0	0.1

● RED DONAHUE

Donahue, Francis Rostell b: 1/23/1873, Waterbury, Conn. d: 8/25/13, Philadelphia, Pa. BR/TR, 6', 187 lbs. Deb: 5/6/1893

YEAR	TM/L	W	L	PCT	G	GS	CG	SH	SV	IP	H	HR	BB	SO	RAT	ERA	ERA+	OAV	OOB	BH	AVG	PB	PR	/A	PD	TPI
1893	NY-N	0	0	—	2	0	0	0	1	5	8	1	3	1	23.4	9.00	52	.348	.464	0	.000	-0	-2	-2	0	-0.1
1895	StL-N	0	1	.000	1	1	1	0	0	8	9	2	3	2	14.6	6.75	72	.281	.361	0	.000	-1	-2	-2	0	-0.2
1896	StL-N	7	24	.226	32	32	28	0	0	267	376	6	98	70	16.4	5.80	75	.329	.389	17	.159	-8	-43	-43	-1	-4.3
1897	StL-N	10	35	.222	46	42	**38**	1	1	348	485	16	106	64	15.9	6.13	72	.327	.380	33	.213	-3	-70	-67	5	-6.1
1898	Phi-N	16	17	.485	35	35	33	1	0	284^{1}	327	7	80	57	13.3	3.55	97	.286	.340	16	.143	-7	2	-3	4	-0.7
1899	Phi-N	21	8	.724	35	31	27	4	0	279	292	6	63	51	11.8	3.39	109	.269	.316	20	.180	-5	15	9	3	0.6
1900	Phi-N	15	10	.600	32	24	21	2	0	240	299	6	50	41	13.4	3.60	100	.304	.344	20	.222	-1	3	0	-1	-0.2
1901	Phi-N	20	13	.606	34	33	33	1	1	295^{1}	299	2	59	88	11.2	2.59	131	.261	.302	11	.097	-9	24	27	-2	1.6
1902	StL-A	22	11	.667	35	34	33	2	0	316^{1}	322	7	65	63	11.2	2.76	128	.264	.306	11	.093	-9	29	27	7	2.2
1903	StL-A	8	7	.533	16	15	14	0	0	131	145	0	22	51	11.5	2.75	106	.279	.309	8	.157	-2	3	2	0	0.1
	Cle-A	7	9	.438	16	15	14	4	0	136^{2}	142	3	12	45	10.5	2.44	117	.267	.291	8	.151	-1	8	6	1	0.7
	Yr	15	16	.484	32	30	28	4	0	267^{2}	287	3	34	96	11.0	2.59	111	.273	.300	16	.154	-3	11	9	2	0.8
1904	Cle-A	19	14	.576	35	32	30	6	0	277	281	2	49	127	10.9	2.40	105	.264	.299	17	.168	-1	6	4	2	0.5
1905	Cle-A	6	12	.333	20	18	14	1	0	137^{2}	132	2	25	45	10.6	3.40	77	.254	.295	4	.075	-5	-11	-12	1	-1.8
1906	Det-A	13	14	.481	28	28	26	3	0	241	260	1	54	82	12.0	2.73	101	.278	.323	10	.123	-4	-1	1	-0	-0.3
Total	13	164	175	.484	367	340	312	25	3	2966^{1}	3377	61	689	787	12.7	3.61	96	.286	.331	175	.152	-56	-40	-52	18	-8.0

● DEACON DONAHUE

Donahue, John Stephen Michael b: 6/23/20, Chicago, Ill. BR/TR, 6', 180 lbs. Deb: 9/16/43

YEAR	TM/L	W	L	PCT	G	GS	CG	SH	SV	IP	H	HR	BB	SO	RAT	ERA	ERA+	OAV	OOB	BH	AVG	PB	PR	/A	PD	TPI
1943	Phi-N	0	0	—	2	0	0	0	0	4	4	0	1	1	13.5	4.50	75	.235	.316	0	—	0	-1	-1	0	0.0
1944	Phi-N	0	2	.000	6	0	0	0	0	9^{1}	18	0	2	2	19.3	7.71	47	.429	.455	0	.000	-0	-4	-4	0	-0.8
Total	2	0	2	.000	8	0	0	0	0	13^{1}	22	0	3	3	17.6	6.75	52	.373	.413	0	.000	-0	-5	-5	0	-0.8

● ATLEY DONALD

Donald, Richard Atley "Swampy" b: 8/19/10, Morton, Miss. d: 10/19/92, West Monroe, La. BL/TR, 6'1", 186 lbs. Deb: 4/21/38

YEAR	TM/L	W	L	PCT	G	GS	CG	SH	SV	IP	H	HR	BB	SO	RAT	ERA	ERA+	OAV	OOB	BH	AVG	PB	PR	/A	PD	TPI
1938	NY-A	0	1	.000	2	2	0	0	0	12	7	0	14	6	16.5	5.25	86	.175	.400	1	.167	-0	-1	-1	0	-0.1
1939	NY-A	13	3	.813	24	20	11	2	1	153	144	12	60	55	12.0	3.71	118	.247	.317	15	.250	3	16	11	-1	1.1
1940	NY-A	8	3	.727	24	11	6	1	0	118^{2}	113	11	59	60	13.2	3.03	133	.249	.339	6	.146	-2	18	13	-3	0.6
1941	*NY-A	9	5	.643	22	20	10	0	0	159	141	11	69	71	12.1	3.57	110	.237	.320	5	.081	-4	10	6	-0	0.1
1942	*NY-A	11	3	.786	20	19	10	1	0	147^{2}	133	6	45	53	10.8	3.11	111	.239	.296	9	.148	-1	9	5	-2	0.1
1943	NY-A	6	4	.600	22	15	2	0	0	119^{1}	134	10	38	57	13.0	4.60	70	.276	.329	6	.128	-2	-17	-18	-2	-1.9
1944	NY-A	13	10	.565	30	19	9	0	0	159	173	13	59	48	13.2	3.34	104	.280	.345	10	.182	-0	2	3	-1	0.2
1945	NY-A	5	4	.556	9	9	6	2	0	63^{2}	62	3	25	19	12.3	2.97	117	.248	.316	5	.208	0	3	4	-2	0.3
Total	8	65	33	.663	153	115	54	6	1	932^{1}	907	66	369	369	12.4	3.52	107	.253	.325	57	.160	-7	39	24	-11	0.4

● ED DONALDS

Donalds, Edward Alexander "Erston" b: 6/22/1885, Bidwell, Ohio d: 7/3/50, Columbus, Ohio BR/TR, 5'11", 180 lbs. Deb: 9/1/12

YEAR	TM/L	W	L	PCT	G	GS	CG	SH	SV	IP	H	HR	BB	SO	RAT	ERA	ERA+	OAV	OOB	BH	AVG	PB	PR	/A	PD	TPI
1912	Cin-N	1	0	1.000	1	0	0	0	0	4	7	0	0	1	15.8	4.50	75	.438	.438	0	.000	-0	-0	-1	0	-0.1

● MIKE DONLIN

Donlin, Michael Joseph "Turkey Mike" b: 5/30/1878, Peoria, Ill. d: 9/24/33, Hollywood, Cal. BL/TL, 5'9", 170 lbs. Deb: 7/19/1899 ♦

YEAR	TM/L	W	L	PCT	G	GS	CG	SH	SV	IP	H	HR	BB	SO	RAT	ERA	ERA+	OAV	OOB	BH	AVG	PB	PR	/A	PD	TPI
1899	StL-N	0	1	.000	3	1	0	0	0	15^{1}	15	1	14	6	17.6	7.63	52	.254	.405	86	.323	1	-6	-6	1	-0.2
1902	Cin-N	0	0	—	1	0	0	0	0	1	1	0	0	0	9.0	0.00	—	.250	.250	41	.287	0	0	-0	0	0.0
Total	2	0	1	.000	4	1	0	0	0	16^{1}	16	1	14	6	17.1	7.16	55	.254	.397	1282	.333	1	-6	-6	1	-0.2

● ED DONNELLY

Donnelly, Edward "Big Ed" or "Ned" (b: Edward O'Donnell)
b: 7/29/1880, Hampton, N.Y. d: 11/28/57, Rutland, Vt. BR/TR, 6'1", 205 lbs. Deb: 9/19/11

YEAR	TM/L	W	L	PCT	G	GS	CG	SH	SV	IP	H	HR	BB	SO	RAT	ERA	ERA+	OAV	OOB	BH	AVG	PB	PR	/A	PD	TPI
1911	Bos-N	3	2	.600	5	4	4	1	0	36^{2}	33	0	9	16	10.8	2.45	156	.236	.291	1	.071	-1	4	6	-0	0.6
1912	Bos-N	5	10	.333	37	18	10	0	0	184^{1}	225	10	72	67	14.7	4.35	82	.304	.370	19	.275	3	-19	-16	1	-0.8
Total	2	8	12	.400	42	22	14	1	0	221	258	10	81	83	14.1	4.03	90	.293	.357	20	.241	1	-15	-10	1	-0.2

● ED DONNELLY

Donnelly, Edward Vincent b: 12/10/32, Allen, Mich. d: 12/25/97, Houston, Tex. BR/TR, 6', 175 lbs. Deb: 8/1/59

YEAR	TM/L	W	L	PCT	G	GS	CG	SH	SV	IP	H	HR	BB	SO	RAT	ERA	ERA+	OAV	OOB	BH	AVG	PB	PR	/A	PD	TPI
1959	Chi-N	1	1	.500	9	0	0	0	0	14^{1}	18	1	9	6	17.0	3.14	126	.305	.397	0	—	0	1	1	0	0.2

● FRANK DONNELLY

Donnelly, Franklin Marion b: 10/7/1869, Tamaroa, Ill. d: 2/3/53, Canton, Ill. 5'6", 180 lbs. Deb: 8/15/1893

YEAR	TM/L	W	L	PCT	G	GS	CG	SH	SV	IP	H	HR	BB	SO	RAT	ERA	ERA+	OAV	OOB	BH	AVG	PB	PR	/A	PD	TPI
1893	Chi-N	3	1	.750	7	5	3	0	**2**	42	51	1	17	6	15.4	5.36	86	.291	.367	8	.444	4	-3	-3	-0	0.1

YEAR	TM/L	W	L	PCT	G	GS	CG	SH	SV	IP	H	HR	BB	SO	RAT	ERA	ERA+	OAV	OOB	BH	AVG	PB	PR	/A	PD	TPI
● **BLIX DONNELLY**	Donnelly, Sylvester Urban b: 1/21/14, Olivia, Minn. d: 6/20/76, Olivia, Minn. BR/TR, 5′10″, 178 lbs. Deb: 5/6/44																									
1944	*StL-N	2	1	.667	27	4	2	1	2	76^1	61	2	34	45	11.4	2.12	166	.218	.307	1	.063	-1	13	12	1	0.5
1945	StL-N	8	10	.444	31	23	9	4	2	166^1	157	10	87	76	13.5	3.52	106	.250	.346	7	.130	-2	5	4	-4	-0.2
1946	StL-N	1	2	.333	13	0	0	0	0	13^2	17	1	10	11	18.4	3.95	87	.347	.467	0	—	0	-1	-1	-0	-0.2
	Phi-N	3	4	.429	12	8	2	0	1	76^1	64	7	24	38	10.6	2.95	116	.220	.284	7	.280	2	4	4	-1	0.5
	Yr	4	6	.400	25	8	2	0	1	90	81	8	34	49	11.7	3.10	111	.238	.310	7	.280	2	3	3	-1	0.3
1947	Phi-N	4	6	.400	38	10	5	1	5	120^2	113	6	46	31	12.1	2.98	134	.265	.340	2	.063	-2	14	14	-0	0.9
1948	Phi-N	5	7	.417	26	19	8	1	2	131^2	125	13	49	46	11.9	3.69	107	.261	.330	10	.222	2	4	4	-3	0.3
1949	Phi-N	2	1	.667	23	10	1	0	0	78^1	84	7	40	36	14.4	5.06	78	.294	.382	4	.174	-1	-9	-10	-2	-0.6
1950	Phi-N	2	4	.333	14	1	0	0	0	21	30	5	10	10	17.1	4.29	94	.330	.396	1	.200	-0	-0	-1	0	-0.1
1951	Bos-N	0	1	.000	6	0	0	0	0	7^1	8	1	6	3	18.4	7.36	50	.286	.429	0	.000	-0	-3	-3	0	-0.4
Total	8	27	36	.429	190	75	27	7	12	691^2	659	52	306	296	12.8	3.49	109	.257	.340	32	.159	-1	27	24	-8	0.7
● **JIM DONOHUE**	Donohue, James Thomas b: 10/31/38, St.Louis, Mo. BR/TR, 6′4″, 190 lbs. Deb: 4/11/61																									
1961	Det-A	1	1	.500	14	0	0	0	1	20^1	23	2	15	20	16.8	3.54	116	.287	.400	0	.000	-0	1	1	-0	0.1
	LA-A	4	6	.400	38	7	0	0	5	100^1	93	16	50	79	12.8	4.31	105	.246	.334	4	.148	-1	-3	2	-0	0.1
	Yr	5	7	.417	52	7	0	0	6	120^2	116	18	65	99	13.5	4.18	106	.253	.346	4	.143	-1	-2	4	-1	0.2
1962	LA-A	1	0	1.000	12	1	0	0	0	24^1	24	4	11	14	13.7	3.70	104	.258	.349	1	.250	0	1	0	-1	0.0
	Min-A	0	1	.000	6	1	0	0	1	10^1	12	2	6	3	15.7	6.97	59	.324	.419	0	.000	-0	-3	-3	1	-0.3
	Yr	1	1	.500	18	2	0	0	1	34^2	36	6	17	17	13.8	4.67	84	.273	.356	1	.167	0	-3	-3	-0	-0.3
Total	2	6	8	.429	70	9	0	0	7	155^1	152	24	82	116	13.7	4.29	101	.259	.351	5	.147	-1	-5	1	-1	-0.1
● **PETE DONOHUE**	Donohue, Peter Joseph b: 11/5/1900, Athens, Tex. d: 2/23/88, Ft.Worth, Tex. BR/TR, 6′2″, 185 lbs. Deb: 7/1/21																									
1921	Cin-N	7	6	.538	21	11	7	0	1	118^1	117	5	26	44	10.9	3.35	107	.263	.304	8	.211	1	6	3	2	0.6
1922	Cin-N	18	9	**.667**	33	30	18	2	1	242	257	7	43	66	11.3	3.12	128	.276	.312	16	.182	-3	26	23	1	2.1
1923	Cin-N	21	15	.583	42	36	19	2	3	274^1	304	3	68	84	12.5	3.38	114	.278	.326	24	.250	3	19	15	1	2.0
1924	Cin-N	16	9	.640	35	31	16	3	0	222^1	248	9	36	72	11.9	3.60	105	.285	.321	14	.192	-0	7	4	-1	0.2
1925	Cin-N	21	14	.600	42	38	**27**	3	2	**301**	310	3	49	78	10.8	3.08	133	.268	.299	32	.294	7	40	34	-3	4.0
1926	Cin-N	**20**	14	.588	47	36	17	**5**	2	$\mathbf{285^2}$	298	6	39	73	10.9	3.37	109	.268	.298	33	.311	9	14	10	-3	1.7
1927	Cin-N	6	16	.273	33	24	12	1	1	190^2	253	3	32	48	13.5	4.11	92	.328	.356	16	.250	1	-4	-7	0	-0.6
1928	Cin-N	7	11	.389	23	18	8	0	0	150	180	10	32	37	12.9	4.74	83	.309	.348	7	.146	-0	-12	-13	1	-1.2
1929	Cin-N	10	13	.435	32	24	7	0	0	177^2	243	12	51	30	15.1	5.42	84	.331	.377	20	.333	4	-14	-17	0	-1.3
1930	Cin-N	1	3	.250	8	5	2	0	1	34^1	53	0	13	4	17.6	6.29	77	.363	.419	1	.100	-1	-5	-6	1	-0.5
	NY-N	7	6	.538	18	11	4	0	1	86^2	135	6	18	26	16.1	6.13	77	.360	.392	9	.273	1	-11	-13	-2	-1.6
	Yr	8	9	.471	26	16	6	0	2	121	188	6	31	30	16.4	6.17	77	.360	.398	10	.233	0	-16	-19	-0	-2.1
1931	NY-N	0	1	.000	4	1	0	0	0	11^1	14	1	4	4	14.3	5.56	66	.311	.367	0	.000	-0	-2	-2	-0	-0.2
	Cle-A	0	0	—	2	0	0	0	0	5^1	9	1	5	4	23.6	8.44	55	.429	.538	0	.000	-0	-2	-2	-0	0.0
1932	Bos-A	0	1	.000	4	2	0	0	0	12^2	18	2	6	1	17.1	7.82	57	.340	.407	0	.000	-0	-5	-5	1	-0.3
Total	12	134	118	.532	344	267	137	16	12	2112^1	2439	68	422	571	12.4	3.87	103	.293	.330	180	.246	21	56	25	-1	4.9
● **LINO DONOSO**	Donoso, Lino (Galeta) b: 9/23/22, Havana, Cuba d: 10/13/90, Veracruz, Mexico BL/TL, 5′11″, 160 lbs. Deb: 6/18/55																									
1955	Pit-N	4	6	.400	25	9	3	0	1	95	106	16	35	38	13.5	5.31	78	.287	.351	5	.185	-1	-13	-13	0	-1.2
1956	Pit-N	0	0	—	3	0	0	0	0	1^2	2	0	1	1	16.2	0.00	—	.250	.333	0	—	0	1	1	0	0.0
Total	2	4	6	.400	28	9	3	0	1	96^2	108	16	36	39	13.5	5.21	79	.286	.350	5	.185	-1	-13	-12	0	-1.2
● **DICK DONOVAN**	Donovan, Richard Edward b: 12/7/27, Boston, Mass. d: 1/6/97, Weymouth, Mass. BL/TR, 6′3″, 205 lbs. Deb: 4/24/50																									
1950	Bos-N	0	2	.000	10	3	0	0	0	29^2	28	4	34	9	19.4	8.19	47	.255	.438	1	.167	1	-13	-14	-0	-0.7
1951	Bos-N	0	0	—	8	2	0	0	0	13^2	17	0	11	4	18.4	5.27	70	.298	.412	1	.333	1	-2	-2	0	0.2
1952	Bos-N	0	2	.000	7	2	0	0	1	13	18	1	12	6	22.2	5.54	65	.346	.485	0	.000	-0	-3	-3	1	-0.4
1954	Det-A	0	0	—	2	0	0	0	0	6	9	1	5	2	21.0	10.50	35	.360	.467	0	.000	-0	-5	-5	-0	0.0
1955	Chi-A☆	15	9	.625	29	24	11	5	0	187	186	17	48	88	11.4	3.32	119	.261	.311	17	.224	5	13	13	1	2.1
1956	Chi-A	12	10	.545	34	31	14	3	0	234^2	212	22	59	120	10.6	3.64	113	.240	.292	20	.222	8	13	12	2	1.9
1957	Chi-A	16	6	**.727**	28	28	**16**	2	0	220^2	203	17	45	88	10.4	2.77	135	.247	.293	12	.145	2	25	24	0	2.5
1958	Chi-A	15	14	.517	34	34	16	4	0	248	240	23	53	127	10.9	3.01	121	.251	.295	9	.112	-1	21	17	-1	1.6
1959	*Chi-A	9	10	.474	31	29	5	1	0	179^2	171	15	58	71	11.7	3.66	103	.247	.310	8	.131	1	4	2	-2	0.1
1960	Chi-A	6	1	.857	33	8	0	0	3	78^2	87	13	25	30	12.8	5.38	70	.283	.337	3	.130	-0	-13	-14	1	-1.1
1961	Was-A★	10	10	.500	23	22	11	2	0	168^2	138	10	35	62	**9.4**	**2.40**	**167**	.224	**.269**	10	.179	2	30	30	-1	3.7
1962	Cle-A★	20	10	.667	34	34	16	**5**	0	250^2	255	23	47	94	10.9	3.59	108	.263	.299	16	.180	6	11	8	-1	1.4
1963	Cle-A	11	13	.458	30	30	7	3	0	206	211	27	28	84	10.7	4.24	85	.265	.295	9	.130	-1	-14	-14	-1	-1.7
1964	Cle-A	7	9	.438	30	23	5	0	1	158^1	181	19	29	83	12.1	4.55	79	.290	.324	7	.146	3	-16	-17	1	-1.2
1965	Cle-A	1	3	.250	12	3	0	0	0	22^2	32	6	6	12	15.1	5.96	58	.333	.373	0	.000	-1	-6	-6	-0	-1.1
Total	15	122	99	.552	345	273	101	25	5	2017^1	1988	198	495	880	11.3	3.67	104	.258	.306	113	.163	24	45	31	-0	7.3
● **TOM DONOVAN**	Donovan, Thomas Joseph b: 1/1/1873, West Troy, N.Y. d: 3/25/33, Watervliet, N.Y. BR/TR, 6′2″, 168 lbs. Deb: 9/10/01 F♦																									
1901	Cle-A	0	0	—	1	0	0	0	0	7	16	0	3	0	27.0	5.14	69	.444	.512	18	.254	0	-1	-1	0	0.0
● **BILL DONOVAN**	Donovan, Willard Earl b: 7/6/16, Maywood, Ill. d: 9/25/97, Maywood, Ill. BB/TL, 6′2″, 198 lbs. Deb: 4/19/42																									
1942	Bos-N	3	6	.333	31	10	2	0	0	89^1	97	2	32	23	13.0	3.43	97	.283	.344	6	.240	1	-1	-1	2	0.3
1943	Bos-N	1	0	1.000	7	0	0	0	0	14^2	17	0	9	1	16.0	1.84	185	.304	.400	1	.333	0	3	3	1	0.3
Total	2	4	6	.400	38	10	2	0	0	104	114	2	41	24	13.4	3.20	105	.286	.352	7	.250	1	1	2	3	0.6
● **BILL DONOVAN**	Donovan, William Edward "Wild Bill" b: 10/13/1876, Lawrence, Mass. d: 12/9/23, Forsyth, N.Y. BR/TR, 5′11″, 190 lbs. Deb: 4/22/1898 MC♦																									
1898	Was-N	1	6	.143	17	7	6	0	0	88	88	0	69	36	16.8	4.30	85	.259	.394	17	.165	-1	-7	-6	-0	-0.5
1899	Bro-N	1	2	.333	5	2	2	0	1	25	35	0	13	11	17.3	4.32	91	.330	.403	3	.231	-0	-1	-1	-0	-0.1
1900	Bro-N	1	2	.333	5	4	2	0	0	31	36	0	18	13	16.5	6.68	58	.290	.393	0	.000	-2	-10	-10	1	-0.8
1901	Bro-N	**25**	15	.625	**45**	38	36	2	**3**	351	324	1	152	226	12.4	2.77	121	.244	.325	23	.170	-1	22	23	-1	2.1
1902	Bro-N	17	15	.531	35	33	30	4	1	297^2	250	1	111	170	11.1	2.78	99	.228	.303	28	.174	-0	-0	-1	1	0.0
1903	Det-A	17	16	.515	35	34	**34**	4	0	307	247	3	95	187	10.2	2.29	127	.220	.284	30	.242	4	23	21	-3	2.4
1904	Det-A	16	16	.500	34	34	30	3	0	293	251	5	94	137	10.9	2.46	104	.232	.300	38	.271	5	5	3	0	1.0
1905	Det-A	18	15	.545	34	32	27	5	0	280^2	236	2	101	135	11.1	2.60	105	.230	.305	25	.192	1	2	4	-3	0.3
1906	Det-A	9	15	.375	25	25	22	0	0	211^2	221	4	72	85	12.8	3.15	88	.272	.337	11	.121	-5	-11	-9	-0	-1.5
1907	*Det-A	25	4	**.862**	32	28	27	3	1	271	222	3	82	123	10.4	2.19	119	.226	.291	29	.266	7	11	12	-6	1.5
1908	*Det-A	18	7	.720	29	28	25	6	0	242^2	210	2	53	141	10.0	2.08	116	.231	.278	13	.159	0	9	9	-6	0.2
1909	*Det-A	8	7	.533	21	17	13	4	2	140^1	121	0	60	76	12.0	2.31	109	.235	.322	9	.200	1	3	3	-2	0.2
1910	Det-A	17	7	.708	26	23	20	3	0	206^2	184	4	61	107	11.0	2.44	108	.243	.305	10	.145	-2	2	4	-6	-0.4
1911	Det-A	10	9	.526	20	19	15	1	0	168^1	160	4	64	81	12.1	3.31	104	.250	.321	12	.200	3	1	3	-5	0.1
1912	Det-A	1	0	1.000	3	1	0	0	0	10	5	0	2	6	7.2	0.90	362	.147	.216	1	.077	-1	3	3	-0	0.1
1915	NY-A	0	3	.000	9	1	0	0	0	33^2	35	1	10	17	12.3	4.81	61	.278	.336	1	.083	-1	-7	-7	-1	-0.7
1916	NY-A	0	0	—	1	0	0	0	0	1	1	0	1	0	18.0	0.00	—	.250	.400	0	—	0	0	0	-0	0.0
1918	Det-A	1	0	1.000	2	1	0	0	0	6	5	0	1	1	9.0	1.50	177	.227	.261	1	.500	0	1	1	-0	0.2
Total	18	185	139	.571	378	327	289	35	8	2964^2	2631	30	1059	1552	11.5	2.69	106	.239	.310	251	.193	9	43	54	-31	4.1
● **JOHN DOPSON**	Dopson, John Robert b: 7/14/63, Baltimore, Md. BL/TR, 6′4″, 225 lbs. Deb: 9/4/85																									
1985	Mon-N	0	2	.000	4	3	0	0	0	13	25	4	4	4	20.1	11.08	31	.379	.414	0	.000	0	-11	-11	-0	-1.3
1988	Mon-N	3	11	.214	26	26	1	0	0	168^2	150	15	58	101	11.2	3.04	118	.235	.300	3	.059	-3	8	10	-3	0.3
1989	Bos-A	12	8	.600	29	28	2	0	0	169^1	166	14	69	95	12.6	3.99	103	.257	.330	0	—	0	-2	2	3	0.5
1990	Bos-A	0	0	—	4	4	0	0	0	17^2	13	2	9	9	11.2	2.04	200	.200	.297	0	—	0	4	4	1	0.0
1991	Bos-A	0	0	—	1	0	0	0	0	1	2	0	1	0	27.0	18.00	24	.500	.600	0	—	0	-2	-2	0	0.0
1992	Bos-A	7	11	.389	25	25	0	0	0	141^1	159	17	38	55	12.7	4.08	103	.287	.335	0	—	0	-2	2	1	-0.1
1993	Bos-A	7	11	.389	34	28	1	1	0	155^2	170	16	59	89	13.4	4.97	93	.281	.347	0	—	0	-11	-6	1	-0.9

YEAR TM/L	W	L	PCT	G	GS	CG	SH	SV	IP	H	HR	BB	SO	RAT	ERA	ERA+	OAV	OOB	BH	AVG	PB	PR	/A	PD	TPI
1994 Cal-A	1	4	.200	21	5	0	0	1	58^2	67	6	26	33	14.7	6.14	80	.288	.366	0	—	0	-9	-8	0	-0.6
Total 8	30	47	.390	144	119	4	1	1	725^1	752	74	264	386	12.7	4.27	98	.268	.333	3	.055	-3	-25	-8	3	-2.1
● JOHN DORAN Doran, John F. b: 1867, Chicago, Ill. TL, 5'4", 160 lbs. Deb: 4/11/1891																									
1891 Lou-a	5	10	.333	15	14	12	1	0	126	160	3	75	55	17.7	5.43	67	.299	.398	10	.189	-2	-24	-25	-0	-2.3
● MIKE DORGAN Dorgan, Michael Cornelius b: 10/2/1853, Middletown, Conn. d: 4/26/09, Hartford, Conn. BR/TR, 5'9", 180 lbs. Deb: 5/8/1877 FM♦																									
1879 Syr-N	0	0	—	2	0	0	0	0	12	13	0	2	8	11.3	2.25	105	.260	.288	72	.267	0	0	0	0	0.0
1880 Pro-N	0	0	—	1	0	0	0	0	8	4	0	0	2	4.5	1.13	196	.138	.138	79	.246	0	1	1	0	0.0
1883 NY-N	0	1	.000	1	1	1	0	0	7	8	0	6	3	18.0	3.86	80	.286	.412	61	.234	0	-1	-1	-0	-0.1
1884 NY-N	8	6	.571	14	14	12	0	0	113	98	5	51	90	11.9	3.50	85	.215	.294	94	.276	2	-7	-7	1	-0.5
Total 4	8	7	.533	18	15	13	0	0	140	123	5	59	103	11.7	3.28	88	.218	.293	802	.274	3	-6	-6	1	-0.6
● HARRY DORISH Dorish, Harry "Fritz" b: 7/13/21, Swoyersville, Pa. BR/TR, 5'11", 206 lbs. Deb: 4/15/47 C																									
1947 Bos-A	7	8	.467	41	9	2	0	2	136	149	6	54	50	13.5	4.70	83	.283	.351	5	.143	-1	-15	-12	1	-1.3
1948 Bos-A	0	1	.000	9	0	0	0	0	14^1	18	1	6	5	15.1	5.65	78	.281	.343	1	.250	-0	-2	-2	-0	-0.1
1949 Bos-A	0	0	—	5	0	0	0	0	7^2	7	1	1	5	9.4	2.35	186	.241	.267	0	—	0	2	2	0	0.0
1950 StL-A	4	9	.308	29	13	4	0	0	109	162	13	36	36	17.1	6.44	77	.337	.394	5	.161	0	-23	-18	-1	-1.8
1951 Chi-A	5	6	.455	32	4	2	1	0	96^2	101	6	31	29	12.3	3.54	114	.272	.328	8	.258	0	6	5	0	0.6
1952 Chi-A	8	4	.667	39	1	1	0	**11**	91	66	4	42	47	10.8	2.47	148	.208	.303	2	.091	-1	**12**	**12**	2	1.9
1953 Chi-A	10	6	.625	55	6	2	0	18	145^2	140	9	52	69	12.2	3.40	118	.254	.325	7	.171	-2	10	10	2	1.3
1954 Chi-A	6	4	.600	37	6	2	1	6	109	88	9	29	48	9.7	2.72	137	.228	.284	3	.111	-2	12	12	-1	0.9
1955 Chi-A	2	0	1.000	13	0	0	0	1	17	16	0	9	6	13.2	1.59	249	.258	.352	1	.333	0	4	4	1	0.6
Bal-A	3	3	.500	35	1	0	0	6	65^2	58	4	28	22	11.9	3.15	121	.238	.319	0	.000	-1	6	5	1	0.4
Yr	5	3	.625	48	1	0	0	7	82^2	74	4	37	28	12.2	2.83	136	.242	.326	1	.077	-1	10	9	1	1.0
1956 Bal-A	0	0	—	13	0	0	0	0	19^2	22	3	3	4	11.4	4.12	95	.297	.325	0	—	0	0	-0	1	0.1
Bos-A	0	2	.000	15	0	0	0	0	22^2	23	1	10	11	13.1	3.57	129	.277	.355	0	—	0	1	3	1	0.3
Yr	0	2	.000	28	0	0	0	0	42^1	45	4	13	15	12.3	3.83	112	.283	.337	0	—	0	2	2	2	0.4
Total 10	45	43	.511	323	40	13	2	44	834^1	850	57	301	332	12.6	3.83	106	.267	.333	32	.157	-6	14	20	6	2.9
● GUS DORNER Dorner, Augustus b: 8/18/1876, Chambersburg, Pa. d: 5/4/56, Chambersburg, Pa. BR/TR, 5'10", 176 lbs. Deb: 9/17/02																									
1902 Cle-A	3	1	.750	4	4	4	1	0	36	33	1	13	5	11.8	1.25	275	.244	.315	5	.385	2	9	9	-0	1.2
1903 Cle-A	3	5	.375	12	8	4	2	0	73^2	83	4	24	28	13.2	4.52	63	.283	.340	2	.080	-2	-13	-14	0	-1.4
1906 Cin-N	0	1	.000	2	1	1	0	0	15	16	0	4	5	12.6	1.20	230	.276	.333	0	.000	-1	2	3	-0	0.1
Bos-N	8	25	.242	34	32	29	0	0	273^1	264	5	103	104	12.6	3.65	74	.260	.338	14	.140	-4	-31	-29	3	-3.5
Yr	8	26	.235	36	33	30	0	0	288^1	280	5	107	109	12.6	3.53	76	.261	.337	14	.133	-5	-29	-27	2	-3.4
1907 Bos-N	12	16	.429	36	31	24	2	0	271^1	253	4	92	85	11.9	3.12	82	.255	.327	12	.130	-3	-19	-17	-3	-2.4
1908 Bos-N	8	19	.296	38	28	14	3	0	216^1	176	3	77	41	11.1	3.54	68	.224	.305	12	.179	-1	-28	-27	2	-3.3
1909 Bos-N	1	2	.333	5	2	0	0	1	24^2	17	1	17	7	13.1	2.55	110	.198	.343	1	.167	-0	0	1	-0	0.0
Total 6	35	69	.337	131	106	76	8	1	910^1	842	18	330	275	12.1	3.37	78	.250	.326	46	.149	-9	-80	-74	1	-9.3
● BERT DORR Dorr, Charles Albert b: 2/2/1862, New York d: 6/16/14, Dickinson, N.Y. Deb: 8/24/1882																									
1882 StL-a	2	6	.250	8	8	8	0	0	66	53	0	1	34	7.4	2.59	108	.205	.208	4	.154	-2	1	2	1	0.1
● CAL DORSETT Dorsett, Calvin Leavelle "Preacher" b: 6/10/13, Lone Oak, Tex. d: 10/22/70, Elk City, Okla. BR/TR, 6', 180 lbs. Deb: 8/19/40																									
1940 Cle-A	0	0	—	1	0	0	0	0	1	1	1	0	0	9.0	9.00	47	.250	.250	0	—	0	-1	-1	-0	0.0
1941 Cle-A	0	1	.000	5	2	0	0	0	11^1	21	0	10	5	24.6	10.32	38	.382	.477	0	.000	-0	-8	-8	-0	-0.6
1947 Cle-A	0	0	—	2	0	0	0	0	1^1	3	1	3	1	40.5	27.00	13	.500	.667	0	—	0	-3	-3	-0	0.0
Total 3	0	1	.000	8	2	0	0	0	13^2	25	2	13	6	25.0	11.85	33	.385	.487	0	.000	-0	-12	-12	-0	-0.6
● JIM DORSEY Dorsey, James Edward b: 8/2/55, Oak Park, Ill. BR/TR, 6'7", 190 lbs. Deb: 9/2/80																									
1980 Cal-A	1	2	.333	4	4	0	0	0	15^2	25	2	8	8	19.5	9.19	43	.368	.442	0	—	0	-9	-9	-0	-1.3
1984 Bos-A	0	0	—	2	0	0	0	0	2^2	6	0	2	4	27.0	10.13	41	.462	.533	0	—	0	-2	-2	0	0.0
1985 Bos-A	0	1	.000	2	1	0	0	0	5^1	12	2	10	2	37.1	20.25	21	.444	.595	0	—	0	-10	-9	-0	-1.2
Total 3	1	3	.250	8	5	0	0	0	23^2	43	4	20	14	24.3	11.79	34	.398	.496	0	—	0	-20	-20	-0	-2.5
● JERRY DORSEY Dorsey, Michael Jeremiah b: 1854, Canada d: 11/3/38, Auburn, N.Y. Deb: 7/9/1884 ♦																									
1884 Bal-U	0	1	.000	1	1	0	0	0	4	7	1	0	3	15.8	9.00	30	.368	.368	0	.000	-1	-3	-3	0	-0.5
● JACK DOSCHER Doscher, John Henry Jr. b: 7/27/1880, Troy, N.Y. d: 5/27/71, Park Ridge, N.J. BL/TL, 6'1", 205 lbs. Deb: 7/2/03 F																									
1903 Chi-N	0	1	.000	1	1	0	0	0	3	6	0	2	5	27.0	12.00	26	.429	.529	0	.000	-0	-3	-3	0	-0.6
Bro-N	0	0	—	3	0	0	0	0	7	8	1	9	4	23.1	7.71	41	.296	.486	0	.000	-0	-3	-4	-0	-0.1
Yr	0	1	.000	4	1	0	0	0	10	14	1	11	9	23.4	9.00	35	.333	.481	0	.000	-1	-6	-6	-0	-0.7
1904 Bro-N	0	0	—	2	0	0	0	0	6^1	1	0	1	2	2.8	0.00	—	.053	.100	1	.500	0	2	2	-0	0.0
1905 Bro-N	1	5	.167	12	7	6	0	0	71	60	1	30	33	11.8	3.17	91	.232	.318	2	.083	-2	-1	-2	-2	-0.5
1906 Bro-N	1	0	1.000	2	1	1	0	0	14	12	0	4	10	10.3	1.29	196	.250	.308	0	.000	-1	2	2	-0	0.0
1908 Cin-N	1	3	.250	7	4	3	0	0	44^1	31	1	22	7	11.4	1.83	126	.196	.306	2	.133	0	3	2	-0	0.2
Total 5	2	10	.167	27	13	10	0	0	145^2	118	3	68	61	12.0	2.84	95	.225	.323	5	.100	-3	-1	-2	-3	-1.0
● RICHARD DOTSON Dotson, Richard Elliott b: 1/10/59, Cincinnati, Ohio BR/TR, 6', 204 lbs. Deb: 9/4/79																									
1979 Chi-A	2	0	1.000	5	5	1	1	0	24^1	28	0	6	13	12.6	3.70	115	.286	.327	0	—	0	1	1	0	0.1
1980 Chi-A	12	10	.545	33	32	8	0	0	198	185	20	87	109	12.6	4.27	94	.247	.331	0	—	0	-5	-5	1	-0.4
1981 Chi-A	9	8	.529	24	24	5	**4**	0	141	145	13	49	73	12.6	3.77	95	.270	.336	0	—	0	-2	-3	-0	-0.4
1982 Chi-A	11	15	.423	34	31	3	1	0	196^2	219	19	73	109	13.6	3.84	105	.282	.348	0	—	0	5	4	-1	0.4
1983 *Chi-A	22	7	**.759**	35	35	8	1	0	240	209	19	106	137	12.1	3.23	130	.240	.328	0	—	0	22	26	4	3.4
1984 Chi-A★	14	15	.483	32	32	14	1	0	245^2	216	24	103	120	11.9	3.59	116	.238	.321	0	—	0	11	15	-0	1.7
1985 Chi-A	3	4	.429	9	9	0	0	0	52^1	53	5	17	33	12.6	4.47	97	.261	.327	0	—	0	-2	-1	-0	-0.1
1986 Chi-A	10	17	.370	34	34	3	1	0	197	226	24	69	110	13.6	5.48	79	.289	.348	0	—	0	-29	-26	-1	-3.1
1987 Chi-A	11	12	.478	31	31	7	2	0	211^1	201	24	86	114	12.2	4.17	110	.249	.321	0	—	0	7	10	2	1.1
1988 NY-A	12	9	.571	32	29	4	0	0	171	178	27	72	77	13.4	5.00	79	.266	.341	0	—	0	-20	-20	-1	-2.3
1989 NY-A	2	5	.286	11	9	1	0	0	51^2	69	8	17	14	15.2	5.57	69	.317	.369	0	—	0	-10	-10	-1	-1.2
Chi-A	3	7	.300	17	17	1	0	0	99^2	112	8	41	55	13.8	3.88	98	.282	.349	0	—	0	-0	-1	0	-0.1
Yr	5	12	.294	28	26	2	0	0	151^1	181	16	58	69	14.2	4.46	86	.293	.354	0	—	0	-10	-11	-1	-1.3
1990 KC-A	0	4	.000	8	7	0	0	0	28^2	43	3	14	9	17.9	8.48	45	.355	.422	0	—	0	-15	-15	-0	-1.7
Total 12	111	113	.496	305	295	55	11	0	1857^1	1884	194	740	973	12.9	4.23	97	.264	.337	0	—	0	-35	-25	2	-2.6
● GARY DOTTER Dotter, Gary Richard b: 8/7/42, St.Louis, Mo. BL/TL, 6'1", 180 lbs. Deb: 9/10/61																									
1961 Min-A	0	0	—	2	0	0	0	0	6	6	0	4	2	15.0	9.00	47	.273	.385	0	.000	-0	-3	-3	0	0.0
1963 Min-A	0	0	—	2	0	0	0	0	2	0	0	0	2	0.0	0.00	—	.000	.000	0	—	0	1	1	0	0.0
1964 Min-A	0	0	—	3	0	0	0	0	4^1	3	1	3	6	12.5	2.08	172	.188	.316	0	—	0	1	1	-0	0.0
Total 3	0	0	—	7	0	0	0	0	12^1	9	1	7	10	11.7	5.11	76	.205	.314	0	.000	-0	-2	-2	0	0.0
● BABE DOTY Doty, Elmer L. b: 12/17/1867, Genoa, Ohio d: 11/20/29, Toledo, Ohio BL/TR, 6', 160 lbs. Deb: 8/18/1890																									
1890 Tol-a	1	0	1.000	1	1	1	0	0	9	9	0	1	4	10.0	1.00	395	.250	.270	0	.000	-0	3	3	-0	0.2
● JIM DOUGHERTY Dougherty, James E. b: 3/8/68, Brentwood, N.Y. BR/TR, 6', 210 lbs. Deb: 4/27/95																									
1995 Hou-N	8	4	.667	56	0	0	0	0	67^2	76	7	25	49	13.8	4.92	79	.292	.361	1	.125	-0	-6	-8	1	-1.1
1996 Hou-N	0	2	.000	12	0	0	0	0	13	14	2	11	6	18.0	9.00	43	.280	.419	0	—	0	-7	-7	0	-0.9
1998 Oak-A	0	2	.000	9	0	0	0	0	12	17	2	7	3	18.8	8.25	55	.340	.431	0	—	0	-5	-5	1	-0.4
Total 3	8	8	.500	77	0	0	0	0	92^2	107	11	43	58	15.1	5.92	67	.297	.380	1	.125	-0	-17	-20	2	-2.4

● TOM DOUGHERTY Dougherty, Thomas James "Sugar Boy" b: 5/30/1881, Chicago, Ill. d: 11/6/53, Milwaukee, Wis. BL/TR, 195 lbs. Deb: 4/24/04

YEAR	TM/L	W	L	PCT	G	GS	CG	SH	SV	IP	H	HR	BB	SO	RAT	ERA	ERA+	OAV	OOB	BH	AVG	PB	PR	/A	PD	TPI
1904	Chi-A	1	0	1.000	1	0	0	0	0	2	0	0	0	0	0.0	0.00	—	.000	.000	0	.000	-0	1	1	0	0.3

● WHAMMY DOUGLAS Douglas, Charles William b: 2/17/35, Carrboro, N.C. BR/TR, 6'2", 185 lbs. Deb: 7/29/57

YEAR	TM/L	W	L	PCT	G	GS	CG	SH	SV	IP	H	HR	BB	SO	RAT	ERA	ERA+	OAV	OOB	BH	AVG	PB	PR	/A	PD	TPI
1957	Pit-N	3	3	.500	11	8	0	0	0	47	48	5	30	28	15.5	3.26	116	.270	.384	1	.063	-1	3	3	-0	0.2

● LARRY DOUGLAS Douglas, Lawrence Howard b: 6/5/1890, Jellico, Tenn. d: 11/4/49, Jellico, Tenn. 6'3", 175 lbs. Deb: 6/17/15

YEAR	TM/L	W	L	PCT	G	GS	CG	SH	SV	IP	H	HR	BB	SO	RAT	ERA	ERA+	OAV	OOB	BH	AVG	PB	PR	/A	PD	TPI
1915	Bal-F	1	0	1.000	2	0	0	0	0	3	3	0	2	1	15.0	3.00	96	.273	.385	0	—	0	-0	-0	0	0.0

● PHIL DOUGLAS Douglas, Phillip Brooks "Shufflin' Phil" b: 6/17/1890, Cedartown, Ga. d: 8/1/52, Sequatchie, Tenn. BR/TR, 6'3", 190 lbs. Deb: 8/30/12

YEAR	TM/L	W	L	PCT	G	GS	CG	SH	SV	IP	H	HR	BB	SO	RAT	ERA	ERA+	OAV	OOB	BH	AVG	PB	PR	/A	PD	TPI
1912	Chi-A	0	1	.000	3	1	0	0	0	12^{1}	21	0	6	7	19.7	7.30	44	.382	.443	0	.000	-0	-5	-6	0	-0.4
1914	Cin-N	11	18	.379	45	25	13	0	1	239^{1}	186	7	92	121	10.9	2.56	115	.223	.308	10	.137	-2	6	10	-2	0.7
1915	Cin-N	1	5	.167	8	7	0	0	0	46^{2}	53	0	23	29	14.7	5.40	53	.299	.380	2	.118	-1	-14	-13	0	-1.6
	Bro-N	5	5	.500	20	13	5	1	0	116^{2}	104	1	17	63	9.7	2.62	106	.241	.278	6	.154	-1	2	2	0	0.1
	Chi-N	1	1	.500	4	4	2	1	0	25	17	0	7	18	9.0	2.16	129	.187	.253	0	.000	-1	2	2	0	0.1
	Yr	7	11	.389	32	24	7	2	0	188^{1}	174	1	47	110	10.6	3.25	86	.247	.295	8	.125	-3	-10	-9	1	-1.4
1917	Chi-N	14	20	.412	**51**	37	20	5	1	293^{1}	269	13	50	151	10.0	2.55	114	.250	.287	11	.126	-4	5	11	4	1.4
1918	*Chi-N	10	9	.526	25	19	11	2	2	156^{2}	145	2	31	51	10.2	2.13	131	.246	.285	14	.255	1	11	12	3	1.9
1919	Chi-N	10	6	.625	25	19	8	4	0	161^{2}	133	0	34	63	9.4	2.00	144	.230	.275	8	.157	-2	16	16	5	2.0
	NY-N	2	4	.333	8	6	4	0	0	51^{1}	53	0	6	21	10.5	2.10	133	.264	.288	0	.000	-2	5	4	0	0.2
	Yr	12	10	.545	33	25	12	4	0	213	186	0	40	84	9.6	2.03	141	.238	.276	8	.121	-4	21	20	5	2.2
1920	NY-N	14	10	.583	46	21	10	3	2	226	225	6	55	71	11.2	2.71	111	.263	.309	11	.151	-4	11	7	1	0.4
1921	*NY-N	15	10	.600	40	27	13	**3**	2	221^{2}	266	17	55	55	13.1	4.22	87	.308	.351	16	.198	0	-11	-14	1	-1.3
1922	NY-N	11	4	.733	24	21	9	1	0	157^{2}	154	6	35	33	**11.0**	**2.63**	**152**	**.257**	**.302**	12	.207	1	26	24	0	2.1
Total	9	94	93	.503	299	200	95	20	8	1708^{1}	1626	52	411	683	10.9	2.80	111	.256	.305	90	.161	-16	53	58	13	5.6

● KIP DOWD Dowd, James Joseph b: 2/16/1889, Holyoke, Mass. d: 12/20/60, Holyoke, Mass. BR/TR, 5'10.5", 160 lbs. Deb: 7/5/10

YEAR	TM/L	W	L	PCT	G	GS	CG	SH	SV	IP	H	HR	BB	SO	RAT	ERA	ERA+	OAV	OOB	BH	AVG	PB	PR	/A	PD	TPI
1910	Pit-N	0	0	—	1	0	0	0	0	2	4	0	2	1	31.5	0.00	—	.400	.538	0	—	0	1	1	-0	0.0

● DAVE DOWLING Dowling, David Barclay b: 8/23/42, Baton Rouge, La. BR/TL, 6'2", 181 lbs. Deb: 10/3/64

YEAR	TM/L	W	L	PCT	G	GS	CG	SH	SV	IP	H	HR	BB	SO	RAT	ERA	ERA+	OAV	OOB	BH	AVG	PB	PR	/A	PD	TPI
1964	StL-N	0	0	—	1	0	0	0	0	1	2	0	0	0	18.0	0.00	—	.400	.400	0	—	0	0	0	-0	0.0
1966	Chi-N	1	0	1.000	1	1	1	0	0	9	10	0	0	3	10.0	2.00	184	.270	.270	0	.000	-0	2	2	-0	0.1
Total	2	1	0	1.000	2	1	1	0	0	10	12	0	0	3	10.8	1.80	205	.286	.286	0	.000	-0	2	2	-0	0.1

● PETE DOWLING Dowling, Henry Peter b: St.Louis, Mo. d: 6/30/05, Hot Lake, Ore. TL , 5'11", Deb: 7/17/1897

YEAR	TM/L	W	L	PCT	G	GS	CG	SH	SV	IP	H	HR	BB	SO	RAT	ERA	ERA+	OAV	OOB	BH	AVG	PB	PR	/A	PD	TPI
1897	Lou-N	1	2	.333	4	4	2	0	0	26	39	0	8	3	18.3	5.88	72	.342	.414	2	.200	-0	-5	-5	-0	-0.4
1898	Lou-N	13	20	.394	36	32	30	0	0	285^{2}	284	7	120	84	13.4	4.16	86	.257	.342	21	.196	1	-17	-18	-1	-1.7
1899	Lou-N	13	17	.433	34	32	29	0	0	289^{2}	321	4	93	88	13.4	3.11	124	.280	.343	27	.233	-1	24	24	-0	2.0
1901	Mil-A	1	3	.250	10	4	3	0	1	49^{2}	71	1	14	25	16.1	5.62	64	.332	.384	4	.211	1	-11	-11	0	-0.6
	Cle-A	11	22	.333	33	30	28	2	0	256^{1}	269	1	104	99	13.6	3.86	92	.267	.344	16	.162	-4	-6	-9	0	-1.2
	Yr	12	25	.324	43	34	31	2	1	306	340	2	118	124	13.9	4.15	86	.277	.348	20	.169	-3	-16	-20	1	-1.8
Total	4	39	64	.379	117	102	92	2	1	907^{1}	984	13	339	299	13.8	3.87	95	.274	.348	70	.199	-3	-14	-19	-1	-1.9

● AL DOWNING Downing, Alphonso Erwin b: 6/28/41, Trenton, N.J. BR/TL, 5'11", 177 lbs. Deb: 7/19/61

YEAR	TM/L	W	L	PCT	G	GS	CG	SH	SV	IP	H	HR	BB	SO	RAT	ERA	ERA+	OAV	OOB	BH	AVG	PB	PR	/A	PD	TPI
1961	NY-A	0	1	.000	5	1	0	0	0	9	7	0	12	12	20.0	8.00	46	.212	.435	0	.000	-0	-4	-4	0	-0.4
1962	NY-A	0	0	—	1	0	0	0	0	1	0	0	0	1	0.0	0.00	—	.000	.000	0	—	0	0	0	0	0.0
1963	*NY-A	13	5	.722	24	22	10	4	0	175^{2}	114	7	80	171	9.9	2.56	137	**.184**	.277	6	.103	-2	21	19	-1	1.5
1964	*NY-A	13	8	.619	37	35	11	1	2	244	201	18	120	**217**	11.8	3.47	104	.223	.314	15	.176	1	4	4	0	0.4
1965	NY-A	12	14	.462	35	32	8	2	0	212	185	16	105	179	12.4	3.40	100	.237	.329	8	.108	-1	1	0	0	0.0
1966	NY-A	10	11	.476	30	30	1	0	0	200	178	23	79	152	11.6	3.56	94	.235	.309	7	.100	-2	-3	-5	-4	-1.1
1967	NY-A★	14	10	.583	31	28	10	4	0	201^{2}	158	13	61	171	10.0	2.63	119	.217	.283	8	.121	1	13	11	-1	1.3
1968	NY-A	3	3	.500	15	12	1	0	0	61^{1}	54	7	20	40	11.0	3.52	82	.237	.301	3	.176	0	-4	-4	-0	-0.4
1969	NY-A	7	5	.583	30	15	5	1	0	130^{2}	117	12	49	85	11.4	3.38	103	.240	.309	6	.136	-0	4	1	-2	-0.1
1970	Oak-A	3	3	.500	10	6	1	0	0	41	39	5	22	26	13.6	3.95	90	.252	.348	2	.182	-0	-1	-2	2	-0.1
	Mil-A	2	10	.167	17	16	1	0	0	94^{1}	79	8	59	53	13.5	3.34	113	.232	.350	2	.083	-2	4	5	0	0.4
	Yr	5	13	.278	27	22	2	0	0	135^{1}	118	13	81	79	13.4	3.52	105	.237	.347	4	.114	-2	3	3	2	0.3
1971	LA-N	20	9	.690	37	36	12	**5**	0	262^{1}	245	16	84	136	11.4	2.68	121	.247	.308	16	.174	2	23	16	-1	1.9
1972	LA-N	9	9	.500	31	30	7	4	0	202^{2}	196	13	67	117	12.0	2.98	112	.254	.319	8	.121	-1	11	8	5	1.1
1973	LA-N	9	9	.500	30	28	5	2	0	193	155	19	68	124	10.4	3.31	104	.219	.289	5	.088	-1	7	3	1	0.2
1974	*LA-N	5	6	.455	21	16	1	1	0	98^{1}	94	7	45	63	13.0	3.66	93	.255	.341	5	.172	-0	-0	-3	1	-0.2
1975	LA-N	2	1	.667	22	6	0	0	1	74^{2}	59	6	28	39	10.7	2.89	118	.215	.293	0	.000	-1	6	4	1	0.2
1976	LA-N	1	2	.333	17	3	0	0	0	46^{2}	43	3	18	30	11.8	3.86	88	.250	.321	0	.000	-1	-2	-2	0	-0.2
1977	LA-N	0	1	.000	12	1	0	0	0	20	22	4	16	23	17.1	6.75	57	.278	.400	0	.000	-0	-6	-7	-0	-0.3
Total	17	123	107	.535	405	317	73	24	3	2268^{1}	1946	177	933	1639	11.5	3.22	105	.232	.311	91	.127	-7	75	44	2	4.2

● DAVE DOWNS Downs, David Ralph b: 6/21/52, Logan, Utah BR/TR, 6'5", 220 lbs. Deb: 9/2/72 F

YEAR	TM/L	W	L	PCT	G	GS	CG	SH	SV	IP	H	HR	BB	SO	RAT	ERA	ERA+	OAV	OOB	BH	AVG	PB	PR	/A	PD	TPI
1972	Phi-N	1	1	.500	4	4	1	1	0	23	25	1	3	5	11.3	2.74	131	.294	.326	2	.250	0	2	2	0	0.2

● KELLY DOWNS Downs, Kelly Robert b: 10/25/60, Ogden, Utah BR/TR, 6'4", 200 lbs. Deb: 7/29/86 F

YEAR	TM/L	W	L	PCT	G	GS	CG	SH	SV	IP	H	HR	BB	SO	RAT	ERA	ERA+	OAV	OOB	BH	AVG	PB	PR	/A	PD	TPI
1986	SF-N	4	4	.500	14	14	1	0	0	88^{1}	78	5	30	64	11.3	2.75	128	.236	.305	5	.172	0	9	8	0	0.6
1987	*SF-N	12	9	.571	41	28	4	3	1	186	185	14	67	137	12.4	3.63	106	.258	.324	8	.143	-0	9	4	-4	0.0
1988	SF-N	13	9	.591	27	26	6	3	0	168	140	11	47	118	10.2	3.32	98	.225	.283	9	.167	2	2	-1	0	0.1
1989	*SF-N	4	8	.333	18	15	0	0	0	82^{2}	82	7	26	49	11.9	4.79	70	.261	.320	2	.091	-1	-12	-13	-1	-1.9
1990	SF-N	3	2	.600	13	9	0	0	0	63	56	2	20	31	11.1	3.43	106	.233	.298	0	.000	-1	3	2	1	0.1
1991	SF-N	10	4	.714	45	11	0	0	0	111^{2}	99	12	53	62	12.5	4.19	85	.239	.329	2	.087	-1	-6	-8	1	-0.9
1992	SF-N	1	2	.333	19	7	0	0	0	62^{1}	65	4	24	33	13.3	3.47	95	.275	.350	0	.000	-1	0	-1	-1	-0.3
	*Oak-A	5	5	.500	18	13	0	0	0	82	72	4	46	38	13.4	3.29	114	.237	.345	0	—	0	6	4	-1	0.6
1993	Oak-A	5	10	.333	42	12	0	0	0	119^{2}	135	14	60	66	14.8	5.64	72	.287	.370	0	—	0	-18	-21	-2	-2.3
Total	8	57	53	.518	237	135	11	6	1	963^{2}	912	73	373	598	12.2	3.86	94	.250	.324	26	.123	-2	-6	-26	-7	-4.0

● TOM DOWSE Dowse, Thomas Joseph b: 8/12/1866, Ireland d: 12/14/46, Riverside, Cal. BR/TR, 5'11", 175 lbs. Deb: 4/21/1890 ♦

YEAR	TM/L	W	L	PCT	G	GS	CG	SH	SV	IP	H	HR	BB	SO	RAT	ERA	ERA+	OAV	OOB	BH	AVG	PB	PR	/A	PD	TPI
1890	Cle-N	0	0	—	1	0	0	0	0	5	6	0	1	0	12.6	5.40	66	.286	.318	33	.208	-0	-1	-1	0	0.0

● JESS DOYLE Doyle, Jesse Herbert b: 4/14/1898, Knoxville, Tenn. d: 4/15/61, Belleville, Ill. BR/TR, 5'11", 175 lbs. Deb: 4/14/25

YEAR	TM/L	W	L	PCT	G	GS	CG	SH	SV	IP	H	HR	BB	SO	RAT	ERA	ERA+	OAV	OOB	BH	AVG	PB	PR	/A	PD	TPI
1925	Det-A	4	7	.364	45	3	0	0	8	118^{1}	158	6	50	31	16.2	5.93	73	.340	.410	8	.242	3	-20	-21	-1	-1.7
1926	Det-A	0	0	—	2	0	0	0	1	4^{1}	6	0	1	2	14.5	4.15	98	.316	.350	1	1.000	0	-0	-0	-0	0.0
1927	Det-A	0	0	—	7	0	0	0	0	12^{1}	16	0	5	5	15.3	8.03	52	.314	.375	1	.333	0	-5	-5	0	0.0
1931	StL-A	0	0	—	1	0	0	0	0	1	3	0	1	0	36.0	27.00	17	.500	.571	0	—	0	-3	-2	-0	0.0
Total	4	4	7	.364	55	3	0	0	9	136	183	6	57	38	16.2	6.22	69	.338	.406	10	.270	4	-28	-29	-1	-1.7

● JOHN DOYLE Doyle, John Aloysius b: 1858, Nova Scotia, Canada d: 12/24/15, Providence, R.I. Deb: 7/26/1882

YEAR	TM/L	W	L	PCT	G	GS	CG	SH	SV	IP	H	HR	BB	SO	RAT	ERA	ERA+	OAV	OOB	BH	AVG	PB	PR	/A	PD	TPI
1882	StL-a	0	3	.000	3	3	3	0	0	24	41	0	3	5	16.5	2.63	107	.353	.370	2	.182	-0	0	0	-1	0.0

● SLOW JOE DOYLE Doyle, Judd Bruce b: 9/15/1881, Clay Center, Kan. d: 11/21/47, Tannersville, N.Y. BR/TR, 5'8", 150 lbs. Deb: 8/25/06

YEAR	TM/L	W	L	PCT	G	GS	CG	SH	SV	IP	H	HR	BB	SO	RAT	ERA	ERA+	OAV	OOB	BH	AVG	PB	PR	/A	PD	TPI
1906	NY-A	2	1	.667	9	6	3	2	0	45^{1}	34	1	13	28	9.5	2.38	124	.211	.274	3	.214	-0	2	3	0	0.2
1907	NY-A	11	11	.500	29	23	15	1	1	193^{2}	169	2	67	94	11.2	2.65	105	.237	.308	8	.138	-1	-2	3	-3	-0.1
1908	NY-A	1	1	.500	12	4	2	1	0	48	42	1	14	20	10.9	2.63	94	.235	.297	3	.214	0	-1	-1	-2	-0.1
1909	NY-A	8	6	.571	17	15	8	3	0	125^{2}	103	3	37	57	10.2	2.58	98	.232	.294	7	.167	0	-1	-1	-4	-0.4
1910	NY-A	0	2	.000	3	2	1	0	0	12^{1}	19	0	5	6	18.2	8.03	33	.365	.431	1	.250	0	-8	-7	1	-0.9
	Cin-N	0	0	—	5	0	0	0	0	11^{1}	16	0	11	4	21.4	6.35	46	.327	.450	0	.000	-0	-4	-4	-1	-0.1
Total	5	22	21	.512	75	50	29	7	1	436^{1}	383	7	147	209	11.2	2.85	95	.240	.308	22	.163	-1	-15	-7	-7	-1.4

● PAUL DOYLE
Doyle, Paul Sinnott b: 10/2/39, Philadelphia, Pa. BL/TL, 5'11", 172 lbs. Deb: 5/28/69

YEAR	TM/L	W	L	PCT	G	GS	CG	SH	SV	IP	H	HR	BB	SO	RAT	ERA	ERA+	OAV	OOB	BH	AVG	PB	PR	/A	PD	TPI
1969	*Atl-N	2	0	1.000	36	0	0	0	4	39	31	4	16	25	10.8	2.08	174	.231	.313	0	.000	-0	7	7	1	0.5
1970	Cal-A	3	1	.750	40	0	0	0	5	42	43	7	21	34	13.9	5.14	70	.267	.355	0	.000	-0	-7	-7	1	-0.7
	SD-N	0	2	.000	9	0	0	0	2	7	9	0	6	2	19.3	6.43	62	.360	.484	0	.000	-0	-2	-2	1	-0.5
1972	Cal-A	0	0	—	2	0	0	0	0	2^1	2	0	3	4	19.3	0.00	—	.250	.455	0	—	0	1	1	0	0.0
Total	3	5	3	.625	87	0	0	0	11	90^1	85	11	46	65	13.2	3.79	96	.259	.352	0	.000	-1	-1	-2	3	-0.7

● CARL DOYLE
Doyle, William Carl b: 7/30/12, Knoxville, Tenn. d: 9/4/51, Knoxville, Tenn. BR/TR, 6'1", 185 lbs. Deb: 8/5/35

YEAR	TM/L	W	L	PCT	G	GS	CG	SH	SV	IP	H	HR	BB	SO	RAT	ERA	ERA+	OAV	OOB	BH	AVG	PB	PR	/A	PD	TPI
1935	Phi-A	2	7	.222	14	9	3	0	0	79^2	86	3	72	34	18.1	5.99	76	.282	.422	4	.133	-2	-14	-13	1	-1.3
1936	Phi-A	0	3	.000	8	6	1	0	0	38^2	66	4	29	12	23.3	10.94	47	.369	.469	4	.267	1	-25	-25	-1	-1.4
1939	Bro-N	1	2	.333	5	1	1	1	1	17^2	8	1	7	7	7.6	1.02	395	.136	.227	1	.167	0	6	6	0	1.1
1940	Bro-N	0	0	—	3	0	0	0	1	5^2	18	3	6	4	44.5	27.00	15	.545	.651	1	1.000	1	-15	-14	0	-0.5
	StL-N	3	3	.500	21	5	1	0	0	81	99	7	41	44	16.2	5.89	68	.294	.380	6	.200	2	-18	-17	-0	-1.0
	Yr	3	3	.500	24	5	1	0	1	86^2	117	10	47	48	17.7	7.27	55	.313	.398	7	.226	2	-33	-32	0	-1.5
Total	4	6	15	.286	51	21	6	1	2	222^2	277	18	155	101	18.1	6.95	63	.303	.414	16	.195	1	-66	-63	-0	-3.1

● TOM DOZIER
Dozier, Thomas Dean b: 9/5/61, San Pablo, Cal. BR/TR, 6'2", 190 lbs. Deb: 5/17/86

YEAR	TM/L	W	L	PCT	G	GS	CG	SH	SV	IP	H	HR	BB	SO	RAT	ERA	ERA+	OAV	OOB	BH	AVG	PB	PR	/A	PD	TPI
1986	Oak-A	0	0	—	4	0	0	0	0	6^1	6	1	5	4	15.6	5.68	68	.261	.393	0	—	0	-1	-1	-0	0.6

● BUZZ DOZIER
Dozier, William Joseph b: 8/31/27, Waco, Tex. BR/TR, 6'3", 185 lbs. Deb: 9/12/47

YEAR	TM/L	W	L	PCT	G	GS	CG	SH	SV	IP	H	HR	BB	SO	RAT	ERA	ERA+	OAV	OOB	BH	AVG	PB	PR	/A	PD	TPI
1947	Was-A	0	0	—	2	0	0	0	0	4^2	2	0	1	2	5.8	0.00	—	.133	.188	0	.000	-0	2	2	0	0.0
1949	Was-A	0	0	—	2	0	0	0	0	6^1	12	0	6	1	25.6	11.37	37	.429	.529	0	.000	-0	-5	-5	-0	-0.1
Total	2	0	0	—	4	0	0	0	0	11	14	0	7	3	17.2	6.55	62	.326	.420	0	.000	-0	-3	-3	-0	-0.1

● DOUG DRABEK
Drabek, Douglas Dean b: 7/25/62, Victoria, Tex. BR/TR, 6'1", 185 lbs. Deb: 5/30/86

YEAR	TM/L	W	L	PCT	G	GS	CG	SH	SV	IP	H	HR	BB	SO	RAT	ERA	ERA+	OAV	OOB	BH	AVG	PB	PR	/A	PD	TPI
1986	NY-A	7	8	.467	27	21	0	0	0	131^2	126	13	50	76	12.2	4.10	100	.251	.323	0	—	0	1	-0	-1	-0.1
1987	Pit-N	11	12	.478	29	28	1	1	0	176^1	165	22	46	120	10.8	3.88	106	.247	.296	7	.119	-1	4	4	1	0.5
1988	Pit-N	15	7	.682	33	32	3	1	0	219^1	194	21	50	127	10.3	3.08	111	.239	.288	13	.171	3	9	8	-1	1.0
1989	Pit-N	14	12	.538	35	34	8	5	0	244^1	215	21	69	123	10.6	2.80	120	.238	.295	8	.104	-2	19	15	-0	1.3
1990	*Pit-N	**22**	6	**.786**	33	33	9	3	0	231^1	190	15	56	131	9.7	2.76	131	.225	.275	18	.214	5	26	22	2	3.4
1991	*Pit-N	15	14	.517	35	35	5	2	0	234^2	245	16	62	142	11.9	3.07	116	.274	.323	15	.179	1	16	13	2	1.9
1992	*Pit-N	15	11	.577	34	34	10	4	0	256^2	218	17	54	177	9.7	2.77	124	.231	.277	14	.157	1	21	19	1	2.1
1993	Hou-N	9	18	.333	34	34	7	2	0	237^2	242	18	60	157	11.5	3.79	102	.267	.315	6	.085	-2	7	2	0	0.1
1994	Hou-N★	12	6	.667	23	23	6	2	0	164^2	132	14	45	121	9.8	2.84	139	.220	.277	14	.241	3	25	20	2	2.7
1995	Hou-N	10	9	.526	31	31	2	1	0	185	205	18	54	143	13.0	4.77	81	.282	.338	14	.233	4	-12	-19	0	-1.3
1996	Hou-N	7	9	.438	30	30	1	0	0	175^1	208	21	60	137	14.1	4.57	85	.298	.359	10	.179	0	-7	-14	0	-1.0
1997	Chi-A	12	11	.522	31	31	0	0	0	169^1	170	30	69	85	12.9	5.74	76	.261	.335	0	.000	-0	-22	-26	-1	-2.9
1998	Bal-A	6	11	.353	23	21	1	0	0	108^2	138	20	29	55	14.2	7.29	62	.312	.361	0	.000	-0	-32	-33	-0	-4.1
Total	13	155	134	.536	398	387	53	21	0	2535	2448	246	704	1594	11.4	3.73	101	.255	.310	119	.166	13	55	14	5	3.6

● MOE DRABOWSKY
Drabowsky, Myron Walter b: 7/21/35, Ozanna, Poland BR/TR, 6'2", 200 lbs. Deb: 8/7/56 C

YEAR	TM/L	W	L	PCT	G	GS	CG	SH	SV	IP	H	HR	BB	SO	RAT	ERA	ERA+	OAV	OOB	BH	AVG	PB	PR	/A	PD	TPI
1956	Chi-N	2	4	.333	9	7	3	0	0	51	37	1	39	36	13.8	2.47	153	.207	.355	4	.250	0	7	7	-0	0.9
1957	Chi-N	13	15	.464	36	33	12	2	0	239^2	214	22	94	170	11.9	3.53	110	.242	.321	15	.183	2	9	9	0	1.2
1958	Chi-N	9	11	.450	22	20	4	1	0	125^2	118	19	73	77	14.0	4.51	87	.245	.350	7	.156	-1	-8	-8	-0	-1.3
1959	Chi-N	5	10	.333	31	23	3	1	0	141^2	138	21	75	70	13.7	4.13	96	.251	.344	5	.111	-1	-3	-3	-0	-0.4
1960	Chi-N	3	1	.750	32	7	0	0	1	50^1	71	3	23	26	17.0	6.44	59	.338	.406	0	.000	-1	-15	-15	-1	-1.3
1961	Mil-N	0	2	.000	16	0	0	0	2	25^1	26	4	18	5	16.0	4.62	81	.277	.398	1	.250	0	-2	-2	0	-0.2
1962	Cin-N	2	6	.250	23	10	1	0	1	83	84	13	31	56	13.1	4.99	81	.267	.344	0	.000	-2	-10	-9	1	-1.0
	KC-A	1	1	.500	10	3	0	0	0	28	29	8	10	19	12.9	5.14	82	.266	.333	1	.167	-0	-4	-3	0	-0.2
1963	KC-A	7	13	.350	26	22	9	2	0	174^1	135	16	64	109	10.7	3.05	128	.214	.295	10	.161	1	11	17	-2	1.8
1964	KC-A	5	13	.278	53	21	1	0	1	168^1	176	24	72	119	13.7	5.29	72	.273	.353	1	.023	-4	-31	-28	4	-3.1
1965	KC-A	1	5	.167	14	5	0	0	0	38^2	44	5	18	25	15.1	4.42	79	.291	.378	1	.091	-1	-4	-4	-0	-0.7
1966	*Bal-A	6	0	1.000	44	3	0	0	7	96	62	10	29	98	8.6	2.81	118	.181	.247	8	.364	4	7	6	-1	0.7
1967	Bal-A	7	5	.583	43	0	0	0	12	95^1	66	7	25	96	8.8	1.60	196	.194	.253	7	.350	2	17	16	0	2.9
1968	Bal-A	4	4	.500	45	0	0	0	7	61^1	35	3	25	46	9.4	1.91	153	.166	.267	2	.286	0	7	7	-0	1.2
1969	KC-A	11	9	.550	52	0	0	0	11	98	68	10	30	76	9.2	2.94	125	.190	.256	4	.235	1	7	8	1	2.0
1970	KC-A	1	2	.333	24	0	0	0	2	35^2	28	3	12	38	10.6	3.28	114	.217	.294	1	.250	0	2	2	0	0.2
	*Bal-A	4	2	.667	21	0	0	0	1	33^1	30	7	15	21	12.4	3.78	96	.233	.317	0	.000	-1	-0	-0	-0	-0.2
	Yr	5	4	.556	45	0	0	0	3	69	58	10	27	59	11.2	3.52	105	.221	.296	1	.111	-0	1	1	-0	0.0
1971	StL-N	6	1	.857	51	0	0	0	8	60^1	45	2	33	49	11.9	3.43	105	.207	.317	1	.167	-0	0	1	-1	0.1
1972	StL-N	1	1	.500	30	0	0	0	2	27^2	29	4	14	22	14.3	2.60	131	.259	.346	0	.000	-0	3	2	-1	0.1
	Chi-A	0	0	—	7	0	0	0	0	7^1	6	0	2	4	9.8	2.45	127	.240	.296	0	.000	-0	0	1	-0	0.0
Total	17	88	105	.456	589	154	33	6	55	1641	1441	182	702	1162	12.1	3.71	101	.236	.321	68	.162	-0	-5	4	-5	2.7

● DICK DRAGO
Drago, Richard Anthony b: 6/25/45, Toledo, Ohio BR/TR, 6'1", 190 lbs. Deb: 4/11/69

YEAR	TM/L	W	L	PCT	G	GS	CG	SH	SV	IP	H	HR	BB	SO	RAT	ERA	ERA+	OAV	OOB	BH	AVG	PB	PR	/A	PD	TPI
1969	KC-A	11	13	.458	41	26	10	2	1	200^2	190	19	65	108	11.5	3.77	98	.248	.308	3	.058	-3	-3	-2	2	-0.3
1970	KC-A	9	15	.375	35	34	7	1	0	240	239	20	72	127	11.9	3.75	100	.266	.325	4	.053	-6	-1	-0	-1	-0.7
1971	KC-A	17	11	.607	35	34	15	4	0	241^1	251	14	46	109	11.4	2.98	115	.276	.318	10	.130	1	13	12	0	1.5
1972	KC-A	12	17	.414	34	33	11	2	0	239^1	230	22	51	135	10.8	3.01	101	.254	.298	4	.059	-2	1	1	-3	-0.5
1973	KC-A	12	14	.462	37	33	10	1	0	212^2	252	16	76	98	14.2	4.23	97	.300	.363	0	—	0	-10	-3	1	-0.2
1974	Bos-A	7	10	.412	33	18	8	0	3	175^2	165	17	56	90	11.6	3.48	110	.251	.315	0	—	0	3	7	-2	0.1
1975	*Bos-A	2	2	.500	40	2	0	0	15	72^2	69	5	31	43	12.4	3.84	106	.247	.323	0	—	0	-1	2	0	-0.1
1976	Cal-A	7	8	.467	43	0	0	0	6	79^1	80	7	31	43	13.2	4.42	75	.264	.342	0	—	0	-8	-10	-2	-1.8
1977	Cal-A	0	1	.000	13	0	0	0	2	21	22	3	3	15	10.7	3.00	130	.272	.298	0	—	0	2	2	-0	0.3
	Bal-A	6	3	.667	36	0	0	0	3	39^2	49	2	15	20	14.7	3.63	104	.308	.371	0	—	0	2	1	-0	0.5
	Yr	6	4	.600	49	0	0	0	5	60^2	71	5	18	35	13.4	3.41	112	.293	.345	0	—	0	4	3	-1	0.8
1978	Bos-A	4	4	.500	37	1	0	0	7	77^1	71	5	32	42	12.5	3.03	136	.246	.329	0	—	0	6	9	-1	1.0
1979	Bos-A	10	6	.625	53	1	0	0	13	89	85	6	21	67	11.0	3.03	145	.254	.304	0	—	0	12	14	-0	2.6
1980	Bos-A	7	7	.500	43	7	1	0	3	132^2	127	17	44	63	11.9	4.14	102	.251	.317	0	.000	-0	-2	1	-1	0.0
1981	Sea-A	4	6	.400	39	0	0	0	5	53^2	71	4	15	27	14.4	5.53	70	.324	.368	0	—	0	-11	-10	0	-1.9
Total	13	108	117	.480	519	189	62	10	58	1875	1901	157	558	987	12.1	3.62	103	.266	.324	21	.077	-11	4	23	-5	0.5

● BRIAN DRAHMAN
Drahman, Brian Stacy b: 11/7/66, Kenton, Ky. BR/TR, 6'3", 205 lbs. Deb: 4/16/91

YEAR	TM/L	W	L	PCT	G	GS	CG	SH	SV	IP	H	HR	BB	SO	RAT	ERA	ERA+	OAV	OOB	BH	AVG	PB	PR	/A	PD	TPI
1991	Chi-A	3	2	.600	28	0	0	0	0	30^2	21	4	13	18	10.0	3.23	123	.193	.279	0	—	0	3	3	-0	0.5
1992	Chi-A	0	0	—	5	0	0	0	0	7	6	0	2	1	10.3	2.57	150	.222	.276	0	—	0	1	1	-0	0.0
1993	Chi-A	0	0	—	5	0	0	0	1	5^1	7	0	2	3	15.2	0.00	—	.333	.391	0	—	0	3	2	0	0.1
1994	Fla-N	0	0	—	9	0	0	0	0	13	15	2	6	7	14.5	6.23	70	.300	.375	0	—	0	-3	-3	0	0.0
Total	4	3	2	.600	47	0	0	0	1	56	49	6	23	29	11.6	3.54	115	.237	.313	0	—	0	4	3	-0	0.6

● LOGAN DRAKE
Drake, Logan Gaffney "L.G." b: 12/26/1900, Spartanburg, S.C. d: 6/1/40, Columbia, S.C. BR/TR, 5'10.5", 165 lbs. Deb: 9/21/22

YEAR	TM/L	W	L	PCT	G	GS	CG	SH	SV	IP	H	HR	BB	SO	RAT	ERA	ERA+	OAV	OOB	BH	AVG	PB	PR	/A	PD	TPI
1922	Cle-A	0	0	—	1	0	0	0	0	3	4	0	2	1	18.0	3.00	134	.364	.462	0	.000	-0	0	0	-0	0.0
1923	Cle-A	0	0	—	4	0	0	0	0	4^1	2	0	4	2	14.5	4.15	95	.133	.350	0	—	0	-0	-0	-0	0.0
1924	Cle-A	0	1	.000	5	1	0	0	0	11^1	18	0	10	8	23.0	10.32	41	.400	.518	0	.000	-0	-8	-8	-0	-0.6
Total	3	0	1	.000	10	1	0	0	0	18^2	24	0	16	11	20.3	7.71	54	.338	.472	0	.000	-0	-7	-7	-1	-0.6

● TOM DRAKE
Drake, Thomas Kendall b: 8/7/12, Birmingham, Ala. d: 7/2/88, Birmingham, Ala. BR/TR, 6'1", 185 lbs. Deb: 4/24/39

YEAR	TM/L	W	L	PCT	G	GS	CG	SH	SV	IP	H	HR	BB	SO	RAT	ERA	ERA+	OAV	OOB	BH	AVG	PB	PR	/A	PD	TPI
1939	Cle-A	0	1	.000	8	1	0	0	0	15	23	2	19	1	26.4	9.00	49	.377	.537	0	.000	-0	-7	-8	0	-0.4
1941	Bro-N	1	1	.500	10	2	0	0	0	24^2	26	2	9	12	12.8	4.38	84	.280	.343	2	.400	0	-2	-2	-0	-0.1
Total	2	1	2	.333	18	3	0	0	0	39^2	49	4	28	13	17.9	6.13	65	.318	.429	2	.286	0	-9	-10	0	-0.5

YEAR	TM/L	W	L	PCT	G	GS	CG	SH	SV	IP	H	HR	BB	SO	RAT	ERA	ERA+	OAV	OOB	BH	AVG	PB	PR	/A	PD	TPI
● **MIKE DRAPER**	Draper, Michael Anthony b: 9/14/66, Hagerstown, Md. BR/TR, 6′2″, 180 lbs. Deb: 4/10/93																									
1993	NY-N	1	1	.500	29	1	0	0	0	42^1	53	2	14	16	14.2	4.25	94	.327	.381	2	.667	1	-1	-1	0	0.0
● **DAVE DRAVECKY**	Dravecky, David Francis b: 2/14/56, Youngstown, Ohio BR/TL, 6′1″, 195 lbs. Deb: 6/15/82																									
1982	SD-N	5	3	.625	31	10	0	0	2	105	86	8	33	59	10.3	2.57	133	.225	.288	3	.130	-0	12	10	2	0.9
1983	SD-N★	14	10	.583	28	28	9	1	0	183^2	181	18	44	74	11.2	3.58	97	.262	.309	6	.098	-1	1	-2	1	-0.3
1984	*SD-N	9	8	.529	50	14	3	2	8	156^2	125	12	51	71	10.3	2.93	122	.222	.291	4	.098	-1	11	11	-2	1.0
1985	SD-N	13	11	.542	34	31	7	2	0	214^2	200	18	57	105	10.8	2.93	120	.249	.300	8	.116	-0	16	14	-1	1.4
1986	SD-N	9	11	.450	26	26	3	1	0	161^1	149	17	54	87	11.4	3.07	119	.246	.309	7	.140	0	12	10	0	1.3
1987	SD-N	3	7	.300	30	10	1	0	0	79	71	10	31	60	12.0	3.76	105	.240	.318	3	.167	0	3	2	0	0.2
	*SF-N	7	5	.583	18	18	4	3	0	112^1	115	8	33	78	12.0	3.20	120	.272	.328	5	.132	0	11	8	1	0.9
	Yr	10	12	.455	48	28	5	3	0	191^1	186	18	64	138	11.9	3.43	113	.257	.319	8	.143	1	14	10	1	1.1
1988	SF-N	2	2	.500	7	7	1	0	0	37	33	4	8	19	10.0	3.16	103	.243	.285	1	.100	-0	1	0	0	0.0
1989	SF-N	2	0	1.000	2	2	0	0	0	13	8	2	4	5	9.0	3.46	97	.182	.265	1	.333	1	0	-0	0	0.1
Total	8	64	57	.529	226	146	28	9	10	1062^2	968	97	315	558	11.0	3.13	115	.245	.304	38	.121	-2	67	54	1	5.5
● **TOM DREES**	Drees, Thomas Kent b: 6/17/63, Des Moines, Iowa BB/TL, 6′6″, 210 lbs. Deb: 9/3/91																									
1991	Chi-A	0	0	—	4	0	0	0	0	7^1	10	4	6	2	19.6	12.27	32	.345	.457	0	—	0	-7	-7	-0	0.1
● **DARREN DREIFORT**	Dreifort, Darren James b: 5/18/72, Wichita, Kan. BR/TR, 6′2″, 205 lbs. Deb: 4/7/94																									
1994	LA-N	0	5	.000	27	0	0	0	6	29	45	0	15	22	19.9	6.21	63	.357	.441	1	1.000	1	-6	-7	1	-1.2
1996	*LA-N	1	4	.200	19	0	0	0	0	23^2	23	2	12	24	13.3	4.94	78	.256	.343	0	.000	-0	-2	-3	1	-0.5
1997	LA-N	5	2	.714	48	0	0	0	4	63	45	3	34	63	11.4	2.86	135	.202	.310	1	.143	-0	9	7	2	1.0
1998	LA-N	8	12	.400	32	26	1	1	0	180	171	12	57	168	11.9	4.00	97	.256	.324	11	.224	3	5	-2	5	0.5
Total	4	14	23	.378	126	26	1	1	10	295^2	284	17	118	277	12.7	4.05	96	.257	.336	13	.217	3	6	-5	8	-0.2
● **CLEM DREISEWERD**	Dreisewerd, Clemens Johann “Steamboat” b: 1/24/16, Old Monroe, Mo. BL/TL, 6′1.5″, 195 lbs. Deb: 8/29/44																									
1944	Bos-A	2	4	.333	7	7	3	0	0	48^2	52	2	9	9	11.3	4.07	84	.268	.300	3	.188	0	-3	-4	-1	-0.5
1945	Bos-A	0	1	.000	2	2	0	0	0	9^2	13	0	2	3	14.9	4.66	73	.325	.372	0	.000	-0	-1	-1	-0	-0.2
1946	*Bos-A	4	1	.800	20	1	0	0	0	47^1	50	3	15	19	12.4	4.18	88	.276	.332	0	.000	-1	-4	-3	1	-0.3
1948	StL-A	0	2	.000	13	0	0	0	1	22^1	28	6	8	6	14.5	5.64	81	.318	.375	0	.000	-1	-3	-3	-0	-0.3
	NY-N	0	0	—	4	0	0	0	1	12^2	17	3	5	2	15.6	5.68	69	.321	.379	1	.250	1	-2	-2	-0	0.0
Total	4	6	8	.429	46	10	3	0	2	140^2	160	14	39	39	12.8	4.54	82	.288	.336	4	.105	-1	-14	-13	-1	-1.3
● **KIRK DRESSENDORFER**	Dressendorfer, Kirk Richard b: 4/8/69, Houston, Tex. BR/TR, 5′11″, 190 lbs. Deb: 4/13/91																									
1991	Oak-A	3	3	.500	7	7	0	0	0	34^2	33	5	21	17	14.0	5.45	70	.244	.346	0	—	0	-5	-6	-0	-0.7
● **BOB DRESSER**	Dresser, Robert Nicholson b: 10/4/1878, Newton, Mass. d: 7/27/24, Duxbury, Mass. BL/TL, Deb: 8/13/02																									
1902	Bos-N	0	1	.000	1	1	1	0	0	9	12	0	0	8	12.0	3.00	94	.316	.316	1	.250	0	-0	-0	-0	0.0
● **ROB DRESSLER**	Dressler, Robert Anthony b: 2/2/54, Portland, Ore. BR/TR, 6′3″, 180 lbs. Deb: 9/7/75																									
1975	SF-N	1	0	1.000	3	2	1	0	0	16^1	17	0	4	6	11.6	1.10	345	.274	.318	0	.000	-0	5	5	0	0.3
1976	SF-N	3	10	.231	25	19	0	0	0	107^2	125	8	35	33	13.5	4.43	82	.291	.347	4	.129	-1	-11	-10	1	-1.1
1978	StL-N	0	1	.000	3	2	0	0	0	13	12	0	4	4	11.1	2.08	169	.267	.327	0	.000	-0	2	2	-0	0.1
1979	Sea-A	3	2	.600	21	11	2	0	0	104	134	11	22	36	13.5	4.93	88	.312	.345	0	—	0	-8	-7	-0	-0.3
1980	Sea-A	4	10	.286	30	14	3	0	0	149^1	161	14	33	50	11.9	3.98	104	.280	.322	0	—	0	1	3	1	0.3
Total	5	11	23	.324	82	48	6	0	0	390^1	449	33	98	129	12.7	4.17	96	.291	.335	4	.105	-1	-12	-7	2	-0.7
● **DAVE DREW**	Drew, David Deb: 5/14/1884 ♦																									
1884	Phi-U	0	1	.000	1	0	0	0	0	7	7	0	0	2	9.0	3.86	60	.241	.241	4	.444	0	-1	-1	-0	-0.1
● **KARL DREWS**	Drews, Karl August b: 2/22/20, Staten Island, N.Y d: 8/15/63, Dania, Fla. BR/TR, 6′4″, 198 lbs. Deb: 9/8/46																									
1946	NY-A	0	1	.000	3	1	0	0	0	6^1	6	0	6	4	18.5	8.53	40	.250	.419	0	.000	-0	-4	-4	-0	-0.5
1947	*NY-A	6	6	.500	30	10	0	0	1	91^2	92	6	55	45	14.9	4.91	72	.264	.373	1	.037	-2	-12	-14	1	-1.9
1948	NY-A	2	3	.400	19	2	0	0	1	38	35	3	31	11	15.6	3.79	108	.248	.384	0	.000	-1	2	1	1	0.2
	StL-A	3	2	.600	20	2	0	0	2	38	43	3	38	11	19.2	8.05	57	.289	.433	0	.000	-0	-16	-15	0	-1.8
	Yr	5	5	.500	39	4	0	0	3	76	78	6	69	22	17.4	5.92	73	.269	.409	0	.000	-1	-14	-14	1	-1.6
1949	StL-A	4	12	.250	31	23	3	1	0	139^2	180	11	66	35	16.4	6.64	68	.317	.397	0	.000	-5	-38	-33	-1	-3.6
1951	Phi-N	1	0	1.000	5	3	1	0	0	23	29	2	7	13	15.7	6.26	61	.296	.367	2	.250	1	-6	-6	0	-0.2
1952	Phi-N	14	15	.483	33	30	15	5	0	228^2	213	13	52	96	10.6	2.72	135	.252	.298	9	.110	-2	26	24	0	2.8
1953	Phi-N	9	10	.474	47	27	6	0	3	185^1	218	26	50	72	13.5	4.52	93	.293	.346	7	.119	-2	-5	-6	2	-0.7
1954	Phi-N	1	0	1.000	8	0	0	0	0	16	18	2	8	6	14.6	5.63	72	.300	.382	0	.000	-1	-3	-3	0	-0.2
	Cin-N	4	4	.500	22	9	1	1	0	60	79	6	19	29	15.0	6.00	70	.326	.380	2	.167	1	-13	-12	0	-1.3
	Yr	5	4	.556	30	9	1	1	0	76	97	8	27	35	14.9	5.92	70	.320	.380	2	.125	1	-16	-15	0	-1.5
Total	8	44	53	.454	218	107	26	7	7	826^2	913	72	332	322	13.9	4.76	84	.284	.357	21	.083	-12	-68	-68	3	-7.2
● **STEVE DREYER**	Dreyer, Steven William b: 11/19/69, Ames, Iowa BR/TR, 6′3″, 180 lbs. Deb: 8/8/93																									
1993	Tex-A	3	3	.500	10	6	0	0	0	41	48	7	20	23	15.1	5.71	73	.291	.371	0	—	0	-6	-7	-0	-0.9
1994	Tex-A	1	1	.500	5	3	0	0	0	17^1	19	1	8	11	14.5	5.71	84	.271	.354	0	—	0	-2	-2	-0	-0.2
Total	2	4	4	.500	15	9	0	0	0	58^1	67	8	28	34	15.0	5.71	76	.285	.366	0	—	0	-8	-9	-1	-1.1
● **DENNY DRISCOLL**	Driscoll, John F. b: 11/19/1855, Lowell, Mass. d: 7/11/1886, Lowell, Mass. BL/TL, 5′10.5″, 160 lbs. Deb: 7/1/1880 ♦																									
1880	Buf-N	1	3	.250	6	4	4	0	0	41^2	48	1	9	17	12.3	3.89	63	.270	.305	10	.154	-1	-7	-7	0	-0.6
1882	Pit-a	13	9	.591	23	23	23	0	0	201	162	0	12	59	7.8	**1.21**	**216**	.206	.218	11	.138	-2	33	31	-4	2.4
1883	Pit-a	18	21	.462	41	40	35	1	0	336^1	427	3	39	79	12.5	3.99	81	.290	.309	27	.182	-5	-26	-29	6	-2.5
1884	Lou-a	6	6	.500	13	13	10	0	0	102	110	3	7	16	10.5	3.44	90	.252	.267	9	.188	-1	-2	-4	2	-0.3
Total	4	38	39	.494	83	80	72	1	0	681	747	7	67	171	10.8	3.08	97	.260	.277	60	.167	-9	-2	-8	4	-1.0
● **MICHAEL DRISCOLL**	Driscoll, Michael Columbus b: 10/19/1892, Rockland, Mass. d: 3/22/53, Foxboro, Mass. BR/TR, 6′1″, 160 lbs. Deb: 7/6/16																									
1916	Phi-A	0	1	.000	1	0	0	0	0	5	6	0	2	0	14.4	5.40	53	.273	.333	0	.000	-0	-1	-1	1	-0.2
● **TOM DROHAN**	Drohan, Thomas F b: 8/26/1887, Fall River, Mass. d: 9/17/26, Kewanee, Ill. BR/TR, 5′10″, 175 lbs. Deb: 5/1/13																									
1913	Was-A	0	0	—	2	0	0	0	0	2	5	1	0	2	22.5	9.00	33	.500	.500	0	—	0	-1	-1	0	0.0
● **DICK DROTT**	Drott, Richard Fred “Hummer” b: 7/1/36, Cincinnati, Ohio d: 8/16/85, Glendale Heights, Ill. BR/TR, 6′, 185 lbs. Deb: 4/16/57																									
1957	Chi-N	15	11	.577	38	32	7	3	0	229	200	22	129	170	13.2	3.58	108	.234	.340	8	.100	-5	8	8	-1	0.2
1958	Chi-N	7	11	.389	39	31	4	0	0	167^1	156	23	99	127	14.0	5.43	72	.245	.352	15	.273	3	-28	-28	1	-2.3
1959	Chi-N	1	2	.333	8	6	1	1	0	27^1	25	5	26	15	16.8	5.93	67	.245	.398	1	.125	-0	-6	-6	-0	-0.6
1960	Chi-N	0	6	.000	23	9	0	0	0	55^1	63	7	42	32	17.6	7.16	53	.296	.419	1	.100	-1	-21	-21	-0	-2.1
1961	Chi-N	1	4	.200	35	8	0	0	0	98	75	13	51	48	11.7	4.22	99	.215	.317	6	.273	1	-2	-0	-2	-0.1
1962	Hou-N	1	0	1.000	6	1	0	0	0	13	12	1	9	10	14.5	7.62	49	.240	.356	0	.000	-0	-5	-6	-0	-0.4
1963	Hou-N	2	12	.143	27	14	2	1	0	97^2	95	13	49	58	13.8	4.98	63	.257	.353	3	.130	-1	-18	-20	-1	-2.8
Total	7	27	46	.370	176	101	14	5	0	687^2	626	84	405	460	13.8	4.78	80	.243	.351	34	.168	-2	-72	-74	-5	-8.1
● **LOUIS DRUCKE**	Drucke, Louis Frank b: 12/3/1888, Waco, Tex. d: 9/22/55, Waco, Tex. BR/TR, 6′1″, 188 lbs. Deb: 9/25/09																									
1909	NY-N	2	1	.667	3	3	2	0	0	24	20	0	13	8	12.4	2.25	114	.227	.327	1	.125	-0	1	1	-0	0.0
1910	NY-N	12	10	.545	34	27	15	0	0	215^1	174	3	82	151	11.2	2.47	120	.228	.312	15	.214	4	14	12	2	1.7
1911	NY-N	4	4	.500	15	10	4	0	0	75^2	83	1	41	42	15.7	4.04	83	.281	.384	2	.087	-1	-5	-6	1	-0.6
1912	NY-N	0	0	—	1	0	0	0	1	2	5	0	1	0	27.0	13.50	25	.417	.462	0	—	0	-2	-2	-0	-0.2
Total	4	18	15	.545	53	40	21	0	1	317	282	4	137	201	12.4	2.90	105	.243	.333	18	.178	2	7	5	2	0.9
● **CARL DRUHOT**	Druhot, Carl A. “Collie” b: 9/1/1882, Ohio d: 2/11/18, Portland, Ore. BL/TL, 5′7″, 150 lbs. Deb: 4/18/06																									
1906	Cin-N	2	2	.500	4	3	1	0	0	25	27	0	7	14	13.0	4.32	64	.270	.330	2	.222	0	-5	-4	-1	-0.7

YEAR	TM/L	W	L	PCT	G	GS	CG	SH	SV	IP	H	HR	BB	SO	RAT	ERA	ERA+	OAV	OOB	BH	AVG	PB	PR	/A	PD	TPI
	StL-N	6	7	.462	15	13	12	1	0	130^1	117	1	46	45	11.6	2.62	100	.238	.310	13	.232	1	0	0	1	0.2
	Yr	8	9	.471	19	16	13	1	0	155^1	144	1	53	59	11.7	2.90	91	.243	.310	15	.231	1	-5	-4	-1	-0.5
1907	StL-N	0	1	.000	1	1	0	0	0	2^1	3	0	4	1	30.9	15.43	16	.600	.800	0	—	0	-3	-3	0	-0.9
Total	2	8	10	.444	20	17	13	1	0	157^2	147	1	57	60	12.1	3.08	86	.247	.321	15	.231	1	-8	-8	-0	-1.4
● TIM DRUMMOND	Drummond, Timothy Darnell b: 12/24/64, LaPlata, Md. BR/TR, 6'3", 170 lbs. Deb: 9/12/87																									
1987	Pit-N	0	0	—	6	0	0	0	0	6	5	0	3	5	12.0	4.50	91	.227	.320	0	.000	-0	-0	-0	0	0.0
1989	Min-A	0	0	—	8	0	0	0	1	16^1	16	0	8	9	14.3	3.86	107	.246	.347	0	—	0	0	1	-0	-0.5
1990	Min-A	3	5	.375	35	4	0	0	1	91	104	8	36	49	13.9	4.35	95	.295	.362	0	—	0	-5	-2	-1	-0.6
Total	3	3	5	.375	49	4	0	0	2	113^1	125	8	47	63	13.9	4.29	97	.284	.357	0	.000	-0	-5	-2	-1	-1.1
● DON DRYSDALE	Drysdale, Donald Scott b: 7/23/36, Van Nuys, Cal. d: 7/3/93, Montreal, Que., Canada BR/TR, 6'6", 216 lbs. Deb: 4/17/56 H																									
1956	*Bro-N	5	5	.500	25	12	2	0	0	99	95	9	31	55	11.7	2.64	150	.255	.317	5	.192	1	12	15	1	1.6
1957	Bro-N	17	9	.654	34	29	9	4	0	221	197	17	61	148	10.8	2.69	155	.236	.294	9	.123	-0	29	**36**	5	**4.7**
1958	LA-N	12	13	.480	44	29	6	1	0	211^2	214	21	72	131	12.8	4.17	98	.263	.333	15	.227	8	-5	-2	3	1.0
1959	*LA-N★	17	13	.567	44	36	15	**4**	2	270^2	237	26	93	**242**	11.6	3.46	122	.233	.308	15	.165	3	15	23	2	3.0
1960	LA-N	15	14	.517	41	36	15	5	2	269	214	27	72	**246**	**9.9**	2.84	140	.215	**.275**	13	.157	2	27	34	4	4.3
1961	LA-N☆	13	10	.565	40	37	10	3	0	244	236	29	83	182	12.5	3.69	118	.254	.329	16	.193	4	9	18	-1	1.8
1962	LA-N★	**25**	9	.735	43	41	19	2	1	**314^1**	272	21	78	**232**	10.3	2.83	128	.230	.283	22	.198	5	**39**	28	1	3.4
1963	*LA-N★	19	17	.528	42	42	17	3	0	315^1	287	25	57	251	10.1	2.63	115	.242	.283	16	.167	5	23	14	3	2.4
1964	LA-N★	18	16	.529	40	40	21	5	0	**321^1**	242	15	68	237	9.0	2.18	148	.207	.256	19	.173	4	**48**	**38**	2	**4.7**
1965	*LA-N★	23	12	.657	44	42	20	7	1	308^1	270	30	66	210	10.2	2.77	118	.232	.280	39	.300	22	26	17	0	4.4
1966	*LA-N	13	16	.448	40	40	11	3	0	273^2	279	21	45	177	11.2	3.42	96	.265	.306	20	.189	4	6	-4	-1	-0.1
1967	LA-N★	13	16	.448	38	38	9	3	0	282	269	19	60	196	10.8	2.74	113	.251	.296	12	.129	-0	20	11	3	1.4
1968	LA-N★	14	12	.538	31	31	12	8	0	239	201	11	56	155	10.1	2.15	129	.231	.286	14	.177	1	22	16	2	2.4
1969	LA-N	5	4	.556	12	12	1	1	0	62^2	71	9	13	24	12.4	4.45	75	.291	.332	3	.136	0	-6	-8	0	-1.0
Total	14	209	166	.557	518	465	167	49	6	3432	3084	280	855	2486	10.7	2.95	121	.239	.294	218	.186	60	266	230	25	34.0
● MONK DUBIEL	Dubiel, Walter John b: 2/12/18, Hartford, Conn. d: 10/23/69, Hartford, Conn. BR/TR, 6', 190 lbs. Deb: 4/19/44																									
1944	NY-A	13	13	.500	30	28	19	3	0	232	217	12	86	79	11.8	3.38	103	.248	.316	15	.181	-2	1	3	0	0.1
1945	NY-A	10	9	.526	26	20	9	1	0	151^1	157	9	62	45	13.0	4.64	75	.266	.335	16	.276	4	-21	-20	-2	-2.1
1948	Phi-N	8	10	.444	37	17	6	2	4	150^1	139	13	58	42	11.9	3.89	101	.248	.320	7	.167	0	1	1	-2	0.0
1949	Chi-N	6	9	.400	32	20	3	1	4	147^2	142	16	54	52	12.0	4.14	97	.250	.317	10	.286	3	-2	-2	1	0.3
1950	Chi-N	6	10	.375	39	12	4	2	2	142^2	152	12	67	51	13.9	4.16	101	.270	.348	9	.200	1	-0	1	2	0.3
1951	Chi-N	2	2	.500	22	0	0	0	1	54^2	46	3	22	19	11.2	2.30	178	.232	.309	0	.000	-1	10	11	0	0.7
1952	Chi-N	0	0	—	1	0	0	0	0	0^2	1	0	0	1	13.5	0.00	—	.333	.333	0	—	0	0	0	0	0.0
Total	7	45	53	.459	187	97	41	9	11	879^1	854	65	349	289	12.4	3.87	98	.254	.325	57	.207	5	-11	-6	-0	-0.7
● BRIAN DuBOIS	DuBois, Brian Andrew b: 4/18/67, Joliet, Ill. BL/TL, 5'10", 195 lbs. Deb: 8/17/89																									
1989	Det-A	0	4	.000	6	5	0	0	1	36	29	2	17	13	12.0	1.75	218	.218	.316	0	—	0	9	8	-0	1.1
1990	Det-A	3	5	.375	12	11	0	0	0	58^1	70	9	22	34	14.3	5.09	78	.310	.373	0	—	0	-8	-7	-1	-1.0
Total	2	3	9	.250	18	16	0	0	1	94^1	99	11	39	47	13.5	3.82	102	.276	.352	0	—	0	1	1	-1	0.1
● JEAN DUBUC	Dubuc, Jean Joseph Octave Arthur "Chauncey" b: 9/15/1888, St.Johnsbury, Vt. d: 8/28/58, Fort Myers, Fla. BR/TR, 5'10.5", 185 lbs. Deb: 6/25/08 C♦																									
1908	Cin-N	5	6	.455	15	9	7	1	0	85^1	62	2	41	32	11.4	2.74	84	.205	.309	4	.138	-1	-4	-4	1	-0.6
1909	Cin-N	2	5	.286	19	5	2	0	1	71^1	72	0	46	19	15.4	3.66	71	.269	.384	3	.167	0	-8	-8	0	-0.8
1912	Det-A	17	10	.630	37	26	23	2	3	250	217	2	109	97	12.0	2.77	118	.235	.321	29	.269	6	15	14	4	2.5
1913	Det-A	15	14	.517	36	28	22	1	2	242^2	228	1	91	73	12.1	2.89	101	.252	.325	36	.267	5	1	1	8	1.9
1914	Det-A	12	14	.462	36	27	15	2	1	224	216	3	76	70	12.0	3.46	81	.257	.324	28	.226	7	-18	-16	3	-0.7
1915	Det-A	17	12	.586	39	33	22	5	2	258	231	6	88	74	11.5	3.21	94	.245	.316	23	.205	0	-8	-5	1	-0.4
1916	Det-A	10	10	.500	36	16	8	1	1	170^1	134	1	84	40	11.8	2.96	97	.233	.336	20	.256	5	-2	-2	4	0.8
1918	*Bos-A	0	1	.000	2	1	1	0	0	10^2	11	1	5	1	13.5	4.22	64	.268	.348	1	.167	0	-2	-2	-0	-0.2
1919	NY-N	6	4	.600	36	5	1	0	3	132	119	4	37	32	10.8	2.66	105	.246	.303	6	.143	-1	4	2	2	0.2
Total	9	84	76	.525	256	150	101	12	13	1444^1	1290	20	577	438	11.9	3.04	96	.244	.324	150	.230	21	-22	-21	23	2.7
● JIM DUCKWORTH	Duckworth, James Raymond b: 5/24/39, National City, Cal. BR/TR, 6'4", 194 lbs. Deb: 4/13/63																									
1963	Was-A	4	12	.250	37	15	2	0	0	120^2	131	13	67	66	15.5	6.04	61	.278	.379	0	.000	-3	-32	-31	-1	-4.1
1964	Was-A	1	6	.143	30	2	0	0	3	56	52	9	25	56	12.9	4.34	85	.244	.332	2	.222	0	-4	-4	0	-0.4
1965	Was-A	2	2	.500	17	8	0	0	0	64	45	11	36	74	11.7	3.94	88	.202	.318	0	.000	-2	-3	-3	-1	-0.5
1966	Was-A	0	3	.000	5	4	0	0	0	14^1	14	2	10	14	15.7	5.02	69	.259	.385	0	.000	-0	-3	-2	-0	-0.6
	KC-A	0	2	.000	8	0	0	0	1	12	14	2	10	10	18.8	9.00	38	.292	.424	0	.000	-0	-7	-7	-0	-1.3
	Yr	0	5	.000	13	4	0	0	1	26^1	28	4	20	24	16.7	6.84	50	.269	.392	0	.000	-1	-10	-10	-1	-1.9
Total	4	7	25	.219	97	29	2	0	4	267	256	37	148	220	14.2	5.26	69	.253	.358	2	.034	-5	-50	-49	-2	-6.9
● CLISE DUDLEY	Dudley, Elzie Clise b: 8/8/03, Graham, N.C. d: 1/12/89, Moncks Corner, S.C BL/TR, 6'1", 195 lbs. Deb: 4/18/29																									
1929	Bro-N	6	14	.300	35	21	8	1	0	156^2	202	9	64	33	15.9	5.69	81	.315	.385	5	.098	-1	-17	-19	2	-1.8
1930	Bro-N	2	4	.333	21	7	2	0	1	66^2	103	3	27	18	17.8	6.35	77	.371	.430	5	.208	-0	-10	-11	1	-0.7
1931	Phi-N	8	14	.364	30	24	8	0	0	179	206	10	56	50	13.5	3.52	121	.287	.343	18	.214	-0	7	14	1	1.8
1932	Phi-N	1	1	.500	13	0	0	0	1	17^2	23	3	8	5	15.8	7.13	62	.329	.397	4	.286	3	-6	-5	0	-0.3
1933	Pit-N	0	0	—	1	0	0	0	0	0^1	6	0	1	0	189.0	135.00	2	.857	.875	0	—	0	-5	-5	0	0.0
Total	5	17	33	.340	100	52	18	1	2	420^1	540	25	156	106	15.3	5.03	90	.315	.378	32	.185	1	-31	-24	4	-1.0
● HAL DUES	Dues, Hal Joseph b: 9/22/54, LaMarque, Tex. BR/TR, 6'3", 180 lbs. Deb: 9/9/77																									
1977	Mon-N	1	1	.500	6	4	0	0	0	23	26	2	9	9	13.7	4.30	88	.265	.327	0	.000	-1	-1	-1	0	-0.1
1978	Mon-N	5	6	.455	25	12	1	0	1	99	85	5	42	36	11.9	2.36	149	.240	.327	6	.194	0	13	13	-0	1.4
1980	Mon-N	0	1	.000	6	1	0	0	0	12^1	17	1	4	2	15.3	6.57	54	.333	.382	0	.000	-0	-4	-4	0	-0.3
Total	3	6	8	.429	37	17	1	0	1	134^1	128	8	55	47	12.5	3.08	116	.254	.333	6	.154	-1	8	7	0	1.0
● LARRY DUFF	Duff, Cecil Elba b: 11/30/1897, Radersburg, Mont. d: 11/10/69, Bend, Ore. BL/TR, 6'1", 175 lbs. Deb: 9/5/22																									
1922	Chi-A	1	1	.500	3	1	0	0	0	12^2	16	1	3	7	13.5	4.97	82	.340	.380	2	.400	0	-1	-1	-0	-0.2
● JIM DUFFALO	Duffalo, James Francis b: 11/25/35, Helvetia, Pa. BR/TR, 6'1", 175 lbs. Deb: 4/12/61																									
1961	SF-N	5	1	.833	24	4	1	0	1	61^2	59	9	32	37	13.6	4.23	90	.257	.352	5	.294	3	-1	-3	-1	0.0
1962	SF-N	1	2	.333	24	2	0	0	0	42	42	3	23	29	13.9	3.64	104	.256	.348	0	.000	-0	1	1	-1	0.0
1963	SF-N	4	2	.667	34	5	0	0	2	75^1	56	3	37	55	11.3	2.87	112	.209	.309	2	.111	-1	4	3	1	0.2
1964	SF-N	5	1	.833	35	3	1	0	3	74	57	9	31	55	10.9	2.92	122	.209	.294	1	.071	-1	5	5	-1	0.3
1965	SF-N	0	1	.000	2	0	0	0	0	0^1	1	0	2	0	81.0	27.00	13	.500	.750	0	—	0	-1	-1	0	-1.6
	Cin-N	0	1	.000	22	0	0	0	0	44^1	33	3	30	34	13.8	3.45	109	.212	.356	0	.000	-1	0	1	1	0.0
	Yr	0	2	.000	24	0	0	0	0	44^2	34	3	32	34	14.3	3.63	103	.215	.364	0	.000	-1	-0	1	1	-1.6
Total	5	15	8	.652	141	14	2	0	6	297^2	248	27	155	210	12.5	3.39	106	.227	.329	8	.127	1	8	7	-1	-1.1
● JOHN DUFFIE	Duffie, John Brown b: 10/4/45, Greenwood, S.C. BR/TR, 6'7", 210 lbs. Deb: 9/18/67																									
1967	LA-N	0	2	.000	2	2	0	0	0	9^2	11	1	4	6	14.0	2.79	111	.282	.349	0	.000	-0	1	0	-0	0.0
● BERNIE DUFFY	Duffy, Bernard Allen b: 8/18/1893, Vinson, Okla. d: 2/9/62, Abilene, Tex. BR/TR, 5'11", 180 lbs. Deb: 9/20/13																									
1913	Pit-N	0	0	—	3	2	0	0	0	11^1	18	0	3	8	16.7	5.56	54	.360	.396	1	.250	0	-3	-3	0	0.0
● DAN DUGAN	Dugan, Daniel Phillip b: 2/22/07, Plainfield, N.J. d: 6/25/68, Green Brook, N.J. BL/TL, 6'1.5", 187 lbs. Deb: 9/5/28																									
1928	Chi-A	0	0	—	1	0	0	0	0	0^1	0	0	0	0	0.0	0.00	—	.000	.000	0	—	0	0	0	0	0.0
1929	Chi-A	1	4	.200	19	2	0	0	1	65	77	8	19	15	13.6	6.65	64	.300	.353	3	.150	-1	-17	-17	-2	-1.4
Total	2	1	4	.200	20	2	0	0	1	65^1	77	8	19	15	13.5	6.61	65	.298	.351	3	.150	-1	-17	-17	-2	-1.4

YEAR	TM/L	W	L	PCT	G	GS	CG	SH	SV	IP	H	HR	BB	SO	RAT	ERA	ERA+	OAV	OOB	BH	AVG	PB	PR	/A	PD	TPI
● **ED DUGAN** Dugan, Edward John b: 1864, Brooklyn, N.Y. Deb: 8/5/1884 F																										
1884	Ric-a	5	14	.263	20	20	20	0	0	166^1	196	5	15	60	11.5	4.49	74	.267	.284	8	.114	-4	-23	-22	-2	-2.4
● **BILL DUGGLEBY** Duggleby, William James "Frosty Bill" b: 3/16/1874, Utica, N.Y. d: 8/30/44, Redfield, N.Y. TR , Deb: 4/21/1898																										
1898	Phi-N	3	3	.500	9	5	4	0	0	54	70	4	18	12	15.7	5.50	62	.311	.378	5	.238	2	-11	-12	1	-0.8
1901	Phi-N	20	12	.625	35	29	26	5	0	284^2	302	9	41	95	11.2	2.88	118	.270	.302	19	.165	-3	14	17	5	1.9
1902	Phi-A	1	1	.500	2	2	2	0	0	17	19	0	4	4	12.2	3.18	116	.284	.324	0	.000	-1	1	1	1	0.1
	Phi-N	11	17	.393	33	27	25	0	1	258^2	282	2	57	60	12.2	3.38	83	.277	.323	17	.173	-1	-17	-16	2	-1.5
1903	Phi-N	13	16	.448	36	30	28	3	2	264^1	318	4	79	57	13.9	3.75	87	.303	.358	24	.231	2	-14	-14	1	-1.0
1904	Phi-N	12	13	.480	32	27	22	2	1	223^2	265	3	53	55	13.2	3.78	71	.292	.338	14	.171	0	-26	-27	0	-2.7
1905	Phi-N	18	17	.514	38	36	27	1	0	289^1	270	10	83	75	11.4	2.46	119	.253	.315	11	.109	-2	18	15	-2	1.3
1906	Phi-N	13	19	.406	42	30	22	5	2	280^1	241	5	66	83	10.2	2.25	116	.227	.280	14	.141	-2	12	11	1	1.2
1907	Phi-N	0	2	.000	5	2	2	0	0	29	43	2	11	8	18.3	7.45	33	.371	.447	1	.111	0	-16	-16	1	-0.9
	Pit-N	2	2	.500	9	3	1	1	0	40^1	34	0	12	4	10.7	2.68	91	.239	.308	2	.154	-0	-1	-1	1	0.0
	Yr	2	4	.333	14	5	3	1	0	69^1	77	2	23	12	13.2	4.67	52	.293	.354	3	.136	0	-17	-17	2	-0.9
Total	8	93	102	.477	241	191	159	17	6	1741^1	1844	39	424	453	12.2	3.18	93	.272	.323	107	.165	-4	-41	-43	11	-2.4
● **MARTIN DUKE** Duke, Martin F. "Duck" (b: Martin F. Duck) b: 1867, Zanesville, Ohio d: 12/31/1898, Minneapolis, Minn. TL , Deb: 8/24/1891																										
1891	Was-a	0	3	.000	4	3	2	0	0	23	36	0	19	5	21.5	7.43	50	.346	.447	1	.111	-1	-9	-9	-0	-0.9
● **JAN DUKES** Dukes, Noble Jan b: 8/16/45, Cheyenne, Wyo. BL/TL, 5'11", 175 lbs. Deb: 9/6/69																										
1969	Was-A	0	2	.000	8	0	0	0	0	11	8	0	4	3	9.8	2.45	141	.216	.293	0	.000	0	1	1	-0	0.2
1970	Was-A	0	0	—	5	0	0	0	0	6^2	6	0	1	4	10.8	2.70	132	.240	.296	0	.000	-0	1	1	0	0.0
1972	Tex-A	0	0	—	3	0	0	0	0	2^1	1	0	5	0	23.1	3.86	78	.167	.545	0	—	0	-0	-0	0	0.0
Total	3	0	2	.000	16	0	0	0	0	20	15	0	10	7	11.7	2.70	128	.221	.329	0	.000	0	2	2	-0	0.2
● **TOM DUKES** Dukes, Thomas Earl b: 8/31/42, Knoxville, Tenn. BR/TR, 6'2", 185 lbs. Deb: 8/15/67																										
1967	Hou-N	0	2	.000	17	0	0	0	1	23^2	25	2	11	23	14.5	5.32	62	.275	.365	1	.500	0	-5	-5	-0	-0.5
1968	Hou-N	2	2	.500	43	0	0	0	4	52^2	62	3	28	37	15.7	4.27	69	.291	.379	0	.000	-0	-8	-8	0	-0.7
1969	SD-N	1	0	1.000	13	0	0	0	1	22^1	26	2	10	15	14.5	7.25	49	.295	.367	0	.000	-0	-9	-9	0	-0.5
1970	SD-N	1	6	.143	53	0	0	0	10	69	62	7	25	56	11.6	4.04	98	.246	.319	0	.000	-1	0	-1	-0	-0.2
1971	*Bal-A	1	5	.167	28	0	0	0	4	38^1	40	4	8	30	11.5	3.52	95	.263	.304	1	.143	0	-0	-1	-1	-0.2
1972	Cal-A	0	1	.000	7	0	0	0	1	11	11	1	0	8	9.8	1.64	178	.262	.279	0	—	0	2	2	-1	0.1
Total	6	5	16	.238	161	0	0	0	21	217	226	19	82	169	13.1	4.35	79	.270	.341	2	.095	-1	-20	-22	-2	-2.0
● **BOB DULIBA** Duliba, Robert John b: 1/9/35, Glen Lyon, Pa. BR/TR, 5'10", 185 lbs. Deb: 8/11/59																										
1959	StL-N	0	1	.000	11	0	0	0	1	22^2	19	2	12	14	12.3	2.78	153	.237	.337	0	.000	-0	3	4	1	0.2
1960	StL-N	4	4	.500	27	0	0	0	0	40^2	49	6	16	23	14.4	4.20	97	.310	.374	1	.200	-0	-2	-0	-0	-0.1
1962	StL-N	2	0	1.000	28	0	0	0	2	39^1	33	3	17	22	11.4	2.06	207	.239	.323	0	.000	-0	8	10	0	0.5
1963	LA-A	1	1	.500	6	0	0	0	1	7^2	3	0	6	4	10.6	1.17	292	.125	.300	0	.000	-0	2	2	-0	0.5
1964	LA-A	6	4	.600	58	0	0	0	9	72^2	80	5	22	33	12.8	3.59	91	.287	.341	0	.000	-1	0	-2	1	-0.4
1965	Bos-A	4	2	.667	39	0	0	0	1	64^1	60	6	22	27	11.5	3.78	99	.248	.311	0	.000	-0	-2	-0	-0	-0.1
1967	KC-A	0	0	—	7	0	0	0	0	9^2	13	3	1	6	13.0	6.52	49	.342	.359	0	—	0	-4	-4	-0	0.0
Total	7	17	12	.586	176	0	0	0	14	257	257	25	96	129	12.4	3.47	108	.268	.335	1	.038	-2	6	8	1	0.6
● **GEORGE DUMONT** Dumont, George Henry "Pea Soup" b: 11/13/1895, Minneapolis, Minn. d: 10/13/56, Minneapolis, Minn. BR/TR, 5'11", 163 lbs. Deb: 9/14/15																										
1915	Was-A	2	1	.667	6	4	3	2	0	40	23	0	12	18	8.3	2.02	147	.169	.247	2	.167	-0	4	4	-1	0.2
1916	Was-A	2	3	.400	17	5	2	0	1	53	37	0	17	21	9.3	3.06	91	.194	.263	1	.071	-0	-1	-2	-1	-0.3
1917	Was-A	5	14	.263	37	23	8	2	2	204^2	171	3	76	65	11.1	2.55	103	.227	.303	2	.034	-5	3	2	-3	-0.7
1918	Was-A	1	1	.500	4	1	1	0	0	14	18	0	6	12	15.4	5.14	53	.295	.358	1	.333	1	-4	-4	0	-0.4
1919	Bos-A	0	4	.000	13	2	0	0	0	35^1	45	1	19	12	16.6	4.33	70	.326	.411	0	.000	-0	-4	-5	0	-0.5
Total	5	10	23	.303	77	35	14	4	3	347	294	4	130	128	11.3	2.85	96	.230	.306	6	.064	-5	-3	-4	-5	-1.7
● **DAN DUMOULIN** Dumoulin, Daniel Lynn b: 8/20/53, Kokomo, Ind. BR/TR, 6', 175 lbs. Deb: 9/5/77																										
1977	Cin-N	0	0	—	5	0	0	0	0	5^1	12	0	3	5	25.3	13.50	29	.462	.517	0	—	0	-6	-6	0	0.0
1978	Cin-N	1	0	1.000	3	0	0	0	0	5	7	0	3	2	19.8	1.80	197	.368	.478	0	—	0	1	1	0	0.2
Total	2	1	0	1.000	8	0	0	0	0	10^1	19	0	6	7	22.6	7.84	48	.422	.500	0	—	0	-5	-5	0	0.2
● **NICK DUMOVICH** Dumovich, Nicholas b: 1/2/02, Sacramento, Cal. d: 12/12/78, Laguna Hills, Cal. BL/TL, 6', 170 lbs. Deb: 4/20/23																										
1923	Chi-N	3	5	.375	28	8	1	0	1	94	118	4	45	23	15.9	4.60	87	.319	.397	7	.241	1	-6	-6	1	-0.2
● **MATT DUNBAR** Dunbar, Matthew Marshall b: 10/15/68, Tallahassee, Fla. BL/TL, 6', 170 lbs. Deb: 4/25/95																										
1995	Fla-N	0	1	.000	8	0	0	0	0	7	12	0	11	5	30.9	11.57	36	.387	.558	0	—	0	-6	-6	1	-0.6
● **ED DUNDON** Dundon, Edward Joseph "Dummy" b: 7/10/1859, Columbus, Ohio d: 8/18/1893, Columbus, Ohio TR , Deb: 6/2/1883 ♦																										
1883	Col-a	3	16	.158	20	19	16	0	0	166^2	213	7	38	31	13.6	4.48	69	.292	.327	15	.161	-3	-22	-26	0	-2.5
1884	Col-a	6	4	.600	11	9	7	0	0	81	85	9	15	37	11.1	3.78	80	.249	.281	12	.140	-1	-5	-7	1	-0.6
Total	2	9	20	.310	31	28	23	0	0	247^2	298	16	53	68	12.8	4.25	72	.278	.312	27	.151	-4	-27	-33	1	-3.1
● **JIM DUNEGAN** Dunegan, James William b: 8/6/47, Burlington, Iowa BR/TR, 6'1", 205 lbs. Deb: 5/28/70																										
1970	Chi-N	0	2	.000	7	0	0	0	0	13^1	13	2	12	3	16.9	4.73	95	.277	.424	1	.250	0	-1	-0	0	0.0
● **WILEY DUNHAM** Dunham, Henry Huston b: 1/30/1877, Piketon, Ohio d: 1/16/34, Cleveland, Ohio 6'1", 180 lbs. Deb: 5/24/02																										
1902	StL-N	2	3	.400	7	5	3	0	1	38	47	1	13	15	14.9	5.68	48	.303	.368	1	.083	-1	-12	-12	-0	-1.6
● **DAVEY DUNKLE** Dunkle, Edward Perks b: 8/30/1872, Philipsburg, Pa. d: 11/19/41, Lock Haven, Pa. BB/TR, 6'2", 220 lbs. Deb: 8/28/1897																										
1897	Phi-N	5	2	.714	7	7	7	0	0	62	72	0	23	9	13.9	3.48	121	.288	.350	4	.174	-1	6	5	-1	0.3
1898	Phi-N	1	4	.200	12	7	4	0	0	68^1	83	1	38	21	17.1	6.98	49	.297	.399	6	.214	-0	-26	-27	-1	-1.7
1899	Was-N	0	2	.000	4	2	2	0	0	26	46	3	14	9	21.1	10.04	39	.383	.452	3	.273	-0	-18	-18	-0	-1.0
1903	Chi-A	4	4	.500	12	7	6	0	1	82	96	1	31	26	14.3	4.06	69	.291	.357	10	.303	2	-10	-11	-2	-1.0
	Was-A	5	9	.357	14	13	10	0	0	108^1	111	4	33	51	12.3	4.24	74	.264	.324	4	.098	-4	-15	-13	-2	-2.0
	Yr	9	13	.409	26	20	16	0	1	190^1	207	5	64	77	13.0	4.16	72	.275	.335	14	.189	-2	-25	-25	-4	-3.0
1904	Was-A	2	9	.182	12	11	7	0	0	74^1	95	1	23	23	14.7	4.96	54	.311	.366	4	.143	-2	-20	-19	-0	-2.7
Total	5	17	30	.362	61	47	36	0	1	421	503	10	162	139	14.7	5.02	65	.295	.364	31	.189	-4	-83	-83	-7	-8.1
● **FRED DUNLAP** Dunlap, Frederick C. "Sure Shot" b: 5/21/1859, Philadelphia, Pa. d: 12/1/02, Philadelphia, Pa. BR/TR, 5'8", 165 lbs. Deb: 5/1/1880 M♦																										
1884	StL-U	0	0	—	1	0	0	0	1	0^2	2	0	0	1	27.0	13.50	18	.500	.500	185	.412	1	-1	-1	0	-0.2
1887	*Det-N	0	0	—	1	0	0	0	0	2	4	0	0	1	18.0	4.50	90	.500	.500	72	.265	0	-0	-0	-0	0.0
Total	2	0	0	—	2	0	0	0	1	2^2	6	0	0	2	20.3	6.75	54	.500	.500	1159	.292	1	-1	-1	-0	-0.2
● **JACK DUNLEAVY** Dunleavy, John Francis b: 9/14/1879, Harrison, N.J. d: 4/11/44, S.Norwalk, Conn. TL , 5'6", 167 lbs. Deb: 5/30/03 ♦																										
1903	StL-N	6	8	.429	14	13	9	0	0	102	101	2	57	51	14.6	4.06	80	.264	.371	48	.249	2	-9	-9	1	-0.8
1904	StL-N	1	4	.200	7	5	5	0	0	55	63	4	23	28	14.2	4.42	61	.275	.344	40	.233	2	-10	-11	1	-0.7
Total	2	7	12	.368	21	18	14	0	0	157	164	6	80	79	14.5	4.18	73	.268	.361	193	.241	4	-19	-20	1	-1.5
● **JIM DUNN** Dunn, James William "Bill" b: 2/25/31, Valdosta, Ga. BR/TR, 6'0.5", 185 lbs. Deb: 8/26/52																										
1952	Pit-N	0	0	—	3	0	0	0	0	5^1	4	0	3	2	11.8	3.38	118	.190	.292	0	.000	-0	0	0	0	0.0
● **JACK DUNN** Dunn, John Joseph b: 10/6/1872, Meadville, Pa. d: 10/22/28, Towson, Md. BR/TR, 5'9", Deb: 5/6/1897 ♦																										
1897	Bro-N	14	9	.609	25	21	21	0	0	216^2	251	6	66	26	13.5	4.57	90	.288	.344	29	.221	-2	-6	-11	1	-1.0
1898	Bro-N	16	21	.432	41	37	31	0	0	322^2	352	10	82	66	12.5	3.60	100	.275	.327	41	.246	0	0	-0	-1	-0.1
1899	Bro-N	23	13	.639	41	34	29	2	2	299^1	323	8	86	48	12.8	3.70	106	.275	.334	30	.246	0	5	7	3	1.0
1900	Bro-N	3	4	.429	10	7	5	0	0	63	88	1	28	6	17.1	5.57	69	.330	.401	6	.231	-0	-13	-12	1	-1.0

YEAR	TM/L	W	L	PCT	G	GS	CG	SH	SV	IP	H	HR	BB	SO	RAT	ERA	ERA+	OAV	OOB	BH	AVG	PB	PR	/A	PD	TPI
	Phi-N	5	5	.500	10	9	9	1	0	80	87	2	29	12	13.6	4.84	75	.276	.347	10	.303	1	-10	-11	-1	-1.0
	Yr	8	9	.471	20	16	14	1	0	143	175	3	57	18	14.9	5.16	72	.299	.366	16	.271	1	-23	-23	1	-2.0
1901	Phi-N	0	1	.000	2	2	0	0	0	4^{2}	11	0	7	1	38.6	21.21	16	.458	.606	1	1.000	1	-9	-9	-0	-1.2
	Bal-A	3	3	.500	9	6	6	0	0	59^{2}	74	2	21	5	14.5	3.62	107	.301	.358	90	.249	0	0	2	1	0.2
1902	NY-N	0	3	.000	3	2	2	0	0	26^{2}	28	0	12	6	13.5	3.71	76	.269	.345	72	.211	0	-3	-3	1	-0.2
1904	NY-N	0	0	—	1	0	0	0	1	4	3	1	3	1	13.5	4.50	61	.167	.286	56	.309	0	-1	-1	-0	0.0
Total	7	64	59	.520	142	118	103	3	3	1076^{2}	1217	30	334	171	13.4	4.11	92	.283	.342	397	.245	1	-36	-38	5	-3.3

● MIKE DUNNE

Dunne, Michael Dennis b: 10/27/62, South Bend, Ind. BR/TR, 6'4", 200 lbs. Deb: 6/5/87

YEAR	TM/L	W	L	PCT	G	GS	CG	SH	SV	IP	H	HR	BB	SO	RAT	ERA	ERA+	OAV	OOB	BH	AVG	PB	PR	/A	PD	TPI
1987	Pit-N	13	6	.684	23	23	5	1	0	163^{1}	143	10	68	72	11.7	3.03	136	.240	.319	5	.094	-1	19	20	2	2.3
1988	Pit-N	7	11	.389	30	28	1	0	0	170	163	15	88	70	13.6	3.92	87	.255	.349	5	.109	-1	-9	-10	0	-1.0
1989	Pit-N	1	1	.500	3	3	0	0	0	14^{1}	21	1	9	4	19.5	7.53	45	.328	.419	1	.250	0	-6	-7	0	-0.7
	Sea-A	2	9	.182	15	15	1	0	0	85^{1}	104	7	37	38	15.1	5.27	76	.307	.378	0	—	0	-13	-12	0	-1.3
1990	SD-N	0	3	.000	10	6	0	0	0	28^{2}	28	4	17	15	14.1	5.65	68	.241	.338	0	.000	-1	-6	-6	1	-0.6
1992	Chi-A	2	0	1.000	4	1	0	0	0	12^{2}	12	0	6	6	13.5	4.26	91	.255	.352	0	—	0	-0	-1	0	-0.1
Total	5	25	30	.455	85	76	7	1	0	474^{1}	471	37	225	205	13.4	4.08	93	.261	.347	11	.101	-1	-16	-15	3	-1.4

● ANDY DUNNING

Dunning, Andrew Jackson b: 8/12/1871, New York, N.Y. d: 6/21/52, New York, N.Y. BR/TR, 6', 175 lbs. Deb: 5/23/1889

YEAR	TM/L	W	L	PCT	G	GS	CG	SH	SV	IP	H	HR	BB	SO	RAT	ERA	ERA+	OAV	OOB	BH	AVG	PB	PR	/A	PD	TPI
1889	Pit-N	0	2	.000	2	2	2	0	0	18	20	1	16	4	18.0	7.00	54	.274	.404	0	.000	-1	-6	-7	0	-0.6
1891	NY-N	0	1	.000	1	1	0	0	0	2	3	1	3	1	27.0	4.50	71	.333	.500	0	—	0	-0	-0	-0	-0.1
Total	2	0	3	.000	3	3	2	0	0	20	23	2	19	5	18.9	6.75	55	.280	.416	0	.000	-1	-6	-7	0	-0.7

● STEVE DUNNING

Dunning, Steven John b: 5/15/49, Denver, Colo. BR/TR, 6'2", 205 lbs. Deb: 6/14/70

YEAR	TM/L	W	L	PCT	G	GS	CG	SH	SV	IP	H	HR	BB	SO	RAT	ERA	ERA+	OAV	OOB	BH	AVG	PB	PR	/A	PD	TPI
1970	Cle-A	4	9	.308	19	17	0	0	0	94^{1}	93	16	54	77	14.4	4.96	80	.261	.364	5	.161	-1	-13	-11	1	-1.2
1971	Cle-A	8	14	.364	31	29	3	1	1	184	173	25	109	132	14.0	4.50	85	.254	.361	10	.182	1	-21	-14	2	-1.2
1972	Cle-A	6	4	.600	16	16	1	0	0	105	98	16	43	52	12.1	3.26	99	.248	.322	9	.273	5	-2	-0	-1	0.5
1973	Cle-A	0	2	.000	4	3	0	0	0	18	17	2	13	10	15.0	6.50	60	.250	.370	0	—	0	-5	-5	-0	-0.5
	Tex-A	2	6	.250	23	12	2	0	0	94^{1}	101	11	52	38	14.7	5.34	70	.275	.367	0	—	0	-16	-17	-0	-1.3
	Yr	2	8	.200	27	15	2	0	0	112^{1}	118	13	65	48	14.7	5.53	68	.271	.367	0	—	0	-21	-22	-0	-1.8
1974	Tex-A	0	0	—	1	0	0	0	0	2^{1}	3	2	3	1	23.1	19.29	18	.333	.500	0	—	0	-4	-4	0	0.1
1976	Cal-A	0	0	—	4	0	0	0	0	6	9	2	6	4	22.5	7.50	44	.310	.429	0	—	0	-3	-3	-0	0.2
	Mon-N	2	6	.250	32	7	1	0	0	91^{1}	93	6	33	72	12.6	4.14	90	.274	.342	2	.133	-0	-6	-4	0	-0.3
1977	Oak-A	1	0	1.000	6	0	0	0	0	18^{1}	17	2	10	4	13.3	3.93	102	.254	.351	0	—	0	0	0	0	0.1
Total	7	23	41	.359	136	84	7	1	1	613^{2}	604	82	323	390	13.8	4.56	82	.261	.355	26	.194	6	-71	-58	3	-3.6

● FRANK DUPEE

Dupee, Frank Oliver b: 4/29/1877, Monkton, Vt. d: 8/14/56, Portland, Me. TL, 6'1", 200 lbs. Deb: 8/24/01

YEAR	TM/L	W	L	PCT	G	GS	CG	SH	SV	IP	H	HR	BB	SO	RAT	ERA	ERA+	OAV	OOB	BH	AVG	PB	PR	/A	PD	TPI
1901	Chi-A	0	1	.000	1	1	0	0	0	0	0	0	3	0	—	∞	—	—	1.000	0	—	0	-3	-3	0	-0.2

● MIKE DUPREE

Dupree, Michael Dennis b: 5/29/53, Kansas City, Kan. BR/TR, 6'1", 185 lbs. Deb: 4/13/76

YEAR	TM/L	W	L	PCT	G	GS	CG	SH	SV	IP	H	HR	BB	SO	RAT	ERA	ERA+	OAV	OOB	BH	AVG	PB	PR	/A	PD	TPI
1976	SD-N	0	0	—	12	0	0	0	0	15^{2}	18	4	7	5	14.4	9.19	36	.286	.357	1	1.000	1	-10	-10	0	0.1

● ROBERTO DURAN

Duran, Roberto Alejandro b: 3/6/73, Moca, D.R. BL/TL, 6', 167 lbs. Deb: 7/6/97

YEAR	TM/L	W	L	PCT	G	GS	CG	SH	SV	IP	H	HR	BB	SO	RAT	ERA	ERA+	OAV	OOB	BH	AVG	PB	PR	/A	PD	TPI
1997	Det-A	0	0	—	13	0	0	0	0	10^{2}	7	0	15	11	21.1	7.59	60	.189	.455	0	—	0	-4	-4	-0	0.0
1998	Det-A	0	1	.000	18	0	0	0	0	15^{1}	9	0	17	12	16.4	5.87	80	.170	.389	0	—	0	-2	-2	0	-0.1
Total	2	0	1	.000	31	0	0	0	0	26	16	0	32	23	18.3	6.58	71	.178	.417	0	—	0	-6	-6	-0	-0.1

● KID DURBIN

Durbin, Blaine Alphonsus b: 9/10/1886, Lamar, Mo. d: 9/11/43, Kirkwood, Mo. BL/TL, 5'8", 155 lbs. Deb: 4/24/07 ♦

YEAR	TM/L	W	L	PCT	G	GS	CG	SH	SV	IP	H	HR	BB	SO	RAT	ERA	ERA+	OAV	OOB	BH	AVG	PB	PR	/A	PD	TPI
1907	Chi-N	0	1	.000	5	1	1	0	1	16^{2}	14	0	10	5	13.5	5.40	46	.233	.352	6	.333	1	-5	-5	0	-0.3

● RYNE DUREN

Duren, Rinold George b: 2/22/29, Cazenovia, Wis. BR/TR, 6'1", 195 lbs. Deb: 9/25/54

YEAR	TM/L	W	L	PCT	G	GS	CG	SH	SV	IP	H	HR	BB	SO	RAT	ERA	ERA+	OAV	OOB	BH	AVG	PB	PR	/A	PD	TPI
1954	Bal-A	0	0	—	1	0	0	0	0	2	3	0	1	2	18.0	9.00	40	.333	.400	0	—	0	-1	-1	-0	0.0
1957	KC-A	0	3	.000	14	6	0	0	1	42^{2}	37	4	30	37	14.6	5.27	75	.236	.365	1	.071	-1	-7	-6	0	-0.5
1958	*NY-A☆	6	4	.600	44	1	0	0	**20**	75^{2}	40	4	43	87	10.7	2.02	175	.157	.296	1	.077	0	15	13	0	2.5
1959	NY-A★	3	6	.333	41	0	0	0	14	76^{2}	49	6	43	96	11.2	1.88	194	.181	.301	0	.000	-1	17	15	-0	2.2
1960	*NY-A	3	4	.429	42	1	0	0	9	49	27	3	49	67	15.2	4.96	72	.160	.369	0	.000	-1	-6	-7	1	-1.3
1961	NY-A	0	1	.000	4	0	0	0	0	5	2	2	4	7	10.8	5.40	69	.125	.300	0	—	0	-1	-1	-0	-0.2
	LA-A☆	6	12	.333	40	14	1	1	2	99	87	13	75	108	15.0	5.18	87	.233	.366	1	.040	-2	-13	-7	-1	-1.5
	Yr	6	13	.316	44	14	1	1	2	104	89	15	79	115	14.8	5.19	86	.229	.363	1	.040	-2	-14	-8	-2	-1.7
1962	LA-A	2	9	.182	42	3	0	0	8	71^{1}	53	1	57	74	14.6	4.42	87	.206	.363	1	.067	-1	-4	-4	-1	-0.9
1963	Phi-N	6	2	.750	33	7	1	0	2	87^{1}	65	6	52	84	12.6	3.30	98	.210	.332	3	.143	1	-0	-1	-1	-0.1
1964	Phi-N	0	0	—	2	0	0	0	0	3	5	0	1	5	21.0	6.00	58	.357	.438	0	—	0	-1	-1	-0	0.0
	Cin-N	0	2	.000	26	0	0	0	1	43^{2}	41	1	15	39	12.2	2.89	125	.248	.322	0	.000	-0	3	4	-1	0.1
	Yr	0	2	.000	28	0	0	0	1	46^{2}	46	1	16	44	12.5	3.09	117	.256	.327	0	.000	-0	2	3	-1	0.1
1965	Phi-N	0	0	—	6	0	0	0	0	11	10	0	4	6	12.3	3.27	106	.270	.357	0	.000	-0	0	0	0	0.0
	Was-A	1	1	.500	16	0	0	0	0	23	24	0	18	18	17.6	6.65	52	.286	.429	0	—	0	-8	-8	-0	-0.7
Total	10	27	44	.380	311	32	2	1	57	589^{1}	443	40	392	630	13.4	3.83	98	.209	.344	7	.061	-5	-5	-6	-4	-0.4

● DON DURHAM

Durham, Donald Gary b: 3/21/49, Yosemite, Ky. BR/TR, 6', 170 lbs. Deb: 7/16/72

YEAR	TM/L	W	L	PCT	G	GS	CG	SH	SV	IP	H	HR	BB	SO	RAT	ERA	ERA+	OAV	OOB	BH	AVG	PB	PR	/A	PD	TPI
1972	StL-N	2	7	.222	10	8	1	0	0	47^{2}	42	1	22	35	12.1	4.34	78	.240	.325	7	.500	4	-5	-5	-1	-0.5
1973	Tex-A	0	4	.000	15	4	0	0	1	40^{1}	49	7	23	23	16.3	7.59	49	.304	.395	0	—	0	-17	-17	-1	-1.6
Total	2	2	11	.154	25	12	1	0	1	88	91	8	45	58	14.0	5.83	61	.271	.359	7	.500	4	-22	-22	-1	-2.1

● ED DURHAM

Durham, Edward Fant "Bull" b: 8/17/08, Chester, S.C. d: 4/27/76, Chester, S.C. BL/TR, 5'11", 170 lbs. Deb: 4/19/29

YEAR	TM/L	W	L	PCT	G	GS	CG	SH	SV	IP	H	HR	BB	SO	RAT	ERA	ERA+	OAV	OOB	BH	AVG	PB	PR	/A	PD	TPI
1929	Bos-A	1	0	1.000	14	1	0	0	0	22^{1}	34	2	14	6	19.3	9.27	46	.374	.457	0	.000	-0	-12	-12	-0	-0.5
1930	Bos-A	4	15	.211	33	12	6	1	1	140	144	9	43	28	12.2	4.69	98	.270	.326	4	.098	-4	-1	-1	-0	-0.6
1931	Bos-A	8	10	.444	38	15	7	2	0	165^{1}	175	9	50	53	12.5	4.25	101	.266	.322	3	.056	-6	2	1	-2	-0.6
1932	Bos-A	6	13	.316	34	22	4	0	0	175^{1}	187	13	49	52	12.3	3.80	118	.274	.327	7	.123	-3	13	14	1	1.0
1933	Chi-A	10	6	.625	24	21	6	0	0	138^{2}	137	12	46	65	12.2	4.48	95	.256	.320	10	.217	0	-3	-4	-1	-0.5
Total	5	29	44	.397	143	71	23	3	1	641^{2}	677	45	202	204	12.5	4.45	99	.271	.329	24	.119	-14	-0	-3	-3	-1.2

● JOHN DURHAM

Durham, John Garfield b: 10/7/1881, Douglass, Kan. d: 5/7/49, Coffeyville, Kan. BR/TR, 6', 175 lbs. Deb: 9/15/02

YEAR	TM/L	W	L	PCT	G	GS	CG	SH	SV	IP	H	HR	BB	SO	RAT	ERA	ERA+	OAV	OOB	BH	AVG	PB	PR	/A	PD	TPI
1902	Chi-A	1	1	.500	3	3	3	0	0	20	21	0	16	3	16.6	5.85	58	.269	.394	1	.067	-1	-5	-5	0	-0.5

● BULL DURHAM

Durham, Louis Raphael (b: Louis Raphael Staub) b: 6/27/1877, New Oxford, Pa. d: 6/28/60, Bentley, Kan. BR/TR, 5'10", Deb: 9/15/04

YEAR	TM/L	W	L	PCT	G	GS	CG	SH	SV	IP	H	HR	BB	SO	RAT	ERA	ERA+	OAV	OOB	BH	AVG	PB	PR	/A	PD	TPI
1904	Bro-N	2	0	1.000	2	2	1	0	0	11	10	0	5	1	12.3	3.27	84	.250	.333	1	.250	0	-1	-1	-0	-0.1
1907	Was-A	0	0	—	2	0	0	0	0	5	10	0	4	1	27.0	12.60	19	.417	.517	0	.000	-0	-6	-6	-0	0.0
1908	NY-N	0	0	—	1	0	0	0	0	2	2	0	1	2	13.5	9.00	27	.250	.333	0	—	0	-1	-1	-0	0.0
1909	NY-N	0	0	—	4	0	0	0	1	11	15	0	2	2	13.9	3.27	78	.326	.354	0	.000	-0	-1	-1	-0	-0.1
Total	4	2	0	1.000	9	2	1	0	1	29	37	0	12	6	15.5	5.28	49	.314	.382	1	.143	-0	-9	-9	-1	-0.2

● RICH DURNING

Durning, Richard Knott b: 10/10/1892, Louisville, Ky. d: 9/23/48, Castle Point, N.Y BL/TL, 6'2", 178 lbs. Deb: 4/16/17

YEAR	TM/L	W	L	PCT	G	GS	CG	SH	SV	IP	H	HR	BB	SO	RAT	ERA	ERA+	OAV	OOB	BH	AVG	PB	PR	/A	PD	TPI
1917	Bro-N	0	0	—	1	0	0	0	0	1	0	0	0	0	0.0	0.00	—	.000	.000	0	—	0	0	0	-0	0.0
1918	Bro-N	0	0	—	1	0	0	0	0	2	3	0	4	0	31.5	13.50	21	.375	.583	0	—	0	-2	-2	0	0.0
Total	2	0	0	—	2	0	0	0	0	3	3	0	4	0	21.0	9.00	31	.273	.467	0	—	0	-2	-2	0	0.0

● JESSE DURYEA

Duryea, James Newton "Cyclone Jim" b: 9/7/1859, Osage, Iowa d: 8/19/42, Algona, Iowa BR/TR, 5'10", 175 lbs. Deb: 4/20/1889

YEAR	TM/L	W	L	PCT	G	GS	CG	SH	SV	IP	H	HR	BB	SO	RAT	ERA	ERA+	OAV	OOB	BH	AVG	PB	PR	/A	PD	TPI
1889	Cin-a	32	19	.627	53	48	38	2	1	401	372	9	127	183	11.6	2.56	153	.238	.302	44	.272	6	**57**	**60**	0	6.7
1890	Cin-N	16	12	.571	33	32	29	2	0	274	270	11	60	108	11.1	2.92	122	.250	.294	15	.152	1	20	19	0	1.7
1891	Cin-N	1	9	.100	10	10	8	0	0	77	101	4	25	23	15.5	5.38	63	.305	.366	1	.031	-5	-17	-17	-0	-2.0
	StL-a	1	1	.500	3	3	2	0	0	24	19	0	10	13	10.9	3.38	125	.211	.290	4	.364	1	1	2	0	0.2
1892	Cin-N	2	5	.286	9	7	5	0	0	68	55	3	26	21	11.1	3.57	91	.212	.292	3	.111	-1	-2	-2	1	-0.2
	Was-N	3	11	.214	18	15	13	1	2	127	102	6	45	48	11.1	2.41	135	.211	.291	6	.120	-2	12	12	4	1.3

YEAR	TM/L	W	L	PCT	G	GS	CG	SH	SV	IP	H	HR	BB	SO	RAT	ERA	ERA+	OAV	OOB	BH	AVG	PB	PR	/A	PD	TPI
	Yr	5	16	.238	27	22	18	1	2	195	157	9	71	69	10.9	2.82	116	.211	.287	9	.117	-3	10	10	4	1.1
1893	Was-N	4	10	.286	17	15	9	0	0	117	182	8	56	20	19.3	7.54	61	.345	.420	13	.277	2	-37	-38	0	-2.9
Total	5	59	67	.468	143	130	104	5	3	1088	1101	41	349	416	12.5	3.45	109	.254	.318	86	.201	3	34	36	5	4.8
● ERV DUSAK	Dusak, Ervin Frank "Four Sack" b: 7/29/20, Chicago, Ill. d: 11/6/94, Glendale Heights, Ill. BR/TR, 6'2", 185 lbs. Deb: 9/18/41 ♦																									
1948	StL-N	0	0	—	1	0	0	0	0	1	0	0	1	0	9.0	0.00	—	.000	.250	65	.209	0	0	0	-0	0.0
1950	StL-N	0	2	.000	14	2	0	0	1	36^1	27	2	27	16	13.6	3.72	116	.211	.353	1	.083	-0	2	2	0	0.1
1951	StL-N	0	0	—	5	0	0	0	0	10	14	0	7	8	18.9	7.20	55	.333	.429	1	.500	1	-4	-4	0	0.2
	Pit-N	0	1	.000	3	1	0	0	0	6^2	10	2	9	2	27.0	12.15	35	.357	.526	12	.308	1	-6	-6	-0	-0.7
	Yr	0	1	.000	8	1	0	0	0	16^2	24	2	16	10	22.1	9.18	44	.343	.471	13	.317	2	-10	-9	-0	-0.5
Total	3	0	3	.000	23	3	0	0	1	54	51	4	44	26	16.2	5.33	79	.254	.393	251	.243	2	-8	-7	-0	-0.4
● CARL DUSER	Duser, Carl Robert b: 7/22/32, Hazleton, Pa. BL/TL, 6'1", 175 lbs. Deb: 9/15/56																									
1956	KC-A	1	1	.500	2	2	0	0	0	6	14	0	2	5	24.0	9.00	48	.452	.485	0	.000	-0	-3	-3	0	-0.8
1958	KC-A	0	0	—	1	0	0	0	0	2	5	0	1	0	27.0	4.50	87	.500	.545	0	—	0	-0	-0	-0	0.0
Total	2	1	1	.500	3	2	0	0	0	8	19	0	3	5	24.8	7.88	54	.463	.500	0	.000	-0	-3	-3	0	-0.8
● BOB DUSTAL	Dustal, Robert Andrew b: 9/28/35, Sayreville, N.J. BR/TR, 6', 172 lbs. Deb: 4/9/63																									
1963	Det-A	0	1	.000	7	0	0	0	0	6	10	0	5	4	22.5	9.00	42	.357	.455	0	—	0	-4	-4	1	-0.5
● MIKE DUVALL	Duvall, Michael Alan b: 10/11/74, Warrenton, Va. BR/TL, 6', 185 lbs. Deb: 9/22/98																									
1998	TB-A	0	0	—	3	0	0	0	0	4	4	0	2	1	13.5	6.75	73	.267	.353	0	—	0	-1	-1	0	-0.3
● BILL DUZEN	Duzen, William George b: 2/21/1870, Buffalo, N.Y. d: 3/11/44, Buffalo, N.Y. BR/TR, 5'11", 165 lbs. Deb: 9/21/1890																									
1890	Buf-P	0	2	.000	2	2	2	0	0	13	20	2	14	5	23.5	13.85	30	.339	.466	1	.250	1	-14	-14	-0	-1.1
● FRANK DWYER	Dwyer, John Francis b: 3/25/1868, Lee, Mass. d: 2/4/43, Pittsfield, Mass. BR/TR, 5'8", 145 lbs. Deb: 9/20/1888 MC																									
1888	Chi-N	4	1	.800	5	5	5	1	0	42	32	1	9	17	8.8	1.07	283	.198	.240	4	.190	-0	8	9	0	1.0
1889	Chi-N	16	13	.552	32	30	27	0	0	276	307	14	72	63	12.6	3.59	116	.273	.321	27	.200	-2	13	17	-2	1.1
1890	Chi-P	3	6	.333	12	6	6	0	1	69^1	98	4	25	17	16.0	6.23	70	.319	.370	14	.264	-0	-15	-15	1	-1.3
1891	Cin-a	13	19	.406	35	31	29	1	0	289	332	10	124	101	14.5	4.52	91	.279	.351	40	.284	2	-25	-13	1	-0.8
	Mil-a	6	4	.600	10	10	10	0	0	86	92	2	21	27	12.2	2.20	200	.264	.314	9	.225	-1	15	21	-0	1.9
	Yr	19	23	.452	45	41	39	1	0	375	424	12	145	128	13.8	3.98	105	.274	.337	49	.271	1	-11	8	1	1.1
1892	StL-N	2	8	.200	10	10	6	0	0	64	90	1	24	16	16.3	5.63	57	.319	.377	2	.080	-1	-17	-17	1	-2.1
	Cin-N	20	10	.667	34	28	25	3	1	268^1	262	6	49	47	10.6	2.31	141	.246	.282	21	.159	-4	29	28	-1	2.2
	Yr	22	18	.550	44	38	31	3	1	332^1	352	7	73	63	11.6	2.95	110	.261	.301	23	.146	-6	12	11	-1	0.1
1893	Cin-N	18	15	.545	37	30	28	1	**2**	287^1	332	17	93	53	13.5	4.13	116	.281	.336	24	.200	-3	17	21	3	1.8
1894	Cin-N	19	21	.475	45	39	34	1	1	348	471	27	106	49	15.3	5.07	110	.320	.371	46	.267	1	10	19	1	1.7
1895	Cin-N	18	15	.545	37	31	23	2	0	280^1	355	10	74	46	14.2	4.24	117	.304	.353	30	.265	2	17	23	-0	2.1
1896	Cin-N	24	11	.686	36	34	30	3	1	288^2	321	8	60	57	12.2	3.15	146	.279	.321	29	.264	4	39	47	-2	4.7
1897	Cin-N	18	13	.581	37	31	22	0	0	247^1	315	5	56	41	13.9	3.78	120	.307	.350	25	.266	0	15	21	-3	1.8
1898	Cin-N	16	10	.615	31	28	24	0	0	240	257	3	42	29	11.8	3.04	126	.272	.314	12	.141	-4	15	21	-2	1.4
1899	Cin-N	0	5	.000	5	5	2	0	0	32^2	48	1	9	2	16.0	5.51	71	.340	.384	4	.364	1	-6	-6	0	-0.6
Total	12	177	151	.540	366	318	271	12	6	2819	3312	109	764	565	13.3	3.84	115	.286	.336	287	.229	-7	114	178	-4	14.9
● BEN DYER	Dyer, Benjamin Franklin b: 2/13/1893, Chicago, Ill. d: 8/7/59, Kenosha, Wis. BR/TR, 5'11", 170 lbs. Deb: 5/23/14 ♦																									
1918	Det-A	0	0	—	2	0	0	0	0	1^2	0	0	0	0	0.0	0.00	—	.000	.000	5	.278	0	1	0	0	0.0
● EDDIE DYER	Dyer, Edwin Hawley b: 10/11/1900, Morgan City, La. d: 4/20/64, Houston, Tex. BL/TL, 5'11.5", 168 lbs. Deb: 7/8/22 M♦																									
1922	StL-N	0	0	—	2	0	0	0	0	3^2	7	0	0	3	17.2	2.45	157	.412	.412	1	.333	1	1	1	0	0.1
1923	StL-N	2	1	.667	4	3	2	1	0	22	30	0	5	7	14.7	4.09	95	.333	.375	12	.267	0	-0	-0	-0	0.0
1924	StL-N	8	11	.421	29	15	7	1	0	136^2	174	6	51	23	15.1	4.61	82	.331	.395	18	.237	1	-11	-13	1	-1.2
1925	StL-N	4	3	.571	27	5	1	0	3	82^1	93	4	24	25	13.6	4.15	104	.278	.340	3	.097	-2	1	2	0	-0.1
1926	StL-N	1	0	1.000	6	0	0	0	0	9^1	7	0	14	4	21.2	11.57	34	.219	.468	1	.500	0	-8	-8	0	-0.7
1927	StL-N	0	0	—	1	0	0	0	0	2	5	1	2	1	31.5	18.00	22	.500	.583	0	—	0	-3	-3	-0	0.0
Total	6	15	15	.500	69	23	10	2	3	256	316	11	96	63	14.9	4.75	84	.313	.380	35	.223	1	-21	-22	1	-1.9
● MIKE DYER	Dyer, Michael Lawrence b: 9/8/66, Upland, Cal. BR/TR, 6'3", 195 lbs. Deb: 6/29/89																									
1989	Min-A	4	7	.364	16	12	1	0	0	71	74	2	37	37	14.3	4.82	86	.273	.365	0	—	0	-7	-5	-1	-1.0
1994	Pit-N	1	1	.500	14	0	0	0	4	15^1	15	1	12	13	17.6	5.87	74	.268	.423	0	.000	-0	-3	-3	-0	-0.5
1995	Pit-N	4	5	.444	55	0	0	0	0	74^2	81	9	30	53	14.0	4.34	99	.281	.359	4	.571	1	-1	-0	1	0.2
1996	Mon-N	5	5	.500	70	1	0	0	2	75^2	79	7	34	51	14.0	4.40	98	.277	.364	0	.000	-1	-2	-1	1	-0.1
Total	4	14	18	.438	155	13	1	0	6	236^2	249	19	113	154	14.3	4.60	93	.277	.367	4	.267	1	-13	-9	0	-1.4
● JIMMY DYGERT	Dygert, James Henry "Sunny Jim" b: 7/5/1884, Utica, N.Y. d: 2/8/36, New Orleans, La. BR/TR, 5'10", 185 lbs. Deb: 9/8/05																									
1905	Phi-A	1	4	.200	6	3	2	0	0	35^1	41	2	11	24	13.8	4.33	61	.291	.351	4	.267	0	-7	-7	2	-0.7
1906	Phi-A	11	13	.458	35	25	15	4	0	213^2	175	1	91	106	11.6	2.70	101	.226	.316	13	.176	-0	-0	1	1	0.1
1907	Phi-A	21	8	.724	42	28	18	5	1	261^2	200	2	85	151	10.4	2.34	111	**.214**	.292	12	.128	-4	6	8	-1	0.3
1908	Phi-A	11	15	.423	41	28	15	5	1	238^2	184	3	97	164	11.0	2.87	89	.220	.309	6	.080	-6	-13	-8	3	-1.3
1909	Phi-A	9	5	.643	32	13	6	1	0	137^1	117	1	50	79	11.7	2.42	99	.242	.327	9	.205	0	1	-0	-1	-0.1
1910	Phi-A	4	4	.500	19	8	6	1	0	99^1	81	0	49	59	12.1	2.54	94	.231	.331	3	.083	-2	-0	-2	-2	-0.6
Total	6	57	49	.538	175	105	62	16	2	986	798	9	383	583	11.3	2.65	97	.227	.312	47	.139	-11	-13	-8	1	-2.3
● JIMMY DYKES	Dykes, James Joseph b: 11/10/1896, Philadelphia, Pa. d: 6/15/76, Philadelphia, Pa. BR/TR, 5'9", 185 lbs. Deb: 5/6/18 MC♦																									
1927	Phi-A	0	0	—	2	0	0	0	1	2	2	0	1	0	13.5	4.50	95	.333	.429	135	.324	1	-0	-0	-0	0.0
● RADHAMES DYKHOFF	Dykhoff, Radhames Alviro b: 9/27/74, Paradera, Aruba BL/TL, 6', 205 lbs. Deb: 6/7/98																									
1998	Bal-A	0	0	—	1	0	0	0	0	1	2	0	1	1	27.0	18.00	25	.400	.500	0	—	0	-1	-1	0	0.1
● ARNOLD EARLEY	Earley, Arnold Carl b: 6/4/33, Lincoln Park, Mich. BL/TL, 6'1", 200 lbs. Deb: 9/27/60																									
1960	Bos-A	0	1	.000	2	0	0	0	0	4	9	1	4	5	29.3	15.75	26	.429	.520	0	.000	0	-5	-5	-0	-0.9
1961	Bos-A	2	4	.333	33	0	0	0	7	49^2	42	3	34	44	13.8	3.99	105	.226	.345	0	.000	-1	0	1	0	0.1
1962	Bos-A	4	5	.444	38	3	0	0	5	68^1	76	8	46	59	16.2	5.80	71	.281	.388	2	.200	0	-14	-13	1	-1.6
1963	Bos-A	3	7	.300	53	4	0	0	1	115^2	124	13	43	97	13.6	4.75	80	.270	.343	5	.278	1	-14	-12	0	-0.9
1964	Bos-A	1	1	.500	25	3	1	0	1	50^1	51	3	18	45	12.5	2.68	144	.266	.332	1	.111	0	5	7	1	0.4
1965	Bos-A	0	1	.000	57	0	0	0	0	74^1	79	5	29	47	13.4	3.63	103	.271	.344	0	.000	-0	-1	1	-0	0.0
1966	Chi-N	2	1	.667	13	0	0	0	0	17^2	14	1	9	12	11.7	3.57	103	.226	.324	0	.000	-0	0	0	-1	-0.1
1967	Hou-N	0	0	—	2	0	0	0	0	1^1	5	1	1	1	40.5	27.00	12	.625	.667	0	—	0	-4	-4	0	0.0
Total	8	12	20	.375	223	10	1	0	14	381^1	400	35	184	310	14.1	4.48	87	.269	.354	8	.157	0	-33	-25	1	-3.0
● TOM EARLEY	Earley, Thomas Francis Aloysius b: 2/19/17, Roxbury, Mass. d: 4/5/88, Nantucket, Mass. BR/TR, 6', 180 lbs. Deb: 9/27/38																									
1938	Bos-N	1	0	1.000	2	1	1	0	0	11	8	2	1	4	8.2	3.27	105	.186	.222	0	.000	-1	1	0	-0	-0.1
1939	Bos-N	1	4	.200	14	2	0	0	1	40	49	1	19	9	15.7	4.72	78	.304	.385	3	.300	1	-4	-5	1	-0.4
1940	Bos-N	2	0	1.000	4	1	1	1	0	16^1	16	1	3	5	11.6	3.86	96	.267	.323	2	.400	1	-0	-0	-0	0.1
1941	Bos-N	6	8	.429	33	13	6	1	3	138^2	120	9	46	54	11.0	2.53	141	.233	.300	11	.234	1	17	16	-1	1.7
1942	Bos-N	6	11	.353	27	18	6	0	1	112^2	120	10	55	28	14.1	4.71	71	.276	.359	4	.118	-1	-18	-17	0	-2.4
1945	Bos-N	2	1	.667	11	2	1	0	0	41	36	4	19	4	12.1	4.61	83	.235	.320	3	.214	1	-4	-4	0	-0.2
Total	6	18	24	.429	91	37	15	2	5	359^2	349	27	143	104	12.5	3.78	94	.256	.330	23	.202	2	-7	-9	-0	-1.3
● BILL EARLEY	Earley, William Albert b: 1/30/56, Cincinnati, Ohio BR/TL, 6'4", 200 lbs. Deb: 9/22/86																									
1986	StL-N	0	0	—	3	0	0	0	0	3	0	0	2	2	6.0	0.00	—	.000	.182	0	—	0	1	1	-0	0.0

● GEORGE EARNSHAW Earnshaw, George Livingston "Moose" b: 2/15/1900, New York, N.Y. d: 12/1/76, Little Rock, Ark. BR/TR, 6'4", 210 lbs. Deb: 6/3/28 C

YEAR	TM/L	W	L	PCT	G	GS	CG	SH	SV	IP	H	HR	BB	SO	RAT	ERA	ERA+	OAV	OOB	BH	AVG	PB	PR	/A	PD	TPI
1928	Phi-A	7	7	.500	26	22	7	3	1	158^1	143	7	100	117	13.9	3.81	105	.240	.351	14	.246	1	4	4	-1	0.2
1929	*Phi-A	**24**	8	.750	44	33	13	3	1	254^2	233	8	125	149	12.8	3.29	129	**.241**	.331	15	.172	-2	27	27	-3	2.4
1930	*Phi-A	22	13	.629	49	39	20	**3**	2	296	299	20	139	193	13.3	4.44	105	.266	.347	26	.228	1	7	8	-1	0.7
1931	*Phi-A	21	7	.750	43	30	23	3	6	281^2	255	16	75	152	10.6	3.67	122	.236	.288	30	.263	6	22	26	0	2.9
1932	Phi-A	19	13	.594	36	33	21	1	0	245^1	262	28	94	109	13.2	4.77	95	.270	.336	26	.286	4	-8	-7	1	-0.3
1933	Phi-A	5	10	.333	21	18	4	0	0	117^2	153	8	58	37	16.2	5.97	72	.311	.385	8	.182	-0	-22	-22	1	-2.2
1934	Chi-A	14	11	.560	33	30	16	2	0	227	242	28	104	97	13.9	4.52	105	.270	.349	16	.203	-0	-1	5	-1	0.5
1935	Chi-A	1	2	.333	3	3	0	0	0	18	26	2	11	8	18.5	9.00	51	.342	.425	2	.286	0	-9	-9	-0	-1.0
	Bro-N	8	12	.400	25	22	6	2	0	166	175	14	53	72	12.4	4.12	96	.270	.325	13	.217	1	-2	-3	0	-0.2
1936	Bro-N	4	9	.308	19	13	4	1	1	93	113	7	30	40	14.1	5.32	78	.297	.354	8	.242	0	-13	-12	-0	-1.5
	StL-N	2	1	.667	20	6	1	0	1	57^2	80	4	20	28	16.1	6.40	62	.333	.392	4	.222	-0	-15	-16	1	-0.7
	Yr	6	10	.375	39	19	5	1	2	150^2	193	11	50	68	14.7	5.73	71	.310	.364	12	.235	0	-29	-28	1	-2.2
Total	9	127	93	.577	319	249	115	18	12	1915^1	1981	142	809	1002	13.2	4.38	100	.265	.339	162	.230	9	-10	0	-2	0.8

● LOGAN EASLEY Easley, Kenneth Logan b: 11/4/61, Salt Lake City, Utah BR/TR, 6'1", 185 lbs. Deb: 4/9/87

YEAR	TM/L	W	L	PCT	G	GS	CG	SH	SV	IP	H	HR	BB	SO	RAT	ERA	ERA+	OAV	OOB	BH	AVG	PB	PR	/A	PD	TPI
1987	Pit-N	1	1	.500	17	0	0	0	1	26^1	23	5	17	21	14.0	5.47	75	.242	.363	0	.000	-0	-4	-4	1	-0.2
1989	Pit-N	1	0	1.000	10	0	0	0	1	12^1	8	1	7	6	11.7	4.38	77	.190	.320	0	.000	-0	-1	-1	-0	-0.2
Total	2	2	1	.667	27	0	0	0	2	38^2	31	6	24	27	13.3	5.12	75	.226	.350	0	.000	-0	-5	-5	1	-0.4

● MAL EASON Eason, Malcolm Wayne "Kid" b: 3/13/1879, Brookville, Pa. d: 4/16/70, Douglas, Ariz. BR/TR, 6', 175 lbs. Deb: 10/1/00 U

YEAR	TM/L	W	L	PCT	G	GS	CG	SH	SV	IP	H	HR	BB	SO	RAT	ERA	ERA+	OAV	OOB	BH	AVG	PB	PR	/A	PD	TPI
1900	Chi-N	1	0	1.000	1	1	1	0	0	9	9	0	3	2	12.0	1.00	361	.257	.316	0	.000	-1	3	3	-0	0.2
1901	Chi-N	8	17	.320	27	25	23	1	0	220^2	246	9	60	68	13.0	3.59	90	.280	.335	12	.138	-5	-7	-9	-2	-1.5
1902	Chi-N	1	1	.500	2	2	2	0	0	18	21	0	2	4	11.5	1.00	270	.292	.311	1	.200	0	4	3	0	0.5
	Bos-N	9	12	.429	27	27	20	2	0	213^1	249	4	61	51	13.6	2.91	97	.291	.347	6	.083	-6	-3	-2	-1	-0.9
	Yr	10	13	.435	29	29	22	2	0	231^1	270	4	63	55	13.4	2.76	102	.291	.344	7	.091	-6	0	1	-0	-0.4
1903	Det-A	2	5	.286	7	6	6	1	0	56^1	60	1	19	21	13.1	3.36	87	.271	.337	2	.100	-2	-2	-3	1	-0.3
1905	Bro-N	5	21	.192	27	27	20	3	0	207	230	5	72	64	13.3	4.30	67	.292	.355	14	.173	-1	-30	-32	1	-3.5
1906	Bro-N	10	17	.370	34	26	18	3	1	227	212	1	74	64	11.7	3.25	78	.256	.323	8	.091	-4	-16	-18	1	-2.5
Total	6	36	73	.330	125	114	90	10	1	951^1	1027	20	291	274	12.9	3.42	84	.279	.339	43	.121	-19	-51	-58	2	-8.0

● CARL EAST East, Carlton William b: 8/27/1894, Marietta, Ga. d: 1/15/53, Whitesburg, Ga. BL/TR, 6'2", 178 lbs. Deb: 8/24/15 ♦

YEAR	TM/L	W	L	PCT	G	GS	CG	SH	SV	IP	H	HR	BB	SO	RAT	ERA	ERA+	OAV	OOB	BH	AVG	PB	PR	/A	PD	TPI
1915	StL-A	0	0	—	1	1	0	0	0	3^1	6	0	2	1	21.6	16.20	18	.400	.471	0	.000	-0	-5	-5	-0	0.0

● HUGH EAST East, Gordon Hugh b: 7/7/19, Birmingham, Ala. d: 11/2/81, Charleston, S.C. BR/TR, 6'2", 185 lbs. Deb: 9/13/41

YEAR	TM/L	W	L	PCT	G	GS	CG	SH	SV	IP	H	HR	BB	SO	RAT	ERA	ERA+	OAV	OOB	BH	AVG	PB	PR	/A	PD	TPI
1941	NY-N	1	1	.500	2	2	0	0	0	15^2	19	0	9	4	16.1	3.45	107	.297	.384	2	.222	0	0	0	-0	0.1
1942	NY-N	0	2	.000	4	1	0	0	0	7^1	15	1	7	2	27.0	9.82	34	.429	.524	1	.500	2	-5	-5	0	-1.0
1943	NY-N	1	3	.250	13	5	1	0	0	40^1	51	4	25	21	17.0	5.36	64	.298	.388	1	.077	-1	-9	-9	-1	-0.9
Total	3	2	6	.250	19	8	1	0	0	63^1	85	5	41	27	17.9	5.40	65	.315	.405	4	.167	1	-14	-13	-1	-1.8

● JAMIE EASTERLY Easterly, James Morris b: 2/17/53, Houston, Tex. BL/TL, 5'9", 180 lbs. Deb: 4/6/74

YEAR	TM/L	W	L	PCT	G	GS	CG	SH	SV	IP	H	HR	BB	SO	RAT	ERA	ERA+	OAV	OOB	BH	AVG	PB	PR	/A	PD	TPI
1974	Atl-N	0	0	—	3	0	0	0	0	2^2	6	0	4	0	33.8	16.88	22	.400	.526	0	—	0	-4	-4	0	0.0
1975	Atl-N	2	9	.182	21	13	0	0	0	68^2	73	5	42	34	15.3	4.98	76	.275	.379	1	.056	-2	-10	-9	-1	-1.5
1976	Atl-N	1	1	.500	4	4	0	0	0	22	23	0	13	11	14.7	4.91	77	.280	.379	1	.111	-0	-3	-3	0	-0.3
1977	Atl-N	2	4	.333	22	5	0	0	1	58^2	72	5	30	37	16.1	6.14	72	.303	.387	4	.267	1	-15	-11	-1	-1.1
1978	Atl-N	3	6	.333	37	6	0	0	1	78	91	9	45	42	15.9	5.65	72	.299	.393	4	.211	0	-18	-14	0	-1.5
1979	Atl-N	0	0	—	4	0	0	0	0	2^2	7	0	3	3	33.8	13.50	30	.467	.556	0	—	0	-3	-3	0	0.0
1981	*Mil-A	3	3	.500	44	0	0	0	4	62	46	0	34	31	11.6	3.19	107	.219	.328	0	—	0	3	2	0	0.2
1982	Mil-A	0	2	.000	28	0	0	0	2	30^2	39	6	15	16	15.8	4.70	81	.312	.386	0	—	0	-2	-3	1	0.0
1983	Mil-A	0	1	.000	12	0	0	0	1	11^2	14	0	10	6	20.1	3.86	97	.350	.500	0	.000	-0	0	-0	-0	0.0
	Cle-A	4	2	.667	41	0	0	0	3	57	69	4	22	39	14.7	3.63	117	.309	.377	0	—	0	3	4	0	0.4
	Yr	4	3	.571	53	0	0	0	4	68^2	83	4	32	45	15.3	3.67	113	.312	.390	0	.000	-0	3	4	0	0.4
1984	Cle-A	3	1	.750	26	1	0	0	2	69^1	74	3	23	42	12.7	3.38	121	.273	.332	0	—	0	5	5	0	0.2
1985	Cle-A	4	1	.800	50	7	0	0	0	98^2	96	9	53	58	14.0	3.92	105	.264	.363	0	—	0	2	2	-0	0.2
1986	Cle-A	0	2	.000	13	0	0	0	0	17^2	27	3	12	9	19.9	7.64	54	.365	.453	0	—	0	-7	-7	-0	-0.6
1987	Cle-A	1	1	.500	16	0	0	0	0	31^2	26	4	13	22	11.4	4.55	99	.218	.301	0	—	0	-0	-0	0	0.0
Total	13	23	33	.411	321	36	0	0	14	611^1	663	48	319	350	14.7	4.62	87	.283	.373	10	.161	-1	-49	-40	-0	-4.0

● JACK EASTON Easton, John S. b: 2/28/1867, Bridgeport, Ohio d: 11/28/03, Steubenville, Ohio Deb: 9/23/1889

YEAR	TM/L	W	L	PCT	G	GS	CG	SH	SV	IP	H	HR	BB	SO	RAT	ERA	ERA+	OAV	OOB	BH	AVG	PB	PR	/A	PD	TPI
1889	Col-a	1	0	1.000	4	1	1	0	1	18	13	0	21	7	18.5	3.50	104	.197	.411	0	.000	-1	1	0	-0	-0.1
1890	Col-a	15	14	.517	37	29	23	0	1	255^2	213	4	125	147	12.6	3.52	102	.220	.321	19	.178	0	10	2	1	0.3
1891	Col-a	5	10	.333	18	16	13	0	0	135^1	145	3	59	52	14.6	4.52	77	.265	.352	15	.238	2	-12	-16	1	-1.1
	StL-a	3	2	.600	7	6	4	0	0	47^2	48	3	23	22	14.2	5.10	83	.253	.346	5	.179	-1	-7	-5	-2	-0.6
	Col-a	0	2	.000	2	2	2	0	0	15	15	2	4	13	12.6	3.60	96	.250	.318	0	.000	-1	0	-0	-1	-0.1
	Yr	8	14	.364	27	24	19	0	0	198	208	8	86	87	13.5	4.59	79	.255	.327	20	.196	-0	-19	-21	-1	-1.8
1892	StL-N	2	0	1.000	5	2	2	0	0	31	38	2	26	4	19.5	6.39	50	.290	.419	3	.176	-0	-11	-11	0	-0.6
1894	Pit-N	0	1	.000	3	1	1	0	0	19^2	26	0	4	1	15.1	4.12	127	.313	.367	0	.000	-1	3	2	-1	-0.1
Total	5	26	29	.473	76	57	46	0	2	522^1	498	14	262	246	14.0	4.12	89	.243	.343	42	.176	-2	-16	-27	-1	-2.3

● RAWLY EASTWICK Eastwick, Rawlins Jackson b: 10/24/50, Camden, N.J. BR/TR, 6'3", 180 lbs. Deb: 9/12/74

YEAR	TM/L	W	L	PCT	G	GS	CG	SH	SV	IP	H	HR	BB	SO	RAT	ERA	ERA+	OAV	OOB	BH	AVG	PB	PR	/A	PD	TPI
1974	Cin-N	0	0	—	8	0	0	0	2	17^2	12	1	5	14	8.7	2.04	171	.188	.246	0	.000	-0	3	3	-0	0.0
1975	*Cin-N	5	3	.625	58	0	0	0	**22**	90	77	6	25	61	10.4	2.60	138	.229	.287	1	.067	-1	10	10	-1	1.1
1976	*Cin-N	11	5	.688	71	0	0	0	**26**	107^2	93	3	27	70	10.2	2.09	168	.232	.284	0	.000	-2	17	17	-2	3.1
1977	Cin-N	2	2	.500	23	0	0	0	7	43^1	40	3	8	17	10.0	2.91	135	.244	.279	1	.167	-0	5	5	-1	0.5
	StL-N	3	7	.300	41	1	0	0	4	53^2	74	6	21	30	15.9	4.70	82	.332	.389	2	.400	1	-5	-5	-1	-0.9
	Yr	5	9	.357	64	1	0	0	11	97	114	9	29	47	13.3	3.90	100	.295	.344	3	.273	1	0	-0	-2	-0.4
1978	NY-A	2	1	.667	8	0	0	0	0	24^2	22	2	4	13	9.9	3.28	110	.232	.270	0	—	0	1	1	-0	0.2
	*Phi-N	2	1	.667	22	0	0	0	0	40^1	31	5	18	14	10.9	4.02	89	.209	.295	0	.000	-0	-2	-2	-1	-0.2
1979	Phi-N	3	6	.333	51	0	0	0	6	82^2	90	8	25	47	12.6	4.90	78	.284	.338	0	.000	-1	-11	-10	-2	-1.4
1980	KC-A	0	1	.000	14	0	0	0	0	22	37	2	8	5	19.2	5.32	76	.363	.420	0	—	0	-3	-3	1	-0.1
1981	Chi-N	0	1	.000	30	0	0	0	1	43^1	43	2	15	24	12.0	2.28	162	.264	.326	0	.000	-0	6	7	0	0.2
Total	8	28	27	.509	326	1	0	0	68	525^1	519	38	156	295	11.7	3.31	112	.258	.314	4	.071	-3	22	22	-7	2.5

● CRAIG EATON Eaton, Craig b: 9/7/54, Glendale, Ohio BR/TR, 5'11", 175 lbs. Deb: 9/5/79

YEAR	TM/L	W	L	PCT	G	GS	CG	SH	SV	IP	H	HR	BB	SO	RAT	ERA	ERA+	OAV	OOB	BH	AVG	PB	PR	/A	PD	TPI
1979	KC-A	0	0	—	5	0	0	0	0	10	8	0	3	4	9.9	2.70	158	.222	.282	0	—	0	2	2	0	0.0

● ZEB EATON Eaton, Zebulon Vance "Red" b: 2/2/20, Cooleemee, N.C. d: 12/17/89, W.Palm Beach, Fla. BR/TR, 5'10", 185 lbs. Deb: 4/18/44

YEAR	TM/L	W	L	PCT	G	GS	CG	SH	SV	IP	H	HR	BB	SO	RAT	ERA	ERA+	OAV	OOB	BH	AVG	PB	PR	/A	PD	TPI
1944	Det-A	0	0	—	6	0	0	0	0	15^2	19	2	8	4	15.5	5.74	62	.322	.403	1	.100	-1	-4	-4	-0	-0.1
1945	*Det-A	4	2	.667	17	3	0	0	0	53^1	48	0	40	15	15.4	4.05	87	.247	.384	8	.250	2	-4	-3	0	-0.1
Total	2	4	2	.667	23	3	0	0	0	69	67	2	48	19	15.4	4.43	80	.265	.388	9	.214	2	-8	-7	-0	-0.2

● GARY EAVE Eave, Gary Louis b: 7/22/63, Monroe, La. BR/TR, 6'4", 200 lbs. Deb: 4/12/88

YEAR	TM/L	W	L	PCT	G	GS	CG	SH	SV	IP	H	HR	BB	SO	RAT	ERA	ERA+	OAV	OOB	BH	AVG	PB	PR	/A	PD	TPI
1988	Atl-N	0	0	—	5	0	0	0	0	5	7	0	3	0	18.0	9.00	41	.333	.417	0	—	0	-3	-3	-0	0.0
1989	Atl-N	2	0	1.000	3	3	0	0	0	20^2	15	0	12	9	12.2	1.31	279	.200	.318	0	.000	-1	5	5	-1	0.4
1990	Sea-A	0	3	.000	8	5	0	0	0	30	27	5	20	16	14.7	4.20	94	.241	.366	0	—	0	-1	-1	0	-0.1
Total	3	2	3	.400	16	8	0	0	0	55^2	49	5	35	25	14.1	3.56	107	.236	.354	0	.000	-1	1	2	-1	0.3

● VALLIE EAVES Eaves, Vallie Ennis "Chief" b: 9/6/11, Allen, Okla. d: 4/19/60, Norman, Okla. BR/TR, 6'2.5", 180 lbs. Deb: 9/12/35

YEAR	TM/L	W	L	PCT	G	GS	CG	SH	SV	IP	H	HR	BB	SO	RAT	ERA	ERA+	OAV	OOB	BH	AVG	PB	PR	/A	PD	TPI
1935	Phi-A	1	2	.333	3	3	1	0	0	14	12	0	15	6	17.4	5.14	88	.240	.415	0	.000	-1	-1	-1	-0	-0.2
1939	Chi-A	0	1	.000	2	1	1	0	0	11^2	11	1	8	5	15.4	4.63	102	.250	.377	2	.333	0	-0	0	-0	0.0
1940	Chi-A	0	2	.000	5	3	0	0	0	18^2	22	2	24	11	22.7	6.75	66	.301	.480	0	.000	-1	-5	-5	-1	-0.5

YEAR	TM/L	W	L	PCT	G	GS	CG	SH	SV	IP	H	HR	BB	SO	RAT	ERA	ERA+	OAV	OOB	BH	AVG	PB	PR	/A	PD	TPI
1941	Chi-N	3	3	.500	12	7	4	0	0	58^{2}	56	4	21	24	12.3	3.53	99	.253	.327	2	.100	-1	1	-0	-1	-0.3
1942	Chi-N	0	0	—	2	0	0	0	0	3	4	0	2	0	21.0	9.00	36	.308	.438	0	—	0	-2	-2	-0	0.0
Total	5	4	8	.333	24	14	6	0	0	106	105	7	70	46	15.4	4.58	86	.262	.379	4	.114	-3	-7	-8	-3	-1.0
● EDDIE EAYRS	Eayrs, Edwin b: 11/10/1890, Blackstone, Mass. d: 11/30/69, Warwick, R.I. BL/TL, 5′7″, 160 lbs. Deb: 6/30/13 ♦																									
1913	Pit-N	0	0	—	2	0	0	0	0	8	8	0	6	5	15.8	2.25	134	.267	.389	1	.167	-0	1	1	-0	0.0
1920	Bos-N	1	2	.333	7	3	0	0	0	26^{1}	36	1	12	7	17.1	5.47	56	.346	.424	80	.328	2	-7	-7	1	-0.5
1921	Bos-N	0	0	—	2	0	0	0	0	4^{2}	9	0	9	1	34.7	17.36	21	.391	.563	1	.067	-2	-7	-7	-0	-0.2
Total	3	1	2	.333	11	3	0	0	0	39	53	1	27	13	18.9	6.23	50	.338	.441	83	.306	0	-13	-13	0	-0.7
● HARRY ECCLES	Eccles, Harry Josiah "Bugs" b: 7/9/1893, Kennedy, N.Y. d: 6/2/55, Jamestown, N.Y. BL/TL, 6′2″, 170 lbs. Deb: 9/13/15																									
1915	Phi-A	0	1	.000	5	1	0	0	1	21	18	2	6	13	10.3	4.71	62	.240	.296	1	.167	-0	-4	-4	-1	-0.3
● DENNIS ECKERSLEY	Eckersley, Dennis Lee b: 10/3/54, Oakland, Cal. BR/TR, 6′2″, 190 lbs. Deb: 4/12/75																									
1975	Cle-A	13	7	.650	34	24	6	2	2	186^{2}	147	16	90	152	11.8	2.60	145	.215	.312	0	—	0	24	24	-3	2.3
1976	Cle-A	13	12	.520	36	30	9	3	1	199^{1}	155	13	78	200	10.7	3.43	102	.214	.295	0	—	0	2	1	-1	0.1
1977	Cle-A★	14	13	.519	33	33	12	3	0	247^{1}	214	31	54	191	10.0	3.53	112	.231	**.278**	0	—	0	15	11	-3	0.9
1978	Bos-A	20	8	.714	35	35	16	3	0	268^{1}	258	30	71	162	11.3	2.99	138	.251	.304	0	—	0	23	34	-2	2.8
1979	Bos-A	17	10	.630	33	33	17	2	0	246^{2}	234	29	59	150	10.9	2.99	**148**	.250	.298	0	—	0	34	**39**	1	4.0
1980	Bos-A	12	14	.462	30	30	8	0	0	197^{2}	188	25	44	121	10.7	4.28	99	.248	.291	0	—	0	-5	-1	-1	-0.4
1981	Bos-A	9	8	.529	23	23	8	2	0	154	160	9	35	79	11.6	4.27	91	.267	.310	0	—	0	-10	-7	-1	-0.8
1982	Bos-A★	13	13	.500	33	33	11	3	0	224^{1}	228	31	43	127	11.0	3.73	115	.261	.297	0	—	0	9	14	-1	1.2
1983	Bos-A	9	13	.409	28	28	2	0	0	176^{1}	223	27	39	77	13.7	5.61	77	.303	.343	0	—	0	-30	-25	-1	-2.7
1984	Bos-A	4	4	.500	9	9	2	0	0	64^{2}	71	10	13	33	11.8	5.01	83	.284	.322	0	—	0	-7	-6	1	-0.9
	*Chi-N	10	8	.556	24	24	2	0	0	160^{1}	152	11	36	81	10.8	3.03	129	.250	.296	6	.109	-3	10	16	1	1.5
1985	Chi-N	11	7	.611	25	25	6	2	0	169^{1}	145	15	19	117	8.9	3.08	129	.229	.255	7	.125	0	10	17	0	1.8
1986	Chi-N	6	11	.353	33	32	1	0	0	201	226	21	43	137	12.2	4.57	88	.285	.324	11	.159	1	-19	-12	-0	-0.8
1987	Oak-A	6	8	.429	54	2	0	0	16	115^{2}	99	11	17	113	9.3	3.03	136	.228	.262	0	—	0	18	14	-1	2.0
1988	*Oak-A★	4	2	.667	60	0	0	0	**45**	72^{2}	52	5	11	70	7.9	2.35	161	.198	.233	0	—	0	13	12	-1	2.1
1989	*Oak-A	4	0	1.000	51	0	0	0	33	57^{2}	32	5	3	55	5.6	1.56	236	.162	.178	0	—	0	15	14	-0	2.4
1990	*Oak-A★	4	2	.667	63	0	0	0	48	73^{1}	41	2	4	73	5.5	0.61	605	.160	.172	0	—	0	27	25	-2	4.7
1991	Oak-A★	5	4	.556	67	0	0	0	43	76	60	11	9	87	8.3	2.96	129	.208	.235	0	—	0	10	7	0	1.6
1992	*Oak-A★	7	1	.875	69	0	0	0	**51**	80	62	5	11	93	8.3	1.91	196	.211	.242	0	—	0	18	16	1	3.5
1993	Oak-A	2	4	.333	64	0	0	0	36	67	67	7	13	80	11.0	4.16	98	.261	.301	0	—	0	1	-1	-1	0.0
1994	Oak-A	5	4	.556	45	0	0	0	19	44^{1}	49	5	13	47	12.8	4.26	104	.275	.328	0	—	0	3	1	-1	0.5
1995	Oak-A	4	6	.400	52	0	0	0	29	50^{1}	53	5	11	40	11.6	4.83	93	.269	.311	0	—	0	-1	-2	-0	-0.3
1996	*StL-N	0	6	.000	63	0	0	0	30	60	65	8	6	49	11.3	3.30	127	.274	.304	0	.000	-0	6	6	-1	1.0
1997	StL-N	1	5	.167	57	0	0	0	36	53	49	9	8	45	10.0	3.91	106	.238	.273	0	—	0	2	1	-1	0.3
1998	*Bos-A	4	1	.800	50	0	0	0	1	39^{2}	46	6	8	22	12.7	4.76	97	.291	.333	0	—	0	-1	-1	-1	-0.1
Total	24	197	171	.535	1071	361	100	20	390	3285^{2}	3076	347	738	2401	10.7	3.50	116	.246	.292	24	.133	-1	164	202	-16	26.7
● AL ECKERT	Eckert, Albert George "Obbie" b: 5/17/06, Milwaukee, Wis. d: 4/20/74, Milwaukee, Wis. BL/TL, 5′10″, 174 lbs. Deb: 4/21/30																									
1930	Cin-N	0	1	.000	2	1	0	0	0	5	7	0	4	1	19.8	7.20	67	.304	.407	0	.000	-0	-1	-1	0	-0.2
1931	Cin-N	0	1	.000	14	1	0	0	0	18^{2}	26	3	9	5	16.9	9.16	41	.325	.393	1	.333	0	-11	-11	-0	-0.5
1935	StL-N	0	0	—	2	0	0	0	0	3	7	0	1	1	24.0	12.00	34	.467	.500	0	—	0	-3	-3	-0	0.0
Total	3	0	2	.000	18	2	0	0	0	26^{2}	40	3	14	7	18.2	9.11	44	.339	.409	1	.250	0	-15	-15	0	-0.7
● CHARLIE ECKERT	Eckert, Charles William "Buzz" b: 8/8/1897, Philadelphia, Pa. d: 8/22/86, Trevose, Pa. BR/TR, 5′10.5″, 165 lbs. Deb: 9/18/19																									
1919	Phi-A	0	1	.000	2	1	1	0	0	16	17	1	3	6	11.3	3.94	87	.270	.303	1	.167	-0	-1	-1	0	-0.1
1920	Phi-A	0	0	—	2	0	0	0	0	5^{2}	8	0	1	1	15.9	4.76	84	.421	.476	0	.000	-0	-1	-0	-0	-0.1
1922	Phi-A	0	2	.000	21	0	0	0	0	50	61	7	23	15	15.3	4.68	91	.319	.395	1	.091	-1	-4	-2	2	-0.1
Total	3	0	3	.000	25	1	1	0	0	71^{2}	86	8	27	22	14.4	4.52	90	.315	.381	2	.111	-2	-5	-4	1	-0.3
● CHRIS EDDY	Eddy, Christopher Mark b: 11/27/69, Dallas, Tex. BL/TL, 6′3″, 200 lbs. Deb: 4/26/95																									
1995	Oak-A	0	0	—	6	0	0	0	0	3^{2}	7	0	2	2	27.0	7.36	61	.438	.550	0	—	0	-1	-1	0	0.3
● DON EDDY	Eddy, Donald Eugene b: 10/25/46, Mason City, Iowa BR/TL, 5′11″, 170 lbs. Deb: 9/7/70																									
1970	Chi-A	0	0	—	7	0	0	0	0	11^{2}	10	0	6	9	12.3	2.31	168	.244	.340	0	—	0	2	2	0	0.0
1971	Chi-A	0	2	.000	22	0	0	0	0	22^{2}	19	3	19	14	15.1	2.38	151	.232	.376	1	1.000	1	3	3	-1	0.3
Total	2	0	2	.000	29	0	0	0	0	34^{1}	29	3	25	23	14.2	2.36	157	.236	.365	1	1.000	1	5	5	-1	0.3
● STEVE EDDY	Eddy, Steven Allen b: 8/21/57, Sterling, Ill. BR/TR, 6′2″, 185 lbs. Deb: 6/13/79																									
1979	Cal-A	1	1	.500	7	4	0	0	0	32^{1}	36	1	20	7	16.1	4.73	86	.290	.397	0	—	0	-2	-2	0	0.0
● JOE EDELEN	Edelen, Benny Joe b: 9/16/55, Durant, Okla. BR/TR, 6′, 165 lbs. Deb: 4/18/81																									
1981	StL-N	1	0	1.000	13	0	0	0	0	17^{1}	29	2	3	10	17.1	9.35	38	.367	.398	1	.333	0	-11	-11	-0	-0.6
	Cin-N	1	0	1.000	5	0	0	0	0	12^{2}	5	1	0	5	3.6	0.71	500	.128	.128	0	.000	-0	4	4	-1	0.2
	Yr	2	0	1.000	18	0	0	0	0	30	34	3	3	15	11.1	5.70	62	.283	.301	1	.200	0	-7	-7	-1	-0.4
1982	Cin-N	0	0	—	9	0	0	0	0	15^{1}	22	2	8	11	17.6	8.80	42	.344	.417	1	.500	0	-9	-9	-0	0.0
Total	2	2	0	1.000	27	0	0	0	0	45^{1}	56	5	11	26	13.5	6.75	53	.308	.351	2	.286	0	-16	-16	-1	-0.4
● ED EDELEN	Edelen, Edward Joseph "Doc" b: 3/16/12, Bryantown, Md. d: 2/1/82, LaPlata, Md. BR/TR, 6′, 191 lbs. Deb: 8/20/32																									
1932	Was-A	0	0	—	2	0	0	0	0	1	0	0	6	0	54.0	27.00	16	.000	.600	0	—	0	-3	-3	-0	0.0
● JOHN EDELMAN	Edelman, John Rogers b: 7/27/35, Philadelphia, Pa. BR/TR, 6′3″, 185 lbs. Deb: 6/2/55																									
1955	Mil-N	0	0	—	5	0	0	0	0	5^{2}	7	0	8	3	23.8	11.12	34	.304	.484	0	—	0	-4	-5	0	0.0
● CHARLIE EDEN	Eden, Charles M. b: 1/18/1855, Lexington, Ky. d: 9/17/20, Cincinnati, Ohio BL/TL, 168 lbs. Deb: 8/17/1877 ♦																									
1884	Pit-a	0	1	.000	2	1	1	0	0	12	12	1	3	3	12.0	6.00	56	.255	.314	33	.270	1	-4	-4	-1	-0.2
1885	Pit-a	1	2	.333	4	1	0	0	0	15^{2}	22	0	3	5	14.4	5.17	62	.314	.342	103	.254	1	-3	-3	-1	-0.5
Total	2	1	3	.250	6	2	1	0	0	27^{2}	34	1	6	8	13.3	5.53	59	.291	.331	244	.261	1	-7	-7	-1	-0.7
● KEN EDENFIELD	Edenfield, Kenneth Edward b: 3/18/67, Jesup, Ga. BR/TR, 6′1″, 165 lbs. Deb: 5/11/95																									
1995	Cal-A	0	0	—	7	0	0	0	0	12^{2}	15	1	5	6	14.2	4.26	110	.300	.364	0	—	0	1	1	-0	0.0
1996	Cal-A	0	0	—	2	0	0	0	0	4^{1}	10	2	2	4	27.0	10.38	48	.435	.500	0	—	0	-3	-3	0	0.0
Total	2	0	0	—	9	0	0	0	0	17	25	3	7	10	17.5	5.82	82	.342	.407	0	—	0	-2	-2	-0	0.0
● TOM EDENS	Edens, Thomas Patrick b: 6/9/61, Ontario, Ore. BR/TR, 6′2″, 188 lbs. Deb: 6/2/87																									
1987	NY-N	0	0	—	2	2	0	0	0	8	15	2	4	4	21.4	6.75	56	.417	.475	0	.000	-0	-2	-3	0	0.0
1990	Mil-A	4	5	.444	35	6	0	0	2	89	89	8	33	40	12.7	4.45	87	.262	.334	0	—	0	-5	-6	-1	-0.6
1991	Min-A	2	2	.500	8	6	0	0	0	33	34	2	10	19	12.0	4.09	104	.256	.308	0	—	0	0	1	0	0.1
1992	Min-A	6	3	.667	52	0	0	0	3	76^{1}	65	1	36	57	12.1	2.83	143	.236	.329	0	—	0	9	10	-1	1.1
1993	Hou-N	1	1	.500	38	0	0	0	0	49	47	4	19	21	12.1	3.12	124	.263	.333	0	.000	-0	5	4	0	0.2
1994	Hou-N	4	1	.800	39	0	0	0	1	50	55	3	17	38	13.3	4.50	88	.289	.354	0	.000	-0	-2	-3	1	-0.2
	Phi-N	1	0	1.000	3	0	0	0	0	4	4	0	1	1	11.3	2.25	191	.267	.313	0	—	0	1	1	0	0.2
	Yr	5	1	.833	42	0	0	0	1	54	59	3	18	39	12.8	4.33	92	.281	.338	0	.000	-0	-1	-2	1	0.0
1995	Chi-N	1	0	1.000	5	0	0	0	0	3	6	0	3	2	27.0	6.00	68	.400	.500	0	—	0	-1	-1	0	-0.2
Total	7	19	12	.613	182	14	0	0	6	312^{1}	315	20	123	182	12.9	3.86	103	.266	.339	0	.000	-1	5	4	1	0.6
● BUTCH EDGE	Edge, Claude Lee b: 7/18/56, Houston, Tex. BR/TR, 6′3″, 203 lbs. Deb: 8/13/79																									
1979	Tor-A	3	4	.429	9	9	1	0	0	51^{2}	60	6	24	19	14.8	5.23	83	.283	.359	0	—	0	-6	-5	-0	-0.6

YEAR	TM/L	W	L	PCT	G	GS	CG	SH	SV	IP	H	HR	BB	SO	RAT	ERA	ERA+	OAV	OOB	BH	AVG	PB	PR	/A	PD	TPI
● **BILL EDGERTON**	Edgerton, William Albert b: 8/16/41, South Bend, Ind. BL/TL, 6′2″, 185 lbs. Deb: 9/3/66																									
1966	KC-A	0	1	.000	6	1	0	0	0	8^1	10	0	7	3	18.4	3.24	105	.303	.425	0	—	0	0	0	0	0.0
1967	KC-A	1	0	1.000	7	0	0	0	0	8^1	11	1	3	6	16.2	2.16	147	.324	.395	0	—	0	1	1	0	0.1
1969	Sea-A	0	1	.000	4	0	0	0	0	4	10	1	0	2	24.8	13.50	27	.455	.478	0	—	0	-4	-4	0	-0.9
Total	3	1	2	.333	17	1	0	0	0	20^2	31	2	10	11	18.7	4.79	70	.348	.426	0	—	0	-3	-3	1	-0.8
● **BRIAN EDMONDSON**	Edmondson, Brian Christopher b: 1/29/73, Fontana, Cal. BR/TR, 6′2″, 165 lbs. Deb: 4/2/98																									
1998	Atl-N	0	1	.000	10	0	0	0	0	16^2	14	2	8	8	11.9	4.32	98	.215	.301	0	.000	-0	-0	-0	0	0.0
	Fla-N	4	3	.571	43	0	0	0	0	59^1	62	8	29	32	14.3	3.79	108	.281	.372	0	.000	-1	3	2	-1	0.0
	Yr	4	4	.500	53	0	0	0	0	76	76	10	37	40	13.7	3.91	105	.266	.356	0	.000	-1	3	2	-1	0.0
● **GEORGE EDMONDSON**	Edmondson, George Henderson "Big Ed" b: 5/18/1896, Waxahachie, Tex. d: 7/11/73, Waco, Tex. BR/TR, 6′1″, 179 lbs. Deb: 8/15/22																									
1922	Cle-A	0	0	—	2	0	0	0	0	2	4	0	0	0	18.0	9.00	45	.444	.444	0	—	0	-1	-1	0	0.0
1923	Cle-A	0	0	—	1	0	0	0	0	4	8	0	3	0	27.0	11.25	35	.444	.545	0	.000	-0	-3	-3	0	0.0
1924	Cle-A	0	0	—	5	1	0	0	0	8	10	1	5	3	16.9	9.00	47	.294	.385	1	.333	0	-4	-4	-0	0.0
Total	3	0	0	—	8	1	0	0	0	14	22	1	8	3	19.9	9.64	43	.361	.443	1	.250	-0	-9	-9	0	0.0
● **PAUL EDMONDSON**	Edmondson, Paul Michael b: 2/12/43, Kansas City, Kan. d: 2/13/70, Santa Barbara, Cal. BR/TR, 6′5″, 195 lbs. Deb: 6/20/69																									
1969	Chi-A	1	6	.143	14	13	1	0	0	87^2	72	5	39	46	11.8	3.70	104	.227	.319	5	.172	-1	-1	2	3	0.4
● **BOB EDMONDSON**	Edmondson, Robert E. b: 4/30/1879, Paris, Ky. d: 8/14/31, Lawrence, Kan. BR/TR, 5′11″, 185 lbs. Deb: 9/15/06 ♦																									
1906	Was-A	0	1	.000	2	1	1	0	0	10	10	0	2	0	10.8	4.50	59	.263	.300	1	.333	0	-2	-2	0	-0.1
● **SAM EDMONSTON**	Edmonston, Samuel Sherwood "Big Sam" b: 8/30/1883, Washington, D.C. d: 4/12/79, Corpus Christi, Tex. BL/TL, 5′11.5″, 185 lbs. Deb: 6/24/07																									
1907	Was-A	0	0	—	1	0	0	0	0	3	8	0	1	0	27.0	9.00	27	.500	.529	0	.000	-0	-2	-2	0	0.0
● **EDWARDS**	Edwards Deb: 9/11/1875																									
1875	Atl-n	0	1	.000	1	1	0	0	0	2	4	0	0	0	18.0	4.50	46	.308	.308	1	.200	-0	-1	-1		-0.2
● **FOSTER EDWARDS**	Edwards, Foster Hamilton "Eddie" b: 9/1/03, Holstein, Iowa d: 1/4/80, Orleans, Mass. BR/TR, 6′3″, 175 lbs. Deb: 7/2/25																									
1925	Bos-N	0	0	—	1	0	0	0	0	2	6	0	1	1	31.5	9.00	45	.545	.583	0	—	0	-1	-1	-0	0.0
1926	Bos-N	2	0	1.000	3	3	1	0	0	25	20	0	13	4	11.9	0.72	492	.230	.330	0	.000	-2	9	8	-0	0.4
1927	Bos-N	2	8	.200	29	11	1	0	0	92	95	2	45	37	14.0	4.99	74	.274	.362	1	.045	-2	-11	-13	-1	-1.5
1928	Bos-N	2	1	.667	21	3	2	0	0	49^1	67	2	23	17	16.8	5.66	69	.327	.400	1	.091	-1	-9	-10	0	-0.6
1930	NY-A	0	0	—	2	0	0	0	0	1^2	5	0	2	1	37.8	21.60	20	.500	.583	0	—	0	-3	-3	-0	0.0
Total	5	6	9	.400	56	17	4	0	0	170	193	4	84	60	14.9	4.76	79	.292	.377	2	.048	-5	-16	-19	-1	-1.7
● **JIM JOE EDWARDS**	Edwards, James Corbette "Little Joe" b: 12/14/1894, Banner, Miss. d: 1/19/65, Sarepta, Miss. BR/TL, 6′2″, 185 lbs. Deb: 5/14/22																									
1922	Cle-A	3	8	.273	25	7	0	0	0	92^2	113	1	40	44	15.3	4.47	90	.313	.389	2	.087	-2	-4	-5	-1	-0.8
1923	Cle-A	10	10	.500	38	21	8	1	1	179^1	200	5	75	68	14.1	3.71	107	.286	.359	7	.119	-5	5	5	-1	-0.1
1924	Cle-A	4	3	.571	10	7	5	1	0	57	64	3	34	15	15.5	2.84	150	.305	.402	3	.150	-1	9	9	0	0.9
1925	Cle-A	0	3	.000	13	3	1	0	0	36	60	0	23	12	21.0	8.25	54	.382	.464	1	.111	-1	-15	-15	1	-1.0
	Chi-A	1	2	.333	9	4	1	1	0	45^1	46	4	23	20	13.9	3.97	105	.263	.352	3	.176	-1	2	1	1	0.0
	Yr	1	5	.167	22	7	2	1	0	81^1	106	4	46	32	16.9	5.86	73	.318	.403	4	.154	-2	-13	-14	2	-1.0
1926	Chi-A	6	9	.400	32	16	8	3	1	142	140	4	63	41	12.9	4.18	92	.264	.343	5	.109	-3	-3	-5	-1	-0.9
1928	Cin-N	2	2	.500	18	1	0	0	2	32	43	1	20	11	17.7	7.59	52	.347	.438	3	.300	0	-13	-13	-1	-1.6
Total	6	26	37	.413	145	59	23	6	4	584^1	666	18	278	211	14.7	4.37	92	.295	.376	24	.130	-13	-19	-23	-1	-3.5
● **SHERMAN EDWARDS**	Edwards, Sherman Stanley b: 7/25/09, Mt.Ida, Ark. d: 3/8/92, ElDorado, Ark. BR/TR, 6′, 165 lbs. Deb: 9/21/34																									
1934	Cin-N	0	0	—	1	0	0	0	0	3	4	0	1	1	15.0	3.00	136	.333	.385	0	.000	-0	0	0	0	0.0
● **WAYNE EDWARDS**	Edwards, Wayne Maurice b: 3/7/64, Burbank, Cal. BL/TL, 6′5″, 185 lbs. Deb: 9/11/89																									
1989	Chi-A	0	0	—	7	0	0	0	0	7^1	7	1	3	9	12.3	3.68	103	.269	.345	0	—	0	0	0	0	0.1
1990	Chi-A	5	3	.625	42	5	0	0	2	95	81	6	41	63	11.8	3.22	119	.234	.321	0	—	0	7	6	0	0.6
1991	Chi-A	0	2	.000	13	0	0	0	0	23^1	22	2	17	12	15.0	3.86	103	.259	.382	0	—	0	1	0	-0	0.0
Total	3	5	5	.500	62	5	0	0	2	125^2	110	9	61	84	12.5	3.37	114	.241	.334	0	—	0	8	7	0	0.7
● **HARRY EELLS**	Eells, Harry Archibald "Slippery" b: 2/14/1881, Ida Grove, Iowa d: 10/15/40, Los Angeles, Cal. BR/TR, 6′1″, 195 lbs. Deb: 4/22/06																									
1906	Cle-A	4	5	.444	14	8	6	1	0	86^1	77	1	48	35	13.3	2.61	100	.242	.347	6	.188	1	1	0	1	0.1
● **WISH EGAN**	Egan, Aloysius Jerome b: 6/16/1881, Evart, Mich. d: 4/13/51, Detroit, Mich. BR/TR, 6′3″, 185 lbs. Deb: 9/3/02																									
1902	Det-A	0	2	.000	3	3	2	0	0	22	23	0	6	0	11.9	2.86	127	.271	.319	2	.250	-0	2	2	1	0.2
1905	StL-N	6	15	.286	23	19	18	0	0	171^1	189	2	39	29	12.4	3.57	83	.285	.333	6	.102	-3	-11	-11	5	-1.1
1906	StL-N	2	9	.182	16	12	7	0	0	86^1	97	3	27	23	13.1	4.59	57	.278	.333	2	.069	-2	-19	-19	1	-2.3
Total	3	8	26	.235	42	34	27	0	0	279^2	309	5	72	52	12.6	3.83	76	.282	.332	10	.104	-5	-28	-28	6	-3.2
● **JIM EGAN**	Egan, James K. "Troy Terrier" b: 1858, Derby, Conn. d: 9/26/1884, New Haven, Conn. TL , Deb: 5/15/1882 ♦																									
1882	Tro-N	4	6	.400	12	10	10	0	0	100	133	2	24	20	14.1	4.14	68	.315	.352	23	.200	-2	-14	-15	-2	-1.4
● **RIP EGAN**	Egan, John Joseph b: 7/9/1871, Philadelphia, Pa. d: 12/22/50, Cranston, R.I. TR , 5′11″, 168 lbs. Deb: 4/30/1894 U																									
1894	Was-N	0	0	—	1	0	0	0	0	5	8	1	2	2	18.0	10.80	49	.364	.417	0	.000	-0	-3	-3	0	0.0
● **DICK EGAN**	Egan, Richard Wallis b: 3/24/37, Berkeley, Cal. BL/TL, 6′4″, 193 lbs. Deb: 4/9/63 C																									
1963	Det-A	0	1	.000	20	0	0	0	0	21	25	4	3	16	12.0	5.14	73	.287	.311	0	—	0	-4	-3	0	-0.1
1964	Det-A	0	0	—	23	0	0	0	2	34^1	33	4	17	21	13.4	4.46	82	.246	.336	0	.000	-0	-3	-3	1	0.0
1966	Cal-A	0	0	—	11	0	0	0	0	14^1	17	2	6	11	14.4	4.40	76	.309	.377	0	.000	-0	-2	-2	-0	0.0
1967	LA-N	1	1	.500	20	0	0	0	0	31^2	34	3	15	20	15.1	6.25	50	.272	.368	0	.000	-0	-10	-11	-1	-0.7
Total	4	1	2	.333	74	0	0	0	2	101^1	109	13	41	68	13.8	5.15	67	.272	.347	0	.000	-1	-18	-19	0	-0.8
● **BRUCE EGLOFF**	Egloff, Bruce Edward b: 4/10/65, Denver, Colo. BR/TR, 6′2″, 215 lbs. Deb: 4/13/91																									
1991	Cle-A	0	0	—	6	0	0	0	0	5^2	8	0	4	8	19.1	4.76	87	.333	.429	0	—	0	-0	-0	0	0.0
● **HOWARD EHMKE**	Ehmke, Howard Jonathan "Bob" b: 4/24/1894, Silver Creek, N.Y. d: 3/17/59, Philadelphia, Pa. BR/TR, 6′3″, 190 lbs. Deb: 4/12/15																									
1915	Buf-F	0	2	.000	18	2	0	0	0	53^2	69	2	25	18	16.6	5.53	51	.325	.409	0	.000	-2	-17	-16	2	-0.6
1916	Det-A	3	1	.750	5	4	4	0	0	37^1	34	0	15	15	11.8	3.13	91	.252	.327	2	.143	-1	-1	-1	1	-0.1
1917	Det-A	10	15	.400	35	25	13	4	2	206	174	3	88	90	11.7	2.97	89	.243	.330	17	.246	2	-7	-7	2	-0.4
1919	Det-A	17	10	.630	33	31	20	2	0	248^2	255	5	107	79	13.3	3.18	100	.274	.353	23	.253	3	1	0	4	0.7
1920	Det-A	15	18	.455	38	33	23	2	3	268^1	250	8	124	98	13.0	3.25	115	.253	.344	25	.238	2	16	14	6	2.4
1921	Det-A	13	14	.481	30	22	13	1	0	196^1	220	15	81	68	14.4	4.54	94	.286	.364	21	.284	2	-6	-6	1	-0.4
1922	Det-A	17	17	.500	45	29	16	1	1	279^2	299	12	101	108	13.6	4.22	92	.281	.356	16	.157	-4	-5	-10	2	-1.3
1923	Bos-A	20	17	.541	43	39	28	2	3	316^2	318	12	119	121	13.0	3.78	109	.272	.349	25	.223	-2	7	12	5	1.6
1924	Bos-A	19	17	.528	45	36	26	4	4	**315**	324	9	81	119	11.9	3.46	126	.265	.316	28	.222	-2	27	32	2	3.3
1925	Bos-A	9	20	.310	34	31	**22**	0	1	260^2	285	8	85	95	13.2	3.73	122	.285	.348	13	.148	-5	19	24	5	2.2
1926	Bos-A	3	10	.231	14	14	7	1	0	97^1	115	3	45	38	15.2	5.46	75	.303	.382	5	.147	-1	-16	-15	1	-1.6
	Phi-A	12	4	.750	20	18	10	1	0	147^1	125	1	50	55	10.9	2.81	148	.232	.302	7	.152	-2	20	22	0	2.1
	Yr	15	14	.517	34	32	17	2	0	244^2	240	4	95	93	12.5	3.86	107	.260	.332	12	.150	-3	4	7	1	0.5
1927	Phi-A	12	10	.545	30	27	10	1	0	189^2	200	13	60	68	13.0	4.22	101	.281	.349	14	.206	-1	-2	1	3	0.2
1928	Phi-A	9	8	.529	23	18	5	1	0	139^1	135	6	44	34	11.8	3.62	111	.254	.316	11	.239	1	7	6	0	0.8
1929	*Phi-A	7	2	.778	11	8	2	0	0	54^2	48	2	15	20	10.5	3.29	129	.233	.288	2	.105	-2	6	6	0	0.7
1930	Phi-A	0	1	.000	3	1	0	0	0	10	22	4	2	4	24.3	11.70	40	.458	.509	1	.333	0	-8	-8	0	-0.5
Total	15	166	166	.500	427	338	199	20	14	2820^2	2873	103	1042	1030	12.9	3.75	104	.271	.343	210	.208	-11	42	52	32	9.1

● RED EHRET
Ehret, Philip Sydney b: 8/31/1868, Louisville, Ky. d: 7/28/40, Cincinnati, Ohio BR/TR, 6', 175 lbs. Deb: 7/7/1888 ♦

YEAR	TM/L	W	L	PCT	G	GS	CG	SH	SV	IP	H	HR	BB	SO	RAT	ERA	ERA+	OAV	OOB	BH	AVG	PB	PR	/A	PD	TPI
1888	KC-a	3	2	.600	7	6	5	0	0	52	58	1	22	12	14.4	3.98	86	.272	.349	12	.190	-1	-5	-3	1	-0.2
1889	Lou-a	10	29	.256	45	38	35	1	0	364	441	11	115	135	14.2	4.80	80	.290	.347	65	.252	2	-38	-38	3	-2.7
1890	*Lou-a	25	14	.641	43	38	35	4	2	359	351	5	79	174	11.2	2.53	152	.248	.296	31	.212	-3	53	53	-3	4.3
1891	Lou-a	13	13	.500	26	24	23	2	0	220^2	225	2	70	76	12.5	3.47	105	.255	.318	22	.242	1	6	5	0	0.5
1892	Pit-N	16	20	.444	39	36	32	0	0	316	290	7	83	101	11.3	2.65	124	.234	.294	34	.258	3	22	23	-4	2.1
1893	Pit-N	18	18	.500	39	35	32	**4**	0	314^1	322	3	115	70	13.2	3.44	133	.257	.331	24	.176	-6	43	39	1	3.0
1894	Pit-N	19	21	.475	46	38	31	1	0	346^2	441	12	128	102	15.0	5.14	102	.306	.367	23	.170	-11	7	4	-1	-0.6
1895	StL-N	6	19	.240	37	32	18	0	0	231^2	360	11	88	55	17.8	6.02	80	.349	.405	21	.219	-3	-32	-30	0	-2.5
1896	Cin-N	18	14	.563	34	33	29	2	0	276^2	298	5	74	60	12.4	3.42	135	.273	.324	20	.196	-3	29	37	1	3.1
1897	Cin-N	8	10	.444	34	19	11	0	2	184^1	256	3	47	43	15.4	4.78	95	.326	.374	13	.197	-3	-10	-5	-1	-0.7
1898	Lou-N	3	7	.300	12	10	9	0	0	89	130	3	20	20	15.5	5.76	62	.338	.375	9	.225	1	-21	-22	-1	-1.9
Total	11	139	167	.454	362	309	260	14	4	2754^1	3172	63	841	848	13.6	4.02	105	.282	.339	274	.217	-22	55	62	-4	4.4

● RUBE EHRHARDT
Ehrhardt, Welton Claude b: 11/20/1894, Beecher, Ill. d: 4/27/80, Chicago Heights, Ill. BR/TR, 6'2", 190 lbs. Deb: 7/18/24

YEAR	TM/L	W	L	PCT	G	GS	CG	SH	SV	IP	H	HR	BB	SO	RAT	ERA	ERA+	OAV	OOB	BH	AVG	PB	PR	/A	PD	TPI
1924	Bro-N	5	3	.625	15	9	6	2	0	83^2	71	5	17	13	9.6	2.26	166	.232	.275	4	.138	-2	15	14	-2	0.8
1925	Bro-N	10	14	.417	36	25	12	0	1	207^2	239	10	62	47	13.2	5.03	83	.293	.345	15	.211	2	-17	-20	4	-1.4
1926	Bro-N	2	5	.286	44	1	0	0	4	97	101	5	35	25	12.6	3.90	98	.275	.338	6	.250	0	-1	-1	-2	-0.2
1927	Bro-N	3	7	.300	46	3	2	0	2	95^2	90	3	37	22	12.2	3.57	111	.264	.341	6	.250	1	4	4	3	0.7
1928	Bro-N	1	3	.250	28	2	1	0	2	54	74	1	27	12	17.0	4.67	85	.352	.429	4	.286	0	-4	-4	0	-0.2
1929	Cin-N	1	2	.333	24	1	1	1	1	49^1	58	2	22	9	14.8	4.74	96	.305	.380	2	.182	-0	-0	-1	1	0.0
Total	6	22	34	.393	193	41	22	3	10	587^1	633	26	200	128	12.9	4.15	97	.284	.345	37	.214	1	-4	-7	5	-0.3

● HACK EIBEL
Eibel, Henry Hack b: 12/6/1893, Brooklyn, N.Y. d: 10/16/45, Macon, Ga. BL/TL, 5'11", 220 lbs. Deb: 6/13/12 ♦

YEAR	TM/L	W	L	PCT	G	GS	CG	SH	SV	IP	H	HR	BB	SO	RAT	ERA	ERA+	OAV	OOB	BH	AVG	PB	PR	/A	PD	TPI
1920	Bos-A	0	0	—	3	0	0	0	0	10^1	10	0	3	5	11.3	3.48	105	.270	.325	8	.186	-0	0	0	-0	0.0

● JUAN EICHELBERGER
Eichelberger, Juan Tyrone b: 10/21/53, St.Louis, Mo. BR/TR, 6'3", 205 lbs. Deb: 9/7/78

YEAR	TM/L	W	L	PCT	G	GS	CG	SH	SV	IP	H	HR	BB	SO	RAT	ERA	ERA+	OAV	OOB	BH	AVG	PB	PR	/A	PD	TPI
1978	SD-N	0	0	—	3	0	0	0	0	3^1	4	0	2	2	16.2	10.80	31	.267	.353	0	—	0	-3	-3	0	0.0
1979	SD-N	1	1	.500	3	3	1	0	0	21	15	1	11	12	11.1	3.43	103	.211	.317	2	.400	1	1	0	-0	0.1
1980	SD-N	4	2	.667	15	13	0	0	0	88^2	73	8	55	43	13.1	3.65	94	.233	.350	3	.111	-1	-1	-2	1	-0.3
1981	SD-N	8	8	.500	25	24	3	1	0	141^1	136	5	74	81	13.6	3.50	93	.259	.353	4	.087	-3	-0	-4	1	-0.6
1982	SD-N	7	14	.333	31	24	8	0	0	177^2	171	23	72	74	12.4	4.20	81	.251	.325	5	.091	-2	-12	-15	-1	-1.9
1983	Cle-A	4	11	.267	28	15	2	0	0	134	132	10	59	56	13.0	4.90	86	.259	.338	0	—	0	-13	-10	-1	-1.1
1988	Atl-N	2	0	1.000	20	0	0	0	0	37^1	44	3	10	13	13.0	3.86	95	.297	.342	0	.000	-0	-2	-1	1	0.0
Total	7	26	36	.419	125	79	14	1	0	603^1	575	50	283	281	12.9	4.10	87	.254	.339	14	.103	-4	-29	-35	-2	-3.8

● MARK EICHHORN
Eichhorn, Mark Anthony b: 11/21/60, San Jose, Cal. BR/TR, 6'3", 210 lbs. Deb: 8/30/82

YEAR	TM/L	W	L	PCT	G	GS	CG	SH	SV	IP	H	HR	BB	SO	RAT	ERA	ERA+	OAV	OOB	BH	AVG	PB	PR	/A	PD	TPI
1982	Tor-A	0	3	.000	7	7	0	0	0	38	40	4	14	16	12.8	5.45	82	.260	.321	0	—	0	-6	-4	-1	-0.5
1986	Tor-A	14	6	.700	69	0	0	0	10	157	105	8	45	166	9.0	1.72	245	.191	.261	0	—	0	**43**	**44**	2	**5.7**
1987	Tor-A	10	6	.625	**89**	0	0	0	4	127^2	110	14	52	96	11.8	3.17	142	.234	.318	0	—	0	18	19	2	2.3
1988	Tor-A	0	3	.000	37	0	0	0	1	66^2	79	3	27	28	15.1	4.18	94	.304	.382	0	—	0	-2	-2	1	0.0
1989	Atl-N	5	5	.500	45	0	0	0	0	68^1	70	6	19	49	11.9	4.35	84	.275	.327	0	.000	-0	-6	-5	2	-0.5
1990	Cal-A	2	5	.286	60	0	0	0	13	84^2	98	2	23	69	13.5	3.08	124	.289	.345	0	—	0	8	7	1	0.9
1991	Cal-A	3	3	.500	70	0	0	0	1	81^2	63	2	13	49	8.6	1.98	207	.219	.257	0	—	0	19	19	2	1.5
1992	Cal-A	2	4	.333	42	0	0	0	2	56^2	51	2	18	42	11.0	2.38	167	.238	.297	0	—	0	10	10	1	1.1
	*Tor-A	2	0	1.000	23	0	0	0	0	31	35	1	7	19	12.8	4.35	94	.285	.333	0	—	0	-1	-1	1	-0.1
	Yr	4	4	.500	65	0	0	0	2	87^2	86	3	25	61	11.6	3.08	130	.253	.308	0	—	0	8	9	2	1.0
1993	*Tor-A	3	1	.750	54	0	0	0	0	72^2	76	3	22	47	12.5	2.72	158	.272	.332	0	—	0	13	13	2	0.8
1994	Bal-A	6	5	.545	43	0	0	0	1	71	62	1	19	35	10.9	2.15	232	.240	.305	0	—	0	**21**	**22**	2	3.2
1996	Cal-A	1	2	.333	24	0	0	0	0	30^1	36	3	11	24	14.5	5.04	99	.308	.377	0	—	0	-0	-0	1	0.0
Total	11	48	43	.527	563	7	0	0	32	885^2	825	49	270	640	11.5	3.00	141	.249	.314	0	.000	-0	116	121	15	14.4

● DAVE EILAND
Eiland, David William b: 7/5/66, Dade City, Fla. BR/TR, 6'3", 205 lbs. Deb: 8/3/88

YEAR	TM/L	W	L	PCT	G	GS	CG	SH	SV	IP	H	HR	BB	SO	RAT	ERA	ERA+	OAV	OOB	BH	AVG	PB	PR	/A	PD	TPI
1988	NY-A	0	0	—	3	3	0	0	0	12^2	15	6	4	7	14.9	6.39	62	.294	.368	0	—	0	-3	-3	0	0.0
1989	NY-A	1	3	.250	6	6	0	0	0	34^1	44	5	13	11	15.5	5.77	67	.328	.396	0	—	0	-7	-7	-1	-0.8
1990	NY-A	2	1	.667	5	5	0	0	0	30^1	31	2	5	16	10.7	3.56	111	.254	.283	0	—	0	1	1	-0	0.1
1991	NY-A	2	5	.286	18	13	0	0	0	72^2	87	10	23	18	14.0	5.33	78	.302	.360	0	—	0	-10	-10	-2	-1.0
1992	SD-N	0	2	.000	7	7	0	0	0	27	33	1	5	10	12.7	5.67	63	.287	.317	1	.111	1	-6	-6	0	-0.4
1993	SD-N	0	3	.000	10	9	0	0	0	48^1	58	5	17	14	14.2	5.21	79	.297	.357	1	.083	-1	-6	-6	0	-0.4
1995	NY-A	1	1	.500	4	1	0	0	0	10	16	1	3	6	18.0	6.30	73	.348	.400	0	—	0	-2	-2	0	-0.3
1998	TB-A	0	1	.000	1	1	0	0	0	2^2	6	0	3	1	30.4	20.25	24	.429	.529	0	—	0	-5	-5	-0	-1.1
Total	8	6	16	.273	54	45	0	0	0	238	290	30	73	83	14.1	5.45	74	.301	.355	2	.095	-0	-39	-37	-2	-3.9

● DAVE EILERS
Eilers, David Louis b: 12/3/36, Oldenburg, Tex. BR/TR, 5'11", 188 lbs. Deb: 7/27/64

YEAR	TM/L	W	L	PCT	G	GS	CG	SH	SV	IP	H	HR	BB	SO	RAT	ERA	ERA+	OAV	OOB	BH	AVG	PB	PR	/A	PD	TPI
1964	Mil-N	0	0	—	6	0	0	0	0	7^2	11	1	1	1	15.3	4.70	75	.333	.371	0	—	0	-1	-1	-0	0.0
1965	Mil-N	0	0	—	6	0	0	0	0	3^2	8	1	0	1	19.6	12.27	29	.421	.421	0	—	0	-4	-4	0	0.0
	NY-N	1	1	.500	11	0	0	0	2	18	20	2	4	9	13.0	4.00	88	.274	.329	1	1.000	0	-1	-1	-0	-0.1
	Yr	1	1	.500	17	0	0	0	2	21^2	28	3	4	10	14.1	5.40	65	.304	.347	1	1.000	0	-4	-5	-0	-0.1
1966	NY-N	1	1	.500	23	0	0	0	0	34^2	39	7	7	14	12.2	4.67	78	.287	.326	0	.000	-0	-4	-4	1	-0.2
1967	Hou-N	6	4	.600	35	0	0	0	1	59^1	68	3	17	27	13.3	3.94	84	.296	.352	0	.000	-1	-4	-4	-0	-0.8
Total	4	8	6	.571	81	0	0	0	3	123^1	146	14	29	52	13.3	4.45	78	.297	.345	1	.111	-0	-13	-14	-0	-1.1

● JOEY EISCHEN
Eischen, Joseph Raymond b: 5/25/70, West Covina, Cal. BL/TL, 6'1", 190 lbs. Deb: 6/19/94

YEAR	TM/L	W	L	PCT	G	GS	CG	SH	SV	IP	H	HR	BB	SO	RAT	ERA	ERA+	OAV	OOB	BH	AVG	PB	PR	/A	PD	TPI
1994	Mon-N	0	0	—	1	0	0	0	0	0^2	4	0	0	1	67.5	54.00	8	.667	.714	0	—	0	-4	-4	0	0.0
1995	LA-N	0	0	—	17	0	0	0	0	20^1	19	1	11	15	14.2	3.10	122	.232	.337	0	.000	-0	2	2	-0	0.0
1996	LA-N	0	1	.000	28	0	0	0	0	43^1	48	4	20	36	15.0	4.78	81	.282	.371	0	.000	-1	-3	-4	-1	-0.2
	Det-A	1	1	.500	24	0	0	0	0	25	27	3	14	15	14.8	3.24	156	.284	.376	0	—	0	5	5	1	0.4
1997	Cin-N	0	0	—	1	0	0	0	0	1^1	2	0	1	2	20.3	6.75	63	.333	.429	0	.000	-0	-0	-0	0	0.0
Total	4	1	2	.333	71	0	0	0	0	90^2	100	8	46	69	15.2	4.37	95	.279	.371	0	.000	-1	1	-2	-0	0.2

● JAKE EISENHART
Eisenhart, Jacob Henry b: 10/3/22, Perkasie, Pa. d: 12/20/87, Huntingdon, Pa. BL/TL, 6'3.5", 195 lbs. Deb: 6/10/44

YEAR	TM/L	W	L	PCT	G	GS	CG	SH	SV	IP	H	HR	BB	SO	RAT	ERA	ERA+	OAV	OOB	BH	AVG	PB	PR	/A	PD	TPI
1944	Cin-N	0	0	—	1	0	0	0	0	0^1	0	0	1	0	27.0	0.00	—	.000	.500	0	—	0	0	0	0	0.0

● HARRY EISENSTAT
Eisenstat, Harry b: 10/10/15, Brooklyn, N.Y. BL/TL, 5'11", 185 lbs. Deb: 5/19/35

YEAR	TM/L	W	L	PCT	G	GS	CG	SH	SV	IP	H	HR	BB	SO	RAT	ERA	ERA+	OAV	OOB	BH	AVG	PB	PR	/A	PD	TPI
1935	Bro-N	0	1	.000	2	0	0	0	0	4^2	9	0	2	2	21.2	13.50	29	.429	.478	0	.000	-0	-5	-5	1	-0.7
1936	Bro-N	1	2	.333	5	2	1	0	0	14^1	22	1	6	5	17.6	5.65	73	.344	.400	1	.333	0	-3	-2	0	-0.4
1937	Bro-N	3	3	.500	13	5	0	0	0	47^2	61	2	11	12	13.8	3.97	102	.308	.348	0	.000	-1	-0	0	1	0.0
1938	Det-A	9	6	.600	32	9	5	0	4	125^1	131	7	29	37	11.6	3.73	134	.266	.308	5	.139	-1	15	18	1	1.8
1939	Det-A	2	2	.500	10	2	1	0	0	29^2	39	3	9	6	14.6	6.98	70	.315	.361	3	.375	1	-8	-7	1	-0.6
	Cle-A	6	7	.462	26	11	4	1	2	103^2	109	8	23	38	11.5	3.30	133	.265	.304	8	.250	1	15	13	-1	1.4
	Yr	8	9	.471	36	13	5	1	2	133^1	148	11	32	44	12.2	4.12	110	.277	.317	11	.275	1	7	6	-0	0.8
1940	Cle-A	1	4	.200	27	3	0	0	4	71^2	78	6	12	27	11.3	3.14	134	.282	.311	6	.273	1	**10**	9	-0	0.7
1941	Cle-A	1	1	.500	21	0	0	0	2	34	43	2	16	11	16.1	4.24	93	.312	.391	2	.333	1	-0	-1	-1	-0.1
1942	Cle-A	2	1	.667	29	1	0	0	0	47^2	58	1	6	19	12.1	2.45	140	.304	.325	1	.250	0	6	5	-0	0.3
Total	8	25	27	.481	165	33	11	1	14	478^2	550	30	114	157	12.6	3.84	114	.287	.328	26	.211	1	30	29	0	2.4

● ED EITELJORGE
Eiteljorge, Edward Henry b: 10/14/1871, Berlin, Germany d: 12/5/42, Greencastle, Ind. BR/TR, 6'2", 190 lbs. Deb: 5/2/1890

YEAR	TM/L	W	L	PCT	G	GS	CG	SH	SV	IP	H	HR	BB	SO	RAT	ERA	ERA+	OAV	OOB	BH	AVG	PB	PR	/A	PD	TPI
1890	Chi-N	0	1	.000	1	1	0	0	0	2	5	0	1	1	27.0	22.50	16	.455	.500	0	.000	-0	-4	-4	-0	-1.0
1891	Was-a	1	5	.167	8	7	6	0	0	61^1	79	3	41	23	18.9	6.16	61	.303	.415	5	.192	-1	-17	-17	2	-1.1
Total	2	1	6	.143	9	8	6	0	0	63^1	84	3	42	24	19.2	6.68	56	.309	.418	5	.185	-1	-21	-21	1	-2.1

YEAR	TM/L	W	L	PCT	G	GS	CG	SH	SV	IP	H	HR	BB	SO	RAT	ERA	ERA+	OAV	OOB	BH	AVG	PB	PR	/A	PD	TPI
● SCOTT ELARTON	Elarton, Vincent Scott b: 2/23/76, Lamar, Colo. BR/TR, 6'7", 240 lbs. Deb: 6/20/98																									
1998	*Hou-N	2	1	.667	28	2	0	0	2	57	40	5	20	56	9.6	3.32	123	.196	.271	0	.000	-1	6	5	-1	0.1
● HEINIE ELDER	Elder, Henry Knox b: 8/23/1890, Seattle, Wash. d: 11/13/58, Long Beach, Cal. BL/TL, 6'2", 200 lbs. Deb: 7/7/13																									
1913	Det-A	0	0	—	1	0	0	0	0	3^{1}	4	0	5	0	24.3	8.10	36	.286	.474	0	.000	-0	-2	-2	-0	0.0
● CAL ELDRED	Eldred, Calvin John b: 11/24/67, Cedar Rapids, Iowa BR/TR, 6'4", 235 lbs. Deb: 9/24/91																									
1991	Mil-A	2	0	1.000	3	3	0	0	0	16	20	2	6	10	14.6	4.50	88	.299	.356	0	—	0	-1	-1	-0	0.0
1992	Mil-A	11	2	.846	14	14	2	1	0	100^{1}	76	4	23	62	9.1	1.79	214	.207	.257	0	—	0	24	23	-0	3.1
1993	Mil-A	16	16	.500	36	36	8	1	0	**258**	232	32	91	180	11.6	4.01	106	.239	.311	0	—	0	9	7	-0	0.7
1994	Mil-A	11	11	.500	25	25	6	0	0	179	158	23	84	98	12.4	4.68	108	.236	.325	0	—	0	2	7	1	0.8
1995	Mil-A	1	1	.500	4	4	0	0	0	23^{2}	24	4	10	18	13.3	3.42	146	.261	.340	0	—	0	3	4	-0	0.3
1996	Mil-A	4	4	.500	15	15	0	0	0	84^{2}	82	8	38	50	13.2	4.46	116	.259	.345	0	—	0	5	7	-1	0.5
1997	Mil-A	13	15	.464	34	34	1	1	0	202	207	31	89	122	13.6	4.99	92	.266	.349	0	.000	-0	-10	-8	-3	-1.3
1998	Mil-N	4	8	.333	23	23	0	0	0	133	157	14	61	86	15.0	4.80	89	.297	.374	4	.125	-0	-8	-7	-1	-0.8
Total	8	62	57	.521	154	154	17	3	0	996^{2}	956	118	402	626	12.6	4.24	106	.252	.330	4	.114	-1	25	30	-5	3.3
● HOD ELLER	Eller, Horace Owen b: 7/5/1894, Muncie, Ind. d: 7/18/61, Indianapolis, Ind BR/TR, 5'11.5", 185 lbs. Deb: 4/16/17																									
1917	Cin-N	10	5	.667	37	11	7	1	1	152^{1}	131	2	37	77	10.1	2.36	111	.239	.290	6	.133	-2	6	4	-2	0.0
1918	Cin-N	16	12	.571	37	22	14	0	1	217^{2}	205	1	59	84	11.2	2.36	113	.253	.309	11	.157	-2	10	8	-4	0.3
1919	*Cin-N	19	9	.679	38	30	16	7	2	248^{1}	216	7	50	137	9.8	2.39	116	.238	.281	26	.280	7	14	11	-3	1.6
1920	Cin-N	13	12	.520	35	23	15	1	0	210^{1}	208	6	52	76	11.3	2.95	103	.266	.315	22	.253	1	4	2	-1	0.2
1921	Cin-N	2	2	.500	13	3	0	0	1	34^{1}	46	3	15	7	16.0	4.98	72	.322	.386	3	.231	0	-5	-5	-1	-0.7
Total	5	60	40	.600	160	89	52	9	5	863	806	19	213	381	10.8	2.62	108	.253	.303	68	.221	5	30	19	-11	1.4
● JOE ELLICK	Ellick, Joseph J. b: 4/3/1854, Cincinnati, Ohio d: 4/21/23, Kansas City, Kan. 5'10", 162 lbs. Deb: 5/13/1875 MU♦																									
1878	Mil-N	0	1	.000	1	0	0	0	0	3	1	0	1	0	6.0	3.00	88	.100	.182	2	.154	-0	-0	-0	-0	-0.1
● BRUCE ELLINGSEN	Ellingsen, Harold Bruce b: 4/26/49, Pocatello, Idaho BL/TL, 6', 180 lbs. Deb: 7/4/74																									
1974	Cle-A	1	1	.500	16	2	0	0	0	42	45	5	17	16	13.3	3.21	112	.278	.346	0	—	0	2	2	-0	0.1
● CLAUD ELLIOTT	Elliott, Claud Judson "Chaucer" or "Old Pardee" b: 11/17/1876, Pardeeville, Wis. d: 6/21/23, Pardeeville, Wis. BR/TR, 6', 190 lbs. Deb: 4/16/04																									
1904	Cin-N	3	1	.750	9	6	4	1	0	57^{2}	53	1	23	19	12.5	2.97	99	.247	.331	5	.208	1	-1	-0	0	0.1
	NY-N	0	1	.000	3	1	1	0	0	15	21	2	3	8	14.4	3.00	91	.328	.358	1	.200	0	-0	-0	-1	-0.1
	Yr	3	2	.600	12	7	5	1	0	72^{2}	74	3	26	27	12.4	2.97	97	.261	.324	6	.207	1	-2	-1	-1	0.0
1905	NY-N	0	1	.000	10	2	2	0	**6**	38	41	3	12	20	12.8	4.03	73	.270	.327	3	.188	-0	-4	-5	1	-0.3
Total	2	3	3	.500	22	9	7	1	6	110^{2}	115	6	38	47	12.8	3.33	87	.267	.333	9	.200	1	-6	-5	0	-0.3
● DONNIE ELLIOTT	Elliott, Donald Glenn b: 9/20/68, Pasadena, Tex. BR/TR, 6'4", 190 lbs. Deb: 4/23/94																									
1994	SD-N	0	1	.000	30	1	0	0	0	33	31	3	21	24	14.5	3.27	125	.250	.363	0	.000	-0	3	3	-0	0.0
1995	SD-N	0	0	—	1	0	0	0	0	2	2	0	1	3	13.5	0.00	—	.250	.333	0	—	0	1	1	-0	0.0
Total	2	0	1	.000	31	1	0	0	0	35	33	3	22	27	14.4	3.09	133	.250	.361	0	.000	-0	4	4	-0	0.0
● HAL ELLIOTT	Elliott, Harold William b: 5/29/1899, Mt.Clemens, Mich. d: 4/25/63, Honolulu, Hawaii BR/TR, 6'1.5", 170 lbs. Deb: 4/19/29																									
1929	Phi-N	3	7	.300	40	8	2	0	2	114^{1}	146	5	59	32	16.1	6.06	86	.313	.390	5	.167	-1	-17	-11	1	-0.8
1930	Phi-N	6	11	.353	**48**	11	2	0	0	117^{1}	191	7	58	37	19.2	7.67	71	.382	.447	3	.094	-3	-35	-29	2	-3.3
1931	Phi-N	0	2	.000	16	4	0	0	2	33	46	5	19	8	18.0	9.55	44	.338	.423	1	.111	-0	-21	-19	0	-1.3
1932	Phi-N	2	4	.333	16	7	0	0	0	57^{2}	70	5	38	13	16.9	5.77	76	.297	.394	3	.167	-0	-12	-9	-1	-0.9
Total	4	11	24	.314	120	30	4	0	4	322^{1}	453	22	174	90	17.6	6.95	73	.338	.415	12	.135	-5	-85	-68	2	-6.3
● GLENN ELLIOTT	Elliott, Herbert Glenn "Lefty" b: 11/11/19, Sapulpa, Okla d: 7/27/69, Portland, Ore. BB/TL, 5'10", 170 lbs. Deb: 4/17/47																									
1947	Bos-N	0	1	.000	11	0	0	0	1	19	18	4	11	8	13.7	4.74	82	.269	.372	1	.500	0	-1	-2	0	0.0
1948	Bos-N	1	0	1.000	1	1	0	0	0	3	5	0	1	2	18.0	3.00	128	.357	.400	0	.000	-0	0	0	-0	0.0
1949	Bos-N	3	4	.429	22	6	1	0	0	68^{1}	70	7	27	15	12.8	3.95	96	.269	.338	1	.059	-1	1	-1	1	-0.2
Total	3	4	5	.444	34	7	1	0	1	90^{1}	93	11	39	25	13.2	4.08	93	.273	.347	2	.095	-1	-0	-3	1	-0.2
● JUMBO ELLIOTT	Elliott, James Thomas b: 10/22/1900, St.Louis, Mo. d: 1/7/70, Terre Haute, Ind. BR/TL, 6'3", 235 lbs. Deb: 4/21/23																									
1923	StL-A	0	0	—	1	0	0	0	0	1	1	0	3	0	36.0	27.00	15	.333	.667	0	—	0	-3	-3	-0	0.0
1925	Bro-N	0	2	.000	3	1	0	0	0	10^{2}	17	0	9	3	22.8	8.44	50	.362	.474	0	.000	-1	-5	-5	-0	-0.8
1927	Bro-N	6	13	.316	30	21	12	2	3	188^{1}	188	5	60	99	11.9	3.30	120	.269	.327	9	.141	-1	13	14	-4	0.8
1928	Bro-N	9	14	.391	41	21	7	2	1	192	194	8	64	74	12.4	3.89	102	.268	.332	12	.176	2	2	2	-3	0.1
1929	Bro-N	1	2	.333	6	3	0	0	0	19	21	2	16	7	18.0	6.63	70	.280	.413	1	.250	0	-4	-4	-0	-0.5
1930	Bro-N	10	7	.588	35	21	6	2	1	198^{1}	204	16	70	59	12.7	3.95	124	.271	.337	10	.147	-2	23	21	-3	1.1
1931	Phi-N	**19**	14	.576	**52**	30	12	2	5	249	288	15	83	99	13.6	4.27	100	.287	.344	11	.122	-6	-11	-1	-5	-1.2
1932	Phi-N	11	10	.524	39	22	8	0	0	166	210	14	47	62	14.0	5.42	81	.300	.346	12	.197	-1	-28	-19	-2	-2.3
1933	Phi-N	6	10	.375	35	21	6	0	2	161^{2}	188	8	49	43	13.4	3.84	99	.295	.348	12	.231	0	-9	-0	-4	-0.4
1934	Phi-N	0	1	.000	3	1	0	0	0	5^{1}	8	0	4	1	21.9	10.13	47	.333	.448	0	.000	-0	-4	-3	-0	-0.5
	Bos-N	1	1	.500	7	3	0	0	0	15^{1}	19	2	9	6	17.0	5.87	65	.284	.377	1	.250	0	-3	-3	-0	-0.4
	Yr	1	2	.333	10	4	0	0	0	20^{2}	27	2	13	7	17.9	6.97	58	.293	.387	1	.200	0	-7	-7	-0	-0.9
Total	10	63	74	.460	252	144	51	8	12	1206^{2}	1338	70	414	453	13.3	4.24	100	.283	.344	68	.163	-8	-29	2	-21	-4.1
● DOCK ELLIS	Ellis, Dock Phillip b: 3/11/45, Los Angeles, Cal. BB/TR, 6'3", 210 lbs. Deb: 6/18/68																									
1968	Pit-N	6	5	.545	26	10	2	0	0	104	82	4	38	52	10.5	2.51	117	.213	.285	2	.069	-1	5	5	0	0.4
1969	Pit-N	11	17	.393	35	33	8	2	0	218^{2}	206	14	76	173	11.8	3.58	97	.250	.316	6	.088	-3	0	-2	1	-0.5
1970	*Pit-N	13	10	.565	30	30	9	4	0	201^{2}	194	9	87	128	13.0	3.21	121	.257	.342	7	.100	-3	19	15	2	1.5
1971	*Pit-N★	19	9	.679	31	31	11	2	0	226^{2}	207	15	63	137	10.8	3.06	111	.239	.292	16	.203	2	10	8	0	1.3
1972	*Pit-N	15	7	.682	25	25	4	1	0	163^{1}	156	6	33	96	10.6	2.70	123	.253	.294	9	.153	-1	14	11	-1	1.3
1973	Pit-N	12	14	.462	28	28	3	1	0	192	176	7	55	122	11.1	3.05	115	.240	.299	7	.108	-3	13	10	1	1.2
1974	Pit-N	12	9	.571	26	26	9	0	0	176^{2}	163	13	41	91	10.7	3.16	109	.242	.292	12	.214	3	9	6	-1	0.9
1975	*Pit-N	8	9	.471	27	24	5	2	0	140	163	9	43	69	13.4	3.79	93	.292	.345	4	.111	0	-3	-4	-1	-0.5
1976	*NY-A	17	8	.680	32	32	8	1	0	211^{2}	195	14	76	65	11.7	3.19	107	.247	.316	0	—	0	8	5	-3	0.3
1977	NY-A	1	1	.500	3	3	1	0	0	19^{2}	18	1	8	5	11.9	1.83	215	.237	.310	0	—	0	5	5	-0	0.5
	Oak-A	1	5	.167	7	7	0	0	0	26	35	5	14	11	17.3	9.69	42	.315	.397	0	—	0	-16	-16	-0	-2.7
	Tex-A	10	6	.625	23	22	7	1	1	167^{1}	158	13	42	90	10.8	2.90	140	.254	.301	0	—	0	21	22	-2	1.8
	Yr	12	12	.500	33	32	8	1	1	213	211	19	64	106	11.6	3.63	112	.260	.314	0	—	0	10	10	-2	-0.4
1978	Tex-A	9	7	.563	22	22	3	0	0	141^{1}	131	15	46	45	11.4	4.20	89	.245	.307	0	—	0	-7	-7	0	-0.7
1979	Tex-A	1	5	.167	10	9	0	0	0	46^{2}	64	5	16	10	15.4	5.98	69	.323	.374	0	—	0	-9	-9	-0	-1.0
	NY-N	3	7	.300	17	14	1	0	0	85	110	9	34	41	15.4	6.04	60	.320	.383	2	.077	-1	-22	-23	0	-2.4
	Pit-N	0	0	—	3	1	0	0	0	7	9	1	2	1	14.1	2.57	151	.346	.393	0	.000	-0	1	1	-0	0.0
	Yr	3	7	.300	20	15	1	0	0	92	119	10	36	42	15.2	5.77	63	.316	.375	2	.074	-2	-21	-22	0	-2.4
Total	12	138	119	.537	345	317	71	14	1	2127^{2}	2067	140	674	1136	11.8	3.46	103	.255	.315	65	.133	-7	49	26	-3	1.4
● JIM ELLIS	Ellis, James Russell b: 3/25/45, Tulare, Cal. BR/TL, 6'2", 185 lbs. Deb: 8/11/67																									
1967	Chi-N	1	1	.500	8	1	0	0	0	16^{2}	20	1	9	8	15.7	3.24	109	.313	.397	1	.200	0	0	1	-0	0.1
1969	StL-N	0	0	—	2	1	0	0	0	5^{1}	7	0	3	0	16.9	1.69	212	.318	.400	0	—	0	1	1	-0	0.0
Total	2	1	1	.500	10	2	0	0	0	22	27	1	12	8	16.0	2.86	124	.314	.398	1	.200	0	1	2	-1	0.1
● ROBERT ELLIS	Ellis, Robert Randolph b: 12/15/70, Baton Rouge, La. BR/TR, 6'5", 220 lbs. Deb: 9/12/96																									
1996	Cal-A	0	0	—	3	0	0	0	0	5	0	0	4	5	7.2	0.00	—	.000	.211	0	—	0	3	3	-0	0.0

YEAR	TM/L	W	L	PCT	G	GS	CG	SH	SV	IP	H	HR	BB	SO	RAT	ERA	ERA+	OAV	OOB	BH	AVG	PB	PR	/A	PD	TPI
● **SAMMY ELLIS** Ellis, Samuel Joseph b: 2/11/41, Youngstown, Ohio BL/TR, 6′1″, 180 lbs. Deb: 4/14/62 C																										
1962	Cin-N	2	2	.500	8	4	0	0	0	28	29	6	29	27	19.0	6.75	60	.269	.428	2	.200	-0	-9	-8	-0	-1.0
1964	Cin-N	10	3	.769	52	5	2	0	14	122^1	101	9	28	125	9.6	2.57	140	.223	.270	2	.083	-0	13	14	0	1.9
1965	Cin-N☆	22	10	.688	44	39	15	2	2	263^2	222	22	104	183	11.3	3.79	99	.226	.304	12	.125	-1	-7	-1	-3	-0.6
1966	Cin-N	12	19	.387	41	36	7	0	0	221	226	35	78	154	12.5	5.29	74	.264	.328	8	.114	-2	-41	-34	-3	-4.7
1967	Cin-N	8	11	.421	32	27	8	1	0	175^2	197	18	67	80	13.7	3.84	98	.286	.353	4	.082	-2	-9	-2	-1	-0.5
1968	Cal-A	9	10	.474	42	24	3	0	2	164	150	22	56	93	11.6	3.95	74	.244	.313	2	.045	-3	-18	-19	-2	-2.8
1969	Chi-A	0	3	.000	10	5	0	0	0	29^1	42	6	16	15	18.1	5.83	66	.336	.415	1	.167	0	-7	-6	0	-0.5
Total	7	63	58	.521	229	140	35	3	18	1004	967	118	378	677	12.3	4.15	88	.253	.323	31	.104	-8	-78	-58	-9	-8.2
● **GEORGE ELLISON** Ellison, George Russell b: 1/24/1895, California d: 1/20/78, San Francisco, Cal. BR/TR, 6′3″, 185 lbs. Deb: 8/21/20																										
1920	Cle-A	0	0	—	1	0	0	0	0	1	0	0	2	1	18.0	0.00	—	.000	.400	0	—	0	0	0	0	0.0
● **DICK ELLSWORTH** Ellsworth, Richard Clark b: 3/22/40, Lusk, Wyo. BL/TL, 6′4″, 195 lbs. Deb: 6/22/58 F																										
1958	Chi-N	0	1	.000	1	1	0	0	0	2^1	4	0	3	0	30.9	15.43	25	.364	.533	0	.000	-0	-3	-3	-0	-0.8
1960	Chi-N	7	13	.350	31	27	6	0	0	176^2	170	12	72	94	12.4	3.72	102	.257	.332	2	.042	-3	1	1	-0	-0.2
1961	Chi-N	10	11	.476	37	31	7	1	0	186^2	213	23	48	91	12.7	3.86	108	.292	.338	2	.036	-5	4	7	3	0.5
1962	Chi-N	9	20	.310	37	33	6	0	1	208^2	241	23	77	113	13.9	5.09	81	.291	.355	7	.113	1	-27	-22	0	-2.5
1963	Chi-N	22	10	.688	37	37	19	4	0	290^2	223	14	75	185	9.3	2.11	**167**	.210	.263	9	.096	-2	38	**45**	2	**5.2**
1964	Chi-N☆	14	18	.438	37	36	16	1	0	256^2	267	34	71	148	12.0	3.75	99	.266	.317	4	.046	-5	-6	-1	2	-0.5
1965	Chi-N	14	15	.483	36	34	8	0	1	222^1	227	22	57	130	11.7	3.81	97	.265	.313	7	.096	-2	-7	-3	2	-0.4
1966	Chi-N	8	22	.267	38	37	9	0	0	269^1	321	28	51	144	12.6	3.98	92	.294	.328	14	.156	-0	-11	-9	2	-0.8
1967	Phi-N	6	7	.462	32	21	3	1	0	125^1	152	6	36	45	13.9	4.38	78	.306	.359	4	.108	-1	-14	-14	2	-1.3
1968	Bos-A	16	7	.696	31	28	10	1	0	196	196	16	37	106	11.0	3.03	104	.260	.301	4	.056	-5	-1	3	-0	-0.2
1969	Bos-A	0	0	—	2	2	0	0	0	12	16	1	4	4	15.0	3.75	101	.320	.370	0	.000	-0	-0	0	-0	0.0
	Cle-A	6	9	.400	34	22	3	1	0	135	162	10	40	48	13.8	4.13	91	.301	.354	6	.133	-1	-8	-6	0	-0.7
	Yr	6	9	.400	36	24	3	1	0	147	178	11	44	52	13.9	4.10	92	.302	.356	6	.125	-2	-8	-5	0	-0.7
1970	Cle-A	3	3	.500	29	1	0	0	2	43^2	49	4	14	13	13.2	4.53	87	.299	.358	0	.000	-0	-4	-3	1	-0.3
	Mil-A	0	0	—	14	0	0	0	1	15^2	11	0	3	9	8.6	1.72	220	.196	.250	0	—	0	3	4	-0	0.0
	Yr	3	3	.500	43	1	0	0	3	59^1	60	4	17	22	11.8	3.79	103	.269	.324	0	.000	-0	-1	1	1	-0.3
1971	Mil-A	0	1	.000	11	0	0	0	0	14^2	22	1	7	10	18.4	4.91	71	.361	.435	0	.000	-0	-2	-2	-0	-0.2
Total	13	115	137	.456	407	310	87	9	5	2155^2	2274	194	595	1140	12.2	3.72	100	.272	.324	59	.088	-25	-37	-2	12	-2.2
● **STEVE ELLSWORTH** Ellsworth, Steven Clark b: 7/30/60, Chicago, Ill. BR/TR, 6′8″, 220 lbs. Deb: 4/7/88 F																										
1988	Bos-A	1	6	.143	8	7	0	0	0	36	47	7	16	16	16.0	6.75	61	.315	.386	0	—	0	-11	-11	-0	-1.8
● **DON ELSTON** Elston, Donald Ray b: 4/6/29, Campbellstown, Ohio d: 1/2/95, Evanston, Ill. BR/TR, 6′, 170 lbs. Deb: 9/17/53																										
1953	Chi-N	0	1	.000	2	1	0	0	0	5	11	1	0	2	19.8	14.40	31	.458	.458	0	.000	-0	-6	-6	-0	-0.8
1957	Bro-N	0	0	—	1	0	0	0	0	1	1	0	0	1	9.0	0.00	—	.250	.250	0	—	0	0	0	0	0.0
	Chi-N	6	7	.462	39	14	2	0	8	144	139	15	55	102	12.4	3.56	109	.259	.334	4	.108	-2	5	5	0	0.3
	Yr	6	7	.462	40	14	2	0	8	145	140	15	55	103	12.4	3.54	109	.259	.333	4	.108	-2	5	5	0	0.3
1958	Chi-N	9	8	.529	**69**	0	0	0	10	97	75	9	39	84	10.7	2.88	136	.214	.294	5	.357	1	**12**	**11**	1	2.4
1959	Chi-N★	10	8	.556	**65**	0	0	0	13	97^2	77	11	46	82	11.6	3.32	119	.218	.313	4	.211	0	7	7	-0	1.3
1960	Chi-N	8	9	.471	60	0	0	0	11	127	109	17	55	85	11.9	3.40	111	.231	.316	3	.125	-1	5	5	-2	0.5
1961	Chi-N	6	7	.462	58	0	0	0	8	93^1	108	11	45	59	15.3	5.59	75	.297	.383	2	.182	-0	-16	-15	0	-2.1
1962	Chi-N	4	8	.333	57	0	0	0	8	66^1	57	6	32	37	12.2	2.44	170	.247	.341	0	.000	-1	11	13	1	2.5
1963	Chi-N	4	1	.800	51	0	0	0	4	70	57	6	21	41	10.3	2.83	124	.226	.291	0	.000	-0	4	5	-1	0.3
1964	Chi-N	2	5	.286	48	0	0	0	1	54^1	68	4	34	26	17.4	5.30	70	.330	.432	1	.167	-0	-11	-10	1	-1.1
Total	9	49	54	.476	450	15	2	0	63	755^2	702	80	327	519	12.6	3.69	106	.251	.335	19	.153	-3	11	17	1	3.3
● **NARCISO ELVIRA** Elvira, Narciso Chicho (Delgado) b: 10/29/67, Veracruz, Mex. BL/TL, 5′10″, 160 lbs. Deb: 9/9/90																										
1990	Mil-A	0	0	—	4	0	0	0	0	5	6	0	5	6	19.8	5.40	72	.300	.440	0	—	0	-1	-1	0	0.1
● **HARRY ELY** Ely, Harry Deb: 9/24/1892																										
1892	Bal-N	0	1	.000	1	1	1	0	0	7	14	0	7	0	29.6	7.71	44	.400	.523	0	.000	-0	-3	-3	-0	-0.4
● **BONES ELY** Ely, William Frederick b: 6/7/1863, N.Girard, Pa. d: 1/10/52, Berkeley, Cal. BR/TR, 6′1″, 155 lbs. Deb: 6/19/1884 ♦																										
1884	Buf-N	0	1	.000	1	1	0	0	0	5	17	1	5	4	39.6	14.40	22	.500	.564	0	.000	-1	-6	-6	-0	-0.7
1886	Lou-a	0	4	.000	6	4	4	0	**1**	44	53	0	26	28	16.2	5.32	68	.280	.367	5	.156	-1	-9	-8	0	-0.7
1890	Syr-a	0	0	—	1	0	0	0	0	2	7	0	0	0	31.5	22.50	16	.538	.538	130	.262	0	-4	-4	0	0.0
1894	StL-N	0	0	—	1	0	0	0	0	1	0	0	3	0	27.0	0.00	—	.000	.500	156	.306	0	1	1	0	0.0
Total	4	0	5	.000	9	5	4	0	1	52	77	1	34	32	19.2	6.75	54	.322	.407	1331	.258	-1	-19	-18	0	-1.4
● **ALAN EMBREE** Embree, Alan Duane b: 1/23/70, Vancouver, Wash. BL/TL, 6′2″, 185 lbs. Deb: 9/15/92																										
1992	Cle-A	0	2	.000	4	4	0	0	0	18	19	3	8	12	14.0	7.00	56	.271	.354	0	—	0	-6	-6	-1	-0.6
1995	*Cle-A	3	2	.600	23	0	0	0	1	24^2	23	2	16	23	14.2	5.11	92	.253	.364	0	—	0	-1	-1	-0	-0.2
1996	*Cle-A	1	1	.500	24	0	0	0	0	31	30	10	21	33	14.8	6.39	77	.259	.372	0	—	0	-5	-5	-0	-0.3
1997	Atl-N	3	1	.750	66	0	0	0	0	46	36	1	20	45	11.3	2.54	164	.221	.314	0	—	0	8	8	0	0.7
1998	Atl-N	1	0	1.000	20	0	0	0	0	18^2	23	2	10	19	15.9	4.34	97	.307	.388	0	.000	-0	-0	-0	0	0.0
	Ari-N	3	2	.600	35	0	0	0	1	35	33	5	13	24	12.1	4.11	105	.248	.320	0	—	0	0	1	-1	0.0
	Yr	4	2	.667	55	0	0	0	1	53^2	56	7	23	43	13.4	4.19	102	.268	.343	0	.000	0	0	1	-0	0.0
Total	5	11	8	.579	172	4	0	0	2	173^1	164	23	88	156	13.3	4.57	96	.253	.346	0	.000	0	-3	-4	-2	-0.4
● **RED EMBREE** Embree, Charles Willard b: 8/30/17, ElMonte, Cal. d: 9/24/96, Eugene, Ore. BR/TR, 6′, 165 lbs. Deb: 9/10/41																										
1941	Cle-A	0	1	.000	1	1	0	0	0	4	7	0	3	4	24.8	6.75	58	.438	.550	0	.000	-0	-1	-1	-0	-0.3
1942	Cle-A	3	4	.429	19	6	2	0	0	63	58	0	31	44	13.0	3.86	89	.242	.333	2	.133	-0	-1	-3	-0	-0.3
1944	Cle-A	0	1	.000	3	1	0	0	0	3^1	2	0	5	4	18.9	13.50	24	.167	.412	0	—	0	-4	-4	0	-0.9
1945	Cle-A	4	4	.500	8	8	5	1	0	70	56	3	26	42	10.5	1.93	168	.215	.287	3	.143	-1	11	10	1	1.2
1946	Cle-A	8	12	.400	28	26	8	0	0	200	170	15	79	87	11.3	3.47	95	.227	.302	13	.186	1	1	-3	-1	-0.3
1947	Cle-A	8	10	.444	27	21	6	0	0	162^2	137	13	67	56	11.3	3.15	110	.233	.313	9	.173	-1	10	6	1	0.5
1948	NY-A	5	3	.625	20	8	4	0	0	76^2	77	6	30	25	12.7	3.76	109	.261	.331	4	.148	-1	5	3	-1	0.0
1949	StL-A	3	13	.188	35	19	4	0	1	127^1	146	13	89	24	16.8	5.37	84	.294	.405	6	.162	-1	-17	-12	-0	-1.4
Total	8	31	48	.392	141	90	29	1	1	707	653	50	330	286	12.6	3.72	98	.246	.331	37	.166	-4	4	-5	-2	-1.5
● **SLIM EMBREY** Embrey, Charles Akin b: 8/17/01, Columbia, Tenn. d: 10/10/47, Nashville, Tenn. BR/TR, 6′2″, 184 lbs. Deb: 10/1/23																										
1923	Chi-A	0	0	—	1	0	0	0	0	2^2	7	0	2	1	30.4	10.13	39	.500	.563	0	—	0	-2	-2	0	0.0
● **CHARLIE EMIG** Emig, Charles Henry b: 4/5/1875, Cincinnati, Ohio d: 10/2/75, Oklahoma City, Okla. TL , Deb: 9/4/1896																										
1896	Lou-N	0	1	.000	1	1	1	0	0	8	12	1	7	1	24.8	7.88	55	.343	.489	0	.000	-1	-3	-3	1	-0.3
● **SLIM EMMERICH** Emmerich, William Peter b: 9/29/19, Allentown, Pa. BR/TR, 6′1″, 170 lbs. Deb: 5/14/45																										
1945	NY-N	4	4	.500	31	7	1	0	0	100	111	8	33	27	13.1	4.86	80	.278	.334	3	.120	-2	-12	-11	-0	-0.9
1946	NY-N	0	0	—	2	0	0	0	0	4	6	1	0	1	13.5	4.50	76	.400	.400	0	—	0	-0	-0	0	0.0
Total	2	4	4	.500	33	7	1	0	0	104	117	9	33	28	13.1	4.85	80	.282	.336	3	.120	-2	-12	-11	-0	-0.9
● **BOB EMSLIE** Emslie, Robert Daniel b: 1/27/1859, Guelph, Ont., Can. d: 4/26/43, St.Thomas, Ont., Canada BR/TR, 5′11″, Deb: 7/25/1883 U																										
1883	Bal-a	9	13	.409	24	23	21	1	0	201^1	188	3	41	62	10.2	3.17	110	.231	.268	16	.165	-3	3	7	2	0.5
1884	Bal-a	32	17	.653	50	50	50	4	0	455^1	419	5	88	264	10.3	2.75	126	.224	.264	37	.190	-5	25	36	-1	2.8
1885	Bal-a	3	10	.231	13	13	11	0	0	107	131	0	30	27	14.0	4.29	76	.298	.350	12	.235	0	-12	-12	-1	-1.2
	Phi-a	0	4	.000	4	4	3	0	0	28^2	37	1	6	9	13.5	6.28	55	.291	.323	1	.083	-1	-10	-9	1	-1.0
	Yr	3	14	.176	17	17	14	0	0	135^2	168	1	36	36	13.5	4.71	70	.294	.336	13	.206	-1	-22	-21	-1	-2.2
Total	3	44	44	.500	91	90	85	5	0	792^1	775	9	165	362	10.9	3.19	108	.239	.279	66	.186	-9	6	22	0	1.1

● LUIS ENCARNACION

Encarnacion, Luis Martin Lora (b: Luis Martin Lora (Encarcnacion)) b: 10/20/63, Santo Domingo, D.R. BR/TR, 5'10", 178 lbs. Deb: 7/27/90

YEAR	TM/L	W	L	PCT	G	GS	CG	SH	SV	IP	H	HR	BB	SO	RAT	ERA	ERA+	OAV	OOB	BH	AVG	PB	PR	/A	PD	TPI
1990	KC-A	0	0	—	4	0	0	0	0	10^1	14	1	4	8	15.7	7.84	49	.311	.367	0	—	0	-5	-5	-0	0.1

● JOE ENGEL

Engel, Joseph William b: 3/12/1893, Washington, D.C. d: 6/12/69, Chattanooga, Tenn BR/TL, 6'1.5", 183 lbs. Deb: 5/30/12

YEAR	TM/L	W	L	PCT	G	GS	CG	SH	SV	IP	H	HR	BB	SO	RAT	ERA	ERA+	OAV	OOB	BH	AVG	PB	PR	/A	PD	TPI
1912	Was-A	2	5	.286	17	10	2	0	1	75	70	2	50	29	14.9	3.96	84	.253	.375	1	.059	-1	-5	-5	1	-0.5
1913	Was-A	8	9	.471	36	24	6	2	0	164^2	124	2	85	70	12.0	3.06	97	.207	.317	3	.061	-5	-2	-2	-1	-0.8
1914	Was-A	7	5	.583	35	15	1	0	3	124^1	108	2	75	41	13.6	2.97	95	.254	.372	3	.107	1	-3	-2	-0	-0.2
1915	Was-A	0	3	.000	11	3	0	0	0	33^2	30	0	19	9	13.9	3.21	93	.261	.380	0	.000	-1	-1	-1	0	-0.1
1917	Cin-N	0	1	.000	1	1	1	0	0	8	12	0	6	2	20.3	5.63	47	.353	.450	0	.000	-0	-3	-3	0	-0.3
1919	Cle-A	0	0	—	1	0	0	0	0	0	0	0	3	0	—	∞	—	—	1.000	0	—	0	-2	-2	0	-0.2
1920	Was-A	0	0	—	1	0	0	0	0	1^2	0	0	4	0	27.0	21.60	17	.000	.556	0	.000	-0	-3	-3	-0	0.0
Total	7	17	23	.425	102	53	10	2	4	407^1	344	6	242	151	13.5	3.38	88	.237	.355	7	.067	-6	-20	-18	-0	-2.1

● STEVE ENGEL

Engel, Steven Michael b: 12/31/61, Cincinnati, Ohio BR/TL, 6'3", 216 lbs. Deb: 7/30/85

YEAR	TM/L	W	L	PCT	G	GS	CG	SH	SV	IP	H	HR	BB	SO	RAT	ERA	ERA+	OAV	OOB	BH	AVG	PB	PR	/A	PD	TPI
1985	Chi-N	1	5	.167	11	8	1	0	1	51^2	61	10	26	29	15.2	5.57	72	.298	.377	3	.188	1	-11	-9	-0	-0.9

● RICK ENGLE

Engle, Richard Douglas b: 4/7/57, Corbin, Ky. BR/TL, 5'11.5", 181 lbs. Deb: 9/2/81

YEAR	TM/L	W	L	PCT	G	GS	CG	SH	SV	IP	H	HR	BB	SO	RAT	ERA	ERA+	OAV	OOB	BH	AVG	PB	PR	/A	PD	TPI
1981	Mon-N	0	0	—	1	0	0	0	0	2	6	0	1	2	31.5	18.00	19	.500	.538	0	—	0	-3	-3	-0	0.0

● JACK ENRIGHT

Enright, Jackson Percy b: 11/29/1895, Fort Worth, Tex. d: 8/18/75, Pompano Beach, Fla BR/TR, 5'11", 177 lbs. Deb: 9/26/17

YEAR	TM/L	W	L	PCT	G	GS	CG	SH	SV	IP	H	HR	BB	SO	RAT	ERA	ERA+	OAV	OOB	BH	AVG	PB	PR	/A	PD	TPI
1917	NY-A	0	1	.000	1	1	0	0	0	5	5	0	3	1	14.4	5.40	50	.294	.400	0	.000	-0	-2	-2	1	-0.2

● TERRY ENYART

Enyart, Terry Gene b: 10/10/50, Ironton, Ohio BR/TL, 6'2", 190 lbs. Deb: 6/17/74

YEAR	TM/L	W	L	PCT	G	GS	CG	SH	SV	IP	H	HR	BB	SO	RAT	ERA	ERA+	OAV	OOB	BH	AVG	PB	PR	/A	PD	TPI
1974	Mon-N	0	0	—	2	0	0	0	0	1^2	4	0	4	2	43.2	16.20	24	.444	.615	0	—	0	-2	-2	-0	0.0

● JOHNNY ENZMANN

Enzmann, John "Gentleman John" b: 3/4/1890, Brooklyn, N.Y. d: 3/14/84, Riverhead, N.Y. BR/TR, 5'10", 165 lbs. Deb: 7/10/14

YEAR	TM/L	W	L	PCT	G	GS	CG	SH	SV	IP	H	HR	BB	SO	RAT	ERA	ERA+	OAV	OOB	BH	AVG	PB	PR	/A	PD	TPI
1914	Bro-N	1	0	1.000	7	1	0	0	0	19	21	1	8	5	15.2	4.74	60	.300	.395	0	.000	-1	-4	-4	1	-0.2
1918	Cle-A	5	7	.417	30	14	8	0	2	136^2	130	2	29	38	10.8	2.37	127	.263	.310	7	.149	-2	6	10	0	0.6
1919	Cle-A	3	2	.600	14	4	2	0	0	55^1	67	0	8	13	12.5	2.28	147	.312	.342	2	.133	-0	6	7	-1	0.4
1920	Phi-N	2	3	.400	16	2	1	0	0	58^2	79	1	16	35	15.3	3.84	89	.320	.373	4	.167	1	-5	-3	-0	-0.2
Total	4	11	12	.478	67	21	11	0	2	269^2	297	4	61	91	12.4	2.84	111	.289	.338	13	.141	-3	3	10	-0	0.6

● AL EPPERLY

Epperly, Albert Paul "Tub" or "Pard" b: 5/7/18, Glidden, Iowa BL/TR, 6'2", 194 lbs. Deb: 4/25/38

YEAR	TM/L	W	L	PCT	G	GS	CG	SH	SV	IP	H	HR	BB	SO	RAT	ERA	ERA+	OAV	OOB	BH	AVG	PB	PR	/A	PD	TPI
1938	Chi-N	2	0	1.000	9	4	1	0	0	27	28	1	15	10	14.3	3.67	104	.264	.355	2	.250	1	0	0	0	0.1
1950	Bro-N	0	0	—	5	0	0	0	0	9	14	1	5	3	19.0	5.00	82	.378	.452	0	—	0	-1	-1	-0	0.0
Total	2	2	0	1.000	14	4	1	0	0	36	42	2	20	13	15.5	4.00	97	.294	.380	2	.250	1	-0	-0	-0	0.1

● GREG ERARDI

Erardi, Joseph Gregory b: 5/31/54, Syracuse, N.Y. BR/TR, 6'1", 190 lbs. Deb: 9/6/77

YEAR	TM/L	W	L	PCT	G	GS	CG	SH	SV	IP	H	HR	BB	SO	RAT	ERA	ERA+	OAV	OOB	BH	AVG	PB	PR	/A	PD	TPI
1977	Sea-A	0	1	.000	5	0	0	0	0	9	12	3	6	5	18.0	6.00	69	.300	.391	0	—	0	-2	-2	-0	-0.2

● EDDIE ERAUTT

Erautt, Edward Lorenz Sebastian b: 9/26/24, Portland, Ore. BR/TR, 6', 186 lbs. Deb: 4/16/47 F

YEAR	TM/L	W	L	PCT	G	GS	CG	SH	SV	IP	H	HR	BB	SO	RAT	ERA	ERA+	OAV	OOB	BH	AVG	PB	PR	/A	PD	TPI
1947	Cin-N	4	9	.308	36	10	2	0	0	119	146	5	53	43	15.2	5.07	81	.307	.379	2	.069	-1	-13	-13	1	-1.3
1948	Cin-N	0	0	—	2	0	0	0	0	3	3	0	1	0	12.0	6.00	65	.250	.308	0	—	0	-1	-1	-0	0.0
1949	Cin-N	4	11	.267	39	9	1	0	1	112^2	99	9	61	43	13.0	3.36	125	.247	.351	4	.174	0	**9**	**10**	-1	1.2
1950	Cin-N	4	2	.667	33	2	1	0	1	65^1	82	9	22	35	15.2	5.65	75	.307	.373	2	.154	0	-11	-10	-0	-0.9
1951	Cin-N	0	0	—	30	0	0	0	0	39^1	50	4	23	20	17.4	5.72	71	.314	.411	0	.000	-0	-8	-7	1	0.0
1953	Cin-N	0	0	—	4	0	0	0	0	4^2	11	1	3	1	27.0	5.79	75	.500	.560	0	.000	-0	-1	-1	0	0.0
	StL-N	3	1	.750	20	1	0	0	0	35^2	43	6	16	15	15.4	6.31	67	.299	.377	1	.167	-0	-8	-8	0	-0.8
	Yr	3	1	.750	24	1	0	0	0	40^1	54	7	19	16	16.7	6.25	68	.325	.401	1	.143	-0	-9	-9	0	-0.8
Total	6	15	23	.395	164	22	4	0	2	379^2	434	34	179	157	14.9	4.86	86	.293	.376	9	.120	-2	-33	-29	0	-1.8

● TODD ERDOS

Erdos, Todd Michael b: 11/21/73, Washington, Pa. BR/TR, 6'1", 205 lbs. Deb: 6/8/97

YEAR	TM/L	W	L	PCT	G	GS	CG	SH	SV	IP	H	HR	BB	SO	RAT	ERA	ERA+	OAV	OOB	BH	AVG	PB	PR	/A	PD	TPI
1997	SD-N	2	0	1.000	11	0	0	0	0	13^2	17	1	4	13	15.1	5.27	74	.293	.359	0	.000	-0	-2	-2	0	-0.3
1998	NY-A	0	0	—	2	0	0	0	0	2	5	0	1	0	27.0	9.00	49	.500	.545	0	—	0	-1	-1	-0	0.0
Total	2	2	0	1.000	13	0	0	0	0	15^2	22	1	5	13	16.7	5.74	69	.324	.387	0	.000	-0	-3	-3	0	-0.3

● JOHN ERICKS

Ericks, John Edward b: 6/16/67, Tinley Park, Ill. BR/TR, 6'7", 220 lbs. Deb: 6/24/95

YEAR	TM/L	W	L	PCT	G	GS	CG	SH	SV	IP	H	HR	BB	SO	RAT	ERA	ERA+	OAV	OOB	BH	AVG	PB	PR	/A	PD	TPI
1995	Pit-N	3	9	.250	19	18	1	0	0	106	108	7	50	80	13.6	4.58	94	.263	.346	3	.097	-2	-5	-3	-1	-0.6
1996	Pit-N	4	5	.444	28	4	0	0	8	46^2	56	11	19	46	14.5	5.79	75	.292	.355	0	.000	-1	-8	-7	-1	-1.6
1997	Pit-N	1	0	1.000	10	0	0	0	6	9^1	7	1	4	6	10.6	1.93	222	.200	.282	0	—	0	2	2	0	0.5
Total	3	8	14	.364	57	22	1	0	14	162	171	19	73	132	13.7	4.78	90	.268	.346	3	.083	-2	-11	-8	-2	-1.7

● DON ERICKSON

Erickson, Don Lee b: 12/13/31, Springfield, Ill. BR/TR, 6', 175 lbs. Deb: 9/1/58

YEAR	TM/L	W	L	PCT	G	GS	CG	SH	SV	IP	H	HR	BB	SO	RAT	ERA	ERA+	OAV	OOB	BH	AVG	PB	PR	/A	PD	TPI
1958	Phi-N	0	1	.000	9	0	0	0	1	11^2	11	3	9	9	15.4	4.63	86	.244	.370	0	.000	-0	-1	-1	-0	-0.1

● ERIC ERICKSON

Erickson, Eric George Adolph b: 3/13/1895, Goteborg, Sweden d: 5/19/65, Jamestown, N.Y. BR/TR, 6'2", 190 lbs. Deb: 10/6/14

YEAR	TM/L	W	L	PCT	G	GS	CG	SH	SV	IP	H	HR	BB	SO	RAT	ERA	ERA+	OAV	OOB	BH	AVG	PB	PR	/A	PD	TPI
1914	NY-N	0	1	.000	1	1	0	0	0	5	8	0	3	3	19.8	0.00	—	.364	.440	0	.000	-0	2	1	-0	0.3
1916	Det-A	0	0	—	8	0	0	0	0	16	13	0	8	7	12.4	2.81	102	.220	.324	0	.000	-1	0	0	-1	-0.1
1918	Det-A	4	5	.444	12	9	8	0	1	94^1	81	2	29	48	10.8	2.48	107	.240	.306	4	.121	-3	3	2	-3	-0.4
1919	Det-A	0	2	.000	3	2	0	0	0	14^2	17	0	10	4	17.2	6.75	47	.293	.406	1	.200	-0	-6	-6	0	-0.7
	Was-A	6	11	.353	20	15	7	1	0	132	130	7	63	86	13.6	3.95	81	.254	.344	7	.146	-1	-11	-11	-3	-1.7
	Yr	6	13	.316	23	17	7	1	0	146^2	147	7	73	90	13.9	4.23	76	.258	.349	8	.151	-2	-16	-17	-3	-2.4
1920	Was-A	12	16	.429	39	27	12	0	1	239^1	231	13	128	87	13.9	3.84	97	.264	.365	23	.277	4	-1	-3	-4	-0.3
1921	Was-A	8	10	.444	32	22	9	3	0	179	181	7	65	71	12.8	3.62	114	.269	.341	9	.150	-3	13	10	-3	0.2
1922	Was-A	4	12	.250	30	17	6	2	2	141^2	144	8	73	61	14.0	4.96	78	.279	.372	6	.133	-2	-14	-17	-2	-2.1
Total	7	34	57	.374	145	93	42	6	4	822	805	37	379	367	13.3	3.85	93	.264	.352	50	.179	-6	-14	-23	-15	-4.8

● HAL ERICKSON

Erickson, Harold James b: 7/17/19, Portland, Ore. BR/TR, 6'5", 230 lbs. Deb: 4/14/53

YEAR	TM/L	W	L	PCT	G	GS	CG	SH	SV	IP	H	HR	BB	SO	RAT	ERA	ERA+	OAV	OOB	BH	AVG	PB	PR	/A	PD	TPI
1953	Det-A	0	1	.000	18	0	0	0	1	32^1	43	4	10	19	15.3	4.73	86	.323	.379	0	.000	-1	-3	-2	-0	-0.2

● PAUL ERICKSON

Erickson, Paul Walford "Li'L Abner" b: 12/14/15, Zion, Ill. BR/TR, 6'2", 200 lbs. Deb: 6/29/41

YEAR	TM/L	W	L	PCT	G	GS	CG	SH	SV	IP	H	HR	BB	SO	RAT	ERA	ERA+	OAV	OOB	BH	AVG	PB	PR	/A	PD	TPI
1941	Chi-N	5	7	.417	32	15	7	1	1	141	126	2	64	85	12.3	3.70	95	.234	.318	7	.152	0	-1	-3	-1	-0.3
1942	Chi-N	1	6	.143	18	7	1	0	0	63	70	4	41	26	15.9	5.43	59	.288	.391	3	.143	-1	-15	-16	0	-1.7
1943	Chi-N	1	3	.250	15	4	0	0	0	42^2	47	4	22	24	15.0	6.12	55	.280	.370	3	.200	0	-13	-13	-1	-1.2
1944	Chi-N	5	9	.357	33	15	5	3	1	124^1	113	5	67	82	13.0	3.55	100	.243	.338	2	.056	-1	1	-0	2	0.0
1945	*Chi-N	7	4	.636	28	9	3	0	3	108^1	94	5	48	53	12.4	3.32	110	.233	.325	5	.156	0	6	4	-0	0.4
1946	Chi-N	9	7	.563	32	14	5	1	0	137	119	2	65	70	12.3	2.43	137	.232	.321	2	.050	-4	15	14	-1	1.0
1947	Chi-N	7	12	.368	40	20	6	0	1	174	179	17	93	82	14.3	4.34	91	.268	.362	15	.250	3	-6	-8	1	-0.4
1948	Chi-N	0	0	—	3	0	0	0	0	5^2	7	0	6	4	20.6	6.35	61	.292	.433	0	.000	-0	-2	-2	0	0.0
	Phi-N	2	0	1.000	4	2	0	0	0	17^1	19	2	17	5	18.7	5.19	76	.292	.439	1	.143	-0	-2	-2	0	-0.2
	NY-N	0	0	—	2	0	0	0	0	1	0	0	2	1	18.0	0.00	—	.000	.400	0	—	0	0	0	0	0.0
	Yr	2	0	1.000	9	2	0	0	0	24	26	2	25	10	19.1	5.25	75	.283	.436	1	.125	-0	-3	-4	0	-0.2
Total	8	37	48	.435	207	86	27	5	6	814^1	774	41	425	432	13.5	3.86	93	.250	.345	38	.147	-2	-16	-26	-0	-2.4

● RALPH ERICKSON

Erickson, Ralph Lief b: 6/25/02, Dubois, Idaho BL/TL, 6'1", 175 lbs. Deb: 9/11/29

YEAR	TM/L	W	L	PCT	G	GS	CG	SH	SV	IP	H	HR	BB	SO	RAT	ERA	ERA+	OAV	OOB	BH	AVG	PB	PR	/A	PD	TPI
1929	Pit-N	0	0	—	1	0	0	0	0	1	2	0	2	0	36.0	27.00	18	.500	.667	0	—	0	-2	-2	-0	0.0
1930	Pit-N	1	0	1.000	7	0	0	0	0	14	21	1	10	2	19.9	7.07	70	.375	.470	1	.250	-0	-3	-3	0	-0.2
Total	2	1	0	1.000	8	0	0	0	0	15	23	1	12	2	21.0	8.40	59	.383	.486	1	.250	-0	-6	-6	-0	-0.2

● ROGER ERICKSON

Erickson, Roger Farrell b: 8/30/56, Springfield, Ill. BR/TR, 6'3", 190 lbs. Deb: 4/6/78

YEAR	TM/L	W	L	PCT	G	GS	CG	SH	SV	IP	H	HR	BB	SO	RAT	ERA	ERA+	OAV	OOB	BH	AVG	PB	PR	/A	PD	TPI
1978	Min-A	14	13	.519	37	37	14	0	0	265^2	268	19	79	121	12.0	3.96	96	.263	.321	0	—	0	-6	-4	0	-0.4
1979	Min-A	3	10	.231	24	21	0	0	0	123	154	17	48	47	14.9	5.63	78	.310	.372	0	—	0	-19	-17	-0	-1.7

YEAR	TM/L	W	L	PCT	G	GS	CG	SH	SV	IP	H	HR	BB	SO	RAT	ERA	ERA+	OAV	OOB	BH	AVG	PB	PR	/A	PD	TPI
1980	Min-A	7	13	.350	32	27	7	0	0	191^1	198	13	56	97	12.1	3.25	134	.268	.322	0	—	0	17	24	-0	2.3
1981	Min-A	3	8	.273	14	14	1	0	0	91^1	93	7	31	44	12.2	3.84	103	.262	.321	0	—	0	-2	1	-0	-0.1
1982	Min-A	4	3	.571	7	7	2	0	0	40^2	56	6	12	12	15.3	4.87	87	.326	.373	0	—	0	-4	-3	1	-0.4
	NY-A	4	5	.444	16	11	0	0	1	70^2	86	5	17	37	13.1	4.46	89	.301	.340	0	—	0	-3	-4	-1	-0.5
	Yr	8	8	.500	23	18	2	0	1	111^1	142	11	29	49	13.8	4.61	89	.308	.349	0	—	0	-7	-7	-1	-0.9
1983	NY-A	0	1	.000	5	0	0	0	0	16^2	13	1	8	7	11.3	4.32	90	.213	.304	0	—	0	-0	-1	0	0.2
Total	6	35	53	.398	135	117	24	0	1	799^1	868	68	251	365	12.8	4.13	99	.277	.334	0	—	0	-18	-4	-1	-0.6
● SCOTT ERICKSON	Erickson, Scott Gavin b: 2/2/68, Long Beach, Cal. BR/TR, 6′4″, 224 lbs. Deb: 6/25/90																									
1990	Min-A	8	4	.667	19	17	1	0	0	113	108	9	51	53	13.1	2.87	145	.256	.343	0	—	0	13	16	-0	1.6
1991	*Min-A	**20**	8	**.714**	32	32	5	3	0	204	189	13	71	108	11.7	3.18	134	.248	.317	0	—	0	21	25	1	3.1
1992	Min-A	13	12	.520	32	32	5	3	0	212	197	18	83	101	12.2	3.40	119	.252	.330	0	—	0	13	15	2	1.8
1993	Min-A	8	19	.296	34	34	1	0	0	218^2	266	17	71	116	14.3	5.19	84	.305	.364	0	—	0	-21	-20	1	-2.0
1994	Min-A	8	11	.421	23	23	2	1	0	144	173	15	59	104	15.1	5.44	90	.299	.372	0	—	0	-10	-9	1	-0.9
1995	Min-A	4	6	.400	15	15	0	0	0	87^2	102	11	32	45	14.2	5.95	80	.291	.357	0	—	0	-12	-12	2	-0.9
	Bal-A	9	4	.692	17	16	7	2	0	108^2	111	7	35	61	12.2	3.89	122	.273	.332	0	—	0	10	10	3	1.3
	Yr	13	10	.565	32	31	7	2	0	196^1	213	18	67	106	12.9	4.81	99	.279	.338	0	—	0	-2	-1	4	0.4
1996	*Bal-A	13	12	.520	34	34	6	0	0	222^1	262	21	66	100	13.7	5.02	98	.297	.354	0	—	0	-1	-2	4	0.2
1997	*Bal-A	16	7	.696	34	33	3	2	0	221^2	218	16	61	131	11.5	3.69	119	.257	.310	0	.000	0	21	17	3	1.9
1998	Bal-A	16	13	.552	36	36	**11**	2	0	**251**^{1}	284	23	69	186	13.1	4.01	113	.281	.335	0	.000	1	18	14	5	1.9
Total	9	115	96	.545	276	272	41	13	0	1783^1	1910	150	598	1005	13.0	4.20	107	.276	.340	0	.000	1	52	56	20	8.0
● DICK ERRICKSON	Errickson, Richard Merriwell "Lief" b: 3/5/14, Vineland, N.J. BL/TR, 6′1″, 175 lbs. Deb: 4/27/38																									
1938	Bos-N	9	7	.563	34	10	6	1	6	122^2	113	1	56	40	12.5	3.15	109	.246	.330	4	.114	-1	9	4	2	0.5
1939	Bos-N	6	9	.400	28	11	3	0	1	128^1	143	6	54	33	13.9	4.00	92	.293	.365	10	.227	1	-1	-4	2	-0.2
1940	Bos-N	12	13	.480	34	29	17	3	4	236^1	241	8	90	34	12.6	3.16	118	.270	.338	13	.157	-2	18	15	1	1.4
1941	Bos-N	6	12	.333	38	23	5	2	1	165^2	192	12	62	45	14.0	4.78	75	.287	.351	8	.178	-0	-21	-22	1	-2.2
1942	Bos-N	2	5	.286	21	4	0	0	1	59^1	76	8	20	15	14.6	5.01	67	.309	.361	2	.125	-1	-11	-11	-1	-1.4
	Chi-N	1	1	.500	13	0	0	0	0	24	39	1	8	9	18.0	4.13	78	.411	.462	0	.000	-1	-2	-2	1	-0.2
	Yr	3	6	.333	34	4	0	0	1	83^1	115	9	28	24	15.6	4.75	69	.337	.389	2	.095	-1	-13	-13	-0	-1.6
Total	5	36	47	.434	168	77	31	6	13	736^1	804	36	290	176	13.5	3.85	93	.282	.350	37	.162	-5	-9	-21	5	-2.1
● CARL ERSKINE	Erskine, Carl Daniel "Oisk" b: 12/13/26, Anderson, Ind. BR/TR, 5′10″, 165 lbs. Deb: 7/25/48																									
1948	Bro-N	6	3	.667	17	9	3	0	0	64	51	5	35	29	12.2	3.23	124	.231	.339	2	.095	-2	5	5	-1	0.4
1949	*Bro-N	8	1	.889	22	3	2	0	0	79^2	68	6	51	49	13.7	4.63	89	.235	.354	3	.115	-2	-5	-5	0	-0.6
1950	Bro-N	7	6	.538	22	13	3	0	1	103	109	15	35	50	12.7	4.72	87	.273	.333	9	.243	2	-7	-7	-1	-0.7
1951	Bro-N	16	12	.571	46	19	7	0	4	189^2	206	23	78	95	13.6	4.46	88	.280	.351	8	.131	-2	-11	-11	-0	-1.8
1952	*Bro-N	14	6	.700	33	26	10	4	2	206^2	167	17	71	131	10.5	2.70	135	.220	.289	10	.152	-0	24	22	2	2.3
1953	*Bro-N	20	6	**.769**	39	33	16	4	3	246^2	213	21	95	187	11.3	3.54	120	.230	.304	20	.215	0	20	20	-2	1.7
1954	Bro-N★	18	15	.545	38	37	12	2	1	260^1	239	31	92	166	11.6	4.15	98	.243	.311	14	.159	-1	-2	-2	-0	-0.4
1955	*Bro-N	11	8	.579	31	29	7	2	1	194^2	185	29	64	84	11.5	3.79	107	.253	.313	15	.203	-0	5	6	-2	0.3
1956	*Bro-N	13	11	.542	31	28	8	1	0	186^1	189	25	57	95	11.9	4.25	93	.264	.320	8	.121	-3	-10	-6	1	-1.0
1957	Bro-N	5	3	.625	15	7	1	0	0	66	62	8	20	26	11.2	3.55	118	.248	.304	2	.091	-2	2	5	-1	0.2
1958	LA-N	4	4	.500	31	9	2	1	0	98^1	115	14	35	54	13.7	5.13	80	.297	.355	1	.037	-3	-13	-11	1	-1.0
1959	LA-N	0	3	.000	10	3	0	0	1	23^1	33	5	13	15	17.7	7.71	55	.320	.397	0	.000	-1	-10	-9	-0	-1.2
Total	12	122	78	.610	335	216	71	14	13	1718^2	1637	199	646	981	12.0	4.00	101	.252	.321	92	.156	-13	-0	6	-4	-1.8
● CHICO ESCARREGA	Escarrega, Ernesto (Acosta) b: 12/27/49, Los Mochis, Mex. BR/TR, 5′11″, 185 lbs. Deb: 4/26/82																									
1982	Chi-A	1	3	.250	38	2	0	0	1	73^2	73	3	16	33	10.9	3.67	110	.263	.303	0	—	0	3	3	-1	0.1
● KELVIM ESCOBAR	Escobar, Kelvim Jose (Bolivar) b: 4/11/76, LaGuaira, Venez. BR/TR, 6′1″, 205 lbs. Deb: 6/29/97																									
1997	Tor-A	3	2	.600	27	0	0	0	14	31	28	1	19	36	13.6	2.90	158	.237	.343	0	—	0	6	6	-0	1.2
1998	Tor-A	7	3	.700	22	10	0	0	0	79^2	72	5	35	72	12.1	3.73	125	.237	.316	0	—	0	8	8	-1	0.7
Total	2	10	5	.667	49	10	0	0	14	110^2	100	6	54	108	12.5	3.50	132	.237	.324	0	—	0	14	14	-2	1.9
● VAUGHN ESHELMAN	Eshelman, Vaughn Michael b: 5/22/69, Philadelphia, Pa. BL/TL, 6′3″, 205 lbs. Deb: 5/2/95																									
1995	Bos-A	6	3	.667	23	14	0	0	0	81^2	86	3	36	41	13.6	4.85	100	.272	.348	0	—	0	-1	0	-1	-0.1
1996	Bos-A	6	3	.667	39	10	0	0	0	87^2	112	13	58	59	17.7	7.08	72	.311	.410	0	—	0	-20	-20	0	-1.6
1997	Bos-A	3	3	.500	21	6	0	0	0	42^2	58	3	17	18	16.2	6.33	73	.330	.395	1	.250	0	-8	-8	-0	-1.0
Total	3	15	9	.625	83	30	0	0	0	212	256	19	111	118	15.8	6.07	81	.300	.384	1	.250	0	-30	-27	-1	-2.7
● DUKE ESPER	Esper, Charles H. (b: Charles Esbacher) b: 7/28/1868, Salem, N.J. d: 8/31/10, Philadelphia, Pa. TL, 5′11.5″, 185 lbs. Deb: 4/18/1890																									
1890	Phi-a	8	9	.471	18	16	14	1	0	143^2	176	1	67	61	15.5	4.89	78	.292	.368	18	.295	4	-16	-17	1	-1.1
	Pit-N	0	2	.000	2	2	2	0	0	17	18	0	10	9	15.4	5.29	62	.265	.367	1	.143	-1	-3	-4	0	-0.3
	Phi-N	5	0	1.000	5	5	4	0	0	41	40	1	16	18	12.3	3.07	119	.248	.316	3	.158	-1	2	3	0	0.2
	Yr	5	2	.714	7	7	6	0	0	58	58	1	26	27	13.0	3.72	95	.252	.328	4	.154	-2	-1	-1	1	-0.1
1891	Phi-N	20	15	.571	39	36	25	1	1	296	302	8	121	108	13.1	3.56	96	.254	.327	27	.220	1	-7	-5	1	-0.4
1892	Phi-N	11	6	.647	21	18	14	0	1	160^1	171	2	58	45	12.9	3.42	95	.262	.323	17	.243	2	-2	-3	-1	-0.2
	Pit-N	2	0	1.000	3	3	1	0	0	18^1	18	0	12	5	14.7	5.40	61	.247	.353	0	.000	-1	-4	-4	-0	-0.5
	Yr	13	6	.684	24	21	15	0	1	178^2	189	2	70	50	13.0	3.63	90	.260	.325	17	.215	0	-7	-7	-1	-0.7
1893	Was-N	12	28	.300	42	36	34	0	0	334^1	442	14	156	78	16.4	4.71	98	.309	.381	41	.287	7	-2	-3	1	0.4
1894	Was-N	5	10	.333	18	14	7	0	0	116	177	8	39	24	16.9	7.45	71	.346	.395	14	.259	1	-27	-28	0	-2.3
	*Bal-N	10	2	.833	16	9	8	0	2	101	107	1	36	25	12.8	3.92	139	.269	.331	10	.222	-1	16	17	1	1.5
	Yr	15	12	.556	34	23	15	0	2	217	284	9	75	49	14.9	5.81	92	.312	.365	24	.242	0	-12	-11	1	-0.8
1895	*Bal-N	10	12	.455	34	25	16	1	1	218^1	248	2	79	39	13.5	3.92	122	.281	.341	16	.178	-6	21	20	-2	0.8
1896	Bal-N	14	5	.737	20	18	14	1	0	155^2	168	3	39	19	12.1	3.58	119	.273	.319	13	.197	-2	13	12	-2	0.7
1897	StL-N	1	6	.143	8	8	7	0	0	61^1	95	5	12	8	15.8	5.28	83	.351	.380	8	.320	1	-7	-6	1	-0.3
1898	StL-N	3	5	.375	10	8	6	0	0	64^2	86	1	22	14	15.0	5.98	63	.316	.367	10	.370	2	-17	-16	0	-1.4
Total	9	101	100	.502	236	198	152	4	5	1727^2	2048	46	667	453	14.3	4.39	96	.288	.351	178	.241	5	-33	-33	1	-2.9
● NINO ESPINOSA	Espinosa, Arnulfo Acevedo (b: Arnulfo Acevedo (Espinosa)) b: 8/15/53, Villa Altagracia, D.R. d: 12/24/87, Villa Altagracia, D.R. BR/TR, 6′1″, 192 lbs. Deb: 9/13/74																									
1974	NY-N	0	0	—	2	1	0	0	0	9	12	1	0	2	12.0	5.00	71	.324	.324	1	.500	0	-1	-1	0	0.0
1975	NY-N	0	1	.000	2	0	0	0	0	3	8	0	1	2	27.0	18.00	19	.471	.500	0	—	0	-5	-5	-0	-1.1
1976	NY-N	4	4	.500	12	5	0	0	0	41^2	41	3	13	30	11.7	3.67	90	.265	.321	0	.000	-1	-1	-2	-1	-0.5
1977	NY-N	10	13	.435	32	29	7	1	0	200	188	17	55	105	11.2	3.42	109	.249	.304	8	.129	-1	11	7	-0	0.6
1978	NY-N	11	15	.423	32	32	6	1	0	203^2	230	24	75	76	13.6	4.73	74	.292	.355	14	.209	2	-26	-28	2	-2.8
1979	Phi-N	14	12	.538	33	33	8	3	0	212	211	20	65	88	11.8	3.65	105	.262	.319	14	.194	2	2	4	0	0.6
1980	Phi-N	3	5	.375	12	12	1	0	0	76^1	73	9	19	13	11.1	3.77	100	.250	.300	3	.115	-1	-1	0	-1	-0.2
1981	Phi-N	2	5	.286	14	14	2	0	0	73^2	98	11	24	22	15.0	6.11	59	.333	.386	4	.200	-0	-21	-20	-1	-1.8
	Tor-A	0	0	—	1	0	0	0	0	1	4	0	0	0	36.0	9.00	44	.667	.667	0	—	0	-1	-1	-0	-0.2
Total	8	44	55	.444	140	126	24	5	0	820^1	865	85	252	338	12.4	4.17	88	.275	.331	44	.171	1	-44	-46	0	-5.4
● ALVARO ESPINOZA	Espinoza, Alvaro Alberto b: 2/19/62, Valencia, Venez. BR/TR, 6′, 181 lbs. Deb: 9/14/84 ♦																									
1991	NY-A	0	0	—	1	0	0	0	0	0^2	0	0	0	0	0.0	0.00	—	.000	.000	123	.256	0	0	0	0	0.0
● MARK ESSER	Esser, Mark Gerald b: 4/1/56, Erie, Pa. BR/TL, 6′1″, 190 lbs. Deb: 4/22/79																									
1979	Chi-A	0	0	—	2	0	0	0	0	1^2	2	0	4	1	32.4	16.20	26	.286	.545	0	—	0	-2	-2	-0	0.0
● BILL ESSICK	Essick, William Earl "Vinegar Bill" b: 12/18/1881, Grand Ridge, Ill. d: 10/12/51, Los Angeles, Cal. TR, 5′10″, 175 lbs. Deb: 9/12/06																									
1906	Cin-N	2	2	.500	6	4	3	0	0	39^1	39	1	16	16	13.0	2.97	93	.273	.354	1	.077	-1	-1	-1	-1	-0.3

YEAR TM/L	W	L	PCT	G	GS	CG	SH	SV	IP	H	HR	BB	SO	RAT	ERA	ERA+	OAV	OOB	BH	AVG	PB	PR	/A	PD	TPI
1907 Cin-N	0	2	.000	3	2	2	0	0	21^2	23	0	8	7	13.3	2.91	89	.274	.344	0	.000	-1	-1	-1	1	-0.1
Total 2	2	4	.333	9	6	5	0	0	61	62	1	24	23	13.1	2.95	91	.273	.350	1	.048	-2	-3	-2	-0	-0.4
● **DICK ESTELLE**	Estelle, Richard Henry b: 1/18/42, Lakewood, N.J. BB/TL, 6'2", 170 lbs. Deb: 9/4/64																								
1964 SF-N	1	2	.333	6	6	0	0	0	41^2	39	3	23	23	13.4	3.02	118	.247	.343	1	.067	-1	2	3	-1	0.0
1965 SF-N	0	0	—	6	1	0	0	0	11^1	12	0	8	6	16.7	3.97	91	.261	.382	0	.000	0	-1	-0	0	0.0
Total 2	1	2	.333	12	7	0	0	0	53	51	3	31	29	14.1	3.23	111	.250	.352	1	.063	-0	2	2	-1	0.0
● **SHAWN ESTES**	Estes, Aaron Shawn b: 2/18/73, San Bernardino, Cal. BB/TL, 6'2", 185 lbs. Deb: 9/16/95																								
1995 SF-N	0	3	.000	3	3	0	0	0	17^1	16	2	5	14	11.4	6.75	60	.229	.289	0	.000	-1	-5	-5	-0	-0.8
1996 SF-N	3	5	.375	11	11	0	0	0	70	63	3	39	60	13.4	3.60	114	.243	.347	3	.158	-0	5	4	0	0.4
1997 *SF-N★	19	5	.792	32	32	3	2	0	201	162	12	100	181	12.1	3.18	130	.223	.324	10	.147	1	23	21	1	2.6
1998 SF-N	7	12	.368	25	25	1	1	0	149^1	150	14	80	136	14.2	5.06	80	.269	.366	8	.190	1	-14	-17	1	-1.6
Total 4	29	25	.537	71	71	4	3	0	437^2	391	31	224	391	13.0	4.03	102	.243	.341	21	.157	1	9	3	2	0.6
● **GEORGE ESTOCK**	Estock, George John b: 11/2/24, Stirling, N.J. BR/TR, 6', 185 lbs. Deb: 4/21/51																								
1951 Bos-N	0	1	.000	37	1	0	0	3	60^1	56	2	37	11	13.9	4.33	85	.258	.366	2	.286	1	-2	-4	0	0.0
● **CHUCK ESTRADA**	Estrada, Charles Leonard b: 2/15/38, San Luis Obispo, Cal. BR/TR, 6'1", 185 lbs. Deb: 4/21/60 C																								
1960 Bal-A★	**18**	11	.621	36	25	12	1	2	208^2	162	18	101	144	12.0	3.58	106	**.218**	.323	9	.141	-0	7	5	-0	0.6
1961 Bal-A	15	9	.625	33	31	6	1	0	212	159	19	132	160	12.8	3.69	104	**.207**	.331	8	.114	-3	8	4	-2	-0.2
1962 Bal-A	9	17	.346	34	33	6	0	0	223^1	199	24	121	165	13.3	3.83	97	.240	.343	10	.152	-0	3	-3	-3	-0.6
1963 Bal-A	3	2	.600	8	7	0	0	0	31^1	26	2	19	16	13.2	4.60	76	.226	.341	1	.100	-1	-3	-4	-1	-0.7
1964 Bal-A	3	2	.600	17	6	0	0	0	54^2	62	8	21	32	14.0	5.27	68	.282	.350	2	.143	-0	-10	-10	-1	-1.0
1966 Chi-N	1	1	.500	9	1	0	0	0	12^1	16	2	5	3	16.1	7.30	50	.314	.386	0	.000	-0	-5	-5	-0	-0.8
1967 NY-N	1	2	.333	9	2	0	0	0	22	28	5	17	15	18.8	9.41	36	.326	.442	0	.000	-1	-15	-15	-0	-1.8
Total 7	50	44	.532	146	105	24	2	2	764^1	652	78	416	535	13.0	4.07	92	.232	.339	30	.129	-5	-15	-28	-8	-4.5
● **OSCAR ESTRADA**	Estrada, Oscar b: 2/15/04, Havana, Cuba d: 1/2/78, Havana, Cuba BL/TL, 5'8", 160 lbs. Deb: 4/21/29																								
1929 StL-A	0	0	—	1	0	0	0	0	1	1	0	1	0	18.0	0.00	—	.250	.400	0	—	0	0	0	0	0.0
● **MARK ETTLES**	Ettles, Mark Edward b: 10/30/66, Perth, Australia BR/TR, 6', 178 lbs. Deb: 6/5/93																								
1993 SD-N	1	0	1.000	14	0	0	0	0	18	23	4	4	9	13.5	6.50	64	.307	.342	0	.000	-0	-5	-5	0	-0.2
● **JOHN EUBANK**	Eubank, John Franklin "Honest John" b: 9/9/1872, Servia, Ind. d: 11/3/58, Bellevue, Mich. BR/TR, 6'2", 215 lbs. Deb: 9/19/05																								
1905 Det-A	1	0	1.000	3	2	0	0	0	17^1	13	0	3	1	8.8	2.08	132	.210	.258	5	.357	1	1	1	-1	0.2
1906 Det-A	4	10	.286	24	12	7	1	2	135	147	0	35	38	12.7	3.53	78	.280	.335	13	.206	0	-13	-12	1	-1.1
1907 Det-A	3	3	.500	15	8	4	1	0	81	88	0	20	17	12.0	2.67	98	.279	.322	4	.129	-1	-1	-1	1	-0.1
Total 3	8	13	.381	42	22	11	2	2	233^1	248	0	58	56	12.1	3.12	87	.275	.325	22	.204	-1	-13	-11	1	-1.0
● **UEL EUBANKS**	Eubanks, Uel Melvin "Poss" b: 2/14/03, Quinlan, Tex. d: 11/21/54, Dallas, Tex. BR/TR, 6'3", 175 lbs. Deb: 7/20/22																								
1922 Chi-N	0	0	—	2	0	0	0	0	1^2	5	0	4	1	48.6	27.00	16	.556	.692	1	1.000	1	-4	-4	0	0.1
● **FRANK EUFEMIA**	Eufemia, Frank Anthony b: 12/23/59, Bronx, N.Y. BR/TR, 5'11", 185 lbs. Deb: 5/21/85																								
1985 Min-A	4	2	.667	39	0	0	0	2	61^2	56	7	21	30	11.2	3.79	116	.250	.314	0	—	0	2	4	1	0.4
● **BART EVANS**	Evans, Bart Steven b: 12/30/70, Springfield, Mo. BR/TR, 6'2", 210 lbs. Deb: 6/16/98																								
1998 KC-A	0	0	—	8	0	0	0	0	9	7	1	0	7	7.0	2.00	245	.206	.206	0	—	0	3	3	0	-0.3
● **CHICK EVANS**	Evans, Charles Franklin b: 10/15/1889, Arlington, Vt. d: 9/2/16, Schenectady, N.Y. BR/TR, Deb: 9/19/09																								
1909 Bos-N	0	3	.000	4	3	1	0	0	21^2	25	0	14	11	16.2	4.57	62	.305	.406	0	.000	-1	-5	-4	-0	-0.7
1910 Bos-N	1	1	.500	13	1	0	0	2	31	28	1	27	12	16.8	5.23	64	.275	.439	1	.100	-1	-8	-7	0	-0.5
Total 2	1	4	.200	17	4	1	0	2	52^2	53	1	41	23	16.6	4.96	63	.288	.425	1	.053	-2	-12	-11	0	-1.2
● **ROY EVANS**	Evans, Roy b: 3/19/1874, Knoxville, Tenn. d: 8/15/15, Galveston, Tex. BR/TR, 6', 180 lbs. Deb: 5/15/1897																								
1897 StL-N	0	0	—	3	0	0	0	0	13	33	1	13	4	31.8	9.69	45	.471	.554	0	.000	0	-8	-8	-0	0.0
Lou-N	5	4	.556	9	8	6	0	0	59^1	66	4	24	20	14.9	4.10	104	.280	.366	3	.130	-2	1	1	-1	-0.1
Yr	5	4	.556	12	8	6	0	0	72^1	99	5	37	24	17.9	5.10	84	.324	.410	3	.115	-2	-6	-7	-1	-0.1
1898 Was-N	3	3	.500	7	6	4	0	0	50^2	50	0	25	11	14.6	3.38	109	.256	.361	1	.053	-2	1	2	-1	-0.1
1899 Was-N	3	4	.429	7	7	6	0	0	54	60	1	25	27	14.2	5.67	69	.280	.356	4	.200	-1	-11	-11	0	-1.1
1902 NY-N	8	13	.381	23	17	17	0	0	176	186	2	58	48	12.9	3.17	89	.271	.336	8	.148	-1	-8	-7	2	-0.7
Bro-N	5	6	.455	13	11	11	2	0	97^1	91	0	33	35	11.7	2.68	103	.247	.313	9	.265	2	1	1	-3	0.0
Yr	13	19	.406	36	28	28	2	0	273^1	277	2	91	83	12.2	3.00	93	.261	.320	17	.193	1	-7	-6	-2	-0.7
1903 Bro-N	5	9	.357	15	12	9	0	0	110	121	1	41	42	13.8	3.27	98	.297	.371	5	.172	0	-0	-1	-1	-0.2
StL-A	0	4	.000	7	7	4	0	0	54	66	1	14	24	13.8	4.17	70	.300	.350	2	.105	-1	-7	-8	0	-0.6
Total 5	29	43	.403	84	68	57	2	0	614^1	673	10	233	211	13.8	3.66	88	.281	.353	32	.159	-4	-30	-30	-5	-2.8
● **RED EVANS**	Evans, Russell Edison b: 11/12/06, Chicago, Ill. d: 6/14/82, Lakeview, Ark. BR/TR, 5'11", 168 lbs. Deb: 4/24/36																								
1936 Chi-A	0	3	.000	17	0	0	0	1	47^1	70	4	22	19	17.5	7.61	68	.338	.402	2	.133	-1	-14	-13	1	-0.7
1939 Bro-N	1	8	.111	24	6	0	0	1	64^1	74	4	26	28	14.0	5.18	78	.284	.348	4	.308	1	-9	-8	1	-0.8
Total 2	1	11	.083	41	6	0	0	2	111^2	144	8	48	47	15.5	6.21	73	.308	.372	6	.214	-0	-23	-21	3	-1.5
● **JAKE EVANS**	Evans, Uriah L. P. "Bloody Jake" b: 9/1856, Baltimore, Md. d: 1/16/07, Baltimore, Md. TR, 5'8", 154 lbs. Deb: 5/1/1879 ♦																								
1880 Tro-N	0	0	—	1	0	0	0	0	4	11	0	0	0	24.8	13.50	19	.524	.524	46	.256	0	-5	-5	0	0.0
1882 Wor-N	0	1	.000	1	1	1	0	0	8	13	1	0	2	14.6	5.63	55	.317	.317	71	.213	-0	-2	-2	-0	-0.2
1883 Cle-N	0	0	—	1	0	0	0	0	3	0	0	0	1	0.0	0.00	—	.000	.000	79	.238	0	1	1	1	0.1
Total 3	0	1	.000	3	1	1	0	0	15	24	1	0	3	14.4	6.60	45	.338	.338	435	.238	-0	-6	-6	1	-0.1
● **ART EVANS**	Evans, William Arthur b: 8/3/11, Elvins, Mo. d: 1/8/52, Wichita, Kan. BB/TL, 6'1.5", 181 lbs. Deb: 6/20/32																								
1932 Chi-A	0	0	—	7	0	0	0	0	18	19	1	10	6	14.5	3.00	144	.257	.345	0	.000	-0	3	3	1	0.0
● **BILL EVANS**	Evans, William James b: 2/10/1894, Reidsville, N.C. d: 12/21/46, Burlington, N.C. BR/TR, 6', 175 lbs. Deb: 8/13/16																								
1916 Pit-N	2	5	.286	13	7	3	0	0	63	57	2	16	21	10.9	3.00	89	.249	.306	3	.150	-1	-3	-2	2	-0.1
1917 Pit-N	0	4	.000	8	2	1	0	0	26^2	24	0	14	5	13.2	3.38	84	.231	.328	1	.111	-0	-2	-2	-0	-0.3
1919 Pit-N	0	4	.000	7	3	2	0	0	36^2	41	1	18	15	14.5	5.65	53	.297	.378	0	.000	-1	-11	-11	1	-1.1
Total 3	2	13	.133	28	12	6	0	0	126^1	122	3	48	41	12.4	3.85	73	.259	.333	4	.100	-2	-16	-15	2	-1.5
● **BILL EVANS**	Evans, William Lawrence b: 3/25/19, Quanah, Texas d: 11/30/83, Grand Junction, Colo. BR/TR, 6'2", 180 lbs. Deb: 4/21/49																								
1949 Chi-A	0	1	.000	4	0	0	0	0	6^1	6	0	8	1	19.9	7.11	59	.261	.452	0	.000	-0	-2	-2	-0	-0.3
1951 Bos-A	0	0	—	9	0	0	0	0	15^1	15	0	8	3	13.5	4.11	109	.268	.359	0	.000	-1	0	1	-0	-0.1
Total 2	0	1	.000	13	0	0	0	0	21^2	21	0	16	4	15.4	4.98	88	.266	.389	0	.000	-1	-2	-1	-1	-0.4
● **LEON EVERITT**	Everitt, Edward Leon b: 1/12/47, Marshall, Tex. BL/TR, 6'1.5", 195 lbs. Deb: 4/21/69																								
1969 SD-N	0	1	.000	5	0	0	0	0	15^2	18	4	12	11	17.8	8.04	44	.300	.425	0	.000	-0	-8	-8	0	-0.4
● **BRYAN EVERSGERD**	Eversgerd, Bryan David b: 2/11/69, Centralia, Ill. BR/TL, 6'1", 190 lbs. Deb: 4/30/94																								
1994 StL-N	2	3	.400	40	1	0	0	0	67^2	75	8	20	47	12.9	4.52	92	.295	.351	0	.000	-1	-2	-3	1	-0.2
1995 Mon-N	0	0	—	25	0	0	0	0	21	22	2	9	8	13.7	5.14	83	.268	.348	0	.000	-0	-2	-2	-0	0.0
1997 Tex-A	0	2	.000	3	0	0	0	0	1^1	5	0	3	2	54.0	20.25	24	.556	.667	0	—	0	-2	-2	0	-2.1
1998 StL-N	0	0	—	8	0	0	0	0	6	9	1	2	4	18.0	9.00	46	.346	.414	0	—	0	-3	-3	0	0.0
Total 4	2	5	.286	76	1	0	0	0	96	111	11	34	61	14.0	5.16	81	.299	.364	0	.000	-1	-10	-10	1	-2.3
● **BOB EWING**	Ewing, George Lemuel "Long Bob" b: 4/24/1873, New Hampshire, O. d: 6/20/47, Wapakoneta, Ohio BR/TR, 6'1.5", 170 lbs. Deb: 4/19/02																								
1902 Cin-N	5	6	.455	15	12	10	0	0	117^2	126	1	47	44	13.5	2.98	100	.273	.344	12	.169	-1	-3	0	-1	-0.2

YEAR	TM/L	W	L	PCT	G	GS	CG	SH	SV	IP	H	HR	BB	SO	RAT	ERA	ERA+	OAV	OOB	BH	AVG	PB	PR	/A	PD	TPI
1903	Cin-N	14	13	.519	29	28	27	1	1	246^2	254	3	64	104	12.0	2.77	128	.265	.317	24	.253	4	14	22	4	2.9
1904	Cin-N	11	13	.458	26	24	22	0	0	212	198	3	58	99	11.0	2.46	119	.253	.308	25	.258	5	7	11	-1	1.6
1905	Cin-N	20	11	.645	40	34	30	4	0	311^2	284	5	79	164	10.8	2.51	132	.246	.301	32	.262	4	17	27	-3	2.7
1906	Cin-N	13	14	.481	33	32	26	2	0	287^2	248	4	60	145	9.7	2.38	116	.238	.281	14	.139	-3	8	12	1	0.8
1907	Cin-N	17	19	.472	41	37	32	2	0	332^2	279	2	85	147	10.0	1.73	150	.231	.286	19	.154	-1	27	**32**	-6	2.9
1908	Cin-N	17	15	.531	37	32	23	4	3	293^2	247	5	57	95	9.5	2.21	105	.241	.284	14	.149	-0	5	3	-3	-0.1
1909	Cin-N	11	12	.478	31	29	14	2	0	218^1	195	1	63	86	10.9	2.43	107	.238	.298	8	.110	-4	4	4	-4	-0.5
1910	Phi-N	16	14	.533	34	32	20	4	0	255^1	235	5	86	102	11.6	3.00	104	.251	.318	20	.222	2	1	4	-2	0.4
1911	Phi-N	0	1	.000	4	3	1	0	0	24	29	2	14	12	16.1	7.88	44	.309	.398	2	.333	0	-12	-12	-0	-0.4
1912	StL-N	0	0	—	1	1	0	0	0	1^1	2	0	1	0	20.3	0.00	—	.333	.429	0	—	0	1	1	0	0.0
Total	11	124	118	.512	291	264	205	19	4	2301	2097	31	614	998	10.8	2.49	116	.247	.302	170	.195	7	69	102	-16	10.1

● JOHN EWING

Ewing, John "Long Jong" b: 6/1/1863, Cincinnati, Ohio d: 4/23/1895, Denver, Colo. TR , Deb: 6/18/1883 F♦

YEAR	TM/L	W	L	PCT	G	GS	CG	SH	SV	IP	H	HR	BB	SO	RAT	ERA	ERA+	OAV	OOB	BH	AVG	PB	PR	/A	PD	TPI
1888	Lou-a	8	13	.381	21	21	21	2	0	191	175	3	34	87	10.2	2.83	109	.235	.276	16	.203	-2	5	5	0	0.4
1889	Lou-a	6	30	.167	40	39	37	1	0	331	407	6	147	155	15.4	4.87	79	.293	.367	23	.172	-6	-37	-37	2	-3.3
1890	NY-P	18	12	.600	35	31	27	1	2	267^1	294	6	104	145	13.9	4.24	107	.267	.339	24	.211	-3	-0	9	0	0.5
1891	NY-N	21	8	**.724**	33	30	28	5	0	269^1	237	2	105	138	11.8	**2.27**	141	.227	.305	23	.204	-2	32	28	0	2.3
Total	4	53	63	.457	129	121	113	9	2	1058^2	1113	17	390	525	13.2	3.68	101	.260	.329	87	.192	-12	-1	3	3	-0.1

● BUCK EWING

Ewing, William b: 10/17/1859, Hoagland, Ohio d: 10/20/06, Cincinnati, Ohio BR/TR, 5'10", 188 lbs. Deb: 9/9/1880 FMH♦

YEAR	TM/L	W	L	PCT	G	GS	CG	SH	SV	IP	H	HR	BB	SO	RAT	ERA	ERA+	OAV	OOB	BH	AVG	PB	PR	/A	PD	TPI
1882	Tro-N	0	0	—	1	0	0	0	0	1	2	0	1	0	27.0	9.00	31	.400	.500	89	.271	0	-1	-1	0	0.0
1884	NY-N	0	1	.000	1	1	1	0	0	8	7	0	4	3	12.4	1.13	265	.241	.333	106	.277	0	2	2	-0	0.2
1885	NY-N	0	1	.000	1	0	0	0	0	2	4	0	3	0	31.5	4.50	59	.444	.583	104	.304	0	-0	-0	-0	-0.2
1888	*NY-N	0	0	—	2	0	0	0	0	7	8	1	4	6	16.7	2.57	107	.174	.255	127	.306	1	0	0	-0	0.0
1889	*NY-N	2	0	1.000	3	2	2	0	0	20	23	0	8	12	13.9	4.05	97	.280	.344	133	.327	2	-0	-0	-0	0.0
1890	NY-P	0	1	.000	1	1	1	0	0	9	11	1	3	2	14.0	4.00	114	.289	.341	119	.338	0	0	1	-0	0.1
Total	6	2	3	.400	9	4	4	0	0	47	55	2	23	23	15.1	3.45	105	.263	.339	1625	.303	4	1	1	-1	0.1

● SCOTT EYRE

Eyre, Scott Alan b: 5/30/72, Inglewood, Cal. BL/TL, 6'1", 160 lbs. Deb: 8/1/97

YEAR	TM/L	W	L	PCT	G	GS	CG	SH	SV	IP	H	HR	BB	SO	RAT	ERA	ERA+	OAV	OOB	BH	AVG	PB	PR	/A	PD	TPI
1997	Chi-A	4	4	.500	11	11	0	0	0	60^2	62	11	31	36	13.9	5.04	87	.267	.356	1	.500	0	-3	-4	-1	-0.5
1998	Chi-A	3	8	.273	33	17	0	0	0	107	114	24	64	73	15.1	5.38	85	.271	.370	0	.000	-0	-9	-10	0	-0.9
Total	2	7	12	.368	44	28	0	0	0	167^2	176	35	95	109	14.7	5.26	85	.270	.365	1	.200	0	-12	-14	-1	-1.4

● GEORGE EYRICH

Eyrich, George Lincoln b: 3/3/25, Reading, Pa. BR/TR, 5'11", 175 lbs. Deb: 6/13/43

YEAR	TM/L	W	L	PCT	G	GS	CG	SH	SV	IP	H	HR	BB	SO	RAT	ERA	ERA+	OAV	OOB	BH	AVG	PB	PR	/A	PD	TPI
1943	Phi-N	0	0	—	9	0	0	0	0	18^2	27	1	9	5	17.4	3.38	100	.342	.409	0	.000	-0	0	-0	-0	0.0

● RED FABER

Faber, Urban Charles b: 9/6/1888, Cascade, Iowa d: 9/25/76, Chicago, Ill. BB/TR, 6'2", 180 lbs. Deb: 4/17/14 CH

YEAR	TM/L	W	L	PCT	G	GS	CG	SH	SV	IP	H	HR	BB	SO	RAT	ERA	ERA+	OAV	OOB	BH	AVG	PB	PR	/A	PD	TPI
1914	Chi-A	10	9	.526	40	19	11	2	**4**	181^1	154	3	64	88	11.4	2.68	100	.239	.319	8	.145	2	1	0	2	0.3
1915	Chi-A	24	14	.632	**50**	32	21	2	2	299^2	264	3	99	182	11.2	2.55	117	.240	.309	11	.131	2	13	14	-0	2.1
1916	Chi-A	17	9	.654	35	25	15	3	1	205^1	167	1	61	87	10.2	2.02	137	.228	.292	6	.095	-3	19	17	2	2.0
1917	*Chi-A	16	13	.552	41	29	16	3	3	248	224	1	85	84	11.6	1.92	138	.247	.319	4	.058	-4	20	20	2	2.2
1918	Chi-A	4	1	.800	11	9	5	1	1	80^2	70	3	23	26	10.4	1.23	223	.245	.301	1	.042	-2	14	14	1	0.8
1919	Chi-A	11	9	.550	25	20	9	0	0	162^1	185	7	45	45	13.2	3.83	83	.287	.341	10	.185	-0	-11	-12	0	-1.3
1920	Chi-A	23	13	.639	40	39	28	2	1	319	332	8	88	108	12.0	2.99	126	.277	.328	11	.106	-4	29	28	-1	2.3
1921	Chi-A	25	15	.625	43	39	**32**	4	1	330^2	293	10	87	124	**10.5**	**2.48**	**171**	**.242**	**.297**	16	.148	-4	**66**	**65**	1	**7.0**
1922	Chi-A	21	17	.553	43	38	**31**	4	2	**352**	334	10	83	148	**10.8**	**2.81**	**145**	.252	**.299**	25	.200	-2	**48**	**49**	1	**4.9**
1923	Chi-A	14	11	.560	32	31	15	2	0	232^1	233	6	62	91	11.7	3.41	116	.259	.311	15	.217	3	15	14	2	1.9
1924	Chi-A	9	11	.450	21	20	9	0	0	161^1	173	5	58	47	13.0	3.85	107	.282	.346	8	.148	-2	7	5	-2	0.2
1925	Chi-A	12	11	.522	34	32	16	1	0	238	266	8	59	71	12.4	3.78	110	.289	.333	8	.104	-4	16	10	1	0.6
1926	Chi-A	15	9	.625	27	25	13	1	0	184^2	203	3	57	65	12.8	3.56	109	.281	.335	9	.150	-0	9	6	-3	0.4
1927	Chi-A	4	7	.364	18	15	6	0	0	110^2	131	2	41	39	14.4	4.55	89	.312	.380	10	.270	2	-5	-6	2	-0.2
1928	Chi-A	13	9	.591	27	27	16	2	0	201^1	223	11	68	43	13.2	3.75	108	.286	.347	8	.114	-3	6	7	1	0.4
1929	Chi-A	13	13	.500	31	31	15	1	0	234	241	10	61	68	12.0	3.88	110	.273	.327	10	.128	-3	9	10	2	0.9
1930	Chi-A	8	13	.381	29	26	10	0	1	169	188	7	49	62	12.9	4.21	110	.283	.337	2	.041	-5	8	8	2	0.6
1931	Chi-A	10	14	.417	44	19	5	1	1	184	210	11	57	49	13.2	3.82	112	.285	.339	4	.075	-3	12	9	-2	0.6
1932	Chi-A	2	11	.154	42	5	0	0	6	106	123	0	38	26	13.8	3.74	116	.290	.350	4	.222	3	**9**	7	-0	1.0
1933	Chi-A	3	4	.429	36	2	0	0	5	86^1	92	2	28	18	12.6	3.44	123	.275	.332	0	.000	-3	8	8	-1	0.3
Total	20	254	213	.544	669	483	273	29	28	4086^2	4106	111	1213	1471	11.9	3.15	119	.266	.323	170	.134	-31	294	274	11	27.0

● ROY FACE

Face, Elroy Leon b: 2/20/28, Stephentown, N.Y. BR/TR, 5'8", 155 lbs. Deb: 4/16/53

YEAR	TM/L	W	L	PCT	G	GS	CG	SH	SV	IP	H	HR	BB	SO	RAT	ERA	ERA+	OAV	OOB	BH	AVG	PB	PR	/A	PD	TPI
1953	Pit-N	6	8	.429	41	13	2	0	0	119	145	19	30	56	13.4	6.58	68	.297	.340	4	.133	-1	-30	-28	-1	-3.0
1955	Pit-N	5	7	.417	42	10	4	0	5	125^2	128	10	40	84	12.0	3.58	115	.268	.325	3	.115	-1	6	7	-1	0.5
1956	Pit-N	12	13	.480	**68**	3	0	0	6	135^1	131	16	42	96	11.6	3.52	107	.256	.314	5	.192	-0	4	4	1	0.8
1957	Pit-N	4	6	.400	59	1	0	0	10	93^2	97	9	24	53	11.7	3.07	123	.270	.318	2	.125	-1	8	7	-2	0.7
1958	Pit-N	5	2	.714	57	0	0	0	**20**	84	77	6	22	47	10.6	2.89	134	.244	.293	0	.000	-1	10	9	1	1.2
1959	Pit-N★	18	1	**.947**	57	0	0	0	10	93^1	91	5	25	69	11.3	2.70	143	.266	.318	3	.231	0	13	12	-0	2.6
1960	*Pit-N★	10	8	.556	**68**	0	0	0	24	114^2	93	11	29	72	9.6	2.90	129	.226	.277	7	.412	2	11	11	1	2.5
1961	Pit-N★	6	12	.333	62	0	0	0	**17**	92	94	12	10	55	10.3	3.82	105	.267	.289	3	.273	0	2	2	2	0.6
1962	Pit-N	8	7	.533	63	0	0	0	**28**	91	74	7	18	45	9.2	1.88	209	.231	.274	1	.083	-1	**21**	**21**	-1	4.5
1963	Pit-N	3	9	.250	56	0	0	0	16	69^2	75	6	19	41	12.5	3.23	102	.285	.340	2	.250	0	0	1	1	0.3
1964	Pit-N	3	3	.500	55	0	0	0	4	79^2	82	11	27	63	12.4	5.20	68	.269	.330	0	.000	-0	-15	-15	0	-1.2
1965	Pit-N	5	2	.714	16	0	0	0	0	20^1	20	1	7	19	12.0	2.66	132	.263	.325	0	.000	-0	2	2	-1	0.6
1966	Pit-N	6	6	.500	54	0	0	0	18	70	68	9	24	67	12.0	2.70	132	.262	.326	0	.000	-1	7	7	1	1.5
1967	Pit-N	7	5	.583	61	0	0	0	17	74^1	62	5	22	41	10.2	2.42	139	.230	.288	0	.000	-1	8	8	-1	1.5
1968	Pit-N	2	4	.333	43	0	0	0	13	52	46	3	7	34	9.5	2.60	113	.238	.272	0	.000	-0	2	2	-0	0.3
	Det-A	0	0	—	2	0	0	0	0	1	2	0	1	1	27.0	0.00	—	.500	.600	0	—	0	0	0	0	0.0
1969	Mon-N	4	2	.667	44	0	0	0	5	59^1	62	11	15	34	11.7	3.94	93	.263	.307	1	.500	0	-2	-2	-1	-0.2
Total	16	104	95	.523	848	27	6	0	193	1375	1347	141	362	877	11.3	3.48	109	.260	.310	31	.160	-4	48	48	0	13.2

● TONY FAETH

Faeth, Anthony Joseph b: 7/9/1893, Aberdeen, S.D. d: 12/22/82, St.Paul, Minn. BR/TR, 6', 180 lbs. Deb: 8/10/19

YEAR	TM/L	W	L	PCT	G	GS	CG	SH	SV	IP	H	HR	BB	SO	RAT	ERA	ERA+	OAV	OOB	BH	AVG	PB	PR	/A	PD	TPI
1919	Cle-A	0	0	—	6	0	0	0	0	18^1	13	0	10	7	11.3	0.49	682	.224	.338	0	.000	-1	6	6	-0	-0.1
1920	Cle-A	0	0	—	13	0	0	0	0	25	31	0	20	14	18.7	4.32	88	.333	.456	0	.000	-1	-1	-1	-0	-0.1
Total	2	0	0	—	19	0	0	0	0	43^1	44	0	30	21	15.6	2.70	134	.291	.412	0	.000	-1	4	4	-0	-0.2

● EVERETT FAGAN

Fagan, Everett Joseph b: 1/13/18, Pottersville, N.J. d: 2/16/83, Morristown, N.J. BR/TR, 6', 195 lbs. Deb: 4/24/43

YEAR	TM/L	W	L	PCT	G	GS	CG	SH	SV	IP	H	HR	BB	SO	RAT	ERA	ERA+	OAV	OOB	BH	AVG	PB	PR	/A	PD	TPI
1943	Phi-A	2	6	.250	18	2	0	0	3	37^1	41	4	14	9	13.7	6.27	54	.283	.354	0	.000	-0	-12	-12	0	-2.5
1946	Phi-A	0	1	.000	20	0	0	0	0	45	47	2	24	12	14.8	4.80	74	.264	.361	4	.286	1	-6	-6	-0	-0.1
Total	2	2	7	.222	38	2	0	0	3	82^1	88	6	38	21	14.3	5.47	64	.272	.358	4	.190	1	-19	-18	0	-2.6

● BILL FAGAN

Fagan, William A. "Clinkers" b: 2/15/1869, Troy, N.Y. d: 3/21/30, Troy, N.Y. TL , 5'11", 165 lbs. Deb: 9/15/1887

YEAR	TM/L	W	L	PCT	G	GS	CG	SH	SV	IP	H	HR	BB	SO	RAT	ERA	ERA+	OAV	OOB	BH	AVG	PB	PR	/A	PD	TPI
1887	NY-a	1	4	.200	6	6	6	0	0	45	55	1	24	12	16.2	4.00	106	.306	.393	3	.143	-2	1	1	0	-0.1
1888	KC-a	5	11	.313	17	17	15	0	0	142^1	179	4	75	49	16.1	5.69	60	.296	.375	14	.215	-1	-42	-36	1	-3.0
Total	2	6	15	.286	23	23	21	0	0	187^1	234	5	99	61	16.1	5.28	69	.298	.379	17	.198	-3	-40	-34	1	-3.1

● FRANK FAHEY

Fahey, Francis Raymond b: 1/22/1896, Milford, Mass. d: 3/19/54, Boston, Mass. BB/TR, 6'1", 190 lbs. Deb: 4/25/18 ♦

YEAR	TM/L	W	L	PCT	G	GS	CG	SH	SV	IP	H	HR	BB	SO	RAT	ERA	ERA+	OAV	OOB	BH	AVG	PB	PR	/A	PD	TPI
1918	Phi-A	0	0	—	3	0	0	0	0	9	5	0	14	1	20.0	6.00	49	.200	.500	3	.176	-0	-3	-3	-1	-0.1

● JERRY FAHR

Fahr, Gerald Warren b: 12/9/24, Marmaduke, Ark. BR/TR, 6'5", 185 lbs. Deb: 4/29/51

YEAR	TM/L	W	L	PCT	G	GS	CG	SH	SV	IP	H	HR	BB	SO	RAT	ERA	ERA+	OAV	OOB	BH	AVG	PB	PR	/A	PD	TPI
1951	Cle-A	0	0	—	5	0	0	0	0	5^2	11	0	2	0	20.6	4.76	80	.500	.542	0	—	0	-0	-1	-0	0.0

● PETE FAHRER

Fahrer, Clarence Willie b: 3/10/1890, Holgate, Ohio d: 6/10/67, Fremont, Mich. BL/TR, 6', 190 lbs. Deb: 8/17/14

YEAR	TM/L	W	L	PCT	G	GS	CG	SH	SV	IP	H	HR	BB	SO	RAT	ERA	ERA+	OAV	OOB	BH	AVG	PB	PR	/A	PD	TPI
1914	Cin-N	0	0	—	5	0	0	0	0	8	8	0	4	2	13.5	1.13	260	.308	.400	0	.000	-0	1	2	0	0.0

YEAR	TM/L	W	L	PCT	G	GS	CG	SH	SV	IP	H	HR	BB	SO	RAT	ERA	ERA+	OAV	OOB	BH	AVG	PB	PR	/A	PD	TPI
● JIM FAIRBANK Fairbank, James Lee "Lee" or "Smoky" b: 3/17/1881, Deansboro, N.Y. d: 12/27/55, Utica, N.Y. BR/TR, 5'9.5", 175 lbs. Deb: 9/18/03																										
1903	Phi-A	1	1	.500	4	1	1	0	0	24	33	1	12	10	16.9	4.88	63	.327	.398	1	.100	-1	-5	-5	1	-0.3
1904	Phi-A	0	1	.000	3	1	1	0	0	17	19	0	13	6	18.0	6.35	42	.284	.415	0	.000	-1	-7	-7	1	-0.4
Total	2	1	2	.333	7	2	2	0	0	41	52	1	25	16	17.3	5.49	53	.310	.405	1	.063	-1	-12	-12	2	-0.7
● RAGS FAIRCLOTH Faircloth, James Lamar b: 8/19/1892, Kenton, Tenn. d: 10/5/53, Tucson, Ariz. BR/TR, 5'11", 160 lbs. Deb: 5/6/19																										
1919	Phi-N	0	0	—	2	0	0	0	0	2	5	0	0	0	22.5	9.00	36	.625	.625	0	—	0	-1	-1	0	0.0
● HECTOR FAJARDO Fajardo, Hector (Nabaratte) b: 11/16/70, Sahuayo, Mexico BR/TR, 6'4", 185 lbs. Deb: 8/10/91																										
1991	Pit-N	0	0	—	2	2	0	0	0	6^1	10	0	7	8	24.2	9.95	36	.357	.486	0	.000	-0	-4	-4	-0	0.0
	Tex-A	0	2	.000	4	3	0	0	0	19	25	2	4	15	14.2	5.68	71	.329	.370	0	—	0	-3	-3	-0	-0.3
1993	Tex-A	0	0	—	1	0	0	0	0	0^2	0	0	0	1	0.0	0.00	—	.000	.000	0	—	0	0	0	0	0.1
1994	Tex-A	5	7	.417	18	12	0	0	0	83^1	95	15	26	45	13.3	6.91	70	.284	.340	0	—	0	-20	-19	-0	-2.2
1995	Tex-A	0	0	—	5	0	0	0	0	15	19	2	5	9	15.0	7.80	62	.311	.373	0	—	0	-5	-5	0	-0.1
Total	4	5	9	.357	30	17	0	0	0	124^1	149	19	42	78	14.1	6.95	67	.297	.356	0	.000	-0	-32	-32	-1	-2.5
● PETE FALCONE Falcone, Peter Frank b: 10/1/53, Brooklyn, N.Y. BL/TL, 6'2", 185 lbs. Deb: 4/13/75																										
1975	SF-N	12	11	.522	34	32	3	1	0	190	171	16	111	131	13.5	4.17	91	.244	.350	4	.062	-5	-12	-8	-1	-1.4
1976	StL-N	12	16	.429	32	32	9	2	0	212	173	12	93	138	11.4	3.23	110	.222	.306	8	.129	-1	6	7	-4	0.3
1977	StL-N	4	8	.333	27	22	1	1	1	124	130	19	61	75	14.1	5.44	71	.273	.359	10	.244	2	-21	-22	-1	-1.8
1978	StL-N	2	7	.222	19	14	0	0	0	75	94	9	48	28	17.3	5.76	61	.319	.417	5	.238	1	-18	-19	-2	-2.1
1979	NY-N	6	14	.300	33	31	1	1	0	184	194	24	76	113	13.3	4.16	88	.276	.347	9	.173	0	-9	-11	-3	-1.3
1980	NY-N	7	10	.412	37	23	1	0	1	157^1	163	16	58	109	12.8	4.52	79	.269	.335	6	.146	-1	-16	-17	-3	-2.1
1981	NY-N	5	3	.625	35	9	3	1	1	95^1	84	3	36	56	11.3	2.55	137	.241	.312	4	.182	1	10	10	-2	0.8
1982	NY-N	8	10	.444	40	23	3	0	2	171	159	24	71	101	12.2	3.84	94	.252	.329	6	.113	-2	-5	-4	-3	-0.9
1983	Atl-N	9	4	.692	33	15	2	0	0	106^2	102	14	60	59	13.8	3.63	107	.256	.355	3	.115	-1	-0	3	-2	0.0
1984	Atl-N	5	7	.417	35	16	2	1	2	120	115	15	57	55	12.9	4.13	93	.252	.335	7	.212	1	-7	-4	-1	-0.4
Total	10	70	90	.438	325	217	25	7	7	1435^1	1385	152	671	865	13.0	4.07	90	.257	.341	62	.149	-6	-71	-63	-20	-8.9
● CHET FALK Falk, Chester Emanuel "Spot" b: 5/15/05, Austin, Tex. d: 1/7/82, Austin, Tex. BL/TL, 6'2", 170 lbs. Deb: 4/20/25 F																										
1925	StL-A	0	0	—	13	0	0	0	0	25	38	2	17	7	19.8	8.28	56	.362	.451	5	.625	2	-11	-10	0	0.3
1926	StL-A	4	4	.500	18	8	3	0	0	74	95	1	27	7	15.6	5.35	80	.338	.408	6	.194	-1	-11	-9	-1	-0.9
1927	StL-A	1	0	1.000	9	0	0	0	0	15^2	25	1	10	2	20.1	5.74	76	.352	.432	1	.200	-0	-3	-2	0	-0.1
Total	3	5	4	.556	40	8	3	0	0	114^2	158	4	54	16	17.1	6.04	73	.346	.422	12	.273	1	-25	-21	0	-0.7
● CY FALKENBERG Falkenberg, Frederick Peter b: 12/17/1880, Chicago, Ill. d: 4/14/61, San Francisco, Cal BR/TR, 6'5", 180 lbs. Deb: 4/21/03																										
1903	Pit-N	1	5	.167	10	6	3	0	0	56	65	0	32	24	15.9	3.86	84	.295	.390	4	.190	-0	-4	-4	2	-0.2
1905	Was-A	7	2	.778	12	10	6	2	0	75^1	71	1	31	35	12.8	3.82	69	.251	.335	4	.125	-2	-10	-10	-1	-1.4
1906	Was-A	14	20	.412	40	36	30	2	1	298^2	277	1	108	178	12.0	2.86	92	.249	.323	18	.170	1	-6	-8	2	-0.5
1907	Was-A	6	17	.261	32	24	17	1	1	233^2	195	0	77	108	10.8	2.35	103	.229	.299	12	.140	-3	5	2	2	0.1
1908	Was-A	6	2	.750	17	8	5	1	0	82^2	70	2	21	34	10.1	1.96	117	.236	.291	6	.222	0	4	3	1	0.4
	Cle-A	2	4	.333	8	7	2	0	0	46^1	52	1	10	17	12.4	3.88	62	.284	.328	2	.118	-1	-8	-8	-1	-1.1
	Yr	8	6	.571	25	15	7	1	0	129	122	3	31	51	10.8	2.65	88	.253	.301	8	.182	-1	-4	-5	0	-0.7
1909	Cle-A	10	9	.526	24	18	13	2	0	165	135	0	50	82	10.4	2.40	107	.231	.297	9	.173	-1	1	3	3	0.5
1910	Cle-A	14	13	.519	37	29	18	3	1	256^2	246	3	75	107	11.5	2.95	88	.261	.320	15	.183	-0	-12	-10	3	-0.8
1911	Cle-A	8	5	.615	15	13	7	0	1	106^2	117	0	24	46	12.2	3.29	104	.282	.326	7	.175	-1	1	1	1	0.1
1913	Cle-A	23	10	.697	39	36	23	6	0	276	238	2	88	166	10.8	2.22	137	.235	.299	10	.119	-2	22	25	-2	2.5
1914	Ind-F	25	16	.610	**49**	43	33	**9**	3	**377^1**	332	5	89	**236**	10.2	2.22	141	.236	.284	21	.168	-4	28	38	3	3.8
1915	New-F	9	11	.450	25	21	14	0	1	172	175	6	47	76	12.1	3.24	79	.268	.326	3	.053	-7	-10	-13	1	-2.1
	Bro-F	3	3	.500	7	7	5	1	0	48	31	1	12	20	8.3	1.50	181	.189	.249	1	.067	-2	7	7	-0	0.6
	Yr	12	14	.462	32	28	19	1	1	220	206	7	59	96	10.9	2.86	91	.250	.301	4	.056	-9	-3	-7	1	-1.5
1917	Phi-A	2	6	.250	15	8	4	0	0	80^2	86	1	26	35	12.5	3.35	82	.293	.350	5	.185	0	-6	-5	1	-0.3
Total	12	130	123	.514	330	266	180	27	8	2275	2090	23	690	1164	11.3	2.68	103	.248	.310	117	.152	-23	13	20	13	1.6
● ED FALLENSTEIN Fallenstein, Edward Joseph "Jack" (b: Edward Joseph Valestin) b: 12/22/08, Newark, N.J. d: 11/24/71, Orange, N.J. BR/TR, 6'3", 180 lbs. Deb: 4/16/31																										
1931	Phi-N	0	0	—	24	0	0	0	0	41^2	56	2	26	15	17.7	7.13	60	.333	.423	1	.200	0	-15	-13	0	0.0
1933	Bos-N	2	1	.667	9	4	1	1	0	35	43	1	13	5	14.7	3.60	85	.305	.368	3	.375	1	-1	-2	-0	-0.1
Total	2	2	1	.667	33	4	1	1	0	76^2	99	3	39	20	16.3	5.52	67	.320	.398	4	.308	1	-16	-16	-0	-0.1
● BOB FALLON Fallon, Robert Joseph b: 2/18/60, Bronx, N.Y. BL/TL, 6'3", 200 lbs. Deb: 4/26/84																										
1984	Chi-A	0	0	—	3	3	0	0	0	14^2	12	0	11	10	14.1	3.68	113	.235	.371	0	—	0	1	1	0	0.0
1985	Chi-A	0	0	—	10	0	0	0	0	16	25	5	9	17	19.1	6.19	70	.362	.436	0	—	0	-4	-3	1	-0.3
Total	2	0	0	—	13	3	0	0	0	30^2	37	5	20	27	16.7	4.99	85	.308	.407	0	—	0	-3	-3	1	-0.3
● STEVE FALTEISEK Falteisek, Steven James b: 1/28/72, Mineola, N.Y. BR/TR, 6'2", 200 lbs. Deb: 7/21/97																										
1997	Mon-N	0	0	—	5	0	0	0	0	8	8	0	3	2	13.5	3.38	124	.286	.375	0	.000	-0	1	1	0	0.0
● CLIFF FANNIN Fannin, Clifford Bryson "Mule" b: 5/13/24, Louisa, Ky. d: 12/11/66, Sandusky, Ohio BL/TR, 6', 170 lbs. Deb: 9/2/45																										
1945	StL-A	0	0	—	5	0	0	0	0	10^1	8	0	5	5	11.3	2.61	135	.222	.317	0	.000	-0	1	1	-0	0.0
1946	StL-A	5	2	.714	27	7	4	1	2	86^2	76	4	42	52	12.4	3.01	124	.236	.326	5	.161	-1	5	7	-0	0.5
1947	StL-A	6	8	.429	26	18	6	2	1	145^2	134	10	77	77	13.1	3.58	108	.245	.340	9	.196	-0	2	5	0	0.5
1948	StL-A	10	14	.417	34	29	10	3	1	213^2	198	14	104	102	12.8	4.17	109	.245	.332	11	.169	-0	3	9	-2	0.7
1949	StL-A	8	14	.364	30	25	5	0	1	143	177	15	93	57	17.0	6.17	73	.308	.404	9	.164	-2	-31	-26	-3	-3.7
1950	StL-A	5	9	.357	25	16	3	0	1	102	116	18	58	42	15.4	6.53	76	.280	.369	6	.176	-2	-22	-18	-0	-2.2
1951	StL-A	0	2	.000	7	1	0	0	0	15^1	20	6	5	11	14.7	6.46	68	.317	.368	1	.250	-0	-4	-4	0	-0.4
1952	StL-A	0	2	.000	10	2	0	0	0	16^1	34	5	9	6	23.7	12.67	31	.453	.512	0	.000	0	-16	-16	-1	-1.7
Total	8	34	51	.400	164	98	28	6	6	733	763	72	393	352	14.2	4.85	89	.269	.358	41	.173	-5	-63	-42	-6	-6.3
● JACK FANNING Fanning, John Jacob b: 1863, S.Orange, N.J. d: 6/10/17, Aberdeen, Wash. TR , 5'9", 163 lbs. Deb: 9/20/1889																										
1889	Ind-N	0	1	.000	1	1	0	0	0	1	3	0	2	0	45.0	18.00	23	.500	.625	0	.000	-0	-2	-2	0	-0.8
1894	Phi-N	1	3	.250	5	4	2	0	0	32^1	45	4	20	7	18.6	8.07	63	.326	.419	2	.154	-1	-10	-11	-0	-0.9
Total	2	1	4	.200	6	5	2	0	0	33^1	48	4	22	7	19.4	8.37	61	.333	.429	2	.143	-1	-11	-12	0	-1.7
● HARRY FANOK Fanok, Harry Michael "The Flame Thrower" b: 5/11/40, Whippany, N.J. BB/TR, 6', 180 lbs. Deb: 4/16/63																										
1963	StL-N	2	1	.667	12	0	0	0	1	25^2	24	3	21	25	16.1	5.26	67	.255	.397	2	.400	1	-6	-5	-0	-0.5
1964	StL-N	0	0	—	4	0	0	0	0	7^2	5	0	3	10	9.4	5.87	65	.179	.258	0	.000	-0	-2	-2	-0	0.0
Total	2	2	1	.667	16	0	0	0	1	33^1	29	3	24	35	14.6	5.40	67	.238	.367	2	.333	1	-8	-7	-0	-0.5
● FRANK FANOVICH Fanovich, Frank Joseph "Lefty" b: 1/11/22, New York, N.Y. BL/TL, 5'11", 180 lbs. Deb: 4/25/49																										
1949	Cin-N	0	2	.000	29	1	0	0	0	43^1	44	2	28	27	15.4	5.40	77	.257	.368	0	.000	-0	-7	-6	0	-0.2
1953	Phi-A	0	3	.000	26	3	0	0	0	61^2	62	5	37	37	15.3	5.55	77	.273	.389	2	.182	-0	-11	-9	-1	-0.5
Total	2	0	5	.000	55	4	0	0	0	105	106	7	65	64	15.3	5.49	77	.266	.380	2	.133	-1	-17	-14	-0	-0.7
● STAN FANSLER Fansler, Stanley Robert b: 2/12/65, Elkins, W.Va. BR/TR, 5'11", 180 lbs. Deb: 9/6/86																										
1986	Pit-N	0	3	.000	5	5	0	0	0	24	20	2	15	13	13.1	3.75	102	.247	.365	1	.167	-0	-0	0	-0	0.0
● HARRY FANWELL Fanwell, Harry Clayton b: 10/16/1886, Patapsco, Md. d: 7/15/65, Baltimore, Md. BL/TR, 6', 175 lbs. Deb: 7/23/10																										
1910	Cle-A	2	9	.182	17	11	5	1	0	92	87	0	38	30	12.8	3.62	71	.260	.347	1	.033	-3	-11	-11	1	-1.4
● ED FARMER Farmer, Edward Joseph b: 10/18/49, Evergreen Park, Ill BR/TR, 6'5", 210 lbs. Deb: 6/9/71																										
1971	Cle-A	5	4	.556	43	4	0	0	4	78^2	77	9	41	48	13.8	4.35	88	.263	.359	1	.071	-1	-8	-5	-0	-0.7

YEAR TM/L	W	L	PCT	G	GS	CG	SH	SV	IP	H	HR	BB	SO	RAT	ERA	ERA+	OAV	OOB	BH	AVG	PB	PR	/A	PD	TPI
1972 Cle-A	2	5	.286	46	1	0	0	7	61^1	51	10	27	33	11.6	4.40	73	.231	.317	1	.143	-0	-9	-8	0	-1.1
1973 Cle-A	0	2	.000	16	0	0	0	1	17^1	25	4	5	10	15.6	4.67	84	.325	.366	0	—	0	-2	-1	-0	-0.2
Det-A	3	0	1.000	24	0	0	0	2	45	52	3	27	28	16.2	5.00	82	.292	.391	0	—	0	-6	-5	-1	-0.4
Yr	3	2	.600	40	0	0	0	3	62^1	77	7	32	38	16.0	4.91	82	.301	.383	0	—	0	-8	-6	-1	-0.6
1974 Phi-N	2	1	.667	14	3	0	0	0	31	41	5	27	20	19.7	8.42	45	.323	.442	1	.111	-1	-17	-16	-0	-1.5
1977 Bal-A	0	0	—	1	0	0	0	0	0	1	0	1	0	—	∞	—	1.000	1.000	0	—	0	-1	-1	0	0.3
1978 Mil-A	1	0	1.000	3	0	0	0	1	11	7	1	4	6	9.0	0.82	459	.175	.250	0	—	0	4	4	-0	0.4
1979 Tex-A	2	0	1.000	11	2	0	0	0	33	30	2	19	25	13.9	4.36	95	.252	.364	0	—	0	-1	-1	-0	0.0
Chi-A	3	7	.300	42	3	0	0	14	81^1	66	2	34	48	11.2	2.43	175	.219	.301	0	—	0	16	16	0	2.5
Yr	5	7	.417	53	5	0	0	14	114^1	96	4	53	73	11.8	2.99	141	.226	.314	0	—	0	16	16	0	2.5
1980 Chi-A★	7	9	.438	64	0	0	0	30	99^2	92	6	56	54	13.5	3.34	121	.244	.343	0	—	0	8	8	1	1.7
1981 Chi-A	3	3	.500	42	0	0	0	10	52^2	53	5	34	42	15.0	4.61	78	.262	.371	0	—	0	-6	-6	1	-0.8
1982 Phi-N	2	6	.250	47	4	0	0	6	76	66	2	50	58	13.7	4.86	75	.234	.349	0	.000	-1	-11	-10	0	-1.3
1983 Phi-N	0	6	.000	12	3	0	0	0	26^2	35	2	20	16	18.9	6.08	59	.307	.415	1	.167	-0	-7	-7	0	-1.5
Oak-A	0	0	—	5	1	0	0	0	10^1	15	1	0	7	13.1	3.48	111	.366	.366	0	—	0	1	0	-0	0.0
Total 11	30	43	.411	370	21	0	0	75	624	611	52	345	395	14.0	4.30	89	.257	.355	4	.085	-3	-38	-31	0	-2.6

● HOWARD FARMER Farmer, Howard Earl b: 11/18/66, Gary, Ind. BR/TR, 6'3", 185 lbs. Deb: 7/2/90 F

YEAR TM/L	W	L	PCT	G	GS	CG	SH	SV	IP	H	HR	BB	SO	RAT	ERA	ERA+	OAV	OOB	BH	AVG	PB	PR	/A	PD	TPI
1990 Mon-N	0	3	.000	6	4	0	0	0	23	26	9	10	14	14.1	7.04	52	.302	.375	2	.400	1	-8	-9	1	-0.8

● MIKE FARMER Farmer, Michael Anthony b: 7/3/68, Gary, Ind. BB/TL, 6'1", 193 lbs. Deb: 5/4/96

YEAR TM/L	W	L	PCT	G	GS	CG	SH	SV	IP	H	HR	BB	SO	RAT	ERA	ERA+	OAV	OOB	BH	AVG	PB	PR	/A	PD	TPI
1996 Col-N	0	1	.000	7	4	0	0	0	28	32	8	13	16	14.5	7.71	68	.286	.360	4	.400	1	-11	-8	-0	-0.2

● JIM FARR Farr, James Alfred b: 5/18/56, Waverly, N.Y. BR/TR, 6'1", 195 lbs. Deb: 9/7/82

YEAR TM/L	W	L	PCT	G	GS	CG	SH	SV	IP	H	HR	BB	SO	RAT	ERA	ERA+	OAV	OOB	BH	AVG	PB	PR	/A	PD	TPI
1982 Tex-A	0	0	—	5	0	0	0	0	18	20	0	7	6	13.5	2.50	155	.278	.342	0	—	0	3	3	-0	0.0

● STEVE FARR Farr, Steven Michael b: 12/12/56, LaPlata, Md. BR/TR, 5'11", 200 lbs. Deb: 5/16/84

YEAR TM/L	W	L	PCT	G	GS	CG	SH	SV	IP	H	HR	BB	SO	RAT	ERA	ERA+	OAV	OOB	BH	AVG	PB	PR	/A	PD	TPI
1984 Cle-A	3	11	.214	31	16	0	0	1	116	106	14	46	83	12.2	4.58	89	.245	.325	0	—	0	-8	-6	1	-0.6
1985 *KC-A	2	1	.667	16	3	0	0	1	37^2	34	2	20	36	13.4	3.11	134	.245	.348	0	—	0	4	4	0	0.4
1986 KC-A	8	4	.667	56	0	0	0	8	109^1	90	10	39	83	10.9	3.13	136	.228	.304	0	—	0	13	14	1	1.5
1987 KC-A	4	3	.571	47	0	0	0	1	91	97	9	44	88	14.1	4.15	110	.270	.353	0	—	0	3	4	-1	0.0
1988 KC-A	5	4	.556	62	1	0	0	20	82^2	74	5	30	72	11.5	2.50	159	.240	.312	0	—	0	13	14	-1	1.8
1989 KC-A	2	5	.286	51	2	0	0	18	63^1	75	5	22	56	13.9	4.12	93	.296	.355	0	—	0	-2	-2	-0	-0.3
1990 KC-A	13	7	.650	57	6	1	1	1	127	99	6	48	94	10.8	1.98	193	.220	.302	0	—	0	**27**	**26**	0	4.1
1991 NY-A	5	5	.500	60	0	0	0	23	70	57	4	20	60	10.5	2.19	189	.219	.288	0	—	0	15	15	1	3.0
1992 NY-A	2	2	.500	50	0	0	0	30	52	34	2	19	37	9.5	1.56	251	.186	.270	0	—	0	14	14	-1	2.3
1993 NY-A	2	2	.500	49	0	0	0	25	47	44	8	28	39	14.2	4.21	99	.253	.363	0	—	0	1	-0	1	0.2
1994 Cle-A	1	1	.500	19	0	0	0	4	15^1	17	3	15	12	20.0	5.28	89	.279	.436	0	—	0	-1	-1	-0	-0.2
Bos-A	1	0	1.000	11	0	0	0	0	13	24	2	3	8	18.7	6.23	81	.407	.435	0	—	0	-2	-2	-0	-0.2
Yr	2	1	.667	30	0	0	0	4	28^1	41	5	18	20	18.7	5.72	85	.333	.418	0	—	0	-3	-3	-0	-0.4
Total 11	48	45	.516	509	28	1	1	132	824^1	751	70	334	668	12.2	3.25	127	.244	.325	0	—	0	78	79	1	12.0

● JOHN FARRELL Farrell, John Edward b: 8/4/62, Monmouth Beach, N.J. BR/TR, 6'4", 210 lbs. Deb: 8/18/87

YEAR TM/L	W	L	PCT	G	GS	CG	SH	SV	IP	H	HR	BB	SO	RAT	ERA	ERA+	OAV	OOB	BH	AVG	PB	PR	/A	PD	TPI
1987 Cle-A	5	1	.833	10	9	1	0	0	69	68	7	22	28	12.4	3.39	133	.256	.324	0	—	0	8	9	-0	0.6
1988 Cle-A	14	10	.583	31	30	4	0	0	210^1	216	15	67	92	12.5	4.24	97	.269	.332	0	—	0	-6	-3	-0	-0.5
1989 Cle-A	9	14	.391	31	31	7	2	0	208	196	14	71	132	11.9	3.63	109	.244	.311	0	—	0	6	8	-2	0.5
1990 Cle-A	4	5	.444	17	17	1	0	0	96^2	108	10	33	44	13.2	4.28	91	.286	.345	0	—	0	-4	-4	-0	-0.3
1993 Cal-A	3	12	.200	21	17	0	0	0	90^2	110	22	44	45	16.0	7.35	61	.301	.387	0	—	0	-30	-29	-0	-3.9
1994 Cal-A	1	2	.333	3	3	0	0	0	13	16	2	8	10	17.3	9.00	54	.308	.410	0	—	0	-6	-6	1	-0.9
1995 Cle-A	0	0	—	1	0	0	0	0	4^2	7	0	0	4	13.5	3.86	122	.368	.368	0	—	0	0	0	-0	0.0
1996 Det-A	0	2	.000	2	2	0	0	0	6^1	11	2	5	0	24.2	14.21	36	.407	.515	0	—	0	-6	-6	-0	-1.2
Total 8	36	46	.439	116	109	13	2	0	698^2	732	72	250	355	13.0	4.56	91	.270	.338	0	—	0	-39	-31	-2	-5.7

● KERBY FARRELL Farrell, Major Kerby b: 9/3/13, Leapwood, Tenn. d: 12/17/75, Nashville, Tenn. BL/TL, 5'11", 172 lbs. Deb: 4/24/43 MC♦

YEAR TM/L	W	L	PCT	G	GS	CG	SH	SV	IP	H	HR	BB	SO	RAT	ERA	ERA+	OAV	OOB	BH	AVG	PB	PR	/A	PD	TPI
1943 Bos-N	0	1	.000	5	0	0	0	0	23	24	1	9	4	12.9	4.30	79	.276	.344	75	.268	1	-2	-2	-0	0.0

● TURK FARRELL Farrell, Richard Joseph b: 4/8/34, Boston, Mass. d: 6/10/77, Great Yarmouth, England BR/TR, 6'4", 220 lbs. Deb: 9/21/56

YEAR TM/L	W	L	PCT	G	GS	CG	SH	SV	IP	H	HR	BB	SO	RAT	ERA	ERA+	OAV	OOB	BH	AVG	PB	PR	/A	PD	TPI
1956 Phi-N	0	1	.000	1	1	0	0	0	4^1	6	0	3	0	20.8	12.46	30	.353	.476	0	.000	-0	-4	-4	0	-0.6
1957 Phi-N	10	2	.833	52	0	0	0	10	83^1	74	2	36	54	12.1	2.38	160	.242	.326	1	.111	0	**14**	13	0	2.2
1958 Phi-N★	8	9	.471	54	0	0	0	11	94	84	7	40	73	11.9	3.35	118	.244	.323	5	.208	0	6	6	-2	1.1
1959 Phi-N	1	6	.143	38	0	0	0	6	57	61	9	25	31	13.6	4.74	87	.288	.363	1	.167	-0	-5	-4	-0	-0.6
1960 Phi-N	10	6	.625	59	0	0	0	11	103^1	88	3	29	70	10.5	2.70	144	.239	.302	3	.200	1	12	14	-1	2.3
1961 Phi-N	2	1	.667	5	0	0	0	0	9^2	10	3	6	10	15.8	6.52	63	.270	.386	1	.500	0	-3	-3	-0	-0.7
LA-N	6	6	.500	50	0	0	0	10	89	107	12	43	80	15.3	5.06	86	.296	.373	0	.000	-2	-10	-7	-2	-1.4
Yr	8	7	.533	55	0	0	0	10	98^2	117	15	49	90	15.2	5.20	83	.293	.372	1	.050	-2	-13	-10	-2	-2.1
1962 Hou-N★	10	20	.333	43	29	11	2	4	241^2	210	21	55	203	10.1	3.02	124	.233	.280	14	.179	2	25	19	-2	2.3
1963 Hou-N	14	13	.519	34	26	12	0	1	202^1	161	12	35	141	8.8	3.02	104	.219	.256	9	.143	1	6	3	-2	0.4
1964 Hou-N★	11	10	.524	32	27	7	0	0	198^1	196	21	52	117	11.4	3.27	105	.261	.311	5	.072	-3	6	3	-1	-0.1
1965 Hou-N★	11	11	.500	33	29	8	3	1	208^1	202	18	35	122	10.4	3.50	96	.252	.286	10	.135	-1	1	-3	-2	-0.6
1966 Hou-N	6	10	.375	32	21	3	0	2	152^2	167	23	28	101	11.5	4.60	74	.278	.310	7	.146	-0	-17	-20	-2	-2.2
1967 Hou-N	1	0	1.000	7	0	0	0	0	11^2	11	0	7	10	14.7	4.63	72	.244	.358	0	.000	-0	-2	-2	-0	-0.2
Phi-N	9	6	.600	50	1	0	0	12	92	76	6	15	68	9.0	2.05	166	.228	.263	2	.105	-0	14	14	-1	2.6
Yr	10	6	.625	57	1	0	0	12	103^2	87	6	22	78	9.5	2.34	145	.229	.273	2	.100	-0	12	12	-1	2.4
1968 Phi-N	4	6	.400	54	0	0	0	12	83	83	7	32	57	12.7	3.47	87	.271	.344	1	.167	-0	-4	-4	-0	-0.7
1969 Phi-N	3	4	.429	46	0	0	0	3	74^1	92	8	27	40	14.5	4.00	89	.307	.366	0	.000	-0	-3	-4	-2	-0.6
Total 14	106	111	.488	590	134	41	5	83	1705	1628	152	468	1177	11.2	3.45	103	.254	.307	59	.135	-3	35	21	-17	3.2

● JEFF FASSERO Fassero, Jeffrey Joseph b: 1/5/63, Springfield, Ill. BL/TL, 6'1", 195 lbs. Deb: 5/4/91

YEAR TM/L	W	L	PCT	G	GS	CG	SH	SV	IP	H	HR	BB	SO	RAT	ERA	ERA+	OAV	OOB	BH	AVG	PB	PR	/A	PD	TPI
1991 Mon-N	2	5	.286	51	0	0	0	8	55^1	39	1	17	42	9.3	2.44	148	.196	.263	0	.000	0	8	7	1	1.1
1992 Mon-N	8	7	.533	70	0	0	0	1	85^2	81	1	34	63	12.3	2.84	122	.249	.324	1	.143	0	6	6	0	1.0
1993 Mon-N	12	5	.706	56	15	1	0	1	149^2	119	7	54	140	10.4	2.29	183	.216	.286	2	.063	-2	**29**	**31**	0	3.1
1994 Mon-N	8	6	.571	21	21	1	0	0	138^2	119	13	40	119	10.4	2.99	141	.229	.286	3	.068	-2	19	19	3	1.9
1995 Mon-N	13	14	.481	30	30	1	0	0	189	207	15	74	164	13.5	4.33	99	.283	.351	4	.070	-3	-3	-1	1	-0.3
1996 Mon-N	15	11	.577	34	34	5	1	0	231^2	217	20	55	222	10.7	3.30	131	.244	.291	6	.094	-1	23	26	3	2.9
1997 *Sea-A	16	9	.640	35	35	2	1	0	234^1	226	21	84	189	12.0	3.61	124	.249	.315	1	.200	0	25	23	1	2.3
1998 Sea-A	13	12	.520	32	32	7	0	0	224^2	223	33	66	176	12.0	3.97	117	.259	.319	0	.000	0	17	17	0	1.6
Total 8	87	69	.558	329	167	17	2	10	1309	1231	111	424	1115	11.5	3.40	126	.247	.309	17	.079	-8	124	129	9	13.7

● FAST Fast b: Milwaukee, Wis. Deb: 7/11/1887

YEAR TM/L	W	L	PCT	G	GS	CG	SH	SV	IP	H	HR	BB	SO	RAT	ERA	ERA+	OAV	OOB	BH	AVG	PB	PR	/A	PD	TPI
1887 Ind-N	0	1	.000	4	2	1	0	**1**	15^2	25	1	8	0	20.1	10.34	40	.347	.427	2	.182	-1	-11	-11	0	-0.6

● DARCY FAST Fast, Darcy Rae b: 3/10/47, Dallas, Ore. BL/TL, 6'3", 195 lbs. Deb: 6/15/68

YEAR TM/L	W	L	PCT	G	GS	CG	SH	SV	IP	H	HR	BB	SO	RAT	ERA	ERA+	OAV	OOB	BH	AVG	PB	PR	/A	PD	TPI
1968 Chi-N	0	1	.000	8	1	0	0	0	10	8	1	8	10	14.4	5.40	59	.216	.356	0	.000	0	-3	-2	0	-0.3

● JACK FASZHOLZ Faszholz, John Edward "Preacher" b: 4/11/27, St.Louis, Mo. BR/TR, 6'3", 205 lbs. Deb: 4/25/53

YEAR TM/L	W	L	PCT	G	GS	CG	SH	SV	IP	H	HR	BB	SO	RAT	ERA	ERA+	OAV	OOB	BH	AVG	PB	PR	/A	PD	TPI
1953 StL-N	0	0	—	4	1	0	0	0	11^2	16	3	1	7	13.9	6.94	61	.327	.353	0	.000	-0	-3	-3	-1	-0.1

● BILL FAUL Faul, William Alvan b: 4/21/40, Cincinnati, Ohio BR/TR, 5'10", 190 lbs. Deb: 9/19/62

YEAR TM/L	W	L	PCT	G	GS	CG	SH	SV	IP	H	HR	BB	SO	RAT	ERA	ERA+	OAV	OOB	BH	AVG	PB	PR	/A	PD	TPI
1962 Det-A	0	0	—	1	0	0	0	0	1^2	4	1	3	2	43.2	32.40	13	.444	.615	0	—	0	-5	-5	-0	0.0
1963 Det-A	5	6	.455	28	10	2	0	1	97	93	14	48	64	13.5	4.64	81	.251	.343	4	.148	0	-11	-10	-2	-1.2
1964 Det-A	0	0	—	1	1	0	0	0	5	5	2	2	1	12.6	10.80	34	.250	.318	0	.000	-0	-4	-4	0	0.0
1965 Chi-N	6	6	.500	17	16	5	3	0	96^2	83	12	18	59	9.7	3.54	104	.232	.275	3	.100	-1	0	2	-2	-0.1

YEAR	TM/L	W	L	PCT	G	GS	CG	SH	SV	IP	H	HR	BB	SO	RAT	ERA	ERA+	OAV	OOB	BH	AVG	PB	PR	/A	PD	TPI
1966	Chi-N	1	4	.200	17	6	1	0	0	51^1	47	12	18	32	12.1	5.08	72	.242	.319	0	.000	-2	-8	-8	-1	-0.9
1970	SF-N	0	0	—	7	0	0	0	1	9^2	15	1	6	6	19.6	7.45	53	.357	.438	0	—	0	-4	-4	-0	-0.1
Total	6	12	16	.429	71	33	8	3	2	261^1	247	42	95	164	12.2	4.72	79	.249	.322	7	.097	-2	-32	-29	-5	-2.3

● JIM FAULKNER

Faulkner, James Leroy "Lefty" b: 7/27/1899, Beatrice, Neb. d: 6/1/62, W.Palm Beach, Fla. BB/TL, 6'3", 190 lbs. Deb: 9/15/27

YEAR	TM/L	W	L	PCT	G	GS	CG	SH	SV	IP	H	HR	BB	SO	RAT	ERA	ERA+	OAV	OOB	BH	AVG	PB	PR	/A	PD	TPI
1927	NY-N	1	0	1.000	3	1	0	0	0	9^2	13	0	5	2	17.7	3.72	104	.317	.404	1	.500	1	0	0	-0	0.1
1928	NY-N	9	8	.529	38	8	3	0	2	117^1	131	5	41	32	13.4	3.53	111	.289	.351	9	.231	1	6	5	1	0.8
1930	Bro-N	0	0	—	2	1	0	0	1	0^1	2	1	1	0	81.0	81.00	6	.667	.750	0	—	0	-3	-3	0	-1.2
Total	3	10	8	.556	43	10	3	0	3	127^1	146	6	47	34	13.9	3.75	104	.293	.359	10	.244	2	3	2	1	-0.3

● BUCK FAUSETT

Fausett, Robert Shaw "Leaky" b: 4/8/08, Sheridan, Ark. d: 5/2/94, College Station, Tex. BL/TR, 5'10", 170 lbs. Deb: 4/18/44 ♦

YEAR	TM/L	W	L	PCT	G	GS	CG	SH	SV	IP	H	HR	BB	SO	RAT	ERA	ERA+	OAV	OOB	BH	AVG	PB	PR	/A	PD	TPI
1944	Cin-N	0	0	—	2	0	0	0	0	10^2	13	0	7	3	18.6	5.91	59	.295	.415	3	.097	-0	-3	-3	0	0.0

● CHARLIE FAUST

Faust, Charles Victor "Victory" b: 10/9/1880, Marion, Kan. d: 6/18/15, Fort Steilacoom, Wash. BR/TR, 6'2", Deb: 10/7/11

YEAR	TM/L	W	L	PCT	G	GS	CG	SH	SV	IP	H	HR	BB	SO	RAT	ERA	ERA+	OAV	OOB	BH	AVG	PB	PR	/A	PD	TPI
1911	NY-N	0	0	—	2	0	0	0	0	2	2	0	0	0	9.0	4.50	75	.250	.250	0	—	0	-0	-0	0	0.1

● CLAY FAUVER

Fauver, Clayton King "Cayt" b: 8/1/1872, N.Eaton, Ohio d: 3/3/42, Chatsworth, Ga. BB/TR, 5'10", Deb: 9/7/1899

YEAR	TM/L	W	L	PCT	G	GS	CG	SH	SV	IP	H	HR	BB	SO	RAT	ERA	ERA+	OAV	OOB	BH	AVG	PB	PR	/A	PD	TPI
1899	Lou-N	1	0	1.000	1	1	1	0	0	9	11	0	2	1	13.0	0.00	—	.297	.333	0	.000	-1	4	4	-0	0.3

● VERN FEAR

Fear, Luvern Carl b: 8/21/24, Everly, Iowa d: 9/6/76, Spencer, Iowa BB/TR, 6', 170 lbs. Deb: 8/3/52

YEAR	TM/L	W	L	PCT	G	GS	CG	SH	SV	IP	H	HR	BB	SO	RAT	ERA	ERA+	OAV	OOB	BH	AVG	PB	PR	/A	PD	TPI
1952	Chi-N	0	0	—	4	0	0	0	0	8	9	1	3	4	14.6	7.88	49	.290	.371	0	.000	-0	-4	-4	-0	0.0

● JACK FEE

Fee, John b: 12/23/1867, Carbondale, Pa. d: 3/3/13, Carbondale, Pa. Deb: 9/14/1889

YEAR	TM/L	W	L	PCT	G	GS	CG	SH	SV	IP	H	HR	BB	SO	RAT	ERA	ERA+	OAV	OOB	BH	AVG	PB	PR	/A	PD	TPI
1889	Ind-N	2	2	.500	7	3	2	0	0	40	39	2	31	10	17.1	4.27	98	.248	.392	3	.143	-2	-1	-0	1	-0.1

● HARRY FELDMAN

Feldman, Harry b: 11/10/19, New York, N.Y. d: 3/16/62, Fort Smith, Ark. BR/TR, 6', 175 lbs. Deb: 9/10/41

YEAR	TM/L	W	L	PCT	G	GS	CG	SH	SV	IP	H	HR	BB	SO	RAT	ERA	ERA+	OAV	OOB	BH	AVG	PB	PR	/A	PD	TPI
1941	NY-N	1	1	.500	3	3	1	1	0	20^1	21	0	6	9	12.0	3.98	93	.280	.333	1	.167	0	-1	-1	-0	-0.1
1942	NY-N	7	1	.875	31	6	2	1	0	114	100	5	73	49	13.7	3.16	106	.236	.350	11	.282	3	2	3	-0	0.5
1943	NY-N	4	5	.444	31	10	1	0	0	104^2	114	7	58	49	15.1	4.30	80	.279	.374	4	.133	-1	-11	-10	0	-0.9
1944	NY-N	11	13	.458	40	27	8	1	2	205^1	214	18	91	70	13.5	4.16	88	.266	.342	15	.205	0	-13	-11	-2	-1.4
1945	NY-N	12	13	.480	35	30	10	3	1	217^2	213	14	69	74	11.7	3.27	120	.251	.308	7	.097	-3	13	16	-2	1.1
1946	NY-N	0	2	.000	3	2	0	0	0	4	9	1	3	3	27.0	18.00	19	.474	.545	0	.000	-0	-6	-6	-0	-2.1
Total	6	35	35	.500	143	78	22	6	3	666	671	45	300	254	13.2	3.80	96	.260	.339	38	.172	-1	-16	-10	-5	-2.9

● HARRY FELIX

Felix, Harry b: 1870, Brooklyn, N.Y. d: 10/17/61, Miami, Fla. BR/TR, 5'7.5", 160 lbs. Deb: 10/5/01

YEAR	TM/L	W	L	PCT	G	GS	CG	SH	SV	IP	H	HR	BB	SO	RAT	ERA	ERA+	OAV	OOB	BH	AVG	PB	PR	/A	PD	TPI
1901	NY-N	0	0	—	1	0	0	0	0	2	3	0	0	0	13.5	0.00	—	.333	.333	0	.000	-0	1	1	-0	0.0
1902	Phi-N	1	3	.250	9	5	3	0	0	45	61	1	11	10	14.4	5.60	50	.323	.360	5	.135	-1	-14	-14	-1	-1.2
Total	2	1	3	.250	10	5	3	0	0	47	64	1	11	10	14.4	5.36	53	.323	.359	5	.132	-1	-13	-13	-1	-1.2

● BOB FELLER

Feller, Robert William Andrew "Rapid Robert" (b: Robert William Feller) b: 11/3/18, Van Meter, Iowa BR/TR, 6', 185 lbs. Deb: 7/19/36 H

YEAR	TM/L	W	L	PCT	G	GS	CG	SH	SV	IP	H	HR	BB	SO	RAT	ERA	ERA+	OAV	OOB	BH	AVG	PB	PR	/A	PD	TPI
1936	Cle-A	5	3	.625	14	8	5	0	1	62	52	1	47	76	15.0	3.34	151	.229	.371	3	.136	-2	12	12	-1	1.1
1937	Cle-A	9	7	.563	26	19	9	0	1	148^2	116	4	106	150	13.6	3.39	136	.218	.351	9	.170	-1	20	20	1	1.9
1938	Cle-A☆	17	11	.607	39	36	20	2	1	277^2	225	13	208	**240**	14.3	4.08	114	**.220**	.356	17	.181	2	22	17	-2	1.4
1939	Cle-A★	**24**	9	.727	39	35	**24**	4	1	**296^2**	227	13	142	**246**	11.3	2.85	154	**.210**	.303	21	.212	5	**58**	**51**	0	**5.6**
1940	Cle-A★	**27**	11	.711	**43**	37	**31**	**4**	4	**320^1**	245	13	118	**261**	**10.3**	**2.61**	161	**.210**	**.285**	18	.157	1	**63**	**57**	-4	**6.1**
1941	Cle-A★	**25**	13	.658	**44**	40	28	**6**	2	**343**	284	15	194	**260**	12.7	3.15	125	.226	.332	18	.150	2	38	30	-1	3.2
1945	Cle-A	5	3	.625	9	9	7	1	0	72	50	1	35	59	10.9	2.50	130	.192	.293	4	.160	-0	7	6	-1	0.5
1946	Cle-A★	**26**	15	.634	**48**	42	**36**	**10**	4	**371^1**	277	11	153	**348**	10.5	2.18	152	.208	.291	16	.129	-2	**55**	46	-1	4.9
1947	Cle-A†	**20**	11	.645	42	37	20	**5**	3	**299**	230	17	127	**196**	**10.9**	2.68	130	.215	.300	18	.184	3	**34**	27	2	3.1
1948	*Cle-A†	19	15	.559	44	38	18	2	3	280^1	255	20	116	**164**	12.0	3.56	114	.241	.317	9	.095	-8	23	15	-1	0.7
1949	Cle-A	15	14	.517	36	28	15	0	0	211	198	18	84	108	12.1	3.75	106	.248	.320	17	.236	4	10	6	-4	0.7
1950	Cle-A★	16	11	.593	35	34	16	3	0	247	230	20	103	119	12.3	3.43	126	.247	.325	10	.120	-2	32	25	-4	1.7
1951	Cle-A	**22**	8	**.733**	33	32	16	4	0	249^2	239	22	95	111	12.3	3.50	108	.253	.325	10	.123	-4	17	8	-3	0.1
1952	Cle-A	9	13	.409	30	30	11	0	0	191^2	219	13	83	81	14.3	4.74	71	.288	.360	7	.117	1	-23	-30	-0	-3.0
1953	Cle-A	10	7	.588	25	25	10	1	0	175^2	163	16	60	60	11.6	3.59	105	.251	.317	6	.107	-2	8	3	1	0.1
1954	Cle-A	13	3	.813	19	19	9	1	0	140	127	13	39	59	10.9	3.09	119	.239	.294	9	.188	1	10	9	-2	0.9
1955	Cle-A	4	4	.500	25	11	2	1	0	83	71	7	31	25	11.2	3.47	115	.235	.308	1	.048	-2	5	5	-1	0.1
1956	Cle-A	0	4	.000	19	4	2	0	1	58	63	7	23	18	13.3	4.97	85	.280	.347	0	.000	-2	-5	-5	-1	-0.6
Total	18	266	162	.621	570	484	279	44	21	3827	3271	224	1764	2581	12.0	3.25	122	.231	.319	193	.151	-7	385	301	-22	28.5

● TERRY FELTON

Felton, Terry Lane b: 10/29/57, Texarkana, Ark. BR/TR, 6'1", 180 lbs. Deb: 9/28/79

YEAR	TM/L	W	L	PCT	G	GS	CG	SH	SV	IP	H	HR	BB	SO	RAT	ERA	ERA+	OAV	OOB	BH	AVG	PB	PR	/A	PD	TPI
1979	Min-A	0	0	—	1	0	0	0	0	2	0	0	0	1	0.0	0.00	—	.000	.000	0	—	0	1	1	-0	-0.2
1980	Min-A	0	3	.000	5	4	0	0	0	17^2	20	2	9	14	15.3	7.13	61	.286	.375	0	—	0	-6	-5	-0	-0.8
1981	Min-A	0	0	—	1	0	0	0	0	1^1	4	1	2	1	40.5	40.50	10	.500	.600	0	—	0	-5	-5	0	-0.1
1982	Min-A	0	13	.000	48	6	0	0	3	117^1	99	18	76	92	13.7	4.99	85	.230	.351	0	—	0	-12	-10	-2	-1.2
Total	4	0	16	.000	55	10	0	0	3	138^1	123	21	87	108	14.0	5.53	77	.240	.355	0	—	0	-22	-20	-3	-2.3

● HOD FENNER

Fenner, Horace Alfred b: 7/12/1897, Martin, Mich. d: 11/20/54, Detroit, Mich. BR/TR, 5'10.5", 165 lbs. Deb: 9/9/21

YEAR	TM/L	W	L	PCT	G	GS	CG	SH	SV	IP	H	HR	BB	SO	RAT	ERA	ERA+	OAV	OOB	BH	AVG	PB	PR	/A	PD	TPI
1921	Chi-A	0	0	—	2	1	0	0	0	7	14	0	3	1	21.9	7.71	55	.452	.500	0	.000	-0	-3	-3	-0	-0.1

● STAN FERENS

Ferens, Stanley "Lefty" b: 3/5/15, Wendel, Pa. d: 10/7/94, Hempfield Township, Pa. BB/TL, 5'11", 170 lbs. Deb: 6/10/42

YEAR	TM/L	W	L	PCT	G	GS	CG	SH	SV	IP	H	HR	BB	SO	RAT	ERA	ERA+	OAV	OOB	BH	AVG	PB	PR	/A	PD	TPI
1942	StL-A	3	4	.429	19	3	1	0	0	69	76	2	21	23	12.7	3.78	98	.279	.331	3	.143	-1	-1	-1	-0	-0.1
1946	StL-A	2	9	.182	34	6	1	0	0	88	100	3	38	28	14.4	4.50	83	.293	.369	4	.167	-1	-10	-8	-1	-1.0
Total	2	5	13	.278	53	9	2	0	0	157	176	5	59	51	13.6	4.18	89	.287	.353	7	.156	-1	-11	-8	-1	-1.1

● CHARLIE FERGUSON

Ferguson, Charles Augustus b: 5/10/1875, Okemos, Mich. d: 5/17/31, Sault Ste.Marie, Mich. TR , 5'11", Deb: 9/20/01

YEAR	TM/L	W	L	PCT	G	GS	CG	SH	SV	IP	H	HR	BB	SO	RAT	ERA	ERA+	OAV	OOB	BH	AVG	PB	PR	/A	PD	TPI
1901	Chi-N	0	0	—	1	0	0	0	0	2	1	0	2	0	13.5	0.00	—	.143	.333	0	.000	-0	1	1	-0	0.0

● CHARLIE FERGUSON

Ferguson, Charles J. b: 4/17/1863, Charlottesville, Va. d: 4/29/1888, Philadelphia, Pa. BB/TR, 6', 165 lbs. Deb: 5/1/1884

YEAR	TM/L	W	L	PCT	G	GS	CG	SH	SV	IP	H	HR	BB	SO	RAT	ERA	ERA+	OAV	OOB	BH	AVG	PB	PR	/A	PD	TPI
1884	Phi-N	21	25	.457	50	47	46	2	1	416^2	443	13	93	194	11.6	3.54	84	.253	.291	50	.246	7	-26	-26	-2	-1.7
1885	Phi-N	26	20	.565	48	45	45	5	0	405	345	5	81	197	9.5	2.22	126	.219	.257	72	.306	17	27	26	1	4.3
1886	Phi-N	30	9	.769	48	45	43	4	**2**	395^2	317	11	69	212	8.8	1.98	167	.210	.244	66	.253	12	**59**	58	5	**6.5**
1887	Phi-N	22	10	.688	37	33	31	2	**1**	297^1	297	13	47	125	10.7	3.00	141	.254	.289	89	.337	14	36	41	1	4.7
Total	4	99	64	.607	183	170	165	13	4	1514^2	1402	42	290	728	10.1	2.67	122	.233	.270	277	.288	49	95	97	6	13.8

● GEORGE FERGUSON

Ferguson, George Cecil "Cecil" b: 8/19/1886, Ellsworth, Ind. d: 9/5/43, Orlando, Fla. BR/TR, 5'10", 165 lbs. Deb: 4/19/06

YEAR	TM/L	W	L	PCT	G	GS	CG	SH	SV	IP	H	HR	BB	SO	RAT	ERA	ERA+	OAV	OOB	BH	AVG	PB	PR	/A	PD	TPI
1906	NY-N	2	0	1.000	22	1	1	1	**7**	52^1	43	1	24	32	11.9	2.58	101	.229	.322	5	.333	2	**0**	**0**	1	0.3
1907	NY-N	3	2	.600	15	5	4	0	1	64	63	2	20	37	12.4	2.11	118	.266	.336	1	.056	-1	3	3	-0	0.0
1908	Bos-N	11	11	.500	37	21	13	3	0	208	168	1	84	98	11.3	2.47	98	.230	.316	11	.169	1	-2	-1	-3	-0.4
1909	Bos-N	5	23	.179	36	30	19	3	0	226^2	235	2	83	87	13.1	3.73	76	.282	.355	15	.205	1	-29	-23	0	-2.5
1910	Bos-N	7	7	.500	26	14	10	1	0	123	110	3	58	40	12.8	3.80	87	.254	.351	7	.175	-1	-11	-7	-0	-0.8
1911	Bos-N	1	3	.250	6	3	0	0	0	24	40	3	12	4	19.5	9.75	39	.388	.452	2	.286	1	-17	-16	-0	-1.9
Total	6	29	46	.387	142	74	47	8	8	698	659	12	281	298	12.6	3.34	83	.261	.343	41	.188	3	-56	-44	-2	-5.3

● ALEX FERGUSON

Ferguson, James Alexander b: 2/16/1897, Montclair, N.J. d: 4/26/76, Sepulveda, Cal. BR/TR, 6', 180 lbs. Deb: 8/16/18

YEAR	TM/L	W	L	PCT	G	GS	CG	SH	SV	IP	H	HR	BB	SO	RAT	ERA	ERA+	OAV	OOB	BH	AVG	PB	PR	/A	PD	TPI
1918	NY-A	0	0	—	1	0	0	0	0	1^2	2	0	2	1	21.6	0.00	—	.333	.500	0	.000	-0	1	1	-0	0.0
1921	NY-A	3	1	.750	17	4	1	0	1	56^1	64	4	27	9	15.2	5.91	72	.296	.385	4	.211	-1	-10	-10	-0	-0.7
1922	Bos-A	9	16	.360	39	27	10	1	2	198^1	201	5	62	44	12.2	4.31	95	.265	.326	6	.092	-6	-6	-4	-1	-1.2
1923	Bos-A	9	13	.409	34	27	11	0	0	198^1	229	5	67	72	13.8	4.04	102	.297	.360	6	.097	-5	-1	2	-1	-0.5
1924	Bos-A	14	17	.452	41	32	15	0	2	237^2	259	6	108	78	14.1	3.79	115	.286	.366	12	.140	-6	12	15	1	1.3
1925	Bos-A	0	2	.000	5	4	0	0	1	15^2	22	6	5	5	16.1	10.91	42	.314	.368	0	.000	-0	-11	-11	-0	-1.2
	NY-A	4	2	.667	21	6	0	0	1	54^1	83	3	42	20	21.0	7.79	55	.358	.460	2	.133	-1	-20	-21	1	-1.9
	*Was-A	5	1	.833	7	6	3	0	0	55^1	52	2	23	24	12.5	3.25	130	.256	.338	1	.050	-3	7	6	-1	0.2

YEAR	TM/L	W	L	PCT	G	GS	CG	SH	SV	IP	H	HR	BB	SO	RAT	ERA	ERA+	OAV	OOB	BH	AVG	PB	PR	/A	PD	TPI
	Yr	9	5	.643	33	16	3	0	2	125^1	157	11	70	49	16.4	6.18	69	.309	.395	3	.077	-4	-25	-26	-1	-2.9
1926	Was-A	3	4	.429	19	4	0	0	1	47^2	69	4	18	16	17.0	7.74	50	.343	.405	2	.182	-0	-20	-21	0	-2.5
1927	Phi-N	8	16	.333	31	31	16	0	0	227	280	15	65	73	13.9	4.84	85	.313	.363	7	.100	-5	-23	-18	0	-2.0
1928	Phi-N	5	10	.333	34	19	5	1	2	134^2	168	14	52	51	15.1	5.88	73	.315	.382	1	.026	-4	-28	-24	2	-2.6
1929	Phi-N	1	2	.333	5	4	1	0	0	12^2	19	2	10	3	20.6	12.08	43	.345	.446	0	.000	-1	-10	-10	0	-1.6
	Bro-N	0	1	.000	3	3	0	0	0	2	7	2	1	1	36.0	22.50	21	.583	.615	1	1.000	0	-4	-4	0	-1.3
	Yr	1	3	.250	8	7	1	0	0	14^2	26	4	11	4	22.7	13.50	38	.388	.474	1	.200	-0	-14	-14	1	-2.9
Total	10	61	85	.418	257	167	62	2	10	1241^2	1455	68	482	397	14.4	4.93	85	.299	.368	42	.106	-33	-115	-99	1	-14.0

● BOB FERGUSON

Ferguson, Robert Lester b: 4/18/19, Birmingham, Ala. BR/TR, 6′1.5″, 180 lbs. Deb: 4/29/44

YEAR	TM/L	W	L	PCT	G	GS	CG	SH	SV	IP	H	HR	BB	SO	RAT	ERA	ERA+	OAV	OOB	BH	AVG	PB	PR	/A	PD	TPI
1944	Cin-N	0	3	.000	9	2	0	0	1	16	24	3	10	9	20.3	9.00	39	.358	.456	1	.333	0	-10	-10	0	-1.6

● BOB FERGUSON

Ferguson, Robert Vavasour b: 1/31/1845, Brooklyn, N.Y. d: 5/3/1894, Brooklyn, N.Y. BB/TR, 5′9.5″, 149 lbs. Deb: 5/18/1871 MU♦

YEAR	TM/L	W	L	PCT	G	GS	CG	SH	SV	IP	H	HR	BB	SO	RAT	ERA	ERA+	OAV	OOB	BH	AVG	PB	PR	/A	PD	TPI
1871	Mut-n	0	0	—	1	0	0	0	0	1	8	0	0	0	72.0	27.00	14	.571	.571	38	.241	-0	-3	-3		0.0
1873	Atl-n	0	1	.000	4	1	1	0	0	19^1	41	2	2	0	20.0	6.05	50	.380	.391	59	.259	1	-6	-6		-0.2
1874	Atl-n	0	1	.000	1	1	1	0	0	9	12	0	3	0	15.0	4.00	51	.273	.319	64	.261	0	-2	-2		-0.1
1875	Har-n	0	0	—	1	0	0	0	0	2	9	1	0	0	40.5	22.50	10	.600	.600	88	.240	0	-5	-4		0.0
1877	Har-N	1	1	.500	3	2	2	0	0	25	38	0	2	1	14.4	3.96	61	.352	.364	65	.256	0	-3	-4	0	-0.2
1883	Phi-N	0	0	—	1	0	0	0	0	1	2	0	0	0	18.0	9.00	34	.286	.286	85	.258	0	-1	-1	0	0.0
Total	4 n	0	2	.000	7	2	2	0	0	31^1	70	3	5	0	21.5	7.18	38	.387	.403	295	.254	1	-15	-15		-0.3
Total	2	1	1	.500	4	2	2	0	0	26	40	0	2	1	14.5	4.15	59	.348	.359	625	.271	0	-4	-5	0	-0.2

● RAMON FERMIN

Fermin, Ramon Antonio (Ventura) b: 11/25/72, San Francisco De Macoris, D.R. BR/TR, 6′3″, 180 lbs. Deb: 8/6/95

YEAR	TM/L	W	L	PCT	G	GS	CG	SH	SV	IP	H	HR	BB	SO	RAT	ERA	ERA+	OAV	OOB	BH	AVG	PB	PR	/A	PD	TPI
1995	Oak-A	0	0	—	1	0	0	0	0	1^1	4	0	1	0	33.8	13.50	33	.500	.556	0	—	0	-1	-1	0	0.2

● ALEX FERNANDEZ

Fernandez, Alexander b: 8/13/69, Miami Beach, Fla. BR/TR, 6′1″, 215 lbs. Deb: 8/2/90

YEAR	TM/L	W	L	PCT	G	GS	CG	SH	SV	IP	H	HR	BB	SO	RAT	ERA	ERA+	OAV	OOB	BH	AVG	PB	PR	/A	PD	TPI
1990	Chi-A	5	5	.500	13	13	3	0	0	87^2	89	6	34	61	12.9	3.80	101	.265	.338	0	—	0	1	0	-0	0.1
1991	Chi-A	9	13	.409	34	32	2	0	0	191^2	186	16	88	145	13.0	4.51	88	.259	.341	0	—	0	-9	-11	1	-1.0
1992	Chi-A	8	11	.421	29	29	4	2	0	187^2	199	21	50	95	12.3	4.27	90	.270	.324	0	—	0	-7	-9	2	-0.6
1993	*Chi-A	18	9	.667	34	34	3	1	0	247^1	221	27	67	169	10.7	3.13	133	.240	.296	0	—	0	33	29	2	3.2
1994	Chi-A	11	7	.611	24	24	4	3	0	170^1	163	25	50	122	11.3	3.86	121	.250	.305	0	—	0	18	15	4	1.9
1995	Chi-A	12	8	.600	30	30	5	2	0	203^2	200	19	65	159	11.7	3.80	117	.255	.313	0	—	0	21	15	0	1.4
1996	Chi-A	16	10	.615	35	35	6	1	0	258	248	34	72	200	11.4	3.45	137	.253	.309	0	—	0	44	37	3	3.6
1997	*Fla-N	17	12	.586	32	32	5	1	0	220^2	193	25	69	183	10.8	3.59	112	.238	.301	10	.152	3	15	11	3	1.9
Total	8	96	75	.561	231	229	32	10	0	1567	1499	173	495	1134	11.6	3.76	113	.253	.313	10	.152	3	116	87	14	10.5

● SID FERNANDEZ

Fernandez, Charles Sidney b: 10/12/62, Honolulu, Hawaii BL/TL, 6′1″, 230 lbs. Deb: 9/20/83

YEAR	TM/L	W	L	PCT	G	GS	CG	SH	SV	IP	H	HR	BB	SO	RAT	ERA	ERA+	OAV	OOB	BH	AVG	PB	PR	/A	PD	TPI
1983	LA-N	0	1	.000	2	1	0	0	0	6	7	0	7	9	22.5	6.00	60	.280	.455	1	1.000	0	-2	-2	0	-0.2
1984	NY-N	6	6	.500	15	15	0	0	0	90	74	8	34	62	10.8	3.50	101	.226	.299	5	.179	-0	1	0	-2	-0.2
1985	NY-N	9	9	.500	26	26	3	0	0	170^1	108	14	80	180	10.0	2.80	123	**.181**	.280	11	.212	2	15	12	-0	1.4
1986	*NY-N★	16	6	.727	32	31	2	1	1	204^1	161	13	91	200	11.2	3.52	100	.216	.303	11	.162	1	4	0	-3	-0.1
1987	NY-N★	12	8	.600	28	27	3	1	0	156	130	16	67	134	11.8	3.81	99	.224	.313	7	.163	1	5	-1	-3	-0.2
1988	*NY-N	12	10	.545	31	31	1	1	0	187	127	15	70	189	9.8	3.03	106	**.191**	.274	14	.250	6	9	4	-3	0.7
1989	NY-N	14	5	.737	35	32	6	2	0	219^1	157	21	75	198	9.8	2.83	115	.198	.272	15	.211	4	16	11	-4	1.0
1990	NY-N	9	14	.391	30	30	2	1	0	179^1	130	18	67	181	10.1	3.46	108	**.200**	.280	11	.190	1	7	6	-2	0.5
1991	NY-N	1	3	.250	8	8	0	0	0	44	36	4	9	31	9.2	2.86	127	.222	.263	2	.154	0	4	4	1	0.4
1992	NY-N	14	11	.560	32	32	5	2	0	214^2	162	12	67	193	9.8	2.73	127	.210	.277	15	.203	2	19	18	-2	2.1
1993	NY-N	5	6	.455	18	18	1	1	0	119^2	82	17	36	81	9.1	2.93	137	.192	.260	3	.094	-1	15	14	-2	0.9
1994	Bal-A	6	6	.500	19	19	2	0	0	115^1	109	27	46	95	12.3	5.15	97	.248	.322	0	—	0	-4	-2	-2	-0.5
1995	Bal-A	0	4	.000	8	7	0	0	0	28	36	9	17	31	17.0	7.39	64	.305	.393	0	—	0	-8	-8	-1	-1.0
	Phi-N	6	1	.857	11	11	0	0	0	64^2	48	11	21	79	9.7	3.34	126	.200	.267	1	.043	-2	6	6	-2	0.3
1996	Phi-N	3	6	.333	11	11	0	0	0	63	50	5	26	77	11.0	3.43	126	.215	.296	2	.105	0	6	6	-1	0.7
1997	Hou-N	1	0	1.000	1	1	0	0	0	5	4	1	2	3	10.8	3.60	111	.211	.286	0	.000	-0	0	0	0	0.0
Total	15	114	96	.543	307	300	25	9	1	1866^2	1421	191	715	1743	10.5	3.36	110	.209	.288	98	.182	15	91	68	-24	5.8

● OSVALDO FERNANDEZ

Fernandez, Osvaldo b: 11/4/68, Holguin, Cuba BR/TR, 6′2″, 190 lbs. Deb: 4/5/96

YEAR	TM/L	W	L	PCT	G	GS	CG	SH	SV	IP	H	HR	BB	SO	RAT	ERA	ERA+	OAV	OOB	BH	AVG	PB	PR	/A	PD	TPI
1996	SF-N	7	13	.350	30	28	2	0	0	171^2	193	20	57	106	13.6	4.61	89	.286	.350	5	.088	-3	-8	-10	1	-1.2
1997	SF-N	3	4	.429	11	11	0	0	0	56^1	74	9	15	31	14.2	4.95	83	.314	.355	0	.000	-1	-5	-5	-1	-0.7
Total	2	10	17	.370	41	39	2	0	0	228	267	29	72	137	13.8	4.70	87	.293	.351	5	.068	-5	-12	-15	0	-1.9

● DON FERRARESE

Ferrarese, Donald Hugh b: 6/19/29, Oakland, Cal. BR/TL, 5′9″, 170 lbs. Deb: 4/11/55

YEAR	TM/L	W	L	PCT	G	GS	CG	SH	SV	IP	H	HR	BB	SO	RAT	ERA	ERA+	OAV	OOB	BH	AVG	PB	PR	/A	PD	TPI
1955	Bal-A	0	0	—	6	0	0	0	0	9	8	0	11	5	19.0	3.00	127	.276	.475	0	.000	-0	1	1	-0	0.0
1956	Bal-A	4	10	.286	36	14	3	1	2	102	86	8	64	81	13.5	5.03	78	.229	.345	1	.036	-3	-10	-13	1	-1.8
1957	Bal-A	1	1	.500	8	2	0	0	0	19	14	1	12	13	12.3	4.74	76	.200	.317	0	.000	-0	-2	-2	0	-0.3
1958	Cle-A	3	4	.429	28	10	2	0	1	94^2	91	5	46	62	13.1	3.71	98	.254	.341	3	.115	-1	1	-1	-1	-0.3
1959	Cle-A	5	3	.625	15	10	4	0	0	76	58	6	51	45	13.0	3.20	115	.219	.347	7	.259	2	6	4	0	0.6
1960	Chi-A	0	1	.000	5	0	0	0	0	4	8	2	9	4	38.3	18.00	21	.400	.586	1	.500	0	-6	-6	-0	-1.2
1961	Phi-N	5	12	.294	42	14	3	1	1	138^2	120	14	68	89	12.3	3.76	108	.234	.325	6	.171	-1	4	5	-3	0.2
1962	Phi-N	0	1	.000	5	0	0	0	0	6^2	9	1	3	6	16.2	8.10	48	.310	.375	1	1.000	0	-3	-3	0	-0.3
	StL-N	1	4	.200	38	0	0	0	1	56^2	55	2	31	45	13.8	2.70	158	.270	.369	1	.200	1	8	10	1	1.0
	Yr	1	5	.167	43	0	0	0	1	63^1	64	3	34	51	14.1	3.27	129	.274	.368	2	.333	1	5	7	1	0.7
Total	8	19	36	.345	183	50	12	2	5	506^2	449	39	295	350	13.3	4.00	98	.241	.347	20	.156	-2	-2	-5	-1	-2.1

● BILL FERRAZZI

Ferrazzi, William Joseph b: 4/19/07, W.Quincy, Mass. d: 8/10/93, Gainesville, Fla. BR/TR, 6′2.5″, 200 lbs. Deb: 9/7/35

YEAR	TM/L	W	L	PCT	G	GS	CG	SH	SV	IP	H	HR	BB	SO	RAT	ERA	ERA+	OAV	OOB	BH	AVG	PB	PR	/A	PD	TPI
1935	Phi-A	1	2	.333	3	2	0	0	0	7	7	0	5	0	15.4	5.14	88	.269	.387	0	.000	0	-1	-0	0	-0.1

● TONY FERREIRA

Ferreira, Anthony Ross b: 10/4/62, Riverside, Cal. BL/TL, 6′1″, 160 lbs. Deb: 9/17/85

YEAR	TM/L	W	L	PCT	G	GS	CG	SH	SV	IP	H	HR	BB	SO	RAT	ERA	ERA+	OAV	OOB	BH	AVG	PB	PR	/A	PD	TPI
1985	KC-A	0	0	—	2	0	0	0	0	5^2	6	0	2	5	12.7	7.94	52	.273	.333	0	—	0	-2	-2	0	0.0

● WES FERRELL

Ferrell, Wesley Cheek b: 2/2/08, Greensboro, N.C. d: 12/9/76, Sarasota, Fla. BR/TR, 6′2″, 195 lbs. Deb: 9/9/27 F♦

YEAR	TM/L	W	L	PCT	G	GS	CG	SH	SV	IP	H	HR	BB	SO	RAT	ERA	ERA+	OAV	OOB	BH	AVG	PB	PR	/A	PD	TPI
1927	Cle-A	0	0	—	1	0	0	0	0	1	3	0	2	0	45.0	27.00	16	.600	.714	0	—	0	-3	-3	-0	0.0
1928	Cle-A	0	2	.000	2	2	1	0	0	16	15	0	5	4	11.3	2.25	184	.242	.299	1	.250	1	3	3	0	0.5
1929	Cle-A	21	10	.677	43	25	18	1	5	242^2	256	7	109	100	13.6	3.60	124	.279	.358	22	.237	4	17	23	3	3.4
1930	Cle-A	25	13	.658	43	35	25	1	3	296^2	299	14	106	143	12.3	3.31	146	.262	.325	35	.297	8	44	50	-3	6.2
1931	Cle-A	22	12	.647	40	35	**27**	2	3	276^1	276	9	130	123	13.3	3.75	123	.255	.336	37	.319	17	19	27	5	5.2
1932	Cle-A	23	13	.639	38	34	26	3	1	287^2	299	17	104	105	12.6	3.66	130	.264	.326	31	.242	5	26	35	1	4.3
1933	Cle-A☆	11	12	.478	28	26	16	1	0	201	225	8	70	41	13.3	4.21	106	.282	.341	38	.271	7	2	5	1	1.6
1934	Bos-A	14	5	.737	26	23	17	3	1	181	205	4	49	67	12.6	3.63	132	.282	.327	22	.282	8	17	24	-2	2.8
1935	Bos-A	**25**	14	.641	41	38	**31**	3	0	**322^1**	336	16	108	110	12.5	3.52	135	.267	.326	52	.347	20	34	44	2	**7.2**
1936	Bos-A	20	15	.571	39	38	**28**	3	0	**301**	330	11	119	106	13.6	4.19	127	.274	.343	36	.267	11	28	38	-3	4.5
1937	Bos-A	3	6	.333	12	11	5	0	0	73^1	111	14	34	31	17.9	7.61	62	.348	.412	12	.364	6	-24	-23	2	-1.5
	Was-A☆	11	13	.458	25	24	21	0	0	207^2	214	11	88	92	13.2	3.94	112	.265	.339	27	.255	5	16	11	-1	1.5
	Yr	14	19	.424	37	35	**26**	0	0	**281**	325	25	122	123	14.4	4.90	92	.288	.359	39	.281	11	-9	-12	1	0.0
1938	Was-A	13	8	.619	23	22	9	0	0	149	193	12	68	36	15.8	5.92	76	.311	.380	11	.224	7	-19	-23	1	-1.9
	NY-A	2	2	.500	5	4	1	0	0	30	52	6	18	7	21.0	8.10	56	.388	.461	2	.167	0	-11	-12	1	-1.1
	Yr	15	10	.600	28	26	10	0	0	179	245	18	86	43	16.6	6.28	72	.324	.393	13	.213	7	-30	-35	2	-3.0
1939	NY-A	1	2	.333	3	3	1	0	0	19^1	14	2	17	6	14.4	4.66	94	.219	.383	1	.125	-0	-0	-1	0	-0.1
1940	Bro-N	0	0	—	1	0	0	0	0	4	4	0	4	4	20.3	6.75	59	.250	.429	0	.000	-0	-1	-1	1	0.0
1941	Bos-N	2	1	.667	4	3	1	0	0	14	13	1	9	10	14.8	5.14	69	.241	.359	2	.500	2	-2	-2	-0	-0.3
Total	15	193	128	.601	374	323	227	17	13	2623	2845	132	1040	985	13.4	4.04	117	.275	.343	329	.280	100	147	195	6	32.3

● TOM FERRICK
Ferrick, Thomas Jerome b: 1/6/15, New York, N.Y. d: 10/15/96, Lima, Pa. BR/TR, 6'2.5", 220 lbs. Deb: 4/19/41 C

YEAR	TM/L	W	L	PCT	G	GS	CG	SH	SV	IP	H	HR	BB	SO	RAT	ERA	ERA+	OAV	OOB	BH	AVG	PB	PR	/A	PD	TPI
1941	Phi-A	8	10	.444	36	4	2	1	7	119^1	130	8	33	30	12.3	3.77	111	.275	.322	9	.205	1	5	6	3	1.2
1942	Cle-A	3	2	.600	31	2	2	0	3	81^1	56	3	32	28	9.7	1.99	173	.200	.282	4	.211	0	**15**	**13**	2	1.1
1946	Cle-A	0	0	—	9	0	0	0	1	18	25	3	4	9	14.5	5.00	66	.321	.354	2	.667	1	-3	-3	0	0.1
	StL-A	4	1	.800	25	1	0	0	5	32^1	26	1	5	13	8.6	2.78	134	.224	.256	0	.000	-1	3	3	0	0.6
	Yr	4	1	.800	34	1	0	0	6	50^1	51	4	9	22	10.7	3.58	100	.263	.296	2	.286	1	-0	0	0	0.7
1947	Was-A	1	7	.125	31	0	0	0	9	60	57	1	20	23	11.6	3.15	118	.256	.317	1	.100	-1	4	4	2	0.7
1948	Was-A	2	5	.286	37	0	0	0	10	73^2	75	3	38	34	13.8	4.15	105	.261	.348	1	.067	-1	1	2	1	0.2
1949	StL-A	6	4	.600	50	0	0	0	6	104^1	102	9	41	34	12.4	3.88	117	.258	.329	3	.143	-1	4	7	2	0.8
1950	StL-A	1	3	.250	16	0	0	0	2	24	24	2	7	6	11.6	4.13	120	.267	.320	1	.250	-0	1	2	1	0.4
	*NY-A	8	4	.667	30	0	0	0	9	56^2	49	5	22	20	11.3	3.65	118	.233	.306	2	.143	0	6	4	1	1.0
	Yr	9	7	.563	46	0	0	0	11	80^2	73	7	29	26	11.4	3.79	118	.243	.310	3	.167	0	7	6	1	1.4
1951	NY-A	1	1	.500	9	0	0	0	1	12	21	4	7	3	21.0	7.50	51	.389	.459	1	1.000	1	-5	-5	-0	-0.7
	Was-A	2	0	1.000	22	0	0	0	2	41^2	36	3	7	17	9.3	2.38	172	.234	.267	2	.286	0	8	8	0	0.5
	Yr	3	1	.750	31	0	0	0	3	53^2	57	7	14	20	11.9	3.52	115	.274	.320	3	.375	1	4	3	0	-0.2
1952	Was-A	4	3	.571	27	0	0	0	1	50^2	53	2	11	28	11.4	3.02	118	.273	.312	1	.200	1	4	3	1	0.6
Total	9	40	40	.500	323	7	4	1	56	674	654	44	227	245	11.8	3.47	117	.256	.317	27	.184	1	42	44	11	6.5

● BOB FERRIS
Ferris, Robert Eugene b: 5/7/55, Arlington, Va. BR/TR, 6'6", 225 lbs. Deb: 9/12/79

YEAR	TM/L	W	L	PCT	G	GS	CG	SH	SV	IP	H	HR	BB	SO	RAT	ERA	ERA+	OAV	OOB	BH	AVG	PB	PR	/A	PD	TPI
1979	Cal-A	0	0	—	2	0	0	0	0	6	5	1	3	2	12.0	1.50	271	.217	.308	0	—	0	2	2	0	0.3
1980	Cal-A	0	2	.000	5	3	0	0	0	15^1	23	2	9	4	18.8	5.87	67	.354	.432	0	—	0	-3	-3	0	-0.4
Total	2	0	2	.000	7	3	0	0	0	21^1	28	3	12	6	16.9	4.64	86	.318	.400	0	—	0	-1	-2	0	-0.1

● DAVE FERRISS
Ferriss, David Meadow "Boo" b: 12/5/21, Shaw, Miss. BL/TR, 6'2", 208 lbs. Deb: 4/29/45 C

YEAR	TM/L	W	L	PCT	G	GS	CG	SH	SV	IP	H	HR	BB	SO	RAT	ERA	ERA+	OAV	OOB	BH	AVG	PB	PR	/A	PD	TPI
1945	Bos-A†	21	10	.677	35	31	26	5	2	264^2	263	6	85	94	12.1	2.96	115	.264	.327	32	.267	11	12	13	5	3.3
1946	*Bos-A☆	25	6	**.806**	40	35	26	6	3	274	274	14	71	106	11.4	3.25	113	.259	.308	24	.209	2	8	13	0	1.7
1947	Bos-A	12	11	.522	33	28	14	1	0	218^1	241	14	92	64	14.0	4.04	96	.287	.362	27	.273	7	-8	-4	-1	0.3
1948	Bos-A	7	3	.700	31	9	1	0	3	115^1	127	7	61	30	15.2	5.23	84	.286	.381	9	.243	2	-12	-11	1	-0.7
1949	Bos-A	0	0	—	4	0	0	0	0	6^2	7	1	4	1	16.2	4.05	108	.292	.414	1	1.000	1	0	0	-0	0.0
1950	Bos-A	0	0	—	1	0	0	0	0	1	2	0	1	1	27.0	18.00	27	.500	.600	0	—	0	-1	-1	0	0.0
Total	6	65	30	.684	144	103	67	12	8	880	914	42	314	296	12.8	3.64	103	.272	.338	93	.250	23	-2	10	5	4.6

● CY FERRY
Ferry, Alfred Joseph b: 9/27/1878, Hudson, N.Y. d: 9/27/38, Pittsfield, Mass. BR/TR, 6'1", 170 lbs. Deb: 5/12/04 F

YEAR	TM/L	W	L	PCT	G	GS	CG	SH	SV	IP	H	HR	BB	SO	RAT	ERA	ERA+	OAV	OOB	BH	AVG	PB	PR	/A	PD	TPI
1904	Det-A	0	1	.000	3	1	1	0	0	13	12	0	11	4	16.6	6.23	41	.245	.393	2	.333	1	-5	-5	0	-0.3
1905	Cle-A	0	0	—	1	1	0	0	0	2	3	1	0	2	22.5	13.50	19	.333	.455	0	.000	-0	-2	-2	0	0.0
Total	2	0	1	.000	4	2	1	0	0	15	15	1	11	6	17.4	7.20	36	.259	.403	2	.286	1	-8	-8	0	-0.3

● JACK FERRY
Ferry, John Francis b: 4/7/1887, Pittsfield, Mass. d: 8/29/54, Pittsfield, Mass. BR/TR, 5'11", 175 lbs. Deb: 9/4/10 F

YEAR	TM/L	W	L	PCT	G	GS	CG	SH	SV	IP	H	HR	BB	SO	RAT	ERA	ERA+	OAV	OOB	BH	AVG	PB	PR	/A	PD	TPI
1910	Pit-N	1	2	.333	6	3	2	0	0	31	26	0	8	12	10.2	2.32	133	.230	.287	3	.333	1	2	3	0	0.4
1911	Pit-N	6	4	.600	26	8	4	1	3	85^2	83	3	27	32	11.8	3.15	109	.260	.322	9	.310	3	2	3	-2	0.4
1912	Pit-N	2	0	1.000	11	3	1	1	1	39	33	1	23	10	13.2	3.00	109	.234	.345	1	.077	-1	2	1	1	0.0
1913	Pit-N	1	0	1.000	4	0	0	0	0	5	4	0	2	2	10.8	5.40	56	.286	.375	0	—	0	-1	-1	0	-0.2
Total	4	10	6	.625	47	14	7	2	4	160^2	146	4	60	56	11.8	3.02	110	.249	.323	13	.255	3	5	5	-1	0.6

● ALEX FERSON
Ferson, Alexander "Colonel" b: 7/14/1866, Philadelphia, Pa. d: 12/5/57, Boston, Mass. BR/TR, 5'9", 165 lbs. Deb: 5/4/1889

YEAR	TM/L	W	L	PCT	G	GS	CG	SH	SV	IP	H	HR	BB	SO	RAT	ERA	ERA+	OAV	OOB	BH	AVG	PB	PR	/A	PD	TPI
1889	Was-N	17	17	.500	36	33	28	1	0	288^1	319	9	105	85	13.6	3.90	101	.272	.338	13	.114	-5	4	1	-2	-0.5
1890	Buf-P	1	7	.125	10	10	7	0	0	71	88	5	40	13	16.4	5.45	75	.291	.376	7	.219	1	-10	-11	0	-0.7
1892	Bal-N	0	1	.000	2	1	1	0	0	9	17	1	6	8	23.0	11.00	31	.386	.460	0	.000	-1	-8	-8	-0	-0.7
Total	3	18	25	.419	48	44	36	1	0	368^1	424	15	151	106	14.4	4.37	91	.279	.349	20	.133	-5	-14	-17	-3	-1.9

● LOU FETTE
Fette, Louis Henry William b: 3/15/07, Alma, Mo. d: 1/3/81, Warrensburg, Mo. BR/TR, 6'1.5", 200 lbs. Deb: 4/26/37

YEAR	TM/L	W	L	PCT	G	GS	CG	SH	SV	IP	H	HR	BB	SO	RAT	ERA	ERA+	OAV	OOB	BH	AVG	PB	PR	/A	PD	TPI
1937	Bos-N	20	10	.667	35	33	23	**5**	0	259	243	5	81	70	11.4	2.88	124	.251	.311	22	.239	3	30	20	0	2.5
1938	Bos-N	11	13	.458	33	32	17	3	1	239^2	235	11	79	83	11.9	3.15	109	.258	.320	16	.188	0	17	7	2	0.9
1939	Bos-N★	10	10	.500	27	26	11	**6**	0	146	123	7	61	35	11.4	2.96	125	.229	.309	3	.061	-4	16	12	3	1.3
1940	Bos-N	0	5	.000	7	5	0	0	0	32^1	38	0	18	2	15.9	5.57	67	.302	.393	3	.375	1	-6	-7	-1	-0.8
	Bro-N	0	0	—	2	0	0	0	0	3	3	0	2	0	15.0	0.00	—	.300	.417	0	—	0	1	1	-0	0.0
	Yr	0	5	.000	9	5	0	0	0	35^1	41	0	20	2	15.5	5.09	73	.299	.389	3	.375	1	-5	-5	-1	-0.8
1945	Bos-N	0	2	.000	5	1	0	0	0	11	16	1	7	4	19.6	5.73	67	.356	.453	0	.000	-0	-2	-2	0	-0.4
Total	5	41	40	.506	109	97	51	14	1	691	658	24	248	194	11.9	3.15	113	.253	.321	44	.186	-0	55	32	4	3.5

● MIKE FETTERS
Fetters, Michael Lee b: 12/19/64, Van Nuys, Cal. BR/TR, 6'4", 212 lbs. Deb: 9/1/89

YEAR	TM/L	W	L	PCT	G	GS	CG	SH	SV	IP	H	HR	BB	SO	RAT	ERA	ERA+	OAV	OOB	BH	AVG	PB	PR	/A	PD	TPI
1989	Cal-A	0	0	—	1	0	0	0	0	3^1	5	1	1	4	16.2	8.10	47	.333	.375	0	—	0	-2	-2	0	0.2
1990	Cal-A	1	1	.500	26	2	0	0	1	67^2	77	9	20	35	13.2	4.12	93	.287	.341	0	—	0	-2	-2	1	0.2
1991	Cal-A	2	5	.286	19	4	0	0	0	44^2	53	4	28	24	16.9	4.84	85	.305	.410	0	—	0	-4	-4	-1	-0.6
1992	Mil-A	5	1	.833	50	0	0	0	2	62^2	38	3	24	43	9.9	1.87	205	.185	.292	0	—	0	14	14	1	1.4
1993	Mil-A	3	3	.500	45	0	0	0	0	59^1	59	4	22	23	12.6	3.34	127	.278	.352	0	—	0	6	6	0	0.6
1994	Mil-A	1	4	.200	42	0	0	0	17	46	41	0	27	31	13.5	2.54	198	.243	.350	0	—	0	12	13	-0	1.8
1995	Mil-A	0	3	.000	40	0	0	0	22	34^2	40	3	20	33	15.6	3.38	148	.286	.375	0	—	0	5	6	-1	0.8
1996	Mil-A	3	3	.500	61	0	0	0	32	61^1	65	4	26	53	13.5	3.38	154	.274	.348	0	—	0	11	12	-0	2.1
1997	Mil-A	1	5	.167	51	0	0	0	6	70^1	62	4	33	62	12.3	3.45	134	.244	.333	0	—	0	9	9	1	0.8
1998	Oak-A	1	6	.143	48	0	0	0	5	47^1	48	3	21	34	13.3	3.99	114	.258	.337	0	—	0	3	3	1	0.7
	Ana-A	1	2	.333	12	0	0	0	0	11^1	14	2	4	9	14.3	5.56	84	.304	.360	0	—	0	-1	-1	1	-0.3
	Yr	2	8	.200	60	0	0	0	5	58^2	62	5	25	43	13.3	4.30	107	.264	.335	0	—	0	2	2	1	0.4
Total	10	18	33	.353	395	6	0	0	85	508^2	502	37	226	351	13.2	3.49	127	.263	.347	0	—	0	53	54	2	7.7

● JOHN FICK
Fick, John Ralph b: 5/18/21, Baltimore, Md. d: 6/9/58, Somers Point, N.J. BL/TL, 5'10", 150 lbs. Deb: 7/29/44

YEAR	TM/L	W	L	PCT	G	GS	CG	SH	SV	IP	H	HR	BB	SO	RAT	ERA	ERA+	OAV	OOB	BH	AVG	PB	PR	/A	PD	TPI
1944	Phi-N	0	0	—	4	0	0	0	0	5^1	3	0	3	2	11.8	3.38	107	.150	.292	0	—	0	0	0	-0	0.0

● MARK FIDRYCH
Fidrych, Mark Steven "The Bird" b: 8/14/54, Worcester, Mass. BR/TR, 6'3", 175 lbs. Deb: 4/20/76

YEAR	TM/L	W	L	PCT	G	GS	CG	SH	SV	IP	H	HR	BB	SO	RAT	ERA	ERA+	OAV	OOB	BH	AVG	PB	PR	/A	PD	TPI
1976	Det-A★	19	9	.679	31	29	**24**	4	0	250^1	217	12	53	97	9.8	**2.34**	**159**	.235	.279	0	—	0	33	**38**	5	**5.0**
1977	Det-A†	6	4	.600	11	11	7	1	0	81	82	2	12	42	10.6	2.89	148	.269	.299	0	—	0	11	13	-1	1.0
1978	Det-A	2	0	1.000	3	3	2	0	0	22	17	1	5	10	9.0	2.45	157	.213	.259	0	—	0	3	3	1	0.3
1979	Det-A	0	3	.000	4	4	0	0	0	14^2	23	3	9	5	20.3	10.43	41	.371	.458	0	—	0	-10	-10	-0	-1.6
1980	Det-A	2	3	.400	9	9	1	0	0	44^1	58	5	20	16	16.0	5.68	72	.309	.378	0	—	0	-8	-8	1	-0.7
Total	5	29	19	.604	58	56	34	5	0	412^1	397	23	99	170	11.0	3.10	126	.255	.302	0	—	0	28	37	5	4.0

● CLARENCE FIEBER
Fieber, Clarence Thomas "Lefty" b: 9/4/13, San Francisco, Cal d: 8/20/85, Redwood City, Cal BL/TL, 6'4", 187 lbs. Deb: 5/18/32

YEAR	TM/L	W	L	PCT	G	GS	CG	SH	SV	IP	H	HR	BB	SO	RAT	ERA	ERA+	OAV	OOB	BH	AVG	PB	PR	/A	PD	TPI
1932	Chi-A	1	0	1.000	3	0	0	0	0	5^1	6	0	3	1	15.2	1.69	256	.273	.360	0	—	0	2	2	0	0.3

● JIM FIELD
Field, James C. b: 4/24/1863, Philadelphia, Pa. d: 5/13/53, Atlantic City, N.J 6'1", 170 lbs. Deb: 6/2/1883 ◆

YEAR	TM/L	W	L	PCT	G	GS	CG	SH	SV	IP	H	HR	BB	SO	RAT	ERA	ERA+	OAV	OOB	BH	AVG	PB	PR	/A	PD	TPI
1890	Roc-a	1	0	1.000	2	1	1	0	1	9^2	7	0	4	2	11.2	2.79	128	.194	.293	38	.202	1	1	1	-0	0.1

● JOCKO FIELDS
Fields, John Joseph b: 10/20/1864, Cork, Ireland d: 10/14/50, Jersey City, N.J. BR/TR, 5'10", 160 lbs. Deb: 5/31/1887 ◆

YEAR	TM/L	W	L	PCT	G	GS	CG	SH	SV	IP	H	HR	BB	SO	RAT	ERA	ERA+	OAV	OOB	BH	AVG	PB	PR	/A	PD	TPI
1887	Pit-N	0	0	—	1	0	0	0	0	1	0	0	2	0	18.0	0.00	—	.000	.286	44	.268	0	0	0	-0	0.0

● LOU FIENE
Fiene, Louis Henry "Big Finn" b: 12/29/1884, Ft.Dodge, Iowa d: 12/22/64, Chicago, Ill. BR/TR, 6', 175 lbs. Deb: 5/7/06

YEAR	TM/L	W	L	PCT	G	GS	CG	SH	SV	IP	H	HR	BB	SO	RAT	ERA	ERA+	OAV	OOB	BH	AVG	PB	PR	/A	PD	TPI
1906	Chi-A	1	1	.500	6	2	1	0	0	31	35	0	9	12	13.9	2.90	87	.287	.356	2	.200	0	-1	-1	0	-0.1
1907	Chi-A	0	1	.000	6	1	1	0	1	26	30	0	7	15	13.5	4.15	58	.291	.348	2	.182	-0	-5	-5	0	-0.3
1908	Chi-A	0	1	.000	1	1	1	0	0	9	9	0	1	3	10.0	4.00	58	.257	.278	0	.000	-0	-2	-2	0	-0.2
1909	Chi-A	2	5	.286	13	6	4	0	0	72	75	1	18	24	12.3	4.13	57	.284	.341	2	.069	-2	-13	-14	1	-1.4
Total	4	3	8	.273	26	10	7	0	1	138	149	1	35	54	12.7	3.85	62	.284	.342	6	.113	-2	-20	-22	2	-2.0

● DANNY FIFE Fife, Danny Wayne b: 10/5/49, Harrisburg, Ill. BR/TR, 6'3", 175 lbs. Deb: 8/18/73

YEAR TM/L	W	L	PCT	G	GS	CG	SH	SV	IP	H	HR	BB	SO	RAT	ERA	ERA+	OAV	OOB	BH	AVG	PB	PR	/A	PD	TPI
1973 Min-A	3	2	.600	10	7	1	0	0	51^2	54	2	29	18	15.0	4.35	91	.270	.371	0	—	0	-3	-2	-0	-0.2
1974 Min-A	0	0	—	4	0	0	0	0	4^2	10	0	4	3	28.9	17.36	21	.417	.517	0	—	0	-7	-7	-0	0.0
Total 2	3	2	.600	14	7	1	0	0	56^1	64	2	33	21	16.1	5.43	72	.286	.387	0	—	0	-10	-9	-0	-0.2

● JACK FIFIELD Fifield, John Proctor b: 10/5/1871, Enfield, N.H. d: 11/27/39, Syracuse, N.Y. BR/TR, 5'11", 160 lbs. Deb: 4/28/1897

YEAR TM/L	W	L	PCT	G	GS	CG	SH	SV	IP	H	HR	BB	SO	RAT	ERA	ERA+	OAV	OOB	BH	AVG	PB	PR	/A	PD	TPI
1897 Phi-N	5	18	.217	27	26	21	0	0	210^2	263	8	80	38	15.0	5.51	76	.303	.368	18	.234	3	-28	-31	1	-2.2
1898 Phi-N	11	9	.550	21	21	18	2	0	171^1	170	2	60	31	13.0	3.31	104	.257	.336	7	.109	-4	6	2	-3	-0.4
1899 Phi-N	3	8	.273	14	11	9	1	1	92^2	110	0	36	8	14.6	4.08	90	.294	.362	9	.257	1	-2	-4	1	-0.3
Was-N	2	4	.333	6	6	6	0	0	47	73	1	17	12	17.6	6.13	64	.353	.407	4	.200	-0	-12	-12	-1	-1.2
Yr	5	12	.294	20	17	15	1	1	139^2	183	1	53	20	15.3	4.77	79	.313	.372	13	.236	1	-14	-16	-0	-1.5
Total 3	21	39	.350	68	64	54	3	1	521^2	616	11	193	89	14.5	4.59	83	.292	.360	38	.194	-0	-36	-44	-2	-4.1

● FRANK FIGGEMEIER Figgemeier, Frank Y. b: 4/22/1874, St.Louis, Mo. d: 4/15/15, St.Louis, Mo. Deb: 9/25/1894

YEAR TM/L	W	L	PCT	G	GS	CG	SH	SV	IP	H	HR	BB	SO	RAT	ERA	ERA+	OAV	OOB	BH	AVG	PB	PR	/A	PD	TPI
1894 Phi-N	0	1	.000	1	1	1	0	0	8	12	1	4	2	21.4	11.25	45	.343	.452	1	.333	0	-5	-5	0	-0.4

● ED FIGUEROA Figueroa, Eduardo (Padilla) b: 10/14/48, Ciales, P.R. BR/TR, 6'1", 190 lbs. Deb: 4/9/74

YEAR TM/L	W	L	PCT	G	GS	CG	SH	SV	IP	H	HR	BB	SO	RAT	ERA	ERA+	OAV	OOB	BH	AVG	PB	PR	/A	PD	TPI
1974 Cal-A	2	8	.200	25	12	5	1	0	105^1	119	3	36	49	13.6	3.67	94	.294	.357	0	—	0	-1	-3	0	-0.2
1975 Cal-A	16	13	.552	33	32	16	2	0	244^2	213	14	84	139	11.1	2.91	122	.233	.301	0	—	0	24	17	1	2.1
1976 *NY-A	19	10	.655	34	34	14	4	0	256^2	237	13	94	119	11.7	3.02	113	.246	.315	0	—	0	14	11	-3	0.9
1977 *NY-A	16	11	.593	32	32	12	2	0	239^1	228	19	75	104	11.5	3.57	110	.252	.312	0	—	0	13	10	-2	0.9
1978 *NY-A	20	9	.690	35	35	12	2	0	253	233	22	77	92	11.1	2.99	121	.248	.307	0	—	0	22	18	-0	2.0
1979 NY-A	4	6	.400	16	16	4	1	0	104^2	109	6	35	42	12.4	4.13	99	.275	.333	0	—	0	1	-1	0	0.1
1980 NY-A	3	3	.500	15	9	0	0	1	58	90	3	24	16	17.8	6.98	56	.363	.421	0	—	0	-19	-20	0	-1.7
Tex-A	0	7	.000	8	8	0	0	0	39^2	62	9	12	9	16.8	5.90	66	.365	.407	0	—	0	-8	-9	1	-1.2
Yr	3	10	.231	23	17	0	0	1	97^2	152	12	36	25	17.3	6.54	60	.360	.410	0	—	0	-27	-29	1	-2.9
1981 Oak-A	0	0	—	2	1	0	0	0	8^1	8	1	6	1	15.1	5.40	64	.258	.378	0	—	0	-2	-2	-0	0.0
Total 8	80	67	.544	200	179	63	12	1	1309^2	1299	90	443	571	12.1	3.51	104	.261	.324	0	—	0	44	23	-4	2.9

● TOM FILER Filer, Thomas Carson b: 12/1/56, Philadelphia, Pa. BR/TR, 6'1", 198 lbs. Deb: 6/8/82

YEAR TM/L	W	L	PCT	G	GS	CG	SH	SV	IP	H	HR	BB	SO	RAT	ERA	ERA+	OAV	OOB	BH	AVG	PB	PR	/A	PD	TPI
1982 Chi-N	1	2	.333	8	8	0	0	0	40^2	50	5	18	15	15.0	5.53	67	.301	.370	1	.083	-0	-9	-8	2	-0.4
1985 Tor-A	7	0	1.000	11	9	0	0	0	48^2	38	6	18	24	10.4	3.88	108	.222	.296	0	—	0	1	2	-1	0.1
1988 Mil-A	5	8	.385	19	16	2	1	0	101^2	108	8	33	39	12.6	4.43	90	.281	.339	0	—	0	-5	-5	3	-0.3
1989 Mil-A	7	3	.700	13	13	0	0	0	72^1	74	6	23	20	12.6	3.61	106	.271	.337	0	—	0	2	2	0	0.3
1990 Mil-A	2	3	.400	7	4	0	0	0	22	26	2	9	8	14.3	6.14	63	.289	.354	0	—	0	-5	-6	-1	-1.0
1992 NY-N	0	1	.000	9	1	0	0	0	22	18	2	6	9	9.8	2.05	170	.222	.276	0	.000	-0	4	3	0	0.1
Total 6	22	17	.564	67	51	2	1	0	307^1	314	29	107	115	12.5	4.25	92	.269	.333	1	.067	-1	-12	-12	5	-1.2

● EDDIE FILES Files, Charles Edward b: 5/19/1883, Portland, Me. d: 5/10/54, Cornish, Maine BR/TR, Deb: 10/3/08

YEAR TM/L	W	L	PCT	G	GS	CG	SH	SV	IP	H	HR	BB	SO	RAT	ERA	ERA+	OAV	OOB	BH	AVG	PB	PR	/A	PD	TPI
1908 Phi-A	0	0	—	2	0	0	0	0	9	8	0	3	6	13.0	6.00	43	.286	.394	0	.000	-0	-4	-3	-0	-0.1

● MARC FILLEY Filley, Marcus Lucius b: 2/28/12, Lansingburgh, N.Y. d: 1/20/95, Yarmouth, Maine BR/TR, 5'11", 172 lbs. Deb: 4/19/34

YEAR TM/L	W	L	PCT	G	GS	CG	SH	SV	IP	H	HR	BB	SO	RAT	ERA	ERA+	OAV	OOB	BH	AVG	PB	PR	/A	PD	TPI
1934 Was-A	0	0	—	1	0	0	0	0	0^1	2	0	0	0	54.0	27.00	16	.667	.667	0	—	0	-1	-1	0	0.0

● DANA FILLINGIM Fillingim, Dana b: 11/6/1893, Columbus, Ga. d: 2/3/61, Tuskegee, Ala. BL/TR, 5'10", 175 lbs. Deb: 8/2/15

YEAR TM/L	W	L	PCT	G	GS	CG	SH	SV	IP	H	HR	BB	SO	RAT	ERA	ERA+	OAV	OOB	BH	AVG	PB	PR	/A	PD	TPI
1915 Phi-A	0	5	.000	8	4	1	0	0	39^1	42	0	32	17	17.2	3.43	85	.313	.449	2	.167	-0	-2	-2	-0	-0.3
1918 Bos-N	7	6	.538	14	13	10	4	0	113	99	0	28	29	10.5	2.23	120	.243	.300	9	.214	0	7	6	-0	0.7
1919 Bos-N	6	13	.316	32	18	9	0	2	186^1	185	2	39	50	10.9	3.38	85	.270	.312	16	.246	1	-10	-11	2	-0.7
1920 Bos-N	12	21	.364	37	31	22	2	0	272	292	8	79	66	12.4	3.11	98	.287	.340	16	.174	-2	1	-2	5	0.2
1921 Bos-N	15	10	.600	44	23	11	**3**	1	239^2	249	10	56	54	11.5	3.45	106	.272	.316	21	.247	5	9	5	-1	0.8
1922 Bos-N	5	9	.357	25	12	5	1	2	117	143	6	37	25	13.9	4.54	88	.311	.363	6	.158	-2	-6	-7	-1	-0.9
1923 Bos-N	1	9	.100	35	12	1	0	0	100^1	141	6	36	27	16.0	5.20	77	.345	.399	7	.226	1	-13	-14	-0	-1.1
1925 Phi-N	1	0	1.000	5	1	0	0	0	8^2	19	0	6	2	26.0	10.38	46	.432	.500	0	.000	0	-6	-5	0	-0.5
Total 8	47	73	.392	200	114	59	10	5	1076^1	1170	32	313	270	12.5	3.56	93	.287	.340	77	.209	4	-21	-30	5	-1.8

● PETE FILSON Filson, William Peter b: 9/28/58, Darby, Pa. BB/TL, 6'2", 195 lbs. Deb: 5/15/82

YEAR TM/L	W	L	PCT	G	GS	CG	SH	SV	IP	H	HR	BB	SO	RAT	ERA	ERA+	OAV	OOB	BH	AVG	PB	PR	/A	PD	TPI
1982 Min-A	0	2	.000	5	3	0	0	0	12^1	17	2	8	10	18.2	8.76	48	.321	.410	0	—	0	-6	-6	-0	-0.9
1983 Min-A	4	1	.800	26	8	0	0	1	90	87	9	29	49	11.7	3.40	125	.252	.312	0	—	0	7	8	-2	0.3
1984 Min-A	6	5	.545	55	7	0	0	1	118^2	106	14	54	59	12.4	4.10	103	.238	.325	0	—	0	-1	1	-1	-0.1
1985 Min-A	4	5	.444	40	6	1	0	2	95^2	93	13	30	42	11.6	3.67	120	.251	.307	0	—	0	5	8	-1	0.6
1986 Min-A	0	0	—	4	0	0	0	0	6^1	13	1	2	4	22.7	5.68	76	.406	.457	0	—	0	-1	-1	-0	0.0
Chi-A	0	1	.000	3	1	0	0	0	11^2	14	4	5	4	14.7	6.17	70	.286	.352	0	—	0	-3	-2	-0	-0.2
Yr	0	1	.000	7	1	0	0	0	18^1	27	5	7	8	17.0	6.00	72	.329	.382	0	—	0	-4	-3	-1	-0.2
1987 NY-A	1	0	1.000	7	2	0	0	0	22	26	2	9	10	14.7	3.27	134	.299	.371	0	—	0	3	3	1	0.2
1990 KC-A	0	4	.000	8	7	0	0	0	35	42	6	13	9	14.7	5.91	65	.282	.348	0	—	0	-8	-8	-1	-0.7
Total 7	15	18	.455	148	34	1	0	4	391^2	398	51	150	187	12.8	4.18	102	.260	.329	0	—	0	-5	3	-4	-0.8

● JOEL FINCH Finch, Joel D b: 8/20/56, South Bend, Ind. BR/TR, 6'2", 175 lbs. Deb: 6/12/79

YEAR TM/L	W	L	PCT	G	GS	CG	SH	SV	IP	H	HR	BB	SO	RAT	ERA	ERA+	OAV	OOB	BH	AVG	PB	PR	/A	PD	TPI
1979 Bos-A	0	3	.000	15	7	0	0	0	57^1	65	5	25	25	14.3	4.87	91	.289	.363	0	.000	-0	-4	-3	1	-0.1

● BILL FINCHER Fincher, William Allen b: 5/26/1894, Atlanta, Ga. d: 5/7/46, Shreveport, La. BR/TR, 6'1", 180 lbs. Deb: 4/23/16

YEAR TM/L	W	L	PCT	G	GS	CG	SH	SV	IP	H	HR	BB	SO	RAT	ERA	ERA+	OAV	OOB	BH	AVG	PB	PR	/A	PD	TPI
1916 StL-A	0	1	.000	12	1	0	0	0	21	22	0	7	5	12.4	2.14	128	.282	.341	1	.250	0	2	1	1	0.2

● TOMMY FINE Fine, Thomas Morgan b: 10/10/14, Cleburne, Tex. BB/TR, 6', 180 lbs. Deb: 4/26/47

YEAR TM/L	W	L	PCT	G	GS	CG	SH	SV	IP	H	HR	BB	SO	RAT	ERA	ERA+	OAV	OOB	BH	AVG	PB	PR	/A	PD	TPI
1947 Bos-A	1	2	.333	9	7	1	0	0	36	41	0	19	10	15.3	5.50	71	.285	.372	3	.333	1	-7	-6	2	-0.2
1950 StL-A	0	1	.000	14	0	0	0	0	36^2	53	6	25	6	19.1	8.10	61	.342	.433	4	.333	1	-14	-13	-0	-0.2
Total 2	1	3	.250	23	7	1	0	0	72^2	94	6	44	16	17.2	6.81	65	.314	.404	7	.333	2	-22	-19	1	-0.4

● ROLLIE FINGERS Fingers, Roland Glen b: 8/25/46, Steubenville, Ohio BR/TR, 6'4", 195 lbs. Deb: 9/15/68 H

YEAR TM/L	W	L	PCT	G	GS	CG	SH	SV	IP	H	HR	BB	SO	RAT	ERA	ERA+	OAV	OOB	BH	AVG	PB	PR	/A	PD	TPI
1968 Oak-A	0	0	—	1	0	0	0	0	1^1	4	1	1	0	40.5	27.00	10	.571	.667	0	—	0	-4	-4	-0	0.0
1969 Oak-A	6	7	.462	60	8	1	1	12	119	116	13	41	61	12.2	3.71	93	.257	.325	5	.200	0	-1	-4	2	-0.2
1970 Oak-A	7	9	.438	45	19	1	0	2	148	137	13	48	79	11.4	3.65	97	.250	.312	4	.103	-0	1	-2	1	-0.2
1971 *Oak-A	4	6	.400	48	8	2	1	17	129^1	94	14	30	98	9.2	2.99	111	.207	.268	7	.212	1	7	5	2	0.8
1972 *Oak-A	11	9	.550	65	0	0	0	21	111^1	85	8	32	113	9.5	2.51	113	.212	.272	6	.316	3	7	4	-0	1.2
1973 *Oak-A★	7	8	.467	62	2	0	0	22	126^2	107	5	39	110	10.7	1.92	185	.226	.290	0	.000	-0	27	23	-1	3.4
1974 *Oak-A★	9	5	.643	**76**	0	0	0	18	119	104	5	29	95	10.1	2.65	125	.240	.289	0	—	0	13	9	2	1.6
1975 *Oak-A☆	10	6	.625	**75**	0	0	0	24	126^2	95	13	33	115	9.5	2.98	122	.213	.276	0	.000	-0	11	9	0	1.4
1976 Oak-A☆	13	11	.542	70	0	0	0	20	134^2	118	3	40	113	11.0	2.47	136	.243	.310	0	—	0	16	13	2	3.0
1977 SD-N	8	9	.471	**78**	0	0	0	**35**	132^1	123	12	36	113	10.9	2.99	118	.248	.300	1	.050	-2	13	8	-0	1.2
1978 SD-N★	6	13	.316	67	0	0	0	**37**	107^1	84	4	29	72	9.6	2.52	132	.212	.267	2	.167	-0	13	10	0	2.4
1979 SD-N	9	9	.500	54	0	0	0	13	83^2	91	7	37	65	13.9	4.52	78	.281	.356	1	.083	-1	-7	-9	-1	-2.2
1980 SD-N	11	9	.550	66	0	0	0	23	103	101	3	32	69	11.6	2.80	123	.263	.320	5	.278	2	9	7	-1	1.9
1981 *Mil-A★	6	3	.667	47	0	0	0	**28**	78	55	3	13	61	8.0	1.04	330	.198	.236	0	—	0	**23**	**21**	0	**4.2**
1982 Mil-A★	5	6	.455	50	0	0	0	29	79^2	63	5	20	71	9.5	2.60	146	.220	.273	0	—	0	13	11	0	2.3
1984 Mil-A	1	2	.333	33	0	0	0	23	46	38	5	13	40	10.0	1.96	197	.213	.267	0	—	0	10	10	-0	1.7
1985 Mil-A	1	6	.143	47	0	0	0	17	55^1	59	9	19	24	12.7	5.04	83	.272	.331	0	—	0	-6	-5	1	-0.8
Total 17	114	118	.491	944	37	4	2	341	1701^1	1474	123	492	1299	10.6	2.90	119	.235	.295	31	.172	2	145	105	6	21.7

● HERMAN FINK Fink, Herman Adam b: 8/22/11, Concord, N.C. d: 8/24/80, Salisbury, N.C. BR/TR, 6'2", 198 lbs. Deb: 9/16/35

YEAR TM/L	W	L	PCT	G	GS	CG	SH	SV	IP	H	HR	BB	SO	RAT	ERA	ERA+	OAV	OOB	BH	AVG	PB	PR	/A	PD	TPI
1935 Phi-A	0	3	.000	5	3	0	0	0	15^2	18	0	10	2	16.7	9.19	49	.290	.397	1	.200	-0	-8	-8	0	-1.2
1936 Phi-A	8	16	.333	34	24	9	0	3	188^2	222	18	78	53	14.3	5.39	95	.294	.360	8	.125	-4	-7	-6	-2	-1.1

YEAR	TM/L					GS	CG	SH	SV	IP	H	HR	BB	SO	RAT	ERA	ERA+	OAV	OOB	BH	AVG	PB	PR	/A	PD	TPI
1937	Phi-A	2	[illegible]	[illegible]	[illegible]	3	1	0	1	80	82	6	35	18	13.3	4.05	116	.263	.339	5	.208	-1	5	6	-0	0.1
Total	3	10	20	[illegible]	[illegible]	[illegible]	10	0	4	284^1	322	24	123	73	14.1	5.22	95	.285	.356	14	.151	-5	-11	-8	-2	-2.2
● PEMBROKE FINLA[illegible]	[illegible]n, Pembroke b: 7/31/1888, Cheraw, S.C. d: 3/6/12, Brooklyn, N.Y. BR/TR, Deb: 6/6/08																									
1908	Bro-N	0	0	—	[illegible]	[illegible]	[illegible]	[illegible]	[illegible]	0^1	0	0	4	0	108.0	135.00	2	.000	.800	0	—	0	-5	-5	0	0.0
1909	Bro-N	0	0	—	[illegible]	[illegible]	[illegible]	[illegible]	[illegible]	7	7	0	4	2	14.1	5.14	50	.212	.297	0	.000	-0	-2	-2	-0	-0.1
Total	2	0	0	—	2	[illegible]	[illegible]	[illegible]	[illegible]	7^1	7	0	8	2	18.4	11.05	23	.206	.357	0	.000	-0	-7	-7	-0	-0.1
● CHUCK FINLEY	Finley, Charles E[illegible] Monroe, La. BL/TL, 6'6", 214 lbs. Deb: 5/29/86																									
1986	*Cal-A	3	1	.750	25	0	0	[illegible]	[illegible]	[illegible]	40	2	23	37	12.4	3.30	124	.235	.330	0	—	0	4	4	1	0.4
1987	Cal-A	2	7	.222	35	3	0	[illegible]	[illegible]	[illegible]	102	7	43	63	14.7	4.67	92	.287	.369	0	—	0	-2	-4	-0	-0.3
1988	Cal-A	9	15	.375	31	31	2	0	[illegible]	[illegible]	191	15	82	111	12.9	4.17	93	.263	.343	0	—	0	-4	-7	-1	-0.8
1989	Cal-A☆	16	9	.640	29	29	9	1	[illegible]	[illegible]	[illegible]	13	82	156	11.5	2.57	148	.233	.312	0	—	0	29	28	-3	3.0
1990	Cal-A★	18	9	.667	32	32	7	2	0	[illegible]	[illegible]	17	81	177	11.2	2.40	159	.243	.309	0	—	0	39	37	-2	4.1
1991	Cal-A	18	9	.667	34	34	4	2	0	[illegible]	[illegible]	[illegible]	101	171	12.4	3.80	108	.244	.331	0	—	0	7	8	-3	0.6
1992	Cal-A	7	12	.368	31	31	4	1	0	204^1	[illegible]	[illegible]	98	124	13.8	3.96	100	.277	.362	0	—	0	-1	0	-3	-0.3
1993	Cal-A	16	14	.533	35	35	**13**	2	0	251^1	[illegible]	[illegible]	[illegible]	187	11.9	3.15	143	.253	.316	0	—	0	33	38	-2	3.7
1994	Cal-A	10	10	.500	25	25	7	2	0	**183^1**	178	[illegible]	[illegible]	148	12.4	4.32	113	.260	.332	0	—	0	10	12	-2	0.8
1995	Cal-A☆	15	12	.556	32	32	2	1	0	203	192	[illegible]	[illegible]	[illegible]	12.9	4.21	111	.249	.335	0	—	0	11	11	-2	1.1
1996	*Cal-A★	15	16	.484	35	35	4	1	0	238	241	27	[illegible]	[illegible]	13.1	4.16	120	.263	.339	0	—	0	22	22	-1	2.4
1997	Ana-A	13	6	.684	25	25	3	1	0	164	152	20	[illegible]	[illegible]	[illegible]	4.23	108	.248	.325	0	.000	-1	6	6	-1	0.5
1998	Ana-A	11	9	.550	34	34	1	1	0	223^1	210	20	109	[illegible]	[illegible]	3.39	139	.246	.336	0	.000	-0	31	32	-0	2.5
Total	13	153	129	.543	403	346	56	14	0	2461^2	2347	231	1024	[illegible]	[illegible]	3.66	119	.254	.332	0	.000	-1	187	187	-19	17.7
● HAPPY FINNERAN	Finneran, Joseph Ignatius "Smokey Joe" b: 10/29/1891, E.Orange, N.J. [illegible] Orange, N.J. BR/TR, 5'10.5", 169 lbs. Deb: 8/20/12																									
1912	Phi-N	0	2	.000	14	4	0	0	1	46^1	50	2	10	10	11.8	[illegible]	144	.282	.324	2	.200	0	5	6	-0	0.3
1913	Phi-N	0	0	—	3	0	0	0	0	5	12	0	2	0	25.2	7.[illegible]	[illegible]	.462	.500	2	.667	1	-2	-2	-0	0.1
1914	Bro-F	12	11	.522	27	23	13	2	1	175^1	153	6	60	54	11.2	3.18	[illegible]	.237	.308	7	.127	-5	-6	-6	-1	-1.3
1915	Bro-F	10	12	.455	37	24	12	1	2	215^1	197	2	87	68	12.2	2.80	[illegible]	.249	.331	11	.149	-5	-2	-2	-1	-0.7
1918	Det-A	0	2	.000	5	2	0	0	1	13^2	22	0	8	2	19.8	9.88	27	[illegible]	.469	0	.000	-0	-11	-11	1	-1.5
	NY-A	3	6	.333	23	13	4	0	0	114^1	134	7	35	34	13.5	3.78	75	[illegible]	.359	9	.231	1	-13	-12	-1	-0.9
	Yr	3	8	.273	28	15	4	0	1	128	156	7	43	36	14.1	4.43	63	.315	[illegible]72	9	.214	0	-23	-23	-0	-2.4
Total	5	25	33	.431	109	66	29	3	5	570	568	17	202	168	12.4	3.30	87	.266	[illegible]	31	.168	-7	-29	-28	-2	-4.0
● GAR FINNVOLD	Finnvold, Anders Gar b: 3/11/68, Boynton Beach, Fla. BR/TR, 6'5", 195 lbs. Deb: 5/10/94																									
1994	Bos-A	0	4	.000	8	8	0	0	0	36^1	45	4	15	17	15.6	5.94	85	.304	.380	0	[illegible]	0	-5	-4	-1	-0.7
● STEVE FIREOVID	Fireovid, Stephen John b: 6/6/57, Bryan, Ohio BB/TR, 6'2", 195 lbs. Deb: 9/6/81																									
1981	SD-N	0	1	.000	5	4	0	0	0	26^1	30	2	7	11	12.6	2.73	119	.294	.339	1	.143	-0	2	2	0	0.0
1983	SD-N	0	0	—	3	0	0	0	0	5	4	0	2	1	10.8	1.80	194	.235	.316	0	—	0	1	1	0	0.0
1984	Phi-N	0	0	—	6	0	0	0	0	5^2	4	0	0	3	6.4	1.59	229	.200	.200	0	—	0	1	1	0	0.0
1985	Chi-A	0	0	—	4	0	0	0	0	7	17	0	2	2	24.4	5.14	84	.472	.500	0	—	0	-1	-1	-0	-0.1
1986	Sea-A	2	0	1.000	10	1	0	0	0	21	28	1	4	10	14.1	4.29	99	.333	.371	0	—	0	-0	-0	-0	0.0
1992	Tex-A	1	0	1.000	3	0	0	0	0	6^2	10	0	4	0	18.9	4.05	94	.370	.452	0	—	0	-0	-0	0	0.3
Total	6	3	1	.750	31	5	0	0	0	71^2	93	3	19	27	14.2	3.39	110	.325	.369	1	.143	-0	3	3	0	0.2
● TED FIRTH	Firth, John E. b: 5/6/1855, Lowell, Mass. d: 6/23/02, Tewksbury, Mass. Deb: 8/15/1884																									
1884	Ric-a	0	1	.000	1	1	1	0	0	9	14	0	5	0	19.0	8.00	41	.326	.396	1	.333	0	-5	-5	-0	-0.4
● CARL FISCHER	Fischer, Charles William b: 11/5/05, Medina, N.Y. d: 12/10/63, Medina, N.Y. BR/TL, 6', 180 lbs. Deb: 7/19/30																									
1930	Was-A	1	1	.500	8	4	1	0	1	33^1	37	0	18	21	15.4	4.86	95	.285	.380	0	.000	-1	-1	-1	1	-0.1
1931	Was-A	13	9	.591	46	23	7	0	3	191	207	12	80	96	13.6	4.38	98	.273	.344	8	.121	-5	-0	-2	-4	-1.0
1932	Was-A	3	2	.600	12	7	1	1	1	50^2	57	4	31	23	15.6	4.97	87	.282	.378	3	.200	1	-3	-4	-2	-0.4
	StL-A	3	7	.300	24	11	4	0	0	97	122	12	45	35	15.5	5.57	87	.310	.380	9	.265	0	-12	-8	-1	-0.7
	Yr	6	9	.400	36	18	5	1	1	147^2	179	16	76	58	15.5	5.36	87	.300	.379	12	.245	1	-15	-11	-3	-1.1
1933	Det-A	11	15	.423	35	22	9	0	3	182^2	176	5	84	93	13.0	3.55	122	.251	.334	9	.145	-3	15	15	-2	1.5
1934	Det-A	6	4	.600	20	15	4	1	1	95	107	5	38	39	13.8	4.36	101	.288	.356	2	.065	-3	1	0	-2	-0.4
1935	Det-A	0	1	.000	3	1	0	0	0	12	16	2	5	7	16.5	6.00	69	.320	.393	0	.000	-0	-2	-2	-0	-0.2
	Chi-A	5	5	.500	24	11	3	1	0	88^2	102	7	39	31	14.5	6.19	75	.283	.356	4	.190	-0	-17	-15	-1	-1.6
	Yr	5	6	.455	27	12	3	1	0	100^2	118	9	44	38	14.7	6.17	74	.286	.358	4	.174	-1	-19	-18	-1	-1.8
1937	Cle-A	0	1	.000	2	0	0	0	0	0^2	2	0	1	1	40.5	27.00	17	.667	.750	0	—	0	-2	-2	0	-1.4
	Was-A	4	5	.444	17	11	2	0	2	72	74	6	31	30	13.1	4.38	101	.270	.344	3	.136	-1	2	0	-2	-0.2
	Yr	4	6	.400	19	11	2	0	2	72^2	76	6	32	31	13.4	4.58	97	.274	.350	3	.136	-1	0	-1	-2	-1.6
Total	7	46	50	.479	191	105	31	3	11	823	900	53	372	376	14.0	4.63	96	.277	.354	38	.145	-12	-18	-18	-14	-4.5
● HANK FISCHER	Fischer, Henry William "Bulldog" b: 1/11/40, Yonkers, N.Y. BR/TR, 6', 190 lbs. Deb: 4/16/62																									
1962	Mil-N	2	3	.400	29	0	0	0	4	37^1	43	4	20	29	15.2	5.30	72	.291	.375	0	.000	-0	-6	-6	-0	-0.9
1963	Mil-N	4	3	.571	31	6	1	0	0	74^1	74	8	28	72	13.0	4.96	65	.262	.340	2	.105	-0	-14	-14	-1	-1.4
1964	Mil-N	11	10	.524	37	28	9	5	2	168^1	177	17	39	99	11.7	4.01	88	.265	.309	8	.154	1	-9	-9	-1	-1.1
1965	Mil-N	8	9	.471	31	19	2	0	0	122^2	126	18	39	79	12.3	3.89	91	.270	.331	4	.108	-1	-5	-5	-2	-1.0
1966	Atl-N	2	3	.400	14	8	0	0	0	48^1	55	3	14	22	13.0	3.91	93	.296	.348	0	.000	-2	-2	-1	-1	-0.4
	Cin-N	0	6	.000	11	9	0	0	0	38	53	3	15	24	16.8	6.63	59	.331	.399	1	.091	-1	-13	-12	-0	-1.7
	Yr	2	9	.182	25	17	0	0	0	86^1	108	6	29	46	14.6	5.11	73	.309	.366	1	.042	-2	-14	-13	-2	-2.1
	Bos-A	2	3	.400	6	5	1	0	0	31	35	4	11	26	13.6	2.90	131	.287	.351	2	.222	0	2	3	0	0.6
1967	Bos-A	1	2	.333	9	2	1	0	1	26^2	24	3	8	18	11.1	2.36	148	.229	.289	1	.143	-0	3	3	-0	0.4
Total	6	30	39	.435	168	77	14	5	7	546^2	587	60	174	369	12.8	4.23	84	.275	.334	18	.118	-3	-43	-41	-5	-5.5
● JEFF FISCHER	Fischer, Jeffrey Thomas b: 8/17/63, W.Palm Beach, Fla. BR/TR, 6'3", 185 lbs. Deb: 6/19/87																									
1987	Mon-N	0	1	.000	4	2	0	0	0	13^2	21	3	5	6	17.1	8.56	49	.362	.413	1	.200	0	-7	-7	-0	-0.4
1989	LA-N	0	0	—	2	0	0	0	0	3^1	7	1	0	2	18.9	13.50	25	.438	.438	0	—	0	-4	-4	-0	0.0
Total	2	0	1	.000	6	2	0	0	0	17	28	4	5	8	17.5	9.53	42	.378	.418	1	.200	0	-11	-10	-0	-0.4
● RUBE FISCHER	Fischer, Reuben Walter b: 9/19/16, Carlock, S.D. BR/TR, 6'4", 190 lbs. Deb: 9/12/41																									
1941	NY-N	1	0	1.000	2	1	1	0	0	11	10	0	6	9	13.1	2.45	151	.238	.333	1	.333	0	1	2	-0	0.1
1943	NY-N	5	10	.333	22	17	4	0	1	130^2	140	4	59	47	13.8	4.61	75	.281	.360	11	.256	3	-18	-17	-2	-1.7
1944	NY-N	6	14	.300	38	18	2	1	2	128^2	128	7	87	39	15.5	5.18	71	.266	.384	5	.125	-2	-22	-22	-2	-3.4
1945	NY-N	3	8	.273	31	4	0	0	1	76^2	90	6	49	27	16.4	5.63	69	.288	.387	4	.211	2	-16	-15	-1	-1.8
1946	NY-N	1	2	.333	15	1	0	0	0	35^2	48	3	21	14	17.4	6.31	55	.316	.399	1	.111	-1	-11	-11	0	-0.9
Total	5	16	34	.320	108	41	7	1	4	382^2	416	20	222	136	15.2	5.10	71	.280	.377	22	.193	2	-66	-63	-5	-7.7
● TODD FISCHER	Fischer, Todd Richard b: 9/15/60, Columbus, Ohio BR/TR, 5'10", 170 lbs. Deb: 5/29/86																									
1986	Cal-A	0	0	—	9	0	0	0	0	17	18	4	8	7	13.8	4.24	97	.286	.366	0	—	0	-0	-0	-0	0.0
● BILL FISCHER	Fischer, William Charles b: 10/11/30, Wausau, Wis. BR/TR, 6', 190 lbs. Deb: 4/21/56 C																									
1956	Chi-A	0	0	—	3	0	0	0	0	1^2	6	0	1	2	37.8	21.60	19	.545	.583	0	—	0	-3	-3	0	0.0
1957	Chi-A	7	8	.467	33	11	3	1	1	124	139	1	35	48	12.8	3.48	107	.291	.344	6	.150	-2	4	3	-1	0.1
1958	Chi-A	2	3	.400	17	3	0	0	0	36^1	43	6	13	16	13.9	6.69	54	.301	.359	1	.143	-0	-12	-12	1	-1.4
	Det-A	2	4	.333	22	0	0	0	2	30^2	46	6	13	16	17.3	7.63	53	.362	.421	0	.000	0	-13	-12	0	-2.2
	Was-A	0	3	.000	3	3	0	0	0	21	24	1	5	10	12.9	3.86	99	.320	.370	1	.200	0	-0	-0	0	0.1
	Yr	4	10	.286	42	6	0	0	2	88	113	13	31	42	14.8	6.34	60	.325	.382	2	.154	0	-25	-25	2	-3.5
1959	Was-A	9	11	.450	34	29	6	1	0	187^1	211	16	43	62	12.4	4.28	92	.281	.324	7	.130	-2	-9	-8	4	-0.5
1960	Was-A	3	5	.375	20	7	1	0	0	77	85	7	17	31	11.9	4.91	79	.281	.320	3	.158	1	-9	-9	1	-0.6

YEAR	TM/L	W	L	PCT	G	GS	CG	SH	SV	IP	H	HR	BB	SO	RAT	ERA	ERA+	OAV				PB	PR	/A	PD	TPI
	Det-A	5	3	.625	20	6	1	0	0	55	50	6	18	24	11.1	3.44	115	[illegible]	[illegible]	[illegible]	.364	2	3	3	0	0.7
	Yr	8	8	.500	40	13	2	0	0	132	135	13	35	55	11.6	4.30	91	[illegible]	[illegible]	[illegible]	.233	3	-6	-6	2	0.1
1961	Det-A	3	2	.600	26	1	0	0	3	46^2	54	10	17	18	13.7	5.01	82	[illegible]	[illegible]	0	.000	-1	-5	-5	-0	-0.6
	KC-A	1	0	1.000	15	0	0	0	2	21	26	2	6	12	13.7	3.86	[illegible]	[illegible]	[illegible]	0	.000	-0	0	1	0	0.0
	Yr	4	2	.667	41	1	0	0	5	67^2	80	12	23	30	13.7	4.66	[illegible]	[illegible]	[illegible]	0	.000	-1	-5	-4	-0	-0.6
1962	KC-A	4	12	.250	34	16	5	0	2	127^2	150	16	8	38	11.2	[illegible]	[illegible]	[illegible]	.305	4	.105	-2	0	4	-1	0.2
1963	KC-A	9	6	.600	45	2	0	0	3	95^2	86	13	29	34	11.1	[illegible]	[illegible]	[illegible]	.305	1	.067	-0	1	3	-1	0.4
1964	Min-A	0	1	.000	9	0	0	0	0	7^1	16	2	5	2	25.8	[illegible]	[illegible]	.471	.538	0	—	0	-3	-3	0	-0.4
Total	9	45	58	.437	281	78	16	2	13	831^1	936	86	210	313	12.5	[illegible]	[illegible]	.287	.333	27	.136	-4	-46	-37	5	-4.2
● LEO FISHEL	Fishel, Leo b: 12/13/1877, Babylon, N.Y. d: 5/19/60, Hempstead, N.Y. BR/[illegible] Deb: 5/3/1899																									
1899	NY-N	0	1	.000	1	1	1	0	0	9	9	0	6	6	[illegible]	[illegible]	63	.257	.395	1	.250	-0	-2	-2	0	-0.2
● FISHER	Fisher b: Johnstown, Pa. Deb: 7/17/1884																									
1884	Phi-U	1	7	.125	8	8	8	0	0	70^2	76	0	13	[illegible]	[illegible]	3.57	65	.257	.288	8	.222	-1	-9	-10	-1	-1.0
● FISHER	Fisher b: Philadelphia, Pa. Deb: 8/6/1885																									
1885	Buf-N	0	1	.000	1	1	1	0	0	9	10	[illegible]	[illegible]	4	12.0	5.00	60	.256	.293	0	.000	-1	-2	-2	0	-0.2
● BRIAN FISHER	Fisher, Brian Kevin b: 3/18/62, Honolulu, Hawaii [illegible], 210 lbs. Deb: 5/7/85																									
1985	NY-A	4	4	.500	55	0	0	0	14	98^1	[illegible]	[illegible]	29	85	9.7	2.38	168	.216	.275	0	—	0	19	18	0	1.8
1986	NY-A	9	5	.643	62	0	0	0	6	96^2	[illegible]	[illegible]	37	67	13.3	4.93	83	.277	.343	0	—	0	-8	-9	-1	-1.4
1987	Pit-N	11	9	.550	37	26	6	3	0	185[illegible]	[illegible]	27	72	117	12.7	4.52	91	.262	.334	11	.190	5	-9	-8	-1	-0.6
1988	Pit-N	8	10	.444	33	22	1	1	1	[illegible]	[illegible]7	13	57	66	13.5	4.61	74	.277	.348	2	.048	-2	-19	-20	-2	-2.7
1989	Pit-N	0	3	.000	9	3	0	0	1	[illegible]	25	2	10	8	18.5	7.94	42	.329	.407	0	.000	-1	-8	-9	-0	-1.5
1990	Hou-N	0	0	—	4	0	0	0	[illegible]	[illegible]	9	1	0	1	16.2	7.20	52	.409	.409	0	—	0	-2	-2	-0	0.0
1992	Sea-A	4	3	.571	22	14	0	0	[illegible]	91^1	80	9	47	26	12.6	4.53	88	.234	.328	0	—	0	-6	-6	-0	-0.5
Total	7	36	34	.514	222	65	7	[illegible]	[illegible]	640	638	70	252	370	12.7	4.39	89	.261	.332	13	.124	2	-33	-36	-5	-4.9
● CHAUNCEY FISHER	Fisher, Cha[illegible]urr "Peach" or "Whoa Bill" b: 1/8/18[illegible]2, [illegible]derson, Ind. d: 4/27/39, Los Angeles, Cal. BR/TR, 5'11", 175 lbs. Deb: 9/20/1893 F																									
1893	Cle-N	0	2	.000	2	[illegible]	[illegible]	0	0	18	26	0	9	9	17.5	5.50	89	.329	.398	2	.250	-0	-2	-1	0	-0.1
1894	Cle-N	0	2	.000	3	[illegible]	0	0	0	11	22	0	5	0	22.9	11.45	48	.407	.467	0	.000	-1	-7	-7	1	-0.8
	Cin-N	2	8	.200	[illegible]	11	10	0	0	91	134	4	44	14	17.6	7.32	76	.338	.405	10	.233	-1	-20	-18	-1	-1.5
	Yr	2	10	.167	14	13	10	0	0	102	156	4	49	14	18.1	7.76	71	.346	.410	10	.213	-2	-28	-25	-1	-2.3
1896	Cin-N	10	7	.5[illegible]	27	15	13	2	2	159^2	199	9	36	25	13.5	4.45	104	.303	.344	14	.246	0	-2	3	-0	0.2
1897	Bro-N	9	7	[illegible]63	20	13	11	1	1	149	184	5	43	31	13.8	4.23	97	.301	.349	12	.203	-1	1	-2	-2	-0.4
1901	NY-N	0	0	—	1	1	0	0	0	4	11	0	2	1	29.3	15.75	21	.500	.542	0	.000	-0	-6	-6	-0	-0.1
	StL-N	*0*	*0*	—	1	0	0	0	0	3	7	0	1	0	24.0	15.00	21	.438	.471	0	.000	-0	-4	-4	0	0.0
	Yr	*0*	0	—	2	1	0	0	0	7	18	0	3	1	27.0	15.43	21	.474	.512	0	.000	-0	-9	-9	0	-0.1
Total	5	21	26	.447	65	44	36	3	3	435^2	583	18	140	80	15.1	5.37	86	.318	.368	38	.218	-3	-39	-35	-2	-2.7
● CLARENCE FISHER	Fisher, Clarence Henry b: 8/27/1898, Letart, W.Va. d: 11/2/65, Point Pleasant, W.Va. BR/TR, 6', 174 lbs. Deb: 9/14/19																									
1919	Was-A	0	0	—	2	0	0	0	0	4	8	0	3	1	24.8	13.50	24	.421	.500	0	—	0	-5	-5	0	0.0
1920	Was-A	0	1	.000	2	0	0	0	0	3^2	5	0	5	0	24.5	9.82	38	.714	.833	0	.000	-0	-2	-2	1	-0.5
Total	2	0	1	.000	4	0	0	0	0	7^2	13	0	8	1	24.7	11.74	29	.500	.618	0	.000	-0	-7	-7	1	-0.5
● DON FISHER	Fisher, Donald Raymond b: 2/6/16, Cleveland, Ohio d: 7/29/73, Mayfield Heights, Ohio BR/TR, 6', 210 lbs. Deb: 8/25/45																									
1945	NY-N	1	0	*1.000*	2	1	1	1	0	18	12	0	7	4	10.5	2.00	196	.190	.292	1	.143	-0	4	4	-0	0.2
● EDDIE FISHER	Fisher, Eddie Gene b: 7/16/36, Shreveport, La. BR/TR, 6'2.5", 200 lbs. Deb: 6/22/59																									
1959	SF-N	2	6	.250	17	5	0	0	1	40	57	8	8	15	14.8	7.87	48	.339	.373	0	.000	-1	-17	-18	-1	-3.1
1960	SF-N	1	0	1.000	3	1	1	0	0	12^2	11	2	2	7	9.2	3.55	98	.244	.277	3	.600	1	0	-0	0	0.1
1961	SF-N	0	2	.000	15	1	0	0	1	33^2	36	7	9	16	12.0	5.35	71	.267	.313	1	.143	0	-5	-6	-0	-0.3
1962	Chi-A	9	5	.643	57	12	2	1	5	182^2	169	17	45	88	10.6	3.10	126	.245	.293	6	.130	-0	18	16	0	1.2
1963	Chi-A	9	8	.529	33	15	2	1	0	120^2	114	14	28	67	10.7	3.95	89	.244	.290	5	.139	-1	-4	-6	1	-0.8
1964	Chi-A	6	3	.667	59	2	0	0	9	125	86	13	32	74	8.7	3.02	114	.192	.250	3	.167	-0	8	6	0	0.5
1965	Chi-A★	15	7	.682	**82**	0	0	0	24	165^1	118	13	43	90	**8.9**	2.40	133	.205	.262	4	.138	0	20	15	1	2.5
1966	Chi-A	1	3	.250	23	0	0	0	6	35^1	27	1	17	18	11.5	2.29	138	.214	.313	0	.000	-0	4	3	0	0.5
	Bal-A	5	3	.625	44	0	0	0	13	71^2	60	4	19	39	10.2	2.64	126	.226	.282	2	.154	0	6	6	-0	0.8
	Yr	6	6	.500	**67**	0	0	0	19	107	87	5	36	57	10.5	2.52	130	.221	.289	2	.133	-0	11	9	-0	1.3
1967	Bal-A	4	3	.571	46	0	0	0	1	89^2	82	7	26	53	11.2	3.61	87	.245	.307	1	.200	0	-4	-5	-1	-0.4
1968	Cle-A	4	2	.667	54	0	0	0	4	94^2	87	8	17	42	10.1	2.85	104	.248	.286	0	.000	-1	1	1	1	0.1
1969	Cal-A	3	2	.600	52	1	0	0	2	96^2	100	9	28	47	12.0	3.63	96	.272	.326	0	.000	-1	-0	-2	0	-0.2
1970	Cal-A	4	4	.500	67	2	0	0	8	130^1	117	15	35	74	10.6	3.04	119	.239	.292	1	.091	-1	10	8	1	0.7
1971	Cal-A	10	8	.556	57	3	0	0	3	119	92	11	50	82	10.9	2.72	119	.211	.295	1	.063	-1	10	7	-0	0.9
1972	Cal-A	4	5	.444	43	1	0	0	4	81^1	73	6	31	32	11.5	3.76	77	.247	.319	2	.118	-1	-6	-8	-0	-1.1
	Chi-A	0	1	.000	6	4	0	0	0	22^1	31	1	9	10	16.1	4.43	70	.348	.408	0	.000	-1	-3	-3	0	-0.2
	Yr	4	6	.400	49	5	0	0	4	103^2	104	7	40	42	12.5	3.91	76	.267	.336	2	.083	-1	-10	-11	-0	-1.3
1973	Chi-A	6	7	.462	26	16	2	0	0	110^2	135	12	38	57	14.3	4.88	81	.301	.360	0	—	0	-13	-11	0	-1.2
	StL-N	2	1	.667	6	0	0	0	0	7	3	1	1	1	6.4	1.29	283	.125	.192	1	1.000	0	2	2	-0	0.8
Total	15	85	70	.548	690	63	7	2	81	1538^2	1398	149	438	812	10.9	3.41	101	.243	.299	30	.122	-5	26	5	3	0.8
● ED FISHER	Fisher, Edward Fredrick b: 10/31/1876, Wayne, Mich. d: 7/24/51, Spokane, Wash. BR/TR, 6'2", 200 lbs. Deb: 9/5/02																									
1902	Det-A	0	0	—	1	0	0	0	0	4	4	0	1	0	11.3	0.00	—	.267	.313	0	.000	-0	2	2	-0	-0.1
● FRITZ FISHER	Fisher, Frederick Brown b: 11/28/41, Adrian, Mich. BL/TL, 6'1", 180 lbs. Deb: 4/19/64																									
1964	Det-A	0	0	—	1	0	0	0	0	0^1	2	0	2	1	108.0	108.00	3	.667	.800	0	—	0	-4	-4	0	0.0
● HARRY FISHER	Fisher, Harry Devereux b: 1/3/26, Newbury, Ont., Can. d: 9/20/81, Waterloo, Ont., Canada BL/TR, 6', 180 lbs. Deb: 9/16/51 ♦																									
1952	Pit-N	1	2	.333	8	3	0	0	0	18^1	17	4	13	5	15.7	6.87	58	.266	.405	5	.333	1	-6	-6	-1	-0.8
● JACK FISHER	Fisher, John Howard "Fat Jack" b: 3/4/39, Frostburg, Md. BR/TR, 6'2", 215 lbs. Deb: 4/14/59																									
1959	Bal-A	1	6	.143	27	7	1	1	2	88^2	76	7	38	52	11.7	3.05	124	.230	.311	3	.130	-1	8	7	-1	0.4
1960	Bal-A	12	11	.522	40	20	8	3	2	197^2	174	13	78	99	11.6	3.41	111	.241	.317	11	.183	2	10	9	0	1.2
1961	Bal-A	10	13	.435	36	25	10	1	1	196	205	17	75	118	13.0	3.90	99	.270	.339	5	.089	-2	3	-1	-3	-0.6
1962	Bal-A	7	9	.438	32	25	4	0	1	152	173	23	56	81	13.7	5.09	73	.284	.346	5	.102	-1	-19	-24	-1	-2.3
1963	SF-N	6	10	.375	36	12	2	0	1	116	132	12	38	57	13.6	4.58	70	.284	.344	3	.103	1	-17	-18	-0	-2.3
1964	NY-N	10	17	.370	40	34	8	1	0	227^2	256	23	56	115	12.7	4.23	85	.283	.331	12	.158	1	-18	-16	-1	-1.8
1965	NY-N	8	24	.250	43	36	10	0	1	253^2	252	22	68	116	11.5	3.94	90	.259	.310	12	.154	0	-11	-12	2	-1.2
1966	NY-N	11	14	.440	38	33	10	2	0	230	229	26	54	127	11.4	3.68	99	.260	.309	6	.090	-2	-2	-1	3	0.0
1967	NY-N	9	18	.333	39	30	7	1	0	220^1	251	21	64	117	13.0	4.70	72	.287	.339	7	.100	-2	-32	-32	1	-3.7
1968	Chi-A	8	13	.381	35	28	2	0	0	180^2	176	14	48	80	11.5	2.99	101	.257	.312	6	.113	-1	-0	1	-0	-0.1
1969	Cin-N	4	4	.500	34	15	0	0	1	113	137	15	30	55	13.7	5.50	68	.295	.345	4	.121	-1	-24	-22	-2	-1.8
Total	11	86	139	.382	400	265	62	9	9	1975^2	2061	193	605	1017	12.4	4.06	88	.269	.326	74	.125	-6	-102	-108	-1	-12.2
● MAURICE FISHER	Fisher, Maurice Wayne b: 2/16/31, Uniondale, Ind. BR/TR, 6'5", 210 lbs. Deb: 4/16/55																									
1955	Cin-N	0	0	—	1	0	0	0	0	2^2	5	1	2	1	23.6	6.75	63	.385	.467	0	.000	-0	-1	-1	-0	0.0
● RAY FISHER	Fisher, Ray Lyle "Pick" b: 10/4/1887, Middlebury, Vt. d: 11/3/82, Ann Arbor, Mich. BR/TR, 5'11.5", 180 lbs. Deb: 7/2/10																									
1910	NY-A	5	3	.625	17	7	3	0	1	92^1	95	0	18	42	11.3	2.92	91	.274	.315	3	.103	-2	-4	-3	1	-0.3
1911	NY-A	10	11	.476	29	22	8	2	0	171^2	178	3	55	99	12.5	3.25	111	.269	.330	7	.119	-3	2	7	4	0.8
1912	NY-A	2	8	.200	17	13	5	0	0	90^1	107	2	32	47	14.0	5.88	61	.312	.374	2	.065	-4	-26	-23	3	-2.2

YEAR	TM/L	W	L	PCT	G	GS	CG	SH	SV	IP	H	HR	BB	SO	RAT	ERA	ERA+	OAV	OOB	BH	AVG	PB	PR	/A	PD	TPI
1913	NY-A	12	16	.429	43	31	14	1	1	246^1	244	3	71	92	11.8	3.18	94	.261	.319	22	.278	3	-7	-5	2	0.0
1914	NY-A	10	12	.455	29	26	17	2	1	209	177	2	61	86	10.4	2.28	121	.241	.303	9	.138	-2	11	11	4	1.3
1915	NY-A	18	11	.621	30	28	20	4	0	247^2	219	7	62	97	10.4	2.11	139	.243	.295	9	.108	-5	23	23	-0	2.1
1916	NY-A	11	8	.579	31	21	9	1	2	179	191	4	51	56	12.4	3.17	91	.285	.339	11	.177	1	-7	-5	-1	-0.6
1917	NY-A	8	9	.471	23	18	12	3	0	144	126	3	43	64	10.7	2.19	123	.243	.304	9	.180	-0	8	8	1	1.1
1919	*Cin-N	14	5	.737	26	20	12	5	1	174^1	141	5	38	41	9.3	2.17	128	.226	.271	16	.271	3	14	12	3	2.1
1920	Cin-N	10	11	.476	33	21	10	1	1	201	189	5	50	56	11.1	2.73	111	.249	.302	17	.243	1	9	7	2	1.1
Total	10	100	94	.515	278	207	110	19	7	1755^2	1667	34	481	680	11.2	2.82	106	.257	.312	105	.179	-8	23	30	19	5.4
● TOM FISHER	Fisher, Thomas Chalmers "Red" b: 11/1/1880, Anderson, Ind. d: 9/3/72, Anderson, Ind. BR/TR, 5'10.5", 185 lbs. Deb: 4/17/04 F																									
1904	Bos-N	6	16	.273	31	21	19	2	0	214	257	5	82	84	14.7	4.25	65	.302	.370	21	.212	3	-36	-35	-5	-3.4
● TOM FISHER	Fisher, Thomas Gene b: 4/4/42, Cleveland, Ohio BR/TR, 6', 180 lbs. Deb: 9/20/67																									
1967	Bal-A	0	0	—	2	0	0	0	0	3^1	2	0	2	1	10.8	0.00	—	.182	.308	0	—	0	1	1	-0	0.0
● CHEROKEE FISHER	Fisher, William Charles b: 12/1845, Philadelphia, Pa. d: 9/26/12, New York, N.Y. BR/TR, 5'9", 164 lbs. Deb: 5/6/1871 ♦																									
1871	Rok-n	4	16	.200	24	24	22	**1**	0	213	295	3	31	15	13.8	4.35	94	.281	.302	28	.228	-3	-3	-6		-0.3
1872	Bal-n	10	1	.909	19	11	9	1	1	110	93	0	11	20	**8.5**	**1.80**	**204**	**.197**	**.216**	52	.231	-1	22	23		1.5
1873	Ath-n	3	4	.429	13	5	5	0	2	84^1	90	1	10	14	**10.7**	**1.81**	**188**	**.227**	**.246**	66	.261	1	13	15		0.8
1874	Har-n	13	23	.361	39	35	31	0	0	322^1	416	1	13	25	12.0	2.32	99	.277	.284	54	.224	-4	-5	-1		-0.5
1875	Phi-n	22	19	.537	41	41	36	2	0	358	345	6	9	18	8.9	1.99	115	.229	.233	41	.232	-1	10	11		0.5
1876	Cin-N	4	20	.167	28	24	22	0	0	229^1	294	6	6	29	11.8	3.02	73	.285	.289	32	.248	-1	-18	-21	-2	-1.9
1878	Pro-N	0	1	.000	1	1	1	0	0	9	14	0	0	2	14.0	4.00	55	.304	.304	0	.000	-0	-2	-2	0	-0.2
Total	5 n	52	63	.452	136	116	103	4	3	1087^2	1239	11	74	92	10.9	2.52	115	.252	.263	241	.237	-8	38	45		2.0
Total	2	4	21	.160	29	25	23	0	0	238^1	308	6	6	31	11.9	3.06	72	.285	.289	32	.235	-2	-20	-23	-2	-2.1
● MAX FISKE	Fiske, Maximilian Patrick "Ski" b: 10/12/1888, Chicago, Ill. d: 5/15/28, Chicago, Ill. BR/TR, 5'11", 185 lbs. Deb: 4/19/14																									
1914	Chi-F	12	12	.500	38	22	7	0	0	198	161	7	59	87	10.3	3.14	85	.231	.298	16	.235	0	-6	-11	-0	-1.2
● PAUL FITTERY	Fittery, Paul Clarence b: 10/10/1887, Lebanon, Pa. d: 1/28/74, Cartersville, Ga. BR/TL, 5'8.5", 156 lbs. Deb: 9/5/14																									
1914	Cin-N	0	2	.000	8	4	2	0	0	43^2	41	0	12	21	11.1	3.09	95	.246	.300	1	.059	-1	-1	-1	0	-0.2
1917	Phi-N	1	1	.500	17	2	1	0	0	55^2	69	1	27	13	16.3	4.53	62	.317	.404	2	.091	-1	-11	-11	1	-0.3
Total	2	1	3	.250	25	6	3	0	0	99^1	110	1	39	34	14.0	3.90	73	.286	.360	3	.077	-2	-13	-11	2	-0.5
● JOHN FITZGERALD	Fitzgerald, John Francis b: 9/15/33, Brooklyn, N.Y. BL/TL, 6'3", 190 lbs. Deb: 9/28/58																									
1958	SF-N	0	0	—	1	1	0	0	0	3	1	1	1	3	6.0	3.00	127	.111	.200	0	.000	-0	0	0	0	0.0
● JOHN FITZGERALD	Fitzgerald, John H. b: 5/30/1870, Natick, Mass. d: 3/31/21, Boston, Mass. Deb: 7/18/1891																									
1891	Bos-a	1	1	.500	6	3	2	0	1	32	49	2	11	16	17.4	5.63	62	.340	.395	1	.071	-2	-7	-8	0	-0.5
● JOHN FITZGERALD	Fitzgerald, John J. Deb: 4/18/1890																									
1890	Roc-a	3	8	.273	11	11	8	1	0	78	77	0	45	35	14.8	4.04	88	.250	.357	6	.194	-0	-1	-4	1	-0.4
● WARREN FITZGERALD	Fitzgerald, Warren B. b: 4/1872, Pennsylvania d: 11/7/30, Phoenix, Ariz. TL , 5'9", 162 lbs. Deb: 6/4/1891																									
1891	Lou-a	14	18	.438	33	32	29	3	0	276	280	6	95	111	12.7	3.59	102	.254	.321	19	.170	0	4	2	-4	-0.1
1892	Lou-N	1	3	.250	4	4	4	0	0	34	45	2	11	3	15.1	4.24	72	.306	.358	2	.133	-0	-4	-4	-1	-0.5
Total	2	15	21	.417	37	36	33	3	0	310	325	8	106	114	12.9	3.66	98	.260	.325	21	.165	-0	1	-2	-4	-0.6
● PAUL FITZKE	Fitzke, Paul Frederick Herman "Bob" b: 7/30/1900, LaCrosse, Wis. d: 6/30/50, Sacramento, Cal. BR/TR, 5'11.5", 185 lbs. Deb: 9/1/24																									
1924	Cle-A	0	0	—	1	0	0	0	0	4	5	0	3	1	18.0	4.50	95	.313	.421	0	.000	-0	-0	-0	-0	0.0
● AL FITZMORRIS	Fitzmorris, Alan James b: 3/21/46, Buffalo, N.Y. BB/TR, 6'2", 190 lbs. Deb: 9/8/69																									
1969	KC-A	1	1	.500	7	0	0	0	2	10^2	9	1	4	3	11.0	4.22	87	.237	.310	0	.000	-0	-1	-1	-0	-0.2
1970	KC-A	8	5	.615	43	11	2	0	1	117^2	112	14	52	47	12.5	4.44	84	.254	.333	9	.290	4	-9	-9	1	-0.5
1971	KC-A	7	5	.583	36	15	2	1	0	127^1	112	6	55	53	11.9	4.17	82	.245	.327	11	.250	2	-10	-10	2	-0.6
1972	KC-A	2	5	.286	38	2	0	0	3	101	99	10	28	51	11.4	3.74	81	.252	.303	4	.174	1	-8	-8	2	-0.3
1973	KC-A	8	3	.727	15	13	3	1	0	89	88	5	25	26	11.4	2.83	145	.259	.310	0	—	0	10	13	2	1.1
1974	KC-A	13	6	.684	34	27	9	4	1	190	189	8	63	53	11.9	2.79	137	.260	.319	0	—	0	17	22	3	2.3
1975	KC-A	16	12	.571	35	35	11	3	0	242	239	16	76	78	11.9	3.57	108	.262	.322	0	—	0	6	7	1	0.8
1976	KC-A	15	11	.577	35	33	8	2	0	220^1	227	6	56	80	11.6	3.06	114	.273	.320	0	—	0	11	11	3	1.6
1977	Cle-A	6	10	.375	29	21	1	0	0	133	164	12	53	54	14.8	5.41	73	.306	.369	0	—	0	-20	-22	-0	-2.0
1978	Cle-A	0	1	.000	7	0	0	0	0	14^1	19	3	7	5	17.0	6.28	59	.333	.415	0	—	0	-4	-4	-0	-0.2
	Cal-A	1	0	1.000	9	2	0	0	0	31^2	26	2	14	8	11.4	1.71	212	.236	.323	0	—	0	7	7	-0	0.5
	Yr	1	1	.500	16	2	0	0	0	46	45	5	21	13	12.9	3.13	117	.268	.349	0	—	0	3	3	-0	0.3
Total	10	77	59	.566	288	159	36	11	7	1277	1284	83	433	458	12.2	3.65	101	.265	.327	24	.242	7	-1	5	12	2.5
● FREDDIE FITZSIMMONS	Fitzsimmons, Frederick Landis "Fat Freddie" b: 7/28/01, Mishawaka, Ind. d: 11/18/79, Yucca Valley, Cal. BR/TR, 5'11", 185 lbs. Deb: 8/12/25 MC																									
1925	NY-N	6	3	.667	10	8	6	1	0	74^2	70	4	18	17	10.6	2.65	152	.248	.293	9	.310	2	13	12	2	1.6
1926	NY-N	14	10	.583	37	26	12	0	0	219	224	7	58	48	11.8	2.88	130	.272	.322	11	.128	-6	23	21	3	1.8
1927	NY-N	17	10	.630	42	31	14	1	3	244^2	260	15	67	78	12.2	3.72	104	.275	.325	18	.207	-0	6	4	2	0.6
1928	NY-N	20	9	.690	40	32	16	1	1	261^1	264	13	65	67	11.5	3.68	106	.268	.316	18	.191	1	9	7	2	0.9
1929	NY-N	15	11	.577	37	31	14	4	1	221^2	242	14	66	55	12.6	4.10	112	.285	.338	15	.183	-2	15	12	4	1.4
1930	NY-N	19	7	**.731**	41	29	17	1	1	224^1	230	26	59	76	11.6	4.25	111	.266	.314	22	.265	5	18	12	7	2.2
1931	NY-N	18	11	.621	35	33	19	4	0	253^2	242	16	62	78	10.8	3.05	121	.251	.296	21	.228	9	23	18	8	**3.7**
1932	NY-N	11	11	.500	35	31	11	0	0	237^2	287	18	83	65	14.1	4.43	84	.299	.356	19	.221	4	-15	-19	7	-0.6
1933	*NY-N	16	11	.593	36	35	13	1	0	251^2	243	14	72	65	11.3	2.90	111	.251	.305	19	.200	3	12	9	6	1.8
1934	NY-N	18	14	.563	38	37	14	3	1	263^1	266	12	51	73	10.9	3.04	127	.261	.297	22	.232	5	30	24	5	3.7
1935	NY-N	4	8	.333	18	15	6	**4**	0	94	104	7	22	23	12.2	4.02	96	.281	.323	8	.258	1	-0	-2	1	0.0
1936	*NY-N	10	7	.588	28	17	7	0	2	141	147	6	39	35	11.9	3.32	117	.274	.323	7	.149	-2	11	9	1	0.8
1937	NY-N	2	2	.500	6	4	1	1	0	27^1	28	3	8	13	11.9	4.61	84	.272	.324	3	.300	2	-2	-2	-0	-0.1
	Bro-N	4	8	.333	13	13	4	0	0	90^2	91	2	32	29	12.3	4.27	95	.263	.327	5	.167	-1	-4	-2	1	-0.3
	Yr	6	10	.375	19	17	5	1	0	118	119	5	40	42	12.2	4.35	92	.265	.327	8	.200	1	-6	-5	1	-0.4
1938	Bro-N	11	8	.579	27	26	12	3	0	202^2	205	8	43	38	11.1	3.02	129	.261	.302	12	.171	-1	17	20	6	2.3
1939	Bro-N	7	9	.438	27	20	5	0	3	151^1	178	6	28	44	12.4	3.87	104	.293	.327	11	.234	3	1	3	5	1.1
1940	Bro-N	16	2	**.889**	20	18	11	4	1	134^1	120	5	25	35	9.8	2.81	142	.233	.269	5	.106	-2	15	18	1	2.2
1941	*Bro-N	6	1	.857	13	12	3	1	0	82^2	78	3	26	19	11.5	2.07	177	.245	.305	4	.143	-0	14	15	2	1.5
1942	Bro-N	0	0	—	1	1	0	0	0	3	6	1	1	0	21.0	15.00	22	.400	.438	1	.500	0	-4	-4	0	0.0
1943	Bro-N	3	4	.429	9	7	1	0	0	44^2	50	6	21	12	14.5	5.44	62	.281	.360	1	.071	-1	-10	-10	0	-1.5
Total	19	217	146	.598	513	426	186	29	13	3223^2	3335	186	846	870	11.8	3.51	111	.268	.316	231	.200	21	174	144	60	23.1
● PATSY FLAHERTY	Flaherty, Patrick Joseph b: 6/29/1876, Mansfield, Pa. d: 1/23/68, Alexandria, La. BL/TL, 5'8", 165 lbs. Deb: 9/8/1899 ♦																									
1899	Lou-N	2	3	.400	5	4	4	0	0	39	41	0	5	5	10.8	2.31	167	.270	.297	5	.208	1	7	7	-1	0.7
1900	Pit-N	0	0	—	4	1	0	0	0	22	30	0	9	5	18.0	6.14	59	.323	.411	1	.111	-1	-6	-6	1	0.0
1903	Chi-A	11	25	.306	40	34	29	2	1	293^2	338	9	50	65	12.3	3.74	75	.288	.324	14	.137	-3	-25	-30	3	-3.4
1904	Chi-A	1	2	.333	5	5	4	0	0	43	36	1	10	14	9.8	2.09	117	.228	.278	4	.333	2	2	2	1	0.5
	Pit-N	19	9	.679	29	28	28	5	0	242	210	3	59	54	10.4	2.05	134	.232	.287	22	.212	5	19	19	5	3.4
1905	Pit-N	10	10	.500	27	20	15	0	1	187^2	197	2	49	44	12.1	3.50	86	.272	.324	15	.197	2	-10	-10	2	-0.6
1907	Bos-N	12	15	.444	27	25	23	0	0	217	197	4	59	34	10.9	2.70	95	.248	.306	22	.191	2	-5	-3	2	0.1
1908	Bos-N	12	18	.400	31	31	21	0	0	244	221	6	81	50	11.4	3.25	74	.236	.303	12	.140	-0	-24	-23	2	-2.6
1910	Phi-N	0	0	—	1	0	0	0	0	0^1	1	0	1	0	54.0	0.00	—	.333	.500	1	.500	0	0	0	0	0.0

YEAR	TM/L	W	L	PCT	G	GS	CG	SH	SV	IP	H	HR	BB	SO	RAT	ERA	ERA+	OAV	OOB	BH	AVG	PB	PR	/A	PD	TPI
1911	Bos-N	0	2	.000	4	2	1	0	0	14	21	0	8	0	20.6	7.07	54	.350	.451	27	.287	1	-6	-5	-0	-0.6
Total	9	67	84	.444	173	150	125	7	2	1302^2	1292	25	331	271	11.6	3.10	89	.259	.312	123	.197	10	-49	-50	14	-2.5
● **MIKE FLANAGAN**	Flanagan, Michael Kendall b: 12/16/51, Manchester, N.H. BL/TL, 6', 195 lbs. Deb: 9/5/75																									
1975	Bal-A	0	1	.000	2	1	0	0	0	9^2	9	0	6	7	14.0	2.79	126	.250	.357	0	—	0	1	1	0	0.3
1976	Bal-A	3	5	.375	20	10	4	0	0	85	83	7	33	56	12.3	4.13	79	.260	.330	0	—	0	-6	-8	0	-0.3
1977	Bal-A	15	10	.600	36	33	15	2	1	235	235	17	70	149	11.8	3.64	104	.266	.321	0	—	0	11	4	-0	0.8
1978	Bal-A☆	19	15	.559	40	40	17	2	0	281^1	271	22	87	167	11.5	4.03	87	.257	.315	0	—	0	-8	-17	-2	-1.5
1979	*Bal-A	**23**	9	.719	39	38	16	**5**	0	265^2	245	23	70	190	10.8	3.08	130	.245	.297	0	—	0	33	27	-0	3.2
1980	Bal-A	16	13	.552	37	37	12	2	0	251^1	278	27	71	128	12.6	4.12	96	.287	.337	0	—	0	-2	-5	0	-0.5
1981	Bal-A	9	6	.600	20	20	3	2	0	116	108	11	37	72	11.4	4.19	87	.244	.305	0	—	0	-7	-7	1	-0.8
1982	Bal-A	15	11	.577	36	35	11	1	0	236	233	24	76	103	11.9	3.97	102	.259	.319	0	—	0	3	2	0	0.2
1983	*Bal-A	12	4	.750	20	20	3	1	0	125^1	135	10	31	50	12.1	3.30	120	.278	.324	0	—	0	11	9	-1	1.1
1984	Bal-A	13	13	.500	34	34	10	2	0	226^2	213	24	81	115	11.7	3.53	110	.250	.316	0	—	0	11	8	-1	0.9
1985	Bal-A	4	5	.444	15	15	1	0	0	86	101	14	28	42	13.7	5.13	79	.297	.354	0	—	0	-9	-10	-0	-0.8
1986	Bal-A	7	11	.389	29	28	2	0	0	172	179	15	66	96	12.9	4.24	98	.270	.337	0	—	0	-1	-2	-2	-0.3
1987	Bal-A	3	6	.333	16	16	4	0	0	94^2	102	9	36	50	13.1	4.94	89	.278	.342	0	—	0	-5	-6	-0	-0.3
	Tor-A	3	2	.600	7	7	0	0	0	49^1	46	3	15	43	11.1	2.37	189	.237	.292	0	—	0	11	12	-0	0.9
	Yr	6	8	.429	23	23	4	0	0	144	148	12	51	93	12.4	4.06	109	.263	.325	0	—	0	6	6	-1	0.6
1988	Tor-A	13	13	.500	34	34	2	1	0	211	220	23	80	99	13.1	4.18	94	.271	.341	0	—	0	-5	-6	1	-0.6
1989	*Tor-A	8	10	.444	30	30	1	1	0	171^2	186	10	47	47	12.5	3.93	96	.283	.335	0	—	0	-1	-3	1	-0.1
1990	Tor-A	2	2	.500	5	5	0	0	0	20^1	28	3	8	5	15.9	5.31	74	.329	.387	0	—	0	-3	-3	0	-0.6
1991	Bal-A	2	7	.222	64	1	0	0	3	98^1	84	6	25	55	10.3	2.38	166	.236	.292	0	—	0	19	17	2	2.0
1992	Bal-A	0	0	—	42	0	0	0	0	34^2	50	3	23	17	20.3	8.05	50	.338	.443	0	—	0	-16	-16	1	0.1
Total	18	167	143	.539	526	404	101	19	4	2770	2806	251	890	1491	12.1	3.90	100	.266	.325	0	—	0	36	-3	-1	3.7
● **RAY FLANIGAN**	Flanigan, Raymond Arthur b: 1/8/23, Morgantown, W.Va. d: 3/28/93, Baltimore, Md. BR/TR, 6', 190 lbs. Deb: 9/20/46																									
1946	Cle-A	0	1	.000	3	1	0	0	0	9	11	1	8	2	19.0	11.00	30	.289	.413	1	.500	1	-7	-8	0	-0.6
● **TOM FLANIGAN**	Flanigan, Thomas Anthony b: 9/6/34, Cincinnati, Ohio BR/TL, 6'3", 175 lbs. Deb: 4/14/54																									
1954	Chi-A	0	0	—	2	0	0	0	0	1^2	1	0	1	0	10.8	0.00	—	.200	.333	0	—	0	1	1	0	0.0
1958	StL-N	0	0	—	1	0	0	0	0	1	2	1	1	0	27.0	9.00	46	.500	.600	0	—	0	-1	-1	-0	0.0
Total	2	0	0	—	3	0	0	0	0	2^2	3	1	2	0	16.9	3.38	115	.333	.455	0	—	0	0	0	0	0.0
● **JACK FLATER**	Flater, John William b: 9/22/1880, Sandymount, Md. d: 3/20/70, Westminster, Md. BR/TR, 5'10", 175 lbs. Deb: 9/18/08																									
1908	Phi-A	1	3	.250	5	3	3	0	0	39^1	35	0	12	8	11.2	2.06	124	.252	.320	2	.133	-0	1	2	2	0.4
● **JOHN FLAVIN**	Flavin, John Thomas b: 5/7/42, Albany, Cal. BL/TL, 6'2", 208 lbs. Deb: 8/25/64																									
1964	Chi-N	0	1	.000	5	1	0	0	0	4^2	11	0	3	5	27.0	13.50	28	.500	.560	0	.000	-0	-5	-5	-0	-1.0
● **FRANK FLEET**	Fleet, Frank H. b: 1848, New York, N.Y. d: 6/13/1900, New York, N.Y. Deb: 10/18/1871 ◆																									
1871	Mut-n	0	1	.000	1	1	1	0	0	9	20	0	3	0	23.0	10.00	38	.370	.404	2	.333	0	-6	-6		-0.3
1873	Res-n	0	3	.000	3	3	2	0	0	24	57	0	0	1	21.4	5.63	60	.399	.399	23	.256	0	-6	-6		-0.4
1875	StL-n	2	1	.667	3	3	3	0	0	27	33	0	3	3	12.0	3.33	60	.277	.295	1	.063	-1	-3	-4		-0.4
	Atl-n	0	1	.000	2	1	1	0	0	15^1	26	0	0	0	15.3	4.70	44	.333	.333	25	.225	-0	-4	-4		-0.2
	Yr	2	2	.500	5	4	4	0	0	42^1	59	0	3	3	13.2	3.83	53	.299	.310	26	.205	-1	-8	-8		-0.6
Total	3 n	2	6	.250	9	8	7	0	0	75^1	136	0	6	4	17.0	5.14	40	.345	.355	86	.231	-1	-24	-26		-1.3
● **DAVE FLEMING**	Fleming, David Anthony b: 11/7/69, Jackson Heights, N.Y. BL/TL, 6'3", 200 lbs. Deb: 8/6/91																									
1991	Sea-A	1	0	1.000	9	3	0	0	0	17^2	19	3	3	11	12.7	6.62	62	.284	.342	0	—	0	-5	-5	1	-0.1
1992	Sea-A	17	10	.630	33	33	7	4	0	228^1	225	13	60	112	11.4	3.39	117	.257	.307	0	—	0	14	15	-0	1.6
1993	Sea-A	12	5	.706	26	26	1	1	0	167^1	189	15	67	75	14.1	4.36	101	.290	.361	0	—	0	-1	1	1	0.1
1994	Sea-A	7	11	.389	23	23	0	0	0	117	152	17	65	65	16.8	6.46	76	.311	.394	0	—	0	-22	-20	-0	-2.5
1995	Sea-A	1	5	.167	16	7	1	0	0	48	57	15	34	26	17.1	7.50	63	.294	.399	0	—	0	-15	-15	-0	-1.5
	KC-A	0	1	.000	9	5	0	0	0	32	27	4	19	14	13.5	3.66	131	.229	.345	0	—	0	4	4	0	0.1
	Yr	1	6	.143	25	12	1	0	0	80	84	19	53	40	15.6	5.96	80	.267	.376	0	—	0	-11	-11	0	-1.4
Total	5	38	32	.543	116	97	9	5	0	610^1	669	67	248	303	13.8	4.67	93	.279	.351	0	—	0	-24	-21	2	-2.3
● **BILL FLEMING**	Fleming, Leslie Fletchard b: 7/31/13, Rowland, Cal. BR/TR, 6', 190 lbs. Deb: 8/21/40																									
1940	Bos-A	1	2	.333	10	6	1	0	0	46^1	53	4	20	24	14.6	4.86	93	.290	.366	0	.000	-2	-2	-2	-1	-0.3
1941	Bos-A	1	1	.500	16	1	0	0	1	41^1	32	4	24	20	12.2	3.92	106	.212	.320	2	.222	1	1	1	1	0.2
1942	Chi-N	5	6	.455	33	14	4	2	2	134^1	117	9	63	59	12.3	3.01	106	.230	.318	2	.051	-4	4	3	-1	-0.3
1943	Chi-N	0	1	.000	11	0	0	0	0	32^1	41	2	12	12	15.6	6.40	52	.311	.381	0	.000	-1	-11	-11	1	-0.3
1944	Chi-N	9	10	.474	39	18	9	1	0	158^1	163	6	62	42	12.8	3.13	113	.269	.337	9	.170	-1	9	7	1	0.8
1946	Chi-N	0	1	.000	14	1	0	0	0	29^1	37	2	12	10	15.3	6.14	54	.301	.368	0	.000	-0	-9	-9	0	-0.3
Total	6	16	21	.432	123	40	14	3	3	442	443	27	193	167	13.2	3.79	94	.260	.339	13	.104	-7	-8	-11	1	-0.2
● **HUCK FLENER**	Flener, Gregory Alan b: 2/25/69, Austin, Tex. BB/TL, 5'11", 185 lbs. Deb: 9/14/93																									
1993	Tor-A	0	0	—	6	0	0	0	0	6^2	7	0	4	2	14.9	4.05	107	.269	.367	0	—	0	0	0	0	0.0
1996	Tor-A	3	2	.600	15	11	0	0	0	70^2	68	9	33	44	13.0	4.58	109	.251	.334	0	—	0	3	3	1	0.2
1997	Tor-A	0	1	.000	8	1	0	0	0	17^1	40	3	6	9	23.9	9.87	46	.444	.479	0	—	0	-10	-10	-1	-0.5
Total	3	3	3	.500	29	12	0	0	0	94^2	115	12	43	55	15.1	5.51	88	.297	.369	0	—	0	-7	-7	0	-0.3
● **VAN FLETCHER**	Fletcher, Alfred Vanoide b: 8/6/24, East Bend, N.C. BR/TR, 6'2", 185 lbs. Deb: 4/12/55																									
1955	Det-A	0	0	—	9	0	0	0	0	12	13	1	2	4	11.3	3.00	128	.260	.288	0	—	0	1	1	-0	0.0
● **PAUL FLETCHER**	Fletcher, Edward Paul b: 1/14/67, Gallipolis, Ohio BR/TR, 6'1", 185 lbs. Deb: 7/11/93																									
1993	Phi-N	0	0	—	1	0	0	0	0	0^1	0	0	0	0	0.0	0.00	—	.000	.000	0	—	0	0	0	0	0.0
1995	Phi-N	1	0	1.000	10	0	0	0	0	13^1	15	2	9	10	16.9	5.40	78	.288	.403	0	—	0	-2	-2	-0	-0.1
1996	Oak-A	0	0	—	1	0	0	0	0	1^1	6	0	1	0	47.3	20.25	24	.667	.700	0	—	0	-2	-2	-0	0.0
Total	3	1	0	1.000	12	0	0	0	0	15	21	2	10	10	19.2	6.60	65	.339	.438	0	—	0	-4	-4	-0	-0.1
● **SAM FLETCHER**	Fletcher, Samuel S. b: Altoona, Pa. TR , 6'2", 210 lbs. Deb: 10/6/09																									
1909	Bro-N	0	1	.000	1	1	1	0	0	9	13	0	2	5	15.0	8.00	32	.351	.385	0	.000	-0	-5	-5	-0	-0.5
1912	Cin-N	0	0	—	2	0	0	0	0	9^2	15	1	11	3	24.2	12.10	28	.366	.500	2	.500	1	-9	-9	0	0.1
Total	2	0	1	.000	3	1	1	0	0	18^2	28	1	13	8	19.8	10.13	30	.359	.451	2	.286	0	-15	-15	0	-0.4
● **TOM FLETCHER**	Fletcher, Thomas Wayne b: 6/28/42, Elmira, N.Y. BB/TL, 6', 170 lbs. Deb: 9/12/62 F																									
1962	Det-A	0	0	—	1	0	0	0	0	2	2	0	2	1	18.0	0.00	—	.250	.400	0	—	0	1	1	0	0.0
● **JOHN FLINN**	Flinn, John Richard b: 9/2/54, Merced, Cal. BR/TR, 6', 175 lbs. Deb: 5/6/78																									
1978	Bal-A	1	1	.500	13	0	0	0	0	15^2	24	3	13	8	21.3	8.04	43	.348	.451	0	—	0	-7	-8	0	-0.5
1979	Bal-A	0	0	—	4	0	0	0	0	2^2	2	0	1	0	10.1	0.00	—	.222	.300	0	—	0	1	1	0	0.1
1980	Mil-A	2	1	.667	20	1	0	0	2	37	31	3	20	15	12.4	3.89	99	.220	.317	0	—	0	1	-0	-0	0.0
1982	Bal-A	2	0	1.000	5	0	0	0	0	13^2	13	1	3	13	10.5	1.32	306	.260	.302	0	—	0	4	4	-0	0.6
Total	4	5	2	.714	42	1	0	0	2	69	70	7	37	36	14.0	4.17	92	.260	.350	0	—	0	-1	-3	-0	0.2
● **HILLY FLITCRAFT**	Flitcraft, Hildreth Milton b: 8/21/23, Woodstown, N.J. BL/TL, 6'2", 180 lbs. Deb: 8/31/42																									
1942	Phi-N	0	0	—	3	0	0	0	0	3^1	6	0	2	1	21.6	8.10	41	.429	.500	0	—	0	-2	-2	0	0.0
● **MORT FLOHR**	Flohr, Moritz Herman "Dutch" b: 8/15/11, Canisteo, N.Y. d: 6/2/94, Hornell, N.Y. BL/TL, 6', 173 lbs. Deb: 6/8/34																									
1934	Phi-A	0	2	.000	14	3	0	0	0	30^2	34	3	33	6	20.0	5.87	75	.296	.456	4	.333	1	-5	-5	1	-0.1

YEAR TM/L	W	L	PCT	G	GS	CG	SH	SV	IP	H	HR	BB	SO	RAT	ERA	ERA+	OAV	OOB	BH	AVG	PB	PR	/A	PD	TPI
● DON FLORENCE	Florence, Donald Emery b: 3/16/67, Manchester, N.H. BR/TL, 6', 195 lbs. Deb: 8/8/95																								
1995 NY-N	3	0	1.000	14	0	0	0	0	12	17	0	6	5	17.3	1.50	270	.340	.411	0	.000	-0	4	3	0	0.8
● JESSE FLORES	Flores, Jesse (Sandoval) b: 11/2/14, Guadalajara, Mexico d: 12/17/91, Orange, Cal. BR/TR, 5'10", 175 lbs. Deb: 4/16/42																								
1942 Chi-N	0	1	.000	4	0	0	0	0	5^1	5	1	2	6	11.8	3.38	95	.227	.292	0	—	0	-0	-0	0	0.0
1943 Phi-A	12	14	.462	31	27	13	0	0	231^1	208	13	70	113	11.0	3.11	109	.240	.301	14	.175	-0	5	7	1	0.9
1944 Phi-A	9	11	.450	27	25	11	2	0	185^2	172	8	49	65	10.9	3.39	103	.245	.298	11	.172	-0	1	2	-1	0.1
1945 Phi-A	7	10	.412	29	24	9	4	1	191^1	180	6	63	52	11.6	3.43	100	.250	.314	9	.148	-2	-1	-0	-3	-0.5
1946 Phi-A	9	7	.563	29	15	8	4	1	155	147	8	38	48	10.8	2.32	153	.249	.295	11	.250	3	20	21	-2	2.3
1947 Phi-A	4	13	.235	28	20	4	0	0	151^1	139	10	59	41	11.8	3.39	112	.244	.315	10	.227	1	5	7	-1	0.8
1950 Cle-A	3	3	.500	28	2	1	1	4	53	53	3	25	27	13.4	3.74	116	.261	.345	0	.000	-2	5	4	-2	0.1
Total 7	44	59	.427	176	113	46	11	6	973	904	49	306	352	11.3	3.18	112	.246	.307	55	.181	-0	35	41	-7	3.7
● BRYCE FLORIE	Florie, Bryce Bettencourt b: 5/21/70, Charleston, S.C. BR/TR, 6', 185 lbs. Deb: 7/17/94																								
1994 SD-N	0	0	—	9	0	0	0	0	9^1	8	0	3	8	10.6	0.96	426	.242	.306	0	—	0	3	3	1	0.1
1995 SD-N	2	2	.500	47	0	0	0	1	68^2	49	8	38	68	11.9	3.01	134	.202	.320	0	.000	-0	9	8	0	0.4
1996 SD-N	2	2	.500	39	0	0	0	0	49^1	45	1	27	51	14.2	4.01	99	.239	.353	0	.000	-0	1	-0	0	0.0
Mil-A	0	1	.000	15	0	0	0	0	19	20	3	13	12	15.6	6.63	78	.270	.379	0	—	0	-3	-3	-0	-0.2
1997 Mil-A	4	4	.500	32	8	0	0	0	75	74	4	42	53	14.3	4.32	107	.262	.364	0	—	0	2	2	-1	0.1
1998 Det-A	8	9	.471	42	16	0	0	0	133	141	16	59	97	13.8	4.80	98	.275	.355	1	.333	1	-2	-1	2	0.1
Total 5	16	18	.471	184	24	0	0	1	354^1	337	32	182	289	13.6	4.24	105	.253	.350	1	.125	0	10	8	1	0.5
● BEN FLOWERS	Flowers, Bennett b: 6/15/27, Wilson, N.C. BR/TR, 6'4", 195 lbs. Deb: 9/29/51																								
1951 Bos-A	0	0	—	1	0	0	0	0	3	2	0	1	2	9.0	0.00	—	.200	.273	0	.000	-0	1	1	-0	0.0
1953 Bos-A	1	4	.200	32	6	1	1	3	79^1	87	6	24	36	12.7	3.86	109	.280	.333	3	.158	-0	1	3	1	0.2
1955 Det-A	0	0	—	4	0	0	0	0	6	5	1	2	2	10.5	6.00	64	.238	.304	0	.000	-0	-1	-1	0	0.0
StL-N	1	0	1.000	4	4	0	0	0	27^1	27	1	12	19	12.8	3.62	112	.255	.331	1	.100	-1	1	1	-0	-0.1
1956 StL-N	1	1	.500	3	3	0	0	0	11^2	15	1	5	5	15.4	6.94	54	.341	.408	0	.000	-0	-4	-4	0	-0.6
Phi-N	0	2	.000	32	0	0	0	0	41	54	9	10	22	14.3	5.71	65	.331	.374	0	.000	0	-9	-9	1	-0.3
Yr	1	3	.250	35	3	0	0	0	52^2	69	10	15	27	14.5	5.98	62	.330	.378	0	.000	-0	-13	-13	1	-0.9
Total 4	3	7	.300	76	13	1	1	3	168^1	190	18	54	86	13.2	4.49	90	.290	.346	4	.111	-2	-10	-9	1	-0.8
● DICKIE FLOWERS	Flowers, Charles Richard b: 1850, Philadelphia, Pa. d: 10/5/1892, Philadelphia, Pa. Deb: 6/3/1871 ♦																								
1871 Tro-n	0	0	—	1	0	0	0	0	1	1	0	0	0	9.0	0.00	—	.333	.333	33	.314	0	0	0		0.0
● WES FLOWERS	Flowers, Charles Wesley b: 8/13/13, Vanndale, Ark. d: 12/31/88, Wynne, Ark. BL/TL, 6'1.5", 190 lbs. Deb: 8/8/40																								
1940 Bro-N	1	1	.500	5	2	0	0	0	21	23	2	10	8	15.4	3.43	117	.299	.400	1	.200	-0	1	1	0	0.1
1944 Bro-N	1	1	.500	9	1	0	0	0	17^1	26	3	13	3	20.8	7.79	46	.333	.435	3	.600	1	-8	-8	-0	-0.7
Total 2	2	2	.500	14	3	0	0	0	38^1	49	5	23	11	17.8	5.40	70	.316	.418	4	.400	1	-7	-7	-0	-0.6
● CARNEY FLYNN	Flynn, Cornelius Francis Xavier b: 1/23/1875, Cincinnati, Ohio d: 2/10/47, Cincinnati, Ohio BL/TL, 5'11", 165 lbs. Deb: 7/17/1894																								
1894 Cin-N	0	2	.000	2	1	0	0	0	7^2	16	4	10	4	31.7	17.61	32	.421	.551	0	.000	-1	-10	-10	-0	-1.4
1896 NY-N	0	2	.000	3	2	1	0	0	10^2	18	0	8	4	26.2	11.81	36	.367	.500	2	.500	2	-9	-9	0	-1.0
Was-N	0	1	.000	4	1	1	0	0	20	43	0	10	3	24.7	8.55	52	.430	.491	2	.250	-0	-9	-9	-1	-0.4
Yr	0	3	.000	7	3	2	0	0	30^2	61	0	18	7	23.8	9.68	45	.396	.466	4	.333	1	-18	-18	-1	-1.4
Total 2	0	5	.000	9	4	2	0	0	38^1	77	4	28	11	26.5	11.27	41	.412	.507	4	.267	1	-29	-29	-1	-2.8
● JOCKO FLYNN	Flynn, John A. b: 6/30/1864, Lawrence, Mass. d: 12/30/07, Lawrence, Mass. TR , 5'6.5", 143 lbs. Deb: 5/1/1886 ♦																								
1886 Chi-N	23	6	**.793**	32	29	28	2	1	257	207	9	63	146	9.5	2.24	162	.210	.257	41	.200	1	31	39	2	4.1
● STU FLYTHE	Flythe, Stuart McGuire b: 12/5/11, Conway, N.C. d: 10/18/63, Durham, N.C. BR/TR, 6'2", 175 lbs. Deb: 5/31/36																								
1936 Phi-A	0	0	—	17	3	0	0	0	39^1	49	4	61	14	25.9	13.04	39	.302	.500	4	.267	0	-35	-35	-0	0.0
● GENE FODGE	Fodge, Gene Arlan "Suds" b: 7/9/31, South Bend, Ind. BR/TR, 6', 175 lbs. Deb: 4/20/58																								
1958 Chi-N	1	1	.500	16	4	1	0	0	39^2	47	5	11	15	13.2	4.76	82	.296	.341	0	.000	-1	-4	-4	0	-0.2
● JIM FOGARTY	Fogarty, James G. b: 2/12/1864, San Francisco, Cal d: 5/20/1891, Philadelphia, Pa. BR/TR, 5'10.5", 180 lbs. Deb: 5/1/1884 FM♦																								
1884 Phi-N	0	0	—	1	0	0	0	0	1	2	0	0	1	18.0	0.00	—	.333	.333	80	.212	0	0	0	0	0.0
1886 Phi-N	0	1	.000	1	0	0	0	0	6	7	1	0	4	10.5	0.00	—	.250	.250	82	.293	0	2	2	0	0.4
1887 Phi-N	0	0	—	1	0	0	0	0	3	3	0	1	0	12.0	9.00	47	.200	.250	129	.261	0	-2	-2	-0	0.0
1889 Phi-N	0	0	—	4	0	0	0	0	4	4	0	2	0	13.5	9.00	48	.250	.333	129	.259	0	-2	-2	-0	0.0
Total 4	0	1	.000	7	0	0	0	0	14	16	1	3	5	12.2	4.50	84	.246	.279	709	.246	2	-1	-1	0	0.4
● CURRY FOLEY	Foley, Charles Joseph b: 1/14/1856, Milltown, Ireland d: 10/20/1898, Boston, Mass. TL , 5'10", 160 lbs. Deb: 5/13/1879 ♦																								
1879 Bos-N	9	9	.500	21	16	16	1	0	161^2	175	1	15	57	10.6	2.51	99	.252	.268	46	.315	5	-0	-0	-2	0.2
1880 Bos-N	14	14	.500	36	28	21	1	0	238	264	1	40	68	11.5	3.89	58	.274	.303	97	.292	8	-40	-43	1	-3.6
1881 Buf-N	3	4	.429	10	6	2	0	0	41	70	1	5	2	16.5	5.27	53	.337	.352	96	.256	1	-11	-11	-0	-1.5
1882 Buf-N	0	0	—	1	0	0	0	0	1	2	0	0	0	18.0	18.00	16	.333	.333	104	.305	0	-2	-2	-0	0.0
1883 Buf-N	1	0	1.000	1	0	0	0	0	1	0	0	4	0	36.0	0.00	—	.000	.667	30	.270	0	0	0	-0	0.3
Total 5	27	27	.500	69	50	39	2	0	442^2	511	3	64	127	11.7	3.54	68	.273	.297	373	.286	14	-53	-56	-2	-4.6
● JOHN FOLEY	Foley, John J b: Hannibal, Mo. TL , Deb: 9/18/1885																								
1885 Pro-N	0	1	.000	1	1	1	0	0	8	6	0	5	2	12.4	4.50	60	.188	.297	0	.000	0	-1	-2	0	-0.2
● TOM FOLEY	Foley, Thomas Michael b: 9/9/59, Columbus, Ga. BL/TR, 6'1", 180 lbs. Deb: 4/9/83 ♦																								
1989 Mon-N	0	0	—	1	0	0	0	0	0^1	1	1	0	0	27.0	27.00	13	.500	.500	86	.229	0	-1	-1	0	0.0
● RICH FOLKERS	Folkers, Richard Nevin b: 10/17/46, Waterloo, Iowa BL/TL, 6'2", 180 lbs. Deb: 6/10/70																								
1970 NY-N	0	2	.000	16	1	0	0	2	29^1	36	6	25	15	18.7	6.44	62	.313	.436	2	.333	0	-8	-8	1	-0.4
1972 StL-N	1	0	1.000	9	0	0	0	0	13^1	12	0	5	7	11.5	3.38	101	.240	.309	0	.000	-0	0	0	0	0.0
1973 StL-N	4	4	.500	34	9	1	0	3	82^1	74	10	34	44	12.1	3.61	101	.239	.321	2	.100	-1	0	0	-0	-0.1
1974 StL-N	6	2	.750	55	0	0	0	2	90	65	4	38	57	10.5	3.00	119	.207	.297	1	.100	-1	6	6	-1	0.3
1975 SD-N	6	11	.353	45	15	4	0	0	142	155	8	39	87	12.4	4.18	83	.278	.327	6	.167	1	-9	-11	-0	-1.1
1976 SD-N	2	3	.400	33	3	0	0	0	59^2	67	10	25	26	14.2	5.28	62	.279	.352	0	.000	-0	-12	-13	-0	-1.1
1977 Mil-A	0	1	.000	3	0	0	0	0	6^1	7	2	4	6	15.6	4.26	95	.269	.367	0	—	0	-0	-0	0	0.0
Total 7	19	23	.452	195	28	5	0	7	423	416	40	170	242	12.6	4.11	86	.258	.332	11	.143	-1	-22	-27	-1	-2.4
● LEW FONSECA	Fonseca, Lewis Albert b: 1/21/1899, Oakland, Cal. d: 11/26/89, Ely, Iowa BR/TR, 5'10.5", 180 lbs. Deb: 4/13/21 M♦																								
1932 Chi-A	0	0	—	1	0	0	0	0	1	0	0	0	0	0.0	0.00	—	.000	.000	5	.135	-0	0	0	-0	0.0
● JOE FONTENOT	Fontenot, Joseph D. b: 3/20/77, Scott, La. BR/TR, 6'2", 185 lbs. Deb: 5/23/98																								
1998 Fla-N	0	7	.000	8	8	0	0	0	42^2	56	5	20	24	17.1	6.33	65	.320	.405	0	.000	-1	-10	-11	1	-1.4
● RAY FONTENOT	Fontenot, Silton Ray b: 8/8/57, Lake Charles, La. BL/TL, 6', 175 lbs. Deb: 6/30/83																								
1983 NY-A	8	2	.800	15	15	3	1	0	97^1	101	3	25	27	11.7	3.33	117	.266	.314	0	—	0	8	6	1	0.8
1984 NY-A	8	9	.471	35	24	0	0	0	169^1	189	8	58	85	13.3	3.61	105	.290	.351	0	—	0	7	3	0	0.4
1985 Chi-N	6	10	.375	38	23	0	0	0	154^2	177	23	45	70	12.9	4.36	91	.294	.343	2	.049	-3	-13	-6	2	-0.8
1986 Chi-N	3	5	.375	42	0	0	0	2	56	57	5	21	24	12.5	3.86	105	.266	.332	1	.167	-0	-1	1	-1	0.1
Min-A	0	0	—	15	0	0	0	0	16^1	27	3	4	10	18.2	9.92	43	.360	.407	0	.000	-0	-10	-10	0	0.0
Total 4	25	26	.490	145	62	3	1	2	493^2	551	42	153	216	12.9	4.03	98	.287	.341	3	.063	-4	-10	-5	2	0.5
● JIM FOOR	Foor, James Emerson b: 1/13/49, St.Louis, Mo. BL/TL, 6'2", 170 lbs. Deb: 4/9/71																								
1971 Det-A	0	0	—	3	0	0	0	0	1	2	0	4	2	54.0	18.00	20	.400	.667	0	—	0	-2	-2	0	0.0

YEAR	TM/L	W	L	PCT	G	GS	CG	SH	SV	IP	H	HR	BB	SO	RAT	ERA	ERA+	OAV	OOB	BH	AVG	PB	PR	/A	PD	TPI
1972	Det-A	1	0	1.000	7	0	0	0	0	3^{2}	6	1	6	2	29.5	14.73	21	.353	.522	0	—	0	-5	-5	0	-1.2
1973	Pit-N	0	0	—	3	0	0	0	0	1^{1}	2	0	1	1	20.3	0.00	—	.286	.375	0	—	0	1	1	0	0.0
Total	3	1	0	1.000	13	0	0	0	0	6	10	1	11	5	31.5	12.00	28	.345	.525	0	—	0	-6	-6	0	-1.2
● DAVY FORCE	Force, David W. "Wee Davy" or "Tom Thumb" b: 7/27/1849, New York, N.Y. d: 6/21/18, Englewood, N.J. BR/TR, 5'4", 130 lbs. Deb: 5/5/1871 ♦																									
1873	Bal-n	1	1	.500	3	1	1	0	0	18	23	0	0	0	11.5	3.50	93	.264	.264	86	.368	1	-0	-0		0.0
1874	Chi-n	0	0	—	1	0	0	0	0	7	22	4	0	0	28.3	15.43	14	.431	.431	92	.313	0	-10	-10		0.0
Total	2 n	1	1	.500	4	1	1	0	0	25	45	4	0	0	16.2	6.84	32	.326	.326	437	.336	2	-13	-13		0.0
● BEN FORD	Ford, Benjamin Cooper b: 8/15/75, Cedar Rapids, Iowa BR/TR, 6'7", 200 lbs. Deb: 8/20/98																									
1998	Ari-N	0	0	—	8	0	0	0	0	10	13	2	3	5	16.2	9.90	43	.295	.367	0	—	0	-6	-6	-0	0.0
● DAVE FORD	Ford, David Alan b: 12/29/56, Cleveland, Ohio BR/TR, 6'4", 190 lbs. Deb: 9/2/78																									
1978	Bal-A	1	0	1.000	2	1	0	0	0	15	10	0	2	5	7.2	0.00	—	.196	.226	0	—	0	6	6	-0	1.1
1979	Bal-A	2	1	.667	9	2	0	0	2	30	23	2	7	7	9.0	2.10	191	.219	.268	0	—	0	7	6	0	1.0
1980	Bal-A	1	3	.250	25	3	1	0	1	69^{2}	66	11	13	22	10.5	4.26	93	.251	.291	0	—	0	-2	-2	-1	-0.2
1981	Bal-A	1	2	.333	15	2	0	0	0	40	61	2	10	12	16.0	6.52	56	.359	.394	0	—	0	-13	-13	-0	-0.9
Total	4	5	6	.455	51	8	1	0	3	154^{2}	160	15	32	46	11.3	4.02	96	.272	.311	0	—	0	-1	-3	-1	1.0
● WHITEY FORD	Ford, Edward Charles "Chairman Of The Board" b: 10/21/28, New York, N.Y. BL/TL, 5'10", 181 lbs. Deb: 7/1/50 CH																									
1950	*NY-A	9	1	.900	20	12	7	2	1	112	87	7	52	59	11.3	2.81	153	.216	.309	7	.194	0	22	18	-0	1.5
1953	*NY-A	18	6	.750	32	30	11	3	0	207	187	13	110	110	13.1	3.00	123	.245	.344	20	.267	6	23	16	0	2.3
1954	NY-A★	16	8	.667	34	28	11	3	1	210^{2}	170	10	101	125	11.6	2.82	122	.227	.319	10	.161	2	21	14	1	1.8
1955	*NY-A★	**18**	7	.720	39	33	**18**	5	2	253^{2}	188	20	113	137	10.7	2.63	143	.208	.297	14	.163	2	38	31	-0	3.1
1956	*NY-A★	19	6	**.760**	31	30	18	2	1	225^{2}	187	13	84	141	11.0	**2.47**	156	.228	.303	17	.218	3	42	35	5	4.5
1957	*NY-A	11	5	.688	24	17	5	0	0	129^{1}	114	10	53	84	11.7	2.57	139	.237	.313	6	.143	-1	17	15	2	1.8
1958	*NY-A☆	14	7	.667	30	29	15	**7**	1	219^{1}	174	14	62	145	**9.8**	**2.01**	**176**	.217	**.276**	15	.205	2	**43**	**37**	1	**3.9**
1959	NY-A★	16	10	.615	35	29	9	2	1	204	194	13	89	114	12.5	3.04	120	.250	.328	15	.231	7	19	14	4	2.8
1960	*NY-A★	12	9	.571	33	29	8	**4**	0	192^{2}	168	15	65	85	10.9	3.08	116	.235	.299	8	.151	2	17	11	1	1.4
1961	*NY-A★	**25**	4	**.862**	39	39	11	3	0	**283**	242	23	92	209	10.7	3.21	116	.229	.292	17	.177	3	26	16	0	1.8
1962	*NY-A	17	8	.680	38	37	7	0	0	257^{2}	243	22	69	160	11.0	2.90	129	.246	.298	10	.118	-1	31	24	4	2.6
1963	*NY-A	**24**	7	**.774**	38	37	13	3	1	**269^{1}**	240	26	56	189	10.0	2.74	128	.241	.283	13	.141	0	27	23	-0	2.5
1964	*NY-A☆	17	6	.739	39	36	12	8	1	244^{2}	212	10	57	172	10.0	2.13	170	.230	.276	8	.119	1	41	40	2	4.2
1965	NY-A	16	13	.552	37	36	9	2	1	244^{1}	241	22	50	162	10.8	3.24	105	.258	.297	15	.183	2	6	4	2	0.9
1966	NY-A	2	5	.286	22	9	0	0	0	73	79	8	24	43	12.7	2.47	135	.277	.333	0	.000	-2	8	7	3	0.8
1967	NY-A	2	4	.333	7	7	2	1	0	44	40	2	9	21	10.0	1.64	191	.247	.287	2	.154	-0	8	7	2	1.3
Total	16	236	106	.690	498	438	156	45	10	3170^{1}	2766	228	1086	1956	11.0	2.75	133	.235	.301	177	.173	27	386	315	26	37.2
● GENE FORD	Ford, Eugene Matthew b: 6/23/12, Ft.Dodge, Iowa d: 9/7/70, Emmetsburg, Iowa BR/TR, 6'2", 195 lbs. Deb: 6/17/36																									
1936	Bos-N	0	0	—	2	1	0	0	0	2	2	0	3	0	22.5	13.50	28	.250	.455	0	—	0	-2	-2	0	0.0
1938	Chi-A	0	0	—	4	0	0	0	0	14	21	1	12	2	21.2	10.29	48	.350	.458	1	.167	-0	-9	-8	0	0.0
Total	2	0	0	—	6	1	0	0	0	16	23	1	15	2	21.4	10.69	44	.338	.458	1	.167	-0	-11	-11	0	0.0
● GENE FORD	Ford, Eugene Wyman b: 4/16/1881, Milton, N.S., Can. d: 8/23/73, Dunedin, Fla. BR/TR, 6', 170 lbs. Deb: 5/5/05 F																									
1905	Det-A	0	1	.000	7	1	1	0	0	35	51	0	14	20	17.2	5.66	48	.340	.404	0	.000	-1	-12	-11	0	-0.4
● WENTY FORD	Ford, Percival Edmund Wentworth b: 11/25/46, Nassau, Bahamas d: 7/8/80, Nassau, Bahamas BR/TR, 5'11", 165 lbs. Deb: 9/10/73																									
1973	Atl-N	1	2	.333	4	2	1	0	0	16^{1}	17	3	8	4	14.3	5.51	71	.279	.371	2	.400	1	-3	-3	0	-0.4
● RUSS FORD	Ford, Russell William b: 4/25/1883, Brandon, Man., Can. d: 1/24/60, Rockingham, N.C. BR/TR, 5'11", 175 lbs. Deb: 4/28/09 F																									
1909	NY-A	0	0	—	1	0	0	0	0	3	4	0	4	2	33.0	9.00	28	.333	.579	0	.000	-0	-2	-2	0	0.0
1910	NY-A	26	6	.813	36	33	29	8	1	299^{2}	194	4	70	209	8.2	1.65	161	.188	.245	20	.208	4	29	34	-3	4.0
1911	NY-A	22	11	.667	37	33	26	1	0	281^{1}	251	3	76	158	10.6	2.27	158	.237	.291	20	.196	-2	34	41	-1	4.3
1912	NY-A	13	21	.382	36	35	30	0	0	291^{2}	317	10	79	112	12.4	3.55	101	.280	.329	32	.286	5	-7	1	1	0.9
1913	NY-A	12	18	.400	33	28	15	1	2	237	244	9	58	72	11.6	2.66	113	.275	.322	12	.162	0	7	9	-4	0.8
1914	Buf-F	21	6	**.778**	35	26	19	5	**6**	247^{1}	190	11	41	123	8.7	1.82	**163**	.214	.254	10	.128	-4	29	31	0	3.1
1915	Buf-F	5	9	.357	21	15	7	0	0	127^{1}	140	7	48	34	13.5	4.52	62	.285	.352	12	.279	3	-25	-24	-0	-2.2
Total	7	99	71	.582	199	170	126	15	9	1487^{1}	1340	44	376	710	10.6	2.59	121	.243	.296	106	.209	5	64	89	-5	10.9
● TOM FORD	Ford, Thomas Walter b: 1866, Chattanooga, Tenn. d: 5/27/17, Chattanooga, Tenn. 5'10.5", 155 lbs. Deb: 5/6/1890																									
1890	Col-a	0	0	—	1	0	0	0	0	2	0	0	3	0	13.5	0.00	—	.000	.333	0	.000	-0	1	1	0	0.0
	Bro-a	0	6	.000	7	6	6	0	0	49	70	2	32	12	18.7	5.14	76	.326	.413	1	.033	-3	-7	-7	0	-0.8
	Yr	0	6	.000	8	6	6	0	0	51	70	2	35	12	18.5	4.94	79	.317	.410	1	.032	-3	-6	-6	1	-0.8
● TOM FORDHAM	Fordham, Thomas James b: 2/20/74, San Diego, Cal. BL/TL, 6'2", 210 lbs. Deb: 8/19/97																									
1997	Chi-A	0	1	.000	7	1	0	0	0	17^{1}	17	2	10	10	14.5	6.23	70	.266	.373	0	—	0	-3	-4	-0	-0.2
1998	Chi-A	1	2	.333	29	5	0	0	0	48	51	7	42	23	17.6	6.75	67	.279	.416	0	.000	-0	-11	-12	1	-0.6
Total	2	1	3	.250	36	6	0	0	0	65^{1}	68	9	52	33	16.8	6.61	68	.275	.405	0	.000	-0	-14	-15	1	-0.8
● HAPPY FOREMAN	Foreman, August b: 7/20/1897, Memphis, Tenn. d: 2/13/53, New York, N.Y. BL/TL, 5'7", 160 lbs. Deb: 9/3/24																									
1924	Chi-A	0	0	—	3	0	0	0	0	4	7	0	4	1	24.8	2.25	183	.467	.579	0	.000	-0	1	1	-0	-0.1
1926	Bos-A	0	0	—	3	0	0	0	0	7^{1}	3	0	5	3	9.8	3.68	111	.130	.286	0	.000	-0	0	0	1	0.0
Total	2	0	0	—	6	0	0	0	0	11^{1}	10	0	9	4	15.1	3.18	129	.263	.404	0	.000	-1	1	1	0	-0.1
● FRANK FOREMAN	Foreman, Francis Isaiah "Monkey" b: 5/1/1863, Baltimore, Md. d: 11/19/57, Baltimore, Md. BL/TL, 6', 160 lbs. Deb: 5/15/1884 F♦																									
1884	CP-U	1	2	.333	3	3	1	0	0	18	23	0	2	10	12.5	4.00	61	.291	.309	1	.091	-2	-3	-3	-0	-0.5
	KC-U	0	1	.000	1	1	1	0	0	8	17	0	2	5	21.4	5.63	40	.405	.432	0	.000	-1	-3	-3	1	-0.3
	Yr	1	3	.250	4	4	2	0	0	26	40	0	4	15	15.2	4.50	53	.331	.352	1	.071	-3	-6	-6	1	-0.8
1885	Bal-a	2	1	.667	3	3	2	0	0	27	33	0	9	11	14.3	6.00	54	.284	.341	4	.286	1	-8	-8	-0	-0.6
1889	Bal-a	23	21	.523	51	48	43	5	0	414	364	8	137	180	11.8	3.52	112	.229	.306	26	.144	-10	15	19	-2	0.5
1890	Cin-N	13	10	.565	25	24	20	0	0	198^{1}	201	6	89	57	14.1	3.95	90	.255	.345	10	.133	-0	-8	-9	-3	-1.1
1891	Was-a	18	20	.474	43	41	39	1	1	345^{1}	381	9	142	170	14.8	3.73	100	.271	.355	34	.222	9	-0	1	-1	0.9
1892	Was-N	2	4	.333	11	7	4	0	0	60	53	3	37	16	14.3	3.30	99	.227	.345	13	.464	8	-0	-0	-1	0.6
	Bal-N	0	3	.000	4	3	2	0	0	25	40	4	11	5	18.7	6.84	50	.348	.409	4	.174	0	-10	-9	0	-0.8
	Yr	2	7	.222	15	10	6	0	0	85	93	7	48	21	15.0	4.34	76	.263	.353	17	.333	8	-10	-10	-1	-0.2
1893	NY-N	0	1	.000	2	1	0	0	0	5^{2}	19	1	10	0	47.6	27.00	17	.528	.638	0	.000	-1	-14	-14	-0	-1.4
1895	Cin-N	11	14	.440	32	27	19	0	1	219	253	11	92	55	14.8	4.11	121	.285	.362	29	.309	4	16	21	-3	1.9
1896	Cin-N	14	7	.667	27	22	17	0	1	185^{2}	212	2	62	33	13.7	3.97	116	.285	.346	18	.243	-1	8	13	-1	1.0
1901	Bos-A	0	1	.000	1	1	1	0	0	8	8	1	2	1	13.5	9.00	39	.258	.343	0	.000	-1	-5	-5	-0	-0.5
	Bal-A	12	6	.667	24	22	18	1	1	191^{1}	225	2	58	41	13.6	3.67	105	.290	.344	26	.325	5	-0	4	-3	0.5
	Yr	12	7	.632	25	23	19	1	1	199^{1}	233	3	60	42	13.5	3.88	99	.288	.341	26	.310	4	-5	-1	-3	0.0
1902	Bal-A	0	2	.000	2	2	2	0	0	16^{1}	28	0	6	2	18.7	6.06	62	.378	.425	3	.429	1	-5	-4	1	-0.3
Total	11	96	93	.508	229	205	169	7	4	1721^{2}	1857	47	659	586	13.9	3.97	100	.268	.344	169	.224	12	-17	1	-14	-0.1
● BROWNIE FOREMAN	Foreman, John Davis b: 8/6/1875, Baltimore, Md. d: 10/10/26, Baltimore, Md. BL/TL, 5'8", 150 lbs. Deb: 7/18/1895 F																									
1895	Pit-N	8	6	.571	19	16	12	0	2	139^{2}	131	0	64	54	13.8	3.22	140	**.244**	.346	3	.065	-6	24	20	2	1.3
1896	Pit-N	3	3	.500	9	9	5	0	0	61^{2}	73	4	35	18	16.9	6.57	64	.292	.396	3	.150	0	-15	-16	1	-1.1
	Cin-N	1	3	.250	4	4	3	1	0	23	41	2	16	9	23.1	11.35	41	.383	.472	2	.200	-0	-18	-17	-0	-1.9
	Yr	4	6	.400	13	13	8	1	0	84^{2}	114	6	51	27	17.8	7.87	55	.312	.400	5	.167	-0	-33	-33	1	-3.0
Total	2	12	12	.500	32	29	20	1	2	224^{1}	245	6	115	81	15.6	4.97	89	.274	.375	8	.105	-6	-9	-13	3	-1.7

● BILL FORMAN Forman, William Orange b: 10/10/1886, Venango, Pa. d: 10/2/58, Uniontown, Pa. BB/TR, 5'11", 180 lbs. Deb: 9/20/09

YEAR	TM/L	W	L	PCT	G	GS	CG	SH	SV	IP	H	HR	BB	SO	RAT	ERA	ERA+	OAV	OOB	BH	AVG	PB	PR	/A	PD	TPI
1909	Was-A	0	2	.000	2	2	1	0	0	11	8	0	7	2	13.9	4.91	50	.211	.362	1	.333	0	-3	-3	1	-0.4
1910	Was-A	0	0	—	1	0	0	0	0	0^2	1	0	0	0	13.5	13.50	18	.333	.333	0	—	0	-1	-1	-0	0.0
Total	2	0	2	.000	3	2	1	0	0	11^2	9	0	7	2	13.9	5.40	45	.220	.360	1	.333	1	-4	-4	1	-0.4

● MIKE FORNIELES Fornieles, Jose Miguel (Torres) b: 1/18/32, Havana, Cuba d: 2/11/98, St.Petersburg, Fla. BR/TR, 5'11", 172 lbs. Deb: 9/2/52

YEAR	TM/L	W	L	PCT	G	GS	CG	SH	SV	IP	H	HR	BB	SO	RAT	ERA	ERA+	OAV	OOB	BH	AVG	PB	PR	/A	PD	TPI
1952	Was-A	2	2	.500	4	2	2	1	0	26^1	13	1	11	12	8.2	1.37	260	.143	.235	0	.000	-1	7	6	-0	0.8
1953	Chi-A	8	7	.533	39	16	5	0	3	153	160	8	61	72	13.1	3.59	112	.270	.340	4	.098	-3	7	7	2	0.6
1954	Chi-A	1	2	.333	15	6	0	0	1	42	41	4	14	18	11.8	4.29	87	.252	.311	3	.273	0	-3	-3	1	-0.1
1955	Chi-A	6	3	.667	26	9	2	0	2	86^1	84	12	29	23	12.0	3.86	102	.255	.319	3	.103	-2	1	1	0	-0.1
1956	Chi-A	0	1	.000	6	0	0	0	0	15^2	22	1	6	6	16.1	4.60	89	.306	.359	1	.200	0	-1	-1	-0	0.0
	Bal-A	4	7	.364	30	11	1	1	1	111	109	7	25	53	10.9	3.97	99	.266	.308	5	.167	-1	2	-1	2	0.1
	Yr	4	8	.333	36	11	1	1	1	126^2	131	8	31	59	11.5	4.05	97	.271	.315	6	.171	-1	2	-2	2	0.1
1957	Bal-A	2	6	.250	15	4	1	1	0	57	57	4	17	43	11.7	4.26	84	.257	.310	5	.278	1	-3	-4	1	-0.4
	Bos-A	8	7	.533	25	18	7	1	2	125^1	136	7	38	64	12.7	3.52	113	.271	.327	6	.136	-2	4	7	-1	0.4
	Yr	10	13	.435	40	22	8	2	2	182^1	193	11	55	107	12.4	3.75	103	.267	.321	11	.177	-1	1	2	-1	0.0
1958	Bos-A	4	6	.400	37	7	1	0	1	110^2	123	10	33	49	13.2	4.96	81	.284	.343	6	.207	-0	-15	-12	-0	-1.1
1959	Bos-A	5	3	.625	46	0	0	0	11	82	77	6	29	54	11.7	3.07	132	.254	.321	3	.158	-1	7	9	-0	1.0
1960	Bos-A	10	5	.667	**70**	0	0	0	**14**	109	86	6	49	64	11.6	2.64	153	.219	.315	6	.400	2	15	17	1	2.9
1961	Bos-A★	9	8	.529	57	2	1	0	15	119^1	121	18	54	70	13.3	4.68	89	.265	.345	5	.156	0	-9	-7	2	-0.9
1962	Bos-A	3	6	.333	42	1	0	0	5	82^1	96	14	37	36	15.4	5.36	77	.303	.390	3	.188	-0	-13	-11	-0	-1.3
1963	Bos-A	0	0	—	9	0	0	0	0	14	16	0	5	5	13.5	6.43	59	.286	.344	1	.333	1	-4	-4	-0	0.0
	Min-A	1	1	.500	11	0	0	0	0	22^2	24	0	13	7	15.5	4.76	76	.273	.379	1	.167	0	-3	-3	1	-0.3
	Yr	1	1	.500	20	0	0	0	0	36^2	40	0	18	12	14.7	5.40	68	.276	.364	2	.222	1	-7	-7	-1	-0.3
Total	12	63	64	.496	432	76	20	4	55	1156^2	1165	98	421	576	12.6	3.96	100	.263	.332	52	.169	-6	-7	2	4	1.6

● KEN FORSCH Forsch, Kenneth Roth b: 9/8/46, Sacramento, Cal. BR/TR, 6'4", 210 lbs. Deb: 9/7/70 F

YEAR	TM/L	W	L	PCT	G	GS	CG	SH	SV	IP	H	HR	BB	SO	RAT	ERA	ERA+	OAV	OOB	BH	AVG	PB	PR	/A	PD	TPI
1970	Hou-N	1	2	.333	4	4	1	0	0	24	28	1	5	13	12.4	5.63	69	.298	.333	0	.000	-1	-4	-5	-0	-0.6
1971	Hou-N	8	8	.500	33	23	7	2	0	188^1	162	8	53	131	10.5	2.53	133	.230	.288	8	.136	-1	20	17	-2	1.1
1972	Hou-N	6	8	.429	30	24	1	0	0	156^1	163	19	62	113	13.0	3.91	86	.273	.341	6	.146	-1	-8	-10	-3	-1.1
1973	Hou-N	9	12	.429	46	26	5	0	4	201^1	197	18	74	149	12.3	4.20	86	.257	.325	4	.065	-4	-12	-13	-2	-1.9
1974	Hou-N	8	7	.533	70	0	0	0	10	103^1	98	3	37	48	12.1	2.79	124	.255	.326	0	.000	-1	10	8	-0	1.2
1975	Hou-N	4	8	.333	34	9	2	0	2	109	114	9	30	54	12.1	3.22	105	.277	.330	1	.045	-1	5	2	-0	0.1
1976	Hou-N★	4	3	.571	52	0	0	0	19	92	76	5	26	49	10.2	2.15	148	.226	.286	1	.091	-0	14	11	1	1.3
1977	Hou-N	5	8	.385	42	5	0	0	8	86	80	2	28	45	11.5	2.72	131	.246	.310	1	.077	-1	11	8	1	1.3
1978	Hou-N	10	6	.625	52	6	4	2	7	133^1	136	2	37	71	11.7	2.70	123	.268	.319	5	.185	0	13	9	1	1.2
1979	Hou-N	11	6	.647	26	24	10	2	0	177^2	155	14	35	58	**9.6**	3.04	116	.236	**.275**	8	.138	0	14	9	2	1.1
1980	*Hou-N	12	13	.480	32	32	6	3	0	222^1	230	15	41	84	11.3	3.20	103	.266	.304	18	.234	4	10	2	1	0.8
1981	Cal-A★	11	7	.611	20	20	10	**4**	0	153	143	7	27	55	10.2	2.88	126	.250	.289	0	—	0	13	13	1	1.6
1982	Cal-A	13	11	.542	37	35	12	4	0	228	225	25	57	73	11.6	3.87	105	.258	.311	0	—	0	5	5	-2	0.3
1983	Cal-A	11	12	.478	31	31	11	1	0	219^1	226	21	61	81	11.9	4.06	99	.266	.318	0	—	0	-0	-1	-1	-0.2
1984	Cal-A	1	1	.500	2	2	1	0	0	16^1	14	2	3	10	9.4	2.20	180	.237	.274	0	—	0	3	3	1	0.5
1986	Cal-A	0	1	.000	10	0	0	0	1	17	24	4	10	13	19.1	9.53	43	.343	.439	0	—	0	-10	-10	0	-0.6
Total	16	114	113	.502	521	241	70	18	51	2127^1	2071	155	586	1047	11.4	3.37	106	.257	.311	52	.136	-5	83	48	-3	6.1

● BOB FORSCH Forsch, Robert Herbert b: 1/13/50, Sacramento, Cal. BR/TR, 6'4", 200 lbs. Deb: 7/7/74 F

YEAR	TM/L	W	L	PCT	G	GS	CG	SH	SV	IP	H	HR	BB	SO	RAT	ERA	ERA+	OAV	OOB	BH	AVG	PB	PR	/A	PD	TPI
1974	StL-N	7	4	.636	19	14	5	2	0	100	84	5	34	39	10.7	2.97	120	.230	.298	7	.241	1	7	7	-0	0.9
1975	StL-N	15	10	.600	34	34	7	4	0	230	213	14	70	108	11.2	2.86	131	.244	.303	24	.308	9	20	23	2	3.7
1976	StL-N	8	10	.444	33	32	2	0	0	194	209	17	71	76	13.1	3.94	90	.277	.341	11	.177	1	-10	-9	1	-0.6
1977	StL-N	20	7	.741	35	35	8	2	0	217^1	210	20	69	95	11.7	3.48	111	.251	.311	12	.167	0	10	9	-1	0.9
1978	StL-N	11	17	.393	34	34	7	3	0	233^2	205	15	97	114	11.8	3.70	95	.238	.318	15	.181	3	-3	-5	1	-0.1
1979	StL-N	11	11	.500	33	32	7	1	0	218^2	215	16	52	92	11.1	3.83	98	.262	.309	8	.110	-0	-2	-2	1	-0.1
1980	StL-N	11	10	.524	31	31	8	0	0	214^2	225	12	33	87	11.0	3.77	98	.273	.304	23	.295	9	-4	-2	2	1.0
1981	StL-N	10	5	.667	20	20	1	0	0	124^1	106	7	29	41	10.1	3.18	112	.232	.284	5	.122	-1	4	5	0	0.5
1982	*StL-N	15	9	.625	36	34	6	2	1	233	238	16	54	69	11.4	3.48	104	.268	.313	15	.205	3	3	4	-2	0.5
1983	StL-N	10	12	.455	34	30	6	2	0	187	190	23	54	56	11.9	4.28	85	.266	.320	13	.241	4	-14	-14	-0	-1.1
1984	StL-N	2	5	.286	16	11	1	0	0	52^1	64	6	19	21	14.3	6.02	58	.303	.361	4	.250	1	-14	-15	0	-1.6
1985	*StL-N	9	6	.600	34	19	3	1	2	136	132	11	47	48	12.0	3.90	91	.258	.323	11	.244	4	-5	-6	-0	-0.2
1986	StL-N	14	10	.583	33	33	3	0	0	230	211	19	68	104	11.0	3.25	112	.247	.304	13	.171	3	12	10	-1	1.3
1987	*StL-N	11	7	.611	33	30	2	1	0	179	189	15	45	89	12.0	4.32	96	.273	.321	17	.298	8	-5	-3	-1	0.4
1988	StL-N	9	4	.692	30	12	1	1	0	108^2	111	8	38	40	12.4	3.73	93	.270	.333	7	.280	2	-3	-3	-2	-0.3
	Hou-N	1	4	.200	6	6	0	0	0	27^2	42	2	6	14	16.3	6.51	51	.359	.400	1	.143	0	-9	-10	-0	-1.5
	Yr	10	8	.556	36	18	1	1	0	136^1	153	10	44	54	13.1	4.29	80	.287	.344	8	.250	2	-13	-13	-2	-1.8
1989	Hou-N	4	5	.444	37	15	0	0	0	108^1	133	10	46	40	15.0	5.32	64	.303	.370	4	.167	-0	-22	-23	-1	-1.9
Total	16	168	136	.553	498	422	67	19	3	2794^2	2777	216	832	1133	11.8	3.76	97	.261	.318	190	.213	48	-35	-33	-3	1.8

● TERRY FORSTER Forster, Terry Jay b: 1/14/52, Sioux Falls, S.D. BL/TL, 6'3", 210 lbs. Deb: 4/11/71

YEAR	TM/L	W	L	PCT	G	GS	CG	SH	SV	IP	H	HR	BB	SO	RAT	ERA	ERA+	OAV	OOB	BH	AVG	PB	PR	/A	PD	TPI
1971	Chi-A	2	3	.400	45	3	0	0	1	49^2	46	5	23	48	12.7	3.99	90	.241	.326	2	.400	1	-3	-2	0	-0.1
1972	Chi-A	6	5	.545	62	0	0	0	29	100	75	0	44	104	11.0	2.25	139	.208	.300	10	.526	4	9	10	1	2.5
1973	Chi-A	6	11	.353	51	12	4	0	16	172^2	174	7	78	120	13.1	3.23	122	.266	.344	0	.000	-0	11	14	5	2.1
1974	Chi-A	7	8	.467	59	1	0	0	**24**	134^1	120	6	48	105	11.8	3.62	103	.245	.322	0	—	0	0	2	3	0.6
1975	Chi-A	3	3	.500	17	1	0	0	4	37	30	0	24	32	13.1	2.19	177	.236	.358	0	—	0	7	7	2	1.4
1976	Chi-A	2	12	.143	29	16	1	0	1	111^1	126	7	41	70	13.6	4.37	82	.288	.351	0	—	0	-10	-10	2	-1.0
1977	Pit-N	6	4	.600	33	6	0	0	1	87^1	90	7	32	58	12.8	4.43	90	.269	.337	9	.346	3	-5	-4	-0	-0.2
1978	*LA-N	5	4	.556	47	0	0	0	22	65^1	56	2	23	46	10.9	1.93	182	.233	.300	4	.500	2	12	11	-0	2.6
1979	LA-N	1	2	.333	17	0	0	0	2	16^1	18	0	11	8	16.0	5.51	66	.295	.403	0	—	0	-3	-3	1	-0.6
1980	LA-N	0	0	—	9	0	0	0	0	11^2	10	0	4	2	10.8	3.09	113	.222	.286	0	—	0	1	1	0	0.0
1981	*LA-N	0	1	.000	21	0	0	0	0	30^2	37	1	15	17	15.3	4.11	81	.308	.385	0	.000	-0	-2	-3	1	0.0
1982	LA-N	5	6	.455	56	0	0	0	3	83	66	3	31	52	11.0	3.04	114	.221	.302	0	.000	-0	5	4	1	0.6
1983	Atl-N	3	2	.600	56	0	0	0	13	79^1	60	3	31	54	10.6	2.16	180	.217	.301	4	.500	2	13	15	1	1.6
1984	Atl-N	2	0	1.000	25	0	0	0	5	26^2	30	1	7	10	12.5	2.70	143	.297	.343	2	.667	1	3	3	0	0.5
1985	Atl-N	2	3	.400	46	0	0	0	1	59^1	49	7	28	37	11.7	2.28	169	.222	.309	0	.000	-0	9	10	-1	0.8
1986	Cal-A	4	1	.800	41	0	0	0	5	41	47	2	17	28	14.7	3.51	117	.297	.376	0	—	0	3	3	1	0.5
Total	16	54	65	.454	614	39	5	0	127	1105^2	1034	51	457	791	12.3	3.23	114	.251	.330	31	.397	11	48	57	16	11.3

● TIM FORTUGNO Fortugno, Timothy Shawn b: 4/11/62, Clinton, Mass. BL/TL, 6'1", 195 lbs. Deb: 7/20/92

YEAR	TM/L	W	L	PCT	G	GS	CG	SH	SV	IP	H	HR	BB	SO	RAT	ERA	ERA+	OAV	OOB	BH	AVG	PB	PR	/A	PD	TPI
1992	Cal-A	1	1	.500	14	5	1	1	1	41^2	37	5	19	31	12.1	5.18	77	.236	.318	0	—	0	-6	-6	-0	-0.3
1994	Cin-N	1	0	1.000	25	0	0	0	0	30	32	2	14	29	14.7	4.20	98	.288	.383	1	.333	0	0	-0	1	0.1
1995	Chi-A	1	3	.250	37	0	0	0	0	38^2	30	7	19	24	11.4	5.59	80	.213	.306	0	—	0	-4	-5	0	-0.4
Total	3	3	4	.429	76	5	1	1	1	110^1	99	14	52	84	12.6	5.06	83	.242	.332	1	.333	0	-9	-11	0	-0.6

● GARY FORTUNE Fortune, Garrett Reese b: 10/11/1894, High Point, N.C. d: 9/23/55, Washington, D.C. BB/TR, 5'11.5", 176 lbs. Deb: 10/5/16

YEAR	TM/L	W	L	PCT	G	GS	CG	SH	SV	IP	H	HR	BB	SO	RAT	ERA	ERA+	OAV	OOB	BH	AVG	PB	PR	/A	PD	TPI
1916	Phi-N	0	1	.000	1	1	0	0	0	5	2	0	4	3	10.8	3.60	74	.118	.286	0	.000	-0	-1	-1	-0	-0.2
1918	Phi-N	0	2	.000	5	2	1	0	0	31	41	2	19	10	17.7	8.13	37	.333	.427	2	.200	0	-18	-18	-0	-1.0
1920	Bos-A	0	2	.000	14	3	1	0	0	41^2	46	0	23	10	14.9	5.83	63	.282	.371	2	.167	-0	-9	-10	-1	-0.5
Total	3	0	5	.000	20	6	2	0	0	77^2	89	2	46	23	15.8	6.61	51	.294	.389	4	.167	-0	-28	-28	-1	-1.7

● JERRY FOSNOW Fosnow, Gerald Eugene b: 9/21/40, Deshler, Ohio BR/TL, 6'4", 195 lbs. Deb: 6/29/64

YEAR	TM/L	W	L	PCT	G	GS	CG	SH	SV	IP	H	HR	BB	SO	RAT	ERA	ERA+	OAV	OOB	BH	AVG	PB	PR	/A	PD	TPI
1964	Min-A	0	1	.000	7	0	0	0	0	10^2	13	3	8	9	17.7	10.97	33	.302	.412	0	—	0	-9	-9	-0	-0.8
1965	Min-A	3	3	.500	29	0	0	0	2	46^2	33	7	25	35	11.4	4.44	80	.193	.299	0	.000	-1	-5	-5	0	-0.6
Total	2	3	4	.429	36	0	0	0	2	57^1	46	10	33	44	12.6	5.65	63	.215	.323	0	.000	-1	-14	-13	0	-1.4

● LARRY FOSS Foss, Larry Curtis b: 4/18/36, Castleton, Kan. BR/TR, 6'2", 187 lbs. Deb: 9/18/61

YEAR	TM/L	W	L	PCT	G	GS	CG	SH	SV	IP	H	HR	BB	SO	RAT	ERA	ERA+	OAV	OOB	BH	AVG	PB	PR	/A	PD	TPI
1961	Pit-N	1	1	.500	3	3	0	0	0	15^1	15	3	11	9	16.4	5.87	68	.273	.412	1	.167	-0	-3	-3	-0	-0.4
1962	NY-N	0	1	.000	5	1	0	0	0	11^2	17	2	7	3	19.3	4.63	90	.362	.455	0	.000	-0	-1	-1	-0	-0.1
Total	2	1	2	.333	8	4	0	0	0	27	32	5	18	12	17.7	5.33	76	.314	.431	1	.143	-0	-4	-4	-0	-0.5

● TONY FOSSAS Fossas, Emilio Antonio (Morejon) b: 9/23/57, Havana, Cuba BL/TL, 6', 187 lbs. Deb: 5/15/88

YEAR	TM/L	W	L	PCT	G	GS	CG	SH	SV	IP	H	HR	BB	SO	RAT	ERA	ERA+	OAV	OOB	BH	AVG	PB	PR	/A	PD	TPI
1988	Tex-A	0	0	—	5	0	0	0	0	5^2	11	0	2	0	20.6	4.76	86	.423	.464	0	—	0	-1	-0	0	-0.2
1989	Mil-A	2	2	.500	51	0	0	0	1	61	57	3	22	42	11.8	3.54	108	.256	.325	0	—	0	2	2	0	0.2
1990	Mil-A	2	3	.400	32	0	0	0	0	29^1	44	5	10	24	16.6	6.44	60	.331	.378	0	—	0	-8	-8	-0	-1.3
1991	Bos-A	3	2	.600	64	0	0	0	1	57	49	3	28	29	12.6	3.47	124	.236	.335	0	—	0	4	5	1	0.5
1992	Bos-A	1	2	.333	60	0	0	0	2	29^2	31	1	14	19	14.0	2.43	174	.279	.365	0	—	0	5	6	1	0.3
1993	Bos-A	1	1	.500	71	0	0	0	0	40	38	4	15	39	12.4	5.17	89	.242	.316	0	—	0	-4	-2	0	-0.5
1994	Bos-A	2	0	1.000	44	0	0	0	1	34	35	6	15	31	13.5	4.76	106	.263	.342	0	—	0	0	1	-0	-0.1
1995	StL-N	3	0	1.000	58	0	0	0	0	36^2	28	1	10	40	9.6	1.47	284	.214	.275	0	—	0	11	11	-0	0.8
1996	*StL-N	0	4	.000	65	0	0	0	2	47	43	7	21	36	12.3	2.68	156	.231	.309	0	.000	-0	8	8	0	0.7
1997	StL-N	2	7	.222	71	0	0	0	0	51^2	62	7	26	41	15.5	3.83	108	.298	.379	0	—	0	2	2	2	0.4
1998	Sea-A	0	3	.000	23	0	0	0	0	11^1	19	1	6	10	19.9	8.74	53	.404	.472	0	—	0	-5	-5	0	-1.1
	Chi-N	0	0	—	8	0	0	0	0	4	8	0	6	6	31.5	9.00	48	.421	.560	0	—	0	-2	-2	0	0.0
	Tex-A	1	0	1.000	10	0	0	0	0	7^1	3	0	4	7	8.6	0.00	—	.120	.241	0	—	0	4	4	-0	0.5
Total	11	17	24	.415	562	0	0	0	7	414^2	428	38	179	324	13.4	3.82	111	.266	.344	0	.000	-0	16	20	3	0.2

● ALAN FOSTER Foster, Alan Benton b: 12/8/46, Pasadena, Cal. BR/TR, 6', 180 lbs. Deb: 4/25/67

YEAR	TM/L	W	L	PCT	G	GS	CG	SH	SV	IP	H	HR	BB	SO	RAT	ERA	ERA+	OAV	OOB	BH	AVG	PB	PR	/A	PD	TPI
1967	LA-N	0	1	.000	4	2	0	0	0	16^2	10	0	3	15	7.0	2.16	143	.169	.210	0	.000	-0	2	2	0	0.1
1968	LA-N	1	1	.500	3	3	0	0	0	15^1	11	1	2	10	7.5	1.72	160	.200	.228	1	.250	0	2	2	-0	0.3
1969	LA-N	3	9	.250	24	15	2	2	0	102^2	119	11	29	59	13.3	4.38	76	.290	.342	2	.074	-1	-9	-12	-0	-1.4
1970	LA-N	10	13	.435	33	33	7	1	0	198^2	200	22	81	83	12.8	4.26	90	.264	.337	7	.109	-2	-5	-9	-1	-1.2
1971	Cle-A	8	12	.400	36	26	3	0	0	181^2	158	19	82	97	12.1	4.16	92	.232	.318	2	.039	-4	-14	-7	-4	-1.6
1972	Cal-A	0	1	.000	8	0	0	0	0	12^2	12	3	6	11	14.2	4.97	59	.245	.351	0	—	0	-3	-3	0	-0.2
1973	StL-N	13	9	.591	35	29	6	2	0	203^2	195	17	63	106	11.6	3.14	116	.254	.315	13	.191	1	12	11	-2	1.1
1974	StL-N	7	10	.412	31	25	5	1	0	162^1	167	16	61	78	12.8	3.88	92	.268	.336	8	.167	-1	-5	-6	-1	-0.7
1975	SD-N	3	1	.750	17	4	1	0	0	44^2	41	1	21	20	12.5	2.42	144	.244	.328	1	.091	-1	6	5	0	0.4
1976	SD-N	3	6	.333	26	11	2	0	0	86^2	75	9	35	22	11.5	3.22	102	.235	.313	1	.056	-0	3	0	-1	-0.1
Total	10	48	63	.432	217	148	26	6	0	1025^1	988	99	383	501	12.2	3.74	96	.254	.324	35	.119	-8	-10	-15	-9	-3.3

● ED FOSTER Foster, Eddy Lee "Slim" b: Georgia d: 3/1/29, Montgomery, Ala. BR/TR, 6'1", Deb: 7/31/08

YEAR	TM/L	W	L	PCT	G	GS	CG	SH	SV	IP	H	HR	BB	SO	RAT	ERA	ERA+	OAV	OOB	BH	AVG	PB	PR	/A	PD	TPI
1908	Cle-A	1	0	1.000	6	1	1	0	2	21	16	1	12	11	12.9	2.14	111	.229	.357	0	.000	-0	1	1	-1	-0.1

● RUBE FOSTER Foster, George b: 1/5/1888, Lehigh, Okla d: 3/1/76, Bokoshe, Okla. BR/TR, 5'7.5", 170 lbs. Deb: 4/10/13

YEAR	TM/L	W	L	PCT	G	GS	CG	SH	SV	IP	H	HR	BB	SO	RAT	ERA	ERA+	OAV	OOB	BH	AVG	PB	PR	/A	PD	TPI
1913	Bos-A	3	3	.500	19	8	4	1	0	68^1	64	1	28	36	12.6	3.16	93	.249	.332	2	.095	-1	-2	-2	-0	-0.3
1914	Bos-A	14	8	.636	32	27	17	5	0	211^2	164	2	52	89	9.5	1.70	158	.218	.274	11	.175	0	24	23	-0	2.6
1915	*Bos-A	19	8	.704	37	33	21	5	1	255^1	217	3	86	82	11.0	2.11	131	.237	.310	23	.277	7	23	19	1	2.8
1916	*Bos-A	14	7	.667	33	19	9	3	2	182^1	173	0	86	53	13.0	3.06	90	.263	.352	11	.177	0	-5	-6	2	-0.5
1917	Bos-A	8	7	.533	17	16	9	1	0	124^2	108	0	53	34	11.9	2.53	102	.243	.329	11	.268	2	2	1	1	0.4
Total	5	58	33	.637	138	103	60	15	3	842^1	726	6	305	294	11.3	2.36	116	.240	.315	58	.215	9	43	35	2	5.0

● KEVIN FOSTER Foster, Kevin Christopher b: 1/13/69, Evanston, Ill. BR/TR, 6'1", 170 lbs. Deb: 9/12/93

YEAR	TM/L	W	L	PCT	G	GS	CG	SH	SV	IP	H	HR	BB	SO	RAT	ERA	ERA+	OAV	OOB	BH	AVG	PB	PR	/A	PD	TPI
1993	Phi-N	0	1	.000	2	1	0	0	0	6^2	13	3	7	6	27.0	14.85	27	.394	.500	0	.000	-0	-8	-8	-0	-0.9
1994	Chi-N	3	4	.429	13	13	0	0	0	81	70	7	35	75	11.8	2.89	144	.234	.316	2	.074	-2	12	11	-1	0.6
1995	Chi-N	12	11	.522	30	28	0	0	0	167^2	149	32	65	146	11.8	4.51	91	.240	.317	15	.250	5	-6	-8	-2	-0.6
1996	Chi-N	7	6	.538	17	16	1	0	0	87	98	16	35	53	14.0	6.21	70	.288	.358	8	.296	5	-19	-18	1	-1.8
1997	Chi-N	10	7	.588	26	25	1	0	0	146^1	141	27	66	118	12.9	4.61	93	.255	.337	6	.128	-1	-7	-5	-2	-0.8
1998	Chi-N	0	0	—	3	0	0	0	0	3^1	8	1	2	3	27.0	16.20	27	.500	.556	0	—	0	-4	-4	-0	0.0
Total	6	32	29	.525	91	83	2	0	0	492	479	86	210	401	12.8	4.79	88	.257	.336	31	.190	7	-33	-32	-4	-3.5

● LARRY FOSTER Foster, Larry Lynn b: 12/24/37, Lansing, Mich. BL/TR, 6', 185 lbs. Deb: 9/18/63

YEAR	TM/L	W	L	PCT	G	GS	CG	SH	SV	IP	H	HR	BB	SO	RAT	ERA	ERA+	OAV	OOB	BH	AVG	PB	PR	/A	PD	TPI
1963	Det-A	0	0	—	1	0	0	0	0	2	4	0	1	1	22.5	13.50	28	.364	.417	0	—	0	-2	-2	0	0.0

● STEVE FOSTER Foster, Stephen Eugene b: 8/16/66, Dallas, Tex. BR/TR, 6', 180 lbs. Deb: 8/22/91

YEAR	TM/L	W	L	PCT	G	GS	CG	SH	SV	IP	H	HR	BB	SO	RAT	ERA	ERA+	OAV	OOB	BH	AVG	PB	PR	/A	PD	TPI
1991	Cin-N	0	0	—	11	0	0	0	0	14	7	1	4	11	7.1	1.93	197	.143	.208	0	—	0	3	3	-0	0.0
1992	Cin-N	1	1	.500	31	1	0	0	2	50	52	4	13	34	11.7	2.88	125	.275	.322	1	.200	0	3	4	1	0.3
1993	Cin-N	2	2	.500	17	0	0	0	0	25^2	23	1	5	16	10.2	1.75	230	.235	.279	0	—	0	7	6	-1	0.9
Total	3	3	3	.500	59	1	0	0	2	89^2	82	6	22	61	10.5	2.41	156	.244	.292	1	.200	0	13	13	0	1.2

● STEVE FOUCAULT Foucault, Steven Raymond b: 10/3/49, Duluth, Minn. BL/TR, 6', 205 lbs. Deb: 4/7/73

YEAR	TM/L	W	L	PCT	G	GS	CG	SH	SV	IP	H	HR	BB	SO	RAT	ERA	ERA+	OAV	OOB	BH	AVG	PB	PR	/A	PD	TPI
1973	Tex-A	2	4	.333	32	0	0	0	8	55^2	54	6	31	28	14.2	3.88	96	.262	.367	0	—	0	-0	-1	1	0.2
1974	Tex-A	8	9	.471	69	0	0	0	12	144^1	123	8	40	106	10.5	2.24	159	.234	.295	0	—	0	22	21	1	2.9
1975	Tex-A	8	4	.667	59	0	0	0	10	107	96	10	55	56	13.0	4.12	91	.249	.349	0	—	0	-4	-4	-1	-0.6
1976	Tex-A	8	8	.500	46	0	0	0	5	75^2	68	9	25	41	11.5	3.33	108	.249	.321	0	—	0	2	2	0	0.6
1977	Det-A	7	7	.500	44	0	0	0	13	74^1	64	7	17	58	9.8	3.15	136	.226	.270	0	—	0	8	9	-1	1.9
1978	Det-A	2	4	.333	24	0	0	0	4	37^1	48	1	21	18	16.9	3.13	123	.324	.412	0	—	0	3	3	-1	0.3
	KC-A	0	0	—	3	0	0	0	0	2^1	5	0	1	0	23.1	3.86	99	.417	.462	0	—	0	-0	-0	0	-0.2
	Yr	2	4	.333	27	0	0	0	4	39^2	53	1	22	18	17.0	3.18	122	.323	.403	0	—	0	3	3	-0	0.1
Total	6	35	36	.493	277	0	0	0	52	496^2	458	41	190	307	12.1	3.21	117	.250	.326	0	—	0	29	30	1	5.1

● KEITH FOULKE Foulke, Keith Charles b: 10/19/72, San Diego, Cal. BR/TR, 6', 195 lbs. Deb: 5/21/97

YEAR	TM/L	W	L	PCT	G	GS	CG	SH	SV	IP	H	HR	BB	SO	RAT	ERA	ERA+	OAV	OOB	BH	AVG	PB	PR	/A	PD	TPI
1997	SF-N	1	5	.167	11	8	0	0	0	44^2	60	9	18	33	16.5	8.26	50	.324	.396	2	.154	-0	-20	-21	0	-2.2
	Chi-A	3	0	1.000	16	0	0	0	3	28^2	28	4	5	21	10.4	3.45	127	.255	.287	0	—	0	4	3	0	0.3
1998	Chi-A	3	2	.600	54	0	0	0	1	65^1	51	9	20	57	10.3	4.13	110	.213	.285	0	—	0	4	3	-1	0.2
Total	2	7	7	.500	81	8	0	0	4	138^2	139	22	43	111	12.3	5.32	82	.260	.325	2	.154	-0	-13	-14	-0	-1.7

● JACK FOURNIER Fournier, John Frank b: 9/28/1889, AuSable, Mich. d: 9/5/73, Tacoma, Wash. BL/TR, 6', 195 lbs. Deb: 4/13/12 ♦

YEAR	TM/L	W	L	PCT	G	GS	CG	SH	SV	IP	H	HR	BB	SO	RAT	ERA	ERA+	OAV	OOB	BH	AVG	PB	PR	/A	PD	TPI
1922	StL-N	0	0	—	1	0	0	0	0	1	0	0	0	0	0.0	0.00	—	.000	.000	119	.295	0	0	0	0	0.0

● HENRY FOURNIER Fournier, Julius Henry "Frenchy" b: 8/8/1865, Syracuse, N.Y. d: 12/8/45, Detroit, Mich. TL, Deb: 8/22/1894

YEAR	TM/L	W	L	PCT	G	GS	CG	SH	SV	IP	H	HR	BB	SO	RAT	ERA	ERA+	OAV	OOB	BH	AVG	PB	PR	/A	PD	TPI
1894	Cin-N	1	3	.250	6	4	4	0	0	45	71	4	20	5	18.6	5.40	103	.353	.417	2	.105	-3	-0	1	0	-0.1

● DAVE FOUTZ Foutz, David Luther "Scissors" b: 9/7/1856, Carroll Co., Md. d: 3/5/1897, Waverly, Md. BR/TR, 6'2", 161 lbs. Deb: 7/29/1884 FM♦

YEAR	TM/L	W	L	PCT	G	GS	CG	SH	SV	IP	H	HR	BB	SO	RAT	ERA	ERA+	OAV	OOB	BH	AVG	PB	PR	/A	PD	TPI
1884	StL-a	15	6	.714	25	25	19	2	0	206^2	167	7	36	95	9.2	2.18	150	.212	.255	27	.227	1	25	25	3	2.5
1885	*StL-a	33	14	.702	47	46	46	2	0	407^2	351	8	92	147	10.2	2.63	125	.227	.278	59	.248	5	28	29	7	3.8
1886	*StL-a	**41**	16	**.719**	59	57	55	11	**1**	504	418	5	144	283	10.2	**2.11**	**163**	.216	.274	116	.280	11	**75**	75	2	**8.1**
1887	*StL-a	25	12	.676	40	38	36	1	0	339^1	369	7	90	94	12.4	3.87	117	.258	.306	151	.357	15	16	25	0	3.1
1888	Bro-a	12	7	.632	23	19	19	0	0	176	146	3	35	73	9.5	2.51	119	.218	.262	156	.277	6	11	9	3	1.5
1889	*Bro-a	3	0	1.000	12	4	3	0	0	59^2	70	2	19	21	13.4	4.37	85	.283	.335	152	.275	3	-3	-4	1	0.1
1890	*Bro-N	2	1	.667	5	2	2	0	**2**	29	29	0	6	4	11.2	1.86	185	.252	.295	154	.303	2	6	5	-1	0.6
1891	Bro-N	3	2	.600	6	5	5	0	0	52	51	1	16	14	11.8	3.29	100	.246	.304	134	.257	1	0	0	-0	0.1
1892	Bro-N	13	8	.619	27	20	17	0	1	203	210	3	63	56	12.3	3.41	93	.256	.313	41	.186	0	-3	-6	3	-0.3
1893	Bro-N	0	0	—	6	0	0	0	0	18	28	2	8	3	18.0	7.50	59	.346	.404	137	.246	1	-6	-6	1	0.1
1894	Bro-N	0	0	—	1	0	0	0	0	2	4	0	1	0	22.5	13.50	37	.400	.455	90	.307	0	-2	-2	-0	0.0
Total	11	147	66	.690	251	216	202	16	4	1997^1	1843	38	510	790	10.9	2.84	124	.235	.286	1253	.276	45	147	148	18	19.6

● JESSE FOWLER Fowler, Jesse Peter "Pete" b: 10/30/1898, Spartanburg, S.C. d: 9/23/73, Columbia, S.C. BR/TL, 5'10.5", 158 lbs. Deb: 7/29/24 F

YEAR	TM/L	W	L	PCT	G	GS	CG	SH	SV	IP	H	HR	BB	SO	RAT	ERA	ERA+	OAV	OOB	BH	AVG	PB	PR	/A	PD	TPI
1924	StL-N	1	1	.500	13	3	0	0	0	32^2	28	0	18	5	13.2	4.41	86	.226	.333	2	.222	0	-2	-2	-1	-0.2

● ART FOWLER Fowler, John Arthur b: 7/3/22, Converse, S.C. BR/TR, 5'11", 180 lbs. Deb: 4/17/54 FC

YEAR	TM/L	W	L	PCT	G	GS	CG	SH	SV	IP	H	HR	BB	SO	RAT	ERA	ERA+	OAV	OOB	BH	AVG	PB	PR	/A	PD	TPI
1954	Cin-N	12	10	.545	40	29	8	1	0	227^{2}	256	20	85	93	13.6	3.83	109	.286	.351	6	.100	-1	6	9	-1	0.5
1955	Cin-N	11	10	.524	46	28	8	3	2	207^{2}	198	20	63	94	11.4	3.90	109	.250	.306	12	.200	-0	3	8	-1	0.6
1956	Cin-N	11	11	.500	45	23	8	0	1	177^{2}	191	15	35	86	11.4	4.05	98	.278	.313	7	.146	-0	-6	-1	1	-0.1
1957	Cin-N	3	0	1.000	33	7	1	0	0	87^{2}	111	11	24	45	14.1	6.47	64	.310	.357	3	.176	0	-25	-23	0	-0.7
1959	LA-N	3	4	.429	36	0	0	0	2	61	70	8	23	47	13.7	5.31	80	.294	.356	1	.083	-1	-9	-7	0	-0.9
1961	LA-A	5	8	.385	53	3	0	0	11	89	68	12	29	78	9.8	3.64	124	.209	.274	1	.077	-1	4	9	-1	1.1
1962	LA-A	4	3	.571	48	0	0	0	5	77	67	6	25	38	10.9	2.81	138	.234	.298	3	.273	1	10	9	-0	0.9
1963	LA-A	5	3	.625	57	0	0	0	10	89^{1}	70	5	19	53	9.0	2.42	142	.219	.263	2	.222	0	12	10	-1	1.0
1964	LA-A	0	2	.000	4	0	0	0	1	7	8	2	5	5	18.0	10.29	32	.296	.424	0	.000	-0	-5	-5	0	-1.3
Total	9	54	51	.514	362	90	25	4	32	1024	1039	99	308	539	11.9	4.03	102	.265	.320	35	.152	-2	-10	7	-3	1.1

● DICK FOWLER Fowler, Richard John b: 3/30/21, Toronto, Ont., Can. d: 5/22/72, Oneonta, N.Y. BR/TR, 6'4.5", 215 lbs. Deb: 9/13/41

YEAR	TM/L	W	L	PCT	G	GS	CG	SH	SV	IP	H	HR	BB	SO	RAT	ERA	ERA+	OAV	OOB	BH	AVG	PB	PR	/A	PD	TPI
1941	Phi-A	1	2	.333	4	3	1	0	0	24	26	4	8	8	12.8	3.38	124	.289	.347	0	.000	-1	2	2	-0	0.1
1942	Phi-A	6	11	.353	31	17	4	0	1	140	159	13	45	38	13.1	4.95	76	.287	.341	8	.160	-1	-20	-18	-2	-2.3
1945	Phi-A	1	2	.333	7	3	2	1	0	37^{1}	41	1	18	21	14.2	4.82	71	.283	.362	8	.444	3	-6	-6	-1	-0.1
1946	Phi-A	9	16	.360	32	28	14	1	0	205^{2}	213	16	75	89	12.7	3.28	108	.263	.327	13	.183	-1	5	6	-1	0.5
1947	Phi-A	12	11	.522	36	31	16	3	0	227^{1}	210	12	85	75	11.8	2.81	136	.249	.319	14	.171	-3	23	25	-2	2.0
1948	Phi-A	15	8	.652	29	26	16	2	2	204^{2}	221	15	76	50	13.2	3.78	113	.281	.348	14	.171	-2	12	12	-1	0.8
1949	Phi-A	15	11	.577	31	28	15	4	1	213^{2}	210	13	115	43	13.8	3.75	110	.262	.357	18	.234	3	11	9	1	1.3
1950	Phi-A	1	5	.167	11	9	2	0	0	66^{2}	75	7	56	15	18.1	6.48	70	.300	.434	5	.192	-1	-14	-14	0	-1.1
1951	Phi-A	5	11	.313	22	22	4	0	0	125	141	11	72	29	15.4	5.62	76	.291	.384	8	.190	-0	-21	-19	-1	-2.1
1952	Phi-A	1	2	.333	18	3	1	0	0	58^{2}	71	4	28	14	15.8	6.44	61	.302	.386	0	.000	-2	-18	-16	1	-0.9
Total	10	66	79	.455	221	170	75	11	4	1303	1367	96	578	382	13.6	4.11	97	.273	.351	88	.186	-6	-27	-19	-6	-1.8

● ALAN FOWLKES Fowlkes, Alan Kim b: 8/8/58, Brawley, Cal. BR/TR, 6'2", 190 lbs. Deb: 4/7/82

YEAR	TM/L	W	L	PCT	G	GS	CG	SH	SV	IP	H	HR	BB	SO	RAT	ERA	ERA+	OAV	OOB	BH	AVG	PB	PR	/A	PD	TPI
1982	SF-N	4	2	.667	21	15	1	0	0	85	111	12	24	50	14.8	5.19	69	.321	.373	3	.115	-1	-15	-15	-0	-1.1
1985	Cal-A	0	0	—	2	0	0	0	0	7	8	4	4	5	15.4	9.00	46	.276	.364	0	—	0	-4	-4	0	0.0
Total	2	4	2	.667	23	15	1	0	0	92	119	16	28	55	14.9	5.48	66	.317	.373	3	.115	-1	-19	-19	-0	-1.1

● CHAD FOX Fox, Chad Douglas b: 9/3/70, Coronado, Cal. BR/TR, 6'3", 175 lbs. Deb: 7/13/97

YEAR	TM/L	W	L	PCT	G	GS	CG	SH	SV	IP	H	HR	BB	SO	RAT	ERA	ERA+	OAV	OOB	BH	AVG	PB	PR	/A	PD	TPI
1997	Atl-N	0	1	.000	30	0	0	0	0	27^{1}	24	4	16	28	13.2	3.29	127	.231	.333	0	—	0	3	3	-1	0.0
1998	Mil-N	1	4	.200	49	0	0	0	0	57	56	4	20	64	12.2	3.95	109	.260	.326	0	.000	-0	2	2	-0	0.1
Total	2	1	5	.167	79	0	0	0	0	84^{1}	80	8	36	92	12.5	3.74	114	.251	.329	0	.000	-0	5	5	-1	0.1

● HENRY FOX Fox, Henry (b: Henry Fuchs) b: 11/18/1874, Scranton, Pa. d: 6/6/27, Scranton, Pa. Deb: 9/4/02

YEAR	TM/L	W	L	PCT	G	GS	CG	SH	SV	IP	H	HR	BB	SO	RAT	ERA	ERA+	OAV	OOB	BH	AVG	PB	PR	/A	PD	TPI
1902	Phi-N	0	0	—	1	0	0	0	1	1	2	0	1	1	27.0	18.00	16	.400	.500	0	—	0	-2	-2	0	-0.3

● HOWIE FOX Fox, Howard Francis b: 3/1/21, Coburg, Ore. d: 10/9/55, San Antonio, Tex. BR/TR, 6'3", 210 lbs. Deb: 9/28/44

YEAR	TM/L	W	L	PCT	G	GS	CG	SH	SV	IP	H	HR	BB	SO	RAT	ERA	ERA+	OAV	OOB	BH	AVG	PB	PR	/A	PD	TPI
1944	Cin-N	0	0	—	2	0	0	0	0	2^{1}	2	0	0	0	7.7	0.00	—	.222	.222	0	.000	-0	1	1	-0	0.0
1945	Cin-N	8	13	.381	45	15	7	0	0	164^{1}	169	6	77	54	13.8	4.93	76	.268	.353	13	.283	3	-21	-21	4	-1.7
1946	Cin-N	0	0	—	4	0	0	0	0	5	12	2	5	1	30.6	18.00	19	.462	.548	0	—	0	-8	-8	0	0.0
1948	Cin-N	6	9	.400	34	24	5	0	1	171	185	11	62	63	13.1	4.53	86	.280	.343	12	.200	1	-11	-12	1	-0.7
1949	Cin-N	6	19	.240	38	30	9	0	0	215	221	13	77	60	12.6	3.98	105	.265	.330	17	.236	2	2	5	6	1.3
1950	Cin-N	11	8	.579	34	22	10	1	1	187	196	14	85	64	13.6	4.33	98	.269	.347	11	.175	-0	-4	-2	3	0.1
1951	Cin-N	9	14	.391	40	30	9	4	2	228	239	15	69	57	12.2	3.83	107	.272	.326	8	.114	-2	3	6	1	0.4
1952	Phi-N	2	7	.222	13	11	2	0	0	62	70	8	26	16	13.9	5.08	72	.287	.356	1	.048	-2	-9	-10	1	-1.3
1954	Bal-A	1	2	.333	38	0	0	0	2	73^{2}	80	2	34	27	14.2	3.67	98	.289	.371	4	.250	1	0	-1	1	0.2
Total	9	43	72	.374	248	132	42	5	6	1108^{1}	1174	71	435	342	13.2	4.33	92	.274	.343	66	.189	2	-46	-42	17	-1.7

● JOHN FOX Fox, John Joseph b: 2/7/1859, Roxbury, Mass. d: 4/18/1893, Boston, Mass. Deb: 6/2/1881

YEAR	TM/L	W	L	PCT	G	GS	CG	SH	SV	IP	H	HR	BB	SO	RAT	ERA	ERA+	OAV	OOB	BH	AVG	PB	PR	/A	PD	TPI
1881	Bos-N	6	8	.429	17	16	12	0	0	124^{1}	144	0	39	30	13.2	3.33	80	.279	.329	21	.178	-4	-8	-9	1	-1.1
1883	Bal-a	6	13	.316	20	19	18	0	0	165^{1}	209	2	32	49	13.1	4.03	86	.289	.320	14	.152	-4	-13	-10	-1	-1.3
1884	Pit-a	1	6	.143	7	7	7	0	0	59	76	2	16	22	14.5	5.64	60	.291	.339	6	.240	0	-16	-15	1	-1.2
1886	Was-N	0	1	.000	1	1	1	0	0	8	11	0	11	3	24.8	9.00	37	.314	.478	1	.333	0	-5	-5	0	-0.4
Total	4	13	28	.317	45	43	38	0	0	356^{2}	440	4	98	104	13.7	4.16	76	.287	.331	42	.176	-8	-42	-40	0	-4.0

● TERRY FOX Fox, Terrence Edward b: 7/31/35, Chicago, Ill. BR/TR, 6', 175 lbs. Deb: 9/4/60

YEAR	TM/L	W	L	PCT	G	GS	CG	SH	SV	IP	H	HR	BB	SO	RAT	ERA	ERA+	OAV	OOB	BH	AVG	PB	PR	/A	PD	TPI
1960	Mil-N	0	0	—	5	0	0	0	0	8^{1}	6	0	6	5	13.0	4.32	79	.200	.333	0	.000	-0	-1	-1	-0	0.0
1961	Det-A	5	2	.714	39	0	0	0	12	57^{1}	42	6	16	32	9.6	1.41	290	.200	.266	2	.167	-0	17	17	1	2.8
1962	Det-A	3	1	.750	44	0	0	0	16	58	48	2	16	23	10.1	1.71	238	.227	.285	2	.250	2	15	15	0	2.1
1963	Det-A	8	6	.571	46	0	0	0	11	80^{1}	81	9	20	35	11.5	3.59	104	.263	.312	1	.091	-0	0	1	0	0.3
1964	Det-A	4	3	.571	32	0	0	0	5	61	77	4	16	28	13.9	3.39	108	.316	.360	3	.250	1	2	2	1	0.4
1965	Det-A	6	4	.600	42	0	0	0	10	77^{2}	59	7	31	34	10.8	2.78	125	.214	.300	0	.000	-1	6	6	2	1.0
1966	Det-A	0	1	.000	4	0	0	0	1	10	9	3	2	6	9.9	6.30	55	.243	.282	0	.000	-0	-3	-3	-0	-0.3
	Phi-N	3	2	.600	36	0	0	0	4	44^{1}	57	3	17	22	15.4	4.47	80	.322	.388	0	.000	-0	-4	-4	-0	-0.6
Total	7	29	19	.604	248	0	0	0	59	397	379	34	124	185	11.7	2.99	125	.254	.316	8	.123	1	31	33	4	5.7

● BILL FOXEN Foxen, William Aloysius b: 5/31/1884, Tenafly, N.J. d: 4/17/37, Brooklyn, N.Y. BL/TL, 5'11.5", 165 lbs. Deb: 5/5/08

YEAR	TM/L	W	L	PCT	G	GS	CG	SH	SV	IP	H	HR	BB	SO	RAT	ERA	ERA+	OAV	OOB	BH	AVG	PB	PR	/A	PD	TPI
1908	Phi-N	7	7	.500	22	16	10	2	0	147^{1}	126	2	53	52	11.4	1.95	124	.240	.319	5	.094	-3	7	8	2	0.6
1909	Phi-N	3	7	.300	18	7	5	1	0	83^{1}	65	0	32	37	10.9	3.35	78	.219	.303	5	.208	3	-7	-7	4	0.0
1910	Phi-N	5	5	.500	16	9	5	0	0	77^{2}	73	2	40	33	13.4	2.55	123	.268	.368	4	.174	-1	4	5	2	0.7
	Chi-N	0	0	—	2	0	0	0	0	5	7	0	3	2	18.0	9.00	32	.350	.435	0	.000	-0	-3	-3	-0	0.0
	Yr	5	5	.500	18	9	5	0	0	82^{2}	80	2	43	35	13.4	2.94	106	.271	.364	4	.160	-1	1	2	1	0.7
1911	Chi-N	1	1	.500	3	1	0	0	0	13	12	0	12	6	16.6	2.08	159	.255	.407	1	.250	1	2	2	1	0.4
Total	4	16	20	.444	61	33	20	3	0	326^{1}	283	4	140	130	12.1	2.56	104	.244	.333	15	.142	0	3	4	8	1.7

● JIMMIE FOXX Foxx, James Emory "Beast" or "Double X" b: 10/22/07, Sudlersville, Md. d: 7/21/67, Miami, Fla. BR/TR, 6', 195 lbs. Deb: 5/1/25 CH♦

YEAR	TM/L	W	L	PCT	G	GS	CG	SH	SV	IP	H	HR	BB	SO	RAT	ERA	ERA+	OAV	OOB	BH	AVG	PB	PR	/A	PD	TPI
1939	Bos-A☆	0	0	—	1	0	0	0	0	1	0	0	0	1	0.0	0.00	—	.000	.000	168	.360	1	1	1	0	0.0
1945	Phi-N	1	0	1.000	9	2	0	0	0	22^{2}	13	0	14	10	11.1	1.59	241	.171	.308	60	.268	2	6	6	-1	0.3
Total	2	1	0	1.000	10	2	0	0	0	23^{2}	13	0	14	11	10.6	1.52	254	.165	.298	2646	.325	3	6	6	-1	0.3

● PAUL FOYTACK Foytack, Paul Eugene b: 11/16/30, Scranton, Pa. BR/TR, 5'11", 180 lbs. Deb: 4/21/53

YEAR	TM/L	W	L	PCT	G	GS	CG	SH	SV	IP	H	HR	BB	SO	RAT	ERA	ERA+	OAV	OOB	BH	AVG	PB	PR	/A	PD	TPI
1953	Det-A	0	0	—	6	0	0	0	0	9^{2}	15	1	9	7	23.3	11.17	36	.375	.500	0	.000	-0	-8	-8	-0	0.0
1955	Det-A	0	1	.000	22	1	0	0	0	49^{2}	48	4	36	38	15.2	5.26	73	.259	.380	1	.091	-1	-7	-8	-0	-0.2
1956	Det-A	15	13	.536	43	33	16	1	1	256	211	24	142	184	12.5	3.59	115	.226	.330	11	.122	-6	16	15	-1	0.8
1957	Det-A	14	11	.560	38	27	8	1	1	212	175	19	104	118	12.0	3.14	123	.226	.321	14	.222	1	15	17	-2	1.7
1958	Det-A	15	13	.536	39	33	16	2	1	230	198	23	77	135	10.9	3.44	117	.233	.299	18	.240	2	8	15	-2	1.8
1959	Det-A	14	14	.500	39	37	11	2	1	240^{1}	239	34	64	110	11.4	4.64	87	.259	.308	9	.111	-4	-21	-16	-2	-2.1
1960	Det-A	2	11	.154	28	13	1	0	2	96^{2}	108	11	49	38	14.6	6.14	64	.286	.369	7	.280	2	-24	-23	-2	-2.8
1961	Det-A	11	10	.524	32	20	6	0	0	169^{2}	152	27	56	89	11.1	3.93	104	.238	.301	12	.222	2	2	3	-3	0.2
1962	Det-A	10	7	.588	29	21	5	1	0	143^{2}	145	18	86	63	14.5	4.39	93	.259	.359	6	.143	-1	-7	-5	0	-0.6
1963	Det-A	0	1	.000	9	0	0	0	1	17^{2}	18	4	8	7	13.2	8.66	43	.265	.342	0	.000	-0	-10	-10	-0	-0.7
	LA-A	5	5	.500	25	8	0	0	0	70^{1}	68	9	29	37	12.4	3.71	92	.255	.328	4	.267	1	-1	-2	-1	-0.2
	Yr	5	6	.455	34	8	0	0	1	88	86	13	37	44	12.6	4.70	74	.256	.330	4	.211	1	-11	-12	-1	-0.9
1964	LA-A	0	1	.000	2	0	0	0	0	2^{1}	4	2	2	1	23.1	15.43	21	.364	.462	0	—	0	-3	-3	-0	-1.0
Total	11	86	87	.497	312	193	63	7	7	1498	1381	176	662	827	12.4	4.14	97	.246	.327	82	.178	-3	-39	-24	-13	-3.1

● KEN FRAILING Frailing, Kenneth Douglas b: 1/19/48, Marion, Wis. BL/TL, 6', 190 lbs. Deb: 9/1/72

YEAR	TM/L	W	L	PCT	G	GS	CG	SH	SV	IP	H	HR	BB	SO	RAT	ERA	ERA+	OAV	OOB	BH	AVG	PB	PR	/A	PD	TPI
1972	Chi-A	1	0	1.000	4	0	0	0	0	3	3	1	1	1	12.0	3.00	104	.250	.308	0	—	0	0	0	0	0.0
1973	Chi-A	0	0	—	10	0	0	0	0	18^{1}	18	1	7	15	12.8	1.96	202	.254	.329	0	—	0	4	4	-0	-0.2

YEAR	TM/L	W	L	PCT	G	GS	CG	SH	SV	IP	H	HR	BB	SO	RAT	ERA	ERA+	OAV	OOB	BH	AVG	PB	PR	/A	PD	TPI
1974	Chi-N	6	9	.400	55	16	1	0	1	125^1	150	11	43	71	13.9	3.88	98	.296	.353	8	.258	1	-4	-1	0	0.0
1975	Chi-N	2	5	.286	41	0	0	0	1	53	61	6	26	39	15.1	5.43	71	.293	.377	1	.143	0	-11	-9	2	-1.0
1976	Chi-N	1	2	.333	6	3	0	0	0	18^2	20	0	5	10	12.1	2.41	160	.274	.321	0	.000	-0	2	3	0	0.4
Total	5	10	16	.385	116	19	1	0	2	218^1	252	19	82	136	13.9	3.96	97	.290	.354	9	.220	1	-8	-3	2	-0.8

● OSSIE FRANCE France, Osman Beverly "O. B." b: 10/4/1858, Greensburg, Ohio d: 5/2/47, Akron, Ohio BL/TL, 5'8", 155 lbs. Deb: 7/14/1890

YEAR	TM/L	W	L	PCT	G	GS	CG	SH	SV	IP	H	HR	BB	SO	RAT	ERA	ERA+	OAV	OOB	BH	AVG	PB	PR	/A	PD	TPI
1890	Chi-N	0	0	—	1	0	0	0	0	2	3	0	2	0	22.5	13.50	27	.333	.455	0	.000	-0	-2	-2	-0	0.0

● EARL FRANCIS Francis, Earl Coleman b: 7/14/35, Slab Fork, W.Va. BR/TR, 6'2", 215 lbs. Deb: 6/30/60

YEAR	TM/L	W	L	PCT	G	GS	CG	SH	SV	IP	H	HR	BB	SO	RAT	ERA	ERA+	OAV	OOB	BH	AVG	PB	PR	/A	PD	TPI
1960	Pit-N	1	0	1.000	7	0	0	0	0	18	14	0	4	8	9.5	2.00	188	.222	.279	0	.000	-1	4	4	-0	0.1
1961	Pit-N	2	8	.200	23	15	0	0	0	102^2	110	4	47	53	13.9	4.21	95	.274	.351	3	.107	-1	-2	-3	0	-0.2
1962	Pit-N	9	8	.529	36	23	5	1	0	176	153	8	83	121	12.2	3.07	128	.235	.323	10	.164	1	17	17	1	1.7
1963	Pit-N	4	6	.400	33	13	0	0	0	97^1	107	6	43	72	14.2	4.53	73	.284	.363	8	.308	3	-13	-13	0	-1.0
1964	Pit-N	0	1	.000	2	1	0	0	0	6^1	7	2	1	6	12.8	8.53	41	.269	.321	0	.000	-0	-4	-4	-0	-0.5
1965	StL-N	0	0	—	2	0	0	0	0	5^1	7	1	3	3	16.9	5.06	76	.318	.400	0	.000	-0	-1	-1	-0	0.0
Total	6	16	23	.410	103	52	5	1	0	405^2	398	21	181	263	13.0	3.77	100	.258	.340	21	.172	2	1	0	1	0.1

● RAY FRANCIS Francis, Ray James b: 3/8/1893, Sherman, Tex. d: 7/6/34, Atlanta, Ga. BL/TL, 6'1.5", 182 lbs. Deb: 4/18/22

YEAR	TM/L	W	L	PCT	G	GS	CG	SH	SV	IP	H	HR	BB	SO	RAT	ERA	ERA+	OAV	OOB	BH	AVG	PB	PR	/A	PD	TPI
1922	Was-A	7	18	.280	39	26	15	2	2	225	265	7	66	64	13.5	4.28	90	.303	.356	13	.167	-2	-6	-10	-1	-1.3
1923	Det-A	5	8	.385	33	6	0	0	1	79^1	95	2	28	27	14.4	4.42	87	.308	.374	3	.143	-2	-4	-5	-0	-0.9
1925	NY-A	0	0	—	4	0	0	0	0	4^2	5	0	3	1	17.4	7.71	55	.278	.409	0	—	0	-2	-2	-0	0.0
	Bos-A	0	2	.000	6	4	0	0	0	28	44	3	13	4	18.6	7.71	59	.373	.439	1	.125	-0	-10	-10	0	-0.6
	Yr	0	2	.000	10	4	0	0	0	32^2	49	3	16	5	18.2	7.71	58	.358	.429	1	.125	-0	-12	-12	-0	-0.6
Total	3	12	28	.300	82	36	15	2	3	337	409	12	110	96	14.2	4.65	84	.310	.368	17	.159	-4	-22	-27	-1	-2.8

● JOHN FRANCO Franco, John Anthony b: 9/17/60, Brooklyn, N.Y. BL/TL, 5'10", 185 lbs. Deb: 4/24/84

YEAR	TM/L	W	L	PCT	G	GS	CG	SH	SV	IP	H	HR	BB	SO	RAT	ERA	ERA+	OAV	OOB	BH	AVG	PB	PR	/A	PD	TPI
1984	Cin-N	6	2	.750	54	0	0	0	4	79^1	74	3	36	55	12.7	2.61	145	.256	.343	0	.000	-0	9	10	1	1.1
1985	Cin-N	12	3	.800	67	0	0	0	12	99	83	5	40	61	11.3	2.18	173	.234	.314	2	.333	0	16	**18**	2	3.3
1986	Cin-N☆	6	6	.500	74	0	0	0	29	101	90	7	44	84	12.1	2.94	132	.242	.325	0	.000	-0	9	10	1	1.8
1987	Cin-N★	8	5	.615	68	0	0	0	32	82	76	6	27	61	11.3	2.52	168	.245	.306	0	.000	-0	14	16	-1	3.3
1988	Cin-N	6	6	.500	70	0	0	0	**39**	86	60	3	27	46	9.1	1.57	228	.198	.264	0	.000	-0	**18**	**19**	1	**4.5**
1989	Cin-N☆	4	8	.333	60	0	0	0	32	80^2	77	3	36	60	12.6	3.12	115	.258	.337	1	.333	0	3	4	1	1.1
1990	NY-N★	5	3	.625	55	0	0	0	**33**	67^2	66	4	21	56	11.6	2.53	148	.252	.307	0	.000	-1	10	9	1	1.9
1991	NY-N	5	9	.357	52	0	0	0	30	55^1	61	2	18	45	13.0	2.93	124	.271	.328	0	.000	-0	5	4	1	1.5
1992	NY-N	6	2	.750	31	0	0	0	15	33	24	1	11	20	9.5	1.64	212	.209	.278	0	.000	-0	7	7	2	2.4
1993	NY-N	4	3	.571	35	0	0	0	10	36^1	46	6	19	29	16.3	5.20	77	.313	.395	0	.000	-0	-5	-5	1	-1.0
1994	NY-N	1	4	.200	47	0	0	0	**30**	50	47	2	19	42	12.1	2.70	155	.244	.315	0	.000	-0	8	8	0	1.6
1995	NY-N	5	3	.625	48	0	0	0	29	51^2	48	4	17	41	11.3	2.44	166	.251	.313	0	—	0	10	9	0	2.3
1996	NY-N	4	3	.571	51	0	0	0	28	54	54	2	21	48	12.5	1.83	219	.260	.328	0	.000	-0	14	13	0	2.7
1997	NY-N	5	3	.625	59	0	0	0	36	60	49	3	20	53	10.5	2.55	158	.226	.294	0	—	0	11	10	1	2.4
1998	NY-N	0	8	.000	61	0	0	0	38	64^2	66	4	29	59	13.8	3.62	115	.267	.354	0	.000	-0	4	4	2	1.0
Total	15	77	68	.531	832	0	0	0	397	1000^2	921	55	385	760	11.9	2.64	147	.247	.319	3	.091	-2	133	138	12	29.9

● TERRY FRANCONA Francona, Terry Jon b: 4/22/59, Aberdeen, S.D. BL/TL, 6'1", 190 lbs. Deb: 8/19/81 FMC♦

YEAR	TM/L	W	L	PCT	G	GS	CG	SH	SV	IP	H	HR	BB	SO	RAT	ERA	ERA+	OAV	OOB	BH	AVG	PB	PR	/A	PD	TPI
1989	Mil-A	0	0	—	1	0	0	0	0	1	0	0	0	1	0.0	0.00	—	.000	.000	54	.232	0	0	0	0	0.0

● CHARLIE FRANK Frank, Charles b: 5/30/1870, Mobile, Ala. d: 5/24/22, Memphis, Tenn. 5'10", 170 lbs. Deb: 8/18/1893 ♦

YEAR	TM/L	W	L	PCT	G	GS	CG	SH	SV	IP	H	HR	BB	SO	RAT	ERA	ERA+	OAV	OOB	BH	AVG	PB	PR	/A	PD	TPI
1894	StL-N	0	0	—	2	0	0	0	0	3	6	1	7	1	39.0	15.00	36	.400	.591	89	.279	0	-3	-3	-0	0.0

● FRED FRANKHOUSE Frankhouse, Frederick Meloy b: 4/9/04, Port Royal, Pa. d: 8/17/89, Port Royal, Pa. BR/TR, 5'11", 175 lbs. Deb: 9/11/27

YEAR	TM/L	W	L	PCT	G	GS	CG	SH	SV	IP	H	HR	BB	SO	RAT	ERA	ERA+	OAV	OOB	BH	AVG	PB	PR	/A	PD	TPI
1927	StL-N	5	1	.833	6	6	5	1	0	50	41	2	16	20	10.4	2.70	146	.218	.283	5	.250	0	7	7	-1	0.7
1928	StL-N	3	2	.600	21	10	1	0	1	84	91	6	36	29	14.1	3.96	101	.277	.358	5	.185	1	0	0	1	0.2
1929	StL-N	7	2	.778	30	12	6	0	1	133^1	149	9	43	37	13.2	4.12	113	.289	.349	15	.288	4	9	8	3	1.0
1930	StL-N	2	3	.400	8	1	0	0	0	19^2	31	1	11	4	19.2	7.32	69	.373	.447	0	.000	-1	-5	-5	0	-1.0
	Bos-N	7	6	.538	27	11	3	1	0	110^2	138	13	43	30	14.9	5.61	88	.313	.377	14	.359	4	-8	-8	-0	-0.4
	Yr	9	9	.500	35	12	3	1	0	130^1	169	14	54	34	15.5	5.87	84	.323	.388	14	.318	3	-13	-13	0	-1.4
1931	Bos-N	8	8	.500	26	15	6	0	1	127^1	125	4	43	50	12.1	4.03	94	.252	.315	6	.150	-0	-2	-3	1	-0.3
1932	Bos-N	4	6	.400	37	6	3	0	0	108^2	113	7	45	35	13.3	3.56	106	.278	.355	3	.100	-1	4	2	3	0.4
1933	Bos-N	16	15	.516	43	30	14	2	2	244^2	249	12	77	83	12.1	3.16	97	.267	.324	19	.237	4	5	-3	4	0.5
1934	Bos-N★	17	9	.654	37	31	13	2	1	233^2	239	10	77	78	12.3	3.20	120	.262	.322	17	.200	2	22	16	-0	1.8
1935	Bos-N	11	15	.423	40	29	10	1	0	230^2	278	12	81	64	14.2	4.76	80	.293	.352	20	.263	6	-19	-25	3	-1.4
1936	Bro-N	13	10	.565	41	31	9	1	2	234^1	236	18	89	84	12.6	3.65	113	.257	.325	13	.143	-4	10	13	1	0.8
1937	Bro-N	10	13	.435	33	25	9	1	0	179^1	214	8	78	64	14.9	4.27	95	.297	.369	11	.190	-0	-7	-5	3	-0.3
1938	Bro-N	3	5	.375	30	8	2	1	0	93^2	92	6	44	32	13.5	4.04	97	.256	.344	4	.154	-1	-3	-1	1	-0.1
1939	Bos-N	0	2	.000	23	0	0	0	4	38	37	3	18	12	13.3	2.61	142	.253	.339	0	.000	-1	6	5	-1	0.2
Total	13	106	97	.522	402	215	81	10	12	1888	2033	111	701	622	13.2	3.92	100	.275	.341	132	.208	12	18	-0	18	2.1

● JACK FRANKLIN Franklin, Jack Wilford b: 10/20/19, Paris, Ill. d: 11/15/91, Panama City, Fla. BR/TR, 5'11.5", 170 lbs. Deb: 6/12/44

YEAR	TM/L	W	L	PCT	G	GS	CG	SH	SV	IP	H	HR	BB	SO	RAT	ERA	ERA+	OAV	OOB	BH	AVG	PB	PR	/A	PD	TPI
1944	Bro-N	0	0	—	1	0	0	0	0	2	2	1	4	0	36.0	13.50	26	.250	.571	0	—	0	-2	-2	-0	0.0

● JAY FRANKLIN Franklin, John William b: 3/16/53, Arlington, Va. BR/TR, 6'2", 180 lbs. Deb: 9/4/71

YEAR	TM/L	W	L	PCT	G	GS	CG	SH	SV	IP	H	HR	BB	SO	RAT	ERA	ERA+	OAV	OOB	BH	AVG	PB	PR	/A	PD	TPI
1971	SD-N	0	1	.000	3	1	0	0	0	5^2	5	3	4	4	14.3	6.35	52	.250	.375	0	.000	-0	-2	-2	0	-0.3

● JOHN FRASCATORE Frascatore, John Vincent b: 2/4/70, Ozone Park, N.Y. BR/TR, 6'1", 200 lbs. Deb: 7/21/94

YEAR	TM/L	W	L	PCT	G	GS	CG	SH	SV	IP	H	HR	BB	SO	RAT	ERA	ERA+	OAV	OOB	BH	AVG	PB	PR	/A	PD	TPI
1994	StL-N	0	1	.000	1	1	0	0	0	3^1	7	2	2	2	24.3	16.20	26	.438	.500	0	.000	-0	-4	-4	0	-0.8
1995	StL-N	1	1	.500	14	4	0	0	0	32^2	39	3	16	21	15.7	4.41	95	.298	.383	0	.000	-0	-1	-1	-1	-0.1
1997	StL-N	5	2	.714	59	0	0	0	0	80	74	5	33	58	12.7	2.47	167	.247	.334	0	.000	-0	15	15	-1	1.0
1998	StL-N	3	4	.429	69	0	0	0	0	95^2	95	11	36	49	12.6	4.14	101	.256	.327	1	.167	-0	1	0	-1	0.0
Total	4	9	8	.529	143	5	0	0	0	211^2	215	21	87	130	13.3	3.74	111	.263	.342	1	.059	-1	11	10	-2	0.1

● CHICK FRASER Fraser, Charles Carrolton b: 3/17/1871, Chicago, Ill. d: 5/8/40, Wendell, Idaho BR/TR, 5'10.5", 188 lbs. Deb: 4/19/1896 C

YEAR	TM/L	W	L	PCT	G	GS	CG	SH	SV	IP	H	HR	BB	SO	RAT	ERA	ERA+	OAV	OOB	BH	AVG	PB	PR	/A	PD	TPI
1896	Lou-N	12	27	.308	43	38	36	0	1	349^1	396	9	166	91	15.2	4.87	89	.283	.371	22	.151	-9	-20	-21	3	-2.2
1897	Lou-N	15	19	.441	35	34	32	0	0	286^1	332	11	133	70	15.3	4.09	104	.288	.372	18	.161	-4	7	6	6	0.7
1898	Lou-N	7	17	.292	26	26	20	1	0	203	230	4	100	58	15.7	5.32	67	.283	.378	13	.167	-2	-39	-39	4	-3.5
	Cle-N	2	3	.400	6	6	6	0	0	42	49	2	12	19	14.4	5.57	65	.290	.358	4	.250	0	-9	-9	0	-0.8
	Yr	9	20	.310	32	32	26	1	0	245	279	6	112	77	14.6	5.36	67	.278	.354	17	.181	-2	-48	-48	4	-4.3
1899	Phi-N	21	12	.636	35	33	29	4	0	270^2	278	1	85	68	12.8	3.36	110	.265	.333	21	.179	-2	15	10	2	1.0
1900	Phi-N	15	9	.625	29	26	22	1	0	223^1	250	7	93	58	14.3	3.14	115	.282	.358	22	.259	4	14	12	3	1.7
1901	Phi-A	22	16	.579	40	37	35	2	0	331	344	6	132	110	13.8	3.81	99	.265	.347	26	.187	-3	-5	-1	2	-0.3
1902	Phi-N	12	13	.480	27	26	24	3	0	224	238	2	74	97	13.1	3.42	82	.272	.339	15	.174	0	-16	-15	-0	-1.5
1903	Phi-N	12	17	.414	31	29	26	1	1	250	260	8	97	104	13.4	4.50	73	.267	.344	19	.204	4	-34	-34	2	-2.7
1904	Phi-N	14	24	.368	42	36	32	2	1	302	287	5	100	127	11.9	3.25	82	.246	.311	17	.155	-1	-17	-19	2	-2.1
1905	Bos-N	14	21	.400	39	37	35	2	0	334^1	320	8	149	130	13.0	3.28	94	.254	.340	35	.224	3	-10	-7	-1	-0.3
1906	Cin-N	10	20	.333	31	28	25	2	0	236	221	1	80	58	11.8	2.67	103	.259	.329	14	.171	-1	-1	2	1	0.2
1907	Chi-N	8	5	.615	22	15	9	2	1	138^1	112	1	46	41	10.5	2.28	110	.229	.299	3	.067	-3	3	3	0	0.0
1908	Chi-N	11	9	.550	26	17	11	2	2	162^2	141	4	61	66	11.5	2.27	104	.244	.323	6	.120	-2	2	2	4	0.4
1909	Chi-N	0	0	—	1	0	0	0	0	3	2	0	4	1	18.0	0.00	—	.222	.462	0	.000	-0	1	1	-0	0.0
Total	14	175	212	.452	433	388	342	22	6	3356	3460	69	1332	1098	13.4	3.68	92	.267	.345	235	.179	-15	-109	-108	29	-9.4

● WILLIE FRASER Fraser, William Patrick b: 5/26/64, New York, N.Y. BR/TR, 6'1", 206 lbs. Deb: 9/10/86

YEAR	TM/L	W	L	PCT	G	GS	CG	SH	SV	IP	H	HR	BB	SO	RAT	ERA	ERA+	OAV	OOB	BH	AVG	PB	PR	/A	PD	TPI
1986	Cal-A	0	0	—	1	1	0	0	0	4^1	6	0	1	2	14.5	8.31	49	.353	.389	0	—	0	-2	-2	-0	0.1
1987	Cal-A	10	10	.500	36	23	5	1	1	176^2	160	26	63	106	11.7	3.92	110	.240	.312	0	—	0	10	7	-3	0.7

YEAR	TM/L	W	L	PCT	G	GS	CG	SH	SV	IP	H	HR	BB	SO	RAT	ERA	ERA+	OAV	OOB	BH	AVG	PB	PR	/A	PD	TPI
1988	Cal-A	12	13	.480	34	32	2	0	0	194^2	203	33	80	86	13.5	5.41	71	.267	.344	0	—	0	-31	-34	-1	-3.7
1989	Cal-A	4	7	.364	44	0	0	0	2	91^2	80	6	23	46	10.6	3.24	118	.235	.293	0	—	0	7	6	0	0.7
1990	Cal-A	5	4	.556	45	0	0	0	2	76	69	4	24	32	11.0	3.08	124	.241	.300	0	—	0	7	6	-1	0.6
1991	Tor-A	0	2	.000	13	1	0	0	0	26^1	33	4	11	12	16.1	6.15	68	.303	.382	0	—	0	-6	-6	-0	-0.7
	StL-N	3	3	.500	35	0	0	0	0	49^1	44	9	21	25	12.4	4.93	75	.242	.330	0	.000	-0	-7	-7	-1	-0.9
1994	Fla-N	2	0	1.000	9	0	0	0	0	12^1	20	1	6	7	19.0	5.84	75	.370	.433	0	—	0	-2	-2	-0	-0.3
1995	Mon-N	2	1	.667	22	0	0	0	2	25^2	25	6	9	12	13.0	5.61	76	.248	.327	0	.000	-0	-4	-4	-0	-0.5
Total	8	38	40	.487	239	57	7	1	7	657	640	89	238	328	12.4	4.47	90	.254	.326	0	.000	-0	-28	-34	-6	-4.0

● VIC FRASIER Frasier, Victor Patrick b: 8/5/04, Ruston, La. d: 1/10/77, Jacksonville, Tex. BR/TR, 6', 182 lbs. Deb: 4/18/31

YEAR	TM/L	W	L	PCT	G	GS	CG	SH	SV	IP	H	HR	BB	SO	RAT	ERA	ERA+	OAV	OOB	BH	AVG	PB	PR	/A	PD	TPI
1931	Chi-A	13	15	.464	46	29	13	2	4	254	258	11	127	87	13.8	4.46	95	.259	.345	18	.209	1	-2	-6	-1	-0.6
1932	Chi-A	3	13	.188	29	21	4	0	0	146	180	14	70	33	15.7	6.23	69	.297	.374	4	.091	-3	-28	-31	2	-2.8
1933	Chi-A	1	1	.500	10	1	0	0	0	20^1	32	2	11	4	19.0	8.85	48	.368	.439	0	.000	-1	-10	-10	1	-0.8
	Det-A	5	5	.500	20	14	4	0	0	104^1	129	9	59	26	16.3	6.64	65	.312	.399	7	.189	-0	-27	-27	0	-2.1
	Yr	6	6	.500	30	15	4	0	0	124^2	161	11	70	30	16.7	7.00	61	.321	.406	7	.171	-1	-38	-37	2	-2.9
1934	Det-A	1	3	.250	8	2	0	0	0	22^2	30	0	12	11	17.1	5.96	74	.313	.394	2	.286	0	-4	-4	2	-0.4
1937	Bos-N	0	0	—	3	0	0	0	0	8	12	1	1	2	14.6	5.63	64	.364	.382	0	.000	-0	-2	-2	0	0.0
1939	Chi-A	0	1	.000	10	1	0	0	0	23^2	45	0	11	7	21.3	10.27	46	.405	.459	2	.286	0	-15	-15	0	-0.5
Total	6	23	38	.377	126	68	21	2	4	579	686	37	291	170	15.4	5.77	75	.293	.373	33	.177	-3	-88	-94	4	-7.2

● GEORGE FRAZIER Frazier, George Allen b: 10/13/54, Oklahoma City, Okla BR/TR, 6'5", 205 lbs. Deb: 5/25/78

YEAR	TM/L	W	L	PCT	G	GS	CG	SH	SV	IP	H	HR	BB	SO	RAT	ERA	ERA+	OAV	OOB	BH	AVG	PB	PR	/A	PD	TPI
1978	StL-N	0	3	.000	14	0	0	0	0	22	22	2	6	8	11.5	4.09	86	.250	.298	1	.333	0	-1	-1	0	-0.2
1979	StL-N	2	4	.333	25	0	0	0	0	32^1	35	3	12	14	13.4	4.45	84	.278	.345	0	.000	-0	-3	-2	-0	-0.4
1980	StL-N	1	4	.200	22	0	0	0	3	23	24	2	7	11	12.1	2.74	135	.273	.326	0	—	0	2	2	0	0.6
1981	*NY-A	0	1	.000	16	0	0	0	3	27^2	26	1	11	17	12.0	1.63	220	.245	.316	0	—	0	6	6	-0	0.4
1982	NY-A	4	4	.500	63	0	0	0	1	111^2	103	7	39	69	11.8	3.47	115	.252	.325	0	—	0	8	6	0	0.5
1983	NY-A	4	4	.500	61	0	0	0	8	115^1	94	5	45	78	11.1	3.43	113	.227	.307	0	—	0	8	6	0	0.7
1984	Cle-A	3	2	.600	22	0	0	0	1	44^1	45	3	14	24	12.0	3.65	112	.259	.314	0	—	0	2	2	-1	0.0
	*Chi-N	6	3	.667	37	0	0	0	3	63^2	53	4	26	58	11.3	4.10	95	.221	.300	2	.286	0	-4	-1	-1	-0.3
1985	Chi-N	7	8	.467	51	0	0	0	2	76	88	11	52	46	16.9	6.39	62	.299	.410	0	.000	-1	-24	-20	-0	-3.8
1986	Chi-N	2	4	.333	35	0	0	0	0	51^2	63	5	34	41	17.1	5.40	75	.310	.412	0	.000	-0	-10	-8	-1	-1.0
	Min-A	1	1	.500	15	0	0	0	6	26^2	23	2	16	25	13.2	4.39	98	.232	.339	0	—	0	-1	-0	0	-0.2
1987	*Min-A	5	5	.500	54	0	0	0	2	81^1	77	9	51	58	14.4	4.98	93	.258	.369	0	—	0	-5	-3	-1	-0.7
Total	10	35	43	.449	415	0	0	0	29	675^2	653	54	313	449	13.1	4.20	96	.257	.342	3	.143	-1	-20	-14	-4	-4.4

● SCOTT FREDRICKSON Fredrickson, Scott Eric b: 8/19/67, Manchester, N.H. BR/TR, 6'3", 215 lbs. Deb: 4/30/93

YEAR	TM/L	W	L	PCT	G	GS	CG	SH	SV	IP	H	HR	BB	SO	RAT	ERA	ERA+	OAV	OOB	BH	AVG	PB	PR	/A	PD	TPI
1993	Col-N	0	1	.000	25	0	0	0	0	29	33	3	17	20	15.8	6.21	77	.287	.383	0	.000	-0	-7	-5	-0	-0.2

● BUCK FREEMAN Freeman, Alexander Vernon b: 7/5/1893, Mart, Tex. d: 2/21/53, Fort Sam Houston, Tex. BB/TR, 5'10", 167 lbs. Deb: 4/13/21

YEAR	TM/L	W	L	PCT	G	GS	CG	SH	SV	IP	H	HR	BB	SO	RAT	ERA	ERA+	OAV	OOB	BH	AVG	PB	PR	/A	PD	TPI
1921	Chi-N	9	10	.474	38	20	6	0	3	177^1	189	12	70	42	13.6	4.11	93	.281	.356	11	.208	0	-6	-6	-1	-0.7
1922	Chi-N	0	1	.000	11	1	0	0	1	25^2	47	0	10	10	20.7	8.77	48	.412	.468	1	.125	-0	-13	-13	1	-0.5
Total	2	9	11	.450	49	21	6	0	4	203	236	12	80	52	14.5	4.70	82	.300	.372	12	.197	-0	-20	-19	-0	-1.2

● HARVEY FREEMAN Freeman, Harvey Bayard "Buck" b: 12/22/1897, Mottville, Mich. d: 1/10/70, Kalamazoo, Mich. BR/TR, 5'10", 160 lbs. Deb: 7/10/21

YEAR	TM/L	W	L	PCT	G	GS	CG	SH	SV	IP	H	HR	BB	SO	RAT	ERA	ERA+	OAV	OOB	BH	AVG	PB	PR	/A	PD	TPI
1921	Phi-A	1	4	.200	18	4	2	0	0	48	65	2	35	5	19.7	7.69	58	.346	.461	1	.083	-2	-18	-17	1	-1.5

● HERSH FREEMAN Freeman, Hershell Baskin "Buster" b: 7/1/28, Gadsden, Ala. BR/TR, 6'3", 220 lbs. Deb: 9/10/52

YEAR	TM/L	W	L	PCT	G	GS	CG	SH	SV	IP	H	HR	BB	SO	RAT	ERA	ERA+	OAV	OOB	BH	AVG	PB	PR	/A	PD	TPI
1952	Bos-A	1	0	1.000	4	1	1	0	0	13^2	13	1	5	5	12.5	3.29	120	.260	.339	2	.500	1	1	1	0	0.2
1953	Bos-A	1	4	.200	18	2	0	0	0	39	50	2	17	15	15.5	5.54	76	.316	.383	1	.091	-1	-7	-6	-0	-0.8
1955	Bos-A	0	0	—	2	0	0	0	0	1^2	1	0	1	1	10.8	0.00	—	.200	.333	0	—	0	1	1	-0	0.0
	Cin-N	7	4	.636	52	0	0	0	11	91^2	94	3	30	37	12.4	2.16	196	.276	.338	3	.167	1	**19**	**21**	1	3.1
1956	Cin-N	14	5	.737	64	0	0	0	18	108^2	112	2	34	50	12.2	3.40	117	.274	.331	1	.056	-1	5	7	-0	1.3
1957	Cin-N	7	2	.778	52	0	0	0	8	83^2	90	14	14	36	11.5	4.52	91	.277	.313	2	.200	0	-6	-4	-1	-0.5
1958	Cin-N	0	0	—	3	0	0	0	0	7^2	4	0	5	7	10.6	3.52	118	.154	.290	0	.000	-0	0	1	0	0.0
	Chi-N	0	1	.000	9	0	0	0	0	13	23	3	3	7	18.0	8.31	47	.354	.382	0	.000	-0	-6	-6	0	-0.4
	Yr	0	1	.000	12	0	0	0	0	20^2	27	3	8	14	15.2	6.53	61	.293	.350	0	.000	-0	-6	-6	0	-0.4
Total	6	30	16	.652	204	3	1	0	37	359	387	25	109	158	12.6	3.74	110	.281	.336	9	.143	-0	6	15	1	2.9

● JIMMY FREEMAN Freeman, Jimmy Lee b: 6/29/51, Carlsbad, N.Mex. BL/TL, 6'4", 180 lbs. Deb: 9/1/72

YEAR	TM/L	W	L	PCT	G	GS	CG	SH	SV	IP	H	HR	BB	SO	RAT	ERA	ERA+	OAV	OOB	BH	AVG	PB	PR	/A	PD	TPI
1972	Atl-N	2	2	.500	6	6	1	0	0	36	40	5	22	18	15.5	6.00	63	.278	.373	1	.077	-0	-10	-9	-1	-1.0
1973	Atl-N	0	2	.000	13	5	0	0	1	37^1	50	7	25	20	18.1	7.71	51	.327	.421	2	.154	-0	-17	-16	-1	-0.9
Total	2	2	4	.333	19	11	1	0	1	73^1	90	12	47	38	16.8	6.87	56	.303	.398	3	.115	-1	-27	-25	-2	-1.9

● BUCK FREEMAN Freeman, John Frank b: 10/30/1871, Catasauqua, Pa. d: 6/25/49, Wilkes-Barre, Pa. BL/TL, 5'9", 169 lbs. Deb: 6/27/1891 ♦

YEAR	TM/L	W	L	PCT	G	GS	CG	SH	SV	IP	H	HR	BB	SO	RAT	ERA	ERA+	OAV	OOB	BH	AVG	PB	PR	/A	PD	TPI
1891	Was-a	3	2	.600	5	4	4	0	0	44	35	0	33	28	14.7	3.89	96	.211	.355	4	.222	0	-1	-1	-0	0.0
1899	Was-N	0	0	—	2	0	0	0	0	7	15	3	3	0	27.0	7.71	51	.429	.512	187	.318	1	-3	-3	0	0.0
Total	2	3	2	.600	7	4	4	0	0	51	50	3	36	28	16.4	4.41	85	.249	.381	1235	.293	1	-4	-4	-0	0.0

● JULIE FREEMAN Freeman, Julius Benjamin b: 11/7/1868, Missouri d: 6/10/21, St.Louis, Mo. BR , Deb: 10/10/1888

YEAR	TM/L	W	L	PCT	G	GS	CG	SH	SV	IP	H	HR	BB	SO	RAT	ERA	ERA+	OAV	OOB	BH	AVG	PB	PR	/A	PD	TPI
1888	StL-a	0	1	.000	1	1	0	0	0	6^1	7	0	4	1	17.1	4.26	77	.269	.387	1	.333	0	-1	-1	-0	-0.1

● MARK FREEMAN Freeman, Mark Price b: 12/7/30, Memphis, Tenn. BR/TR, 6'4", 220 lbs. Deb: 4/18/59

YEAR	TM/L	W	L	PCT	G	GS	CG	SH	SV	IP	H	HR	BB	SO	RAT	ERA	ERA+	OAV	OOB	BH	AVG	PB	PR	/A	PD	TPI
1959	KC-A	0	0	—	3	0	0	0	0	3^2	6	0	3	1	22.1	9.82	41	.375	.474	0	—	0	-2	-2	-0	0.0
	NY-A	0	0	—	1	1	0	0	0	7	6	0	2	4	11.6	2.57	142	.240	.321	0	.000	-0	1	1	-0	0.0
	Yr	0	0	—	4	1	0	0	0	10^2	12	0	5	5	15.2	5.06	74	.286	.375	0	.000	-0	-1	-2	-0	0.0
1960	Chi-N	3	3	.500	30	8	1	0	1	76^2	70	10	33	50	12.7	5.63	67	.240	.327	3	.150	-0	-16	-16	-2	-1.4
Total	2	3	3	.500	34	9	1	0	1	87^1	82	10	38	55	13.0	5.56	68	.246	.334	3	.136	-1	-17	-17	-2	-1.4

● MARVIN FREEMAN Freeman, Marvin b: 4/10/63, Chicago, Ill. BR/TR, 6'7", 222 lbs. Deb: 9/16/86

YEAR	TM/L	W	L	PCT	G	GS	CG	SH	SV	IP	H	HR	BB	SO	RAT	ERA	ERA+	OAV	OOB	BH	AVG	PB	PR	/A	PD	TPI
1986	Phi-N	2	0	1.000	3	3	0	0	0	16	6	0	10	8	9.0	2.25	171	.120	.267	0	.000	-1	3	3	-0	0.2
1988	Phi-N	2	3	.400	11	11	0	0	0	51^2	55	2	43	37	17.2	6.10	58	.276	.407	3	.214	0	-15	-15	0	-1.2
1989	Phi-N	0	0	—	1	1	0	0	0	3	2	0	5	0	21.0	6.00	59	.182	.438	0	.000	-0	-1	-1	-0	0.0
1990	Phi-N	0	2	.000	16	3	0	0	1	32^1	34	5	14	26	14.2	5.57	69	.264	.349	0	.000	-1	-6	-6	0	-0.5
	Atl-N	1	0	1.000	9	0	0	0	0	15^2	7	0	3	12	6.9	1.72	234	.130	.203	0	—	0	4	4	-0	0.2
	Yr	1	2	.333	25	3	0	0	1	48	41	5	17	38	11.3	4.31	90	.220	.293	0	.000	-1	-3	-2	-0	-0.3
1991	Atl-N	1	0	1.000	34	0	0	0	1	48	37	2	13	34	9.8	3.00	130	.214	.277	0	.000	-1	4	5	-1	0.0
1992	*Atl-N	7	5	.583	58	0	0	0	3	64^1	61	7	29	41	12.7	3.22	114	.251	.333	2	.500	1	2	3	-1	0.5
1993	Atl-N	2	0	1.000	21	0	0	0	0	23^2	24	1	10	25	13.3	6.08	66	.261	.340	0	—	0	-5	-5	-1	-0.5
1994	Col-N	10	2	.833	19	18	0	0	0	112^2	113	10	23	67	11.3	2.80	178	.262	.307	4	.111	-0	18	27	1	2.8
1995	Col-N	3	7	.300	22	18	0	0	0	94^2	122	15	41	61	15.7	5.89	91	.318	.386	2	.087	-1	-18	-5	-1	-0.7
1996	Col-N	7	9	.438	26	23	0	0	0	129^2	151	21	57	71	14.9	6.04	86	.294	.372	5	.122	-2	-26	-12	1	-1.4
	Chi-A	0	0	—	1	1	0	0	0	2	4	0	1	1	22.5	13.50	35	.364	.417	0	—	0	-2	-2	-0	0.0
Total	10	35	28	.556	221	78	0	0	5	593^2	616	63	249	383	13.5	4.64	98	.269	.346	16	.114	-5	-44	-6	-2	-0.6

● JAKE FREEZE Freeze, Carl Alexander b: 4/25/1900, Huntington, Ark. d: 4/9/83, San Angelo, Tex. BR/TR, 5'8", 150 lbs. Deb: 7/1/25

YEAR	TM/L	W	L	PCT	G	GS	CG	SH	SV	IP	H	HR	BB	SO	RAT	ERA	ERA+	OAV	OOB	BH	AVG	PB	PR	/A	PD	TPI
1925	Chi-A	0	0	—	2	0	0	0	0	3^2	5	1	3	1	19.6	2.45	169	.333	.444	0	.000	-0	1	1	-0	0.0

● DAVE FREISLEBEN Freisleben, David James b: 10/31/51, Coraopolis, Pa. BR/TR, 5'11", 200 lbs. Deb: 4/26/74

YEAR	TM/L	W	L	PCT	G	GS	CG	SH	SV	IP	H	HR	BB	SO	RAT	ERA	ERA+	OAV	OOB	BH	AVG	PB	PR	/A	PD	TPI
1974	SD-N	9	14	.391	33	31	6	2	0	211^2	194	13	112	130	13.3	3.66	97	.241	.339	11	.172	2	-1	-2	-0	0.0
1975	SD-N	5	14	.263	36	27	4	1	0	181	206	11	82	77	14.7	4.28	81	.289	.368	4	.083	-1	-13	-16	0	-1.7
1976	SD-N	10	13	.435	34	24	6	3	1	172	163	10	66	81	12.2	3.51	93	.248	.321	7	.189	1	-0	-5	2	-0.2
1977	SD-N	7	9	.438	33	23	1	0	0	138^2	140	21	71	72	13.8	4.61	77	.266	.356	5	.135	0	-11	-16	-2	-1.9

YEAR	TM/L	W	L	PCT	G	GS	CG	SH	SV	IP	H	HR	BB	SO	RAT	ERA	ERA+	OAV	OOB	BH	AVG	PB	PR	/A	PD	TPI
1978	SD-N	0	3	.000	12	4	0	0	0	26^2	41	3	15	16	18.9	6.08	55	.363	.438	0	.000	-1	-7	-8	-0	-0.9
	Cle-A	1	4	.200	12	10	0	0	0	44^1	52	4	31	19	17.3	7.11	53	.299	.411	0	—	0	-16	-17	-0	-1.6
1979	Tor-A	2	3	.400	42	2	0	0	3	91	101	5	53	35	15.4	4.95	88	.294	.391	0	—	0	-7	-6	-1	-0.4
Total	6	34	60	.362	202	121	17	6	4	865^1	897	67	430	430	14.1	4.30	83	.269	.357	27	.141	2	-56	-71	-2	-6.7

● TONY FREITAS Freitas, Antonio b: 5/5/08, Mill Valley, Cal. d: 3/13/94, Orangevale, Cal. BR/TL, 5'8", 161 lbs. Deb: 5/31/32

YEAR	TM/L	W	L	PCT	G	GS	CG	SH	SV	IP	H	HR	BB	SO	RAT	ERA	ERA+	OAV	OOB	BH	AVG	PB	PR	/A	PD	TPI
1932	Phi-A	12	5	.706	23	18	10	1	0	150^1	150	11	48	31	12.1	3.83	118	.263	.325	8	.148	-1	11	12	1	1.1
1933	Phi-A	2	4	.333	19	9	2	0	1	64^1	90	8	24	15	16.2	7.27	59	.337	.396	1	.063	-1	-21	-21	0	-1.8
1934	Cin-N	6	12	.333	30	18	5	0	1	152^2	194	6	25	37	13.1	4.01	102	.311	.341	9	.191	0	1	1	2	0.4
1935	Cin-N	5	10	.333	31	18	5	0	2	143^2	174	6	38	51	13.4	4.57	87	.295	.340	6	.130	-0	-9	-9	-0	-0.8
1936	Cin-N	0	2	.000	4	0	0	0	0	7	6	0	2	1	10.3	1.29	297	.240	.296	0	.000	-0	2	2	-0	0.5
Total	5	25	33	.431	107	63	22	1	4	518	614	31	137	135	13.2	4.48	94	.296	.343	24	.145	-2	-16	-16	4	-0.6

● LARRY FRENCH French, Lawrence Herbert b: 11/1/07, Visalia, Cal. d: 2/9/87, San Diego, Cal. BR/TL, 6'1", 195 lbs. Deb: 4/18/29

YEAR	TM/L	W	L	PCT	G	GS	CG	SH	SV	IP	H	HR	BB	SO	RAT	ERA	ERA+	OAV	OOB	BH	AVG	PB	PR	/A	PD	TPI
1929	Pit-N	7	5	.583	30	13	6	0	1	123	130	10	62	49	14.3	4.90	97	.276	.364	8	.190	-1	-3	-2	1	-0.1
1930	Pit-N	17	18	.486	42	35	21	3	1	274^2	325	20	89	90	13.8	4.36	114	.295	.351	22	.242	1	19	19	-1	1.9
1931	Pit-N	15	13	.536	39	33	20	1	1	275^2	301	9	70	73	12.1	3.26	118	.278	.322	17	.179	-1	18	18	-1	1.5
1932	Pit-N	18	16	.529	**47**	33	19	3	4	274^1	301	17	62	72	11.9	3.02	126	.276	.316	19	.207	1	26	24	-4	2.5
1933	Pit-N	18	13	.581	47	35	21	5	1	291^1	290	9	55	88	10.8	2.72	122	.257	.294	15	.149	-2	20	19	-4	1.4
1934	Pit-N	12	18	.400	49	35	16	3	1	263^2	299	8	59	103	12.3	3.58	115	.281	.321	16	.190	-0	14	16	-3	1.3
1935	*Chi-N	17	10	.630	42	30	16	**4**	2	246^1	279	10	44	90	11.9	2.96	133	.286	.318	12	.141	-4	29	27	1	2.4
1936	Chi-N	18	9	.667	43	28	16	**4**	3	252^1	262	16	54	104	11.5	3.39	118	.266	.308	18	.212	0	18	17	-3	1.3
1937	Chi-N	16	10	.615	42	28	11	4	0	208	229	17	65	100	12.8	3.98	100	.274	.327	9	.127	-4	-2	0	2	-0.2
1938	*Chi-N	10	19	.345	43	27	10	3	0	201^1	210	17	62	83	12.2	3.80	101	.271	.326	13	.210	2	-0	1	1	0.4
1939	Chi-N	15	8	.652	36	21	10	2	1	194	205	7	50	98	11.9	3.29	120	.269	.314	14	.192	1	13	14	2	1.8
1940	Chi-N★	14	14	.500	40	33	18	3	2	246	240	12	64	107	11.3	3.29	114	.256	.306	14	.165	1	15	12	2	1.7
1941	Chi-N	5	14	.263	26	18	6	1	0	138	161	10	43	60	13.4	4.63	76	.285	.338	9	.191	1	-15	-17	-1	-2.1
	*Bro-N	0	0	—	6	1	0	0	0	15^2	16	1	4	8	12.1	3.45	106	.267	.323	1	.250	0	0	0	-0	0.0
	Yr	5	14	.263	32	19	6	1	0	153^2	177	11	47	68	13.2	4.51	78	.282	.333	10	.196	1	-15	-17	-1	-2.1
1942	Bro-N	15	4	**.789**	38	14	8	4	0	147^2	127	1	36	62	10.2	1.83	178	.233	.287	12	.300	4	24	24	-1	3.4
Total	14	197	171	.535	570	384	198	40	17	3152	3375	164	819	1187	12.1	3.44	114	.272	.320	199	.188	0	178	171	-7	17.2

● BILL FRENCH French, William b: Baltimore, Md. Deb: 4/14/1873 ♦

YEAR	TM/L	W	L	PCT	G	GS	CG	SH	SV	IP	H	HR	BB	SO	RAT	ERA	ERA+	OAV	OOB	BH	AVG	PB	PR	/A	PD	TPI
1873	Mar-n	0	1	.000	1	1	1	0	0	9	30	0	0	0	30.0	12.00	27	.462	.462	4	.222	-0	-9	-9		-0.5

● BENNY FREY Frey, Benjamin Rudolph b: 4/6/06, Dexter, Mich. d: 11/1/37, Spring Arbor Township, Mich. BR/TR, 5'10", 165 lbs. Deb: 9/18/29

YEAR	TM/L	W	L	PCT	G	GS	CG	SH	SV	IP	H	HR	BB	SO	RAT	ERA	ERA+	OAV	OOB	BH	AVG	PB	PR	/A	PD	TPI
1929	Cin-N	1	2	.333	3	3	2	0	0	24	29	2	8	1	13.9	4.13	111	.302	.356	3	.375	1	2	1	1	0.3
1930	Cin-N	11	18	.379	44	28	14	2	1	245	295	15	62	43	13.2	4.70	103	.305	.349	25	.284	4	7	3	6	1.3
1931	Cin-N	8	12	.400	34	17	7	1	2	133^2	166	2	36	19	13.7	4.92	76	.319	.365	14	.318	4	-16	-18	4	-1.6
1932	StL-N	0	2	.000	2	0	0	0	0	3	6	0	2	0	24.0	12.00	33	.600	.667	0	.000	-0	-3	-3	-0	-1.2
	Cin-N	4	10	.286	28	15	5	0	0	131^1	159	10	30	27	13.0	4.32	89	.299	.338	9	.205	-0	-6	-7	3	-0.4
	Yr	4	12	.250	30	15	5	0	0	134^1	165	10	32	27	13.3	4.49	86	.305	.345	9	.200	-0	-9	-9	2	-1.6
1933	Cin-N	6	4	.600	37	9	1	1	0	132	144	4	21	12	11.3	3.82	89	.281	.309	11	.262	3	-7	-6	2	0.1
1934	Cin-N	11	16	.407	39	30	12	2	2	245^1	288	10	42	33	12.2	3.52	116	.289	.319	14	.171	-0	15	15	4	1.9
1935	Cin-N	6	10	.375	38	13	3	1	3	114^1	164	6	32	24	15.7	6.85	58	.335	.381	11	.344	4	-36	-36	2	-3.9
1936	Cin-N	10	8	.556	31	12	5	0	0	131^1	164	5	30	20	13.3	4.25	90	.296	.332	11	.250	2	-3	-6	0	-0.5
Total	8	57	82	.410	256	127	49	7	8	1160	1415	54	263	179	13.1	4.50	90	.303	.341	98	.255	17	-47	-55	21	-4.0

● STEVE FREY Frey, Steven Francis b: 7/29/63, Meadowbrook, Pa. BR/TL, 5'9", 170 lbs. Deb: 5/10/89

YEAR	TM/L	W	L	PCT	G	GS	CG	SH	SV	IP	H	HR	BB	SO	RAT	ERA	ERA+	OAV	OOB	BH	AVG	PB	PR	/A	PD	TPI
1989	Mon-N	3	2	.600	20	0	0	0	0	21^1	29	4	11	15	17.3	5.48	64	.326	.406	0	—	0	-5	-5	-0	-1.0
1990	Mon-N	8	2	.800	51	0	0	0	9	55^2	44	4	29	29	12.0	2.10	174	.219	.320	0	.000	-0	10	10	-0	1.9
1991	Mon-N	0	1	.000	31	0	0	0	1	39^2	43	3	23	21	15.2	4.99	72	.281	.379	0	.000	0	-6	-6	-1	-0.2
1992	Cal-A	4	2	.667	51	0	0	0	4	45^1	39	6	22	24	12.5	3.57	111	.238	.335	0	—	0	2	2	0	0.3
1993	Cal-A	2	3	.400	55	0	0	0	13	48^1	41	1	26	22	13.0	2.98	151	.230	.338	0	—	0	7	8	-0	0.9
1994	SF-N	1	0	1.000	44	0	0	0	0	31	37	6	15	20	15.7	4.94	81	.322	.409	0	—	0	-2	-3	-0	-0.1
1995	SF-N	0	1	.000	9	0	0	0	0	6^1	7	1	2	5	12.8	4.26	96	.280	.333	0	—	0	-0	-0	-0	0.0
	Sea-A	0	3	.000	13	0	0	0	0	11^1	16	0	6	7	18.3	4.76	99	.356	.442	0	—	0	-0	-0	1	0.0
	Phi-N	0	0	—	9	0	0	0	1	10^2	3	1	2	2	4.2	0.84	501	.091	.143	0	.000	-0	4	4	-0	0.0
1996	Phi-N	0	1	.000	31	0	0	0	0	34^1	38	4	18	12	14.7	4.72	91	.295	.381	0	—	0	-2	-2	1	0.0
Total	8	18	15	.545	314	0	0	0	28	304	297	30	154	157	13.7	3.76	106	.262	.356	0	.000	-0	8	8	-1	1.8

● BERNIE FRIBERG Friberg, Bernard Albert (b: Gustaf Bernhard Friberg)
b: 8/18/1899, Manchester, N.H. d: 12/8/58, Lynn, Mass. BR/TR, 5'11", 178 lbs. Deb: 8/20/19 ♦

YEAR	TM/L	W	L	PCT	G	GS	CG	SH	SV	IP	H	HR	BB	SO	RAT	ERA	ERA+	OAV	OOB	BH	AVG	PB	PR	/A	PD	TPI
1925	Phi-N	0	0	—	1	0	0	0	0	4	4	0	3	1	15.8	4.50	106	.286	.412	82	.270	0	-0	0	-0	0.0

● MARION FRICANO Fricano, Marion John b: 7/15/23, Brant, N.Y. d: 5/18/76, Tijuana, Mex. BR/TR, 6', 170 lbs. Deb: 9/6/52

YEAR	TM/L	W	L	PCT	G	GS	CG	SH	SV	IP	H	HR	BB	SO	RAT	ERA	ERA+	OAV	OOB	BH	AVG	PB	PR	/A	PD	TPI
1952	Phi-A	1	0	1.000	2	0	0	0	0	5	5	0	1	0	10.8	1.80	220	.238	.273	0	—	0	1	1	0	0.2
1953	Phi-A	9	12	.429	39	23	10	0	0	211	206	21	90	67	12.9	3.88	110	.257	.337	10	.145	-3	3	10	-2	0.4
1954	Phi-A	5	11	.313	37	20	4	0	1	151^2	163	17	64	43	13.7	5.16	76	.275	.349	4	.098	-3	-24	-21	-2	-2.5
1955	KC-A	0	0	—	10	0	0	0	0	20	19	2	9	5	12.6	3.15	133	.253	.333	2	.667	1	2	2	0	0.1
Total	4	15	23	.395	88	43	14	0	1	387^2	393	40	164	115	13.2	4.32	96	.264	.341	16	.142	-5	-19	-8	-3	-1.8

● SKIPPER FRIDAY Friday, Grier William b: 10/26/1897, Gastonia, N.C. d: 8/25/62, Gastonia, N.C. BR/TR, 5'11", 170 lbs. Deb: 6/17/23

YEAR	TM/L	W	L	PCT	G	GS	CG	SH	SV	IP	H	HR	BB	SO	RAT	ERA	ERA+	OAV	OOB	BH	AVG	PB	PR	/A	PD	TPI
1923	Was-A	0	1	.000	7	2	1	0	0	30	35	2	22	9	17.7	6.90	55	.313	.434	2	.222	0	-10	-10	1	-0.2

● CY FRIED Fried, Arthur Edwin b: 7/23/1897, San Antonio, Tex. d: 10/10/70, San Antonio, Tex. BL/TL, 5'11.5", 150 lbs. Deb: 9/17/20

YEAR	TM/L	W	L	PCT	G	GS	CG	SH	SV	IP	H	HR	BB	SO	RAT	ERA	ERA+	OAV	OOB	BH	AVG	PB	PR	/A	PD	TPI
1920	Det-A	0	0	—	2	0	0	0	0	1^2	3	0	4	0	37.8	16.20	23	.500	.700	0	—	0	-2	-2	0	0.0

● BOB FRIEDRICHS Friedrichs, Robert George b: 8/30/06, Cincinnati, Ohio d: 4/15/97, Jasper, Ind. BR/TR, 5'11.5", 165 lbs. Deb: 5/17/32

YEAR	TM/L	W	L	PCT	G	GS	CG	SH	SV	IP	H	HR	BB	SO	RAT	ERA	ERA+	OAV	OOB	BH	AVG	PB	PR	/A	PD	TPI
1932	Was-A	0	0	—	2	0	0	0	0	4	4	0	7	2	27.0	11.25	38	.250	.500	0	.000	-0	-3	-3	-0	0.0

● BILL FRIEL Friel, William Edward b: 4/1/1876, Renovo, Pa. d: 12/24/59, St.Louis, Mo. BL/TR, 5'10", 165 lbs. Deb: 5/3/01 FUC♦

YEAR	TM/L	W	L	PCT	G	GS	CG	SH	SV	IP	H	HR	BB	SO	RAT	ERA	ERA+	OAV	OOB	BH	AVG	PB	PR	/A	PD	TPI
1902	StL-A	0	0	—	1	0	0	0	0	4	4	0	0	0	9.0	4.50	78	.267	.267	64	.240	0	-0	-0	-0	0.0

● DANNY FRIEND Friend, Daniel Sebastian b: 4/18/1873, Cincinnati, Ohio d: 6/1/42, Chillicothe, Ohio TL , 5'9", 175 lbs. Deb: 9/10/1895

YEAR	TM/L	W	L	PCT	G	GS	CG	SH	SV	IP	H	HR	BB	SO	RAT	ERA	ERA+	OAV	OOB	BH	AVG	PB	PR	/A	PD	TPI
1895	Chi-N	2	2	.500	5	5	5	0	0	41	50	5	14	10	14.7	5.27	97	.296	.360	4	.235	-1	-2	-1	0	-0.1
1896	Chi-N	18	14	.563	36	33	28	1	0	290^2	298	11	139	86	14.7	4.74	96	.263	.363	30	.238	-1	-12	-6	-2	-0.8
1897	Chi-N	12	11	.522	24	24	23	0	0	203	244	5	86	58	15.4	4.52	99	.295	.373	25	.284	2	-5	-1	-2	-0.1
1898	Chi-N	0	2	.000	2	2	2	0	0	17	20	1	10	4	16.4	5.29	68	.290	.387	2	.286	0	-3	-3	2	-0.1
Total	4	32	29	.525	67	64	58	1	0	551^2	612	22	249	158	15.0	4.71	96	.279	.368	61	.256	0	-22	-12	-2	-1.1

● BOB FRIEND Friend, Robert Bartmess "Warrior" b: 11/24/30, Lafayette, Ind. BR/TR, 6', 190 lbs. Deb: 4/28/51

YEAR	TM/L	W	L	PCT	G	GS	CG	SH	SV	IP	H	HR	BB	SO	RAT	ERA	ERA+	OAV	OOB	BH	AVG	PB	PR	/A	PD	TPI
1951	Pit-N	6	10	.375	34	22	3	1	0	149^2	173	12	68	41	14.5	4.27	99	.293	.366	4	.091	-2	-5	-1	0	-0.3
1952	Pit-N	7	17	.292	35	23	6	1	0	185	186	15	84	75	13.3	4.18	95	.258	.338	3	.058	-4	-9	-4	1	-0.8
1953	Pit-N	8	11	.421	32	24	8	0	0	170^2	193	18	57	66	13.3	4.90	91	.286	.344	7	.135	-2	-12	-8	1	-0.9
1954	Pit-N	7	12	.368	35	20	4	2	2	170^1	204	16	58	73	13.9	5.07	83	.302	.358	14	.275	5	-19	-17	-1	-1.2
1955	Pit-N	14	9	.609	44	20	9	2	2	200^1	178	18	52	98	10.4	**2.83**	**145**	.242	.294	10	.164	-2	**27**	**29**	3	3.3
1956	Pit-N★	17	17	.500	49	42	19	4	3	**314^1**	310	25	85	166	11.4	3.46	109	.258	.308	16	.165	-1	11	11	-1	0.9
1957	Pit-N	14	18	.438	40	38	17	3	0	**277**	273	28	68	143	11.1	3.38	112	.257	.303	16	.184	1	15	13	-1	1.4
1958	Pit-N★	**22**	14	.611	38	38	16	1	0	274	299	25	61	135	12.0	3.68	105	.281	.322	10	.106	-4	8	6	-0	0.3
1959	Pit-N	8	19	.296	35	35	7	2	0	234^2	267	19	52	104	12.5	4.03	96	.283	.325	12	.164	0	-2	-4	0	-0.4
1960	*Pit-N★	18	12	.600	38	37	16	4	1	275^2	266	18	45	183	10.2	3.00	125	.251	.281	6	.068	-5	23	23	0	1.9

YEAR	TM/L	W	L	PCT	G	GS	CG	SH	SV	IP	H	HR	BB	SO	RAT	ERA	ERA+	OAV	OOB	BH	AVG	PB	PR	/A	PD	TPI
1961	Pit-N	14	19	.424	41	35	10	1	1	236	271	16	45	108	12.2	3.85	104	.289	.324	11	.139	-3	5	4	-1	0.1
1962	Pit-N	18	14	.563	39	36	13	**5**	1	261^2	280	23	53	144	11.5	3.06	129	.273	.310	11	.121	-3	26	25	0	2.5
1963	Pit-N	17	16	.515	39	38	12	4	0	268^2	236	13	44	144	9.5	2.34	141	.233	.269	9	.105	-3	28	28	-1	3.1
1964	Pit-N	13	18	.419	35	35	13	3	0	240^1	253	10	50	128	11.5	3.33	105	.271	.310	5	.070	-3	5	5	2	0.4
1965	Pit-N	8	12	.400	34	34	8	2	0	222	221	17	47	74	11.2	3.24	108	.260	.305	3	.042	-5	7	7	0	0.0
1966	NY-A	1	4	.200	12	8	0	0	0	44^2	61	2	9	22	14.1	4.84	69	.330	.361	0	.000	-1	-7	-7	1	-0.8
	NY-N	5	8	.385	22	12	2	1	1	86	101	11	16	30	12.3	4.40	83	.289	.322	1	.034	-3	-8	-7	-2	-1.5
Total	16	197	230	.461	602	497	163	36	11	3611	3772	286	894	1734	11.7	3.58	107	.269	.315	138	.121	-36	94	100	2	8.0

● PETE FRIES Fries, Peter Martin b: 10/30/1857, Scranton, Pa. d: 7/30/37, Chicago, Ill. BL/TL, 5'8", 160 lbs. Deb: 8/10/1883 ♦

YEAR	TM/L	W	L	PCT	G	GS	CG	SH	SV	IP	H	HR	BB	SO	RAT	ERA	ERA+	OAV	OOB	BH	AVG	PB	PR	/A	PD	TPI
1883	Col-a	0	3	.000	3	3	3	0	0	25	34	1	14	7	17.3	6.48	48	.304	.381	3	.300	1	-9	-9	0	-0.7

● JOHN FRILL Frill, John Edmond b: 4/3/1879, Reading, Pa. d: 9/28/18, Westerly, R.I. BR/TL, 5'10.5", 170 lbs. Deb: 4/16/10

YEAR	TM/L	W	L	PCT	G	GS	CG	SH	SV	IP	H	HR	BB	SO	RAT	ERA	ERA+	OAV	OOB	BH	AVG	PB	PR	/A	PD	TPI
1910	NY-A	2	2	.500	10	5	3	1	1	48^1	55	1	5	27	11.4	4.47	59	.289	.311	2	.111	-1	-10	-10	0	-0.9
1912	StL-A	0	1	.000	3	3	0	0	0	4^1	16	1	1	2	37.4	20.77	16	.571	.600	1	.500	0	-8	-8	0	-1.3
	Cin-N	1	0	1.000	3	2	0	0	0	15	19	0	1	4	13.2	6.00	56	.345	.379	1	.250	0	-4	-4	0	-0.2
Total	2	3	3	.500	16	10	3	1	1	67^2	90	2	7	33	13.4	5.85	49	.330	.356	4	.167	-1	-23	-22	0	-2.4

● DANNY FRISELLA Frisella, Daniel Vincent "Bear" b: 3/4/46, San Francisco, Cal. d: 1/1/77, Phoenix, Ariz. BL/TR, 6', 195 lbs. Deb: 7/27/67

YEAR	TM/L	W	L	PCT	G	GS	CG	SH	SV	IP	H	HR	BB	SO	RAT	ERA	ERA+	OAV	OOB	BH	AVG	PB	PR	/A	PD	TPI
1967	NY-N	1	6	.143	14	11	0	0	0	74	68	6	33	51	12.3	3.41	100	.249	.330	2	.087	-1	-0	-0	-0	-0.1
1968	NY-N	2	4	.333	19	4	0	0	2	50^2	53	5	17	47	12.4	3.91	77	.270	.329	1	.083	-1	-5	-5	0	-0.7
1969	NY-N	0	0	—	3	0	0	0	0	4^2	8	1	3	5	21.2	7.71	47	.381	.458	0	.000	-0	-2	-2	-0	0.0
1970	NY-N	8	3	.727	30	1	0	0	1	65^2	49	4	34	54	11.4	3.02	133	.204	.303	4	.308	1	8	7	-0	1.3
1971	NY-N	8	5	.615	53	0	0	0	12	90^2	76	6	30	93	10.8	1.99	172	.227	.296	3	.231	1	15	14	1	2.6
1972	NY-N	5	8	.385	39	0	0	0	9	67^1	63	8	20	46	11.1	3.34	101	.243	.297	2	.286	0	1	0	1	0.2
1973	Atl-N	1	2	.333	42	0	0	0	8	45	40	5	23	27	12.8	4.20	94	.241	.337	1	.500	0	-3	-1	-0	-0.1
1974	Atl-N	3	4	.429	36	1	0	0	6	41^2	37	4	28	27	14.0	5.18	73	.240	.357	0	.000	0	-7	-7	-0	-1.2
1975	SD-N	1	6	.143	65	0	0	0	9	97^2	86	7	51	67	12.8	3.13	111	.242	.340	1	.200	0	5	4	-0	0.3
1976	StL-N	0	0	—	18	0	0	0	1	22^2	19	3	13	11	12.7	3.97	89	.232	.337	0	.000	-0	-1	-1	-0	0.0
	Mil-A	5	2	.714	32	0	0	0	9	49^1	30	4	34	43	11.9	2.74	128	.175	.316	0	—	0	4	4	0	0.8
Total	10	34	40	.459	351	17	0	0	57	609^1	529	53	286	471	12.1	3.32	106	.235	.323	14	.179	1	14	13	0	3.1

● EMIL FRISK Frisk, John Emil b: 10/15/1874, Kalkaska, Mich. d: 1/27/22, Seattle, Wash. BL/TR, 6'1", 190 lbs. Deb: 9/2/1899 ♦

YEAR	TM/L	W	L	PCT	G	GS	CG	SH	SV	IP	H	HR	BB	SO	RAT	ERA	ERA+	OAV	OOB	BH	AVG	PB	PR	/A	PD	TPI
1899	Cin-N	3	6	.333	9	9	9	0	0	68^1	81	1	17	17	13.7	3.95	99	.295	.349	7	.280	1	-1	-0	-0	0.1
1901	Det-A	5	4	.556	11	7	6	0	0	74^2	94	1	26	22	14.7	4.34	89	.304	.362	15	.313	2	-6	-4	3	0.1
Total	2	8	10	.444	20	16	15	0	0	143	175	2	43	39	14.2	4.15	94	.300	.356	135	.267	3	-6	-4	2	0.2

● CHARLIE FRITZ Fritz, Charles Cornelius b: 6/18/1882, Mobile, Ala. d: 7/30/43, Mobile, Ala. TL , Deb: 10/5/07

YEAR	TM/L	W	L	PCT	G	GS	CG	SH	SV	IP	H	HR	BB	SO	RAT	ERA	ERA+	OAV	OOB	BH	AVG	PB	PR	/A	PD	TPI
1907	Phi-A	0	0	—	1	1	0	0	0	3	0	0	3	1	12.0	3.00	87	.000	.333	0	.000	-0	-0	-0	-0	0.0

● BILL FROATS Froats, William John b: 10/20/30, New York, N.Y. d: 2/9/98, Minneapolis, Minn. BL/TL, 6', 180 lbs. Deb: 4/22/55

YEAR	TM/L	W	L	PCT	G	GS	CG	SH	SV	IP	H	HR	BB	SO	RAT	ERA	ERA+	OAV	OOB	BH	AVG	PB	PR	/A	PD	TPI
1955	Det-A	0	0	—	1	0	0	0	0	2	0	0	2	0	9.0	0.00	—	.000	.333	0	—	0	1	1	0	0.0

● SAM FROCK Frock, Samuel William b: 12/23/1882, Baltimore, Md. d: 11/3/25, Baltimore, Md. BR/TR, 6', 168 lbs. Deb: 9/21/07

YEAR	TM/L	W	L	PCT	G	GS	CG	SH	SV	IP	H	HR	BB	SO	RAT	ERA	ERA+	OAV	OOB	BH	AVG	PB	PR	/A	PD	TPI
1907	Bos-N	1	2	.333	5	3	3	1	0	33^1	28	1	11	12	11.1	2.97	86	.243	.320	1	.071	-1	-2	-2	-2	-0.4
1909	Pit-N	2	1	.667	8	4	3	0	1	36^1	44	0	4	11	12.6	2.48	110	.299	.331	2	.143	-1	0	1	0	0.0
1910	Pit-N	0	0	—	1	0	0	0	0	2	2	0	2	1	22.5	4.50	69	.400	.625	0	—	0	-0	-0	0	0.0
	Bos-N	12	19	.387	45	29	13	2	2	255^1	245	8	91	170	12.0	3.21	104	.262	.330	16	.190	-3	-5	3	1	0.2
	Yr	12	19	.387	46	29	13	2	2	257^1	247	8	93	171	12.0	3.22	103	.263	.332	16	.190	-3	-5	3	2	0.2
1911	Bos-N	0	1	.000	4	1	1	0	0	16	29	0	5	8	19.7	5.63	68	.426	.473	1	.200	-0	-4	-3	0	-0.2
Total	4	15	23	.395	63	37	20	3	3	343	348	9	113	202	12.4	3.23	99	.274	.339	20	.171	-5	-11	-1	0	-0.4

● TODD FROHWIRTH Frohwirth, Todd Gerard b: 9/28/62, Milwaukee, Wis. BR/TR, 6'4", 205 lbs. Deb: 8/10/87

YEAR	TM/L	W	L	PCT	G	GS	CG	SH	SV	IP	H	HR	BB	SO	RAT	ERA	ERA+	OAV	OOB	BH	AVG	PB	PR	/A	PD	TPI
1987	Phi-N	1	0	1.000	10	0	0	0	0	11	12	0	2	9	11.5	0.00	—	.293	.326	0	.000	-0	5	5	0	0.4
1988	Phi-N	1	2	.333	12	0	0	0	0	12	16	2	11	11	20.3	8.25	43	.327	.450	0	—	0	-6	-6	1	-1.4
1989	Phi-N	1	0	1.000	45	0	0	0	0	62^2	56	4	18	39	11.1	3.59	99	.240	.303	0	.000	-0	-1	-0	-0	0.0
1990	Phi-N	0	1	.000	5	0	0	0	0	1	3	0	6	1	81.0	18.00	21	.500	.750	0	—	0	-2	-2	0	-1.3
1991	Bal-A	7	3	.700	51	0	0	0	3	96^1	64	2	29	77	8.8	1.87	211	.190	.256	0	—	0	**24**	**22**	3	2.9
1992	Bal-A	4	3	.571	65	0	0	0	4	106	97	4	41	58	12.0	2.46	163	.247	.323	0	—	0	17	18	3	1.5
1993	Bal-A	6	7	.462	70	0	0	0	3	96^1	91	7	44	50	12.9	3.83	117	.256	.343	0	—	0	5	7	2	0.7
1994	Bos-A	0	3	.000	22	0	0	0	1	26^2	40	3	17	13	19.9	10.80	47	.339	.431	0	—	0	-18	-17	1	-1.9
1996	Cal-A	0	0	—	4	0	0	0	0	5^2	10	1	4	1	23.8	11.12	45	.370	.469	0	—	0	-4	-4	-0	0.0
Total	9	20	19	.513	284	0	0	0	11	417^2	389	23	172	259	12.4	3.60	114	.250	.329	0	.000	-0	21	24	9	0.9

● ART FROMME Fromme, Arthur Henry b: 9/3/1883, Quincy, Ill. d: 8/24/56, Los Angeles, Cal. BR/TR, 6', 178 lbs. Deb: 9/14/06

YEAR	TM/L	W	L	PCT	G	GS	CG	SH	SV	IP	H	HR	BB	SO	RAT	ERA	ERA+	OAV	OOB	BH	AVG	PB	PR	/A	PD	TPI
1906	StL-N	1	2	.333	3	3	3	1	0	25	19	0	10	11	10.8	1.44	183	.221	.309	2	.222	0	3	3	1	0.5
1907	StL-N	5	13	.278	23	16	13	2	0	145^2	138	3	67	67	12.9	2.90	86	.256	.343	10	.182	1	-7	-6	0	-0.7
1908	StL-N	5	13	.278	20	14	9	2	0	116	102	1	50	62	11.9	2.72	87	.218	.296	5	.139	-1	-5	-5	-0	-0.9
1909	Cin-N	19	13	.594	37	34	22	4	2	279^1	195	2	101	126	9.6	1.90	137	.201	.278	18	.191	2	22	22	2	3.1
1910	Cin-N	3	4	.429	11	5	1	0	0	49^1	44	2	39	10	15.3	2.92	100	.260	.402	2	.133	-1	1	-0	0	-0.1
1911	Cin-N	10	11	.476	38	26	11	1	0	208	190	8	79	107	12.3	3.46	96	.248	.331	14	.189	-1	-1	-3	1	-0.4
1912	Cin-N	16	18	.471	43	37	23	3	0	296	285	7	88	120	11.7	2.74	123	.260	.321	9	.087	-9	22	21	-0	1.2
1913	Cin-N	1	4	.200	9	7	2	0	0	56	55	1	21	24	12.7	4.18	78	.274	.351	3	.143	-0	-6	-6	-1	-0.6
	NY-N	11	6	.647	26	12	3	0	0	112^1	112	5	29	50	11.5	4.01	78	.260	.310	6	.171	-0	-10	-11	1	-1.4
	Yr	12	10	.545	35	19	5	0	0	168^1	167	6	50	74	11.7	4.06	78	.263	.319	9	.161	-1	-16	-17	1	-2.0
1914	NY-N	9	5	.643	38	12	3	1	2	138	142	7	44	57	12.6	3.20	83	.283	.349	7	.226	1	-6	-8	3	-0.4
1915	NY-N	0	1	.000	4	1	0	0	0	12^1	15	1	2	4	12.4	5.84	44	.306	.333	1	.333	1	-4	-4	0	-0.3
Total	10	80	90	.471	252	167	90	14	4	1438	1297	37	530	638	11.7	2.90	100	.246	.320	77	.162	-8	8	2	8	-0.0

● DAVE FROST Frost, Carl David b: 11/17/52, Long Beach, Cal. BR/TR, 6'6", 235 lbs. Deb: 9/11/77

YEAR	TM/L	W	L	PCT	G	GS	CG	SH	SV	IP	H	HR	BB	SO	RAT	ERA	ERA+	OAV	OOB	BH	AVG	PB	PR	/A	PD	TPI
1977	Chi-A	1	1	.500	4	3	0	0	0	23^2	30	0	3	15	12.9	3.04	134	.323	.351	0	—	0	3	3	-0	0.2
1978	Cal-A	5	4	.556	11	10	2	1	0	80^1	71	6	24	30	10.9	2.58	140	.240	.301	0	—	0	11	9	1	1.5
1979	*Cal-A	16	10	.615	36	33	12	2	1	239^1	226	17	77	107	11.6	3.57	114	.251	.314	0	—	0	17	13	-1	1.2
1980	Cal-A	4	8	.333	15	15	2	0	0	78^1	97	8	21	28	13.8	5.29	74	.308	.355	0	—	0	-11	-12	-1	-1.6
1981	Cal-A	1	8	.111	12	9	0	0	0	47^1	44	3	19	16	12.2	5.51	66	.250	.327	0	—	0	-10	-10	0	-1.6
1982	KC-A	6	6	.500	21	14	0	0	0	81^2	103	7	30	26	15.0	5.51	74	.313	.376	0	—	0	-13	-13	-1	-1.8
Total	6	33	37	.471	99	84	16	3	1	550^2	571	41	174	222	12.4	4.10	96	.271	.330	0	—	0	-3	-9	-3	-2.1

● JOHNSON FRY Fry, Johnson "Jay" b: 11/21/01, Huntington, W.Va. d: 4/7/59, Carmi, Ill. BR/TR, 6'1", 150 lbs. Deb: 8/24/23

YEAR	TM/L	W	L	PCT	G	GS	CG	SH	SV	IP	H	HR	BB	SO	RAT	ERA	ERA+	OAV	OOB	BH	AVG	PB	PR	/A	PD	TPI
1923	Cle-A	0	0	—	1	0	0	0	0	3^2	6	0	4	0	24.5	12.27	32	.353	.476	1	1.000	1	-3	-3	-0	0.1

● CHARLIE FRYE Frye, Charles Andrew b: 7/17/14, Hickory, N.C. d: 5/25/45, Hickory, N.C. BR/TR, 6'1", 175 lbs. Deb: 7/28/40

YEAR	TM/L	W	L	PCT	G	GS	CG	SH	SV	IP	H	HR	BB	SO	RAT	ERA	ERA+	OAV	OOB	BH	AVG	PB	PR	/A	PD	TPI
1940	Phi-N	0	6	.000	15	5	1	0	0	50^1	58	3	26	18	15.0	4.65	84	.291	.373	5	.263	1	-4	-4	-1	-0.4

● WOODIE FRYMAN Fryman, Woodrow Thompson b: 4/15/40, Ewing, Ky. BR/TL, 6'2", 205 lbs. Deb: 4/15/66

YEAR	TM/L	W	L	PCT	G	GS	CG	SH	SV	IP	H	HR	BB	SO	RAT	ERA	ERA+	OAV	OOB	BH	AVG	PB	PR	/A	PD	TPI
1966	Pit-N	12	9	.571	36	28	9	3	1	181^2	182	13	47	105	11.4	3.81	94	.261	.309	10	.159	-1	-4	-5	-2	-0.8
1967	Pit-N	3	8	.273	28	18	3	1	1	113^1	121	12	44	74	13.4	4.05	83	.276	.348	4	.118	-1	-9	-9	2	-0.7
1968	Phi-N☆	12	14	.462	34	32	10	5	0	213^2	198	12	64	151	11.3	2.78	108	.246	.306	6	.085	-2	5	5	-1	0.2
1969	Phi-N	12	15	.444	36	35	10	1	0	228^1	243	15	89	150	13.5	4.41	80	.270	.343	9	.118	-2	-21	-22	-1	-2.6
1970	Phi-N	8	6	.571	27	20	4	3	0	127^2	122	11	43	97	11.7	4.09	98	.253	.315	5	.128	-2	-1	-1	-0	-0.3
1971	Phi-N	10	7	.588	37	17	3	2	2	149^1	133	7	46	104	11.0	3.38	104	.242	.304	7	.189	0	1	2	2	0.6
1972	Phi-N	4	10	.286	23	17	3	2	1	119^2	131	15	39	69	12.9	4.36	82	.279	.337	5	.152	1	-12	-10	1	-1.0

YEAR	TM/L	W	L	PCT	G	GS	CG	SH	SV	IP	H	HR	BB	SO	RAT	ERA	ERA+	OAV	OOB	BH	AVG	PB	PR	/A	PD	TPI
	*Det-A	10	3	.769	16	14	6	1	0	113^2	93	6	31	72	10.4	2.06	153	.220	.285	5	.125	-2	13	14	-1	1.4
1973	Det-A	6	13	.316	34	29	1	0	0	169^2	200	23	64	119	14.2	5.36	76	.294	.357	0	—	0	-29	-24	1	-2.4
1974	Det-A	6	9	.400	27	22	4	1	0	141^2	120	16	67	92	12.1	4.32	88	.233	.326	0	—	0	-11	-8	-1	-1.0
1975	Mon-N	9	12	.429	38	20	7	3	3	157	141	10	68	118	12.3	3.32	115	.239	.323	10	.204	1	5	9	1	1.4
1976	Mon-N☆	13	13	.500	34	32	4	2	2	216^1	218	14	76	123	12.6	3.37	110	.263	.332	7	.109	-3	3	8	-0	0.6
1977	Cin-N	5	5	.500	17	12	0	0	1	75^1	83	13	45	57	15.5	5.38	73	.292	.393	7	.318	2	-12	-12	1	-1.2
1978	Chi-N	2	4	.333	13	9	0	0	0	55^2	64	6	37	28	16.3	5.17	78	.309	.414	1	.063	-1	-10	-7	1	-0.7
	Mon-N	5	7	.417	19	17	4	3	1	94^2	93	4	37	53	12.6	3.61	98	.260	.334	2	.059	-2	-0	-1	-0	-0.4
	Yr	7	11	.389	32	26	4	3	1	150^1	157	10	74	81	14.0	4.19	89	.276	.362	3	.060	-3	-10	-8	1	-1.1
1979	Mon-N	3	6	.333	44	0	0	0	10	58	52	4	22	44	11.9	2.79	131	.248	.328	0	.000	-1	6	6	1	1.0
1980	Mon-N	7	4	.636	61	0	0	0	17	80	61	1	30	59	10.5	2.25	158	.209	.287	2	.167	-0	12	12	-1	2.0
1981	*Mon-N	5	3	.625	35	0	0	0	7	43	38	1	14	25	11.1	1.88	185	.247	.314	2	.667	1	8	8	0	1.8
1982	Mon-N	9	4	.692	60	0	0	0	12	69^2	66	3	26	46	12.0	3.75	97	.259	.330	2	.222	0	-1	-1	1	0.0
1983	Mon-N	0	3	.000	6	0	0	0	0	3	8	1	1	1	27.0	21.00	17	.571	.600	0	—	0	-6	-6	0	-3.8
Total	18	141	155	.476	625	322	68	27	58	2411^1	2367	187	890	1587	12.4	3.77	96	.259	.329	84	.138	-12	-63	-43	4	-5.9
● CHARLIE FUCHS	Fuchs, Charles Thomas b: 11/18/12, Union Hill, N.J. d: 6/10/69, Weehawken, N.J. BB/TR, 5'8", 168 lbs. Deb: 4/17/42																									
1942	Det-A	3	3	.500	9	4	1	1	0	36^2	43	5	19	15	15.5	6.63	60	.285	.368	1	.077	-1	-12	-11	1	-1.5
1943	Phi-N	2	7	.222	17	9	4	1	1	77^2	76	4	34	12	13.1	4.29	79	.266	.350	2	.091	-2	-8	-8	1	-1.1
	StL-A	0	0	—	13	0	0	0	0	35^2	42	4	11	9	13.6	4.04	82	.294	.348	0	.000	-1	-3	-3	-0	-0.1
1944	Bro-N	1	0	1.000	8	0	0	0	0	15^2	25	2	9	5	20.1	5.74	62	.347	.427	0	.000	0	-4	-4	1	-0.2
Total	3	6	10	.375	47	13	5	2	1	165^2	186	15	73	41	14.4	4.89	72	.285	.363	3	.070	-4	-27	-25	0	-2.9
● MIGUEL FUENTES	Fuentes, Miguel (Pinet) b: 5/10/46, Loiza Aldea, P.R. d: 1/29/70, Loiza Aldea, P.R. BR/TR, 6', 160 lbs. Deb: 9/1/69																									
1969	Sea-A	1	3	.250	8	4	1	0	0	26	29	1	16	14	15.6	5.19	70	.284	.381	2	.333	0	-5	-5	-1	-0.6
● OSCAR FUHR	Fuhr, Oscar Lawrence b: 8/22/1893, Defiance, Mo. d: 3/27/75, Dallas, Tex. BL/TL, 6'0.5", 176 lbs. Deb: 4/19/21																									
1921	Chi-N	0	0	—	1	0	0	0	0	4	11	1	0	2	24.8	9.00	42	.500	.500	0	.000	0	-2	-2	0	0.0
1924	Bos-A	3	6	.333	23	10	4	1	0	80^1	100	1	39	30	16.1	5.94	74	.310	.392	4	.182	-1	-15	-14	1	-1.3
1925	Bos-A	0	6	.000	39	5	0	0	0	91^1	138	7	30	27	16.9	6.60	69	.364	.415	5	.250	0	-22	-21	1	-1.0
Total	3	3	12	.200	63	15	4	1	0	175^2	249	9	69	59	16.7	6.35	70	.344	.407	9	.209	-1	-40	-37	2	-2.3
● JOHN FULGHAM	Fulgham, John Thomas b: 6/9/56, St.Louis, Mo. BR/TR, 6'2", 205 lbs. Deb: 6/19/79																									
1979	StL-N	10	6	.625	20	19	10	2	0	146	123	10	26	75	9.4	2.53	149	.227	.267	6	.143	1	20	20	-2	2.0
1980	StL-N	4	6	.400	15	14	4	1	0	85^1	66	7	32	48	10.4	3.38	109	.219	.296	0	.000	-3	2	3	-0	0.0
Total	2	14	12	.538	35	33	14	3	0	231^1	189	17	58	123	9.8	2.84	132	.224	.277	6	.087	-2	22	23	-2	2.0
● ED FULLER	Fuller, Edward Ashton b: 3/22/1868, Washington, D.C. d: 3/16/35, Hyattsville, Md. BR/TR, 6', 158 lbs. Deb: 7/17/1886																									
1886	Was-N	0	1	.000	2	1	1	0	0	13	15	0	5	3	13.8	6.92	47	.375	.444	1	.143	-0	-5	-5	-0	-0.3
● CURT FULLERTON	Fullerton, Curtis Hooper b: 9/13/1898, Ellsworth, Me. d: 1/2/75, Winthrop, Mass. BL/TR, 6', 162 lbs. Deb: 4/14/21																									
1921	Bos-A	0	1	.000	4	1	1	0	0	15^1	22	3	10	4	19.4	8.80	48	.355	.452	0	.000	-0	-8	-8	-1	-0.5
1922	Bos-A	1	4	.200	31	3	0	0	0	64^1	70	4	35	17	15.4	5.46	75	.290	.391	2	.250	1	-10	-10	1	-0.4
1923	Bos-A	2	15	.118	37	15	6	0	1	143^1	167	9	71	37	15.3	5.09	81	.300	.385	11	.297	2	-18	-16	-2	-1.6
1924	Bos-A	7	12	.368	33	20	9	0	2	152	166	1	73	33	14.5	4.32	101	.283	.368	3	.071	-3	-2	1	-0	-0.3
1925	Bos-A	0	3	.000	4	2	0	0	0	22^2	22	1	9	3	13.1	3.18	143	.259	.344	2	.200	-0	3	3	1	0.4
1933	Bos-A	0	2	.000	6	2	2	0	0	25^1	36	1	13	10	17.8	8.53	51	.364	.442	2	.222	0	-12	-12	-1	-0.7
Total	6	10	37	.213	115	43	18	0	3	423	483	19	211	104	15.2	5.11	83	.296	.384	20	.182	-1	-46	-40	-1	-3.1
● CHICK FULMER	Fulmer, Charles John b: 2/12/1851, Philadelphia, Pa. d: 2/15/40, Philadelphia, Pa. BR/TR, 6', 158 lbs. Deb: 8/23/1871 FU♦																									
1873	Phi-n	0	0	—	2	0	0	0	0	5	7	0	1	0	14.4	3.60	92	.304	.333	66	.280	0	-0	-0		0.0
● CHRIS FULMER	Fulmer, Christopher b: 7/4/1858, Tamaqua, Pa. d: 11/9/31, Tamaqua, Pa. BR/TR, 5'8", 165 lbs. Deb: 8/4/1884 ♦																									
1886	Bal-a	0	0	—	1	0	0	0	0	2	2	0	1	0	13.5	4.50	76	.250	.333	66	.244	0	-0	-0	-0	0.0
● BILL FULTON	Fulton, William David b: 10/22/63, Pittsburgh, Pa. BR/TR, 6'3", 195 lbs. Deb: 9/12/87																									
1987	NY-A	1	0	1.000	3	0	0	0	0	4^2	9	4	1	2	21.2	11.57	38	.409	.458	0	—	0	-4	-4	0	-0.6
● FRANK FUNK	Funk, Franklin Ray b: 8/30/35, Washington, D.C. BR/TR, 6', 175 lbs. Deb: 9/3/60 C																									
1960	Cle-A	4	2	.667	9	0	0	0	1	31^2	27	3	9	18	10.2	1.99	188	.248	.305	1	.111	-0	7	6	0	1.2
1961	Cle-A	11	11	.500	56	0	0	0	11	92^1	79	9	31	64	11.1	3.31	119	.234	.306	1	.059	-1	7	6	0	1.4
1962	Cle-A	2	1	.667	47	0	0	0	6	80^2	62	11	32	49	10.9	3.24	120	.212	.298	1	.067	-1	7	6	-0	0.1
1963	Mil-N	3	3	.500	25	0	0	0	0	43^2	42	3	13	19	11.5	2.68	120	.258	.316	0	.000	-0	3	3	-1	0.2
Total	4	20	17	.541	137	0	0	0	18	248^1	210	26	85	150	11.0	3.01	125	.233	.305	3	.067	-3	23	21	-1	2.9
● TOM FUNK	Funk, Thomas James b: 3/13/62, Kansas City, Mo. BL/TL, 6'2", 210 lbs. Deb: 7/24/86																									
1986	Hou-N	0	0	—	8	0	0	0	0	8^1	10	1	6	2	17.3	6.48	56	.286	.390	0	.000	-0	-3	-3	0	0.0
● EDDIE FUSSELBACK	Fusselback, Edward L. b: 7/17/1856, Philadelphia, Pa. d: 4/14/26, Philadelphia, Pa. 5'6", 156 lbs. Deb: 5/3/1882 ♦																									
1882	StL-a	1	2	.333	4	2	2	0	1	23	34	0	2	3	14.1	4.70	60	.321	.333	31	.228	0	-5	-5	-1	-0.6
● CHRIS FUSSELL	Fussell, Christopher Wren b: 5/19/76, Oregon, Ohio BR/TR, 6'2", 200 lbs. Deb: 9/15/98																									
1998	Bal-A	0	1	.000	3	2	0	0	0	9^2	11	1	9	8	18.6	8.38	54	.306	.444	0	—	0	-4	-4	0	-0.2
● FRED FUSSELL	Fussell, Frederick Morris "Moonlight Ace" b: 10/7/1895, Sheridan, Mo. d: 10/23/66, Syracuse, N.Y. BL/TL, 5'10", 155 lbs. Deb: 9/23/22																									
1922	Chi-N	1	1	.500	3	2	1	0	0	19	24	0	8	4	15.2	4.74	89	.333	.400	0	.000	-1	-1	-1	0	-0.1
1923	Chi-N	3	5	.375	28	2	1	0	3	76^1	90	2	31	38	14.6	5.54	72	.298	.369	4	.200	-0	-13	-13	0	-1.2
1928	Pit-N	8	9	.471	28	20	9	2	1	159^2	183	6	41	43	12.7	3.61	113	.295	.340	7	.121	-3	7	8	-3	0.2
1929	Pit-N	2	2	.500	21	3	0	0	1	39^2	68	8	8	18	17.5	8.62	55	.389	.418	4	.250	2	-17	-17	-0	-1.3
Total	4	14	17	.452	80	27	11	2	5	294^2	365	16	88	103	14.0	4.86	85	.312	.363	15	.150	-2	-25	-23	-2	-2.4
● MIKE FYHRIE	Fyhrie, Michael Edwin b: 12/9/69, Long Beach, Cal. BR/TR, 6'2", 190 lbs. Deb: 9/14/96																									
1996	NY-N	0	1	.000	2	0	0	0	0	2^1	4	0	3	0	27.0	15.43	26	.364	.500	0	—	0	-3	-3	0	-0.9
● FRANK GABLER	Gabler, Frank Harold "The Great Gabbo" b: 11/6/11, E.Highlands, Cal. d: 11/1/67, Long Beach, Cal. BR/TR, 6'1", 175 lbs. Deb: 4/19/35																									
1935	NY-N	2	1	.667	26	1	0	0	0	60	79	6	20	24	14.9	5.70	68	.315	.365	2	.125	-1	-11	-12	0	-0.6
1936	*NY-N	9	8	.529	43	14	5	0	6	161^2	170	11	34	46	11.5	3.12	125	.274	.315	10	.208	2	16	14	-1	1.5
1937	NY-N	0	0	—	6	0	0	0	0	9	20	1	2	3	22.0	10.00	39	.455	.478	0	—	0	-6	-6	-0	0.0
	Bos-N	4	7	.364	19	9	2	1	2	76	84	7	16	19	11.8	5.09	70	.283	.319	4	.182	0	-10	-13	-0	-1.6
	Yr	4	7	.364	25	9	2	1	2	85	104	8	18	22	12.9	5.61	64	.305	.340	4	.182	0	-16	-19	-0	-1.6
1938	Bos-N	0	0	—	1	0	0	0	0	0^1	3	0	1	0	108.0	81.00	4	1.000	1.000	0	—	0	-3	-3	0	0.0
	Chi-A	1	7	.125	18	7	3	0	0	69^1	101	12	34	17	17.7	9.09	54	.348	.418	5	.238	0	-33	-32	-1	-2.9
Total	4	16	23	.410	113	31	10	1	8	376^1	457	37	107	109	13.6	5.26	76	.303	.351	21	.196	1	-47	-53	-2	-3.6
● GABE GABLER	Gabler, John Richard b: 10/2/30, Kansas City, Mo. BB/TR, 6'2", 165 lbs. Deb: 9/18/59																									
1959	NY-A	1	1	.500	3	1	0	0	0	19^1	21	1	10	11	14.9	2.79	130	.284	.376	0	.000	-1	2	2	0	0.1
1960	NY-A	3	3	.500	21	4	0	0	1	52	46	2	32	19	13.5	4.15	86	.242	.351	1	.091	-0	-2	-3	0	-0.4
1961	Was-A	3	8	.273	29	9	0	0	4	92^2	104	5	37	33	13.8	4.86	83	.283	.351	5	.200	1	-9	-9	1	-0.8
Total	3	7	12	.368	53	14	0	0	5	164	171	8	79	63	13.8	4.39	87	.271	.354	6	.143	-0	-8	-10	1	-1.1
● KEN GABLES	Gables, Kenneth Harlin "Coral" b: 1/31/19, Walnut Grove, Mo. d: 1/2/60, Walnut Grove, Mo. BR/TR, 5'11", 210 lbs. Deb: 4/18/45																									
1945	Pit-N	11	7	.611	29	16	6	0	1	138^2	139	5	46	49	12.3	4.15	95	.256	.319	4	.103	-3	-5	-3	-2	-0.9
1946	Pit-N	2	4	.333	32	7	0	0	1	100^2	113	3	52	39	14.8	5.27	67	.281	.365	6	.250	1	-21	-20	-2	-1.2

YEAR	TM/L	W	L	PCT	G	GS	CG	SH	SV	IP	H	HR	BB	SO	RAT	ERA	ERA+	OAV	OOB	BH	AVG	PB	PR	/A	PD	TPI
1947	Pit-N	0	0	—	1	0	0	0	0	0^{1}	3	1	0	0	81.0	54.00	8	.750	.750	0	—	0	-2	-2	0	0.0
Total	3	13	11	.542	62	23	6	0	2	239^{2}	255	9	98	88	13.4	4.69	80	.269	.340	10	.159	-1	-28	-25	-4	-2.1

● JOHN GADDY Gaddy, John Wilson "Sheriff" b: 2/5/14, Wadesboro, N.C. d: 5/3/66, Albemarle, N.C. BR/TR, 6'0.5", 182 lbs. Deb: 9/27/38

YEAR	TM/L	W	L	PCT	G	GS	CG	SH	SV	IP	H	HR	BB	SO	RAT	ERA	ERA+	OAV	OOB	BH	AVG	PB	PR	/A	PD	TPI
1938	Bro-N	2	0	1.000	2	2	1	0	0	13	13	0	4	3	12.5	0.69	564	.255	.321	0	.000	-1	4	5	-0	0.7

● GARY GAETTI Gaetti, Gary Joseph b: 8/19/58, Centralia, Ill. BR/TR, 6', 200 lbs. Deb: 9/20/81 ♦

YEAR	TM/L	W	L	PCT	G	GS	CG	SH	SV	IP	H	HR	BB	SO	RAT	ERA	ERA+	OAV	OOB	BH	AVG	PB	PR	/A	PD	TPI
1997	StL-N	0	0	—	1	0	0	0	0	0^{1}	1	0	0	0	54.0	0.00	—	.500	.667	126	.251	0	0	0	0	0.0
1998	StL-N	0	0	—	1	0	0	0	0	1	2	0	0	0	18.0	0.00	—	.400	.400	81	.265	0	0	0	-0	0.0
Total	2	0	0	—	2	0	0	0	0	1^{1}	3	0	0	0	27.0	0.00	—	.429	.500	2223	.257	1	1	1	-0	0.0

● BRENT GAFF Gaff, Brent Allen b: 10/5/58, Fort Wayne, Ind. BR/TR, 6'2", 200 lbs. Deb: 7/7/82

YEAR	TM/L	W	L	PCT	G	GS	CG	SH	SV	IP	H	HR	BB	SO	RAT	ERA	ERA+	OAV	OOB	BH	AVG	PB	PR	/A	PD	TPI
1982	NY-N	0	3	.000	7	5	0	0	0	31^{2}	41	3	10	14	14.8	4.55	80	.323	.377	0	.000	-0	-3	-3	-0	-0.3
1983	NY-N	1	0	1.000	4	0	0	0	0	10^{1}	18	0	1	4	16.5	6.10	59	.360	.373	0	.000	-0	-3	-3	-0	-0.3
1984	NY-N	3	2	.600	47	0	0	0	1	84^{1}	77	4	36	42	12.2	3.63	97	.247	.327	0	.000	-1	-0	-1	0	-0.1
Total	3	4	5	.444	58	5	0	0	1	126^{1}	136	7	47	60	13.2	4.06	88	.278	.344	0	.000	-1	-7	-7	0	-0.7

● CHARLIE GAGUS Gagus, Charles Frederick (b: Charles Frederick Geggus) b: 3/25/1862, San Francisco, Cal d: 1/16/17, San Francisco, Cal Deb: 8/7/1884

YEAR	TM/L	W	L	PCT	G	GS	CG	SH	SV	IP	H	HR	BB	SO	RAT	ERA	ERA+	OAV	OOB	BH	AVG	PB	PR	/A	PD	TPI
1884	Was-U	10	9	.526	23	21	19	0	0	177^{1}	143	2	38	156	9.2	2.54	95	.206	.247	38	.247	-3	-2	-3	1	-0.4

● EDDIE GAILLARD Gaillard, Julian Edward b: 8/13/70, Camden, N.J. BR/TR, 6'1", 180 lbs. Deb: 8/11/97

YEAR	TM/L	W	L	PCT	G	GS	CG	SH	SV	IP	H	HR	BB	SO	RAT	ERA	ERA+	OAV	OOB	BH	AVG	PB	PR	/A	PD	TPI
1997	Det-A	1	0	1.000	16	0	0	0	1	20^{1}	16	2	10	12	11.5	5.31	86	.211	.302	0	—	0	-2	-2	-1	-0.1
1998	TB-A	0	0	—	6	0	0	0	0	7^{2}	4	3	3	5	8.2	5.87	83	.148	.233	0	—	0	-1	-1	-0	-0.3
Total	2	1	0	1.000	22	0	0	0	1	28	20	5	13	17	10.6	5.46	85	.194	.284	0	—	0	-3	-2	-1	-0.4

● NEMO GAINES Gaines, Willard Roland b: 12/23/1897, Alexandria, Va. d: 1/26/79, Warrenton, Va. BL/TL, 6', 180 lbs. Deb: 6/26/21

YEAR	TM/L	W	L	PCT	G	GS	CG	SH	SV	IP	H	HR	BB	SO	RAT	ERA	ERA+	OAV	OOB	BH	AVG	PB	PR	/A	PD	TPI
1921	Was-A	0	0	—	4	0	0	0	0	4^{2}	5	0	2	1	13.5	0.00	—	.294	.368	0	.000	-0	2	2	-0	0.0

● FRED GAISER Gaiser, Frederick Jacob b: 8/31/1885, Stuttgart, Germany d: 10/9/18, Trenton, N.J. Deb: 9/3/08

YEAR	TM/L	W	L	PCT	G	GS	CG	SH	SV	IP	H	HR	BB	SO	RAT	ERA	ERA+	OAV	OOB	BH	AVG	PB	PR	/A	PD	TPI
1908	StL-N	0	0	—	1	0	0	0	0	2^{1}	4	0	3	2	27.0	7.71	31	.444	.583	0	.000	-0	-1	-1	0	0.0

● STEVE GAJKOWSKI Gajkowski, Stephen Robert b: 12/30/69, Seattle, Wash. BR/TR, 6'2", 200 lbs. Deb: 5/25/98

YEAR	TM/L	W	L	PCT	G	GS	CG	SH	SV	IP	H	HR	BB	SO	RAT	ERA	ERA+	OAV	OOB	BH	AVG	PB	PR	/A	PD	TPI
1998	Sea-A	0	0	—	9	0	0	0	0	8^{2}	14	3	4	3	20.8	7.27	64	.389	.476	0	—	0	-3	-3	-0	0.0

● DAN GAKELER Gakeler, Daniel Michael b: 5/1/64, Mt.Holly, N.J. BR/TR, 6'6", 215 lbs. Deb: 6/9/91

YEAR	TM/L	W	L	PCT	G	GS	CG	SH	SV	IP	H	HR	BB	SO	RAT	ERA	ERA+	OAV	OOB	BH	AVG	PB	PR	/A	PD	TPI
1991	Det-A	1	4	.200	31	7	0	0	2	73^{2}	73	5	39	43	13.8	5.74	72	.256	.348	0	—	0	-13	-13	0	-0.9

● BOB GALASSO Galasso, Robert Joseph b: 1/13/52, Connellsville, Pa. BL/TR, 6'1", 205 lbs. Deb: 7/24/77

YEAR	TM/L	W	L	PCT	G	GS	CG	SH	SV	IP	H	HR	BB	SO	RAT	ERA	ERA+	OAV	OOB	BH	AVG	PB	PR	/A	PD	TPI
1977	Sea-A	0	6	.000	11	7	0	0	0	35	57	8	8	21	17.5	9.00	46	.365	.407	0	—	0	-19	-19	-0	-2.5
1979	Mil-A	3	1	.750	31	0	0	0	3	51^{1}	64	5	26	28	15.8	4.38	95	.299	.375	0	—	0	-1	-1	-0	-0.1
1981	Sea-A	1	1	.500	13	1	0	0	1	31^{2}	32	2	13	14	12.8	4.83	80	.264	.336	0	—	0	-4	-3	-0	-0.3
Total	3	4	8	.333	55	8	0	0	4	118	153	15	47	63	15.5	5.87	69	.312	.375	0	—	0	-24	-24	-1	-2.9

● MILT GALATZER Galatzer, Milton b: 5/4/07, Chicago, Ill. d: 1/29/76, San Francisco, Cal BL/TL, 5'10", 168 lbs. Deb: 6/25/33 ♦

YEAR	TM/L	W	L	PCT	G	GS	CG	SH	SV	IP	H	HR	BB	SO	RAT	ERA	ERA+	OAV	OOB	BH	AVG	PB	PR	/A	PD	TPI
1936	Cle-A	0	0	—	1	0	0	0	0	6	7	0	5	3	18.0	4.50	112	.292	.414	23	.237	0	0	0	0	0.0

● RICH GALE Gale, Richard Blackwell b: 1/19/54, Littleton, N.H. BR/TR, 6'7", 225 lbs. Deb: 4/30/78 C

YEAR	TM/L	W	L	PCT	G	GS	CG	SH	SV	IP	H	HR	BB	SO	RAT	ERA	ERA+	OAV	OOB	BH	AVG	PB	PR	/A	PD	TPI
1978	KC-A	14	8	.636	31	30	9	3	0	192^{1}	171	10	100	88	12.8	3.09	124	.244	.340	0	—	0	14	16	-2	1.5
1979	KC-A	9	10	.474	34	31	2	1	0	181^{2}	197	19	99	103	14.9	5.65	75	.278	.369	0	—	0	-29	-28	-1	-2.5
1980	*KC-A	13	9	.591	32	28	6	1	1	190^{2}	169	16	78	97	11.8	3.92	103	.239	.316	0	—	0	2	3	-1	0.2
1981	KC-A	6	6	.500	19	15	2	0	0	101^{2}	107	14	38	47	13.0	5.40	67	.270	.336	0	—	0	-20	-20	-2	-2.3
1982	SF-N	7	14	.333	33	29	2	0	0	170^{1}	193	9	81	102	14.7	4.23	85	.294	.376	6	.125	1	-12	-12	1	-1.2
1983	Cin-N	4	6	.400	33	7	0	0	1	89^{2}	103	8	43	53	14.8	5.82	65	.286	.364	3	.150	1	-22	-20	-1	-2.1
1984	Bos-A	2	3	.400	13	4	0	0	0	43^{2}	57	6	18	28	15.7	5.56	75	.315	.380	0	—	0	-8	-7	-0	-0.7
Total	7	55	56	.495	195	144	21	5	2	970	997	82	457	518	13.7	4.54	86	.269	.351	9	.132	2	-73	-69	-5	-7.1

● DENNY GALEHOUSE Galehouse, Dennis Ward b: 12/7/11, Marshallville, Ohio BR/TR, 6'1", 195 lbs. Deb: 4/30/34

YEAR	TM/L	W	L	PCT	G	GS	CG	SH	SV	IP	H	HR	BB	SO	RAT	ERA	ERA+	OAV	OOB	BH	AVG	PB	PR	/A	PD	TPI
1934	Cle-A	0	0	—	1	0	0	0	0	1	2	0	1	0	27.0	18.00	25	.500	.600	0	—	-0	-2	-1	-0	0.0
1935	Cle-A	1	0	1.000	5	1	1	0	0	13	16	1	9	8	18.0	9.00	50	.314	.426	1	.250	-0	-7	-6	0	-0.4
1936	Cle-A	8	7	.533	36	15	5	0	1	148^{1}	161	5	68	71	14.0	4.85	104	.280	.358	8	.170	-0	3	3	-2	0.0
1937	Cle-A	9	14	.391	36	29	7	0	3	200^{2}	238	11	83	78	14.4	4.57	101	.302	.369	15	.208	-1	1	1	1	0.0
1938	Cle-A	7	8	.467	36	12	5	1	3	114	119	12	65	66	14.6	4.34	107	.275	.371	6	.154	-1	6	4	0	0.3
1939	Bos-A	9	10	.474	30	18	6	1	0	146^{2}	160	6	52	68	13.1	4.54	104	.276	.337	3	.064	-3	1	3	0	0.1
1940	Bos-A	6	6	.500	25	20	5	0	0	120	155	10	41	53	14.7	5.18	87	.313	.366	3	.077	-4	-11	-9	1	-1.0
1941	StL-A	9	10	.474	30	24	11	2	0	190^{1}	183	10	68	61	12.1	3.64	118	.253	.320	13	.191	-0	11	14	1	1.3
1942	StL-A	12	12	.500	32	28	12	3	1	192^{1}	193	5	79	75	12.9	3.60	103	.262	.337	14	.194	1	1	2	1	0.4
1943	StL-A	11	11	.500	31	28	14	2	1	224	217	8	74	114	11.7	2.77	120	.255	.315	9	.125	-3	13	14	-3	0.7
1944	*StL-A	9	10	.474	24	19	6	2	0	153	162	6	44	80	12.2	3.12	115	.266	.316	3	.063	-4	5	8	-2	0.3
1946	StL-A	8	12	.400	30	24	11	2	0	180	194	9	52	90	12.3	3.65	102	.273	.322	5	.091	-3	-3	2	-2	-0.4
1947	StL-A	1	3	.250	9	4	0	0	1	32^{1}	42	3	16	11	16.1	6.12	63	.311	.384	0	.000	-1	-9	-8	0	-1.0
	Bos-A	11	7	.611	21	21	11	3	0	149	150	7	34	38	11.1	3.32	117	.260	.301	5	.096	-4	6	9	-1	0.6
	Yr	12	10	.545	30	25	11	3	1	181^{1}	192	10	50	49	12.0	3.82	102	.269	.317	5	.083	-5	-2	1	-1	-0.4
1948	Bos-A	8	8	.500	27	15	6	1	3	137^{1}	152	10	46	38	13.1	4.00	110	.282	.341	7	.167	-0	4	6	-2	0.5
1949	Bos-A	0	0	—	2	0	0	0	0	2	4	1	3	0	31.5	13.50	32	.400	.538	0	—	0	-2	-2	0	0.0
Total	15	109	118	.480	375	258	100	17	13	2004	2148	104	735	851	13.0	3.97	105	.275	.338	92	.138	-25	20	40	-8	1.4

● DOUG GALLAGHER Gallagher, Douglas Eugene b: 2/21/40, Fremont, Ohio BR/TL, 6'3.5", 195 lbs. Deb: 4/9/62

YEAR	TM/L	W	L	PCT	G	GS	CG	SH	SV	IP	H	HR	BB	SO	RAT	ERA	ERA+	OAV	OOB	BH	AVG	PB	PR	/A	PD	TPI
1962	Det-A	0	4	.000	9	2	0	0	1	25	31	2	15	14	16.6	4.68	87	.290	.377	2	.333	1	-2	-2	0	-0.1

● ED GALLAGHER Gallagher, Edward Michael "Lefty" b: 11/28/10, Dorchester, Mass. d: 12/22/81, Hyannis, Mass. BB/TL, 6'2", 197 lbs. Deb: 7/8/32

YEAR	TM/L	W	L	PCT	G	GS	CG	SH	SV	IP	H	HR	BB	SO	RAT	ERA	ERA+	OAV	OOB	BH	AVG	PB	PR	/A	PD	TPI
1932	Bos-A	0	3	.000	9	3	0	0	0	23^{2}	30	3	28	6	22.1	12.55	36	.323	.479	0	.000	-1	-21	-21	0	-2.1

● BILL GALLAGHER Gallagher, William John b: Philadelphia, Pa. TL , Deb: 5/2/1883 ♦

YEAR	TM/L	W	L	PCT	G	GS	CG	SH	SV	IP	H	HR	BB	SO	RAT	ERA	ERA+	OAV	OOB	BH	AVG	PB	PR	/A	PD	TPI
1883	Bal-a	0	5	.000	7	5	4	0	0	51^{2}	79	0	6	19	14.8	5.40	64	.331	.347	10	.164	-1	-12	-11	-1	-0.9
1884	Phi-U	1	2	.333	3	3	3	0	0	25	32	3	4	12	13.0	3.24	72	.291	.316	1	.091	-2	-2	-3	0	-0.4
Total	2	1	7	.125	10	8	7	0	0	76^{2}	111	3	10	31	14.2	4.70	66	.318	.337	11	.138	-3	-14	-14	-1	-1.3

● BERT GALLIA Gallia, Melvin Allys b: 10/14/1891, Beeville, Tex. d: 3/19/76, Devine, Tex. BR/TR, 6', 165 lbs. Deb: 9/4/12

YEAR	TM/L	W	L	PCT	G	GS	CG	SH	SV	IP	H	HR	BB	SO	RAT	ERA	ERA+	OAV	OOB	BH	AVG	PB	PR	/A	PD	TPI
1912	Was-A	0	0	—	2	0	0	0	0	2	0	0	3	0	13.5	0.00	—	.000	.333	0	—	0	1	1	-0	0.0
1913	Was-A	1	5	.167	31	4	0	0	3	96	85	2	46	46	12.9	4.13	72	.222	.317	2	.087	-2	-13	-12	2	-0.8
1914	Was-A	0	0	—	2	0	0	0	0	6	3	0	4	4	10.5	4.50	63	.120	.241	0	.000	-0	-1	-1	-0	-0.1
1915	Was-A	17	11	.607	43	29	14	3	1	259^{2}	220	2	64	130	10.0	2.29	130	.234	.286	14	.165	-2	19	20	-2	1.7
1916	Was-A	17	13	.567	49	31	13	1	2	283^{2}	278	3	99	120	12.2	2.76	101	.266	.334	18	.194	1	2	1	-3	-0.2
1917	Was-A	9	13	.409	42	23	9	1	1	207^{2}	191	1	93	84	12.5	2.99	88	.258	.344	14	.209	2	-8	-8	-1	-0.8
1918	StL-A	8	6	.571	19	17	10	1	0	124	126	1	61	48	14.0	3.48	79	.268	.359	6	.130	-3	-10	-10	0	-1.4
1919	StL-A	12	14	.462	34	25	14	1	1	222^{1}	220	10	92	83	13.0	3.60	92	.264	.343	11	.153	-2	-9	-7	2	-0.8
1920	StL-A	0	1	.000	2	1	0	0	0	3^{2}	8	0	3	0	27.0	7.36	53	.400	.478	0	.000	-0	-1	-1	-0	-0.3
	Phi-N	2	6	.250	18	5	1	0	2	72	79	2	29	35	13.9	4.50	76	.287	.362	4	.174	-1	-11	-9	-1	-1.1
Total	9	66	69	.489	242	135	61	7	10	1277	1210	21	494	550	12.3	3.14	94	.256	.331	69	.167	-7	-31	-28	-3	-3.8

● PHIL GALLIVAN Gallivan, Philip Joseph b: 5/29/07, Seattle, Wash. d: 11/24/69, St.Paul, Minn. BR/TR, 6', 170 lbs. Deb: 4/21/31

YEAR	TM/L	W	L	PCT	G	GS	CG	SH	SV	IP	H	HR	BB	SO	RAT	ERA	ERA+	OAV	OOB	BH	AVG	PB	PR	/A	PD	TPI
1931	Bro-N	0	1	.000	6	1	0	0	0	15^{1}	23	2	7	1	17.6	5.28	72	.354	.417	0	.000	-0	-2	-3	1	-0.1
1932	Chi-A	1	3	.250	13	3	1	0	0	33^{1}	49	4	24	12	20.0	7.56	57	.338	.435	3	.375	1	-11	-12	-0	-1.1

YEAR	TM/L	W	L	PCT	G	GS	CG	SH	SV	IP	H	HR	BB	SO	RAT	ERA	ERA+	OAV	OOB	BH	AVG	PB	PR	/A	PD	TPI
1934	Chi-A	4	7	.364	35	7	3	0	1	126^{2}	155	14	64	55	15.6	5.61	84	.295	.373	9	.225	0	-16	-12	-1	-0.9
Total	3	5	11	.313	54	11	4	0	1	175^{1}	227	20	95	68	16.6	5.95	77	.309	.389	12	.235	1	-30	-27	-1	-2.1

● BALVINO GALVEZ Galvez, Balvino (Jerez) b: 3/31/64, San Pedro De Macoris, D.R. BR/TR, 6', 170 lbs. Deb: 5/7/86

YEAR	TM/L	W	L	PCT	G	GS	CG	SH	SV	IP	H	HR	BB	SO	RAT	ERA	ERA+	OAV	OOB	BH	AVG	PB	PR	/A	PD	TPI
1986	LA-N	0	1	.000	10	0	0	0	0	20^{2}	19	3	12	11	13.5	3.92	88	.241	.341	0	.000	-0	-0	-1	0	-0.1

● JIM GALVIN Galvin, James Francis "Pud', "Gentle Jeems" or "The Little Steam Engine"
b: 12/25/1856, St.Louis, Mo. d: 3/7/02, Pittsburgh, Pa. BR/TR, 5'8", 190 lbs. Deb: 5/22/1875 MUH

YEAR	TM/L	W	L	PCT	G	GS	CG	SH	SV	IP	H	HR	BB	SO	RAT	ERA	ERA+	OAV	OOB	BH	AVG	PB	PR	/A	PD	TPI
1875	StL-n	4	2	.667	8	7	7	0	1	62	53	0	1	8	7.8	**1.16**	**173**	.209	.212	6	.130	-1	7	6		0.5
1879	Buf-N	37	27	.578	66	66	65	6	0	593	585	3	31	136	9.3	2.28	115	.243	.253	66	.249	5	14	22	3	2.8
1880	Buf-N	20	35	.364	58	54	46	5	0	458^{2}	528	5	32	128	11.0	2.71	91	.273	.284	51	.212	-4	-17	-13	1	-1.5
1881	Buf-N	28	24	.538	56	53	48	5	0	474	546	4	46	136	11.2	2.37	117	.274	.291	50	.212	-1	21	21	7	2.6
1882	Buf-N	28	23	.549	52	51	48	3	0	445^{1}	476	8	40	162	10.4	3.17	93	.256	.272	44	.214	-5	-13	-12	1	-1.6
1883	Buf-N	46	29	.613	**76**	75	**72**	**5**	0	**656^{1}**	676	9	50	279	10.0	2.72	117	.251	.265	71	.220	-4	31	34	-0	2.6
1884	Buf-N	46	22	.676	72	72	71	**12**	0	636^{1}	566	23	63	369	8.9	1.99	158	.227	.246	49	.179	-14	70	82	7	6.8
1885	Buf-N	13	19	.406	33	32	31	3	1	284	356	8	37	93	12.5	4.09	73	.292	.313	23	.189	-2	-40	-35	4	-3.0
	Pit-a	3	7	.300	11	11	9	0	0	88^{1}	97	2	7	27	10.6	3.67	88	.266	.280	4	.105	-4	-4	-4	-1	-0.7
1886	Pit-a	29	21	.580	50	50	49	2	0	434^{2}	457	3	75	72	11.2	2.67	127	.263	.296	49	.253	2	38	35	3	3.6
1887	Pit-N	28	21	.571	49	48	47	3	0	440^{2}	490	12	67	76	11.6	3.29	118	.269	.299	41	.212	-2	38	29	8	3.0
1888	Pit-N	23	25	.479	50	50	49	6	0	437^{1}	446	9	53	107	10.4	2.63	101	.255	.280	25	.143	-6	10	2	4	-0.1
1889	Pit-N	23	16	.590	41	40	38	4	0	341	392	19	78	77	12.7	4.17	90	.280	.322	28	.187	-1	-6	-16	1	-1.3
1890	Pit-P	12	13	.480	26	25	23	1	0	217	275	3	49	35	13.8	4.35	90	.296	.337	20	.206	-1	-3	-11	4	-0.7
1891	Pit-N	15	14	.517	33	30	23	2	0	246^{2}	256	10	62	46	12.1	2.88	114	.258	.310	18	.165	-4	13	11	0	0.7
1892	Pit-N	5	6	.455	12	12	10	0	0	96	104	0	28	29	12.4	2.63	126	.265	.314	5	.122	-3	7	7	-0	0.4
	StL-N	5	6	.455	12	12	10	0	0	92	102	4	26	27	12.8	3.23	99	.270	.322	2	.051	-5	1	-0	-2	-0.6
	Yr	10	12	.455	24	24	20	0	0	188	206	4	54	56	12.6	2.92	111	.268	.318	7	.087	-7	8	7	-2	-0.2
Total	14	361	308	.540	697	681	639	57	1	5941^{1}	6352	122	744	1799	10.8	2.87	109	.261	.284	546	.202	-48	160	162	39	13.0

● LOU GALVIN Galvin, Louis J. b: 4/1862, St.Paul, Minn. d: 6/17/1895, Deb: 10/1/1884

YEAR	TM/L	W	L	PCT	G	GS	CG	SH	SV	IP	H	HR	BB	SO	RAT	ERA	ERA+	OAV	OOB	BH	AVG	PB	PR	/A	PD	TPI
1884	StP-U	0	2	.000	3	3	3	0	0	25	21	0	10	17	11.2	2.88	46	.212	.284	2	.222	-1	-1	-4	-1	-0.4

● BOB GAMBLE Gamble, Robert J. b: 2/1867, Hazleton, Pa. TR, 5'10", 155 lbs. Deb: 5/2/1888

YEAR	TM/L	W	L	PCT	G	GS	CG	SH	SV	IP	H	HR	BB	SO	RAT	ERA	ERA+	OAV	OOB	BH	AVG	PB	PR	/A	PD	TPI
1888	Phi-a	0	1	.000	1	1	1	0	0	9	10	0	3	2	13.0	8.00	37	.270	.325	1	.333	0	-5	-5	-0	-0.4

● GUSSIE GANNON Gannon, James Edward b: 11/26/1873, Erie, Pa. d: 4/12/66, Erie, Pa. BL/TL, 5'11", 154 lbs. Deb: 6/15/1895

YEAR	TM/L	W	L	PCT	G	GS	CG	SH	SV	IP	H	HR	BB	SO	RAT	ERA	ERA+	OAV	OOB	BH	AVG	PB	PR	/A	PD	TPI
1895	Pit-N	0	0	—	1	0	0	0	0	5	7	0	2	0	16.2	1.80	251	.333	.391	0	.000	-0	2	2	-0	-0.1

● JOE GANNON Gannon, Joseph b: St.Louis, Mo. Deb: 8/28/1898

YEAR	TM/L	W	L	PCT	G	GS	CG	SH	SV	IP	H	HR	BB	SO	RAT	ERA	ERA+	OAV	OOB	BH	AVG	PB	PR	/A	PD	TPI
1898	StL-N	0	1	.000	1	1	1	0	0	9	13	0	5	2	19.0	11.00	34	.333	.422	0	.000	-1	-7	-7	-0	-0.5

● JIM GANTNER Gantner, James Elmer b: 1/5/53, Fond Du Lac, Wis. BL/TR, 6', 180 lbs. Deb: 9/3/76 C♦

YEAR	TM/L	W	L	PCT	G	GS	CG	SH	SV	IP	H	HR	BB	SO	RAT	ERA	ERA+	OAV	OOB	BH	AVG	PB	PR	/A	PD	TPI
1979	Mil-A	0	0	—	1	0	0	0	0	1	2	0	0	0	18.0	0.00	—	.400	.400	59	.284	0	0	0	0	0.0

● KEITH GARAGOZZO Garagozzo, Keith John b: 10/25/69, Camden, N.J. BL/TL, 6', 170 lbs. Deb: 4/5/94

YEAR	TM/L	W	L	PCT	G	GS	CG	SH	SV	IP	H	HR	BB	SO	RAT	ERA	ERA+	OAV	OOB	BH	AVG	PB	PR	/A	PD	TPI
1994	Min-A	0	0	—	7	0	0	0	0	9^{1}	9	3	13	3	21.2	9.64	50	.273	.478	0	—	0	-5	-5	0	0.0

● GENE GARBER Garber, Henry Eugene b: 11/13/47, Lancaster, Pa. BR/TR, 5'10", 175 lbs. Deb: 6/17/69

YEAR	TM/L	W	L	PCT	G	GS	CG	SH	SV	IP	H	HR	BB	SO	RAT	ERA	ERA+	OAV	OOB	BH	AVG	PB	PR	/A	PD	TPI
1969	Pit-N	0	0	—	2	1	0	0	0	5	6	3	1	3	12.6	5.40	65	.333	.368	0	.000	-0	-1	-1	-0	0.0
1970	Pit-N	0	3	.000	14	0	0	0	0	22^{1}	22	4	10	7	13.7	5.24	74	.275	.370	2	.667	1	-3	-3	1	-0.2
1972	Pit-N	0	0	—	4	0	0	0	0	6^{1}	7	3	3	3	14.2	7.11	47	.269	.345	0	.000	-0	-3	-3	0	0.0
1973	KC-A	9	9	.500	48	8	4	0	11	152^{2}	164	14	49	60	12.7	4.24	97	.283	.341	0	—	0	-7	-2	1	-0.2
1974	KC-A	1	2	.333	17	0	0	0	1	28	35	3	13	14	15.8	4.82	79	.313	.389	0	—	0	-4	-3	-0	-0.7
	Phi-N	4	0	1.000	34	0	0	0	4	48	39	1	31	27	13.3	2.06	183	.236	.360	0	.000	-0	8	9	0	0.9
1975	Phi-N	10	12	.455	**71**	0	0	0	14	110	104	13	27	69	10.9	3.60	104	.254	.304	2	.167	-0	0	2	-0	0.3
1976	*Phi-N	9	3	.750	59	0	0	0	11	92^{2}	78	4	30	92	10.9	2.82	126	.228	.298	2	.286	1	7	8	1	1.4
1977	*Phi-N	8	6	.571	64	0	0	0	19	103^{1}	82	6	23	78	9.3	2.35	170	.220	.270	0	.000	-1	18	19	2	3.2
1978	Phi-N	2	1	.667	22	0	0	0	3	38^{2}	26	1	11	24	9.3	1.40	256	.191	.267	0	.000	-0	9	9	-0	0.8
	Atl-N	4	4	.500	43	0	0	0	22	78^{1}	58	11	13	61	8.4	2.53	160	.204	.244	1	.091	-0	9	13	1	2.2
	Yr	6	5	.545	65	0	0	0	25	117	84	12	24	85	8.5	2.15	181	.199	.245	1	.071	-1	18	**23**	1	3.0
1979	Atl-N	6	16	.273	68	0	0	0	25	106	121	10	24	56	12.7	4.33	94	.283	.328	3	.300	1	-7	-3	1	-0.6
1980	Atl-N	5	5	.500	68	0	0	0	7	82^{1}	95	6	24	51	13.0	3.83	98	.288	.336	1	.500	0	-2	-1	2	0.1
1981	Atl-N	4	6	.400	35	0	0	0	2	58^{2}	49	2	20	34	10.6	2.61	137	.214	.277	0	.000	-1	6	6	2	1.3
1982	*Atl-N	8	10	.444	69	0	0	0	30	119^{1}	100	4	32	68	10.1	2.34	160	.231	.288	2	.133	0	17	18	2	3.9
1983	Atl-N	4	5	.444	43	0	0	0	9	60^{2}	72	8	23	45	14.4	4.60	84	.300	.366	0	.000	0	-7	-5	2	-0.6
1984	Atl-N	3	6	.333	62	0	0	0	11	106	103	7	24	55	11.0	3.06	126	.254	.299	2	.143	-0	6	9	1	1.0
1985	Atl-N	6	6	.500	59	0	0	0	1	97^{1}	98	8	25	66	11.6	3.61	107	.263	.313	1	.200	0	-0	3	1	0.4
1986	Atl-N	5	5	.500	61	0	0	0	24	78	76	3	20	56	11.2	2.54	157	.260	.310	1	.167	0	10	12	1	2.4
1987	Atl-N	8	10	.444	49	0	0	0	10	69^{1}	87	7	28	48	15.1	4.41	98	.311	.375	0	.000	-0	-3	-1	2	0.0
	KC-A	0	0	—	13	0	0	0	8	14^{1}	13	1	1	3	9.4	2.51	181	.245	.273	0	—	0	3	3	0	0.3
1988	KC-A	0	4	.000	26	0	0	0	6	32^{2}	29	4	13	20	12.1	3.58	111	.238	.321	0	—	0	1	1	0	0.2
Total	19	96	113	.459	931	9	4	0	218	1510	1464	123	445	940	11.6	3.34	116	.257	.314	17	.148	-0	59	92	20	16.1

● BOB GARBER Garber, Robert Mitchell b: 9/10/28, Hunker, Pa. BR/TR, 6'1", 190 lbs. Deb: 5/13/56

YEAR	TM/L	W	L	PCT	G	GS	CG	SH	SV	IP	H	HR	BB	SO	RAT	ERA	ERA+	OAV	OOB	BH	AVG	PB	PR	/A	PD	TPI
1956	Pit-N	0	0	—	2	0	0	0	0	4	3	1	3	3	13.5	2.25	168	.200	.333	0	—	0	1	1	-0	0.0

● RICH GARCES Garces, Richard Aron (Mendoza) b: 5/18/71, Maracay, Venez. BR/TR, 6', 215 lbs. Deb: 9/18/90

YEAR	TM/L	W	L	PCT	G	GS	CG	SH	SV	IP	H	HR	BB	SO	RAT	ERA	ERA+	OAV	OOB	BH	AVG	PB	PR	/A	PD	TPI
1990	Min-A	0	0	—	5	0	0	0	2	5^{2}	4	0	4	1	12.7	1.59	261	.200	.333	0	—	0	1	2	0	-0.2
1993	Min-A	0	0	—	3	0	0	0	0	4	4	0	2	3	13.5	0.00	—	.250	.333	0	—	0	2	2	-0	0.0
1995	Chi-N	0	0	—	7	0	0	0	0	11	11	0	3	6	11.5	3.27	125	.256	.304	0	.000	-0	1	1	-0	0.0
	Fla-N	0	2	.000	11	0	0	0	0	13^{1}	14	1	8	16	14.9	5.40	78	.264	.361	0	—	0	-2	-2	-0	-0.3
	Yr	0	2	.000	18	0	0	0	0	24^{1}	25	1	11	22	13.3	4.44	94	.260	.336	0	.000	-0	-1	-1	-0	-0.3
1996	Bos-A	3	2	.600	37	0	0	0	0	44	42	5	33	55	15.3	4.91	103	.251	.375	0	—	0	0	1	1	0.0
1997	Bos-A	0	1	.000	12	0	0	0	0	13^{2}	14	2	9	12	15.8	4.61	100	.255	.369	0	—	0	-0	0	0	-0.1
1998	Bos-A	1	1	.500	30	0	0	0	1	46	36	6	27	34	12.7	3.33	139	.213	.328	0	—	0	7	7	-0	0.2
Total	6	4	6	.400	105	0	0	0	3	137^{2}	125	14	86	127	14.0	3.99	117	.239	.350	0	.000	-0	10	10	-0	-0.4

● MIKE GARCIA Garcia, Edward Miguel "The Big Bear" b: 11/17/23, San Gabriel, Cal. d: 1/13/86, Fairview Park, O. BR/TR, 6'1", 200 lbs. Deb: 10/3/48

YEAR	TM/L	W	L	PCT	G	GS	CG	SH	SV	IP	H	HR	BB	SO	RAT	ERA	ERA+	OAV	OOB	BH	AVG	PB	PR	/A	PD	TPI
1948	Cle-A	0	0	—	1	0	0	0	0	2	3	0	0	1	13.5	0.00	—	.333	.333	0	—	0	1	1	0	0.0
1949	Cle-A	14	5	.737	41	20	8	5	2	175^{2}	154	6	60	94	11.1	**2.36**	**169**	.241	.308	12	.235	3	36	32	1	3.6
1950	Cle-A	11	11	.500	33	29	11	0	0	184	191	15	74	76	13.0	3.86	112	.266	.334	13	.200	-1	15	10	2	1.1
1951	Cle-A	20	13	.606	47	30	15	1	6	254	239	10	82	118	11.5	3.15	120	.246	.307	18	.212	2	27	18	1	2.4
1952	Cle-A☆	22	11	.667	46	36	19	**6**	4	292^{1}	284	9	87	143	11.6	2.37	141	.253	.310	13	.137	-2	42	32	2	3.6
1953	Cle-A★	18	9	.667	38	35	21	3	0	271^{2}	260	18	81	134	11.4	3.25	116	.250	.307	24	.250	4	23	15	-0	1.7
1954	*Cle-A†	19	8	.704	45	34	13	**5**	5	258^{2}	220	6	71	129	**10.2**	**2.64**	**139**	.229	**.284**	11	.136	-2	**31**	**30**	0	2.9
1955	Cle-A	11	13	.458	38	31	6	2	3	210^{2}	230	17	56	120	12.3	4.02	99	.278	.327	15	.217	2	-1	-1	-1	0.0
1956	Cle-A	11	12	.478	35	30	8	4	0	197^{2}	213	18	74	119	13.3	3.78	111	.272	.339	7	.115	-3	8	9	-0	0.6
1957	Cle-A	12	8	.600	38	27	9	1	0	211^{1}	221	14	73	110	12.8	3.75	99	.269	.333	12	.160	-1	1	-1	-2	-0.4
1958	Cle-A	1	0	1.000	6	1	0	0	0	8	15	2	7	2	25.9	9.00	41	.395	.500	0	.000	-0	-5	-5	0	-0.5
1959	Cle-A	3	6	.333	29	8	1	0	1	72	72	4	31	49	12.9	4.00	92	.265	.340	1	.071	-1	-1	-3	0	-0.4
1960	Chi-A	0	0	—	15	0	0	0	2	17^{2}	23	2	10	8	16.8	4.58	82	.338	.423	1	.333	0	-1	-2	0	0.0
1961	Was-A	0	1	.000	16	0	0	0	0	19	23	1	13	14	17.5	4.74	85	.287	.394	0	—	0	-2	-2	-1	-0.1
Total	14	142	97	.594	428	281	111	27	23	2174^{2}	2148	122	719	1117	12.0	3.27	117	.257	.319	127	.182	1	174	134	2	14.5

YEAR	TM/L	W	L	PCT	G	GS	CG	SH	SV	IP	H	HR	BB	SO	RAT	ERA	ERA+	OAV	OOB	BH	AVG	PB	PR	/A	PD	TPI
● **MIGUEL GARCIA** Garcia, Miguel Angel (Silfontes) b: 4/3/67, Caracas, Venez. BL/TL, 5′11″, 173 lbs. Deb: 4/30/87																										
1987	Cal-A	0	0	—	1	0	0	0	0	1^2	3	0	3	0	32.4	16.20	27	.375	.545	0	—	0	-2	-2	0	0.1
	Pit-N	0	0	—	1	0	0	0	0	0^2	0	0	0	0	0.0	0.00	—	.000	.000	0	—	0	0	0	-0	0.0
1988	Pit-N	0	0	—	1	0	0	0	0	2	3	1	2	2	27.0	4.50	76	.375	.545	0	—	0	-0	-0	-0	0.0
1989	Pit-N	0	2	.000	11	0	0	0	0	16	25	2	7	9	18.0	8.44	40	.357	.416	1	1.000	0	-9	-9	0	-1.0
Total	3	0	2	.000	14	0	0	0	0	20^1	31	3	12	11	19.5	8.41	41	.352	.436	1	1.000	0	-11	-11	0	-0.9
● **RALPH GARCIA** Garcia, Ralph b: 12/14/48, Los Angeles, Cal. BR/TR, 6′, 195 lbs. Deb: 9/26/72																										
1972	SD-N	0	0	—	3	0	0	0	0	5	4	0	3	3	12.6	1.80	183	.211	.318	0	—	0	1	1	0	0.0
1974	SD-N	0	0	—	8	0	0	0	0	10^1	15	1	7	9	19.2	6.10	58	.357	.449	0	—	0	-3	-3	0	0.0
Total	2	0	0	—	11	0	0	0	0	15^1	19	1	10	12	17.0	4.70	74	.311	.408	0	—	0	-2	-2	0	0.0
● **RAMON GARCIA** Garcia, Ramon (Garcia) b: 3/5/24, LaEsperanza, Cuba BR/TR, 5′10″, 170 lbs. Deb: 4/19/48																										
1948	Was-A	0	0	—	4	0	0	0	0	3^2	11	0	4	2	39.3	17.18	25	.524	.615	1	1.000	0	-5	-5	0	0.1
● **RAMON GARCIA** Garcia, Ramon Antonio (Fortunato) b: 12/9/69, Guanare, Venez. BR/TR, 6′2″, 200 lbs. Deb: 5/31/91																										
1991	Chi-A	4	4	.500	16	15	0	0	0	78^1	79	13	31	40	12.9	5.40	74	.269	.343	0	—	0	-11	-12	1	-0.9
1996	Mil-A	4	4	.500	37	2	0	0	4	75^2	84	17	21	40	13.2	6.66	78	.287	.347	0	—	0	-14	-12	0	-1.5
1997	*Hou-N	9	8	.529	42	20	1	1	1	158^2	155	20	52	120	12.3	3.69	108	.262	.331	4	.111	-0	9	5	1	0.6
Total	3	17	16	.515	95	37	1	1	5	312^2	318	50	104	200	12.6	4.84	88	.270	.338	4	.111	-0	-16	-20	2	-1.8
● **ART GARDINER** Gardiner, Arthur Cecil b: 12/26/1899, Brooklyn, N.Y. d: 10/21/54, Copiague, N.Y. BR/TR, Deb: 9/25/23																										
1923	Phi-N	0	0	—	1	0	0	0	0	0	1	0	1	0	—	—	—	1.000	1.000	0	—	0	0	0	0	0.0
● **MIKE GARDINER** Gardiner, Michael James b: 10/19/65, Sarnia, Ont., Can. BB/TR, 6′, 200 lbs. Deb: 9/8/90																										
1990	Sea-A	0	2	.000	5	3	0	0	0	12^2	22	1	5	6	20.6	10.66	37	.379	.446	0	—	0	-10	-9	0	-1.2
1991	Bos-A	9	10	.474	22	22	0	0	0	130	140	18	47	91	12.9	4.85	89	.274	.335	0	—	0	-11	-8	-0	-1.3
1992	Bos-A	4	10	.286	28	18	0	0	0	130^2	126	12	58	79	12.8	4.75	89	.253	.333	0	—	0	-12	-8	0	-0.9
1993	Mon-N	2	3	.400	24	2	0	0	0	38	40	3	19	21	14.2	5.21	80	.268	.355	0	.000	-0	-5	-4	-0	-0.6
	Det-A	0	0	—	10	0	0	0	0	11^1	12	0	7	4	15.1	3.97	108	.279	.380	0	—	0	0	0	0	0.0
1994	Det-A	2	2	.500	38	1	0	0	5	58^2	53	10	23	31	11.7	4.14	117	.233	.304	0	—	0	4	5	-1	0.2
1995	Det-A	0	0	—	9	0	0	0	0	12^1	27	5	2	7	21.2	14.59	33	.458	.475	0	—	0	-14	-13	0	0.0
Total	6	17	27	.386	136	46	0	0	5	393^2	420	49	161	239	13.4	5.21	83	.272	.342	0	.000	-0	-46	-38	-1	-3.8
● **CHRIS GARDNER** Gardner, Christopher John b: 3/30/69, Long Beach, Cal. BR/TR, 6′, 175 lbs. Deb: 9/10/91																										
1991	Hou-N	1	2	.333	5	4	0	0	0	24^2	19	5	14	12	12.0	4.01	87	.218	.327	0	.000	-0	-1	-1	1	-0.1
● **GID GARDNER** Gardner, Frank Washington b: 6/9/1859, Attleboro, Mass. d: 8/1/14, Cambridge, Mass. 165 lbs. Deb: 8/23/1879 ♦																										
1879	Tro-N	0	2	.000	2	2	2	0	0	14	27	0	0	3	17.4	5.79	43	.365	.365	1	.167	-0	-5	-5	-1	-0.6
1880	Cle-N	1	8	.111	9	9	9	0	0	77	80	2	20	21	11.7	2.57	91	.254	.299	6	.188	-0	-2	-2	-0	-0.2
1883	Bal-a	1	0	1.000	2	0	0	0	0	7	9	1	1	2	12.9	5.14	68	.290	.313	44	.273	1	-1	-1	-0	-0.1
1884	CP-U	0	1	.000	1	1	0	0	0	6	10	0	1	4	16.5	6.00	41	.345	.367	38	.255	-0	-2	-2	0	-0.2
1885	Bal-a	0	1	.000	1	1	1	0	0	9	16	2	6	3	23.0	10.00	33	.372	.460	37	.218	0	-7	-7	0	-0.5
Total	5	2	12	.143	15	13	12	0	0	113	142	5	28	33	13.6	3.90	64	.289	.328	178	.233	0	-17	-17	-1	-1.6
● **HARRY GARDNER** Gardner, Harry Ray b: 6/1/1887, Quincy, Mich. d: 8/2/61, Canby, Ore. BR/TR, 6′2″, 180 lbs. Deb: 4/17/11																										
1911	Pit-N	1	1	.500	13	3	2	0	2	42	39	2	20	24	13.1	4.50	76	.244	.335	3	.214	0	-5	-5	-1	-0.3
1912	Pit-N	0	0	—	1	0	0	0	0	0^1	3	0	1	0	108.0	0.00	—	.500	.571	0	—	0	0	0	0	0.0
Total	2	1	1	.500	14	3	2	0	2	42^1	42	2	21	24	13.8	4.46	77	.253	.344	3	.214	0	-5	-5	-1	-0.3
● **JIM GARDNER** Gardner, James Anderson b: 10/4/1874, Pittsburgh, Pa. d: 4/24/05, Pittsburgh, Pa. TR , Deb: 6/20/1895																										
1895	Pit-N	8	2	.800	11	10	8	0	0	85^1	99	1	27	31	13.9	2.64	171	.286	.348	9	.265	1	20	18	-1	1.6
1897	Pit-N	5	5	.500	14	11	8	0	0	95^1	115	4	32	35	14.7	5.19	80	.296	.363	12	.158	-1	-9	-11	-0	-0.9
1898	Pit-N	10	13	.435	25	22	19	1	0	185^1	179	3	48	41	11.4	3.21	111	.252	.306	14	.154	-2	8	7	-2	0.4
1899	Pit-N	1	0	1.000	6	3	0	0	0	32^1	52	1	13	2	18.1	7.52	51	.361	.414	3	.231	1	-13	-13	-2	-0.4
1902	Chi-N	1	2	.333	3	3	2	0	0	25	23	0	10	6	11.9	2.88	94	.245	.317	2	.200	0	-0	-0	0	0.0
Total	5	25	22	.532	59	49	37	1	0	423^1	468	9	130	115	13.2	3.85	100	.278	.338	40	.179	-1	6	1	-4	0.7
● **MARK GARDNER** Gardner, Mark Allan b: 3/1/62, Los Angeles, Cal. BR/TR, 6′1″, 205 lbs. Deb: 5/16/89																										
1989	Mon-N	0	3	.000	7	4	0	0	0	26^1	26	2	11	21	13.3	5.13	69	.250	.333	1	.167	-0	-5	-5	-0	-0.5
1990	Mon-N	7	9	.438	27	26	3	3	0	152^2	129	13	61	135	11.7	3.42	107	.230	.315	5	.114	-1	6	4	2	0.5
1991	Mon-N	9	11	.450	27	27	0	0	0	168^1	139	17	75	107	11.7	3.85	94	.230	.319	5	.091	-2	-3	-4	-2	-0.9
1992	Mon-N	12	10	.545	33	30	0	0	0	179^2	179	15	60	132	12.4	4.36	80	.259	.327	7	.140	1	-17	-18	-1	-2.1
1993	KC-A	4	6	.400	17	16	0	0	0	91^2	92	17	36	54	13.0	6.19	74	.271	.348	0	—	0	-19	-16	-2	-1.9
1994	Fla-N	4	4	.500	20	14	0	0	0	92^1	97	14	30	57	12.5	4.87	90	.276	.335	1	.040	-2	-7	-5	-1	-0.7
1995	Fla-N	5	5	.500	39	11	1	1	1	102^1	109	14	43	87	13.8	4.49	94	.272	.350	4	.190	-0	-3	-3	-1	-0.4
1996	SF-N	12	7	.632	30	28	4	1	0	179^1	200	28	57	145	13.3	4.42	93	.283	.344	11	.162	0	-4	-7	-2	-0.8
1997	SF-N	12	9	.571	30	30	2	1	0	180^1	188	28	57	136	12.3	4.29	96	.272	.329	7	.115	-2	-2	-3	1	-0.4
1998	SF-N	13	6	.684	33	33	4	2	0	212	203	29	65	151	11.6	4.33	94	.253	.314	12	.164	1	-2	-6	1	-0.3
Total	10	78	70	.527	263	219	14	8	1	1385	1362	177	495	1025	12.4	4.37	90	.260	.329	53	.132	-5	-56	-64	-5	-7.5
● **GLENN GARDNER** Gardner, Miles Glenn b: 1/25/16, Burnsville, N.C. d: 7/7/64, Rochester, N.Y. BR/TR, 5′11″, 180 lbs. Deb: 7/21/45																										
1945	StL-N	3	1	.750	17	4	2	1	1	54^2	50	2	27	20	12.7	3.29	114	.242	.329	7	.333	2	3	3	-1	0.3
● **ROB GARDNER** Gardner, Richard Frank b: 12/19/44, Binghamton, N.Y. BR/TL, 6′1″, 176 lbs. Deb: 9/1/65																										
1965	NY-N	0	2	.000	5	4	0	0	0	28	23	4	7	19	9.6	3.21	110	.217	.265	0	.000	-1	1	1	0	0.0
1966	NY-N	4	8	.333	41	17	3	0	1	133^2	147	15	64	74	14.4	5.12	71	.285	.367	7	.171	-0	-22	-22	0	-1.9
1967	Chi-N	0	2	.000	18	5	0	0	0	31^2	33	2	6	16	11.1	3.98	89	.260	.293	0	.000	-0	-2	-2	0	-0.1
1968	Cle-A	0	0	—	5	0	0	0	0	2^2	5	0	2	6	23.6	6.75	44	.417	.500	0	—	0	-1	-1	-0	0.0
1970	NY-A	1	0	1.000	1	1	0	0	0	7^1	8	2	4	6	14.7	4.91	72	.276	.364	1	.333	1	-1	-1	0	-0.1
1971	Oak-A	0	0	—	4	1	0	0	0	7^2	8	1	3	5	12.9	2.35	142	.267	.333	1	.500	0	1	1	0	0.1
	NY-A	0	0	—	2	0	0	0	0	3	3	0	2	2	15.0	3.00	108	.273	.385	0	—	0	0	0	-0	0.0
	Yr	0	0	—	6	1	0	0	0	10^2	11	1	5	7	13.5	2.53	131	.268	.348	1	.500	0	1	1	0	0.1
1972	NY-A	8	5	.615	20	14	1	0	0	97	91	9	28	58	11.0	3.06	96	.243	.296	3	.107	-1	-0	-1	-1	-0.4
1973	Oak-A	0	0	—	3	0	0	0	0	7^1	10	2	4	2	17.2	4.91	72	.370	.452	0	—	0	-1	-1	-0	0.4
	Mil-A	1	1	.500	10	0	0	0	1	12^2	17	0	13	5	22.0	9.95	38	.327	.470	0	—	0	-9	-9	0	-1.2
	Yr	1	1	.500	13	0	0	0	1	20	27	2	17	7	20.2	8.10	45	.342	.464	0	—	0	-10	-10	0	-0.8
Total	8	14	18	.438	109	42	4	0	2	331	345	35	133	193	13.1	4.35	78	.269	.339	12	.138	-2	-34	-35	-0	-3.2
● **WES GARDNER** Gardner, Wesley Brian b: 4/29/61, Benton, Ark. BR/TR, 6′4″, 197 lbs. Deb: 7/29/84																										
1984	NY-N	1	1	.500	21	0	0	0	1	25^1	34	0	8	19	14.9	6.39	55	.321	.368	0	.000	-0	-8	-8	-0	-0.7
1985	NY-N	0	2	.000	9	0	0	0	0	12	18	1	8	11	19.5	5.25	66	.375	.464	0	—	0	-2	-2	0	-0.3
1986	Bos-A	0	0	—	1	0	0	0	0	1	1	0	0	1	9.0	9.00	46	.333	.333	0	—	0	-1	-1	0	0.0
1987	Bos-A	3	6	.333	49	1	0	0	10	89^2	98	17	42	70	14.3	5.42	84	.279	.359	0	—	0	-10	-9	-1	-1.2
1988	*Bos-A	8	6	.571	36	18	1	0	2	149	119	17	64	106	11.2	3.50	117	.220	.305	0	—	0	8	10	-0	0.8
1989	Bos-A	3	7	.300	22	16	0	0	0	86	97	10	47	81	15.2	5.97	69	.287	.376	0	—	0	-20	-18	-1	-2.2
1990	Bos-A	3	7	.300	34	9	0	0	0	77^1	77	6	35	58	13.3	4.89	83	.259	.341	0	—	0	-8	-7	-0	-1.0
1991	SD-N	0	1	.000	14	0	0	0	1	20^1	27	1	12	9	17.3	7.08	54	.310	.394	0	.000	-0	-8	-7	0	-0.4
	KC-A	0	0	—	3	0	0	0	0	5^2	5	0	2	3	11.1	1.59	259	.208	.269	0	—	0	2	2	0	0.0
Total	8	18	30	.375	189	44	1	0	14	466^1	476	52	218	358	13.5	4.90	84	.265	.347	0	.000	-0	-47	-40	-2	-5.0

YEAR	TM/L	W	L	PCT	G	GS	CG	SH	SV	IP	H	HR	BB	SO	RAT	ERA	ERA+	OAV	OOB	BH	AVG	PB	PR	/A	PD	TPI
● **BILL GARDNER** Gardner, William A. b: 9/1868, Baltimore, Md. Deb: 8/9/1887																										
1887	Bal-a	0	1	.000	3	2	1	0	0	13	23	0	10	3	23.5	11.08	37	.426	.523	3	.273	0	-10	-10	-0	-0.5
● **BILL GARFIELD** Garfield, William Milton b: 10/26/1867, Sheffield, Ohio d: 12/16/41, Danville, Ill. BR/TR, 5'11.5", 160 lbs. Deb: 7/10/1889																										
1889	Pit-N	0	2	.000	4	2	2	0	0	29	45	2	17	4	19.6	7.76	48	.344	.423	0	.000	-2	-12	-13	0	-0.8
1890	Cle-N	1	7	.125	9	8	7	0	0	70	91	3	35	16	17.2	4.89	73	.305	.393	4	.154	-1	-10	-10	-0	-1.0
Total	2	1	9	.100	13	10	9	0	0	99	136	5	52	20	17.9	5.73	63	.317	.402	4	.103	-3	-22	-23	-0	-1.8
● **BOB GARIBALDI** Garibaldi, Robert Roy b: 3/3/42, Stockton, Cal. BL/TR, 6'4", 210 lbs. Deb: 7/15/62																										
1962	SF-N	0	0	—	9	0	0	0	1	12^1	13	1	5	9	13.1	5.11	74	.265	.333	0	.000	-0	-2	-2	0	0.0
1963	SF-N	0	1	.000	4	0	0	0	1	8	8	0	4	4	14.6	1.13	284	.276	.382	0	.000	-0	2	2	0	0.3
1966	SF-N	0	0	—	1	0	0	0	0	1	1	0	0	0	9.0	0.00	—	.250	.250	0	—	0	0	0	-0	0.0
1969	SF-N	0	1	.000	1	1	0	0	0	5	6	0	2	1	14.4	1.80	194	.316	.381	0	.000	-0	1	1	0	0.2
Total	4	0	2	.000	15	1	0	0	2	26^1	28	1	11	14	13.7	3.08	116	.277	.354	0	.000	-0	2	1	0	0.5
● **LOU GARLAND** Garland, Louis Lyman b: 7/16/05, Archie, Mo. d: 8/30/90, Idaho Falls, Idaho BR/TR, 6'2.5", 200 lbs. Deb: 8/31/31																										
1931	Chi-A	0	2	.000	7	2	0	0	0	16^2	30	2	14	4	24.3	10.26	41	.400	.500	0	.000	-0	-11	-11	1	-1.0
● **WAYNE GARLAND** Garland, Marcus Wayne b: 10/26/50, Nashville, Tenn. BR/TR, 6', 195 lbs. Deb: 9/13/73																										
1973	Bal-A	0	1	.000	4	1	0	0	0	16	14	1	7	10	11.8	3.94	95	.233	.313	0	—	0	-0	-0	-0	0.0
1974	*Bal-A	5	5	.500	20	6	0	0	1	91	68	5	26	40	9.6	2.97	116	.211	.276	0	—	0	7	5	-1	0.6
1975	Bal-A	2	5	.286	29	1	0	0	4	87^1	80	7	31	46	11.5	3.71	95	.252	.321	0	—	0	-2	-2	-0	0.0
1976	Bal-A	20	7	.741	38	25	14	4	1	232^1	224	10	64	113	11.4	2.67	122	.255	.309	0	—	0	22	15	2	2.1
1977	Cle-A	13	19	.406	38	38	21	1	0	282^2	281	23	88	118	11.8	3.60	110	.261	.318	0	—	0	14	11	-0	1.1
1978	Cle-A	2	3	.400	6	6	0	0	0	29^2	43	6	16	13	18.2	7.89	47	.347	.426	0	—	0	-14	-14	0	-1.8
1979	Cle-A	4	10	.286	18	14	2	0	0	94^2	120	11	34	40	14.9	5.23	81	.318	.379	0	—	0	-11	-10	-1	-1.4
1980	Cle-A	6	9	.400	25	20	4	1	0	150^1	163	18	48	55	13.0	4.61	88	.276	.337	0	—	0	-10	-9	-1	-0.9
1981	Cle-A	3	7	.300	12	10	2	1	0	56	89	8	14	15	16.6	5.79	63	.374	.409	0	—	0	-13	-13	0	-2.0
Total	9	55	66	.455	190	121	43	7	6	1040	1082	89	328	450	12.4	3.89	96	.272	.330	0	—	0	-4	-18	-2	-2.3
● **MIKE GARMAN** Garman, Michael Douglas b: 9/16/49, Caldwell, Idaho BR/TR, 6'3", 215 lbs. Deb: 9/22/69																										
1969	Bos-A	1	0	1.000	2	2	0	0	0	12^1	13	0	10	10	16.8	4.38	87	.277	.404	2	.400	1	-1	-1	0	0.0
1971	Bos-A	1	1	.500	3	3	0	0	0	18^2	15	3	9	6	12.1	3.86	96	.217	.316	2	.333	0	-1	-0	-1	-0.1
1972	Bos-A	0	1	.000	3	1	0	0	0	3^1	4	1	2	1	16.2	10.80	30	.286	.375	0	—	0	-3	-3	-0	-0.7
1973	Bos-A	0	0	—	12	0	0	0	0	22	32	1	15	9	19.2	5.32	76	.352	.443	0	—	0	-4	-3	-0	-0.4
1974	StL-N	7	2	.778	64	0	0	0	6	81^2	66	4	27	45	10.5	2.64	135	.227	.297	1	.100	-1	9	8	0	1.0
1975	StL-N	3	8	.273	66	0	0	0	10	79	73	3	48	48	13.9	2.39	157	.245	.352	0	.000	-0	11	12	-1	1.8
1976	Chi-N	2	4	.333	47	2	0	0	1	76^1	79	7	35	37	13.8	4.95	78	.273	.358	0	.000	-1	-12	-9	0	-0.8
1977	*LA-N	4	4	.500	49	0	0	0	12	62^2	60	7	22	29	12.1	2.73	140	.254	.323	0	.000	-1	8	8	-1	1.1
1978	LA-N	0	1	.000	10	0	0	0	0	16^1	15	3	3	5	9.9	4.41	80	.259	.295	0	—	0	-2	-2	-0	-0.1
	Mon-N	4	6	.400	47	0	0	0	13	61^1	54	5	31	23	12.5	4.40	80	.238	.329	0	.000	-1	-6	-6	-0	-1.3
	Yr	4	7	.364	57	0	0	0	13	77^2	69	8	34	28	11.9	4.40	80	.242	.323	0	.000	-1	-7	-8	-1	-1.4
Total	9	22	27	.449	303	8	0	0	42	433^2	411	34	202	213	12.9	3.63	102	.254	.340	5	.119	-2	-0	4	-3	0.5
● **WILLIE GARONI** Garoni, William b: 7/28/1877, Ft.Lee, N.J. d: 9/9/14, Ft.Lee, N.J. BR/TR, 6'1", 165 lbs. Deb: 9/7/1899																										
1899	NY-N	0	1	.000	3	1	1	0	0	10	12	0	2	2	12.6	4.50	83	.300	.333	0	.000	-1	-1	-1	0	-0.1
● **SCOTT GARRELTS** Garrelts, Scott William b: 10/30/61, Urbana, Ill. BR/TR, 6'4", 195 lbs. Deb: 10/2/82																										
1982	SF-N	0	0	—	1	0	0	0	0	2	3	0	2	4	22.5	13.50	27	.333	.455	0	—	0	-2	-2	0	0.0
1983	SF-N	2	2	.500	5	5	1	1	0	35^2	33	4	19	16	13.6	2.52	140	.254	.358	2	.222	0	4	4	0	0.5
1984	SF-N	2	3	.400	21	3	0	0	0	43	45	6	34	32	16.7	5.65	62	.274	.402	1	.100	-0	-10	-10	-1	-1.2
1985	SF-N☆	9	6	.600	74	0	0	0	13	105^2	76	2	58	106	11.7	2.30	149	.198	.308	2	.222	1	15	13	2	2.4
1986	SF-N	13	9	.591	53	18	2	0	10	173^2	144	17	74	125	11.4	3.11	113	.231	.314	8	.178	2	12	8	2	1.5
1987	*SF-N	11	7	.611	64	0	0	0	12	106^1	70	10	55	127	10.6	3.22	119	.192	.298	2	.200	1	10	7	-1	1.3
1988	SF-N	5	9	.357	65	0	0	0	13	98	80	3	46	86	11.8	3.58	91	.226	.318	1	.077	-1	-1	-3	-1	-0.7
1989	*SF-N	14	5	.737	30	29	2	1	0	193^1	149	11	46	119	**9.1**	**2.28**	**148**	.212	**.260**	9	.136	1	26	23	-0	2.3
1990	SF-N	12	11	.522	31	31	4	2	0	182	190	16	70	80	13.0	4.15	88	.272	.341	4	.061	-3	-7	-10	-1	-1.6
1991	SF-N	1	1	.500	8	3	0	0	0	19^2	25	5	9	8	15.6	6.41	56	.313	.382	0	.000	-0	-6	-6	-0	-0.6
Total	10	69	53	.566	352	89	9	4	48	959^1	815	74	413	703	11.6	3.29	107	.232	.315	29	.125	-1	41	24	1	3.9
● **CLARENCE GARRETT** Garrett, Clarence Raymond "Laz" b: 3/6/1891, Reader, W.Va. d: 2/11/77, Moundsville, W.Va. BR/TR, 6'5.5", 185 lbs. Deb: 9/13/15																										
1915	Cle-A	2	2	.500	4	4	2	0	0	23^1	19	1	6	5	10.0	2.31	132	.224	.283	0	.000	-0	2	2	1	0.4
● **GREG GARRETT** Garrett, Gregory b: 3/12/48, Atascadero, Cal. BB/TL, 6', 200 lbs. Deb: 4/24/70																										
1970	Cal-A	5	6	.455	32	7	0	0	0	74^2	48	6	44	53	11.2	2.65	136	.190	.312	1	.067	-1	9	8	-0	1.0
1971	Cin-N	0	1	.000	2	1	0	0	0	8^2	7	0	10	2	17.7	1.04	323	.250	.447	1	.333	0	2	2	-0	0.3
Total	2	5	7	.417	34	8	0	0	0	83^1	55	6	54	55	11.9	2.48	144	.196	.327	2	.111	-1	11	10	-0	1.3
● **CLIFF GARRISON** Garrison, Clifford William b: 8/13/06, Bellemont, Okla. d: 8/25/94, Woodland, Cal. BR/TR, 6', 180 lbs. Deb: 4/16/28																										
1928	Bos-A	0	0	—	6	0	0	0	0	16	22	2	6	0	15.8	7.88	52	.361	.418	0	.000	-0	-7	-7	1	0.0
● **JIM GARRY** Garry, James Thomas b: 9/21/1869, Great Barrington, Mass. d: 1/15/17, Pittsfield, Mass. TL , Deb: 5/2/1893																										
1893	Bos-N	0	1	.000	1	0	0	0	0	1	5	0	4	2	81.0	63.00	8	.625	.750	0	.000	-0	-6	-6	0	-2.1
● **NED GARVER** Garver, Ned Franklin b: 12/25/25, Ney, Ohio BR/TR, 5'10.5", 180 lbs. Deb: 4/28/48																										
1948	StL-A	7	11	.389	38	24	7	0	5	198	200	14	95	75	13.5	3.41	134	.268	.352	19	.288	4	19	25	1	2.7
1949	StL-A	12	17	.414	41	32	16	1	3	223^2	245	14	102	70	14.1	3.98	114	.277	.354	14	.187	1	5	14	0	1.8
1950	StL-A	13	18	.419	37	31	**22**	2	0	260	264	18	108	85	13.0	3.39	**146**	.264	.338	26	.286	4	**34**	**45**	2	**5.7**
1951	StL-A★	20	12	.625	33	30	**24**	1	0	246	237	17	96	84	12.4	3.73	118	.255	.328	29	.305	7	11	18	1	3.1
1952	StL-A	7	10	.412	21	21	7	2	0	148^2	130	14	55	60	11.4	3.69	106	.235	.309	9	.184	0	-0	4	-0	0.4
	Det-A	1	0	1.000	1	1	1	0	0	9	9	1	3	3	12.0	2.00	190	.265	.324	0	.000	0	2	2	0	0.3
	Yr	8	10	.444	22	22	8	2	0	157^2	139	15	58	63	11.2	3.60	109	.235	.304	9	.176	0	1	5	0	0.7
1953	Det-A	11	11	.500	30	26	13	0	1	198^1	228	16	66	69	13.4	4.45	91	.290	.347	11	.153	-1	-10	-8	1	-0.8
1954	Det-A	14	11	.560	35	32	16	3	1	246^1	216	20	62	93	10.3	2.81	131	.236	.287	13	.165	-0	25	24	2	2.5
1955	Det-A	12	16	.429	33	32	16	1	0	230^2	251	21	67	83	12.6	3.98	97	.279	.333	17	.224	5	-1	-4	0	0.1
1956	Det-A	0	2	.000	6	3	1	0	0	17^2	15	2	13	6	14.8	4.08	101	.234	.372	0	.000	-0	0	0	1	0.0
1957	KC-A	6	13	.316	24	23	6	1	0	145^1	120	13	55	61	11.1	3.84	103	.223	.301	8	.182	0	-1	2	-0	0.2
1958	KC-A	12	11	.522	31	28	10	3	1	201	192	24	66	72	11.6	4.03	97	.244	.304	12	.174	0	-6	-3	5	0.3
1959	KC-A	10	13	.435	32	30	9	2	1	201^1	214	22	42	61	11.6	3.71	108	.270	.309	20	.282	6	3	7	-0	1.3
1960	KC-A	4	9	.308	28	15	5	2	0	122^1	110	15	35	50	10.8	3.83	104	.240	.296	2	.074	-1	1	2	-0	0.1
1961	LA-A	0	3	.000	12	2	0	0	0	29	40	2	16	9	17.4	5.59	81	.348	.427	0	.000	-1	-5	-3	1	-0.3
Total	14	129	157	.451	402	330	153	18	12	2477^1	2471	213	881	881	12.3	3.73	112	.260	.325	180	.218	24	78	122	14	17.4
● **JERRY GARVIN** Garvin, Theodore Jared b: 10/21/55, Oakland, Cal. BL/TL, 6'3", 195 lbs. Deb: 4/10/77																										
1977	Tor-A	10	18	.357	34	34	12	1	0	244^2	247	33	85	127	12.4	4.19	100	.264	.328	0	—	0	-4	0	5	0.4
1978	Tor-A	4	12	.250	26	22	3	0	0	144^2	189	20	48	67	15.0	5.54	71	.319	.374	0	—	0	-29	-26	1	-2.5
1979	Tor-A	0	1	.000	8	1	0	0	0	22^2	15	2	10	14	10.7	2.78	156	.197	.307	0	—	0	4	4	-0	0.1
1980	Tor-A	4	7	.364	61	0	0	0	8	82^2	70	6	27	52	10.6	2.29	188	.233	.296	0	—	0	16	19	1	2.7
1981	Tor-A	1	2	.333	35	4	0	0	0	53	46	3	23	25	11.7	3.40	116	.240	.321	0	—	0	2	3	0	0.2
1982	Tor-A	1	1	.500	32	4	0	0	0	58^1	81	10	26	35	16.7	7.25	62	.335	.401	0	—	0	-21	-18	2	-1.0
Total	6	20	41	.328	196	65	15	1	8	606	648	74	219	320	13.0	4.43	94	.277	.342	0	—	0	-32	-18	9	-0.1

YEAR	TM/L	W	L	PCT	G	GS	CG	SH	SV	IP	H	HR	BB	SO	RAT	ERA	ERA+	OAV	OOB	BH	AVG	PB	PR	/A	PD	TPI
● **NED GARVIN**	Garvin, Virgil Lee b: 1/1/1874, Navasota, Tex. d: 6/16/08, Fresno, Cal. TR, 6'3.5", 160 lbs. Deb: 7/13/1896																									
1896	Phi-N	0	1	.000	2	1	1	0	0	13	19	0	7	4	18.0	7.62	57	.339	.413	0	.000	-1	-5	-5	-0	-0.4
1899	Chi-N	9	13	.409	24	23	22	4	0	199	202	1	42	69	11.6	2.85	132	.263	.311	11	.155	-5	22	20	1	1.5
1900	Chi-N	10	18	.357	30	28	25	1	0	246^{1}	225	4	63	107	11.2	2.41	150	.243	.304	14	.154	-5	**35**	33	4	3.1
1901	Mil-A	8	20	.286	37	27	22	1	2	257^{1}	258	4	90	122	12.7	3.46	104	.258	.328	10	.108	-9	6	4	4	-0.2
1902	Chi-A	10	10	.500	23	19	16	2	0	175^{1}	169	3	43	55	11.3	2.21	153	.254	.307	9	.153	-2	27	23	3	2.4
	Bro-N	1	1	.500	2	2	2	1	0	18	15	0	4	7	9.5	1.00	276	.227	.271	1	.143	-0	4	4	0	0.4
1903	Bro-N	15	18	.455	38	34	30	2	2	298	277	2	84	154	11.3	3.08	104	.248	.308	8	.075	-8	6	4	8	0.2
1904	Bro-N	5	15	.250	23	22	16	2	0	181^{2}	141	6	78	86	11.1	1.68	163	.218	.308	8	.127	-4	21	21	4	2.4
	NY-A	0	1	.000	2	2	0	0	0	12	14	0	2	8	12.0	2.25	121	.292	.320	0	.000	-1	0	1	1	0.1
Total	7	58	97	.374	181	158	134	13	4	1400^{2}	1320	20	413	612	11.6	2.72	125	.249	.312	61	.122	-35	117	104	24	9.5
● **HARRY GASPAR**	Gaspar, Harry Lambert b: 4/28/1883, Kingsley, Iowa d: 5/14/40, Orange, Cal. BR/TR, 6', 180 lbs. Deb: 4/21/09																									
1909	Cin-N	19	11	.633	44	29	19	4	2	260	228	0	57	65	10.2	2.01	129	.242	.291	10	.122	-3	17	17	-5	1.1
1910	Cin-N	15	17	.469	48	31	16	4	**7**	275	257	6	75	74	11.4	2.59	113	.255	.317	10	.115	-3	14	10	-2	0.6
1911	Cin-N	11	17	.393	44	32	11	2	4	253^{2}	272	9	69	76	12.6	3.30	100	.283	.340	13	.153	-2	3	0	-1	-0.4
1912	Cin-N	1	3	.250	7	6	2	1	0	36^{2}	38	0	16	13	13.5	4.17	81	.277	.357	3	.250	0	-3	-3	0	-0.3
Total	4	46	48	.489	143	98	48	11	13	825^{1}	795	15	217	228	11.5	2.69	110	.261	.318	36	.135	-9	31	24	-8	1.0
● **CHARLIE GASSAWAY**	Gassaway, Charles Cason "Sheriff" b: 8/12/18, Gassaway, Tenn. d: 1/15/92, Miami, Fla. BL/TL, 6'2.5", 210 lbs. Deb: 9/25/44																									
1944	Chi-N	0	1	.000	2	2	0	0	0	11^{2}	20	3	10	7	23.1	7.71	46	.385	.484	1	.250	0	-5	-5	-0	-0.4
1945	Phi-A	4	7	.364	24	11	4	0	0	118	114	4	55	50	13.0	3.74	92	.252	.336	6	.154	-2	-5	-4	-1	-0.7
1946	Cle-A	1	1	.500	13	6	0	0	0	50^{2}	54	2	26	23	14.9	3.91	85	.273	.368	1	.067	-1	-2	-3	0	-0.2
Total	3	5	9	.357	39	19	4	0	0	180^{1}	188	9	91	80	14.2	4.04	84	.268	.357	8	.138	-3	-12	-13	-2	-1.3
● **MILT GASTON**	Gaston, Nathaniel Milton b: 1/27/1896, Ridgefield Park, N.J. d: 4/26/96, Hyannis, Mass. BR/TR, 6'1", 185 lbs. Deb: 4/20/24 F																									
1924	NY-A	5	3	.625	29	2	0	0	1	86	92	3	44	24	14.9	4.50	92	.286	.382	6	.222	-1	-3	-3	-1	-0.5
1925	StL-A	15	14	.517	42	29	16	0	1	238^{2}	284	8	101	84	14.7	4.41	106	.305	.376	21	.262	2	-0	7	-2	0.8
1926	StL-A	10	18	.357	32	28	14	1	0	214^{1}	227	13	101	39	13.9	4.33	99	.283	.366	13	.167	-2	-7	-1	-1	-0.3
1927	StL-A	13	17	.433	37	30	21	0	1	254	275	18	100	77	13.4	5.00	87	.281	.350	25	.260	5	-24	-18	1	-1.2
1928	Was-A	6	12	.333	28	22	8	3	0	148^{2}	179	3	53	45	14.0	5.51	73	.302	.360	7	.143	-3	-24	-25	1	-2.7
1929	Bos-A	12	19	.387	39	29	20	1	2	243^{2}	265	15	81	83	12.9	3.73	115	.289	.348	15	.192	0	14	15	-1	1.6
1930	Bos-A	13	20	.394	38	34	20	2	2	273	272	15	98	99	12.2	3.92	117	.259	.323	20	.204	-4	22	21	1	1.9
1931	Bos-A	2	13	.133	23	18	4	0	0	119	137	4	41	33	13.5	4.46	96	.291	.348	6	.158	-2	-1	-2	-0	-0.4
1932	Chi-A	7	17	.292	28	25	7	1	1	166^{2}	183	10	73	44	13.9	4.00	108	.279	.352	14	.233	2	9	6	2	1.1
1933	Chi-A	8	12	.400	30	25	7	1	0	167	177	9	60	39	12.8	4.85	87	.272	.334	8	.154	-0	-11	-11	-1	-1.2
1934	Chi-A	6	19	.240	29	28	10	1	0	194	247	16	84	48	15.4	5.85	81	.313	.379	10	.147	-3	-29	-24	3	-2.5
Total	11	97	164	.372	355	270	127	10	8	2105	2338	114	836	615	13.7	4.55	97	.287	.355	145	.200	-5	-54	-35	0	-3.4
● **WELCOME GASTON**	Gaston, Welcome Thornburg b: 12/19/1872, Guernsey Co., Ohio d: 12/13/44, Columbus, Ohio TL, Deb: 10/6/1898																									
1898	Bro-N	1	1	.500	2	2	2	0	0	16	17	0	9	0	14.6	2.81	128	.270	.361	1	.125	-0	1	1	-0	0.1
1899	Bro-N	0	0	—	1	0	0	0	0	3	3	0	4	0	24.0	3.00	130	.250	.471	1	1.000	1	0	0	0	0.1
Total	2	1	1	.500	3	2	2	0	0	19	20	0	13	0	16.1	2.84	128	.267	.382	2	.222	1	2	2	-0	0.2
● **HANK GASTRIGHT**	Gastright, Henry Carl (b: Henry Carl Gastreich) b: 3/29/1865, Covington, Ky. d: 10/9/37, Cold Spring, Ky. BR/TR, 6'2", 190 lbs. Deb: 4/19/1889																									
1889	Col-a	10	16	.385	32	26	21	0	0	222^{2}	255	8	104	115	14.7	4.57	79	.279	.355	17	.181	-4	-18	-23	-0	-2.4
1890	Col-a	30	14	.682	48	45	41	4	0	401^{1}	312	8	135	199	10.4	2.94	122	.208	.281	36	.213	3	42	29	-4	2.4
1891	Col-a	12	19	.387	35	33	28	1	0	283^{2}	280	7	136	109	13.5	3.78	92	.249	.336	23	.197	2	-2	-10	1	-0.6
1892	Was-N	3	3	.500	11	8	6	0	0	79^{2}	94	3	38	32	15.3	5.08	64	.282	.361	4	.138	0	-16	-16	-1	-1.1
1893	Pit-N	3	1	.750	9	5	3	0	0	59	74	3	39	12	17.7	6.25	73	.297	.399	1	.042	-4	-10	-11	1	-0.8
	Bos-N	12	4	.750	19	18	16	0	0	156	179	9	76	27	15.2	5.13	96	.279	.364	13	.191	-3	-8	-3	-2	-0.6
	Yr	15	5	**.750**	28	23	19	0	0	215	253	12	115	39	15.8	5.44	89	.283	.371	14	.152	-6	-19	-15	-1	-1.4
1894	Bro-N	2	6	.250	16	8	6	1	2	93	135	1	55	20	19.0	6.39	77	.335	.422	7	.171	-3	-11	-15	-1	-1.2
1896	Cin-N	0	0	—	1	0	0	0	0	6	8	0	1	0	13.5	4.50	102	.320	.346	0	.000	-0	-0	0	-0	0.0
Total	7	72	63	.533	171	143	121	6	2	1301^{1}	1337	39	584	514	13.7	4.20	92	.258	.339	101	.186	-8	-23	-51	-7	-4.3
● **AUBREY GATEWOOD**	Gatewood, Aubrey Lee b: 11/17/38, Little Rock, Ark. BR/TR, 6'1", 170 lbs. Deb: 9/11/63																									
1963	LA-A	1	1	.500	4	3	1	0	0	24	12	0	16	13	10.5	1.50	228	.148	.289	0	.000	-1	6	5	-0	0.3
1964	LA-A	3	3	.500	15	7	0	0	0	60^{1}	59	4	12	25	10.7	2.24	147	.258	.298	2	.100	-1	9	7	-0	0.5
1965	Cal-A	4	5	.444	46	3	0	0	0	92	91	5	37	37	12.6	3.42	99	.266	.339	3	.214	1	0	-0	-1	0.0
1970	Atl-N	0	0	—	3	0	0	0	0	2	4	0	2	0	31.5	4.50	95	.364	.500	0	—	0	-0	-0	0	0.0
Total	4	8	9	.471	68	13	1	0	0	178^{1}	166	9	67	75	11.9	2.78	122	.250	.322	5	.119	-1	15	12	-1	0.8
● **CHIPPY GAW**	Gaw, George Joseph b: 3/13/1892, W.Newton, Mass. d: 5/26/68, Boston, Mass. BR/TR, 5'11", 180 lbs. Deb: 4/20/20																									
1920	Chi-N	1	1	.500	6	1	0	0	0	13	16	1	3	4	13.8	4.85	66	.320	.370	1	.250	-0	-2	-2	-0	-0.4
● **DALE GEAR**	Gear, Dale Dudley b: 2/2/1872, Lone Elm, Kan. d: 9/23/51, Topeka, Kan. BR/TR, 5'11", 165 lbs. Deb: 8/15/1896 ♦																									
1896	Cle-N	0	2	.000	3	2	2	0	0	23	35	1	6	6	16.8	5.48	83	.347	.394	6	.400	2	-3	-2	-0	0.0
1901	Was-A	4	11	.267	24	16	14	1	1	163	199	9	22	35	12.4	4.03	91	.297	.324	47	.236	0	-7	-7	2	-0.3
Total	2	4	13	.235	27	18	16	1	1	186	234	10	28	41	13.0	4.21	90	.304	.333	57	.239	2	-9	-9	2	-0.3
● **DINTY GEARIN**	Gearin, Dennis John b: 10/15/1897, Providence, R.I. d: 3/11/59, Providence, R.I. BL/TL, 5'4", 148 lbs. Deb: 8/6/23																									
1923	*NY-N	1	1	.500	6	2	1	0	0	24	23	1	10	9	12.4	3.38	113	.264	.340	2	.286	0	2	1	-0	0.1
1924	NY-N	1	2	.333	6	3	2	0	0	29	30	3	16	4	14.3	2.48	148	.275	.368	3	.333	0	4	4	-0	0.4
	Bos-N	0	1	.000	1	1	0	0	0	0	3	0	2	0	—	∞	—	1.000	1.000	0	—	0	-5	-5	0	-0.4
	Yr	1	3	.250	7	4	2	0	0	29	33	3	18	4	15.8	4.03	91	.295	.392	3	.333	0	-1	-1	-0	0.0
Total	2	2	4	.333	13	6	3	0	0	53	56	4	28	13	14.3	3.74	100	.281	.370	5	.313	1	1	0	-1	0.1
● **BOB GEARY**	Geary, Robert Norton "Speed" b: 5/10/1891, Cincinnati, Ohio d: 1/3/80, Cincinnati, Ohio BR/TR, 5'11", 168 lbs. Deb: 4/25/18																									
1918	Phi-A	2	5	.286	16	7	6	2	4	87	94	0	31	22	13.2	2.69	109	.289	.357	4	.148	-1	1	2	-1	0.1
1919	Phi-A	0	3	.000	9	2	1	0	0	32^{1}	32	1	18	9	13.9	4.73	72	.264	.360	5	.500	2	-5	-5	0	-0.2
1921	Cin-N	1	1	.500	10	1	0	0	0	29	38	1	2	10	12.4	4.34	82	.333	.345	2	.250	0	-2	-2	-0	-0.2
Total	3	3	9	.250	35	10	7	2	4	148^{1}	164	2	51	41	13.2	3.46	92	.293	.355	11	.244	1	-6	-5	-1	-0.3
● **BOB GEBHARD**	Gebhard, Robert Henry b: 1/3/43, Lamberton, Minn. BR/TR, 6'2", 210 lbs. Deb: 8/2/71 C																									
1971	Min-A	1	2	.333	17	0	0	0	0	18	17	0	11	13	14.5	3.00	118	.243	.354	0	—	0	1	1	1	0.3
1972	Min-A	0	1	.000	13	0	0	0	1	21	36	3	13	13	21.9	8.57	37	.371	.455	0	—	0	-13	-13	1	-0.6
1974	Mon-N	0	0	—	1	0	0	0	0	2	5	1	0	0	22.5	4.50	85	.500	.500	0	—	0	-0	-0	0	0.0
Total	3	1	3	.250	31	0	0	0	1	41	58	4	24	26	18.7	5.93	57	.328	.417	0	—	0	-12	-12	1	-0.3
● **PETE GEBRIAN**	Gebrian, Peter "Gabe" b: 8/10/23, Bayonne, N.J. BR/TR, 6', 170 lbs. Deb: 5/6/47																									
1947	Chi-A	2	3	.400	27	4	0	0	5	66^{1}	61	7	33	17	13.0	4.48	82	.247	.340	0	.000	-2	-6	-6	-1	-0.8
● **JIM GEDDES**	Geddes, James Lee b: 3/23/49, Columbus, Ohio BR/TR, 6'2", 200 lbs. Deb: 4/28/72																									
1972	Chi-A	0	0	—	5	1	0	0	0	10^{1}	12	1	10	3	20.0	6.97	45	.293	.442	0	.000	-0	-4	-4	-0	0.0
1973	Chi-A	0	0	—	6	1	0	0	0	15^{2}	14	0	14	7	17.8	2.87	138	.255	.431	0	—	0	2	2	0	0.0
Total	2	0	0	—	11	2	0	0	0	26	26	1	24	10	18.7	4.50	81	.271	.435	0	.000	-0	-3	-3	0	0.0
● **JOE GEDEON**	Gedeon, Elmer Joseph b: 12/5/1893, Sacramento, Cal. d: 5/19/41, San Francisco, Cal BR/TR, 6', 167 lbs. Deb: 5/13/13 ♦																									
1913	Was-A	0	0	—	1	0	0	0	1	0^{1}	0	0	0	0	0.0	0.00	—	.000	.000	13	.183	0	0	0	0	0.1

YEAR	TM/L	W	L	PCT	G	GS	CG	SH	SV	IP	H	HR	BB	SO	RAT	ERA	ERA+	OAV	OOB	BH	AVG	PB	PR	/A	PD	TPI
● COUNT GEDNEY	Gedney, Alfred W. b: 5/10/1849, Brooklyn, N.Y. d: 3/26/22, Hackensack, N.J. 5′9″, 140 lbs. Deb: 4/27/1872 ♦																									
1875	Mut-n	1	0	1.000	2	1	1	0	0	11	7	0	1	2	6.5	0.82	285	.167	.186	55	.206	-0	2	2		0.2
● JOHNNY GEE	Gee, John Alexander "Whiz" b: 12/7/15, Syracuse, N.Y. d: 1/23/88, Cortland, N.Y. BL/TL, 6′9″, 225 lbs. Deb: 9/17/39																									
1939	Pit-N	1	2	.333	3	3	1	0	0	19^2	20	0	10	16	13.7	4.12	93	.253	.337	0	.000	-1	-0	-1	1	-0.1
1941	Pit-N	0	2	.000	3	2	0	0	0	7^1	10	0	5	2	18.4	6.14	59	.294	.385	1	.333	0	-2	-2	-0	-0.5
1943	Pit-N	4	4	.500	15	10	2	0	0	82	89	5	27	18	12.7	4.28	81	.280	.336	3	.115	-1	-8	-7	-3	-1.0
1944	Pit-N	0	0	—	4	0	0	0	0	11^1	20	0	5	3	19.9	7.15	52	.377	.431	1	.500	0	-4	-4	-0	0.0
	NY-N	0	0	—	4	0	0	0	0	4^2	5	0	0	3	9.6	0.00	—	.263	.263	0	—	0	2	2	0	0.0
	Yr	0	0	—	8	0	0	0	0	16	25	0	5	6	16.9	5.06	73	.347	.390	1	.500	0	-3	-2	0	0.0
1945	NY-N	0	0	—	2	0	0	0	1	3	5	0	2	1	21.0	9.00	43	.385	.467	0	.000	-0	-2	-2	0	-0.1
1946	NY-N	2	4	.333	13	6	1	0	0	47^1	60	3	15	22	14.6	3.99	86	.308	.363	3	.231	0	-3	-3	-1	-0.4
Total	6	7	12	.368	44	21	4	0	1	175^1	209	8	64	65	14.1	4.41	80	.294	.354	8	.157	-1	-18	-17	-3	-2.1
● BILLY GEER	Geer, William Henry Harrison (b: George Harrison Geer) b: 8/13/1849, Syracuse, N.Y. TR , 5′8″, 160 lbs. Deb: 10/15/1874 ♦																									
1884	Bro-a	0	0	—	2	0	0	0	0	5	14	0	3	1	30.6	12.60	26	.609	.654	82	.210	0	-5	-5	-0	0.0
● HENRY GEHRING	Gehring, Henry b: 1/24/1881, St.Paul, Minn. d: 4/18/12, Kansas City, Mo. BR/TR, Deb: 7/16/07																									
1907	Was-A	3	7	.300	15	9	8	2	0	87	92	1	14	31	11.1	3.31	73	.274	.305	9	.205	3	-7	-9	-2	-0.8
1908	Was-A	0	1	.000	3	1	0	0	0	5	9	0	2	0	23.4	14.40	16	.450	.542	3	.600	2	-7	-7	0	-0.9
Total	2	3	8	.273	18	10	8	2	0	92	101	1	16	31	11.7	3.91	62	.284	.320	12	.245	5	-14	-15	-2	-1.7
● PAUL GEHRMAN	Gehrman, Paul Arthur "Dutch" b: 5/3/12, Marquam, Ore. d: 10/23/86, Bend, Ore. BR/TR, 6′, 195 lbs. Deb: 9/15/37																									
1937	Cin-N	0	1	.000	2	1	0	0	0	9^1	11	0	5	1	15.4	2.89	129	.282	.364	0	.000	-0	1	1	0	0.1
● GARY GEIGER	Geiger, Gary Merle b: 4/4/37, Sand Ridge, Ill. d: 4/24/96, Murphysboro, Ill. BL/TR, 6′, 168 lbs. Deb: 4/15/58 ♦																									
1958	Cle-A	0	0	—	1	0	0	0	0	2	2	0	1	2	13.5	9.00	41	.286	.375	45	.231	0	-1	-1	0	0.0
● EMIL GEIS	Geis, Emil Michael b: 3/1861, Villmar, Germany BR/TR, 5′11″, 170 lbs. Deb: 7/19/1882																									
1882	Bal-a	4	9	.308	13	13	10	1	0	95^2	84	2	22	10	10.0	4.80	57	.220	.263	6	.146	-2	-22	-22	-3	-2.5
● BILL GEIS	Geis, William J. (b: William J. Geiss) b: 7/15/1858, Chicago, Ill. d: 9/18/24, Chicago, Ill. 5′10″, 164 lbs. Deb: 5/1/1884 F♦																									
1884	Det-N	0	0	—	1	0	0	0	0	5	14	0	2	1	28.8	14.40	20	.424	.457	50	.177	-0	-6	-6	0	0.0
● DAVE GEISEL	Geisel, John David b: 1/18/55, Windber, Pa. BL/TL, 6′3″, 210 lbs. Deb: 6/13/78																									
1978	Chi-N	1	0	1.000	18	1	0	0	0	23^1	27	0	11	15	14.7	4.24	95	.278	.352	0	.000	-0	-2	-1	-0	-0.1
1979	Chi-N	0	0	—	7	0	0	0	0	15	10	0	4	5	9.0	0.60	686	.189	.259	0	.000	-0	5	6	-0	0.0
1981	Chi-N	2	0	1.000	11	2	0	0	0	16	11	0	10	7	11.8	0.56	657	.204	.328	0	.000	-0	5	6	-0	0.7
1982	Tor-A	1	1	.500	16	2	0	0	0	31^2	32	6	17	22	14.5	3.98	113	.260	.359	0	—	0	0	2	-0	-0.3
1983	Tor-A	0	3	.000	47	0	0	0	5	52^1	47	4	31	50	13.8	4.64	93	.240	.349	0	—	0	-3	-2	-1	-0.4
1984	Sea-A	1	1	.500	20	3	0	0	3	43^1	47	2	9	28	12.0	4.15	96	.273	.317	0	—	0	-1	-1	-1	0.0
1985	Sea-A	0	0	—	12	0	0	0	0	27	35	3	15	17	16.7	6.33	67	.310	.391	0	—	0	-7	-6	-0	-0.1
Total	7	5	5	.500	131	8	0	0	8	208^2	209	15	97	144	13.5	4.01	104	.259	.343	0	.000	-1	-2	4	-3	-0.2
● VERN GEISHERT	Geishert, Vernon William b: 1/10/46, Madison, Wis. BR/TR, 6′1″, 215 lbs. Deb: 8/26/69																									
1969	Cal-A	1	1	.500	11	3	0	0	1	31	32	4	7	18	11.6	4.65	75	.267	.313	0	.000	-1	-4	-4	0	-0.3
● EMIL GEISS	Geiss, Emil August b: 3/20/1867, Chicago, Ill. d: 10/4/11, Chicago, Ill. BR/TR, 5′11″, 170 lbs. Deb: 5/18/1887 F♦																									
1887	Chi-N	0	1	.000	1	1	1	0	0	9	17	0	3	4	20.0	8.00	56	.395	.435	1	.083	-1	-4	-4	0	-0.3
● CHARLIE GELBERT	Gelbert, Charles Magnus b: 1/26/06, Scranton, Pa. d: 1/13/67, Easton, Pa. BR/TR, 5′11″, 170 lbs. Deb: 4/16/29 ♦																									
1940	Was-A	0	0	—	2	0	0	0	0	4	5	2	3	1	18.0	9.00	46	.278	.381	20	.370	1	-2	-2	0	0.0
● JOHN GELNAR	Gelnar, John Richard b: 6/25/43, Granite, Okla BR/TR, 6′1.5″, 190 lbs. Deb: 8/4/64																									
1964	Pit-N	0	0	—	7	0	0	0	0	9	11	2	1	4	12.0	5.00	70	.314	.333	0	—	0	-1	-1	-0	0.0
1967	Pit-N	0	1	.000	10	1	0	0	0	19	30	4	11	5	20.4	8.05	42	.375	.462	1	.167	0	-10	-10	0	-0.5
1969	Sea-A	3	10	.231	39	10	0	0	3	108^2	103	7	26	69	11.1	3.31	110	.250	.302	1	.053	-2	4	4	-0	0.3
1970	Mil-A	4	3	.571	53	0	0	0	4	92^1	98	7	23	48	12.3	4.19	90	.277	.330	1	.083	-1	-5	-4	1	-0.2
1971	Mil-A	0	0	—	2	0	0	0	0	1^1	3	0	1	0	27.0	13.50	26	.429	.500	0	—	0	-1	-1	0	0.0
Total	5	7	14	.333	111	11	0	0	7	230^1	245	20	62	126	12.5	4.18	88	.276	.332	3	.081	-2	-14	-13	1	-0.4
● JOE GENEWICH	Genewich, Joseph Edward b: 1/15/1897, Elmira, N.Y. d: 12/21/85, Lockport, N.Y. BR/TR, 6′, 174 lbs. Deb: 9/3/22																									
1922	Bos-N	0	2	.000	6	2	1	0	0	23	29	2	11	4	15.7	7.04	57	.319	.392	1	.167	-0	-8	-8	-0	-0.6
1923	Bos-N	13	14	.481	43	24	12	1	1	227^1	272	15	46	54	12.9	3.72	107	.303	.341	19	.247	2	7	7	2	1.1
1924	Bos-N	10	19	.345	34	27	11	2	1	200^1	258	4	65	43	14.9	5.21	73	.329	.386	10	.167	-2	-30	-31	-0	-4.0
1925	Bos-N	12	10	.545	34	21	10	0	0	169	185	4	41	34	12.4	3.99	100	.279	.327	15	.273	1	5	0	-1	0.1
1926	Bos-N	8	16	.333	37	26	12	2	2	216	239	6	63	59	12.8	3.88	92	.288	.342	11	.164	-1	-1	-8	1	-0.8
1927	Bos-N	11	8	.579	40	19	7	0	1	181	199	7	54	38	12.7	3.83	97	.279	.332	11	.193	-1	2	-2	0	-0.3
1928	Bos-N	3	7	.300	13	11	4	0	0	80^2	88	14	18	15	12.2	4.13	95	.280	.325	1	.038	-3	-1	-2	1	-0.4
	NY-N	11	4	.733	26	18	10	2	3	158^1	136	10	54	37	10.9	3.18	123	.232	.298	13	.203	-1	14	13	1	1.1
	Yr	14	11	.560	39	29	14	2	3	239	224	24	72	52	11.2	3.50	112	.248	.304	14	.156	-4	13	11	2	0.7
1929	NY-N	3	7	.300	21	9	1	0	1	85	133	9	30	19	17.4	6.78	68	.359	.409	12	.375	3	-19	-21	0	-1.7
1930	NY-N	2	5	.286	18	9	3	0	3	61	71	6	20	13	13.6	5.61	84	.297	.354	3	.150	-1	-4	-6	2	-0.5
Total	9	73	92	.442	272	166	71	7	12	1401^2	1610	77	402	316	13.1	4.29	91	.293	.345	96	.207	-4	-35	-58	5	-6.0
● GARY GENTRY	Gentry, Gary Edward b: 10/6/46, Phoenix, Ariz. BR/TR, 6′, 183 lbs. Deb: 4/10/69																									
1969	*NY-N	13	12	.520	35	35	6	3	0	233^2	192	24	81	154	10.7	3.43	107	.222	.293	6	.081	-4	4	6	1	0.3
1970	NY-N	9	9	.500	32	29	5	2	1	188^1	155	19	86	134	11.9	3.68	109	.224	.318	4	.068	-2	8	7	-2	0.2
1971	NY-N	12	11	.522	32	31	8	3	0	203^1	167	16	82	155	11.3	3.23	105	.224	.305	5	.074	-5	5	4	-1	-0.2
1972	NY-N	7	10	.412	32	26	3	0	0	164	153	20	75	120	12.8	4.01	84	.250	.338	5	.104	-1	-10	-12	2	-1.1
1973	Atl-N	4	6	.400	16	14	3	0	1	86^2	74	7	35	42	11.4	3.43	115	.231	.308	7	.233	1	2	5	-1	0.5
1974	Atl-N	0	0	—	3	1	0	0	0	6^2	4	1	2	0	9.5	1.35	280	.167	.259	0	.000	-0	2	2	-0	0.0
1975	Atl-N	1	1	.500	7	2	0	0	0	20	25	3	8	10	14.8	4.95	76	.313	.375	0	.000	-1	-3	-3	0	-0.3
Total	7	46	49	.484	157	138	25	8	2	902^2	770	90	369	615	11.6	3.56	103	.231	.312	27	.095	-12	8	9	-1	-0.6
● RUFE GENTRY	Gentry, James Ruffus b: 5/18/18, Daisy Station, N.C. d: 7/3/97, Winston-Salem, N.C BR/TR, 6′1″, 180 lbs. Deb: 9/10/43 F																									
1943	Det-A	1	3	.250	4	4	2	0	0	29^1	30	2	12	8	13.5	3.68	96	.268	.349	0	.000	-1	-1	-1	-0	-0.2
1944	Det-A	12	14	.462	37	30	10	3	0	203^2	211	9	108	68	14.3	4.24	84	.273	.365	15	.197	-1	-18	-15	1	-1.8
1946	Det-A	0	0	—	2	0	0	0	0	3	4	0	7	1	33.0	15.00	24	.333	.579	0	—	0	-4	-4	-0	0.0
1947	Det-A	0	0	—	1	0	0	0	0	0^1	1	0	2	0	81.0	81.00	5	.500	.750	0	—	0	-3	-3	0	0.0
1948	Det-A	0	0	—	4	0	0	0	0	6^2	5	0	5	1	14.9	2.70	162	.208	.367	1	1.000	0	1	1	-0	0.0
Total	5	13	17	.433	48	34	12	3	0	243	251	11	134	78	14.5	4.37	82	.272	.368	16	.184	-1	-25	-21	0	-2.0
● CHRIS GEORGE	George, Christopher Sean b: 9/24/66, Pittsburgh, Pa. BR/TR, 6′2″, 200 lbs. Deb: 10/1/91																									
1991	Mil-A	0	0	—	2	1	0	0	0	6	8	0	0	2	12.0	3.00	132	.333	.333	0	—	0	1	1	-0	0.1
● LEFTY GEORGE	George, Thomas Edward b: 8/13/1886, Pittsburgh, Pa. d: 5/13/55, York, Pa. BL/TL, 6′, 155 lbs. Deb: 4/14/11																									
1911	StL-A	4	9	.308	27	13	6	1	0	116^1	136	3	51	23	15.2	4.18	81	.256	.332	5	.114	-3	-11	-10	-1	-1.4
1912	Cle-A	0	5	.000	11	5	2	0	0	44^1	69	1	18	18	18.1	4.87	70	.373	.434	3	.214	1	-8	-7	0	-0.6
1915	Cin-N	2	2	.500	5	3	2	1	0	28	24	1	8	11	11.9	3.86	74	.242	.330	4	.333	2	-3	-3	1	-0.2
1918	Bos-N	1	5	.167	9	5	4	0	0	54^1	56	0	21	22	13.3	2.32	116	.281	.359	2	.091	-2	3	2	2	0.3
Total	4	7	21	.250	52	26	14	2	0	243	285	5	98	74	14.9	3.85	82	.281	.355	14	.152	-2	-19	-19	1	-1.9

YEAR	TM/L	W	L	PCT	G	GS	CG	SH	SV	IP	H	HR	BB	SO	RAT	ERA	ERA+	OAV	OOB	BH	AVG	PB	PR	/A	PD	TPI
● **BILL GEORGE**	George, William M. b: 1/27/1865, Bellaire, Ohio d: 8/23/16, Wheeling, W.Va. BR/TL, 5′8″, 165 lbs. Deb: 5/11/1887 ♦																									
1887	NY-N	3	9	.250	13	13	11	0	0	108	126	1	89	49	19.1	5.25	72	.292	.428	9	.170	-4	-14	-18	2	-1.6
1888	*NY-N	2	1	.667	4	3	3	1	0	33^{2}	18	0	11	26	8.0	1.34	205	.149	.226	9	.231	1	6	5	-0	0.5
1889	Col-a	0	0	—	2	0	0	0	0	8	11	1	3	3	15.8	7.88	46	.314	.368	4	.235	-0	-4	-4	0	0.0
Total	3	5	10	.333	19	16	14	1	0	149^{2}	155	2	103	78	16.4	4.51	78	.264	.387	26	.210	-3	-12	-16	2	-1.1
● **OSCAR GEORGY**	Georgy, Oscar John b: 11/25/16, New Orleans, La. BR/TR, 6′3.5″, 180 lbs. Deb: 6/4/38																									
1938	NY-N	0	0	—	1	0	0	0	0	1	2	0	1	0	27.0	18.00	21	.400	.500	0	—	0	-2	-2	-0	0.0
● **DAVE GERARD**	Gerard, David Frederick b: 8/6/36, New York, N.Y. BR/TR, 6′2″, 205 lbs. Deb: 4/10/62																									
1962	Chi-N	2	3	.400	39	0	0	0	3	58^{2}	67	10	28	30	14.7	4.91	84	.289	.368	3	.375	1	-6	-5	-0	-0.4
● **GEORGE GERBERMAN**	Gerberman, George Alois b: 3/8/42, ElCampo, Tex. BR/TR, 6′, 180 lbs. Deb: 9/23/62																									
1962	Chi-N	0	0	—	1	1	0	0	0	5^{1}	3	1	5	1	13.5	1.69	246	.158	.333	0	.000	0	1	1	-0	0.0
● **RUSTY GERHARDT**	Gerhardt, Allen Russell b: 8/13/50, Baltimore, Md. BB/TL, 5′9″, 175 lbs. Deb: 7/27/74																									
1974	SD-N	2	1	.667	23	1	0	0	1	35^{2}	44	1	17	22	15.9	7.07	50	.308	.389	1	.167	-0	-14	-14	-0	-1.2
● **AL GERHEAUSER**	Gerheauser, Albert "Lefty" b: 6/24/17, St.Louis, Mo. d: 5/28/72, Springfield, Mo. BL/TL, 6′3″, 190 lbs. Deb: 4/24/43																									
1943	Phi-N	10	19	.345	38	31	11	2	0	215	222	10	70	92	12.3	3.60	94	.263	.321	8	.113	-3	-5	-5	-1	-1.1
1944	Phi-N	8	16	.333	30	29	10	2	0	182^{2}	210	8	65	66	13.6	4.58	79	.285	.344	15	.231	3	-20	-20	-2	-2.1
1945	Pit-N	5	10	.333	32	14	5	0	1	140^{1}	170	5	54	55	14.4	3.91	101	.304	.366	12	.250	3	-2	1	2	0.5
1946	Pit-N	2	2	.500	35	3	1	0	0	81^{2}	92	2	25	32	13.0	3.97	89	.286	.339	7	.333	2	-5	-4	1	0.1
1948	StL-A	0	3	.000	14	2	0	0	0	23^{1}	32	0	10	10	16.6	7.33	62	.317	.384	2	.333	0	-8	-7	-0	-0.8
Total	5	25	50	.333	149	79	27	4	1	643	726	25	224	255	13.4	4.13	88	.283	.342	44	.209	5	-40	-36	-0	-3.4
● **STEVE GERKIN**	Gerkin, Stephen Paul "Splinter" b: 11/19/12, Grafton, W.Va. d: 11/9/78, Bay Pines, Fla. BR/TR, 6′1″, 162 lbs. Deb: 5/13/45																									
1945	Phi-A	0	12	.000	21	12	3	0	0	102	112	4	27	25	12.5	3.62	95	.285	.336	2	.059	-4	-3	-2	0	-0.6
● **LES GERMAN**	German, Lester Stanley b: 6/1/1869, Baltimore, Md. d: 6/10/34, Germantown, Md. BR/TR, 5′8″, 165 lbs. Deb: 8/27/1890																									
1890	Bal-a	5	11	.313	17	16	15	0	0	132^{1}	147	2	54	37	14.6	4.83	84	.273	.353	6	.118	-2	-14	-11	-2	-1.4
1893	NY-N	8	8	.500	20	18	14	0	0	152	162	6	70	35	14.3	4.14	112	.265	.349	23	.311	2	9	9	-1	0.8
1894	NY-N	9	8	.529	23	15	10	0	1	134	178	7	66	17	17.1	5.78	91	.316	.397	17	.298	0	-7	-8	2	-0.5
1895	NY-N	7	11	.389	25	18	16	0	0	178^{1}	243	7	78	36	16.7	5.96	78	.320	.390	29	.261	3	-23	-26	-0	-1.7
1896	NY-N	0	0	—	1	0	0	0	0	2^{2}	9	0	1	0	33.8	13.50	31	.529	.556	0	.000	-0	-3	-3	-0	0.0
	Was-N	2	20	.091	28	20	14	0	1	166^{2}	240	6	74	20	17.2	6.32	70	.334	.400	16	.229	0	-36	-35	1	-3.3
	Yr	2	20	.091	29	20	14	0	1	169^{1}	249	6	75	20	17.5	6.43	68	.339	.404	16	.225	-0	-39	-38	1	-3.3
1897	Was-N	3	5	.375	15	5	4	0	0	83^{2}	117	2	33	2	16.9	5.59	78	.328	.395	15	.341	2	-12	-12	-1	-0.7
Total	6	34	63	.351	129	92	73	0	2	849^{2}	1096	30	376	147	16.2	5.49	83	.307	.382	106	.260	5	-86	-86	-0	-6.8
● **ED GERNER**	Gerner, Edwin Frederick "Lefty" b: 7/22/1897, Philadelphia, Pa. d: 5/15/70, Philadelphia, Pa. BL/TL, 5′8.5″, 175 lbs. Deb: 5/14/19																									
1919	Cin-N	1	0	1.000	5	1	0	0	0	17	22	0	3	2	14.3	3.18	87	.333	.380	1	.167	0	-0	-1	1	0.0
● **LEFTY GERVAIS**	Gervais, Lucien Edward b: 7/6/1890, Grover, Wis. d: 10/19/50, Los Angeles, Cal. BL/TL, 5′10″, 165 lbs. Deb: 4/17/13																									
1913	Bos-N	0	1	.000	5	2	1	0	0	15^{2}	18	0	4	1	12.6	5.74	57	.383	.431	0	.000	-0	-4	-4	-0	-0.3
● **CHARLIE GESSNER**	Gessner, Charles J. b: Philadelphia, Pa. Deb: 7/19/1886																									
1886	Phi-a	0	1	.000	1	1	1	0	0	8	13	0	5	0	22.5	9.00	39	.351	.455	1	.250	-0	-5	-5	-0	-0.4
● **AL GETTEL**	Gettel, Allen Jones b: 9/17/17, Norfolk, Va. BR/TR, 6′3.5″, 200 lbs. Deb: 4/20/45																									
1945	NY-A	9	8	.529	27	17	9	0	3	154^{2}	141	11	53	67	11.7	3.90	89	.243	.314	16	.281	2	-9	-7	-1	-0.8
1946	NY-A	6	7	.462	26	11	5	2	0	103	89	6	40	54	11.4	2.97	116	.229	.305	4	.125	-2	6	5	0	0.5
1947	Cle-A	11	10	.524	31	21	9	2	0	149	122	12	62	64	11.3	3.20	109	.229	.313	15	.294	4	8	5	1	1.1
1948	Cle-A	0	1	.000	5	2	0	0	0	7^{2}	15	2	10	4	30.5	17.61	23	.385	.520	0	.000	-0	-11	-12	-0	-1.2
	Chi-A	8	10	.444	22	19	7	0	1	148	154	7	60	49	13.3	4.01	106	.268	.342	13	.241	0	5	4	-1	0.4
	Yr	8	11	.421	27	21	7	0	1	155^{2}	169	9	70	53	14.0	4.68	91	.275	.353	13	.228	-0	-7	-7	-1	-0.8
1949	Chi-A	2	5	.286	19	7	1	1	1	63	69	12	26	22	13.9	6.43	65	.283	.357	3	.167	-0	-16	-16	-1	-1.6
	Was-A	0	2	.000	16	1	0	0	1	34^{2}	43	4	24	7	17.4	5.45	78	.314	.416	0	.000	-1	-5	-5	1	-0.3
	Yr	2	7	.222	35	8	1	1	2	97^{2}	112	16	50	29	14.9	6.08	69	.292	.374	3	.115	-1	-20	-20	-0	-1.9
1951	NY-N	1	2	.333	30	1	0	0	0	57^{1}	52	12	25	36	12.1	4.87	80	.240	.318	1	.083	-1	-6	-6	1	-0.3
1955	StL-N	1	0	1.000	8	0	0	0	0	17	26	6	10	7	19.1	9.00	45	.361	.439	3	.500	1	-9	-9	-1	-0.4
Total	7	38	45	.458	184	79	31	5	6	734^{1}	711	72	310	310	12.7	4.28	88	.255	.334	55	.228	3	-37	-40	-1	-2.6
● **CHARLIE GETTIG**	Gettig, Charles Henry b: 12/1870, Baltimore, Md. d: 4/11/35, Baltimore, Md. BR, 5′10″, 172 lbs. Deb: 8/5/1896 ♦																									
1896	NY-N	1	0	1.000	4	1	1	0	1	14	20	0	8	5	19.3	9.64	44	.333	.429	3	.333	1	-8	-8	0	-0.5
1897	NY-N	1	1	.500	3	2	2	0	0	19	23	0	9	7	16.1	5.21	80	.295	.382	15	.200	-0	-2	-2	0	-0.2
1898	NY-N	6	3	.667	17	8	7	0	0	115	141	1	39	14	14.7	3.83	91	.299	.363	49	.250	2	-3	-5	1	0.0
1899	NY-N	7	8	.467	18	15	12	0	0	128	161	3	54	25	15.4	4.43	85	.307	.376	24	.247	1	-8	-10	-1	-0.8
Total	4	15	12	.556	42	26	22	0	1	276	345	4	110	51	15.4	4.50	82	.304	.374	91	.241	4	-21	-25	1	-1.5
● **TOM GETTINGER**	Gettinger, Lewis Thomas Leyton (b: Lewis Thomas Leyton Gittinger) b: 12/11/1868, Frederick, Md. d: 7/26/43, Pensacola, Fla. BL/TL, 5′10″, 180 lbs. Deb: 9/21/1889 ♦																									
1895	Lou-N	0	0	—	2	0	0	0	0	6^{1}	13	1	1	0	19.9	7.11	65	.419	.438	70	.269	0	-2	-2	0	0.0
● **CHARLIE GETZIEN**	Getzien, Charles H. "Pretzels" b: 2/14/1864, Germany d: 6/19/32, Chicago, Ill. BR/TR, 5′10″, 172 lbs. Deb: 8/13/1884																									
1884	Det-N	5	12	.294	17	17	17	1	0	147^{1}	118	2	25	107	8.7	1.95	148	.204	.237	6	.109	-4	17	15	-2	1.0
1885	Det-N	12	25	.324	37	37	37	1	0	330	360	8	92	110	12.3	3.03	94	.264	.311	29	.212	-1	-8	-7	-2	-0.9
1886	Det-N	30	11	.732	43	43	42	1	0	386^{2}	388	6	85	172	11.0	3.03	110	.250	.288	29	.176	-3	12	12	-2	0.4
1887	*Det-N	29	13	**.690**	43	42	41	2	0	366^{2}	373	24	106	135	11.8	3.73	109	.254	.305	29	.186	-2	14	13	0	0.8
1888	Det-N	19	25	.432	46	46	45	2	0	404	411	13	54	202	10.5	3.05	91	.251	.279	41	.246	10	-9	-13	-2	-0.6
1889	Ind-N	18	22	.450	45	44	36	0	1	349	395	27	100	139	13.0	4.54	92	.277	.328	25	.180	2	-20	-14	-3	-1.3
1890	Bos-N	23	17	.575	40	40	39	4	0	350	342	5	82	140	11.0	3.19	118	.248	.292	34	.231	5	15	22	-2	2.2
1891	Bos-N	4	5	.444	11	9	7	0	0	89	112	4	23	29	13.7	3.84	95	.296	.337	7	.171	1	-5	-2	1	0.0
	Cle-N	0	1	.000	1	1	1	0	0	9	12	1	4	4	16.0	8.00	43	.308	.372	0	.000	-1	-5	-5	-1	-0.4
	Yr	4	6	.400	12	10	8	0	0	98	124	5	27	33	13.9	4.22	86	.297	.340	7	.156	0	-10	-6	0	-0.4
1892	StL-N	5	8	.385	13	13	12	0	0	108	159	5	31	32	16.3	5.67	56	.329	.377	9	.200	0	-29	-30	-1	-2.7
Total	9	145	139	.511	296	292	277	11	1	2539^{2}	2670	95	602	1070	11.7	3.46	99	.259	.302	209	.198	8	-17	-9	-13	-1.5
● **RUBE GEYER**	Geyer, Jacob Bowman b: 3/26/1884, Allegheny, Pa. d: 10/12/62, Ford Township, Minn. BR/TR, 5′10″, 170 lbs. Deb: 4/24/10																									
1910	StL-N	0	1	.000	4	0	0	0	0	4	5	0	3	5	18.0	4.50	66	.294	.400	0	.000	-0	-1	-1	-0	-0.2
1911	StL-N	9	6	.600	29	11	7	1	0	148^{2}	141	7	56	46	12.3	3.27	103	.259	.335	13	.228	1	2	2	-1	0.1
1912	StL-N	7	14	.333	41	18	5	0	0	181	191	4	84	61	13.9	3.28	104	.288	.371	11	.208	-0	3	3	0	0.3
1913	StL-N	1	5	.167	30	4	2	0	1	78^{2}	83	6	38	21	14.1	5.26	61	.282	.368	2	.091	-2	-18	-18	-1	-1.5
Total	4	17	26	.395	104	33	14	1	1	412^{1}	420	17	181	133	13.4	3.67	92	.276	.358	26	.195	-1	-14	-14	-2	-1.3
● **TONY GHELFI**	Ghelfi, Anthony Paul b: 8/23/61, LaCrosse, Wis. BR/TR, 6′3″, 185 lbs. Deb: 9/1/83																									
1983	Phi-N	1	1	.500	3	3	0	0	0	14^{1}	15	2	6	14	13.2	3.14	114	.268	.339	1	.250	0	1	1	1	0.2
● **BOB GIALLOMBARDO**	Giallombardo, Robert Paul b: 5/20/37, Brooklyn, N.Y. BL/TL, 6′, 175 lbs. Deb: 6/21/58																									
1958	LA-N	1	1	.500	6	5	0	0	0	26^{1}	29	3	15	14	15.0	3.76	109	.284	.376	1	.167	-0	1	1	0	0.1
● **JOE GIARD**	Giard, Joseph Oscar "Peco" b: 10/7/1898, Ware, Mass. d: 7/10/56, Worcester, Mass. BL/TL, 5′10.5″, 170 lbs. Deb: 4/18/25																									
1925	StL-A	10	5	.667	30	21	9	4	0	160^{2}	179	13	87	43	15.2	5.04	93	.295	.388	3	.057	-6	-12	-7	2	-0.9

YEAR	TM/L	W	L	PCT	G	GS	CG	SH	SV	IP	H	HR	BB	SO	RAT	ERA	ERA+	OAV	OOB	BH	AVG	PB	PR	/A	PD	TPI
1926	StL-A	3	10	.231	22	15	2	0	0	90	113	7	67	18	18.1	7.00	61	.318	.428	8	.276	0	-30	-27	-1	-3.2
1927	NY-A	0	0	—	16	0	0	0	0	27	38	1	19	10	19.0	8.00	48	.352	.449	2	.286	0	-12	-12	-0	0.0
Total	3	13	15	.464	68	36	11	4	0	277^{2}	330	21	173	71	16.5	5.96	75	.309	.408	13	.146	-6	-53	-46	1	-4.1

● JOE GIBBON Gibbon, Joseph Charles b: 4/10/35, Hickory, Miss. BR/TL, 6′4″, 210 lbs. Deb: 4/17/60

YEAR	TM/L	W	L	PCT	G	GS	CG	SH	SV	IP	H	HR	BB	SO	RAT	ERA	ERA+	OAV	OOB	BH	AVG	PB	PR	/A	PD	TPI
1960	*Pit-N	4	2	.667	27	9	0	0	0	80^{1}	87	5	31	60	13.2	4.03	93	.277	.342	4	.211	1	-2	-3	0	-0.1
1961	Pit-N	13	10	.565	30	29	7	3	0	195^{1}	185	16	57	145	11.3	3.32	120	.251	.309	8	.136	-2	16	15	-0	1.4
1962	Pit-N	3	4	.429	19	8	0	0	0	57	53	4	24	26	12.2	3.63	108	.250	.326	3	.176	-0	2	2	1	0.3
1963	Pit-N	5	12	.294	37	22	5	0	1	147^{1}	147	7	54	110	12.6	3.30	100	.258	.328	4	.093	-2	-0	-0	1	-0.1
1964	Pit-N	10	7	.588	28	24	3	0	0	146^{2}	145	10	54	97	12.6	3.68	95	.262	.334	12	.255	3	-2	-3	1	0.1
1965	Pit-N	4	9	.308	31	15	1	0	1	105^{2}	85	7	34	63	10.5	4.51	78	.221	.291	3	.115	-0	-11	-12	0	-1.4
1966	SF-N	4	6	.400	37	10	1	0	1	81	86	4	16	48	11.6	3.67	100	.275	.314	3	.200	0	-1	0	1	0.2
1967	SF-N	6	2	.750	28	10	3	1	1	82	65	4	33	63	11.1	3.07	107	.220	.305	1	.042	-1	3	2	2	0.3
1968	SF-N	1	2	.333	29	0	0	0	1	40	33	3	19	22	12.1	1.57	187	.234	.333	0	.000	-0	6	6	0	0.5
1969	SF-N	1	3	.250	16	0	0	0	2	20	15	1	13	9	13.0	3.60	97	.211	.341	0	.000	-0	-0	-0	1	0.0
	Pit-N	5	1	.833	35	0	0	0	9	51^{1}	38	5	17	35	10.0	1.93	181	.208	.282	0	.000	-1	9	9	1	1.4
	Yr	6	4	.600	51	0	0	0	11	71^{1}	53	6	30	44	10.7	2.40	146	.208	.296	0	.000	-1	9	9	2	1.4
1970	*Pit-N	0	1	.000	41	0	0	0	5	41	44	2	24	26	15.4	4.83	81	.280	.383	0	.000	-0	-4	-4	0	-0.2
1971	Cin-N	5	6	.455	50	0	0	0	11	64^{1}	54	3	32	34	12.2	2.94	114	.239	.336	0	.000	-0	4	3	1	0.7
1972	Cin-N	0	0	—	2	0	0	0	0	0^{1}	3	1	1	1	108.0	54.00	6	.750	.800	0	—	0	-2	-2	0	0.0
	Hou-N	0	0	—	9	0	0	0	0	7^{1}	13	2	5	4	23.3	9.82	34	.394	.487	0	—	0	-5	-5	1	0.1
	Yr	0	0	—	11	0	0	0	0	7^{2}	16	3	6	5	27.0	11.74	29	.432	.523	0	—	0	-7	-7	1	0.1
Total	13	61	65	.484	419	127	20	4	32	1119^{2}	1053	74	414	743	12.1	3.52	102	.251	.323	38	.144	-3	12	8	11	3.2

● NORWOOD GIBSON Gibson, Norwood Ringold "Gibby" b: 3/11/1877, Peoria, Ill. d: 7/7/59, Peoria, Ill. BR/TR, 5′10″, 165 lbs. Deb: 4/29/03

YEAR	TM/L	W	L	PCT	G	GS	CG	SH	SV	IP	H	HR	BB	SO	RAT	ERA	ERA+	OAV	OOB	BH	AVG	PB	PR	/A	PD	TPI
1903	Bos-A	13	9	.591	24	21	17	2	0	183^{1}	166	2	65	76	11.7	3.19	95	.241	.313	17	.266	5	-5	-3	0	0.1
1904	Bos-A	17	14	.548	33	32	29	1	0	273	216	8	81	112	9.9	2.21	121	.219	.281	6	.065	-6	12	14	-3	0.6
1905	Bos-A	4	7	.364	23	17	9	0	0	134	118	9	55	67	12.0	3.69	73	.238	.321	4	.095	-2	-15	-15	-2	-1.6
1906	Bos-A	0	2	.000	5	2	1	0	0	18^{2}	25	2	7	3	15.4	5.30	52	.325	.381	1	.200	0	-5	-5	-0	-0.5
Total	4	34	32	.515	85	72	56	3	0	609	525	21	208	258	11.1	2.93	95	.233	.303	28	.138	-4	-14	-9	-5	-1.4

● PAUL GIBSON Gibson, Paul Marshall b: 1/4/60, Southampton, N.Y. BR/TL, 6′, 185 lbs. Deb: 4/8/88

YEAR	TM/L	W	L	PCT	G	GS	CG	SH	SV	IP	H	HR	BB	SO	RAT	ERA	ERA+	OAV	OOB	BH	AVG	PB	PR	/A	PD	TPI
1988	Det-A	4	2	.667	40	1	0	0	0	92	83	6	34	50	11.6	2.93	130	.240	.312	0	—	0	11	9	0	0.7
1989	Det-A	4	8	.333	45	13	0	0	0	132	129	11	57	77	13.1	4.64	82	.259	.342	0	—	0	-11	-12	-0	-1.0
1990	Det-A	5	4	.556	61	0	0	0	3	97^{1}	99	10	44	56	13.3	3.05	130	.269	.349	0	—	0	9	10	0	0.9
1991	Det-A	5	7	.417	68	0	0	0	8	96	112	10	48	52	15.3	4.59	90	.297	.381	0	—	0	-5	-5	-0	-0.7
1992	NY-N	0	1	.000	43	1	0	0	0	62	70	7	25	49	13.8	5.23	66	.287	.353	0	.000	-0	-12	-12	-1	-0.3
1993	NY-N	1	1	.500	8	0	0	0	0	8^{2}	14	1	2	12	16.6	5.19	77	.350	.381	0	—	0	-1	-1	0	-0.2
	NY-A	2	0	1.000	20	0	0	0	0	35^{1}	31	4	9	25	10.2	3.06	136	.238	.288	0	—	0	5	4	0	0.4
1994	NY-A	1	1	.500	30	0	0	0	0	29	26	5	17	21	13.7	4.97	92	.236	.344	0	—	0	-1	-1	0	0.1
1996	NY-A	0	0	—	4	0	0	0	0	4^{1}	6	1	0	3	12.5	6.23	79	.316	.316	0	—	0	-1	-1	0	0.0
Total	8	22	24	.478	319	15	0	0	11	556^{2}	570	55	236	345	13.2	4.07	97	.267	.344	0	.000	-0	-6	-9	-1	-0.1

● BOB GIBSON Gibson, Robert (b: Pack Robert Gibson) b: 11/9/35, Omaha, Neb. BR/TR, 6′1.5″, 195 lbs. Deb: 4/15/59 CH

YEAR	TM/L	W	L	PCT	G	GS	CG	SH	SV	IP	H	HR	BB	SO	RAT	ERA	ERA+	OAV	OOB	BH	AVG	PB	PR	/A	PD	TPI
1959	StL-N	3	5	.375	13	9	2	1	0	75^{2}	77	4	39	48	13.9	3.33	127	.273	.363	3	.115	-1	5	8	-0	0.7
1960	StL-N	3	6	.333	27	12	2	0	0	86^{2}	97	7	48	69	15.2	5.61	73	.284	.374	5	.179	-0	-18	-15	1	-1.3
1961	StL-N	13	12	.520	35	27	10	2	1	211^{1}	186	13	119	166	13.2	3.24	136	.239	.344	13	.197	2	19	27	1	3.3
1962	StL-N★	15	13	.536	32	30	15	**5**	1	233^{2}	174	15	95	208	10.7	2.85	**150**	.204	.291	20	.263	6	28	37	1	**5.0**
1963	StL-N	18	9	.667	36	33	14	2	0	254^{2}	224	19	96	204	11.8	3.39	105	.233	.311	18	.207	7	-3	4	-2	1.0
1964	*StL-N	19	12	.613	40	36	17	2	1	287^{1}	250	25	86	245	10.8	3.01	127	.232	.294	15	.156	1	17	26	-1	2.7
1965	StL-N★	20	12	.625	38	36	20	6	1	299	243	34	103	270	10.7	3.07	125	.222	.295	25	.240	8	16	26	-2	3.6
1966	StL-N†	21	12	.636	35	35	20	**5**	0	280^{1}	210	20	78	225	9.4	2.44	147	.207	.267	20	.200	3	36	36	-1	4.4
1967	*StL-N★	13	7	.650	24	24	10	2	0	175^{1}	151	10	40	147	10.0	2.98	110	.231	.278	8	.133	1	8	6	0	0.8
1968	*StL-N☆	22	9	.710	34	34	28	**13**	0	304^{2}	198	11	62	**268**	**7.9**	**1.12**	**258**	**.184**	**.233**	16	.170	4	**63**	**60**	-3	**7.3**
1969	StL-N★	20	13	.606	35	35	**28**	4	0	314	251	12	95	269	10.2	2.18	164	.219	.285	29	.246	8	49	49	-2	**6.0**
1970	StL-N★	**23**	7	**.767**	34	34	23	3	0	294	262	13	88	274	10.8	3.12	132	.237	.296	33	.303	12	30	32	-1	4.2
1971	StL-N	16	13	.552	31	31	20	**5**	0	245^{2}	215	14	76	185	10.9	3.04	118	.232	.296	15	.172	2	12	15	0	2.1
1972	StL-N★	19	11	.633	34	34	23	4	0	278	226	14	88	208	10.3	2.46	138	.224	.288	20	.194	7	31	29	2	4.2
1973	StL-N	12	10	.545	25	25	13	1	0	195	159	12	57	142	10.1	2.77	132	.224	.284	12	.185	2	19	19	-1	2.3
1974	StL-N	11	13	.458	33	33	9	1	0	240	236	24	104	129	12.9	3.83	93	.259	.338	17	.210	3	-6	-7	-1	-0.6
1975	StL-N	3	10	.231	22	14	1	0	2	109	120	10	62	60	15.4	5.04	75	.287	.384	5	.179	0	-17	-16	-0	-1.7
Total	17	251	174	.591	528	482	255	56	6	3884^{1}	3279	257	1336	3117	10.9	2.91	127	.228	.299	274	.206	65	290	335	-10	44.0

● BOB GIBSON Gibson, Robert Louis b: 6/19/57, Philadelphia, Pa. BR/TR, 6′, 195 lbs. Deb: 4/13/83

YEAR	TM/L	W	L	PCT	G	GS	CG	SH	SV	IP	H	HR	BB	SO	RAT	ERA	ERA+	OAV	OOB	BH	AVG	PB	PR	/A	PD	TPI
1983	Mil-A	3	4	.429	27	7	0	0	2	80^{2}	71	6	46	46	13.2	3.90	96	.237	.340	0	—	0	1	-2	-1	0.2
1984	Mil-A	2	5	.286	18	9	1	1	0	69	61	10	47	54	14.1	4.96	78	.236	.354	0	—	0	-7	-9	0	-0.4
1985	Mil-A	6	7	.462	41	1	0	0	11	92^{1}	86	10	49	53	13.3	3.90	107	.260	.357	0	—	0	3	3	-0	0.4
1986	Mil-A	1	2	.333	11	1	0	0	0	26^{2}	23	3	23	11	15.5	4.73	92	.232	.377	0	—	0	-2	-1	-0	-0.3
1987	NY-N	0	0	—	1	0	0	0	0	1	0	0	1	2	9.0	0.00	—	.000	.250	0	—	0	0	0	0	0.0
Total	5	12	18	.400	98	18	1	1	13	269^{2}	241	29	166	166	13.7	4.24	94	.243	.353	0	—	0	-5	-8	-1	-0.1

● ROBERT GIBSON Gibson, Robert Murray b: 8/20/1869, Duncansville, Pa. d: 12/19/49, Pittsburgh, Pa. BR/TR, 6′3″, 185 lbs. Deb: 6/4/1890

YEAR	TM/L	W	L	PCT	G	GS	CG	SH	SV	IP	H	HR	BB	SO	RAT	ERA	ERA+	OAV	OOB	BH	AVG	PB	PR	/A	PD	TPI
1890	Chi-N	1	0	1.000	1	1	1	0	0	9	6	0	2	1	8.0	0.00	—	.182	.229	0	.000	-0	4	4	0	0.4
	Pit-N	0	3	.000	3	3	2	0	0	12	24	0	23	3	37.5	17.25	19	.400	.581	3	.231	-0	-18	-19	-1	-2.5
	Yr	1	3	.250	4	4	3	0	0	21	30	0	25	4	24.9	9.86	35	.323	.479	3	.176	-1	-15	-15	-0	-2.1

● SAM GIBSON Gibson, Samuel Braxton b: 8/5/1899, King, N.C. d: 1/31/83, High Point, N.C. BL/TR, 6′2″, 198 lbs. Deb: 4/19/26

YEAR	TM/L	W	L	PCT	G	GS	CG	SH	SV	IP	H	HR	BB	SO	RAT	ERA	ERA+	OAV	OOB	BH	AVG	PB	PR	/A	PD	TPI
1926	Det-A	12	9	.571	35	24	16	2	2	196^{1}	199	6	75	61	12.8	3.48	117	.269	.341	18	.250	2	12	13	0	1.4
1927	Det-A	11	12	.478	33	26	11	0	0	184^{2}	201	9	86	76	14.4	3.80	111	.285	.369	14	.212	-1	7	8	-1	0.6
1928	Det-A	5	8	.385	20	18	5	1	0	119^{2}	155	4	53	29	16.2	5.42	76	.322	.397	12	.286	2	-18	-17	-1	-1.5
1930	NY-A	0	1	.000	2	2	0	0	0	6	14	1	6	3	30.0	15.00	29	.424	.513	1	.333	0	-7	-7	0	-0.8
1932	NY-N	4	8	.333	41	5	1	1	3	81^{2}	107	7	30	39	15.3	4.85	77	.322	.382	5	.263	0	-9	-10	-1	-1.4
Total	5	32	38	.457	131	75	33	4	5	588^{1}	676	27	250	208	14.5	4.28	95	.295	.370	50	.248	3	-15	-14	-3	-1.7

● GEORGE GICK Gick, George Edward b: 10/18/15, Dunnington, Ind. BB/TR, 6′, 190 lbs. Deb: 10/3/37

YEAR	TM/L	W	L	PCT	G	GS	CG	SH	SV	IP	H	HR	BB	SO	RAT	ERA	ERA+	OAV	OOB	BH	AVG	PB	PR	/A	PD	TPI
1937	Chi-A	0	0	—	1	0	0	0	1	2	0	0	0	1	0.0	0.00	—	.000	.000	0	—	0	1	1	-0	0.1
1938	Chi-A	0	0	—	1	0	0	0	0	1	0	0	0	1	9.0	0.00	—	.000	.250	0	—	0	1	1	0	0.0
Total	2	0	0	—	2	0	0	0	1	3	0	0	0	2	3.0	0.00	—	.000	.100	0	—	0	2	2	-0	0.1

● BRETT GIDEON Gideon, Byron Brett b: 8/8/63, Ozona, Tex. BR/TR, 6′2″, 200 lbs. Deb: 7/5/87

YEAR	TM/L	W	L	PCT	G	GS	CG	SH	SV	IP	H	HR	BB	SO	RAT	ERA	ERA+	OAV	OOB	BH	AVG	PB	PR	/A	PD	TPI
1987	Pit-N	1	5	.167	29	0	0	0	3	36^{2}	34	6	10	31	11.0	4.66	88	.243	.298	1	1.000	1	-2	-2	-0	-0.3
1989	Mon-N	0	0	—	4	0	0	0	0	4^{2}	5	1	5	2	19.3	1.93	183	.294	.455	0	—	0	1	1	-0	0.0
1990	Mon-N	0	0	—	1	0	0	0	0	1	2	0	4	0	54.0	9.00	41	.500	.750	0	—	0	-1	-1	0	0.0
Total	3	1	5	.167	34	0	0	0	3	42^{1}	41	7	19	33	13.0	4.46	90	.255	.337	1	1.000	1	-2	-2	-0	-0.3

● JIM GIDEON Gideon, James Leslie b: 9/26/53, Taylor, Tex. BR/TR, 6′3″, 190 lbs. Deb: 9/14/75

YEAR	TM/L	W	L	PCT	G	GS	CG	SH	SV	IP	H	HR	BB	SO	RAT	ERA	ERA+	OAV	OOB	BH	AVG	PB	PR	/A	PD	TPI
1975	Tex-A	0	0	—	1	1	0	0	0	5^{2}	7	1	5	2	19.1	7.94	47	.292	.414	0	—	0	-3	-3	-0	0.0

● FLOYD GIEBELL Giebell, Floyd George b: 12/10/09, Pennsboro, W.Va. BL/TR, 6′2.5″, 172 lbs. Deb: 4/21/39

YEAR	TM/L	W	L	PCT	G	GS	CG	SH	SV	IP	H	HR	BB	SO	RAT	ERA	ERA+	OAV	OOB	BH	AVG	PB	PR	/A	PD	TPI
1939	Det-A	1	1	.500	9	0	0	0	0	15^{1}	19	1	12	9	18.2	2.93	167	.317	.431	0	.000	-0	3	3	-0	0.3
1940	Det-A	2	0	1.000	2	2	2	1	0	18	14	2	4	11	9.0	1.00	476	.206	.250	0	.000	-1	7	8	-0	0.7

YEAR	TM/L	W	L	PCT	G	GS	CG	SH	SV	IP	H	HR	BB	SO	RAT	ERA	ERA+	OAV	OOB	BH	AVG	PB	PR	/A	PD	TPI
1941	Det-A	0	0	—	17	2	0	0	0	34^1	45	3	26	10	18.6	6.03	75	.313	.418	2	.333	0	-7	-6	-0	0.0
Total	3	3	1	.750	28	4	2	1	0	67^2	78	6	42	30	16.0	3.99	117	.287	.382	2	.143	-1	2	5	-1	1.0
● PAUL GIEL Giel, Paul Robert b: 2/29/32, Winona, Minn. BR/TR, 5′11″, 185 lbs. Deb: 7/10/54																										
1954	NY-N	0	0	—	6	0	0	0	0	4^1	8	0	2	4	20.8	8.31	49	.421	.476	0	—	0	-2	-2	-0	0.0
1955	NY-N	4	4	.500	34	2	0	0	0	82^1	70	8	50	47	13.3	3.39	119	.233	.346	1	.053	-2	6	6	-1	0.3
1958	SF-N	4	5	.444	29	9	0	0	0	92	89	12	55	55	14.3	4.70	81	.259	.365	2	.074	-2	-8	-9	1	-0.8
1959	Pit-N	0	0	—	4	0	0	0	0	7^2	17	0	6	3	27.0	14.09	27	.472	.548	0	—	0	-9	-9	0	0.0
1960	Pit-N	2	0	1.000	16	0	0	0	0	33	35	3	15	21	13.6	5.73	65	.276	.352	0	.000	-1	-7	-7	-1	-0.5
1961	Min-A	1	0	1.000	12	0	0	0	0	19^1	24	6	17	14	19.1	9.78	43	.289	.410	1	.500	0	-12	-12	0	-0.5
	KC-A	0	0	—	1	0	0	0	0	1^2	6	1	3	1	48.6	37.80	11	.600	.692	0	—	0	-6	-6	-0	0.0
	Yr	1	0	1.000	13	0	0	0	0	21	30	7	20	15	21.4	12.00	35	.319	.439	1	.500	0	-19	-18	0	-0.5
Total	6	11	9	.550	102	11	0	0	0	240^1	249	30	148	145	15.0	5.39	73	.271	.374	4	.073	-4	-38	-39	-0	-1.5
● BOB GIGGIE Giggie, Robert Thomas b: 8/13/33, Dorchester, Mass. BR/TR, 6′1″, 200 lbs. Deb: 4/18/59																										
1959	Mil-N	1	0	1.000	13	0	0	0	1	20	24	2	10	15	15.3	4.05	87	.316	.395	0	.000	-0	-0	-1	1	0.0
1960	Mil-N	0	0	—	3	0	0	0	0	4^1	5	0	4	5	18.7	4.15	83	.278	.409	0	—	0	-0	-0	-0	0.0
	KC-A	1	0	1.000	10	0	0	0	0	18^2	24	1	15	8	18.8	5.79	69	.333	.448	0	.000	-0	-4	-4	0	-0.2
1962	KC-A	1	1	.500	4	2	0	0	0	14^1	17	5	3	4	13.2	6.28	67	.293	.339	0	.000	-0	-4	-3	-1	-0.5
Total	3	3	1	.750	30	2	0	0	1	57^1	70	8	32	32	16.2	5.18	74	.313	.401	0	.000	-1	-8	-8	0	-0.7
● BILL GILBERT Gilbert, Alfred Gideon b: 3/13/1868, Havre De Grace, Md 6′, 180 lbs. Deb: 9/15/1892																										
1892	Bal-N	0	1	.000	2	1	1	0	0	14	14	1	17	5	19.9	5.79	59	.250	.425	2	.333	1	-4	-4	-1	-0.2
● JOE GILBERT Gilbert, Joe Dennis b: 4/20/52, Jasper, Tex. BR/TL, 6′1″, 167 lbs. Deb: 4/30/72																										
1972	Mon-N	0	1	.000	22	0	0	0	0	33	41	3	18	25	16.1	8.45	42	.306	.388	0	.000	-0	-18	-18	-1	-0.6
1973	Mon-N	1	2	.333	21	0	0	0	1	29	30	1	19	17	15.2	4.97	77	.270	.377	0	.000	0	-4	-4	0	-0.4
Total	2	1	3	.250	43	0	0	0	1	62	71	4	37	42	15.7	6.82	54	.290	.383	0	.000	-0	-23	-22	-0	-1.0
● BILL GILBRETH Gilbreth, William Freeman b: 9/3/47, Abilene, Tex. BL/TL, 6′, 180 lbs. Deb: 6/25/71																										
1971	Det-A	2	1	.667	9	5	2	0	0	30	28	4	21	14	15.3	4.80	75	.264	.395	2	.182	-0	-4	-4	0	-0.4
1972	Det-A	0	0	—	2	0	0	0	0	5	10	1	4	2	25.2	16.20	19	.476	.560	0	.000	-0	-7	-7	0	0.0
1974	Cal-A	0	0	—	3	0	0	0	0	1^1	2	0	1	0	20.3	13.50	25	.400	.500	0	—	0	-1	-1	0	0.0
Total	3	2	1	.667	14	5	2	0	0	36^1	40	5	26	16	16.8	6.69	53	.303	.425	2	.167	-0	-13	-13	0	-0.4
● BOB GILKS Gilks, Robert James b: 7/2/1864, Cincinnati, Ohio d: 8/21/44, Brunswick, Ga. BR/TR, 5′8″, 178 lbs. Deb: 8/25/1887 ♦																										
1887	Cle-a	7	5	.583	13	13	12	1	0	108	104	1	42	28	12.9	3.08	141	.245	.326	26	.313	2	15	15	2	1.6
1888	Cle-a	0	2	.000	4	2	2	0	1	21	26	1	8	3	15.0	8.14	38	.292	.357	111	.229	0	-12	-12	-0	-0.9
1890	Cle-N	2	2	.500	4	3	3	0	0	31^2	34	0	9	5	13.4	4.26	84	.266	.333	116	.213	-0	-2	-2	-1	-0.3
Total	3	9	9	.500	21	18	17	1	1	160^2	164	2	59	36	13.3	3.98	101	.256	.332	320	.231	2	0	1	1	0.4
● ED GILL Gill, Edward James b: 8/7/1895, Somerville, Mass. d: 10/10/95, Brockton, Mass. BL/TR, 5′10″, 165 lbs. Deb: 7/5/19																										
1919	Was-A	1	1	.500	16	2	0	0	0	37^1	38	0	21	7	14.7	4.82	67	.260	.361	0	.000	-1	-7	-7	-1	-0.5
● GEORGE GILL Gill, George Lloyd b: 2/13/09, Catchings, Miss. BR/TR, 6′1″, 185 lbs. Deb: 5/4/37																										
1937	Det-A	11	4	.733	31	10	4	1	1	127^2	146	11	42	40	13.3	4.51	104	.285	.340	7	.140	-3	2	2	1	0.1
1938	Det-A	12	9	.571	24	23	13	1	0	164	195	15	50	30	13.6	4.12	121	.296	.348	6	.105	-4	12	16	-1	1.3
1939	Det-A	0	1	.000	3	1	0	0	0	8^2	14	1	3	1	17.7	8.31	59	.368	.415	0	.000	-0	-4	-3	0	-0.3
	StL-A	1	12	.077	27	11	5	0	0	95	139	10	34	24	16.7	7.11	68	.343	.398	4	.154	-2	-26	-24	1	-2.6
	Yr	1	13	.071	30	12	5	0	0	103^2	153	11	37	25	16.8	7.21	68	.345	.400	4	.143	-2	-30	-27	1	-2.9
Total	3	24	26	.480	85	45	22	2	1	395^1	494	37	129	95	14.3	5.05	96	.306	.360	17	.126	-9	-16	-9	2	-1.5
● HADDIE GILL Gill, Harold Edward b: 1/23/1899, Brockton, Mass. d: 8/1/32, Brockton, Mass. BL/TL, 5′11″, 165 lbs. Deb: 8/16/23																										
1923	Cin-N	0	0	—	1	0	0	0	0	1	1	0	1	1	18.0	0.00	—	.333	.500	0	—	0	0	0	0	0.0
● CLARAL GILLENWATER Gillenwater, Claral Lewis b: 5/20/1900, Sims, Ind. d: 2/26/78, Bradenton, Fla. BR/TR, 6′, 187 lbs. Deb: 8/20/23																										
1923	Chi-A	1	3	.250	5	3	1	1	0	21^1	28	2	6	2	14.8	5.48	72	.337	.389	0	.000	-1	-4	-4	0	-0.6
● TOM GILLES Gilles, Thomas Bradford b: 7/2/62, Peoria, Ill. BR/TR, 6′1″, 185 lbs. Deb: 6/7/90																										
1990	Tor-A	1	0	1.000	2	0	0	0	0	1^1	2	0	0	1	13.5	6.75	58	.333	.333	0	—	0	-0	-0	0	-0.3
● DUKE GILLESPIE Gillespie, John Patrick "Silent John" b: 2/25/1900, Oakland, Cal. d: 2/15/54, Vallejo, Cal. BR/TR, 5′11.5″, 172 lbs. Deb: 4/12/22																										
1922	Cin-N	3	3	.500	31	4	1	0	0	77^2	84	2	29	21	13.6	4.52	88	.294	.367	2	.133	-1	-4	-5	1	-0.3
● BOB GILLESPIE Gillespie, Robert William "Bunch" b: 10/8/18, Columbus, Ohio BR/TR, 6′4″, 187 lbs. Deb: 5/11/44																										
1944	Det-A	0	1	.000	7	0	0	0	0	11	7	0	12	4	15.5	6.55	54	.194	.396	0	.000	-0	-4	-4	0	-0.3
1947	Chi-A	5	8	.385	25	17	1	0	0	118	133	4	53	36	14.3	4.73	77	.291	.366	2	.061	-3	-13	-14	3	-1.4
1948	Chi-A	0	4	.000	25	6	1	0	0	72	81	3	33	19	14.4	5.13	83	.287	.364	0	.000	-2	-7	-7	-0	-0.6
1950	Bos-A	0	0	—	1	0	0	0	0	1^1	2	1	4	0	40.5	20.25	24	.333	.600	0	—	0	-2	-2	-0	0.0
Total	4	5	13	.278	58	23	2	0	0	202^1	223	8	102	59	14.5	5.07	76	.286	.369	2	.039	-5	-26	-27	3	-2.3
● PAUL GILLIFORD Gilliford, Paul Gant "Gorilla" b: 1/12/45, Bryn Mawr, Pa. BR/TL, 5′11″, 210 lbs. Deb: 9/20/67																										
1967	Bal-A	0	0	—	2	0	0	0	0	3	6	1	1	2	21.0	12.00	26	.429	.467	0	—	0	-3	-3	0	0.0
● JACK GILLIGAN Gilligan, John Patrick b: 10/18/1884, Chicago, Ill. d: 11/19/80, Modesto, Cal. BB/TR, 6′, 190 lbs. Deb: 9/16/09																										
1909	StL-A	1	2	.333	3	3	3	0	0	23	28	1	9	4	15.3	5.48	44	.315	.390	1	.111	-1	-8	-8	-1	-1.0
1910	StL-A	0	3	.000	9	5	2	0	0	39^1	37	0	28	10	15.1	3.66	68	.253	.377	3	.200	-0	-5	-5	0	-0.4
Total	2	1	5	.167	12	8	5	0	0	62^1	65	1	37	14	15.2	4.33	57	.277	.382	4	.167	-1	-13	-13	-0	-1.4
● GEORGE GILLPATRICK Gillpatrick, George F. b: 2/28/1875, Holden, Mo. d: 12/15/41, Kansas City, Mo. Deb: 5/22/1898																										
1898	StL-N	0	2	.000	7	3	1	0	0	35	42	0	19	12	16.2	6.94	55	.296	.387	2	.125	-2	-13	-12	-1	-0.8
● FRANK GILMORE Gilmore, Frank T. "Shadow" b: 4/27/1864, Webster, Mass. d: 7/21/29, Hartford, Conn. BR , Deb: 9/11/1886																										
1886	Was-N	4	4	.500	9	9	9	1	0	75	57	3	22	75	9.5	2.52	130	.200	.257	0	.000	-4	7	6	-1	0.1
1887	Was-N	7	20	.259	28	27	27	1	0	234^2	247	7	92	114	13.5	3.87	105	.262	.336	6	.065	-11	5	5	-3	-0.8
1888	Was-N	1	9	.100	12	11	10	0	0	95^2	131	4	29	23	15.7	6.59	43	.323	.378	1	.024	-5	-40	-40	-2	-3.7
Total	3	12	33	.267	49	47	46	2	0	405^1	435	14	143	212	13.3	4.26	85	.266	.333	7	.043	-20	-28	-29	-6	-4.4
● LEN GILMORE Gilmore, Leonard Preston "Meow" b: 11/3/17, Fairview Park, Ind. BR/TR, 6′3″, 175 lbs. Deb: 10/1/44																										
1944	Pit-N	0	1	.000	1	1	1	0	0	8	13	2	0	0	14.6	7.88	47	.361	.361	0	.000	-0	-4	-4	1	-0.3
● JOHN GILROY Gilroy, John M. b: 10/26/1869, Washington, D.C. d: 8/4/1897, Norfolk, Va. Deb: 8/30/1895																										
1895	Was-N	1	4	.200	8	4	2	0	0	41^1	63	3	24	2	19.8	6.53	73	.344	.431	7	.241	-1	-8	-8	1	-0.7
1896	Was-N	0	0	—	1	0	0	0	0	2	0	0	1	0	4.5	0.00	—	.000	.143	0	.000	-0	1	1	0	0.0
Total	2	1	4	.200	9	4	2	0	0	43^1	63	3	25	2	19.1	6.23	77	.333	.422	7	.233	-1	-7	-7	1	-0.7
● HAL GILSON Gilson, Harold "Lefty" b: 2/9/42, Los Angeles, Cal. BR/TL, 6′5″, 195 lbs. Deb: 4/14/68																										
1968	StL-N	0	2	.000	13	0	0	0	2	21^2	27	1	11	19	15.8	4.57	63	.310	.388	0	.000	-0	-4	-4	-1	-0.6
	Hou-N	0	0	—	2	0	0	0	0	3^2	7	0	1	1	22.1	7.36	40	.412	.474	0	—	0	-2	-2	0	0.0
	Yr	0	2	.000	15	0	0	0	2	25^1	34	1	12	20	16.7	4.97	58	.327	.402	0	.000	-0	-6	-6	-1	-0.6
● BILLY GING Ging, William Joseph b: 11/7/1872, Elmira, N.Y. d: 9/14/50, Elmira, N.Y. BR/TR, 5′10″, 170 lbs. Deb: 9/25/1899																										
1899	Bos-N	1	0	1.000	1	1	1	0	0	8	5	0	5	2	11.3	1.13	370	.179	.303	0	.000	-0	2	3	-0	0.2

YEAR	TM/L	W	L	PCT	G	GS	CG	SH	SV	IP	H	HR	BB	SO	RAT	ERA	ERA+	OAV	OOB	BH	AVG	PB	PR	/A	PD	TPI
● JOE GINGRAS	Gingras, Joseph Elzead John b: 1/10/1894, New York, N.Y. d: 9/6/47, Jersey City, N.J. BR/TR, 6'2", 188 lbs. Deb: 6/18/15																									
1915	KC-F	0	0	—	2	0	0	0	0	4	6	0	1	2	15.8	6.75	39	.353	.389	0	.000	-0	-2	-2	-0	0.0
● CHARLIE GIRARD	Girard, Charles August b: 12/16/1884, Brooklyn, N.Y. d: 8/6/36, Brooklyn, N.Y. BR/TR, 5'10", 175 lbs. Deb: 9/14/10																									
1910	Phi-N	1	2	.333	7	1	0	0	1	26^2	33	2	12	11	15.9	6.41	49	.308	.388	1	.125	-0	-10	-10	-1	-1.2
● DAVE GIUSTI	Giusti, David John b: 11/27/39, Seneca Falls, N.Y. BR/TR, 5'11", 195 lbs. Deb: 4/13/62																									
1962	Hou-N	2	3	.400	22	5	0	0	0	73^2	82	7	30	43	13.7	5.62	66	.280	.347	7	.292	3	-14	-15	1	-0.6
1964	Hou-N	0	0	—	8	0	0	0	0	25^2	24	1	8	16	11.2	3.16	108	.253	.311	2	.286	1	1	1	1	0.2
1965	Hou-N	8	7	.533	38	13	4	1	3	131^1	132	13	46	92	12.3	4.32	78	.259	.321	6	.171	2	-11	-14	1	-1.2
1966	Hou-N	15	14	.517	34	33	9	4	0	210	215	23	54	131	11.7	4.20	81	.260	.310	17	.230	5	-14	-18	-1	-1.9
1967	Hou-N	11	15	.423	37	33	8	1	1	221^2	231	20	58	157	11.9	4.18	79	.265	.313	13	.155	3	-20	-21	-2	-2.2
1968	Hou-N	11	14	.440	37	34	12	2	1	251	226	15	67	186	10.6	3.19	93	.239	.293	15	.183	2	-6	-7	3	-0.1
1969	StL-N	3	7	.300	22	12	2	1	0	99^2	96	7	37	62	12.1	3.61	99	.255	.323	5	.200	1	-0	-0	1	0.2
1970	*Pit-N	9	3	.750	66	1	0	0	26	103	98	7	39	85	12.0	3.06	128	.259	.328	3	.188	2	11	10	0	1.7
1971	*Pit-N	5	6	.455	58	0	0	0	**30**	86	79	5	31	55	11.6	2.93	115	.241	.308	1	.059	-1	5	4	-1	0.7
1972	*Pit-N	7	4	.636	54	0	0	0	22	74^2	59	3	20	54	9.5	1.93	172	.219	.273	0	.000	-1	13	12	1	2.5
1973	Pit-N★	9	2	.818	67	0	0	0	20	98^2	89	9	37	64	11.5	2.37	148	.241	.310	4	.308	1	14	13	-2	1.8
1974	*Pit-N	7	5	.583	64	2	0	0	12	105^2	101	2	40	53	12.0	3.32	104	.258	.327	1	.111	-0	3	1	1	0.3
1975	*Pit-N	5	4	.556	61	0	0	0	17	91^2	79	3	42	38	11.9	2.95	120	.237	.322	3	.300	1	7	6	0	0.9
1976	Pit-N	5	4	.556	40	0	0	0	6	58^1	59	5	27	24	13.3	4.32	81	.267	.347	0	.000	-0	-5	-5	0	-0.9
1977	Oak-A	3	3	.500	40	0	0	0	6	60^1	54	4	20	28	11.0	2.98	135	.245	.308	0	—	0	7	7	0	0.9
	Chi-N	0	2	.000	20	0	0	0	1	25^1	30	2	14	15	15.6	6.04	73	.297	.383	0	.000	-0	-6	-5	-0	-0.4
Total	15	100	93	.518	668	133	35	9	145	1716^2	1654	126	570	1103	11.7	3.60	95	.253	.315	77	.187	18	-14	-33	2	1.9
● BRIAN GIVENS	Givens, Brian Allen b: 11/6/65, Lompoc, Cal. BR/TL, 6'6", 220 lbs. Deb: 6/24/95																									
1995	Mil-A	5	7	.417	19	19	0	0	0	107^1	116	11	54	73	14.5	4.95	101	.275	.361	0	—	0	-3	0	-1	-0.1
1996	Mil-A	1	3	.250	4	4	0	0	0	14	32	3	7	10	25.1	12.86	40	.438	.488	0	—	0	-12	-12	-1	-2.3
Total	2	6	10	.375	23	23	0	0	0	121^1	148	14	61	83	15.7	5.86	85	.299	.379	0	—	0	-15	-12	-2	-2.4
● DAN GLADDEN	Gladden, Clinton Daniel b: 7/7/57, San Jose, Cal. BR/TR, 5'11", 180 lbs. Deb: 9/5/83 ♦																									
1988	Min-A	0	0	—	1	0	0	0	0	1	0	0	0	0	0.0	0.00	—	.000	.000	155	.269	0	0	0	0	0.0
1989	Min-A	0	0	—	1	0	0	0	0	1	2	0	1	0	27.0	9.00	46	.400	.500	136	.295	0	-1	-1	0	0.0
Total	2	0	0	—	2	0	0	0	0	2	2	0	1	0	13.5	4.50	91	.250	.333	1215	.270	1	-0	-0	0	0.0
● FRED GLADDING	Gladding, Fred Earl b: 6/28/36, Flat Rock, Mich. BL/TR, 6', 225 lbs. Deb: 7/1/61 C																									
1961	Det-A	1	0	1.000	8	0	0	0	0	16^1	18	1	11	11	17.1	3.31	124	.286	.408	0	.000	-0	1	1	-0	0.0
1962	Det-A	0	0	—	6	0	0	0	0	5	3	0	2	4	9.0	0.00	—	.176	.263	0	—	0	2	2	0	0.0
1963	Det-A	1	1	.500	22	0	0	0	7	27^1	19	1	14	24	10.9	1.98	189	.198	.300	0	.000	-0	5	5	0	0.7
1964	Det-A	7	4	.636	42	0	0	0	7	67^1	57	7	27	59	11.5	3.07	119	.233	.314	0	.000	-1	4	4	1	0.7
1965	Det-A	6	2	.750	46	0	0	0	5	70	63	6	29	43	12.3	2.83	123	.239	.323	0	.000	-1	5	5	-1	0.5
1966	Det-A	5	0	1.000	51	0	0	0	2	74	62	6	29	57	11.2	3.28	106	.230	.307	0	.000	-0	1	2	-1	0.0
1967	Det-A	6	4	.600	42	1	0	0	12	77	62	6	19	64	9.9	1.99	164	.227	.287	0	.000	-2	11	11	-0	1.6
1968	Hou-N	0	0	—	7	0	0	0	2	4^1	8	0	3	2	24.9	14.54	20	.421	.522	0	—	0	-6	-6	-0	-0.6
1969	Hou-N	4	8	.333	57	0	0	0	**29**	72^2	83	2	27	40	13.7	4.21	84	.289	.352	1	.100	-1	-5	-5	0	-1.4
1970	Hou-N	7	4	.636	63	0	0	0	18	71	84	4	24	46	14.1	4.06	96	.293	.354	0	.000	-1	-0	-1	1	-0.2
1971	Hou-N	4	5	.444	48	0	0	0	12	51^1	51	0	22	17	14.0	2.10	160	.268	.365	0	.000	-0	8	7	-1	1.5
1972	Hou-N	5	6	.455	42	0	0	0	14	48^2	38	1	12	18	9.6	2.77	121	.222	.281	0	.000	-1	4	3	-1	0.8
1973	Hou-N	2	0	1.000	16	0	0	0	1	16	18	4	4	9	12.4	4.50	81	.290	.333	0	—	0	-1	-2	0	-0.2
Total	13	48	34	.585	450	1	0	0	109	601	566	38	223	394	12.2	3.13	113	.252	.327	1	.016	-6	29	28	-2	3.4
● FRED GLADE	Glade, Frederick Monroe "Lucky" b: 1/25/1876, Dubuque, Iowa d: 11/21/34, Grand Island, Neb. BR/TR, 6', 190 lbs. Deb: 5/27/02																									
1902	Chi-N	0	1	.000	1	1	1	0	0	8	13	0	3	3	19.1	9.00	30	.361	.425	1	.333	1	-6	-6	0	-0.4
1904	StL-A	18	15	.545	35	34	30	6	1	289	248	2	58	156	9.9	2.27	109	.233	.281	19	.186	1	10	7	1	1.1
1905	StL-A	6	25	.194	32	32	28	2	0	275	257	3	58	127	10.7	2.81	90	.249	.296	9	.092	-6	-5	-8	4	-1.2
1906	StL-A	15	14	.517	35	32	28	4	1	266^2	215	4	59	96	9.6	2.36	109	.224	.276	13	.137	-4	10	7	-3	0.0
1907	StL-A	13	9	.591	24	22	18	2	0	202	187	2	45	71	10.7	2.67	94	.248	.298	15	.205	2	-3	-4	-4	-0.6
1908	NY-A	0	4	.000	5	5	2	0	0	32	30	0	14	11	13.5	4.22	59	.275	.378	0	.000	-1	-6	-6	-1	-0.9
Total	6	52	68	.433	132	126	107	14	2	1072^2	950	11	237	464	10.4	2.62	97	.240	.291	57	.150	-7	0	-10	-3	-2.0
● JOHN GLAISER	Glaiser, John Burke "Bert" b: 7/28/1894, Yoakum, Tex. d: 3/7/59, Houston, Tex. BL/TR, 5'8", 165 lbs. Deb: 4/20/20																									
1920	Det-A	0	0	—	9	1	0	0	1	17	23	1	8	3	16.9	6.35	59	.354	.432	0	.000	-0	-5	-5	1	0.0
● TOM GLASS	Glass, Thomas Joseph b: 4/29/1898, Greensboro, N.C. d: 12/15/81, Greensboro, N.C. BR/TR, 6'3", 170 lbs. Deb: 6/12/25																									
1925	Phi-A	1	0	1.000	2	0	0	0	0	5	9	0	0	2	16.2	5.40	86	.409	.409	0	.000	-0	-1	-0	-0	-0.1
● JACK GLASSCOCK	Glasscock, John Wesley "Pebbly Jack" b: 7/22/1859, Wheeling, W.Va. d: 2/24/47, Wheeling, W.Va. BR/TR, 5'8", 160 lbs. Deb: 5/1/1879 M♦																									
1884	Cle-N	0	0	—	2	0	0	0	0	5	8	0	2	1	18.0	5.40	58	.333	.385	70	.249	0	-1	-1	1	0.1
1887	Ind-N	0	0	—	1	0	0	0	0	1	0	0	0	1	0.0	0.00	—	.000	.000	142	.294	0	0	0	0	0.0
1888	Ind-N	0	0	—	1	0	0	0	0	0^1	1	0	2	1	108.0	54.00	5	1.000	1.000	119	.269	0	-2	-2	0	0.0
1889	Ind-N	0	0	—	1	0	0	0	0	0^2	3	0	3	0	81.0	0.00	—	.600	.750	205	.352	0	0	0	-0	0.0
Total	4	0	0	—	5	0	0	0	0	7	12	0	7	3	25.7	6.43	53	.364	.488	2040	.290	1	-2	-2	1	0.1
● KEITH GLAUBER	Glauber, Keith H. b: 1/18/72, Brooklyn, N.Y. BR/TR, 6'2", 190 lbs. Deb: 9/8/98																									
1998	Cin-N	0	0	—	3	0	0	0	0	7^2	6	0	1	4	8.2	2.35	184	.214	.241	0	.000	-0	2	2	-0	-0.1
● LUKE GLAVENICH	Glavenich, Luke Frank b: 1/17/1893, Jackson, Cal. d: 5/22/35, Stockton, Cal. BR/TR, 5'9.5", 189 lbs. Deb: 4/12/13																									
1913	Cle-A	0	0	—	1	0	0	0	0	1	3	0	3	1	54.0	9.00	34	.500	.667	0	—	0	-1	-1	-0	0.0
● TOM GLAVINE	Glavine, Thomas Michael b: 3/25/66, Concord, Mass. BL/TL, 6'1", 190 lbs. Deb: 8/17/87																									
1987	Atl-N	2	4	.333	9	9	0	0	0	50^1	55	5	33	20	16.3	5.54	78	.279	.391	2	.125	-0	-8	-7	1	-0.7
1988	Atl-N	7	17	.292	34	34	1	0	0	195^1	201	12	63	84	12.5	4.56	81	.270	.333	11	.183	1	-24	-19	2	-1.9
1989	Atl-N	14	8	.636	29	29	6	4	0	186	172	20	40	90	10.4	3.68	99	.243	.285	10	.149	0	-4	-1	1	0.1
1990	Atl-N	10	12	.455	33	33	1	0	0	214^1	232	18	78	129	13.1	4.28	94	.281	.343	7	.113	0	-12	-6	1	-0.4
1991	*Atl-N★	**20**	11	.645	34	34	**9**	1	0	246^2	201	17	69	192	9.9	2.55	**152**	.222	.279	17	.230	4	31	**37**	3	**5.5**
1992	*Atl-N★	**20**	8	.714	33	33	7	**5**	0	225	197	6	70	129	10.8	2.76	133	.235	.295	19	.247	4	19	22	-0	3.3
1993	*Atl-N☆	**22**	6	.786	36	36	4	2	0	239^1	236	16	90	120	12.3	3.20	126	.259	.327	14	.173	1	22	22	0	2.5
1994	Atl-N	13	9	.591	25	25	2	0	0	165^1	173	10	70	140	13.3	3.97	107	.268	.341	10	.179	1	4	5	2	0.9
1995	*Atl-N	16	7	.696	29	29	3	1	0	198^2	182	9	66	127	11.5	3.08	138	.246	.312	14	.222	3	24	26	3	3.5
1996	*Atl-N★	15	10	.600	36	36	1	0	0	235^1	222	14	85	181	11.7	2.98	148	.249	.314	22	.289	6	32	37	4	4.8
1997	*Atl-N☆	14	7	.667	33	33	5	2	0	240	197	20	79	152	10.5	2.96	141	.226	.294	14	.222	4	33	32	0	3.0
1998	*Atl-N★	**20**	6	.769	33	33	4	3	0	229^1	202	13	74	157	10.9	2.47	171	.238	.300	17	.239	3	45	45	3	5.6
Total	12	173	105	.622	364	364	43	18	0	2425^2	2270	160	817	1521	11.6	3.31	122	.249	.313	157	.205	28	163	195	20	26.2
● RALPH GLAZE	Glaze, Daniel Ralph b: 3/13/1882, Denver, Col. d: 10/31/68, Atascadero, Cal. BR/TR, 5'9", 165 lbs. Deb: 6/1/06																									
1906	Bos-A	4	6	.400	19	10	7	0	0	123	110	4	32	56	10.8	3.59	77	.242	.299	10	.182	0	-12	-11	0	-0.8
1907	Bos-A	9	13	.409	32	21	11	1	0	182^1	150	4	48	68	10.0	2.32	111	.227	.283	11	.180	0	5	5	-4	0.2
1908	Bos-A	2	2	.500	10	3	2	0	0	34^2	43	1	5	13	12.5	3.38	73	.253	.274	1	.077	-1	-4	-4	-1	-0.6
Total	3	15	21	.417	61	34	20	1	0	340	303	9	85	137	10.5	2.89	91	.236	.288	22	.171	-1	-11	-10	-4	-1.2
● WHITEY GLAZNER	Glazner, Charles Franklin b: 9/17/1893, Sycamore, Ala. d: 6/6/89, Orlando, Fla. BR/TR, 5'9", 165 lbs. Deb: 9/26/20																									
1920	Pit-N	0	0	—	2	0	0	0	0	8^2	9	0	2	1	11.4	3.12	103	.300	.344	0	.000	-0	0	0	-0	-0.1

YEAR	TM/L	W	L	PCT	G	GS	CG	SH	SV	IP	H	HR	BB	SO	RAT	ERA	ERA+	OAV	OOB	BH	AVG	PB	PR	/A	PD	TPI
1921	Pit-N	14	5	.737	36	25	15	0	1	234	214	5	58	88	10.9	2.77	139	**.250**	.306	10	.132	-3	26	28	-4	1.4
1922	Pit-N	11	12	.478	34	26	10	1	1	193	238	9	52	77	13.6	4.38	93	.309	.354	16	.246	3	-6	-7	0	-0.4
1923	Pit-N	2	1	.667	7	4	1	1	1	30	29	5	11	8	12.0	3.30	122	.250	.315	4	.333	2	2	2	0	0.4
	Phi-N	7	14	.333	28	23	12	2	1	161^1	195	11	63	51	14.7	4.69	98	.304	.371	9	.170	-1	-12	-1	-0	-0.3
	Yr	9	15	.375	35	27	13	3	2	191^1	224	16	74	59	14.3	4.47	101	.296	.363	13	.200	1	-10	0	0	0.1
1924	Phi-N	7	16	.304	35	24	8	2	0	156^2	210	14	63	41	15.9	5.92	75	.339	.403	8	.157	-4	-36	-25	1	-3.4
Total	5	41	48	.461	142	102	46	6	4	783^2	895	44	249	266	13.4	4.21	99	.295	.353	47	.181	-3	-25	-3	-3	-2.4

● JOE GLEASON Gleason, Joseph Paul b: 7/9/1895, Phelps, N.Y. d: 9/8/90, Phelps, N.Y. BR/TR, 5'10.5", 175 lbs. Deb: 9/11/20

YEAR	TM/L	W	L	PCT	G	GS	CG	SH	SV	IP	H	HR	BB	SO	RAT	ERA	ERA+	OAV	OOB	BH	AVG	PB	PR	/A	PD	TPI
1920	Was-A	0	0	—	3	0	0	0	0	8	14	2	6	2	23.6	13.50	28	.326	.420	0	.000	1	-9	-9	0	0.1
1922	Was-A	2	2	.500	8	5	3	0	0	40^2	53	3	18	12	15.9	4.65	83	.319	.389	2	.143	-0	-3	-4	-0	-0.3
Total	2	2	2	.500	11	5	3	0	0	48^2	67	5	24	14	17.2	6.10	63	.321	.396	2	.125	0	-11	-12	0	-0.2

● BILL GLEASON Gleason, William b: 1868, Cleveland, Ohio d: 12/2/1893, Cleveland, Ohio Deb: 4/24/1890

YEAR	TM/L	W	L	PCT	G	GS	CG	SH	SV	IP	H	HR	BB	SO	RAT	ERA	ERA+	OAV	OOB	BH	AVG	PB	PR	/A	PD	TPI
1890	Cle-P	0	1	.000	1	1	0	0	0	4	14	1	6	0	45.0	27.00	15	.538	.625	0	.000	-0	-10	-10	-0	-1.2

● KID GLEASON Gleason, William J. b: 10/26/1866, Camden, N.J. d: 1/2/33, Philadelphia, Pa. BB/TR, 5'7", 158 lbs. Deb: 4/20/1888 FMC◆

YEAR	TM/L	W	L	PCT	G	GS	CG	SH	SV	IP	H	HR	BB	SO	RAT	ERA	ERA+	OAV	OOB	BH	AVG	PB	PR	/A	PD	TPI
1888	Phi-N	7	16	.304	24	23	23	0	0	199^2	199	11	53	89	11.9	2.84	105	.252	.309	17	.205	0	0	3	-3	0.0
1889	Phi-N	9	15	.375	29	21	15	0	1	205	242	8	97	64	15.3	5.58	78	.285	.364	25	.253	2	-36	-28	1	-2.3
1890	Phi-N	38	17	.691	60	55	54	6	**2**	506	479	8	167	222	11.8	2.63	139	.242	.306	47	.210	-6	53	58	-0	4.6
1891	Phi-N	24	22	.522	53	44	40	1	1	418	431	10	165	100	13.1	3.51	97	.256	.328	53	.248	6	-8	-5	-3	-0.2
1892	StL-N	20	24	.455	47	45	43	2	0	400	389	11	151	133	12.4	3.33	96	.245	.314	50	.215	8	-2	-6	5	0.7
1893	StL-N	21	22	.488	48	45	37	1	1	380^1	436	18	187	86	15.0	4.61	103	.279	.360	51	.256	4	2	5	1	0.8
1894	StL-N	2	6	.250	8	8	6	0	0	58	75	2	21	9	15.4	6.05	89	.310	.372	7	.250	-0	-5	-4	1	-0.3
	*Bal-N	15	5	.750	21	20	19	0	0	172	224	3	44	35	14.2	4.45	123	.312	.354	30	.349	4	17	19	-2	1.8
	Yr	17	11	.607	29	28	25	0	0	230	299	5	65	44	14.4	4.85	112	.310	.356	37	.325	4	12	15	-0	1.5
1895	*Bal-N	2	4	.333	9	5	3	0	1	50^1	77	4	21	6	18.1	6.97	68	.345	.409	130	.309	2	-12	-12	-0	-1.0
Total	8	138	131	.513	299	266	240	10	6	2389^1	2552	75	906	744	13.3	3.79	103	.265	.333	1944	.261	20	10	29	-0	4.1

● JERRY DON GLEATON Gleaton, Jerry Don b: 9/14/57, Brownwood, Tex. BL/TL, 6'3", 210 lbs. Deb: 7/11/79

YEAR	TM/L	W	L	PCT	G	GS	CG	SH	SV	IP	H	HR	BB	SO	RAT	ERA	ERA+	OAV	OOB	BH	AVG	PB	PR	/A	PD	TPI
1979	Tex-A	0	1	.000	5	2	0	0	0	9^2	15	0	2	2	16.8	6.52	64	.375	.419	0	—	0	-2	-3	0	-0.2
1980	Tex-A	0	0	—	5	0	0	0	0	7	5	0	4	2	11.6	2.57	151	.208	.321	0	—	0	1	1	0	0.1
1981	Sea-A	4	7	.364	20	13	1	0	0	85^1	88	10	38	31	13.5	4.75	81	.273	.354	0	—	0	-10	-8	-1	-1.2
1982	Sea-A	0	0	—	3	0	0	0	0	4^2	7	3	2	1	19.3	13.50	31	.333	.417	0	—	0	-5	-5	-0	-0.1
1984	Chi-A	1	2	.333	11	1	0	0	2	18^1	20	2	6	4	13.3	3.44	121	.286	.351	0	—	0	1	1	-1	-0.1
1985	Chi-A	1	0	1.000	31	0	0	0	1	29^2	37	3	13	22	15.2	5.76	75	.316	.385	0	—	0	-5	-5	-0	-0.2
1987	KC-A	4	4	.500	48	0	0	0	5	50^2	38	4	28	44	11.7	4.26	107	.216	.324	0	—	0	1	2	1	0.2
1988	KC-A	0	4	.000	42	0	0	0	3	38	33	2	17	29	12.6	3.55	112	.232	.327	0	—	0	2	2	-0	0.1
1989	KC-A	0	0	—	15	0	0	0	0	14^1	20	0	6	9	16.3	5.65	68	.345	.406	0	—	0	-3	-3	-0	0.0
1990	Det-A	1	3	.250	57	0	0	0	13	82^2	62	5	25	56	9.8	2.94	135	.213	.282	0	—	0	9	9	-0	0.6
1991	Det-A	3	2	.600	47	0	0	0	2	75^1	74	7	39	47	13.5	4.06	102	.269	.360	0	—	0	0	1	0	0.0
1992	Pit-N	1	0	1.000	23	0	0	0	0	31^2	34	4	19	18	15.1	4.26	81	.283	.381	0	.000	0	-3	-3	0	-0.1
Total	12	15	23	.395	307	16	1	0	26	447^1	433	40	199	265	12.9	4.25	95	.261	.345	0	.000	0	-14	-10	-0	-0.9

● MARTIN GLENDON Glendon, Martin J. b: 2/8/1877, Milwaukee, Wis. d: 11/6/50, Norwood Park, Ill. 5'8", 165 lbs. Deb: 4/18/02

YEAR	TM/L	W	L	PCT	G	GS	CG	SH	SV	IP	H	HR	BB	SO	RAT	ERA	ERA+	OAV	OOB	BH	AVG	PB	PR	/A	PD	TPI
1902	Cin-N	0	1	.000	1	1	0	0	0	3	5	0	4	0	27.0	12.00	25	.357	.500	0	.000	-0	-3	-3	0	-0.7
1903	Cle-A	1	2	.333	3	3	3	0	0	27^2	20	0	7	9	8.8	0.98	292	.202	.255	0	.000	-1	6	6	1	0.6
Total	2	1	3	.250	4	4	3	0	0	30^2	25	0	11	9	10.6	2.05	140	.221	.290	0	.000	-1	3	3	1	-0.1

● BOB GLENN Glenn, Burdette b: 6/16/1894, W.Sunbury, Pa. d: 6/3/77, Richmond, Cal. Deb: 7/27/20

YEAR	TM/L	W	L	PCT	G	GS	CG	SH	SV	IP	H	HR	BB	SO	RAT	ERA	ERA+	OAV	OOB	BH	AVG	PB	PR	/A	PD	TPI
1920	StL-N	0	0	—	2	0	0	0	0	2	2	0	0	0	9.0	0.00	—	.222	.222	0	—	0	1	1	0	0.0

● SAL GLIATTO Gliatto, Salvador Michael b: 5/7/02, Chicago, Ill. d: 11/2/95, Tyler, Tex. BB/TR, 5'8.5", 150 lbs. Deb: 4/19/30

YEAR	TM/L	W	L	PCT	G	GS	CG	SH	SV	IP	H	HR	BB	SO	RAT	ERA	ERA+	OAV	OOB	BH	AVG	PB	PR	/A	PD	TPI
1930	Cle-A	0	0	—	8	0	0	0	2	15	21	1	9	7	19.2	6.60	73	.328	.427	0	.000	-0	-3	-3	-0	-0.2

● GEORGE GLINATSIS Glinatsis, George b: 6/29/69, Youngstown, Ohio BR/TR, 6'4", 195 lbs. Deb: 7/18/94

YEAR	TM/L	W	L	PCT	G	GS	CG	SH	SV	IP	H	HR	BB	SO	RAT	ERA	ERA+	OAV	OOB	BH	AVG	PB	PR	/A	PD	TPI
1994	Sea-A	0	1	.000	2	2	0	0	0	5^1	9	2	6	1	25.3	13.50	36	.429	.556	0	—	0	-5	-5	-0	-0.7

● ED GLYNN Glynn, Edward Paul b: 6/3/53, Flushing, N.Y. BR/TL, 6'2", 180 lbs. Deb: 9/19/75

YEAR	TM/L	W	L	PCT	G	GS	CG	SH	SV	IP	H	HR	BB	SO	RAT	ERA	ERA+	OAV	OOB	BH	AVG	PB	PR	/A	PD	TPI
1975	Det-A	0	2	.000	3	1	0	0	0	14^2	11	1	8	8	11.7	4.30	93	.220	.328	0	—	0	-1	-0	0	-0.1
1976	Det-A	1	3	.250	5	4	1	0	0	23^2	22	3	20	17	16.0	6.08	61	.265	.408	0	—	0	-7	-6	-1	-1.0
1977	Det-A	2	1	.667	8	3	0	0	0	27^1	36	3	12	13	15.8	5.27	81	.316	.381	0	—	0	-4	-3	-0	-0.7
1978	Det-A	0	0	—	10	0	0	0	0	14^2	11	3	4	9	9.2	3.07	126	.208	.263	0	—	0	1	1	1	0.1
1979	NY-N	1	4	.200	46	0	0	0	7	60	57	3	40	32	14.9	3.00	121	.259	.378	0	.000	-0	5	4	-1	0.3
1980	NY-N	3	3	.500	38	0	0	0	1	52^1	49	5	23	32	12.4	4.13	86	.246	.324	0	.000	-1	-3	-3	1	-0.4
1981	Cle-A	0	0	—	4	0	0	0	0	7^2	5	0	4	4	10.6	1.17	309	.192	.300	0	—	0	2	2	-0	0.0
1982	Cle-A	5	2	.714	47	0	0	0	4	49^2	43	6	30	54	13.2	4.17	98	.232	.340	0	—	0	-1	-0	-0	-0.1
1983	Cle-A	0	2	.000	11	0	0	0	0	12^1	22	2	6	13	20.4	5.84	73	.373	.431	0	—	0	-2	-2	-0	-0.5
1985	Mon-N	0	0	—	3	0	0	0	0	2^1	5	0	4	2	34.7	19.29	18	.455	.600	0	—	0	-4	-4	-0	0.0
Total	10	12	17	.414	175	8	1	0	12	264^2	261	26	151	184	14.1	4.25	90	.261	.359	0	.000	-1	-13	-12	-2	-2.4

● JOT GOAR Goar, Joshua Mercer b: 1/31/1870, New Lisbon, Ind. d: 4/4/47, New Castle, Ind. BR/TR, 5'9", 160 lbs. Deb: 4/18/1896

YEAR	TM/L	W	L	PCT	G	GS	CG	SH	SV	IP	H	HR	BB	SO	RAT	ERA	ERA+	OAV	OOB	BH	AVG	PB	PR	/A	PD	TPI
1896	Pit-N	0	1	.000	3	0	0	0	0	13^1	36	1	8	3	30.4	16.88	25	.486	.542	1	.167	-1	-19	-19	-1	-1.0
1898	Cin-N	0	0	—	1	0	0	0	0	2	4	0	1	0	22.5	9.00	43	.400	.455	0	—	0	-1	-1	0	0.0
Total	2	0	1	.000	4	0	0	0	0	15^1	40	1	9	3	29.3	15.85	26	.476	.532	1	.167	-1	-20	-20	-0	-1.0

● GEORGE GOETZ Goetz, George Burt b: Greencastle, Pa. 6'2", 180 lbs. Deb: 6/17/1889

YEAR	TM/L	W	L	PCT	G	GS	CG	SH	SV	IP	H	HR	BB	SO	RAT	ERA	ERA+	OAV	OOB	BH	AVG	PB	PR	/A	PD	TPI
1889	Bal-a	1	0	1.000	1	1	0	0	0	9	12	0	0	2	12.0	4.00	99	.308	.308	0	.000	-1	-0	-0	0	0.0

● JOHN GOETZ Goetz, John Hardy b: 10/24/37, Goetzville, Mich. BR/TR, 6', 185 lbs. Deb: 4/16/60

YEAR	TM/L	W	L	PCT	G	GS	CG	SH	SV	IP	H	HR	BB	SO	RAT	ERA	ERA+	OAV	OOB	BH	AVG	PB	PR	/A	PD	TPI
1960	Chi-N	0	0	—	4	0	0	0	0	6^1	10	2	4	6	19.9	12.79	30	.370	.452	0	.000	-0	-6	-6	0	0.0

● BILL GOGOLEWSKI Gogolewski, William Joseph b: 10/26/47, Oshkosh, Wis. BL/TR, 6'4", 190 lbs. Deb: 9/3/70

YEAR	TM/L	W	L	PCT	G	GS	CG	SH	SV	IP	H	HR	BB	SO	RAT	ERA	ERA+	OAV	OOB	BH	AVG	PB	PR	/A	PD	TPI
1970	Was-A	2	2	.500	8	5	0	0	0	33^2	33	2	25	19	15.8	4.81	74	.260	.386	0	.000	-0	-4	-5	1	-0.5
1971	Was-A	6	5	.545	27	17	4	1	0	124^1	112	5	39	70	11.1	2.75	120	.241	.302	5	.156	0	10	8	-0	0.7
1972	Tex-A	4	11	.267	36	21	2	1	2	150^2	136	9	58	95	11.9	4.24	71	.239	.316	5	.125	-1	-20	-21	-0	-2.2
1973	Tex-A	3	6	.333	49	1	0	0	6	123^2	139	10	48	77	13.7	4.22	88	.286	.351	0	—	0	-6	-7	2	-0.3
1974	Cle-A	0	0	—	5	0	0	0	0	13^2	15	1	2	3	11.9	4.61	78	.283	.321	0	—	0	-2	-2	1	0.1
1975	Chi-A	0	0	—	19	0	0	0	2	55	61	5	28	37	14.7	5.24	74	.292	.378	0	—	0	-9	-8	1	0.0
Total	6	15	24	.385	144	44	6	2	10	501	496	32	200	301	12.7	4.02	85	.260	.334	10	.127	-1	-30	-34	5	-2.2

● GREG GOHR Gohr, Gregory James b: 10/29/67, Santa Clara, Cal. BR/TR, 6'3", 205 lbs. Deb: 4/7/93

YEAR	TM/L	W	L	PCT	G	GS	CG	SH	SV	IP	H	HR	BB	SO	RAT	ERA	ERA+	OAV	OOB	BH	AVG	PB	PR	/A	PD	TPI
1993	Det-A	0	0	—	16	0	0	0	0	22^2	26	1	14	23	16.7	5.96	72	.289	.396	0	—	0	-4	-4	-0	0.0
1994	Det-A	2	2	.500	8	6	0	0	0	34	36	3	21	21	15.1	4.50	108	.263	.361	0	—	0	1	1	-1	0.0
1995	Det-A	1	0	1.000	10	0	0	0	0	10^1	9	0	3	12	10.5	0.87	546	.243	.300	0	—	0	4	4	-0	0.4
1996	Det-A	4	8	.333	17	16	0	0	0	91^2	129	24	34	60	16.3	7.17	70	.328	.386	0	—	0	-22	-22	-1	-2.3
	Cal-A	1	1	.500	15	0	0	0	1	24	34	7	10	15	16.5	7.50	67	.337	.396	0	—	0	-7	-7	0	-0.5
	Yr	5	9	.357	32	16	0	0	1	115^2	163	31	44	75	16.1	7.24	70	.326	.381	0	—	0	-29	-28	-1	-2.8
Total	4	8	11	.421	66	22	0	0	1	182^2	234	35	82	131	15.8	6.21	79	.309	.380	0	—	0	-27	-27	-2	-2.4

● JIM GOLDEN Golden, James Edward b: 3/20/36, Eldon, Mo. BL/TR, 6', 175 lbs. Deb: 9/30/60

YEAR	TM/L	W	L	PCT	G	GS	CG	SH	SV	IP	H	HR	BB	SO	RAT	ERA	ERA+	OAV	OOB	BH	AVG	PB	PR	/A	PD	TPI
1960	LA-N	1	0	1.000	1	1	0	0	0	7	6	1	4	4	12.9	6.43	62	.240	.345	1	.333	0	-2	-2	-0	-0.2
1961	LA-N	1	1	.500	28	0	0	0	0	42	52	7	20	18	15.4	5.79	75	.306	.379	0	.000	-0	-8	-7	-0	-0.3

YEAR	TM/L	W	L	PCT	G	GS	CG	SH	SV	IP	H	HR	BB	SO	RAT	ERA	ERA+	OAV	OOB	BH	AVG	PB	PR	/A	PD	TPI
1962	Hou-N	7	11	.389	37	18	5	2	1	152^2	163	13	50	88	12.6	4.07	92	.270	.326	12	.222	4	-2	-6	1	-0.2
1963	Hou-N	0	1	.000	3	1	0	0	0	6^1	12	0	2	5	19.9	5.68	55	.429	.467	0	—	0	-2	-2	0	-0.3
Total	4	9	13	.409	69	20	5	2	1	208	233	21	76	115	13.4	4.54	85	.282	.343	13	.217	4	-14	-16	0	-1.0

● MIKE GOLDEN Golden, Michael Henry b: 9/11/1851, Shirley, Mass. d: 1/11/29, Rockford, Ill. BR/TR, 5'8", 168 lbs. Deb: 5/5/1875 ♦

YEAR	TM/L	W	L	PCT	G	GS	CG	SH	SV	IP	H	HR	BB	SO	RAT	ERA	ERA+	OAV	OOB	BH	AVG	PB	PR	/A	PD	TPI
1875	Wes-n	1	12	.077	13	13	13	0	0	113	111	0	12	20	9.8	1.83	133	.225	.243	6	.130	-4	5	8		0.3
	Chi-n	6	7	.462	14	14	12	1	0	119	129	0	8	14	10.4	1.89	120	.247	.258	40	.258	1	4	5		0.4
	Yr	7	19	.269	27	27	25	1	0	232	240	0	20	34	10.1	1.86	126	.236	.251	46	.229	-3	9	13		0.7
1878	Mil-N	3	13	.188	22	18	15	0	0	161	217	1	33	52	14.0	4.14	63	.295	.325	44	.206	-2	-33	-27	0	-2.2

● ROY GOLDEN Golden, Roy Kramer b: 7/12/1888, Madisonville, O. d: 10/4/61, Norwood, Ohio BR/TR, 6'1", 195 lbs. Deb: 9/7/10

YEAR	TM/L	W	L	PCT	G	GS	CG	SH	SV	IP	H	HR	BB	SO	RAT	ERA	ERA+	OAV	OOB	BH	AVG	PB	PR	/A	PD	TPI
1910	StL-N	2	3	.400	7	6	3	0	0	42^2	44	3	33	31	16.7	4.43	67	.286	.418	4	.267	1	-7	-7	1	-0.6
1911	StL-N	4	9	.308	30	25	6	0	0	148^2	127	6	129	81	15.8	5.02	67	.240	.394	5	.114	-1	-27	-27	-0	-2.2
Total	2	6	12	.333	37	31	9	0	0	191^1	171	9	162	112	16.0	4.89	67	.250	.399	9	.153	-1	-33	-34	1	-2.8

● FRED GOLDSMITH Goldsmith, Fred Ernest b: 5/15/1856, New Haven, Conn. d: 3/28/39, Berkley, Mich. BR/TR, 6'1", 195 lbs. Deb: 10/23/1875 U♦

YEAR	TM/L	W	L	PCT	G	GS	CG	SH	SV	IP	H	HR	BB	SO	RAT	ERA	ERA+	OAV	OOB	BH	AVG	PB	PR	/A	PD	TPI
1879	Tro-N	2	4	.333	8	7	7	0	0	63	61	0	1	31	8.9	1.57	159	.237	.240	9	.237	0	6	6	-0	0.6
1880	Chi-N	21	3	**.875**	26	24	22	4	1	210^1	189	2	18	90	8.9	1.75	138	.231	.247	37	.261	2	14	16	2	1.9
1881	Chi-N	24	13	.649	39	39	37	5	0	330	328	4	44	76	10.1	2.59	106	.247	.271	38	.241	3	7	5	5	1.1
1882	Chi-N	28	17	.622	45	45	45	4	0	405	377	7	38	109	9.2	2.42	119	.236	.254	42	.230	-1	22	20	-2	1.4
1883	Chi-N	25	19	.568	46	45	40	2	0	383^1	456	14	39	82	11.6	3.15	101	.277	.294	52	.221	-0	-0	2	1	0.2
1884	Chi-N	9	11	.450	21	21	20	1	0	188	245	11	29	34	13.1	4.26	74	.298	.322	11	.136	-2	-27	-24	-3	-2.4
	Bal-a	3	1	.750	4	4	3	0	0	30	29	0	2	11	9.6	2.70	128	.238	.256	2	.143	-0	2	3	1	0.3
Total	6	112	68	.622	189	185	174	16	1	1609^2	1685	38	171	433	10.4	2.73	106	.256	.275	191	.224	-1	24	28	4	3.1

● HAL GOLDSMITH Goldsmith, Harold Eugene b: 8/18/1898, Peconic, N.Y. d: 10/20/85, Riverhead, N.Y. BR/TR, 6', 174 lbs. Deb: 6/23/26

YEAR	TM/L	W	L	PCT	G	GS	CG	SH	SV	IP	H	HR	BB	SO	RAT	ERA	ERA+	OAV	OOB	BH	AVG	PB	PR	/A	PD	TPI
1926	Bos-N	5	7	.417	19	15	5	0	0	101	135	2	28	16	14.6	4.37	81	.333	.377	8	.211	0	-6	-9	1	-0.8
1927	Bos-N	1	3	.250	22	5	1	0	1	71^2	83	4	26	13	13.7	3.52	106	.289	.348	5	.238	0	3	2	0	0.1
1928	Bos-N	0	0	—	4	0	0	0	0	8^1	14	2	1	1	16.2	3.24	121	.359	.375	0	.000	-0	1	1	0	0.0
1929	StL-N	0	0	—	2	0	0	0	0	4	3	1	1	0	9.0	6.75	69	.214	.267	0	.000	-0	-1	-1	-0	0.0
Total	4	6	10	.375	47	20	6	0	1	185	235	9	56	30	14.2	4.04	90	.315	.364	13	.210	0	-3	-8	1	-0.7

● IZZY GOLDSTEIN Goldstein, Isidore b: 6/6/08, Odessa, Russia d: 9/24/93, Delray Beach, Fla. BB/TR, 6', 160 lbs. Deb: 4/24/32

YEAR	TM/L	W	L	PCT	G	GS	CG	SH	SV	IP	H	HR	BB	SO	RAT	ERA	ERA+	OAV	OOB	BH	AVG	PB	PR	/A	PD	TPI
1932	Det-A	3	2	.600	16	6	2	0	0	56^1	63	2	41	14	17.1	4.47	105	.276	.393	5	.294	1	0	1	0	0.2

● DAVE GOLTZ Goltz, David Allan b: 6/23/49, Pelican Rapids, Minn. BR/TR, 6'4", 215 lbs. Deb: 7/18/72

YEAR	TM/L	W	L	PCT	G	GS	CG	SH	SV	IP	H	HR	BB	SO	RAT	ERA	ERA+	OAV	OOB	BH	AVG	PB	PR	/A	PD	TPI
1972	Min-A	3	3	.500	15	11	2	0	1	91	75	5	26	38	10.0	2.67	120	.224	.280	3	.103	-1	4	5	-0	0.3
1973	Min-A	6	4	.600	32	10	1	0	1	106^1	138	11	32	65	14.6	5.25	75	.318	.368	0	—	0	-17	-15	1	-1.3
1974	Min-A	10	10	.500	28	24	5	1	1	174^1	192	14	45	89	12.6	3.25	115	.282	.333	0	—	0	7	9	1	1.1
1975	Min-A	14	14	.500	32	32	15	1	0	243	235	18	72	128	11.6	3.67	104	.255	.313	0	—	0	3	4	1	0.5
1976	Min-A	14	14	.500	36	35	13	4	0	249^1	239	14	91	133	12.1	3.36	107	.254	.323	0	—	0	4	6	0	0.6
1977	Min-A	**20**	11	.645	39	39	19	2	0	303	284	23	91	186	11.2	3.36	119	.247	.304	0	—	0	24	21	-1	2.0
1978	Min-A	15	10	.600	29	29	13	2	0	220^1	209	12	67	116	11.3	2.49	153	.253	.309	0	—	0	31	32	0	3.7
1979	Min-A	14	13	.519	36	35	12	1	0	250^2	282	22	69	132	12.6	4.16	105	.288	.336	0	—	0	1	6	-1	0.5
1980	LA-N	7	11	.389	35	27	2	2	1	171^1	198	12	59	91	13.5	4.31	81	.299	.356	6	.128	0	-13	-15	-0	-1.5
1981	*LA-N	2	7	.222	26	8	0	0	1	77	83	4	25	48	12.6	4.09	81	.288	.345	1	.059	-1	-5	-7	1	-0.8
1982	LA-N	0	1	.000	2	1	0	0	0	3^2	6	0	0	3	14.7	4.91	71	.353	.353	0	.000	-0	-1	-1	0	-0.1
	*Cal-A	8	5	.615	28	7	1	0	3	86	82	4	32	49	12.0	4.08	99	.252	.320	0	—	0	-0	-0	-2	-0.2
1983	Cal-A	0	6	.000	15	6	0	0	0	63^2	81	10	37	27	16.8	6.22	65	.315	.403	0	—	0	-15	-16	-0	-1.2
Total	12	113	109	.509	353	264	83	13	8	2039^2	2104	149	646	1105	12.2	3.69	104	.269	.327	10	.106	-1	23	31	0	3.6

● WAYNE GOMES Gomes, Wayne Maurice b: 1/15/73, Hampton, Va. BR/TR, 6', 215 lbs. Deb: 6/13/97

YEAR	TM/L	W	L	PCT	G	GS	CG	SH	SV	IP	H	HR	BB	SO	RAT	ERA	ERA+	OAV	OOB	BH	AVG	PB	PR	/A	PD	TPI
1997	Phi-N	5	1	.833	37	0	0	0	0	42^2	45	4	24	24	14.8	5.27	80	.274	.370	0	.000	0	-5	-5	-1	-0.7
1998	Phi-N	9	6	.600	71	0	0	0	1	93^1	94	9	35	86	12.7	4.24	103	.258	.328	0	.000	-0	-0	1	-1	0.1
Total	2	14	7	.667	108	0	0	0	1	136	139	13	59	110	13.4	4.57	95	.263	.342	0	.000	-0	-5	-4	-2	-0.6

● LUIS GOMEZ Gomez, Luis (Sanchez) b: 8/19/51, Guadalajara, Mex. BR/TR, 5'9", 150 lbs. Deb: 4/28/74 ♦

YEAR	TM/L	W	L	PCT	G	GS	CG	SH	SV	IP	H	HR	BB	SO	RAT	ERA	ERA+	OAV	OOB	BH	AVG	PB	PR	/A	PD	TPI
1981	Atl-N	0	0	—	1	0	0	0	0	1	3	0	2	0	45.0	27.00	13	.500	.625	7	.200	0	-3	-3	-0	0.0

● PAT GOMEZ Gomez, Patrick Alexander b: 3/17/68, Roseville, Cal. BL/TL, 5'11", 185 lbs. Deb: 4/6/93

YEAR	TM/L	W	L	PCT	G	GS	CG	SH	SV	IP	H	HR	BB	SO	RAT	ERA	ERA+	OAV	OOB	BH	AVG	PB	PR	/A	PD	TPI
1993	SD-N	1	2	.333	27	1	0	0	0	31^2	35	2	19	26	15.3	5.12	81	.292	.388	0	.000	-1	-4	-3	-1	-0.4
1994	SF-N	0	1	.000	26	0	0	0	0	33^1	23	2	20	14	11.6	3.78	106	.211	.333	0	.000	-0	2	1	-1	-0.1
1995	SF-N	0	0	—	18	0	0	0	0	14	16	2	12	15	18.0	5.14	79	.276	.400	0	.000	-0	-1	-2	-0	0.0
Total	3	1	3	.250	71	1	0	0	0	79	74	6	51	55	14.2	4.56	89	.258	.370	0	.000	-1	-4	-4	-1	-0.5

● RUBEN GOMEZ Gomez, Ruben (Colon) b: 7/13/27, Arroyo, P.R. BR/TR, 6', 175 lbs. Deb: 4/17/53

YEAR	TM/L	W	L	PCT	G	GS	CG	SH	SV	IP	H	HR	BB	SO	RAT	ERA	ERA+	OAV	OOB	BH	AVG	PB	PR	/A	PD	TPI
1953	NY-N	13	11	.542	29	26	13	3	0	204	166	17	101	113	12.0	3.40	126	.218	.313	15	.208	-0	20	20	2	2.3
1954	*NY-N	17	9	.654	37	32	10	4	0	221^2	202	20	109	106	12.9	2.88	140	.244	.337	14	.173	0	29	28	2	3.2
1955	NY-N	9	10	.474	33	31	9	3	1	185^1	207	20	63	79	13.5	4.56	88	.285	.348	18	.300	4	-11	-11	3	-0.4
1956	NY-N	7	17	.292	40	31	4	2	0	196^1	191	19	77	76	12.7	4.58	83	.259	.337	11	.183	-0	-18	-17	2	-1.7
1957	NY-N	15	13	.536	38	36	16	1	0	238^1	233	28	71	92	11.7	3.78	104	.254	.311	16	.184	1	3	4	2	0.8
1958	SF-N	10	12	.455	42	30	8	1	1	207^2	204	21	77	112	12.5	4.38	87	.261	.334	14	.200	1	-10	-13	2	-0.9
1959	Phi-N	3	8	.273	20	12	2	1	1	72^1	90	12	24	37	14.2	6.10	67	.300	.352	3	.176	0	-17	-16	2	-2.0
1960	Phi-N	0	3	.000	22	1	0	0	1	52^1	68	7	9	24	13.4	5.33	73	.321	.351	1	.083	-1	-9	-8	-1	-0.6
1962	Cle-A	1	2	.333	15	4	0	0	1	45^1	50	5	25	21	15.3	4.37	89	.292	.389	3	.231	0	-2	-2	1	-0.1
	Min-A	1	1	.500	6	2	1	0	0	19^1	17	3	11	8	13.0	4.66	88	.254	.359	0	.000	-0	-1	-1	0	-0.1
	Yr	2	3	.400	21	6	1	0	1	64^2	67	8	36	29	14.3	4.45	88	.276	.369	3	.167	-0	-3	-4	1	-0.2
1967	Phi-N	0	0	—	7	0	0	0	0	11^1	8	2	7	9	11.9	3.97	86	.211	.333	0	—	0	-1	-1	1	0.1
Total	10	76	86	.469	289	205	63	15	5	1454	1436	154	574	677	12.7	4.09	97	.259	.334	95	.199	6	-17	-18	14	0.6

● LEFTY GOMEZ Gomez, Vernon Louis "Goofy" b: 11/26/08, Rodeo, Cal. d: 2/17/89, Greenbrae, Cal. BL/TL, 6'2", 173 lbs. Deb: 4/29/30 H

YEAR	TM/L	W	L	PCT	G	GS	CG	SH	SV	IP	H	HR	BB	SO	RAT	ERA	ERA+	OAV	OOB	BH	AVG	PB	PR	/A	PD	TPI
1930	NY-A	2	5	.286	15	6	2	0	1	60	66	12	28	22	14.3	5.55	78	.280	.358	3	.150	-2	-6	-8	1	-0.8
1931	NY-A	21	9	.700	40	26	17	1	3	243	206	7	85	150	10.9	2.67	149	.226	.295	11	.133	-3	46	35	-1	3.5
1932	*NY-A	24	7	.774	37	31	21	1	1	265^1	266	23	105	176	12.7	4.21	97	.259	.329	18	.173	-1	8	-4	-3	-0.8
1933	NY-A★	16	10	.615	35	30	14	4	2	234^2	218	16	106	**163**	12.4	3.18	122	.240	.319	9	.112	-3	29	18	-4	1.1
1934	NY-A★	**26**	5	**.839**	38	33	**25**	**6**	1	**281^2**	223	12	96	**158**	**10.2**	**2.33**	174	**.215**	**.282**	13	.131	-3	**68**	54	-2	4.8
1935	NY-A★	12	15	.444	34	30	15	2	1	246	223	18	86	138	11.4	3.18	127	.242	.309	10	.120	-6	35	24	1	1.6
1936	*NY-A☆	13	7	.650	31	30	10	0	0	188^2	184	6	122	105	14.6	4.39	106	.254	.362	10	.145	-3	14	6	-1	0.1
1937	*NY-A★	**21**	11	.656	34	34	25	**6**	0	278^1	233	10	93	**194**	10.6	**2.33**	191	**.223**	.287	21	.200	-1	**71**	**65**	-3	**6.5**
1938	*NY-A★	18	12	.600	32	32	20	**4**	0	239	239	7	99	129	12.8	3.35	135	.260	.332	13	.151	-2	38	31	2	3.3
1939	*NY-A☆	12	8	.600	26	26	14	2	0	198	173	11	84	102	11.8	3.41	128	.235	.316	11	.151	-2	27	21	-1	1.5
1940	NY-A	3	3	.500	9	5	0	0	0	27^1	37	2	18	14	18.4	6.59	61	.325	.421	0	.000	-1	-7	-8	-1	-1.5
1941	NY-A	15	5	**.750**	23	23	8	2	0	156^1	151	10	103	76	14.7	3.74	105	.250	.360	9	.153	-1	7	3	-4	-0.1
1942	NY-A	6	4	.600	13	13	2	0	0	80	67	4	65	41	15.1	4.27	80	.237	.383	5	.152	-1	-5	-7	-2	-1.1
1943	Was-A	0	1	.000	1	1	0	0	0	4^2	4	0	5	0	17.4	5.79	55	.250	.429	0	.000	-0	-1	-1	1	-0.2
Total	14	189	102	.649	368	320	173	28	9	2503	2290	138	1095	1468	12.2	3.34	125	.242	.321	133	.147	-30	322	229	-15	17.9

● JOE GONZALES Gonzales, Joe Madrid "Smokey" b: 3/19/15, San Francisco, Cal d: 11/16/96, Torrance, Cal. BR/TR, 5'9", 175 lbs. Deb: 8/28/37

YEAR	TM/L	W	L	PCT	G	GS	CG	SH	SV	IP	H	HR	BB	SO	RAT	ERA	ERA+	OAV	OOB	BH	AVG	PB	PR	/A	PD	TPI
1937	Bos-A	1	2	.333	8	2	2	0	0	31	37	1	11	11	13.9	4.35	109	.291	.348	0	.000	-2	1	1	0	0.0

● RENE GONZALES Gonzales, Rene Adrian b: 9/3/60, Austin, Tex. BR/TR, 6'3", 201 lbs. Deb: 7/27/84 ♦

YEAR	TM/L	W	L	PCT	G	GS	CG	SH	SV	IP	H	HR	BB	SO	RAT	ERA	ERA+	OAV	OOB	BH	AVG	PB	PR	/A	PD	TPI
1993	Cal-A	0	0	—	1	0	0	0	0	1	0	0	0	0	0.0	0.00	—	.000	.000	84	.251	0	0	1	0	0.0

YEAR	TM/L	W	L	PCT	G	GS	CG	SH	SV	IP	H	HR	BB	SO	RAT	ERA	ERA+	OAV	OOB	BH	AVG	PB	PR	/A	PD	TPI
● VINCE GONZALES	Gonzales, Wenceslao (O'Reilly) b: 9/28/25, Quivican, Cuba d: 3/11/81, Ciudad Del Carmen, Campeche, Mexico BL/TL, 6'1", 165 lbs. Deb: 4/13/55																									
1955	Was-A	0	0	—	1	0	0	0	0	2	6	0	3	1	40.5	27.00	14	.500	.600	0	—	0	-5	-5	-0	0.0
● GABE GONZALEZ	Gonzalez, Gabriel b: 5/24/72, Long Beach, Cal. BB/TL, 6'1", 160 lbs. Deb: 4/1/98																									
1998	Fla-N	0	0	—	3	0	0	0	0	1	1	0	1	0	27.0	9.00	45	.333	.600	0	—	0	-1	-1	0	0.0
● JEREMI GONZALEZ	Gonzalez, Geremis Segundo (Acosta) b: 1/8/75, Maracaibo, Venezuela BR/TR, 6'2", 200 lbs. Deb: 5/27/97																									
1997	Chi-N	11	9	.550	23	23	1	1	0	144	126	16	69	93	12.3	4.25	101	.236	.326	4	.100	-1	-1	1	-2	-0.2
1998	Chi-N	7	7	.500	20	20	1	1	0	110	124	13	41	70	13.7	5.32	82	.281	.346	6	.188	0	-13	-12	-1	-1.4
Total	2	18	16	.529	43	43	2	2	0	254	250	29	110	163	12.9	4.71	92	.256	.335	10	.139	-1	-14	-11	-2	-1.6
● GERMAN GONZALEZ	Gonzalez, German Jose (Caraballo) b: 3/7/62, Rio Caribe, Venez. BR/TR, 6', 170 lbs. Deb: 8/5/88																									
1988	Min-A	0	0	—	16	0	0	0	1	21^1	20	4	8	19	12.2	3.38	121	.244	.319	0	—	0	1	2	0	-0.1
1989	Min-A	3	2	.600	22	0	0	0	0	29	32	2	11	25	14.6	4.66	89	.274	.356	0	—	0	-2	-2	-0	-0.3
Total	2	3	2	.600	38	0	0	0	1	50^1	52	6	19	44	13.6	4.11	100	.261	.341	0	—	0	-1	-0	0	-0.4
● JULIO GONZALEZ	Gonzalez, Julio Enrique (Herrera) b: 12/20/20, Banes, Cuba d: 2/15/91, Banes, Cuba BR/TR, 5'11", 150 lbs. Deb: 8/9/49																									
1949	Was-A	0	0	—	13	0	0	0	0	34^1	33	3	27	5	16.0	4.72	90	.256	.389	1	.200	0	-2	-2	-0	0.0
● LARIEL GONZALEZ	Gonzalez, Lariel Alfonso b: 5/25/76, San Cristobal, D.R. BR/TR, 6'4", 228 lbs. Deb: 9/22/98																									
1998	Col-N	0	0	—	1	0	0	0	0	1	0	0	0	0	0.0	0.00	—	.000	.000	0	—	0	0	1	-0	0.0
● RALPH GOOD	Good, Ralph Nelson "Holy" b: 4/25/1886, Monticello, Me. d: 11/24/65, Waterville, Maine BR/TR, 6', 165 lbs. Deb: 7/1/10																									
1910	Bos-N	0	0	—	2	0	0	0	0	9	6	0	2	4	10.0	2.00	166	.188	.278	0	.000	-0	1	1	0	0.0
● WILBUR GOOD	Good, Wilbur David "Lefty" b: 9/28/1885, Punxsutawney, Pa. d: 12/30/63, Brooksville, Fla. BL/TL, 5'6", 165 lbs. Deb: 8/18/05 ♦																									
1905	NY-A	0	2	.000	5	2	0	0	0	19	18	1	14	13	15.2	4.74	62	.250	.372	3	.375	1	-4	-4	0	-0.3
● HERB GOODALL	Goodall, Herbert Frank b: 3/10/1870, Mansfield, Pa. d: 1/20/38, Mansfield, Pa. BR/TR, 5'9", 180 lbs. Deb: 4/29/1890																									
1890	Lou-a	8	5	.615	18	13	8	1	**4**	109	94	2	51	46	12.8	3.39	114	.225	.324	19	.422	6	6	6	1	1.2
● JOHN GOODELL	Goodell, John Henry William "Lefty" b: 4/5/07, Muskogee, Okla. d: 9/21/93, Mesquite, Tex. BR/TL, 5'10", 165 lbs. Deb: 4/19/28																									
1928	Chi-A	0	0	—	2	0	0	0	0	3	6	0	2	0	27.0	18.00	23	.500	.600	0	—	0	-5	-5	0	0.0
● DWIGHT GOODEN	Gooden, Dwight Eugene "Doc" b: 11/16/64, Tampa, Fla. BR/TR, 6'3", 210 lbs. Deb: 4/7/84																									
1984	NY-N★	17	9	.654	31	31	7	3	0	218	161	7	73	**276**	**9.7**	2.60	136	**.202**	**.270**	14	.200	1	24	23	1	2.9
1985	NY-N☆	**24**	4	.857	35	35	**16**	8	0	**276^2**	198	13	69	**268**	8.8	**1.53**	**226**	.201	.254	21	.226	6	**63**	**59**	2	**7.3**
1986	*NY-N★	17	6	.739	33	33	12	2	0	250	197	17	80	200	10.1	2.84	124	.215	.280	7	.086	-3	24	19	2	1.7
1987	NY-N	15	7	**.682**	25	25	7	3	0	179^2	162	11	53	148	10.9	3.21	118	.244	.301	14	.219	2	17	11	-0	1.5
1988	*NY-N★	18	9	.667	34	34	10	3	0	248^1	242	8	57	175	11.1	3.19	101	.256	.303	16	.178	3	7	1	5	0.9
1989	NY-N	9	4	.692	19	17	0	0	1	118^1	93	9	47	101	10.8	2.89	113	.211	.290	8	.200	2	8	5	0	0.7
1990	NY-N	19	7	.731	34	34	2	1	0	232^2	229	10	70	223	11.8	3.83	98	.258	.317	14	.187	4	-1	-2	2	0.3
1991	NY-N	13	7	.650	27	27	3	1	0	190	185	12	56	150	11.6	3.60	101	.257	.313	15	.238	4	2	1	1	0.6
1992	NY-N	10	13	.435	31	31	3	0	0	206	197	11	70	145	11.8	3.67	95	.255	.319	19	.264	7	-4	-5	1	0.3
1993	NY-N	12	15	.444	29	29	7	2	0	208^2	188	16	61	149	11.1	3.45	116	.242	.304	14	.200	4	14	13	-0	2.0
1994	NY-N	3	4	.429	7	7	0	0	0	41^1	46	9	15	40	13.5	6.31	66	.282	.346	2	.167	-0	-10	-10	1	-1.3
1996	NY-A	11	7	.611	29	29	1	1	0	170^2	169	19	88	126	14.0	5.01	99	.259	.355	0	—	0	-0	-1	1	-0.1
1997	*NY-A	9	5	.643	20	19	0	0	0	106^1	116	14	53	66	14.9	4.91	91	.283	.374	0	.000	-0	-4	-5	1	-0.5
1998	*Cle-A	8	6	.571	23	23	0	0	0	134	135	13	51	83	13.1	3.76	127	.262	.339	0	.000	-0	13	15	-0	1.3
Total	14	185	103	.642	377	374	68	24	1	2580^2	2318	169	843	2150	11.3	3.33	113	.240	.305	144	.196	28	154	122	15	17.6
● ART GOODWIN	Goodwin, Arthur Ingram b. 2/27/1877, Whiteley Twnshp, Pa. d: 6/19/43, Franklin Township, Pa. TR , 5'8", 195 lbs. Deb: 10/7/05																									
1905	NY-A	0	0	—	1	0	0	0	0	0^1	2	0	2	0	108.0	81.00	4	.667	.800	0	—	0	-3	-3	0	0.0
● CLYDE GOODWIN	Goodwin, Clyde Samuel b: 11/12/1886, Athens, Ohio d: 10/12/63, Dayton, Ohio BR/TR, 5'11", 145 lbs. Deb: 9/18/06																									
1906	Was-A	0	2	.000	4	3	1	0	0	22^1	20	0	13	9	13.7	4.43	59	.244	.354	1	.200	-0	-4	-4	-1	-0.4
● JIM GOODWIN	Goodwin, James Patrick b: 8/15/26, St.Louis, Mo. BL/TL, 6'1", 170 lbs. Deb: 4/24/48																									
1948	Chi-A	0	0	—	8	1	0	0	1	10^1	9	0	12	3	19.2	8.71	49	.237	.431	1	.500	0	-5	-5	0	-0.1
● MARV GOODWIN	Goodwin, Marvin Mardo b: 1/16/1891, Gordonsville, Va. d: 10/21/25, Houston, Tex. BR/TR, 5'11", 168 lbs. Deb: 9/7/16																									
1916	Was-A	0	0	—	3	0	0	0	0	5^2	5	0	3	1	12.7	3.18	88	.217	.308	0	.000	-0	-0	-0	-0	0.0
1917	StL-N	6	4	.600	14	12	6	3	0	85^1	70	1	19	38	9.4	2.21	122	.222	.266	4	.174	-0	5	5	2	0.7
1919	StL-N	11	9	.550	33	17	7	0	0	179	163	3	33	48	10.3	2.51	111	.245	.289	12	.200	1	8	6	-1	0.7
1920	StL-N	3	8	.273	32	12	3	0	1	116^1	153	1	28	23	14.4	4.95	60	.314	.357	7	.200	-0	-23	-25	-3	-2.5
1921	StL-N	1	2	.333	14	4	1	0	1	36^1	47	1	9	7	14.1	3.72	99	.315	.358	0	.000	-1	0	-0	0	0.0
1922	StL-N	0	0	—	2	0	0	0	0	4	3	0	3	0	13.5	2.25	172	.250	.400	0	—	0	1	1	0	0.0
1925	Cin-N	0	2	.000	4	3	2	0	0	20^2	26	2	5	4	13.9	4.79	86	.317	.364	1	.250	0	-1	-2	1	0.0
Total	7	21	25	.457	102	48	19	3	2	447^1	467	8	100	121	11.7	3.30	90	.269	.315	24	.186	0	-11	-17	0	-1.1
● RAY GORDINIER	Gordinier, Raymond Cornelius "Gordy" b: 4/11/1892, Rochester, N.Y. d: 11/15/60, Rochester, N.Y. BB/TR, 5'8.5", 170 lbs. Deb: 9/17/21																									
1921	Bro-N	1	0	1.000	3	3	0	0	0	12	10	0	8	4	13.5	5.25	74	.227	.346	1	.250	0	-2	-2	0	-0.1
1922	Bro-N	0	0	—	5	0	0	0	0	11^1	13	3	8	5	16.7	8.74	47	.289	.396	0	.000	-0	-6	-6	-0	0.0
Total	2	1	0	1.000	8	3	0	0	0	23^1	23	3	16	9	15.0	6.94	57	.258	.371	1	.167	-0	-8	-8	0	-0.1
● DON GORDON	Gordon, Donald Thomas b: 10/10/59, New York, N.Y. BR/TR, 6'1", 175 lbs. Deb: 4/10/86																									
1986	Tor-A	0	1	.000	14	0	0	0	1	21^2	28	1	8	13	15.4	7.06	60	.311	.374	0	—	0	-7	-7	-1	-0.4
1987	Tor-A	0	0	—	5	0	0	0	0	11	8	2	3	3	9.0	4.09	110	.200	.256	0	—	0	0	0	-0	0.0
	Cle-A	0	3	.000	21	0	0	0	1	39^2	49	3	12	20	14.7	4.08	111	.295	.357	0	—	0	2	2	1	0.2
	Yr	0	3	.000	26	0	0	0	1	50^2	57	5	15	23	13.5	4.09	111	.277	.338	0	—	0	2	2	1	0.2
1988	Cle-A	3	4	.429	38	0	0	0	1	59^1	65	5	19	20	13.2	4.40	93	.284	.347	0	—	0	-3	-2	1	-0.2
Total	3	3	8	.273	78	0	0	0	3	131^2	150	11	42	56	13.7	4.72	91	.286	.348	0	—	0	-8	-6	1	-0.4
● TOM GORDON	Gordon, Thomas b: 11/18/67, Sebring, Fla. BR/TR, 5'9", 180 lbs. Deb: 9/8/88																									
1988	KC-A	0	2	.000	5	2	0	0	0	15^2	16	1	7	18	13.2	5.17	77	.267	.343	0	—	0	-2	-2	0	-0.2
1989	KC-A	17	9	.654	49	16	1	1	1	163	122	10	86	153	11.5	3.64	106	.210	.312	0	—	0	4	4	3	0.8
1990	KC-A	12	11	.522	32	32	6	1	0	195^1	192	17	99	175	13.5	3.73	103	.257	.347	0	—	0	4	2	1	0.3
1991	KC-A	9	14	.391	45	14	1	0	1	158	129	16	87	167	12.5	3.87	106	.221	.325	0	—	0	4	4	0	0.6
1992	KC-A	6	10	.375	40	11	0	0	0	117^2	116	9	55	98	13.4	4.59	88	.258	.344	0	—	0	-9	-7	1	-1.0
1993	KC-A	12	6	.667	48	14	2	0	1	155^2	125	11	77	143	11.7	3.58	128	.223	.318	0	—	0	13	17	1	1.5
1994	KC-A	11	7	.611	24	24	0	0	0	155^1	136	15	87	126	13.1	4.35	115	.237	.340	0	—	0	8	11	2	1.3
1995	KC-A	12	12	.500	31	31	2	0	0	189	204	12	89	119	14.1	4.43	108	.279	.360	0	—	0	6	7	1	0.9
1996	Bos-A	12	9	.571	34	34	4	1	0	215^2	249	28	105	171	14.9	5.59	91	.284	.363	0	—	0	-14	-12	1	-1.1
1997	Bos-A	6	10	.375	42	25	2	1	11	182^2	155	10	78	159	11.6	3.74	124	.226	.308	0	—	0	17	18	0	1.5
1998	*Bos-A★	7	4	.636	73	0	0	0	**46**	79^1	55	2	25	78	9.1	2.72	170	.191	.256	0	—	0	17	17	-1	3.5
Total	11	104	94	.525	423	203	18	4	60	1627^1	1499	131	795	1407	12.8	4.14	108	.244	.333	0	—	0	47	59	8	8.1
● RICK GORECKI	Gorecki, Richard John b: 8/27/73, Evergreen Park, Ill. BR/TR, 6'3", 167 lbs. Deb: 9/10/97																									
1997	LA-N	1	0	1.000	4	1	0	0	0	6	9	3	6	6	22.5	15.00	26	.346	.469	0	—	0	-7	-7	-0	-1.0
1998	TB-A	1	2	.333	3	3	0	0	0	16^2	15	1	10	7	13.5	4.86	101	.259	.368	0	—	0	-0	0	-0	-0.3
Total	2	2	2	.500	7	4	0	0	0	22^2	24	4	16	13	15.9	7.54	61	.286	.400	0	—	0	-8	-7	-0	-1.3

● CHARLIE GORIN Gorin, Charles Perry b: 2/6/28, Waco, Tex. BL/TL, 5′10″, 165 lbs. Deb: 5/29/54

YEAR	TM/L	W	L	PCT	G	GS	CG	SH	SV	IP	H	HR	BB	SO	RAT	ERA	ERA+	OAV	OOB	BH	AVG	PB	PR	/A	PD	TPI
1954	Mil-N	0	1	.000	5	0	0	0	0	9^2	5	0	6	12	10.2	1.86	200	.152	.282	0	.000	-0	2	2	-0	0.1
1955	Mil-N	0	0	—	2	0	0	0	0	0^1	1	0	3	0	108.0	54.00	7	.500	.800	0	—	0	-2	-2	0	0.0
Total	2	0	1	.000	7	0	0	0	0	10	6	0	9	12	13.5	3.60	103	.171	.341	0	.000	-0	1	0	-0	0.1

● JACK GORMAN Gorman, John F. "Stooping Jack" b: 1859, St.Louis, Mo. d: 9/9/1889, St.Louis, Mo. Deb: 7/1/1883 ♦

YEAR	TM/L	W	L	PCT	G	GS	CG	SH	SV	IP	H	HR	BB	SO	RAT	ERA	ERA+	OAV	OOB	BH	AVG	PB	PR	/A	PD	TPI
1884	Pit-a	1	2	.333	3	3	3	0	0	25	22	0	5	10	10.1	4.68	72	.212	.255	4	.148	-0	-4	-4	0	-0.4

● TOM GORMAN Gorman, Thomas Aloysius b: 1/4/25, New York, N.Y. d: 12/26/92, Valley Stream, N.Y. BR/TR, 6′1″, 190 lbs. Deb: 7/16/52

YEAR	TM/L	W	L	PCT	G	GS	CG	SH	SV	IP	H	HR	BB	SO	RAT	ERA	ERA+	OAV	OOB	BH	AVG	PB	PR	/A	PD	TPI
1952	*NY-A	6	2	.750	12	6	1	1	1	60^2	63	8	22	31	12.9	4.60	72	.272	.340	2	.087	-1	-6	-9	-0	-1.2
1953	*NY-A	4	5	.444	40	1	0	0	6	77	65	5	32	38	12.0	3.39	109	.226	.317	2	.133	-1	5	3	-0	0.2
1954	NY-A	0	0	—	23	0	0	0	2	36^2	30	1	14	31	11.0	2.21	156	.222	.300	0	.000	-1	6	5	0	0.0
1955	KC-A	7	6	.538	57	0	0	0	18	109	98	11	36	46	11.4	3.55	118	.246	.314	2	.083	-1	5	8	-1	0.9
1956	KC-A	9	10	.474	52	13	1	0	3	171^1	168	23	68	56	12.5	3.83	113	.258	.330	2	.051	-4	6	9	-0	0.6
1957	KC-A	5	9	.357	38	12	3	1	3	124^2	125	18	33	66	11.5	3.83	103	.261	.310	4	.121	-2	-1	2	-0	0.0
1958	KC-A	4	4	.500	50	1	0	0	8	89^2	86	8	20	44	10.9	3.51	111	.258	.306	2	.118	-1	3	4	-1	0.2
1959	KC-A	1	0	1.000	17	0	0	0	1	20^1	24	3	14	9	17.3	7.08	57	.293	.402	0	—	0	-7	-7	-1	-0.5
Total	8	36	36	.500	289	33	5	2	42	689^1	659	77	239	321	12.0	3.77	105	.254	.321	14	.090	-10	11	14	-4	0.2

● TOM GORMAN Gorman, Thomas David "Big Tom" b: 3/16/16, New York, N.Y. d: 8/11/86, Closter, N.J. BR/TL, 6′2″, 200 lbs. Deb: 9/14/39 U

YEAR	TM/L	W	L	PCT	G	GS	CG	SH	SV	IP	H	HR	BB	SO	RAT	ERA	ERA+	OAV	OOB	BH	AVG	PB	PR	/A	PD	TPI
1939	NY-N	0	0	—	4	0	0	0	0	5	7	0	1	2	14.4	7.20	55	.350	.381	0	.000	-0	-2	-2	0	0.0

● TOM GORMAN Gorman, Thomas Patrick b: 12/16/57, Portland, Ore. BL/TL, 6′4″, 200 lbs. Deb: 9/2/81

YEAR	TM/L	W	L	PCT	G	GS	CG	SH	SV	IP	H	HR	BB	SO	RAT	ERA	ERA+	OAV	OOB	BH	AVG	PB	PR	/A	PD	TPI
1981	Mon-N	0	0	—	9	0	0	0	0	15	12	0	6	13	11.4	4.20	83	.222	.311	0	—	0	-1	-1	1	0.1
1982	Mon-N	1	0	1.000	5	0	0	0	0	7	8	0	4	6	15.4	5.14	71	.286	.375	0	—	0	-1	-1	0	-0.1
	NY-N	0	1	.000	3	1	0	0	0	9^1	8	0	0	7	7.7	0.96	376	.235	.235	0	.000	-0	3	3	0	0.3
	Yr	1	1	.500	8	1	0	0	0	16^1	16	0	4	13	11.0	2.76	132	.254	.299	0	.000	-0	2	2	0	0.2
1983	NY-N	1	4	.200	25	4	0	0	0	49^1	45	3	15	30	10.9	4.93	74	.245	.302	1	.250	0	-7	-7	0	-0.7
1984	NY-N	6	0	1.000	36	0	0	0	0	57^2	51	6	13	40	10.1	2.97	119	.238	.285	0	.000	-0	4	4	0	0.3
1985	NY-N	4	4	.500	34	2	0	0	0	52^2	56	8	18	32	12.6	5.13	67	.277	.336	0	.000	-1	-9	-10	1	-1.3
1986	Phi-N	0	1	.000	8	0	0	0	0	11^2	21	0	5	8	20.1	7.71	50	.382	.433	0	.000	-0	-5	-5	0	-0.4
1987	SD-N	0	0	—	6	0	0	0	0	11	11	1	5	8	13.1	4.09	97	.262	.340	0	—	0	-0	-0	-0	0.0
Total	7	12	10	.545	126	7	0	0	0	213^2	212	18	66	144	11.8	4.34	83	.261	.318	1	.071	-1	-17	-18	2	-1.8

● JOE GORMLEY Gormley, Joseph b: 12/20/1866, Summit Hill, Pa. d: 7/2/50, Summit Hill, Pa. BL/TL, Deb: 6/16/1891

YEAR	TM/L	W	L	PCT	G	GS	CG	SH	SV	IP	H	HR	BB	SO	RAT	ERA	ERA+	OAV	OOB	BH	AVG	PB	PR	/A	PD	TPI
1891	Phi-N	0	1	.000	1	1	1	0	0	8	10	0	5	2	16.9	5.63	61	.294	.385	0	.000	-1	-2	-2	0	-0.2

● HANK GORNICKI Gornicki, Henry Frank b: 1/14/11, Niagara Falls, N.Y d: 2/16/96, Riviera Beach, Fla BR/TR, 6′1″, 145 lbs. Deb: 4/17/41

YEAR	TM/L	W	L	PCT	G	GS	CG	SH	SV	IP	H	HR	BB	SO	RAT	ERA	ERA+	OAV	OOB	BH	AVG	PB	PR	/A	PD	TPI
1941	StL-N	1	0	1.000	4	1	1	1	0	11^1	6	0	9	6	12.7	3.18	118	.158	.333	1	.250	0	1	1	-0	0.0
	Chi-N	0	0	—	1	0	0	0	0	2	3	0	0	2	13.5	4.50	78	.375	.375	0	—	0	-0	-0	0	0.0
	Yr	1	0	1.000	5	1	1	1	0	13^1	9	0	9	8	12.2	3.38	110	.191	.321	1	.250	0	0	1	0	0.0
1942	Pit-N	5	6	.455	25	14	7	2	2	112	89	2	40	48	10.4	2.57	132	.215	.286	4	.114	-1	9	10	-1	0.8
1943	Pit-N	9	13	.409	42	18	4	1	4	147	165	10	47	63	13.1	3.98	87	.286	.342	7	.175	-1	-10	-8	-1	-1.4
1946	Pit-N	0	0	—	7	0	0	0	0	12^2	12	0	11	4	16.3	3.55	99	.255	.397	0	.000	-0	-0	-0	-0	-0.1
Total	4	15	19	.441	79	33	12	4	6	285	275	12	107	123	12.2	3.38	102	.254	.323	12	.146	-2	-0	2	-2	-0.7

● JOHNNY GORSICA Gorsica, John Joseph Perry (b: John Joseph Perry Gorczyca) b: 3/29/15, Bayonne, N.J. BR/TR, 6′2″, 180 lbs. Deb: 4/22/40

YEAR	TM/L	W	L	PCT	G	GS	CG	SH	SV	IP	H	HR	BB	SO	RAT	ERA	ERA+	OAV	OOB	BH	AVG	PB	PR	/A	PD	TPI
1940	*Det-A	7	7	.500	29	20	5	2	0	160	170	10	57	68	13.0	4.33	110	.272	.337	12	.194	0	1	8	5	1.1
1941	Det-A	9	11	.450	33	21	8	1	2	171	193	14	55	59	13.2	4.47	102	.281	.336	17	.298	4	-6	1	4	0.9
1942	Det-A	3	2	.600	28	0	0	0	4	53	63	2	26	19	15.6	4.75	83	.310	.397	1	.100	-0	-6	-5	4	-0.1
1943	Det-A	4	5	.444	35	4	1	0	5	96^1	88	3	40	45	12.1	3.36	105	.247	.327	4	.174	0	-1	2	3	0.5
1944	Det-A	6	14	.300	34	19	8	1	4	162	192	5	32	47	12.7	4.11	87	.296	.333	7	.135	-1	-12	-10	3	-1.0
1946	Det-A	0	0	—	14	0	0	0	1	23^2	28	5	11	14	14.8	4.56	80	.301	.375	2	.667	1	-3	-2	-0	0.0
1947	Det-A	2	0	1.000	31	0	0	0	1	57^2	44	5	26	20	11.2	3.75	101	.208	.300	2	.200	0	-0	0	1	0.2
Total	7	31	39	.443	204	64	22	4	17	723^2	778	44	247	272	13.0	4.18	98	.276	.338	45	.207	4	-28	-7	20	1.6

● RICH GOSSAGE Gossage, Richard Michael "Goose" b: 7/5/51, Colorado Springs, Colo. BR/TR, 6′3″, 217 lbs. Deb: 4/16/72

YEAR	TM/L	W	L	PCT	G	GS	CG	SH	SV	IP	H	HR	BB	SO	RAT	ERA	ERA+	OAV	OOB	BH	AVG	PB	PR	/A	PD	TPI
1972	Chi-A	7	1	.875	36	1	0	0	2	80	72	2	44	57	13.5	4.27	73	.247	.353	0	.000	-2	-11	-10	-1	-1.3
1973	Chi-A	0	4	.000	20	4	1	0	0	49^2	57	9	37	33	17.6	7.43	53	.311	.435	0	—	0	-20	-19	-0	-1.4
1974	Chi-A	4	6	.400	39	3	0	0	1	89^1	92	4	47	64	14.2	4.13	90	.272	.364	0	—	0	-5	-4	0	-0.5
1975	Chi-A★	9	8	.529	62	0	0	0	**26**	141^2	99	3	70	130	11.1	1.84	210	.201	.306	0	—	0	**30**	**32**	1	5.2
1976	Chi-A☆	9	17	.346	31	29	15	0	1	224	214	16	90	135	12.6	3.94	91	.254	.333	0	—	0	-10	-9	-1	-1.1
1977	Pit-N★	11	9	.550	72	0	0	0	26	133	78	9	49	151	8.7	1.62	245	.170	.253	5	.217	1	**34**	35	-1	**6.4**
1978	*NY-A★	10	11	.476	63	0	0	0	**27**	134^1	87	9	59	122	9.9	2.01	180	.187	.281	0	—	0	**26**	**24**	-1	4.7
1979	NY-A	5	3	.625	36	0	0	0	18	58^1	48	5	19	41	10.3	2.62	155	.227	.291	0	—	0	10	9	-1	1.8
1980	*NY-A★	6	2	.750	64	0	0	0	**33**	99	74	5	37	103	10.2	2.27	173	.211	.288	0	—	0	19	18	-1	2.7
1981	*NY-A†	3	2	.600	32	0	0	0	20	46^2	22	2	14	48	7.1	0.77	463	.141	.216	0	—	0	15	15	0	3.1
1982	NY-A☆	4	5	.444	56	0	0	0	30	93	63	5	28	102	8.8	2.23	179	.196	.261	0	—	0	19	18	-1	2.9
1983	NY-A	13	5	.722	57	0	0	0	22	87^1	82	5	25	90	11.1	2.27	172	.248	.303	0	—	0	17	16	-2	3.7
1984	*SD-N★	10	6	.625	62	0	0	0	25	102^1	75	6	36	84	9.9	2.90	123	.204	.277	4	.182	0	8	8	-1	1.4
1985	SD-N★	5	3	.625	50	0	0	0	26	79	64	1	17	52	9.3	1.82	194	.226	.272	0	.000	-1	16	15	-1	2.3
1986	SD-N	5	7	.417	45	0	0	0	21	64^2	69	8	20	63	12.7	4.45	82	.273	.331	0	.000	-1	-5	-6	-1	-1.5
1987	SD-N	5	4	.556	40	0	0	0	11	52	47	4	19	44	11.4	3.12	127	.244	.311	0	.000	-0	6	5	-1	0.8
1988	Chi-N	4	4	.500	46	0	0	0	13	43^2	50	3	15	30	14.0	4.33	83	.291	.358	0	.000	-0	-4	-4	-0	-0.8
1989	SF-N	2	1	.667	31	0	0	0	4	43^2	32	2	27	24	12.2	2.68	126	.212	.331	0	.000	-0	4	3	-1	0.2
	NY-A	1	0	1.000	11	0	0	0	1	14^1	14	0	3	6	11.3	3.77	103	.275	.327	0	—	0	0	0	0	0.0
1991	Tex-A	4	2	.667	44	0	0	0	1	40^1	33	4	16	28	11.6	3.57	113	.228	.317	0	—	0	2	2	-1	0.2
1992	Oak-A	0	2	.000	30	0	0	0	0	38	32	5	19	26	12.6	2.84	132	.230	.331	0	—	0	5	4	-0	0.6
1993	Oak-A	4	5	.444	39	0	0	0	1	47^2	49	6	26	40	14.3	4.53	90	.266	.360	0	—	0	-1	-2	-1	0.0
1994	Sea-A	3	0	1.000	36	0	0	0	1	47^1	44	6	15	29	11.8	4.18	117	.251	.321	0	—	0	3	4	-1	0.1
Total	22	124	107	.537	1002	37	16	0	310	1809^1	1497	119	732	1502	11.3	3.01	125	.228	.310	9	.106	-3	158	154	-14	29.5

● JIM GOTT Gott, James William b: 8/3/59, Hollywood, Cal. BR/TR, 6′4″, 220 lbs. Deb: 4/9/82

YEAR	TM/L	W	L	PCT	G	GS	CG	SH	SV	IP	H	HR	BB	SO	RAT	ERA	ERA+	OAV	OOB	BH	AVG	PB	PR	/A	PD	TPI
1982	Tor-A	5	10	.333	30	23	1	1	0	136	134	15	66	82	13.4	4.43	101	.255	.341	0	—	0	-5	1	-0	0.0
1983	Tor-A	9	14	.391	34	30	6	1	0	176^2	195	15	68	121	13.7	4.74	91	.280	.349	0	—	0	-13	-9	-1	-1.1
1984	Tor-A	7	6	.538	35	12	1	1	2	109^2	93	7	49	73	11.9	4.02	102	.233	.322	0	—	0	-0	1	-1	-0.3
1985	SF-N	7	10	.412	26	26	2	0	0	148^1	144	10	51	78	11.9	3.88	89	.254	.317	10	.196	4	-5	-7	1	-0.3
1986	SF-N	0	0	—	9	2	0	0	1	13	16	0	13	9	20.1	7.62	46	.314	.453	0	.000	0	-6	-6	-0	-0.1
1987	SF-N	1	0	1.000	30	3	0	0	0	56	53	4	32	63	14.0	4.50	85	.244	.347	1	.100	1	-3	-4	0	0.0
	Pit-N	0	2	.000	25	0	0	0	13	31	28	0	8	27	10.5	1.45	283	.233	.281	0	.000	-0	9	9	-0	1.2
	Yr	1	2	.333	55	3	0	0	13	87	81	4	40	90	12.5	3.41	115	.238	.318	1	.091	0	6	5	-0	1.2
1988	Pit-N	6	6	.500	67	0	0	0	34	77^1	68	9	22	76	10.7	3.49	97	.243	.303	0	.000	-0	-0	-1	-0	-0.2
1989	Pit-N	0	0	—	1	0	0	0	0	0^2	1	0	1	1	27.0	0.00	—	.333	.500	0	—	0	0	0	0	0.0
1990	LA-N	3	5	.375	50	0	0	0	3	62	59	5	34	44	13.5	2.90	126	.257	.352	0	.000	-0	6	5	-0	0.6
1991	LA-N	4	3	.571	55	0	0	0	2	76	63	5	32	73	11.4	2.96	121	.223	.305	1	.500	0	6	5	1	0.6
1992	LA-N	3	3	.500	68	0	0	0	6	88	72	4	41	75	11.7	2.45	140	.225	.315	1	.500	0	10	10	1	0.9
1993	LA-N	4	8	.333	62	0	0	0	25	77^2	71	6	17	67	10.3	2.32	165	.248	.293	0	.000	-0	15	13	0	2.5
1994	LA-N	5	3	.625	37	0	0	0	2	36^1	46	3	20	29	17.1	5.94	66	.322	.416	0	—	0	-7	-8	0	-1.6
1995	Pit-N	2	4	.333	25	0	0	0	3	31^1	38	2	12	19	14.6	6.03	71	.288	.352	0	.000	-0	-6	-6	0	-1.1
Total	14	56	74	.431	554	96	10	3	91	1120	1081	85	466	837	12.6	3.87	101	.254	.331	13	.178	5	1	2	0	1.1

YEAR TM/L		W	L	PCT	G	GS	CG	SH	SV	IP	H	HR	BB	SO	RAT	ERA	ERA+	OAV	OOB	BH	AVG	PB	PR	/A	PD	TPI
● **TED GOULAIT**	Goulait, Theodore Lee b: 8/12/1889, St.Clair, Mich. d: 7/15/36, St.Clair, Mich. BR/TR, 5'9.5", 172 lbs. Deb: 9/28/12																									
1912	NY-N	0	0	—	1	1	1	0	0	7	11	0	4	6	19.3	6.43	53	.367	.441	1	.500	0	-2	-2	0	0.0
● **AL GOULD**	Gould, Albert Frank "Pudgy" b: 1/20/1893, Muscatine, Iowa d: 8/8/82, San Jose, Cal. BR/TR, 5'6.5", 160 lbs. Deb: 7/11/16																									
1916	Cle-A	5	6	.455	30	9	6	1	1	106^2	101	0	40	41	12.2	2.53	119	.256	.329	3	.103	-2	4	6	-1	0.3
1917	Cle-A	4	4	.500	27	7	1	0	0	94	95	1	52	24	14.4	3.64	78	.281	.382	5	.208	1	-10	-8	2	-0.5
Total	2	9	10	.474	57	16	7	1	1	200^2	196	1	92	65	13.2	3.05	96	.267	.354	8	.151	-1	-7	-3	1	-0.2
● **CHARLIE GOULD**	Gould, Charles Harvey b: 8/21/1847, Cincinnati, Ohio d: 4/10/17, Flushing, N.Y. BR/TR, 6', 172 lbs. Deb: 5/5/1871 M♦																									
1876	Cin-N	0	0	—	2	0	0	0	0	4^1	10	0	0	0	20.8	0.00	—	.400	.400	65	.252	0	1	1	-0	0.0
● **LARRY GOWELL**	Gowell, Lawrence Clyde b: 5/2/48, Lewiston, Me. BR/TR, 6'2", 182 lbs. Deb: 9/21/72																									
1972	NY-A	0	1	.000	2	1	0	0	0	7	3	0	2	7	6.4	1.29	229	.143	.217	1	1.000	1	1	1	0	0.3
● **MAURO GOZZO**	Gozzo, Mauro Paul b: 3/7/66, New Britain, Conn. BR/TR, 6'3", 212 lbs. Deb: 8/8/89																									
1989	Tor-A	4	1	.800	9	3	0	0	0	31^2	35	1	9	10	12.8	4.83	78	.289	.344	0	—	0	-3	-4	-0	-0.5
1990	Cle-A	0	0	—	2	0	0	0	0	3	2	0	2	2	12.0	0.00	—	.182	.308	0	—	0	1	1	-0	0.0
1991	Cle-A	0	0	—	2	2	0	0	0	4^2	9	0	7	3	30.9	19.29	22	.450	.593	0	—	0	-8	-8	-0	0.0
1992	Min-A	0	0	—	2	0	0	0	0	1^2	7	2	0	1	37.8	27.00	15	.583	.583	0	—	0	-4	-4	-0	-0.2
1993	NY-N	0	1	.000	10	0	0	0	1	14	11	1	5	6	10.3	2.57	156	.212	.281	0	—	0	2	2	-1	0.1
1994	NY-N	3	5	.375	23	8	0	0	0	69	86	5	28	33	15.0	4.83	86	.304	.369	4	.250	1	-5	-5	-0	-0.4
Total	6	7	7	.500	48	13	0	0	1	124	150	9	51	55	14.7	5.30	76	.301	.368	4	.250	1	-17	-17	-2	-1.0
● **AL GRABOWSKI**	Grabowski, Alfons Francis b: 9/6/01, Syracuse, N.Y. d: 10/29/66, Memphis, N.Y. BL/TL, 5'11.5", 175 lbs. Deb: 9/11/29 F																									
1929	StL-N	3	2	.600	6	6	4	2	0	50	44	0	8	22	9.4	2.52	185	.227	.257	4	.250	2	12	12	-0	1.2
1930	StL-N	6	4	.600	33	8	1	0	1	107	120	7	49	43	14.5	4.79	105	.290	.369	12	.364	3	2	3	-0	0.4
Total	2	9	6	.600	39	14	5	2	1	157	164	7	57	65	12.8	4.07	120	.270	.335	16	.327	4	14	15	-0	1.6
● **REGGIE GRABOWSKI**	Grabowski, Reginald John b: 7/16/07, Syracuse, N.Y. d: 4/2/55, Syracuse, N.Y. BR/TR, 6'0.5", 185 lbs. Deb: 4/15/32 F																									
1932	Phi-N	2	2	.500	14	2	0	0	0	34^1	38	2	22	15	16.3	3.67	120	.273	.380	0	.000	-1	1	3	-1	0.2
1933	Phi-N	1	3	.250	10	5	4	1	0	48	38	4	10	9	9.2	2.44	157	.220	.266	2	.125	-1	5	7	-1	0.4
1934	Phi-N	1	3	.250	27	5	0	0	0	65^1	114	13	23	13	19.3	9.23	51	.384	.433	1	.056	-2	-38	-33	-1	-2.0
Total	3	4	8	.333	51	12	4	1	0	147^2	190	19	55	37	15.3	5.73	76	.312	.375	3	.075	-3	-32	-23	-3	-1.4
● **MIKE GRACE**	Grace, Michael James b: 6/20/70, Joliet, Ill. BR/TR, 6'4", 210 lbs. Deb: 9/1/95																									
1995	Phi-N	1	1	.500	2	2	0	0	0	11^1	10	0	4	7	11.1	3.18	133	.238	.304	0	.000	-0	1	1	0	0.2
1996	Phi-N	7	2	.778	12	12	1	1	0	80	72	9	16	49	10.0	3.49	124	.238	.279	4	.138	-0	6	7	1	0.9
1997	Phi-N	3	2	.600	6	6	1	1	0	39	32	3	10	26	9.9	3.46	123	.230	.287	1	.083	-1	3	3	-1	0.3
1998	Phi-N	4	7	.364	21	15	0	0	0	90^1	116	10	30	46	15.3	5.48	80	.312	.376	2	.087	-1	-13	-11	-1	-1.4
Total	4	15	12	.556	41	35	2	2	0	220^2	230	22	60	128	12.2	4.28	101	.269	.324	7	.106	-2	-2	1	-0	0.0
● **JOHN GRAFF**	Graff, John F. b: Philadelphia, Pa. Deb: 7/19/1893																									
1893	Was-N	0	1	.000	2	1	1	0	0	12	21	2	13	4	26.3	11.25	41	.368	.493	1	.200	-0	-9	-9	-0	-0.5
● **PEACHES GRAHAM**	Graham, George Frederick b: 3/23/1877, Aledo, Ill. d: 7/25/39, Long Beach, Cal. BR/TR, 5'9", 180 lbs. Deb: 9/14/02 F♦																									
1903	Chi-N	0	1	.000	1	1	0	0	0	5	9	0	3	4	23.4	5.40	58	.429	.520	0	.000	-0	-1	-1	0	-0.2
● **SKINNY GRAHAM**	Graham, Kyle b: 8/14/1899, Oak Grove, Ala. d: 12/1/73, Oak Grove, Ala. BR/TR, 6'2", 172 lbs. Deb: 9/3/24																									
1924	Bos-N	0	4	.000	5	4	1	0	0	33	33	0	11	15	12.0	3.82	100	.287	.349	0	.000	-1	0	0	-0	-0.1
1925	Bos-N	7	12	.368	34	23	5	0	1	157	177	6	62	32	13.9	4.41	91	.296	.365	6	.136	-2	-3	-7	-2	-1.1
1926	Bos-N	3	3	.500	15	4	1	0	0	36^1	54	3	19	7	18.6	7.93	45	.370	.449	2	.167	-1	-17	-18	0	-2.4
1929	Det-A	1	3	.250	13	6	2	0	1	51^2	70	2	33	7	18.5	5.57	77	.340	.438	2	.105	-1	-8	-7	-1	0.7
Total	4	11	22	.333	67	37	9	0	2	278	334	11	125	61	15.1	5.02	79	.314	.390	10	.122	-5	-27	-32	-3	-4.3
● **OSCAR GRAHAM**	Graham, Oscar M. b: 7/20/1878, Plattsmouth, Neb. d: 10/15/31, Moline, Ill. BL/TL, 6'0.5", Deb: 4/16/07																									
1907	Was-A	4	9	.308	20	14	6	0	0	104	116	3	29	44	13.4	3.98	61	.284	.347	11	.229	3	-17	-18	0	-1.7
● **BILL GRAHAM**	Graham, William Albert b: 1/21/37, Flemingsburg, Ky. BR/TR, 6'3", 217 lbs. Deb: 10/2/66																									
1966	Det-A	0	0	—	1	0	0	0	0	2	2	0	0	2	9.0	0.00	—	.250	.250	0	—	0	1	1	-0	0.0
1967	NY-N	1	2	.333	5	3	1	0	0	27^1	20	3	11	14	10.2	2.63	129	.200	.279	1	.125	-0	2	2	-1	0.1
Total	2	1	2	.333	6	3	1	0	0	29^1	22	3	11	16	10.1	2.45	138	.204	.277	1	.125	-0	3	3	-1	0.1
● **BILL GRAHAME**	Grahame, William James b: 7/22/1884, Owosso, Mich. d: 2/15/36, Holt, Mich. TL, 6', Deb: 4/18/08																									
1908	StL-A	6	7	.462	21	13	7	0	0	117^1	104	0	32	47	11.4	2.30	104	.240	.310	5	.119	-3	1	1	-0	-0.2
1909	StL-A	8	14	.364	34	21	13	3	1	187^1	171	3	60	82	11.3	3.12	77	.256	.322	10	.159	-0	-13	-15	1	-1.7
1910	StL-A	0	8	.000	9	6	1	0	0	43	46	2	13	12	13.2	3.56	70	.297	.366	2	.154	-0	-5	-5	-2	-1.1
Total	3	14	29	.326	64	40	21	3	1	347^2	321	5	105	141	11.6	2.90	83	.256	.323	17	.144	-3	-17	-19	-1	-3.0
● **JOE GRAHE**	Grahe, Joseph Milton b: 8/14/67, W.Palm Beach, Fla. BR/TR, 6', 200 lbs. Deb: 8/4/90																									
1990	Cal-A	3	4	.429	8	8	0	0	0	43^1	51	3	23	25	16.0	4.98	77	.293	.385	0	—	0	-5	-6	1	-0.7
1991	Cal-A	3	7	.300	18	10	1	0	0	73	84	2	33	40	14.8	4.81	85	.288	.366	0	—	0	-6	-6	0	-0.7
1992	Cal-A	5	6	.455	46	7	0	0	21	94^2	85	5	39	39	12.4	3.52	113	.246	.332	0	—	0	4	5	0	0.7
1993	Cal-A	4	1	.800	45	0	0	0	11	56^2	54	5	25	31	12.9	2.86	158	.251	.335	0	—	0	9	10	1	1.0
1994	Cal-A	2	5	.286	40	0	0	0	13	43^1	68	5	18	26	19.1	6.65	74	.362	.434	0	—	0	-9	-8	1	-1.5
1995	Col-N	4	3	.571	17	9	0	0	0	56^2	69	6	27	27	15.7	5.08	106	.301	.382	5	.417	1	-6	2	1	0.4
Total	6	21	26	.447	174	34	1	0	45	367^2	411	26	165	188	14.7	4.46	98	.285	.367	5	.417	1	-12	-3	4	-0.8
● **TOMMY GRAMLY**	Gramly, Bert Thomas b: 4/19/45, Dallas, Tex. BR/TR, 6'3", 175 lbs. Deb: 4/18/68																									
1968	Cle-A	0	1	.000	3	0	0	0	0	3^1	3	0	2	1	13.5	2.70	110	.250	.357	0	—	0	0	0	-0	0.0
● **HANK GRAMPP**	Grampp, Henry Erchardt b: 9/28/03, New York, N.Y. d: 3/24/86, New York, N.Y. BR/TR, 6'1", 185 lbs. Deb: 6/2/27																									
1927	Chi-N	0	0	—	2	0	0	0	0	3	4	0	1	3	15.0	9.00	43	.333	.385	0	—	0	-2	-2	0	0.0
1929	Chi-N	0	1	.000	1	1	0	0	0	2	4	0	3	0	36.0	27.00	17	.500	.667	0	—	0	-5	-5	-0	-1.2
Total	2	0	1	.000	3	1	0	0	0	5	8	0	4	3	23.4	16.20	26	.400	.520	0	—	0	-7	-7	0	-1.2
● **JACK GRANEY**	Graney, John Gladstone b: 6/10/1886, St.Thomas, Ont., Can. d: 4/20/78, Louisiana, Mo. BL/TL, 5'9", 180 lbs. Deb: 4/30/08 ♦																									
1908	Cle-A	0	0	—	2	0	0	0	0	3^1	6	0	1	0	18.9	5.40	44	.400	.438	0	—	0	-1	-1	-0	0.0
● **JEFF GRANGER**	Granger, Jeffrey Adam b: 12/16/71, San Pedro, Cal. BR/TL, 6'4", 200 lbs. Deb: 9/16/93																									
1993	KC-A	0	0	—	1	0	0	0	0	1	3	0	2	1	45.0	27.00	17	.500	.625	0	—	0	-3	-2	0	-0.3
1994	KC-A	0	1	.000	2	2	0	0	0	9^1	13	2	6	3	18.3	6.75	74	.325	.413	0	—	0	-2	-2	0	-0.2
1996	KC-A	0	0	—	15	0	0	0	0	16^1	21	3	10	11	18.2	6.61	76	.313	.418	0	—	0	-3	-3	0	0.0
1997	Pit-N	0	0	—	9	0	0	0	0	5	10	3	8	4	32.4	18.00	24	.417	.563	0	—	0	-8	-8	-0	0.0
Total	4	0	1	.000	27	2	0	0	0	31^2	47	8	26	19	21.3	9.09	54	.343	.455	0	—	0	-15	-15	-0	-0.5
● **WAYNE GRANGER**	Granger, Wayne Allan b: 3/15/44, Springfield, Mass. BR/TR, 6'2", 165 lbs. Deb: 6/5/68																									
1968	*StL-N	4	2	.667	34	0	0	0	4	44	40	2	12	27	11.0	2.25	129	.238	.297	1	.200	0	4	3	2	0.7
1969	Cin-N	9	6	.600	**90**	0	0	0	27	144^2	143	10	40	68	11.8	2.80	134	.262	.320	2	.095	-0	13	15	1	2.3
1970	*Cin-N	6	5	.545	67	0	0	0	**35**	84^2	79	5	27	38	11.4	2.66	152	.252	.313	1	.100	-1	13	13	2	2.8
1971	Cin-N	7	6	.538	**70**	0	0	0	11	100	94	8	28	51	11.1	3.33	101	.251	.304	1	.143	1	2	0	3	0.5
1972	Min-A	4	6	.400	63	0	0	0	19	89^2	83	7	28	45	11.3	3.01	107	.243	.304	2	.200	0	0	2	-0	0.3
1973	StL-N	2	4	.333	33	0	0	0	5	46^2	50	3	21	14	14.1	4.24	86	.284	.367	0	.000	-0	-3	-3	-0	-0.5
	NY-A	0	1	.000	7	0	0	0	0	15^1	19	1	3	10	13.5	1.76	208	.279	.319	0	—	0	4	3	-1	0.2

YEAR	TM/L	W	L	PCT	G	GS	CG	SH	SV	IP	H	HR	BB	SO	RAT	ERA	ERA+	OAV	OOB	BH	AVG	PB	PR	/A	PD	TPI
1974	Chi-A	0	0	—	5	0	0	0	0	7^2	16	1	3	4	22.3	8.22	45	.432	.475	0	—	0	-4	-4	0	0.0
1975	Hou-N	2	5	.286	55	0	0	0	5	74	76	7	23	30	12.5	3.65	92	.264	.327	0	.000	-1	-0	-2	1	-0.2
1976	Mon-N	1	0	1.000	27	0	0	0	2	32	32	3	16	16	14.1	3.66	102	.264	.360	0	.000	-0	-1	0	-0	0.0
Total	9	35	35	.500	451	0	0	0	108	638^2	632	47	201	303	12.0	3.14	113	.260	.322	7	.103	-1	27	28	8	6.1

● GEORGE GRANT Grant, George Addison b: 1/6/03, E.Tallassee, Ala. d: 3/25/86, Montgomery, Ala. BR/TR, 5′11.5″, 175 lbs. Deb: 9/17/23

YEAR	TM/L	W	L	PCT	G	GS	CG	SH	SV	IP	H	HR	BB	SO	RAT	ERA	ERA+	OAV	OOB	BH	AVG	PB	PR	/A	PD	TPI
1923	StL-A	0	0	—	4	0	0	0	0	8^2	15	0	3	2	18.7	5.19	80	.395	.439	0	.000	-0	-1	-1	0	0.0
1924	StL-A	1	2	.333	22	2	0	0	0	51^1	69	4	25	11	16.7	6.31	72	.325	.399	0	.000	-2	-12	-10	-1	-0.8
1925	StL-A	0	2	.000	12	0	0	0	0	16^1	26	2	8	7	18.7	6.06	77	.400	.466	1	.250	-0	-3	-3	0	-0.2
1927	Cle-A	4	6	.400	25	3	2	0	1	74^2	85	1	40	19	15.1	4.46	94	.300	.387	2	.095	-2	-3	-2	0	-0.4
1928	Cle-A	10	8	.556	28	18	6	1	0	155^1	196	7	76	39	15.9	5.04	82	.319	.395	11	.183	-2	-17	-15	2	-1.5
1929	Cle-A	0	2	.000	12	0	0	0	0	24	41	2	23	5	24.0	10.50	42	.414	.525	0	.000	-0	-17	-16	0	-1.1
1931	Pit-N	0	0	—	11	0	0	0	0	17	28	0	7	6	19.1	7.41	52	.364	.424	0	.000	-0	-7	-7	0	0.0
Total	7	15	20	.429	114	23	8	1	1	347^1	460	16	182	89	16.7	5.65	75	.331	.410	14	.135	-8	-59	-54	3	-4.0

● JIM GRANT Grant, James Ronald b: 8/4/1894, Coalville, Iowa d: 11/30/85, Des Moines, Iowa BR/TL, 5′11″, 180 lbs. Deb: 4/21/23

YEAR	TM/L	W	L	PCT	G	GS	CG	SH	SV	IP	H	HR	BB	SO	RAT	ERA	ERA+	OAV	OOB	BH	AVG	PB	PR	/A	PD	TPI
1923	Phi-N	0	0	—	2	0	0	0	0	4	10	0	4	0	33.8	13.50	34	.588	.682	0	.000	-0	-4	-4	0	0.0

● MUDCAT GRANT Grant, James Timothy "Jim" b: 8/13/35, Lacoochee, Fla. BR/TR, 6′1″, 186 lbs. Deb: 4/17/58

YEAR	TM/L	W	L	PCT	G	GS	CG	SH	SV	IP	H	HR	BB	SO	RAT	ERA	ERA+	OAV	OOB	BH	AVG	PB	PR	/A	PD	TPI
1958	Cle-A	10	11	.476	44	28	11	1	4	204	173	20	104	111	12.3	3.84	95	.228	.321	5	.076	-4	-2	-4	-2	-1.0
1959	Cle-A	10	7	.588	38	19	6	1	3	165^1	140	23	81	85	12.1	4.14	89	.232	.325	11	.200	1	-5	-8	-0	-0.7
1960	Cle-A	9	8	.529	33	19	5	0	0	159^2	147	26	78	75	12.8	4.40	85	.243	.332	16	.281	4	-9	-12	-1	-0.9
1961	Cle-A	15	9	.625	35	35	11	3	0	244^2	207	32	109	146	11.7	3.86	102	.227	.312	15	.170	1	4	2	1	0.3
1962	Cle-A	7	10	.412	26	23	6	1	0	149^2	128	24	81	90	12.6	4.27	91	.233	.331	8	.151	-0	-5	-7	-0	-0.7
1963	Cle-A☆	13	14	.481	38	32	10	2	1	229^1	213	30	87	157	11.9	3.69	98	.243	.314	13	.188	3	-2	-2	-3	-0.2
1964	Cle-A	3	4	.429	13	9	1	0	0	62	82	11	25	43	15.7	5.95	60	.324	.387	6	.273	4	-16	-16	0	-1.2
	Min-A	11	9	.550	26	23	10	1	1	166	162	21	36	75	10.7	2.82	127	.248	.288	10	.167	0	15	14	0	1.7
	Yr	14	13	.519	39	32	11	1	1	228	244	32	61	118	12.0	3.67	98	.269	.315	16	.195	4	-1	-2	1	0.5
1965	*Min-A★	**21**	7	**.750**	41	39	14	**6**	0	270^1	252	34	61	142	10.4	3.30	108	.247	.289	15	.155	2	5	8	1	1.1
1966	Min-A	13	13	.500	35	35	10	3	0	249	248	23	49	110	11.0	3.25	111	.260	.300	15	.192	2	5	10	2	1.4
1967	Min-A	5	6	.455	27	14	2	0	0	95^1	121	10	17	50	13.1	4.72	73	.315	.346	5	.179	0	-16	-13	-2	-1.7
1968	LA-N	6	4	.600	37	4	1	0	3	94^2	77	1	19	35	9.7	2.09	132	.226	.279	4	.129	0	9	7	1	0.9
1969	Mon-N	1	6	.143	11	10	1	0	0	50^2	64	7	14	20	14.0	4.80	77	.299	.345	2	.125	-1	-7	-6	0	-0.8
	StL-N	7	5	.583	30	3	1	0	7	63^1	62	9	22	35	12.2	4.12	87	.252	.319	5	.294	2	-4	-4	-1	-0.7
	Yr	8	11	.421	41	13	2	0	7	114	126	16	36	55	12.9	4.42	82	.273	.328	7	.212	1	-10	-10	-1	-1.5
1970	Oak-A	6	2	.750	72	0	0	0	24	123^1	104	8	30	54	10.0	1.82	194	.235	.288	2	.222	2	**26**	**24**	1	2.6
	Pit-N	2	1	.667	8	0	0	0	0	12	8	2	2	4	7.5	2.25	173	.190	.227	0	.000	-0	2	2	0	0.5
1971	Pit-N	5	3	.625	42	0	0	0	7	75	79	8	28	22	13.0	3.60	94	.274	.341	2	.250	1	-1	-2	1	-0.1
	*Oak-A	1	0	1.000	15	0	0	0	3	27^1	25	3	6	13	10.2	1.98	169	.243	.284	1	.333	0	5	4	-0	0.3
Total	14	145	119	.549	571	293	89	18	53	2441^2	2292	292	849	1267	11.7	3.63	100	.248	.313	135	.178	16	5	-3	-3	0.8

● MARK GRANT Grant, Mark Andrew b: 10/24/63, Aurora, Ill. BR/TR, 6′2″, 205 lbs. Deb: 4/27/84

YEAR	TM/L	W	L	PCT	G	GS	CG	SH	SV	IP	H	HR	BB	SO	RAT	ERA	ERA+	OAV	OOB	BH	AVG	PB	PR	/A	PD	TPI
1984	SF-N	1	4	.200	11	10	0	0	1	53^2	56	6	19	32	12.7	6.37	55	.272	.336	0	.000	-2	-17	-17	-0	-1.6
1986	SF-N	0	1	.000	4	1	0	0	0	10	6	0	5	5	9.9	3.60	98	.176	.282	0	.000	-0	0	-0	-0	0.0
1987	SF-N	1	2	.333	16	8	0	0	1	61	66	6	21	32	13.0	3.54	109	.282	.344	1	.083	-0	4	2	-1	0.0
	SD-N	6	7	.462	17	17	2	1	0	102^1	104	16	52	58	13.7	4.66	85	.263	.348	3	.094	-1	-7	-8	-1	-1.0
	Yr	7	9	.438	33	25	2	1	1	163^1	170	22	73	90	13.4	4.24	92	.269	.345	4	.091	-1	-3	-6	-1	-1.0
1988	SD-N	2	8	.200	33	11	0	0	0	97^2	97	14	36	61	12.4	3.69	92	.268	.338	0	.000	-1	-3	-3	0	-0.4
1989	SD-N	8	2	.800	50	0	0	0	2	116^1	105	11	32	69	10.8	3.33	105	.248	.305	1	.050	-0	2	2	-0	0.1
1990	SD-N	1	1	.500	26	0	0	0	0	39	47	5	19	29	15.2	4.85	79	.305	.382	1	.500	0	-5	-4	1	-0.1
	Atl-N	1	2	.333	33	1	0	0	3	52^1	61	4	18	40	13.8	4.64	87	.293	.352	1	.250	1	-5	-4	-0	-0.2
	Yr	2	3	.400	59	1	0	0	3	91^1	108	9	37	69	14.4	4.73	83	.296	.362	2	.333	1	-10	-8	0	-0.3
1992	Sea-A	2	4	.333	23	10	0	0	0	81	100	6	22	42	13.8	3.89	102	.311	.358	0	—	0	0	1	-1	-0.1
1993	Hou-N	0	0	—	6	0	0	0	0	11	11	0	5	6	13.1	0.82	473	.275	.356	0	—	0	4	4	1	0.1
	Col-N	0	1	.000	14	0	0	0	1	14^1	23	4	6	8	18.2	12.56	38	.377	.433	0	—	0	-14	-12	0	-0.9
	Yr	0	1	.000	20	0	0	0	1	25^1	34	4	11	14	16.0	7.46	59	.333	.398	0	—	0	-10	-9	1	-0.8
Total	8	22	32	.407	233	58	2	1	8	638^2	676	72	235	382	13.0	4.31	87	.277	.343	7	.067	-3	-39	-40	-2	-4.1

● RICK GRAPENTHIN Grapenthin, Richard Ray b: 4/16/58, Linn Grove, Iowa BR/TR, 6′2″, 205 lbs. Deb: 5/3/83

YEAR	TM/L	W	L	PCT	G	GS	CG	SH	SV	IP	H	HR	BB	SO	RAT	ERA	ERA+	OAV	OOB	BH	AVG	PB	PR	/A	PD	TPI
1983	Mon-N	0	1	.000	1	0	0	0	0	4	4	2	1	3	11.3	9.00	40	.267	.313	0	.000	-0	-2	-2	0	-0.4
1984	Mon-N	1	2	.333	13	1	0	0	2	23	19	3	7	9	10.2	3.52	97	.235	.295	1	.200	0	0	-0	0	0.0
1985	Mon-N	0	0	—	5	0	0	0	0	7	13	0	8	4	28.3	14.14	24	.394	.524	1	1.000	1	-8	-8	-0	0.0
Total	3	1	3	.250	19	1	0	0	2	34	36	5	16	16	14.0	6.35	54	.279	.363	2	.286	0	-10	-11	0	-0.4

● LOU GRASMICK Grasmick, Louis Junior b: 9/11/24, Baltimore, Md. BR/TR, 6′, 195 lbs. Deb: 4/22/48

YEAR	TM/L	W	L	PCT	G	GS	CG	SH	SV	IP	H	HR	BB	SO	RAT	ERA	ERA+	OAV	OOB	BH	AVG	PB	PR	/A	PD	TPI
1948	Phi-N	0	0	—	2	0	0	0	0	5	3	1	8	2	19.8	7.20	55	.176	.440	1	1.000	0	-2	-2	0	0.1

● DON GRATE Grate, Donald "Buckeye" b: 8/27/23, Greenfield, Ohio BR/TR, 6′2.5″, 180 lbs. Deb: 7/6/45

YEAR	TM/L	W	L	PCT	G	GS	CG	SH	SV	IP	H	HR	BB	SO	RAT	ERA	ERA+	OAV	OOB	BH	AVG	PB	PR	/A	PD	TPI
1945	Phi-N	0	1	.000	4	2	0	0	0	8^1	18	0	12	6	32.4	17.28	22	.439	.566	0	.000	-0	-12	-12	-0	-1.2
1946	Phi-N	1	0	1.000	3	0	0	0	0	8	4	0	2	2	6.8	1.13	305	.160	.222	0	.000	0	2	2	-0	0.2
Total	2	1	1	.500	7	2	0	0	0	16^1	22	0	14	8	19.8	9.37	39	.333	.450	0	.000	-0	-10	-10	-1	-1.0

● MARK GRATER Grater, Mark Anthony b: 1/19/64, Rochester, Pa. BR/TR, 5′10″, 205 lbs. Deb: 6/12/91

YEAR	TM/L	W	L	PCT	G	GS	CG	SH	SV	IP	H	HR	BB	SO	RAT	ERA	ERA+	OAV	OOB	BH	AVG	PB	PR	/A	PD	TPI
1991	StL-N	0	0	—	3	0	0	0	0	3	5	0	2	0	21.0	0.00	—	.385	.467	0	—	0	1	1	-0	0.0
1993	Det-A	0	0	—	6	0	0	0	0	5	6	0	4	4	18.0	5.40	79	.286	.400	0	—	0	-1	-1	-0	0.0
Total	2	0	0	—	9	0	0	0	0	8	11	0	6	4	19.1	3.38	121	.324	.425	0	—	0	1	1	-0	0.0

● DANNY GRAVES Graves, Daniel Peter b: 8/7/73, Saigon, South Vietnam BR/TR, 5′11″, 200 lbs. Deb: 7/13/96

YEAR	TM/L	W	L	PCT	G	GS	CG	SH	SV	IP	H	HR	BB	SO	RAT	ERA	ERA+	OAV	OOB	BH	AVG	PB	PR	/A	PD	TPI
1996	Cle-A	2	0	1.000	15	0	0	0	0	29^2	29	2	10	22	11.8	4.55	107	.246	.305	0	—	0	1	1	-0	0.1
1997	Cle-A	0	0	—	5	0	0	0	0	11^1	15	2	9	4	19.1	4.76	98	.326	.436	0	—	0	-0	-0	-0	-0.1
	Cin-N	0	0	—	10	0	0	0	0	14^2	26	0	11	7	22.7	6.14	69	.413	.500	0	.000	-0	-3	-3	0	0.0
1998	Cin-N	2	1	.667	62	0	0	0	8	81^1	76	6	28	44	11.7	3.32	130	.251	.318	0	.000	-0	8	9	1	0.5
Total	3	4	1	.800	92	0	0	0	8	137	146	10	58	77	13.5	4.01	112	.275	.349	0	.000	-1	6	7	-0	0.5

● FRANK GRAVES Graves, Frank M. b: 11/2/1860, Cincinnati, Ohio 6′, 163 lbs. Deb: 5/10/1886 ♦

YEAR	TM/L	W	L	PCT	G	GS	CG	SH	SV	IP	H	HR	BB	SO	RAT	ERA	ERA+	OAV	OOB	BH	AVG	PB	PR	/A	PD	TPI
1886	StL-N	0	0	—	1	0	0	0	0	7	10	0	1	2	14.1	9.00	36	.323	.344	21	.152	-0	-4	-4	-0	0.0

● CHARLIE GRAY Gray, Charles b: 1867, Indianapolis, Ind. Deb: 4/23/1890

YEAR	TM/L	W	L	PCT	G	GS	CG	SH	SV	IP	H	HR	BB	SO	RAT	ERA	ERA+	OAV	OOB	BH	AVG	PB	PR	/A	PD	TPI
1890	Pit-N	1	4	.200	5	4	3	0	0	31	48	0	24	10	21.2	7.55	44	.343	.442	3	.200	-0	-14	-15	-1	-1.7

● DAVE GRAY Gray, David Alexander b: 1/7/43, Ogden, Utah BR/TR, 6′1″, 190 lbs. Deb: 6/14/64

YEAR	TM/L	W	L	PCT	G	GS	CG	SH	SV	IP	H	HR	BB	SO	RAT	ERA	ERA+	OAV	OOB	BH	AVG	PB	PR	/A	PD	TPI
1964	Bos-A	0	0	—	9	1	0	0	0	13	18	3	20	17	26.3	9.00	43	.321	.500	1	1.000	0	-8	-7	0	0.1

● CHUMMY GRAY Gray, George Edward b: 7/17/1873, Rockland, Me. d: 8/14/13, Rockland, Maine TR, 5′11.5″, 163 lbs. Deb: 9/14/1899

YEAR	TM/L	W	L	PCT	G	GS	CG	SH	SV	IP	H	HR	BB	SO	RAT	ERA	ERA+	OAV	OOB	BH	AVG	PB	PR	/A	PD	TPI
1899	Pit-N	3	3	.500	9	7	6	0	0	70^2	85	1	24	9	14.4	3.44	111	.297	.360	1	.038	-3	3	3	2	0.1

● JEFF GRAY Gray, Jeffrey Edward b: 4/10/63, Richmond, Va. BR/TR, 6′1″, 175 lbs. Deb: 6/21/88

YEAR	TM/L	W	L	PCT	G	GS	CG	SH	SV	IP	H	HR	BB	SO	RAT	ERA	ERA+	OAV	OOB	BH	AVG	PB	PR	/A	PD	TPI
1988	Cin-N	0	0	—	5	0	0	0	0	9^1	12	0	4	5	15.4	3.86	93	.333	.400	0	.000	-0	-0	-0	0	0.0
1990	*Bos-A	2	4	.333	41	0	0	0	9	50^2	53	3	15	50	12.3	4.44	92	.268	.322	0	—	0	-3	-2	-0	-0.3
1991	Bos-A	2	3	.400	50	0	0	0	1	61^2	39	7	10	41	7.3	2.34	184	.181	.220	0	—	0	12	13	1	1.1
Total	3	4	7	.364	96	0	0	0	10	121^2	104	10	29	96	10.0	3.33	125	.231	.281	0	.000	-0	9	11	1	0.8

YEAR	TM/L	W	L	PCT	G	GS	CG	SH	SV	IP	H	HR	BB	SO	RAT	ERA	ERA+	OAV	OOB	BH	AVG	PB	PR	/A	PD	TPI
● **JOHNNY GRAY**	Gray, John Leonard b: 12/11/26, W.Palm Beach, Fla. BR/TR, 6'4", 226 lbs. Deb: 7/18/54																									
1954	Phi-A	3	12	.200	18	16	5	0	0	105	111	10	91	51	17.3	6.51	60	.273	.406	1	.029	-4	-33	-30	0	-3.9
1955	KC-A	0	3	.000	8	5	0	0	0	26^2	28	2	24	11	17.9	6.41	65	.277	.421	1	.125	-0	-7	-7	-1	-0.7
1957	Cle-A	1	3	.250	7	3	1	1	0	20	21	1	13	3	15.3	5.85	64	.288	.395	0	.000	-1	-5	-5	-0	-0.9
1958	Phi-N	0	0	—	15	0	0	0	0	17^1	12	3	14	10	13.5	4.15	95	.222	.382	0	.000	-0	-0	-0	-0	0.0
Total	4	4	18	.182	48	24	6	1	0	169	172	16	142	75	16.8	6.18	64	.271	.405	2	.043	-5	-45	-42	-1	-5.5
● **DOLLY GRAY**	Gray, Samuel David "Sam" b: 10/15/1897, Van Alstyne, Tex. d: 4/16/53, McKinney, Tex. BR/TR, 5'11", 175 lbs. Deb: 4/19/24																									
1924	Phi-A	8	7	.533	34	19	8	2	2	151^2	169	5	89	54	15.7	3.98	108	.284	.383	10	.175	-2	4	5	-1	0.2
1925	Phi-A	16	8	.667	32	28	14	4	3	203^2	199	11	63	80	11.7	3.27	142	.260	.319	12	.179	-2	25	31	-3	2.8
1926	Phi-A	11	12	.478	38	18	5	0	0	150^2	164	9	50	82	13.0	3.64	114	.279	.340	11	.216	1	6	9	-2	1.1
1927	Phi-A	9	6	.600	37	13	3	1	3	133^1	153	4	51	49	14.0	4.59	93	.295	.362	8	.190	-1	-7	-5	0	-0.6
1928	StL-A	20	12	.625	35	31	21	2	3	262^2	256	11	86	102	11.8	3.19	132	.260	.320	19	.188	-2	25	30	3	3.5
1929	StL-A	18	15	.545	43	37	23	**4**	1	**305**	336	18	96	109	12.8	3.72	119	.285	.340	19	.184	-2	18	24	-1	2.0
1930	StL-A	4	15	.211	27	24	7	0	0	167^2	215	17	52	51	14.5	6.28	78	.316	.368	11	.204	-2	-30	-26	-1	-2.5
1931	StL-A	11	24	.314	43	37	13	0	2	258	323	20	54	88	13.3	5.09	91	.297	.332	14	.177	-1	-20	-13	-1	-1.7
1932	StL-A	7	12	.368	52	18	7	3	4	206^2	250	9	53	79	13.2	4.53	107	.294	.336	13	.210	-0	-1	7	-1	0.5
1933	StL-A	7	4	.636	38	6	0	0	4	112	131	7	45	36	14.2	4.10	114	.301	.368	7	.219	1	2	7	-1	0.7
Total	10	111	115	.491	379	231	101	16	22	1951^1	2196	111	639	730	13.2	4.18	108	.286	.343	124	.191	-10	23	68	-7	6.0
● **TED GRAY**	Gray, Ted Glenn b: 12/31/24, Detroit, Mich. BB/TL, 5'11", 175 lbs. Deb: 5/15/46																									
1946	Det-A	0	2	.000	3	2	0	0	1	11^2	17	4	5	5	17.0	8.49	43	.340	.400	0	.000	-0	-6	-6	-0	-1.0
1948	Det-A	6	2	.750	26	11	3	1	0	85^1	73	2	72	60	15.6	4.22	104	.236	.385	7	.241	1	1	1	-0	0.1
1949	Det-A	10	10	.500	34	27	8	3	1	195	163	11	103	96	12.5	3.51	119	.227	.328	8	.127	-3	15	14	1	1.1
1950	Det-A★	10	7	.588	27	21	7	0	1	149^1	139	22	72	102	12.8	4.40	107	.248	.335	7	.140	-2	3	5	-2	0.1
1951	Det-A	7	14	.333	34	28	9	1	1	197^1	194	17	95	131	13.5	4.06	103	.256	.343	9	.143	-3	1	3	-1	-0.2
1952	Det-A	12	17	.414	35	32	13	2	0	224	212	21	101	138	12.7	4.14	92	.249	.331	13	.171	-2	-12	-8	1	-1.1
1953	Det-A	10	15	.400	30	28	8	0	0	176	166	25	76	115	12.7	4.60	88	.252	.336	14	.230	2	-12	-10	-1	-1.2
1954	Det-A	3	5	.375	19	10	2	0	0	72	70	8	56	29	16.0	5.38	69	.268	.401	1	.045	-2	-13	-13	-1	-1.7
1955	Chi-A	0	0	—	2	1	0	0	0	3	9	0	2	1	33.0	18.00	22	.500	.550	0	—	0	-5	-5	0	0.0
	Cle-A	0	0	—	2	0	0	0	0	2	5	1	2	1	31.5	18.00	22	.455	.538	0	—	0	-3	-3	0	0.0
	NY-A	0	0	—	1	1	0	0	0	3	3	0	0	1	9.0	3.00	125	.300	.300	0	.000	-0	0	0	-0	0.0
	Bal-A	1	2	.333	9	1	0	0	0	15^1	21	3	11	8	18.8	8.22	46	.344	.444	0	.000	-0	-7	-8	1	-1.2
	Yr	1	2	.333	14	3	0	0	0	23^1	38	4	15	11	20.4	9.64	40	.376	.457	0	.000	-0	-15	-15	1	-1.2
Total	9	59	74	.444	222	162	50	7	4	1134	1072	114	595	687	13.5	4.37	94	.251	.346	59	.159	-10	-38	-30	-4	-5.1
● **DOLLY GRAY**	Gray, William Denton b: 12/3/1878, Houghton, Mich. d: 4/4/56, Yuba City, Cal. BL/TL, 6'2", 160 lbs. Deb: 4/13/09																									
1909	Was-A	5	19	.208	36	26	19	0	0	218	210	1	77	87	12.2	3.59	68	.258	.329	13	.146	-1	-27	-28	-1	-3.2
1910	Was-A	8	19	.296	34	29	21	3	0	229	216	3	65	84	11.4	2.63	95	.249	.309	21	.247	4	-3	-4	2	0.2
1911	Was-A	2	13	.133	28	15	6	0	0	121	160	4	40	42	15.1	5.06	65	.331	.385	10	.227	1	-23	-24	1	-2.3
Total	3	15	51	.227	98	70	46	3	0	568	586	8	182	213	12.5	3.52	75	.271	.333	44	.202	3	-53	-56	2	-5.3
● **ELI GRBA**	Grba, Eli b: 8/9/34, Chicago, Ill. BR/TR, 6'2", 207 lbs. Deb: 7/10/59																									
1959	NY-A	2	5	.286	19	6	0	0	0	50^1	52	6	39	23	16.3	6.44	57	.269	.392	3	.214	1	-14	-16	-0	-1.8
1960	*NY-A	6	4	.600	24	9	1	0	1	80^2	65	9	46	32	12.6	3.68	97	.226	.337	5	.238	2	2	-1	-1	0.1
1961	LA-A	11	13	.458	40	30	8	0	2	211^2	197	26	114	105	13.5	4.25	106	.242	.340	15	.234	4	-5	6	-1	0.9
1962	LA-A	8	9	.471	40	29	1	0	1	176^1	185	19	75	90	13.4	4.54	85	.267	.340	12	.207	3	-11	-13	1	-0.8
1963	LA-A	1	2	.333	12	1	0	0	0	17^1	14	2	10	5	13.0	4.67	73	.222	.338	0	.000	-0	-2	-2	0	-0.4
Total	5	28	33	.459	135	75	10	0	4	536^1	513	62	284	255	13.6	4.48	90	.250	.345	35	.219	10	-31	-27	-1	-2.0
● **GREASON**	Greason TL , Deb: 8/27/1873																									
1873	Was-n	1	6	.143	7	7	7	0	0	63	112	3	7	3	17.0	5.43	62	.357	.371	4	.143	-2	-15	-15		-1.1
● **BILL GREASON**	Greason, William Henry "Booster" b: 9/3/24, Atlanta, Ga. BR/TR, 5'10", 170 lbs. Deb: 5/31/54																									
1954	StL-N	0	1	.000	3	2	0	0	0	4	8	4	4	2	27.0	13.50	30	.421	.522	0	.000	-0	-4	-4	0	-0.8
● **CHRIS GREEN**	Green, Christopher De Wayne b: 9/5/60, Los Angeles, Cal. BL/TL, 6'2", 214 lbs. Deb: 4/17/84																									
1984	Pit-N	0	0	—	4	0	0	0	0	3	5	0	1	3	18.0	6.00	60	.417	.462	0	—	0	-1	-1	0	0.0
● **ED GREEN**	Green, Edward M. b: 1850, Philadelphia, Pa. Deb: 4/22/1890																									
1890	Phi-a	7	15	.318	25	22	20	1	1	191	267	4	94	56	17.3	5.80	66	.321	.393	15	.119	-4	-41	-42	3	-3.6
● **FRED GREEN**	Green, Fred Allen b: 9/14/33, Titusville, N.J. d: 12/22/96, Titusville, N.J. BR/TL, 6'4", 190 lbs. Deb: 4/15/59 F																									
1959	Pit-N	1	2	.333	17	1	0	0	1	37^1	37	2	15	20	12.5	3.13	123	.259	.329	0	.000	-1	3	3	0	0.2
1960	*Pit-N	8	4	.667	45	0	0	0	3	70	61	4	33	49	12.2	3.21	117	.243	.333	3	.375	3	4	4	-1	1.0
1961	Pit-N	0	0	—	13	0	0	0	0	20^2	27	2	9	4	15.7	4.79	83	.321	.387	0	.000	-0	-2	-2	1	0.0
1962	Was-A	0	1	.000	5	0	0	0	0	7	7	3	6	2	16.7	6.43	63	.250	.382	0	—	0	-2	-2	0	-0.2
1964	Pit-N	0	0	—	8	0	0	0	0	7^1	10	1	0	2	12.3	1.23	286	.323	.323	0	—	0	2	2	-0	0.0
Total	5	9	7	.563	88	1	0	0	4	142^1	142	12	63	77	13.0	3.48	110	.264	.343	3	.176	2	6	5	0	1.0
● **DALLAS GREEN**	Green, George Dallas b: 8/4/34, Newport, Del. BL/TR, 6'5", 210 lbs. Deb: 6/18/60 M																									
1960	Phi-N	3	6	.333	23	10	5	1	0	108^2	100	10	44	51	12.1	4.06	96	.248	.325	7	.206	0	-4	-2	-1	-0.1
1961	Phi-N	2	4	.333	42	10	1	1	1	128	160	8	47	51	14.7	4.85	84	.315	.375	5	.152	0	-12	-11	0	-0.4
1962	Phi-N	6	6	.500	37	10	2	0	1	129^1	145	10	43	58	13.4	3.83	101	.289	.352	2	.063	-1	2	1	2	0.2
1963	Phi-N	7	5	.583	40	14	4	0	2	120	134	10	38	68	13.1	3.23	100	.286	.342	3	.086	-1	1	0	1	0.0
1964	Phi-N	2	1	.667	25	0	0	0	0	42	63	4	14	21	16.9	5.79	60	.362	.416	0	.000	-0	-10	-11	-1	-0.8
1965	Was-A	0	0	—	6	2	0	0	0	14^1	14	0	3	6	10.7	3.14	111	.241	.279	0	.000	-0	1	1	0	0.0
1966	NY-N	0	0	—	4	0	0	0	0	5	6	2	2	1	14.4	5.40	67	.333	.400	0	—	0	-1	-1	0	0.0
1967	Phi-N	0	0	—	8	0	0	0	0	15	25	2	6	12	19.2	9.00	38	.362	.421	0	.000	-0	-9	-9	1	0.0
Total	8	20	22	.476	185	46	12	2	4	562^1	647	46	197	268	13.7	4.26	88	.294	.356	17	.120	-3	-33	-33	3	-1.1
● **HARVEY GREEN**	Green, Harvey George "Buck" b: 2/9/15, Kenosha, Wis. d: 7/24/70, Franklin, La. BB/TR, 6'2.5", 185 lbs. Deb: 9/12/35																									
1935	Bro-N	0	0	—	2	0	0	0	0	1	2	0	3	0	54.0	9.00	44	.400	.667	0	—	0	-1	-1	-0	0.0
● **TYLER GREEN**	Green, Tyler Scott b: 2/18/70, Springfield, Ohio BR/TR, 6'5", 185 lbs. Deb: 4/9/93																									
1993	Phi-N	0	0	—	3	2	0	0	0	7^1	16	1	5	7	25.8	7.36	54	.444	.512	0	.000	-0	-3	-3	-0	-0.1
1995	Phi-N★	8	9	.471	26	25	4	2	0	140^2	157	15	66	85	14.5	5.31	80	.290	.371	8	.182	2	-18	-17	-1	-1.7
1997	Phi-N	4	4	.500	14	14	0	0	0	76^2	72	8	45	58	13.9	4.93	86	.247	.350	8	.308	3	-6	-6	-1	-0.3
1998	Phi N	6	12	.333	27	27	0	0	0	159^1	142	23	85	113	13.3	5.03	87	.239	.343	6	.146	-0	-14	-12	-2	-1.3
Total	4	18	25	.419	70	68	4	2	0	384	387	47	201	263	14.1	5.16	83	.265	.359	22	.195	4	-41	-37	-3	-3.4
● **TOMMY GREENE**	Greene, Ira Thomas b: 4/6/67, Lumberton, N.C. BR/TR, 6'5", 227 lbs. Deb: 9/10/89 ♦																									
1989	Atl-N	1	2	.333	4	4	1	1	0	26^1	22	5	6	17	9.6	4.10	89	.234	.280	1	.100	-1	-2	-1	-0	-0.2
1990	Atl-N	1	0	1.000	5	2	0	0	0	12^1	14	3	9	4	17.5	8.03	50	.286	.407	0	.000	-0	-6	-5	-0	-0.4
	Phi-N	2	3	.400	10	7	0	0	0	39	36	5	17	17	12.2	4.15	92	.247	.325	2	.182	0	-2	-1	-0	-0.2
	Yr	3	3	.500	15	9	0	0	0	51^1	50	8	26	21	13.3	5.08	76	.255	.342	2	.167	0	-7	-7	-1	-0.6
1991	Phi-N	13	7	.650	36	27	3	2	0	207^2	177	19	66	154	10.7	3.38	108	.230	.294	19	.268	7	7	7	-3	1.1
1992	Phi-N	3	3	.500	13	12	0	0	0	64^1	75	5	34	39	15.2	5.32	66	.291	.373	3	.125	-1	-13	-13	-1	-1.3
1993	*Phi-N	16	4	.800	31	30	7	2	0	200	175	12	62	167	10.8	3.42	116	.233	.294	16	.222	6	14	12	-1	1.6
1994	Phi-N	2	0	1.000	7	7	0	0	0	35^2	37	5	22	28	14.9	4.54	94	.272	.373	5	.385	2	-1	-1	-0	0.1
1995	Phi-N	0	5	.000	11	6	0	0	0	33^2	45	6	20	24	18.2	8.29	51	.319	.415	0	.000	-0	-15	-15	-0	-1.9

YEAR TM/L		W	L	PCT	G	GS	CG	SH	SV	IP	H	HR	BB	SO	RAT	ERA	ERA+	OAV	OOB	BH	AVG	PB	PR	/A	PD	TPI
1997	Hou-N	0	1	.000	2	2	0	0	0	9	10	2	5	11	15.0	7.00	57	.286	.375	1	.333	1	-3	-3	-0	-0.2
Total	8	38	25	.603	119	97	11	5	0	628	591	62	241	461	12.1	4.14	92	.249	.320	65	.230	14	-21	-22	-6	-1.4

● JUNE GREENE Greene, Julius Foust b: 6/25/1899, Ramseur, N.C. d: 3/19/74, Glendora, Cal. BL/TR, 6'2.5", 185 lbs. Deb: 4/20/28 ♦

YEAR TM/L		W	L	PCT	G	GS	CG	SH	SV	IP	H	HR	BB	SO	RAT	ERA	ERA+	OAV	OOB	BH	AVG	PB	PR	/A	PD	TPI
1928	Phi-N	0	0	—	1	0	0	0	0	2	5	0	0	0	22.5	9.00	47	.556	.556	3	.500	2	-1	-1	0	0.2
1929	Phi-N	0	0	—	5	0	0	0	0	13^2	33	2	9	4	29.6	19.76	26	.465	.542	4	.211	0	-23	-22	0	0.0
Total	2	0	0	—	6	0	0	0	0	15^2	38	2	9	4	28.7	18.38	28	.475	.543	7	.280	2	-24	-23	1	0.2

● NELSON GREENE Greene, Nelson George "Lefty" b: 9/20/1900, Philadelphia, Pa. d: 4/6/83, Lebanon, Pa. BL/TL, 6', 185 lbs. Deb: 4/28/24

YEAR TM/L		W	L	PCT	G	GS	CG	SH	SV	IP	H	HR	BB	SO	RAT	ERA	ERA+	OAV	OOB	BH	AVG	PB	PR	/A	PD	TPI
1924	Bro-N	0	1	.000	4	1	0	0	0	9	14	1	2	3	16.0	4.00	94	.350	.381	0	.000	-0	-0	-0	0	0.0
1925	Bro-N	2	0	1.000	11	0	0	0	1	22	45	4	7	4	21.3	10.64	39	.417	.452	2	.286	0	-16	-16	0	-1.3
Total	2	2	1	.667	15	1	0	0	1	31	59	5	9	7	19.7	8.71	47	.399	.433	2	.250	-0	-16	-16	1	-1.3

● KENT GREENFIELD Greenfield, Kent b: 7/1/02, Guthrie, Ky. d: 3/14/78, Guthrie, Ky. BR/TR, 6'1", 180 lbs. Deb: 9/28/24

YEAR TM/L		W	L	PCT	G	GS	CG	SH	SV	IP	H	HR	BB	SO	RAT	ERA	ERA+	OAV	OOB	BH	AVG	PB	PR	/A	PD	TPI
1924	NY-N	0	1	.000	1	1	0	0	0	3	9	1	1	1	30.0	15.00	24	.500	.526	0	—	0	-4	-4	-0	-0.8
1925	NY-N	12	8	.600	29	20	12	0	0	171^2	195	4	64	66	13.7	3.88	104	.288	.352	5	.081	-6	7	3	1	-0.2
1926	NY-N	13	12	.520	39	28	8	1	1	222^2	206	17	82	74	11.8	3.96	95	.251	.322	6	.092	-5	-3	-5	-2	-1.2
1927	NY-N	2	2	.500	12	1	0	0	0	20	39	3	13	4	24.3	9.45	41	.411	.491	0	.000	-0	-12	-12	0	-2.0
	Bos-N	11	14	.440	27	26	11	1	0	190	203	3	59	59	12.6	3.84	97	.282	.341	11	.172	-2	2	-3	-0	-0.5
	Yr	13	16	.448	39	27	11	1	0	210	242	6	72	63	13.7	4.37	85	.297	.357	11	.167	-2	-11	-15	-0	-2.5
1928	Bos-N	3	11	.214	32	20	5	0	0	143^2	173	6	60	30	14.9	5.32	73	.307	.378	2	.053	-4	-21	-23	1	-2.2
1929	Bos-N	0	0	—	6	2	0	0	0	15^2	33	1	15	7	28.7	10.91	43	.465	.568	0	.000	-1	-11	-11	1	0.0
	Bro-N	0	0	—	6	0	0	0	0	8^2	13	1	3	1	16.6	8.31	56	.382	.432	0	.000	-0	-3	-4	0	0.0
	Yr	0	0	—	12	2	0	0	0	24^1	46	2	18	8	23.7	9.99	47	.430	.512	0	.000	-1	-14	-14	1	0.0
Total	6	41	48	.461	152	98	36	2	1	775^1	871	36	297	242	13.8	4.54	85	.290	.358	24	.101	-18	-46	-58	-0	-6.9

● JOHN GREENING Greening, John A. (b: John A. Greenig) b: Philadelphia, Pa. Deb: 5/9/1888

YEAR TM/L		W	L	PCT	G	GS	CG	SH	SV	IP	H	HR	BB	SO	RAT	ERA	ERA+	OAV	OOB	BH	AVG	PB	PR	/A	PD	TPI
1888	Was-N	0	1	.000	1	1	1	0	0	9	17	2	4	2	21.0	11.00	25	.405	.457	0	.000	-0	-8	-8	-0	-0.6

● BOB GREENWOOD Greenwood, Robert Chandler "Greenie" b: 3/13/28, Cananea, Mexico BR/TR, 6'5", 200 lbs. Deb: 4/21/54

YEAR TM/L		W	L	PCT	G	GS	CG	SH	SV	IP	H	HR	BB	SO	RAT	ERA	ERA+	OAV	OOB	BH	AVG	PB	PR	/A	PD	TPI
1954	Phi-N	1	2	.333	11	4	0	0	0	36^2	28	2	18	9	11.3	3.19	127	.209	.303	0	.000	-1	4	3	0	0.2
1955	Phi-N	0	0	—	1	0	0	0	0	2^1	7	1	0	0	27.0	15.43	26	.500	.500	0	.000	-0	-3	-3	-0	0.0
Total	2	1	2	.333	12	4	0	0	0	39	35	3	18	9	12.2	3.92	103	.236	.319	0	.000	-1	1	0	0	0.2

● KENNY GREER Greer, Kenneth William b: 5/12/67, Boston, Mass. BR/TR, 6'2", 210 lbs. Deb: 9/29/93

YEAR TM/L		W	L	PCT	G	GS	CG	SH	SV	IP	H	HR	BB	SO	RAT	ERA	ERA+	OAV	OOB	BH	AVG	PB	PR	/A	PD	TPI
1993	NY-N	1	0	1.000	1	0	0	0	0	1	0	0	0	2	0.0	0.00	—	.000	.000	0	—	0	0	0	0	0.5
1995	SF-N	0	2	.000	8	0	0	0	0	12	15	3	5	7	15.8	5.25	78	.288	.362	0	.000	-0	-1	-2	-0	-0.2
Total	2	1	2	.333	9	0	0	0	0	13	15	3	5	9	14.5	4.85	84	.273	.344	0	.000	-0	-1	-1	-0	0.3

● DAVE GREGG Gregg, David Charles "Highpockets" b: 3/14/1891, Chehalis, Wash. d: 11/12/65, Clarkston, Wash. BR/TR, 6'1", 185 lbs. Deb: 6/15/13 F

YEAR TM/L		W	L	PCT	G	GS	CG	SH	SV	IP	H	HR	BB	SO	RAT	ERA	ERA+	OAV	OOB	BH	AVG	PB	PR	/A	PD	TPI
1913	Cle-A	0	0	—	1	0	0	0	0	1	2	0	0	0	27.0	18.00	17	.400	.500	0	—	0	-2	-2	0	0.0

● HAL GREGG Gregg, Harold Dana "Skeets" b: 7/11/21, Anaheim, Cal. d: 5/13/91, Bishop, Cal. BR/TR, 6'3.5", 195 lbs. Deb: 8/18/43

YEAR TM/L		W	L	PCT	G	GS	CG	SH	SV	IP	H	HR	BB	SO	RAT	ERA	ERA+	OAV	OOB	BH	AVG	PB	PR	/A	PD	TPI
1943	Bro-N	0	3	.000	5	4	0	0	0	18^2	21	2	21	7	20.3	9.64	35	.304	.467	0	.000	0	-13	-13	-0	-1.6
1944	Bro-N	9	16	.360	39	31	6	0	2	197^2	201	12	137	92	15.8	5.46	65	.258	.376	14	.206	-0	-41	-42	0	-4.7
1945	Bro-N†	18	13	.581	42	34	13	2	2	254^1	221	5	120	139	12.3	3.47	108	.232	.323	20	.220	3	9	8	-0	1.2
1946	Bro-N	6	4	.600	26	16	4	1	2	117^1	103	3	44	54	11.4	2.99	113	.236	.308	4	.125	-1	5	5	-2	0.1
1947	*Bro-N	4	5	.444	37	16	2	1	1	104^1	115	6	55	59	15.0	5.87	70	.272	.361	9	.265	2	-21	-20	0	-1.4
1948	Pit-N	2	4	.333	22	8	1	0	1	74^1	72	3	34	25	13.2	4.60	88	.255	.342	6	.273	2	-5	-4	-0	-0.2
1949	Pit-N	1	1	.500	8	1	0	0	0	18^2	20	1	8	9	14.0	3.38	125	.303	.387	0	.000	-0	1	2	-0	0.1
1950	Pit-N	0	1	.000	5	1	0	0	0	5^1	10	2	7	3	30.4	13.50	32	.400	.545	0	.000	-0	-6	-5	0	-0.8
1952	NY-N	0	1	.000	16	4	1	0	1	36^1	42	7	17	13	15.1	4.71	79	.286	.367	1	.125	-0	-4	-4	1	-0.2
Total	9	40	48	.455	200	115	27	4	9	827	805	41	443	401	13.9	4.54	82	.253	.350	54	.205	4	-73	-74	-3	-7.5

● VEAN GREGG Gregg, Sylveanus Augustus b: 4/13/1885, Chehalis, Wash. d: 7/29/64, Aberdeen, Wash. BR/TL, 6'1", 185 lbs. Deb: 4/12/11 F

YEAR TM/L		W	L	PCT	G	GS	CG	SH	SV	IP	H	HR	BB	SO	RAT	ERA	ERA+	OAV	OOB	BH	AVG	PB	PR	/A	PD	TPI
1911	Cle-A	23	7	.767	34	26	22	5	0	244^2	172	2	86	125	**9.9**	**1.80**	**189**	**.205**	.286	14	.165	-4	42	44	0	4.7
1912	Cle-A	20	13	.606	37	34	26	1	2	271^1	242	4	90	184	11.3	2.59	132	.246	.316	17	.175	-3	22	25	-2	2.4
1913	Cle-A	20	13	.606	44	34	23	3	3	285^2	258	2	124	166	12.4	2.24	136	.246	.334	13	.131	-4	22	25	-3	2.1
1914	Cle-A	9	3	.750	17	12	6	1	0	96^2	88	0	48	56	12.9	3.07	94	.251	.347	6	.176	1	-4	-2	-0	-0.3
	Bos-A	3	4	.429	12	9	4	0	0	68^1	71	0	37	24	14.2	3.95	68	.283	.375	4	.211	0	-9	-10	-1	-1.0
	Yr	12	7	.632	29	21	10	1	0	165	159	0	85	80	13.3	3.44	82	.263	.354	10	.189	1	-13	-12	-2	-1.3
1915	Bos-A	4	2	.667	18	9	3	1	3	75	71	2	32	43	13.0	3.36	83	.260	.348	7	.350	2	-4	-5	0	-0.2
1916	Bos-A	2	5	.286	21	7	3	0	0	77^2	71	0	30	41	12.1	3.01	92	.259	.339	2	.111	-1	-2	-2	-0	-0.3
1918	Phi-A	9	14	.391	30	25	17	3	2	199^1	180	4	67	63	11.4	3.12	94	.251	.320	12	.169	-3	-7	-4	-1	-0.9
1925	Was-A	2	2	.500	26	5	1	0	2	74^1	87	3	38	18	15.4	4.12	103	.318	.404	3	.214	0	2	1	-1	0.0
Total	8	92	63	.594	239	161	105	14	12	1393	1240	17	552	720	11.9	2.70	117	.248	.328	78	.171	-12	63	73	-8	6.5

● FRANK GREGORY Gregory, Frank Ernst b: 7/25/1888, Spring Valley Township, Wis. d: 11/5/55, Beloit, Wis. BR/TR, 5'11", 185 lbs. Deb: 9/5/12

YEAR TM/L		W	L	PCT	G	GS	CG	SH	SV	IP	H	HR	BB	SO	RAT	ERA	ERA+	OAV	OOB	BH	AVG	PB	PR	/A	PD	TPI
1912	Cin-N	2	0	1.000	4	2	1	0	0	15^2	19	0	7	4	15.5	4.60	73	.297	.375	1	.200	0	-2	-2	-1	-0.3

● LEE GREGORY Gregory, Grover Leroy b: 6/2/38, Bakersfield, Cal. BL/TL, 6'1", 180 lbs. Deb: 4/17/64

YEAR TM/L		W	L	PCT	G	GS	CG	SH	SV	IP	H	HR	BB	SO	RAT	ERA	ERA+	OAV	OOB	BH	AVG	PB	PR	/A	PD	TPI
1964	Chi-N	0	0	—	11	0	0	0	0	18	23	3	5	8	14.0	3.50	106	.333	.378	1	.077	0	0	0	0	0.0

● HOWIE GREGORY Gregory, Howard Watterson b: 11/18/1886, Hannibal, Mo. d: 5/30/70, Tulsa, Okla. BL/TR, 6', 175 lbs. Deb: 4/16/11

YEAR TM/L		W	L	PCT	G	GS	CG	SH	SV	IP	H	HR	BB	SO	RAT	ERA	ERA+	OAV	OOB	BH	AVG	PB	PR	/A	PD	TPI
1911	StL-A	0	1	.000	3	1	0	0	0	7	11	0	4	1	19.3	5.14	66	.393	.469	0	.000	-0	-1	-1	-0	-0.2

● PAUL GREGORY Gregory, Paul Edwin "Pop" b: 6/9/08, Tomnolen, Miss. BR/TR, 6'2", 180 lbs. Deb: 4/20/32

YEAR TM/L		W	L	PCT	G	GS	CG	SH	SV	IP	H	HR	BB	SO	RAT	ERA	ERA+	OAV	OOB	BH	AVG	PB	PR	/A	PD	TPI
1932	Chi-A	5	3	.625	33	9	3	0	0	117^2	125	8	51	39	13.6	4.51	96	.273	.348	3	.079	-3	-0	-2	3	-0.1
1933	Chi-A	4	11	.267	23	17	5	0	0	103^2	124	10	47	18	14.9	4.95	86	.296	.368	5	.143	-1	-8	-8	1	-1.0
Total	2	9	14	.391	56	26	8	0	0	221^1	249	18	98	57	14.2	4.72	91	.284	.358	8	.110	-4	-8	-11	4	-1.1

● BILL GREIF Greif, William Briley b: 4/25/50, Ft.Stockton, Tex. BR/TR, 6'5", 205 lbs. Deb: 7/19/71

YEAR TM/L		W	L	PCT	G	GS	CG	SH	SV	IP	H	HR	BB	SO	RAT	ERA	ERA+	OAV	OOB	BH	AVG	PB	PR	/A	PD	TPI
1971	Hou-N	1	1	.500	7	3	0	0	0	16	18	1	8	14	15.8	5.06	66	.290	.389	1	.333	0	-3	-3	-0	-0.3
1972	SD-N	5	16	.238	34	22	2	1	2	125^1	143	18	47	91	14.2	5.60	59	.287	.357	1	.030	-3	-30	-32	-2	-5.3
1973	SD-N	10	17	.370	36	31	9	3	1	199^1	181	20	62	120	11.2	3.21	108	.246	.309	6	.098	-2	10	6	-1	0.5
1974	SD-N	9	19	.321	43	35	7	1	1	226	244	17	95	137	14.1	4.66	76	.279	.359	4	.071	-2	-26	-28	0	-3.2
1975	SD-N	4	6	.400	59	1	0	0	9	72	74	7	38	43	14.6	3.88	90	.269	.368	0	.000	-0	-2	-3	-2	-0.7
1976	SD-N	1	3	.250	5	5	0	0	0	22^1	27	2	11	5	15.3	8.06	41	.297	.373	0	.000	-1	-11	-12	0	-1.7
	StL-N	1	5	.167	47	0	0	0	6	54^2	60	5	26	32	14.5	4.12	86	.290	.374	0	.000	0	-4	-4	-1	-0.5
	Yr	2	8	.200	52	5	0	0	6	77	87	7	37	37	14.7	5.26	66	.291	.373	0	.000	-1	-15	-15	-0	-2.2
Total	6	31	67	.316	231	97	18	5	19	715^2	747	70	287	442	13.5	4.41	78	.272	.349	12	.072	-7	-66	-76	-5	-11.2

● SETH GREISINGER Greisinger, Seth Adam b: 7/29/75, Kansas City, Kan. BR/TR, 6'4", 190 lbs. Deb: 6/3/98

YEAR TM/L		W	L	PCT	G	GS	CG	SH	SV	IP	H	HR	BB	SO	RAT	ERA	ERA+	OAV	OOB	BH	AVG	PB	PR	/A	PD	TPI
1998	Det-A	6	9	.400	21	21	0	0	0	130	142	17	48	66	13.4	5.12	92	.282	.350	1	.250	0	-7	-6	-2	-0.7

● BILL GREVELL Grevell, William J. b: 3/5/1898, Williamstown, N.J. d: 6/21/23, Philadelphia, Pa. BR/TR, 5'11", 170 lbs. Deb: 5/14/19

YEAR TM/L		W	L	PCT	G	GS	CG	SH	SV	IP	H	HR	BB	SO	RAT	ERA	ERA+	OAV	OOB	BH	AVG	PB	PR	/A	PD	TPI
1919	Phi-A	0	0	—	5	2	0	0	0	12	15	0	18	3	25.5	14.25	24	.306	.500	0	.000	-1	-15	-14	1	0.0

● LEE GRIFFETH Griffeth, Leon Clifford b: 5/20/25, Carmel, N.Y. BB/TL, 5'11.5", 180 lbs. Deb: 6/25/46

YEAR TM/L		W	L	PCT	G	GS	CG	SH	SV	IP	H	HR	BB	SO	RAT	ERA	ERA+	OAV	OOB	BH	AVG	PB	PR	/A	PD	TPI
1946	Phi-A	0	0	—	10	0	0	0	0	15^1	13	1	6	4	12.3	2.93	121	.232	.328	0	.000	0	1	1	-0	0.0

● HANK GRIFFIN Griffin, James Linton "Pepper" b: 7/11/1886, Whitehouse, Tex. d: 2/11/50, Terrell, Tex. BR/TR, 6', 165 lbs. Deb: 5/5/11

YEAR TM/L		W	L	PCT	G	GS	CG	SH	SV	IP	H	HR	BB	SO	RAT	ERA	ERA+	OAV	OOB	BH	AVG	PB	PR	/A	PD	TPI
1911	Chi-N	0	0	—	1	1	0	0	0	1	1	1	3	1	36.0	18.00	18	.250	.571	0	—	0	-2	-2	0	0.0

YEAR	TM/L	W	L	PCT	G	GS	CG	SH	SV	IP	H	HR	BB	SO	RAT	ERA	ERA+	OAV	OOB	BH	AVG	PB	PR	/A	PD	TPI
	Bos-N	0	6	.000	15	6	1	0	0	82^2	96	3	34	30	14.8	5.23	73	.305	.383	7	.233	-0	-17	-13	0	-0.8
	Yr	0	6	.000	16	7	1	0	0	83^2	97	4	37	31	15.1	5.38	71	.304	.387	7	.233	-0	-18	-14	0	-0.8
1912	Bos-N	0	0	—	3	0	0	0	0	1^2	3	0	3	0	37.8	27.00	13	.750	.875	0	—	0	-4	-4	-0	0.0
Total	2	0	6	.000	19	7	1	0	0	85^1	100	4	40	31	15.5	5.80	66	.310	.397	7	.233	-0	-23	-19	0	-0.8

● **MARTY GRIFFIN** Griffin, Martin John b: 9/2/01, San Francisco, Cal d: 11/19/51, Los Angeles, Cal. BR/TR, 6'2", 200 lbs. Deb: 7/25/28

YEAR	TM/L	W	L	PCT	G	GS	CG	SH	SV	IP	H	HR	BB	SO	RAT	ERA	ERA+	OAV	OOB	BH	AVG	PB	PR	/A	PD	TPI
1928	Bos-A	0	3	.000	11	3	0	0	0	37^2	42	0	17	9	14.1	5.02	82	.300	.376	4	.308	1	-4	-4	-0	-0.2

● **MIKE GRIFFIN** Griffin, Michael Leroy b: 6/26/57, Colusa, Cal. BR/TR, 6'5", 197 lbs. Deb: 9/17/79

YEAR	TM/L	W	L	PCT	G	GS	CG	SH	SV	IP	H	HR	BB	SO	RAT	ERA	ERA+	OAV	OOB	BH	AVG	PB	PR	/A	PD	TPI
1979	NY-A	0	0	—	3	0	0	0	1	4^1	5	0	2	5	14.5	4.15	98	.313	.389	0	—	0	0	-0	-0	0.2
1980	NY-A	2	4	.333	13	9	0	0	0	54	64	6	23	25	14.7	4.83	81	.287	.356	0	—	0	-5	-5	-0	-0.4
1981	NY-A	0	0	—	2	0	0	0	0	4^1	5	0	1	4	10.4	2.08	172	.278	.278	0	—	0	1	1	0	0.1
	Chi-N	2	5	.286	16	9	0	0	1	52	64	4	9	20	12.6	4.50	82	.302	.330	2	.154	-0	-6	-5	0	-0.6
1982	SD-N	0	1	.000	7	0	0	0	0	10^1	9	0	3	4	10.5	3.48	98	.237	.293	0	.000	-0	0	-0	-0	0.0
1987	Bal-A	3	5	.375	23	6	1	0	1	74^1	78	9	33	42	13.8	4.36	101	.269	.350	0	—	0	1	0	-1	0.2
1989	Cin-N	0	0	—	3	0	0	0	0	4^1	10	0	3	1	27.0	12.46	29	.500	.565	1	1.000	0	-4	-4	0	0.1
Total	6	7	15	.318	67	24	1	0	3	203^2	235	19	73	101	13.8	4.60	87	.288	.349	3	.200	-0	-13	-13	-1	-0.4

● **PAT GRIFFIN** Griffin, Patrick Richard b: 5/6/1893, Niles, Ohio d: 6/7/27, Youngstown, Ohio BR/TR, 6'2", 180 lbs. Deb: 7/23/14

YEAR	TM/L	W	L	PCT	G	GS	CG	SH	SV	IP	H	HR	BB	SO	RAT	ERA	ERA+	OAV	OOB	BH	AVG	PB	PR	/A	PD	TPI
1914	Cin-N	0	0	—	1	0	0	0	0	1	3	0	2	0	45.0	9.00	33	.750	.833	0	—	0	-1	-1	0	0.0

● **TOM GRIFFIN** Griffin, Thomas James b: 2/22/48, Los Angeles, Cal. BR/TR, 6'3", 210 lbs. Deb: 4/10/69

YEAR	TM/L	W	L	PCT	G	GS	CG	SH	SV	IP	H	HR	BB	SO	RAT	ERA	ERA+	OAV	OOB	BH	AVG	PB	PR	/A	PD	TPI
1969	Hou-N	11	10	.524	31	31	6	3	0	188^1	156	19	93	200	12.2	3.54	100	.220	.317	9	.145	2	1	0	-2	0.1
1970	Hou-N	3	13	.188	23	20	2	1	0	111^1	118	9	72	72	15.6	5.74	68	.275	.383	2	.061	-2	-21	-23	-1	-3.1
1971	Hou-N	0	6	.000	10	6	0	0	0	37^2	44	4	20	29	15.8	4.78	70	.288	.377	1	.111	-0	-5	-6	1	-0.8
1972	Hou-N	5	4	.556	39	5	1	1	3	94^1	92	7	38	83	12.7	3.24	104	.258	.334	7	.280	3	2	1	-1	0.4
1973	Hou-N	4	6	.400	25	12	4	0	0	99^2	83	10	46	69	11.8	4.15	87	.229	.320	3	.107	0	-5	-6	0	-0.5
1974	Hou-N	14	10	.583	34	34	8	3	0	211	202	14	89	110	12.6	3.54	98	.250	.328	20	.294	8	2	-2	1	0.7
1975	Hou-N	3	8	.273	17	13	3	1	0	79^1	89	11	46	56	15.5	5.33	63	.288	.384	3	.136	-0	-15	-17	1	-2.1
1976	Hou-N	5	3	.625	20	2	0	0	0	41^2	44	4	37	33	17.7	6.05	53	.278	.418	0	.000	-0	-12	-13	0	-2.3
	SD-N	4	3	.571	11	11	2	0	0	70^1	56	0	42	36	12.7	2.94	111	.222	.336	2	.077	-2	4	3	-0	0.0
	Yr	9	6	.600	31	13	2	0	0	112	100	4	79	69	14.5	4.10	79	.242	.364	2	.065	-2	-7	-11	-0	-2.3
1977	SD-N	6	9	.400	38	20	0	0	0	151^1	144	17	88	79	14.1	4.46	79	.254	.359	6	.133	1	-9	-16	-2	-1.4
1978	Cal-A	3	4	.429	24	4	0	0	0	56	63	8	31	35	15.3	4.02	90	.279	.368	0	—	0	-2	-3	1	-0.2
1979	SF-N	5	6	.455	59	3	0	0	2	94^1	83	9	46	82	12.7	3.91	89	.237	.333	1	.071	-1	-2	-4	2	-0.4
1980	SF-N	5	1	.833	42	4	0	0	0	107^2	80	8	49	79	11.5	2.76	128	.212	.315	2	.111	0	10	9	0	0.5
1981	SF-N	8	8	.500	22	22	3	1	0	129^1	121	8	57	83	12.9	3.76	91	.249	.336	8	.195	2	-4	-5	2	-0.2
1982	Pit-N	1	3	.250	6	4	0	0	0	22^1	32	5	15	8	19.3	8.87	42	.330	.425	2	.222	0	-13	-13	0	-1.8
Total	14	77	94	.450	401	191	29	10	5	1494^2	1407	133	769	1054	13.4	4.07	86	.249	.345	66	.163	12	-69	-94	1	-11.1

● **CLARK GRIFFITH** Griffith, Clark Calvin "The Old Fox"
b: 11/20/1869, Clear Creek, Mo. d: 10/27/55, Washington, D.C. BR/TR, 5'6.5", 156 lbs. Deb: 4/11/1891 MH♦

YEAR	TM/L	W	L	PCT	G	GS	CG	SH	SV	IP	H	HR	BB	SO	RAT	ERA	ERA+	OAV	OOB	BH	AVG	PB	PR	/A	PD	TPI
1891	StL-a	11	8	.579	27	17	12	0	0	186^1	195	8	58	68	12.9	3.33	126	.260	.326	12	.156	-3	8	18	0	1.2
	Bos-a	3	1	.750	7	4	3	0	0	40	47	3	15	20	15.1	5.62	62	.283	.360	4	.174	2	-8	-9	-1	-0.6
	Yr	14	9	.609	34	21	15	0	0	226^1	242	11	73	88	12.7	3.74	109	.260	.317	16	.160	-1	-0	9	-1	0.6
1893	Chi-N	1	2	.333	4	2	2	0	0	19^2	24	1	5	9	13.7	5.03	92	.293	.341	2	.182	-1	-1	-1	1	-0.1
1894	Chi-N	21	14	.600	36	30	28	0	0	261^1	328	12	85	71	14.7	4.92	114	.303	.362	33	.232	-0	12	20	1	1.9
1895	Chi-N	26	14	.650	42	41	39	0	0	353	434	11	91	79	13.9	3.93	130	.298	.348	46	.319	5	34	46	1	4.5
1896	Chi-N	23	11	.676	36	35	35	0	0	317^2	370	3	70	81	12.8	3.54	128	.289	.331	36	.267	3	29	35	1	3.3
1897	Chi-N	21	18	.538	41	38	**38**	1	1	343^2	410	3	86	102	13.4	3.72	120	.293	.342	38	.235	3	23	28	3	3.0
1898	Chi-N	24	10	.706	38	38	36	4	0	325^2	305	1	64	97	10.8	**1.88**	**191**	.246	.294	20	.164	-2	63	62	1	5.8
1899	Chi-N	22	14	.611	38	38	35	0	0	319^2	329	5	65	73	11.5	2.79	134	.266	.310	31	.258	6	38	34	6	4.5
1900	Chi-N	14	13	.519	30	30	27	**4**	0	248	245	6	51	61	11.3	3.05	118	.258	.306	24	.253	5	18	15	-1	1.8
1901	Chi-A	24	7	**.774**	35	30	26	**5**	1	266^2	275	4	50	67	11.1	2.67	131	.263	.299	27	.303	14	30	24	0	3.7
1902	Chi-A	15	9	.625	28	24	20	3	0	213	247	11	47	51	13.1	4.18	81	.290	.339	20	.217	2	-14	-19	-1	-1.7
1903	NY-A	14	11	.560	25	24	22	2	0	213	201	3	33	69	10.1	2.70	116	.249	.283	11	.159	2	6	10	-3	1.0
1904	NY-A	7	5	.583	16	11	8	1	0	100^1	91	3	16	36	10.0	2.87	94	.243	.281	6	.143	-1	-3	-2	-1	-0.4
1905	NY-A	9	6	.600	25	7	4	2	1	101^2	82	1	15	46	8.7	1.68	174	.223	.255	7	.219	1	11	14	-2	2.1
1906	NY-A	2	2	.500	17	2	1	0	2	59^2	58	0	15	16	11.6	3.02	98	.258	.316	2	.111	-1	-2	-0	1	0.0
1907	NY-A	0	0	—	4	0	0	0	0	8^1	15	0	6	5	22.7	8.64	32	.395	.477	0	.000	-0	-6	-5	0	0.0
1909	Cin-N	0	1	.000	1	1	1	0	0	6	11	0	2	3	19.5	6.00	43	.379	.419	0	.000	-0	-2	-2	1	-0.3
1912	Was-A	0	0	—	1	0	0	0	0	0	1	0	0	0	—	∞	—	1.000	1.000	0	.000	-0	-1	-1	0	-0.1
1913	Was-A	0	0	—	1	0	0	0	0	1	1	0	0	0	9.0	0.00	—	.250	.250	1	1.000	1	0	0	-0	0.0
1914	Was-A	0	0	—	1	0	0	0	0	1	1	0	0	1	9.0	0.00	—	.250	.250	1	1.000	1	0	0	-0	0.1
Total	20	237	146	.619	453	372	337	22	6	3385^2	3670	76	774	955	12.3	3.31	121	.274	.322	321	.233	35	233	266	7	29.7

● **FRANK GRIFFITH** Griffith, Frank Wesley b: 11/18/1872, Gilman, Ill. d: 12/13/08, BL/TL, Deb: 8/13/1892

YEAR	TM/L	W	L	PCT	G	GS	CG	SH	SV	IP	H	HR	BB	SO	RAT	ERA	ERA+	OAV	OOB	BH	AVG	PB	PR	/A	PD	TPI
1892	Chi-N	0	1	.000	1	1	0	0	0	4	3	1	6	3	20.3	11.25	30	.200	.429	0	.000	-0	-4	-4	-0	-0.6
1894	Cle-N	1	2	.333	7	6	3	0	0	42^1	64	5	37	15	23.4	9.99	55	.344	.474	8	.333	2	-22	-21	-0	-0.9
Total	2	1	3	.250	8	7	3	0	0	46^1	67	6	43	18	23.1	10.10	52	.333	.470	8	.320	2	-25	-25	-0	-1.5

● **HAL GRIGGS** Griggs, Harold Lloyd b: 8/24/28, Shannon, Ga. BR/TR, 6', 170 lbs. Deb: 4/18/56

YEAR	TM/L	W	L	PCT	G	GS	CG	SH	SV	IP	H	HR	BB	SO	RAT	ERA	ERA+	OAV	OOB	BH	AVG	PB	PR	/A	PD	TPI
1956	Was-A	1	6	.143	34	12	1	0	0	98^2	120	14	76	48	18.0	6.02	72	.307	.421	0	.000	-1	-20	-19	1	-1.2
1957	Was-A	0	1	.000	2	2	0	0	0	13^2	11	1	7	12	11.9	3.29	118	.229	.327	1	.250	0	1	1	0	0.1
1958	Was-A	3	11	.214	32	21	3	0	0	137	138	20	74	69	14.1	5.52	69	.262	.355	5	.122	-2	-27	-26	-0	-2.6
1959	Was-A	2	8	.200	37	10	2	1	2	97^2	103	8	52	43	14.4	5.25	75	.270	.359	1	.056	-2	-15	-15	-0	-1.6
Total	4	6	26	.188	105	45	6	1	3	347	372	43	209	172	15.2	5.50	73	.276	.375	7	.089	-5	-61	-58	1	-5.3

● **GUIDO GRILLI** Grilli, Guido John b: 1/9/39, Memphis, Tenn. BL/TL, 6', 188 lbs. Deb: 4/12/66

YEAR	TM/L	W	L	PCT	G	GS	CG	SH	SV	IP	H	HR	BB	SO	RAT	ERA	ERA+	OAV	OOB	BH	AVG	PB	PR	/A	PD	TPI
1966	Bos-A	0	1	.000	6	0	0	0	0	4^2	5	1	9	4	27.0	7.71	49	.278	.519	1	.500	0	-2	-2	0	-0.4
	KC-A	0	1	.000	16	0	0	0	1	15^2	19	0	11	8	19.0	6.89	49	.302	.429	0	—	0	-6	-6	-1	-0.5
	Yr	0	2	.000	22	0	0	0	1	20^1	24	1	20	12	20.8	7.08	49	.296	.452	1	.500	0	-8	-8	-1	-0.9

● **STEVE GRILLI** Grilli, Stephen Joseph b: 5/2/49, Brooklyn, N.Y. BR/TR, 6'2", 170 lbs. Deb: 9/19/75

YEAR	TM/L	W	L	PCT	G	GS	CG	SH	SV	IP	H	HR	BB	SO	RAT	ERA	ERA+	OAV	OOB	BH	AVG	PB	PR	/A	PD	TPI
1975	Det-A	0	0	—	3	0	0	0	0	6^2	3	0	6	5	12.2	1.35	297	.136	.321	0	—	0	2	2	0	-0.2
1976	Det-A	3	1	.750	36	0	0	0	3	66	63	5	41	36	14.9	4.64	80	.258	.376	0	—	0	-8	-7	2	-0.3
1977	Det-A	1	2	.333	30	2	0	0	0	72^2	71	8	49	49	15.2	4.83	89	.265	.384	0	—	0	-6	-4	-1	-0.3
1979	Tor-A	0	0	—	1	0	0	0	0	2^1	1	0	0	1	3.9	0.00	—	.143	.143	0	—	0	1	1	-0	-0.1
Total	4	4	3	.571	70	2	0	0	3	147^2	138	13	96	91	14.7	4.51	89	.255	.375	0	—	0	-12	-8	1	-0.9

● **JOHN GRIM** Grim, John Helm b: 8/9/1867, Lebanon, Ky. d: 7/28/61, Indianapolis, Ind BR/TR, 6'2", 175 lbs. Deb: 9/29/1888 ♦

YEAR	TM/L	W	L	PCT	G	GS	CG	SH	SV	IP	H	HR	BB	SO	RAT	ERA	ERA+	OAV	OOB	BH	AVG	PB	PR	/A	PD	TPI
1890	Roc-a	0	0	—	1	0	0	0	0	3^1	3	0	4	3	18.9	0.00	—	.231	.412	51	.266	0	1	1	-0	0.0

● **BOB GRIM** Grim, Robert Anton b: 3/8/30, New York, N.Y. d: 10/23/96, Shawnee, Kan. BR/TR, 6'1", 185 lbs. Deb: 4/18/54

YEAR	TM/L	W	L	PCT	G	GS	CG	SH	SV	IP	H	HR	BB	SO	RAT	ERA	ERA+	OAV	OOB	BH	AVG	PB	PR	/A	PD	TPI
1954	NY-A	20	6	.769	37	20	8	1	0	199	175	9	85	108	11.9	3.26	106	.244	.327	10	.143	-1	10	4	-1	0.2
1955	*NY-A	7	5	.583	26	11	1	1	4	92^1	81	9	42	63	12.3	4.19	89	.238	.326	3	.120	-1	-2	-5	0	-0.7
1956	NY-A	6	1	.857	26	6	1	0	5	74^2	64	3	31	48	11.7	2.77	139	.235	.318	1	.063	-0	11	9	-1	0.8
1957	*NY-A★	12	8	.600	46	0	0	0	**19**	72	60	5	36	52	12.0	2.63	137	.239	.334	1	.111	1	9	8	0	2.6
1958	NY-A	0	1	.000	11	0	0	0	0	16^1	12	3	10	11	12.7	5.51	64	.211	.338	0	.000	-0	-3	-4	-0	-0.2
	KC-A	7	6	.538	26	14	5	1	0	113^2	118	7	41	54	12.8	3.56	110	.269	.336	6	.188	-0	3	4	-1	0.3
	Yr	7	7	.500	37	14	5	1	0	130	130	10	51	65	12.7	3.81	101	.262	.335	6	.182	-1	-1	1	-1	0.1
1959	KC-A	6	10	.375	40	9	3	1	4	125^1	124	10	57	65	13.2	4.09	98	.260	.343	3	.094	-1	-3	-1	-2	-0.4

YEAR	TM/L	W	L	PCT	G	GS	CG	SH	SV	IP	H	HR	BB	SO	RAT	ERA	ERA+	OAV	OOB	BH	AVG	PB	PR	/A	PD	TPI
1960	Cle-A	0	1	.000	3	0	0	0	0	2^{1}	6	0	1	2	27.0	11.57	32	.500	.538	0	—	0	-2	-2	0	-0.7
	Cin-N	2	2	.500	26	0	0	0	2	30^{1}	32	3	10	22	12.5	4.45	86	.274	.331	0	.000	-0	-2	-2	-0	-0.3
	StL-N	1	0	1.000	15	0	0	0	0	20^{2}	22	1	9	15	13.5	3.05	134	.272	.344	0	.000	-0	2	2	0	0.1
	Yr	3	2	.600	41	0	0	0	2	51	54	4	19	37	12.9	3.88	101	.267	.330	0	.000	-0	-1	0	-0	-0.2
1962	KC-A	0	1	.000	12	0	0	0	3	13	14	0	8	3	15.2	6.23	68	.292	.393	0	.000	-0	-3	-3	1	-0.3
Total	8	61	41	.598	268	60	18	4	37	759^{2}	708	50	330	443	12.5	3.61	104	.252	.334	24	.127	-4	19	11	-4	1.4

● BURLEIGH GRIMES

Grimes, Burleigh Arland "Ol' Stubblebeard"
b: 8/18/1893, Emerald, Wis. d: 12/6/85, Clear Lake, Wis. BR/TR, 5'10", 175 lbs. Deb: 9/10/16 MCH

YEAR	TM/L	W	L	PCT	G	GS	CG	SH	SV	IP	H	HR	BB	SO	RAT	ERA	ERA+	OAV	OOB	BH	AVG	PB	PR	/A	PD	TPI
1916	Pit-N	2	3	.400	6	5	4	0	0	45^{2}	40	1	10	20	9.9	2.36	114	.241	.284	3	.176	-0	1	2	1	0.2
1917	Pit-N	3	16	.158	37	17	8	1	0	194	186	5	70	72	12.2	3.53	80	.260	.331	16	.232	2	-18	-15	1	-1.2
1918	Bro-N	19	9	.679	**40**	30	19	7	1	269^{2}	210	3	76	113	9.7	2.14	130	.216	.276	18	.200	0	19	19	4	2.6
1919	Bro-N	10	11	.476	25	21	13	1	0	181^{1}	179	2	60	82	12.2	3.47	86	.256	.321	17	.246	1	-11	-10	1	-0.9
1920	*Bro-N	23	11	**.676**	40	33	25	5	2	303^{2}	271	5	67	131	10.1	2.22	144	.238	.282	34	.306	10	31	33	3	5.4
1921	Bro-N	**22**	13	.629	37	35	**30**	2	0	302^{1}	313	6	76	**136**	11.7	2.83	138	.274	.322	27	.237	2	32	**36**	4	**4.5**
1922	Bro-N	17	14	.548	36	34	18	1	1	259	324	17	84	99	14.4	4.76	85	.308	.363	22	.237	4	-19	-20	4	-1.2
1923	Bro-N	21	18	.538	39	38	**33**	2	0	**327**	356	9	100	119	12.9	3.58	108	.280	.338	30	.238	3	15	11	5	2.0
1924	Bro-N	22	13	.629	38	36	**30**	1	1	**310^{2}**	351	15	91	135	13.0	3.82	98	.287	.339	37	.298	6	1	-3	5	0.9
1925	Bro-N	12	19	.387	33	31	19	0	0	246^{2}	305	15	102	73	15.1	5.04	83	.309	.377	24	.250	5	-21	-23	8	-1.2
1926	Bro-N	12	13	.480	30	29	18	1	0	225^{1}	238	4	88	64	13.2	3.71	103	.276	.346	18	.222	1	3	3	3	0.6
1927	NY-N	19	8	.704	39	34	15	2	2	259^{2}	274	12	87	102	12.7	3.54	109	.276	.337	18	.188	-0	11	9	5	1.3
1928	Pit-N	**25**	14	.641	**48**	37	**28**	**4**	3	**330^{2}**	311	11	77	97	10.8	2.99	136	.248	.297	42	.321	11	37	39	6	6.1
1929	Pit-N	17	7	.708	33	29	18	2	2	232^{2}	245	11	70	62	12.3	3.13	**152**	.269	.324	26	.286	6	**41**	**42**	3	**4.7**
1930	Bos-N	3	5	.375	11	9	1	0	0	49	72	4	22	15	17.8	7.35	67	.353	.424	3	.188	-0	-13	-13	0	-1.6
	*StL-N	13	6	.684	22	19	10	1	0	152^{1}	174	5	43	58	13.1	3.01	166	.293	.345	15	.263	2	33	34	1	4.0
	Yr	16	11	.593	33	28	11	1	0	201^{1}	246	9	65	73	14.1	4.07	123	.307	.362	18	.247	2	20	21	2	2.4
1931	*StL-N	17	9	.654	29	28	17	3	0	212^{1}	240	11	59	67	13.1	3.65	108	.286	.340	14	.184	-2	5	7	3	0.8
1932	*Chi-N	6	11	.353	30	18	5	1	1	141^{1}	174	8	50	36	14.3	4.78	79	.297	.354	11	.250	1	-14	-16	1	-1.5
1933	Chi-N	3	6	.333	17	7	3	1	3	69^{2}	71	2	29	12	13.0	3.49	94	.277	.353	3	.150	-1	-1	-2	1	-0.2
	StL-N	0	1	.000	4	3	0	0	1	13^{2}	15	1	8	4	15.8	5.27	66	.263	.364	1	.200	0	-3	-3	-1	-0.3
	Yr	3	7	.300	21	10	3	1	4	83^{1}	86	3	37	16	13.4	3.78	87	.274	.352	4	.160	-0	-4	-4	-0	-0.5
1934	StL-N	2	1	.667	4	0	0	0	0	7^{2}	5	1	2	1	8.2	3.52	120	.179	.233	0	—	0	0	1	0	0.2
	Pit-N	1	2	.333	8	4	0	0	0	27^{1}	36	0	10	9	15.5	7.24	57	.310	.370	1	.143	-0	-10	-10	1	-0.9
	Yr	3	3	.500	12	4	0	0	0	35	41	1	12	10	13.9	6.43	64	.285	.344	1	.143	-0	-9	-9	1	-0.7
	NY-A	1	2	.333	10	0	0	0	1	18	22	0	14	5	18.5	5.50	74	.319	.440	0	.000	-0	-2	-3	1	-0.4
Total	19	270	212	.560	616	497	314	35	18	4179^{2}	4412	148	1295	1512	12.5	3.53	107	.273	.331	380	.248	52	118	122	58	23.9

● JOHN GRIMES

Grimes, John Thomas b: 4/17/1869, Woodstock, Md. d: 1/17/64, San Francisco, Cal BR/TR, 5'11", 160 lbs. Deb: 7/28/1897

YEAR	TM/L	W	L	PCT	G	GS	CG	SH	SV	IP	H	HR	BB	SO	RAT	ERA	ERA+	OAV	OOB	BH	AVG	PB	PR	/A	PD	TPI
1897	StL-N	0	2	.000	3	1	1	0	0	19^{2}	24	0	8	4	17.4	5.95	74	.300	.404	2	.286	1	-4	-3	1	-0.1

● JASON GRIMSLEY

Grimsley, Jason Alan b: 8/7/67, Cleveland, Tex. BR/TR, 6'3", 180 lbs. Deb: 9/8/89

YEAR	TM/L	W	L	PCT	G	GS	CG	SH	SV	IP	H	HR	BB	SO	RAT	ERA	ERA+	OAV	OOB	BH	AVG	PB	PR	/A	PD	TPI
1989	Phi-N	1	3	.250	4	4	0	0	0	18^{1}	19	2	19	7	18.7	5.89	60	.268	.422	0	.000	-1	-5	-5	0	-0.9
1990	Phi-N	3	2	.600	11	11	0	0	0	57^{1}	47	1	43	41	14.4	3.30	116	.227	.365	3	.188	0	3	3	1	0.4
1991	Phi-N	1	7	.125	12	12	0	0	0	61	54	4	41	42	14.5	4.87	75	.242	.367	1	.059	-1	-8	-8	1	-0.9
1993	Cle-A	3	4	.429	10	6	0	0	0	42^{1}	52	3	20	27	15.5	5.31	81	.302	.378	0	—	0	-5	-5	-0	-0.7
1994	Cle-A	5	2	.714	14	13	1	0	0	82^{2}	91	7	34	59	14.3	4.57	103	.283	.362	0	—	0	2	1	-0	0.1
1995	Cle-A	0	0	—	15	2	0	0	1	34	37	4	32	25	18.8	6.09	77	.289	.438	0	—	0	-5	-5	1	0.0
1996	Cal-A	5	7	.417	35	20	2	1	0	130^{1}	150	14	74	82	16.4	6.84	73	.286	.388	0	—	0	-27	-27	2	-1.8
Total	7	18	25	.419	101	68	3	1	1	426	450	35	263	283	15.6	5.39	82	.273	.382	4	.105	-1	-44	-45	4	-3.8

● ROSS GRIMSLEY

Grimsley, Ross Albert I b: 6/4/22, Americus, Kan. d: 2/6/94, Memphis, Tenn. BL/TL, 6', 175 lbs. Deb: 9/3/51 F

YEAR	TM/L	W	L	PCT	G	GS	CG	SH	SV	IP	H	HR	BB	SO	RAT	ERA	ERA+	OAV	OOB	BH	AVG	PB	PR	/A	PD	TPI
1951	Chi-A	0	0	—	7	0	0	0	0	14	12	1	10	8	14.1	3.86	105	.235	.361	0	.000	-0	0	0	-1	-0.1

● ROSS GRIMSLEY

Grimsley, Ross Albert II b: 1/7/50, Topeka, Kan. BL/TL, 6'3", 200 lbs. Deb: 5/16/71 F

YEAR	TM/L	W	L	PCT	G	GS	CG	SH	SV	IP	H	HR	BB	SO	RAT	ERA	ERA+	OAV	OOB	BH	AVG	PB	PR	/A	PD	TPI
1971	Cin-N	10	7	.588	26	26	6	3	0	161^{1}	151	15	43	67	10.9	3.57	94	.250	.302	6	.118	-1	-2	-4	-1	-0.6
1972	*Cin-N	14	8	.636	30	28	4	1	1	197^{2}	194	18	50	79	11.1	3.05	105	.260	.307	8	.121	-2	9	4	-0	0.1
1973	*Cin-N	13	10	.565	38	36	8	1	1	242^{1}	245	24	68	90	11.6	3.23	105	.266	.317	5	.061	-6	12	5	-2	-0.4
1974	*Bal-A	18	13	.581	40	39	17	4	1	295^{2}	267	26	76	158	10.5	3.07	112	.244	.295	0	—	0	18	12	0	1.4
1975	Bal-A	10	13	.435	35	32	8	1	0	197	210	29	47	89	11.8	4.07	86	.276	.319	0	—	0	-6	-12	0	-1.1
1976	Bal-A	8	7	.533	28	19	2	0	0	136^{2}	143	8	35	41	11.8	3.95	83	.270	.317	0	—	0	-7	-10	-1	-1.1
1977	Bal-A	14	10	.583	34	34	11	2	0	218^{1}	230	24	74	53	12.6	3.96	96	.277	.337	0	—	0	2	-4	2	-0.2
1978	Mon-N☆	20	11	.645	36	36	19	3	0	263	237	17	67	84	10.5	3.05	116	.243	.293	13	.144	-1	15	14	1	1.6
1979	Mon-N	10	9	.526	32	27	2	0	0	151^{1}	199	18	41	42	14.5	5.35	68	.322	.367	11	.200	1	-27	-28	-0	-3.1
1980	Mon-N	2	4	.333	11	7	0	0	0	41^{1}	61	5	12	11	16.1	6.31	56	.351	.396	2	.222	0	-12	-13	0	-1.6
	Cle-A	4	5	.444	14	11	2	0	0	74^{2}	103	11	24	18	15.4	6.75	60	.331	.381	0	—	0	-23	-22	-1	-2.3
1982	Bal-A	1	2	.333	21	0	0	0	0	60	65	7	22	18	13.1	5.25	77	.283	.345	0	—	0	-8	-8	0	-0.3
Total	11	124	99	.556	345	295	79	15	3	2039^{1}	2105	202	559	750	11.8	3.81	92	.270	.320	45	.127	-10	-29	-67	-1	-7.6

● DAN GRINER

Griner, Donald Dexter "Rusty" b: 3/7/1888, Centerville, Tenn. d: 6/3/50, Bishopville, S.C. BL/TR, 6'1.5", 200 lbs. Deb: 8/17/12

YEAR	TM/L	W	L	PCT	G	GS	CG	SH	SV	IP	H	HR	BB	SO	RAT	ERA	ERA+	OAV	OOB	BH	AVG	PB	PR	/A	PD	TPI
1912	StL-N	3	4	.429	12	7	2	0	0	54	59	3	15	20	12.8	3.17	108	.278	.335	1	.077	-0	1	2	-1	0.0
1913	StL-N	10	22	.313	34	34	18	1	0	225	279	12	66	79	14.2	5.08	64	.312	.366	21	.259	5	-47	-46	2	-5.0
1914	StL-N	9	13	.409	37	17	11	2	2	179	163	3	57	74	11.2	2.51	111	.254	.318	14	.255	4	5	6	-1	1.0
1915	StL-N	5	11	.313	37	17	9	3	3	150^{1}	137	4	46	46	11.4	2.81	99	.259	.328	14	.269	4	-1	-0	-2	0.2
1916	StL-N	0	0	—	4	0	0	0	1	11	15	0	3	3	15.5	4.09	65	.341	.396	1	.250	0	-2	-2	0	0.0
1918	Bro-N	1	5	.167	11	6	3	1	0	54^{1}	47	0	15	22	11.4	2.15	129	.267	.348	1	.071	-1	4	4	0	0.4
Total	6	28	55	.337	135	81	43	7	6	673^{2}	700	22	202	244	12.5	3.49	86	.280	.342	52	.237	12	-39	-37	-2	-3.4

● LEE GRISSOM

Grissom, Lee Theo b: 10/23/07, Sherman, Tex. d: 10/4/98, Corning, Cal. BB/TL, 6'3", 200 lbs. Deb: 9/2/34 F

YEAR	TM/L	W	L	PCT	G	GS	CG	SH	SV	IP	H	HR	BB	SO	RAT	ERA	ERA+	OAV	OOB	BH	AVG	PB	PR	/A	PD	TPI
1934	Cin-N	0	1	.000	4	1	0	0	0	7	13	0	7	4	25.7	15.43	26	.382	.488	0	.000	-0	-9	-9	-0	-1.0
1935	Cin-N	1	1	.500	3	3	1	0	0	21	31	0	4	13	15.0	3.86	103	.333	.361	0	.000	-1	0	0	0	0.0
1936	Cin-N	1	1	.500	6	4	0	0	0	24^{1}	33	1	9	13	15.5	6.29	61	.320	.375	0	.000	-1	-6	-7	0	-0.6
1937	Cin-N★	12	17	.414	50	30	14	**5**	6	223^{2}	193	7	93	149	11.7	3.26	114	.232	.313	7	.109	-3	16	12	-2	0.9
1938	Cin-N	2	3	.400	14	7	0	0	0	51	60	4	22	16	14.8	5.29	69	.300	.375	3	.188	-0	-9	-9	-0	-0.9
1939	*Cin-N	9	7	.563	33	21	3	0	0	153^{2}	145	14	56	53	11.8	4.10	93	.249	.316	4	.085	-2	-3	-5	-2	-0.8
1940	NY-A	0	0	—	5	0	0	0	0	4^{2}	4	0	2	1	11.6	0.00	—	.250	.333	0	—	0	2	2	0	0.0
	Bro-N	2	5	.286	14	10	3	1	0	73^{2}	59	3	34	56	11.4	2.81	142	.215	.302	5	.217	0	9	10	-1	0.8
1941	Bro-N	0	0	—	4	1	0	0	1	11^{1}	10	2	8	5	14.3	2.38	154	.238	.360	1	.500	0	2	2	-0	0.1
	Phi-N	2	13	.133	29	18	2	0	0	131^{1}	120	4	70	74	13.2	3.97	93	.242	.338	6	.167	-1	-5	-4	-1	-0.5
	Yr	2	13	.133	33	19	2	0	1	142^{2}	130	6	78	79	13.2	3.85	96	.242	.340	7	.184	-0	-3	-2	-1	-0.4
Total	8	29	48	.377	162	95	23	6	7	701^{2}	668	35	305	384	12.6	3.89	97	.250	.329	26	.127	-8	-3	-8	-6	-2.0

● MARV GRISSOM

Grissom, Marvin Edward b: 3/31/18, Los Molinos, Cal. BR/TR, 6'3", 195 lbs. Deb: 9/10/46 FC

YEAR	TM/L	W	L	PCT	G	GS	CG	SH	SV	IP	H	HR	BB	SO	RAT	ERA	ERA+	OAV	OOB	BH	AVG	PB	PR	/A	PD	TPI
1946	NY-N	0	2	.000	4	3	0	0	0	18^{2}	17	1	13	9	14.9	4.34	79	.254	.383	1	.200	-0	-2	-2	1	-0.1
1949	Det-A	2	4	.333	27	2	0	0	0	39^{1}	56	6	34	17	20.8	6.41	65	.335	.450	2	.222	1	-10	-10	0	-1.2
1952	Chi-A	12	10	.545	28	24	7	1	0	166	156	6	79	97	12.9	3.74	98	.250	.337	8	.151	-1	-1	-2	-2	-0.5
1953	Bos-A	2	6	.250	13	11	1	1	0	59^{1}	61	5	30	31	14.0	4.70	89	.266	.354	0	.000	-3	-5	-3	-1	-0.7
	NY-N	4	2	.667	21	7	3	0	0	84^{1}	83	6	31	46	12.3	3.95	109	.255	.321	2	.074	-2	3	3	1	0.1
1954	*NY-N★	10	7	.588	56	3	1	1	19	122^{1}	100	13	50	64	11.6	2.35	171	.226	.314	5	.156	-1	23	23	-0	3.6
1955	NY-N	5	4	.556	55	0	0	0	8	89^{1}	76	6	41	49	12.4	2.92	138	.237	.334	2	.154	-1	11	11	0	1.2
1956	NY-N	1	1	.500	43	2	0	0	7	80^{2}	71	3	16	49	9.8	1.56	242	.241	.282	1	.091	-0	**20**	**20**	-1	0.8
1957	NY-N	4	4	.500	55	0	0	0	14	82^{2}	74	6	23	51	10.8	2.61	151	.243	.301	2	.167	0	12	12	1	1.7

YEAR	TM/L	W	L	PCT	G	GS	CG	SH	SV	IP	H	HR	BB	SO	RAT	ERA	ERA+	OAV	OOB	BH	AVG	PB	PR	/A	PD	TPI
1958	SF-N	7	5	.583	51	0	0	0	10	65^1	71	11	26	46	14.1	3.99	95	.287	.367	0	.000	-1	-0	-1	-0	-0.3
1959	StL-N	0	0	—	3	0	0	0	0	2	6	2	0	0	27.0	22.50	19	.500	.500	0	—	0	-4	-4	0	0.0
Total	10	47	45	.511	356	52	12	3	58	810	771	65	343	459	12.7	3.41	115	.254	.335	23	.122	-7	47	47	-0	4.6

● CONNIE GROB Grob, Conrad George b: 11/9/32, Cross Plains, Wis. d: 9/28/97, Madison, Wis. BL/TR, 6'0.5", 180 lbs. Deb: 4/22/56

YEAR	TM/L	W	L	PCT	G	GS	CG	SH	SV	IP	H	HR	BB	SO	RAT	ERA	ERA+	OAV	OOB	BH	AVG	PB	PR	/A	PD	TPI
1956	Was-A	4	5	.444	37	1	0	0	1	79^1	121	14	26	27	16.8	7.83	55	.353	.400	6	.333	1	-32	-31	1	-2.8

● JOHNNY GRODZICKI Grodzicki, John "Grod" b: 2/26/17, Nanticoke, Pa. BR/TR, 6'1.5", 200 lbs. Deb: 4/18/41 C

YEAR	TM/L	W	L	PCT	G	GS	CG	SH	SV	IP	H	HR	BB	SO	RAT	ERA	ERA+	OAV	OOB	BH	AVG	PB	PR	/A	PD	TPI
1941	StL-N	2	1	.667	5	1	0	0	0	13^1	6	0	11	10	11.5	1.35	279	.130	.298	0	.000	0	3	4	-0	0.8
1946	StL-N	0	0	—	3	0	0	0	0	4	4	1	4	2	18.0	9.00	38	.250	.400	0	—	0	-2	-2	0	0.0
1947	StL-N	0	1	.000	16	0	0	0	0	23^1	21	5	19	8	15.4	5.40	77	.253	.392	0	.000	-0	-3	-3	0	-0.1
Total	3	2	2	.500	24	1	0	0	0	40^2	31	6	34	20	14.4	4.43	89	.214	.363	0	.000	0	-3	-2	0	0.7

● STEVE GROMEK Gromek, Stephen Joseph b: 1/15/20, Hamtramck, Mich. BB/TR, 6'2", 180 lbs. Deb: 8/18/41

YEAR	TM/L	W	L	PCT	G	GS	CG	SH	SV	IP	H	HR	BB	SO	RAT	ERA	ERA+	OAV	OOB	BH	AVG	PB	PR	/A	PD	TPI
1941	Cle-A	1	1	.500	9	2	1	0	2	23^1	25	0	11	19	13.9	4.24	93	.266	.343	1	.167	-0	-0	-1	-1	-0.2
1942	Cle-A	2	0	1.000	14	0	0	0	0	44^1	46	2	23	14	14.0	3.65	94	.267	.354	5	.333	3	0	-1	-1	0.2
1943	Cle-A	0	0	—	3	0	0	0	0	4	6	0	0	4	13.5	9.00	35	.353	.353	2	1.000	1	-3	-3	-0	0.1
1944	Cle-A	10	9	.526	35	21	12	2	1	203^2	160	5	70	115	10.3	2.56	129	**.219**	.290	19	.260	5	20	17	-3	1.8
1945	Cle-A†	19	9	.679	33	30	21	3	1	251	229	6	66	101	10.7	2.55	128	.243	.295	21	.231	3	23	20	-3	2.2
1946	Cle-A	5	15	.250	29	21	5	2	4	153^2	159	20	47	75	12.2	4.33	76	.264	.321	11	.196	0	-14	-18	-1	-2.2
1947	Cle-A	3	5	.375	29	7	0	0	4	84^1	77	8	36	39	12.2	3.74	93	.240	.318	7	.318	2	-0	-2	-0	-0.1
1948	*Cle-A	9	3	.750	38	9	4	1	2	130	109	10	51	50	11.5	2.84	143	.226	.307	6	.146	-1	21	18	-1	1.3
1949	Cle-A	4	6	.400	27	12	3	0	0	92	86	8	40	22	12.5	3.33	120	.250	.332	4	.167	-0	9	7	0	0.7
1950	Cle-A	10	7	.588	31	13	4	1	0	113^1	94	10	36	43	10.6	3.65	119	.226	.292	6	.158	-2	12	9	-0	0.9
1951	Cle-A	7	4	.636	27	8	4	0	1	107^1	98	6	29	40	11.0	2.77	137	.238	.295	8	.296	3	16	12	1	1.5
1952	Cle-A	7	7	.500	29	13	3	1	1	122^2	109	14	28	65	10.2	3.67	91	.232	.278	3	.100	-0	0	-4	-3	-0.8
1953	Cle-A	1	1	.500	5	1	0	0	0	11	11	0	3	8	12.3	3.27	115	.268	.333	0	.000	-0	1	1	-0	0.0
	Det-A	6	8	.429	19	17	6	1	1	125^2	138	17	36	59	13.0	4.51	90	.276	.335	3	.073	-4	-7	-6	-1	-1.1
	Yr	7	9	.438	24	18	6	1	1	136^2	149	17	39	67	12.9	4.41	92	.275	.333	3	.070	-4	-6	-6	-1	-1.1
1954	Det-A	18	16	.529	36	32	17	4	1	252^2	236	26	57	102	10.9	2.74	135	.246	.297	15	.190	2	28	27	-3	3.4
1955	Det-A	13	10	.565	28	25	8	2	0	181	183	26	37	73	11.4	3.98	97	.261	.307	9	.167	4	-0	-3	-2	-0.1
1956	Det-A	8	6	.571	40	13	4	0	4	141	142	25	47	64	12.6	4.28	96	.263	.332	4	.148	2	-2	-3	-2	-0.3
1957	Det-A	0	1	.000	15	1	0	0	1	23^2	32	3	13	11	17.5	6.08	63	.333	.418	0	.000	-0	-6	-6	-1	-0.4
Total	17	123	108	.532	447	225	92	17	23	2064^2	1940	186	630	904	11.5	3.41	108	.247	.309	124	.197	15	96	63	-21	6.9

● BOB GROOM Groom, Robert b: 9/12/1884, Belleville, Ill. d: 2/19/48, Belleville, Ill. BR/TR, 6'2", 175 lbs. Deb: 4/13/09

YEAR	TM/L	W	L	PCT	G	GS	CG	SH	SV	IP	H	HR	BB	SO	RAT	ERA	ERA+	OAV	OOB	BH	AVG	PB	PR	/A	PD	TPI
1909	Was-A	7	26	.212	44	31	17	1	0	260^2	218	2	105	131	11.6	2.87	85	.229	.314	8	.091	-6	-11	-13	4	-1.8
1910	Was-A	12	17	.414	34	30	22	3	0	257^2	244	8	77	98	11.5	2.76	90	.260	.322	11	.120	-6	-7	-8	-2	-1.6
1911	Was-A	13	17	.433	37	32	20	2	2	254^2	280	9	67	135	12.5	3.82	86	.282	.332	11	.134	-4	-13	-15	1	-1.9
1912	Was-A	24	13	.649	43	40	28	2	1	316	287	3	94	179	11.0	2.62	127	.246	.305	12	.117	-7	24	25	-2	1.9
1913	Was-A	16	16	.500	37	36	17	4	0	264^1	258	8	81	156	11.7	3.23	91	.254	.312	15	.163	1	-9	-8	2	-0.7
1914	StL-F	13	20	.394	42	34	23	1	1	280^2	281	9	75	167	11.5	3.24	94	.262	.312	15	.160	-4	-11	-6	-0	-1.1
1915	StL-F	11	11	.500	37	26	11	4	2	209	200	6	73	111	11.8	3.27	88	.261	.327	10	.152	-3	-13	-9	0	-1.2
1916	StL-A	13	9	.591	41	26	8	1	4	217^1	174	1	98	92	11.4	2.57	107	.226	.315	7	.111	-2	6	4	2	0.4
1917	StL-A	8	19	.296	38	28	11	4	3	232^2	193	3	95	82	11.3	2.94	88	.233	.315	8	.111	-4	-7	-9	-1	-1.6
1918	Cle-A	2	2	.500	14	5	0	0	0	43^1	70	0	18	8	18.5	7.06	43	.380	.438	1	.083	-1	-21	-20	0	-1.8
Total	10	119	150	.442	367	288	157	22	13	2336^1	2205	49	783	1159	11.7	3.10	93	.254	.319	98	.128	-35	-61	-58	2	-9.4

● BUDDY GROOM Groom, Wedsel Gary b: 7/10/65, Dallas, Tex. BL/TL, 6'2", 200 lbs. Deb: 6/20/92

YEAR	TM/L	W	L	PCT	G	GS	CG	SH	SV	IP	H	HR	BB	SO	RAT	ERA	ERA+	OAV	OOB	BH	AVG	PB	PR	/A	PD	TPI
1992	Det-A	0	5	.000	12	7	0	0	1	38^2	48	4	22	15	16.3	5.82	68	.320	.407	0	—	0	-8	-8	-0	-1.0
1993	Det-A	0	2	.000	19	3	0	0	0	36^2	48	4	13	15	15.5	6.14	70	.322	.384	0	—	0	-7	-8	0	-0.3
1994	Det-A	0	1	.000	40	0	0	0	1	32	31	4	13	27	12.9	3.94	123	.256	.338	0	—	0	3	3	0	0.0
1995	Det-A	1	3	.250	23	4	0	0	1	40^2	55	6	26	23	18.4	7.52	63	.322	.417	0	—	0	-13	-13	-1	-1.1
	Fla-N	1	2	.333	14	0	0	0	0	15	26	2	6	12	19.2	7.20	59	.400	.451	0	—	0	-5	-5	0	-0.8
1996	Oak-A	5	0	1.000	72	1	0	0	2	77^1	85	8	34	57	14.2	3.84	128	.281	.360	0	—	0	10	9	-1	0.6
1997	Oak-A	2	2	.500	78	0	0	0	3	64^2	75	9	24	45	13.8	5.15	88	.292	.352	0	—	0	-4	-5	0	-0.1
1998	Oak-A	3	1	.750	75	0	0	0	0	57^1	62	4	20	36	13.0	4.24	108	.274	.336	0	—	0	3	2	-1	0.3
Total	7	12	16	.429	333	15	0	0	8	362^1	430	41	158	230	14.9	5.14	89	.298	.372	0	—	0	-22	-23	-3	-2.4

● DON GROSS Gross, Donald John b: 6/30/31, Weidman, Mich. BL/TL, 5'11", 186 lbs. Deb: 7/21/55

YEAR	TM/L	W	L	PCT	G	GS	CG	SH	SV	IP	H	HR	BB	SO	RAT	ERA	ERA+	OAV	OOB	BH	AVG	PB	PR	/A	PD	TPI
1955	Cin-N	4	5	.444	17	11	2	1	0	67^1	79	11	16	33	12.8	4.14	102	.298	.340	3	.158	-1	-1	1	0	0.0
1956	Cin-N	3	0	1.000	19	7	2	0	0	69^1	69	4	20	47	11.7	1.95	204	.257	.310	2	.105	-1	14	16	1	0.7
1957	Cin-N	7	9	.438	43	16	5	0	1	148^1	152	21	33	73	11.4	4.31	95	.264	.307	5	.109	-2	-7	-3	-0	-0.6
1958	Pit-N	5	7	.417	40	3	0	0	7	74^2	67	5	38	59	12.8	3.98	97	.241	.334	1	.056	-1	-0	-1	1	-0.2
1959	Pit-N	1	1	.500	21	0	0	0	2	33	28	3	10	15	10.6	3.55	109	.228	.291	0	.000	-0	1	1	1	0.2
1960	Pit-N	0	0	—	5	0	0	0	0	5^1	5	1	0	3	8.4	3.38	111	.238	.238	0	—	0	0	0	-0	0.0
Total	6	20	22	.476	145	37	9	1	10	398	400	45	117	230	11.8	3.73	108	.261	.316	11	.106	-5	8	14	2	0.1

● GREG GROSS Gross, Gregory Eugene b: 8/1/52, York, Pa. BL/TL, 5'11", 175 lbs. Deb: 9/5/73 ♦

YEAR	TM/L	W	L	PCT	G	GS	CG	SH	SV	IP	H	HR	BB	SO	RAT	ERA	ERA+	OAV	OOB	BH	AVG	PB	PR	/A	PD	TPI
1986	Phi-N	0	0	—	1	0	0	0	0	0^2	1	0	1	2	27.0	0.00	—	.333	.500	25	.248	0	0	0	0	0.0
1989	Hou-N	0	0	—	1	0	0	0	0	1	3	0	1	1	36.0	18.00	19	.500	.571	15	.200	0	-2	-2	0	0.0
Total	2	0	0	—	2	0	0	0	0	1^2	4	0	2	3	32.4	10.80	33	.444	.545	1073	.287	0	-1	-1	0	0.0

● KEVIN GROSS Gross, Kevin Frank b: 6/8/61, Downey, Cal. BR/TR, 6'5", 215 lbs. Deb: 6/25/83

YEAR	TM/L	W	L	PCT	G	GS	CG	SH	SV	IP	H	HR	BB	SO	RAT	ERA	ERA+	OAV	OOB	BH	AVG	PB	PR	/A	PD	TPI
1983	Phi-N	4	6	.400	17	17	1	1	0	96	100	13	35	66	12.9	3.56	100	.265	.333	3	.091	-1	1	0	0	-0.1
1984	Phi-N	8	5	.615	44	14	1	0	1	129	140	8	44	84	13.2	4.12	88	.277	.341	2	.067	-2	-8	-7	1	-0.7
1985	Phi-N	15	13	.536	38	31	6	2	0	205^2	194	11	81	151	12.3	3.41	108	.251	.328	9	.138	0	4	6	1	1.0
1986	Phi-N	12	12	.500	37	36	7	2	0	241^2	240	28	94	154	12.7	4.02	96	.259	.333	15	.188	3	-8	-5	-1	-0.2
1987	Phi-N	9	16	.360	34	33	3	1	0	200^2	205	26	87	110	13.5	4.35	97	.267	.350	12	.190	2	-6	-2	-2	-0.3
1988	Phi-N★	12	14	.462	33	33	5	1	0	231^2	209	18	89	162	12.0	3.69	96	.239	.317	13	.173	1	-6	-3	-0	-0.3
1989	Mon-N	11	12	.478	31	31	4	3	0	201^1	188	20	88	158	12.6	4.38	81	.247	.330	9	.141	1	-20	-19	-0	-2.0
1990	Mon-N	9	12	.429	31	26	2	1	0	163^1	171	9	65	111	13.2	4.57	80	.272	.344	10	.200	4	-14	-17	-2	-1.8
1991	LA-N	10	11	.476	46	10	0	0	3	115^2	123	10	50	95	13.6	3.58	100	.275	.351	7	.280	2	1	0	-0	0.3
1992	LA-N	8	13	.381	34	30	4	3	0	204^2	182	11	77	158	11.5	3.17	109	.241	.313	6	.095	-1	8	6	-1	0.4
1993	LA-N	13	13	.500	33	32	3	0	0	202^1	224	15	74	150	13.5	4.14	92	.281	.346	13	.203	5	-2	-7	2	-0.1
1994	LA-N	9	7	.563	25	23	1	0	1	157^1	162	11	43	124	11.8	3.60	109	.263	.314	7	.149	1	11	6	2	0.8
1995	Tex-A	9	15	.375	31	30	4	0	0	183^2	200	27	89	106	14.6	5.54	87	.279	.365	0	—	0	-17	-15	-1	-1.7
1996	Tex-A	11	8	.579	28	19	1	0	0	129^1	151	19	50	78	14.3	5.22	100	.293	.360	0	—	0	-3	0	0	-0.3
1997	Ana-A	2	1	.667	12	3	0	0	0	25^1	30	4	20	20	18.1	6.75	68	.313	.436	0	.000	-0	-6	-6	0	-0.6
Total	15	142	158	.473	474	368	42	14	5	2487^2	2519	230	986	1727	13.0	4.11	94	.264	.338	106	.161	14	-66	-63	0	-5.6

● KIP GROSS Gross, Kip Lee b: 8/24/64, Scottsbluff, Neb. BR/TR, 6'2", 195 lbs. Deb: 4/21/90

YEAR	TM/L	W	L	PCT	G	GS	CG	SH	SV	IP	H	HR	BB	SO	RAT	ERA	ERA+	OAV	OOB	BH	AVG	PB	PR	/A	PD	TPI
1990	Cin-N	0	0	—	5	0	0	0	0	6^1	6	0	2	3	11.4	4.26	93	.273	.333	0	—	0	-0	-0	-0	0.0
1991	Cin-N	6	4	.600	29	9	1	0	0	85^2	93	8	40	40	14.0	3.47	110	.279	.357	2	.091	-1	2	3	0	0.2
1992	LA-N	1	1	.500	16	1	0	0	0	23^2	32	1	10	14	16.0	4.18	82	.323	.385	2	1.000	1	-2	-2	1	0.0
1993	LA-N	0	0	—	10	0	0	0	0	15	13	0	4	12	10.2	0.60	636	.236	.288	0	—	0	6	5	-0	0.0
Total	4	7	5	.583	60	10	1	0	0	130^2	144	9	56	69	13.8	3.31	113	.283	.354	4	.167	-0	6	6	0	0.2

● WAYNE GROSS Gross, Wayne Dale b: 1/14/52, Riverside, Cal. BL/TR, 6'2", 210 lbs. Deb: 8/21/76 ♦

YEAR	TM/L	W	L	PCT	G	GS	CG	SH	SV	IP	H	HR	BB	SO	RAT	ERA	ERA+	OAV	OOB	BH	AVG	PB	PR	/A	PD	TPI
1983	Oak-A	0	0	—	1	0	0	0	0	2^1	2	0	1	0	15.4	0.00	—	.222	.364	79	.233	0	1	1	-0	0.0

YEAR	TM/L	W	L	PCT	G	GS	CG	SH	SV	IP	H	HR	BB	SO	RAT	ERA	ERA+	OAV	OOB	BH	AVG	PB	PR	/A	PD	TPI
● **HARLEY GROSSMAN**	Grossman, Harley Joseph b: 5/5/30, Evansville, Ind. BR/TR, 6', 170 lbs. Deb: 4/22/52																									
1952	Was-A	0	0	—	1	0	0	0	0	0^1	2	1	0	0	54.0	54.00	7	.667	.667	0	—	0	-2	-2	0	0.0
● **ERNIE GROTH**	Groth, Ernest John "Dango" b: 12/24/1884, Cedarburg, Wis. d: 5/23/50, Milwaukee, Wis. BR/TR, 5'11", 175 lbs. Deb: 9/6/04																									
1904	Chi-N	0	2	.000	3	2	2	0	1	16	22	1	6	9	16.3	5.63	47	.310	.372	0	.000	-1	-5	-5	-0	-0.7
● **ERNEST GROTH**	Groth, Ernest William b: 5/3/22, Beaver Falls, Pa. BR/TR, 5'9", 185 lbs. Deb: 9/11/47																									
1947	Cle-A	0	0	—	2	0	0	0	0	1^1	0	0	1	1	6.8	0.00	—	.000	.250	0	—	0	1	1	0	0.0
1948	Cle-A	0	0	—	1	0	0	0	0	1	1	0	2	0	27.0	9.00	45	.250	.500	0	—	0	-1	-1	-0	0.0
1949	Chi-A	0	1	.000	3	0	0	0	0	5	2	2	3	1	10.8	5.40	77	.125	.300	0	—	0	-1	-1	-0	-0.1
Total	3	0	1	.000	6	0	0	0	0	7^1	3	2	6	2	12.3	4.91	82	.130	.333	0	—	0	-1	-1	-0	-0.1
● **MATT GROTT**	Grott, Matthew Allen b: 12/5/67, LaPorte, Ind. BL/TL, 6'1", 210 lbs. Deb: 5/4/95																									
1995	Cin-N	0	0	—	2	0	0	0	0	1^2	6	1	0	2	32.4	21.60	19	.545	.545	0	—	0	-3	-3	0	0.0
● **ORVAL GROVE**	Grove, Orval Leroy b: 8/29/19, Mineral, Kan. d: 4/20/92, Carmichael, Cal. BR/TR, 6'3", 196 lbs. Deb: 5/28/40																									
1940	Chi-A	0	0	—	3	0	0	0	0	6	4	0	4	1	12.0	3.00	147	.182	.308	0	.000	-0	1	1	-0	0.0
1941	Chi-A	0	0	—	2	0	0	0	0	7	9	2	5	5	18.0	10.29	40	.321	.424	0	.000	-0	-5	-5	0	0.0
1942	Chi-A	4	6	.400	12	8	4	0	0	66^1	77	1	33	21	15.1	5.16	70	.283	.363	5	.227	1	-11	-11	1	-1.3
1943	Chi-A	15	9	.625	32	25	18	3	2	216^1	192	9	72	76	11.1	2.75	122	.239	.304	12	.182	2	13	14	1	1.9
1944	Chi-A☆	14	15	.483	34	33	11	2	0	234^2	237	11	71	105	12.1	3.72	92	.263	.322	8	.104	-3	-8	-8	4	-0.8
1945	Chi-A	14	12	.538	33	30	16	4	1	217	233	12	68	54	12.7	3.44	96	.273	.330	7	.099	-4	-2	-3	2	-0.6
1946	Chi-A	8	13	.381	33	26	10	1	0	205^1	213	10	78	60	12.9	3.02	113	.272	.340	7	.108	-2	11	9	2	0.8
1947	Chi-A	6	8	.429	25	19	6	1	0	135^2	158	10	70	33	15.4	4.44	82	.296	.382	7	.146	-0	-11	-12	-1	-1.2
1948	Chi-A	2	10	.167	32	11	1	0	1	87^2	110	6	42	18	15.9	6.16	69	.315	.393	2	.095	-2	-18	-19	2	-2.2
1949	Chi-A	0	0	—	1	0	0	0	0	0^2	4	1	1	1	81.0	54.00	8	.667	.750	0	—	0	-4	-4	0	0.0
Total	10	63	73	.463	207	152	66	11	4	1176^2	1237	62	444	374	13.1	3.78	93	.272	.340	48	.129	-9	-33	-37	10	-3.4
● **LEFTY GROVE**	Grove, Robert Moses b: 3/6/1900, Lonaconing, Md. d: 5/22/75, Norwalk, Ohio BL/TL, 6'3", 190 lbs. Deb: 4/14/25 H																									
1925	Phi-A	10	12	.455	45	18	5	0	1	197	207	11	131	**116**	15.7	4.75	98	.278	.390	8	.123	-6	-8	-2	2	-0.6
1926	Phi-A	13	13	.500	45	33	20	1	6	258	227	6	101	**194**	11.7	**2.51**	**166**	.244	.322	8	.099	-5	**43**	**48**	-1	4.0
1927	Phi-A	20	13	.606	51	28	14	1	9	262^1	251	6	79	**174**	11.4	3.19	134	.252	.309	10	.125	-3	28	31	-1	3.3
1928	Phi-A	**24**	8	.750	39	31	24	4	4	261^3	228	10	64	**183**	10.1	2.58	156	.229	.277	15	.170	1	**43**	**42**	-3	**4.6**
1929	*Phi-A	20	6	**.769**	42	37	19	2	4	275^1	278	8	81	**170**	11.8	**2.81**	**151**	.262	.316	22	.216	1	**44**	**43**	-3	3.5
1930	*Phi-A	**28**	5	**.848**	**50**	32	22	2	**9**	291	273	8	60	**209**	**10.5**	**2.54**	**184**	**.247**	**.288**	22	.200	0	**68**	**69**	0	**7.3**
1931	*Phi-A	**31**	4	**.886**	41	30	**27**	**4**	5	288^2	249	10	62	**175**	**9.7**	**2.06**	**218**	.229	**.271**	23	.200	-2	**74**	**78**	-2	**8.7**
1932	Phi-A	25	10	.714	44	30	**27**	**4**	7	291^2	269	13	79	188	**10.8**	**2.84**	**159**	.241	**.292**	18	.168	0	**53**	**55**	-2	**5.9**
1933	Phi-A★	**24**	8	**.750**	45	28	**21**	2	6	275^1	280	12	83	114	12.0	3.20	134	.261	.316	9	.086	-7	33	33	0	2.9
1934	Bos-A	8	8	.500	22	12	5	0	0	109^1	149	5	32	43	15.0	6.50	74	.320	.365	6	.162	-0	-24	-21	-1	-2.5
1935	Bos-A☆	20	12	.625	35	30	23	2	1	273	269	6	65	121	**11.1**	**2.70**	**176**	.257	.302	7	.079	-5	**53**	**62**	2	6.4
1936	Bos-A★	17	12	.586	35	30	22	**6**	2	253^1	237	14	65	130	**10.9**	**2.81**	**189**	.246	**.297**	11	.138	-3	**63**	**71**	0	**7.0**
1937	Bos-A☆	17	9	.654	32	32	21	3	0	262	269	9	83	153	12.1	3.02	157	.261	.317	13	.143	-3	46	50	-1	4.0
1938	Bos-A★	14	4	.778	24	21	12	1	1	163^2	169	8	52	99	12.2	**3.08**	**160**	.263	.319	8	.148	-1	31	34	-0	3.1
1939	Bos-A☆	15	4	**.789**	23	23	17	2	0	191	180	8	58	81	11.3	**2.54**	**186**	.249	.305	9	.134	-1	44	46	-3	3.7
1940	Bos-A	7	6	.538	22	21	9	1	0	153^1	159	20	50	62	12.3	3.99	113	.269	.328	8	.151	-1	7	9	0	0.5
1941	Bos-A	7	7	.500	21	21	10	0	0	134	155	8	42	54	13.4	4.37	95	.287	.340	5	.111	-1	-3	-3	-2	-0.6
Total	17	300	141	.680	616	457	298	35	55	3940^2	3849	162	1187	2266	11.6	3.06	148	.255	.311	202	.148	-37	595	643	-15	61.2
● **CHARLIE GROVER**	Grover, Charles Byrd "Bugs" b: 6/20/1890, Gallopis, Ohio d: 5/24/71, Emmett Township, Mich. BL/TR, 6'1.5", 185 lbs. Deb: 9/9/13																									
1913	Det-A	0	0	—	2	1	0	0	0	10^2	9	0	7	2	13.5	3.38	86	.265	.390	0	.000	-0	-1	-1	0	0.0
● **TOM GRUBBS**	Grubbs, Thomas Dillard "Judge" b: 2/22/1894, Mt.Sterling, Ky. d: 1/28/86, Lexington, Ky. BR/TR, 6'2", 165 lbs. Deb: 10/3/20																									
1920	NY-N	0	1	.000	1	1	0	0	0	5	9	0	0	0	16.2	7.20	42	.409	.409	0	.000	-0	-2	-2	-0	-0.4
● **HENRY GRUBER**	Gruber, Henry John b: 12/14/1863, Hamden, Conn. d: 9/26/32, New Haven, Conn. BR/TR, 5'9", 155 lbs. Deb: 7/28/1887																									
1887	Det-N	4	3	.571	7	7	7	0	0	62^1	63	3	21	12	12.1	2.74	148	.262	.322	4	.167	1	9	9	-1	0.7
1888	Det-N	11	14	.440	27	25	25	3	0	240	196	8	41	71	9.0	2.29	121	.213	.249	13	.141	-1	15	13	1	1.1
1889	Cle-N	7	16	.304	25	23	23	0	1	205	198	6	94	74	13.2	3.64	111	.246	.331	7	.101	-1	8	9	-0	0.7
1890	Cle-P	22	23	.489	48	44	39	1	0	383^1	464	15	204	110	16.0	4.27	93	.286	.371	36	.221	6	-2	-13	1	-0.5
1891	Cle-N	17	22	.436	44	40	35	1	0	348^2	407	10	119	79	13.8	4.13	84	.281	.338	23	.163	1	-30	-26	2	-2.0
Total	5	61	78	.439	151	139	129	5	1	1239^1	1328	42	479	346	13.4	3.67	99	.264	.332	83	.170	5	1	-7	3	0.0
● **KEN GRUNDT**	Grundt, Kenneth Allan b: 8/26/69, Melrose Park, Ill. BL/TL, 6'4", 195 lbs. Deb: 8/8/96																									
1996	Bos-A	0	0	—	1	0	0	0	0	0^1	1	0	0	0	27.0	27.00	19	.500	.500	0	—	0	-1	-1	0	-0.1
1997	Bos-A	0	0	—	2	0	0	0	0	3	5	0	0	0	15.0	9.00	51	.357	.357	0	—	0	-1	-1	0	0.0
Total	2	0	0	—	3	0	0	0	0	3^1	6	0	0	0	16.2	10.80	43	.375	.375	0	—	0	-2	-2	0	-0.1
● **AL GRUNWALD**	Grunwald, Alfred Henry "Stretch" b: 2/13/30, Los Angeles, Cal. BL/TL, 6'4", 210 lbs. Deb: 4/18/55																									
1955	Pit-N	0	0	—	3	0	0	0	0	7^2	7	1	7	2	16.4	4.70	88	.241	.389	2	.500	1	-1	-0	0	0.1
1959	KC-A	0	1	.000	6	1	0	0	1	11^1	18	1	11	9	23.0	7.94	50	.360	.475	0	.000	-1	-5	-5	0	-0.5
Total	2	0	1	.000	9	1	0	0	1	19	25	2	18	11	20.4	6.63	61	.316	.443	2	.250	0	-6	-5	-0	-0.4
● **MIKE GRZANICH**	Grzanich, Michael Edward b: 8/24/72, Canton, Ill. BR/TR, 6'1", 180 lbs. Deb: 5/14/98																									
1998	Hou-N	0	0	—	1	0	0	0	0	1	1	0	2	1	27.0	18.00	23	.333	.600	0	—	0	-2	-2	0	0.0
● **JOE GRZENDA**	Grzenda, Joseph Charles b: 6/8/37, Scranton, Pa. BR/TL, 6'2", 180 lbs. Deb: 4/26/61																									
1961	Det-A	1	0	1.000	4	0	0	0	0	5^2	9	2	2	0	17.5	7.94	52	.375	.423	1	1.000	0	-2	-2	0	-0.3
1964	KC-A	0	2	.000	20	0	0	0	0	25	34	2	13	17	17.3	5.40	71	.324	.403	0	.000	-0	-5	-4	1	-0.2
1966	KC-A	0	2	.000	21	0	0	0	0	22	28	1	12	14	16.4	3.27	104	.337	.421	0	.000	-0	0	0	1	0.1
1967	NY-N	0	0	—	11	0	0	0	0	16^2	14	0	8	9	12.4	2.16	157	.237	.338	0	.000	-0	2	2	-1	-0.1
1969	*Min-A	4	1	.800	38	0	0	0	3	48^2	52	4	17	24	12.9	3.88	94	.281	.345	0	.000	0	-1	-1	1	0.0
1970	Was-A	3	6	.333	49	3	0	0	6	84^2	86	8	34	38	13.1	5.00	71	.267	.343	0	.000	-1	-12	-14	0	-1.6
1971	Was-A	5	2	.714	46	0	0	0	5	70^1	54	2	17	56	9.2	1.92	172	.217	.270	1	.143	-0	12	11	-0	1.2
1972	StL-N	1	0	1.000	30	0	0	0	0	35	46	1	17	15	17.0	5.66	60	.326	.410	0	.000	-0	-9	-9	0	-0.2
Total	8	14	13	.519	219	3	0	0	14	308	323	20	120	173	13.2	4.00	88	.277	.349	2	.067	-2	-15	-17	3	-1.1
● **CECILIO GUANTE**	Guante, Cecilio (Magallane) b: 2/1/60, Villa Mella, D.R. BR/TR, 6'3", 205 lbs. Deb: 5/1/82																									
1982	Pit-N	0	0	—	10	0	0	0	0	27	28	1	5	26	11.7	3.33	111	.264	.310	0	.000	-1	1	1	-0	-0.1
1983	Pit-N	2	6	.250	49	0	0	0	9	100^1	90	5	46	82	12.4	3.32	112	.241	.327	2	.091	-1	3	4	-1	0.2
1984	Pit-N	2	3	.400	27	0	0	0	2	41^1	32	3	16	30	10.9	2.61	138	.224	.311	0	.000	-0	4	5	-1	0.5
1985	Pit-N	4	6	.400	63	0	0	0	5	109	84	5	40	92	10.7	2.72	131	.214	.295	1	.059	-1	10	10	-1	0.8
1986	Pit-N	5	2	.714	52	0	0	0	4	78	65	11	29	63	11.2	3.35	115	.225	.302	0	.000	-0	3	4	-2	0.2
1987	NY-A	3	2	.600	23	0	0	0	1	44	42	8	20	46	12.9	5.73	77	.247	.330	0	—	0	-6	-7	-1	-0.7
1988	NY-A	5	6	.455	56	0	0	0	11	75	59	10	22	61	10.3	2.88	137	.213	.283	0	—	0	9	9	-2	1.3
	Tex-A	0	0	—	7	0	0	0	1	4^2	8	1	4	4	23.1	1.93	212	.400	.500	0	—	0	1	1	-0	-0.1
	Yr	5	6	.455	63	0	0	0	12	79^2	67	11	26	65	10.5	2.82	140	.221	.283	0	—	0	10	10	-2	1.2
1989	Tex-A	6	6	.500	50	0	0	0	2	69	66	7	36	69	13.8	3.91	101	.249	.348	0	—	0	-0	0	-1	-0.1
1990	Cle-A	2	3	.400	26	1	0	0	0	46^2	38	10	18	30	11.4	5.01	78	.220	.304	0	—	0	-6	-6	0	-0.5
Total	9	29	34	.460	363	1	0	0	35	595	512	61	236	503	11.7	3.48	110	.232	.313	3	.061	-3	20	23	-8	1.5
● **EDDIE GUARDADO**	Guardado, Edward Adrian b: 10/2/70, Stockton, Cal. BR/TL, 6', 193 lbs. Deb: 6/13/93																									
1993	Min-A	3	8	.273	19	16	0	0	0	94^2	123	13	36	46	15.2	6.18	70	.319	.379	0	—	0	-20	-19	-1	-1.9

YEAR	TM/L	W	L	PCT	G	GS	CG	SH	SV	IP	H	HR	BB	SO	RAT	ERA	ERA+	OAV	OOB	BH	AVG	PB	PR	/A	PD	TPI
1994	Min-A	0	2	.000	4	4	0	0	0	17	26	3	4	8	15.9	8.47	57	.351	.385	0	—	0	-7	-7	-1	-0.7
1995	Min-A	4	9	.308	51	5	0	0	2	91^1	99	13	45	71	14.2	5.12	93	.280	.361	0	—	0	-4	-4	-1	-0.6
1996	Min-A	6	5	.545	**83**	0	0	0	4	73^2	61	12	33	74	11.9	5.25	97	.228	.320	0	—	0	-2	-1	-0	-0.3
1997	Min-A	0	4	.000	69	0	0	0	1	46	45	7	17	54	12.5	3.91	119	.251	.323	0	—	0	3	4	0	0.3
1998	Min-A	3	1	.750	79	0	0	0	0	65^2	66	10	28	53	12.9	4.52	104	.265	.339	0	—	0	1	1	-1	0.0
Total	6	16	29	.356	305	25	0	0	7	388^1	420	58	163	306	13.7	5.31	89	.279	.351	0	—	0	-29	-26	-3	-3.2

● MARK GUBICZA

Gubicza, Mark Steven b: 8/14/62, Philadelphia, Pa. BR/TR, 6'5", 220 lbs. Deb: 4/6/84

YEAR	TM/L	W	L	PCT	G	GS	CG	SH	SV	IP	H	HR	BB	SO	RAT	ERA	ERA+	OAV	OOB	BH	AVG	PB	PR	/A	PD	TPI
1984	KC-A	10	14	.417	29	29	4	2	0	189	172	13	75	111	12.0	4.05	99	.243	.320	0	—	0	-1	-0	2	0.1
1985	*KC-A	14	10	.583	29	28	0	0	0	177^1	160	14	77	99	12.3	4.06	102	.238	.321	0	—	0	2	2	2	0.4
1986	KC-A	12	6	.667	35	24	3	2	0	180^2	155	8	84	118	12.2	3.64	117	.233	.324	0	—	0	11	12	3	1.3
1987	KC-A	13	18	.419	35	35	10	2	0	241^2	231	18	120	166	13.3	3.98	114	.259	.350	0	—	0	13	15	4	2.0
1988	KC-A★	20	8	.714	35	35	8	4	0	269^2	237	11	83	183	10.9	2.70	147	.234	.296	0	—	0	38	38	3	4.2
1989	KC-A★	15	11	.577	36	36	8	2	0	255	252	10	63	173	11.3	3.04	127	.259	.307	0	—	0	24	23	2	2.5
1990	KC-A	4	7	.364	16	16	2	0	0	94	101	5	38	71	13.7	4.50	85	.283	.358	0	—	0	-6	-7	0	-0.6
1991	KC-A	9	12	.429	26	26	0	0	0	133	168	10	42	89	14.6	5.68	72	.308	.364	0	—	0	-23	-23	2	-2.9
1992	KC-A	7	6	.538	18	18	2	1	0	111^1	110	8	36	81	11.9	3.72	109	.259	.318	0	—	0	3	4	0	0.3
1993	KC-A	5	8	.385	49	6	0	0	2	104^1	128	2	43	80	14.9	4.66	98	.307	.374	0	—	0	-4	-1	-1	-0.2
1994	KC-A	7	9	.438	22	22	0	0	0	130	158	11	26	59	12.7	4.50	111	.301	.334	0	—	0	4	7	1	0.6
1995	KC-A	12	14	.462	33	33	3	2	0	213^1	222	21	62	81	12.2	3.75	127	.272	.328	0	—	0	23	24	2	2.8
1996	KC-A	4	12	.250	19	19	2	1	0	119^1	132	22	34	55	13.0	5.13	98	.284	.343	0	—	0	-2	-2	0	-0.1
1997	Ana-A	0	1	.000	2	2	0	0	0	4^2	13	2	3	5	30.9	25.07	18	.481	.533	0	—	0	-11	-11	0	-1.4
Total	14	132	136	.493	384	329	42	16	2	2223^1	2239	155	786	1371	12.5	3.96	108	.264	.330	0	—	0	69	82	21	9.0

● MARV GUDAT

Gudat, Marvin John b: 8/27/05, Goliad, Tex. d: 3/1/54, Los Angeles, Cal. BL/TL, 5'11", 162 lbs. Deb: 5/21/29 ♦

YEAR	TM/L	W	L	PCT	G	GS	CG	SH	SV	IP	H	HR	BB	SO	RAT	ERA	ERA+	OAV	OOB	BH	AVG	PB	PR	/A	PD	TPI
1929	Cin-N	1	1	.500	7	2	2	0	0	26^2	29	0	4	0	11.1	3.38	135	.282	.308	2	.200	-0	4	4	-1	0.1
1932	*Chi-N	0	0	—	1	0	0	0	0	1	1	0	0	2	9.0	0.00	—	.250	.250	24	.255	0	0	0	0	0.0
Total	2	1	1	.500	8	2	2	0	0	27^2	30	0	4	2	11.1	3.25	139	.280	.306	26	.250	-0	4	4	-1	0.1

● WHITEY GUESE

Guese, Theodore b: 1/24/1872, New Bremen, Ohio d: 4/8/51, Wapakoneta, Ohio BR/TR, 6'0.5", 200 lbs. Deb: 7/13/01

YEAR	TM/L	W	L	PCT	G	GS	CG	SH	SV	IP	H	HR	BB	SO	RAT	ERA	ERA+	OAV	OOB	BH	AVG	PB	PR	/A	PD	TPI
1901	Cin-N	1	4	.200	6	5	4	0	0	44^1	62	5	14	11	16.0	6.09	53	.328	.383	3	.200	1	-14	-14	-2	-1.3

● LEE GUETTERMAN

Guetterman, Arthur Lee b: 11/22/58, Chattanooga, Tenn. BL/TL, 6'8", 227 lbs. Deb: 9/12/84

YEAR	TM/L	W	L	PCT	G	GS	CG	SH	SV	IP	H	HR	BB	SO	RAT	ERA	ERA+	OAV	OOB	BH	AVG	PB	PR	/A	PD	TPI
1984	Sea-A	0	0	—	3	0	0	0	0	4^1	9	0	2	2	22.8	4.15	96	.450	.500	0	—	0	-0	-0	0	0.0
1986	Sea-A	0	4	.000	41	4	1	0	0	76	108	7	30	38	16.8	7.34	58	.347	.412	0	—	0	-27	-26	0	-1.2
1987	Sea-A	11	4	.733	25	17	2	1	0	113^1	117	13	35	42	12.2	3.81	124	.267	.324	0	—	0	8	11	1	1.2
1988	NY-A	1	2	.333	20	2	0	0	0	40^2	49	2	14	15	14.2	4.65	85	.306	.366	0	—	0	-3	-3	-0	-0.2
1989	NY-A	5	5	.500	70	0	0	0	13	103	98	6	26	51	10.8	2.45	158	.258	.305	0	—	0	16	16	2	2.1
1990	NY-A	11	7	.611	64	0	0	0	2	93	80	6	26	48	10.3	3.39	117	.236	.290	0	—	0	5	6	1	1.2
1991	NY-A	3	4	.429	64	0	0	0	6	88	91	6	25	35	12.2	3.68	112	.268	.323	0	—	0	4	4	0	0.4
1992	NY-A	1	1	.500	15	0	0	0	0	22^2	35	5	13	5	19.1	9.53	41	.354	.429	0	—	0	-14	-14	0	-1.0
	NY-N	3	4	.429	43	0	0	0	2	43^1	57	5	14	15	15.0	5.82	60	.324	.377	0	.000	-0	-11	-11	-1	-1.9
1993	StL-N	3	3	.500	40	0	0	0	1	46	41	1	16	19	11.5	2.93	135	.240	.312	1	.500	1	6	5	-1	0.6
1995	Sea-A	0	0	—	23	0	0	0	0	17	21	1	11	11	18.5	6.88	69	.300	.417	0	—	0	-4	-4	1	0.0
1996	Sea-A	0	2	.000	17	0	0	0	0	11	11	0	10	6	17.2	4.09	121	.275	.420	0	—	0	1	1	0	0.2
Total	11	38	36	.514	425	23	3	1	25	658^1	717	52	222	287	13.1	4.33	95	.282	.343	1	.250	0	-19	-15	4	1.4

● RON GUIDRY

Guidry, Ronald Ames b: 8/28/50, Lafayette, La. BL/TL, 5'11", 162 lbs. Deb: 7/27/75

YEAR	TM/L	W	L	PCT	G	GS	CG	SH	SV	IP	H	HR	BB	SO	RAT	ERA	ERA+	OAV	OOB	BH	AVG	PB	PR	/A	PD	TPI
1975	NY-A	0	1	.000	10	1	0	0	0	15^2	15	0	9	15	14.4	3.45	107	.259	.368	0	—	0	1	0	-1	0.0
1976	*NY-A	0	0	—	7	0	0	0	0	16	20	1	4	12	13.5	5.63	61	.294	.333	0	—	0	-4	-4	0	0.1
1977	*NY-A	16	7	.696	31	25	9	5	1	210^2	174	12	65	176	10.2	2.82	140	.224	.284	0	—	0	29	26	-1	2.6
1978	*NY-A★	**25**	3	**.893**	35	35	16	**9**	0	273^2	187	13	72	248	**8.6**	**1.74**	**208**	**.193**	**.250**	0	—	0	**61**	**57**	2	**6.2**
1979	*NY-A★	18	8	.692	33	30	15	2	2	236^1	203	20	71	201	10.4	**2.78**	146	.236	.294	0	—	0	38	34	-0	3.5
1980	*NY-A	17	10	.630	37	29	5	3	1	219^2	215	19	80	166	12.1	3.56	110	.260	.326	0	—	0	11	9	2	1.3
1981	*NY-A	11	5	.688	23	21	0	0	0	127	100	12	26	104	**9.0**	2.76	129	.214	**.257**	0	—	0	13	11	1	1.5
1982	NY-A☆	14	8	.636	34	33	6	1	0	222	216	22	69	162	11.6	3.81	105	.254	.311	0	—	0	6	4	-2	0.2
1983	NY-A†	21	9	.700	31	31	**21**	3	0	250^1	232	26	60	156	10.6	3.42	114	.244	.291	0	—	0	18	13	-0	1.4
1984	NY-A	10	11	.476	29	28	5	1	0	195^2	223	24	44	127	12.4	4.51	84	.287	.327	0	—	0	-11	-16	-0	-1.5
1985	NY-A	**22**	6	**.786**	34	33	11	2	0	259	243	28	42	143	9.9	3.27	122	.248	.279	0	—	0	25	21	-1	2.0
1986	NY-A	9	12	.429	30	30	5	0	0	192^1	202	28	38	140	11.3	3.98	103	.265	.301	0	—	0	4	2	-1	0.1
1987	NY-A	5	8	.385	22	17	2	0	0	117^2	111	14	38	96	11.5	3.67	119	.248	.308	0	—	0	10	9	-0	0.9
1988	NY-A	2	3	.400	12	10	0	0	0	56	57	7	15	32	11.9	4.18	94	.259	.312	0	—	0	-1	-1	-0	-0.1
Total	14	170	91	.651	368	323	95	26	4	2392	2198	226	633	1778	10.7	3.29	119	.244	.294	0	—	0	201	167	-3	18.2

● SKIP GUINN

Guinn, Drannon Eugene b: 10/25/44, St.Charles, Mo. BR/TL, 5'10", 180 lbs. Deb: 5/7/68

YEAR	TM/L	W	L	PCT	G	GS	CG	SH	SV	IP	H	HR	BB	SO	RAT	ERA	ERA+	OAV	OOB	BH	AVG	PB	PR	/A	PD	TPI
1968	Atl-N	0	0	—	3	0	0	0	0	5	3	0	3	4	10.8	3.60	83	.167	.286	0	—	0	-0	-0	-0	0.0
1969	Hou-N	1	2	.333	28	0	0	0	0	27	34	3	21	33	18.7	6.67	53	.304	.418	0	.000	-0	-9	-9	-0	-1.0
1971	Hou-N	0	0	—	4	0	0	0	1	4^2	1	0	3	3	7.7	0.00	—	.067	.222	0	—	0	2	2	-0	0.1
Total	3	1	2	.333	35	0	0	0	1	36^2	38	3	27	40	16.2	5.40	64	.262	.382	0	.000	-0	-8	-8	-0	-0.9

● LEFTY GUISE

Guise, Witt Orison b: 9/18/09, Driggs, Ark. d: 8/13/68, Little Rock, Ark. BL/TL, 6'2", 172 lbs. Deb: 9/13/40

YEAR	TM/L	W	L	PCT	G	GS	CG	SH	SV	IP	H	HR	BB	SO	RAT	ERA	ERA+	OAV	OOB	BH	AVG	PB	PR	/A	PD	TPI
1940	Cin-N	0	0	—	2	0	0	0	0	7^2	8	0	5	1	16.4	1.17	323	.296	.424	1	.333	0	2	2	0	0.0

● DON GULLETT

Gullett, Donald Edward b: 1/6/51, Lynn, Ky. BR/TL, 6', 190 lbs. Deb: 4/10/70 C

YEAR	TM/L	W	L	PCT	G	GS	CG	SH	SV	IP	H	HR	BB	SO	RAT	ERA	ERA+	OAV	OOB	BH	AVG	PB	PR	/A	PD	TPI
1970	*Cin-N	5	2	.714	44	2	0	0	6	77^2	54	4	44	76	11.4	2.43	166	.196	.306	4	.211	1	14	14	-1	1.4
1971	Cin-N	16	6	**.727**	35	31	4	3	0	217^2	196	14	64	107	10.8	2.65	127	.242	.299	9	.120	-2	20	17	-2	1.2
1972	*Cin-N	9	10	.474	31	16	2	0	2	134^2	127	15	43	96	11.4	3.94	81	.250	.309	8	.211	2	-7	-11	-2	-1.5
1973	*Cin-N	18	8	.692	45	30	7	4	2	228^1	198	24	69	153	10.6	3.51	97	.232	.292	12	.188	3	4	-3	-0	0.0
1974	Cin-N	17	11	.607	36	35	10	3	0	243	201	22	88	183	10.8	3.04	115	.222	.292	19	.237	4	16	12	-0	1.7
1975	*Cin-N	15	4	**.789**	22	22	8	3	0	159^2	127	11	56	98	10.4	2.42	148	.218	.289	14	.226	3	21	21	-1	2.6
1976	*Cin-N	11	3	.786	23	20	4	0	1	126	119	8	48	64	11.9	3.00	117	.253	.322	8	.182	-0	7	7	-0	0.8
1977	*NY-A	14	4	.778	22	22	7	1	0	158^1	137	14	69	116	11.8	3.58	110	.232	.314	0	—	0	8	6	-2	0.5
1978	NY-A	4	2	.667	8	8	2	0	0	44^2	46	3	20	28	13.5	3.63	100	.269	.349	0	—	0	1	-0	0	0.0
Total	9	109	50	.686	266	186	44	14	11	1390	1205	115	501	921	11.1	3.11	113	.233	.302	74	.194	10	83	63	-8	6.7

● BILL GULLICKSON

Gullickson, William Lee b: 2/20/59, Marshall, Minn. BR/TR, 6'3", 215 lbs. Deb: 9/26/79

YEAR	TM/L	W	L	PCT	G	GS	CG	SH	SV	IP	H	HR	BB	SO	RAT	ERA	ERA+	OAV	OOB	BH	AVG	PB	PR	/A	PD	TPI
1979	Mon-N	0	0	—	1	0	0	0	0	1	2	0	0	0	18.0	0.00	—	.500	.500	0	—	0	0	0	0	0.0
1980	Mon-N	10	5	.667	24	19	5	2	0	141	127	6	50	120	11.4	3.00	119	.238	.305	7	.175	0	9	9	0	1.0
1981	*Mon-N	7	9	.438	22	22	3	2	0	157^1	142	3	34	115	10.3	2.80	125	.239	.284	7	.152	0	12	12	-1	1.1
1982	Mon-N	12	14	.462	34	34	6	0	0	236^2	231	25	61	155	11.3	3.57	102	.254	.304	10	.122	-2	1	2	-4	-0.4
1983	Mon-N	17	12	.586	34	34	10	1	0	242^1	230	19	59	120	10.9	3.75	96	.251	.299	11	.134	1	-3	-4	-1	-0.5
1984	Mon-N	12	9	.571	32	32	3	0	0	226^2	230	27	37	100	10.6	3.61	95	.265	.295	8	.110	-2	-1	-5	-4	-1.1
1985	Mon-N	14	12	.538	29	29	4	1	0	181^1	187	8	47	68	11.7	3.52	96	.271	.318	12	.188	2	1	-3	-1	-0.3
1986	Cin-N	15	12	.556	37	37	6	2	0	244^2	245	24	60	121	11.3	3.38	114	.264	.310	6	.076	-4	9	13	-2	0.7
1987	Cin-N	10	11	.476	27	27	3	1	0	165	172	33	39	89	11.6	4.85	87	.267	.310	11	.208	2	-14	-11	-2	-1.2
	NY-A	4	2	.667	8	8	1	0	0	48	46	7	11	28	10.9	4.88	90	.253	.299	0	—	0	-2	-3	-1	-0.2
1990	Hou-N	10	14	.417	32	32	2	1	0	193^1	221	21	61	73	13.2	3.82	97	.287	.341	9	.158	2	-1	-2	-3	-0.4
1991	Det-A	**20**	9	.690	35	35	4	0	0	226^1	256	22	44	91	12.1	3.90	107	.288	.324	0	—	0	5	6	-3	0.5
1992	Det-A	14	13	.519	34	34	4	1	0	221^2	228	35	50	64	11.3	4.34	91	.267	.308	0	—	0	-10	-10	-0	-1.1
1993	Det-A	13	9	.591	28	28	2	0	0	159^1	186	28	44	70	13.2	5.37	80	.291	.340	0	—	0	-19	-19	0	-2.1

YEAR	TM/L	W	L	PCT	G	GS	CG	SH	SV	IP	H	HR	BB	SO	RAT	ERA	ERA+	OAV	OOB	BH	AVG	PB	PR	/A	PD	TPI
1994	Det-A	4	5	.444	21	19	1	0	0	115^1	156	24	25	65	14.4	5.93	82	.322	.361	0	—	0	-14	-14	1	-0.9
Total	14	162	136	.544	398	390	54	11	0	2560	2659	282	622	1279	11.7	3.93	97	.268	.314	81	.141	-1	-26	-29	-20	-4.9

● AD GUMBERT Gumbert, Addison Courtney b: 10/10/1868, Pittsburgh, Pa. d: 4/23/25, Pittsburgh, Pa. BR/TR, 5′10″, 200 lbs. Deb: 9/15/1888 F

YEAR	TM/L	W	L	PCT	G	GS	CG	SH	SV	IP	H	HR	BB	SO	RAT	ERA	ERA+	OAV	OOB	BH	AVG	PB	PR	/A	PD	TPI
1888	Chi-N	3	3	.500	6	6	5	0	0	48^2	44	0	10	16	10.9	3.14	96	.234	.291	8	.333	2	-2	-1	-1	0.0
1889	Chi-N	16	13	.552	31	28	25	2	0	246^1	258	16	76	91	12.7	3.62	115	.261	.323	44	.288	11	11	15	-1	2.2
1890	Bos-P	23	12	.657	39	33	27	1	0	277^1	338	18	86	81	14.1	3.96	111	.288	.342	35	.241	5	8	14	2	1.7
1891	Chi-N	17	11	.607	32	31	24	1	0	256^1	282	5	90	73	13.4	3.58	93	.269	.332	32	.305	12	-7	-7	1	0.6
1892	Chi-N	22	19	.537	46	45	39	0	0	382^2	399	11	107	118	12.2	3.41	97	.258	.312	42	.236	4	-5	-4	1	0.1
1893	Pit-N	11	7	.611	22	20	16	2	0	162^2	207	5	78	40	16.0	5.15	88	.301	.376	21	.221	1	-9	-11	-2	-0.9
1894	Pit-N	15	14	.517	37	31	26	0	0	269	372	13	84	65	15.5	6.02	87	.324	.373	33	.292	5	-21	-23	1	-1.3
1895	Bro-N	11	16	.407	33	26	20	0	1	234	288	11	69	45	14.2	5.08	87	.298	.352	35	.361	11	-8	-18	-1	-0.7
1896	Bro-N	0	4	.000	5	4	2	0	0	31	34	2	11	3	13.1	3.77	109	.276	.336	2	.182	-0	2	1	1	0.2
	Phi-N	5	3	.625	11	10	7	1	0	77^1	99	0	23	14	14.7	4.54	95	.308	.362	9	.265	1	-2	-2	-1	-0.1
	Yr	5	7	.417	16	14	9	1	0	108^1	133	2	34	17	14.2	4.32	99	.300	.355	11	.244	1	1	-1	0	0.1
Total	9	123	102	.547	262	234	191	7	1	1985^1	2321	81	634	546	13.8	4.27	97	.283	.341	261	.273	52	-31	-33	1	1.8

● HARRY GUMBERT Gumbert, Harry Edward "Gunboat" b: 11/5/09, Elizabeth, Pa. d: 1/4/95, Wimberley, Tex. BR/TR, 6′2″, 185 lbs. Deb: 9/12/35

YEAR	TM/L	W	L	PCT	G	GS	CG	SH	SV	IP	H	HR	BB	SO	RAT	ERA	ERA+	OAV	OOB	BH	AVG	PB	PR	/A	PD	TPI
1935	NY-N	1	2	.333	6	3	1	0	0	23^2	35	1	10	11	17.1	6.08	63	.330	.388	0	.000	-1	-5	-6	-0	-0.7
1936	*NY-N	11	3	.786	39	15	3	0	0	140^2	157	7	54	52	13.6	3.90	100	.281	.346	11	.250	2	2	-0	3	0.5
1937	*NY-N	10	11	.476	34	24	10	1	1	200^1	194	11	62	65	11.7	3.68	106	.257	.317	13	.181	-1	5	5	8	1.1
1938	NY-N	15	13	.536	38	33	14	1	0	235^2	238	13	84	84	12.6	4.01	94	.261	.328	13	.155	-3	-6	-6	8	-0.2
1939	NY-N	18	11	.621	36	34	14	2	0	243^2	257	21	81	81	12.5	4.32	91	.271	.329	18	.200	-0	-11	-11	6	-0.5
1940	NY-N	12	14	.462	35	30	14	2	2	237	230	17	81	77	11.9	3.76	103	.252	.316	17	.195	2	2	3	4	0.9
1941	NY-N	1	1	.500	5	5	1	0	0	32^1	34	3	18	9	14.5	4.45	83	.266	.356	2	.167	-0	-3	-3	1	-0.1
	StL-N	11	5	.688	33	17	8	3	1	144^1	139	7	30	53	10.6	2.74	137	.251	.291	17	.321	6	14	16	4	2.7
	Yr	12	6	.667	38	22	9	3	1	176^2	173	10	48	62	11.3	3.06	123	.254	.304	19	.292	5	11	14	4	2.6
1942	*StL-N	9	5	.643	38	19	5	0	5	163	156	3	59	52	11.9	3.26	105	.250	.315	6	.111	-2	1	3	5	0.5
1943	StL-N	10	5	.667	21	19	7	3	0	133	115	4	32	40	9.9	2.84	118	.237	.284	7	.156	-2	8	8	2	0.8
1944	StL-N	4	2	.667	10	7	3	0	1	61^1	60	1	19	16	11.6	2.49	141	.258	.313	4	.190	-0	8	7	1	0.8
	Cin-N	10	8	.556	24	19	11	2	2	155^1	157	7	40	40	11.5	3.30	106	.262	.310	5	.096	-2	5	3	2	0.4
	Yr	14	10	.583	34	26	14	2	3	216^2	217	8	59	56	11.5	3.07	114	.261	.311	9	.123	-2	13	10	3	1.2
1946	Cin-N	6	8	.429	36	10	5	0	4	119	112	8	42	44	11.7	3.25	103	.248	.314	8	.250	1	2	1	1	0.4
1947	Cin-N	10	10	.500	46	0	0	0	10	90^1	88	3	47	43	13.5	3.89	106	.260	.351	6	.273	1	2	2	0	0.6
1948	Cin-N	10	8	.556	**61**	0	0	0	**17**	106^1	123	5	34	25	13.3	3.47	113	.291	.344	1	.040	-1	6	5	4	1.2
1949	Cin-N	4	3	.571	29	0	0	0	2	40^2	58	5	8	12	14.8	5.53	76	.341	.374	0	.000	-0	-7	-6	1	-0.9
	Pit-N	1	4	.200	16	0	0	0	3	27^2	30	5	18	5	15.6	5.86	72	.270	.372	1	.250	0	-6	-5	1	-0.8
	Yr	5	7	.417	45	0	0	0	5	68^1	88	10	26	17	15.0	5.66	74	.312	.370	1	.167	-0	-12	-11	2	-1.7
1950	Pit-N	0	0	—	1	0	0	0	0	1^2	3	0	2	0	27.0	5.40	81	.333	.455	1	1.000	0	-0	-0	0	0.1
Total	15	143	113	.559	508	235	96	14	48	2156	2186	121	721	709	12.2	3.68	102	.263	.323	130	.184	-2	18	17	50	6.8

● BILLY GUMBERT Gumbert, William Skeen b: 8/8/1865, Pittsburgh, Pa. d: 4/13/46, Pittsburgh, Pa. BR/TR, 6′1.5″, 200 lbs. Deb: 6/19/1890 F

YEAR	TM/L	W	L	PCT	G	GS	CG	SH	SV	IP	H	HR	BB	SO	RAT	ERA	ERA+	OAV	OOB	BH	AVG	PB	PR	/A	PD	TPI
1890	Pit-N	4	6	.400	10	10	8	0	0	79^1	96	0	31	18	15.3	5.22	63	.290	.365	9	.243	3	-15	-17	1	-1.3
1892	Pit-N	3	2	.600	6	3	2	0	0	39^2	30	0	23	3	12.3	1.36	242	.201	.312	2	.111	-1	8	9	-1	0.8
1893	Lou-N	0	0	—	1	1	0	0	0	0^2	2	0	5	0	94.5	27.00	16	.500	.778	1	1.000	1	-2	-2	-0	0.1
Total	3	7	8	.467	17	14	10	0	0	119^2	128	0	59	21	14.7	4.06	81	.264	.355	12	.214	3	-8	-10	-1	-0.4

● DAVE GUMPERT Gumpert, David Lawrence b: 5/5/58, South Haven, Mich. BR/TR, 6′1″, 190 lbs. Deb: 7/25/82

YEAR	TM/L	W	L	PCT	G	GS	CG	SH	SV	IP	H	HR	BB	SO	RAT	ERA	ERA+	OAV	OOB	BH	AVG	PB	PR	/A	PD	TPI
1982	Det-A	0	0	—	5	1	0	0	1	2	7	1	2	0	40.5	27.00	15	.700	.750	0	—	0	-5	-5	-0	-0.5
1983	Det-A	0	2	.000	26	0	0	0	2	44^1	43	1	7	14	10.2	2.64	148	.257	.287	0	—	0	7	6	-1	0.2
1985	Chi-N	1	0	1.000	9	0	0	0	0	10^1	12	0	7	4	16.5	3.48	115	.279	.380	0	.000	-0	0	1	-0	0.0
1986	Chi-N	2	0	1.000	38	0	0	0	2	59^2	60	4	28	45	13.4	4.37	92	.267	.350	0	.000	-1	-4	-2	-1	-0.2
1987	KC-A	0	0	—	8	0	0	0	0	19^1	27	3	6	13	15.4	6.05	75	.333	.379	0	—	0	-3	-3	0	-0.1
Total	5	3	2	.600	86	1	0	0	5	135^2	149	9	50	76	13.3	4.31	95	.283	.347	0	.000	-1	-6	-4	-2	-0.6

● RANDY GUMPERT Gumpert, Randall Pennington b: 1/23/18, Monocacy, Pa. BR/TR, 6′3″, 205 lbs. Deb: 6/13/36

YEAR	TM/L	W	L	PCT	G	GS	CG	SH	SV	IP	H	HR	BB	SO	RAT	ERA	ERA+	OAV	OOB	BH	AVG	PB	PR	/A	PD	TPI
1936	Phi-A	1	2	.333	22	3	2	0	2	62^1	74	2	32	9	15.3	4.76	107	.295	.375	6	.273	0	2	**2**	-1	0.1
1937	Phi-A	0	0	—	10	1	0	0	0	12	16	1	15	5	24.0	12.00	39	.333	.500	1	.333	0	-10	-10	0	0.0
1938	Phi-A	0	2	.000	4	2	0	0	0	12^1	24	1	10	1	24.8	10.95	44	.393	.479	1	.250	0	-8	-8	1	-0.9
1946	NY-A	11	3	.786	33	12	4	0	1	132^2	113	8	32	63	9.8	2.31	150	.229	.276	6	.128	-2	18	17	-1	1.4
1947	NY-A	4	1	.800	24	6	2	0	0	56^1	71	4	28	25	15.8	5.43	65	.311	.387	1	.071	-1	-11	-12	0	-1.1
1948	NY-A	1	0	1.000	15	0	0	0	0	25	27	0	6	12	12.2	2.88	142	.267	.315	0	—	0	4	3	0	0.1
	Chi-A	2	6	.250	16	11	6	1	0	97^1	103	6	13	31	10.9	3.79	112	.275	.303	4	.138	-2	5	5	-1	0.1
	Yr	3	6	.333	31	11	6	1	0	122^1	130	6	19	43	11.1	3.60	117	.273	.303	4	.138	-2	9	8	-1	0.2
1949	Chi-A	13	16	.448	34	32	18	3	1	234	223	22	83	78	11.8	3.81	110	.253	.318	16	.190	-1	10	9	1	1.0
1950	Chi-A	5	12	.294	40	17	6	1	0	155^1	165	15	58	48	13.2	4.75	94	.275	.343	3	.071	-4	-3	-5	-0	-0.8
1951	Chi-A☆	9	8	.529	33	16	7	1	2	141^2	156	20	34	45	12.1	4.32	93	.272	.314	15	.333	3	-3	-4	-3	-0.5
1952	Bos-A	1	0	1.000	10	1	0	0	1	19^2	15	1	5	6	9.6	4.12	96	.205	.266	0	.000	-1	-1	-0	-0	-0.1
	Was-A	4	9	.308	20	12	2	0	0	104	112	12	30	29	12.7	4.24	84	.273	.330	7	.206	0	-7	-8	-1	-0.9
	Yr	5	9	.357	30	13	2	0	1	123^2	127	13	35	35	12.2	4.22	86	.262	.318	7	.179	-0	-8	-8	-1	-1.0
Total	10	51	59	.464	261	113	47	6	7	1052^2	1099	92	346	352	12.5	4.17	98	.268	.328	60	.182	-8	-4	-10	-5	-1.6

● ERIC GUNDERSON Gunderson, Eric Andrew b: 3/29/66, Portland, Ore. BR/TL, 6′, 195 lbs. Deb: 4/11/90

YEAR	TM/L	W	L	PCT	G	GS	CG	SH	SV	IP	H	HR	BB	SO	RAT	ERA	ERA+	OAV	OOB	BH	AVG	PB	PR	/A	PD	TPI
1990	SF-N	1	2	.333	7	4	0	0	0	19^2	24	2	11	14	16.0	5.49	66	.293	.376	0	.000	-1	-4	-4	0	-0.6
1991	SF-N	0	0	—	2	0	0	0	1	3^1	6	0	1	2	18.9	5.40	66	.353	.389	0	—	0	-1	-1	0	0.0
1992	Sea-A	2	1	.667	9	0	0	0	0	9^1	12	1	5	2	17.4	8.68	46	.324	.419	0	—	0	-5	-5	0	-1.3
1994	NY-N	0	0	—	14	0	0	0	0	9	5	0	4	4	9.0	0.00	—	.185	.290	0	—	0	4	4	-0	0.0
1995	NY-N	1	1	.500	30	0	0	0	0	24^1	25	2	8	19	12.6	3.70	109	.269	.333	0	—	0	1	1	1	0.1
	Bos-A	2	1	.667	19	0	0	0	0	12^1	13	0	9	9	17.5	5.11	95	.295	.436	0	—	0	-1	-0	0	-0.2
1996	Bos-A	0	1	.000	28	0	0	0	0	17^1	21	5	8	7	16.1	8.31	61	.300	.387	0	—	0	-6	-6	-1	-0.5
1997	Tex-A	2	1	.667	60	0	0	0	1	49^2	45	5	15	31	11.2	3.26	147	.241	.304	0	—	0	7	8	-1	0.0
1998	Tex-A	0	3	.000	68	1	0	0	0	67^2	88	13	19	41	14.4	5.19	93	.315	.361	0	—	0	-4	-3	0	-0.1
Total	8	8	10	.444	237	5	0	0	2	212^2	239	28	80	129	13.9	4.78	95	.286	.355	0	.000	-0	-8	-5	-0	-2.6

● RED GUNKEL Gunkel, Woodward William b: 4/15/1894, Sheffield, Ill. d: 4/19/54, Chicago, Ill. BB/TR, 5′8″, 158 lbs. Deb: 6/18/16

YEAR	TM/L	W	L	PCT	G	GS	CG	SH	SV	IP	H	HR	BB	SO	RAT	ERA	ERA+	OAV	OOB	BH	AVG	PB	PR	/A	PD	TPI
1916	Cle-A	0	0	—	1	0	0	0	0	1	0	0	1	1	18.0	0.00	—	.000	.500	0	—	0	0	0	-0	0.0

● LARRY GURA Gura, Lawrence Cyril b: 11/26/47, Joliet, Ill. BB/TL, 6′1″, 185 lbs. Deb: 4/30/70

YEAR	TM/L	W	L	PCT	G	GS	CG	SH	SV	IP	H	HR	BB	SO	RAT	ERA	ERA+	OAV	OOB	BH	AVG	PB	PR	/A	PD	TPI
1970	Chi-N	1	3	.250	20	3	1	0	1	38	35	6	23	21	14.0	3.79	119	.254	.364	0	.000	-1	1	3	0	0.2
1971	Chi-N	0	0	—	6	0	0	0	1	3	6	0	1	2	21.0	6.00	66	.400	.438	0	.000	-0	-1	-1	-0	-0.1
1972	Chi-N	0	0	—	7	0	0	0	0	12^1	11	3	3	13	10.2	3.65	104	.250	.298	0	.000	-0	-0	0	0	0.0
1973	Chi-N	2	4	.333	21	7	0	0	0	64^2	79	10	11	43	12.7	4.87	81	.296	.326	3	.200	0	-9	-7	1	-0.4
1974	NY-A	5	1	.833	8	8	4	2	0	56	54	2	12	17	10.6	2.41	146	.248	.287	0	—	0	8	7	-0	0.8
1975	NY-A	7	8	.467	26	20	5	0	0	151^1	173	13	41	65	12.9	3.51	105	.295	.344	0	—	0	5	3	-0	0.3
1976	*KC-A	4	0	1.000	20	2	1	1	1	62^2	47	4	20	22	9.8	2.30	152	.213	.281	0	—	0	9	8	1	0.6
1977	*KC-A	8	5	.615	52	6	1	1	10	106^1	108	8	28	46	11.6	3.13	129	.265	.314	0	—	0	11	11	0	1.4
1978	*KC-A	16	4	.800	35	26	8	2	0	221^2	183	13	60	81	10.0	2.72	141	.229	.286	0	—	0	26	27	2	2.6
1979	KC-A	13	12	.520	39	33	7	1	0	233^2	226	29	73	85	11.8	4.47	95	.253	.315	0	—	0	-7	-5	1	-0.5
1980	*KC-A☆	18	10	.643	36	36	16	4	0	283^1	272	20	76	113	11.2	2.95	137	.255	.307	0	—	0	34	35	1	3.3
1981	*KC-A	11	8	.579	23	23	12	2	0	172^1	139	11	35	61	9.3	2.72	133	.223	.269	0	—	0	18	17	0	1.9
1982	KC-A	18	12	.600	37	37	8	3	0	248	251	31	64	98	11.6	4.03	101	.261	.311	0	—	0	1	1	2	0.4

YEAR	TM/L	W	L	PCT	G	GS	CG	SH	SV	IP	H	HR	BB	SO	RAT	ERA	ERA+	OAV	OOB	BH	AVG	PB	PR	/A	PD	TPI
1983	KC-A	11	18	.379	34	31	5	0	0	200^1	220	23	76	57	13.7	4.90	83	.284	.354	0	—	0	-19	-18	3	-2.0
1984	KC-A	12	9	.571	31	25	3	0	0	168^2	175	26	67	68	13.1	5.18	78	.269	.341	0	—	0	-22	-22	1	-2.3
1985	KC-A	0	0	—	3	0	0	0	1	4^1	7	1	4	2	22.8	12.46	33	.368	.478	0	—	0	-4	-4	0	-0.2
	Chi-N	0	3	.000	5	4	0	0	0	20^1	34	4	6	7	18.1	8.41	47	.370	.414	0	.000	-0	-11	-10	0	-1.2
Total	16	126	97	.565	403	261	71	16	14	2047	2020	204	600	801	11.7	3.76	105	.260	.317	3	.091	-2	39	46	11	4.8

● CHARLIE GUTH

Guth, Charles J. b: 1856, Chicago, Ill. d: 7/5/1883, Cambridge, Mass. Deb: 9/30/1880

YEAR	TM/L	W	L	PCT	G	GS	CG	SH	SV	IP	H	HR	BB	SO	RAT	ERA	ERA+	OAV	OOB	BH	AVG	PB	PR	/A	PD	TPI
1880	Chi-N	1	0	1.000	1	1	1	0	0	9	12	0	1	7	13.0	5.00	48	.293	.310	1	.250	0	-3	-3	-0	-0.2

● MARK GUTHRIE

Guthrie, Mark Andrew b: 9/22/65, Buffalo, N.Y. BB/TL, 6′4″, 206 lbs. Deb: 7/25/89

YEAR	TM/L	W	L	PCT	G	GS	CG	SH	SV	IP	H	HR	BB	SO	RAT	ERA	ERA+	OAV	OOB	BH	AVG	PB	PR	/A	PD	TPI
1989	Min-A	2	4	.333	13	8	0	0	0	57^1	66	7	21	38	13.8	4.55	91	.292	.355	0	—	0	-4	-3	-0	-0.7
1990	Min-A	7	9	.438	24	21	3	1	0	144^2	154	8	39	101	12.1	3.79	109	.276	.325	0	—	0	2	6	1	0.2
1991	*Min-A	7	5	.583	41	12	0	0	2	98	116	11	41	72	14.5	4.32	99	.303	.372	0	—	0	-2	-1	-1	-0.1
1992	Min-A	2	3	.400	54	0	0	0	5	75	59	7	23	76	9.8	2.88	141	.215	.276	0	—	0	9	10	-0	0.7
1993	Min-A	2	1	.667	22	0	0	0	0	21	20	2	16	15	15.4	4.71	92	.267	.396	0	—	0	-1	-1	0	-0.1
1994	Min-A	4	2	.667	50	2	0	0	1	51^1	65	8	18	38	14.9	6.14	79	.316	.376	0	—	0	-8	-7	0	-0.7
1995	Min-A	5	3	.625	36	0	0	0	0	42^1	47	5	16	48	13.6	4.46	107	.290	.358	0	—	0	1	1	-1	0.1
	*LA-N	0	2	.000	24	0	0	0	0	19^2	19	1	9	19	13.3	3.66	104	.241	.326	0	.000	-0	1	0	0	0.0
1996	*LA-N	2	3	.400	66	0	0	0	1	73	65	3	22	56	10.8	2.22	174	.240	.299	0	.000	-0	16	13	-0	0.8
1997	LA-N	1	4	.200	62	0	0	0	1	69^1	71	12	30	42	13.1	5.32	72	.271	.346	1	.250	0	-9	-11	0	-0.7
1998	LA-N	2	1	.667	53	0	0	0	0	54	56	3	24	45	13.7	3.50	111	.267	.347	0	.000	-0	4	2	0	0.1
Total	10	34	37	.479	445	43	3	1	10	705^2	738	67	259	550	12.8	4.03	103	.273	.339	1	.111	-0	10	11	-1	-0.4

● JOHNNY GUZMAN

Guzman, Dionini Ramon (Estrella) b: 1/21/71, Hatillo Palma, D.R. BR/TL, 5′10″, 155 lbs. Deb: 6/8/91

YEAR	TM/L	W	L	PCT	G	GS	CG	SH	SV	IP	H	HR	BB	SO	RAT	ERA	ERA+	OAV	OOB	BH	AVG	PB	PR	/A	PD	TPI
1991	Oak-A	1	0	1.000	5	0	0	0	0	5	11	0	2	3	23.4	9.00	43	.500	.542	0	—	0	-3	-3	0	-0.5
1992	Oak-A	0	0	—	2	0	0	0	0	3	8	0	0	0	27.0	12.00	31	.471	.500	0	—	0	-3	-3	-0	0.0
Total	2	1	0	1.000	7	0	0	0	0	8	19	0	2	3	24.8	10.13	38	.487	.524	0	—	0	-5	-6	0	-0.5

● JOSE GUZMAN

Guzman, Jose Alberto (Mirabal) b: 4/9/63, Santa Isabel, P.R. BR/TR, 6′2″, 195 lbs. Deb: 9/10/85

YEAR	TM/L	W	L	PCT	G	GS	CG	SH	SV	IP	H	HR	BB	SO	RAT	ERA	ERA+	OAV	OOB	BH	AVG	PB	PR	/A	PD	TPI
1985	Tex-A	3	2	.600	5	5	0	0	0	32^2	27	3	14	24	11.3	2.76	153	.214	.293	0	—	0	5	5	0	0.7
1986	Tex-A	9	15	.375	29	29	2	0	0	172^1	199	23	60	87	13.8	4.54	95	.293	.355	0	—	0	-7	-5	0	-0.6
1987	Tex-A	14	14	.500	37	30	6	0	0	208^1	196	30	82	143	12.1	4.67	96	.251	.324	0	—	0	-5	-4	1	-0.4
1988	Tex-A	11	13	.458	30	30	6	2	0	206^2	180	20	82	157	11.6	3.70	110	.231	.308	0	—	0	6	9	-0	0.7
1991	Tex-A	13	7	.650	25	25	5	1	0	169^2	152	10	84	125	12.7	3.08	131	.239	.331	0	—	0	19	18	2	2.2
1992	Tex-A	16	11	.593	33	33	5	0	0	224	229	17	73	179	12.3	3.66	104	.268	.329	0	—	0	7	3	-0	0.4
1993	Chi-N	12	10	.545	30	30	2	1	0	191	188	25	74	163	12.5	4.34	92	.258	.329	7	.111	-3	-6	-7	0	-1.0
1994	Chi-N	2	2	.500	4	4	0	0	0	19^2	22	1	13	11	16.5	9.15	45	.289	.400	0	.000	-1	-11	-11	-0	-1.7
Total	8	80	74	.519	193	186	26	4	0	1224^1	1193	129	482	889	12.5	4.05	101	.256	.329	7	.099	-3	8	8	3	0.3

● JUAN GUZMAN

Guzman, Juan Andres (Correa) b: 10/28/66, Santo Domingo, D.R. BR/TR, 5′11″, 195 lbs. Deb: 6/7/91

YEAR	TM/L	W	L	PCT	G	GS	CG	SH	SV	IP	H	HR	BB	SO	RAT	ERA	ERA+	OAV	OOB	BH	AVG	PB	PR	/A	PD	TPI
1991	*Tor-A	10	3	.769	23	23	1	0	0	138^2	98	6	66	123	10.9	2.99	141	.197	.296	0	—	0	17	19	-2	1.4
1992	*Tor-A★	16	5	.762	28	28	1	0	0	180^2	135	6	72	165	10.4	2.64	155	.207	.287	0	—	0	26	29	-2	3.1
1993	*Tor-A	14	3	.824	33	33	2	1	0	221	211	17	110	194	13.2	3.99	108	.252	.341	0	—	0	8	8	-2	0.3
1994	Tor-A	12	11	.522	25	25	2	0	0	147^1	165	20	76	124	14.9	5.68	85	.282	.367	0	—	0	-14	-14	-2	-1.9
1995	Tor-A	4	14	.222	24	24	3	0	0	135^1	151	13	73	94	15.1	6.32	75	.281	.370	0	—	0	-24	-24	-2	-2.7
1996	Tor-A	11	8	.579	27	27	4	1	0	187^2	158	20	53	165	**10.5**	**2.93**	**171**	**.228**	**.290**	0	—	0	43	43	-1	3.8
1997	Tor-A	3	6	.333	13	13	0	0	0	60	48	14	31	52	12.2	4.95	93	.213	.314	0	—	0	-3	-2	-1	-0.4
1998	Tor-A	6	12	.333	22	22	2	0	0	145	133	19	65	113	12.7	4.41	105	.239	.325	0	.000	-0	4	4	-1	0.3
	Bal-A	4	4	.500	11	11	0	0	0	66	60	4	33	55	13.0	4.23	107	.241	.335	0	—	0	3	2	-1	0.2
	Yr	10	16	.385	33	33	2	0	0	211	193	23	98	168	12.5	4.35	106	.237	.321	0	.000	-0	7	6	-2	0.5
Total	8	80	66	.548	206	206	15	2	0	1281^2	1159	119	579	1085	12.4	4.08	111	.240	.325	0	.000	-0	60	65	-12	4.1

● SANTIAGO GUZMAN

Guzman, Santiago Donovan (b: Santiago Donovan (Guzman))
b: 7/25/49, San Pedro De Macoris, D.R. BR/TR, 6′2″, 180 lbs. Deb: 9/30/69

YEAR	TM/L	W	L	PCT	G	GS	CG	SH	SV	IP	H	HR	BB	SO	RAT	ERA	ERA+	OAV	OOB	BH	AVG	PB	PR	/A	PD	TPI
1969	StL-N	0	1	.000	1	1	0	0	0	7^1	9	2	3	7	14.7	4.91	73	.321	.387	1	.333	0	-1	-1	-0	-0.1
1970	StL-N	1	1	.500	8	3	1	0	0	13^2	14	1	13	9	17.8	7.24	57	.275	.422	1	.200	-0	-5	-5	-0	-0.6
1971	StL-N	0	0	—	2	1	0	0	0	10	6	0	2	13	7.2	0.00	—	.162	.205	0	.000	-0	4	4	-0	0.0
1972	StL-N	0	0	—	1	0	0	0	0	1	1	1	0	0	9.0	9.00	38	.250	.250	0	—	0	-1	-1	0	0.0
Total	4	1	2	.333	12	5	1	0	0	32	30	4	18	29	13.5	4.50	85	.250	.348	2	.222	0	-3	-2	-1	-0.7

● BRUNO HAAS

Haas, Bruno Philip "Boon" b: 5/5/1891, Worcester, Mass. d: 6/5/52, Sarasota, Fla. BB/TL, 5′10″, 180 lbs. Deb: 6/23/15 ♦

YEAR	TM/L	W	L	PCT	G	GS	CG	SH	SV	IP	H	HR	BB	SO	RAT	ERA	ERA+	OAV	OOB	BH	AVG	PB	PR	/A	PD	TPI
1915	Phi-A	0	1	.000	6	2	1	0	0	14^1	23	0	28	7	32.0	11.93	25	.404	.600	1	.056	-1	-14	-14	0	-0.9

● MOOSE HAAS

Haas, Bryan Edmund b: 4/22/56, Baltimore, Md. BR/TR, 6′, 180 lbs. Deb: 9/8/76

YEAR	TM/L	W	L	PCT	G	GS	CG	SH	SV	IP	H	HR	BB	SO	RAT	ERA	ERA+	OAV	OOB	BH	AVG	PB	PR	/A	PD	TPI
1976	Mil-A	0	1	.000	5	2	0	0	0	16	12	0	12	9	13.5	3.94	89	.207	.343	0	—	0	-1	-1	1	0.1
1977	Mil-A	10	12	.455	32	32	6	0	0	197^2	195	21	84	113	12.8	4.33	94	.261	.338	0	—	0	-6	-6	-2	-0.8
1978	Mil-A	2	3	.400	7	6	2	0	1	30^2	33	6	8	32	12.0	6.16	61	.273	.318	0	—	0	-8	-8	-0	-1.2
1979	Mil-A	11	11	.500	29	28	8	1	0	184^2	198	26	59	95	12.5	4.78	87	.275	.330	0	—	0	-12	-13	-1	-1.4
1980	Mil-A	16	15	.516	33	33	14	3	0	252^1	246	25	56	146	10.8	3.10	125	.258	.300	0	—	0	26	21	-0	2.4
1981	*Mil-A	11	7	.611	24	22	5	0	0	137^1	146	10	40	64	12.3	4.46	77	.275	.327	0	—	0	-12	-16	-1	-1.9
1982	*Mil-A	11	8	.579	32	27	3	0	1	193^1	232	15	39	104	12.8	4.47	85	.302	.339	0	—	0	-8	-15	-2	-1.3
1983	Mil-A	13	3	.813	25	25	7	3	0	179	170	12	42	75	10.7	3.27	114	.251	.296	0	—	0	16	9	-1	0.7
1984	Mil-A	9	11	.450	31	30	4	0	0	189^1	205	15	43	84	11.8	3.99	96	.279	.318	0	—	0	-0	-3	3	0.2
1985	Mil-A	8	8	.500	27	26	6	1	0	161^2	165	21	25	78	10.6	3.84	108	.260	.289	0	—	0	5	6	-1	0.4
1986	Oak-A	7	2	.778	12	12	1	0	0	72^1	58	4	19	40	9.7	2.74	141	.218	.273	0	—	0	12	9	-0	1.2
1987	Oak-A	2	2	.500	9	9	0	0	0	40^2	57	7	9	13	14.6	5.75	72	.335	.369	0	—	0	-6	-7	-0	-0.6
Total	12	100	83	.546	266	252	56	8	2	1655	1717	162	436	853	11.8	4.01	97	.269	.317	0	—	0	6	-23	-5	-2.2

● DAVE HAAS

Haas, Robert David b: 10/19/65, Independence, Mo. BR/TR, 6′1″, 200 lbs. Deb: 9/8/91

YEAR	TM/L	W	L	PCT	G	GS	CG	SH	SV	IP	H	HR	BB	SO	RAT	ERA	ERA+	OAV	OOB	BH	AVG	PB	PR	/A	PD	TPI
1991	Det-A	1	0	1.000	11	0	0	0	0	10^2	8	1	12	6	17.7	6.75	62	.242	.457	0	—	0	-3	-3	-0	-0.3
1992	Det-A	5	3	.625	12	11	1	1	0	61^2	68	8	16	29	12.4	3.94	100	.276	.323	0	—	0	-0	0	-0	0.0
1993	Det-A	1	2	.333	20	0	0	0	0	28	45	9	8	17	17.0	6.11	70	.375	.414	0	—	0	-6	-6	0	-0.5
Total	3	7	5	.583	43	11	1	1	0	100^1	121	18	36	52	14.3	4.84	84	.303	.364	0	—	0	-9	-9	-0	-0.8

● BOB HABENICHT

Habenicht, Robert Julius "Hobby" b: 2/13/26, St.Louis, Mo. d: 12/24/80, Richmond, Va. BR/TR, 6′2″, 185 lbs. Deb: 4/17/51

YEAR	TM/L	W	L	PCT	G	GS	CG	SH	SV	IP	H	HR	BB	SO	RAT	ERA	ERA+	OAV	OOB	BH	AVG	PB	PR	/A	PD	TPI
1951	StL-N	0	0	—	3	0	0	0	0	5	5	0	9	1	25.2	7.20	55	.278	.519	0	.000	0	-2	-2	0	0.0
1953	StL-A	0	0	—	1	0	0	0	0	1^2	1	0	1	1	16.2	5.40	78	.167	.375	0	—	0	-0	-0	-0	0.0
Total	2	0	0	—	4	0	0	0	0	6^2	6	0	10	2	23.0	6.75	60	.250	.486	0	.000	0	-2	-2	0	0.0

● JOHN HABYAN

Habyan, John Gabriel b: 1/29/64, Bay Shore, N.Y. BR/TR, 6′2″, 195 lbs. Deb: 9/29/85

YEAR	TM/L	W	L	PCT	G	GS	CG	SH	SV	IP	H	HR	BB	SO	RAT	ERA	ERA+	OAV	OOB	BH	AVG	PB	PR	/A	PD	TPI
1985	Bal-A	1	0	1.000	2	0	0	0	0	2^2	3	0	0	2	10.1	0.00	—	.250	.250	0	—	0	1	1	0	0.6
1986	Bal-A	1	3	.250	6	5	0	0	0	26^1	24	3	18	14	14.4	4.44	93	.250	.368	0	—	0	-1	-1	-0	-0.1
1987	Bal-A	6	7	.462	27	13	0	0	1	116^1	110	20	40	64	11.8	4.80	92	.248	.313	0	—	0	-4	-5	1	-0.4
1988	Bal-A	1	0	1.000	7	0	0	0	0	14^2	22	2	4	4	16.0	4.30	91	.355	.394	0	—	0	-1	-1	0	0.2
1990	NY-A	0	0	—	6	0	0	0	0	8^2	10	0	2	4	13.5	2.08	191	.294	.351	0	—	0	2	2	-0	0.0
1991	NY-A	4	2	.667	66	0	0	0	2	90	73	2	20	70	9.5	2.30	180	.225	.275	0	—	0	18	18	0	1.2
1992	NY-A	5	6	.455	56	0	0	0	7	72^2	84	6	21	44	13.3	3.84	102	.295	.347	0	—	0	1	1	1	0.2
1993	NY-A	2	1	.667	36	0	0	0	1	42^1	45	5	16	29	13.0	4.04	103	.276	.341	0	—	0	1	1	-0	0.2
	KC-A	0	0	—	12	0	0	0	0	14	14	1	4	10	11.6	4.50	102	.259	.310	0	—	0	-0	0	0	-0.2
	Yr	2	1	.667	48	0	0	0	1	56^1	59	6	20	39	12.6	4.15	103	.269	.331	0	—	0	1	1	0	0.0
1994	StL-N	1	0	1.000	52	0	0	0	1	47^1	50	2	20	46	13.3	3.23	128	.275	.347	0	—	0	5	5	1	0.2
1995	StL-N	3	2	.600	31	0	0	0	0	40^2	32	0	15	35	10.6	2.88	146	.222	.300	0	.000	-0	6	6	1	0.7

YEAR	TM/L	W	L	PCT	G	GS	CG	SH	SV	IP	H	HR	BB	SO	RAT	ERA	ERA+	OAV	OOB	BH	AVG	PB	PR	/A	PD	TPI
	Cal-A	1	2	.333	28	0	0	0	0	32^2	36	2	12	25	13.5	4.13	114	.279	.345	0	—	0	2	2	-1	0.1
1996	Col-N	1	1	.500	19	0	0	0	0	24	34	4	14	25	18.4	7.13	73	.347	.434	0	.000	-0	-8	-5	-0	-0.4
Total	11	26	24	.520	348	18	0	0	12	532^1	537	47	186	372	12.4	3.85	110	.265	.330	0	.000	-0	22	24	2	2.3

● WARREN HACKER Hacker, Warren Louis b: 11/21/24, Marissa, Ill. BR/TR, 6'1", 185 lbs. Deb: 9/24/48

YEAR	TM/L	W	L	PCT	G	GS	CG	SH	SV	IP	H	HR	BB	SO	RAT	ERA	ERA+	OAV	OOB	BH	AVG	PB	PR	/A	PD	TPI
1948	Chi-N	0	1	.000	3	1	0	0	0	3	7	0	3	0	30.0	21.00	19	.438	.526	0	—	0	-6	-6	0	-1.3
1949	Chi-N	5	8	.385	30	12	3	0	0	125^2	141	7	53	40	14.2	4.23	95	.283	.356	7	.184	-1	-3	-3	1	-0.3
1950	Chi-N	0	1	.000	5	3	1	0	1	15^1	20	3	8	5	16.4	5.28	80	.313	.389	0	.000	-1	-2	-2	1	-0.1
1951	Chi-N	0	0	—	2	0	0	0	0	1^1	3	0	0	2	27.0	13.50	30	.500	.571	0	—	0	-1	-1	0	0.0
1952	Chi-N	15	9	.625	33	20	12	5	1	185	144	17	31	84	**8.6**	2.58	149	**.212**	**.247**	7	.121	-2	24	26	-4	2.8
1953	Chi-N	12	19	.387	39	32	9	0	2	221^2	225	35	54	106	11.4	4.38	101	.254	.299	17	.218	0	-2	2	-3	0.0
1954	Chi-N	6	13	.316	39	18	4	1	2	158^2	157	28	37	80	11.2	4.25	99	.257	.304	13	.236	1	-3	-1	-1	-0.1
1955	Chi-N	11	15	.423	35	30	13	0	3	213	202	38	43	80	10.4	4.27	96	.245	.285	18	.250	2	-5	-4	-4	-0.6
1956	Chi-N	3	13	.188	34	24	4	0	0	168	190	28	44	65	12.6	4.66	81	.285	.330	8	.148	-2	-17	-17	-3	-1.9
1957	Cin-N	3	2	.600	15	6	0	0	0	43^1	50	5	13	18	13.7	5.19	79	.294	.355	1	.125	-0	-6	-5	-0	-0.6
	Phi-N	4	4	.500	20	10	1	0	0	74	72	10	18	33	11.1	4.50	85	.257	.304	6	.261	1	-5	-6	-1	-0.5
	Yr	7	6	.538	35	16	1	0	0	117^1	122	15	31	51	11.8	4.76	82	.267	.315	7	.226	1	-11	-11	-1	-1.1
1958	Phi-N	0	1	.000	9	1	0	0	0	17	24	2	8	4	16.9	7.41	53	.329	.395	0	.000	-0	-7	-7	-0	-0.4
1961	Chi-A	3	3	.500	42	0	0	0	8	57^1	62	8	8	40	11.1	3.77	104	.272	.300	1	.111	-1	2	1	-1	-0.1
Total	12	62	89	.411	306	157	47	6	17	1283^1	1297	181	320	557	11.5	4.21	96	.259	.307	78	.195	-2	-32	-22	-15	-3.1

● JIM HACKETT Hackett, James Joseph "Sunny Jim" b: 10/1/1877, Jacksonville, Ill. d: 3/28/61, Douglas, Mich. BR/TR, 6'2", 185 lbs. Deb: 9/14/02 ♦

YEAR	TM/L	W	L	PCT	G	GS	CG	SH	SV	IP	H	HR	BB	SO	RAT	ERA	ERA+	OAV	OOB	BH	AVG	PB	PR	/A	PD	TPI
1902	StL-N	0	3	.000	4	3	3	0	0	30^1	46	0	16	7	18.7	6.23	44	.348	.423	6	.286	1	-12	-12	-0	-0.9
1903	StL-N	1	3	.250	7	6	5	0	1	48^1	47	0	18	21	12.7	3.72	88	.249	.324	80	.228	1	-2	-2	0	-0.1
Total	2	1	6	.143	11	9	8	0	1	78^2	93	0	34	28	15.0	4.69	65	.290	.365	86	.231	2	-14	-14	-0	-1.0

● HARVEY HADDIX Haddix, Harvey "The Kitten" b: 9/18/25, Medway, Ohio d: 1/8/94, Springfield, Ohio BL/TL, 5'9.5", 170 lbs. Deb: 8/20/52 C

YEAR	TM/L	W	L	PCT	G	GS	CG	SH	SV	IP	H	HR	BB	SO	RAT	ERA	ERA+	OAV	OOB	BH	AVG	PB	PR	/A	PD	TPI
1952	StL-N	2	2	.500	7	6	3	0	0	42	31	4	10	31	9.2	2.79	133	.201	.259	3	.214	0	4	4	-1	0.4
1953	StL-N☆	20	9	.690	36	33	19	**6**	1	253	220	24	69	163	10.4	3.06	139	.232	.287	28	.289	10	35	34	1	4.7
1954	StL-N†	18	13	.581	43	35	13	3	4	259^2	247	26	77	184	11.3	3.57	115	.249	.305	18	.194	3	14	16	-0	2.0
1955	StL-N★	12	16	.429	37	30	9	2	1	208	216	27	62	150	12.2	4.46	91	.268	.325	12	.164	0	-10	-9	1	-0.9
1956	StL-N	1	0	1.000	4	4	1	1	0	23^2	28	3	10	16	14.5	5.32	71	.298	.365	2	.222	1	-4	-4	-0	-0.1
	Phi-N	12	8	.600	31	26	11	2	2	206^2	196	23	55	154	11.2	3.48	107	.247	.301	22	.237	4	7	5	-1	0.9
	Yr	13	8	.619	35	30	12	3	2	230^1	224	26	65	170	11.5	3.67	102	.253	.308	24	.235	5	3	1	-1	0.8
1957	Phi-N	10	13	.435	27	25	8	1	0	170^2	176	18	39	136	11.4	4.06	94	.264	.306	21	.309	7	-3	-5	-2	-0.1
1958	Cin-N	8	7	.533	29	26	8	1	0	184	191	28	43	110	11.8	3.52	118	.268	.315	11	.180	3	9	13	-1	1.2
1959	Pit-N	12	12	.500	31	29	14	2	0	224^1	189	26	49	149	**9.6**	3.13	124	.228	**.273**	12	.145	-0	20	18	-0	1.8
1960	*Pit-N	11	10	.524	29	28	4	0	1	172^1	189	13	38	101	11.9	3.97	94	.277	.316	17	.254	4	-4	-4	3	0.3
1961	Pit-N	10	6	.625	29	22	5	2	0	156	159	15	41	99	11.7	4.10	97	.266	.316	8	.143	0	-1	-2	0	-0.1
1962	Pit-N	9	6	.600	28	20	4	0	0	141^1	146	17	42	101	12.1	4.20	94	.264	.319	13	.250	4	-4	-4	-1	0.0
1963	Pit-N	3	4	.429	49	1	0	0	1	70	67	7	20	70	11.7	3.34	99	.256	.318	2	.182	1	-0	-0	0	0.0
1964	Bal-A	5	5	.500	49	0	0	0	10	89^2	68	4	23	90	9.3	2.31	155	.211	.268	0	.000	-2	13	13	1	1.5
1965	Bal-A	3	2	.600	24	0	0	0	1	33^2	31	5	23	21	15.0	3.48	100	.248	.373	0	.000	-0	-0	-0	-0	0.0
Total	14	136	113	.546	453	285	99	20	21	2235	2154	240	601	1575	11.3	3.63	108	.252	.305	169	.212	35	75	74	1	11.6

● GEORGE HADDOCK Haddock, George Silas "Gentleman George"
b: 12/25/1866, Portsmouth, N.H. d: 4/18/26, Boston, Mass. BR/TR, 5'11", 155 lbs. Deb: 9/27/1888

YEAR	TM/L	W	L	PCT	G	GS	CG	SH	SV	IP	H	HR	BB	SO	RAT	ERA	ERA+	OAV	OOB	BH	AVG	PB	PR	/A	PD	TPI
1888	Was-N	0	2	.000	2	2	2	0	0	16	9	0	2	3	6.8	2.25	125	.148	.188	1	.200	0	1	1	1	0.2
1889	Was-N	11	19	.367	33	31	30	0	0	276^1	299	10	123	106	14.0	4.20	94	.268	.345	25	.223	7	-6	-8	0	0.0
1890	Buf-P	9	26	.257	35	34	31	0	0	290^2	366	15	149	123	16.4	5.76	71	.295	.377	36	.247	7	-49	-54	4	-3.4
1891	Bos-a	34	11	.756	51	47	37	**5**	1	379^2	330	8	137	169	11.4	2.49	140	.226	.299	45	.243	9	**52**	42	6	5.3
1892	Bro-N	29	13	.690	46	44	39	3	1	381^1	340	11	163	153	12.2	3.14	101	.229	.311	28	.177	-1	6	1	2	0.2
1893	Bro-N	8	9	.471	23	20	12	0	0	151	193	10	89	37	17.2	5.60	79	.302	.393	24	.282	4	-16	-20	-3	-1.5
1894	Phi-N	4	3	.571	10	7	5	0	0	56	63	0	34	7	15.8	5.79	88	.281	.378	5	.172	-1	-3	-4	1	-0.4
	Was-N	0	4	.000	4	4	4	0	0	29	50	2	17	1	21.1	8.69	61	.373	.447	3	.188	-1	-11	-11	-0	-1.0
	Yr	4	7	.364	14	11	9	0	0	85	113	2	51	8	17.5	6.78	76	.315	.401	8	.178	-1	-14	-15	1	-1.4
Total	7	95	87	.522	204	189	160	8	2	1580	1650	56	714	599	13.8	4.07	93	.259	.340	167	.227	25	-25	-53	11	-0.6

● BUMP HADLEY Hadley, Irving Darius b: 7/5/04, Lynn, Mass. d: 2/15/63, Lynn, Mass. BR/TR, 5'11", 190 lbs. Deb: 4/20/26

YEAR	TM/L	W	L	PCT	G	GS	CG	SH	SV	IP	H	HR	BB	SO	RAT	ERA	ERA+	OAV	OOB	BH	AVG	PB	PR	/A	PD	TPI
1926	Was-A	0	0	—	1	0	0	0	0	3	6	0	2	0	24.0	12.00	32	.429	.500	0	—	0	-3	-3	-0	0.0
1927	Was-A	14	6	.700	30	27	13	0	0	198^2	177	2	86	60	12.3	2.85	142	.244	.332	19	.271	2	28	27	0	2.6
1928	Was-A	12	13	.480	33	31	16	3	0	231^2	236	4	100	80	13.4	3.54	113	.268	.348	17	.210	1	13	12	-0	1.3
1929	Was-A	6	16	.273	37	27	7	1	0	195^1	196	10	85	98	13.2	5.62	75	.263	.342	6	.097	-4	-30	-30	1	-3.1
1930	Was-A	15	11	.577	42	34	15	1	2	260^1	242	6	105	162	12.2	3.73	123	.247	.323	21	.226	1	27	25	-1	2.2
1931	Was-A	11	10	.524	**55**	11	2	1	8	179^2	145	4	92	124	11.9	3.06	140	**.218**	.314	9	.167	-1	26	25	2	2.7
1932	Chi-A	1	1	.500	3	2	1	0	1	18^2	17	2	8	13	12.1	3.86	112	.262	.342	1	.167	-0	1	1	0	0.1
	StL-A	13	20	.394	40	33	12	1	1	229^2	244	21	163	132	16.3	5.53	88	.274	.391	22	.282	4	-27	-17	-3	-1.9
	Yr	14	21	.400	43	35	13	1	2	248^1	261	23	171	145	15.9	5.40	89	.273	.388	23	.274	4	-25	-16	-3	-1.8
1933	StL-A	15	20	.429	45	36	19	2	3	**316^2**	309	17	141	149	12.9	3.92	119	.256	.335	17	.156	-4	13	26	-3	1.9
1934	StL-A	10	16	.385	39	32	7	2	1	213	212	14	127	79	14.6	4.35	115	.257	.361	13	.203	-1	3	15	-0	1.5
1935	Was-A	10	15	.400	35	32	13	0	0	230^1	268	18	102	77	14.6	4.92	88	.292	.366	15	.195	1	-12	-15	1	-1.2
1936	*NY-A	14	4	.778	31	17	8	1	1	173^2	194	12	89	74	14.7	4.35	107	.283	.366	16	.235	2	13	6	1	0.7
1937	*NY-A	11	8	.579	29	25	6	0	0	178^1	199	16	83	70	14.4	5.30	84	.281	.358	11	.169	1	-13	-17	1	-1.4
1938	NY-A	9	8	.529	29	17	8	1	1	167^1	165	13	66	61	12.6	3.60	126	.254	.325	5	.093	-1	22	17	3	1.6
1939	*NY-A	12	6	.667	26	18	7	1	2	154	132	10	85	65	12.9	2.98	146	.237	.342	11	.177	-1	28	24	2	2.6
1940	NY-A	3	5	.375	25	2	0	0	2	80	88	4	52	39	15.9	5.74	70	.276	.379	3	.111	-1	-12	-15	0	-1.4
1941	NY-N	1	0	1.000	3	2	0	0	0	13	19	1	9	4	19.4	6.23	59	.345	.438	0	.000	-0	-4	-4	-0	-0.3
	Phi-A	4	6	.400	25	9	1	0	3	102^1	131	13	47	31	15.8	5.01	84	.310	.381	4	.129	-1	-10	-9	-1	-0.9
Total	16	161	165	.494	528	355	135	14	25	2945^2	2980	167	1442	1318	13.7	4.24	105	.263	.350	190	.189	-1	65	69	2	7.0

● MICKEY HAEFNER Haefner, Milton Arnold b: 10/9/12, Lenzburg, Ill. d: 1/3/95, New Athens, Ill. BL/TL, 5'8", 160 lbs. Deb: 4/22/43

YEAR	TM/L	W	L	PCT	G	GS	CG	SH	SV	IP	H	HR	BB	SO	RAT	ERA	ERA+	OAV	OOB	BH	AVG	PB	PR	/A	PD	TPI
1943	Was-A	11	5	.688	36	13	8	1	6	165^1	126	4	60	65	10.3	2.29	140	.208	.283	6	.133	0	19	17	-0	1.8
1944	Was-A	12	15	.444	31	28	18	3	1	228	221	7	71	86	11.7	3.04	107	.251	.310	11	.157	-1	10	5	1	0.6
1945	Was-A	16	14	.533	37	28	19	1	3	238^1	226	10	69	83	11.4	3.47	89	.247	.305	20	.244	4	-3	-10	1	-0.7
1946	Was-A	14	11	.560	33	27	17	2	1	227^2	220	10	80	85	12.1	2.85	118	.251	.317	15	.203	4	17	13	-1	1.7
1947	Was-A	10	14	.417	31	28	14	4	1	193	195	8	85	77	13.2	3.64	102	.264	.343	8	.136	-1	1	2	-1	0.0
1948	Was-A	5	13	.278	28	20	4	0	0	147^2	151	7	61	45	13.3	4.02	108	.265	.342	7	.163	-1	4	5	2	0.7
1949	Was-A	5	5	.500	19	12	4	1	0	91^2	85	7	53	23	13.7	4.42	96	.249	.353	5	.200	1	-2	-2	1	0.0
	Chi-A	4	6	.400	14	12	4	1	1	80^1	84	9	41	17	14.6	4.37	95	.275	.370	6	.261	2	-2	-2	0	0.0
	Yr	9	11	.450	33	24	8	2	1	172	169	16	94	40	14.0	4.40	96	.260	.358	11	.229	2	-4	-3	1	0.0
1950	Chi-A	1	6	.143	24	9	2	0	0	70^2	83	11	45	17	16.6	5.73	78	.299	.400	4	.200	0	-9	-10	-1	-0.8
	Bos-N	0	2	.000	8	2	1	0	0	24	23	3	12	10	13.1	5.63	68	.247	.333	2	.286	1	-4	-5	-0	-0.3
Total	8	78	91	.462	261	179	91	13	13	1466^2	1414	76	577	508	12.5	3.50	102	.252	.326	84	.188	8	31	13	1	3.0

● BUD HAFEY Hafey, Daniel Albert b: 8/6/12, Berkeley, Cal. d: 7/27/86, Sacramento, Cal. BR/TR, 6', 185 lbs. Deb: 4/21/35 F♦

YEAR	TM/L	W	L	PCT	G	GS	CG	SH	SV	IP	H	HR	BB	SO	RAT	ERA	ERA+	OAV	OOB	BH	AVG	PB	PR	/A	PD	TPI
1939	Phi-N	0	0	—	2	0	0	0	0	1^1	7	0	1	1	54.0	33.75	12	.700	.727	9	.176	-0	-4	-4	0	0.0

● LEO HAFFORD Hafford, Leo Edgar b: 9/17/1883, Somerville, Mass. d: 10/2/11, Willimantic, Conn. TR , 6', 170 lbs. Deb: 4/15/06

YEAR	TM/L	W	L	PCT	G	GS	CG	SH	SV	IP	H	HR	BB	SO	RAT	ERA	ERA+	OAV	OOB	BH	AVG	PB	PR	/A	PD	TPI
1906	Cin-N	1	1	.500	3	1	1	0	0	19	13	0	11	5	11.8	0.95	291	.191	.313	2	.222	-0	4	4	-1	0.3

YEAR	TM/L	W	L	PCT	G	GS	CG	SH	SV	IP	H	HR	BB	SO	RAT	ERA	ERA+	OAV	OOB	BH	AVG	PB	PR	/A	PD	TPI
● **FRANK HAFNER** Hafner, Francis R. b: 8/14/1867, Hannibal, Mo. d: 3/2/57, Hannibal, Mo. TR , Deb: 5/5/1888																										
1888	KC-a	0	2	.000	2	2	2	0	0	18	24	2	16	5	20.5	7.00	49	.308	.432	0	.000	-1	-8	-7	-0	-0.6
● **ART HAGAN** Hagan, Arthur Charles b: 3/17/1863, Providence, R.I. d: 3/25/36, Providence, R.I. TR , Deb: 6/30/1883																										
1883	Phi-N	1	14	.067	17	16	15	0	0	137	207	2	33	39	15.8	5.45	57	.342	.376	6	.102	-5	-35	-36	-1	-3.3
	Buf-N	0	2	.000	2	2	1	0	0	15	17	0	6	7	13.8	3.60	88	.270	.333	0	.000	-1	-1	-1	0	-0.2
	Yr	1	16	.059	19	18	16	0	0	152	224	2	39	46	15.6	5.27	59	.335	.371	6	.091	-7	-36	-37	-1	-3.5
1884	Buf-N	1	2	.333	3	3	3	0	0	26	53	1	4	4	19.7	5.88	54	.384	.401	4	.308	0	-8	-8	-1	-0.7
Total	2	2	18	.100	22	21	19	0	0	178	277	3	43	50	16.2	5.36	58	.343	.376	10	.127	-6	-44	-45	-2	-4.2
● **CASEY HAGEMAN** Hageman, Kurt Moritz b: 5/12/1887, Mt.Oliver, Pa. d: 4/1/64, New Bedford, Pa. BR/TR, 5′10.5″, 186 lbs. Deb: 9/18/11																										
1911	Bos-A	0	2	.000	2	2	2	0	0	17	16	2	5	8	11.6	2.12	155	.262	.328	0	.000	-0	2	2	-1	0.1
1912	Bos-A	0	0	—	2	1	0	0	0	1^1	5	0	3	1	54.0	27.00	13	.500	.615	0	—	0	-4	-3	-0	0.0
1914	StL-N	2	4	.333	12	7	2	0	0	55^1	43	0	20	21	11.1	2.44	115	.215	.302	2	.125	-1	2	2	1	0.3
	Chi-N	1	1	.500	16	1	0	0	1	46^2	44	0	12	17	11.4	3.47	80	.254	.314	7	.467	3	-4	-4	-1	0.0
	Yr	3	5	.375	28	8	2	0	1	102	87	0	32	38	10.8	2.91	96	.230	.295	9	.290	2	-1	-1	-0	0.3
Total	3	3	7	.300	32	11	4	0	1	120^1	108	2	40	47	11.7	3.07	93	.243	.318	9	.257	2	-3	-3	-1	0.4
● **KEVIN HAGEN** Hagen, Kevin Eugene b: 3/8/60, Renton, Wash. BR/TR, 6′2″, 185 lbs. Deb: 6/4/83																										
1983	StL-N	2	2	.500	9	4	0	0	0	22^1	34	0	7	7	16.5	4.84	75	.362	.406	0	.000	-1	-3	-3	0	-0.5
1984	StL-N	1	0	1.000	4	0	0	0	0	7^1	9	0	1	2	12.3	2.45	141	.300	.323	0	—	0	1	1	-0	0.1
Total	2	3	2	.600	13	4	0	0	0	29^2	43	0	8	9	15.5	4.25	84	.347	.386	0	.000	-1	-2	-2	-0	-0.4
● **RIP HAGERMAN** Hagerman, Zerah Zequiel b: 6/20/1888, Lyndon, Kan. d: 1/30/30, Albuquerque, N.Mex BR/TR, 6′2″, 200 lbs. Deb: 4/16/09																										
1909	Chi-N	4	4	.500	13	7	4	1	0	79	64	0	28	32	10.7	1.82	139	.225	.298	3	.130	-0	7	6	-0	0.5
1914	Cle-A	9	15	.375	37	26	12	3	0	198	189	3	118	112	14.2	3.09	93	.265	.374	1	.016	-5	-8	-4	-3	-1.4
1915	Cle-A	6	14	.300	29	22	7	0	0	151	156	4	77	69	14.2	3.52	87	.277	.370	4	.105	-2	-10	-8	-3	-1.5
1916	Cle-A	0	0	—	2	0	0	0	0	3^2	5	1	2	1	22.1	12.27	25	.333	.474	0	.000	-0	-4	-4	-0	0.0
Total	4	19	33	.365	81	55	23	4	0	431^2	414	8	225	214	13.6	3.09	93	.263	.360	8	.065	-9	-14	-10	-6	-2.4
● **NOODLES HAHN** Hahn, Frank George b: 4/29/1879, Nashville, Tenn. d: 2/6/60, Candler, N.C. BL/TL, 5′9″, 160 lbs. Deb: 4/18/1899																										
1899	Cin-N	23	8	.742	38	34	32	4	0	309	280	3	68	**145**	10.4	2.68	146	.242	.289	16	.147	-4	40	43	-4	2.8
1900	Cin-N	16	20	.444	39	37	29	**4**	0	311^1	306	4	89	**132**	11.6	3.27	112	.256	.312	24	.209	0	15	14	-0	1.4
1901	Cin-N	22	19	.537	42	42	**41**	2	0	**375^1**	370	12	69	**239**	10.7	2.71	118	.256	.294	24	.170	-1	26	20	-0	1.9
1902	Cin-N	23	12	.657	36	36	35	6	0	321	282	2	58	142	9.7	1.77	170	.236	.275	22	.185	0	36	44	-2	4.6
1903	Cin-N	22	12	.647	34	34	34	5	0	296	297	3	47	127	10.7	2.52	141	.262	.297	18	.161	-2	25	34	-1	3.2
1904	Cin-N	16	18	.471	35	34	33	2	0	297^2	258	3	35	98	9.1	2.06	143	.234	.262	17	.172	1	23	29	-0	3.3
1905	Cin-N	5	3	.625	13	8	5	1	0	77	85	0	9	17	11.2	2.81	118	.272	.297	4	.167	-1	2	4	-2	0.1
1906	NY-A	3	2	.600	6	6	3	1	0	42	38	0	6	17	10.1	3.86	77	.245	.287	4	.333	1	-5	-4	-1	-0.4
Total	8	130	94	.580	243	231	212	25	0	2029^1	1916	27	381	917	10.4	2.55	133	.249	.289	129	.176	-5	161	187	-11	16.9
● **FRED HAHN** Hahn, Frederick Aloys b: 2/16/29, Nyack, N.Y. d: 8/16/84, Valhalla, N.Y. BR/TL, 6′3″, 174 lbs. Deb: 4/19/52																										
1952	StL-N	0	0	—	1	0	0	0	0	2	2	0	1	0	13.5	0.00	—	.250	.333	0	—	0	1	1	0	0.0
● **HAL HAID** Haid, Harold Augustine b: 12/21/1897, Barberton, Ohio d: 8/13/52, Los Angeles, Cal. BR/TR, 5′10.5″, 150 lbs. Deb: 9/5/19																										
1919	StL-A	0	0	—	1	0	0	0	0	2	5	0	3	1	36.0	18.00	18	.556	.667	0	—	0	-3	-3	0	0.0
1928	StL-N	2	2	.500	27	0	0	0	**5**	47	39	1	11	21	9.8	2.30	174	.218	.267	3	.375	1	9	9	0	1.0
1929	StL-N	9	9	.500	38	12	8	0	4	154^2	171	8	66	41	14.1	4.07	115	.284	.360	4	.082	-4	11	10	-1	0.6
1930	StL-N	3	2	.600	20	0	0	0	2	33	38	1	14	13	15.0	4.09	123	.297	.379	0	.000	-0	3	3	1	0.5
1931	Bos-N	0	2	.000	27	0	0	0	1	56	59	3	16	20	12.5	4.50	84	.263	.321	1	.125	-1	-4	-4	2	0.0
1933	Chi-A	0	0	—	6	0	0	0	0	14^2	18	2	13	7	20.3	7.98	53	.310	.452	1	.250	0	-6	-6	0	0.0
Total	6	14	15	.483	119	12	8	0	12	307^1	330	15	123	103	13.7	4.16	106	.275	.349	9	.125	-3	10	9	2	2.1
● **JESSE HAINES** Haines, Jesse Joseph "Pop" b: 7/22/1893, Clayton, Ohio d: 8/5/78, Dayton, Ohio BR/TR, 6′, 190 lbs. Deb: 7/20/18 CH																										
1918	Cin-N	0	0	—	1	0	0	0	0	5	5	0	1	2	10.8	1.80	148	.294	.333	1	1.000	0	1	0	0	0.1
1920	StL-N	13	20	.394	**47**	37	19	4	2	301^2	303	9	80	120	11.7	2.98	100	.270	.324	19	.176	-1	5	0	-5	-0.7
1921	StL-N	18	12	.600	37	29	13	**3**	0	244^1	261	15	56	84	12.0	3.50	105	.286	.333	17	.181	-3	8	5	2	0.4
1922	StL-N	11	9	.550	29	26	11	2	0	183	207	10	45	62	12.6	3.84	101	.284	.329	12	.167	-2	5	1	1	0.0
1923	StL-N	20	13	.606	37	36	23	1	0	266	283	7	75	73	12.3	3.11	125	.275	.328	20	.202	-2	26	23	0	2.4
1924	StL-N	8	19	.296	35	31	16	1	0	222^2	275	14	66	69	14.0	4.41	86	.309	.360	14	.189	-2	-13	-15	-1	-1.9
1925	StL-N	13	14	.481	29	25	15	0	0	207	234	11	52	63	12.5	4.57	95	.290	.334	13	.176	-2	-7	-6	-1	-0.9
1926	*StL-N	13	4	.765	33	20	14	3	1	183	186	10	48	46	11.6	3.25	120	.265	.314	13	.213	-1	12	13	-3	0.7
1927	StL-N	24	10	.706	38	36	**25**	**6**	1	300^2	273	11	77	89	10.6	2.72	145	.245	.297	23	.202	-1	40	41	1	4.3
1928	*StL-N	20	8	.714	33	28	20	1	0	240^1	238	14	72	77	11.8	3.18	126	.266	.324	16	.184	-1	22	22	-3	1.9
1929	StL-N	13	10	.565	28	25	12	0	0	179^2	230	21	73	59	15.3	5.71	82	.313	.376	11	.159	-3	-20	-21	-4	-2.7
1930	*StL-N	13	8	.619	29	24	14	0	1	182	215	15	54	68	13.4	4.30	117	.298	.348	16	.246	1	14	14	-3	1.2
1931	StL-N	12	3	.800	19	17	8	2	0	122^1	134	2	28	27	11.9	3.02	131	.278	.318	6	.133	-2	12	13	-1	1.0
1932	StL-N	3	5	.375	20	10	4	1	0	85^1	116	4	16	27	14.0	4.75	83	.326	.357	5	.185	0	-8	-8	-1	-0.7
1933	StL-N	9	6	.600	32	10	5	0	1	115^1	113	3	37	37	11.8	2.50	139	.252	.311	2	.067	-2	11	13	-2	1.2
1934	*StL-N	4	4	.500	37	6	0	0	1	90	86	6	19	17	10.9	3.50	121	.262	.311	3	.158	-1	**6**	**7**	2	0.7
1935	StL-N	6	5	.545	30	12	3	0	2	115^1	110	4	28	24	10.8	3.59	114	.252	.299	9	.273	1	6	7	-2	0.5
1936	StL-N	7	5	.583	25	9	4	0	1	99^1	110	4	21	19	12.0	3.90	101	.284	.323	5	.167	-1	1	1	-0	0.0
1937	StL-N	3	3	.500	16	6	2	0	0	65^2	81	5	23	18	14.4	4.52	88	.303	.361	4	.182	-0	-4	-4	-1	-0.5
Total	19	210	158	.571	555	387	208	24	10	3208^2	3460	165	871	981	12.3	3.64	108	.280	.330	209	.186	-22	114	104	-21	7.0
● **JIM HAISLIP** Haislip, James Clifton "Slim" b: 8/4/1891, Farmersville, Tex. d: 1/22/70, Dallas, Tex. BR/TR, 6′1″, 186 lbs. Deb: 8/27/13																										
1913	Phi-N	0	0	—	1	0	0	0	0	3	4	0	3	0	21.0	6.00	56	.400	.538	0	.000	-0	-1	-1	-0	0.0
● **JOHN HALAMA** Halama, John Thadeuz b: 2/22/72, Brooklyn, N.Y. BL/TL, 6′5″, 200 lbs. Deb: 4/2/98																										
1998	Hou-N	1	1	.500	6	6	0	0	0	32^1	37	0	13	21	14.5	5.85	70	.296	.371	0	.000	-0	-6	-6	0	-0.4
● **ED HALBRITER** Halbriter, Edward L. b: 2/2/1860, Auburn, N.Y. d: 8/9/36, Los Angeles, Cal. Deb: 5/23/1882																										
1882	Phi-a	0	1	.000	1	1	1	0	0	8	17	1	4	4	23.6	7.88	38	.405	.457	0	.000	-1	-5	-4	-0	-0.4
● **DAD HALE** Hale, Ray Luther b: 2/18/1880, Allegan, Mich. d: 2/1/46, Allegan, Mich. BR/TR, 5′10″, 180 lbs. Deb: 4/21/02																										
1902	Bos-N	1	3	.250	8	5	3	0	0	40	57	1	16	11	16.6	6.07	46	.333	.394	0	.000	-1	-15	-14	-0	-1.4
	Bal-A	0	1	.000	3	2	1	0	0	14	21	0	6	6	18.0	4.50	84	.344	.412	0	.000	-1	-1	-1	-1	-0.2
Total	1	1	4	.200	11	7	4	0	0	54	78	1	22	17	17.0	5.67	54	.336	.398	0	.000	-2	-16	-16	-1	-1.6
● **ED HALICKI** Halicki, Edward Louis b: 10/4/50, Newark, N.J. BR/TR, 6′7″, 220 lbs. Deb: 7/8/74																										
1974	SF-N	1	8	.111	16	11	2	0	0	74^1	84	6	31	40	14.2	4.24	90	.275	.345	6	.240	1	-5	-4	-1	-0.3
1975	SF-N	9	13	.409	24	23	7	2	0	159^2	143	6	59	153	11.6	3.49	109	.240	.312	6	.113	-2	2	5	-1	0.5
1976	SF-N	12	14	.462	32	31	8	4	0	186^1	171	10	61	130	11.3	3.62	100	.246	.309	9	.170	1	-3	0	-0	0.1
1977	SF-N	16	12	.571	37	37	7	2	0	257^2	241	27	70	168	11.1	3.32	118	.244	.298	15	.176	3	17	17	-3	1.7
1978	SF-N	9	10	.474	29	28	9	4	1	199	166	11	45	105	9.9	2.85	121	.221	**.271**	9	.136	-2	16	13	-2	0.8
1979	SF-N	5	8	.385	33	19	3	1	0	125^2	134	12	47	81	13.2	4.58	76	.266	.333	7	.206	1	-12	-15	0	-1.3
1980	SF-N	0	0	—	11	2	0	0	0	25	29	5	10	14	14.0	5.40	65	.293	.358	1	.167	-0	-5	-5	0	0.0
	Cal-A	3	1	.750	10	6	0	0	0	35^1	39	5	11	16	12.7	4.84	81	.279	.331	0	—	0	-3	-4	-1	-0.4
Total	7	55	66	.455	192	157	36	13	1	1063	1007	82	334	707	11.6	3.62	102	.247	.308	53	.165	3	8	8	-7	1.1
● **DREW HALL** Hall, Andrew Clark b: 3/27/63, Louisville, Ky. BL/TL, 6′4″, 205 lbs. Deb: 9/14/86																										
1986	Chi-N	1	2	.333	5	4	1	0	1	23^2	24	3	10	21	12.9	4.56	89	.267	.340	1	.143	0	-2	-1	-0	-0.2

YEAR	TM/L	W	L	PCT	G	GS	CG	SH	SV	IP	H	HR	BB	SO	RAT	ERA	ERA+	OAV	OOB	BH	AVG	PB	PR	/A	PD	TPI
1987	Chi-N	1	1	.500	21	0	0	0	0	32^2	40	4	14	20	14.9	6.89	62	.308	.375	0	.000	-0	-10	-9	-0	-0.6
1988	Chi-N	1	1	.500	19	0	0	0	1	22^1	26	4	9	22	14.5	7.66	47	.295	.367	0	.000	0	-10	-10	0	-0.9
1989	Tex-A	2	1	.667	38	0	0	0	0	58^1	42	3	33	45	12.0	3.70	107	.207	.326	0	—	0	1	2	0	0.1
1990	Mon-N	4	7	.364	42	0	0	0	3	58^1	52	6	29	40	12.5	5.09	72	.242	.332	0	.000	-0	-8	-9	1	-1.7
Total	5	9	12	.429	125	4	1	0	5	195^1	184	20	95	148	13.0	5.21	75	.253	.343	1	.063	-1	-30	-29	-0	-3.3
● CHARLEY HALL	Hall, Charles Louis "Sea Lion" (b: Carlos Clolo) b: 7/27/1885, Ventura, Cal. d: 12/6/43, Ventura, Cal. BL/TR, 6'1", 187 lbs. Deb: 7/12/06																									
1906	Cin-N	4	8	.333	14	9	9	1	1	95	86	1	50	49	13.6	3.32	83	.258	.368	6	.128	-1	-7	-6	0	-0.9
1907	Cin-N	4	2	.667	11	8	5	0	0	68	51	0	43	25	13.0	2.51	103	.226	.359	7	.269	1	-0	1	-1	0.1
1909	Bos-A	6	4	.600	11	7	3	0	0	59^2	59	0	17	27	11.9	2.56	98	.271	.332	3	.158	-1	-1	-0	-0	-0.2
1910	Bos-A	12	9	.571	35	16	13	0	2	188^2	142	6	73	95	10.7	1.91	134	.207	.292	17	.207	3	13	14	0	2.0
1911	Bos-A	8	7	.533	32	10	6	0	**4**	146^1	149	3	72	83	13.9	3.75	87	.279	.370	9	.141	-1	-7	-8	-2	-1.0
1912	*Bos-A	15	8	.652	34	20	9	2	2	191	178	3	70	83	11.9	3.02	113	.257	.329	20	.267	5	6	8	1	1.6
1913	Bos-A	5	4	.556	35	4	2	0	2	105	97	1	46	48	12.7	3.43	86	.235	.319	9	.214	1	-6	-6	-1	-0.5
1916	StL-N	0	4	.000	10	5	2	0	1	42^2	45	1	14	15	12.4	5.48	48	.280	.337	2	.143	-1	-14	-13	0	-1.3
1918	Det-A	0	1	.000	6	1	0	0	0	13^1	14	1	6	2	13.5	6.75	39	.269	.345	0	.000	-0	-6	-6	-1	-0.5
Total	9	54	47	.535	188	80	49	3	12	909^2	821	16	391	427	12.4	3.09	95	.248	.334	73	.197	7	-21	-17	-2	-0.7
● BERT HALL	Hall, Herbert Ernest b: 10/15/1888, Portland, Ore. d: 7/18/48, Seattle, Wash. BR/TR, 5'10", 178 lbs. Deb: 8/21/11																									
1911	Phi-N	0	1	.000	7	1	0	0	0	18	19	0	13	8	16.5	4.00	86	.297	.423	1	.333	0	-1	-1	-1	-0.1
● HERB HALL	Hall, Herbert Silas "Iron Duke" b: 6/5/1893, Steeleville, Ill. d: 7/1/70, Fresno, Cal. BB/TR, 6'4", 220 lbs. Deb: 4/28/18																									
1918	Det-A	0	0	—	3	0	0	0	0	6	12	0	7	1	31.5	15.00	18	.500	.636	0	.000	-0	-8	-8	0	0.0
● JOHN HALL	Hall, John Sylvester b: 1/9/24, Muskogee, Okla. d: 1/17/95, Midwest City, Okla. BR/TR, 6'2.5", 170 lbs. Deb: 4/21/48																									
1948	Bro-N	0	0	—	3	0	0	0	0	4^1	4	1	2	2	12.5	6.23	64	.267	.353	0	—	0	-1	-1	0	0.0
● MARC HALL	Hall, Marcus b: 8/12/1887, Joplin, Mo. d: 2/24/15, Joplin, Mo. BR/TR, 6'1.5", 190 lbs. Deb: 8/20/10																									
1910	StL-A	1	7	.125	8	7	5	0	0	46^1	50	0	31	25	16.3	4.27	58	.289	.406	1	.067	-2	-9	-9	1	-1.5
1913	Det-A	10	12	.455	30	21	8	1	0	165	154	1	79	69	12.8	3.27	89	.255	.344	4	.089	-3	-6	-6	0	-1.1
1914	Det-A	4	6	.400	25	8	1	0	0	90^1	88	1	27	18	11.5	2.69	104	.267	.322	1	.043	-2	1	1	0	-0.1
Total	3	15	25	.375	63	36	14	1	0	301^2	292	2	137	112	12.9	3.25	87	.264	.348	6	.072	-7	-15	-15	1	-2.7
● DARREN HALL	Hall, Michael Darren b: 7/14/64, Marysville, Ohio BR/TR, 6'3", 205 lbs. Deb: 4/30/94																									
1994	Tor-A	2	3	.400	30	0	0	0	17	31^2	26	3	14	28	11.7	3.41	141	.226	.315	0	—	0	5	5	1	1.2
1995	Tor-A	0	2	.000	17	0	0	0	3	16^1	21	2	9	11	16.5	4.41	107	.309	.390	0	—	0	1	1	-0	0.1
1996	LA-N	0	2	.000	9	0	0	0	0	12	13	2	5	12	13.5	6.00	64	.271	.340	0	—	0	-2	-3	-0	-0.4
1997	LA-N	3	2	.600	63	0	0	0	2	54^2	58	3	26	39	13.8	2.30	167	.283	.364	0	—	0	12	9	1	1.0
1998	LA-N	0	3	.000	11	0	0	0	0	11^1	17	2	5	8	18.3	10.32	38	.347	.418	0	—	0	-8	-8	-0	-1.8
Total	5	5	12	.294	130	0	0	0	22	126	135	12	59	98	14.0	3.93	107	.278	.359	0	—	0	7	4	1	0.1
● DICK HALL	Hall, Richard Wallace b: 9/27/30, St.Louis, Mo. BR/TR, 6'6", 200 lbs. Deb: 4/15/52 ♦																									
1955	Pit-N	6	6	.500	15	13	4	0	1	94^1	92	8	28	46	11.6	3.91	105	.253	.310	7	.175	1	1	2	-2	0.2
1956	Pit-N	0	7	.000	19	9	1	0	1	62^1	64	8	21	27	12.3	4.76	79	.270	.329	10	.345	2	-7	-7	-1	-0.5
1957	Pit-N	0	0	—	8	0	0	0	0	10	17	4	5	7	20.7	10.80	35	.362	.434	0	.000	-0	-8	-8	-0	-0.1
1959	Pit-N	0	0	—	2	1	0	0	0	8^2	12	1	1	3	13.5	3.12	124	.333	.351	0	.000	-0	1	1	-0	0.0
1960	KC-A	8	13	.381	29	28	9	1	0	182^1	183	28	38	79	11.1	4.05	98	.261	.301	6	.107	-2	-4	-1	-1	-0.4
1961	Bal-A	7	5	.583	29	13	4	2	4	122^1	102	10	30	92	9.7	3.09	124	.227	.275	5	.139	-0	13	10	1	1.1
1962	Bal-A	6	6	.500	43	6	1	0	6	118^1	102	9	19	71	9.2	2.28	162	.230	.262	4	.167	1	22	19	-0	2.1
1963	Bal-A	5	5	.500	47	3	0	0	12	111^2	91	12	16	74	8.9	2.98	116	.224	.260	13	.464	6	8	6	1	1.4
1964	Bal-A	9	1	.900	45	0	0	0	7	87^2	58	8	16	52	7.6	1.85	193	.188	.228	2	.125	-0	17	17	-0	2.1
1965	Bal-A	11	8	.579	48	0	0	0	12	93^2	84	8	11	79	9.1	3.07	113	.243	.266	5	.333	3	4	4	-1	1.0
1966	Bal-A	6	2	.750	32	0	0	0	7	66	59	8	8	44	9.5	3.95	84	.233	.265	2	.167	0	-4	-5	-0	-0.6
1967	Phi-N	10	8	.556	48	1	1	0	8	86	83	5	12	49	10.2	2.20	155	.255	.286	1	.071	-1	11	12	1	2.7
1968	Phi-N	4	1	.800	32	0	0	0	0	46	53	6	5	31	11.5	4.89	61	.296	.319	1	.333	0	-10	-10	-0	-1.1
1969	*Bal-A	5	2	.714	39	0	0	0	6	65^2	49	3	9	31	8.1	1.92	186	.213	.246	2	.286	1	12	12	-1	1.5
1970	*Bal-A	10	5	.667	32	0	0	0	3	61^1	51	8	6	30	8.4	3.08	118	.229	.249	1	.083	-1	4	4	-1	0.7
1971	*Bal-A	6	6	.500	27	0	0	0	1	43^1	52	4	11	26	13.3	4.98	67	.302	.348	2	.400	1	-7	-8	-1	-2.1
Total	16	93	75	.554	495	74	20	3	68	1259^2	1152	130	236	741	10.0	3.32	110	.244	.283	150	.210	10	55	48	-7	8.0
● BOB HALL	Hall, Robert Lewis b: 12/22/23, Swissvale, Pa. d: 3/12/83, St.Petersburg, Fla BR/TR, 6'2", 195 lbs. Deb: 4/23/49																									
1949	Bos-N	6	4	.600	31	6	2	0	0	74^1	77	7	41	43	14.4	4.36	87	.272	.366	8	.364	3	-3	-5	-2	-0.5
1950	Bos-N	0	2	.000	21	4	0	0	0	50^1	58	8	33	22	16.6	6.97	55	.293	.399	1	.083	-1	-16	-17	-0	-0.7
1953	Pit-N	3	12	.200	37	17	6	1	1	152	172	17	72	68	14.5	5.39	83	.286	.364	6	.158	0	-19	-15	-1	-1.4
Total	3	9	18	.333	89	27	8	1	1	276^2	307	32	146	133	14.9	5.40	77	.284	.371	15	.208	2	-37	-38	-3	-2.6
● TOM HALL	Hall, Tom Edward b: 11/23/47, Thomasville, N.C. BL/TL, 6', 155 lbs. Deb: 6/9/68																									
1968	Min-A	2	1	.667	8	4	0	0	0	29^2	27	1	12	18	12.1	2.43	127	.239	.317	0	.000	-1	2	2	-0	0.1
1969	*Min-A	8	7	.533	31	18	5	2	0	140^2	129	12	50	92	11.5	3.33	110	.243	.308	8	.186	1	5	5	-2	0.4
1970	*Min-A	11	6	.647	52	11	1	0	4	155^1	94	11	66	184	9.4	2.55	146	.173	.265	8	.182	-0	20	20	-2	1.9
1971	Min-A	4	7	.364	48	11	0	0	9	129^2	104	13	58	137	11.2	3.33	107	.216	.300	9	.265	2	2	3	1	0.6
1972	*Cin-N	10	1	.909	47	7	1	1	8	124^1	77	13	56	134	9.8	2.61	123	.173	.269	3	.100	-1	12	8	-2	0.6
1973	*Cin-N	8	5	.615	54	7	0	0	8	103^2	74	13	48	96	10.6	3.47	98	.202	.295	1	.045	-2	2	-1	-2	-0.5
1974	Cin-N	3	1	.750	40	1	0	0	1	64	54	9	30	48	11.8	4.08	86	.232	.319	0	.000	-1	-3	-4	-0	-0.3
1975	Cin-N	0	0	—	2	0	0	0	0	2	2	0	2	3	18.0	0.00	—	.250	.400	0	—	0	1	1	0	0.0
	NY-N	4	3	.571	34	4	0	0	1	60^2	58	10	31	48	13.6	4.75	73	.254	.351	2	.400	1	-8	-9	-0	-0.9
	Yr	4	3	.571	36	4	0	0	1	62^2	60	10	33	51	13.8	4.60	75	.254	.353	2	.400	1	-7	-8	-0	-0.9
1976	NY-N	1	1	.500	5	0	0	0	0	4^2	5	0	5	2	19.3	5.79	57	.250	.400	0	—	0	-1	-1	0	-0.5
	*KC-A	1	1	.500	31	0	0	0	1	30^1	28	4	18	25	13.6	4.45	79	.246	.348	0	—	0	-3	-3	1	-0.2
1977	KC-A	0	0	—	6	0	0	0	0	7^2	4	2	6	10	11.7	3.52	115	.154	.313	0	—	0	0	0	0	0.0
Total	10	52	33	.612	358	63	7	3	32	852^2	656	88	382	797	11.0	3.27	107	.211	.299	31	.161	-1	28	22	-8	1.2
● BILL HALL	Hall, William Bernard "Beanie" b: 2/22/1894, Charleston, W.Va. d: 8/15/47, Newport, Ky. BR/TR, 6'2", 250 lbs. Deb: 7/4/13																									
1913	Bro-N	0	0	—	3	0	0	0	0	4^2	4	0	5	3	19.3	5.79	57	.267	.476	0	.000	-0	-1	-1	-0	0.0
● JOHN HALLA	Halla, John Arthur b: 5/13/1884, St.Louis, Mo. d: 9/30/47, ElSegundo, Cal. BL/TL, 5'11", 175 lbs. Deb: 8/18/05																									
1905	Cle-A	0	0	—	3	0	0	0	0	12^2	12	0	0	4	9.2	2.84	92	.250	.265	1	.200	-0	-0	-0	-0	0.0
● ROY HALLADAY	Halladay, Harry Leroy b: 5/14/77, Denver, Colo. BR/TR, 6'6", 205 lbs. Deb: 9/20/98																									
1998	Tor-A	1	0	1.000	2	2	1	0	0	14	9	2	2	13	7.1	1.93	241	.176	.208	0	—	0	4	4	0	0.3
● BILL HALLAHAN	Hallahan, William Anthony "Wild Bill" b: 8/4/02, Binghamton, N.Y. d: 7/8/81, Binghamton, N.Y. BR/TL, 5'10.5", 170 lbs. Deb: 4/16/25																									
1925	StL-N	1	0	1.000	6	0	0	0	0	15^1	14	0	11	8	14.7	3.52	123	.259	.385	1	.333	0	1	1	0	0.1
1926	*StL-N	1	4	.200	19	3	0	0	0	56^2	45	1	32	28	12.4	3.65	107	.260	.379	4	.250	0	**1**	**2**	-1	0.1
1929	StL-N	4	4	.500	20	12	5	0	0	93^2	94	6	60	52	14.8	4.42	106	.269	.376	4	.154	-1	3	3	1	0.2
1930	*StL-N	15	9	.625	35	32	13	2	2	237^1	233	15	126	**177**	13.6	4.66	108	.260	.351	10	.123	-6	8	9	-0	0.2
1931	*StL-N	**19**	9	.679	37	30	16	3	4	248^2	242	10	112	**159**	12.8	3.29	120	.259	.339	8	.099	-4	16	18	-2	1.2
1932	StL-N	12	7	.632	25	22	13	1	1	176^1	169	10	69	108	12.1	3.11	126	.253	.323	12	.214	2	15	16	-1	1.7
1933	StL-N★	16	13	.552	36	32	16	2	0	244^1	245	6	98	93	12.6	3.50	99	.260	.330	12	.150	-0	-4	-1	-3	-0.5
1934	*StL-N	8	12	.400	32	26	10	2	0	162^2	195	2	66	70	14.4	4.26	99	.294	.358	10	.182	-1	-4	-1	-0	-0.2
1935	StL-N	15	8	.652	40	23	8	2	1	181^1	196	7	57	73	12.6	3.42	120	.275	.329	8	.143	-2	12	14	-1	1.3

YEAR	TM/L	W	L	PCT	G	GS	CG	SH	SV	IP	H	HR	BB	SO	RAT	ERA	ERA+	OAV	OOB	BH	AVG	PB	PR	/A	PD	TPI
1936	StL-N	2	2	.500	9	6	1	0	0	37	58	4	17	16	18.2	6.32	62	.360	.421	5	.556	3	-9	-10	0	-0.6
	Cin-N	5	9	.357	23	19	5	2	0	135	150	3	57	32	13.9	4.33	88	.287	.359	9	.191	1	-5	-8	1	-0.5
	Yr	7	11	.389	32	25	6	2	0	172	208	7	74	48	14.8	4.76	81	.305	.373	14	.250	3	-14	-17	1	-1.1
1937	Cin-N	3	9	.250	21	9	2	0	0	63	90	3	29	18	17.3	6.14	61	.345	.414	2	.095	-1	-16	-17	0	-2.7
1938	Phi-N	1	8	.111	21	10	1	0	0	89	107	4	45	22	15.6	5.46	71	.295	.376	5	.192	-0	-17	-16	-0	-1.4
Total	12	102	94	.520	324	224	90	14	8	1740^1	1838	71	779	856	13.6	4.03	102	.274	.351	90	.162	-9	2	12	-6	-1.1

● JACK HALLETT Hallett, Jack Price b: 11/13/14, Toledo, Ohio d: 6/11/82, Toledo, Ohio BR/TR, 6'4", 215 lbs. Deb: 9/13/40

YEAR	TM/L	W	L	PCT	G	GS	CG	SH	SV	IP	H	HR	BB	SO	RAT	ERA	ERA+	OAV	OOB	BH	AVG	PB	PR	/A	PD	TPI
1940	Chi-A	1	1	.500	2	2	1	0	0	14	15	1	6	9	14.1	6.43	69	.273	.355	2	.400	0	-3	-3	0	-0.3
1941	Chi-A	5	5	.500	22	6	3	0	0	74^2	96	7	38	25	16.5	6.03	68	.306	.386	4	.154	0	-16	-16	-0	-1.8
1942	Pit-N	0	1	.000	3	3	2	0	0	22^1	23	0	8	16	12.5	4.84	70	.274	.337	3	.375	2	-4	-4	0	0.0
1943	Pit-N	1	2	.333	9	4	2	1	0	47^2	36	0	11	11	9.1	1.70	205	.212	.264	4	.286	2	9	9	-1	0.7
1946	Pit-N	5	7	.417	35	9	3	1	0	115	107	0	39	64	11.4	3.29	107	.267	.332	6	.231	0	2	3	0	0.4
1948	NY-N	0	0	—	2	0	0	0	0	4	3	0	4	3	15.8	4.50	87	.214	.389	0	.000	-0	-0	-0	-0	0.0
Total	6	12	16	.429	73	24	11	2	0	277^2	280	8	106	128	12.7	4.05	92	.270	.340	19	.237	4	-12	-10	-1	-1.0

● BILL HALLMAN Hallman, William Wilson b: 3/31/1867, Pittsburgh, Pa. d: 9/11/20, Philadelphia, Pa. BR/TR, 5'8", 160 lbs. Deb: 4/23/1888 M♦

YEAR	TM/L	W	L	PCT	G	GS	CG	SH	SV	IP	H	HR	BB	SO	RAT	ERA	ERA+	OAV	OOB	BH	AVG	PB	PR	/A	PD	TPI
1896	Phi-N	0	0	—	1	0	0	0	0	2	4	0	2	0	27.0	18.00	24	.400	.500	150	.320	0	-3	-3	-0	0.0

● CHARLIE HALLSTROM Hallstrom, Charles E. "Swedish Wonder" b: 1/22/1864, Jonkoping, Sweden d: 5/6/49, Chicago, Ill. Deb: 9/23/1885

YEAR	TM/L	W	L	PCT	G	GS	CG	SH	SV	IP	H	HR	BB	SO	RAT	ERA	ERA+	OAV	OOB	BH	AVG	PB	PR	/A	PD	TPI
1885	Pro-N	0	1	.000	1	1	1	0	0	9	18	3	6	0	24.0	11.00	24	.409	.480	0	.000	-1	-8	-8	-0	-0.6

● SHANE HALTER Halter, Shane David b: 11/8/69, LaPlata, Md. BR/TR, 5'10", 160 lbs. Deb: 4/6/97 ♦

YEAR	TM/L	W	L	PCT	G	GS	CG	SH	SV	IP	H	HR	BB	SO	RAT	ERA	ERA+	OAV	OOB	BH	AVG	PB	PR	/A	PD	TPI
1998	KC-A	0	0	—	1	0	0	0	0	1	1	0	0	0	9.0	0.00	—	.333	.333	45	.221	0	1	1	0	0.0

● DOC HAMANN Hamann, Elmer Joseph b: 12/21/1900, New Ulm, Minn. d: 1/11/73, Milwaukee, Wis. BR/TR, 6'1", 180 lbs. Deb: 9/21/22

YEAR	TM/L	W	L	PCT	G	GS	CG	SH	SV	IP	H	HR	BB	SO	RAT	ERA	ERA+	OAV	OOB	BH	AVG	PB	PR	/A	PD	TPI
1922	Cle-A	0	0	—	1	0	0	0	0	0	3	0	3	0	—	∞	—	1.000	1.000	0	—	0	-6	-6	0	-0.5

● ROGER HAMBRIGHT Hambright, Roger Dee b: 3/26/49, Sunnyside, Wash. BR/TR, 5'10", 180 lbs. Deb: 7/19/71

YEAR	TM/L	W	L	PCT	G	GS	CG	SH	SV	IP	H	HR	BB	SO	RAT	ERA	ERA+	OAV	OOB	BH	AVG	PB	PR	/A	PD	TPI
1971	NY-A	3	1	.750	18	0	0	0	2	26^2	22	5	10	14	10.8	4.39	74	.224	.296	1	.500	0	-3	-3	0	-0.5

● JOHN HAMILL Hamill, John Alexander Charles b: 12/18/1860, New York, N.Y. d: 12/6/11, Bristol, R.I. BR/TR, 5'8", 158 lbs. Deb: 5/1/1884

YEAR	TM/L	W	L	PCT	G	GS	CG	SH	SV	IP	H	HR	BB	SO	RAT	ERA	ERA+	OAV	OOB	BH	AVG	PB	PR	/A	PD	TPI
1884	Was-a	2	17	.105	19	19	18	1	0	156^2	197	8	43	50	14.1	4.48	68	.287	.333	7	.099	-3	-21	-25	-1	-2.6

● DAVE HAMILTON Hamilton, David Edward b: 12/13/47, Seattle, Wash. BL/TL, 6', 190 lbs. Deb: 5/29/72

YEAR	TM/L	W	L	PCT	G	GS	CG	SH	SV	IP	H	HR	BB	SO	RAT	ERA	ERA+	OAV	OOB	BH	AVG	PB	PR	/A	PD	TPI
1972	*Oak-A	6	6	.500	25	14	1	0	0	101^1	94	7	31	55	11.2	2.93	97	.249	.307	4	.154	2	1	-1	-0	0.1
1973	Oak-A	6	4	.600	16	11	1	0	0	69^2	74	8	24	34	12.8	4.39	81	.274	.336	0	—	0	-4	-7	-1	-0.8
1974	Oak-A	7	4	.636	29	18	1	1	0	117	104	10	48	69	12.1	3.15	105	.241	.324	0	—	0	6	2	-0	0.2
1975	Oak-A	1	2	.333	11	4	0	0	0	35^2	42	4	18	20	15.1	4.04	90	.290	.368	0	—	0	-1	-2	-0	-0.1
	Chi-A	6	5	.545	30	1	0	0	6	69^2	63	4	29	51	11.9	2.84	136	.246	.323	0	—	0	7	8	0	1.3
	Yr	7	7	.500	41	5	0	0	6	105^1	105	8	47	71	13.0	3.25	117	.261	.339	0	—	0	6	6	0	1.2
1976	Chi-A	6	6	.500	45	1	0	0	10	90^1	81	4	45	62	13.0	3.59	99	.243	.340	0	—	0	-1	-0	-1	-0.1
1977	Chi-A	4	5	.444	55	0	0	0	9	67^1	71	6	33	45	13.9	3.61	113	.270	.351	0	—	0	3	4	0	0.5
1978	StL-N	0	0	—	13	0	0	0	0	14	16	5	6	8	14.1	6.43	55	.296	.367	0	.000	-0	-4	-5	0	0.0
	Pit-N	0	2	.000	16	0	0	0	1	26^1	23	2	12	15	12.0	3.42	108	.221	.302	0	.000	-1	0	1	-0	0.0
	Yr	0	2	.000	29	0	0	0	1	40^1	39	7	18	23	12.7	4.46	81	.247	.324	0	.000	-1	-4	-4	-0	0.0
1979	Oak-A	3	4	.429	40	7	1	0	5	82^2	80	5	43	52	13.5	3.70	109	.261	.353	0	—	0	5	3	1	0.4
1980	Oak-A	0	3	.000	21	1	0	0	0	30	44	6	28	23	22.5	11.40	33	.344	.472	0	—	0	-25	-25	-0	-2.2
Total	9	39	41	.488	301	57	4	1	31	704	692	61	317	434	13.1	3.85	93	.259	.341	4	.121	1	-12	-22	-2	-0.7

● EARL HAMILTON Hamilton, Earl Andrew b: 7/19/1891, Gibson City, Ill. d: 11/17/68, Anaheim, Cal. BL/TL, 5'8", 160 lbs. Deb: 4/14/11

YEAR	TM/L	W	L	PCT	G	GS	CG	SH	SV	IP	H	HR	BB	SO	RAT	ERA	ERA+	OAV	OOB	BH	AVG	PB	PR	/A	PD	TPI
1911	StL-A	5	12	.294	32	17	10	1	0	177	191	4	69	55	13.4	3.97	85	.284	.354	6	.107	-1	-12	-12	1	-1.0
1912	StL-A	11	14	.440	41	26	17	1	2	249^2	228	2	86	139	11.6	3.24	102	.248	.319	13	.178	-0	2	2	-2	0.1
1913	StL-A	13	12	.520	31	24	19	3	1	217^1	197	3	83	101	12.0	2.57	114	.241	.318	10	.135	-2	9	9	-1	0.7
1914	StL-A	16	18	.471	44	35	20	5	2	302^1	265	5	100	111	11.2	2.50	108	.239	.307	15	.176	4	8	7	-4	0.7
1915	StL-A	9	17	.346	35	28	13	1	0	204	203	4	69	63	12.5	2.87	100	.274	.346	7	.113	-2	2	-0	-2	-0.4
1916	StL-A	0	0	—	1	0	0	0	0	4	4	0	4	0	18.0	9.00	31	.250	.400	0	—	0	-3	-3	-0	0.0
	Det-A	1	2	.333	5	5	3	0	0	37^1	34	0	22	7	14.5	2.65	108	.254	.375	1	.077	-1	1	1	1	0.1
	StL-A	5	7	.417	22	12	3	0	0	91^1	97	2	26	25	12.3	3.05	90	.284	.339	0	.000	-1	-2	-3	-1	-0.7
	Yr	6	9	.400	28	17	6	0	0	132^2	135	2	52	32	12.8	3.12	89	.273	.344	1	.027	-2	-4	-5	-1	-0.6
1917	StL-A	0	9	.000	27	8	2	0	1	83	86	1	41	19	14.0	3.14	83	.274	.361	7	.368	3	-4	-5	-1	-0.3
1918	Pit-N	6	0	1.000	6	6	6	1	0	54	47	0	13	20	10.0	0.83	344	.242	.290	6	.286	1	12	12	-0	1.7
1919	Pit-N	8	11	.421	28	19	9	1	1	160^1	167	3	49	39	12.4	3.31	91	.280	.340	7	.135	-2	-7	-5	2	-0.7
1920	Pit-N	10	13	.435	39	23	12	0	3	230^1	223	2	69	74	11.5	3.24	99	.258	.314	10	.149	-3	-3	-1	-0	-0.4
1921	Pit-N	13	15	.464	35	30	12	2	0	225	237	5	58	59	12.1	3.36	114	.272	.323	12	.160	-0	11	12	4	1.6
1922	Pit-N	11	7	.611	33	14	9	1	2	160	183	6	40	34	12.6	3.99	102	.296	.339	9	.155	-2	2	1	-1	-0.1
1923	Pit-N	7	9	.438	28	15	5	0	1	141	148	6	42	42	12.2	3.77	106	.271	.324	9	.173	-2	4	4	2	0.5
1924	Phi-N	0	1	.000	3	0	0	0	0	6	9	0	2	2	18.0	10.50	42	.391	.462	0	.000	-0	-4	-4	0	-0.6
Total	14	115	147	.439	410	262	140	16	13	2342^2	2319	43	773	790	12.1	3.16	102	.264	.329	112	.153	-9	13	15	-4	1.2

● JACK HAMILTON Hamilton, Jack Edwin b: 12/25/38, Burlington, Iowa BR/TR, 6', 200 lbs. Deb: 4/13/62

YEAR	TM/L	W	L	PCT	G	GS	CG	SH	SV	IP	H	HR	BB	SO	RAT	ERA	ERA+	OAV	OOB	BH	AVG	PB	PR	/A	PD	TPI
1962	Phi-N	9	12	.429	41	26	4	1	2	182	185	18	107	101	14.7	5.09	76	.268	.370	3	.056	-4	-23	-25	2	-2.7
1963	Phi-N	2	1	.667	19	1	0	0	1	30	22	3	17	23	11.7	5.40	60	.200	.307	0	.000	-0	-7	-7	1	-0.7
1964	Det-A	0	1	.000	5	1	0	0	0	15	24	2	8	5	19.8	8.40	44	.364	.440	0	.000	-0	-8	-8	1	-0.5
1965	Det-A	1	1	.500	4	1	0	0	0	4^1	6	1	4	3	20.8	14.54	24	.316	.435	0	—	0	-5	-5	0	-1.8
1966	NY-N	6	13	.316	57	13	3	1	13	148^2	138	13	88	93	14.0	3.93	92	.248	.356	5	.132	-1	-5	-5	1	-0.7
1967	NY-N	2	0	1.000	17	1	0	0	1	31^1	24	2	16	22	11.8	3.73	91	.205	.306	1	.200	1	-1	-1	-0	0.0
	Cal-A	9	6	.600	26	20	0	0	0	119^1	104	6	63	74	12.7	3.24	97	.239	.337	6	.158	-0	-0	-1	-0	-0.2
1968	Cal-A	3	1	.750	21	2	1	0	2	38	34	0	15	18	11.6	3.32	88	.246	.320	1	.143	-0	-1	-2	-0	-0.2
1969	Cle-A	0	2	.000	20	0	0	0	1	30^2	37	2	23	13	17.6	4.40	86	.316	.429	0	.000	-0	-3	-2	-0	-0.2
	Chi-A	0	3	.000	8	0	0	0	0	12^1	23	1	7	5	21.9	11.68	33	.411	.476	0	—	0	-11	-11	-0	-2.1
	Yr	0	5	.000	28	0	0	0	1	43	60	3	30	18	18.8	6.49	58	.345	.441	0	.000	-0	-14	-13	-0	-2.3
Total	8	32	40	.444	218	65	8	2	20	611^2	597	48	348	357	14.1	4.53	78	.259	.359	16	.107	-6	-66	-67	4	-9.1

● JEFF HAMILTON Hamilton, Jeffrey Robert b: 3/19/64, Flint, Mich. BR/TR, 6'3", 207 lbs. Deb: 6/28/86 ♦

YEAR	TM/L	W	L	PCT	G	GS	CG	SH	SV	IP	H	HR	BB	SO	RAT	ERA	ERA+	OAV	OOB	BH	AVG	PB	PR	/A	PD	TPI
1989	LA-N	0	1	.000	1	0	0	0	0	1^2	2	0	1	2	16.2	5.40	63	.286	.375	134	.245	0	-0	-0	0	-0.2

● JOEY HAMILTON Hamilton, Johns Joseph b: 9/9/70, Statesboro, Ga. BR/TR, 6'4", 220 lbs. Deb: 5/24/94

YEAR	TM/L	W	L	PCT	G	GS	CG	SH	SV	IP	H	HR	BB	SO	RAT	ERA	ERA+	OAV	OOB	BH	AVG	PB	PR	/A	PD	TPI
1994	SD-N	9	6	.600	16	16	1	1	0	108^2	98	7	29	61	11.0	2.98	138	.241	.302	0	.000	-4	15	14	0	1.4
1995	SD-N	6	9	.400	31	30	2	2	0	204^1	189	17	56	123	11.3	3.08	131	.246	.307	7	.108	-2	25	21	-1	1.2
1996	*SD-N	15	9	.625	34	33	3	1	0	211^2	206	19	83	184	12.7	4.17	95	.256	.332	11	.162	1	1	-5	0	-0.3
1997	SD-N	12	7	.632	31	29	1	0	0	192^2	199	22	69	124	13.1	4.25	91	.271	.344	7	.130	1	-1	-8	-2	-0.8
1998	*SD-N	13	13	.500	34	34	0	0	0	217^1	220	15	106	147	13.8	4.27	90	.267	.356	10	.141	0	-1	-11	-0	-1.1
Total	5	55	44	.556	146	142	7	4	0	934^2	912	80	343	639	12.5	3.83	103	.258	.331	35	.117	-3	39	12	-3	0.4

● STEVE HAMILTON Hamilton, Steve Absher b: 11/30/35, Columbia, Ky. BL/TL, 6'7", 195 lbs. Deb: 4/23/61 C

YEAR	TM/L	W	L	PCT	G	GS	CG	SH	SV	IP	H	HR	BB	SO	RAT	ERA	ERA+	OAV	OOB	BH	AVG	PB	PR	/A	PD	TPI
1961	Cle-A	0	0	—	2	0	0	0	0	3	2	0	3	4	15.0	3.00	131	.200	.385	1	1.000	0	0	0	0	0.1
1962	Was-A	3	8	.273	41	10	1	0	2	107^1	103	10	39	83	12.2	3.77	107	.248	.317	2	.077	-1	2	3	1	0.3
1963	Was-A	0	1	.000	3	0	0	0	0	2	5	0	2	1	31.5	13.50	27	.556	.636	0	—	0	-2	-2	0	-0.9
	*NY-A	5	1	.833	34	0	0	0	5	62^1	49	3	24	63	10.7	2.60	135	.220	.298	4	.286	1	7	6	1	0.9
	Yr	5	2	.714	37	0	0	0	5	64^1	54	3	26	64	11.3	2.94	120	.232	.312	4	.286	1	5	4	1	0.0
1964	*NY-A	7	2	.778	30	3	1	0	3	60^1	55	6	15	49	10.4	3.28	110	.246	.293	4	.200	1	2	2	0	0.4

YEAR	TM/L	W	L	PCT	G	GS	CG	SH	SV	IP	H	HR	BB	SO	RAT	ERA	ERA+	OAV	OOB	BH	AVG	PB	PR	/A	PD	TPI
1965	NY-A	3	1	.750	46	1	0	0	5	58^1	47	2	16	51	9.7	1.39	245	.214	.267	1	.167	0	13	13	-2	1.0
1966	NY-A	8	3	.727	44	3	1	1	3	90	69	8	22	57	9.4	3.00	111	.218	.276	1	.053	-2	4	3	-1	0.1
1967	NY-A	2	4	.333	44	0	0	0	4	62	57	7	23	55	11.8	3.48	90	.250	.321	1	.111	-0	-2	-2	0	-0.3
1968	NY-A	2	2	.500	40	0	0	0	11	50^2	37	0	13	42	9.1	2.13	136	.211	.270	0	.000	0	5	4	0	0.7
1969	NY-A	3	4	.429	38	0	0	0	2	57	39	7	21	39	9.5	3.32	105	.194	.270	0	.000	-1	2	1	-1	-0.1
1970	NY-A	4	3	.571	35	0	0	0	3	45^1	36	3	16	33	10.5	2.78	126	.222	.296	0	.000	-1	5	4	0	0.5
	Chi-A	0	0	—	3	0	0	0	0	3	4	0	1	3	15.0	6.00	65	.333	.385	0	—	0	-1	-1	0	0.0
	Yr	4	3	.571	38	0	0	0	3	48^1	40	3	17	36	10.6	2.98	119	.227	.295	0	.000	-1	4	3	1	0.5
1971	*SF-N	2	2	.500	39	0	0	0	4	44^2	29	4	11	38	8.3	3.02	112	.186	.244	0	.000	-0	2	2	-0	0.1
1972	Chi-N	1	0	1.000	22	0	0	0	0	17	24	1	8	13	17.5	4.76	80	.333	.407	0	.000	-0	-2	-2	-0	-0.1
Total	12	40	31	.563	421	17	3	1	42	663	556	51	214	531	10.6	3.05	114	.229	.295	14	.125	-2	36	32	-1	2.7

● LUKE HAMLIN Hamlin, Luke Daniel "Hot Potato" b: 7/3/04, Ferris Center, Mich. d: 2/18/78, Clare, Mich. BL/TR, 6'2", 168 lbs. Deb: 9/18/33

YEAR	TM/L	W	L	PCT	G	GS	CG	SH	SV	IP	H	HR	BB	SO	RAT	ERA	ERA+	OAV	OOB	BH	AVG	PB	PR	/A	PD	TPI
1933	Det-A	1	0	1.000	3	3	0	0	0	16^2	20	3	10	10	16.2	4.86	89	.294	.385	2	.400	1	-1	-1	-1	0.0
1934	Det-A	2	3	.400	20	5	1	0	1	75^1	87	11	44	30	15.7	5.38	82	.289	.380	6	.231	-0	-7	-8	-0	-0.5
1937	Bro-N	11	13	.458	39	25	11	1	1	185^2	183	4	48	93	11.2	3.59	113	.252	.298	11	.186	-1	7	9	-3	0.7
1938	Bro-N	12	15	.444	44	30	10	3	6	237^1	243	14	65	97	11.8	3.68	106	.263	.313	11	.141	-3	3	6	-4	0.0
1939	Bro-N	20	13	.606	40	36	19	2	0	269^2	255	27	54	88	10.3	3.64	111	.248	.285	13	.126	-5	8	12	-5	0.4
1940	Bro-N	9	8	.529	33	25	9	2	0	182^1	183	17	34	91	10.8	3.06	131	.256	.292	5	.086	-4	16	19	-4	0.8
1941	Bro-N	8	8	.500	30	20	5	1	1	136	139	14	41	58	12.0	4.24	87	.261	.316	6	.146	-1	-9	-9	-2	-1.2
1942	Pit-N	4	4	.500	23	14	6	1	0	112	128	3	19	38	11.9	3.94	86	.281	.312	9	.243	1	-8	-7	-2	-0.6
1944	Phi-A	6	12	.333	29	23	9	2	0	190	204	13	38	58	11.6	3.74	93	.271	.309	13	.232	3	-7	-6	-5	-0.7
Total	9	73	76	.490	261	181	70	12	9	1405	1442	106	353	563	11.6	3.77	103	.262	.308	76	.164	-8	2	16	-25	-1.1

● PETE HAMM Hamm, Peter Whitfield b: 9/20/47, Buffalo, N.Y. BR/TR, 6'5", 210 lbs. Deb: 7/29/70

YEAR	TM/L	W	L	PCT	G	GS	CG	SH	SV	IP	H	HR	BB	SO	RAT	ERA	ERA+	OAV	OOB	BH	AVG	PB	PR	/A	PD	TPI
1970	Min-A	0	2	.000	10	0	0	0	0	16^1	17	3	7	3	13.2	5.51	68	.262	.333	0	.000	-0	-3	-3	-1	-0.4
1971	Min-A	2	4	.333	13	8	1	0	0	44	55	7	18	16	15.1	6.75	53	.309	.376	3	.273	1	-16	-16	0	-1.8
Total	2	2	6	.250	23	8	1	0	0	60^1	72	10	25	19	14.6	6.41	56	.296	.364	3	.250	1	-19	-19	-0	-2.2

● ATLEE HAMMAKER Hammaker, Charlton Atlee b: 1/24/58, Carmel, Cal. BB/TL, 6'3", 200 lbs. Deb: 8/13/81

YEAR	TM/L	W	L	PCT	G	GS	CG	SH	SV	IP	H	HR	BB	SO	RAT	ERA	ERA+	OAV	OOB	BH	AVG	PB	PR	/A	PD	TPI
1981	KC-A	1	3	.250	10	6	0	0	0	39	44	2	12	11	12.9	5.54	65	.286	.337	0	—	0	-8	-8	-1	-0.8
1982	SF-N	12	8	.600	29	27	4	1	0	175	189	16	28	102	11.3	4.11	87	.278	.309	4	.068	-4	-10	-10	1	-1.4
1983	SF-N★	10	9	.526	23	23	8	3	0	172^1	147	9	32	127	**9.5**	**2.25**	**157**	.228	**.267**	6	.102	-1	26	25	1	2.7
1984	SF-N	2	0	1.000	6	6	0	0	0	33	32	2	9	24	11.2	2.18	161	.256	.306	2	.182	1	5	5	0	0.4
1985	SF-N	5	12	.294	29	29	1	1	0	170^2	161	17	47	100	11.0	3.74	92	.247	.298	4	.085	-3	-3	-6	1	-0.7
1987	*SF-N	10	10	.500	31	27	2	0	0	168^1	159	22	57	107	11.7	3.58	107	.248	.313	7	.123	-1	9	5	-1	0.3
1988	SF-N	9	9	.500	43	17	3	1	5	144^2	136	11	41	65	11.2	3.73	87	.248	.304	4	.121	-0	-5	-8	2	-0.8
1989	*SF-N	6	6	.500	28	9	0	0	0	76^2	78	5	23	30	12.0	3.76	90	.271	.327	7	.368	2	-2	-3	-1	-0.3
1990	SF-N	4	5	.444	25	6	0	0	0	67^1	69	7	21	28	12.0	4.28	85	.273	.328	1	.059	-1	-4	-5	-1	-0.7
	SD-N	0	4	.000	9	1	0	0	0	19^1	16	1	6	16	10.2	4.66	82	.213	.272	1	.500	0	-2	-2	-0	-0.3
	Yr	4	9	.308	34	7	0	0	0	86^2	85	8	27	44	11.6	4.36	84	.256	.312	2	.105	-0	-5	-7	-1	-1.0
1991	SD-N	0	1	.000	1	1	0	0	0	4^2	8	0	3	1	21.2	5.79	66	.364	.440	0	.000	-0	-1	-1	0	-0.2
1994	Chi-A	0	0	—	2	0	0	0	0	1^1	1	0	0	1	6.8	0.00	—	.200	.200	0	—	0	1	1	0	0.0
1995	Chi-A	0	0	—	13	0	0	0	0	6^1	11	2	8	3	28.4	12.79	35	.393	.541	0	—	0	-6	-6	0	0.3
Total	12	59	67	.468	249	152	18	6	5	1078^2	1051	94	287	615	11.3	3.66	97	.255	.306	36	.118	-7	1	-13	1	-1.5

● CHRIS HAMMOND Hammond, Christopher Andrew b: 1/21/66, Atlanta, Ga. BL/TL, 6'1", 195 lbs. Deb: 7/16/90 F

YEAR	TM/L	W	L	PCT	G	GS	CG	SH	SV	IP	H	HR	BB	SO	RAT	ERA	ERA+	OAV	OOB	BH	AVG	PB	PR	/A	PD	TPI
1990	Cin-N	0	2	.000	3	3	0	0	0	11^1	13	2	12	4	19.9	6.35	62	.302	.455	0	.000	-0	-3	-3	0	-0.5
1991	Cin-N	7	7	.500	20	18	0	0	0	99^2	92	4	48	50	12.8	4.06	94	.250	.340	12	.353	5	-4	-3	0	0.1
1992	Cin-N	7	10	.412	28	26	0	0	0	147^1	149	13	55	79	12.6	4.21	85	.266	.334	6	.136	2	-12	-10	-0	-0.9
1993	Fla-N	11	12	.478	32	32	1	0	0	191	207	18	66	108	12.9	4.66	93	.277	.337	12	.190	4	-13	-7	0	-0.3
1994	Fla-N	4	4	.500	13	13	1	1	0	73^1	79	5	23	40	12.6	3.07	142	.281	.338	3	.136	0	9	11	-2	0.9
1995	Fla-N	9	6	.600	25	24	3	2	0	161	157	17	47	126	11.9	3.80	111	.256	.318	13	.271	6	7	7	-0	1.2
1996	Fla-N	5	8	.385	38	9	0	0	0	81	104	14	27	50	15.0	6.56	62	.315	.374	1	.067	-1	-21	-22	0	-3.1
1997	Bos-A	3	4	.429	29	8	0	0	1	65^1	81	5	27	48	15.2	5.92	78	.310	.379	0	—	0	-10	-9	0	-0.9
1998	Fla-N	0	2	.000	3	3	0	0	0	13^2	20	3	8	8	19.1	6.59	62	.357	.446	1	.200	0	-4	-4	-1	-0.5
Total	9	46	55	.455	191	136	5	3	1	843^2	902	81	313	513	13.2	4.54	90	.277	.344	48	.205	16	-51	-41	-2	-4.0

● GRANNY HAMNER Hamner, Granville Wilbur b: 4/26/27, Richmond, Va. d: 9/12/93, Philadelphia, Pa. BR/TR, 5'10", 163 lbs. Deb: 9/14/44 F♦

YEAR	TM/L	W	L	PCT	G	GS	CG	SH	SV	IP	H	HR	BB	SO	RAT	ERA	ERA+	OAV	OOB	BH	AVG	PB	PR	/A	PD	TPI
1956	Phi-N	0	1	.000	3	1	0	0	0	8^1	10	0	2	4	13.0	4.32	86	.294	.333	90	.224	1	-1	-1	-0	0.0
1957	Phi-N	0	0	—	1	0	0	0	0	1	1	0	0	1	9.0	0.00	—	.250	.250	114	.227	0	0	0	0	0.0
1962	KC-A	0	1	.000	3	0	0	0	0	4	10	0	6	0	36.0	9.00	47	.476	.593	0	—	0	-2	-2	0	-0.4
Total	3	0	2	.000	7	1	0	0	0	13^1	21	0	8	5	19.6	5.40	72	.356	.433	1529	.262	1	-2	-2	-0	-0.4

● RALPH HAMNER Hamner, Ralph Conant "Bruz" b: 9/12/16, Gibsland, La. BR/TR, 6'3", 165 lbs. Deb: 4/28/46

YEAR	TM/L	W	L	PCT	G	GS	CG	SH	SV	IP	H	HR	BB	SO	RAT	ERA	ERA+	OAV	OOB	BH	AVG	PB	PR	/A	PD	TPI
1946	Chi-A	2	7	.222	25	7	1	0	1	71^1	80	2	39	29	15.6	4.42	77	.276	.371	3	.167	0	-7	-8	-1	-1.0
1947	Chi-N	1	2	.333	3	3	2	0	0	25	24	0	16	14	14.4	2.52	157	.267	.377	1	.125	-0	4	4	-1	0.4
1948	Chi-N	5	9	.357	27	17	5	0	0	111^1	110	12	69	53	14.9	4.69	83	.259	.369	6	.182	1	-9	-10	2	-0.8
1949	Chi-N	0	2	.000	6	1	0	0	0	12^1	22	1	8	3	22.6	8.76	46	.407	.492	0	.000	-0	-6	-6	1	-0.8
Total	4	8	20	.286	61	28	8	0	1	220	236	15	132	99	15.5	4.58	82	.275	.378	10	.164	0	-18	-20	1	-2.2

● MIKE HAMPTON Hampton, Michael William b: 9/9/72, Brooksville, Fla. BR/TL, 5'10", 180 lbs. Deb: 4/17/93

YEAR	TM/L	W	L	PCT	G	GS	CG	SH	SV	IP	H	HR	BB	SO	RAT	ERA	ERA+	OAV	OOB	BH	AVG	PB	PR	/A	PD	TPI
1993	Sea-A	1	3	.250	13	3	0	0	1	17	28	3	17	8	23.8	9.53	46	.368	.484	0	—	0	-10	-10	-0	-2.0
1994	Hou-N	2	1	.667	44	0	0	0	0	41^1	46	4	16	24	13.9	3.70	107	.282	.354	0	.000	-0	2	1	2	0.2
1995	Hou-N	9	8	.529	24	24	0	0	0	150^2	141	13	49	115	11.6	3.35	116	.247	.310	7	.146	1	14	9	0	1.0
1996	Hou-N	10	10	.500	27	27	2	1	0	160^1	175	12	49	101	12.7	3.59	108	.280	.335	10	.238	4	11	5	2	1.1
1997	*Hou-N	15	10	.600	34	34	7	2	0	223	217	16	77	139	11.9	3.83	104	.257	.321	10	.137	1	9	4	5	0.9
1998	*Hou-N	11	7	.611	32	32	1	1	0	211^2	227	18	81	137	13.3	3.36	121	.278	.347	16	.262	7	20	17	3	2.4
Total	6	48	39	.552	174	120	10	4	1	804	834	66	289	524	12.8	3.68	108	.269	.335	43	.191	12	47	26	12	3.6

● LEE HANCOCK Hancock, Leland David b: 6/27/67, N.Hollywood, Cal. BL/TL, 6'4", 215 lbs. Deb: 9/3/95

YEAR	TM/L	W	L	PCT	G	GS	CG	SH	SV	IP	H	HR	BB	SO	RAT	ERA	ERA+	OAV	OOB	BH	AVG	PB	PR	/A	PD	TPI
1995	Pit-N	0	0	—	11	0	0	0	0	14	10	0	2	6	7.7	1.93	223	.192	.222	0	—	0	4	4	-0	0.0
1996	Pit-N	0	0	—	13	0	0	0	0	18^1	21	5	10	13	16.2	6.38	68	.276	.375	0	—	0	-4	-4	1	0.1
Total	2	0	0	—	24	0	0	0	0	32^1	31	5	12	19	12.5	4.45	97	.242	.317	0	—	0	-1	-0	1	0.1

● GARRY HANCOCK Hancock, Ronald Garry b: 1/23/54, Tampa, Fla. BL/TL, 6', 175 lbs. Deb: 7/16/78 ♦

YEAR	TM/L	W	L	PCT	G	GS	CG	SH	SV	IP	H	HR	BB	SO	RAT	ERA	ERA+	OAV	OOB	BH	AVG	PB	PR	/A	PD	TPI
1984	Oak-A	0	0	—	1	0	0	0	0	1^1	0	0	0	0	0.0	0.00	—	.000	.000	13	.217	0	1	1	0	0.0

● RYAN HANCOCK Hancock, Ryan Lee b: 11/11/71, Santa Clara, Cal. BR/TR, 6'2", 220 lbs. Deb: 6/8/96

YEAR	TM/L	W	L	PCT	G	GS	CG	SH	SV	IP	H	HR	BB	SO	RAT	ERA	ERA+	OAV	OOB	BH	AVG	PB	PR	/A	PD	TPI
1996	Cal-A	4	1	.800	11	4	0	0	0	27^2	34	2	17	19	17.2	7.48	67	.306	.408	1	1.000	0	-8	-8	0	-1.0

● RICH HAND Hand, Richard Allen b: 7/10/48, Bellevue, Wash. BR/TR, 6'1", 195 lbs. Deb: 4/9/70

YEAR	TM/L	W	L	PCT	G	GS	CG	SH	SV	IP	H	HR	BB	SO	RAT	ERA	ERA+	OAV	OOB	BH	AVG	PB	PR	/A	PD	TPI
1970	Cle-A	6	13	.316	35	25	3	1	3	159^2	132	27	69	110	11.6	3.83	103	.228	.314	6	.146	-1	-2	2	0	0.1
1971	Cle-A	2	6	.250	15	12	0	0	0	60^2	74	6	38	26	17.2	5.79	66	.311	.414	2	.125	-0	-16	-13	-1	-1.7
1972	Tex-A	10	14	.417	30	28	2	1	0	170^2	139	12	103	109	12.9	3.32	91	.226	.340	8	.154	1	-5	-6	-0	-0.7
1973	Tex-A	2	3	.400	8	7	1	0	0	41^2	49	2	19	14	15.1	5.40	69	.290	.368	0	—	0	-7	-8	-1	-0.8
	Cal-A	4	3	.571	16	6	0	0	0	54^2	58	5	21	19	13.2	3.62	98	.274	.342	0	—	0	1	-0	1	0.2
	Yr	6	6	.500	24	13	1	0	0	96^1	107	7	40	33	13.8	4.39	82	.277	.347	0	—	0	-6	-8	0	-0.6
Total	4	24	39	.381	104	78	6	2	3	487^1	452	52	250	278	13.2	4.01	88	.249	.345	16	.147	-0	-29	-25	-1	-2.9

● JIM HANDIBOE Handiboe, James Edward "Nick" b: 7/17/1866, Columbus, Ohio d: 11/8/42, Columbus, Ohio BR/TR, 5'11", 160 lbs. Deb: 5/28/1886

YEAR	TM/L	W	L	PCT	G	GS	CG	SH	SV	IP	H	HR	BB	SO	RAT	ERA	ERA+	OAV	OOB	BH	AVG	PB	PR	/A	PD	TPI
1886	Pit-a	7	7	.500	14	14	12	1	0	114	82	1	33	83	10.0	3.32	102	.195	.273	5	.114	-2	2	1	-0	-0.2

● VERN HANDRAHAN
Handrahan, James Vernon b: 11/27/38, Charlottetown, P.E.I., Canada BL/TR, 6'2", 185 lbs. Deb: 4/14/64

YEAR	TM/L	W	L	PCT	G	GS	CG	SH	SV	IP	H	HR	BB	SO	RAT	ERA	ERA+	OAV	OOB	BH	AVG	PB	PR	/A	PD	TPI
1964	KC-A	0	1	.000	18	1	0	0	0	35^2	33	9	25	18	15.1	6.06	63	.252	.380	2	.222	0	-10	-9	0	-0.2
1966	KC-A	0	1	.000	16	1	0	0	1	25^1	20	5	15	18	12.8	4.26	80	.227	.346	0	.000	-0	-2	-2	0	-0.1
Total	2	0	2	.000	34	2	0	0	1	61	53	14	40	36	14.2	5.31	69	.242	.366	2	.167	-0	-12	-11	0	-0.3

● BILL HANDS
Hands, William Alfred b: 5/6/40, Hackensack, N.J. BR/TR, 6'2", 185 lbs. Deb: 6/3/65

YEAR	TM/L	W	L	PCT	G	GS	CG	SH	SV	IP	H	HR	BB	SO	RAT	ERA	ERA+	OAV	OOB	BH	AVG	PB	PR	/A	PD	TPI
1965	SF-N	0	2	.000	4	2	0	0	0	6	13	0	6	5	28.5	16.50	22	.433	.528	0	.000	-0	-9	-9	0	-2.0
1966	Chi-N	8	13	.381	41	26	0	0	2	159	168	17	59	93	13.1	4.58	80	.272	.340	2	.041	-3	-17	-16	1	-2.2
1967	Chi-N	7	8	.467	49	11	3	1	6	150	134	9	48	84	11.0	2.46	144	.239	.301	4	.105	-1	15	18	-0	1.9
1968	Chi-N	16	10	.615	38	34	11	4	0	258^2	221	26	36	148	9.2	2.89	109	.231	.264	5	.061	-5	3	8	-0	0.2
1969	Chi-N	20	14	.588	41	41	18	3	0	300	268	21	73	181	10.4	2.49	162	.237	.287	9	.092	-5	37	**51**	1	5.5
1970	Chi-N	18	15	.545	39	38	12	2	1	265	278	20	76	170	12.2	3.70	122	.269	.322	10	.133	1	10	24	1	3.0
1971	Chi-N	12	18	.400	36	35	14	1	0	242^1	248	27	50	128	11.1	3.42	115	.260	.298	6	.083	-3	1	14	-0	1.3
1972	Chi-N	11	8	.579	32	28	6	3	0	189	168	12	47	96	10.3	3.00	127	.237	.286	1	.018	-4	10	17	-2	1.0
1973	Min-A	7	10	.412	39	15	3	1	2	142	138	14	41	78	11.5	3.49	114	.252	.307	0	—	0	5	7	-1	0.7
1974	Min-A	4	5	.444	35	10	0	0	3	115^1	130	9	25	74	12.4	4.45	84	.284	.327	0	—	0	-11	-9	-1	-0.9
	Tex-A	2	0	1.000	2	2	1	1	0	14	11	0	3	4	9.0	1.93	185	.208	.250	0	—	0	3	3	0	0.4
	Yr	6	5	.545	37	12	1	1	3	129^1	141	9	28	78	11.8	4.18	89	.274	.311	0	—	0	-8	-7	-1	-0.5
1975	Tex-A	6	7	.462	18	18	4	1	0	109^2	118	12	28	67	12.2	4.02	93	.271	.319	0	—	0	-3	-3	0	-0.3
Total	11	111	110	.502	374	260	72	17	14	1951	1895	167	492	1128	11.2	3.35	114	.253	.302	37	.078	-20	44	104	-0	8.6

● CHRIS HANEY
Haney, Christopher Deane b: 11/16/68, Baltimore, Md. BL/TL, 6'3", 195 lbs. Deb: 6/21/91 F

YEAR	TM/L	W	L	PCT	G	GS	CG	SH	SV	IP	H	HR	BB	SO	RAT	ERA	ERA+	OAV	OOB	BH	AVG	PB	PR	/A	PD	TPI
1991	Mon-N	3	7	.300	16	16	0	0	0	84^2	94	6	43	51	14.7	4.04	90	.280	.363	2	.074	-2	-3	-4	1	-0.5
1992	Mon-N	2	3	.400	9	6	1	1	0	38	40	6	10	27	12.8	5.45	64	.270	.333	2	.222	0	-8	-8	-0	-1.0
	KC-A	2	3	.400	7	7	1	1	0	42	35	5	16	27	10.9	3.86	105	.226	.298	0	—	0	0	1	-1	-0.2
1993	KC-A	9	9	.500	23	23	1	1	0	124	141	13	53	65	14.3	6.02	76	.286	.359	0	—	0	-23	-20	0	-2.4
1994	KC-A	2	2	.500	6	6	0	0	0	28^1	36	2	11	18	15.2	7.31	68	.333	.400	0	—	0	-8	-7	1	-0.9
1995	KC-A	3	4	.429	16	13	1	0	0	81^1	78	7	33	31	12.5	3.65	131	.262	.339	0	—	0	10	10	0	0.7
1996	KC-A	10	14	.417	35	35	4	1	0	228	267	29	51	115	12.8	4.70	107	.291	.332	0	—	0	7	8	-2	0.5
1997	KC-A	1	2	.333	8	3	0	0	0	24^2	29	1	5	16	13.1	4.38	108	.290	.336	0	—	0	1	1	0	0.0
1998	KC-A	6	6	.500	33	12	0	0	0	97^1	125	18	36	51	15.3	7.03	70	.316	.380	0	—	0	-26	-23	1	-2.3
	Chi-N	0	0	—	5	0	0	0	0	5	3	2	1	4	7.2	7.20	61	.167	.211	0	—	0	-2	-2	0	0.0
Total	8	38	50	.432	158	121	8	4	0	753^1	848	89	259	405	13.5	5.13	90	.286	.348	4	.111	-1	-52	-44	1	-6.1

● DON HANKINS
Hankins, Donald Wayne b: 2/9/02, Pendleton, Ind. d: 5/16/63, Winston-Salem, N.C BR/TR, 6'3", 183 lbs. Deb: 4/23/27

YEAR	TM/L	W	L	PCT	G	GS	CG	SH	SV	IP	H	HR	BB	SO	RAT	ERA	ERA+	OAV	OOB	BH	AVG	PB	PR	/A	PD	TPI
1927	Det-A	2	1	.667	20	1	0	0	2	42^2	67	1	13	10	16.9	6.33	67	.383	.426	1	.143	-1	-10	-10	0	-0.7

● FRANK HANKINSON
Hankinson, Frank Edward b: 4/29/1856, New York, N.Y. d: 4/5/11, Palisades Park, N.J BR/TR, 5'11", 168 lbs. Deb: 5/1/1878 ♦

YEAR	TM/L	W	L	PCT	G	GS	CG	SH	SV	IP	H	HR	BB	SO	RAT	ERA	ERA+	OAV	OOB	BH	AVG	PB	PR	/A	PD	TPI
1878	Chi-N	0	1	.000	1	1	1	0	0	9	11	0	0	4	11.0	6.00	40	.282	.282	64	.267	0	-4	-4	-0	-0.3
1879	Chi-N	15	10	.600	26	25	25	2	0	230^2	248	0	27	69	10.7	2.50	103	.255	.275	31	.181	-4	-0	2	4	0.2
1880	Cle-N	1	1	.500	4	2	2	0	1	25	20	0	3	8	8.3	1.08	218	.215	.240	55	.209	-0	4	4	1	0.4
1885	NY-a	0	0	—	1	0	0	0	0	2	2	1	1	0	13.5	4.50	66	.500	.600	81	.224	0	-0	-0	-0	0.0
Total	4	16	12	.571	32	28	28	2	1	266^2	281	1	31	81	10.5	2.50	102	.253	.274	747	.228	-4	-0	1	5	0.3

● JIM HANLEY
Hanley, James Patrick b: 10/13/1885, Providence, R.I. d: 5/1/61, Elmhurst, N.Y. BR/TL, 5'11", 165 lbs. Deb: 7/3/13

YEAR	TM/L	W	L	PCT	G	GS	CG	SH	SV	IP	H	HR	BB	SO	RAT	ERA	ERA+	OAV	OOB	BH	AVG	PB	PR	/A	PD	TPI
1913	NY-A	0	0	—	1	0	0	0	0	4	5	0	4	2	20.3	6.75	44	.313	.450	0	.000	-0	-2	-2	0	0.0

● PRESTON HANNA
Hanna, Preston Lee b: 9/10/54, Pensacola, Fla. BR/TR, 6'1", 195 lbs. Deb: 9/13/75

YEAR	TM/L	W	L	PCT	G	GS	CG	SH	SV	IP	H	HR	BB	SO	RAT	ERA	ERA+	OAV	OOB	BH	AVG	PB	PR	/A	PD	TPI
1975	Atl-N	0	0	—	4	0	0	0	0	5^2	7	0	5	2	22.2	1.59	238	.304	.467	0	—	0	1	1	-0	0.0
1976	Atl-N	0	0	—	5	0	0	0	0	8	11	0	4	3	16.9	4.50	84	.333	.405	0	.000	-0	-1	-1	-0	0.0
1977	Atl-N	2	6	.250	17	9	1	0	1	60	69	6	34	37	15.8	4.95	90	.285	.378	1	.071	-0	-7	-3	1	-0.3
1978	Atl-N	7	13	.350	29	28	0	0	0	140^1	132	10	93	90	14.6	5.13	79	.251	.367	9	.184	1	-24	-17	-0	-2.1
1979	Atl-N	1	1	.500	6	4	0	0	0	24^1	27	1	15	15	15.5	2.96	137	.284	.382	0	.000	-0	2	3	1	0.3
1980	Atl-N	2	0	1.000	32	2	0	0	0	79^1	63	3	44	35	12.5	3.18	118	.224	.335	2	.143	0	4	5	-1	0.0
1981	Atl-N	2	1	.667	20	1	0	0	0	35^1	45	2	23	22	17.3	6.37	56	.341	.439	1	.250	0	-11	-11	2	-0.7
1982	Atl-N	3	0	1.000	20	1	0	0	0	36	36	3	28	17	16.0	3.75	99	.277	.405	2	.400	1	-1	-0	-1	0.0
	Oak-A	0	4	.000	23	2	1	0	0	48^1	54	3	33	32	16.4	5.59	70	.287	.396	0	—	0	-8	-9	-0	-0.7
Total	8	17	25	.405	156	47	2	0	1	437^1	444	28	279	253	15.1	4.61	86	.269	.378	15	.161	1	-45	-31	1	-3.5

● GERRY HANNAHS
Hannahs, Gerald Ellis b: 3/6/53, Binghamton, N.Y. BL/TL, 6'3", 210 lbs. Deb: 9/8/76

YEAR	TM/L	W	L	PCT	G	GS	CG	SH	SV	IP	H	HR	BB	SO	RAT	ERA	ERA+	OAV	OOB	BH	AVG	PB	PR	/A	PD	TPI
1976	Mon-N	2	0	1.000	3	3	0	0	0	16	20	2	12	10	18.0	6.75	55	.323	.432	3	.375	1	-6	-5	-0	-0.5
1977	Mon-N	1	5	.167	8	7	0	0	0	37	43	7	17	21	14.6	4.86	78	.291	.364	0	.000	-0	-4	-4	-0	-0.7
1978	LA-N	0	0	—	1	0	0	0	0	2	3	0	0	5	13.5	9.00	39	.333	.333	0	—	0	-1	-1	0	0.0
1979	LA-N	0	2	.000	4	2	0	0	1	16	10	2	13	6	12.9	3.38	108	.175	.329	1	.250	0	1	0	0	0.1
Total	4	3	7	.300	16	12	0	0	1	71	76	11	42	42	15.0	5.07	74	.275	.371	4	.211	1	-10	-10	-1	-1.1

● JIM HANNAN
Hannan, James John b: 1/7/40, Jersey City, N.J. BR/TR, 6'3", 205 lbs. Deb: 4/17/62

YEAR	TM/L	W	L	PCT	G	GS	CG	SH	SV	IP	H	HR	BB	SO	RAT	ERA	ERA+	OAV	OOB	BH	AVG	PB	PR	/A	PD	TPI
1962	Was-A	2	4	.333	42	3	0	0	4	68	56	6	49	39	13.9	3.31	122	.230	.360	1	.091	-1	5	5	0	0.5
1963	Was-A	2	2	.500	13	2	0	0	0	27^2	23	2	17	14	13.0	4.88	76	.228	.339	0	.000	-0	-4	-4	0	-0.5
1964	Was-A	4	7	.364	49	7	0	0	3	106	108	13	45	67	13.0	4.16	89	.266	.339	3	.150	-1	-6	-5	-1	-0.7
1965	Was-A	1	1	.500	4	1	1	1	0	14^2	18	0	6	5	15.3	4.91	71	.340	.417	0	.000	-0	-2	-2	-1	-0.4
1966	Was-A	3	9	.250	30	18	2	0	0	114	125	9	59	68	14.8	4.26	81	.288	.377	2	.067	-2	-10	-10	-0	-1.2
1967	Was-A	1	1	.500	8	2	0	0	0	21^2	28	3	7	14	15.0	5.40	59	.315	.371	0	.000	-0	-5	-5	0	-0.5
1968	Was-A	10	6	.625	25	22	4	1	0	140^1	147	4	50	75	12.9	3.01	97	.272	.338	3	.064	-2	-1	-2	-0	-0.5
1969	Was-A	7	6	.538	35	28	1	1	0	158^1	138	17	91	72	13.1	3.64	95	.238	.343	6	.115	-2	-0	-3	-1	-0.5
1970	Was-A	9	11	.450	42	17	1	1	0	128	119	17	54	61	12.2	4.01	89	.250	.328	4	.129	-0	-4	-6	1	-0.9
1971	Det-A	1	0	1.000	7	0	0	0	0	11	7	1	7	6	12.3	3.27	110	.189	.333	0	.000	-0	0	0	1	0.1
	Mil-A	1	1	.500	21	1	0	0	0	32^1	38	7	21	17	16.7	5.01	69	.295	.397	0	.000	-0	-6	-6	-0	-0.4
	Yr	2	1	.667	28	1	0	0	0	43^1	45	8	28	23	15.4	4.57	77	.269	.378	0	.000	-1	-5	-5	0	-0.3
Total	10	41	48	.461	276	101	9	4	7	822	807	79	406	438	13.4	3.88	89	.261	.350	19	.091	-9	-34	-38	-1	-5.0

● LOY HANNING
Hanning, Loy Vernon b: 10/18/17, Bunker, Mo. d: 6/24/86, Anaconda, Mo. BR/TR, 6'2", 175 lbs. Deb: 9/20/39

YEAR	TM/L	W	L	PCT	G	GS	CG	SH	SV	IP	H	HR	BB	SO	RAT	ERA	ERA+	OAV	OOB	BH	AVG	PB	PR	/A	PD	TPI
1939	StL-A	0	1	.000	4	1	0	0	0	10	6	1	4	8	9.0	3.60	135	.158	.238	0	.000	-0	1	1	0	0.1
1942	StL-A	1	1	.500	11	0	0	0	0	17^1	26	2	12	9	20.3	7.79	48	.356	.453	1	.250	0	-8	-8	1	-0.7
Total	2	1	2	.333	15	1	0	0	0	27^1	32	3	16	17	16.1	6.26	66	.288	.383	1	.200	-0	-7	-6	1	-0.6

● GREG HANSELL
Hansell, Gregory Michael b: 3/12/71, Bellflower, Cal. BR/TR, 6'5", 215 lbs. Deb: 4/28/95

YEAR	TM/L	W	L	PCT	G	GS	CG	SH	SV	IP	H	HR	BB	SO	RAT	ERA	ERA+	OAV	OOB	BH	AVG	PB	PR	/A	PD	TPI
1995	LA-N	0	1	.000	20	0	0	0	0	19^1	29	5	6	13	17.2	7.45	51	.349	.407	0	—	0	-7	-8	-0	-0.4
1996	Min-A	3	0	1.000	50	0	0	0	3	74^1	83	14	31	46	14.0	5.69	90	.285	.358	0	—	0	-6	-5	-1	-0.3
1997	Mil-A	0	0	—	3	0	0	0	0	4^2	5	1	1	5	13.5	9.64	48	.263	.333	0	—	0	-3	-3	-0	-0.1
Total	3	3	1	.750	73	0	0	0	3	98^1	117	20	38	64	14.6	6.22	77	.298	.367	0	—	0	-15	-15	-1	-0.8

● ANDY HANSEN
Hansen, Andrew Viggo "Swede" b: 11/12/24, Lake Worth, Fla. BR/TR, 6'3", 190 lbs. Deb: 6/30/44

YEAR	TM/L	W	L	PCT	G	GS	CG	SH	SV	IP	H	HR	BB	SO	RAT	ERA	ERA+	OAV	OOB	BH	AVG	PB	PR	/A	PD	TPI
1944	NY-N	3	3	.500	23	4	0	0	1	52^2	63	3	32	15	16.7	6.49	56	.301	.402	2	.167	0	-17	-17	1	-1.6
1945	NY-N	4	3	.571	23	13	4	0	3	92^2	98	7	28	37	12.4	4.66	84	.273	.329	0	.000	-3	-9	-8	2	-0.7
1947	NY-N	1	5	.167	27	9	1	0	0	82^1	78	8	38	18	12.7	4.37	93	.248	.330	4	.190	-0	-3	-3	1	-0.1
1948	NY-N	5	3	.625	36	9	3	0	1	100	96	4	36	27	11.9	2.97	133	.255	.320	1	.050	-0	11	11	-1	0.7
1949	NY-N	2	6	.250	33	2	0	0	1	66^1	58	7	28	26	11.7	4.61	86	.234	.312	0	.000	-1	-4	-5	0	-0.5
1950	NY-N	0	1	.000	31	1	0	0	3	57	64	8	26	19	14.4	5.53	74	.279	.355	0	.000	-1	-9	-9	-0	-0.4
1951	Phi-N	3	1	.750	24	0	0	0	0	39	34	4	7	11	9.7	2.54	152	.228	.268	1	.333	1	6	6	1	0.7
1952	Phi-N	5	6	.455	43	0	0	0	4	77^1	76	6	27	18	12.3	3.26	112	.259	.328	2	.182	1	4	3	1	0.7

YEAR TM/L		W	L	PCT	G	GS	CG	SH	SV	IP	H	HR	BB	SO	RAT	ERA	ERA+	OAV	OOB	BH	AVG	PB	PR	/A	PD	TPI
1953	Phi-N	0	2	.000	30	1	0	0	3	51^1	60	6	24	17	14.9	4.03	104	.296	.373	2	.286	0	1	1	1	0.1
Total	9	23	30	.434	270	39	8	0	16	618^2	627	53	246	188	12.9	4.22	93	.263	.335	12	.102	-3	-19	-20	5	-1.1
● SNIPE HANSEN	Hansen, Roy Emil Frederick b: 2/21/07, Chicago, Ill. d: 9/11/78, Chicago, Ill. BB/TL, 6'3", 195 lbs. Deb: 7/5/30																									
1930	Phi-N	0	7	.000	22	9	1	0	0	84^1	123	8	38	25	17.4	6.72	81	.364	.431	3	.111	-2	-16	-12	-1	-1.0
1932	Phi-N	10	10	.500	39	23	5	0	2	191	215	13	51	56	12.8	3.72	118	.278	.328	8	.127	-4	3	15	-2	0.9
1933	Phi-N	6	14	.300	32	22	8	0	1	168^1	199	12	30	47	12.5	4.44	86	.294	.328	9	.155	-3	-21	-12	-1	-1.7
1934	Phi-N	6	12	.333	50	16	5	2	3	151	194	15	61	40	15.4	5.42	87	.307	.371	10	.233	-0	-23	-12	1	-1.1
1935	Phi-N	0	1	.000	2	1	0	0	0	4^1	8	0	5	0	27.0	12.46	36	.421	.542	0	.000	-0	-4	-4	0	-0.7
	StL-A	0	1	.000	10	0	0	0	0	26^2	44	2	9	8	18.2	8.78	55	.364	.412	1	.143	-1	-13	-12	-1	-0.5
Total	5	22	45	.328	155	71	19	2	6	625^2	783	50	194	176	14.3	5.01	90	.306	.358	31	.155	-10	-73	-36	-3	-4.1
● ROY HANSEN	Hansen, Roy Inglof "Ing" b: 3/6/1898, Beloit, Wis. d: 2/9/77, Beloit, Wis. BR/TR, 6', 165 lbs. Deb: 5/28/18																									
1918	Was-A	1	0	1.000	5	0	0	0	0	9	10	0	3	2	14.0	3.00	91	.278	.350	0	—	0	-0	-0	0	0.0
● F. C. HANSFORD	Hansford, F. C. TL, 6', 180 lbs. Deb: 6/9/1898																									
1898	Bro-N	0	0	—	1	0	0	0	0	7	10	0	5	0	19.3	3.86	93	.333	.429	0	.000	-1	-0	-0	-0	-0.1
● DON HANSKI	Hanski, Donald Thomas (b: Donald Thomas Hanyzewski) b: 2/27/16, LaPorte, Ind. d: 9/2/57, Worth, Ill. BL/TL, 5'11", 180 lbs. Deb: 5/6/43 ♦																									
1943	Chi-A	0	0	—	1	0	0	0	0	1	1	0	1	0	18.0	0.00	—	.333	.500	5	.238	0	0	0	-0	0.0
1944	Chi-A	0	0	—	2	0	0	0	0	3	5	0	2	0	21.0	12.00	29	.357	.438	0	.000	-0	-3	-3	-0	0.0
Total	2	0	0	—	3	0	0	0	0	4	6	0	3	0	20.3	9.00	38	.353	.450	5	.227	-0	-2	-2	-0	0.0
● OLLIE HANSON	Hanson, Earl Sylvester b: 1/19/1896, Holbrook, Mass. d: 8/19/51, Clifton, N.J. BR/TR, 5'11", 178 lbs. Deb: 4/27/21																									
1921	Chi-N	0	2	.000	2	2	1	0	0	9	9	0	6	2	16.0	7.00	55	.265	.390	0	.000	-0	-3	-3	0	-0.6
● ERIK HANSON	Hanson, Erik Brian b: 5/18/65, Kinnelon, N.J. BR/TR, 6'6", 210 lbs. Deb: 9/5/88																									
1988	Sea-A	2	3	.400	6	6	0	0	0	41^2	35	4	12	36	10.4	3.24	128	.230	.291	0	—	0	3	4	-0	0.4
1989	Sea-A	9	5	.643	17	17	1	0	0	113^1	103	7	32	75	11.1	3.18	127	.243	.304	0	—	0	9	11	0	1.1
1990	Sea-A	18	9	.667	33	33	5	1	0	236	205	15	68	211	10.5	3.24	122	.232	.289	0	—	0	17	19	-0	2.0
1991	Sea-A	8	8	.500	27	27	2	1	0	174^2	182	16	56	143	12.4	3.81	108	.269	.327	0	—	0	5	6	-1	0.4
1992	Sea-A	8	17	.320	31	30	6	1	0	186^2	209	14	57	112	13.2	4.82	82	.287	.345	0	—	0	-18	-18	0	-2.1
1993	Sea-A	11	12	.478	31	30	7	0	0	215	215	17	60	163	11.7	3.47	127	.263	.317	0	—	0	20	22	1	2.2
1994	Cin-N	5	5	.500	22	21	0	0	0	122^2	137	10	23	101	12.0	4.11	101	.283	.320	6	.154	-1	1	0	0	0.0
1995	*Bos-A☆	15	5	.750	29	29	1	1	0	186^2	187	17	59	139	11.9	4.24	115	.258	.314	0	—	0	10	13	-0	1.1
1996	Tor-A	13	17	.433	35	35	4	1	0	214^2	243	26	102	156	14.5	5.41	92	.289	.367	0	—	0	-10	-10	-3	-1.3
1997	Tor-A	0	0	—	3	2	0	0	0	15	15	3	6	18	12.6	7.80	59	.254	.323	0	—	0	-5	-5	-0	0.0
1998	Tor-A	0	3	.000	11	8	0	0	0	49	73	10	29	21	18.9	6.24	74	.348	.429	0	—	0	-9	-9	1	-0.4
Total	11	89	84	.514	245	238	26	5	0	1555^1	1604	139	504	1175	12.4	4.15	105	.267	.327	6	.154	-1	24	34	-3	3.4
● ED HANYZEWSKI	Hanyzewski, Edward Michael b: 9/18/20, Union Mills, Ind. d: 10/8/91, Fargo, N.D. BR/TR, 6'1", 200 lbs. Deb: 5/12/42																									
1942	Chi-N	1	1	.500	6	1	0	0	0	19	17	2	8	6	11.8	3.79	84	.254	.333	1	.200	-0	-1	-1	0	-0.1
1943	Chi-N	8	7	.533	33	16	3	0	0	130	120	2	45	55	11.6	2.56	130	.243	.309	2	.049	-4	12	11	2	1.0
1944	Chi-N	2	5	.286	14	7	3	0	0	58^1	61	6	20	19	12.7	4.47	79	.261	.322	1	.059	-1	-6	-6	3	-0.4
1945	Chi-N	0	0	—	2	1	0	0	0	4^2	7	1	1	0	15.4	5.79	63	.350	.381	0	.000	0	-1	-1	0	0.0
1946	Chi-N	1	0	1.000	3	0	0	0	0	6	8	0	5	1	21.0	4.50	74	.348	.483	0	.000	-0	-1	-1	0	-0.1
Total	5	12	13	.480	58	25	6	0	0	218	213	11	79	81	12.2	3.30	102	.254	.321	4	.062	-5	4	2	5	0.4
● MEL HARDER	Harder, Melvin Leroy "Chief" b: 10/15/09, Beemer, Neb. BR/TR, 6'1", 195 lbs. Deb: 4/24/28 MC																									
1928	Cle-A	0	2	.000	23	1	0	0	1	49	64	4	32	15	17.6	6.61	63	.335	.430	0	.000	-1	-14	-13	-1	-0.7
1929	Cle-A	1	0	1.000	11	0	0	0	0	17^2	24	2	5	4	16.3	5.60	79	.333	.400	0	.000	-0	-3	-2	-0	-0.2
1930	Cle-A	11	10	.524	36	19	7	0	2	175^1	205	9	68	45	14.2	4.21	115	.295	.361	9	.143	-4	9	12	-1	0.8
1931	Cle-A	13	14	.481	40	24	9	0	1	194	229	8	72	63	14.2	4.36	106	.289	.352	19	.253	1	0	6	0	0.8
1932	Cle-A	15	13	.536	39	32	17	1	0	254^2	277	9	68	90	12.3	3.75	127	.272	.319	17	.181	-0	21	28	3	2.9
1933	Cle-A	15	17	.469	43	31	14	2	4	253	254	10	67	81	11.5	2.95	**151**	.259	.309	16	.190	-1	**37**	**42**	8	**5.7**
1934	Cle-A★	20	12	.625	44	29	17	**6**	4	255^1	246	6	81	91	11.8	2.61	**174**	.254	.316	14	.161	-1	54	**55**	2	**6.4**
1935	Cle-A★	22	11	.667	42	35	17	4	2	287^1	313	6	53	95	11.5	3.29	137	.275	.307	21	.206	-1	37	39	5	4.4
1936	Cle-A★	15	15	.500	36	30	13	0	1	224^2	294	13	71	84	14.9	5.17	97	.313	.365	11	.138	-4	-3	-3	0	-0.7
1937	Cle-A★	15	12	.556	38	30	13	0	2	233^2	269	9	86	95	13.8	4.28	108	.288	.350	15	.174	-1	9	9	2	0.9
1938	Cle-A	17	10	.630	38	29	15	2	4	240	257	16	62	102	12.2	3.83	121	.271	.319	10	.114	-5	26	22	2	1.8
1939	Cle-A	15	9	.625	29	26	12	1	1	208	213	15	64	67	12.1	3.50	126	.269	.326	10	.139	-2	26	21	-2	1.8
1940	Cle-A	12	11	.522	31	25	5	0	0	186^1	200	16	59	76	12.8	4.06	104	.278	.337	11	.177	-1	7	3	1	0.4
1941	Cle-A	5	4	.556	15	10	1	0	1	68^2	76	8	37	21	15.1	5.24	75	.279	.370	2	.080	-2	-8	-10	1	-1.2
1942	Cle-A	13	14	.481	29	29	13	4	0	198^2	179	8	82	74	12.0	3.44	100	.240	.317	8	.119	-3	5	0	1	-0.2
1943	Cle-A	8	7	.533	19	18	6	1	0	135^1	126	7	61	40	12.5	3.06	102	.254	.337	10	.213	2	4	1	-0	0.2
1944	Cle-A	12	10	.545	30	27	12	2	0	196^1	211	5	69	64	13.0	3.71	89	.278	.341	16	.216	1	-6	-9	-1	-0.9
1945	Cle-A	3	7	.300	11	11	2	0	0	76	93	3	23	16	13.7	3.67	88	.303	.352	2	.080	-2	-3	-4	1	-0.6
1946	Cle-A	5	4	.556	13	12	4	1	0	92^1	85	4	31	21	11.3	3.41	97	.249	.311	3	.086	-2	1	-1	-2	-0.5
1947	Cle-A	6	4	.600	15	15	4	1	0	80	91	3	27	17	13.4	4.50	77	.289	.347	5	.179	0	-7	-9	-1	-1.1
Total	20	223	186	.545	582	433	181	25	23	3426^1	3706	161	1118	1161	12.8	3.80	113	.276	.334	199	.165	-27	190	182	18	20.0
● JIM HARDIN	Hardin, James Warren b: 8/6/43, Morris Chapel, Tenn. d: 3/9/91, Key West, Fla. BR/TR, 6', 175 lbs. Deb: 6/23/67																									
1967	Bal-A	8	3	.727	19	14	5	2	0	111	85	5	27	64	9.3	2.27	139	.211	.266	5	.135	-0	12	11	-1	1.0
1968	Bal-A	18	13	.581	35	35	16	2	0	244	188	20	70	160	9.9	2.51	117	.212	.277	7	.085	-3	13	11	-0	1.1
1969	Bal-A	6	7	.462	30	20	3	1	1	137^2	128	18	43	64	11.6	3.60	99	.248	.313	7	.156	2	0	-0	-1	0.0
1970	Bal-A	6	5	.545	36	19	3	2	1	145^1	150	13	26	78	11.0	3.53	103	.267	.301	3	.067	-1	3	2	-2	-0.2
1971	Bal-A	0	0	—	6	0	0	0	0	5^2	12	0	3	3	23.8	4.76	70	.480	.536	0	—	0	-1	-1	0	0.0
	NY-A	0	2	.000	12	3	0	0	0	28^1	35	3	9	14	14.3	5.08	64	.313	.369	0	.000	-0	-5	-6	-0	-0.5
	Yr	0	2	.000	18	3	0	0	0	34	47	3	12	17	15.9	5.03	65	.343	.400	0	.000	-0	-6	-7	-0	-0.5
1972	Atl-N	5	2	.714	26	9	1	0	2	79^2	93	11	24	25	13.4	4.41	86	.287	.340	2	.095	1	-8	-5	-1	-0.5
Total	6	43	32	.573	164	100	28	7	4	751^2	691	70	202	408	11.0	3.18	104	.244	.300	24	.103	-3	14	11	-5	0.9
● CHARLIE HARDING	Harding, Charles Harold "Slim" b: 1/3/1891, Nashville, Tenn. d: 10/30/71, Bold Spring, Tenn BR/TR, 6'2.5", 172 lbs. Deb: 9/18/13																									
1913	Det-A	0	0	—	1	0	0	0	0	2	3	0	1	0	18.0	4.50	65	.375	.444	0	—	0	-0	-0	0	0.0
● ALEX HARDY	Hardy, David Alexander "Dooney" b: 1877, Toronto, Ont., Canada d: 4/22/40, Toronto, Ont., Can. TL, Deb: 9/4/02																									
1902	Chi-N	2	2	.500	4	4	4	1	0	35	29	0	12	12	10.5	3.60	75	.227	.293	3	.214	0	-3	-3	-1	-0.4
1903	Chi-N	1	1	.500	3	3	1	0	0	12^2	21	0	7	4	20.6	6.39	49	.375	.453	1	.167	0	-4	-5	0	-0.5
Total	2	3	3	.500	7	7	5	1	0	47^2	50	0	19	16	13.2	4.34	65	.272	.343	4	.200	1	-8	-8	-0	-0.9
● RED HARDY	Hardy, Francis Joseph b: 1/6/23, Marmarth, N.Dak. BR/TR, 5'11", 175 lbs. Deb: 6/20/51																									
1951	NY-N	0	0	—	2	0	0	0	0	1^1	4	0	1	0	40.5	6.75	58	.571	.667	0	—	0	-0	-0	0	0.0
● HARRY HARDY	Hardy, Harry b: 11/5/1875, Steubenville, Ohio d: 9/4/43, Steubenville, Ohio BL/TL, 5'6", 155 lbs. Deb: 9/26/05																									
1905	Was-A	1	1	.500	3	2	2	0	0	24	20	0	6	10	9.8	1.88	141	.227	.277	1	.111	-1	2	2	-1	-0.1
1906	Was-A	0	3	.000	5	3	2	0	0	20	35	0	12	4	21.1	9.00	29	.385	.456	0	.000	-1	-14	-14	1	-1.7
Total	2	1	4	.200	8	5	4	0	0	44	55	0	18	14	14.9	5.11	52	.307	.371	1	.067	-2	-12	-12	-0	-1.8
● LARRY HARDY	Hardy, Howard Lawrence b: 1/10/48, Goose Creek, Tex. BR/TR, 5'10", 180 lbs. Deb: 4/28/74																									
1974	SD-N	9	4	.692	76	1	0	0	2	101^2	129	9	44	57	15.3	4.69	76	.317	.384	0	.000	-1	-12	-13	1	-1.5
1975	SD-N	0	0	—	3	0	0	0	0	2^2	8	3	2	3	33.8	13.50	26	.500	.556	0	—	0	-3	-3	-0	0.0

YEAR	TM/L	W	L	PCT	G	GS	CG	SH	SV	IP	H	HR	BB	SO	RAT	ERA	ERA+	OAV	OOB	BH	AVG	PB	PR	/A	PD	TPI
1976	Hou-N	0	0	—	15	0	0	0	3	21^2	34	2	10	10	18.3	7.06	45	.362	.423	0	.000	-0	-9	-9	0	-0.3
Total	3	9	4	.692	94	1	0	0	5	126	171	14	56	70	16.2	5.29	66	.331	.396	0	.000	-1	-24	-25	1	-1.8

● JACK HARDY

Hardy, John Graydon b: 10/8/59, St.Petersburg, Fla. BR/TR, 6'2", 175 lbs. Deb: 5/23/89

YEAR	TM/L	W	L	PCT	G	GS	CG	SH	SV	IP	H	HR	BB	SO	RAT	ERA	ERA+	OAV	OOB	BH	AVG	PB	PR	/A	PD	TPI
1989	Chi-A	0	0	—	5	0	0	0	0	12^1	14	1	5	4	14.6	6.57	58	.286	.364	0	—	0	-4	-4	1	0.2

● STEVE HARGAN

Hargan, Steven Lowell b: 9/8/42, Ft.Wayne, Ind. BR/TR, 6'3", 180 lbs. Deb: 8/3/65

YEAR	TM/L	W	L	PCT	G	GS	CG	SH	SV	IP	H	HR	BB	SO	RAT	ERA	ERA+	OAV	OOB	BH	AVG	PB	PR	/A	PD	TPI
1965	Cle-A	4	3	.571	17	8	1	0	2	60^1	55	2	28	37	12.5	3.43	101	.246	.332	1	.053	-1	0	0	0	-0.1
1966	Cle-A	13	10	.565	38	21	7	3	0	192	173	9	45	132	10.3	2.48	138	.241	.286	7	.121	-2	20	20	0	2.3
1967	Cle-A☆	14	13	.519	30	29	15	**6**	0	223	180	9	72	141	10.3	2.62	125	.224	.290	11	.164	1	15	16	1	2.3
1968	Cle-A	8	15	.348	32	27	4	2	0	158^1	139	11	81	78	12.8	4.15	71	.241	.340	9	.176	1	-21	-21	-2	-3.1
1969	Cle-A	5	14	.263	32	23	1	1	0	143^2	145	14	81	76	14.3	5.70	66	.265	.363	7	.159	-1	-33	-31	2	-3.6
1970	Cle-A	11	3	.786	23	19	8	1	0	142^2	101	14	53	72	9.9	2.90	136	.201	.281	5	.111	-2	13	17	1	1.5
1971	Cle-A	1	13	.071	37	16	1	0	1	113^1	138	18	56	52	15.9	6.19	62	.304	.388	2	.063	-3	-34	-30	-2	-3.8
1972	Cle-A	0	3	.000	12	1	0	0	0	20	23	1	15	10	17.1	5.85	55	.291	.404	0	.000	-0	-6	-6	1	-0.8
1974	Tex-A	12	9	.571	37	27	8	2	0	186^2	202	15	48	98	12.3	3.95	90	.275	.324	0	—	0	-7	-8	2	-0.7
1975	Tex-A	9	10	.474	33	26	8	1	0	189^1	203	17	62	93	12.9	3.80	99	.275	.336	0	—	0	-1	-1	2	0.1
1976	Tex-A	8	8	.500	35	8	2	1	1	124^1	127	8	38	63	12.2	3.62	99	.261	.318	0	—	0	-1	-0	-0	-0.1
1977	Tor-A	1	3	.250	6	5	1	0	0	29^1	36	2	14	11	15.3	5.22	80	.308	.382	0	—	0	-4	-3	0	-0.4
	Tex-A	1	0	1.000	6	0	0	0	0	12^1	22	2	5	10	19.7	8.76	47	.393	.443	0	—	0	-6	-6	-0	-0.5
	Yr	2	3	.400	12	5	1	0	0	41^2	58	4	19	21	16.6	6.26	66	.335	.401	0	—	0	-10	-10	0	-0.9
	Atl-N	0	3	.000	16	5	0	0	0	36^2	49	3	16	18	16.0	6.87	65	.325	.389	0	.000	-1	-12	-10	1	-0.7
Total	12	87	107	.448	354	215	56	17	4	1632	1593	125	614	891	12.4	3.92	91	.257	.328	42	.129	-7	-77	-64	6	-7.6

● ALAN HARGESHEIMER

Hargesheimer, Alan Robert b: 11/21/54, Chicago, Ill. BR/TR, 6'3", 195 lbs. Deb: 7/14/80

YEAR	TM/L	W	L	PCT	G	GS	CG	SH	SV	IP	H	HR	BB	SO	RAT	ERA	ERA+	OAV	OOB	BH	AVG	PB	PR	/A	PD	TPI
1980	SF-N	4	6	.400	15	13	0	0	0	75	82	3	32	40	13.7	4.32	82	.285	.356	4	.182	1	-6	-7	-1	-0.8
1981	SF-N	1	2	.333	6	3	0	0	0	18^2	20	1	9	6	14.5	4.34	79	.299	.390	1	.200	0	-2	-2	0	-0.2
1983	Chi-N	0	0	—	5	0	0	0	0	4	6	0	2	5	18.0	9.00	42	.375	.444	0	—	0	-2	-2	-0	0.0
1986	KC-A	0	1	.000	5	1	0	0	0	13	18	1	7	4	18.0	6.23	68	.340	.426	0	—	0	-3	-3	-0	-0.3
Total	4	5	9	.357	31	17	0	0	0	110^2	126	5	50	55	14.5	4.72	77	.297	.374	5	.185	1	-13	-14	-1	-1.3

● TIM HARIKKALA

Harikkala, Timothy Allan b: 7/15/71, W.Palm Beach, Fla. BR/TR, 6'2", 185 lbs. Deb: 5/27/95

YEAR	TM/L	W	L	PCT	G	GS	CG	SH	SV	IP	H	HR	BB	SO	RAT	ERA	ERA+	OAV	OOB	BH	AVG	PB	PR	/A	PD	TPI
1995	Sea-A	0	0	—	1	0	0	0	0	3^1	7	1	1	1	21.6	16.20	29	.412	.444	0	—	0	-4	-4	-0	0.0
1996	Sea-A	0	1	.000	1	1	0	0	0	4^1	4	1	2	1	14.5	12.46	40	.250	.368	0	—	0	-4	-4	0	-0.5
Total	2	0	1	.000	2	1	0	0	0	7^2	11	2	3	2	17.6	14.09	34	.333	.405	0	—	0	-8	-8	0	-0.5

● MIKE HARKEY

Harkey, Michael Anthony b: 10/25/66, San Diego, Cal. BR/TR, 6'5", 220 lbs. Deb: 9/5/88

YEAR	TM/L	W	L	PCT	G	GS	CG	SH	SV	IP	H	HR	BB	SO	RAT	ERA	ERA+	OAV	OOB	BH	AVG	PB	PR	/A	PD	TPI
1988	Chi-N	0	3	.000	5	5	0	0	0	34^2	33	0	15	18	13.0	2.60	139	.248	.333	1	.091	-1	3	4	-1	0.2
1990	Chi-N	12	6	.667	27	27	2	1	0	173^2	153	14	59	94	11.3	3.26	125	.234	.305	14	.250	3	10	16	-1	1.8
1991	Chi-N	0	2	.000	4	4	0	0	0	18^2	21	3	6	15	13.0	5.30	73	.273	.325	2	.400	1	-3	-3	0	-0.2
1992	Chi-N	4	0	1.000	7	7	0	0	0	38	34	4	15	21	11.8	1.89	190	.243	.321	4	.267	1	7	7	-0	0.9
1993	Chi-N	10	10	.500	28	28	1	0	0	157^1	187	17	43	67	13.3	5.26	76	.305	.353	5	.093	-2	-21	-22	-1	-2.8
1994	Col-N	1	6	.143	24	13	0	0	0	91^2	125	10	35	39	15.8	5.79	86	.336	.395	4	.182	-1	-16	-8	1	-0.5
1995	Oak-A	4	6	.400	14	12	0	0	0	66	75	12	31	28	14.9	6.27	71	.292	.375	0	—	0	-11	-13	1	-1.5
	Cal-A	4	3	.571	12	8	1	0	0	61^1	80	12	16	28	14.2	4.55	103	.311	.354	0	—	0	1	1	-2	0.0
	Yr	8	9	.471	26	20	1	0	0	127^1	155	24	47	56	14.3	5.44	84	.299	.358	0	—	0	-10	-12	-1	-1.5
1997	LA-N	1	0	1.000	10	0	0	0	0	14^2	12	3	5	6	10.4	4.30	90	.211	.274	0	.000	-0	-0	-1	-0	-0.1
Total	8	36	36	.500	131	104	4	1	0	656	720	75	225	316	13.2	4.49	94	.281	.344	30	.183	1	-31	-19	-4	-2.2

● JOHN HARKINS

Harkins, John Joseph "Pa" b: 4/12/1859, New Brunswick, N.J d: 11/20/40, New Brunswick, N.J BR/TR, 6'1", 205 lbs. Deb: 5/2/1884

YEAR	TM/L	W	L	PCT	G	GS	CG	SH	SV	IP	H	HR	BB	SO	RAT	ERA	ERA+	OAV	OOB	BH	AVG	PB	PR	/A	PD	TPI
1884	Cle-N	12	32	.273	46	45	42	3	0	391	399	7	108	192	11.7	3.68	86	.249	.297	47	.205	-4	-30	-23	-1	-2.4
1885	Bro-a	14	20	.412	34	34	33	1	0	293	303	7	56	141	11.2	3.75	88	.250	.287	42	.264	5	-16	-15	4	-0.5
1886	Bro-a	15	16	.484	34	33	33	0	0	292^1	286	6	114	118	12.5	3.60	97	.244	.313	32	.225	3	-5	-4	2	0.2
1887	Bro-a	10	14	.417	24	24	22	0	0	199	262	6	77	36	15.6	6.02	72	.309	.369	23	.235	-0	-38	-38	-1	-3.2
1888	Bal-a	0	1	.000	1	1	1	0	0	8	12	0	3	2	16.9	6.75	44	.333	.385	0	.000	-0	-3	-3	0	-0.3
Total	5	51	83	.381	139	137	131	4	0	1183^1	1262	26	358	489	12.5	4.09	85	.259	.312	144	.228	4	-93	-81	5	-6.2

● SPEC HARKNESS

Harkness, Frederick Harvey b: 12/13/1887, Los Angeles, Cal. d: 5/16/52, Compton, Cal. BR/TR, 5'11", 180 lbs. Deb: 6/13/10

YEAR	TM/L	W	L	PCT	G	GS	CG	SH	SV	IP	H	HR	BB	SO	RAT	ERA	ERA+	OAV	OOB	BH	AVG	PB	PR	/A	PD	TPI
1910	Cle-A	10	7	.588	26	16	6	1	1	136^1	132	2	55	60	12.5	3.04	85	.268	.345	7	.140	-1	-8	-7	-1	-1.1
1911	Cle-A	2	2	.500	12	6	3	0	0	53^1	62	1	21	25	14.0	4.22	81	.310	.376	6	.316	1	-5	-5	-2	-0.4
Total	2	12	9	.571	38	22	9	1	1	189^2	194	3	76	85	13.0	3.37	84	.280	.354	13	.188	-0	-13	-12	-3	-1.5

● DICK HARLEY

Harley, Henry Risk b: 8/18/1874, Springfield, Ohio d: 5/16/61, Springfield, Ohio BR/TR, Deb: 4/15/05

YEAR	TM/L	W	L	PCT	G	GS	CG	SH	SV	IP	H	HR	BB	SO	RAT	ERA	ERA+	OAV	OOB	BH	AVG	PB	PR	/A	PD	TPI
1905	Bos-N	2	5	.286	9	4	4	1	0	65^2	72	5	19	19	12.6	4.66	67	.286	.338	1	.045	-2	-12	-11	2	-1.1

● LARRY HARLOW

Harlow, Larry Duane b: 11/13/51, Colorado Springs, Colo. BL/TL, 6'2", 185 lbs. Deb: 9/20/75 ◆

YEAR	TM/L	W	L	PCT	G	GS	CG	SH	SV	IP	H	HR	BB	SO	RAT	ERA	ERA+	OAV	OOB	BH	AVG	PB	PR	/A	PD	TPI
1978	Bal-A	0	0	—	1	0	0	0	0	0^2	2	1	4	1	81.0	67.50	5	.500	.750	112	.243	0	-5	-5	0	0.0

● BILL HARMAN

Harman, William Bell b: 1/2/19, Bridgewater, Va. BR/TR, 6'4", 200 lbs. Deb: 6/17/41 ◆

YEAR	TM/L	W	L	PCT	G	GS	CG	SH	SV	IP	H	HR	BB	SO	RAT	ERA	ERA+	OAV	OOB	BH	AVG	PB	PR	/A	PD	TPI
1941	Phi-N	0	0	—	5	0	0	0	0	13	15	0	8	3	15.9	4.85	76	.319	.418	1	.071	-0	-2	-2	-0	-0.1

● BOB HARMON

Harmon, Robert Green "Hickory Bob" b: 10/15/1887, Liberal, Mo. d: 11/27/61, Monroe, La. BB/TR, 6', 187 lbs. Deb: 6/23/09

YEAR	TM/L	W	L	PCT	G	GS	CG	SH	SV	IP	H	HR	BB	SO	RAT	ERA	ERA+	OAV	OOB	BH	AVG	PB	PR	/A	PD	TPI
1909	StL-N	6	11	.353	21	17	10	0	0	159	155	6	65	48	12.7	3.68	69	.265	.342	13	.255	4	-19	-20	-0	-1.7
1910	StL-N	13	15	.464	43	33	15	0	2	236	227	1	133	87	14.0	4.46	67	.258	.360	14	.184	2	-37	-39	2	-3.8
1911	StL-N	23	16	.590	51	41	28	2	4	348	290	10	181	144	12.4	3.13	108	.235	.336	17	.153	0	11	10	1	1.1
1912	StL-N	18	18	.500	43	34	15	3	0	268	284	4	116	73	13.5	3.93	87	.281	.357	23	.232	1	-15	-15	4	-1.3
1913	StL-N	8	21	.276	42	27	16	1	2	273^1	291	6	99	66	13.0	3.92	83	.286	.353	24	.261	5	-22	-21	2	-1.4
1914	Pit-N	13	17	.433	37	30	19	2	3	245	226	3	55	61	10.6	2.53	105	.252	.300	12	.140	-1	7	3	-1	0.1
1915	Pit-N	16	17	.485	37	32	25	5	1	269^2	242	6	62	86	10.2	2.50	109	.247	.294	14	.147	1	7	7	4	1.4
1916	Pit-N	8	11	.421	31	17	10	2	0	172^2	175	4	39	62	11.2	2.81	95	.267	.309	6	.109	-3	-4	-2	3	-0.2
1918	Pit-N	2	7	.222	16	9	5	0	0	82^1	76	3	12	7	9.6	2.62	109	.254	.283	4	.148	-1	1	2	0	0.2
Total	9	107	133	.446	321	240	143	15	12	2054	1966	43	762	634	12.1	3.33	90	.260	.331	127	.184	7	-71	-76	14	-5.6

● PETE HARNISCH

Harnisch, Peter Thomas b: 9/23/66, Commack, N.Y. BB/TR, 6', 207 lbs. Deb: 9/13/88

YEAR	TM/L	W	L	PCT	G	GS	CG	SH	SV	IP	H	HR	BB	SO	RAT	ERA	ERA+	OAV	OOB	BH	AVG	PB	PR	/A	PD	TPI
1988	Bal-A	0	2	.000	2	2	0	0	0	13	13	1	9	10	15.2	5.54	70	.260	.373	0	—	0	-2	-2	0	-0.3
1989	Bal-A	5	9	.357	18	17	2	0	0	103^1	97	10	64	70	14.5	4.62	82	.249	.362	0	—	0	-8	-9	-1	-1.1
1990	Bal-A	11	11	.500	31	31	3	0	0	188^2	189	17	86	122	13.2	4.34	87	.261	.341	0	—	0	-9	-11	-2	-1.4
1991	Hou-N★	12	9	.571	33	33	4	2	0	216^2	169	14	83	172	10.7	2.70	130	**.212**	.291	6	.097	-1	24	19	-3	1.3
1992	Hou-N	9	10	.474	34	34	0	0	0	206^2	182	18	64	164	10.9	3.70	91	.233	.296	11	.164	2	-5	-8	-3	-0.8
1993	Hou-N	16	9	.640	33	33	5	**4**	0	217^2	171	20	79	185	10.6	2.98	130	**.214**	.290	7	.104	-1	26	22	-4	1.8
1994	Hou-N	8	5	.615	17	17	1	0	0	95	100	13	39	62	13.5	5.40	73	.269	.343	6	.171	1	-13	-15	-1	-1.7
1995	NY-N	2	8	.200	18	18	0	0	0	110	111	13	24	82	11.3	3.68	110	.261	.305	3	.091	-2	6	4	-1	0.1
1996	NY-N	8	12	.400	31	31	2	1	0	194^2	195	30	61	114	12.2	4.21	95	.260	.322	5	.091	-2	0	-4	-3	-0.9
1997	NY-N	0	1	.000	6	5	0	0	0	25^2	35	5	11	12	16.5	8.06	50	.327	.395	0	.000	-1	-11	-12	0	-0.4
	Mil-A	1	1	.500	4	3	0	0	0	14	13	1	12	10	16.1	5.14	90	.245	.385	0	—	0	-1	-1	-0	-0.1
1998	Cin-N	14	7	.667	32	32	2	1	0	209	176	24	64	157	10.6	3.14	138	.228	.293	7	.106	-3	25	27	-1	2.1
Total	11	86	84	.506	259	256	19	8	0	1594^1	1451	166	596	1160	11.8	3.79	101	.241	.314	45	.115	-8	32	10	-17	-1.4

● JACK HARPER

Harper, Charles William b: 4/2/1878, Galloway, Pa. d: 9/30/50, Jamestown, N.Y. BR/TR, 6', 178 lbs. Deb: 9/18/1899

YEAR	TM/L	W	L	PCT	G	GS	CG	SH	SV	IP	H	HR	BB	SO	RAT	ERA	ERA+	OAV	OOB	BH	AVG	PB	PR	/A	PD	TPI
1899	Cle-N	1	4	.200	5	5	5	0	0	37	44	3	12	14	14.4	3.89	95	.295	.360	2	.182	1	-0	-1	-0	0.0
1900	StL-N	0	1	.000	1	1	0	0	0	3	4	0	2	0	18.0	12.00	30	.308	.400	0	.000	-0	-3	-3	0	-0.6
1901	StL-N	23	13	.639	39	37	28	1	0	308^2	294	7	99	128	11.9	3.62	88	.249	.316	20	.172	1	-10	-15	1	-1.3

YEAR	TM/L	W	L	PCT	G	GS	CG	SH	SV	IP	H	HR	BB	SO	RAT	ERA	ERA+	OAV	OOB	BH	AVG	PB	PR	/A	PD	TPI
1902	StL-A	15	11	.577	29	26	20	2	0	222^1	224	8	81	74	12.7	4.13	85	.262	.332	17	.205	-0	-14	-15	1	-1.4
1903	Cin-N	8	9	.471	17	15	13	0	0	135	143	2	70	45	14.9	4.33	82	.271	.367	14	.250	2	-16	-12	1	-1.0
1904	Cin-N	23	9	.719	35	35	31	6	0	293^2	262	2	85	125	10.9	2.30	128	.234	.293	18	.159	-2	14	21	-5	1.4
1905	Cin-N	9	13	.409	26	23	15	1	1	179^1	189	2	69	70	13.3	3.86	86	.271	.344	10	.167	1	-17	-11	-0	-1.3
1906	Cin-N	1	4	.200	5	5	3	0	0	36^2	38	1	20	10	14.7	4.17	66	.286	.387	3	.273	1	-6	-6	-1	-0.7
	Chi-N	0	0	—	1	1	0	0	0	1	0	0	0	0	0.0	0.00	—	.000	.000	0	—	0	0	0	0	0.0
	Yr	1	4	.200	6	6	3	0	0	37^2	38	1	20	10	13.9	4.06	68	.275	.367	3	.273	1	-6	-5	-1	-0.7
Total	8	80	64	.556	158	148	115	10	1	1216^2	1198	25	438	466	12.5	3.55	92	.256	.327	84	.186	3	-51	-39	-3	-4.9

● GEORGE HARPER
Harper, George B. b: 8/17/1866, Milwaukee, Wis. d: 12/11/31, Stockton, Cal. BR/TR, 5'10", 165 lbs. Deb: 7/11/1894

YEAR	TM/L	W	L	PCT	G	GS	CG	SH	SV	IP	H	HR	BB	SO	RAT	ERA	ERA+	OAV	OOB	BH	AVG	PB	PR	/A	PD	TPI
1894	Phi-N	6	6	.500	12	9	7	0	0	86^1	128	3	49	24	18.7	5.32	96	.340	.418	6	.150	-4	0	-2	-1	-0.5
1896	Bro-N	4	8	.333	16	11	7	0	0	86	106	4	39	22	15.5	5.55	74	.300	.375	6	.162	0	-11	-14	1	-1.3
Total	2	10	14	.417	28	20	14	0	0	172^1	234	7	88	46	17.1	5.43	85	.321	.397	12	.156	-4	-11	-16	0	-1.8

● HARRY HARPER
Harper, Harry Clayton b: 4/24/1895, Hackensack, N.J. d: 4/23/63, New York, N.Y. BL/TL, 6'2", 165 lbs. Deb: 6/27/13

YEAR	TM/L	W	L	PCT	G	GS	CG	SH	SV	IP	H	HR	BB	SO	RAT	ERA	ERA+	OAV	OOB	BH	AVG	PB	PR	/A	PD	TPI
1913	Was-A	0	0	—	4	0	0	0	0	12^2	10	1	5	9	11.4	3.55	83	.204	.291	1	.250	0	-1	-1	0	0.0
1914	Was-A	2	1	.667	23	3	1	0	2	57	45	1	35	50	13.4	3.47	81	.211	.336	3	.250	0	-5	-4	-1	-0.4
1915	Was-A	4	4	.500	19	10	5	2	2	86^1	66	1	40	54	11.2	1.77	168	.222	.317	0	.000	-4	11	11	-2	0.5
1916	Was-A	14	10	.583	36	34	13	2	0	249^2	209	4	101	149	11.5	2.45	114	.235	.319	18	.207	1	10	9	-4	0.5
1917	Was-A	11	12	.478	31	31	10	4	0	179^1	145	1	106	99	12.8	3.01	87	.230	.345	7	.117	-3	-7	-8	-3	-1.6
1918	Was-A	11	10	.524	35	32	14	3	1	244	182	1	104	78	10.8	2.18	125	.212	.303	11	.134	-4	16	15	-5	0.3
1919	Was-A	6	21	.222	35	31	8	0	0	208	220	3	97	87	14.1	3.72	86	.284	.370	11	.169	-2	-11	-12	-1	-1.8
1920	Bos-A	5	14	.263	27	22	11	1	0	162^2	163	9	66	71	12.8	3.04	120	.275	.349	6	.120	-3	14	11	-3	0.5
1921	*NY-A	4	3	.571	8	7	4	0	0	52^2	52	3	25	22	13.5	3.76	113	.263	.351	2	.125	-1	3	3	-2	0.0
1923	Bro-N	0	1	.000	1	1	0	0	0	3^2	8	2	3	4	27.0	14.73	26	.421	.500	0	.000	-0	-4	-4	-0	-0.7
Total	10	57	76	.429	219	171	66	12	5	1256	1100	26	582	623	12.3	2.87	105	.243	.335	59	.147	-16	26	21	-21	-2.7

● JACK HARPER
Harper, John Wesley b: 8/5/1893, Hendricks, W.Va. d: 6/18/27, Halstead, Kan. BR/TR, 5'11", 180 lbs. Deb: 4/17/15

YEAR	TM/L	W	L	PCT	G	GS	CG	SH	SV	IP	H	HR	BB	SO	RAT	ERA	ERA+	OAV	OOB	BH	AVG	PB	PR	/A	PD	TPI
1915	Phi-A	0	0	—	3	0	0	0	0	8^2	5	0	1	3	6.2	3.12	94	.161	.188	0	.000	-0	-0	-0	0	0.0

● BILL HARPER
Harper, William Homer "Blue Sleeve" b: 6/14/1889, Bertrand, Mo. d: 6/17/51, Somerville, Tenn. BB/TR, 6'1", 180 lbs. Deb: 6/10/11

YEAR	TM/L	W	L	PCT	G	GS	CG	SH	SV	IP	H	HR	BB	SO	RAT	ERA	ERA+	OAV	OOB	BH	AVG	PB	PR	/A	PD	TPI
1911	StL-A	0	0	—	2	0	0	0	0	8	9	0	4	6	15.8	6.75	50	.300	.400	0	.000	-0	-3	-3	0	0.0

● SLIM HARRELL
Harrell, Oscar Martin b: 7/31/1890, Grandview, Tex. d: 4/30/71, Hillsboro, Tex. BR/TR, 6'3", 180 lbs. Deb: 6/21/12

YEAR	TM/L	W	L	PCT	G	GS	CG	SH	SV	IP	H	HR	BB	SO	RAT	ERA	ERA+	OAV	OOB	BH	AVG	PB	PR	/A	PD	TPI
1912	Phi-A	0	0	—	1	0	0	0	0	3	4	0	0	1	12.0	0.00	—	.364	.364	0	.000	-0	1	1	-0	0.0

● RAY HARRELL
Harrell, Raymond James "Cowboy" b: 2/16/12, Petrolia, Tex. d: 1/28/84, Alexandria, La. BR/TR, 6'1", 185 lbs. Deb: 4/16/35

YEAR	TM/L	W	L	PCT	G	GS	CG	SH	SV	IP	H	HR	BB	SO	RAT	ERA	ERA+	OAV	OOB	BH	AVG	PB	PR	/A	PD	TPI
1935	StL-N	1	1	.500	11	1	0	0	0	29^2	39	4	11	13	15.2	6.67	61	.320	.376	0	.000	-1	-9	-8	-0	-0.6
1937	StL-N	3	7	.300	35	15	1	1	1	96^2	99	7	59	41	14.9	5.87	68	.263	.366	1	.045	-2	-21	-20	-1	-2.1
1938	StL-N	2	3	.400	32	3	1	0	2	63	78	6	29	32	15.7	4.86	81	.308	.386	0	.000	-1	-7	-6	0	-0.6
1939	Chi-N	0	2	.000	4	2	0	0	0	17^1	29	2	6	5	18.2	8.31	47	.387	.432	0	.000	-1	-8	-8	0	-0.8
	Phi-N	3	7	.300	22	10	4	0	0	94^2	101	6	56	35	15.3	5.42	74	.270	.371	3	.115	-1	-16	-15	-3	-1.7
	Yr	3	9	.250	26	12	4	0	0	112	130	8	62	40	15.8	5.87	68	.290	.381	3	.097	-2	-24	-23	-3	-2.5
1940	Pit-N	0	0	—	3	0	0	0	0	3^1	5	0	2	3	18.9	8.10	47	.333	.412	0	—	0	-2	-2	-0	0.0
1945	NY-N	0	0	—	12	0	0	0	0	25^1	34	1	14	7	17.4	4.97	79	.343	.430	1	.200	1	-3	-3	0	0.1
Total	6	9	20	.310	119	31	6	1	3	330	385	26	177	136	15.6	5.70	70	.293	.381	5	.069	-5	-66	-63	-3	-5.7

● BILL HARRELSON
Harrelson, William Charles b: 11/17/45, Tahlequah, Okla. BB/TR, 6'5", 215 lbs. Deb: 7/31/68

YEAR	TM/L	W	L	PCT	G	GS	CG	SH	SV	IP	H	HR	BB	SO	RAT	ERA	ERA+	OAV	OOB	BH	AVG	PB	PR	/A	PD	TPI
1968	Cal-A	1	6	.143	10	5	1	0	0	33^2	28	4	26	22	14.7	5.08	57	.226	.364	1	.100	-0	-8	-8	-0	-1.7

● DENNY HARRIGER
Harriger, Dennis Scott b: 7/21/69, Kittanning, Pa. BR/TR, 5'11", 185 lbs. Deb: 6/16/98

YEAR	TM/L	W	L	PCT	G	GS	CG	SH	SV	IP	H	HR	BB	SO	RAT	ERA	ERA+	OAV	OOB	BH	AVG	PB	PR	/A	PD	TPI
1998	Det-A	0	3	.000	4	2	0	0	0	12	17	1	8	3	18.8	6.75	70	.327	.417	0	—	0	-3	-3	-0	-0.6

● ANDY HARRINGTON
Harrington, Andrew Francis b: 11/13/1888, Wakefield, Mass. d: 11/12/38, Malden, Mass. BR/TR, 6', 193 lbs. Deb: 9/8/13

YEAR	TM/L	W	L	PCT	G	GS	CG	SH	SV	IP	H	HR	BB	SO	RAT	ERA	ERA+	OAV	OOB	BH	AVG	PB	PR	/A	PD	TPI
1913	Cin-N	0	0	—	1	0	0	0	0	4	6	0	1	1	15.8	9.00	36	.353	.389	1	.500	0	-3	-3	-0	0.0

● BILL HARRINGTON
Harrington, William Womble b: 10/3/27, Sanford, N.C. BR/TR, 5'11", 160 lbs. Deb: 4/16/53

YEAR	TM/L	W	L	PCT	G	GS	CG	SH	SV	IP	H	HR	BB	SO	RAT	ERA	ERA+	OAV	OOB	BH	AVG	PB	PR	/A	PD	TPI
1953	Phi-A	0	0	—	1	0	0	0	0	2	5	0	0	0	22.5	13.50	32	.500	.500	0	—	0	-2	-2	-0	0.0
1955	KC-A	3	3	.500	34	1	0	0	2	76^2	69	6	41	26	13.1	4.11	102	.246	.347	2	.118	-1	-1	1	-1	-0.1
1956	KC-A	2	2	.500	23	1	0	0	1	37^2	40	3	26	14	15.8	6.45	67	.274	.384	0	.000	-1	-10	-9	-0	-0.9
Total	3	5	5	.500	58	2	0	0	3	116^1	114	9	67	40	14.2	5.03	84	.261	.362	2	.083	-1	-13	-10	-1	-1.0

● BEN HARRIS
Harris, Ben Franklin b: 12/17/1889, Donelson, Tenn. d: 4/29/27, St.Louis, Mo. BR/TR, 6', 220 lbs. Deb: 4/19/14

YEAR	TM/L	W	L	PCT	G	GS	CG	SH	SV	IP	H	HR	BB	SO	RAT	ERA	ERA+	OAV	OOB	BH	AVG	PB	PR	/A	PD	TPI
1914	KC-F	7	7	.500	31	14	5	0	1	154	179	7	41	40	13.2	4.09	68	.303	.354	9	.200	1	-21	-22	1	-1.7
1915	KC-F	0	0	—	1	0	0	0	0	2	1	0	0	0	4.5	0.00	—	.143	.143	0	—	0	1	1	0	0.0
Total	2	7	7	.500	32	14	5	0	1	156	180	7	41	40	13.1	4.04	69	.301	.352	9	.200	1	-20	-22	1	-1.7

● LUM HARRIS
Harris, Chalmer Luman b: 1/17/15, New Castle, Ala. d: 11/11/96, Pell City, Ala. BR/TR, 6'1", 180 lbs. Deb: 4/19/41 MC

YEAR	TM/L	W	L	PCT	G	GS	CG	SH	SV	IP	H	HR	BB	SO	RAT	ERA	ERA+	OAV	OOB	BH	AVG	PB	PR	/A	PD	TPI
1941	Phi-A	4	4	.500	33	10	5	0	2	131^2	134	16	51	49	12.8	4.78	88	.260	.329	11	.275	2	-9	-9	-1	-0.4
1942	Phi-A	11	15	.423	26	20	10	1	0	166	146	14	70	60	11.8	3.74	101	.234	.313	10	.161	-2	-2	1	-1	-0.1
1943	Phi-A	7	21	.250	32	27	15	1	1	216^1	241	17	63	55	12.8	4.20	81	.279	.330	12	.171	-1	-22	-19	-0	-2.4
1944	Phi-A	10	9	.526	23	22	12	2	0	174^1	193	8	26	33	11.3	3.30	105	.281	.308	10	.169	-1	2	3	-1	0.2
1946	Phi-A	3	14	.176	34	12	4	0	0	125^1	153	11	48	33	14.4	5.24	68	.308	.369	8	.222	1	-24	-24	3	-2.4
1947	Was-A	0	0	—	3	0	0	0	0	6^1	7	0	7	2	19.9	2.84	131	.318	.483	0	.000	-0	1	1	1	0.0
Total	6	35	63	.357	151	91	46	4	3	820	874	66	265	232	12.6	4.16	88	.273	.329	51	.190	-0	-54	-47	1	-5.1

● BUBBA HARRIS
Harris, Charles b: 2/15/26, Sulligent, Ala. BR/TR, 6'4", 204 lbs. Deb: 4/29/48

YEAR	TM/L	W	L	PCT	G	GS	CG	SH	SV	IP	H	HR	BB	SO	RAT	ERA	ERA+	OAV	OOB	BH	AVG	PB	PR	/A	PD	TPI
1948	Phi-A	5	2	.714	45	0	0	0	5	93^2	89	2	35	32	12.0	4.13	104	.249	.317	3	.125	-1	2	2	-0	0.0
1949	Phi-A	1	1	.500	37	0	0	0	3	84^1	92	12	42	18	14.4	5.44	75	.286	.370	3	.125	-2	-12	-12	2	-0.3
1951	Phi-A	0	0	—	3	0	0	0	0	4	4	0	5	2	22.5	9.00	48	.250	.455	0	—	0	-2	-2	0	0.0
	Cle-A	0	0	—	2	0	0	0	0	4	5	0	4	1	20.3	4.50	84	.333	.474	0	—	0	-0	-0	0	0.0
	Yr	0	0	—	5	0	0	0	0	8	9	0	9	3	20.3	6.75	60	.281	.439	0	—	0	-2	-2	0	0.0
Total	3	6	3	.667	87	0	0	0	8	186	190	14	86	53	13.5	4.84	87	.267	.349	6	.125	-3	-12	-13	2	-0.3

● GREG HARRIS
Harris, Greg Allen b: 11/2/55, Lynwood, Cal. BB/TR, 6', 175 lbs. Deb: 5/20/81

YEAR	TM/L	W	L	PCT	G	GS	CG	SH	SV	IP	H	HR	BB	SO	RAT	ERA	ERA+	OAV	OOB	BH	AVG	PB	PR	/A	PD	TPI
1981	NY-N	3	5	.375	16	14	0	0	1	68^2	65	8	28	54	12.5	4.46	78	.245	.322	4	.182	0	-7	-7	-1	-0.9
1982	Cin-N	2	6	.250	34	10	1	0	1	91^1	96	12	37	67	13.3	4.83	77	.274	.346	3	.167	-0	-12	-11	0	-0.9
1983	Cin-N	0	0	—	1	0	0	0	0	1	2	0	3	1	54.0	27.00	14	.500	.750	0	.000	-0	-3	-3	0	0.0
1984	Mon-N	0	1	.000	15	0	0	0	2	17^2	10	0	7	15	9.7	2.04	168	.172	.284	0	.000	-0	3	3	0	0.2
	*SD-N	2	1	.667	19	1	0	0	1	36^2	28	3	18	30	11.8	2.70	132	.209	.312	3	.375	1	4	4	-0	0.4
	Yr	2	2	.500	34	1	0	0	3	54^1	38	3	25	45	10.8	2.48	142	.196	.294	3	.333	1	7	6	-0	0.6
1985	Tex-A	5	4	.556	58	0	0	0	11	113	74	7	43	111	9.7	2.47	171	.186	.274	0	—	0	21	22	1	2.1
1986	Tex-A	10	8	.556	73	0	0	0	20	111^1	103	12	42	95	11.8	2.83	152	.251	.322	0	—	0	17	18	1	3.3
1987	Tex-A	5	10	.333	42	19	0	0	0	140^2	157	18	56	106	13.9	4.86	92	.281	.351	0	—	0	-6	-6	0	-0.5
1988	Phi-N	4	6	.400	66	1	0	0	1	107	80	7	52	71	11.4	2.36	151	.209	.311	3	.333	1	13	14	-0	1.5
1989	Phi-N	2	2	.500	44	0	0	0	1	75^1	64	7	43	51	13.0	3.58	99	.234	.342	1	.167	1	-1	-0	1	0.1
	Bos-A	2	2	.500	15	0	0	0	0	28	21	1	15	25	11.6	2.57	159	.208	.310	0	—	0	4	5	0	0.3
1990	*Bos-A	13	9	.591	34	30	1	0	0	184^1	186	13	77	117	13.1	4.00	102	.265	.342	0	—	0	-2	1	3	0.2
1991	Bos-A	11	12	.478	53	21	1	0	2	173	157	13	69	127	12.0	3.85	112	.243	.321	0	—	0	5	9	2	1.2
1992	Bos-A	4	9	.308	70	2	1	0	4	107^2	82	6	60	73	12.2	2.51	168	.215	.327	0	—	0	17	20	0	2.4
1993	Bos-A	6	7	.462	**80**	0	0	0	8	112^1	95	7	60	103	13.2	3.77	123	.232	.344	0	—	0	7	11	-0	1.1
1994	Bos-A	3	4	.429	35	0	0	0	2	45^2	60	8	23	44	16.6	8.28	61	.321	.398	0	—	0	-18	-16	0	-2.3

YEAR	TM/L	W	L	PCT	G	GS	CG	SH	SV	IP	H	HR	BB	SO	RAT	ERA	ERA+	OAV	OOB	BH	AVG	PB	PR	/A	PD	TPI
	NY-A	0	1	.000	3	0	0	0	0	5	4	1	3	4	16.2	5.40	85	.222	.391	0	—	0	-0	-0	-0	0.0
	Yr	3	5	.375	38	0	0	0	2	50^2	64	9	26	48	16.3	7.99	62	.309	.391	0	—	0	-18	-17	0	-2.3
1995	Mon-N	2	3	.400	45	0	0	0	0	48^1	45	6	16	47	11.5	2.61	165	.245	.308	1	.333	1	8	9	-0	0.9
Total	15	74	90	.451	703	98	4	0	54	1467	1329	129	652	1141	12.5	3.69	112	.243	.330	15	.221	3	49	71	7	9.1

● GREG HARRIS Harris, Gregory Wade b: 12/1/63, Greensboro, N.C. BR/TR, 6'2", 187 lbs. Deb: 9/14/88

YEAR	TM/L	W	L	PCT	G	GS	CG	SH	SV	IP	H	HR	BB	SO	RAT	ERA	ERA+	OAV	OOB	BH	AVG	PB	PR	/A	PD	TPI
1988	SD-N	2	0	1.000	3	1	1	0	0	18	13	0	3	15	8.0	1.50	226	.200	.235	0	.000	-1	4	4	-0	0.3
1989	SD-N	8	9	.471	56	8	0	0	6	135	106	8	52	106	10.7	2.60	134	.215	.293	1	.053	-1	13	13	1	1.8
1990	SD-N	8	8	.500	73	0	0	0	9	117^1	92	6	49	97	11.1	2.30	166	.220	.307	1	.083	-0	19	20	0	2.9
1991	SD-N	9	5	.643	20	20	3	2	0	133	116	16	27	95	9.7	2.23	170	.233	.274	3	.083	-1	21	23	-1	2.2
1992	SD-N	4	8	.333	20	20	1	0	0	118	113	13	35	66	11.4	4.12	87	.252	.309	4	.129	1	-8	-7	0	-0.6
1993	SD-N	10	9	.526	22	22	4	0	0	152	151	18	39	83	11.4	3.67	113	.257	.307	9	.170	1	6	8	1	1.1
	Col-N	1	8	.111	13	13	0	0	0	73^1	88	15	30	40	15.0	6.50	73	.299	.372	1	.050	-2	-20	-14	0	-1.6
	Yr	11	17	.393	35	35	4	0	0	225^1	239	33	69	123	12.5	4.59	94	.270	.325	10	.137	-0	-14	-6	1	-0.5
1994	Col-N	3	12	.200	29	19	1	0	1	130	154	22	52	82	14.6	6.65	75	.300	.370	7	.175	-0	-35	-24	1	-2.4
1995	Min-A	0	5	.000	7	6	0	0	0	32^2	50	5	16	21	18.2	8.82	54	.355	.420	0	—	0	-15	-15	0	-1.7
Total	8	45	64	.413	243	109	10	2	16	909^1	883	103	303	605	11.9	3.98	102	.255	.319	26	.119	-3	-14	7	3	2.0

● HERB HARRIS Harris, Herbert Benjamin "Hub" or "Lefty" b: 4/24/13, Chicago, Ill. d: 1/18/91, Crystal Lake, Ill. BL/TL, 6'1", 175 lbs. Deb: 7/21/36

YEAR	TM/L	W	L	PCT	G	GS	CG	SH	SV	IP	H	HR	BB	SO	RAT	ERA	ERA+	OAV	OOB	BH	AVG	PB	PR	/A	PD	TPI
1936	Phi-N	0	0	—	4	0	0	0	0	7	14	0	5	0	25.7	10.29	44	.438	.526	0	.000	-0	-5	-4	0	0.0

● PEP HARRIS Harris, Hernando Petrocelli b: 9/23/72, Lancaster, S.C. BR/TR, 6'2", 185 lbs. Deb: 8/14/96

YEAR	TM/L	W	L	PCT	G	GS	CG	SH	SV	IP	H	HR	BB	SO	RAT	ERA	ERA+	OAV	OOB	BH	AVG	PB	PR	/A	PD	TPI
1996	Cal-A	2	0	1.000	11	3	0	0	0	32^1	31	4	17	20	14.2	3.90	128	.254	.359	0	—	0	4	4	0	0.2
1997	Ana-A	5	4	.556	61	0	0	0	0	79^2	82	7	38	56	13.8	3.62	126	.274	.360	0	—	0	8	8	1	0.9
1998	Ana-A	3	1	.750	49	0	0	0	0	60	55	7	23	34	11.7	4.35	108	.239	.308	0	—	0	2	2	1	0.2
Total	3	10	5	.667	121	3	0	0	0	172	168	18	78	110	13.1	3.92	120	.258	.342	0	—	0	14	15	2	1.3

● JOE HARRIS Harris, Joseph White b: 2/1/1882, Melrose, Mass. d: 4/12/66, Melrose, Mass. BR/TR, 6'1", 198 lbs. Deb: 9/22/05

YEAR	TM/L	W	L	PCT	G	GS	CG	SH	SV	IP	H	HR	BB	SO	RAT	ERA	ERA+	OAV	OOB	BH	AVG	PB	PR	/A	PD	TPI
1905	Bos-A	1	2	.333	3	3	3	0	0	23	16	0	8	14	9.4	2.35	115	.198	.270	1	.111	-1	1	1	-0	0.0
1906	Bos-A	2	21	.087	30	24	20	1	2	235	211	5	67	99	10.9	3.52	78	.243	.303	13	.160	-2	-22	-20	6	-1.5
1907	Bos-A	0	7	.000	12	5	3	0	0	59	57	0	13	24	10.8	3.05	84	.256	.300	4	.190	-0	-3	-3	0	-0.4
Total	3	3	30	.091	45	32	26	1	2	317	284	5	88	137	10.8	3.35	81	.242	.300	18	.162	-3	-24	-22	6	-1.9

● LENNY HARRIS Harris, Leonard Anthony b: 10/28/64, Miami, Fla. BL/TR, 5'10", 205 lbs. Deb: 9/7/88 ♦

YEAR	TM/L	W	L	PCT	G	GS	CG	SH	SV	IP	H	HR	BB	SO	RAT	ERA	ERA+	OAV	OOB	BH	AVG	PB	PR	/A	PD	TPI
1998	Cin-N	0	0	—	1	0	0	0	0	1	0	0	0	1	0.0	0.00	—	.000	.000	36	.295	0	0	0	0	0.0

● MICKEY HARRIS Harris, Maurice Charles b: 1/30/17, New York, N.Y. d: 4/15/71, Farmington, Mich. BL/TL, 6', 195 lbs. Deb: 4/23/40

YEAR	TM/L	W	L	PCT	G	GS	CG	SH	SV	IP	H	HR	BB	SO	RAT	ERA	ERA+	OAV	OOB	BH	AVG	PB	PR	/A	PD	TPI
1940	Bos-A	4	2	.667	13	9	3	0	0	68^1	83	8	26	36	14.6	5.00	90	.292	.356	6	.273	2	-5	-4	0	-0.1
1941	Bos-A	8	14	.364	35	22	11	1	1	194	189	6	86	111	12.9	3.25	128	.250	.328	6	.109	2	19	20	-1	2.2
1946	*Bos-A☆	17	9	.654	34	30	15	0	0	222^2	236	18	76	131	12.7	3.64	101	.268	.329	18	.231	4	-3	1	-1	0.3
1947	Bos-A	5	4	.556	15	6	1	0	0	51^2	42	3	23	35	11.3	2.44	159	.225	.310	5	.417	3	7	8	0	1.7
1948	Bos-A	7	10	.412	20	17	6	1	0	113^2	120	10	59	42	14.3	5.30	83	.273	.360	2	.063	-1	-13	-12	-2	-1.7
1949	Bos-A	2	3	.400	7	6	2	0	0	37^2	53	3	20	14	17.7	5.02	87	.323	.400	1	.083	-1	-3	-3	0	-0.4
	Was-A	2	12	.143	23	19	4	0	0	129	151	8	55	54	14.4	5.16	82	.292	.360	8	.205	1	-14	-13	-2	-1.2
	Yr	4	15	.211	30	25	6	0	0	166^2	204	11	75	68	15.1	5.13	83	.299	.368	9	.176	1	-17	-16	-2	-1.6
1950	Was-A	5	9	.357	**53**	0	0	0	**15**	98	93	10	46	41	12.9	4.78	94	.247	.330	4	.235	1	-2	-3	-1	-0.5
1951	Was-A	6	8	.429	41	0	0	0	4	87^1	87	6	43	47	13.5	3.81	107	.260	.347	3	.188	0	3	3	-1	0.4
1952	Was-A	0	0	—	1	0	0	0	0	1	1	1	0	0	9.0	9.00	40	.250	.250	0	—	0	-1	-1	-0	0.0
	Cle-A	3	0	1.000	29	0	0	0	1	46^2	42	6	21	23	12.3	4.63	72	.249	.335	1	.200	-0	-5	-7	0	-0.4
	Yr	3	0	1.000	30	0	0	0	1	47^2	43	7	21	23	12.3	4.72	71	.249	.333	1	.200	-0	-6	-7	-0	-0.4
Total	9	59	71	.454	271	109	42	2	21	1050	1097	79	455	534	13.4	4.18	98	.267	.342	54	.188	11	-16	-9	-7	0.3

● REGGIE HARRIS Harris, Reginald Allen b: 8/12/68, Waynesboro, Va. BR/TR, 6'1", 180 lbs. Deb: 7/4/90

YEAR	TM/L	W	L	PCT	G	GS	CG	SH	SV	IP	H	HR	BB	SO	RAT	ERA	ERA+	OAV	OOB	BH	AVG	PB	PR	/A	PD	TPI
1990	Oak-A	1	0	1.000	16	1	0	0	0	41^1	25	5	21	31	10.5	3.48	107	.176	.291	0	—	0	2	1	-0	0.2
1991	Oak-A	0	0	—	2	0	0	0	0	3	5	0	3	2	24.0	12.00	32	.455	.571	0	—	0	-3	-3	-0	0.0
1996	Bos-A	0	0	—	4	0	0	0	0	4^1	7	2	5	4	27.0	12.46	41	.389	.542	0	—	0	-4	-4	-0	0.0
1997	Phi-N	1	3	.250	50	0	0	0	0	54^1	55	1	43	45	17.1	5.30	80	.263	.401	0	—	0	-7	-6	-1	-0.5
1998	Hou-N	0	0	—	6	0	0	0	0	6	6	1	2	2	12.0	6.00	68	.261	.320	0	—	0	-1	-1	-0	0.0
Total	5	2	3	.400	78	1	0	0	0	109	98	9	74	84	14.9	5.12	79	.243	.371	0	—	0	-12	-13	-2	-0.3

● BOB HARRIS Harris, Robert Arthur b: 5/1/17, Gillette, Wyo. d: 8/8/89, North Platte, Neb. BR/TR, 6', 185 lbs. Deb: 9/19/38

YEAR	TM/L	W	L	PCT	G	GS	CG	SH	SV	IP	H	HR	BB	SO	RAT	ERA	ERA+	OAV	OOB	BH	AVG	PB	PR	/A	PD	TPI
1938	Det-A	1	0	1.000	3	1	1	0	0	10	14	0	4	7	16.2	7.20	69	.318	.375	1	.333	0	-3	-2	0	-0.1
1939	Det-A	1	1	.500	5	1	0	0	0	18	18	4	8	9	13.0	4.00	122	.269	.347	2	.400	0	1	2	0	0.2
	StL-A	3	12	.200	28	16	6	0	0	126	162	5	71	48	16.6	5.71	85	.321	.405	7	.189	-0	-15	-12	3	-0.9
	Yr	4	13	.235	33	17	6	0	0	144	180	9	79	57	16.2	5.50	89	.315	.398	9	.214	-0	-14	-10	3	-0.7
1940	StL-A	11	15	.423	35	28	8	1	1	193^2	225	24	85	49	14.5	4.93	93	.290	.362	15	.250	3	-12	-7	-0	-0.6
1941	StL-A	12	14	.462	34	29	9	2	1	186^2	237	18	85	57	15.6	5.21	83	.312	.383	7	.115	-3	-22	-19	-2	-2.6
1942	StL-A	1	5	.167	6	6	0	0	0	33^2	37	2	17	9	14.4	5.61	66	.268	.348	0	.000	-1	-7	-7	-1	-1.2
	Phi-A	1	5	.167	16	8	2	1	0	78	77	5	24	26	11.7	2.88	131	.253	.308	7	.269	1	7	8	2	0.9
	Yr	2	10	.167	22	14	2	1	0	111^2	114	7	41	35	12.5	3.71	101	.258	.321	7	.194	0	-1	1	2	-0.3
Total	5	30	52	.366	127	89	26	4	2	646	770	58	294	205	14.9	4.96	89	.297	.370	39	.193	1	-51	-38	3	-4.3

● GENE HARRIS Harris, Tyrone Eugene b: 12/5/64, Sebring, Fla. BR/TR, 5'11", 190 lbs. Deb: 4/5/89

YEAR	TM/L	W	L	PCT	G	GS	CG	SH	SV	IP	H	HR	BB	SO	RAT	ERA	ERA+	OAV	OOB	BH	AVG	PB	PR	/A	PD	TPI
1989	Mon-N	1	1	.500	11	0	0	0	0	20	16	1	10	11	11.7	4.95	71	.242	.342	0	.000	-0	-3	-3	2	-0.2
	Sea-A	1	4	.200	10	6	0	0	1	33^1	47	3	15	14	17.0	6.48	62	.353	.423	0	—	0	-10	-9	-1	-1.4
1990	Sea-A	1	2	.333	25	0	0	0	0	38	31	5	30	43	14.7	4.74	84	.217	.356	0	—	0	-4	-3	-0	-0.3
1991	Sea-A	0	0	—	8	0	0	0	1	13^1	15	1	10	6	16.9	4.05	102	.273	.385	0	—	0	0	0	-0	0.0
1992	Sea-A	0	0	—	8	0	0	0	0	9	8	3	6	6	14.0	7.00	57	.235	.350	0	—	0	-3	-3	-0	0.0
	SD-N	0	2	.000	14	1	0	0	0	21^1	15	0	9	19	10.5	2.95	121	.195	.287	1	.333	0	1	1	0	0.2
1993	SD-N	6	6	.500	59	0	0	0	23	59^1	57	3	37	39	14.4	3.03	136	.254	.363	0	.000	-0	7	7	1	1.9
1994	SD-N	1	1	.500	13	0	0	0	0	12^1	21	2	8	9	21.2	8.03	51	.389	.468	0	.000	-0	-5	-5	-0	-0.8
	Det-A	0	0	—	11	0	0	0	1	11^1	13	1	4	10	14.3	7.15	68	.271	.340	0	—	0	-3	-3	0	-0.1
1995	Phi-N	2	2	.500	21	0	0	0	0	19	19	2	8	9	12.8	4.26	99	.260	.333	0	—	0	-0	-0	1	0.0
	Bal-A	0	0	—	3	0	0	0	0	4	4	0	1	4	11.3	4.50	106	.267	.313	0	—	0	0	0	0	0.0
Total	7	12	18	.400	183	7	0	0	26	241	246	21	138	170	14.5	4.71	86	.267	.365	1	.167	-0	-20	-18	1	-0.7

● BUDDY HARRIS Harris, Walter Francis b: 12/5/48, Philadelphia, Pa. BR/TR, 6'7", 245 lbs. Deb: 9/10/70

YEAR	TM/L	W	L	PCT	G	GS	CG	SH	SV	IP	H	HR	BB	SO	RAT	ERA	ERA+	OAV	OOB	BH	AVG	PB	PR	/A	PD	TPI
1970	Hou-N	0	0	—	2	0	0	0	0	6^1	6	3	0	2	8.5	5.68	68	.240	.240	0	.000	-0	-1	-1	-0	0.0
1971	Hou-N	1	1	.500	20	0	0	0	0	30^2	33	3	16	21	14.4	6.46	52	.275	.360	0	.000	-0	-10	-11	-1	-0.7
Total	2	1	1	.500	22	0	0	0	0	37	39	6	16	23	13.4	6.32	55	.269	.342	0	.000	-0	-11	-12	-1	-0.7

● BILL HARRIS Harris, William Milton b: 6/23/1900, Wylie, Tex. d: 8/21/65, Indian Trail, N.C. BR/TR, 6'1", 180 lbs. Deb: 4/22/23

YEAR	TM/L	W	L	PCT	G	GS	CG	SH	SV	IP	H	HR	BB	SO	RAT	ERA	ERA+	OAV	OOB	BH	AVG	PB	PR	/A	PD	TPI
1923	Cin-N	3	2	.600	22	3	1	0	0	69^2	79	3	18	18	12.9	5.17	75	.292	.342	6	.353	1	-9	-10	0	-0.5
1924	Cin-N	0	0	—	3	0	0	0	0	7	10	0	2	5	15.4	9.00	42	.323	.364	1	1.000	0	-4	-4	0	0.1
1931	Pit-N	2	2	.500	4	4	3	1	0	31	21	0	9	10	8.7	0.87	442	.194	.256	1	.091	-1	10	10	0	1.3
1932	Pit-N	10	9	.526	37	17	4	0	2	168	178	6	38	63	11.9	3.64	105	.271	.317	10	.182	-1	4	3	-2	0.1
1933	Pit-N	4	4	.500	31	0	0	0	5	58^2	68	1	14	19	12.7	3.22	103	.289	.332	0	.000	-1	1	1	-1	-0.1
1934	Pit-N	0	0	—	11	2	0	0	0	19	28	2	7	8	17.1	6.63	62	.350	.409	1	.500	0	-5	-5	0	0.1
1938	Bos-A	5	5	.500	13	11	5	1	1	80^1	83	5	21	26	11.8	4.03	122	.268	.316	6	.214	-0	7	8	-0	0.8
Total	7	24	22	.522	121	37	13	2	8	433^2	467	17	109	149	12.2	3.92	101	.276	.324	25	.203	-1	4	2	-2	1.8

YEAR TM/L		W	L	PCT	G	GS	CG	SH	SV	IP	H	HR	BB	SO	RAT	ERA	ERA+	OAV	OOB	BH	AVG	PB	PR	/A	PD	TPI
● BILL HARRIS Harris, William Thomas b: 12/3/31, Duguayville, N.B., Canada BL/TR, 5'8", 187 lbs. Deb: 9/27/57																										
1957	Bro-N	0	1	.000	1	1	0	0	0	7	9	1	1	3	12.9	3.86	108	.321	.345	1	.500	0	0	0	0	0.1
1959	LA-N	0	0	—	1	0	0	0	0	1^2	0	0	3	0	16.2	0.00	—	.000	.375	0	—	0	1	1	0	0.0
Total	2	0	1	.000	2	1	0	0	0	8^2	9	1	4	3	13.5	3.12	134	.273	.351	1	.500	0	1	1	0	0.1
● BOB HARRISON Harrison, Robert Lee b: 9/22/30, St.Louis, Mo. BL/TR, 5'11", 178 lbs. Deb: 9/23/55																										
1955	Bal-A	0	0	—	1	0	0	0	0	2	3	0	4	0	31.5	9.00	42	.500	.700	0	—	0	-1	-1	-0	0.0
1956	Bal-A	0	0	—	1	1	0	0	0	1^2	3	0	5	0	43.2	16.20	24	.375	.615	0	—	0	-2	-2	-0	0.0
Total	2	0	0	—	2	1	0	0	0	3^2	6	0	9	0	36.8	12.27	31	.429	.652	0	—	0	-3	-3	-0	0.0
● RORIC HARRISON Harrison, Roric Edward b: 9/20/46, Los Angeles, Cal. BR/TR, 6'3", 195 lbs. Deb: 4/18/72																										
1972	Bal-A	3	4	.429	39	2	0	0	4	94	68	2	34	62	10.1	2.30	134	.209	.292	2	.118	1	8	8	-1	0.7
1973	Atl-N	11	8	.579	38	22	3	0	5	177^1	161	15	98	130	13.3	4.16	94	.242	.342	3	.056	-2	-10	-5	-1	-0.8
1974	Atl-N	6	11	.353	20	20	3	0	0	126	148	12	49	46	14.3	4.71	80	.294	.360	7	.184	2	-15	-13	-2	-1.6
1975	Atl-N	3	4	.429	15	7	2	0	1	54^2	58	7	19	22	12.7	4.77	79	.266	.325	3	.200	1	-7	-6	0	-0.7
	Cle-A	7	7	.500	19	19	4	0	0	126	137	9	46	52	13.4	4.79	79	.275	.341	0	—	0	-14	-14	-1	-1.5
1978	Min-A	0	1	.000	9	0	0	0	0	12	18	0	11	7	21.8	7.50	51	.346	.460	0	—	0	-5	-5	-0	-0.5
Total	5	30	35	.462	140	70	12	0	10	590	590	45	257	319	13.1	4.24	87	.261	.340	15	.121	2	-43	-35	-5	-4.4
● TOM HARRISON Harrison, Thomas James b: 1/18/45, Trail, B.C., Canada BR/TR, 6'3", 200 lbs. Deb: 5/7/65 ♦																										
1965	KC-A	0	0	—	1	0	0	0	0	1	2	0	1	0	27.0	9.00	39	.667	.750	0	—	0	-1	-1	-0	0.0
● SLIM HARRISS Harriss, William Jennings Bryan b: 12/11/1896, Brownwood, Tex. d: 9/19/63, Temple, Tex. BR/TR, 6'6", 180 lbs. Deb: 4/19/20																										
1920	Phi-A	9	14	.391	31	25	11	1	0	192	226	5	57	60	13.5	4.08	99	.305	.359	7	.106	-7	-6	-1	3	-0.5
1921	Phi-A	11	16	.407	39	28	14	0	2	227^2	258	16	73	92	13.4	4.27	104	.290	.350	12	.148	-7	0	5	-1	-0.2
1922	Phi-A	9	20	.310	47	32	13	0	3	229^2	262	19	94	102	14.1	5.02	85	.290	.359	13	.176	-4	-25	-19	1	-2.5
1923	Phi-A	10	16	.385	46	28	9	0	6	209^1	221	9	95	89	13.7	4.00	103	.280	.359	4	.066	-8	-0	3	5	0.0
1924	Phi-A	6	10	.375	36	12	4	1	2	123	138	5	62	45	14.9	4.68	92	.291	.377	7	.167	-3	-6	-5	4	-0.5
1925	Phi-A	19	12	.613	46	33	15	2	1	252^2	263	8	95	95	13.0	3.49	133	.268	.336	18	.205	-3	25	33	4	3.6
1926	Phi-A	3	5	.375	12	10	2	0	0	57	66	0	22	13	13.9	4.11	102	.289	.352	1	.059	-2	-1	0	0	-0.1
	Bos-A	6	10	.375	21	18	6	1	0	113	135	0	33	34	13.5	4.46	91	.311	.362	7	.206	-0	-6	-5	1	-0.5
	Yr	9	15	.375	33	28	8	1	0	170	201	0	55	47	13.7	4.34	95	.304	.359	8	.157	-2	-6	-4	1	-0.6
1927	Bos-A	14	21	.400	44	27	11	1	1	217^2	253	8	66	77	13.6	4.18	101	.298	.355	8	.121	-5	-1	1	1	-0.2
1928	Bos-A	8	11	.421	27	15	4	1	1	128^1	141	5	33	37	12.3	4.63	89	.287	.335	5	.139	-3	-8	-7	-2	-1.3
Total	9	95	135	.413	349	228	89	7	16	1750^1	1963	75	630	644	13.5	4.25	100	.290	.354	82	.145	-40	-27	3	15	-2.2
● EARL HARRIST Harrist, Earl "Irish" b: 8/20/19, Dubach, La. d: 9/1/98, Simsboro, La. BR/TR, 6', 178 lbs. Deb: 8/18/45																										
1945	Cin-N	2	4	.333	14	5	1	0	0	62^1	60	2	27	15	12.7	3.61	104	.249	.327	0	.000	-2	1	1	-1	-0.2
1947	Chi-A	3	8	.273	33	4	0	0	5	93^2	85	3	49	55	13.2	3.56	103	.248	.347	5	.208	-0	2	1	1	0.2
1948	Chi-A	1	3	.250	11	1	0	0	0	23	23	4	13	14	15.3	5.87	73	.267	.382	0	.000	-1	-4	-4	0	-0.7
	Was-A	3	3	.500	23	4	0	0	0	60^2	70	1	37	21	16.3	4.60	94	.293	.394	3	.167	-1	-2	-2	-1	-0.3
	Yr	4	6	.400	34	5	0	0	0	83^2	93	5	50	35	15.7	4.95	87	.284	.383	3	.136	-2	-6	-6	-1	-1.0
1952	StL-A	2	8	.200	36	9	1	0	5	116^2	119	7	47	49	13.6	4.01	98	.269	.352	3	.097	-2	-4	-1	1	-0.3
1953	Chi-A	1	0	1.000	7	0	0	0	0	8^1	9	1	5	1	15.1	7.56	53	.290	.389	0	.000	-0	-3	-3	-0	-0.4
	Det-A	0	2	.000	8	1	0	0	0	18^2	25	2	15	7	19.3	8.68	47	.333	.444	0	.000	-0	-10	-10	1	-0.8
	Yr	1	2	.333	15	1	0	0	0	27	34	3	20	8	18.0	8.33	49	.321	.429	0	.000	-0	-13	-13	1	-1.2
Total	5	12	28	.300	132	24	2	0	10	383^1	391	20	193	162	14.2	4.34	90	.268	.361	11	.115	-7	-21	-18	0	-2.5
● JACK HARSHMAN Harshman, John Elvin b: 7/12/27, San Diego, Cal. BL/TL, 6'2", 185 lbs. Deb: 9/16/48 ♦																										
1952	NY-N	0	2	.000	2	2	0	0	0	6^1	12	2	6	6	25.6	14.21	26	.429	.529	0	.000	-0	-7	-7	0	-1.5
1954	Chi-A	14	8	.636	35	21	9	4	1	177	157	7	96	134	13.1	2.95	127	.238	.339	8	.143	3	15	15	-1	2.1
1955	Chi-A	11	7	.611	32	23	9	0	0	179^1	144	16	97	116	12.3	3.36	117	.224	.330	11	.183	4	12	12	-0	1.4
1956	Chi-A	15	11	.577	34	30	15	4	0	226^2	183	14	102	143	11.4	3.10	132	.221	.308	12	.169	6	27	25	-2	3.0
1957	Chi-A	8	8	.500	30	26	6	0	1	151^1	142	16	82	83	13.6	4.10	91	.250	.349	10	.222	5	-5	-6	-3	-0.3
1958	Bal-A	12	15	.444	34	29	17	3	4	236^1	204	20	75	161	10.7	2.89	124	.231	.294	16	.195	8	23	18	1	3.4
1959	Bal-A	0	6	.000	14	8	0	0	0	47^1	58	6	28	24	16.7	6.85	55	.319	.415	2	.200	1	-16	-16	1	-1.5
	Bos-A	2	3	.400	8	2	0	0	0	24^2	29	2	10	14	14.2	6.57	62	.284	.348	1	.143	0	-7	-7	-1	-1.2
	Cle-A	5	1	.833	13	6	5	1	1	66	46	6	13	35	8.0	2.59	142	.179	.219	7	.206	2	9	8	-0	0.9
	Yr	7	10	.412	35	16	5	1	1	138	133	14	51	73	12.0	4.76	79	.244	.308	10	.196	3	-14	-15	1	-1.8
1960	Cle-A	2	4	.333	15	8	0	0	0	54^1	50	7	30	25	13.3	3.98	94	.243	.339	3	.176	-0	-1	-1	-1	-0.2
Total	8	69	65	.515	217	155	61	12	7	1169^1	1025	96	539	741	12.2	3.50	109	.235	.323	76	.179	29	50	41	-5	6.1
● OSCAR HARSTAD Harstad, Oscar Theander b: 5/24/1892, Parkland, Wash. d: 11/14/85, Corvallis, Ore. BR/TR, 6', 174 lbs. Deb: 4/23/15																										
1915	Cle-A	3	5	.375	32	7	4	0	1	82	81	1	35	35	12.8	3.40	90	.270	.348	2	.125	-1	-4	-3	2	-0.2
● BILLY HART Hart, Robert Lee b: 5/16/1866, Palmyra, Mo. d: 5/14/44, Hannibal, Mo. 5'8", Deb: 7/13/1890																										
1890	StL-a	12	8	.600	26	24	20	0	0	201^1	188	6	66	95	12.1	3.67	118	.240	.312	15	.192	-1	5	15	-3	0.8
● BILL HART Hart, William Franklin b: 7/19/1865, Louisville, Ky. d: 9/19/36, Cincinnati, Ohio TR, 5'10", 163 lbs. Deb: 7/26/1886 U																										
1886	Phi-a	9	13	.409	22	22	22	2	0	186	183	7	66	78	12.4	3.19	110	.234	.299	10	.137	-5	5	6	1	0.3
1887	Phi-a	1	2	.333	3	3	3	0	0	26	28	1	17	4	15.9	4.50	95	.272	.380	1	.077	-2	-1	-1	0	-0.2
1892	Bro-N	9	12	.429	28	23	16	2	1	195	188	3	96	65	13.4	3.28	97	.243	.332	24	.192	3	0	-2	3	0.3
1895	Pit-N	14	17	.452	36	29	24	0	1	261^2	293	4	135	85	15.2	4.75	95	.279	.369	25	.236	-2	1	-7	6	-0.3
1896	StL-N	12	29	.293	42	41	37	0	1	336	411	11	141	65	15.2	5.12	85	.299	.370	30	.186	-5	-28	-29	6	-2.5
1897	StL-N	9	27	.250	39	38	31	0	0	294^2	395	10	148	67	17.1	6.26	70	.318	.398	39	.250	-1	-64	-61	3	-5.2
1898	Pit-N	5	9	.357	16	15	13	1	1	125	141	4	44	19	13.8	4.82	74	.282	.348	12	.240	0	-17	-18	0	-1.6
1901	Cle-A	7	11	.389	20	19	16	0	0	157^2	180	3	57	48	14.1	3.77	94	.283	.352	14	.219	-2	-2	-4	2	-0.3
Total	8	66	120	.355	206	190	162	5	3	1582	1819	43	704	431	14.8	4.65	86	.281	.359	155	.207	-14	-105	-114	22	-9.5
● CHUCK HARTENSTEIN Hartenstein, Charles Oscar "Twiggy" b: 5/26/42, Seguin, Tex. BR/TR, 5'11", 165 lbs. Deb: 9/11/65 C♦																										
1966	Chi-N	0	0	—	5	0	0	0	0	9^1	8	0	3	4	11.6	1.93	191	.222	.300	0	—	0	2	2	0	0.0
1967	Chi-N	9	5	.643	45	0	0	0	10	73	74	4	17	20	11.3	3.08	115	.278	.324	1	.063	-1	2	4	-0	0.7
1968	Chi-N	2	4	.333	28	0	0	0	1	35^2	41	3	11	17	13.4	4.54	70	.291	.346	0	.000	-0	-6	-5	-0	-1.0
1969	Pit-N	5	4	.556	56	0	0	0	10	95^2	84	9	27	44	10.8	3.95	88	.241	.303	1	.071	-1	-4	-5	1	-0.5
1970	Pit-N	1	1	.500	17	0	0	0	1	23^2	25	3	8	14	12.5	4.56	85	.278	.337	0	.000	-0	-1	-2	1	-0.1
	StL-N	0	0	—	6	0	0	0	0	13^1	24	1	5	9	19.6	8.78	47	.375	.420	0	.000	0	-7	-7	0	0.0
	Yr	1	1	.500	23	0	0	0	1	37	49	4	13	23	15.1	6.08	65	.316	.369	0	.000	-0	-8	-9	1	-0.1
	Bos-A	0	3	.000	17	0	0	0	1	19	21	6	12	12	16.1	8.05	49	.288	.395	0	.000	0	-9	-9	-1	-1.3
1977	Tor-A	0	2	.000	13	0	0	0	0	27^1	40	8	6	15	15.5	6.59	64	.348	.385	0	—	0	-8	-7	-0	-0.5
Total	6	17	19	.472	187	0	0	0	23	297	317	34	89	135	12.6	4.52	80	.280	.337	2	.054	-2	-31	-29	2	-2.7
● FRANK HARTER Harter, Franklin Pierce "Chief" b: 9/19/1886, Keyesport, Ill. d: 4/14/59, Breese, Ill. BR/TR, 5'11", 165 lbs. Deb: 8/31/12																										
1912	Cin-N	1	2	.333	6	3	1	0	0	29^1	25	1	11	12	11.0	3.07	110	.234	.305	1	.091	-1	1	1	-1	-0.1
1913	Cin-N	1	1	.500	17	2	0	0	0	46^2	47	3	19	10	12.7	3.86	84	.272	.344	2	.143	-1	-3	-3	-1	-0.3
1914	Ind-F	1	2	.333	6	1	1	0	0	24^2	33	0	7	8	14.6	4.01	78	.330	.374	0	.000	-1	-3	-2	-0	-0.4
Total	3	3	5	.375	29	6	2	0	0	100^2	105	4	37	30	12.7	3.67	89	.276	.341	3	.091	-3	-5	-5	-2	-0.8
● DEAN HARTGRAVES Hartgraves, Dean Charles b: 8/12/66, Bakersfield, Cal. BR/TL, 6', 185 lbs. Deb: 5/3/95																										
1995	Hou-N	2	0	1.000	40	0	0	0	0	36^1	30	2	16	24	11.4	3.22	120	.227	.311	0	.000	-0	4	3	0	0.1
1996	Hou-N	0	0	—	19	0	0	0	0	19	18	1	16	16	16.6	5.21	74	.257	.402	0	—	0	-2	-3	0	0.0
	Atl-N	1	0	1.000	20	0	0	0	0	18^2	16	3	7	14	11.6	4.34	101	.232	.312	0	.000	-0	-0	0	0	0.0
	Yr	1	0	1.000	39	0	0	0	0	37^2	34	4	23	30	13.9	4.78	86	.241	.352	0	.000	-0	-2	-3	0	0.0

YEAR	TM/L	W	L	PCT	G	GS	CG	SH	SV	IP	H	HR	BB	SO	RAT	ERA	ERA+	OAV	OOB	BH	AVG	PB	PR	/A	PD	TPI
1998	SF-N	0	0	—	5	0	0	0	0	5^2	10	1	4	4	22.2	9.53	43	.385	.467	0	—	0	-3	-3	-0	0.0
Total	3	3	0	1.000	84	0	0	0	0	79^2	74	7	43	58	13.4	4.41	91	.249	.348	0	.000	-0	-2	-4	-0	0.1
● **MIKE HARTLEY**	Hartley, Michael Edward b: 8/31/61, Hawthorne, Cal. BR/TR, 6′1″, 197 lbs. Deb: 9/10/89																									
1989	LA-N	0	1	.000	5	0	0	0	0	6	2	0	0	4	3.0	1.50	228	.100	.100	0	.000	-0	1	1	0	0.2
1990	LA-N	6	3	.667	32	6	1	1	1	79^1	58	7	30	76	10.2	2.95	124	.200	.280	1	.077	-1	7	6	-0	0.6
1991	LA-N	2	0	1.000	40	0	0	0	1	57	53	7	37	44	14.7	4.42	81	.245	.363	0	.000	-0	-5	-5	0	-0.2
	Phi-N	2	1	.667	18	0	0	0	1	26^1	21	4	10	19	11.6	3.76	98	.219	.312	0	.000	-0	-0	-0	-1	-0.1
	Yr	4	1	.800	58	0	0	0	2	83^1	74	11	47	63	13.4	4.21	86	.234	.339	0	.000	-1	-5	-6	-1	-0.3
1992	Phi-N	7	6	.538	46	0	0	0	0	55	54	5	23	53	12.9	3.44	102	.255	.333	0	.000	-0	0	0	-0	0.0
1993	Min-A	1	2	.333	53	0	0	0	1	81	86	4	36	57	14.3	4.00	109	.281	.370	0	—	0	3	3	-2	0.0
1995	Bos-A	0	0	—	5	0	0	0	0	7	8	1	2	2	15.4	9.00	54	.308	.400	0	—	0	-3	-3	-0	0.0
	Bal-A	1	0	1.000	3	0	0	0	0	7	5	0	1	4	7.7	1.29	369	.217	.250	0	—	0	3	3	0	0.4
	Yr	1	0	1.000	8	0	0	0	0	14	13	1	3	6	10.3	5.14	94	.245	.286	0	—	0	-1	-1	0	0.4
Total	6	19	13	.594	202	6	1	1	4	318^2	287	28	139	259	12.6	3.70	104	.241	.330	1	.043	-2	6	5	-3	0.9
● **CHARLIE HARTMAN**	Hartman, Charles Otto b: 8/10/1888, Los Angeles, Cal. d: 10/22/60, Los Angeles, Cal. Deb: 6/24/08																									
1908	Bos-A	0	0	—	1	0	0	0	0	2	1	0	2	1	13.5	4.50	55	.143	.333	0	—	0	-0	-0	0	0.0
● **BOB HARTMAN**	Hartman, Robert Louis b: 8/28/37, Kenosha, Wis. BR/TL, 5′11″, 185 lbs. Deb: 4/26/59																									
1959	Mil-N	0	0	—	3	0	0	0	0	1^2	6	0	2	1	43.2	27.00	13	.545	.615	0	—	0	-4	-4	-0	0.0
1962	Cle-A	0	1	.000	8	2	0	0	0	17^1	14	1	8	11	11.4	3.12	124	.209	.293	0	.000	-1	2	1	-0	0.0
Total	2	0	1	.000	11	2	0	0	0	19	20	1	10	12	14.2	5.21	74	.256	.341	0	.000	-1	-3	-3	-0	0.0
● **RAY HARTRANFT**	Hartranft, Raymond Joseph b: 9/19/1890, Quakertown, Pa. d: 2/10/55, Spring City, Pa. BL/TL, 6′1″, 195 lbs. Deb: 6/16/13																									
1913	Phi-N	0	0	—	1	0	0	0	0	1	3	0	1	1	36.0	9.00	37	.500	.571	0	—	0	-1	-1	0	0.0
● **JEFF HARTSOCK**	Hartsock, Jeffrey Roger b: 11/19/66, Fairfield, Ohio BR/TR, 6′, 190 lbs. Deb: 9/12/92																									
1992	Chi-N	0	0	—	4	0	0	0	0	9^1	15	2	4	6	18.3	6.75	53	.375	.432	0	.000	-0	-3	-3	0	0.0
● **CLINT HARTUNG**	Hartung, Clinton Clarence "Floppy" or "The Hondo Hurricane" b: 8/10/22, Hondo, Tex. BR/TR, 6′4″, 215 lbs. Deb: 4/15/47 ♦																									
1947	NY-N	9	7	.563	23	20	8	1	0	138	140	15	69	54	13.8	4.57	89	.263	.350	29	.309	9	-8	-8	-1	0.1
1948	NY-N	8	8	.500	36	19	6	2	1	153^1	146	15	72	42	13.1	4.75	83	.258	.347	10	.179	2	-14	-14	-0	-1.2
1949	NY-N	9	11	.450	33	25	8	0	0	154^2	156	16	86	48	14.3	5.00	80	.260	.357	12	.190	4	-17	-18	2	-1.5
1950	NY-N	3	3	.500	20	8	1	0	0	65^1	87	10	44	23	18.3	6.61	62	.326	.425	13	.302	4	-18	-18	2	-0.8
Total	4	29	29	.500	112	72	23	3	1	511^1	529	56	271	167	14.3	5.02	80	.269	.361	90	.238	19	-56	-57	3	-3.4
● **PAUL HARTZELL**	Hartzell, Paul Franklin b: 11/2/53, Bloomsburg, Pa. BR/TR, 6′5″, 200 lbs. Deb: 4/10/76																									
1976	Cal-A	7	4	.636	37	15	7	2	2	166	166	6	43	51	11.9	2.77	120	.266	.323	0	—	0	14	10	1	1.3
1977	Cal-A	8	12	.400	41	23	6	0	4	189^1	200	14	38	79	11.5	3.57	110	.274	.313	0	—	0	10	7	1	0.8
1978	Cal-A	6	10	.375	54	12	5	0	6	157	168	8	41	55	12.3	3.44	105	.278	.329	0	—	0	6	3	1	0.7
1979	Min-A	6	10	.375	28	26	4	0	0	163	193	18	44	44	13.3	5.36	82	.301	.350	0	—	0	-21	-18	1	-1.4
1980	Bal-A	0	2	.000	6	0	0	0	0	17^2	22	3	9	5	15.8	6.62	60	.310	.387	0	—	0	-5	-5	-1	-0.6
1984	Mil-A	0	1	.000	4	1	0	0	0	10^1	17	0	6	3	20.0	7.84	49	.370	.442	0	—	0	-4	-5	0	-0.4
Total	6	27	39	.409	170	77	22	2	12	703^1	766	49	181	237	12.4	3.90	98	.282	.332	0	—	0	-0	-7	3	0.4
● **BRYAN HARVEY**	Harvey, Bryan Stanley b: 6/2/63, Soddy-Daisy, Tenn. BR/TR, 6′2″, 212 lbs. Deb: 5/16/87																									
1987	Cal-A	0	0	—	3	0	0	0	0	5	6	0	2	3	14.4	0.00	—	.300	.364	0	—	0	2	2	-0	0.0
1988	Cal-A	7	5	.583	50	0	0	0	17	76	59	4	20	67	9.5	2.13	181	.214	.269	0	—	0	15	15	-2	2.7
1989	Cal-A	3	3	.500	51	0	0	0	25	55	36	6	41	78	12.6	3.44	111	.183	.324	0	—	0	3	2	0	0.5
1990	Cal-A	4	4	.500	54	0	0	0	25	64^1	45	4	35	82	11.2	3.22	119	.201	.309	0	—	0	5	4	-0	0.9
1991	Cal-A☆	2	4	.333	67	0	0	0	**46**	78^2	51	6	17	101	7.9	1.60	256	.178	.227	0	—	0	22	22	-0	3.7
1992	Cal-A	0	4	.000	25	0	0	0	13	28^2	22	4	11	34	10.4	2.83	141	.208	.282	0	—	0	4	4	-1	0.7
1993	Fla-N★	1	5	.167	59	0	0	0	45	69	45	4	13	73	7.6	1.70	255	.186	.227	0	—	0	18	20	-1	3.9
1994	Fla-N	0	0	—	12	0	0	0	6	10^1	12	1	4	10	13.9	5.23	84	.279	.340	0	—	0	-1	-1	0	-0.1
1995	Fla-N	0	0	—	1	0	0	0	0	0	2	1	1	0	—	∞	—	1.000	1.000	0	—	0	-3	-3	0	-0.3
Total	9	17	25	.405	322	0	0	0	177	387	278	30	144	448	9.9	2.49	161	.199	.275	0	—	0	65	65	-3	12.0
● **ZAZA HARVEY**	Harvey, Ervin King b: 1/5/1879, Saratoga, Cal. d: 6/3/54, Santa Monica, Cal. BL/TL, 6′, 190 lbs. Deb: 5/3/00 ♦																									
1900	Chi-N	0	0	—	1	0	0	0	0	4	3	0	1	0	9.0	0.00	—	.214	.267	0	.000	-1	2	2	-0	-0.1
1901	Chi-A	3	7	.300	16	9	5	0	1	92	91	2	34	27	12.7	3.62	96	.255	.328	10	.250	2	0	-1	2	0.2
Total	2	3	7	.300	17	9	5	0	1	96	94	2	35	27	12.6	3.47	101	.253	.326	86	.332	2	2	0	2	0.1
● **SHIGETOSHI HASEGAWA**	Hasegawa, Shigetoshi b: 8/1/68, Kobe, Japan BR/TR, 5′11″, 160 lbs. Deb: 4/5/97																									
1997	Ana-A	3	7	.300	50	7	0	0	0	116^2	118	14	46	83	12.9	3.93	116	.269	.343	0	—	0	8	8	2	0.8
1998	Ana-A	8	3	.727	61	0	0	0	5	97^1	86	14	32	73	11.1	3.14	149	.241	.307	0	—	0	16	17	1	1.8
Total	2	11	10	.524	111	7	0	0	5	214	204	28	78	156	12.1	3.57	129	.257	.327	0	—	0	24	25	2	2.6
● **HERB HASH**	Hash, Herbert Howard b: 2/13/11, Woolwine, Va. BR/TR, 6′1″, 180 lbs. Deb: 4/19/40																									
1940	Bos-A	7	7	.500	34	12	3	1	3	120	123	11	84	36	15.9	4.95	91	.266	.385	7	.175	-0	-8	-6	1	-0.6
1941	Bos-A	1	0	1.000	4	0	0	0	1	8^1	7	1	7	3	15.1	5.40	77	.226	.368	0	.000	-0	-1	-1	0	-0.2
Total	2	8	7	.533	38	12	3	1	4	128^1	130	12	91	39	15.8	4.98	90	.264	.384	7	.167	-1	-9	-7	1	-0.8
● **ANDY HASSLER**	Hassler, Andrew Earl b: 10/18/51, Texas City, Tex. BL/TL, 6′5″, 220 lbs. Deb: 5/30/71																									
1971	Cal-A	0	3	.000	6	4	0	0	0	18^2	25	0	15	13	19.8	3.86	84	.333	.451	0	.000	-1	-1	-1	0	-0.2
1973	Cal-A	0	4	.000	7	4	1	0	0	31^2	33	0	19	19	15.6	3.69	96	.262	.372	0	—	0	0	-1	-0	0.3
1974	Cal-A	7	11	.389	23	22	10	2	1	162	132	10	79	76	12.2	2.61	132	.225	.326	0	—	0	18	15	0	1.7
1975	Cal-A	3	12	.200	30	18	6	1	0	133^1	158	12	53	82	14.6	5.94	60	.303	.373	0	—	0	-32	-35	1	-2.9
1976	Cal-A	0	6	.000	14	4	0	0	0	47^1	50	3	17	16	12.7	5.13	65	.284	.347	0	—	0	-8	-10	-0	-0.7
	*KC-A	5	6	.455	19	14	4	1	0	99^2	89	2	39	45	11.6	2.89	121	.242	.314	0	—	0	7	7	1	0.7
	Yr	5	12	.294	33	18	4	1	0	147	139	5	56	61	11.9	3.61	95	.254	.323	0	—	0	-2	-3	1	0.0
1977	*KC-A	9	6	.600	29	27	3	1	0	156^1	166	7	75	83	14.2	4.20	96	.270	.354	0	—	0	-2	-3	0	-0.2
1978	KC-A	1	4	.200	11	9	1	0	0	58^1	76	1	24	26	15.7	4.32	88	.317	.383	0	—	0	-4	-3	-1	-0.3
	Bos-A	2	1	.667	13	2	0	0	1	30	38	0	13	23	15.3	3.00	137	.302	.367	0	—	0	3	4	-0	0.3
	Yr	3	5	.375	24	11	1	0	1	88^1	114	1	37	49	15.4	3.87	101	.308	.371	0	—	0	-1	0	-1	0.0
1979	Bos-A	1	2	.333	8	0	0	0	0	15^1	23	0	7	7	18.2	8.80	50	.365	.437	0	—	0	-8	-7	-0	-1.4
	NY-N	4	5	.444	29	8	1	0	4	80^1	74	5	42	53	13.0	3.70	98	.252	.345	0	.000	-2	0	-1	1	-0.2
1980	Pit-N	0	0	—	6	0	0	0	0	11^2	9	2	4	4	10.0	3.86	94	.243	.317	0	.000	-0	-0	-0	1	0.0
	Cal-A	5	1	.833	41	0	0	0	10	83	67	8	37	75	11.4	2.49	158	.214	.299	0	—	0	14	13	-1	1.3
1981	Cal-A	4	3	.571	42	0	0	0	5	75^2	72	8	33	44	12.5	3.21	114	.262	.341	0	—	0	4	4	1	0.4
1982	*Cal-A	2	1	.667	54	0	0	0	4	71^1	58	5	40	38	12.9	2.78	146	.232	.347	0	—	0	10	10	2	0.7
1983	Cal-A	0	5	.000	42	0	0	0	4	36^1	42	2	17	20	14.6	5.45	74	.302	.378	0	—	0	-6	-6	1	-0.7
1984	StL-N	1	0	1.000	3	0	0	0	0	2^1	4	2	2	1	23.1	11.57	30	.364	.462	0	—	0	-2	-2	0	-0.7
1985	StL-N	0	1	.000	10	0	0	0	0	10	9	0	4	5	11.7	1.80	196	.225	.295	0	—	0	2	2	-0	0.2
Total	14	44	71	.383	387	112	26	5	29	1123^1	1125	67	520	630	13.4	3.83	97	.264	.349	0	.000	-3	-5	-15	4	-1.7
● **CHARLIE HASTINGS**	Hastings, Charles Morton b: 11/11/1870, Ironton, Ohio d: 8/3/34, Parkersburg, W.Va. 5′11″, 179 lbs. Deb: 5/3/1893																									
1893	Cle-N	4	5	.444	15	9	6	0	1	92	128	5	33	14	16.2	4.70	104	.320	.379	7	.179	0	-0	2	-2	0.0
1896	Pit-N	5	10	.333	17	13	9	0	1	104	126	1	44	19	15.3	5.88	71	.296	.372	8	.216	-0	-18	-19	1	-2.0
1897	Pit-N	5	4	.556	16	10	9	0	0	118	138	3	47	42	14.6	4.58	91	.289	.362	10	.233	3	-3	-5	-1	-0.1
1898	Pit-N	4	10	.286	19	13	12	0	0	137^1	142	2	52	40	13.4	3.41	104	.265	.341	10	.233	2	3	2	1	0.5
Total	4	18	29	.383	67	45	36	0	2	451^1	534	11	176	115	14.7	4.55	91	.291	.362	35	.216	5	-18	-21	-1	-1.6

YEAR	TM/L	W	L	PCT	G	GS	CG	SH	SV	IP	H	HR	BB	SO	RAT	ERA	ERA+	OAV	OOB	BH	AVG	PB	PR	/A	PD	TPI
● **BOB HASTY** Hasty, Robert Keller b: 5/3/1896, Canton, Ga. d: 5/28/72, Dallas, Ga. BR/TR, 6'3", 210 lbs. Deb: 9/11/19																										
1919	Phi-A	0	2	.000	2	2	1	0	0	12	15	1	4	5	14.3	5.25	65	.306	.358	1	.333	0	-3	-2	-1	-0.4
1920	Phi-A	1	3	.250	19	4	1	0	0	71^2	91	5	28	12	14.9	5.02	80	.323	.384	6	.250	0	-10	-8	2	-0.2
1921	Phi-A	5	16	.238	35	22	9	0	0	179^1	238	8	40	46	14.1	4.87	92	.331	.368	20	.294	2	-12	-8	0	-0.5
1922	Phi-A	9	14	.391	28	26	14	1	0	192^1	225	20	41	33	12.6	4.26	100	.298	.336	15	.200	-2	-5	-0	-2	-0.4
1923	Phi-A	13	15	.464	44	36	10	1	1	243^1	274	11	72	56	13.1	4.44	93	.291	.347	17	.193	-3	-12	-9	-1	-1.2
1924	Phi-A	1	3	.250	18	4	0	0	0	52^2	57	4	30	15	15.0	5.64	76	.282	.378	1	.077	-1	-8	-8	2	-0.5
Total	6	29	53	.354	146	94	35	2	1	751^1	900	49	215	167	13.5	4.65	91	.305	.355	60	.221	-3	-49	-35	-0	-3.2
● **MICKEY HATCHER** Hatcher, Michael Vaughn b: 3/15/55, Cleveland, Ohio BR/TR, 6'2", 200 lbs. Deb: 8/3/79 C♦																										
1989	LA-N	0	0	—	1	0	0	0	0	1	0	0	3	0	36.0	9.00	38	.000	.667	66	.295	0	-1	-1	0	0.0
● **GIL HATFIELD** Hatfield, Gilbert "Colonel" b: 1/27/1855, Hoboken, N.J. d: 5/27/21, Hoboken, N.J. TR, 5'9.5", 168 lbs. Deb: 9/24/1885 F♦																										
1889	NY-N	2	4	.333	6	5	5	0	0	52	53	2	25	28	13.7	3.98	99	.256	.339	23	.184	-0	0	-0	0	0.0
1890	NY-P	1	1	.500	3	0	0	0	1	7^2	8	1	4	3	15.3	3.52	129	.258	.361	80	.279	0	1	1	-0	0.2
1891	Was-a	0	0	—	4	0	0	0	0	18	29	1	14	3	21.5	11.00	34	.349	.443	128	.256	1	-15	-15	-0	0.0
Total	3	3	5	.375	13	5	5	0	1	77^2	90	4	43	34	15.6	5.56	71	.280	.369	295	.248	1	-14	-14	-0	0.2
● **JOHN HATFIELD** Hatfield, John Van Buskirk b: 7/20/1847, New Jersey d: 2/20/09, Long Island City, N.Y. 5'10", 165 lbs. Deb: 5/18/1871 FM♦																										
1874	Mut-n	0	1	.000	3	0	0	0	0	8	11	0	0	0	12.4	2.25	99	.314	.314	66	.226	-0	-0	-0		0.1
● **HILLY HATHAWAY** Hathaway, Hillary Houston b: 9/12/69, Jacksonville, Fla. BL/TL, 6'4", 195 lbs. Deb: 9/8/92																										
1992	Cal-A	0	0	—	2	1	0	0	0	5^2	8	1	3	1	17.5	7.94	50	.333	.407	0	—	0	-3	-2	-0	0.0
1993	Cal-A	4	3	.571	11	11	0	0	0	57^1	71	6	26	11	16.0	5.02	90	.326	.410	0	—	0	-4	-3	1	-0.5
Total	2	4	3	.571	13	12	0	0	0	63	79	7	29	12	16.1	5.29	84	.326	.409	0	—	0	-7	-6	0	-0.5
● **RAY HATHAWAY** Hathaway, Ray Wilson b: 10/13/16, Greenville, Ohio BR/TR, 6', 165 lbs. Deb: 4/20/45																										
1945	Bro-N	0	1	.000	4	1	0	0	0	9	11	1	6	3	17.0	4.00	94	.297	.395	0	.000	-0	-0	-0	0	0.0
● **JOE HATTEN** Hatten, Joseph Hilarian b: 11/17/16, Bancroft, Iowa d: 12/16/88, Redding, Cal. BR/TL, 6', 176 lbs. Deb: 4/21/46																										
1946	Bro-N	14	11	.560	42	30	13	1	2	222	207	10	110	85	13.1	2.84	119	.253	.347	6	.076	-6	14	13	-2	0.6
1947	*Bro-N	17	8	.680	42	32	11	3	0	225^1	211	9	105	76	12.8	3.63	114	.252	.339	17	.205	0	11	12	3	1.5
1948	Bro-N	13	10	.565	42	30	11	1	0	208^2	228	9	94	73	14.0	3.58	112	.283	.360	13	.206	1	9	10	4	1.5
1949	*Bro-N	12	8	.600	37	29	11	2	2	187^1	194	15	69	58	12.7	4.18	98	.271	.337	12	.179	-1	-3	-2	0	-0.3
1950	Bro-N	2	2	.500	23	8	2	1	0	68^2	82	10	31	29	14.8	4.59	89	.294	.365	2	.111	-1	-3	-4	-1	-0.4
1951	Bro-N	1	0	1.000	11	6	0	0	0	49^1	55	3	21	22	13.9	4.56	86	.281	.350	2	.133	-1	-3	-3	1	-0.1
	Chi-N	2	6	.250	23	6	1	0	0	75^1	82	8	37	23	14.3	5.14	80	.281	.364	4	.235	0	-10	-9	-0	-0.8
	Yr	3	6	.333	34	12	1	0	0	124^2	137	11	58	45	14.1	4.91	82	.281	.358	6	.188	-1	-13	-12	1	-0.9
1952	Chi-N	4	4	.500	13	8	2	0	0	50^1	65	6	25	15	16.3	6.08	63	.314	.391	1	.067	-1	-13	-12	1	-1.7
Total	7	65	49	.570	233	149	51	8	4	1087	1124	70	492	381	13.5	3.87	101	.271	.351	57	.160	-8	1	5	6	0.3
● **CLYDE HATTER** Hatter, Clyde Melno b: 8/7/08, Poplar Hills, Ky. d: 10/16/37, Yosemite, Ky. BR/TL, 5'11", 170 lbs. Deb: 4/23/35																										
1935	Det-A	0	0	—	8	2	0	0	0	33^1	44	2	30	15	20.3	7.56	55	.319	.444	3	.300	0	-12	-13	-1	-0.1
1937	Det-A	1	0	1.000	3	0	0	0	0	9^1	17	0	11	4	28.0	11.57	40	.415	.547	0	.000	-0	-7	-7	-0	-0.6
Total	2	1	0	1.000	11	2	0	0	0	42^2	61	2	41	19	21.9	8.44	51	.341	.468	3	.231	0	-19	-20	-1	-0.7
● **CHRIS HAUGHEY** Haughey, Christopher Francis "Bud" b: 10/3/25, Astoria, N.Y. BR/TR, 6'1", 180 lbs. Deb: 10/3/43																										
1943	Bro-N	0	1	.000	1	0	0	0	0	7	5	0	10	0	19.3	3.86	87	.238	.484	0	.000	-0	-0	-0	-0	-0.1
● **GARY HAUGHT** Haught, Gary Allen b: 9/29/70, Tacoma, Wash. BB/TR, 6'1", 190 lbs. Deb: 7/16/97																										
1997	Oak-A	0	0	—	6	0	0	0	0	11^1	12	3	6	11	15.9	7.15	63	.279	.392	0	—	0	-3	-3	0	0.1
● **PHIL HAUGSTAD** Haugstad, Philip Donald b: 2/23/24, Black River Falls, Wis. d: 10/21/98, Black River Falls, Wis. BR/TR, 6'2", 165 lbs. Deb: 9/1/47																										
1947	Bro-N	1	0	1.000	6	1	0	0	0	12^2	14	1	4	4	12.8	2.84	145	.298	.353	0	.000	-0	2	2	-0	0.1
1948	Bro-N	0	0	—	1	0	0	0	0	1	1	0	0	0	9.0	0.00	—	.333	.333	0	—	0	0	0	0	0.0
1951	Bro-N	0	1	.000	21	1	0	0	0	30^2	28	4	24	22	16.1	6.46	61	.233	.374	0	.000	0	-9	-9	0	-0.2
1952	Cin-N	0	0	—	9	0	0	0	0	12	8	1	13	2	16.5	6.75	56	.190	.393	0	.000	-0	-4	-4	0	0.0
Total	4	1	1	.500	37	2	0	0	0	56^1	51	6	41	28	15.3	5.59	70	.241	.374	0	.000	-0	-10	-10	1	-0.1
● **TOM HAUSMAN** Hausman, Thomas Matthew b: 3/31/53, Mobridge, S.D. BR/TR, 6'5", 200 lbs. Deb: 4/26/75																										
1975	Mil-A	3	6	.333	29	9	1	0	0	112	110	7	47	46	13.1	4.10	93	.258	.340	0	—	0	-4	-3	1	-0.2
1976	Mil-A	0	0	—	3	0	0	0	0	3^1	3	0	3	1	16.2	5.40	65	.250	.400	0	—	0	-1	-1	0	0.2
1978	NY-N	3	3	.500	10	10	0	0	0	51^2	58	6	9	16	11.8	4.70	74	.287	.321	3	.176	1	-6	-7	0	-0.7
1979	NY-N	2	6	.250	19	10	1	0	2	78^2	65	6	19	33	10.1	2.75	133	.226	.284	3	.115	-1	9	8	0	0.7
1980	NY-N	6	5	.545	55	4	0	0	1	122	125	12	26	53	11.4	3.98	89	.266	.309	1	.063	-1	-5	-6	1	-0.5
1981	NY-N	0	1	.000	20	0	0	0	0	33	28	2	7	13	9.5	2.18	160	.235	.278	0	.000	0	5	5	0	0.2
1982	NY-N	1	2	.333	21	0	0	0	0	36^2	44	4	6	16	12.8	4.42	82	.295	.331	0	.000	-0	-3	-3	-1	-0.3
	Atl-N	0	0	—	3	0	0	0	0	3^2	6	0	4	2	24.5	4.91	76	.500	.625	0	—	0	-1	-0	0	0.0
	Yr	1	2	.333	24	0	0	0	0	40^1	50	4	10	18	13.4	4.46	82	.299	.339	0	.000	-0	-4	-4	0	-0.3
Total	7	15	23	.395	160	33	2	0	3	441	439	37	121	180	11.8	3.80	96	.262	.317	7	.111	-2	-7	-8	2	-0.6
● **CLEM HAUSMANN** Hausmann, Clemens Raymond b: 8/17/19, Houston, Tex. d: 8/29/72, Baytown, Tex. BR/TR, 5'9", 165 lbs. Deb: 4/28/44																										
1944	Bos-A	4	7	.364	32	12	3	0	2	137	139	6	69	43	13.9	3.42	99	.266	.355	3	.079	-3	0	-0	-0	-0.3
1945	Bos-A	5	7	.417	31	13	4	2	2	125	131	5	60	30	13.9	5.04	68	.270	.352	4	.103	-3	-23	-23	2	-2.2
1949	Phi-A	0	0	—	1	0	0	0	0	1	0	0	2	0	18.0	9.00	46	.000	.500	0	—	0	-1	-1	0	0.0
Total	3	9	14	.391	64	25	7	2	4	263	270	11	131	73	13.9	4.21	81	.267	.354	7	.091	-5	-24	-23	2	-2.5
● **BRAD HAVENS** Havens, Bradley David b: 11/17/59, Highland Park, Mich BL/TL, 6'1", 196 lbs. Deb: 6/5/81																										
1981	Min-A	3	6	.333	14	12	1	1	0	78	76	6	24	43	11.7	3.58	110	.257	.315	0	—	0	1	3	-1	0.0
1982	Min-A	10	14	.417	33	32	4	1	0	208^2	201	32	80	129	12.1	4.31	98	.250	.318	0	—	0	-6	-2	-3	-0.5
1983	Min-A	5	8	.385	16	14	1	0	0	80^1	110	11	38	40	16.6	8.18	52	.333	.402	0	—	0	-37	-35	-2	-4.7
1985	Bal-A	0	1	.000	8	1	0	0	0	14^1	20	4	10	19	18.8	8.79	46	.333	.429	0	—	0	-7	-8	-0	-0.3
1986	Bal-A	3	3	.500	46	0	0	0	1	71	64	7	29	57	11.8	4.56	91	.248	.324	0	—	0	-3	-3	1	-0.1
1987	LA-N	0	0	—	31	1	0	0	1	35^1	30	2	23	23	13.8	4.33	92	.227	.346	0	.000	-0	-1	-1	-1	-0.1
1988	LA-N	0	0	—	9	0	0	0	0	9^2	15	1	4	8	17.7	4.66	72	.357	.413	0	.000	-0	-1	-1	1	0.1
	Cle-A	2	3	.400	28	0	0	0	1	57^1	62	7	17	30	12.4	3.14	131	.273	.324	0	—	0	5	6	-0	0.4
1989	Cle-A	0	0	—	7	0	0	0	0	13^1	18	3	7	6	16.9	4.05	98	.353	.431	0	—	0	-0	-0	1	0.0
	Det-A	1	2	.333	13	1	0	0	0	22^2	28	3	14	15	17.9	5.56	69	.308	.417	0	—	0	-4	-4	0	-0.4
	Yr	1	2	.333	20	1	0	0	0	36	46	6	21	21	17.5	5.00	77	.319	.417	0	—	0	-4	-5	1	-0.4
Total	8	24	37	.393	205	61	6	2	3	590^2	624	76	246	370	13.3	4.81	86	.272	.344	0	.000	-0	-54	-46	-4	-5.6
● **RYAN HAWBLITZEL** Hawblitzel, Ryan Wade b: 4/30/71, West Palm Beach, Fla. BR/TR, 6'2", 170 lbs. Deb: 6/9/96																										
1996	Col-N	0	1	.000	8	0	0	0	0	15	18	2	6	7	14.4	6.00	87	.290	.353	0	.000	-0	-3	-1	0	-0.1
● **ED HAWK** Hawk, Edward b: 5/11/1890, Neosho, Mo. d: 3/26/36, Neosho, Mo. BL/TR, 5'11", 175 lbs. Deb: 9/7/11																										
1911	StL-A	0	4	.000	5	4	4	0	0	37^2	38	1	8	14	11.9	3.35	101	.253	.309	2	.154	-1	-0	0	0	-0.1
● **BILL HAWKE** Hawke, William Victor "Dick" b: 4/28/1870, Elsmere, Del. d: 12/11/02, Wilmington, Del. BR/TR, 5'8.5", 169 lbs. Deb: 7/28/1892																										
1892	StL-N	5	5	.500	14	11	10	1	0	97^1	108	2	45	55	14.9	3.70	86	.270	.355	4	.089	-4	-4	-5	0	-0.9
1893	StL-N	0	1	.000	1	1	0	0	0	5^1	9	0	3	1	20.3	5.06	93	.360	.429	1	.333	0	-0	-0	-0	0.0
	Bal-N	11	16	.407	29	29	22	1	0	225	248	8	108	69	14.6	4.76	100	.271	.354	16	.172	-4	-2	-0	0	-0.4
	Yr	11	17	.393	30	30	22	1	0	230^1	257	8	111	70	14.7	4.77	100	.274	.356	17	.177	-4	-3	-1	0	-0.4

YEAR TM/L	W	L	PCT	G	GS	CG	SH	SV	IP	H	HR	BB	SO	RAT	ERA	ERA+	OAV	OOB	BH	AVG	PB	PR	/A	PD	TPI
1894 *Bal-N	16	9	.640	32	25	17	0	3	206	264	9	78	68	15.5	5.81	94	.308	.374	28	.304	2	-11	-8	1	-0.5
Total 3	32	31	.508	76	66	49	2	3	533^2	629	19	234	193	15.0	4.98	95	.286	.363	49	.210	-7	-18	-15	1	-1.8
● **LA TROY HAWKINS**	Hawkins, La Troy b: 12/21/72, Gary, Ind. BR/TR, 6'5", 195 lbs. Deb: 4/29/95																								
1995 Min-A	2	3	.400	6	6	1	0	0	27	39	3	12	9	17.3	8.67	55	.339	.406	0	—	0	-12	-12	0	-1.6
1996 Min-A	1	1	.500	7	6	0	0	0	26^1	42	8	9	24	17.4	8.20	62	.372	.418	0	—	0	-9	-9	0	-0.5
1997 Min-A	6	12	.333	20	20	0	0	0	103^1	134	19	47	58	16.1	5.84	80	.317	.390	0	.000	-0	-15	-14	0	-1.9
1998 Min-A	7	14	.333	33	33	0	0	0	190^1	227	27	61	105	13.9	5.25	89	.299	.355	0	.000	-0	-13	-12	1	-1.0
Total 4	16	30	.348	66	65	1	0	0	347	442	57	129	196	15.1	5.91	80	.313	.375	0	.000	-0	-49	-46	2	-5.0
● **ANDY HAWKINS**	Hawkins, Melton Andrew b: 1/21/60, Waco, Tex. BR/TR, 6'3", 223 lbs. Deb: 7/17/82																								
1982 SD-N	2	5	.286	15	10	1	0	0	63^2	66	4	27	25	13.4	4.10	84	.274	.352	0	.000	-2	-4	-5	-1	-0.7
1983 SD-N	5	7	.417	21	19	4	1	0	119^2	106	8	48	59	12.0	2.93	119	.244	.326	2	.065	-1	9	7	1	0.7
1984 *SD-N	8	9	.471	36	22	2	1	0	146	143	13	72	77	13.4	4.68	76	.254	.341	8	.195	1	-18	-18	-1	-2.0
1985 SD-N	18	8	.692	33	33	5	2	0	228^2	229	18	65	69	11.7	3.15	112	.267	.321	6	.078	-4	11	10	-1	0.6
1986 SD-N	10	8	.556	37	35	3	1	0	209^1	218	24	75	117	12.8	4.30	85	.268	.334	10	.149	-1	-14	-15	-2	-1.4
1987 SD-N	3	10	.231	24	20	0	0	0	117^2	131	16	49	51	13.9	5.05	78	.287	.358	5	.156	-0	-13	-14	0	-1.4
1988 SD-N	14	11	.560	33	33	4	2	0	217^2	196	16	76	91	11.5	3.35	101	.244	.314	7	.113	-2	2	1	-3	-0.3
1989 NY-A	15	15	.500	34	34	5	2	0	208^1	238	23	76	98	13.8	4.80	81	.290	.355	0	—	0	-21	-21	-3	-2.9
1990 NY-A	5	12	.294	28	26	2	1	0	157^2	156	20	82	74	13.7	5.37	74	.260	.351	0	—	0	-26	-24	-2	-2.5
1991 NY-A	0	2	.000	4	3	0	0	0	12^2	23	5	6	5	20.6	9.95	42	.383	.439	0	—	0	-8	-8	1	-0.9
Oak-A	4	4	.500	15	14	1	0	0	77	68	5	36	40	12.7	4.79	80	.237	.332	0	—	0	-6	-8	0	-0.7
Yr	4	6	.400	19	17	1	0	0	89^2	91	10	42	45	13.9	5.52	70	.262	.350	0	—	0	-14	-16	1	-1.6
Total 10	84	91	.480	280	249	27	10	0	1558^1	1574	152	612	706	12.9	4.22	87	.265	.338	38	.117	-8	-86	-96	-11	-11.5
● **WYNN HAWKINS**	Hawkins, Wynn Firth "Hawk" b: 2/20/36, E.Palestine, Ohio BR/TR, 6'3", 195 lbs. Deb: 4/22/60																								
1960 Cle-A	4	4	.500	15	9	1	0	0	66	68	10	39	39	14.7	4.23	88	.269	.369	2	.100	-1	-3	-4	1	-0.4
1961 Cle-A	7	9	.438	30	21	3	1	1	133	139	16	59	51	13.5	4.06	97	.270	.347	4	.108	-2	-1	-2	-1	-0.5
1962 Cle-A	1	0	1.000	3	0	0	0	0	3^2	9	1	1	0	24.5	7.36	53	.429	.455	0	—	0	-1	-1	-0	-0.3
Total 3	12	13	.480	48	30	4	1	1	202^2	216	27	99	90	14.1	4.17	93	.274	.357	6	.105	-2	-5	-7	-1	-1.2
● **PINK HAWLEY**	Hawley, Emerson P. b: 12/5/1872, Beaver Dam, Wis. d: 9/19/38, Beaver Dam, Wis. BL/TR, 5'10", 185 lbs. Deb: 8/13/1892																								
1892 StL-N	6	14	.300	20	20	18	0	0	166^1	160	4	63	63	12.7	3.19	100	.243	.319	12	.169	-2	2	0	-2	-0.4
1893 StL-N	5	17	.227	31	24	21	0	1	227	249	6	103	73	14.7	4.60	103	.270	.356	26	.286	7	2	3	-3	0.6
1894 StL-N	19	27	.413	53	41	36	0	0	392^2	481	14	149	120	14.9	4.90	110	.298	.365	43	.264	2	18	22	2	2.1
1895 Pit-N	31	22	.585	**56**	50	44	**4**	1	**444**^{1}	449	7	122	142	12.2	3.18	142	.258	.319	57	.308	14	**79**	66	2	**7.4**
1896 Pit-N	22	21	.512	49	43	37	2	0	378	382	2	157	137	13.5	3.57	118	.260	.343	39	.239	2	33	26	3	2.8
1897 Pit-N	18	18	.500	40	39	33	0	0	311^1	362	7	94	88	13.9	4.80	87	.288	.350	30	.231	-2	-17	-22	0	-2.0
1898 Cin-N	27	11	.711	43	37	32	3	0	331	357	5	91	69	12.8	3.37	114	.273	.331	24	.185	-4	9	17	-5	0.7
1899 Cin-N	14	17	.452	34	29	25	0	1	250^1	289	7	65	46	13.4	4.24	92	.289	.344	22	.218	-1	-11	-9	-2	-1.2
1900 NY-N	18	18	.500	41	38	**34**	2	0	329^1	377	7	89	80	13.3	3.53	103	.287	.341	25	.203	-2	6	3	4	0.5
1901 Mil-A	7	14	.333	26	23	17	0	0	182^1	228	3	41	50	13.7	4.59	78	.302	.346	19	.260	2	-19	-20	1	-1.5
Total 10	167	179	.483	393	344	297	11	3	3012^2	3334	62	974	868	13.5	3.96	107	.277	.342	297	.241	15	103	89	-0	9.0
● **SCOTT HAWLEY**	Hawley, Marvin Hiram b: Painesville, Ohio d: 4/28/04, Alliance, Ohio Deb: 9/22/1894																								
1894 Bos-N	0	1	.000	1	1	1	0	0	7	10	0	7	1	24.4	7.71	74	.333	.487	0	.000	-1	-2	-2	0	-0.2
● **HAL HAYDEL**	Haydel, John Harold b: 7/9/44, Houma, La. BR/TR, 6', 190 lbs. Deb: 9/7/70																								
1970 Min-A	2	0	1.000	4	0	0	0	0	9	7	2	4	4	11.0	3.00	124	.226	.314	2	.667	2	1	1	-0	0.4
1971 Min-A	4	2	.667	31	0	0	0	1	40	33	3	20	29	12.4	4.27	83	.243	.348	1	.333	0	-4	-3	0	-0.5
Total 2	6	2	.750	35	0	0	0	1	49	40	5	24	33	12.1	4.04	89	.240	.342	3	.500	2	-3	-2	-0	-0.1
● **LEFTY HAYDEN**	Hayden, Eugene Franklin b: 4/14/35, San Francisco, Cal BL/TL, 6'2", 175 lbs. Deb: 6/26/58																								
1958 Cin-N	0	0	—	3	0	0	0	0	3^2	5	0	1	3	14.7	4.91	84	.313	.353	0	—	0	-0	-0	-0	0.0
● **BEN HAYES**	Hayes, Ben Joseph b: 8/4/57, Niagara Falls, N.Y. BR/TR, 6'1", 180 lbs. Deb: 6/25/82																								
1982 Cin-N	2	0	1.000	26	0	0	0	2	45^2	37	3	22	38	11.6	1.97	188	.219	.309	0	.000	-0	8	9	-1	0.3
1983 Cin-N	4	6	.400	60	0	0	0	7	69^1	82	8	37	44	15.6	6.49	59	.301	.387	0	.000	-1	-22	-21	0	-3.2
Total 2	6	6	.500	86	0	0	0	9	115	119	11	59	82	14.0	4.70	80	.270	.357	0	.000	-1	-14	-12	-1	-2.9
● **JIM HAYES**	Hayes, James Millard "Whitey" b: 2/25/12, Montevallo, Ala. d: 11/27/93, Decatur, Ga. BL/TR, 6'1", 168 lbs. Deb: 7/13/35																								
1935 Was-A	2	4	.333	7	4	1	0	0	28	38	0	23	9	19.6	8.36	52	.322	.433	2	.250	-0	-12	-13	-1	-2.0
● **HEATH HAYNES**	Haynes, Heath Burnett b: 11/30/68, Wheeling, W.Va. BR/TR, 6', 175 lbs. Deb: 6/1/94																								
1994 Mon-N	0	0	—	4	0	0	0	0	3^2	3	0	3	1	14.7	0.00	—	.231	.375	0	—	0	2	2	-0	0.0
● **JIMMY HAYNES**	Haynes, Jimmy Wayne b: 9/5/72, LaGrange, Ga. BR/TR, 6'4", 185 lbs. Deb: 9/13/95																								
1995 Bal-A	2	1	.667	4	3	0	0	0	24	11	2	12	22	8.6	2.25	211	.136	.247	0	—	0	7	7	-0	0.8
1996 Bal-A	3	6	.333	26	11	0	0	1	89	122	14	58	65	18.4	8.29	59	.333	.427	0	—	0	-33	-33	0	-2.7
1997 Oak-A	3	6	.333	13	13	0	0	0	73^1	74	7	40	65	14.2	4.42	102	.262	.358	0	.000	-0	1	1	1	0.1
1998 Oak-A	11	9	.550	33	33	1	1	0	194^1	229	25	88	134	14.9	5.09	89	.298	.374	0	.000	-0	-10	-12	-2	-1.1
Total 4	19	22	.463	76	60	1	1	1	380^2	436	48	198	286	15.2	5.53	84	.291	.377	0	.000	-0	-35	-37	-1	-2.9
● **JOE HAYNES**	Haynes, Joseph Walton b: 9/21/17, Lincolnton, Ga. d: 1/6/67, Hopkins, Minn. BR/TR, 6'2.5", 190 lbs. Deb: 4/24/39 C																								
1939 Was-A	8	12	.400	27	20	10	1	0	173	186	10	78	64	13.8	5.36	81	.276	.352	14	.209	0	-14	-19	-1	-1.9
1940 Was-A	3	6	.333	22	7	1	0	0	63^1	85	4	34	23	17.1	6.54	64	.327	.407	2	.105	-2	-15	-17	-1	-2.1
1941 Chi-A	0	0	—	8	0	0	0	0	28	30	0	11	18	13.2	3.86	106	.280	.347	3	.273	0	1	1	-0	0.0
1942 Chi-A	8	5	.615	**40**	1	1	0	6	103	88	6	47	35	12.1	2.62	137	.234	.324	5	.179	0	12	11	0	1.5
1943 Chi-A	7	2	.778	35	2	1	0	3	109^1	114	2	32	37	12.2	2.96	113	.263	.316	9	.265	2	4	5	-1	0.5
1944 Chi-A	5	6	.455	33	12	8	0	2	154^1	148	5	43	44	11.1	2.57	134	.254	.306	10	.200	1	15	15	0	1.3
1945 Chi-A	5	5	.500	14	13	8	1	1	104	92	5	29	34	10.6	3.55	94	.237	.291	7	.175	-2	-2	-3	1	-0.4
1946 Chi-A	7	9	.438	32	23	9	0	2	177^1	203	14	60	60	13.6	3.76	91	.289	.349	14	.246	3	-5	-7	1	-0.2
1947 Chi-A	14	6	.700	29	22	7	2	0	182	174	5	61	50	11.7	**2.42**	**151**	.250	.312	17	.262	2	26	25	0	2.9
1948 Chi-A☆	9	10	.474	27	22	6	0	0	149^2	167	13	52	40	13.3	3.97	107	.284	.344	8	.160	-1	5	5	-2	0.2
1949 Was-A	2	9	.182	37	10	0	0	2	96^1	106	6	55	19	15.3	6.26	68	.283	.380	6	.240	1	-22	-21	1	-2.0
1950 Was-A	7	5	.583	27	10	1	1	0	101^2	124	14	46	15	15.5	5.84	77	.305	.382	7	.200	1	-14	-15	1	-1.3
1951 Was-A	1	4	.200	26	3	1	0	2	73	85	9	37	18	15.2	4.56	90	.290	.372	7	.333	2	-4	-4	-1	-0.4
1952 Was-A	0	3	.000	22	2	0	0	3	66	70	2	35	18	14.5	4.50	79	.275	.364	2	.105	-1	-6	-7	-1	-0.5
Total 14	76	82	.481	379	147	53	5	21	1581	1672	95	620	475	13.2	4.01	96	.272	.342	111	.213	7	-20	-31	-2	-2.1
● **RAY HAYWARD**	Hayward, Raymond Alton b: 4/27/61, Enid, Okla. BL/TL, 6'1", 190 lbs. Deb: 9/20/86																								
1986 SD-N	0	2	.000	3	3	0	0	0	10	16	1	4	6	18.0	9.00	41	.340	.392	0	.000	-0	-6	-6	-0	-1.0
1987 SD-N	0	0	—	4	0	0	0	0	6	12	3	3	2	22.5	16.50	24	.444	.500	0	.000	-0	-8	-8	1	0.0
1988 Tex-A	4	6	.400	12	12	1	1	0	62^2	63	6	35	37	14.1	5.46	75	.276	.373	0	—	0	-10	-10	1	-1.3
Total 3	4	8	.333	19	15	1	1	0	78^2	91	10	42	45	15.2	6.75	60	.301	.387	0	.000	-1	-25	-24	1	-2.3
● **BILL HAYWOOD**	Haywood, William Kiernan b: 4/21/37, Colon, Panama BR/TR, 6'3", 205 lbs. Deb: 7/28/68																								
1968 Was-A	0	0	—	14	0	0	0	0	23	27	1	12	10	16.0	4.70	62	.314	.410	0	—	0	-4	-5	-0	0.0
● **ED HEAD**	Head, Edward Marvin b: 1/25/18, Selma, La. d: 1/31/80, Bastrop, La. BR/TR, 6'1", 175 lbs. Deb: 7/27/40																								
1940 Bro-N	1	2	.333	13	5	2	0	0	39^1	40	0	18	13	13.3	4.12	97	.260	.337	2	.182	-0	-1	-1	-1	-0.2
1942 Bro-N	10	6	.625	36	15	5	1	4	136^2	118	11	47	78	11.1	3.56	92	.231	.300	13	.333	4	-4	-4	0	-0.1
1943 Bro-N	9	10	.474	47	18	7	3	6	169^2	166	8	66	83	12.3	3.66	92	.250	.318	7	.152	2	-5	-6	1	-0.7

YEAR	TM/L	W	L	PCT	G	GS	CG	SH	SV	IP	H	HR	BB	SO	RAT	ERA	ERA+	OAV	OOB	BH	AVG	PB	PR	/A	PD	TPI
1944	Bro-N	4	3	.571	9	8	5	1	0	63^1	54	2	19	17	10.4	2.70	132	.232	.290	5	.263	1	6	6	-1	0.6
1946	Bro-N	3	2	.600	13	7	3	1	1	56	56	3	24	17	12.9	3.21	105	.267	.342	5	.313	2	1	1	-1	0.2
Total	5	27	23	.540	118	53	22	6	11	465	434	24	174	208	11.8	3.48	98	.245	.314	32	.244	5	-2	-4	-1	-0.2
● **RALPH HEAD**	Head, Ralph b: 8/30/1893, Tallapoosa, Ga. d: 10/8/62, Muscadine, Ala. BR/TR, 5'10", 175 lbs. Deb: 4/18/23																									
1923	Phi-N	2	9	.182	35	13	5	0	0	132^1	185	13	57	24	16.5	6.66	69	.341	.404	3	.071	-5	-39	-30	-1	-2.6
● **TOM HEALEY**	Healey, Thomas F. b: 1853, Cranston, R.I. d: 2/6/1891, Lewiston, Maine TR , Deb: 6/13/1878																									
1878	Pro-N	0	3	.000	3	3	3	0	0	24	27	1	7	2	12.8	3.00	74	.278	.327	2	.222	0	-2	-2	-0	-0.2
	Ind-N	6	4	.600	11	10	9	0	1	89	98	1	13	18	11.2	2.22	91	.270	.295	8	.178	-1	1	-2	-0	-0.3
	Yr	6	7	.462	14	13	12	0	**1**	113	125	2	20	20	11.5	2.39	87	.272	.302	10	.185	-1	-1	-4	-0	-0.5
● **JOHN HEALY**	Healy, John J. "Egyptian" or "Long John" b: 10/27/1866, Cairo, Ill. d: 3/16/1899, St.Louis, Mo. BR/TR, 6'2", 158 lbs. Deb: 9/11/1885																									
1885	StL-N	1	7	.125	8	8	8	0	0	66	54	0	20	32	10.1	3.00	92	.210	.267	1	.042	-3	-1	-2	1	-0.4
1886	StL-N	17	23	.425	43	41	39	3	0	353^2	315	5	118	213	11.0	2.88	112	.230	.291	14	.097	-12	17	14	-2	0.0
1887	Ind-N	12	29	.293	41	41	40	3	0	341	415	24	108	75	14.2	5.17	80	.294	.350	24	.174	-4	-42	-39	-4	-4.0
1888	Ind-N	12	24	.333	37	37	36	1	0	321^1	347	13	87	124	12.6	3.89	76	.267	.320	30	.229	4	-37	-33	1	-2.8
1889	Was-N	1	11	.083	13	12	10	0	0	101	139	2	38	49	16.2	6.24	63	.317	.378	10	.222	1	-25	-26	2	-2.0
	Chi-N	1	4	.200	5	5	5	0	0	46	48	4	18	22	13.7	4.50	92	.261	.340	2	.100	-2	-2	-2	-0	-0.3
	Yr	2	15	.118	18	17	15	0	0	147	187	6	56	71	15.1	5.69	70	.298	.360	12	.185	-1	-27	-27	1	-2.3
1890	Tol-a	22	21	.512	46	46	44	2	0	389	326	5	127	225	11.0	2.89	137	.221	.293	34	.218	7	42	46	-2	4.7
1891	Bal-a	8	10	.444	23	22	19	0	0	170^1	179	6	57	54	12.7	3.75	100	.261	.322	9	.141	-2	-1	-0	-5	-0.6
1892	Bal-N	3	6	.333	9	8	5	0	0	68^1	82	4	21	24	13.8	4.74	72	.286	.339	6	.222	0	-11	-10	-0	-1.0
	Lou-N	1	1	.500	2	2	2	0	0	18^1	15	0	5	4	9.8	1.96	156	.214	.267	2	.286	1	3	2	-1	0.3
	Yr	4	7	.364	11	10	7	0	0	86^2	97	4	26	28	12.8	4.15	81	.270	.319	8	.235	1	-8	-8	-1	-0.7
Total	8	78	136	.364	227	222	208	9	0	1875	1920	63	599	822	12.4	3.84	94	.257	.318	132	.174	-9	-57	-50	-10	-6.1
● **CHARLIE HEARD**	Heard, Charles b: 1/30/1872, Philadelphia, Pa. d: 2/20/45, Philadelphia, Pa. BR/TR, 6'2", 190 lbs. Deb: 7/14/1890 ♦																									
1890	Pit-N	0	6	.000	6	6	5	0	0	44	75	5	32	13	22.3	8.39	39	.366	.456	8	.186	-1	-24	-25	-1	-2.3
● **JAY HEARD**	Heard, Jehosie b: 1/17/20, Atlanta, Ga. BL/TL, 5'7", 155 lbs. Deb: 4/24/54																									
1954	Bal-A	0	0	—	2	0	0	0	0	3^1	6	1	3	2	24.3	13.50	27	.375	.474	0	—	0	-4	-4	0	0.0
● **BUNNY HEARN**	Hearn, Bunn b: 5/21/1891, Chapel Hill, N.C. d: 10/10/59, Wilson, N.C. BL/TL, 5'11", 190 lbs. Deb: 9/17/10																									
1910	StL-N	1	3	.250	5	5	4	0	0	39	49	2	16	14	15.2	5.08	59	.322	.391	2	.133	-0	-9	-9	-1	-0.9
1911	StL-N	0	0	—	2	0	0	0	0	2^2	7	1	0	1	23.6	13.50	25	.538	.538	0	.000	-0	-3	-3	-0	0.0
1913	NY-N	1	1	.500	2	2	1	0	0	13	13	0	7	8	13.8	2.77	113	.277	.370	2	.400	1	1	1	-0	0.1
1915	Pit-F	6	11	.353	29	17	8	1	0	175^2	187	6	37	49	11.6	3.38	80	.285	.326	10	.189	-0	-13	-13	-1	-1.3
1918	Bos-N	5	6	.455	17	12	9	1	0	126^1	119	2	29	30	10.5	2.49	108	.256	.300	8	.178	-1	4	3	1	0.2
1920	Bos-N	0	3	.000	11	4	2	0	0	43	54	3	11	9	13.8	5.65	54	.329	.375	2	.143	-1	-12	-12	0	-0.9
Total	6	13	24	.351	66	40	24	2	0	399^2	429	14	100	111	12.0	3.56	78	.287	.333	24	.180	-2	-32	-34	-1	-2.8
● **BUNNY HEARN**	Hearn, Elmer Lafayette b: 1/13/04, Brooklyn, N.Y. d: 3/31/74, Venice, Fla. BL/TL, 5'8", 160 lbs. Deb: 4/13/26																									
1926	Bos-N	4	9	.308	34	12	3	0	2	117^1	121	2	56	40	13.6	4.22	84	.276	.358	3	.100	-2	-5	-9	2	-0.9
1927	Bos-N	0	2	.000	8	0	0	0	0	12^2	16	0	9	5	17.8	4.26	87	.327	.431	2	.400	1	-0	-1	0	0.0
1928	Bos-N	1	0	1.000	7	0	0	0	0	10	6	0	8	8	13.5	6.30	62	.167	.333	0	.000	-0	-3	-3	-0	-0.3
1929	Bos-N	2	0	1.000	10	1	0	0	0	18^1	18	2	9	12	13.3	4.42	106	.277	.365	0	.000	0	1	1	1	0.1
Total	4	7	11	.389	59	13	3	0	2	158^1	161	4	82	65	13.9	4.38	85	.273	.363	5	.132	-2	-8	-12	2	-1.1
● **JIM HEARN**	Hearn, James Tolbert b: 4/11/21, Atlanta, Ga. d: 6/10/98, Boca Grande, Fla. BR/TR, 6'3", 205 lbs. Deb: 4/17/47																									
1947	StL-N	12	7	.632	37	21	4	1	1	162	151	9	63	57	11.9	3.22	128	.248	.319	8	.145	-1	15	16	-1	1.5
1948	StL-N	8	6	.571	34	13	3	0	1	89^2	92	9	35	27	12.9	4.22	97	.271	.342	5	.200	-0	-3	-1	-2	-0.4
1949	StL-N	1	3	.250	17	4	0	0	0	42	48	3	23	18	15.6	5.14	81	.294	.388	1	.100	-0	-5	-5	0	-0.4
1950	StL-N	0	1	.000	6	0	0	0	0	9	12	1	6	4	18.0	10.00	43	.333	.429	1	1.000	0	-6	-6	-0	-0.5
	NY-N	11	3	.786	16	16	11	5	0	125	72	8	38	54	7.9	1.94	211	.169	.237	6	.136	-0	31	30	0	3.3
	Yr	11	4	.733	22	16	11	**5**	0	134	84	9	44	58	8.6	**2.49**	165	.182	.253	7	.156	0	25	24	0	2.8
1951	*NY-N	17	9	.654	34	34	11	0	0	211^1	204	21	82	66	12.3	3.62	108	.251	.321	12	.162	-0	8	7	5	1.3
1952	NY-N☆	14	7	.667	37	34	11	1	1	223^2	208	16	97	89	12.5	3.78	98	.245	.326	14	.182	4	-1	-2	4	0.6
1953	NY-N	9	12	.429	36	32	6	0	0	196^2	206	22	84	77	13.4	4.53	95	.266	.341	9	.136	0	-5	-5	2	-0.3
1954	NY-N	8	8	.500	29	18	3	2	1	130	137	10	66	45	14.2	4.15	97	.272	.359	5	.111	-1	-1	-2	1	-0.1
1955	NY-N	14	16	.467	39	33	11	1	0	226^2	225	27	66	86	11.7	3.73	108	.260	.314	12	.156	1	8	7	2	1.2
1956	NY-N	5	11	.313	30	19	2	0	1	129^1	124	17	44	66	11.9	3.97	95	.254	.319	4	.098	-3	-3	-3	-0	-0.6
1957	Phi-N	5	1	.833	36	4	1	0	3	74	79	6	18	46	12.0	3.65	104	.274	.321	0	.000	-2	2	1	1	0.0
1958	Phi-N	5	3	.625	39	1	0	0	0	73^1	88	6	27	33	14.1	4.17	95	.292	.351	0	.000	-1	-2	-2	-1	-0.4
1959	Phi-N	0	2	.000	6	0	0	0	0	11	15	2	6	1	17.2	5.73	72	.333	.412	0	.000	0	-2	-2	0	-0.3
Total	13	109	89	.551	396	229	63	10	8	1703^2	1661	157	655	669	12.4	3.81	105	.255	.326	77	.141	-3	35	35	11	4.9
● **SPENCER HEATH**	Heath, Spencer Paul b: 11/5/1894, Chicago, Ill. d: 1/25/30, Chicago, Ill. BB/TR, 6', 170 lbs. Deb: 5/4/20																									
1920	Chi-A	0	0	—	4	0	0	0	0	7	19	1	2	0	27.0	15.43	24	.475	.500	0	.000	-1	-9	-9	-0	-0.1
● **JEFF HEATHCOCK**	Heathcock, Ronald Jeffrey b: 11/18/59, Covina, Cal. BR/TR, 6'4", 205 lbs. Deb: 9/3/83																									
1983	Hou-N	2	1	.667	6	3	0	0	1	28	19	1	4	12	7.7	3.21	106	.181	.218	0	.000	-1	1	1	0	0.0
1985	Hou-N	3	1	.750	14	7	1	0	1	56^1	50	9	13	25	10.2	3.36	103	.239	.287	1	.063	0	1	1	0	0.1
1987	Hou-N	4	2	.667	19	2	0	0	1	42^2	44	4	9	15	11.4	3.16	124	.277	.320	0	.000	-1	4	4	-0	0.4
1988	Hou-N	0	5	.000	17	1	0	0	0	31	33	2	16	12	14.5	5.81	57	.275	.365	0	.000	-0	-8	-9	0	-1.3
Total	4	9	9	.500	56	13	1	0	3	158	146	16	42	64	10.9	3.76	94	.246	.300	1	.029	-2	-1	-4	0	-0.8
● **MIKE HEATHCOTT**	Heathcott, Michael Joseph b: 5/16/69, Chicago, Ill. BR/TR, 6'3", 180 lbs. Deb: 8/28/98																									
1998	Chi-A	0	0	—	1	0	0	0	0	3	2	0	1	3	9.0	3.00	152	.182	.250	0	—	0	1	1	-0	0.0
● **NEAL HEATON**	Heaton, Neal b: 3/3/60, Holtsville, N.Y. BL/TL, 6'1", 205 lbs. Deb: 9/3/82																									
1982	Cle-A	0	2	.000	8	4	0	0	0	31	32	1	16	14	13.9	5.23	78	.260	.345	0	—	0	-4	-4	-0	-0.2
1983	Cle-A	11	7	.611	39	16	4	3	7	149^1	157	11	44	75	12.2	4.16	102	.269	.321	0	—	0	-2	1	-2	-0.2
1984	Cle-A	12	15	.444	38	34	4	1	0	198^2	231	21	75	75	13.9	5.21	78	.293	.354	0	—	0	-27	-25	-3	-3.3
1985	Cle-A	9	17	.346	36	33	5	1	0	207^2	244	19	80	82	14.3	4.90	84	.298	.365	0	—	0	-17	-18	-3	-2.1
1986	Cle-A	3	6	.333	12	12	2	0	0	74^1	73	8	34	24	13.1	4.24	98	.254	.335	0	—	0	-1	-1	-0	-0.1
	Min-A	4	9	.308	21	17	3	0	1	124^1	128	18	47	66	12.7	3.98	108	.273	.340	0	—	0	3	4	-1	0.3
	Yr	7	15	.318	33	29	5	0	1	198^2	201	26	81	90	12.8	4.08	104	.266	.337	0	—	0	2	4	-1	0.2
1987	Mon-N	13	10	.565	32	32	3	1	0	193^1	207	25	37	105	11.5	4.52	93	.273	.310	14	.209	2	-9	-7	-1	-0.7
1988	Mon-N	3	10	.231	32	11	0	0	2	97^1	98	14	43	43	13.3	4.99	72	.271	.354	3	.143	-0	-17	-15	-0	-2.0
1989	Pit-N	6	7	.462	42	18	1	0	0	147^1	127	12	55	67	11.5	3.05	110	.233	.311	9	.214	1	7	5	1	0.5
1990	Pit-N☆	12	9	.571	30	24	0	0	0	146	143	17	38	68	11.3	3.45	105	.263	.314	2	.047	-2	6	3	-0	0.1
1991	Pit-N	3	3	.500	42	1	0	0	0	68^2	72	6	21	34	12.7	4.33	83	.275	.338	4	.286	2	-5	-6	-1	-0.4
1992	KC-A	3	1	.750	31	0	0	0	0	41	43	5	22	29	14.5	4.17	97	.274	.367	0	—	0	-1	-1	-0	-0.2
	Mil-A	0	0	—	1	0	0	0	0	1	0	0	1	2	9.0	0.00	—	.000	.250	0	—	0	0	0	0	0.1
	Yr	3	1	.750	32	0	0	0	0	42	43	5	23	31	14.1	4.07	99	.262	.353	0	—	0	-1	-0	-0	-0.1
1993	NY-A	1	0	1.000	18	0	0	0	0	27	34	6	11	15	16.0	6.00	69	.301	.378	0	—	0	-5	-6	0	0.1
Total	12	80	96	.455	382	202	22	6	10	1507	1589	163	524	699	12.8	4.37	91	.273	.337	32	.171	2	-72	-68	-11	-8.1
● **DAVE HEAVERLO**	Heaverlo, David Wallace b: 8/25/50, Ellensburg, Wash. BR/TR, 6'1", 210 lbs. Deb: 4/14/75																									
1975	SF-N	3	1	.750	42	0	0	0	1	64	62	2	31	35	13.2	2.39	159	.262	.349	2	.500	1	9	10	1	0.7
1976	SF-N	4	4	.500	61	0	0	0	1	75	85	2	15	40	12.2	4.44	82	.289	.328	1	.333	0	-8	-7	1	-0.6

YEAR TM/L	W	L	PCT	G	GS	CG	SH	SV	IP	H	HR	BB	SO	RAT	ERA	ERA+	OAV	OOB	BH	AVG	PB	PR	/A	PD	TPI
1977 SF-N	5	1	.833	56	0	0	0	1	98^2	92	10	21	58	10.6	2.55	153	.251	.297	0	.000	-0	15	15	2	1.0
1978 Oak-A	3	6	.333	69	0	0	0	10	130	141	11	41	71	12.8	3.25	112	.281	.339	0	—	0	7	6	3	0.8
1979 Oak-A	4	11	.267	62	0	0	0	9	85^2	97	7	42	40	15.0	4.20	96	.294	.380	0	.000	-0	0	-2	0	-0.2
1980 Sea-A	6	3	.667	60	0	0	0	4	78^2	75	9	35	42	13.2	3.89	106	.253	.342	0	—	0	1	2	-2	0.1
1981 Oak-A	1	0	1.000	6	0	0	0	0	5^2	7	0	3	2	15.9	1.59	219	.292	.370	0	—	0	1	1	-0	0.4
Total 7	26	26	.500	356	0	0	0	26	537^2	559	41	188	288	12.8	3.41	113	.273	.339	3	.231	0	26	26	4	2.2
● **WALLY HEBERT** Hebert, Wallace Andrew "Preacher" b: 8/21/07, Lake Charles, La. BL/TL, 6'1", 195 lbs. Deb: 5/1/31																									
1931 StL-A	6	7	.462	23	13	5	0	0	103	128	11	43	26	15.2	5.07	91	.306	.375	9	.209	-1	-8	-5	-2	-0.8
1932 StL-A	1	12	.077	35	15	2	0	1	108^1	145	6	45	29	16.0	6.48	75	.322	.386	12	.353	2	-24	-20	0	-1.7
1933 StL-A	4	6	.400	33	10	3	0	0	88^1	114	4	35	19	15.3	5.30	88	.308	.369	9	.391	3	-10	-6	-1	-0.4
1943 Pit-N	10	11	.476	34	23	12	1	0	184	197	3	45	41	11.9	2.98	117	.272	.316	13	.220	1	8	10	1	1.4
Total 4	21	36	.368	125	61	22	1	1	483^2	584	24	168	115	14.1	4.63	91	.298	.355	43	.270	5	-34	-21	-1	-1.5
● **GUY HECKER** Hecker, Guy Jackson b: 4/3/1856, Youngsville, Pa. d: 12/3/38, Wooster, Ohio BR/TR, 6', 190 lbs. Deb: 5/2/1882 MU♦																									
1882 Lou-a	6	6	.500	13	11	10	0	0	104	75	0	5	33	**6.9**	1.30	191	**.188**	**.199**	94	.276	4	16	14	3	2.1
1883 Lou-a	28	23	.549	53	52	51	3	0	469	526	4	75	164	11.5	3.34	90	.266	.292	90	.271	12	-2	-18	4	-0.2
1884 Lou-a	**52**	20	.722	**75**	73	**72**	6	0	**670^2**	526	4	56	**385**	**8.0**	**1.80**	**172**	.204	**.226**	94	.297	28	108	**96**	7	**12.6**
1885 Lou-a	30	23	.566	53	53	51	2	0	480	454	6	54	209	9.9	2.18	148	.237	.265	81	.273	9	57	56	5	**6.6**
1886 Lou-a	26	23	.531	49	48	45	2	0	420^2	390	6	118	133	11.1	2.87	127	.231	.285	117	.341	18	27	36	1	5.2
1887 Lou-a	18	12	.600	34	32	32	2	1	285^1	325	9	50	58	12.1	4.16	105	.272	.307	118	.319	11	4	7	5	1.8
1888 Lou-a	8	17	.320	26	25	25	0	0	223^1	251	5	43	63	12.3	3.39	91	.274	.313	48	.227	2	-8	-8	1	-0.4
1889 Lou-a	5	13	.278	19	16	15	0	0	151^1	215	7	47	33	15.9	5.59	69	.324	.373	93	.284	4	-29	-29	1	-2.2
1890 Pit-N	2	9	.182	14	12	11	0	0	119^2	160	9	44	32	15.6	5.11	64	.311	.369	77	.226	2	-21	-24	-1	-1.6
Total 9	175	146	.545	336	322	312	15	1	2924	2922	50	492	1110	10.7	2.93	113	.247	.281	812	.282	90	153	127	25	23.9
● **HARRY HEDGPETH** Hedgpeth, Harry Malcolm b: 9/4/1888, Fayetteville, N.C. d: 7/30/66, Richmond, Va. BL/TL, 6'1.5", 194 lbs. Deb: 10/3/13																									
1913 Was-A	0	0	—	1	0	0	0	1	1	1	0	0	0	9.0	0.00	—	.250	.250	0	—	0	0	0	0	0.1
● **MIKE HEDLUND** Hedlund, Michael David "Red" b: 8/11/46, Dallas, Tex. BR/TR, 6'1", 190 lbs. Deb: 5/8/65																									
1965 Cle-A	0	0	—	6	0	0	0	0	5^1	6	0	5	4	18.6	5.06	69	.286	.423	0	.000	-0	-1	-1	-0	0.0
1968 Cle-A	0	0	—	3	0	0	0	0	1^2	6	0	2	0	48.6	10.80	27	.545	.643	0	—	0	-1	-1	0	0.0
1969 KC-A	3	6	.333	34	16	1	0	2	125	123	8	40	74	11.8	3.24	114	.259	.318	5	.152	-1	5	6	1	0.6
1970 KC-A	2	3	.400	9	0	0	0	0	15	18	6	7	5	15.0	7.20	52	.300	.373	0	.000	-0	-6	-6	-0	-1.7
1971 KC-A	15	8	.652	32	30	7	1	0	205^2	168	15	72	76	10.5	2.71	126	.227	.296	6	.088	-4	17	16	3	1.8
1972 KC-A	5	7	.417	29	16	1	0	0	113	119	10	41	52	13.1	4.78	63	.275	.343	6	.188	-0	-22	-22	1	-2.2
Total 6	25	24	.510	113	62	9	1	2	465^2	440	39	167	211	11.9	3.56	96	.253	.321	17	.123	-5	-7	-8	5	-1.5
● **DANNY HEEP** Heep, Daniel William b: 7/3/57, San Antonio, Tex. BL/TL, 5'11", 185 lbs. Deb: 8/31/79 ♦																									
1988 *LA-N	0	0	—	1	0	0	0	0	2	2	1	0	0	9.0	9.00	37	.222	.222	36	.242	0	-1	-1	-0	0.0
1990 *Bos-A	0	0	—	1	0	0	0	0	1	4	0	0	0	36.0	9.00	45	.667	.667	12	.174	0	-1	-1	0	0.0
Total 2	0	0	—	2	0	0	0	0	3	6	1	0	0	18.0	9.00	40	.400	.400	503	.257	0	-2	-2	-0	0.0
● **BOB HEFFNER** Heffner, Robert Frederic b: 9/13/38, Allentown, Pa. BR/TR, 6'4", 205 lbs. Deb: 6/19/63																									
1963 Bos-A	4	9	.308	20	19	3	1	0	124^2	131	15	36	77	12.2	4.26	89	.267	.319	5	.116	-1	-9	-7	-0	-0.8
1964 Bos-A	7	9	.438	55	10	1	1	6	158^2	152	20	44	112	11.3	4.08	94	.251	.305	7	.159	0	-8	-4	-1	-0.5
1965 Bos-A	0	2	.000	27	1	0	0	0	49	59	9	18	42	14.3	7.16	52	.304	.366	0	.000	-1	-20	-19	-1	-0.9
1966 Cle-A	0	1	.000	5	1	0	0	0	13	12	1	3	7	10.4	3.46	99	.240	.283	0	.000	0	-0	-0	-1	0.0
1968 Cal-A	0	0	—	7	0	0	0	0	8	6	0	6	3	13.5	2.25	129	.240	.387	0	—	0	1	1	-0	0.0
Total 5	11	21	.344	114	31	4	2	6	353^1	360	45	107	241	12.0	4.51	84	.264	.320	12	.128	-1	-36	-29	-2	-2.2
● **BRONSON HEFLIN** Heflin, Bronson Wayne b: 8/29/71, Clarksville, Tenn. BR/TR, 6'3", 195 lbs. Deb: 8/1/96																									
1996 Phi-N	0	0	—	3	0	0	0	0	6^2	11	1	3	4	18.9	6.75	64	.367	.424	0	—	0	-2	-2	-0	0.0
● **RANDY HEFLIN** Heflin, Randolph Rutherford b: 9/11/18, Fredericksburg, Va. BL/TR, 6', 185 lbs. Deb: 6/9/45																									
1945 Bos-A	4	10	.286	20	14	6	2	0	102	102	3	61	39	14.7	4.06	84	.272	.380	3	.086	-3	-8	-7	1	-1.1
1946 Bos-A	0	1	.000	5	1	0	0	0	14^2	16	0	12	6	17.8	2.45	149	.296	.433	2	.667	1	2	2	1	0.3
Total 2	4	11	.267	25	15	6	2	0	116^2	118	3	73	45	15.1	3.86	89	.275	.387	5	.132	-2	-6	-5	2	-0.8
● **JAKE HEHL** Hehl, Herman Jacob b: 12/8/1899, Brooklyn, N.Y. d: 7/4/61, Brooklyn, N.Y. BR/TR, 5'11", 180 lbs. Deb: 6/20/18																									
1918 Bro-N	0	0	—	1	0	0	0	0	1	0	0	0	0	9.0	0.00	—	.000	.250	0	—	0	0	0	0	0.0
● **EMMET HEIDRICK** Heidrick, R. Emmet "Snags" b: 7/9/1876, Queenstown, Pa. d: 1/20/16, Clarion, Pa. BL/TR, 6', 185 lbs. Deb: 9/14/1898 ♦																									
1902 StL-A	0	0	—	1	0	0	0	0	1	0	0	0	0	0.0	0.00	—	.000	.000	129	.289	0	0	0	-0	0.0
● **FRANK HEIFER** Heifer, Franklin "Heck" b: 1/18/1854, Reading, Pa. d: 8/29/1893, Reading, Pa. 5'10.5", 175 lbs. Deb: 6/4/1875 ♦																									
1875 Bos-n	0	0	—	2	0	0	0	1	2^1	6	0	0	0	23.1	15.43	14	.462	.462	14	.280	1	-3	-3		-0.3
● **FRED HEIMACH** Heimach, Frederick Amos "Lefty" b: 1/27/01, Camden, N.J. d: 6/1/73, Ft.Myers, Fla. BL/TL, 6', 175 lbs. Deb: 10/1/20																									
1920 Phi-A	0	1	.000	1	1	0	0	0	5	13	0	1	0	25.2	14.40	28	.542	.560	0	.000	-0	-6	-6	1	-0.7
1921 Phi-A	1	0	1.000	1	1	1	1	0	9	7	0	1	1	8.0	0.00	—	.226	.250	1	.250	-0	4	4	1	0.6
1922 Phi-A	7	11	.389	37	19	7	0	1	171^2	220	18	63	47	15.0	5.03	85	.316	.375	15	.250	2	-19	-15	1	-1.0
1923 Phi-A	6	12	.333	40	19	10	0	0	208^1	238	14	69	63	13.5	4.32	95	.292	.352	30	.254	2	-8	-5	0	-0.1
1924 Phi-A	14	12	.538	40	26	10	0	0	198	243	2	60	60	14.0	4.73	91	.306	.357	29	.322	6	-11	-10	2	-0.3
1925 Phi-A	0	1	.000	10	0	0	0	0	20^1	24	2	9	6	15.0	3.98	117	.312	.391	1	.167	-0	1	2	0	0.1
1926 Phi-A	1	0	1.000	13	1	0	0	0	31^2	28	1	5	8	9.4	2.84	147	.239	.270	1	.100	-1	4	5	2	0.2
Bos-A	2	9	.182	20	13	6	0	0	102	119	5	42	17	14.2	5.65	72	.303	.370	13	.295	2	-18	-18	3	-1.1
Yr	3	9	.250	33	14	6	0	0	133^2	147	6	47	25	13.1	4.98	82	.288	.348	14	.259	2	-14	-13	5	-0.9
1928 NY-A	2	3	.400	13	9	5	0	0	68	66	3	16	25	11.0	3.31	114	.250	.295	5	.167	-1	6	3	0	0.1
1929 NY-A	11	6	.647	35	10	3	3	4	134^2	141	4	29	26	11.6	4.01	96	.272	.314	9	.184	1	4	-2	2	-0.1
1930 Bro-N	0	2	.000	9	0	0	0	1	7^1	14	0	3	1	20.9	4.91	100	.424	.472	1	.250	-0	0	0	0	0.0
1931 Bro-N	9	7	.563	31	10	7	1	1	135^1	145	6	23	43	11.2	3.46	110	.274	.306	12	.197	1	6	5	4	1.0
1932 Bro-N	9	4	.692	36	15	7	0	0	167^2	203	7	28	30	12.7	3.97	96	.299	.333	9	.164	1	-2	-3	1	0.0
1933 Bro-N	0	1	.000	10	3	0	0	0	29^2	49	2	11	7	18.8	10.01	32	.374	.431	2	.200	-0	-22	-22	-0	-0.7
Total 13	62	69	.473	296	127	56	5	7	1288^2	1510	64	360	334	13.2	4.46	90	.296	.346	128	.236	12	-61	-61	16	-2.0
● **GORMAN HEIMUELLER** Heimueller, Gorman John b: 9/24/55, Los Angeles, Cal. BL/TL, 6'4", 195 lbs. Deb: 7/12/83																									
1983 Oak-A	3	5	.375	16	14	2	1	0	83^2	93	8	29	31	13.2	4.41	87	.286	.346	0	—	0	-3	-5	2	0.0
1984 Oak-A	0	1	.000	6	0	0	0	0	14^2	21	2	7	3	17.2	6.14	61	.344	.412	0	—	0	-3	-4	0	0.2
Total 2	3	6	.333	22	14	2	1	0	98^1	114	10	36	34	13.8	4.67	82	.295	.357	0	—	0	-7	-9	3	0.2
● **DON HEINKEL** Heinkel, Donald Elliott b: 10/20/59, Racine, Wis. BL/TR, 6', 185 lbs. Deb: 4/7/88																									
1988 Det-A	0	0	—	21	0	0	0	1	36^1	30	4	12	30	10.7	3.96	96	.219	.287	0	—	0	0	-1	-0	0.1
1989 StL-N	1	1	.500	7	5	0	0	0	26^1	40	2	7	16	16.1	5.81	62	.348	.385	0	.000	-0	-7	-6	0	-0.4
Total 2	1	1	.500	28	5	0	0	1	62^2	70	6	19	46	12.9	4.74	79	.278	.331	0	.000	-0	-7	-7	0	-0.3
● **KEN HEINTZELMAN** Heintzelman, Kenneth Alphonse b: 10/14/15, Peruque, Mo. BR/TL, 5'11.5", 185 lbs. Deb: 10/3/37 F																									
1937 Pit-N	1	0	1.000	1	1	1	0	0	9	6	0	3	4	10.0	2.00	193	.207	.303	0	.000	-1	2	2	-1	0.1
1938 Pit-N	0	0	—	1	0	0	0	0	2	1	0	3	1	18.0	9.00	42	.167	.444	0	—	0	-1	-1	0	0.0
1939 Pit-N	1	1	.500	17	2	1	1	0	35^2	35	2	18	18	13.4	5.05	76	.250	.335	2	.222	0	-4	-5	-0	-0.2
1940 Pit-N	8	8	.500	39	16	5	2	3	165	193	7	56	71	14.3	4.47	85	.292	.359	9	.167	-1	-11	-12	3	-1.0
1941 Pit-N	11	11	.500	35	24	13	2	0	196	206	8	83	81	13.3	3.44	105	.272	.345	8	.127	-2	4	4	1	0.3
1942 Pit-N	8	11	.421	27	18	5	3	0	130	143	9	63	39	14.3	4.57	74	.281	.361	3	.086	-2	-18	-17	-2	-2.6

YEAR	TM/L	W	L	PCT	G	GS	CG	SH	SV	IP	H	HR	BB	SO	RAT	ERA	ERA+	OAV	OOB	BH	AVG	PB	PR	/A	PD	TPI
1946	Pit-N	8	12	.400	32	24	6	2	1	157^2	165	7	86	57	14.3	3.77	94	.271	.362	6	.136	-1	-6	-4	2	-0.4
1947	Pit-N	0	0	—	2	1	0	0	0	4	9	2	6	2	33.8	20.25	21	.409	.536	0	—	0	-7	-7	-0	0.0
	Phi-N	7	10	.412	24	19	8	0	1	136	144	12	46	55	12.7	4.04	99	.277	.338	5	.116	-2	0	-0	-3	-0.5
	Yr	7	10	.412	26	20	8	0	1	140	153	14	52	57	13.3	4.50	89	.282	.347	5	.116	-2	-7	-8	-3	-0.5
1948	Phi-N	6	11	.353	27	16	5	2	2	130	117	10	45	57	11.3	4.29	92	.241	.307	5	.135	-1	-5	-5	-1	-0.8
1949	Phi-N	17	10	.630	33	32	15	**5**	0	250	239	19	93	65	12.0	3.02	130	.255	.323	13	.157	-1	28	26	-3	2.2
1950	*Phi-N	3	9	.250	23	17	4	1	0	125^1	122	10	54	39	12.6	4.09	99	.250	.325	2	.053	-3	1	-1	-2	-0.6
1951	Phi-N	6	12	.333	35	12	3	0	2	118^1	119	13	53	55	13.4	4.18	92	.267	.350	3	.107	-1	-3	-4	-1	-0.8
1952	Phi-N	1	3	.250	23	1	0	0	1	42^2	41	1	12	20	11.2	3.16	115	.266	.319	0	.000	-0	3	2	-1	0.1
Total	13	77	98	.440	319	183	66	18	10	1501^2	1540	100	630	564	13.1	3.93	96	.267	.341	56	.127	-16	-18	-23	-7	-4.2

● **CLARENCE HEISE** Heise, Clarence Edward "Lefty" b: 8/7/07, Topeka, Kan. BL/TL, 5'10", 172 lbs. Deb: 4/22/34

YEAR	TM/L	W	L	PCT	G	GS	CG	SH	SV	IP	H	HR	BB	SO	RAT	ERA	ERA+	OAV	OOB	BH	AVG	PB	PR	/A	PD	TPI
1934	StL-N	0	0	—	1	0	0	0	0	2	3	1	0	1	13.5	4.50	94	.300	.300	0	—	0	-0	-0	-0	0.0

● **JIM HEISE** Heise, James Edward b: 10/2/32, Scottdale, Pa. BR/TR, 6'1", 185 lbs. Deb: 6/29/57

YEAR	TM/L	W	L	PCT	G	GS	CG	SH	SV	IP	H	HR	BB	SO	RAT	ERA	ERA+	OAV	OOB	BH	AVG	PB	PR	/A	PD	TPI
1957	Was-A	0	3	.000	8	2	0	0	0	19	25	2	16	8	19.4	8.05	48	.329	.446	0	.000	-0	-9	-9	-0	-1.2

● **ROY HEISER** Heiser, Le Roy Barton b: 6/22/42, Baltimore, Md. BR/TR, 6'4", 190 lbs. Deb: 9/2/61

YEAR	TM/L	W	L	PCT	G	GS	CG	SH	SV	IP	H	HR	BB	SO	RAT	ERA	ERA+	OAV	OOB	BH	AVG	PB	PR	/A	PD	TPI
1961	Was-A	0	0	—	3	0	0	0	0	5^2	6	1	9	1	25.4	6.35	63	.261	.485	0	.000	-0	-1	-1	-0	-0.1

● **CRESE HEISMANN** Heismann, Christian Ernest b: 4/16/1880, Cincinnati, Ohio d: 11/19/51, Cincinnati, Ohio BL/TL, 6', 150 lbs. Deb: 9/25/01

YEAR	TM/L	W	L	PCT	G	GS	CG	SH	SV	IP	H	HR	BB	SO	RAT	ERA	ERA+	OAV	OOB	BH	AVG	PB	PR	/A	PD	TPI
1901	Cin-N	0	1	.000	3	2	1	0	0	13^2	18	1	6	6	17.8	5.93	54	.316	.409	2	.400	1	-4	-4	-1	-0.2
1902	Cin-N	2	1	.667	5	3	2	0	0	33	33	1	10	15	13.1	2.45	122	.260	.338	3	.214	0	1	2	0	0.2
	Bal-A	0	3	.000	3	3	2	0	0	16	20	1	12	2	19.1	8.44	45	.308	.430	1	.143	-1	-9	-8	-0	-1.2
Total	2	2	5	.286	11	8	5	0	0	62^2	71	3	28	23	15.7	4.74	69	.285	.380	6	.231	1	-11	-10	-1	-1.2

● **HARRY HEITMANN** Heitmann, Henry Anton b: 10/6/1896, Albany, N.Y. d: 12/15/58, Brooklyn, N.Y. BR/TR, 6', 175 lbs. Deb: 7/27/18

YEAR	TM/L	W	L	PCT	G	GS	CG	SH	SV	IP	H	HR	BB	SO	RAT	ERA	ERA+	OAV	OOB	BH	AVG	PB	PR	/A	PD	TPI
1918	Bro-N	0	1	.000	1	1	0	0	0	0^1	4	0	0	0	108.0	108.00	3	1.000	1.000	0	—	0	-4	-4	0	-3.0

● **MEL HELD** Held, Melvin Nicholas "Country" b: 4/12/29, Edon, Ohio BR/TR, 6'1", 178 lbs. Deb: 4/27/56

YEAR	TM/L	W	L	PCT	G	GS	CG	SH	SV	IP	H	HR	BB	SO	RAT	ERA	ERA+	OAV	OOB	BH	AVG	PB	PR	/A	PD	TPI
1956	Bal-A	0	0	—	4	0	0	0	0	7	7	1	3	4	12.9	5.14	76	.318	.400	0	—	0	-1	-1	0	0.0

● **RICK HELLING** Helling, Ricky Allen b: 12/15/70, Devils Lake, N.D. BR/TR, 6'3", 215 lbs. Deb: 4/10/94

YEAR	TM/L	W	L	PCT	G	GS	CG	SH	SV	IP	H	HR	BB	SO	RAT	ERA	ERA+	OAV	OOB	BH	AVG	PB	PR	/A	PD	TPI
1994	Tex-A	3	2	.600	9	9	1	1	0	52	62	14	18	25	13.8	5.88	82	.295	.351	0	—	0	-6	-6	-1	-0.6
1995	Tex-A	0	2	.000	3	3	0	0	0	12^1	17	2	8	5	19.7	6.57	73	.340	.450	0	—	0	-3	-2	-0	-0.4
1996	Tex-A	1	2	.333	6	2	0	0	0	20^1	23	7	9	16	14.2	7.52	70	.280	.352	0	—	0	-6	-5	-0	-0.7
	Fla-N	2	1	.667	5	4	0	0	0	27^2	14	2	7	26	6.8	1.95	208	.143	.200	1	.111	-0	7	7	-1	0.6
1997	Fla-N	2	6	.250	31	8	0	0	0	76	61	12	48	53	13.4	4.38	92	.232	.359	1	.091	-1	-2	-3	-1	-0.4
	Tex-A	3	3	.500	10	8	0	0	0	55	47	5	21	46	11.5	4.58	104	.235	.314	0	.000	-0	-0	1	-1	0.0
1998	*Tex-A	**20**	7	.741	33	33	4	2	0	216^1	209	27	78	164	12.0	4.41	110	.253	.318	1	.200	0	6	10	-4	0.7
Total	5	31	23	.574	97	67	5	3	0	459^2	433	69	189	335	12.4	4.64	100	.250	.327	3	.107	-1	-4	1	-8	-0.8

● **HORACE HELMBOLD** Helmbold, Horace b: Philadelphia, Pa. Deb: 10/11/1890

YEAR	TM/L	W	L	PCT	G	GS	CG	SH	SV	IP	H	HR	BB	SO	RAT	ERA	ERA+	OAV	OOB	BH	AVG	PB	PR	/A	PD	TPI
1890	Phi-a	0	1	.000	1	1	1	0	0	7	17	0	6	3	29.6	14.14	27	.447	.523	0	.000	-1	-8	-8	0	-0.7

● **RUSS HEMAN** Heman, Russell Fredrick b: 2/10/33, Olive, Cal. BR/TR, 6'4", 200 lbs. Deb: 4/20/61

YEAR	TM/L	W	L	PCT	G	GS	CG	SH	SV	IP	H	HR	BB	SO	RAT	ERA	ERA+	OAV	OOB	BH	AVG	PB	PR	/A	PD	TPI
1961	Cle-A	0	0	—	6	0	0	0	1	10	8	0	8	4	15.3	3.60	109	.216	.370	0	.000	-0	0	0	0	0.0
	LA-A	0	0	—	6	0	0	0	0	10	4	1	2	2	6.3	1.80	251	.125	.200	0	.000	-0	2	3	0	0.0
	Yr	0	0	—	12	0	0	0	1	20	12	1	10	6	10.3	2.70	156	.171	.284	0	.000	-0	3	3	0	0.0

● **GEORGE HEMMING** Hemming, George Earl "Old Wax Figger"
b: 12/15/1868, Carrollton, Ohio d: 6/3/30, Springfield, Mass. BR/TR, 5'11", 170 lbs. Deb: 4/21/1890

YEAR	TM/L	W	L	PCT	G	GS	CG	SH	SV	IP	H	HR	BB	SO	RAT	ERA	ERA+	OAV	OOB	BH	AVG	PB	PR	/A	PD	TPI
1890	Cle-P	0	1	.000	3	1	1	0	0	21	25	1	19	3	19.7	6.86	58	.284	.422	2	.182	-1	-6	-7	1	-0.2
	Bro-P	8	4	.667	19	11	11	0	3	123	117	3	59	32	13.1	3.80	117	.240	.325	9	.158	-4	6	9	0	0.3
	Yr	8	5	.615	22	12	12	0	**3**	144	142	4	78	35	13.9	4.25	103	.246	.338	11	.162	-5	-0	2	1	0.1
1891	Bro-N	8	15	.348	27	22	19	1	1	199^2	231	11	84	83	14.7	4.96	67	.279	.353	13	.159	-1	-36	-37	1	-3.3
1892	Cin-N	0	1	.000	1	0	0	0	0	6	10	1	2	0	18.0	7.50	44	.357	.400	1	.333	0	-3	-3	0	-0.3
	Lou-N	2	2	.500	4	4	4	0	0	35	36	1	17	12	13.6	4.63	66	.255	.335	1	.077	-1	-5	-6	0	-0.6
	Yr	2	3	.400	5	4	4	0	0	41	46	2	19	12	14.3	5.05	61	.272	.346	2	.125	-1	-8	-9	0	-0.9
1893	Lou-N	18	17	.514	41	32	32	1	1	332	369	7	176	79	15.2	5.10	86	.273	.363	32	.203	-2	-16	-26	2	-2.0
1894	Lou-N	13	19	.406	35	32	32	1	1	294^1	358	7	133	66	15.3	4.37	117	.297	.371	33	.252	2	31	24	-1	1.9
	*Bal-N	4	0	1.000	6	6	4	0	0	45^1	48	0	26	4	15.1	3.57	153	.268	.367	6	.286	1	9	9	-0	0.7
	Yr	17	19	.472	41	38	36	1	1	339^2	406	7	159	70	15.0	4.27	121	.291	.365	39	.257	3	40	33	1	2.6
1895	Bal-N	20	13	.606	34	31	26	1	0	262^1	288	10	96	43	13.4	4.05	118	.275	.339	33	.282	3	21	21	-3	1.9
1896	Bal-N	15	6	.714	25	21	20	3	0	202	233	9	54	33	12.9	4.19	102	.287	.333	25	.258	4	4	2	-3	0.2
1897	Lou-N	3	4	.429	9	8	7	0	0	67	80	5	25	7	14.2	5.10	83	.294	.356	5	.179	-1	-6	-6	1	-0.5
Total	8	91	82	.526	204	168	156	7	6	1587^2	1795	55	691	362	14.4	4.53	98	.279	.353	160	.223	-0	-1	-19	-2	-1.9

● **BERNIE HENDERSON** Henderson, Bernard "Barnyard" b: 4/12/1899, Douglassville, Tex d: 6/6/66, Linden, Tex. BR/TR, 5'9", 175 lbs. Deb: 9/5/21

YEAR	TM/L	W	L	PCT	G	GS	CG	SH	SV	IP	H	HR	BB	SO	RAT	ERA	ERA+	OAV	OOB	BH	AVG	PB	PR	/A	PD	TPI
1921	Cle-A	0	1	.000	2	1	0	0	0	3	5	0	0	1	15.0	9.00	47	.333	.333	0	.000	0	-2	-2	-0	-0.4

● **ED HENDERSON** Henderson, Edward J. (b: Eugene J. Ball) b: 12/25/1884, Newark, N.J. d: 1/15/64, New York, N.Y. BL/TL, 5'9", 168 lbs. Deb: 5/15/14

YEAR	TM/L	W	L	PCT	G	GS	CG	SH	SV	IP	H	HR	BB	SO	RAT	ERA	ERA+	OAV	OOB	BH	AVG	PB	PR	/A	PD	TPI
1914	Pit-F	0	1	.000	6	1	1	0	0	16	14	2	8	4	12.4	3.94	73	.241	.333	0	.000	-0	-2	-2	-1	-0.2
	Ind-F	1	0	1.000	2	1	1	0	0	10	8	0	4	1	13.5	4.50	69	.229	.357	0	.000	-1	-2	-2	-0	-0.2
	Yr	1	1	.500	8	2	2	0	0	26	22	2	12	5	12.8	4.15	71	.237	.343	0	.000	-1	-4	-3	-1	-0.4

● **HARDIE HENDERSON** Henderson, James Harding b: 10/31/1862, Philadelphia, Pa. d: 2/6/03, Philadelphia, Pa. BR/TR, Deb: 5/2/1883 U

YEAR	TM/L	W	L	PCT	G	GS	CG	SH	SV	IP	H	HR	BB	SO	RAT	ERA	ERA+	OAV	OOB	BH	AVG	PB	PR	/A	PD	TPI
1883	Phi-N	0	1	.000	1	1	1	0	0	9	26	0	2	2	28.0	19.00	16	.481	.500	2	.250	0	-16	-16	-0	-0.9
	Bal-a	10	32	.238	45	42	38	0	0	358^1	383	4	87	145	11.8	4.02	87	.256	.297	31	.162	-6	-28	-21	-2	-2.6
1884	Bal-a	27	23	.540	52	52	50	4	0	439^1	382	9	116	346	10.5	2.62	132	.216	.271	46	.227	2	31	41	1	4.4
1885	Bal-a	25	35	.417	61	61	59	0	0	539^1	539	7	117	263	11.3	3.19	102	.253	.298	51	.223	3	4	4	-0	0.7
1886	Bal-a	3	15	.167	19	19	19	0	0	171^1	188	0	66	88	13.8	4.62	74	.252	.320	16	.235	2	-22	-23	2	-1.4
	Bro-a	10	4	.714	14	14	14	0	0	124	112	2	51	49	11.8	2.90	120	.232	.306	9	.180	-1	8	8	0	0.6
	Yr	13	19	.406	33	33	33	0	0	295^1	300	2	117	137	12.7	3.90	88	.242	.308	25	.212	1	-15	-15	2	-0.8
1887	Bro-a	5	8	.385	13	12	12	0	0	111^2	127	3	63	28	15.7	3.95	109	.281	.375	5	.122	-3	4	4	1	0.2
1888	Pit-N	1	3	.250	5	5	4	0	0	35^1	43	0	20	9	16.6	5.35	50	.289	.380	5	.278	1	-10	-11	0	-0.9
Total	6	81	121	.401	210	206	197	4	0	1788^1	1800	25	522	930	11.9	3.50	98	.247	.302	165	.204	-2	-30	-13	2	0.1

● **JOE HENDERSON** Henderson, Joseph Lee b: 7/4/46, Lake Cormorant, Miss. BL/TR, 6'2", 195 lbs. Deb: 6/7/74

YEAR	TM/L	W	L	PCT	G	GS	CG	SH	SV	IP	H	HR	BB	SO	RAT	ERA	ERA+	OAV	OOB	BH	AVG	PB	PR	/A	PD	TPI
1974	Chi-A	1	0	1.000	5	3	0	0	0	15	21	2	11	12	19.2	8.40	44	.328	.427	0	.000	-0	-8	-8	0	-0.5
1976	Cin-N	2	0	1.000	4	0	0	0	0	11	9	0	8	7	13.9	0.00	—	.225	.354	0	—	0	4	4	0	0.9
1977	Cin-N	0	2	.000	7	0	0	0	0	9	17	2	6	8	23.0	12.00	33	.386	.460	0	.000	-0	-8	-8	-0	-1.5
Total	3	3	2	.600	16	3	0	0	0	35	47	4	25	27	18.5	6.69	55	.318	.416	0	.000	-0	-12	-12	-0	-1.1

● **ROD HENDERSON** Henderson, Rodney Wood b: 3/11/71, Greensburg, Ky. BR/TR, 6'4", 195 lbs. Deb: 4/19/94

YEAR	TM/L	W	L	PCT	G	GS	CG	SH	SV	IP	H	HR	BB	SO	RAT	ERA	ERA+	OAV	OOB	BH	AVG	PB	PR	/A	PD	TPI
1994	Mon-N	0	1	.000	3	2	0	0	0	6^2	9	1	7	3	21.6	9.45	45	.333	.471	0	.000	-0	-4	-4	0	-0.5
1998	Mil-N	0	0	—	2	0	0	0	0	3^2	5	2	0	1	14.7	9.82	44	.313	.353	0	—	0	-2	-2	-0	0.0
Total	2	0	1	.000	5	2	0	0	0	10^1	14	3	7	4	19.2	9.58	44	.326	.431	0	.000	-0	-6	-6	0	-0.5

● **BILL HENDERSON** Henderson, William Maxwell b: 11/4/01, Pensacola, Fla. d: 10/6/66, Pensacola, Fla. BR/TR, 6', 190 lbs. Deb: 6/20/30

YEAR	TM/L	W	L	PCT	G	GS	CG	SH	SV	IP	H	HR	BB	SO	RAT	ERA	ERA+	OAV	OOB	BH	AVG	PB	PR	/A	PD	TPI
1930	NY-A	0	0	—	3	0	0	0	0	8	7	1	4	2	12.4	4.50	96	.250	.344	1	.500	0	0	-0	0	0.0

● BOB HENDLEY
Hendley, Charles Robert b: 4/30/39, Macon, Ga. BR/TL, 6'2", 190 lbs. Deb: 6/23/61

YEAR	TM/L	W	L	PCT	G	GS	CG	SH	SV	IP	H	HR	BB	SO	RAT	ERA	ERA+	OAV	OOB	BH	AVG	PB	PR	/A	PD	TPI
1961	Mil-N	5	7	.417	19	13	3	0	0	97	96	8	39	44	12.5	3.90	96	.262	.333	1	.032	-3	1	-2	1	-0.4
1962	Mil-N	11	13	.458	35	29	7	2	1	200	188	17	59	112	11.1	3.60	105	.247	.301	7	.119	1	8	4	1	0.6
1963	Mil-N	9	9	.500	41	24	7	3	3	169^1	153	16	64	105	11.6	3.93	82	.244	.315	5	.106	-1	-12	-13	1	-1.4
1964	SF-N	10	11	.476	30	29	4	1	0	163^1	161	18	59	104	12.2	3.64	98	.258	.325	5	.106	-1	-2	-1	-2	-0.5
1965	SF-N	0	0	—	8	2	0	0	0	15	27	6	13	8	24.6	12.60	29	.397	.500	0	.000	-0	-15	-15	0	0.0
	Chi-N	4	4	.500	18	10	2	0	0	62	59	9	25	38	12.3	4.35	85	.244	.317	0	.000	-1	-6	-5	1	-0.7
	Yr	4	4	.500	26	12	2	0	0	77	86	15	38	46	14.6	5.96	62	.277	.357	0	.000	-2	-21	-20	1	-0.7
1966	Chi-N	4	5	.444	43	6	0	0	7	89^2	98	10	39	65	13.8	3.91	94	.285	.358	3	.167	1	-3	-2	1	-0.1
1967	Chi-N	2	0	1.000	7	0	0	0	1	12^1	17	4	3	10	14.6	6.57	54	.315	.351	0	.000	-1	-4	-4	-0	-0.8
	NY-N	3	3	.500	15	13	2	0	0	70^2	65	11	28	36	12.0	3.44	99	.241	.314	2	.111	-0	-1	-0	-2	-0.2
	Yr	5	3	.625	22	13	2	0	1	83	82	15	31	46	12.4	3.90	87	.253	.320	2	.083	-1	-5	-5	-2	-1.0
Total	7	48	52	.480	216	126	25	6	12	879^1	864	99	329	522	12.3	3.97	90	.257	.325	23	.095	-6	-34	-38	0	-3.5

● ED HENDRICKS
Hendricks, Edward "Big Ed" b: 6/20/1885, Zeeland, Mich. d: 11/28/30, Jackson, Mich. BL/TL, 6'3", 200 lbs. Deb: 9/15/10

YEAR	TM/L	W	L	PCT	G	GS	CG	SH	SV	IP	H	HR	BB	SO	RAT	ERA	ERA+	OAV	OOB	BH	AVG	PB	PR	/A	PD	TPI
1910	NY-N	0	1	.000	4	1	1	0	1	12	12	0	4	2	12.0	3.75	79	.261	.320	0	.000	-1	-1	-1	-1	-0.2

● ELLIE HENDRICKS
Hendricks, Elrod Jerome b: 12/22/40, Charlotte Amalie, V.I. BL/TR, 6'1", 175 lbs. Deb: 4/13/68 C♦

YEAR	TM/L	W	L	PCT	G	GS	CG	SH	SV	IP	H	HR	BB	SO	RAT	ERA	ERA+	OAV	OOB	BH	AVG	PB	PR	/A	PD	TPI
1978	Bal-A	0	0	—	1	0	0	0	0	2^1	1	0	1	0	7.7	0.00	—	.125	.222	6	.333	0	1	1	-0	0.0

● DON HENDRICKSON
Hendrickson, Donald William b: 7/14/13, Kewanna, Ind. d: 1/19/77, Norfolk, Va. BR/TR, 6'2", 204 lbs. Deb: 7/4/45

YEAR	TM/L	W	L	PCT	G	GS	CG	SH	SV	IP	H	HR	BB	SO	RAT	ERA	ERA+	OAV	OOB	BH	AVG	PB	PR	/A	PD	TPI
1945	Bos-N	4	8	.333	37	2	1	0	5	73^1	74	8	39	14	14.0	4.91	78	.261	.353	3	.167	-0	-9	-9	-1	-1.5
1946	Bos-N	0	1	.000	2	0	0	0	0	2	4	0	2	2	27.0	4.50	76	.364	.462	0	.000	-0	-0	-0	-0	-0.1
Total	2	4	9	.308	39	2	1	0	5	75^1	78	8	41	16	14.3	4.90	78	.265	.357	3	.158	-0	-9	-9	-1	-1.6

● CLAUDE HENDRIX
Hendrix, Claude Raymond b: 4/13/1889, Olathe, Kan. d: 3/22/44, Allentown, Pa. BR/TR, 6', 195 lbs. Deb: 6/7/11

YEAR	TM/L	W	L	PCT	G	GS	CG	SH	SV	IP	H	HR	BB	SO	RAT	ERA	ERA+	OAV	OOB	BH	AVG	PB	PR	/A	PD	TPI
1911	Pit-N	4	6	.400	22	12	6	1	1	118^2	85	1	53	57	10.5	2.73	126	.204	.295	4	.098	-1	9	9	4	1.0
1912	Pit-N	24	9	**.727**	39	32	25	4	1	288^2	256	6	105	176	11.5	2.59	126	.246	.320	39	.322	16	26	22	5	4.3
1913	Pit-N	14	15	.483	42	25	17	2	3	241	216	3	89	138	11.6	2.84	106	.248	.321	27	.273	10	10	5	2	1.7
1914	Chi-F	**29**	10	.744	**49**	37	**34**	6	5	362	262	6	77	189	**8.6**	1.69	157	**.203**	**.251**	30	.231	4	**48**	**39**	6	**5.4**
1915	Chi-F	16	15	.516	40	31	26	5	4	285	256	7	84	107	10.8	3.00	84	.241	.298	30	.265	11	-9	-15	-4	-1.0
1916	Chi-N	8	16	.333	36	24	15	3	2	218	193	4	67	117	11.0	2.68	108	.242	.306	16	.200	2	-2	5	2	1.1
1917	Chi-N	10	12	.455	40	21	13	1	1	215	202	3	72	81	11.6	2.60	112	.257	.322	22	.256	3	3	7	-2	1.0
1918	*Chi-N	20	7	**.741**	32	27	21	3	0	233	229	2	54	86	11.1	2.78	100	.259	.305	24	.264	8	-0	0	1	1.1
1919	Chi-N	10	14	.417	33	25	15	2	0	206^1	208	3	42	69	11.3	2.62	110	.266	.311	15	.192	-0	7	6	1	0.8
1920	Chi-N	9	12	.429	27	23	12	0	0	203^2	216	6	54	72	12.1	3.58	90	.273	.322	15	.181	-2	-10	-8	-1	-1.0
Total	10	144	116	.554	360	257	184	27	17	2371^1	2123	41	697	1092	10.9	2.65	110	.243	.303	222	.241	50	82	71	14	14.4

● LAFAYETTE HENION
Henion, Lafayette Marion b: 6/7/1899, Eureka, Cal. d: 7/22/55, San Luis Obispo, Cal. BR/TR, 5'11", 154 lbs. Deb: 9/10/19

YEAR	TM/L	W	L	PCT	G	GS	CG	SH	SV	IP	H	HR	BB	SO	RAT	ERA	ERA+	OAV	OOB	BH	AVG	PB	PR	/A	PD	TPI
1919	Bro-N	0	0	—	1	0	0	0	0	3	2	0	2	2	12.0	6.00	50	.200	.333	0	.000	-0	-1	-1	-0	0.0

● TOM HENKE
Henke, Thomas Anthony b: 12/21/57, Kansas City, Mo. BR/TR, 6'5", 215 lbs. Deb: 9/10/82

YEAR	TM/L	W	L	PCT	G	GS	CG	SH	SV	IP	H	HR	BB	SO	RAT	ERA	ERA+	OAV	OOB	BH	AVG	PB	PR	/A	PD	TPI
1982	Tex-A	1	0	1.000	8	0	0	0	0	15^2	14	0	8	9	13.2	1.15	337	.246	.348	0	—	0	5	5	0	0.7
1983	Tex-A	1	0	1.000	8	0	0	0	1	16	16	1	4	17	11.3	3.38	119	.262	.308	0	—	0	1	1	0	0.2
1984	Tex-A	1	1	.500	25	0	0	0	2	28^1	36	0	20	25	18.1	6.35	65	.313	.419	0	—	0	-7	-7	-0	-0.7
1985	*Tor-A	3	3	.500	28	0	0	0	13	40	29	4	8	42	8.3	2.02	208	.206	.248	0	—	0	9	10	-0	1.9
1986	Tor-A	9	5	.643	63	0	0	0	27	91^1	63	6	32	118	9.5	3.35	126	.191	.265	0	—	0	8	9	-2	1.5
1987	Tor-A★	0	6	.000	72	0	0	0	**34**	94	62	10	25	128	8.3	2.49	180	.188	.245	0	—	0	**21**	**21**	1	2.9
1988	Tor-A	4	4	.500	52	0	0	0	25	68	60	6	24	66	11.4	2.91	135	.237	.308	0	—	0	8	8	0	1.4
1989	*Tor-A	8	3	.727	64	0	0	0	20	89	66	5	25	116	9.4	1.92	196	.205	.266	0	—	0	19	18	0	2.9
1990	Tor-A	2	4	.333	61	0	0	0	32	74^2	58	8	19	75	9.4	2.17	182	.213	.267	0	—	0	14	15	-1	2.0
1991	*Tor-A	0	2	.000	49	0	0	0	32	50^1	33	4	11	53	7.9	2.32	181	.184	.232	0	—	0	10	11	-1	1.1
1992	*Tor-A	3	2	.600	57	0	0	0	34	55^2	40	5	22	46	10.0	2.26	180	.197	.276	0	—	0	10	11	-1	1.7
1993	Tex-A	5	5	.500	66	0	0	0	40	74^1	55	7	27	79	10.0	2.91	143	.205	.280	0	—	0	12	10	1	2.3
1994	Tex-A	3	6	.333	37	0	0	0	15	38	33	6	12	39	10.7	3.79	127	.232	.292	0	—	0	4	4	-0	1.2
1995	StL-N★	1	1	.500	52	0	0	0	36	54^1	42	2	18	48	9.9	1.82	230	.209	.274	0	.000	-0	14	14	-0	2.1
Total	14	41	42	.494	642	0	0	0	311	789^2	607	64	255	861	9.9	2.67	155	.211	.278	0	.000	-0	129	130	-3	21.2

● WELDON HENLEY
Henley, Weldon b: 10/25/1880, Jasper, Ga. d: 11/16/60, Palatka, Fla. BR/TR, 6', 175 lbs. Deb: 4/23/03

YEAR	TM/L	W	L	PCT	G	GS	CG	SH	SV	IP	H	HR	BB	SO	RAT	ERA	ERA+	OAV	OOB	BH	AVG	PB	PR	/A	PD	TPI
1903	Phi-A	12	10	.545	29	21	13	1	0	186^1	186	3	67	86	12.8	3.91	78	.259	.333	9	.132	-3	-20	-18	-1	-2.3
1904	Phi-A	15	17	.469	36	34	31	5	0	295^2	245	3	76	130	10.3	2.53	106	.226	.289	24	.222	2	2	5	4	1.2
1905	Phi-A	4	11	.267	25	19	13	1	0	183^2	155	4	67	82	11.3	2.60	102	.231	.309	11	.169	-1	1	1	4	0.4
1907	Bro-N	1	5	.167	7	7	5	0	0	56	54	2	21	11	12.2	3.05	77	.273	.345	4	.200	1	-4	-4	2	-0.2
Total	4	32	43	.427	97	81	62	7	0	721^2	640	12	231	309	11.4	2.94	93	.240	.310	48	.184	-2	-20	-16	9	-0.9

● MIKE HENNEMAN
Henneman, Michael Alan b: 12/11/61, St.Charles, Mo. BR/TR, 6'4", 195 lbs. Deb: 5/11/87

YEAR	TM/L	W	L	PCT	G	GS	CG	SH	SV	IP	H	HR	BB	SO	RAT	ERA	ERA+	OAV	OOB	BH	AVG	PB	PR	/A	PD	TPI
1987	*Det-A	11	3	.786	55	0	0	0	7	96^2	86	8	30	75	11.1	2.98	142	.238	.301	0	.000	-0	16	13	0	1.9
1988	Det-A	9	6	.600	65	0	0	0	22	91^1	72	7	24	58	9.7	1.87	204	.218	.275	0	—	0	**21**	**20**	-1	3.9
1989	Det-A☆	11	4	.733	60	0	0	0	8	90	84	4	51	69	14.0	3.70	103	.251	.358	0	—	0	2	1	0	0.2
1990	Det-A	8	6	.571	69	0	0	0	22	94^1	90	4	33	50	12.0	3.05	130	.253	.321	0	—	0	9	9	1	1.7
1991	Det-A	10	2	.833	60	0	0	0	21	84^1	81	2	34	61	12.3	2.88	144	.258	.330	0	—	0	11	12	-0	1.9
1992	Det-A	2	6	.250	60	0	0	0	24	77^1	75	6	20	58	11.1	3.96	100	.256	.304	0	—	0	-0	-0	1	0.0
1993	Det-A	5	3	.625	63	0	0	0	24	71^2	69	4	32	58	12.9	2.64	162	.251	.333	0	—	0	13	13	-1	2.0
1994	Det-A	1	3	.250	30	0	0	0	8	34^2	43	5	17	27	16.1	5.19	93	.297	.378	0	—	0	-2	-1	0	-0.2
1995	Det-A	0	1	.000	29	0	0	0	18	29^2	24	0	9	24	10.1	1.53	310	.222	.282	0	—	0	10	10	1	1.4
	Hou-N	0	1	.000	21	0	0	0	8	21	21	1	4	19	11.6	3.00	129	.266	.318	0	—	0	3	2	-0	0.2
1996	*Tex-A	0	7	.000	49	0	0	0	31	42	41	6	17	34	12.4	5.79	91	.258	.330	0	—	0	-4	-3	-0	-0.7
Total	10	57	42	.576	561	0	0	0	193	732^2	686	47	271	533	12.0	3.21	130	.249	.320	0	.000	-0	80	77	-1	12.3

● GEORGE HENNESSEY
Hennessey, George "Three Star" b: 10/28/07, Slatington, Pa. d: 1/15/88, Princeton, N.J. BR/TR, 5'10", 168 lbs. Deb: 9/2/37

YEAR	TM/L	W	L	PCT	G	GS	CG	SH	SV	IP	H	HR	BB	SO	RAT	ERA	ERA+	OAV	OOB	BH	AVG	PB	PR	/A	PD	TPI
1937	StL-A	0	1	.000	5	0	0	0	0	7	15	2	6	4	27.0	10.29	47	.500	.583	0	—	0	-4	-4	0	-0.5
1942	Phi-N	1	1	.500	5	1	0	0	0	17	11	1	10	2	11.1	2.65	125	.180	.296	0	.000	-1	1	1	-0	0.0
1945	Chi-N	0	0	—	2	0	0	0	0	3^2	7	0	1	2	19.6	7.36	50	.438	.471	0	—	0	-1	-2	0	0.0
Total	3	1	2	.333	12	1	0	0	0	27^2	33	3	17	8	16.3	5.20	72	.308	.403	0	.000	-1	-5	-5	-0	-0.5

● PHIL HENNIGAN
Hennigan, Phillip Winston b: 4/10/46, Jasper, Tex. BR/TR, 5'11.5", 185 lbs. Deb: 9/2/69

YEAR	TM/L	W	L	PCT	G	GS	CG	SH	SV	IP	H	HR	BB	SO	RAT	ERA	ERA+	OAV	OOB	BH	AVG	PB	PR	/A	PD	TPI
1969	Cle-A	2	1	.667	9	0	0	0	0	16^1	14	0	4	10	10.5	3.31	114	.241	.302	0	.000	-0	1	1	-1	0.1
1970	Cle-A	6	3	.667	42	1	0	0	3	71^2	69	7	44	43	14.7	4.02	99	.263	.377	1	.143	1	-2	-0	1	0.1
1971	Cle-A	4	3	.571	57	0	0	0	14	82	80	13	51	69	14.7	4.94	77	.261	.371	0	.000	-0	-13	-10	-1	-1.3
1972	Cle-A	5	3	.625	38	1	0	0	5	67^1	54	8	18	44	9.9	2.67	120	.226	.286	1	.083	-0	3	4	-1	0.4
1973	NY-N	0	4	.000	30	0	0	0	3	43^1	50	6	16	22	13.9	6.23	58	.289	.353	1	.333	0	-12	-13	-1	-1.3
Total	5	17	14	.548	176	2	0	0	25	280^2	267	34	133	188	13.2	4.26	86	.257	.347	3	.100	1	-25	-18	-2	-2.0

● PETE HENNING
Henning, Ernest Herman b: 12/28/1887, Crown Point, Ind. d: 11/4/39, Dyer, Ind. BR/TR, 5'11", 185 lbs. Deb: 4/17/14

YEAR	TM/L	W	L	PCT	G	GS	CG	SH	SV	IP	H	HR	BB	SO	RAT	ERA	ERA+	OAV	OOB	BH	AVG	PB	PR	/A	PD	TPI
1914	KC-F	5	10	.333	28	14	7	0	2	138	153	5	58	45	14.2	4.83	58	.291	.369	8	.182	0	-30	-31	0	-3.1
1915	KC-F	9	15	.375	40	20	15	1	2	207	181	5	76	73	11.3	3.17	83	.235	.307	14	.206	-1	-10	-13	4	-1.2
Total	2	14	25	.359	68	34	22	1	4	345	334	10	134	118	12.5	3.83	70	.258	.332	22	.196	-1	-40	-44	4	-4.3

● RICK HENNINGER
Henninger, Richard Lee b: 1/11/48, Hastings, Neb. BR/TR, 6'6", 225 lbs. Deb: 9/3/73

YEAR	TM/L	W	L	PCT	G	GS	CG	SH	SV	IP	H	HR	BB	SO	RAT	ERA	ERA+	OAV	OOB	BH	AVG	PB	PR	/A	PD	TPI
1973	Tex-A	1	0	1.000	6	2	0	0	0	23	23	1	11	6	13.3	2.74	136	.261	.343	0	—	0	3	3	-1	0.1

YEAR	TM/L	W	L	PCT	G	GS	CG	SH	SV	IP	H	HR	BB	SO	RAT	ERA	ERA+	OAV	OOB	BH	AVG	PB	PR	/A	PD	TPI
● **RANDY HENNIS** Hennis, Randall Philip b: 12/16/65, Clearlake, Cal. BR/TR, 6'6", 220 lbs. Deb: 9/17/90																										
1990	Hou-N	0	0	—	3	1	0	0	0	9^2	1	0	3	4	4.7	0.00	—	.033	.147	0	.000	-0	4	4	-0	0.0
● **OSCAR HENRIQUEZ** Henriquez, Oscar Eduardo b: 1/28/74, LaGuaira, Venez. BR/TR, 6'6", 220 lbs. Deb: 9/7/97																										
1997	Hou-N	0	1	.000	4	0	0	0	0	4	2	0	3	3	13.5	4.50	89	.167	.375	0	—	0	-0	-0	0	0.0
1998	Fla-N	0	0	—	15	0	0	0	0	20	26	4	12	19	17.5	8.55	48	.306	.398	0	.000	-0	-10	-10	-1	-0.1
Total	2	0	1	.000	19	0	0	0	0	24	28	4	15	22	16.9	7.88	52	.289	.395	0	.000	-0	-10	-10	-1	-0.1
● **DWAYNE HENRY** Henry, Dwayne Allen b: 2/16/62, Elkton, Md. BR/TR, 6'3", 205 lbs. Deb: 9/7/84																										
1984	Tex-A	0	1	.000	3	0	0	0	0	4^1	5	0	7	2	24.9	8.31	50	.294	.500	0	—	0	-2	-2	-0	-0.5
1985	Tex-A	2	2	.500	16	0	0	0	3	21	16	0	7	20	9.9	2.57	164	.211	.277	0	—	0	4	4	-0	0.8
1986	Tex-A	1	0	1.000	19	0	0	0	0	19^1	14	1	22	17	17.2	4.66	92	.209	.411	0	—	0	-1	-1	0	0.0
1987	Tex-A	0	0	—	5	0	0	0	0	10	12	2	9	7	18.9	9.00	50	.293	.420	0	—	0	-5	-5	0	0.0
1988	Tex-A	0	1	.000	11	0	0	0	1	10^1	15	1	9	10	23.5	8.71	47	.326	.466	0	—	0	-5	-5	-0	-0.6
1989	Atl-N	0	2	.000	12	0	0	0	1	12^2	12	2	5	16	12.1	4.26	86	.250	.321	0	—	0	-1	-1	-0	-0.2
1990	Atl-N	2	2	.500	34	0	0	0	0	38^1	41	3	25	34	15.5	5.63	72	.273	.377	0	—	0	-8	-7	-1	-0.7
1991	Hou-N	3	2	.600	52	0	0	0	2	67^2	51	7	39	51	12.2	3.19	110	.219	.336	0	.000	-0	4	2	-1	0.1
1992	Cin-N	3	3	.500	60	0	0	0	0	83^2	59	4	44	72	11.2	3.33	108	.199	.304	1	.250	0	2	2	0	0.2
1993	Cin-N	0	1	.000	3	0	0	0	0	4^2	6	0	4	2	19.3	3.86	104	.273	.385	0	.000	-0	0	0	-0	0.0
	Sea-A	2	1	.667	31	1	0	0	2	54	56	6	35	35	15.5	6.67	66	.273	.384	0	—	0	-14	-14	-2	-0.9
1995	Det-A	1	0	1.000	10	0	0	0	5	8^2	11	0	10	9	21.8	6.23	76	.306	.457	0	—	0	-1	-1	-0	-0.3
Total	11	14	15	.483	256	1	0	0	14	334^2	298	26	216	275	14.1	4.65	84	.241	.357	1	.167	-0	-29	-27	-3	-2.1
● **EARL HENRY** Henry, Earl Clifford "Hook" b: 6/10/17, Roseville, Ohio BL/TL, 5'11", 172 lbs. Deb: 9/23/44																										
1944	Cle-A	1	1	.500	2	2	1	0	0	17^2	18	0	3	5	10.7	4.58	72	.269	.300	0	.000	-0	-2	-3	0	-0.3
1945	Cle-A	0	3	.000	15	1	0	0	0	21^2	20	0	20	10	17.0	5.40	60	.253	.410	2	.500	1	-5	-5	1	-0.5
Total	2	1	4	.200	17	3	1	0	0	39^1	38	0	23	15	14.2	5.03	65	.260	.365	2	.222	0	-7	-8	1	-0.8
● **BUTCH HENRY** Henry, Floyd Bluford b: 10/7/68, ElPaso, Tex. BL/TL, 6'1", 205 lbs. Deb: 4/9/92																										
1992	Hou-N	6	9	.400	28	28	2	1	0	165^2	185	16	41	96	12.3	4.02	84	.285	.329	8	.148	1	-10	-12	1	-0.9
1993	Col-N	2	8	.200	20	15	1	0	0	84^2	117	14	24	39	15.1	6.59	72	.331	.375	2	.091	-1	-24	-17	-0	-1.9
	Mon-N	1	1	.500	10	1	0	0	0	18^1	18	1	4	8	10.8	3.93	106	.250	.289	0	.000	-0	0	0	-1	0.0
	Yr	3	9	.250	30	16	1	0	0	103	135	15	28	47	14.2	6.12	76	.313	.354	2	.083	-2	-24	-17	-1	-1.9
1994	Mon-N	8	3	.727	24	15	0	0	1	107^1	97	10	20	70	10.0	2.43	174	.241	.280	9	.290	3	21	21	-0	2.4
1995	Mon-N	7	9	.438	21	21	1	0	0	126^2	133	11	28	60	11.6	2.84	151	.275	.317	2	.048	-4	19	20	2	2.2
1997	Bos-A	7	3	.700	36	5	0	0	6	84^1	89	6	19	51	11.5	3.52	132	.277	.318	0	—	0	10	10	1	1.3
1998	Bos-A	0	0	—	2	2	0	0	0	9	8	2	3	6	12.0	4.00	115	.235	.316	0	—	0	1	1	0	0.0
Total	6	31	33	.484	141	87	4	2	7	596	647	60	139	330	12.0	3.78	109	.279	.322	21	.139	-2	17	23	3	3.1
● **DUTCH HENRY** Henry, Frank John b: 5/12/02, Cleveland, Ohio d: 8/23/68, Cleveland, Ohio BL/TL, 6'1", 175 lbs. Deb: 9/16/21																										
1921	StL-A	0	0	—	1	0	0	0	0	2	2	0	0	1	9.0	4.50	100	.250	.250	1	1.000	0	-0	-0	0	0.0
1922	StL-A	0	0	—	4	0	0	0	0	5	7	0	5	3	21.6	5.40	77	.280	.400	0	—	0	-1	-1	0	0.0
1923	Bro-N	4	6	.400	17	9	5	2	0	94^1	105	9	28	28	12.9	3.91	99	.281	.334	8	.229	1	1	-0	0	0.0
1924	Bro-N	1	2	.333	16	4	0	0	0	46	69	0	15	11	16.4	5.67	66	.352	.398	5	.250	1	-9	-10	0	-0.5
1927	NY-N	11	6	.647	45	15	7	1	4	163^2	184	6	31	40	11.8	4.23	91	.278	.311	13	.236	1	-6	-7	-2	-0.7
1928	NY-N	3	6	.333	17	8	4	0	1	64	82	4	25	23	15.2	3.80	103	.325	.388	3	.158	-1	1	1	0	0.1
1929	NY-N	5	6	.455	27	9	4	0	1	101^1	129	10	31	27	14.3	3.82	120	.316	.366	7	.250	2	10	9	-1	0.8
	Chi-A	1	0	1.000	2	1	1	0	0	15	20	1	7	2	16.2	6.00	71	.308	.375	1	.143	0	-3	-3	-1	-0.2
1930	Chi-A	2	17	.105	35	16	4	0	0	155	211	12	48	35	15.3	4.88	95	.331	.381	12	.235	1	-4	-4	3	-0.1
Total	8	27	43	.386	164	62	25	3	6	646^1	809	42	190	170	14.0	4.39	95	.308	.356	50	.231	6	-10	-16	0	-0.6
● **JIM HENRY** Henry, James Francis b: 6/26/10, Danville, Pa. d: 8/15/76, Memphis, Tenn. BR/TR, 6'2", 175 lbs. Deb: 4/23/36																										
1936	Bos-A	5	1	.833	21	8	2	0	0	76^1	75	10	40	36	13.8	4.60	116	.255	.348	3	.115	-1	4	6	0	0.3
1937	Bos-A	1	0	1.000	3	2	1	0	0	15^1	15	2	11	8	15.3	5.28	90	.263	.382	0	.000	-0	-1	-1	-0	-0.1
1939	Phi-N	0	1	.000	9	1	0	0	1	23	24	3	8	7	12.9	5.09	79	.276	.344	0	.000	-1	-3	-3	-1	-0.3
Total	3	6	2	.750	33	11	3	0	1	114^2	114	15	59	51	13.8	4.79	104	.260	.352	3	.083	-2	-0	2	-1	-0.1
● **JOHN HENRY** Henry, John Michael b: 9/2/1863, Springfield, Mass. d: 6/11/39, Hartford, Conn. TL, Deb: 8/13/1884 ♦																										
1884	Cle-N	1	4	.200	5	5	5	1	0	42	46	2	26	23	15.4	3.64	87	.257	.351	4	.154	-1	-3	-2	1	-0.3
1885	Bal-a	2	7	.222	9	9	9	0	0	71	71	0	13	31	10.9	4.31	76	.247	.284	9	.265	1	-8	-8	2	-0.5
1886	Was-N	1	3	.250	4	4	4	0	0	27^2	35	1	15	19	16.3	4.23	78	.285	.362	5	.357	1	-3	-3	-0	-0.3
Total	3	4	14	.222	18	18	18	1	0	140^2	152	3	54	73	13.3	4.09	79	.258	.322	53	.243	1	-14	-13	2	-1.1
● **DOUG HENRY** Henry, Richard Douglas b: 12/10/63, Sacramento, Cal. BR/TR, 6'4", 205 lbs. Deb: 7/15/91																										
1991	Mil-A	2	1	.667	32	0	0	0	15	36	16	1	14	28	7.5	1.00	397	.133	.224	0	—	0	12	12	-1	1.9
1992	Mil-A	1	4	.200	68	0	0	0	29	65	64	6	24	52	12.2	4.02	96	.256	.321	0	—	0	-1	-1	0	-0.1
1993	Mil-A	4	4	.500	54	0	0	0	17	55	67	7	25	38	15.5	5.56	76	.300	.378	0	—	0	-8	-8	0	-1.4
1994	Mil-A	2	3	.400	25	0	0	0	0	31^1	32	7	23	20	16.1	4.60	109	.271	.394	0	.000	-0	1	2	-0	0.2
1995	NY-N	3	6	.333	51	0	0	0	4	67	48	7	25	62	9.9	2.96	137	.198	.276	1	1.000	0	9	8	0	1.1
1996	NY-N	2	8	.200	58	0	0	0	9	75	82	7	36	58	14.3	4.68	86	.273	.353	0	.000	-1	-4	-6	-1	-0.9
1997	*SF-N	4	5	.444	75	0	0	0	3	70^2	70	5	41	69	14.3	4.71	88	.261	.361	0	.000	-0	-4	-5	-1	-0.7
1998	*Hou-N	8	2	.800	59	0	0	0	2	71	55	9	35	59	11.4	3.04	134	.216	.310	0	.000	-0	9	8	-1	0.9
Total	8	26	33	.441	422	0	0	0	79	471	434	49	223	386	12.7	3.92	105	.244	.331	1	.067	-1	16	10	-3	1.0
● **BILL HENRY** Henry, William Francis b: 2/15/42, Long Beach, Cal. BL/TL, 6'3", 195 lbs. Deb: 9/13/66																										
1966	NY-A	0	0	—	2	0	0	0	0	3	0	0	2	3	6.0	0.00	—	.000	.200	0	—	0	1	1	0	0.0
● **BILL HENRY** Henry, William Rodman b: 10/15/27, Alice, Tex. BL/TL, 6'2", 180 lbs. Deb: 4/17/52																										
1952	Bos-A	5	4	.556	13	10	5	0	0	76^2	75	7	36	23	13.3	3.87	102	.254	.339	8	.258	2	-2	1	-1	0.1
1953	Bos-A	5	5	.500	21	12	4	1	1	85^2	86	4	33	56	12.9	3.26	129	.260	.334	6	.188	-0	7	9	-1	0.9
1954	Bos-A	3	7	.300	24	13	3	1	0	95^2	104	9	49	38	14.5	4.52	91	.270	.354	4	.118	-1	-8	-4	-1	-0.7
1955	Bos-A	2	4	.333	17	7	0	1	0	59^2	56	7	21	23	11.6	3.32	129	.247	.310	2	.105	-1	4	6	0	0.5
1958	Chi-N	5	4	.556	44	0	0	0	6	81^1	63	8	17	58	9.0	2.88	136	.214	.259	4	.235	1	10	9	-1	1.1
1959	Chi-N	9	8	.529	**65**	0	0	0	12	134^1	111	19	26	115	9.2	2.68	147	.227	.267	6	.194	0	19	**19**	-1	2.5
1960	Cin-N★	1	5	.167	51	0	0	0	17	67^2	62	8	20	58	11.4	3.19	120	.247	.313	0	.000	-1	4	5	1	0.6
1961	*Cin-N	2	1	.667	47	0	0	0	16	53^1	50	8	15	53	11.0	2.19	185	.244	.295	0	.000	-1	11	11	0	1.2
1962	Cin-N	4	2	.667	40	0	0	0	11	37^1	40	5	20	35	14.7	4.58	88	.280	.372	1	.333	0	-3	-2	-1	-0.5
1963	Cin-N	1	3	.250	47	0	0	0	14	52	55	4	11	45	11.6	4.15	81	.279	.321	1	.167	-0	-5	-5	-0	-0.7
1964	Cin-N	2	2	.500	37	0	0	0	6	52	31	2	12	28	8.0	0.87	418	.170	.234	3	.500	1	15	16	-0	1.7
1965	Cin-N	2	0	1.000	3	0	0	0	0	5	3	0	1	5	7.2	0.00	—	.176	.222	0	—	0	2	2	-0	0.9
	SF-N	2	2	.500	35	0	0	0	4	42	40	2	8	35	10.5	3.64	99	.248	.288	1	.200	0	-0	-0	-0	-0.1
	Yr	4	2	.667	38	0	0	0	4	47	43	2	9	40	10.1	3.26	111	.242	.282	1	.200	0	1	2	-1	0.8
1966	SF-N	1	1	.500	35	0	0	0	1	22	15	3	10	15	10.6	2.45	149	.190	.289	0	.000	-0	3	3	-0	0.2
1967	SF-N	2	0	1.000	28	1	0	0	2	21^2	16	1	9	23	11.2	2.08	158	.198	.293	0	.000	-0	3	3	-0	0.3
1968	SF-N	0	2	.000	7	1	0	0	0	5	4	0	3	0	14.4	5.40	55	.250	.400	0	—	0	-1	-1	0	-0.5
	Pit-N	0	0	—	10	0	0	0	0	16^2	29	2	3	9	18.4	8.10	36	.382	.420	0	.000	-0	-9	-10	-1	-0.1
	Yr	0	2	.000	17	1	0	0	0	21^2	33	2	6	9	17.0	7.48	39	.355	.406	0	.000	-0	-11	-11	-1	-0.6
1969	Hou-N	0	0	—	3	0	0	0	0	5	5	0	2	2	7.2	0.00	—	.111	.200	0	—	0	2	2	-0	0.0
Total	16	46	50	.479	527	44	12	2	90	913	842	89	296	621	11.5	3.26	119	.244	.308	36	.177	-0	51	63	-6	7.4

YEAR	TM/L	W	L	PCT	G	GS	CG	SH	SV	IP	H	HR	BB	SO	RAT	ERA	ERA+	OAV	OOB	BH	AVG	PB	PR	/A	PD	TPI
● ROY HENSHAW Henshaw, Roy Knikelbine b: 7/29/11, Chicago, Ill. d: 6/8/93, LaGrange, Ill. BR/TL, 5′8″, 155 lbs. Deb: 4/15/33																										
1933	Chi-N	2	1	.667	21	0	0	0	0	38^2	32	0	20	16	12.6	4.19	78	.230	.335	2	.200	-0	-4	-4	-1	-0.4
1935	*Chi-N	13	5	.722	31	18	7	3	1	142^2	135	6	68	53	13.1	3.28	120	.249	.337	13	.255	2	12	10	-3	1.0
1936	Chi-N	6	5	.545	39	14	6	2	1	129^1	152	8	56	69	14.8	3.97	100	.296	.370	6	.136	-2	1	0	-2	-0.4
1937	Bro-N	5	12	.294	42	16	5	0	2	156^1	176	14	69	98	14.3	5.07	80	.278	.352	8	.167	-2	-20	-18	0	-1.9
1938	StL-N	5	11	.313	27	15	4	0	0	130	132	7	48	34	12.5	4.02	99	.266	.332	9	.220	-0	-3	-1	-1	-0.2
1942	Det-A	2	4	.333	23	2	0	0	1	61^2	63	3	27	24	13.3	4.09	97	.269	.347	1	.083	-1	-3	-1	-1	-0.2
1943	Det-A	0	2	.000	26	3	0	0	2	71^1	75	2	33	33	14.0	3.79	93	.276	.360	2	.111	-1	-4	-2	0	-0.2
1944	Det-A	0	0	—	7	1	0	0	0	12^1	17	0	6	10	16.8	8.76	41	.315	.383	0	.000	-1	-7	-7	0	0.0
Total	8	33	40	.452	216	69	22	5	7	742^1	782	40	327	337	13.7	4.16	94	.271	.349	41	.179	-5	-29	-22	-8	-2.3
● PHIL HENSIEK Hensiek, Philip Frank "Sid" b: 10/13/01, St.Louis, Mo. d: 2/21/72, St.Louis, Mo. BR/TR, 6′, 160 lbs. Deb: 8/15/35																										
1935	Was-A	0	3	.000	6	1	0	0	1	13	21	2	9	6	20.8	9.69	45	.356	.441	2	.667	1	-8	-8	-0	-1.4
● CHUCK HENSLEY Hensley, Charles Floyd b: 3/11/59, Tulare, Cal. BL/TL, 6′3″, 190 lbs. Deb: 5/10/86																										
1986	SF-N	0	0	—	11	0	0	0	1	7^1	5	2	2	6	8.6	2.45	143	.179	.233	0	—	0	1	1	0	0.0
● PAT HENTGEN Hentgen, Patrick George b: 11/13/68, Detroit, Mich. BR/TR, 6′2″, 200 lbs. Deb: 9/3/91																										
1991	Tor-A	0	0	—	3	1	0	0	0	7^1	5	1	3	3	12.3	2.45	171	.208	.345	0	—	0	1	1	0	-0.2
1992	Tor-A	5	2	.714	28	2	0	0	0	50^1	49	7	32	39	14.5	5.36	76	.254	.360	0	—	0	-8	-7	-1	-1.2
1993	*Tor-A☆	19	9	.679	34	32	3	0	0	216^1	215	27	74	122	12.3	3.87	112	.258	.323	0	—	0	11	11	-2	1.1
1994	Tor-A★	13	8	.619	24	24	6	3	0	174^2	158	21	59	147	11.3	3.40	142	.240	.306	0	—	0	27	28	0	2.9
1995	Tor-A	10	14	.417	30	30	2	0	0	200^2	236	24	90	135	14.8	5.11	92	.290	.364	0	—	0	-9	-9	-2	-1.0
1996	Tor-A	20	10	.667	35	35	**10**	**3**	0	**265^2**	238	20	94	177	11.4	3.22	155	.241	.310	0	—	0	**52**	**53**	-1	**5.2**
1997	Tor-A★	15	10	.600	35	35	**9**	**3**	0	**264**	253	31	71	160	11.3	3.68	125	.254	.308	0	.000	-1	26	27	-0	2.1
1998	Tor-A	12	11	.522	29	29	0	0	0	177^2	208	28	69	94	14.3	5.17	90	.293	.360	0	.000	-0	-10	-10	-1	-1.2
Total	8	94	64	.595	218	188	30	9	0	1356^2	1362	159	492	877	12.5	4.05	115	.261	.329	0	.000	-1	90	92	-5	7.7
● BILL HEPLER Hepler, William Lewis b: 9/25/45, Covington, Va. BL/TL, 6′, 160 lbs. Deb: 4/23/66																										
1966	NY-N	3	3	.500	37	3	0	0	0	69	71	3	51	25	16.3	3.52	103	.274	.399	3	.214	0	1	1	-1	0.0
● RON HERBEL Herbel, Ronald Samuel b: 1/16/38, Denver, Colo. BR/TR, 6′1″, 195 lbs. Deb: 9/10/63																										
1963	SF-N	0	0	—	2	0	0	0	0	1^1	1	0	1	1	13.5	6.75	47	.200	.333	0	—	0	-1	-1	0	0.0
1964	SF-N	9	9	.500	40	22	7	2	1	161	162	7	61	98	12.6	3.07	116	.259	.328	0	.000	-4	8	9	2	0.7
1965	SF-N	12	9	.571	47	21	1	0	1	170^2	172	16	47	106	11.7	3.85	94	.261	.313	1	.020	-4	-6	-5	2	-0.8
1966	SF-N	4	5	.444	32	18	0	0	1	129^2	149	15	39	55	13.2	4.16	88	.291	.344	1	.026	-4	-8	-7	-1	-0.9
1967	SF-N	4	5	.444	42	11	1	1	1	125^2	125	10	35	52	11.6	3.08	107	.268	.322	3	.107	0	4	3	4	0.6
1968	SF-N	0	0	—	28	2	0	0	0	42^2	55	5	15	18	15.0	3.38	87	.309	.366	0	.000	-0	-2	-2	1	0.0
1969	SF-N	4	1	.800	39	4	2	0	1	87^1	92	7	23	34	12.0	4.02	87	.275	.323	0	.000	-2	-4	-5	0	-0.4
1970	SD-N	7	5	.583	64	1	0	0	9	111	114	14	39	53	12.7	4.95	80	.266	.333	0	.000	-1	-11	-12	-0	-1.5
	NY-N	2	2	.500	12	0	0	0	1	13	14	1	2	8	11.1	1.38	291	.275	.302	0	—	0	4	4	-0	1.1
	Yr	9	7	.563	**76**	1	0	0	10	124	128	15	41	61	12.3	4.57	87	.262	.319	0	.000	-1	-7	-8	-1	-0.4
1971	Atl-N	0	1	.000	25	0	0	0	1	51^2	61	6	23	22	15.3	5.23	71	.300	.383	1	.091	-1	-10	-9	0	-0.3
Total	9	42	37	.532	331	79	11	3	16	894	945	81	285	447	12.6	3.83	94	.273	.332	6	.029	-15	-25	-25	7	-1.5
● ERNIE HERBERT Herbert, Ernie Albert "Tex" b: 1/30/1887, Hale, Mo. d: 1/13/68, Dallas, Tex. BR/TR, 5′10″, 165 lbs. Deb: 7/27/13																										
1913	Cin-N	0	0	—	6	0	0	0	0	17^1	12	0	5	5	9.3	2.08	156	.179	.247	1	.250	0	2	2	-1	-0.1
1914	StL-F	1	0	1.000	18	1	0	0	1	50^1	56	2	27	24	15.6	3.58	85	.293	.392	7	.538	2	-4	-3	-2	-0.1
1915	StL-F	1	0	1.000	11	1	1	0	0	48	48	1	18	23	12.9	3.38	85	.253	.327	5	.278	1	-3	-3	-1	0.0
Total	3	2	0	1.000	35	2	1	0	1	115^2	116	3	50	52	13.5	3.27	92	.259	.344	13	.371	3	-5	-3	-4	-0.2
● FRED HERBERT Herbert, Frederick (b: Herbert Frederick Kemman) b: 3/4/1887, LaGrange, Ill. d: 5/29/63, Tice, Fla. BR/TR, 6′, 185 lbs. Deb: 9/25/15																										
1915	NY-N	1	1	.500	2	2	1	0	0	17	12	0	4	6	8.5	1.06	242	.197	.246	1	.167	-0	3	3	0	0.4
● RAY HERBERT Herbert, Raymond Ernest b: 12/15/29, Detroit, Mich. BR/TR, 5′11″, 185 lbs. Deb: 8/27/50																										
1950	Det-A	1	2	.333	8	3	1	0	1	22^1	20	1	12	5	12.9	3.63	129	.244	.340	2	.286	0	2	3	1	0.4
1951	Det-A	4	0	1.000	5	0	0	0	0	12^2	8	0	9	9	12.1	1.42	294	.190	.333	0	.000	-0	4	4	-0	1.1
1953	Det-A	4	6	.400	43	3	0	0	6	87^2	109	5	46	37	15.9	5.24	78	.308	.387	3	.158	-0	-12	-11	3	-1.0
1954	Det-A	3	6	.333	42	4	0	0	0	84^1	114	6	50	44	17.7	5.87	63	.334	.422	3	.176	2	-20	-20	2	-1.6
1955	KC-A	1	8	.111	23	11	2	0	0	87^2	99	10	40	30	14.4	6.26	67	.292	.368	4	.190	0	-22	-20	2	-1.6
1958	KC-A	8	8	.500	42	16	5	0	3	175	161	20	55	108	11.3	3.50	112	.248	.311	10	.192	1	5	8	2	1.1
1959	KC-A	11	11	.500	37	26	10	2	1	183^2	196	24	62	99	12.7	4.85	83	.275	.334	12	.211	2	-20	-17	-1	-1.8
1960	KC-A	14	15	.483	37	33	14	0	1	252^2	256	17	72	122	11.9	3.28	121	.267	.323	13	.171	1	17	20	3	2.5
1961	KC-A	3	6	.333	13	12	1	0	0	83^2	103	10	30	34	14.5	5.38	78	.303	.363	3	.107	-1	-13	-11	0	-1.1
	Chi-A	9	6	.600	21	20	4	0	0	137^2	142	15	36	50	11.6	4.05	97	.265	.311	12	.226	4	-0	-2	1	0.3
	Yr	12	12	.500	34	32	5	0	0	221^1	245	25	66	84	12.6	4.55	88	.278	.328	15	.185	3	-13	-13	-1	-0.8
1962	Chi-A★	20	9	**.690**	35	35	12	2	0	236^2	228	13	74	115	11.5	3.27	119	.255	.312	16	.195	5	18	17	3	2.8
1963	Chi-A	13	10	.565	33	33	14	**7**	0	224^2	230	12	35	105	10.7	3.24	108	.265	.295	14	.222	6	10	7	2	1.5
1964	Chi-A	6	7	.462	20	19	1	1	0	111^2	117	14	17	40	11.0	3.47	100	.275	.306	5	.139	-1	2	-0	-1	-0.2
1965	Phi-N	5	8	.385	25	19	4	1	1	130^2	162	13	19	51	12.5	3.86	90	.309	.334	11	.268	3	-5	-6	0	-0.2
1966	Phi-N	2	5	.286	23	2	0	0	2	50^1	55	7	14	15	12.5	4.29	84	.293	.345	1	.077	-1	-4	-4	-0	-0.6
Total	14	104	107	.493	407	236	68	13	15	1881^1	2000	167	571	864	12.4	4.01	96	.276	.331	109	.192	20	-38	-35	18	1.6
● FELIX HEREDIA Heredia, Felix (Perez) b: 6/18/76, Barahona, D.R. BL/TL, 6′, 160 lbs. Deb: 8/9/96																										
1996	Fla-N	1	1	.500	21	0	0	0	0	16^2	21	1	10	10	16.7	4.32	94	.313	.403	0	—	0	-0	-0	-1	-0.1
1997	*Fla-N	5	3	.625	56	0	0	0	0	56^2	53	3	30	54	14.0	4.29	94	.241	.345	1	.500	0	-1	-2	-2	-0.3
1998	Fla-N	0	3	.000	41	2	0	0	2	41	38	1	32	38	15.6	5.49	75	.241	.372	0	.000	-0	-6	-6	-0	-0.5
	*Chi-N	3	0	1.000	30	0	0	0	0	17^2	19	1	6	16	12.7	4.08	107	.279	.338	0	—	0	0	1	-1	0.0
	Yr	3	3	.500	71	2	0	0	2	58^2	57	2	38	54	14.6	5.06	82	.249	.356	0	.000	-0	-5	-6	-1	-0.5
Total	3	9	7	.563	148	2	0	0	2	132	131	6	78	118	14.7	4.64	88	.255	.360	1	.200	0	-6	-8	-3	-0.9
● GIL HEREDIA Heredia, Gilbert b: 10/26/65, Nogales, Ariz. BR/TR, 6′1″, 190 lbs. Deb: 9/1/91																										
1991	SF-N	0	2	.000	7	4	0	0	0	33	27	4	7	13	9.3	3.82	94	.233	.276	3	.429	1	-0	-1	-1	0.0
1992	SF-N	2	3	.400	13	4	0	0	0	30	32	3	16	15	14.7	5.40	61	.278	.371	1	.167	0	-6	-7	-1	-1.2
	Mon-N	0	0	—	7	1	0	0	0	14^2	12	1	4	7	9.8	1.84	188	.250	.308	0	.000	-0	3	3	0	0.0
	Yr	2	3	.400	20	5	0	0	0	44^2	44	4	20	22	12.9	4.23	79	.268	.348	1	.111	-0	-4	-4	-1	-1.2
1993	Mon-N	4	2	.667	20	9	1	0	2	57^1	66	4	14	40	12.9	3.92	106	.293	.340	2	.154	-0	1	2	1	0.2
1994	Mon-N	6	3	.667	39	3	0	0	0	75^1	85	7	13	62	11.9	3.46	122	.281	.314	5	.313	1	6	6	0	0.8
1995	Mon-N	5	6	.455	40	18	0	0	1	119	137	7	21	74	12.3	4.31	100	.291	.329	6	.182	-0	-2	-0	1	0.0
1996	Tex-A	2	5	.286	44	0	0	0	1	73^1	91	12	14	43	13.0	5.89	89	.301	.334	0	—	0	-7	-5	-0	-0.5
1998	Oak-A	3	3	.500	8	6	0	0	0	42^2	43	4	3	27	10.3	2.74	166	.256	.282	0	—	0	9	9	1	1.2
Total	7	22	24	.478	178	45	1	0	4	445^1	493	42	92	281	12.1	4.18	103	.282	.323	17	.218	2	3	5	1	0.5
● UBALDO HEREDIA Heredia, Ubaldo Jose (Martinez) b: 5/4/56, Ciudad Bolivar, Ven. BR/TR, 6′2″, 180 lbs. Deb: 5/12/87																										
1987	Mon-N	0	1	.000	2	2	0	0	0	10	10	2	3	6	12.6	5.40	78	.263	.333	0	.000	-0	-1	-1	0	-0.1
● WILSON HEREDIA Heredia, Wilson b: 3/30/72, LaRomana, D.R. BR/TR, 6′, 175 lbs. Deb: 4/27/95																										
1995	Tex-A	0	1	.000	6	0	0	0	0	12	9	2	15	6	18.0	3.75	129	.225	.436	0	—	0	1	1	-0	-0.1
1997	Tex-A	1	0	1.000	10	0	0	0	0	19^2	14	2	16	8	13.7	3.20	149	.197	.345	0	—	0	3	3	0	0.1
Total	2	1	1	.500	16	0	0	0	0	31^2	23	4	31	14	15.3	3.41	141	.207	.380	0	—	0	4	5	-0	0.0

YEAR	TM/L	W	L	PCT	G	GS	CG	SH	SV	IP	H	HR	BB	SO	RAT	ERA	ERA+	OAV	OOB	BH	AVG	PB	PR	/A	PD	TPI
● ART HERMAN	Herman, Arthur b: 5/11/1871, Louisville, Ky. d: 9/20/55, Los Angeles, Cal. Deb: 6/29/1896																									
1896	Lou-N	4	6	.400	14	12	9	0	0	94^1	122	4	36	13	15.3	5.63	77	.310	.371	5	.139	-4	-13	-14	-1	-1.4
1897	Lou-N	0	1	.000	3	2	1	0	0	18	23	1	5	4	14.0	4.00	107	.307	.350	2	.333	1	1	1	0	0.2
Total	2	4	7	.364	17	14	10	0	0	112^1	145	5	41	17	15.1	5.37	80	.310	.368	7	.167	-2	-13	-13	-1	-1.2
● DUSTIN HERMANSON	Hermanson, Dustin Michael b: 12/21/72, Springfield, Ohio BR/TR, 6'3", 195 lbs. Deb: 5/8/95																									
1995	SD-N	3	1	.750	26	0	0	0	0	31^2	35	8	22	19	16.5	6.82	59	.280	.392	0	—	0	-9	-10	0	-1.1
1996	SD-N	1	0	1.000	8	0	0	0	0	13^2	18	3	4	11	14.5	8.56	46	.340	.386	0	—	0	-7	-7	0	-0.4
1997	Mon-N	8	8	.500	32	28	1	1	0	158^1	134	15	66	136	11.4	3.69	113	.234	.314	5	.104	-0	9	9	-0	0.7
1998	Mon-N	14	11	.560	32	30	1	0	0	187	163	21	56	154	10.7	3.13	131	.234	.294	6	.115	3	23	20	0	2.8
Total	4	26	20	.565	98	58	2	1	0	390^2	350	47	148	320	11.6	3.85	107	.242	.314	11	.110	2	16	12	1	2.0
● JESUS HERNAIZ	Hernaiz, Jesus Rafael (Rodriguez) b: 1/8/45, Santurce, P.R. BR/TR, 6'2", 175 lbs. Deb: 6/14/74																									
1974	Phi-N	2	3	.400	27	0	0	0	1	41^1	53	6	25	16	17.0	5.88	64	.323	.413	0	.000	-0	-10	-10	-0	-1.2
● LIVAN HERNANDEZ	Hernandez, Eisler Livan b: 2/20/75, Villa Clara, Cuba BR/TR, 6'2", 220 lbs. Deb: 9/24/96 F																									
1996	Fla-N	0	0	—	1	0	0	0	0	3	3	0	2	2	15.0	0.00	—	.273	.385	1	1.000	0	1	1	-0	0.0
1997	*Fla-N	9	3	.750	17	17	0	0	0	96^1	81	5	38	72	11.4	3.18	127	.229	.310	5	.172	1	11	9	1	1.2
1998	Fla-N	10	12	.455	33	33	9	0	0	234^1	265	37	104	162	14.4	4.72	87	.289	.365	16	.195	2	-13	-16	1	-1.1
Total	3	19	15	.559	51	50	9	0	0	333^2	349	42	144	236	13.5	4.23	96	.272	.350	22	.196	3	-1	-6	1	0.1
● FERNANDO HERNANDEZ	Hernandez, Fernando b: 6/16/71, Santiago, D.R. BR/TR, 6'2", 185 lbs. Deb: 4/3/97																									
1997	Det-A	0	0	—	2	0	0	0	0	1^1	5	0	3	2	60.8	40.50	11	.556	.692	0	—	0	-5	-5	0	0.0
● XAVIER HERNANDEZ	Hernandez, Francis Xavier b: 8/16/65, Port Arthur, Tex. BL/TR, 6'2", 185 lbs. Deb: 6/4/89																									
1989	Tor-A	1	0	1.000	7	0	0	0	0	22^2	25	2	8	7	13.5	4.76	79	.278	.343	0	—	0	-2	-3	-1	-0.1
1990	Hou-N	2	1	.667	34	1	0	0	0	62^1	60	8	24	24	12.7	4.62	80	.256	.336	1	.333	0	-6	-6	-1	-0.4
1991	Hou-N	2	7	.222	32	6	0	0	3	63	66	6	32	55	14.0	4.71	74	.263	.346	0	.000	-0	-7	-8	0	-1.2
1992	Hou-N	9	1	.900	77	0	0	0	7	111	81	5	42	96	10.2	2.11	159	.200	.281	0	.000	-1	17	15	-2	1.3
1993	Hou-N	4	5	.444	72	0	0	0	9	96^2	75	6	28	101	9.7	2.61	149	.212	.272	0	.000	-1	15	14	-1	1.2
1994	NY-A	4	4	.500	31	0	0	0	6	40	48	7	21	37	16.0	5.85	78	.300	.388	0	—	0	-5	-6	1	-1.0
1995	*Cin-N	7	2	.778	59	0	0	0	3	90	95	8	31	84	13.0	4.60	89	.273	.339	0	.000	-1	-4	-5	-0	-0.6
1996	Cin-N	0	0	—	3	0	0	0	0	3^1	8	2	2	3	27.0	13.50	31	.471	.526	0	—	0	-3	-3	-0	0.0
	Hou-N	5	5	.500	58	0	0	0	6	74^2	69	11	26	78	11.7	4.22	92	.245	.313	0	.000	-0	-0	-3	-0	-0.4
	Yr	5	5	.500	61	0	0	0	6	78	77	13	28	81	12.3	4.62	84	.258	.325	0	.000	-0	-3	-6	-0	-0.4
1997	Tex-A	0	4	.000	44	0	0	0	0	49^1	51	7	22	36	13.7	4.56	105	.262	.342	0	—	0	0	1	0	0.1
1998	Tex-A	6	6	.500	46	0	0	0	1	58	43	5	30	41	11.5	3.57	136	.207	.310	0	—	0	7	8	-1	1.4
Total	10	40	35	.533	463	7	0	0	35	671	621	67	266	562	12.2	3.90	101	.244	.321	1	.027	-3	12	4	-4	0.3
● EVELIO HERNANDEZ	Hernandez, Gregorio Evelio (Lopez) b: 12/24/30, Guanabacoa, Havana, Cuba BR/TR, 6'1", 195 lbs. Deb: 9/12/56																									
1956	Was-A	1	1	.500	4	4	1	0	0	22^2	24	2	8	9	12.7	4.76	91	.276	.337	2	.182	-0	-2	-1	-0	-0.1
1957	Was-A	0	0	—	14	2	0	0	0	36	38	2	20	15	14.5	4.25	92	.268	.358	0	.000	-1	-2	-1	-1	-0.1
Total	2	1	1	.500	18	6	1	0	0	58^2	62	4	28	24	13.8	4.45	91	.271	.350	2	.118	-1	-3	-3	-1	-0.2
● WILLIE HERNANDEZ	Hernandez, Guillermo (Villanueva) b: 11/14/54, Aguada, P.R. BL/TL, 6'3", 180 lbs. Deb: 4/9/77																									
1977	Chi-N	8	7	.533	67	1	0	0	4	110	94	11	28	78	10.1	3.03	145	.234	.285	1	.063	-1	11	17	3	2.3
1978	Chi-N	8	2	.800	54	0	0	0	3	59^2	57	6	35	38	14.0	3.77	107	.263	.368	0	.000	-0	-1	2	1	0.3
1979	Chi-N	4	4	.500	51	2	0	0	0	79	85	8	39	53	14.6	5.01	82	.281	.370	2	.250	0	-11	-8	-0	-0.7
1980	Chi-N	1	9	.100	53	7	0	0	0	108^1	115	8	45	75	13.5	4.40	89	.276	.349	4	.211	0	-10	-6	2	-0.3
1981	Chi-N	0	0	—	12	0	0	0	2	13^2	14	0	8	13	14.5	3.95	94	.280	.379	0	—	0	-1	-0	0	0.0
1982	Chi-N	4	6	.400	75	0	0	0	10	75	74	3	24	54	11.9	3.00	124	.268	.329	0	.000	-0	5	6	2	1.2
1983	Chi-N	1	0	1.000	11	1	0	0	1	19^2	16	0	6	18	10.1	3.20	118	.222	.282	1	.500	0	1	1	0	0.1
	*Phi-N	8	4	.667	63	0	0	0	7	95^2	93	9	26	75	11.3	3.29	108	.254	.305	5	.385	2	4	3	-0	0.5
	Yr	9	4	.692	74	1	0	0	8	115^1	109	9	32	93	11.1	3.28	110	.249	.301	6	.400	2	4	4	0	0.6
1984	*Det-A★	9	3	.750	**80**	0	0	0	32	140^1	96	6	36	112	8.7	1.92	204	.194	.254	0	—	0	**32**	**31**	-1	3.9
1985	Det-A★	8	10	.444	74	0	0	0	31	106^2	82	13	14	76	8.2	2.70	151	.210	.239	0	.000	-0	17	16	-2	3.3
1986	Det-A☆	8	7	.533	64	0	0	0	24	88^2	87	13	21	77	11.5	3.55	116	.251	.304	0	—	0	6	6	1	1.2
1987	*Det-A	3	4	.429	45	0	0	0	8	49	53	8	20	30	13.4	3.67	115	.276	.344	0	—	0	4	3	-1	0.4
1988	Det-A	6	5	.545	63	0	0	0	10	67^2	50	8	31	59	11.3	3.06	125	.208	.309	0	—	0	7	6	1	1.2
1989	Det-A	2	2	.500	32	0	0	0	15	31^1	36	4	16	30	15.2	5.74	66	.293	.379	0	—	0	-6	-7	0	-1.3
Total	13	70	63	.526	744	11	0	0	147	1044^2	952	97	349	788	11.4	3.38	118	.245	.311	13	.206	1	57	70	6	12.1
● JEREMY HERNANDEZ	Hernandez, Jeremy Stuart b: 7/6/66, Burbank, Cal. BR/TR, 6'6", 195 lbs. Deb: 9/2/91																									
1991	SD-N	0	0	—	9	0	0	0	2	14^1	8	0	5	9	8.2	0.00	—	.157	.232	0	.000	-0	6	6	0	0.2
1992	SD-N	1	4	.200	26	0	0	0	1	36^2	39	4	11	25	12.5	4.17	86	.291	.349	0	.000	-0	-3	-2	0	-0.3
1993	SD-N	0	2	.000	21	0	0	0	0	34^1	41	2	7	26	12.6	4.72	88	.301	.336	0	.000	-0	-3	-2	0	-0.1
	Cle-A	6	5	.545	49	0	0	0	8	77^1	75	12	27	44	11.9	3.14	138	.261	.325	0	—	0	10	10	-0	1.5
1994	Fla-N	3	3	.500	21	0	0	0	9	23^1	16	0	14	13	12.3	2.70	162	.205	.340	0	.000	-0	4	4	-0	1.3
1995	Fla-N	0	0	—	7	0	0	0	0	7	12	2	3	5	20.6	11.57	36	.400	.471	0	.000	-0	-6	-6	-0	0.0
Total	5	10	14	.417	133	0	0	0	20	193	191	20	67	122	12.2	3.64	113	.267	.333	0	.000	-1	9	10	-0	2.6
● MANNY HERNANDEZ	Hernandez, Manuel Antonio (Montas) b: 5/7/61, LaRomana, D.R. BR/TR, 6', 150 lbs. Deb: 6/5/86																									
1986	Hou-N	2	3	.400	9	4	0	0	0	27^2	33	2	12	9	14.6	3.90	92	.306	.375	0	.000	-1	-1	-1	-0	-0.2
1987	Hou-N	0	4	.000	6	3	0	0	0	21^2	25	1	5	12	12.9	5.40	73	.301	.348	0	.000	-1	-3	-4	0	-0.6
1989	NY-N	0	0	—	1	0	0	0	0	1	0	0	0	1	0.0	0.00	—	.000	.000	0	—	0	0	0	0	0.0
Total	3	2	7	.222	16	7	0	0	0	50^1	58	3	17	22	13.6	4.47	83	.299	.358	0	.000	-1	-3	-4	0	-0.8
● ORLANDO HERNANDEZ	Hernandez, Orlando P. "El Duque" b: 10/11/69, Villa Clara, Cuba BR/TR, 6'2", 210 lbs. Deb: 6/3/98 F																									
1998	*NY-A	12	4	.750	21	21	3	1	0	141	113	11	52	131	10.9	3.13	142	.222	.302	0	.000	-1	24	21	1	2.1
● RAMON HERNANDEZ	Hernandez, Ramon (Gonzalez) b: 8/31/40, Carolina, P.R. BB/TL, 5'9", 170 lbs. Deb: 4/11/67																									
1967	Atl-N	0	2	.000	46	0	0	0	5	51^2	60	5	14	28	13.2	4.18	79	.296	.347	0	.000	-0	-5	-5	1	-0.3
1968	Chi-N	0	0	—	8	0	0	0	0	9	14	1	0	3	15.0	9.00	35	.350	.366	0	—	0	-6	-6	0	0.0
1971	Pit-N	0	1	.000	10	0	0	0	4	12^1	5	0	2	7	5.1	0.73	463	.122	.163	1	.500	0	4	4	0	0.6
1972	*Pit-N	5	0	1.000	53	0	0	0	14	70	50	3	22	47	9.6	1.67	199	.194	.265	2	.167	0	14	13	0	1.6
1973	Pit-N	4	5	.444	59	0	0	0	11	89^2	71	5	25	64	10.0	2.41	146	.218	.282	1	.125	0	12	11	1	1.4
1974	*Pit-N	5	2	.714	58	0	0	0	2	68^2	68	3	18	33	11.5	2.75	125	.258	.310	1	.250	1	7	5	-1	0.6
1975	*Pit-N	7	2	.778	46	0	0	0	5	64	62	0	28	43	12.7	2.95	120	.252	.328	0	.000	-0	5	4	1	0.7
1976	Pit-N	2	2	.500	37	0	0	0	3	43	42	3	16	17	12.3	3.56	98	.262	.333	0	.000	-0	-0	-0	-1	-0.1
	Chi-N	0	0	—	2	0	0	0	0	1^2	2	0	0	1	10.8	0.00	—	.333	.333	0	—	0	1	1	0	0.0
	Yr	2	2	.500	39	0	0	0	3	44^2	44	3	16	18	12.1	3.43	102	.257	.321	0	.000	-0	0	0	-0	-0.1
1977	Chi-N	0	0	—	6	0	0	0	1	7^2	11	1	3	4	16.4	8.22	53	.306	.359	0	.000	-0	-4	-3	0	-0.1
	Bos-A	0	1	.000	12	0	0	0	1	12^2	14	2	7	8	15.6	5.68	79	.280	.379	0	—	0	-2	-2	-0	-0.2
Total	9	23	15	.605	337	0	0	0	46	430^1	399	23	135	255	11.5	3.03	115	.245	.308	5	.125	1	25	22	1	4.2
● ROBERTO HERNANDEZ	Hernandez, Roberto Manuel (Rodriguez) b: 11/11/64, Santurce, P.R. BR/TR, 6'4", 235 lbs. Deb: 9/2/91																									
1991	Chi-A	1	0	1.000	9	3	0	0	0	15	18	1	7	6	15.0	7.80	51	.290	.362	0	—	0	-6	-6	-0	-0.4
1992	Chi-A	7	3	.700	43	0	0	0	12	71	45	4	20	68	8.7	1.65	234	.180	.252	0	—	0	18	17	-0	2.8
1993	*Chi-A	3	4	.429	70	0	0	0	38	78^2	66	6	20	71	9.8	2.29	183	.228	.277	0	—	0	18	17	0	2.7
1994	Chi-A	4	4	.500	45	0	0	0	14	47^2	44	5	19	50	12.1	4.91	95	.238	.312	0	—	0	-1	-1	-1	-0.3
1995	Chi-A	3	7	.300	60	0	0	0	32	59^2	63	9	28	84	14.2	3.92	114	.266	.351	0	—	0	5	4	-0	1.1
1996	Chi-A★	6	5	.545	72	0	0	0	38	84^2	65	2	38	85	10.9	1.91	248	.208	.293	0	—	0	29	27	-1	5.0

YEAR	TM/L	W	L	PCT	G	GS	CG	SH	SV	IP	H	HR	BB	SO	RAT	ERA	ERA+	OAV	OOB	BH	AVG	PB	PR	/A	PD	TPI
1997	Chi-A	5	1	.833	46	0	0	0	27	48	38	5	24	47	11.8	2.44	180	.216	.313	0	—	0	11	10	0	2.2
	*SF-N	5	2	.714	28	0	0	0	4	32^{2}	29	2	14	35	11.8	2.48	167	.238	.316	1	.500	0	6	6	-0	1.3
1998	TB-A	2	6	.250	67	0	0	0	26	71^{1}	55	5	41	55	12.7	4.04	121	.212	.330	0	—	0	5	7	-0	1.0
Total	8	36	32	.529	440	3	0	0	191	508^{2}	423	39	211	501	11.5	3.01	147	.223	.306	1	.500	0	86	80	-3	15.4

● RUDY HERNANDEZ

Hernandez, Rudolph Albert (Fuentes) b: 12/10/31, Santiago, D.R. BR/TR, 6'3", 185 lbs. Deb: 7/3/60

YEAR	TM/L	W	L	PCT	G	GS	CG	SH	SV	IP	H	HR	BB	SO	RAT	ERA	ERA+	OAV	OOB	BH	AVG	PB	PR	/A	PD	TPI
1960	Was-A	4	1	.800	21	0	0	0	0	34^{2}	34	2	21	22	14.5	4.41	88	.262	.368	1	.167	-0	-2	-2	-0	-0.3
1961	Was-A	0	1	.000	7	0	0	0	0	9	8	0	3	4	11.0	3.00	134	.250	.314	0	—	0	1	1	0	0.1
Total	2	4	2	.667	28	0	0	0	0	43^{2}	42	2	24	26	13.8	4.12	95	.259	.358	1	.167	-0	-1	-1	-0	-0.2

● WALT HERRELL

Herrell, Walter William "Reds" b: 2/19/1889, Rockville, Md. d: 1/23/49, Front Royal, Va. Deb: 6/10/11

YEAR	TM/L	W	L	PCT	G	GS	CG	SH	SV	IP	H	HR	BB	SO	RAT	ERA	ERA+	OAV	OOB	BH	AVG	PB	PR	/A	PD	TPI
1911	Was-A	0	0	—	1	0	0	0	0	2	5	0	2	0	31.5	18.00	18	.556	.636	0	.000	-0	-3	-3	0	0.0

● BOBBY HERRERA

Herrera, Procopio Rodriguez "Tito" (b: Procopio Rodriguez (Herrera)) b: 7/26/26, Nuevo Laredo, Mex BR/TR, 6', 184 lbs. Deb: 4/19/51

YEAR	TM/L	W	L	PCT	G	GS	CG	SH	SV	IP	H	HR	BB	SO	RAT	ERA	ERA+	OAV	OOB	BH	AVG	PB	PR	/A	PD	TPI
1951	StL-A	0	0	—	3	0	0	0	0	2^{1}	6	2	4	1	42.4	27.00	16	.462	.611	0	—	0	-6	-6	-0	0.0

● TROY HERRIAGE

Herriage, William Troy "Dutch" b: 12/20/30, Tipton, Okla. BR/TR, 6'1", 170 lbs. Deb: 4/25/56

YEAR	TM/L	W	L	PCT	G	GS	CG	SH	SV	IP	H	HR	BB	SO	RAT	ERA	ERA+	OAV	OOB	BH	AVG	PB	PR	/A	PD	TPI
1956	KC-A	1	13	.071	31	16	1	0	0	103	135	16	64	59	17.9	6.64	65	.321	.418	3	.120	-1	-28	-26	-2	-3.3

● TOM HERRIN

Herrin, Thomas Edward b: 9/12/29, Shreveport, La. BR/TR, 6'3", 190 lbs. Deb: 4/13/54

YEAR	TM/L	W	L	PCT	G	GS	CG	SH	SV	IP	H	HR	BB	SO	RAT	ERA	ERA+	OAV	OOB	BH	AVG	PB	PR	/A	PD	TPI
1954	Bos-A	1	2	.333	14	1	0	0	0	28^{1}	34	3	22	8	17.8	7.31	56	.315	.431	1	.125	-0	-11	-10	1	-0.9

● ART HERRING

Herring, Arthur L "Red" or "Sandy" b: 3/10/06, Altus, Okla. d: 12/2/95, Marion, Ind. BR/TR, 5'7", 168 lbs. Deb: 9/12/29

YEAR	TM/L	W	L	PCT	G	GS	CG	SH	SV	IP	H	HR	BB	SO	RAT	ERA	ERA+	OAV	OOB	BH	AVG	PB	PR	/A	PD	TPI
1929	Det-A	2	1	.667	4	4	2	0	0	32	38	0	19	15	16.3	4.78	90	.302	.397	3	.214	1	-2	-2	0	0.0
1930	Det-A	3	3	.500	23	6	1	0	0	77^{2}	97	2	36	16	15.8	5.33	90	.315	.392	3	.130	-2	-6	-5	-0	-0.5
1931	Det-A	7	13	.350	35	16	9	0	1	165	186	8	67	64	14.2	4.31	106	.281	.355	11	.200	-1	1	5	2	0.6
1932	Det-A	1	2	.333	12	0	0	0	2	22^{1}	25	2	15	12	16.5	5.24	90	.284	.394	0	.000	-0	-2	-1	0	-0.2
1933	Det-A	1	2	.333	24	3	1	0	0	61	61	6	20	20	12.1	3.84	112	.264	.325	1	.077	-1	3	3	-1	0.0
1934	Bro-N	2	4	.333	14	4	2	0	0	49^{1}	63	2	29	15	16.8	6.20	63	.307	.393	2	.143	1	-12	-13	-0	-1.3
1939	Chi-A	0	0	—	7	0	0	0	0	14^{1}	13	2	5	8	11.9	5.65	84	.250	.328	0	.000	-0	-2	-1	0	0.0
1944	Bro-N	3	4	.429	12	6	3	1	1	55^{1}	59	3	17	19	12.5	3.42	104	.277	.333	3	.200	0	1	1	0	0.2
1945	Bro-N	7	4	.636	22	15	7	2	2	124	103	11	43	34	10.8	3.48	108	.222	.292	4	.095	-2	4	4	1	0.2
1946	Bro-N	7	2	.778	35	2	0	0	5	86	91	2	29	34	12.7	3.35	101	.277	.338	4	.182	0	1	0	2	0.2
1947	Pit-N	1	3	.250	11	0	0	0	2	10^{2}	18	3	4	6	18.6	8.44	50	.360	.407	0	.000	-0	-5	-5	-0	-1.8
Total	11	34	38	.472	199	56	25	3	13	697^{2}	754	41	284	243	13.6	4.32	96	.276	.349	31	.149	-4	-18	-14	4	-2.6

● HERB HERRING

Herring, Herbert Lee b: 7/22/1891, Danville, Ark. d: 4/22/64, Tucson, Ariz. BR/TR, 5'11", 178 lbs. Deb: 9/4/12

YEAR	TM/L	W	L	PCT	G	GS	CG	SH	SV	IP	H	HR	BB	SO	RAT	ERA	ERA+	OAV	OOB	BH	AVG	PB	PR	/A	PD	TPI
1912	Was-A	0	0	—	1	0	0	0	0	1	1	0	1	0	18.0	0.00	—	.250	.400	0	—	0	0	0	-0	0.0

● LEFTY HERRING

Herring, Silas Clarke b: 3/4/1880, Philadelphia, Pa. d: 2/11/65, Massapequa, N.Y. BL/TL, 5'11", 160 lbs. Deb: 5/16/1899 ♦

YEAR	TM/L	W	L	PCT	G	GS	CG	SH	SV	IP	H	HR	BB	SO	RAT	ERA	ERA+	OAV	OOB	BH	AVG	PB	PR	/A	PD	TPI
1899	Was-N	0	0	—	2	0	0	0	0	2	0	0	2	0	9.0	0.00	—	.000	.250	1	1.000		1	1	0	0.1

● BILL HERRING

Herring, William Francis "Smoke" b: 10/31/1893, New York, N.Y. d: 9/10/62, Honesdale, Pa. BR/TR, 6'3", 185 lbs. Deb: 6/26/15

YEAR	TM/L	W	L	PCT	G	GS	CG	SH	SV	IP	H	HR	BB	SO	RAT	ERA	ERA+	OAV	OOB	BH	AVG	PB	PR	/A	PD	TPI
1915	Bro-F	0	0	—	3	0	0	0	0	3	5	1	2	3	24.0	15.00	18	.385	.500	0	—	0	-4	-4	-0	0.0

● LEROY HERRMANN

Herrmann, Leroy George b: 2/27/06, Steward, Ill. d: 7/3/72, Livermore, Cal. BR/TR, 5'10", 185 lbs. Deb: 7/30/32

YEAR	TM/L	W	L	PCT	G	GS	CG	SH	SV	IP	H	HR	BB	SO	RAT	ERA	ERA+	OAV	OOB	BH	AVG	PB	PR	/A	PD	TPI
1932	Chi-N	2	1	.667	7	0	0	0	0	12^{1}	18	0	9	5	19.2	6.39	59	.346	.443	1	.500	0	-4	-4	-0	-0.7
1933	Chi-N	0	1	.000	9	1	0	0	1	21	26	3	8	4	16.3	5.57	59	.299	.384	1	.167	-0	-5	-5	-1	-0.4
1935	Cin-N	3	5	.375	29	8	2	0	0	108	124	9	31	30	13.6	3.58	111	.297	.357	8	.267	1	5	5	-0	0.4
Total	3	5	7	.417	45	9	2	0	1	141^{2}	168	12	48	39	14.5	4.13	93	.302	.370	10	.263	1	-4	-4	-1	-0.7

● MARTY HERRMANN

Herrmann, Martin John "Lefty" b: 1/10/1893, Oldenburg, Ind. d: 9/11/56, Cincinnati, Ohio BL/TL, 5'10", 150 lbs. Deb: 7/10/18 F

YEAR	TM/L	W	L	PCT	G	GS	CG	SH	SV	IP	H	HR	BB	SO	RAT	ERA	ERA+	OAV	OOB	BH	AVG	PB	PR	/A	PD	TPI
1918	Bro-N	0	0	—	1	0	0	0	0	1	0	0	1	0	9.0	0.00	—	.000	.250	0	—	0	0	0	-0	0.0

● FRANK HERSHEY

Hershey, Frank b: 12/13/1877, Gorham, N.Y. d: 12/15/49, Canandaigua, N.Y. TR , 175 lbs. Deb: 4/20/05

YEAR	TM/L	W	L	PCT	G	GS	CG	SH	SV	IP	H	HR	BB	SO	RAT	ERA	ERA+	OAV	OOB	BH	AVG	PB	PR	/A	PD	TPI
1905	Bos-N	0	1	.000	1	1	0	0	0	4	5	0	2	1	15.8	6.75	46	.313	.389	0	.000	-0	-2	-2	-0	-0.3

● OREL HERSHISER

Hershiser, Orel Leonard Quinton b: 9/16/58, Buffalo, N.Y. BR/TR, 6'3", 192 lbs. Deb: 9/1/83

YEAR	TM/L	W	L	PCT	G	GS	CG	SH	SV	IP	H	HR	BB	SO	RAT	ERA	ERA+	OAV	OOB	BH	AVG	PB	PR	/A	PD	TPI
1983	LA-N	0	0	—	8	0	0	0	1	8	7	1	6	5	14.6	3.38	106	.233	.361	0	—	0	0	0	0	0.0
1984	LA-N	11	8	.579	45	20	8	**4**	2	189^{2}	160	9	50	150	10.2	2.66	133	.225	.279	10	.200	2	20	18	1	2.1
1985	*LA-N	19	3	**.864**	36	34	9	5	0	239^{2}	179	8	68	157	9.5	2.03	171	.206	.268	15	.197	3	42	39	2	4.2
1986	LA-N	14	14	.500	35	35	8	1	0	231^{1}	213	13	86	153	11.8	3.85	90	.243	.314	17	.239	4	-3	-10	1	-0.6
1987	LA-N★	16	16	.500	37	35	10	1	1	**264^{2}**	247	17	74	190	11.2	3.06	130	.247	.305	19	.211	4	30	27	1	**3.6**
1988	*LA-N★	**23**	8	.742	35	34	**15**	**8**	1	**267**	208	18	73	178	9.6	2.26	147	.213	.271	11	.129	-0	**35**	**32**	6	4.5
1989	LA-N☆	15	15	.500	35	33	8	4	0	**256^{2}**	226	9	77	178	10.7	2.31	148	.240	.299	14	.182	3	**34**	**31**	4	**4.6**
1990	LA-N	1	1	.500	4	4	0	0	0	25^{1}	26	1	4	16	11.0	4.26	86	.260	.295	0	.000	-1	-1	-2	-0	-0.2
1991	LA-N	7	2	.778	21	21	0	0	0	112	112	3	32	73	12.0	3.46	104	.259	.317	8	.258	3	3	1	2	0.6
1992	LA-N	10	15	.400	33	33	1	0	0	210^{2}	209	15	69	130	12.2	3.67	94	.257	.322	15	.221	4	-4	-5	3	0.2
1993	LA-N	12	14	.462	33	33	5	1	0	215^{2}	201	17	72	141	11.7	3.59	106	.246	.312	26	.356	10	11	5	3	1.9
1994	LA-N	6	6	.500	21	21	1	0	0	135^{1}	146	15	42	72	12.6	3.79	103	.279	.335	9	.205	2	6	2	2	0.6
1995	*Cle-A	16	6	.727	26	26	1	1	0	167^{1}	151	21	51	111	11.1	3.87	121	.244	.306	0	—	0	16	15	2	2.0
1996	*Cle-A	15	9	.625	33	33	1	0	0	206	238	21	58	125	13.5	4.24	115	.287	.343	0	—	0	17	15	4	1.9
1997	*Cle-A	14	6	.700	32	32	1	0	0	195^{1}	199	26	69	107	12.9	4.47	105	.272	.344	0	.000	-0	2	5	1	0.5
1998	SF-N	11	10	.524	34	34	0	0	0	202	200	22	85	126	13.3	4.41	92	.259	.343	10	.152	1	-4	-8	2	-0.4
Total	16	190	133	.588	468	428	68	25	5	2926^{2}	2722	216	916	1912	11.5	3.33	115	.246	.310	154	.208	34	202	165	33	25.5

● JOE HESKETH

Hesketh, Joseph Thomas b: 2/15/59, Lackawanna, N.Y. BR/TL, 6'2", 170 lbs. Deb: 8/7/84

YEAR	TM/L	W	L	PCT	G	GS	CG	SH	SV	IP	H	HR	BB	SO	RAT	ERA	ERA+	OAV	OOB	BH	AVG	PB	PR	/A	PD	TPI
1984	Mon-N	2	2	.500	11	5	1	1	1	45	38	2	15	32	10.6	1.80	190	.233	.298	1	.100	0	9	8	-0	0.8
1985	Mon-N	10	5	.667	25	25	2	1	0	155^{1}	125	10	45	113	9.8	2.49	136	.222	.280	4	.091	-1	19	16	-1	1.3
1986	Mon-N	6	5	.545	15	15	0	0	0	82^{2}	92	11	31	67	13.6	5.01	74	.283	.349	0	.000	-2	-12	-12	-1	-1.7
1987	Mon-N	0	0	—	18	0	0	0	1	28^{2}	23	2	15	31	12.6	3.14	134	.211	.317	0	.000	-0	3	3	-1	-0.1
1988	Mon-N	4	3	.571	60	0	0	0	9	72^{2}	63	1	35	64	12.1	2.85	126	.242	.332	0	.000	0	5	6	1	0.9
1989	Mon-N	6	4	.600	43	0	0	0	3	48^{1}	54	5	26	44	14.9	5.77	61	.292	.379	1	.500	0	-12	-12	1	-2.3
1990	Mon-N	1	0	1.000	2	0	0	0	0	3	2	0	2	3	12.0	0.00	—	.200	.333	0	—	0	1	1	0	0.4
	Atl-N	0	2	.000	31	0	0	0	5	31	30	5	12	21	12.5	5.81	69	.248	.321	0	.000	-0	-7	-6	-0	-0.6
	Yr	1	2	.333	33	0	0	0	5	34	32	5	14	24	12.4	5.29	76	.244	.322	0	.000	-0	-6	-5	-0	-0.2
	Bos-A	0	4	.000	12	2	0	0	0	25^{2}	37	2	11	26	16.8	3.51	116	.333	.393	0	—	0	1	2	-0	0.1
1991	Bos-A	12	4	.750	39	17	0	0	0	153^{1}	142	19	53	104	11.4	3.29	131	.250	.314	0	—	0	14	17	1	1.6
1992	Bos-A	8	9	.471	30	25	1	0	1	148^{2}	162	15	58	104	13.4	4.36	97	.276	.343	0	—	0	-7	-2	0	-0.2
1993	Bos-A	3	4	.429	28	5	0	0	1	53^{1}	62	4	29	34	15.4	5.06	91	.294	.379	0	—	0	-4	-3	-0	-0.5
1994	Bos-A	8	5	.615	25	20	0	0	0	114	117	9	46	83	13.0	4.26	118	.267	.340	0	—	0	7	10	-2	0.8
Total	11	60	47	.561	339	114	4	2	21	961^{2}	947	85	378	726	12.5	3.78	107	.259	.330	6	.070	-2	16	26	-2	0.5

● OTTO HESS

Hess, Otto C. b: 10/10/1878, Bern, Switzerland d: 2/25/26, Tucson, Ariz. BL/TL, 6'1", 170 lbs. Deb: 8/3/02 ♦

YEAR	TM/L	W	L	PCT	G	GS	CG	SH	SV	IP	H	HR	BB	SO	RAT	ERA	ERA+	OAV	OOB	BH	AVG	PB	PR	/A	PD	TPI
1902	Cle-A	2	4	.333	7	4	4	0	0	43^{2}	67	0	23	13	18.8	5.98	58	.351	.423	1	.071	-1	-12	-12	1	-1.3
1904	Cle-A	8	7	.533	21	16	15	4	0	151^{1}	134	2	31	64	10.1	1.67	152	.238	.284	12	.120	-3	16	15	-0	1.1
1905	Cle-A	10	15	.400	26	25	22	4	0	213^{2}	179	1	72	109	11.0	3.16	83	.229	.302	44	.254	5	-12	-13	1	-0.9
1906	Cle-A	20	17	.541	43	36	33	7	**3**	333^{2}	274	4	85	167	10.3	1.83	143	.227	.291	31	.201	1	32	**29**	-2	3.3
1907	Cle-A	6	6	.500	17	14	7	0	1	93^{1}	84	1	37	36	12.8	2.89	87	.243	.337	4	.133	0	-4	-4	-1	-0.6
1908	Cle-A	0	0	—	4	0	0	0	0	7	11	0	1	2	15.4	5.14	46	.407	.429	0	.000	-1	-2	-2	0	0.0
1912	Bos-N	12	17	.414	33	31	21	0	0	254	270	3	90	80	13.3	3.76	95	.283	.354	23	.245	3	-10	-5	-4	-0.6
1913	Bos-N	7	17	.292	29	27	19	2	0	218^{1}	231	12	70	80	12.7	3.83	86	.279	.340	26	.313	8	-15	-13	1	-0.5
1914	Bos-N	5	6	.455	14	11	7	1	1	89	89	2	33	24	12.8	3.03	91	.271	.347	11	.234	1	-2	-3	2	0.0

YEAR	TM/L	W	L	PCT	G	GS	CG	SH	SV	IP	H	HR	BB	SO	RAT	ERA	ERA+	OAV	OOB	BH	AVG	PB	PR	/A	PD	TPI
1915	Bos-N	0	1	.000	4	1	1	0	0	14	16	0	6	5	15.4	3.86	67	.286	.375	2	.400	1	-2	-2	-0	-0.1
Total	10	70	90	.438	198	165	129	18	5	1418	1355	25	448	580	12.0	2.98	98	.257	.324	154	.216	14	-11	-12	-2	0.4

● GEORGE HESSELBACHER
Hesselbacher, George Edward b: 1/18/1895, Philadelphia, Pa. d: 2/18/80, Rydal, Pa. BR/TR, 6'2", 175 lbs. Deb: 6/29/16

YEAR	TM/L	W	L	PCT	G	GS	CG	SH	SV	IP	H	HR	BB	SO	RAT	ERA	ERA+	OAV	OOB	BH	AVG	PB	PR	/A	PD	TPI
1916	Phi-A	0	4	.000	6	4	2	0	0	26	37	3	22	6	20.4	7.27	39	.349	.461	1	.125	-0	-13	-13	1	-1.6

● LARRY HESTERFER
Hesterfer, Lawrence b: 6/9/1878, Newark, N.J. d: 9/22/43, Cedar Grove, N.J. BR/TL, 5'8", 145 lbs. Deb: 9/5/01

YEAR	TM/L	W	L	PCT	G	GS	CG	SH	SV	IP	H	HR	BB	SO	RAT	ERA	ERA+	OAV	OOB	BH	AVG	PB	PR	/A	PD	TPI
1901	NY-N	0	1	.000	1	1	1	0	0	6	15	0	3	2	27.0	7.50	44	.469	.514	0	.000	0	-3	-3	-0	-0.3

● JOHNNY HETKI
Hetki, John Edward b: 5/12/22, Leavenworth, Kan. BR/TR, 6'1", 205 lbs. Deb: 9/14/45

YEAR	TM/L	W	L	PCT	G	GS	CG	SH	SV	IP	H	HR	BB	SO	RAT	ERA	ERA+	OAV	OOB	BH	AVG	PB	PR	/A	PD	TPI
1945	Cin-N	1	2	.333	5	2	2	0	0	32^2	28	1	11	9	10.7	3.58	105	.235	.300	1	.091	-1	1	1	1	0.0
1946	Cin-N	6	6	.500	32	11	4	0	1	126^1	121	3	31	41	10.9	2.99	112	.253	.300	11	.333	3	6	5	-1	0.7
1947	Cin-N	3	4	.429	37	5	2	0	0	96	110	7	48	33	14.9	5.81	71	.287	.368	6	.222	1	-19	-18	0	-1.1
1948	Cin-N	0	1	.000	3	0	0	0	0	6^2	8	0	3	3	14.9	9.45	41	.286	.355	0	.000	0	-4	-4	-0	-0.5
1950	Cin-N	1	2	.333	22	1	0	0	0	53	53	9	27	21	14.1	5.09	83	.265	.361	2	.222	0	-6	-5	-0	-0.3
1952	StL-A	0	1	.000	3	1	0	0	0	9^1	15	2	2	4	16.4	3.86	101	.357	.386	0	.000	0	-0	0	0	0.0
1953	Pit-N	3	6	.333	54	2	0	0	3	118^1	120	9	33	37	11.7	3.95	113	.266	.318	5	.208	1	4	7	0	0.7
1954	Pit-N	4	4	.500	58	1	0	0	9	83	102	11	30	27	14.3	4.99	84	.297	.353	2	.222	-0	-8	-7	-1	-0.9
Total	8	18	26	.409	214	23	8	0	13	525^1	557	42	185	175	12.8	4.39	91	.272	.335	27	.235	5	-26	-23	-2	-1.4

● ERIC HETZEL
Hetzel, Eric Paul b: 9/25/63, Crowley, La. BR/TR, 6'3", 175 lbs. Deb: 7/1/89

YEAR	TM/L	W	L	PCT	G	GS	CG	SH	SV	IP	H	HR	BB	SO	RAT	ERA	ERA+	OAV	OOB	BH	AVG	PB	PR	/A	PD	TPI
1989	Bos-A	2	3	.400	12	11	0	0	0	50^1	61	7	28	33	16.3	6.26	66	.296	.386	0	—	0	-13	-12	-1	-1.2
1990	Bos-A	1	4	.200	9	8	0	0	0	35	39	3	21	20	15.7	5.91	69	.281	.379	0	—	0	-8	-7	-0	-1.0
Total	2	3	7	.300	21	19	0	0	0	85^1	100	10	49	53	16.0	6.12	67	.290	.383	0	—	0	-21	-19	-2	-2.2

● ED HEUSSER
Heusser, Edward Burlton "The Wild Elk Of The Wasatch"
b: 5/7/09, Salt Lake County, Utah d: 3/1/56, Aurora, Col. BB/TR, 6'0.5", 187 lbs. Deb: 4/25/35

YEAR	TM/L	W	L	PCT	G	GS	CG	SH	SV	IP	H	HR	BB	SO	RAT	ERA	ERA+	OAV	OOB	BH	AVG	PB	PR	/A	PD	TPI
1935	StL-N	5	5	.500	33	11	2	0	2	123^1	125	5	27	39	11.2	2.92	140	.263	.305	4	.118	-1	15	16	-1	1.0
1936	StL-N	7	3	.700	42	3	0	0	3	104^1	130	6	38	26	14.8	5.43	73	.310	.373	7	.269	3	-16	-17	-0	-1.3
1938	Phi-N	0	0	—	1	0	0	0	0	1	2	1	1	0	27.0	27.00	14	.400	.500	0	—	0	-3	-3	-0	0.0
1940	Phi-A	6	13	.316	41	6	2	0	5	110	144	11	42	39	15.4	4.99	89	.308	.368	5	.167	1	-7	-7	1	-0.9
1943	Cin-N	4	3	.571	26	10	2	1	0	91	97	4	23	28	11.9	3.46	96	.275	.319	5	.185	-1	-1	-1	-1	-0.3
1944	Cin-N	13	11	.542	30	23	17	4	2	192^2	165	9	42	42	9.7	**2.38**	**146**	.231	.275	15	.217	1	26	24	-1	2.9
1945	Cin-N	11	16	.407	31	30	18	4	1	223	248	10	60	56	12.6	3.71	101	.280	.328	19	.247	4	2	1	0	0.6
1946	Cin-N	7	14	.333	29	21	9	1	2	167^2	167	11	39	47	11.1	3.22	104	.260	.304	11	.208	2	4	2	-2	0.2
1948	Phi-N	3	2	.600	33	0	0	0	3	74	89	9	28	22	14.2	4.99	79	.299	.359	3	.158	-1	-8	-9	0	-0.6
Total	9	56	67	.455	266	104	50	10	18	1087	1167	66	300	299	12.3	3.69	101	.274	.324	69	.206	8	11	6	-5	1.6

● JOE HEVING
Heving, Joseph William b: 9/2/1900, Covington, Ky. d: 4/11/70, Covington, Ky. BR/TR, 6'1", 185 lbs. Deb: 4/29/30 F

YEAR	TM/L	W	L	PCT	G	GS	CG	SH	SV	IP	H	HR	BB	SO	RAT	ERA	ERA+	OAV	OOB	BH	AVG	PB	PR	/A	PD	TPI
1930	NY-N	7	5	.583	41	2	0	0	6	89^2	109	7	27	37	13.8	5.22	91	.309	.360	5	.227	-0	-2	-5	4	-0.3
1931	NY-N	1	6	.143	22	0	0	0	3	42^1	48	4	11	26	13.0	4.89	76	.277	.328	1	.125	-0	-5	-6	1	-0.9
1933	Chi-A	7	5	.583	40	6	3	1	6	118	113	6	27	47	10.8	2.67	159	.249	.295	8	.211	0	21	21	0	2.1
1934	Chi-A	1	7	.125	33	2	0	0	4	88	133	12	48	40	18.8	7.26	65	.343	.419	5	.185	1	-27	-25	1	-1.9
1937	Cle-A	8	4	.667	40	0	0	0	5	72^2	92	6	30	35	15.4	4.83	95	.311	.378	5	.263	0	-2	-2	1	-0.1
1938	Cle-A	1	1	.500	3	0	0	0	0	6	10	0	5	0	22.5	9.00	52	.370	.469	0	.000	-0	-3	-3	-0	-0.7
	Bos-A	8	1	.889	16	11	7	1	2	82	94	5	22	34	12.8	3.73	132	.283	.330	4	.133	-1	10	11	2	1.1
	Yr	9	2	.818	19	11	7	1	2	88	104	5	27	34	13.5	4.09	120	.290	.341	4	.129	-2	7	8	2	0.4
1939	Bos-A	11	3	.786	46	5	1	0	7	107	124	8	34	43	13.5	3.70	128	.295	.350	6	.188	-1	**11**	**12**	0	1.4
1940	Bos-A	12	7	.632	39	7	4	0	3	119	129	7	42	55	13.2	4.01	112	.272	.335	8	.200	0	5	6	0	0.9
1941	Cle-A	5	2	.714	27	3	2	1	5	70^2	63	2	31	18	12.1	2.29	172	.240	.323	0	.000	-1	15	13	2	1.5
1942	Cle-A	5	3	.625	27	2	0	0	3	46^1	52	4	25	13	15.3	4.86	71	.278	.369	0	.000	-1	-6	-7	0	-1.3
1943	Cle-A	1	1	.500	30	1	0	0	9	72	58	1	34	34	11.8	2.75	113	.230	.326	1	.071	-0	4	3	2	0.3
1944	Cle-A	8	3	.727	**63**	1	0	0	10	119^2	106	2	41	46	11.2	1.96	169	.239	.307	4	.182	-1	**20**	18	1	2.0
1945	Bos-N	1	0	1.000	3	0	0	0	0	5^1	5	0	3	1	15.2	3.38	114	.294	.429	0	.000	-0	0	0	1	0.1
Total	13	76	48	.613	430	40	17	3	63	1038^2	1136	64	380	429	13.3	3.90	108	.279	.344	47	.170	-4	40	36	14	4.2

● JAKE HEWITT
Hewitt, Charles Jacob b: 6/6/1870, Maidsville, W.Va. d: 5/18/59, Morgantown, W.Va. BL/TL, 5'7", 150 lbs. Deb: 8/6/1895

YEAR	TM/L	W	L	PCT	G	GS	CG	SH	SV	IP	H	HR	BB	SO	RAT	ERA	ERA+	OAV	OOB	BH	AVG	PB	PR	/A	PD	TPI
1895	Pit-N	1	0	1.000	4	2	1	0	2	13	13	0	2	4	11.1	4.15	109	.255	.296	1	.167	-1	1	1	-0	0.0

● GREG HEYDEMAN
Heydeman, Gregory George b: 1/2/52, Carmel, Cal. BR/TR, 6', 180 lbs. Deb: 9/2/73

YEAR	TM/L	W	L	PCT	G	GS	CG	SH	SV	IP	H	HR	BB	SO	RAT	ERA	ERA+	OAV	OOB	BH	AVG	PB	PR	/A	PD	TPI
1973	LA-N	0	0	—	1	0	0	0	0	2	2	0	1	1	18.0	4.50	76	.222	.364	0	—	0	-0	-0	-0	0.0

● JOHN HEYNER
Heyner, John b: Hyde Park, Ill. Deb: 8/19/1890

YEAR	TM/L	W	L	PCT	G	GS	CG	SH	SV	IP	H	HR	BB	SO	RAT	ERA	ERA+	OAV	OOB	BH	AVG	PB	PR	/A	PD	TPI
1890	Pit-N	0	0	—	1	0	0	0	0	4	7	2	5	1	27.0	13.50	24	.368	.500	0	.000	-0	-4	-5	0	0.0

● GREG HIBBARD
Hibbard, James Gregory b: 9/13/64, New Orleans, La. BL/TL, 6', 190 lbs. Deb: 5/31/89

YEAR	TM/L	W	L	PCT	G	GS	CG	SH	SV	IP	H	HR	BB	SO	RAT	ERA	ERA+	OAV	OOB	BH	AVG	PB	PR	/A	PD	TPI
1989	Chi-A	6	7	.462	23	23	2	0	0	137^1	142	5	41	55	12.1	3.21	118	.268	.323	0	—	0	10	9	1	0.9
1990	Chi-A	14	9	.609	33	33	3	1	0	211	202	11	55	92	11.2	3.16	121	.255	.308	0	—	0	18	16	-1	1.6
1991	Chi-A	11	11	.500	32	29	5	0	0	194	196	23	57	71	11.8	4.31	92	.266	.320	0	—	0	-5	-7	-1	-0.8
1992	Chi-A	10	7	.588	31	28	0	0	1	176	187	17	57	69	12.8	4.40	88	.277	.340	0	—	0	-9	-11	2	-0.7
1993	Chi-N	15	11	.577	31	31	1	0	0	191	209	19	47	82	12.2	3.96	101	.286	.332	6	.092	-3	2	1	-1	-0.3
1994	Sea-A	1	5	.167	15	14	0	0	0	80^2	115	11	31	39	16.5	6.69	73	.328	.385	0	—	0	-17	-16	1	-0.9
Total	6	57	50	.533	165	158	11	1	1	990	1051	86	288	408	12.4	4.05	98	.275	.330	6	.092	-3	-1	-9	1	-0.2

● JOHN HIBBARD
Hibbard, John Denison b: 12/2/1864, Chicago, Ill. d: 11/17/37, Hollywood, Cal. TL, Deb: 7/31/1884

YEAR	TM/L	W	L	PCT	G	GS	CG	SH	SV	IP	H	HR	BB	SO	RAT	ERA	ERA+	OAV	OOB	BH	AVG	PB	PR	/A	PD	TPI
1884	Chi-N	1	1	.500	2	2	2	1	0	17	18	1	9	4	14.3	2.65	118	.300	.391	0	.000	-1	1	1	-0	0.0

● BRYAN HICKERSON
Hickerson, Bryan David b: 10/13/63, Bemidji, Minn. BL/TL, 6'2", 203 lbs. Deb: 7/25/91

YEAR	TM/L	W	L	PCT	G	GS	CG	SH	SV	IP	H	HR	BB	SO	RAT	ERA	ERA+	OAV	OOB	BH	AVG	PB	PR	/A	PD	TPI
1991	SF-N	2	2	.500	17	6	0	0	0	50	53	3	17	43	12.6	3.60	99	.275	.333	0	.000	-1	0	-0	-1	-0.3
1992	SF-N	5	3	.625	61	1	0	0	0	87^1	74	7	21	68	9.9	3.09	107	.236	.286	0	.000	-0	4	2	-2	-0.1
1993	SF-N	7	5	.583	47	15	0	0	0	120^1	137	14	39	69	13.2	4.26	92	.291	.347	4	.143	-0	-3	-5	-2	-0.6
1994	SF-N	4	8	.333	28	14	0	0	1	98^1	118	20	38	59	14.4	5.40	74	.301	.364	5	.185	1	-13	-15	-2	-1.7
1995	Chi-N	2	3	.400	38	0	0	0	1	31^2	36	3	15	28	14.5	6.82	60	.283	.359	1	.500	1	-9	-10	-0	-1.3
	Col-N	1	0	1.000	18	0	0	0	0	16^2	33	5	13	12	25.4	11.88	45	.407	.495	1	1.000	1	-14	-12	-1	-0.6
	Yr	3	3	.500	56	0	0	0	1	48^1	69	8	28	40	18.2	8.57	53	.332	.414	2	.667	1	-24	-22	-1	-1.9
Total	5	21	21	.500	209	36	0	0	2	404^1	451	52	143	279	13.3	4.72	81	.286	.347	11	.149	1	-35	-40	-7	-4.6

● JIM HICKEY
Hickey, James Robert "Sid" b: 10/22/20, N.Abington, Mass. d: 9/20/97, Manchester, Conn. BR/TR, 6'1", 204 lbs. Deb: 4/25/42

YEAR	TM/L	W	L	PCT	G	GS	CG	SH	SV	IP	H	HR	BB	SO	RAT	ERA	ERA+	OAV	OOB	BH	AVG	PB	PR	/A	PD	TPI
1942	Bos-N	0	1	.000	1	1	0	0	0	1^1	4	1	2	0	40.5	20.25	16	.500	.600	0	.000	-0	-3	-3	-0	-1.0
1944	Bos-N	0	0	—	8	0	0	0	0	9^1	15	0	5	3	20.3	4.82	79	.366	.447	0	.000	-0	-1	-1	0	0.0
Total	2	0	1	.000	9	1	0	0	0	10^2	19	1	7	3	22.8	6.75	56	.388	.474	0	.000	-0	-4	-4	0	-1.0

● JACK HICKEY
Hickey, John William b: 11/3/1881, Minneapolis, Minn. d: 12/28/41, Seattle, Wash. BR/TL, 5'10", 170 lbs. Deb: 4/16/04

YEAR	TM/L	W	L	PCT	G	GS	CG	SH	SV	IP	H	HR	BB	SO	RAT	ERA	ERA+	OAV	OOB	BH	AVG	PB	PR	/A	PD	TPI
1904	Cle-A	0	1	.000	2	2	1	0	0	12^1	14	0	11	5	18.2	7.30	35	.286	.417	0	.000	-1	-6	-7	0	-0.5

● KEVIN HICKEY
Hickey, Kevin John b: 2/25/57, Chicago, Ill. BL/TL, 6'1", 200 lbs. Deb: 4/14/81

YEAR	TM/L	W	L	PCT	G	GS	CG	SH	SV	IP	H	HR	BB	SO	RAT	ERA	ERA+	OAV	OOB	BH	AVG	PB	PR	/A	PD	TPI
1981	Chi-A	0	2	.000	41	0	0	0	3	44^1	38	3	18	17	11.6	3.65	98	.232	.311	0	—	0	0	-0	1	0.2
1982	Chi-A	4	4	.500	60	0	0	0	6	78	73	4	30	38	12.1	3.00	134	.256	.331	0	—	0	9	9	2	1.2
1983	Chi-A	1	2	.333	23	0	0	0	5	20^2	23	5	11	8	14.8	5.23	80	.264	.347	0	—	0	-3	-2	-0	-0.7
1989	Bal-A	2	3	.400	51	0	0	0	2	49^1	38	3	23	28	11.3	2.92	130	.220	.315	0	—	0	5	5	-0	0.5
1990	Bal-A	1	3	.250	37	0	0	0	1	26^1	26	3	13	17	13.3	5.13	74	.265	.351	0	—	0	-4	-4	-0	-0.5
1991	Bal-A	1	0	1.000	19	0	0	0	0	14	15	3	6	10	13.5	9.00	44	.278	.350	0	—	0	-8	-8	-0	-0.5
Total	6	9	14	.391	231	0	0	0	17	232^2	213	21	101	118	12.3	3.91	99	.247	.329	0	—	0	1	-1	2	0.2

YEAR	TM/L	W	L	PCT	G	GS	CG	SH	SV	IP	H	HR	BB	SO	RAT	ERA	ERA+	OAV	OOB	BH	AVG	PB	PR	/A	PD	TPI
● CHARLIE HICKMAN	Hickman, Charles Taylor "Cheerful Charlie" or "Piano Legs" b: 3/4/1876, Taylortown, Dunkard Township, Pa. d: 4/19/34, Morgantown, W.Va. BR/TR, 5'11.5", 215 lbs. Deb: 9/8/1897 ♦																									
1897	*Bos-N	0	0	—	2	0	0	0	1	7^{2}	10	0	5	0	17.6	5.87	76	.313	.405	2	.667	2	-1	-1	0	0.1
1898	Bos-N	1	2	.333	6	3	3	1	2	33	22	0	13	9	9.5	2.18	169	.188	.269	15	.259	0	5	6	-1	0.4
1899	Bos-N	6	0	1.000	11	9	5	2	1	66^{1}	52	3	40	14	13.6	4.48	93	.216	.346	25	.397	6	-5	-2	-1	0.2
1901	NY-N	3	5	.375	9	9	6	0	0	65	76	1	26	11	14.5	4.57	72	.290	.361	113	.278	2	-9	-9	1	-0.7
1902	Cle-A	0	1	.000	1	1	1	0	0	8	11	0	5	1	19.1	7.88	44	.324	.425	161	.378	1	-4	-4	-0	-0.3
1907	Was-A	0	0	—	1	0	0	0	0	5	4	0	5	2	16.2	3.60	67	.222	.391	55	.278	0	-1	-1	1	0.1
Total	6	10	8	.556	30	22	15	3	4	185	175	4	94	37	13.7	4.28	86	.249	.347	1176	.295	11	-14	-12	-1	-0.2
● ERNIE HICKMAN	Hickman, Ernest P. b: 1856, E.St.Louis, Ill. d: 11/19/1891, E.St.Louis, Ill Deb: 6/7/1884																									
1884	KC-U	4	13	.235	17	17	15	0	0	137^{1}	172	5	36	68	13.6	4.52	49	.287	.328	12	.167	-7	-32	-35	-1	-3.6
● JIM HICKMAN	Hickman, James Lucius b: 5/10/37, Henning, Tenn. BR/TR, 6'4", 205 lbs. Deb: 4/14/62 ♦																									
1967	LA-N	0	0	—	1	0	0	0	0	2	2	1	0	0	9.0	4.50	69	.286	.286	16	.163	0	-0	-0	-0	0.0
● JESSE HICKMAN	Hickman, Jesse Owens b: 2/18/39, Lecompte, La. BR/TR, 6'2", 186 lbs. Deb: 6/5/65																									
1965	KC-A	0	1	.000	12	0	0	0	0	15^{1}	9	3	8	16	10.0	5.87	59	.184	.298	0	—	0	-4	-4	-0	-0.3
1966	KC-A	0	0	—	1	0	0	0	0	1	0	0	1	0	9.0	0.00	—	.000	.333	0	—	0	0	0	-0	0.0
Total	2	0	1	.000	13	0	0	0	0	16^{1}	9	3	9	16	9.9	5.51	63	.176	.300	0	—	0	-4	-4	-0	-0.3
● KIRBY HIGBE	Higbe, Walter Kirby b: 4/8/15, Columbia, S.C. d: 5/6/85, Columbia, S.C. BR/TR, 5'11", 190 lbs. Deb: 10/3/37																									
1937	Chi-N	1	0	1.000	1	0	0	0	0	5	4	1	1	2	9.0	5.40	74	.182	.217	0	.000	-0	-1	-1	-0	-0.2
1938	Chi-N	0	0	—	2	2	0	0	0	10	10	1	6	4	14.4	5.40	71	.263	.364	0	.000	-0	-2	-2	1	0.0
1939	Chi-N	2	1	.667	9	2	0	0	0	22^{2}	12	0	22	16	13.5	3.18	124	.158	.347	2	.286	1	2	2	-0	0.3
	Phi-N	10	14	.417	34	26	14	1	2	187^{1}	208	10	101	79	15.3	4.85	83	.283	.378	11	.167	-2	-19	-18	-4	-2.6
	Yr	12	15	.444	43	28	14	1	2	210	220	10	123	95	15.1	4.67	86	.272	.374	13	.178	-2	-18	-16	-4	-2.3
1940	Phi-N☆	14	19	.424	41	36	20	1	1	283	242	12	121	**137**	11.6	3.72	105	.232	.313	17	.165	-2	4	6	-1	0.4
1941	*Bro-N	**22**	9	.710	**48**	39	19	2	3	298	244	17	132	121	11.5	3.14	117	.220	.306	21	.188	1	16	17	-5	1.3
1942	Bro-N	16	11	.593	38	32	13	2	0	221^{2}	180	17	106	115	11.7	3.25	100	.223	.315	8	.104	-4	2	0	-1	-0.6
1943	Bro-N	13	10	.565	35	27	8	1	0	185	189	4	95	108	14.1	3.70	91	.264	.354	9	.138	-2	-6	-7	-1	-1.1
1946	Bro-N★	17	8	.680	42	29	11	3	1	210^{2}	178	6	107	134	12.2	3.03	111	.229	.323	10	.130	-4	9	8	1	0.6
1947	Bro-N	2	0	1.000	4	3	0	0	0	15^{2}	18	0	12	10	17.8	5.17	80	.295	.419	1	.200	0	-2	-2	0	-0.2
	Pit-N	11	17	.393	46	30	10	1	5	225	204	22	110	99	12.7	3.72	113	.240	.329	10	.139	-1	8	13	-4	0.9
	Yr	13	17	.433	50	33	10	1	5	240^{2}	222	22	122	109	13.0	3.81	111	.243	.334	11	.143	-1	7	11	-4	0.7
1948	Pit-N	8	7	.533	56	8	3	0	10	158	140	11	83	86	12.9	3.36	121	.240	.337	10	.208	1	10	12	-1	1.2
1949	Pit-N	0	2	.000	7	1	0	0	0	15^{1}	25	2	12	5	21.7	13.50	31	.379	.474	0	.000	-0	-16	-16	0	-1.6
	NY-N	2	0	1.000	37	2	0	0	2	80^{1}	72	12	41	38	12.8	3.47	115	.242	.335	1	.067	-0	5	5	-1	0.0
	Yr	2	2	.500	44	3	0	0	2	95^{2}	97	14	53	43	14.2	5.08	79	.266	.361	1	.056	-1	-11	-11	-1	-1.6
1950	NY-N	0	3	.000	18	1	0	0	0	34^{2}	37	2	30	17	17.4	4.93	83	.285	.419	1	.250	0	-3	-3	-1	-0.1
Total	12	118	101	.539	418	238	98	11	24	1952^{1}	1763	117	979	971	12.8	3.69	102	.241	.333	101	.153	-14	7	14	-16	-1.7
● IRV HIGGINBOTHAM	Higginbotham, Irving Clinton b: 4/26/1882, Homer, Neb. d: 6/12/59, Seattle, Wash. BR/TR, 6'1", 196 lbs. Deb: 8/11/06																									
1906	StL-N	1	4	.200	7	6	4	0	0	47^{1}	50	1	11	14	11.8	3.23	81	.266	.310	4	.222	0	-3	-3	1	-0.2
1908	StL-N	3	8	.273	19	11	7	1	0	107	113	0	33	38	12.5	3.20	74	.270	.328	5	.132	-1	-10	-10	-1	-1.3
1909	StL-N	1	0	1.000	3	1	1	0	0	11^{1}	5	0	2	2	5.6	1.59	159	.143	.189	0	.000	-0	1	1	-1	0.0
	Chi-N	5	2	.714	19	6	4	0	1	78	64	0	20	32	10.0	2.19	116	.213	.269	6	.231	1	4	3	-1	0.2
	Yr	6	2	.750	22	7	5	0	1	89^{1}	69	0	22	34	9.5	2.12	120	.205	.260	6	.207	0	5	4	-2	0.2
Total	3	10	14	.417	48	24	16	1	1	243^{2}	232	1	66	86	11.3	2.81	88	.246	.300	15	.176	-1	-8	-9	-2	-1.3
● DENNIS HIGGINS	Higgins, Dennis Dean b: 8/4/39, Jefferson City, Mo. BR/TR, 6'4", 190 lbs. Deb: 4/12/66																									
1966	Chi-A	1	0	1.000	42	1	0	0	5	93	66	9	33	86	10.1	2.52	126	.202	.286	3	.176	0	9	7	1	0.2
1967	Chi-A	1	2	.333	9	0	0	0	0	12^{1}	13	0	10	8	19.0	5.84	53	.271	.426	0	.000	-0	-4	-4	0	-0.9
1968	Was-A	4	4	.500	59	0	0	0	13	99^{2}	81	8	46	66	11.7	3.25	90	.226	.319	2	.133	-0	-3	-4	-1	-0.6
1969	Was-A	10	9	.526	55	0	0	0	16	85^{1}	79	7	56	71	14.6	3.48	100	.252	.371	1	.091	-1	1	-0	-1	-0.2
1970	Cle-A	4	6	.400	58	0	0	0	11	90^{1}	82	8	54	82	13.7	3.99	99	.248	.358	3	.250	1	-3	-0	1	0.1
1971	StL-N	1	0	1.000	3	0	0	0	0	7	6	0	2	6	10.3	3.86	93	.240	.296	0	.000	-0	-0	-0	0	0.0
1972	StL-N	1	2	.333	15	1	0	0	1	22^{2}	19	0	22	20	16.3	3.97	86	.226	.387	0	.000	-0	-1	-1	-0	-0.2
Total	7	22	23	.489	241	2	0	0	46	410^{1}	346	32	223	339	12.8	3.42	98	.233	.340	9	.155	0	-0	-3	-1	-1.6
● EDDIE HIGGINS	Higgins, Thomas Edward "Doc" or "Irish" b: 3/18/1888, Nevada, Ill. d: 2/14/59, Elgin, Ill. BR/TR, 6'0.5", 174 lbs. Deb: 5/14/09																									
1909	StL-N	3	3	.500	16	5	5	0	0	66	68	4	17	15	11.7	4.50	56	.273	.322	4	.190	-0	-14	-14	0	-1.2
1910	StL-N	0	1	.000	2	0	0	0	0	10^{1}	15	0	7	1	19.2	4.35	68	.349	.440	2	.400	1	-2	-2	1	0.0
Total	2	3	4	.429	18	5	5	0	0	76^{1}	83	4	24	16	12.7	4.48	58	.284	.341	6	.231	1	-15	-16	1	-1.2
● ED HIGH	High, Edward T. "Lefty" b: 12/26/1876, Baltimore, Md. d: 2/10/26, Baltimore, Md. TL , Deb: 7/4/01																									
1901	Det-A	1	0	1.000	4	1	1	0	0	18	21	0	6	4	14.0	3.50	110	.288	.350	0	.000	-1	0	1	-0	0.0
● TEDDY HIGUERA	Higuera, Teodoro Valenzuela (Valenzuela) b: 11/9/58, Los Mochis, Mexico BB/TL, 5'10", 178 lbs. Deb: 4/23/85																									
1985	Mil-A	15	8	.652	32	30	7	2	0	212^{1}	186	22	63	127	10.7	3.90	107	.235	.293	0	—	0	6	6	-3	0.4
1986	Mil-A★	20	11	.645	34	34	15	4	0	248^{1}	226	26	74	207	11.0	2.79	155	.241	.299	0	—	0	38	42	-1	4.8
1987	Mil-A	18	10	.643	35	35	14	3	0	261^{2}	236	24	87	240	11.2	3.85	119	.241	.304	0	—	0	18	21	-2	1.6
1988	Mil-A	16	9	.640	31	31	8	1	0	227^{1}	168	15	59	192	**9.2**	2.45	162	.207	**.265**	0	—	0	**38**	38	1	4.3
1989	Mil-A	9	6	.600	22	22	2	1	0	135^{1}	125	9	48	91	11.8	3.46	111	.248	.318	0	—	0	6	6	-2	0.4
1990	Mil-A	11	10	.524	27	27	4	1	0	170	167	16	50	129	11.6	3.76	103	.256	.312	0	—	0	3	2	-1	0.2
1991	Mil-A	3	2	.600	7	6	0	0	0	36^{1}	37	2	10	33	11.9	4.46	89	.262	.316	0	—	0	-1	-2	-0	-0.2
1993	Mil-A	1	3	.250	8	8	0	0	0	30	43	4	16	27	18.0	7.20	59	.333	.411	0	—	0	-10	-10	-1	-1.1
1994	Mil-A	1	5	.167	17	12	0	0	0	58^{2}	74	13	36	35	17.2	7.06	71	.311	.406	0	—	0	-15	-13	0	-1.1
Total	9	94	64	.595	213	205	50	12	0	1380	1262	131	443	1081	11.3	3.61	116	.243	.306	0	—	0	83	90	-9	9.3
● WHITEY HILCHER	Hilcher, Walter Frank b: 2/28/09, Chicago, Ill. d: 11/21/62, Minneapolis, Minn. BR/TR, 6', 174 lbs. Deb: 9/17/31																									
1931	Cin-N	0	1	.000	2	1	0	0	0	12	16	0	4	5	15.8	3.00	125	.320	.382	0	.000	-1	1	1	-0	0.0
1932	Cin-N	0	3	.000	11	2	0	0	0	18^{2}	24	3	10	4	16.4	7.71	50	.316	.395	1	.333	1	-8	-8	0	-1.0
1935	Cin-N	2	0	1.000	4	2	1	1	0	19^{1}	19	0	5	9	11.2	2.79	142	.264	.312	1	.167	-0	3	3	1	0.3
1936	Cin-N	1	2	.333	14	1	0	0	0	35	44	3	14	10	15.2	6.17	62	.299	.364	0	.000	-1	-8	-9	-1	-0.8
Total	4	3	6	.333	31	6	1	1	0	85	103	6	33	28	14.6	5.29	73	.299	.363	2	.095	-2	-13	-14	-0	-1.5
● ORAL HILDEBRAND	Hildebrand, Oral Clyde b: 4/7/07, Indianapolis, Ind. d: 9/8/77, Southport, Ind. BR/TR, 6'3", 175 lbs. Deb: 9/8/31																									
1931	Cle-A	2	1	.667	5	2	2	0	0	26^{2}	25	0	13	6	13.8	4.39	105	.243	.345	2	.182	-1	-0	1	-0	0.0
1932	Cle-A	8	6	.571	27	15	7	0	0	129^{1}	124	7	62	49	12.9	3.69	129	.249	.333	7	.146	-3	11	15	-2	0.9
1933	Cle-A☆	16	11	.593	36	31	15	**6**	0	220^{1}	205	8	88	90	12.0	3.76	118	.245	.318	16	.190	-1	13	17	-0	1.6
1934	Cle-A	11	9	.550	33	28	10	1	1	198	225	14	99	72	14.9	4.50	101	.282	.364	13	.171	-1	-0	1	0	0.0
1935	Cle-A	9	8	.529	34	20	8	0	5	171^{1}	171	12	63	49	12.4	3.94	114	.263	.331	9	.164	-2	10	11	-0	0.8
1936	Cle-A	10	11	.476	36	21	9	0	4	174^{2}	197	10	83	65	14.6	4.90	103	.283	.362	12	.190	0	3	3	-1	0.2
1937	StL-A	8	17	.320	30	27	12	1	1	201^{1}	228	18	87	75	14.2	5.14	94	.284	.356	14	.200	-1	-12	-7	-1	-0.8
1938	StL-A	8	10	.444	23	23	10	0	0	163	194	18	73	66	14.9	5.69	87	.297	.370	15	.254	1	-16	-13	-3	-1.3
1939	*NY-A	10	4	.714	21	15	7	1	2	126^{2}	102	11	41	50	10.2	3.06	143	.219	.284	8	.182	-1	22	18	-1	1.6
1940	NY-A	1	1	.500	13	0	0	0	0	19^{1}	19	1	14	5	15.8	1.86	217	.268	.395	0	.000	-0	5	5	-0	0.4
Total	10	83	78	.516	258	182	80	9	13	1430^{2}	1490	99	623	527	13.4	4.35	107	.267	.343	96	.187	-9	36	50	-8	3.4
● TOM HILGENDORF	Hilgendorf, Thomas Eugene b: 3/10/42, Clinton, Iowa BB/TL, 6'1", 190 lbs. Deb: 8/15/69																									
1969	StL-N	0	0	—	6	0	0	0	2	6^{1}	3	0	2	2	7.1	1.42	251	.150	.227	1	1.000	1	2	2	-0	0.2

YEAR	TM/L	W	L	PCT	G	GS	CG	SH	SV	IP	H	HR	BB	SO	RAT	ERA	ERA+	OAV	OOB	BH	AVG	PB	PR	/A	PD	TPI
1970	StL-N	0	4	.000	23	0	0	0	3	20^2	22	0	13	13	15.2	3.92	105	.272	.372	0	.000	-0	0	0	0	0.1
1972	Cle-A	3	1	.750	19	5	1	0	0	47	51	4	21	25	14.2	2.68	120	.283	.365	1	.077	-1	2	3	0	0.2
1973	Cle-A	5	3	.625	48	1	1	0	6	94^2	87	9	36	58	12.0	3.14	125	.242	.316	0	—	0	7	8	1	0.8
1974	Cle-A	4	3	.571	35	0	0	0	3	48^1	58	6	17	23	14.2	4.84	75	.302	.362	0	—	0	-7	-7	0	-0.9
1975	Phi-N	7	3	.700	53	0	0	0	0	96^2	81	6	38	52	11.2	2.14	174	.230	.307	3	.250	1	16	17	1	1.9
Total	6	19	14	.576	184	6	2	0	14	313^2	302	25	127	173	12.5	3.04	122	.255	.331	5	.185	1	20	24	2	2.3

● CARMEN HILL
Hill, Carmen Proctor "Specs" or "Bunker" b: 10/1/1895, Royalton, Minn. d: 1/1/90, Indianapolis, Ind. BR/TR, 6'1", 180 lbs. Deb: 8/24/15

YEAR	TM/L	W	L	PCT	G	GS	CG	SH	SV	IP	H	HR	BB	SO	RAT	ERA	ERA+	OAV	OOB	BH	AVG	PB	PR	/A	PD	TPI
1915	Pit-N	2	1	.667	8	3	2	1	0	47	42	0	13	24	10.9	1.15	238	.255	.317	2	.154	0	8	8	1	0.7
1916	Pit-N	0	0	—	2	0	0	0	0	6^1	11	0	5	5	24.2	8.53	31	.611	.708	0	—	0	-4	-4	-0	0.0
1918	Pit-N	2	3	.400	6	4	3	0	0	43^2	24	0	17	15	8.5	1.24	232	.160	.246	2	.167	0	7	8	0	1.1
1919	Pit-N	0	0	—	4	0	0	0	0	5	12	0	1	1	23.4	9.00	33	.480	.500	0	—	0	-3	-3	0	0.0
1922	NY-N	2	1	.667	8	4	0	0	0	28^1	33	0	5	6	12.1	4.76	84	.295	.325	2	.182	-0	-2	-2	1	-0.2
1926	Pit-N	3	3	.500	6	6	4	1	0	39^2	42	2	9	8	12.0	3.40	116	.288	.338	3	.176	-1	2	2	1	0.4
1927	*Pit-N	22	11	.667	43	31	22	2	3	277^2	260	12	80	95	11.2	3.24	127	.249	.305	22	.212	2	21	27	1	3.2
1928	Pit-N	16	10	.615	36	31	16	1	2	237	229	16	81	73	11.9	3.53	115	.259	.324	20	.233	2	12	14	-3	1.3
1929	Pit-N	2	3	.400	27	3	0	0	3	79	94	4	35	28	14.7	3.99	120	.297	.366	1	.036	-3	6	7	0	0.1
	StL-N	0	0	—	3	1	0	0	0	8^2	10	2	8	1	19.7	8.31	56	.303	.452	0	.000	-0	-3	-4	0	0.0
	Yr	2	3	.400	30	4	0	0	3	87^2	104	6	43	29	15.2	4.41	108	.297	.376	1	.032	-4	**3**	**3**	0	0.1
1930	StL-N	0	1	.000	4	2	0	0	0	14^2	12	2	13	8	15.3	7.36	68	.240	.397	1	.333	0	-4	-4	-0	-0.2
Total	10	49	33	.598	147	85	47	5	8	787	769	38	267	264	12.0	3.44	116	.261	.326	53	.191	-0	40	49	1	6.4

● RED HILL
Hill, Clifford Joseph b: 1/20/1893, Marshall, Tex. d: 8/11/38, ElPaso, Tex. BB/TL, Deb: 4/21/17

YEAR	TM/L	W	L	PCT	G	GS	CG	SH	SV	IP	H	HR	BB	SO	RAT	ERA	ERA+	OAV	OOB	BH	AVG	PB	PR	/A	PD	TPI
1917	Phi-A	0	0	—	1	0	0	0	0	2^2	5	0	1	0	20.3	6.75	41	.385	.429	0	—	0	-1	-1	0	0.0

● DAVE HILL
Hill, David Burnham b: 11/11/37, New Orleans, La. BR/TL, 6'2", 170 lbs. Deb: 8/22/57

YEAR	TM/L	W	L	PCT	G	GS	CG	SH	SV	IP	H	HR	BB	SO	RAT	ERA	ERA+	OAV	OOB	BH	AVG	PB	PR	/A	PD	TPI
1957	KC-A	0	0	—	2	0	0	0	0	2^1	6	3	3	1	34.7	27.00	15	.462	.563	0	—	0	-6	-6	-0	0.0

● DONNIE HILL
Hill, Donald Earl b: 11/12/60, Pomona, Cal. BB/TR, 5'10", 160 lbs. Deb: 7/25/83 ♦

YEAR	TM/L	W	L	PCT	G	GS	CG	SH	SV	IP	H	HR	BB	SO	RAT	ERA	ERA+	OAV	OOB	BH	AVG	PB	PR	/A	PD	TPI
1990	Cal-A	0	0	—	1	0	0	0	0	1	0	0	1	1	9.0	0.00		.000	.250	93	.264	0	0	0	0	0.0

● GARRY HILL
Hill, Garry Alton b: 11/3/46, Rutherfordton, N.C. BR/TR, 6'2", 195 lbs. Deb: 6/12/69

YEAR	TM/L	W	L	PCT	G	GS	CG	SH	SV	IP	H	HR	BB	SO	RAT	ERA	ERA+	OAV	OOB	BH	AVG	PB	PR	/A	PD	TPI
1969	Atl-N	0	1	.000	1	1	0	0	0	2^1	6	1	1	2	27.0	15.43	23	.462	.500	0	—	0	-3	-3	0	-0.8

● HERBERT HILL
Hill, Herbert Lee b: 8/19/1891, Hutchins, Tex. d: 9/2/70, Farmers Branch, Tex. BR/TR, 5'11.5", 175 lbs. Deb: 7/17/15

YEAR	TM/L	W	L	PCT	G	GS	CG	SH	SV	IP	H	HR	BB	SO	RAT	ERA	ERA+	OAV	OOB	BH	AVG	PB	PR	/A	PD	TPI
1915	Cle-A	0	0	—	1	0	0	0	0	2	1	0	2	0	13.5	0.00	—	.250	.500	0	—	0	1	1	-0	0.0

● KEN HILL
Hill, Kenneth Wade b: 12/14/65, Lynn, Mass. BR/TR, 6'2", 175 lbs. Deb: 9/3/88

YEAR	TM/L	W	L	PCT	G	GS	CG	SH	SV	IP	H	HR	BB	SO	RAT	ERA	ERA+	OAV	OOB	BH	AVG	PB	PR	/A	PD	TPI
1988	StL-N	0	1	.000	4	1	0	0	0	14	16	0	6	6	14.1	5.14	68	.286	.355	0	.000	-0	-3	-3	0	-0.2
1989	StL-N	7	15	.318	33	33	2	1	0	196^2	186	9	99	112	13.3	3.80	96	.252	.344	9	.153	-0	-7	-4	0	-0.4
1990	StL-N	5	6	.455	17	14	1	0	0	78^2	79	7	33	58	12.9	5.49	69	.264	.339	4	.211	1	-15	-15	0	-1.7
1991	StL-N	11	10	.524	30	30	0	0	0	181^1	147	15	67	121	10.9	3.57	104	.224	.302	5	.100	-1	2	3	0	0.2
1992	Mon-N	16	9	.640	33	33	3	3	0	218	187	13	75	150	10.9	2.68	129	.230	.298	11	.177	5	20	19	1	3.0
1993	Mon-N	9	7	.563	28	28	2	0	0	183^2	163	7	74	90	11.9	3.23	129	.238	.318	6	.115	-1	16	19	3	1.8
1994	Mon-N★	**16**	5	.762	23	23	2	1	0	154^2	145	12	44	85	11.3	3.32	127	.248	.307	7	.146	-0	15	16	2	2.1
1995	StL-N	6	7	.462	18	18	0	0	0	110^1	125	16	45	50	13.9	5.06	83	.286	.353	6	.194	1	-11	-11	1	-0.9
	*Cle-A	4	1	.800	12	11	1	0	0	74^2	77	5	32	48	13.3	3.98	118	.268	.344	0	—	0	6	6	2	0.4
1996	*Tex-A	16	10	.615	35	35	7	**3**	0	250^2	250	19	95	170	12.6	3.63	144	.263	.334	0	—	0	38	45	2	3.9
1997	Tex-A	5	8	.385	19	19	0	0	0	111	129	11	56	68	15.2	5.19	92	.298	.381	0	—	0	-8	-5	3	-0.2
	Ana-A	4	4	.500	12	12	1	0	0	79	65	8	39	38	12.0	3.65	125	.223	.316	1	.500	1	8	8	0	0.8
	Yr	9	12	.429	31	31	1	0	0	190	194	19	95	106	13.7	4.55	103	.265	.350	1	.500	1	0	3	3	0.6
1998	Ana-A	9	6	.600	19	19	0	0	0	103	123	6	47	57	15.1	4.98	94	.311	.388	0	.000	-0	-4	-3	2	-0.2
Total	11	108	89	.548	283	276	19	8	0	1755^2	1692	128	712	1053	12.5	3.83	110	.255	.331	49	.150	4	60	74	17	8.6

● MILT HILL
Hill, Milton Giles b: 8/22/65, Atlanta, Ga. BR/TR, 6', 180 lbs. Deb: 8/1/91

YEAR	TM/L	W	L	PCT	G	GS	CG	SH	SV	IP	H	HR	BB	SO	RAT	ERA	ERA+	OAV	OOB	BH	AVG	PB	PR	/A	PD	TPI
1991	Cin-N	1	1	.500	22	0	0	0	0	33^1	36	1	8	20	11.9	3.78	101	.295	.338	0	.000	-0	-0	0	-1	-0.1
1992	Cin-N	0	0	—	14	0	0	0	1	20	15	1	5	10	9.4	3.15	114	.211	.273	0	—	0	1	1	-0	0.0
1993	Cin-N	3	0	1.000	19	0	0	0	0	28^2	34	5	9	23	13.5	5.65	71	.301	.352	0	.000	-0	-5	-5	-1	-0.6
1994	Atl-N	0	0	—	10	0	0	0	0	11^1	18	3	6	10	19.1	7.94	53	.367	.436	0	—	0	-5	-5	-0	0.0
	Sea-A	1	0	1.000	13	0	0	0	0	23^2	30	4	11	16	15.6	6.46	76	.306	.376	0	—	0	-4	-4	-0	-0.2
Total	4	5	1	.833	78	0	0	0	1	117	133	14	39	79	13.3	5.08	80	.294	.351	0	.000	-0	-14	-13	-2	-0.9

● BILL HILL
Hill, William Cicero "Still Bill" b: 8/2/1874, Chattanooga, Tenn. d: 1/28/38, Cincinnati, Ohio BL/TL, 6'1", 201 lbs. Deb: 4/18/1896 F

YEAR	TM/L	W	L	PCT	G	GS	CG	SH	SV	IP	H	HR	BB	SO	RAT	ERA	ERA+	OAV	OOB	BH	AVG	PB	PR	/A	PD	TPI
1896	Lou-N	9	28	.243	43	39	32	0	2	319^2	353	14	155	104	14.8	4.31	100	.278	.364	24	.207	-5	2	1	4	0.0
1897	Lou-N	7	17	.292	27	26	20	1	0	199	209	6	69	55	13.3	3.62	118	.268	.341	7	.095	-8	15	14	2	0.8
1898	Cin-N	13	14	.481	33	32	26	2	0	262	261	3	119	75	13.6	3.98	96	.258	.346	13	.133	-7	-11	-4	1	-0.9
1899	Cle-N	3	6	.333	11	10	7	0	0	72^1	96	0	39	26	17.3	6.97	53	.318	.403	4	.129	-2	-25	-26	0	-2.6
	Bal-N	3	4	.429	8	7	6	0	0	61	64	1	18	17	12.5	3.25	122	.269	.328	7	.292	1	4	5	1	0.6
	Bro-N	1	0	1.000	2	1	1	0	1	11	11	0	6	3	13.9	0.82	478	.262	.354	3	.600	2	4	4	-0	0.6
	Yr	7	10	.412	21	18	14	0	1	144^1	171	1	63	46	14.6	4.93	78	.290	.359	14	.233	0	-17	-18	1	-1.4
Total	4	36	69	.343	124	115	92	3	3	925	994	24	406	280	14.2	4.16	99	.273	.355	58	.167	-20	-11	-6	7	-1.5

● HOMER HILLEBRAND
Hillebrand, Homer Hiller Henry b: 10/10/1879, Freeport, Ill. d: 1/20/74, Elsinore, Cal. BR/TL, 5'8", 165 lbs. Deb: 4/24/05 ♦

YEAR	TM/L	W	L	PCT	G	GS	CG	SH	SV	IP	H	HR	BB	SO	RAT	ERA	ERA+	OAV	OOB	BH	AVG	PB	PR	/A	PD	TPI
1905	Pit-N	5	2	.714	10	6	4	0	1	60^2	43	0	19	37	9.5	2.82	107	.198	.269	26	.236	1	1	1	-1	0.2
1906	Pit-N	3	2	.600	7	5	4	1	0	53	42	1	21	32	10.9	2.21	121	.220	.300	5	.238	1	3	3	1	0.5
1908	Pit-N	0	0	—	1	0	0	0	0	1	1	0	0	1	9.0	0.00	—	.333	.333	0	—	0	0	0	-0	0.0
Total	3	8	4	.667	18	11	8	1	1	114^2	86	1	40	70	10.1	2.51	113	.209	.284	31	.237	2	4	4	1	0.7

● SHAWN HILLEGAS
Hillegas, Shawn Patrick b: 8/21/64, Dos Palos, Cal. BR/TR, 6'2", 208 lbs. Deb: 8/9/87

YEAR	TM/L	W	L	PCT	G	GS	CG	SH	SV	IP	H	HR	BB	SO	RAT	ERA	ERA+	OAV	OOB	BH	AVG	PB	PR	/A	PD	TPI
1987	LA-N	4	3	.571	12	10	0	0	0	58	52	5	31	51	12.9	3.57	111	.241	.336	0	.000	-1	3	3	-1	0.1
1988	LA-N	3	4	.429	11	10	0	0	0	56^2	54	5	17	30	11.8	4.13	81	.250	.314	2	.133	0	-4	-5	-1	-0.7
	Chi-A	3	2	.600	6	6	0	0	0	40	30	4	18	26	11.0	3.15	126	.207	.299	0	—	0	4	4	-0	0.4
1989	Chi-A	7	11	.389	50	13	0	0	3	119^2	132	12	51	76	14.0	4.74	80	.279	.353	0	—	0	-11	-12	-1	-1.8
1990	Chi-A	0	0	—	7	0	0	0	0	11^1	4	0	5	5	7.1	0.79	481	.111	.220	0	—	0	4	4	0	0.1
1991	Cle-A	3	4	.429	51	3	0	0	7	83	67	7	46	66	12.5	4.34	96	.223	.330	0	—	0	-2	-2	-0	-0.2
1992	NY-A	1	8	.111	21	9	1	1	0	78^1	96	12	33	46	14.8	5.51	71	.306	.372	0	—	0	-14	-14	-1	-1.5
	Oak-A	0	0	—	5	0	0	0	0	7^2	8	1	4	3	14.1	2.35	159	.276	.364	0	—	0	1	1	-0	0.2
	Yr	1	8	.111	26	9	1	1	0	86	104	13	37	49	14.8	5.23	75	.301	.368	0	—	0	-12	-13	-1	-1.3
1993	Oak-A	3	6	.333	18	11	0	0	0	60^2	78	8	33	29	17.1	6.97	58	.317	.406	0	—	0	-18	-20	-1	-2.3
Total	7	24	38	.387	181	62	1	1	10	515^1	521	54	238	332	13.5	4.61	84	.264	.347	2	.069	-1	-37	-41	-6	-5.7

● FRANK HILLER
Hiller, Frank Walter "Dutch" b: 7/13/20, Newark, N.J. d: 1/8/87, West Chester, Pa. BR/TR, 6', 200 lbs. Deb: 5/25/46

YEAR	TM/L	W	L	PCT	G	GS	CG	SH	SV	IP	H	HR	BB	SO	RAT	ERA	ERA+	OAV	OOB	BH	AVG	PB	PR	/A	PD	TPI
1946	NY-A	0	2	.000	3	1	0	0	0	11^1	13	2	6	4	15.1	4.76	72	.295	.380	1	.250	0	-2	-2	-0	-0.3
1948	NY-A	5	2	.714	22	5	1	0	0	62^1	59	8	30	25	13.0	4.04	101	.244	.330	6	.375	2	2	0	0	0.2
1949	NY-A	0	2	.000	4	0	0	0	1	7^2	9	0	7	3	18.8	5.87	69	.290	.421	1	.500	0	-1	-2	-0	-0.4
1950	Chi-N	12	5	.706	38	17	9	2	1	153	153	16	32	55	11.1	3.53	119	.258	.300	5	.114	-3	10	11	1	1.0
1951	Chi-N	6	12	.333	24	21	6	2	1	141^1	147	17	31	50	11.9	4.84	85	.268	.317	6	.125	-2	-14	-12	1	-1.4
1952	Cin-N	5	8	.385	28	15	6	1	1	124^1	129	7	37	50	12.5	4.63	81	.271	.331	5	.167	1	-12	-12	0	-1.1
1953	NY-N	2	1	.667	19	1	0	0	0	33^2	43	6	15	10	16.6	6.15	70	.303	.385	2	.500	1	-7	-7	1	-0.4
Total	7	30	32	.484	138	60	22	5	4	533^2	553	56	158	197	12.4	4.42	92	.266	.325	26	.176	-1	-24	-22	3	-2.4

YEAR	TM/L	W	L	PCT	G	GS	CG	SH	SV	IP	H	HR	BB	SO	RAT	ERA	ERA+	OAV	OOB	BH	AVG	PB	PR	/A	PD	TPI
● JOHN HILLER Hiller, John Frederick b: 4/8/43, Toronto, Ont., Canada BR/TL, 6′, 195 lbs. Deb: 9/6/65																										
1965	Det-A	0	0	—	5	0	0	0	1	6	5	0	1	4	9.0	0.00	—	.227	.261	0	—	0	2	2	-0	0.1
1966	Det-A	0	0	—	1	0	0	0	0	2	2	0	2	1	18.0	9.00	39	.286	.444	0	—	0	-1	-1	-0	0.0
1967	Det-A	4	3	.571	23	6	2	2	3	65	57	4	9	49	9.1	2.63	124	.233	.260	2	.133	-0	4	5	-0	0.5
1968	*Det-A	9	6	.600	39	12	4	1	2	128	92	9	51	78	10.1	2.39	126	.200	.280	3	.081	-2	8	9	-0	0.8
1969	Det-A	4	4	.500	40	8	1	1	4	99^1	97	13	44	74	12.9	3.99	94	.257	.336	6	.286	2	-4	-3	-1	-0.2
1970	Det-A	6	6	.500	47	5	1	1	3	104	82	12	46	89	11.3	3.03	123	.219	.307	0	.000	-2	8	8	-1	0.6
1972	*Det-A	1	2	.333	24	3	1	0	3	44^1	39	4	13	26	11.2	2.03	155	.232	.299	0	.000	-0	5	5	1	0.5
1973	Det-A	10	5	.667	**65**	0	0	0	**38**	125^1	89	7	39	124	9.2	1.44	285	.198	.262	0	—	0	**33**	**37**	0	**6.7**
1974	Det-A☆	17	14	.548	59	0	0	0	13	150	127	10	62	134	11.5	2.64	144	.231	.312	0	—	0	16	19	-2	3.9
1975	Det-A	2	3	.400	36	0	0	0	14	70^2	52	6	36	87	11.2	2.17	185	.205	.303	0	—	0	13	15	-0	1.5
1976	Det-A	12	8	.600	56	1	1	1	13	121	93	7	67	117	12.0	2.38	156	.219	.329	0	.000	-0	15	**18**	-1	3.3
1977	Det-A	8	14	.364	45	8	3	0	7	124	120	15	61	115	13.2	3.56	121	.258	.345	0	—	0	7	10	-1	1.6
1978	Det-A	9	4	.692	51	0	0	0	15	92^1	64	6	35	74	9.6	2.34	165	.202	.281	0	—	0	15	16	-1	2.6
1979	Det-A	4	7	.364	43	0	0	0	9	79^1	83	14	55	46	15.7	5.22	83	.274	.385	0	—	0	-9	-8	-0	-1.2
1980	Det-A	1	0	1.000	11	0	0	0	0	30^2	38	3	14	18	15.3	4.40	93	.309	.380	0	—	0	-1	-1	-0	-0.1
Total	15	87	76	.534	545	43	13	6	125	1242	1040	110	535	1036	11.5	2.83	133	.229	.312	11	.109	-3	112	130	-8	20.6
● DAVE HILLMAN Hillman, Darius Dutton b: 9/14/27, Dungannon, Va. BR/TR, 5′11″, 168 lbs. Deb: 4/30/55																										
1955	Chi-N	0	0	—	25	3	0	0	0	57^2	63	10	25	23	13.9	5.31	77	.283	.357	1	.100	0	-8	-8	0	0.0
1956	Chi-N	0	2	.000	2	2	0	0	0	12^1	11	0	5	6	11.7	2.19	172	.216	.286	0	.000	-1	2	2	0	0.3
1957	Chi-N	6	11	.353	32	14	1	0	1	103^1	115	13	37	53	13.2	4.35	89	.280	.340	0	.000	-2	-5	-6	-0	-1.1
1958	Chi-N	4	8	.333	31	16	3	0	1	125^2	132	12	31	65	11.7	3.15	124	.265	.308	6	.146	-1	11	11	-0	0.8
1959	Chi-N	8	11	.421	39	24	4	1	0	191	178	17	43	88	10.5	3.53	112	.248	.292	9	.150	1	9	9	1	1.0
1960	Bos-A	0	3	.000	16	3	0	0	0	36^2	41	6	12	14	13.0	5.65	72	.281	.335	0	.000	-0	-7	-7	0	-0.5
1961	Bos-A	3	2	.600	28	1	0	0	0	78	70	8	23	39	10.7	2.77	151	.242	.298	0	.000	-2	11	12	0	0.5
1962	Cin-N	0	0	—	2	0	0	0	0	3^2	8	0	1	0	22.1	9.82	41	.421	.450	0	—	0	-2	-2	-0	0.0
	NY-N	0	0	—	13	1	0	0	1	15^2	21	5	8	8	17.2	6.32	66	.333	.417	0	.000	-0	-4	-4	0	-0.1
	Yr	0	0	—	15	1	0	0	1	19^1	29	5	9	8	18.2	6.98	59	.354	.424	0	.000	-0	-7	-6	-0	-0.1
Total	8	21	37	.362	188	64	8	1	3	624	639	71	185	296	11.9	3.87	103	.264	.317	16	.098	-5	6	8	1	0.9
● ERIC HILLMAN Hillman, John Eric b: 4/27/66, Gary, Ind. BL/TL, 6′10″, 225 lbs. Deb: 5/18/92																										
1992	NY-N	2	2	.500	11	8	0	0	0	52^1	67	9	10	16	13.6	5.33	65	.318	.354	1	.077	-1	-11	-11	-1	-0.9
1993	NY-N	2	9	.182	27	22	3	1	0	145	173	12	24	60	12.5	3.97	101	.299	.331	7	.159	-0	1	1	-1	0.0
1994	NY-N	0	3	.000	11	6	0	0	0	34^2	45	9	11	20	15.1	7.79	54	.321	.379	0	.000	-1	-14	-14	-0	-1.1
Total	3	4	14	.222	49	36	3	1	0	232	285	30	45	96	13.1	4.85	81	.306	.344	8	.123	-2	-23	-24	-1	-2.0
● CHARLIE HILSEY Hilsey, Charles T. b: 3/23/1864, Philadelphia, Pa. d: 10/31/18, Philadelphia, Pa. 5′7″, 180 lbs. Deb: 9/27/1883 ♦																										
1883	Phi-N	0	3	.000	3	3	3	0	0	26	36	1	4	8	13.8	5.54	56	.305	.328	1	.100	-1	-7	-7	-0	-0.7
1884	Phi-a	2	1	.667	3	3	3	0	0	27	29	0	5	10	11.3	4.67	73	.257	.288	5	.208	0	-4	-4	1	-0.3
Total	2	2	4	.333	6	6	6	0	0	53	65	1	9	18	12.6	5.09	64	.281	.308	6	.176	-1	-11	-11	0	-1.0
● HOWARD HILTON Hilton, Howard James b: 1/3/64, Oxnard, Cal. BR/TR, 6′3″, 230 lbs. Deb: 4/9/90																										
1990	StL-N	0	0	—	2	0	0	0	0	3	2	0	3	2	15.0	0.00	—	.182	.357	0	—	0	1	1	-0	0.0
● SAM HINDS Hinds, Samuel Russell b: 7/11/53, Frederick, Md. BR/TR, 6′6″, 215 lbs. Deb: 5/21/77																										
1977	Mil-A	0	3	.000	29	1	0	0	2	72^1	72	5	40	46	14.2	4.73	86	.266	.364	0	—	0	-5	-5	-0	-0.3
● PAUL HINES Hines, Paul A. b: 3/1/1852, Washington, D.C. d: 7/10/35, Hyattsville, Md. BR/TR, 5′9.5″, 173 lbs. Deb: 4/20/1872 ♦																										
1884	*Pro-N	0	0	—	1	0	0	0	0	1	3	0	0	0	27.0	0.00	—	.500	.500	148	.302	0	0	0	-0	0.0
● PAUL HINRICHS Hinrichs, Paul Edwin "Herky" b: 8/31/25, Marengo, Iowa BR/TR, 6′, 180 lbs. Deb: 5/16/51																										
1951	Bos-A	0	0	—	4	0	0	0	0	3^1	7	1	4	1	29.7	21.60	21	.412	.524	0	—	0	-6	-6	0	0.0
● DUTCH HINRICHS Hinrichs, William Louis b: 4/27/1889, Orange, Cal. d: 8/18/72, Kingsburg, Cal. BR/TR, 6′3″, 195 lbs. Deb: 6/25/10																										
1910	Was-A	0	1	.000	3	0	0	0	1	7	10	0	3	5	16.7	2.57	97	.357	.419	0	.000	-1	-0	-0	-0	-0.1
● JERRY HINSLEY Hinsley, Jerry Dean b: 4/9/44, Hugo, Okla. BR/TR, 5′11″, 165 lbs. Deb: 4/18/64																										
1964	NY-N	0	2	.000	9	2	0	0	0	15^1	21	0	7	11	16.4	8.22	44	.313	.378	0	.000	-0	-8	-8	-1	-1.0
1967	NY-N	0	0	—	2	0	0	0	0	5	6	0	4	3	18.0	3.60	94	.316	.435	0	—	0	-0	-0	0	0.0
Total	2	0	2	.000	11	2	0	0	0	20^1	27	0	11	14	16.8	7.08	50	.314	.392	0	.000	-0	-8	-8	-1	-1.0
● RICH HINTON Hinton, Richard Michael b: 5/22/47, Tucson, Ariz. BL/TL, 6′2″, 185 lbs. Deb: 7/17/71																										
1971	Chi-A	3	4	.429	18	2	0	0	0	24^1	27	1	6	15	12.6	4.44	81	.310	.362	0	.000	-0	-3	-2	1	-0.5
1972	NY-A	1	0	1.000	7	3	0	0	0	16^2	20	2	8	13	15.1	4.86	61	.299	.373	0	.000	-0	-3	-4	-0	-0.3
	Tex-A	0	1	.000	5	0	0	0	0	11^1	7	1	10	4	13.5	2.38	126	.171	.333	1	.500	1	1	1	0	0.2
	Yr	1	1	.500	12	3	0	0	0	28	27	3	18	17	14.5	3.86	77	.245	.352	1	.200	1	-2	-3	-0	-0.1
1975	Chi-A	1	0	1.000	15	0	0	0	0	37^1	41	3	15	30	13.5	4.82	80	.270	.335	0	—	0	-4	-4	1	0.0
1976	Cin-N	1	2	.333	12	1	0	0	0	17^2	30	4	11	8	20.9	7.64	46	.380	.456	0	.000	-0	-8	-8	-0	-1.3
1978	Chi-A	2	6	.250	29	4	2	0	1	80^2	78	5	28	48	12.0	4.02	95	.261	.328	0	—	0	-2	-2	-1	-0.3
1979	Chi-A	1	2	.333	16	2	0	0	2	41^2	57	4	8	27	14.5	6.05	70	.331	.368	0	—	0	-8	-8	1	-0.6
	Sea-A	0	2	.000	14	1	0	0	0	20	23	4	5	7	13.5	5.40	81	.284	.341	0	—	0	-3	-2	-0	-0.2
	Yr	1	4	.200	30	3	0	0	2	61^2	80	8	13	34	13.9	5.84	73	.310	.348	0	—	0	-11	-11	0	-0.8
Total	6	9	17	.346	116	13	2	0	3	249^2	283	24	91	152	13.7	4.87	78	.289	.354	1	.143	0	-31	-30	0	-3.0
● HERB HIPPAUF Hippauf, Herbert August b: 5/9/39, New York, N.Y. d: 7/17/95, Santa Clara, Cal. BR/TL, 6′, 180 lbs. Deb: 4/27/66																										
1966	Atl-N	0	1	.000	3	0	0	0	0	2^2	6	0	1	1	23.6	13.50	27	.462	.500	0	—	0	-3	-3	-0	-0.9
● HARLEY HISNER Hisner, Harley Parnell b: 11/6/26, Maples, Ind. BR/TR, 6′1″, 185 lbs. Deb: 9/30/51																										
1951	Bos-A	0	1	.000	1	1	0	0	0	6	7	0	4	3	16.5	4.50	99	.292	.393	1	.500	0	-0	-0	0	0.0
● STERLING HITCHCOCK Hitchcock, Sterling Alex b: 4/29/71, Fayetteville, N.C. BL/TL, 6′1″, 192 lbs. Deb: 9/11/92																										
1992	NY-A	0	2	.000	3	3	0	0	0	13	23	2	6	6	20.8	8.31	47	.377	.441	0	—	0	-6	-6	0	-0.7
1993	NY-A	1	2	.333	6	6	0	0	0	31	32	4	14	26	13.6	4.65	89	.271	.353	0	—	0	-1	-2	-0	-0.1
1994	NY-A	4	1	.800	23	5	1	0	2	49^1	48	3	29	37	14.0	4.20	109	.265	.367	0	—	0	3	2	-0	0.2
1995	*NY-A	11	10	.524	27	27	4	1	0	168^1	155	22	68	121	12.2	4.70	98	.245	.323	0	—	0	0	-2	-3	-0.3
1996	Sea-A	13	9	.591	35	35	0	0	0	196^2	245	27	73	132	14.9	5.35	92	.309	.372	0	—	0	-8	-9	-1	-0.9
1997	SD-N	10	11	.476	32	28	1	0	0	161	172	24	55	106	12.9	5.20	75	.276	.339	5	.100	-1	-18	-24	-1	-2.9
1998	*SD-N	9	7	.563	39	27	2	1	1	176^1	169	29	48	158	11.5	3.93	97	.251	.309	7	.140	-1	6	-2	-2	-0.4
Total	7	48	42	.533	165	131	8	2	3	795^2	844	111	293	586	13.2	4.82	90	.274	.342	12	.120	-2	-24	-43	-7	-5.1
● BRUCE HITT Hitt, Bruce Smith b: 3/14/1897, Comanche, Tex. d: 11/10/73, Portland, Ore. BR/TR, 6′1″, 190 lbs. Deb: 9/23/17																										
1917	StL-N	0	0	—	2	0	0	0	0	4	7	1	1	1	18.0	9.00	30	.368	.400	0	.000	-0	-3	-3	0	0.0
● ROY HITT Hitt, Roy Wesley "Rhino" b: 6/22/1887, Carleton, Neb. d: 2/8/56, Pomona, Cal. BL/TL, 5′10″, 200 lbs. Deb: 4/27/07																										
1907	Cin-N	6	10	.375	21	18	14	2	0	153^1	143	2	56	63	12.4	3.40	76	.258	.339	10	.179	-0	-16	-14	-1	-1.5
● LLOYD HITTLE Hittle, Lloyd Eldon "Red" b: 2/21/24, Lodi, Cal. BR/TL, 5′10.5″, 164 lbs. Deb: 6/12/49																										
1949	Was-A	5	7	.417	36	9	3	2	0	109	123	2	57	32	14.9	4.21	101	.285	.369	4	.143	-2	-0	1	-1	-0.2
1950	Was-A	2	4	.333	11	4	1	0	0	43^1	60	1	17	9	16.0	4.98	90	.326	.383	1	.077	-1	-2	-2	1	-0.3
Total	2	7	11	.389	47	13	4	2	0	152^1	183	3	74	41	15.2	4.43	98	.298	.373	5	.122	-3	-2	-2	0	-0.5

YEAR	TM/L	W	L	PCT	G	GS	CG	SH	SV	IP	H	HR	BB	SO	RAT	ERA	ERA+	OAV	OOB	BH	AVG	PB	PR	/A	PD	TPI
● **MYRIL HOAG** Hoag, Myril Oliver b: 3/9/08, Davis, Cal. d: 7/28/71, High Springs, Fla BR/TR, 5'11", 180 lbs. Deb: 4/15/31 ♦																										
1939	StL-A★	0	0	—	1	0	0	0	0	1	0	0	0	0	0.0	0.00	—	.000	.000	142	.295	0	1	1	0	0.0
1945	Cle-A	0	0	—	2	0	0	0	0	3	3	0	1	0	12.0	0.00	—	.300	.364	27	.211	0	1	1	0	0.0
Total	2	0	0	—	3	0	0	0	0	4	3	0	1	0	9.0	0.00	—	.214	.267	854	.271	1	2	2	0	0.0
● **ED HOBAUGH** Hobaugh, Edward Russell b: 6/27/34, Kittanning, Pa. BR/TR, 6', 176 lbs. Deb: 4/19/61																										
1961	Was-A	7	9	.438	26	18	3	0	0	126^1	142	12	64	67	14.7	4.42	91	.281	.363	4	.098	-2	-6	-6	0	-0.8
1962	Was-A	2	1	.667	26	2	0	0	1	69^1	66	9	25	37	11.8	3.76	107	.258	.324	2	.167	0	2	2	-1	0.0
1963	Was-A	0	0	—	9	1	0	0	0	16	20	3	6	11	15.8	6.19	60	.308	.384	1	.500	2	-5	-4	0	0.2
Total	3	9	10	.474	61	21	3	0	1	211^2	228	24	95	115	13.9	4.34	92	.276	.352	7	.127	-1	-8	-8	-0	-0.6
● **GLEN HOBBIE** Hobbie, Glen Frederick b: 4/24/36, Witt, Ill. BR/TR, 6'2", 195 lbs. Deb: 9/20/57																										
1957	Chi-N	0	0	—	2	0	0	0	0	4^1	6	0	5	3	22.8	10.38	37	.333	.478	0	.000	-0	-3	-3	0	0.0
1958	Chi-N	10	6	.625	55	16	2	1	2	168^1	163	13	93	91	14.1	3.74	105	.252	.353	7	.146	-2	4	3	4	0.5
1959	Chi-N	16	13	.552	46	33	10	3	0	234	204	15	106	138	12.2	3.69	107	.236	.324	9	.114	-3	7	7	1	0.5
1960	Chi-N	16	20	.444	46	36	16	4	1	258^2	253	27	101	134	12.6	3.97	95	.256	.330	13	.151	1	-6	-5	4	-0.2
1961	Chi-N	7	13	.350	36	29	7	2	2	198^2	207	26	54	103	12.1	4.26	98	.268	.321	11	.167	2	-5	-2	3	0.4
1962	Chi-N	5	14	.263	42	23	5	0	0	162	198	19	62	87	14.6	5.22	79	.304	.367	6	.122	-1	-23	-19	1	-2.1
1963	Chi-N	7	10	.412	36	24	4	1	0	165^1	172	17	49	94	12.4	3.92	90	.270	.328	4	.080	-2	-12	-8	-1	-1.1
1964	Chi-N	0	3	.000	8	4	0	0	0	27^1	39	4	10	14	16.5	7.90	47	.325	.382	0	.000	0	-13	-13	0	-1.2
	StL-N	1	2	.333	13	5	1	0	1	44^1	41	4	15	18	11.6	4.26	89	.241	.306	2	.154	1	-4	-2	1	0.0
	Yr	1	5	.167	21	9	1	0	1	71^2	80	8	25	32	13.3	5.65	67	.275	.334	2	.111	1	-17	-15	1	-1.2
Total	8	62	81	.434	284	170	45	11	6	1263	1283	125	495	682	12.9	4.20	93	.264	.337	52	.131	-5	-55	-42	13	-3.2
● **JOHN HOBBS** Hobbs, John Douglas b: 11/11/56, Philadelphia, Pa. BR/TL, 6'3", 190 lbs. Deb: 8/31/81																										
1981	Min-A	0	0	—	4	0	0	0	0	5^2	5	0	6	1	20.6	3.18	124	.238	.448	0	—	0	0	0	-0	-0.1
● **HARRY HOCH** Hoch, Harry Keller b: 1/9/1887, Woodside, Del. d: 10/26/81, Lewes, Del. BR/TR, 5'10.5", 165 lbs. Deb: 4/16/08																										
1908	Phi-N	2	1	.667	3	3	2	0	0	26	20	0	13	4	12.1	2.77	88	.211	.318	1	.200	1	-1	-1	0	0.0
1914	StL-A	0	2	.000	15	2	1	0	0	54	55	1	27	13	14.0	3.00	90	.284	.377	1	.056	-2	-2	-2	2	-0.1
1915	StL-A	0	4	.000	12	3	1	0	0	40	52	2	26	9	18.2	7.20	40	.311	.413	2	.200	0	-19	-19	-0	-1.7
Total	3	2	7	.222	30	8	4	0	0	120	127	3	66	26	15.0	4.35	62	.279	.378	4	.121	-1	-22	-22	2	-1.8
● **CHUCK HOCKENBERY** Hockenbery, Charles Marion b: 12/15/50, LaCrosse, Wis. BB/TR, 6'1", 195 lbs. Deb: 7/4/75																										
1975	Cal-A	0	5	.000	16	4	0	0	1	41	48	3	19	15	15.4	5.27	67	.296	.380	0	—	0	-7	-8	-0	-0.9
● **GEORGE HOCKETTE** Hockette, George Edward "Lefty" b: 4/7/08, Perth, Miss. d: 1/20/74, Plantation, Fla. BL/TL, 6', 174 lbs. Deb: 9/17/34																										
1934	Bos-A	2	1	.667	3	3	3	2	0	27^1	22	3	6	14	9.2	1.65	292	.218	.262	3	.273	0	9	10	-0	1.1
1935	Bos-A	2	3	.400	23	4	0	0	0	61	83	6	12	11	14.2	5.16	92	.329	.362	2	.143	-1	-5	-3	3	0.0
Total	2	4	4	.500	26	7	3	2	0	88^1	105	9	18	25	12.6	4.08	117	.297	.333	5	.200	-0	4	7	3	1.1
● **SHOVEL HODGE** Hodge, Clarence Clemet b: 7/6/1893, Mount Andrew, Ala. d: 12/31/67, Ft.Walton Beach, Fla. BL/TR, 6'4", 190 lbs. Deb: 9/6/20																										
1920	Chi-A	1	1	.500	4	2	1	0	0	19^2	15	0	12	5	12.4	2.29	165	.224	.342	0	.000	-1	3	3	-1	0.1
1921	Chi-A	6	8	.429	36	10	5	0	2	142^2	191	7	54	25	15.8	6.56	65	.335	.397	17	.327	3	-36	-37	3	-2.5
1922	Chi-A	7	6	.538	35	8	2	0	1	139	154	3	65	37	14.3	4.14	98	.300	.381	12	.207	-1	-2	-1	2	-0.1
Total	3	14	15	.483	75	20	8	0	3	301^1	360	10	131	67	14.9	5.17	80	.313	.387	29	.250	1	-34	-35	4	-2.5
● **ED HODGE** Hodge, Ed Oliver b: 4/19/58, Bellflower, Cal. BL/TL, 6'2", 192 lbs. Deb: 5/1/84																										
1984	Min-A	4	3	.571	25	15	0	0	0	100	116	13	29	59	13.1	4.77	88	.291	.340	0	—	0	-9	-6	-2	-0.7
● **ELI HODKEY** Hodkey, Aloysius Joseph b: 11/3/17, Lorain, Ohio BL/TL, 6'4", 185 lbs. Deb: 9/12/46																										
1946	Phi-N	0	1	.000	2	1	0	0	0	4^1	9	0	5	0	29.1	12.46	28	.391	.500	0	.000	-0	-4	-4	-0	-0.8
● **CHARLIE HODNETT** Hodnett, Charles b: 1861, Iowa Deb: 5/3/1883																										
1883	StL-a	2	2	.500	4	4	3	0	0	32	28	1	7	6	9.8	1.41	248	.220	.261	2	.182	-0	7	7	-0	0.8
1884	StL-U	12	2	.857	14	14	12	1	0	121	121	0	16	41	10.2	2.01	119	.243	.267	12	.207	-1	6	5	-2	0.1
Total	2	14	4	.778	18	18	15	1	0	153	149	1	23	47	10.1	1.88	139	.239	.266	14	.203	-1	13	12	-2	0.9
● **GEORGE HODSON** Hodson, George S. b: 6/1870, Pennsylvania TR , Deb: 8/9/1894																										
1894	Bos-N	4	4	.500	12	11	8	0	0	74	103	4	35	12	17.4	5.84	97	.326	.402	3	.100	-4	-4	-1	-1	-0.5
1895	Phi-N	1	2	.333	4	2	1	0	0	17	27	4	9	6	19.1	9.53	50	.355	.424	0	.000	-1	-9	-9	-1	-1.1
Total	2	5	6	.455	16	13	9	0	0	91	130	8	44	18	17.7	6.53	84	.332	.406	3	.086	-5	-13	-10	-2	-1.6
● **BILLY HOEFT** Hoeft, William Frederick b: 5/17/32, Oshkosh, Wis. BL/TL, 6'3", 205 lbs. Deb: 4/18/52																										
1952	Det-A	2	7	.222	34	10	1	0	4	125	123	14	63	67	13.8	4.32	88	.260	.353	6	.150	-1	-9	-7	1	-0.5
1953	Det-A	9	14	.391	29	27	9	0	2	197^2	223	24	58	90	13.0	4.83	84	.283	.335	11	.172	0	-18	-17	-2	-1.8
1954	Det-A	7	15	.318	34	25	10	4	1	175	180	22	59	114	12.5	4.58	81	.266	.328	10	.192	4	-17	-17	-2	-1.7
1955	Det-A☆	16	7	.696	32	29	17	**7**	0	220	187	17	75	133	11.0	2.99	129	.229	.298	17	.207	3	24	21	-3	2.1
1956	Det-A	20	14	.588	38	34	18	4	0	248	276	22	104	172	14.0	4.06	101	.287	.360	20	.250	6	3	1	-3	0.5
1957	Det-A	9	11	.450	34	28	10	1	1	207	188	15	69	111	11.4	3.48	111	.244	.310	10	.149	2	7	9	-2	0.8
1958	Det-A	10	9	.526	36	21	6	0	3	143	148	15	49	94	12.5	4.15	97	.268	.328	12	.273	3	-6	-2	-2	-0.1
1959	Det-A	1	1	.500	2	2	0	0	0	9	6	0	4	2	11.0	5.00	81	.188	.297	1	.333	0	-1	-1	0	-0.2
	Bos-A	0	3	.000	5	3	0	0	0	17^2	22	1	8	8	15.8	5.60	72	.319	.397	0	.000	-0	-3	-3	0	-0.5
	Bal-A	1	1	.500	16	3	0	0	0	41	50	6	19	30	15.1	5.71	66	.307	.379	3	.250	1	-8	-9	-0	-0.3
	Yr	2	5	.286	23	8	0	0	0	67^2	78	7	31	40	14.5	5.59	70	.290	.363	4	.222	0	-13	-13	0	-1.0
1960	Bal-A	2	1	.667	19	0	0	0	0	18^2	18	2	14	14	15.4	4.34	88	.240	.360	0	.000	-0	-1	-1	0	-0.1
1961	Bal-A	7	4	.636	35	12	3	1	3	138	106	7	55	100	10.6	2.02	190	.216	.296	7	.179	1	**31**	28	1	2.4
1962	Bal-A	4	8	.333	57	4	0	0	7	113^2	103	7	43	73	11.6	4.59	81	.243	.315	3	.158	3	-8	-11	0	-1.0
1963	SF-N	2	0	1.000	23	0	0	0	4	24^1	26	5	10	8	13.3	4.44	72	.271	.340	1	1.000	1	-3	-3	-0	-0.4
1964	Mil-N	4	0	1.000	42	0	0	0	4	73^1	76	9	18	47	11.7	3.80	93	.271	.318	2	.222	1	-2	-2	0	0.0
1965	Chi-N	2	2	.500	29	2	1	0	1	51^1	41	3	20	44	10.7	2.81	131	.215	.289	3	.273	1	4	5	-1	0.4
1966	Chi-N	1	2	.333	36	0	0	0	3	41	43	4	14	30	12.7	4.61	80	.264	.326	1	.250	0	-5	-4	1	-0.3
	SF-N	0	2	.000	4	0	0	0	0	3^2	4	0	3	3	17.2	7.36	50	.250	.368	0	—	0	-2	-2	-0	-0.7
	Yr	1	4	.200	40	0	0	0	3	44^2	47	4	17	33	12.9	4.84	76	.261	.325	1	.250	0	-6	-6	0	-1.0
Total	15	97	101	.490	505	200	75	17	33	1847^1	1820	173	685	1140	12.4	3.94	98	.259	.327	107	.202	24	-15	-15	-11	-1.4
● **ART HOELSKOETTER** Hoelskoetter, Arthur "Holley" or "Hoss" (a.k.a. Arthur H. Hostetter) b: 9/30/1882, St.Louis, Mo. d: 8/3/54, St.Louis, Mo. BR/TR, 6'2", Deb: 9/10/05 ♦																										
1905	StL-N	0	1	.000	1	1	1	0	0	6	6	1	5	4	16.5	1.50	199	.273	.407	20	.241	0	1	1	0	0.2
1906	StL-N	1	4	.200	12	3	2	0	0	58^1	53	1	34	20	13.6	4.63	57	.240	.344	71	.224	1	-13	-13	-1	-1.1
1907	StL-N	0	0	—	2	0	0	0	0	11	9	0	10	8	17.2	5.73	44	.209	.382	98	.247	0	-4	-4	-1	0.0
Total	3	1	5	.167	15	4	3	0	0	75^1	68	2	49	32	14.3	4.54	58	.238	.355	225	.236	1	-16	-16	-1	-0.9
● **JOE HOERNER** Hoerner, Joseph Walter b: 11/12/36, Dubuque, Iowa d: 10/4/96, Hermann, Mo. BR/TL, 6'1", 200 lbs. Deb: 9/27/63																										
1963	Hou-N	0	0	—	1	0	0	0	0	3	2	0	0	2	6.0	0.00	—	.182	.182	0	.000	-0	1	1	0	0.0
1964	Hou-N	0	0	—	7	0	0	0	0	11	13	3	6	4	15.5	4.91	70	.310	.396	0	.000	-0	-2	-2	0	0.0
1966	StL-N	5	1	.833	57	0	0	0	13	76	57	5	21	63	9.7	1.54	233	.212	.279	1	.125	1	17	17	-1	2.0
1967	*StL-N	4	4	.500	57	0	0	0	15	66	52	5	20	50	10.0	2.59	127	.225	.290	2	.182	0	6	5	-0	0.9
1968	*StL-N	8	2	.800	47	0	0	0	17	48^2	34	2	12	42	8.5	1.48	196	.192	.243	0	.000	-1	8	8	-0	2.3
1969	StL-N	2	3	.400	45	0	0	0	15	53^1	44	5	9	35	9.1	2.87	125	.230	.269	0	.000	-1	4	4	0	0.6
1970	Phi-N☆	9	5	.643	44	0	0	0	9	57^2	53	5	20	39	11.5	2.65	150	.247	.314	2	.200	1	9	9	-2	2.1
1971	Phi-N	4	5	.444	49	0	0	0	9	73	57	6	21	57	9.7	1.97	179	.215	.275	1	.100	-1	12	13	-0	1.8

YEAR	TM/L	W	L	PCT	G	GS	CG	SH	SV	IP	H	HR	BB	SO	RAT	ERA	ERA+	OAV	OOB	BH	AVG	PB	PR	/A	PD	TPI
1972	Phi-N	0	2	.000	15	0	0	0	3	21^{2}	21	2	5	12	11.2	2.08	173	.259	.310	0	.000	-0	3	4	-1	0.4
	Atl-N	1	3	.250	25	0	0	0	2	23^{1}	34	4	8	19	16.6	6.56	58	.351	.406	0	.000	-0	-8	-7	-0	-1.4
	Yr	1	5	.167	40	0	0	0	5	45	55	6	13	31	13.8	4.40	84	.301	.350	0	.000	-1	-5	-4	-1	-1.0
1973	Atl-N	2	2	.500	20	0	0	0	2	12^{2}	17	1	4	10	14.9	6.39	61	.333	.382	0	—	0	-4	-3	-0	-1.1
	KC-A	2	0	1.000	22	0	0	0	4	19^{1}	28	0	13	15	19.1	5.12	80	.329	.418	0	—	0	-3	-2	-0	-0.9
1974	KC-A	2	3	.400	30	0	0	0	2	35^{1}	32	3	12	24	12.2	3.82	100	.244	.327	0	—	0	-1	-0	-1	-0.5
1975	Phi-N	0	0	—	25	0	0	0	0	21	25	3	8	20	14.6	2.57	145	.298	.366	0	.000	-0	2	3	-1	-0.1
1976	Tex-A	0	4	.000	41	0	0	0	8	35	41	3	19	15	15.4	5.14	70	.315	.403	0	—	0	-6	-6	-1	-1.1
1977	Cin-N	0	0	—	8	0	0	0	0	5^{2}	9	3	3	5	23.8	12.71	31	.375	.500	0	—	0	-6	-6	-0	0.0
Total	14	39	34	.534	493	0	0	0	99	562^{2}	519	50	181	412	11.5	2.99	119	.249	.314	6	.102	-1	35	36	-7	5.0
● LEFTY HOERST Hoerst, Frank Joseph b: 8/11/17, Philadelphia, Pa. BL/TL, 6'3", 192 lbs. Deb: 4/26/40																										
1940	Phi-N	1	0	1.000	6	0	0	0	0	12	12	1	8	3	15.0	5.25	74	.250	.357	0	.000	-0	-2	-2	1	-0.1
1941	Phi-N	3	10	.231	37	11	1	0	0	105^{2}	111	7	50	33	13.8	5.20	71	.275	.357	4	.182	0	-18	-18	2	-1.7
1942	Phi-N	4	16	.200	33	22	5	0	1	150^{2}	162	11	78	52	14.4	5.20	64	.271	.357	7	.152	-0	-32	-32	2	-3.7
1946	Phi-N	1	6	.143	18	7	2	0	0	68^{1}	77	4	36	17	15.0	4.61	74	.288	.375	1	.059	-1	-9	-9	-1	-1.1
1947	Phi-N	1	1	.500	4	1	0	0	0	11^{1}	19	1	3	0	17.5	7.94	50	.358	.393	2	.500	1	-5	-5	0	-0.6
Total	5	10	33	.233	98	41	8	0	1	348	381	24	175	105	14.5	5.17	68	.279	.362	14	.154	-1	-66	-65	4	-7.2
● CHET HOFF Hoff, Chester Cornelius "Red" b: 5/8/1891, Ossining, N.Y. d: 9/17/98, Daytona Beach, Fla. BL/TL, 5'9", 162 lbs. Deb: 9/6/11																										
1911	NY-A	0	1	.000	5	1	0	0	0	20^{2}	21	0	7	10	12.2	2.18	165	.262	.322	2	.286	0	3	3	1	0.2
1912	NY-A	0	1	.000	5	1	0	0	0	15^{2}	20	0	6	14	14.9	6.89	52	.303	.361	1	.200	-0	-6	-6	-0	-0.3
1913	NY-A	0	0	—	2	0	0	0	0	3	0	0	1	2	3.0	0.00	—	.000	.111	0	.000	-0	1	1	-0	0.0
1915	StL-A	2	2	.500	11	3	2	0	0	43^{2}	26	0	24	23	10.5	1.24	232	.169	.285	3	.176	-1	8	8	1	0.7
Total	4	2	4	.333	23	5	2	0	0	83	67	0	38	49	11.5	2.49	127	.218	.305	6	.200	-1	6	6	1	0.6
● BILL HOFFER Hoffer, William Leopold "Chick" or "Wizard" b: 11/8/1870, Cedar Rapids, Iowa d: 7/21/59, Cedar Rapids, Ia. BR/TR, 5'9", 155 lbs. Deb: 4/26/1895																										
1895	*Bal-N	31	6	**.838**	41	38	32	**4**	0	314	296	9	124	80	12.6	3.21	148	.245	.325	27	.214	-3	55	54	-2	4.3
1896	*Bal-N	25	7	**.781**	35	35	32	3	0	309	317	1	95	93	12.3	3.38	127	.263	.323	38	.304	11	34	31	2	3.6
1897	*Bal-N	22	11	.667	38	33	29	1	0	303^{1}	350	5	104	62	14.0	4.30	97	.287	.351	33	.237	2	0	-4	0	-0.3
1898	Bal-N	0	4	.000	4	4	4	0	0	34^{1}	62	0	16	5	20.7	7.34	49	.387	.446	5	.208	0	-14	-14	-0	-1.2
	Pit-N	3	0	1.000	4	3	3	0	0	31	26	0	15	11	11.9	1.74	204	.226	.315	1	.091	-1	6	6	-0	0.5
	Yr	3	4	.429	8	7	7	0	0	65^{1}	88	0	31	16	16.4	4.68	76	.319	.388	6	.171	-0	-8	-8	-0	-0.7
1899	Pit-N	8	10	.444	23	19	15	2	0	163^{2}	169	5	64	44	13.4	3.63	105	.266	.343	18	.198	-1	4	3	-0	0.2
1901	Cle-A	3	8	.273	16	10	10	0	**3**	99	113	2	35	19	13.5	4.55	78	.283	.343	6	.136	-1	-10	-11	0	-1.1
Total	6	92	46	.667	161	142	125	10	3	1254^{1}	1333	22	453	314	13.2	3.75	112	.270	.339	128	.229	6	76	65	-1	6.0
● DANNY HOFFMAN Hoffman, Daniel John b: 3/2/1880, Canton, Conn. d: 3/14/22, Manchester, Conn. BL/TL, 5'9", 175 lbs. Deb: 4/20/03 ♦																										
1903	Phi-A	0	0	—	1	0	0	0	0	3	2	0	2	0	12.0	3.00	102	.182	.308	61	.246	0	-0	0	-0	0.0
● FRANK HOFFMAN Hoffman, Frank J. "The Texas Wonder" b: Houston, Tex. TR , Deb: 8/13/1888																										
1888	KC-a	3	9	.250	12	12	12	0	0	104	102	3	42	38	13.0	2.77	124	.248	.326	6	.154	-1	3	8	0	0.7
● GUY HOFFMAN Hoffman, Guy Alan b: 7/9/56, Ottawa, Ill. BL/TL, 5'9", 185 lbs. Deb: 7/4/79																										
1979	Chi-A	0	5	.000	24	0	0	0	2	30^{1}	30	0	23	18	16.0	5.34	80	.261	.388	0	—	0	-4	-4	0	-0.6
1980	Chi-A	1	0	1.000	23	1	0	0	1	37^{2}	38	1	17	24	13.1	2.63	153	.268	.346	0	—	0	6	6	-1	0.1
1983	Chi-A	1	0	1.000	11	0	0	0	0	6	14	1	2	2	24.0	7.50	56	.483	.516	0	—	0	-2	-2	-0	-0.6
1986	Chi-N	6	2	.750	32	8	1	0	0	84	92	6	29	47	13.2	3.86	105	.288	.351	1	.067	-1	-1	2	-1	-0.1
1987	Cin-N	9	10	.474	36	22	0	0	0	158^{2}	160	20	49	87	12.1	4.37	97	.265	.325	5	.111	-2	-5	-2	-2	-0.6
1988	Tex-A	0	0	—	11	0	0	0	0	22^{1}	22	5	8	9	12.5	5.24	78	.247	.316	0	—	0	-3	-3	0	-0.1
Total	6	17	17	.500	137	31	1	0	3	339	356	33	128	187	13.1	4.25	98	.274	.343	6	.100	-2	-10	-3	-4	-1.9
● TREVOR HOFFMAN Hoffman, Trevor William b: 10/13/67, Bellflower, Cal. BR/TR, 6', 205 lbs. Deb: 4/6/93 F																										
1993	Fla-N	2	2	.500	28	0	0	0	2	35^{2}	24	5	19	26	10.9	3.28	132	.185	.289	0	.000	-0	3	4	0	0.5
	SD-N	2	4	.333	39	0	0	0	3	54^{1}	56	5	20	53	12.8	4.31	96	.264	.330	1	.200	-0	-2	-1	-0	-0.2
	Yr	4	6	.400	67	0	0	0	5	90	80	10	39	79	12.0	3.90	108	.233	.313	1	.143	-0	1	3	0	0.3
1994	SD-N	4	4	.500	47	0	0	0	20	56	39	4	20	68	9.5	2.57	160	.193	.266	0	.000	-0	10	10	0	1.8
1995	SD-N	7	4	.636	55	0	0	0	31	53^{1}	48	10	14	52	10.5	3.88	104	.235	.284	1	.500	1	2	1	-1	0.2
1996	*SD-N	9	5	.643	70	0	0	0	42	88	50	6	31	111	8.5	2.25	176	.161	.241	0	.000	-1	19	17	-0	3.7
1997	SD-N	6	4	.600	70	0	0	0	37	81^{1}	59	9	24	111	9.2	2.66	146	.200	.260	1	.333	0	14	11	-1	2.1
1998	*SD-N★	4	2	.667	66	0	0	0	**53**	73	41	2	21	86	7.8	1.48	258	.165	.232	0	.000	-0	22	19	-1	3.7
Total	6	34	25	.576	375	0	0	0	188	441^{2}	317	41	149	507	9.6	2.77	144	.198	.268	3	.115	-1	69	60	-3	11.8
● BILL HOFFMAN Hoffman, William Joseph b: 3/3/18, Philadelphia, Pa. BL/TL, 5'9", 170 lbs. Deb: 8/13/39																										
1939	Phi-N	0	0	—	3	0	0	0	0	6	8	2	7	1	27.0	13.50	30	.333	.529	0	.000	-0	-6	-6	-0	0.0
● JOHN HOFFORD Hofford, John William b: 5/25/1863, Philadelphia, Pa. d: 12/16/15, Philadelphia, Pa. Deb: 9/26/1885																										
1885	Pit-a	0	3	.000	3	3	3	0	0	25	28	1	9	21	13.3	3.60	89	.275	.333	1	.125	-1	-1	-1	0	-0.1
1886	Pit-a	3	6	.333	9	9	9	0	0	81	88	1	40	25	14.4	4.33	78	.261	.343	10	.294	3	-8	-9	1	-0.4
Total	2	3	9	.250	12	12	12	0	0	106	116	2	49	46	14.2	4.16	80	.264	.341	11	.262	2	-9	-10	1	-0.5
● GEORGE HOGAN Hogan, George A. b: 9/25/1885, Marion, Ohio d: 2/22/22, Bartlesville, Okla BR/TR, 6', 160 lbs. Deb: 4/18/14 F																										
1914	KC-F	0	1	.000	4	1	0	0	0	13	12	1	7	7	13.8	4.15	67	.255	.364	0	.000	-1	-2	-2	0	-0.2
● EDDIE HOGAN Hogan, Robert Edward b: 4/1860, St.Louis, Mo. BR , 5'7", 153 lbs. Deb: 7/5/1882 ♦																										
1882	StL-a	0	1	.000	1	1	1	0	0	8	10	0	0	4	11.3	1.13	249	.286	.286	1	.333	0	1	1	-1	0.1
● BRAD HOGG Hogg, Carter Bradley b: 3/26/1888, Buena Vista, Ga. d: 4/2/35, Buena Vista, Ga. BR/TR, 6', 185 lbs. Deb: 9/1/11																										
1911	Bos-N	0	3	.000	8	3	2	0	1	25^{2}	33	0	14	8	16.8	6.66	57	.337	.425	4	.444	1	-9	-8	0	-0.7
1912	Bos-N	1	1	.500	10	1	0	0	1	31	37	2	16	12	16.0	6.97	51	.308	.399	1	.091	-1	-12	-12	-1	-0.8
1915	Chi-N	1	0	1.000	2	2	1	1	0	13	12	1	6	0	13.2	2.08	134	.245	.339	0	.000	-0	1	1	0	0.1
1918	Phi-N	13	13	.500	29	25	17	3	1	228	201	3	61	81	10.6	2.53	119	.245	.302	18	.228	3	6	12	2	2.0
1919	Phi-N	5	12	.294	22	19	13	0	0	150^{1}	163	7	55	48	13.4	4.43	73	.292	.360	17	.283	3	-25	-20	-2	-2.1
Total	5	20	29	.408	71	50	33	4	3	448	446	13	152	149	12.3	3.70	85	.271	.338	40	.247	5	-40	-27	-0	-1.5
● BILL HOGG Hogg, William Johnston "Buffalo Bill" b: 9/11/1881, Port Huron, Mich. d: 12/8/09, New Orleans, La. BR/TR, 6', 200 lbs. Deb: 4/25/05																										
1905	NY-A	9	13	.409	39	22	9	3	1	205	178	1	101	125	12.8	3.20	92	.236	.336	4	.060	-6	-13	-6	-5	-1.8
1906	NY-A	14	13	.519	28	25	15	3	0	206	171	5	72	107	11.1	2.93	101	.229	.307	9	.125	-5	-5	1	-5	-0.9
1907	NY-A	10	8	.556	25	21	13	0	0	166^{2}	173	3	83	64	14.1	3.08	91	.270	.359	11	.183	-0	-10	-5	-2	-0.8
1908	NY-A	4	16	.200	24	21	6	0	0	152^{1}	155	4	63	72	13.1	3.01	82	.262	.337	4	.093	-3	-10	-9	-2	-1.7
Total	4	37	50	.425	116	89	43	6	1	730	677	13	319	368	12.7	3.06	92	.248	.334	28	.116	-14	-38	-20	-13	-5.2
● CHIEF HOGSETT Hogsett, Elon Chester b: 11/2/03, Brownell, Kan. BL/TL, 6', 190 lbs. Deb: 9/18/29																										
1929	Det-A	1	2	.333	4	4	2	1	0	28^{2}	34	0	9	9	13.8	2.83	152	.312	.370	2	.200	-0	5	5	0	0.4
1930	Det-A	9	8	.529	33	17	4	0	1	146	174	9	63	54	15.2	5.42	88	.300	.377	17	.293	3	-13	-10	2	-0.6
1931	Det-A	3	9	.250	22	12	5	0	2	112^{1}	150	8	33	47	15.1	5.93	77	.324	.375	11	.234	0	-19	-17	0	-1.5
1932	Det-A	11	9	.550	47	15	7	0	7	178	201	8	66	56	13.8	3.54	133	.286	.351	14	.246	3	19	23	2	2.9
1933	Det-A	6	10	.375	45	2	0	0	9	116	137	7	56	39	15.3	4.50	96	.296	.377	8	.211	-0	-3	-2	1	-0.3
1934	*Det-A	3	2	.600	26	0	0	0	3	50^{1}	61	4	19	23	14.5	4.29	102	.303	.367	3	.231	-0	1	1	1	0.1
1935	*Det-A	6	6	.500	40	0	0	0	5	96^{2}	109	1	49	39	15.2	3.54	118	.288	.377	6	.261	2	10	7	3	1.2
1936	Det-A	0	1	.000	3	0	0	0	0	4	8	1	1	1	20.3	9.00	55	.400	.429	0	—	0	-2	-2	0	-0.3
	StL-A	13	15	.464	39	29	10	0	1	215^{1}	278	15	90	67	16.0	5.52	97	.310	.383	10	.143	-2	-11	-3	1	-0.5

YEAR	TM/L	W	L	PCT	G	GS	CG	SH	SV	IP	H	HR	BB	SO	RAT	ERA	ERA+	OAV	OOB	BH	AVG	PB	PR	/A	PD	TPI
	Yr	13	16	.448	42	29	10	0	1	219^1	286	16	91	68	16.1	5.58	96	.312	.384	10	.143	-2	-13	-5	1	-0.8
1937	StL-A	6	19	.240	37	26	8	1	2	177^1	245	19	75	68	16.5	6.29	77	.328	.393	13	.210	0	-33	-29	-1	-3.3
1938	Was-A	5	6	.455	31	9	1	0	3	91	107	12	36	33	14.9	6.03	75	.292	.368	7	.304	3	-13	-15	0	-1.3
1944	Det-A	0	0	—	3	0	0	0	0	6^1	7	1	4	5	18.5	0.00	—	.250	.382	0	.000	-0	2	3	-0	0.0
Total	11	63	87	.420	330	114	37	2	33	1222	1511	85	501	441	15.3	5.02	94	.305	.376	91	.226	8	-57	-42	9	-3.2
● CAL HOGUE	Hogue, Calvin Grey b: 10/24/27, Dayton, Ohio BR/TR, 6', 185 lbs. Deb: 7/15/52																									
1952	Pit-N	1	8	.111	19	12	3	0	0	83^2	79	7	68	34	16.2	4.84	82	.258	.399	6	.250	1	-10	-8	-2	-0.8
1953	Pit-N	1	1	.500	3	2	2	0	0	19	19	4	16	10	17.1	5.21	86	.250	.387	0	.000	-1	-2	-2	0	-0.2
1954	Pit-N	0	1	.000	3	2	0	0	0	11	11	1	12	7	18.8	4.91	85	.282	.451	0	.000	-0	-1	-1	0	-0.1
Total	3	2	10	.167	25	16	5	0	0	113^2	109	12	96	51	16.6	4.91	83	.259	.402	6	.188	0	-13	-10	-1	-1.1
● BOBBY HOGUE	Hogue, Robert Clinton b: 4/5/21, Miami, Fla. d: 12/22/87, Miami, Fla. BR/TR, 5'10", 195 lbs. Deb: 4/24/48																									
1948	Bos-N	8	2	.800	40	1	0	0	2	86^1	88	4	19	43	11.4	3.23	119	.265	.309	2	.095	-1	7	6	-1	0.4
1949	Bos-N	2	2	.500	33	0	0	0	3	72	78	4	25	23	13.1	3.13	121	.280	.343	6	.286	1	7	5	2	0.6
1950	Bos-N	3	5	.375	36	1	0	0	7	62^2	69	8	31	15	14.9	5.03	77	.280	.370	3	.231	1	-6	-8	1	-1.0
1951	Bos-N	0	0	—	3	0	0	0	0	5	4	1	3	0	12.6	5.40	68	.235	.350	1	.500	0	-1	-1	-0	0.0
	StL-A	1	1	.500	18	0	0	0	0	29^2	31	1	23	11	16.4	5.16	85	.279	.403	2	.667	1	-3	-3	1	0.0
	*NY-A	1	0	1.000	7	0	0	0	0	7^1	4	0	3	2	8.6	0.00	—	.174	.269	0	—	0	3	3	0	0.4
	Yr	2	1	.667	25	0	0	0	1	37	35	1	26	13	14.8	4.14	104	.261	.381	2	.667	1	-0	1	1	0.4
1952	NY-A	3	5	.375	27	0	0	0	4	47^1	52	6	25	12	14.8	5.32	62	.294	.384	3	.273	0	-9	-11	-1	-1.9
	StL-A	0	1	.000	8	1	0	0	0	16^1	10	1	13	2	12.7	2.76	142	.179	.333	0	.000	-0	2	2	0	0.1
	Yr	3	6	.333	35	1	0	0	4	63^2	62	7	38	14	14.1	4.66	74	.265	.368	3	.231	0	-7	-8	-1	-1.8
Total	5	18	16	.529	172	3	0	0	17	326^2	336	25	142	108	13.4	3.97	96	.271	.350	17	.233	3	0	-6	1	-1.4
● WALLY HOLBOROW	Holborow, Walter Albert b: 11/30/13, New York, N.Y. d: 7/14/86, Ft.Lauderdale, Fla. BR/TR, 5'11", 187 lbs. Deb: 9/27/44																									
1944	Was-A	0	0	—	1	0	0	0	0	3	0	0	2	1	6.0	0.00	—	.000	.182	0	—	0	1	1	0	0.0
1945	Was-A	1	1	.500	15	1	1	1	0	31^1	20	0	16	14	10.3	2.30	135	.189	.295	0	.000	-0	4	3	-1	0.1
1948	Phi-A	1	2	.333	5	1	1	0	0	17^1	32	1	7	3	20.3	5.71	75	.421	.470	2	.500	1	-3	-3	1	-0.2
Total	3	2	3	.400	21	2	2	1	0	51^2	52	1	25	18	13.4	3.31	106	.272	.356	2	.333	1	2	1	-0	-0.1
● KEN HOLCOMBE	Holcombe, Kenneth Edward b: 8/23/18, Burnsville, N.C. BR/TR, 5'11.5", 169 lbs. Deb: 4/27/45																									
1945	NY-A	3	3	.500	23	2	0	0	0	55^1	43	2	27	20	11.4	1.79	194	.226	.323	2	.133	-1	10	10	-0	1.0
1948	Cin-N	0	0	—	2	0	0	0	0	2^1	3	0	0	2	11.6	7.71	51	.300	.300	0	—	0	-1	-1	-0	0.0
1950	Chi-A	3	10	.231	24	15	5	0	1	96	122	10	45	37	15.7	4.59	98	.307	.378	5	.156	-2	-0	-1	-0	-0.3
1951	Chi-A	11	12	.478	28	23	12	2	0	159^1	142	9	68	39	11.9	3.78	107	.241	.321	11	.250	1	6	4	2	0.9
1952	Chi-A	0	5	.000	7	7	1	0	0	35	38	3	18	12	14.9	6.17	59	.286	.379	0	.000	-1	-10	-10	0	-1.3
	StL-A	0	2	.000	12	1	0	0	0	21	20	1	9	7	12.4	3.86	101	.263	.341	1	.333	0	-0	0	0	0.1
	Yr	0	7	.000	19	8	1	0	0	56	58	4	27	19	13.7	5.30	71	.275	.357	1	.077	-1	-10	-10	1	-1.2
1953	Bos-A	1	0	1.000	3	0	0	0	1	6	9	0	3	1	18.0	6.00	70	.333	.400	0	.000	-0	-1	-1	0	-0.2
Total	6	18	32	.360	99	48	18	2	2	375	377	25	170	118	13.2	3.98	101	.265	.345	19	.179	-3	3	2	3	0.2
● DAVID HOLDRIDGE	Holdridge, David Allen b: 2/5/69, Wayne, Mich. BR/TR, 6'3", 190 lbs. Deb: 8/8/98																									
1998	Sea-A	0	0	—	7	0	0	0	0	6^2	6	0	4	6	13.5	4.05	114	.231	.333	0	—	0	0	0	-0	0.0
● FRED HOLDSWORTH	Holdsworth, Fredrick William b: 5/29/52, Detroit, Mich. BR/TR, 6'1", 190 lbs. Deb: 7/27/72																									
1972	Det-A	0	1	.000	2	2	0	0	0	7	13	0	2	5	19.3	12.86	24	.419	.455	1	.333	0	-8	-8	-0	-0.8
1973	Det-A	0	1	.000	5	2	0	0	0	14^2	13	3	6	9	11.7	6.75	61	.236	.311	0	—	0	-5	-4	-0	-0.7
1974	Det-A	0	3	.000	8	5	0	0	0	35^2	40	4	14	16	13.9	4.29	89	.286	.355	0	—	0	-3	-2	-1	-0.5
1976	Bal-A	4	1	.800	16	0	0	0	2	39^2	24	0	13	24	8.4	2.04	160	.179	.252	0	—	0	7	5	-0	0.9
1977	Bal-A	0	1	.000	12	0	0	0	0	14^1	17	0	16	4	21.3	6.28	60	.333	.500	0	—	0	-4	-4	-0	0.2
	Mon-N	3	3	.500	14	6	0	0	0	42^1	35	6	18	21	11.3	3.19	119	.230	.312	0	.000	-1	3	3	0	0.3
1978	Mon-N	0	0	—	6	0	0	0	0	8^2	16	3	8	3	24.9	7.27	48	.381	.480	0	—	0	-4	-4	-0	0.0
1980	Mil-A	0	0	—	9	0	0	0	0	19^2	24	2	9	12	15.1	4.58	85	.286	.355	0	—	0	-1	-2	0	0.2
Total	7	7	10	.412	72	15	0	0	2	182	182	18	86	94	13.4	4.40	84	.264	.347	1	.077	-1	-13	-15	-2	-0.4
● WALTER HOLKE	Holke, Walter Henry "Union Man" b: 12/25/1892, St.Louis, Mo. d: 10/12/54, St.Louis, Mo. BB/TL, 6'1.5", 185 lbs. Deb: 10/6/14 C♦																									
1923	Phi-N	0	0	—	1	0	0	0	0	0^1	1	0	0	0	27.0	0.00	—	.500	.500	175	.311	0	0	0	0	0.0
● AL HOLLAND	Holland, Alfred Willis b: 8/16/52, Roanoke, Va. BR/TL, 5'11", 207 lbs. Deb: 9/5/77																									
1977	Pit-N	0	0	—	2	0	0	0	0	2^1	4	0	0	1	15.4	7.71	52	.400	.400	0	—	0	-1	-1	0	0.0
1979	SF-N	0	0	—	3	0	0	0	0	7	3	0	5	7	10.3	0.00	—	.125	.276	0	—	0	3	3	-0	0.0
1980	SF-N	5	3	.625	54	0	0	0	7	82^1	71	2	34	65	11.6	1.75	202	.233	.312	1	.200	1	17	16	0	2.0
1981	SF-N	7	5	.583	47	3	0	0	7	100^2	87	4	44	78	11.9	2.41	142	.233	.317	1	.063	-1	12	11	-1	1.3
1982	SF-N	7	3	.700	58	7	0	0	5	129^2	115	12	40	97	10.8	3.33	108	.231	.289	2	.059	-3	4	4	0	0.0
1983	*Phi-N	8	4	.667	68	0	0	0	25	91^2	63	8	30	100	9.1	2.26	158	.188	.255	0	.000	-1	14	13	-2	2.1
1984	Phi-N☆	5	10	.333	68	0	0	0	29	98^1	82	14	30	61	10.3	3.39	107	.225	.286	0	.000	-1	2	3	-2	0.3
1985	Phi-N	0	1	.000	3	0	0	0	1	4	5	0	4	1	20.3	4.50	82	.333	.474	0	—	0	-0	-0	0	-0.1
	Pit-N	1	3	.250	38	0	0	0	4	58^2	48	5	17	47	10.0	3.38	106	.227	.285	2	.400	2	1	1	-1	0.2
	Yr	1	4	.200	41	0	0	0	5	62^2	53	5	21	48	10.6	3.45	104	.233	.298	2	.400	2	1	1	-1	0.1
	Cal-A	0	1	.000	15	0	0	0	0	24^1	17	4	10	14	10.0	1.48	278	.193	.276	0	—	0	7	7	-0	0.3
1986	NY-A	1	0	1.000	25	1	0	0	0	40^2	44	5	9	37	11.7	5.09	80	.268	.306	0	—	0	-4	-5	-1	-0.2
1987	NY-A	0	0	—	3	0	0	0	0	6^1	9	1	9	5	25.6	14.21	31	.321	.486	0	—	0	-7	-7	0	0.0
Total	10	34	30	.531	384	11	0	0	78	646	548	55	232	513	10.9	2.98	121	.227	.296	6	.083	-2	48	46	-6	5.9
● MUL HOLLAND	Holland, Howard Arthur b: 1/6/03, Franklin, Va. d: 2/16/69, Winchester, Va. BR/TR, 6'4", 185 lbs. Deb: 5/25/26																									
1926	Cin-N	0	0	—	3	0	0	0	0	6^2	3	0	5	0	10.8	1.35	273	.136	.296	1	.500	0	2	2	1	0.1
1927	NY-N	1	0	1.000	2	0	0	0	0	2	0	0	3	0	13.5	0.00	—	.000	.333	0	—	0	1	1	-0	0.4
1929	StL-N	0	1	.000	8	0	0	0	0	14^1	13	3	7	5	13.2	9.42	50	.232	.328	1	.250	0	-7	-8	-0	-0.4
Total	3	1	1	.500	13	0	0	0	0	23	16	3	15	5	12.5	6.26	69	.190	.320	2	.333	1	-5	-5	0	0.1
● BILL HOLLAND	Holland, William David "Dutch" b: 6/4/15, Varina, N.C. BL/TL, 6'1", 190 lbs. Deb: 9/17/39																									
1939	Was-A	0	1	.000	3	0	0	0	0	4	6	1	5	2	24.8	11.25	39	.400	.550	0	—	0	-3	-3	0	-0.6
● ED HOLLEY	Holley, Edward Edgar b: 7/23/1899, Benton, Ky. d: 10/26/86, Paducah, Ky. BR/TR, 6'1.5", 195 lbs. Deb: 5/24/28																									
1928	Chi-N	0	0	—	13	1	0	0	0	31	31	1	16	10	14.2	3.77	102	.265	.363	0	.000	-0	1	0	-1	-0.1
1932	Phi-N	11	14	.440	34	30	16	2	0	228	247	15	55	87	12.2	3.95	112	.273	.319	12	.132	-6	-2	12	-2	0.4
1933	Phi-N	13	15	.464	30	28	12	3	0	206^2	219	18	62	56	12.8	3.53	108	.273	.335	12	.162	-2	-4	7	-3	0.4
1934	Phi-N	1	8	.111	15	13	2	0	0	72^2	85	10	31	14	14.9	7.18	66	.294	.370	5	.208	-1	-25	-20	-1	-2.2
	Pit-N	0	3	.000	5	4	0	0	0	9^1	20	1	6	2	27.0	15.43	27	.426	.509	2	1.000	2	-12	-12	0	-2.4
	Yr	1	11	.083	20	17	2	0	0	82	105	11	37	16	15.8	8.12	57	.309	.380	7	.269	1	-37	-32	-1	-4.6
Total	4	25	40	.385	97	76	30	5	0	547^2	602	45	170	169	13.1	4.40	95	.279	.339	31	.158	-8	-42	-13	-6	-3.9
● BUG HOLLIDAY	Holliday, James Wear b: 2/8/1867, St.Louis, Mo. d: 2/15/10, Cincinnati, Ohio BR/TR, 5'11", 151 lbs. Deb: 4/17/1889 U♦																									
1892	Cin-N	0	0	—	1	0	0	0	0	4	13	0	1	0	31.5	11.25	29	.520	.538	176	.292	0	-4	-4	0	0.0
1896	Cin-N	0	0	—	1	0	0	0	0	1	4	0	2	0	63.0	0.00	—	.571	.700	27	.321	0	0	1	-0	0.0
Total	2	0	0	—	2	0	0	0	0	5	17	0	3	0	37.8	9.00	39	.531	.583	1134	.311	1	-3	-3	-0	0.0
● CARL HOLLING	Holling, Carl b: 7/9/1896, Dana, Cal. d: 7/18/62, Santa Rosa, Cal. BR/TR, 6'1", 172 lbs. Deb: 4/19/21																									
1921	Det-A	3	7	.300	35	11	4	0	4	136	162	8	58	38	14.8	4.30	99	.305	.378	13	.271	1	-0	-0	2	0.2
1922	Det-A	1	1	.500	5	1	0	0	0	9^1	21	1	5	2	27.0	15.43	25	.525	.596	0	.000	-0	-12	-12	0	-1.9
Total	2	4	8	.333	40	12	4	0	4	145^1	183	9	63	40	15.6	5.02	85	.320	.394	13	.260	1	-12	-12	2	-1.7

YEAR	TM/L	W	L	PCT	G	GS	CG	SH	SV	IP	H	HR	BB	SO	RAT	ERA	ERA+	OAV	OOB	BH	AVG	PB	PR	/A	PD	TPI
● **AL HOLLINGSWORTH**	Hollingsworth, Albert Wayne "Boots" b: 2/25/08, St.Louis, Mo. d: 4/28/96, Austin, Tex. BL/TL, 6', 174 lbs. Deb: 4/16/35 C																									
1935	Cin-N	6	13	.316	38	22	8	0	0	173^1	165	5	76	89	12.6	3.89	102	.243	.321	8	.148	-2	2	2	1	0.0
1936	Cin-N	9	10	.474	29	25	9	0	0	184	204	4	66	76	13.5	4.16	92	.281	.345	23	.315	7	-3	-7	-2	-0.1
1937	Cin-N	9	15	.375	43	24	11	1	5	202^1	224	8	73	74	13.3	3.91	95	.278	.339	19	.250	3	0	-4	1	-0.1
1938	Cin-N	2	2	.500	9	4	1	0	0	34	43	2	12	13	14.6	7.15	51	.307	.362	3	.250	1	-13	-13	0	-1.2
	Phi-N	5	16	.238	24	21	11	1	0	174^1	177	4	77	80	13.1	3.82	102	.264	.340	15	.224	-0	-1	1	-2	-0.1
	Yr	7	18	.280	33	25	12	1	0	208^1	220	6	89	93	13.3	4.36	88	.272	.344	18	.228	1	-13	-12	-2	-1.3
1939	Phi-N	1	9	.100	15	10	3	0	0	60	78	2	27	24	15.8	5.85	69	.317	.385	2	.100	-1	-13	-12	-0	-1.9
	Bro-N	1	2	.333	8	5	1	0	0	27^1	33	1	11	11	14.8	5.27	76	.311	.381	1	.125	-1	-4	-4	1	-0.3
	Yr	2	11	.154	23	15	4	0	0	87^1	111	3	38	35	15.5	5.67	71	.315	.384	3	.107	-2	-17	-16	1	-2.2
1940	Was-A	1	0	1.000	3	2	0	0	0	18	18	0	11	7	14.5	5.50	76	.261	.363	1	.167	0	-2	-3	1	0.0
1942	StL-A	10	6	.625	33	18	7	1	4	161	173	4	52	60	12.7	2.96	125	.272	.329	10	.179	0	12	13	0	1.4
1943	StL-A	6	13	.316	35	20	9	1	3	154	169	7	51	63	13.0	4.21	79	.281	.339	7	.140	-1	-16	-15	-1	-2.0
1944	*StL-A	5	7	.417	26	10	3	2	1	92^2	108	3	37	22	14.2	4.47	81	.291	.357	2	.071	-2	-11	-9	-1	-1.4
1945	StL-A	12	9	.571	26	22	15	1	1	173^1	164	4	68	64	12.0	2.70	130	.251	.322	12	.197	1	13	16	2	2.2
1946	StL-A	0	0	—	5	0	0	0	0	11	23	1	4	3	22.1	6.55	57	.411	.450	0	.000	-0	-4	-3	-1	-0.1
	Chi-A	3	2	.600	21	2	0	0	1	55	63	2	22	22	13.9	4.58	74	.288	.353	0	.000	-1	-7	-7	-0	-0.8
	Yr	3	2	.600	26	2	0	0	1	66	86	3	26	25	15.3	4.91	71	.313	.372	0	.000	-1	-10	-11	-1	-0.9
Total	11	70	104	.402	315	185	78	7	15	1520^1	1642	47	587	608	13.3	3.99	93	.275	.341	103	.196	3	-44	-44	-2	-4.4
● **BONNIE HOLLINGSWORTH**	Hollingsworth, John Burnette b: 12/26/1895, Jacksboro, Tenn. d: 1/4/90, Knoxville, Tenn. BR/TR, 5'10", 170 lbs. Deb: 5/30/22																									
1922	Pit-N	0	0	—	9	0	0	0	0	13^2	17	0	8	7	17.1	7.90	52	.315	.413	0	—	0	-6	-6	-0	0.0
1923	Was-A	3	7	.300	17	8	1	0	0	72^2	72	3	50	26	15.5	4.09	92	.272	.393	2	.091	-1	-1	-3	-1	-0.5
1924	Bro-N	1	0	1.000	3	1	1	0	0	8^2	8	0	10	7	18.7	6.23	60	.267	.450	0	.000	-1	-2	-2	0	-0.3
1928	Bos-N	0	2	.000	7	2	0	0	0	22^1	30	2	13	10	17.3	5.24	75	.341	.426	1	.167	-0	-3	-3	0	-0.2
Total	4	4	9	.308	36	11	2	0	0	117^1	127	5	81	50	16.3	4.91	78	.291	.406	3	.097	-2	-12	-14	-1	-1.0
● **JESSIE HOLLINS**	Hollins, Jessie Edward b: 1/27/70, Conroe, Tex. BR/TR, 6'3", 190 lbs. Deb: 9/19/92																									
1992	Chi-N	0	0	—	4	0	0	0	0	4^2	8	1	5	0	25.1	13.50	27	.400	.520	0	—	0	-5	-5	-0	0.0
● **JOHN HOLLISON**	Hollison, John Henry "Swede" b: 5/3/1870, Chicago, Ill. d: 8/19/69, Chicago, Ill. BR/TL, 5'8", 162 lbs. Deb: 8/13/1892																									
1892	Chi-N	0	0	—	1	0	0	0	0	4	1	1	0	2	2.3	2.25	148	.077	.077	0	.000	-0	0	0	0	0.0
● **BOBO HOLLOMAN**	Holloman, Alva Lee b: 3/7/25, Thomaston, Ga. d: 5/1/87, Athens, Ga. BR/TR, 6'2", 207 lbs. Deb: 4/18/53																									
1953	StL-A	3	7	.300	22	10	1	1	0	65^1	69	2	50	25	16.5	5.23	80	.275	.397	2	.105	-2	-9	-8	-0	-1.2
● **JIM HOLLOWAY**	Holloway, James Madison b: 9/22/08, Plaquemine, La. d: 4/15/97, Baton Rouge, La. BR/TR, 6'1", 165 lbs. Deb: 5/17/29																									
1929	Phi-N	0	0	—	3	0	0	0	0	4^2	10	2	5	1	28.9	13.50	38	.455	.556	1	1.000	0	-5	-4	-0	0.0
● **KEN HOLLOWAY**	Holloway, Kenneth Eugene (b: Kenneth Eugene Hollaway) b: 8/8/1897, Barwick, Ga. d: 9/25/68, Thomasville, Ga. BR/TR, 6', 185 lbs. Deb: 8/27/22																									
1922	Det-A	0	0	—	1	0	0	0	0	1	1	0	0	1	9.0	0.00	—	.250	.250	0	—	0	0	0	0	0.0
1923	Det-A	11	10	.524	42	24	7	1	1	194	232	12	75	55	14.7	4.45	87	.302	.372	8	.123	-5	-10	-13	1	-1.5
1924	Det-A	14	6	.700	49	13	5	0	3	181^1	209	6	61	46	13.7	4.07	101	.299	.361	11	.190	-1	3	1	2	0.2
1925	Det-A	13	4	.765	38	14	6	0	2	157^2	170	8	67	29	13.6	4.62	93	.282	.356	11	.229	-0	-4	-6	-2	-0.8
1926	Det-A	4	6	.400	36	12	3	0	2	139	192	2	42	43	15.7	5.12	79	.343	.397	11	.239	0	-17	-16	0	-1.0
1927	Det-A	11	12	.478	36	23	11	1	6	183^1	210	10	61	36	13.5	4.07	103	.299	.359	8	.129	-5	1	3	2	0.0
1928	Det-A	4	8	.333	30	11	5	0	2	120^1	137	2	32	32	13.0	4.34	95	.291	.343	4	.121	-2	-4	-3	1	-0.4
1929	Cle-A	6	5	.545	25	11	6	2	0	119	118	2	37	32	11.9	3.03	147	.264	.323	7	.171	-2	16	19	-2	1.2
1930	Cle-A	1	1	.500	12	2	0	0	2	30	49	5	14	8	18.9	8.40	57	.374	.434	0	.000	-2	-13	-12	1	-0.9
	NY-A	0	0	—	16	0	0	0	0	34^1	52	3	8	11	15.7	5.24	82	.374	.408	3	.231	-0	-2	-4	-0	0.0
	Yr	1	1	.500	28	2	0	0	2	64^1	101	8	22	19	17.2	6.72	68	.374	.421	3	.120	-3	-15	-16	1	-0.9
Total	9	64	52	.552	285	110	43	4	18	1160	1370	50	397	293	14.0	4.40	95	.303	.364	63	.167	-18	-29	-30	4	-3.2
● **JEFF HOLLY**	Holly, Jeffrey Owen b: 3/1/53, San Pedro, Cal. BL/TL, 6'5", 210 lbs. Deb: 5/1/77																									
1977	Min-A	2	3	.400	18	5	0	0	0	48^1	57	8	12	32	13.0	6.89	58	.300	.345	0	—	0	-15	-16	-1	-1.3
1978	Min-A	1	1	.500	15	1	0	0	0	35^1	28	1	18	12	11.7	3.57	107	.222	.319	0	—	0	1	1	0	0.0
1979	Min-A	0	0	—	6	0	0	0	0	6^1	10	0	3	5	18.5	7.11	62	.385	.448	0	—	0	-2	-2	0	0.0
Total	3	3	4	.429	39	6	0	0	0	90	95	9	33	49	12.9	5.60	70	.278	.343	0	—	0	-16	-17	-0	-1.3
● **BRAD HOLMAN**	Holman, Bradley Thomas b: 2/9/68, Kansas City, Mo. BR/TR, 6'5", 200 lbs. Deb: 7/4/93 F																									
1993	Sea-A	1	3	.250	19	0	0	0	3	36^1	27	1	16	17	11.9	3.72	118	.208	.318	0	—	0	2	3	-1	0.2
● **BRIAN HOLMAN**	Holman, Brian Scott b: 1/25/65, Denver, Colo. BR/TR, 6'4", 185 lbs. Deb: 6/25/88 F																									
1988	Mon-N	4	8	.333	18	16	1	1	0	100^1	101	3	34	58	12.1	3.23	111	.264	.324	3	.107	-1	2	4	-1	0.2
1989	Mon-N	1	2	.333	10	3	0	0	0	31^2	34	2	15	23	14.2	4.83	73	.270	.352	1	.125	-0	-5	-5	-0	-0.5
	Sea-A	8	10	.444	23	22	6	2	0	159^2	160	9	62	82	12.9	3.44	117	.261	.335	0	—	0	8	10	1	1.2
1990	Sea-A	11	11	.500	28	28	3	0	0	189^2	188	17	66	121	12.3	4.03	98	.260	.327	0	.000	-0	-3	-2	-1	-0.3
1991	Sea-A	13	14	.481	30	30	5	3	0	195^1	199	16	77	108	13.2	3.69	112	.268	.345	0	—	0	9	9	2	1.4
Total	4	37	45	.451	109	99	15	6	0	676^2	682	47	254	392	12.8	3.71	106	.263	.335	4	.108	-1	12	18	-0	2.0
● **SCOTT HOLMAN**	Holman, Randy Scott b: 9/18/58, Santa Paula, Cal. BR/TR, 6'1", 190 lbs. Deb: 9/20/80																									
1980	NY-N	0	0	—	4	0	0	0	0	7	6	0	1	3	9.0	1.29	276	.250	.280	0	—	0	2	2	-0	0.0
1982	NY-N	2	1	.667	4	4	1	0	0	26^2	23	2	7	11	10.1	2.36	154	.232	.283	2	.222	0	4	4	1	0.5
1983	NY-N	1	7	.125	35	10	0	0	0	101	90	7	52	44	12.7	3.74	97	.242	.336	5	.217	0	-1	-1	2	0.2
Total	3	3	8	.273	43	14	1	0	0	134^2	119	9	60	58	12.0	3.34	108	.240	.324	7	.219	1	4	4	2	0.7
● **SHAWN HOLMAN**	Holman, Shawn Leroy b: 11/10/64, Sewickley, Pa. BR/TR, 6'2", 185 lbs. Deb: 9/5/89																									
1989	Det-A	0	0	—	5	0	0	0	0	10	8	0	11	9	17.1	1.80	212	.211	.388	0	—	0	2	2	-0	0.0
● **DARREN HOLMES**	Holmes, Darren Lee b: 4/25/66, Asheville, N.C. BR/TR, 6', 199 lbs. Deb: 9/1/90																									
1990	LA-N	0	1	.000	14	0	0	0	0	17^1	15	1	11	19	13.5	5.19	70	.238	.351	0	—	0	-3	-3	-0	-0.2
1991	Mil-A	1	4	.200	40	0	0	0	3	76^1	90	6	27	59	13.9	4.72	84	.295	.354	0	—	0	-5	-6	1	-0.2
1992	Mil-A	4	4	.500	41	0	0	0	6	42^1	35	1	11	31	10.2	2.55	150	.224	.284	0	—	0	7	6	0	1.3
1993	Col-N	3	3	.500	62	0	0	0	25	66^2	56	6	20	60	10.5	4.05	118	.222	.285	0	—	0	-0	5	-0	0.8
1994	Col-N	0	3	.000	29	0	0	0	3	28^1	35	5	24	33	19.1	6.35	78	.313	.438	0	.000	-0	-7	-4	-0	-0.5
1995	*Col-N	6	1	.857	68	0	0	0	14	66^2	59	3	28	61	11.9	3.24	166	.237	.317	0	.000	-0	7	16	1	2.2
1996	Col-N	5	4	.556	62	0	0	0	1	77	78	8	28	73	12.5	3.97	131	.259	.324	0	.000	-0	2	11	-1	1.1
1997	Col-N	9	2	.818	42	6	0	0	3	89^1	113	12	36	70	15.0	5.34	97	.314	.376	3	.158	-0	-11	-2	1	-0.1
1998	NY-A	0	3	.000	34	0	0	0	2	51^1	53	4	14	31	12.1	3.33	134	.270	.325	0	—	0	8	6	-0	0.4
Total	9	28	25	.528	392	6	0	0	57	515^1	534	46	199	437	13.0	4.23	112	.268	.337	3	.130	-0	-3	29	1	4.8
● **CHICK HOLMES**	Holmes, Elwood Marter b: 3/22/1896, Beverly, N.J. d: 4/15/54, Camden, N.J. TR , Deb: 6/27/18																									
1918	Phi-A	0	0	—	2	0	0	0	0	2	4	0	1	0	27.0	13.50	22	.400	.500	0	—	0	-2	-2	-0	0.0
● **JIM HOLMES**	Holmes, James Scott b: 8/2/1882, Lawrenceburg, Ky. d: 3/10/60, Jacksonville, Fla. Deb: 9/8/06																									
1906	Phi-A	0	1	.000	3	1	0	0	0	9	10	0	8	1	19.0	4.00	68	.286	.432	3	.600	1	-1	-1	0	0.0
1908	Bro-N	1	4	.200	13	1	1	0	0	40	37	0	20	10	13.5	3.37	69	.270	.375	1	.077	-1	-4	-5	-2	-0.9
Total	2	1	5	.167	16	2	1	0	0	49	47	0	28	11	14.5	3.49	69	.273	.387	4	.222	0	-6	-6	-2	-0.9
● **DUCKY HOLMES**	Holmes, James William b: 1/28/1869, Des Moines, Iowa d: 8/6/32, Truro, Iowa BL/TR, 5'6", 170 lbs. Deb: 8/8/1895 ♦																									
1895	Lou-N	1	0	1.000	2	1	1	0	0	14	16	1	4	0	13.5	5.79	80	.281	.339	60	.373	1	-2	-2	0	0.0

YEAR	TM/L	W	L	PCT	G	GS	CG	SH	SV	IP	H	HR	BB	SO	RAT	ERA	ERA+	OAV	OOB	BH	AVG	PB	PR	/A	PD	TPI
1896	Lou-N	0	1	.000	2	1	0	0	0	12	26	0	8	3	25.5	7.50	58	.433	.500	38	.270	0	-4	-4	0	-0.2
Total	2	1	1	.500	4	2	1	0	0	26	42	1	12	3	19.0	6.58	68	.359	.423	1014	.282	1	-6	-6	0	-0.2
● HERM HOLSHOUSER	Holshouser, Herman Alexander b: 1/20/07, Rockwell, N.C. d: 7/26/94, Concord, N.C. BR/TR, 6′, 170 lbs. Deb: 4/15/30																									
1930	StL-A	0	1	.000	25	1	0	0	1	62^1	103	8	28	37	19.3	7.80	63	.376	.439	2	.125	-1	-22	-20	-0	-0.4
● CHRIS HOLT	Holt, Christopher Michael b: 9/18/71, Dallas, Tex. BR/TR, 6′4″, 205 lbs. Deb: 9/1/96																									
1996	Hou-N	0	1	.000	4	0	0	0	0	4^2	5	0	3	0	15.4	5.79	67	.263	.364	0	.000	-0	-1	-1	0	-0.2
1997	Hou-N	8	12	.400	33	32	0	0	0	209^2	211	17	61	95	12.0	3.52	113	.263	.321	6	.090	-3	16	11	0	0.7
Total	2	8	13	.381	37	32	0	0	0	214^1	216	17	64	95	12.1	3.57	112	.263	.323	6	.088	-3	15	10	0	0.5
● VERN HOLTGRAVE	Holtgrave, Lavern George "Woody" b: 10/18/42, Aviston, Ill. BR/TR, 6′1″, 183 lbs. Deb: 9/26/65																									
1965	Det-A	0	0	—	1	0	0	0	0	3	4	0	2	2	18.0	6.00	58	.308	.400	0	—	0	-1	-1	-0	0.0
● BRIAN HOLTON	Holton, Brian John b: 11/29/59, McKeesport, Pa. BR/TR, 6′, 193 lbs. Deb: 9/9/85																									
1985	LA-N	1	1	.500	3	0	0	0	0	4	9	0	1	1	22.5	9.00	39	.450	.476	0	—	0	-2	-2	0	-1.0
1986	LA-N	2	3	.400	12	3	0	0	0	24^1	28	1	6	24	12.9	4.44	78	.292	.340	0	.000	-1	-2	-3	0	-0.5
1987	LA-N	3	2	.600	53	1	0	0	2	83^1	87	11	32	58	12.9	3.89	102	.269	.335	1	.200	0	2	1	1	0.1
1988	*LA-N	7	3	.700	45	0	0	0	1	84^2	69	1	26	49	10.2	1.70	196	.228	.292	0	.000	-1	16	15	-0	1.7
1989	Bal-A	5	7	.417	39	12	0	0	0	116^1	140	11	39	51	13.9	4.02	94	.300	.355	0	—	0	-2	-3	-0	-0.3
1990	Bal-A	2	3	.400	33	0	0	0	0	58	68	7	21	27	13.8	4.50	84	.292	.350	0	—	0	-4	-5	1	-0.3
Total	6	20	19	.513	185	16	0	0	3	370^2	401	31	125	210	12.8	3.62	102	.278	.337	1	.050	-1	8	3	1	-0.3
● MIKE HOLTZ	Holtz, Michael James b: 10/10/72, Arlington, Va. BL/TL, 5′9″, 172 lbs. Deb: 7/11/96																									
1996	Cal-A	3	3	.500	30	0	0	0	0	29^1	21	1	19	31	13.2	2.45	204	.204	.344	0	—	0	8	8	0	1.5
1997	Ana-A	3	4	.429	66	0	0	0	2	43^1	38	7	15	40	11.4	3.32	137	.228	.299	0	.000	-0	6	6	1	0.9
1998	Ana-A	2	2	.500	53	0	0	0	1	30^1	38	0	15	29	16.0	4.75	99	.322	.403	0	—	0	-0	-0	-1	-0.1
Total	3	8	9	.471	149	0	0	0	3	103	97	8	49	100	13.3	3.50	135	.250	.343	0	.000	-0	14	14	0	2.3
● KEN HOLTZMAN	Holtzman, Kenneth Dale b: 11/3/45, St.Louis, Mo. BR/TL, 6′2″, 175 lbs. Deb: 9/4/65																									
1965	Chi-N	0	0	—	3	0	0	0	0	4	2	1	3	3	11.3	2.25	164	.143	.294	0	—	0	1	1	0	0.0
1966	Chi-N	11	16	.407	34	33	9	0	0	220^2	194	27	68	171	10.8	3.79	97	.235	.296	9	.123	-3	-5	-3	-2	-0.8
1967	Chi-N	9	0	1.000	12	12	3	0	0	92^2	76	11	44	62	11.8	2.53	140	.222	.314	7	.200	1	9	10	0	1.1
1968	Chi-N	11	14	.440	34	32	6	3	1	215	201	17	76	151	11.8	3.35	94	.248	.317	10	.125	-2	-9	-4	1	-0.7
1969	Chi-N	17	13	.567	39	39	12	6	0	261^1	248	18	93	176	11.9	3.58	112	.247	.314	15	.150	-1	0	13	-1	1.2
1970	Chi-N	17	11	.607	39	38	15	1	0	287^2	271	30	94	202	11.5	3.38	133	.248	.309	21	.200	1	21	36	0	3.4
1971	Chi-N	9	15	.375	30	29	9	3	0	195	213	18	64	143	12.9	4.48	88	.276	.333	9	.130	-1	-22	-12	-1	-1.5
1972	*Oak-A☆	19	11	.633	39	37	16	4	0	265^1	232	23	52	134	9.8	2.51	113	.236	.278	16	.178	2	16	10	0	1.4
1973	*Oak-A★	21	13	.618	40	40	16	4	0	297^1	275	22	66	157	10.4	2.97	120	.243	.287	0	—	0	28	19	-1	2.0
1974	*Oak-A	19	17	.528	39	38	9	3	0	255^1	273	14	51	117	11.5	3.07	108	.272	.309	0	—	0	16	7	0	1.0
1975	*Oak-A	18	14	.563	39	38	13	2	0	266^1	217	16	108	122	11.2	3.14	115	.222	.303	0	.000	-0	19	14	3	1.9
1976	Bal-A	5	4	.556	13	13	6	1	0	97^2	100	4	35	25	12.5	2.86	115	.271	.336	0	—	0	7	5	1	0.5
	NY-A	9	7	.563	21	21	10	2	0	149	165	14	35	41	12.1	4.17	82	.283	.323	0	—	0	-11	-12	-1	-1.3
	Yr	14	11	.560	34	34	16	3	0	246^2	265	18	70	66	12.2	3.65	92	.277	.326	0	—	0	-4	-8	1	-0.8
1977	NY-A	2	3	.400	18	11	0	0	0	71^2	105	7	24	14	16.3	5.78	68	.362	.413	0	—	0	-14	-15	2	-0.6
1978	NY-A	1	0	1.000	5	3	0	0	0	17^2	21	2	9	3	15.3	4.08	89	.313	.395	0	—	0	-1	-1	1	0.2
	Chi-N	0	3	.000	23	6	0	0	2	53	61	10	35	36	16.5	6.11	66	.286	.390	2	.200	0	-15	-12	-0	-0.8
1979	Chi-N	6	9	.400	23	20	3	2	0	117^2	133	15	53	44	14.7	4.59	90	.287	.368	10	.233	2	-11	-6	-2	-0.7
Total	15	174	150	.537	451	410	127	31	3	2867^1	2787	249	910	1601	11.8	3.49	104	.255	.315	99	.163	-1	31	48	1	6.3
● MARK HOLZEMER	Holzemer, Mark Harold b: 8/20/69, Littleton, Colo. BL/TL, 6′, 165 lbs. Deb: 8/21/93																									
1993	Cal-A	0	3	.000	5	4	0	0	0	23^1	34	2	13	10	19.3	8.87	51	.340	.431	0	—	0	-12	-11	0	-1.3
1995	Cal-A	0	1	.000	12	0	0	0	0	8^1	11	1	7	5	20.5	5.40	87	.306	.432	0	—	0	-1	-1	-1	-0.1
1996	Cal-A	1	0	1.000	25	0	0	0	0	24^2	35	7	8	20	16.8	8.76	57	.327	.390	0	—	0	-10	-10	1	-0.3
1997	Sea-A	0	0	—	14	0	0	0	1	9	9	0	8	7	17.0	6.00	75	.250	.386	0	—	0	-1	-2	1	0.0
1998	Oak-A	1	0	1.000	13	0	0	0	0	9^2	13	1	3	3	15.8	5.59	82	.333	.395	0	—	0	-1	-1	-0	0.0
Total	5	2	4	.333	69	4	0	0	1	75	102	11	39	45	17.9	7.68	61	.321	.408	0	—	0	-25	-25	0	-1.7
● RICK HONEYCUTT	Honeycutt, Frederick Wayne b: 6/29/54, Chattanooga, Tenn. BL/TL, 5′11″, 190 lbs. Deb: 8/24/77																									
1977	Sea-A	0	1	.000	10	3	0	0	0	29	26	7	11	17	12.4	4.34	95	.239	.325	0	—	0	-1	-1	-1	0.0
1978	Sea-A	5	11	.313	26	24	4	1	0	134^1	150	12	49	50	13.5	4.89	78	.285	.349	0	—	0	-17	-16	1	-1.5
1979	Sea-A	11	12	.478	33	28	8	1	0	194	201	22	67	83	12.7	4.04	108	.268	.333	0	—	0	4	7	-1	0.6
1980	Sea-A☆	10	17	.370	30	30	9	1	0	203^1	221	22	60	79	12.6	3.94	105	.280	.333	0	—	0	2	4	-0	0.5
1981	Tex-A	11	6	.647	20	20	8	2	0	127^2	120	12	17	40	9.7	3.31	105	.246	.272	0	—	0	5	2	1	0.5
1982	Tex-A	5	17	.227	30	26	4	1	0	164	201	20	54	64	14.2	5.27	73	.305	.360	0	—	0	-22	-25	1	-2.5
1983	Tex-A★	14	8	.636	25	25	5	2	0	174^2	168	9	37	56	10.9	**2.42**	**165**	.262	.308	0	—	0	**32**	31	3	**4.3**
	*LA-N	2	3	.400	9	7	1	0	0	39	46	6	13	18	14.1	5.77	62	.297	.359	1	.083	-1	-9	-9	2	-1.0
1984	LA-N	10	9	.526	29	28	6	2	0	183^2	180	11	51	75	11.4	2.84	124	.258	.310	8	.143	-0	15	14	2	1.6
1985	*LA-N	8	12	.400	31	25	1	0	1	142	141	9	49	67	12.1	3.42	102	.261	.323	5	.132	0	3	1	3	0.4
1986	LA-N	11	9	.550	32	28	0	0	0	171	164	9	45	100	11.2	3.32	104	.249	.300	3	.070	0	8	3	2	0.5
1987	LA-N	2	12	.143	27	20	1	1	0	115^2	133	10	45	92	14.0	4.59	86	.278	.343	7	.233	2	-7	-8	-0	-0.7
	Oak-A	1	4	.200	7	4	0	0	0	23^2	25	3	9	10	13.7	5.32	77	.275	.353	0	—	0	-2	-3	-0	-0.5
1988	*Oak-A	3	2	.600	55	0	0	0	7	79^2	74	6	25	47	11.5	3.50	108	.253	.318	0	—	0	4	2	1	0.4
1989	*Oak-A	2	2	.500	64	0	0	0	12	76^2	56	5	26	52	9.7	2.35	157	.207	.279	0	—	0	13	11	1	1.0
1990	*Oak-A	2	2	.500	63	0	0	0	7	63^1	46	2	22	38	9.8	2.70	138	.204	.278	0	.000	-0	8	7	1	0.6
1991	Oak-A	2	4	.333	43	0	0	0	0	37^2	37	3	20	26	14.1	3.58	107	.261	.360	0	—	0	2	1	0	0.4
1992	*Oak-A	1	4	.200	54	0	0	0	3	39	41	2	10	32	12.5	3.69	101	.272	.329	0	—	0	1	0	-1	0.2
1993	Oak-A	1	4	.200	52	0	0	0	1	41^2	30	2	20	21	11.0	2.81	145	.211	.313	0	—	0	7	6	-0	1.0
1994	Tex-A	1	2	.333	42	0	0	0	1	25	37	4	9	18	17.3	7.20	67	.349	.410	0	—	0	-7	-7	1	-0.6
1995	Oak-A	5	1	.833	49	0	0	0	2	44^2	37	5	9	21	9.5	2.42	185	.231	.276	0	—	0	11	10	-0	1.2
	NY-A	0	0	—	3	0	0	0	0	1	2	1	1	0	27.0	27.00	17	.400	.500	0	—	0	-2	-2	0	0.0
	Yr	5	1	.833	52	0	0	0	2	45^2	39	6	10	21	9.7	2.96	151	.234	.277	0	—	0	9	8	-0	1.2
1996	*StL-N	2	1	.667	61	0	0	0	4	47^1	42	3	7	30	9.3	2.85	147	.240	.269	0	.000	1	7	7	1	0.6
1997	StL-N	0	0	—	2	0	0	0	0	2	5	0	1	2	27.0	13.50	31	.500	.545	0	—	0	-2	-2	-0	0.0
Total	21	109	143	.433	797	268	47	11	38	2160	2183	185	657	1038	12.0	3.72	104	.264	.322	24	.132	2	54	32	15	7.0
● DON HOOD	Hood, Donald Harris b: 10/16/49, Florence, S.C. BL/TL, 6′2″, 180 lbs. Deb: 7/16/73																									
1973	*Bal-A	3	2	.600	8	4	1	1	1	32^1	31	1	6	18	10.6	3.90	96	.256	.297	0	—	0	-0	-1	-1	-0.1
1974	Bal-A	1	1	.500	20	2	0	0	1	57^1	47	1	20	26	10.5	3.45	100	.223	.290	0	—	0	1	-0	-0	0.0
1975	Cle-A	6	10	.375	29	19	2	0	0	135^1	136	16	57	51	12.8	4.39	86	.268	.342	0	—	0	-9	-9	-2	-1.1
1976	Cle-A	3	5	.375	33	6	0	0	1	77^2	89	5	41	32	15.5	4.87	72	.296	.387	0	—	0	-12	-12	0	-1.1
1977	Cle-A	2	1	.667	41	5	1	0	0	105	87	3	49	62	12.0	3.00	131	.224	.317	0	—	0	12	11	-2	0.4
1978	Cle-A	5	6	.455	36	19	1	0	0	154^2	166	13	77	73	14.2	4.48	83	.278	.361	0	—	0	-12	-13	0	-0.7
1979	Cle-A	1	0	1.000	13	0	0	0	1	22	13	1	14	7	11.5	3.68	116	.169	.304	0	—	0	1	1	0	0.1
	NY-A	3	1	.750	27	6	0	0	1	67^1	62	3	30	22	12.6	3.07	132	.252	.338	0	—	0	9	7	1	0.5
	Yr	4	1	.800	40	6	0	0	2	89^1	75	4	44	29	12.2	3.22	128	.231	.327	0	—	0	10	9	1	0.6
1980	StL-N	4	6	.400	33	8	1	0	0	82^1	90	2	34	35	13.8	3.39	109	.288	.362	4	.200	-0	2	3	1	0.4
1982	KC-A	4	0	1.000	30	3	0	0	1	66^2	71	7	22	31	12.8	3.51	116	.276	.338	0	—	0	4	4	0	0.3
1983	KC-A	2	3	.400	27	0	0	0	0	47^2	48	5	14	17	12.1	2.27	180	.273	.333	0	—	0	10	10	1	1.1
Total	10	34	35	.493	297	72	6	1	6	848^1	840	57	364	374	13.0	3.79	101	.263	.342	4	.200	-0	5	2	-0	-0.2

YEAR TM/L	W	L	PCT	G	GS	CG	SH	SV	IP	H	HR	BB	SO	RAT	ERA	ERA+	OAV	OOB	BH	AVG	PB	PR	/A	PD	TPI
● **WALLY HOOD**	Hood, Wallace James Jr. b: 9/24/25, Los Angeles, Cal. BR/TR, 6'1", 190 lbs. Deb: 9/23/49 F																								
1949 NY-A	0	0	—	2	0	0	0	0	2^1	0	0	1	2	3.9	0.00	—	.000	.143	0		0	1	1	-0	0.0
● **CHRIS HOOK**	Hook, Christopher Wayne b: 8/4/68, San Diego, Cal. BR/TR, 6'5", 230 lbs. Deb: 4/30/95																								
1995 SF-N	5	1	.833	45	0	0	0	0	52^1	55	7	29	40	15.0	5.50	74	.274	.373	0	.000	-0	-8	-8	-0	-0.9
1996 SF-N	0	1	.000	10	0	0	0	0	13^1	16	3	14	4	21.6	7.43	55	.308	.471	1	.500	0	-5	-5	0	-0.2
Total 2	5	2	.714	55	0	0	0	0	65^2	71	10	43	44	16.3	5.89	69	.281	.395	1	.200	0	-12	-13	0	-1.1
● **JAY HOOK**	Hook, James Wesley b: 11/18/36, Waukegan, Ill. BL/TR, 6'2", 182 lbs. Deb: 9/3/57																								
1957 Cin-N	0	1	.000	3	2	0	0	0	10	6	0	8	6	12.6	4.50	91	.176	.333	0	.000	-0	-1	-0	0	-0.1
1958 Cin-N	0	1	.000	1	1	0	0	0	3	3	2	2	5	15.0	12.00	35	.250	.357	0	.000	-0	-3	-3	-0	-0.6
1959 Cin-N	5	5	.500	17	15	4	0	0	79	79	11	39	37	13.8	5.13	79	.266	.357	3	.125	-1	-10	-9	-1	-1.2
1960 Cin-N	11	18	.379	36	33	10	2	0	222	222	31	73	103	12.2	4.50	85	.263	.325	6	.083	-3	-18	-17	-1	-2.4
1961 Cin-N	1	3	.250	22	5	0	0	0	62^2	83	14	22	36	15.8	7.76	52	.322	.386	2	.133	-1	-26	-26	-1	-1.6
1962 NY-N	8	19	.296	37	34	13	0	0	213^2	230	31	71	113	13.0	4.84	86	.273	.335	14	.203	2	-21	-16	-0	-1.5
1963 NY-N	4	14	.222	41	20	3	0	1	152^2	168	21	53	89	13.6	5.48	64	.281	.348	9	.237	2	-37	-34	-1	-3.7
1964 NY-N	0	1	.000	3	2	0	0	0	9^2	17	2	7	5	22.3	9.31	38	.395	.480	0	.000	-0	-6	-6	0	-0.5
Total 8	29	62	.319	160	112	30	2	1	752^2	808	112	275	394	13.3	5.23	75	.276	.344	34	.151	-2	-123	-110	-4	-11.6
● **BUCK HOOKER**	Hooker, William Edward b: 8/28/1880, Richmond, Va. d: 7/2/29, Richmond, Va. TR, 5'6", Deb: 9/5/02																								
1902 Cin-N	0	1	.000	1	1	1	0	0	8	11	1	0	0	12.4	4.50	67	.324	.324	0	.000	-0	-2	-1	-0	-0.2
1903 Cin-N	0	0	—	1	0	0	0	0	2^1	2	0	2	0	15.4	0.00	—	.250	.400	0	.000	-0	1	1	-0	0.0
Total 2	0	1	.000	2	1	1	0	0	10^1	13	1	2	0	13.1	3.48	90	.310	.341	0	.000	-1	-1	-0	-0	-0.2
● **HARRY HOOPER**	Hooper, Harry Bartholomew b: 8/24/1887, Bell Station, Cal. d: 12/18/74, Santa Cruz, Cal. BL/TR, 5'10", 168 lbs. Deb: 4/16/09 H◆																								
1913 Bos-A	0	0	—	1	0	0	0	0	2	2	0	1	0	13.5	0.00	—	.333	.429	169	.288	0	1	1	-0	0.0
● **BOB HOOPER**	Hooper, Robert Nelson b: 5/30/22, Leamington, Ont., Canada d: 3/17/80, New Brunswick, N.J BR/TR, 5'11", 195 lbs. Deb: 4/19/50																								
1950 Phi-A	15	10	.600	45	20	3	0	5	170^1	181	15	91	58	14.4	5.02	91	.272	.361	7	.125	-2	-8	-9	3	-1.0
1951 Phi-A	12	10	.545	38	23	9	0	5	189	192	13	61	64	12.2	4.38	98	.267	.327	15	.208	-1	-5	-2	1	-0.2
1952 Phi-A	8	15	.348	43	14	4	0	6	144^1	158	13	68	40	14.3	5.18	76	.279	.361	8	.195	1	-24	-20	3	-2.6
1953 Cle-A	5	4	.556	43	0	0	0	7	69^1	50	4	38	16	11.7	4.02	93	.206	.318	1	.083	-1	-0	-2	1	-0.3
1954 Cle-A	0	0	—	17	0	0	0	2	34^2	39	3	16	12	14.5	4.93	74	.289	.368	0	.000	-1	-5	-5	-0	-0.1
1955 Cin-N	0	2	.000	8	0	0	0	0	13	20	2	6	6	18.0	7.62	56	.357	.419	0	.000	-0	-5	-5	0	-0.6
Total 6	40	41	.494	194	57	16	0	25	620^2	640	50	280	196	13.5	4.80	87	.268	.348	31	.166	-4	-48	-42	8	-4.8
● **LEON HOOTEN**	Hooten, Michael Leon b: 4/4/48, Downey, Cal. BR/TR, 5'11", 180 lbs. Deb: 4/13/74																								
1974 Oak-A	0	0	—	6	0	0	0	0	8^1	6	1	4	1	11.9	3.24	102	.207	.324	0	—	0	0	0	0	0.0
● **BURT HOOTON**	Hooton, Burt Carlton b: 2/7/50, Greenville, Tex. BR/TR, 6'1", 210 lbs. Deb: 6/17/71																								
1971 Chi-N	2	0	1.000	3	3	2	1	0	21^1	8	2	10	22	7.6	2.11	186	.111	.220	0	.000	-1	3	4	-0	0.3
1972 Chi-N	11	14	.440	33	31	9	3	0	218^1	201	13	81	132	11.7	2.80	136	.246	.315	9	.125	-1	16	24	1	2.8
1973 Chi-N	14	17	.452	42	34	9	2	0	239^2	248	12	73	134	12.2	3.68	107	.270	.327	9	.129	-0	-1	7	-1	0.7
1974 Chi-N	7	11	.389	48	21	3	1	1	176^1	214	16	51	94	13.7	4.80	79	.299	.348	3	.060	-4	-23	-19	3	-1.9
1975 Chi-N	0	2	.000	3	3	0	0	0	11	18	2	4	5	18.0	8.18	47	.383	.431	0	.000	-0	-6	-5	1	-0.7
LA-N	18	7	.720	31	30	12	4	0	223^2	172	16	64	148	9.5	2.82	121	.210	.267	9	.129	1	20	14	-2	1.4
Yr	18	9	.667	34	33	12	4	0	234^2	190	18	68	153	9.9	3.07	111	.219	.276	9	.123	0	14	9	-1	0.7
1976 LA-N	11	15	.423	33	33	8	4	0	226^2	203	16	60	116	10.5	3.26	104	.241	.292	6	.097	-2	6	3	-2	0.0
1977 *LA-N	12	7	.632	32	31	6	2	1	223^1	184	14	60	153	10.0	2.62	146	.225	.281	11	.164	-0	32	30	0	2.4
1978 *LA-N	19	10	.655	32	32	10	3	0	236	196	17	61	104	9.8	2.71	130	.226	.277	10	.149	1	23	21	1	2.6
1979 LA-N	11	10	.524	29	29	12	1	0	212	191	11	63	129	10.9	2.97	122	.244	.302	11	.147	-1	18	16	-0	1.4
1980 LA-N	14	8	.636	34	33	4	2	1	206^2	194	22	64	118	11.2	3.66	96	.249	.306	4	.063	-3	-1	-4	-0	-0.7
1981 *LA-N★	11	6	.647	23	23	5	4	0	142^1	124	3	33	74	10.1	2.28	146	.237	.285	8	.190	1	19	16	-1	2.1
1982 LA-N	4	7	.364	21	21	2	2	0	120^2	130	5	33	51	12.3	4.03	86	.275	.325	3	.086	-1	-6	-8	0	-0.7
1983 LA-N	9	8	.529	33	27	2	0	0	160	156	21	59	87	12.2	4.22	85	.254	.321	8	.160	1	-11	-11	-0	-1.1
1984 LA-N	3	6	.333	54	6	0	0	4	110	109	5	43	62	12.4	3.44	103	.263	.333	1	.071	-1	2	1	-0	0.0
1985 Tex-A	5	8	.385	29	20	2	0	0	124	149	18	40	62	13.7	5.23	81	.297	.349	0	—	0	-15	-14	-1	-1.4
Total 15	151	136	.526	480	377	86	29	7	2652	2497	193	799	1491	11.3	3.38	108	.250	.306	92	.123	-9	77	77	-4	7.2
● **JOHN HOOVER**	Hoover, John Nicklaus b: 11/22/62, Fresno, Cal. BR/TR, 6'2", 190 lbs. Deb: 5/23/90																								
1990 Tex-A	0	0	—	2	0	0	0	0	4^2	8	0	3	0	21.2	11.57	34	.364	.440	0	—	0	-4	-4	-0	0.0
● **DICK HOOVER**	Hoover, Richard Lloyd b: 12/11/25, Columbus, Ohio d: 4/12/81, Lake Placid, Fla. BL/TL, 6', 170 lbs. Deb: 4/16/52																								
1952 Bos-N	0	0	—	2	0	0	0	0	4^2	8	1	3	0	21.2	7.71	47	.348	.423	0	—	0	-2	-2	-0	0.0
● **JOHN HOPE**	Hope, John Alan b: 12/21/70, Ft.Lauderdale, Fla. BR/TR, 6'3", 195 lbs. Deb: 8/29/93																								
1993 Pit-N	0	2	.000	7	7	0	0	0	38	47	2	8	8	13.5	4.03	101	.313	.356	1	.077	-1	0	0	0	0.0
1994 Pit-N	0	0	—	9	0	0	0	0	14	18	1	4	6	15.4	5.79	75	.310	.375	1	.333	0	-2	-2	0	0.0
1995 Pit-N	0	0	—	3	0	0	0	0	2^1	8	0	4	2	57.9	30.86	14	.615	.750	0	—	0	-7	-7	-0	0.0
1996 Pit-N	1	3	.250	5	4	0	0	0	19^1	17	5	11	13	14.0	6.98	62	.243	.361	1	.200	0	-6	-6	0	-0.9
Total 4	1	5	.167	24	11	0	0	0	73^2	90	8	27	29	15.4	5.99	70	.309	.385	3	.143	-1	-15	-15	1	-0.9
● **SAM HOPE**	Hope, Samuel b: 12/4/1878, Brooklyn, N.Y. d: 6/30/46, Greenport, N.Y. BR/TR, 5'10", Deb: 8/5/07																								
1907 Phi-A	0	0	—	1	0	0	0	0	0^1	3	0	0	0	81.0	0.00	—	.750	.750	0	—	0	0	0	0	0.0
● **PAUL HOPKINS**	Hopkins, Paul Henry b: 9/25/04, Chester, Conn. BR/TR, 6', 175 lbs. Deb: 9/29/27																								
1927 Was-A	1	0	1.000	2	1	0	0	0	9	13	1	4	5	17.0	5.00	81	.361	.425	2	.667	1	-1	-1	0	0.0
1929 Was-A	0	1	.000	7	0	0	0	0	16^1	15	1	9	5	13.2	2.20	192	.250	.348	0	.000	-1	4	4	-0	0.1
StL-A	0	0	—	2	0	0	0	0	2	0	0	2	1	9.0	0.00	—	.000	.286	0	—	0	1	1	-0	0.0
Yr	0	1	.000	9	0	0	0	0	18^1	15	1	11	6	12.8	1.96	217	.231	.342	0	.000	-1	5	5	-0	0.1
Total 2	1	1	.500	11	1	0	0	0	27^1	28	2	15	11	14.2	2.96	142	.277	.371	2	.333	1	4	4	-0	0.1
● **LEFTY HOPPER**	Hopper, Clarence F. b: 5/27/1874, Jersey City, N.J. TL, Deb: 10/10/1898																								
1898 Bro-N	0	2	.000	2	2	2	0	0	11	14	0	5	5	15.5	4.91	73	.304	.373	0	.000	-1	-2	-2	0	-0.3
● **JIM HOPPER**	Hopper, James McDaniel b: 9/1/19, Charlotte, N.C. d: 1/23/82, Charlotte, N.C. BR/TR, 6'1", 175 lbs. Deb: 4/21/46																								
1946 Pit-N	0	1	.000	2	1	0	0	0	4	6	1	3	1	20.3	11.25	31	.316	.409	0	—	0	-3	-3	0	-0.7
● **BILL HOPPER**	Hopper, William Booth "Bird Dog" b: 10/26/1890, Jackson, Tenn. d: 1/14/65, Allen Park, Mich. BR/TR, 6', 175 lbs. Deb: 9/11/13																								
1913 StL-N	0	3	.000	3	3	2	0	0	24	20	2	8	3	11.6	3.75	86	.230	.316	3	.375	1	-1	-1	-0	0.0
1914 StL-N	0	0	—	3	0	0	0	0	5	6	0	5	1	19.8	3.60	78	.286	.423	0	—	0	-0	-0	0	0.0
1915 Was-A	0	1	.000	13	0	0	0	1	31^1	39	0	16	8	16.1	4.60	65	.348	.434	1	.200	0	-6	-6	1	-0.1
Total 3	0	4	.000	19	3	2	0	1	60^1	65	2	29	12	14.6	4.18	73	.295	.387	4	.308	1	-8	-7	1	-0.1
● **JOHN HORAN**	Horan, Patrick J. b: 1863, Ireland 5'10.5", 160 lbs. Deb: 5/17/1884																								
1884 CP-U	3	6	.333	13	10	9	0	0	98	94	0	24	55	10.8	3.49	70	.236	.279	6	.088	-8	-11	-11	-1	-1.4
● **JOE HORLEN**	Horlen, Joel Edward b: 8/14/37, San Antonio, Tex. BR/TR, 6', 175 lbs. Deb: 9/4/61																								
1961 Chi-A	1	3	.250	5	4	0	0	0	17^2	25	2	13	11	19.4	6.62	59	.338	.437	0	.000	-1	-5	-5	0	-1.0
1962 Chi-A	7	6	.538	20	19	5	1	0	108^2	108	10	43	63	12.7	4.89	80	.262	.335	2	.053	-3	-11	-12	2	-1.3
1963 Chi-A	11	7	.611	33	21	3	0	0	124	122	10	55	61	13.0	3.27	107	.261	.341	9	.225	1	5	3	1	0.7
1964 Chi-A	13	9	.591	32	28	9	2	0	210^2	142	11	55	138	**8.6**	1.88	184	**.190**	**.250**	11	.159	-1	41	37	3	4.2
1965 Chi-A	13	13	.500	34	34	7	4	0	219	203	16	39	125	10.1	2.88	111	.245	.281	9	.132	0	14	8	-0	0.9

YEAR	TM/L	W	L	PCT	G	GS	CG	SH	SV	IP	H	HR	BB	SO	RAT	ERA	ERA+	OAV	OOB	BH	AVG	PB	PR	/A	PD	TPI
1966	Chi-A	10	13	.435	37	29	4	2	1	211	185	14	53	124	10.4	2.43	130	.233	.286	4	.067	-4	24	17	6	2.2
1967	Chi-A☆	19	7	**.731**	35	35	13	**6**	0	258	188	13	58	103	**8.7**	**2.06**	**151**	.203	**.253**	14	.169	1	**34**	**30**	3	3.5
1968	Chi-A	12	14	.462	35	35	4	1	0	223^2	197	16	70	102	11.3	2.37	127	.238	.308	7	.104	-1	15	16	2	2.1
1969	Chi-A	13	16	.448	36	35	7	2	0	235^2	237	20	77	121	12.2	3.78	102	.261	.323	14	.182	-1	-4	2	-1	0.0
1970	Chi-A	6	16	.273	28	26	4	0	0	172^1	198	18	41	77	12.7	4.86	80	.287	.331	6	.115	-2	-22	-18	4	-1.9
1971	Chi-A	8	9	.471	34	18	3	0	2	137^1	150	12	30	82	12.1	4.26	84	.284	.329	4	.100	-2	-12	-10	1	-1.4
1972	*Oak-A	3	4	.429	32	6	0	0	1	84	74	3	20	58	10.5	3.00	95	.236	.291	3	.176	-0	1	-1	1	-0.1
Total	12	116	117	.498	361	290	59	18	4	2002	1829	145	554	1065	11.0	3.11	109	.243	.300	83	.134	-12	78	66	22	7.9

● TRADER HORNE Horne, Berlyn Dale "Sonny" b: 4/12/1899, Bachman, Ohio d: 2/3/83, Franklin, Ohio BB/TR, 5'9", 155 lbs. Deb: 4/24/29

YEAR	TM/L	W	L	PCT	G	GS	CG	SH	SV	IP	H	HR	BB	SO	RAT	ERA	ERA+	OAV	OOB	BH	AVG	PB	PR	/A	PD	TPI
1929	Chi-N	1	1	.500	11	1	0	0	0	23	24	3	21	6	17.6	5.09	91	.273	.413	2	.400	0	-1	-1	0	0.0

● JACK HORNER Horner, William Frank b: 9/21/1863, Baltimore, Md. d: 7/14/10, New Orleans, La. BR , Deb: 5/7/1894

YEAR	TM/L	W	L	PCT	G	GS	CG	SH	SV	IP	H	HR	BB	SO	RAT	ERA	ERA+	OAV	OOB	BH	AVG	PB	PR	/A	PD	TPI
1894	Bal-N	0	1	.000	2	1	1	0	1	11	15	0	7	2	18.8	9.00	61	.319	.418	1	.167	-0	-4	-4	0	-0.3

● JOE HORNUNG Hornung, Michael Joseph "Ubbo Ubbo" b: 6/12/1857, Carthage, N.Y. d: 10/30/31, Howard Beach, N.Y. BR/TR, 5'8.5", 164 lbs. Deb: 5/1/1879 U♦

YEAR	TM/L	W	L	PCT	G	GS	CG	SH	SV	IP	H	HR	BB	SO	RAT	ERA	ERA+	OAV	OOB	BH	AVG	PB	PR	/A	PD	TPI
1880	Buf-N	0	0	—	1	0	0	0	0	3	2	0	1	0	9.0	6.00	41	.167	.231	91	.266	0	-1	-1	0	0.0

● HANSON HORSEY Horsey, Hanson b: 11/26/1889, Galena, Md. d: 12/1/49, Millington, Md. BR/TR, 5'11", 165 lbs. Deb: 4/27/12

YEAR	TM/L	W	L	PCT	G	GS	CG	SH	SV	IP	H	HR	BB	SO	RAT	ERA	ERA+	OAV	OOB	BH	AVG	PB	PR	/A	PD	TPI
1912	Cin-N	0	0	—	1	0	0	0	0	4	14	0	3	0	38.3	22.50	15	.609	.654	0	.000	-0	-8	-9	-0	-0.1

● VINCE HORSMAN Horsman, Vincent Stanley Joseph b: 3/9/67, Halifax, N.S., Can. BR/TL, 6'2", 180 lbs. Deb: 9/5/91

YEAR	TM/L	W	L	PCT	G	GS	CG	SH	SV	IP	H	HR	BB	SO	RAT	ERA	ERA+	OAV	OOB	BH	AVG	PB	PR	/A	PD	TPI
1991	Tor-A	0	0	—	4	0	0	0	0	4	2	0	3	2	11.3	0.00	—	.167	.333	0	—	0	2	2	-0	-0.2
1992	Oak-A	2	1	.667	58	0	0	0	1	43^1	39	3	21	18	12.5	2.49	150	.252	.341	0	—	0	7	6	-0	0.5
1993	Oak-A	2	0	1.000	40	0	0	0	0	25	25	2	15	17	15.5	5.40	75	.255	.371	0	—	0	-3	-4	-0	-0.3
1994	Oak-A	0	1	.000	33	0	0	0	0	29^1	29	2	11	20	12.6	4.91	90	.266	.339	0	—	0	-0	-2	1	0.4
1995	Min-A	0	0	—	6	0	0	0	0	9	12	2	4	4	16.0	7.00	68	.333	.400	0	—	0	-2	-2	-0	0.0
Total	5	4	2	.667	141	0	0	0	1	110^2	107	9	54	61	13.4	4.07	101	.261	.353	0	—	0	3	0	-1	0.4

● OSCAR HORSTMANN Horstmann, Oscar Theodore b: 6/2/1891, Alma, Mo. d: 5/11/77, Salina, Kan. BR/TR, 5'11", 165 lbs. Deb: 4/18/17

YEAR	TM/L	W	L	PCT	G	GS	CG	SH	SV	IP	H	HR	BB	SO	RAT	ERA	ERA+	OAV	OOB	BH	AVG	PB	PR	/A	PD	TPI
1917	StL-N	9	4	.692	35	11	4	1	1	138^2	111	5	54	50	11.0	3.44	78	.225	.307	9	.196	1	-11	-12	-0	-1.1
1918	StL-N	0	2	.000	9	2	0	0	0	23	29	0	14	6	16.8	5.48	49	.349	.443	0	.000	-0	-7	-7	1	-0.5
1919	StL-N	0	1	.000	6	2	0	0	0	15	14	0	12	5	15.6	3.00	93	.264	.400	1	.500	0	-0	-0	0	0.0
Total	3	9	7	.563	50	15	4	1	1	176^2	154	5	80	61	12.1	3.67	74	.245	.334	10	.192	1	-18	-19	1	-1.6

● ELMER HORTON Horton, Elmer E. "Herky Jerky" b: 9/4/1869, Hamilton, Ohio d: 8/12/20, Vienna, N.Y. Deb: 9/24/1896

YEAR	TM/L	W	L	PCT	G	GS	CG	SH	SV	IP	H	HR	BB	SO	RAT	ERA	ERA+	OAV	OOB	BH	AVG	PB	PR	/A	PD	TPI
1896	Pit-N	0	2	.000	2	2	2	0	0	15	22	0	9	3	19.2	9.60	44	.338	.427	0	.000	-1	-9	-9	-1	-0.9
1898	Bro-N	0	1	.000	1	1	1	0	0	9	16	0	6	0	22.0	10.00	36	.381	.458	1	.250	-0	-6	-6	-0	-0.5
Total	2	0	3	.000	3	3	3	0	0	24	38	0	15	3	20.3	9.75	41	.355	.439	1	.091	-1	-15	-15	-1	-1.4

● RICKY HORTON Horton, Ricky Neal b: 7/30/59, Poughkeepsie, N.Y. BL/TL, 6'2", 195 lbs. Deb: 4/7/84

YEAR	TM/L	W	L	PCT	G	GS	CG	SH	SV	IP	H	HR	BB	SO	RAT	ERA	ERA+	OAV	OOB	BH	AVG	PB	PR	/A	PD	TPI
1984	StL-N	9	4	.692	37	18	1	1	1	125^2	140	14	39	76	12.9	3.44	101	.285	.339	2	.065	-2	2	0	3	0.2
1985	*StL-N	3	2	.600	49	3	0	0	1	89^2	84	5	34	59	12.1	2.91	121	.251	.326	1	.063	-0	7	6	2	0.5
1986	StL-N	4	3	.571	42	9	1	0	3	100^1	77	7	26	49	9.3	2.24	162	.218	.273	1	.056	0	16	16	2	1.3
1987	*StL-N	8	3	.727	67	6	0	0	7	125	127	15	42	55	12.2	3.82	109	.263	.323	5	.172	0	4	5	2	0.7
1988	Chi-A	6	10	.375	52	9	1	0	2	109^1	120	6	36	28	13.3	4.86	82	.291	.355	0	—	0	-11	-11	1	-1.3
	*LA-N	1	1	.500	12	0	0	0	0	9	11	2	2	8	13.0	5.00	67	.306	.342	0	—	0	-2	-2	1	-0.3
1989	LA-N	0	0	—	23	0	0	0	0	26^2	35	1	11	12	15.9	5.06	67	.343	.412	0	.000	-0	-5	-5	-0	0.0
	StL-N	0	3	.000	11	8	0	0	0	45^2	50	2	10	14	12.4	4.73	77	.282	.332	3	.273	1	-6	-6	0	-0.2
	Yr	0	3	.000	34	8	0	0	0	72^1	85	3	21	26	13.6	4.85	73	.301	.356	3	.250	1	-11	-10	0	-0.2
1990	StL-N	1	1	.500	32	0	0	0	1	42	52	3	22	18	16.1	4.93	77	.315	.399	0	.000	-0	-5	-5	2	-0.1
Total	7	32	27	.542	325	53	3	1	15	673^1	696	55	222	319	12.5	3.76	100	.273	.334	12	.109	-1	0	-1	12	0.8

● DAVE HOSKINS Hoskins, David Taylor b: 8/3/25, Greenwood, Miss. d: 4/2/70, Flint, Mich. BL/TR, 6'1", 180 lbs. Deb: 4/18/53

YEAR	TM/L	W	L	PCT	G	GS	CG	SH	SV	IP	H	HR	BB	SO	RAT	ERA	ERA+	OAV	OOB	BH	AVG	PB	PR	/A	PD	TPI
1953	Cle-A	9	3	.750	26	7	3	0	1	112^2	102	9	38	55	11.5	3.99	94	.243	.312	15	.259	4	0	-3	0	0.1
1954	Cle-A	0	1	.000	14	1	0	0	0	26^2	29	3	10	9	13.2	3.04	121	.284	.348	0	.000	-1	2	2	-0	0.0
Total	2	9	4	.692	40	8	3	0	1	139^1	131	12	48	64	11.8	3.81	98	.251	.319	15	.227	3	2	-1	0	0.1

● GENE HOST Host, Eugene Earl "Twinkles" or "Slick" b: 1/1/33, Leeper, Pa. d: 10/20/98, Nashville, Tenn. BB/TL, 5'11", 190 lbs. Deb: 9/16/56

YEAR	TM/L	W	L	PCT	G	GS	CG	SH	SV	IP	H	HR	BB	SO	RAT	ERA	ERA+	OAV	OOB	BH	AVG	PB	PR	/A	PD	TPI
1956	Det-A	0	0	—	1	1	0	0	0	4^2	9	2	2	5	21.2	7.71	53	.409	.458	0	.000	-0	-2	-2	-0	0.0
1957	KC-A	0	2	.000	11	2	0	0	0	23^2	29	5	14	9	16.4	7.23	55	.315	.406	0	.000	-1	-9	-9	0	-0.7
Total	2	0	2	.000	12	3	0	0	0	28^1	38	7	16	14	17.2	7.31	55	.333	.415	0	.000	-1	-11	-10	0	-0.7

● BYRON HOUCK Houck, Byron Simon "Duke" b: 8/28/1891, Prosper, Minn. d: 6/17/69, Santa Cruz, Cal. BR/TR, 6', 175 lbs. Deb: 5/15/12

YEAR	TM/L	W	L	PCT	G	GS	CG	SH	SV	IP	H	HR	BB	SO	RAT	ERA	ERA+	OAV	OOB	BH	AVG	PB	PR	/A	PD	TPI
1912	Phi-A	8	8	.500	30	17	10	0	1	180^2	148	1	74	75	11.7	2.94	105	.234	.326	4	.065	-7	8	3	-1	-0.5
1913	Phi-A	14	6	.700	41	19	4	1	0	176	147	3	122	71	14.1	4.14	67	.214	.337	5	.083	-4	-24	-27	-2	-3.4
1914	Phi-A	0	0	—	3	3	0	0	0	11	14	0	6	4	16.4	3.27	80	.318	.400	1	.333	0	-1	-1	-0	0.0
	Bro-F	2	6	.250	17	9	3	0	0	92	95	4	43	45	13.7	3.13	92	.272	.355	7	.233	2	-2	-3	-3	-0.3
1918	StL-A	2	4	.333	27	2	0	0	2	71^2	58	0	29	29	10.9	2.39	115	.225	.303	3	.150	-1	**3**	**3**	-1	0.1
Total	4	26	24	.520	118	50	17	1	3	531^1	462	8	274	224	12.8	3.30	87	.234	.334	20	.114	-9	-16	-24	-6	-4.1

● CHARLIE HOUGH Hough, Charles Oliver b: 1/5/48, Honolulu, Hawaii BR/TR, 6'2", 190 lbs. Deb: 8/12/70 C

YEAR	TM/L	W	L	PCT	G	GS	CG	SH	SV	IP	H	HR	BB	SO	RAT	ERA	ERA+	OAV	OOB	BH	AVG	PB	PR	/A	PD	TPI
1970	LA-N	0	0	—	8	0	0	0	2	17	18	7	11	8	15.4	5.29	72	.265	.367	1	.333	0	-2	-3	0	0.0
1971	LA-N	0	0	—	4	0	0	0	0	4^1	3	1	3	4	12.5	4.15	78	.200	.333	0	—	0	-0	-0	0	0.0
1972	LA-N	0	0	—	2	0	0	0	0	2^2	2	0	2	4	16.9	3.38	99	.200	.385	0	—	0	0	-0	0	0.0
1973	LA-N	4	2	.667	37	0	0	0	5	71^2	52	3	45	70	12.9	2.76	124	.207	.341	3	.214	0	7	5	0	0.6
1974	*LA-N	9	4	.692	49	0	0	0	1	96	65	12	40	63	10.2	3.75	91	.196	.291	0	.000	-1	-1	-4	-0	-0.6
1975	LA-N	3	7	.300	38	0	0	0	4	61	43	3	34	34	12.5	2.95	115	.195	.323	2	.333	1	5	3	-1	0.5
1976	LA-N	12	8	.600	77	0	0	0	18	142^2	102	6	77	81	11.8	2.21	153	.200	.314	6	.286	2	**20**	**19**	-1	**3.3**
1977	*LA-N	6	12	.333	70	1	0	0	22	127^1	98	10	70	105	12.4	3.32	115	.213	.326	4	.182	1	8	7	-1	1.2
1978	*LA-N	5	5	.500	55	0	0	0	7	93^1	69	6	48	66	11.8	3.28	107	.205	.313	4	.333	1	3	2	-0	0.4
1979	LA-N	7	5	.583	42	14	0	0	0	151^1	152	16	66	76	13.4	4.76	76	.264	.348	6	.158	-0	-17	-19	0	-1.4
1980	LA-N	1	3	.250	19	1	0	0	1	32^1	37	4	21	25	16.7	5.57	63	.291	.400	1	.500	0	-7	-7	-1	-0.9
	Tex-A	2	2	.500	16	2	2	1	0	61^1	54	2	37	47	13.8	3.96	98	.240	.355	0	—	0	0	-0	-0	0.1
1981	Tex-A	4	1	.800	21	5	2	0	1	82	61	4	31	69	10.4	2.96	117	.207	.290	0	—	0	6	5	-1	0.2
1982	Tex-A	16	13	.552	34	34	12	2	0	228	217	21	72	128	11.7	3.95	98	.251	.314	0	—	0	3	-2	1	0.2
1983	Tex-A	15	13	.536	34	33	11	3	0	252	219	22	95	152	11.3	3.18	126	.238	.311	0	—	0	25	23	4	2.9
1984	Tex-A	16	14	.533	36	36	**17**	1	0	266	260	26	94	164	12.3	3.76	110	.255	.324	0	—	0	7	12	3	1.5
1985	Tex-A	14	16	.467	34	34	14	1	0	250^1	198	23	83	141	10.4	3.31	128	.215	.285	0	—	0	23	26	1	2.9
1986	Tex-A★	17	10	.630	33	33	7	2	0	230^1	188	32	89	146	11.2	3.79	113	.221	.302	0	—	0	10	13	1	1.5
1987	Tex-A	18	13	.581	40	40	13	0	0	**285^1**	238	36	124	223	12.0	3.79	118	.223	.314	0	—	0	21	22	3	2.4
1988	Tex-A	15	16	.484	34	34	10	0	0	252	202	20	126	174	12.1	3.32	123	.221	.324	0	—	0	18	21	4	2.9
1989	Tex-A	10	13	.435	30	30	5	1	0	182	168	28	95	94	13.3	4.35	91	.245	.342	0	—	0	-9	-8	-2	-1.0
1990	Tex-A	12	12	.500	32	32	5	0	0	218^2	190	24	119	114	13.2	4.07	96	.235	.342	0	—	0	-4	-4	-0	-0.4
1991	Chi-A	9	10	.474	31	29	4	1	0	199^1	167	21	94	107	12.3	4.02	99	.229	.326	0	—	0	2	-1	0	0.1
1992	Chi-A	7	12	.368	27	27	4	0	0	176^1	160	19	66	76	11.9	3.93	98	.239	.314	0	—	0	0	-1	-1	-0.2
1993	Fla-N	9	16	.360	34	34	0	0	0	204^1	202	20	71	126	12.4	4.27	101	.259	.328	2	.032	-5	-5	1	2	-0.2
1994	Fla-N	5	9	.357	21	21	1	1	0	113^2	118	17	52	65	14.3	5.15	85	.274	.366	4	.121	-1	-12	-10	0	-1.1
Total	25	216	216	.500	858	440	107	13	61	3801^1	3283	383	1665	2362	12.1	3.75	106	.233	.322	33	.146	-2	101	98	13	14.9

● PAT HOUSE House, Patrick Lory b: 9/1/40, Boise, Idaho BL/TL, 6'3", 185 lbs. Deb: 9/6/67

YEAR	TM/L	W	L	PCT	G	GS	CG	SH	SV	IP	H	HR	BB	SO	RAT	ERA	ERA+	OAV	OOB	BH	AVG	PB	PR	/A	PD	TPI
1967	Hou-N	1	0	1.000	6	0	0	0	1	4	3	0	0	2	9.0	4.50	74	.214	.267	0	—	0	-1	-1	0	-0.1

YEAR	TM/L	W	L	PCT	G	GS	CG	SH	SV	IP	H	HR	BB	SO	RAT	ERA	ERA+	OAV	OOB	BH	AVG	PB	PR	/A	PD	TPI
1968	Hou-N	1	1	.500	18	0	0	0	0	16^{1}	21	0	6	6	16.0	7.71	38	.323	.397	0	—	0	-9	-9	-0	-1.1
Total	2	2	1	.667	24	0	0	0	1	20^{1}	24	0	6	8	14.6	7.08	43	.304	.375	0	—	0	-9	-9	0	-1.2
● **TOM HOUSE**	House, Thomas Ross b: 4/29/47, Seattle, Wash. BL/TL, 5′11″, 190 lbs. Deb: 6/23/71 C																									
1971	Atl-N	1	0	1.000	11	1	0	0	0	20^{2}	20	2	3	11	10.5	3.05	122	.263	.300	2	.400	1	1	2	0	0.1
1972	Atl-N	0	0	—	8	0	0	0	2	9^{1}	7	1	6	7	13.5	2.89	131	.226	.368	0	.000	-0	1	1	0	0.0
1973	Atl-N	4	2	.667	52	0	0	0	4	67^{1}	58	13	31	42	12.2	4.68	84	.243	.335	2	.200	0	-8	-6	-0	-0.5
1974	Atl-N	6	2	.750	56	0	0	0	11	102^{2}	74	5	27	64	9.1	1.93	196	.203	.264	4	.400	1	19	21	1	2.4
1975	Atl-N	7	7	.500	58	0	0	0	11	79^{1}	79	2	36	36	13.3	3.18	119	.262	.344	1	.111	-0	4	5	1	1.1
1976	Bos-A	1	3	.250	36	0	0	0	4	43^{2}	39	4	19	27	12.4	4.33	90	.241	.328	0	—	0	-4	-2	1	-0.2
1977	Bos-A	1	0	1.000	8	0	0	0	0	7^{2}	15	0	6	6	24.7	12.91	35	.405	.488	0	—	0	-8	-7	-0	-0.9
	Sea-A	4	5	.444	26	11	1	0	1	89^{1}	94	12	19	39	11.8	3.93	105	.268	.313	0	—	0	1	2	-1	0.1
	Yr	5	5	.500	34	11	1	0	1	97	109	12	25	45	12.8	4.64	89	.281	.331	0	—	0	-6	-5	-1	-0.8
1978	Sea-A	5	4	.556	34	9	3	0	0	116	130	10	35	29	13.2	4.66	82	.289	.347	0	—	0	-12	-11	-0	-0.8
Total	8	29	23	.558	289	21	4	0	33	536	516	49	182	261	12.1	3.79	102	.256	.324	9	.257	1	-5	5	1	1.3
● **FRED HOUSE**	House, Willard Edwin b: 10/3/1890, Cabool, Mo. d: 11/16/23, Kansas City, Mo. BR/TR, 6′3″, 190 lbs. Deb: 4/22/13																									
1913	Det-A	1	2	.333	19	2	0	0	0	53^{2}	64	1	17	16	13.9	5.20	56	.325	.384	0	.000	-1	-14	-14	1	-0.7
● **CHARLIE HOUSEHOLDER**	Householder, Charles F. b: 1856, Harrisburg, Pa. BR/TR, 5′7″, 150 lbs. Deb: 4/20/1884 ♦																									
1884	CP-U	0	0	—	2	0	0	0	0	3	4	0	0	3	12.0	3.00	81	.308	.308	74	.239	-0	-0	-0	-0	0.0
● **FRANK HOUSEMAN**	Houseman, Frank b: Holland Deb: 9/2/1886																									
1886	Bal-a	0	1	.000	1	1	1	0	0	8	6	0	1	5	9.0	3.38	101	.182	.229	1	.250	-0	0	0	0	0.0
● **JOE HOUSER**	Houser, Joseph William b: 7/3/1891, Steubenville, Ohio d: 1/3/53, Orlando, Fla. BL/TL, 5′9.5″, 160 lbs. Deb: 4/24/14																									
1914	Buf-F	0	1	.000	7	2	0	0	0	23	21	1	20	6	16.0	5.48	54	.250	.394	1	.143	-0	-7	-6	1	-0.2
● **ART HOUTTEMAN**	Houtteman, Arthur Joseph b: 8/7/27, Detroit, Mich. BR/TR, 6′2″, 188 lbs. Deb: 4/29/45																									
1945	Det-A	0	2	.000	13	0	0	0	0	25^{1}	27	1	11	9	13.9	5.33	66	.270	.348	0	.000	-1	-6	-5	1	-0.4
1946	Det-A	0	1	.000	1	1	0	0	0	8	15	1	0	2	16.9	9.00	41	.385	.385	1	.500	0	-5	-5	-0	-0.4
1947	Det-A	7	2	.778	23	9	7	2	0	110^{2}	106	6	36	58	11.6	3.42	110	.247	.306	12	.300	2	4	4	-0	0.5
1948	Det-A	2	16	.111	43	20	4	0	10	164^{1}	186	11	52	74	13.1	4.66	94	.287	.342	11	.196	-2	-7	-5	4	-0.4
1949	Det-A	15	10	.600	34	25	13	2	0	203^{2}	227	19	59	85	12.9	3.71	112	.282	.335	19	.244	1	11	10	5	1.7
1950	Det-A★	19	12	.613	41	34	21	**4**	4	274^{2}	257	29	99	88	11.9	3.54	132	.251	.322	14	.151	-3	32	35	3	3.5
1952	Det-A	8	20	.286	35	28	10	2	1	221	218	19	65	109	11.7	4.36	87	.253	.309	7	.101	-4	-17	-14	1	-1.9
1953	Det-A	2	6	.250	16	9	3	1	1	68^{2}	87	11	29	28	15.7	5.90	69	.309	.381	3	.158	0	-15	-14	-0	-1.4
	Cle-A	7	7	.500	22	13	6	1	3	109	113	4	25	40	11.8	3.80	99	.269	.318	5	.147	-1	2	-1	0	-0.2
	Yr	9	13	.409	38	22	9	2	4	177^{2}	200	15	54	68	13.1	4.61	84	.283	.339	8	.151	-1	-12	-15	-0	-1.6
1954	*Cle-A	15	7	.682	32	25	11	1	0	188	198	14	59	68	12.4	3.35	110	.273	.330	18	.277	5	8	7	2	1.4
1955	Cle-A	10	6	.625	35	12	3	1	0	124^{1}	126	15	44	53	12.5	3.98	100	.265	.330	6	.158	-1	-0	0	2	0.2
1956	Cle-A	2	2	.500	22	4	0	0	1	46^{2}	60	5	31	19	18.3	6.56	64	.317	.424	2	.167	-1	-12	-12	0	-1.0
1957	Cle-A	0	0	—	3	0	0	0	0	4	6	1	3	3	20.3	6.75	55	.353	.450	0	—	0	-1	-1	-0	0.0
	Bal-A	0	0	—	5	1	0	0	0	6^{2}	20	0	3	3	31.1	17.55	20	.513	.548	1	.500	0	-10	-10	0	0.1
	Yr	0	0	—	8	1	0	0	0	10^{2}	26	1	6	6	27.0	13.50	27	.464	.516	1	.500	0	-12	-12	0	0.1
Total	12	87	91	.489	325	181	78	14	20	1555	1646	136	516	639	12.7	4.14	99	.272	.333	99	.193	-4	-16	-11	17	1.7
● **ED HOVLIK**	Hovlik, Edward Charles b: 8/20/1891, Cleveland, Ohio d: 3/19/55, Painesville, Ohio BR/TR, 6′, 180 lbs. Deb: 7/14/18 F																									
1918	Was-A	2	1	.667	8	2	1	0	0	28	25	0	10	10	11.3	1.29	212	.272	.343	1	.125	-1	5	4	-1	0.4
1919	Was-A	0	0	—	3	0	0	0	0	5^{2}	12	0	9	3	33.4	12.71	25	.480	.618	0	.000	-0	-6	-6	0	0.0
Total	2	2	1	.667	11	2	1	0	0	33^{2}	37	0	19	13	15.0	3.21	88	.316	.412	1	.100	-1	-1	-1	-0	0.4
● **JOE HOVLIK**	Hovlik, Joseph b: 8/16/1884, Czechoslovakia d: 11/3/51, Oxford Junction, Ia BR/TR, 5′10.5″, 194 lbs. Deb: 7/10/09 F																									
1909	Was-A	0	0	—	3	0	0	0	0	6	13	0	3	1	25.5	4.50	54	.419	.486	0	.000	0	-1	-1	0	0.1
1910	Was-A	0	0	—	1	0	0	0	0	1^{2}	6	0	0	0	37.8	16.20	15	.500	.538	0	—	0	-3	-3	-0	0.0
1911	Chi-A	2	0	1.000	12	3	1	1	0	47	47	1	20	24	12.8	3.06	105	.257	.330	1	.077	-0	1	1	1	0.1
Total	3	2	0	1.000	16	3	1	1	0	54^{2}	66	1	23	25	15.0	3.62	86	.292	.363	1	.067	-0	-2	-3	1	0.2
● **BRUCE HOWARD**	Howard, Bruce Ernest b: 3/23/43, Salisbury, Md. BB/TR, 6′2″, 180 lbs. Deb: 9/4/63 F																									
1963	Chi-A	2	1	.667	7	0	0	0	1	17	12	0	14	9	13.8	2.65	132	.207	.361	1	.250	0	2	2	-0	0.3
1964	Chi-A	2	1	.667	3	3	1	1	0	22^{1}	10	0	8	17	7.7	0.81	429	.139	.235	0	.000	-1	7	7	-0	0.9
1965	Chi-A	9	8	.529	30	22	1	1	0	148	123	13	72	120	11.9	3.47	92	.224	.316	6	.146	2	-0	-4	-1	-0.4
1966	Chi-A	9	5	.643	27	21	4	2	0	149	110	14	44	85	9.4	2.30	138	.202	.263	3	.070	-1	19	14	0	1.3
1967	Chi-A	3	10	.231	30	17	1	0	0	112^{2}	102	9	52	76	12.5	3.43	90	.240	.327	5	.179	1	-3	-4	1	-0.3
1968	Bal-A	0	2	.000	10	5	0	0	0	31	30	2	26	19	16.8	3.77	78	.268	.414	2	.286	2	-3	-3	0	0.1
	Was-A	1	4	.200	13	7	0	0	0	48^{2}	62	7	23	23	15.7	5.36	54	.330	.403	0	.000	-2	-13	-13	1	-1.4
	Yr	1	6	.143	23	12	0	0	0	79^{2}	92	9	49	42	15.9	4.74	62	.302	.398	2	.087	0	-16	-16	1	-1.3
Total	6	26	31	.456	120	75	7	4	1	528^{2}	449	45	239	349	11.8	3.18	99	.231	.317	17	.116	2	9	-2	1	0.5
● **CHRIS HOWARD**	Howard, Christian b: 11/18/65, Lynn, Mass. BR/TL, 6′, 185 lbs. Deb: 9/21/93																									
1993	Chi-A	1	0	1.000	3	0	0	0	0	2^{1}	2	0	3	1	19.3	0.00	—	.286	.500	0	—	0	1	1	-0	0.4
1994	Bos-A	1	0	1.000	37	0	0	0	1	39^{2}	35	5	12	22	10.7	3.63	139	.233	.290	0	—	0	5	6	-0	-0.1
1995	Tex-A	0	0	—	4	0	0	0	0	4	3	0	1	2	9.0	0.00	—	.231	.286	0	—	0	2	2	-0	0.0
Total	3	2	0	1.000	44	0	0	0	1	46	40	5	16	25	11.0	3.13	159	.235	.301	0	—	0	8	9	-1	0.3
● **DAVID HOWARD**	Howard, David Wayne b: 2/26/67, Sarasota, Fla. BB/TR, 6′, 175 lbs. Deb: 4/14/91 F♦																									
1994	KC-A	0	0	—	1	0	0	0	0	2	2	0	5	0	31.5	4.50	111	.286	.583	19	.229	0	0	0	-0	0.0
● **EARL HOWARD**	Howard, Earl Nycum b: 6/25/1893, Everett, Pa. d: 4/4/37, Everett, Pa. BR/TR, 6′1″, 160 lbs. Deb: 4/18/18																									
1918	StL-N	0	0	—	1	0	0	0	0	2	0	0	2	0	9.0	0.00	—	.000	.286	0	—	0	1	1	1	0.1
● **FRED HOWARD**	Howard, Fred Irving b: 9/2/56, Portland, Maine BR/TR, 6′3″, 190 lbs. Deb: 5/26/79																									
1979	Chi-A	1	5	.167	28	6	0	0	0	68	73	5	32	36	14.0	3.57	119	.283	.364	0	—	0	5	5	-1	0.3
● **DEL HOWARD**	Howard, George Elmer b: 12/24/1877, Kenney, Ill. d: 12/24/56, Seattle, Wash. BL/TR, 6′, 180 lbs. Deb: 4/15/05 F♦																									
1905	Pit-N	0	0	—	1	0	0	0	0	6	4	1	1	0	9.0	0.00	—	.200	.273	127	.292	0	2	2	0	0.0
● **LEE HOWARD**	Howard, Lee Vincent b: 11/11/23, Staten Island, N.Y BL/TL, 6′2″, 175 lbs. Deb: 9/22/46																									
1946	Pit-N	0	1	.000	3	2	1	0	0	13^{1}	14	0	9	6	15.5	2.03	174	.286	.397	0	.000	-1	2	2	-0	0.1
1947	Pit-N	0	0	—	2	0	0	0	0	2^{2}	4	1	0	2	13.5	3.38	125	.333	.333	0	—	0	0	0	-0	0.0
Total	2	0	1	.000	5	2	1	0	0	16	18	1	9	8	15.2	2.25	162	.295	.386	0	.000	-1	2	2	-0	0.1
● **CAL HOWE**	Howe, Calvin Earl b: 11/27/24, Rock Falls, Ill. BL/TL, 6′3″, 205 lbs. Deb: 9/26/52																									
1952	Chi-N	0	0	—	1	0	0	0	0	2	0	0	1	2	4.5	0.00	—	.000	.143	0	—	0	1	1	-0	0.0
● **LES HOWE**	Howe, Lester Curtis "Lucky" b: 8/24/1895, Brooklyn, N.Y. d: 7/16/76, Woodmere, N.Y. BR/TR, 5′11.5″, 170 lbs. Deb: 8/18/23																									
1923	Bos-A	1	0	1.000	12	2	0	0	0	30	23	0	7	7	9.3	2.40	171	.211	.265	0	.000	-1	5	6	0	0.1
1924	Bos-A	1	0	1.000	4	0	0	0	0	7^{1}	11	1	2	3	17.2	7.36	59	.423	.483	1	.500	0	-3	-2	0	-0.2
Total	2	2	0	1.000	16	2	0	0	0	37^{1}	34	1	9	10	10.8	3.38	123	.252	.308	1	.125	-1	3	3	0	-0.1
● **STEVE HOWE**	Howe, Steven Roy b: 3/10/58, Pontiac, Mich. BL/TL, 6′1″, 180 lbs. Deb: 4/11/80																									
1980	LA-N	7	9	.438	59	0	0	0	17	84^{2}	83	1	22	39	11.4	2.66	132	.256	.307	1	.091	-1	9	8	1	1.8
1981	*LA-N	5	3	.625	41	0	0	0	8	54	51	2	18	32	11.5	2.50	133	.254	.315	0	.000	0	6	5	-1	0.8

YEAR	TM/L	W	L	PCT	G	GS	CG	SH	SV	IP	H	HR	BB	SO	RAT	ERA	ERA+	OAV	OOB	BH	AVG	PB	PR	/A	PD	TPI
1982	LA-N★	7	5	.583	66	0	0	0	13	99^1	87	3	17	49	9.4	2.08	166	.240	.274	0	.000	-1	17	15	-0	2.1
1983	LA-N	4	7	.364	46	0	0	0	18	68^2	55	2	12	52	8.9	1.44	249	.217	.256	1	.125	0	17	16	1	3.6
1985	LA-N	1	1	.500	19	0	0	0	3	22	30	2	5	11	14.7	4.91	71	.319	.360	0	—	0	-3	-4	0	-0.4
	Min-A	2	3	.400	13	0	0	0	0	19	28	1	7	10	16.6	6.16	72	.333	.385	0	—	0	-4	-4	-0	-1.1
1987	Tex-A	3	3	.500	24	0	0	0	1	31^1	33	2	8	19	12.6	4.31	104	.280	.341	0	—	0	1	1	0	0.1
1991	NY-A	3	1	.750	37	0	0	0	3	48^1	39	1	7	34	9.1	1.68	247	.222	.263	0	—	0	13	13	0	1.1
1992	NY-A	3	0	1.000	20	0	0	0	6	22	9	1	3	12	4.9	2.45	160	.122	.156	0	—	0	4	4	1	0.7
1993	NY-A	3	5	.375	51	0	0	0	4	50^2	58	7	10	19	12.6	4.97	83	.297	.341	0	—	0	-4	-5	1	-0.5
1994	NY-A	3	0	1.000	40	0	0	0	15	40	28	2	7	18	7.9	1.80	254	.194	.232	0	—	0	13	12	-0	1.6
1995	*NY-A	6	3	.667	56	0	0	0	2	49	66	7	17	28	16.0	4.96	93	.324	.387	0	—	0	-1	-2	1	-0.2
1996	NY-A	0	1	.000	25	0	0	0	1	17	19	1	6	5	13.8	6.35	78	.284	.351	0	—	0	-3	-3	0	-0.1
Total	12	47	41	.534	497	0	0	0	91	606	586	32	139	328	11.0	3.03	128	.255	.303	2	.074	-1	64	58	3	9.5

● HARRY HOWELL

Howell, Henry Harry b: 11/14/1876, New Jersey d: 5/22/56, Spokane, Wash. BR/TR, 5'9", Deb: 10/10/1898 U♦

YEAR	TM/L	W	L	PCT	G	GS	CG	SH	SV	IP	H	HR	BB	SO	RAT	ERA	ERA+	OAV	OOB	BH	AVG	PB	PR	/A	PD	TPI
1898	Bro-N	2	0	1.000	2	2	2	0	0	18	15	0	11	2	13.5	5.00	72	.224	.342	2	.250	0	-3	-3	0	-0.2
1899	Bal-N	13	8	.619	28	25	21	0	1	209^1	248	1	69	58	14.1	3.91	101	.294	.355	12	.146	-3	-1	1	1	-0.2
1900	*Bro-N	6	5	.545	21	10	7	2	0	110^1	131	4	36	26	13.9	3.75	102	.294	.351	12	.286	4	-1	1	1	0.5
1901	Bal-A	14	21	.400	37	34	32	1	0	294^2	333	5	79	93	12.8	3.67	106	.281	.330	41	.218	1	0	7	-1	0.6
1902	Bal-A	9	15	.375	26	23	19	1	0	199	243	5	48	33	13.5	4.12	92	.301	.346	93	.268	5	-12	-8	4	0.1
1903	NY-A	9	6	.600	25	15	13	0	0	155^2	140	4	44	62	11.0	3.53	89	.240	.300	23	.217	2	-10	-7	3	-0.1
1904	StL-A	13	21	.382	34	33	32	2	0	299^2	254	1	60	122	9.8	2.19	113	.230	.278	25	.221	5	14	10	9	2.9
1905	StL-A	15	22	.405	38	37	**35**	4	0	323	252	2	101	198	10.2	1.98	129	.217	.286	26	.193	3	24	20	18	**4.9**
1906	StL-A	15	14	.517	35	33	30	6	1	276^2	233	1	61	140	9.9	2.11	122	.231	.282	13	.126	-3	18	14	8	2.1
1907	StL-A	16	15	.516	42	35	26	2	3	316^1	258	3	88	118	10.1	1.93	130	.225	.285	27	.237	6	21	20	8	3.7
1908	StL-A	18	18	.500	41	32	27	2	1	324^1	279	1	70	117	10.2	1.89	127	.240	.293	22	.183	1	18	18	0	2.3
1909	StL-A	1	1	.500	10	3	0	0	0	37^1	42	0	8	16	12.8	3.13	77	.294	.344	6	.176	0	-3	-3	-0	-0.2
1910	StL-A	0	0	—	1	0	0	0	0	3^1	7	0	2	1	24.3	10.80	23	.467	.529	0	.000	-0	-3	-3	0	0.0
Total	13	131	146	.473	340	282	244	20	6	2567^2	2435	27	677	986	11.2	2.74	108	.252	.307	302	.217	21	63	64	51	16.4

● JAY HOWELL

Howell, Jay Canfield b: 11/26/55, Miami, Fla. BR/TR, 6'3", 205 lbs. Deb: 8/10/80

YEAR	TM/L	W	L	PCT	G	GS	CG	SH	SV	IP	H	HR	BB	SO	RAT	ERA	ERA+	OAV	OOB	BH	AVG	PB	PR	/A	PD	TPI
1980	Cin-N	0	0	—	5	0	0	0	0	3^1	8	0	0	1	24.3	13.50	26	.471	.500	0	—	0	-4	-4	-0	0.0
1981	Chi-N	2	0	1.000	10	2	0	0	0	22^1	23	3	10	10	14.1	4.84	76	.277	.368	0	.000	0	-3	-3	1	-0.1
1982	NY-A	2	3	.400	6	6	0	0	0	28	42	1	13	21	17.7	7.71	52	.341	.404	0	—	0	-11	-12	-0	-1.6
1983	NY-A	1	5	.167	19	12	2	0	0	82	89	7	35	61	13.9	5.38	72	.275	.351	0	—	0	-12	-14	0	-0.7
1984	NY-A	9	4	.692	61	1	0	0	7	103^2	86	5	34	109	10.4	2.69	141	.223	.286	0	—	0	15	13	2	1.9
1985	Oak-A☆	9	8	.529	63	0	0	0	29	98	98	5	31	68	11.9	2.85	135	.261	.319	0	—	0	14	11	0	2.5
1986	Oak-A	3	6	.333	38	0	0	0	16	53^1	53	3	23	42	13.0	3.38	115	.262	.341	0	—	0	5	3	-0	0.7
1987	Oak-A★	3	4	.429	36	0	0	0	16	44^1	48	6	21	35	14.2	5.89	70	.277	.359	0	—	0	-7	-9	-0	-1.4
1988	*LA-N	5	3	.625	50	0	0	0	21	65	44	1	21	70	9.1	2.08	160	.188	.258	0	.000	-0	10	9	-0	1.6
1989	LA-N★	5	3	.625	56	0	0	0	28	79^2	60	3	22	55	9.3	1.58	216	.211	.268	0	.000	-0	17	16	-0	2.7
1990	LA-N	5	5	.500	45	0	0	0	16	66	59	5	20	59	11.6	2.18	168	.242	.315	0	.000	-0	12	11	-0	2.0
1991	LA-N	6	5	.545	44	0	0	0	16	51	39	3	11	40	9.0	3.18	113	.213	.262	0	—	0	3	2	0	0.6
1992	LA-N	1	3	.250	41	0	0	0	4	46^2	41	2	18	36	11.6	1.54	223	.230	.305	0	—	0	10	10	0	1.0
1993	Atl-N	3	3	.500	54	0	0	0	0	58^1	48	3	16	37	9.9	2.31	173	.229	.283	0	—	0	11	11	-0	1.0
1994	Tex-A	4	1	.800	40	0	0	0	2	43	44	10	16	22	12.8	5.44	89	.262	.330	0	—	0	-3	-3	0	-0.3
Total	15	58	53	.523	568	21	2	0	155	844^2	782	57	291	666	11.6	3.34	114	.246	.313	0	.000	-1	56	43	2	9.9

● KEN HOWELL

Howell, Kenneth b: 11/28/60, Detroit, Mich. BR/TR, 6'3", 228 lbs. Deb: 6/25/84

YEAR	TM/L	W	L	PCT	G	GS	CG	SH	SV	IP	H	HR	BB	SO	RAT	ERA	ERA+	OAV	OOB	BH	AVG	PB	PR	/A	PD	TPI
1984	LA-N	5	5	.500	32	1	0	0	6	51^1	51	1	9	54	10.7	3.33	106	.267	.303	0	.000	-1	1	1	0	0.2
1985	*LA-N	4	7	.364	56	0	0	0	12	86	66	8	35	85	10.6	3.77	92	.208	.287	0	.000	-0	-2	-3	0	-0.4
1986	LA-N	6	12	.333	62	0	0	0	12	97^2	86	7	63	104	14.0	3.87	89	.239	.357	0	.000	-1	-2	-5	-1	-1.1
1987	LA-N	3	4	.429	40	2	0	0	1	55	54	7	29	60	13.6	4.91	81	.265	.356	1	.250	0	-5	-6	-0	-0.7
1988	LA-N	0	1	.000	4	1	0	0	0	12^2	16	0	4	12	14.2	6.39	52	.320	.370	0	.000	-0	-4	-4	-0	-0.3
1989	Phi-N	12	12	.500	33	32	1	1	0	204	155	11	86	164	10.7	3.44	103	.215	.300	6	.092	-2	1	2	-1	-0.1
1990	Phi-N	8	7	.533	18	18	2	0	0	106^2	106	12	49	70	13.3	4.64	82	.260	.343	2	.067	-1	-10	-10	-1	-1.4
Total	7	38	48	.442	245	54	3	1	31	613^1	534	46	275	549	12.0	3.95	91	.237	.323	9	.079	-5	-20	-24	-3	-3.8

● DIXIE HOWELL

Howell, Millard b: 1/7/20, Bowman, Ky. d: 3/18/60, Hollywood, Fla. BL/TR, 6'2", 210 lbs. Deb: 9/14/40

YEAR	TM/L	W	L	PCT	G	GS	CG	SH	SV	IP	H	HR	BB	SO	RAT	ERA	ERA+	OAV	OOB	BH	AVG	PB	PR	/A	PD	TPI
1940	Cle-A	0	0	—	3	0	0	0	0	5	2	0	4	2	10.8	1.80	234	.143	.333	0	—	0	1	1	0	0.0
1949	Cin-N	0	1	.000	5	1	0	0	0	13^1	21	3	8	7	19.6	8.10	52	.362	.439	1	.111	-0	-6	-6	0	-0.4
1955	Chi-A	8	3	.727	35	0	0	0	9	73^2	70	1	25	25	11.6	2.93	135	.250	.311	8	.381	2	8	8	1	1.7
1956	Chi-A	5	6	.455	34	1	0	0	4	64^1	79	3	36	28	16.4	4.62	89	.309	.398	4	.235	2	-3	-4	0	-0.4
1957	Chi-A	6	5	.545	37	0	0	0	6	68^1	64	6	30	37	12.4	3.29	113	.255	.335	5	.185	4	4	3	1	1.0
1958	Chi-A	0	0	—	1	0	0	0	0	1^2	0	0	0	0	0.0	0.00	—	.000	.000	0	—	0	1	1	0	0.0
Total	6	19	15	.559	115	2	0	0	19	226^1	236	13	103	99	13.6	3.78	104	.273	.352	18	.243	8	5	4	2	1.9

● ROLAND HOWELL

Howell, Roland Boatner "Billiken" b: 1/3/1892, Napoleonville, La. d: 3/31/73, Baton Rouge, La. BR/TR, 6'4", 210 lbs. Deb: 6/14/12

YEAR	TM/L	W	L	PCT	G	GS	CG	SH	SV	IP	H	HR	BB	SO	RAT	ERA	ERA+	OAV	OOB	BH	AVG	PB	PR	/A	PD	TPI
1912	StL-N	0	0	—	3	0	0	0	0	1^2	5	0	5	0	54.0	27.00	13	.556	.714	0	—	0	-4	-4	-0	0.0

● BOB HOWRY

Howry, Bobby Dean b: 8/4/73, Phoenix, Ariz. BL/TR, 6'5", 215 lbs. Deb: 6/21/98

YEAR	TM/L	W	L	PCT	G	GS	CG	SH	SV	IP	H	HR	BB	SO	RAT	ERA	ERA+	OAV	OOB	BH	AVG	PB	PR	/A	PD	TPI
1998	Chi-A	0	3	.000	44	0	0	0	9	54^1	37	7	19	51	9.6	3.15	145	.194	.274	0	—	0	9	8	-0	0.8

● PETER HOY

Hoy, Peter Alexander b: 6/29/66, Brockville, Ont., Canada BL/TR, 6'7", 220 lbs. Deb: 4/11/92

YEAR	TM/L	W	L	PCT	G	GS	CG	SH	SV	IP	H	HR	BB	SO	RAT	ERA	ERA+	OAV	OOB	BH	AVG	PB	PR	/A	PD	TPI
1992	Bos-A	0	0	—	5	0	0	0	0	3^2	8	0	2	2	24.5	7.36	57	.471	.526	0	—	0	-1	-1	0	0.0

● TEX HOYLE

Hoyle, Roland Edison b: 7/17/21, Carbondale, Pa. d: 7/4/94, Carbondale, Pa. BR/TR, 6'4", 170 lbs. Deb: 4/18/52

YEAR	TM/L	W	L	PCT	G	GS	CG	SH	SV	IP	H	HR	BB	SO	RAT	ERA	ERA+	OAV	OOB	BH	AVG	PB	PR	/A	PD	TPI
1952	Phi-A	0	0	—	3	0	0	0	0	2^1	9	2	1	1	38.6	27.00	15	.563	.588	0	—	0	-6	-6	0	0.0

● LA MARR HOYT

Hoyt, Dewey La Marr b: 1/1/55, Columbia, S.C. BR/TR, 6'1", 222 lbs. Deb: 9/14/79

YEAR	TM/L	W	L	PCT	G	GS	CG	SH	SV	IP	H	HR	BB	SO	RAT	ERA	ERA+	OAV	OOB	BH	AVG	PB	PR	/A	PD	TPI
1979	Chi-A	0	0	—	2	0	0	0	0	3	2	0	0	0	6.0	0.00	—	.200	.200	0	—	0	1	1	-0	0.0
1980	Chi-A	9	3	.750	24	13	3	1	0	112^1	123	8	41	55	13.3	4.57	88	.281	.345	0	—	0	-7	-7	-2	-0.8
1981	Chi-A	9	3	.750	43	1	0	0	10	90^2	80	10	28	60	11.0	3.57	100	.240	.305	0	—	0	1	0	-1	0.0
1982	Chi-A	**19**	15	.559	39	32	14	2	0	239^2	248	17	48	124	11.2	3.53	114	.266	.303	0	—	0	14	13	-1	1.6
1983	*Chi-A	**24**	10	.706	36	36	11	1	0	260^2	236	27	31	148	**9.3**	3.66	114	.238	**.262**	0	—	0	12	15	5	2.3
1984	Chi-A	13	18	.419	34	34	11	1	0	235^2	244	31	43	126	11.2	4.47	93	.266	.302	0	—	0	-13	-8	1	-0.9
1985	SD-N★	16	8	.667	31	31	8	3	0	210^1	210	20	20	83	9.9	3.47	102	.261	.281	4	.063	-4	3	2	1	-0.1
1986	SD-N	8	11	.421	35	25	1	0	0	159	170	27	68	85	13.6	5.15	71	.276	.351	6	.130	-1	-25	-26	-2	-3.1
Total	8	98	68	.590	244	172	48	8	10	1311^1	1313	140	279	681	11.0	3.99	98	.260	.302	10	.091	-5	-13	-10	1	-1.0

● WAITE HOYT

Hoyt, Waite Charles "Schoolboy" b: 9/9/1899, Brooklyn, N.Y. d: 8/25/84, Cincinnati, Ohio BR/TR, 6', 180 lbs. Deb: 7/24/18 H

YEAR	TM/L	W	L	PCT	G	GS	CG	SH	SV	IP	H	HR	BB	SO	RAT	ERA	ERA+	OAV	OOB	BH	AVG	PB	PR	/A	PD	TPI
1918	NY-N	0	0	—	1	0	0	0	0	1	0	0	0	2	0.0	0.00	—	.000	.000	0	.000	-0	0	0	0	0.0
1919	Bos-A	4	6	.400	13	11	6	1	0	105^1	99	1	22	28	10.3	3.25	93	.262	.303	5	.132	-3	-0	-3	1	-0.4
1920	Bos-A	6	6	.500	22	11	6	2	1	121^1	123	2	47	45	12.7	4.38	83	.270	.339	5	.116	-3	-8	-10	1	-1.1
1921	*NY-A	19	13	.594	43	32	21	1	3	282^1	301	3	81	102	12.3	3.09	137	.276	.329	22	.222	-2	37	36	-1	3.3
1922	*NY-A	19	12	.613	37	31	17	3	0	265	271	13	76	95	12.1	3.43	117	.269	.326	20	.217	1	18	17	-2	1.7
1923	*NY-A	17	9	.654	37	28	19	1	1	238^2	227	9	66	60	11.2	3.02	131	.253	.307	16	.190	-2	26	24	-1	2.1
1924	NY-A	18	13	.581	46	32	14	2	4	247	295	8	76	71	13.6	3.79	110	.300	.352	10	.133	-5	12	10	-0	0.6
1925	NY-A	11	14	.440	46	30	17	1	6	243	283	14	78	86	13.4	4.00	107	.292	.346	24	.304	6	11	7	3	1.3
1926	*NY-A	16	12	.571	40	28	12	1	4	217^2	224	4	62	79	11.9	3.85	100	.264	.316	16	.211	-0	4	0	-3	-0.3
1927	*NY-A	**22**	7	**.759**	36	32	23	3	1	256^1	242	10	54	86	10.5	2.63	146	.251	.294	22	.222	0	43	35	-0	3.5
1928	*NY-A	23	7	.767	42	31	19	3	**8**	273	279	16	60	67	11.2	3.36	112	.272	.313	28	.257	2	21	12	-1	1.2
1929	NY-A	10	9	.526	30	25	12	0	1	201^2	219	9	69	57	13.0	4.24	91	.279	.339	17	.224	1	0	-9	-2	-0.7

YEAR	TM/L	W	L	PCT	G	GS	CG	SH	SV	IP	H	HR	BB	SO	RAT	ERA	ERA+	OAV	OOB	BH	AVG	PB	PR	/A	PD	TPI
1930	NY-A	2	2	.500	8	7	2	0	0	47^{2}	64	7	9	10	13.8	4.53	95	.317	.346	1	.063	-2	1	-1	-0	-0.3
	Det-A	9	8	.529	26	20	8	1	4	135^{2}	176	7	47	25	14.9	4.78	100	.313	.368	9	.196	-2	-2	0	-3	-0.5
	Yr	11	10	.524	34	27	10	1	4	183^{1}	240	14	56	35	14.6	4.71	99	.314	.363	10	.161	-4	-1	-1	-3	-0.8
1931	Det-A	3	8	.273	16	12	5	0	0	92	124	2	32	10	15.5	5.87	78	.319	.374	4	.133	-2	-15	-13	-0	-1.5
	*Phi-A	10	5	.667	16	14	9	2	0	111	130	9	37	30	13.5	4.22	107	.298	.353	13	.302	3	2	3	1	0.7
	Yr	13	13	.500	32	26	14	2	0	203	254	11	69	40	14.3	4.97	91	.307	.360	17	.233	0	-13	-10	0	-0.8
1932	Bro-N	1	3	.250	8	4	0	0	1	26^{2}	38	3	12	7	16.9	7.76	49	.342	.407	0	.000	-1	-12	-12	1	-1.5
	NY-N	5	7	.417	18	12	3	0	0	97^{1}	103	6	25	29	12.3	3.42	109	.275	.328	3	.097	-2	5	3	1	0.2
	Yr	6	10	.375	26	16	3	0	1	124	141	9	37	36	13.3	4.35	86	.290	.347	3	.081	-3	-7	-9	2	-1.3
1933	Pit-N	5	7	.417	36	8	4	1	4	117	118	3	19	44	10.6	2.92	114	.262	.293	5	.156	-1	5	5	1	0.5
1934	Pit-N	15	6	.714	48	15	8	3	5	190^{2}	184	6	43	105	10.8	2.93	141	.252	.296	10	.179	-1	24	25	-1	2.5
1935	Pit-N	7	11	.389	39	11	5	0	6	164	187	8	27	63	11.8	3.40	121	.285	.315	14	.259	2	11	13	-0	1.5
1936	Pit-N	7	5	.583	22	9	6	0	1	116^{2}	115	5	20	37	10.6	2.70	150	.255	.291	6	.154	-1	17	18	1	1.6
1937	Pit-N	1	2	.333	11	0	0	0	2	28	31	3	6	21	11.9	4.50	86	.270	.306	1	.083	-1	-2	-2	-1	-0.4
	Bro-N	7	7	.500	27	19	10	1	0	167	180	5	30	44	11.3	3.23	125	.270	.301	4	.083	-2	13	15	-1	0.8
	Yr	8	9	.471	38	19	10	1	2	195	211	8	36	65	11.4	3.42	117	.270	.302	5	.083	-3	11	13	-2	0.4
1938	Bro-N	0	3	.000	6	1	0	0	0	16^{1}	24	1	5	3	16.0	4.96	79	.333	.377	0	.000	-0	-2	-2	-0	-0.4
Total	21	237	182	.566	674	423	226	26	52	3762^{1}	4037	154	1003	1206	12.2	3.59	112	.276	.325	255	.198	-17	210	173	-7	14.4

● AL HRABOSKY

Hrabosky, Alan Thomas b: 7/21/49, Oakland, Cal. BR/TL, 5′11″, 185 lbs. Deb: 6/16/70

YEAR	TM/L	W	L	PCT	G	GS	CG	SH	SV	IP	H	HR	BB	SO	RAT	ERA	ERA+	OAV	OOB	BH	AVG	PB	PR	/A	PD	TPI
1970	StL-N	2	1	.667	16	1	0	0	0	19	22	2	7	12	13.7	4.74	87	.286	.345	0	.000	-0	-1	-1	-1	-0.3
1971	StL-N	0	0	—	1	0	0	0	0	2	2	0	0	2	9.0	0.00	—	.250	.250	0	—	0	1	1	-0	0.0
1972	StL-N	1	0	1.000	5	0	0	0	0	7	2	0	3	9	6.4	0.00	—	.087	.192	0	.000	-0	3	3	-0	0.3
1973	StL-N	2	4	.333	44	0	0	0	5	56	45	2	21	57	10.9	2.09	174	.220	.298	0	.000	-0	10	10	-1	1.1
1974	StL-N	8	1	.889	65	0	0	0	9	88^{1}	71	3	38	82	11.2	2.95	121	.221	.306	4	.308	1	7	6	-1	0.7
1975	StL-N	13	3	.813	65	0	0	0	**22**	97^{1}	72	3	33	82	9.8	1.66	226	.205	.275	3	.200	1	**21**	**23**	-2	4.8
1976	StL-N	8	6	.571	68	0	0	0	13	95^{1}	89	5	39	73	12.5	3.30	107	.252	.333	0	.000	0	2	2	-0	0.4
1977	StL-N	6	5	.545	65	0	0	0	10	86^{1}	82	12	41	68	13.1	4.38	88	.256	.346	0	.000	-1	-5	-5	-1	-0.9
1978	*KC-A	8	7	.533	58	0	0	0	20	75	52	6	35	60	10.6	2.88	133	.200	.297	0	—	0	7	8	-0	1.8
1979	KC-A	9	4	.692	58	0	0	0	11	65	67	3	41	39	15.1	3.74	114	.272	.378	0	—	0	3	4	-2	0.5
1980	Atl-N	4	2	.667	45	0	0	0	3	59^{2}	50	8	31	31	12.2	3.62	103	.223	.318	0	.000	-0	-0	1	-2	-0.1
1981	Atl-N	1	1	.500	24	0	0	0	1	33^{2}	24	1	9	13	8.8	1.07	335	.207	.264	0	.000	-0	9	9	-1	0.5
1982	Atl-N	2	1	.667	31	0	0	0	3	37^{1}	41	5	17	20	14.0	5.54	67	.285	.360	1	.333	0	-8	-8	-1	-0.7
Total	13	64	35	.646	545	1	0	0	97	722	619	50	315	548	11.8	3.10	121	.234	.318	8	.143	0	49	52	-11	8.1

● CARL HUBBELL

Hubbell, Carl Owen "King Carl" or "The Mealticket"
b: 6/22/03, Carthage, Mo. d: 11/21/88, Scottsdale, Ariz. BR/TL, 6′, 170 lbs. Deb: 7/26/28 H

YEAR	TM/L	W	L	PCT	G	GS	CG	SH	SV	IP	H	HR	BB	SO	RAT	ERA	ERA+	OAV	OOB	BH	AVG	PB	PR	/A	PD	TPI
1928	NY-N	10	6	.625	20	14	8	1	1	124	117	7	21	37	10.2	2.83	138	.248	.284	5	.106	-3	16	15	2	1.7
1929	NY-N	18	11	.621	39	35	19	1	1	268	273	17	67	106	11.6	3.69	124	.265	.313	12	.129	-6	30	26	5	2.3
1930	NY-N	17	12	.586	37	32	17	3	2	241^{2}	263	11	58	117	12.4	3.87	122	.278	.327	13	.151	-5	29	23	-1	1.7
1931	NY-N	14	12	.538	36	30	21	4	3	248	211	14	67	155	**10.2**	2.65	139	**.227**	**.282**	20	.241	4	34	29	-2	3.1
1932	NY-N	18	11	.621	40	32	22	0	2	284	260	20	40	137	**9.6**	2.50	148	.238	**.268**	26	.241	4	43	38	6	**4.8**
1933	*NY-N★	**23**	12	.657	45	33	22	**10**	5	**308^{2}**	256	6	47	156	**8.9**	**1.66**	**193**	.227	**.260**	20	.183	1	**58**	**53**	7	**7.5**
1934	NY-N★	21	12	.636	49	35	**25**	5	**8**	313	286	17	37	118	**9.3**	**2.30**	**168**	.239	**.263**	23	.197	-1	**61**	**54**	4	6.0
1935	NY-N☆	23	12	.657	42	35	24	1	0	302^{2}	314	27	49	150	10.9	3.27	118	.263	.294	26	.239	4	25	20	4	2.9
1936	*NY-N★	**26**	6	**.813**	42	34	25	3	3	304	265	7	57	123	**9.7**	**2.31**	**169**	.236	**.276**	25	.227	1	**58**	**54**	1	**5.5**
1937	*NY-N★	**22**	8	**.733**	39	32	18	4	4	261^{2}	261	18	55	**159**	11.0	3.20	122	.257	.298	21	.216	1	21	20	-1	2.1
1938	NY-N☆	13	10	.565	24	22	13	1	1	179	171	16	33	104	**10.4**	3.07	123	.249	**.285**	9	.155	-2	14	14	-1	1.3
1939	NY-N	11	9	.550	29	18	10	0	2	154	150	11	24	62	**10.3**	2.75	143	.249	**.280**	8	.151	-1	20	20	1	2.5
1940	NY-N★	11	12	.478	31	27	11	2	0	214^{1}	220	22	59	86	11.8	3.65	106	.259	.309	15	.185	-0	5	5	1	0.6
1941	NY-N☆	11	9	.550	26	22	11	1	1	164	169	10	53	75	12.3	3.57	104	.266	.325	8	.140	-2	1	2	-3	-0.2
1942	NY-N☆	11	8	.579	24	20	11	0	0	157^{1}	158	17	34	61	11.0	3.95	85	.259	.299	11	.183	-0	-11	-10	-1	-1.3
1943	NY-N	4	4	.500	12	11	3	0	0	66	87	7	24	31	15.1	4.91	70	.322	.378	4	.200	-0	-11	-11	-1	-1.3
Total	16	253	154	.622	535	432	260	36	33	3590^{1}	3461	227	725	1677	10.6	2.98	130	.251	.291	246	.191	-5	394	355	22	39.2

● BILL HUBBELL

Hubbell, Wilbert William b: 6/17/1897, San Francisco, Cal. d: 8/3/80, Lakewood, Colo. BR/TR, 6′1.5″, 195 lbs. Deb: 9/24/19

YEAR	TM/L	W	L	PCT	G	GS	CG	SH	SV	IP	H	HR	BB	SO	RAT	ERA	ERA+	OAV	OOB	BH	AVG	PB	PR	/A	PD	TPI
1919	NY-N	1	1	.500	2	2	2	0	0	18^{1}	19	0	2	3	11.3	1.96	143	.260	.299	1	.125	-1	2	2	-0	0.1
1920	NY-N	0	1	.000	14	0	0	0	2	30	26	2	15	8	12.6	2.10	143	.239	.336	1	.200	-0	3	3	1	0.2
	Phi-N	9	9	.500	24	18	9	1	2	150	176	3	42	26	13.3	3.84	89	.301	.352	7	.132	-3	-12	-7	-2	-1.3
	Yr	9	10	.474	38	18	9	1	4	180	202	5	57	34	13.1	3.55	94	.291	.348	8	.138	-3	-8	-4	-1	-1.1
1921	Phi-N	9	16	.360	36	30	15	1	2	220^{1}	269	18	38	43	12.7	4.33	98	.306	.337	12	.160	-2	-13	-2	-1	-0.4
1922	Phi-N	7	15	.318	35	26	11	1	1	189	257	14	41	33	14.4	5.00	93	.317	.353	12	.171	-2	-19	-7	0	-0.8
1923	Phi-N	1	6	.143	22	5	1	0	0	55	102	13	17	8	19.8	8.35	55	.394	.435	4	.235	0	-27	-23	0	-2.3
1924	Phi-N	10	9	.526	36	22	9	2	2	179	233	9	45	30	14.1	4.83	92	.324	.365	13	.220	-1	-19	-7	0	-0.7
1925	Phi-N	0	0	—	2	0	0	0	0	2^{2}	5	0	1	0	20.3	0.00	—	.385	.429	0	.000	-0	1	1	1	0.0
	Bro-N	3	6	.333	33	5	3	0	1	86^{2}	120	8	24	16	15.2	5.30	79	.337	.382	3	.150	0	-10	-11	1	-0.8
	Yr	3	6	.333	35	5	3	0	1	89^{1}	125	8	25	16	15.3	5.14	82	.339	.384	3	.143	0	-9	-9	2	-0.8
Total	7	40	63	.388	204	108	50	5	10	931	1207	67	225	167	14.0	4.68	89	.317	.359	53	.172	-8	-93	-52	0	-6.0

● EARL HUCKLEBERRY

Huckleberry, Earl Eugene b: 5/23/10, Konawa, Okla. BR/TR, 5′11″, 165 lbs. Deb: 9/13/35

YEAR	TM/L	W	L	PCT	G	GS	CG	SH	SV	IP	H	HR	BB	SO	RAT	ERA	ERA+	OAV	OOB	BH	AVG	PB	PR	/A	PD	TPI
1935	Phi-A	1	0	1.000	1	1	0	0	0	6^{2}	8	1	4	2	16.2	9.45	48	.296	.387	0	.000	-0	-4	-4	-0	-0.4

● JOHN HUDEK

Hudek, John Raymond b: 8/8/66, Tampa, Fla. BB/TR, 6′1″, 200 lbs. Deb: 4/23/94

YEAR	TM/L	W	L	PCT	G	GS	CG	SH	SV	IP	H	HR	BB	SO	RAT	ERA	ERA+	OAV	OOB	BH	AVG	PB	PR	/A	PD	TPI
1994	Hou-N★	0	2	.000	42	0	0	0	16	39^{1}	24	5	18	39	9.8	2.97	133	.174	.274	0	—	0	5	4	-0	0.5
1995	Hou-N	2	2	.500	19	0	0	0	7	20	19	3	5	29	10.8	5.40	72	.247	.293	1	1.000	1	-3	-3	1	-0.7
1996	Hou-N	2	0	1.000	15	0	0	0	2	16	12	2	5	14	9.6	2.81	137	.207	.270	0	—	0	2	2	1	0.3
1997	Hou-N	1	3	.250	40	0	0	0	4	40^{2}	38	8	33	36	16.4	5.98	67	.252	.396	0	—	0	-8	-9	0	-0.9
1998	NY-N	1	4	.200	28	0	0	0	0	27	23	2	19	28	14.7	4.00	104	.237	.373	0	—	0	1	0	0	0.1
	Cin-N	4	2	.667	30	0	0	0	0	37	27	6	28	40	13.9	2.43	178	.206	.354	0	.000	-0	7	8	-1	1.1
	Yr	5	6	.455	58	0	0	0	0	64	50	8	47	68	13.9	3.09	138	.216	.352	0	.000	-0	8	8	-0	1.2
Total	5	10	13	.435	174	0	0	0	29	180	143	26	108	186	12.9	3.95	103	.219	.337	1	.250	0	5	2	1	0.4

● WILLIS HUDLIN

Hudlin, George Willis "Ace" b: 5/23/06, Wagoner, Okla. BR/TR, 6′, 190 lbs. Deb: 8/15/26 C

YEAR	TM/L	W	L	PCT	G	GS	CG	SH	SV	IP	H	HR	BB	SO	RAT	ERA	ERA+	OAV	OOB	BH	AVG	PB	PR	/A	PD	TPI
1926	Cle-A	1	3	.250	8	2	1	0	0	32^{1}	25	1	13	6	11.1	2.78	146	.227	.320	1	.125	0	4	5	2	0.7
1927	Cle-A	18	12	.600	43	30	18	1	0	264^{2}	291	3	83	65	13.1	4.01	105	.283	.343	24	.250	2	4	6	3	1.1
1928	Cle-A	14	14	.500	42	26	10	0	7	220^{1}	231	7	90	62	13.4	4.04	103	.279	.355	14	.194	-0	0	2	2	0.5
1929	Cle-A	17	15	.531	40	33	22	2	1	280^{1}	299	7	73	60	12.0	3.34	133	.272	.318	19	.196	-3	28	34	7	**3.9**
1930	Cle-A	13	16	.448	37	33	13	1	1	216^{2}	255	12	76	60	13.8	4.57	106	.293	.351	16	.219	-1	2	6	5	1.0
1931	Cle-A	15	14	.517	44	34	15	1	4	254^{1}	313	14	88	83	14.2	4.60	100	.301	.356	20	.200	1	-6	1	4	0.5
1932	Cle-A	12	8	.600	33	21	12	0	2	181^{2}	204	10	59	65	13.1	4.71	101	.278	.332	13	.203	1	-5	1	1	0.2
1933	Cle-A	5	13	.278	34	17	6	0	1	147^{1}	161	7	61	44	13.7	3.97	112	.275	.346	6	.146	-1	5	8	4	1.1
1934	Cle-A	15	10	.600	36	26	15	1	4	195	210	8	65	58	12.9	4.75	96	.277	.338	14	.206	3	-6	-4	5	0.2
1935	Cle-A	15	11	.577	36	29	14	3	5	231^{2}	252	8	61	45	12.3	3.69	122	.277	.324	24	.279	6	20	21	0	2.7
1936	Cle-A	1	5	.167	27	7	1	0	0	64	112	1	31	20	20.4	9.00	56	.397	.460	2	.111	-1	-28	-28	1	-2.0
1937	Cle-A	12	11	.522	35	23	10	2	2	175^{2}	213	8	43	31	13.2	4.10	112	.295	.337	10	.169	-1	10	10	3	1.3
1938	Cle-A	8	8	.500	29	15	8	0	1	127	158	13	45	27	14.5	4.89	95	.303	.361	5	.116	-2	-1	-4	1	-0.5
1939	Cle-A	9	10	.474	27	20	7	0	3	143	175	6	42	28	13.7	4.91	90	.303	.352	9	.188	1	-5	-8	5	-0.4
1940	Cle-A	2	1	.667	4	4	2	0	0	23^{2}	31	3	2	8	12.5	4.94	85	.316	.330	1	.125	-0	-1	-2	-0	-0.2
	Was-A	1	2	.333	8	6	1	0	0	37^{1}	50	9	5	9	13.7	6.51	64	.314	.343	1	.100	-1	-9	-10	0	-0.7
	StL-A	0	1	.000	6	1	0	0	0	11^{1}	19	0	8	4	21.4	11.12	41	.358	.443	1	.500	0	-8	-8	0	-0.6
	Yr	3	4	.429	18	11	3	0	0	72^{1}	100	12	15	21	14.3	6.72	63	.321	.352	3	.150	-1	-19	-20	0	-1.5

YEAR	TM/L	W	L	PCT	G	GS	CG	SH	SV	IP	H	HR	BB	SO	RAT	ERA	ERA+	OAV	OOB	BH	AVG	PB	PR	/A	PD	TPI
	NY-N	0	1	.000	1	1	0	0	0	5	9	1	1	1	18.0	10.80	36	.409	.435	0	.000	-0	-4	-4	0	-0.5
1944	StL-A	0	1	.000	1	0	0	0	0	2	3	0	0	1	13.5	4.50	80	.300	.300	0	—	0	-0	-0	-0	-0.1
Total	16	158	156	.503	491	328	155	11	31	2613^1	3011	118	846	677	13.4	4.41	102	.289	.345	180	.201	4	-0	26	42	8.2

● CHARLIE HUDSON
Hudson, Charles b: 8/18/49, Ada, Okla. BL/TL, 6'3", 185 lbs. Deb: 5/21/72

YEAR	TM/L	W	L	PCT	G	GS	CG	SH	SV	IP	H	HR	BB	SO	RAT	ERA	ERA+	OAV	OOB	BH	AVG	PB	PR	/A	PD	TPI
1972	StL-N	1	0	1.000	12	0	0	0	0	12^1	10	0	7	4	13.1	5.11	67	.233	.353	0	—	0	-2	-2	0	-0.2
1973	Tex-A	4	2	.667	25	4	1	1	1	62^1	59	3	31	34	13.0	4.62	81	.254	.342	0	—	0	-6	-6	0	-0.5
1975	Cal-A	0	1	.000	3	1	0	0	0	5^2	7	0	4	0	17.5	9.53	37	.304	.407	0	—	0	-4	-4	0	-0.2
Total	3	5	3	.625	40	5	1	1	1	80^1	76	3	42	38	13.3	5.04	73	.255	.349	0	—	0	-11	-12	0	-0.9

● CHARLES HUDSON
Hudson, Charles Lynn b: 3/16/59, Ennis, Tex. BB/TR, 6'3", 185 lbs. Deb: 5/31/83

YEAR	TM/L	W	L	PCT	G	GS	CG	SH	SV	IP	H	HR	BB	SO	RAT	ERA	ERA+	OAV	OOB	BH	AVG	PB	PR	/A	PD	TPI
1983	*Phi-N	8	8	.500	26	26	3	0	0	169^1	158	13	53	101	11.2	3.35	106	.248	.305	5	.093	-2	5	4	-1	0.1
1984	Phi-N	9	11	.450	30	30	1	1	0	173^2	181	12	52	94	12.2	4.04	90	.265	.319	5	.089	-2	-9	-8	-2	-1.3
1985	Phi-N	8	13	.381	38	26	3	0	0	193	188	23	74	122	12.3	3.78	97	.252	.320	8	.140	-1	-4	-2	-2	-0.5
1986	Phi-N	7	10	.412	33	23	0	0	0	144	165	20	58	82	13.9	4.94	78	.291	.357	2	.047	-3	-20	-17	-0	-2.2
1987	NY-A	11	7	.611	35	16	6	2	0	154^2	137	19	57	100	11.5	3.61	122	.239	.311	0	—	0	15	13	-2	1.3
1988	NY-A	6	6	.500	28	12	1	0	2	106^1	93	9	36	58	11.3	4.49	88	.235	.306	0	—	0	-6	-6	-0	-0.7
1989	Det-A	1	5	.167	18	7	0	0	0	66^2	75	14	31	23	14.6	6.35	60	.288	.369	0	—	0	-18	-19	-1	-1.5
Total	7	50	60	.455	208	140	14	3	2	1007^2	997	110	361	580	12.2	4.14	92	.258	.324	20	.095	-8	-37	-35	-8	-4.8

● HAL HUDSON
Hudson, Hal Campbell "Bud" or "Lefty" b: 5/4/27, Grosse Pointe, Mich. BL/TL, 5'10", 175 lbs. Deb: 4/20/52

YEAR	TM/L	W	L	PCT	G	GS	CG	SH	SV	IP	H	HR	BB	SO	RAT	ERA	ERA+	OAV	OOB	BH	AVG	PB	PR	/A	PD	TPI
1952	StL-A	0	0	—	3	0	0	0	0	5^2	9	0	6	0	23.8	12.71	31	.360	.484	0	.000	-0	-6	-6	-0	0.0
	Chi-A	0	0	—	2	0	0	0	0	4	7	0	1	4	18.0	2.25	162	.389	.421	0	—	0	1	1	-0	0.0
	Yr	0	0	—	5	0	0	0	0	9^2	16	0	7	4	21.4	8.38	45	.372	.460	0	.000	-0	-5	-5	-0	0.0
1953	Chi-A	0	0	—	1	0	0	0	0	0^2	0	0	0	0	0.0	0.00	—	.000	.000	0	—	0	0	0	0	0.0
Total	2	0	0	—	6	0	0	0	0	10^1	16	0	7	4	20.0	7.84	49	.364	.451	0	.000	-0	-5	-5	-0	0.0

● JESSE HUDSON
Hudson, Jesse James b: 7/22/48, Mansfield, La. BL/TL, 6'2", 165 lbs. Deb: 9/19/69

YEAR	TM/L	W	L	PCT	G	GS	CG	SH	SV	IP	H	HR	BB	SO	RAT	ERA	ERA+	OAV	OOB	BH	AVG	PB	PR	/A	PD	TPI
1969	NY-N	0	0	—	1	0	0	0	0	2	2	0	2	3	18.0	4.50	81	.250	.400	0	—	0	-0	-0	0	0.0

● JOE HUDSON
Hudson, Joseph Paul b: 9/29/70, Philadelphia, Pa. BR/TR, 6'1", 175 lbs. Deb: 6/10/95

YEAR	TM/L	W	L	PCT	G	GS	CG	SH	SV	IP	H	HR	BB	SO	RAT	ERA	ERA+	OAV	OOB	BH	AVG	PB	PR	/A	PD	TPI
1995	*Bos-A	0	1	.000	39	0	0	0	1	46	53	2	23	29	15.3	4.11	118	.301	.388	0	—	0	3	4	-0	0.0
1996	Bos-A	3	5	.375	36	0	0	0	1	45	57	4	32	19	17.8	5.40	94	.318	.422	0	—	0	-2	-2	-0	-0.3
1997	Bos-A	3	1	.750	26	0	0	0	0	35^2	39	1	14	14	14.4	3.53	131	.289	.373	0	—	0	4	4	1	0.5
1998	Mil-N	0	0	—	1	0	0	0	0	0^1	2	0	4	0	162.0	162.00	3	1.000	1.000	0	—	0	-6	-6	0	0.0
Total	4	6	7	.462	102	0	0	0	2	127	151	7	73	62	16.3	4.82	101	.307	.403	0	—	0	-1	1	0	0.2

● NAT HUDSON
Hudson, Nathaniel P. b: 1/12/1859, Chicago, Ill. d: 3/14/28, Chicago, Ill. BR/TR, Deb: 4/18/1886

YEAR	TM/L	W	L	PCT	G	GS	CG	SH	SV	IP	H	HR	BB	SO	RAT	ERA	ERA+	OAV	OOB	BH	AVG	PB	PR	/A	PD	TPI
1886	*StL-a	16	10	.615	29	27	25	0	**1**	234^1	224	3	62	100	11.1	3.03	113	.243	.293	35	.233	1	11	11	-1	0.9
1887	StL-a	4	4	.500	9	9	7	0	0	67	91	2	20	15	15.4	4.97	91	.305	.357	12	.250	-0	-5	-3	-2	-0.4
1888	StL-a	25	10	**.714**	39	37	36	5	0	333	283	8	59	130	9.6	2.54	128	.222	.264	50	.255	5	19	27	-1	2.7
1889	StL-a	3	2	.600	9	5	4	0	0	60	71	2	15	13	13.5	4.20	101	.285	.336	13	.250	0	-2	0	-1	0.0
Total	4	48	26	.649	86	78	72	5	1	694^1	669	15	156	258	11.0	3.08	114	.244	.291	110	.247	6	23	34	-4	3.2

● REX HUDSON
Hudson, Rex Haughton b: 8/11/53, Tulsa, Okla. BB/TR, 5'11", 165 lbs. Deb: 7/27/74

YEAR	TM/L	W	L	PCT	G	GS	CG	SH	SV	IP	H	HR	BB	SO	RAT	ERA	ERA+	OAV	OOB	BH	AVG	PB	PR	/A	PD	TPI
1974	LA-N	0	0	—	1	0	0	0	0	2	6	2	0	0	27.0	22.50	15	.500	.500	0	—	0	-4	-4	-0	0.0

● SID HUDSON
Hudson, Sidney Charles b: 1/3/15, Coalfield, Tenn. BR/TR, 6'4", 180 lbs. Deb: 4/18/40 C

YEAR	TM/L	W	L	PCT	G	GS	CG	SH	SV	IP	H	HR	BB	SO	RAT	ERA	ERA+	OAV	OOB	BH	AVG	PB	PR	/A	PD	TPI
1940	Was-A	17	16	.515	38	31	19	3	1	252	272	20	81	96	12.7	4.57	91	.274	.330	22	.237	2	-5	-11	1	-1.0
1941	Was-A★	13	14	.481	33	33	17	3	0	249^2	242	12	97	108	12.3	3.46	117	.253	.322	16	.186	-0	19	16	2	1.8
1942	Was-A☆	10	17	.370	35	31	19	1	2	239^1	266	9	70	72	12.8	4.36	84	.276	.328	19	.213	1	-19	-19	3	-1.5
1946	Was-A	8	11	.421	31	15	6	1	1	142^1	160	9	37	35	12.7	3.60	93	.280	.328	12	.279	3	-2	-4	2	0.0
1947	Was-A	6	9	.400	20	17	5	1	0	106	113	8	58	37	14.6	5.60	66	.272	.363	12	.308	2	-22	-22	1	-2.4
1948	Was-A	4	16	.200	39	29	4	0	1	182	217	11	107	53	16.3	5.88	74	.299	.394	14	.237	2	-32	-31	3	-2.4
1949	Was-A	8	17	.320	40	27	11	2	1	209	234	11	91	54	14.2	4.22	101	.283	.357	16	.239	2	-1	1	4	0.6
1950	Was-A	14	14	.500	30	30	17	0	0	237^2	261	17	98	75	13.8	4.09	110	.284	.356	20	.215	-1	13	11	3	1.3
1951	Was-A	5	12	.294	23	19	8	0	0	138^2	168	8	52	43	14.5	5.13	80	.302	.365	12	.273	2	-15	-16	3	-1.3
1952	Was-A	3	4	.429	7	7	6	0	0	62^2	59	4	29	24	12.6	2.73	130	.257	.340	4	.167	-0	7	6	2	0.8
	Bos-A	7	9	.438	21	18	7	0	0	134^1	145	9	36	50	12.6	3.62	109	.276	.330	8	.174	-1	1	5	4	0.8
	Yr	10	13	.435	28	25	13	0	0	197	204	13	65	74	12.6	3.34	114	.270	.333	12	.171	-1	7	11	6	1.6
1953	Bos-A	6	9	.400	30	17	4	0	2	156	164	13	49	60	12.5	3.52	120	.269	.327	7	.140	-2	8	12	1	0.9
1954	Bos-A	3	4	.429	33	5	0	0	5	71^1	83	5	30	27	14.5	4.42	93	.296	.369	2	.154	-1	-5	-2	0	-0.3
Total	12	104	152	.406	380	279	123	11	13	2181	2384	136	835	734	13.5	4.28	95	.278	.345	164	.220	9	-54	-55	28	-2.7

● AL HUENKE
Huenke, Albert A. b: 6/26/1891, New Bremen, Ohio d: 9/20/74, St.Marys, Ohio BR/TR, 6', 175 lbs. Deb: 10/6/14

YEAR	TM/L	W	L	PCT	G	GS	CG	SH	SV	IP	H	HR	BB	SO	RAT	ERA	ERA+	OAV	OOB	BH	AVG	PB	PR	/A	PD	TPI
1914	NY-N	0	0	—	1	0	0	0	0	2	2	0	0	2	9.0	4.50	59	.250	.250	0	.000	-0	-0	-0	-0	0.0

● PHIL HUFFMAN
Huffman, Phillip Lee b: 6/20/58, Freeport, Tex. BR/TR, 6'2", 180 lbs. Deb: 4/10/79

YEAR	TM/L	W	L	PCT	G	GS	CG	SH	SV	IP	H	HR	BB	SO	RAT	ERA	ERA+	OAV	OOB	BH	AVG	PB	PR	/A	PD	TPI
1979	Tor-A	6	18	.250	31	31	2	1	0	173	220	25	68	56	15.0	5.77	75	.304	.364	0	—	0	-30	-28	0	-3.2
1985	Bal-A	0	0	—	2	1	0	0	0	4^2	7	1	5	2	23.1	15.43	26	.350	.480	0	—	0	-6	-6	0	0.0
Total	2	6	18	.250	33	32	2	1	0	177^2	227	26	73	58	15.2	6.03	72	.305	.367	0	—	0	-36	-33	0	-3.2

● ED HUGHES
Hughes, Edward J. b: 10/5/1880, Chicago, Ill. d: 10/11/27, McHenry, Ill. BR/TR, 6'1", 180 lbs. Deb: 8/29/02 F♦

YEAR	TM/L	W	L	PCT	G	GS	CG	SH	SV	IP	H	HR	BB	SO	RAT	ERA	ERA+	OAV	OOB	BH	AVG	PB	PR	/A	PD	TPI
1905	Bos-A	3	2	.600	6	4	2	0	0	33^1	38	0	9	8	13.0	4.59	59	.288	.338	3	.214	-0	-7	-7	-2	-1.1
1906	Bos-A	0	0	—	2	0	0	0	0	10	15	0	3	3	16.2	5.40	51	.349	.391	0	.000	-0	-3	-3	-0	-0.1
Total	2	3	2	.600	8	4	2	0	0	43^1	53	0	12	11	13.7	4.78	57	.303	.351	4	.190	-1	-10	-10	-2	-1.2

● JAY HUGHES
Hughes, James Jay b: 1/22/1874, Sacramento, Cal. d: 6/2/24, Sacramento, Cal. BR/TR, 185 lbs. Deb: 4/18/1898 F

YEAR	TM/L	W	L	PCT	G	GS	CG	SH	SV	IP	H	HR	BB	SO	RAT	ERA	ERA+	OAV	OOB	BH	AVG	PB	PR	/A	PD	TPI
1898	Bal-N	23	12	.657	38	35	31	5	0	300^2	268	4	100	81	11.6	3.20	112	.237	.309	37	.226	4	14	13	2	1.9
1899	Bro-N	**28**	6	**.824**	35	35	30	3	0	291^2	250	6	119	99	11.8	2.68	146	.231	.316	27	.252	5	38	40	2	4.7
1901	Bro-N	17	12	.586	31	29	24	0	0	250^2	265	3	102	96	13.6	3.27	103	.269	.345	16	.176	-1	2	2	1	0.2
1902	Bro-N	15	10	.600	30	29	26	0	0	245	223	3	51	92	10.4	2.87	96	.243	.289	19	.209	4	-2	-3	1	0.3
Total	4	83	40	.675	134	128	111	8	0	1088	1006	16	372	368	11.8	3.00	114	.245	.315	99	.219	13	51	52	7	7.1

● JIM HUGHES
Hughes, James Michael b: 7/2/51, Los Angeles, Cal. BR/TR, 6'3", 190 lbs. Deb: 9/14/74

YEAR	TM/L	W	L	PCT	G	GS	CG	SH	SV	IP	H	HR	BB	SO	RAT	ERA	ERA+	OAV	OOB	BH	AVG	PB	PR	/A	PD	TPI
1974	Min-A	0	2	.000	2	2	1	0	0	10^1	8	2	4	8	10.5	5.23	71	.216	.293	0	—	0	-2	-2	0	-0.3
1975	Min-A	16	14	.533	37	34	12	2	0	249^2	241	17	127	130	13.7	3.82	100	.255	.351	0	—	0	-1	0	1	0.0
1976	Min-A	9	14	.391	37	26	3	0	0	177	190	17	73	87	13.8	4.98	72	.281	.358	0	—	0	-29	-28	-1	-3.5
1977	Min-A	0	0	—	2	0	0	0	0	4^1	4	0	1	1	10.4	2.08	192	.250	.294	0	—	0	1	1	-0	0.1
Total	4	25	30	.455	78	62	16	2	0	441^1	443	36	205	226	13.6	4.30	87	.265	.352	0	—	0	-31	-28	-1	-3.7

● JIM HUGHES
Hughes, James Robert b: 3/21/23, Chicago, Ill. BR/TR, 6'1", 200 lbs. Deb: 9/13/52

YEAR	TM/L	W	L	PCT	G	GS	CG	SH	SV	IP	H	HR	BB	SO	RAT	ERA	ERA+	OAV	OOB	BH	AVG	PB	PR	/A	PD	TPI
1952	Bro-N	2	1	.667	6	0	0	0	0	18^2	16	0	11	8	13.0	1.45	252	.235	.342	0	.000	-0	5	5	-1	0.6
1953	*Bro-N	4	3	.571	48	0	0	0	9	85^2	80	6	41	49	12.8	3.47	123	.245	.332	4	.286	1	8	8	-1	0.7
1954	Bro-N	8	4	.667	**60**	0	0	0	**24**	86^2	76	7	44	58	12.5	3.22	127	.239	.331	3	.188	-0	8	8	-1	1.4
1955	Bro-N	0	2	.000	24	0	0	0	6	42^2	41	10	19	20	12.7	4.22	96	.256	.335	0	.000	-2	-1	-1	0	-0.2
1956	Bro-N	0	0	—	5	0	0	0	0	12	10	3	4	8	10.5	5.25	76	.233	.298	0	.000	-0	-2	-2	-0	-0.1
	Chi-N	1	3	.250	25	1	0	0	0	45^1	43	4	30	20	15.3	5.16	73	.259	.385	2	.286	1	-7	-7	-1	-0.5
	Yr	1	3	.250	30	1	0	0	0	57^1	53	7	34	28	14.3	5.18	74	.254	.368	2	.222	0	-9	-9	-1	-0.6
1957	Chi-A	0	0	—	4	0	0	0	0	5	12	0	3	2	27.0	10.80	35	.462	.517	0	—	0	-4	-4	0	0.0
Total	6	15	13	.536	172	1	0	0	39	296	278	30	152	165	13.2	3.83	106	.251	.344	9	.170	-1	7	7	-3	1.9

YEAR	TM/L	W	L	PCT	G	GS	CG	SH	SV	IP	H	HR	BB	SO	RAT	ERA	ERA+	OAV	OOB	BH	AVG	PB	PR	/A	PD	TPI
● **MICKEY HUGHES**	Hughes, Michael J. b: 10/25/1866, New York, N.Y. d: 4/10/31, Jersey City, N.J. TR, 5'6", 165 lbs. Deb: 4/22/1888 F																									
1888	Bro-a	25	13	.658	40	40	40	2	0	363	281	5	98	159	9.5	2.13	140	.206	.262	19	.137	-7	38	34	-1	2.4
1889	*Bro-a	9	8	.529	20	17	13	0	0	153	172	6	86	54	15.6	4.35	86	.275	.369	12	.176	-3	-9	-11	-0	-1.2
1890	Bro-N	4	4	.500	9	8	6	0	0	66^1	77	1	30	22	15.1	5.16	67	.282	.362	1	.038	-4	-12	-13	0	-1.4
	Phi-a	1	3	.250	6	5	4	0	0	41^1	64	0	21	15	19.6	5.44	70	.344	.425	2	.125	-1	-7	-7	-1	-0.7
Total	3	39	28	.582	75	70	63	2	0	623^2	594	12	235	250	12.3	3.22	102	.243	.315	34	.137	-14	10	4	-1	-0.9
● **DICK HUGHES**	Hughes, Richard Henry b: 2/13/38, Stephens, Ark. BR/TR, 6'3", 195 lbs. Deb: 9/11/66																									
1966	StL-N	2	1	.667	6	2	1	1	1	21	12	0	7	20	9.0	1.71	209	.162	.253	2	.400	1	4	4	0	0.8
1967	*StL-N	16	6	**.727**	37	27	12	3	3	222^1	164	22	48	161	**8.8**	2.67	123	**.203**	**.252**	10	.128	-1	17	15	-2	1.2
1968	*StL-N	2	2	.500	25	5	0	0	4	64	45	7	21	49	9.3	3.52	82	.202	.270	0	.000	-1	-4	-4	1	-0.4
Total	3	20	9	.690	68	34	13	4	8	307^1	221	29	76	230	8.9	2.78	116	.200	.256	12	.122	-2	18	15	-1	1.6
● **TOM HUGHES**	Hughes, Thomas Edward b: 9/13/34, Ancon, C.Z. BL/TR, 6'2", 180 lbs. Deb: 9/13/59																									
1959	StL-N	0	2	.000	2	2	0	0	0	4	9	2	2	2	24.8	15.75	27	.409	.458	0	.000	-0	-5	-5	-0	-1.5
● **TOM HUGHES**	Hughes, Thomas James "Long Tom" b: 11/29/1878, Chicago, Ill. d: 2/8/56, Chicago, Ill. BR/TR, 6'1", 175 lbs. Deb: 9/7/00 F																									
1900	Chi-N	1	1	.500	3	3	3	0	0	21	31	0	7	12	16.7	5.14	70	.341	.394	0	.000	-0	-3	-4	0	-0.3
1901	Chi-N	10	23	.303	37	35	32	1	0	308^1	309	4	115	225	12.9	3.24	100	.259	.333	14	.119	-8	3	-0	-2	-1.0
1902	Bal-A	7	5	.583	13	13	12	1	0	108^1	120	2	32	45	12.8	3.90	97	.281	.334	6	.140	-2	-4	-2	1	-0.3
	Bos-A	3	3	.500	9	8	4	0	0	49^1	51	0	24	15	13.9	3.28	109	.267	.352	11	.367	2	2	2	-0	0.4
	Yr	10	8	.556	22	21	16	1	0	157^2	171	2	56	60	13.0	3.71	100	.276	.337	17	.233	0	-2	0	1	0.1
1903	*Bos-A	20	7	.741	33	31	25	5	0	244^2	232	5	60	112	11.1	2.57	118	.249	.301	26	.280	7	11	13	-4	1.5
1904	NY-A	7	11	.389	19	18	12	1	0	136^1	141	3	48	75	12.8	3.70	73	.268	.334	13	.241	1	-17	-15	-3	-2.0
	Was-A	3	12	.200	16	14	14	0	1	124^1	133	4	34	48	12.5	3.47	77	.274	.330	13	.228	3	-12	-11	-1	-1.1
	Yr	10	23	.303	35	32	26	1	1	260^2	274	7	82	123	12.5	3.59	75	.269	.328	26	.234	4	-29	-26	-3	-3.1
1905	Was-A	17	20	.459	39	35	26	6	0	291^1	239	3	79	149	10.1	2.35	113	.225	.285	22	.212	4	10	10	-4	1.3
1906	Was-A	7	17	.292	30	24	18	1	0	204	230	5	81	90	13.9	3.62	73	.287	.355	14	.212	3	-21	-22	-4	-2.6
1907	Was-A	7	14	.333	34	23	18	2	**4**	211	206	1	47	102	11.3	3.11	78	.258	.309	19	.237	3	-13	-16	-1	-1.3
1908	Was-A	18	15	.545	43	31	24	3	4	276^1	224	3	77	165	10.0	2.21	103	.227	.287	17	.195	2	6	2	1	0.6
1909	Was-A	4	7	.364	22	13	7	2	1	120^1	113	1	33	77	11.3	2.69	90	.246	.303	3	.083	-2	-3	-3	-0	-0.6
1911	Was-A	11	17	.393	34	27	17	2	0	223	251	7	77	86	13.4	3.47	95	.288	.348	15	.185	-3	-3	-5	-2	-0.9
1912	Was-A	13	10	.565	31	26	11	1	0	196	201	8	78	108	13.1	2.94	113	.270	.344	13	.194	1	8	9	0	1.0
1913	Was-A	4	12	.250	36	12	4	0	6	129^2	129	6	61	59	14.2	4.30	69	.253	.350	4	.111	-1	-20	-19	1	-2.4
Total	13	132	174	.431	399	313	227	25	16	2644	2610	52	853	1368	12.1	3.09	93	.259	.323	190	.198	12	-57	-64	-18	-7.7
● **TOM HUGHES**	Hughes, Thomas L. "Salida Tom" b: 1/28/1884, Coal Creek, Colo. d: 11/1/61, Los Angeles, Cal. BR/TR, 6'2", 175 lbs. Deb: 9/18/06																									
1906	NY-A	1	0	1.000	3	1	1	0	0	15	11	2	1	5	7.2	4.20	71	.208	.222	1	.200	0	-3	-2	-1	-0.2
1907	NY-A	2	0	1.000	4	3	2	0	0	27	16	0	11	10	9.7	2.67	105	.174	.276	1	.143	-0	-0	0	-1	-0.1
1909	NY-A	7	8	.467	24	15	9	2	2	118^2	109	3	37	69	11.4	2.65	95	.249	.313	5	.128	0	-2	-2	-1	-0.2
1910	NY-A	7	9	.438	23	15	11	0	1	151^2	153	2	37	64	11.5	3.50	76	.271	.320	9	.164	-1	-17	-14	1	-1.4
1914	Bos-N	2	0	1.000	2	2	1	0	0	17	14	0	4	11	9.5	2.65	104	.226	.273	0	.000	-1	0	0	1	0.0
1915	Bos-N	16	14	.533	**50**	25	17	4	**9**	280^1	208	4	58	171	8.9	2.12	122	.213	.265	9	.100	-3	20	15	-2	1.1
1916	Bos-N	16	3	**.842**	40	13	7	1	5	161	121	2	51	97	10.1	2.35	106	.215	.290	10	.192	2	5	2	-1	0.4
1917	Bos-N	5	3	.625	11	8	6	2	0	74	54	1	30	40	10.6	1.95	131	.216	.307	0	.000	-3	6	5	-0	0.2
1918	Bos-N	0	2	.000	3	3	1	0	0	18^1	17	0	6	9	11.3	3.44	78	.250	.311	2	.333	1	-1	-2	0	0.0
Total	9	56	39	.589	160	85	55	9	17	863	703	14	235	476	10.1	2.56	102	.229	.291	37	.130	-4	8	4	-4	-0.2
● **TOMMY HUGHES**	Hughes, Thomas Owen b: 10/7/19, Wilkes-Barre, Pa. d: 11/28/90, Wilkes-Barre, Pa. BR/TR, 6'1", 190 lbs. Deb: 4/19/41																									
1941	Phi-N	9	14	.391	34	24	5	2	0	170	187	12	82	59	14.5	4.45	83	.280	.362	11	.200	0	-15	-14	1	-1.6
1942	Phi-N	12	18	.400	40	31	19	0	1	253	224	8	99	77	11.5	3.06	108	.238	.310	8	.100	-5	7	7	3	0.5
1946	Phi-N	6	9	.400	29	13	3	2	1	111	123	5	44	34	13.6	4.38	78	.281	.349	3	.097	-1	-12	-12	-1	-1.7
1947	Phi-N	4	11	.267	29	15	4	1	1	127	121	5	59	44	12.8	3.47	115	.265	.350	2	.050	-4	8	8	0	0.5
1948	Cin-N	0	4	.000	12	4	0	0	0	27	43	3	24	7	22.3	9.00	43	.364	.472	1	.143	-0	-15	-15	-0	-1.9
Total	5	31	56	.356	144	87	31	5	3	688	698	33	308	221	13.2	3.92	91	.266	.344	25	.117	-10	-27	-26	2	-4.2
● **VERN HUGHES**	Hughes, Vernon Alexander "Lefty" b: 4/15/1893, Etna, Pa. d: 9/26/61, Sewickley, Pa. BL/TL, 5'10", 155 lbs. Deb: 7/6/14																									
1914	Bal-F	0	0	—	3	0	0	0	0	5^2	5	0	3	0	12.7	3.18	95	.250	.348	0	.000	-0	-0	-0	-0	0.0
● **BILL HUGHES**	Hughes, William Nesbert b: 11/18/1896, Philadelphia, Pa. d: 2/25/63, Birmingham, Ala. BR/TR, 5'10.5", 155 lbs. Deb: 9/15/21																									
1921	Pit-N	0	0	—	1	0	0	0	0	2	3	0	1	2	22.5	4.50	85	.375	.500	0	—	0	-0	-0	0	0.0
● **BILL HUGHES**	Hughes, William R. b: 11/25/1866, Blandinsville, Ill. d: 8/25/43, Santa Ana, Cal. BL/TL, Deb: 9/28/1884 ♦																									
1885	Phi-a	0	2	.000	2	2	2	0	0	16^2	18	0	10	4	16.2	4.86	71	.269	.380	3	.188	0	-3	-3	-0	-0.2
● **JIM HUGHEY**	Hughey, James Ulysses "Coldwater Jim" b: 3/8/1869, Wakeshma, Mich. d: 3/29/45, Coldwater, Mich. TR, 6', Deb: 9/29/1891																									
1891	Mil-a	1	0	1.000	2	1	1	0	0	15	18	0	3	9	12.6	3.00	146	.286	.318	1	.143	-1	1	2	0	0.1
1893	Chi-N	0	1	.000	2	1	1	0	0	9	14	0	3	4	18.0	11.00	42	.341	.400	0	.000	0	-6	-6	0	-0.4
1896	Pit-N	6	8	.429	25	14	11	0	0	155	171	3	67	48	14.2	4.99	84	.278	.355	14	.215	-1	-11	-14	-3	-1.3
1897	Pit-N	6	10	.375	25	17	13	0	1	149^1	193	3	45	38	14.8	5.06	82	.310	.364	8	.127	-5	-12	-15	-2	-1.7
1898	StL-N	7	24	.226	35	33	31	0	0	283^2	325	2	71	74	12.9	3.93	96	.285	.333	11	.113	-5	-10	-5	-1	-1.0
1899	Cle-N	4	30	.118	36	34	32	0	0	283	403	9	88	54	16.3	5.41	68	.334	.389	18	.162	-6	-49	-54	-4	-5.7
1900	StL-N	5	7	.417	20	12	11	0	0	112^2	147	4	40	23	15.4	5.19	70	.314	.375	7	.171	0	-19	-19	-2	-1.8
Total	7	29	80	.266	145	113	100	0	1	1007^2	1271	21	317	250	14.7	4.87	80	.306	.363	59	.153	-17	-106	-110	-11	-11.8
● **TEX HUGHSON**	Hughson, Cecil Carlton b: 2/9/16, Buda, Tex. d: 8/6/93, Austin, Tex. BR/TR, 6'3", 198 lbs. Deb: 4/16/41																									
1941	Bos-A	5	3	.625	12	8	4	0	0	61	70	3	13	22	12.4	4.13	101	.289	.328	1	.059	-1	0	0	0	-0.1
1942	Bos-A☆	**22**	6	.786	38	30	**22**	4	4	**281**	258	10	75	**113**	10.7	2.59	144	.245	.296	18	.176	-1	33	**35**	1	3.8
1943	Bos-A★	12	15	.444	35	32	**20**	4	2	266	242	23	73	114	10.7	2.64	126	.247	.300	9	.105	-4	19	20	1	1.7
1944	Bos-A★	18	5	**.783**	28	23	19	2	5	203^1	172	4	41	112	**9.5**	2.26	151	.225	**.267**	10	.152	-1	26	26	-0	3.0
1946	*Bos-A	20	11	.645	39	35	21	6	3	278	252	15	51	172	9.9	2.75	133	.238	.274	12	.132	-2	23	28	-2	2.7
1947	Bos-A	12	11	.522	29	26	13	3	0	189^1	173	17	71	119	11.7	3.33	117	.244	.314	2	.033	-6	8	12	-0	0.7
1948	Bos-A	3	1	.750	15	0	0	0	0	19^1	21	0	7	6	13.0	5.12	86	.276	.337	0	.000	-0	-2	-2	-1	-0.4
1949	Bos-A	4	2	.667	29	2	0	0	3	77^2	82	5	41	35	14.4	5.33	82	.268	.356	1	.045	-3	-10	-8	-2	-1.0
Total	8	96	54	.640	225	156	99	19	17	1375^2	1270	77	372	693	10.8	2.94	125	.245	.297	53	.119	-15	99	111	-3	10.4
● **RICK HUISMAN**	Huisman, Richard Allen b: 5/17/69, Oak Park, Ill. BR/TR, 6'3", 200 lbs. Deb: 9/4/95																									
1995	KC-A	0	0	—	7	0	0	0	0	9^2	14	2	1	12	14.0	7.45	64	.333	.349	0	—	0	-3	-3	-0	0.0
1996	KC-A	2	1	.667	22	0	0	0	1	29^1	25	4	18	23	13.2	4.60	109	.231	.341	0	—	0	1	1	0	0.1
Total	2	2	1	.667	29	0	0	0	1	39	39	6	19	35	13.4	5.31	93	.260	.343	0	—	0	-2	-2	0	0.1
● **MARK HUISMANN**	Huismann, Mark Lawrence b: 5/11/58, Littleton, Colo. BR/TR, 6'3", 195 lbs. Deb: 8/16/83																									
1983	KC-A	2	1	.667	13	0	0	0	0	30^2	29	1	17	20	13.5	5.58	73	.250	.346	0	—	0	-5	-5	-1	-0.5
1984	*KC-A	3	3	.500	38	0	0	0	3	75	84	7	21	54	12.7	4.20	96	.286	.335	0	—	0	-2	-1	0	-0.1
1985	KC-A	1	0	1.000	9	0	0	0	0	18^2	14	1	3	9	8.2	1.93	216	.219	.254	0	—	0	5	5	0	0.2
1986	KC-A	0	1	.000	10	0	0	0	1	17^1	18	1	6	13	12.5	4.15	102	.269	.329	0	—	0	0	0	0	0.0
	Sea-A	3	3	.500	36	1	0	0	4	80	80	18	19	59	11.2	3.71	114	.256	.301	0	—	0	4	5	0	0.4
	Yr	3	4	.429	46	1	0	0	5	97^1	98	19	25	72	11.5	3.79	112	.258	.305	0	—	0	4	5	0	0.4
1987	Sea-A	0	0	—	6	0	0	0	0	14^2	10	1	4	15	9.8	4.91	96	.196	.281	0	—	0	-1	-0	0	0.0
	Cle-A	2	3	.400	20	0	0	0	2	35^1	38	6	8	23	11.7	5.09	89	.271	.311	0	—	0	-3	-2	-0	-0.3
	Yr	2	3	.400	26	0	0	0	2	50	48	7	12	38	10.8	5.04	91	.247	.291	0	—	0	-3	-3	0	-0.3
1988	Det-A	1	0	1.000	5	0	0	0	0	5^1	6	0	2	6	13.5	5.06	75	.286	.348	0	—	0	-1	-1	0	0.0

YEAR	TM/L	W	L	PCT	G	GS	CG	SH	SV	IP	H	HR	BB	SO	RAT	ERA	ERA+	OAV	OOB	BH	AVG	PB	PR	/A	PD	TPI
1989	Bal-A	0	0	—	8	0	0	0	1	11^1	13	0	0	13	10.3	6.35	60	.277	.277	0	—	0	-3	-3	1	0.1
1990	Pit-N	1	0	1.000	2	0	0	0	0	3	6	2	1	2	24.0	9.00	40	.462	.533	0	—	0	-2	-2	-0	-0.5
1991	Pit-N	0	0	—	5	0	0	0	0	5	7	0	2	5	16.2	7.20	50	.304	.360	0	—	0	-2	-2	0	0.0
Total	9	13	11	.542	152	1	0	0	11	296^1	305	37	83	219	11.9	4.40	95	.266	.318	0	—	0	-9	-7	1	-0.7

● HARRY HULIHAN Hulihan, Harry Joseph b: 4/18/1899, Rutland, Vt. d: 9/11/80, Rutland, Vt. BR/TL, 5'11", 170 lbs. Deb: 8/16/22

YEAR	TM/L	W	L	PCT	G	GS	CG	SH	SV	IP	H	HR	BB	SO	RAT	ERA	ERA+	OAV	OOB	BH	AVG	PB	PR	/A	PD	TPI
1922	Bos-N	2	3	.400	7	6	2	0	0	40	40	0	26	16	15.7	3.15	127	.274	.398	2	.154	-0	4	4	-1	0.3

● HANK HULVEY Hulvey, James Hensel b: 7/18/1897, Mount Sidney, Va. d: 4/9/82, Mount Sidney, Va. BB/TR, 6', 180 lbs. Deb: 9/5/23

YEAR	TM/L	W	L	PCT	G	GS	CG	SH	SV	IP	H	HR	BB	SO	RAT	ERA	ERA+	OAV	OOB	BH	AVG	PB	PR	/A	PD	TPI
1923	Phi-A	0	1	.000	1	1	0	0	0	7	10	1	2	2	15.4	7.71	53	.357	.400	1	.500	0	-3	-3	0	-0.3

● TOM HUME Hume, Thomas Hubert b: 3/29/53, Cincinnati, Ohio BR/TR, 6'1", 185 lbs. Deb: 5/25/77 C

YEAR	TM/L	W	L	PCT	G	GS	CG	SH	SV	IP	H	HR	BB	SO	RAT	ERA	ERA+	OAV	OOB	BH	AVG	PB	PR	/A	PD	TPI
1977	Cin-N	3	3	.500	14	5	0	0	0	43	54	5	17	22	14.9	7.12	55	.305	.366	2	.200	1	-15	-15	-0	-1.7
1978	Cin-N	8	11	.421	42	23	3	0	1	174	198	12	50	90	13.0	4.14	86	.289	.341	3	.067	-3	-11	-11	0	-1.4
1979	*Cin-N	10	9	.526	57	12	2	0	17	163	162	12	33	80	10.8	2.76	**135**	.262	.300	8	.174	0	18	18	0	2.4
1980	Cin-N	9	10	.474	78	0	0	0	25	137	121	6	38	68	10.6	2.56	140	.240	.297	3	.188	1	16	15	3	3.0
1981	Cin-N	9	4	.692	51	0	0	0	13	67^2	63	7	31	27	12.6	3.46	103	.259	.345	0	.000	-0	0	-0	-0	0.1
1982	Cin-N★	2	6	.250	46	0	0	0	17	63^2	57	2	21	22	11.2	3.11	119	.245	.310	0	.000	-1	3	4	-1	0.6
1983	Cin-N	3	5	.375	48	0	0	0	9	66	66	8	41	34	15.0	4.77	80	.264	.374	0	.000	-1	-8	-7	1	-1.0
1984	Cin-N	4	13	.235	54	8	0	0	3	113^1	142	14	41	59	14.6	5.64	67	.309	.367	3	.136	-0	-26	-23	1	-3.3
1985	Cin-N	3	5	.375	56	0	0	0	3	80	65	7	35	50	11.6	3.26	116	.224	.314	0	.000	-1	3	5	-0	0.4
1986	Phi-N	4	1	.800	48	1	0	0	4	94^1	89	5	34	51	12.0	2.77	139	.252	.323	0	.000	-1	10	11	1	0.6
1987	Phi-N	1	4	.200	38	6	0	0	0	70^2	75	10	41	29	15.3	5.60	76	.277	.380	3	.200	0	-12	-11	0	-0.6
	Cin-N	1	0	1.000	11	0	0	0	0	13^1	14	0	2	4	11.5	4.05	105	.292	.333	0	—	0	0	0	-0	0.0
	Yr	2	4	.333	49	6	0	0	0	84	89	10	43	33	14.3	5.36	79	.274	.360	3	.200	0	-12	-10	0	-0.6
Total	11	57	71	.445	543	55	5	0	92	1086	1106	88	384	536	12.5	3.85	97	.268	.334	22	.120	-5	-22	-14	5	-0.9

● BILL HUMPHREY Humphrey, Byron William b: 6/17/11, Vienna, Mo. d: 2/13/92, Springfield, Mo. BR/TR, 6', 180 lbs. Deb: 4/24/38

YEAR	TM/L	W	L	PCT	G	GS	CG	SH	SV	IP	H	HR	BB	SO	RAT	ERA	ERA+	OAV	OOB	BH	AVG	PB	PR	/A	PD	TPI
1938	Bos-A	0	0	—	2	0	0	0	0	2	5	0	1	0	27.0	9.00	55	.500	.545	0	—	0	-1	-1	-0	0.0

● BOB HUMPHREYS Humphreys, Robert William b: 8/18/35, Covington, Va. BR/TR, 5'11", 170 lbs. Deb: 9/8/62

YEAR	TM/L	W	L	PCT	G	GS	CG	SH	SV	IP	H	HR	BB	SO	RAT	ERA	ERA+	OAV	OOB	BH	AVG	PB	PR	/A	PD	TPI
1962	Det-A	0	1	.000	4	0	0	0	1	5	8	3	2	3	18.0	7.20	57	.381	.435	0	—	0	-2	-2	0	-0.4
1963	StL-N	0	1	.000	9	0	0	0	0	10^2	11	4	7	8	16.0	5.06	70	.282	.404	0	—	0	-2	-2	0	-0.2
1964	*StL-N	2	0	1.000	28	0	0	0	2	42^2	32	3	15	36	10.1	2.53	150	.213	.289	1	.250	1	5	6	-0	0.4
1965	Chi-N	2	0	1.000	41	0	0	0	0	65^2	59	6	27	38	12.1	3.15	117	.244	.325	0	.000	-0	3	4	-1	0.4
1966	Was-A	7	3	.700	58	1	0	0	3	111^2	91	6	28	88	9.9	2.82	123	.229	.287	2	.167	1	8	8	-0	0.8
1967	Was-A	6	2	.750	48	2	0	0	4	105^2	93	13	41	54	11.6	4.17	76	.238	.314	2	.133	1	-11	-12	-1	-1.1
1968	Was-A	5	7	.417	56	0	0	0	2	92^2	78	13	30	56	10.5	3.69	79	.233	.296	2	.400	1	-7	-8	-0	-0.9
1969	Was-A	3	3	.500	47	0	0	0	5	79^2	69	3	38	43	12.2	3.05	114	.233	.322	1	.077	-1	5	4	0	0.3
1970	Was-A	0	0	—	5	0	0	0	0	6^2	4	1	9	6	17.6	1.35	263	.200	.448	0	—	0	2	2	0	0.0
	Mil-A	2	4	.333	23	1	0	0	3	45^2	37	3	22	32	12.0	3.15	120	.222	.319	0	.000	-1	3	3	-0	0.4
	Yr	2	4	.333	28	1	0	0	3	52^1	41	4	31	38	12.7	2.92	129	.219	.336	0	.000	-1	5	5	0	0.4
Total	9	27	21	.563	319	4	0	0	20	566	482	55	219	364	11.4	3.36	101	.234	.312	8	.131	1	3	3	-2	-0.7

● BERT HUMPHRIES Humphries, Albert b: 9/26/1880, California, Pa. d: 9/21/45, Orlando, Fla. BR/TR, 5'11.5", 182 lbs. Deb: 4/16/10

YEAR	TM/L	W	L	PCT	G	GS	CG	SH	SV	IP	H	HR	BB	SO	RAT	ERA	ERA+	OAV	OOB	BH	AVG	PB	PR	/A	PD	TPI
1910	Phi-N	0	0	—	5	0	0	0	2	9^2	13	0	3	3	15.8	4.66	67	.317	.378	0	.000	0	-2	-2	0	0.0
1911	Phi-N	3	1	.750	11	5	2	0	1	41	56	1	10	13	15.8	4.17	83	.339	.398	5	.333	3	-4	-3	-1	-0.1
	Cin-N	4	3	.571	14	7	3	0	0	65	62	3	18	16	11.9	2.35	141	.266	.335	1	.063	-1	8	7	0	0.6
	Yr	7	4	.636	25	12	5	0	1	106	118	4	28	29	12.9	3.06	110	.292	.347	6	.194	2	4	4	-0	0.5
1912	Cin-N	9	11	.450	30	15	9	1	2	158^2	162	6	36	58	11.7	3.23	104	.270	.319	2	.137	-2	3	2	1	-0.1
1913	Chi-N	16	4	**.800**	28	20	13	2	1	181	169	10	24	61	9.7	2.69	118	.250	.277	12	.194	1	10	10	-2	0.9
1914	Chi-N	10	11	.476	34	21	8	2	0	171	162	5	37	62	10.6	2.68	104	.250	.293	13	.236	2	2	2	2	0.6
1915	Chi-N	8	13	.381	31	22	10	4	3	171^2	183	6	23	45	11.1	2.31	120	.280	.309	8	.174	0	8	9	-2	0.9
Total	6	50	43	.538	153	90	45	9	9	798	807	31	151	258	11.1	2.79	110	.267	.309	46	.186	3	26	25	-3	2.8

● JOHNNY HUMPHRIES Humphries, John William b: 6/23/15, Clifton Forge, Va d: 6/24/65, New Orleans, La. BR/TR, 6'1", 185 lbs. Deb: 5/8/38

YEAR	TM/L	W	L	PCT	G	GS	CG	SH	SV	IP	H	HR	BB	SO	RAT	ERA	ERA+	OAV	OOB	BH	AVG	PB	PR	/A	PD	TPI
1938	Cle-A	9	8	.529	**45**	6	1	0	6	103^1	105	6	63	56	14.7	5.23	89	.264	.367	3	.103	-1	-5	-7	-1	-1.1
1939	Cle-A	2	4	.333	15	1	0	0	2	28^1	30	0	32	12	20.0	8.26	53	.294	.467	0	.000	-1	-11	-12	-0	-2.2
1940	Cle-A	0	2	.000	19	1	1	0	1	33^2	35	5	29	17	17.6	8.29	51	.269	.410	0	.000	-1	-15	-15	-1	-1.0
1941	Chi-A	4	2	.667	14	6	4	4	1	73^1	63	2	22	25	10.6	1.84	223	.230	.290	2	.087	-1	19	18	-1	1.2
1942	Chi-A	12	12	.500	28	28	17	2	0	228^1	227	9	59	71	11.5	2.68	134	.257	.309	18	.225	5	25	23	-2	2.7
1943	Chi-A	11	11	.500	28	27	8	2	0	188^1	198	7	54	51	12.3	3.30	101	.268	.322	20	.290	5	-0	1	-2	0.6
1944	Chi-A	8	10	.444	30	20	8	0	1	169	170	9	57	42	12.3	3.67	93	.267	.331	10	.189	0	-5	-5	-3	-0.8
1945	Chi-A	6	14	.300	22	21	10	1	1	153	172	11	48	33	13.1	4.24	78	.282	.337	8	.148	-3	-15	-16	-4	-2.5
1946	Phi-N	0	0	—	10	1	0	0	0	24^2	24	1	9	10	12.4	4.01	85	.258	.330	2	.250	0	-2	-2	-1	-0.1
Total	9	52	63	.452	211	111	49	9	12	1002	1024	50	373	317	12.8	3.78	97	.265	.334	63	.191	4	-9	-13	-14	-3.2

● BEN HUNT Hunt, Benjamin Franklin "High Pockets" b: 11/10/1888, Eufaula, Okla. d: 9/27/27, Greybull, Wyo. BL/TL, 6'5", 190 lbs. Deb: 8/24/10

YEAR	TM/L	W	L	PCT	G	GS	CG	SH	SV	IP	H	HR	BB	SO	RAT	ERA	ERA+	OAV	OOB	BH	AVG	PB	PR	/A	PD	TPI
1910	Bos-A	2	3	.400	7	7	3	0	0	46^2	45	4	20	19	12.5	4.05	63	.266	.344	1	.056	-2	-8	-8	-1	-1.0
1913	StL-N	0	1	.000	2	1	0	0	0	8	6	0	9	6	18.0	3.38	96	.240	.457	0	.000	-0	-0	-0	1	0.0
Total	2	2	4	.333	9	8	3	0	0	54^2	51	4	29	25	13.3	3.95	67	.263	.362	1	.050	-2	-8	-8	-0	-1.0

● KEN HUNT Hunt, Kenneth Raymond b: 12/14/38, Ogden, Utah BR/TR, 6'4", 200 lbs. Deb: 4/16/61

YEAR	TM/L	W	L	PCT	G	GS	CG	SH	SV	IP	H	HR	BB	SO	RAT	ERA	ERA+	OAV	OOB	BH	AVG	PB	PR	/A	PD	TPI
1961	*Cin-N	9	10	.474	29	22	4	0	0	136^1	130	13	66	75	13.3	3.96	103	.257	.349	7	.179	0	1	2	-1	0.1

● GEORGE HUNTER Hunter, George Henry b: 7/8/1887, Buffalo, N.Y. d: 1/11/68, Harrisburg, Pa. BB/TL, 5'8.5", 165 lbs. Deb: 5/4/09 F◆

YEAR	TM/L	W	L	PCT	G	GS	CG	SH	SV	IP	H	HR	BB	SO	RAT	ERA	ERA+	OAV	OOB	BH	AVG	PB	PR	/A	PD	TPI
1909	Bro-N	4	10	.286	16	13	10	0	0	113^1	104	2	38	43	11.5	2.46	105	.254	.322	28	.228	2	2	2	0	0.5

● CATFISH HUNTER Hunter, James Augustus "Jim" b: 4/8/46, Hertford, N.C. BR/TR, 6', 195 lbs. Deb: 5/13/65 H

YEAR	TM/L	W	L	PCT	G	GS	CG	SH	SV	IP	H	HR	BB	SO	RAT	ERA	ERA+	OAV	OOB	BH	AVG	PB	PR	/A	PD	TPI
1965	KC-A	8	8	.500	32	20	3	2	0	133	124	21	46	82	11.6	4.26	82	.246	.311	6	.150	-1	-12	-11	-2	-1.5
1966	KC-A☆	9	11	.450	30	25	4	0	0	176^2	158	17	64	103	11.4	4.02	84	.239	.308	9	.153	1	-12	-12	-3	-1.5
1967	KC-A★	13	17	.433	35	35	13	5	0	259^2	209	16	84	196	10.2	2.81	113	.219	.284	18	.196	4	12	11	-5	1.2
1968	Oak-A	13	13	.500	36	34	11	2	1	234	210	29	69	172	10.9	3.35	84	.238	.296	19	.232	5	-10	-14	-3	-1.3
1969	Oak-A	12	15	.444	38	35	10	3	0	247	210	34	85	150	10.9	3.35	103	.234	.304	19	.224	4	7	2	-1	0.6
1970	Oak-A★	18	14	.563	40	40	9	1	0	262^1	253	32	74	178	11.5	3.81	93	.250	.307	18	.200	4	-3	-8	-2	-0.7
1971	*Oak-A	21	11	.656	37	37	16	4	0	273^2	225	27	80	181	10.2	2.96	113	.223	.282	36	.350	13	15	11	-4	2.4
1972	*Oak-A☆	21	7	**.750**	38	37	16	5	0	295^1	200	21	70	191	8.3	2.04	139	.189	.242	23	.219	3	33	26	-3	2.7
1973	*Oak-A★	21	5	**.808**	36	36	11	3	0	256^1	222	39	69	124	10.3	3.34	106	.232	.284	1	1.000	1	14	6	-4	0.2
1974	*Oak-A★	**25**	12	.676	41	41	23	6	0	318^1	268	25	46	143	**9.0**	**2.49**	133	.229	**.260**	0	—	0	**40**	29	-4	3.0
1975	NY-A★	**23**	14	.622	39	39	**30**	7	0	**328**	248	25	83	177	**9.2**	2.58	143	**.208**	**.263**	0	—	0	44	40	-4	3.9
1976	*NY-A★	17	15	.531	36	36	21	2	0	298^2	268	28	68	173	10.2	3.53	97	.241	.286	0	.000	-0	-0	-4	-2	-0.6
1977	*NY-A	9	9	.500	22	22	8	1	0	143^1	137	29	47	52	11.7	4.71	84	.250	.313	0	—	0	-10	-12	-3	-1.6
1978	*NY-A	12	6	.667	21	20	5	1	0	118	98	16	35	56	10.2	3.58	101	.226	.286	0	—	0	2	0	-1	0.0
1979	NY-A	2	9	.182	19	19	1	0	0	105	128	15	34	34	14.0	5.31	77	.312	.366	0	—	0	-13	-14	-1	-1.4
Total	15	224	166	.574	500	476	181	42	1	3449^1	2958	374	954	2012	10.3	3.26	104	.231	.287	149	.226	33	109	51	-40	5.4

● JIM HUNTER Hunter, James Mac Gregor b: 6/22/64, Jersey City, N.J. BR/TR, 6'3", 205 lbs. Deb: 5/17/91

YEAR	TM/L	W	L	PCT	G	GS	CG	SH	SV	IP	H	HR	BB	SO	RAT	ERA	ERA+	OAV	OOB	BH	AVG	PB	PR	/A	PD	TPI
1991	Mil-A	0	5	.000	8	6	0	0	0	31	45	3	17	14	19.2	7.26	55	.349	.440	0	—	0	-11	-11	1	-1.4

● RICH HUNTER Hunter, Richard Thomas b: 9/25/74, Pasadena, Cal. BR/TR, 6'1", 185 lbs. Deb: 4/6/96

YEAR	TM/L	W	L	PCT	G	GS	CG	SH	SV	IP	H	HR	BB	SO	RAT	ERA	ERA+	OAV	OOB	BH	AVG	PB	PR	/A	PD	TPI
1996	Phi-N	3	7	.300	14	14	0	0	0	69^1	84	10	33	32	15.8	6.49	66	.303	.387	3	.167	0	-18	-17	0	-1.9

YEAR	TM/L	W	L	PCT	G	GS	CG	SH	SV	IP	H	HR	BB	SO	RAT	ERA	ERA+	OAV	OOB	BH	AVG	PB	PR	/A	PD	TPI
● **LEM HUNTER** Hunter, Robert Lemuel b: 1/16/1863, Warren, Ohio d: 11/9/56, W.Lafayette, Ohio Deb: 9/1/1883 ♦																										
1883	Cle-N	0	0	—	1	0	0	0	0	6^1	10	0	2	4	17.1	1.42	222	.370	.414	1	.250	-0	1	1	0	0.0
● **WILLARD HUNTER** Hunter, Willard Mitchell b: 3/8/34, Newark, N.J. BR/TL, 6'2", 180 lbs. Deb: 4/16/62																										
1962	LA-N	0	0	—	1	0	0	0	0	2	6	1	4	1	45.0	40.50	9	.545	.667	0	—	0	-8	-8	0	0.0
	NY-N	1	6	.143	27	6	1	0	0	63	67	9	34	40	14.6	5.57	75	.270	.360	3	.231	0	-11	-10	-1	-1.0
	Yr	1	6	.143	28	6	1	0	0	65	73	10	38	41	15.5	6.65	63	.281	.375	3	.231	0	-20	-18	-1	-1.0
1964	NY-N	3	3	.500	41	0	0	0	5	49	54	4	9	22	11.9	4.41	81	.284	.323	1	1.000	0	-5	-5	-0	-0.6
Total	2	4	9	.308	69	6	1	0	5	114	127	14	47	63	14.0	5.68	69	.283	.355	4	.286	1	-24	-22	-1	-1.6
● **WALT HUNTZINGER** Huntzinger, Walter Henry "Shakes" b: 2/6/1899, Pottsville, Pa. d: 8/11/81, Upper Darby, Pa. BR/TR, 6', 150 lbs. Deb: 9/29/23																										
1923	NY-N	0	1	.000	2	1	0	0	0	8	9	0	1	2	11.3	7.88	49	.290	.313	0	.000	-0	-3	-4	-0	-0.4
1924	NY-N	1	1	.500	12	2	0	0	1	32^1	41	3	9	6	13.9	4.45	82	.318	.362	4	.500	1	-2	-3	-0	-0.1
1925	NY-N	5	1	.833	26	1	0	0	0	64^1	68	3	17	19	11.9	3.50	115	.281	.328	1	.091	-1	**6**	**4**	-1	0.1
1926	StL-N	0	4	.000	9	4	2	0	0	34	35	4	14	9	13.0	4.24	92	.267	.338	0	.000	-1	-2	-1	1	-0.2
	Chi-N	1	1	.500	11	0	0	0	2	28^2	26	0	8	4	11.6	0.94	408	.260	.333	1	.143	-1	9	9	0	0.7
	Yr	1	5	.167	20	4	2	0	2	62^2	61	4	22	13	12.4	2.73	142	.264	.336	1	.067	-2	8	8	1	0.5
Total	4	7	8	.467	60	8	2	0	3	167^1	179	10	49	40	12.4	3.60	108	.283	.337	6	.167	-1	8	6	-1	0.1
● **TOM HURD** Hurd, Thomas Carr "Whitey" b: 5/27/24, Danville, Va. d: 9/5/82, Waterloo, Iowa BR/TR, 5'9", 155 lbs. Deb: 7/30/54																										
1954	Bos-A	2	0	1.000	16	0	0	0	1	29^2	21	2	12	14	10.0	3.03	135	.198	.280	1	.333	0	2	4	0	0.3
1955	Bos-A	8	6	.571	43	0	0	0	5	80^2	72	7	38	48	12.4	3.01	142	.242	.330	1	.071	-1	8	11	-0	1.9
1956	Bos-A	3	4	.429	40	0	0	0	5	76	84	5	47	34	15.9	5.33	87	.289	.393	6	.500	2	-10	-6	-1	-0.5
Total	3	13	10	.565	99	0	0	0	11	186^1	177	14	97	96	13.4	3.96	111	.255	.350	8	.276	1	1	9	-1	1.7
● **BRUCE HURST** Hurst, Bruce Vee b: 3/24/58, St.George, Utah BL/TL, 6'3", 215 lbs. Deb: 4/12/80																										
1980	Bos-A	2	2	.500	12	7	0	0	0	30^2	39	4	16	16	16.7	9.10	46	.307	.393	0	—	0	-17	-17	-0	-2.0
1981	Bos-A	2	0	1.000	5	5	0	0	0	23	23	1	12	11	14.1	4.30	90	.258	.353	0	—	0	-2	-1	-1	-0.2
1982	Bos-A	3	7	.300	28	19	0	0	0	117	161	16	40	53	15.7	5.77	75	.333	.388	0	—	0	-22	-19	1	-1.7
1983	Bos-A	12	12	.500	33	32	6	2	0	211^1	241	22	62	115	13.0	4.09	106	.290	.342	0	—	0	-1	6	1	0.7
1984	Bos-A	12	12	.500	33	33	9	2	0	218	232	25	88	136	13.5	3.92	106	.271	.343	0	—	0	2	6	0	0.6
1985	Bos-A	11	13	.458	35	31	6	1	0	229^1	243	31	70	189	12.4	4.51	95	.273	.328	0	—	0	-9	-6	0	-0.5
1986	*Bos-A	13	8	.619	25	25	11	4	0	174^1	169	18	50	167	11.5	2.99	139	.256	.311	0	—	0	23	23	-1	2.5
1987	Bos-A☆	15	13	.536	33	33	15	3	0	238^2	239	35	76	190	11.9	4.41	103	.262	.320	0	—	0	1	3	0	0.3
1988	*Bos-A	18	6	.750	33	32	7	1	0	216^2	222	21	65	166	12.0	3.66	113	.264	.318	0	—	0	7	11	0	1.1
1989	SD-N	15	11	.577	33	33	**10**	2	0	244^2	214	16	66	179	10.3	2.69	130	.237	.289	5	.071	-2	22	22	1	2.3
1990	SD-N	11	9	.550	33	33	9	**4**	0	223^2	188	21	63	162	10.1	3.14	122	.228	.284	6	.090	-2	16	17	0	1.2
1991	SD-N	15	8	.652	31	31	4	0	0	221^2	201	17	59	141	10.7	3.29	115	.241	.293	9	.134	-0	10	13	-1	1.1
1992	SD-N	14	9	.609	32	32	6	4	0	217^1	223	22	51	131	11.3	3.85	93	.267	.309	11	.159	1	-8	-7	-1	-0.6
1993	SD-N	0	1	.000	2	2	0	0	0	4^1	9	0	3	3	24.9	12.46	33	.409	.480	0	—	0	-4	-4	0	-0.7
	Col-N	0	1	.000	3	3	0	0	0	8^2	6	1	3	6	9.3	5.19	92	.194	.265	0	.000	-0	-1	-0	0	0.0
	Yr	0	2	.000	5	5	0	0	0	13	15	1	6	9	14.5	7.62	60	.283	.356	0	.000	-0	-5	-4	0	-0.7
1994	Tex-A	2	1	.667	8	8	0	0	0	38	53	8	16	24	16.3	7.11	68	.342	.404	0	—	0	-10	-10	-1	-0.7
Total	15	145	113	.562	379	359	83	23	0	2417^1	2463	258	740	1689	12.0	3.92	103	.265	.321	31	.113	-3	7	37	2	3.4
● **JAMES HURST** Hurst, James Lavon b: 6/1/67, Plantation, Fla. BL/TL, 6', 160 lbs. Deb: 4/4/94																										
1994	Tex-A	0	0	—	8	0	0	0	0	10^2	17	1	8	5	21.1	10.13	48	.362	.455	0	—	0	-6	-6	0	0.0
● **JONATHAN HURST** Hurst, Jonathan b: 10/20/66, New York, N.Y. BR/TR, 6'3", 175 lbs. Deb: 6/9/92																										
1992	Mon-N	1	1	.500	3	3	0	0	0	16^1	18	1	7	4	14.3	5.51	63	.281	.361	0	.000	-0	-4	-4	-0	-0.5
1994	NY-N	0	1	.000	7	0	0	0	0	10	15	5	5	6	18.0	12.60	33	.341	.408	0	—	0	-9	-9	-0	-0.8
Total	2	1	2	.333	10	3	0	0	0	26^1	33	6	12	10	15.7	8.20	46	.306	.380	0	.000	-0	-13	-13	-0	-1.3
● **BILL HURST** Hurst, William Hansel b: 4/28/70, Miami Beach, Fla. BR/TR, 6'7", 220 lbs. Deb: 9/18/96																										
1996	Fla-N	0	0	—	2	0	0	0	0	2	3	0	1	1	18.0	0.00	—	.333	.400	0	—	0	1	1	-0	0.0
● **EDWIN HURTADO** Hurtado, Edwin Amilgar b: 2/1/70, Barquisimeto, Venez. BR/TR, 6'3", 215 lbs. Deb: 5/22/95																										
1995	Tor-A	5	2	.714	14	10	1	0	0	77^2	81	11	40	33	14.6	5.45	86	.275	.371	0	—	0	-6	-6	-1	-0.5
1996	Sea-A	2	5	.286	16	4	0	0	2	47^2	61	10	30	36	17.2	7.74	64	.324	.417	0	—	0	-15	-15	1	-1.7
1997	Sea-A	1	2	.333	13	1	0	0	0	19	25	5	15	10	19.9	9.00	50	.329	.452	0	—	0	-9	-10	1	-1.2
Total	3	8	9	.471	43	15	1	0	2	144^1	167	26	85	79	16.2	6.67	71	.299	.398	0	—	0	-30	-31	1	-3.4
● **BILL HUSTED** Husted, William J. b: 10/11/1866, Gloucester, N.J. d: 5/17/41, Gloucester, N.J. Deb: 4/29/1890																										
1890	Phi-P	5	10	.333	18	17	12	0	0	129	148	2	67	33	15.3	4.88	88	.276	.361	6	.107	-6	-9	-9	-2	-1.3
● **BERT HUSTING** Husting, Berthold Juneau "Pete" b: 3/6/1878, Fond Du Lac, Wis. d: 9/3/48, Milwaukee, Wis. BR/TR, Deb: 8/16/00																										
1900	Pit-N	0	0	—	2	0	0	0	0	8	10	2	5	7	18.0	5.63	65	.303	.410	0	.000	-1	-2	-2	1	0.0
1901	Mil-A	9	15	.375	34	26	19	0	1	217^1	234	5	95	67	14.2	4.27	84	.272	.353	19	.202	-1	-14	-16	5	-1.1
1902	Bos-A	0	1	.000	1	1	1	0	0	8	15	0	8	4	25.9	9.00	40	.395	.500	1	.250	1	-5	-5	0	-0.4
	Phi-A	14	5	.737	32	27	17	1	0	204	240	7	91	44	15.0	3.79	97	.293	.370	13	.159	-3	-5	-3	2	-0.3
	Yr	14	6	.700	33	28	18	1	0	212	255	7	99	48	15.4	3.99	92	.298	.377	14	.163	-3	-10	-8	3	-0.7
Total	3	23	21	.523	69	54	37	1	1	437^1	499	14	199	122	14.8	4.16	87	.285	.366	33	.180	-4	-26	-26	8	-1.8
● **JOHNNY HUTCHINGS** Hutchings, John Richard Joseph b: 4/14/16, Chicago, Ill. d: 4/27/63, Indianapolis, Ind. BB/TR, 6'2", 250 lbs. Deb: 4/26/40																										
1940	*Cin-N	2	1	.667	19	4	0	0	0	54	53	3	18	18	12.0	3.50	108	.260	.323	2	.154	0	2	2	-1	0.0
1941	Cin-N	0	0	—	8	0	0	0	0	11	12	0	4	5	13.1	4.09	88	.279	.340	0	—	0	-1	-1	0	0.0
	Bos-N	1	6	.143	36	7	1	1	2	95^2	110	6	22	36	12.8	4.14	86	.287	.333	4	.148	0	-5	-6	0	-0.4
	Yr	1	6	.143	44	7	1	1	2	106^2	122	6	26	41	12.8	4.13	86	.286	.333	4	.148	0	-6	-7	0	-0.4
1942	Bos-N	1	0	1.000	20	3	0	0	0	65^2	66	2	34	27	14.0	4.39	76	.260	.352	1	.050	-2	-8	-8	-1	-0.4
1944	Bos-N	1	4	.200	14	7	1	0	1	56^2	55	3	26	26	13.0	3.97	96	.252	.335	1	.067	-1	-2	-1	-1	-0.2
1945	Bos-N	7	6	.538	57	12	3	2	3	185	173	21	75	99	12.3	3.75	102	.244	.320	13	.241	2	1	2	0	0.3
1946	Bos-N	0	1	.000	1	1	0	0	0	3	5	1	1	1	18.0	9.00	38	.357	.400	0	.000	-0	-2	-2	-0	-0.5
Total	6	12	18	.400	155	34	5	3	6	471	474	36	180	212	12.7	3.96	93	.260	.330	21	.162	-1	-15	-14	-2	-1.2
● **FRED HUTCHINSON** Hutchinson, Frederick Charles b: 8/12/19, Seattle, Wash. d: 11/12/64, Bradenton, Fla. BL/TR, 6'2", 200 lbs. Deb: 5/2/39 M♦																										
1939	Det-A	3	6	.333	13	12	3	0	0	84^2	95	9	51	22	15.5	5.21	94	.287	.382	13	.382	3	-6	-3	-0	0.0
1940	*Det-A	3	7	.300	17	10	1	0	1	76	85	6	26	32	13.4	5.68	84	.281	.342	8	.267	0	-11	-8	0	-0.8
1946	Det-A	14	11	.560	28	26	16	3	2	207	184	14	66	138	10.9	3.09	118	.236	.295	28	.315	8	10	13	3	2.8
1947	Det-A	18	10	.643	33	25	18	3	2	219^2	211	14	61	113	11.2	3.03	124	.251	.304	32	.302	11	16	18	2	3.7
1948	Det-A	13	11	.542	33	28	15	0	0	221	223	32	48	92	**11.1**	4.32	101	.258	**.297**	23	.205	4	-1	1	3	0.9
1949	Det-A	15	7	.682	33	21	9	4	1	188^2	167	18	52	54	**10.5**	2.96	141	.237	**.290**	18	.247	4	26	25	2	3.4
1950	Det-A	17	8	.680	39	26	10	1	0	231^2	269	18	48	71	12.5	3.96	118	.290	.329	31	.326	10	16	19	2	2.9
1951	Det-A★	10	10	.500	31	20	9	2	2	188^1	204	11	27	53	11.1	3.68	113	.275	.302	16	.188	-2	9	10	2	1.0
1952	Det-A	2	1	.667	12	1	0	0	0	37^1	40	4	9	12	12.1	3.38	113	.276	.323	1	.056	-1	1	2	2	0.2
1953	Det-A	0	0	—	3	0	0	0	0	9^2	9	0	0	4	8.4	2.79	146	.243	.243	1	.167	0	1	1	-0	0.0
Total	10	95	71	.572	242	169	81	13	7	1464	1487	126	388	591	11.6	3.73	113	.262	.311	171	.263	39	62	79	15	14.1
● **IRA HUTCHINSON** Hutchinson, Ira Kendall b: 8/31/10, Chicago, Ill. d: 8/21/73, Chicago, Ill. BR/TR, 5'10.5", 180 lbs. Deb: 9/24/33																										
1933	Chi-A	0	0	—	1	1	0	0	0	4	7	1	3	2	22.5	13.50	31	.368	.455	1	.500	0	-4	-4	-0	0.0
1937	Bos-N	4	6	.400	31	8	1	0	1	91^2	99	4	35	29	13.3	3.73	96	.286	.353	3	.115	-1	2	-1	1	-0.2
1938	Bos-N	9	8	.529	36	12	4	1	4	151	150	3	61	38	12.8	2.74	125	.258	.332	9	.173	-1	18	12	1	1.3
1939	Bro-N	5	2	.714	41	1	0	0	1	105^2	103	9	51	46	13.2	4.34	93	.265	.352	1	.037	-3	-5	-4	1	-0.4

YEAR	TM/L	W	L	PCT	G	GS	CG	SH	SV	IP	H	HR	BB	SO	RAT	ERA	ERA+	OAV	OOB	BH	AVG	PB	PR	/A	PD	TPI
1940	StL-N	4	2	.667	20	2	1	0	1	63^1	68	3	19	19	12.4	3.13	128	.271	.322	4	.222	0	5	6	0	0.6
1941	StL-N	1	5	.167	29	0	0	0	5	46^2	32	3	19	19	10.2	3.86	98	.196	.288	2	.250	0	-1	-0	0	0.0
1944	Bos-N	9	7	.563	40	8	1	1	1	119^2	136	8	53	22	14.4	4.21	91	.296	.373	4	.138	-1	-8	-5	1	-0.7
1945	Bos-N	2	3	.400	11	0	0	0	1	28^2	33	2	8	4	13.2	5.02	76	.277	.328	0	.000	-1	-4	-4	1	-0.7
Total	8	34	33	.507	209	32	7	2	13	610^2	628	33	249	179	13.1	3.76	100	.270	.344	24	.140	-7	2	-1	5	-0.1

● BILL HUTCHISON

Hutchison, William Forrest "Wild Bill" b: 12/17/1859, New Haven, Conn. d: 3/19/26, Kansas City, Mo. BR/TR, 5'9", 175 lbs. Deb: 6/10/1884

YEAR	TM/L	W	L	PCT	G	GS	CG	SH	SV	IP	H	HR	BB	SO	RAT	ERA	ERA+	OAV	OOB	BH	AVG	PB	PR	/A	PD	TPI
1884	KC-U	1	1	.500	2	2	2	0	0	17	14	0	1	5	7.9	2.65	84	.209	.221	2	.250	-0	-0	-1	2	0.0
1889	Chi-N	16	17	.485	37	36	33	3	0	318	306	11	117	136	12.2	3.54	118	.245	.314	21	.158	-5	17	22	5	1.8
1890	Chi-N	**42**	25	.627	**71**	66	**65**	5	**2**	**603**	505	20	199	289	10.7	2.70	135	.220	.286	53	.203	-4	58	64	5	5.9
1891	Chi-N	**44**	19	.698	**66**	58	**56**	4	1	**561**	508	26	178	261	11.1	2.81	119	.232	.292	45	.185	-1	34	33	-2	2.7
1892	Chi-N	**36**	36	.500	**75**	70	**67**	5	1	**622**	571	11	190	**314**	11.2	2.76	120	.234	.293	57	.217	3	36	39	4	4.6
1893	Chi-N	16	24	.400	44	40	38	2	0	348^1	420	9	156	80	15.2	4.75	97	.289	.364	41	.253	1	-3	-5	-3	-0.5
1894	Chi-N	14	16	.467	36	34	28	0	0	277^2	373	9	140	59	17.2	6.06	93	.318	.398	42	.309	5	-23	-14	-2	-0.7
1895	Chi-N	13	21	.382	38	35	30	2	0	291	371	13	129	85	15.9	4.73	108	.305	.378	25	.198	-7	2	12	-0	0.4
1897	StL-N	1	4	.200	6	5	2	0	0	40	55	5	22	5	17.8	6.07	73	.324	.407	5	.278	1	-8	-7	-1	-0.7
Total	9	183	163	.529	375	346	321	21	4	3078	3123	104	1132	1234	12.7	3.59	111	.255	.323	291	.216	-7	112	139	7	13.5

● HERB HUTSON

Hutson, George Herbert b: 7/17/49, Savannah, Ga. BR/TR, 6'2", 205 lbs. Deb: 4/10/74

YEAR	TM/L	W	L	PCT	G	GS	CG	SH	SV	IP	H	HR	BB	SO	RAT	ERA	ERA+	OAV	OOB	BH	AVG	PB	PR	/A	PD	TPI
1974	Chi-N	0	2	.000	20	2	0	0	0	28^2	24	3	15	22	12.6	3.45	110	.233	.336	0	.000	-0	1	1	-1	0.0

● MARK HUTTON

Hutton, Mark Steven b: 2/6/70, South Adelaide, Australia BR/TR, 6'6", 240 lbs. Deb: 7/23/93

YEAR	TM/L	W	L	PCT	G	GS	CG	SH	SV	IP	H	HR	BB	SO	RAT	ERA	ERA+	OAV	OOB	BH	AVG	PB	PR	/A	PD	TPI
1993	NY-A	1	1	.500	7	4	0	0	0	22	24	2	17	12	17.2	5.73	72	.293	.420	0	—	0	-3	-4	-0	-0.3
1994	NY-A	0	0	—	2	0	0	0	0	3^2	4	0	0	1	9.8	4.91	93	.250	.250	0	—	0	-0	-0	-0	0.2
1996	NY-A	0	2	.000	12	2	0	0	0	30^1	32	3	18	25	15.1	5.04	98	.269	.370	0	—	0	-0	-0	-1	-0.1
	Fla-N	5	1	.833	13	9	0	0	0	56^1	47	6	18	31	10.9	3.67	111	.222	.292	6	.316	2	3	2	-1	0.4
1997	Fla-N	3	1	.750	32	0	0	0	0	47^2	50	7	19	29	13.4	3.78	107	.286	.362	0	—	0	2	1	1	0.2
	Col-N	0	1	.000	8	1	0	0	0	12^2	22	3	7	10	23.4	7.11	73	.407	.508	0	.000	-0	-4	-3	-0	-0.2
	Yr	3	2	.600	40	1	0	0	0	60^1	72	10	26	39	15.2	4.48	95	.308	.386	0	.000	-0	-2	-1	1	0.0
1998	Cin-N	0	1	.000	10	2	0	0	0	17	24	2	17	3	22.2	7.41	58	.348	.483	1	1.000	0	-6	-6	1	-0.2
Total	5	9	7	.563	84	18	0	0	0	189^2	203	23	96	111	14.8	4.75	91	.279	.372	7	.304	3	-8	-9	-1	-0.0

● TOM HUTTON

Hutton, Thomas George b: 4/20/46, Los Angeles, Cal. BL/TL, 5'11", 180 lbs. Deb: 9/16/66 ◆

YEAR	TM/L	W	L	PCT	G	GS	CG	SH	SV	IP	H	HR	BB	SO	RAT	ERA	ERA+	OAV	OOB	BH	AVG	PB	PR	/A	PD	TPI
1980	Mon-N	0	0	—	1	0	0	0	0	1	3	1	1	1	36.0	27.00	13	.500	.571	12	.218	0	-3	-3	0	0.0

● DICK HYDE

Hyde, Richard Elde b: 8/3/28, Hindsboro, Ill. BR/TR, 5'11", 170 lbs. Deb: 4/23/55

YEAR	TM/L	W	L	PCT	G	GS	CG	SH	SV	IP	H	HR	BB	SO	RAT	ERA	ERA+	OAV	OOB	BH	AVG	PB	PR	/A	PD	TPI
1955	Was-A	0	0	—	3	0	0	0	0	2	2	0	1	1	13.5	4.50	85	.286	.375	0	—	0	-0	-0	-0	0.0
1957	Was-A	4	3	.571	52	2	0	0	1	109^1	104	4	56	46	13.7	4.12	95	.261	.361	3	.167	-0	-4	-3	1	-0.1
1958	Was-A	10	3	.769	53	0	0	0	18	103	82	1	35	49	10.4	1.75	218	.220	.291	0	.000	-2	**23**	**24**	2	3.9
1959	Was-A	2	5	.286	37	0	0	0	4	54^1	56	5	27	29	14.1	4.97	79	.269	.359	0	.000	-1	-7	-6	2	-0.7
1960	Was-A	0	1	.000	9	0	0	0	0	8^2	11	2	5	4	17.7	4.15	94	.355	.459	0	—	0	-0	-0	-0	0.0
1961	Bal-A	1	2	.333	15	0	0	0	0	21	18	1	13	15	13.7	5.57	69	.228	.344	1	1.000	0	-4	-4	1	-0.3
Total	6	17	14	.548	169	2	0	0	23	298^1	273	13	137	144	12.8	3.56	109	.249	.339	4	.093	-2	8	10	6	2.8

● JIM HYNDMAN

Hyndman, James William b: 7/1865, Ontario, Canada Deb: 7/23/1886 ◆

YEAR	TM/L	W	L	PCT	G	GS	CG	SH	SV	IP	H	HR	BB	SO	RAT	ERA	ERA+	OAV	OOB	BH	AVG	PB	PR	/A	PD	TPI
1886	Phi-a	0	1	.000	1	1	0	0	0	2	5	1	5	1	49.5	27.00	13	.455	.647	0	.000	-1	-5	-5	0	-1.2

● PAT HYNES

Hynes, Patrick J. b: 3/12/1884, St.Louis, Mo. d: 3/12/07, St.Louis, Mo. TL , Deb: 9/27/03 ◆

YEAR	TM/L	W	L	PCT	G	GS	CG	SH	SV	IP	H	HR	BB	SO	RAT	ERA	ERA+	OAV	OOB	BH	AVG	PB	PR	/A	PD	TPI
1903	StL-N	0	1	.000	1	1	1	0	0	9	10	0	6	1	16.0	4.00	82	.294	.400	0	.000	-0	-1	-1	-1	-0.2
1904	StL-A	1	0	1.000	5	2	1	0	0	26	35	1	7	6	14.5	6.23	40	.321	.362	60	.236	0	-10	-11	-1	-0.5
Total	2	1	1	.500	6	3	2	0	0	35	45	1	13	7	14.9	5.66	47	.315	.372	60	.233	0	-11	-12	-2	-0.7

● HAM IBURG

Iburg, Herman Edward b: 10/29/1877, San Francisco, Cal d: 2/11/45, San Francisco, Cal BR/TR, 5'11", 165 lbs. Deb: 4/17/02

YEAR	TM/L	W	L	PCT	G	GS	CG	SH	SV	IP	H	HR	BB	SO	RAT	ERA	ERA+	OAV	OOB	BH	AVG	PB	PR	/A	PD	TPI
1902	Phi-N	11	18	.379	30	29	20	1	0	236	286	1	62	106	13.7	3.89	72	.299	.349	12	.138	-5	-29	-28	0	-3.5

● GARY IGNASIAK

Ignasiak, Gary Raymond b: 9/1/49, Anchorville, Mich. BR/TL, 5'11", 185 lbs. Deb: 9/20/73 F

YEAR	TM/L	W	L	PCT	G	GS	CG	SH	SV	IP	H	HR	BB	SO	RAT	ERA	ERA+	OAV	OOB	BH	AVG	PB	PR	/A	PD	TPI
1973	Det-A	0	0	—	3	0	0	0	0	4^2	5	0	3	4	15.4	3.86	106	.278	.381	0	—	0	-0	0	0	0.0

● MIKE IGNASIAK

Ignasiak, Michael James b: 3/12/66, Mt.Clemens, Mich. BB/TR, 5'11", 175 lbs. Deb: 8/22/91 F

YEAR	TM/L	W	L	PCT	G	GS	CG	SH	SV	IP	H	HR	BB	SO	RAT	ERA	ERA+	OAV	OOB	BH	AVG	PB	PR	/A	PD	TPI
1991	Mil-A	2	1	.667	4	1	0	0	0	12^2	7	2	8	10	10.7	5.68	70	.163	.294	0	—	0	-2	-2	-0	-0.4
1993	Mil-A	1	1	.500	27	0	0	0	0	37	32	2	21	28	13.4	3.65	116	.241	.353	0	—	0	3	2	-1	0.1
1994	Mil-A	3	1	.750	23	5	0	0	0	47^2	51	5	13	24	12.3	4.53	111	.276	.327	0	—	0	1	3	-1	-0.1
1995	Mil-A	4	1	.800	25	0	0	0	0	39^2	51	5	23	26	17.2	5.90	84	.325	.418	0	—	0	-5	-4	-1	-0.6
Total	4	10	4	.714	79	6	0	0	0	137	141	14	65	88	13.9	4.80	98	.272	.359	0	—	0	-3	-1	-2	-1.0

● BLAISE ILSLEY

Ilsley, Blaise Francis b: 4/9/64, Alpena, Mich. BL/TL, 6'1", 195 lbs. Deb: 4/4/94

YEAR	TM/L	W	L	PCT	G	GS	CG	SH	SV	IP	H	HR	BB	SO	RAT	ERA	ERA+	OAV	OOB	BH	AVG	PB	PR	/A	PD	TPI
1994	Chi-N	0	0	—	10	0	0	0	0	15	25	2	9	9	20.4	7.80	53	.385	.459	0	.000	-0	-6	-6	0	0.0

● DOC IMLAY

Imlay, Harry Miller b: 1/12/1889, Allentown, N.J. d: 10/7/48, Bordentown, N.J. BR/TR, 5'11", 168 lbs. Deb: 7/7/13

YEAR	TM/L	W	L	PCT	G	GS	CG	SH	SV	IP	H	HR	BB	SO	RAT	ERA	ERA+	OAV	OOB	BH	AVG	PB	PR	/A	PD	TPI
1913	Phi-N	0	0	—	9	0	0	0	0	13^2	19	1	7	7	17.1	7.24	46	.358	.433	0	.000	-0	-6	-6	0	0.0

● BOB INGERSOLL

Ingersoll, Robert Randolph b: 1/8/1883, Rapid City, S.D. d: 1/13/27, Minneapolis, Minn. BR/TR, 5'11.5", 175 lbs. Deb: 4/23/14

YEAR	TM/L	W	L	PCT	G	GS	CG	SH	SV	IP	H	HR	BB	SO	RAT	ERA	ERA+	OAV	OOB	BH	AVG	PB	PR	/A	PD	TPI
1914	Cin-N	0	0	—	4	0	0	0	0	6	5	0	5	2	16.5	3.00	98	.250	.423	1	1.000	0	-0	-0	-0	0.0

● BERT INKS

Inks, Albert John b: 1/27/1871, Ligonier, Ind. d: 10/3/41, Ligonier, Ind. BL/TL, 6'3", 175 lbs. Deb: 9/2/1891

YEAR	TM/L	W	L	PCT	G	GS	CG	SH	SV	IP	H	HR	BB	SO	RAT	ERA	ERA+	OAV	OOB	BH	AVG	PB	PR	/A	PD	TPI
1891	Bro-N	3	10	.231	13	13	11	1	0	96^1	99	2	43	47	13.8	4.02	82	.256	.339	10	.286	2	-7	-8	-0	-0.7
1892	Bro-N	4	2	.667	9	8	4	1	0	58	48	0	33	25	13.2	3.88	82	.216	.328	10	.400	3	-4	-5	0	-0.1
	Was-N	1	2	.333	3	3	3	0	0	21	29	0	10	11	17.6	5.14	63	.315	.394	3	.300	1	-4	-4	-0	-0.4
	Yr	5	4	.556	12	11	7	1	0	79	77	0	43	36	13.9	4.22	76	.242	.336	13	.371	4	-8	-9	-0	-0.5
1894	Bal-N	9	4	.692	22	14	10	0	1	133	181	4	54	30	16.6	5.55	98	.321	.391	18	.316	2	-3	-1	-1	-0.1
	Lou-N	2	6	.250	8	8	8	0	0	59^2	87	2	34	8	18.4	6.49	79	.336	.415	12	.444	3	-8	-9	0	-0.6
	Yr	11	10	.524	30	22	18	0	1	192^2	268	6	88	38	16.7	5.84	92	.321	.387	30	.357	5	-11	-11	-1	-0.7
1895	Lou-N	7	20	.259	28	27	21	0	0	205^1	294	3	78	42	17.0	6.40	72	.331	.394	21	.250	-0	-37	-40	1	-3.6
1896	Phi-N	0	1	.000	3	1	0	0	0	10^1	21	1	5	2	23.5	7.84	55	.412	.474	1	.200	-0	-4	-4	-1	-0.4
	Cin-N	1	1	.500	3	3	2	0	0	20	21	0	9	2	13.9	4.50	102	.269	.352	0	.000	-1	-0	0	-1	-0.1
	Yr	1	2	.333	6	4	2	0	0	30^1	42	1	14	4	16.9	5.64	80	.323	.393	1	.083	-1	-4	-4	-1	-0.5
Total	5	27	46	.370	89	77	59	2	1	603^2	780	12	266	167	16.2	5.52	81	.307	.382	75	.300	9	-68	-72	-2	-6.0

● JEFF INNIS

Innis, Jeffrey David b: 7/5/62, Decatur, Ill. BR/TR, 6', 170 lbs. Deb: 5/16/87

YEAR	TM/L	W	L	PCT	G	GS	CG	SH	SV	IP	H	HR	BB	SO	RAT	ERA	ERA+	OAV	OOB	BH	AVG	PB	PR	/A	PD	TPI
1987	NY-N	0	1	.000	17	1	0	0	0	25^2	29	5	4	28	11.9	3.16	120	.279	.312	0	.000	-0	3	2	-0	0.0
1988	NY-N	1	1	.500	12	0	0	0	0	19	19	0	2	14	9.9	1.89	170	.250	.269	0	—	0	3	3	-1	0.2
1989	NY-N	0	1	.000	29	0	0	0	0	39^2	38	2	8	16	10.7	3.18	103	.255	.297	0	.000	-0	1	0	1	0.1
1990	NY-N	1	3	.250	18	0	0	0	1	26^1	19	4	10	12	10.3	2.39	156	.209	.294	0	—	0	4	4	0	0.6
1991	NY-N	0	2	.000	69	0	0	0	0	84^2	66	2	23	47	9.5	2.66	137	.219	.274	0	.000	-0	10	9	3	0.5
1992	NY-N	6	9	.400	76	0	0	0	1	88	85	4	36	39	13.0	2.86	121	.266	.351	0	.000	-0	6	6	2	1.2
1993	NY-N	2	3	.400	67	0	0	0	3	76^2	81	5	38	36	14.7	4.11	98	.278	.373	0	—	0	-1	-1	1	0.0
Total	7	10	20	.333	288	1	0	0	5	360	337	22	121	192	11.8	3.05	119	.253	.322	0	.000	-1	27	23	6	2.6

● DANE IORG

Iorg, Dane Charles b: 5/11/50, Eureka, Cal. BL/TR, 6', 180 lbs. Deb: 4/9/77 F◆

YEAR	TM/L	W	L	PCT	G	GS	CG	SH	SV	IP	H	HR	BB	SO	RAT	ERA	ERA+	OAV	OOB	BH	AVG	PB	PR	/A	PD	TPI
1986	SD-N	0	0	—	2	0	0	0	0	3	5	2	1	2	18.0	12.00	30	.357	.400	24	.226	0	-3	-3	-0	0.0

YEAR	TM/L	W	L	PCT	G	GS	CG	SH	SV	IP	H	HR	BB	SO	RAT	ERA	ERA+	OAV	OOB	BH	AVG	PB	PR	/A	PD	TPI
● HOOKS IOTT		Iott, Clarence Eugene b: 12/3/19, Mountain Grove, Mo. d: 8/17/80, St.Petersburg, Fla BB/TL, 6'2", 200 lbs. Deb: 9/6/41																								
1941	StL-A	0	0	—	2	0	0	0	0	2	2	0	1	1	13.5	9.00	48	.250	.333	0	—	0	-1	-1	0	0.0
1947	StL-A	0	1	.000	4	0	0	0	0	8^1	15	4	14	6	31.3	16.20	24	.375	.537	0	.000	-0	-12	-11	0	-1.1
	NY-N	3	8	.273	20	9	2	1	0	71^1	67	3	52	46	15.1	5.93	69	.251	.375	3	.143	1	-15	-15	-0	-1.9
Total	2	3	9	.250	26	9	2	1	0	81^2	84	7	67	53	16.8	7.05	58	.267	.397	3	.130	1	-27	-27	0	-3.0
● HIDEKI IRABU		Irabu, Hideki b: 5/5/69, Hyogo, Japan BR/TR, 6'4", 240 lbs. Deb: 7/10/97																								
1997	NY-A	5	4	.556	13	9	0	0	0	53^1	69	15	20	56	15.2	7.09	63	.311	.370	0	.000	-0	-15	-16	-0	-2.1
1998	NY-A	13	9	.591	29	28	2	1	0	173	148	27	76	126	12.1	4.06	110	.233	.324	1	.250	0	11	7	-2	0.7
Total	2	18	13	.581	42	37	2	1	0	226^1	217	42	96	182	12.8	4.77	93	.253	.335	1	.200	0	-4	-8	-2	-1.4
● DARYL IRVINE		Irvine, Daryl Keith b: 11/15/64, Harrisonburg, Va. BR/TR, 6'3", 195 lbs. Deb: 4/28/90																								
1990	Bos-A	1	1	.500	11	0	0	0	0	17^1	15	0	10	9	13.0	4.67	87	.246	.352	0	—	0	-1	-1	0	-0.4
1991	Bos-A	0	0	—	9	0	0	0	0	18	25	2	9	8	18.0	6.00	72	.321	.404	0	—	0	-4	-3	0	-0.2
1992	Bos-A	3	4	.429	21	0	0	0	0	28	31	1	14	10	15.1	6.11	69	.287	.379	0	—	0	-7	-6	0	-1.5
Total	3	4	5	.444	41	0	0	0	0	63^1	71	3	33	27	15.3	5.68	74	.287	.380	0	—	0	-12	-10	1	-2.1
● ARTHUR IRWIN		Irwin, Arthur Albert "Doc" or "Sandy" b: 2/14/1858, Toronto, Ont., Can. d: 7/16/21, AtSea Atlantic Ocean N.Y. To Boston BL/TR, 5'8.5", 158 lbs. Deb: 5/1/1880 FMU♦																								
1884	*Pro-N	0	0	—	1	0	0	0	0	3	5	0	1	0	18.0	3.00	95	.357	.400	97	.240	0	-0	-0	0	0.0
1889	Was-N	0	0	—	1	0	0	0	0	1	1	0	0	0	9.0	0.00	—	.250	.250	73	.233	0	0	0	-0	0.0
Total	2	0	0	—	2	0	0	0	0	4	6	0	1	0	15.8	2.25	139	.333	.368	934	.241	0	0	0	-0	0.0
● BILL IRWIN		Irwin, William Franklin "Phil" b: 9/16/1859, Neville, Ohio d: 8/7/33, Ft.Thomas, Ky. BR/TR, 6', 195 lbs. Deb: 8/30/1886																								
1886	Cin-a	0	2	.000	2	2	2	0	0	17	18	2	8	6	13.8	5.82	60	.247	.321	0	.000	-0	-4	-4	0	-0.4
● FRANK ISBELL		Isbell, William Frank "Bald Eagle" b: 8/21/1875, Delevan, N.Y. d: 7/15/41, Wichita, Kan. BL/TR, 5'11", 190 lbs. Deb: 5/1/1898 ♦																								
1898	Chi-N	4	7	.364	13	9	7	0	0	81	86	0	42	16	15.0	3.56	101	.270	.368	37	.233	-0	0	0	-0	0.0
1901	Chi-A	0	0	—	1	0	0	0	0	1	2	0	0	0	18.0	9.00	39	.400	.400	143	.257	0	-1	-1	0	0.0
1902	Chi-A	0	0	—	1	1	0	0	0	1	3	0	1	1	36.0	9.00	38	.500	.571	130	.252	0	-1	-1	1	0.1
1906	*Chi-A	0	0	—	1	0	0	0	0	2	1	0	0	2	4.5	0.00	—	.143	.143	153	.279	0	1	1	-0	0.0
1907	Chi-A	0	0	—	1	0	0	0	1	0^1	0	0	0	0	0.0	0.00	—	.000	.000	118	.243	0	0	0	0	0.1
Total	5	4	7	.364	17	10	7	0	1	85^1	92	0	43	19	15.0	3.59	99	.273	.367	1056	.250	1	-0	-0	1	0.2
● JASON ISRINGHAUSEN		Isringhausen, Jason Derik b: 9/7/72, Brighton, Ill. BR/TR, 6'3", 195 lbs. Deb: 7/17/95																								
1995	NY-N	9	2	.818	14	14	1	0	0	93	88	6	31	55	11.7	2.81	144	.254	.319	4	.148	1	14	13	-1	1.4
1996	NY-N	6	14	.300	27	27	2	1	0	171^2	190	13	73	114	14.2	4.77	84	.284	.361	13	.255	6	-11	-15	0	-0.9
1997	NY-N	2	2	.500	6	6	0	0	0	29^2	40	3	22	25	19.1	7.58	53	.336	.444	1	.143	-0	-11	-12	-1	-1.3
Total	3	17	18	.486	47	47	3	1	0	294^1	318	22	126	194	13.9	4.43	91	.280	.358	18	.212	6	-8	-13	-1	-0.8
● AL JACKSON		Jackson, Alvin Neil b: 12/25/35, Waco, Tex. BL/TL, 5'10", 169 lbs. Deb: 6/1/59 C																								
1959	Pit-N	0	0	—	8	3	0	0	0	18	30	1	8	13	19.0	6.50	60	.405	.463	1	.200	0	-5	-5	-0	0.0
1961	Pit-N	1	0	1.000	3	2	1	0	0	23^2	20	2	4	15	9.1	3.42	117	.233	.267	0	.000	-1	2	1	1	0.1
1962	NY-N	8	20	.286	36	33	12	4	0	231^1	244	16	78	118	12.7	4.40	95	.273	.335	5	.068	-5	-12	-5	4	-0.6
1963	NY-N	13	17	.433	37	34	11	0	1	227	237	25	84	142	13.2	3.96	88	.267	.338	16	.203	2	-17	-12	2	-1.2
1964	NY-N	11	16	.407	40	31	11	3	0	213^1	229	18	60	112	12.4	4.26	84	.272	.323	11	.153	2	-17	-16	0	-1.6
1965	NY-N	8	20	.286	37	31	7	3	1	205^1	217	17	61	120	12.5	4.34	81	.271	.329	7	.117	-1	-18	-18	2	-2.2
1966	StL-N	13	15	.464	36	30	11	3	0	232^2	222	18	45	90	10.4	2.51	143	.250	.288	13	.176	2	28	28	4	4.2
1967	StL-N	9	4	.692	38	11	1	1	1	107	117	7	29	43	12.4	3.95	83	.279	.327	8	.258	2	-7	-8	2	-0.4
1968	NY-N	3	7	.300	25	9	0	0	3	92^2	88	5	17	59	10.4	3.69	82	.249	.287	7	.250	1	-7	-7	1	-0.6
1969	NY-N	0	0	—	9	0	0	0	0	11	18	1	4	10	18.8	10.64	34	.353	.411	0	.000	-0	-9	-9	0	0.0
	Cin-N	1	0	1.000	33	0	0	0	3	27^1	27	5	17	16	15.5	5.27	71	.260	.379	1	.250	0	-5	-5	-0	-0.3
	Yr	1	0	1.000	42	0	0	0	3	38^1	45	6	21	26	16.2	6.81	55	.285	.379	1	.200	0	-14	-13	-0	-0.3
Total	10	67	99	.404	302	184	54	14	10	1389^1	1449	115	407	738	12.3	3.98	91	.268	.324	69	.159	3	-67	-56	16	-2.6
● CHARLIE JACKSON		Jackson, Charles Bernard b: 8/4/1876, Versailles, Ohio d: 11/23/57, Scottsbluff, Neb. TR, Deb: 8/11/05																								
1905	Det-A	0	2	.000	2	2	1	0	0	11	14	1	7	3	17.2	5.73	48	.311	.404	1	.250	0	-4	-4	-0	-0.6
● DANNY JACKSON		Jackson, Danny Lynn b: 1/5/62, San Antonio, Tex. BR/TL, 6', 205 lbs. Deb: 9/11/83																								
1983	KC-A	1	1	.500	4	3	0	0	0	19	26	1	6	9	15.2	5.21	78	.325	.372	0	—	0	-2	-2	0	-0.2
1984	KC-A	2	6	.250	15	11	1	0	0	76	84	4	35	40	14.7	4.26	94	.285	.370	0	—	0	-2	-2	-0	-0.3
1985	*KC-A	14	12	.538	32	32	4	3	0	208	209	7	76	114	12.6	3.42	122	.261	.329	0	—	0	17	17	-1	1.8
1986	KC-A	11	12	.478	32	27	4	1	1	185^2	177	13	79	115	12.6	3.20	133	.256	.335	0	—	0	20	22	-1	2.3
1987	KC-A	9	18	.333	36	34	11	2	0	224	219	11	109	152	13.5	4.02	113	.258	.347	0	—	0	11	13	-2	1.2
1988	Cin-N☆	**23**	8	.742	35	35	**15**	6	0	260^2	206	13	71	161	9.6	2.73	131	.218	.275	13	.144	-0	21	25	2	3.2
1989	Cin-N	6	11	.353	20	20	1	0	0	115^2	122	10	57	70	14.0	5.60	64	.271	.354	8	.222	1	-27	-26	-1	-3.3
1990	*Cin-N	6	6	.500	22	21	0	0	0	117^1	119	11	40	76	12.3	3.61	109	.266	.329	2	.054	-2	2	4	-1	0.1
1991	Chi-N	1	5	.167	17	14	0	0	0	70^2	89	8	48	31	17.6	6.75	58	.309	.409	2	.087	-1	-24	-23	-1	-1.9
1992	Chi-N	4	9	.308	19	19	0	0	0	113	117	5	48	51	13.4	4.22	85	.270	.346	3	.083	-2	-9	-8	-1	-1.2
	*Pit-N	4	4	.500	15	15	0	0	0	88^1	94	1	29	46	12.6	3.36	102	.276	.334	2	.083	-1	1	1	0	0.0
	Yr	8	13	.381	34	34	0	0	0	201^1	211	6	77	97	12.9	3.84	92	.269	.336	5	.083	-3	-8	-7	-1	-1.2
1993	*Phi-N	12	11	.522	32	32	2	1	0	210^1	214	12	80	120	12.8	3.77	105	.263	.332	5	.077	-2	6	5	-2	0.0
1994	Phi-N★	14	6	.700	25	25	4	1	0	179^1	183	13	46	129	11.6	3.26	131	.266	.314	9	.158	1	19	20	1	2.3
1995	StL-N	2	12	.143	19	19	2	1	0	100^2	120	10	48	52	15.6	5.90	71	.303	.387	5	.161	0	-19	-19	-1	-2.3
1996	*StL-N	1	1	.500	13	4	0	0	0	36^1	33	3	16	27	12.4	4.46	94	.243	.327	3	.333	1	-1	-1	0	0.1
1997	StL-N	1	2	.333	4	4	0	0	0	18^2	26	3	8	13	17.4	7.71	54	.347	.424	1	.143	-0	-7	-7	-1	-0.9
	SD-N	1	7	.125	13	9	0	0	0	49	72	8	20	19	17.4	7.53	51	.353	.419	1	.077	-0	-18	-20	-1	-2.7
	Yr	2	9	.182	17	13	0	0	0	67^2	98	11	28	32	17.2	7.58	52	.346	.411	2	.100	-1	-25	-27	-1	-3.6
Total	15	112	131	.461	353	324	44	15	1	2072^2	2110	133	816	1225	12.9	4.01	100	.266	.338	54	.126	-6	-13	-0	-7	-1.8
● DARRELL JACKSON		Jackson, Darrell Preston b: 4/3/56, Los Angeles, Cal. BB/TL, 5'10", 150 lbs. Deb: 6/16/78																								
1978	Min-A	4	6	.400	19	15	1	1	0	92^1	89	9	48	54	13.5	4.48	85	.256	.350	0	—	0	-7	-7	-1	-0.8
1979	Min-A	4	4	.500	24	8	1	0	0	69^1	89	5	26	43	15.1	4.28	102	.319	.379	0	—	0	-1	1	1	0.0
1980	Min-A	9	9	.500	32	25	1	0	1	172	161	15	69	90	12.1	3.87	113	.250	.325	0	—	0	3	9	-0	0.9
1981	Min-A	3	3	.500	14	5	0	0	0	32^2	35	1	19	26	15.2	4.41	90	.282	.382	0	—	0	-3	-2	-1	-0.4
1982	Min-A	0	5	.000	13	7	0	0	0	44^2	51	6	24	16	15.3	6.25	68	.297	.386	0	—	0	-11	-10	-0	-1.1
Total	5	20	27	.426	102	60	3	1	1	411	425	36	186	229	13.5	4.38	96	.272	.352	0	—	0	-18	-8	-2	-1.4
● DARRIN JACKSON		Jackson, Darrin Jay b: 8/22/62, Los Angeles, Cal. BR/TR, 6', 185 lbs. Deb: 6/17/85 ♦																								
1991	SD-N	0	0	—	1	0	0	0	0	2	3	0	2	0	22.5	9.00	42	.375	.500	94	.262	0	-1	-1	-0	0.0
● GRANT JACKSON		Jackson, Grant Dwight "Buck" b: 9/28/42, Fostoria, Ohio BB/TL, 6', 190 lbs. Deb: 9/3/65 C																								
1965	Phi-N	1	1	.500	6	2	0	0	0	13^2	17	4	5	15	14.5	7.24	48	.304	.361	0	.000	-0	-6	-6	0	-0.8
1966	Phi-N	0	0	—	2	0	0	0	0	1^2	2	0	3	0	27.0	5.40	67	.333	.556	0	—	0	-0	-0	0	0.0
1967	Phi-N	2	3	.400	43	4	0	0	1	84^1	86	3	43	83	14.0	3.84	89	.267	.357	2	.133	-0	-4	-4	-2	-0.4
1968	Phi-N	1	6	.143	33	6	1	0	1	61	59	4	20	49	11.7	2.95	102	.248	.306	3	.300	1	0	0	0	0.2
1969	Phi-N☆	14	18	.438	38	35	13	4	1	253	237	16	92	180	11.9	3.34	106	.249	.318	12	.140	-0	7	6	-2	0.5
1970	Phi-N	5	15	.250	32	23	1	0	0	149^2	170	17	61	104	14.0	5.29	75	.288	.356	4	.091	-2	-21	-22	0	-2.7
1971	*Bal-A	4	3	.571	29	9	0	0	0	77^2	72	7	20	51	10.9	3.13	107	.249	.302	2	.091	0	3	2	-0	0.2
1972	Bal-A	1	1	.500	32	0	0	0	8	41	33	1	9	34	9.2	2.63	117	.217	.261	0	.000	-0	2	2	0	0.2
1973	*Bal-A	8	0	1.000	45	0	0	0	9	80^1	54	5	24	47	8.7	1.90	196	.198	.263	0	—	0	17	16	-0	2.0
1974	*Bal-A	6	4	.600	49	0	0	0	12	66^2	48	7	22	56	9.6	2.57	135	.198	.268	0	—	0	8	7	-1	1.1

YEAR	TM/L	W	L	PCT	G	GS	CG	SH	SV	IP	H	HR	BB	SO	RAT	ERA	ERA+	OAV	OOB	BH	AVG	PB	PR	/A	PD	TPI
1975	Bal-A	4	3	.571	41	0	0	0	7	48^1	42	3	21	39	11.9	3.35	105	.241	.327	0	—	0	2	1	-0	0.1
1976	Bal-A	1	1	.500	13	0	0	0	3	19^1	19	1	9	14	14.0	5.12	64	.268	.366	0	—	0	-3	-4	-0	-0.5
	*NY-A	6	0	1.000	21	2	1	1	1	58^2	38	1	16	25	8.4	1.69	202	.186	.249	0	—	0	12	11	-1	1.0
	Yr	7	1	.875	34	2	1	1	4	78	57	2	25	39	9.6	2.54	133	.205	.273	0	—	0	8	7	-2	0.5
1977	Pit-N	5	3	.625	49	2	0	0	4	91	81	11	39	41	12.0	3.86	103	.240	.321	6	.333	2	1	1	-1	0.2
1978	Pit-N	7	5	.583	60	0	0	0	5	77^1	89	5	32	45	14.2	3.26	114	.298	.367	3	.250	1	3	4	0	0.7
1979	*Pit-N	8	5	.615	72	0	0	0	14	82	67	9	35	39	11.4	2.96	131	.230	.317	0	.000	-1	7	8	-1	1.3
1980	Pit-N	8	4	.667	61	0	0	0	9	71	71	4	20	31	11.5	2.92	125	.275	.327	0	.000	-1	5	6	-0	0.9
1981	Pit-N	1	2	.333	35	0	0	0	4	32^1	30	1	10	17	11.1	2.51	143	.248	.305	0	.000	-0	4	4	-1	0.3
	Mon-N	1	0	1.000	10	0	0	0	0	10^2	14	2	9	4	19.4	7.59	46	.333	.451	0	—	0	-5	-5	0	-0.4
	Yr	2	2	.500	45	0	0	0	4	43	44	3	19	21	13.2	3.77	95	.267	.342	0	.000	-0	-1	-1	-1	-0.1
1982	KC-A	3	1	.750	20	0	0	0	0	38^1	42	7	21	15	15.3	5.17	79	.271	.365	0	—	0	-5	-5	-0	-0.5
	Pit-N	0	0	—	1	0	0	0	0	0^2	1	1	0	0	13.5	13.50	27	.333	.333	0	—	0	-1	-1	-0	0.0
Total	18	86	75	.534	692	83	16	5	79	1358^2	1272	109	511	889	11.9	3.46	104	.251	.322	32	.136	-2	26	22	-9	3.4

● JOHN JACKSON Jackson, John Lewis b: 7/15/09, Wynnefield, Pa. d: 10/22/56, Somers Point, N.J. BR/TR, 6'2", 180 lbs. Deb: 6/20/33

YEAR	TM/L	W	L	PCT	G	GS	CG	SH	SV	IP	H	HR	BB	SO	RAT	ERA	ERA+	OAV	OOB	BH	AVG	PB	PR	/A	PD	TPI
1933	Phi-N	2	2	.500	10	7	1	0	0	54	74	3	35	11	19.0	6.00	64	.329	.430	3	.143	-1	-16	-13	-2	-1.2

● LARRY JACKSON Jackson, Lawrence Curtis b: 6/2/31, Nampa, Idaho d: 8/28/90, Boise, Idaho BR/TR, 6'2", 190 lbs. Deb: 4/17/55

YEAR	TM/L	W	L	PCT	G	GS	CG	SH	SV	IP	H	HR	BB	SO	RAT	ERA	ERA+	OAV	OOB	BH	AVG	PB	PR	/A	PD	TPI
1955	StL-N	9	14	.391	37	25	4	1	2	177^1	189	25	72	88	13.7	4.31	94	.277	.353	3	.053	-6	-5	-5	0	-1.1
1956	StL-N	2	2	.500	51	1	0	0	9	85^1	75	5	45	50	12.8	4.11	92	.240	.337	1	.091	-0	-3	-3	2	-0.1
1957	StL-N★	15	9	.625	41	22	6	2	1	210^1	196	21	57	96	11.0	3.47	114	.248	.302	13	.181	0	10	12	4	1.7
1958	StL-N★	13	13	.500	49	23	11	1	8	198	211	21	51	124	12.4	3.68	112	.272	.325	9	.150	-2	6	10	-2	0.8
1959	StL-N	14	13	.519	40	37	12	3	0	256	271	13	64	145	11.9	3.30	128	.270	.316	9	.112	-3	18	27	-0	2.2
1960	StL-N★	18	13	.581	43	38	14	3	0	**282**	277	22	70	171	11.2	3.48	118	.257	.304	20	.211	2	9	19	-2	2.0
1961	StL-N	14	11	.560	33	28	12	3	0	211	203	20	56	113	11.2	3.75	117	.252	.303	13	.176	0	7	15	2	1.8
1962	StL-N	16	11	.593	36	35	11	2	0	252^1	267	25	64	112	12.0	3.75	114	.269	.318	15	.169	2	6	15	1	1.7
1963	Chi-N★	14	18	.438	37	37	13	4	0	275	256	11	54	153	10.3	2.55	137	.245	.286	17	.195	2	22	29	2	4.1
1964	Chi-N	**24**	11	.686	40	38	19	3	0	297^2	265	17	58	148	9.8	3.14	118	.235	.273	20	.175	1	13	19	7	3.0
1965	Chi-N	14	21	.400	39	39	12	4	0	257^1	268	28	57	131	11.5	3.85	96	.267	.310	11	.128	1	-9	-5	3	-0.2
1966	Chi-N	0	2	.000	3	2	0	0	0	8	14	3	4	5	20.3	13.50	27	.368	.429	0	.000	-0	-9	-9	0	-1.5
	Phi-N	15	13	.536	35	33	12	5	0	247	243	22	58	107	11.1	2.99	120	.259	.306	13	.146	-0	17	17	1	2.0
	Yr	15	15	.500	38	35	12	**5**	0	255	257	25	62	112	11.4	3.32	108	.264	.311	13	.141	-1	8	8	2	0.5
1967	Phi-N	13	15	.464	40	37	11	4	0	261^2	242	17	54	139	10.4	3.10	110	.241	.284	14	.161	0	4	4	4	1.5
1968	Phi-N	13	17	.433	34	34	12	2	0	243^2	229	9	60	127	10.8	2.77	109	.248	.297	12	.141	-0	6	6	2	0.9
Total	14	194	183	.515	558	429	149	37	20	3262^2	3206	259	824	1709	11.3	3.40	113	.256	.306	170	.156	-5	95	155	25	18.8

● MIKE JACKSON Jackson, Michael Ray b: 12/22/64, Houston, Tex. BR/TR, 6', 200 lbs. Deb: 8/11/86

YEAR	TM/L	W	L	PCT	G	GS	CG	SH	SV	IP	H	HR	BB	SO	RAT	ERA	ERA+	OAV	OOB	BH	AVG	PB	PR	/A	PD	TPI
1986	Phi-N	0	0	—	9	0	0	0	0	13^1	12	2	4	3	12.2	3.38	114	.250	.333	0	—	0	1	1	-0	0.0
1987	Phi-N	3	10	.231	55	7	0	0	1	109^1	88	16	56	93	12.1	4.20	101	.219	.319	2	.118	-0	-1	0	-1	-0.1
1988	Sea-A	6	5	.545	62	0	0	0	4	99^1	74	10	43	76	10.8	2.63	158	.209	.298	0	—	0	15	17	-0	1.8
1989	Sea-A	4	6	.400	65	0	0	0	7	99^1	81	8	54	94	12.8	3.17	127	.223	.333	0	—	0	8	9	-1	0.9
1990	Sea-A	5	7	.417	63	0	0	0	3	77^1	64	8	44	69	12.8	4.54	87	.229	.338	0	—	0	-5	-5	1	-0.7
1991	Sea-A	7	7	.500	72	0	0	0	14	88^2	64	5	34	74	10.6	3.25	127	.201	.290	0	—	0	8	9	-1	1.4
1992	SF-N	6	6	.500	67	0	0	0	2	82	76	7	33	80	12.4	3.73	89	.252	.333	0	.000	-0	-2	-4	-0	-0.6
1993	SF-N	6	6	.500	**81**	0	0	0	1	77^1	58	7	24	70	9.9	3.03	129	.204	.273	2	.667	2	9	8	0	1.3
1994	SF-N	3	2	.600	36	0	0	0	4	42^1	23	4	11	51	7.7	1.49	269	.164	.235	0	.000	-0	**13**	12	0	1.5
1995	*Cin-N	6	1	.857	40	0	0	0	2	49	38	5	19	41	10.7	2.39	172	.213	.293	1	.250	0	10	9	-1	1.2
1996	Sea-A	1	1	.500	73	0	0	0	6	72	61	11	24	70	11.4	3.63	136	.225	.302	0	—	0	11	11	1	0.5
1997	*Cle-A	2	5	.286	71	0	0	0	15	75	59	3	29	74	11.0	3.24	145	.215	.300	0	—	0	11	12	2	1.5
1998	*Cle-A	1	1	.500	69	0	0	0	40	64	43	4	13	55	8.4	1.55	309	.195	.252	0	—	0	**22**	**23**	1	3.1
Total	13	50	57	.467	763	7	0	0	99	949	741	90	388	850	11.1	3.21	130	.216	.304	5	.185	1	98	101	1	11.8

● MIKE JACKSON Jackson, Michael Warren b: 3/27/46, Paterson, N.J. BL/TL, 6'3", 190 lbs. Deb: 5/10/70

YEAR	TM/L	W	L	PCT	G	GS	CG	SH	SV	IP	H	HR	BB	SO	RAT	ERA	ERA+	OAV	OOB	BH	AVG	PB	PR	/A	PD	TPI
1970	Phi-N	1	1	.500	5	0	0	0	0	6^1	6	0	4	4	14.2	1.42	281	.286	.400	1	1.000	0	2	2	0	0.6
1971	StL-N	0	0	—	1	0	0	0	0	0^2	1	0	1	0	27.0	0.00	—	.333	.500	0	.000	-0	0	0	0	0.0
1972	KC-A	1	2	.333	7	3	0	0	0	19^2	24	0	14	15	17.4	6.41	47	.320	.427	0	.000	-1	-7	-7	1	-1.0
1973	KC-A	0	0	—	9	0	0	0	0	22^1	25	3	20	13	18.5	6.85	60	.301	.442	0	—	0	-8	-7	-0	0.0
	Cle-A	0	0	—	1	0	0	0	0	0^2	1	0	0	1	13.5	0.00	—	.333	.333	0	—	0	0	0	0	0.0
	Yr	0	0	—	10	0	0	0	0	23	26	3	20	14	18.0	6.65	62	.295	.426	0	—	0	-7	-7	-0	0.0
Total	4	2	3	.400	23	3	0	0	0	49^2	57	3	39	33	17.6	5.80	63	.308	.431	1	.143	-0	-12	-12	1	-0.4

● ROY LEE JACKSON Jackson, Roy Lee b: 5/1/54, Opelika, Ala. BR/TR, 6'2", 194 lbs. Deb: 9/13/77

YEAR	TM/L	W	L	PCT	G	GS	CG	SH	SV	IP	H	HR	BB	SO	RAT	ERA	ERA+	OAV	OOB	BH	AVG	PB	PR	/A	PD	TPI
1977	NY-N	0	2	.000	4	4	0	0	0	24	25	2	15	13	16.1	6.00	62	.263	.381	0	.000	-1	-6	-6	-1	-0.6
1978	NY-N	0	0	—	4	2	0	0	0	12^2	21	2	6	6	20.6	9.24	38	.429	.509	2	.667	1	-8	-8	0	0.1
1979	NY-N	1	0	1.000	8	0	0	0	0	16^1	11	1	5	10	9.4	2.20	165	.200	.279	1	1.000	0	3	3	0	0.2
1980	NY-N	1	7	.125	24	8	1	0	1	70^2	78	4	20	58	12.5	4.20	84	.287	.336	3	.188	1	-5	-5	-1	-0.6
1981	Tor-A	1	2	.333	39	0	0	0	7	62	65	5	25	27	13.2	2.61	151	.275	.347	0	—	0	7	9	0	0.6
1982	Tor-A	8	8	.500	48	2	0	0	6	97	77	7	31	71	10.2	3.06	146	.218	.284	0	—	0	11	15	0	2.4
1983	Tor-A	8	3	.727	49	0	0	0	7	92	92	6	41	48	13.3	4.50	96	.267	.351	0	—	0	-4	-2	0	-0.5
1984	Tor-A	7	8	.467	54	0	0	0	10	86	73	12	31	58	11.0	3.56	115	.230	.301	0	—	0	4	5	0	0.9
1985	SD-N	2	3	.400	22	2	0	0	2	40	32	4	13	28	10.3	2.70	131	.224	.293	0	.000	-1	4	4	0	0.4
1986	Min-A	0	1	.000	28	0	0	0	1	58^1	57	7	16	32	11.7	3.86	112	.256	.314	0	—	0	2	3	-1	-0.1
Total	10	28	34	.452	280	18	1	0	34	559	531	50	203	351	12.1	3.77	107	.254	.325	6	.194	1	8	17	-1	2.8

● TONY JACOBS Jacobs, Anthony Robert b: 8/5/25, Dixmoor, Ill. d: 12/21/80, Nashville, Tenn. BB/TR, 5'9", 150 lbs. Deb: 9/19/48

YEAR	TM/L	W	L	PCT	G	GS	CG	SH	SV	IP	H	HR	BB	SO	RAT	ERA	ERA+	OAV	OOB	BH	AVG	PB	PR	/A	PD	TPI
1948	Chi-N	0	0	—	1	0	0	0	0	2	3	1	0	2	13.5	4.50	87	.333	.333	0	—	0	-0	-0	0	0.0
1955	StL-N	0	0	—	1	0	0	0	0	2	6	1	1	1	31.5	18.00	23	.500	.538	0	.000	-0	-3	-3	0	0.0
Total	2	0	0	—	2	0	0	0	0	4	9	2	1	3	22.5	11.25	35	.429	.455	0	.000	-0	-3	-3	0	0.0

● ART JACOBS Jacobs, Arthur Edward b: 8/28/02, Luckey, Ohio d: 6/8/67, Inglewood, Cal. BL/TL, 5'10", 170 lbs. Deb: 6/18/39

YEAR	TM/L	W	L	PCT	G	GS	CG	SH	SV	IP	H	HR	BB	SO	RAT	ERA	ERA+	OAV	OOB	BH	AVG	PB	PR	/A	PD	TPI
1939	Cin-N	0	0	—	1	0	0	0	1	1	2	0	1	0	27.0	9.00	43	.400	.500	0	—	0	-1	-1	-0	-0.1

● BUCKY JACOBS Jacobs, Newton Smith b: 3/21/13, Altavista, Va. d: 6/15/90, Richmond, Va. BR/TR, 5'11", 155 lbs. Deb: 6/27/37

YEAR	TM/L	W	L	PCT	G	GS	CG	SH	SV	IP	H	HR	BB	SO	RAT	ERA	ERA+	OAV	OOB	BH	AVG	PB	PR	/A	PD	TPI
1937	Was-A	1	1	.500	11	1	0	0	0	22^1	26	0	11	8	14.9	4.84	92	.295	.374	0	.000	-1	-1	-1	0	-0.1
1939	Was-A	0	0	—	2	0	0	0	0	3	1	0	0	1	3.0	0.00	—	.100	.100	0	—	0	2	1	-0	0.0
1940	Was-A	0	1	.000	9	0	0	0	0	15	16	1	9	6	16.2	6.00	69	.271	.386	0	.000	-0	-3	-3	1	-0.1
Total	3	1	2	.333	22	1	0	0	0	40^1	43	1	20	15	14.5	4.91	88	.274	.363	0	.000	-1	-2	-3	2	-0.2

● ELMER JACOBS Jacobs, William Elmer b: 8/10/1892, Salem, Mo. d: 2/10/58, Salem, Mo. BR/TR, 6', 165 lbs. Deb: 4/23/14

YEAR	TM/L	W	L	PCT	G	GS	CG	SH	SV	IP	H	HR	BB	SO	RAT	ERA	ERA+	OAV	OOB	BH	AVG	PB	PR	/A	PD	TPI
1914	Phi-N	1	3	.250	14	7	1	0	0	50^2	65	2	20	17	15.6	4.80	61	.342	.413	0	.000	-2	-11	-10	0	-0.9
1916	Pit-N	6	10	.375	34	17	8	0	0	153	151	2	38	46	11.4	2.94	91	.258	.308	3	.075	-2	-5	-4	-2	-0.8
1917	Pit-N	6	19	.240	38	25	10	1	2	227^1	214	3	76	58	11.7	2.81	101	.262	.329	12	.179	-1	-2	1	2	0.1
1918	Pit-N	0	1	.000	8	4	0	0	0	23^1	31	0	14	2	17.4	5.79	50	.344	.433	2	.286	0	-8	-8	1	-0.2
	Phi-N	9	5	.643	18	14	12	4	1	123	91	3	42	33	10.0	2.41	124	.210	.285	6	.158	-1	5	8	-2	0.6
	Yr	9	6	.600	26	18	12	4	1	146^1	122	3	56	35	11.2	2.95	101	.233	.312	8	.178	-1	-3	0	-1	0.4
1919	Phi-N	6	10	.375	17	15	13	0	0	128^2	150	5	44	37	14.0	3.85	84	.304	.368	8	.178	-1	-13	-9	1	-1.1
	StL-N	3	6	.333	17	8	4	1	1	85^1	81	2	25	31	11.7	2.53	110	.264	.329	8	.348	3	4	2	-0	0.6
	Yr	9	16	.360	34	23	17	1	1	214	231	7	69	68	12.8	3.32	92	.287	.347	16	.235	2	-10	-6	1	-0.5
1920	StL-N	4	8	.333	23	9	1	0	1	77^2	91	2	33	21	14.9	5.21	57	.296	.374	5	.192	-0	-18	-19	1	-2.7
1924	Chi-N	11	12	.478	38	22	13	1	1	190^1	181	9	72	50	12.1	3.74	104	.258	.329	6	.111	-4	3	4	1	0.1

YEAR	TM/L	W	L	PCT	G	GS	CG	SH	SV	IP	H	HR	BB	SO	RAT	ERA	ERA+	OAV	OOB	BH	AVG	PB	PR	/A	PD	TPI
1925	Chi-N	2	3	.400	18	4	1	1	1	55^2	63	9	22	19	13.9	5.17	84	.274	.340	3	.231	-0	-6	-5	0	-0.4
1927	Chi-A	2	4	.333	25	8	2	1	0	74^1	105	3	37	22	17.7	4.60	88	.354	.432	3	.150	-1	-4	-5	2	-0.3
Total	9	50	81	.382	250	133	65	9	7	1189^1	1223	40	423	336	12.8	3.55	91	.275	.343	56	.161	-8	-57	-44	5	-5.0

● BEANY JACOBSON Jacobson, Albert L. (b: Albin L. Jacobson) b: 6/5/1881, Port Washington, Wis. d: 1/31/33, Decatur, Ill. BL/TL, 6', 170 lbs. Deb: 4/30/04

YEAR	TM/L	W	L	PCT	G	GS	CG	SH	SV	IP	H	HR	BB	SO	RAT	ERA	ERA+	OAV	OOB	BH	AVG	PB	PR	/A	PD	TPI
1904	Was-A	5	23	.179	33	30	23	1	0	253^2	276	6	57	75	11.9	3.55	75	.278	.319	8	.091	-6	-27	-25	2	-3.0
1905	Was-A	7	8	.467	22	17	12	0	0	144^1	139	1	35	50	11.2	3.30	80	.255	.305	7	.159	1	-10	-11	-2	-1.1
1906	StL-A	9	9	.500	24	15	12	0	0	155	146	3	27	53	10.3	2.50	103	.252	.290	5	.091	-4	3	1	-0	-0.3
1907	StL-A	1	6	.143	7	7	6	0	0	57^1	55	1	26	16	12.7	2.98	84	.255	.335	4	.222	-0	-3	-3	-0	-0.4
	Bos-A	0	0	—	2	1	0	0	0	2	2	0	3	1	22.5	9.00	29	.250	.455	0	—	0	-1	-1	0	0.0
	Yr	1	6	.143	9	8	6	0	0	59^1	57	1	29	17	13.0	3.19	79	.254	.340	4	.222	-0	-4	-4	-0	-0.4
Total	4	22	46	.324	88	70	53	1	0	612^1	618	11	148	195	11.4	3.19	82	.264	.311	24	.117	-9	-38	-38	-1	-4.8

● LARRY JACOBUS Jacobus, Stuart Louis b: 12/18/1893, Cincinnati, Ohio d: 8/19/65, N.College Hill, O. BB/TR, 6'2", 186 lbs. Deb: 7/15/18

YEAR	TM/L	W	L	PCT	G	GS	CG	SH	SV	IP	H	HR	BB	SO	RAT	ERA	ERA+	OAV	OOB	BH	AVG	PB	PR	/A	PD	TPI
1918	Cin-N	0	1	.000	5	0	0	0	0	17^1	25	0	1	8	13.5	5.71	47	.368	.377	0	.000	-1	-6	-6	-0	-0.4

● JASON JACOME Jacome, Jason James b: 11/24/70, Tulsa, Okla. BL/TL, 6'1", 155 lbs. Deb: 7/2/94

YEAR	TM/L	W	L	PCT	G	GS	CG	SH	SV	IP	H	HR	BB	SO	RAT	ERA	ERA+	OAV	OOB	BH	AVG	PB	PR	/A	PD	TPI
1994	NY-N	4	3	.571	8	8	1	1	0	54	54	3	17	30	11.8	2.67	157	.269	.326	1	.063	-1	9	9	1	1.0
1995	NY-N	0	4	.000	5	5	0	0	0	21	33	3	15	11	21.0	10.29	39	.359	.454	0	.000	-1	-14	-15	-0	-2.0
	KC-A	4	6	.400	15	14	1	0	0	84	101	15	21	39	13.2	5.36	89	.300	.343	0	—	0	-6	-5	2	-0.4
1996	KC-A	0	4	.000	49	2	0	0	1	47^2	67	5	22	32	17.2	4.72	106	.337	.408	0	—	0	1	2	2	0.3
1997	KC-A	0	0	—	7	0	0	0	0	6^2	13	2	5	3	25.7	9.45	50	.448	.543	0	—	0	-4	-4	1	0.1
	Cle-A	2	0	1.000	21	4	0	0	0	42^2	45	8	15	24	12.7	5.27	89	.269	.330	0	—	0	-3	-3	0	-0.1
	Yr	2	0	1.000	28	4	0	0	0	49^1	58	10	20	27	14.2	5.84	80	.294	.359	0	—	0	-7	-6	1	0.0
1998	Cle-A	0	1	.000	1	1	0	0	0	5	10	2	3	2	23.4	14.40	33	.435	.500	0	—	0	-5	-5	-0	-0.7
Total	5	10	18	.357	106	34	2	1	1	261	323	38	98	141	14.7	5.34	86	.308	.370	1	.043	-2	-22	-21	5	-1.8

● PAT JACQUEZ Jacquez, Patrick Thomas b: 4/23/47, Stockton, Cal. BR/TR, 6', 200 lbs. Deb: 4/18/71

YEAR	TM/L	W	L	PCT	G	GS	CG	SH	SV	IP	H	HR	BB	SO	RAT	ERA	ERA+	OAV	OOB	BH	AVG	PB	PR	/A	PD	TPI
1971	Chi-A	0	0	—	2	0	0	0	0	2	4	0	2	1	27.0	4.50	80	.444	.545	0	.000	-0	-0	-0	0	0.0

● JAKE JAECKEL Jaeckel, Paul Henry b: 4/1/42, E.Los Angeles, Cal. BR/TR, 5'10", 170 lbs. Deb: 9/19/64

YEAR	TM/L	W	L	PCT	G	GS	CG	SH	SV	IP	H	HR	BB	SO	RAT	ERA	ERA+	OAV	OOB	BH	AVG	PB	PR	/A	PD	TPI
1964	Chi-N	1	0	1.000	4	0	0	0	1	8	4	0	3	2	7.9	0.00	—	.160	.250	0	.000	-0	3	3	-0	0.5

● CHARLIE JAEGER Jaeger, Charles Thomas b: 4/17/1875, Ottawa, Ill. d: 9/27/42, Ottawa, Ill. BR/TR, Deb: 9/9/04

YEAR	TM/L	W	L	PCT	G	GS	CG	SH	SV	IP	H	HR	BB	SO	RAT	ERA	ERA+	OAV	OOB	BH	AVG	PB	PR	/A	PD	TPI
1904	Det-A	3	3	.500	8	6	5	0	0	49	49	0	15	13	12.9	2.57	99	.261	.335	1	.059	-2	0	-0	-1	-0.3

● JOE JAEGER Jaeger, Joseph Peter "Zip" b: 3/3/1895, St.Cloud, Minn. d: 12/13/63, Hampton, Iowa BR/TR, 6'1", 190 lbs. Deb: 7/28/20

YEAR	TM/L	W	L	PCT	G	GS	CG	SH	SV	IP	H	HR	BB	SO	RAT	ERA	ERA+	OAV	OOB	BH	AVG	PB	PR	/A	PD	TPI
1920	Chi-N	0	0	—	2	0	0	0	0	3	6	0	4	0	30.0	12.00	27	.500	.625	0	.000	-0	-3	-3	0	0.0

● SIG JAKUCKI Jakucki, Sigmund "Jack" b: 8/20/09, Camden, N.J. d: 5/28/79, Galveston, Tex. BR/TR, 6'2.5", 198 lbs. Deb: 8/30/36

YEAR	TM/L	W	L	PCT	G	GS	CG	SH	SV	IP	H	HR	BB	SO	RAT	ERA	ERA+	OAV	OOB	BH	AVG	PB	PR	/A	PD	TPI
1936	StL-A	0	3	.000	7	2	0	0	0	20^2	32	2	12	9	19.6	8.71	62	.348	.429	0	.000	-1	-8	-8	0	-0.9
1944	*StL-A	13	9	.591	35	24	12	4	3	198	211	17	54	67	12.2	3.55	101	.268	.318	11	.151	-2	-3	1	1	0.1
1945	StL-A	12	10	.545	30	24	15	1	2	192^1	188	9	65	55	11.9	3.51	100	.257	.318	13	.186	0	-3	0	0	0.1
Total	3	25	22	.532	72	50	27	5	5	411	431	28	131	131	12.4	3.79	96	.268	.325	24	.161	-2	-14	-6	1	-0.7

● LEFTY JAMERSON Jamerson, Charles Dewey "Charlie" b: 1/26/1900, Enfield, Ill. d: 8/4/80, Mocksville, N.C. BL/TL, 6'1", 195 lbs. Deb: 8/16/24

YEAR	TM/L	W	L	PCT	G	GS	CG	SH	SV	IP	H	HR	BB	SO	RAT	ERA	ERA+	OAV	OOB	BH	AVG	PB	PR	/A	PD	TPI
1924	Bos-A	0	0	—	1	0	0	0	0	1	1	0	3	0	36.0	18.00	24	.250	.571	0	—	0	-2	-2	-0	0.0

● JEFF JAMES James, Jeffrey Lynn "Jesse" b: 9/29/41, Indianapolis, Ind. BR/TR, 6'3", 195 lbs. Deb: 4/13/68

YEAR	TM/L	W	L	PCT	G	GS	CG	SH	SV	IP	H	HR	BB	SO	RAT	ERA	ERA+	OAV	OOB	BH	AVG	PB	PR	/A	PD	TPI
1968	Phi-N	4	4	.500	29	13	1	1	0	116	112	8	46	83	12.6	4.27	70	.256	.332	4	.121	-1	-17	-16	0	-1.2
1969	Phi-N	2	2	.500	6	5	1	0	0	31^2	36	5	14	21	14.2	5.40	66	.288	.360	2	.182	-0	-6	-7	-0	-0.8
Total	2	6	6	.500	35	18	2	1	0	147^2	148	13	60	104	12.9	4.51	69	.263	.338	6	.136	-1	-23	-23	-0	-2.0

● JOHNNY JAMES James, John Phillip b: 7/23/33, Bonners Ferry, Idaho BL/TR, 5'10", 160 lbs. Deb: 9/6/58

YEAR	TM/L	W	L	PCT	G	GS	CG	SH	SV	IP	H	HR	BB	SO	RAT	ERA	ERA+	OAV	OOB	BH	AVG	PB	PR	/A	PD	TPI
1958	NY-A	0	0	—	1	0	0	0	0	3	2	0	4	1	18.0	0.00	—	.250	.500	0	.000	-0	1	1	0	0.0
1960	NY-A	5	1	.833	28	0	0	0	2	43^1	38	3	26	29	13.9	4.36	82	.248	.368	0	.000	-0	-2	-4	0	-0.5
1961	NY-A	0	0	—	1	0	0	0	0	1^1	1	0	0	2	6.8	0.00	—	.250	.250	0	—	0	1	1	0	0.0
	LA-A	0	2	.000	36	3	0	0	0	71^1	66	12	54	41	15.4	5.30	85	.246	.377	0	.000	-1	-10	-6	-0	-0.3
	Yr	0	2	.000	37	3	0	0	0	72^2	67	12	54	43	15.2	5.20	86	.246	.375	0	.000	-1	-10	-6	-0	-0.3
Total	3	5	3	.625	66	3	0	0	2	119	107	15	84	73	14.8	4.76	87	.247	.375	0	.000	-2	-11	-8	0	-0.8

● MIKE JAMES James, Michael Elmo b: 8/15/67, Ft.Walton Beach, Fla. BR/TR, 6'4", 215 lbs. Deb: 4/29/95

YEAR	TM/L	W	L	PCT	G	GS	CG	SH	SV	IP	H	HR	BB	SO	RAT	ERA	ERA+	OAV	OOB	BH	AVG	PB	PR	/A	PD	TPI
1995	Cal-A	3	0	1.000	46	0	0	0	1	55^2	49	6	26	36	12.6	3.88	121	.238	.332	0	—	0	5	5	-0	0.2
1996	Cal-A	5	5	.500	69	0	0	0	1	81	62	7	42	65	12.7	2.67	188	.214	.333	0	—	0	21	21	1	2.3
1997	Ana-A	5	5	.500	58	0	0	0	7	62^2	69	3	28	57	14.6	4.31	106	.283	.368	0	—	0	2	2	0	0.3
1998	Ana-A	0	0	—	11	0	0	0	0	14	10	0	7	12	10.9	1.93	243	.208	.309	0	—	0	4	4	-0	0.0
Total	4	13	10	.565	184	0	0	0	9	213^1	190	16	103	170	13.1	3.42	140	.241	.342	0	—	0	32	32	1	2.8

● RICK JAMES James, Richard Lee b: 10/11/47, Sheffield, Ala. BR/TR, 6'2.5", 205 lbs. Deb: 9/20/67

YEAR	TM/L	W	L	PCT	G	GS	CG	SH	SV	IP	H	HR	BB	SO	RAT	ERA	ERA+	OAV	OOB	BH	AVG	PB	PR	/A	PD	TPI
1967	Chi-N	0	1	.000	3	1	0	0	0	4^2	9	1	2	2	21.2	13.50	26	.529	.579	0	.000	-0	-5	-5	-0	-0.9

● BOB JAMES James, Robert Harvey b: 8/15/58, Glendale, Cal. BR/TR, 6'4", 230 lbs. Deb: 9/7/78

YEAR	TM/L	W	L	PCT	G	GS	CG	SH	SV	IP	H	HR	BB	SO	RAT	ERA	ERA+	OAV	OOB	BH	AVG	PB	PR	/A	PD	TPI
1978	Mon-N	0	1	.000	4	1	0	0	0	4	4	1	4	3	18.0	9.00	39	.267	.421	0	—	0	-2	-2	0	-0.5
1979	Mon-N	0	0	—	2	0	0	0	0	2	2	0	3	1	22.5	13.50	27	.250	.455	0	—	0	-2	-2	-0	0.0
1982	Mon-N	0	0	—	7	0	0	0	0	9	10	0	8	11	18.0	6.00	61	.294	.429	0	—	0	-2	-2	-0	0.0
	Det-A	0	2	.000	12	1	0	0	0	19^2	22	4	8	20	13.7	5.03	81	.278	.345	0	—	0	-2	-2	-0	-0.2
1983	Det-A	0	0	—	4	0	0	0	0	4	5	2	3	4	18.0	11.25	35	.313	.421	0	—	0	-3	-3	-0	0.0
	Mon-N	1	0	1.000	27	0	0	0	7	50	37	3	23	56	11.3	2.88	125	.210	.312	2	.286	0	4	4	1	0.4
1984	Mon-N	6	6	.500	62	0	0	0	10	96	92	6	45	91	13.2	3.66	94	.251	.339	2	.143	-0	-1	-2	-1	-0.5
1985	Chi-A	8	7	.533	69	0	0	0	32	110	90	5	23	88	9.4	2.13	203	.226	.271	0	—	0	25	**27**	-1	4.8
1986	Chi-A	5	4	.556	49	0	0	0	14	58^1	61	8	23	32	13.6	5.25	82	.268	.345	0	—	0	-7	-6	-1	-1.4
1987	Chi-A	4	6	.400	43	0	0	0	10	54	54	10	17	34	12.5	4.67	98	.256	.323	0	—	0	-1	-1	0	-0.3
Total	8	24	26	.480	279	2	0	0	73	407	377	39	157	340	12.2	3.80	105	.246	.323	4	.190	0	8	9	-2	2.3

● LEFTY JAMES James, William A. b: 7/1/1889, Glen Roy, Ohio d: 5/3/33, Glen Roy, Ohio BL/TL, 5'11.5", 175 lbs. Deb: 4/13/12

YEAR	TM/L	W	L	PCT	G	GS	CG	SH	SV	IP	H	HR	BB	SO	RAT	ERA	ERA+	OAV	OOB	BH	AVG	PB	PR	/A	PD	TPI
1912	Cle-A	0	1	.000	3	1	0	0	1	6	8	0	4	2	21.0	7.50	45	.348	.483	0	.000	-0	-3	-3	-0	-0.5
1913	Cle-A	2	3	.400	11	4	3	0	0	39	42	0	9	18	12.5	3.00	101	.273	.325	3	.231	-0	0	0	-1	-0.1
1914	Cle-A	0	3	.000	17	6	1	0	0	50^2	44	0	32	16	13.9	3.20	90	.251	.373	0	.000	-1	-3	-2	1	-0.1
Total	3	2	7	.222	31	11	4	0	1	95^2	94	0	45	36	13.7	3.39	88	.267	.361	3	.107	-1	-6	-4	0	-0.7

● BILL JAMES James, William Henry "Big Bill" b: 1/20/1887, Detroit, Mich. d: 5/24/42, Venice, Cal. BB/TR, 6'4", 195 lbs. Deb: 6/12/11

YEAR	TM/L	W	L	PCT	G	GS	CG	SH	SV	IP	H	HR	BB	SO	RAT	ERA	ERA+	OAV	OOB	BH	AVG	PB	PR	/A	PD	TPI
1911	Cle-A	2	4	.333	8	6	4	0	0	51^2	58	1	32	21	16.0	4.88	70	.284	.387	1	.059	-1	-9	-8	-1	-1.0
1912	Cle-A	0	0	—	3	0	0	0	0	13^2	15	0	9	5	15.8	4.61	74	.288	.393	0	.000	-0	-2	-2	-1	-0.1
1914	StL-A	15	14	.517	44	35	20	3	1	284	269	4	109	109	12.2	2.85	95	.257	.330	10	.112	-3	-3	-5	5	-0.4
1915	StL-A	6	10	.375	34	22	8	0	1	170^1	155	2	92	58	13.4	3.59	80	.255	.359	8	.190	1	-12	-14	2	-1.0
	Det-A	7	3	.700	11	9	3	1	0	67	57	1	33	24	12.1	2.42	125	.243	.336	6	.286	2	4	4	1	1.0
	Yr	13	13	.500	45	31	11	1	1	237^1	212	3	125	82	12.8	3.26	89	.249	.345	14	.222	2	-9	-9	3	0.0
1916	Det-A	8	12	.400	30	20	8	0	1	151^2	141	1	79	61	13.7	3.68	78	.255	.360	3	.068	-3	-14	-14	-0	-2.1
1917	Det-A	13	10	.565	34	23	10	2	1	198	163	2	96	62	12.3	2.09	127	.229	.330	12	.211	2	13	12	-0	1.7
1918	Det-A	6	11	.353	19	18	8	1	0	122	127	3	68	42	14.8	3.76	71	.279	.379	5	.109	-3	-13	-15	2	-2.1
1919	Det-A	1	0	1.000	2	1	0	0	0	9^1	12	0	7	3	18.3	5.79	55	.324	.432	1	.250	0	-3	-3	0	-0.3
	Bos-A	3	5	.375	13	7	4	0	0	72^2	74	2	39	12	14.4	4.09	74	.280	.379	3	.143	-1	-7	-9	0	-0.9

YEAR	TM/L	W	L	PCT	G	GS	CG	SH	SV	IP	H	HR	BB	SO	RAT	ERA	ERA+	OAV	OOB	BH	AVG	PB	PR	/A	PD	TPI
	*Chi-A	3	2	.600	5	5	3	2	0	39^1	39	0	14	11	12.6	2.52	126	.281	.355	2	.143	-1	3	3	-1	0.2
	Yr	7	7	.500	20	13	7	2	0	121^1	125	2	60	26	13.9	3.71	83	.282	.370	6	.154	-2	-6	-8	-0	-1.0
Total	8	64	71	.474	203	146	68	9	4	1179^2	1110	16	578	408	13.2	3.20	88	.258	.352	51	.142	-8	-44	-49	8	-5.0

● BILL JAMES

James, William Lawrence "Seattle Bill" b: 3/12/1892, Iowa Hill, Cal. d: 3/10/71, Oroville, Cal. BR/TR, 6'3", 196 lbs. Deb: 4/17/13

YEAR	TM/L	W	L	PCT	G	GS	CG	SH	SV	IP	H	HR	BB	SO	RAT	ERA	ERA+	OAV	OOB	BH	AVG	PB	PR	/A	PD	TPI
1913	Bos-N	6	10	.375	24	14	10	1	0	135^2	134	4	57	73	13.1	2.79	118	.264	.347	12	.255	1	6	8	0	1.0
1914	*Bos-N	26	7	**.788**	46	37	30	4	3	332^1	261	7	118	156	10.6	1.90	145	.225	.304	33	.256	4	**33**	**32**	-1	**3.6**
1915	Bos-N	5	4	.556	13	9	4	0	0	68^1	68	3	22	23	12.1	3.03	86	.269	.332	1	.048	-2	-2	-3	1	-0.5
1919	Bos-N	0	0	—	1	0	0	0	0	5^1	6	0	2	1	13.5	3.38	85	.273	.333	0	.000	-0	-0	-0	0	0.0
Total	4	37	21	.638	84	60	44	5	3	541^2	469	14	199	253	11.5	2.28	126	.242	.319	46	.231	4	37	35	1	4.1

● CHARLIE JAMIESON

Jamieson, Charles Devine "Cuckoo" b: 2/7/1893, Paterson, N.J. d: 10/27/69, Paterson, N.J. BL/TL, 5'8.5", 165 lbs. Deb: 9/20/15 ◆

YEAR	TM/L	W	L	PCT	G	GS	CG	SH	SV	IP	H	HR	BB	SO	RAT	ERA	ERA+	OAV	OOB	BH	AVG	PB	PR	/A	PD	TPI
1916	Was-A	0	0	—	1	0	0	0	0	4	2	0	3	2	11.3	4.50	62	.143	.294	36	.248	0	-1	-1	0	0.0
1917	Was-A	0	0	—	1	0	0	0	0	2^1	10	0	2	1	46.3	38.57	7	.625	.667	6	.171	0	-9	-9	-0	0.0
1918	Phi-A	2	1	.667	5	2	1	0	0	23	24	0	13	2	15.3	4.30	68	.261	.364	84	.202	0	-4	-4	-0	-0.5
1919	Cle-A	0	0	—	4	1	0	0	0	13	12	0	8	0	13.8	5.54	60	.250	.357	6	.353	0	-3	-3	-0	0.1
1922	Cle-A	0	0	—	2	0	0	0	0	5^2	7	0	4	2	17.5	3.18	126	.318	.423	183	.323	1	1	1	-0	0.0
Total	5	2	1	.667	13	3	1	0	0	48	55	0	30	7	16.3	6.19	51	.286	.388	1990	.303	2	-17	-16	-1	-0.4

● JERRY JANESKI

Janeski, Gerard Joseph b: 4/18/46, Pasadena, Cal. BR/TR, 6'4", 205 lbs. Deb: 4/10/70

YEAR	TM/L	W	L	PCT	G	GS	CG	SH	SV	IP	H	HR	BB	SO	RAT	ERA	ERA+	OAV	OOB	BH	AVG	PB	PR	/A	PD	TPI
1970	Chi-A	10	17	.370	35	35	4	1	0	205^2	247	22	63	79	13.8	4.77	82	.300	.353	5	.076	-4	-24	-20	1	-2.6
1971	Was-A	1	5	.167	23	10	0	0	1	61^2	72	5	34	19	15.9	4.96	67	.304	.398	3	.214	1	-10	-11	1	-1.0
1972	Tex-A	0	1	.000	4	1	0	0	0	12^2	11	0	7	7	12.8	2.84	106	.229	.327	0	.000	-0	0	0	0	0.0
Total	3	11	23	.324	62	46	4	1	1	280	330	27	104	105	14.2	4.72	79	.298	.362	8	.098	-4	-34	-31	2	-3.6

● LARRY JANSEN

Jansen, Lawrence Joseph b: 7/16/20, Verboort, Ore. BR/TR, 6'2", 190 lbs. Deb: 4/17/47 C

YEAR	TM/L	W	L	PCT	G	GS	CG	SH	SV	IP	H	HR	BB	SO	RAT	ERA	ERA+	OAV	OOB	BH	AVG	PB	PR	/A	PD	TPI
1947	NY-N	21	5	**.808**	42	30	20	1	1	248	241	23	57	104	10.9	3.16	129	.262	.306	16	.186	-0	25	25	-0	2.4
1948	NY-N	18	12	.600	42	36	15	4	2	277	283	25	54	126	11.0	3.61	109	.265	.303	13	.137	-2	11	10	2	1.0
1949	NY-N	15	16	.484	37	35	17	3	0	259^2	271	36	62	113	11.6	3.85	104	.263	.306	16	.165	-0	6	4	3	0.6
1950	NY-N★	19	13	.594	40	35	21	**5**	3	275	238	31	55	161	**9.6**	3.01	136	.232	**.271**	16	.167	-0	35	33	2	3.8
1951	*NY-N☆	**23**	11	.676	39	34	18	3	0	278^2	254	26	56	145	10.1	3.04	129	.239	.279	9	.094	-5	29	27	3	2.9
1952	NY-N	11	11	.500	34	27	8	1	2	167^1	183	16	47	74	12.7	4.09	91	.281	.335	8	.178	3	-7	-7	2	-0.4
1953	NY-N	11	16	.407	36	26	6	0	1	184^2	185	24	55	88	11.8	4.14	104	.256	.311	8	.133	-1	3	3	-1	0.2
1954	NY-N	2	2	.500	13	7	0	0	0	40^2	57	5	15	15	16.2	5.98	68	.337	.395	4	.286	1	-9	-9	1	-0.5
1956	Cin-N	2	3	.400	8	7	2	0	1	34^2	39	5	9	16	12.7	5.19	77	.281	.329	0	.000	-1	-5	-5	-0	-0.8
Total	9	122	89	.578	291	237	107	17	10	1765^2	1751	191	410	842	11.1	3.58	112	.258	.302	90	.150	-6	87	82	11	9.2

● MARTY JANZEN

Janzen, Martin Thomas b: 5/31/73, Homestead, Fla. BR/TR, 6'3", 197 lbs. Deb: 5/12/96

YEAR	TM/L	W	L	PCT	G	GS	CG	SH	SV	IP	H	HR	BB	SO	RAT	ERA	ERA+	OAV	OOB	BH	AVG	PB	PR	/A	PD	TPI
1996	Tor-A	4	6	.400	15	11	0	0	0	73^2	95	16	38	47	16.5	7.33	68	.317	.397	0	—	0	-19	-19	-1	-2.1
1997	Tor-A	2	1	.667	12	0	0	0	0	25	23	4	13	17	13.0	3.60	127	.250	.343	0	—	0	3	3	-0	0.2
Total	2	6	7	.462	27	11	0	0	0	98^2	118	20	51	64	15.6	6.39	77	.301	.384	0	—	0	-16	-16	-1	-1.9

● KEVIN JARVIS

Jarvis, Kevin Thomas b: 8/1/69, Lexington, Ky. BL/TR, 6'2", 200 lbs. Deb: 4/6/94

YEAR	TM/L	W	L	PCT	G	GS	CG	SH	SV	IP	H	HR	BB	SO	RAT	ERA	ERA+	OAV	OOB	BH	AVG	PB	PR	/A	PD	TPI
1994	Cin-N	1	1	.500	6	3	0	0	0	17^2	22	4	5	10	13.8	7.13	58	.301	.346	1	.250	0	-6	-6	0	-0.5
1995	Cin-N	3	4	.429	19	11	1	1	0	79	91	13	32	33	14.4	5.70	72	.292	.363	3	.143	-0	-13	-14	0	-1.1
1996	Cin-N	8	9	.471	24	20	2	1	0	120^1	152	17	43	63	14.7	5.98	71	.305	.362	6	.167	-0	-24	-23	-1	-2.8
1997	Cin-N	0	1	.000	9	0	0	0	1	13^1	21	4	7	12	19.6	10.13	42	.344	.420	0	.000	-0	-9	-9	-0	-0.7
	Min-A	0	0	—	6	2	0	0	0	13	23	4	8	9	21.5	12.46	37	.371	.443	0	—	0	-11	-11	-0	0.0
	Det-A	0	3	.000	17	3	0	0	1	41^2	55	9	14	27	14.9	5.40	85	.318	.369	0	—	0	-4	-4	-0	-0.2
	Yr	0	3	.000	23	5	0	0	1	54^2	78	13	22	36	16.5	7.08	65	.332	.389	0	—	0	-15	-15	-1	-0.2
Total	4	12	18	.400	81	39	3	2	1	285	364	51	109	154	15.1	6.38	67	.308	.370	10	.161	-0	-67	-67	-2	-5.3

● RAY JARVIS

Jarvis, Raymond Arnold b: 5/10/46, Providence, R.I. BR/TR, 6'2", 198 lbs. Deb: 4/15/69

YEAR	TM/L	W	L	PCT	G	GS	CG	SH	SV	IP	H	HR	BB	SO	RAT	ERA	ERA+	OAV	OOB	BH	AVG	PB	PR	/A	PD	TPI
1969	Bos-A	5	6	.455	29	12	2	0	1	100^1	105	8	43	36	13.5	4.75	80	.274	.352	2	.069	-2	-13	-11	1	-1.2
1970	Bos-A	0	1	.000	15	0	0	0	0	16	17	1	14	8	18.6	3.94	101	.274	.423	0	—	0	-0	0	0	0.0
Total	2	5	7	.417	44	12	2	0	1	116^1	122	9	57	44	14.2	4.64	82	.274	.363	2	.069	-2	-13	-11	1	-1.2

● PAT JARVIS

Jarvis, Robert Patrick b: 3/18/41, Carlyle, Ill. BR/TR, 5'10.5", 180 lbs. Deb: 8/4/66

YEAR	TM/L	W	L	PCT	G	GS	CG	SH	SV	IP	H	HR	BB	SO	RAT	ERA	ERA+	OAV	OOB	BH	AVG	PB	PR	/A	PD	TPI
1966	Atl-N	6	2	.750	10	9	3	1	0	62^1	46	1	12	41	8.5	2.31	157	.206	.250	0	.000	-2	9	9	-1	0.8
1967	Atl-N	15	10	.600	32	30	7	1	0	194	195	15	62	118	12.1	3.66	91	.260	.320	6	.085	-3	-6	-7	-2	-1.4
1968	Atl-N	16	12	.571	34	34	14	1	0	256	202	15	50	157	8.9	2.60	115	.214	.255	12	.141	0	11	11	-3	1.0
1969	*Atl-N	13	11	.542	37	33	4	1	0	217^1	204	25	73	123	11.5	4.43	81	.246	.308	8	.113	-2	-20	-20	-0	-2.3
1970	Atl-N	16	16	.500	36	34	11	1	0	254	240	21	72	173	11.1	3.61	119	.247	.299	15	.183	-0	12	19	2	2.4
1971	Atl-N	6	14	.300	35	23	3	3	1	162^1	162	16	51	68	12.0	4.10	90	.261	.320	5	.106	-2	-12	-7	1	-1.0
1972	Atl-N	11	7	.611	37	6	0	0	2	98^2	94	7	44	56	12.6	4.10	92	.260	.341	3	.125	-0	-7	-3	1	-0.5
1973	Mon-N	2	1	.667	28	0	0	0	0	39^1	37	6	16	19	12.4	3.20	119	.250	.327	0	.000	-0	2	3	-0	0.1
Total	8	85	73	.538	249	169	42	8	3	1284	1180	106	380	755	11.0	3.58	101	.243	.300	49	.121	-10	-11	3	-3	-0.9

● HI JASPER

Jasper, Henry W. b: 11/15/1880, St.Louis, Mo. d: 5/22/37, St.Louis, Mo. BR/TR, 5'11", 180 lbs. Deb: 4/19/14

YEAR	TM/L	W	L	PCT	G	GS	CG	SH	SV	IP	H	HR	BB	SO	RAT	ERA	ERA+	OAV	OOB	BH	AVG	PB	PR	/A	PD	TPI
1914	Chi-A	1	0	1.000	16	0	0	0	0	32^1	22	0	20	19	12.0	3.34	80	.210	.341	0	.000	-1	-2	-2	1	0.0
1915	Chi-A	0	1	.000	3	2	1	0	0	15^2	8	2	9	15	9.8	4.60	65	.157	.283	2	.286	0	-3	-3	1	0.0
1916	StL-N	5	6	.455	21	9	2	0	1	107	97	0	42	37	12.3	3.28	81	.254	.339	7	.212	1	-8	-8	2	-0.5
1919	Cle-A	4	5	.444	12	10	5	0	0	82^2	83	1	28	25	12.1	3.59	93	.269	.330	3	.103	-2	-3	-2	1	-0.4
Total	4	10	12	.455	52	21	8	0	1	237^2	210	3	99	96	12.0	3.48	84	.248	.333	12	.162	-2	-16	-15	5	-0.9

● LARRY JASTER

Jaster, Larry Edward b: 1/13/44, Midland, Mich. BL/TL, 6'3.5", 205 lbs. Deb: 9/17/65

YEAR	TM/L	W	L	PCT	G	GS	CG	SH	SV	IP	H	HR	BB	SO	RAT	ERA	ERA+	OAV	OOB	BH	AVG	PB	PR	/A	PD	TPI
1965	StL-N	3	0	1.000	4	3	3	0	0	28	21	1	7	10	9.0	1.61	239	.206	.257	2	.200	0	6	7	-1	0.7
1966	StL-N	11	5	.688	26	21	6	**5**	0	151^2	124	17	45	92	10.3	3.26	110	.227	.291	8	.178	1	6	5	-1	0.6
1967	*StL-N	9	7	.563	34	23	2	1	3	152^1	141	12	44	87	11.0	3.01	109	.244	.300	5	.100	-1	6	5	-2	0.1
1968	*StL-N	9	13	.409	31	21	3	1	0	154^1	153	13	38	70	11.5	3.50	83	.262	.313	6	.140	0	-9	-10	-2	-1.6
1969	Mon-N	1	6	.143	24	11	1	0	0	77	95	17	28	39	14.6	5.49	67	.302	.362	8	.421	3	-16	-16	-2	-1.2
1970	Atl-N	1	1	.500	14	0	0	0	0	22^1	33	5	8	9	16.5	6.85	63	.359	.410	0	.000	-0	-7	-6	1	-0.5
1972	Atl-N	1	1	.500	5	1	0	0	0	12^1	12	4	8	6	14.6	5.11	74	.267	.377	0	.000	-0	-2	-2	-0	-0.3
Total	7	35	33	.515	138	80	15	7	3	598	579	69	178	313	11.6	3.64	93	.256	.314	29	.170	3	-16	-17	-7	-2.2

● AL JAVERY

Javery, Alva William "Beartracks" b: 6/5/18, Worcester, Mass. d: 8/16/77, Putnam, Conn. BR/TR, 6'3", 183 lbs. Deb: 4/23/40

YEAR	TM/L	W	L	PCT	G	GS	CG	SH	SV	IP	H	HR	BB	SO	RAT	ERA	ERA+	OAV	OOB	BH	AVG	PB	PR	/A	PD	TPI
1940	Bos-N	2	4	.333	29	4	1	0	1	83^1	99	2	36	42	14.8	5.51	68	.293	.364	2	.087	-1	-15	-17	-2	-1.4
1941	Bos-N	10	11	.476	34	23	9	1	1	160^2	181	5	65	54	14.1	4.31	83	.283	.355	6	.103	-4	-12	-13	1	-1.8
1942	Bos-N	12	16	.429	42	37	19	5	0	261	251	8	78	85	11.4	3.03	110	.251	.307	9	.105	-5	8	9	2	0.6
1943	Bos-N★	17	16	.515	41	35	19	5	0	**303**	288	13	99	134	11.6	3.21	106	.248	.309	17	.163	-3	6	7	2	0.7
1944	Bos-N☆	10	19	.345	40	33	11	3	3	254	248	12	118	137	13.0	3.54	108	.262	.345	12	.152	-3	2	8	-2	0.3
1945	Bos-N	2	7	.222	17	14	2	1	0	77^1	92	4	51	18	16.6	6.28	61	.295	.394	6	.207	-0	-21	-21	1	-2.0
1946	Bos-N	0	1	.000	2	1	0	0	0	3^1	5	0	5	0	27.0	13.50	25	.417	.588	0	.000	-0	-4	-4	-0	-0.9
Total	7	53	74	.417	205	147	61	15	5	1142^2	1164	44	452	470	12.9	3.80	94	.264	.335	52	.137	-15	-37	-31	2	-4.5

● JOEY JAY

Jay, Joseph Richard b: 8/15/35, Middletown, Conn. BB/TR, 6'4", 228 lbs. Deb: 7/21/53

YEAR	TM/L	W	L	PCT	G	GS	CG	SH	SV	IP	H	HR	BB	SO	RAT	ERA	ERA+	OAV	OOB	BH	AVG	PB	PR	/A	PD	TPI
1953	Mil-N	1	0	1.000	3	1	1	1	0	10	6	0	5	4	9.9	0.00	—	.188	.297	0	.000	-0	5	4	-0	0.3
1954	Mil-N	1	0	1.000	15	1	0	0	0	18	21	2	16	13	19.0	6.50	57	.304	.442	0	—	0	-5	-6	-0	-0.3
1955	Mil-N	0	0	—	12	1	0	0	0	19	23	2	13	3	17.1	4.74	79	.324	.429	2	.667	1	-1	-2	-1	0.0
1957	Mil-N	0	0	—	1	0	0	0	1	0^2	0	0	0	0	0.0	0.00	—	.000	.000	0	—	0	0	0	0	0.1
1958	Mil-N	7	5	.583	18	12	6	3	0	96^2	60	8	43	74	9.7	2.14	164	.177	.272	3	.094	-1	19	15	0	1.7
1959	Mil-N	6	11	.353	34	19	4	1	0	136^1	130	11	64	88	13.1	4.09	87	.248	.336	3	.086	-1	-2	-8	2	-0.9

YEAR	TM/L	W	L	PCT	G	GS	CG	SH	SV	IP	H	HR	BB	SO	RAT	ERA	ERA+	OAV	OOB	BH	AVG	PB	PR	/A	PD	TPI
1960	Mil-N	9	8	.529	32	11	3	0	1	133^1	128	10	59	90	13.0	3.24	106	.254	.339	7	.156	0	8	3	-0	0.3
1961	*Cin-N☆	**21**	10	.677	34	34	14	**4**	0	247^1	217	25	92	157	11.4	3.53	115	.236	.309	8	.090	-5	14	15	-1	1.0
1962	Cin-N	21	14	.600	39	37	16	4	0	273	269	26	100	155	12.3	3.76	107	.260	.327	15	.167	3	6	8	-2	1.0
1963	Cin-N	7	18	.280	30	22	4	1	1	170	172	19	73	116	13.1	4.29	78	.266	.343	8	.160	0	-19	-18	-0	-2.5
1964	Cin-N	11	11	.500	34	23	10	0	2	183	167	17	36	134	10.1	3.39	107	.245	.285	3	.057	-3	3	5	-2	0.0
1965	Cin-N	9	8	.529	37	24	4	1	1	155^2	150	21	63	102	12.5	4.22	89	.252	.328	2	.041	-3	-12	-8	-0	-1.2
1966	Cin-N	6	2	.750	12	10	1	1	0	73^2	78	8	23	44	12.7	3.91	100	.275	.335	3	.115	-1	-2	-0	-1	-0.2
	Atl-N	0	4	.000	9	8	0	0	1	29^2	39	4	20	19	18.2	7.89	46	.315	.414	1	.125	-0	-14	-14	-0	-1.7
	Yr	6	6	.500	21	18	1	1	1	103^1	117	12	43	63	14.0	5.05	76	.285	.354	4	.118	-1	-17	-14	-1	-1.9
Total	13	99	91	.521	310	203	63	16	7	1546^1	1460	153	607	999	12.2	3.77	99	.251	.325	55	.114	-10	-1	-5	-6	-2.4

● DOMINGO JEAN

Jean, Domingo (Luisa) b: 1/9/69, San Pedro De Macoris, D.R. BR/TR, 6'2", 175 lbs. Deb: 8/8/93

YEAR	TM/L	W	L	PCT	G	GS	CG	SH	SV	IP	H	HR	BB	SO	RAT	ERA	ERA+	OAV	OOB	BH	AVG	PB	PR	/A	PD	TPI
1993	NY-A	1	1	.500	10	6	0	0	0	40^1	37	7	19	20	12.5	4.46	93	.237	.320	0	—	0	-1	-1	-0	0.0

● TEX JEANES

Jeanes, Ernest Lee b: 12/19/1900, Maypearl, Tex. d: 4/5/73, Longview, Tex. BR/TR, 6', 176 lbs. Deb: 4/20/21 ♦

YEAR	TM/L	W	L	PCT	G	GS	CG	SH	SV	IP	H	HR	BB	SO	RAT	ERA	ERA+	OAV	OOB	BH	AVG	PB	PR	/A	PD	TPI
1922	Cle-A	0	0	—	1	0	0	0	0	0	0	0	1	0	—	—	—	—	1.000	0	.000	0	0	0	0	0.0
1927	NY-N	0	0	—	1	0	0	0	0	1	2	0	2	0	36.0	9.00	43	.400	.571	6	.300	0	-1	-1	-0	0.0
Total	2	0	0	—	2	0	0	0	0	1	2	0	3	0	45.0	9.00	43	.400	.625	20	.274	0	-1	-1	-0	0.0

● GEORGE JEFFCOAT

Jeffcoat, George Edward b: 12/24/13, New Brookland, S.C d: 10/13/78, Leesville, S.C. BR/TR, 5'11.5", 175 lbs. Deb: 4/20/36 F

YEAR	TM/L	W	L	PCT	G	GS	CG	SH	SV	IP	H	HR	BB	SO	RAT	ERA	ERA+	OAV	OOB	BH	AVG	PB	PR	/A	PD	TPI
1936	Bro-N	5	6	.455	40	5	3	0	3	95^2	84	7	63	46	14.6	4.52	92	.239	.366	3	.130	-1	-5	-4	-1	-0.6
1937	Bro-N	1	3	.250	21	3	1	1	0	54^1	58	4	27	29	14.2	5.13	79	.274	.358	0	.000	-2	-7	-7	-0	-0.6
1939	Bro-N	0	0	—	1	0	0	0	0	2	2	0	0	1	9.0	0.00	—	.286	.286	0	—	0	1	1	-0	0.0
1943	Bos-N	1	2	.333	8	1	0	0	0	17^2	15	1	10	10	12.7	3.06	112	.217	.316	2	.500	1	1	1	0	0.2
Total	4	7	11	.389	70	9	4	1	3	169^2	159	12	100	86	14.2	4.51	89	.248	.358	5	.128	-2	-11	-9	-1	-1.0

● HAL JEFFCOAT

Jeffcoat, Harold Bentley b: 9/6/24, W.Columbia, S.C. BR/TR, 5'10.5", 185 lbs. Deb: 4/20/48 F♦

YEAR	TM/L	W	L	PCT	G	GS	CG	SH	SV	IP	H	HR	BB	SO	RAT	ERA	ERA+	OAV	OOB	BH	AVG	PB	PR	/A	PD	TPI
1954	Chi-N	5	6	.455	43	3	1	0	7	104	110	12	58	35	14.9	5.19	81	.276	.373	8	.258	2	-13	-11	1	-0.8
1955	Chi-N	8	6	.571	50	1	0	0	6	100^2	107	5	53	32	14.7	2.95	139	.276	.369	4	.174	1	12	13	1	1.9
1956	Cin-N	8	2	.800	38	16	2	0	2	171	189	12	55	55	13.1	3.84	104	.281	.340	8	.148	-1	-1	3	3	0.3
1957	Cin-N	12	13	.480	37	31	10	1	0	207	236	29	46	63	12.6	4.52	91	.294	.338	14	.203	6	-15	-9	-1	-0.6
1958	Cin-N	6	8	.429	49	0	0	0	9	75	76	8	26	35	12.5	3.72	111	.268	.333	5	.556	2	2	4	2	1.1
1959	Cin-N	0	1	.000	17	0	0	0	1	21^2	21	3	10	12	12.9	3.32	122	.253	.333	1	1.000	1	2	2	0	0.2
	StL-N	0	1	.000	11	0	0	0	0	17^2	33	4	9	7	21.4	9.17	46	.402	.462	0	.000	-0	-10	-10	0	-0.5
	Yr	0	2	.000	28	0	0	0	1	39^1	54	7	19	19	16.7	5.95	70	.327	.397	1	.250	0	-9	-8	0	-0.3
Total	6	39	37	.513	245	51	13	1	25	697	772	73	257	239	13.6	4.22	97	.285	.352	487	.248	10	-24	-10	5	1.6

● MIKE JEFFCOAT

Jeffcoat, James Michael b: 8/3/59, Pine Bluff, Ark. BL/TL, 6'2", 187 lbs. Deb: 8/21/83

YEAR	TM/L	W	L	PCT	G	GS	CG	SH	SV	IP	H	HR	BB	SO	RAT	ERA	ERA+	OAV	OOB	BH	AVG	PB	PR	/A	PD	TPI
1983	Cle-A	1	3	.250	11	2	0	0	0	32^2	32	1	13	9	12.7	3.31	128	.256	.331	0	—	0	3	3	-0	0.3
1984	Cle-A	5	2	.714	63	1	0	0	1	75^1	82	7	24	41	12.8	2.99	137	.281	.338	0	—	0	8	9	1	0.9
1985	Cle-A	0	0	—	9	0	0	0	0	9^2	8	1	6	4	13.0	2.79	148	.235	.350	0	—	0	1	1	1	0.1
	SF-N	0	2	.000	19	1	0	0	0	22	27	4	6	10	14.3	5.32	65	.307	.365	0	.000	0	-4	-5	1	-0.3
1987	Tex-A	0	1	.000	2	2	0	0	0	7	11	4	4	1	19.3	12.86	35	.355	.429	0	—	0	-7	-7	-0	-0.7
1988	Tex-A	0	2	.000	5	2	0	0	0	10	19	1	5	5	23.4	11.70	35	.432	.510	0	—	0	-9	-8	0	-1.4
1989	Tex-A	9	6	.600	22	22	2	2	0	130^2	139	7	33	64	12.1	3.58	111	.270	.319	0	—	0	4	6	0	0.5
1990	Tex-A	5	6	.455	44	12	1	0	5	110^2	122	12	28	58	12.4	4.47	88	.283	.330	0	—	0	-7	-7	-1	-0.8
1991	Tex-A	5	3	.625	70	0	0	0	1	79^2	104	8	25	43	15.0	4.63	87	.320	.376	1	1.000	1	-5	-5	0	-0.4
1992	Tex-A	0	1	.000	6	3	0	0	0	19^2	28	2	5	6	15.1	7.32	52	.350	.388	0	—	0	-7	-8	0	-0.3
1994	Fla-N	0	0	—	4	0	0	0	0	2^2	4	2	0	1	13.5	10.13	43	.364	.364	0	—	0	-2	-2	-0	0.0
Total	10	25	26	.490	255	45	3	2	7	500	576	49	149	242	13.3	4.37	91	.292	.346	1	.500	1	-23	-22	0	-2.1

● JESSE JEFFERSON

Jefferson, Jesse Harrison b: 3/3/49, Midlothian, Va. BR/TR, 6'3", 195 lbs. Deb: 6/23/73

YEAR	TM/L	W	L	PCT	G	GS	CG	SH	SV	IP	H	HR	BB	SO	RAT	ERA	ERA+	OAV	OOB	BH	AVG	PB	PR	/A	PD	TPI
1973	Bal-A	6	5	.545	18	15	3	0	0	100^2	104	15	46	52	13.4	4.11	91	.267	.345	0	—	0	-3	-4	1	-0.3
1974	Bal-A	1	0	1.000	20	2	0	0	0	57^1	55	2	38	31	14.6	4.40	79	.261	.373	0	—	0	-5	-6	0	0.1
1975	Bal-A	0	2	.000	4	0	0	0	0	7^2	5	0	8	4	15.3	2.35	149	.227	.433	0	—	0	1	1	0	0.3
	Chi-A	5	9	.357	22	21	1	0	0	107^2	100	10	94	67	16.4	5.10	76	.249	.394	0	—	0	-16	-15	0	-1.7
	Yr	5	11	.313	26	21	1	0	0	115^1	105	10	102	71	16.3	4.92	78	.248	.397	0	—	0	-15	-14	1	-1.4
1976	Chi-A	2	5	.286	19	9	0	0	0	62^1	86	3	42	30	18.8	8.52	42	.339	.436	0	—	0	-35	-34	1	-3.3
1977	Tor-A	9	17	.346	33	33	8	0	0	217	224	23	83	114	12.8	4.31	97	.269	.336	0	—	0	-6	-3	0	-0.3
1978	Tor-A	7	16	.304	31	30	9	2	0	211^2	214	28	86	97	12.9	4.38	90	.267	.340	0	—	0	-15	-11	0	-1.2
1979	Tor-A	2	10	.167	34	10	2	0	1	116	150	19	45	43	15.3	5.51	79	.328	.390	0	—	0	-17	-15	1	-1.4
1980	Tor-A	4	13	.235	29	18	2	2	0	121^2	130	12	52	53	13.6	5.47	79	.281	.357	0	—	0	-19	-16	1	-2.1
	Pit-N	1	0	1.000	1	1	0	0	0	6^2	3	0	2	4	6.8	1.35	270	.143	.217	0	.000	-0	2	2	0	0.3
1981	Cal-A	2	4	.333	26	5	0	0	0	77	80	4	24	27	12.4	3.62	101	.269	.328	0	—	0	0	0	-1	-0.1
Total	9	39	81	.325	237	144	25	4	1	1085^2	1151	116	520	522	14.0	4.81	83	.277	.360	0	.000	-0	-112	-101	3	-9.7

● FERGIE JENKINS

Jenkins, Ferguson Arthur b: 12/13/43, Chatham, Ont., Can. BR/TR, 6'5", 210 lbs. Deb: 9/10/65 H

YEAR	TM/L	W	L	PCT	G	GS	CG	SH	SV	IP	H	HR	BB	SO	RAT	ERA	ERA+	OAV	OOB	BH	AVG	PB	PR	/A	PD	TPI
1965	Phi-N	2	1	.667	7	0	0	0	1	12^1	7	2	2	10	6.6	2.19	158	.159	.196	0	.000	-0	2	2	-0	0.4
1966	Phi-N	0	0	—	1	0	0	0	0	2^1	3	0	1	2	15.4	3.86	93	.273	.333	0	—	0	-0	-0	-0	0.0
	Chi-N	6	8	.429	60	12	2	1	5	182	147	24	51	148	9.9	3.31	111	.219	.277	7	.137	1	6	7	-2	0.5
	Yr	6	8	.429	61	12	2	1	5	184^1	150	24	52	150	10.0	3.32	111	.220	.278	7	.137	1	6	7	-2	0.5
1967	Chi-N★	20	13	.606	38	38	**20**	3	0	289^1	230	30	83	236	9.9	2.80	127	.217	.277	14	.151	1	19	24	2	3.1
1968	Chi-N	20	15	.571	40	40	20	3	0	308	255	26	65	260	9.4	2.63	120	.222	.266	16	.160	2	12	18	-1	2.3
1969	Chi-N	21	15	.583	43	42	23	7	1	311^1	284	27	71	**273**	10.5	3.21	125	.242	.290	15	.139	-1	13	28	0	3.2
1970	Chi-N	22	16	.579	40	39	**24**	3	0	313	265	30	60	274	**9.5**	3.39	133	.224	**.265**	14	.124	-3	23	39	-1	4.0
1971	Chi-N★	**24**	13	.649	39	39	**30**	3	0	**325**	304	29	37	263	9.6	2.77	142	.246	.271	28	.243	10	25	42	2	6.4
1972	Chi-N☆	20	12	.625	36	36	23	5	0	289^1	253	32	62	184	10.0	3.20	119	.234	.280	20	.183	1	8	19	3	2.7
1973	Chi-N	14	16	.467	38	38	7	2	0	271	267	35	57	170	10.9	3.89	101	.259	.301	10	.119	-1	-7	2	3	0.4
1974	Tex-A	**25**	12	.676	41	41	**29**	6	0	328^1	286	27	45	225	9.3	2.82	126	.232	.264	1	.500	0	29	27	-0	3.0
1975	Tex-A	17	18	.486	37	37	22	4	0	270	261	37	56	157	10.9	3.93	95	.251	.295	0	—	0	-5	-5	1	-0.6
1976	Bos-A	12	11	.522	30	29	12	2	0	209	201	20	43	142	10.7	3.27	119	.253	.296	0	—	0	6	15	-1	0.9
1977	Bos-A	10	10	.500	28	28	11	1	0	193	190	30	36	105	10.5	3.68	122	.257	.291	0	—	0	8	17	1	1.3
1978	Tex-A	18	8	.692	34	30	16	4	0	249	228	21	41	157	9.8	3.04	123	.245	.279	0	—	0	20	20	2	2.2
1979	Tex-A	16	14	.533	37	37	10	3	0	259	252	40	81	164	11.7	4.07	102	.256	.314	0	—	0	4	2	4	0.7
1980	Tex-A	12	12	.500	29	29	12	0	0	198	190	22	52	129	11.2	3.77	103	.250	.301	0	—	0	6	3	1	0.5
1981	Tex-A	5	8	.385	19	16	1	0	0	106	122	14	40	63	13.8	4.50	77	.290	.351	0	—	0	-10	-12	2	-1.1
1982	Chi-N	14	15	.483	34	34	4	1	0	217^1	221	19	68	134	12.2	3.15	119	.264	.323	10	.149	-1	11	14	-0	1.6
1983	Chi-N	6	9	.400	33	29	1	1	0	167^1	176	19	46	96	12.3	4.30	88	.275	.329	13	.245	3	-13	-10	-1	-0.6
Total	19	284	226	.557	664	594	267	49	7	4500^2	4142	484	997	3192	10.4	3.34	115	.243	.289	148	.165	13	157	254	14	30.9

● JACK JENKINS

Jenkins, Warren Washington b: 12/22/42, Covington, Va. BR/TR, 6'2", 195 lbs. Deb: 9/13/62

YEAR	TM/L	W	L	PCT	G	GS	CG	SH	SV	IP	H	HR	BB	SO	RAT	ERA	ERA+	OAV	OOB	BH	AVG	PB	PR	/A	PD	TPI
1962	Was-A	0	1	.000	3	1	1	0	0	13^1	12	4	7	10	12.8	4.05	100	.245	.339	0	.000	-0	-0	-0	-0	-0.1
1963	Was-A	0	2	.000	4	2	0	0	0	12^1	16	2	12	5	20.4	5.84	64	.340	.475	1	.333	0	-3	-3	0	-0.4
1969	LA-N	0	0	—	1	0	0	0	0	1	0	0	0	1	0.0	0.00	—	.000	.000	0	—	0	0	0	0	0.0
Total	3	0	3	.000	8	3	1	0	0	26^2	28	6	19	16	15.9	4.73	82	.283	.398	1	.143	-0	-3	-3	0	-0.5

● WILLIE JENSEN

Jensen, William Christian b: 11/17/1889, Philadelphia, Pa. d: 3/27/17, Philadelphia, Pa. BL/TR, 5'11.5", 170 lbs. Deb: 9/10/12

YEAR	TM/L	W	L	PCT	G	GS	CG	SH	SV	IP	H	HR	BB	SO	RAT	ERA	ERA+	OAV	OOB	BH	AVG	PB	PR	/A	PD	TPI
1912	Det-A	1	2	.333	5	4	1	0	0	33	43	1	18	8	17.2	4.91	66	.339	.429	0	.000	-2	-6	-6	-0	-0.7
1914	Phi-A	0	1	.000	1	1	1	0	0	9	7	1	2	1	9.0	2.00	131	.226	.273	0	.000	0	1	1	0	0.1
Total	2	1	3	.250	6	5	2	0	0	42	50	2	20	9	15.4	4.29	73	.316	.400	0	.000	-2	-5	-5	-0	-0.6

YEAR	TM/L	W	L	PCT	G	GS	CG	SH	SV	IP	H	HR	BB	SO	RAT	ERA	ERA+	OAV	OOB	BH	AVG	PB	PR	/A	PD	TPI
● MIKE JERZEMBECK Jerzembeck, Michael Joseph b: 5/18/72, Queens, N.Y. BR/TR, 6′1″, 185 lbs. Deb: 8/8/98																										
1998	NY-A	0	1	.000	3	2	0	0	0	6^1	9	2	4	1	18.5	12.79	35	.346	.433	0	—	0	-6	-6	-0	-0.7
● VIRGIL JESTER Jester, Virgil Milton b: 7/23/27, Denver, Colo. BR/TR, 5′11″, 188 lbs. Deb: 6/18/52																										
1952	Bos-N	3	5	.375	19	8	4	1	0	73	80	5	23	25	12.8	3.33	108	.283	.339	4	.211	1	3	2	-1	0.2
1953	Mil-N	0	0	—	2	0	0	0	0	2	4	1	4	0	36.0	22.50	17	.400	.571	0	—	0	-4	-4	0	0.0
Total	2	3	5	.375	21	8	4	1	0	75	84	6	27	25	13.4	3.84	94	.287	.349	4	.211	1	-1	-2	-1	0.2
● GERMAN JIMENEZ Jimenez, German (Camarena) b: 12/5/62, Santiago, Mex. BL/TL, 5′11″, 200 lbs. Deb: 6/28/88																										
1988	Atl-N	1	6	.143	15	9	0	0	0	55^2	65	4	12	26	12.6	5.01	73	.294	.333	1	.059	-1	-10	-8	-1	-1.2
● JOSE JIMENEZ Jimenez, Jose b: 7/7/73, San Pedro De Macoris, D.R. BR/TR, 6′3″, 170 lbs. Deb: 9/9/98																										
1998	StL-N	3	0	1.000	4	3	0	0	0	21^1	22	0	8	12	12.7	2.95	142	.262	.326	0	.000	-1	3	3	0	0.3
● JUAN JIMENEZ Jimenez, Juan Antonio (Martes) b: 3/8/49, LaTorre, La Vega, D.R. BR/TR, 6′1″, 165 lbs. Deb: 9/9/74																										
1974	Pit-N	0	0	—	4	0	0	0	0	4	6	0	2	2	18.0	6.75	51	.353	.421	0	—	0	-1	-1	-0	0.0
● MIGUEL JIMENEZ Jimenez, Miguel Anthony b: 8/19/69, New York, N.Y. BR/TR, 6′2″, 205 lbs. Deb: 9/12/93																										
1993	Oak-A	1	0	1.000	5	4	0	0	0	27	27	5	16	13	14.7	4.00	102	.262	.367	0	—	0	1	0	-1	0.2
1994	Oak-A	1	4	.200	8	7	0	0	0	34	38	9	32	22	18.8	7.41	60	.275	.415	0	—	0	-10	-11	0	-1.1
Total	2	2	4	.333	13	11	0	0	0	61	65	14	48	35	17.0	5.90	72	.270	.395	0	—	0	-9	-11	-1	-0.9
● TOMMY JOHN John, Thomas Edward b: 5/22/43, Terre Haute, Ind. BR/TL, 6′3″, 185 lbs. Deb: 9/6/63																										
1963	Cle-A	0	2	.000	6	3	0	0	0	20^1	23	1	6	9	12.8	2.21	164	.284	.333	0	.000	-1	3	3	-0	0.2
1964	Cle-A	2	9	.182	25	14	2	1	0	94^1	97	10	35	65	12.6	3.91	92	.262	.326	5	.208	0	-3	-3	1	-0.3
1965	Chi-A	14	7	.667	39	27	6	1	3	183^2	162	12	58	126	10.9	3.09	103	.237	.298	10	.169	2	8	2	3	0.8
1966	Chi-A	14	11	.560	34	33	10	**5**	0	223	195	13	57	138	10.5	2.62	121	.235	.290	10	.145	2	20	14	1	1.8
1967	Chi-A	10	13	.435	31	29	9	**6**	0	178^1	143	12	47	110	9.8	2.47	126	.219	.277	8	.157	-0	15	13	6	2.3
1968	Chi-A★	10	5	.667	25	25	5	1	0	177^1	135	10	49	117	9.9	1.98	153	.212	.280	12	.194	2	20	21	6	2.9
1969	Chi-A	9	11	.450	33	33	6	2	0	232^1	230	16	90	128	12.4	3.25	119	.261	.330	9	.114	-2	9	16	7	1.9
1970	Chi-A	12	17	.414	37	37	10	3	0	269^1	253	19	101	138	12.1	3.27	119	.251	.324	17	.202	1	13	19	4	2.5
1971	Chi-A	13	16	.448	38	35	10	3	0	229^1	244	17	58	131	12.0	3.61	99	.274	.321	10	.145	-1	-4	-1	-1	-0.3
1972	LA-N	11	5	.688	29	29	4	1	0	186^2	172	14	40	117	10.4	2.89	115	.244	.287	10	.159	-1	12	9	4	1.1
1973	LA-N	16	7	**.696**	36	31	4	2	0	218	202	16	50	116	10.6	3.10	111	.246	.293	15	.203	2	14	8	7	1.8
1974	LA-N	13	3	.813	22	22	5	3	0	153	133	4	42	78	10.4	2.59	131	.235	.289	6	.118	-1	18	14	2	1.5
1976	LA-N	10	10	.500	31	31	6	2	0	207	207	7	61	91	11.7	3.09	110	.261	.314	7	.109	-2	10	7	-1	0.3
1977	*LA-N	20	7	.741	31	31	11	3	0	220^1	225	12	50	123	11.4	2.78	138	.267	.311	14	.177	1	28	26	2	3.4
1978	*LA-N☆	17	10	.630	33	30	7	0	1	213	230	11	53	124	12.2	3.30	106	.271	.318	8	.121	-1	7	5	2	0.7
1979	NY-A☆	21	9	.700	37	36	17	3	0	276^1	268	9	65	111	11.0	2.96	137	.260	.306	0	—	0	**38**	34	2	3.8
1980	*NY-A★	22	9	.710	36	36	16	**6**	0	265^1	270	13	56	78	11.3	3.43	114	.268	.311	0	—	0	18	15	1	1.7
1981	*NY-A	9	8	.529	20	20	7	0	0	140^1	135	10	39	50	11.4	2.63	136	.256	.311	0	—	0	16	15	1	1.9
1982	NY-A	10	10	.500	30	26	9	2	0	186^2	190	11	34	54	10.9	3.66	109	.266	.302	0	—	0	8	7	2	0.8
	*Cal-A	4	2	.667	7	7	1	0	0	35	49	4	5	14	13.9	3.86	105	.336	.358	0	—	0	1	1	1	0.2
	Yr	14	12	.538	37	33	10	2	0	221^2	239	15	39	68	11.3	3.69	108	.274	.305	0	—	0	9	7	2	1.0
1983	Cal-A	11	13	.458	34	34	9	0	0	234^2	287	20	49	65	13.0	4.33	93	.304	.340	0	—	0	-7	-8	1	-0.7
1984	Cal-A	7	13	.350	32	29	4	1	0	181^1	223	15	56	47	14.0	4.52	88	.306	.359	0	—	0	-11	-11	0	-1.0
1985	Cal-A	2	4	.333	12	6	0	0	0	38^1	51	3	15	17	15.7	4.70	87	.329	.392	0	—	0	-2	-3	1	-0.2
	Oak-A	2	6	.250	11	11	0	0	0	48	66	6	13	8	15.0	6.19	62	.332	.376	0	—	0	-11	-12	1	-1.6
	Yr	4	10	.286	23	17	0	0	0	86^1	117	9	28	25	15.2	5.53	72	.328	.378	0	—	0	-13	-15	2	-1.8
1986	NY-A	5	3	.625	13	10	1	0	0	70^2	73	8	15	28	11.5	2.93	140	.275	.319	0	—	0	10	9	1	1.0
1987	NY-A	13	6	.684	33	33	3	1	0	187^2	212	12	47	63	12.7	4.03	109	.288	.336	0	—	0	9	7	-1	0.6
1988	NY-A	9	8	.529	35	32	0	0	0	176^1	221	11	46	81	13.9	4.49	88	.308	.355	0	—	0	-10	-11	2	-0.7
1989	NY-A	2	7	.222	10	10	0	0	0	63^2	87	6	22	18	15.8	5.80	67	.336	.394	0	—	0	-14	-14	2	-1.4
Total	26	288	231	.555	760	700	162	46	4	4710^1	4783	302	1259	2245	11.7	3.34	110	.265	.316	141	.157	1	214	179	55	25.0
● AUGIE JOHNS Johns, Augustus Francis "Lefty" b: 9/10/1899, St.Louis, Mo. d: 9/12/75, San Antonio, Tex. BL/TL, 5′8.5″, 170 lbs. Deb: 4/16/26																										
1926	Det-A	6	4	.600	35	14	3	1	1	112^2	117	6	69	40	15.3	5.35	76	.271	.377	4	.143	-1	-17	-16	-2	-1.6
1927	Det-A	0	0	—	1	0	0	0	0	1	1	0	1	1	18.0	9.00	47	.333	.500	0	—	0	-1	-1	0	0.0
Total	2	6	4	.600	36	14	3	1	1	113^2	118	6	70	41	15.3	5.38	75	.271	.378	4	.143	-1	-17	-17	-2	-1.6
● DOUG JOHNS Johns, Douglas Alan b: 12/19/67, South Bend, Ind. BR/TL, 6′2″, 185 lbs. Deb: 7/8/95																										
1995	Oak-A	5	3	.625	11	9	1	1	0	54^2	44	5	26	25	12.3	4.61	97	.226	.332	0	—	0	1	-1	1	0.0
1996	Oak-A	6	12	.333	40	23	1	0	1	158	187	21	69	71	14.9	5.98	82	.297	.372	0	—	0	-17	-19	2	-1.5
1998	Bal-A	3	3	.500	31	10	0	0	1	86^2	108	9	32	34	15.0	4.57	99	.321	.387	2	1.000	1	1	-0	2	0.3
Total	3	14	18	.438	82	42	2	1	2	299^1	339	35	127	130	14.5	5.32	89	.292	.369	2	1.000	1	-16	-20	5	-1.2
● OLLIE JOHNS Johns, Oliver Tracy b: 8/21/1879, Trenton, Ohio d: 6/17/61, Hamilton, Ohio BL/TL, Deb: 9/24/05																										
1905	Cin-N	1	0	1.000	4	1	1	0	1	18	31	1	4	8	17.5	3.50	94	.369	.398	1	.200	-0	-1	-0	-0	-0.1
● ABE JOHNSON Johnson, Abraham b: Chicago, Ill. Deb: 7/16/1893																										
1893	Chi-N	0	0	—	1	0	0	0	1	1	2	0	2	0	45.0	36.00	13	.400	.625	0	—	0	-3	-3	-0	-0.5
● RANKIN JOHNSON Johnson, Adam Rankin Jr. b: 3/1/17, Hayden, Ariz. BR/TR, 6′3″, 177 lbs. Deb: 4/17/41 F																										
1941	Phi-A	1	0	1.000	7	0	0	0	0	10	14	0	3	0	15.3	3.60	116	.326	.370	0	.000	-0	1	1	0	0.1
● RANKIN JOHNSON Johnson, Adam Rankin Sr. "Tex" b: 2/4/1888, Burnet, Tex. d: 7/2/72, Williamsport, Pa. BR/TR, 6′1.5″, 185 lbs. Deb: 4/20/14 F																										
1914	Bos-A	3	9	.250	16	13	4	2	0	99^1	92	2	34	24	11.7	3.08	87	.265	.336	4	.133	-1	-4	-4	-2	-0.8
	Chi-F	9	5	.643	16	14	12	2	0	120	88	5	29	60	9.1	**1.58**	169	.209	.267	4	.108	-3	17	14	-1	1.1
1915	Chi-F	2	4	.333	11	6	3	0	1	57	58	2	23	19	12.9	4.42	57	.270	.343	1	.045	-3	-11	-12	-2	-1.7
	Bal-F	7	11	.389	23	19	12	2	1	150^2	143	3	58	62	12.1	3.35	86	.255	.326	8	.157	-2	-10	-8	-3	-1.4
	Yr	9	15	.375	34	25	15	2	2	207^2	201	5	81	81	12.3	3.64	76	.259	.330	9	.123	-5	-21	-20	-5	-3.1
1918	StL-N	1	1	.500	6	1	0	0	0	23	20	0	7	4	10.6	2.74	99	.263	.325	1	.250	0	0	-0	1	0.1
Total	3	22	30	.423	72	53	31	6	2	450	401	12	151	169	11.2	2.92	93	.248	.315	18	.125	-9	-7	-10	-7	-2.7
● ART JOHNSON Johnson, Arthur Gilbert b: 2/15/1897, Warren, Pa. d: 6/7/82, Sarasota, Fla. BB/TL, 6′1″, 167 lbs. Deb: 9/18/27																										
1927	NY-N	0	0	—	1	0	0	0	0	3	1	0	1	0	6.0	0.00	—	.125	.222	0	—	0	1	1	-0	0.0
● ART JOHNSON Johnson, Arthur Henry "Lefty" b: 7/16/16, Winchester, Mass. BL/TL, 6′2″, 185 lbs. Deb: 9/22/40																										
1940	Bos-N	0	1	.000	2	1	0	0	0	6	10	0	3	1	21.0	10.50	35	.345	.424	0	.000	-0	-4	-5	0	-0.6
1941	Bos-N	7	15	.318	43	18	6	0	1	183^1	189	7	71	70	13.0	3.53	101	.270	.342	8	.145	-2	2	1	0	-0.1
1942	Bos-N	0	0	—	4	0	0	0	0	6^1	4	0	5	0	14.2	1.42	235	.190	.370	0	.000	-0	1	1	-0	0.0
Total	3	7	16	.304	49	19	6	0	1	195^2	203	7	79	71	13.3	3.68	97	.271	.346	8	.140	-2	-1	-2	1	-0.7
● BEN JOHNSON Johnson, Benjamin Franklin b: 5/16/31, Greenwood, S.C. BR/TR, 6′2″, 190 lbs. Deb: 9/6/59																										
1959	Chi-N	0	0	—	4	2	0	0	0	16^2	17	1	4	6	11.3	2.16	183	.262	.304	0	.000	-0	3	3	-0	-0.1
1960	Chi-N	2	1	.667	17	0	0	0	1	29^1	39	3	11	9	15.6	4.91	77	.355	.418	0	.000	-0	-4	-4	1	-0.3
Total	2	2	1	.667	21	2	0	0	1	46	56	4	15	15	14.1	3.91	98	.320	.377	0	.000	-1	-0	-0	0	-0.4
● CHET JOHNSON Johnson, Chester Lillis "Chesty Chet" b: 8/1/17, Redmond, Wash. d: 4/10/83, Seattle, Wash. BL/TL, 6′, 175 lbs. Deb: 9/12/46 F																										
1946	StL-A	0	0	—	5	3	0	0	0	18	20	0	13	8	16.5	5.00	75	.286	.398	0	.000	-1	-3	-3	-1	-0.2
● BART JOHNSON Johnson, Clair Barth b: 1/3/50, Torrance, Cal. BR/TR, 6′5″, 215 lbs. Deb: 9/8/69																										
1969	Chi-A	1	3	.250	4	3	0	0	0	22^1	22	2	6	18	11.3	3.22	120	.259	.308	1	.167	0	1	2	-0	0.3

YEAR	TM/L	W	L	PCT	G	GS	CG	SH	SV	IP	H	HR	BB	SO	RAT	ERA	ERA+	OAV	OOB	BH	AVG	PB	PR	/A	PD	TPI
1970	Chi-A	4	7	.364	18	15	2	1	0	89^{2}	92	11	46	71	14.1	4.82	81	.268	.358	8	.276	2	-11	-9	-0	-0.8
1971	Chi-A	12	10	.545	53	16	4	0	14	178	148	9	111	153	13.4	2.93	122	.227	.345	11	.193	0	10	13	-1	1.7
1972	Chi-A	0	3	.000	9	0	0	0	1	13^{2}	18	2	13	9	21.1	9.22	34	.327	.464	0	.000	-0	-9	-9	0	-2.0
1973	Chi-A	3	3	.500	22	9	0	0	0	80^{2}	76	6	40	56	13.2	4.13	96	.252	.343	0	—	0	-3	-2	-0	-0.4
1974	Chi-A	10	4	.714	18	18	8	2	0	121^{2}	105	6	32	76	10.2	2.74	136	.229	.281	0	—	0	12	13	-2	1.3
1976	Chi-A	9	16	.360	32	32	8	3	0	211^{1}	231	20	62	91	12.5	4.73	75	.282	.334	0	—	0	-28	-27	0	-2.9
1977	Chi-A	4	5	.444	29	4	0	0	2	92	114	5	38	46	15.1	4.01	102	.302	.369	0	—	0	0	1	-0	0.1
Total	8	43	51	.457	185	97	22	6	17	809^{1}	806	61	348	520	13.0	3.94	95	.261	.339	20	.215	3	-28	-19	-4	-2.7
● **CONNIE JOHNSON**	Johnson, Clifford b: 12/27/22, Stone Mountain, Ga BR/TR, 6'4", 200 lbs. Deb: 4/17/53																									
1953	Chi-A	4	4	.500	14	10	2	1	0	60^{2}	55	4	38	44	14.1	3.56	113	.238	.351	1	.050	-2	3	3	-1	0.1
1955	Chi-A	7	4	.636	17	16	5	2	0	99	95	5	52	72	13.5	3.45	114	.251	.343	5	.152	-1	6	5	-1	0.3
1956	Chi-A	0	1	.000	5	2	0	0	0	12^{1}	11	1	7	6	13.1	3.65	112	.234	.333	0	.000	-0	1	1	0	0.0
	Bal-A	9	10	.474	26	25	9	2	0	183^{2}	165	12	62	130	11.2	3.43	114	.239	.303	15	.259	3	15	10	-3	1.0
	Yr	9	11	.450	31	27	9	2	0	196	176	13	69	136	11.3	3.44	114	.239	.305	15	.246	3	16	11	-3	1.0
1957	Bal-A	14	11	.560	35	30	14	3	0	242	212	17	66	177	10.5	3.20	112	.235	.289	12	.135	-4	16	11	-4	0.2
1958	Bal-A	6	9	.400	26	17	4	0	1	118^{1}	116	13	32	68	11.3	3.88	93	.260	.310	7	.206	1	-1	-4	-2	-0.5
Total	5	40	39	.506	123	100	34	8	1	716	654	52	257	497	11.5	3.44	109	.243	.310	40	.169	-3	38	26	-10	1.1
● **DANE JOHNSON**	Johnson, Dane Edward b: 2/10/63, Coral Gables, Fla. BR/TR, 6'5", 205 lbs. Deb: 5/30/94																									
1994	Chi-A	2	1	.667	15	0	0	0	0	12^{1}	16	2	11	7	19.7	6.57	71	.327	.450	0	—	0	-2	-3	-0	-0.5
1996	Tor-A	0	0	—	10	0	0	0	0	9	5	0	5	7	10.0	3.00	167	.161	.278	0	—	0	2	2	0	0.0
1997	Oak-A	4	1	.800	38	0	0	0	2	45^{2}	49	4	31	43	16.2	4.53	100	.272	.385	0	—	0	0	-0	-1	0.0
Total	3	6	2	.750	63	0	0	0	2	67	70	6	47	57	16.0	4.70	98	.269	.385	0	—	0	-0	-1	-1	-0.5
● **DAVE JOHNSON**	Johnson, David Charles b: 10/4/48, Abilene, Tex. BR/TR, 6'1", 183 lbs. Deb: 7/2/74																									
1974	Bal-A	2	2	.500	11	0	0	0	2	15^{1}	17	1	5	6	12.9	2.93	118	.274	.328	0	—	0	1	1	-0	0.2
1975	Bal-A	0	1	.000	6	0	0	0	0	8^{2}	8	0	7	4	15.6	4.15	84	.250	.385	0	—	0	-0	-1	0	0.0
1977	Min-A	2	5	.286	30	6	0	0	0	72^{2}	86	7	23	33	14.1	4.58	87	.299	.361	0	—	0	-4	-5	0	-0.4
1978	Min-A	0	2	.000	6	1	0	0	0	12	15	1	9	7	18.0	7.50	51	.313	.421	0	—	0	-5	-5	0	-0.7
Total	4	4	10	.286	53	7	0	0	2	108^{2}	126	9	44	50	14.5	4.64	83	.293	.365	0	—	0	-8	-10	-0	-0.9
● **DAVE JOHNSON**	Johnson, David Wayne b: 10/24/59, Baltimore, Md. BR/TR, 5'11", 183 lbs. Deb: 5/29/87																									
1987	Pit-N	0	0	—	5	0	0	0	0	6^{1}	13	1	2	4	21.3	9.95	41	.448	.484	0	—	0	-4	-4	0	0.0
1989	Bal-A	4	7	.364	14	14	4	0	0	89^{1}	90	11	28	26	12.3	4.23	90	.265	.328	0	—	0	-3	-4	-2	-0.7
1990	Bal-A	13	9	.591	30	29	3	0	0	180	196	30	43	68	12.1	4.10	93	.280	.324	0	—	0	-4	-6	-3	-0.9
1991	Bal-A	4	8	.333	22	14	0	0	0	84	127	18	24	38	16.6	7.07	56	.349	.395	0	—	0	-28	-29	-1	-3.5
1993	Det-A	1	1	.500	6	0	0	0	0	8^{1}	13	3	5	7	21.6	12.96	33	.342	.444	0	—	0	-8	-8	-0	-1.5
Total	5	22	25	.468	77	57	7	0	0	368	439	63	102	143	13.5	5.11	75	.298	.349	0	—	0	-47	-52	-6	-6.6
● **DON JOHNSON**	Johnson, Donald Roy b: 11/12/26, Portland, Ore. BR/TR, 6'3", 200 lbs. Deb: 4/20/47																									
1947	NY-A	4	3	.571	15	8	2	0	0	54^{1}	57	2	23	16	13.4	3.64	97	.270	.345	0	.000	-2	0	-1	-1	-0.3
1950	NY-A	1	0	1.000	8	0	0	0	0	18	35	2	12	9	23.5	10.00	43	.398	.470	0	.000	-0	-11	-11	-0	-0.6
	StL-A	5	6	.455	25	12	4	1	1	96	126	14	55	31	17.1	6.09	81	.325	.410	2	.069	-3	-16	-12	-1	-1.5
	Yr	6	6	.500	33	12	4	1	1	114	161	16	67	40	18.1	6.71	72	.338	.421	2	.063	-4	-27	-24	-1	-2.1
1951	StL-A	0	1	.000	6	3	0	0	0	15	27	4	18	8	27.6	12.60	35	.391	.523	1	.333	0	-14	-14	0	-0.7
	Was-A	7	11	.389	21	20	8	1	0	143^{2}	138	9	58	52	12.4	3.95	104	.255	.329	4	.085	-5	3	2	-0	-0.3
	Yr	7	12	.368	27	23	8	1	0	158^{2}	165	13	76	60	13.8	4.76	87	.270	.352	5	.100	-5	-11	-11	-0	-1.0
1952	Was-A	0	5	.000	29	6	0	0	2	69	80	4	33	37	15.3	4.43	80	.287	.370	1	.077	-1	-6	-7	-0	-0.6
1954	Chi-A	8	7	.533	46	16	3	3	7	144	129	14	43	68	10.8	3.13	119	.243	.300	1	.029	-3	10	10	0	0.7
1955	Bal-A	2	4	.333	31	5	0	0	1	68	89	4	35	27	16.4	5.82	65	.333	.411	0	.000	-1	-14	-15	0	-1.3
1958	SF-N	0	1	.000	17	0	0	0	1	23	31	2	8	14	16.0	6.26	61	.323	.387	0	.000	-0	-6	-6	-0	-0.3
Total	7	27	38	.415	198	70	17	5	12	631	712	55	285	262	14.4	4.78	84	.288	.364	9	.058	-16	-54	-55	-2	-4.9
● **EARL JOHNSON**	Johnson, Earl Douglas "Lefty" b: 4/2/19, Redmond, Wash. d: 12/3/94, Seattle, Wash. BL/TL, 6'3", 190 lbs. Deb: 7/20/40 F																									
1940	Bos-A	6	2	.750	17	10	2	0	0	70^{1}	69	0	39	26	14.1	4.09	110	.260	.359	2	.074	-3	2	3	1	0.1
1941	Bos-A	4	5	.444	17	12	4	0	0	93^{2}	90	4	51	46	13.8	4.52	92	.247	.344	10	.294	2	-4	-4	2	0.1
1946	*Bos-A	5	4	.556	29	5	0	0	3	80	78	5	39	40	13.4	3.71	99	.250	.337	5	.227	2	-2	-0	-0	0.1
1947	Bos-A	12	11	.522	45	17	6	3	8	142^{1}	129	7	62	65	12.2	2.97	131	.246	.328	12	.273	1	12	14	2	2.8
1948	Bos-A	10	4	.714	35	3	1	0	5	91^{1}	98	7	42	45	13.8	4.53	97	.276	.353	3	.097	-3	-2	-1	2	-0.3
1949	Bos-A	3	6	.333	19	3	0	0	0	49^{1}	65	1	29	20	17.9	7.48	58	.327	.422	0	.000	-1	-18	-17	-1	-2.7
1950	Bos-A	0	0	—	11	0	0	0	0	13^{2}	18	0	8	6	17.8	7.24	68	.333	.429	0	.000	-0	-4	-4	1	0.0
1951	Det-A	0	0	—	6	0	0	0	1	5^{2}	9	0	2	2	17.5	6.35	66	.375	.423	0	—	0	-1	-1	0	0.0
Total	8	40	32	.556	179	50	13	3	17	546^{1}	556	24	272	250	13.9	4.30	96	.265	.353	32	.187	-2	-18	-10	7	0.1
● **WALT JOHNSON**	Johnson, Ellis Walter b: 12/8/1892, Minneapolis, Minn. d: 1/4/65, Minneapolis, Minn. BR/TR, 6'0.5", 180 lbs. Deb: 7/6/12																									
1912	Chi-A	0	0	—	3	0	0	0	0	11^{2}	11	0	7	7	14.7	3.86	83	.262	.380	0	.000	-0	-1	-1	-0	0.0
1915	Chi-A	0	0	—	1	0	0	0	0	2	3	0	0	3	13.5	9.00	33	.333	.333	0	—	0	-1	-1	-0	0.0
1917	Phi-A	0	2	.000	4	2	0	0	0	13^{2}	15	0	5	8	13.2	7.24	38	.294	.357	0	.000	0	-7	-7	0	-0.8
Total	3	0	2	.000	8	2	0	0	0	27^{1}	29	0	12	18	13.8	5.93	50	.284	.365	0	.000	0	-9	-9	-0	-0.8
● **ERNIE JOHNSON**	Johnson, Ernest Thorwald b: 6/16/24, Brattleboro, Vt. BR/TR, 6'4", 195 lbs. Deb: 4/28/50																									
1950	Bos-N	2	0	1.000	16	1	0	0	0	20^{2}	37	1	13	15	21.8	6.97	55	.394	.467	1	.500	0	-6	-7	1	-0.4
1952	Bos-N	6	3	.667	29	10	2	1	1	92	100	7	31	45	13.0	4.11	88	.270	.329	2	.091	-0	-4	-5	1	-0.4
1953	Mil-N	4	3	.571	36	1	0	0	0	81	79	4	22	36	11.6	2.67	147	.263	.320	1	.071	-1	15	11	0	0.7
1954	Mil-N	5	2	.714	40	4	1	0	2	99^{1}	77	11	34	68	10.1	2.81	133	.219	.290	3	.231	0	14	10	1	0.8
1955	Mil-N	5	7	.417	40	2	0	0	4	92	81	5	55	43	13.5	3.42	110	.240	.349	2	.100	-1	6	3	-0	0.3
1956	Mil-N	4	3	.571	36	0	0	0	6	51	54	9	21	26	13.4	3.71	93	.270	.342	1	.250	0	0	-1	0	-0.2
1957	*Mil-N	7	3	.700	30	0	0	0	4	65	67	9	26	44	13.0	3.88	90	.265	.336	6	.353	3	0	-3	1	0.0
1958	Mil-N	3	1	.750	15	0	0	0	1	23^{1}	35	4	10	13	17.7	8.10	43	.357	.422	0	.000	0	-11	-12	0	-1.8
1959	Bal-A	4	1	.800	31	1	0	0	1	50^{1}	57	6	19	29	14.1	4.11	92	.286	.357	2	.333	0	-1	-2	0	-0.1
Total	9	40	23	.635	273	19	3	1	19	574^{2}	587	56	231	319	13.0	3.77	98	.266	.340	18	.180	2	13	-5	5	-1.1
● **FRED JOHNSON**	Johnson, Frederick Edward "Deacon" or "Cactus" b: 3/10/1894, Tolar, Tex. d: 6/14/73, Kerrville, Tex. BR/TR, 6', 185 lbs. Deb: 9/27/22																									
1922	NY-N	0	2	.000	2	2	1	0	0	18	20	3	1	8	10.5	4.00	100	.294	.304	0	.000	-1	0	0	-0	-0.1
1923	NY-N	2	0	1.000	3	2	1	0	0	17	11	2	7	5	9.5	4.24	90	.177	.261	0	.000	-1	-0	-1	1	-0.1
1938	StL-A	3	7	.300	17	6	3	0	3	69	91	7	27	24	15.5	5.61	89	.316	.377	6	.240	-0	-6	-5	-2	-0.8
1939	StL-A	0	1	.000	5	2	1	0	0	14	23	0	9	2	20.6	6.43	76	.383	.464	0	.000	-1	-3	-2	1	-0.1
Total	4	5	10	.333	27	12	6	0	3	118	145	12	44	39	14.5	5.26	88	.303	.363	6	.154	-2	-9	-8	0	-1.1
● **CHIEF JOHNSON**	Johnson, George Howard "Murphy" or "Big Murph" b: 3/30/1886, Winnebago, Neb. d: 6/11/22, Des Moines, Iowa BR/TR, 5'11.5", 190 lbs. Deb: 4/16/13																									
1913	Cin-N	14	16	.467	44	31	13	3	0	269	251	8	86	107	11.5	3.01	108	.256	.320	10	.114	-3	6	7	0	0.5
1914	Cin-N	0	0	—	1	1	0	0	0	4	6	0	2	1	18.0	6.75	43	.333	.400	0	—	0	-2	-2	-0	0.0
	KC-F	9	10	.474	20	19	12	2	0	134	157	2	33	78	13.0	3.16	88	.298	.345	6	.122	-2	-4	-6	-3	-1.2
1915	KC-F	17	17	.500	46	34	19	4	2	281^{1}	253	5	71	118	10.6	2.75	96	.242	.295	11	.126	-4	-1	-4	2	-0.6
Total	3	40	43	.482	111	85	44	9	2	688^{1}	667	15	192	304	11.5	2.95	98	.259	.315	27	.121	-9	-1	-4	-1	-1.3
● **HANK JOHNSON**	Johnson, Henry Ward b: 5/21/06, Bradenton, Fla. d: 8/20/82, Bradenton, Fla. BR/TR, 5'11.5", 175 lbs. Deb: 4/17/25																									
1925	NY-A	1	3	.250	24	4	2	1	0	67	88	3	37	25	17.9	6.85	62	.319	.414	1	.059	-1	-18	-19	1	-1.0
1926	NY-A	0	0	—	1	0	0	0	1	1	2	0	2	0	36.0	18.00	21	.400	.571	0	—	0	-2	-2	-0	-0.3
1928	NY-A	14	9	.609	31	22	10	1	0	199	188	16	104	110	13.7	4.30	88	.250	.351	19	.241	2	-6	-12	0	-1.1

YEAR	TM/L	W	L	PCT	G	GS	CG	SH	SV	IP	H	HR	BB	SO	RAT	ERA	ERA+	OAV	OOB	BH	AVG	PB	PR	/A	PD	TPI
1929	NY-A	3	3	.500	12	8	2	0	0	42^2	37	5	39	24	16.0	5.06	76	.237	.390	1	.071	-1	-4	-6	-1	-0.9
1930	NY-A	14	11	.560	44	15	7	1	2	175^1	177	12	104	115	14.5	4.67	92	.265	.366	17	.266	5	-0	-7	2	-0.3
1931	NY-A	13	8	.619	40	23	8	0	4	196^1	176	13	102	106	12.8	4.72	84	.234	.326	15	.195	2	-7	-16	-3	-1.7
1932	NY-A	2	2	.500	5	4	2	0	0	31^1	34	7	15	27	14.1	4.88	83	.266	.343	3	.231	0	-1	-3	0	-0.3
1933	Bos-A	8	6	.571	25	21	7	0	1	155^1	156	13	74	65	13.5	4.06	108	.263	.348	12	.231	3	4	6	-2	0.6
1934	Bos-A	6	8	.429	31	14	7	1	1	124^1	162	12	53	66	15.9	5.36	90	.316	.385	10	.233	1	-12	-8	-1	-0.8
1935	Bos-A	2	1	.667	13	2	0	0	1	31	41	3	14	14	16.0	5.52	86	.331	.399	0	.000	-1	-4	-3	-1	-0.4
1936	Phi-A	0	2	.000	3	3	0	0	0	11^2	16	4	10	6	20.8	7.71	66	.296	.415	1	.250	-0	-3	-3	-0	-0.4
1939	Cin-N	0	3	.000	20	0	0	0	1	31^1	30	1	13	10	12.4	2.01	191	.268	.344	2	.400	1	7	6	-1	0.5
Total	12	63	56	.529	249	116	45	4	11	1066^1	1107	89	567	568	14.4	4.75	88	.268	.361	81	.215	9	-47	-67	-6	-6.1

● JIM JOHNSON

Johnson, James Brian b: 11/3/45, Muskegon, Mich. BL/TL, 5'11", 175 lbs. Deb: 4/13/70

YEAR	TM/L	W	L	PCT	G	GS	CG	SH	SV	IP	H	HR	BB	SO	RAT	ERA	ERA+	OAV	OOB	BH	AVG	PB	PR	/A	PD	TPI
1970	SF-N	1	0	1.000	3	0	0	0	0	6^2	8	0	5	2	17.6	8.10	49	.320	.433	0	.000	0	-3	-3	0	-0.4

● JASON JOHNSON

Johnson, Jason Michael b: 10/27/73, Santa Barbara, Cal. BR/TR, 6'6", 220 lbs. Deb: 8/27/97

YEAR	TM/L	W	L	PCT	G	GS	CG	SH	SV	IP	H	HR	BB	SO	RAT	ERA	ERA+	OAV	OOB	BH	AVG	PB	PR	/A	PD	TPI
1997	Pit-N	0	0	—	3	0	0	0	0	6	10	2	1	3	16.5	6.00	71	.400	.423	0	.000	-0	-1	-1	-0	0.0
1998	TB-A	2	5	.286	13	13	0	0	0	60	74	9	27	36	15.6	5.70	86	.306	.382	0	.000	-0	-7	-5	-1	-0.6
Total	2	2	5	.286	16	13	0	0	0	66	84	11	28	39	15.7	5.73	85	.315	.386	0	.000	-0	-8	-7	-1	-0.6

● JERRY JOHNSON

Johnson, Jerry Michael b: 12/3/43, Miami, Fla. BR/TR, 6'3", 200 lbs. Deb: 7/17/68

YEAR	TM/L	W	L	PCT	G	GS	CG	SH	SV	IP	H	HR	BB	SO	RAT	ERA	ERA+	OAV	OOB	BH	AVG	PB	PR	/A	PD	TPI
1968	Phi-N	4	4	.500	16	11	2	0	0	80^2	82	5	29	40	12.6	3.24	93	.264	.330	2	.080	-0	-2	-2	1	-0.2
1969	Phi-N	6	13	.316	33	21	4	2	1	147^1	151	18	57	82	12.9	4.28	83	.268	.338	9	.209	2	-11	-12	-1	-1.4
1970	StL-N	2	0	1.000	7	0	0	0	1	11^1	6	1	3	5	7.1	3.18	130	.146	.205	0	.000	0	1	1	-0	0.2
	SF-N	3	4	.429	33	1	0	0	3	65^1	67	5	38	44	14.6	4.27	93	.266	.364	1	.067	-1	-2	-2	-0	-0.4
	Yr	5	4	.556	40	1	0	0	4	76^2	73	6	41	49	13.5	4.11	97	.249	.343	1	.063	-1	-1	-1	-1	-0.2
1971	*SF-N	12	9	.571	67	0	0	0	18	109	93	9	48	85	11.7	2.97	114	.230	.313	2	.154	-0	6	5	-0	1.2
1972	SF-N	8	6	.571	48	0	0	0	8	73^1	73	4	40	57	13.9	4.42	79	.261	.353	0	.000	-1	-8	-8	0	-1.6
1973	Cle-A	5	6	.455	39	1	0	0	5	59^2	70	7	39	45	16.4	6.18	63	.299	.399	0	—	0	-16	-15	0	-2.8
1974	Hou-N	2	1	.667	34	0	0	0	0	45	47	2	24	32	14.2	4.80	72	.276	.366	0	.000	-0	-6	-7	0	-0.4
1975	SD-N	3	1	.750	21	4	0	0	0	54	60	3	31	18	15.2	5.17	67	.282	.373	1	.083	-0	-9	-10	-1	-0.8
1976	SD-N	1	3	.250	24	1	0	0	0	39	39	0	26	27	15.0	5.31	62	.260	.369	0	.000	-0	-8	-9	-0	-0.9
1977	Tor-A	2	4	.333	43	0	0	0	5	86	91	9	54	54	15.2	4.60	91	.279	.382	0	—	0	-5	-4	-0	-0.4
Total	10	48	51	.485	365	39	6	2	41	770^2	779	63	389	489	13.7	4.31	83	.265	.352	15	.123	-2	-60	-62	-1	-7.5

● JOHNNY JOHNSON

Johnson, John Clifford "Swede" b: 9/29/14, Belmore, Ohio d: 6/26/91, Iron Mountain, Mich. BL/TL, 6', 182 lbs. Deb: 4/19/44

YEAR	TM/L	W	L	PCT	G	GS	CG	SH	SV	IP	H	HR	BB	SO	RAT	ERA	ERA+	OAV	OOB	BH	AVG	PB	PR	/A	PD	TPI
1944	NY-A	0	2	.000	22	1	0	0	3	26^2	25	0	24	11	16.9	4.05	86	.243	.391	3	.500	1	-2	-2	-1	-0.1
1945	Chi-A	3	0	1.000	29	0	0	0	4	69^2	85	2	35	38	15.6	4.26	78	.306	.385	4	.286	2	-7	-7	-1	-0.3
Total	2	3	2	.600	51	1	0	0	7	96^1	110	2	59	49	16.0	4.20	80	.289	.387	7	.350	3	-9	-9	-2	-0.4

● YOUNGY JOHNSON

Johnson, John Godfred b: 7/22/1877, San Francisco, Cal. d: 8/28/36, Berkeley, Cal. TR , Deb: 4/29/1897

YEAR	TM/L	W	L	PCT	G	GS	CG	SH	SV	IP	H	HR	BB	SO	RAT	ERA	ERA+	OAV	OOB	BH	AVG	PB	PR	/A	PD	TPI
1897	Phi-N	1	2	.333	5	2	1	0	0	29	39	0	12	7	16.4	4.66	90	.320	.390	1	.077	-2	-1	-1	-0	-0.3
1899	NY-N	0	0	—	1	0	0	0	0	2	0	0	2	1	9.0	0.00	—	.000	.250	0	.000	-0	1	1	0	0.0
Total	2	1	2	.333	6	2	1	0	0	31	39	0	14	8	16.0	4.35	96	.305	.382	1	.071	-2	-0	-1	-0	-0.3

● JOHN HENRY JOHNSON

Johnson, John Henry b: 8/21/56, Houston, Tex. BL/TL, 6'2", 190 lbs. Deb: 4/10/78

YEAR	TM/L	W	L	PCT	G	GS	CG	SH	SV	IP	H	HR	BB	SO	RAT	ERA	ERA+	OAV	OOB	BH	AVG	PB	PR	/A	PD	TPI
1978	Oak-A	11	10	.524	33	30	7	2	0	186	164	18	82	91	11.9	3.39	107	.238	.319	0	—	0	8	5	-3	0.4
1979	Oak-A	2	8	.200	14	13	1	0	0	84^2	89	13	36	50	13.4	4.36	93	.269	.342	0	—	0	-1	-3	-1	-0.2
	Tex-A	2	6	.250	17	12	1	0	0	82^1	79	12	36	46	12.7	4.92	84	.255	.334	0	—	0	-6	-7	-1	-0.6
	Yr	4	14	.222	31	25	2	0	0	167	168	25	72	96	13.0	4.63	88	.261	.336	0	—	0	-8	-10	-1	-0.8
1980	Tex-A	2	2	.500	33	0	0	0	4	38^2	27	2	15	44	10.0	2.33	167	.199	.283	0	—	0	7	7	0	0.9
1981	Tex-A	3	1	.750	24	0	0	0	2	23^2	19	2	6	8	9.9	2.66	130	.232	.292	0	—	0	3	2	1	0.6
1983	Bos-A	3	2	.600	34	1	0	0	1	53^1	58	3	20	51	13.3	3.71	117	.283	.350	0	—	0	2	4	-0	0.2
1984	Bos-A	1	2	.333	30	3	0	0	1	63^2	64	7	27	57	12.9	3.53	118	.260	.333	0	—	0	3	4	-0	0.0
1986	Mil-A	2	1	.667	19	0	0	0	1	44	43	2	10	42	10.8	2.66	163	.251	.293	0	—	0	7	8	-1	0.3
1987	Mil-A	0	1	.000	10	2	0	0	0	26^1	42	1	18	18	20.5	9.57	48	.365	.451	0	—	0	-15	-15	0	-0.5
Total	8	26	33	.441	214	61	9	2	9	602^2	585	60	250	407	12.5	3.90	102	.256	.331	0	—	0	8	6	-5	1.1

● JOHN JOHNSON

Johnson, John Louis (b: John Louis Mercer) b: 11/18/1869, Pekin, Ill. d: 1/28/41, Kansas City, Mo. TL , 5'10", 165 lbs. Deb: 9/11/1894

YEAR	TM/L	W	L	PCT	G	GS	CG	SH	SV	IP	H	HR	BB	SO	RAT	ERA	ERA+	OAV	OOB	BH	AVG	PB	PR	/A	PD	TPI
1894	Phi-N	1	1	.500	4	3	2	0	0	32^2	44	3	15	10	16.5	6.06	84	.319	.390	3	.188	-1	-3	-3	0	-0.2

● JONATHAN JOHNSON

Johnson, Jonathan Kent b: 7/16/74, LaGrange, Ga. BR/TR, 6', 180 lbs. Deb: 9/27/98

YEAR	TM/L	W	L	PCT	G	GS	CG	SH	SV	IP	H	HR	BB	SO	RAT	ERA	ERA+	OAV	OOB	BH	AVG	PB	PR	/A	PD	TPI
1998	Tex-A	0	0	—	1	1	0	0	0	4^1	5	0	5	3	20.8	8.31	58	.313	.476	0	—	0	-2	-2	0	0.0

● JOE JOHNSON

Johnson, Joseph Richard b: 10/30/61, Brookline, Mass. BR/TR, 6'2", 195 lbs. Deb: 7/25/85

YEAR	TM/L	W	L	PCT	G	GS	CG	SH	SV	IP	H	HR	BB	SO	RAT	ERA	ERA+	OAV	OOB	BH	AVG	PB	PR	/A	PD	TPI
1985	Atl-N	4	4	.500	15	14	1	0	0	85^2	95	9	24	34	12.8	4.10	94	.285	.339	1	.043	-1	-5	-2	-2	-0.5
1986	Atl-N	6	7	.462	17	15	2	0	0	87	101	8	35	49	14.3	4.97	80	.289	.358	3	.115	-1	-12	-10	2	-1.2
	Tor-A	7	2	.778	16	15	0	0	0	88	94	3	22	39	12.2	3.89	109	.281	.331	0	—	0	3	3	-1	0.1
1987	Tor-A	3	5	.375	14	14	0	0	0	66^2	77	10	18	27	13.1	5.13	88	.289	.339	0	—	0	-5	-5	-0	-0.5
Total	3	20	18	.526	62	58	3	0	0	327^1	367	30	99	149	13.1	4.48	92	.286	.342	4	.082	-2	-19	-13	-2	-2.1

● KEN JOHNSON

Johnson, Kenneth Travis b: 6/16/33, W.Palm Beach, Fla. BR/TR, 6'4", 210 lbs. Deb: 9/13/58

YEAR	TM/L	W	L	PCT	G	GS	CG	SH	SV	IP	H	HR	BB	SO	RAT	ERA	ERA+	OAV	OOB	BH	AVG	PB	PR	/A	PD	TPI
1958	KC-A	0	0	—	2	0	0	0	0	2^1	6	1	3	1	34.7	27.00	14	.429	.529	0	—	0	-6	-6	0	0.0
1959	KC-A	1	1	.500	2	2	0	0	0	11	11	2	5	8	13.1	4.09	98	.268	.348	0	.000	-0	-0	-0	0	0.0
1960	KC-A	5	10	.333	42	6	2	0	3	120^1	120	16	45	83	12.9	4.26	93	.263	.338	5	.167	-1	-5	-4	2	-0.3
1961	KC-A	0	4	.000	6	1	0	0	0	9^1	11	2	7	4	17.4	10.61	39	.297	.409	0	.000	-0	-7	-7	1	-2.1
	*Cin-N	6	2	.750	15	11	3	1	1	83	71	11	22	42	10.3	3.25	125	.229	.284	6	.240	1	7	7	1	0.9
1962	Hou-N	7	16	.304	33	31	5	1	0	197	195	18	46	178	11.3	3.84	97	.257	.305	4	.077	-3	2	-2	1	-0.4
1963	Hou-N	11	17	.393	37	32	6	1	1	224	204	12	50	148	10.5	2.65	119	.242	.291	5	.068	-4	16	12	2	1.4
1964	Hou-N	11	16	.407	35	35	7	1	0	218	209	15	44	117	10.7	3.63	94	.250	.293	6	.079	-2	-2	-5	1	-0.6
1965	Hou-N	3	2	.600	8	8	1	0	0	51^2	52	4	11	28	11.7	4.18	80	.267	.319	2	.111	-0	-4	-5	1	-0.3
	Mil-N	13	8	.619	29	26	8	1	2	179^2	165	15	37	123	10.3	3.21	110	.240	.282	7	.115	-2	7	6	-3	0.2
	Yr	16	10	.615	37	34	9	1	2	231^1	217	19	48	151	10.4	3.42	102	.244	.285	9	.114	-2	3	2	-2	-0.1
1966	Atl-N	14	8	.636	32	31	11	2	0	215^2	213	24	46	105	10.8	3.30	110	.262	.301	10	.143	0	7	8	0	0.8
1967	Atl-N	13	9	.591	29	29	6	0	0	210^1	191	19	38	85	10.1	2.74	121	.244	.285	9	.127	-0	15	14	-2	1.2
1968	Atl-N	5	8	.385	31	16	1	0	0	135	145	10	25	57	11.9	3.47	86	.279	.324	7	.175	-0	-7	-7	-1	-0.8
1969	Atl-N	0	1	.000	9	2	0	0	1	29	32	4	9	20	12.7	4.97	73	.283	.336	0	.000	-0	-4	-4	0	-0.2
	NY-A	1	2	.333	12	0	0	0	0	26	19	1	11	21	10.4	3.46	100	.202	.286	0	.000	-0	0	0	1	0.1
	Chi-N	1	2	.333	9	1	0	0	1	19	17	2	13	18	14.2	2.84	142	.230	.345	0	.000	-0	2	2	-0	0.3
1970	Mon-N	0	0	—	3	0	0	0	0	6	9	1	1	4	18.0	7.50	55	.321	.387	0	—	0	-2	-2	0	0.0
Total	13	91	106	.462	334	231	50	7	9	1737^1	1670	157	413	1042	11.1	3.46	101	.253	.302	61	.114	-12	18	8	5	0.2

● KEN JOHNSON

Johnson, Kenneth Wandersee "Hook" b: 1/14/23, Topeka, Kan. BL/TL, 6'1", 185 lbs. Deb: 9/18/47

YEAR	TM/L	W	L	PCT	G	GS	CG	SH	SV	IP	H	HR	BB	SO	RAT	ERA	ERA+	OAV	OOB	BH	AVG	PB	PR	/A	PD	TPI
1947	StL-N	1	0	1.000	2	1	1	0	0	10	2	0	5	8	7.2	0.00	—	.063	.211	2	.500	1	5	5	0	0.5
1948	StL-N	2	4	.333	13	4	0	0	0	45^1	43	1	30	20	14.7	4.76	86	.262	.379	6	.300	2	-4	-3	-0	-0.3
1949	StL-N	0	1	.000	14	2	0	0	0	33^2	29	1	35	18	17.9	6.42	65	.250	.435	2	.250	0	-9	-8	1	-0.1
1950	StL-N	0	0	—	2	0	0	0	0	2	1	0	3	1	18.0	0.00	—	.167	.444	0	—	0	1	1	0	0.0
	*Phi-N	4	1	.800	14	8	3	1	0	60^2	61	3	43	32	15.6	4.01	101	.260	.376	3	.158	-0	1	0	0	0.0
	Yr	4	1	.800	16	8	3	1	0	62^2	62	3	46	33	15.7	3.88	105	.257	.378	3	.158	-0	2	1	0	0.0
1951	Phi-N	5	8	.385	20	18	4	3	0	106^1	103	8	68	58	14.7	4.57	84	.259	.371	5	.143	-1	-7	-9	-0	-1.0
1952	Det-A	0	0	—	9	1	0	0	0	11^1	12	1	11	10	18.3	6.35	60	.273	.418	1	.333	0	-3	-3	0	0.0
Total	6	12	14	.462	74	34	8	4	0	269^1	251	14	195	147	15.2	4.58	87	.252	.379	19	.213	1	-17	-18	1	-0.9

YEAR	TM/L	W	L	PCT	G	GS	CG	SH	SV	IP	H	HR	BB	SO	RAT	ERA	ERA+	OAV	OOB	BH	AVG	PB	PR	/A	PD	TPI
● **LLOYD JOHNSON**	Johnson, Lloyd William "Eppa" b: 12/24/10, Santa Rosa, Cal. d: 10/8/80, Stockton, Cal. BL/TL, 6'4", 204 lbs. Deb: 4/21/34																									
1934	Pit-N	0	0	—	1	0	0	0	0	1	1	0	0	0	9.0	0.00	—	.333	.333	0	—	0	0	0	-0	0.0
● **MIKE JOHNSON**	Johnson, Michael Keith b: 10/3/75, Edmonton, Alberta, Canada BL/TR, 6'2", 175 lbs. Deb: 4/6/97																									
1997	Bal-A	0	1	.000	14	5	0	0	2	39^2	52	12	16	29	15.7	7.94	55	.317	.381	0	—	0	-15	-16	-0	-0.4
	Mon-N	2	5	.286	11	11	0	0	0	50	54	8	21	28	13.5	5.94	71	.277	.347	1	.077	-1	-10	-10	0	-1.2
1998	Mon-N	0	2	.000	2	2	0	0	0	7^1	16	4	2	4	23.3	14.73	28	.432	.475	1	.333	0	-9	-9	-0	-1.4
Total	2	2	8	.200	27	18	0	0	2	97	122	24	39	61	15.1	7.42	58	.308	.373	2	.125	-1	-33	-34	-0	-3.0
● **MIKE JOHNSON**	Johnson, Michael Norton b: 3/2/51, Slayton, Minn. BR/TR, 6'1", 185 lbs. Deb: 7/25/74																									
1974	SD-N	0	2	.000	18	0	0	0	0	21^1	29	1	15	15	19.0	4.64	77	.326	.429	0	—	0	-2	-3	-0	-0.2
● **RANDY JOHNSON**	Johnson, Randall David b: 9/10/63, Walnut Creek, Cal. BR/TL, 6'10", 225 lbs. Deb: 9/15/88																									
1988	Mon-N	3	0	1.000	4	4	1	0	0	26	23	3	7	25	10.4	2.42	148	.225	.275	1	.111	-0	3	3	-1	0.3
1989	Mon-N	0	4	.000	7	6	0	0	0	29^2	29	2	26	26	16.7	6.67	53	.264	.404	1	.143	-0	-10	-10	-0	-1.2
	Sea-A	7	9	.438	22	22	2	0	0	131	118	11	70	104	13.1	4.40	92	.244	.344	0	—	0	-7	-5	0	-0.6
1990	Sea-A☆	14	11	.560	33	33	5	2	0	219^2	174	26	120	194	12.3	3.65	109	.216	.321	0	—	0	6	8	-1	0.6
1991	Sea-A	13	10	.565	33	33	2	1	0	201^1	151	15	152	228	14.1	3.98	104	.213	.361	0	—	0	3	3	-1	0.2
1992	Sea-A	12	14	.462	31	31	6	2	0	210^1	154	13	144	**241**	13.5	3.77	105	**.206**	.347	0	—	0	4	5	-1	0.4
1993	Sea-A★	19	8	.704	35	34	10	3	1	255^1	185	22	99	**308**	10.6	3.24	136	**.203**	.292	0	—	0	31	33	1	3.1
1994	Sea-A★	13	6	.684	23	23	**9**	**4**	0	172	132	14	72	**204**	11.0	3.19	153	.216	.304	0	—	0	31	32	2	3.3
1995	*Sea-A★	18	2	**.900**	30	30	6	3	0	214^1	159	12	65	**294**	**9.7**	**2.48**	**191**	**.201**	**.267**	0	—	0	**53**	**54**	1	**4.6**
1996	Sea-A	5	0	1.000	14	8	0	0	1	61^1	48	8	25	85	11.0	3.67	135	.211	.294	0	—	0	9	9	0	0.6
1997	*Sea-A★	20	4	**.833**	30	29	5	2	0	213	147	20	77	291	9.9	2.28	197	**.194**	.277	0	—	0	54	52	-1	5.5
1998	Sea-A	9	10	.474	23	23	6	2	0	160	146	19	60	213	12.2	4.33	107	.240	.320	1	.143	-0	6	5	1	0.6
	*Hou-N	10	1	.909	11	11	4	4	0	84^1	57	4	26	116	9.2	1.28	317	.191	.262	2	.063	-2	28	26	-1	3.2
Total	11	143	79	.644	296	287	56	23	2	1978^1	1523	169	943	2329	11.6	3.36	129	.212	.312	5	.091	-3	209	215	-1	20.6
● **BOB JOHNSON**	Johnson, Robert Dale b: 4/25/43, Aurora, Ill. BL/TR, 6'4", 220 lbs. Deb: 9/19/69																									
1969	NY-N	0	0	—	2	0	0	0	1	1^2	1	0	1	1	10.8	0.00	—	.167	.286	0	—	0	1	1	-0	0.1
1970	KC-A	8	13	.381	40	26	10	1	4	214	178	18	82	206	11.4	3.07	122	.228	.310	6	.105	-1	15	16	-1	1.3
1971	*Pit-N	9	10	.474	31	27	7	1	0	174^2	170	19	55	101	12.0	3.45	98	.259	.323	3	.063	-1	0	-1	-1	-0.4
1972	*Pit-N	4	4	.500	31	11	1	0	3	115^2	98	14	46	79	11.5	2.96	112	.231	.312	5	.143	-0	6	5	-2	0.1
1973	Pit-N	4	2	.667	50	2	0	0	4	92	98	12	34	68	13.4	3.62	97	.276	.348	0	.000	-1	0	-1	-2	-0.4
1974	Cle-A	3	4	.429	14	10	0	0	0	72	75	12	37	36	14.4	4.38	83	.273	.365	0	—	0	-6	-6	-0	-0.6
1977	Atl-N	0	1	.000	15	0	0	0	0	22^1	24	7	14	16	16.1	7.25	61	.270	.381	1	.333	0	-8	-7	-1	-0.3
Total	7	28	34	.452	183	76	18	2	12	692^1	644	82	269	507	12.3	3.48	102	.249	.327	15	.096	-4	9	6	-7	-0.2
● **ROY JOHNSON**	Johnson, Roy J "Hardrock" b: 10/1/1895, Madill, Okla. d: 1/10/86, Scottsdale, Ariz. BR/TR, 6', 185 lbs. Deb: 8/7/18 MC																									
1918	Phi-A	1	5	.167	10	8	3	0	0	50	47	0	34	12	14.9	3.42	86	.254	.376	1	.067	-2	-4	-3	-0	-0.5
● **JING JOHNSON**	Johnson, Russell Conwell b: 10/9/1894, Parker Ford, Pa. d: 12/6/50, Pottstown, Pa. BR/TR, 5'9", 172 lbs. Deb: 6/27/16																									
1916	Phi-A	2	9	.182	12	12	8	0	0	84^1	90	3	39	25	13.8	3.74	76	.288	.368	2	.074	-1	-8	-8	3	-0.8
1917	Phi-A	9	12	.429	34	23	13	0	0	191	184	3	56	55	11.5	2.78	99	.260	.319	12	.203	2	-2	-1	2	0.4
1919	Phi-A	9	15	.375	34	25	12	0	0	202	222	8	62	67	12.8	3.61	95	.291	.346	14	.194	0	-9	-4	5	0.1
1927	Phi-A	4	2	.667	17	3	2	0	0	51^2	42	2	16	16	10.8	3.48	122	.235	.312	2	.167	-0	4	4	1	0.5
1928	Phi-A	0	0	—	3	0	0	0	0	10^2	13	1	5	3	15.2	5.06	79	.310	.383	2	.500	1	-1	-1	0	0.1
Total	5	24	38	.387	100	63	35	0	0	539^2	551	17	178	166	12.4	3.35	95	.275	.338	32	.184	2	-17	-10	10	0.3
● **SI JOHNSON**	Johnson, Silas Kenneth b: 10/5/06, Danway, Ill. d: 5/12/94, Sheridan, Ill. BR/TR, 5'11.5", 185 lbs. Deb: 5/2/28																									
1928	Cin-N	0	0	—	3	0	0	0	0	10^1	9	0	5	1	12.2	4.35	91	.250	.341	1	.250	0	-0	-0	0	0.0
1929	Cin-N	0	0	—	1	0	0	0	0	2	2	0	1	0	13.5	4.50	101	.250	.333	0	—	0	0	0	-0	0.0
1930	Cin-N	3	1	.750	35	3	0	0	0	78^1	86	5	31	47	13.9	4.94	98	.286	.360	4	.235	-0	0	-1	-0	-0.1
1931	Cin-N	11	19	.367	42	33	14	0	0	262^1	273	5	74	95	12.1	3.77	99	.269	.323	13	.149	-3	3	-1	-5	-0.9
1932	Cin-N	13	15	.464	42	27	14	2	2	245	246	8	57	94	11.2	3.27	118	.259	.302	10	.125	-4	17	16	-0	1.3
1933	Cin-N	7	18	.280	34	28	14	4	1	211^1	212	7	54	51	11.5	3.49	97	.263	.312	3	.042	-7	-4	-2	-1	-1.1
1934	Cin-N	7	22	.241	46	31	9	0	3	215^2	264	15	84	89	14.8	5.22	78	.297	.362	10	.139	-3	-28	-27	-3	-3.7
1935	Cin-N	5	11	.313	30	20	4	1	0	130	155	14	59	40	15.0	6.23	64	.293	.367	1	.024	-4	-32	-33	-1	-3.7
1936	Cin-N	0	0	—	2	0	0	0	0	4	7	1	0	2	15.8	13.50	28	.368	.368	0	—	0	-4	-4	-0	0.0
	StL-N	5	3	.625	12	9	3	1	0	61^2	82	4	11	21	13.7	4.38	90	.314	.344	4	.190	-0	-2	-3	-1	-0.5
	Yr	5	3	.625	14	9	3	1	0	65^2	89	5	11	23	13.8	4.93	80	.318	.346	4	.190	-0	-7	-7	-1	-0.5
1937	StL-N	12	12	.500	38	21	12	1	1	192^1	222	14	43	64	12.4	3.32	120	.292	.330	9	.138	-3	13	14	-2	1.2
1938	StL-N	0	3	.000	6	3	0	0	0	15^2	27	0	6	4	19.0	7.47	53	.380	.429	0	.000	-0	-6	-6	0	-1.0
1940	Phi-N	5	14	.263	37	14	5	0	1	138^1	145	13	42	58	12.3	4.88	80	.268	.323	6	.140	-2	-16	-15	-2	-2.3
1941	Phi-N	5	12	.294	39	21	6	1	2	163^1	207	8	54	80	14.4	4.52	82	.309	.362	7	.149	-2	-16	-15	-1	-1.7
1942	Phi-N	8	19	.296	39	26	10	1	0	195^1	198	6	72	78	12.5	3.69	90	.266	.332	6	.103	-4	-8	-8	-3	-1.7
1943	Phi-N	8	3	.727	21	14	9	1	2	113	110	4	25	46	10.8	3.27	103	.252	.292	6	.182	0	1	1	-0	0.1
1946	Phi-N	0	0	—	1	0	0	0	0	3	7	1	0	2	21.0	3.00	114	.538	.538	1	1.000	0	0	0	-0	0.0
	Bos-N	6	5	.545	28	12	5	1	1	127	134	8	35	41	12.3	2.76	124	.272	.325	5	.135	-2	9	9	-1	0.5
	Yr	6	5	.545	29	12	5	1	1	130	141	9	35	43	12.5	2.77	124	.279	.330	6	.158	-1	9	10	-1	0.5
1947	Bos-N	6	8	.429	36	10	3	0	2	112^2	124	7	34	27	12.7	4.23	92	.275	.327	1	.033	-3	-2	-4	3	-0.5
Total	17	101	165	.380	492	272	108	13	15	2281^1	2510	120	687	840	12.8	4.09	92	.279	.333	87	.123	-37	-76	-79	-17	-14.1
● **SYL JOHNSON**	Johnson, Sylvester W (Born Sylvester Johnson) b: 12/31/1900, Portland, Ore. d: 2/20/85, Portland, Ore. BR/TR, 5'11", 180 lbs. Deb: 4/24/22 C																									
1922	Det-A	7	3	.700	29	8	3	0	1	97	99	7	30	29	12.3	3.71	105	.273	.336	8	.222	-0	4	2	-2	0.0
1923	Det-A	12	7	.632	37	18	7	0	0	176^1	181	12	47	93	11.8	3.98	97	.274	.325	10	.161	-1	0	-2	-5	-0.8
1924	Det-A	5	4	.556	29	9	2	0	3	104	117	8	42	55	14.2	4.93	83	.287	.360	7	.206	-0	-8	-9	-1	-0.9
1925	Det-A	0	2	.000	6	0	0	0	0	13	11	1	10	5	14.5	3.46	124	.250	.389	0	.000	-1	1	1	0	0.1
1926	StL-N	0	3	.000	19	6	1	0	1	49	54	3	15	10	13.0	4.22	92	.297	.357	0	.000	-2	-2	-2	-1	-0.4
1927	StL-N	0	0	—	2	0	0	0	0	3	3	1	0	2	9.0	6.00	66	.250	.250	0	—	0	-1	-1	0	0.0
1928	*StL-N	8	4	.667	34	6	2	0	3	120	117	6	33	66	11.6	3.90	103	.259	.315	6	.158	-0	1	1	-1	0.0
1929	StL-N	13	7	.650	42	19	12	3	3	182^1	186	11	56	80	12.3	3.60	129	.265	.325	7	.117	-2	23	21	-4	1.4
1930	*StL-N	12	10	.545	32	24	9	2	2	187^2	215	13	38	92	12.3	4.65	108	.293	.332	15	.214	-0	7	8	-3	0.4
1931	*StL-N	11	9	.550	32	24	12	2	2	186	186	9	29	82	10.5	3.00	131	.255	.286	14	.233	2	18	19	-3	1.8
1932	StL-N	5	14	.263	32	22	7	0	2	164^2	199	14	35	70	13.0	4.92	80	.299	.338	10	.196	-1	-19	-18	-1	-2.0
1933	StL-N	3	3	.500	35	1	0	0	3	84	89	7	16	28	11.6	4.29	81	.271	.311	5	.238	0	-9	-8	-2	-0.7
1934	Cin-N	0	0	—	2	0	0	0	0	6^2	9	2	0	0	12.2	2.70	151	.310	.310	1	.500	1	1	1	-0	0.1
	Phi-N	5	9	.357	42	10	4	3	3	133^2	122	14	24	54	9.9	3.50	135	.242	.277	8	.195	-1	8	18	-4	1.4
	Yr	5	9	.357	44	10	4	3	3	140^1	131	16	24	54	10.0	3.46	136	.245	.279	9	.209	1	9	19	-4	1.5
1935	Phi-N	10	8	.556	37	18	8	1	6	174^2	182	15	31	89	11.1	3.56	128	.265	.299	14	.241	1	9	19	-3	1.7
1936	Phi-N	5	7	.417	39	8	1	0	7	111	129	10	29	48	13.1	4.30	106	.288	.335	9	.250	-0	-3	3	-2	0.1
1937	Phi-N	4	10	.286	32	15	4	0	3	138	155	19	22	46	11.7	5.02	86	.288	.318	7	.146	-3	-17	-11	-1	-1.3
1938	Phi-N	2	7	.222	22	6	2	0	0	83	87	4	11	21	10.6	4.23	92	.267	.291	1	.034	-3	-4	-3	-2	-0.8
1939	Phi-N	8	8	.500	22	13	6	0	2	111	112	10	15	37	10.4	3.81	105	.264	.291	5	.152	-1	1	2	-1	0.1
1940	Phi-N	2	2	.500	17	2	2	0	2	40^2	37	6	5	13	9.3	4.20	93	.236	.259	0	.000	-1	-2	-1	-0	-0.3
Total	19	112	117	.489	542	209	82	11	43	2165^2	2290	172	488	920	11.7	4.06	104	.273	.316	127	.181	-10	8	43	-36	-0.1
● **TOM JOHNSON**	Johnson, Thomas Raymond b: 4/2/51, St.Paul, Minn. BR/TR, 6'1", 185 lbs. Deb: 9/10/74																									
1974	Min-A	2	0	1.000	4	0	0	0	1	7	4	0	0	4	5.1	0.00	—	.167	.167	0	—	0	3	3	-0	1.0
1975	Min-A	1	2	.333	18	0	0	0	3	38^2	40	4	21	17	14.7	4.19	91	.263	.360	0	—	0	-2	-2	0	-0.1

YEAR	TM/L	W	L	PCT	G	GS	CG	SH	SV	IP	H	HR	BB	SO	RAT	ERA	ERA+	OAV	OOB	BH	AVG	PB	PR	/A	PD	TPI
1976	Min-A	3	1	.750	18	1	0	0	0	48^1	44	2	8	37	9.7	2.61	137	.243	.275	0	—	0	5	5	0	0.4
1977	Min-A	16	7	.696	71	0	0	0	15	146^2	152	11	47	87	12.5	3.13	127	.272	.334	0	—	0	15	14	1	2.4
1978	Min-A	1	4	.200	18	0	0	0	3	32^2	42	2	17	21	16.8	5.51	69	.318	.404	0	—	0	-6	-6	0	-1.0
Total	5	23	14	.622	129	1	0	0	22	273^1	282	19	93	166	12.6	3.39	114	.269	.334	0	—	0	15	14	1	2.7

● VIC JOHNSON

Johnson, Victor Oscar b: 8/3/20, Eau Claire, Wis. BR/TL, 6′, 160 lbs. Deb: 5/3/44

YEAR	TM/L	W	L	PCT	G	GS	CG	SH	SV	IP	H	HR	BB	SO	RAT	ERA	ERA+	OAV	OOB	BH	AVG	PB	PR	/A	PD	TPI
1944	Bos-A	0	3	.000	7	5	0	0	0	27^1	42	0	15	7	18.8	6.26	54	.362	.435	0	.000	-1	-9	-9	1	-0.9
1945	Bos-A	6	4	.600	26	9	4	1	2	85^1	90	4	46	21	14.6	4.01	85	.276	.369	5	.167	-1	-6	-6	1	-0.7
1946	Cle-A	0	1	.000	9	1	0	0	0	13^2	20	1	8	3	18.4	9.22	36	.357	.438	0	.000	-0	-9	-9	1	-0.6
Total	3	6	8	.429	42	15	4	1	2	126^1	152	5	69	31	15.9	5.06	67	.305	.392	5	.119	-3	-23	-23	2	-2.2

● WALTER JOHNSON

Johnson, Walter Perry "Barney" or "The Big Train"
b: 11/6/1887, Humboldt, Kan. d: 12/10/46, Washington, D.C. BR/TR, 6′1″, 200 lbs. Deb: 8/2/07 MH♦

YEAR	TM/L	W	L	PCT	G	GS	CG	SH	SV	IP	H	HR	BB	SO	RAT	ERA	ERA+	OAV	OOB	BH	AVG	PB	PR	/A	PD	TPI
1907	Was-A	5	9	.357	14	12	11	2	0	110^1	100	1	20	71	10.0	1.88	129	.244	.282	4	.111	-2	8	7	-2	0.4
1908	Was-A	14	14	.500	36	30	23	6	1	256^1	194	0	53	160	9.1	1.65	139	.211	.262	13	.165	3	21	18	-4	2.0
1909	Was-A	13	25	.342	40	36	27	4	1	296^1	247	1	84	164	10.5	2.22	110	.221	.284	13	.129	-3	9	7	-2	0.4
1910	Was-A	25	17	.595	**45**	42	**38**	8	1	**370**	262	1	76	**313**	8.5	1.36	183	.205	.257	24	.175	1	48	**46**	-1	5.8
1911	Was-A	25	13	.658	40	37	**36**	**6**	1	322^1	292	8	70	207	10.3	1.90	173	.238	.283	30	.234	3	**52**	**50**	4	6.4
1912	Was-A	33	12	.733	50	37	34	7	2	369	259	2	76	**303**	**8.6**	**1.39**	**240**	**.196**	**.248**	38	.264	9	**79**	**80**	1	**11.2**
1913	Was-A	**36**	7	**.837**	48	36	**29**	**11**	2	**346**	232	9	38	**243**	**7.3**	**1.14**	**258**	**.187**	**.217**	35	.261	10	**69**	**70**	0	**10.9**
1914	Was-A	**28**	18	.609	**51**	40	**33**	**9**	1	**371^2**	287	3	74	**225**	9.0	1.72	164	.217	.265	30	.221	8	42	**45**	2	**7.3**
1915	Was-A	**27**	13	.675	47	39	**35**	**7**	4	**336^2**	258	1	56	**203**	**8.9**	1.55	**192**	.214	**.260**	34	.231	6	**52**	**53**	2	**7.7**
1916	Was-A	**25**	20	.556	48	38	**36**	3	1	**369^2**	290	0	82	**228**	9.3	1.90	147	.220	.270	32	.225	8	38	**37**	-5	5.1
1917	Was-A	23	16	.590	47	34	30	8	3	326	248	3	68	**188**	9.1	2.21	119	.211	.263	33	.254	10	16	15	-1	3.0
1918	Was-A	**23**	13	.639	39	29	29	**8**	3	326	241	2	70	**162**	**8.8**	**1.27**	**215**	.210	**.260**	40	.267	6	**55**	**53**	-3	**7.6**
1919	Was-A	20	14	.588	39	29	27	**7**	2	290^1	235	0	51	**147**	9.1	**1.49**	**216**	**.219**	**.259**	24	.192	2	**56**	**56**	0	**7.2**
1920	Was-A	8	10	.444	21	15	12	4	3	143^2	135	5	27	78	10.5	3.13	119	.245	.286	17	.266	4	11	10	-1	1.4
1921	Was-A	17	14	.548	35	32	25	1	1	264	265	7	92	**143**	12.2	3.51	117	.263	.326	30	.270	4	23	18	-3	2.0
1922	Was-A	15	16	.484	41	31	23	4	4	280	283	8	99	105	12.5	2.99	129	.267	.334	22	.204	-1	33	27	1	2.8
1923	Was-A	17	12	.586	42	34	18	3	4	261	263	9	73	**130**	12.3	3.48	108	.269	.333	18	.194	1	15	8	-2	0.7
1924	*Was-A	**23**	7	**.767**	38	38	20	**6**	0	277^2	233	10	77	**158**	**10.4**	**2.72**	148	**.224**	**.284**	32	.283	7	**47**	41	-1	**4.5**
1925	*Was-A	20	7	.741	30	29	16	3	0	229	217	7	78	108	11.9	3.07	138	**.250**	.317	42	.433	17	34	30	-4	**4.3**
1926	Was-A	15	16	.484	33	33	22	2	0	260^2	259	13	73	125	11.6	3.63	107	.263	.317	20	.194	1	11	7	-5	0.3
1927	Was-A	5	6	.455	18	15	7	1	0	107^2	113	7	26	48	12.2	5.10	80	.278	.332	16	.348	6	-11	-12	0	-0.5
Total	21	417	279	.599	802	666	531	110	34	5914^1	4913	97	1363	3509	9.9	2.17	147	.227	.279	547	.235	99	706	668	-23	90.5

● BILL JOHNSON

Johnson, William Charles b: 10/6/60, Wilmington, Del. BR/TR, 6′5″, 205 lbs. Deb: 9/6/83

YEAR	TM/L	W	L	PCT	G	GS	CG	SH	SV	IP	H	HR	BB	SO	RAT	ERA	ERA+	OAV	OOB	BH	AVG	PB	PR	/A	PD	TPI
1983	Chi-N	1	0	1.000	10	0	0	0	0	12^1	17	0	3	4	14.6	4.38	87	.347	.385	0	—	0	-1	-1	0	0.0
1984	Chi-N	0	0	—	4	0	0	0	0	5^1	4	0	1	3	8.4	1.69	232	.235	.278	0	—	0	1	1	0	0.0
Total	2	1	0	1.000	14	0	0	0	0	17^2	21	0	4	7	12.7	3.57	107	.318	.357	0	—	0	0	1	1	0.0

● JEFF JOHNSON

Johnson, William Jeffrey b: 8/4/66, Durham, N.C. BR/TL, 6′3″, 200 lbs. Deb: 6/5/91

YEAR	TM/L	W	L	PCT	G	GS	CG	SH	SV	IP	H	HR	BB	SO	RAT	ERA	ERA+	OAV	OOB	BH	AVG	PB	PR	/A	PD	TPI
1991	NY-A	6	11	.353	23	23	0	0	0	127	156	15	33	62	13.8	5.95	70	.305	.354	0	—	0	-26	-26	1	-2.8
1992	NY-A	2	3	.400	13	8	0	0	0	52^2	71	4	23	14	16.4	6.66	59	.329	.398	0	—	0	-16	-16	-0	-1.3
1993	NY-A	0	2	.000	2	2	0	0	0	2^2	12	1	2	0	47.3	30.38	14	.600	.636	0	—	0	-8	-8	-0	-2.6
Total	3	8	16	.333	38	33	0	0	0	182^1	239	20	58	76	15.1	6.52	63	.320	.375	0	—	0	-50	-49	1	-6.7

● JOEL JOHNSTON

Johnston, Joel Raymond b: 3/8/67, West Chester, Pa. BR/TR, 6′4″, 220 lbs. Deb: 9/5/91

YEAR	TM/L	W	L	PCT	G	GS	CG	SH	SV	IP	H	HR	BB	SO	RAT	ERA	ERA+	OAV	OOB	BH	AVG	PB	PR	/A	PD	TPI
1991	KC-A	1	0	1.000	13	0	0	0	0	22^1	9	0	9	21	7.3	0.40	1022	.120	.214	0	—	0	9	9	-0	0.3
1992	KC-A	0	0	—	5	0	0	0	0	2^2	3	2	2	0	16.9	13.50	30	.273	.385	0	—	0	-3	-3	-0	-0.2
1993	Pit-N	2	4	.333	33	0	0	0	2	53^1	38	7	19	31	9.6	3.38	120	.203	.277	2	.333	1	4	4	-1	0.5
1994	Pit-N	0	0	—	4	0	0	0	0	3^1	14	0	4	5	54.0	29.70	15	.583	.667	0	—	0	-9	-9	-0	0.0
1995	Bos-A	0	1	.000	4	0	0	0	0	4	2	1	3	4	13.5	11.25	43	.143	.333	0	—	0	-3	-3	-0	-0.8
Total	5	3	5	.375	59	0	0	0	2	85^2	66	10	37	61	11.1	4.31	96	.212	.302	2	.333	1	-2	-2	-1	-0.2

● JOHN JOHNSTONE

Johnstone, John William b: 11/25/68, Liverpool, N.Y. BR/TR, 6′3″, 195 lbs. Deb: 9/3/93

YEAR	TM/L	W	L	PCT	G	GS	CG	SH	SV	IP	H	HR	BB	SO	RAT	ERA	ERA+	OAV	OOB	BH	AVG	PB	PR	/A	PD	TPI
1993	Fla-N	0	2	.000	7	0	0	0	0	10^2	16	1	7	5	19.4	5.91	73	.340	.426	0	—	0	-2	-2	-0	-0.3
1994	Fla-N	1	2	.333	17	0	0	0	0	21^1	23	4	16	23	16.9	5.91	74	.264	.385	0	—	0	-4	-4	0	-0.4
1995	Fla-N	0	0	—	4	0	0	0	0	4^2	7	1	2	3	17.4	3.86	109	.333	.391	0	—	0	0	0	-0	0.0
1996	Hou-N	1	0	1.000	9	0	0	0	0	13	17	2	5	5	15.2	5.54	70	.321	.379	0	—	0	-2	-2	-0	-0.2
1997	SF-N	0	0	—	13	0	0	0	0	18^2	15	1	7	15	12.5	3.38	122	.234	.347	0	.000	-0	2	2	0	0.0
	Oak-A	0	0	—	5	0	0	0	0	6^1	7	0	7	4	19.9	2.84	159	.292	.452	0	—	0	1	1	-0	0.0
1998	SF-N	6	5	.545	70	0	0	0	0	88	72	10	38	86	11.4	3.07	132	.223	.307	0	.000	-0	11	10	-1	1.0
Total	6	8	9	.471	125	0	0	0	0	162^2	157	19	82	141	13.6	3.87	107	.254	.347	0	.000	-0	6	5	-1	0.1

● ROY JOINER

Joiner, Roy Merrill "Pop" b: 10/30/06, Red Bluff, Cal. d: 12/26/89, Red Bluff, Cal. BL/TL, 6′, 170 lbs. Deb: 4/30/34

YEAR	TM/L	W	L	PCT	G	GS	CG	SH	SV	IP	H	HR	BB	SO	RAT	ERA	ERA+	OAV	OOB	BH	AVG	PB	PR	/A	PD	TPI
1934	Chi-N	0	1	.000	20	2	0	0	0	34	61	3	8	9	18.3	8.21	47	.391	.421	2	.200	-0	-16	-16	-0	-0.5
1935	Chi-N	0	0	—	2	0	0	0	0	3^1	6	0	2	0	21.6	5.40	73	.429	.500	0	.000	-0	-1	-1	0	0.0
1940	NY-N	3	2	.600	30	2	0	0	1	53	66	8	17	25	14.9	3.40	114	.308	.373	3	.273	1	3	3	0	0.3
Total	3	3	3	.500	52	4	0	0	1	90^1	133	11	27	34	16.4	5.28	74	.346	.397	5	.227	0	-13	-14	0	-0.2

● DAVE JOLLY

Jolly, David "Gabby" b: 10/14/24, Stony Point, N.C. d: 5/27/63, Durham, N.C. BR/TR, 6′, 165 lbs. Deb: 5/9/53

YEAR	TM/L	W	L	PCT	G	GS	CG	SH	SV	IP	H	HR	BB	SO	RAT	ERA	ERA+	OAV	OOB	BH	AVG	PB	PR	/A	PD	TPI
1953	Mil-N	0	1	.000	24	0	0	0	0	38^1	34	4	27	23	14.6	3.52	111	.239	.365	1	.500	1	3	2	0	0.1
1954	Mil-N	11	6	.647	47	1	0	0	10	111^1	87	6	64	62	12.4	2.43	154	.215	.326	9	.290	3	20	16	0	3.0
1955	Mil-N	2	3	.400	36	0	0	0	1	58^1	58	6	51	23	17.0	5.71	66	.258	.397	1	.167	0	-11	-13	1	-0.9
1956	Mil-N	2	3	.400	29	0	0	0	7	45^2	39	7	35	20	14.6	3.74	92	.228	.359	0	.000	-0	0	-1	-1	-0.3
1957	Mil-N	1	1	.500	23	0	0	0	1	37^2	37	4	21	27	14.6	5.02	70	.264	.372	3	.600	1	-5	-6	0	-0.2
Total	5	16	14	.533	159	1	0	0	19	291^1	255	27	198	155	14.2	3.77	98	.236	.357	14	.292	5	8	-3	0	1.7

● COWBOY JONES

Jones, Albert Edward "Bronco" b: 8/23/1874, Golden, Colo. d: 2/9/58, Inglewood, Cal. BL/TL, 5′11″, 160 lbs. Deb: 6/24/1898

YEAR	TM/L	W	L	PCT	G	GS	CG	SH	SV	IP	H	HR	BB	SO	RAT	ERA	ERA+	OAV	OOB	BH	AVG	PB	PR	/A	PD	TPI
1898	Cle-N	4	4	.500	9	9	7	0	0	72	76	0	29	26	13.6	3.00	121	.269	.345	2	.071	-3	5	5	-2	0.0
1899	StL-N	6	5	.545	12	12	9	0	0	85^1	111	1	22	28	14.7	3.59	111	.314	.364	5	.172	0	3	4	2	0.6
1900	StL-N	13	19	.406	39	36	29	3	0	292^2	334	10	82	68	13.4	3.57	102	.286	.343	21	.179	-3	4	2	5	0.4
1901	StL-N	2	6	.250	10	9	7	0	0	76^1	97	4	22	25	14.4	4.48	71	.307	.358	4	.148	0	-10	-11	2	-0.8
Total	4	25	34	.424	70	66	52	3	0	526^1	618	15	155	147	13.8	3.63	100	.292	.349	32	.159	-5	2	-0	6	0.2

● ALEX JONES

Jones, Alexander b: 12/25/1869, Pittsburgh, Pa. d: 4/4/41, Woodville, Pa. BL/TL, 5′6″, 135 lbs. Deb: 9/25/1889

YEAR	TM/L	W	L	PCT	G	GS	CG	SH	SV	IP	H	HR	BB	SO	RAT	ERA	ERA+	OAV	OOB	BH	AVG	PB	PR	/A	PD	TPI
1889	Pit-N	1	0	1.000	1	1	1	0	0	9	7	0	1	10	8.0	3.00	125	.206	.229	1	.200	0	1	1	0	0.1
1892	Lou-N	5	11	.313	18	16	13	1	0	146^2	130	3	56	44	12.0	3.31	93	.228	.307	8	.145	-1	-0	-4	2	-0.3
	Was-N	0	3	.000	4	4	3	0	0	27	33	0	14	7	16.3	4.00	81	.289	.377	3	.273	0	-2	-2	-1	-0.2
	Yr	5	14	.263	22	20	16	1	0	173^2	163	3	70	51	12.2	3.42	91	.235	.307	11	.167	-1	-3	-6	1	-0.5
1894	Phi-N	1	0	1.000	1	1	1	0	0	9	10	0	0	2	10.0	2.00	255	.278	.278	1	.250	-0	3	3	0	0.2
1903	Det-A	0	1	.000	2	2	0	0	0	8^2	19	0	6	2	26.0	12.46	23	.432	.500	0	.000	-1	-9	-9	-0	-0.8
Total	4	7	15	.318	26	24	18	1	0	200^1	199	3	77	65	12.9	3.73	86	.249	.324	13	.165	-1	-7	-12	1	-1.0

● AL JONES

Jones, Alfornia b: 2/10/59, Charleston, Miss. BR/TR, 6′4″, 210 lbs. Deb: 8/6/83

YEAR	TM/L	W	L	PCT	G	GS	CG	SH	SV	IP	H	HR	BB	SO	RAT	ERA	ERA+	OAV	OOB	BH	AVG	PB	PR	/A	PD	TPI
1983	Chi-A	0	0	—	2	0	0	0	0	2^1	3	0	2	2	19.3	3.86	109	.375	.500	0	—	0	0	0	-0	0.0
1984	Chi-A	1	1	.500	20	0	0	0	5	20^1	23	3	11	15	15.5	4.43	94	.299	.393	0	—	0	-1	-1	0	-0.3
1985	Chi-A	1	0	1.000	5	0	0	0	0	6	3	0	3	2	9.0	1.50	288	.167	.286	0	—	0	2	2	0	0.3
Total	3	2	1	.667	27	0	0	0	5	28^2	29	3	16	19	14.4	3.77	111	.282	.383	0	—	0	1	1	0	0.0

YEAR	TM/L	W	L	PCT	G	GS	CG	SH	SV	IP	H	HR	BB	SO	RAT	ERA	ERA+	OAV	OOB	BH	AVG	PB	PR	/A	PD	TPI
● **ART JONES**	Jones, Arthur Lennox b: 2/7/06, Kershaw, S.C. d: 11/25/80, Columbia, S.C. BR/TR, 6′, 165 lbs. Deb: 4/23/32																									
1932	Bro-N	0	0	—	1	0	0	0	0	1	2	0	1	0	27.0	18.00	21	.667	.750	0	—	0	-2	-2	0	0.0
● **BARRY JONES**	Jones, Barry Louis b: 2/15/63, Centerville, Ind. BR/TR, 6′4″, 225 lbs. Deb: 7/18/86																									
1986	Pit-N	3	4	.429	26	0	0	0	3	37^{1}	29	3	21	29	12.1	2.89	132	.215	.321	1	.200	0	3	4	1	0.8
1987	Pit-N	2	4	.333	32	0	0	0	1	43^{1}	55	6	23	28	16.2	5.61	73	.314	.394	0	.000	-0	-7	-7	0	-0.9
1988	Pit-N	1	1	.500	42	0	0	0	2	56^{1}	57	3	21	31	12.6	3.04	112	.271	.341	0	.000	-0	3	2	0	0.0
	Chi-A	2	2	.500	17	0	0	0	1	26	15	3	17	17	11.1	2.42	164	.170	.305	0	—	0	4	4	0	0.7
1989	Chi-A	3	2	.600	22	0	0	0	1	30^{1}	22	2	8	17	9.2	2.37	160	.208	.270	0	—	0	5	5	1	0.9
1990	Chi-A	11	4	.733	65	0	0	0	1	74	62	2	33	45	11.7	2.31	165	.235	.322	0	—	0	13	12	2	2.7
1991	Mon-N	4	9	.308	**77**	0	0	0	13	88^{2}	76	8	33	46	11.2	3.35	108	.246	.321	0	.000	-0	3	3	1	0.5
1992	Phi-N	5	6	.455	44	0	0	0	0	54^{1}	65	3	24	19	15.1	4.64	75	.305	.381	0	.000	-0	-7	-7	1	-1.3
	NY-N	2	0	1.000	17	0	0	0	1	15^{1}	20	0	11	11	18.2	9.39	37	.317	.419	0	—	0	-10	-10	0	-1.3
	Yr	7	6	.538	61	0	0	0	1	69^{2}	85	3	35	30	15.5	5.68	61	.304	.381	0	.000	-0	-17	-17	1	-2.6
1993	Chi-A	0	1	.000	6	0	0	0	0	7^{1}	14	2	3	7	20.9	8.59	49	.412	.459	0	—	0	-3	-4	-0	-0.3
Total	8	33	33	.500	348	0	0	0	23	433	415	32	194	250	12.8	3.66	102	.260	.342	1	.063	-1	4	3	5	1.8
● **CALVIN JONES**	Jones, Calvin Douglas b: 9/26/63, Compton, Cal. BR/TR, 6′3″, 185 lbs. Deb: 6/14/91																									
1991	Sea-A	2	2	.500	27	0	0	0	2	46^{1}	33	0	29	42	12.2	2.53	163	.209	.335	0	—	0	8	8	0	0.7
1992	Sea-A	3	5	.375	38	1	0	0	0	61^{2}	50	8	47	49	14.4	5.69	70	.226	.367	0	—	0	-12	-12	-0	-1.4
Total	2	5	7	.417	65	1	0	0	2	108	83	8	76	91	13.5	4.33	93	.219	.354	0	—	0	-4	-4	0	-0.7
● **DEACON JONES**	Jones, Carroll Elmer b: 12/20/1892, Arcadia, Kan. d: 12/28/52, Pittsburg, Kan. BR/TR, 6′1″, 174 lbs. Deb: 9/23/16																									
1916	Det-A	0	0	—	1	0	0	0	0	7	7	0	5	2	15.4	2.57	111	.269	.387	0	.000	-0	0	0	-0	0.0
1917	Det-A	4	4	.500	24	6	2	0	0	77	69	0	26	28	11.8	2.92	91	.256	.334	0	.000	-1	-2	-2	1	-0.2
1918	Det-A	3	2	.600	21	4	1	0	0	67	60	0	38	15	13.3	3.09	86	.244	.347	5	.185	-1	-2	-3	1	-0.2
Total	3	7	6	.538	46	10	3	0	0	151	136	0	69	45	12.6	2.98	89	.251	.343	5	.114	-2	-4	-5	2	-0.4
● **BUMPUS JONES**	Jones, Charles Leander b: 1/1/1870, Cedarville, Ohio d: 6/25/38, Xenia, Ohio BR/TR, Deb: 10/15/1892																									
1892	Cin-N	1	0	1.000	1	1	1	0	0	9	0	0	4	3	4.0	0.00	—	.000	.129	0	.000	-0	3	3	-1	0.3
1893	Cin-N	1	3	.250	6	5	2	0	0	28^{2}	37	1	23	6	20.4	10.05	48	.303	.433	4	.250	1	-17	-17	-1	-1.5
	NY-N	0	1	.000	1	1	0	0	0	4	5	0	10	1	36.0	11.25	41	.294	.571	0	—	0	-3	-3	1	-0.4
	Yr	1	4	.200	7	6	2	0	0	32^{2}	42	1	33	7	20.9	10.19	47	.292	.427	4	.250	1	-20	-20	-0	-1.9
Total	2	2	4	.333	8	7	3	0	0	41^{2}	42	1	37	10	18.4	7.99	56	.253	.407	4	.222	1	-17	-16	-1	-1.6
● **CHARLEY JONES**	Jones, Charles Wesley "Baby" (b: Benjamin Wesley Rippay) b: 4/30/1850, Alamance Co., N.C. BR/TR, 5′11.5″, 202 lbs. Deb: 5/4/1875 U♦																									
1887	NY-a	0	0	—	2	0	0	0	0	3	2	0	4	0	18.0	3.00	142	.286	.545	63	.255	0	0	0	-0	0.0
● **DALE JONES**	Jones, Dale Eldon "Nubs" b: 12/17/18, Marquette, Neb. d: 11/8/80, Orlando, Fla. BR/TR, 6′1″, 172 lbs. Deb: 9/7/41																									
1941	Phi-N	0	1	.000	2	1	0	0	0	8^{1}	13	0	6	2	20.5	7.56	49	.342	.432	1	.333	0	-4	-4	-1	-0.4
● **JACK JONES**	Jones, Daniel Albion "Jumping Jack" b: 10/23/1860, Litchfield, Conn. d: 10/19/36, Wallingford, Conn. TR, Deb: 7/9/1883																									
1883	Det-N	6	5	.545	12	12	9	1	0	92^{2}	103	0	19	33	11.8	3.50	89	.259	.293	8	.190	-2	-4	-4	-2	-0.6
	Phi-a	5	2	.714	7	7	7	0	0	65	58	1	6	28	8.9	2.63	132	.223	.241	6	.240	0	5	6	-0	0.5
Total	1	11	7	.611	19	19	16	1	0	157^{2}	161	1	25	61	10.6	3.14	104	.245	.273	14	.209	-1	1	2	-2	-0.1
● **DICK JONES**	Jones, Decatur Poindexter b: 5/22/02, Meadville, Miss. d: 8/2/94, Burlingame, Cal. BL/TR, 6′, 184 lbs. Deb: 9/11/26																									
1926	Was-A	2	1	.667	4	3	1	0	0	21	20	0	11	3	13.3	4.29	90	.263	.356	2	.200	-0	-1	-1	0	-0.1
1927	Was-A	0	0	—	2	0	0	0	0	3^{1}	8	0	5	1	35.1	21.60	19	.444	.565	0	—	0	-6	-6	-0	0.0
Total	2	2	1	.667	6	3	1	0	0	24^{1}	28	0	16	4	16.3	6.66	58	.298	.400	2	.200	-0	-7	-7	-0	-0.1
● **DOUG JONES**	Jones, Douglas Reid b: 6/24/57, Lebanon, Ind. BR/TR, 6′2″, 195 lbs. Deb: 4/9/82																									
1982	Mil-A	0	0	—	4	0	0	0	0	2^{2}	5	1	1	1	20.3	10.13	37	.385	.429	0	—	0	-2	-2	0	0.0
1986	Cle-A	1	0	1.000	11	0	0	0	1	18	18	0	6	12	12.5	2.50	166	.257	.325	0	—	0	3	3	0	0.2
1987	Cle-A	6	5	.545	49	0	0	0	8	91^{1}	101	4	24	87	12.9	3.15	143	.281	.336	0	—	0	13	14	1	1.8
1988	Cle-A★	3	4	.429	51	0	0	0	37	83^{1}	69	1	16	72	9.4	2.27	181	.218	.260	0	—	0	16	17	0	2.8
1989	Cle-A★	7	10	.412	59	0	0	0	32	80^{2}	76	4	13	65	10.0	2.34	169	.251	.284	0	—	0	14	14	1	4.0
1990	Cle-A☆	5	5	.500	66	0	0	0	43	84^{1}	66	5	22	55	9.6	2.56	153	.218	.275	0	—	0	13	13	-1	2.4
1991	Cle-A	4	8	.333	36	4	0	0	7	63^{1}	87	7	17	48	14.8	5.54	75	.320	.360	0	—	0	-10	-10	1	-1.8
1992	Hou-N★	11	8	.579	80	0	0	0	36	111^{2}	96	5	17	93	9.5	1.85	181	.235	.274	0	.000	-0	20	19	-1	4.2
1993	Hou-N	4	10	.286	71	0	0	0	26	85^{1}	102	7	21	66	13.5	4.54	85	.298	.348	0	—	0	-5	-6	-0	-1.3
1994	Phi-N★	2	4	.333	47	0	0	0	27	54	55	2	6	38	10.2	2.17	198	.255	.275	1	1.000	0	12	**13**	0	2.5
1995	Bal-A	0	4	.000	52	0	0	0	22	46^{2}	55	6	16	42	14.1	5.01	95	.286	.348	0	—	0	-2	-1	0	-0.3
1996	Chi-N	2	2	.500	28	0	0	0	2	32^{1}	41	4	7	26	13.6	5.01	86	.306	.345	0	—	0	-3	-2	-0	-0.3
	Mil-A	5	0	1.000	24	0	0	0	1	31^{2}	31	3	13	34	13.1	3.41	152	.254	.336	0	—	0	6	6	0	0.9
1997	Mil-A	6	6	.500	75	0	0	0	36	80^{1}	62	4	9	82	8.3	2.02	229	.215	.246	0	—	0	23	23	-0	4.9
1998	Mil-N	3	4	.429	46	0	0	0	12	54	65	15	11	43	13.3	5.17	83	.298	.343	0	.000	-0	-6	-5	0	-0.8
	*Cle-A	1	2	.333	23	0	0	0	1	31^{1}	34	2	6	28	11.5	3.45	139	.279	.313	0	—	0	4	5	1	0.5
Total	14	60	72	.455	722	4	0	0	291	951	963	70	205	792	11.4	3.23	129	.262	.307	1	.143	0	97	99	0	19.7
● **EARL JONES**	Jones, Earl Leslie "Lefty" b: 6/11/19, Fresno, Cal. d: 1/24/89, Fresno, Cal. BL/TL, 5′10.5″, 190 lbs. Deb: 7/6/45																									
1945	StL-A	0	0	—	10	0	0	0	1	28^{1}	18	0	18	13	11.4	2.54	139	.184	.310	2	.200	1	3	3	-1	0.1
● **ELIJAH JONES**	Jones, Elijah Albert "Bumpus" b: 1/27/1882, Oxford, Mich. d: 4/29/43, Pontiac, Mich. BR/TR, 5′11.5″, Deb: 4/13/07																									
1907	Det-A	0	1	.000	4	1	1	0	1	16	23	0	4	9	15.8	5.06	51	.338	.384	0	.000	-1	-4	-4	-0	-0.4
1909	Det-A	1	1	.500	2	2	0	0	0	10	10	0	0	2	9.0	2.70	93	.278	.278	1	.250	0	-0	-0	-0	-0.1
Total	2	1	2	.333	6	3	1	0	1	26	33	0	4	11	13.2	4.15	62	.317	.349	1	.125	-0	-5	-5	-1	-0.5
● **GARY JONES**	Jones, Gareth Howell b: 6/12/45, Huntington Park, Cal. BL/TL, 6′, 191 lbs. Deb: 9/25/70 F																									
1970	NY-A	0	0	—	2	0	0	0	0	2	3	0	1	2	18.0	0.00	—	.375	.444	0	—	0	1	1	-0	0.0
1971	NY-A	0	0	—	12	0	0	0	0	14	19	1	7	10	16.7	9.00	36	.317	.388	0	.000	-0	-9	-9	-0	0.0
Total	2	0	0	—	14	0	0	0	0	16	22	1	8	12	16.9	7.88	41	.324	.395	0	.000	-0	-8	-8	-0	0.0
● **GORDON JONES**	Jones, Gordon Bassett b: 4/2/30, Portland, Ore. d: 4/25/94, Lodi, Cal. BR/TR, 6′, 190 lbs. Deb: 8/6/54 C																									
1954	StL-N	4	4	.500	11	10	4	2	0	81	78	3	19	48	10.9	2.00	206	.248	.293	3	.125	-1	19	19	-0	1.7
1955	StL-N	1	4	.200	15	9	0	0	0	57	66	10	28	46	15.0	5.84	70	.286	.365	1	.071	-1	-11	-11	-1	-1.1
1956	StL-N	0	2	.000	5	1	0	0	0	11^{1}	14	2	5	6	15.1	5.56	68	.311	.380	0	.000	-0	-2	-2	0	-0.4
1957	NY-N	0	1	.000	10	0	0	0	0	11^{2}	16	1	3	5	15.4	6.17	64	.320	.370	1	.500	0	-3	-3	-1	-0.2
1958	SF-N	3	1	.750	11	1	0	0	1	30^{1}	33	2	5	8	11.6	2.37	161	.284	.320	0	.000	-1	5	5	1	0.6
1959	SF-N	3	2	.600	31	0	0	0	2	43^{2}	45	6	19	29	13.4	4.33	88	.280	.359	0	.000	-0	-2	-3	-0	-0.4
1960	Bal-A	1	1	.500	29	0	0	0	2	55	59	9	13	30	11.9	4.42	86	.281	.326	2	.400	1	-3	-4	0	-0.1
1961	Bal-A	0	0	—	3	0	0	0	1	5	5	3	0	4	9.0	5.40	71	.250	.250	0	—	0	-1	-1	-0	0.0
1962	KC-A	3	2	.600	21	0	0	0	6	32^{2}	31	10	14	28	12.4	6.34	67	.252	.328	0	.000	-1	-9	-8	-0	-1.4
1964	Hou-N	0	1	.000	34	0	0	0	0	50	58	3	14	28	13.0	4.14	83	.290	.336	1	.250	0	-3	-4	-0	-0.1
1965	Hou-N	0	0	—	1	0	0	0	0	1	0	0	0	0	0.0	0.00	—	.000	.000	0	—	0	0	0	-0	0.0
Total	11	15	18	.455	171	21	4	2	12	378^{2}	405	49	120	232	12.6	4.16	94	.275	.332	8	.119	-3	-10	-11	-2	-1.4
● **HENRY JONES**	Jones, Henry b: Pittsburgh, Pa. Deb: 4/22/1890																									
1890	Pit-N	2	1	.667	5	4	2	0	0	31	35	1	14	13	14.2	3.48	95	.276	.348	2	.222	-0	0	-1	-1	-0.1
● **JIMMY JONES**	Jones, James Condia b: 4/20/64, Dallas, Tex. BR/TR, 6′2″, 190 lbs. Deb: 9/21/86																									
1986	SD-N	2	0	1.000	3	3	1	1	0	18	10	1	3	15	6.5	2.50	146	.164	.203	1	.167	-0	2	2	-0	0.2

YEAR	TM/L	W	L	PCT	G	GS	CG	SH	SV	IP	H	HR	BB	SO	RAT	ERA	ERA+	OAV	OOB	BH	AVG	PB	PR	/A	PD	TPI
1987	SD-N	9	7	.563	30	22	2	1	0	145^2	154	14	54	51	13.2	4.14	96	.270	.339	8	.163	1	-1	-3	1	0.0
1988	SD-N	9	14	.391	29	29	3	0	0	179	192	14	44	82	12.0	4.12	82	.277	.323	9	.164	2	-13	-14	1	-1.4
1989	NY-A	2	1	.667	11	6	0	0	0	48	56	7	16	25	13.9	5.25	74	.293	.354	0	—	0	-7	-7	1	-0.3
1990	NY-A	1	2	.333	17	7	0	0	0	50	72	8	23	25	17.3	6.30	63	.344	.412	0	—	0	-13	-13	-1	-0.8
1991	Hou-N	6	8	.429	26	22	1	1	0	135^1	143	9	51	88	13.1	4.39	80	.270	.337	7	.184	2	-11	-13	1	-1.0
1992	Hou-N	10	6	.625	25	23	0	0	0	139^1	135	13	39	69	11.6	4.07	83	.258	.315	6	.167	2	-9	-11	-1	-1.1
1993	Mon-N	4	1	.800	12	6	0	0	0	39^2	47	6	9	21	12.7	6.35	66	.285	.322	1	.111	0	-10	-10	-0	-1.0
Total	8	43	39	.524	153	118	7	3	0	755	809	72	239	376	12.7	4.46	81	.275	.333	32	.166	7	-62	-69	3	-5.4
● **JIM JONES**	Jones, James Tilford "Sheriff" b: 12/25/1876, London, Ky. d: 5/6/53, London, Ky. BR/TR, 5'10", 162 lbs. Deb: 6/29/1897 ♦																									
1897	Lou-N	0	0	—	1	0	0	0	0	6^2	19	1	5	0	35.1	18.90	23	.500	.578	1	.250	1	-11	-11	-0	0.0
1901	NY-N	0	1	.000	1	1	1	0	0	5	6	0	2	3	14.4	10.80	31	.300	.364	19	.209	0	-4	-4	0	-0.5
Total	2	0	1	.000	2	1	1	0	0	11^2	25	1	7	3	26.2	15.43	25	.431	.507	79	.230	1	-15	-15	-0	-0.5
● **JEFF JONES**	Jones, Jeffrey Allen b: 7/29/56, Detroit, Mich. BR/TR, 6'3", 210 lbs. Deb: 4/10/80																									
1980	Oak-A	1	3	.250	35	0	0	0	5	44^1	32	2	26	34	12.0	2.84	133	.204	.321	0	—	0	6	5	1	0.6
1981	*Oak-A	4	1	.800	33	0	0	0	3	61	51	7	40	43	13.9	3.39	102	.233	.359	0	—	0	2	1	-1	0.0
1982	Oak-A	3	1	.750	18	2	0	0	0	37	44	6	26	18	17.3	5.11	76	.306	.415	0	—	0	-4	-5	-0	-0.5
1983	Oak-A	1	1	.500	13	1	0	0	0	29^2	43	7	8	14	16.1	5.76	67	.339	.387	0	—	0	-6	-6	-0	-0.4
1984	Oak-A	0	3	.000	13	0	0	0	0	33	31	4	12	19	11.7	3.55	106	.258	.326	0	—	0	2	1	-0	0.4
Total	5	9	9	.500	112	3	0	0	8	205	201	26	112	128	14.0	3.95	94	.262	.361	0	—	0	-1	-5	-0	0.1
● **BROADWAY JONES**	Jones, Jesse Frank b: 11/15/1898, Millsboro, Del. d: 9/7/77, Lewes, Del. BR/TR, 5'9", 154 lbs. Deb: 7/4/23																									
1923	Phi-N	0	0	—	3	0	0	0	0	8	5	0	7	1	13.5	9.00	51	.185	.353	1	.500	0	-4	-4	-0	0.0
● **JOHNNY JONES**	Jones, John Paul "Admiral" b: 8/25/1892, Arcadia, La. d: 6/5/80, Ruston, La. BR/TR, 6'1", 151 lbs. Deb: 4/24/19																									
1919	NY-N	0	0	—	2	0	0	0	1	6^2	9	0	3	3	17.6	5.40	52	.310	.394	0	.000	-0	-2	-2	0	-0.1
1920	Bos-N	1	0	1.000	3	1	0	0	0	9^2	16	1	5	6	19.6	6.52	47	.372	.438	1	.250	1	-4	-4	0	-0.3
Total	2	1	0	1.000	5	1	0	0	1	16^1	25	1	8	9	18.7	6.06	49	.347	.420	1	.143	0	-5	-6	0	-0.4
● **STACY JONES**	Jones, Joseph Stacy b: 5/26/67, Gadsden, Ala. BR/TR, 6'6", 225 lbs. Deb: 7/30/91																									
1991	Bal-A	0	0	—	4	1	0	0	0	11	11	1	5	10	13.1	4.09	97	.256	.333	0	—	0	0	-0	0	0.3
1996	Chi-A	0	0	—	2	0	0	0	0	2	0	0	1	1	4.5	0.00	—	.000	.143	0	—	0	1	1	-0	0.0
Total	2	0	0	—	6	1	0	0	0	13	11	1	6	11	11.8	3.46	118	.224	.309	0	—	0	1	1	0	0.3
● **KEN JONES**	Jones, Kenneth Frederick "Broadway" b: 4/13/03, Dover, N.J. d: 5/15/91, Hartford, Conn. BR/TR, 6'3", 193 lbs. Deb: 5/19/24																									
1924	Det-A	0	0	—	1	0	0	0	0	2	1	0	1	0	9.0	0.00	—	.143	.250	0	—	0	1	1	-0	0.0
1930	Bos-N	0	1	.000	8	1	0	0	0	19^2	28	1	4	4	14.6	5.95	83	.359	.390	1	.200	-0	-2	-2	0	-0.1
Total	2	0	1	.000	9	1	0	0	0	21^2	29	1	5	4	14.1	5.40	90	.341	.378	1	.200	-0	-1	-1	0	-0.1
● **MIKE JONES**	Jones, Michael b: 7/6/1865, Hamilton, Ont., Canada d: 3/24/1894, Hamilton, Ont., Canada BL/TL, 5'11.5", 168 lbs. Deb: 8/12/1890																									
1890	Lou-a	2	0	1.000	3	3	2	0	0	22	21	2	9	6	12.3	3.27	118	.244	.316	4	.444	2	1	1	-0	0.2
● **MIKE JONES**	Jones, Michael Carl b: 7/30/59, Penfield, N.Y. BL/TL, 6'6", 215 lbs. Deb: 9/6/80																									
1980	KC-A	0	1	.000	3	1	0	0	0	4^2	6	0	5	2	21.2	11.57	35	.333	.478	0	—	0	-4	-4	-0	-0.7
1981	*KC-A	6	3	.667	12	11	0	0	0	75^2	74	7	28	29	12.4	3.21	112	.256	.326	0	—	0	4	3	0	0.4
1984	*KC-A	2	3	.400	23	12	0	0	0	81	86	10	36	43	13.7	4.89	82	.270	.346	0	—	0	-8	-8	-1	-0.5
1985	KC-A	3	3	.500	33	1	0	0	0	64	62	6	39	32	14.2	4.78	87	.257	.361	0	—	0	-5	-4	-0	-0.4
Total	4	11	10	.524	71	25	0	0	0	225^1	228	23	108	106	13.5	4.43	88	.263	.347	0	—	0	-13	-13	-1	-1.2
● **ODELL JONES**	Jones, Odell b: 1/13/53, Tulare, Cal. BR/TR, 6'3", 175 lbs. Deb: 9/11/75																									
1975	Pit-N	0	0	—	2	0	0	0	0	3	1	0	0	2	3.0	0.00	—	.100	.100	0	—	0	1	1	0	0.0
1977	Pit-N	3	7	.300	34	15	1	0	0	108	118	14	31	66	12.7	5.08	78	.278	.332	4	.143	-1	-14	-13	-2	-1.4
1978	Pit-N	2	0	1.000	3	1	0	0	0	9	7	0	4	10	11.0	2.00	185	.206	.289	0	.000	-0	2	2	-0	0.4
1979	Sea-A	3	11	.214	25	19	3	0	0	118^2	151	16	58	72	16.1	6.07	72	.317	.395	0	—	0	-24	-23	-2	-2.4
1981	Pit-N	4	5	.444	13	8	0	0	0	54^1	51	3	23	30	12.3	3.31	108	.250	.326	2	.200	-0	1	2	0	0.3
1983	Tex-A	3	6	.333	42	0	0	0	10	67	56	4	22	50	10.7	3.09	130	.223	.291	0	—	0	7	7	-1	1.0
1984	Tex-A	2	4	.333	33	0	0	0	2	59^1	62	7	23	28	13.2	3.64	114	.281	.354	0	—	0	2	3	1	0.3
1986	Bal-A	2	2	.500	21	0	0	0	0	49^1	58	4	23	32	14.8	3.83	108	.305	.380	0	—	0	2	2	-0	0.1
1988	Mil-A	5	0	1.000	28	2	0	0	1	80^2	75	8	29	48	11.7	4.35	91	.251	.319	0	—	0	-3	-3	-1	-0.3
Total	9	24	35	.407	201	45	4	0	13	549^1	579	56	213	338	13.2	4.42	92	.275	.344	6	.154	-1	-27	-23	-5	-2.0
● **OSCAR JONES**	Jones, Oscar Winfield "Flip Flap" b: 1/21/1879, London Grove, Pa. d: 10/8/46, Perkasie, Pa. BR/TR, 5'7", 163 lbs. Deb: 4/20/03																									
1903	Bro-N	19	14	.576	38	36	31	4	0	324^1	320	4	77	95	11.5	2.94	109	.260	.313	32	.256	3	12	9	-3	0.7
1904	Bro-N	17	25	.405	46	41	38	0	0	377	387	7	92	96	11.8	2.75	100	.270	.321	24	.175	-1	-0	0	-7	-0.8
1905	Bro-N	8	15	.348	29	20	14	0	1	174	197	6	56	66	13.6	4.66	62	.285	.347	13	.200	-0	-32	-34	-4	-4.3
Total	3	44	54	.449	113	97	83	4	1	875^1	904	17	225	257	12.1	3.20	92	.269	.324	69	.211	2	-20	-25	-14	-4.4
● **PERCY JONES**	Jones, Percy Lee b: 10/28/1899, Harwood, Tex. d: 3/18/79, Dallas, Tex. BR/TL, 5'11.5", 175 lbs. Deb: 8/6/20																									
1920	Chi-N	0	0	—	4	0	0	0	0	7	15	1	3	0	24.4	11.57	28	.455	.514	0	.000	-0	-7	-7	-0	0.0
1921	Chi-N	3	5	.375	32	3	1	0	0	98^2	116	2	39	46	14.5	4.56	84	.295	.365	6	.222	-0	-9	-8	-2	-0.8
1922	Chi-N	8	9	.471	44	24	7	2	1	162	197	10	68	45	15.0	4.78	88	.314	.385	4	.085	-4	-12	-10	0	-1.3
1925	Chi-N	6	6	.500	28	13	6	1	0	124	123	12	71	60	14.4	4.65	93	.263	.366	6	.154	-3	-5	-4	2	-0.4
1926	Chi-N	12	7	.632	30	20	10	2	2	160^1	151	3	90	80	13.8	3.09	125	.256	.359	13	.260	3	13	13	-1	1.6
1927	Chi-N	7	8	.467	30	11	5	1	0	112^2	123	3	72	37	16.1	4.07	95	.285	.394	14	.350	3	-2	-3	2	0.1
1928	Chi-N	10	6	.625	39	19	9	1	3	154	167	4	56	41	13.4	4.03	95	.288	.358	11	.196	-0	-1	-3	-0	-0.4
1929	Bos-N	7	15	.318	35	22	11	1	0	188^1	219	15	84	69	14.7	4.64	101	.298	.373	9	.148	-3	2	1	1	-0.1
1930	Pit-N	0	1	.000	9	2	0	0	0	19	26	3	11	3	18.9	6.63	75	.329	.430	0	.000	-0	-4	-3	-1	-0.2
Total	9	53	57	.482	251	114	49	8	6	1026	1137	53	494	381	14.7	4.34	95	.289	.374	63	.194	-5	-24	-24	1	-1.5
● **RANDY JONES**	Jones, Randall Leo b: 1/12/50, Fullerton, Cal. BR/TL, 6', 178 lbs. Deb: 6/16/73																									
1973	SD-N	7	6	.538	20	19	6	1	0	139^2	129	13	37	77	10.8	3.16	110	.241	.291	8	.167	0	8	5	0	0.4
1974	SD-N	8	22	.267	40	34	4	1	2	208^1	217	16	78	124	13.0	4.45	80	.270	.339	10	.154	-1	-19	-21	2	-2.6
1975	SD-N★	20	12	.625	37	36	18	6	0	285	242	17	56	103	**9.4**	**2.24**	**155**	.232	.271	11	.133	-1	44	39	5	**4.9**
1976	SD-N★	**22**	14	.611	40	40	**25**	5	0	**315^1**	274	15	50	93	**9.4**	2.74	119	.234	**.267**	6	.058	-6	27	19	8	2.3
1977	SD-N	6	12	.333	27	25	1	0	0	147^1	173	12	36	44	12.8	4.58	77	.291	.332	5	.116	-1	-11	-17	4	-1.6
1978	SD-N	13	14	.481	37	36	7	2	0	253	263	6	64	71	11.6	2.88	115	.272	.317	15	.183	1	20	12	2	1.6
1979	SD-N	11	12	.478	39	39	6	0	0	263	257	17	64	112	11.1	3.63	97	.259	.306	15	.174	0	3	-3	4	0.2
1980	SD-N	5	13	.278	24	24	4	3	0	154^1	165	14	29	53	11.3	3.91	88	.276	.310	3	.067	-3	-5	-8	3	-0.9
1981	NY-N	1	8	.111	13	12	0	0	0	59^1	65	8	38	14	15.8	4.85	72	.274	.377	2	.118	-1	-9	-9	2	-1.2
1982	NY-N	7	10	.412	28	20	2	1	0	107^2	130	11	51	44	15.5	4.60	79	.304	.384	4	.148	0	-12	-12	3	-1.4
Total	10	100	123	.448	305	285	73	19	2	1933	1915	129	503	735	11.3	3.42	101	.260	.309	79	.132	-12	44	6	32	1.7
● **BOBBY JONES**	Jones, Robert Joseph b: 2/10/70, Fresno, Cal. BR/TR, 6'4", 225 lbs. Deb: 8/14/93																									
1993	NY-N	2	4	.333	9	9	0	0	0	61^2	61	6	22	35	12.4	3.65	110	.262	.331	1	.050	-2	3	2	-0	0.0
1994	NY-N	12	7	.632	24	24	1	1	0	160	157	10	56	80	12.2	3.15	133	.257	.324	5	.109	-2	19	18	2	2.0
1995	NY-N	10	10	.500	30	30	3	1	0	195^2	209	20	53	127	12.4	4.19	97	.274	.327	9	.161	-1	-0	-3	-0	-0.4
1996	NY-N	12	8	.600	31	31	3	1	0	195^2	219	26	46	116	12.3	4.42	91	.288	.331	7	.117	-1	-4	-9	0	-0.8
1997	NY-N★	15	9	.625	30	30	2	1	0	193^1	177	24	63	125	11.3	3.63	111	.242	.304	8	.129	-0	12	9	2	1.1
1998	NY-N	9	9	.500	30	30	0	0	0	195^1	192	23	53	115	11.7	4.05	103	.262	.319	9	.188	1	4	2	1	0.4
Total	6	60	47	.561	154	154	9	4	0	1001^2	1015	109	293	598	12.0	3.90	105	.265	.322	39	.134	-4	33	20	5	2.3

YEAR	TM/L	W	L	PCT	G	GS	CG	SH	SV	IP	H	HR	BB	SO	RAT	ERA	ERA+	OAV	OOB	BH	AVG	PB	PR	/A	PD	TPI
● BOBBY JONES	Jones, Robert Mitchell b: 4/11/72, Orange, N.J. BR/TL, 6', 185 lbs. Deb: 5/18/97																									
1997	Col-N	1	1	.500	4	4	0	0	0	19^1	30	2	12	5	19.6	8.38	62	.380	.462	1	.200	0	-9	-7	-0	-0.6
1998	Col-N	7	8	.467	35	20	1	0	0	141^1	153	12	66	109	14.3	5.22	97	.282	.366	8	.178	-1	-16	-3	-1	-0.4
Total	2	8	9	.471	39	24	1	0	0	160^2	183	14	78	114	15.0	5.60	91	.294	.378	9	.180	-1	-25	-9	-1	-1.0
● SAM JONES	Jones, Samuel "Toothpick Sam" b: 12/14/25, Stewartsville, Ohio d: 11/5/71, Morgantown, W.Va. BR/TR, 6'4", 200 lbs. Deb: 9/22/51																									
1951	Cle-A	0	1	.000	2	1	0	0	0	8^2	4	0	5	4	9.3	2.08	182	.143	.273	0	.000	-0	2	2	-0	0.1
1952	Cle-A	2	3	.400	14	4	0	0	1	36	38	6	37	28	19.8	7.25	46	.270	.434	1	.100	-1	-14	-16	-1	-2.1
1955	Chi-N★	14	20	.412	36	34	12	4	0	241^2	175	22	185	**198**	13.9	4.10	100	**.206**	.357	14	.182	-2	-2	-0	-0	-0.2
1956	Chi-N	9	14	.391	33	28	8	2	0	188^2	155	21	115	**176**	13.3	3.91	96	.221	.338	10	.175	0	-3	-3	-1	-0.4
1957	StL-N	12	9	.571	28	27	10	2	0	182^2	164	17	71	154	11.9	3.60	110	.239	.316	10	.159	-1	6	7	0	0.7
1958	StL-N	14	13	.519	35	35	14	2	0	250	204	23	107	**225**	11.4	2.88	143	.223	.309	9	.100	-6	30	**35**	-0	2.9
1959	SF-N★	**21**	15	.583	50	35	16	**4**	4	270^2	232	18	109	209	11.6	**2.83**	135	**.228**	.307	11	.129	-2	**34**	30	-2	3.4
1960	SF-N	18	14	.563	39	35	13	3	0	234	200	18	91	190	11.3	3.19	109	.230	.306	16	.200	1	15	7	-2	0.9
1961	SF-N	8	8	.500	37	17	2	0	1	128^1	134	12	57	105	14.0	4.49	85	.264	.348	5	.139	-1	-7	-10	-2	-1.3
1962	Det-A	2	4	.333	30	6	1	0	1	81^1	77	13	35	73	12.6	3.65	111	.254	.335	2	.095	-1	3	4	-0	0.2
1963	StL-N	2	0	1.000	11	0	0	0	2	11	15	0	5	8	16.4	9.00	39	.319	.385	0	.000	0	-7	-7	-0	-1.4
1964	Bal-A	0	0	—	7	0	0	0	0	10^1	5	1	5	6	8.7	2.61	137	.152	.263	0	—	0	1	1	-0	0.0
Total	12	102	101	.502	322	222	76	17	9	1643^1	1403	151	822	1376	12.5	3.59	108	.230	.328	78	.149	-11	58	50	-8	2.8
● SAM JONES	Jones, Samuel Pond "Sad Sam" b: 7/26/1892, Woodsfield, Ohio d: 7/6/66, Barnesville, Ohio BR/TR, 6', 170 lbs. Deb: 6/13/14																									
1914	Cle-A	0	0	—	1	0	0	0	0	3^1	2	0	2	0	10.8	2.70	107	.200	.333	1	.500	0	0	0	0	0.0
1915	Cle-A	4	9	.308	48	9	2	0	4	145^2	131	0	63	42	12.0	3.65	84	.252	.334	5	.156	-0	-11	-10	0	-0.9
1916	Bos-A	0	1	.000	12	0	0	0	1	27	25	0	10	7	11.7	3.67	76	.272	.343	2	.333	0	-3	-3	-0	-0.1
1917	Bos-A	0	1	.000	9	1	0	0	1	16^1	15	1	6	5	11.6	4.41	59	.259	.328	0	.000	-1	-3	-3	1	-0.3
1918	*Bos-A	16	5	**.762**	24	21	16	5	0	184	151	1	70	44	11.2	2.25	119	.230	.312	10	.175	2	11	9	-1	1.1
1919	Bos-A	12	20	.375	35	31	21	5	1	245	258	4	95	67	13.2	3.75	81	.278	.350	11	.136	-0	-14	-20	3	-2.2
1920	Bos-A	13	16	.448	37	33	21	3	0	274	302	9	79	86	12.6	3.94	93	.288	.340	20	.217	1	-4	-9	-1	-0.8
1921	Bos-A	23	16	.590	40	38	25	**5**	1	298^2	318	1	78	98	12.1	3.22	131	.279	.329	24	.240	5	35	33	-3	4.0
1922	*NY-A	13	13	.500	45	28	20	0	**8**	260	270	16	76	81	12.1	3.67	109	.275	.329	23	.264	8	11	10	-1	1.6
1923	*NY-A	21	8	.724	39	27	18	3	4	243	239	11	69	68	11.6	3.63	109	.257	.312	19	.224	2	10	8	1	1.1
1924	NY-A	9	6	.600	36	21	8	3	3	178^2	187	6	76	53	13.3	3.63	115	.276	.350	9	.176	-0	12	11	-1	0.7
1925	NY-A	15	21	.417	43	31	14	1	2	246^2	267	14	104	92	13.6	4.63	92	.281	.354	13	.162	-3	-7	-10	0	-1.5
1926	*NY-A	9	8	.529	39	23	6	1	5	161	186	6	80	69	15.1	4.98	77	.298	.381	10	.204	1	-17	-20	-1	-2.0
1927	StL-A	8	14	.364	30	26	11	0	0	189^2	211	13	102	72	15.0	4.32	101	.282	.371	6	.109	-2	-4	1	-2	-0.3
1928	Was-A	17	7	.708	30	27	19	4	0	224^2	209	5	78	63	11.6	2.84	141	.252	.319	20	.253	6	30	29	1	3.5
1929	Was-A	9	9	.500	24	24	8	1	0	153^2	156	5	49	36	12.2	3.92	108	.264	.324	8	.157	0	5	5	-1	0.4
1930	Was-A	15	7	.682	25	25	14	1	0	183^1	195	4	61	60	12.7	4.07	113	.277	.337	9	.148	-1	12	11	-1	0.8
1931	Was-A	9	10	.474	25	24	8	1	1	148	185	10	47	58	14.4	4.32	99	.304	.358	15	.313	4	1	-0	-0	0.3
1932	Chi-A	10	15	.400	30	28	10	0	0	200^1	217	9	75	64	13.3	4.22	102	.270	.335	11	.193	2	6	2	3	0.7
1933	Chi-A	10	12	.455	27	25	11	2	0	176^2	181	13	65	60	12.7	3.36	126	.265	.333	9	.155	-0	18	17	-1	1.8
1934	Chi-A	8	12	.400	27	26	11	1	0	183^1	217	16	60	60	13.7	5.11	93	.289	.343	12	.200	2	-12	-8	-2	-0.7
1935	Chi-A	8	7	.533	21	19	7	0	0	140	162	8	51	38	13.8	4.05	114	.284	.343	8	.167	0	6	9	0	0.9
Total	22	229	217	.513	647	487	250	36	31	3883	4084	152	1396	1223	12.9	3.84	104	.274	.339	245	.197	25	81	61	-8	8.1
● SHELDON JONES	Jones, Sheldon Leslie "Available" b: 2/2/22, Tecumseh, Neb. d: 4/18/91, Greenville, N.C. BR/TR, 6', 180 lbs. Deb: 9/9/46																									
1946	NY-N	1	2	.333	6	4	1	0	0	28	21	4	17	24	12.5	3.21	107	.208	.328	2	.250	0	1	1	-0	0.1
1947	NY-N	2	2	.500	15	6	0	0	0	55^2	51	2	29	24	13.4	3.88	105	.250	.352	2	.125	-1	1	1	-1	-0.1
1948	NY-N	16	8	.667	55	21	8	1	5	201^1	204	16	90	82	13.4	3.35	117	.263	.344	13	.203	1	14	13	0	1.6
1949	NY-N	15	12	.556	42	27	11	1	0	207^1	198	19	88	79	12.8	3.34	119	.248	.331	8	.121	-3	16	15	-0	1.4
1950	NY-N	13	16	.448	40	28	11	2	2	199	188	26	90	97	12.9	4.61	89	.249	.335	6	.105	-2	-10	-11	-2	-1.9
1951	*NY-N	6	11	.353	41	12	2	0	4	120^1	119	12	52	58	13.1	4.26	92	.260	.340	3	.097	-1	-4	-5	0	-0.7
1952	Bos-N	1	4	.200	39	1	0	0	1	70	81	8	31	40	14.5	4.76	76	.286	.359	1	.125	-0	-8	-9	0	-0.6
1953	Chi-N	0	2	.000	22	2	0	0	0	38^1	47	3	16	9	16.0	5.40	82	.299	.382	0	.000	-1	-5	-4	0	-0.3
Total	8	54	57	.486	260	101	33	4	12	920	909	90	413	413	13.3	3.96	100	.258	.342	35	.136	-7	4	1	-3	-0.5
● SHERMAN JONES	Jones, Sherman Jarvis "Roadblock" b: 2/10/35, Winton, N.C. BL/TR, 6'4", 205 lbs. Deb: 8/2/60																									
1960	SF-N	1	1	.500	16	0	0	0	1	32	37	3	11	10	13.8	3.09	112	.291	.353	2	.286	0	2	1	-1	0.1
1961	*Cin-N	1	1	.500	24	2	0	0	2	55	51	6	27	32	13.1	4.42	92	.256	.351	2	.182	0	-2	-2	-0	-0.1
1962	NY-N	0	4	.000	8	3	0	0	0	23^1	31	3	8	11	15.8	7.71	54	.326	.390	3	.429	1	-10	-9	0	-1.2
Total	3	2	6	.250	48	5	0	0	3	110^1	119	12	46	53	13.9	4.73	83	.283	.360	7	.280	1	-10	-10	-1	-1.2
● STEVE JONES	Jones, Steven Howell b: 4/22/41, Huntington Park, Cal. BL/TL, 5'10", 175 lbs. Deb: 8/15/67 F																									
1967	Chi-A	2	2	.500	11	3	0	0	0	25^2	21	1	12	17	11.6	4.21	74	.223	.311	1	.250	0	-3	-3	-0	-0.5
1968	Was-A	1	2	.333	7	0	0	0	0	10^2	8	3	7	11	12.7	5.91	49	.205	.326	0	.000	-0	-3	-4	-0	-1.0
1969	KC-A	2	3	.400	20	4	0	0	0	44^2	45	3	24	31	14.5	4.23	87	.260	.360	1	.125	0	-3	-3	0	-0.2
Total	3	5	7	.417	38	7	0	0	0	81	74	7	43	59	13.3	4.44	76	.242	.341	2	.154	1	-9	-9	-1	-1.7
● RICK JONES	Jones, Thomas Fredrick b: 4/16/55, Jacksonville, Fla. BL/TL, 6'5", 190 lbs. Deb: 4/18/76																									
1976	Bos-A	5	3	.625	24	14	1	0	0	104^1	133	6	26	45	13.8	3.36	116	.311	.352	0	—	0	2	6	-0	0.4
1977	Sea-A	1	4	.200	10	10	0	0	0	42^1	47	10	37	16	17.9	5.10	81	.283	.414	0	—	0	-5	-5	0	-0.4
1978	Sea-A	0	2	.000	3	2	0	0	0	12^1	17	1	7	11	17.5	5.84	65	.315	.393	0	—	0	-3	-3	-0	-0.4
Total	3	6	9	.400	37	26	1	0	0	159	197	17	70	72	15.2	4.02	99	.304	.373	0	—	0	-6	-1	-0	-0.4
● TIM JONES	Jones, Timmothy Byron b: 1/24/54, Sacramento, Cal. BB/TR, 6'5", 220 lbs. Deb: 9/4/77																									
1977	Pit-N	1	0	1.000	3	1	0	0	0	10	4	0	3	5	6.3	0.00	—	.118	.189	0	.000	-0	4	4	-0	0.4
● TODD JONES	Jones, Todd Barton Givin b: 4/24/68, Marietta, Ga. BL/TR, 6'3", 200 lbs. Deb: 7/7/93																									
1993	Hou-N	1	2	.333	27	0	0	0	2	37^1	28	4	15	25	10.6	3.13	124	.214	.299	0	—	0	4	3	-0	0.2
1994	Hou-N	5	2	.714	48	0	0	0	5	72^2	52	3	26	63	9.8	2.72	145	.202	.278	2	.400	1	12	10	-1	0.9
1995	Hou-N	6	5	.545	68	0	0	0	15	99^2	89	8	52	96	13.3	3.07	126	.237	.339	1	.200	0	12	9	-1	1.1
1996	Hou-N	6	3	.667	51	0	0	0	17	57^1	61	5	32	44	15.4	4.40	88	.274	.377	0	.000	-0	-1	-3	-0	-0.7
1997	Det-A	5	4	.556	68	0	0	0	31	70	60	3	35	70	12.3	3.09	148	.231	.324	0	—	0	11	12	-1	2.1
1998	Det-A	1	4	.200	65	0	0	0	28	63^1	58	7	36	57	13.6	4.97	95	.249	.354	0	—	0	-2	-2	0	-0.2
Total	6	24	20	.545	327	0	0	0	98	400^1	348	30	196	355	12.6	3.51	118	.235	.331	3	.273	1	36	28	-3	3.4
● TIM JONES	Jones, William Timothy b: 12/1/62, Sumter, S.C. BL/TR, 5'10", 175 lbs. Deb: 7/26/88 ♦																									
1990	StL-N	0	0	—	1	0	0	0	0	1^1	1	0	2	0	20.3	6.75	57	.167	.375	28	.219	0	-0	-0	0	0.0
● CLAUDE JONNARD	Jonnard, Claude Alfred b: 11/23/1897, Nashville, Tenn. d: 8/27/59, Nashville, Tenn. BR/TR, 6'1", 165 lbs. Deb: 10/1/21 F																									
1921	NY-N	0	0	—	1	0	0	0	1	4	4	0	0	7	9.0	0.00	—	.267	.267	0	.000	-0	2	2	-0	0.1
1922	NY-N	6	1	.857	33	0	0	0	**5**	96	96	7	28	44	11.9	3.84	104	.272	.331	1	.042	-3	3	2	-2	-0.3
1923	*NY-N	4	3	.571	**45**	1	1	0	**5**	96	105	6	35	45	13.1	3.28	116	.279	.340	1	.038	-3	8	6	-1	0.1
1924	*NY-N	3	5	.375	34	3	1	0	5	89^2	80	2	24	40	10.6	2.41	152	.229	.282	1	.045	-3	**15**	**13**	-0	0.9
1926	StL-A	0	2	.000	12	3	0	0	1	36	46	1	24	13	17.5	6.00	71	.313	.409	0	.000	-1	-8	-7	1	-0.3
1929	Chi-N	0	1	.000	12	2	0	0	0	27^2	41	4	11	11	17.2	7.48	62	.320	.379	2	.200	1	-9	-9	0	-0.2
Total	6	13	12	.520	137	9	2	0	17	349^1	372	20	122	160	12.9	3.79	104	.272	.334	5	.056	-9	10	6	-1	0.3
● CHARLIE JORDAN	Jordan, Charles T. "Kid" b: 10/4/1871, Baltimore, Md. d: 6/1/28, Hazleton, Pa. Deb: 7/31/1896																									
1896	Phi-N	0	0	—	2	0	0	0	0	4^2	9	0	2	3	21.2	7.71	56	.409	.458	1	.500	0	-2	-2	0	0.0

YEAR TM/L	W	L	PCT	G	GS	CG	SH	SV	IP	H	HR	BB	SO	RAT	ERA	ERA+	OAV	OOB	BH	AVG	PB	PR	/A	PD	TPI
● HARRY JORDAN Jordan, Harry J. b: 2/14/1873, Pittsburgh, Pa. d: 3/1/20, Pittsburgh, Pa. Deb: 9/25/1894																									
1894 Pit-N	1	0	1.000	1	1	1	0	0	9	10	0	2	1	13.0	4.00	131	.278	.333	0	.000	-0	1	1	-0	0.1
1895 Pit-N	0	2	.000	2	2	2	0	0	17	24	0	6	4	16.4	4.24	107	.329	.387	2	.286	-0	1	1	-0	0.0
Total 2	1	2	.333	3	3	3	0	0	26	34	0	8	5	15.2	4.15	115	.312	.370	2	.200	-0	2	2	-1	0.1
● MILT JORDAN Jordan, Milton Mignot b: 5/24/27, Mineral Springs, Pa. d: 5/13/93, Ithaca, N.Y. BR/TR, 6'2.5", 207 lbs. Deb: 4/16/53																									
1953 Det-A	0	1	.000	8	1	0	0	0	17	26	3	5	4	16.4	5.82	70	.366	.408	1	.500	0	-3	-3	0	-0.1
● NILES JORDAN Jordan, Niles Chapman b: 12/1/25, Lyman, Wash. BL/TL, 5'11", 180 lbs. Deb: 8/26/51																									
1951 Phi-N	2	3	.400	5	5	2	1	0	36^2	35	4	8	11	10.6	3.19	121	.250	.291	1	.077	-1	3	3	-1	0.2
1952 Cin-N	0	1	.000	3	1	0	0	0	6^1	14	1	3	2	24.2	9.95	38	.452	.500	0	.000	-0	-4	-4	0	-0.6
Total 2	2	4	.333	8	6	2	1	0	43	49	5	11	13	12.6	4.19	92	.287	.330	1	.071	-1	-1	-2	-1	-0.4
● RIP JORDAN Jordan, Raymond Willis "Lanky" b: 9/28/1889, Portland, Me. d: 6/5/60, Meriden, Conn. BL/TR, 6', 172 lbs. Deb: 6/25/12																									
1912 Chi-A	0	0	—	4	0	0	0	0	12^1	13	2	3	1	12.4	5.11	63	.289	.347	0	.000	-1	-2	-3	-0	-0.1
1919 Was-A	0	0	—	1	1	0	0	0	4	6	1	2	2	18.0	11.25	29	.353	.421	0	.000	-0	-4	-4	-0	0.0
Total 2	0	0	—	5	1	0	0	0	16^1	19	3	5	3	13.8	6.61	48	.306	.368	0	.000	-1	-6	-6	-1	-0.1
● RICARDO JORDAN Jordan, Ricardo b: 6/27/70, Boynton Beach, Fla BL/TL, 5'11", 165 lbs. Deb: 6/23/95																									
1995 Tor-A	1	0	1.000	15	0	0	0	1	15	18	3	13	10	19.8	6.60	71	.305	.446	0	—	0	-3	-3	0	-0.2
1996 Phi-N	2	2	.500	26	0	0	0	0	25	18	0	12	17	10.8	1.80	239	.202	.297	0	.000	-0	7	7	-0	1.0
1997 NY-N	1	2	.333	22	0	0	0	0	27	31	1	15	19	16.0	5.33	76	.304	.403	0	.000	-0	-3	-4	0	-0.4
1998 Cin-N	1	0	1.000	6	0	0	0	0	3^1	4	2	7	1	29.7	24.30	18	.308	.550	0	—	0	-7	-7	0	-1.7
Total 4	5	4	.556	69	0	0	0	1	70^1	71	6	47	47	15.6	5.25	82	.270	.389	0	.000	-0	-7	-7	-0	-1.3
● ORVILLE JORGENS Jorgens, Orville Edward b: 6/4/08, Rockford, Ill. d: 1/11/92, Colorado Springs, Colo. BR/TR, 6'1", 180 lbs. Deb: 4/19/35 F																									
1935 Phi-N	10	15	.400	**53**	24	6	0	2	188^1	216	12	96	57	15.3	4.83	94	.283	.370	6	.097	-5	-17	-6	3	-0.9
1936 Phi-N	8	8	.500	39	21	4	0	0	167^1	196	16	69	58	14.6	4.79	95	.290	.361	12	.200	-1	-14	-5	1	-0.4
1937 Phi-N	3	4	.429	52	9	1	0	3	140^2	159	12	68	34	14.8	4.41	98	.298	.383	5	.143	-1	-8	-1	2	0.0
Total 3	21	27	.438	144	54	11	0	5	496^1	571	40	233	149	14.9	4.70	95	.290	.370	23	.146	-7	-39	-12	5	-1.3
● ADDIE JOSS Joss, Adrian b: 4/12/1880, Woodland, Wis. d: 4/14/11, Toledo, Ohio BR/TR, 6'3", 185 lbs. Deb: 4/26/02 H																									
1902 Cle-A	17	13	.567	32	29	28	**5**	0	269^1	225	2	75	106	10.5	2.77	124	.228	.291	12	.117	-5	24	20	6	2.0
1903 Cle-A	18	13	.581	32	31	31	3	0	283^2	232	3	37	120	**8.8**	2.19	130	.223	**.256**	22	.193	0	24	21	4	2.7
1904 Cle-A	14	10	.583	25	24	20	5	0	192^1	160	0	30	83	9.2	**1.59**	159	.227	.266	10	.132	-4	22	20	0	2.2
1905 Cle-A	20	12	.625	33	32	31	3	0	286	246	4	46	132	9.5	2.01	131	.234	.273	13	.134	-0	20	20	5	2.7
1906 Cle-A	21	9	.700	34	31	28	9	1	282	220	3	43	106	8.5	1.72	152	.218	.252	21	.210	2	30	28	2	3.7
1907 Cle-A	**27**	11	.711	42	38	34	6	2	338^2	279	3	54	127	9.0	1.83	137	.227	.263	13	.114	-5	27	25	9	3.4
1908 Cle-A	24	11	.686	42	35	29	9	2	325	232	2	30	130	**7.3**	**1.16**	**205**	**.197**	**.218**	15	.155	2	44	44	2	5.9
1909 Cle-A	14	13	.519	33	28	24	4	0	242^2	198	0	31	67	8.6	1.71	150	.226	.255	8	.100	-3	21	23	0	2.4
1910 Cle-A	5	5	.500	13	12	9	1	0	107^1	96	2	18	49	9.7	2.26	114	.245	.282	4	.111	-1	3	4	2	0.4
Total 9	160	97	.623	286	260	234	45	5	2327	1888	19	364	920	8.9	1.89	142	.223	.260	118	.144	-14	216	206	30	25.4
● MIKE JOYCE Joyce, Michael Lewis b: 2/12/41, Detroit, Mich. BR/TR, 6'2", 193 lbs. Deb: 7/2/62																									
1962 Chi-A	2	1	.667	25	1	0	0	2	43^1	40	2	14	9	11.2	3.32	118	.247	.307	3	.429	1	3	3	0	0.3
1963 Chi-A	0	0	—	6	0	0	0	0	10^2	13	1	8	7	17.7	8.44	42	.289	.396	0	—	0	-6	-6	-0	0.0
Total 2	2	1	.667	31	1	0	0	2	54	53	3	22	16	12.5	4.33	88	.256	.328	3	.429	1	-3	-3	0	0.3
● DICK JOYCE Joyce, Richard Edward b: 11/18/43, Portland, Me. BL/TL, 6'5", 225 lbs. Deb: 9/3/65																									
1965 KC-A	0	1	.000	5	3	0	0	0	13	12	0	4	7	11.1	2.77	126	.240	.296	0	.000	-0	1	1	-0	0.0
● BOB JOYCE Joyce, Robert Emmett b: 1/14/15, Stockton, Cal. d: 12/10/81, San Francisco, Cal BR/TR, 6'1", 180 lbs. Deb: 5/4/39																									
1939 Phi-A	3	5	.375	30	6	1	0	0	107^2	156	13	37	25	16.2	6.69	70	.337	.387	3	.086	-3	-25	-24	1	-1.6
1946 NY-N	3	4	.429	14	7	2	0	0	60^2	79	3	20	24	14.7	5.34	64	.315	.365	3	.158	0	-13	-13	1	-1.2
Total 2	6	9	.400	44	13	3	0	0	168^1	235	16	57	49	15.7	6.20	69	.329	.380	6	.111	-3	-38	-37	2	-2.8
● MIKE JUDD Judd, Michael Galen b: 6/30/75, San Diego, Cal. BR/TR, 6'2", 200 lbs. Deb: 9/28/97																									
1997 LA-N	0	0	—	1	0	0	0	0	2^2	4	0	0	4	13.5	0.00	—	.364	.364	0	.000	-0	1	1	-0	0.0
1998 LA-N	0	0	—	7	0	0	0	0	11^1	19	4	9	14	23.0	15.09	26	.373	.475	0	.000	-0	-14	-14	1	0.0
Total 2	0	0	—	8	0	0	0	0	14	23	4	9	18	21.2	12.21	32	.371	.458	0	.000	-0	-12	-13	0	0.0
● RALPH JUDD Judd, Ralph Wesley b: 12/7/01, Perrysburg, Ohio d: 5/6/57, Lapeer, Mich. BL/TR, 5'10", 170 lbs. Deb: 10/2/27																									
1927 Was-A	0	0	—	1	0	0	0	1	4	8	0	2	2	22.5	6.75	60	.400	.455	0	.000	-0	-1	-1	-0	-0.1
1929 NY-N	3	0	1.000	18	0	0	0	0	50^2	49	4	11	21	10.7	2.66	172	.261	.302	0	.000	-2	12	11	0	0.4
1930 NY-N	0	0	—	2	0	0	0	0	7^2	13	0	3	0	18.8	5.87	81	.394	.444	0	.000	-1	-1	-1	-0	-0.1
Total 3	3	0	1.000	21	0	0	0	1	62^1	70	4	16	23	12.4	3.32	138	.290	.335	0	.000	-3	10	9	0	0.2
● OSCAR JUDD Judd, Thomas William Oscar "Ossie" b: 2/14/08, London, Ont., Can. d: 12/27/95, Ingersoll, Ont., Can. BL/TL, 6'0.5", 180 lbs. Deb: 4/16/41																									
1941 Bos-A	0	0	—	7	0	0	0	1	12^1	15	1	10	5	18.2	8.76	48	.300	.417	2	.500	2	-6	-6	0	0.1
1942 Bos-A	8	10	.444	31	19	11	0	2	150^1	135	3	90	70	13.6	3.89	96	.239	.346	18	.269	6	-4	-3	-0	0.3
1943 Bos-A☆	11	6	.647	23	20	8	1	0	155^1	131	2	69	53	11.8	2.90	114	.230	.317	14	.259	4	7	7	2	1.4
1944 Bos-A	1	1	.500	9	6	1	0	0	30	30	1	15	9	13.5	3.60	94	.261	.346	2	.182	1	-1	-1	-0	0.0
1945 Bos-A	0	1	.000	2	1	0	0	0	6^1	10	1	3	5	18.5	8.53	40	.333	.394	1	.500	0	-4	-4	0	-0.4
Phi-N	5	4	.556	23	9	3	1	2	82^2	80	3	40	36	13.2	3.81	101	.254	.340	8	.267	3	-0	0	1	0.4
1946 Phi-N	11	12	.478	30	24	12	1	2	173^1	169	6	90	65	13.5	3.53	97	.260	.350	25	.316	8	-2	-2	4	1.1
1947 Phi-N	4	15	.211	32	19	8	1	0	146^2	155	6	69	54	13.9	4.60	87	.279	.361	12	.188	2	-9	-10	1	-0.7
1948 Phi-N	0	2	.000	4	1	0	0	0	14^1	19	1	11	7	18.8	6.91	57	.317	.423	1	.167	0	-5	-5	-0	-0.5
Total 8	40	51	.440	161	99	43	4	7	771^1	744	24	397	304	13.4	3.90	93	.256	.347	83	.262	26	-23	-22	8	1.7
● JEFF JUDEN Juden, Jeffrey Daniel b: 1/19/71, Salem, Mass. BR/TR, 6'8", 265 lbs. Deb: 9/15/91																									
1991 Hou-N	0	2	.000	4	3	0	0	0	18	19	3	7	11	13.0	6.00	58	.275	.342	0	.000	-1	-5	-5	-1	-0.6
1993 Hou-N	0	1	.000	2	0	0	0	0	5	4	1	4	7	14.4	5.40	72	.222	.364	0	—	0	-1	-1	-0	-0.2
1994 Phi-N	1	4	.200	6	5	0	0	0	27^2	29	4	12	22	13.7	6.18	69	.276	.356	1	.111	-0	-6	-6	-0	-0.9
1995 Phi-N	2	4	.333	13	10	1	0	0	62^2	53	6	31	47	12.8	4.02	105	.235	.340	1	.056	-1	1	1	-0	0.0
1996 SF-N	4	0	1.000	36	0	0	0	0	41^2	39	7	20	35	13.0	4.10	100	.250	.339	0	.000	-0	1	-0	-0	-0.1
Mon-N	1	0	1.000	22	0	0	0	0	32^2	22	1	14	26	11.0	2.20	196	.188	.296	0	—	0	7	8	-1	0.2
Yr	5	0	1.000	58	0	0	0	0	74^1	61	8	34	61	12.0	3.27	128	.221	.315	0	.000	-0	8	8	-1	0.1
1997 Mon-N	11	5	.688	22	22	3	0	0	130	125	17	57	107	13.2	4.22	99	.255	.344	6	.140	0	-0	-0	-2	-0.2
*Cle-A	0	1	.000	8	5	0	0	0	31^1	32	6	15	29	13.8	5.46	86	.264	.350	0	—	0	-3	-3	-0	-0.1
1998 Mil-N	7	11	.389	24	24	2	0	0	138^1	149	20	66	109	14.6	5.53	78	.277	.367	5	.122	-1	-20	-19	-1	-2.3
Ana-A	1	3	.250	8	6	0	0	0	40	33	7	18	39	11.9	6.75	69	.217	.308	0	—	0	-9	-9	-0	-0.8
Total 7	27	31	.466	145	75	6	0	0	527^1	505	72	244	432	13.3	4.85	88	.254	.345	13	.109	-3	-35	-34	-5	-5.0
● HOWIE JUDSON Judson, Howard Kolls b: 2/16/26, Hebron, Ill. BR/TR, 6'1", 195 lbs. Deb: 4/22/48																									
1948 Chi-A	4	5	.444	40	5	1	0	8	107^1	102	7	56	38	13.5	4.78	89	.255	.351	3	.103	-2	-6	-6	0	-0.7
1949 Chi-A	1	14	.067	26	12	3	0	1	108	114	13	70	36	15.4	4.58	91	.274	.380	2	.065	-3	-5	-5	0	-0.8
1950 Chi-A	2	3	.400	46	3	1	0	0	112	105	10	63	34	13.7	3.94	114	.252	.353	2	.100	-1	**8**	**7**	-2	0.1
1951 Chi-A	5	6	.455	27	14	3	0	1	121^2	124	9	55	43	13.4	3.77	107	.264	.343	4	.121	-2	5	4	0	0.1
1952 Chi-A	0	1	.000	21	0	0	0	1	34	30	4	22	15	13.8	4.24	86	.244	.359	0	.000	-0	-2	-2	-0	-0.1
1953 Cin-N	0	1	.000	10	6	0	0	0	38^2	58	8	11	11	16.1	5.59	78	.341	.381	1	.111	1	-6	-5	0	0.0
1954 Cin-N	5	7	.417	37	8	0	0	3	93^1	86	9	42	27	12.6	3.95	106	.251	.338	2	.083	-2	1	2	-2	0.0
Total 7	17	37	.315	207	48	8	0	14	615	619	60	319	204	13.9	4.29	98	.265	.356	14	.093	-9	-4	-6	-3	-1.4

YEAR	TM/L	W	L	PCT	G	GS	CG	SH	SV	IP	H	HR	BB	SO	RAT	ERA	ERA+	OAV	OOB	BH	AVG	PB	PR	/A	PD	TPI
● KEN JUNGELS	Jungels, Kenneth Peter "Curly" b: 6/23/16, Aurora, Ill. d: 9/9/75, West Bend, Wis. BR/TR, 6'1", 180 lbs. Deb: 9/15/37																									
1937	Cle-A	0	0	—	2	0	0	0	0	3	3	0	1	0	12.0	0.00	—	.273	.333	0	—	0	2	2	0	0.0
1938	Cle-A	1	0	1.000	9	0	0	0	0	15^1	21	1	18	7	24.1	8.80	53	.339	.500	0	.000	-1	-7	-7	-0	-0.4
1940	Cle-A	0	0	—	2	0	0	0	0	3^1	3	0	1	1	10.8	2.70	156	.273	.333	0	.000	-0	1	1	0	0.0
1941	Cle-A	0	0	—	6	0	0	0	0	13^2	17	4	8	6	17.1	7.24	54	.293	.388	0	.000	-0	-5	-5	-0	-0.1
1942	Pit-N	0	0	—	6	0	0	0	0	13^2	12	0	4	7	10.5	6.59	51	.235	.291	1	.500	0	-5	-5	0	0.0
Total	5	1	0	1.000	25	0	0	0	0	49	56	5	32	21	16.7	6.80	60	.290	.399	1	.100	-1	-14	-15	-0	-0.5
● MIKE JUREWICZ	Jurewicz, Michael Allen b: 9/20/45, Buffalo, N.Y. BB/TL, 6'3", 205 lbs. Deb: 9/7/65																									
1965	NY-A	0	0	—	2	0	0	0	0	2^1	5	0	1	2	23.1	7.71	44	.417	.462	0	—	0	-1	-1	-0	0.0
● AL JURISICH	Jurisich, Alvin Joseph b: 8/25/21, New Orleans, La. d: 11/3/81, New Orleans, La. BR/TR, 6'2", 193 lbs. Deb: 4/26/44																									
1944	*StL-N	7	9	.438	30	14	5	2	1	130	102	7	65	53	11.9	3.39	104	.221	.323	8	.178	-1	3	2	-1	0.0
1945	StL-N	3	3	.500	27	6	1	0	0	71^2	61	7	41	42	12.9	5.15	73	.232	.338	2	.087	-2	-11	-11	-1	-1.1
1946	Phi-N	4	3	.571	13	10	2	1	1	68^1	71	9	31	34	13.6	3.69	93	.263	.341	3	.130	-0	-2	-2	-1	-0.4
1947	Phi-N	1	7	.125	34	12	5	0	3	118^1	110	15	52	48	12.4	4.94	81	.258	.340	1	.032	-3	-12	-12	-2	-1.2
Total	4	15	22	.405	104	42	13	3	5	388^1	344	38	189	177	12.5	4.24	87	.242	.334	14	.115	-6	-21	-24	-5	-2.7
● WALT JUSTIS	Justis, Walter Newton "Smoke" b: 8/17/1883, Moores Hill, Ind. d: 10/4/41, Greendale, Ind. BR/TR, 5'11.5", 195 lbs. Deb: 8/1/05																									
1905	Det-A	0	0	—	2	0	0	0	0	3^1	4	0	6	0	29.7	8.10	34	.308	.550	0	—	0	-2	-2	-0	0.0
● HEROLD JUUL	Juul, Earl Herold b: 5/21/1893, Chicago, Ill. d: 1/4/42, Chicago, Ill. BR/TR, 5'9.5", 150 lbs. Deb: 4/24/14																									
1914	Bro-F	0	3	.000	9	3	0	0	0	29	26	0	31	16	18.0	6.21	46	.248	.423	2	.222	-0	-11	-11	-0	-1.0
● HERB JUUL	Juul, Herbert Victor b: 2/2/1886, Chicago, Ill. d: 11/14/28, Chicago, Ill. BL/TL, 5'11", 150 lbs. Deb: 7/11/11 ◆																									
1911	Cin-N	0	0	—	1	0	0	0	0	4	3	0	4	2	15.8	4.50	74	.231	.412	0	.000	-0	-0	-1	-0	0.0
● JIM KAAT	Kaat, James Lee b: 11/7/38, Zeeland, Mich. BL/TL, 6'4", 217 lbs. Deb: 8/2/59 C◆																									
1959	Was-A	0	2	.000	3	2	0	0	0	5	7	1	4	2	23.4	12.60	31	.350	.500	0	.000	-0	-5	-5	0	-1.4
1960	Was-A	1	5	.167	13	9	0	0	0	50	48	8	31	25	15.1	5.58	70	.255	.375	2	.143	-1	-9	-9	0	-1.0
1961	Min-A	9	17	.346	36	29	8	1	0	200^2	188	12	82	122	12.6	3.90	109	.248	.331	15	.238	3	3	8	3	1.6
1962	Min-A☆	18	14	.563	39	35	16	**5**	1	269	243	23	75	173	11.2	3.14	130	.243	.307	18	.180	3	25	28	6	**4.2**
1963	Min-A	10	10	.500	31	27	7	1	1	178^1	195	24	38	105	12.2	4.19	87	.274	.319	8	.131	-0	-11	-11	4	-0.7
1964	Min-A	17	11	.607	36	34	13	0	1	243	231	23	60	171	11.1	3.22	111	.251	.304	14	.169	5	11	10	3	1.9
1965	*Min-A	18	11	.621	45	42	7	2	2	264^1	267	25	63	154	11.4	2.83	126	.258	.304	23	.247	6	19	21	3	3.5
1966	Min-A★	**25**	13	.658	41	41	**19**	3	0	**304^2**	271	29	55	205	9.7	2.75	131	.235	.271	23	.195	4	23	**29**	0	**4.1**
1967	Min-A	16	13	.552	42	38	13	2	0	263^1	269	21	42	211	10.9	3.04	114	.260	.295	17	.172	3	6	12	1	1.8
1968	Min-A	14	12	.538	30	29	9	2	0	208	192	16	40	130	10.2	2.94	105	.243	.282	12	.156	0	1	3	-0	0.4
1969	Min-A	14	13	.519	40	32	10	0	1	242^1	252	23	75	139	12.5	3.49	105	.265	.325	18	.207	6	3	4	-3	0.8
1970	*Min-A	14	10	.583	45	34	4	1	0	230^1	244	26	58	120	11.9	3.56	105	.273	.319	15	.197	3	4	4	2	0.9
1971	Min-A	13	14	.481	39	38	15	4	0	260^1	275	16	47	137	11.3	3.32	107	.268	.304	15	.161	-0	4	7	-0	0.7
1972	Min-A	10	2	.833	15	15	5	0	0	113^1	94	6	20	64	9.1	2.06	155	.227	.263	13	.289	5	13	14	-0	2.3
1973	Min-A	11	12	.478	29	28	7	2	0	181^2	206	26	39	93	12.3	4.41	90	.282	.322	0	—	0	-12	-9	-1	-1.2
	Chi-A	4	1	.800	7	7	3	1	0	42^2	44	4	4	16	10.1	4.22	94	.260	.277	0	—	0	-2	-1	-1	-0.2
	Yr	15	13	.536	36	35	10	3	0	224^1	250	30	43	109	11.8	4.37	90	.276	.309	0	—	0	-14	-10	-2	-1.4
1974	Chi-A	21	13	.618	42	39	15	3	0	277^1	263	18	63	142	10.8	2.92	128	.250	.296	0	.000	-0	21	25	-2	2.8
1975	Chi-A★	20	14	.588	43	41	12	1	0	303^2	321	20	77	142	12.1	3.11	124	.274	.324	0	—	0	22	26	-2	2.5
1976	*Phi-N	12	14	.462	38	35	7	1	0	227^2	241	21	32	83	10.8	3.48	102	.274	.300	14	.177	2	1	2	-3	0.1
1977	Phi-N	6	11	.353	35	27	2	0	0	160^1	211	20	40	55	14.2	5.39	74	.320	.361	10	.189	1	-26	-25	-2	-2.4
1978	Phi-N	8	5	.615	26	24	2	1	0	140^1	150	9	32	48	12.0	4.10	87	.280	.326	7	.146	-1	-8	-8	-2	-1.0
1979	Phi-N	1	0	1.000	3	1	0	0	0	8^1	9	1	5	2	15.1	4.32	89	.281	.378	0	.000	0	-1	-0	-0	0.0
	NY-A	2	3	.400	40	1	0	0	2	58^1	64	4	14	23	12.3	3.86	106	.287	.335	0	—	0	2	1	-1	0.0
1980	NY-A	0	1	.000	4	0	0	0	0	5	8	0	4	1	21.6	7.20	54	.381	.480	0	—	0	-2	-2	1	-0.3
	StL-N	8	7	.533	49	14	6	1	4	129^2	140	6	33	36	12.0	3.82	97	.281	.325	5	.143	1	-3	-2	-2	-0.3
1981	StL-N	6	6	.500	41	1	0	0	4	53	60	2	17	8	13.1	3.40	105	.299	.353	3	.375	1	1	1	1	0.4
1982	*StL-N	5	3	.625	62	2	0	0	2	75	79	6	23	35	12.5	4.08	89	.276	.334	0	.000	-1	-4	-4	1	-0.5
1983	StL-N	0	0	—	24	0	0	0	0	34^2	48	5	10	19	15.1	3.89	93	.327	.369	0	.000	-0	-1	-1	0	0.0
Total	25	283	237	.544	898	625	180	31	18	4530^1	4620	395	1083	2461	11.6	3.45	107	.264	.311	232	.185	41	74	119	6	19.0
● GEORGE KAHLER	Kahler, George Runnells "Krum" b: 9/6/1889, Athens, Ohio d: 2/7/24, Battle Creek, Va. BR/TR, 6', 183 lbs. Deb: 8/13/10																									
1910	Cle-A	6	4	.600	12	12	8	2	0	95^1	80	0	46	38	12.3	1.60	161	.237	.335	5	.143	-2	10	10	-1	0.8
1911	Cle-A	9	8	.529	30	17	10	0	1	154^1	153	1	66	97	13.5	3.27	104	.270	.360	9	.167	-2	1	3	-1	-0.1
1912	Cle-A	12	19	.387	41	32	17	3	1	246^1	263	1	121	104	14.4	3.69	92	.291	.382	9	.112	-5	-10	-8	-4	-1.7
1913	Cle-A	5	11	.313	24	15	5	0	0	117^2	118	1	32	43	11.8	3.14	97	.266	.322	2	.061	-3	-3	-1	-4	-0.9
1914	Cle-A	0	1	.000	2	1	1	0	0	14	17	0	7	3	15.4	3.86	75	.309	.387	0	.000	-0	-2	-2	-0	-0.2
Total	5	32	43	.427	109	77	41	5	2	627^2	631	3	272	285	13.4	3.17	101	.274	.358	25	.121	-13	-4	2	-9	-2.1
● DON KAINER	Kainer, Donald Wayne b: 9/3/55, Houston, Tex. BR/TR, 6'3", 205 lbs. Deb: 9/6/80																									
1980	Tex-A	0	0	—	4	3	0	0	0	19^2	22	0	9	10	15.6	1.83	213	.289	.386	0	—	0	5	5	1	0.1
● DON KAISER	Kaiser, Clyde Donald "Tiger" b: 2/3/35, Byng, Okla. BR/TR, 6'5", 195 lbs. Deb: 7/20/55																									
1955	Chi-N	0	0	—	11	0	0	0	0	18^1	20	2	5	11	12.8	5.40	76	.274	.329	0	.000	-0	-3	-3	-0	-0.1
1956	Chi-N	4	9	.308	27	22	5	1	0	150^1	144	15	52	74	11.8	3.59	105	.247	.310	2	.043	-5	3	3	-0	-0.3
1957	Chi-N	2	6	.250	20	13	1	0	0	72	91	4	28	23	14.9	5.00	77	.316	.377	2	.105	-1	-9	-9	2	-0.8
Total	3	6	15	.286	58	35	6	1	0	240^2	255	21	85	108	12.8	4.15	92	.270	.332	4	.059	-6	-9	-9	1	-1.2
● JEFF KAISER	Kaiser, Jeffrey Patrick b: 7/24/60, Wyandotte, Mich. BR/TL, 6'3", 195 lbs. Deb: 4/11/85																									
1985	Oak-A	0	0	—	15	0	0	0	0	16^2	25	6	20	10	24.8	14.58	26	.342	.489	0	—	0	-19	-20	1	0.1
1987	Cle-A	0	0	—	2	0	0	0	0	3^1	4	1	3	2	21.6	16.20	28	.286	.444	0	—	0	-4	-4	0	0.0
1988	Cle-A	0	0	—	3	0	0	0	0	2^2	2	0	1	0	10.1	0.00	—	.286	.375	0	—	0	1	1	0	0.0
1989	Cle-A	0	1	.000	6	0	0	0	0	3^2	5	1	5	4	24.5	7.36	54	.313	.476	0	—	0	-1	-1	-0	-0.5
1990	Cle-A	0	0	—	5	0	0	0	0	12^2	16	2	7	9	16.3	3.55	110	.308	.390	0	—	0	0	1	0	0.0
1991	Det-A	0	1	.000	10	0	0	0	2	5	6	1	5	4	19.8	9.00	46	.286	.423	0	—	0	-3	-3	0	-0.7
1993	Cin-N	0	0	—	3	0	0	0	0	3^1	4	0	2	4	16.2	2.70	149	.286	.375	0	—	0	0	0	-0	0.0
	NY-N	0	0	—	6	0	0	0	0	4^2	6	1	3	5	17.4	11.57	35	.353	.450	0	—	0	-4	-4	0	0.0
	Yr	0	0	—	9	0	0	0	0	8	10	1	5	9	16.9	7.88	51	.323	.417	0	—	0	-3	-3	0	0.0
Total	7	0	2	.000	50	0	0	0	2	52	68	12	46	38	20.1	9.17	43	.318	.443	0	—	0	-30	-30	1	-1.1
● BOB KAISER	Kaiser, Robert Thomas b: 4/29/50, Cincinnati, Ohio BB/TL, 5'10", 175 lbs. Deb: 9/3/71																									
1971	Cle-A	0	0	—	5	0	0	0	0	6	8	2	3	4	19.5	4.50	85	.333	.448	0	—	0	-1	-0	0	0.0
● GEORGE KAISERLING	Kaiserling, George b: 5/12/1893, Steubenville, Ohio d: 3/2/18, Steubenville, Ohio BR/TR, 6', 175 lbs. Deb: 4/20/14																									
1914	Ind-F	17	10	.630	37	33	20	1	0	275^1	288	8	72	75	12.3	3.11	100	.274	.330	11	.112	-7	-7	0	-3	-1.0
1915	New-F	15	15	.500	41	29	16	5	2	261^1	246	1	73	75	11.3	2.24	114	.257	.316	12	.152	-3	14	9	-1	0.6
Total	2	32	25	.561	78	62	36	6	2	536^2	534	9	145	150	11.8	2.68	106	.266	.323	23	.130	-10	8	9	-5	-0.4
● BILL KALFASS	Kalfass, William Philip "Lefty" b: 3/3/16, New York, N.Y. d: 9/8/68, Brooklyn, N.Y. BR/TL, 6'3.5", 190 lbs. Deb: 9/15/37																									
1937	Phi-A	1	0	1.000	3	1	1	0	0	12	10	0	10	9	15.0	3.00	157	.233	.377	0	.000	-1	2	2	-0	0.1
● RUDY KALLIO	Kallio, Rudolph b: 12/14/1892, Portland, Ore. d: 4/6/79, Newport, Ore. BR/TR, 5'10", 160 lbs. Deb: 4/25/18																									
1918	Det-A	8	13	.381	30	22	10	2	0	181^1	178	0	76	70	12.7	3.62	73	.261	.336	9	.161	-1	-17	-19	-0	-2.3
1919	Det-A	0	0	—	12	1	0	0	1	22^1	28	0	8	3	14.9	5.64	57	.326	.389	0	.000	-1	-6	-6	-0	-0.2

YEAR TM/L	W	L	PCT	G	GS	CG	SH	SV	IP	H	HR	BB	SO	RAT	ERA	ERA+	OAV	OOB	BH	AVG	PB	PR	/A	PD	TPI
1925 Bos-A	1	4	.200	7	4	0	0	0	18^{2}	28	0	9	2	18.3	7.71	59	.364	.437	2	.333	0	-7	-7	-0	-1.3
Total 3	9	17	.346	49	27	10	2	1	222^{1}	234	0	93	75	13.4	4.17	69	.277	.351	11	.167	-1	-30	-32	-1	-3.8

● SCOTT KAMIENIECKI Kamieniecki, Scott Andrew b: 4/19/64, Mt.Clemens, Mich. BR/TR, 6', 195 lbs. Deb: 6/18/91

YEAR TM/L	W	L	PCT	G	GS	CG	SH	SV	IP	H	HR	BB	SO	RAT	ERA	ERA+	OAV	OOB	BH	AVG	PB	PR	/A	PD	TPI
1991 NY-A	4	4	.500	9	9	0	0	0	55^{1}	54	8	22	34	12.8	3.90	106	.256	.335	0	—	0	1	1	1	0.2
1992 NY-A	6	14	.300	28	28	4	0	0	188	193	13	74	88	13.0	4.36	90	.269	.342	0	—	0	-9	-9	-1	-0.9
1993 NY-A	10	7	.588	30	20	2	0	1	154^{1}	163	17	59	72	13.1	4.08	102	.277	.346	0	—	0	4	1	1	0.4
1994 NY-A	8	6	.571	22	16	1	0	0	117^{1}	115	13	59	71	13.6	3.76	122	.261	.353	0	—	0	14	11	0	1.3
1995 *NY-A	7	6	.538	17	16	1	0	0	89^{2}	83	8	49	43	13.6	4.01	115	.246	.346	0	—	0	7	6	-1	0.8
1996 NY-A	1	2	.333	7	5	0	0	0	22^{2}	36	6	19	15	22.6	11.12	44	.364	.475	0	—	0	-15	-16	0	-1.5
1997 *Bal-A	10	6	.625	30	30	0	0	0	179^{1}	179	20	67	109	12.5	4.01	110	.261	.330	0	.000	-0	11	8	2	0.7
1998 Bal-A	2	6	.250	12	11	0	0	0	54^{2}	67	7	26	25	16.0	6.75	67	.313	.398	0	—	0	-13	-14	1	-1.3
Total 8	48	51	.485	155	135	8	0	1	861^{1}	890	92	375	457	13.5	4.42	97	.270	.350	0	.000	-0	-0	-11	3	-0.3

● BOB KAMMEYER Kammeyer, Robert Lynn b: 12/2/50, Kansas City, Kan. BR/TR, 6'4", 210 lbs. Deb: 7/3/78

YEAR TM/L	W	L	PCT	G	GS	CG	SH	SV	IP	H	HR	BB	SO	RAT	ERA	ERA+	OAV	OOB	BH	AVG	PB	PR	/A	PD	TPI
1978 NY-A	0	0	—	7	0	0	0	0	21^{2}	24	1	6	11	13.3	5.82	62	.276	.337	0	—	0	-5	-5	1	0.1
1979 NY-A	0	0	—	1	0	0	0	0	0	7	2	0	0	—	∞	—	1.000	1.000	0	—	0	-8	-8	0	-0.6
Total 2	0	0	—	8	0	0	0	0	21^{2}	31	3	6	11	16.6	9.14	40	.330	.388	0	—	0	-13	-13	1	-0.5

● IKE KAMP Kamp, Alphonse Francis b: 9/5/1900, Roxbury, Mass. d: 2/25/55, Boston, Mass. BB/TL, 6', 170 lbs. Deb: 9/16/24

YEAR TM/L	W	L	PCT	G	GS	CG	SH	SV	IP	H	HR	BB	SO	RAT	ERA	ERA+	OAV	OOB	BH	AVG	PB	PR	/A	PD	TPI
1924 Bos-N	0	1	.000	1	1	0	0	0	7	9	0	5	4	18.0	5.14	74	.360	.467	0	.000	-0	-1	-1	0	-0.1
1925 Bos-N	2	4	.333	24	4	1	0	0	58^{1}	68	0	35	20	15.9	5.09	79	.301	.395	2	.167	-0	-5	-7	0	-0.6
Total 2	2	5	.286	25	5	1	0	0	65^{1}	77	0	40	24	16.1	5.10	78	.307	.402	2	.154	-0	-6	-8	1	-0.7

● HARRY KANE Kane, Harry "Klondike" (b: Harry Cohen) b: 7/27/1883, Hamburg, Ark. d: 9/15/32, Portland, Ore. BL/TL, Deb: 8/8/02

YEAR TM/L	W	L	PCT	G	GS	CG	SH	SV	IP	H	HR	BB	SO	RAT	ERA	ERA+	OAV	OOB	BH	AVG	PB	PR	/A	PD	TPI
1902 StL-A	0	1	.000	4	1	1	0	0	23	34	2	16	7	19.6	5.48	64	.343	.435	1	.111	-1	-5	-5	-0	-0.3
1903 Det-A	0	2	.000	3	3	2	0	0	18	26	0	8	10	17.5	8.50	34	.338	.407	1	.143	-0	-11	-11	-1	-1.0
1905 Phi-N	1	1	.500	2	2	2	1	0	17	12	0	8	12	10.6	1.59	184	.203	.299	1	.167	-0	3	3	-0	0.2
1906 Phi-N	1	3	.250	6	3	2	0	0	28	28	0	18	14	15.8	3.86	68	.255	.374	0	.000	-1	-4	-4	0	-0.6
Total 4	2	7	.222	15	9	7	1	0	86	100	2	50	43	16.1	4.81	62	.290	.386	3	.100	-2	-17	-17	-1	-1.7

● ERV KANTLEHNER Kantlehner, Erving Leslie "Peanuts" b: 7/31/1892, San Jose, Cal. d: 2/3/90, Santa Barbara, Cal. BL/TL, 6', 190 lbs. Deb: 4/17/14

YEAR TM/L	W	L	PCT	G	GS	CG	SH	SV	IP	H	HR	BB	SO	RAT	ERA	ERA+	OAV	OOB	BH	AVG	PB	PR	/A	PD	TPI
1914 Pit-N	3	2	.600	21	5	3	2	0	67	51	0	39	26	12.5	3.09	86	.218	.337	1	.067	-0	-2	-3	-0	-0.3
1915 Pit-N	5	12	.294	29	18	10	1	3	163	135	1	58	64	10.9	2.26	121	.230	.304	15	.288	3	9	8	1	1.4
1916 Pit-N	5	15	.250	34	21	7	2	2	165	151	1	57	49	11.6	3.16	85	.249	.317	8	.174	-0	-10	-9	1	-1.0
Phi-N	0	0	—	3	0	0	0	0	4	7	0	3	2	22.5	9.00	29	.500	.588	0	—	0	-3	-3	0	0.0
Yr	5	15	.250	37	21	7	2	2	169	158	1	60	51	11.6	3.30	81	.253	.318	8	.174	-0	-13	-12	1	-1.0
Total 3	13	29	.310	87	44	20	5	5	399	344	2	157	141	11.5	2.84	95	.239	.318	24	.212	2	-6	-6	2	0.1

● MATT KARCHNER Karchner, Matthew Dean b: 6/28/67, Berwick, Pa. BR/TR, 6'4", 245 lbs. Deb: 7/18/95

YEAR TM/L	W	L	PCT	G	GS	CG	SH	SV	IP	H	HR	BB	SO	RAT	ERA	ERA+	OAV	OOB	BH	AVG	PB	PR	/A	PD	TPI
1995 Chi-A	4	2	.667	31	0	0	0	0	32	33	2	12	24	12.9	1.69	264	.275	.346	0	—	0	11	10	0	2.0
1996 Chi-A	7	4	.636	50	0	0	0	1	59^{1}	61	10	41	46	15.8	5.76	82	.266	.382	0	—	0	-5	-7	-1	-1.1
1997 Chi-A	3	1	.750	52	0	0	0	15	52^{2}	50	4	26	30	13.0	2.91	151	.258	.345	0	—	0	10	9	-0	1.0
1998 Chi-A	2	4	.333	32	0	0	0	11	36^{2}	33	2	19	30	14.0	5.15	88	.243	.356	0	—	0	-2	-2	0	-0.4
*Chi-N	3	1	.750	29	0	0	0	0	28	30	6	14	22	14.8	5.14	85	.263	.354	0	—	0	-3	-2	0	-0.3
Total 4	19	12	.613	194	0	0	0	27	208^{2}	207	24	112	152	14.2	4.23	107	.261	.360	0	—	0	10	7	-1	1.2

● PAUL KARDOW Kardow, Paul Otto "Tex" b: 9/19/15, Humble, Tex. d: 4/27/68, San Antonio, Tex. BR/TR, 6'6", 210 lbs. Deb: 7/1/36

YEAR TM/L	W	L	PCT	G	GS	CG	SH	SV	IP	H	HR	BB	SO	RAT	ERA	ERA+	OAV	OOB	BH	AVG	PB	PR	/A	PD	TPI
1936 Cle-A	0	0	—	2	0	0	0	0	2	1	0	2	0	13.5	4.50	112	.167	.375	0	—	0	0	0	-0	0.0

● ED KARGER Karger, Edwin "Loose" b: 5/6/1883, San Angelo, Tex. d: 9/9/57, Delta, Colo. BR/TL, 5'11", 185 lbs. Deb: 4/15/06

YEAR TM/L	W	L	PCT	G	GS	CG	SH	SV	IP	H	HR	BB	SO	RAT	ERA	ERA+	OAV	OOB	BH	AVG	PB	PR	/A	PD	TPI
1906 Pit-N	2	3	.400	6	2	0	0	0	28	21	0	9	8	10.3	1.93	139	.204	.281	1	.091	-1	2	2	1	0.5
StL-N	5	16	.238	25	20	17	0	1	191^{2}	193	0	43	73	11.4	2.72	97	.271	.319	17	.233	4	-2	-2	3	0.6
Yr	7	19	.269	31	22	17	0	1	219^{2}	214	0	52	81	11.2	2.62	100	.262	.312	18	.214	3	0	0	4	1.1
1907 StL-N	15	19	.441	39	32	29	6	1	314	257	2	65	137	9.5	2.04	123	.223	.270	20	.179	1	15	16	4	2.6
1908 StL-N	4	9	.308	22	15	9	1	0	141^{1}	148	1	50	34	12.7	3.06	77	.260	.322	13	.241	3	-11	-11	-1	-0.8
1909 Cin-N	1	3	.250	9	5	1	0	0	34^{1}	26	0	30	8	15.2	4.46	58	.217	.382	3	.273	2	-7	-7	-0	-0.6
Bos-A	5	2	.714	12	6	3	0	0	68	71	0	22	17	12.7	3.18	79	.273	.337	3	.125	-0	-5	-5	-0	-0.6
1910 Bos-A	11	7	.611	27	25	16	1	1	183^{1}	162	5	53	81	10.8	3.19	80	.230	.289	20	.294	6	-14	-13	-2	-0.9
1911 Bos-A	5	8	.385	25	18	6	1	0	131	134	4	42	57	12.4	3.37	97	.272	.334	11	.234	3	-0	-1	-0	0.2
Total 6	48	67	.417	165	123	81	9	3	1091^{2}	1012	12	314	415	11.2	2.79	94	.246	.305	88	.220	18	-22	-20	5	1.0

● ANDY KARL Karl, Anton Andrew b: 4/8/14, Mt.Vernon, N.Y. d: 4/8/89, LaJolla, Cal. BR/TR, 6'1.5", 175 lbs. Deb: 4/24/43

YEAR TM/L	W	L	PCT	G	GS	CG	SH	SV	IP	H	HR	BB	SO	RAT	ERA	ERA+	OAV	OOB	BH	AVG	PB	PR	/A	PD	TPI
1943 Bos-A	1	1	.500	11	0	0	0	1	26	31	0	13	6	15.2	3.46	96	.310	.389	2	.286	0	-0	-0	1	0.1
Phi-N	1	2	.333	9	2	0	0	0	26^{2}	44	0	11	4	18.6	7.09	48	.383	.437	2	.250	1	-11	-11	0	-1.0
1944 Phi-N	3	2	.600	38	0	0	0	2	89	76	1	21	26	9.9	2.33	155	.237	.287	3	.200	1	**13**	**13**	1	0.9
1945 Phi-N	8	8	.500	**67**	2	1	0	**15**	180^{2}	175	7	50	51	11.4	2.99	128	.253	.306	7	.143	-2	**16**	**17**	1	1.6
1946 Phi-N	3	7	.300	39	0	0	0	5	65^{1}	84	6	22	15	14.7	4.96	69	.321	.375	1	.100	-0	-11	-11	1	-1.8
1947 Bos-N	2	3	.400	27	0	0	0	3	35	41	2	13	5	13.9	3.86	101	.318	.380	1	.167	-0	1	0	2	0.2
Total 5	18	23	.439	191	4	1	0	26	422^{2}	451	16	130	107	12.5	3.51	104	.279	.334	16	.168	-0	7	7	6	0.0

● SCOTT KARL Karl, Randall Scott b: 8/9/71, Fontana, Cal. BL/TL, 6'2", 195 lbs. Deb: 5/4/95

YEAR TM/L	W	L	PCT	G	GS	CG	SH	SV	IP	H	HR	BB	SO	RAT	ERA	ERA+	OAV	OOB	BH	AVG	PB	PR	/A	PD	TPI
1995 Mil-A	6	7	.462	25	18	1	0	0	124	141	10	50	59	14.1	4.14	120	.288	.358	0	—	0	8	12	0	0.8
1996 Mil-A	13	9	.591	32	32	3	1	0	207^{1}	220	29	72	121	13.2	4.86	107	.271	.338	0	—	0	3	7	-1	0.4
1997 Mil-A	10	13	.435	32	32	1	0	0	193^{1}	212	23	67	119	13.2	4.47	103	.279	.340	0	.000	-0	2	3	-0	0.3
1998 Mil-N	10	11	.476	33	33	0	0	0	192^{1}	219	21	66	102	13.5	4.40	98	.290	.350	4	.071	-2	-4	-2	2	-0.2
Total 4	39	40	.494	122	115	5	1	0	717	792	83	255	401	13.4	4.51	106	.281	.345	4	.067	-3	9	20	1	1.3

● BILL KARNS Karns, William Arthur b: 12/28/1875, Richmond, Iowa d: 11/15/41, Seattle, Wash. BL/TL, Deb: 8/1/01

YEAR TM/L	W	L	PCT	G	GS	CG	SH	SV	IP	H	HR	BB	SO	RAT	ERA	ERA+	OAV	OOB	BH	AVG	PB	PR	/A	PD	TPI
1901 Bal-A	1	0	1.000	3	1	1	0	0	17	30	0	9	5	20.6	6.35	61	.380	.443	1	.143	-1	-5	-5	-0	-0.3

● RYAN KARP Karp, Ryan Jason b: 4/5/70, Los Angeles, Cal. BL/TL, 6'4", 220 lbs. Deb: 6/23/95

YEAR TM/L	W	L	PCT	G	GS	CG	SH	SV	IP	H	HR	BB	SO	RAT	ERA	ERA+	OAV	OOB	BH	AVG	PB	PR	/A	PD	TPI
1995 Phi-N	0	0	—	1	0	0	0	0	2	1	0	3	2	18.0	4.50	94	.143	.400	0	—	0	-0	-0	-0	0.0
1997 Phi-N	1	1	.500	15	1	0	0	0	15	12	2	9	18	13.8	5.40	79	.218	.348	0	—	0	-2	-2	-0	-0.2
Total 2	1	1	.500	16	1	0	0	0	17	13	2	12	20	14.3	5.29	80	.210	.355	0	—	0	-2	-2	-0	-0.2

● HERB KARPEL Karpel, Herbert "Lefty" b: 12/27/17, Brooklyn, N.Y. d: 1/24/95, San Diego, Cal. BL/TL, 5'9.5", 180 lbs. Deb: 4/19/46

YEAR TM/L	W	L	PCT	G	GS	CG	SH	SV	IP	H	HR	BB	SO	RAT	ERA	ERA+	OAV	OOB	BH	AVG	PB	PR	/A	PD	TPI
1946 NY-A	0	0	—	2	0	0	0	0	1^{2}	4	0	0	0	21.6	10.80	32	.500	.500	0	—	0	-1	-1	-0	0.0

● BENN KARR Karr, Benjamin Joyce "Baldy" b: 11/28/1893, Mt.Pleasant, Miss. d: 12/8/68, Memphis, Tenn. BL/TR, 6', 175 lbs. Deb: 4/20/20

YEAR TM/L	W	L	PCT	G	GS	CG	SH	SV	IP	H	HR	BB	SO	RAT	ERA	ERA+	OAV	OOB	BH	AVG	PB	PR	/A	PD	TPI
1920 Bos-A	3	8	.273	26	2	0	0	1	91^{2}	109	3	24	21	13.2	4.81	76	.304	.349	21	.280	6	-10	-12	-1	-0.8
1921 Bos-A	8	7	.533	26	7	5	0	0	117^{2}	123	8	38	37	12.4	3.67	115	.283	.342	16	.258	1	8	7	-0	0.9
1922 Bos-A	5	12	.294	41	13	7	0	1	183^{1}	212	10	45	41	12.9	4.47	92	.302	.348	21	.214	-1	-9	-7	-1	-0.7
1925 Cle-A	11	12	.478	32	24	12	1	0	197^{2}	248	8	80	41	15.2	4.78	92	.317	.385	24	.261	4	-8	-8	2	-0.2
1926 Cle-A	5	6	.455	30	7	4	0	1	113^{1}	137	9	41	23	14.6	5.00	81	.291	.355	10	.222	2	-12	-12	1	-0.8
1927 Cle-A	3	3	.500	22	5	1	0	2	76^{2}	92	5	32	17	14.7	5.05	83	.315	.385	4	.200	1	-8	-7	2	-0.3
Total 6	35	48	.422	177	58	29	1	5	780^{1}	921	43	260	180	13.9	4.60	90	.303	.362	96	.245	12	-40	-39	2	-1.9

● STEVE KARSAY Karsay, Stefan Andrew b: 3/24/72, Flushing, N.Y. BR/TR, 6'3", 210 lbs. Deb: 8/17/93

YEAR TM/L	W	L	PCT	G	GS	CG	SH	SV	IP	H	HR	BB	SO	RAT	ERA	ERA+	OAV	OOB	BH	AVG	PB	PR	/A	PD	TPI
1993 Oak-A	3	3	.500	8	8	0	0	0	49	49	4	16	33	12.3	4.04	101	.258	.322	0	—	0	2	0	-1	0.3
1994 Oak-A	1	1	.500	4	4	1	0	0	28	26	1	8	15	11.3	2.57	172	.252	.313	0	—	0	7	6	0	0.7
1997 Oak-A	3	12	.200	24	24	0	0	0	132^{2}	166	20	47	92	15.1	5.77	78	.304	.369	0	—	0	-18	-18	-1	-1.8

YEAR	TM/L	W	L	PCT	G	GS	CG	SH	SV	IP	H	HR	BB	SO	RAT	ERA	ERA+	OAV	OOB	BH	AVG	PB	PR	/A	PD	TPI
1998	Cle-A	0	2	.000	11	1	0	0	0	24^1	31	3	6	13	14.4	5.92	81	.310	.361	0	—	0	-3	-3	-0	-0.2
Total	4	7	18	.280	47	37	1	0	0	234	272	28	77	153	14.0	5.04	88	.290	.352	0	—	0	-13	-15	-2	-1.0

● TAKASHI KASHIWADA Kashiwada, Takashi b: 5/14/71, Tokyo, Japan BL/TL, 5'11", 165 lbs. Deb: 5/1/97

YEAR	TM/L	W	L	PCT	G	GS	CG	SH	SV	IP	H	HR	BB	SO	RAT	ERA	ERA+	OAV	OOB	BH	AVG	PB	PR	/A	PD	TPI
1997	NY-N	3	1	.750	35	0	0	0	0	31^1	35	4	18	19	16.1	4.31	94	.289	.394	0	.000	-0	-0	-1	0	-0.1

● JACK KATOLL Katoll, John "Big Jack" b: 6/24/1872, Germany d: 6/18/55, Hartland, Ill. BR/TR, 5'11", 195 lbs. Deb: 9/9/1898

YEAR	TM/L	W	L	PCT	G	GS	CG	SH	SV	IP	H	HR	BB	SO	RAT	ERA	ERA+	OAV	OOB	BH	AVG	PB	PR	/A	PD	TPI
1898	Chi-N	0	1	.000	2	1	1	0	0	11	8	0	1	3	7.4	0.82	438	.200	.220	0	.000	-1	3	3	-0	0.2
1899	Chi-N	1	1	.500	2	2	2	0	0	18	17	0	4	1	11.0	6.00	62	.250	.301	0	.000	-1	-4	-5	-0	-0.4
1901	Chi-A	11	10	.524	27	25	19	0	0	208	231	3	53	59	12.8	2.81	124	.278	.330	10	.125	-4	20	15	2	1.1
1902	Chi-A	0	0	—	1	0	0	0	0	1	1	0	0	2	9.0	0.00	—	.250	.250	0	.000	-0	0	0	0	0.0
	Bal-A	5	10	.333	15	13	13	0	0	123	175	5	32	25	15.3	4.02	94	.334	.375	10	.175	-0	-6	-3	4	0.0
	Yr	5	10	.333	16	13	13	0	0	124	176	5	32	27	15.2	3.99	94	.333	.374	10	.172	-0	-6	-3	4	0.0
Total	4	17	22	.436	47	41	35	0	0	361	432	8	90	90	13.4	3.32	109	.294	.341	20	.134	-6	13	11	6	0.9

● BOB KATZ Katz, Robert Clyde b: 1/30/11, Lancaster, Pa. d: 12/14/62, St.Joseph, Mich. BR/TR, 5'11.5", 190 lbs. Deb: 5/12/44

YEAR	TM/L	W	L	PCT	G	GS	CG	SH	SV	IP	H	HR	BB	SO	RAT	ERA	ERA+	OAV	OOB	BH	AVG	PB	PR	/A	PD	TPI
1944	Cin-N	0	1	.000	6	2	0	0	0	18^1	17	0	7	4	11.8	3.93	89	.254	.324	0	.000	-1	-1	-1	1	0.0

● CURT KAUFMAN Kaufman, Curt Gerrard b: 7/19/57, Omaha, Neb. BR/TR, 6'2", 175 lbs. Deb: 9/10/82

YEAR	TM/L	W	L	PCT	G	GS	CG	SH	SV	IP	H	HR	BB	SO	RAT	ERA	ERA+	OAV	OOB	BH	AVG	PB	PR	/A	PD	TPI
1982	NY-A	1	0	1.000	7	0	0	0	0	8^2	9	2	6	1	15.6	5.19	77	.265	.375	0	—	0	-1	-1	-0	-0.1
1983	NY-A	0	0	—	4	0	0	0	0	8^2	10	0	4	8	14.5	3.12	125	.303	.378	0	—	0	1	1	-0	0.1
1984	Cal-A	2	3	.400	29	1	0	0	1	69	68	13	20	41	11.5	4.57	87	.254	.306	0	—	0	-4	-5	0	-0.3
Total	3	3	3	.500	40	1	0	0	1	86^1	87	15	30	50	12.2	4.48	88	.260	.321	0	—	0	-5	-5	0	-0.3

● TONY KAUFMANN Kaufmann, Anthony Charles b: 12/16/1900, Chicago, Ill. d: 6/4/82, Elgin, Ill. BR/TR, 5'11", 165 lbs. Deb: 9/23/21 C♦

YEAR	TM/L	W	L	PCT	G	GS	CG	SH	SV	IP	H	HR	BB	SO	RAT	ERA	ERA+	OAV	OOB	BH	AVG	PB	PR	/A	PD	TPI
1921	Chi-N	1	0	1.000	2	1	1	0	1	13	12	0	3	6	10.4	4.15	92	.240	.283	2	.400	1	-1	-0	-1	0.0
1922	Chi-N	7	13	.350	37	14	4	1	3	153	161	15	57	45	13.1	4.06	103	.273	.343	9	.200	1	1	2	-1	0.3
1923	Chi-N	14	10	.583	33	24	18	2	3	206^1	209	14	67	72	12.5	3.10	129	.264	.330	16	.216	3	21	21	-1	2.4
1924	Chi-N	16	11	.593	34	26	16	3	0	208^1	218	21	66	79	12.4	4.02	97	.272	.330	24	.316	6	-3	-3	-1	0.1
1925	Chi-N	13	13	.500	31	23	14	2	2	196	221	9	77	49	14.0	4.50	96	.292	.363	15	.192	1	-5	-4	-0	-0.3
1926	Chi-N	9	7	.563	26	22	14	1	2	169^2	169	6	44	52	11.6	3.02	127	.262	.316	15	.250	2	15	15	-2	1.4
1927	Chi-N	3	3	.500	9	6	3	0	0	53^1	75	8	19	21	16.5	6.41	60	.338	.400	5	.313	3	-15	-15	2	-1.0
	Phi-N	0	3	.000	5	5	1	0	0	18^2	37	2	8	4	21.7	10.61	39	.425	.474	1	.143	0	-14	-13	-0	-1.6
	StL-N	0	0	—	1	0	0	0	0	0^1	4	0	1	0	135.0	81.00	5	1.000	1.000	0	—	0	-3	-3	0	0.0
	Yr	3	6	.333	15	11	4	0	0	72^1	116	10	28	25	17.9	7.84	50	.366	.417	6	.261	3	-32	-31	1	-2.6
1928	StL-N	0	0	—	4	1	0	0	0	4^2	8	1	4	2	25.1	9.64	41	.444	.565	0	—	0	-3	-3	-0	0.0
1930	StL-N	0	1	.000	2	1	0	0	0	10^1	15	2	4	2	16.5	7.84	64	.357	.413	1	.333	0	-3	-3	-0	-0.2
1931	StL-N	1	1	.500	15	1	0	0	1	49	65	3	17	13	15.2	6.06	65	.319	.374	2	.111	-1	-12	-12	0	-0.6
1935	StL-N	0	0	—	3	0	0	0	0	3^2	4	0	1	0	12.3	2.45	167	.286	.333	0	—	0	1	1	0	0.0
Total	11	64	62	.508	202	124	71	9	12	1086^1	1198	81	368	345	13.3	4.18	97	.284	.347	91	.220	17	-22	-17	-5	0.5

● GREG KEAGLE Keagle, Gregory Charles b: 6/28/71, Corning, N.Y. BR/TR, 6'1", 185 lbs. Deb: 4/1/96

YEAR	TM/L	W	L	PCT	G	GS	CG	SH	SV	IP	H	HR	BB	SO	RAT	ERA	ERA+	OAV	OOB	BH	AVG	PB	PR	/A	PD	TPI
1996	Det-A	3	6	.333	26	6	0	0	0	87^2	104	13	68	70	18.6	7.39	68	.298	.425	0	—	0	-23	-23	-0	-1.9
1997	Det-A	3	5	.375	11	10	0	0	0	45^1	58	9	18	33	16.1	6.55	70	.309	.384	0	.000	-0	-10	-10	-0	-1.4
1998	Det-A	0	5	.000	9	7	0	0	0	38^2	46	5	20	25	16.3	5.59	84	.295	.389	0	—	0	-4	-4	0	-0.4
Total	3	6	16	.273	46	23	0	0	0	171^2	208	27	106	128	17.4	6.76	72	.300	.406	0	.000	-0	-37	-36	-1	-3.7

● STEVE KEALEY Kealey, Steven William b: 5/13/47, Torrance, Cal. BR/TR, 6', 185 lbs. Deb: 9/9/68

YEAR	TM/L	W	L	PCT	G	GS	CG	SH	SV	IP	H	HR	BB	SO	RAT	ERA	ERA+	OAV	OOB	BH	AVG	PB	PR	/A	PD	TPI
1968	Cal-A	0	1	.000	6	0	0	0	0	10	10	0	5	4	13.5	2.70	108	.256	.341	0	—	0	0	0	-1	0.0
1969	Cal-A	2	0	1.000	15	3	1	1	0	36^2	48	4	13	17	15.2	3.93	89	.322	.380	0	.000	-1	-1	-2	-1	-0.3
1970	Cal-A	1	0	1.000	17	0	0	0	1	21^2	19	2	6	14	10.4	4.15	87	.260	.316	1	.250	0	-1	-1	-1	-0.1
1971	Chi-A	2	2	.500	54	1	0	0	6	77^1	69	10	26	50	11.1	3.84	93	.239	.302	2	.200	1	-3	-2	-0	-0.1
1972	Chi-A	3	2	.600	40	0	0	0	4	57^1	50	4	12	37	9.7	3.30	95	.234	.274	0	.000	-0	-2	-1	-1	-0.2
1973	Chi-A	0	0	—	7	0	0	0	0	11^1	23	2	7	4	23.8	15.09	26	.418	.484	0	—	0	-14	-14	-0	0.0
Total	6	8	5	.615	139	4	1	1	11	214^1	219	22	69	126	12.1	4.28	80	.267	.325	3	.115	-0	-21	-20	-3	-0.7

● ED KEAS Keas, Edward James b: 2/2/1863, Dubuque, Iowa d: 1/12/40, Dubuque, Iowa Deb: 8/25/1888

YEAR	TM/L	W	L	PCT	G	GS	CG	SH	SV	IP	H	HR	BB	SO	RAT	ERA	ERA+	OAV	OOB	BH	AVG	PB	PR	/A	PD	TPI
1888	Cle-a	3	3	.500	6	6	6	0	0	51	53	1	12	18	11.6	2.29	135	.259	.303	2	.087	-2	4	5	1	0.3

● RAY KEATING Keating, Raymond Herbert b: 7/21/1891, Bridgeport, Conn. d: 12/28/63, Sacramento, Cal. BR/TR, 5'11", 185 lbs. Deb: 9/12/12

YEAR	TM/L	W	L	PCT	G	GS	CG	SH	SV	IP	H	HR	BB	SO	RAT	ERA	ERA+	OAV	OOB	BH	AVG	PB	PR	/A	PD	TPI
1912	NY-A	0	3	.000	6	5	3	0	0	35^2	36	0	18	21	13.9	5.80	62	.265	.355	6	.375	1	-10	-9	0	-0.5
1913	NY-A	6	12	.333	28	21	9	2	0	151^1	147	3	51	83	11.9	3.21	93	.253	.316	3	.070	-3	-5	-4	-2	-0.9
1914	NY-A	8	11	.421	34	25	14	0	0	210	198	1	67	109	11.6	2.96	93	.253	.316	12	.169	-0	-5	-5	2	-0.2
1915	NY-A	3	6	.333	11	10	8	1	0	79^1	66	3	45	37	12.9	3.63	81	.228	.337	4	.154	-1	-6	-6	1	-0.6
1916	NY-A	5	6	.455	14	11	6	0	0	91	91	4	37	35	12.9	3.07	94	.272	.349	7	.241	1	-2	-2	2	0.1
1918	NY-A	2	2	.500	15	6	1	0	0	48^1	39	0	30	16	13.2	3.91	72	.238	.362	3	.188	-0	-6	-6	0	-0.5
1919	Bos-N	7	11	.389	22	14	9	1	0	136	129	2	45	48	11.6	2.98	96	.261	.325	7	.152	-1	-1	-2	2	-0.2
Total	7	31	51	.378	130	92	50	4	0	751^2	706	13	293	349	12.2	3.29	88	.254	.329	42	.170	-2	-35	-33	5	-2.8

● BOB KEATING Keating, Robert M. b: 9/22/1862, Springfield, Mass d: 1/19/22, Springfield, Mass. BL/TL, 6'4", 190 lbs. Deb: 8/27/1887

YEAR	TM/L	W	L	PCT	G	GS	CG	SH	SV	IP	H	HR	BB	SO	RAT	ERA	ERA+	OAV	OOB	BH	AVG	PB	PR	/A	PD	TPI
1887	Bal-a	0	1	.000	1	1	1	0	0	9	16	0	6	0	22.0	11.00	37	.372	.449	1	.250	-0	-7	-7	0	-0.4

● CACTUS KECK Keck, Frank Joseph b: 1/13/1899, St.Louis, Mo. d: 2/6/81, Kirkwood, Mo. BR/TR, 5'11", 170 lbs. Deb: 5/26/22

YEAR	TM/L	W	L	PCT	G	GS	CG	SH	SV	IP	H	HR	BB	SO	RAT	ERA	ERA+	OAV	OOB	BH	AVG	PB	PR	/A	PD	TPI
1922	Cin-N	7	6	.538	27	15	5	1	1	131	138	4	29	27	11.8	3.37	119	.276	.322	7	.159	-1	11	9	-3	0.3
1923	Cin-N	3	6	.333	35	6	1	0	2	87	84	5	32	16	12.3	3.72	104	.254	.325	1	.059	-1	3	1	1	0.1
Total	2	10	12	.455	62	21	6	1	3	218	222	9	61	43	12.0	3.51	112	.267	.323	8	.131	-2	13	10	-3	0.4

● DAVE KEEFE Keefe, David Edwin b: 1/9/1897, Williston, Vt. d: 2/4/78, Kansas City, Mo. BL/TR, 5'9", 165 lbs. Deb: 4/21/17 C

YEAR	TM/L	W	L	PCT	G	GS	CG	SH	SV	IP	H	HR	BB	SO	RAT	ERA	ERA+	OAV	OOB	BH	AVG	PB	PR	/A	PD	TPI
1917	Phi-A	1	0	1.000	3	0	0	0	0	5	5	0	4	1	16.2	1.80	153	.278	.409	0	.000	-0	0	1	0	0.1
1919	Phi-A	0	1	.000	1	1	1	0	0	9	8	0	3	5	11.0	4.00	86	.242	.306	0	.000	-0	-1	-1	0	-0.1
1920	Phi-A	6	7	.462	31	13	7	1	0	130^1	129	2	30	41	11.4	2.97	136	.262	.313	10	.250	-0	12	15	1	1.5
1921	Phi-A	2	9	.182	44	12	4	0	1	173	214	19	64	68	14.7	4.68	95	.311	.374	10	.175	-3	-8	-4	-2	-0.7
1922	Cle-A	0	0	—	18	1	0	0	0	36^1	47	2	12	11	14.6	6.19	65	.333	.386	2	.333	1	-9	-9	-0	0.0
Total	5	9	17	.346	97	27	12	1	1	353^2	403	23	113	126	13.4	4.15	101	.294	.352	22	.206	-3	-5	2	-1	0.8

● GEORGE KEEFE Keefe, George W. b: 1/7/1867, Washington, D.C. d: 8/24/35, Washington, D.C. BL/TL, 5'9", 168 lbs. Deb: 7/30/1886

YEAR	TM/L	W	L	PCT	G	GS	CG	SH	SV	IP	H	HR	BB	SO	RAT	ERA	ERA+	OAV	OOB	BH	AVG	PB	PR	/A	PD	TPI
1886	Was-N	0	3	.000	4	4	4	0	0	31^1	28	0	15	5	12.4	5.17	64	.233	.319	0	.000	-2	-6	-7	-1	-0.7
1887	Was-N	0	1	.000	1	1	1	0	0	8	16	1	4	0	24.8	9.00	45	.364	.440	0	.000	-1	-4	-4	-0	-0.4
1888	Was-N	6	7	.462	13	13	13	1	0	114	87	2	43	52	10.6	2.84	99	.206	.286	9	.214	1	0	-0	1	0.2
1889	Was-N	8	18	.308	30	28	24	0	0	230	266	6	143	90	16.2	5.13	77	.281	.378	16	.163	-2	-28	-30	-2	-2.8
1890	Buf-P	6	16	.273	25	22	22	0	0	196	280	11	138	55	19.4	6.52	63	.321	.417	16	.203	1	-50	-53	-1	-3.9
1891	Was-a	0	3	.000	5	4	4	0	1	37	44	0	17	11	15.1	2.68	140	.286	.360	2	.143	-0	4	4	1	0.3
Total	6	20	48	.294	78	72	68	1	1	616^1	721	20	360	213	16.0	5.05	74	.282	.374	43	.172	-3	-85	-90	-4	-7.3

● JOHN KEEFE Keefe, John Thomas b: 5/5/1867, Fitchburg, Mass. d: 8/9/37, Fitchburg, Mass. TL , Deb: 4/28/1890

YEAR	TM/L	W	L	PCT	G	GS	CG	SH	SV	IP	H	HR	BB	SO	RAT	ERA	ERA+	OAV	OOB	BH	AVG	PB	PR	/A	PD	TPI
1890	Syr-a	17	24	.415	43	41	36	2	0	352^1	355	9	148	120	13.5	4.32	82	.254	.336	30	.191	-5	-17	-31	0	-3.1

● BOBBY KEEFE Keefe, Robert Francis b: 6/16/1882, Folsom, Cal. d: 12/7/64, Sacramento, Cal. BR/TR, 5'11", 155 lbs. Deb: 4/15/07

YEAR	TM/L	W	L	PCT	G	GS	CG	SH	SV	IP	H	HR	BB	SO	RAT	ERA	ERA+	OAV	OOB	BH	AVG	PB	PR	/A	PD	TPI
1907	NY-A	3	5	.375	19	3	0	0	3	57^2	60	1	20	20	12.6	2.50	112	.270	.333	1	.053	-2	0	2	0	0.1
1911	Cin-N	12	13	.480	39	26	15	0	3	234^1	196	7	76	105	10.6	2.69	123	.229	.294	6	.086	-2	19	16	-5	0.8
1912	Cin-N	1	3	.250	17	6	0	0	2	68^2	78	0	33	29	15.1	5.24	64	.289	.375	3	.167	-1	-14	-14	0	-0.9
Total	3	16	21	.432	75	35	15	0	8	360^2	334	8	129	154	11.8	3.14	103	.248	.317	10	.093	-5	5	4	-5	0.0

YEAR	TM/L	W	L	PCT	G	GS	CG	SH	SV	IP	H	HR	BB	SO	RAT	ERA	ERA+	OAV	OOB	BH	AVG	PB	PR	/A	PD	TPI
● TIM KEEFE	Keefe, Timothy John "Smiling Tim" or "Sir Timothy" b: 1/1/1857, Cambridge, Mass. d: 4/23/33, Cambridge, Mass. BR/TR, 5'10.5", 185 lbs. Deb: 8/6/1880 UH																									
1880	Tro-N	6	6	.500	12	12	12	0	0	105	68	0	16	39	**7.2**	**0.86**	**294**	**.178**	**.212**	10	.233	-0	18	19	1	2.2
1881	Tro-N	18	27	.400	45	45	45	4	0	402	442	4	81	103	11.7	3.25	91	.274	.309	35	.230	4	-21	-13	-0	-0.9
1882	Tro-N	17	26	.395	43	42	41	1	0	375	368	4	81	116	10.8	2.50	113	.244	.283	43	.228	5	17	14	5	2.2
1883	NY-a	41	27	.603	**68**	68	**68**	5	0	**619**	488	6	108	**359**	**8.7**	2.41	138	**.203**	**.237**	57	.220	4	61	64	6	6.6
1884	*NY-a	37	17	.685	58	58	56	4	0	483	380	5	71	334	8.7	2.25	138	**.204**	.239	50	.238	12	53	47	-0	5.5
1885	NY-N	32	13	.711	46	46	45	7	0	400	300	6	102	227	9.0	**1.58**	**169**	.203	.255	27	.163	-1	55	49	0	4.7
1886	NY-N	**42**	20	.677	**64**	64	**62**	2	0	**535**	479	9	102	297	9.8	2.56	126	.231	.267	35	.171	1	45	39	1	3.7
1887	NY-N	35	19	.648	56	56	54	2	0	476^2	428	11	108	189	**10.3**	3.12	121	**.230**	**.276**	42	.220	8	51	35	3	3.8
1888	*NY-N	**35**	12	**.745**	51	51	48	**8**	0	434^1	317	5	90	**335**	**8.7**	**1.74**	**157**	**.196**	.243	23	.127	-6	**54**	**48**	1	4.2
1889	*NY-N	28	13	.683	47	45	39	3	1	364	319	9	151	225	12.1	3.31	119	**.228**	.312	23	.154	-4	28	25	2	2.1
1890	NY-P	17	11	.607	30	30	23	1	0	229	225	6	89	89	12.7	3.38	134	.246	.318	10	.109	-5	22	30	1	2.4
1891	NY-N	2	5	.286	8	7	4	0	0	55	70	1	27	30	16.5	5.24	61	.299	.381	2	.095	-1	-12	-12	0	-1.2
	Phi-N	3	6	.333	11	10	9	0	1	78^1	82	2	30	34	13.3	3.91	87	.259	.331	5	.172	0	-5	-4	0	-0.4
	Yr	5	11	.313	19	17	13	0	1	133^1	152	3	57	64	14.4	4.45	75	.274	.346	7	.140	-1	-16	-17	1	-1.6
1892	Phi-N	19	16	.543	39	38	31	2	0	313^1	264	4	100	127	10.8	2.36	138	.219	.286	10	.085	-7	32	31	-1	2.2
1893	Phi-N	10	7	.588	22	22	17	0	0	178	202	3	80	56	14.9	4.40	104	.277	.359	18	.228	0	5	4	-2	0.1
Total	14	342	225	.603	600	594	554	39	2	5047^2	4432	75	1236	2560	10.3	2.62	125	.226	.275	390	.187	11	404	375	18	37.2
● ED KEEGAN	Keegan, Edward Charles b: 7/8/39, Camden, N.J. BR/TR, 6'3", 165 lbs. Deb: 8/24/59																									
1959	Phi-N	0	3	.000	3	3	0	0	0	9	19	2	13	3	33.0	18.00	23	.432	.569	0	.000	-0	-14	-14	-0	-2.6
1961	KC-A	0	0	—	6	0	0	0	1	6	6	0	5	3	16.5	4.50	93	.261	.393	0	—	0	-0	-0	-0	0.0
1962	Phi-N	0	0	—	4	0	0	0	0	8	6	1	5	5	13.5	2.25	172	.214	.353	0	—	0	2	1	-0	0.0
Total	3	0	3	.000	13	3	0	0	1	23	31	3	23	11	21.9	9.00	45	.326	.467	0	.000	-0	-13	-13	-1	-2.6
● BOB KEEGAN	Keegan, Robert Charles "Smiley" b: 8/4/20, Rochester, N.Y. BR/TR, 6'2.5", 207 lbs. Deb: 5/24/53																									
1953	Chi-A	7	5	.583	22	11	4	2	1	98^2	80	4	33	32	10.5	2.74	147	.223	.293	9	.321	2	14	14	1	1.9
1954	Chi-A★	16	9	.640	31	27	14	2	2	209^2	211	16	82	61	12.6	3.09	121	.266	.336	9	.120	-2	15	15	-1	1.4
1955	Chi-A	2	5	.286	18	11	1	0	0	58^2	83	4	28	29	17.2	5.83	68	.336	.406	6	.333	2	-12	-12	0	-1.1
1956	Chi-A	5	7	.417	20	16	4	0	0	105^1	119	15	35	32	13.3	3.93	104	.286	.344	4	.125	-1	3	2	-0	0.1
1957	Chi-A	10	8	.556	30	20	6	2	2	142^2	131	22	37	36	10.7	3.53	106	.243	.294	4	.103	-1	4	3	-1	0.1
1958	Chi-A	0	2	.000	14	2	0	0	0	29^2	44	9	18	8	18.8	6.07	60	.358	.440	0	.000	-1	-8	-8	1	-0.5
Total	6	40	36	.526	135	87	29	6	5	644^2	668	70	233	198	12.7	3.66	105	.270	.335	32	.163	-2	16	14	-1	1.9
● BURT KEELEY	Keeley, Burton Elwood "Speed" b: 11/2/1879, Wilmington, Ill. d: 5/3/52, Ely, Minn. BR/TR, 5'9", 170 lbs. Deb: 4/18/08																									
1908	Was-A	6	11	.353	28	15	12	1	1	169	173	3	48	68	12.0	2.98	77	.259	.313	5	.102	-3	-11	-13	2	-1.5
1909	Was-A	0	0	—	2	0	0	0	0	7	12	0	1	0	18.0	11.57	21	.364	.400	1	.500	0	-7	-7	1	0.1
Total	2	6	11	.353	30	15	12	1	1	176	185	3	49	68	12.2	3.32	69	.264	.317	6	.118	-3	-18	-20	2	-1.4
● VIC KEEN	Keen, Howard Victor b: 3/16/1899, Bel Air, Md. d: 12/10/76, Salisbury, Md. BR/TR, 5'9", 165 lbs. Deb: 8/13/18																									
1918	Phi-A	0	1	.000	1	1	0	0	0	8	9	1	1	1	11.3	3.38	87	.300	.323	0	.000	-0	-1	-0	-1	-0.1
1921	Chi-N	0	3	.000	5	4	1	0	0	25	29	0	9	9	14.0	4.68	82	.319	.386	0	.000	-0	-2	-2	0	-0.3
1922	Chi-N	1	2	.333	7	2	2	0	1	34^2	36	4	10	11	12.2	3.89	108	.275	.331	4	.333	1	1	1	-0	0.2
1923	Chi-N	12	8	.600	35	17	10	0	1	177	169	8	57	46	11.7	3.00	133	.255	.319	8	.151	-3	20	20	-2	1.6
1924	Chi-N	15	14	.517	40	28	15	0	3	234^2	242	17	80	75	12.5	3.80	103	.272	.335	12	.156	-4	2	3	-3	-0.5
1925	Chi-N	2	6	.250	30	8	1	0	1	83^1	125	8	41	19	17.9	6.26	69	.359	.427	6	.240	0	-18	-18	1	-1.4
1926	*StL-N	10	9	.526	26	21	12	1	0	152	179	15	42	29	13.1	4.56	86	.295	.342	3	.057	-6	-12	-11	-2	-2.0
1927	StL-N	2	1	.667	21	0	0	0	0	33^2	39	3	8	12	13.1	4.81	82	.293	.343	1	.250	0	-3	-3	0	-0.2
Total	8	42	44	.488	165	81	41	1	6	748^1	828	56	248	202	13.1	4.11	97	.287	.346	34	.148	-12	-15	-11	-6	-2.7
● KID KEENAN	Keenan, Harry Leon b: 1875, Louisville, Ky. d: 6/11/03, Covington, Ky. TR, Deb: 8/11/1891																									
1891	Cin-a	0	1	.000	1	1	1	0	0	8	6	0	4	5	12.4	0.00	—	.200	.314	2	.500	0	3	4	-0	0.5
● JIM KEENAN	Keenan, James William b: 2/10/1858, New Haven, Conn. d: 9/21/26, Cincinnati, Ohio BR/TR, 5'10", 186 lbs. Deb: 5/17/1875 ♦																									
1884	Ind-a	0	0	—	1	0	0	0	0	3	2	0	0	0	6.0	3.00	110	.182	.182	73	.293	0	0	0	-0	0.0
1885	Cin-a	0	0	—	1	0	0	0	0	8	7	0	1	0	9.0	1.13	290	.233	.258	35	.265	0	2	2	0	0.0
1886	Cin-a	0	1	.000	2	0	0	0	0	8	8	0	3	2	12.4	3.38	104	.258	.324	40	.270	0	0	0	-0	0.0
Total	3	0	1	.000	4	0	0	0	0	19	17	0	4	2	9.9	2.37	142	.236	.276	452	.241	1	2	2	-0	0.0
● JIMMIE KEENAN	Keenan, James William "Sparkplug" b: 5/25/1898, Avon, N.Y. d: 6/5/80, Seminole, Fla. BL/TL, 5'7", 155 lbs. Deb: 9/9/20																									
1920	Phi-N	0	0	—	1	0	0	0	0	3	3	0	1	2	12.0	3.00	114	.333	.400	0	.000	-0	0	0	0	0.0
1921	Phi-N	1	2	.333	15	2	0	0	0	32^1	48	3	15	7	17.8	6.68	63	.364	.432	0	.000	-1	-10	-9	-1	-0.9
Total	2	1	2	.333	16	2	0	0	0	35^1	51	3	16	9	17.3	6.37	65	.362	.430	0	.000	-2	-10	-9	-1	-0.9
● JEFF KEENER	Keener, Jeffrey Bruce b: 1/14/59, Pana, Ill. BL/TR, 6', 170 lbs. Deb: 6/8/82																									
1982	StL-N	1	1	.500	19	0	0	0	0	22^1	19	1	19	25	15.3	1.61	224	.235	.380	0	—	0	5	5	0	0.4
1983	StL-N	0	0	—	4	0	0	0	0	4^1	6	0	1	4	16.6	8.31	44	.333	.400	0	—	0	-2	-2	0	0.0
Total	2	1	1	.500	23	0	0	0	0	26^2	25	1	20	29	15.5	2.70	134	.253	.383	0	—	0	3	3	0	0.4
● JOE KEENER	Keener, Joseph Donald b: 4/21/53, San Pedro, Cal. BR/TR, 6'4", 200 lbs. Deb: 9/18/76																									
1976	Mon-N	0	1	.000	2	2	0	0	0	4^1	7	0	8	1	33.2	10.38	36	.389	.593	0	.000	-0	-3	-3	0	-0.6
● HARRY KEENER	Keener, Joshua Harry "Beans" b: 9/1869, Easton, Pa. d: 3/5/12, Easton, Pa. TR, Deb: 6/27/1896																									
1896	Phi-N	3	11	.214	16	13	11	0	0	113^1	144	5	39	28	15.2	5.88	73	.307	.371	16	.314	2	-19	-20	0	-1.6
● RICKEY KEETON	Keeton, Rickey b: 3/18/57, Cincinnati, Ohio BR/TR, 6'2", 190 lbs. Deb: 5/27/80																									
1980	Mil-A	2	2	.500	5	5	0	0	0	28^1	35	4	9	8	14.0	4.76	81	.307	.358	0	—	0	-2	-3	0	-0.3
1981	Mil-A	1	0	1.000	17	0	0	0	0	35^1	47	4	11	9	14.8	5.09	67	.329	.377	0	—	0	-6	-7	0	-0.2
Total	2	3	2	.600	22	5	0	0	0	63^2	82	8	20	17	14.4	4.95	73	.319	.368	0	—	0	-8	-9	0	-0.5
● FRANK KEFFER	Keffer, Frank b: Harrisburg, Pa. Deb: 4/19/1890																									
1890	Syr-a	1	1	.500	2	1	1	0	0	16	15	0	9	4	13.5	5.63	63	.242	.338	1	.143	-1	-3	-4	0	-0.4
● CHET KEHN	Kehn, Chester Lawrence b: 10/30/21, San Diego, Cal. d: 4/5/84, San Diego, Cal. BR/TR, 5'11", 168 lbs. Deb: 4/30/42																									
1942	Bro-N	0	0	—	3	1	0	0	0	7^2	8	2	4	3	14.1	7.04	46	.267	.353	2	1.000	1	-3	-3	0	0.2
● KATSY KEIFER	Keifer, Sherman Carl b: 9/3/1891, California, Pa. d: 2/19/27, Outwood, Ky. BB/TL, Deb: 10/8/14																									
1914	Ind-F	1	0	1.000	1	1	1	0	0	9	6	0	2	2	8.0	2.00	156	.194	.242	1	.333	0	1	1	0	0.2
● MIKE KEKICH	Kekich, Michael Dennis b: 4/2/45, San Diego, Cal. BR/TL, 6'1", 200 lbs. Deb: 6/9/65																									
1965	LA-N	0	1	.000	5	1	0	0	0	10^1	10	2	13	9	20.0	9.58	34	.263	.451	0	.000	-0	-7	-7	-0	-0.7
1968	LA-N	2	10	.167	25	20	1	1	0	115	116	9	46	84	12.8	3.91	71	.267	.339	3	.081	-2	-12	-15	-1	-1.8
1969	NY-A	4	6	.400	28	13	1	0	1	105	91	11	49	66	12.2	4.54	77	.236	.325	3	.111	-1	-11	-12	-1	-1.3
1970	NY-A	6	3	.667	26	14	1	0	0	98^2	103	12	55	63	14.5	4.83	73	.267	.360	3	.094	-1	-12	-14	-1	-1.4
1971	NY-A	10	9	.526	37	24	3	0	0	170^1	167	13	82	93	13.4	4.07	79	.257	.344	8	.154	-0	-11	-16	1	-1.5
1972	NY-A	10	13	.435	29	28	2	0	0	175^1	172	13	76	78	12.9	3.70	80	.263	.344	8	.136	-1	-12	-15	-1	-2.1
1973	NY-A	1	1	.500	5	4	0	0	0	14^2	20	1	14	4	22.1	9.20	40	.351	.493	0	—	0	-9	-9	-0	-1.0
	Cle-A	1	4	.200	16	6	0	0	0	50	73	6	35	26	19.4	7.02	56	.349	.443	0	—	0	-18	-17	-1	-1.6
	Yr	2	5	.286	21	10	0	0	0	64^2	93	7	49	30	19.8	7.52	51	.346	.447	0	—	0	-27	-26	-2	-2.6
1975	Tex-A	0	0	—	23	0	0	0	2	31^1	33	2	21	19	15.5	3.73	101	.282	.391	0	—	0	0	0	1	0.1

YEAR	TM/L	W	L	PCT	G	GS	CG	SH	SV	IP	H	HR	BB	SO	RAT	ERA	ERA+	OAV	OOB	BH	AVG	PB	PR	/A	PD	TPI
1977	Sea-A	5	4	.556	41	2	0	0	3	90	90	11	51	55	14.4	5.60	73	.265	.365	0	—	0	-15	-15	-0	-1.4
Total	9	39	51	.433	235	112	8	1	6	860^2	875	80	442	497	13.9	4.59	72	.268	.358	25	.120	-5	-108	-121	-4	-12.7
● GEORGE KELB Kelb, George Francis "Pugger" or "Lefty" b: 7/17/1870, Toledo, Ohio d: 10/20/36, Toledo, Ohio BL/TL, Deb: 4/17/1898																										
1898	Cle-N	0	1	.000	3	1	1	0	0	16^1	23	0	1	8	15.4	4.41	82	.329	.373	1	.200	-0	-1	-1	0	-0.1
● HAL KELLEHER Kelleher, Harold Joseph b: 6/24/13, Philadelphia, Pa. d: 8/27/89, Cape May Court House, N.J. BR/TR, 6', 165 lbs. Deb: 9/17/35																										
1935	Phi-N	2	0	1.000	3	3	2	1	0	25	26	0	12	12	14.0	1.80	252	.260	.345	3	.375	1	6	8	0	0.7
1936	Phi-N	0	5	.000	14	4	1	0	0	44	60	2	29	13	18.8	5.32	85	.331	.432	2	.167	-0	-6	-4	0	-0.4
1937	Phi-N	2	4	.333	27	2	1	0	0	58^1	72	3	31	20	17.0	6.63	65	.308	.404	3	.176	-0	-18	-15	-0	-1.4
1938	Phi-N	0	0	—	6	0	0	0	0	7^1	16	0	9	4	30.7	18.41	21	.432	.543	1	.500	0	-12	-12	0	0.1
Total	4	4	9	.308	50	9	4	1	0	134^2	174	5	81	49	17.8	5.95	74	.315	.413	9	.231	0	-30	-23	0	-1.0
● RON KELLER Keller, Ronald Lee b: 6/3/43, Indianapolis, Ind. BR/TR, 6'2", 200 lbs. Deb: 7/9/66																										
1966	Min-A	0	0	—	2	0	0	0	0	5^1	7	1	1	1	13.5	5.06	71	.318	.348	0	.000	-0	-1	-1	0	0.0
1968	Min-A	0	1	.000	7	1	0	0	0	16	18	2	4	11	12.9	2.81	110	.305	.359	0	.000	-0	0	0	0	0.0
Total	2	0	1	.000	9	1	0	0	0	21^1	25	3	5	12	13.1	3.38	95	.309	.356	0	.000	-0	-1	-0	0	0.0
● AL KELLETT Kellett, Alfred Henry b: 10/30/01, Red Bank, N.J. d: 7/14/60, New York, N.Y. BR/TR, 6'3", 200 lbs. Deb: 7/1/23																										
1923	Phi-A	0	1	.000	5	0	0	0	0	10	11	0	8	1	17.1	6.30	65	.282	.404	1	.333	0	-3	-2	1	-0.1
1924	Bos-A	0	0	—	1	0	0	0	0	0	0	0	2	0	—	∞	—	—	1.000	0	—	0	-2	-2	0	-0.2
Total	2	0	1	.000	6	0	0	0	0	10	11	0	10	1	18.9	8.10	51	.282	.429	1	.333	0	-5	-4	1	-0.3
● HARRY KELLEY Kelley, Harry Leroy b: 2/13/06, Parkin, Ark. d: 3/23/58, Parkin, Ark. BR/TR, 5'9.5", 170 lbs. Deb: 4/16/25																										
1925	Was-A	1	1	.500	6	1	0	0	0	16	30	0	12	7	23.6	9.00	47	.405	.488	0	.000	-1	-8	-8	1	-0.8
1926	Was-A	0	0	—	7	1	0	0	0	10	17	0	8	6	23.4	8.10	48	.405	.510	0	.000	-0	-5	-5	-0	0.0
1936	Phi-A	15	12	.556	35	27	20	1	3	235^1	250	21	75	82	12.5	3.86	132	.275	.332	18	.198	-1	31	32	-2	2.9
1937	Phi-A	13	21	.382	41	29	14	0	0	205	267	16	79	68	15.3	5.36	88	.306	.365	16	.225	1	-17	-15	-1	-1.9
1938	Phi-A	0	2	.000	4	3	0	0	0	8	17	0	10	3	30.4	16.88	29	.436	.551	0	.000	-0	-11	-11	-0	-1.8
	Was-A	9	8	.529	38	14	7	2	1	148^1	162	12	46	44	12.7	4.49	100	.276	.330	12	.250	1	5	0	0	0.2
	Yr	9	10	.474	42	17	7	2	1	156^1	179	12	56	47	13.6	5.12	88	.286	.346	12	.240	1	-6	-10	0	-1.6
1939	Was-A	4	3	.571	15	3	2	0	1	53^2	69	2	14	20	14.4	4.70	93	.314	.363	4	.267	1	-0	-2	-0	-0.2
Total	6	42	47	.472	146	78	43	3	5	676^1	812	51	244	230	14.2	4.86	98	.296	.356	50	.216	0	-5	-8	-2	-1.6
● DICK KELLEY Kelley, Richard Anthony b: 1/8/40, Boston, Mass d: 12/12/91, Northridge, Cal. BR/TL, 6', 175 lbs. Deb: 4/15/64																										
1964	Mil-N	0	0	—	2	0	0	0	0	2	2	0	3	2	22.5	18.00	20	.250	.455	0	—	0	-3	-3	-0	0.0
1965	Mil-N	1	1	.500	21	4	0	0	0	45	37	5	20	31	11.4	3.00	117	.226	.310	0	.000	-1	3	3	-0	0.0
1966	Atl-N	7	5	.583	20	13	2	2	0	81	75	6	21	50	11.0	3.22	113	.247	.302	1	.036	-3	3	4	-2	0.1
1967	Atl-N	2	9	.182	39	9	1	1	2	98	88	8	42	75	12.0	3.77	88	.247	.328	4	.250	1	-4	-5	1	-0.3
1968	Atl-N	2	4	.333	31	11	1	1	1	98	86	4	45	73	12.1	2.76	109	.238	.324	1	.043	-1	3	3	1	0.2
1969	SD-N	4	8	.333	27	23	1	1	0	136	113	11	61	96	11.8	3.57	99	.230	.321	5	.106	-2	0	-1	2	-0.1
1971	SD-N	2	3	.400	48	1	0	0	2	59^2	52	5	23	42	11.9	3.47	95	.232	.315	1	.333	0	-0	-1	0	-0.1
Total	7	18	30	.375	188	61	5	5	5	519^2	453	39	215	369	11.8	3.39	100	.237	.319	12	.096	-5	1	-1	2	-0.2
● TOM KELLEY Kelley, Thomas Henry b: 1/5/44, Manchester, Conn. BR/TR, 6', 191 lbs. Deb: 5/5/64																										
1964	Cle-A	0	0	—	6	0	0	0	0	9^2	9	1	9	7	17.7	5.59	64	.237	.396	0	—	0	-2	-2	0	0.0
1965	Cle-A	2	1	.667	4	4	1	0	0	30	19	3	13	31	9.6	2.40	145	.186	.278	2	.222	0	4	4	-0	0.4
1966	Cle-A	4	8	.333	31	7	1	0	0	95^1	97	14	42	64	13.1	4.34	79	.264	.340	4	.143	-1	-10	-10	-1	-1.4
1967	Cle-A	0	0	—	1	0	0	0	0	1	0	0	2	0	18.0	0.00	—	.000	.500	0	—	0	0	0	0	0.0
1971	Atl-N	9	5	.643	28	20	5	0	0	143	140	8	69	68	13.2	2.96	125	.262	.347	2	.047	-4	8	12	-1	0.7
1972	Atl-N	5	7	.417	27	14	2	1	0	116^1	122	12	65	59	14.5	4.56	83	.272	.364	3	.088	-2	-14	-10	-3	-1.4
1973	Atl-N	0	1	.000	7	0	0	0	0	12^2	13	0	7	5	14.2	2.84	138	.289	.385	0	.000	-0	1	2	-0	0.1
Total	7	20	22	.476	104	45	9	1	0	408	400	38	207	234	13.4	3.75	97	.260	.349	11	.095	-6	-13	-4	-5	-1.6
● ALEX KELLNER Kellner, Alexander Raymond b: 8/26/24, Tucson, Ariz. d: 5/3/96, Tucson, Ariz. BR/TL, 6', 200 lbs. Deb: 4/29/48 F																										
1948	Phi-A	0	0	—	13	1	0	0	0	23	21	0	16	14	15.3	7.83	55	.239	.368	0	.000	-1	-9	-9	-0	-0.1
1949	Phi-A☆	20	12	.625	38	27	19	0	1	245	243	18	129	94	13.7	3.75	110	.261	.352	20	.217	1	12	10	-0	1.3
1950	Phi-A	8	20	.286	36	29	15	0	2	225^1	253	28	112	85	14.7	5.47	83	.282	.363	16	.200	-1	-22	-23	-2	-2.7
1951	Phi-A	11	14	.440	33	29	11	1	2	209^2	218	20	93	94	13.5	4.46	96	.272	.350	18	.228	-1	-8	-4	-1	-0.6
1952	Phi-A	12	14	.462	34	33	14	2	0	231^1	223	21	86	105	12.2	4.36	91	.252	.321	17	.207	0	-18	-10	-2	-1.2
1953	Phi-A	11	12	.478	25	25	14	2	0	201^2	210	8	51	81	11.8	3.93	109	.269	.317	15	.217	1	2	8	-2	0.8
1954	Phi-A	6	17	.261	27	27	8	1	0	173^2	204	16	88	69	15.4	5.39	72	.301	.387	10	.182	-0	-32	-29	0	-3.3
1955	KC-A	11	8	.579	30	24	6	3	0	162^2	164	18	60	75	12.7	4.20	99	.265	.335	12	.214	2	-4	-1	-0	0.2
1956	KC-A	7	4	.636	20	17	5	0	0	91^2	103	15	33	44	13.5	4.32	100	.289	.353	6	.200	-0	-2	0	0	0.0
1957	KC-A	6	5	.545	28	21	3	0	0	132^2	141	18	41	72	12.5	4.27	93	.278	.335	11	.234	4	-7	-5	0	0.1
1958	KC-A	0	2	.000	7	6	0	0	0	33^2	40	5	8	22	12.8	5.88	66	.315	.356	1	.091	-0	-8	-7	0	-0.4
	Cin-N	7	3	.700	18	7	4	0	0	82	74	8	20	42	10.6	2.30	180	.243	.296	10	.357	3	15	17	-2	2.1
1959	StL-N	2	1	.667	12	4	0	0	0	37	31	9	10	19	10.2	3.16	134	.220	.276	2	.222	0	3	4	-0	0.3
Total	12	101	112	.474	321	250	99	9	5	1849^1	1925	184	747	816	13.2	4.41	95	.270	.343	138	.215	7	-78	-47	-8	-3.5
● WALT KELLNER Kellner, Walter Joseph b: 4/26/29, Tucson, Ariz. BR/TR, 6', 200 lbs. Deb: 9/6/52 F																										
1952	Phi-A	0	0	—	1	0	0	0	1	4	4	0	3	2	15.8	6.75	59	.250	.368	0	.000	-0	-1	-1	-0	-0.1
1953	Phi-A	0	0	—	2	0	0	0	0	3	1	0	4	4	18.0	6.00	71	.111	.429	0	—	0	-1	-1	0	0.0
Total	2	0	0	—	3	0	0	0	1	7	5	0	7	6	16.7	6.43	64	.200	.394	0	.000	-0	-2	-2	0	-0.1
● AL KELLOGG Kellogg, Albert C. b: 9/9/1886, Providence, R.I. d: 7/21/53, Portland, Ore. TL, 6'3", 208 lbs. Deb: 9/25/08																										
1908	Phi-A	0	2	.000	3	3	2	0	0	17	20	1	9	8	15.9	5.82	44	.294	.385	1	.125	-0	-6	-6	0	-0.7
● WIN KELLUM Kellum, Winford Ansley b: 4/11/1876, Waterford, Ont., Canada d: 8/10/51, Big Rapids, Mich. BB/TL, 5'10", 190 lbs. Deb: 4/26/01																										
1901	Bos-A	2	3	.400	6	6	5	0	0	48	61	3	7	8	13.3	6.38	55	.305	.338	3	.167	-1	-14	-15	1	-1.2
1904	Cin-N	15	10	.600	31	24	22	1	2	224^2	206	1	46	70	10.5	2.60	113	.244	.291	13	.159	2	3	8	1	1.1
1905	StL-N	3	3	.500	11	7	5	1	0	74	70	1	10	19	9.9	2.92	102	.255	.283	5	.200	1	1	0	1	0.2
Total	3	20	16	.556	48	37	32	2	2	346^2	337	5	63	97	10.7	3.19	95	.255	.297	21	.168	2	-10	-6	3	0.1
● BRYAN KELLY Kelly, Bryan Keith b: 2/24/59, Silver Spring, Md. BR/TR, 6'2", 195 lbs. Deb: 9/2/86																										
1986	Det-A	1	2	.333	6	4	0	0	0	20	21	4	10	18	13.9	4.50	92	.269	.352	0	—	0	-1	-1	0	-0.1
1987	Det-A	0	1	.000	5	0	0	0	0	10^2	12	2	7	10	16.0	5.06	83	.286	.388	0	—	0	-1	-1	-0	-0.1
Total	2	1	3	.250	11	4	0	0	0	30^2	33	6	17	28	14.7	4.70	89	.275	.365	0	—	0	-1	-2	0	-0.2
● ED KELLY Kelly, Edward Leo b: 12/10/1888, Pawtucket, R.I. d: 11/4/28, Red Lodge, Mont. BR/TR, 5'11.5", 173 lbs. Deb: 4/14/14																										
1914	Bos-A	0	0	—	3	0	0	0	0	2^1	1	0	1	4	7.7	0.00	—	.100	.182	0	.000	-0	1	1	0	0.0
● GEORGE KELLY Kelly, George Lange "Highpockets" b: 9/10/1895, San Francisco, Cal. d: 10/13/84, Burlingame, Cal. BR/TR, 6'4", 190 lbs. Deb: 8/18/15 FCH♦																										
1917	NY-N	1	0	1.000	1	0	0	0	0	5	4	0	1	2	9.0	0.00	—	.211	.250	0	.000	-0	2	1	-0	0.3
● HERB KELLY Kelly, Herbert Barrett "Moke" b: 6/4/1892, Mobile, Ala. d: 5/18/73, Torrance, Cal. BL/TL, 5'9", 160 lbs. Deb: 9/25/14																										
1914	Pit-N	0	2	.000	5	2	2	0	0	25^2	24	1	7	6	10.9	2.45	108	.253	.304	2	.222	0	1	1	-0	0.0
1915	Pit-N	1	1	.500	5	1	0	0	0	11	10	0	4	6	12.3	4.09	67	.250	.333	1	.500	1	-2	-2	1	-0.1
Total	2	1	3	.250	10	3	2	0	0	36^2	34	1	11	12	11.3	2.95	91	.252	.313	3	.273	1	-1	-1	1	-0.1
● MIKE KELLY Kelly, Michael J. b: 11/9/02, St.Louis, Mo. BR/TR, 6'1", 178 lbs. Deb: 9/3/26																										
1926	Phi-N	0	0	—	4	0	0	0	0	6^2	9	0	4	2	18.9	9.45	44	.346	.452	0	.000	-0	-4	-4	-0	-0.1

YEAR	TM/L	W	L	PCT	G	GS	CG	SH	SV	IP	H	HR	BB	SO	RAT	ERA	ERA+	OAV	OOB	BH	AVG	PB	PR	/A	PD	TPI
● **KING KELLY**	Kelly, Michael Joseph b: 12/31/1857, Troy, N.Y. d: 11/8/1894, Boston, Mass. BR/TR, 5'10", 170 lbs. Deb: 5/1/1878 MH♦																									
1880	Chi-N	0	0	—	1	0	0	0	0	3	3	0	1	1	12.0	0.00	—	.250	.308	100	.291	0	1	1	-0	0.0
1883	Chi-N	0	0	—	1	0	0	0	0	1	1	0	0	0	9.0	0.00	—	.333	.333	109	.255	0	0	0	0	0.0
1884	Chi-N	0	1	.000	2	0	0	0	0	5^1	12	2	2	1	23.6	8.44	37	.400	.438	160	.354	1	-3	-3	-0	-0.4
1887	Bos-N	1	0	1.000	3	0	0	0	0	13	17	1	14	0	21.5	3.46	117	.298	.437	156	.322	1	1	1	0	0.1
1890	Bos-P	1	0	1.000	1	0	0	0	0	2	1	0	2	2	13.5	4.50	98	.143	.333	111	.326	0	-0	-0	-0	0.0
1891	Cin-a	0	1	.000	3	0	0	0	0	15^1	21	2	7	0	17.0	5.28	78	.313	.387	84	.297	1	-3	-2	0	0.0
1892	*Bos-N	0	0	—	1	0	0	0	0	6	8	0	4	0	22.5	1.50	234	.308	.455	53	.189	0	1	1	-0	0.0
Total	7	2	2	.500	12	0	0	0	0	45^2	63	5	30	4	19.1	4.14	92	.312	.411	1813	.308	4	-3	-2	-0	-0.3
● **REN KELLY**	Kelly, Reynolds Joseph b: 11/18/1899, San Francisco, Cal d: 8/24/63, Millbrae, Cal. BR/TR, 6', 183 lbs. Deb: 9/18/23 F																									
1923	Phi-A	0	0	—	1	0	0	0	0	7	7	0	4	1	14.1	2.57	160	.259	.355	0	.000	-0	1	1	-0	-0.1
● **BOB KELLY**	Kelly, Robert Edward b: 10/4/27, Cleveland, Ohio BR/TR, 6', 180 lbs. Deb: 5/4/51																									
1951	Chi-N	7	4	.636	35	11	4	0	0	123^2	130	8	55	48	13.5	4.66	88	.275	.352	5	.161	-1	-10	-8	-0	-0.7
1952	Chi-N	4	9	.308	31	15	3	2	0	125^1	114	7	46	50	11.7	3.59	107	.236	.306	8	.216	0	2	4	1	0.5
1953	Chi-N	0	1	.000	14	0	0	0	0	17	27	2	9	6	19.6	9.53	47	.375	.451	0	.000	-0	-10	-10	0	-0.5
	Cin-N	1	2	.333	28	5	0	0	2	66^1	71	7	26	29	13.2	4.34	100	.276	.343	2	.118	-1	-0	0	0	-0.1
	Yr	1	3	.250	42	5	0	0	2	83^1	98	9	35	35	14.4	5.40	81	.297	.364	2	.111	-1	-10	-9	1	-0.6
1958	Cin-N	0	0	—	2	1	0	0	0	2	3	0	3	1	27.0	4.50	92	.500	.667	0	—	0	-0	-0	0	0.0
	Cle-A	0	2	.000	13	3	0	0	0	27^2	29	4	13	12	14.0	5.20	70	.282	.368	1	.250	0	-4	-5	0	-0.3
Total	4	12	18	.400	123	35	7	2	2	362	374	28	152	146	13.2	4.50	90	.268	.343	16	.178	-1	-22	-18	1	-1.1
● **BILL KELSO**	Kelso, William Eugene b: 2/19/40, Kansas City, Mo. BR/TR, 6'4", 215 lbs. Deb: 7/31/64																									
1964	LA-A	2	0	1.000	10	1	1	1	0	23^2	19	3	9	21	11.0	2.28	144	.218	.299	0	.000	-0	4	3	0	0.2
1966	Cal-A	1	1	.500	5	0	0	0	0	11^1	11	1	6	11	14.3	2.38	141	.244	.346	0	.000	-0	1	1	-0	0.2
1967	Cal-A	5	3	.625	69	1	0	0	11	112	85	6	63	91	12.2	2.97	106	.219	.333	2	.105	-1	3	2	1	0.2
1968	Cin-N	4	1	.800	35	0	0	0	1	54	56	6	15	39	12.3	4.00	79	.277	.336	0	.000	-1	-6	-5	-1	-0.7
Total	4	12	5	.706	119	2	1	1	12	201	171	16	93	162	12.2	3.13	102	.237	.331	2	.059	-2	2	1	-0	-0.1
● **RUSS KEMMERER**	Kemmerer, Russell Paul "Rusty" or "Dutch" b: 11/1/31, Pittsburgh, Pa. BR/TR, 6'3", 200 lbs. Deb: 6/27/54																									
1954	Bos-A	5	3	.625	19	9	2	1	0	75^1	71	4	41	37	13.6	3.82	108	.257	.357	3	.143	-0	-1	2	0	0.2
1955	Bos-A	1	1	.500	7	2	0	0	0	17^1	18	3	15	13	17.1	7.27	59	.269	.402	0	.000	-0	-6	-6	-0	-0.6
1957	Bos-A	0	0	—	1	0	0	0	0	4	5	0	2	1	15.8	4.50	89	.333	.412	0	.000	-0	-0	-0	-0	0.0
	Was-A	7	11	.389	39	26	6	0	0	172^1	214	20	71	81	15.0	4.96	79	.309	.375	3	.067	-1	-22	-20	-3	-2.3
	Yr	7	11	.389	40	26	6	0	0	176^1	219	20	73	82	15.0	4.95	79	.309	.375	3	.065	-1	-23	-21	-3	-2.3
1958	Was-A	6	15	.286	40	30	6	0	0	224^1	234	25	74	111	12.5	4.61	83	.270	.330	11	.159	-2	-21	-20	0	-1.9
1959	Was-A	8	17	.320	37	28	8	0	0	206	221	20	71	89	12.9	4.50	87	.276	.338	8	.133	-1	-15	-13	0	-1.5
1960	Was-A	0	2	.000	3	3	0	0	0	17^1	18	2	10	10	15.1	7.79	50	.269	.372	0	.000	0	-8	-8	1	-0.6
	Chi-A	6	3	.667	36	7	2	1	2	120^2	111	5	45	76	11.7	2.98	127	.248	.318	0	.000	-3	12	11	0	0.5
	Yr	6	5	.545	39	10	2	1	2	138	129	7	55	86	12.1	3.59	106	.250	.323	0	.000	-3	4	3	1	-0.1
1961	Chi-A	3	3	.500	47	2	0	0	2	96^2	102	10	26	35	11.9	4.38	89	.278	.326	3	.200	1	-4	-5	1	-0.1
1962	Chi-A	2	1	.667	20	0	0	0	0	28	30	3	11	17	13.2	3.86	101	.270	.336	1	.500	1	0	0	1	0.2
	Hou-N	5	3	.625	36	2	0	0	3	68	72	10	15	23	11.9	4.10	91	.272	.318	3	.333	1	-1	-3	0	-0.2
1963	Hou-N	0	0	—	17	0	0	0	1	36^2	48	1	8	12	13.7	5.65	56	.320	.354	2	.286	0	-10	-10	1	0.0
Total	9	43	59	.422	302	109	24	2	8	1066^2	1144	103	389	505	13.1	4.46	86	.277	.342	34	.128	-5	-76	-72	1	-6.3
● **DUTCH KEMNER**	Kemner, Herman John b: 3/4/1899, Quincy, Ill. d: 1/16/88, Quincy, Ill. BR/TR, 5'10.5", 175 lbs. Deb: 4/19/29																									
1929	Cin-N	0	0	—	9	0	0	0	1	15^1	19	0	8	10	15.8	7.63	60	.328	.409	1	.250	0	-5	-5	0	-0.1
● **ED KENNA**	Kenna, Edward Benninghaus "The Pitching Poet" b: 10/17/1877, Charleston, W.Va. d: 3/22/12, Grant, Fla. TR , 6', 180 lbs. Deb: 5/5/02																									
1902	Phi-A	1	1	.500	2	1	1	0	0	17	19	1	11	5	16.4	5.29	69	.284	.392	1	.125	-0	-3	-3	0	-0.3
● **VERN KENNEDY**	Kennedy, Lloyd Vernon b: 3/20/07, Kansas City, Mo. d: 1/28/93, Mendon, Mo. BL/TR, 6', 175 lbs. Deb: 9/18/34																									
1934	Chi-A	0	2	.000	3	3	1	0	0	19^1	21	1	9	7	14.0	3.72	127	.300	.380	2	.286	0	2	2	1	0.3
1935	Chi-A	11	11	.500	31	25	16	2	1	211^2	211	17	95	65	13.2	3.91	118	.262	.343	18	.247	1	13	17	2	1.8
1936	Chi-A☆	21	9	.700	35	34	20	1	0	274^1	282	13	147	99	14.2	4.63	112	.268	.360	32	.283	5	13	17	1	2.0
1937	Chi-A	14	13	.519	32	30	15	1	0	221	238	16	124	114	14.9	5.09	90	.273	.366	20	.230	2	-12	-12	0	-1.0
1938	Det-A☆	12	9	.571	33	26	11	0	2	190^1	215	13	113	53	15.6	5.06	99	.287	.381	23	.291	3	-6	-1	2	0.3
1939	Det-A	0	3	.000	4	4	1	0	0	21	25	4	9	9	15.0	6.43	76	.301	.376	2	.286	0	-4	-4	1	-0.3
	StL-A	9	17	.346	33	27	12	1	0	191^2	229	18	115	55	16.2	5.73	85	.297	.389	10	.149	-2	-24	-18	-1	-2.3
	Yr	9	20	.310	37	31	13	1	0	212^2	254	22	124	64	16.0	5.80	84	.297	.387	12	.162	-2	-28	-22	0	-2.6
1940	StL-A	12	17	.414	34	32	18	0	0	222^1	263	18	122	70	15.7	5.59	82	.298	.385	25	.298	6	-30	-25	2	-1.8
1941	StL-A	2	4	.333	6	6	2	0	0	45	44	5	27	6	14.2	4.40	98	.259	.360	6	.400	2	-1	-1	0	0.2
	Was-A	1	7	.125	17	7	2	0	0	66^1	77	5	39	22	16.0	5.70	71	.297	.393	3	.143	-1	-11	-12	0	-1.3
	Yr	3	11	.214	23	13	4	0	0	111^1	121	10	66	28	15.3	5.17	80	.282	.380	9	.250	2	-13	-13	0	-1.1
1942	Cle-A	4	8	.333	28	12	4	0	1	108	99	1	50	37	12.5	4.08	84	.244	.328	6	.200	1	-5	-8	0	-0.6
1943	Cle-A	10	7	.588	28	17	8	1	0	146^2	130	4	59	63	11.7	2.45	127	.242	.319	12	.231	1	14	11	1	1.5
1944	Cle-A	2	5	.286	12	10	2	0	0	59	66	0	37	17	15.7	5.03	66	.289	.389	2	.087	-2	-11	-11	1	-1.3
	Phi-N	1	5	.167	12	7	3	0	0	55^1	60	3	20	23	13.0	4.23	85	.269	.329	6	.286	1	-4	-4	0	-0.3
1945	Phi-N	0	3	.000	12	3	0	0	0	36	43	2	14	13	14.3	5.50	70	.297	.358	2	.182	0	-7	-7	1	-0.4
	Cin-N	5	12	.294	24	20	11	1	1	157^2	170	10	69	38	13.8	4.00	94	.280	.356	12	.226	2	-3	-4	1	-0.1
	Yr	5	15	.250	36	23	11	1	1	193^2	213	12	83	51	13.9	4.28	88	.283	.356	14	.219	2	-10	-11	2	-0.5
Total	12	104	132	.441	344	263	126	7	5	2025^2	2173	130	1049	691	14.4	4.67	94	.277	.363	181	.244	19	-77	-63	13	-3.3
● **MONTE KENNEDY**	Kennedy, Monty Calvin b: 5/11/22, Amelia, Va. d: 3/1/97, Midlothian, Va. BR/TL, 6'2", 185 lbs. Deb: 4/18/46																									
1946	NY-N	9	10	.474	38	27	10	1	1	186^2	153	14	116	71	13.2	3.42	101	.224	.340	15	.234	2	-0	0	-0	0.2
1947	NY-N	9	12	.429	34	24	9	0	0	148^1	158	8	88	60	15.2	4.85	84	.272	.372	8	.167	-1	-13	-13	-0	-1.6
1948	NY-N	3	9	.250	25	16	7	1	0	114^1	118	10	57	63	14.0	4.01	98	.264	.351	4	.129	-1	-1	-1	-1	-0.3
1949	NY-N	12	14	.462	38	32	14	4	1	223^1	208	13	100	95	12.5	3.43	116	.242	.323	12	.145	-1	15	14	-2	1.1
1950	NY-N	5	4	.556	36	17	5	0	2	114^1	120	14	53	41	13.9	4.72	87	.269	.351	2	.056	-3	-7	-8	-0	-0.9
1951	*NY-N	1	2	.333	29	5	1	0	0	68	68	0	31	22	13.1	2.25	174	.270	.350	3	.200	0	13	13	-0	0.5
1952	NY-N	3	4	.429	31	6	2	1	0	83^1	73	6	31	48	11.4	3.02	122	.230	.303	2	.091	-1	7	6	1	0.4
1953	NY-N	0	0	—	18	0	0	0	0	22^2	30	2	19	11	19.9	7.15	60	.337	.459	0	.000	-0	-7	-7	0	0.0
Total	8	42	55	.433	249	127	48	7	4	961	928	67	495	411	13.5	3.84	101	.253	.344	46	.153	-5	6	4	-4	-0.6
● **TED KENNEDY**	Kennedy, Theodore A. b: 2/1865, Henry, Ill. d: 10/31/07, St.Louis, Mo. BL , Deb: 6/12/1885																									
1885	Chi-N	7	2	.778	9	9	8	0	0	78^2	91	5	28	36	13.6	3.43	88	.288	.346	3	.083	-4	-5	-4	-0	-0.7
1886	Phi-a	5	15	.250	20	19	19	0	0	172^2	196	4	65	68	14.0	4.53	77	.271	.338	3	.044	-9	-21	-20	1	-2.4
	Lou-a	0	4	.000	4	4	4	0	0	32	53	1	16	14	19.7	5.34	68	.351	.417	1	.077	-1	-7	-6	-1	-0.7
	Yr	5	19	.208	24	23	23	0	0	204^2	249	5	81	82	14.6	4.66	76	.282	.343	4	.049	-10	-28	-26	0	-3.1
Total	2	12	21	.364	33	32	31	0	0	283^1	340	10	109	118	14.5	4.32	78	.286	.350	7	.060	-14	-33	-29	-0	-3.8
● **BILL KENNEDY**	Kennedy, William Aulton "Lefty" b: 3/14/21, Carnesville, Ga. d: 4/9/83, Seattle, Wash. BL/TL, 6'2", 195 lbs. Deb: 4/26/48																									
1948	Cle-A	1	0	1.000	6	3	0	0	0	11^1	16	0	13	12	23.0	11.12	37	.333	.475	2	.667	1	-9	-9	0	-0.5
	StL-A	7	8	.467	26	20	3	0	0	132	132	10	104	77	16.4	4.70	97	.259	.389	11	.250	1	-6	-2	-1	-0.2
	Yr	8	8	.500	32	23	3	0	0	143^1	148	10	117	89	17.0	5.21	87	.265	.397	13	.277	2	-15	-11	-1	-0.7
1949	StL-A	4	11	.267	48	16	2	0	1	153^2	172	12	73	69	14.5	4.69	97	.285	.365	6	.150	-2	-8	-3	-2	-0.5
1950	StL-A	0	0	—	1	0	0	0	0	2	1	0	2	1	13.5	0.00	—	.143	.333	0	—	0	1	1	-0	0.0
1951	StL-A	1	5	.167	19	5	1	0	0	56	76	4	37	29	18.3	5.79	76	.332	.427	2	.125	-2	-10	-9	1	-0.8
1952	Chi-A	2	2	.500	**47**	1	0	0	5	70^2	54	4	38	46	11.8	2.80	130	.213	.318	3	.231	0	7	7	-1	0.4

YEAR	TM/L	W	L	PCT	G	GS	CG	SH	SV	IP	H	HR	BB	SO	RAT	ERA	ERA+	OAV	OOB	BH	AVG	PB	PR	/A	PD	TPI
1953	Bos-A	0	0	—	16	0	0	0	2	24^1	24	2	17	14	15.5	3.70	114	.255	.375	1	.500	0	1	1	-0	0.0
1956	Cin-N	0	0	—	1	0	0	0	0	2	6	1	0	0	27.0	18.00	22	.667	.667	0	—	0	-3	-3	-0	0.0
1957	Cin-N	0	2	.000	8	0	0	0	3	12^2	16	1	5	8	15.6	6.39	64	.314	.386	0	.000	0	-4	-3	0	-0.6
Total	8	15	28	.349	172	45	6	0	11	464^2	497	34	289	256	15.5	4.73	92	.275	.379	25	.208	-1	-31	-20	-2	-2.2
● **BILL KENNEDY**	Kennedy, William Gorman b: 12/22/18, Alexandria, Va. d: 8/20/95, Alexandria, Va. BL/TL, 6'1", 175 lbs. Deb: 5/1/42																									
1942	Was-A	0	1	.000	8	2	1	0	2	18	21	1	10	4	15.5	8.00	46	.296	.383	0	.000	-1	-9	-9	1	-0.6
1946	Was-A	1	2	.333	21	2	0	0	3	39	40	1	29	18	15.9	6.00	56	.270	.390	1	.125	-0	-11	-11	-0	-1.1
1947	Was-A	0	0	—	2	0	0	0	0	6^2	10	1	5	1	20.3	8.10	46	.370	.469	0	.000	-0	-3	-3	0	0.0
Total	3	1	3	.250	31	4	1	0	5	63^2	71	3	44	23	16.3	6.79	51	.289	.397	1	.071	-1	-23	-23	0	-1.7
● **BRICKYARD KENNEDY**	Kennedy, William Park b: 10/7/1867, Bellaire, Ohio d: 9/23/15, Bellaire, Ohio BR/TR, 5'11", 160 lbs. Deb: 4/26/1892																									
1892	Bro-N	13	8	.619	26	21	18	0	1	191	189	3	95	108	13.6	3.86	82	.248	.334	14	.165	-1	-12	-15	-0	-1.5
1893	Bro-N	25	20	.556	46	44	40	2	1	382^2	376	15	168	107	13.0	3.72	119	.249	.327	39	.248	2	40	30	5	3.2
1894	Bro-N	24	20	.545	48	41	34	0	2	360^2	445	15	149	107	15.1	4.92	101	.300	.368	49	.304	4	16	1	3	0.6
1895	Bro-N	19	12	.613	39	33	26	2	1	279^2	335	13	93	39	14.0	5.12	86	.292	.349	39	.307	4	-10	-22	-1	-1.6
1896	Bro-N	17	20	.459	42	38	28	1	1	305^2	334	12	130	76	14.0	4.42	93	.276	.352	23	.189	-7	-2	-10	3	-1.3
1897	Bro-N	18	20	.474	44	40	36	2	1	343^1	370	6	149	81	13.8	3.91	105	.273	.348	40	.272	4	16	8	2	1.2
1898	Bro-N	16	22	.421	40	39	38	0	0	339^1	360	12	123	73	12.9	3.37	107	.270	.334	34	.252	3	9	8	6	1.6
1899	Bro-N	22	9	.710	40	33	27	2	2	277^1	297	11	86	55	12.5	2.79	140	.273	.329	27	.248	4	33	35	0	3.7
1900	Bro-N	20	13	.606	42	35	26	2	0	292	316	5	111	75	13.4	3.91	98	.276	.344	37	.301	7	-7	-2	1	0.5
1901	Bro-N	3	5	.375	14	8	6	0	0	85^1	80	1	24	28	11.1	3.06	110	.246	.300	6	.167	-1	3	3	-0	0.0
1902	NY-N	1	4	.200	6	6	4	1	0	38^2	44	0	16	9	14.0	3.96	71	.286	.353	4	.267	1	-5	-5	-1	-0.6
1903	*Pit-N	9	6	.600	18	15	10	1	0	125^1	130	0	57	39	13.6	3.45	94	.277	.357	21	.362	8	-2	-3	-1	0.3
Total	12	187	159	.540	405	353	293	13	9	3021	3276	93	1201	797	13.5	3.96	102	.273	.343	333	.261	27	78	33	15	6.1
● **ART KENNEY**	Kenney, Arthur Joseph b: 4/29/16, Milford, Mass. BL/TL, 6', 175 lbs. Deb: 7/1/38																									
1938	Bos-N	0	0	—	2	0	0	0	0	2^1	3	0	8	2	42.4	15.43	22	.300	.611	0	—	0	-3	-3	0	0.0
● **ED KENT**	Kent, Edward C. b: 1859, New York BR/TR, 5'6.5", 152 lbs. Deb: 8/14/1884																									
1884	Tol-a	0	1	.000	1	1	1	0	0	9	14	0	3	4	18.0	6.00	57	.298	.353	0	.000	-1	-3	-3	0	-0.2
● **MAURY KENT**	Kent, Maurice Allen b: 9/17/1885, Marshalltown, Ia. d: 4/19/66, Iowa City, Iowa BR/TR, 6', 168 lbs. Deb: 4/15/12																									
1912	Bro-N	5	5	.500	20	9	2	1	0	93	107	3	46	24	14.9	4.84	69	.296	.377	8	.229	1	-15	-15	1	-1.3
1913	Bro-N	0	0	—	3	0	0	0	0	7^1	5	0	3	1	9.8	2.45	134	.192	.276	0	.000	-0	1	1	-0	-0.1
Total	2	5	5	.500	23	9	2	1	0	100^1	112	3	49	25	14.5	4.66	72	.289	.371	8	.211	1	-14	-15	1	-1.4
● **MATT KEOUGH**	Keough, Matthew Lon b: 7/3/55, Pomona, Cal. BR/TR, 6'3", 190 lbs. Deb: 9/3/77 F																									
1977	Oak-A	1	3	.250	7	6	0	0	0	42^2	39	4	22	23	13.1	4.85	83	.247	.343	0	—	0	-4	-4	-1	-0.3
1978	Oak-A★	8	15	.348	32	32	6	0	0	197^1	178	9	85	108	12.2	3.24	112	.241	.323	0	—	0	11	9	2	1.1
1979	Oak-A	2	17	.105	30	28	7	1	0	176^2	220	18	78	95	15.5	5.04	80	.315	.389	0	—	0	-16	-20	2	-1.3
1980	Oak-A	16	13	.552	34	32	20	2	0	250	218	24	94	121	11.4	2.92	129	.236	.310	0	—	0	31	24	-1	3.0
1981	*Oak-A	10	6	.625	19	19	10	2	0	140^1	125	11	45	60	10.9	3.40	102	.239	.299	0	—	0	4	1	-2	0.2
1982	Oak-A	11	18	.379	34	34	10	2	0	209^1	233	38	101	75	14.6	5.72	68	.284	.366	0	—	0	-38	-42	-3	-4.8
1983	Oak-A	2	3	.400	14	4	0	0	0	44	50	7	31	28	16.6	5.52	70	.284	.391	0	—	0	-7	-8	-1	-0.6
	NY-A	3	4	.429	12	12	0	0	0	55^2	59	12	20	26	13.1	5.17	75	.266	.332	0	—	0	-7	-8	-0	-0.7
	Yr	5	7	.417	26	16	0	0	0	99^2	109	19	51	54	14.6	5.33	73	.273	.358	0	—	0	-14	-16	-1	-1.3
1985	StL-N	0	1	.000	4	1	0	0	0	10	10	0	4	10	13.5	4.50	79	.278	.366	0	.000	-0	-1	-1	0	-0.1
1986	Chi-N	2	2	.500	19	2	0	0	0	29	36	4	12	19	15.2	4.97	81	.316	.386	2	.400	1	-4	-3	-0	-0.3
	Hou-N	3	2	.600	10	5	0	0	0	35	22	5	18	25	10.5	3.09	117	.180	.291	4	.364	1	2	2	-1	0.4
	Yr	5	4	.556	29	7	0	0	0	64	58	9	30	44	12.5	3.94	96	.245	.332	6	.375	2	-2	-1	-1	0.1
Total	9	58	84	.408	215	175	53	7	0	1190	1190	132	510	590	13.1	4.17	91	.262	.341	6	.333	2	-28	-50	-5	-3.4
● **KURT KEPSHIRE**	Kepshire, Kurt David b: 7/3/59, Bridgeport, Conn. BL/TR, 6'1", 180 lbs. Deb: 7/4/84																									
1984	StL-N	6	5	.545	17	16	2	2	0	109	100	7	44	71	11.9	3.30	105	.249	.323	2	.056	-2	3	2	-2	-0.2
1985	StL-N	10	9	.526	32	29	0	0	0	153^1	155	16	71	67	13.3	4.75	74	.264	.343	6	.118	-1	-20	-21	-2	-2.6
1986	StL-N	0	1	.000	2	1	0	0	0	8	8	2	4	6	13.5	4.50	81	.258	.343	0	.000	-0	-1	-1	0	-0.1
Total	3	16	15	.516	51	46	2	2	0	270^1	263	25	119	144	12.7	4.16	84	.258	.335	8	.091	-3	-17	-20	-3	-2.9
● **CHARLIE KERFELD**	Kerfeld, Charles Patrick b: 9/28/63, Knob Noster, Mo. BR/TR, 6'6", 225 lbs. Deb: 7/27/85																									
1985	Hou-N	4	2	.667	11	6	0	0	0	44^1	44	2	25	30	14.0	4.06	85	.268	.365	0	.000	-1	-2	-3	-1	-0.6
1986	*Hou-N	11	2	.846	61	0	0	0	7	93^2	71	5	42	77	11.0	2.59	139	.213	.305	1	.111	-0	12	10	-1	1.5
1987	Hou-N	0	2	.000	21	0	0	0	0	29^2	34	3	21	17	17.0	6.67	59	.309	.424	0	.000	-0	-9	-9	-0	-0.6
1990	Hou-N	0	2	.000	5	0	0	0	0	3^1	9	0	6	4	40.5	16.20	23	.529	.652	0	—	0	-5	-5	-0	-2.1
	Atl-N	3	1	.750	25	0	0	0	2	30^2	31	2	23	27	15.8	5.58	72	.270	.391	0	—	0	-6	-5	-1	-0.7
	Yr	3	3	.500	30	0	0	0	2	34	40	2	29	31	18.3	6.62	60	.303	.429	0	—	0	-11	-10	-1	-2.8
Total	4	18	9	.667	123	6	0	0	9	201^2	189	12	117	155	13.8	4.20	88	.256	.360	1	.038	-2	-10	-11	-2	-2.5
● **GUS KERIAZAKOS**	Keriazakos, Constantine Nicholas b: 7/28/31, W.Orange, N.J. d: 5/4/96, Hilton Head, S.C. BR/TR, 6'3", 187 lbs. Deb: 10/1/50																									
1950	Chi-A	0	1	.000	1	1	0	0	0	2^1	7	0	5	1	46.3	19.29	23	.500	.632	1	1.000	0	-4	-4	-0	-0.9
1954	Was-A	2	3	.400	22	3	2	0	0	59^2	59	4	30	33	13.4	3.77	94	.262	.349	1	.067	-1	-0	-1	-0	-0.2
1955	KC-A	0	1	.000	5	1	0	0	0	11^2	15	4	7	8	17.0	12.34	34	.333	.423	0	.000	-0	-11	-11	-0	-0.8
Total	3	2	5	.286	28	5	2	0	0	73^2	81	8	42	42	15.0	5.62	65	.285	.377	2	.105	-1	-15	-16	-0	-1.9
● **BILL KERKSIECK**	Kerksieck, Wayman William b: 12/6/13, Ulm, Ark. d: 3/11/70, Stuttgart, Ark. BR/TR, 6'1", 183 lbs. Deb: 6/21/39																									
1939	Phi-N	0	2	.000	23	2	1	0	0	62^2	81	13	32	13	16.2	7.18	56	.328	.405	1	.083	-0	-23	-22	-1	-0.7
● **JIM KERN**	Kern, James Lester b: 3/15/49, Gladwin, Mich. BR/TR, 6'5", 205 lbs. Deb: 9/6/74																									
1974	Cle-A	0	1	.000	4	3	1	0	0	15^1	16	1	14	11	17.6	4.70	77	.262	.400	0	—	0	-2	-2	-0	-0.1
1975	Cle-A	1	2	.333	13	7	0	0	0	71^2	60	5	45	55	13.8	3.77	100	.233	.357	0	—	0	0	0	0	0.0
1976	Cle-A	10	7	.588	50	2	0	0	15	117^2	91	2	50	111	11.2	2.37	147	.222	.314	0	—	0	15	15	-0	2.6
1977	Cle-A★	8	10	.444	60	0	0	0	18	92	85	3	47	91	13.5	3.42	115	.260	.363	0	—	0	6	5	0	1.3
1978	Cle-A★	10	10	.500	58	0	0	0	13	99^1	77	4	58	95	12.5	3.08	121	.224	.342	0	.000	-0	8	7	1	1.7
1979	Tex-A★	13	5	.722	71	0	0	0	29	143	99	5	62	136	10.3	1.57	264	.199	.290	0	—	0	**42**	**41**	-1	**6.7**
1980	Tex-A	3	11	.214	38	1	0	0	2	63^1	65	4	45	40	15.9	4.83	81	.279	.400	0	—	0	-6	-7	0	-1.1
1981	Tex-A	1	2	.333	23	0	0	0	6	30	21	0	22	20	13.2	2.70	128	.204	.349	0	—	0	3	3	-0	0.6
1982	Cin-N	3	5	.375	50	0	0	0	2	76	61	3	48	43	13.1	2.84	130	.222	.342	0	.000	-0	6	7	1	0.8
	Chi-A	2	1	.667	13	1	0	0	3	28	20	3	12	23	10.3	5.14	78	.204	.291	0	—	0	-3	-3	0	-0.4
1983	Chi-A	0	0	—	1	0	0	0	0	0^2	1	0	0	0	13.5	0.00	—	.333	.333	0	—	0	0	0	0	-0.2
1984	Phi-N	0	1	.000	8	0	0	0	0	13^1	20	3	10	8	20.3	10.13	36	.339	.435	0	.000	-0	-10	-10	-0	-0.7
	Mil-A	1	0	1.000	6	0	0	0	0	4^2	6	0	3	4	17.4	0.00	—	.300	.391	0	—	0	2	2	-0	0.6
1985	Mil-A	0	1	.000	5	0	0	0	0	11	14	1	5	3	15.5	6.55	64	.318	.388	0	—	0	-3	-3	1	-0.2
1986	Cle-A	1	1	.500	16	0	0	0	0	27^1	34	1	23	11	19.8	7.90	52	.298	.429	0	—	0	-11	-11	0	-0.6
Total	13	53	57	.482	416	14	1	0	88	793^1	670	35	444	651	13.0	3.32	115	.235	.344	0	.000	-1	48	45	1	11.0
● **DICKIE KERR**	Kerr, Richard Henry b: 7/3/1893, St.Louis, Mo. d: 5/4/63, Houston, Tex. BL/TL, 5'7", 155 lbs. Deb: 4/25/19																									
1919	*Chi-A	13	7	.650	39	17	10	1	0	212^1	208	2	64	79	11.6	2.88	110	.259	.316	17	.250	5	8	7	1	1.2
1920	Chi-A	21	9	.700	45	27	19	3	**5**	253^2	266	7	72	72	12.1	3.37	112	.278	.331	14	.156	-4	12	11	3	1.1
1921	Chi-A	19	17	.528	44	37	25	3	1	308^2	357	12	96	80	13.5	4.72	90	.295	.352	25	.238	5	-15	-17	-0	-1.2
1925	Chi-A	0	1	.000	12	2	0	0	0	36^2	45	3	18	4	15.7	5.15	81	.304	.383	4	.333	1	-3	-4	0	0.0
Total	4	53	34	.609	140	83	54	7	6	811^1	876	24	250	235	12.7	3.84	99	.281	.338	60	.218	7	2	-2	4	1.1

YEAR TM/L	W	L	PCT	G	GS	CG	SH	SV	IP	H	HR	BB	SO	RAT	ERA	ERA+	OAV	OOB	BH	AVG	PB	PR	/A	PD	TPI
● JOE KERRIGAN Kerrigan, Joseph Thomas b: 11/30/54, Philadelphia, Pa. BR/TR, 6'5", 205 lbs. Deb: 7/9/76 C																									
1976 Mon-N	2	6	.250	38	0	0	0	1	56^2	63	3	23	22	14.0	3.81	98	.289	.362	0	.000	-0	-2	-1	1	-0.1
1977 Mon-N	3	5	.375	66	0	0	0	11	89^1	80	4	33	43	11.7	3.22	118	.241	.315	0	.000	-1	7	6	1	0.6
1978 Bal-A	3	1	.750	26	2	0	0	3	71^2	75	10	36	41	14.2	4.77	73	.273	.361	0	—	0	-8	-10	2	-0.5
1980 Bal-A	0	0	—	1	0	0	0	0	2^1	3	0	0	1	11.6	3.86	103	.273	.273	0	—	0	0	0	0	0.1
Total 4	8	12	.400	131	2	0	0	15	220	221	17	92	107	13.1	3.89	95	.264	.342	0	.000	-1	-3	-5	3	0.1
● RICK KESTER Kester, Richard Lee b: 7/7/46, Iola, Kan. BR/TR, 6', 190 lbs. Deb: 8/18/68																									
1968 Atl-N	0	0	—	5	0	0	0	0	6^1	8	0	3	9	15.6	5.68	53	.308	.379	0	—	0	-2	-2	-0	0.0
1969 Atl-N	0	0	—	1	0	0	0	0	2	5	1	0	2	22.5	13.50	27	.455	.455	0	—	0	-2	-2	-0	0.0
1970 Atl-N	0	0	—	15	0	0	0	0	32^1	36	3	19	20	15.3	5.57	77	.283	.377	0	.000	-1	-5	-5	-1	-0.2
Total 3	0	0	—	21	0	0	0	0	40^2	49	4	22	31	15.7	5.98	68	.299	.382	0	.000	-1	-10	-9	-1	-0.2
● GUS KETCHUM Ketchum, Augustus Franklin b: 3/21/1897, Royse City, Tex. d: 9/6/80, Oklahoma City, Okla. BR/TR, 5'9.5", 170 lbs. Deb: 8/7/22																									
1922 Phi-A	0	1	.000	6	0	0	0	0	16	19	2	8	4	15.8	5.63	76	.302	.389	0	.000	-1	-3	-2	-1	-0.3
● HENRY KEUPPER Keupper, Henry J. b: 6/24/1887, Staunton, Ill. d: 8/14/60, Marion, Ill. BL/TL, 6'1", 185 lbs. Deb: 4/19/14																									
1914 StL-F	8	20	.286	42	25	12	1	0	213	256	3	49	70	13.1	4.27	71	.291	.332	17	.250	1	-33	-29	2	-3.1
● JIMMY KEY Key, James Edward b: 4/22/61, Huntsville, Ala. BR/TL, 6'1", 190 lbs. Deb: 4/6/84																									
1984 Tor-A	4	5	.444	63	0	0	0	10	62	70	8	32	44	15.0	4.65	88	.286	.371	0	—	0	-5	-4	1	-0.7
1985 *Tor-A★	14	6	.700	35	32	3	0	0	212^2	188	22	50	85	10.2	3.00	140	.237	.284	0	—	0	27	28	4	2.9
1986 Tor-A	14	11	.560	36	35	4	2	0	232	222	24	74	141	11.6	3.57	118	.256	.317	0	—	0	16	17	3	1.8
1987 Tor-A	17	8	.680	36	36	8	1	0	261	210	24	66	161	**9.6**	**2.76**	**163**	**.221**	**.273**	0	—	0	**49**	**50**	2	4.4
1988 Tor-A	12	5	.706	21	21	2	2	0	131^1	127	13	30	65	11.1	3.29	119	.250	.298	0	—	0	10	9	-0	1.1
1989 *Tor-A	13	14	.481	33	33	5	1	0	216	226	18	27	118	10.7	3.88	97	.270	.295	0	—	0	0	-3	2	0.0
1990 Tor-A	13	7	.650	27	27	0	0	0	154^2	169	20	22	88	11.2	4.25	93	.281	.307	0	—	0	-6	-5	0	-0.7
1991 *Tor-A★	16	12	.571	33	33	2	2	0	209^1	207	12	44	125	10.9	3.05	138	.254	.295	0	—	0	24	27	3	3.5
1992 *Tor-A	13	13	.500	33	33	4	2	0	216^2	205	24	59	117	11.1	3.53	116	.248	.301	0	—	0	10	13	0	1.4
1993 NY-A★	18	6	**.750**	34	34	4	2	0	236^2	219	26	43	173	10.0	3.00	138	.246	.282	0	—	0	35	30	0	3.0
1994 NY-A★	**17**	4	.810	25	25	1	0	0	168	177	10	52	97	12.4	3.27	140	.273	.330	0	—	0	29	24	3	3.2
1995 NY-A	1	2	.333	5	5	0	0	0	30^1	40	3	6	14	13.6	5.64	82	.323	.354	0	—	0	-3	-3	0	-0.2
1996 *NY-A	12	11	.522	30	30	0	0	0	169^1	171	21	58	116	12.3	4.68	106	.266	.329	0	—	0	6	5	1	0.7
1997 *Bal-A	16	10	.615	34	34	1	1	0	212^1	210	24	82	141	12.6	3.43	128	.261	.333	0	.000	-0	27	23	2	2.6
1998 Bal-A	6	3	.667	25	11	0	0	0	79^1	77	5	23	53	11.7	4.20	108	.258	.317	0	—	0	4	3	0	0.4
Total 15	186	117	.614	470	389	34	13	10	2591^2	2518	254	668	1538	11.2	3.51	121	.255	.305	0	.000	-0	222	216	21	23.4
● BRIAN KEYSER Keyser, Brian Lee b: 10/31/66, Castro Valley, Cal. BR/TR, 6'1", 180 lbs. Deb: 6/2/95																									
1995 Chi-A	5	6	.455	23	10	0	0	0	92^1	114	10	27	48	13.9	4.97	90	.306	.356	0	—	0	-3	-5	1	-0.3
1996 Chi-A	1	2	.333	28	0	0	0	1	59^2	78	3	28	19	16.0	4.98	95	.328	.398	0	—	0	0	-2	2	0.2
Total 2	6	8	.429	51	10	0	0	1	152	192	13	55	67	14.7	4.97	92	.314	.373	0	—	0	-3	-7	3	-0.1
● DANA KIECKER Kiecker, Dana Ervin b: 2/25/61, Sleepy Eye, Minn. BR/TR, 6'3", 180 lbs. Deb: 4/12/90																									
1990 *Bos-A	8	9	.471	32	25	0	0	0	152	145	7	54	93	12.3	3.97	103	.253	.328	0	—	0	-1	2	2	0.0
1991 Bos-A	2	3	.400	18	5	0	0	0	40^1	56	6	23	21	18.1	7.36	58	.344	.431	0	—	0	-15	-14	1	-1.6
Total 2	10	12	.455	50	30	0	0	0	192^1	201	13	77	114	13.5	4.68	88	.273	.351	0	—	0	-16	-12	3	-1.6
● JOE KIEFER Kiefer, Joseph William "Harlem Joe" or "Smoke" b: 7/19/1899, W.Leyden, N.Y. d: 7/5/75, Utica, N.Y. BR/TR, 5'11", 190 lbs. Deb: 10/1/20																									
1920 Chi-A	0	1	.000	2	1	0	0	0	4^2	7	0	5	1	25.1	15.43	24	.333	.481	0	.000	-0	-6	-6	-0	-0.9
1925 Bos-A	0	2	.000	2	2	0	0	0	15	20	0	9	4	18.0	6.00	76	.351	.448	0	.000	-1	-3	-2	1	-0.3
1926 Bos-A	0	2	.000	11	1	0	0	0	30	29	2	16	4	14.1	4.80	85	.266	.370	1	.143	-0	-3	-2	0	-0.1
Total 3	0	5	.000	15	4	0	0	0	49^2	56	2	30	9	16.3	6.16	68	.299	.407	1	.077	-1	-11	-11	1	-1.3
● MARK KIEFER Kiefer, Mark Andrew b: 11/13/68, Orange, Cal. BR/TR, 6'4", 175 lbs. Deb: 9/20/93																									
1993 Mil-A	0	0	—	6	0	0	0	1	9^1	3	0	5	7	8.7	0.00	—	.097	.243	0	—	0	4	4	0	0.2
1994 Mil-A	1	0	1.000	7	0	0	0	0	10^2	15	4	8	8	19.4	8.44	60	.357	.460	0	—	0	-4	-4	-0	-0.5
1995 Mil-A	4	1	.800	24	0	0	0	0	49^2	37	6	27	41	11.6	3.44	145	.203	.306	0	—	0	7	8	-1	0.4
1996 Mil-A	0	0	—	7	0	0	0	0	10	15	1	5	5	18.0	8.10	64	.366	.435	0	—	0	-3	-3	-0	-0.1
Total 4	5	1	.833	44	0	0	0	1	79^2	70	11	45	61	13.1	4.29	115	.236	.339	0	—	0	4	6	-2	-0.0
● JOHN KIELY Kiely, John Francis b: 10/4/64, Boston, Mass. BR/TR, 6'3", 210 lbs. Deb: 7/26/91																									
1991 Det-A	0	1	.000	7	0	0	0	0	6^2	13	0	9	1	31.1	14.85	28	.448	.590	0	—	0	-8	-8	-0	-1.1
1992 Det-A	4	2	.667	39	0	0	0	0	55	44	2	28	18	11.8	2.13	186	.224	.321	0	—	0	11	11	2	1.4
1993 Det-A	0	2	.000	8	0	0	0	0	11^2	13	2	13	5	20.8	7.71	56	.295	.466	0	—	0	-4	-4	1	-0.5
Total 3	4	5	.444	54	0	0	0	0	73^1	70	4	50	24	15.0	4.17	96	.260	.380	0	—	0	-1	-1	3	-0.2
● LEO KIELY Kiely, Leo Patrick "Kiki" b: 11/30/29, Hoboken, N.J. d: 1/18/84, Montclair, N.J. BL/TL, 6'2", 180 lbs. Deb: 6/27/51																									
1951 Bos-A	7	7	.500	17	16	4	0	0	113^1	106	9	39	46	11.7	3.34	134	.251	.317	5	.143	-1	10	14	1	1.7
1954 Bos-A	5	8	.385	28	19	4	1	0	131	153	12	58	59	14.6	3.50	117	.295	.367	9	.180	0	3	9	1	0.7
1955 Bos-A	3	3	.500	33	4	0	0	6	90	91	5	37	36	12.8	2.80	153	.269	.341	5	.192	-0	12	15	1	1.3
1956 Bos-A	2	2	.500	23	0	0	0	3	31^1	47	1	14	9	18.1	5.17	89	.362	.432	1	.167	-0	-4	-2	0	-0.3
1958 Bos-A	5	2	.714	47	0	0	0	12	81	77	3	18	26	10.8	3.00	134	.254	.300	0	.000	-2	7	9	1	1.0
1959 Bos-A	3	3	.500	41	0	0	0	7	55^2	67	8	18	30	13.9	4.20	97	.299	.354	0	.000	-1	-2	-1	1	-0.1
1960 KC-A	1	2	.333	20	0	0	0	1	20^2	21	1	5	6	11.8	1.74	229	.266	.318	0	.000	-0	5	5	1	0.9
Total 7	26	27	.491	209	39	8	1	29	523	562	39	189	212	13.1	3.37	125	.279	.343	20	.144	-4	31	49	5	5.2
● DARRYL KILE Kile, Darryl Andrew b: 12/2/68, Garden Grove, Cal. BR/TR, 6'5", 185 lbs. Deb: 4/8/91																									
1991 Hou-N	7	11	.389	37	22	0	0	0	153^2	144	16	84	100	13.7	3.69	95	.246	.347	0	.000	-3	-0	-3	-2	-0.8
1992 Hou-N	5	10	.333	22	22	2	0	0	125^1	124	8	63	90	13.7	3.95	85	.261	.352	5	.156	1	-6	-8	-2	-1.1
1993 Hou-N☆	15	8	.652	32	26	4	2	0	171^2	152	12	69	141	12.4	3.51	110	.239	.327	5	.094	-1	10	7	-2	0.6
1994 Hou-N	9	6	.600	24	24	0	0	0	147^2	153	13	82	105	14.9	4.57	86	.275	.377	7	.149	1	-6	-10	-1	-0.9
1995 Hou-N	4	12	.250	25	21	0	0	0	127	114	5	73	113	14.1	4.96	78	.240	.355	4	.111	0	-11	-15	2	-1.5
1996 Hou-N	12	11	.522	35	33	4	0	0	219	233	16	97	219	14.2	4.19	92	.276	.362	10	.137	1	1	-8	1	-0.6
1997 *Hou-N☆	19	7	.731	34	34	6	4	0	255^2	208	19	94	205	11.0	2.57	155	.225	.303	11	.124	0	46	40	2	4.1
1998 Col-N	13	17	.433	36	35	4	1	0	230^1	257	28	96	158	14.1	5.20	97	.287	.361	18	.254	3	-25	-4	0	-0.1
Total 8	84	82	.506	245	217	20	7	0	1430^1	1385	117	658	1131	13.4	4.01	100	.257	.346	60	.137	1	9	-2	-2	-0.3
● JOHN KILEY Kiley, John Frederick b: 7/1/1859, Dedham, Mass. d: 12/18/40, Norwood, Mass. BL/TL, 5'7", 147 lbs. Deb: 5/1/1884 ♦																									
1891 Bos-N	0	1	.000	1	1	1	0	0	8	13	3	5	1	20.3	6.75	54	.351	.429	0	.000	0	-3	-3	0	-0.2
● PAUL KILGUS Kilgus, Paul Nelson b: 2/2/62, Bowling Green, Ky. BL/TL, 6'1", 185 lbs. Deb: 6/7/87																									
1987 Tex-A	2	7	.222	25	12	0	0	0	89^1	95	14	31	42	12.9	4.13	108	.271	.334	0	—	0	3	3	-1	0.2
1988 Tex-A	12	15	.444	32	32	5	3	0	203^1	190	18	71	88	12.0	4.16	98	.243	.314	0	—	0	-4	-2	1	-0.1
1989 *Chi-N	6	10	.375	35	23	0	0	2	145^2	164	9	49	61	13.5	4.39	86	.283	.344	3	.073	-3	-14	-10	0	-1.3
1990 Tor-A	0	0	—	11	0	0	0	0	16^1	19	2	7	7	14.9	6.06	65	.306	.386	0	—	0	-4	-4	0	-0.1
1991 Bal-A	0	2	.000	38	0	0	0	1	62	60	8	24	32	12.6	5.08	78	.256	.333	0	—	0	-7	-8	2	0.2
1993 StL-N	1	0	1.000	22	1	0	0	1	28^2	18	1	8	21	8.5	0.63	631	.180	.248	1	.200	0	11	11	0	0.4
Total 6	21	34	.382	163	68	5	3	4	545^1	546	52	190	251	12.5	4.19	96	.259	.327	4	.087	-2	-15	-9	2	-0.7
● MIKE KILKENNY Kilkenny, Michael David b: 4/11/45, Bradford, Ont., Can. BR/TL, 6'3.5", 175 lbs. Deb: 4/11/69																									
1969 Det-A	8	6	.571	39	15	6	4	2	128^1	99	13	63	97	11.6	3.37	111	.211	.310	2	.054	-2	4	5	-0	0.3
1970 Det-A	7	6	.538	36	21	3	0	0	129	141	10	70	105	14.9	5.16	72	.279	.369	3	.077	-3	-21	-21	0	-2.1

YEAR	TM/L	W	L	PCT	G	GS	CG	SH	SV	IP	H	HR	BB	SO	RAT	ERA	ERA+	OAV	OOB	BH	AVG	PB	PR	/A	PD	TPI
1971	Det-A	4	5	.444	30	11	2	0	1	86^1	83	8	44	47	13.4	5.00	72	.247	.338	2	.083	-2	-15	-14	-0	-1.6
1972	Det-A	0	0	—	1	0	0	0	0	1	1	1	0	0	9.0	9.00	35	.250	.250	0	—	0	-1	-1	0	0.0
	Oak-A	0	0	—	1	0	0	0	0	1	0	0	0	0	0.0	0.00	—	.000	.000	0	—	0	0	0	-0	0.0
	SD-N	0	0	—	5	0	0	0	0	4^1	7	1	3	5	20.8	8.31	40	.350	.435	0	—	0	-2	-2	0	0.0
	Cle-A	4	1	.800	22	7	1	0	1	58	51	5	39	44	14.0	3.41	94	.237	.354	1	.071	-1	-2	-1	1	-0.2
	Yr	4	1	.800	24	7	1	0	1	60	52	6	39	44	13.6	3.45	95	.234	.349	1	.071	-1	-3	-2	1	-0.3
1973	Cle-A	0	0	—	5	0	0	0	0	2	5	1	5	3	49.5	22.50	17	.455	.647	0	—	0	-4	-4	0	0.0
Total	5	23	18	.561	139	54	12	4	4	410	387	39	224	301	13.6	4.43	82	.248	.345	8	.070	-8	-41	-37	1	-3.6
● EVANS KILLEEN	Killeen, Evans Henry b: 2/27/36, Brooklyn, N.Y. BR/TR, 6′, 190 lbs. Deb: 9/7/59																									
1959	KC-A	0	0	—	4	0	0	0	0	5^2	4	0	4	1	12.7	4.76	84	.211	.348	0	—	0	-1	-0	-0	0.0
● HENRY KILLEEN	Killeen, Henry b: 5/1872, Troy, N.Y. 5′9″, 150 lbs. Deb: 9/11/1891																									
1891	Cle-N	0	1	.000	1	1	1	0	0	8^2	11	1	8	3	19.7	6.23	56	.297	.422	0	.000	-0	-3	-3	0	-0.2
● FRANK KILLEN	Killen, Frank Bissell "Lefty" b: 11/30/1870, Pittsburgh, Pa. d: 12/3/39, Pittsburgh, Pa. BL/TL, 6′1″, 200 lbs. Deb: 8/27/1891																									
1891	Mil-a	7	4	.636	11	11	11	2	0	96^2	73	1	51	38	11.8	1.68	262	.202	.306	8	.229	1	22	29	-0	3.0
1892	Was-N	29	26	.527	60	52	46	2	0	459^2	448	15	182	147	12.7	3.31	98	.245	.320	37	.199	10	-1	-3	3	1.0
1893	Pit-N	**36**	14	.720	55	48	38	2	0	415	401	12	140	99	12.1	3.64	125	.246	.312	47	.275	14	47	42	1	5.2
1894	Pit-N	14	11	.560	28	28	20	1	0	204	261	3	86	62	15.5	4.50	116	.308	.375	21	.262	0	19	17	1	1.5
1895	Pit-N	5	5	.500	13	11	6	0	0	95	113	2	57	25	16.2	5.49	82	.291	.383	13	.342	4	-8	-10	1	-0.4
1896	Pit-N	**30**	18	.625	**52**	50	**44**	**5**	0	**432^1**	476	7	119	134	12.7	3.41	123	.277	.329	40	.231	9	46	38	2	4.2
1897	Pit-N	17	23	.425	42	41	**38**	1	0	337^1	417	4	76	99	13.4	4.46	94	.301	.341	32	.248	4	-5	-10	-1	-0.6
1898	Pit-N	10	11	.476	23	23	17	0	0	177^2	201	3	41	48	12.8	3.75	95	.283	.332	17	.262	2	-3	-4	-0	-0.2
	Was-N	6	9	.400	17	16	15	0	0	128^1	149	4	29	43	12.6	3.58	102	.288	.328	15	.273	3	0	1	-0	0.5
	Yr	16	20	.444	40	39	32	0	0	306	350	7	70	91	12.4	3.68	98	.282	.322	32	.267	5	-2	-3	-1	0.3
1899	Was-N	0	2	.000	2	2	1	0	0	12	18	0	4	3	17.3	6.00	65	.346	.404	1	.200	-0	-3	-3	-1	-0.4
	Bos-N	7	5	.583	12	12	11	0	0	99^1	108	3	26	23	12.4	4.26	98	.276	.326	7	.171	-2	-4	-1	-0	-0.3
	Yr	7	7	.500	14	14	12	0	0	111^1	126	3	30	26	12.9	4.45	93	.284	.333	8	.174	-3	-7	-4	-1	-0.7
1900	Chi-N	3	3	.500	6	6	6	0	0	54	65	1	11	4	13.0	4.67	77	.297	.336	3	.150	-1	-6	-6	-0	-0.6
Total	10	164	131	.556	321	300	253	13	0	2511^1	2730	55	822	725	13.0	3.78	109	.272	.332	241	.241	44	104	92	5	12.9
● ED KILLIAN	Killian, Edwin Henry "Twilight Ed" b: 11/12/1876, Racine, Wis. d: 7/18/28, Detroit, Mich. BL/TL, 5′11″, 170 lbs. Deb: 8/25/03																									
1903	Cle-A	3	4	.429	9	8	7	3	0	61^2	61	1	13	18	11.4	2.48	115	.257	.307	5	.179	-1	3	3	-0	0.2
1904	Det-A	15	20	.429	40	34	32	4	0	331^2	293	0	93	124	10.9	2.44	104	.238	.301	18	.143	-3	6	4	-5	-0.5
1905	Det-A	23	14	.622	39	37	33	**8**	0	313^1	263	0	102	110	10.9	2.27	120	.230	.300	32	.271	6	13	16	-4	2.3
1906	Det-A	10	6	.625	21	16	14	0	2	149^2	165	0	54	47	13.5	3.43	81	.283	.348	9	.170	-1	-12	-11	-2	-1.5
1907	*Det-A	25	13	.658	42	34	29	3	0	314	286	2	91	96	11.1	1.78	147	.245	.306	39	.320	10	27	29	-2	4.6
1908	*Det-A	12	9	.571	27	23	15	0	1	180^2	170	3	53	47	11.5	2.99	81	.252	.314	10	.137	-3	-12	-11	3	-1.4
1909	Det-A	11	9	.550	25	19	14	3	1	173^1	150	1	49	54	10.6	1.71	147	.236	.297	10	.161	-1	15	15	-1	1.6
1910	Det-A	4	3	.571	11	9	5	1	0	74	75	2	27	20	13.1	3.04	87	.268	.345	4	.148	-1	-4	-3	-1	-0.5
Total	8	103	78	.569	214	180	149	22	4	1598^1	1463	9	482	516	11.3	2.38	110	.246	.310	127	.209	6	35	41	-12	4.8
● JACK KILLILAY	Killilay, John William b: 5/24/1887, Leavenworth, Kan. d: 10/21/68, Tulsa, Okla. BR/TR, 5′11″, 165 lbs. Deb: 5/13/11																									
1911	Bos-A	4	2	.667	14	7	1	0	0	61	65	0	36	28	16.4	3.54	93	.302	.425	1	.042	-2	-1	-2	0	-0.4
● MATT KILROY	Kilroy, Matthew Aloysius "Matches" b: 6/21/1866, Philadelphia, Pa. d: 3/2/40, Philadelphia, Pa. BL/TL, 5′9″, 175 lbs. Deb: 4/17/1886 F																									
1886	Bal-a	29	34	.460	**68**	68	**66**	5	0	583	476	10	182	**513**	10.5	3.37	102	.210	.274	38	.174	-5	5	4	6	0.4
1887	Bal-a	**46**	19	.708	**69**	69	**66**	**6**	0	**589^1**	585	9	157	217	11.6	3.07	134	.253	.306	59	.247	9	**80**	67	10	**7.3**
1888	Bal-a	17	21	.447	40	40	35	2	0	321	347	5	79	135	12.6	4.04	74	.266	.319	26	.179	-0	-35	-38	-1	-3.7
1889	Bal-a	29	25	.537	59	56	**55**	5	0	480^2	476	8	142	217	12.1	2.85	139	.250	.312	57	.274	10	54	59	8	**6.9**
1890	Bos-P	9	15	.375	30	27	18	0	1	217^2	268	14	87	48	15.3	4.26	103	.290	.361	20	.215	-0	-1	3	1	0.3
1891	Cin-a	1	4	.200	7	6	4	0	0	45^1	51	1	19	6	15.5	2.98	138	.274	.366	3	.150	-1	4	6	0	0.5
1892	Was-N	1	1	.500	4	3	2	0	0	26^1	20	0	15	1	12.6	2.39	136	.202	.319	2	.200	-0	3	3	2	0.3
1893	Lou-N	3	2	.600	5	5	5	1	0	35	57	2	23	4	21.6	9.00	49	.354	.447	7	.438	3	-17	-18	1	-1.4
1894	Lou-N	0	5	.000	8	7	3	0	0	37	46	2	20	11	16.5	3.89	131	.301	.389	2	.118	-2	6	5	1	0.4
1898	Chi-N	6	7	.462	13	11	10	0	0	100^1	119	2	30	18	14.4	4.31	83	.292	.357	22	.229	2	-8	-8	1	-0.6
Total	10	141	133	.515	303	292	264	19	1	2435^2	2445	53	754	1170	12.3	3.47	109	.252	.314	236	.222	15	92	83	28	10.4
● MIKE KILROY	Kilroy, Michael Joseph b: 11/4/1872, Philadelphia, Pa. d: 10/2/60, Philadelphia, Pa. BR/TR, 5′11″, 180 lbs. Deb: 9/1/1888 F																									
1888	Bal-a	0	1	.000	1	1	1	0	0	9	12	1	5	1	17.0	8.00	37	.308	.386	0	.000	-1	-5	-5	-0	-0.4
1891	Phi-N	0	2	.000	3	1	0	0	0	10	15	1	4	3	18.9	9.90	34	.333	.412	2	.400	1	-7	-7	-0	-0.9
Total	2	0	3	.000	4	2	1	0	0	19	27	2	9	4	18.0	9.00	36	.321	.400	2	.222	0	-12	-12	-0	-1.3
● NEWT KIMBALL	Kimball, Newell W. b: 3/27/15, Logan, Utah BR/TR, 6′2.5″, 190 lbs. Deb: 5/7/37																									
1937	Chi-N	0	0	—	2	0	0	0	0	5	12	1	1	0	23.4	10.80	37	.444	.464	0	.000	-0	-4	-4	0	0.0
1938	Chi-N	0	0	—	1	0	0	0	0	1	3	0	0	1	27.0	9.00	43	.500	.500	0	—	0	-1	-1	0	0.0
1940	Bro-N	3	1	.750	21	0	0	0	1	33^2	29	2	15	21	11.8	3.21	125	.238	.321	0	.000	-1	2	3	-0	0.2
	StL-N	1	0	1.000	2	1	1	0	0	14	11	1	6	6	10.9	2.57	155	.208	.288	2	.333	1	2	2	-0	0.2
	Yr	4	1	.800	23	1	1	0	1	47^2	40	3	21	27	11.5	3.02	132	.229	.311	2	.182	0	4	5	-1	0.4
1941	Bro-N	3	1	.750	15	5	1	0	1	52	43	0	29	17	12.5	3.63	101	.225	.327	3	.214	0	-0	0	-0	0.0
1942	Bro-N	2	0	1.000	14	1	0	0	0	29^1	27	0	19	8	14.4	3.68	89	.265	.385	1	.200	-0	-1	-1	-2	-0.2
1943	Bro-N	1	1	.500	5	0	0	0	1	11	9	0	5	2	11.5	1.64	205	.214	.298	0	.000	-0	2	2	-0	0.4
	Phi-N	1	6	.143	34	6	2	0	2	89^2	85	4	42	33	12.8	4.12	82	.253	.338	3	.188	1	-7	-7	-2	-0.7
	Yr	2	7	.222	39	6	2	0	3	100^2	94	4	47	35	12.7	3.84	88	.249	.333	3	.158	1	-5	-5	-2	-0.3
Total	6	11	9	.550	94	13	4	0	5	235^2	219	8	117	88	12.9	3.78	94	.249	.339	9	.180	1	-6	-6	-4	-0.1
● SAM KIMBER	Kimber, Samuel Jackson b: 10/29/1852, Philadelphia, Pa. d: 11/7/25, Philadelphia, Pa. BR/TR, 5′10.5″, 165 lbs. Deb: 5/1/1884																									
1884	Bro-a	18	20	.474	41	41	41	4	0	361^1	364	6	72	122	11.2	3.81	87	.247	.289	21	.148	-5	-23	-20	-1	-2.2
1885	Pro-N	0	1	.000	1	1	1	0	0	8	15	1	5	4	22.5	11.25	24	.405	.476	0	.000	-0	-7	-8	0	-0.6
Total	2	18	21	.462	42	42	42	4	0	369^1	379	7	77	126	11.5	3.97	83	.251	.294	21	.145	-6	-30	-27	-1	-2.8
● HARRY KIMBERLIN	Kimberlin, Harry Lydle "Murphy" or "Mule Trader" b: 3/13/09, Sullivan, Mo. BR/TR, 6′3″, 175 lbs. Deb: 7/11/36																									
1936	StL-A	0	0	—	13	0	0	0	0	20	24	3	16	4	18.0	5.40	100	.296	.412	0	.000	-0	-1	-0	-0	-0.1
1937	StL-A	0	2	.000	3	2	1	0	0	15^1	16	2	9	5	14.7	2.35	206	.254	.347	1	.200	0	4	4	-0	0.5
1938	StL-A	0	0	—	1	1	1	0	0	8	8	1	3	1	12.4	3.38	147	.286	.355	0	.000	-0	1	1	-0	0.0
1939	StL-A	1	2	.333	17	3	0	0	0	41	59	6	19	11	17.6	5.49	89	.326	.396	3	.333	0	-4	-3	0	-0.1
Total	4	1	4	.200	34	6	2	0	0	84^1	107	12	47	21	16.6	4.70	106	.303	.388	4	.250	0	0	3	-1	0.3
● HAL KIME	Kime, Harold Lee "Lefty" b: 3/15/1899, W.Salem, Ohio d: 5/16/39, Columbus, Ohio BL/TL, 5′9″, 160 lbs. Deb: 6/19/20																									
1920	StL-N	0	0	—	4	0	0	0	0	7	9	0	2	1	15.4	2.57	116	.333	.400	0	.000	-0	0	0	0	0.0
● CHAD KIMSEY	Kimsey, Clyde Elias b: 8/6/06, Copperhill, Tenn. d: 12/3/42, Pryor, Okla. BL/TR, 6′2″, 200 lbs. Deb: 4/21/29																									
1929	StL-A	3	6	.333	24	3	1	0	1	64^1	83	2	19	13	14.3	5.04	88	.340	.388	8	.267	3	-6	-4	3	0.0
1930	StL-A	6	10	.375	42	4	1	0	1	113^1	139	8	45	32	14.8	6.35	77	.312	.377	24	.343	7	-21	-19	1	-1.3
1931	StL-A	4	6	.400	42	1	0	0	7	94^1	121	1	27	27	14.3	4.39	106	.312	.360	10	.270	5	-0	**3**	2	1.0
1932	StL-A	4	2	.667	33	0	0	0	3	78^1	85	3	33	13	13.6	4.02	121	.281	.352	6	.333	1	4	7	1	0.7
	Chi-A	1	1	.500	7	0	0	0	2	11	8	0	5	6	11.5	2.45	176	.211	.318	0	.000	-0	2	2	1	0.5
	Yr	5	3	.625	40	0	0	0	5	89^1	93	3	38	19	13.3	3.83	125	.274	.348	6	.300	1	6	**10**	2	1.2
1933	Chi-A	4	1	.800	28	2	0	0	0	96	124	7	36	19	15.4	5.53	77	.318	.381	5	.152	-2	-13	-14	1	-0.7
1936	Det-A	2	3	.400	22	0	0	0	3	52	58	2	29	11	15.2	4.85	102	.284	.376	5	.313	2	1	1	2	0.4
Total	6	24	29	.453	198	10	2	0	17	509^1	618	23	194	121	14.5	5.07	92	.307	.371	58	.282	16	-33	-24	11	0.6

● **ELLIS KINDER** Kinder, Ellis Raymond "Old Folks" b: 7/26/14, Atkins, Ark. d: 10/16/68, Jackson, Tenn. BR/TR, 6', 195 lbs. Deb: 4/30/46

YEAR	TM/L	W	L	PCT	G	GS	CG	SH	SV	IP	H	HR	BB	SO	RAT	ERA	ERA+	OAV	OOB	BH	AVG	PB	PR	/A	PD	TPI
1946	StL-A	3	3	.500	33	7	1	0	1	86^2	78	8	36	59	11.8	3.32	112	.241	.318	1	.053	-1	2	4	-1	0.1
1947	StL-A	8	15	.348	34	26	10	2	1	194^1	201	11	82	110	13.1	4.49	86	.264	.336	8	.129	-4	-17	-13	-3	-2.1
1948	Bos-A	10	7	.588	28	22	10	1	0	178	183	10	63	53	12.5	3.74	117	.266	.330	6	.097	-4	11	13	-3	0.4
1949	Bos-A	23	6	**.793**	43	30	19	**6**	4	252	251	21	99	138	12.6	3.36	130	.260	.330	12	.130	-4	24	28	-4	2.1
1950	Bos-A	14	12	.538	48	23	11	1	9	207	212	23	78	95	12.7	4.26	115	.263	.328	13	.183	-1	7	15	-2	1.4
1951	Bos-A	11	2	.846	**63**	2	1	0	**14**	127	108	9	46	84	10.9	2.55	175	.230	.298	4	.118	-3	**22**	**27**	-2	2.7
1952	Bos-A	5	6	.455	23	10	4	0	4	97^2	85	11	28	50	10.5	2.58	153	.234	.290	0	.000	-4	12	15	-0	1.3
1953	Bos-A	10	6	.625	**69**	0	0	0	**27**	107	84	8	38	39	10.4	1.85	227	.215	.288	11	.379	3	**26**	**28**	0	**5.9**
1954	Bos-A	8	8	.500	48	2	0	0	15	107	106	7	36	67	11.9	3.62	114	.260	.321	5	.185	0	3	6	-2	0.9
1955	Bos-A	5	5	.500	43	0	0	0	18	66^2	57	5	15	31	9.9	2.84	151	.229	.275	3	.250	0	8	11	-1	2.1
1956	StL-N	2	0	1.000	22	0	0	0	6	25^2	23	3	9	4	11.2	3.51	108	.245	.311	0	.000	-0	1	1	-1	0.0
	Chi-A	3	1	.750	29	0	0	0	3	29^2	33	2	8	19	12.4	2.73	150	.277	.323	0	.000	-0	5	5	-1	0.6
1957	Chi-A	0	0	—	1	0	0	0	0	1	0	0	1	0	9.0	0.00	—	.000	.250	0	—	—	0	0	-0	0.0
Total	12	102	71	.590	484	122	56	10	102	1479^2	1421	118	539	749	12.0	3.43	125	.252	.318	63	.142	-19	101	139	-17	15.4

● **SILVER KING** King, Charles Frederick (b: Charles Frederick Koenig) b: 1/11/1868, St.Louis, Mo. d: 5/21/38, St.Louis, Mo. BR/TR, 6', 170 lbs. Deb: 9/28/1886

YEAR	TM/L	W	L	PCT	G	GS	CG	SH	SV	IP	H	HR	BB	SO	RAT	ERA	ERA+	OAV	OOB	BH	AVG	PB	PR	/A	PD	TPI
1886	KC-N	1	3	.250	5	5	5	0	0	39	43	1	9	23	12.0	4.85	78	.243	.280	1	.045	-2	-7	-5	1	-0.5
1887	*StL-a	32	12	.727	46	44	43	2	1	390	401	4	109	128	12.2	3.78	120	.260	.316	46	.207	-4	22	33	-3	2.0
1888	*StL-a	**45**	21	.682	**66**	65	**64**	**6**	0	**585^2**	437	6	76	258	**8.3**	**1.64**	**198**	.200	**.237**	43	.208	9	**92**	105	-1	**11.4**
1889	StL-a	35	16	.686	56	53	47	2	1	458	462	15	125	188	11.9	3.14	134	.254	.309	43	.228	1	36	55	-3	4.5
1890	Chi-P	30	22	.577	56	56	48	**4**	0	461	420	5	163	185	11.7	**2.69**	**161**	**.232**	.301	31	.168	-6	**79**	**84**	6	**7.1**
1891	Pit-N	14	29	.326	48	44	40	3	1	384^1	382	7	144	160	12.7	3.11	105	.250	.321	25	.169	-1	10	7	-2	0.4
1892	NY-N	22	24	.478	51	47	45	1	0	410^1	392	15	171	170	12.8	3.29	98	.242	.322	34	.209	6	-0	-3	-1	0.1
1893	NY-N	3	4	.429	7	7	4	0	0	49	69	4	26	13	17.8	8.63	54	.322	.401	3	.176	1	-22	-22	-0	-2.0
	Cin-N	5	6	.455	17	15	8	1	1	105	119	2	56	30	15.6	4.89	98	.277	.369	6	.162	-0	-3	-1	-0	-0.1
	Yr	8	10	.444	24	22	12	1	1	154	188	6	82	43	16.2	6.08	78	.291	.377	9	.167	1	-24	-23	-0	-2.1
1896	Was-N	10	7	.588	22	16	12	0	1	145^1	179	3	43	35	14.0	4.09	108	.300	.351	16	.276	3	4	5	-3	0.5
1897	Was-N	6	9	.400	23	19	12	0	1	154	196	7	45	32	14.7	4.79	91	.307	.363	11	.193	0	-8	-8	1	-0.5
Total	10	203	153	.570	397	371	328	19	6	3181^2	3100	69	967	1222	11.9	3.18	122	.247	.308	259	.198	7	204	251	-6	22.9

● **CLYDE KING** King, Clyde Edward b: 5/23/25, Goldsboro, N.C. BB/TR, 6'1", 175 lbs. Deb: 6/21/44 MC

YEAR	TM/L	W	L	PCT	G	GS	CG	SH	SV	IP	H	HR	BB	SO	RAT	ERA	ERA+	OAV	OOB	BH	AVG	PB	PR	/A	PD	TPI
1944	Bro-N	2	1	.667	14	3	1	0	0	43^2	42	1	12	14	11.3	3.09	115	.256	.311	2	.200	-0	3	2	-1	0.0
1945	Bro-N	5	5	.500	42	2	0	0	3	112^1	131	8	48	29	14.3	4.09	92	.295	.364	4	.125	-2	-4	-4	1	-0.5
1947	Bro-N	6	5	.545	29	9	2	0	0	87^2	85	11	29	31	11.7	2.77	149	.252	.311	3	.115	-1	13	13	-1	1.3
1948	Bro-N	0	1	.000	9	0	0	0	0	12^1	14	3	6	5	15.3	8.03	50	.286	.375	0	.000	-0	-6	-6	0	-0.4
1951	Bro-N	14	7	.667	48	3	1	0	6	121^1	118	15	50	33	12.7	4.15	94	.263	.341	4	.138	0	-3	-3	0	-0.5
1952	Bro-N	2	0	1.000	23	0	0	0	0	42^2	56	5	12	17	14.6	5.06	72	.318	.365	0	.000	-1	-6	-7	1	-0.3
1953	Cin-N	3	6	.333	35	4	0	0	2	76	78	15	32	21	13.3	5.21	84	.271	.348	0	.000	-1	-8	-7	-0	-0.9
Total	7	32	25	.561	200	21	4	0	11	496	524	58	189	150	13.1	4.14	95	.275	.343	13	.114	-4	-11	-11	-0	-1.3

● **CURTIS KING** King, Curtis Albert b: 10/25/70, Norristown, Pa. BR/TR, 6'5", 205 lbs. Deb: 8/1/97

YEAR	TM/L	W	L	PCT	G	GS	CG	SH	SV	IP	H	HR	BB	SO	RAT	ERA	ERA+	OAV	OOB	BH	AVG	PB	PR	/A	PD	TPI
1997	StL-N	4	2	.667	30	0	0	0	0	29^1	38	0	11	13	15.3	2.76	150	.325	.388	0	.000	-0	5	5	0	0.8
1998	StL-N	2	0	1.000	36	0	0	0	2	51	50	5	20	28	12.9	3.53	119	.262	.341	0	.000	-1	4	4	1	0.2
Total	2	6	2	.750	66	0	0	0	2	80^1	88	5	31	41	13.8	3.25	128	.286	.359	0	.000	-1	9	8	1	1.0

● **ERIC KING** King, Eric Steven b: 4/10/64, Oxnard, Cal. BR/TR, 6'2", 215 lbs. Deb: 5/15/86

YEAR	TM/L	W	L	PCT	G	GS	CG	SH	SV	IP	H	HR	BB	SO	RAT	ERA	ERA+	OAV	OOB	BH	AVG	PB	PR	/A	PD	TPI
1986	Det-A	11	4	.733	33	16	3	1	3	138^1	108	11	63	79	11.6	3.51	117	.216	.313	0	—	0	10	9	0	1.0
1987	*Det-A	6	9	.400	55	4	0	0	9	116	111	15	60	89	13.6	4.89	86	.251	.345	0	—	0	-6	-9	2	-0.8
1988	Det-A	4	1	.800	23	5	0	0	3	68^2	60	5	34	45	13.0	3.41	112	.233	.334	0	—	0	4	3	-1	0.2
1989	Chi-A	9	10	.474	25	25	1	1	0	159^1	144	13	64	72	12.0	3.39	112	.244	.322	0	—	0	9	7	-0	0.8
1990	Chi-A	12	4	.750	25	25	2	2	0	151	135	10	40	70	10.8	3.28	117	.237	.294	0	—	0	11	9	-1	0.9
1991	Cle-A	6	11	.353	25	24	2	1	0	150^2	166	7	44	59	12.7	4.60	90	.279	.332	0	—	0	-8	-7	-2	-1.0
1992	Det-A	4	6	.400	17	14	0	0	1	79^1	90	12	28	45	13.5	5.22	76	.285	.345	0	—	0	-11	-11	-1	-1.4
Total	7	52	45	.536	203	113	8	5	16	863^1	814	73	333	459	12.3	3.97	100	.249	.324	0	—	0	8	2	-3	-0.3

● **KEVIN KING** King, Kevin Ray b: 2/11/69, Atwater, Cal. BL/TL, 6'4", 170 lbs. Deb: 9/2/93

YEAR	TM/L	W	L	PCT	G	GS	CG	SH	SV	IP	H	HR	BB	SO	RAT	ERA	ERA+	OAV	OOB	BH	AVG	PB	PR	/A	PD	TPI
1993	Sea-A	0	1	.000	13	0	0	0	0	11^2	9	3	4	8	10.8	6.17	71	.231	.318	0	—	0	-2	-2	-0	-0.3
1994	Sea-A	0	2	.000	19	0	0	0	0	15^1	21	0	17	6	22.9	7.04	69	.333	.481	0	—	0	-4	-4	0	-0.5
1995	Sea-A	0	0	—	2	0	0	0	0	3^2	7	0	1	3	22.1	12.27	39	.412	.474	0	—	0	-3	-3	-0	-0.1
Total	3	0	3	.000	34	0	0	0	0	30^2	37	3	22	17	18.2	7.34	64	.311	.431	0	—	0	-9	-9	-0	-0.9

● **NELLIE KING** King, Nelson Joseph b: 3/15/28, Shenandoah, Pa. BR/TR, 6'6", 185 lbs. Deb: 4/15/54

YEAR	TM/L	W	L	PCT	G	GS	CG	SH	SV	IP	H	HR	BB	SO	RAT	ERA	ERA+	OAV	OOB	BH	AVG	PB	PR	/A	PD	TPI
1954	Pit-N	0	0	—	4	0	0	0	0	7	10	0	1	3	14.1	5.14	81	.400	.423	0	—	0	-1	-1	0	0.0
1955	Pit-N	1	3	.250	17	4	0	0	0	54^1	60	2	14	21	12.6	2.98	138	.286	.336	0	.000	-2	6	7	-0	0.3
1956	Pit-N	4	1	.800	38	0	0	0	5	60	54	8	19	25	11.1	3.15	120	.241	.303	0	.000	-1	4	4	-1	0.2
1957	Pit-N	2	1	.667	36	0	0	0	1	52	69	7	16	23	15.1	4.50	84	.337	.390	0	.000	-1	-4	-4	-0	-0.3
Total	4	7	5	.583	95	4	0	0	6	173^1	193	17	50	72	12.9	3.58	109	.291	.345	0	.000	-3	6	6	-1	0.2

● **BRIAN KINGMAN** Kingman, Brian Paul b: 7/27/54, Los Angeles, Cal. BR/TR, 6'2", 200 lbs. Deb: 6/28/79

YEAR	TM/L	W	L	PCT	G	GS	CG	SH	SV	IP	H	HR	BB	SO	RAT	ERA	ERA+	OAV	OOB	BH	AVG	PB	PR	/A	PD	TPI
1979	Oak-A	8	7	.533	18	17	5	1	0	112^2	113	10	33	58	11.9	4.31	94	.258	.314	0	—	0	-1	-3	-2	-0.5
1980	Oak-A	8	20	.286	32	30	10	1	0	211^1	209	21	82	116	12.6	3.83	98	.256	.326	0	—	0	5	-2	-2	-0.2
1981	*Oak-A	3	6	.333	18	15	3	1	0	100^1	112	10	32	52	13.3	3.95	88	.286	.347	0	—	0	-3	-5	-2	-0.4
1982	Oak-A	4	12	.250	23	20	3	0	1	122^2	131	11	57	46	14.3	4.48	87	.279	.365	0	—	0	-5	-8	-3	-0.8
1983	SF-N	0	0	—	3	0	0	0	0	4^2	10	0	1	1	21.2	7.71	46	.417	.440	0	—	0	-2	-2	-0	0.0
Total	5	23	45	.338	94	82	21	3	1	551^2	575	52	205	273	13.0	4.13	92	.269	.338	0	—	0	-7	-20	-9	-1.9

● **DAVE KINGMAN** Kingman, David Arthur b: 12/21/48, Pendleton, Ore. BR/TR, 6'6", 210 lbs. Deb: 7/30/71 ♦

YEAR	TM/L	W	L	PCT	G	GS	CG	SH	SV	IP	H	HR	BB	SO	RAT	ERA	ERA+	OAV	OOB	BH	AVG	PB	PR	/A	PD	TPI
1973	SF-N	0	0	—	2	0	0	0	0	4	3	0	6	4	20.3	9.00	42	.200	.429	62	.203	1	-2	-2	-0	0.0

● **DENNIS KINNEY** Kinney, Dennis Paul b: 2/26/52, Toledo, Ohio BL/TL, 6'1", 190 lbs. Deb: 4/9/78

YEAR	TM/L	W	L	PCT	G	GS	CG	SH	SV	IP	H	HR	BB	SO	RAT	ERA	ERA+	OAV	OOB	BH	AVG	PB	PR	/A	PD	TPI
1978	Cle-A	0	2	.000	18	0	0	0	5	38^2	37	3	14	19	12.1	4.42	84	.259	.329	0	—	0	-3	-3	-0	-0.2
	SD-N	0	1	.000	7	0	0	0	0	7	6	3	4	2	12.9	6.43	52	.222	.323	0	.000	-0	-2	-2	-0	-0.4
1979	SD-N	0	0	—	13	0	0	0	0	18	17	2	8	11	13.0	3.50	101	.250	.338	0	.000	-0	0	0	-0	0.0
1980	SD-N	4	6	.400	50	0	0	0	1	82^2	79	3	37	40	12.7	4.25	81	.252	.333	1	.083	-0	-6	-7	-0	-1.0
1981	Det-A	0	0	—	6	0	0	0	0	3^2	5	0	4	3	22.1	9.82	38	.313	.450	0	—	0	-3	-2	0	-0.2
1982	Oak-A	0	0	—	3	0	0	0	0	4^1	9	1	4	0	27.0	8.31	47	.474	.565	0	—	0	-2	-2	0	0.4
Total	5	4	9	.308	97	0	0	0	6	154^1	153	12	71	75	13.2	4.55	78	.261	.344	1	.071	-1	-15	-17	-1	-1.4

● **WALT KINNEY** Kinney, Walter William b: 9/9/1893, Denison, Tex. d: 7/1/71, Escondido, Cal. BL/TL, 6'2", 186 lbs. Deb: 7/26/18

YEAR	TM/L	W	L	PCT	G	GS	CG	SH	SV	IP	H	HR	BB	SO	RAT	ERA	ERA+	OAV	OOB	BH	AVG	PB	PR	/A	PD	TPI
1918	Bos-A	0	0	—	5	0	0	0	0	15	5	0	8	4	9.0	1.80	149	.106	.263	0	.000	-1	2	1	-0	-0.1
1919	Phi-A	9	15	.375	43	21	13	0	2	202^2	199	7	91	97	13.2	3.64	94	.262	.347	25	.284	5	-9	-5	3	0.5
1920	Phi-A	2	4	.333	10	8	5	1	0	61	59	3	28	19	13.0	3.10	130	.261	.345	9	.346	2	5	6	0	0.8
1923	Phi-A	0	1	.000	5	1	0	0	0	12	11	0	9	9	15.0	7.50	55	.229	.351	1	.167	1	-5	-5	-0	-0.3
Total	4	11	20	.355	63	30	18	1	2	290^2	274	10	136	129	13.0	3.59	99	.254	.343	35	.280	7	-8	-2	2	0.9

● **MIKE KINNUNEN** Kinnunen, Michael John b: 4/1/58, Seattle, Wash. BL/TL, 6'1", 185 lbs. Deb: 6/12/80

YEAR	TM/L	W	L	PCT	G	GS	CG	SH	SV	IP	H	HR	BB	SO	RAT	ERA	ERA+	OAV	OOB	BH	AVG	PB	PR	/A	PD	TPI
1980	Min-A	0	0	—	21	0	0	0	0	24^2	29	1	9	8	14.2	5.11	85	.290	.355	0	—	0	-3	-2	0	-0.2
1986	Bal-A	0	0	—	9	0	0	0	0	7	8	1	5	1	16.7	6.43	64	.308	.419	0	—	0	-2	-2	0	0.1
1987	Bal-A	0	0	—	18	0	0	0	0	20	27	3	16	14	19.3	4.95	89	.338	.448	0	—	0	-1	-1	-0	0.1
Total	3	0	0	—	48	0	0	0	0	51^2	64	5	30	23	16.5	5.23	83	.311	.401	0	—	0	-6	-5	0	0.0

YEAR	TM/L	W	L	PCT	G	GS	CG	SH	SV	IP	H	HR	BB	SO	RAT	ERA	ERA+	OAV	OOB	BH	AVG	PB	PR	/A	PD	TPI
● ED KINSELLA	Kinsella, Edward William "Rube" b: 1/15/1882, Lexington, Ill. d: 1/17/76, Bloomington, Ill. BR/TR, 6'1.5", 175 lbs. Deb: 9/16/05																									
1905	Pit-N	0	1	.000	3	2	2	0	0	17	19	0	3	11	12.2	2.65	113	.292	.333	0	.000	-0	1	1	-1	-0.1
1910	StL-A	1	3	.250	10	5	2	0	0	50	62	0	16	10	14.4	3.78	65	.321	.379	3	.250	2	-7	-7	1	-0.3
Total	2	1	4	.200	13	7	4	0	0	67	81	0	19	21	13.8	3.49	75	.314	.368	3	.200	2	-6	-7	0	-0.4
● MATT KINZER	Kinzer, Matthew Roy b: 6/17/63, Indianapolis, Ind. BR/TR, 6'2", 210 lbs. Deb: 5/18/89																									
1989	StL-N	0	2	.000	8	1	0	0	0	13^1	25	3	4	8	19.6	12.83	28	.403	.439	0	.000	-0	-14	-14	-0	-1.8
1990	Det-A	0	0	—	1	0	0	0	0	1^2	3	0	3	1	32.4	16.20	24	.375	.545	0	—	0	-2	-2	-0	-0.1
Total	2	0	2	.000	9	1	0	0	0	15	28	3	7	9	21.0	13.20	28	.400	.455	0	.000	-0	-16	-16	-1	-1.9
● HARRY KINZY	Kinzy, Henry Hershel "Slim" b: 7/19/10, Hallsville, Tex. BR/TR, 6'4", 185 lbs. Deb: 6/8/34																									
1934	Chi-A	0	1	.000	13	2	1	0	0	34^1	38	1	31	12	19.1	4.98	95	.290	.440	3	.300	1	-2	-1	-0	0.0
● FRED KIPP	Kipp, Fred Leo b: 10/1/31, Piqua, Kan. BL/TL, 6'4", 200 lbs. Deb: 9/10/57																									
1957	Bro-N	0	0	—	1	0	0	0	0	4	6	2	0	3	13.5	9.00	46	.333	.333	0	.000	-0	-2	-2	0	0.0
1958	LA-N	6	6	.500	40	9	0	0	0	102^1	107	16	45	58	13.5	5.01	82	.273	.349	9	.250	1	-12	-10	1	-0.9
1959	LA-N	0	0	—	2	0	0	0	0	2^2	2	0	3	1	16.9	0.00	—	.222	.417	0	—	0	1	1	0	0.0
1960	NY-A	0	1	.000	4	0	0	0	0	4^1	4	0	0	2	8.3	6.23	57	.250	.250	0	—	0	-1	-1	0	-0.3
Total	4	6	7	.462	47	9	0	0	0	113^1	119	18	48	64	13.3	5.08	80	.274	.347	9	.243	1	-14	-13	1	-1.2
● BOB KIPPER	Kipper, Robert Wayne b: 7/8/64, Aurora, Ill. BR/TL, 6'2", 200 lbs. Deb: 4/12/85																									
1985	Cal-A	0	1	.000	2	1	0	0	0	3^1	7	1	3	0	27.0	21.60	19	.467	.556	0	—	0	-6	-6	0	-1.2
	Pit-N	1	2	.333	5	4	0	0	0	24^2	21	4	7	13	10.2	5.11	70	.221	.275	2	.250	0	-4	-4	0	-0.4
1986	Pit-N	6	8	.429	20	19	0	0	0	114	123	17	34	81	12.6	4.03	95	.271	.324	1	.030	-3	-4	-2	-1	-0.7
1987	Pit-N	5	9	.357	24	20	1	1	0	110^2	117	25	52	83	13.9	5.94	69	.271	.352	8	.242	2	-23	-22	-0	-2.3
1988	Pit-N	2	6	.250	50	0	0	0	0	65	54	7	26	39	11.4	3.74	91	.234	.317	0	.000	-0	-2	-2	1	-0.2
1989	Pit-N	3	4	.429	52	0	0	0	4	83	55	5	33	58	9.5	2.93	115	.188	.270	1	.111	-0	5	4	-1	0.3
1990	Pit-N	5	2	.714	41	1	0	0	3	62^2	44	7	26	35	10.5	3.02	120	.195	.286	1	.143	-0	5	4	-0	0.5
1991	*Pit-N	2	2	.500	52	0	0	0	4	60	66	7	22	38	13.2	4.65	77	.276	.337	0	.000	-0	-6	-7	-1	-0.6
1992	Min-A	3	3	.500	25	0	0	0	0	38^2	40	8	14	22	13.3	4.42	92	.268	.343	0	—	0	-2	-2	0	-0.2
Total	8	27	37	.422	271	45	1	1	11	562	527	81	217	369	12.1	4.34	86	.247	.320	13	.137	-1	-37	-39	-2	-4.8
● THORNTON KIPPER	Kipper, Thornton John b: 9/27/28, Bagley, Wis. BR/TR, 6'3", 190 lbs. Deb: 6/7/53																									
1953	Phi-N	3	3	.500	20	3	0	0	0	45^2	59	8	12	15	14.0	4.73	89	.319	.360	1	.091	-1	-2	-3	-0	-0.4
1954	Phi-N	0	0	—	11	0	0	0	1	13^2	22	0	12	5	23.0	7.90	51	.379	.493	0	.000	-0	-6	-6	0	-0.1
1955	Phi-N	0	1	.000	24	0	0	0	0	39^2	47	4	22	15	15.9	4.99	80	.301	.391	1	.333	0	-4	-5	-1	-0.1
Total	3	3	4	.429	55	3	0	0	1	99	128	12	46	35	16.0	5.27	78	.321	.394	2	.125	-1	-12	-13	-1	-0.6
● CLAY KIRBY	Kirby, Clayton Laws b: 6/25/48, Washington, D.C. d: 10/11/91, Arlington, Va. BR/TR, 6'3", 185 lbs. Deb: 4/11/69																									
1969	SD-N	7	20	.259	35	35	2	0	0	215^2	204	18	100	113	12.9	3.80	93	.252	.339	4	.061	-2	-5	-6	-2	-1.1
1970	SD-N	10	16	.385	36	34	6	1	0	214^2	198	29	120	154	13.7	4.53	88	.248	.352	11	.149	-0	-11	-13	-2	-1.6
1971	SD-N	15	13	.536	38	36	13	2	0	267^1	213	20	103	231	10.7	2.83	117	.216	.292	8	.093	-3	19	14	-0	1.1
1972	SD-N	12	14	.462	34	34	9	2	0	238^2	197	21	116	175	11.9	3.13	105	.226	.318	5	.068	-4	9	4	-1	-0.1
1973	SD-N	8	18	.308	34	31	4	2	0	191^2	214	30	66	129	13.2	4.79	72	.282	.341	5	.093	-3	-24	-28	-2	-3.8
1974	Cin-N	12	9	.571	36	35	7	1	0	230^2	210	15	91	160	11.8	3.28	106	.242	.316	7	.095	-3	9	5	-2	-0.1
1975	Cin-N	10	6	.625	26	19	1	0	0	110^2	113	13	54	48	14.0	4.72	76	.263	.352	6	.188	1	-13	-14	-2	-1.9
1976	Mon-N	1	8	.111	22	15	0	0	0	78^2	81	10	63	51	16.7	5.72	65	.273	.403	1	.056	-1	-19	-18	-1	-2.0
Total	8	75	104	.419	261	239	42	8	0	1548	1430	156	713	1061	12.6	3.84	92	.246	.331	47	.098	-15	-37	-56	-13	-9.5
● JOHN KIRBY	Kirby, John F. b: 1/13/1865, St.Louis, Mo. d: 10/6/31, St.Louis, Mo. TR , 5'8", 172 lbs. Deb: 8/1/1884																									
1884	KC-U	0	1	.000	2	2	1	0	0	11	13	0	2	1	12.3	4.09	55	.277	.306	1	.143	-1	-2	-2	1	-0.2
1885	StL-N	5	8	.385	14	14	14	0	0	129^1	118	0	44	46	11.3	3.55	77	.241	.303	3	.060	-6	-10	-12	-2	-1.6
1886	StL-N	11	26	.297	41	41	38	1	0	325	329	9	134	129	12.8	3.30	98	.252	.322	15	.110	-9	1	-3	-1	-1.2
1887	Ind-N	1	6	.143	8	8	5	0	0	62	70	3	43	7	16.7	6.10	68	.272	.381	4	.138	-2	-14	-13	-1	-1.3
	Cle-a	0	5	.000	5	5	5	0	0	41	62	1	28	6	20.2	9.00	48	.339	.432	3	.167	-1	-21	-21	-0	-1.7
1888	KC-a	1	4	.200	5	5	5	0	0	43	48	0	7	11	11.7	4.19	82	.273	.304	1	.063	-2	-5	-4	-0	-0.5
Total	5	18	50	.265	75	75	68	1	0	611^1	640	13	258	200	13.3	4.09	80	.260	.332	27	.105	-21	-53	-55	-3	-6.5
● LA RUE KIRBY	Kirby, La Rue b: 12/30/1889, Eureka, Mich. d: 6/10/61, Lansing, Mich. BB/TR, 6', 185 lbs. Deb: 8/7/12 ♦																									
1912	NY-N	1	0	1.000	3	1	1	0	0	11	13	1	6	2	16.4	5.73	59	.295	.392	1	.200	0	-3	-3	0	-0.2
1915	StL-F	0	0	—	1	0	0	0	0	7	7	1	2	7	11.6	5.14	56	.269	.321	38	.213	0	-2	-2	-0	0.0
Total	2	1	0	1.000	4	1	1	0	0	18	20	2	8	9	14.5	5.50	58	.286	.367	87	.230	0	-5	-5	-0	-0.2
● MIKE KIRCHER	Kircher, Michael Andrew (b: Wolfgang Andrew Kerscher) b: 9/30/1897, Rochester, N.Y. d: 6/26/72, Rochester, N.Y. BB/TR, 6', 180 lbs. Deb: 8/8/19																									
1919	Phi-A	0	0	—	2	0	0	0	0	8	15	0	3	2	20.3	7.88	44	.429	.474	0	.000	-0	-4	-4	-1	-0.1
1920	StL-N	2	1	.667	9	3	1	0	0	36^2	50	0	5	5	14.0	5.40	55	.333	.363	3	.273	0	-9	-10	-1	-0.9
1921	StL-N	0	1	.000	3	0	0	0	0	3^1	4	0	1	2	16.2	8.10	45	.364	.462	0	—	0	-2	-2	0	-0.4
Total	3	2	2	.500	14	3	1	0	0	48	69	0	9	9	15.2	6.00	52	.352	.389	3	.214	-0	-15	-15	-2	-1.4
● BILL KIRK	Kirk, William Partlemore b: 7/19/35, Coatesville, Pa. BL/TL, 6', 165 lbs. Deb: 9/23/61																									
1961	KC-A	0	0	—	1	1	0	0	0	3	6	2	1	3	21.0	12.00	35	.375	.412	0	—	0	-3	-3	-0	0.0
● DON KIRKWOOD	Kirkwood, Donald Paul b: 9/24/49, Pontiac, Mich. BR/TR, 6'3", 188 lbs. Deb: 9/13/74																									
1974	Cal-A	0	0	—	3	0	0	0	0	7^1	12	0	6	4	22.1	8.59	40	.375	.474	0	—	0	-4	-4	-0	0.2
1975	Cal-A	6	5	.545	44	2	0	0	7	84	85	6	28	49	12.1	3.11	114	.270	.329	0	—	0	6	4	-0	0.8
1976	Cal-A	6	12	.333	28	26	4	0	0	157^2	167	12	57	78	12.8	4.62	72	.278	.341	0	—	0	-19	-23	1	-2.1
1977	Cal-A	1	0	1.000	13	0	0	0	1	17^2	20	3	9	10	14.8	5.09	77	.290	.372	0	—	0	-2	-2	1	0.0
	Chi-A	1	1	.500	16	0	0	0	0	40	49	3	10	24	13.5	5.17	79	.310	.355	0	—	0	-5	-5	0	-0.2
	Yr	2	1	.667	29	0	0	0	1	57^2	69	6	19	34	13.9	5.15	78	.304	.360	0	—	0	-7	-7	1	-0.2
1978	Tor-A	4	5	.444	16	9	3	0	0	68	76	6	25	29	13.4	4.24	93	.289	.351	0	—	0	-4	-2	0	-0.4
Total	5	18	23	.439	120	37	7	0	8	374^2	409	30	135	194	13.1	4.37	82	.284	.347	0	—	0	-28	-33	2	-1.7
● HARRY KIRSCH	Kirsch, Harry Louis "Casey" b: 10/17/1887, Pittsburgh, Pa. d: 12/25/25, Overbrook, Pa. BR/TR, 5'11", 170 lbs. Deb: 4/16/10																									
1910	Cle-A	0	0	—	2	0	0	0	0	3	5	0	1	5	18.0	6.00	43	.385	.429	0	—	0	-1	-1	-0	0.0
● GARLAND KISER	Kiser, Garland Routhard b: 7/8/68, Charlotte, N.C. BL/TL, 6'3", 190 lbs. Deb: 9/9/91																									
1991	Cle-A	0	0	—	7	0	0	0	0	4^2	7	0	4	3	23.1	9.64	43	.368	.500	0	—	0	-3	-3	-0	0.0
● RUBE KISINGER	Kisinger, Charles Samuel b: 12/13/1876, Adrian, Mich. d: 7/14/41, Huron, Ohio BR/TR, 6', 190 lbs. Deb: 9/10/02																									
1902	Det-A	2	3	.400	5	5	5	0	0	43^1	48	0	14	7	13.5	3.12	117	.281	.346	3	.158	-1	2	3	-0	0.2
1903	Det-A	7	9	.438	16	14	13	2	0	118^2	118	0	27	33	11.1	2.96	98	.259	.303	6	.128	-3	0	-1	1	-0.3
Total	2	9	12	.429	21	19	18	2	0	162	166	0	41	40	11.8	3.00	103	.265	.315	9	.136	-4	2	2	1	-0.1
● BRUCE KISON	Kison, Bruce Eugene b: 2/18/50, Pasco, Wash. BR/TR, 6'4", 178 lbs. Deb: 7/4/71 C																									
1971	*Pit-N	6	5	.545	18	13	2	1	0	95^1	93	6	36	60	12.7	3.40	100	.259	.337	2	.065	-1	1	-0	1	0.0
1972	*Pit-N	9	7	.563	32	18	6	1	3	152	123	11	69	102	11.9	3.26	102	.220	.316	10	.189	2	3	1	-1	0.2
1973	Pit-N	3	0	1.000	7	7	0	0	0	43^2	36	4	24	26	12.6	3.09	114	.232	.339	1	.083	0	3	2	0	0.2
1974	*Pit-N	9	8	.529	40	16	1	0	2	129	123	8	57	71	13.3	3.49	99	.247	.338	4	.108	-0	2	-1	1	0.0
1975	*Pit-N	12	11	.522	33	29	6	0	0	192	160	10	92	89	12.0	3.23	109	.227	.320	7	.119	-2	8	7	2	0.8
1976	Pit-N	14	9	.609	31	29	6	1	1	193	180	10	52	98	11.0	3.08	113	.247	.299	12	.203	4	9	9	1	1.5
1977	Pit-N	9	10	.474	33	32	3	1	0	193	209	25	55	122	12.6	4.90	81	.278	.333	18	.261	5	-21	-20	1	-1.3

YEAR	TM/L	W	L	PCT	G	GS	CG	SH	SV	IP	H	HR	BB	SO	RAT	ERA	ERA+	OAV	OOB	BH	AVG	PB	PR	/A	PD	TPI
1978	Pit-N	6	6	.500	28	11	0	0	0	96	81	3	39	62	11.7	3.19	116	.229	.314	4	.138	1	4	5	1	0.8
1979	*Pit-N	13	7	.650	33	25	3	1	0	172^1	157	13	45	105	10.8	3.19	122	.246	.300	8	.145	0	10	13	1	1.6
1980	Cal-A	3	6	.333	13	13	2	1	0	73^1	73	5	32	28	13.3	4.91	80	.264	.346	0	—	0	-7	-8	-1	-0.8
1981	Cal-A	1	1	.500	11	4	0	0	0	44	40	8	14	19	11.0	3.48	105	.241	.300	0	—	0	1	1	1	0.1
1982	*Cal-A	10	5	.667	33	16	3	1	1	142	120	15	44	86	10.7	3.17	128	.226	.292	0	—	0	14	14	2	1.6
1983	Cal-A	11	5	.688	26	17	4	1	2	126^2	128	13	43	83	12.4	4.05	99	.264	.330	0	—	0	0	-1	1	0.1
1984	Cal-A	4	5	.444	20	7	0	0	2	65^1	72	10	28	66	14.6	5.37	74	.280	.364	0	—	0	-10	-10	-1	-1.3
1985	Bos-A	5	3	.625	22	9	0	0	1	92	98	9	32	56	12.8	4.11	104	.274	.335	0	—	0	0	2	2	0.0
Total	15	115	88	.567	380	246	36	8	12	1809^2	1693	150	662	1073	12.1	3.66	102	.248	.321	66	.163	8	18	14	11	3.5

● BILL KISSINGER Kissinger, William Francis "Shang" b: 8/15/1871, Dayton, Ky. d: 4/20/29, Cincinnati, Ohio BR/TR, 185 lbs. Deb: 5/30/1895 ♦

YEAR	TM/L	W	L	PCT	G	GS	CG	SH	SV	IP	H	HR	BB	SO	RAT	ERA	ERA+	OAV	OOB	BH	AVG	PB	PR	/A	PD	TPI
1895	Bal-N	1	0	1.000	2	2	1	0	0	11^1	18	0	2	3	15.9	3.97	120	.353	.377	1	.200	-0	1	1	-0	0.0
	StL-N	4	12	.250	24	14	9	0	0	140^2	222	8	51	31	18.0	6.72	72	.352	.408	24	.247	-2	-30	-29	0	-2.4
	Yr	5	12	.294	26	16	10	0	0	152	240	8	53	34	17.8	6.51	74	.352	.406	25	.245	-2	-29	-28	0	-2.4
1896	StL-N	2	9	.182	20	12	11	0	1	136	209	5	55	22	18.0	6.49	67	.349	.411	22	.301	1	-32	-32	2	-1.7
1897	StL-N	0	4	.000	7	4	2	0	0	31^1	51	2	15	5	21.3	11.49	38	.362	.451	13	.333	2	-25	-25	0	-2.0
Total	3	7	25	.219	53	32	23	0	1	319^1	500	15	123	61	18.2	6.99	66	.352	.413	60	.280	1	-86	-85	2	-6.1

● FRANK KITSON Kitson, Frank R. b: 9/11/1869, Hopkins, Mich. d: 4/14/30, Allegan, Mich. BL/TR, 5'11", 165 lbs. Deb: 5/19/1898

YEAR	TM/L	W	L	PCT	G	GS	CG	SH	SV	IP	H	HR	BB	SO	RAT	ERA	ERA+	OAV	OOB	BH	AVG	PB	PR	/A	PD	TPI
1898	Bal-N	8	5	.615	17	13	13	1	0	119^1	123	0	35	32	12.5	3.24	110	.265	.327	27	.314	4	5	4	0	0.8
1899	Bal-N	22	16	.579	40	37	34	2	0	326^2	327	6	65	75	11.1	2.78	142	.260	.303	27	.201	-2	39	43	-2	3.8
1900	*Bro-N	15	13	.536	40	30	21	2	**4**	253^1	283	12	56	55	12.4	4.19	92	.282	.326	32	.294	5	-14	-10	-5	-0.9
1901	Bro-N	19	11	.633	38	32	26	5	2	280^2	312	9	67	127	12.5	2.98	112	.279	.326	35	.263	5	11	12	-3	1.5
1902	Bro-N	19	13	.594	32	31	29	3	0	268^2	256	4	52	109	10.6	2.85	97	.251	.292	32	.276	8	-2	-2	2	0.7
1903	Det-A	15	16	.484	31	28	28	2	0	257^2	277	8	38	102	11.2	2.58	113	.274	.303	21	.181	-1	11	9	-2	0.7
1904	Det-A	9	13	.409	26	24	19	0	0	199^2	211	7	38	69	11.5	3.07	83	.272	.312	15	.208	1	-10	-11	-0	-1.2
1905	Det-A	12	14	.462	33	27	21	3	1	225^2	230	3	57	78	11.9	3.47	79	.266	.319	16	.184	-1	-20	-18	-2	-2.4
1906	Was-A	6	14	.300	30	21	15	1	0	197	196	2	57	59	11.8	3.65	72	.262	.320	22	.244	8	-21	-22	-0	-1.3
1907	Was-A	0	3	.000	5	3	2	0	0	32	41	1	9	11	14.6	3.94	61	.313	.366	1	.100	-0	-5	-5	-1	-0.6
	NY-A	4	0	1.000	12	4	3	0	0	61	75	0	17	14	14.2	3.10	90	.305	.360	7	.280	1	-4	-2	-1	-0.2
	Yr	4	3	.571	17	7	5	0	0	93	116	1	26	25	14.1	3.39	79	.306	.357	8	.229	0	-9	-7	-2	-0.8
Total	10	129	118	.522	304	250	211	19	7	2221^2	2331	52	491	731	11.8	3.18	99	.270	.315	235	.240	27	-11	-5	-15	0.9

● MALACHI KITTRIDGE Kittridge, Malachi Jeddidah "Jeddidah" b: 10/12/1869, Clinton, Mass. d: 6/23/28, Gary, Ind. BR/TR, 5'7", 170 lbs. Deb: 4/19/1890 M♦

YEAR	TM/L	W	L	PCT	G	GS	CG	SH	SV	IP	H	HR	BB	SO	RAT	ERA	ERA+	OAV	OOB	BH	AVG	PB	PR	/A	PD	TPI
1896	Chi-N	0	0	—	1	0	0	0	0	1^2	2	0	1	0	16.2	5.40	84	.286	.375	48	.223	-0	-0	-0	-0	0.0

● HUGO KLAERNER Klaerner, Hugo Emil "Dutch" b: 10/15/08, Fredericksburg, Tex. d: 2/3/82, Fredericksburg, Tex. BR/TR, 5'11", 190 lbs. Deb: 9/10/34

YEAR	TM/L	W	L	PCT	G	GS	CG	SH	SV	IP	H	HR	BB	SO	RAT	ERA	ERA+	OAV	OOB	BH	AVG	PB	PR	/A	PD	TPI
1934	Chi-A	0	2	.000	3	3	1	0	0	17^1	24	4	16	9	20.8	10.90	43	.329	.449	2	.333	1	-12	-12	1	-0.8

● FRED KLAGES Klages, Frederick Albert Anthony b: 10/31/43, Ambridge, Pa. BR/TR, 6'2", 185 lbs. Deb: 9/11/66

YEAR	TM/L	W	L	PCT	G	GS	CG	SH	SV	IP	H	HR	BB	SO	RAT	ERA	ERA+	OAV	OOB	BH	AVG	PB	PR	/A	PD	TPI
1966	Chi-A	1	0	1.000	3	3	0	0	0	15^2	9	0	7	6	9.2	1.72	184	.167	.262	3	.500	1	3	3	0	0.3
1967	Chi-A	4	4	.500	11	9	0	0	0	44^2	43	6	16	17	12.1	3.83	81	.256	.324	0	.000	-1	-3	-4	-1	-0.8
Total	2	5	4	.556	14	12	0	0	0	60^1	52	6	23	23	11.3	3.28	95	.234	.309	3	.167	-0	0	-1	-1	-0.5

● AL KLAWITTER Klawitter, Albert "Dutch" b: 4/12/1888, Wilkes-Barre, Pa. d: 5/2/50, Milwaukee, Wis. BR/TR, 5'11.5", 187 lbs. Deb: 9/20/09

YEAR	TM/L	W	L	PCT	G	GS	CG	SH	SV	IP	H	HR	BB	SO	RAT	ERA	ERA+	OAV	OOB	BH	AVG	PB	PR	/A	PD	TPI
1909	NY-N	1	1	.500	6	3	2	0	1	27	24	1	13	6	12.3	2.00	128	.247	.336	3	.333	1	2	2	1	0.4
1910	NY-N	0	0	—	1	0	0	0	0	1	2	0	2	0	36.0	9.00	33	.400	.571	0	—	0	-1	-1	-0	0.0
1913	Det-A	1	2	.333	8	3	1	0	0	32	39	0	15	10	15.2	5.91	49	.305	.378	0	.000	-2	-11	-11	0	-1.0
Total	3	2	3	.400	15	6	3	0	1	60	65	1	30	16	14.3	4.20	66	.283	.365	3	.150	-0	-9	-10	1	-0.6

● TOM KLAWITTER Klawitter, Thomas Carl b: 6/24/58, LaCrosse, Wis. BR/TL, 6'2", 190 lbs. Deb: 4/14/85

YEAR	TM/L	W	L	PCT	G	GS	CG	SH	SV	IP	H	HR	BB	SO	RAT	ERA	ERA+	OAV	OOB	BH	AVG	PB	PR	/A	PD	TPI
1985	Min-A	0	0	—	7	2	0	0	0	9^1	7	2	13	5	19.3	6.75	65	.226	.455	0	—	0	-3	-2	0	-0.3

● HAL KLEINE Kleine, Harold John b: 6/8/23, St.Louis, Mo. d: 12/10/57, St.Louis, Mo. BL/TL, 6'2", 193 lbs. Deb: 4/26/44

YEAR	TM/L	W	L	PCT	G	GS	CG	SH	SV	IP	H	HR	BB	SO	RAT	ERA	ERA+	OAV	OOB	BH	AVG	PB	PR	/A	PD	TPI
1944	Cle-A	1	2	.333	11	6	1	0	0	40^2	38	0	36	13	16.4	5.75	57	.248	.392	2	.143	-1	-11	-11	-1	-0.9
1945	Cle-A	0	0	—	3	0	0	0	0	7	8	0	7	5	19.3	3.86	84	.286	.429	1	.333	1	-0	-0	-0	0.0
Total	2	1	2	.333	14	6	1	0	0	47^2	46	0	43	18	16.8	5.48	60	.254	.397	3	.176	-0	-11	-12	-1	-0.9

● TED KLEINHANS Kleinhans, Theodore Otto (b: Traugott Otto Kleinhans) b: 4/8/1899, Deer Park, Wis. d: 7/24/85, Redington Beach, Fla. BR/TL, 6', 170 lbs. Deb: 4/20/34

YEAR	TM/L	W	L	PCT	G	GS	CG	SH	SV	IP	H	HR	BB	SO	RAT	ERA	ERA+	OAV	OOB	BH	AVG	PB	PR	/A	PD	TPI
1934	Phi-N	0	0	—	5	0	0	0	0	6	11	1	3	2	21.0	9.00	52	.379	.438	0	.000	-0	-3	-3	0	0.0
	Cin-N	2	6	.250	24	9	0	0	0	80	107	2	38	23	16.4	5.74	71	.321	.392	3	.130	-1	-15	-15	1	-1.2
	Yr	2	6	.250	29	9	0	0	0	86	118	3	41	25	16.7	5.97	69	.326	.396	3	.125	-1	-18	-18	2	-1.2
1936	NY-A	1	1	.500	19	0	0	0	1	29^1	36	0	23	10	18.1	5.83	80	.300	.413	1	.167	-0	-3	-4	-0	-0.3
1937	Cin-N	1	2	.333	7	3	1	0	0	27^1	29	1	12	13	13.8	2.30	162	.271	.350	2	.250	0	5	4	-1	0.4
1938	Cin-N	0	0	—	1	0	0	0	0	1	2	0	0	0	18.0	9.00	41	.400	.400	0	—	0	-1	-1	-0	0.0
Total	4	4	9	.308	56	12	1	0	1	143^2	185	4	76	48	16.5	5.26	79	.311	.391	6	.158	-1	-16	-17	1	-1.1

● NUB KLEINKE Kleinke, Norbert George b: 5/19/11, Fond Du Lac, Wis. d: 3/16/50, Off Marin Coast, Cal. BR/TR, 6'1", 170 lbs. Deb: 4/25/35

YEAR	TM/L	W	L	PCT	G	GS	CG	SH	SV	IP	H	HR	BB	SO	RAT	ERA	ERA+	OAV	OOB	BH	AVG	PB	PR	/A	PD	TPI
1935	StL-N	0	0	—	4	2	0	0	0	12^2	19	1	3	5	15.6	4.97	82	.358	.393	0	.000	-0	-1	-1	-0	0.0
1937	StL-N	1	1	.500	5	2	1	0	0	20^2	25	0	7	9	13.9	4.79	83	.321	.376	0	.000	-1	-2	-2	0	-0.2
Total	2	1	1	.500	9	4	1	0	0	33^1	44	1	10	14	14.6	4.86	83	.336	.383	0	.000	-1	-3	-3	0	-0.2

● ED KLEPFER Klepfer, Edward Lloyd "Big Ed" b: 3/17/1888, Summerville, Pa. d: 8/9/50, Tulsa, Okla. BR/TR, 6', 185 lbs. Deb: 7/4/11

YEAR	TM/L	W	L	PCT	G	GS	CG	SH	SV	IP	H	HR	BB	SO	RAT	ERA	ERA+	OAV	OOB	BH	AVG	PB	PR	/A	PD	TPI
1911	NY-A	0	0	—	2	0	0	0	0	4	5	0	2	4	15.8	6.75	53	.250	.318	0	.000	-0	-2	-1	0	0.0
1913	NY-A	0	1	.000	8	1	0	0	0	24^2	38	2	12	10	19.0	7.66	39	.373	.448	1	.167	0	-13	-13	0	-0.4
1915	Chi-A	1	0	1.000	3	2	1	0	0	12^2	11	0	5	3	11.4	2.84	105	.234	.308	0	.000	-0	0	0	-0	0.0
	Cle-A	1	6	.143	8	7	2	0	0	43	47	0	11	13	12.1	2.09	146	.283	.328	2	.167	-0	4	5	1	0.8
	Yr	2	6	.250	11	9	3	0	0	55^2	58	0	16	16	12.0	2.26	134	.272	.323	2	.133	-0	4	5	0	0.8
1916	Cle-A	6	6	.500	31	13	4	1	2	143	136	0	46	62	11.7	2.52	119	.262	.327	1	.025	-4	5	8	-0	0.2
1917	Cle-A	14	4	.778	41	27	9	0	1	213	208	0	55	66	11.1	2.37	120	.264	.312	2	.032	-6	7	11	-2	0.1
1919	Cle-A	0	0	—	5	0	0	0	0	7^1	12	1	6	7	22.1	7.36	45	.375	.474	0	.000	-0	-3	-3	0	0.0
Total	6	22	17	.564	98	50	16	1	3	447^2	457	3	137	165	12.1	2.81	104	.273	.330	6	.048	-11	-2	6	-1	0.7

● ED KLIEMAN Klieman, Edward Frederick "Specs" or "Babe" b: 3/21/18, Norwood, Ohio d: 11/15/79, Homosassa, Fla. BR/TR, 6'1", 190 lbs. Deb: 9/24/43

YEAR	TM/L	W	L	PCT	G	GS	CG	SH	SV	IP	H	HR	BB	SO	RAT	ERA	ERA+	OAV	OOB	BH	AVG	PB	PR	/A	PD	TPI
1943	Cle-A	0	1	.000	1	1	1	0	0	9	8	0	5	2	13.0	1.00	311	.286	.394	0	.000	-0	2	2	-0	0.2
1944	Cle-A	11	13	.458	47	19	5	1	5	178^1	185	4	70	44	13.2	3.38	98	.274	.348	6	.105	-3	1	-2	1	-0.5
1945	Cle-A	5	8	.385	38	12	4	1	4	126^1	123	3	49	33	12.5	3.85	84	.261	.336	8	.200	1	-7	-8	3	-0.5
1946	Cle-A	0	0	—	9	0	0	0	0	15	18	0	10	2	16.8	6.60	50	.290	.389	0	.000	-0	-5	-5	-1	-0.1
1947	Cle-A	5	4	.556	**58**	0	0	0	**17**	92	78	5	39	21	11.6	3.03	115	.231	.315	2	.105	-1	7	5	2	0.7
1948	*Cle-A	3	2	.600	44	0	0	0	4	79^2	62	3	46	18	12.4	2.60	156	.229	.345	2	.143	-0	**15**	**13**	1	0.9
1949	Was-A	0	0	—	2	0	0	0	0	3	8	0	3	1	33.0	18.00	24	.500	.579	1	1.000	0	-5	-5	-0	0.0
	Chi-A	2	0	1.000	18	0	0	0	3	33	33	2	15	9	13.1	3.00	139	.273	.353	2	.250	0	4	4	1	0.4
	Yr	2	0	1.000	20	0	0	0	3	36	41	2	18	10	14.8	4.25	98	.299	.381	3	.333	1	-0	-0	1	0.4
1950	Phi-A	0	0	—	5	0	0	0	0	5^2	10	0	2	0	22.2	9.53	48	.357	.438	0	.000	-0	-3	-3	-0	0.0
Total	8	26	28	.481	222	32	10	2	33	542	525	17	239	130	13.0	3.49	100	.261	.345	21	.146	-3	10	1	6	1.1

● RON KLIMKOWSKI Klimkowski, Ronald Bernard b: 3/1/44, Jersey City, N.J. BR/TR, 6'2", 190 lbs. Deb: 9/15/69

YEAR	TM/L	W	L	PCT	G	GS	CG	SH	SV	IP	H	HR	BB	SO	RAT	ERA	ERA+	OAV	OOB	BH	AVG	PB	PR	/A	PD	TPI
1969	NY-A	0	0	—	3	1	0	0	0	14	6	0	5	3	7.1	0.64	541	.130	.216	0	.000	-0	5	4	-0	-0.1
1970	NY-A	6	7	.462	45	3	1	1	1	98^1	80	7	33	40	10.6	2.65	132	.223	.294	1	.053	-2	12	9	0	1.1
1971	Oak-A	2	2	.500	26	0	0	0	2	45^1	37	3	23	25	12.1	3.38	99	.220	.318	2	.400	1	0	-0	1	0.2

YEAR	TM/L	W	L	PCT	G	GS	CG	SH	SV	IP	H	HR	BB	SO	RAT	ERA	ERA+	OAV	OOB	BH	AVG	PB	PR	/A	PD	TPI
1972	NY-A	0	3	.000	16	2	0	0	1	31^1	32	3	15	11	13.8	4.02	73	.271	.358	0	.000	-1	-3	-4	0	-0.5
Total	4	8	12	.400	90	6	1	1	4	189	155	13	76	79	11.2	2.90	116	.224	.306	3	.091	-2	13	10	1	0.7

● BOBBY KLINE

Kline, John Robert b: 1/27/29, St.Petersburg, Fla BR/TR, 6′, 179 lbs. Deb: 4/11/55 ♦

YEAR	TM/L	W	L	PCT	G	GS	CG	SH	SV	IP	H	HR	BB	SO	RAT	ERA	ERA+	OAV	OOB	BH	AVG	PB	PR	/A	PD	TPI
1955	Was-A	0	0	—	1	0	0	0	0	1	4	1	1	0	45.0	27.00	14	.667	.714	31	.221	0	-3	-3	0	0.0

● BOB KLINE

Kline, Robert George "Junior" b: 12/9/09, Enterprise, Ohio d: 3/16/87, Westerville, Ohio BR/TR, 6′3″, 200 lbs. Deb: 9/17/30

YEAR	TM/L	W	L	PCT	G	GS	CG	SH	SV	IP	H	HR	BB	SO	RAT	ERA	ERA+	OAV	OOB	BH	AVG	PB	PR	/A	PD	TPI
1930	Bos-A	0	0	—	1	0	0	0	0	1	1	0	0	0	9.0	0.00	—	.333	.333	0	—	0	1	1	-0	0.0
1931	Bos-A	5	5	.500	28	10	3	0	0	98	110	3	35	25	13.6	4.41	98	.298	.364	9	.333	2	-0	-1	2	0.3
1932	Bos-A	11	13	.458	47	19	4	1	2	172	203	10	76	31	14.7	5.28	85	.294	.365	7	.130	-3	-15	-15	3	-1.8
1933	Bos-A	7	8	.467	46	8	1	0	4	127	127	5	67	16	14.2	4.54	97	.265	.362	6	.176	-1	-4	-2	3	0.0
1934	Phi-A	6	2	.750	20	0	0	0	1	39^2	50	6	13	14	14.3	6.35	69	.314	.366	3	.333	1	-8	-9	1	-1.3
	Was-A	1	0	1.000	6	0	0	0	0	4	10	0	4	1	33.8	15.75	27	.500	.600	0	—	0	-5	-5	0	-1.0
	Yr	7	2	.778	26	0	0	0	1	43^2	60	6	17	15	16.1	7.21	61	.335	.396	3	.333	1	-13	-14	2	-2.3
Total	5	30	28	.517	148	37	8	1	7	441^2	501	24	195	87	14.4	5.05	87	.291	.367	25	.202	-1	-32	-32	9	-3.8

● RON KLINE

Kline, Ronald Lee b: 3/9/32, Callery, Pa. BR/TR, 6′3″, 205 lbs. Deb: 4/21/52

YEAR	TM/L	W	L	PCT	G	GS	CG	SH	SV	IP	H	HR	BB	SO	RAT	ERA	ERA+	OAV	OOB	BH	AVG	PB	PR	/A	PD	TPI
1952	Pit-N	0	7	.000	27	11	0	0	0	78^2	74	3	66	27	16.7	5.49	73	.253	.401	0	.000	-2	-15	-13	-1	-1.4
1955	Pit-N	6	13	.316	36	19	2	1	2	136^2	161	13	53	48	14.4	4.15	99	.298	.366	5	.132	-2	-2	-1	2	0.0
1956	Pit-N	14	18	.438	44	39	9	2	2	264	263	26	81	125	11.9	3.38	112	.263	.321	10	.127	-3	12	12	-0	1.1
1957	Pit-N	9	16	.360	40	31	11	2	0	205	214	28	61	88	12.1	4.04	94	.268	.321	4	.061	-6	-4	-6	-1	-1.3
1958	Pit-N	13	16	.448	32	32	11	2	0	237^1	220	25	92	109	11.8	3.53	110	.252	.323	2	.027	-6	11	9	1	0.4
1959	Pit-N	11	13	.458	33	29	7	0	0	186	186	23	70	91	12.5	4.26	91	.263	.331	8	.136	-2	-6	-8	-1	-1.1
1960	StL-N	4	9	.308	34	17	1	0	1	117^2	133	21	43	54	13.5	6.04	68	.284	.344	5	.143	-2	-30	-25	1	-2.6
1961	LA-A	3	6	.333	26	12	0	0	1	104^2	119	16	44	70	14.1	4.90	92	.288	.358	3	.097	-2	-10	-5	1	-0.5
	Det-A	5	3	.625	10	8	3	1	0	56^1	53	3	17	27	11.2	2.72	151	.245	.300	3	.167	0	8	9	-1	1.1
	Yr	8	9	.471	36	20	3	1	1	161	172	19	61	97	13.0	4.14	106	.272	.336	6	.122	-2	-2	4	0	0.6
1962	Det-A	3	6	.333	36	4	0	0	2	77^1	88	9	28	47	13.7	4.31	94	.284	.347	2	.125	-1	-3	-2	1	-0.3
1963	Was-A	3	8	.273	62	1	0	0	17	93^2	85	3	30	49	11.3	2.79	133	.249	.316	1	.091	-0	9	10	-1	1.4
1964	Was-A	10	7	.588	61	0	0	0	14	81^1	81	4	21	40	11.5	2.32	159	.262	.313	1	.167	0	12	12	-0	3.0
1965	Was-A	7	6	.538	74	0	0	0	**29**	99^1	106	7	32	52	12.7	2.63	132	.275	.333	0	.000	-1	9	9	-1	1.6
1966	Was-A	6	4	.600	63	0	0	0	23	90^1	79	12	17	46	9.6	2.39	145	.237	.274	1	.167	0	10	11	-2	1.6
1967	Min-A	7	1	.875	54	0	0	0	5	71^2	71	10	15	36	10.9	3.77	92	.261	.302	0	.000	-1	-4	-2	-1	-0.4
1968	Pit-N	12	5	.706	56	0	0	0	7	112^2	94	3	31	48	10.1	1.68	174	.234	.293	0	.000	-1	**16**	**16**	-1	2.4
1969	Pit-N	1	3	.250	20	0	0	0	3	31	37	3	5	15	12.5	5.81	60	.296	.328	0	.000	-1	-8	-8	-0	-1.2
	SF-N	0	2	.000	7	0	0	0	0	11	16	1	6	7	18.0	4.09	86	.364	.440	0	—	0	-1	-1	-0	-0.1
	Yr	1	5	.167	27	0	0	0	3	42	53	4	11	22	13.7	5.36	65	.310	.352	0	.000	-1	-8	-9	-0	-1.3
	Bos-A	0	1	.000	16	0	0	0	1	17	24	4	17	7	21.7	4.76	80	.329	.456	0	—	0	-2	-2	0	-0.1
1970	Atl-N	0	0	—	5	0	0	0	1	6^1	9	4	2	3	15.6	7.11	60	.321	.367	0	—	0	-2	-2	-0	-0.1
Total	17	114	144	.442	736	203	44	8	108	2078	2113	218	731	989	12.5	3.75	101	.266	.331	45	.092	-28	1	13	-5	3.5

● STEVE KLINE

Kline, Steven Jack b: 10/6/47, Wenatchee, Wash. BR/TR, 6′3″, 205 lbs. Deb: 7/10/70

YEAR	TM/L	W	L	PCT	G	GS	CG	SH	SV	IP	H	HR	BB	SO	RAT	ERA	ERA+	OAV	OOB	BH	AVG	PB	PR	/A	PD	TPI
1970	NY-A	6	6	.500	16	15	5	0	0	100^1	99	8	24	49	11.0	3.41	103	.254	.298	5	.179	2	3	1	1	0.4
1971	NY-A	12	13	.480	31	30	15	1	0	222^1	206	21	37	81	9.8	2.96	109	.244	.276	9	.136	-0	13	7	3	1.1
1972	NY-A	16	9	.640	32	32	11	4	0	236^1	210	11	44	58	10.1	2.40	123	.237	.281	7	.092	-3	17	14	2	1.5
1973	NY-A	4	7	.364	14	13	2	1	0	74	76	5	31	19	13.1	4.01	91	.270	.344	0	—	0	-2	-3	-0	-0.2
1974	NY-A	2	2	.500	4	4	0	0	0	26	26	3	5	6	11.1	3.46	102	.263	.305	0	—	0	0	0	-0	0.1
	Cle-A	3	8	.273	16	11	1	0	0	71	70	9	31	17	13.3	5.07	71	.266	.352	0	—	0	-11	-11	1	-1.5
	Yr	5	10	.333	20	15	1	0	0	97	96	12	36	23	12.6	4.64	77	.264	.337	0	—	0	-11	-11	1	-1.4
1977	Atl-N	0	0	—	16	0	0	0	1	20^1	21	4	12	10	14.6	6.64	67	.259	.355	0	—	0	-6	-5	-0	-0.1
Total	6	43	45	.489	129	105	34	6	1	750^1	708	61	184	240	10.9	3.26	101	.249	.298	21	.124	-1	14	3	5	1.3

● STEVE KLINE

Kline, Steven James b: 8/22/72, Sunbury, Pa. BB/TL, 6′2″, 200 lbs. Deb: 4/2/97

YEAR	TM/L	W	L	PCT	G	GS	CG	SH	SV	IP	H	HR	BB	SO	RAT	ERA	ERA+	OAV	OOB	BH	AVG	PB	PR	/A	PD	TPI
1997	Cle-A	3	1	.750	20	1	0	0	0	26^1	42	6	13	17	19.1	5.81	81	.365	.434	0	—	0	-4	-3	-1	-0.7
	Mon-N	1	3	.250	26	0	0	0	0	26^1	31	4	10	20	14.4	6.15	68	.304	.372	0	.000	-0	-6	-6	0	-0.8
1998	Mon-N	3	6	.333	78	0	0	0	1	71^2	62	4	41	76	13.3	2.76	149	.228	.335	0	.000	-0	12	11	0	1.2
Total	2	7	10	.412	124	1	0	0	1	124^1	135	14	64	113	14.8	4.13	103	.276	.366	0	.000	-1	2	2	-0	-0.3

● BILL KLING

Kling, William b: 1/14/1867, Kansas City, Mo. d: 8/26/34, Kansas City, Mo. BL/TR, 6′, 190 lbs. Deb: 8/13/1891 F

YEAR	TM/L	W	L	PCT	G	GS	CG	SH	SV	IP	H	HR	BB	SO	RAT	ERA	ERA+	OAV	OOB	BH	AVG	PB	PR	/A	PD	TPI
1891	Phi-N	4	2	.667	12	7	4	0	0	75	91	2	32	26	15.0	4.32	79	.289	.358	6	.194	1	-8	-8	-1	-0.5
1892	Bal-N	0	2	.000	2	2	0	0	0	11	17	1	7	7	21.3	11.45	30	.340	.441	1	.250	1	-10	-10	-0	-1.1
1895	Lou-N	0	0	—	1	0	0	0	0	1	0	0	1	0	9.0	0.00	—	.000	.250	0	.000	-0	1	1	-0	0.0
Total	3	4	4	.500	15	9	4	0	0	87	108	3	40	33	15.7	5.17	66	.293	.369	7	.194	1	-18	-17	-1	-1.6

● SCOTT KLINGENBECK

Klingenbeck, Scott Edward b: 2/3/71, Cincinnati, Ohio BR/TR, 6′2″, 205 lbs. Deb: 6/2/94

YEAR	TM/L	W	L	PCT	G	GS	CG	SH	SV	IP	H	HR	BB	SO	RAT	ERA	ERA+	OAV	OOB	BH	AVG	PB	PR	/A	PD	TPI
1994	Bal-A	1	0	1.000	1	1	0	0	0	7	6	1	4	5	14.1	3.86	130	.240	.367	0	—	0	1	1	-0	0.0
1995	Bal-A	2	2	.500	6	5	0	0	0	31^1	32	6	18	15	14.4	4.88	97	.269	.365	0	—	0	-1	-0	1	0.0
	Min-A	0	2	.000	18	4	0	0	0	48^1	69	16	24	27	18.1	8.57	56	.338	.418	0	—	0	-21	-20	-1	-0.8
	Yr	2	4	.333	24	9	0	0	0	79^2	101	22	42	42	16.6	7.12	67	.313	.398	0	—	0	-21	-21	-0	-0.8
1996	Min-A	1	1	.500	10	3	0	0	0	28^2	42	5	10	15	16.6	7.85	65	.339	.393	0	—	0	-9	-9	0	-0.5
1998	Cin-N	1	3	.250	4	4	0	0	0	22^2	26	6	7	13	13.5	5.96	73	.286	.343	0	.000	-1	-4	-4	0	-0.6
Total	4	5	8	.385	39	17	0	0	0	138	175	34	63	75	16.0	6.91	69	.311	.387	0	.000	-1	-34	-33	0	-1.9

● BOB KLINGER

Klinger, Robert Harold b: 6/4/08, Allenton, Mo. d: 8/19/77, Villa Ridge, Mo. BR/TR, 6′, 180 lbs. Deb: 4/19/38

YEAR	TM/L	W	L	PCT	G	GS	CG	SH	SV	IP	H	HR	BB	SO	RAT	ERA	ERA+	OAV	OOB	BH	AVG	PB	PR	/A	PD	TPI
1938	Pit-N	12	5	.706	28	21	10	1	1	159^1	152	7	42	58	11.3	2.99	127	.253	.308	10	.167	-2	14	14	0	1.3
1939	Pit-N	14	17	.452	37	33	10	2	0	225	251	11	81	64	13.4	4.36	88	.284	.346	17	.202	0	-11	-13	3	-1.3
1940	Pit-N	8	13	.381	39	22	3	0	3	142	196	5	53	48	16.1	5.39	71	.329	.388	6	.143	-2	-24	-25	1	-3.4
1941	Pit-N	9	4	.692	35	9	3	0	4	116^2	127	5	30	36	12.2	3.93	92	.276	.322	8	.250	2	-4	-4	0	-0.3
1942	Pit-N	8	11	.421	37	19	8	1	1	152^2	151	6	45	58	11.7	3.24	104	.252	.307	8	.200	1	1	2	1	0.5
1943	Pit-N	11	8	.579	33	25	14	3	0	195	185	6	58	65	11.2	2.72	128	.252	.307	16	.246	3	14	16	0	1.9
1946	*Bos-A	3	2	.600	28	1	0	0	**9**	57	49	1	25	16	11.8	2.37	155	.238	.323	5	.313	1	7	8	-0	1.1
1947	Bos-A	1	1	.500	28	0	0	0	5	42	42	5	24	12	14.4	3.86	101	.253	.351	1	.111	-1	-1	0	-0	-0.1
Total	8	66	61	.520	265	130	48	7	23	1089^2	1153	46	358	357	12.6	3.68	100	.271	.331	71	.204	3	-3	-0	5	-0.3

● JOE KLINK

Klink, Joseph Charles b: 2/3/62, Johnstown, Pa. BL/TL, 5′11″, 175 lbs. Deb: 4/9/87

YEAR	TM/L	W	L	PCT	G	GS	CG	SH	SV	IP	H	HR	BB	SO	RAT	ERA	ERA+	OAV	OOB	BH	AVG	PB	PR	/A	PD	TPI
1987	Min-A	0	1	.000	12	0	0	0	0	23	37	4	11	17	18.8	6.65	69	.359	.421	0	—	0	-6	-5	-0	-0.3
1990	*Oak-A	0	0	—	40	0	0	0	1	39^2	34	1	18	19	11.8	2.04	182	.233	.317	0	—	0	8	7	-1	-0.1
1991	Oak-A	10	3	.769	62	0	0	0	2	62	60	4	21	34	12.5	4.35	88	.259	.333	0	—	0	-2	-4	0	-0.7
1993	Fla-N	0	2	.000	59	0	0	0	0	37^2	37	0	24	22	14.6	5.02	86	.266	.374	0	.000	-0	-4	-3	-1	-0.2
1996	Sea-A	0	0	—	3	0	0	0	0	2^1	3	1	1	2	15.4	3.86	128	.300	.364	0	—	0	0	0	-0	0.0
Total	5	10	6	.625	176	0	0	0	3	164^2	171	10	75	94	13.7	4.26	95	.271	.354	0	.000	-0	-3	-4	-2	-1.3

● JOHNNY KLIPPSTEIN

Klippstein, John Calvin b: 10/17/27, Washington, D.C. BR/TR, 6′1″, 185 lbs. Deb: 5/3/50

YEAR	TM/L	W	L	PCT	G	GS	CG	SH	SV	IP	H	HR	BB	SO	RAT	ERA	ERA+	OAV	OOB	BH	AVG	PB	PR	/A	PD	TPI
1950	Chi-N	2	9	.182	33	11	3	0	1	104^2	112	9	64	51	15.5	5.25	80	.279	.383	11	.333	4	-13	-12	-1	-0.8
1951	Chi-N	6	6	.500	35	11	1	1	2	123^2	125	10	53	56	13.4	4.29	95	.263	.344	4	.108	-2	-5	-3	0	-0.4
1952	Chi-N	9	14	.391	41	25	7	2	3	202^2	208	17	89	110	13.5	4.44	87	.265	.344	11	.175	1	-16	-13	1	-1.2
1953	Chi-N	10	11	.476	48	19	5	0	6	167^2	169	15	107	113	15.2	4.83	92	.258	.369	9	.155	-1	-10	-7	-2	-1.0
1954	Chi-N	4	11	.267	36	21	4	0	1	148	155	13	96	69	15.5	5.29	79	.272	.381	6	.133	-2	-20	-18	1	-1.7
1955	Cin-N	9	10	.474	39	14	3	2	0	138	120	13	60	68	12.0	3.39	125	.233	.318	2	.065	-2	10	13	-0	1.4
1956	Cin-N	12	11	.522	37	29	11	0	1	211	219	26	82	86	13.3	4.09	97	.275	.350	7	.099	-4	-8	-3	1	-0.6
1957	Cin-N	8	11	.421	46	18	3	1	3	146	146	17	68	99	13.4	5.05	81	.261	.344	3	.073	-3	-19	-15	-1	-2.3
1958	Cin-N	3	2	.600	12	4	0	0	1	33	37	5	14	22	14.2	4.91	84	.285	.359	1	.125	-0	-4	-3	-1	-0.5

YEAR	TM/L	W	L	PCT	G	GS	CG	SH	SV	IP	H	HR	BB	SO	RAT	ERA	ERA+	OAV	OOB	BH	AVG	PB	PR	/A	PD	TPI
	LA-N	3	5	.375	45	0	0	0	9	90	81	12	44	73	12.7	3.80	108	.248	.341	1	.050	-2	2	3	-0	0.1
	Yr	6	7	.462	57	4	0	0	10	123	118	17	58	95	13.0	4.10	100	.258	.344	2	.071	-2	-2	0	-1	-0.4
1959	*LA-N	4	0	1.000	28	0	0	0	2	45^{2}	48	8	33	30	16.4	5.91	72	.276	.397	1	.143	-0	-10	-9	-0	-0.8
1960	Cle-A	5	5	.500	49	0	0	0	**14**	74^{1}	53	8	35	46	10.8	2.91	129	.205	.303	2	.143	-0	8	7	0	1.2
1961	Was-A	2	2	.500	42	1	0	0	0	71^{2}	83	13	43	41	16.3	6.78	59	.297	.399	1	.143	-0	-22	-22	1	-1.1
1962	Cin-N	7	6	.538	40	7	0	0	4	108^{2}	113	13	64	67	15.0	4.47	90	.278	.381	3	.125	0	-6	-5	0	-0.5
1963	Phi-N	5	6	.455	49	1	0	0	8	112	80	3	46	86	10.4	1.93	168	.204	.293	1	.038	-2	17	16	-1	1.6
1964	Phi-N	2	1	.667	11	0	0	0	1	22^{1}	22	6	8	13	12.9	4.03	86	.250	.327	0	.000	-0	-1	-1	1	-0.2
	Min-A	0	4	.000	33	0	0	0	2	45^{2}	44	4	20	39	12.8	1.97	181	.260	.342	0	.000	0	8	8	1	0.9
1965	*Min-A	9	3	.750	56	0	0	0	5	76^{1}	59	8	31	59	11.0	2.24	159	.217	.304	0	.000	-1	10	11	-1	1.7
1966	Min-A	1	1	.500	26	0	0	0	3	39^{2}	35	2	20	26	12.9	3.40	106	.238	.337	0	.000	-0	0	1	-0	0.0
1967	Det-A	0	0	—	5	0	0	0	0	6^{2}	6	1	1	4	9.5	5.40	60	.250	.280	0	—	0	-2	-2	-0	0.0
Total	18	101	118	.461	711	161	37	6	66	1967^{2}	1915	203	978	1158	13.6	4.24	94	.258	.350	63	.125	-14	-80	-54	-0	-4.2

● FRED KLOBEDANZ

Klobedanz, Frederick Augustus "Duke" b: 6/13/1871, Waterbury, Conn. d: 4/12/40, Waterbury, Conn. BL/TL, 5′11″, 190 lbs. Deb: 8/20/1896

YEAR	TM/L	W	L	PCT	G	GS	CG	SH	SV	IP	H	HR	BB	SO	RAT	ERA	ERA+	OAV	OOB	BH	AVG	PB	PR	/A	PD	TPI
1896	Bos-N	6	4	.600	10	9	9	0	0	80^{2}	69	5	31	26	11.9	3.01	151	.229	.316	13	.317	2	12	14	-1	1.5
1897	*Bos-N	26	7	**.788**	38	37	30	2	0	309^{1}	344	13	125	92	14.3	4.60	97	.279	.357	48	.324	9	-10	-4	-4	0.1
1898	Bos-N	19	10	.655	35	33	25	0	0	270^{2}	281	13	99	51	13.0	3.89	95	.266	.336	27	.213	0	-8	-6	-1	-0.6
1899	Bos-N	1	4	.200	5	5	4	0	0	33^{1}	39	2	9	8	13.5	4.86	86	.291	.345	2	.182	1	-4	-3	1	-0.2
1902	Bos-N	1	0	1.000	1	1	1	0	0	8	9	0	2	4	13.5	1.13	251	.281	.343	1	.500	1	1	2	-0	0.3
Total	5	53	25	.679	89	85	69	2	0	702	742	33	266	181	13.5	4.12	101	.269	.343	91	.277	13	-8	2	-6	1.1

● STAN KLOPP

Klopp, Stanley Harold "Betz" b: 12/22/10, Womelsdorf, Pa. d: 3/11/80, Robesonia, Pa. BR/TR, 6′1.5″, 180 lbs. Deb: 4/30/44

YEAR	TM/L	W	L	PCT	G	GS	CG	SH	SV	IP	H	HR	BB	SO	RAT	ERA	ERA+	OAV	OOB	BH	AVG	PB	PR	/A	PD	TPI
1944	Bos-N	1	2	.333	24	0	0	0	0	46^{1}	47	1	33	17	15.5	4.27	89	.272	.388	2	.286	0	-3	-2	-1	-0.2

● BRENT KNACKERT

Knackert, Brent Bradley b: 8/1/69, Los Angeles, Cal. BR/TR, 6′3″, 185 lbs. Deb: 4/10/90

YEAR	TM/L	W	L	PCT	G	GS	CG	SH	SV	IP	H	HR	BB	SO	RAT	ERA	ERA+	OAV	OOB	BH	AVG	PB	PR	/A	PD	TPI
1990	Sea-A	1	1	.500	24	2	0	0	0	37^{1}	50	5	21	28	17.6	6.51	61	.313	.399	0	—	0	-11	-11	-0	-0.5
1996	Bos-A	0	1	.000	8	0	0	0	0	10	16	1	7	5	20.7	9.00	56	.356	.442	0	—	0	-4	-4	1	-0.3
Total	2	1	2	.333	32	2	0	0	0	47^{1}	66	6	28	33	18.3	7.04	60	.322	.409	0	—	0	-15	-15	0	-0.8

● CHRIS KNAPP

Knapp, Robert Christian b: 9/16/53, Cherry Point, N.C. BR/TR, 6′5″, 195 lbs. Deb: 9/4/75

YEAR	TM/L	W	L	PCT	G	GS	CG	SH	SV	IP	H	HR	BB	SO	RAT	ERA	ERA+	OAV	OOB	BH	AVG	PB	PR	/A	PD	TPI
1975	Chi-A	0	0	—	2	0	0	0	0	2	2	0	4	3	27.0	4.50	86	.250	.500	0	—	0	-0	-0	0	-0.1
1976	Chi-A	3	1	.750	11	6	1	0	0	52^{1}	54	5	32	41	15.0	4.82	74	.273	.377	0	—	0	-8	-7	-0	-0.6
1977	Chi-A	12	7	.632	27	26	4	0	0	146^{1}	166	16	61	103	14.4	4.80	85	.283	.357	0	—	0	-12	-12	-1	-1.4
1978	Cal-A	14	8	.636	30	29	6	0	0	188^{1}	178	25	67	126	11.8	4.21	86	.250	.317	0	—	0	-9	-13	-2	-1.5
1979	*Cal-A	5	5	.500	20	18	3	0	0	98	109	8	35	36	13.4	5.51	74	.275	.337	0	—	0	-14	-16	-0	-1.3
1980	Cal-A	2	11	.154	32	20	1	0	1	117^{1}	133	18	51	46	14.7	6.14	64	.289	.369	0	—	0	-27	-29	-1	-2.9
Total	6	36	32	.529	122	99	15	0	1	604^{1}	642	72	250	355	13.6	4.99	77	.272	.347	0	—	0	-70	-76	-5	-7.8

● FRANK KNAUSS

Knauss, Frank H. b: 1868, Cleveland, Ohio BL/TL, 5′10″, 170 lbs. Deb: 6/25/1890

YEAR	TM/L	W	L	PCT	G	GS	CG	SH	SV	IP	H	HR	BB	SO	RAT	ERA	ERA+	OAV	OOB	BH	AVG	PB	PR	/A	PD	TPI
1890	Col-a	17	12	.586	37	34	28	3	2	275^{2}	206	3	106	148	10.9	2.81	128	**.202**	.290	24	.226	5	33	24	-1	2.5
1891	Cle-N	0	3	.000	3	3	1	0	0	15	23	2	8	6	21.0	7.20	48	.338	.438	1	.167	-0	-6	-6	0	-0.9
1892	Cin-N	0	0	—	1	0	0	0	0	8	13	0	5	2	20.3	3.38	97	.351	.429	1	.333	0	-0	-0	0	0.1
1894	Cle-N	0	1	.000	2	2	1	0	0	11	7	0	14	2	19.6	5.73	95	.179	.429	0	.000	-1	-0	-0	1	0.0
1895	NY-N	0	0	—	1	1	0	0	0	3^{2}	9	0	2	1	27.0	17.18	27	.450	.500	0	.000	-0	-5	-5	-0	0.0
Total	5	17	16	.515	44	40	30	3	2	313^{1}	258	5	135	159	12.1	3.30	111	.218	.312	26	.217	4	20	12	-0	1.7

● RUDY KNEISCH

Kneisch, Rudolph Frank b: 4/10/1899, Baltimore, Md. d: 4/6/65, Baltimore, Md. BR/TL, 5′10.5″, 175 lbs. Deb: 9/21/26

YEAR	TM/L	W	L	PCT	G	GS	CG	SH	SV	IP	H	HR	BB	SO	RAT	ERA	ERA+	OAV	OOB	BH	AVG	PB	PR	/A	PD	TPI
1926	Det-A	0	1	.000	2	2	1	0	0	17	18	2	6	4	13.8	2.65	153	.273	.351	0	.000	-1	3	3	0	0.1

● PHIL KNELL

Knell, Philip Louis b: 3/12/1865, San Francisco, Cal d: 6/5/44, Santa Monica, Cal. BR/TL, 5′7.5″, 154 lbs. Deb: 7/6/1888

YEAR	TM/L	W	L	PCT	G	GS	CG	SH	SV	IP	H	HR	BB	SO	RAT	ERA	ERA+	OAV	OOB	BH	AVG	PB	PR	/A	PD	TPI
1888	Pit-N	1	2	.333	3	3	3	0	0	26^{1}	20	1	18	15	14.7	3.76	71	.217	.374	1	.091	-1	-3	-3	-0	-0.4
1890	Phi-P	22	11	.667	35	31	30	2	0	286^{2}	287	10	166	99	15.1	3.83	112	.249	.358	29	.220	-1	13	14	0	1.1
1891	Col-a	28	27	.509	58	52	47	**5**	0	462	363	4	226	228	12.5	2.92	118	**.209**	.319	34	.158	-9	41	28	5	2.2
1892	Was-N	9	13	.409	22	21	17	1	0	170	156	4	76	74	12.9	3.65	89	.234	.323	8	.118	-5	-7	-8	-0	-1.2
	Phi-N	5	5	.500	11	9	7	0	0	80	87	0	35	43	15.0	4.05	80	.266	.357	3	.088	-3	-7	-7	-2	-1.1
	Yr	14	18	.438	33	30	24	1	0	250	243	4	111	117	13.1	3.78	86	.242	.324	11	.108	-7	-14	-15	-2	-2.3
1894	Pit-N	0	0	—	1	0	0	0	0	7	11	0	6	0	23.1	11.57	45	.355	.474	0	.000	-1	-5	-5	1	0.0
	Lou-N	7	21	.250	32	28	25	0	0	247	330	9	104	67	16.3	5.32	96	.317	.387	31	.274	0	0	-6	-2	-0.6
	Yr	7	21	.250	33	28	25	0	0	254	341	9	110	67	16.5	5.49	93	.318	.388	31	.267	-0	-5	-11	-2	-0.6
1895	Lou-N	0	6	.000	10	6	3	0	0	56^{2}	75	3	21	19	16.2	6.51	71	.314	.383	6	.231	0	-11	-12	1	-0.8
	Cle-N	7	5	.583	20	13	9	0	0	116^{2}	149	7	53	30	16.0	5.40	92	.306	.381	11	.200	-3	-8	-5	0	-0.6
	Yr	7	11	.389	30	19	12	0	0	173^{1}	224	10	74	49	15.8	5.76	85	.306	.374	17	.210	-3	-19	-17	1	-1.4
Total	6	79	90	.467	192	163	141	8	0	1452^{1}	1478	38	705	575	14.4	4.05	99	.256	.351	123	.187	-21	14	-5	2	-1.4

● CHARLIE KNEPPER

Knepper, Charles b: 2/18/1871, Anderson, Ind. d: 2/6/46, Muncie, Ind. BR/TR, 6′4″, 190 lbs. Deb: 5/26/1899

YEAR	TM/L	W	L	PCT	G	GS	CG	SH	SV	IP	H	HR	BB	SO	RAT	ERA	ERA+	OAV	OOB	BH	AVG	PB	PR	/A	PD	TPI
1899	Cle-N	4	22	.154	27	26	26	0	0	219^{2}	307	11	77	43	16.3	5.78	64	.329	.390	12	.135	-5	-47	-51	-1	-5.0

● BOB KNEPPER

Knepper, Robert Wesley b: 5/25/54, Akron, Ohio BL/TL, 6′2″, 200 lbs. Deb: 9/10/76

YEAR	TM/L	W	L	PCT	G	GS	CG	SH	SV	IP	H	HR	BB	SO	RAT	ERA	ERA+	OAV	OOB	BH	AVG	PB	PR	/A	PD	TPI
1976	SF-N	1	2	.333	4	4	0	0	0	25	26	0	7	11	11.9	3.24	112	.277	.327	1	.111	-0	1	1	0	0.1
1977	SF-N	11	9	.550	27	27	6	2	0	166	151	14	72	100	12.3	3.36	116	.242	.323	10	.182	1	10	10	-1	1.2
1978	SF-N	17	11	.607	36	35	16	**6**	0	260	218	10	85	147	10.6	2.63	131	.229	.295	5	.063	-3	**27**	24	-2	1.9
1979	SF-N	9	12	.429	34	34	6	2	0	207^{1}	241	30	77	123	13.9	4.64	75	.289	.352	12	.182	3	-21	-27	-1	-2.2
1980	SF-N	9	16	.360	35	33	8	1	0	215^{1}	242	15	61	103	13.0	4.10	86	.281	.335	10	.152	-0	-12	-13	2	-1.3
1981	*Hou-N★	9	5	.643	22	22	6	5	0	156^{2}	128	5	38	75	9.8	2.18	151	.226	.280	7	.149	1	23	19	-1	1.8
1982	Hou-N	5	15	.250	33	29	4	0	1	180	193	14	60	108	12.8	4.45	75	.278	.338	3	.058	-2	-17	-23	1	-2.5
1983	Hou-N	6	13	.316	35	29	4	3	0	203	202	12	71	125	12.3	3.19	107	.261	.326	12	.182	3	10	5	1	0.9
1984	Hou-N	15	10	.600	35	34	11	3	0	233^{2}	223	26	55	140	10.7	3.20	104	.251	.296	13	.171	4	10	3	-1	0.6
1985	Hou-N	15	13	.536	37	37	4	0	0	241	253	21	54	131	11.6	3.55	98	.271	.313	11	.141	0	1	-2	-3	-0.5
1986	*Hou-N	17	12	.586	40	38	8	**5**	0	258	232	19	62	143	10.4	3.14	115	.242	.290	9	.099	-3	17	13	2	1.3
1987	Hou-N	8	17	.320	33	31	1	0	0	177^{2}	226	26	54	76	14.4	5.27	74	.313	.364	5	.098	-1	-23	-27	2	-3.2
1988	Hou-N★	14	5	.737	27	27	3	2	0	175	156	13	67	103	11.6	3.14	106	.243	.316	6	.125	-1	6	4	2	0.5
1989	Hou-N	4	10	.286	22	20	0	0	0	113	135	12	60	45	15.7	5.89	57	.303	.388	7	.226	5	-30	-31	1	-2.9
	SF-N	3	2	.600	13	6	1	1	0	52	55	4	15	19	12.3	3.46	97	.270	.323	1	.083	1	0	-1	-1	-0.1
	Yr	7	12	.368	35	26	1	1	0	165	190	16	75	64	14.5	5.13	66	.290	.364	8	.186	6	-30	-32	0	-3.0
1990	SF-N	3	3	.500	12	7	0	0	0	44^{1}	56	7	19	24	15.4	5.68	64	.311	.380	3	.231	1	-9	-10	0	-1.1
Total	15	146	155	.485	445	413	78	30	1	2708	2737	228	857	1473	12.1	3.68	95	.264	.323	115	.137	7	-8	-55	1	-5.5

● LOU KNERR

Knerr, Wallace Luther b: 8/21/21, Strasburg, Pa. d: 3/23/80, Denver, Pa. BR/TR, 6′1″, 210 lbs. Deb: 4/17/45

YEAR	TM/L	W	L	PCT	G	GS	CG	SH	SV	IP	H	HR	BB	SO	RAT	ERA	ERA+	OAV	OOB	BH	AVG	PB	PR	/A	PD	TPI
1945	Phi-A	5	11	.313	27	17	5	0	0	130	142	6	74	41	15.0	4.22	81	.283	.376	9	.191	-1	-12	-11	0	-1.4
1946	Phi-A	3	16	.158	30	22	6	0	0	148^{1}	171	13	67	58	14.5	5.40	66	.288	.361	9	.180	0	-31	-31	-0	-3.5
1947	Was-A	0	0	—	6	0	0	0	0	9	17	1	8	5	25.0	11.00	34	.405	.500	1	1.000	0	-7	-7	0	0.1
Total	3	8	27	.229	63	39	11	0	0	287^{1}	330	20	149	104	15.1	5.04	69	.290	.373	19	.194	-1	-51	-49	0	-4.8

● ELMER KNETZER

Knetzer, Elmer Ellsworth "Baron" b: 7/22/1885, Carrick, Pa. d: 10/3/75, Pittsburgh, Pa. BR/TR, 5′10″, 180 lbs. Deb: 9/11/09

YEAR	TM/L	W	L	PCT	G	GS	CG	SH	SV	IP	H	HR	BB	SO	RAT	ERA	ERA+	OAV	OOB	BH	AVG	PB	PR	/A	PD	TPI
1909	Bro-N	1	3	.250	5	4	3	0	0	35^{2}	33	2	22	7	13.9	3.03	86	.252	.359	0	.000	-2	-2	-2	1	-0.3
1910	Bro-N	7	5	.583	20	15	10	3	0	132^{2}	122	1	60	56	12.4	3.19	95	.255	.339	2	.053	-3	-2	-2	-2	-0.6
1911	Bro-N	11	12	.478	35	20	11	3	0	204	202	1	93	66	13.1	3.49	96	.277	.359	6	.097	-4	-2	-3	-1	-0.8
1912	Bro-N	7	9	.438	33	16	4	1	0	140^{1}	135	6	70	61	13.4	4.55	74	.254	.345	5	.135	-1	-18	-19	-0	-2.0
1914	Pit-F	20	12	.625	37	30	20	3	1	272	257	9	88	146	11.5	2.88	100	.254	.315	9	.099	-9	0	-0	2	-0.8
1915	Pit-F	18	14	.563	41	33	22	3	3	279	256	5	89	120	11.2	2.58	105	.251	.311	12	.132	-7	5	4	-0	-0.3

YEAR	TM/L	W	L	PCT	G	GS	CG	SH	SV	IP	H	HR	BB	SO	RAT	ERA	ERA+	OAV	OOB	BH	AVG	PB	PR	/A	PD	TPI
1916	Bos-N	0	2	.000	2	0	0	0	0	5	11	0	2	2	23.4	7.20	35	.524	.565	0	—	0	-3	-3	1	-0.8
	Cin-N	5	12	.294	36	16	12	0	1	171^{1}	161	6	48	70	11.1	2.89	90	.252	.307	8	.154	-1	-5	-6	3	-0.4
	Yr	5	14	.263	38	16	12	0	1	176^{1}	172	6	50	72	11.5	3.01	86	.261	.316	8	.154	-1	-8	-8	3	-1.2
1917	Cin-N	0	0	—	11	0	0	0	1	27^{1}	29	0	12	7	14.2	2.96	88	.282	.368	0	.000	-0	-1	-1	0	0.0
Total	8	69	69	.500	220	134	82	13	6	1267^{1}	1206	30	484	535	12.1	3.15	93	.258	.330	42	.109	-25	-27	-32	2	-6.0

● LON KNIGHT Knight, Alonzo P. b: 6/16/1853, Philadelphia, Pa. d: 4/23/32, Philadelphia, Pa. BR/TR, 5′11.5″, 165 lbs. Deb: 9/4/1875 MU♦

YEAR	TM/L	W	L	PCT	G	GS	CG	SH	SV	IP	H	HR	BB	SO	RAT	ERA	ERA+	OAV	OOB	BH	AVG	PB	PR	/A	PD	TPI
1875	Ath-n	6	5	.545	13	13	12	0	0	107	114	0	12	15	10.6	2.27	105	.259	.278	6	.128	-3	-1	1		-0.1
1876	Phi-N	10	22	.313	34	32	27	0	0	282	383	0	34	12	13.3	2.62	93	.297	.315	60	.250	-1	-10	-6	-1	-0.6
1884	Phi-a	0	1	.000	2	1	1	0	0	14	24	0	4	2	18.6	9.00	38	.348	.392	131	.271	0	-9	-9	0	-0.4
1885	Phi-a	0	0	—	1	0	0	0	0	5	4	0	2	1	10.8	1.80	191	.103	.146	25	.210	-0	1	1	0	0.0
	Pro-N	0	0	—	1	0	0	0	0	4	4	1	4	1	18.0	6.75	40	.235	.381	13	.160	-0	-2	-2	-0	0.0
Total	3	10	23	.303	38	33	28	0	0	305	415	1	44	16	13.6	2.95	84	.293	.315	549	.245	-1	-20	-16	-1	-1.0

● JACK KNIGHT Knight, Elma Russell b: 1/12/1895, Pittsboro, Miss. d: 7/30/76, San Antonio, Tex. BL/TR, 6′, 175 lbs. Deb: 9/20/22

YEAR	TM/L	W	L	PCT	G	GS	CG	SH	SV	IP	H	HR	BB	SO	RAT	ERA	ERA+	OAV	OOB	BH	AVG	PB	PR	/A	PD	TPI
1922	StL-N	0	0	—	1	1	0	0	0	4	9	0	3	1	27.0	9.00	43	.474	.545	1	.500	0	-2	-2	0	0.0
1925	Phi-N	7	6	.538	33	11	4	0	3	105^{1}	161	14	36	19	16.9	6.84	70	.354	.402	9	.205	-1	-30	-24	-1	-2.7
1926	Phi-N	3	12	.200	35	15	5	0	2	142^{2}	206	14	48	29	16.0	6.62	63	.347	.396	12	.214	0	-44	-39	5	-3.1
1927	Bos-N	0	0	—	3	0	0	0	0	3	6	0	2	0	24.0	15.00	25	.429	.500	0	—	0	-4	-4	1	0.1
Total	4	10	18	.357	72	27	9	0	5	255	382	28	89	49	16.7	6.85	64	.353	.403	22	.216	0	-80	-70	4	-5.7

● GEORGE KNIGHT Knight, George Henry b: 11/24/1855, Lakeville, Conn. d: 10/4/12, Lakeville, Conn. Deb: 9/28/1875

YEAR	TM/L	W	L	PCT	G	GS	CG	SH	SV	IP	H	HR	BB	SO	RAT	ERA	ERA+	OAV	OOB	BH	AVG	PB	PR	/A	PD	TPI
1875	NH-n	1	0	1.000	1	1	1	0	0	9	12	0	0	0	12.0	3.00	69	.293	.293	0	.000	-1	-1	-1		-0.1

● JOE KNIGHT Knight, Joseph William "Quiet Joe"
b: 9/28/1859, Port Stanley, Ont., Canada d: 10/16/38, Lynhurst, Ont., Canada BL/TL, 5′11″, 185 lbs. Deb: 5/16/1884 ♦

YEAR	TM/L	W	L	PCT	G	GS	CG	SH	SV	IP	H	HR	BB	SO	RAT	ERA	ERA+	OAV	OOB	BH	AVG	PB	PR	/A	PD	TPI
1884	Phi-N	2	4	.333	6	6	6	0	0	51	66	2	21	8	15.4	5.47	55	.293	.354	6	.250	1	-14	-14	-0	-1.2

● HUB KNOLLS Knolls, Oscar Edward b: 12/18/1883, Valparaiso, Ind. d: 7/1/46, Chicago, Ill. TR, 6′2″, 190 lbs. Deb: 5/1/06

YEAR	TM/L	W	L	PCT	G	GS	CG	SH	SV	IP	H	HR	BB	SO	RAT	ERA	ERA+	OAV	OOB	BH	AVG	PB	PR	/A	PD	TPI
1906	Bro-N	0	0	—	2	0	0	0	0	6^{2}	13	0	2	3	20.3	4.05	62	.382	.417	1	1.000	1	-1	-1	-1	0.0

● JACK KNOTT Knott, John Henry b: 3/2/07, Dallas, Tex. d: 10/13/81, Brownwood, Tex. BR/TR, 6′2.5″, 200 lbs. Deb: 4/13/33

YEAR	TM/L	W	L	PCT	G	GS	CG	SH	SV	IP	H	HR	BB	SO	RAT	ERA	ERA+	OAV	OOB	BH	AVG	PB	PR	/A	PD	TPI
1933	StL-A	1	8	.111	20	9	0	0	0	82^{2}	88	11	33	19	13.4	5.01	93	.269	.340	7	.304	1	-7	-3	-1	-0.3
1934	StL-A	10	3	.769	45	10	2	0	4	138	149	17	67	56	14.2	4.96	101	.278	.359	4	.133	-1	-7	1	1	0.0
1935	StL-A	11	8	.579	48	19	7	2	**7**	187^{2}	219	8	78	45	14.3	4.60	104	.287	.353	7	.115	-5	-3	4	1	0.0
1936	StL-A	9	17	.346	47	23	9	0	6	192^{2}	272	15	93	60	17.2	7.29	74	.330	.401	4	.070	-5	-48	-41	-1	-4.9
1937	StL-A	8	18	.308	38	22	8	0	2	191^{1}	220	25	91	74	14.9	4.89	99	.291	.370	8	.140	-4	-6	-1	-2	-0.7
1938	StL-A	1	2	.333	7	4	0	0	0	30	35	3	15	8	15.0	4.80	104	.285	.362	1	.100	-1	-0	1	-0	-0.1
	Chi-A	5	10	.333	20	18	9	0	0	131	135	8	54	35	13.0	4.05	121	.271	.342	5	.125	-2	11	12	1	1.0
	Yr	6	12	.333	27	22	9	0	0	161	170	11	69	43	13.4	4.19	117	.273	.346	6	.120	-3	11	13	1	0.9
1939	Chi-A	11	6	.647	25	23	8	0	0	149^{2}	157	13	41	56	12.0	4.15	114	.269	.318	8	.151	-3	8	10	-1	0.6
1940	Chi-A	11	9	.550	25	23	4	2	0	158	166	12	52	44	12.5	4.56	97	.265	.324	5	.088	-4	-3	-2	-1	-0.7
1941	Phi-A	13	11	.542	27	26	11	0	0	194^{1}	212	20	81	54	13.7	4.40	95	.279	.350	5	.077	-3	-5	-5	-3	-1.0
1942	Phi-A	2	10	.167	20	14	4	0	0	95^{1}	127	7	36	31	15.5	5.57	68	.310	.367	4	.138	-1	-20	-19	1	-2.0
1946	Phi-A	0	1	.000	3	1	0	0	0	6^{1}	7	1	1	2	12.8	5.68	62	.280	.333	0	—	0	-2	-2	-0	-0.2
Total	11	82	103	.443	325	192	62	4	19	1557	1787	140	642	484	14.2	4.97	95	.287	.355	58	.120	-29	-83	-46	-5	-8.3

● ED KNOUFF Knouff, Edward "Fred" b: 6/1868, Philadelphia, Pa. d: 9/14/1900, Philadelphia, Pa. BR/TR, 210 lbs. Deb: 7/1/1885 ♦

YEAR	TM/L	W	L	PCT	G	GS	CG	SH	SV	IP	H	HR	BB	SO	RAT	ERA	ERA+	OAV	OOB	BH	AVG	PB	PR	/A	PD	TPI
1885	Phi-a	7	6	.538	14	13	12	0	0	106	103	0	44	43	13.2	3.65	94	.228	.309	9	.188	-2	-5	-2	1	-0.3
1886	Bal-a	0	1	.000	1	1	1	0	0	9	2	0	5	8	10.0	2.00	171	.067	.263	0	.000	-0	1	1	1	0.2
1887	Bal-a	2	6	.250	9	9	6	0	0	63	79	0	41	27	19.0	7.57	54	.295	.413	9	.290	0	-23	-24	0	-2.0
	StL-a	4	2	.667	6	6	6	1	0	50	40	0	36	18	14.2	4.50	101	.225	.364	10	.179	-1	-1	0	-0	-0.1
	Yr	6	8	.429	15	15	12	1	0	113	119	0	77	45	15.8	6.21	69	.259	.369	19	.218	-1	-24	-24	0	-2.1
1888	StL-a	5	4	.556	9	9	9	0	0	81	66	0	37	25	12.3	2.67	122	.214	.314	3	.097	-2	4	5	-2	0.1
	Cle-a	0	1	.000	2	2	1	0	0	9	8	0	3	2	12.0	1.00	309	.229	.308	1	.167	0	2	2	1	0.3
	Yr	5	5	.500	11	11	10	0	0	90	74	0	40	27	11.5	2.50	130	.211	.293	4	.108	-2	6	7	-1	0.4
1889	Phi-a	2	0	1.000	3	3	2	0	0	25	37	2	9	5	16.9	3.96	96	.333	.388	3	.250	0	-0	-0	-1	0.0
Total	5	20	20	.500	44	43	37	1	0	343	335	2	175	128	14.4	4.17	89	.242	.344	35	.187	-4	-22	-18	0	-1.8

● DAROLD KNOWLES Knowles, Darold Duane b: 12/9/41, Brunswick, Mo. BL/TL, 6′, 190 lbs. Deb: 4/18/65 C

YEAR	TM/L	W	L	PCT	G	GS	CG	SH	SV	IP	H	HR	BB	SO	RAT	ERA	ERA+	OAV	OOB	BH	AVG	PB	PR	/A	PD	TPI
1965	Bal-A	0	1	.000	5	1	0	0	0	14^{2}	14	2	10	12	16.6	9.20	38	.250	.391	0	.000	-0	-9	-9	0	-0.6
1966	Phi-N	6	5	.545	69	0	0	0	13	100^{1}	98	4	46	88	13.5	3.05	118	.260	.351	4	.250	0	6	6	2	1.1
1967	Was-A	6	8	.429	61	1	0	0	14	113^{1}	91	5	52	85	11.7	2.70	117	.228	.322	1	.063	-1	7	6	2	1.0
1968	Was-A	1	1	.500	32	0	0	0	4	41^{1}	38	0	12	37	11.1	2.18	134	.241	.298	1	.250	1	4	3	0	0.4
1969	Was-A★	9	2	.818	53	0	0	0	13	84^{1}	73	8	31	59	11.5	2.24	155	.236	.314	1	.077	0	13	11	0	1.9
1970	Was-A	2	14	.125	71	0	0	0	27	119^{1}	100	4	58	71	12.2	2.04	175	.231	.328	1	.050	-1	22	20	2	**3.5**
1971	Was-A	2	2	.500	12	0	0	0	2	15^{1}	17	2	6	16	13.5	3.52	94	.266	.329	0	.000	-0	-0	-0	-0	-0.1
	*Oak-A	5	2	.714	43	0	0	0	7	52^{2}	40	3	16	40	10.1	3.59	93	.221	.295	1	.125	-0	-1	-1	1	-0.2
	Yr	7	4	.636	55	0	0	0	9	68	57	5	22	56	10.9	3.57	93	.233	.304	1	.100	-1	-1	-2	1	-0.3
1972	Oak-A	5	1	.833	54	0	0	0	11	65^{2}	49	1	37	36	11.8	1.37	207	.212	.321	3	.250	1	12	11	3	1.9
1973	*Oak-A	6	8	.429	52	5	1	1	9	99	87	7	49	46	12.6	3.09	115	.246	.343	0	—	0	8	5	2	0.9
1974	Oak-A	3	3	.500	45	1	0	0	3	53^{1}	61	6	35	18	16.5	4.22	79	.296	.403	0	—	0	-4	-5	1	-0.3
1975	Chi-N	6	9	.400	58	0	0	0	15	88^{1}	107	3	36	63	14.9	5.81	66	.298	.367	1	.067	-1	-21	-19	3	-3.5
1976	Chi-N	5	7	.417	58	0	0	0	9	71^{2}	61	6	22	39	10.7	2.89	134	.242	.308	1	.143	1	5	8	2	1.8
1977	Tex-A	5	2	.714	42	0	0	0	4	50^{1}	50	3	23	14	13.4	3.22	127	.272	.359	0	—	0	5	5	1	0.8
1978	Mon-N	3	3	.500	60	0	0	0	6	72	63	5	30	34	11.6	2.38	148	.250	.330	1	.167	-0	10	9	2	1.1
1979	StL-N	2	5	.286	48	0	0	0	6	48^{2}	54	5	17	22	13.1	4.07	92	.277	.335	0	.000	-0	-2	-2	-1	-0.3
1980	StL-N	0	1	.000	2	0	0	0	0	1^{2}	3	1	0	1	16.2	10.80	34	.375	.375	0	—	0	-1	-1	-0	-0.6
Total	16	66	74	.471	765	8	1	1	143	1092	1006	65	480	681	12.6	3.12	112	.250	.336	15	.120	-2	53	45	20	8.8

● TOM KNOWLSON Knowlson, Thomas Herbert "Doc" b: 4/23/1895, Pittsburgh, Pa. d: 4/11/43, Miami Shores, Fla. BB/TR, 5′11″, 178 lbs. Deb: 7/3/15

YEAR	TM/L	W	L	PCT	G	GS	CG	SH	SV	IP	H	HR	BB	SO	RAT	ERA	ERA+	OAV	OOB	BH	AVG	PB	PR	/A	PD	TPI
1915	Phi-A	4	6	.400	18	9	8	0	0	100^{2}	99	1	60	24	14.8	3.49	84	.273	.386	3	.083	-3	-6	-6	-0	-0.9

● BILL KNOWLTON Knowlton, William Young b: 8/18/1892, Philadelphia, Pa. d: 2/25/44, Philadelphia, Pa. BR/TR, Deb: 9/3/20

YEAR	TM/L	W	L	PCT	G	GS	CG	SH	SV	IP	H	HR	BB	SO	RAT	ERA	ERA+	OAV	OOB	BH	AVG	PB	PR	/A	PD	TPI
1920	Phi-A	0	1	.000	1	1	0	0	0	5^{2}	9	0	3	5	23.8	4.76	84	.346	.469	0	.000	-0	-1	-0	0	-0.1

● KURT KNUDSEN Knudsen, Kurt David b: 2/20/67, Arlington Heights, Ill. BR/TR, 6′3″, 200 lbs. Deb: 5/16/92

YEAR	TM/L	W	L	PCT	G	GS	CG	SH	SV	IP	H	HR	BB	SO	RAT	ERA	ERA+	OAV	OOB	BH	AVG	PB	PR	/A	PD	TPI
1992	Det-A	2	3	.400	48	1	0	0	5	70^{2}	70	9	41	51	14.3	4.58	86	.264	.365	0	—	0	-5	-5	0	-0.4
1993	Det-A	3	2	.600	30	0	0	0	2	37^{2}	41	9	16	29	14.6	4.78	90	.281	.367	0	—	0	-2	-2	-0	-0.3
1994	Det-A	1	0	1.000	4	0	0	0	0	5^{1}	7	2	11	1	30.4	13.50	36	.304	.529	0	—	0	-5	-5	-0	-0.7
Total	3	6	5	.545	82	1	0	0	7	113^{2}	118	20	68	81	15.1	5.07	81	.272	.377	0	—	0	-12	-12	-0	-1.4

● MARK KNUDSON Knudson, Mark Richard b: 10/28/60, Denver, Colo. BR/TR, 6′5″, 215 lbs. Deb: 7/8/85

YEAR	TM/L	W	L	PCT	G	GS	CG	SH	SV	IP	H	HR	BB	SO	RAT	ERA	ERA+	OAV	OOB	BH	AVG	PB	PR	/A	PD	TPI
1985	Hou-N	0	2	.000	2	2	0	0	0	11	21	0	3	4	19.6	9.00	38	.429	.462	0	.000	0	-7	-7	-0	-0.9
1986	Hou-N	1	5	.167	9	7	0	0	0	42^{2}	48	5	15	20	13.5	4.22	85	.279	.340	0	.000	-1	-2	-3	-1	-0.5
	Mil-A	0	1	.000	4	1	0	0	0	17^{2}	22	7	5	9	13.8	7.64	57	.286	.329	0	—	0	-7	-7	-0	-0.4
1987	Mil-A	4	4	.500	15	8	1	0	0	62	88	7	14	26	14.8	5.37	85	.331	.364	0	—	0	-6	-6	-1	-0.9
1988	Mil-A	0	0	—	5	0	0	0	0	16	17	1	2	7	10.7	1.13	354	.279	.302	0	—	0	5	5	0	0.0
1989	Mil-A	8	5	.615	40	7	1	0	0	123^{2}	110	15	29	47	10.3	3.35	115	.237	.286	0	—	0	7	7	-1	0.5
1990	Mil-A	10	9	.526	30	27	4	2	0	168^{1}	187	14	40	56	12.3	4.12	94	.282	.325	0	—	0	-4	-5	-2	-0.6
1991	Mil-A	1	3	.250	12	7	0	0	0	35	54	8	15	23	18.0	7.97	50	.355	.417	0	—	0	-15	-16	-0	-1.5

YEAR TM/L	W	L	PCT	G	GS	CG	SH	SV	IP	H	HR	BB	SO	RAT	ERA	ERA+	OAV	OOB	BH	AVG	PB	PR	/A	PD	TPI
1993 Col-N	0	0	—	4	0	0	0	0	5^{2}	16	4	5	3	33.4	22.24	21	.471	.538	0	.000	-0	-11	-11	-0	0.0
Total 8	24	29	.453	121	59	6	2	0	482	563	61	128	195	13.1	4.72	84	.290	.337	0	.000	-1	-40	-41	-5	-4.3
● KEVIN KOBEL Kobel, Kevin Richard b: 10/2/53, Buffalo, N.Y. BR/TL, 6'1", 195 lbs. Deb: 9/8/73																									
1973 Mil-A	0	1	.000	2	1	0	0	0	8^{1}	9	2	8	4	18.4	8.64	44	.273	.415	0	—	0	-4	-5	-0	-0.4
1974 Mil-A	6	14	.300	34	24	3	2	0	169^{1}	166	16	54	74	11.8	3.99	91	.258	.317	0	—	0	-7	-7	1	-0.7
1976 Mil-A	0	1	.000	3	0	0	0	0	4	6	3	3	1	22.5	11.25	31	.375	.500	0	—	0	-3	-3	0	-0.7
1978 NY-N	5	6	.455	32	11	1	0	0	108^{1}	95	9	30	51	10.6	2.91	120	.239	.295	4	.160	0	8	7	-1	0.6
1979 NY-N	6	8	.429	30	27	1	1	0	161^{2}	169	14	46	67	12.1	3.51	104	.274	.328	9	.196	0	4	2	0	0.3
1980 NY-N	1	4	.200	14	1	0	0	0	24^{1}	36	5	11	8	17.4	7.03	51	.353	.416	0	.000	-0	-9	-9	-0	-1.7
Total 6	18	34	.346	115	64	5	3	0	476	481	49	152	205	12.1	3.88	93	.266	.326	13	.178	0	-12	-15	0	-2.6
● ALAN KOCH Koch, Alan Goodman b: 3/25/38, Decatur, Ala. BR/TR, 6'4", 195 lbs. Deb: 7/26/63																									
1963 Det-A	1	1	.500	7	1	0	0	0	10	21	3	9	5	27.9	10.80	35	.467	.564	2	.667	1	-8	-8	0	-1.2
1964 Det-A	0	0	—	3	0	0	0	0	4	6	1	3	1	20.3	6.75	54	.375	.474	0	—	0	-1	-1	-0	0.0
Was-A	3	10	.231	32	14	1	0	0	114	110	18	43	67	12.3	4.89	76	.253	.325	8	.250	2	-16	-15	-2	-1.6
Yr	3	10	.231	35	14	1	0	0	118	116	19	46	68	12.6	4.96	75	.258	.331	8	.250	2	-17	-17	-2	-1.6
Total 2	4	11	.267	42	15	1	0	0	128	137	22	55	73	13.8	5.41	68	.277	.354	10	.286	3	-25	-24	-2	-2.8
● DICK KOECHER Koecher, Richard Finlay "Highpockets" b: 3/30/26, Philadelphia, Pa. BL/TL, 6'5", 196 lbs. Deb: 9/29/46																									
1946 Phi-N	0	1	.000	1	1	0	0	0	2^{2}	7	0	1	2	27.0	10.13	34	.467	.500	0	.000	-0	-2	-2	-0	-0.5
1947 Phi-N	0	2	.000	3	2	1	0	0	17	20	1	10	4	16.4	4.76	84	.299	.397	0	.000	-1	-1	-1	0	-0.2
1948 Phi-N	0	1	.000	3	0	0	0	0	6	4	0	3	2	10.5	3.00	132	.235	.350	0	—	0	1	1	-0	0.1
Total 3	0	4	.000	7	3	1	0	0	25^{2}	31	1	14	8	16.1	4.91	80	.313	.404	0	.000	-1	-3	-3	0	-0.6
● MARK KOENIG Koenig, Mark Anthony b: 7/19/04, San Francisco, Cal. d: 4/22/93, Willows, Cal. BB/TR, 6', 180 lbs. Deb: 9/8/25 ♦																									
1930 Det-A	0	1	.000	2	1	0	0	0	9	11	0	8	6	20.0	10.00	48	.314	.455	64	.240	0	-5	-5	-0	-0.4
1931 Det-A	0	0	—	3	0	0	0	0	7	7	0	11	3	23.1	6.43	71	.280	.500	92	.253	0	-2	-1	0	0.0
Total 2	0	1	.000	5	1	0	0	0	16	18	0	19	9	21.4	8.44	56	.300	.475	1190	.279	0	-7	-7	-0	-0.4
● WILL KOENIGSMARK Koenigsmark, William Thomas b: 2/27/1896, Waterloo, Ill. d: 7/1/72, Waterloo, Ill. BR/TR, 6'4", 180 lbs. Deb: 9/10/19																									
1919 StL-N	0	0	—	1	0	0	0	0	0	2	0	1	0	—	∞	—	1.000	1.000	0	—	0	-2	-2	0	-0.2
● ELMER KOESTNER Koestner, Elmer Joseph "Bob" b: 11/30/1885, Piper City, Ill. d: 10/27/59, Fairbury, Ill. BR/TR, 6'1.5", 175 lbs. Deb: 4/23/10																									
1910 Cle-A	5	10	.333	27	13	8	1	2	145	145	0	63	44	13.3	3.04	85	.282	.367	15	.313	2	-8	-7	-2	-0.7
1914 Chi-N	0	0	—	4	0	0	0	0	6^{1}	6	0	4	6	14.2	2.84	98	.261	.370	0	.000	-0	-0	-0	-0	0.0
Cin-N	0	0	—	5	1	0	0	0	18^{1}	18	0	9	6	13.3	4.42	66	.265	.351	2	.400	1	-3	-3	0	0.1
Yr	0	0	—	9	1	0	0	0	24^{2}	24	0	13	12	13.5	4.01	72	.264	.356	2	.333	1	-3	-3	0	0.1
Total 2	5	10	.333	36	14	8	1	2	169^{2}	169	0	76	56	13.3	3.18	83	.279	.365	17	.315	3	-12	-10	-2	-0.6
● JOE KOHLMAN Kohlman, Joseph James "Blackie" b: 1/28/13, Philadelphia, Pa. d: 3/16/74, Philadelphia, Pa. BR/TR, 6', 160 lbs. Deb: 9/26/37																									
1937 Was-A	1	0	1.000	2	2	1	0	0	13	15	0	3	3	12.5	4.15	107	.283	.321	1	.200	-0	1	0	-0	0.0
1938 Was-A	0	0	—	7	0	0	0	0	14^{1}	12	1	11	5	14.4	6.28	72	.240	.377	0	.000	-0	-2	-3	0	0.0
Total 2	1	0	1.000	9	2	1	0	0	27^{1}	27	1	14	8	13.5	5.27	85	.262	.350	1	.125	-1	-2	-2	-0	0.0
● EDDIE KOLB Kolb, Edward William b: 7/20/1880, Cincinnati, Ohio BR/TR, Deb: 10/15/1899																									
1899 Cle-N	0	1	.000	1	1	1	0	0	8	18	0	5	1	27.0	10.13	36	.439	.511	1	.250	-0	-6	-6	-1	-0.5
● RAY KOLP Kolp, Raymond Carl "Jockey" b: 10/1/1894, New Berlin, Ohio d: 7/29/67, New Orleans, La. BR/TR, 5'10.5", 187 lbs. Deb: 4/16/21																									
1921 StL-A	8	7	.533	37	18	5	1	0	166^{2}	208	12	51	43	14.0	4.97	90	.314	.363	7	.127	-5	-13	-9	1	-1.1
1922 StL-A	14	4	.778	32	18	9	1	0	169^{2}	199	10	36	54	12.7	3.93	106	.292	.332	17	.298	5	2	4	-4	0.4
1923 StL-A	5	12	.294	34	17	11	1	1	171^{1}	178	11	54	44	12.5	3.89	107	.273	.335	6	.111	-4	2	5	-2	-0.1
1924 StL-A	5	7	.417	25	12	5	1	0	96^{2}	131	4	25	29	14.9	5.68	79	.329	.375	6	.200	-0	-16	-13	-1	-1.4
1927 Cin-N	3	3	.500	24	5	2	1	3	82^{1}	86	5	29	28	12.7	3.06	124	.278	.342	6	.200	-0	8	7	0	0.5
1928 Cin-N	13	10	.565	44	23	12	1	3	209	219	9	55	61	12.0	3.19	124	.280	.330	15	.214	3	19	18	1	2.2
1929 Cin-N	8	10	.444	30	16	4	1	0	145^{1}	151	8	39	27	11.8	4.03	113	.278	.328	8	.163	-2	11	9	1	0.8
1930 Cin-N	7	12	.368	37	19	5	2	3	168^{1}	180	10	34	40	11.4	4.22	114	.278	.314	12	.245	1	14	11	-1	1.1
1931 Cin-N	4	9	.308	30	10	2	0	1	107	144	8	39	24	15.7	4.96	75	.332	.392	4	.125	-1	-13	-15	-1	-1.8
1932 Cin-N	6	10	.375	32	19	7	2	1	159^{2}	176	13	27	42	11.6	3.89	99	.280	.313	9	.184	-1	-0	-1	-2	-0.4
1933 Cin-N	6	9	.400	30	14	4	0	3	150^{1}	168	7	23	28	11.5	3.53	96	.290	.318	7	.156	-1	-3	-2	1	-0.2
1934 Cin-N	0	2	.000	28	2	0	0	3	61^{2}	78	1	12	19	13.4	4.52	90	.312	.348	1	.083	-1	-3	-3	2	-0.1
Total 12	79	95	.454	383	173	66	11	18	1688	1918	98	424	439	12.7	4.08	102	.292	.338	98	.184	-7	8	13	-6	-0.1
● HAL KOLSTAD Kolstad, Harold Everette b: 6/1/35, Rice Lake, Wis. BR/TR, 5'9", 190 lbs. Deb: 4/22/62																									
1962 Bos-A	0	2	.000	27	2	0	0	2	61^{1}	65	11	35	36	15.0	5.43	76	.269	.366	1	.056	-2	-10	-9	0	-0.5
1963 Bos-A	0	2	.000	7	0	0	0	0	11	16	4	6	6	19.6	13.09	29	.340	.436	0	.000	-0	-12	-11	-0	-1.7
Total 2	0	4	.000	34	2	0	0	2	72^{1}	81	15	41	42	15.7	6.59	62	.280	.377	1	.053	-2	-22	-20	0	-2.2
● ED KONETCHY Konetchy, Edward Joseph "Big Ed" b: 9/3/1885, LaCrosse, Wis. d: 5/27/47, Ft.Worth, Tex. BR/TR, 6'2.5", 195 lbs. Deb: 6/29/07 ♦																									
1910 StL-N	0	0	—	1	0	0	0	0	4	4	0	1	0	11.3	4.50	66	.267	.313	157	.302	0	-1	-1	-0	0.0
1913 StL-N	1	0	1.000	1	0	0	0	0	4^{2}	1	0	4	3	9.6	0.00	—	.071	.278	139	.276	0	2	2	-0	0.4
1918 Bos-N	0	1	.000	1	1	1	0	0	8	14	1	2	3	18.0	6.75	40	.378	.410	103	.236	0	-4	-4	-0	-0.4
Total 3	1	1	.500	3	1	1	0	0	16^{2}	19	1	7	6	14.0	4.32	67	.288	.356	2150	.281	1	-3	-3	-1	0.0
● DOUG KONIECZNY Konieczny, Douglas James b: 9/27/51, Detroit, Mich. BR/TR, 6'4", 220 lbs. Deb: 9/11/73																									
1973 Hou-N	0	1	.000	2	2	0	0	0	13	12	0	4	6	11.1	5.54	66	.279	.340	0	.000	-0	-3	-3	-0	-0.2
1974 Hou-N	0	3	.000	6	3	0	0	0	16	18	0	12	8	18.0	7.88	44	.290	.421	0	.000	-1	-8	-8	-0	-1.3
1975 Hou-N	6	13	.316	32	29	4	1	0	171	184	15	87	89	14.3	4.47	75	.280	.365	8	.160	1	-16	-21	-2	-2.2
1977 Hou-N	1	1	.500	4	4	0	0	0	21	26	1	8	7	15.0	6.00	59	.302	.368	1	.143	-0	-5	-6	0	-0.5
Total 4	7	18	.280	44	38	4	1	0	221	240	16	111	110	14.5	4.93	69	.283	.368	9	.138	-0	-31	-37	-2	-4.2
● ALEX KONIKOWSKI Konikowski, Alexander James "Whitey" b: 6/8/28, Throop, Pa. d: 9/28/97, Seymour, Conn. BR/TR, 6'1", 187 lbs. Deb: 6/16/48																									
1948 NY-N	2	3	.400	22	1	0	0	0	33^{1}	46	7	17	9	17.0	7.56	52	.346	.420	0	.000	-0	-13	-13	1	-1.7
1951 *NY-N	0	0	—	3	0	0	0	0	4	2	0	0	5	4.5	0.00	—	.154	.154	0	—	0	2	2	0	0.0
1954 NY-N	0	0	—	10	0	0	0	1	12	10	1	12	6	16.5	7.50	54	.244	.415	0	.000	-0	-5	-5	-0	0.0
Total 3	2	3	.400	35	1	0	0	1	49^{1}	58	8	29	20	15.9	6.93	57	.310	.403	0	.000	-0	-16	-16	0	-1.7
● JIM KONSTANTY Konstanty, Casimir James b: 3/2/17, Strykersville, N.Y. d: 6/11/76, Oneonta, N.Y. BR/TR, 6'1.5", 202 lbs. Deb: 6/18/44																									
1944 Cin-N	6	4	.600	20	12	5	1	0	112^{2}	113	11	33	19	11.7	2.80	125	.266	.320	10	.294	2	10	9	1	1.0
1946 Bos-N	0	1	.000	10	1	0	0	0	15^{1}	17	2	7	9	14.1	5.28	65	.283	.358	0	.000	0	-3	-3	1	-0.1
1948 Phi-N	1	0	1.000	6	0	0	0	2	9^{2}	7	0	2	7	8.4	0.93	424	.233	.281	0	.000	-0	3	3	-0	0.4
1949 Phi-N	9	5	.643	53	0	0	0	7	97	98	9	29	43	11.9	3.25	121	.280	.337	3	.176	-0	9	8	1	1.2
1950 *Phi-N★	16	7	.696	**74**	0	0	0	**22**	152	108	11	50	56	9.4	2.66	152	.205	.274	4	.108	-2	**25**	**23**	-1	3.6
1951 Phi-N	4	11	.267	58	1	0	0	9	115^{2}	127	9	31	27	12.3	4.05	95	.282	.328	3	.158	-0	-1	-3	1	-0.2
1952 Phi-N	5	3	.625	42	2	2	1	6	80	87	9	21	16	12.1	3.94	93	.274	.319	1	.071	-0	-2	-3	-0	-0.3
1953 Phi-N	14	10	.583	48	19	7	0	5	170^{2}	198	18	42	45	12.8	4.43	95	.290	.334	11	.220	-0	-3	-4	0	-0.5
1954 Phi-N	2	3	.400	33	1	0	0	3	50^{1}	62	7	12	11	13.2	3.75	108	.316	.356	0	.000	-2	2	2	0	0.0
NY-A	1	1	.500	9	0	0	0	2	18^{1}	11	0	6	3	8.3	0.98	350	.183	.258	0	.000	-0	6	5	0	0.6
1955 NY-A	7	2	.778	45	0	0	0	11	73^{2}	68	5	24	19	11.2	2.32	161	.247	.308	1	.125	-0	13	12	-0	1.7
1956 NY-A	0	0	—	8	0	0	0	2	11	15	3	6	6	17.2	4.91	79	.319	.396	0	.000	-0	-1	-1	-0	-0.1
StL-N	1	1	.500	27	0	0	0	5	39^{1}	46	4	6	7	11.9	4.58	83	.301	.327	0	—	0	-4	-3	-1	-0.3
Total 11	66	48	.579	433	36	14	2	74	945^{2}	957	88	269	268	11.7	3.46	112	.268	.320	33	.163	-5	54	44	2	7.0

YEAR	TM/L	W	L	PCT	G	GS	CG	SH	SV	IP	H	HR	BB	SO	RAT	ERA	ERA+	OAV	OOB	BH	AVG	PB	PR	/A	PD	TPI
● **DENNIS KONUSZEWSKI** Konuszewski, Dennis John b: 2/4/71, Bridgeport, Mich. BR/TR, 6'3", 210 lbs. Deb: 8/4/95																										
1995	Pit-N	0	0	—	1	0	0	0	0	0^1	3	0	1	0	108.0	54.00	8	1.000	1.000	0	—	0	-2	-2	0	0.0
● **ERNIE KOOB** Koob, Ernest Gerald b: 9/11/1892, Keeler, Mich. d: 11/12/41, Lemay, Mo. BL/TL, 5'10", 160 lbs. Deb: 6/23/15																										
1915	StL-A	4	5	.444	28	13	6	0	1	133^2	119	2	50	37	12.1	2.36	122	.254	.339	5	.135	-1	9	8	-2	0.2
1916	StL-A	11	8	.579	33	20	10	2	2	166^2	153	1	56	26	11.6	2.54	108	.252	.321	0	.000	-1	5	4	-4	0.0
1917	StL-A	6	14	.300	39	18	3	1	1	133^2	139	1	57	47	13.6	3.91	67	.280	.361	4	.114	-1	-18	-19	1	-2.9
1919	StL-A	2	4	.333	25	4	0	0	0	66	77	3	23	11	13.9	4.64	72	.296	.358	0	.000	-2	-10	-10	0	-1.0
Total	4	23	31	.426	125	55	19	3	4	500	488	7	186	121	12.6	3.13	90	.266	.342	9	.070	-5	-15	-18	-4	-3.7
● **CAL KOONCE** Koonce, Calvin Lee b: 11/18/40, Fayetteville, N.C. d: 10/28/93, Winston-Salem, N.C. BR/TR, 6'1", 185 lbs. Deb: 4/14/62																										
1962	Chi-N	10	10	.500	35	30	3	1	0	190^2	200	17	86	84	13.8	3.97	105	.271	.353	6	.094	-4	-0	4	-1	-0.1
1963	Chi-N	2	6	.250	21	13	0	0	0	72^2	75	9	32	44	13.5	4.58	77	.273	.353	2	.105	-0	-10	-9	1	-0.8
1964	Chi-N	3	0	1.000	6	2	0	0	0	31	30	1	7	17	10.7	2.03	183	.254	.296	0	.000	-1	5	6	2	0.6
1965	Chi-N	7	9	.438	38	23	3	1	0	173	181	17	52	88	12.4	3.69	100	.271	.329	5	.102	-0	-3	-0	-0	0.0
1966	Chi-N	5	5	.500	45	5	0	0	2	108^2	113	13	35	65	12.3	3.81	97	.268	.325	3	.130	0	-2	-2	1	0.0
1967	Chi-N	2	2	.500	34	0	0	0	2	51	52	2	21	28	13.1	4.59	77	.268	.343	0	.000	-1	-7	-6	1	-0.5
	NY-N	3	3	.500	11	6	2	1	0	45	45	2	7	24	10.4	2.80	121	.259	.287	2	.154	-0	3	3	1	0.5
	Yr	5	5	.500	45	6	2	1	2	96	97	4	28	52	11.7	3.75	93	.262	.314	2	.100	-1	-4	-3	2	0.0
1968	NY-N	6	4	.600	55	2	0	0	11	97	80	4	32	50	10.5	2.41	125	.235	.303	0	.000	-1	6	7	-1	0.8
1969	NY-N	6	3	.667	40	0	0	0	7	83	85	8	42	48	14.1	4.99	73	.269	.360	4	.235	0	-13	-12	1	-1.3
1970	NY-N	0	2	.000	13	0	0	0	0	22	25	2	14	10	16.4	3.27	123	.301	.408	0	.000	-0	2	2	0	0.2
	Bos-A	3	4	.429	23	8	1	0	2	76^1	64	7	29	37	11.3	3.54	112	.231	.311	2	.095	-0	2	4	2	0.5
1971	Bos-A	0	1	.000	13	1	0	0	0	21	22	3	11	9	14.1	5.57	66	.278	.367	0	.000	0	-5	-4	1	-0.1
Total	10	47	49	.490	334	90	9	3	24	971^1	972	85	368	504	12.6	3.78	98	.264	.335	24	.100	-6	-23	-9	9	-0.2
● **JERRY KOOSMAN** Koosman, Jerome Martin b: 12/23/42, Appleton, Minn. BR/TL, 6'2", 208 lbs. Deb: 4/14/67																										
1967	NY-N	0	2	.000	9	3	0	0	0	22^1	22	3	19	11	16.5	6.04	56	.259	.394	0	.000	0	-7	-7	0	-0.5
1968	NY-N★	19	12	.613	35	34	17	7	0	263^2	221	16	69	178	10.2	2.08	145	.228	.285	7	.077	-3	26	27	-1	3.0
1969	*NY-N★	17	9	.654	32	32	16	6	0	241	187	14	68	180	9.7	2.28	160	.216	.277	4	.048	-7	35	37	-1	3.1
1970	NY-N	12	7	.632	30	29	5	1	0	212	189	22	71	118	11.1	3.14	128	.237	.300	6	.086	-2	21	21	-3	1.2
1971	NY-N	6	11	.353	26	24	4	0	0	165^2	160	12	51	96	11.5	3.04	112	.256	.313	8	.160	0	8	7	-1	0.6
1972	NY-N	11	12	.478	34	24	4	1	1	163	155	14	52	147	11.8	4.14	81	.250	.314	4	.085	-3	-12	-14	0	-2.2
1973	*NY-N	14	15	.483	35	35	12	3	0	263	234	18	76	156	10.7	2.84	127	.242	.300	8	.103	-3	24	23	-1	2.0
1974	NY-N	15	11	.577	35	35	13	0	0	265	258	16	85	188	11.9	3.36	106	.257	.320	16	.186	2	8	6	-0	0.8
1975	NY-N	14	13	.519	36	34	11	4	2	239^2	234	19	98	173	12.6	3.42	101	.261	.337	14	.179	1	5	1	-1	0.2
1976	NY-N	21	10	.677	34	32	17	3	0	247^1	205	19	66	200	9.9	2.69	122	.226	.279	17	.215	3	22	17	0	2.4
1977	NY-N	8	20	.286	32	32	6	1	0	226^2	195	17	81	192	11.1	3.49	107	.232	.302	8	.111	-3	10	6	-2	0.2
1978	NY-N	3	15	.167	38	32	3	0	2	235^1	221	17	84	160	12.0	3.75	93	.255	.327	6	.086	-3	-4	-7	2	-0.7
1979	Min-A	20	13	.606	37	36	10	2	0	263^2	268	19	83	157	12.1	3.38	130	.268	.326	0	—	0	24	29	2	3.6
1980	Min-A	16	13	.552	38	34	8	0	2	243^1	252	24	69	149	12.1	4.03	108	.272	.326	0	—	0	0	9	1	0.8
1981	Min-A	3	9	.250	19	13	2	1	5	94^1	98	8	34	55	12.6	4.20	94	.272	.335	0	—	0	-6	-3	0	-0.4
	Chi-A	1	4	.200	8	3	1	0	0	27	27	2	7	21	11.3	3.33	107	.260	.306	0	—	0	1	1	-0	0.1
	Yr	4	13	.235	27	16	3	1	5	121^1	125	10	41	76	12.3	4.01	96	.267	.325	0	—	0	-5	-2	-0	-0.3
1982	Chi-A	11	7	.611	42	19	3	1	3	173^1	194	9	38	88	12.1	3.84	105	.287	.327	0	—	0	4	4	0	0.4
1983	*Chi-A	11	7	.611	37	24	2	1	2	169^2	176	19	53	90	12.5	4.77	88	.266	.326	0	—	0	-13	-11	0	-1.1
1984	Phi-N	14	15	.483	36	34	3	1	0	224	232	8	60	137	11.9	3.25	112	.267	.317	8	.108	-8	8	9	-1	0.8
1985	Phi-N	6	4	.600	19	18	3	1	0	99^1	107	14	34	60	13.0	4.62	80	.276	.340	3	.088	-2	-11	-10	-0	-1.2
Total	19	222	209	.515	612	527	140	33	17	3839^1	3635	290	1198	2556	11.5	3.36	110	.252	.313	109	.119	-22	145	143	-6	13.1
● **HOWIE KOPLITZ** Koplitz, Howard Dean b: 5/4/38, Oshkosh, Wis. BR/TR, 5'11", 195 lbs. Deb: 9/8/61																										
1961	Det-A	2	0	1.000	4	1	1	0	0	12	16	0	8	9	18.0	2.25	182	.327	.421	0	.000	-1	2	2	-0	0.3
1962	Det-A	3	0	1.000	10	6	1	0	0	37^2	54	5	10	10	15.3	5.26	77	.342	.381	3	.231	1	-5	-5	0	-0.3
1964	Was-A	0	0	—	6	1	0	0	0	17	20	3	13	9	17.5	4.76	78	.290	.402	0	.000	-0	-2	-2	0	0.0
1965	Was-A	4	7	.364	33	11	0	0	1	106^2	97	11	48	59	12.5	4.05	86	.249	.336	3	.100	-1	-7	-7	1	-0.7
1966	Was-A	0	0	—	1	0	0	0	0	2	0	0	1	0	4.5	0.00	—	.000	.200	0	—	0	1	1	0	0.0
Total	5	9	7	.563	54	19	2	0	1	175^1	187	19	80	87	13.9	4.21	87	.280	.359	6	.118	-1	-11	-11	1	-0.7
● **GEORGE KORINCE** Korince, George Eugene "Moose" b: 1/10/46, Ottawa, Ont., Canada BR/TR, 6'3", 210 lbs. Deb: 9/10/66																										
1966	Det-A	0	0	—	2	0	0	0	0	3	1	0	3	2	15.0	0.00	—	.091	.333	0	—	0	1	1	-0	0.0
1967	Det-A	1	0	1.000	9	0	0	0	0	14	10	1	11	11	13.5	5.14	63	.204	.350	0	.000	-0	-3	-3	0	-0.2
Total	2	1	0	1.000	11	0	0	0	0	17	11	1	14	13	13.8	4.24	78	.183	.347	0	.000	-0	-2	-2	-0	-0.2
● **JIM KORWAN** Korwan, James "Long Jim" b: 3/4/1874, Brooklyn, N.Y. d: 7/24/1899, Brooklyn, N.Y. BR/TR, 6'1", 181 lbs. Deb: 4/24/1894																										
1894	Bro-N	0	0	—	1	0	0	0	0	5	9	1	5	2	25.2	14.40	34	.391	.500	0	.000	-0	-5	-5	0	0.0
1897	Chi-N	1	2	.333	5	4	3	0	0	34	47	1	28	12	20.1	5.82	77	.324	.437	0	.000	-2	-6	-5	2	-0.4
Total	2	1	2	.333	6	4	3	0	0	39	56	2	33	14	20.8	6.92	66	.333	.446	0	.000	-2	-11	-10	2	-0.4
● **BILL KOSKI** Koski, William John "T-Bone" b: 2/6/32, Madera, Cal. BR/TR, 6'4", 185 lbs. Deb: 4/28/51																										
1951	Pit-N	0	1	.000	13	1	0	0	0	27	26	2	28	6	18.0	6.67	63	.257	.419	0	.000	-1	-8	-7	-1	-0.4
● **DAVE KOSLO** Koslo, George Bernard (b: George Bernard Koslowski) b: 3/31/20, Menasha, Wis. d: 12/1/75, Menasha, Wis. BL/TL, 5'11", 180 lbs. Deb: 9/12/41																										
1941	NY-N	1	2	.333	4	3	2	0	0	23^2	17	0	10	12	10.3	1.90	194	.202	.287	1	.111	-1	5	5	-1	0.5
1942	NY-N	3	6	.333	19	11	3	1	0	78	79	7	32	42	12.9	5.08	66	.261	.333	3	.120	-0	-15	-15	-1	-1.7
1946	NY-N	14	19	.424	40	35	17	3	1	265^1	251	15	101	121	12.1	3.63	95	.249	.320	11	.125	-3	-6	-6	2	-0.8
1947	NY-N	15	10	.600	39	31	10	3	0	217^1	223	23	82	86	12.8	4.39	93	.259	.326	10	.128	-1	-8	-8	-1	-1.0
1948	NY-N	8	10	.444	35	18	5	3	3	149	168	7	62	58	14.0	3.87	102	.290	.359	5	.114	-1	2	1	-1	-0.1
1949	NY-N	11	14	.440	38	23	15	0	4	212	193	13	43	64	**10.0**	**2.50**	**159**	.239	**.278**	10	.145	1	**36**	35	0	4.2
1950	NY-N	13	15	.464	40	22	7	1	3	186^2	190	18	68	56	12.7	3.91	105	.268	.337	8	.123	-1	5	4	-0	0.4
1951	*NY-N	10	9	.526	39	16	5	2	3	149^2	153	18	45	54	12.0	3.31	118	.258	.313	5	.100	-1	11	10	2	1.3
1952	NY-N	10	7	.588	41	17	8	2	5	166^1	154	10	47	67	11.0	3.19	116	.242	.296	2	.037	-4	10	9	1	0.7
1953	NY-N	6	12	.333	37	12	2	0	2	111^2	135	8	36	36	13.9	4.76	90	.296	.349	1	.033	-3	-6	-6	1	-1.1
1954	Bal-A	0	1	.000	3	1	0	0	0	14^1	20	1	3	3	14.4	3.14	114	.333	.365	0	.000	-0	1	1	-0	0.0
	Mil-N	1	1	.500	12	0	0	0	1	17^1	13	0	9	7	11.4	3.12	120	.228	.333	0	.000	-0	2	1	-1	0.1
1955	Mil-N	0	1	.000	1	0	0	0	0	0	1	1	0	0	—	∞	—	1.000	1.000	0	—	0	-1	-1	0	-0.1
Total	12	92	107	.462	348	189	74	15	22	1501^1	1507	121	530	606	12.2	3.68	105	.260	.321	56	.109	-15	34	32	2	2.4
● **JOE KOSTAL** Kostal, Joseph William "Cudgey" b: 3/17/1876, Chicago, Ill. d: 10/17/33, Guelph, Ont., Can. BR/TR, 5'6", 130 lbs. Deb: 7/14/1896																										
1896	Lou-N	0	0	—	2	0	0	0	0	2	4	0	0	0	18.0	0.00	—	.400	.400	0	—	0	1	1	-0	0.0
● **SANDY KOUFAX** Koufax, Sanford (b: Sanford Braun) b: 12/30/35, Brooklyn, N.Y. BR/TL, 6'2", 210 lbs. Deb: 6/24/55 H																										
1955	Bro-N	2	2	.500	12	5	2	2	0	41^2	33	2	28	30	13.4	3.02	134	.216	.341	0	.000	-2	5	5	-0	0.2
1956	Bro-N	2	4	.333	16	10	0	0	0	58^2	66	10	29	30	14.6	4.91	81	.286	.365	2	.118	-0	-7	-6	-1	-0.7
1957	Bro-N	5	4	.556	34	13	2	0	0	104^1	83	14	51	122	11.7	3.88	107	.216	.311	0	.000	-3	-0	3	-2	-0.3
1958	LA-N	11	11	.500	40	26	5	0	1	158^2	132	19	105	131	13.5	4.48	91	**.220**	.337	6	.122	-2	-9	-7	-0	-1.1
1959	*LA-N	8	6	.571	35	23	6	1	2	153^1	136	23	92	173	13.4	4.05	104	.235	.340	6	.111	-1	-2	3	-1	0.0
1960	LA-N	8	13	.381	37	26	7	2	1	175	133	20	100	197	12.0	3.91	102	**.207**	.315	7	.123	-2	-3	1	-1	-0.2
1961	LA-N★	18	13	.581	42	35	15	2	1	255^2	212	27	96	**269**	10.9	3.52	123	**.222**	.295	5	.065	-5	15	23	-3	1.8
1962	LA-N☆	14	7	.667	28	26	11	2	1	184^1	134	13	57	216	**9.4**	**2.54**	143	**.197**	**.261**	6	.087	-3	29	22	-2	1.9
1963	*LA-N☆	**25**	5	.833	40	40	20	**11**	0	311	214	18	58	**306**	**8.0**	**1.88**	161	**.189**	**.230**	7	.064	-4	**49**	39	-4	3.0
1964	LA-N☆	19	5	**.792**	29	28	15	**7**	1	223	154	13	53	223	**8.4**	**1.74**	**187**	**.191**	**.241**	7	.095	-2	45	37	-4	3.5

YEAR TM/L		W	L	PCT	G	GS	CG	SH	SV	IP	H	HR	BB	SO	RAT	ERA	ERA+	OAV	OOB	BH	AVG	PB	PR	/A	PD	TPI
1965	*LA-N★	**26**	8	**.765**	43	41	**27**	8	2	**335^{2}**	216	26	71	**382**	**7.8**	**2.04**	160	**.179**	**.228**	20	.177	5	**56**	46	-2	5.0
1966	*LA-N★	**27**	9	.750	41	41	**27**	**5**	0	**323**	241	19	77	**317**	8.9	**1.73**	**191**	.205	.253	9	.076	-5	**67**	**56**	-4	5.4
Total	12	165	87	.655	397	314	137	40	9	2324^{1}	1754	204	817	2396	10.0	2.76	131	.205	.276	75	.097	-25	243	221	-25	18.5
● JOE KOUKALIK	Koukalik, Joseph b: 3/3/1880, Chicago, Ill. d: 12/27/45, Chicago, Ill. 5'8", 160 lbs. Deb: 9/1/04																									
1904	Bro-N	0	1	.000	1	1	1	0	0	8	10	0	4	1	15.8	1.13	244	.333	.412	0	.000	-0	1	1	-0	0.1
● LOU KOUPAL	Koupal, Louis Laddie b: 12/19/1898, Tabor, S.D. d: 12/8/61, San Gabriel, Cal. BR/TR, 5'11", 175 lbs. Deb: 4/17/25																									
1925	Pit-N	0	0	—	6	0	0	0	0	9	14	1	7	0	21.0	9.00	50	.378	.477	0	.000	-0	-5	-5	0	0.0
1926	Pit-N	0	2	.000	6	2	1	0	0	19^{2}	22	0	8	7	14.2	3.20	123	.289	.365	1	.250	0	1	2	-0	0.2
1928	Bro-N	1	0	1.000	17	1	1	0	1	37^{1}	43	0	15	10	14.2	2.41	165	.303	.373	1	.111	-1	7	6	1	0.2
1929	Bro-N	0	1	.000	18	3	0	0	4	40^{1}	49	3	25	17	16.5	5.36	86	.308	.402	1	.071	-2	-3	-3	-1	-0.3
	Phi-N	5	5	.500	15	12	3	0	2	86^{2}	106	5	29	18	14.2	4.78	109	.305	.362	4	.125	-2	-1	4	-1	0.1
	Yr	5	6	.455	33	15	3	0	6	127	155	8	54	35	15.0	4.96	101	.306	.375	5	.109	-4	-3	1	-1	-0.2
1930	Phi-N	0	4	.000	13	4	1	0	0	36^{2}	52	4	17	11	17.2	8.59	64	.344	.414	1	.083	-1	-15	-13	-1	-1.3
1937	StL-A	4	9	.308	26	13	6	0	0	105^{2}	150	10	55	24	17.5	6.56	74	.339	.412	3	.094	-3	-23	-20	-0	-2.3
Total	6	10	21	.323	101	35	12	0	7	335^{1}	436	23	156	87	16.0	5.58	86	.322	.394	11	.106	-9	-38	-29	-2	-3.4
● FABIAN KOWALIK	Kowalik, Fabian Lorenz b: 4/22/08, Falls City, Tex. d: 8/14/54, Karnes City, Tex. BR/TR, 5'11", 185 lbs. Deb: 9/4/32																									
1932	Chi-A	0	1	.000	2	1	0	0	0	10^{1}	16	2	4	2	18.3	6.97	62	.340	.404	5	.385	1	-3	-3	-0	-0.1
1935	*Chi-N	2	2	.500	20	2	1	0	1	55	60	2	19	20	12.9	4.42	89	.280	.339	3	.200	-0	-2	-3	1	-0.2
1936	Chi-N	0	2	.000	6	0	0	0	1	16	24	1	7	1	17.4	6.75	59	.358	.419	0	.000	-1	-5	-5	0	-0.6
	Phi-N	1	5	.167	22	8	2	0	0	77	100	5	31	19	15.5	5.38	84	.308	.372	13	.228	-0	-12	-7	-2	-0.7
	Bos-N	0	1	.000	1	1	1	0	0	9	18	0	2	0	20.0	8.00	48	.419	.444	2	.400	1	-4	-4	0	-0.3
	Yr	1	8	.111	29	9	3	0	1	102	142	6	40	20	16.1	5.82	75	.325	.382	15	.224	-0	-20	-16	-1	-1.6
Total	3	3	11	.214	51	12	4	0	2	167^{1}	218	10	63	42	15.3	5.43	78	.313	.373	23	.242	-0	-26	-22	-1	-1.9
● JOE KRAEMER	Kraemer, Joseph Wayne b: 9/10/64, Olympia, Wash. BL/TL, 6'2", 185 lbs. Deb: 8/22/89																									
1989	Chi-N	0	1	.000	1	1	0	0	0	3^{2}	7	0	2	5	22.1	4.91	77	.368	.429	0	.000	-0	-1	-0	-0	-0.1
1990	Chi-N	0	0	—	18	0	0	0	0	25	31	2	14	16	16.9	7.20	57	.310	.405	0	—	0	-9	-9	0	0.0
Total	2	0	1	.000	19	1	0	0	0	28^{2}	38	2	16	21	17.6	6.91	58	.319	.409	0	.000	-0	-10	-9	0	-0.1
● JOE KRAKAUSKAS	Krakauskas, Joseph Victor Lawrence b: 3/28/15, Montreal, Que., Can d: 7/8/60, Hamilton, Ont., Can BL/TL, 6'1", 203 lbs. Deb: 9/9/37																									
1937	Was-A	4	1	.800	5	4	3	0	0	40	33	0	22	18	12.4	2.70	164	.226	.327	2	.125	-0	9	8	-1	0.7
1938	Was-A	7	5	.583	29	10	5	1	0	121^{1}	99	4	88	104	14.1	3.12	145	.220	.352	6	.182	1	23	19	-1	1.6
1939	Was-A	11	17	.393	39	29	12	0	1	217^{1}	230	13	114	110	14.3	4.60	95	.276	.364	16	.208	3	1	-6	-2	-0.6
1940	Was-A	1	6	.143	32	10	2	0	2	109	137	7	73	68	17.3	6.44	65	.309	.406	8	.250	1	-25	-28	1	-1.4
1941	Cle-A	1	2	.333	12	5	0	0	0	41^{2}	39	3	29	25	14.7	4.10	96	.245	.362	1	.077	-1	0	-1	1	-0.1
1942	Cle-A	0	0	—	3	0	0	0	0	7	7	1	4	2	14.1	3.86	89	.259	.355	0	.000	-0	-0	-0	1	0.0
1946	Cle-A	2	5	.286	29	5	0	0	1	47^{1}	60	2	25	20	16.2	5.51	60	.314	.394	0	.000	-1	-11	-12	1	-1.7
Total	7	26	36	.419	149	63	22	1	4	583^{2}	605	30	355	347	14.9	4.53	93	.269	.369	33	.180	2	-4	-20	-1	-1.5
● JACK KRALICK	Kralick, John Francis b: 6/1/35, Youngstown, Ohio BL/TL, 6'2", 180 lbs. Deb: 4/15/59																									
1959	Was-A	0	0	—	6	0	0	0	0	12^{1}	13	5	6	7	13.9	6.57	60	.289	.373	0	.000	-0	-4	-4	1	0.1
1960	Was-A	8	6	.571	35	18	7	2	1	151	139	12	45	71	11.2	3.04	128	.245	.305	5	.122	-1	14	14	-1	1.1
1961	Min-A	13	11	.542	33	33	11	2	0	242	257	21	64	137	12.0	3.61	118	.274	.323	13	.151	-2	11	17	2	1.5
1962	Min-A	12	11	.522	39	37	7	1	0	242^{2}	239	30	61	139	11.2	3.86	106	.258	.305	18	.202	3	3	6	1	0.9
1963	Min-A	1	4	.200	5	5	1	1	0	25^{2}	28	2	8	13	13.0	3.86	94	.280	.339	1	.167	1	-1	-1	0	0.0
	Cle-A	13	9	.591	28	27	10	3	0	197^{1}	187	19	41	116	10.4	2.92	124	.249	.288	11	.183	1	16	15	-1	1.7
	Yr	14	13	.519	33	32	11	4	0	223	215	21	49	129	10.7	3.03	120	.252	.293	12	.182	2	15	15	-1	1.7
1964	Cle-A☆	12	7	.632	30	29	8	3	0	190^{2}	196	17	51	119	12.1	3.21	112	.267	.322	10	.156	-1	9	8	0	0.7
1965	Cle-A	5	11	.313	30	16	1	0	0	86	106	9	21	34	13.5	4.92	71	.298	.340	3	.143	-1	-14	-14	-1	-2.5
1966	Cle-A	3	4	.429	27	4	0	0	0	68^{1}	69	9	20	31	11.9	3.82	90	.268	.324	1	.077	-1	-3	-3	1	-0.3
1967	Cle-A	0	2	.000	2	0	0	0	0	2	4	0	1	1	22.5	9.00	36	.444	.500	0	—	0	-1	-1	1	-0.9
Total	9	67	65	.508	235	169	45	12	1	1218	1238	124	318	668	11.7	3.56	108	.264	.314	62	.162	0	30	38	3	2.3
● STEVE KRALY	Kraly, Steve Charles "Lefty" b: 4/18/29, Whiting, Ind. BL/TL, 5'10", 152 lbs. Deb: 8/9/53																									
1953	NY-A	0	2	.000	5	3	0	0	1	25	19	2	16	8	13.3	3.24	114	.209	.339	0	.000	-1	2	1	0	0.0
● JACK KRAMER	Kramer, John Henry b: 1/5/18, New Orleans, La. d: 5/18/95, Metairie, La. BR/TR, 6'2", 190 lbs. Deb: 4/25/39																									
1939	StL-A	9	16	.360	40	31	10	2	0	211^{2}	269	18	127	68	17.0	5.83	84	.318	.409	9	.136	-1	-28	-23	-1	-2.3
1940	StL-A	3	7	.300	16	9	1	0	0	64^{2}	86	4	26	12	15.6	6.26	73	.327	.388	1	.050	-1	-14	-12	0	-1.6
1941	StL-A	4	3	.571	29	3	0	0	2	59^{1}	69	5	40	20	16.5	5.16	83	.289	.391	0	.000	1	-7	-6	0	-0.5
1943	StL-A	0	0	—	3	0	0	0	0	9	11	0	8	4	20.0	8.00	42	.297	.435	1	.500	1	-5	-5	-0	0.1
1944	*StL-A	17	13	.567	33	31	18	1	0	257	233	3	75	124	10.8	2.49	145	.241	.297	14	.165	1	27	32	3	4.3
1945	StL-A†	10	15	.400	29	25	15	3	2	193	190	13	73	99	12.3	3.36	105	.254	.320	9	.148	-0	0	4	1	0.5
1946	StL-A★	13	11	.542	31	28	13	3	0	194^{2}	190	6	68	69	11.9	3.19	117	.257	.319	8	.136	-1	7	12	-0	1.2
1947	StL-A☆	11	16	.407	33	28	9	1	1	199^{1}	206	16	89	77	13.4	4.97	78	.270	.348	7	.113	-2	-28	-24	1	-3.0
1948	Bos-A	18	5	**.783**	29	29	14	2	0	205	233	12	64	72	13.0	4.35	101	.284	.336	11	.151	-1	-1	1	-3	-0.2
1949	Bos-A	6	8	.429	21	18	7	2	1	111^{2}	126	8	49	24	14.2	5.16	85	.286	.358	9	.257	3	-12	-10	-1	-0.9
1950	NY-N	3	6	.333	35	9	1	0	1	86^{2}	91	6	39	27	13.7	3.53	116	.268	.346	2	.100	1	6	5	0	0.6
1951	NY-N	0	0	—	4	1	0	0	0	4^{2}	11	0	3	2	27.0	15.43	25	.524	.583	0	—	0	-6	-6	0	0.0
	NY-A	1	3	.250	19	3	0	0	0	40^{2}	46	1	21	15	14.8	4.65	82	.280	.362	1	.100	-0	-2	-4	-1	-0.5
Total	12	95	103	.480	322	215	88	14	7	1637^{1}	1761	92	682	613	13.5	4.24	96	.276	.347	72	.144	0	-63	-35	0	-2.3
● RANDY KRAMER	Kramer, Randall John b: 9/20/60, Palo Alto, Cal. BR/TR, 6'2", 170 lbs. Deb: 9/11/88																									
1988	Pit-N	1	2	.333	5	1	0	0	0	10	12	1	1	7	12.6	5.40	63	.316	.350	0	.000	-0	-2	-2	-0	-0.6
1989	Pit-N	5	9	.357	35	15	1	1	2	111^{1}	90	10	61	52	12.8	3.96	85	.224	.337	5	.152	-0	-6	-7	-1	-1.0
1990	Pit-N	0	1	.000	12	2	0	0	0	25^{2}	27	3	9	15	13.3	4.91	74	.273	.345	0	.000	-1	-3	-4	1	-0.1
	Chi-N	0	2	.000	10	2	0	0	0	20^{1}	20	3	12	12	14.6	3.98	102	.253	.359	0	.000	-0	-0	0	-0	0.0
	Yr	0	3	.000	22	4	0	0	0	46	47	6	21	27	13.5	4.50	85	.261	.342	0	.000	-1	-4	-3	0	-0.1
1992	Sea-A	0	1	.000	4	4	0	0	0	16^{1}	30	2	7	6	20.9	7.71	51	.400	.458	0	—	0	-7	-7	-0	-0.4
Total	4	6	15	.286	66	24	1	1	2	183^{2}	179	19	90	92	13.8	4.51	78	.259	.354	5	.122	-1	-18	-20	-2	-2.1
● TOM KRAMER	Kramer, Thomas Joseph b: 1/9/68, Cincinnati, Ohio BB/TR, 6', 185 lbs. Deb: 9/12/91																									
1991	Cle-A	0	0	—	4	0	0	0	0	4^{2}	10	1	6	4	30.9	17.36	24	.476	.593	0	—	0	-7	-7	-0	0.0
1993	Cle-A	7	3	.700	39	16	1	0	0	121	126	19	59	71	13.9	4.02	108	.269	.353	0	—	0	4	4	-1	0.2
Total	2	7	3	.700	43	16	1	0	0	125^{2}	136	20	65	75	14.5	4.51	96	.278	.364	0	—	0	-3	-3	-1	0.2
● GENE KRAPP	Krapp, Eugene Hamlet "Rubber Arm" b: 5/12/1887, Rochester, N.Y. d: 4/13/23, Detroit, Mich. BR/TR, 5'5", 165 lbs. Deb: 4/14/11																									
1911	Cle-A	13	9	.591	35	26	14	1	1	222	188	1	138	132	13.7	3.41	100	.232	.353	17	.230	4	-1	0	4	0.8
1912	Cle-A	2	5	.286	9	7	4	0	0	58^{2}	57	0	42	22	15.8	4.60	74	.273	.404	7	.318	1	-8	-8	2	-0.5
1914	Buf-F	16	14	.533	36	29	18	1	0	252^{2}	198	4	115	106	11.6	2.49	119	.210	.304	11	.143	-2	11	13	5	1.8
1915	Buf-F	9	19	.321	38	30	14	1	0	231	188	6	123	93	12.3	3.51	80	.230	.333	9	.129	-3	-20	-18	7	-1.7
Total	4	40	47	.460	118	92	50	3	1	764^{1}	631	11	418	353	12.7	3.23	95	.227	.335	44	.181	-1	-19	-13	19	0.4
● JACK KRAUS	Kraus, John William "Tex" or "Texas Jack" b: 4/26/18, San Antonio, Tex. d: 1/2/76, San Antonio, Tex. BR/TL, 6'4", 190 lbs. Deb: 4/25/43																									
1943	Phi-N	9	15	.375	34	25	10	1	2	199^{2}	197	7	78	48	12.4	3.16	107	.259	.328	4	.067	-5	5	5	1	0.2
1945	Phi-N	4	9	.308	19	13	0	0	0	81^{2}	96	3	40	28	15.4	5.40	71	.293	.376	3	.120	-1	-15	-14	0	-2.0
1946	NY-N	2	1	.667	17	1	0	0	0	25	25	4	15	7	14.8	6.12	56	.260	.366	0	.000	-0	-8	-7	1	-0.8
Total	3	15	25	.375	70	39	10	1	2	306^{1}	318	14	133	83	13.4	4.00	88	.268	.345	7	.080	-6	-17	-17	2	-2.6

● **HARRY KRAUSE** Krause, Harry William "Hal" b: 7/12/1887, San Francisco, Cal. d: 10/23/40, San Francisco, Cal BB/TL, 5'10", 165 lbs. Deb: 4/20/08

YEAR	TM/L	W	L	PCT	G	GS	CG	SH	SV	IP	H	HR	BB	SO	RAT	ERA	ERA+	OAV	OOB	BH	AVG	PB	PR	/A	PD	TPI
1908	Phi-A	1	1	.500	4	2	2	0	0	21	20	0	4	10	11.6	2.57	100	.247	.307	0	.000	-1	-0	-0	-1	-0.2
1909	Phi-A	18	8	.692	32	21	16	7	0	213	151	2	49	139	9.0	**1.39**	**173**	.204	.266	12	.156	-1	26	**24**	-3	2.6
1910	Phi-A	6	6	.500	16	11	9	2	0	112^1	99	4	42	60	11.9	2.88	82	.254	.339	8	.211	1	-5	-6	-2	-0.8
1911	Phi-A	11	8	.579	27	19	12	1	2	169	155	2	47	85	11.2	3.04	104	.251	.313	15	.254	2	6	2	-3	0.1
1912	Phi-A	0	2	.000	4	2	0	0	0	5^1	10	0	2	3	21.9	13.50	23	.435	.500	1	.250	0	-6	-6	0	-1.6
	Cle-A	0	1	.000	2	2	0	0	0	4^2	11	0	2	1	25.1	11.57	29	.500	.542	0	—	0	-4	-4	-0	-0.7
	Yr	0	3	.000	6	4	0	0	0	10	21	0	4	4	22.5	12.60	26	.457	.500	1	.250	0	-10	-10	-0	-2.3
Total	5	36	26	.581	85	57	39	10	2	525^1	446	8	146	298	10.7	2.50	107	.238	.305	36	.195	1	16	10	-9	-0.6

● **LEW KRAUSSE** Krausse, Lewis Bernard Jr. b: 4/25/43, Media, Pa. BR/TR, 5'11", 186 lbs. Deb: 6/16/61 F

YEAR	TM/L	W	L	PCT	G	GS	CG	SH	SV	IP	H	HR	BB	SO	RAT	ERA	ERA+	OAV	OOB	BH	AVG	PB	PR	/A	PD	TPI
1961	KC-A	2	5	.286	12	8	2	1	0	55^2	49	3	46	32	15.5	4.85	86	.243	.386	2	.118	-1	-5	-4	-1	-0.6
1964	KC-A	0	2	.000	5	4	0	0	0	14^2	22	1	9	9	20.3	7.36	52	.349	.446	0	.000	0	-6	-6	-0	-0.7
1965	KC-A	2	4	.333	7	5	0	0	0	25	29	1	8	22	13.3	5.04	69	.284	.336	0	.000	-1	-4	-4	-1	-1.0
1966	KC-A	14	9	.609	36	22	4	1	3	177^2	144	8	63	87	10.8	2.99	114	.222	.297	8	.154	0	9	8	-3	0.8
1967	KC-A	7	17	.292	48	19	0	0	6	160	140	17	67	96	11.9	4.27	75	.236	.317	6	.146	1	-19	-19	-0	-2.9
1968	Oak-A	10	11	.476	36	25	2	0	4	185	147	16	62	105	10.3	3.11	91	.217	.286	9	.161	3	-3	-6	-2	-0.6
1969	Oak-A	7	7	.500	43	16	4	2	7	140	134	23	48	85	12.0	4.44	77	.256	.325	8	.167	4	-13	-16	-1	-1.3
1970	Mil-A	13	18	.419	37	35	8	1	0	216	235	33	67	130	12.8	4.75	80	.275	.330	9	.138	1	-25	-23	-0	-3.0
1971	Mil-A	8	12	.400	43	22	1	0	0	180^1	164	23	62	92	11.5	2.94	118	.239	.307	1	.023	-3	10	11	-1	0.7
1972	Bos-A	1	3	.250	24	7	0	0	1	60^2	74	9	28	35	15.6	6.38	50	.308	.387	2	.125	-0	-22	-21	1	-1.5
1973	StL-N	0	0	—	1	0	0	0	0	2	2	0	1	1	13.5	0.00	—	.250	.333	0	—	0	1	1	0	0.0
1974	Atl-N	4	3	.571	29	4	0	0	0	66^2	65	3	32	27	13.4	4.18	90	.258	.346	2	.333	2	-4	-3	-1	-0.2
Total	12	68	91	.428	321	167	21	5	21	1283^2	1205	137	493	721	12.2	4.00	85	.248	.322	47	.133	6	-81	-84	-9	-10.3

● **LEW KRAUSSE** Krausse, Lewis Bernard Sr. b: 6/8/12, Media, Pa. d: 9/6/88, Sarasota, Fla. BR/TR, 6'0.5", 167 lbs. Deb: 6/11/31 F

YEAR	TM/L	W	L	PCT	G	GS	CG	SH	SV	IP	H	HR	BB	SO	RAT	ERA	ERA+	OAV	OOB	BH	AVG	PB	PR	/A	PD	TPI
1931	Phi-A	1	0	1.000	3	1	1	0	0	11	6	2	6	1	9.8	4.09	110	.150	.261	0	.000	0	0	0	0	0.1
1932	Phi-A	4	1	.800	20	3	2	1	0	57	64	3	24	16	13.9	4.58	99	.281	.349	2	.133	-0	-1	-0	1	0.0
Total	2	5	1	.833	23	4	3	1	0	68	70	5	30	17	13.2	4.50	100	.261	.336	2	.118	0	-0	0	1	0.1

● **KEN KRAVEC** Kravec, Kenneth Peter b: 7/29/51, Cleveland, Ohio BL/TL, 6'2", 185 lbs. Deb: 9/4/75

YEAR	TM/L	W	L	PCT	G	GS	CG	SH	SV	IP	H	HR	BB	SO	RAT	ERA	ERA+	OAV	OOB	BH	AVG	PB	PR	/A	PD	TPI
1975	Chi-A	0	1	.000	2	1	0	0	0	4^1	1	0	8	1	18.7	6.23	62	.071	.409	0	—	0	-1	1	1	-0.2
1976	Chi-A	1	5	.167	9	8	1	0	0	49^2	49	3	32	38	14.9	4.89	73	.257	.366	0	—	0	-8	-7	-0	-0.8
1977	Chi-A	11	8	.579	26	25	6	1	0	166^2	161	12	57	125	12.1	4.10	99	.250	.317	0	—	0	-1	-0	0	0.0
1978	Chi-A	11	16	.407	30	30	7	2	0	203	188	22	95	154	13.0	4.08	93	.245	.336	0	—	0	-7	-6	-1	-0.8
1979	Chi-A	15	13	.536	36	35	10	3	1	250	208	20	111	132	12.0	3.74	113	.233	.327	0	—	0	13	14	-1	1.3
1980	Chi-A	3	6	.333	20	15	0	0	0	81^2	100	13	44	37	16.4	6.94	58	.298	.387	0	—	0	-26	-26	0	-2.4
1981	Chi-N	1	6	.143	24	12	0	0	0	78^1	80	5	39	50	14.1	5.06	73	.268	.361	0	.000	-1	-14	-12	1	-1.1
1982	Chi-N	1	1	.500	13	2	0	0	0	25	27	3	18	20	16.2	6.12	61	.267	.378	0	.000	-0	-7	-7	-0	-0.5
Total	8	43	56	.434	160	128	24	6	1	858^2	814	78	404	557	13.2	4.47	89	.251	.341	0	.000	-1	-51	-46	-0	-4.5

● **RAY KRAWCZYK** Krawczyk, Raymond Allen b: 10/9/59, Pittsburgh, Pa. BR/TR, 6'1", 186 lbs. Deb: 6/29/84

YEAR	TM/L	W	L	PCT	G	GS	CG	SH	SV	IP	H	HR	BB	SO	RAT	ERA	ERA+	OAV	OOB	BH	AVG	PB	PR	/A	PD	TPI
1984	Pit-N	0	0	—	4	0	0	0	0	5^1	7	0	4	3	18.6	3.38	107	.350	.458	0	—	0	0	0	-0	0.0
1985	Pit-N	0	2	.000	8	0	0	0	0	8^1	20	1	6	9	29.2	14.04	25	.455	.529	0	—	0	-10	-10	0	-1.9
1986	Pit-N	0	1	.000	12	0	0	0	0	12^1	17	3	10	7	19.7	7.30	53	.321	.429	0	—	0	-5	-5	-0	-0.4
1988	Cal-A	0	1	.000	14	1	0	0	1	24^1	29	2	8	17	14.4	4.81	80	.299	.364	0	—	0	-2	-3	1	0.1
1989	Mil-A	0	0	—	1	0	0	0	0	2	4	0	1	6	22.5	13.50	28	.400	.455	0	—	0	-2	-2	0	0.0
Total	5	0	4	.000	39	1	0	0	1	52^1	77	6	29	42	18.7	7.05	54	.344	.426	0	—	0	-19	-19	0	-2.2

● **FRANK KREEGER** Kreeger, Frank Deb: 7/28/1884 ♦

YEAR	TM/L	W	L	PCT	G	GS	CG	SH	SV	IP	H	HR	BB	SO	RAT	ERA	ERA+	OAV	OOB	BH	AVG	PB	PR	/A	PD	TPI
1884	KC-U	0	1	.000	1	1	0	0	0	7	9	0	5	3	18.0	0.00	—	.290	.389	0	.000	-1	2	2	0	0.1

● **RAY KREMER** Kremer, Remy Peter "Wiz" b: 3/23/1893, Oakland, Cal. d: 2/8/65, Pinole, Cal. BR/TR, 6'1", 190 lbs. Deb: 4/18/24

YEAR	TM/L	W	L	PCT	G	GS	CG	SH	SV	IP	H	HR	BB	SO	RAT	ERA	ERA+	OAV	OOB	BH	AVG	PB	PR	/A	PD	TPI
1924	Pit-N	18	10	.643	**41**	30	17	**4**	1	259^1	262	7	51	64	11.0	3.19	120	.265	.304	13	.151	-4	19	19	-2	1.3
1925	*Pit-N	17	8	.680	40	27	14	0	2	214^2	232	19	47	62	12.1	3.69	121	.278	.323	14	.197	1	14	18	-3	1.6
1926	Pit-N	**20**	6	**.769**	37	26	18	3	5	231^1	221	9	51	74	10.7	**2.61**	**151**	.252	.296	21	.253	2	**31**	**34**	-3	**3.7**
1927	*Pit-N	19	8	.704	35	28	18	3	2	226	205	9	53	63	10.3	**2.47**	**166**	.244	.289	14	.169	-1	36	41	-3	4.3
1928	Pit-N	15	13	.536	34	31	17	1	0	219	253	15	68	61	13.4	4.64	87	.297	.352	14	.179	0	-16	-14	-4	-1.9
1929	Pit-N	18	10	.643	34	27	14	0	0	221^2	226	21	60	66	11.7	4.26	112	.271	.320	11	.128	-2	11	13	-3	0.8
1930	Pit-N	**20**	12	.625	39	38	18	1	0	**276**	366	29	63	58	14.0	5.02	99	.322	.359	16	.157	-4	-2	-1	-4	-0.9
1931	Pit-N	11	15	.423	30	30	15	1	0	230	246	6	65	58	12.4	3.33	116	.271	.323	17	.227	4	14	13	-6	1.2
1932	Pit-N	4	3	.571	11	10	3	1	0	56^2	61	5	16	6	12.4	4.29	89	.270	.321	2	.105	-1	-3	-3	-2	-0.6
1933	Pit-N	1	0	1.000	7	0	0	0	0	20	36	2	9	4	20.2	10.35	32	.387	.441	0	.000	-1	-16	-16	1	-0.7
Total	10	143	85	.627	308	247	134	14	10	1954^2	2108	122	483	516	12.1	3.76	113	.278	.323	122	.178	-7	90	104	-27	8.8

● **JIM KREMMEL** Kremmel, James Louis b: 2/28/48, Belleville, Ill. BL/TL, 6', 175 lbs. Deb: 7/4/73

YEAR	TM/L	W	L	PCT	G	GS	CG	SH	SV	IP	H	HR	BB	SO	RAT	ERA	ERA+	OAV	OOB	BH	AVG	PB	PR	/A	PD	TPI
1973	Tex-A	0	2	.000	4	2	0	0	0	9	15	1	6	6	23.0	9.00	41	.366	.469	0	—	0	-5	-5	-0	-0.9
1974	Chi-N	0	2	.000	23	2	0	0	0	31	37	3	18	22	16.3	5.23	73	.303	.397	0	.000	-0	-6	-5	-0	-0.3
Total	2	0	4	.000	27	4	0	0	0	40	52	4	24	28	17.8	6.07	62	.319	.416	0	.000	-0	-11	-10	-0	-1.2

● **RED KRESS** Kress, Ralph b: 1/2/07, Columbia, Cal. d: 11/29/62, Los Angeles, Cal. BR/TR, 5'11.5", 165 lbs. Deb: 9/24/27 C♦

YEAR	TM/L	W	L	PCT	G	GS	CG	SH	SV	IP	H	HR	BB	SO	RAT	ERA	ERA+	OAV	OOB	BH	AVG	PB	PR	/A	PD	TPI
1935	Was-A	0	0	—	3	0	0	0	0	5^2	8	0	5	5	20.6	12.71	34	.333	.448	75	.298	1	-5	-5	0	0.1
1946	NY-N	0	0	—	1	0	0	0	0	3^2	5	1	1	1	17.2	12.27	28	.333	.412	0	.000	0	-4	-4	1	0.1
Total	2	0	0	—	4	0	0	0	0	9^1	13	1	6	6	19.3	12.54	32	.333	.435	1454	.286	1	-9	-9	1	0.2

● **LOU KRETLOW** Kretlow, Louis Henry "Lena" b: 6/27/21, Apache, Okla. BR/TR, 6'2", 185 lbs. Deb: 9/26/46

YEAR	TM/L	W	L	PCT	G	GS	CG	SH	SV	IP	H	HR	BB	SO	RAT	ERA	ERA+	OAV	OOB	BH	AVG	PB	PR	/A	PD	TPI
1946	Det-A	1	0	1.000	1	1	1	0	0	9	7	2	2	4	9.0	3.00	122	.206	.250	2	.500	1	1	1	-0	0.2
1948	Det-A	2	1	.667	5	2	1	0	0	23^1	21	1	11	9	12.3	4.63	94	.233	.317	4	.500	1	-1	-1	0	0.0
1949	Det-A	3	2	.600	25	10	1	0	0	76	85	5	69	40	18.4	6.16	68	.290	.427	0	.000	-4	-17	-17	2	-1.1
1950	StL-A	0	2	.000	9	2	0	0	0	14^1	25	2	18	10	28.3	11.93	41	.403	.549	0	.000	-0	-12	-11	-0	-1.3
	Chi-A	0	0	—	11	1	0	0	0	21^1	17	1	27	14	18.6	3.80	118	.221	.423	0	.000	-1	2	2	-1	-0.1
	Yr	0	2	.000	20	3	0	0	0	35^2	42	3	45	24	22.0	7.07	66	.298	.468	0	.000	-1	-10	-9	-1	-1.4
1951	Chi-A	6	9	.400	26	18	7	1	0	137	129	7	74	89	13.5	4.20	96	.250	.347	4	.083	-5	-1	-3	-0	-0.8
1952	Chi-A	4	4	.500	19	11	4	2	1	79	52	5	56	63	12.4	2.96	123	.186	.323	1	.050	-1	6	6	-1	0.4
1953	Chi-A	0	0	—	9	3	0	0	0	20^2	12	2	30	15	18.7	3.48	116	.171	.426	0	.000	-0	1	1	1	0.1
	StL-A	1	5	.167	22	11	0	0	0	81	93	5	52	37	16.1	5.11	82	.286	.385	5	.200	-1	-10	-8	-2	-0.8
	Yr	1	5	.167	31	14	0	0	0	101^2	105	7	82	52	16.6	4.78	87	.265	.391	5	.172	-1	-9	-7	-1	-0.7
1954	Bal-A	6	11	.353	32	20	5	0	0	166^2	169	12	82	82	13.6	4.37	82	.269	.354	8	.157	-0	-12	-15	0	-1.3
1955	Bal-A	0	4	.000	15	5	0	0	0	38^1	50	3	27	26	18.3	8.22	46	.316	.419	1	.091	-1	-18	-19	1	-1.6
1956	KC-A	4	9	.308	25	20	3	0	0	118^2	121	17	74	61	14.8	5.31	82	.262	.364	2	.061	-3	-15	-13	-1	-1.5
Total	10	27	47	.365	199	104	22	3	1	785^1	781	62	522	450	15.0	4.87	82	.261	.372	27	.114	-13	-76	-77	-1	-7.8

● **RICK KREUGER** Kreuger, Richard Allen b: 11/3/48, Grand Rapids, Mich. BR/TL, 6'2", 185 lbs. Deb: 9/6/75

YEAR	TM/L	W	L	PCT	G	GS	CG	SH	SV	IP	H	HR	BB	SO	RAT	ERA	ERA+	OAV	OOB	BH	AVG	PB	PR	/A	PD	TPI
1975	Bos-A	0	0	—	2	0	0	0	0	4	3	0	1	1	9.0	4.50	90	.200	.250	0	—	0	-0	-0	0	-0.1
1976	Bos-A	2	1	.667	8	4	1	0	0	31	31	3	16	12	13.6	4.06	96	.272	.362	0	—	0	-2	-1	1	0.0
1977	Bos-A	0	1	.000	1	0	0	0	0	0	2	0	0	0	—	∞	—	1.000	1.000	0	—	0	-2	-2	0	-0.2
1978	Cle-A	0	0	—	6	0	0	0	0	9^1	6	1	3	7	8.7	3.86	97	.194	.265	0	—	0	-0	-0	0	0.0
Total	4	2	2	.500	17	4	1	0	0	44^1	42	4	20	20	12.6	4.47	87	.259	.341	0	—	0	-4	-3	1	-0.3

● **FRANK KREUTZER** Kreutzer, Franklin James b: 2/7/39, Buffalo, N.Y. BR/TL, 6'1", 190 lbs. Deb: 9/20/62

YEAR	TM/L	W	L	PCT	G	GS	CG	SH	SV	IP	H	HR	BB	SO	RAT	ERA	ERA+	OAV	OOB	BH	AVG	PB	PR	/A	PD	TPI
1962	Chi-A	0	0	—	1	0	0	0	0	1^1	0	0	1	1	6.8	0.00	—	.000	.200	0	—	0	1	1	0	0.0

YEAR	TM/L	W	L	PCT	G	GS	CG	SH	SV	IP	H	HR	BB	SO	RAT	ERA	ERA+	OAV	OOB	BH	AVG	PB	PR	/A	PD	TPI
1963	Chi-A	1	0	1.000	1	1	0	0	0	5	3	1	1	0	7.2	1.80	195	.188	.235	0	.000	-0	1	1	0	0.2
1964	Chi-A	3	1	.750	17	2	0	0	1	40^1	37	1	18	32	12.3	3.35	103	.239	.318	1	.125	-0	1	0	1	0.1
	Was-A	2	6	.250	13	9	0	0	0	45^1	48	6	23	27	14.3	4.76	78	.267	.353	0	.000	-1	-6	-5	0	-1.0
	Yr	5	7	.417	30	11	0	0	1	85^2	85	7	41	59	13.3	4.10	87	.253	.336	1	.053	-1	-5	-5	1	-0.9
1965	Was-A	2	6	.250	33	14	2	1	0	85^1	73	7	54	65	13.6	4.32	80	.232	.348	1	.045	-1	-8	-8	-2	-1.0
1966	Was-A	0	5	.000	9	6	0	0	0	31^1	30	9	10	24	11.8	6.03	57	.236	.297	2	.250	0	-9	-9	0	-1.2
1969	Was-A	0	0	—	4	0	0	0	0	2	3	0	2	2	22.5	4.50	77	.333	.455	0	—	0	-0	-0	0	0.0
Total	6	8	18	.308	78	32	2	1	1	210^2	194	24	109	151	13.1	4.40	80	.241	.334	4	.078	-2	-20	-21	-1	-2.9

● KURT KRIEGER Krieger, Kurt Ferdinand "Dutch" b: 9/16/26, Traisen, Austria d: 8/16/70, St.Louis, Mo. BR/TR, 6'3", 212 lbs. Deb: 4/21/49

YEAR	TM/L	W	L	PCT	G	GS	CG	SH	SV	IP	H	HR	BB	SO	RAT	ERA	ERA+	OAV	OOB	BH	AVG	PB	PR	/A	PD	TPI
1949	StL-N	0	0	—	1	0	0	0	0	1	0	0	1	0	9.0	0.00	—	.000	.250	0	—	0	0	0	-0	0.0
1951	StL-N	0	0	—	2	0	0	0	0	4	6	1	5	3	24.8	15.75	25	.353	.500	0	—	0	-5	-5	0	0.0
Total	2	0	0	—	3	0	0	0	0	5	6	1	6	3	21.6	12.60	32	.300	.462	0	—	0	-5	-5	0	0.0

● HOWIE KRIST Krist, Howard Wilbur "Spud" b: 2/28/16, W.Henrietta, N.Y. d: 4/23/89, Buffalo, N.Y. BL/TR, 6'1", 175 lbs. Deb: 9/12/37

YEAR	TM/L	W	L	PCT	G	GS	CG	SH	SV	IP	H	HR	BB	SO	RAT	ERA	ERA+	OAV	OOB	BH	AVG	PB	PR	/A	PD	TPI
1937	StL-N	3	1	.750	6	4	1	0	0	27^2	34	0	10	6	14.3	4.23	94	.304	.361	0	.000	-1	-1	-1	-1	-0.3
1938	StL-N	0	0	—	2	0	0	0	0	1^1	1	0	0	1	6.8	0.00	—	.250	.250	0	—	0	1	1	0	0.0
1941	StL-N	10	0	1.000	37	8	2	0	2	114	107	10	35	36	11.3	4.03	93	.246	.304	9	.237	1	-5	-3	-1	-0.3
1942	StL-N	13	3	.813	34	8	3	0	1	118^1	103	2	43	47	11.3	2.51	136	.233	.304	6	.143	-1	11	12	-2	1.2
1943	*StL-N	11	5	.688	34	17	9	2	3	164^1	141	5	62	57	11.3	2.90	116	.233	.309	10	.167	-2	9	8	-5	0.1
1946	StL-N	0	2	.000	15	0	0	0	0	18^2	22	3	8	3	14.9	6.75	51	.306	.383	0	—	0	-7	-7	0	-0.7
Total	6	37	11	.771	128	37	15	2	6	444^1	408	20	158	150	11.6	3.32	106	.244	.313	25	.168	-3	7	10	-9	0.0

● RICK KRIVDA Krivda, Rick Michael b: 1/19/70, McKeesport, Pa. BR/TL, 6'1", 180 lbs. Deb: 7/7/95

YEAR	TM/L	W	L	PCT	G	GS	CG	SH	SV	IP	H	HR	BB	SO	RAT	ERA	ERA+	OAV	OOB	BH	AVG	PB	PR	/A	PD	TPI
1995	Bal-A	2	7	.222	13	13	1	0	0	75^1	76	9	25	53	12.5	4.54	105	.266	.333	0	—	0	1	2	-1	0.1
1996	Bal-A	3	5	.375	22	11	0	0	0	81^2	89	14	39	54	14.2	4.96	99	.283	.363	0	—	0	0	-0	-1	-0.1
1997	Bal-A	4	2	.667	10	10	0	0	0	50	67	7	18	29	15.3	6.30	70	.328	.383	0	—	0	-10	-11	0	-0.9
1998	Cle-A	2	0	1.000	11	1	0	0	0	25	24	2	16	10	14.4	3.24	147	.250	.357	0	—	0	4	4	-0	0.3
	Cin-N	0	2	.000	16	1	0	0	0	26^1	41	7	19	19	21.5	11.28	38	.366	.470	0	.000	-0	-21	-20	-0	-1.4
Total	4	11	16	.407	72	36	1	0	0	258^1	297	39	117	165	14.7	5.57	84	.293	.371	0	.000	-0	-25	-25	-2	-2.0

● GUS KROCK Krock, August H. b: 5/9/1866, Milwaukee, Wis. d: 3/22/05, Pasadena, Cal. TL, 6', 196 lbs. Deb: 4/24/1888

YEAR	TM/L	W	L	PCT	G	GS	CG	SH	SV	IP	H	HR	BB	SO	RAT	ERA	ERA+	OAV	OOB	BH	AVG	PB	PR	/A	PD	TPI
1888	Chi-N	25	14	.641	39	39	39	4	0	339^2	295	20	45	161	9.2	2.44	124	.227	.258	22	.164	-3	16	22	-3	1.6
1889	Chi-N	3	3	.500	7	7	5	0	0	60^2	86	10	14	16	15.1	4.90	85	.323	.362	4	.167	-1	-6	-5	0	-0.5
	Ind-N	2	2	.500	4	4	3	0	0	32	48	2	14	10	17.4	7.31	57	.336	.395	5	.357	1	-12	-11	-1	-0.9
	Was-N	2	4	.333	6	6	6	0	0	48	65	1	22	17	16.5	5.25	75	.314	.383	2	.087	-2	-7	-7	-0	-0.8
	Yr	7	9	.438	17	17	14	0	0	140^2	199	13	50	43	16.0	5.57	73	.322	.374	11	.180	-2	-24	-23	-1	-2.2
1890	Buf-P	0	3	.000	4	3	3	0	0	25	43	1	15	5	20.9	6.12	67	.364	.436	1	.083	-1	-5	-6	0	-0.5
Total	3	32	26	.552	60	59	56	4	0	505^1	537	34	110	209	11.7	3.49	97	.264	.306	34	.164	-7	-14	-6	-4	-1.1

● RUBE KROH Kroh, Floyd Myron b: 8/25/1886, Friendship, N.Y. d: 3/17/44, New Orleans, La. BL/TL, 6'2", 186 lbs. Deb: 9/30/06

YEAR	TM/L	W	L	PCT	G	GS	CG	SH	SV	IP	H	HR	BB	SO	RAT	ERA	ERA+	OAV	OOB	BH	AVG	PB	PR	/A	PD	TPI
1906	Bos-A	1	0	1.000	1	1	1	1	0	9	2	0	4	5	6.0	0.00	—	.074	.194	0	.000	-0	3	3	0	0.4
1907	Bos-A	1	4	.200	7	5	1	0	0	34^1	33	0	8	8	11.3	2.62	98	.256	.309	3	.273	0	-0	-0	-0	0.0
1908	Chi-N	0	0	—	2	1	0	0	0	12	9	0	4	11	9.8	1.50	157	.200	.265	0	.000	-0	1	1	0	0.0
1909	Chi-N	9	4	.692	17	13	10	2	0	120^1	97	2	30	51	9.6	1.65	154	.224	.276	6	.150	-0	13	12	1	1.4
1910	Chi-N	3	1	.750	6	4	1	0	0	34^1	33	1	15	16	13.1	4.46	65	.254	.340	3	.250	0	-5	-6	1	-0.6
1912	Bos-N	0	0	—	3	1	0	0	0	6^1	8	0	6	1	19.9	5.68	63	.364	.500	1	.500	0	-2	-1	0	0.1
Total	6	14	9	.609	36	25	13	3	0	216^1	182	3	67	92	10.6	2.29	115	.232	.296	13	.181	-0	9	8	2	1.3

● GARY KROLL Kroll, Gary Melvin b: 7/8/41, Culver City, Cal. BR/TR, 6'6", 220 lbs. Deb: 7/26/64

YEAR	TM/L	W	L	PCT	G	GS	CG	SH	SV	IP	H	HR	BB	SO	RAT	ERA	ERA+	OAV	OOB	BH	AVG	PB	PR	/A	PD	TPI
1964	Phi-N	0	0	—	2	0	0	0	0	3	3	0	2	2	15.0	3.00	116	.250	.357	0	—	0	0	0	-0	0.0
	NY-N	0	1	.000	8	2	0	0	0	21^2	19	1	15	24	14.5	4.15	86	.241	.368	1	.333	0	-1	-1	1	0.1
	Yr	0	1	.000	10	2	0	0	0	24^2	22	1	17	26	14.6	4.01	89	.242	.367	1	.333	0	-1	-1	1	0.1
1965	NY-N	6	6	.500	32	11	1	0	1	87	83	12	41	62	13.4	4.45	79	.249	.342	3	.115	-1	-9	-9	-0	-1.2
1966	Hou-N	0	0	—	10	0	0	0	0	23^2	26	2	11	22	14.1	3.80	90	.280	.356	0	.000	-0	-1	-1	0	0.0
1969	Cle-A	0	0	—	19	0	0	0	0	24	16	3	22	28	14.3	4.13	91	.188	.355	0	—	0	-1	-1	-0	0.0
Total	4	6	7	.462	71	13	1	0	1	159^1	147	18	91	138	13.8	4.24	84	.244	.350	4	.125	-1	-12	-12	1	-1.1

● MARC KROON Kroon, Marc Jason b: 4/2/73, Bronx, N.Y. BB/TR, 6'2", 195 lbs. Deb: 7/7/95

YEAR	TM/L	W	L	PCT	G	GS	CG	SH	SV	IP	H	HR	BB	SO	RAT	ERA	ERA+	OAV	OOB	BH	AVG	PB	PR	/A	PD	TPI
1995	SD-N	0	1	.000	2	0	0	0	0	1^2	1	0	2	2	16.2	10.80	37	.200	.429	0	—	0	-1	-1	-0	-0.6
1997	SD-N	0	1	.000	12	0	0	0	0	11^1	14	2	5	12	15.9	6.35	61	.280	.357	0	—	0	-3	-3	-0	-0.3
1998	SD-N	0	0	—	2	0	0	0	0	2^1	0	0	1	2	3.9	0.00	—	.000	.125	0	—	0	1	1	-0	0.0
	Cin-N	0	0	—	4	0	0	0	0	5^1	7	0	8	4	27.0	13.50	32	.333	.533	0	—	0	-5	-5	0	0.0
	Yr	0	0	—	6	0	0	0	0	7^2	7	0	9	6	20.0	9.39	44	.250	.447	0	—	0	-4	-4	0	0.0
Total	3	0	2	.000	20	0	0	0	0	20^2	22	2	16	20	17.4	7.84	51	.265	.396	0	—	0	-8	-9	-0	-0.9

● BILL KRUEGER Krueger, William Culp b: 4/24/58, Waukegan, Ill. BL/TL, 6'5", 210 lbs. Deb: 4/10/83

YEAR	TM/L	W	L	PCT	G	GS	CG	SH	SV	IP	H	HR	BB	SO	RAT	ERA	ERA+	OAV	OOB	BH	AVG	PB	PR	/A	PD	TPI
1983	Oak-A	7	6	.538	17	16	2	0	0	109^2	104	7	53	58	13.0	3.61	107	.252	.340	0	—	0	5	3	-2	0.2
1984	Oak-A	10	10	.500	26	24	1	0	0	142	156	9	85	61	15.4	4.75	79	.285	.383	0	—	0	-12	-16	-2	-1.7
1985	Oak-A	9	10	.474	32	23	2	0	0	151^1	165	13	69	56	14.0	4.52	85	.276	.353	0	—	0	-6	-11	-1	-1.0
1986	Oak-A	1	2	.333	11	3	0	0	1	34^1	40	4	13	10	13.9	6.03	64	.301	.363	0	—	0	-7	-8	1	-0.5
1987	Oak-A	0	3	.000	9	0	0	0	0	5^2	9	0	8	2	27.0	9.53	43	.360	.515	0	—	0	-3	-3	-0	-1.4
	LA-N	0	0	—	2	0	0	0	0	2^1	3	0	1	2	15.4	0.00	—	.250	.308	0	—	0	1	1	-0	0.0
1988	LA-N	0	0	—	1	1	0	0	0	2^1	4	0	2	1	27.0	11.57	29	.364	.500	0	—	0	-2	-2	0	0.0
1989	Mil-A	3	2	.600	34	5	0	0	3	93^2	96	9	33	72	12.4	3.84	100	.264	.325	0	—	0	0	-0	-0	0.0
1990	Mil-A	6	8	.429	30	17	0	0	0	129	137	10	54	64	13.5	3.98	97	.276	.351	0	—	0	-1	-2	-1	-0.2
1991	Sea-A	11	8	.579	35	25	1	0	0	175	194	15	60	91	13.3	3.60	114	.289	.351	0	—	0	10	10	1	1.1
1992	Min-A	10	6	.625	27	27	2	2	0	161^1	166	18	46	86	12.0	4.30	94	.263	.317	0	—	0	-6	-4	-3	-0.8
	Mon-N	0	2	.000	9	2	0	0	0	17^1	23	0	7	13	16.1	6.75	51	.315	.383	0	.000	-0	-6	-6	-0	-0.7
1993	Det-A	6	4	.600	32	7	0	0	0	82	90	6	30	60	13.6	3.40	126	.285	.354	0	—	0	8	8	-0	0.9
1994	Det-A	0	2	.000	16	2	0	0	0	19^2	26	3	17	17	20.1	9.61	50	.321	.444	0	—	0	-11	-10	0	-0.8
	SD-N	3	2	.600	8	7	1	0	0	41	42	5	7	30	11.0	4.83	85	.259	.294	6	.500	3	-3	-3	0	-0.1
1995	SD-N	0	0	—	6	0	0	0	0	7^2	13	1	4	6	20.0	7.04	57	.371	.436	0	—	0	-2	-3	-0	0.0
	Sea-A	2	1	.667	6	5	0	0	0	20	37	4	4	10	18.4	5.85	81	.407	.432	0	—	0	-3	-2	-0	-0.3
Total	13	68	66	.507	301	164	9	2	4	1194^1	1305	104	493	639	13.7	4.35	91	.280	.352	6	.400	2	-38	-50	-8	-5.3

● ABE KRUGER Kruger, Abraham b: 2/14/1885, Morris Run, Pa. d: 7/4/62, Elmira, N.Y. BR/TR, 6'2", 190 lbs. Deb: 10/6/08

YEAR	TM/L	W	L	PCT	G	GS	CG	SH	SV	IP	H	HR	BB	SO	RAT	ERA	ERA+	OAV	OOB	BH	AVG	PB	PR	/A	PD	TPI
1908	Bro-N	0	1	.000	2	1	0	0	0	6^1	5	0	3	2	15.6	4.26	55	.238	.407	0	.000	-0	-1	-1	1	-0.1

● MIKE KRUKOW Krukow, Michael Edward b: 1/21/52, Long Beach, Cal. BR/TR, 6'5", 205 lbs. Deb: 9/6/76

YEAR	TM/L	W	L	PCT	G	GS	CG	SH	SV	IP	H	HR	BB	SO	RAT	ERA	ERA+	OAV	OOB	BH	AVG	PB	PR	/A	PD	TPI
1976	Chi-N	0	0	—	2	0	0	0	0	4^1	6	0	2	1	16.6	8.31	46	.333	.400	0	.000	-0	-2	-2	-0	0.0
1977	Chi-N	8	14	.364	34	33	1	1	0	172	195	16	61	106	13.6	4.40	100	.281	.341	11	.200	-0	-9	-0	1	0.0
1978	Chi-N	9	3	.750	27	20	3	1	0	138	125	11	53	81	11.9	3.91	103	.243	.320	11	.244	3	-5	2	-0	0.4
1979	Chi-N	9	9	.500	28	28	0	0	0	164^2	172	13	81	119	14.0	4.21	98	.275	.361	16	.314	5	-9	-2	-2	0.1
1980	Chi-N	10	15	.400	34	34	3	0	0	205	200	13	80	130	12.6	4.39	89	.258	.334	16	.246	2	-18	-11	-3	-1.3
1981	Chi-N	9	9	.500	25	25	2	1	0	144^1	146	11	55	101	12.7	3.68	100	.264	.333	9	.180	-0	-3	0	0	0.1
1982	Phi-N	13	11	.542	33	33	7	2	0	208	211	8	82	138	12.8	3.12	118	.268	.339	13	.181	-0	11	13	2	1.5
1983	SF-N	11	11	.500	31	31	2	1	0	184^1	189	17	76	136	13.1	3.95	89	.261	.333	16	.254	5	-7	-9	-2	-0.6
1984	SF-N	11	12	.478	35	33	3	1	1	199^1	234	22	78	141	14.3	4.56	77	.290	.356	10	.139	-1	-22	-23	-2	-2.7
1985	SF-N	8	11	.421	28	28	6	1	0	194^2	176	19	49	150	10.5	3.38	102	.238	.288	12	.218	5	5	1	-0	0.6
1986	SF-N★	20	9	.690	34	34	10	2	0	245	204	24	55	178	9.7	3.05	115	.223	.271	12	.146	0	18	13	-1	1.4
1987	*SF-N	5	6	.455	30	28	3	0	0	163	182	24	46	104	12.7	4.80	80	.288	.338	9	.167	1	-13	-17	1	-0.8

YEAR	TM/L	W	L	PCT	G	GS	CG	SH	SV	IP	H	HR	BB	SO	RAT	ERA	ERA+	OAV	OOB	BH	AVG	PB	PR	/A	PD	TPI
1988	SF-N	7	4	.636	20	20	1	0	0	124^2	111	13	31	75	10.6	3.54	92	.236	.291	3	.073	-0	-1	-4	-0	-0.4
1989	SF-N	4	3	.571	8	8	0	0	0	43	37	5	18	18	11.7	3.98	85	.236	.318	1	.063	-1	-2	-3	0	-0.5
Total	14	124	117	.515	369	355	41	10	1	2190^1	2188	196	767	1478	12.3	3.90	96	.260	.325	139	.193	17	-57	-42	-5	-2.2

● **AL KRUMM** Krumm, Albert b: 1/1865, Pennsylvania TR , Deb: 5/17/1889

YEAR	TM/L	W	L	PCT	G	GS	CG	SH	SV	IP	H	HR	BB	SO	RAT	ERA	ERA+	OAV	OOB	BH	AVG	PB	PR	/A	PD	TPI
1889	Pit-N	0	1	.000	1	1	1	0	0	9	8	0	10	4	18.0	10.00	37	.229	.400	0	.000	-1	-6	-6	-0	-0.5

● **JEFF KUBENKA** Kubenka, Jeffrey S. b: 8/24/74, Weimar, Tex. BR/TL, 6'2", 191 lbs. Deb: 9/6/98

YEAR	TM/L	W	L	PCT	G	GS	CG	SH	SV	IP	H	HR	BB	SO	RAT	ERA	ERA+	OAV	OOB	BH	AVG	PB	PR	/A	PD	TPI
1998	LA-N	1	0	1.000	6	0	0	0	0	9^1	4	0	8	10	11.6	0.96	404	.138	.324	0	—	0	3	3	0	0.3

● **TIM KUBINSKI** Kubinski, Timothy Mark b: 1/20/72, Pullman, Wash. BL/TL, 6'4", 205 lbs. Deb: 7/16/97

YEAR	TM/L	W	L	PCT	G	GS	CG	SH	SV	IP	H	HR	BB	SO	RAT	ERA	ERA+	OAV	OOB	BH	AVG	PB	PR	/A	PD	TPI
1997	Oak-A	0	0	—	11	0	0	0	0	12^2	12	2	6	10	13.5	5.68	80	.255	.352	0	—	0	-2	-2	0	0.1

● **JOHNNY KUCAB** Kucab, John Albert b: 12/17/19, Olyphant, Pa. d: 5/26/77, Youngstown, Ohio BR/TR, 6'2", 185 lbs. Deb: 9/14/50

YEAR	TM/L	W	L	PCT	G	GS	CG	SH	SV	IP	H	HR	BB	SO	RAT	ERA	ERA+	OAV	OOB	BH	AVG	PB	PR	/A	PD	TPI
1950	Phi-A	1	1	.500	4	2	2	0	0	26	29	4	8	8	12.8	3.46	131	.282	.333	1	.111	-0	3	3	-1	0.1
1951	Phi-A	4	3	.571	30	1	0	0	4	74^2	76	9	23	23	12.1	4.22	101	.265	.322	0	.000	-2	-1	0	-2	-0.3
1952	Phi-A	0	1	.000	25	0	0	0	2	51^1	64	5	20	17	14.9	5.26	75	.312	.376	2	.200	-0	-9	-7	-0	-0.2
Total	3	5	5	.500	59	3	2	0	6	152	169	18	51	48	13.1	4.44	95	.284	.343	3	.086	-2	-7	-4	-2	-0.4

● **JACK KUCEK** Kucek, John Andrew Charles b: 6/8/53, Warren, Ohio BR/TR, 6'2", 200 lbs. Deb: 8/8/74

YEAR	TM/L	W	L	PCT	G	GS	CG	SH	SV	IP	H	HR	BB	SO	RAT	ERA	ERA+	OAV	OOB	BH	AVG	PB	PR	/A	PD	TPI
1974	Chi-A	1	4	.200	9	7	0	0	0	37^2	48	3	21	25	16.7	5.26	71	.320	.407	0	—	0	-7	-6	1	-0.8
1975	Chi-A	0	0	—	2	0	0	0	0	3^2	9	0	4	2	31.9	4.91	79	.500	.591	0	—	0	-0	-0	-0	0.0
1976	Chi-A	0	0	—	2	0	0	0	0	4^2	9	2	4	2	25.1	9.64	37	.429	.520	0	—	0	-3	-3	-0	0.0
1977	Chi-A	0	1	.000	8	3	0	0	0	34^2	35	4	10	25	12.2	3.63	112	.267	.329	0	—	0	2	2	1	0.1
1978	Chi-A	2	3	.400	10	5	3	0	1	52	42	5	27	30	11.9	3.29	116	.220	.317	0	—	0	3	3	-0	0.2
1979	Chi-A	0	0	—	1	0	0	0	0	0^2	0	0	3	0	40.5	0.00	—	.000	.500	0	—	0	0	0	0	0.0
	Phi-N	1	0	1.000	4	0	0	0	0	4^1	6	2	1	2	14.5	8.31	46	.333	.368	0	—	0	-2	-2	-0	-0.4
1980	Tor-A	3	8	.273	23	12	0	0	1	68	83	9	41	35	16.5	6.75	64	.300	.392	0	—	0	-21	-19	-1	-2.7
Total	7	7	16	.304	59	27	3	0	2	205^2	232	25	111	121	15.2	5.12	78	.287	.376	0	—	0	-29	-26	0	-3.6

● **JOHNNY KUCKS** Kucks, John Charles b: 7/27/33, Hoboken, N.J. BR/TR, 6'3", 184 lbs. Deb: 4/17/55

YEAR	TM/L	W	L	PCT	G	GS	CG	SH	SV	IP	H	HR	BB	SO	RAT	ERA	ERA+	OAV	OOB	BH	AVG	PB	PR	/A	PD	TPI
1955	*NY-A	8	7	.533	29	13	3	1	0	126^2	122	8	44	49	11.9	3.41	110	.252	.317	2	.050	-4	8	5	-0	0.1
1956	*NY-A☆	18	9	.667	34	31	12	3	0	224^1	223	19	72	67	12.2	3.85	100	.261	.326	11	.143	-2	8	0	0	-0.1
1957	*NY-A	8	10	.444	37	23	4	1	2	179^1	169	13	59	78	11.8	3.56	101	.251	.319	6	.109	-2	4	0	3	0.2
1958	*NY-A	8	8	.500	34	15	4	1	4	126	132	14	39	46	12.6	3.93	90	.269	.331	5	.125	-1	-2	-6	1	-0.7
1959	NY-A	0	1	.000	9	1	0	0	0	16^2	21	5	9	9	16.2	8.64	42	.323	.405	0	.000	-0	-9	-9	0	-0.5
	KC-A	8	11	.421	33	23	6	1	1	151^1	163	10	42	51	12.9	3.87	104	.278	.339	4	.085	-3	-0	2	1	0.1
	Yr	8	12	.400	42	24	6	1	1	168	184	15	51	60	13.2	4.34	91	.282	.345	4	.082	-3	-9	-7	2	-0.4
1960	KC-A	4	10	.286	31	17	1	0	0	114	140	22	43	38	14.5	6.00	66	.306	.367	4	.133	-1	-27	-26	-0	-2.8
Total	6	54	56	.491	207	123	30	7	7	938^1	970	91	308	338	12.6	4.10	92	.269	.333	32	.110	-12	-18	-32	5	-3.7

● **BERT KUCZYNSKI** Kuczynski, Bernard Carl b: 1/8/20, Philadelphia, Pa. d: 1/19/97, Allentown, Pa. BR/TR, 6', 195 lbs. Deb: 6/2/43

YEAR	TM/L	W	L	PCT	G	GS	CG	SH	SV	IP	H	HR	BB	SO	RAT	ERA	ERA+	OAV	OOB	BH	AVG	PB	PR	/A	PD	TPI
1943	Phi-A	0	1	.000	6	1	0	0	0	24^2	36	2	9	8	17.1	4.01	85	.336	.398	0	.000	-0	-2	-2	-0	-0.1

● **FRED KUHAULUA** Kuhaulua, Fred Mahele b: 2/23/53, Honolulu, Hawaii BL/TL, 5'11", 175 lbs. Deb: 8/2/77

YEAR	TM/L	W	L	PCT	G	GS	CG	SH	SV	IP	H	HR	BB	SO	RAT	ERA	ERA+	OAV	OOB	BH	AVG	PB	PR	/A	PD	TPI
1977	Cal-A	0	0	—	3	1	0	0	0	6^1	15	1	7	3	31.3	15.63	25	.455	.550	0	—	0	-8	-8	0	0.0
1981	SD-N	1	0	1.000	5	4	0	0	0	29^1	28	1	9	16	11.4	2.45	133	.257	.314	1	.111	-0	3	3	-1	-0.1
Total	2	1	0	1.000	8	5	0	0	0	35^2	43	2	16	19	14.9	4.79	70	.303	.373	1	.111	-0	-5	-6	-1	-0.1

● **BUB KUHN** Kuhn, Bernard Daniel b: 10/12/1899, Vicksburg, Mich. d: 11/20/56, Detroit, Mich. BL/TR, 6'1.5", 182 lbs. Deb: 9/1/24

YEAR	TM/L	W	L	PCT	G	GS	CG	SH	SV	IP	H	HR	BB	SO	RAT	ERA	ERA+	OAV	OOB	BH	AVG	PB	PR	/A	PD	TPI
1924	Cle-A	0	1	.000	1	0	0	0	0	1	4	1	0	0	36.0	27.00	16	.667	.667	0	—	0	-3	-3	0	-1.2

● **JOHN KULL** Kull, John A. (b: John A Kolonauski) b: 6/24/1882, Shenandoah, Pa. d: 3/30/36, Schuylkill Haven, Pa. BL/TL, 6'2", 190 lbs. Deb: 10/2/09

YEAR	TM/L	W	L	PCT	G	GS	CG	SH	SV	IP	H	HR	BB	SO	RAT	ERA	ERA+	OAV	OOB	BH	AVG	PB	PR	/A	PD	TPI
1909	Phi-A	1	0	1.000	1	0	0	0	0	3	3	0	5	4	27.0	3.00	80	.250	.500	1	1.000	0	-0	-0	0	0.0

● **MIKE KUME** Kume, John Michael b: 5/19/26, Premier, W.Va. BR/TR, 6'1", 195 lbs. Deb: 8/26/55

YEAR	TM/L	W	L	PCT	G	GS	CG	SH	SV	IP	H	HR	BB	SO	RAT	ERA	ERA+	OAV	OOB	BH	AVG	PB	PR	/A	PD	TPI
1955	KC-A	0	2	.000	6	4	0	0	0	23^2	35	1	15	7	20.2	7.99	52	.354	.453	1	.125	-0	-11	-10	-0	-0.8

● **JEFF KUNKEL** Kunkel, Jeffrey William b: 3/25/62, W.Palm Beach, Fla. BR/TR, 6'2", 180 lbs. Deb: 7/23/84 F ♦

YEAR	TM/L	W	L	PCT	G	GS	CG	SH	SV	IP	H	HR	BB	SO	RAT	ERA	ERA+	OAV	OOB	BH	AVG	PB	PR	/A	PD	TPI
1988	Tex-A	0	0	—	1	0	0	0	0	1	0	0	0	1	0.0	0.00	—	.000	.000	35	.227	0	0	0	0	0.0
1989	Tex-A	0	0	—	1	0	0	0	0	1^2	4	1	3	0	37.8	21.60	18	.444	.583	79	.270	0	-3	-3	0	0.0
Total	2	0	0	—	2	0	0	0	0	2^2	4	1	3	1	23.6	13.50	30	.333	.467	192	.221	1	-3	-3	0	0.0

● **BILL KUNKEL** Kunkel, William Gustave James b: 7/7/36, Hoboken, N.J. d: 5/4/85, Red Bank, N.J. BR/TR, 6'1", 187 lbs. Deb: 4/15/61 FU

YEAR	TM/L	W	L	PCT	G	GS	CG	SH	SV	IP	H	HR	BB	SO	RAT	ERA	ERA+	OAV	OOB	BH	AVG	PB	PR	/A	PD	TPI
1961	KC-A	3	4	.429	58	2	0	0	4	88^2	103	11	32	46	13.7	5.18	81	.289	.348	1	.125	-0	-11	-10	0	-0.8
1962	KC-A	0	0	—	9	0	0	0	0	7^2	8	3	4	6	14.1	3.52	120	.258	.343	0	—	0	0	1	-0	0.0
1963	NY-A	3	2	.600	22	0	0	0	0	46^1	42	3	13	31	10.7	2.72	129	.239	.291	2	.333	1	5	4	-1	0.4
Total	3	6	6	.500	89	2	0	0	4	142^2	153	17	49	83	12.7	4.29	92	.272	.330	3	.214	1	-6	-5	-1	-0.4

● **EARL KUNZ** Kunz, Earl Dewey "Pinches" b: 12/25/1899, Sacramento, Cal. d: 4/14/63, Sacramento, Cal. BR/TR, 5'10", 170 lbs. Deb: 4/19/23

YEAR	TM/L	W	L	PCT	G	GS	CG	SH	SV	IP	H	HR	BB	SO	RAT	ERA	ERA+	OAV	OOB	BH	AVG	PB	PR	/A	PD	TPI
1923	Pit-N	1	2	.333	21	2	1	0	1	45^2	48	2	24	12	14.2	5.52	73	.293	.383	1	.083	-1	-8	-8	-1	-0.7

● **RYAN KUROSAKI** Kurosaki, Ryan Yoshitomo b: 7/3/52, Honolulu, Hawaii BR/TR, 5'10", 160 lbs. Deb: 5/20/75

YEAR	TM/L	W	L	PCT	G	GS	CG	SH	SV	IP	H	HR	BB	SO	RAT	ERA	ERA+	OAV	OOB	BH	AVG	PB	PR	/A	PD	TPI
1975	StL-N	0	0	—	7	0	0	0	0	13	15	3	7	6	15.2	7.62	49	.283	.367	0	.000	-0	-6	-6	-0	0.0

● **HAL KURTZ** Kurtz, Harold James "Bud" b: 8/20/43, Washington, D.C. BR/TR, 6'3", 205 lbs. Deb: 4/18/68

YEAR	TM/L	W	L	PCT	G	GS	CG	SH	SV	IP	H	HR	BB	SO	RAT	ERA	ERA+	OAV	OOB	BH	AVG	PB	PR	/A	PD	TPI
1968	Cle-A	1	0	1.000	28	0	0	0	1	38	37	2	15	16	13.5	5.21	57	.255	.345	0	.000	-0	-9	-10	-1	-0.4

● **ED KUSEL** Kusel, Edward D. b: 2/15/1886, Cleveland, Ohio d: 10/20/48, Cleveland, Ohio TR , 6', 165 lbs. Deb: 9/18/09

YEAR	TM/L	W	L	PCT	G	GS	CG	SH	SV	IP	H	HR	BB	SO	RAT	ERA	ERA+	OAV	OOB	BH	AVG	PB	PR	/A	PD	TPI
1909	StL-A	0	3	.000	3	3	3	0	0	24	43	1	1	2	16.5	7.13	34	.384	.389	3	.300	1	-12	-13	-1	-1.2

● **EMIL KUSH** Kush, Emil Benedict b: 11/4/16, Chicago, Ill. d: 11/26/69, River Grove, Ill. BR/TR, 5'11", 185 lbs. Deb: 9/21/41

YEAR	TM/L	W	L	PCT	G	GS	CG	SH	SV	IP	H	HR	BB	SO	RAT	ERA	ERA+	OAV	OOB	BH	AVG	PB	PR	/A	PD	TPI
1941	Chi-N	0	0	—	2	0	0	0	0	4	2	0	0	2	4.5	2.25	156	.143	.143	0	.000	-0	1	1	-0	0.0
1942	Chi-N	0	0	—	1	0	0	0	0	2	1	0	1	1	9.0	0.00	—	.167	.286	0	.000	-0	1	1	0	0.0
1946	Chi-N	9	2	.818	40	6	1	1	2	129^2	120	4	43	50	11.5	3.05	109	.253	.319	8	.211	0	5	4	2	0.6
1947	Chi-N	8	3	.727	47	1	1	0	5	91	80	8	53	44	13.5	3.36	117	.247	.358	5	.250	1	7	6	1	0.9
1948	Chi-N	1	4	.200	34	1	0	0	3	72	70	5	37	31	13.6	4.38	89	.253	.345	2	.154	0	-3	-4	1	-0.2
1949	Chi-N	3	3	.500	26	0	0	0	2	47^2	51	7	24	22	14.5	3.78	107	.283	.374	3	.333	1	1	1	1	0.4
Total	6	21	12	.636	150	8	2	1	12	346^1	324	24	158	150	12.8	3.48	106	.254	.341	18	.220	2	12	9	5	1.7

● **CRAIG KUSICK** Kusick, Craig Robert b: 9/30/48, Milwaukee, Wis. BR/TR, 6'3", 232 lbs. Deb: 9/8/73 ♦

YEAR	TM/L	W	L	PCT	G	GS	CG	SH	SV	IP	H	HR	BB	SO	RAT	ERA	ERA+	OAV	OOB	BH	AVG	PB	PR	/A	PD	TPI
1979	Tor-A	0	0	—	1	0	0	0	0	3^2	3	1	0	0	7.4	4.91	88	.214	.214	11	.204	0	-0	-0	-0	0.0

● **MARTY KUTYNA** Kutyna, Marion John b: 11/14/32, Philadelphia, Pa. BR/TR, 6', 190 lbs. Deb: 9/19/59

YEAR	TM/L	W	L	PCT	G	GS	CG	SH	SV	IP	H	HR	BB	SO	RAT	ERA	ERA+	OAV	OOB	BH	AVG	PB	PR	/A	PD	TPI
1959	KC-A	0	0	—	4	0	0	0	1	7^1	7	0	1	1	9.8	0.00	—	.250	.276	0	—	0	3	3	0	0.1
1960	KC-A	3	2	.600	51	0	0	0	4	61^2	64	7	32	20	14.0	3.94	101	.274	.361	1	.200	-0	-0	0	0	0.0
1961	Was-A	6	8	.429	50	6	0	0	3	143	147	12	48	64	12.4	3.97	101	.271	.332	7	.206	-0	1	1	3	0.4
1962	Was-A	5	6	.455	54	0	0	0	0	78	83	9	27	25	12.7	4.04	100	.275	.334	1	.125	-0	-1	-0	1	0.1
Total	4	14	16	.467	159	6	0	0	8	290	301	28	108	110	12.8	3.88	103	.272	.338	9	.191	-0	3	4	4	0.6

● **JERRY KUTZLER** Kutzler, Jerry Scott b: 3/25/65, Waukegan, Ill. BL/TR, 6'1", 175 lbs. Deb: 4/28/90

YEAR	TM/L	W	L	PCT	G	GS	CG	SH	SV	IP	H	HR	BB	SO	RAT	ERA	ERA+	OAV	OOB	BH	AVG	PB	PR	/A	PD	TPI
1990	Chi-A	2	1	.667	7	7	0	0	0	31^1	38	2	14	21	14.9	6.03	63	.304	.374	0	—	0	-7	-8	-0	-0.7

● BOB KUZAVA Kuzava, Robert Leroy "Sarge" b: 5/28/23, Wyandotte, Mich. BB/TL, 6′2″, 204 lbs. Deb: 9/21/46

YEAR	TM/L	W	L	PCT	G	GS	CG	SH	SV	IP	H	HR	BB	SO	RAT	ERA	ERA+	OAV	OOB	BH	AVG	PB	PR	/A	PD	TPI
1946	Cle-A	1	0	1.000	2	2	0	0	0	12	9	0	11	4	15.8	3.00	110	.191	.356	1	.200	-0	1	0	0	0.1
1947	Cle-A	1	1	.500	4	4	1	1	0	21^2	22	1	9	9	13.3	4.15	84	.265	.344	1	.111	-1	-1	-2	1	-0.1
1949	Chi-A	10	6	.625	29	18	9	1	0	156^2	139	6	91	83	13.3	4.02	104	.240	.344	2	.036	-6	3	3	-2	-0.6
1950	Chi-A	1	3	.250	10	7	1	0	0	44^1	43	5	27	21	14.2	5.68	79	.257	.361	1	.083	-0	-5	-6	0	-0.5
	Was-A	8	7	.533	22	22	8	1	0	155	156	8	75	84	13.5	3.95	114	.263	.346	5	.100	-2	11	9	-1	0.5
	Yr	9	10	.474	32	29	9	1	0	199^1	199	13	102	105	13.6	4.33	104	.261	.350	6	.097	-2	5	3	-1	0.0
1951	Was-A	3	3	.500	8	8	3	0	0	52^1	57	5	28	22	15.0	5.50	74	.284	.377	3	.176	-0	-8	-8	0	-0.8
	*NY-A	8	4	.667	23	8	4	1	5	82^1	76	5	27	50	11.4	2.40	159	.241	.303	3	.136	0	16	13	-1	1.8
	Yr	11	7	.611	31	16	7	1	5	134^2	133	10	55	72	12.6	3.61	109	.257	.329	6	.154	0	8	5	-1	1.0
1952	*NY-A	8	8	.500	28	12	6	1	3	133	115	7	63	67	12.1	3.45	96	.240	.329	4	.093	-1	3	-2	-2	-0.5
1953	*NY-A	6	5	.545	33	6	2	2	4	92^1	92	9	34	48	12.3	3.31	111	.264	.330	1	.048	-1	7	4	-2	0.2
1954	NY-A	1	3	.250	20	3	0	0	1	39^2	46	3	18	22	14.5	5.45	63	.297	.370	0	.000	-0	-8	-9	-1	-1.0
	Bal-A	1	3	.250	4	4	0	0	0	23^2	30	0	11	15	15.6	4.18	86	.323	.394	0	.000	-1	-1	-2	-1	-0.4
	Yr	2	6	.250	24	7	0	0	1	63^1	76	3	29	37	14.9	4.97	70	.304	.376	0	.000	-1	-9	-10	-1	-1.4
1955	Bal-A	0	1	.000	6	1	0	0	0	12^1	10	0	4	5	10.2	3.65	105	.222	.286	0	.000	-0	0	0	-1	0.0
	Phi-N	1	0	1.000	17	4	0	0	0	32^1	47	5	12	13	16.4	7.24	55	.333	.386	1	.143	-0	-11	-12	0	-0.3
1957	Pit-N	0	0	—	4	0	0	0	0	2	3	0	3	1	27.0	9.00	42	.333	.500	0	—	0	-1	-1	-0	0.0
	StL-N	0	0	—	3	0	0	0	0	2^1	4	0	2	2	23.1	3.86	103	.364	.462	0	—	0	0	0	0	0.0
	Yr	0	0	—	7	0	0	0	0	4^1	7	0	5	3	24.9	6.23	62	.350	.480	0	—	0	-1	-1	0	0.0
Total	10	49	44	.527	213	99	34	7	13	862	849	54	415	446	13.3	4.05	97	.260	.345	22	.086	-14	5	-12	-8	-1.6

● CLEM LABINE Labine, Clement Walter b: 8/6/26, Lincoln, R.I. BR/TR, 6′, 180 lbs. Deb: 4/18/50

YEAR	TM/L	W	L	PCT	G	GS	CG	SH	SV	IP	H	HR	BB	SO	RAT	ERA	ERA+	OAV	OOB	BH	AVG	PB	PR	/A	PD	TPI
1950	Bro-N	0	0	—	1	0	0	0	0	2	2	0	1	0	13.5	4.50	91	.286	.375	0	—	0	-0	-0	-0	0.0
1951	Bro-N	5	1	.833	14	6	5	2	0	65^1	52	4	20	39	9.9	2.20	178	.223	.285	3	.143	-1	13	12	-1	0.9
1952	Bro-N	8	4	.667	25	9	0	0	0	77	76	3	47	43	14.5	5.14	71	.259	.364	1	.045	-2	-12	-13	1	-1.9
1953	*Bro-N	11	6	.647	37	7	0	0	7	110^1	92	9	30	44	10.0	2.77	154	.225	.278	2	.071	-1	19	18	0	2.7
1954	Bro-N	7	6	.538	47	2	0	0	5	108^1	101	7	56	43	13.1	4.15	98	.247	.339	1	.033	-2	-1	-1	1	-0.2
1955	*Bro-N	13	5	.722	**60**	8	1	0	11	144^1	121	12	55	67	11.0	3.24	125	.229	.301	3	.097	1	13	13	3	2.1
1956	*Bro-N☆	10	6	.625	62	3	1	0	**19**	115^2	111	11	39	75	11.9	3.35	119	.253	.318	2	.087	-1	5	8	1	1.3
1957	Bro-N★	5	7	.417	58	0	0	0	**17**	104^2	104	8	27	67	11.4	3.44	121	.259	.307	2	.100	-1	5	8	2	1.3
1958	LA-N	6	6	.500	52	2	0	0	14	104	112	8	33	43	12.6	4.15	99	.283	.340	1	.056	-1	-2	-1	0	-0.2
1959	*LA-N	5	10	.333	56	0	0	0	9	84^2	91	11	25	37	12.4	3.93	108	.282	.335	0	.000	-2	0	3	1	0.5
1960	LA-N	0	1	.000	13	0	0	0	1	17	26	1	8	15	18.0	5.82	68	.356	.420	1	.500	1	-4	-4	-0	-0.2
	Det-A	0	3	.000	14	0	0	0	2	19^1	19	2	12	6	14.4	5.12	77	.257	.360	0	.000	-0	-3	-2	0	-0.4
	*Pit-N	3	0	1.000	15	0	0	0	3	30^1	29	0	11	21	12.2	1.48	253	.254	.325	0	.000	-0	8	8	0	0.9
1961	Pit-N	4	1	.800	56	1	0	0	8	92^2	102	4	31	49	13.1	3.69	108	.284	.344	1	.100	-0	4	3	-1	0.1
1962	NY-N	0	0	—	3	0	0	0	0	4	5	1	1	2	13.5	11.25	37	.278	.316	0	—	0	-3	-3	0	0.0
Total	13	77	56	.579	513	38	7	2	96	1079^2	1043	81	396	551	12.1	3.63	112	.256	.323	17	.075	-11	41	50	8	6.9

● BOB LACEY Lacey, Robert Joseph b: 8/25/53, Fredericksburg, Va. BR/TL, 6′5″, 210 lbs. Deb: 5/13/77

YEAR	TM/L	W	L	PCT	G	GS	CG	SH	SV	IP	H	HR	BB	SO	RAT	ERA	ERA+	OAV	OOB	BH	AVG	PB	PR	/A	PD	TPI
1977	Oak-A	6	8	.429	64	0	0	0	7	121^2	100	13	43	69	10.6	3.03	133	.234	.304	0	—	0	14	13	3	2.0
1978	Oak-A	8	9	.471	**74**	0	0	0	5	119^2	126	10	35	60	12.2	3.01	121	.270	.323	0	—	0	10	8	2	1.4
1979	Oak-A	1	5	.167	42	0	0	0	4	47^2	66	7	24	33	17.2	5.85	69	.327	.401	0	—	0	-9	-10	0	-1.2
1980	Oak-A	3	2	.600	47	1	1	1	6	79^2	68	7	21	45	10.2	2.94	128	.234	.288	0	—	0	10	7	-0	0.6
1981	Cle-A	0	0	—	14	0	0	0	0	21^1	36	5	3	11	16.5	7.59	48	.371	.390	0	—	0	-9	-9	-0	0.0
	Tex-A	0	0	—	1	0	0	0	0	1	1	1	0	0	9.0	9.00	39	.250	.250	0	—	0	-1	-1	0	0.0
	Yr	0	0	—	15	0	0	0	0	22^1	37	6	3	11	16.1	7.66	47	.356	.374	0	—	0	-10	-10	0	0.0
1983	Cal-A	1	2	.333	8	0	0	0	0	8^2	12	1	0	7	12.5	5.19	77	.343	.343	0	—	0	-1	-1	-0	-0.3
1984	SF-N	1	3	.250	34	1	0	0	0	51	55	5	13	26	12.0	3.88	90	.276	.321	2	.333	1	-2	-2	0	-0.1
Total	7	20	29	.408	284	2	1	1	22	450^2	464	49	139	251	12.1	3.67	103	.269	.325	2	.333	1	12	6	5	2.4

● MARCEL LACHEMANN Lachemann, Marcel Ernest b: 6/13/41, Los Angeles, Cal. BR/TR, 6′, 185 lbs. Deb: 6/4/69 FMC

YEAR	TM/L	W	L	PCT	G	GS	CG	SH	SV	IP	H	HR	BB	SO	RAT	ERA	ERA+	OAV	OOB	BH	AVG	PB	PR	/A	PD	TPI
1969	Oak-A	4	1	.800	28	0	0	0	2	43^1	43	1	19	16	13.3	3.95	87	.261	.344	0	.000	-0	-2	-2	1	-0.3
1970	Oak-A	3	3	.500	41	0	0	0	3	58^1	58	6	18	39	12.0	2.78	127	.266	.328	0	.000	-1	6	5	1	0.6
1971	Oak-A	0	0	—	1	0	0	0	0	0^1	2	0	1	0	81.0	54.00	6	1.000	1.000	0	—	0	-2	-2	0	0.0
Total	3	7	4	.636	70	0	0	0	5	102	103	7	38	55	12.8	3.44	102	.268	.340	0	.000	-1	3	1	2	0.3

● AL LACHOWICZ Lachowicz, Allen Robert b: 9/6/60, Pittsburgh, Pa. BR/TR, 6′3″, 198 lbs. Deb: 9/13/83

YEAR	TM/L	W	L	PCT	G	GS	CG	SH	SV	IP	H	HR	BB	SO	RAT	ERA	ERA+	OAV	OOB	BH	AVG	PB	PR	/A	PD	TPI
1983	Tex-A	0	1	.000	2	1	0	0	0	8	9	0	2	8	12.4	2.25	178	.281	.324	0	—	0	2	2	0	0.2

● LACKEY Lackey b: Columbus, Ohio Deb: 10/2/1890

YEAR	TM/L	W	L	PCT	G	GS	CG	SH	SV	IP	H	HR	BB	SO	RAT	ERA	ERA+	OAV	OOB	BH	AVG	PB	PR	/A	PD	TPI
1890	Phi-a	0	0	—	1	0	0	0	0	2	1	0	3	1	18.0	9.00	43	.143	.400	0	.000	-0	-1	-1	-0	0.0

● FRANK LaCORTE LaCorte, Frank Joseph b: 10/13/51, San Jose, Cal. BR/TR, 6′1″, 180 lbs. Deb: 9/8/75

YEAR	TM/L	W	L	PCT	G	GS	CG	SH	SV	IP	H	HR	BB	SO	RAT	ERA	ERA+	OAV	OOB	BH	AVG	PB	PR	/A	PD	TPI
1975	Atl-N	0	3	.000	3	2	0	0	0	13^2	13	1	6	10	12.5	5.27	72	.245	.322	0	.000	-1	-3	-2	0	-0.5
1976	Atl-N	3	12	.200	19	17	1	0	0	105^1	97	6	53	79	13.3	4.70	81	.249	.348	3	.091	-2	-14	-11	-0	-1.6
1977	Atl-N	1	8	.111	14	7	0	0	0	37	67	10	29	28	23.8	11.68	38	.394	.488	2	.200	-0	-32	-30	0	-5.3
1978	Atl-N	0	1	.000	2	2	0	0	0	14^2	9	0	4	7	8.0	3.68	110	.180	.241	0	.000	-0	-0	1	-0	0.0
1979	Atl-N	0	0	—	6	0	0	0	0	8^1	9	2	5	6	15.1	7.56	54	.273	.368	0	.000	-0	-4	-3	-0	0.0
	Hou-N	1	2	.333	12	3	0	0	0	27	21	3	10	24	10.3	5.00	70	.208	.279	0	.000	-0	-4	-4	-1	-0.5
	Yr	1	2	.333	18	3	0	0	0	35^1	30	5	15	30	11.5	5.60	65	.224	.302	0	.000	-0	-7	-8	-1	-0.5
1980	*Hou-N	8	5	.615	55	0	0	0	11	83	61	4	43	66	11.3	2.82	117	.210	.311	1	.167	0	7	4	-2	0.6
1981	*Hou-N	4	2	.667	37	0	0	0	5	42	41	1	21	40	13.3	3.64	90	.258	.344	1	.333	0	-1	-2	-0	-0.3
1982	Hou-N	1	5	.167	55	0	0	0	7	76^1	71	5	46	51	13.8	4.48	74	.247	.350	0	.000	-1	-7	-10	-2	-1.2
1983	Hou-N	4	4	.500	37	0	0	0	3	53^1	35	8	28	48	11.0	5.06	67	.190	.304	1	.200	0	-9	-10	-0	-1.5
1984	Cal-A	1	2	.333	13	1	0	0	0	29^1	33	9	13	13	14.1	7.06	56	.282	.354	0	—	0	-10	-10	-0	-0.9
Total	10	23	44	.343	253	32	1	0	26	490	457	49	258	372	13.3	5.01	72	.249	.345	8	.104	-4	-75	-77	-7	-11.2

● MIKE LaCOSS LaCoss, Michael James (b: Michael James Marks) b: 5/30/56, Glendale, Cal. BR/TR, 6′4″, 190 lbs. Deb: 7/18/78

YEAR	TM/L	W	L	PCT	G	GS	CG	SH	SV	IP	H	HR	BB	SO	RAT	ERA	ERA+	OAV	OOB	BH	AVG	PB	PR	/A	PD	TPI
1978	Cin-N	4	8	.333	16	15	2	1	0	96	104	5	46	31	14.2	4.50	79	.288	.370	2	.067	-2	-10	-10	-1	-1.4
1979	*Cin-N★	14	8	.636	35	32	6	1	0	205^2	202	13	79	73	12.4	3.50	107	.263	.333	9	.129	-1	5	5	1	0.5
1980	Cin-N	10	12	.455	34	29	4	2	0	169^1	207	9	68	59	14.7	4.62	77	.303	.367	5	.091	-3	-19	-20	1	-2.5
1981	Cin-N	4	7	.364	20	13	1	1	1	78	102	7	30	22	15.3	6.12	58	.325	.386	0	.000	-2	-23	-22	0	-3.0
1982	Hou-N	6	6	.500	41	8	0	0	0	115	107	3	54	51	12.9	2.90	115	.252	.342	6	.250	2	9	5	-1	0.7
1983	Hou-N	5	7	.417	38	17	2	0	1	138	142	10	56	53	13.0	4.43	77	.273	.346	3	.086	-2	-12	-16	1	-1.4
1984	Hou-N	7	5	.583	39	18	2	1	3	132	132	3	55	86	12.8	4.02	83	.261	.334	4	.129	-1	-6	-10	0	-0.9
1985	KC-A	1	1	.500	21	0	0	0	1	40^2	49	2	29	26	17.3	5.09	82	.304	.411	0	—	0	-4	-4	0	-0.2
1986	SF-N	10	13	.435	37	31	4	1	0	204^1	179	14	70	86	11.2	3.57	99	.240	.310	14	.230	6	3	-1	1	0.5
1987	*SF-N	13	10	.565	39	26	2	1	0	171	184	16	63	79	13.1	3.68	104	.283	.348	3	.060	-2	8	3	4	0.5
1988	SF-N	7	7	.500	19	19	1	1	0	114^1	99	5	47	70	11.6	3.62	90	.234	.312	8	.242	3	-2	-5	3	0.1
1989	*SF-N	10	10	.500	45	18	1	0	6	150^1	143	3	65	78	12.9	3.17	106	.255	.340	3	.073	-1	5	3	-1	0.3
1990	SF-N	6	4	.600	13	12	1	0	0	77^2	75	5	39	39	13.2	3.94	92	.259	.347	1	.043	-1	-1	-3	-1	-0.5
1991	SF-N	1	5	.167	18	5	0	0	0	47^1	61	4	24	30	16.5	7.23	50	.314	.395	2	.222	1	-19	-19	-0	-2.1
Total	14	98	103	.488	415	243	26	9	12	1739^2	1786	99	725	783	13.1	4.02	88	.270	.345	60	.125	-4	-66	-93	8	-9.4

● KERRY LACY Lacy, Kerry Ardeen b: 8/7/72, Chattanooga, Tenn. BR/TR, 6′2″, 195 lbs. Deb: 8/16/96

YEAR	TM/L	W	L	PCT	G	GS	CG	SH	SV	IP	H	HR	BB	SO	RAT	ERA	ERA+	OAV	OOB	BH	AVG	PB	PR	/A	PD	TPI
1996	Bos-A	2	0	1.000	11	0	0	0	0	10^2	15	2	8	9	20.3	3.38	150	.333	.444	0	—	0	2	2	0	0.3
1997	Bos-A	1	1	.500	33	0	0	0	3	45^2	60	7	22	18	16.2	6.11	76	.314	.385	0	—	0	-8	-7	-1	-0.5
Total	2	3	1	.750	44	0	0	0	3	56^1	75	9	30	27	16.9	5.59	84	.318	.397	0	—	0	-6	-5	-1	-0.2

YEAR	TM/L	W	L	PCT	G	GS	CG	SH	SV	IP	H	HR	BB	SO	RAT	ERA	ERA+	OAV	OOB	BH	AVG	PB	PR	/A	PD	TPI
● **PETE LADD**	Ladd, Peter Linwood b: 7/17/56, Portland, Maine BR/TR, 6'3", 240 lbs. Deb: 8/17/79																									
1979	Hou-N	1	1	.500	10	0	0	0	0	12^1	8	1	8	6	13.1	2.92	120	.178	.327	0	.000	-0	1	1	0	0.1
1982	*Mil-A	1	3	.250	16	0	0	0	3	18	16	5	6	12	11.0	4.00	95	.239	.301	0	—	0	0	-0	-1	-0.1
1983	Mil-A	3	4	.429	44	0	0	0	25	49^1	30	3	16	41	8.6	2.55	146	.172	.246	0	—	0	8	6	-0	1.6
1984	Mil-A	4	9	.308	54	1	0	0	3	91	94	16	38	75	13.2	5.24	73	.266	.339	0	—	0	-13	-14	-2	-1.9
1985	Mil-A	0	0	—	29	0	0	0	2	45^2	58	5	10	22	13.8	4.53	92	.315	.357	0	—	0	-2	-2	-0	0.0
1986	Sea-A	8	6	.571	52	0	0	0	6	70^2	69	10	18	53	11.5	3.82	111	.258	.313	0	—	0	3	3	-1	0.5
Total	6	17	23	.425	205	1	0	0	39	287	275	40	96	209	11.9	4.14	96	.252	.318	0	.000	-0	-2	-6	-4	0.2
● **DOYLE LADE**	Lade, Doyle Marion "Porky" b: 2/17/21, Fairbury, Neb. BR/TR, 5'10", 183 lbs. Deb: 9/18/46																									
1946	Chi-N	0	2	.000	3	2	0	0	0	15^1	15	0	3	8	11.2	4.11	81	.238	.284	1	.200	-0	-1	-1	0	-0.2
1947	Chi-N	11	10	.524	34	25	7	1	0	187^1	202	15	79	62	13.5	3.94	100	.276	.347	13	.217	2	2	0	2	0.5
1948	Chi-N	5	6	.455	19	12	6	0	0	87^1	99	4	31	29	13.5	4.02	97	.283	.343	5	.156	-1	-1	-1	1	-0.1
1949	Chi-N	4	5	.444	36	13	5	1	1	129^2	141	14	58	43	14.0	5.00	81	.274	.350	7	.219	2	-14	-14	0	-0.7
1950	Chi-N	5	6	.455	34	12	2	0	2	117^2	126	14	50	36	13.6	4.74	89	.275	.349	10	.286	3	-8	-7	3	0.0
Total	5	25	29	.463	126	64	20	2	3	537^1	583	47	221	178	13.6	4.39	91	.275	.346	36	.220	6	-21	-23	7	-0.5
● **STEVE LADEW**	Ladew, Stephen b: St.Louis, Mo. Deb: 9/27/1889 ♦																									
1889	KC-a	0	0	—	1	0	0	0	0	2	1	0	3	0	18.0	4.50	93	.143	.400	0	.000	-0	-0	-0	0	0.0
● **FLIP LAFFERTY**	Lafferty, Frank Bernard b: 5/4/1854, Scranton, Pa. d: 2/8/10, Wilmington, Del. TR , Deb: 9/15/1876 ♦																									
1876	Phi-N	0	1	.000	1	1	1	0	0	9	5	0	0	0	5.0	0.00	—	.152	.152	0	.000	-1	2	2	0	0.2
● **ED LAFITTE**	Lafitte, Edward Francis "Doc" b: 4/7/1886, New Orleans, La. d: 4/12/71, Jenkintown, Pa. BR/TR, 6'2", 188 lbs. Deb: 4/16/09																									
1909	Det-A	0	1	.000	3	1	1	0	1	14	22	2	2	11	16.1	3.86	65	.344	.373	1	.250	0	-2	-2	0	-0.2
1911	Det-A	11	8	.579	29	20	15	0	1	172^1	205	2	52	63	13.7	3.92	88	.302	.356	11	.157	-2	-11	-9	-2	-1.3
1912	Det-A	0	0	—	1	0	0	0	0	1^2	2	0	2	0	21.6	16.20	20	.333	.500	0	—	0	-2	-2	0	0.0
1914	Bro-F	18	15	.545	42	33	23	0	2	290^2	260	7	127	137	12.5	2.63	109	.248	.338	26	.257	3	8	8	3	1.5
1915	Bro-F	6	9	.400	17	15	7	0	1	117^2	126	6	57	34	14.1	3.90	70	.288	.371	14	.264	2	-15	-15	-2	-1.9
	Buf-F	2	2	.500	14	5	1	1	1	50^1	53	1	22	17	13.8	3.40	82	.286	.368	2	.118	-1	-4	-3	0	-0.4
	Yr	8	11	.421	31	20	8	1	2	168	179	7	79	51	13.9	3.75	73	.287	.369	16	.229	1	-19	-19	-2	-2.3
Total	5	37	35	.514	106	74	47	1	6	646^2	668	18	262	262	13.3	3.33	90	.276	.353	54	.220	1	-26	-24	-0	-2.3
● **ED LAGGER**	Lagger, Edwin Joseph b: 7/14/12, Joliet, Ill. d: 11/10/81, Joliet, Ill. BR/TR, 6'3", 200 lbs. Deb: 6/15/34																									
1934	Phi-A	0	0	—	8	0	0	0	0	18	27	1	14	2	21.0	11.00	40	.342	.447	0	.000	-1	-13	-13	1	0.0
● **LERRIN LaGROW**	LaGrow, Lerrin Harris b: 7/8/48, Phoenix, Ariz. BR/TR, 6'5", 220 lbs. Deb: 7/28/70																									
1970	Det-A	0	1	.000	10	0	0	0	0	12^1	16	2	6	7	16.1	7.30	51	.308	.379	0	.000	-0	-5	-5	-0	-0.4
1972	*Det-A	0	1	.000	16	0	0	0	2	27^1	22	0	6	9	9.2	1.32	239	.222	.267	0	—	0	5	6	-0	0.3
1973	Det-A	1	5	.167	21	3	0	0	3	54	54	8	23	33	13.0	4.33	94	.263	.341	0	—	0	-3	-1	1	-0.2
1974	Det-A	8	19	.296	37	34	11	0	0	216^1	245	21	80	85	13.6	4.66	82	.287	.350	0	—	0	-25	-21	3	-2.2
1975	Det-A	7	14	.333	32	26	7	2	0	164^1	183	15	66	75	13.7	4.38	92	.280	.348	0	—	0	-11	-7	-2	-1.1
1976	StL-N	0	1	.000	8	2	1	0	0	24^1	21	0	7	10	10.7	1.48	239	.241	.305	0	.000	-1	5	6	0	0.2
1977	Chi-A	7	3	.700	66	0	0	0	25	98^2	81	10	35	63	10.7	2.46	166	.230	.302	0	—	0	17	18	1	2.7
1978	Chi-A	6	5	.545	52	0	0	0	16	88	85	9	38	41	12.9	4.40	86	.260	.342	0	—	0	-6	-6	2	-0.8
1979	Chi-A	0	3	.000	11	2	0	0	1	17^2	27	2	16	9	22.4	9.17	46	.346	.463	0	—	0	-10	-10	-0	-1.5
	LA-N	5	1	.833	31	0	0	0	4	37	38	2	18	22	13.6	3.41	107	.270	.352	1	.333	0	1	1	-0	0.2
1980	Phi-N	0	2	.000	25	0	0	0	3	39	42	5	17	21	13.6	4.15	91	.276	.349	1	.250	0	-2	-2	-0	-0.1
Total	10	34	55	.382	309	67	19	2	54	779	814	74	312	375	13.1	4.11	94	.271	.342	2	.154	-0	-33	-21	2	-2.9
● **JEFF LAHTI**	Lahti, Jeffrey Allen b: 10/8/56, Oregon City, Ore. BR/TR, 6', 180 lbs. Deb: 6/27/82																									
1982	*StL-N	5	4	.556	33	1	0	0	0	56^2	53	3	21	22	12.1	3.81	95	.245	.318	1	.077	-1	-1	-1	2	-0.2
1983	StL-N	3	3	.500	53	0	0	0	0	74	64	2	29	26	11.4	3.16	114	.240	.316	0	.000	-1	4	4	1	0.3
1984	StL-N	4	2	.667	63	0	0	0	1	84^2	69	6	34	45	11.2	3.72	93	.225	.306	1	.167	-0	-1	-2	0	-0.1
1985	*StL-N	5	2	.714	52	0	0	0	19	68^1	63	3	26	41	11.7	1.84	192	.251	.321	0	.000	-1	13	13	-0	1.9
1986	StL-N	0	0	—	4	0	0	0	0	2^1	3	0	1	3	15.4	0.00	—	.333	.400	0	—	0	1	1	-0	0.0
Total	5	17	11	.607	205	1	0	0	20	286	252	14	111	137	11.6	3.12	114	.240	.316	2	.053	-3	15	14	2	1.9
● **EDDIE LAKE**	Lake, Edward Erving "Sparky" b: 3/18/16, Antioch, Cal. d: 6/7/95, Castro Valley, Cal. BR/TR, 5'7", 160 lbs. Deb: 9/26/39 ♦																									
1944	Bos-A	0	0	—	6	0	0	0	0	19^1	20	2	11	7	15.8	4.19	81	.278	.395	26	.206	1	-2	-2	0	0.1
● **JOE LAKE**	Lake, Joseph Henry b: 1/6/1881, Brooklyn, N.Y. d: 6/30/50, Brooklyn, N.Y. BR/TR, 6', 185 lbs. Deb: 4/21/08																									
1908	NY-A	9	22	.290	38	27	19	2	0	269^1	252	6	77	118	11.2	3.17	78	.242	.298	21	.188	0	-23	-21	-4	-2.8
1909	NY-A	14	11	.560	31	26	17	3	1	215^1	180	2	59	117	10.2	1.88	135	.225	.283	14	.173	1	14	16	5	2.7
1910	StL-A	11	17	.393	35	29	24	1	2	261^1	243	2	77	141	11.1	2.20	112	.248	.304	21	.231	2	9	8	1	1.2
1911	StL-A	10	15	.400	30	25	14	2	0	215^1	245	3	40	69	12.1	3.30	102	.282	.316	21	.262	2	1	2	6	1.0
1912	StL-A	1	7	.125	11	6	4	0	0	57	70	0	16	28	13.7	4.42	75	.314	.363	3	.150	-1	-7	-7	2	-0.8
	Det-A	9	11	.450	26	14	11	0	1	162^2	190	3	39	86	12.8	3.10	105	.296	.340	9	.145	-3	4	3	0	0.1
	Yr	10	18	.357	37	20	15	0	1	219^2	260	3	55	114	13.0	3.44	95	.301	.345	12	.146	-5	-3	-4	2	-0.7
1913	Det-A	8	7	.533	28	12	6	0	1	137	149	3	24	35	11.4	3.28	89	.278	.309	12	.267	4	-5	-6	3	0.2
Total	6	62	90	.408	199	139	95	8	5	1318	1329	19	332	594	11.5	2.85	99	.261	.309	101	.206	4	-7	-5	12	1.6
● **AL LAKEMAN**	Lakeman, Albert Wesley "Moose" b: 12/31/18, Cincinnati, Ohio d: 5/25/76, Spartanburg, S.C. BR/TR, 6'2", 195 lbs. Deb: 4/19/42 C♦																									
1948	Phi-N	0	0	—	1	0	0	0	0	0^2	1	1	0	0	13.5	13.50	29	.333	.333	11	.162	0	-1	-1	-0	0.0
● **JACK LAMABE**	Lamabe, John Alexander b: 10/3/36, Farmingdale, N.Y. BR/TR, 6'1", 198 lbs. Deb: 4/17/62																									
1962	Pit-N	3	1	.750	46	0	0	0	2	78	70	4	40	56	12.7	2.88	136	.238	.329	0	.000	-1	9	9	1	0.5
1963	Bos-A	7	4	.636	65	2	0	0	6	151^1	139	8	46	93	11.2	3.15	120	.247	.308	3	.094	-1	8	11	1	0.8
1964	Bos-A	9	13	.409	39	25	3	0	1	177^1	235	25	57	109	14.9	5.89	65	.318	.369	6	.115	-1	-45	-40	-0	-4.6
1965	Bos-A	0	3	.000	14	0	0	0	0	25^1	34	5	14	17	18.1	8.17	46	.340	.436	0	.000	-0	-13	-13	0	-1.4
	Hou-N	0	2	.000	3	2	0	0	0	12^2	17	3	3	6	14.2	4.26	79	.315	.351	1	.250	0	-1	-1	-0	-0.2
1966	Chi-A	7	9	.438	34	17	3	2	0	121^1	116	9	35	67	11.3	3.93	81	.251	.305	2	.057	-2	-7	-10	-0	-1.5
1967	Chi-A	1	0	1.000	3	0	0	0	0	5	7	0	1	3	14.4	1.80	172	.318	.348	0	—	0	1	1	0	0.1
	NY-N	0	3	.000	16	2	0	0	1	31^2	24	4	8	23	9.1	3.98	85	.200	.250	0	.000	-0	-2	-2	-0	-0.2
	*StL-N	3	4	.429	23	1	1	1	4	47^2	43	2	10	30	10.0	2.83	116	.244	.285	2	.200	0	3	2	-0	0.4
	Yr	3	7	.300	39	3	1	1	5	79^1	67	6	18	53	9.6	3.29	101	.226	.270	2	.133	-0	1	0	-0	0.2
1968	Chi-N	3	2	.600	42	0	0	0	1	61^1	68	7	24	30	13.6	4.26	74	.289	.358	1	.200	0	-9	-7	-1	-0.6
Total	7	33	41	.446	285	49	7	3	15	711^2	753	67	238	434	12.7	4.24	85	.272	.333	15	.096	-6	-55	-51	0	-6.7
● **AL LaMACCHIA**	LaMacchia, Alfred Anthony b: 7/22/21, St.Louis, Mo. BR/TR, 5'10.5", 190 lbs. Deb: 9/27/43																									
1943	StL-A	0	1	.000	1	1	0	0	0	4	9	0	2	2	24.8	11.25	30	.450	.500	0	.000	-0	-4	-4	-0	-0.6
1945	StL-A	2	0	1.000	5	0	0	0	0	9	6	0	3	2	9.0	2.00	176	.207	.281	0	.000	-0	1	2	0	0.3
1946	StL-A	0	0	—	8	0	0	0	0	15	17	2	7	3	14.4	6.00	62	.279	.353	0	.000	-0	-4	-4	-0	0.0
	Was-A	0	1	.000	2	0	0	0	0	2^2	6	1	2	0	27.0	16.88	20	.462	.533	0	—	0	-4	-4	-0	-1.1
	Yr	0	1	.000	10	0	0	0	0	17^2	23	3	9	3	16.3	7.64	48	.311	.386	0	.000	-0	-8	-8	-0	-1.1
Total	3	2	2	.500	16	1	0	0	0	30^2	38	3	14	7	15.3	6.46	55	.309	.380	0	.000	-1	-10	-10	-1	-1.4
● **FRANK LaMANNA**	LaManna, Frank "Hank" b: 8/22/19, Waterton, Pa. d: 9/1/80, Syracuse, N.Y. BR/TR, 6'2.5", 195 lbs. Deb: 4/16/40																									
1940	Bos-N	1	0	1.000	5	1	1	0	0	13^1	13	1	8	3	14.2	4.73	79	.271	.375	1	.200	0	-1	-1	0	-0.1
1941	Bos-N	5	4	.556	35	4	0	0	1	72^2	77	5	56	23	16.6	5.33	67	.285	.410	9	.281	1	-14	-14	1	-1.4
1942	Bos-N	0	1	.000	5	0	0	0	0	6^2	5	1	3	2	10.8	5.40	62	.208	.296	0	.000	-0	-2	-2	-0	-0.3
Total	3	6	5	.545	45	5	1	0	1	92^2	95	7	67	28	15.8	5.24	68	.278	.398	10	.256	1	-17	-17	1	-1.8

YEAR	TM/L	W	L	PCT	G	GS	CG	SH	SV	IP	H	HR	BB	SO	RAT	ERA	ERA+	OAV	OOB	BH	AVG	PB	PR	/A	PD	TPI
● FRANK LAMANSKE	Lamanske, Frank James “Lefty” b: 9/30/06, Oglesby, Ill. d: 8/4/71, Olney, Ill. BL/TL, 5′11″, 170 lbs. Deb: 4/27/35																									
1935	Bro-N	0	0	—	2	0	0	0	0	3^2	5	0	1	1	14.7	7.36	54	.313	.353	0	.000	-0	-1	-1	0	0.0
● WAYNE LaMASTER	LaMaster, Noble Wayne b: 2/13/07, Speed, Ind. d: 8/4/89, New Albany, Ind. BL/TL, 5′8″, 170 lbs. Deb: 4/19/37																									
1937	Phi-N	15	19	.441	50	30	10	1	4	220^1	255	24	82	135	13.8	5.31	82	.290	.352	15	.190	-2	-34	-24	-4	-3.9
1938	Phi-N	4	7	.364	18	12	1	1	0	63^2	80	8	31	35	16.1	7.77	50	.301	.380	9	.409	4	-28	-27	1	-3.4
	Bro-N	0	1	.000	3	0	0	0	0	11^1	17	0	3	3	15.9	4.76	82	.340	.377	1	.167	-0	-1	-1	-0	-0.1
	Yr	4	8	.333	21	12	1	1	0	75	97	8	34	38	15.7	7.32	53	.304	.371	10	.357	4	-29	-29	1	-3.5
Total	2	19	27	.413	71	42	11	2	4	295^1	352	32	116	173	14.4	5.82	72	.295	.360	25	.234	1	-64	-53	-4	-7.4
● JOHN LAMB	Lamb, John Andrew b: 7/20/46, Sharon, Conn. BR/TR, 6′3″, 180 lbs. Deb: 8/12/70																									
1970	Pit-N	0	1	.000	23	0	0	0	3	32^1	23	2	13	24	10.6	2.78	140	.209	.304	0	.000	-0	5	4	-1	0.1
1971	Pit-N	0	0	—	2	0	0	0	0	4^1	3	0	1	1	8.3	0.00	—	.188	.235	0	.000	-0	2	2	0	0.0
1973	Pit-N	0	1	.000	22	0	0	0	2	29^2	37	3	10	11	14.3	6.07	58	.308	.362	0	.000	-0	-8	-8	0	-0.4
Total	3	0	2	.000	47	0	0	0	5	66^1	63	5	24	36	12.1	4.07	91	.256	.327	0	.000	-1	-2	-3	-1	-0.3
● RAY LAMB	Lamb, Raymond Richard b: 12/28/44, Glendale, Cal. BR/TR, 6′1″, 175 lbs. Deb: 8/1/69																									
1969	LA-N	0	1	.000	10	0	0	0	1	15	12	2	7	11	11.4	1.80	185	.235	.328	0	.000	-0	3	3	0	0.2
1970	LA-N	6	1	.857	35	0	0	0	0	57	59	4	27	32	14.2	3.79	101	.277	.369	0	.000	-0	2	0	-1	-0.1
1971	Cle-A	6	12	.333	43	21	3	1	1	158^1	147	11	69	91	12.3	3.35	114	.247	.326	4	.093	-2	2	8	-2	0.5
1972	Cle-A	5	6	.455	34	9	0	0	0	107^2	101	5	29	64	11.0	3.09	104	.248	.299	0	.000	-1	-0	1	-1	-0.1
1973	Cle-A	3	3	.500	32	1	0	0	2	86	98	7	42	60	14.9	4.60	85	.291	.373	0	—	0	-8	-7	-0	-0.5
Total	5	20	23	.465	154	31	3	1	4	424	417	29	174	258	12.7	3.54	104	.260	.335	4	.058	-4	-1	7	-4	0.0
● CLAYTON LAMBERT	Lambert, Clayton Patrick b: 3/26/17, Summit, Ill. d: 4/3/81, Ogden, Utah BR/TR, 6′2″, 185 lbs. Deb: 4/22/46																									
1946	Cin-N	2	2	.500	23	4	2	0	1	52^2	48	3	20	20	11.8	4.27	78	.251	.325	2	.154	-1	-5	-5	-1	-0.6
1947	Cin-N	0	0	—	3	0	0	0	0	5^2	12	3	6	1	28.6	15.88	26	.444	.545	0	.000	-0	-7	-7	0	0.0
Total	2	2	2	.500	26	4	2	0	1	58^1	60	6	26	21	13.4	5.40	63	.275	.355	2	.143	-1	-12	-13	-1	-0.6
● GENE LAMBERT	Lambert, Eugene Marion b: 4/26/21, Crenshaw, Miss. BR/TR, 5′11″, 175 lbs. Deb: 9/14/41																									
1941	Phi-N	0	1	.000	2	1	0	0	0	9	11	0	2	3	13.0	2.00	185	.297	.333	0	.000	-0	2	2	-0	0.1
1942	Phi-N	0	0	—	1	0	0	0	0	1	3	0	0	1	27.0	9.00	37	.500	.500	0	—	0	-1	-1	0	0.0
Total	2	0	1	.000	3	1	0	0	0	10	14	0	2	4	14.4	2.70	136	.326	.356	0	.000	-0	1	1	0	0.1
● OTIS LAMBETH	Lambeth, Otis Samuel b: 5/13/1890, Berlin, Kan. d: 6/5/76, Moran, Kan. BR/TR, 6′, 175 lbs. Deb: 7/16/16																									
1916	Cle-A	4	4	.500	15	9	3	0	1	74	69	1	38	28	13.4	2.92	103	.256	.354	3	.111	-1	-1	1	-2	-0.3
1917	Cle-A	7	6	.538	26	10	2	0	2	97^1	97	2	30	27	12.8	3.14	90	.274	.349	6	.188	-0	-5	-3	-1	-0.6
1918	Cle-A	0	0	—	2	0	0	0	0	7	10	0	6	3	20.6	6.43	47	.370	.485	1	1.000	0	-3	-3	0	0.0
Total	3	11	10	.524	43	19	5	0	3	178^1	176	3	74	58	13.3	3.18	92	.270	.357	10	.167	-1	-9	-5	-3	-0.9
● FRED LAMLINE	Lamline, Frederick Arthur “Dutch” (b: Frederick Arthur Lamlein) b: 8/14/1887, Port Huron, Mich. d: 9/20/70, Port Huron, Mich. BR/TR, 5′11″, 171 lbs. Deb: 9/18/12																									
1912	Chi-A	0	0	—	1	0	0	0	0	2	7	0	2	1	40.5	31.50	10	.583	.643	0	—	0	-6	-6	0	0.0
1915	StL-N	0	0	—	4	0	0	0	0	19	21	0	3	11	12.3	1.42	196	.300	.347	1	.125	-0	3	3	0	0.0
Total	2	0	0	—	5	0	0	0	0	21	28	0	5	12	15.0	4.29	66	.341	.393	1	.125	-0	-3	-3	0	0.0
● DENNIS LAMP	Lamp, Dennis Patrick b: 9/23/52, Los Angeles, Cal. BR/TR, 6′3″, 210 lbs. Deb: 8/21/77																									
1977	Chi-N	0	2	.000	11	3	0	0	0	30	43	3	8	12	15.9	6.30	70	.344	.393	3	.375	1	-8	-6	0	-0.3
1978	Chi-N	7	15	.318	37	36	6	3	0	223^2	221	16	56	73	11.3	3.30	122	.258	.307	15	.205	0	7	18	3	2.1
1979	Chi-N	11	10	.524	38	32	6	1	0	200^1	223	14	46	86	12.3	3.50	117	.287	.331	9	.155	-1	5	14	4	1.6
1980	Chi-N	10	14	.417	41	37	2	1	0	202^2	259	16	82	83	15.2	5.20	75	.317	.380	6	.098	-3	-36	-29	2	-3.2
1981	Chi-A	7	6	.538	27	10	3	0	0	127	103	4	43	71	10.4	2.41	148	.222	.289	0	—	0	18	16	1	1.7
1982	Chi-A	11	8	.579	44	27	3	2	5	189^2	206	9	59	78	12.9	3.99	101	.279	.337	0	—	0	2	1	2	0.2
1983	*Chi-A	7	7	.500	49	5	1	0	15	116^1	123	6	29	44	12.1	3.71	113	.275	.325	0	—	0	5	6	0	0.8
1984	Tor-A	8	8	.500	56	4	0	0	9	85	97	9	38	45	14.4	4.55	90	.285	.359	0	—	0	-5	-4	1	-0.7
1985	*Tor-A	11	0	1.000	53	1	0	0	2	105^2	96	7	27	68	10.5	3.32	127	.247	.296	0	—	0	10	10	2	1.2
1986	Tor-A	2	6	.250	40	2	0	0	2	73	93	5	23	30	14.3	5.05	83	.309	.358	0	—	0	-7	-7	0	-0.7
1987	Oak-A	1	3	.250	36	5	0	0	0	56^2	76	5	22	36	15.7	5.08	81	.326	.387	0	—	0	-4	-6	-0	-0.1
1988	Bos-A	7	6	.538	46	0	0	0	0	82^2	92	3	19	49	12.3	3.48	118	.284	.328	0	—	0	4	6	1	1.0
1989	Bos-A	4	2	.667	42	0	0	0	2	112^1	96	4	27	61	9.9	2.32	176	.235	.283	0	—	0	19	22	2	1.2
1990	*Bos-A	3	5	.375	47	1	0	0	0	105^2	114	10	30	49	12.5	4.68	87	.279	.333	0	—	0	-9	-7	0	-0.5
1991	Bos-A	6	3	.667	51	0	0	0	0	92	100	8	31	57	13.1	4.70	92	.275	.337	0	—	0	-6	-4	-0	-0.4
1992	Pit-N	1	1	.500	21	0	0	0	0	28	33	3	9	15	14.1	5.14	67	.292	.355	0	.000	-0	-5	-5	0	-0.4
Total	16	96	96	.500	639	163	21	7	35	1830^2	1975	122	549	857	12.6	3.93	103	.278	.333	33	.164	-3	-11	26	18	3.5
● HENRY LAMPE	Lampe, Henry Joseph b: 9/19/1872, Boston, Mass. d: 9/16/36, Dorchester, Mass. BR/TL, 5′11.5″, 175 lbs. Deb: 5/14/1894																									
1894	Bos-N	0	1	.000	2	1	0	0	0	5^1	17	5	7	1	40.5	11.81	48	.531	.615	0	.000	-0	-4	-4	0	-0.4
1895	Phi-N	0	2	.000	7	3	2	0	0	44	68	3	33	18	20.9	7.57	63	.347	.443	2	.125	-1	-14	-14	-0	-0.5
Total	2	0	3	.000	9	4	2	0	0	49^1	85	8	40	19	23.0	8.03	61	.373	.468	2	.111	-1	-17	-17	0	-0.9
● DICK LANAHAN	Lanahan, Richard Anthony b: 9/27/11, Washington, D.C. d: 3/12/75, Rochester, Minn. BL/TL, 6′, 186 lbs. Deb: 9/15/35																									
1935	Was-A	0	3	.000	3	3	0	0	0	20^2	27	2	17	10	20.0	5.66	76	.314	.438	1	.167	-0	-3	-3	-0	-0.4
1937	Was-A	0	1	.000	6	2	0	0	0	11^1	16	2	13	2	23.8	12.71	35	.320	.469	0	.000	0	-10	-10	0	-0.6
1940	Pit-N	6	8	.429	40	8	4	0	2	108	121	8	42	45	13.7	4.25	90	.279	.345	4	.118	-2	-5	-5	0	-0.8
1941	Pit-N	0	1	.000	7	0	0	0	0	12	13	1	3	5	13.5	5.25	69	.283	.353	0	.000	-0	-2	-2	-0	-0.2
Total	4	6	13	.316	56	13	4	0	2	152	177	13	75	62	15.3	5.15	76	.288	.371	5	.119	-2	-20	-21	0	-2.0
● LES LANCASTER	Lancaster, Lester Wayne b: 4/21/62, Dallas, Tex. BR/TR, 6′2″, 200 lbs. Deb: 4/7/87																									
1987	Chi-N	8	3	.727	27	18	0	0	0	132^1	138	14	51	78	12.9	4.90	87	.268	.335	4	.082	-2	-12	-9	-1	-1.0
1988	Chi-N	4	6	.400	44	3	1	0	5	85^2	89	4	34	36	13.0	3.78	95	.273	.343	1	.050	-1	-3	-2	1	-0.3
1989	*Chi-N	4	2	.667	42	0	0	0	8	72^2	60	2	15	56	9.3	1.36	276	.226	.267	2	.182	0	17	**19**	-1	2.0
1990	Chi-N	9	5	.643	55	6	1	1	6	109	121	11	40	65	13.4	4.62	88	.283	.346	1	.050	-1	-10	-7	1	-0.8
1991	Chi-N	9	7	.563	64	11	1	0	3	156	150	13	49	102	11.7	3.52	110	.256	.317	5	.179	0	3	6	-1	0.5
1992	Det-A	3	4	.429	41	1	0	0	0	86^2	101	11	51	35	16.1	6.33	62	.294	.389	0	—	0	-23	-23	-1	-1.7
1993	StL-N	4	1	.800	50	0	0	0	0	61^1	56	5	21	36	11.4	2.93	135	.242	.308	0	.000	-0	8	7	-1	0.4
Total	7	41	28	.594	323	39	3	1	22	703^2	715	60	261	408	12.6	4.05	98	.265	.333	13	.098	-4	-21	-7	-2	-0.9
● GARY LANCE	Lance, Gary Dean b: 9/21/48, Greenville, S.C. BB/TR, 6′3″, 195 lbs. Deb: 9/28/77																									
1977	KC-A	0	1	.000	1	0	0	0	0	2	2	0	2	0	18.0	4.50	90	.286	.444	0	—	0	-0	-0	-0	-0.1
● DOC LANDIS	Landis, Samuel H. b: 8/16/1854, Philadelphia, Pa. BR , 5′11″, 172 lbs. Deb: 5/2/1882																									
1882	Phi-a	1	1	.500	2	2	2	0	0	17	16	1	1	13	9.0	3.18	94	.232	.243	2	.167	-0	-1	-0	-0	-0.1
	Bal-a	11	28	.282	42	40	35	0	0	343	416	7	46	62	12.1	3.38	81	.281	.302	29	.166	-6	-27	-24	-2	-2.8
	Yr	12	29	.293	44	42	37	0	0	360	432	8	47	75	12.0	3.38	82	.278	.300	31	.166	-7	-28	-25	-3	-2.9
● BILL LANDIS	Landis, William Henry b: 10/8/42, Hanford, Cal. BL/TL, 6′2″, 178 lbs. Deb: 9/28/63																									
1963	KC-A	0	0	—	1	0	0	0	0	1^2	0	0	1	3	5.4	0.00	—	.000	.167	0	—	0	1	1	-0	0.0
1967	Bos-A	1	0	1.000	18	1	0	0	0	25^2	24	6	11	23	12.3	5.26	66	.253	.330	0	.000	-0	-6	-5	-1	-0.3
1968	Bos-A	3	3	.500	38	1	0	0	3	60	48	4	30	59	12.0	3.15	100	.223	.324	0	.000	-1	-1	0	-1	-0.2
1969	Bos-A	5	5	.500	45	5	0	0	1	82^1	82	7	49	50	14.6	5.25	72	.269	.375	0	.000	-0	-15	-13	0	-1.5
Total	4	9	8	.529	102	7	0	0	4	169^2	154	17	91	135	13.3	4.46	79	.248	.349	0	.000	-1	-21	-17	-2	-2.0

YEAR TM/L	W	L	PCT	G	GS	CG	SH	SV	IP	H	HR	BB	SO	RAT	ERA	ERA+	OAV	OOB	BH	AVG	PB	PR	/A	PD	TPI
● **LARRY LANDRETH** Landreth, Larry Robert b: 3/11/55, Stratford, Ont., Can BR/TR, 6'1", 175 lbs. Deb: 9/16/76																									
1976 Mon-N	1	2	.333	3	3	0	0	0	11	13	1	10	7	18.8	4.09	91	.310	.442	0	.000	-0	-1	-0	-0	-0.2
1977 Mon-N	0	2	.000	4	1	0	0	0	9^{1}	16	0	8	5	23.1	9.64	39	.381	.480	0	.000	-0	-6	-6	-0	-1.1
Total 2	1	4	.200	7	4	0	0	0	20^{1}	29	1	18	12	20.8	6.64	57	.345	.461	0	.000	-1	-7	-6	-1	-1.3
● **JOE LANDRUM** Landrum, Joseph Butler b: 12/13/28, Columbia, S.C. BR/TR, 5'11", 180 lbs. Deb: 7/13/50 F																									
1950 Bro-N	0	0	—	7	0	0	0	1	6^{2}	12	2	1	5	18.9	8.10	51	.414	.452	0	—	0	-3	-3	0	-0.1
1952 Bro-N	1	3	.250	9	5	2	0	0	38	46	3	10	17	13.5	5.21	70	.301	.348	1	.125	-0	-6	-7	-0	-0.7
Total 2	1	3	.250	16	5	2	0	1	44^{2}	58	5	11	22	14.3	5.64	66	.319	.364	1	.125	-0	-9	-10	0	-0.8
● **BILL LANDRUM** Landrum, Thomas William b: 8/17/57, Columbia, S.C. BR/TR, 6'2", 200 lbs. Deb: 8/31/86 F																									
1986 Cin-N	0	0	—	10	0	0	0	0	13^{1}	23	0	4	14	18.2	6.75	57	.390	.429	0	.000	-0	-4	-4	-0	0.0
1987 Cin-N	3	2	.600	44	2	0	0	2	65	68	3	34	42	14.1	4.71	90	.292	.382	1	.200	0	-5	-3	1	-0.2
1988 Chi-N	1	0	1.000	7	0	0	0	0	12^{1}	19	1	3	6	16.1	5.84	62	.365	.400	0	.000	-0	-3	-3	-0	-0.3
1989 Pit-N	2	3	.400	56	0	0	0	26	81	60	2	28	51	9.8	1.67	201	.205	.275	0	.000	-0	16	15	-0	1.8
1990 *Pit-N	7	3	.700	54	0	0	0	13	71^{2}	69	4	21	39	11.3	2.13	169	.262	.317	1	.111	0	13	12	-0	2.0
1991 *Pit-N	4	4	.500	61	0	0	0	17	76^{1}	76	4	19	45	11.2	3.18	112	.252	.297	0	.000	-0	4	3	-1	0.3
1992 Mon-N	1	1	.500	18	0	0	0	0	20	27	3	9	7	17.1	7.20	48	.325	.404	0	—	0	-8	-8	-0	-0.8
1993 Cin-N	0	2	.000	18	0	0	0	0	21^{2}	18	1	6	14	10.0	3.74	108	.231	.286	0	—	0	1	1	1	0.1
Total 8	18	15	.545	268	2	0	0	58	361^{1}	360	18	124	218	12.1	3.39	109	.265	.327	2	.080	-1	14	12	-0	2.9
● **JERRY LANE** Lane, Gerald Hal b: 2/7/26, Ashland, N.Y. d: 7/24/88, Chattanooga, Tenn BR/TR, 6'0.5", 205 lbs. Deb: 7/7/53																									
1953 Was-A	1	4	.200	20	2	0	0	0	56^{2}	64	3	16	26	12.9	4.92	79	.288	.339	1	.111	0	-6	-6	-0	-0.5
1954 Cin-N	1	0	1.000	3	0	0	0	0	10^{2}	9	0	3	2	10.1	1.69	248	.237	.293	0	.000	-0	3	3	-1	0.2
1955 Cin-N	0	2	.000	8	0	0	0	1	11	11	2	6	5	13.9	4.91	86	.289	.386	0	—	0	-1	-1	0	-0.1
Total 3	2	6	.250	31	2	0	0	1	78^{1}	84	5	25	33	12.6	4.48	89	.282	.340	1	.077	0	-4	-4	-1	-0.4
● **SAM LANFORD** Lanford, Lewis Grover b: 1/8/1886, Woodruff, S.C. d: 9/14/70, Woodruff, S.C. BR/TR, 5'9", 155 lbs. Deb: 8/19/07																									
1907 Was-A	0	1	.000	2	1	0	0	0	7	10	0	5	2	23.1	5.14	47	.333	.474	1	.333	0	-2	-2	-0	-0.3
● **WALT LANFRANCONI** Lanfranconi, Walter Oswald b: 11/9/16, Barre, Vt. d: 8/18/86, Barre, Vt. BR/TR, 5'7.5", 155 lbs. Deb: 9/12/41																									
1941 Chi-N	0	1	.000	2	1	0	0	0	6	7	0	2	1	13.5	3.00	117	.280	.333	0	.000	-0	0	0	-0	0.0
1947 Bos-N	4	4	.500	36	4	1	0	1	64	65	2	27	18	12.9	2.95	132	.272	.346	0	.000	-1	**8**	**7**	1	0.8
Total 2	4	5	.444	38	5	1	0	1	70	72	2	29	19	13.0	2.96	131	.273	.345	0	.000	-1	8	7	1	0.8
● **MARTY LANG** Lang, Martin John b: 9/27/05, Hooper, Neb. d: 1/13/68, Lakewood, Colo. BR/TL, 5'11", 160 lbs. Deb: 7/4/30																									
1930 Pit-N	0	0	—	2	0	0	0	0	1^{2}	9	2	3	2	64.8	54.00	9	.692	.750	0	—	0	-9	-9	-0	0.0
● **CHIP LANG** Lang, Robert David b: 8/21/52, Pittsburgh, Pa. BR/TR, 6'4", 205 lbs. Deb: 9/8/75																									
1975 Mon-N	0	0	—	1	1	0	0	0	1^{2}	2	0	3	2	27.0	10.80	35	.333	.556	0	—	0	-1	-1	-0	0.0
1976 Mon-N	1	3	.250	29	2	0	0	0	62^{1}	56	3	34	30	13.4	4.19	89	.242	.347	1	.167	-0	-5	-3	0	-0.2
Total 2	1	3	.250	30	3	0	0	0	64	58	3	37	32	13.8	4.36	85	.245	.354	1	.167	-0	-6	-5	0	-0.2
● **ERV LANGE** Lange, Erwin Henry b: 8/12/1887, Forest Park, Ill. d: 4/24/71, Maywood, Ill. BR/TR, 5'10", 170 lbs. Deb: 4/19/14																									
1914 Chi-F	12	11	.522	36	22	10	2	2	190	162	3	55	87	10.4	2.23	119	.224	.282	9	.176	2	14	9	-3	0.9
● **FRANK LANGE** Lange, Frank Herman "Seagan" b: 10/28/1883, Columbia, Wis. d: 12/26/45, Madison, Wis. BR/TR, 5'11", 180 lbs. Deb: 5/16/10																									
1910 Chi-A	9	4	.692	23	15	6	1	0	130^{2}	93	2	54	98	10.7	1.65	145	.204	.301	13	.255	3	13	11	-2	1.2
1911 Chi-A	8	8	.500	29	22	8	1	0	161^{2}	151	3	77	104	12.9	3.23	100	.251	.339	22	.289	8	2	-0	-1	0.7
1912 Chi-A	10	10	.500	31	20	11	2	3	165^{1}	165	4	68	96	12.9	3.27	98	.270	.347	14	.215	2	1	1	-1	0.0
1913 Chi-A	1	3	.250	12	3	0	0	0	40^{2}	46	0	20	20	14.8	4.87	60	.295	.379	3	.167	1	-9	-9	1	-0.6
Total 4	28	25	.528	95	60	25	4	3	498^{1}	455	9	219	318	12.5	2.96	100	.249	.335	52	.248	14	7	1	-2	1.3
● **DICK LANGE** Lange, Richard Otto b: 9/1/48, Harbor Beach, Mich. BR/TR, 5'10", 185 lbs. Deb: 9/9/72																									
1972 Cal-A	0	0	—	2	1	0	0	0	7^{2}	7	0	2	8	10.6	4.70	62	.233	.281	0	.000	-0	-1	-2	0	0.0
1973 Cal-A	2	1	.667	17	4	1	0	0	52^{2}	61	9	21	27	14.2	4.44	80	.292	.359	0	—	0	-4	-5	0	-0.3
1974 Cal-A	3	8	.273	21	18	1	0	0	113^{2}	111	10	47	57	12.8	3.80	90	.248	.325	0	—	0	-2	-5	-1	-0.5
1975 Cal-A	4	6	.400	30	8	1	0	1	102	119	12	53	45	15.3	5.21	68	.292	.374	0	—	0	-16	-19	-0	-1.7
Total 4	9	15	.375	70	31	3	0	1	276	298	31	123	137	13.9	4.47	78	.272	.349	0	.000	-0	-24	-30	-1	-2.5
● **RICK LANGFORD** Langford, James Rick b: 3/20/52, Farmville, Va. BR/TR, 6', 180 lbs. Deb: 6/13/76																									
1976 Pit-N	0	1	.000	12	1	0	0	0	23	27	2	14	17	16.0	6.26	56	.307	.402	1	.200	0	-7	-7	0	-0.2
1977 Oak-A	8	19	.296	37	31	6	1	0	208^{1}	223	18	73	141	12.9	4.02	100	.273	.334	0	—	0	1	0	1	0.1
1978 Oak-A	7	13	.350	37	24	4	2	0	175^{2}	169	15	56	92	11.7	3.43	106	.253	.314	0	—	0	6	4	1	0.6
1979 Oak-A	12	16	.429	34	29	14	1	0	218^{2}	233	22	57	101	12.1	4.28	94	.273	.322	0	—	0	-2	-6	2	0.0
1980 Oak-A	19	12	.613	35	33	**28**	2	0	**290**	276	29	64	102	10.6	3.26	116	.255	.297	0	—	0	25	16	1	2.2
1981 *Oak-A	12	10	.545	24	24	**18**	2	0	195^{1}	190	14	58	84	11.6	2.99	116	.255	.311	0	—	0	14	10	-2	1.0
1982 Oak-A	11	16	.407	32	31	15	2	0	237^{1}	265	33	49	79	12.0	4.21	93	.281	.318	0	.000	-0	-4	-8	1	-0.8
1983 Oak-A	0	4	.000	7	7	0	0	0	20	43	4	10	2	24.7	12.15	32	.448	.509	0	—	0	-18	-18	-0	-2.7
1984 Oak-A	0	0	—	3	2	0	0	0	8^{2}	15	2	2	2	17.7	8.31	45	.366	.395	0	—	0	-4	-4	-0	0.0
1985 Oak-A	3	5	.375	23	3	0	0	0	59	60	8	15	21	11.4	3.51	110	.261	.306	0	—	0	4	2	-0	0.3
1986 Oak-A	1	10	.091	16	11	0	0	0	55	69	13	18	30	14.4	7.36	53	.300	.353	0	—	0	-19	-21	-1	-3.5
Total 11	73	106	.408	260	196	85	10	0	1491	1570	160	416	671	12.1	4.01	95	.271	.322	1	.167	0	-3	-32	3	-3.0
● **MARK LANGSTON** Langston, Mark Edward b: 8/20/60, San Diego, Cal. BR/TL, 6'2", 190 lbs. Deb: 4/7/84																									
1984 Sea-A	17	10	.630	35	33	5	2	0	225	188	16	118	**204**	12.6	3.40	117	.230	.332	0	—	0	15	15	1	1.8
1985 Sea-A	7	14	.333	24	24	2	0	0	126^{2}	122	22	91	72	15.3	5.47	77	.255	.376	0	—	0	-19	-18	2	-2.3
1986 Sea-A	12	14	.462	37	36	9	0	0	239^{1}	234	30	123	**245**	13.6	4.85	87	.255	.346	0	—	0	-18	-16	-1	-1.6
1987 Sea-A★	19	13	.594	35	35	14	3	0	272	242	30	114	**262**	11.9	3.84	123	.238	.318	0	—	0	19	27	1	2.7
1988 Sea-A	15	11	.577	35	35	9	3	0	261^{1}	222	32	110	235	11.5	3.34	125	.233	.314	0	—	0	18	24	3	2.5
1989 Sea-A	4	5	.444	10	10	2	1	0	73^{1}	60	3	19	60	10.2	3.56	113	.221	.282	0	—	0	3	4	-0	0.3
Mon-N	12	9	.571	24	24	6	4	0	176^{2}	138	13	93	175	11.8	2.39	147	.218	.318	11	.172	0	22	22	-0	2.7
1990 Cal-A	10	17	.370	33	33	5	1	0	223	215	13	104	195	13.1	4.40	87	.259	.345	0	—	0	-12	-14	2	-1.3
1991 Cal-A☆	19	8	.704	34	34	7	0	0	246^{1}	190	30	96	183	10.5	3.00	137	.215	.293	0	—	0	30	30	1	3.2
1992 Cal-A★	13	14	.481	32	32	9	2	0	229	206	14	74	174	11.2	3.66	109	.242	.307	0	.000	-0	7	8	2	1.1
1993 Cal-A★	16	11	.593	35	35	7	0	0	256^{1}	220	22	85	196	10.7	3.20	141	.234	.298	0	—	0	32	37	3	3.9
1994 Cal-A	7	8	.467	18	18	2	1	0	119^{1}	121	19	54	109	13.2	4.68	105	.268	.346	0	—	0	2	3	2	0.5
1995 Cal-A	15	7	.682	31	31	2	1	0	200^{1}	212	21	64	142	12.5	4.63	101	.272	.330	0	—	0	2	1	2	0.4
1996 Cal-A	6	5	.545	18	18	2	0	0	123^{1}	116	18	45	83	11.9	4.82	104	.247	.316	0	—	0	2	3	2	0.4
1997 Ana-A	2	4	.333	9	9	0	0	0	47^{2}	61	8	29	30	17.0	5.85	78	.316	.405	0	—	0	-7	-7	1	-0.6
1998 *SD-N	4	6	.400	22	16	0	0	0	81^{1}	107	11	41	56	16.5	5.86	65	.325	.402	2	.083	-0	-15	-18	-1	-1.9
Total 15	178	156	.533	432	423	81	18	0	2901	2654	302	1260	2421	12.3	3.94	108	.245	.327	13	.144	-1	81	100	21	11.8
● **MAX LANIER** Lanier, Hubert Max b: 8/18/15, Denton, N.C. BR/TL, 5'10", 187 lbs. Deb: 4/20/38 F																									
1938 StL-N	0	3	.000	18	3	1	0	0	45	57	1	28	14	17.4	4.20	94	.317	.414	1	.100	-0	-2	-1	-0	-0.1
1939 StL-N	2	1	.667	7	6	2	0	0	37^{2}	29	0	13	14	10.3	2.39	172	.220	.295	4	.286	1	6	7	-0	0.6
1940 StL-N	9	6	.600	35	11	4	2	3	105	113	1	38	49	13.0	3.34	119	.276	.339	6	.200	-0	6	8	1	1.1
1941 StL-N	10	8	.556	35	18	8	2	3	153	126	4	59	93	10.9	2.82	133	.225	.300	10	.192	-1	14	16	2	2.0
1942 *StL-N	13	8	.619	34	20	8	2	2	161	137	4	60	93	11.1	2.96	116	.234	.308	12	.255	2	6	8	1	1.4
1943 *StL-N☆	15	7	.682	32	25	14	2	3	213^{1}	195	3	75	123	11.5	1.90	**177**	.246	.312	12	.164	-2	**35**	**35**	0	3.5
1944 *StL-N†	17	12	.586	33	30	16	5	0	224^{1}	192	5	71	141	10.7	2.65	133	.234	.297	14	.182	-0	24	22	-0	2.6
1945 StL-N	2	2	.500	4	3	3	0	0	26	22	0	8	16	10.4	1.73	216	.222	.280	2	.182	-0	6	6	-0	0.8

YEAR	TM/L	W	L	PCT	G	GS	CG	SH	SV	IP	H	HR	BB	SO	RAT	ERA	ERA+	OAV	OOB	BH	AVG	PB	PR	/A	PD	TPI
1946	StL-N	6	0	1.000	6	6	6	2	0	56	45	1	19	36	10.4	1.93	179	.228	.300	5	.200	-0	9	9	-0	1.0
1949	StL-N	5	4	.556	15	15	4	1	0	92	92	5	35	37	12.4	3.82	109	.261	.328	2	.074	-2	2	4	-1	0.1
1950	StL-N	11	9	.550	27	27	10	2	0	181^1	173	13	68	89	12.0	3.13	137	.249	.317	11	.162	-1	20	24	0	2.3
1951	StL-N	11	9	.550	31	23	9	2	1	160	149	14	50	59	11.2	3.26	122	.248	.306	8	.151	-2	12	12	0	1.3
1952	NY-N	7	12	.368	37	16	6	1	5	137	124	11	65	47	12.6	3.94	94	.244	.333	11	.268	3	-3	-4	3	0.0
1953	NY-N	0	0	—	3	0	0	0	0	5^1	8	1	3	2	18.6	6.75	64	.381	.458	0	.000	-0	-1	-1	0	0.0
	StL-A	0	1	.000	10	1	0	0	0	22^1	28	2	19	8	18.9	7.25	58	.322	.443	1	.167	-0	-8	-8	-0	-0.3
Total	14	108	82	.568	327	204	91	21	17	1619^1	1490	65	611	821	11.8	3.01	125	.247	.318	99	.185	-3	127	136	5	16.3

● FRANK LANKFORD Lankford, Frank Greenfield b: 3/26/71, Atlanta, Ga. BR/TR, 6'2", 190 lbs. Deb: 3/31/98

YEAR	TM/L	W	L	PCT	G	GS	CG	SH	SV	IP	H	HR	BB	SO	RAT	ERA	ERA+	OAV	OOB	BH	AVG	PB	PR	/A	PD	TPI
1998	LA-N	0	2	.000	12	0	0	0	1	19^2	23	2	7	7	14.6	5.95	65	.287	.360	0	.000	-0	-4	-4	1	-0.3

● JOHNNY LANNING Lanning, John Young "Tobacco Chewin' Johnny"
b: 9/6/10, Asheville, N.C. d: 11/8/89, Asheville, N.C. BR/TR, 6'1", 185 lbs. Deb: 4/17/36 F

YEAR	TM/L	W	L	PCT	G	GS	CG	SH	SV	IP	H	HR	BB	SO	RAT	ERA	ERA+	OAV	OOB	BH	AVG	PB	PR	/A	PD	TPI
1936	Bos-N	7	11	.389	28	20	3	1	0	153	154	9	55	33	12.3	3.65	105	.263	.326	7	.135	-2	6	3	-2	0.0
1937	Bos-N	5	7	.417	32	11	4	1	2	116^2	107	10	40	37	11.4	3.93	91	.236	.300	4	.121	-1	-0	-5	-0	-0.5
1938	Bos-N	8	7	.533	32	18	4	1	0	138	146	5	52	39	13.0	3.72	92	.267	.332	9	.188	-1	1	-4	-1	-0.6
1939	Bos-N	5	6	.455	37	6	3	0	4	129	120	6	53	45	12.2	3.42	108	.252	.329	6	.143	-1	7	4	0	0.2
1940	Pit-N	8	4	.667	38	7	2	0	2	115^2	119	8	39	42	12.3	4.05	94	.268	.327	7	.200	1	-3	-3	-0	-0.2
1941	Pit-N	11	11	.500	34	23	9	0	1	175^2	175	6	47	41	11.4	3.13	116	.256	.304	6	.107	-2	10	9	1	1.1
1942	Pit-N	6	8	.429	34	8	2	1	1	119^1	125	7	26	31	11.5	3.32	102	.274	.314	4	.138	-0	-0	1	-0	0.0
1943	Pit-N	4	1	.800	12	2	0	0	2	27	23	0	9	11	10.7	2.33	149	.223	.286	1	.167	-0	3	3	-1	0.6
1945	Pit-N	0	0	—	1	0	0	0	0	2	8	1	0	0	36.0	36.00	11	.571	.571	0	—	0	-7	-7	0	0.0
1946	Pit-N	4	5	.444	27	9	3	0	1	91	97	3	31	16	12.8	3.07	115	.269	.329	3	.143	-0	3	5	1	0.5
1947	Bos-N	0	0	—	3	0	0	0	0	3^2	4	0	6	0	24.5	9.82	40	.400	.625	0	—	0	-2	-2	0	0.0
Total	11	58	60	.492	278	104	30	4	13	1071	1078	55	358	295	12.1	3.58	101	.261	.321	47	.146	-7	19	5	-1	1.1

● RED LANNING Lanning, Lester Alfred b: 5/13/1895, Harvard, Ill. d: 6/13/62, Bristol, Conn. BL/TL, 5'9", 165 lbs. Deb: 6/20/16 ♦

YEAR	TM/L	W	L	PCT	G	GS	CG	SH	SV	IP	H	HR	BB	SO	RAT	ERA	ERA+	OAV	OOB	BH	AVG	PB	PR	/A	PD	TPI
1916	Phi-A	0	3	.000	6	3	1	0	0	24^1	38	1	17	9	21.1	8.14	35	.362	.460	6	.182	1	-14	-14	0	-1.4

● TOM LANNING Lanning, Thomas Newton b: 4/22/07, Asheville, N.C. d: 11/4/67, Marietta, Ga. BL/TL, 6'1", 165 lbs. Deb: 9/14/38 F

YEAR	TM/L	W	L	PCT	G	GS	CG	SH	SV	IP	H	HR	BB	SO	RAT	ERA	ERA+	OAV	OOB	BH	AVG	PB	PR	/A	PD	TPI
1938	Phi-N	0	1	.000	3	1	0	0	0	7	9	0	2	2	14.1	6.43	60	.300	.344	1	1.000	0	-2	-2	-0	-0.2

● GENE LANSING Lansing, Eugene Hewitt "Jigger" b: 1/11/1898, Albany, N.Y. d: 1/18/45, Rensselaer, N.Y. BR/TR, 6'1", 185 lbs. Deb: 4/27/22

YEAR	TM/L	W	L	PCT	G	GS	CG	SH	SV	IP	H	HR	BB	SO	RAT	ERA	ERA+	OAV	OOB	BH	AVG	PB	PR	/A	PD	TPI
1922	Bos-N	0	1	.000	15	1	0	0	0	40^2	46	1	22	14	15.0	5.98	67	.301	.389	0	.000	-1	-8	-9	-0	-0.3

● PAUL LaPALME LaPalme, Paul Edmore "Lefty" b: 12/14/23, Springfield, Mass. BL/TL, 5'10", 184 lbs. Deb: 5/28/51

YEAR	TM/L	W	L	PCT	G	GS	CG	SH	SV	IP	H	HR	BB	SO	RAT	ERA	ERA+	OAV	OOB	BH	AVG	PB	PR	/A	PD	TPI
1951	Pit-N	1	5	.167	22	8	1	1	0	54^1	79	6	31	24	18.4	6.29	67	.333	.413	1	.100	-0	-14	-12	-1	-1.3
1952	Pit-N	1	2	.333	31	2	0	0	0	59^2	56	6	37	25	14.2	3.92	102	.253	.363	1	.100	-0	-1	0	1	0.0
1953	Pit-N	8	16	.333	35	24	7	1	2	176^1	191	20	64	86	13.0	4.59	97	.272	.333	5	.085	-5	-6	-2	-2	-0.9
1954	Pit-N	4	10	.286	33	15	2	0	0	120^2	147	15	54	57	15.0	5.52	76	.302	.372	5	.143	-0	-19	-18	-0	-1.8
1955	StL-N	4	3	.571	56	0	0	0	3	91^2	76	10	34	39	10.9	2.75	148	.228	.301	4	.211	0	13	13	1	1.1
1956	StL-N	0	0	—	1	0	0	0	0	0^2	4	0	2	0	81.0	81.00	5	.667	.750	0	—	0	-6	-6	-0	0.0
	Cin-N	2	4	.333	11	2	0	0	0	27	26	7	4	4	10.0	4.67	85	.257	.286	2	.500	1	-3	-2	-0	-0.3
	Yr	2	4	.333	12	2	0	0	0	27^2	30	7	6	4	11.7	6.51	61	.280	.319	2	.500	1	-8	-8	-0	-0.3
	Chi-A	3	1	.750	29	0	0	0	2	45^2	31	2	27	23	11.4	2.36	173	.195	.312	0	.000	-1	9	9	1	0.7
1957	Chi-A	1	4	.200	35	0	0	0	7	40^1	35	5	19	19	12.3	3.35	112	.235	.325	2	.500	1	2	2	1	0.5
Total	7	24	45	.348	253	51	10	2	14	616^1	645	71	272	277	13.4	4.42	95	.269	.345	20	.136	-4	-25	-16	-0	-2.0

● ANDY LAPIHUSKA Lapihuska, Andrew "Apples" b: 11/1/22, Delmont, N.J. d: 2/17/96, Millville, R.I. BL/TR, 5'10.5", 175 lbs. Deb: 9/12/42

YEAR	TM/L	W	L	PCT	G	GS	CG	SH	SV	IP	H	HR	BB	SO	RAT	ERA	ERA+	OAV	OOB	BH	AVG	PB	PR	/A	PD	TPI
1942	Phi-N	0	2	.000	3	2	0	0	0	20^2	17	0	13	8	13.9	5.23	63	.221	.348	2	.286	0	-4	-4	0	-0.3
1943	Phi-N	0	0	—	1	0	0	0	0	2^1	5	1	3	0	30.9	23.14	15	.417	.533	0	.000	-0	-5	-5	-0	0.0
Total	2	0	2	.000	4	2	0	0	0	23	22	1	16	8	15.7	7.04	47	.247	.374	2	.222	0	-10	-10	0	-0.3

● DAVE LaPOINT LaPoint, David Jeffrey b: 7/29/59, Glens Falls, N.Y. BL/TL, 6'3", 215 lbs. Deb: 9/10/80

YEAR	TM/L	W	L	PCT	G	GS	CG	SH	SV	IP	H	HR	BB	SO	RAT	ERA	ERA+	OAV	OOB	BH	AVG	PB	PR	/A	PD	TPI
1980	Mil-A	1	0	1.000	5	3	0	0	1	15	17	2	13	5	18.0	6.00	64	.293	.423	0	—	0	-3	-4	-1	-0.1
1981	StL-N	1	0	1.000	3	2	0	0	0	10^2	12	1	2	4	12.7	4.22	84	.293	.341	0	.000	-1	-1	-1	0	-0.1
1982	*StL-N	9	3	.750	42	21	0	0	0	152^2	170	8	52	81	13.3	3.42	106	.290	.350	2	.053	-3	3	3	-3	-0.4
1983	StL-N	12	9	.571	37	29	1	0	0	191^1	191	12	84	113	13.1	3.95	92	.267	.347	9	.153	1	-7	-7	-1	-0.7
1984	StL-N	12	10	.545	33	33	2	1	0	193	205	9	77	130	13.2	3.96	88	.278	.347	4	.068	-3	-8	-11	-2	-1.6
1985	SF-N	7	17	.292	31	31	2	1	0	206^2	215	18	74	122	12.6	3.57	96	.269	.331	10	.167	2	0	-3	-2	-0.4
1986	Det-A	3	6	.333	16	8	0	0	0	67^2	85	11	32	36	15.6	5.72	72	.307	.379	0	—	0	-12	-12	-1	-1.4
	SD-N	1	4	.200	24	4	0	0	0	61^1	67	8	24	41	13.5	4.26	86	.276	.343	0	.000	-1	-4	-4	-0	-0.4
1987	StL-N	1	1	.500	6	2	0	0	0	16	26	4	5	8	17.4	6.75	62	.351	.392	0	.000	-0	-5	-5	0	-0.5
	Chi-A	6	3	.667	14	12	2	1	0	82^2	69	7	31	43	11.0	2.94	156	.224	.297	0	—	0	14	15	2	1.5
1988	Chi-A	10	11	.476	25	25	1	1	0	161^1	151	10	47	79	11.2	3.40	117	.245	.300	0	—	0	10	10	-2	1.0
	Pit-N	4	2	.667	8	8	1	0	0	52	54	4	10	19	11.1	2.77	123	.271	.306	1	.063	-1	4	4	0	0.3
1989	NY-A	6	9	.400	20	20	0	0	0	113^2	146	12	45	51	15.3	5.62	69	.310	.373	0	—	0	-22	-22	-2	-2.6
1990	NY-A	7	10	.412	28	27	2	0	0	157^2	180	11	57	67	13.6	4.11	97	.292	.353	0	—	0	-4	-2	-0	-0.3
1991	Phi-N	0	1	.000	2	2	0	0	0	5	10	0	6	3	30.6	16.20	23	.435	.567	0	.000	-0	-7	-7	0	-1.0
Total	12	80	86	.482	294	227	11	4	1	1486^2	1598	117	559	802	13.2	4.02	93	.277	.343	26	.104	-6	-40	-46	-12	-6.7

● ANDY LARKIN Larkin, Andrew Dane b: 6/27/74, Chelan, Wash. BR/TR, 6'4", 180 lbs. Deb: 9/29/96

YEAR	TM/L	W	L	PCT	G	GS	CG	SH	SV	IP	H	HR	BB	SO	RAT	ERA	ERA+	OAV	OOB	BH	AVG	PB	PR	/A	PD	TPI
1996	Fla-N	0	0	—	1	1	0	0	0	5	3	0	4	2	14.4	1.80	226	.176	.364	0	.000	-0	1	1	-0	0.0
1998	Fla-N	3	8	.273	17	14	0	0	0	74^2	101	12	55	43	19.3	9.64	42	.329	.437	4	.138	-1	-45	-46	-0	-5.2
Total	2	3	8	.273	18	15	0	0	0	79^2	104	12	59	45	19.0	9.15	45	.321	.433	4	.129	-1	-44	-45	-0	-5.2

● TERRY LARKIN Larkin, Frank S. d: 9/16/1894, Brooklyn, N.Y. BR/TR, Deb: 5/20/1876 ♦

YEAR	TM/L	W	L	PCT	G	GS	CG	SH	SV	IP	H	HR	BB	SO	RAT	ERA	ERA+	OAV	OOB	BH	AVG	PB	PR	/A	PD	TPI
1876	NY-N	0	1	.000	1	1	1	0	0	9	9	0	0	0	9.0	3.00	71	.231	.231	0	.000	-1	-1	-1	-0	-0.1
1877	Har-N	29	25	.537	56	56	55	4	0	501	510	2	53	96	10.1	2.14	114	**.245**	.264	52	.228	6	37	16	-1	1.8
1878	Chi-N	29	26	.527	56	56	56	1	0	506	511	4	31	163	9.6	2.24	108	.246	.257	65	.288	13	4	10	-4	1.8
1879	Chi-N	31	23	.574	58	58	57	4	0	513^1	514	5	30	142	9.5	2.44	105	.240	**.250**	50	.219	1	3	7	-7	0.1
1880	Tro-N	0	5	.000	5	5	3	0	0	38	83	1	10	5	22.0	8.76	29	.421	.449	3	.150	-0	-27	-26	0	-2.4
Total	5	89	80	.527	176	176	172	9	0	1567^1	1627	12	124	406	10.1	2.43	102	.249	.263	215	.235	19	17	9	-12	1.2

● PAT LARKIN Larkin, Patrick Clibborn b: 6/14/60, Arcadia, Cal. BL/TL, 6', 180 lbs. Deb: 7/16/83

YEAR	TM/L	W	L	PCT	G	GS	CG	SH	SV	IP	H	HR	BB	SO	RAT	ERA	ERA+	OAV	OOB	BH	AVG	PB	PR	/A	PD	TPI
1983	SF-N	0	0	—	5	0	0	0	0	10^1	13	1	3	6	15.7	4.35	81	.317	.391	0	.000	-0	-1	-1	-0	0.0

● STEVE LARKIN Larkin, Stephen Patrick b: 12/9/10, Cincinnati, Ohio d: 5/2/69, Norristown, Pa. BR/TR, 6'1", 195 lbs. Deb: 5/6/34

YEAR	TM/L	W	L	PCT	G	GS	CG	SH	SV	IP	H	HR	BB	SO	RAT	ERA	ERA+	OAV	OOB	BH	AVG	PB	PR	/A	PD	TPI
1934	Det-A	0	0	—	2	1	0	0	0	6	8	0	5	8	19.5	1.50	293	.296	.406	1	.333	1	2	2	0	0.1

● DAVE LaROCHE LaRoche, David Eugene b: 5/14/48, Colorado Springs, Colo. BL/TL, 6'2", 200 lbs. Deb: 5/11/70 C

YEAR	TM/L	W	L	PCT	G	GS	CG	SH	SV	IP	H	HR	BB	SO	RAT	ERA	ERA+	OAV	OOB	BH	AVG	PB	PR	/A	PD	TPI
1970	Cal-A	4	1	.800	38	0	0	0	4	49^2	41	6	21	44	12.0	3.44	105	.224	.317	2	.250	1	1	1	0	0.2
1971	Cal-A	5	1	.833	56	0	0	0	9	72	55	3	27	63	10.4	2.50	129	.212	.289	1	.091	-0	8	6	-1	0.5
1972	Min-A	5	7	.417	62	0	0	0	10	95^1	72	9	39	79	11.0	2.83	113	.209	.300	1	.091	0	2	4	0	0.7
1973	Chi-N	4	1	.800	45	0	0	0	4	54^1	55	7	29	34	14.1	5.80	68	.274	.368	2	.500	1	-13	-11	1	-0.9
1974	Chi-N	5	6	.455	49	4	0	0	5	92	103	9	47	49	15.0	4.79	80	.286	.373	9	.333	3	-12	-10	-0	-1.0
1975	Cle-A	5	3	.625	61	0	0	0	17	82^1	61	5	57	94	13.1	2.19	173	.210	.344	0	—	0	15	15	1	2.1
1976	Cle-A☆	1	4	.200	61	0	0	0	21	96^1	57	2	49	104	10.0	2.24	156	.175	.285	0	—	0	14	13	-1	1.3
1977	Cle-A	2	2	.500	13	0	0	0	4	18^2	15	3	7	18	10.6	5.30	74	.234	.310	0	—	0	-3	-3	-0	-0.6
	Cal-A★	6	5	.545	46	0	0	0	13	81^1	64	8	37	61	11.4	3.10	126	.218	.310	0	—	0	9	7	-0	1.2
	Yr	8	7	.533	59	0	0	0	17	100	79	11	44	79	11.3	3.51	112	.220	.309	0	—	0	6	5	-0	0.6

YEAR	TM/L	W	L	PCT	G	GS	CG	SH	SV	IP	H	HR	BB	SO	RAT	ERA	ERA+	OAV	OOB	BH	AVG	PB	PR	/A	PD	TPI
1978	Cal-A	10	9	.526	59	0	0	0	25	95^2	73	7	48	70	11.6	2.82	128	.215	.316	0	—	0	10	8	-0	2.3
1979	*Cal-A	7	11	.389	53	1	0	0	10	85^2	107	13	32	59	14.8	5.57	73	.314	.376	0	—	0	-13	-14	1	-2.5
1980	Cal-A	3	5	.375	52	9	1	0	4	128	122	14	39	89	11.5	4.08	96	.256	.317	0	—	0	-1	-2	-1	-0.2
1981	*NY-A	4	1	.800	26	1	0	0	0	47	38	3	16	24	10.5	2.49	144	.229	.301	0	—	0	6	6	-1	0.6
1982	NY-A	4	2	.667	25	0	0	0	0	50	54	4	11	31	11.9	3.42	117	.273	.314	0	—	0	4	3	-1	0.3
1983	NY-A	0	0	—	1	0	0	0	0	1	2	1	0	0	18.0	18.00	22	.400	.400	0	—	0	-2	-2	0	0.2
Total	14	65	58	.528	647	15	1	0	126	1049^1	919	94	459	819	12.1	3.53	105	.239	.325	15	.246	4	26	22	-1	4.2

● JOHN LaROSE

LaRose, Henry John b: 10/25/51, Pawtucket, R.I. BL/TL, 6'1", 185 lbs. Deb: 9/20/78

YEAR	TM/L	W	L	PCT	G	GS	CG	SH	SV	IP	H	HR	BB	SO	RAT	ERA	ERA+	OAV	OOB	BH	AVG	PB	PR	/A	PD	TPI
1978	Bos-A	0	0	—	1	0	0	0	0	2	3	1	3	0	27.0	22.50	18	.375	.545	0	—	0	-4	-4	0	-0.5

● DON LARSEN

Larsen, Don James b: 8/7/29, Michigan City, Ind. BR/TR, 6'4", 227 lbs. Deb: 4/18/53

YEAR	TM/L	W	L	PCT	G	GS	CG	SH	SV	IP	H	HR	BB	SO	RAT	ERA	ERA+	OAV	OOB	BH	AVG	PB	PR	/A	PD	TPI
1953	StL-A	7	12	.368	38	22	7	2	2	192^2	201	11	64	96	12.6	4.16	101	.267	.328	23	.284	5	-3	1	-1	0.8
1954	Bal-A	3	21	.125	29	28	12	1	0	201^2	213	18	89	80	13.5	4.37	82	.274	.349	22	.250	8	-15	-18	0	-1.0
1955	*NY-A	9	2	.818	19	13	5	1	2	97	81	8	51	44	12.4	3.06	122	.229	.329	6	.146	2	10	7	-1	0.9
1956	*NY-A	11	5	.688	38	20	6	1	1	179^2	133	19	96	107	11.8	3.26	119	.204	.313	19	.241	6	18	12	-1	1.5
1957	*NY-A	10	4	.714	27	20	4	1	0	139^2	113	12	87	81	12.9	3.74	96	.220	.333	14	.250	5	1	-2	-0	0.1
1958	*NY-A	9	6	.600	19	19	5	3	0	114^1	100	4	52	55	12.3	3.07	115	.233	.322	15	.306	9	9	6	-1	1.4
1959	NY-A	6	7	.462	25	18	3	1	3	124^2	122	14	76	69	14.4	4.33	84	.260	.365	12	.255	4	-7	-10	-0	-0.6
1960	KC-A	1	10	.091	22	15	0	0	0	83^2	97	11	42	43	15.0	5.38	74	.293	.373	6	.207	0	-14	-13	-1	-1.6
1961	KC-A	1	0	1.000	8	1	0	0	0	15	21	2	11	13	19.8	4.20	100	.344	.452	6	.300	1	-0	-0	0	0.2
	Chi-A	7	2	.778	25	3	0	0	2	74^1	64	5	29	53	11.4	4.12	95	.231	.306	8	.320	3	-1	-2	0	0.1
	Yr	8	2	.800	33	4	0	0	2	89^1	85	7	40	66	12.7	4.13	96	.251	.332	14	.311	4	-1	-2	1	0.3
1962	*SF-N	5	4	.556	49	0	0	0	11	86^1	83	9	47	58	13.8	4.38	87	.256	.354	5	.200	1	-4	-6	0	-0.6
1963	SF-N	7	7	.500	46	0	0	0	3	62	46	8	30	44	11.0	3.05	105	.203	.296	2	.182	0	2	1	0	0.3
1964	SF-N	0	1	.000	6	0	0	0	0	10^1	10	0	6	6	13.9	4.35	82	.256	.356	0	.000	-0	-1	-1	-0	-0.1
	Hou-N	4	8	.333	30	10	2	1	1	103^1	92	4	20	58	9.8	2.26	151	.233	.272	3	.097	0	15	13	0	1.6
	Yr	4	9	.308	36	10	2	1	1	113^2	102	4	26	64	10.2	2.45	140	.235	.280	3	.094	0	14	12	0	1.5
1965	Hou-N	0	0	—	1	1	0	0	0	5^1	8	0	3	1	18.6	5.06	66	.348	.423	0	.000	-0	-1	-1	1	0.0
	Bal-A	1	2	.333	27	1	0	0	1	54	53	4	20	40	12.3	2.67	130	.255	.323	3	.273	1	5	5	1	0.5
1967	Chi-N	0	0	—	3	0	0	0	0	4	5	1	2	1	15.8	9.00	39	.333	.412	0	—	0	-3	-2	0	0.0
Total	14	81	91	.471	412	171	44	11	26	1548	1442	130	725	849	12.8	3.78	99	.247	.332	144	.242	46	10	-9	-1	3.5

● DAN LARSON

Larson, Daniel James b: 7/4/54, Los Angeles, Cal. BR/TR, 6', 180 lbs. Deb: 7/18/76

YEAR	TM/L	W	L	PCT	G	GS	CG	SH	SV	IP	H	HR	BB	SO	RAT	ERA	ERA+	OAV	OOB	BH	AVG	PB	PR	/A	PD	TPI
1976	Hou-N	5	8	.385	13	13	5	0	0	92^1	81	3	28	42	10.7	3.02	106	.236	.296	9	.290	4	5	2	0	0.7
1977	Hou-N	1	7	.125	32	10	1	0	1	97^2	108	13	45	44	14.3	5.81	61	.280	.358	6	.214	1	-21	-24	0	-1.7
1978	Phi-N	0	0	—	1	0	0	0	0	1	1	1	1	2	18.0	9.00	40	.250	.400	0	—	0	-1	-1	0	0.0
1979	Phi-N	1	1	.500	3	3	0	0	0	19	17	1	9	9	12.8	4.26	90	.250	.346	0	.000	-1	-1	-1	0	-0.1
1980	Phi-N	0	5	.000	12	7	0	0	0	45^2	46	4	24	17	13.8	3.15	120	.271	.361	2	.154	0	2	3	-1	0.3
1981	Phi-N	3	0	1.000	5	4	1	0	0	28	27	4	15	15	13.5	4.18	87	.260	.353	1	.111	0	-2	-2	-0	-0.2
1982	Chi-N	0	4	.000	12	6	0	0	0	39^2	51	4	18	22	16.1	5.67	66	.327	.403	3	.273	0	-9	-9	1	-0.6
Total	7	10	25	.286	78	43	7	0	1	323^1	331	30	140	151	13.3	4.40	80	.269	.346	21	.216	4	-26	-31	1	-1.6

● AL LARY

Lary, Alfred Allen b: 9/26/28, Northport, Ala. BR/TR, 6'3", 185 lbs. Deb: 9/6/54 F♦

YEAR	TM/L	W	L	PCT	G	GS	CG	SH	SV	IP	H	HR	BB	SO	RAT	ERA	ERA+	OAV	OOB	BH	AVG	PB	PR	/A	PD	TPI
1954	Chi-N	0	0	—	1	1	0	0	0	6	3	0	7	4	15.0	3.00	140	.150	.370	1	.500	0	1	1	0	0.0
1962	Chi-N	0	1	.000	15	3	0	0	0	34	42	5	15	18	15.1	7.15	58	.311	.380	1	.167	0	-12	-11	-0	-0.3
Total	2	0	1	.000	16	4	0	0	0	40	45	5	22	22	15.1	6.52	64	.290	.379	2	.250	1	-11	-11	-0	-0.3

● FRANK LARY

Lary, Frank Strong "Mule" or "The Yankee Killer" b: 4/10/30, Northport, Ala. BR/TR, 5'11", 180 lbs. Deb: 9/14/54 F

YEAR	TM/L	W	L	PCT	G	GS	CG	SH	SV	IP	H	HR	BB	SO	RAT	ERA	ERA+	OAV	OOB	BH	AVG	PB	PR	/A	PD	TPI
1954	Det-A	0	0	—	3	0	0	0	0	3^2	4	0	3	5	17.2	2.45	150	.286	.412	0	—	0	1	1	-0	0.0
1955	Det-A	14	15	.483	36	31	16	2	1	235	232	10	89	98	12.5	3.10	124	.262	.334	16	.195	1	22	19	1	2.5
1956	Det-A	**21**	13	.618	41	38	20	3	1	**294**	289	20	116	165	12.8	3.15	131	.257	.333	19	.184	0	33	31	-0	3.4
1957	Det-A	11	16	.407	40	35	12	2	3	237^2	250	23	72	107	12.6	3.98	97	.276	.337	9	.123	-3	-5	-3	0	-0.6
1958	Det-A	16	15	.516	39	34	**19**	3	1	**260**^{1}	249	20	68	131	11.4	2.90	139	.251	.307	15	.170	-1	25	33	-0	3.6
1959	Det-A	17	10	.630	32	32	11	3	0	223	225	23	46	137	11.4	3.55	114	.261	.307	10	.125	-2	8	13	-0	1.2
1960	Det-A★	15	15	.500	38	36	**15**	2	1	**274**^{1}	262	25	62	149	11.3	3.51	113	.249	.302	17	.183	4	11	14	-2	1.6
1961	Det-A★	23	9	.719	36	36	**22**	4	0	275^1	252	24	66	146	10.6	3.24	127	.243	.293	25	.231	4	24	26	4	3.7
1962	Det-A	2	6	.250	17	14	2	1	0	80	98	17	21	41	13.8	5.74	71	.297	.346	4	.167	1	-16	-15	-1	-1.3
1963	Det-A	4	9	.308	16	14	6	0	0	107^1	90	15	26	46	10.1	3.27	114	.226	.281	8	.229	1	4	6	1	0.9
1964	Det-A	0	2	.000	6	4	0	0	0	18	24	3	10	6	18.5	7.00	52	.316	.416	0	.000	-1	-7	-7	-1	-0.8
	NY-N	2	3	.400	13	8	3	1	1	57^1	62	7	14	27	12.6	4.55	79	.279	.333	2	.118	1	-6	-6	-0	-0.5
	Mil-N	1	0	1.000	5	2	0	0	0	12^1	15	4	0	4	10.9	4.38	80	.306	.306	0	.000	-0	-1	-1	1	0.0
	Yr	3	3	.500	18	10	3	1	1	69^2	77	11	14	31	11.8	4.52	79	.279	.314	2	.100	0	-8	-7	0	-0.5
1965	NY-N	1	3	.250	14	7	0	0	1	57^1	48	2	16	23	10.2	2.98	118	.233	.291	4	.211	0	4	3	0	0.3
	Chi-A	1	0	1.000	14	1	0	0	2	26^2	23	4	7	14	10.8	4.05	79	.230	.294	1	.500	0	-2	-3	0	-0.1
Total	12	128	116	.525	350	292	126	21	11	2162^1	2123	197	616	1099	11.8	3.49	113	.257	.316	130	.177	5	95	112	3	13.9

● FRED LASHER

Lasher, Frederick Walter b: 8/19/41, Poughkeepsie, N.Y. BR/TR, 6'4", 210 lbs. Deb: 4/12/63

YEAR	TM/L	W	L	PCT	G	GS	CG	SH	SV	IP	H	HR	BB	SO	RAT	ERA	ERA+	OAV	OOB	BH	AVG	PB	PR	/A	PD	TPI
1963	Min-A	0	0	—	11	0	0	0	0	11^1	12	1	11	10	18.3	4.76	76	.286	.434	0	.000	-0	-1	-1	0	0.0
1967	Det-A	2	1	.667	17	0	0	0	9	30	25	1	11	28	11.1	3.90	84	.221	.296	1	.111	-0	-2	-2	-0	-0.4
1968	*Det-A	5	1	.833	34	0	0	0	5	48^2	37	5	22	32	10.9	3.33	90	.215	.304	1	.111	-0	-2	-2	1	-0.2
1969	Det-A	2	1	.667	32	0	0	0	0	44	34	5	22	26	11.9	3.07	122	.224	.330	0	.000	-0	3	3	0	0.2
1970	Det-A	1	3	.250	12	0	0	0	3	9	10	0	12	8	23.0	5.00	75	.278	.469	0	.000	-0	-1	-1	0	-0.6
	Cle-A	1	7	.125	43	1	0	0	5	57^2	57	6	30	44	14.0	4.06	98	.264	.361	0	.000	-1	-2	-1	-1	-0.3
	Yr	2	10	.167	55	1	0	0	8	66^2	67	6	42	52	15.1	4.18	94	.264	.375	0	.000	-1	-3	-2	-1	-0.9
1971	Cal-A	0	0	—	2	0	0	0	0	1^1	4	0	2	0	40.5	27.00	12	.667	.750	0	—	0	-3	-4	-0	0.0
Total	6	11	13	.458	151	1	0	0	22	202	179	18	110	148	13.2	3.88	91	.243	.347	2	.063	-2	-10	-8	0	-1.3

● BILL LASKEY

Laskey, William Alan b: 12/20/57, Toledo, Ohio BR/TR, 6'5", 190 lbs. Deb: 4/23/82

YEAR	TM/L	W	L	PCT	G	GS	CG	SH	SV	IP	H	HR	BB	SO	RAT	ERA	ERA+	OAV	OOB	BH	AVG	PB	PR	/A	PD	TPI
1982	SF-N	13	12	.520	32	31	7	1	0	189^1	186	14	43	88	11.0	3.14	115	.261	.304	8	.129	-2	10	10	0	1.0
1983	SF-N	13	10	.565	25	25	1	0	0	148^1	151	18	45	81	12.1	4.19	84	.266	.323	5	.106	0	-9	-11	-1	-1.6
1984	SF-N	9	14	.391	35	34	2	0	0	207^2	222	20	50	71	12.0	4.33	81	.273	.320	4	.063	-3	-17	-19	-3	-2.5
1985	SF-N	5	11	.313	19	19	0	0	0	114	110	10	39	42	11.8	3.55	97	.255	.317	4	.133	1	0	-1	0	-0.1
	Mon-N	0	5	.000	11	7	0	0	0	34^1	55	9	14	18	18.6	9.44	36	.362	.423	1	.143	-0	-22	-23	1	-2.7
	Yr	5	16	.238	30	26	0	0	0	148^1	165	19	53	60	13.3	4.91	70	.281	.343	5	.135	0	-22	-25	1	-2.8
1986	SF-N	1	1	.500	20	0	0	0	1	27^1	28	5	13	8	13.5	4.28	82	.275	.357	0	.000	-0	-2	-2	0	-0.1
1988	Cle-A	1	0	1.000	17	0	0	0	1	24^1	32	0	6	17	14.1	5.18	79	.320	.358	0	—	0	-3	-3	0	-0.3
Total	6	42	53	.442	159	116	10	1	2	745^1	784	76	210	325	12.2	4.14	85	.272	.325	22	.105	-4	-44	-50	-2	-6.3

● BILL LASLEY

Lasley, Willard Almond b: 7/13/02, Gallipolis, Ohio d: 8/21/90, Seattle, Wash. BB/TR, 6', 175 lbs. Deb: 9/19/24

YEAR	TM/L	W	L	PCT	G	GS	CG	SH	SV	IP	H	HR	BB	SO	RAT	ERA	ERA+	OAV	OOB	BH	AVG	PB	PR	/A	PD	TPI
1924	StL-A	0	0	—	2	0	0	0	0	4	7	0	2	0	20.3	6.75	67	.412	.474	0	.000	-0	-1	-1	-0	0.0

● TOM LASORDA

Lasorda, Thomas Charles b: 9/22/27, Norristown, Pa. BL/TL, 5'10", 175 lbs. Deb: 8/5/54 MCH

YEAR	TM/L	W	L	PCT	G	GS	CG	SH	SV	IP	H	HR	BB	SO	RAT	ERA	ERA+	OAV	OOB	BH	AVG	PB	PR	/A	PD	TPI
1954	Bro-N	0	0	—	4	0	0	0	0	9	8	2	5	5	13.0	5.00	82	.242	.342	0	.000	-0	-1	-1	-0	0.0
1955	Bro-N	0	0	—	4	1	0	0	0	4	5	1	6	4	27.0	13.50	30	.313	.522	0	—	0	-4	-4	-0	0.0
1956	KC-A	0	4	.000	18	5	0	0	1	45^1	40	6	45	28	17.5	6.15	70	.240	.409	1	.077	-1	-10	-9	0	-0.8
Total	3	0	4	.000	26	6	0	0	1	58^1	53	9	56	37	17.4	6.48	66	.245	.409	1	.071	-2	-15	-14	0	-0.8

● BILL LATHAM

Latham, William Carol b: 8/29/60, Birmingham, Ala. BL/TL, 6'2", 190 lbs. Deb: 4/15/85

YEAR	TM/L	W	L	PCT	G	GS	CG	SH	SV	IP	H	HR	BB	SO	RAT	ERA	ERA+	OAV	OOB	BH	AVG	PB	PR	/A	PD	TPI
1985	NY-N	1	3	.250	7	3	0	0	0	22^2	21	1	7	10	11.1	3.97	87	.250	.308	1	.333	1	-1	-1	1	-0.1
1986	Min-A	0	1	.000	7	2	0	0	0	16	24	1	6	8	17.4	7.31	59	.358	.419	0	—	0	-6	-5	-1	-0.5
Total	2	1	4	.200	14	5	0	0	0	38^2	45	2	13	18	13.7	5.35	71	.298	.358	1	.333	1	-7	-7	0	-0.6

● BILL LATHROP Lathrop, William George b: 8/12/1891, Hanover, Wis. d: 11/20/58, Janesville, Wis. BR/TR, 6'2.5", 184 lbs. Deb: 7/29/13

YEAR	TM/L	W	L	PCT	G	GS	CG	SH	SV	IP	H	HR	BB	SO	RAT	ERA	ERA+	OAV	OOB	BH	AVG	PB	PR	/A	PD	TPI
1913	Chi-A	0	1	.000	6	0	0	0	0	17	16	0	12	9	15.4	4.24	69	.262	.392	0	.000	-1	-2	-2	0	-0.2
1914	Chi-A	1	2	.333	19	1	0	0	0	47^2	41	0	19	7	11.7	2.64	102	.241	.325	0	.000	-1	1	0	1	-0.1
Total	2	1	3	.250	25	1	0	0	0	64^2	57	0	31	16	12.7	3.06	90	.247	.343	0	.000	-2	-2	-2	1	-0.3

● BARRY LATMAN Latman, Arnold Barry b: 5/21/36, Los Angeles, Cal. BR/TR, 6'3", 210 lbs. Deb: 9/10/57

YEAR	TM/L	W	L	PCT	G	GS	CG	SH	SV	IP	H	HR	BB	SO	RAT	ERA	ERA+	OAV	OOB	BH	AVG	PB	PR	/A	PD	TPI
1957	Chi-A	1	2	.333	7	2	0	0	1	12^1	12	2	13	9	19.0	8.03	47	.267	.441	0	.000	-0	-6	-6	0	-1.3
1958	Chi-A	3	0	1.000	13	3	1	1	0	47^2	27	1	17	28	8.5	0.76	481	.162	.243	1	.083	-0	16	15	-1	0.8
1959	Chi-A	8	5	.615	37	21	5	2	0	156	138	15	72	97	12.3	3.75	100	.235	.323	6	.128	-1	2	0	-3	-0.4
1960	Cle-A	7	7	.500	31	20	4	0	0	147^1	146	19	72	94	13.7	4.03	93	.258	.348	9	.220	1	-3	-5	-1	-0.4
1961	Cle-A☆	13	5	.722	45	18	4	2	5	176^2	163	23	54	108	11.3	4.02	98	.244	.306	4	.073	-3	-0	-2	-3	-0.8
1962	Cle-A	8	13	.381	45	21	7	1	5	179^1	179	23	72	117	12.8	4.17	93	.261	.336	10	.189	2	-4	-6	-1	-0.5
1963	Cle-A	7	12	.368	38	21	4	2	2	149^1	146	23	52	133	12.3	4.94	73	.257	.325	8	.182	2	-22	-22	3	-2.1
1964	LA-A	6	10	.375	40	18	2	1	2	138	128	15	52	81	12.2	3.85	85	.244	.321	5	.125	-1	-3	-9	-1	-1.1
1965	Cal-A	1	1	.500	18	0	0	0	0	31^2	30	3	16	18	13.1	2.84	120	.254	.343	0	.000	-0	2	2	-1	0.0
1966	Hou-N	2	7	.222	31	9	1	1	1	103	88	5	35	74	11.4	2.71	126	.233	.310	4	.154	0	10	8	-0	0.7
1967	Hou-N	3	6	.333	39	1	0	0	0	77^2	73	13	34	70	13.1	4.52	73	.252	.342	1	.091	-1	-10	-10	0	-1.2
Total	11	59	68	.465	344	134	28	10	16	1219	1130	142	489	829	12.3	3.91	94	.246	.325	48	.145	-1	-17	-34	-8	-6.3

● BILL LATTIMORE Lattimore, William Hershel "Slothful Bill"
b: 5/25/1884, Roxton, Tex. d: 10/30/19, Colorado Springs, Colo. BL/TL, 5'9", 165 lbs. Deb: 4/17/08

YEAR	TM/L	W	L	PCT	G	GS	CG	SH	SV	IP	H	HR	BB	SO	RAT	ERA	ERA+	OAV	OOB	BH	AVG	PB	PR	/A	PD	TPI
1908	Cle-A	1	2	.333	4	4	1	1	0	24	24	0	7	5	11.6	4.50	53	.247	.298	4	.444	1	-6	-6	-1	-0.6

● CHUCK LAUER Lauer, John Charles b: 1865, Pittsburgh, Pa. TR , Deb: 7/17/1884 ♦

YEAR	TM/L	W	L	PCT	G	GS	CG	SH	SV	IP	H	HR	BB	SO	RAT	ERA	ERA+	OAV	OOB	BH	AVG	PB	PR	/A	PD	TPI
1884	Pit-a	0	2	.000	3	3	2	0	0	19	23	0	9	8	16.6	7.58	44	.277	.368	5	.114	-1	-9	-9	-1	-0.8

● GEORGE LAUZERIQUE Lauzerique, George Albert b: 7/22/47, Havana, Cuba BR/TR, 6'1", 180 lbs. Deb: 9/17/67

YEAR	TM/L	W	L	PCT	G	GS	CG	SH	SV	IP	H	HR	BB	SO	RAT	ERA	ERA+	OAV	OOB	BH	AVG	PB	PR	/A	PD	TPI
1967	KC-A	0	2	.000	3	2	0	0	0	16	11	2	6	10	10.1	2.25	142	.193	.281	0	.000	-0	2	2	0	0.2
1968	Oak-A	0	0	—	1	0	0	0	0	1	0	0	1	0	9.0	0.00	—	.000	.333	0	—	0	0	0	0	0.0
1969	Oak-A	3	4	.429	19	8	1	0	0	61^1	58	14	27	39	12.8	4.70	73	.250	.333	2	.100	-1	-7	-9	1	-0.9
1970	Mil-A	1	2	.333	11	4	1	0	0	35	41	7	14	24	14.4	6.94	55	.295	.364	2	.200	1	-13	-12	-0	-0.9
Total	4	4	8	.333	34	14	2	0	0	113^1	110	23	48	73	12.9	5.00	70	.256	.336	4	.121	-0	-18	-19	1	-1.6

● GARY LAVELLE Lavelle, Gary Robert b: 1/3/49, Scranton, Pa. BB/TL, 6'1", 200 lbs. Deb: 9/10/74

YEAR	TM/L	W	L	PCT	G	GS	CG	SH	SV	IP	H	HR	BB	SO	RAT	ERA	ERA+	OAV	OOB	BH	AVG	PB	PR	/A	PD	TPI
1974	SF-N	0	3	.000	10	0	0	0	0	16^2	14	1	10	12	13.0	2.16	176	.222	.329	0	.000	-0	3	3	-0	0.5
1975	SF-N	6	3	.667	65	0	0	0	8	82^1	80	3	48	51	14.3	2.95	129	.260	.365	1	.111	-0	6	8	0	1.0
1976	SF-N	10	6	.625	65	0	0	0	12	110^1	102	6	52	71	12.7	2.69	135	.246	.333	1	.077	-1	10	11	-2	1.7
1977	SF-N★	7	7	.500	73	0	0	0	20	118^1	106	4	37	93	10.9	2.05	190	.239	.298	0	.000	-2	24	24	1	3.5
1978	SF-N	13	10	.565	67	0	0	0	14	97^2	96	3	44	63	13.1	3.32	104	.263	.345	1	.067	-1	3	1	0	0.3
1979	SF-N	7	9	.438	70	0	0	0	20	96^2	86	5	42	80	12.1	2.51	139	.247	.332	1	.250	0	13	11	0	2.1
1980	SF-N	6	8	.429	62	0	0	0	9	100	106	4	36	66	12.8	3.42	103	.275	.336	0	.000	-1	2	1	0	0.1
1981	SF-N	2	6	.250	34	3	0	0	4	65^2	58	3	23	45	11.4	3.84	89	.244	.316	3	.273	1	-3	-3	1	-0.2
1982	SF-N	10	7	.588	68	0	0	0	8	104^2	97	6	29	76	10.9	2.67	135	.247	.300	2	.154	0	11	11	2	2.1
1983	SF-N☆	7	4	.636	56	0	0	0	20	87	73	4	19	68	9.5	2.59	137	.229	.272	0	.000	-2	10	9	2	1.5
1984	SF-N	5	4	.556	77	0	0	0	12	101	92	5	42	71	12.0	2.76	127	.246	.324	0	.000	-0	9	8	-1	0.8
1985	*Tor-A	5	7	.417	69	0	0	0	8	72^2	54	5	36	50	11.1	3.10	136	.214	.313	0	—	0	8	9	-0	1.4
1987	Tor-A	2	3	.400	23	0	0	0	1	27^2	36	2	19	17	17.9	5.53	81	.313	.410	0	—	0	-3	-3	0	-0.5
	Oak-A	0	0	—	6	0	0	0	0	4^1	4	0	3	6	14.5	8.31	50	.267	.389	0	—	0	-2	-2	-0	0.3
	Yr	2	3	.400	29	0	0	0	1	32	40	2	22	23	17.4	5.91	75	.305	.405	0	—	0	-5	-5	0	-0.2
Total	13	80	77	.510	745	3	0	0	136	1085	1004	51	440	769	12.1	2.93	125	.249	.325	9	.081	-6	92	89	4	14.6

● JIMMY LAVENDER Lavender, James Sanford b: 3/25/1884, Barnesville, Ga. d: 1/12/60, Cartersville, Ga. BR/TR, 5'11", 165 lbs. Deb: 4/23/12

YEAR	TM/L	W	L	PCT	G	GS	CG	SH	SV	IP	H	HR	BB	SO	RAT	ERA	ERA+	OAV	OOB	BH	AVG	PB	PR	/A	PD	TPI
1912	Chi-N	16	13	.552	42	31	15	3	3	251^2	240	8	89	109	12.1	3.04	109	.257	.328	13	.149	-3	10	8	1	0.6
1913	Chi-N	10	14	.417	40	20	10	0	2	204	206	6	98	91	14.0	3.66	87	.267	.359	8	.118	-4	-10	-11	-2	-1.8
1914	Chi-N	11	11	.500	37	28	11	2	0	214^1	191	11	87	87	12.1	3.07	91	.247	.331	11	.175	2	-7	-7	3	-0.1
1915	Chi-N	10	16	.385	41	24	13	1	4	220	178	5	67	117	10.4	2.58	108	.228	.298	9	.134	-2	4	5	3	0.7
1916	Chi-N	10	14	.417	36	25	9	4	2	188	163	3	62	91	11.2	2.82	103	.240	.312	8	.151	-2	-4	2	-1	-0.1
1917	Phi-N	6	8	.429	28	14	7	0	1	129^1	119	5	44	52	11.6	3.55	79	.250	.317	5	.139	-1	-12	-11	-2	-1.5
Total	6	63	76	.453	224	142	65	10	12	1207^1	1097	38	447	547	11.9	3.09	97	.249	.325	54	.144	-9	-19	-12	2	-2.2

● RON LAW Law, Ronald David b: 3/14/46, Hamilton, Ont., Can. BR/TR, 6'2", 165 lbs. Deb: 6/29/69

YEAR	TM/L	W	L	PCT	G	GS	CG	SH	SV	IP	H	HR	BB	SO	RAT	ERA	ERA+	OAV	OOB	BH	AVG	PB	PR	/A	PD	TPI
1969	Cle-A	3	4	.429	35	1	0	0	1	52^1	68	2	34	29	17.9	4.99	76	.325	.424	1	.143	-0	-8	-7	0	-0.9

● VANCE LAW Law, Vance Aaron b: 10/1/56, Boise, Idaho BR/TR, 6'2", 190 lbs. Deb: 6/1/80 F♦

YEAR	TM/L	W	L	PCT	G	GS	CG	SH	SV	IP	H	HR	BB	SO	RAT	ERA	ERA+	OAV	OOB	BH	AVG	PB	PR	/A	PD	TPI
1986	Mon-N	0	0	—	3	0	0	0	0	4	3	0	2	0	11.3	2.25	164	.214	.313	81	.225	1	1	1	0	0.0
1987	Mon-N	0	0	—	3	0	0	0	0	3^1	5	0	0	2	13.5	5.40	78	.333	.333	119	.273	1	-0	-0	0	0.0
1991	Oak-A	0	0	—	1	0	0	0	0	0^2	1	0	1	0	27.0	0.00	—	.333	.500	28	.209	0	0	0	0	0.0
Total	3	0	0	—	7	0	0	0	0	8	9	0	3	2	13.5	3.38	116	.281	.343	972	.256	2	0	0	0	0.0

● VERN LAW Law, Vernon Sanders "Deacon" b: 3/12/30, Meridian, Idaho BR/TR, 6'2", 195 lbs. Deb: 6/11/50 FC

YEAR	TM/L	W	L	PCT	G	GS	CG	SH	SV	IP	H	HR	BB	SO	RAT	ERA	ERA+	OAV	OOB	BH	AVG	PB	PR	/A	PD	TPI
1950	Pit-N	7	9	.438	27	17	5	1	0	128	137	11	49	57	13.4	4.92	89	.272	.341	3	.073	-2	-11	-8	-2	-1.2
1951	Pit-N	6	9	.400	28	14	2	1	2	114	109	9	51	41	13.1	4.50	94	.253	.341	11	.344	5	-7	-3	-1	0.0
1954	Pit-N	9	13	.409	39	18	7	0	3	161^2	201	20	56	57	14.5	5.51	76	.311	.368	12	.231	3	-26	-24	-1	-2.5
1955	Pit-N	10	10	.500	43	24	8	1	1	200^2	221	19	61	82	12.7	3.81	108	.280	.333	16	.254	3	5	7	0	1.0
1956	Pit-N	8	16	.333	39	32	6	0	2	195^2	218	24	49	60	12.6	4.32	87	.281	.329	10	.175	1	-12	-12	-1	-1.3
1957	Pit-N	10	8	.556	31	25	9	3	1	172^2	172	18	32	55	10.7	2.87	132	.256	.291	12	.190	1	19	18	-2	1.7
1958	Pit-N	14	12	.538	35	29	6	1	3	202^1	235	16	39	56	12.2	3.96	98	.297	.331	12	.194	6	-0	-2	-0	0.3
1959	Pit-N	18	9	.667	34	33	20	2	1	266	245	25	53	110	10.2	2.98	130	.243	.282	16	.167	1	29	26	1	2.8
1960	*Pit-N★	20	9	.690	35	35	**18**	3	0	271^2	266	25	40	120	10.3	3.08	122	.257	.287	17	.181	3	21	20	1	2.6
1961	Pit-N	3	4	.429	11	10	1	0	0	59^1	72	10	18	20	13.8	4.70	85	.305	.357	5	.263	1	-4	-5	1	-0.3
1962	Pit-N	10	7	.588	23	20	7	2	0	139^1	156	21	27	78	11.9	3.94	100	.276	.310	14	.311	5	0	-0	1	0.6
1963	Pit-N	4	5	.444	18	12	1	1	0	76^2	91	11	13	31	12.2	4.93	67	.296	.325	5	.217	1	-14	-14	1	-1.3
1964	Pit-N	12	13	.480	35	29	7	5	0	192	203	18	32	93	11.1	3.61	97	.270	.300	19	.311	8	-2	-2	1	0.6
1965	Pit-N	17	9	.654	29	28	13	4	0	217^1	182	17	35	101	9.1	2.15	163	.229	.264	20	.244	4	33	33	1	4.6
1966	Pit-N	12	8	.600	31	28	8	4	0	177^2	203	19	24	88	11.7	4.05	88	.292	.320	16	.242	5	-9	-9	2	-0.4
1967	Pit-N	2	6	.250	25	10	1	0	0	97	122	5	18	43	13.1	4.18	81	.308	.340	3	.111	-0	-9	-9	-0	-0.7
Total	16	162	147	.524	483	364	119	28	13	2672	2833	268	597	1092	11.7	3.77	101	.272	.314	191	.216	45	14	15	2	6.5

● BROOKS LAWRENCE Lawrence, Brooks Ulysses "Bull" b: 1/30/25, Springfield, Ohio BR/TR, 6', 205 lbs. Deb: 6/24/54

YEAR	TM/L	W	L	PCT	G	GS	CG	SH	SV	IP	H	HR	BB	SO	RAT	ERA	ERA+	OAV	OOB	BH	AVG	PB	PR	/A	PD	TPI
1954	StL-N	15	6	.714	35	18	8	0	1	158^2	141	17	72	72	12.5	3.74	110	.243	.335	10	.189	0	6	6	0	0.8
1955	StL-N	3	8	.273	46	10	2	1	1	96	102	11	58	52	15.7	6.56	62	.278	.387	2	.095	-2	-27	-27	1	-2.8
1956	Cin-N☆	19	10	.655	49	30	11	1	0	218^2	210	26	71	96	11.6	3.99	100	.256	.317	11	.157	-1	-5	-0	3	0.2
1957	Cin-N	16	13	.552	49	32	12	1	4	250^1	234	26	76	121	11.4	3.52	117	.247	.309	14	.171	-0	10	16	-0	1.8
1958	Cin-N	8	13	.381	46	23	6	2	5	181	194	12	55	74	12.6	4.13	100	.275	.331	6	.113	-2	-4	0	-0	-0.2
1959	Cin-N	7	12	.368	43	14	3	0	10	128^1	144	17	45	64	13.5	4.77	85	.281	.344	6	.150	-1	-12	-10	-0	-1.6
1960	Cin-N	1	0	1.000	7	0	0	0	1	7^2	9	1	8	2	20.0	10.57	36	.310	.459	0	—	0	-6	-6	0	-0.8
Total	7	69	62	.527	275	127	42	5	22	1040^2	1034	110	385	481	12.6	4.25	96	.261	.332	49	.154	-5	-38	-20	4	-2.6

● BOB LAWRENCE Lawrence, Robert Andrew "Larry" b: 12/14/1899, Brooklyn, N.Y. d: 11/6/83, Jamaica, N.Y. BR/TR, 5'11", 180 lbs. Deb: 7/19/24

YEAR	TM/L	W	L	PCT	G	GS	CG	SH	SV	IP	H	HR	BB	SO	RAT	ERA	ERA+	OAV	OOB	BH	AVG	PB	PR	/A	PD	TPI
1924	Chi-A	0	0	—	1	0	0	0	0	1	1	0	1	1	18.0	9.00	46	.250	.400	0	—	0	-1	-1	0	0.0

YEAR	TM/L	W	L	PCT	G	GS	CG	SH	SV	IP	H	HR	BB	SO	RAT	ERA	ERA+	OAV	OOB	BH	AVG	PB	PR	/A	PD	TPI
● **SEAN LAWRENCE** Lawrence, Sean Christopher b: 9/2/70, Oak Park, Ill. BL/TL, 6′4″, 215 lbs. Deb: 8/25/98																										
1998	Pit-N	2	1	.667	7	3	0	0	0	19^2	25	4	10	12	16.0	7.32	59	.313	.389	0	.000	-1	-7	-7	-0	-0.9
● **ROXIE LAWSON** Lawson, Alfred Voyle b: 4/13/06, Donnellson, Iowa d: 4/9/77, Stockport, Iowa BR/TR, 6′, 170 lbs. Deb: 8/3/30																										
1930	Cle-A	1	2	.333	7	4	2	0	0	33^2	46	1	23	10	18.4	6.15	79	.324	.418	1	.091	-1	-6	-5	-0	-0.4
1931	Cle-A	0	2	.000	17	3	0	0	0	55^2	72	5	36	20	17.5	7.60	61	.304	.396	2	.143	-0	-20	-18	-1	-0.6
1933	Det-A	0	1	.000	4	2	0	0	0	16	17	2	17	6	19.1	7.31	59	.270	.425	0	.000	-1	-5	-5	0	-0.3
1935	Det-A	3	1	.750	7	4	4	2	2	40	34	3	24	16	13.0	1.57	265	.233	.341	4	.308	1	13	12	-1	1.2
1936	Det-A	8	6	.571	41	8	3	0	3	128	139	13	71	34	15.0	5.48	90	.281	.376	10	.222	1	-6	-8	1	-0.6
1937	Det-A	18	7	.720	37	29	15	0	1	217^1	236	17	115	68	14.6	5.26	89	.271	.357	21	.259	3	-15	-14	-1	-1.2
1938	Det-A	8	9	.471	27	16	5	0	1	127	154	13	82	39	16.7	5.46	92	.299	.395	2	.044	-5	-9	-6	1	-1.1
1939	Det-A	1	1	.500	2	1	0	0	0	11^1	7	1	7	4	11.1	4.76	103	.167	.286	0	.000	-1	-0	0	0	0.0
	StL-A	3	7	.300	36	14	5	0	0	150^2	181	10	83	43	15.9	5.32	92	.307	.394	8	.186	-1	-12	-8	-1	-0.5
	Yr	4	8	.333	38	15	5	0	0	162	188	11	90	47	15.6	5.28	92	.297	.387	8	.170	-2	-12	-7	-0	-0.5
1940	StL-A	5	3	.625	30	2	0	0	4	72	77	5	54	18	16.4	5.13	89	.278	.396	1	.045	-3	-6	-4	-0	-0.7
Total	9	47	39	.547	208	83	34	2	11	851^2	963	70	512	258	15.7	5.37	89	.285	.380	49	.173	-6	-67	-57	-2	-4.2
● **AL LAWSON** Lawson, Alfred William b: 3/24/1869, London, England d: 11/29/54, San Antonio, Tex. BR/TR, 5′11″, 161 lbs. Deb: 5/13/1890																										
1890	Bos-N	0	1	.000	1	1	1	0	0	9	12	0	4	1	16.0	4.00	94	.308	.372	0	.000	-0	-0	-0	0	0.0
	Pit-N	0	2	.000	2	2	1	0	0	10	15	0	10	2	22.5	9.00	37	.333	.455	0	.000	-1	-6	-6	0	-0.9
	Yr	0	3	.000	3	3	2	0	0	19	27	0	14	3	19.4	6.63	53	.321	.418	0	.000	-1	-6	-7	0	-0.9
● **BOB LAWSON** Lawson, Robert Baker b: 8/23/1876, Brookneal, Va. d: 10/28/52, Durham, N.C. BR/TR, 5′10″, 170 lbs. Deb: 5/7/01																										
1901	Bos-N	2	2	.500	6	4	4	0	0	46	45	0	28	12	14.9	3.33	109	.254	.365	4	.148	-0	-0	1	1	0.2
1902	Bal-A	0	2	.000	3	2	1	0	0	13	21	0	3	5	18.0	4.85	78	.362	.413	1	.167	-0	-2	-2	1	-0.2
Total	2	2	4	.333	9	6	5	0	0	59	66	0	31	17	15.6	3.66	100	.281	.376	5	.152	-1	-2	-0	1	0.0
● **STEVE LAWSON** Lawson, Steven George b: 12/28/50, Oakland, Cal. BR/TL, 6′1″, 175 lbs. Deb: 8/3/72																										
1972	Tex-A	0	0	—	13	0	0	0	1	16	13	1	10	13	12.9	2.81	107	.213	.324	1	1.000	0	0	0	-0	0.0
● **BILL LAXTON** Laxton, William Harry b: 1/5/48, Camden, N.J. BL/TL, 6′1″, 190 lbs. Deb: 9/15/70																										
1970	Phi-N	0	0	—	2	0	0	0	0	2	2	2	2	2	22.5	13.50	30	.250	.455	0	—	0	-2	-2	-0	0.0
1971	SD-N	0	2	.000	18	0	0	0	0	27^2	32	4	26	23	19.2	6.83	48	.305	.447	0	—	0	-10	-11	0	-0.7
1974	SD-N	0	1	.000	30	1	0	0	0	44^2	37	5	38	40	15.7	4.03	88	.226	.380	1	.200	0	-2	-2	-0	-0.1
1976	Det-A	0	5	.000	26	3	0	0	2	94^2	77	13	51	74	12.7	4.09	91	.221	.331	0	—	0	-6	-4	-2	-0.4
1977	Sea-A	3	2	.600	43	0	0	0	3	72^2	62	10	39	49	13.0	4.95	83	.233	.340	0	—	0	-7	-7	-1	-0.6
	Cle-A	0	0	—	2	0	0	0	0	1^2	2	0	2	1	21.6	5.40	73	.286	.444	0	—	0	-0	-0	0	0.0
	Yr	3	2	.600	45	0	0	0	3	74^1	64	10	41	50	12.7	4.96	83	.228	.326	0	—	0	-7	-7	-1	-0.6
Total	5	3	10	.231	121	4	0	0	5	243^1	212	34	158	189	14.2	4.73	79	.236	.359	1	.200	0	-28	-26	-3	-1.8
● **TIM LAYANA** Layana, Timothy Joseph b: 3/2/64, Inglewood, Cal. BR/TR, 6′2″, 195 lbs. Deb: 4/9/90																										
1990	Cin-N	5	3	.625	55	0	0	0	2	80	71	7	44	53	13.2	3.49	113	.244	.347	0	.000	-1	3	4	0	0.4
1991	Cin-N	0	2	.000	22	0	0	0	0	20^2	23	1	11	14	14.8	6.97	55	.277	.362	0	.000	-0	-8	-7	0	-0.6
1993	SF-N	0	0	—	1	0	0	0	0	2	7	1	1	1	36.0	22.50	17	.538	.571	0	—	0	-4	-4	0	0.0
Total	3	5	5	.500	78	0	0	0	2	102^2	101	9	56	68	13.9	4.56	86	.261	.357	0	.000	-1	-9	-7	1	-0.2
● **DANNY LAZAR** Lazar, John Daniel b: 11/14/43, East Chicago, Ind. BL/TL, 6′1″, 190 lbs. Deb: 6/21/68																										
1968	Chi-A	0	1	.000	8	1	0	0	0	13^1	14	1	4	11	12.2	4.05	75	.269	.321	0	.000	0	-2	-2	0	-0.1
1969	Chi-A	0	0	—	9	3	0	0	0	20^2	21	5	11	9	14.4	6.53	59	.280	.379	0	.000	-0	-7	-6	-0	-0.1
Total	2	0	1	.000	17	4	0	0	0	34	35	6	15	20	13.5	5.56	63	.276	.357	0	.000	-0	-8	-8	-0	-0.2
● **JACK LAZORKO** Lazorko, Jack Thomas b: 3/30/56, Hoboken, N.J. BR/TR, 5′11″, 200 lbs. Deb: 6/4/84																										
1984	Mil-A	0	1	.000	15	1	0	0	1	39^2	37	7	22	24	13.6	4.31	89	.245	.345	0	—	0	-1	-2	0	0.2
1985	Sea-A	0	0	—	15	0	0	0	1	20^1	23	1	8	7	15.0	3.54	119	.291	.378	0	—	0	1	2	1	0.0
1986	Det-A	0	0	—	3	0	0	0	0	6^2	8	0	4	3	16.2	4.05	102	.296	.387	0	—	0	0	0	0	0.0
1987	Cal-A	5	6	.455	26	11	2	0	0	117^2	108	20	44	55	11.8	4.59	94	.248	.320	0	—	0	-2	-4	2	0.0
1988	Cal-A	0	1	.000	10	3	0	0	0	37^2	37	5	16	19	12.9	3.35	115	.255	.333	0	—	0	3	2	0	0.2
Total	5	5	8	.385	69	15	2	0	2	222	213	33	94	108	12.7	4.22	98	.254	.334	0	—	0	1	-2	3	0.4
● **CHARLIE LEA** Lea, Charles William b: 12/25/56, Orleans, France BR/TR, 6′4″, 197 lbs. Deb: 6/12/80																										
1980	Mon-N	7	5	.583	21	19	0	0	0	104	103	5	55	56	13.8	3.72	96	.262	.356	3	.081	-2	-1	-2	-1	-0.5
1981	Mon-N	5	4	.556	16	11	2	2	0	64^1	63	4	26	31	12.6	4.62	76	.268	.344	2	.133	-0	-8	-8	-0	-1.1
1982	Mon-N	12	10	.545	27	27	4	2	0	177^2	145	16	56	115	10.2	3.24	112	.222	.283	8	.123	-1	7	8	-1	0.7
1983	Mon-N	16	11	.593	33	33	8	4	0	222	195	15	84	137	11.4	3.12	115	.238	.309	8	.114	-2	12	11	-1	1.0
1984	Mon-N★	15	10	.600	30	30	8	0	0	224^1	198	19	68	123	10.8	2.89	119	.239	.299	8	.111	-3	17	13	0	1.2
1987	Mon-N	0	1	.000	1	1	0	0	0	1	4	1	2	1	54.0	36.00	12	.571	.667	0	—	0	-4	-4	0	-1.5
1988	Min-A	7	7	.500	24	23	0	0	0	130	156	19	50	72	14.6	4.85	84	.301	.368	0	—	0	-13	-11	-1	-1.3
Total	7	62	48	.564	152	144	22	8	0	923^1	864	79	341	535	11.9	3.54	102	.250	.320	29	.112	-7	11	8	-4	-1.5
● **RICK LEACH** Leach, Richard Max b: 5/4/57, Ann Arbor, Mich. BL/TL, 6′, 195 lbs. Deb: 4/30/81 ♦																										
1984	Tor-A	0	0	—	1	0	0	0	0	1	2	1	2	0	36.0	27.00	15	.400	.571	23	.261	0	-3	-3	0	0.0
● **TERRY LEACH** Leach, Terry Hester b: 3/13/54, Selma, Ala. BR/TR, 6′, 215 lbs. Deb: 8/12/81																										
1981	NY-N	1	1	.500	21	1	0	0	0	35^1	26	2	12	16	9.7	2.55	137	.205	.273	0	.000	1	4	4	1	0.3
1982	NY-N	2	1	.667	21	1	1	1	3	45^1	46	2	18	30	12.7	4.17	87	.271	.340	1	.125	-0	-3	-3	-0	-0.2
1985	NY-N	3	4	.429	22	4	1	1	1	55^2	48	3	14	30	10.2	2.91	119	.235	.288	2	.167	1	4	3	1	0.6
1986	NY-N	0	0	—	6	0	0	0	0	6^2	6	0	3	4	12.2	2.70	131	.222	.300	0	—	0	1	1	0	0.0
1987	NY-N	11	1	.917	44	12	1	1	0	131^1	132	14	29	61	11.1	3.22	117	.262	.304	2	.061	-2	13	8	1	0.6
1988	*NY-N	7	2	.778	52	0	0	0	3	92	95	5	24	51	11.9	2.54	127	.268	.320	2	.143	0	9	7	2	0.9
1989	NY-N	0	0	—	10	0	0	0	0	21^1	19	1	4	2	10.1	4.22	77	.244	.289	0	.000	-0	-2	-2	1	0.0
	KC-A	5	6	.455	30	3	0	0	0	73^2	78	4	36	34	14.0	4.15	93	.278	.362	0	—	0	-2	-3	1	-0.2
1990	Min-A	2	5	.286	55	0	0	0	2	81^2	84	2	21	46	11.7	3.20	130	.268	.316	0	—	0	6	9	1	0.8
1991	*Min-A	1	2	.333	50	0	0	0	0	67^1	82	3	14	32	12.8	3.61	118	.299	.333	0	—	0	4	5	1	0.2
1992	Chi-A	6	5	.545	51	0	0	0	0	73^2	57	2	20	22	9.9	1.95	197	.215	.280	0	—	0	16	16	1	2.3
1993	Chi-A	0	0	—	14	0	0	0	1	16	15	0	2	3	10.1	2.81	149	.250	.286	0	—	0	3	2	-1	0.0
Total	11	38	27	.585	376	21	3	3	10	700	688	38	197	331	11.5	3.15	119	.259	.313	7	.097	-1	53	47	8	5.3
● **LUIS LEAL** Leal, Luis Enrique (Alvarado) b: 3/21/57, Barquisimeto, Ven. BR/TR, 6′3″, 205 lbs. Deb: 5/25/80																										
1980	Tor-A	3	4	.429	13	10	1	0	0	59^2	72	6	31	26	15.7	4.53	95	.314	.398	0	—	0	-3	-1	-1	-0.2
1981	Tor-A	7	13	.350	29	19	3	0	1	129^2	127	8	44	71	12.2	3.68	107	.254	.321	0	—	0	-0	4	-1	0.4
1982	Tor-A	12	15	.444	38	38	10	0	0	249^2	250	24	79	111	12.0	3.93	114	.262	.320	0	—	0	4	15	-1	1.2
1983	Tor-A	13	12	.520	35	35	7	1	0	217^1	216	23	65	116	11.9	4.31	100	.257	.315	0	—	0	-6	-0	-1	-0.3
1984	Tor-A	13	8	.619	35	35	6	2	0	222^1	221	27	77	134	12.2	3.89	105	.258	.323	0	—	0	3	5	0	0.4
1985	Tor-A	3	6	.333	15	14	0	0	0	67^1	82	13	24	33	14.6	5.75	73	.303	.366	0	—	0	-12	-12	0	-1.3
Total	6	51	58	.468	165	151	27	3	1	946	968	101	320	491	12.5	4.14	103	.265	.328	0	—	0	-15	11	-2	0.2
● **KING LEAR** Lear, Charles Bernard b: 1/23/1891, Greencastle, Pa. d: 10/31/76, Waynesboro, Pa. BR/TR, 6′, 175 lbs. Deb: 5/2/14																										
1914	Cin-N	1	2	.333	17	4	3	1	1	55^2	55	3	19	20	12.3	3.07	95	.271	.339	3	.188	1	-2	-1	-0	0.0
1915	Cin-N	6	10	.375	40	15	9	0	0	167^2	169	7	45	46	11.8	3.01	95	.270	.324	8	.170	-1	-5	-3	-4	-0.8
Total	2	7	12	.368	57	19	12	1	1	223^1	224	10	64	66	11.9	3.02	95	.270	.328	11	.175	-0	-6	-4	-4	-0.8

YEAR	TM/L	W	L	PCT	G	GS	CG	SH	SV	IP	H	HR	BB	SO	RAT	ERA	ERA+	OAV	OOB	BH	AVG	PB	PR	/A	PD	TPI
● FRANK LEARY	Leary, Francis Patrick b: 2/26/1881, Wayland, Mass. d: 10/4/07, Natick, Mass. TR , Deb: 4/30/07																									
1907	Cin-N	0	1	.000	2	1	0	0	0	8	7	0	6	4	14.6	1.13	231	.269	.406	0	.000	-0	1	1	0	0.2
● JACK LEARY	Leary, John J. b: 1858, New Haven, Conn. TL , 5'11", 186 lbs. Deb: 8/21/1880 ♦																									
1880	Bos-N	0	1	.000	1	1	0	0	0	3	8	0	0	1	24.0	15.00	15	.727	.727	0	.000	-0	-4	-4	0	-0.8
1881	Det-N	0	2	.000	2	2	1	0	0	13	13	0	2	2	10.4	4.15	70	.255	.283	3	.273	1	-2	-2	-0	-0.2
1882	Pit-a	1	0	1.000	3	2	1	0	0	18^2	28	0	3	5	14.9	6.27	42	.326	.348	75	.292	1	-7	-8	0	-0.2
	Bal-a	2	1	.667	3	3	3	0	0	26	29	1	8	2	12.8	1.38	199	.264	.314	4	.222	0	4	4	-0	0.4
	Yr	3	1	.750	6	5	4	0	0	44^2	57	1	11	7	13.7	3.43	79	.291	.329	79	.287	1	-4	-4	0	0.2
1884	Alt-U	0	3	.000	3	3	2	0	0	24	31	0	2	7	12.4	5.25	51	.292	.306	3	.091	-2	-7	-7	-0	-0.7
	CP-U	0	2	.000	2	1	1	0	0	10	14	0	5	6	17.1	5.40	45	.311	.380	7	.175	-1	-3	-3	-0	-0.5
	Yr	0	5	.000	5	4	3	0	0	34	45	0	7	13	13.8	5.29	49	.298	.329	10	.137	-3	-11	-10	-0	-1.2
Total	4	3	9	.250	14	12	8	0	0	94^2	123	1	20	23	13.6	4.56	59	.301	.333	125	.232	-2	-21	-20	-0	-2.0
● TIM LEARY	Leary, Timothy James b: 12/23/58, Santa Monica, Cal. BR/TR, 6'3", 205 lbs. Deb: 4/12/81																									
1981	NY-N	0	0	—	1	1	0	0	0	2	0	0	1	3	4.5	0.00	—	.000	.143	0	.000	-0	1	1	0	0.0
1983	NY-N	1	1	.500	2	2	1	0	0	10^2	15	0	4	9	16.0	3.38	107	.319	.373	1	.333	0	0	0	0	0.1
1984	NY-N	3	3	.500	20	7	0	0	0	53^2	61	2	18	29	13.6	4.02	88	.285	.346	3	.300	2	-3	-3	-1	-0.2
1985	Mil-A	1	4	.200	5	5	0	0	0	33^1	40	5	8	29	13.2	4.05	103	.296	.340	0	—	0	0	0	1	0.1
1986	Mil-A	12	12	.500	33	30	3	2	0	188^1	216	20	53	110	13.2	4.21	103	.289	.342	0	—	0	-1	3	1	0.3
1987	LA-N	3	11	.214	39	12	0	0	1	107^2	121	15	36	61	13.3	4.76	83	.285	.344	7	.304	2	-8	-10	1	-0.9
1988	*LA-N	17	11	.607	35	34	9	6	0	228^2	201	13	56	180	10.4	2.91	114	.234	.285	18	.269	6	14	11	2	2.0
1989	LA-N	6	7	.462	19	17	2	0	0	117^1	107	9	37	59	11.2	3.38	101	.247	.309	2	.061	-2	2	1	1	-0.1
	Cin-N	2	7	.222	14	14	0	0	0	89^2	98	8	31	64	13.2	3.71	97	.278	.342	5	.192	2	-2	-1	0	0.1
	Yr	8	14	.364	33	31	2	0	0	207	205	17	68	123	12.0	3.52	99	.259	.320	7	.119	-1	-1	-1	1	0.0
1990	NY-A	9	19	.321	31	31	6	1	0	208	202	18	78	138	12.4	4.11	97	.257	.330	0	—	0	-5	-3	2	-0.2
1991	NY-A	4	10	.286	28	18	1	0	0	120^2	150	20	57	83	15.7	6.49	64	.312	.389	0	—	0	-32	-31	-0	-3.1
1992	NY-A	5	6	.455	18	15	2	0	0	97	84	9	57	34	13.5	5.57	70	.245	.359	0	—	0	-18	-18	-1	-1.8
	Sea-A	3	4	.429	8	8	1	0	0	44	47	3	30	12	16.8	4.91	81	.280	.404	0	—	0	-5	-5	1	-0.6
	Yr	8	10	.444	26	23	3	0	0	141	131	12	87	46	14.2	5.36	73	.251	.364	0	—	0	-22	-22	-0	-2.4
1993	Sea-A	11	9	.550	33	27	0	0	0	169^1	202	21	58	68	14.2	5.05	87	.300	.362	0	—	0	-14	-12	1	-1.1
1994	Tex-A	1	1	.500	6	3	0	0	0	21	26	4	11	9	16.3	8.14	59	.306	.392	0	—	0	-8	-8	0	-0.5
Total	13	78	105	.426	292	224	25	9	1	1491^1	1570	147	535	888	13.0	4.36	89	.273	.340	36	.221	9	-78	-76	7	-5.9
● GEORGE LeCLAIR	LeClair, George Lewis "Frenchy" b: 10/18/1886, Milton, Vt. d: 10/10/18, Farnham, Que., Can. BR/TR, 5'9", 170 lbs. Deb: 6/5/14																									
1914	Pit-F	5	2	.714	22	7	5	1	0	103^1	99	0	25	49	10.9	4.01	72	.262	.309	5	.147	-2	-13	-13	0	-1.0
1915	Pit-F	1	2	.333	14	3	1	0	1	45^2	43	1	13	10	11.0	3.35	81	.253	.306	2	.154	-1	-3	-3	1	-0.3
	Buf-F	0	0	—	1	0	0	0	0	3	4	0	1	2	15.0	6.00	47	.333	.385	0	—	0	-1	-1	-0	0.0
	Bal-F	1	8	.111	18	9	6	1	1	84	76	2	22	30	10.5	2.46	116	.246	.296	2	.083	-2	2	4	0	0.2
	Yr	2	10	.167	33	12	7	1	2	132^2	123	3	36	42	10.8	2.85	99	.251	.302	4	.108	-3	-2	-1	1	-0.1
Total	2	7	12	.368	55	19	12	2	2	236	222	3	61	91	10.8	3.36	85	.255	.305	9	.127	-5	-15	-14	1	-1.1
● RAZOR LEDBETTER	Ledbetter, Ralph Overton b: 12/8/1894, Rutherford College, N.C. d: 2/1/69, W.Palm Beach, Fla. BR/TR, 6'3", 190 lbs. Deb: 4/16/15																									
1915	Det-A	0	0	—	1	0	0	0	0	1	1	0	0	0	9.0	0.00	—	.333	.333	0	—	0	0	0	0	0.0
● DON LEE	Lee, Donald Edward b: 2/26/34, Globe, Ariz. BR/TR, 6'4", 210 lbs. Deb: 4/23/57 F																									
1957	Det-A	1	3	.250	11	6	0	0	0	38^2	48	6	18	19	15.6	4.66	83	.308	.383	2	.167	-0	-4	-3	-0	-0.4
1958	Det-A	0	0	—	1	0	0	0	0	2	1	1	1	0	13.5	9.00	45	.143	.333	0	—	0	-1	-1	-0	0.0
1960	Was-A	8	7	.533	44	20	1	0	3	165	160	16	64	88	12.4	3.44	113	.258	.330	5	.116	-0	8	8	1	0.8
1961	Min-A	3	6	.333	37	10	4	0	3	115	93	12	35	65	10.3	3.52	120	.221	.288	2	.067	-3	6	9	2	0.6
1962	Min-A	3	3	.500	9	9	1	0	0	52	51	8	24	28	14.2	4.50	91	.256	.357	4	.211	0	-3	-2	0	-0.2
	LA-A	8	8	.500	27	22	4	2	2	153^1	153	12	39	74	11.4	3.11	124	.256	.305	9	.184	-0	15	13	-2	1.1
	Yr	11	11	.500	36	31	5	2	2	205^1	204	20	63	102	11.8	3.46	113	.254	.310	13	.191	0	12	10	-2	0.9
1963	LA-A	8	11	.421	40	22	3	2	1	154	148	12	51	89	12.2	3.68	93	.251	.320	7	.156	-1	-1	-4	-1	-0.7
1964	LA-A	5	4	.556	33	8	0	0	2	89^1	99	6	25	73	12.6	2.72	121	.279	.328	6	.261	2	9	6	-1	0.7
1965	Cal-A	0	1	.000	10	0	0	0	0	14	21	4	5	12	17.4	6.43	53	.350	.409	1	.333	1	-5	-5	-0	-0.3
	Hou-N	0	0	—	7	0	0	0	0	8	8	0	3	3	13.5	3.38	99	.267	.353	0	.000	-0	0	-0	0	0.0
1966	Hou-N	2	0	1.000	9	0	0	0	0	18	17	1	4	9	10.5	2.50	137	.250	.292	1	1.000	1	2	2	1	0.3
	Chi-N	2	1	.667	16	0	0	0	0	19	28	3	12	7	18.9	7.11	52	.346	.430	0	—	0	-7	-7	-0	-1.0
	Yr	4	1	.800	25	0	0	0	0	37	45	4	16	16	14.8	4.86	73	.302	.370	1	1.000	1	-5	-5	1	-0.7
Total	9	40	44	.476	244	97	13	4	11	828^1	827	81	281	467	12.4	3.61	104	.260	.326	37	.164	-1	20	14	1	0.9
● MARK LEE	Lee, Mark Linden b: 6/14/53, Inglewood, Cal. BR/TR, 6'4", 225 lbs. Deb: 4/23/78																									
1978	SD-N	5	1	.833	56	0	0	0	2	85	74	2	36	31	11.9	3.28	101	.240	.324	0	.000	-1	3	0	2	0.1
1979	SD-N	2	4	.333	46	1	0	0	5	65	88	3	25	25	15.9	4.29	82	.332	.394	2	.333	1	-4	-6	1	-0.4
1980	Pit-N	0	1	.000	4	0	0	0	0	5^2	5	0	3	2	12.7	4.76	76	.227	.320	0	—	0	-1	-1	0	0.0
1981	Pit-N	0	2	.000	12	0	0	0	2	19^2	17	1	5	5	10.1	2.75	131	.233	.282	1	.500	0	2	2	1	0.4
Total	4	7	8	.467	118	1	0	0	9	175^1	184	6	69	63	13.2	3.64	94	.275	.347	3	.231	1	-0	-4	4	0.1
● MARK LEE	Lee, Mark Owen b: 7/20/64, Williston, N.Dak. BL/TL, 6'3", 198 lbs. Deb: 9/8/88																									
1988	KC-A	0	0	—	4	0	0	0	0	5	6	0	1	0	12.6	3.60	111	.300	.333	0	—	0	0	0	0	0.0
1990	Mil-A	1	0	1.000	11	0	0	0	0	21^1	20	1	4	14	10.1	2.11	184	.256	.293	0	—	0	4	4	-0	0.2
1991	Mil-A	2	5	.286	62	0	0	0	1	67^2	72	10	31	43	13.8	3.86	103	.283	.364	0	—	0	2	1	1	0.3
1995	Bal-A	2	0	1.000	39	0	0	0	1	33^1	31	5	18	27	13.5	4.86	98	.246	.345	0	—	0	-1	-0	-1	-0.1
Total	4	5	5	.500	116	0	0	0	2	127^1	129	16	54	84	13.1	3.82	109	.270	.346	0	—	0	6	5	-1	0.4
● MIKE LEE	Lee, Michael Randall b: 5/19/41, Bell, Cal. BL/TL, 6'5", 220 lbs. Deb: 5/6/60																									
1960	Cle-A	0	0	—	7	0	0	0	0	9	6	1	11	6	18.0	2.00	187	.207	.439	0	—	0	2	2	-0	0.0
1963	LA-A	1	1	.500	6	4	0	0	0	26	30	3	14	11	15.6	3.81	90	.300	.391	0	.000	-1	-1	-1	1	-0.1
Total	2	1	1	.500	13	4	0	0	0	35	36	4	25	17	16.2	3.34	105	.279	.404	0	.000	-1	1	1	1	-0.1
● BOB LEE	Lee, Robert Dean "Moose" or "Horse" b: 11/26/37, Ottumwa, Iowa BR/TR, 6'3", 230 lbs. Deb: 4/15/64																									
1964	LA-A	6	5	.545	64	5	0	0	19	137	87	6	58	111	9.6	1.51	217	.182	.272	0	.000	-2	**32**	27	-2	2.5
1965	Cal-A☆	9	7	.563	69	0	0	0	23	131^1	95	11	42	89	9.5	1.92	177	.205	.272	3	.143	1	22	22	-1	3.4
1966	Cal-A	5	4	.556	61	0	0	0	16	101^2	90	8	31	46	10.8	2.74	122	.237	.297	0	.000	-0	8	7	-1	0.7
1967	LA-N	0	0	—	4	0	0	0	0	6^2	6	2	3	2	13.5	5.40	57	.222	.323	0	—	0	-2	-2	-0	0.0
	Cin-N	3	3	.500	27	1	0	0	2	50^2	51	0	25	33	13.5	4.44	84	.262	.345	3	.375	1	-6	-4	-1	-0.5
	Yr	3	3	.500	31	1	0	0	2	57^1	57	2	28	35	13.3	4.55	81	.254	.337	3	.375	1	-8	-6	-1	-0.5
1968	Cin-N	2	4	.333	44	1	0	0	3	65^1	73	4	37	34	15.3	5.10	62	.302	.396	1	.200	0	-15	-14	-1	-1.6
Total	5	25	23	.521	269	7	0	0	63	492^2	402	31	196	315	11.0	2.70	125	.225	.304	7	.104	-1	40	36	-6	4.5
● ROY LEE	Lee, Roy Edwin b: 9/28/17, Elmira, N.Y. d: 11/11/85, St.Louis, Mo. BL/TL, 5'11.5", 175 lbs. Deb: 9/23/45																									
1945	NY-N	0	2	.000	3	1	0	0	0	7	8	3	3	0	14.1	11.57	34	.267	.333	0	.000	-0	-6	-6	-0	-1.3
● TOM LEE	Lee, Thomas Frank b: 6/8/1862, Philadelphia, Pa. d: 3/4/1886, Milwaukee, Wis. Deb: 6/14/1884																									
1884	Chi-N	1	4	.200	5	5	5	0	0	45^1	55	12	15	14	13.9	3.77	83	.272	.323	3	.125	-2	-4	-3	-0	-0.4
	Bal-U	5	8	.385	15	14	12	0	0	122	121	1	29	81	11.1	3.39	79	.242	.283	23	.280	-2	-13	-10	0	-0.9
Total	1	6	12	.333	20	19	17	0	0	167^1	176	13	44	95	11.8	3.50	80	.250	.295	26	.245	-4	-17	-13	0	-1.3
● THORNTON LEE	Lee, Thornton Starr "Lefty" b: 9/13/06, Sonoma, Cal. d: 6/9/97, Tucson, Ariz. BL/TL, 6'3", 205 lbs. Deb: 9/19/33 F																									
1933	Cle-A	1	1	.500	3	2	2	0	0	17^1	13	1	11	7	12.5	4.15	107	.203	.320	3	.375	1	0	1	-0	0.2
1934	Cle-A	1	1	.500	24	6	0	0	0	85^2	105	8	44	41	16.0	5.04	90	.308	.392	2	.095	-1	-5	-5	0	-0.2

YEAR TM/L	W	L	PCT	G	GS	CG	SH	SV	IP	H	HR	BB	SO	RAT	ERA	ERA+	OAV	OOB	BH	AVG	PB	PR	/A	PD	TPI
1935 Cle-A	7	10	.412	32	20	8	1	1	180^2	179	6	71	81	12.7	4.04	112	.259	.331	12	.197	-1	8	9	2	0.8
1936 Cle-A	3	5	.375	43	8	2	0	3	127	138	2	67	49	14.7	4.89	103	.271	.358	5	.122	-2	**2**	2	2	0.1
1937 Chi-A	12	10	.545	30	25	13	2	0	204^2	209	17	60	80	11.9	3.52	131	.260	.312	15	.211	1	25	25	-1	2.2
1938 Chi-A	13	12	.520	33	30	18	1	1	245^1	252	12	94	77	12.8	3.49	140	.263	.331	25	.258	6	36	**38**	-2	3.8
1939 Chi-A	15	11	.577	33	29	15	2	3	235	260	14	70	81	12.8	4.21	112	.285	.338	15	.165	-3	11	14	0	1.1
1940 Chi-A	12	13	.480	28	27	24	1	0	228	223	13	56	87	11.1	3.47	127	.254	.300	23	.274	4	23	24	-3	2.4
1941 Chi-A★	22	11	.667	35	34	**30**	3	1	300^1	258	18	92	130	**10.6**	**2.37**	**173**	.232	**.293**	29	.254	5	**59**	**58**	-2	**6.6**
1942 Chi-A	2	6	.250	11	8	6	1	0	76	82	4	31	25	13.6	3.32	109	.278	.351	6	.200	0	3	2	-2	0.1
1943 Chi-A	5	9	.357	19	19	7	1	0	127	129	8	50	35	13.0	4.18	80	.266	.340	3	.071	-4	-12	-12	-3	-1.9
1944 Chi-A	3	9	.250	15	14	6	0	0	113^1	105	3	25	39	10.4	3.02	114	.246	.290	4	.095	-3	5	5	2	0.4
1945 Chi-A†	15	12	.556	29	28	19	1	0	228^1	208	6	76	108	11.6	2.44	136	.245	.314	14	.179	-1	23	22	-1	2.4
1946 Chi-A	2	4	.333	7	7	2	0	0	43^1	39	1	23	23	13.1	3.53	97	.244	.342	4	.267	1	-0	-1	-0	-0.1
1947 Chi-A	3	7	.300	21	11	2	1	1	86^2	86	5	56	57	15.0	4.47	82	.261	.372	6	.207	0	-7	-8	0	-0.8
1948 NY-N	1	3	.250	11	4	1	0	0	32^2	41	3	12	17	14.9	4.41	89	.304	.365	1	.091	-1	-2	-2	0	-0.2
Total 16	117	124	.485	374	272	155	14	10	2331^1	2327	121	838	937	12.4	3.56	119	.260	.326	167	.200	1	169	172	-7	16.9

● BILL LEE Lee, William Crutcher "Big Bill" b: 10/21/09, Plaquemine, La. d: 6/15/77, Plaquemine, La. BR/TR, 6'3", 195 lbs. Deb: 4/29/34

YEAR TM/L	W	L	PCT	G	GS	CG	SH	SV	IP	H	HR	BB	SO	RAT	ERA	ERA+	OAV	OOB	BH	AVG	PB	PR	/A	PD	TPI
1934 Chi-N	13	14	.481	35	29	16	4	1	214^1	218	9	74	104	12.3	3.40	114	.263	.325	10	.132	-2	16	11	2	1.2
1935 *Chi-N	20	6	**.769**	39	32	18	3	1	252	241	11	84	100	11.8	2.96	133	.251	.314	24	.235	2	30	27	-0	2.7
1936 Chi-N	18	11	.621	43	33	20	**4**	1	258^2	238	14	93	102	11.6	3.31	121	.246	.314	12	.138	-3	21	19	1	1.7
1937 Chi-N	14	15	.483	42	34	17	2	3	272^1	289	14	73	108	12.0	3.54	113	.273	.320	15	.172	-1	11	13	3	1.5
1938 *Chi-N★	**22**	9	**.710**	44	37	19	**9**	2	291	281	18	74	121	11.0	**2.66**	**144**	.252	.299	20	.198	1	**37**	**38**	1	**4.0**
1939 Chi-N★	19	15	.559	37	36	20	1	0	282^1	295	18	85	105	12.1	3.44	114	.272	.325	13	.126	-4	15	16	5	1.7
1940 Chi-N	9	17	.346	37	30	9	1	0	211^1	246	12	70	70	13.5	5.03	75	.294	.350	10	.132	-2	-28	-30	-1	-3.5
1941 Chi-N	8	14	.364	28	22	12	0	1	167^1	179	6	43	62	12.0	3.76	93	.270	.316	11	.186	1	-2	-5	1	-0.3
1942 Chi-N	13	13	.500	32	30	18	1	0	219^2	221	4	67	75	11.8	3.85	83	.258	.312	11	.159	1	-13	-16	1	-1.5
1943 Chi-N	3	7	.300	13	12	4	0	0	78^1	83	4	27	18	12.6	3.56	94	.273	.332	7	.269	1	-2	-2	-1	-0.2
Phi-N	1	5	.167	13	7	2	0	3	60^2	70	4	21	17	13.6	4.60	73	.298	.358	1	.059	-2	-8	-8	-1	-1.1
Yr	4	12	.250	26	19	6	0	3	139	153	8	48	35	13.1	4.01	84	.284	.344	8	.186	-0	-10	-10	-2	-1.3
1944 Phi-N	10	11	.476	31	28	11	3	1	208^1	199	9	57	50	11.2	3.15	115	.248	.300	14	.194	-0	11	11	2	1.2
1945 Phi-N	3	6	.333	13	13	2	0	0	77^1	107	0	30	13	15.9	4.66	82	.318	.374	4	.167	-1	-7	-7	0	-0.7
Bos-N	6	3	.667	16	13	6	1	0	106^1	112	6	36	12	12.5	2.79	137	.279	.338	4	.129	-1	12	12	1	1.0
Yr	9	9	.500	29	26	8	1	0	183^2	219	6	66	25	14.0	3.58	107	.297	.354	8	.145	-1	5	5	1	0.3
1946 Bos-N	10	9	.526	25	21	8	0	0	140	148	7	45	32	12.5	4.18	82	.273	.330	8	.170	-1	-12	-12	1	-1.4
1947 Chi-N	0	2	.000	14	2	0	0	0	24	26	2	14	9	15.4	4.50	88	.268	.366	1	.333	0	-1	-1	0	-0.1
Total 14	169	157	.518	462	379	182	29	13	2864	2953	138	893	998	12.2	3.54	106	.266	.322	165	.168	-10	78	66	14	6.2

● BILL LEE Lee, William Francis "Spaceman" b: 12/28/46, Burbank, Cal. BL/TL, 6'3", 210 lbs. Deb: 6/25/69

YEAR TM/L	W	L	PCT	G	GS	CG	SH	SV	IP	H	HR	BB	SO	RAT	ERA	ERA+	OAV	OOB	BH	AVG	PB	PR	/A	PD	TPI
1969 Bos-A	1	3	.250	20	1	0	0	0	52	56	9	28	45	14.9	4.50	84	.281	.376	0	.000	-1	-5	-4	-0	-0.4
1970 Bos-A	2	2	.500	11	5	0	0	1	37	48	3	14	19	15.1	4.62	86	.320	.378	0	.000	-1	-4	-3	1	-0.3
1971 Bos-A	9	2	.818	47	3	0	0	2	102	102	7	46	74	13.1	2.74	135	.256	.335	5	.217	0	8	11	0	1.3
1972 Bos-A	7	4	.636	47	0	0	0	5	84^1	75	5	32	43	11.5	3.20	100	.248	.322	3	.188	1	-1	0	3	0.5
1973 Bos-A☆	17	11	.607	38	33	18	1	1	284^2	275	20	76	120	11.3	2.75	146	.257	.309	0	—	0	34	40	1	4.0
1974 Bos-A	17	15	.531	38	37	16	1	0	282^1	320	25	67	95	12.5	3.51	110	.290	.333	0	—	0	3	11	4	1.3
1975 *Bos-A	17	9	.654	41	34	17	4	0	260	274	20	69	78	12.0	3.95	103	.273	.322	0	—	0	-5	4	2	0.5
1976 Bos-A	5	7	.417	24	14	1	0	3	96	124	13	28	29	14.5	5.63	70	.307	.356	0	—	0	-22	-18	1	-2.1
1977 Bos-A	9	5	.643	27	16	4	0	3	128	155	14	29	31	12.9	4.43	101	.306	.344	0	—	0	-5	1	2	0.1
1978 Bos-A	10	10	.500	28	24	8	1	0	177	198	20	59	44	13.2	3.46	119	.285	.343	0	—	0	6	13	0	0.8
1979 Mon-N	16	10	.615	33	33	6	3	0	222	230	20	46	59	11.2	3.04	121	.265	.303	16	.216	2	17	15	1	2.0
1980 Mon-N	4	6	.400	24	18	2	0	0	118	156	13	22	34	13.8	4.96	72	.319	.352	9	.220	1	-18	-18	-0	-1.4
1981 *Mon-N	5	6	.455	31	7	0	0	6	88^2	90	6	14	34	10.8	2.94	119	.265	.298	8	.364	3	5	5	3	1.4
1982 Mon-N	0	0	—	7	0	0	0	0	12^1	19	1	1	8	14.6	4.38	83	.352	.364	0	—	0	-1	-1	0	0.0
Total 14	119	90	.569	416	225	72	10	19	1944^1	2122	176	531	713	12.4	3.62	107	.280	.329	41	.208	5	12	55	16	7.7

● WATTY LEE Lee, Wyatt Arnold b: 8/12/1879, Lynch Station, Va. d: 3/6/36, Washington, D.C. BL/TL, 5'10.5", 171 lbs. Deb: 4/30/01 ♦

YEAR TM/L	W	L	PCT	G	GS	CG	SH	SV	IP	H	HR	BB	SO	RAT	ERA	ERA+	OAV	OOB	BH	AVG	PB	PR	/A	PD	TPI
1901 Was-A	16	16	.500	36	33	25	2	0	262	328	14	45	63	13.2	4.40	83	.303	.337	33	.256	4	-21	-21	2	-1.5
1902 Was-A	5	6	.455	13	10	10	0	0	98	118	5	20	24	13.4	5.05	73	.298	.344	100	.256	3	-16	-15	1	-1.0
1903 Was-A	8	12	.400	22	20	15	2	0	166^2	169	5	40	70	11.7	3.08	102	.262	.313	48	.208	1	-2	1	3	0.6
1904 Pit-N	1	2	.333	5	3	1	0	0	22^2	34	0	9	5	18.3	8.74	31	.337	.407	4	.333	1	-15	-15	0	-1.5
Total 4	30	36	.455	76	66	51	4	0	549^1	649	24	114	162	13.0	4.29	81	.292	.334	185	.242	10	-55	-50	5	-3.4

● SAM LEEVER Leever, Samuel "Deacon" or "The Goshen Schoolmaster"
b: 12/23/1871, Goshen, Ohio d: 5/19/53, Goshen, Ohio BR/TR, 5'10.5", 175 lbs. Deb: 5/26/1898

YEAR TM/L	W	L	PCT	G	GS	CG	SH	SV	IP	H	HR	BB	SO	RAT	ERA	ERA+	OAV	OOB	BH	AVG	PB	PR	/A	PD	TPI
1898 Pit-N	1	0	1.000	5	3	2	0	0	33	26	0	5	15	8.7	2.45	145	.215	.252	3	.250	0	4	4	-0	0.1
1899 Pit-N	21	23	.477	**51**	39	35	4	**3**	**379**	353	7	122	121	11.5	3.18	120	.247	.311	33	.226	3	28	27	1	3.0
1900 *Pit-N	15	13	.536	30	29	25	3	0	232^2	236	2	48	84	11.3	2.71	134	.263	.306	18	.205	0	26	24	-1	2.4
1901 Pit-N	14	5	.737	21	20	18	2	0	176	182	2	39	82	11.7	2.86	114	.265	.311	13	.183	-0	9	8	2	0.8
1902 Pit-N	15	7	.682	28	26	23	4	2	222	203	2	31	86	9.8	2.39	114	.243	.277	16	.178	-0	10	9	-4	0.3
1903 *Pit-N	25	7	**.781**	36	34	30	**7**	1	284^1	255	2	60	90	10.1	**2.06**	**157**	.238	.282	19	.165	-4	38	37	-0	3.4
1904 Pit-N	18	11	.621	34	32	26	1	0	253^1	224	2	54	63	10.1	2.17	127	.237	.282	26	.263	7	16	16	-1	2.4
1905 Pit-N	20	5	**.800**	33	29	20	3	1	229^2	199	3	54	81	10.4	2.70	111	.231	.286	9	.102	-4	8	8	0	0.4
1906 Pit-N	22	7	.759	36	31	25	6	0	260^1	232	3	48	76	9.9	2.32	115	.243	.284	20	.211	2	9	10	-5	0.7
1907 Pit-N	14	9	.609	31	24	17	5	0	216^2	182	3	46	65	9.8	1.66	147	.229	.278	11	.151	-1	20	19	-5	1.3
1908 Pit-N	15	7	.682	38	20	14	4	2	192^2	179	1	41	28	10.6	2.10	110	.249	.295	9	.148	0	6	4	-4	0.1
1909 Pit-N	8	1	.889	19	4	2	0	2	70	74	0	14	23	11.8	2.83	96	.276	.322	4	.167	0	-2	-1	0	-0.1
1910 Pit-N	6	5	.545	26	8	4	0	2	111	104	2	25	33	10.9	2.76	112	.259	.313	2	.065	-3	3	4	1	0.2
Total 13	194	100	.660	388	299	241	39	13	2660^2	2449	29	587	847	10.6	2.47	123	.245	.293	183	.184	1	175	169	-15	15.0

● BILL LEFEBVRE Lefebvre, Wilfred Henry "Lefty" b: 11/11/15, Natick, R.I. BL/TL, 5'11.5", 180 lbs. Deb: 6/10/38 ♦

YEAR TM/L	W	L	PCT	G	GS	CG	SH	SV	IP	H	HR	BB	SO	RAT	ERA	ERA+	OAV	OOB	BH	AVG	PB	PR	/A	PD	TPI
1938 Bos-A	0	0	—	1	0	0	0	0	4	8	2	0	0	20.3	13.50	37	.400	.429	1	1.000	1	-4	-4	-0	0.1
1939 Bos-A	1	1	.500	5	3	0	0	0	26^1	35	2	14	8	16.7	5.81	81	.333	.412	3	.300	1	-3	-3	-1	-0.2
1943 Was-A	2	0	1.000	6	3	1	0	0	32^1	33	3	16	10	13.6	4.45	72	.268	.353	4	.286	2	-4	-4	-0	-0.1
1944 Was-A	2	4	.333	24	4	2	0	3	69^2	86	3	21	18	14.0	4.52	72	.305	.355	16	.258	3	-8	-10	-0	-0.3
Total 4	5	5	.500	36	10	3	0	3	132^1	162	10	51	36	14.6	5.03	71	.306	.369	24	.276	7	-20	-21	-1	-0.5

● CRAIG LEFFERTS Lefferts, Craig Lindsay b: 9/29/57, Munich, W.Germany BL/TL, 6'1", 210 lbs. Deb: 4/7/83

YEAR TM/L	W	L	PCT	G	GS	CG	SH	SV	IP	H	HR	BB	SO	RAT	ERA	ERA+	OAV	OOB	BH	AVG	PB	PR	/A	PD	TPI
1983 Chi-N	3	4	.429	56	5	0	0	1	89	80	13	29	60	11.2	3.13	121	.243	.308	2	.111	-1	5	6	0	0.5
1984 *SD-N	3	4	.429	62	0	0	0	10	105^2	88	4	24	56	9.6	2.13	167	.229	.276	5	.294	1	17	17	-1	1.4
1985 SD-N	7	6	.538	60	0	0	0	2	83^1	75	7	30	48	11.3	3.35	106	.244	.312	1	.250	0	2	2	-0	0.2
1986 SD-N	9	8	.529	**83**	0	0	0	4	107^2	98	7	44	72	12.0	3.09	118	.253	.331	1	.125	1	7	7	2	1.3
1987 SD-N	2	2	.500	33	0	0	0	2	51^1	56	9	15	39	12.8	4.38	90	.272	.327	1	.333	0	-2	-2	-1	-0.2
*SF-N	3	3	.500	44	0	0	0	4	47^1	36	4	18	18	10.3	3.23	119	.216	.292	1	.250	1	4	3	-1	0.4
Yr	5	5	.500	77	0	0	0	6	98^2	92	13	33	57	11.4	3.83	102	.245	.306	2	.286	1	3	1	-1	0.2
1988 SF-N	3	8	.273	64	0	0	0	11	92^1	74	7	23	58	9.6	2.92	112	.225	.278	0	.000	-1	5	3	-1	0.3
1989 *SF-N	2	4	.333	70	0	0	0	20	107	93	11	22	71	9.8	2.69	125	.233	.275	0	.000	-1	10	8	-1	0.5
1990 SD-N	7	5	.583	56	0	0	0	23	78^2	68	10	22	60	10.4	2.52	152	.228	.283	1	.250	0	11	11	0	2.3
1991 SD-N	1	6	.143	54	0	0	0	23	69	74	5	14	48	11.6	3.91	97	.285	.324	0	.000	-1	-2	-1	0	-0.2
1992 SD-N	13	9	.591	27	27	0	0	0	163^1	180	16	35	81	11.8	3.69	97	.285	.322	4	.077	-3	-3	-2	-1	-0.6
Bal-A	1	3	.250	5	5	1	0	0	33	34	3	6	23	10.9	4.09	98	.268	.301	0	—	0	-1	-0	-1	-0.2
1993 Tex-A	3	9	.250	52	8	0	0	0	83^1	102	17	28	58	14.1	6.05	69	.304	.360	0	—	0	-16	-18	0	-2.0

YEAR	TM/L	W	L	PCT	G	GS	CG	SH	SV	IP	H	HR	BB	SO	RAT	ERA	ERA+	OAV	OOB	BH	AVG	PB	PR	/A	PD	TPI
1994	Cal-A	1	1	.500	30	0	0	0	1	34^2	50	7	12	27	16.1	4.67	105	.350	.400	0	—	0	0	1	-1	-0.1
Total	12	58	72	.446	696	45	1	0	101	1145^2	1108	120	322	719	11.3	3.43	108	.257	.311	16	.121	-3	39	36	-4	3.6

● PHIL LEFTWICH

Leftwich, Philip Dale b: 5/19/69, Lynchburg, Va. BR/TR, 6′5″, 205 lbs. Deb: 7/29/93

YEAR	TM/L	W	L	PCT	G	GS	CG	SH	SV	IP	H	HR	BB	SO	RAT	ERA	ERA+	OAV	OOB	BH	AVG	PB	PR	/A	PD	TPI
1993	Cal-A	4	6	.400	12	12	1	0	0	80^2	81	5	27	31	12.4	3.79	119	.262	.327	0	—	0	5	6	-0	0.6
1994	Cal-A	5	10	.333	20	20	1	0	0	114	127	16	42	67	13.6	5.68	86	.283	.349	0	—	0	-11	-10	-0	-1.2
1996	Cal-A	0	1	.000	2	2	0	0	0	7^1	12	1	3	4	18.4	7.36	68	.375	.429	0	—	0	-2	-2	0	-0.2
Total	3	9	17	.346	34	34	2	0	0	202	220	22	72	102	13.3	4.99	95	.279	.344	0	—	0	-8	-6	-0	-0.8

● REGIS LEHENY

Leheny, Regis Francis b: 1/5/08, Pittsburgh, Pa. d: 11/2/76, Pittsburgh, Pa. BL/TL, 6′0.5″, 180 lbs. Deb: 5/21/32

YEAR	TM/L	W	L	PCT	G	GS	CG	SH	SV	IP	H	HR	BB	SO	RAT	ERA	ERA+	OAV	OOB	BH	AVG	PB	PR	/A	PD	TPI
1932	Bos-A	0	0	—	2	0	0	0	0	2^2	5	0	3	1	27.0	16.88	27	.417	.533	0	.000	-0	-4	-4	0	0.0

● JIM LEHEW

Lehew, James Anthony b: 8/19/37, Baltimore, Md. BR/TR, 6′, 185 lbs. Deb: 9/13/61

YEAR	TM/L	W	L	PCT	G	GS	CG	SH	SV	IP	H	HR	BB	SO	RAT	ERA	ERA+	OAV	OOB	BH	AVG	PB	PR	/A	PD	TPI
1961	Bal-A	0	0	—	2	0	0	0	0	2	1	0	0	0	4.5	0.00	—	.167	.167	0	—	0	1	1	0	0.0
1962	Bal-A	0	0	—	6	0	0	0	0	9^2	10	0	3	2	12.1	1.86	199	.303	.361	0	.000	-0	2	2	0	0.0
Total	2	0	0	—	8	0	0	0	0	11^2	11	0	3	2	10.8	1.54	241	.282	.333	0	.000	-0	3	3	0	0.0

● KEN LEHMAN

Lehman, Kenneth Karl b: 6/10/28, Seattle, Wash. BL/TL, 6′, 186 lbs. Deb: 9/5/52

YEAR	TM/L	W	L	PCT	G	GS	CG	SH	SV	IP	H	HR	BB	SO	RAT	ERA	ERA+	OAV	OOB	BH	AVG	PB	PR	/A	PD	TPI
1952	*Bro-N	1	2	.333	4	3	0	0	0	15^1	19	1	6	7	14.7	5.28	69	.297	.357	0	.000	0	-3	-3	0	-0.4
1956	Bro-N	2	3	.400	25	4	0	0	0	49^1	65	11	23	29	16.1	5.66	70	.325	.395	3	.300	1	-10	-9	1	-0.7
1957	Bro-N	0	0	—	3	0	0	0	0	7	7	0	1	3	10.3	0.00	—	.259	.286	1	.500	0	3	3	0	0.0
	Bal-A	8	3	.727	30	3	1	0	6	68	57	1	22	32	10.5	2.78	129	.232	.295	4	.200	1	8	6	-1	1.2
1958	Bal-A	2	1	.667	31	1	1	0	0	62	64	5	18	36	12.2	3.48	103	.276	.333	1	.071	-1	2	1	0	-0.1
1961	Phi-N	1	1	.500	41	2	0	0	1	63^1	61	6	25	27	12.4	4.26	96	.260	.333	0	.000	-1	-2	-1	1	0.0
Total	5	14	10	.583	134	13	2	0	7	265	273	24	95	134	12.6	3.91	97	.272	.337	9	.161	1	-2	-3	2	0.0

● NORM LEHR

Lehr, Norman Carl Michael "King" b: 5/28/01, Rochester, N.Y. d: 7/17/68, Livonia, N.Y. BR/TR, 6′, 168 lbs. Deb: 5/20/26

YEAR	TM/L	W	L	PCT	G	GS	CG	SH	SV	IP	H	HR	BB	SO	RAT	ERA	ERA+	OAV	OOB	BH	AVG	PB	PR	/A	PD	TPI
1926	Cle-A	0	0	—	4	0	0	0	0	14^2	11	0	4	4	9.2	3.07	132	.216	.273	0	.000	-1	2	2	1	0.0

● HANK LEIBER

Leiber, Henry Edward b: 1/17/11, Phoenix, Ariz. d: 11/8/93, Tucson, Ariz. BR/TR, 6′1.5″, 205 lbs. Deb: 4/16/33 ♦

YEAR	TM/L	W	L	PCT	G	GS	CG	SH	SV	IP	H	HR	BB	SO	RAT	ERA	ERA+	OAV	OOB	BH	AVG	PB	PR	/A	PD	TPI
1942	NY-N	0	1	.000	1	1	1	0	0	9	9	0	5	5	15.0	6.00	56	.290	.405	32	.218	0	-3	-3	0	-0.2

● CHARLIE LEIBRANDT

Leibrandt, Charles Louis b: 10/4/56, Chicago, Ill. BR/TL, 6′3″, 200 lbs. Deb: 9/17/79

YEAR	TM/L	W	L	PCT	G	GS	CG	SH	SV	IP	H	HR	BB	SO	RAT	ERA	ERA+	OAV	OOB	BH	AVG	PB	PR	/A	PD	TPI
1979	*Cin-N	0	0	—	3	0	0	0	0	4^1	2	0	2	1	8.3	0.00	—	.154	.267	0	—	0	2	2	0	0.0
1980	Cin-N	10	9	.526	36	27	5	2	0	173^2	200	15	54	62	13.3	4.25	84	.292	.346	11	.196	1	-13	-13	1	-1.1
1981	Cin-N	1	1	.500	7	4	1	1	0	30	28	0	15	9	12.9	3.60	99	.262	.352	0	.000	-0	-0	-0	0	0.0
1982	Cin-N	5	7	.417	36	11	0	0	2	107^2	130	4	48	34	15.0	5.10	73	.308	.381	2	.080	-1	-18	-17	-0	-2.0
1984	*KC-A	11	7	.611	23	23	0	0	0	143^2	158	11	38	53	12.5	3.63	111	.277	.326	0	—	0	6	6	-2	0.6
1985	*KC-A	17	9	.654	33	33	8	3	0	237^2	223	17	68	108	11.1	2.69	155	.248	.302	0	—	0	38	39	4	4.5
1986	KC-A	14	11	.560	35	34	8	1	0	231^1	238	18	63	108	11.9	4.09	104	.268	.319	0	—	0	2	4	2	0.6
1987	KC-A	16	11	.593	35	35	8	3	0	240^1	235	23	74	151	11.6	3.41	134	.253	.308	0	—	0	28	31	4	3.5
1988	KC-A	13	12	.520	35	35	7	2	0	243	244	20	62	125	11.5	3.19	125	.264	.313	0	—	0	21	22	2	2.3
1989	KC-A	5	11	.313	33	27	3	1	0	161	196	13	54	73	14.1	5.14	75	.304	.360	0	—	0	-23	-23	-0	-2.1
1990	Atl-N	9	11	.450	24	24	5	2	0	162^1	164	9	35	76	11.3	3.16	128	.261	.304	9	.180	1	11	16	1	2.1
1991	*Atl-N	15	13	.536	36	36	1	1	0	229^2	212	18	56	128	10.7	3.49	111	.245	.294	3	.043	-4	5	10	4	1.2
1992	*Atl-N	15	7	.682	32	31	5	2	0	193	191	9	42	104	11.1	3.36	109	.258	.302	7	.121	-1	3	6	3	0.9
1993	Tex-A	9	10	.474	26	26	1	0	0	150^1	169	15	45	89	13.1	4.55	91	.284	.339	0	—	0	-4	-7	5	-0.1
Total	14	140	119	.541	394	346	52	18	2	2308	2390	172	656	1121	12.0	3.71	108	.268	.321	32	.120	-5	60	77	25	10.4

● LEFTY LEIFIELD

Leifield, Albert Peter b: 9/5/1883, Trenton, Ill. d: 10/10/70, Alexandria, Va. BL/TL, 6′1″, 165 lbs. Deb: 9/3/05 C

YEAR	TM/L	W	L	PCT	G	GS	CG	SH	SV	IP	H	HR	BB	SO	RAT	ERA	ERA+	OAV	OOB	BH	AVG	PB	PR	/A	PD	TPI
1905	Pit-N	5	2	.714	8	7	6	1	0	56	52	0	14	10	11.3	2.89	104	.248	.307	7	.350	3	1	1	1	0.5
1906	Pit-N	18	13	.581	37	31	24	8	1	255^2	214	3	68	111	10.4	1.87	143	.231	.294	11	.125	-3	22	23	1	2.7
1907	Pit-N	20	16	.556	40	33	24	6	1	286	270	1	100	112	12.0	2.33	105	.256	.328	15	.147	0	5	3	4	0.8
1908	Pit-N	15	14	.517	34	26	18	5	2	218^2	168	1	86	87	10.9	2.10	110	.212	.299	17	.227	3	6	5	-0	1.0
1909	*Pit-N	19	8	.704	32	26	13	3	0	201^2	172	4	54	43	10.4	2.37	115	.229	.286	14	.192	2	5	8	-2	1.0
1910	Pit-N	15	13	.536	40	30	13	3	2	218^1	197	6	67	64	11.3	2.64	117	.253	.320	11	.183	0	10	11	3	1.7
1911	Pit-N	16	16	.500	42	37	26	2	1	318	301	7	82	111	11.3	2.63	131	.260	.318	24	.235	6	27	28	-1	3.2
1912	Pit-N	1	2	.333	6	1	1	0	0	23^2	29	0	10	8	15.6	4.18	78	.302	.380	1	.143	0	-2	-2	1	-0.1
	Chi-N	7	2	.778	13	9	4	1	0	70^2	68	0	21	23	11.7	2.42	137	.258	.319	3	.115	-1	8	7	1	0.8
	Yr	8	4	.667	19	10	5	1	0	94^1	97	0	31	31	12.5	2.86	116	.268	.331	4	.121	-1	6	5	2	0.7
1913	Chi-N	0	1	.000	6	1	0	0	1	21^1	28	0	5	4	13.9	5.48	58	.329	.367	0	.000	-1	-5	-5	1	-0.3
1918	StL-A	2	6	.250	15	6	3	1	0	67	61	1	19	22	11.0	2.55	107	.252	.312	1	.053	-2	2	1	1	0.1
1919	StL-A	6	4	.600	19	9	6	2	0	92	96	4	25	18	12.2	2.93	113	.270	.325	3	.100	-2	3	4	1	0.2
1920	StL-A	0	0	—	4	0	0	0	0	9	17	0	3	3	20.0	7.00	56	.405	.444	0	.000	-0	-3	-3	-0	-0.1
Total	12	124	97	.561	296	216	138	32	7	1838	1673	27	554	616	11.3	2.47	116	.248	.313	107	.175	6	77	81	10	11.5

● DAVE LEIPER

Leiper, David Paul b: 6/18/62, Whittier, Cal. BL/TL, 6′1″, 160 lbs. Deb: 9/2/84

YEAR	TM/L	W	L	PCT	G	GS	CG	SH	SV	IP	H	HR	BB	SO	RAT	ERA	ERA+	OAV	OOB	BH	AVG	PB	PR	/A	PD	TPI
1984	Oak-A	1	0	1.000	8	0	0	0	0	7	12	2	5	3	21.9	9.00	42	.353	.436	0	—	0	-4	-4	0	-0.5
1986	Oak-A	2	2	.500	33	0	0	0	1	31^2	28	3	18	15	13.6	4.83	80	.252	.366	0	—	0	-2	-3	0	-0.3
1987	Oak-A	2	1	.667	45	0	0	0	1	52^1	49	6	18	33	11.7	3.78	109	.246	.312	0	—	0	4	2	1	0.3
	SD-N	1	0	1.000	12	0	0	0	1	16	16	2	5	10	11.8	4.50	88	.267	.323	0	—	0	-1	-1	-0	-0.1
1988	SD-N	3	0	1.000	35	0	0	0	1	54	45	1	14	33	9.8	2.17	157	.231	.282	1	.500	0	8	7	0	0.5
1989	SD-N	0	1	.000	22	0	0	0	0	28^2	40	2	20	7	19.5	5.02	70	.333	.437	0	.000	-0	-5	-5	1	-0.1
1994	Oak-A	0	0	—	26	0	0	0	1	18^2	13	0	6	14	9.6	1.93	229	.206	.286	0	—	0	6	5	-0	0.4
1995	Oak-A	1	1	.500	24	0	0	0	0	22^2	23	3	13	10	14.7	3.57	125	.258	.359	0	—	0	3	2	-0	0.2
	Mon-N	0	2	.000	26	0	0	0	2	22	16	2	6	12	9.0	2.86	150	.200	.256	0	.000	-0	3	3	0	0.4
1996	Phi-N	2	0	1.000	26	0	0	0	0	21	31	4	7	10	16.3	6.43	67	.348	.396	0	—	0	-5	-5	0	-0.4
	Mon-N	0	1	.000	7	0	0	0	0	4	9	0	2	3	24.8	11.25	38	.474	.524	0	—	0	-3	-3	0	-0.6
	Yr	2	1	.667	33	0	0	0	0	25	40	4	9	13	17.6	7.20	60	.370	.419	0	—	0	-8	-8	0	-1.0
Total	8	12	8	.600	264	0	0	0	7	278	282	25	114	150	13.0	3.98	99	.266	.342	1	.250	0	4	-1	2	-0.2

● JACK LEIPER

Leiper, John Henry Thomas b: 12/23/1867, Chester, Pa. d: 8/23/60, West Goshen, Pa. BL/TL, 5′11″, Deb: 9/4/1891

YEAR	TM/L	W	L	PCT	G	GS	CG	SH	SV	IP	H	HR	BB	SO	RAT	ERA	ERA+	OAV	OOB	BH	AVG	PB	PR	/A	PD	TPI
1891	Col-a	2	2	.500	6	5	4	0	0	45	41	3	39	19	16.8	5.40	64	.234	.385	3	.143	-2	-8	-10	-1	-0.8

● JOHN LEISTER

Leister, John William b: 1/3/61, San Antonio, Tex. BR/TR, 6′2″, 200 lbs. Deb: 5/28/87

YEAR	TM/L	W	L	PCT	G	GS	CG	SH	SV	IP	H	HR	BB	SO	RAT	ERA	ERA+	OAV	OOB	BH	AVG	PB	PR	/A	PD	TPI
1987	Bos-A	0	2	.000	8	6	0	0	0	30^1	49	9	12	16	18.1	9.20	49	.368	.421	0	—	0	-16	-16	-1	-0.9
1990	Bos-A	0	0	—	2	1	0	0	0	5^2	7	0	4	3	17.5	4.76	86	.304	.407	0	—	0	-1	-0	-0	-0.2
Total	2	0	2	.000	10	7	0	0	0	36	56	9	16	19	18.0	8.50	53	.359	.419	0	—	0	-17	-16	-1	-1.1

● AL LEITER

Leiter, Alois Terry b: 10/23/65, Toms River, N.J. BL/TL, 6′3″, 215 lbs. Deb: 9/15/87 F

YEAR	TM/L	W	L	PCT	G	GS	CG	SH	SV	IP	H	HR	BB	SO	RAT	ERA	ERA+	OAV	OOB	BH	AVG	PB	PR	/A	PD	TPI
1987	NY-A	2	2	.500	4	4	0	0	0	22^2	24	2	15	28	15.5	6.35	69	.273	.379	0	—	0	-5	-5	-0	-0.7
1988	NY-A	4	4	.500	14	14	0	0	0	57^1	49	7	33	60	13.7	3.92	100	.231	.348	0	—	0	0	0	1	0.1
1989	NY-A	1	2	.333	4	4	0	0	0	26^2	23	1	21	22	15.5	6.08	64	.235	.380	0	—	0	-6	-7	-0	-0.6
	Tor-A	0	0	—	1	1	0	0	0	6^2	9	1	2	4	14.9	4.05	93	.310	.355	0	—	0	-0	-0	-0	0.0
	Yr	1	2	.333	5	5	0	0	0	33^1	32	2	23	26	14.9	5.67	68	.246	.359	0	—	0	-7	-7	-1	-0.6
1990	Tor-A	0	0	—	4	0	0	0	0	6^1	1	0	2	5	4.3	0.00	—	.050	.136	0	—	0	3	3	0	-0.1
1991	Tor-A	0	0	—	3	0	0	0	0	1^2	3	0	5	1	43.2	27.00	16	.429	.667	0	—	0	-4	-4	0	-0.2
1992	Tor-A	0	0	—	1	0	0	0	0	1	1	0	2	0	27.0	9.00	45	.200	.429	0	—	0	-1	-1	0	-0.2
1993	*Tor-A	9	6	.600	34	12	1	1	2	105	93	8	56	66	13.1	4.11	105	.240	.342	0	—	0	2	2	-1	0.2
1994	Tor-A	6	7	.462	20	20	1	0	0	111^2	125	6	65	100	15.5	5.08	95	.285	.380	0	—	0	-3	-3	-0	-0.3
1995	Tor-A	11	11	.500	28	28	2	1	0	183	162	15	108	153	13.6	3.64	129	.238	.347	0	—	0	22	22	-2	2.1
1996	Fla-N★	16	12	.571	33	33	2	1	0	215^1	153	14	119	200	11.8	2.93	139	**.202**	.319	7	.100	-2	31	27	-1	2.9

YEAR TM/L	W	L	PCT	G	GS	CG	SH	SV	IP	H	HR	BB	SO	RAT	ERA	ERA+	OAV	OOB	BH	AVG	PB	PR	/A	PD	TPI
1997 *Fla-N	11	9	.550	27	27	0	0	0	151^{1}	133	13	91	132	14.0	4.34	93	.241	.360	5	.104	-1	-2	-5	-2	-0.9
1998 NY-N	17	6	.739	28	28	4	2	0	193	151	8	71	174	10.9	2.47	169	.216	.298	6	.105	0	38	36	-2	3.9
Total 12	77	59	.566	201	171	10	5	2	1081^{2}	927	75	590	945	13.1	3.74	115	.233	.340	18	.103	-3	74	65	-8	6.2

● MARK LEITER
Leiter, Mark Edward b: 4/13/63, Joliet, Ill. BR/TR, 6'3", 210 lbs. Deb: 7/24/90 F

YEAR TM/L	W	L	PCT	G	GS	CG	SH	SV	IP	H	HR	BB	SO	RAT	ERA	ERA+	OAV	OOB	BH	AVG	PB	PR	/A	PD	TPI
1990 NY-A	1	1	.500	8	3	0	0	0	26^{1}	33	5	9	21	15.0	6.84	58	.314	.379	0	—	0	-9	-8	1	-0.5
1991 Det-A	9	7	.563	38	15	1	0	1	134^{2}	125	16	50	103	12.1	4.21	99	.245	.319	0	—	0	-2	-1	-1	-0.2
1992 Det-A	8	5	.615	35	14	1	0	0	112	116	9	43	75	13.0	4.18	95	.277	.348	0	—	0	-3	-3	0	-0.3
1993 Det-A	6	6	.500	27	13	1	0	0	106^{2}	111	17	44	70	13.3	4.73	91	.267	.341	0	—	0	-5	-5	-1	-0.6
1994 Cal-A	4	7	.364	40	7	0	0	2	95^{1}	99	13	35	71	13.5	4.72	104	.265	.343	0	—	0	1	2	1	0.2
1995 SF-N	10	12	.455	30	29	7	1	0	195^{2}	185	19	55	129	11.8	3.82	107	.254	.321	6	.098	-2	8	6	-3	0.1
1996 SF-N	4	10	.286	23	22	1	0	0	135^{1}	151	25	50	118	14.0	5.19	79	.283	.355	6	.143	-0	-15	-17	-2	-1.7
Mon-N	4	2	.667	12	12	1	0	0	69^{2}	68	12	19	46	12.1	4.39	98	.254	.320	2	.080	-1	-1	-1	-1	-0.1
Yr	8	12	.400	35	34	2	0	0	205	219	37	69	164	13.0	4.92	85	.269	.332	8	.119	-2	-16	-17	-1	-1.8
1997 Phi-N	10	17	.370	31	31	3	0	0	182^{2}	216	25	64	148	14.2	5.67	75	.292	.355	6	.118	-1	-30	-29	1	-3.6
1998 Phi-N	7	5	.583	69	0	0	0	23	88^{2}	67	8	47	84	12.4	3.55	123	.216	.334	0	.000	-0	7	8	0	1.3
Total 9	63	72	.467	313	146	15	1	26	1147	1171	149	416	865	13.0	4.60	92	.266	.339	20	.110	-5	-48	-48	-2	-5.4

● BILL LEITH
Leith, William "Shady Bill" b: 5/31/1873, Matteawan, N.Y. d: 7/16/40, Beacon, N.Y. TL , Deb: 9/25/1899

YEAR TM/L	W	L	PCT	G	GS	CG	SH	SV	IP	H	HR	BB	SO	RAT	ERA	ERA+	OAV	OOB	BH	AVG	PB	PR	/A	PD	TPI
1899 Was-N	0	0	—	1	0	0	0	0	2	4	0	2	1	31.5	18.00	22	.400	.538	0	.000	-0	-3	-3	-0	0.0

● DOC LEITNER
Leitner, George Aloysius b: 9/14/1865, Piermont, N.Y. d: 5/18/37, New York, N.Y. BR/TR, 5'11.5", 185 lbs. Deb: 8/10/1887

YEAR TM/L	W	L	PCT	G	GS	CG	SH	SV	IP	H	HR	BB	SO	RAT	ERA	ERA+	OAV	OOB	BH	AVG	PB	PR	/A	PD	TPI
1887 Ind-N	2	6	.250	8	8	8	0	0	65	69	6	41	27	15.2	5.68	73	.259	.358	4	.148	-3	-12	-11	-2	-1.3

● DUMMY LEITNER
Leitner, George Michael b: 6/19/1872, Parkton, Md. d: 2/20/60, Baltimore, Md. BL/TR, 5'7", 120 lbs. Deb: 6/29/01

YEAR TM/L	W	L	PCT	G	GS	CG	SH	SV	IP	H	HR	BB	SO	RAT	ERA	ERA+	OAV	OOB	BH	AVG	PB	PR	/A	PD	TPI
1901 Phi-A	0	0	—	1	0	0	0	0	2	1	0	1	1	9.0	0.00	—	.143	.250	0	.000	-0	1	1	-0	0.0
NY-N	0	2	.000	2	2	2	0	0	18	27	0	4	3	16.0	4.50	73	.342	.381	1	.143	-0	-2	-2	-0	-0.3
1902 Cle-A	0	0	—	1	1	0	0	0	8	11	0	1	0	13.5	4.50	77	.324	.343	1	.250	0	-1	-1	0	0.0
Chi-A	0	0	—	1	0	0	0	0	4	9	0	2	0	29.3	13.50	25	.450	.542	0	.000	-0	-4	-4	0	0.0
Yr	0	0	—	2	1	0	0	0	12	20	0	3	0	18.8	7.50	46	.370	.424	1	.143	-0	-5	-5	1	0.0
Total 2	0	2	.000	5	3	2	0	0	32	48	0	8	4	16.6	5.34	63	.343	.391	2	.133	-1	-7	-7	0	-0.3

● BILL LELIVELT
Lelivelt, William John b: 10/21/1884, Chicago, Ill. d: 2/14/68, Chicago, Ill. BR/TR, 5'10", 168 lbs. Deb: 7/19/09 F

YEAR TM/L	W	L	PCT	G	GS	CG	SH	SV	IP	H	HR	BB	SO	RAT	ERA	ERA+	OAV	OOB	BH	AVG	PB	PR	/A	PD	TPI
1909 Det-A	0	1	.000	4	2	1	0	1	20	27	0	2	4	13.0	4.50	56	.325	.341	2	.333	1	-4	-4	0	-0.2
1910 Det-A	0	1	.000	1	1	1	0	0	9	6	0	3	2	9.0	1.00	263	.207	.281	1	.500	1	2	2	0	0.3
Total 2	0	2	.000	5	3	2	0	1	29	33	0	5	6	11.8	3.41	75	.295	.325	3	.375	2	-3	-3	0	0.1

● DAVE LEMANCZYK
Lemanczyk, David Lawrence b: 8/17/50, Syracuse, N.Y. BR/TR, 6'4", 235 lbs. Deb: 4/15/73

YEAR TM/L	W	L	PCT	G	GS	CG	SH	SV	IP	H	HR	BB	SO	RAT	ERA	ERA+	OAV	OOB	BH	AVG	PB	PR	/A	PD	TPI
1973 Det-A	0	0	—	1	0	0	0	0	2^{1}	4	0	0	0	15.4	11.57	35	.364	.364	0	—	0	-2	-2	-0	-0.1
1974 Det-A	2	1	.667	22	3	0	0	0	78^{2}	79	12	44	52	14.3	4.00	95	.261	.358	0	—	0	-3	-2	1	-0.1
1975 Det-A	2	7	.222	26	6	4	0	0	109	120	8	46	67	14.0	4.46	90	.281	.355	0	—	0	-8	-5	0	-0.7
1976 Det-A	4	6	.400	20	10	1	0	0	81^{1}	86	7	34	51	13.3	5.09	73	.271	.342	0	—	0	-14	-12	1	-1.6
1977 Tor-A	13	16	.448	34	34	11	0	0	252	278	20	87	105	13.2	4.25	99	.282	.343	0	—	0	-5	-1	0	-0.2
1978 Tor-A	4	14	.222	29	20	3	0	0	136^{2}	170	16	65	62	15.7	6.26	63	.313	.389	0	—	0	-38	-35	-1	-4.2
1979 Tor-A☆	8	10	.444	22	20	11	3	0	143	137	12	45	63	11.8	3.71	117	.258	.324	0	—	0	8	10	0	1.0
1980 Tor-A	2	5	.286	10	8	0	0	0	43^{1}	57	4	15	10	15.0	5.40	80	.322	.375	0	—	0	-7	-5	1	-0.8
Cal-A	2	4	.333	21	2	0	0	0	66^{2}	81	8	27	19	14.9	4.32	91	.301	.369	0	—	0	-2	-3	-2	-0.3
Yr	4	9	.308	31	10	0	0	0	110	138	12	42	29	14.9	4.75	86	.308	.370	0	—	0	-9	-8	-1	-1.1
Total 8	37	63	.370	185	103	30	3	0	913	1012	87	363	429	13.8	4.62	88	.284	.354	0	—	0	-72	-56	0	-7.0

● DENNY LEMASTER
Lemaster, Denver Clayton b: 2/25/39, Corona, Cal. BR/TL, 6'1", 185 lbs. Deb: 7/15/62

YEAR TM/L	W	L	PCT	G	GS	CG	SH	SV	IP	H	HR	BB	SO	RAT	ERA	ERA+	OAV	OOB	BH	AVG	PB	PR	/A	PD	TPI
1962 Mil-N	3	4	.429	17	12	4	1	0	86^{2}	75	11	32	69	11.4	3.01	126	.233	.308	4	.121	-1	9	8	-2	0.3
1963 Mil-N	11	14	.440	46	31	10	1	1	237	199	30	85	190	10.8	3.04	106	.227	.296	14	.189	3	7	5	-3	0.5
1964 Mil-N	17	11	.607	39	35	9	3	1	221	216	27	75	185	12.0	4.15	85	.252	.315	9	.134	0	-15	-15	0	-1.8
1965 Mil-N	7	13	.350	32	23	4	1	0	146^{1}	140	12	58	111	12.4	4.43	80	.251	.325	4	.089	-1	-14	-15	-0	-2.0
1966 Atl-N	11	8	.579	27	27	10	3	0	171	170	25	41	139	11.2	3.74	97	.258	.303	7	.119	-1	-2	-2	-2	-0.5
1967 Atl-N†	9	9	.500	31	31	8	2	0	215^{1}	184	20	72	148	10.8	3.34	99	.229	.295	7	.104	-2	1	-1	-1	-0.3
1968 Hou-N	10	15	.400	33	32	7	2	0	224	231	11	72	146	12.3	2.81	105	.262	.321	2	.031	-3	4	4	-3	-0.3
1969 Hou-N	13	17	.433	38	37	11	1	1	244^{2}	232	20	72	173	11.2	3.16	112	.246	.300	15	.170	3	12	10	-1	1.4
1970 Hou-N	7	12	.368	39	21	3	0	3	162	169	22	65	103	13.1	4.56	85	.268	.338	8	.178	2	-9	-12	-2	-1.2
1971 Hou-N	0	2	.000	42	0	0	0	2	60	59	4	22	28	12.3	3.45	98	.262	.331	1	.167	-0	0	-1	-0	0.0
1972 Mon-N	2	0	1.000	13	0	0	0	0	19^{2}	28	2	6	13	16.0	7.78	46	.329	.380	1	.333	1	-9	-9	-1	-0.9
Total 11	90	105	.462	357	249	66	14	8	1787^{2}	1703	184	600	1305	11.7	3.58	96	.249	.312	72	.130	1	-18	-28	-13	-4.8

● DICK LeMAY
LeMay, Richard Paul b: 8/28/38, Cincinnati, Ohio BL/TL, 6'3", 190 lbs. Deb: 6/13/61

YEAR TM/L	W	L	PCT	G	GS	CG	SH	SV	IP	H	HR	BB	SO	RAT	ERA	ERA+	OAV	OOB	BH	AVG	PB	PR	/A	PD	TPI
1961 SF-N	3	6	.333	27	5	1	0	3	83^{1}	65	11	36	54	11.3	3.56	107	.217	.309	2	.077	-2	4	2	-0	0.1
1962 SF-N	0	1	.000	9	0	0	0	1	9^{1}	9	2	9	5	17.4	7.71	49	.265	.419	0	—	0	-4	-4	0	-0.4
1963 Chi-N	0	1	.000	9	1	0	0	0	15^{1}	26	1	4	10	17.6	5.28	66	.394	.429	0	.000	-0	-3	-3	-0	-0.2
Total 3	3	8	.273	45	6	1	0	4	108	100	14	49	69	12.8	4.17	91	.250	.338	2	.071	-1	-3	-5	-0	-0.5

● BOB LEMON
Lemon, Robert Granville b: 9/22/20, San Bernardino, Cal. BL/TR, 6', 185 lbs. Deb: 9/9/41 MCH♦

YEAR TM/L	W	L	PCT	G	GS	CG	SH	SV	IP	H	HR	BB	SO	RAT	ERA	ERA+	OAV	OOB	BH	AVG	PB	PR	/A	PD	TPI
1946 Cle-A	4	5	.444	32	5	1	0	1	94	77	1	68	39	13.9	2.49	133	.229	.359	16	.180	2	11	9	4	1.3
1947 Cle-A	11	5	.688	37	15	6	1	3	167^{1}	150	7	97	65	13.5	3.44	101	.242	.348	18	.321	9	5	1	4	1.6
1948 *Cle-A☆	20	14	.588	43	37	**20**	**10**	2	**293^{2}**	231	12	129	147	11.1	2.82	144	.216	.302	34	.286	14	**48**	40	8	**6.8**
1949 Cle-A☆	22	10	.688	37	33	22	2	1	279^{2}	211	19	137	138	11.4	2.99	133	.211	.309	29	.269	16	37	31	6	**5.7**
1950 Cle-A★	**23**	11	.676	44	37	**22**	3	3	**288**	281	28	146	**170**	13.4	3.84	113	.257	.345	37	.272	17	23	16	5	3.7
1951 Cle-A★	17	14	.548	42	34	17	1	2	263^{1}	244	19	124	132	12.6	3.52	108	.244	.328	21	.206	5	18	8	4	1.7
1952 Cle-A★	22	11	.667	42	36	**28**	5	4	**309^{2}**	236	15	105	131	10.1	2.50	134	**.208**	.279	28	.226	7	40	29	7	4.6
1953 Cle-A☆	21	15	.583	41	36	23	5	1	**286^{2}**	283	16	110	98	12.7	3.36	112	.262	.336	26	.232	8	20	13	8	3.2
1954 *Cle-A★	**23**	7	.767	36	33	**21**	2	0	258^{1}	228	12	92	110	11.3	2.72	135	.237	.307	21	.214	6	29	27	4	**4.1**
1955 Cle-A	**18**	10	.643	35	31	5	0	2	211^{1}	218	17	74	100	12.6	3.88	103	.266	.330	19	.244	6	2	3	2	1.1
1956 Cle-A	20	14	.588	39	35	**21**	2	3	255^{1}	230	23	89	94	11.5	3.03	139	.239	.307	18	.194	5	32	33	4	**5.2**
1957 Cle-A	6	11	.353	21	17	2	0	0	117^{1}	129	9	64	45	15.3	4.60	81	.287	.385	3	.065	-3	-11	-12	3	-1.5
1958 Cle-A	0	1	.000	11	1	0	0	0	25^{1}	41	3	16	8	20.6	5.33	68	.376	.460	3	.231	0	-4	-5	1	-0.1
Total 13	207	128	.618	460	350	188	31	22	2850	2559	181	1251	1277	12.2	3.23	119	.241	.324	274	.232	90	251	193	60	37.4

● DAVE LEMONDS
Lemonds, David Lee b: 7/5/48, Charlotte, N.C. BL/TL, 6'1.5", 180 lbs. Deb: 6/30/69

YEAR TM/L	W	L	PCT	G	GS	CG	SH	SV	IP	H	HR	BB	SO	RAT	ERA	ERA+	OAV	OOB	BH	AVG	PB	PR	/A	PD	TPI
1969 Chi-N	0	1	.000	2	1	0	0	0	4^{2}	5	0	5	0	19.3	3.86	104	.313	.476	0	.000	-0	-0	0	0	0.0
1972 Chi-A	4	7	.364	31	18	0	0	0	94^{2}	87	6	38	69	12.0	2.95	106	.247	.322	3	.120	-1	1	2	-0	0.1
Total 2	4	8	.333	33	19	0	0	0	99^{1}	92	6	43	69	12.3	2.99	106	.250	.330	3	.115	-1	1	2	-0	0.1

● MARK LEMONGELLO
Lemongello, Mark b: 7/21/55, Jersey City, N.J. BR/TR, 6'1", 180 lbs. Deb: 9/14/76

YEAR TM/L	W	L	PCT	G	GS	CG	SH	SV	IP	H	HR	BB	SO	RAT	ERA	ERA+	OAV	OOB	BH	AVG	PB	PR	/A	PD	TPI
1976 Hou-N	3	1	.750	4	4	1	0	0	29	26	2	7	9	10.2	2.79	114	.236	.282	0	.000	-1	2	1	1	0.2
1977 Hou-N	9	14	.391	34	30	5	0	0	214^{2}	237	20	52	83	12.2	3.48	102	.281	.325	6	.087	-4	10	2	-1	-0.2
1978 Hou-N	9	14	.391	33	30	9	1	1	210^{1}	204	20	66	77	11.9	3.94	84	.259	.323	11	.172	1	-8	-15	-0	-1.4
1979 Tor-A	1	9	.100	18	10	2	0	0	83	97	14	34	40	14.5	6.29	69	.299	.371	0	—	0	-19	-18	1	-1.8
Total 4	22	38	.367	89	74	17	1	1	537	564	56	159	209	12.4	4.06	88	.273	.329	17	.121	-3	-15	-30	1	-3.2

● ED LENNON
Lennon, Edward Francis b: 8/17/1897, Philadelphia, Pa. d: 9/13/47, Philadelphia, Pa. BR/TR, 5'11", 170 lbs. Deb: 6/30/28

YEAR TM/L	W	L	PCT	G	GS	CG	SH	SV	IP	H	HR	BB	SO	RAT	ERA	ERA+	OAV	OOB	BH	AVG	PB	PR	/A	PD	TPI
1928 Phi-N	0	0	—	5	0	0	0	0	12^{1}	19	0	10	6	21.2	8.76	49	.373	.475	0	.000	-1	-7	-6	-0	-0.1

YEAR	TM/L	W	L	PCT	G	GS	CG	SH	SV	IP	H	HR	BB	SO	RAT	ERA	ERA+	OAV	OOB	BH	AVG	PB	PR	/A	PD	TPI
● DANILO LEON	Leon, Danilo Enrique (Lineco) b: 4/3/67, LaConcepcion, Venez. BR/TR, 6'1", 170 lbs. Deb: 6/6/92																									
1992	Tex-A	1	1	.500	15	0	0	0	0	18^{1}	18	5	10	15	15.2	5.89	64	.254	.369	0	—	0	-4	-4	0	-0.4
● IZZY LEON	Leon, Isidoro (Becerra) b: 1/4/11, Cruces, Las Villas, Cuba BR/TR, 5'10", 160 lbs. Deb: 6/21/45																									
1945	Phi-N	0	4	.000	14	4	0	0	0	38^{2}	49	3	19	11	15.8	5.35	72	.312	.386	1	.111	-0	-7	-7	0	-0.6
● MAX LEON	Leon, Maximino (Molino) b: 2/4/50, Pozo Hondo, Aculo, Mexico BR/TR, 6', 170 lbs. Deb: 7/18/73																									
1973	Atl-N	2	2	.500	12	1	1	0	0	27	30	6	9	18	14.0	5.33	74	.278	.350	2	.286	0	-5	-4	-0	-0.6
1974	Atl-N	4	7	.364	34	2	1	1	3	75	68	5	14	38	10.0	2.64	143	.242	.280	2	.133	-1	8	9	1	1.4
1975	Atl-N	2	1	.667	50	1	0	0	6	85	90	5	33	53	13.8	4.13	91	.274	.352	3	.333	1	-5	-3	1	0.0
1976	Atl-N	2	4	.333	30	0	0	0	3	36	32	2	15	16	12.3	2.75	138	.234	.318	0	.000	-0	3	4	-1	0.7
1977	Atl-N	4	4	.500	31	9	0	0	1	81^{2}	89	9	25	44	13.6	3.97	112	.280	.349	6	.316	1	-1	4	0	0.5
1978	Atl-N	0	0	—	5	0	0	0	0	5^{2}	6	1	4	1	17.5	6.35	64	.273	.407	0	—	0	-2	-1	-0	0.0
Total	6	14	18	.438	162	13	2	1	13	310^{1}	315	28	100	170	12.7	3.71	107	.264	.332	13	.250	1	-1	9	1	2.0
● DENNIS LEONARD	Leonard, Dennis Patrick b: 5/8/51, Brooklyn, N.Y. BR/TR, 6'1", 190 lbs. Deb: 9/4/74																									
1974	KC-A	0	4	.000	5	4	0	0	0	22	28	0	12	8	17.6	5.32	72	.329	.430	0	—	0	-4	-4	1	-0.5
1975	KC-A	15	7	.682	32	30	8	0	0	212^{1}	212	18	90	146	13.2	3.77	102	.263	.344	0	—	0	0	2	0	0.2
1976	*KC-A	17	10	.630	35	34	16	2	0	259	247	16	70	150	11.4	3.51	100	.255	.313	0	—	0	0	-0	-4	-0.5
1977	*KC-A	**20**	12	.625	38	37	21	5	1	292^{2}	246	18	79	244	10.2	3.04	133	.227	.285	0	—	0	33	32	-2	3.1
1978	*KC-A	21	17	.553	40	40	20	4	0	294^{2}	283	27	78	183	11.3	3.33	115	.254	.308	0	—	0	14	16	0	1.9
1979	KC-A	14	12	.538	32	32	12	**5**	0	236	226	33	56	126	10.8	4.08	104	.253	.299	0	—	0	4	5	0	0.3
1980	*KC-A	20	11	.645	38	38	9	3	0	280^{1}	271	30	80	155	11.3	3.79	107	.253	.306	0	—	0	8	8	-0	0.8
1981	*KC-A	13	11	.542	26	26	9	2	0	**201^{2}**	202	15	41	107	11.0	2.99	121	.258	.298	0	—	0	15	14	0	1.7
1982	KC-A	10	6	.625	21	21	2	0	0	130^{2}	145	20	46	58	13.3	5.10	80	.279	.340	0	—	0	-15	-15	1	-1.5
1983	KC-A	6	3	.667	10	10	1	0	0	63	69	3	19	31	12.6	3.71	110	.277	.328	0	—	0	2	3	0	0.3
1985	KC-A	0	0	—	2	0	0	0	0	2	1	0	0	1	4.5	0.00	—	.143	.143	0	—	0	1	1	-0	0.0
1986	KC-A	8	13	.381	33	30	5	2	0	192^{2}	207	22	51	114	12.2	4.44	96	.275	.324	0	—	0	-6	-4	0	-0.4
Total	12	144	106	.576	312	302	103	23	1	2187	2137	202	622	1323	11.6	3.70	106	.257	.312	0	—	0	52	58	-3	5.4
● ELMER LEONARD	Leonard, Elmer Ellsworth "Tiny" b: 11/12/1888, Napa, Cal. d: 5/27/81, Napa, Cal. BR/TR, 6'3.5", 210 lbs. Deb: 6/22/11																									
1911	Phi-A	2	2	.500	5	1	1	0	0	19	26	0	10	10	18.0	2.84	111	.329	.418	2	.286	1	1	1	-1	0.1
● DUTCH LEONARD	Leonard, Emil John b: 3/25/09, Auburn, Ill. d: 4/17/83, Springfield, Ill. BR/TR, 6', 175 lbs. Deb: 8/31/33 C																									
1933	Bro-N	2	3	.400	10	3	2	0	0	40	42	0	10	6	11.7	2.93	110	.261	.304	0	.000	-1	2	1	0	0.0
1934	Bro-N	14	11	.560	44	20	11	2	5	183^{2}	210	12	33	58	12.1	3.28	119	.286	.320	12	.179	-1	16	13	1	1.7
1935	Bro-N	2	9	.182	43	11	4	0	**8**	137^{2}	152	11	29	41	11.9	3.92	101	.280	.318	1	.026	-4	1	1	-1	-0.5
1936	Bro-N	0	0	—	16	0	0	0	1	32	34	2	5	8	11.0	3.66	113	.262	.289	2	.400	0	1	2	1	0.1
1938	Was-A	12	15	.444	33	31	15	3	0	223^{1}	221	11	53	68	**11.3**	3.43	132	.256	**.305**	19	.232	3	34	27	0	3.1
1939	Was-A	20	8	.714	34	34	21	2	0	269^{1}	273	16	59	88	11.3	3.54	123	.262	.305	21	.221	0	32	24	2	2.4
1940	Was-A☆	14	19	.424	35	35	23	2	0	289	328	19	78	124	12.7	3.49	120	.286	.332	16	.158	-5	29	22	5	2.2
1941	Was-A	18	13	.581	34	33	19	4	0	256	271	6	54	91	11.5	3.45	117	.270	.309	9	.102	-5	20	17	-1	1.2
1942	Was-A	2	2	.500	6	5	1	1	0	35	28	1	5	15	8.5	4.11	89	.214	.243	1	.100	-0	-2	-2	-0	-0.2
1943	Was-A★	11	13	.458	31	30	15	2	1	219^{2}	218	9	46	51	11.0	3.28	98	.257	.298	7	.104	-4	0	-2	2	-0.5
1944	Was-A☆	14	14	.500	32	31	17	3	0	229^{1}	222	8	37	62	10.3	3.06	106	.252	.284	18	.228	2	9	5	1	0.9
1945	Was-A†	17	7	.708	31	29	12	4	1	216	208	5	35	96	10.2	2.13	146	.248	.279	18	.231	1	30	23	0	2.8
1946	Was-A	10	10	.500	26	23	7	2	0	161^{2}	182	9	36	62	12.4	3.56	94	.281	.323	9	.170	-1	-1	-4	3	-0.2
1947	Phi-N	17	12	.586	32	29	19	3	0	235	224	14	57	103	10.8	2.68	149	.258	.306	14	.175	-1	36	35	3	4.3
1948	Phi-N	12	17	.414	34	31	16	1	0	225^{2}	226	9	54	92	11.3	2.51	157	.265	.312	12	.145	-3	36	36	4	4.6
1949	Chi-N	7	16	.304	33	28	10	1	0	180	198	4	43	83	12.4	4.15	97	.272	.319	12	.203	0	-2	-2	1	-0.1
1950	Chi-N	5	1	.833	35	1	0	0	6	74	70	7	27	28	12.0	3.77	111	.248	.318	1	.063	-2	3	4	0	0.2
1951	Chi-N☆	10	6	.625	41	1	0	0	3	81^{2}	69	3	28	30	10.9	2.64	155	.234	.305	0	.000	-3	12	13	2	2.4
1952	Chi-N	2	2	.500	45	0	0	0	11	66^{2}	56	3	24	37	11.2	2.16	178	.235	.313	2	.200	-0	12	13	2	1.4
1953	Chi-N	2	3	.400	45	0	0	0	8	62^{2}	72	9	24	27	13.9	4.60	97	.289	.354	3	.300	1	-2	-1	0	0.0
Total	20	191	181	.513	640	375	192	30	44	3218^{1}	3304	158	737	1170	11.5	3.25	119	.265	.309	177	.168	-21	267	224	24	25.8
● DUTCH LEONARD	Leonard, Hubert Benjamin b: 4/16/1892, Birmingham, Ohio d: 7/11/52, Fresno, Cal. BL/TL, 5'10.5", 185 lbs. Deb: 4/12/13																									
1913	Bos-A	14	17	.452	42	28	14	3	1	259^{1}	245	0	94	144	11.9	2.39	123	.253	.321	15	.181	1	16	16	-2	1.8
1914	Bos-A	19	5	.792	36	25	17	7	3	224^{2}	139	3	60	176	**8.3**	**0.96**	**280**	**.180**	**.246**	10	.147	-1	**44**	43	-3	4.6
1915	*Bos-A	15	7	.682	32	21	10	2	0	183^{1}	130	3	67	116	10.4	2.36	118	**.208**	.299	14	.264	5	12	9	-4	1.1
1916	*Bos-A	18	12	.600	48	34	17	6	6	274	244	6	66	144	10.4	2.36	117	.247	.300	17	.200	2	14	12	-6	0.9
1917	Bos-A	16	17	.485	37	36	26	4	1	294^{1}	257	4	72	144	10.2	2.17	119	.236	.286	9	.087	-6	16	13	-5	0.3
1918	Bos-A	8	6	.571	16	16	12	3	0	125^{2}	119	0	53	47	12.5	2.72	99	.254	.332	8	.186	0	1	-1	-2	-0.2
1919	Det-A	14	13	.519	29	28	18	4	0	217^{1}	212	7	65	102	11.8	2.77	115	.254	.313	11	.155	-3	11	10	-4	0.5
1920	Det-A	10	17	.370	28	27	10	3	0	191^{1}	192	8	63	76	12.4	4.33	86	.271	.338	12	.211	2	-11	-13	-1	-1.5
1921	Det-A	11	13	.458	36	32	16	1	1	245	273	15	63	120	12.7	3.75	114	.286	.336	14	.171	-4	15	14	-3	0.6
1924	Det-A	3	2	.600	9	7	3	0	1	51^{1}	68	1	18	26	15.3	4.56	90	.327	.383	4	.211	-0	-2	-3	-0	-0.3
1925	Det-A	11	4	.733	18	18	9	0	0	125^{2}	143	7	43	65	13.4	4.51	95	.289	.347	10	.200	-1	-2	-3	-2	-0.6
Total	11	139	113	.552	331	272	152	33	13	2192	2022	54	664	1160	11.3	2.76	115	.249	.311	124	.173	-5	114	98	-32	7.2
● DAVE LEONHARD	Leonhard, David Paul b: 1/22/41, Arlington, Va. BR/TR, 5'11", 165 lbs. Deb: 9/21/67																									
1967	Bal-A	0	0	—	3	2	0	0	1	14^{1}	11	1	6	9	11.3	3.14	100	.200	.290	0	.000	-1	0	0	0	0.0
1968	Bal-A	7	7	.500	28	18	5	2	1	126^{1}	95	10	57	61	11.0	3.13	93	.216	.309	4	.129	-1	-2	-3	1	-0.3
1969	*Bal-A	7	4	.636	37	3	1	1	1	94	78	8	38	37	11.1	2.49	143	.228	.305	2	.095	-0	12	11	-1	1.2
1970	Bal-A	0	0	—	23	0	0	0	1	28^{1}	32	5	18	14	15.9	5.08	72	.294	.394	0	.000	0	-4	-5	1	0.1
1971	*Bal-A	2	3	.400	12	6	1	1	1	54	51	5	19	18	11.8	2.83	118	.252	.320	5	.278	1	4	3	1	0.5
1972	Bal-A	0	0	—	14	0	0	0	0	20	20	3	12	7	14.4	4.50	68	.260	.360	1	1.000	1	-3	-3	0	0.1
Total	6	16	14	.533	117	29	7	4	5	337	287	32	150	146	11.8	3.15	103	.234	.320	12	.156	1	6	4	3	1.6
● RUDY LEOPOLD	Leopold, Rudolph Matas b: 7/27/05, Grand Cane, La. d: 9/3/65, Baton Rouge, La. BL/TL, 6', 160 lbs. Deb: 7/4/28																									
1928	Chi-A	0	0	—	2	0	0	0	0	2^{1}	3	0	0	0	11.6	3.86	105	.273	.273	0	.000	-0	0	0	-0	0.0
● RANDY LERCH	Lerch, Randy Louis b: 10/9/54, Sacramento, Cal. BL/TL, 6'5", 190 lbs. Deb: 9/14/75																									
1975	Phi-N	0	0	—	3	0	0	0	0	7	6	1	1	8	9.0	6.43	58	.231	.259	0	—	0	-2	-2	-0	0.0
1976	Phi-N	0	0	—	1	0	0	0	1	3	3	0	0	0	9.0	3.00	118	.250	.250	1	1.000	1	0	0	-0	0.1
1977	Phi-N	10	6	.625	32	28	3	0	0	168^{2}	207	20	75	81	15.1	5.07	79	.312	.383	9	.167	-0	-22	-20	2	-1.5
1978	*Phi-N	11	8	.579	33	28	5	0	0	184	183	15	70	96	12.4	3.96	90	.263	.332	15	.250	7	-8	-8	1	0.0
1979	Phi-N	10	13	.435	37	35	6	1	0	214	228	20	60	92	12.2	3.74	102	.281	.333	11	.153	1	-0	2	2	0.4
1980	Phi-N	4	14	.222	30	22	2	0	0	150	178	15	55	57	14.0	5.16	73	.302	.362	12	.267	3	-26	-23	1	-2.1
1981	*Mil-A	7	9	.438	23	18	1	0	0	110^{2}	134	8	43	53	14.4	4.31	79	.303	.365	0	—	0	-8	-11	0	-1.2
1982	Mil-A	8	7	.533	21	20	1	1	0	108^{2}	123	12	51	33	14.7	4.97	76	.286	.366	0	—	0	-11	-14	-1	-1.5
	Mon-N	2	0	1.000	6	4	0	0	0	23^{2}	26	0	8	4	12.9	3.42	106	.289	.347	2	.250	0	0	1	-0	0.1
1983	Mon-N	1	3	.250	19	5	0	0	0	38^{2}	45	6	18	24	14.9	6.75	53	.292	.370	2	.222	1	-13	-14	-0	-1.2
	SF-N	1	0	1.000	7	0	0	0	0	10^{2}	9	1	8	6	14.3	3.38	105	.231	.362	0	—	0	0	0	0	0.0
	Yr	2	3	.400	26	5	0	0	0	49^{1}	54	7	26	30	14.6	6.02	59	.277	.362	2	.222	1	-13	-13	-0	-1.2
1984	SF-N	5	3	.625	37	4	0	0	2	72^{1}	80	3	36	48	14.6	4.23	83	.287	.370	2	.133	1	-5	-6	1	-0.5
1986	Phi-N	1	1	.500	4	0	0	0	0	8	10	0	7	5	19.1	7.88	49	.286	.405	1	.333	1	-4	-4	-0	-0.7
Total	11	60	64	.484	253	164	18	2	3	1099^{1}	1232	101	432	507	13.7	4.53	82	.289	.356	55	.206	15	-98	-98	4	-8.1
● JOHN LEROY	Leroy, John Michael b: 4/19/75, Bellevue, Wash. BR/TR, 6'3", 175 lbs. Deb: 9/26/97																									
1997	Atl-N	1	0	1.000	1	0	0	0	0	2	1	0	3	3	18.0	0.00	—	.143	.400	0	—	0	1	1	-0	0.5

● **LOUIS LeROY** LeRoy, Louis Paul "Chief" b: 2/18/1879, Omro, Wis. d: 10/10/44, Shawano, Wis. BR/TR, 5'10", 180 lbs. Deb: 9/22/05

YEAR TM/L	W	L	PCT	G	GS	CG	SH	SV	IP	H	HR	BB	SO	RAT	ERA	ERA+	OAV	OOB	BH	AVG	PB	PR	/A	PD	TPI
1905 NY-A	1	1	.500	3	3	2	0	0	24	26	2	1	8	10.5	3.75	78	.277	.292	1	.125	-0	-3	-2	-0	-0.2
1906 NY-A	2	0	1.000	11	2	1	0	1	44^2	33	0	12	28	9.5	2.22	134	.209	.273	2	.143	-1	2	4	1	0.2
1910 Bos-A	0	0	—	1	0	0	0	0	4	7	1	2	3	20.3	11.25	23	.389	.450	0	.000	-0	-4	-4	0	0.0
Total 3	3	1	.750	15	5	3	0	1	72^2	66	3	15	39	10.4	3.22	91	.244	.292	3	.130	-1	-4	-2	1	0.0

● **BARRY LERSCH** Lersch, Barry Lee b: 9/7/44, Denver, Colo. BB/TR, 6', 180 lbs. Deb: 4/8/69

YEAR TM/L	W	L	PCT	G	GS	CG	SH	SV	IP	H	HR	BB	SO	RAT	ERA	ERA+	OAV	OOB	BH	AVG	PB	PR	/A	PD	TPI
1969 Phi-N	0	3	.000	10	0	0	0	2	17^2	20	6	10	13	15.8	7.13	50	.286	.383	0	.000	-0	-7	-7	1	-1.2
1970 Phi-N	6	3	.667	42	11	3	0	3	138	119	17	47	92	10.9	3.26	122	.232	.297	2	.065	-2	12	11	-1	0.5
1971 Phi-N	5	14	.263	38	30	3	0	0	214^1	203	28	50	113	10.7	3.78	93	.252	.298	10	.169	2	-7	-6	-1	-0.4
1972 Phi-N	4	6	.400	36	8	3	1	0	100^2	86	8	33	48	10.9	3.04	118	.231	.299	0	.000	-2	5	6	-0	0.3
1973 Phi-N	3	6	.333	42	4	0	0	1	98^1	105	10	27	51	12.3	4.39	86	.279	.330	3	.176	0	-8	-7	-0	-0.6
1974 StL-N	0	0	—	1	0	0	0	0	1^1	3	1	5	0	54.0	40.50	9	.429	.667	0	—	0	-5	-5	0	0.0
Total 6	18	32	.360	169	53	9	1	6	570^1	536	70	172	317	11.3	3.82	97	.250	.308	15	.113	-3	-11	-8	-1	-1.4

● **DON LESHNOCK** Leshnock, Donald Lee b: 11/25/46, Youngstown, Ohio BR/TL, 6'3", 195 lbs. Deb: 6/7/72

YEAR TM/L	W	L	PCT	G	GS	CG	SH	SV	IP	H	HR	BB	SO	RAT	ERA	ERA+	OAV	OOB	BH	AVG	PB	PR	/A	PD	TPI
1972 Det-A	0	0	—	1	0	0	0	0	1	2	0	0	2	18.0	0.00	—	.400	.400	0	—	0	0	0	0	0.0

● **CURT LESKANIC** Leskanic, Curtis John b: 4/2/68, Homestead, Pa. BR/TR, 6', 180 lbs. Deb: 6/27/93

YEAR TM/L	W	L	PCT	G	GS	CG	SH	SV	IP	H	HR	BB	SO	RAT	ERA	ERA+	OAV	OOB	BH	AVG	PB	PR	/A	PD	TPI
1993 Col-N	1	5	.167	18	8	0	0	0	57	59	7	27	30	13.9	5.37	89	.266	.351	2	.154	0	-8	-4	-0	-0.4
1994 Col-N	1	1	.500	8	3	0	0	0	22^1	27	2	10	17	14.9	5.64	88	.314	.385	1	.167	0	-4	-2	-0	-0.1
1995 *Col-N	6	3	.667	**76**	0	0	0	10	98	83	7	33	107	10.7	3.40	159	.226	.289	1	.143	-0	9	22	2	2.3
1996 Col-N	7	5	.583	70	0	0	0	6	73^2	82	12	38	76	14.9	6.23	84	.285	.372	1	.333	0	-16	-8	-1	-1.3
1997 Col-N	4	0	1.000	55	0	0	0	2	58^1	59	8	24	53	12.8	5.55	93	.271	.343	0	.000	-0	-9	-2	-0	-0.2
1998 Col-N	6	4	.600	66	0	0	0	2	75^2	75	9	40	55	13.8	4.40	115	.258	.349	0	.000	-0	-1	6	-0	0.6
Total 6	25	18	.581	293	11	0	0	20	385	385	45	172	338	13.1	4.89	105	.261	.341	5	.156	-0	-30	11	0	0.9

● **BRAD LESLEY** Lesley, Bradley Jay b: 9/11/58, Turlock, Cal. BR/TR, 6'6", 230 lbs. Deb: 7/31/82

YEAR TM/L	W	L	PCT	G	GS	CG	SH	SV	IP	H	HR	BB	SO	RAT	ERA	ERA+	OAV	OOB	BH	AVG	PB	PR	/A	PD	TPI
1982 Cin-N	0	2	.000	28	0	0	0	4	38^1	27	1	13	29	9.4	2.58	143	.197	.267	0	.000	-0	4	5	-0	0.3
1983 Cin-N	0	0	—	5	0	0	0	0	8^1	9	1	0	5	9.7	2.16	176	.290	.290	0	—	0	1	2	-0	0.0
1984 Cin-N	0	1	.000	16	0	0	0	2	19^1	17	3	14	7	14.4	5.12	74	.246	.373	1	.500	0	-3	-3	0	-0.2
1985 Mil-A	1	0	1.000	5	0	0	0	0	6^1	8	2	2	5	14.2	9.95	42	.296	.345	0	—	0	-4	-4	0	-0.5
Total 4	1	3	.250	54	0	0	0	6	72^1	61	7	29	46	11.2	3.86	98	.231	.307	1	.333	0	-2	-1	-0	-0.4

● **WALT LEVERENZ** Leverenz, Walter Fred "Tiny" b: 7/21/1887, Chicago, Ill. d: 3/19/73, Atascadero, Cal. BL/TL, 5'10", 175 lbs. Deb: 4/18/13

YEAR TM/L	W	L	PCT	G	GS	CG	SH	SV	IP	H	HR	BB	SO	RAT	ERA	ERA+	OAV	OOB	BH	AVG	PB	PR	/A	PD	TPI
1913 StL-A	6	17	.261	30	27	13	2	1	202^2	159	3	89	87	11.5	2.58	114	.222	.318	12	.176	-1	8	8	-1	0.6
1914 StL-A	1	12	.077	27	16	5	0	0	111^1	107	5	63	41	14.1	3.80	71	.264	.368	6	.182	-0	-13	-14	-1	-1.7
1915 StL-A	1	2	.333	5	1	0	0	0	9	11	0	8	3	20.0	8.00	36	.333	.476	0	.000	-0	-5	-5	0	-1.4
Total 3	8	31	.205	62	44	18	2	1	323	277	8	160	131	12.7	3.15	91	.240	.341	18	.176	-1	-10	-11	-3	-2.5

● **DIXIE LEVERETT** Leverett, Gorham Vance b: 3/29/1894, Georgetown, Tex. d: 2/20/57, Beaverton, Ore. BR/TR, 5'11", 190 lbs. Deb: 5/6/22

YEAR TM/L	W	L	PCT	G	GS	CG	SH	SV	IP	H	HR	BB	SO	RAT	ERA	ERA+	OAV	OOB	BH	AVG	PB	PR	/A	PD	TPI
1922 Chi-A	13	10	.565	33	27	16	4	2	223^2	224	11	79	60	12.3	3.34	122	.264	.329	21	.253	3	18	18	-1	1.9
1923 Chi-A	10	13	.435	38	24	9	0	3	192^2	212	6	64	64	13.2	4.06	97	.280	.341	16	.267	4	-2	-2	-1	0.1
1924 Chi-A	2	3	.400	21	11	4	0	0	99	123	2	41	29	15.2	5.82	71	.314	.383	6	.188	-1	-17	-19	0	-0.8
1926 Chi-A	1	1	.500	6	3	1	0	0	24	31	1	7	12	14.3	6.00	64	.316	.362	1	.143	-0	-5	-6	0	-0.4
1929 Bos-N	3	7	.300	24	12	3	0	1	97^2	135	5	30	28	15.7	6.36	74	.339	.393	6	.188	-0	-18	-18	-0	-1.6
Total 5	29	34	.460	122	77	33	4	6	637	725	25	221	193	13.6	4.51	92	.291	.353	50	.234	6	-25	-27	-1	-0.8

● **HOD LEVERETTE** Leverette, Horace Wilbur "Levy" b: 2/4/1889, Shreveport, La. d: 4/10/58, St.Petersburg, Fla BR/TR, 6', 180 lbs. Deb: 4/22/20

YEAR TM/L	W	L	PCT	G	GS	CG	SH	SV	IP	H	HR	BB	SO	RAT	ERA	ERA+	OAV	OOB	BH	AVG	PB	PR	/A	PD	TPI
1920 StL-A	0	2	.000	3	2	0	0	0	10^1	9	1	12	0	18.3	5.23	75	.250	.438	0	.000	-1	-2	-1	1	-0.2

● **ALAN LEVINE** Levine, Alan Brian b: 5/22/68, Park Ridge, Ill. BL/TR, 6'3", 180 lbs. Deb: 6/22/96

YEAR TM/L	W	L	PCT	G	GS	CG	SH	SV	IP	H	HR	BB	SO	RAT	ERA	ERA+	OAV	OOB	BH	AVG	PB	PR	/A	PD	TPI
1996 Chi-A	0	1	.000	16	0	0	0	0	18^1	22	1	7	12	14.7	5.40	88	.289	.357	0	—	0	-1	-1	1	0.1
1997 Chi-A	2	2	.500	25	0	0	0	0	27^1	35	4	16	22	17.5	6.91	63	.313	.408	0	—	0	-7	-8	0	-0.8
1998 Tex-A	0	1	.000	30	0	0	0	0	58	68	6	16	19	13.0	4.50	108	.294	.340	0	—	0	1	2	-0	0.0
Total 3	2	4	.333	71	0	0	0	0	103^2	125	11	39	53	14.5	5.30	89	.298	.362	0	—	0	-7	-7	1	-0.7

● **DUTCH LEVSEN** Levsen, Emil Henry b: 4/29/1898, Wyoming, Iowa d: 3/12/72, St.Louis Park, Minn. BR/TR, 6', 180 lbs. Deb: 9/28/23

YEAR TM/L	W	L	PCT	G	GS	CG	SH	SV	IP	H	HR	BB	SO	RAT	ERA	ERA+	OAV	OOB	BH	AVG	PB	PR	/A	PD	TPI
1923 Cle-A	0	0	—	3	0	0	0	0	4^1	4	0	0	1	8.3	0.00	—	.267	.267	0	.000	-0	2	2	1	0.1
1924 Cle-A	1	1	.500	4	1	1	0	0	16^1	22	0	4	3	14.3	4.41	97	.333	.371	0	.000	-1	-0	-0	0	-0.1
1925 Cle-A	1	2	.333	4	3	2	0	0	24^1	30	1	16	9	17.4	5.55	80	.313	.416	2	.250	0	-3	-3	-1	-0.3
1926 Cle-A	16	13	.552	33	31	18	2	0	237^1	235	11	85	53	12.4	3.41	119	.261	.330	17	.205	-0	16	17	-1	1.8
1927 Cle-A	3	7	.300	25	13	2	1	0	80^1	96	1	37	15	15.1	5.49	77	.303	.379	5	.200	-1	-12	-11	1	-1.2
1928 Cle-A	0	3	.000	11	3	0	0	0	41^1	39	4	31	7	15.7	5.44	76	.258	.391	0	.000	-2	-6	-6	-0	-0.6
Total 6	21	26	.447	80	51	23	3	0	404	426	17	173	88	13.6	4.17	99	.276	.354	24	.178	-4	-4	-2	1	-0.3

● **DENNIS LEWALLYN** Lewallyn, Dennis Dale b: 8/11/53, Pensacola, Fla. BR/TR, 6'4", 200 lbs. Deb: 9/21/75

YEAR TM/L	W	L	PCT	G	GS	CG	SH	SV	IP	H	HR	BB	SO	RAT	ERA	ERA+	OAV	OOB	BH	AVG	PB	PR	/A	PD	TPI
1975 LA-N	0	0	—	2	0	0	0	0	3	1	0	0	0	3.0	0.00	—	.100	.100	0	—	0	1	1	0	0.0
1976 LA-N	1	1	.500	4	2	0	0	0	16^2	12	1	6	4	9.7	2.16	157	.207	.281	0	.000	-1	2	2	0	0.2
1977 LA-N	3	1	.750	5	1	0	0	1	17	22	1	4	8	13.8	4.24	90	.306	.342	0	.000	-1	-1	-1	-0	-0.3
1978 LA-N	0	0	—	1	0	0	0	0	2	2	0	0	0	9.0	0.00	—	.250	.250	0	—	0	1	1	-0	0.0
1979 LA-N	0	1	.000	7	0	0	0	0	12^1	19	0	5	1	18.2	5.11	71	.358	.424	1	.500	0	-2	-2	0	-0.1
1980 Tex-A	0	0	—	4	0	0	0	0	5^2	7	0	4	1	17.5	7.94	49	.304	.407	0	—	0	-2	-3	0	0.1
1981 Cle-A	0	0	—	7	0	0	0	0	13^1	16	1	2	11	12.2	5.40	67	.296	.321	0	—	0	-3	-3	-0	0.0
1982 Cle-A	0	1	.000	4	0	0	0	0	10^1	13	3	1	3	12.2	6.97	59	.310	.326	0	—	0	-3	-3	-0	-0.3
Total 8	4	4	.500	34	3	0	0	1	80^1	92	6	22	28	12.9	4.48	82	.287	.335	1	.077	-1	-6	-7	0	-0.4

● **DAN LEWANDOWSKI** Lewandowski, Daniel William b: 1/6/28, Buffalo, N.Y. d: 7/19/96, Hamilton, Ont., Can. BR/TR, 6', 180 lbs. Deb: 9/22/51

YEAR TM/L	W	L	PCT	G	GS	CG	SH	SV	IP	H	HR	BB	SO	RAT	ERA	ERA+	OAV	OOB	BH	AVG	PB	PR	/A	PD	TPI
1951 StL-N	0	1	.000	2	0	0	0	0	1	3	0	1	1	36.0	9.00	44	.500	.571	0	—	0	-1	-1	0	-0.4

● **LEWIS** Lewis b: Brooklyn, N.Y. Deb: 7/12/1890 ♦

YEAR TM/L	W	L	PCT	G	GS	CG	SH	SV	IP	H	HR	BB	SO	RAT	ERA	ERA+	OAV	OOB	BH	AVG	PB	PR	/A	PD	TPI
1890 Buf-P	0	1	.000	1	1	0	0	0	3	13	3	7	1	60.0	60.00	7	.591	.690	1	.200	-0	-19	-19	1	-2.0

● **TED LEWIS** Lewis, Edward Morgan "Parson" b: 12/25/1872, Machynlleth, Wales d: 5/24/36, Durham, N.H. BR/TR, 5'10.5", 158 lbs. Deb: 7/6/1896

YEAR TM/L	W	L	PCT	G	GS	CG	SH	SV	IP	H	HR	BB	SO	RAT	ERA	ERA+	OAV	OOB	BH	AVG	PB	PR	/A	PD	TPI
1896 Bos-N	1	4	.200	6	5	4	0	0	41^2	37	2	27	12	13.8	3.24	140	.236	.348	2	.111	-2	5	6	1	0.4
1897 *Bos-N	21	12	.636	38	34	30	2	1	290	316	11	125	65	14.0	3.85	116	.275	.351	28	.248	-2	15	20	-5	1.2
1898 Bos-N	26	8	**.765**	41	33	29	1	2	313^1	267	9	109	72	11.1	2.90	127	.229	.300	37	.282	4	25	28	-1	2.9
1899 Bos-N	17	11	.607	29	25	23	2	0	234^2	245	10	73	60	12.5	3.49	119	.269	.328	25	.260	0	10	17	-4	1.4
1900 Bos-N	13	12	.520	30	22	19	1	0	209	215	11	86	66	13.1	4.13	100	.265	.339	10	.137	-4	-10	-0	-3	-0.6
1901 Bos-A	16	17	.485	39	34	31	1	1	316^1	299	14	91	103	11.3	3.53	100	.247	.304	21	.174	-2	5	0	-2	-0.4
Total 6	94	64	.595	183	153	136	7	4	1405	1379	57	511	378	12.4	3.53	113	.255	.324	123	.223	-5	49	71	-13	4.9

● **DUFFY LEWIS** Lewis, George Edward b: 4/18/1888, San Francisco, Cal d: 6/17/79, Salem, N.H. BL/TL, 5'10.5", 165 lbs. Deb: 4/16/10 C♦

YEAR TM/L	W	L	PCT	G	GS	CG	SH	SV	IP	H	HR	BB	SO	RAT	ERA	ERA+	OAV	OOB	BH	AVG	PB	PR	/A	PD	TPI
1913 Bos-A	0	0	—	1	0	0	0	0	1	3	0	0	1	27.0	18.00	16	.500	.500	164	.298	0	-2	-2	-0	0.0

● **JIM LEWIS** Lewis, James Martin b: 10/12/55, Miami, Fla. BR/TR, 6'3", 190 lbs. Deb: 9/12/79

YEAR TM/L	W	L	PCT	G	GS	CG	SH	SV	IP	H	HR	BB	SO	RAT	ERA	ERA+	OAV	OOB	BH	AVG	PB	PR	/A	PD	TPI
1979 Sea-A	0	0	—	2	0	0	0	0	2^1	10	1	1	0	42.4	15.43	28	.625	.647	0	—	0	-3	-3	-0	-0.1
1982 NY-A	0	0	—	1	0	0	0	0	0^2	3	0	3	0	81.0	54.00	7	.500	.667	0	—	0	-4	-4	0	0.1
1983 Min-A	0	0	—	6	0	0	0	0	18	24	5	7	8	16.0	6.50	65	.324	.390	0	—	0	-5	-5	0	-0.2
1985 Sea-A	0	1	.000	2	1	0	0	0	4^2	8	1	1	1	21.2	7.71	55	.421	.500	0	—	0	-2	-2	-0	-0.4
Total 4	0	1	.000	11	1	0	0	0	25^2	45	7	12	9	21.0	8.77	48	.391	.462	0	—	0	-13	-13	-0	-0.6

YEAR TM/L	W	L	PCT	G	GS	CG	SH	SV	IP	H	HR	BB	SO	RAT	ERA	ERA+	OAV	OOB	BH	AVG	PB	PR	/A	PD	TPI
● **JIM LEWIS** Lewis, James Steven b: 7/20/64, Jackson, Mich. BR/TR, 6'2", 200 lbs. Deb: 8/9/91																									
1991 SD-N	0	0	—	12	0	0	0	0	13	14	2	11	10	17.3	4.15	91	.275	.403	0	.000	-0	-1	-1	1	0.0
● **RICHIE LEWIS** Lewis, Richie Todd b: 1/25/66, Muncie, Ind. BR/TR, 5'10", 175 lbs. Deb: 7/31/92																									
1992 Bal-A	1	1	.500	2	2	0	0	0	6^{2}	13	1	7	4	27.0	10.80	37	.406	.513	0	—	0	-5	-5	0	-1.1
1993 Fla-N	6	3	.667	57	0	0	0	0	77^{1}	68	7	43	65	13.0	3.26	133	.239	.340	1	.500	0	7	9	1	1.0
1994 Fla-N	1	4	.200	45	0	0	0	0	54	62	7	38	45	16.8	5.67	77	.284	.393	0	.000	-0	-9	-8	-0	-0.7
1995 Fla-N	0	1	.000	21	1	0	0	0	36	30	9	15	32	11.5	3.75	112	.224	.307	0	.000	0	2	2	-0	0.0
1996 Det-A	4	6	.400	72	0	0	0	2	90^{1}	78	9	65	78	14.6	4.18	121	.238	.370	0	.000	-0	8	9	-1	0.7
1997 Oak-A	2	0	1.000	14	0	0	0	0	18^{2}	24	7	15	12	19.3	9.64	47	.316	.435	0	—	0	-11	-11	0	-0.9
Cin-N	0	0	—	4	0	0	0	0	5^{2}	4	3	3	4	11.1	6.35	67	.200	.304	1	1.000	0	-1	-1	-0	0.0
1998 Bal-A	0	0	—	2	1	0	0	0	4^{2}	8	2	5	4	25.1	15.43	29	.421	.542	0	—	0	-6	-6	-0	0.2
Total 7	14	15	.483	217	4	0	0	2	293^{1}	287	45	191	244	14.9	4.88	93	.258	.371	2	.200	1	-15	-11	-1	-0.8
● **SCOTT LEWIS** Lewis, Scott Allen b: 12/5/65, Grants Pass, Ore. BR/TR, 6'3", 178 lbs. Deb: 9/25/90																									
1990 Cal-A	1	1	.500	2	2	1	0	0	16^{1}	10	2	2	9	6.6	2.20	173	.172	.200	0	—	0	3	3	-0	0.3
1991 Cal-A	3	5	.375	16	11	0	0	0	60^{1}	81	9	21	37	15.5	6.27	65	.316	.373	0	—	0	-15	-14	-0	-1.6
1992 Cal-A	4	0	1.000	21	2	0	0	0	38^{1}	36	3	14	18	12.2	3.99	100	.255	.331	0	—	0	-0	-0	1	0.1
1993 Cal-A	1	2	.333	15	4	0	0	0	32	37	3	12	10	14.3	4.22	107	.311	.383	0	—	0	0	1	-1	0.0
1994 Cal-A	0	1	.000	20	0	0	0	0	31	46	5	10	10	16.8	6.10	80	.359	.414	0	—	0	-4	-4	0	-0.1
Total 5	9	9	.500	74	19	1	0	0	178	210	22	59	84	14.0	5.01	85	.299	.360	0	—	0	-16	-15	-0	-1.3
● **BERT LEWIS** Lewis, William Burton b: 10/3/1895, Tonawanda, N.Y. d: 3/24/50, Tonawanda, N.Y. BR/TR, 6'2", 176 lbs. Deb: 4/19/24																									
1924 Phi-N	0	0	—	12	0	0	0	0	18	23	1	7	3	15.5	6.00	74	.315	.383	0	.000	-1	-4	-3	0	-0.1
● **TERRY LEY** Ley, Terrence Richard b: 2/21/47, Portland, Ore. BL/TL, 6', 190 lbs. Deb: 8/20/71																									
1971 NY-A	0	0	—	6	0	0	0	0	9	9	1	9	7	20.0	5.00	65	.257	.435	0	—	0	-2	-2	0	0.0
● **AL LIBKE** Libke, Albert Walter b: 9/12/18, Tacoma, Wash. BL/TR, 6'4", 215 lbs. Deb: 4/19/45 ♦																									
1945 Cin-N	0	0	—	4	0	0	0	0	4^{1}	3	0	3	2	12.5	0.00	—	.200	.333	127	.283	1	2	2	0	0.0
1946 Cin-N	0	0	—	1	1	0	0	0	5	4	0	3	2	12.6	3.60	93	.235	.350	109	.253	0	-0	-0	-0	0.0
Total 2	0	0	—	5	1	0	0	0	9^{1}	7	0	6	4	12.5	1.93	183	.219	.342	236	.268	2	2	2	0	0.0
● **DON LIDDLE** Liddle, Donald Eugene b: 5/25/25, Mt.Carmel, Ill. BL/TL, 5'10", 165 lbs. Deb: 4/17/53																									
1953 Mil-N	7	6	.538	31	15	4	0	2	128^{2}	119	6	55	63	12.3	3.08	127	.248	.328	3	.088	-2	17	12	-1	0.9
1954 *NY-N	9	4	.692	28	19	4	3	0	126^{2}	100	5	55	44	11.2	3.06	132	.223	.312	7	.189	2	14	14	-1	1.4
1955 NY-N	10	4	.714	33	13	4	0	1	106^{1}	97	18	61	56	13.7	4.23	95	.246	.353	5	.185	1	-2	-2	-1	-0.2
1956 NY-N	1	2	.333	11	5	1	0	1	41^{1}	45	5	14	21	13.1	3.92	97	.278	.339	2	.167	-0	-1	-1	0	0.0
StL-N	1	2	.333	14	2	0	0	0	24^{2}	36	8	18	14	19.7	8.39	45	.353	.450	0	.000	-0	-13	-13	-0	-1.4
Yr	2	4	.333	25	7	1	0	1	66	81	13	32	35	15.4	5.59	68	.302	.377	2	.143	-0	-13	-13	0	-1.4
Total 4	28	18	.609	117	54	13	3	4	427^{2}	397	42	203	198	12.8	3.75	106	.250	.339	17	.152	1	16	10	-2	0.7
● **CORY LIDLE** Lidle, Cory Fulton b: 3/22/72, Hollywood, Cal. BR/TR, 5'11", 175 lbs. Deb: 5/8/97																									
1997 NY-N	7	2	.778	54	2	0	0	2	81^{2}	86	7	20	54	12.0	3.53	114	.274	.323	0	.000	-0	6	5	-1	0.4
● **DUTCH LIEBER** Lieber, Charles Edwin b: 2/1/10, Alameda, Cal. d: 12/31/61, Sawtelle, Cal. BR/TR, 6'0.5", 180 lbs. Deb: 4/18/35																									
1935 Phi-A	1	1	.500	18	1	0	0	2	46^{2}	45	1	19	14	12.5	3.09	147	.263	.340	2	.143	-1	7	8	0	0.3
1936 Phi-A	0	1	.000	3	0	0	0	0	11^{2}	17	0	6	1	17.7	7.71	66	.362	.434	0	.000	-0	-3	-3	1	-0.2
Total 2	1	2	.333	21	1	0	0	2	58^{1}	62	1	25	15	13.6	4.01	116	.284	.361	2	.118	-2	4	4	1	0.1
● **JON LIEBER** Lieber, Jonathan Ray b: 4/2/70, Council Bluffs, Iowa BL/TR, 6'3", 220 lbs. Deb: 5/15/94																									
1994 Pit-N	6	7	.462	17	17	1	0	0	108^{2}	116	12	25	71	11.8	3.73	116	.271	.313	4	.103	-2	6	7	-1	0.5
1995 Pit-N	4	7	.364	21	12	0	0	0	72^{2}	103	7	14	45	15.0	6.32	68	.346	.383	1	.048	-2	-17	-16	1	-2.2
1996 Pit-N	9	5	.643	51	15	0	0	1	142	156	19	28	94	11.9	3.99	109	.279	.316	7	.194	2	4	6	2	0.8
1997 Pit-N	11	14	.440	33	32	1	0	0	188^{1}	193	23	51	160	11.7	4.49	95	.263	.312	7	.121	-0	-6	-4	0	-0.5
1998 Pit-N	8	14	.364	29	28	2	0	1	171	182	23	40	138	11.8	4.11	105	.269	.313	8	.167	0	2	4	-1	0.4
Total 5	38	47	.447	151	104	4	0	2	682^{2}	750	84	158	508	12.1	4.36	99	.278	.321	27	.134	-2	-12	-4	0	-1.0
● **GLENN LIEBHARDT** Liebhardt, Glenn Ignatius "Sandy" b: 7/31/10, Cleveland, Ohio d: 3/14/92, Winston-Salem, N.C. BR/TR, 5'10.5", 170 lbs. Deb: 4/22/30 F																									
1930 Phi-A	0	1	.000	5	0	0	0	0	9	14	2	8	2	22.0	11.00	42	.359	.468	0	.000	-0	-6	-6	-0	-0.6
1936 StL-A	0	0	—	24	0	0	0	0	55^{1}	98	4	27	20	20.7	8.78	61	.375	.438	0	.000	-2	-23	-21	-2	-0.3
1938 StL-A	0	0	—	2	0	0	0	0	3	4	1	0	1	12.0	6.00	83	.308	.308	0	—	0	-0	-0	0	0.0
Total 3	0	1	.000	31	0	0	0	0	67^{1}	116	7	35	23	20.5	8.96	59	.371	.437	0	.000	-2	-30	-28	-2	-0.9
● **GLENN LIEBHARDT** Liebhardt, Glenn John b: 3/10/1883, Milton, Ind. d: 7/13/56, Cleveland, Ohio BR/TR, 5'10", 175 lbs. Deb: 10/2/06 F																									
1906 Cle-A	2	0	1.000	2	2	2	0	0	18	13	0	1	9	7.0	1.50	175	.206	.219	0	.000	-1	2	2	0	0.2
1907 Cle-A	18	14	.563	38	34	27	4	1	280^{1}	254	1	85	110	11.2	2.05	122	.244	.307	14	.161	-1	15	14	1	1.6
1908 Cle-A	15	16	.484	38	26	19	3	0	262	222	2	81	146	10.5	2.20	109	.235	.297	14	.175	0	6	6	1	0.7
1909 Cle-A	1	5	.167	12	4	1	0	1	52^{1}	54	0	16	15	12.2	2.92	87	.314	.376	0	.000	-2	-3	-2	-2	-0.6
Total 4	36	35	.507	90	66	49	7	2	612^{2}	543	3	183	280	10.9	2.17	113	.244	.306	28	.147	-4	21	20	0	1.9
● **KERRY LIGTENBERG** Ligtenberg, Kerry Dale b: 5/11/71, Rapid City, S.Dak. BR/TR, 6'2", 185 lbs. Deb: 8/12/97																									
1997 *Atl-N	1	0	1.000	15	0	0	0	1	15	12	4	4	19	9.6	3.00	139	.211	.262	0	—	0	2	2	-0	0.1
1998 *Atl-N	3	2	.600	75	0	0	0	30	73	51	6	24	79	9.2	2.71	156	.193	.260	0	—	0	12	12	-2	1.4
Total 2	4	2	.667	90	0	0	0	31	88	63	10	28	98	9.3	2.76	153	.196	.261	0	—	0	14	14	-2	1.5
● **GENE LILLARD** Lillard, Robert Eugene b: 11/12/13, Santa Barbara, Cal d: 4/12/91, Goleta, Cal. BR/TR, 5'10.5", 178 lbs. Deb: 5/8/36 F♦																									
1939 Chi-N	3	5	.375	20	7	2	0	0	55	68	2	36	31	17.5	6.55	60	.309	.413	1	.100	1	-16	-16	0	-1.9
1940 StL-N	0	1	.000	2	1	0	0	0	4^{2}	8	1	4	2	25.1	13.50	30	.364	.481	0	—	0	-5	-5	0	-0.8
Total 2	3	6	.333	22	8	2	0	0	59^{2}	76	3	40	33	18.1	7.09	56	.314	.420	8	.182	1	-21	-21	0	-2.7
● **JIM LILLIE** Lillie, James J. "Grasshopper" (b: James J. Lilly) b: 7/27/1861, New Haven, Conn. d: 11/9/1890, Kansas City, Mo. Deb: 5/17/1883 ♦																									
1883 Buf-N	0	1	.000	3	0	0	0	0	12	16	0	2	4	13.5	3.00	106	.302	.327	47	.234	0	0	0	0	0.0
1884 Buf-N	0	1	.000	2	1	0	0	0	13	22	0	5	4	18.7	6.23	51	.324	.370	105	.223	-0	-5	-4	0	-0.2
1886 KC-N	0	0	—	1	0	0	0	0	6	8	0	1	0	13.5	4.50	84	.348	.375	73	.175	-0	-1	-0	0	0.0
Total 3	0	2	.000	6	1	0	0	0	31	46	0	8	8	15.7	4.65	71	.319	.355	332	.219	-0	-5	-5	1	-0.2
● **DEREK LILLIQUIST** Lilliquist, Derek Jansen b: 2/20/66, Winter Park, Fla. BL/TL, 6', 214 lbs. Deb: 4/13/89																									
1989 Atl-N	8	10	.444	32	30	0	0	0	165^{2}	202	16	34	79	12.9	3.97	92	.301	.337	12	.190	0	-9	-6	-1	-0.7
1990 Atl-N	2	8	.200	12	11	0	0	0	61^{2}	75	10	19	34	13.9	6.28	64	.301	.353	8	.348	4	-17	-15	-1	-1.9
SD-N	3	3	.500	16	7	1	1	0	60^{1}	61	6	23	29	12.8	4.33	88	.266	.339	3	.150	0	-4	-3	-2	-0.5
Yr	5	11	.313	28	18	1	1	0	122	136	16	42	63	13.3	5.31	74	.282	.342	11	.256	4	-21	-19	-3	-2.4
1991 SD-N	0	2	.000	6	2	0	0	0	14^{1}	25	3	4	7	18.2	8.79	43	.379	.414	0	.000	-0	-8	-8	0	-0.9
1992 Cle-A	5	3	.625	71	0	0	0	6	61^{2}	39	5	18	47	8.6	1.75	223	.186	.257	0	—	0	15	15	0	2.1
1993 Cle-A	4	4	.500	56	2	0	0	10	64	64	5	19	40	11.8	2.25	192	.263	.319	0	—	0	15	15	-0	2.0
1994 Cle-A	1	3	.250	36	0	0	0	1	29^{1}	34	6	8	15	13.2	4.91	96	.304	.355	0	—	0	-0	-1	-1	-0.1
1995 Bos-A	2	1	.667	28	0	0	0	0	23	27	7	9	9	14.1	6.26	78	.303	.367	0	—	0	-4	-4	-0	-0.5
1996 Cin-N	0	0	—	5	0	0	0	0	3^{2}	5	1	0	1	12.3	7.36	57	.357	.357	0	—	0	-1	-1	0	0.0
Total 8	25	34	.424	262	52	1	1	17	483^{2}	532	59	134	261	12.6	4.13	96	.283	.333	23	.213	4	-13	-8	-4	-0.5
● **JOSE LIMA** Lima, Jose Desiderio Rodriguez (b: Jose Desiderio Rodriguez (Lima)) b: 9/30/72, Santiago, D.R. BR/TR, 6'2", 170 lbs. Deb: 4/20/94																									
1994 Det-A	0	1	.000	3	1	0	0	0	6^{2}	11	2	3	7	18.9	13.50	36	.355	.412	0	—	0	-6	-6	-0	-0.7

YEAR	TM/L	W	L	PCT	G	GS	CG	SH	SV	IP	H	HR	BB	SO	RAT	ERA	ERA+	OAV	OOB	BH	AVG	PB	PR	/A	PD	TPI
1995	Det-A	3	9	.250	15	15	0	0	0	73^2	85	10	18	37	13.1	6.11	78	.288	.338	0	—	0	-11	-11	-2	-1.6
1996	Det-A	5	6	.455	39	4	0	0	3	72^2	87	13	22	59	14.1	5.70	89	.296	.355	0	—	0	-6	-5	2	-0.5
1997	*Hou-N	1	6	.143	52	1	0	0	2	75	79	9	16	63	12.0	5.28	76	.271	.321	0	.000	-0	-9	-11	-1	-1.1
1998	Hou-N	16	8	.667	33	33	3	1	0	233^1	229	34	32	169	10.3	3.70	110	.256	.287	11	.139	-1	14	9	1	0.8
Total	5	25	30	.455	142	54	3	1	5	461^1	491	68	91	335	11.8	4.80	90	.272	.314	11	.134	-1	-19	-24	-0	-3.1
● **EZRA LINCOLN** Lincoln, Ezra Perry b: 11/17/1868, Raynham, Mass. d: 5/7/51, Taunton, Mass. BL/TL, 5′11″, 160 lbs. Deb: 5/2/1890																										
1890	Cle-N	3	11	.214	15	15	13	0	0	118	157	1	53	22	16.1	4.42	81	.310	.376	8	.157	-3	-11	-11	0	-1.2
	Syr-a	0	3	.000	3	3	2	0	0	20	33	1	4	6	17.1	10.35	34	.359	.392	0	.000	-1	-14	-15	-0	-1.5
Total	1	3	14	.176	18	18	15	0	0	138	190	2	57	28	16.2	5.28	68	.317	.378	8	.136	-4	-26	-26	0	-2.7
● **VIVE LINDAMAN** Lindaman, Vivan Alexander b: 10/28/1877, Charles City, Iowa d: 2/13/27, Charles City, Iowa BR/TR, 6′1″, 200 lbs. Deb: 4/14/06																										
1906	Bos-N	12	23	.343	39	36	32	2	0	307^1	303	4	90	115	11.8	2.43	111	.264	.324	14	.132	-2	7	9	-2	0.7
1907	Bos-N	11	15	.423	34	28	24	2	1	260	252	10	108	90	13.0	3.63	70	.265	.349	11	.122	-2	-34	-31	-2	-3.5
1908	Bos-N	12	16	.429	43	30	21	2	1	270^2	246	7	70	68	10.8	2.36	102	.249	.306	15	.176	0	0	2	-3	-0.2
1909	Bos-N	1	6	.143	15	6	6	1	0	66	75	1	28	13	14.2	4.64	61	.299	.371	6	.273	1	-15	-13	-1	-1.4
Total	4	36	60	.375	131	100	83	7	2	904	876	22	296	286	12.0	2.92	88	.263	.329	46	.152	-3	-41	-34	-8	-4.4
● **PAUL LINDBLAD** Lindblad, Paul Aaron b: 8/9/41, Chanute, Kan. BL/TL, 6′1″, 195 lbs. Deb: 9/15/65																										
1965	KC-A	0	1	.000	4	0	0	0	0	7^1	12	3	0	12	16.0	11.05	32	.353	.371	0	.000	-0	-6	-6	0	-0.7
1966	KC-A	5	10	.333	38	14	0	0	1	121	138	14	37	69	13.2	4.17	82	.292	.348	5	.147	0	-10	-10	0	-1.2
1967	KC-A	5	8	.385	46	10	1	1	6	115^2	106	15	35	83	11.4	3.58	89	.241	.306	7	.206	2	-4	-5	-0	-0.5
1968	Oak-A	4	3	.571	47	1	0	0	2	56^1	51	6	14	42	10.4	2.40	118	.237	.284	3	.375	1	4	3	0	0.6
1969	Oak-A	9	6	.600	60	0	0	0	9	78^1	72	8	33	64	12.3	4.14	83	.240	.319	4	.333	1	-4	-6	-0	-1.1
1970	Oak-A	8	2	.800	62	0	0	0	3	63^1	52	7	28	42	11.4	2.70	131	.222	.305	0	.000	-1	7	6	-0	0.9
1971	Oak-A	1	0	1.000	8	0	0	0	0	16	18	1	2	4	11.8	3.94	85	.295	.328	1	.333	0	-1	-1	0	0.0
	Was-A	6	4	.600	43	0	0	0	8	83^2	58	6	29	50	9.6	2.58	128	.196	.272	3	.158	0	8	7	1	1.1
	Yr	7	4	.636	51	0	0	0	8	99^2	76	7	31	54	9.8	2.80	118	.212	.279	4	.182	1	7	6	1	1.1
1972	Tex-A	5	8	.385	**66**	0	0	0	9	99^2	95	7	29	51	11.2	2.62	115	.257	.311	3	.200	0	5	4	-1	0.6
1973	*Oak-A	1	5	.167	36	3	0	0	2	78	89	8	28	33	13.8	3.69	96	.292	.357	0	—	0	1	-1	-1	-0.2
1974	Oak-A	4	4	.500	45	2	0	0	6	100^2	85	4	30	46	10.5	2.06	161	.231	.292	0	—	0	17	14	0	1.3
1975	*Oak-A	9	1	.900	68	0	0	0	7	122^1	105	6	43	58	10.9	2.72	133	.237	.305	0	.000	-0	14	12	1	1.2
1976	Oak-A	6	5	.545	65	0	0	0	5	114^2	111	5	24	37	10.8	3.06	110	.253	.296	0	—	0	6	4	1	0.7
1977	Tex-A	4	5	.444	42	1	0	0	4	98^2	103	16	29	46	12.1	4.20	97	.270	.324	0	—	0	-2	-1	0	-0.2
1978	Tex-A	1	1	.500	18	0	0	0	2	39^2	41	2	15	25	13.2	3.63	103	.279	.354	0	—	0	1	0	-0	0.0
	*NY-A	0	0	—	7	1	0	0	0	18^1	21	4	8	9	14.2	4.42	82	.284	.354	0	—	0	-1	-2	0	0.2
	Yr	1	1	.500	25	1	0	0	2	58	62	6	23	34	13.2	3.88	95	.276	.343	0	—	0	-1	-1	0	0.2
Total	14	68	63	.519	655	32	1	1	64	1213^2	1157	112	384	671	11.6	3.29	104	.253	.314	26	.195	4	35	17	2	2.7
● **LYMAN LINDE** Linde, Lyman Gilbert b: 9/30/20, Rolling Prairie, Wis. d: 10/24/95, Beaver Dam, Wis. BR/TR, 5′11″, 185 lbs. Deb: 9/11/47																										
1947	Cle-A	0	0	—	1	0	0	0	0	0^2	3	0	1	0	54.0	27.00	13	.600	.667	0	—	0	-2	-2	0	0.0
1948	Cle-A	0	0	—	3	0	0	0	0	10	9	1	4	0	11.7	5.40	75	.243	.317	0	.000	-0	-1	-1	-0	-0.1
Total	2	0	0	—	4	0	0	0	0	10^2	12	1	5	0	14.3	6.75	60	.286	.362	0	.000	-0	-3	-3	-0	-0.1
● **JOHNNY LINDELL** Lindell, John Harlan b: 8/30/16, Greeley, Colo. d: 8/27/85, Newport Beach, Cal. BR/TR, 6′4.5″, 217 lbs. Deb: 4/18/41 ♦																										
1942	NY-A	2	1	.667	23	2	0	0	1	52^2	52	3	22	28	12.8	3.76	92	.254	.329	6	.250	1	-1	-2	-0	0.0
1953	Pit-N	5	16	.238	27	23	13	1	0	175^2	173	17	116	102	15.1	4.71	95	.262	.377	26	.286	6	-8	-5	3	1.1
	Phi-N	1	1	.500	5	3	2	0	0	23^1	22	0	23	16	17.4	4.24	99	.259	.417	7	.389	2	0	-0	-0	0.2
	Yr	6	17	.261	32	26	15	1	0	199	195	17	139	118	15.1	4.66	95	.259	.375	33	.303	8	-8	-5	2	1.3
Total	2	8	18	.308	55	28	15	1	1	251^2	247	20	161	146	14.8	4.47	95	.260	.371	762	.273	9	-9	-7	2	1.3
● **ERNIE LINDEMANN** Lindemann, Ernest b: 6/10/1883, New York, N.Y. d: 12/27/51, Brooklyn, N.Y. BR/TR, Deb: 6/28/07																										
1907	Bos-N	0	0	—	1	1	0	0	0	6^1	6	0	4	3	14.2	5.68	45	.286	.400	1	.500	0	-2	-2	0	0.1
● **CARL LINDQUIST** Lindquist, Carl Emil b: 5/9/19, Morris Run, Pa. BR/TR, 6′2″, 185 lbs. Deb: 9/27/43																										
1943	Bos-N	0	2	.000	2	2	0	0	0	13	17	3	4	1	14.5	6.23	55	.315	.362	0	.000	-1	-4	-4	0	-0.5
1944	Bos-N	0	0	—	5	0	0	0	0	8^2	8	1	2	4	10.4	3.12	123	.222	.263	0	.000	-0	0	1	-0	0.0
Total	2	0	2	.000	7	2	0	0	0	21^2	25	4	6	5	12.9	4.98	72	.278	.323	0	.000	-1	-4	-3	-0	-0.5
● **JIM LINDSEY** Lindsey, James Kendrick b: 1/24/1898, Greensburg, La. d: 10/25/63, Jackson, La. BR/TR, 6′1″, 175 lbs. Deb: 5/1/22																										
1922	Cle-A	4	5	.444	29	5	0	0	1	83^2	105	4	24	29	14.2	6.02	67	.324	.376	4	.167	-1	-18	-19	-1	-1.9
1924	Cle-A	0	0	—	3	0	0	0	0	3	8	0	3	0	33.0	21.00	20	.500	.579	0	.000	-1	-6	-6	0	0.0
1929	StL-N	1	1	.500	2	2	1	0	0	16^1	20	1	2	8	12.7	5.51	85	.290	.319	1	.200	-0	-1	-2	-0	-0.2
1930	*StL-N	7	5	.583	39	6	3	0	5	105^2	131	6	46	50	15.4	4.43	113	.312	.385	8	.286	1	6	7	-3	0.5
1931	*StL-N	6	4	.600	35	2	1	1	7	74^2	77	2	45	32	14.7	2.77	142	.270	.370	1	.111	-0	**9**	**10**	-0	1.3
1932	StL-N	3	3	.500	33	5	0	0	3	89^1	96	6	38	31	13.7	4.94	80	.279	.354	3	.143	-1	-10	-10	-1	-0.9
1933	StL-N	0	0	—	1	0	0	0	0	2	2	0	1	1	13.5	4.50	77	.286	.375	0	—	0	-0	-0	-0	0.0
1934	Cin-N	0	0	—	4	0	0	0	0	4	4	0	2	2	15.8	4.50	91	.286	.412	0	—	0	-0	-0	0	0.0
	StL-N	0	1	.000	11	0	0	0	1	14	21	2	3	7	15.4	6.43	66	.328	.358	0	.000	-0	-4	-3	-0	-0.3
	Yr	0	1	.000	15	0	0	0	1	18	25	2	5	9	15.0	6.00	70	.316	.357	0	.000	-0	-4	-4	-0	-0.3
1937	Bro-N	0	1	.000	20	0	0	0	2	38^1	43	4	12	15	13.1	3.52	115	.295	.352	1	.167	-0	2	2	-1	0.0
Total	9	21	20	.512	177	20	5	1	19	431	507	25	176	175	14.5	4.70	91	.300	.370	18	.186	-3	-23	-21	-6	-1.5
● **AXEL LINDSTROM** Lindstrom, Axel Olaf b: 8/26/1895, Gustavsberg, Sweden d: 6/24/40, Asheville, N.C. BR/TR, 5′10″, 180 lbs. Deb: 10/3/16																										
1916	Phi-A	0	0	—	1	0	0	0	1	4	2	0	0	1	6.8	4.50	63	.182	.250	1	.500	0	-1	-1	-0	0.0
● **DICK LINES** Lines, Richard George b: 8/17/38, Montreal, Que., Can. BR/TL, 6′1″, 175 lbs. Deb: 4/16/66																										
1966	Was-A	5	2	.714	53	0	0	0	2	83	63	4	24	49	9.5	2.28	152	.213	.274	0	.000	-1	11	11	2	1.1
1967	Was-A	2	5	.286	54	0	0	0	4	85^2	83	6	24	54	11.2	3.36	94	.245	.295	1	.111	-1	-1	-2	0	-0.1
Total	2	7	7	.500	107	0	0	0	6	168^2	146	10	48	103	10.4	2.83	117	.230	.285	1	.053	-1	9	9	2	1.0
● **FRED LINK** Link, Edward Theodore "Laddie" b: 3/11/1886, Columbus, Ohio d: 5/22/39, Houston, Tex. BL/TL, 6′, 170 lbs. Deb: 4/15/10																										
1910	Cle-A	5	6	.455	22	13	6	1	1	127^2	121	0	50	55	12.5	3.17	82	.259	.340	7	.167	-1	-9	-8	-1	-1.0
	StL-A	0	1	.000	3	3	0	0	0	17	24	0	13	5	20.1	4.24	58	.375	.487	1	.167	-0	-3	-3	-0	-0.2
	Yr	5	7	.417	25	16	6	1	1	144^2	145	0	63	60	13.0	3.30	78	.270	.347	8	.167	-1	-12	-12	-2	-1.2
● **ED LINKE** Linke, Edward Karl "Babe" b: 11/9/11, Chicago, Ill. d: 6/21/88, Chicago, Ill. BR/TR, 5′11″, 180 lbs. Deb: 4/27/33																										
1933	Was-A	1	0	1.000	3	2	0	0	0	16	15	0	11	6	14.6	5.06	83	.250	.366	1	.167	0	-1	-2	-0	-0.1
1934	Was-A	2	2	.500	7	4	2	0	0	34^2	38	1	9	9	12.2	4.15	104	.277	.322	2	.182	0	1	1	0	0.1
1935	Was-A	11	7	.611	40	22	10	1	3	178	211	6	80	51	14.8	5.01	86	.296	.367	20	.294	6	-11	-14	-1	-0.8
1936	Was-A	1	5	.167	13	6	1	0	0	52	73	4	14	11	15.1	7.10	67	.330	.370	6	.400	5	-12	-13	1	-0.7
1937	Was-A	6	1	.857	36	7	0	0	3	128^2	158	11	59	61	15.5	5.60	79	.304	.379	10	.217	1	-14	-17	-0	-0.8
1938	StL-A	1	7	.125	21	2	0	0	0	39^2	60	6	33	18	21.1	7.94	63	.357	.463	2	.200	0	-14	-13	1	-2.0
Total	6	22	22	.500	120	43	13	1	6	449	555	28	206	156	15.4	5.61	79	.305	.377	41	.263	12	-51	-58	0	-4.3
● **ROYCE LINT** Lint, Royce James b: 1/1/21, Birmingham, Ala. BL/TL, 6′1″, 165 lbs. Deb: 4/13/54																										
1954	StL-N	2	3	.400	30	4	1	1	0	70^1	75	9	30	36	13.4	4.86	85	.273	.344	1	.100	1	-6	-6	1	-0.2
● **DOUG LINTON** Linton, Douglas Warren b: 2/9/65, Santa Ana, Cal. BR/TR, 6′1″, 190 lbs. Deb: 8/3/92																										
1992	Tor-A	1	3	.250	8	3	0	0	0	24	31	5	17	16	18.0	8.63	47	.323	.425	0	—	0	-12	-12	-0	-1.7
1993	Tor-A	0	1	.000	4	1	0	0	0	11	11	0	9	4	17.2	6.55	66	.256	.396	0	—	0	-3	-3	-0	-0.2
	Cal-A	2	0	1.000	19	0	0	0	0	25^2	35	8	14	19	17.2	7.71	58	.324	.402	0	—	0	-10	-9	-0	-0.6

YEAR	TM/L	W	L	PCT	G	GS	CG	SH	SV	IP	H	HR	BB	SO	RAT	ERA	ERA+	OAV	OOB	BH	AVG	PB	PR	/A	PD	TPI
	Yr	2	1	.667	23	1	0	0	0	36^{2}	46	8	23	23	16.9	7.36	60	.299	.390	0	—	0	-12	-12	-0	-0.8
1994	NY-N	6	2	.750	32	3	0	0	0	50^{1}	74	4	20	29	16.8	4.47	93	.341	.397	0	.000	-1	-1	-2	-1	-0.4
1995	KC-A	0	1	.000	7	2	0	0	0	22^{1}	22	4	10	13	13.7	7.25	66	.256	.347	0	—	0	-6	-6	0	-0.2
1996	KC-A	7	9	.438	21	18	0	0	0	104	111	13	26	87	12.5	5.02	100	.271	.327	0	—	0	-0	-0	-1	-0.1
Total	5	16	16	.500	91	27	0	0	0	237^{1}	284	34	96	168	14.8	5.84	79	.296	.366	0	.000	-1	-33	-32	-2	-3.2

● FRANK LINZY
Linzy, Frank Alfred b: 9/15/40, Ft.Gibson, Okla BR/TR, 6'1", 190 lbs. Deb: 8/14/63

YEAR	TM/L	W	L	PCT	G	GS	CG	SH	SV	IP	H	HR	BB	SO	RAT	ERA	ERA+	OAV	OOB	BH	AVG	PB	PR	/A	PD	TPI
1963	SF-N	0	0	—	8	1	0	0	0	16^{2}	22	0	10	14	17.8	4.86	66	.324	.418	0	.000	-0	-3	-3	0	0.0
1965	SF-N	9	3	.750	57	0	0	0	21	81^{2}	76	2	23	35	11.2	1.43	251	.250	.309	4	.222	1	**19**	**20**	5	4.9
1966	SF-N	7	11	.389	51	0	0	0	16	100^{1}	107	4	34	57	12.8	2.96	124	.273	.334	3	.150	0	7	8	1	1.7
1967	SF-N	7	7	.500	57	0	0	0	17	95^{2}	67	4	34	38	9.5	1.51	218	.203	.277	0	.000	-2	20	19	3	3.9
1968	SF-N	9	8	.529	57	0	0	0	12	94^{2}	76	1	27	36	9.9	2.09	141	.218	.277	0	.000	-1	9	9	4	2.3
1969	SF-N	14	9	.609	58	0	0	0	11	116^{1}	129	5	38	62	13.2	3.64	96	.283	.342	8	.267	3	-1	-2	3	0.3
1970	SF-N	2	1	.667	20	0	0	0	1	25^{2}	33	2	11	16	15.8	7.01	57	.327	.398	0	.000	-0	-8	-9	0	-1.0
	StL-N	3	5	.375	47	0	0	0	2	61^{1}	66	3	23	19	13.1	3.67	112	.282	.346	0	.000	-1	3	3	1	0.4
	Yr	5	6	.455	67	0	0	0	3	87	99	5	34	35	13.8	4.66	88	.293	.358	0	.000	-1	-6	-6	1	-0.6
1971	StL-N	4	3	.571	50	0	0	0	6	59^{1}	49	2	27	24	11.5	2.12	170	.226	.311	2	.500	1	9	10	1	1.5
1972	Mil-A	2	2	.500	47	0	0	0	12	77^{1}	70	4	27	24	11.5	3.03	100	.248	.318	1	.111	-0	0	0	1	0.1
1973	Mil-A	2	6	.250	42	1	0	0	13	63	68	7	21	21	12.9	3.57	105	.282	.342	0	—	0	2	1	0	0.2
1974	Phi-N	3	2	.600	22	0	0	0	0	24^{2}	27	1	7	12	12.4	3.28	115	.284	.333	0	—	0	1	1	1	0.3
Total	11	62	57	.521	516	2	0	0	111	816^{2}	790	35	282	358	12.0	2.85	122	.257	.323	18	.149	0	58	57	20	14.6

● ANGELO LiPETRI
LiPetri, Michael Angelo b: 7/6/30, Brooklyn, N.Y. BR/TR, 6'1.5", 180 lbs. Deb: 4/25/56

YEAR	TM/L	W	L	PCT	G	GS	CG	SH	SV	IP	H	HR	BB	SO	RAT	ERA	ERA+	OAV	OOB	BH	AVG	PB	PR	/A	PD	TPI
1956	Phi-N	0	0	—	6	0	0	0	0	11	7	2	3	8	9.0	3.27	114	.175	.250	0	.000	-0	1	1	0	0.0
1958	Phi-N	0	0	—	4	0	0	0	0	4	6	1	0	1	15.8	11.25	35	.353	.389	0	—	0	-3	-3	0	0.0
Total	2	0	0	—	10	0	0	0	0	15	13	3	3	9	10.8	5.40	70	.228	.290	0	.000	-0	-3	-3	0	0.0

● TOM LIPP
Lipp, Thomas Charles (b: Thomas Charles Lieb) b: 6/4/1870, Baltimore, Md. d: 5/30/32, Baltimore, Md. 5'11.5", 170 lbs. Deb: 9/18/1897

YEAR	TM/L	W	L	PCT	G	GS	CG	SH	SV	IP	H	HR	BB	SO	RAT	ERA	ERA+	OAV	OOB	BH	AVG	PB	PR	/A	PD	TPI
1897	Phi-N	0	1	.000	1	1	0	0	0	3	8	0	2	1	30.0	15.00	28	.471	.526	1	1.000	0	-4	-4	-0	-0.7

● NIG LIPSCOMB
Lipscomb, Gerard b: 2/24/11, Rutherfordton, N.C d: 2/27/78, Huntersville, N.C. BR/TR, 6', 175 lbs. Deb: 4/23/37 ♦

YEAR	TM/L	W	L	PCT	G	GS	CG	SH	SV	IP	H	HR	BB	SO	RAT	ERA	ERA+	OAV	OOB	BH	AVG	PB	PR	/A	PD	TPI
1937	StL-A	0	0	—	3	0	0	0	0	9^{2}	13	3	5	1	16.8	6.52	74	.333	.409	31	.323	1	-2	-2	-0	0.0

● FELIPE LIRA
Lira, Antonio Felipe b: 4/26/72, Santa Teresa, Venez. BR/TR, 6', 170 lbs. Deb: 4/27/95

YEAR	TM/L	W	L	PCT	G	GS	CG	SH	SV	IP	H	HR	BB	SO	RAT	ERA	ERA+	OAV	OOB	BH	AVG	PB	PR	/A	PD	TPI
1995	Det-A	9	13	.409	37	22	0	0	1	146^{1}	151	17	56	89	13.2	4.31	110	.271	.346	0	—	0	7	7	-1	0.9
1996	Det-A	6	14	.300	32	32	3	2	0	194^{2}	204	30	66	113	12.9	5.22	97	.269	.336	0	—	0	-5	-4	2	-0.1
1997	Det-A	5	7	.417	20	15	1	1	0	92	101	15	45	64	14.5	5.77	79	.277	.360	0	—	0	-12	-12	2	-1.2
	Sea-A	0	4	.000	8	3	0	0	0	18^{2}	31	3	10	9	21.7	9.16	49	.365	.455	0	—	0	-10	-10	-0	-1.6
	Yr	5	11	.313	28	18	1	1	0	110^{2}	132	18	55	73	15.5	6.34	72	.291	.373	0	—	0	-22	-22	2	-2.8
1998	Sea-A	1	0	1.000	7	0	0	0	0	15^{2}	22	5	5	16	15.5	4.60	101	.319	.365	0	—	0	0	0	0	0.0
Total	4	21	38	.356	104	72	4	3	1	467^{1}	509	70	182	291	13.8	5.18	93	.278	.350	0	—	0	-20	-18	3	-2.0

● HOD LISENBEE
Lisenbee, Horace Milton b: 9/23/1898, Clarksville, Tenn d: 11/14/87, Clarksville, Tenn. BR/TR, 5'11", 170 lbs. Deb: 4/23/27

YEAR	TM/L	W	L	PCT	G	GS	CG	SH	SV	IP	H	HR	BB	SO	RAT	ERA	ERA+	OAV	OOB	BH	AVG	PB	PR	/A	PD	TPI
1927	Was-A	18	9	.667	39	34	17	**4**	0	242	221	6	78	105	11.2	3.57	114	.245	.307	11	.133	-5	15	13	-2	0.6
1928	Was-A	2	6	.250	16	9	3	0	0	77	102	4	32	13	16.2	6.08	66	.326	.397	4	.174	-0	-17	-18	-1	-1.6
1929	Bos-A	0	0	—	5	0	0	0	0	8^{2}	10	1	4	2	14.5	5.19	82	.294	.368	0	.000	-0	-1	-1	0	0.0
1930	Bos-A	10	17	.370	37	31	15	0	0	237^{1}	254	20	86	47	13.1	4.40	105	.280	.346	20	.267	1	7	6	-4	0.3
1931	Bos-A	5	12	.294	41	17	6	0	0	164^{2}	190	13	49	42	13.2	5.19	83	.281	.332	12	.226	0	-15	-16	-2	-1.5
1932	Bos-A	0	4	.000	19	6	3	0	0	73^{1}	87	9	25	13	13.9	5.65	80	.296	.353	1	.048	-2	-10	-9	-1	-0.7
1936	Phi-A	1	7	.125	19	7	4	0	0	85^{2}	115	9	24	17	14.6	6.20	82	.322	.365	3	.120	-1	-11	-10	-1	-0.9
1945	Cin-N	1	3	.250	31	3	0	0	1	80^{1}	97	12	16	14	12.9	5.49	68	.294	.330	0	.000	-3	-15	-15	-1	-1.1
Total	8	37	58	.389	207	107	48	4	1	969	1076	74	314	253	13.1	4.81	90	.282	.340	51	.169	-10	-47	-51	-11	-4.9

● AD LISKA
Liska, Adolph James b: 7/10/06, Dwight, Neb. d: 11/30/98, Portland, Ore. BR/TR, 5'11.5", 160 lbs. Deb: 4/17/29

YEAR	TM/L	W	L	PCT	G	GS	CG	SH	SV	IP	H	HR	BB	SO	RAT	ERA	ERA+	OAV	OOB	BH	AVG	PB	PR	/A	PD	TPI
1929	Was-A	3	9	.250	24	10	4	0	0	94^{1}	87	1	42	33	12.6	4.77	89	.249	.335	5	.172	-1	-6	-6	3	-0.4
1930	Was-A	9	7	.563	32	16	7	1	1	150^{2}	140	6	71	40	12.9	3.29	140	.250	.340	5	.096	-4	23	22	6	2.2
1931	Was-A	0	1	.000	2	1	0	0	0	4	9	0	1	2	22.5	6.75	64	.450	.476	0	.000	-0	-1	-1	0	-0.2
1932	Phi-N	2	0	1.000	8	0	0	0	1	26^{2}	22	0	10	6	11.1	1.69	261	.239	.320	0	.000	-1	6	8	1	0.7
1933	Phi-N	3	1	.750	45	1	0	0	1	75^{2}	96	5	26	23	14.5	4.52	84	.310	.363	1	.071	-1	-10	-6	4	-0.1
Total	5	17	18	.486	111	28	11	1	3	351^{1}	354	12	150	104	13.1	3.87	112	.266	.344	11	.107	-7	13	19	14	2.2

● MARK LITTELL
Littell, Mark Alan b: 1/17/53, Cape Girardeau, Mo. BL/TR, 6'3", 210 lbs. Deb: 6/14/73

YEAR	TM/L	W	L	PCT	G	GS	CG	SH	SV	IP	H	HR	BB	SO	RAT	ERA	ERA+	OAV	OOB	BH	AVG	PB	PR	/A	PD	TPI
1973	KC-A	1	3	.250	8	7	1	0	0	38	44	5	23	16	15.9	5.68	72	.288	.381	0	—	0	-8	-7	-0	-0.9
1975	KC-A	1	2	.333	7	3	1	0	0	24^{1}	19	1	15	19	12.6	3.70	104	.229	.347	0	—	0	0	0	1	0.1
1976	*KC-A	8	4	.667	60	1	0	0	16	104	68	1	60	92	11.1	2.08	169	.188	.304	0	.000	-0	**17**	16	-1	2.4
1977	*KC-A	8	4	.667	48	5	0	0	12	104^{2}	73	6	55	106	11.1	3.61	112	.198	.304	0	.000	-0	5	5	-1	0.5
1978	StL-N	4	8	.333	72	2	0	0	11	106^{1}	80	8	59	130	12.1	2.79	126	.213	.326	0	.000	-0	9	9	-1	1.0
1979	StL-N	9	4	.692	63	0	0	0	13	82^{1}	60	2	39	67	10.8	2.19	172	.203	.296	0	.000	-1	14	14	-1	2.5
1980	StL-N	0	2	.000	14	0	0	0	2	10^{2}	14	2	7	7	17.7	9.28	40	.318	.412	0	.000	-0	-7	-7	-0	-1.4
1981	StL-N	1	3	.250	28	1	0	0	2	41	36	2	31	22	14.7	4.39	81	.237	.366	2	.250	0	-4	-4	-1	-0.4
1982	StL-N	0	1	.000	16	0	0	0	0	20^{2}	22	1	15	7	16.1	5.23	69	.272	.385	0	.000	-0	-4	-4	-1	-0.2
Total	9	32	31	.508	316	19	2	0	56	532	416	28	304	466	12.3	3.32	112	.217	.326	2	.059	-2	23	24	-4	3.6

● JEFF LITTLE
Little, Donald Jeffrey b: 12/25/54, Fremont, Ohio BR/TL, 6'6", 220 lbs. Deb: 9/6/80

YEAR	TM/L	W	L	PCT	G	GS	CG	SH	SV	IP	H	HR	BB	SO	RAT	ERA	ERA+	OAV	OOB	BH	AVG	PB	PR	/A	PD	TPI
1980	StL-N	1	1	.500	7	2	0	0	0	18^{2}	18	0	9	17	13.0	3.86	96	.250	.333	1	.167	-0	-1	-0	-0	-0.1
1982	Min-A	2	0	1.000	33	0	0	0	0	36^{1}	33	6	27	26	14.9	4.21	101	.244	.370	0	—	0	-1	0	-1	-0.2
Total	2	3	1	.750	40	2	0	0	0	55	51	6	36	43	14.2	4.09	99	.246	.358	1	.167	-0	-1	-0	-1	-0.3

● JOHN LITTLEFIELD
Littlefield, John Andrew b: 1/5/54, Covina, Cal. BR/TR, 6'2", 200 lbs. Deb: 6/8/80

YEAR	TM/L	W	L	PCT	G	GS	CG	SH	SV	IP	H	HR	BB	SO	RAT	ERA	ERA+	OAV	OOB	BH	AVG	PB	PR	/A	PD	TPI
1980	StL-N	5	5	.500	52	0	0	0	9	66	71	2	20	22	12.5	3.14	118	.282	.337	0	.000	-1	3	4	0	0.6
1981	SD-N	2	3	.400	42	0	0	0	2	64	53	5	28	21	11.5	3.66	89	.235	.322	0	.000	-0	-1	-3	-0	-0.3
Total	2	7	8	.467	94	0	0	0	11	130	124	7	48	43	12.0	3.39	102	.259	.330	0	.000	-1	2	1	-0	0.3

● DICK LITTLEFIELD
Littlefield, Richard Bernard b: 3/18/26, Detroit, Mich. d: 11/20/97, Detroit, Mich. BL/TL, 6', 180 lbs. Deb: 7/7/50

YEAR	TM/L	W	L	PCT	G	GS	CG	SH	SV	IP	H	HR	BB	SO	RAT	ERA	ERA+	OAV	OOB	BH	AVG	PB	PR	/A	PD	TPI
1950	Bos-A	2	2	.500	15	2	0	0	1	23^{1}	27	6	24	13	20.1	9.26	53	.297	.448	0	.000	-1	-12	-11	1	-1.6
1951	Chi-A	1	1	.500	4	2	0	0	0	9^{2}	9	1	17	7	24.2	8.38	48	.243	.481	0	.000	0	-5	-5	-0	-0.7
1952	Det-A	0	3	.000	28	1	0	0	1	47^{2}	46	4	25	32	13.4	4.34	88	.257	.348	1	.143	-0	-4	-3	-1	-0.3
	StL-A	2	3	.400	7	5	3	0	0	46^{1}	35	4	17	34	10.1	2.72	144	.205	.277	1	.063	-2	5	6	-1	0.3
	Yr	2	6	.250	35	6	3	0	1	94	81	8	42	66	11.8	3.54	109	.231	.314	2	.087	-2	1	3	-2	0.0
1953	StL-A	7	12	.368	36	22	2	0	0	152^{1}	153	17	84	104	14.2	5.08	83	.264	.361	8	.190	-1	-18	-15	-1	-1.8
1954	Bal-A	0	0	—	3	0	0	0	0	6	8	0	6	5	22.5	10.50	34	.333	.484	0	.000	-0	-5	-5	-0	0.0
	Pit-N	10	11	.476	23	21	7	1	0	155	140	10	85	92	13.2	3.60	116	.239	.337	8	.163	0	8	10	-3	1.0
1955	Pit-N	5	12	.294	35	17	4	1	0	130	148	15	68	70	15.1	5.12	80	.290	.375	6	.176	0	-16	-15	-2	-1.8
1956	Pit-N	0	0	—	6	2	0	0	0	12^{2}	14	2	6	10	14.2	4.26	88	.286	.364	0	.000	-0	-1	-1	-0	-0.1
	StL-N	0	2	.000	3	2	0	0	0	9^{2}	9	2	4	5	12.1	7.45	51	.237	.310	0	.000	-0	-4	-4	-0	-0.7
	NY-N	4	4	.500	31	7	0	0	2	97	78	16	39	65	10.9	4.08	93	.231	.310	2	.083	-2	-3	-3	0	-0.4
	Yr	4	6	.400	40	11	0	0	2	119^{1}	101	20	49	80	11.3	4.37	86	.238	.316	2	.071	-2	-8	-8	-1	-1.2
1957	Chi-N	2	3	.400	48	2	0	0	4	65^{2}	76	12	37	51	15.6	5.35	72	.295	.385	2	.182	0	-11	-11	-1	-1.0
1958	Mil-N	0	1	.000	4	0	0	0	1	6^{1}	7	2	1	7	12.8	4.26	83	.280	.333	0	—	0	-0	-1	-0	-0.1
Total	9	33	54	.379	243	83	16	2	9	761^{2}	750	91	413	495	13.9	4.71	86	.260	.355	28	.145	-5	-65	-56	-9	-7.2

YEAR	TM/L	W	L	PCT	G	GS	CG	SH	SV	IP	H	HR	BB	SO	RAT	ERA	ERA+	OAV	OOB	BH	AVG	PB	PR	/A	PD	TPI
● **CARLISLE LITTLEJOHN**	Littlejohn, Charles Carlisle b: 10/6/01, Irene, Tex. d: 10/27/77, Kansas City, Mo. BR/TR, 5'10", 175 lbs. Deb: 5/11/27																									
1927	StL-N	3	1	.750	14	2	1	0	0	42	47	4	14	16	13.1	4.50	88	.292	.349	5	.417	2	-3	-3	-1	-0.2
1928	StL-N	2	1	.667	12	2	1	0	0	32	36	2	14	6	14.1	3.66	109	.286	.357	0	.000	-2	1	1	-0	-0.1
Total	2	5	2	.714	26	4	2	0	0	74	83	6	28	22	13.5	4.14	96	.289	.352	5	.217	-0	-2	-1	-1	-0.3
● **GREG LITTON**	Litton, Jon Gregory b: 7/13/64, New Orleans, La. BR/TR, 6', 190 lbs. Deb: 5/2/89 ♦																									
1991	SF-N	0	0	—	1	0	0	0	0	1	1	0	3	0	36.0	9.00	40	.250	.571	23	.181	0	-1	-1	0	0.0
● **BUDDY LIVELY**	Lively, Everett Adrian "Red" b: 2/14/25, Birmingham, Ala. BR/TR, 6'0.5", 200 lbs. Deb: 4/17/47 F																									
1947	Cin-N	4	7	.364	38	17	3	1	0	123	126	16	63	52	13.8	4.68	88	.265	.351	6	.188	2	-9	-8	-0	-0.5
1948	Cin-N	0	0	—	10	0	0	0	0	22^{2}	13	0	11	12	9.9	2.38	164	.165	.275	0	.000	-0	4	4	-1	-0.1
1949	Cin-N	4	6	.400	31	10	3	1	1	103^{1}	91	11	53	30	12.5	3.92	107	.245	.339	4	.154	0	1	3	-1	0.2
Total	3	8	13	.381	79	27	6	2	1	249	230	27	127	94	12.9	4.16	99	.248	.339	10	.167	1	-3	-1	-2	-0.4
● **JACK LIVELY**	Lively, Henry Everett b: 5/29/1885, Joppa, Ala. d: 12/5/67, Arab, Ala. BR/TR, 5'9", 185 lbs. Deb: 4/16/11 F																									
1911	Det-A	7	5	.583	18	14	10	0	0	113^{2}	143	1	34	45	14.6	4.59	75	.313	.369	11	.256	3	-16	-14	-1	-1.1
● **WES LIVENGOOD**	Livengood, Wesley Amos b: 7/18/10, Salisbury, N.C. d: 9/2/96, Winston-Salem, N.C. BR/TR, 6'2", 172 lbs. Deb: 5/30/39																									
1939	Cin-N	0	0	—	5	0	0	0	0	5^{2}	9	3	3	4	19.1	9.53	40	.360	.429	0	—	0	-4	-4	0	0.0
● **JAKE LIVINGSTONE**	Livingstone, Jacob M. b: 1/1/1880, St.Petersburg, Russia d: 3/22/49, Wassaic, N.Y. Deb: 9/6/01																									
1901	NY-N	0	0	—	2	0	0	0	0	12	26	0	7	6	27.0	9.00	37	.433	.514	1	.167	0	-8	-8	-0	0.0
● **CLEM LLEWELLYN**	Llewellyn, Clement Manly "Lew" b: 8/1/1895, Dobson, N.C. d: 11/26/69, Concord, N.C. BL/TR, 6'2", 195 lbs. Deb: 6/18/22																									
1922	NY-A	0	0	—	1	0	0	0	0	1	1	0	0	0	9.0	0.00	—	.250	.250	0	—	0	0	0	-0	0.0
● **GRAEME LLOYD**	Lloyd, Graeme John b: 4/9/67, Victoria, Australia BL/TL, 6'7", 234 lbs. Deb: 4/11/93																									
1993	Mil-A	3	4	.429	55	0	0	0	0	63^{2}	64	5	13	31	11.3	2.83	150	.256	.301	0	—	0	11	10	1	1.1
1994	Mil-A	2	3	.400	43	0	0	0	3	47	49	4	15	31	12.8	5.17	97	.269	.335	0	—	0	-2	-1	-0	-0.1
1995	Mil-A	0	5	.000	33	0	0	0	4	32	28	4	8	13	10.1	4.50	111	.246	.295	0	—	0	1	2	0	0.1
1996	Mil-A	2	4	.333	52	0	0	0	0	51	49	3	17	24	11.8	2.82	184	.254	.318	0	—	0	12	13	-0	1.1
	*NY-A	0	2	.000	13	0	0	0	0	5^{2}	12	1	5	6	27.0	17.47	28	.429	.515	0	—	0	-8	-8	-0	-2.1
	Yr	2	6	.250	65	0	0	0	0	56^{2}	61	4	22	30	13.2	4.29	120	.274	.339	0	—	0	4	5	-0	-1.0
1997	*NY-A	1	1	.500	46	0	0	0	1	49	55	6	20	26	14.0	3.31	134	.293	.364	0	—	0	7	6	0	0.3
1998	*NY-A	3	0	1.000	50	0	0	0	0	37^{2}	26	3	6	20	8.1	1.67	266	.191	.236	0	—	0	12	12	-0	0.8
Total	6	11	19	.367	292	0	0	0	8	286	283	26	84	151	11.9	3.62	130	.259	.318	0	—	0	33	34	0	1.2
● **ESTEBAN LOAIZA**	Loaiza, Esteban Antonio Veyna b: 12/31/71, Tijuana, Mexico BR/TR, 6'4", 190 lbs. Deb: 4/29/95																									
1995	Pit-N	8	9	.471	32	31	1	0	0	172^{2}	205	21	55	85	13.8	5.16	83	.300	.357	10	.192	1	-19	-17	1	-1.3
1996	Pit-N	2	3	.400	10	10	1	1	0	52^{2}	65	11	19	32	14.7	4.96	88	.308	.371	2	.118	-1	-4	-3	1	-0.3
1997	Pit-N	11	11	.500	33	32	1	0	0	196^{1}	214	17	56	122	12.9	4.13	104	.279	.338	10	.167	-0	2	3	-1	0.2
1998	Pit-N	6	5	.545	21	14	0	0	0	91^{2}	96	13	30	53	12.7	4.52	96	.275	.338	7	.241	1	-3	-2	2	0.0
	Tex-A	3	6	.333	14	14	1	0	0	79^{1}	103	15	22	55	14.4	5.90	82	.316	.363	0	—	0	-11	-9	-0	-1.0
Total	4	30	34	.469	110	101	4	1	0	592^{2}	683	77	182	347	13.5	4.80	91	.293	.350	29	.184	1	-35	-28	2	-2.4
● **HARRY LOCHHEAD**	Lochhead, Robert Henry b: 3/29/1876, Stockton, Cal. d: 8/22/09, Stockton, Cal. BR/TR, 5'11", 172 lbs. Deb: 4/16/1899 ♦																									
1899	Cle-N	0	0	—	1	0	0	0	0	3^{2}	4	0	2	0	14.7	0.00	—	.286	.375	129	.238	0	2	2	-0	0.0
● **CHUCK LOCKE**	Locke, Charles Edward b: 5/5/32, Malden, Mo. BR/TR, 5'11", 185 lbs. Deb: 9/16/55																									
1955	Bal-A	0	0	—	2	0	0	0	0	3	0	0	1	1	3.0	0.00	—	.000	.100	0	—	0	1	1	0	0.0
● **BOBBY LOCKE**	Locke, Lawrence Donald b: 3/3/34, Rowes Run, Pa. BR/TR, 5'11", 185 lbs. Deb: 6/18/59																									
1959	Cle-A	3	2	.600	24	7	0	0	2	77^{2}	66	6	41	40	12.7	3.13	118	.233	.336	8	.333	3	6	5	0	0.7
1960	Cle-A	3	5	.375	32	11	2	2	2	123	121	10	37	53	11.7	3.37	111	.255	.311	9	.237	3	7	5	2	0.8
1961	Cle-A	4	4	.500	37	4	0	0	2	95^{1}	112	12	40	37	14.5	4.53	87	.300	.371	4	.211	0	-5	-6	1	-0.4
1962	StL-N	0	0	—	1	0	0	0	0	2	1	0	2	1	13.5	0.00	—	.143	.333	0	—	0	1	1	0	0.0
	Phi-N	1	0	1.000	5	0	0	0	0	15^{2}	16	4	10	9	14.9	5.74	67	.262	.366	2	.286	0	-3	-3	1	-0.1
	Yr	1	0	1.000	6	0	0	0	0	17^{2}	17	4	12	10	14.8	5.09	77	.250	.363	2	.286	0	-2	-2	1	-0.1
1963	Phi-N	0	0	—	9	0	0	0	0	10^{2}	10	0	5	7	12.7	5.91	55	.244	.326	0	.000	-0	-3	-3	-0	0.0
1964	Phi-N	0	0	—	8	0	0	0	0	19^{1}	21	2	6	11	12.6	2.79	124	.276	.329	0	.000	-0	2	1	0	0.0
1965	Cin-N	0	1	.000	11	0	0	0	0	17^{1}	20	2	8	8	14.5	5.71	66	.299	.373	0	.000	0	-4	-4	1	-0.1
1967	Cal-A	3	0	1.000	9	1	0	0	2	19^{1}	14	1	3	7	8.4	2.33	135	.203	.247	2	.667	1	2	2	0	0.5
1968	Cal-A	2	3	.400	29	0	0	0	2	36^{1}	51	3	13	21	16.1	6.44	45	.331	.387	0	.000	-0	-14	-14	-1	-2.2
Total	9	16	15	.516	165	23	2	2	10	416^{2}	432	40	165	194	13.1	4.02	91	.269	.340	25	.255	8	-12	-17	4	-0.8
● **RON LOCKE**	Locke, Ronald Thomas b: 4/4/42, Wakefield, R.I. BR/TL, 5'11", 168 lbs. Deb: 4/23/64																									
1964	NY-N	1	2	.333	25	3	0	0	0	41^{1}	46	3	22	17	15.0	3.48	103	.289	.379	0	.000	-0	0	0	-0	0.0
● **BOB LOCKER**	Locker, Robert Awtry b: 3/15/38, George, Iowa BB/TR, 6'3", 200 lbs. Deb: 4/14/65																									
1965	Chi-A	5	2	.714	51	0	0	0	2	91^{1}	71	6	30	69	10.1	3.15	101	.216	.285	0	.000	-2	3	0	3	0.2
1966	Chi-A	9	8	.529	56	0	0	0	12	95	73	2	23	70	9.6	2.46	129	.206	.264	4	.250	1	10	7	3	2.0
1967	Chi-A	7	5	.583	**77**	0	0	0	20	124^{2}	102	5	23	80	9.7	2.09	148	.222	.274	0	.000	-1	16	14	5	2.3
1968	Chi-A	5	4	.556	70	0	0	0	10	90^{1}	78	4	27	62	10.6	2.29	132	.234	.293	0	.000	-1	7	7	2	1.2
1969	Chi-A	2	3	.400	17	0	0	0	4	22	26	6	6	15	13.1	6.55	59	.292	.337	0	.000	-0	-7	-7	0	-1.6
	Sea-A	3	3	.500	51	0	0	0	6	78^{1}	69	3	26	46	11.3	2.18	166	.234	.302	1	.083	-0	13	13	2	1.3
	Yr	5	6	.455	68	0	0	0	10	100^{1}	95	9	32	61	11.7	3.14	117	.247	.310	1	.077	-1	5	6	2	-0.3
1970	Mil-A	0	1	.000	28	0	0	0	3	31^{2}	37	1	10	19	14.8	3.41	111	.306	.382	0	.000	-0	1	1	-0	0.0
	Oak-A	3	3	.500	38	0	0	0	4	56^{1}	49	1	19	33	11.0	2.88	123	.232	.299	1	.167	-0	5	4	1	0.5
	Yr	3	4	.429	66	0	0	0	7	88	86	2	29	52	11.9	3.07	118	.254	.315	1	.143	-0	6	5	0	0.5
1971	*Oak-A	7	2	.778	47	0	0	0	6	72^{1}	68	3	19	46	10.9	2.86	116	.249	.300	0	.000	-0	5	4	1	0.6
1972	*Oak-A	6	1	.857	56	0	0	0	10	78	69	1	16	47	10.0	2.65	107	.235	.280	0	.000	0	4	2	-1	0.2
1973	Chi-N	10	6	.625	63	0	0	0	18	106^{1}	96	6	42	76	12.0	2.54	155	.244	.323	1	.067	-1	13	17	2	3.1
1975	Chi-N	0	1	.000	22	0	0	0	0	32^{2}	38	3	16	14	15.4	4.96	77	.306	.394	0	—	0	-5	-4	1	-0.1
Total	10	57	39	.594	576	0	0	0	95	879	776	41	257	577	10.9	2.75	122	.237	.300	7	.074	-4	64	58	18	9.7
● **SKIP LOCKWOOD**	Lockwood, Claude Edward b: 8/17/46, Boston, Mass. BR/TR, 6', 190 lbs. Deb: 4/23/65 ♦																									
1969	Sea-A	0	1	.000	6	3	0	0	0	23	24	3	6	10	11.7	3.52	103	.279	.326	0	.000	-1	0	0	0	0.0
1970	Mil-A	5	12	.294	27	26	3	1	0	173^{2}	173	22	79	93	13.4	4.30	88	.266	.351	12	.226	2	-11	-10	-1	-0.8
1971	Mil-A	10	15	.400	33	32	5	1	0	208	191	13	91	115	12.4	3.33	104	.246	.329	5	.081	-1	3	3	-3	-0.1
1972	Mil-A	8	15	.348	29	27	5	3	0	170	148	11	71	106	11.8	3.60	84	.232	.313	7	.132	-1	-10	-11	-3	-1.8
1973	Mil-A	5	12	.294	37	15	3	0	0	154^{2}	164	10	59	87	13.3	3.90	96	.280	.352	0	—	0	-1	-2	0	-0.2
1974	Cal-A	2	5	.286	37	2	0	0	1	81^{1}	81	8	32	39	13.1	4.32	80	.264	.343	0	—	0	-6	-8	-0	-0.7
1975	NY-N	1	3	.250	24	0	0	0	2	48^{1}	28	3	25	61	10.1	1.49	232	.174	.289	1	.167	-0	11	11	-1	0.9
1976	NY-N	10	7	.588	56	0	0	0	19	94^{1}	62	6	34	108	9.3	2.67	123	.186	.266	6	.333	3	9	7	-0	1.7
1977	NY-N	4	8	.333	63	0	0	0	20	104	87	5	31	84	10.6	3.38	111	.227	.291	3	.200	-0	6	4	-2	0.4
1978	NY-N	7	13	.350	57	0	0	0	15	90^{2}	78	10	31	73	10.8	3.57	98	.236	.302	2	.182	1	0	-1	-2	-0.3
1979	NY-N	2	5	.286	27	0	0	0	9	42^{1}	33	3	14	42	10.0	1.49	245	.224	.292	0	.000	-0	11	10	-1	2.0
1980	Bos-A	3	1	.750	24	1	0	0	2	45^{2}	61	4	17	11	15.4	5.32	79	.321	.377	0	—	0	-7	-6	-1	-0.6
Total	12	57	97	.370	420	106	16	5	68	1236	1130	98	490	829	12.0	3.55	99	.246	.323	40	.154	3	4	-3	-13	0.5
● **MILO LOCKWOOD**	Lockwood, Milo Hathaway b: 4/7/1858, Solon, Ohio d: 10/9/1897, Economy, Pa. 5'10", 160 lbs. Deb: 4/17/1884 ♦																									
1884	Was-U	1	9	.100	11	10	6	0	0	67^{2}	99	4	15	48	15.2	7.45	32	.319	.351	14	.209	-2	-38	-38	1	-3.8

● BILLY LOES Loes, William b: 12/13/29, Long Island City, N.Y. BR/TR, 6'1", 170 lbs. Deb: 5/18/50

YEAR	TM/L	W	L	PCT	G	GS	CG	SH	SV	IP	H	HR	BB	SO	RAT	ERA	ERA+	OAV	OOB	BH	AVG	PB	PR	/A	PD	TPI
1950	Bro-N	0	0	—	10	0	0	0	0	12^{2}	16	5	5	2	14.9	7.82	52	.314	.375	0	.000	0	-5	-5	-0	0.0
1952	*Bro-N	13	8	.619	39	21	8	4	1	187^{1}	154	12	71	115	11.0	2.69	135	.224	.299	5	.093	-3	22	20	-0	1.8
1953	*Bro-N	14	8	.636	32	25	9	1	0	162^{2}	165	21	53	75	12.2	4.54	94	.261	.322	7	.125	-2	-5	-5	3	-0.5
1954	Bro-N	13	5	.722	28	21	6	0	0	147^{2}	154	14	60	97	13.1	4.14	99	.269	.339	6	.118	-2	-1	-1	-1	-0.4
1955	*Bro-N	10	4	.714	22	19	6	0	0	128	116	16	46	85	11.5	3.59	113	.240	.308	4	.091	-3	6	7	-0	0.4
1956	Bro-N	0	1	.000	1	1	0	0	0	1^{1}	5	1	1	2	40.5	40.50	10	.556	.600	0	—	0	-5	-5	0	-1.6
	Bal-A	2	7	.222	21	6	1	0	3	56^{2}	65	4	23	22	14.3	4.76	82	.291	.363	3	.176	-1	-4	-5	1	-0.8
1957	Bal-A★	12	7	.632	31	18	8	3	4	155^{1}	142	8	37	86	10.6	3.24	111	.245	.295	4	.080	-3	9	6	2	0.6
1958	Bal-A	3	9	.250	32	10	1	0	5	114	106	10	44	44	12.5	3.63	99	.252	.334	2	.067	-2	2	-0	0	-0.3
1959	Bal-A	4	7	.364	37	0	0	0	14	64^{1}	58	5	25	34	12.0	4.06	93	.239	.317	1	.125	-0	-1	-2	1	-0.3
1960	SF-N	3	2	.600	37	0	0	0	5	45^{2}	40	9	17	28	12.0	4.93	71	.247	.333	1	.250	0	-6	-7	1	-0.8
1961	SF-N	6	5	.545	26	18	3	1	0	114^{2}	114	13	39	55	12.4	4.24	90	.258	.325	5	.156	-0	-3	-5	0	-0.5
Total	11	80	63	.559	316	139	42	9	32	1190^{1}	1135	118	421	645	12.0	3.89	99	.252	.321	38	.110	-17	9	-5	6	-2.4

● CARLTON LOEWER Loewer, Carlton Ernest b: 9/24/73, Lafayette, La. BR/TR, 6'6", 220 lbs. Deb: 6/14/98

YEAR	TM/L	W	L	PCT	G	GS	CG	SH	SV	IP	H	HR	BB	SO	RAT	ERA	ERA+	OAV	OOB	BH	AVG	PB	PR	/A	PD	TPI
1998	Phi-N	7	8	.467	21	21	1	0	0	122^{2}	154	18	39	58	14.4	6.09	72	.312	.366	3	.086	-1	-25	-24	-1	-2.6

● FRANK LOFTUS Loftus, Francis Patrick b: 3/10/1898, Scranton, Pa. d: 10/27/80, Belchertown, Mass. BR/TR, 5'9", 190 lbs. Deb: 9/26/26

YEAR	TM/L	W	L	PCT	G	GS	CG	SH	SV	IP	H	HR	BB	SO	RAT	ERA	ERA+	OAV	OOB	BH	AVG	PB	PR	/A	PD	TPI
1926	Was-A	0	0	—	1	0	0	0	0	1	3	0	2	0	45.0	9.00	43	.600	.714	0	—	0	-1	-1	-0	0.0

● BOB LOGAN Logan, Robert Dean "Lefty" b: 2/10/10, Thompson, Neb. d: 5/20/78, Indianapolis, Ind. BR/TL, 5'10", 170 lbs. Deb: 4/18/35

YEAR	TM/L	W	L	PCT	G	GS	CG	SH	SV	IP	H	HR	BB	SO	RAT	ERA	ERA+	OAV	OOB	BH	AVG	PB	PR	/A	PD	TPI
1935	Bro-N	0	1	.000	2	0	0	0	0	2^{2}	2	0	1	1	10.1	3.38	118	.182	.250	0	—	0	0	0	0	0.1
1937	Det-A	0	0	—	1	0	0	0	0	0^{2}	1	0	1	1	27.0	0.00	—	.333	.500	0	—	0	0	0	0	0.0
	Chi-N	0	0	—	4	0	0	0	1	6^{1}	6	0	4	2	14.2	1.42	280	.261	.370	0	.000	-0	2	2	-0	0.0
1938	Chi-N	0	2	.000	14	0	0	0	2	22^{2}	18	0	17	10	14.3	2.78	138	.222	.364	0	.000	-0	3	3	-0	0.2
1941	Cin-N	0	1	.000	2	0	0	0	0	3^{1}	5	0	5	0	27.0	8.10	44	.333	.500	0	—	0	-2	-2	0	-0.4
1945	Bos-N	7	11	.389	34	25	5	1	1	187	213	9	53	53	12.9	3.18	121	.283	.331	13	.213	1	13	14	0	1.4
Total	5	7	15	.318	57	25	5	1	4	222^{2}	245	9	81	67	13.3	3.15	122	.277	.339	13	.200	1	16	17	0	1.3

● BILL LOHRMAN Lohrman, William Le Roy b: 5/22/13, Brooklyn, N.Y. BR/TR, 6'1", 185 lbs. Deb: 6/19/34

YEAR	TM/L	W	L	PCT	G	GS	CG	SH	SV	IP	H	HR	BB	SO	RAT	ERA	ERA+	OAV	OOB	BH	AVG	PB	PR	/A	PD	TPI
1934	Phi-N	0	1	.000	4	0	0	0	1	6	5	0	1	2	9.0	4.50	105	.217	.250	1	.500	0	-0	0	0	0.1
1937	NY-N	1	0	1.000	2	1	1	0	1	10	5	0	2	3	6.3	0.90	432	.152	.200	0	.000	-0	3	3	0	0.4
1938	NY-N	9	6	.600	31	14	3	0	0	152	152	9	33	52	11.1	3.32	114	.253	.294	4	.082	-4	8	8	2	0.5
1939	NY-N	12	13	.480	38	24	9	1	1	185^{2}	200	15	45	70	12.0	4.07	96	.282	.327	14	.233	4	-3	-3	-0	0.0
1940	NY-N	10	15	.400	31	28	11	4	1	195	200	19	43	73	11.4	3.78	103	.264	.306	8	.123	-2	1	2	2	0.2
1941	NY-N	9	10	.474	33	20	6	2	3	159	184	7	40	61	12.7	4.02	92	.286	.327	11	.229	4	-7	-6	0	-0.3
1942	StL-N	1	1	.500	5	0	0	0	0	12^{2}	11	0	2	6	9.2	1.42	241	.244	.277	2	.667	1	3	3	0	0.5
	NY-N	13	4	.765	26	19	12	2	0	158	143	11	33	41	10.1	2.56	131	.240	.282	7	.121	-3	13	14	-1	1.1
	Yr	14	5	.737	31	19	12	2	0	170^{2}	154	11	35	47	10.1	2.48	136	.240	.281	9	.148	-2	16	17	-1	1.6
1943	NY-N	5	6	.455	17	12	3	0	1	80^{1}	110	7	25	16	15.3	5.15	67	.324	.374	1	.037	-3	-16	-15	-1	-2.3
	Bro-N	0	2	.000	6	2	2	0	0	27^{2}	29	2	10	5	13.0	3.58	94	.274	.342	1	.143	0	-1	-1	-0	0.0
	Yr	5	8	.385	23	14	5	0	1	108	139	9	35	21	14.6	4.75	72	.311	.362	2	.059	-3	-16	-16	-1	-2.3
1944	Bro-N	0	0	—	3	0	0	0	0	2^{2}	4	0	4	1	27.0	0.00	—	.500	.667	0	—	0	1	1	-0	0.0
	Cin-N	0	1	.000	2	1	0	0	0	1^{2}	5	0	2	0	37.8	27.00	13	.500	.583	0	—	0	-4	-4	-0	-1.6
	Yr	0	1	.000	5	1	0	0	0	4^{1}	9	0	6	1	31.2	10.38	34	.500	.625	0	—	0	-3	-3	-0	-1.6
Total	9	60	59	.504	198	121	47	9	8	990^{2}	1048	70	240	330	11.8	3.69	101	.271	.315	49	.153	-3	-1	2	3	-1.4

● RICH LOISELLE Loiselle, Richard Frank b: 1/12/72, Neenah, Wis. BR/TR, 6'5", 225 lbs. Deb: 9/7/96

YEAR	TM/L	W	L	PCT	G	GS	CG	SH	SV	IP	H	HR	BB	SO	RAT	ERA	ERA+	OAV	OOB	BH	AVG	PB	PR	/A	PD	TPI
1996	Pit-N	1	0	1.000	5	3	0	0	0	20^{2}	22	3	8	9	13.1	3.05	143	.268	.333	2	.250	1	3	3	0	0.2
1997	Pit-N	1	5	.167	72	0	0	0	29	72^{2}	76	7	24	66	12.5	3.10	138	.269	.328	0	.000	-0	9	10	-1	1.3
1998	Pit-N	2	7	.222	54	0	0	0	19	55	56	2	36	48	15.4	3.44	126	.262	.373	0	—	0	5	5	0	1.2
Total	3	4	12	.250	131	3	0	0	48	148^{1}	154	12	68	123	13.7	3.22	134	.266	.346	2	.222	0	16	18	0	2.7

● MICKEY LOLICH Lolich, Michael Stephen b: 9/12/40, Portland, Ore. BB/TL, 6', 210 lbs. Deb: 5/12/63

YEAR	TM/L	W	L	PCT	G	GS	CG	SH	SV	IP	H	HR	BB	SO	RAT	ERA	ERA+	OAV	OOB	BH	AVG	PB	PR	/A	PD	TPI
1963	Det-A	5	9	.357	33	18	4	0	0	144^{1}	145	13	56	103	12.8	3.55	105	.265	.338	2	.056	-1	1	3	-1	0.2
1964	Det-A	18	9	.667	44	33	12	6	2	232	196	26	64	192	10.3	3.26	112	.225	.282	7	.109	1	9	10	-2	1.0
1965	Det-A	15	9	.625	43	37	7	3	3	243^{2}	216	23	72	226	11.1	3.44	101	.236	.301	5	.058	-6	1	1	-2	-0.7
1966	Det-A	14	14	.500	40	33	5	1	3	203^{2}	204	24	83	173	12.9	4.77	73	.257	.331	9	.141	1	-30	-29	-3	-4.0
1967	Det-A	14	13	.519	31	30	11	**6**	0	204	165	14	56	174	10.1	3.04	107	.221	.282	12	.197	3	4	5	-2	0.7
1968	*Det-A	17	9	.654	39	32	8	4	1	220	178	23	65	197	10.4	3.19	94	.219	.286	8	.114	0	-5	-4	-2	-0.8
1969	Det-A☆	19	11	.633	37	36	15	1	1	280^{2}	214	22	122	271	11.2	3.14	119	.210	.304	8	.088	-3	15	18	-0	1.6
1970	Det-A	14	19	.424	40	39	13	3	0	272^{2}	272	27	109	230	12.7	3.80	98	.260	.333	11	.134	1	-2	-2	1	0.0
1971	Det-A★	**25**	14	.641	45	45	**29**	4	0	**376**	336	36	92	**308**	10.4	2.92	123	.237	.287	15	.130	1	23	28	-4	2.6
1972	*Det-A★	22	14	.611	41	41	23	4	0	327^{1}	282	29	74	250	10.1	2.50	126	.234	.284	6	.067	-0	20	23	-4	2.2
1973	Det-A	16	15	.516	42	42	17	3	0	308^{2}	315	35	79	214	11.6	3.82	107	.266	.315	0	—	0	-0	9	-1	0.7
1974	Det-A	16	21	.432	41	41	27	3	0	308	310	38	78	202	11.4	4.15	92	.268	.316	0	—	0	-18	-12	-4	-1.7
1975	Det-A	12	18	.400	32	32	19	1	0	240^{2}	260	19	64	139	12.1	3.78	106	.279	.325	0	—	0	-0	6	-2	0.5
1976	NY-N	8	13	.381	31	30	5	2	0	192^{2}	184	14	52	120	11.0	3.22	102	.252	.302	7	.130	0	6	2	-1	0.1
1978	SD-N	2	1	.667	20	2	0	0	1	34^{2}	30	0	11	13	10.9	1.56	214	.240	.307	0	.000	-0	8	7	-0	0.6
1979	SD-N	0	2	.000	27	5	0	0	0	49^{1}	59	4	22	20	14.8	4.74	74	.304	.375	0	.000	-0	-6	-7	0	-0.3
Total	16	217	191	.532	586	496	195	41	11	3638^{1}	3366	347	1099	2832	11.3	3.44	104	.246	.306	90	.110	-4	25	58	-25	2.7

● TIM LOLLAR Lollar, William Timothy b: 3/17/56, Poplar Bluff, Mo. BL/TL, 6'3", 200 lbs. Deb: 6/28/80

YEAR	TM/L	W	L	PCT	G	GS	CG	SH	SV	IP	H	HR	BB	SO	RAT	ERA	ERA+	OAV	OOB	BH	AVG	PB	PR	/A	PD	TPI
1980	NY-A	1	0	1.000	14	1	0	0	2	32^{1}	33	3	20	13	14.8	3.34	117	.280	.384	0	—	0	2	2	0	0.1
1981	SD-N	2	8	.200	24	11	0	0	1	76^{2}	87	4	51	38	16.6	6.10	53	.293	.402	3	.167	1	-22	-24	2	-2.6
1982	SD-N	16	9	.640	34	34	4	2	0	232^{2}	192	20	87	150	10.9	3.13	109	.224	.298	21	.247	9	12	8	0	1.8
1983	SD-N	7	12	.368	30	30	1	0	0	175^{2}	170	22	85	135	13.3	4.61	76	.258	.347	14	.241	6	-19	-22	-2	-1.8
1984	*SD-N	11	13	.458	31	31	3	2	0	195^{2}	168	18	105	131	12.6	3.91	91	.234	.333	15	.221	7	-7	-7	-2	-0.4
1985	Chi-A	3	5	.375	18	13	0	0	0	83	83	10	58	61	15.4	4.66	93	.266	.383	0	—	0	-5	-3	-0	-0.3
	Bos-A	5	5	.500	16	10	1	0	1	67	57	9	40	44	13.2	4.57	94	.230	.339	0	.000	-0	-3	-2	-1	-0.4
	Yr	8	10	.444	34	23	1	0	1	150	140	19	98	105	14.3	4.62	93	.248	.360	0	.000	-0	-8	-5	-1	-0.7
1986	Bos-A	2	0	1.000	32	1	0	0	0	43	51	7	34	28	18.4	6.91	60	.304	.429	1	1.000	0	-13	-13	1	-0.4
Total	7	47	52	.475	199	131	9	4	4	906	841	93	480	600	13.3	4.27	85	.249	.345	54	.234	23	-55	-63	-3	-4.0

● VIC LOMBARDI Lombardi, Victor Alvin b: 9/20/22, Reedley, Cal. d: 12/7/97, Fresno, Cal. BL/TL, 5'7", 158 lbs. Deb: 4/18/45

YEAR	TM/L	W	L	PCT	G	GS	CG	SH	SV	IP	H	HR	BB	SO	RAT	ERA	ERA+	OAV	OOB	BH	AVG	PB	PR	/A	PD	TPI
1945	Bro-N	10	11	.476	38	24	9	0	4	203^{2}	195	11	86	64	12.6	3.31	113	.252	.331	13	.183	-1	11	10	-1	0.9
1946	Bro-N	13	10	.565	41	25	13	2	3	193	170	10	84	60	11.9	2.89	117	.235	.316	14	.230	2	11	10	0	1.4
1947	*Bro-N	12	11	.522	33	20	7	3	3	174^{2}	156	12	65	72	11.5	2.99	138	.241	.312	16	.242	2	21	22	1	3.0
1948	Pit-N	10	9	.526	38	17	9	0	4	163	156	9	67	54	12.4	3.70	110	.255	.330	10	.208	1	5	7	1	0.9
1949	Pit-N	5	5	.500	34	12	4	0	1	134	149	14	68	64	14.8	4.57	92	.286	.372	17	.347	5	-8	-5	1	0.3
1950	Pit-N	0	5	.000	39	2	0	0	1	76^{1}	93	14	48	26	16.9	6.60	66	.310	.409	4	.250	1	-21	-19	0	-1.0
Total	6	50	51	.495	223	100	42	5	16	944^{2}	919	70	418	340	12.9	3.68	106	.257	.337	74	.238	10	19	25	3	5.5

● LOU LOMBARDO Lombardo, Louis b: 11/18/28, Carlstadt, N.J. BL/TL, 6'2", 210 lbs. Deb: 9/22/48

YEAR	TM/L	W	L	PCT	G	GS	CG	SH	SV	IP	H	HR	BB	SO	RAT	ERA	ERA+	OAV	OOB	BH	AVG	PB	PR	/A	PD	TPI
1948	NY-N	0	0	—	2	0	0	0	0	5^{1}	5	1	5	0	18.6	6.75	58	.250	.423	0	.000	-0	-2	-2	0	0.0

● KEVIN LOMON Lomon, Kevin Dale b: 11/20/71, Fort Smith, Ark. BR/TR, 6'1", 195 lbs. Deb: 4/27/95

YEAR	TM/L	W	L	PCT	G	GS	CG	SH	SV	IP	H	HR	BB	SO	RAT	ERA	ERA+	OAV	OOB	BH	AVG	PB	PR	/A	PD	TPI
1995	NY-N	0	1	.000	6	0	0	0	0	9^{1}	17	0	5	6	21.2	6.75	60	.405	.468	0	—	0	-3	-3	-0	-0.3
1996	Atl-N	0	0	—	6	0	0	0	0	7^{1}	7	0	3	1	13.5	4.91	90	.259	.355	0	—	0	-1	-0	1	0.0
Total	2	0	1	.000	12	0	0	0	0	16^{2}	24	0	8	7	17.8	5.94	71	.348	.423	0	—	0	-3	-3	0	-0.3

● **JIM LONBORG** Lonborg, James Reynold b: 4/16/42, Santa Maria, Cal. BR/TR, 6'5", 210 lbs. Deb: 4/23/65

YEAR TM/L	W	L	PCT	G	GS	CG	SH	SV	IP	H	HR	BB	SO	RAT	ERA	ERA+	OAV	OOB	BH	AVG	PB	PR	/A	PD	TPI
1965 Bos-A	9	17	.346	32	31	7	1	0	185^1	193	20	65	113	12.7	4.47	83	.262	.324	8	.136	0	-21	-15	-2	-2.1
1966 Bos-A	10	10	.500	45	23	3	1	2	181^2	173	18	55	131	11.6	3.86	98	.249	.310	5	.093	-2	-9	-1	-1	-0.4
1967 *Bos-A☆	**22**	9	.710	39	39	15	2	0	273^1	228	23	83	**246**	10.9	3.16	110	.225	.296	14	.141	-1	2	10	-2	0.7
1968 Bos-A	6	10	.375	23	17	4	1	0	113^1	89	11	59	73	12.6	4.29	74	.216	.330	11	.282	3	-16	-14	-2	-1.8
1969 Bos-A	7	11	.389	29	23	4	0	0	143^2	148	15	65	100	13.8	4.51	84	.270	.355	4	.098	-1	-14	-11	-0	-1.4
1970 Bos-A	4	1	.800	9	4	0	0	0	34	33	3	9	21	11.1	3.18	125	.260	.309	4	.444	2	2	3	0	0.7
1971 Bos-A	10	7	.588	27	26	5	1	0	167^2	167	15	67	100	13.3	4.13	89	.259	.342	9	.170	0	-13	-8	1	-0.7
1972 Mil-A	14	12	.538	33	30	11	2	1	223	197	17	76	143	11.5	2.83	107	.238	.311	10	.145	-1	6	5	-2	0.3
1973 Phi-N	13	16	.448	38	30	6	0	0	199^1	218	25	80	106	13.9	4.88	78	.279	.353	8	.136	0	-27	-24	-1	-3.2
1974 Phi-N	17	13	.567	39	39	16	3	0	283	280	22	70	121	11.3	3.21	118	.261	.310	9	.096	-4	13	18	-4	1.0
1975 Phi-N	8	6	.571	27	26	6	2	0	159^1	161	12	45	72	11.9	4.12	90	.257	.312	1	.023	-3	-9	-7	0	-0.8
1976 *Phi-N	18	10	.643	33	32	8	1	1	222	210	18	50	118	10.7	3.08	115	.249	.294	11	.164	1	10	11	-3	1.2
1977 *Phi-N	11	4	.733	25	25	4	1	0	157^2	157	15	50	76	12.1	4.11	97	.261	.323	5	.104	-2	-4	-2	-1	-0.5
1978 Phi-N	8	10	.444	22	22	1	0	0	113^2	132	16	45	48	14.2	5.23	68	.293	.359	6	.176	1	-21	-21	-0	-2.9
1979 Phi-N	0	1	.000	4	1	0	0	0	7^1	14	3	4	7	23.3	11.05	35	.389	.463	0	.000	-0	-6	-6	-0	-0.7
Total 15	157	137	.534	425	368	90	15	4	2464^1	2400	233	823	1475	12.2	3.86	94	.255	.322	105	.136	-5	-106	-63	-18	-10.6

● **JOEY LONG** Long, Joey J. b: 7/15/70, Sidney, O. BR/TL, 6'2", 220 lbs. Deb: 4/25/97

YEAR TM/L	W	L	PCT	G	GS	CG	SH	SV	IP	H	HR	BB	SO	RAT	ERA	ERA+	OAV	OOB	BH	AVG	PB	PR	/A	PD	TPI
1997 SD-N	0	0	—	10	0	0	0	0	11	17	1	8	8	21.3	8.18	47	.340	.441	0	—	0	-5	-5	0	0.0

● **LEP LONG** Long, Lester b: 7/12/1888, Summit, N.J. d: 10/21/58, Birmingham, Ala. BR/TR, 5'10", 153 lbs. Deb: 6/29/11

YEAR TM/L	W	L	PCT	G	GS	CG	SH	SV	IP	H	HR	BB	SO	RAT	ERA	ERA+	OAV	OOB	BH	AVG	PB	PR	/A	PD	TPI
1911 Phi-A	0	0	—	4	0	0	0	0	8	15	0	5	4	22.5	4.50	70	.405	.476	0	.000	-0	-1	-1	0	0.0

● **RED LONG** Long, Nelson b: 9/28/1876, Burlington, Ont., Canada d: 8/11/29, Hamilton, Ont., Can BR/TR, 6'1", 190 lbs. Deb: 9/11/02

YEAR TM/L	W	L	PCT	G	GS	CG	SH	SV	IP	H	HR	BB	SO	RAT	ERA	ERA+	OAV	OOB	BH	AVG	PB	PR	/A	PD	TPI
1902 Bos-N	0	0	—	1	1	1	0	0	8	4	0	3	5	9.0	1.13	251	.148	.258	0	.000	-0	1	2	-0	0.0

● **BOB LONG** Long, Robert Earl b: 11/11/54, Jasper, Tenn. BR/TR, 6'3", 178 lbs. Deb: 9/2/81

YEAR TM/L	W	L	PCT	G	GS	CG	SH	SV	IP	H	HR	BB	SO	RAT	ERA	ERA+	OAV	OOB	BH	AVG	PB	PR	/A	PD	TPI
1981 Pit-N	1	2	.333	5	3	0	0	0	19^2	23	2	10	8	15.1	5.95	60	.299	.379	0	.000	-0	-5	-5	-1	-0.8
1985 Sea-A	0	0	—	28	0	0	0	0	38^1	30	7	17	29	11.5	3.76	112	.210	.302	0	—	0	2	2	-0	0.0
Total 2	1	2	.333	33	3	0	0	0	58	53	9	27	37	12.7	4.50	89	.241	.329	0	.000	-0	-4	-3	-1	-0.8

● **TOM LONG** Long, Thomas Francis "Little Hawk" b: 4/22/1898, Memphis, Tenn. d: 9/16/73, Louisville, Ky. BL/TL, 5'9", 154 lbs. Deb: 4/26/24

YEAR TM/L	W	L	PCT	G	GS	CG	SH	SV	IP	H	HR	BB	SO	RAT	ERA	ERA+	OAV	OOB	BH	AVG	PB	PR	/A	PD	TPI
1924 Bro-N	0	0	—	1	0	0	0	0	2	2	0	2	0	18.0	9.00	42	.333	.500	0	—	0	-1	-1	-0	0.0

● **BILL LONG** Long, William Douglas b: 2/29/60, Cincinnati, Ohio BR/TR, 6', 185 lbs. Deb: 7/21/85

YEAR TM/L	W	L	PCT	G	GS	CG	SH	SV	IP	H	HR	BB	SO	RAT	ERA	ERA+	OAV	OOB	BH	AVG	PB	PR	/A	PD	TPI
1985 Chi-A	0	1	.000	4	3	0	0	0	14	25	4	5	13	19.3	10.29	42	.391	.435	0	—	0	-10	-9	0	-0.5
1987 Chi-A	8	8	.500	29	23	5	2	1	169	179	20	28	72	11.2	4.37	105	.272	.304	0	—	0	2	4	0	0.2
1988 Chi-A	8	11	.421	47	18	3	0	2	174	187	21	43	77	12.1	4.03	98	.280	.327	0	—	0	-1	-1	-0	-0.1
1989 Chi-A	5	5	.500	30	8	0	0	1	98^2	101	8	37	51	13.0	3.92	97	.265	.336	0	—	0	-0	-1	0	0.0
1990 Chi-A	0	1	.000	4	0	0	0	0	5^2	6	2	2	2	12.7	6.35	60	.261	.320	0	—	0	-2	-2	0	-0.2
Chi-N	6	1	.857	42	0	0	0	5	55^2	66	8	21	32	14.2	4.37	93	.301	.365	0	.000	-0	-4	-2	0	-0.2
1991 Mon-N	0	0	—	3	0	0	0	0	1^2	4	0	4	0	43.2	10.80	33	.500	.667	0	—	0	-1	-1	-0	0.0
Total 6	27	27	.500	159	52	8	2	9	518^2	568	63	140	247	12.5	4.37	95	.281	.331	0	.000	-0	-16	-13	1	-0.8

● **BRIAN LOONEY** Looney, Brian James b: 9/26/69, New Haven, Conn. BL/TL, 5'10", 180 lbs. Deb: 9/26/93

YEAR TM/L	W	L	PCT	G	GS	CG	SH	SV	IP	H	HR	BB	SO	RAT	ERA	ERA+	OAV	OOB	BH	AVG	PB	PR	/A	PD	TPI
1993 Mon-N	0	0	—	3	1	0	0	0	6	8	0	2	7	15.0	3.00	139	.308	.357	0	.000	-0	1	1	0	0.0
1994 Mon-N	0	0	—	1	0	0	0	0	2	4	1	0	2	22.5	22.50	19	.400	.455	0	—	0	-4	-4	-0	0.0
1995 Bos-A	0	1	.000	3	1	0	0	0	4^2	12	1	4	2	30.9	17.36	28	.545	.615	0	—	0	-7	-6	0	-1.1
Total 3	0	1	.000	7	2	0	0	0	12^2	24	2	6	11	22.0	11.37	39	.414	.477	0	.000	-0	-10	-10	-1	-1.1

● **BRADEN LOOPER** Looper, Braden La Vern b: 10/28/74, Weatherford, Okla. BR/TR, 6'4", 210 lbs. Deb: 3/31/98

YEAR TM/L	W	L	PCT	G	GS	CG	SH	SV	IP	H	HR	BB	SO	RAT	ERA	ERA+	OAV	OOB	BH	AVG	PB	PR	/A	PD	TPI
1998 StL-N	0	1	.000	4	0	0	0	0	3^1	5	1	1	4	16.2	5.40	77	.357	.400	0	—	0	-0	-0	-0	-0.1

● **PETE LOOS** Loos, Ivan b: 3/23/1878, Philadelphia, Pa. d: 2/23/56, Darby, Pa. TR , Deb: 5/2/01

YEAR TM/L	W	L	PCT	G	GS	CG	SH	SV	IP	H	HR	BB	SO	RAT	ERA	ERA+	OAV	OOB	BH	AVG	PB	PR	/A	PD	TPI
1901 Phi-A	0	1	.000	1	1	0	0	0	1	2	0	4	0	54.0	27.00	14	.400	.667	0	—	0	-3	-3	0	-1.2

● **ED LOPAT** Lopat, Edmund Walter (b: Edmund Walter Lopatynski) b: 6/21/18, New York, N.Y. d: 6/15/92, Darien, Conn. BL/TL, 5'10", 185 lbs. Deb: 4/30/44 MC

YEAR TM/L	W	L	PCT	G	GS	CG	SH	SV	IP	H	HR	BB	SO	RAT	ERA	ERA+	OAV	OOB	BH	AVG	PB	PR	/A	PD	TPI
1944 Chi-A	11	10	.524	27	25	13	1	0	210	217	12	59	75	11.9	3.26	105	.265	.316	25	.309	6	4	4	1	1.2
1945 Chi-A	10	13	.435	26	24	17	1	1	199^1	226	8	56	74	13.0	4.11	81	.285	.336	24	.293	5	-16	-17	-1	-1.4
1946 Chi-A	13	13	.500	29	29	20	2	0	231	216	18	48	89	10.3	2.73	125	.248	.288	22	.253	6	20	18	1	2.8
1947 Chi-A	16	13	.552	31	31	22	3	0	252^2	241	17	73	109	11.3	2.81	130	.253	.307	19	.198	0	25	24	-1	2.6
1948 NY-A	17	11	.607	33	31	13	3	0	226^2	246	16	66	83	12.5	3.65	112	.284	.336	14	.173	-1	16	11	2	1.2
1949 *NY-A	15	10	.600	31	30	14	4	1	215^1	222	19	69	70	12.4	3.26	124	.269	.330	20	.263	7	22	19	0	2.7
1950 *NY-A	18	8	.692	35	32	15	3	1	236^1	244	19	65	72	11.9	3.47	124	.266	.317	19	.232	8	29	22	1	2.9
1951 *NY-A★	21	9	.700	31	31	20	4	0	234^2	209	12	71	93	**10.9**	2.91	131	.239	**.298**	15	.179	1	31	24	2	3.0
1952 *NY-A	10	5	.667	20	19	10	2	0	149^1	127	11	53	56	11.1	2.53	131	.234	.307	9	.173	1	19	13	0	1.4
1953 *NY-A	16	4	**.800**	25	24	9	3	0	178^1	169	13	32	50	10.3	**2.42**	**152**	.250	.288	12	.190	1	31	25	1	2.9
1954 NY-A	12	4	.750	26	23	7	0	0	170	189	14	33	54	12.1	3.55	97	.288	.328	1	.018	-5	3	-2	-1	-0.8
1955 NY-A	4	8	.333	16	12	3	1	0	86^2	101	12	16	24	12.3	3.74	100	.294	.328	4	.138	-1	2	0	-1	-0.2
Bal-A	3	4	.429	10	7	1	0	0	49	57	8	9	10	12.7	4.22	90	.294	.335	3	.176	0	-1	-2	1	-0.2
Yr	7	12	.368	26	19	4	1	0	135^2	158	20	25	34	12.3	3.91	96	.293	.328	7	.152	-1	1	-2	-0	-0.4
Total 12	166	112	.597	340	318	164	27	3	2439^1	2464	179	650	859	11.6	3.21	116	.264	.315	187	.211	29	186	138	4	18.1

● **ART LOPATKA** Lopatka, Arthur Joseph b: 5/28/19, Chicago, Ill. BB/TL, 5'10", 170 lbs. Deb: 9/12/45

YEAR TM/L	W	L	PCT	G	GS	CG	SH	SV	IP	H	HR	BB	SO	RAT	ERA	ERA+	OAV	OOB	BH	AVG	PB	PR	/A	PD	TPI
1945 StL-N	1	0	1.000	4	1	1	0	0	11^2	7	0	3	5	8.5	1.54	243	.159	.229	1	.250	0	3	3	-0	0.2
1946 Phi-N	0	1	.000	4	1	0	0	0	5^1	13	1	4	4	28.7	16.88	20	.448	.515	0	—	0	-8	-8	0	-1.2
Total 2	1	1	.500	8	2	1	0	0	17	20	1	7	9	14.8	6.35	57	.274	.346	1	.250	0	-5	-5	-0	-1.0

● **ALBIE LOPEZ** Lopez, Albert Anthony b: 8/18/71, Mesa, Ariz. BR/TR, 6'2", 205 lbs. Deb: 7/6/93

YEAR TM/L	W	L	PCT	G	GS	CG	SH	SV	IP	H	HR	BB	SO	RAT	ERA	ERA+	OAV	OOB	BH	AVG	PB	PR	/A	PD	TPI
1993 Cle-A	3	1	.750	9	9	0	0	0	49^2	49	7	32	25	14.9	5.98	72	.262	.373	0	—	0	-9	-9	-0	-0.6
1994 Cle-A	1	2	.333	4	4	1	1	0	17	20	3	6	18	14.3	4.24	111	.290	.355	0	—	0	1	1	-0	0.1
1995 Cle-A	0	0	—	6	2	0	0	0	23	17	4	7	22	9.8	3.13	150	.205	.275	0	—	0	4	4	-0	-0.1
1996 Cle-A	5	4	.556	13	10	0	0	0	62	80	14	22	45	15.1	6.39	77	.311	.370	0	—	0	-10	-10	-0	-1.2
1997 Cle-A	3	7	.300	37	6	0	0	0	76^2	101	11	40	63	17.0	6.93	68	.321	.404	0	.000	-0	-20	-19	1	-2.0
1998 TB-A	7	4	.636	54	0	0	0	1	79^2	73	7	32	62	12.2	2.60	189	.249	.329	0	.000	-0	18	20	1	2.6
Total 6	19	18	.514	123	31	1	1	1	308	340	46	139	235	14.3	5.11	92	.282	.362	0	.000	-0	-16	-13	0	-1.2

● **AURELIO LOPEZ** Lopez, Aurelio Alejandro (Rios) b: 9/21/48, Tecamachalco, Mexico d: 9/22/92, Matehuala, Mex. BR/TR, 6', 220 lbs. Deb: 9/1/74

YEAR TM/L	W	L	PCT	G	GS	CG	SH	SV	IP	H	HR	BB	SO	RAT	ERA	ERA+	OAV	OOB	BH	AVG	PB	PR	/A	PD	TPI
1974 KC-A	0	0	—	8	1	0	0	0	16	21	0	10	5	17.4	5.63	68	.344	.437	0	—	0	-4	-3	0	0.0
1978 StL-N	4	2	.667	25	4	0	0	0	65	52	4	32	46	11.8	4.29	82	.218	.313	3	.214	0	-5	-6	-1	-0.6
1979 Det-A	10	5	.667	61	0	0	0	21	127	95	12	51	106	10.6	2.41	179	.210	.294	0	—	0	25	27	-0	3.7
1980 Det-A	13	6	.684	67	1	0	0	21	124	125	15	45	97	12.6	3.77	109	.263	.330	0	—	0	4	5	-1	0.7
1981 Det-A	5	2	.714	29	3	0	0	3	81^2	70	8	31	53	11.4	3.64	104	.233	.309	0	—	0	0	1	0	0.1
1982 Det-A	3	1	.750	19	0	0	0	3	41	41	8	19	26	13.2	5.27	77	.268	.349	0	—	0	-5	-5	0	-0.6
1983 Det-A☆	9	8	.529	57	0	0	0	18	115^1	87	12	49	90	10.7	2.81	139	.210	.295	0	—	0	16	14	-1	2.5
1984 *Det-A	10	1	.909	71	0	0	0	14	137^2	109	16	52	94	10.7	2.94	133	.221	.298	0	—	0	16	15	-2	1.3
1985 Det-A	3	7	.300	51	0	0	0	5	86^1	82	15	41	53	12.9	4.80	85	.250	.335	0	—	0	-6	-7	-0	-0.8
1986 *Hou-N	3	3	.500	45	0	0	0	7	78	64	6	25	44	10.3	3.46	104	.221	.283	0	.000	-1	2	1	-2	-0.2
1987 Hou-N	2	1	.667	26	0	0	0	1	38	39	6	12	21	12.6	4.50	87	.273	.338	0	.000	-0	-2	-2	-0	-0.2
Total 11	62	36	.633	459	9	0	0	93	910	785	102	367	635	11.5	3.56	111	.234	.313	3	.125	-1	41	39	-8	5.9

● RAMON LOPEZ
Lopez, Jose Ramon (Hevia) b: 5/26/33, Las Villas, Cuba d: 9/4/82, Miami, Fla. BR/TR, 6', 175 lbs. Deb: 8/21/66

YEAR	TM/L	W	L	PCT	G	GS	CG	SH	SV	IP	H	HR	BB	SO	RAT	ERA	ERA+	OAV	OOB	BH	AVG	PB	PR	/A	PD	TPI
1966	Cal-A	0	1	.000	4	1	0	0	0	7	4	1	4	2	10.3	5.14	65	.154	.267	0	—	0	-1	-1	-0	-0.2

● MARCELINO LOPEZ
Lopez, Marcelino Pons b: 9/23/43, Havana, Cuba BR/TL, 6'3", 210 lbs. Deb: 4/14/63

YEAR	TM/L	W	L	PCT	G	GS	CG	SH	SV	IP	H	HR	BB	SO	RAT	ERA	ERA+	OAV	OOB	BH	AVG	PB	PR	/A	PD	TPI
1963	Phi-N	1	0	1.000	4	2	0	0	0	6	8	0	7	2	22.5	6.00	54	.333	.484	0	.000	-0	-2	-2	0	-0.3
1965	Cal-A	14	13	.519	35	32	8	1	1	215^1	185	12	82	122	11.3	2.93	116	.230	.305	14	.203	3	13	11	4	2.3
1966	Cal-A	7	14	.333	37	32	6	2	1	199	188	20	68	132	12.0	3.93	85	.251	.321	11	.190	2	-11	-13	2	-1.0
1967	Cal-A	0	2	.000	4	3	0	0	0	9	11	1	9	6	20.0	9.00	35	.324	.465	1	.500	0	-6	-6	-0	-1.1
	Bal-A	1	0	1.000	4	4	0	0	0	17^2	15	1	10	15	12.7	2.55	124	.227	.329	0	.000	-0	1	1	-1	0.0
	Yr	1	2	.333	8	7	0	0	0	26^2	26	2	19	21	15.2	4.73	67	.257	.375	1	.143	0	-4	-5	-1	-1.1
1969	*Bal-A	5	3	.625	27	4	0	0	0	69^1	65	3	34	57	13.1	4.41	81	.252	.344	3	.214	1	-6	-7	-1	-0.7
1970	*Bal-A	1	1	.500	25	3	0	0	0	60^2	47	2	37	49	12.5	2.08	176	.217	.331	1	.077	0	11	11	-1	0.2
1971	Mil-A	2	7	.222	31	11	0	0	0	67^2	64	5	60	42	16.5	4.66	75	.251	.394	1	.059	-1	-9	-9	1	-1.2
1972	Cle-A	0	0	—	4	2	0	0	0	8^1	8	0	10	1	19.4	5.40	60	.276	.462	0	.000	-0	-2	-2	-0	0.0
Total	8	31	40	.437	171	93	14	3	2	653	591	44	317	426	12.7	3.62	94	.243	.334	31	.171	4	-11	-15	4	-1.8

● BRIS LORD
Lord, Bristol Robotham "The Human Eyeball" b: 9/21/1883, Upland, Pa. d: 11/13/64, Annapolis, Md. BR/TR, 5'9", 185 lbs. Deb: 4/21/05 ♦

YEAR	TM/L	W	L	PCT	G	GS	CG	SH	SV	IP	H	HR	BB	SO	RAT	ERA	ERA+	OAV	OOB	BH	AVG	PB	PR	/A	PD	TPI
1907	Phi-A	0	0	—	1	0	0	0	0	1	3	0	0	0	27.0	9.00	29	.500	.500	31	.182	0	-1	-1	-0	0.0

● LEFTY LORENZEN
Lorenzen, Adolph Andreas b: 1/12/1893, Davenport, Iowa d: 3/5/63, Davenport, Iowa BL/TL, 5'10", 164 lbs. Deb: 9/12/13

YEAR	TM/L	W	L	PCT	G	GS	CG	SH	SV	IP	H	HR	BB	SO	RAT	ERA	ERA+	OAV	OOB	BH	AVG	PB	PR	/A	PD	TPI
1913	Det-A	0	0	—	1	0	0	0	0	2	4	0	3	0	31.5	18.00	16	.667	.778	1	.500	0	-3	-3	1	0.1

● ANDREW LORRAINE
Lorraine, Andrew Jason b: 8/11/72, Los Angeles, Cal. BL/TL, 6'3", 195 lbs. Deb: 7/17/94

YEAR	TM/L	W	L	PCT	G	GS	CG	SH	SV	IP	H	HR	BB	SO	RAT	ERA	ERA+	OAV	OOB	BH	AVG	PB	PR	/A	PD	TPI
1994	Cal-A	0	2	.000	4	3	0	0	0	18^2	30	7	11	10	19.8	10.61	46	.366	.441	0	—	0	-12	-12	0	-1.0
1995	Chi-A	0	0	—	5	0	0	0	0	8	3	0	2	5	6.8	3.38	132	.111	.200	0	—	0	1	1	-0	0.0
1997	Oak-A	3	1	.750	12	6	0	0	0	29^2	45	2	15	18	18.5	6.37	71	.354	.427	0	—	0	-6	-6	-0	-0.6
1998	Sea-A	0	0	—	4	0	0	0	0	3^2	3	0	4	0	17.2	2.45	189	.250	.438	0	—	0	1	1	-0	0.0
Total	4	3	3	.500	25	9	0	0	0	60	81	9	32	33	17.3	7.05	66	.327	.408	0	—	0	-16	-16	-0	-1.6

● JOE LOTZ
Lotz, Joseph Peter "Smokey" b: 1/2/1891, Remsen, Iowa d: 1/1/71, Castro Valley, Cal. BR/TR, 5'8.5", 175 lbs. Deb: 7/15/16

YEAR	TM/L	W	L	PCT	G	GS	CG	SH	SV	IP	H	HR	BB	SO	RAT	ERA	ERA+	OAV	OOB	BH	AVG	PB	PR	/A	PD	TPI
1916	StL-N	0	3	.000	12	3	1	0	0	40	31	1	17	18	11.0	4.27	62	.225	.314	4	.333	1	-7	-7	-1	-0.5

● ART LOUDELL
Loudell, Arthur (b: Arthur Laudel) b: 4/10/1882, Latham, Mo. d: 2/19/61, Kansas City, Mo. BR/TR, 5'11", 173 lbs. Deb: 8/13/10

YEAR	TM/L	W	L	PCT	G	GS	CG	SH	SV	IP	H	HR	BB	SO	RAT	ERA	ERA+	OAV	OOB	BH	AVG	PB	PR	/A	PD	TPI
1910	Det-A	1	1	.500	5	2	1	0	0	21^1	23	0	14	12	15.6	3.38	78	.284	.389	1	.143	-0	-2	-2	-1	-0.3

● LARRY LOUGHLIN
Loughlin, Larry John b: 8/16/41, Tacoma, Wash. BL/TL, 6'1", 190 lbs. Deb: 5/27/67

YEAR	TM/L	W	L	PCT	G	GS	CG	SH	SV	IP	H	HR	BB	SO	RAT	ERA	ERA+	OAV	OOB	BH	AVG	PB	PR	/A	PD	TPI
1967	Phi-N	0	0	—	3	0	0	0	0	5^1	9	1	4	5	21.9	15.19	22	.375	.464	1	1.000	1	-7	-7	-0	0.1

● DON LOUN
Loun, Donald Nelson b: 11/9/40, Frederick, Md. BR/TL, 6'2", 185 lbs. Deb: 9/23/64

YEAR	TM/L	W	L	PCT	G	GS	CG	SH	SV	IP	H	HR	BB	SO	RAT	ERA	ERA+	OAV	OOB	BH	AVG	PB	PR	/A	PD	TPI
1964	Was-A	1	1	.500	2	2	1	1	0	13	13	0	3	3	11.1	2.08	178	.250	.291	0	.000	-0	2	2	0	0.4

● SLIM LOVE
Love, Edward Haughton b: 8/1/1890, Love, Miss. d: 11/30/42, Memphis, Tenn. BL/TL, 6'7", 195 lbs. Deb: 9/8/13

YEAR	TM/L	W	L	PCT	G	GS	CG	SH	SV	IP	H	HR	BB	SO	RAT	ERA	ERA+	OAV	OOB	BH	AVG	PB	PR	/A	PD	TPI
1913	Was-A	1	0	1.000	5	1	0	0	1	16^2	14	0	6	5	10.8	1.62	182	.226	.294	1	.200	0	2	2	-1	0.1
1916	NY-A	2	0	1.000	20	1	0	0	0	47^2	46	2	23	21	13.0	4.91	59	.274	.361	0	.000	-2	-11	-11	-0	-0.6
1917	NY-A	6	5	.545	33	9	2	0	1	130^1	115	0	57	82	11.9	2.35	114	.251	.335	6	.167	-1	5	5	-2	0.1
1918	NY-A	13	12	.520	38	29	13	1	1	228^2	207	3	116	95	13.1	3.07	92	.253	.353	17	.230	2	-7	-6	-5	-0.9
1919	Det-A	6	4	.600	22	8	4	0	1	89^2	92	3	40	46	13.9	3.01	106	.275	.363	6	.222	0	2	2	-2	0.0
1920	Det-A	0	0	—	1	0	0	0	0	4^1	6	0	4	2	20.8	8.31	45	.375	.500	0	—	0	-2	-2	0	0.0
Total	6	28	21	.571	119	48	19	1	4	517^1	480	8	246	251	12.9	3.04	94	.259	.351	30	.192	-0	-11	-10	-9	-1.3

● VANCE LOVELACE
Lovelace, Vance Odell b: 8/9/63, Tampa, Fla. BL/TL, 6'5", 205 lbs. Deb: 9/10/88

YEAR	TM/L	W	L	PCT	G	GS	CG	SH	SV	IP	H	HR	BB	SO	RAT	ERA	ERA+	OAV	OOB	BH	AVG	PB	PR	/A	PD	TPI
1988	Cal-A	0	0	—	3	0	0	0	0	1^1	2	1	3	0	33.8	13.50	29	.400	.625	0	—	0	-1	-1	0	0.1
1989	Cal-A	0	0	—	1	0	0	0	0	1	0	0	1	1	9.0	0.00	—	.000	.250	0	—	0	0	0	0	0.1
1990	Sea-A	0	0	—	5	0	0	0	0	2^1	3	0	6	1	38.6	3.86	103	.300	.588	0	—	0	0	0	-0	0.0
Total	3	0	0	—	9	0	0	0	0	4^2	5	1	10	2	30.9	5.79	67	.278	.552	0	—	0	-1	-1	-0	0.2

● LYNN LOVENGUTH
Lovenguth, Lynn Richard b: 11/29/22, Camden, N.Y. BL/TR, 5'10.5", 170 lbs. Deb: 4/18/55

YEAR	TM/L	W	L	PCT	G	GS	CG	SH	SV	IP	H	HR	BB	SO	RAT	ERA	ERA+	OAV	OOB	BH	AVG	PB	PR	/A	PD	TPI
1955	Phi-N	0	1	.000	14	0	0	0	0	18	17	1	10	14	14.5	4.50	88	.258	.372	0	.000	-0	-1	-1	-0	-0.1
1957	StL-N	0	1	.000	2	1	0	0	0	9	6	0	6	6	12.0	2.00	198	.182	.308	0	.000	-0	2	2	-0	0.1
Total	2	0	2	.000	16	1	0	0	0	27	23	1	16	20	13.7	3.67	108	.232	.350	0	.000	-1	1	1	-1	0.0

● JOHN LOVETT
Lovett, John b: 5/6/1877, Monday, Ohio d: 12/5/37, Murray City, Ohio Deb: 5/22/03

YEAR	TM/L	W	L	PCT	G	GS	CG	SH	SV	IP	H	HR	BB	SO	RAT	ERA	ERA+	OAV	OOB	BH	AVG	PB	PR	/A	PD	TPI
1903	StL-N	0	0	—	3	1	0	0	0	5	6	0	5	3	21.6	5.40	60	.300	.462	1	.333	-0	-1	-1	-0	0.0

● LEN LOVETT
Lovett, Leonard Walker b: 7/17/1852, Lancaster Co., Pa d: 11/18/22, Newark, Del. BR/TR, Deb: 8/4/1873 ♦

YEAR	TM/L	W	L	PCT	G	GS	CG	SH	SV	IP	H	HR	BB	SO	RAT	ERA	ERA+	OAV	OOB	BH	AVG	PB	PR	/A	PD	TPI
1873	Res-n	0	1	.000	1	1	1	0	0	9	22	0	1	1	23.0	7.00	48	.400	.411	2	.400	0	-4	-4		-0.2

● TOM LOVETT
Lovett, Thomas Joseph b: 12/7/1863, Providence, R.I. d: 3/19/28, Providence, R.I. BR , 5'8", 162 lbs. Deb: 6/4/1885

YEAR	TM/L	W	L	PCT	G	GS	CG	SH	SV	IP	H	HR	BB	SO	RAT	ERA	ERA+	OAV	OOB	BH	AVG	PB	PR	/A	PD	TPI
1885	Phi-a	7	8	.467	16	16	15	1	0	138^2	130	3	38	56	11.2	3.70	93	.236	.291	13	.224	-0	-7	-4	-1	-0.5
1889	*Bro-a	17	10	.630	29	28	23	1	0	229	234	3	65	92	12.1	4.32	86	.256	.311	19	.190	-1	-12	-15	-0	-1.5
1890	*Bro-N	30	11	**.732**	44	41	39	4	0	372	327	14	141	124	11.7	2.78	124	.229	.306	33	.201	-1	33	27	-0	2.3
1891	Bro-N	23	19	.548	44	43	39	3	0	365^2	361	14	129	129	12.6	3.69	90	.248	.318	25	.163	-5	-14	-16	-2	-2.0
1893	Bro-N	3	5	.375	14	8	6	0	1	96	134	2	35	15	16.4	6.56	67	.321	.381	9	.180	-2	-20	-23	-1	-1.6
1894	Bos-N	8	6	.571	15	13	10	0	0	104	155	12	36	23	16.8	5.97	95	.341	.394	7	.143	-5	-7	-3	-1	-0.8
Total	6	88	59	.599	162	149	132	9	1	1305^1	1341	48	444	439	12.7	3.94	94	.257	.322	106	.185	-13	-28	-34	-5	-4.1

● PETE LOVRICH
Lovrich, Peter b: 10/16/42, Blue Island, Ill. BR/TR, 6'4", 200 lbs. Deb: 4/26/63

YEAR	TM/L	W	L	PCT	G	GS	CG	SH	SV	IP	H	HR	BB	SO	RAT	ERA	ERA+	OAV	OOB	BH	AVG	PB	PR	/A	PD	TPI
1963	KC-A	1	1	.500	20	1	0	0	0	20^2	25	5	10	16	15.7	7.84	50	.291	.371	0	—	0	-10	-9	-1	-0.9

● GROVER LOWDERMILK
Lowdermilk, Grover Cleveland "Slim" b: 1/15/1885, Sandborn, Ind. d: 3/31/68, Odin, Ill. BR/TR, 6'4", 190 lbs. Deb: 7/3/09 F

YEAR	TM/L	W	L	PCT	G	GS	CG	SH	SV	IP	H	HR	BB	SO	RAT	ERA	ERA+	OAV	OOB	BH	AVG	PB	PR	/A	PD	TPI
1909	StL-N	0	2	.000	7	3	1	0	0	29	28	0	30	14	18.9	6.21	41	.292	.473	1	.100	-1	-12	-12	-0	-0.8
1911	StL-N	0	1	.000	11	2	1	1	0	33^1	37	1	33	15	19.4	7.29	46	.301	.456	1	.111	-1	-14	-14	0	-0.4
1912	Chi-N	0	1	.000	2	1	1	0	0	13	17	1	14	8	21.5	9.69	34	.304	.443	0	.000	-1	-9	-9	-0	-0.6
1915	StL-A	9	17	.346	38	29	14	1	0	222^1	183	1	133	130	13.4	3.12	92	.234	.357	9	.125	-3	-4	-6	0	-1.0
	Det-A	4	1	.800	7	5	0	0	0	28	17	0	24	18	13.5	4.18	73	.185	.359	1	.125	-0	-4	-4	0	-0.6
	Yr	13	18	.419	45	34	14	1	0	250^1	200	1	157	148	12.9	3.24	89	.225	.342	10	.125	-3	-8	-10	0	-1.6
1916	Det-A	0	0	—	1	0	0	0	0	0^1	0	0	3	0	81.0	0.00	—	.000	.750	0	—	0	0	0	0	0.0
	Cle-A	1	5	.167	10	9	2	0	0	51^1	52	0	45	28	17.5	3.16	95	.277	.424	3	.167	-0	-2	-1	0	-0.1
	Yr	1	5	.167	11	9	2	0	0	51^2	52	0	48	28	17.9	3.14	96	.275	.429	3	.167	-0	-2	-1	0	-0.1
1917	StL-A	2	1	.667	3	2	2	1	0	19	16	0	4	9	9.5	1.42	183	.225	.267	0	.000	-1	3	2	0	0.3
1918	StL-A	2	6	.250	13	11	4	0	0	80	74	1	38	25	12.9	3.15	87	.255	.347	7	.250	1	-3	-4	2	0.1
1919	StL-A	0	0	—	7	0	0	0	0	12	6	0	4	6	11.3	0.75	442	.176	.349	0	.000	-0	3	3	-0	0.0
	*Chi-A	5	5	.500	20	11	5	0	0	96^2	95	0	43	43	13.2	2.79	114	.268	.353	3	.088	-3	5	4	1	0.2
	Yr	5	5	.500	27	11	5	0	0	108^2	101	0	47	49	12.6	2.57	125	.256	.342	3	.086	-4	8	8	1	0.2
1920	Chi-A	0	0	—	3	0	0	0	0	5^1	9	0	5	0	23.6	6.75	56	.409	.519	0	—	0	-2	-2	1	0.0
Total	9	23	39	.371	122	73	30	3	0	590^1	534	4	376	296	14.4	3.58	82	.253	.375	25	.131	-8	-40	-41	5	-2.9

● LOU LOWDERMILK
Lowdermilk, Louis Bailey b: 2/23/1887, Sandborn, Ind. d: 12/27/75, Centralia, Ill. BR/TL, 6'1", 180 lbs. Deb: 4/20/11 F

YEAR	TM/L	W	L	PCT	G	GS	CG	SH	SV	IP	H	HR	BB	SO	RAT	ERA	ERA+	OAV	OOB	BH	AVG	PB	PR	/A	PD	TPI
1911	StL-N	3	4	.429	16	3	3	0	0	65	72	0	29	20	14.7	3.46	98	.304	.391	2	.111	-1	-0	-1	-2	-0.3
1912	StL-N	1	1	.500	4	1	1	0	1	15	14	0	9	2	13.8	3.00	114	.246	.348	1	.250	0	1	1	0	0.1
Total	2	4	5	.444	20	4	4	0	1	80	86	0	38	22	14.5	3.37	100	.293	.383	3	.136	-1	0	0	-2	-0.2

● DEREK LOWE
Lowe, Derek Christopher b: 6/1/73, Dearborn, Mich. BR/TR, 6'6", 170 lbs. Deb: 4/26/97

YEAR TM/L	W	L	PCT	G	GS	CG	SH	SV	IP	H	HR	BB	SO	RAT	ERA	ERA+	OAV	OOB	BH	AVG	PB	PR	/A	PD	TPI
1997 Sea-A	2	4	.333	12	9	0	0	0	53	59	11	20	39	13.8	6.96	65	.282	.351	0	.000	-0	-14	-15	-0	-1.4
Bos-A	0	2	.000	8	0	0	0	0	16	15	0	3	13	11.3	3.38	137	.268	.328	0	.000	-0	2	2	0	0.3
Yr	2	6	.250	20	9	0	0	0	69	74	11	23	52	12.9	6.13	74	.276	.338	0	.000	-0	-12	-12	0	-1.1
1998 *Bos-A	3	9	.250	63	10	0	0	4	123	126	5	42	77	12.6	4.02	115	.267	.332	0	.000	-0	9	8	2	0.9
Total 2	5	15	.250	83	19	0	0	4	192	200	16	65	129	12.8	4.78	96	.271	.337	0	.000	-0	-4	-4	2	-0.2

● GEORGE LOWE
Lowe, George Wesley "Doc" b: 4/25/1895, Ridgefield Park, N.J. d: 9/2/81, Somers Point, N.J. BR/TR, 6'2", 180 lbs. Deb: 7/28/20

YEAR TM/L	W	L	PCT	G	GS	CG	SH	SV	IP	H	HR	BB	SO	RAT	ERA	ERA+	OAV	OOB	BH	AVG	PB	PR	/A	PD	TPI
1920 Cin-N	0	0	—	1	0	0	0	0	2	1	0	1	0	9.0	0.00	—	.167	.286	0	—	0	1	1	-0	0.0

● SEAN LOWE
Lowe, Jonathan Sean b: 3/29/71, Dallas, Tex. BR/TR, 6'2", 205 lbs. Deb: 8/29/97

YEAR TM/L	W	L	PCT	G	GS	CG	SH	SV	IP	H	HR	BB	SO	RAT	ERA	ERA+	OAV	OOB	BH	AVG	PB	PR	/A	PD	TPI
1997 StL-N	0	2	.000	6	4	0	0	0	17^1	27	2	10	8	19.7	9.35	44	.360	.442	1	.333	0	-10	-10	-0	-0.9
1998 StL-N	0	3	.000	4	1	0	0	0	5^1	11	1	5	2	27.0	15.19	28	.440	.533	0	.000	-0	-6	-7	0	-2.4
Total 2	0	5	.000	10	5	0	0	0	22^2	38	3	15	10	21.4	10.72	39	.380	.466	1	.200	0	-16	-17	-0	-3.3

● BOBBY LOWE
Lowe, Robert Lincoln "Link" b: 7/10/1868, Pittsburgh, Pa. d: 12/8/51, Detroit, Mich. BR/TR, 5'10", 150 lbs. Deb: 4/19/1890 M♦

YEAR TM/L	W	L	PCT	G	GS	CG	SH	SV	IP	H	HR	BB	SO	RAT	ERA	ERA+	OAV	OOB	BH	AVG	PB	PR	/A	PD	TPI
1891 Bos-N	0	0	—	1	0	0	0	0	1	3	0	1	0	36.0	9.00	41	.500	.571	129	.260	0	-1	-1	-0	0.0

● TURK LOWN
Lown, Omar Joseph b: 5/30/24, Brooklyn, N.Y. BR/TR, 6'1", 185 lbs. Deb: 4/24/51

YEAR TM/L	W	L	PCT	G	GS	CG	SH	SV	IP	H	HR	BB	SO	RAT	ERA	ERA+	OAV	OOB	BH	AVG	PB	PR	/A	PD	TPI
1951 Chi-N	4	9	.308	31	18	3	1	0	127	125	14	90	39	15.3	5.46	75	.260	.378	8	.205	1	-21	-19	0	-1.6
1952 Chi-N	4	11	.267	33	19	5	0	0	156^2	154	13	93	73	14.4	4.37	88	.257	.359	7	.140	-0	-11	-9	1	-0.7
1953 Chi-N	8	7	.533	49	12	2	0	3	148^1	166	20	84	76	15.3	5.16	86	.282	.373	6	.125	-2	-14	-12	2	-1.0
1954 Chi-N	0	2	.000	15	0	0	0	0	22	23	1	15	16	15.5	6.14	68	.261	.369	0	—	0	-5	-5	1	-0.3
1956 Chi-N	9	8	.529	61	0	0	0	13	110^2	95	10	78	74	14.2	3.58	105	.240	.366	5	.217	2	2	2	-1	0.6
1957 Chi-N	5	7	.417	**67**	0	0	0	12	93	74	10	51	51	12.1	3.77	103	.221	.324	2	.200	0	1	1	2	0.3
1958 Chi-N	0	0	—	4	0	0	0	0	4	2	0	3	4	11.3	4.50	87	.154	.313	0	—	0	-0	-0	-0	0.0
Cin-N	0	2	.000	11	0	0	0	0	11^2	12	2	12	9	18.5	5.40	77	.273	.429	0	.000	-0	-2	-2	-0	-0.3
Yr	0	2	.000	15	0	0	0	0	15^2	14	2	15	13	16.7	5.17	79	.246	.403	0	.000	-0	-2	-2	-0	-0.3
Chi-A	3	3	.500	27	0	0	0	8	40^2	49	1	28	40	17.0	3.98	91	.308	.412	3	.333	1	-1	-2	0	-0.2
1959 *Chi-A	9	2	.818	60	0	0	0	**15**	93^1	73	12	42	63	11.3	2.89	130	.215	.305	3	.250	1	10	9	1	1.4
1960 Chi-A	2	3	.400	45	0	0	0	5	67^1	60	6	34	39	12.6	3.88	98	.239	.330	1	.200	1	-0	-1	0	0.0
1961 Chi-A	7	5	.583	59	0	0	0	11	101	87	13	35	50	10.9	2.76	142	.238	.304	0	.000	-2	14	13	-1	1.5
1962 Chi-A	4	2	.667	42	0	0	0	6	56^1	58	3	25	40	13.4	3.04	129	.269	.347	0	.000	-0	6	5	1	0.8
Total 11	55	61	.474	504	49	10	1	73	1032	978	105	590	574	13.8	4.12	96	.252	.352	35	.164	1	-21	-18	7	0.5

● SAM LOWRY
Lowry, Samuel Joseph b: 3/25/20, Philadelphia, Pa. d: 12/1/92, Philadelphia, Pa. BR/TR, 5'11", 170 lbs. Deb: 9/19/42

YEAR TM/L	W	L	PCT	G	GS	CG	SH	SV	IP	H	HR	BB	SO	RAT	ERA	ERA+	OAV	OOB	BH	AVG	PB	PR	/A	PD	TPI
1942 Phi-A	0	0	—	1	0	0	0	0	3	3	0	1	0	12.0	6.00	63	.250	.308	0	.000	-0	-1	-1	-0	0.0
1943 Phi-A	0	0	—	5	0	0	0	0	18	18	1	9	3	13.5	5.00	68	.269	.355	1	.167	-0	-3	-3	0	0.0
Total 2	0	0	—	6	0	0	0	0	21	21	1	10	3	13.3	5.14	67	.266	.348	1	.143	-0	-4	-4	0	0.0

● MIKE LOYND
Loynd, Michael Wallace b: 3/26/64, St.Louis, Mo. BR/TR, 6'4", 210 lbs. Deb: 7/24/86

YEAR TM/L	W	L	PCT	G	GS	CG	SH	SV	IP	H	HR	BB	SO	RAT	ERA	ERA+	OAV	OOB	BH	AVG	PB	PR	/A	PD	TPI
1986 Tex-A	2	2	.500	9	8	0	0	1	42	49	4	19	33	15.0	5.36	80	.290	.368	0	—	0	-6	-5	0	-0.5
1987 Tex-A	1	5	.167	26	8	0	0	1	69^1	82	14	38	48	15.7	6.10	73	.287	.372	0	—	0	-13	-13	-1	-1.0
Total 2	3	7	.300	35	16	0	0	2	111^1	131	18	57	81	15.4	5.82	76	.288	.371	0	—	0	-18	-17	-1	-1.5

● PAT LUBY
Luby, John Perkins b: 6/1869, Charleston, S.C. d: 4/24/1899, Charleston, S.C. TR, 6', 185 lbs. Deb: 6/16/1890

YEAR TM/L	W	L	PCT	G	GS	CG	SH	SV	IP	H	HR	BB	SO	RAT	ERA	ERA+	OAV	OOB	BH	AVG	PB	PR	/A	PD	TPI
1890 Chi-N	20	9	.690	34	31	26	0	1	267^2	226	6	95	85	11.3	3.19	115	.222	.298	31	.267	8	11	14	-2	1.7
1891 Chi-N	8	11	.421	30	24	18	0	1	206	221	11	94	52	14.6	4.76	70	.264	.352	24	.245	7	-32	-33	-0	-1.8
1892 Chi-N	11	16	.407	31	27	24	1	0	252^1	248	10	103	66	12.9	3.07	108	.247	.323	31	.190	1	6	7	1	0.8
1895 Lou-N	1	5	.167	11	6	5	0	0	71^1	115	5	19	12	17.8	6.81	68	.357	.405	15	.283	3	-16	-17	1	-0.7
Total 4	40	41	.494	106	88	73	1	2	797^1	810	32	311	215	13.2	3.88	92	.254	.331	101	.235	18	-31	-29	-1	0.0

● RED LUCAS
Lucas, Charles Frederick "The Nashville Narcissus"
b: 4/28/02, Columbia, Tenn. d: 7/9/86, Nashville, Tenn. BL/TR, 5'9.5", 170 lbs. Deb: 4/19/23 ♦

YEAR TM/L	W	L	PCT	G	GS	CG	SH	SV	IP	H	HR	BB	SO	RAT	ERA	ERA+	OAV	OOB	BH	AVG	PB	PR	/A	PD	TPI
1923 NY-N	0	0	—	3	0	0	0	1	5^1	9	0	4	3	21.9	0.00	—	.346	.433	0	.000	-0	2	2	1	0.1
1924 Bos-N	1	4	.200	27	4	1	0	0	83^2	112	5	18	30	14.6	5.16	74	.332	.377	11	.333	2	-12	-12	1	-0.4
1926 Cin-N	8	5	.615	39	11	7	1	2	154	161	6	30	34	11.3	3.68	100	.277	.314	23	.303	6	2	0	-1	0.9
1927 Cin-N	18	11	.621	37	23	19	4	2	239^2	231	6	39	51	10.1	3.38	112	.256	.287	47	.313	7	14	11	-1	2.3
1928 Cin-N	13	9	.591	27	19	13	**4**	1	167^1	164	9	42	35	11.1	3.39	117	.258	.304	23	.315	6	11	11	-0	1.9
1929 Cin-N	19	12	.613	32	32	**28**	2	0	270	267	14	58	72	**10.9**	3.60	127	**.257**	**.297**	41	.293	11	33	29	0	4.0
1930 Cin-N	14	16	.467	33	28	18	1	1	210^2	270	15	44	53	13.5	5.38	90	.315	.349	38	.336	15	-10	-13	-3	-0.3
1931 Cin-N	14	13	.519	29	29	**24**	3	0	238	261	10	39	56	11.3	3.59	104	.280	.309	43	.281	11	7	4	1	1.6
1932 Cin-N	13	17	.433	31	31	**28**	0	0	269^1	261	10	35	63	9.9	2.94	131	.249	.274	43	.287	13	28	27	-0	4.4
1933 Cin-N	10	16	.385	29	29	21	3	0	219^2	248	13	18	40	11.0	3.40	100	.289	.305	35	.287	12	-2	-0	0	1.4
1934 Pit-N	10	9	.526	29	21	12	1	0	172^2	198	14	40	44	12.5	4.38	94	.283	.324	23	.219	3	-6	-5	-3	-0.5
1935 Pit-N	8	6	.571	20	19	8	2	0	125^2	136	10	23	29	11.5	3.44	119	.272	.307	21	.318	8	8	9	-1	1.6
1936 Pit-N	15	4	.789	27	22	12	0	0	175^2	178	7	26	53	10.6	3.18	128	.257	.287	26	.241	4	16	17	-1	2.0
1937 Pit-N	8	10	.444	20	20	9	1	0	126^1	150	12	23	20	12.4	4.27	90	.290	.322	22	.268	5	-5	-6	-2	-0.4
1938 Pit-N	6	3	.667	13	13	4	0	0	84	90	5	16	19	11.5	3.54	107	.283	.319	5	.109	-2	2	2	-1	-0.1
Total 15	157	135	.538	396	301	204	22	7	2542	2736	136	455	602	11.4	3.72	107	.275	.308	404	.281	98	92	77	-9	18.5

● GARY LUCAS
Lucas, Gary Paul b: 11/8/54, Riverside, Cal. BL/TL, 6'5", 200 lbs. Deb: 4/16/80

YEAR TM/L	W	L	PCT	G	GS	CG	SH	SV	IP	H	HR	BB	SO	RAT	ERA	ERA+	OAV	OOB	BH	AVG	PB	PR	/A	PD	TPI
1980 SD-N	5	8	.385	46	18	0	0	3	150	138	8	43	85	10.9	3.24	106	.250	.306	6	.171	-0	6	3	1	0.3
1981 SD-N	7	7	.500	**57**	0	0	0	13	90	78	1	36	53	11.7	2.00	163	.247	.330	1	.100	-1	**15**	13	0	2.3
1982 SD-N	1	10	.091	65	0	0	0	16	97^1	89	5	29	64	11.0	3.24	106	.245	.303	0	.000	-1	4	2	1	0.2
1983 SD-N	5	8	.385	62	0	0	0	17	91	85	9	34	60	11.8	2.87	122	.245	.312	0	.000	-1	8	6	-1	0.8
1984 Mon-N	0	3	.000	55	0	0	0	8	53	54	4	20	42	12.6	2.72	126	.267	.333	0	.000	-0	5	4	2	0.5
1985 Mon-N	6	2	.750	49	0	0	0	1	67^2	63	6	24	31	11.6	3.19	106	.251	.316	0	.000	-1	3	1	-0	0.1
1986 *Cal-A	4	1	.800	27	0	0	0	2	45^2	45	1	6	31	10.1	3.15	130	.253	.277	0	—	0	5	5	1	0.6
1987 Cal-A	1	5	.167	48	0	0	0	3	74^1	66	7	35	44	12.5	3.63	118	.241	.331	0	—	0	7	6	1	0.5
Total 8	29	44	.397	409	18	0	0	63	669	618	41	227	410	11.5	3.01	118	.249	.314	7	.087	-4	53	40	4	5.3

● RAY LUCAS
Lucas, Ray Wesley "Luke" b: 10/2/08, Springfield, Ohio d: 10/9/69, Harrison, Mich. BR/TR, 6'2", 175 lbs. Deb: 9/28/29

YEAR TM/L	W	L	PCT	G	GS	CG	SH	SV	IP	H	HR	BB	SO	RAT	ERA	ERA+	OAV	OOB	BH	AVG	PB	PR	/A	PD	TPI
1929 NY-N	0	0	—	3	0	0	0	1	8	3	0	3	1	6.8	0.00	—	.111	.200	1	.500	0	4	4	0	0.2
1930 NY-N	0	0	—	6	0	0	0	0	10^1	9	2	10	1	17.4	6.97	68	.265	.444	0	.000	-0	-2	-3	1	0.0
1931 NY-N	0	0	—	1	0	0	0	0	2	1	1	1	0	9.0	4.50	82	.143	.250	0	—	0	-0	-0	-0	0.0
1933 Bro-N	0	0	—	2	0	0	0	0	5	6	0	4	0	19.8	7.20	45	.316	.458	0	—	0	-2	-2	0	0.0
1934 Bro-N	1	1	.500	10	2	0	0	0	30^2	39	2	14	3	16.4	6.75	58	.328	.412	2	.333	1	-9	-10	1	-0.3
Total 5	1	1	.500	22	2	0	0	1	56	58	5	32	5	15.3	5.79	71	.282	.391	3	.333	1	-10	-11	2	-0.1

● JOE LUCEY
Lucey, Joseph Earl "Scootch" b: 3/27/1897, Holyoke, Mass. d: 7/30/80, Holyoke, Mass. BR/TR, 6', 168 lbs. Deb: 7/6/20 ♦

YEAR TM/L	W	L	PCT	G	GS	CG	SH	SV	IP	H	HR	BB	SO	RAT	ERA	ERA+	OAV	OOB	BH	AVG	PB	PR	/A	PD	TPI
1925 Bos-A	0	1	.000	7	2	0	0	0	11	18	0	14	2	26.2	9.00	50	.360	.500	2	.133	-1	-6	-5	1	-0.4

● CON LUCID
Lucid, Cornelius Cecil b: 2/24/1874, Dublin, Ireland d: 6/25/31, Houston, Tex. 5'7", 170 lbs. Deb: 5/1/1893

YEAR TM/L	W	L	PCT	G	GS	CG	SH	SV	IP	H	HR	BB	SO	RAT	ERA	ERA+	OAV	OOB	BH	AVG	PB	PR	/A	PD	TPI
1893 Lou-N	0	1	.000	2	1	0	0	0	6	10	0	10	0	31.5	15.00	29	.357	.538	1	.333	0	-7	-7	-0	-0.7
1894 Bro-N	5	3	.625	10	9	7	0	0	71^1	87	6	44	15	17.7	6.56	75	.298	.406	7	.212	-2	-10	-13	-2	-1.3
1895 Bro-N	10	7	.588	21	19	12	2	0	137	164	4	72	24	16.0	5.52	80	.292	.380	13	.245	2	-11	-17	-1	-1.4
Phi-N	6	3	.667	10	10	7	1	0	69^2	80	3	35	19	16.0	5.94	81	.284	.380	10	.345	4	-9	-9	-2	-0.7
Yr	16	10	.615	31	29	19	3	0	206^2	244	7	107	43	15.7	5.66	80	.287	.373	23	.280	6	-20	-26	-2	-2.1
1896 Phi-N	1	4	.200	5	5	5	0	0	42	75	2	17	3	20.1	8.36	52	.383	.437	2	.125	-2	-19	-19	-1	-1.7
1897 StL-N	1	5	.167	6	6	5	0	0	49	66	0	26	4	16.9	3.67	120	.319	.395	3	.176	-0	3	4	1	0.4
Total 5	23	23	.500	54	50	36	3	0	375	482	15	204	65	17.1	6.02	76	.308	.397	36	.238	2	-52	-60	-5	-5.4

● LOU LUCIER Lucier, Louis Joseph b: 3/23/18, Northbridge, Mass. BR/TR, 5'8", 160 lbs. Deb: 4/23/43

YEAR TM/L	W	L	PCT	G	GS	CG	SH	SV	IP	H	HR	BB	SO	RAT	ERA	ERA+	OAV	OOB	BH	AVG	PB	PR	/A	PD	TPI
1943 Bos-A	3	4	.429	16	9	3	0	0	74	94	1	33	23	15.7	3.89	85	.322	.394	4	.200	-0	-5	-5	3	-0.1
1944 Bos-A	0	0	—	3	0	0	0	0	5^{1}	7	0	7	2	23.6	5.06	67	.292	.452	0	.000	-0	-1	-1	-0	0.0
Phi-N	0	0	—	1	0	0	0	0	2	3	0	2	1	22.5	13.50	27	.333	.455	0	—	0	-2	-2	-0	0.0
1945 Phi-N	0	1	.000	13	0	0	0	1	20^{1}	14	1	5	5	8.4	2.21	173	.194	.247	1	.250	0	4	4	1	0.3
Total 3	3	5	.375	33	9	3	0	1	101^{2}	118	2	47	31	14.8	3.81	90	.297	.374	5	.200	-0	-4	-4	4	0.2

● WILLIE LUDOLPH Ludolph, William Francis "Wee Willie" b: 1/21/1900, San Francisco, Cal d: 4/8/52, Oakland, Cal. BR/TR, 6'1.5", 170 lbs. Deb: 5/28/24

YEAR TM/L	W	L	PCT	G	GS	CG	SH	SV	IP	H	HR	BB	SO	RAT	ERA	ERA+	OAV	OOB	BH	AVG	PB	PR	/A	PD	TPI
1924 Det-A	0	0	—	3	0	0	0	0	5^{2}	5	0	2	1	12.7	4.76	86	.250	.348	0	.000	-0	-0	-0	0	0.0

● ERIC LUDWICK Ludwick, Eric David b: 12/14/71, Whiteman Afb, Mo. BR/TR, 6'5", 210 lbs. Deb: 9/1/96

YEAR TM/L	W	L	PCT	G	GS	CG	SH	SV	IP	H	HR	BB	SO	RAT	ERA	ERA+	OAV	OOB	BH	AVG	PB	PR	/A	PD	TPI
1996 StL-N	0	1	.000	6	1	0	0	0	10	11	4	3	12	13.5	9.00	46	.275	.341	0	.000	-0	-5	-5	-0	-0.5
1997 StL-N	0	1	.000	5	0	0	0	0	6^{2}	12	1	6	7	24.3	9.45	44	.400	.500	0	—	0	-4	-4	-0	-0.5
Oak-A	1	4	.200	6	5	0	0	0	24	32	7	16	14	18.4	8.25	55	.330	.430	0	.000	-0	-10	-10	-0	-1.6
1998 Fla-N	1	4	.200	13	6	0	0	0	32^{2}	46	7	17	27	17.4	7.44	55	.333	.406	0	.000	-1	-12	-12	-0	-1.6
Total 3	2	10	.167	30	12	0	0	0	73^{1}	101	19	42	60	17.8	8.10	52	.331	.415	0	.000	-1	-31	-31	-0	-4.2

● STEVE LUEBBER Luebber, Stephen Lee b: 7/9/49, Clinton, Mo. BR/TR, 6'3", 195 lbs. Deb: 6/27/71

YEAR TM/L	W	L	PCT	G	GS	CG	SH	SV	IP	H	HR	BB	SO	RAT	ERA	ERA+	OAV	OOB	BH	AVG	PB	PR	/A	PD	TPI
1971 Min-A	2	5	.286	18	12	0	0	1	68	73	7	37	35	15.1	5.03	71	.278	.375	1	.053	-2	-12	-11	0	-1.3
1972 Min-A	0	0	—	2	0	0	0	0	2^{1}	3	0	2	1	19.3	0.00	—	.333	.455	0	—	0	1	1	0	0.0
1976 Min-A	4	5	.444	38	12	2	1	2	119^{1}	109	9	62	45	13.0	4.00	89	.248	.342	0	—	0	-6	-6	-1	-0.6
1979 Tor-A	0	0	—	1	0	0	0	0	0	2	0	1	0	—	∞	—	1.000	1.000	0	—	0	-1	-1	0	-0.1
1981 Bal-A	0	0	—	7	0	0	0	0	16^{2}	26	3	4	12	16.7	7.56	48	.366	.408	0	—	0	-7	-7	0	0.0
Total 5	6	10	.375	66	24	2	1	3	206^{1}	213	19	106	93	14.2	4.62	77	.271	.362	1	.053	-2	-26	-24	-1	-2.0

● LARRY LUEBBERS Luebbers, Larry Christopher b: 10/11/69, Cincinnati, Ohio BR/TR, 6'6", 190 lbs. Deb: 7/3/93

YEAR TM/L	W	L	PCT	G	GS	CG	SH	SV	IP	H	HR	BB	SO	RAT	ERA	ERA+	OAV	OOB	BH	AVG	PB	PR	/A	PD	TPI
1993 Cin-N	2	5	.286	14	14	0	0	0	77^{1}	74	7	38	38	13.2	4.54	89	.261	.350	6	.250	1	-4	-4	-1	-0.3

● DICK LUEBKE Luebke, Richard Raymond b: 4/8/35, Chicago, Ill. d: 12/4/74, San Diego, Cal. BR/TL, 6'4", 200 lbs. Deb: 8/11/62

YEAR TM/L	W	L	PCT	G	GS	CG	SH	SV	IP	H	HR	BB	SO	RAT	ERA	ERA+	OAV	OOB	BH	AVG	PB	PR	/A	PD	TPI
1962 Bal-A	0	1	.000	10	0	0	0	0	13^{1}	12	0	6	7	12.2	2.70	137	.250	.333	0	—	0	2	1	-0	0.1

● RICK LUECKEN Luecken, Richard Fred b: 11/15/60, McAllen, Tex. BR/TR, 6'6", 210 lbs. Deb: 6/6/89

YEAR TM/L	W	L	PCT	G	GS	CG	SH	SV	IP	H	HR	BB	SO	RAT	ERA	ERA+	OAV	OOB	BH	AVG	PB	PR	/A	PD	TPI
1989 KC-A	2	1	.667	19	0	0	0	1	23^{2}	23	3	13	16	13.7	3.42	112	.258	.353	0	—	0	1	1	-0	0.1
1990 Atl-N	1	4	.200	36	0	0	0	1	53	73	5	30	35	18.0	5.77	70	.336	.424	1	.333	1	-12	-10	0	-0.9
Tor-A	0	0	—	1	0	0	0	0	1	2	1	1	0	27.0	9.00	44	.500	.600	0	—	0	-1	-1	0	0.0
Total 2	3	5	.375	56	0	0	0	2	77^{2}	98	9	44	51	16.8	5.10	78	.316	.406	1	.333	1	-11	-10	-0	-0.8

● HENRY LUFF Luff, Henry T. b: 9/14/1856, Philadelphia, Pa. d: 10/11/16, Philadelphia, Pa. 5'11", 175 lbs. Deb: 4/21/1875 ♦

YEAR TM/L	W	L	PCT	G	GS	CG	SH	SV	IP	H	HR	BB	SO	RAT	ERA	ERA+	OAV	OOB	BH	AVG	PB	PR	/A	PD	TPI
1875 NH-n	1	6	.143	10	7	5	0	0	68^{2}	98	2	3	5	13.2	3.28	63	.295	.301	45	.271	3	-8	-9		-0.5

● URBANO LUGO Lugo, Rafael Urbano (Colina) b: 8/12/62, Punto Fijo, Venez. BR/TR, 6', 190 lbs. Deb: 4/28/85

YEAR TM/L	W	L	PCT	G	GS	CG	SH	SV	IP	H	HR	BB	SO	RAT	ERA	ERA+	OAV	OOB	BH	AVG	PB	PR	/A	PD	TPI
1985 Cal-A	3	4	.429	20	10	1	0	0	83	86	10	29	42	12.9	3.69	111	.274	.343	0	—	0	4	4	0	0.3
1986 Cal-A	1	1	.500	6	3	0	0	0	21^{1}	21	4	6	9	11.4	3.80	108	.266	.318	0	—	0	1	1	-0	0.1
1987 Cal-A	0	2	.000	7	5	0	0	0	28	42	8	18	24	19.3	9.32	46	.339	.423	0	—	0	-15	-16	-0	-0.9
1988 Cal-A	0	0	—	1	0	0	0	0	2	2	1	1	1	13.5	9.00	43	.250	.333	0	—	0	-1	-1	-0	0.0
1989 Mon-N	0	0	—	3	0	0	0	0	4	4	1	0	3	9.0	6.75	52	.250	.250	0	—	0	-1	-1	0	0.0
1990 Det-A	2	0	1.000	13	1	0	0	0	24^{1}	30	9	13	12	17.0	7.03	56	.313	.411	0	—	0	-8	-8	1	-0.6
Total 6	6	7	.462	50	19	1	0	0	162^{2}	185	33	67	91	14.3	5.31	77	.290	.364	0	—	0	-21	-22	0	-1.1

● WILD BILL LUHRSEN Luhrsen, William Ferdinand b: 4/14/1884, Buckley, Ill. d: 8/15/73, Little Rock, Ark. BR/TR, 5'9", 165 lbs. Deb: 8/23/13

YEAR TM/L	W	L	PCT	G	GS	CG	SH	SV	IP	H	HR	BB	SO	RAT	ERA	ERA+	OAV	OOB	BH	AVG	PB	PR	/A	PD	TPI
1913 Pit-N	3	1	.750	5	3	2	0	0	29	25	3	16	11	13.3	2.48	122	.248	.361	0	.000	-1	2	2	1	0.2

● AL LUKENS Lukens, Albert P. b: 11/1868, Pennsylvania 5'9", 168 lbs. Deb: 6/23/1894

YEAR TM/L	W	L	PCT	G	GS	CG	SH	SV	IP	H	HR	BB	SO	RAT	ERA	ERA+	OAV	OOB	BH	AVG	PB	PR	/A	PD	TPI
1894 Phi-N	0	1	.000	3	2	1	0	0	15	26	0	10	0	23.4	10.20	50	.377	.476	0	.000	-2	-8	-8	-0	-0.5

● RALPH LUMENTI Lumenti, Raphael Anthony b: 12/21/36, Milford, Mass. BL/TL, 6'3", 185 lbs. Deb: 9/7/57

YEAR TM/L	W	L	PCT	G	GS	CG	SH	SV	IP	H	HR	BB	SO	RAT	ERA	ERA+	OAV	OOB	BH	AVG	PB	PR	/A	PD	TPI
1957 Was-A	0	1	.000	3	2	0	0	0	9^{1}	9	1	5	8	14.5	6.75	58	.250	.357	0	.000	-0	-3	-3	0	-0.3
1958 Was-A	1	2	.333	8	4	0	0	0	21	21	2	36	20	24.9	8.57	44	.266	.500	2	.250	0	-11	-11	0	-1.3
1959 Was-A	0	0	—	2	0	0	0	0	3	2	0	1	2	9.0	0.00	—	.200	.273	0	—	0	1	1	-0	0.0
Total 3	1	3	.250	13	6	0	0	0	33^{1}	32	3	42	30	20.5	7.29	53	.256	.450	2	.200	-0	-13	-13	0	-1.6

● MEMO LUNA Luna, Guillermo Romero b: 6/25/30, Tacubaya, Mexico BL/TL, 6', 168 lbs. Deb: 4/20/54

YEAR TM/L	W	L	PCT	G	GS	CG	SH	SV	IP	H	HR	BB	SO	RAT	ERA	ERA+	OAV	OOB	BH	AVG	PB	PR	/A	PD	TPI
1954 StL-N	0	1	.000	1	1	0	0	0	0^{2}	2	0	2	0	54.0	27.00	15	.667	.800	0	—	0	-2	-2	-0	-1.2

● JACK LUNDBOM Lundbom, John Frederick b: 3/10/1877, Manistee, Mich. d: 10/31/49, Manistee, Mich. BR/TR, 6'0.5", 187 lbs. Deb: 5/9/02

YEAR TM/L	W	L	PCT	G	GS	CG	SH	SV	IP	H	HR	BB	SO	RAT	ERA	ERA+	OAV	OOB	BH	AVG	PB	PR	/A	PD	TPI
1902 Cle-A	1	1	.500	8	3	1	0	0	34	48	1	16	7	17.2	6.62	52	.333	.404	4	.267	1	-11	-12	-0	-0.6

● CARL LUNDGREN Lundgren, Carl Leonard b: 2/16/1880, Marengo, Ill. d: 8/21/34, Marengo, Ill. BR/TR, 5'11", 175 lbs. Deb: 6/19/02

YEAR TM/L	W	L	PCT	G	GS	CG	SH	SV	IP	H	HR	BB	SO	RAT	ERA	ERA+	OAV	OOB	BH	AVG	PB	PR	/A	PD	TPI
1902 Chi-N	9	9	.500	18	18	17	1	0	160	158	2	45	68	11.8	1.97	137	.258	.315	7	.106	-4	14	13	-3	0.7
1903 Chi-N	11	9	.550	27	20	16	0	**3**	193	191	1	60	67	12.0	2.94	107	.262	.323	7	.115	-1	7	4	-2	0.0
1904 Chi-N	17	9	.654	31	27	25	2	1	242	203	2	77	106	10.6	2.60	102	.226	.290	20	.222	4	4	2	-1	0.4
1905 Chi-N	13	5	.722	23	19	16	3	0	169^{1}	132	3	53	69	10.3	2.23	134	.220	.293	11	.180	1	15	14	1	1.6
1906 Chi-N	17	6	.739	27	24	21	5	2	207^{2}	160	3	89	103	11.1	2.21	119	.221	.313	12	.179	2	10	10	-1	1.2
1907 Chi-N	18	7	.720	28	25	21	7	0	207	130	0	92	84	9.7	1.17	212	**.185**	.282	7	.106	-3	**30**	30	-0	3.6
1908 Chi-N	6	9	.400	23	15	9	1	0	138^{2}	149	5	56	38	13.3	4.22	56	.284	.353	7	.149	-1	-29	-29	-2	-3.3
1909 Chi-N	0	1	.000	2	1	0	0	0	4^{1}	6	0	4	0	20.8	4.15	61	.353	.476	1	.500	0	-1	-1	-0	-0.2
Total 8	91	55	.623	179	149	125	19	6	1322	1129	16	476	535	11.2	2.42	113	.235	.308	72	.157	-2	50	44	-8	4.0

● DEL LUNDGREN Lundgren, Ebin Delmar b: 9/21/1899, Lindsborg, Kan. d: 10/19/84, Lindsborg, Kan. BR/TR, 5'8", 160 lbs. Deb: 4/27/24

YEAR TM/L	W	L	PCT	G	GS	CG	SH	SV	IP	H	HR	BB	SO	RAT	ERA	ERA+	OAV	OOB	BH	AVG	PB	PR	/A	PD	TPI
1924 Pit-N	0	1	.000	8	1	0	0	0	16^{2}	25	0	3	4	15.7	6.48	59	.403	.439	0	.000	-1	-5	-5	0	-0.3
1926 Bos-A	0	2	.000	18	2	0	0	0	31	35	2	28	11	19.2	7.55	54	.307	.455	0	.000	-0	-12	-12	0	-0.7
1927 Bos-A	5	12	.294	30	17	5	2	0	136^{1}	160	7	87	39	16.6	6.27	67	.302	.405	7	.159	-2	-32	-31	-2	-3.5
Total 3	5	15	.250	56	20	5	2	0	184	220	9	118	54	16.9	6.51	64	.312	.416	7	.137	-3	-49	-48	-2	-4.5

● DOLF LUQUE Luque, Adolfo Domingo De Guzman "The Pride Of Havana" b: 8/4/1890, Havana, Cuba d: 7/3/57, Havana, Cuba BR/TR, 5'7", 160 lbs. Deb: 5/20/14 C

YEAR TM/L	W	L	PCT	G	GS	CG	SH	SV	IP	H	HR	BB	SO	RAT	ERA	ERA+	OAV	OOB	BH	AVG	PB	PR	/A	PD	TPI
1914 Bos-N	0	1	.000	2	1	1	0	0	8^{2}	5	0	4	1	9.3	4.15	66	.167	.265	0	.000	-0	-1	-1	-1	-0.2
1915 Bos-N	0	0	—	2	1	0	0	0	5	6	0	4	3	18.0	3.60	72	.286	.400	0	.000	-0	-0	-1	-0	0.0
1918 Cin-N	6	3	.667	12	10	9	1	0	83	84	1	32	26	12.7	3.80	70	.277	.348	9	.321	5	-10	-10	-0	-0.6
1919 *Cin-N	10	3	.769	30	9	6	2	3	106	89	2	36	40	10.8	2.63	105	.237	.308	4	.125	-0	3	2	1	0.3
1920 Cin-N	13	9	.591	37	23	10	1	1	207^{2}	168	5	60	72	10.1	2.51	121	**.225**	.286	17	.266	4	14	12	-2	1.5
1921 Cin-N	17	19	.472	41	36	25	**3**	3	304	318	13	64	102	11.3	3.38	106	.273	.312	30	.270	6	14	7	1	1.3
1922 Cin-N	13	23	.361	39	33	18	0	0	261	266	7	72	79	11.7	3.31	121	.268	.318	18	.209	2	23	20	0	2.6
1923 Cin-N	**27**	8	**.771**	41	37	28	**6**	2	322	279	2	88	151	10.4	**1.93**	**200**	**.235**	.291	21	.202	2	**74**	**69**	1	**7.4**
1924 Cin-N	10	15	.400	31	28	13	2	0	219^{1}	229	5	53	86	11.7	3.16	119	.271	.316	13	.178	-1	17	15	1	1.6
1925 Cin-N	16	18	.471	36	36	22	**4**	0	291	263	7	78	140	**10.6**	**2.63**	**156**	**.239**	**.291**	26	.255	5	**53**	**48**	4	**6.1**
1926 Cin-N	13	16	.448	34	31	16	1	0	233^{2}	231	7	77	83	11.9	3.43	108	.260	.321	27	.346	8	10	7	2	1.8
1927 Cin-N	13	12	.520	29	27	17	2	0	230^{2}	225	10	56	76	11.0	3.20	118	.260	.305	18	.217	2	18	15	4	2.1
1928 Cin-N	11	10	.524	33	29	11	1	1	234^{1}	254	12	84	72	13.1	3.57	111	.284	.347	8	.119	-1	11	10	-2	0.5
1929 Cin-N	5	16	.238	32	22	8	1	0	176	213	7	56	43	13.9	4.50	101	.310	.364	15	.278	4	4	1	0	0.5
1930 Bro-N	14	8	.636	31	24	16	2	2	199	221	18	58	62	12.6	4.30	114	.287	.337	18	.240	1	15	14	1	1.5
1931 Bro-N	7	6	.538	19	15	5	0	0	102^{2}	122	6	27	25	13.1	4.56	84	.297	.342	4	.133	0	-8	-9	-1	-1.0
1932 NY-N	6	7	.462	38	5	1	0	5	110	128	4	32	32	13.1	4.01	93	.290	.338	1	.040	-2	-2	-4	1	-0.5
1933 *NY-N	8	2	.800	35	0	0	0	4	80^{1}	75	4	19	23	10.5	2.69	119	.251	.296	5	.263	1	6	5	0	0.7

YEAR	TM/L	W	L	PCT	G	GS	CG	SH	SV	IP	H	HR	BB	SO	RAT	ERA	ERA+	OAV	OOB	BH	AVG	PB	PR	/A	PD	TPI
1934	NY-N	4	3	.571	26	0	0	0	7	42^1	54	3	17	12	15.3	3.83	101	.316	.381	2	.286	1	1	0	1	0.2
1935	NY-N	1	0	1.000	2	0	0	0	0	3^2	1	0	1	2	4.9	0.00	—	.077	.143	1	1.000	0	2	2	-0	0.5
Total	20	194	179	.520	550	367	206	26	28	3220^1	3231	113	918	1130	11.7	3.24	117	.265	.318	237	.227	37	245	200	13	26.3

● JOHNNY LUSH

Lush, John Charles b: 10/8/1885, Williamsport, Pa. d: 11/18/46, Beverly Hills, Cal BL/TL, 5'9.5", 165 lbs. Deb: 4/22/04 ♦

YEAR	TM/L	W	L	PCT	G	GS	CG	SH	SV	IP	H	HR	BB	SO	RAT	ERA	ERA+	OAV	OOB	BH	AVG	PB	PR	/A	PD	TPI
1904	Phi-N	0	6	.000	7	6	3	0	0	42^2	52	0	27	27	18.1	3.59	75	.301	.415	102	.276	2	-4	-4	1	-0.3
1905	Phi-N	2	0	1.000	2	2	1	0	0	17	12	0	8	8	11.1	1.59	184	.194	.296	5	.313	1	3	3	0	0.4
1906	Phi-N	18	15	.545	37	35	24	5	0	281	254	2	119	151	12.5	2.37	110	.236	.321	56	.264	7	8	8	3	2.1
1907	Phi-N	3	5	.375	8	8	5	2	0	57^1	48	0	21	20	11.3	2.98	81	.227	.306	8	.200	1	-3	-4	1	-0.4
	StL-N	7	10	.412	20	19	15	3	0	144	132	2	42	71	11.4	2.50	100	.246	.311	23	.280	5	-0	-0	-0	0.8
	Yr	10	15	.400	28	27	20	5	0	201^1	180	2	63	91	11.2	2.64	94	.240	.306	31	.254	6	-4	-4	0	0.4
1908	StL-N	11	18	.379	38	32	23	3	1	250^2	221	6	57	93	10.4	2.12	111	.231	.283	15	.169	1	7	7	0	1.0
1909	StL-N	11	18	.379	34	28	21	2	0	221^1	215	1	69	66	12.0	3.13	81	.260	.324	22	.239	4	-13	-15	-1	-1.4
1910	StL-N	14	13	.519	36	25	13	1	1	225^1	235	6	70	54	12.5	3.20	93	.276	.336	21	.226	4	-4	-5	-2	-0.4
Total	7	66	85	.437	182	155	105	16	2	1239^1	1169	17	413	490	11.9	2.68	97	.249	.318	252	.254	24	-7	-11	1	1.8

● SPARKY LYLE

Lyle, Albert Walter b: 7/22/44, DuBois, Pa. BL/TL, 6'1", 192 lbs. Deb: 7/4/67

YEAR	TM/L	W	L	PCT	G	GS	CG	SH	SV	IP	H	HR	BB	SO	RAT	ERA	ERA+	OAV	OOB	BH	AVG	PB	PR	/A	PD	TPI
1967	Bos-A	1	2	.333	27	0	0	0	5	43^1	33	3	14	42	10.2	2.28	153	.213	.287	2	.250	1	5	6	-0	0.6
1968	Bos-A	6	1	.857	49	0	0	0	11	65^2	67	6	14	52	11.1	2.74	115	.261	.299	1	.125	-0	2	3	-1	0.3
1969	Bos-A	8	3	.727	71	0	0	0	17	102^2	91	8	48	93	12.3	2.54	150	.240	.327	2	.118	-1	12	14	1	2.1
1970	Bos-A	1	7	.125	63	0	0	0	20	67^1	62	5	34	51	13.0	3.88	102	.244	.336	0	.000	-1	-1	1	-1	-0.1
1971	Bos-A	6	4	.600	50	0	0	0	16	52^1	41	5	23	37	11.0	2.75	134	.228	.315	3	1.000	1	4	5	0	1.6
1972	NY-A	9	5	.643	59	0	0	0	**35**	107^2	84	3	29	75	9.4	1.92	153	.216	.271	4	.190	1	**14**	**12**	-1	2.7
1973	NY-A★	5	9	.357	51	0	0	0	27	82^1	66	4	18	63	9.2	2.51	146	.216	.259	0	—	0	12	11	-0	2.6
1974	NY-A	9	3	.750	66	0	0	0	15	114	93	6	43	89	10.8	1.66	213	.226	.300	0	.000	-0	**25**	**24**	-1	3.0
1975	NY-A	5	7	.417	49	0	0	0	6	89^1	94	1	36	65	13.3	3.12	118	.275	.347	0	—	0	6	6	0	0.8
1976	*NY-A☆	7	8	.467	64	0	0	0	**23**	103^2	82	5	42	61	10.8	2.26	151	.225	.305	0	—	0	15	13	-1	2.5
1977	*NY-A★	13	5	.722	**72**	0	0	0	26	137	131	7	33	68	10.9	2.17	182	.257	.305	0	—	0	**29**	**27**	-1	**4.4**
1978	*NY-A	9	3	.750	59	0	0	0	9	111^2	116	6	33	33	12.3	3.47	104	.278	.337	0	—	0	4	2	0	0.3
1979	Tex-A	5	8	.385	67	0	0	0	13	95	78	9	28	48	10.0	3.13	133	.226	.284	0	—	0	11	11	-1	1.6
1980	Tex-A	3	2	.600	49	0	0	0	8	80^2	97	9	28	43	13.9	4.69	83	.306	.362	0	—	0	-6	-7	-0	-0.5
	Phi-N	0	0	—	10	0	0	0	2	14	11	0	6	6	10.9	1.93	196	.220	.304	0	—	0	3	3	-1	0.0
1981	*Phi-N	9	6	.600	48	0	0	0	2	75	85	4	33	29	14.3	4.44	82	.301	.377	2	.400	1	-8	-7	1	-1.1
1982	Phi-N	3	3	.500	34	0	0	0	2	36^2	50	3	12	12	15.2	5.15	71	.327	.376	1	.500	1	-6	-6	1	-0.8
	Chi-A	0	0	—	11	0	0	0	1	12	11	0	7	6	13.5	3.00	134	.262	.367	0	—	0	1	1	-0	0.0
Total	16	99	76	.566	899	0	0	0	238	1390^1	1292	84	481	873	11.6	2.88	127	.251	.316	15	.192	2	121	119	-4	20.0

● JIM LYLE

Lyle, James Charles b: 7/24/1900, Lake, Miss. d: 10/10/77, Williamsport, Pa. BR/TR, 6'1", 180 lbs. Deb: 10/2/25

YEAR	TM/L	W	L	PCT	G	GS	CG	SH	SV	IP	H	HR	BB	SO	RAT	ERA	ERA+	OAV	OOB	BH	AVG	PB	PR	/A	PD	TPI
1925	Was-A	0	0	—	1	0	0	0	0	3	5	0	1	3	18.0	6.00	70	.333	.375	0	—	0	-1	-1	-0	0.0

● ADRIAN LYNCH

Lynch, Adrian Ryan b: 2/9/1897, Laurens, Iowa d: 3/16/34, Davenport, Iowa BB/TR, 6'1.5", 185 lbs. Deb: 8/4/20

YEAR	TM/L	W	L	PCT	G	GS	CG	SH	SV	IP	H	HR	BB	SO	RAT	ERA	ERA+	OAV	OOB	BH	AVG	PB	PR	/A	PD	TPI
1920	StL-A	2	0	1.000	5	3	1	0	0	22^1	23	1	17	8	16.5	5.24	75	.277	.406	2	.222	0	-4	-3	-1	-0.3

● ED LYNCH

Lynch, Edward Francis b: 2/25/56, Brooklyn, N.Y. BR/TR, 6'6", 230 lbs. Deb: 8/31/80

YEAR	TM/L	W	L	PCT	G	GS	CG	SH	SV	IP	H	HR	BB	SO	RAT	ERA	ERA+	OAV	OOB	BH	AVG	PB	PR	/A	PD	TPI
1980	NY-N	1	1	.500	5	4	0	0	0	19^1	24	0	5	9	14.0	5.12	69	.304	.353	2	.333	0	-3	-3	0	-0.3
1981	NY-N	4	5	.444	17	13	0	0	0	80^1	79	6	21	27	11.3	2.91	120	.254	.303	3	.143	1	5	5	-1	0.6
1982	NY-N	4	8	.333	43	12	0	0	2	139^1	145	6	40	51	12.0	3.55	102	.273	.325	0	.000	-3	1	1	-1	-0.4
1983	NY-N	10	10	.500	30	27	1	0	0	174^2	208	17	41	44	13.0	4.28	85	.302	.344	8	.154	-1	-13	-13	-1	-1.5
1984	NY-N	9	8	.529	40	13	0	0	2	124	169	14	24	62	14.3	4.50	79	.324	.359	6	.222	1	-13	-13	-1	-1.8
1985	NY-N	10	8	.556	31	29	6	1	0	191	188	19	27	65	10.2	3.44	100	.256	.283	4	.077	-2	3	0	-4	-0.6
1986	NY-N	0	0	—	1	0	0	0	0	1^2	2	0	0	1	10.8	0.00	—	.286	.286	0	—	0	1	1	-0	0.0
	Chi-N	7	5	.583	23	13	1	1	0	99^2	105	10	23	57	11.6	3.79	107	.279	.322	1	.033	-2	-1	3	-1	0.0
	Yr	7	5	.583	24	13	1	1	0	101^1	107	10	23	58	11.6	3.73	108	.279	.321	1	.033	-2	-0	3	-1	0.0
1987	Chi-N	2	9	.182	58	8	0	0	4	110^1	130	17	48	80	14.7	5.38	79	.295	.367	3	.188	-0	-16	-14	1	-1.2
Total	8	47	54	.465	248	119	8	2	8	940^1	1050	89	229	396	12.4	4.00	92	.284	.329	27	.114	-6	-35	-33	-8	-5.2

● JACK LYNCH

Lynch, John H. b: 2/5/1857, New York, N.Y d: 4/20/23, Bronx, N.Y. BR/TR, 5'8", 185 lbs. Deb: 5/2/1881

YEAR	TM/L	W	L	PCT	G	GS	CG	SH	SV	IP	H	HR	BB	SO	RAT	ERA	ERA+	OAV	OOB	BH	AVG	PB	PR	/A	PD	TPI
1881	Buf-N	10	9	.526	20	19	17	0	0	165^2	203	2	29	32	12.6	3.59	77	.297	.325	13	.167	-3	-15	-15	1	-1.5
1883	NY-a	13	15	.464	29	29	29	1	0	255	263	6	25	119	10.2	4.09	82	.250	.267	20	.187	-3	-22	-21	-1	-2.1
1884	NY-a	37	15	.712	55	53	53	5	0	496	420	10	42	292	8.6	2.67	117	.215	.236	30	.152	-7	32	25	-5	1.0
1885	NY-a	23	21	.523	44	43	43	1	0	379	410	17	42	177	10.8	3.61	82	.263	.283	30	.196	2	-15	-27	-5	-2.8
1886	NY-a	20	30	.400	51	50	50	1	0	432^2	485	10	116	193	12.8	3.95	86	.271	.320	27	.160	-6	-24	-26	-3	-3.1
1887	NY-a	7	14	.333	21	21	21	0	0	187	245	8	36	45	13.7	5.10	83	.305	.338	14	.169	-4	-17	-18	2	-1.5
1890	Bro-a	0	1	.000	1	1	1	0	0	9	22	1	5	1	27.0	12.00	32	.449	.500	3	.750	2	-8	-8	1	-0.4
Total	7	110	105	.512	221	216	214	8	0	1924^1	2048	54	295	859	11.1	3.69	89	.260	.289	137	.173	-18	-69	-91	-10	-10.4

● MIKE LYNCH

Lynch, Michael Joseph b: 6/28/1880, Holyoke, Mass. d: 4/2/27, Garrison, N.Y. BR/TR, 6'2", 170 lbs. Deb: 6/21/04

YEAR	TM/L	W	L	PCT	G	GS	CG	SH	SV	IP	H	HR	BB	SO	RAT	ERA	ERA+	OAV	OOB	BH	AVG	PB	PR	/A	PD	TPI
1904	Pit-N	15	11	.577	27	24	24	1	0	222^2	200	1	91	95	12.4	2.71	101	.243	.330	20	.230	4	1	1	-2	0.2
1905	Pit-N	17	8	.680	33	22	13	0	2	206^1	191	3	107	106	13.2	3.79	79	.254	.351	11	.136	-1	-18	-18	0	-2.2
1906	Pit-N	6	5	.545	18	12	7	0	0	119	101	2	31	48	10.6	2.42	110	.232	.295	8	.205	-0	3	3	-1	0.2
1907	Pit-N	2	2	.500	7	4	2	0	0	36	37	0	22	9	15.0	2.25	108	.282	.390	3	.250	1	1	1	1	0.3
	NY-N	3	6	.333	12	10	7	0	1	72	68	3	30	34	12.3	3.38	73	.249	.323	8	.296	2	-7	-7	0	-0.6
	Yr	5	8	.385	19	14	9	0	1	108	105	3	52	43	13.1	3.00	82	.259	.344	11	.282	3	-6	-6	2	-0.3
Total	4	43	32	.573	97	72	53	1	3	656	597	9	281	292	12.4	3.05	91	.248	.333	50	.203	5	-21	-20	-1	-2.1

● TOM LYNCH

Lynch, Thomas S. b: 1863, Peru, Ill. d: 5/13/03, Peru, Ill. BL , 5'11", 175 lbs. Deb: 8/5/1884

YEAR	TM/L	W	L	PCT	G	GS	CG	SH	SV	IP	H	HR	BB	SO	RAT	ERA	ERA+	OAV	OOB	BH	AVG	PB	PR	/A	PD	TPI
1884	Chi-N	0	0	—	1	1	0	0	0	7	7	1	3	2	12.9	2.57	122	.241	.313	0	.000	-1	0	0	0	0.0

● RED LYNN

Lynn, Japhet Monroe b: 12/27/13, Kenney, Tex. d: 10/27/77, Bellville, Tex. BR/TR, 6', 162 lbs. Deb: 4/25/39

YEAR	TM/L	W	L	PCT	G	GS	CG	SH	SV	IP	H	HR	BB	SO	RAT	ERA	ERA+	OAV	OOB	BH	AVG	PB	PR	/A	PD	TPI
1939	Det-A	0	1	.000	4	0	0	0	0	8^1	11	2	3	3	16.2	8.64	57	.324	.395	0	.000	-0	-4	-3	0	-0.4
	NY-N	1	0	1.000	26	0	0	0	1	49^2	44	3	21	22	12.1	3.08	127	.240	.325	0	.000	-1	5	5	-1	-0.1
1940	NY-N	4	3	.571	33	0	0	0	3	42^1	40	3	24	25	13.8	3.83	101	.247	.348	0	.000	-1	0	0	-1	-0.1
1944	Chi-N	5	4	.556	22	7	4	1	1	84^1	80	4	37	35	12.6	4.06	87	.251	.331	6	.207	0	-4	-5	1	-0.3
Total	3	10	8	.556	85	7	4	1	5	184^2	175	12	85	85	12.9	3.95	96	.251	.336	6	.146	-1	-3	-4	-1	-0.9

● AL LYONS

Lyons, Albert Harold b: 7/18/18, St.Joseph, Mo. d: 12/20/65, Inglewood, Cal. BR/TR, 6'2", 195 lbs. Deb: 4/19/44

YEAR	TM/L	W	L	PCT	G	GS	CG	SH	SV	IP	H	HR	BB	SO	RAT	ERA	ERA+	OAV	OOB	BH	AVG	PB	PR	/A	PD	TPI
1944	NY-A	0	0	—	11	0	0	0	0	39^2	43	2	24	14	15.7	4.54	77	.291	.397	9	.346	2	-5	-5	-1	0.2
1946	NY-A	0	1	.000	2	1	0	0	0	8^1	11	0	6	4	19.4	5.40	64	.314	.429	0	.000	-1	-2	-2	0	-0.2
1947	NY-A	1	0	1.000	6	0	0	0	0	11	18	2	9	7	22.1	9.00	39	.367	.466	4	.667	2	-6	-7	0	-0.3
	Pit-N	1	2	.333	13	0	0	0	0	28^1	36	4	12	16	15.6	7.31	58	.300	.368	2	.200	1	-10	-10	1	-0.7
1948	Bos-N	1	0	1.000	7	0	0	0	0	12^2	17	1	8	5	17.8	7.82	49	.309	.397	2	.167	0	-5	-6	1	-0.2
Total	4	3	3	.500	39	1	0	0	0	100	125	9	59	46	16.9	6.30	59	.307	.400	17	.293	5	-29	-28	2	-1.2

● CURT LYONS

Lyons, Curt Russell b: 10/17/74, Greencastle, Ind. BR/TR, 6'5", 230 lbs. Deb: 9/19/96

YEAR	TM/L	W	L	PCT	G	GS	CG	SH	SV	IP	H	HR	BB	SO	RAT	ERA	ERA+	OAV	OOB	BH	AVG	PB	PR	/A	PD	TPI
1996	Cin-N	2	0	1.000	3	3	0	0	0	16	17	1	7	14	14.1	4.50	94	.274	.357	0	.000	-1	-1	-0	-0	-0.1

● GEORGE LYONS

Lyons, George Tony "Smooth" b: 1/25/1891, Bible Grove, Ill. d: 8/12/81, Nevada, Mo. BR/TR, 5'11", 180 lbs. Deb: 9/6/20

YEAR	TM/L	W	L	PCT	G	GS	CG	SH	SV	IP	H	HR	BB	SO	RAT	ERA	ERA+	OAV	OOB	BH	AVG	PB	PR	/A	PD	TPI
1920	StL-N	2	1	.667	7	2	1	0	0	23^1	21	2	9	5	12.0	3.09	97	.262	.344	1	.143	-0	0	-0	1	0.0
1924	StL-A	3	2	.600	26	6	2	0	0	77^2	97	2	45	25	17.0	5.21	87	.323	.420	5	.250	-0	-8	-6	1	-0.2
Total	2	5	3	.625	33	8	3	0	0	101	118	4	54	30	15.9	4.72	88	.311	.405	6	.222	-0	-8	-7	2	-0.2

YEAR	TM/L	W	L	PCT	G	GS	CG	SH	SV	IP	H	HR	BB	SO	RAT	ERA	ERA+	OAV	OOB	BH	AVG	PB	PR	/A	PD	TPI
● HARRY LYONS	Lyons, Harry P. b: 3/25/1866, Chester, Pa. d: 6/30/12, Mauricetown, N.J. BR/TR, 5'10.5", 157 lbs. Deb: 8/29/1887 ♦																									
1890	Roc-a	0	0	—	1	0	0	0	0	3^{2}	8	0	1	2	22.1	12.27	29	.421	.450	152	.260	0	-3	-4	0	0.0
● HERSH LYONS	Lyons, Herschel Englebert b: 7/23/15, Fresno, Cal. BR/TR, 5'11", 195 lbs. Deb: 4/17/41																									
1941	StL-N	0	0	—	1	0	0	0	0	1^{1}	1	0	3	1	27.0	0.00	—	.200	.500	0	—	0	1	1	0	0.0
● STEVE LYONS	Lyons, Stephen John b: 6/3/60, Tacoma, Wash. BL/TR, 6'3", 195 lbs. Deb: 4/15/85 ♦																									
1990	Chi-A	0	0	—	1	0	0	0	0	2	2	0	4	1	27.0	4.50	85	.250	.500	28	.192	0	-0	-0	0	0.0
1991	Bos-A	0	0	—	1	0	0	0	0	1	2	0	0	1	18.0	0.00	—	.400	.400	51	.241	0	0	0	0	0.0
Total	2	0	0	—	2	0	0	0	0	3	4	0	4	2	24.0	3.00	133	.308	.471	545	.252	0	0	0	0	0.0
● TED LYONS	Lyons, Theodore Amar b: 12/28/1900, Lake Charles, La. d: 7/25/86, Sulphur, La. BB/TR, 5'11", 200 lbs. Deb: 7/2/23 MCH♦																									
1923	Chi-A	2	1	.667	9	1	0	0	0	22^{2}	30	2	15	6	18.3	6.35	62	.323	.422	1	.200	0	-6	-6	1	-0.6
1924	Chi-A	12	11	.522	41	22	12	0	3	216^{1}	279	10	72	52	14.7	4.87	85	.322	.375	17	.221	0	-15	-18	-3	-1.9
1925	Chi-A	**21**	11	.656	43	32	19	**5**	3	262^{2}	274	7	83	45	12.3	3.26	128	.278	.335	18	.186	-3	33	26	2	2.7
1926	Chi-A	18	16	.529	39	31	24	3	2	283^{2}	268	6	106	51	11.9	3.01	128	.252	.320	22	.212	-0	32	27	4	3.3
1927	Chi-A	**22**	14	.611	39	34	**30**	2	2	**307^{2}**	291	7	67	71	10.5	2.84	143	.251	.292	28	.255	5	**45**	**41**	0	**5.1**
1928	Chi-A	15	14	.517	39	27	21	0	6	240	276	11	68	60	13.0	3.98	102	.295	.344	23	.253	1	2	2	2	0.5
1929	Chi-A	14	20	.412	37	31	21	1	2	259^{1}	276	11	76	57	12.3	4.10	105	.278	.331	20	.220	1	4	5	3	1.0
1930	Chi-A	22	15	.595	42	36	**29**	1	1	**297^{2}**	331	12	57	69	11.8	3.78	122	.285	.319	38	.311	8	29	28	3	4.1
1931	Chi-A	4	6	.400	22	12	7	0	0	101	117	6	33	16	13.4	4.01	106	.296	.350	5	.152	-1	4	3	-1	0.0
1932	Chi-A	10	15	.400	33	26	19	1	2	230^{2}	243	10	71	58	12.4	3.28	132	.272	.327	19	.260	5	31	27	-1	3.0
1933	Chi-A	10	21	.323	36	27	14	2	1	228	260	10	74	74	13.2	4.38	97	.280	.333	26	.286	6	-3	-4	0	0.2
1934	Chi-A	11	13	.458	30	24	21	0	1	205^{1}	249	15	66	53	13.9	4.87	97	.293	.345	20	.206	1	-8	-3	2	0.0
1935	Chi-A	15	8	.652	23	22	19	3	0	190^{2}	194	15	56	54	11.9	3.02	153	.262	.317	18	.220	-0	30	34	-1	3.6
1936	Chi-A	10	13	.435	26	24	15	1	0	182	227	21	45	48	13.6	5.14	101	.305	.347	11	.157	-3	-2	1	1	0.0
1937	Chi-A	12	7	.632	22	22	11	0	0	169^{1}	182	21	45	45	12.1	4.15	111	.278	.326	12	.211	1	9	9	0	1.0
1938	Chi-A	9	11	.450	23	23	17	1	0	194^{2}	238	13	52	54	13.4	3.70	132	.299	.342	14	.194	-1	24	26	2	2.3
1939	Chi-A☆	14	6	.700	21	21	16	0	0	172^{2}	162	7	26	65	**9.9**	2.76	171	.247	**.276**	18	.295	4	36	38	-1	4.3
1940	Chi-A	12	8	.600	22	22	17	**4**	0	186^{1}	188	17	37	72	10.9	3.24	137	.252	.287	18	.240	2	24	25	-2	2.3
1941	Chi-A	12	10	.545	22	22	19	2	0	187^{1}	199	9	37	63	11.5	3.70	111	.269	.308	20	.270	4	9	8	1	1.3
1942	Chi-A	14	6	.700	20	20	20	1	0	180^{1}	167	11	26	50	9.7	**2.10**	**172**	.245	.275	16	.239	4	31	30	1	**4.0**
1946	Chi-A	1	4	.200	5	5	5	0	0	42^{2}	38	2	9	10	9.9	2.32	147	.235	.275	0	.000	-1	6	5	0	0.5
Total	21	260	230	.531	594	484	356	27	23	4161	4489	223	1121	1073	12.2	3.67	118	.276	.324	364	.233	32	313	302	12	36.7
● TOBY LYONS	Lyons, Thomas A. b: 3/27/1869, Cambridge, Mass. d: 8/27/20, Boston, Mass. Deb: 4/18/1890																									
1890	Syr-a	0	2	.000	3	3	2	0	0	22^{1}	40	1	21	6	25.0	10.48	34	.377	.484	4	.333	1	-16	-17	0	-1.0
● RICK LYSANDER	Lysander, Richard Eugene b: 2/21/53, Huntington Park, Cal. BR/TR, 6'2", 190 lbs. Deb: 4/12/80																									
1980	Oak-A	0	0	—	5	0	0	0	0	13^{2}	24	3	4	5	18.4	7.90	48	.381	.418	0	—	0	-6	-6	0	0.4
1983	Min-A	5	12	.294	61	4	1	1	3	125	132	8	43	58	12.7	3.38	126	.275	.337	0	—	0	9	12	1	1.4
1984	Min-A	4	3	.571	36	0	0	0	5	56^{2}	62	2	27	22	14.1	3.49	120	.283	.362	0	—	0	3	4	0	0.3
1985	Min-A	0	2	.000	35	1	0	0	3	61	72	3	22	26	13.9	6.05	73	.305	.364	0	—	0	-13	-11	-1	-0.7
Total	4	9	17	.346	137	5	1	1	11	256^{1}	290	16	96	111	13.6	4.28	99	.291	.354	0	—	0	-6	-1	0	1.4
● BILL LYSTON	Lyston, William Edward b: 1863, Near Baltimore, Md. d: 8/4/44, Baltimore, Md. TR , Deb: 8/29/1891																									
1891	Col-a	0	1	.000	1	1	1	0	0	6	10	0	6	1	25.5	10.50	33	.357	.486	0	.000	-0	-5	-5	-0	-0.5
1894	Cle-N	0	0	—	1	1	0	0	0	3^{2}	5	1	4	0	22.1	9.82	56	.313	.450	0	.000	-0	-2	-2	-0	0.0
Total	2	0	1	.000	2	2	1	0	0	9^{2}	15	1	10	1	24.2	10.24	41	.341	.473	0	.000	-0	-6	-7	-0	-0.5
● DUKE MAAS	Maas, Duane Fredrick b: 1/31/29, Utica, Mich. d: 12/7/76, Mt.Clemens, Mich. BR/TR, 5'10", 170 lbs. Deb: 4/21/55																									
1955	Det-A	5	6	.455	18	16	5	2	0	86^{2}	91	7	50	42	14.8	4.88	79	.271	.369	5	.167	0	-9	-10	0	-1.1
1956	Det-A	0	7	.000	26	7	0	0	0	63^{1}	81	9	32	34	16.9	6.54	63	.313	.401	3	.188	0	-17	-17	-0	-1.7
1957	Det-A	10	14	.417	45	26	8	2	6	219^{1}	210	23	65	116	11.4	3.28	118	.252	.309	6	.085	-4	12	14	0	1.2
1958	KC-A	4	5	.444	10	7	3	1	1	55^{1}	49	3	13	19	10.2	3.90	100	.241	.290	3	.176	0	-1	0	0	0.1
	*NY-A	7	3	.700	22	13	2	1	0	101^{1}	93	9	36	50	11.6	3.82	92	.242	.310	3	.088	-2	-1	-3	-1	-0.6
	Yr	11	8	.579	32	20	5	2	1	156^{2}	142	12	49	69	11.1	3.85	95	.241	.302	6	.118	-1	-1	-3	-1	-0.5
1959	NY-A	14	8	.636	38	21	3	1	4	138	149	14	53	67	13.3	4.43	82	.278	.345	5	.125	-1	-9	-12	1	-1.9
1960	*NY-A	5	1	.833	35	1	0	0	4	70^{1}	70	6	35	28	13.6	4.09	87	.265	.353	0	.000	-1	-2	-4	1	-0.4
1961	NY-A	0	0	—	1	0	0	0	0	0^{1}	2	0	0	0	54.0	54.00	7	1.000	1.000	0	—	0	-2	-2	0	0.0
Total	7	45	44	.506	195	91	21	7	15	734^{2}	745	71	284	356	12.8	4.19	90	.264	.336	25	.117	-7	-27	-34	0	-4.4
● BOB MABE	Mabe, Robert Lee b: 10/8/29, Danville, Va. BR/TR, 5'11", 165 lbs. Deb: 4/18/58																									
1958	StL-N	3	9	.250	31	13	4	0	0	111^{2}	113	11	41	74	12.7	4.51	91	.260	.330	1	.042	-2	-7	-5	0	-0.6
1959	Cin-N	4	2	.667	18	1	0	0	3	29^{2}	29	6	19	8	14.6	5.46	74	.254	.361	0	.000	-1	-5	-5	-0	-1.0
1960	Bal-A	0	0	—	2	0	0	0	0	0^{2}	4	0	1	0	67.5	27.00	14	.571	.625	0	—	0	-2	-2	-0	0.0
Total	3	7	11	.389	51	14	4	0	3	142	146	17	61	82	13.4	4.82	85	.263	.340	1	.032	-3	-14	-11	-0	-1.6
● MAC MacARTHUR	MacArthur, Malcolm b: 1/19/1862, Glasgow, Scotland d: 10/18/32, Detroit, Mich. TR , 5'9.5", 164 lbs. Deb: 5/2/1884																									
1884	Ind-a	1	5	.167	6	6	6	0	0	52	57	1	21	19	13.8	5.02	66	.263	.333	2	.095	-2	-10	-10	0	-1.0
● FRANK MacCORMACK	MacCormack, Frank Louis b: 9/21/54, Jersey City, N.J. BR/TR, 6'4", 210 lbs. Deb: 6/14/76																									
1976	Det-A	0	5	.000	9	8	0	0	0	32^{2}	35	1	34	14	19.3	5.79	64	.294	.455	0	.000	-0	-8	-8	-0	-1.1
1977	Sea-A	0	0	—	3	3	0	0	0	7	4	0	12	4	24.4	3.86	107	.174	.500	0	—	0	0	0	0	0.1
Total	2	0	5	.000	12	11	0	0	0	39^{2}	39	1	46	18	20.2	5.45	69	.275	.464	0	.000	-0	-8	-7	-0	-1.0
● ROB MacDONALD	MacDonald, Robert Joseph b: 4/27/65, East Orange, N.J. BL/TL, 6'3", 208 lbs. Deb: 8/14/90																									
1990	Tor-A	0	0	—	4	0	0	0	0	2^{1}	0	0	2	0	7.7	0.00	—	.000	.250	0	—	0	1	1	-0	-0.1
1991	*Tor-A	3	3	.500	45	0	0	0	0	53^{2}	51	5	25	24	12.7	2.85	148	.252	.335	0	—	0	7	8	-1	0.5
1992	Tor-A	1	0	1.000	27	0	0	0	0	47^{1}	50	4	16	26	12.7	4.37	93	.270	.332	0	—	0	-2	-2	-1	-0.3
1993	Det-A	3	3	.500	68	0	0	0	3	65^{2}	67	8	33	39	13.8	5.35	80	.268	.356	0	—	0	-7	-8	1	-0.6
1995	NY-A	1	1	.500	33	0	0	0	0	46^{1}	50	7	22	41	14.2	4.86	95	.282	.365	0	—	0	-1	-1	-0	-0.1
1996	NY-N	0	2	.000	20	0	0	0	0	19	16	2	9	12	11.8	4.26	94	.235	.325	0	—	0	-0	-1	-0	-0.1
Total	6	8	9	.471	197	0	0	0	3	234^{1}	234	26	107	142	13.2	4.34	98	.264	.345	0	—	0	-2	-2	-2	-0.7
● BILL MACDONALD	Macdonald, William Paul b: 3/28/29, Alameda, Cal. d: 5/4/91, Shasta Lake, Cal. BR/TR, 5'10", 170 lbs. Deb: 5/6/50																									
1950	Pit-N	8	10	.444	32	20	6	2	1	153	138	17	88	60	13.4	4.29	102	.243	.346	6	.122	-2	-3	2	-3	-0.3
1953	Pit-N	0	1	.000	4	1	0	0	0	7^{1}	12	0	8	4	25.8	12.27	36	.400	.538	0	—	0	-7	-6	-0	-0.7
Total	2	8	11	.421	36	21	6	2	1	160^{1}	150	17	96	64	13.9	4.66	94	.251	.356	6	.122	-2	-9	-5	-3	-1.0
● JIMMY MACE	Mace, Harry L. b: Washington, D.C. 5'11", 185 lbs. Deb: 5/5/1891																									
1891	Was-a	0	1	.000	3	1	1	0	0	16	18	0	8	3	15.2	7.31	51	.273	.360	0	.000	-1	-6	-6	-0	-0.4
● DANNY MacFAYDEN	MacFayden, Daniel Knowles "Deacon Danny" b: 6/10/05, N.Truro, Mass. d: 8/26/72, Brunswick, Me. BR/TR, 5'11", 170 lbs. Deb: 8/25/26																									
1926	Bos-A	0	1	.000	3	1	1	0	0	13	10	0	7	1	11.8	4.85	84	.217	.321	1	.333	0	-1	-1	1	0.0
1927	Bos-A	5	8	.385	34	16	6	1	2	160^{1}	176	9	59	42	13.5	4.27	99	.294	.363	13	.283	4	-2	-1	-2	0.2
1928	Bos-A	9	15	.375	33	28	9	0	0	195	215	12	78	61	13.8	4.75	87	.289	.361	9	.143	-1	-15	-14	-1	-1.6
1929	Bos-A	10	18	.357	32	26	14	**4**	0	221	225	8	81	61	12.7	3.62	118	.271	.340	13	.176	-3	15	16	2	1.7
1930	Bos-A	11	14	.440	36	33	18	1	2	269^{1}	293	9	93	76	13.1	4.21	109	.281	.343	13	.141	-4	13	12	2	0.7
1931	Bos-A	16	12	.571	35	32	17	2	0	230^{2}	263	4	79	74	13.6	4.02	107	.281	.341	10	.123	-5	9	7	2	0.5
1932	Bos-A	1	10	.091	12	11	6	0	0	77^{2}	91	3	33	29	14.5	5.10	88	.289	.358	3	.120	-2	-5	-5	0	-0.7
	NY-A	7	5	.583	17	15	9	0	1	121^{1}	137	11	37	33	13.1	3.93	104	.281	.334	5	.102	-3	7	2	-2	-0.3

YEAR	TM/L	W	L	PCT	G	GS	CG	SH	SV	IP	H	HR	BB	SO	RAT	ERA	ERA+	OAV	OOB	BH	AVG	PB	PR	/A	PD	TPI
	Yr	8	15	.348	29	26	15	0	1	199	228	14	70	62	13.6	4.39	97	.284	.342	8	.108	-4	2	-3	-1	-1.0
1933	NY-A	3	2	.600	25	6	2	0	0	90^1	120	8	37	28	15.8	5.88	66	.319	.383	1	.029	-4	-16	-20	-0	-1.3
1934	NY-A	4	3	.571	22	11	4	0	0	96	110	5	31	41	13.4	4.50	90	.288	.345	4	.103	-2	-0	-5	-1	-0.5
1935	Cin-N	1	2	.333	7	4	1	0	0	36	39	1	13	13	13.0	4.75	84	.281	.342	1	.091	-1	-3	-3	1	-0.2
	Bos-N	5	13	.278	28	20	7	1	0	151^2	200	8	34	46	14.2	5.10	74	.314	.354	8	.157	-1	-18	-22	2	-2.1
	Yr	6	15	.286	35	24	8	1	0	187^2	239	9	47	59	14.0	5.04	76	.308	.352	9	.145	-2	-21	-25	3	-2.3
1936	Bos-N	17	13	.567	37	31	21	2	0	266^2	268	5	66	86	11.4	2.87	134	.259	.307	8	.096	-5	34	29	3	2.7
1937	Bos-N	14	14	.500	32	32	16	2	0	246	250	5	60	70	11.4	2.93	123	.268	.313	13	.157	-2	27	18	1	1.8
1938	Bos-N	14	9	.609	29	29	19	5	0	219^2	208	6	64	58	11.3	2.95	116	.247	.304	9	.117	-4	20	12	-1	0.6
1939	Bos-N	8	14	.364	33	28	8	0	2	191^2	221	11	59	46	13.3	3.90	95	.291	.345	12	.179	-1	0	-4	1	-0.4
1940	Pit-N	5	4	.556	35	8	0	0	2	91^1	112	5	27	24	14.1	3.55	107	.302	.356	5	.179	-0	3	3	1	0.3
1941	Was-A	0	1	.000	5	0	0	0	0	7	12	1	5	3	21.9	10.29	39	.375	.459	0	—	0	-5	-5	0	-0.5
1943	Bos-N	2	1	.667	10	1	0	0	0	21^1	31	1	9	5	17.3	5.91	58	.344	.410	1	.250	0	-6	-6	-0	-0.8
Total	17	132	159	.454	465	332	158	18	9	2706	2981	112	872	797	13.0	3.96	101	.281	.340	129	.142	-34	58	11	10	0.1

● JULIO MACHADO
Machado, Julio Segundo (Rondon) b: 12/1/65, Zulia, Venezuela BR/TR, 5'9", 165 lbs. Deb: 9/7/89

YEAR	TM/L	W	L	PCT	G	GS	CG	SH	SV	IP	H	HR	BB	SO	RAT	ERA	ERA+	OAV	OOB	BH	AVG	PB	PR	/A	PD	TPI
1989	NY-N	0	1	.000	10	0	0	0	0	11	9	0	3	14	9.8	3.27	100	.214	.267	0	—	0	0	-0	-0	0.0
1990	NY-N	4	1	.800	27	0	0	0	0	34^1	32	4	17	27	13.4	3.15	119	.248	.345	0	—	0	2	2	-0	0.3
	Mil-A	0	0	—	10	0	0	0	3	13	9	0	8	12	11.8	0.69	559	.191	.309	0	—	0	5	5	-0	0.2
1991	Mil-A	3	3	.500	54	0	0	0	3	88^2	65	12	55	98	12.5	3.45	115	.211	.336	0	—	0	6	5	-1	0.4
Total	3	7	5	.583	101	0	0	0	6	147	115	16	83	151	12.4	3.12	123	.219	.331	0	—	0	14	12	-1	0.9

● CHUCK MACHEMEHL
Machemehl, Charles Walter b: 4/20/47, Brenham, Tex. BR/TR, 6'4", 200 lbs. Deb: 4/6/71

YEAR	TM/L	W	L	PCT	G	GS	CG	SH	SV	IP	H	HR	BB	SO	RAT	ERA	ERA+	OAV	OOB	BH	AVG	PB	PR	/A	PD	TPI
1971	Cle-A	0	2	.000	14	0	0	0	3	18^1	16	2	15	9	15.2	6.38	60	.246	.387	1	.500	0	-6	-5	0	-0.7

● DENNY MACK
Mack, Dennis Joseph (b: Dennis Joseph McGee) b: 1851, Easton, Pa. d: 4/10/1888, Wilkes-Barre, Pa. BR/TR, 5'7", 164 lbs. Deb: 5/6/1871 MU♦

YEAR	TM/L	W	L	PCT	G	GS	CG	SH	SV	IP	H	HR	BB	SO	RAT	ERA	ERA+	OAV	OOB	BH	AVG	PB	PR	/A	PD	TPI
1871	Rok-n	0	1	.000	3	1	1	0	0	13	20	0	3	1	15.9	3.46	118	.299	.329	30	.246	-0	1	1		0.1

● FRANK MACK
Mack, Frank George "Stubby" b: 2/2/1900, Oklahoma City, Okla. d: 7/2/71, Clearwater, Fla. BR/TR, 6'1.5", 180 lbs. Deb: 8/16/22

YEAR	TM/L	W	L	PCT	G	GS	CG	SH	SV	IP	H	HR	BB	SO	RAT	ERA	ERA+	OAV	OOB	BH	AVG	PB	PR	/A	PD	TPI
1922	Chi-A	2	2	.500	8	4	1	1	0	34^1	36	2	16	11	13.6	3.67	111	.281	.361	3	.250	1	1	2	-1	0.1
1923	Chi-A	0	1	.000	11	0	0	0	0	23^1	23	0	11	6	13.1	4.24	93	.284	.370	0	.000	-1	-1	-1	0	-0.1
1925	Chi-A	0	0	—	8	0	0	0	0	13^1	24	1	13	6	25.0	9.45	44	.444	.552	1	.333	0	-7	-8	-0	0.0
Total	3	2	3	.400	27	4	1	1	0	71	83	3	40	23	15.6	4.94	82	.316	.406	4	.190	0	-7	-7	-1	0.0

● TONY MACK
Mack, Tony Lynn b: 4/30/61, Lexington, Ky. BR/TR, 5'10", 177 lbs. Deb: 7/27/85

YEAR	TM/L	W	L	PCT	G	GS	CG	SH	SV	IP	H	HR	BB	SO	RAT	ERA	ERA+	OAV	OOB	BH	AVG	PB	PR	/A	PD	TPI
1985	Cal-A	0	1	.000	1	1	0	0	0	2^1	8	0	0	0	30.9	15.43	27	.571	.571	0	—	0	-3	-3	-0	-0.7

● BILL MACK
Mack, William Francis b: 2/12/1885, Elmira, N.Y. d: 9/30/71, Elmira, N.Y. BL/TL, 6'1", 155 lbs. Deb: 7/14/08

YEAR	TM/L	W	L	PCT	G	GS	CG	SH	SV	IP	H	HR	BB	SO	RAT	ERA	ERA+	OAV	OOB	BH	AVG	PB	PR	/A	PD	TPI
1908	Chi-N	0	0	—	2	0	0	0	0	6	5	1	1	2	10.5	3.00	78	.263	.333	2	.667	1	-0	-0	-0	0.2

● KEN MacKENZIE
MacKenzie, Kenneth Purvis b: 3/10/34, Gore Bay, Ont., Can. BR/TL, 6', 185 lbs. Deb: 5/2/60

YEAR	TM/L	W	L	PCT	G	GS	CG	SH	SV	IP	H	HR	BB	SO	RAT	ERA	ERA+	OAV	OOB	BH	AVG	PB	PR	/A	PD	TPI
1960	Mil-N	0	1	.000	9	0	0	0	0	8^1	9	2	3	9	13.0	6.48	53	.281	.343	0	.000	-0	-3	-3	-0	-0.3
1961	Mil-N	0	1	.000	5	0	0	0	0	7	8	1	2	5	14.1	5.14	73	.296	.367	0	.000	-0	-1	-1	0	-0.1
1962	NY-N	5	4	.556	42	1	0	0	1	80	87	10	34	51	13.9	4.95	84	.280	.356	1	.083	-1	-9	-7	1	-0.7
1963	NY-N	3	1	.750	34	0	0	0	3	58	63	11	12	41	11.9	4.97	70	.267	.308	0	.000	-1	-11	-10	-1	-0.9
	StL-N	0	0	—	8	0	0	0	0	9	9	1	3	7	12.0	4.00	89	.250	.308	0	—	0	-1	-0	-0	0.0
	Yr	3	1	.750	42	0	0	0	3	67	72	12	15	48	11.7	4.84	72	.262	.300	0	.000	-1	-12	-10	-1	-0.9
1964	SF-N	0	0	—	10	0	0	0	1	9	9	1	3	3	12.0	5.00	71	.265	.324	0	—	0	-1	-1	0	0.0
1965	Hou-N	0	3	.000	21	0	0	0	0	37	46	7	6	26	12.6	3.89	86	.299	.325	3	.273	1	-1	-2	-0	-0.1
Total	6	8	10	.444	129	1	0	0	5	208^1	231	33	63	142	13.0	4.80	78	.278	.334	4	.111	-2	-27	-24	-1	-2.1

● JOHN MACKINSON
Mackinson, John Joseph b: 10/29/23, Orange, N.J. d: 10/17/89, Reseda, Cal. BR/TR, 5'10.5", 160 lbs. Deb: 4/16/53

YEAR	TM/L	W	L	PCT	G	GS	CG	SH	SV	IP	H	HR	BB	SO	RAT	ERA	ERA+	OAV	OOB	BH	AVG	PB	PR	/A	PD	TPI
1953	Phi-A	0	0	—	1	0	0	0	0	1^1	1	0	2	0	20.3	0.00	—	.200	.429	0	—	0	1	1	0	0.0
1955	StL-N	0	1	.000	8	1	0	0	0	20^2	24	3	10	8	15.2	7.84	52	.296	.380	0	.000	-0	-9	-9	-0	-0.4
Total	2	0	1	.000	9	1	0	0	0	22	25	3	12	8	15.5	7.36	55	.291	.384	0	.000	-0	-8	-8	-0	-0.4

● BILLY MacLEOD
MacLeod, William Daniel b: 5/13/42, Gloucester, Mass. BL/TL, 6'2", 190 lbs. Deb: 9/13/62

YEAR	TM/L	W	L	PCT	G	GS	CG	SH	SV	IP	H	HR	BB	SO	RAT	ERA	ERA+	OAV	OOB	BH	AVG	PB	PR	/A	PD	TPI
1962	Bos-A	0	1	.000	2	0	0	0	0	1^2	4	0	1	2	27.0	5.40	76	.444	.500	0	—	0	-0	-0	-0	-0.1

● MAX MACON
Macon, Max Cullen b: 10/14/15, Pensacola, Fla. d: 8/5/89, Jupiter, Fla. BL/TL, 6'3", 175 lbs. Deb: 4/21/38 ♦

YEAR	TM/L	W	L	PCT	G	GS	CG	SH	SV	IP	H	HR	BB	SO	RAT	ERA	ERA+	OAV	OOB	BH	AVG	PB	PR	/A	PD	TPI
1938	StL-N	4	11	.267	38	12	5	1	2	129^1	133	9	61	39	13.8	4.11	96	.268	.352	11	.306	2	-5	-2	1	0.0
1940	Bro-N	1	0	1.000	2	0	0	0	0	2	5	2	0	1	22.5	22.50	18	.455	.455	1	1.000	0	-4	-4	-0	-1.3
1942	Bro-N	5	3	.625	14	8	4	1	1	84	67	3	33	27	10.9	1.93	169	.220	.300	12	.279	4	13	12	-0	1.6
1943	Bro-N	7	5	.583	25	9	0	0	0	77	91	4	32	21	14.8	5.96	56	.291	.364	9	.164	-1	-22	-22	1	-3.2
1944	Bos-N	0	0	—	1	0	0	0	0	3	10	2	1	1	33.0	21.00	18	.556	.579	100	.273	0	-6	-6	0	0.0
1947	Bos-N	0	0	—	1	0	0	0	0	2	1	0	1	1	9.0	0.00	—	.167	.286	0	.000	-0	1	1	0	0.0
Total	6	17	19	.472	81	29	9	2	3	297^1	307	20	128	90	13.5	4.24	85	.267	.345	133	.265	5	-23	-21	1	-2.9

● HARRY MacPHERSON
MacPherson, Harry William b: 7/10/26, N.Andover, Mass. BR/TR, 5'10", 150 lbs. Deb: 8/14/44

YEAR	TM/L	W	L	PCT	G	GS	CG	SH	SV	IP	H	HR	BB	SO	RAT	ERA	ERA+	OAV	OOB	BH	AVG	PB	PR	/A	PD	TPI
1944	Bos-N	0	0	—	1	0	0	0	0	1	0	0	1	1	9.0	0.00	—	.000	.250	0	—	0	0	0	0	0.0

● JIMMY MACULLAR
Macullar, James F. "Little Mac" b: 1/16/1855, Boston, Mass. d: 4/8/24, Baltimore, Md. BR/TL, 5'6", 155 lbs. Deb: 5/5/1879 MU♦

YEAR	TM/L	W	L	PCT	G	GS	CG	SH	SV	IP	H	HR	BB	SO	RAT	ERA	ERA+	OAV	OOB	BH	AVG	PB	PR	/A	PD	TPI
1885	Bal-a	0	0	—	1	0	0	0	0	1	0	0	0	0	0.0	0.00	—	.000	.000	61	.191	0	0	0	0	0.0
1886	Bal-a	0	0	—	1	0	0	0	0	2	4	0	0	1	18.0	9.00	38	.400	.400	55	.205	0	-1	-1	-0	0.0
Total	2	0	0	—	2	0	0	0	0	3	4	0	0	1	12.0	6.00	56	.308	.308	319	.207	0	-1	-1	-0	0.0

● KEITH MacWHORTER
MacWhorter, Keith b: 12/30/55, Worcester, Mass. BR/TR, 6'4", 190 lbs. Deb: 5/10/80

YEAR	TM/L	W	L	PCT	G	GS	CG	SH	SV	IP	H	HR	BB	SO	RAT	ERA	ERA+	OAV	OOB	BH	AVG	PB	PR	/A	PD	TPI
1980	Bos-A	0	3	.000	14	2	0	0	0	42^1	46	3	18	21	14.0	5.53	76	.280	.359	0	—	0	-7	-6	0	-0.5

● LEN MADDEN
Madden, Leonard Joseph "Lefty" b: 7/2/1890, Toledo, Ohio d: 9/9/49, Toledo, Ohio BL/TL, 6'2", 165 lbs. Deb: 8/31/12

YEAR	TM/L	W	L	PCT	G	GS	CG	SH	SV	IP	H	HR	BB	SO	RAT	ERA	ERA+	OAV	OOB	BH	AVG	PB	PR	/A	PD	TPI
1912	Chi-N	0	1	.000	6	2	0	0	0	12^1	16	1	9	5	19.0	2.92	114	.302	.413	1	.250	0	1	1	-0	0.0

● MIKE MADDEN
Madden, Michael Anthony b: 1/13/58, Denver, Colo. BL/TL, 6'1", 190 lbs. Deb: 4/5/83

YEAR	TM/L	W	L	PCT	G	GS	CG	SH	SV	IP	H	HR	BB	SO	RAT	ERA	ERA+	OAV	OOB	BH	AVG	PB	PR	/A	PD	TPI
1983	Hou-N	9	5	.643	28	13	0	0	0	94^2	76	4	45	44	11.6	3.14	108	.231	.325	1	.045	-1	5	3	0	0.3
1984	Hou-N	2	3	.400	17	7	0	0	0	40^2	46	1	35	29	17.9	5.53	60	.297	.426	2	.333	1	-9	-10	-1	-1.1
1985	Hou-N	0	0	—	13	0	0	0	0	19	29	1	11	16	18.9	4.26	81	.363	.440	0	—	0	-1	-2	-0	0.0
1986	Hou-N	1	2	.333	13	6	0	0	0	39^2	47	3	22	30	15.7	4.08	88	.297	.383	0	.000	-0	-2	-2	-0	-0.2
Total	4	12	10	.545	71	26	0	0	0	194	198	9	113	119	14.5	3.94	87	.274	.373	3	.081	-1	-7	-11	-1	-1.0

● KID MADDEN
Madden, Michael Joseph b: 10/22/1866, Portland, Me. d: 3/16/1896, Portland, Maine TL, 5'7.5", 130 lbs. Deb: 5/6/1887

YEAR	TM/L	W	L	PCT	G	GS	CG	SH	SV	IP	H	HR	BB	SO	RAT	ERA	ERA+	OAV	OOB	BH	AVG	PB	PR	/A	PD	TPI
1887	Bos-N	21	14	.600	37	37	36	3	0	321	317	20	122	81	12.9	3.79	107	.251	.327	32	.242	4	10	10	-2	0.9
1888	Bos-N	7	11	.389	20	18	17	1	0	165	142	6	24	53	9.9	2.95	97	.228	.273	11	.164	-2	-2	-2	1	-0.3
1889	Bos-N	10	10	.500	22	19	18	1	1	178	194	7	71	64	14.2	4.40	95	.269	.348	25	.291	2	-8	-5	0	-0.2
1890	Bos-P	3	2	.600	10	7	5	1	1	62	85	2	25	24	17.1	4.79	92	.313	.387	7	.184	-1	-4	-3	1	-0.2
1891	Bos-a	0	1	1.000	1	1	1	0	0	8	10	2	6	6	21.4	6.75	52	.294	.442	2	.667	1	-3	-3	0	-0.2
	Bal-a	13	12	.520	32	27	20	1	1	224	239	4	88	56	14.1	4.10	91	.264	.345	29	.271	5	-9	-9	4	-0.1
	Yr	13	13	.500	33	28	21	1	1	232	249	6	94	62	14.2	4.19	89	.264	.346	31	.282	6	-12	-12	4	-0.3
Total	5	54	50	.519	122	109	97	7	3	958	987	41	336	284	13.2	3.92	97	.259	.332	106	.245	10	-15	-11	4	-0.1

● MORRIS MADDEN
Madden, Morris De Wayne b: 8/31/60, Laurens, S.C. BL/TL, 6', 155 lbs. Deb: 6/11/87

YEAR	TM/L	W	L	PCT	G	GS	CG	SH	SV	IP	H	HR	BB	SO	RAT	ERA	ERA+	OAV	OOB	BH	AVG	PB	PR	/A	PD	TPI
1987	Det-A	0	0	—	2	0	0	0	0	1^2	4	0	3	0	37.8	16.20	26	.444	.583	0	—	0	-2	-2	-0	0.0
1988	Pit-N	0	0	—	5	0	0	0	0	5^2	5	0	7	3	19.1	0.00	—	.294	.500	0	—	0	2	2	0	0.0

YEAR	TM/L	W	L	PCT	G	GS	CG	SH	SV	IP	H	HR	BB	SO	RAT	ERA	ERA+	OAV	OOB	BH	AVG	PB	PR	/A	PD	TPI
1989	Pit-N	2	2	.500	9	3	0	0	0	14	17	0	13	6	19.3	7.07	47	.327	.462	0	.000	-0	-6	-6	-1	-1.5
Total	3	2	2	.500	16	3	0	0	0	21^1	26	0	23	9	20.7	5.91	58	.333	.485	0	.000	-0	-6	-6	-1	-1.5
● **NICK MADDOX** Maddox, Nicholas b: 11/9/1886, Govans, Md. d: 11/27/54, Pittsburgh, Pa. BL/TR, 6′, 175 lbs. Deb: 9/13/07																										
1907	Pit-N	5	1	.833	6	6	6	1	0	54	32	0	13	38	8.2	0.83	292	.178	.249	5	.250	2	10	10	-0	1.5
1908	Pit-N	23	8	.742	36	32	22	4	1	260^2	209	5	90	70	10.7	2.28	101	.223	.298	25	.266	8	2	1	-1	0.9
1909	*Pit-N	13	8	.619	31	27	17	4	0	203^1	173	2	39	56	10.0	2.21	123	.232	.283	15	.224	4	9	11	-1	1.4
1910	Pit-N	2	3	.400	20	7	2	0	0	87^1	73	0	28	29	10.9	3.40	91	.246	.321	6	.214	1	-4	-3	-0	-0.1
Total	4	43	20	.683	93	72	47	9	1	605^1	487	7	170	193	10.3	2.29	112	.225	.292	51	.244	15	17	19	-2	3.7
● **GREG MADDUX** Maddux, Gregory Alan b: 4/14/66, San Angelo, Tex. BR/TR, 6′, 170 lbs. Deb: 9/3/86 F																										
1986	Chi-N	2	4	.333	6	5	1	0	0	31	44	3	11	20	16.3	5.52	73	.336	.392	4	.333	1	-6	-5	0	-0.8
1987	Chi-N	6	14	.300	30	27	1	1	0	155^2	181	17	74	101	15.0	5.61	76	.294	.374	5	.119	-2	-26	-23	6	-2.2
1988	Chi-N☆	18	8	.692	34	34	9	3	0	249	230	13	81	140	11.6	3.18	113	.244	.309	19	.198	2	7	12	2	1.7
1989	*Chi-N	19	12	.613	35	35	7	1	0	238^1	222	13	82	135	11.7	2.95	128	.249	.317	17	.210	2	15	21	3	3.4
1990	Chi-N	15	15	.500	35	35	8	2	0	237	242	11	71	144	12.0	3.46	118	.265	.321	12	.145	-2	9	16	8	2.6
1991	Chi-N	15	11	.577	37	37	7	2	0	**263**	232	18	66	198	10.4	3.35	116	.237	.289	18	.205	3	10	15	5	2.4
1992	Chi-N★	**20**	11	.645	35	35	9	4	0	**268**	201	7	70	199	9.6	2.18	**165**	.210	.273	15	.170	2	**39**	**42**	6	**6.2**
1993	*Atl-N	20	10	.667	36	36	**8**	1	0	**267**	228	14	52	197	**9.6**	**2.36**	**170**	.232	**.274**	15	.165	-1	**50**	**49**	7	**6.1**
1994	Atl-N★	**16**	6	.727	25	25	**10**	**3**	0	**202**	150	4	31	156	**8.3**	**1.56**	**272**	**.207**	**.245**	14	.222	2	**60**	**60**	3	**7.3**
1995	*Atl-N☆	**19**	2	**.905**	28	28	**10**	**3**	0	**209^2**	147	8	23	181	**7.5**	**1.63**	**261**	.197	**.225**	11	.153	-0	**59**	**61**	6	**6.8**
1996	*Atl-N☆	15	11	.577	35	35	5	1	0	245	225	11	28	172	9.4	2.72	162	.241	.265	10	.147	-1	41	46	10	5.6
1997	*Atl-N★	19	4	**.826**	33	33	5	2	0	232^2	200	9	20	177	8.7	2.20	190	.236	.258	7	.104	-1	52	51	3	5.1
1998	*Atl-N★	18	9	.667	34	34	9	**5**	0	251	201	13	45	204	**9.1**	**2.22**	**190**	.220	**.262**	18	.240	4	**56**	**56**	7	**7.2**
Total	13	202	117	.633	403	399	89	28	0	2849^1	2503	141	654	2024	10.2	2.75	146	.236	.286	165	.178	9	364	404	67	51.4
● **MIKE MADDUX** Maddux, Michael Ausley b: 8/27/61, Dayton, Ohio BL/TR, 6′2″, 190 lbs. Deb: 6/3/86 F																										
1986	Phi-N	3	7	.300	16	16	0	0	0	78	88	6	34	44	14.4	5.42	71	.286	.362	1	.045	-1	-15	-14	-1	-1.7
1987	Phi-N	2	0	1.000	7	2	0	0	0	17	17	0	5	15	11.6	2.65	160	.254	.306	0	.000	-0	3	3	-0	0.3
1988	Phi-N	4	3	.571	25	11	0	0	0	88^2	91	6	34	59	13.2	3.76	95	.275	.351	3	.130	-0	-3	-2	1	0.0
1989	Phi-N	1	3	.250	16	4	2	1	1	43^2	52	3	14	26	14.0	5.15	69	.304	.364	0	.000	-1	-8	-8	2	-0.6
1990	LA-N	0	1	.000	11	2	0	0	0	20^2	24	3	4	11	12.6	6.53	56	.293	.333	0	.000	-0	-6	-7	-0	-0.3
1991	SD-N	7	2	.778	64	1	0	0	5	98^2	78	4	27	57	9.7	2.46	154	.221	.278	1	.077	-0	13	15	1	1.5
1992	SD-N	2	2	.500	50	1	0	0	5	79^2	71	2	24	60	10.7	2.37	151	.236	.292	1	.111	-0	10	11	2	0.8
1993	NY-N	3	8	.273	58	0	0	0	5	75	67	3	27	57	11.8	3.60	111	.243	.319	0	.000	-0	4	3	1	0.6
1994	NY-N	2	1	.667	27	0	0	0	2	44	45	7	13	32	11.9	5.11	82	.263	.315	0	.000	-0	-4	-5	1	-0.2
1995	Pit-N	1	0	1.000	8	0	0	0	0	9	14	0	3	4	17.0	9.00	48	.359	.405	0	—	0	-5	-5	0	-0.5
	*Bos-A	4	1	.800	36	4	0	0	1	89^2	86	5	15	65	10.3	3.61	135	.247	.282	0	—	0	11	13	0	0.5
1996	Bos-A	3	2	.600	23	7	0	0	0	64^1	76	12	27	32	15.1	4.48	113	.295	.372	0	—	0	4	4	1	0.4
1997	Sea-A	1	0	1.000	6	0	0	0	0	10^2	20	1	8	7	24.5	10.13	44	.400	.492	0	—	0	-7	-7	-0	-0.5
1998	Mon-N	3	4	.429	51	0	0	0	1	55^2	50	3	15	33	10.7	3.72	110	.243	.297	0	.000	-0	3	2	0	0.3
Total	13	36	34	.514	398	48	2	1	20	774^2	779	55	250	502	12.2	4.00	101	.263	.326	6	.067	-4	-0	5	8	0.6
● **TONY MADIGAN** Madigan, William J. "Tice" b: 7/1868, Washington, D.C. d: 12/4/54, Washington, D.C. TR, 5′5.5″, 126 lbs. Deb: 7/10/1886																										
1886	Was-N	1	13	.071	14	13	13	0	0	114^2	154	3	44	29	15.5	4.87	68	.310	.366	4	.083	-4	-20	-20	0	-2.2
● **DAVE MADISON** Madison, David Pledger b: 2/1/21, Brooksville, Miss. d: 12/8/85, Macon, Miss. BR/TR, 6′3″, 190 lbs. Deb: 9/26/50																										
1950	NY-A	0	0	—	1	0	0	0	0	3	3	1	1	1	12.0	6.00	72	.273	.333	0	—	0	-0	-1	-0	0.0
1952	StL-A	4	2	.667	31	4	0	0	0	78	78	7	48	35	15.0	4.38	89	.264	.374	2	.118	-1	-6	-4	0	-0.4
	Det-A	1	1	.500	10	1	0	0	0	15	16	1	10	7	16.2	7.80	49	.291	.409	0	.000	0	-7	-7	-0	-0.8
	Yr	5	3	.625	41	5	0	0	0	93	94	8	58	42	14.8	4.94	79	.265	.370	2	.105	-1	-13	-11	-0	-1.2
1953	Det-A	3	4	.429	32	1	0	0	0	62	76	7	44	27	17.9	6.82	60	.303	.413	1	.091	-1	-19	-19	0	-1.9
Total	3	8	7	.533	74	6	0	0	0	158	173	16	103	70	16.2	5.70	70	.282	.392	3	.100	-2	-33	-30	0	-3.1
● **ALEX MADRID** Madrid, Alexander b: 4/18/63, Springerville, Ariz BR/TR, 6′3″, 200 lbs. Deb: 7/20/87																										
1987	Mil-A	0	0	—	3	0	0	0	0	5^1	11	1	1	1	20.3	15.19	30	.440	.462	0	—	0	-6	-6	-0	-0.1
1988	Phi-N	1	1	.500	5	2	1	0	0	16^1	15	0	6	2	11.6	2.76	129	.246	.313	0	.000	-0	1	1	-0	0.1
1989	Phi-N	1	2	.333	6	3	0	0	0	24^2	32	3	14	13	17.1	5.47	65	.314	.402	0	.000	-0	-5	-5	-1	-0.7
Total	3	2	3	.400	14	5	1	0	0	46^1	58	4	21	16	15.5	5.63	65	.309	.381	0	.000	-1	-11	-10	-1	-0.7
● **CALVIN MADURO** Maduro, Calvin Gregory b: 9/5/74, Santa Cruz, Aruba BR/TR, 6′, 175 lbs. Deb: 9/8/96																										
1996	Phi-N	0	1	.000	4	2	0	0	0	15^1	13	1	3	11	10.6	3.52	122	.232	.295	0	.000	-0	1	1	-0	0.0
1997	Phi-N	3	7	.300	15	13	0	0	0	71	83	12	41	31	16.1	7.23	59	.294	.390	1	.050	-2	-24	-24	-1	-2.8
Total	2	3	8	.273	19	15	0	0	0	86^1	96	13	44	42	15.1	6.57	65	.284	.375	1	.042	-2	-23	-22	-1	-2.8
● **HECTOR MAESTRI** Maestri, Hector Anibal (Garcia) b: 4/19/35, Havana, Cuba BR/TR, 5′10″, 158 lbs. Deb: 9/24/60																										
1960	Was-A	0	0	—	1	0	0	0	0	2	1	0	1	1	9.0	0.00	—	.167	.286	0	—	0	1	1	-0	0.0
1961	Was-A	0	1	.000	1	1	0	0	0	6	6	1	2	2	12.0	1.50	268	.250	.308	0	.000	-0	2	2	-0	0.3
Total	2	0	1	.000	2	1	0	0	0	8	7	1	3	3	11.3	1.13	354	.233	.303	0	.000	-0	3	3	-0	0.3
● **BILL MAGEE** Magee, William J. b: 7/6/1875, Canada BR/TR, 5′10″, 154 lbs. Deb: 5/18/1897																										
1897	Lou-N	4	12	.250	22	16	13	1	0	155^1	186	6	99	44	17.1	5.39	79	.294	.398	13	.210	-2	-19	-19	1	-1.6
1898	Lou-N	16	15	.516	38	33	29	3	0	295^1	294	8	129	55	13.5	4.05	88	.258	.343	14	.126	-9	-15	-16	-2	-2.3
1899	Lou-N	3	7	.300	12	10	6	1	0	71	91	1	28	13	16.2	5.20	74	.311	.388	3	.111	-2	-11	-11	1	-1.2
	Phi-N	3	5	.375	9	9	7	0	0	70	82	0	32	4	15.6	5.66	65	.292	.378	5	.161	-2	-14	-15	-1	-1.5
	Was-N	1	4	.200	8	7	4	0	0	42	54	3	28	11	19.1	8.57	46	.312	.428	5	.333	1	-22	-22	1	-1.7
	Yr	7	16	.304	29	26	17	1	0	183	227	4	88	28	15.8	6.15	62	.298	.375	13	.178	-2	-47	-48	1	-4.4
1901	StL-N	0	0	—	1	1	0	0	0	8	8	0	4	3	13.5	4.50	71	.258	.343	2	.500	1	-1	-1	-0	0.1
	NY-N	0	4	.000	6	5	4	0	0	42^1	56	4	11	14	15.1	5.95	56	.316	.370	2	.143	-1	-12	-12	0	-1.0
	Yr	0	4	.000	7	6	4	0	0	50^1	64	4	15	17	14.8	5.72	57	.308	.366	4	.222	1	-13	-14	-0	-0.9
1902	NY-N	0	0	—	2	1	0	0	0	5	5	0	1	2	10.8	3.60	78	.263	.300	0	.000	-0	-0	-0	-0	0.0
	Phi-N	2	4	.333	8	7	6	0	0	53^2	61	1	18	15	13.8	3.69	76	.285	.349	4	.211	-0	-5	-5	-0	-0.6
	Yr	2	4	.333	10	8	6	0	0	58^2	66	1	19	17	13.5	3.68	76	.283	.345	4	.200	-1	-6	-6	-0	-0.6
Total	5	29	51	.363	106	89	69	5	0	742^2	837	23	350	161	15.1	4.93	75	.283	.370	48	.169	-13	-99	-102	-0	-9.8
● **SAL MAGLIE** Maglie, Salvatore Anthony "The Barber" b: 4/26/17, Niagara Falls, N.Y d: 12/28/92, Niagara Falls, N.Y BR/TR, 6′2″, 180 lbs. Deb: 8/9/45 C																										
1945	NY-N	5	4	.556	13	10	7	3	0	84^1	72	2	22	32	10.2	2.35	167	.231	.286	5	.167	-1	14	15	0	1.4
1950	NY-N	18	4	**.818**	47	16	12	**5**	1	206	169	14	86	96	11.6	2.71	**151**	.226	.314	8	.121	-1	33	32	3	3.3
1951	*NY-N★	**23**	6	.793	42	37	22	3	4	298	254	27	86	146	10.4	2.93	**134**	**.230**	.289	17	.152	-3	**34**	**33**	1	2.9
1952	NY-N☆	18	8	.692	35	31	12	5	1	216	199	16	75	112	11.7	2.92	127	.244	.312	5	.072	-3	20	19	1	1.9
1953	NY-N	8	9	.471	27	24	9	3	0	145^1	158	19	47	80	12.8	4.15	103	.278	.334	13	.271	2	2	2	-2	0.3
1954	*NY-N	14	6	.700	34	32	9	1	2	218^1	222	21	70	117	12.2	3.26	124	.262	.320	8	.127	-2	20	19	0	1.4
1955	NY-N	9	5	.643	23	21	6	0	0	129^2	142	18	48	71	13.4	3.75	107	.278	.344	5	.125	-2	4	4	-2	0.0
	Cle-A	0	2	.000	10	2	0	0	2	25^2	26	0	7	11	11.9	3.86	103	.252	.306	0	.000	-0	0	0	-1	-0.1
1956	Cle-A	0	0	—	2	0	0	0	0	5	6	1	2	2	14.4	3.60	117	.300	.364	0	—	0	0	0	-0	0.0
	*Bro-N	13	5	.722	28	26	9	3	0	191	154	21	52	108	9.9	2.87	**138**	.222	.281	9	.129	-3	19	23	-2	1.5
1957	Bro-N	6	6	.500	19	17	4	1	1	101^1	94	12	26	50	11.0	2.93	142	.245	.300	1	.034	-3	11	14	-1	1.2
	NY-A	2	0	1.000	6	3	1	1	3	26	22	1	7	9	10.4	1.73	207	.227	.286	2	.250	0	6	5	-0	0.6
1958	NY-A	1	1	.500	7	3	0	0	0	23^1	27	3	9	7	13.9	4.63	76	.300	.364	1	.143	1	-2	-3	0	-0.1
	StL-N	2	6	.250	10	10	2	0	0	53	46	14	25	21	12.4	4.75	87	.232	.324	2	.125	-1	-5	-4	-1	-0.6
Total	10	119	62	.657	303	232	93	25	14	1723	1591	169	562	862	11.5	3.15	127	.245	.309	76	.135	-16	156	160	-2	13.7

● MIKE MAGNANTE

Magnante, Michael Anthony b: 6/17/65, Glendale, Cal. BL/TL, 6'1", 190 lbs. Deb: 4/22/91

YEAR	TM/L	W	L	PCT	G	GS	CG	SH	SV	IP	H	HR	BB	SO	RAT	ERA	ERA+	OAV	OOB	BH	AVG	PB	PR	/A	PD	TPI
1991	KC-A	0	1	.000	38	0	0	0	0	55	55	3	23	42	12.8	2.45	168	.262	.335	0	—	0	10	10	-0	0.1
1992	KC-A	4	9	.308	44	12	0	0	0	89^1	115	5	35	31	15.3	4.94	82	.325	.389	0	—	0	-10	-9	2	-1.2
1993	KC-A	1	2	.333	7	6	0	0	0	35^1	37	3	11	16	12.5	4.08	112	.282	.343	0	—	0	1	2	0	0.0
1994	KC-A	2	3	.400	36	1	0	0	0	47	55	5	16	21	13.6	4.60	109	.289	.345	0	—	0	1	2	0	0.0
1995	KC-A	1	1	.500	28	0	0	0	0	44^2	45	6	16	28	12.7	4.23	113	.268	.339	0	—	0	2	3	1	0.1
1996	KC-A	2	2	.500	38	0	0	0	0	54	58	5	24	32	14.3	5.67	88	.282	.368	0	—	0	-4	-4	2	-0.1
1997	*Hou-N	3	1	.750	40	0	0	0	1	47^2	39	2	11	43	9.4	2.27	176	.223	.269	0	.000	-0	10	9	-0	0.7
1998	Hou-N	4	7	.364	48	0	0	0	2	51^2	56	2	26	39	15.0	4.88	83	.276	.369	2	1.000	1	-4	-5	2	-0.6
Total	8	17	26	.395	279	19	0	0	3	424^2	460	31	162	252	13.5	4.22	104	.281	.350	2	.400	1	7	9	7	-1.0

● JIM MAGNUSON

Magnuson, James Robert b: 8/18/46, Marinette, Wis. d: 5/30/91, Green Bay, Wis. BR/TL, 6'2", 190 lbs. Deb: 6/28/70

YEAR	TM/L	W	L	PCT	G	GS	CG	SH	SV	IP	H	HR	BB	SO	RAT	ERA	ERA+	OAV	OOB	BH	AVG	PB	PR	/A	PD	TPI
1970	Chi-A	1	5	.167	13	6	0	0	0	44^2	45	7	16	20	12.5	4.84	81	.263	.330	0	.000	-1	-6	-5	-0	-0.7
1971	Chi-A	1	1	.500	15	4	0	0	0	30	30	0	16	11	14.4	4.50	80	.265	.366	0	.000	-0	-3	-3	-0	-0.3
1973	NY-A	0	1	.000	8	0	0	0	0	27^1	38	2	9	9	15.5	4.28	86	.342	.392	0	—	0	-1	-2	0	0.0
Total	3	2	7	.222	36	10	0	0	0	102	113	9	41	40	13.9	4.59	82	.286	.358	0	.000	-2	-10	-10	0	-1.0

● JOE MAGRANE

Magrane, Joseph David b: 7/2/64, Des Moines, Iowa BR/TL, 6'6", 230 lbs. Deb: 4/25/87

YEAR	TM/L	W	L	PCT	G	GS	CG	SH	SV	IP	H	HR	BB	SO	RAT	ERA	ERA+	OAV	OOB	BH	AVG	PB	PR	/A	PD	TPI
1987	*StL-N	9	7	.563	27	26	4	2	0	170^1	157	9	60	101	12.0	3.54	117	.245	.320	7	.135	1	10	12	-0	1.1
1988	StL-N	5	9	.357	24	24	4	3	0	165^1	133	6	51	100	10.1	**2.18**	**160**	.217	.280	8	.167	1	23	24	2	2.5
1989	StL-N	18	9	.667	34	33	9	3	0	234^2	219	5	72	127	11.4	2.91	124	.251	.313	11	.138	1	15	19	-1	2.1
1990	StL-N	10	17	.370	31	31	3	2	0	203^1	204	10	59	100	12.0	3.59	106	.264	.322	7	.127	-0	5	5	1	0.8
1992	StL-N	1	2	.333	5	5	0	0	0	31^1	34	2	15	20	14.6	4.02	84	.279	.367	2	.200	1	-2	-2	-0	-0.1
1993	StL-N	8	10	.444	22	20	0	0	0	116	127	15	37	38	13.1	4.97	80	.286	.348	4	.114	-1	-12	-13	0	-1.8
	Cal-A	3	2	.600	8	8	0	0	0	48	48	4	21	24	12.9	3.94	114	.265	.342	0	—	0	2	3	2	0.4
1994	Cal-A	2	6	.250	20	11	1	0	0	74	89	18	51	33	17.8	7.30	67	.300	.412	0	—	0	-21	-20	-0	-1.8
1996	Chi-A	1	5	.167	19	8	0	0	0	53^2	70	10	25	21	16.4	6.88	69	.318	.395	0	—	0	-11	-13	-0	-1.2
Total	8	57	67	.460	190	166	21	10	0	1096^2	1081	79	391	564	12.4	3.81	103	.260	.330	39	.139	3	10	15	3	2.0

● PETE MAGRINI

Magrini, Peter Alexander b: 6/8/42, San Francisco, Cal. BR/TR, 6', 195 lbs. Deb: 4/13/66

YEAR	TM/L	W	L	PCT	G	GS	CG	SH	SV	IP	H	HR	BB	SO	RAT	ERA	ERA+	OAV	OOB	BH	AVG	PB	PR	/A	PD	TPI
1966	Bos-A	0	1	.000	3	1	0	0	0	7^1	8	0	8	3	20.9	9.82	39	.308	.486	0	.000	-0	-5	-5	-0	-0.6

● ART MAHAFFEY

Mahaffey, Arthur b: 6/4/38, Cincinnati, Ohio BR/TR, 6'2", 200 lbs. Deb: 7/30/60

YEAR	TM/L	W	L	PCT	G	GS	CG	SH	SV	IP	H	HR	BB	SO	RAT	ERA	ERA+	OAV	OOB	BH	AVG	PB	PR	/A	PD	TPI
1960	Phi-N	7	3	.700	14	12	5	1	0	93^1	78	9	34	56	10.9	2.31	168	.229	.301	3	.100	-2	15	16	-1	1.5
1961	Phi-N★	11	19	.367	36	32	12	3	0	219^1	205	27	70	158	11.6	4.10	99	.249	.314	8	.127	-2	-2	-1	-2	-0.4
1962	Phi-N★	19	14	.576	41	39	20	2	0	274	253	36	81	177	11.4	3.94	98	.246	.309	13	.141	1	0	-2	-4	-0.6
1963	Phi-N	7	10	.412	26	22	6	1	0	149	143	18	48	97	11.8	3.99	81	.255	.319	10	.200	2	-12	-12	-1	-1.2
1964	Phi-N	12	9	.571	34	29	2	2	0	157^1	161	17	82	80	14.2	4.52	77	.269	.362	6	.120	0	-17	-18	-2	-2.4
1965	Phi-N	2	5	.286	22	9	1	0	0	71	82	11	32	52	15.3	6.21	56	.294	.381	2	.095	-1	-21	-22	-1	-2.1
1966	StL-N	1	4	.200	12	5	0	0	1	35	37	7	21	19	15.2	6.43	56	.276	.378	0	.000	-1	-11	-11	-1	-1.6
Total	7	59	64	.480	185	148	46	9	1	999	959	125	368	639	12.3	4.17	89	.255	.328	42	.134	-2	-47	-50	-11	-6.8

● ROY MAHAFFEY

Mahaffey, Lee Roy "Popeye" b: 2/9/03, Belton, S.C. d: 7/23/69, Anderson, S.C. BR/TR, 6', 180 lbs. Deb: 8/31/26

YEAR	TM/L	W	L	PCT	G	GS	CG	SH	SV	IP	H	HR	BB	SO	RAT	ERA	ERA+	OAV	OOB	BH	AVG	PB	PR	/A	PD	TPI
1926	Pit-N	0	0	—	4	0	0	0	0	4^2	5	0	1	3	13.5	0.00	—	.294	.368	0	.000	-0	2	2	-0	-0.1
1927	Pit-N	1	0	1.000	2	1	0	0	0	9^1	9	0	9	4	20.3	7.71	53	.300	.500	2	.400	0	-4	-4	-0	-0.3
1930	Phi-A	9	5	.643	33	16	6	0	0	152^2	186	16	53	38	14.3	5.01	93	.298	.357	7	.119	-5	-6	-6	-1	-1.0
1931	*Phi-A	15	4	.789	30	20	8	0	2	162^1	161	9	82	59	13.6	4.21	107	.258	.347	12	.190	1	3	5	-3	0.3
1932	Phi-A	13	13	.500	37	28	13	0	0	222^2	245	27	96	106	14.0	5.09	89	.274	.348	15	.172	-1	-15	-14	-2	-1.6
1933	Phi-A	13	10	.565	33	23	9	0	0	179^1	198	5	74	66	13.9	5.17	83	.275	.346	14	.215	-0	-18	-18	-2	-2.0
1934	Phi-A	6	7	.462	37	14	3	0	2	129	142	10	55	37	13.8	5.37	82	.276	.347	13	.271	2	-13	-14	-2	-1.1
1935	Phi-A	8	4	.667	27	17	5	0	0	136	153	11	42	39	13.2	3.90	116	.283	.341	9	.176	-2	8	10	-1	0.4
1936	StL-A	2	6	.250	21	9	1	0	1	60	82	6	40	13	18.5	8.10	66	.315	.409	1	.063	-1	-20	-18	-2	-2.2
Total	9	67	49	.578	224	128	45	0	5	1056	1181	84	452	365	14.1	5.01	90	.280	.353	73	.184	-7	-63	-57	-13	-7.6

● LOU MAHAFFEY

Mahaffey, Louis Wood b: 1/3/1874, Kentucky d: 10/26/49, Torrance, Cal. BR , 5'9", 170 lbs. Deb: 4/26/1898

YEAR	TM/L	W	L	PCT	G	GS	CG	SH	SV	IP	H	HR	BB	SO	RAT	ERA	ERA+	OAV	OOB	BH	AVG	PB	PR	/A	PD	TPI
1898	Lou-N	0	1	.000	1	1	1	0	0	9	10	0	5	1	15.0	3.00	119	.278	.366	0	.000	-0	1	1	-0	0.0

● ART MAHAN

Mahan, Arthur Leo b: 6/8/13, Somerville, Mass. BL/TL, 5'11", 178 lbs. Deb: 4/30/40 ♦

YEAR	TM/L	W	L	PCT	G	GS	CG	SH	SV	IP	H	HR	BB	SO	RAT	ERA	ERA+	OAV	OOB	BH	AVG	PB	PR	/A	PD	TPI
1940	Phi-N	0	0	—	1	0	0	0	0	1	1	0	0	0	9.0	0.00	—	.333	.333	133	.244	0	0	0	-0	0.0

● RON MAHAY

Mahay, Ronald Matthew b: 6/28/71, Crestwood, Ill. BL/TL, 6'2", 185 lbs. Deb: 5/21/95 ♦

YEAR	TM/L	W	L	PCT	G	GS	CG	SH	SV	IP	H	HR	BB	SO	RAT	ERA	ERA+	OAV	OOB	BH	AVG	PB	PR	/A	PD	TPI
1997	Bos-A	3	0	1.000	28	0	0	0	0	25	19	3	11	22	10.8	2.52	184	.204	.288	0	—	0	6	6	-0	0.5
1998	Bos-A	1	1	.500	29	0	0	0	1	26	26	2	15	14	14.9	3.46	133	.263	.371	0	—	0	3	3	-1	0.2
Total	2	4	1	.800	57	0	0	0	1	51	45	5	26	36	12.9	3.00	154	.234	.332	4	.200	0	9	9	-1	0.7

● MICKEY MAHLER

Mahler, Michael James b: 7/30/52, Montgomery, Ala. BB/TL, 6'3", 189 lbs. Deb: 9/13/77 F

YEAR	TM/L	W	L	PCT	G	GS	CG	SH	SV	IP	H	HR	BB	SO	RAT	ERA	ERA+	OAV	OOB	BH	AVG	PB	PR	/A	PD	TPI
1977	Atl-N	1	2	.333	5	5	0	0	0	23	31	4	9	14	16.0	6.26	71	.326	.390	3	.500	2	-6	-5	-0	-0.4
1978	Atl-N	4	11	.267	34	21	1	0	0	134^2	130	16	66	92	13.6	4.68	87	.255	.349	4	.098	-2	-16	-9	-1	-1.3
1979	Atl-N	5	11	.313	26	18	1	0	0	100	123	11	47	71	15.6	5.85	69	.304	.381	3	.111	-1	-24	-20	-0	-2.9
1980	Pit-N	0	0	—	2	0	0	0	0	1	4	1	3	1	63.0	63.00	6	.571	.700	0	—	0	-7	-7	0	0.0
1981	Cal-A	0	0	—	6	0	0	0	0	6^1	1	0	2	5	4.3	0.00	—	.056	.150	0	—	0	3	3	0	0.0
1982	Cal-A	2	0	1.000	6	0	0	0	0	8	9	0	6	5	16.9	1.13	360	.300	.417	0	—	0	3	3	-0	0.6
1985	Mon-N	1	4	.200	9	7	1	1	1	48^1	40	3	24	32	12.1	3.54	96	.229	.325	3	.188	1	0	-1	-1	-0.1
	Det-A	1	2	.333	3	2	0	0	0	20^2	19	2	4	14	10.0	1.74	234	.241	.277	0	—	0	6	5	-0	0.8
1986	Tex-A	0	2	.000	29	5	0	0	3	63	71	3	29	28	14.7	4.14	104	.295	.377	0	—	0	0	1	-0	0.0
	Tor-A	0	0	—	2	0	0	0	0	1	1	0	0	0	18.0	0.00	—	.200	.333	0	—	0	0	0	0	0.0
	Yr	0	2	.000	31	5	0	0	3	64	72	3	29	28	14.3	4.08	105	.285	.360	0	—	0	1	2	0	0.0
Total	8	14	32	.304	122	58	3	1	4	406	429	40	190	262	14.1	4.68	86	.274	.359	13	.144	-1	-41	-29	-3	-3.3

● RICK MAHLER

Mahler, Richard Keith b: 8/5/53, Austin, Tex. BR/TR, 6'1", 202 lbs. Deb: 4/20/79 F

YEAR	TM/L	W	L	PCT	G	GS	CG	SH	SV	IP	H	HR	BB	SO	RAT	ERA	ERA+	OAV	OOB	BH	AVG	PB	PR	/A	PD	TPI
1979	Atl-N	0	0	—	15	0	0	0	0	22	28	4	11	12	16.0	6.14	66	.311	.386	1	.500	0	-6	-5	-0	0.0
1980	Atl-N	0	0	—	2	0	0	0	0	3^2	2	0	0	1	4.9	2.45	152	.154	.154	0	—	0	0	1	0	0.0
1981	Atl-N	8	6	.571	34	14	1	0	2	112^1	109	5	43	54	12.3	2.80	128	.258	.328	4	.148	-1	9	10	1	1.2
1982	*Atl-N	9	10	.474	39	33	5	2	0	205^1	213	18	62	105	12.1	4.21	89	.272	.327	11	.190	2	-14	-11	2	-0.6
1983	Atl-N	0	0	—	10	0	0	0	0	14^1	16	0	9	7	15.7	5.02	77	.296	.397	0	.000	-0	-2	-2	-0	0.0
1984	Atl-N	13	10	.565	38	29	9	1	0	222	209	13	62	106	11.1	3.12	123	.251	.305	21	.296	5	12	18	2	2.6
1985	Atl-N	17	15	.531	39	39	6	1	0	266^2	272	24	79	107	11.9	3.48	111	.268	.322	14	.156	1	3	11	1	1.3
1986	Atl-N	14	18	.438	39	39	7	1	0	237^2	283	25	95	137	14.4	4.88	81	.301	.367	16	.193	2	-31	-24	2	-2.6
1987	Atl-N	8	13	.381	39	28	3	1	0	197	212	24	85	95	13.7	4.98	87	.283	.357	11	.169	1	-20	-14	2	-1.0
1988	Atl-N	9	16	.360	39	34	5	0	0	249	279	17	42	131	11.9	3.69	100	.282	.317	9	.125	-2	-7	-0	1	-0.1
1989	Cin-N	9	13	.409	40	31	5	2	0	220^2	242	15	51	102	12.4	3.83	94	.282	.329	11	.177	2	-8	-6	-0	-0.4
1990	*Cin-N	7	6	.538	35	16	2	1	4	134^2	134	16	39	68	11.8	4.28	92	.261	.317	4	.114	-1	-7	-5	-0	-0.6
1991	Mon-N	1	3	.250	10	6	0	0	0	37^1	37	2	15	17	12.5	3.62	100	.268	.340	1	.111	-0	0	0	1	0.0
	Atl-N	1	1	.500	13	2	0	0	0	28^2	33	2	13	10	15.1	5.65	69	.282	.364	1	.200	0	-6	-6	0	-0.3
	Yr	2	4	.333	23	8	0	0	0	66	70	4	28	27	13.6	4.50	83	.273	.350	2	.143	-0	-6	-6	1	-0.3
Total	13	96	111	.464	392	271	43	9	6	1951^1	2069	165	606	952	12.5	3.99	96	.275	.332	104	.179	7	-77	-33	10	-0.5

● PAT MAHOMES

Mahomes, Patrick Lavon b: 8/9/70, Bryan, Tex. BR/TR, 6'4", 210 lbs. Deb: 4/12/92

YEAR	TM/L	W	L	PCT	G	GS	CG	SH	SV	IP	H	HR	BB	SO	RAT	ERA	ERA+	OAV	OOB	BH	AVG	PB	PR	/A	PD	TPI
1992	Min-A	3	4	.429	14	13	0	0	0	69^2	73	5	37	44	14.2	5.04	80	.279	.368	0	—	0	-9	-8	-1	-1.0
1993	Min-A	1	5	.167	12	5	0	0	0	37^1	47	8	16	23	15.4	7.71	56	.309	.379	0	—	0	-14	-14	0	-1.8
1994	Min-A	9	5	.643	21	21	0	0	0	120	121	22	62	53	13.8	4.72	103	.269	.359	0	—	0	1	2	-1	0.1

YEAR	TM/L	W	L	PCT	G	GS	CG	SH	SV	IP	H	HR	BB	SO	RAT	ERA	ERA+	OAV	OOB	BH	AVG	PB	PR	/A	PD	TPI
1995	Min-A	4	10	.286	47	7	0	0	3	94^2	100	22	47	67	14.2	6.37	75	.271	.356	0	—	0	-17	-17	0	-2.1
1996	Min-A	1	4	.200	20	5	0	0	0	45	63	10	27	30	18.0	7.20	71	.330	.413	0	—	0	-11	-10	0	-0.9
	Bos-A	2	0	1.000	11	0	0	0	2	12^1	9	3	6	6	10.9	5.84	87	.209	.306	0	—	0	-1	-1	-0	-0.2
	Yr	3	4	.429	31	5	0	0	2	57^1	72	13	33	36	16.5	6.91	74	.305	.390	0	—	0	-12	-11	0	-1.1
1997	Bos-A	1	0	1.000	10	0	0	0	0	10	15	2	10	5	24.3	8.10	57	.366	.509	0	—	0	-4	-4	-0	-0.4
Total	6	21	28	.429	135	51	0	0	5	389	428	72	205	228	14.8	5.88	80	.284	.372	0	—	0	-55	-52	-2	-6.3
● AL MAHON Mahon, Alfred Gwinn "Lefty" b: 9/23/09, Albion, Neb. d: 12/26/77, New Haven, Conn. BL/TL, 5'11", 160 lbs. Deb: 4/22/30																										
1930	Phi-A	0	0	—	3	0	0	0	0	4^1	11	0	7	0	37.4	22.85	20	.579	.692	0	.000	0	-9	-9	0	0.0
● CHRIS MAHONEY Mahoney, Christopher John b: 6/11/1885, Milton, Mass. d: 7/15/54, Visalia, Cal. BR/TR, 5'9", 160 lbs. Deb: 7/12/10																										
1910	Bos-A	0	1	.000	2	1	0	0	1	11	16	1	5	6	17.2	3.27	78	.327	.389	1	.143	-0	-1	-1	1	-0.1
● MIKE MAHONEY Mahoney, George W. "Big Mike" b: 12/5/1873, Boston, Mass. d: 1/3/40, Boston, Mass. BR, 6'4", 220 lbs. Deb: 5/18/1897 ♦																										
1897	Bos-N	0	0	—	1	0	0	0	0	1	3	0	1	1	36.0	18.00	25	.500	.571	1	.500	0	-2	-2	0	0.0
● BOB MAHONEY Mahoney, Robert Paul b: 6/20/28, LeRoy, Minn. BR/TR, 6'1", 185 lbs. Deb: 5/3/51																										
1951	Chi-A	0	0	—	3	0	0	0	0	6^2	5	1	5	3	13.5	5.40	75	.208	.345	0	—	0	-1	-1	-0	0.0
	StL-A	2	5	.286	30	4	0	0	0	81	86	7	41	30	14.1	4.44	99	.274	.358	4	.222	-0	-3	-0	-1	-0.1
	Yr	2	5	.286	33	4	0	0	0	87^2	91	8	46	33	14.1	4.52	97	.269	.357	4	.222	-0	-4	-1	-1	-0.1
1952	StL-A	0	0	—	3	0	0	0	0	3	8	0	4	1	36.0	18.00	22	.500	.600	0	—	0	-5	-5	-0	0.0
Total	2	2	5	.286	36	4	0	0	0	90^2	99	8	50	34	14.8	4.96	88	.280	.369	4	.222	-0	-9	-6	-1	-0.1
● DUSTER MAILS Mails, John Walter "Walter" or "The Great" b: 10/1/1894, San Quentin, Cal. d: 7/5/74, San Francisco, Cal BL/TL, 6', 195 lbs. Deb: 9/28/15																										
1915	Bro-N	0	1	.000	2	0	0	0	0	5	6	2	5	3	19.8	3.60	77	.333	.478	0	.000	-0	-0	-0	0	-0.1
1916	Bro-N	0	1	.000	11	0	0	0	0	17^1	15	1	9	13	12.5	3.63	74	.242	.338	1	.250	0	-2	-2	-0	-0.1
1920	*Cle-A	7	0	1.000	9	8	6	2	0	63^1	54	1	18	25	10.2	1.85	206	.230	.285	4	.200	0	14	14	-1	1.3
1921	Cle-A	14	8	.636	34	24	10	2	2	194^1	210	4	89	87	13.9	3.94	108	.283	.361	6	.094	-4	8	7	-3	0.0
1922	Cle-A	4	7	.364	26	13	4	1	0	104	122	8	40	54	14.4	5.28	76	.291	.359	5	.161	-0	-14	-15	0	-1.3
1925	StL-N	7	7	.500	21	16	9	0	0	131	145	11	58	49	14.4	4.60	94	.279	.360	6	.133	-2	-5	-4	-1	-0.7
1926	StL-N	0	1	.000	1	0	0	0	0	1	2	0	1	1	27.0	0.00	—	.400	.500	0	—	0	0	0	0	0.5
Total	7	32	25	.561	104	61	29	5	2	516	554	27	220	232	13.7	4.10	100	.277	.352	22	.133	-7	0	0	-5	-0.4
● WOODY MAIN Main, Forrest Harry b: 2/12/22, Delano, Cal. d: 6/27/92, Whittier, Cal. BR/TR, 6'3.5", 195 lbs. Deb: 4/21/48																										
1948	Pit-N	1	1	.500	17	0	0	0	0	27	35	4	19	12	18.0	8.33	49	.324	.425	0	.000	-0	-13	-13	0	-0.8
1950	Pit-N	1	0	1.000	12	0	0	0	1	20^1	21	2	11	12	14.6	4.87	90	.256	.351	2	.400	0	-2	-1	0	0.0
1952	Pit-N	2	12	.143	48	11	2	0	2	153^1	149	14	52	79	11.8	4.46	90	.253	.314	2	.054	-3	-12	-8	-3	-1.3
1953	Pit-N	0	0	—	2	0	0	0	0	4	5	1	2	4	15.8	11.25	40	.294	.368	0	—	0	-3	-3	-0	0.0
Total	4	4	13	.235	79	11	2	0	3	204^2	210	21	84	107	13.0	5.14	79	.264	.335	4	.091	-3	-30	-25	-3	-2.1
● ALEX MAIN Main, Miles Grant b: 5/13/1884, Montrose, Mich. d: 12/29/65, Royal Oak, Mich. BL/TR, 6'5", 195 lbs. Deb: 4/18/14																										
1914	Det-A	6	6	.500	32	12	5	1	3	138^1	131	2	59	55	12.6	2.67	105	.259	.340	4	.100	-2	1	2	4	0.4
1915	KC-F	13	14	.481	35	28	18	2	3	230	181	4	75	91	10.2	2.54	103	.222	.291	15	.197	-0	5	2	3	0.6
1918	Phi-N	2	2	.500	8	4	1	1	0	35	30	1	16	14	13.1	4.63	65	.240	.349	1	.091	-1	-7	-6	0	-0.8
Total	3	21	22	.488	75	44	24	4	6	403^1	342	7	150	160	11.3	2.77	98	.236	.313	20	.157	-3	-1	-2	7	0.2
● JIM MAINS Mains, James Royal b: 6/12/22, Bridgton, Maine d: 3/17/69, Bridgton, Maine BR/TR, 6'2", 190 lbs. Deb: 8/22/43																										
1943	Phi-A	0	1	.000	1	1	1	0	0	8	9	0	3	4	13.5	5.63	60	.281	.343	0	.000	0	-2	-2	-0	-0.2
● WILLARD MAINS Mains, Willard Eben "Grasshopper" b: 7/7/1868, N.Windham, Maine d: 5/23/23, Bridgton, Maine TR, 6'2", 190 lbs. Deb: 8/3/1888																										
1888	Chi-N	1	1	.500	2	2	1	0	0	11	8	0	6	5	12.3	4.91	62	.211	.333	1	.143	-0	-3	-2	-0	-0.4
1891	Cin-a	12	12	.500	30	23	19	0	0	204	196	3	107	76	13.9	2.69	153	.244	.342	22	.244	1	23	32	3	3.5
	Mil-a	0	2	.000	2	2	1	0	0	10	14	1	10	2	21.6	10.80	41	.318	.444	3	.600	1	-8	-7	0	-0.9
	Yr	12	14	.462	32	25	20	0	0	214	210	4	117	78	13.8	3.07	135	.244	.335	25	.263	2	16	25	3	2.6
1896	Bos-N	3	2	.600	8	5	3	0	1	42^2	43	1	31	13	16.0	5.48	83	.261	.384	6	.273	-0	-5	-4	-0	-0.4
Total	3	16	17	.485	42	32	24	0	1	267^2	261	5	154	96	14.5	3.53	118	.249	.353	32	.258	1	8	19	3	1.8
● FRANK MAKOSKY Makosky, Frank b: 1/20/10, Boonton, N.J. d: 1/10/87, Stroudsburg, Pa. BR/TR, 6'1", 185 lbs. Deb: 4/30/37																										
1937	NY-A	5	2	.714	26	1	1	0	3	58	64	6	24	27	13.7	4.97	90	.277	.345	5	.313	1	-2	-3	2	-0.1
● TOM MAKOWSKI Makowski, Thomas Anthony b: 12/22/50, Buffalo, N.Y. BR/TL, 5'11", 185 lbs. Deb: 5/1/75																										
1975	Det-A	0	0	—	3	0	0	0	0	9^1	10	2	9	3	18.3	4.82	83	.278	.422	0	—	0	-1	-1	0	-0.1
● JOHN MALARKEY Malarkey, John S. "Liz" b: 5/4/1872, Springfield, Ohio d: 10/29/49, Cincinnati, Ohio TR, 5'11", 155 lbs. Deb: 9/21/1894																										
1894	Was-N	2	1	.667	3	3	3	0	0	26	42	1	5	3	16.3	4.15	127	.359	.385	1	.071	-2	3	3	-1	0.0
1895	Was-N	0	8	.000	22	8	5	0	2	100^2	135	3	60	32	18.1	5.99	80	.316	.410	5	.135	-4	-14	-13	-1	-1.2
1896	Was-N	0	1	.000	1	1	0	0	0	7	9	1	3	0	15.4	1.29	343	.310	.375	1	.500	1	2	2	0	0.4
1899	Chi-N	0	1	.000	1	1	1	0	0	9	19	0	5	7	25.0	13.00	29	.422	.490	1	.200	0	-9	-9	0	-0.6
1902	Bos-N	8	10	.444	21	19	17	1	1	170^1	158	0	58	39	11.4	2.59	109	.246	.309	13	.210	2	4	4	2	0.9
1903	Bos-N	11	16	.407	32	27	25	2	0	253	266	5	96	98	13.3	3.09	104	.272	.344	14	.161	1	5	3	2	0.6
Total	6	21	37	.362	80	59	51	3	3	566	629	10	227	179	13.9	3.64	96	.281	.353	35	.169	-2	-8	-9	2	0.1
● BILL MALARKEY Malarkey, William John b: 11/26/1878, Port Byron, Ill. d: 12/12/56, Phoenix, Ariz. BR/TR, 5'10", 185 lbs. Deb: 4/16/08																										
1908	NY-N	0	2	.000	15	0	0	0	2	35	31	1	10	12	10.8	2.57	94	.242	.302	0	.000	-1	-1	-1	-0	-0.2
● CARLOS MALDONADO Maldonado, Carlos Cesar (Delgado) b: 10/18/66, Chepo, Panama BB/TR, 6'2", 210 lbs. Deb: 9/16/90																										
1990	KC-A	0	0	—	4	0	0	0	0	6	9	0	4	9	19.5	9.00	43	.346	.433	0	—	0	-3	-3	-0	0.1
1991	KC-A	0	0	—	5	0	0	0	0	7^2	11	0	9	1	23.5	8.22	50	.333	.476	0	—	0	-4	-3	-0	-0.1
1993	Mil-A	2	2	.500	29	0	0	0	1	37^1	40	2	17	18	13.7	4.58	93	.282	.358	0	—	0	-1	-1	0	-0.1
Total	3	2	2	.500	38	0	0	0	1	51	60	2	30	28	15.9	5.65	74	.299	.390	0	—	0	-8	-8	-1	-0.1
● CY MALIS Malis, Cyrus Sol b: 2/26/07, Philadelphia, Pa. d: 1/12/71, N.Hollywood, Cal. BR/TR, 5'11", 175 lbs. Deb: 8/17/34																										
1934	Phi-N	0	0	—	1	0	0	0	0	3^2	4	0	2	1	14.7	4.91	96	.267	.353	0	—	0	-0	-0	-0	0.0
● MAL MALLETTE Mallette, Malcolm Francis b: 1/30/22, Syracuse, N.Y. BL/TL, 6'2", 200 lbs. Deb: 9/25/50																										
1950	Bro-N	0	0	—	2	0	0	0	0	1^1	2	0	1	2	20.3	0.00	—	.333	.429	0	—	0	1	1	0	0.0
● ROB MALLICOAT Mallicoat, Robbin Dale b: 11/16/64, St.Helens, Ore. BL/TL, 6'3", 180 lbs. Deb: 9/11/87																										
1987	Hou-N	0	0	—	4	1	0	0	0	6^2	8	0	6	4	18.9	6.75	58	.320	.452	0	—	0	-2	-2	0	0.0
1991	Hou-N	0	2	.000	24	0	0	0	1	23^1	22	2	13	18	14.3	3.86	91	.259	.370	0	.000	-0	-0	-1	-1	-0.2
1992	Hou-N	0	0	—	23	0	0	0	0	23^2	26	2	19	20	19.0	7.23	47	.283	.431	0	.000	-0	-10	-10	-0	0.0
Total	3	0	2	.000	51	1	0	0	1	53^2	56	4	38	42	16.9	5.70	61	.277	.409	0	.000	-0	-12	-13	-1	-0.2
● ALEX MALLOY Malloy, Archibald Alexander "Lick" b: 10/31/1886, Laurinburg, N.C. d: 3/1/61, Ferris, Tex. BR/TR, 6'2", 180 lbs. Deb: 9/10/10																										
1910	StL-A	0	6	.000	7	6	4	0	0	52^2	47	0	17	27	11.3	2.56	97	.261	.332	1	.063	-1	-0	-1	0	-0.2
● HERM MALLOY Malloy, Herman "Tug" b: 6/1/1885, Massillon, Ohio d: 5/9/42, Massillon, Ohio BR/TR, 6', Deb: 10/6/07																										
1907	Det-A	0	1	.000	1	1	1	0	0	8	13	1	5	6	20.3	5.63	46	.371	.450	1	.250	0	-3	-3	-0	-0.3
1908	Det-A	0	2	.000	3	2	2	0	0	17	20	1	4	8	13.8	3.71	65	.278	.333	3	.333	1	-2	-2	1	-0.1
Total	2	0	3	.000	4	3	3	0	0	25	33	2	9	14	15.8	4.32	57	.308	.373	4	.308	1	-5	-5	1	-0.4
● BOB MALLOY Malloy, Robert Paul b: 5/28/18, Canonsburg, Pa. BR/TR, 5'11", 185 lbs. Deb: 5/4/43																										
1943	Cin-N	0	0	—	6	0	0	0	0	10	14	1	8	4	19.8	6.30	53	.778	.846	2	.667	1	-3	-3	-0	0.1

YEAR	TM/L	W	L	PCT	G	GS	CG	SH	SV	IP	H	HR	BB	SO	RAT	ERA	ERA+	OAV	OOB	BH	AVG	PB	PR	/A	PD	TPI
1944	Cin-N	1	1	.500	9	0	0	0	0	23^1	22	0	11	4	12.7	3.09	113	.265	.351	0	.000	-1	1	1	0	0.0
1946	Cin-N	2	5	.286	27	3	1	0	2	72	71	2	26	24	12.4	2.75	122	.265	.334	5	.278	1	5	5	-1	0.5
1947	Cin-N	0	0	—	1	0	0	0	0	1	3	1	0	1	27.0	18.00	23	.600	.600	0	—	0	-2	-2	0	0.0
1949	StL-A	1	1	.500	5	0	0	0	0	9^2	6	0	7	2	12.1	2.79	162	.200	.351	0	.000	-0	2	2	0	0.3
Total	5	4	7	.364	48	3	1	0	2	116	116	4	52	35	13.2	3.26	106	.287	.371	7	.226	1	3	3	-1	0.9

● BOB MALLOY

Malloy, Robert William b: 11/24/64, Arlington, Va. BR/TR, 6′5″, 200 lbs. Deb: 5/26/87

YEAR	TM/L	W	L	PCT	G	GS	CG	SH	SV	IP	H	HR	BB	SO	RAT	ERA	ERA+	OAV	OOB	BH	AVG	PB	PR	/A	PD	TPI
1987	Tex-A	0	0	—	2	2	0	0	0	11	13	6	3	8	13.1	6.55	68	.271	.314	0	—	0	-3	-3	-0	0.0
1990	Mon-N	0	0	—	1	0	0	0	0	2	1	0	1	1	9.0	0.00	—	.143	.250	0	—	0	1	1	-0	0.0
Total	2	0	0	—	3	2	0	0	0	13	14	6	4	9	12.5	5.54	78	.255	.305	0	—	0	-2	-2	-0	0.0

● CHUCK MALONE

Malone, Charles Ray b: 7/8/65, Harrisburg, Ark. BR/TR, 6′7″, 250 lbs. Deb: 9/6/90

YEAR	TM/L	W	L	PCT	G	GS	CG	SH	SV	IP	H	HR	BB	SO	RAT	ERA	ERA+	OAV	OOB	BH	AVG	PB	PR	/A	PD	TPI
1990	Phi-N	1	0	1.000	7	0	0	0	0	7^1	3	1	11	7	17.2	3.68	104	.130	.412	0	—	0	0	0	-0	0.0

● MARTIN MALONE

Malone, Martin Deb: 6/20/1872

YEAR	TM/L	W	L	PCT	G	GS	CG	SH	SV	IP	H	HR	BB	SO	RAT	ERA	ERA+	OAV	OOB	BH	AVG	PB	PR	/A	PD	TPI
1872	Eck-n	0	3	.000	3	3	3	0	0	27	85	1	0	0	28.3	10.33	33	.445	.445	5	.313	1	-20	-21		-1.2

● PAT MALONE

Malone, Perce Leigh b: 9/25/02, Altoona, Pa. d: 5/13/43, Altoona, Pa. BL/TR, 6′, 200 lbs. Deb: 4/12/28

YEAR	TM/L	W	L	PCT	G	GS	CG	SH	SV	IP	H	HR	BB	SO	RAT	ERA	ERA+	OAV	OOB	BH	AVG	PB	PR	/A	PD	TPI
1928	Chi-N	18	13	.581	42	25	16	2	2	250^2	218	15	99	155	11.6	2.84	136	.236	.314	18	.189	1	32	28	0	3.3
1929	*Chi-N	**22**	10	.688	40	30	19	**5**	2	267	283	12	102	**166**	13.2	3.57	129	.276	.345	22	.210	2	34	31	-3	3.0
1930	Chi-N	**20**	9	.690	45	35	**22**	1	4	271^2	290	14	96	142	13.0	3.94	124	.271	.334	26	.248	5	31	28	-2	2.8
1931	Chi-N	16	9	.640	36	30	12	2	0	228^1	229	9	88	112	12.7	3.90	99	.258	.328	17	.215	2	-1	-1	0	0.0
1932	*Chi-N	15	17	.469	37	33	17	2	0	237	222	13	78	120	11.6	3.38	111	.244	.308	14	.179	0	13	10	-3	0.9
1933	Chi-N	10	14	.417	31	26	13	2	0	186^1	186	10	59	72	12.1	3.91	84	.258	.318	10	.159	-2	-12	-13	-1	-1.9
1934	Chi-N	14	7	.667	34	21	8	1	0	191	200	14	55	111	12.2	3.53	110	.270	.322	11	.172	-2	11	7	-1	0.4
1935	NY-A	3	5	.375	29	2	0	0	3	56^1	53	7	33	25	13.9	5.43	75	.252	.357	0	.000	-3	-6	-9	-0	-1.4
1936	*NY-A	12	4	.750	35	9	5	0	**9**	134^2	144	4	60	72	13.9	3.81	122	.273	.352	10	.196	-1	18	13	-2	1.2
1937	NY-A	4	4	.500	28	9	3	0	6	92	109	5	35	49	14.5	5.48	81	.291	.357	1	.030	-5	-9	-11	-2	-1.5
Total	10	134	92	.593	357	220	115	15	26	1915	1934	103	705	1024	12.6	3.74	111	.262	.330	129	.188	-2	112	85	-14	6.8

● CHARLIE MALONEY

Maloney, Charles Michael b: 5/22/1886, Cambridge, Mass. d: 1/17/67, Arlington, Mass. BR/TR, 5′8″, 155 lbs. Deb: 8/10/08

YEAR	TM/L	W	L	PCT	G	GS	CG	SH	SV	IP	H	HR	BB	SO	RAT	ERA	ERA+	OAV	OOB	BH	AVG	PB	PR	/A	PD	TPI
1908	Bos-N	0	0	—	1	0	0	0	0	2	3	0	1	0	18.0	4.50	54	.429	.500	0	—	0	-0	-0	0	0.0

● JIM MALONEY

Maloney, James William b: 6/2/40, Fresno, Cal. BL/TR, 6′2″, 207 lbs. Deb: 7/27/60

YEAR	TM/L	W	L	PCT	G	GS	CG	SH	SV	IP	H	HR	BB	SO	RAT	ERA	ERA+	OAV	OOB	BH	AVG	PB	PR	/A	PD	TPI
1960	Cin-N	2	6	.250	11	10	2	1	0	63^2	61	5	37	48	14.1	4.66	82	.255	.360	2	.111	-0	-6	-6	-0	-0.7
1961	*Cin-N	6	7	.462	27	11	1	0	2	94^2	86	16	59	57	13.9	4.37	93	.242	.352	11	.379	4	-4	-3	-1	-0.1
1962	Cin-N	9	7	.563	22	17	3	0	1	115^1	90	11	66	105	12.3	3.51	115	.214	.323	8	.186	0	6	7	-1	0.7
1963	Cin-N	23	7	.767	33	33	13	6	0	250^1	183	17	88	265	10.0	2.77	121	.202	.276	15	.169	1	14	16	-2	1.8
1964	Cin-N	15	10	.600	31	31	11	2	0	216	175	16	83	214	10.8	2.71	133	.222	.297	11	.151	1	20	22	-2	2.4
1965	Cin-N★	20	9	.690	33	33	14	5	0	255^1	189	13	110	244	10.7	2.54	148	.206	.295	20	.225	7	28	34	-1	4.6
1966	Cin-N	16	8	.667	32	32	10	**5**	0	224^2	174	18	90	216	11.0	2.80	139	.214	.300	18	.222	3	20	27	-0	3.2
1967	Cin-N	15	11	.577	30	29	6	3	0	196^1	181	8	72	153	11.7	3.25	115	.247	.317	11	.159	-0	3	11	-1	1.3
1968	Cin-N	16	10	.615	33	32	8	5	0	207	183	17	80	181	11.5	3.61	88	.239	.313	18	.243	6	-14	-10	-2	-0.8
1969	Cin-N	12	5	.706	30	27	6	3	0	178^2	135	11	86	102	11.2	2.77	136	.208	.302	11	.200	6	16	20	-1	2.4
1970	Cin-N	0	1	.000	7	3	0	0	1	16^2	26	3	15	7	23.2	11.34	36	.366	.489	0	.000	-0	-14	-14	0	-0.8
1971	Cal-A	0	3	.000	13	4	0	0	0	30^1	35	3	24	13	17.8	5.04	64	.294	.417	1	.200	0	-5	-6	-0	-0.6
Total	12	134	84	.615	302	262	74	30	4	1849	1518	138	810	1605	11.5	3.19	115	.224	.310	126	.201	26	64	98	-10	13.4

● SEAN MALONEY

Maloney, Sean Patrick b: 5/25/71, South Kingstown, R.I. BR/TR, 6′7″, 210 lbs. Deb: 4/28/97

YEAR	TM/L	W	L	PCT	G	GS	CG	SH	SV	IP	H	HR	BB	SO	RAT	ERA	ERA+	OAV	OOB	BH	AVG	PB	PR	/A	PD	TPI
1997	Mil-A	0	0	—	3	0	0	0	0	7	7	1	2	5	14.1	5.14	90	.304	.407	0	—	0	-0	-0	-0	0.0
1998	LA-N	0	1	.000	11	0	0	0	0	12^2	13	2	5	11	14.2	4.97	78	.265	.357	0	.000	-0	-1	-2	0	-0.1
Total	2	0	1	.000	14	0	0	0	0	19^2	20	3	7	16	14.2	5.03	82	.278	.373	0	.000	-0	-1	-2	0	-0.1

● PAUL MALOY

Maloy, Paul Augustus "Biff" b: 6/4/1892, Bascom, Ohio d: 3/18/76, Sandusky, Ohio BR/TR, 5′11″, 185 lbs. Deb: 7/11/13

YEAR	TM/L	W	L	PCT	G	GS	CG	SH	SV	IP	H	HR	BB	SO	RAT	ERA	ERA+	OAV	OOB	BH	AVG	PB	PR	/A	PD	TPI
1913	Bos-A	0	0	—	2	0	0	0	0	2	2	0	1	0	22.5	9.00	33	.286	.500	0	—	0	-1	-1	-0	0.0

● GORDON MALTZBERGER

Maltzberger, Gordon Ralph "Maltzy" b: 9/4/12, Utopia, Tex. d: 12/11/74, Rialto, Cal. BR/TR, 6′, 170 lbs. Deb: 4/27/43 C

YEAR	TM/L	W	L	PCT	G	GS	CG	SH	SV	IP	H	HR	BB	SO	RAT	ERA	ERA+	OAV	OOB	BH	AVG	PB	PR	/A	PD	TPI
1943	Chi-A	7	4	.636	37	0	0	0	**14**	98^2	86	8	24	48	10.2	2.46	136	.236	.287	3	.120	0	9	10	0	1.5
1944	Chi-A	10	5	.667	46	0	0	0	**12**	91^1	81	2	19	49	10.0	2.96	116	.235	.277	3	.136	-1	5	5	-1	0.8
1946	Chi-A	2	0	1.000	19	0	0	0	2	39^2	30	3	6	17	8.4	1.59	215	.205	.242	0	.000	-0	8	8	-1	0.4
1947	Chi-A	1	4	.200	33	0	0	0	5	63^2	61	4	25	22	12.3	3.39	108	.257	.331	1	.143	1	2	2	1	0.3
Total	4	20	13	.606	135	0	0	0	33	293^1	258	17	74	136	10.3	2.70	128	.236	.288	7	.117	0	25	24	0	3.0

● AL MAMAUX

Mamaux, Albert Leon b: 5/30/1894, Pittsburgh, Pa. d: 1/2/63, Santa Monica, Cal. BR/TR, 6′0.5″, 168 lbs. Deb: 9/23/13

YEAR	TM/L	W	L	PCT	G	GS	CG	SH	SV	IP	H	HR	BB	SO	RAT	ERA	ERA+	OAV	OOB	BH	AVG	PB	PR	/A	PD	TPI
1913	Pit-N	0	0	—	1	0	0	0	0	3	2	0	2	2	12.0	3.00	101	.167	.286	0	.000	-0	0	0	0	0.0
1914	Pit-N	5	2	.714	13	6	4	2	0	63	41	1	24	30	9.6	1.71	155	.186	.272	5	.250	1	8	7	1	1.0
1915	Pit-N	21	8	.724	38	30	17	8	0	251^2	182	3	96	152	10.3	2.04	134	.208	.293	15	.163	-2	20	19	-3	1.5
1916	Pit-N	21	15	.583	45	37	26	1	2	310	264	3	136	163	11.9	2.53	106	.239	.327	21	.191	1	3	5	0	0.9
1917	Pit-N	2	11	.154	16	13	5	0	0	85^2	92	1	50	22	15.2	5.25	54	.278	.378	7	.226	0	-24	-23	-1	-3.2
1918	Bro-N	0	1	.000	2	1	0	0	0	8	14	0	2	2	18.0	6.75	41	.438	.471	0	.000	-0	-4	-4	1	-0.4
1919	Bro-N	10	12	.455	30	22	16	2	0	199^1	174	2	66	80	11.0	2.66	112	.245	.312	11	.175	0	6	7	-1	0.7
1920	*Bro-N	12	8	.600	41	17	9	2	4	190^2	172	2	63	101	11.3	2.69	119	.255	.322	10	.167	-0	9	11	-1	1.0
1921	Bro-N	3	3	.500	12	1	0	0	1	43	36	1	13	21	10.5	3.14	124	.240	.305	2	.182	-0	3	4	1	0.5
1922	Bro-N	1	4	.200	37	7	1	0	3	87^2	97	7	33	35	13.6	3.70	110	.290	.358	4	.235	3	4	4	0	0.5
1923	Bro-N	0	2	.000	5	1	0	0	0	13	20	0	6	5	18.0	8.31	47	.385	.448	1	.500	0	-6	-6	0	-0.8
1924	NY-A	1	1	.500	14	2	0	0	0	38	44	2	20	12	15.4	5.68	73	.308	.396	1	.077	-1	-6	-6	-1	-0.5
Total	12	76	67	.531	254	137	78	15	10	1293	1138	22	511	625	11.7	2.90	104	.245	.325	77	.182	2	13	17	-3	1.2

● HAL MANDERS

Manders, Harold Carl b: 6/14/17, Waukee, Iowa BR/TR, 6′, 187 lbs. Deb: 8/12/41

YEAR	TM/L	W	L	PCT	G	GS	CG	SH	SV	IP	H	HR	BB	SO	RAT	ERA	ERA+	OAV	OOB	BH	AVG	PB	PR	/A	PD	TPI
1941	Det-A	1	0	1.000	8	0	0	0	0	15^1	13	0	8	7	12.9	2.35	194	.236	.344	0	.000	-1	3	4	-0	0.1
1942	Det-A	2	0	1.000	18	0	0	0	0	33	39	4	15	14	15.0	4.09	97	.307	.385	1	.250	0	-2	-1	0	0.0
1946	Det-A	0	0	—	2	0	0	0	0	6	8	1	2	3	16.5	10.50	35	.364	.440	1	.500	0	-5	-5	-0	0.0
	Chi-N	0	1	.000	2	1	0	0	0	6	11	1	3	4	22.5	9.00	37	.423	.500	0	.000	-0	-4	-4	-0	-0.6
Total	3	3	1	.750	30	1	0	0	0	60^1	71	6	28	28	15.4	4.77	84	.309	.393	2	.167	-0	-7	-5	-1	-0.5

● LEO MANGUM

Mangum, Leo Allan "Blackie" b: 5/24/1896, Durham, N.C. d: 7/9/74, Lima, Ohio BR/TR, 6′1″, 187 lbs. Deb: 7/11/24

YEAR	TM/L	W	L	PCT	G	GS	CG	SH	SV	IP	H	HR	BB	SO	RAT	ERA	ERA+	OAV	OOB	BH	AVG	PB	PR	/A	PD	TPI
1924	Chi-A	1	4	.200	13	7	1	0	0	47	69	3	25	12	18.2	7.09	58	.359	.436	1	.071	-1	-15	-15	0	-1.4
1925	Chi-A	1	0	1.000	7	0	0	0	0	15	25	0	6	6	18.6	7.80	53	.373	.425	2	.500	1	-6	-6	-0	-0.3
1928	NY-N	0	0	—	1	1	0	0	0	3	6	0	5	1	33.0	15.00	26	.500	.647	1	1.000	0	-4	-4	1	0.1
1932	Bos-N	0	0	—	7	0	0	0	0	10^1	17	1	0	3	14.8	5.23	72	.333	.333	0	.000	-0	-2	-2	1	0.1
1933	Bos-N	4	3	.571	25	5	2	1	0	84	93	2	11	28	11.1	3.32	92	.280	.303	2	.091	-2	0	-2	2	-0.2
1934	Bos-N	5	3	.625	29	3	1	0	1	94^1	127	9	23	28	14.3	5.72	67	.315	.352	9	.281	2	-17	-20	1	-1.2
1935	Bos-N	0	0	—	3	0	0	0	0	4^2	6	0	2	0	15.4	3.86	98	.300	.364	0	—	0	0	-0	-0	0.0
Total	7	11	10	.524	85	16	4	1	1	258^1	343	15	72	78	14.5	5.37	68	.318	.362	15	.200	0	-43	-49	4	-2.9

● ERNIE MANNING

Manning, Ernest Devon "Ed" b: 10/9/1890, Florala, Ala. d: 4/28/73, Pensacola, Fla. BL/TR, 6′, 175 lbs. Deb: 5/3/14

YEAR	TM/L	W	L	PCT	G	GS	CG	SH	SV	IP	H	HR	BB	SO	RAT	ERA	ERA+	OAV	OOB	BH	AVG	PB	PR	/A	PD	TPI
1914	StL-A	0	0	—	4	0	0	0	0	10	11	0	3	3	12.6	3.60	75	.297	.350	0	.000	-0	-1	-1	0	0.0

● JIM MANNING

Manning, James Benjamin b: 7/21/43, L'Anse, Mich. BR/TR, 6′1″, 185 lbs. Deb: 4/15/62

YEAR	TM/L	W	L	PCT	G	GS	CG	SH	SV	IP	H	HR	BB	SO	RAT	ERA	ERA+	OAV	OOB	BH	AVG	PB	PR	/A	PD	TPI
1962	Min-A	0	0	—	5	1	0	0	0	7	14	0	1	3	20.6	5.14	79	.389	.421	0	.000	-0	-1	-1	0	0.0

● JACK MANNING

Manning, John E. b: 12/20/1853, Braintree, Mass. d: 8/15/29, Boston, Mass. BR/TR, 5′8.5″, 158 lbs. Deb: 4/23/1873 M◆

YEAR	TM/L	W	L	PCT	G	GS	CG	SH	SV	IP	H	HR	BB	SO	RAT	ERA	ERA+	OAV	OOB	BH	AVG	PB	PR	/A	PD	TPI
1874	Bal-n	4	16	.200	22	20	17	0	0	176^2	222	2	12	12	11.9	2.09	106	.266	.277	61	.351	7	2	2		0.8

YEAR TM/L	W	L	PCT	G	GS	CG	SH	SV	IP	H	HR	BB	SO	RAT	ERA	ERA+	OAV	OOB	BH	AVG	PB	PR	/A	PD	TPI
1875 Bos-n	16	2	.889	27	18	8	1	6	144	152	1	14	34	10.4	2.38	90	.247	.263	94	.270	4	-2	-4		-0.3
1876 Bos-N	18	5	.783	34	20	13	0	**5**	197^1	213	1	32	24	11.2	2.14	105	.252	.279	76	.264	3	4	2	0	0.4
1877 Cin-N	0	4	.000	10	4	2	0	1	44	83	1	7	6	18.4	6.95	38	.379	.398	80	.317	4	-20	-21	0	-1.3
1878 Bos-N	1	0	1.000	3	1	1	0	0	11^1	24	1	5	2	23.0	14.29	17	.393	.439	63	.254	0	-15	-15	0	-0.9
Total 2 n	20	18	.526	49	38	25	1	6	320^2	374	3	26	46	11.2	2.22	99	.258	.271	199	.290	11	-1	-1		0.5
Total 3	19	9	.679	47	25	16	0	6	252^2	320	3	44	32	13.0	3.53	66	.284	.311	725	.257	7	-32	-34	1	-1.8

● **RUBE MANNING** Manning, Walter S. b: 4/29/1883, Chambersburg, Pa. d: 4/23/30, Williamsport, Pa. BR/TR, 6', 180 lbs. Deb: 9/25/07

YEAR TM/L	W	L	PCT	G	GS	CG	SH	SV	IP	H	HR	BB	SO	RAT	ERA	ERA+	OAV	OOB	BH	AVG	PB	PR	/A	PD	TPI
1907 NY-A	0	1	.000	1	1	1	0	0	9	8	0	3	3	12.0	3.00	93	.242	.324	0	.000	-0	-0	-0	-0	-0.1
1908 NY-A	13	16	.448	41	26	19	2	1	245	228	4	86	113	12.2	2.94	84	.256	.334	17	.187	0	-15	-13	-1	-1.6
1909 NY-A	7	11	.389	26	21	11	2	1	173	167	2	48	71	11.7	3.17	80	.265	.326	11	.183	-0	-13	-12	-1	-1.4
1910 NY-A	2	4	.333	16	9	4	0	0	75	80	4	25	25	13.1	3.72	71	.283	.349	5	.192	0	-10	-9	-1	-0.7
Total 4	22	32	.407	84	57	35	4	2	502	483	10	162	212	12.1	3.14	81	.263	.333	33	.183	-0	-39	-34	-3	-3.8

● **RAMON MANON** Manon, Ramon (Reyes) b: 1/20/68, Santo Domingo, D.R. BR/TR, 6', 150 lbs. Deb: 4/19/90

YEAR TM/L	W	L	PCT	G	GS	CG	SH	SV	IP	H	HR	BB	SO	RAT	ERA	ERA+	OAV	OOB	BH	AVG	PB	PR	/A	PD	TPI
1990 Tex-A	0	0	—	1	0	0	0	0	2	3	0	3	0	27.0	13.50	29	.333	.500	0	—	0	-2	-2	0	0.0

● **TOM MANSELL** Mansell, Thomas E. "Brick" b: 1/1/1855, Auburn, N.Y. d: 10/6/34, Auburn, N.Y. BL/TR, 5'8", 160 lbs. Deb: 5/1/1879 F♦

YEAR TM/L	W	L	PCT	G	GS	CG	SH	SV	IP	H	HR	BB	SO	RAT	ERA	ERA+	OAV	OOB	BH	AVG	PB	PR	/A	PD	TPI
1883 Det-N	0	0	—	1	0	0	0	0	6^2	21	2	5	3	35.1	18.90	16	.553	.605	29	.221	0	-12	-12	-0	0.0

● **LOU MANSKE** Manske, Louis Hugo b: 7/4/1884, Milwaukee, Wis. d: 4/27/63, Milwaukee, Wis. BL/TL, 6', Deb: 8/31/06

YEAR TM/L	W	L	PCT	G	GS	CG	SH	SV	IP	H	HR	BB	SO	RAT	ERA	ERA+	OAV	OOB	BH	AVG	PB	PR	/A	PD	TPI
1906 Pit-N	0	0	—	2	1	0	0	0	8	12	0	5	6	19.1	5.63	48	.387	.472	0	.000	-1	-3	-3	-0	-0.1

● **MATT MANTEI** Mantei, Matthew Bruce b: 7/7/73, Tampa, Fla. BR/TR, 6'1", 180 lbs. Deb: 6/18/95

YEAR TM/L	W	L	PCT	G	GS	CG	SH	SV	IP	H	HR	BB	SO	RAT	ERA	ERA+	OAV	OOB	BH	AVG	PB	PR	/A	PD	TPI
1995 Fla-N	0	1	.000	12	0	0	0	0	13^1	12	1	13	15	16.9	4.73	89	.245	.403	0	—	0	-1	-1	0	0.0
1996 Fla-N	1	0	1.000	14	0	0	0	0	18^1	13	2	21	25	17.2	6.38	64	.197	.398	0	.000	-0	-4	-5	1	-0.2
1998 Fla-N	3	4	.429	42	0	0	0	9	54^2	38	1	23	63	11.2	2.96	138	.203	.313	1	.333	0	8	7	-0	1.0
Total 3	4	5	.444	68	0	0	0	9	86^1	63	4	57	103	13.3	3.96	104	.209	.349	1	.250	0	2	1	1	0.8

● **BARRY MANUEL** Manuel, Barry Paul b: 8/12/65, Mamou, La. BR/TR, 5'11", 180 lbs. Deb: 9/6/91

YEAR TM/L	W	L	PCT	G	GS	CG	SH	SV	IP	H	HR	BB	SO	RAT	ERA	ERA+	OAV	OOB	BH	AVG	PB	PR	/A	PD	TPI
1991 Tex-A	1	0	1.000	8	0	0	0	0	16	7	0	6	5	7.3	1.13	358	.143	.236	0	—	0	5	5	1	0.4
1992 Tex-A	1	0	1.000	3	0	0	0	0	5^2	6	2	1	9	12.7	4.76	80	.261	.320	0	—	0	-1	-1	-0	0.1
1996 Mon-N	4	1	.800	53	0	0	0	0	86	70	10	26	62	10.8	3.24	133	.219	.293	0	.000	-0	9	10	-1	0.4
1997 NY-N	0	1	.000	19	0	0	0	0	25^2	35	6	13	21	17.2	5.26	77	.324	.402	0	.000	-0	-3	-4	-1	-0.2
1998 Ari-N	1	0	1.000	13	0	0	0	0	15^2	17	5	14	12	18.4	7.47	58	.266	.405	0	—	0	-6	-6	-0	-0.4
Total 5	7	2	.778	96	0	0	0	0	149	135	23	60	109	12.4	3.87	109	.240	.324	0	.000	-1	5	6	-1	0.3

● **MOXIE MANUEL** Manuel, Mark Garfield b: 10/16/1881, Metropolis, Ill. d: 4/26/24, Memphis, Tenn. BR/TR, 5'11", 170 lbs. Deb: 9/25/05

YEAR TM/L	W	L	PCT	G	GS	CG	SH	SV	IP	H	HR	BB	SO	RAT	ERA	ERA+	OAV	OOB	BH	AVG	PB	PR	/A	PD	TPI
1905 Was-A	0	0	—	3	1	1	0	0	10	9	0	3	3	11.7	5.40	49	.243	.317	1	.250	0	-3	-3	0	0.0
1908 Chi-A	3	4	.429	18	6	3	0	1	60^1	52	0	25	25	11.8	3.28	71	.243	.328	1	.063	-1	-6	-6	0	-0.9
Total 2	3	4	.429	21	7	4	0	1	70^1	61	0	28	28	11.8	3.58	66	.243	.326	2	.100	-1	-9	-10	0	-0.9

● **DICK MANVILLE** Manville, Richard Wesley b: 12/25/26, Des Moines, Iowa BR/TR, 6'4", 192 lbs. Deb: 4/30/50

YEAR TM/L	W	L	PCT	G	GS	CG	SH	SV	IP	H	HR	BB	SO	RAT	ERA	ERA+	OAV	OOB	BH	AVG	PB	PR	/A	PD	TPI
1950 Bos-N	0	0	—	1	0	0	0	0	2	0	0	3	2	13.5	0.00	—	.000	.300	0	—	0	1	1	-0	0.0
1952 Chi-N	0	0	—	11	0	0	0	0	17	25	2	12	6	19.6	7.94	48	.362	.457	1	.500	0	-8	-8	0	0.1
Total 2	0	0	—	12	0	0	0	0	19	25	2	15	8	18.9	7.11	54	.329	.440	1	.500	0	-7	-7	0	0.1

● **JOSIAS MANZANILLO** Manzanillo, Josias (Adams) b: 10/16/67, San Pedro De Macoris, D.R. BR/TR, 6', 190 lbs. Deb: 10/5/91 F

YEAR TM/L	W	L	PCT	G	GS	CG	SH	SV	IP	H	HR	BB	SO	RAT	ERA	ERA+	OAV	OOB	BH	AVG	PB	PR	/A	PD	TPI
1991 Bos-A	0	0	—	1	0	0	0	0	1	2	0	3	1	45.0	18.00	24	.400	.625	0	—	0	-2	-2	0	-0.1
1993 Mil-A	1	1	.500	10	1	0	0	1	17	22	1	10	10	18.0	9.53	45	.314	.415	0	—	0	-10	-10	1	-1.0
NY-N	0	0	—	6	0	0	0	0	12	8	1	9	11	12.8	3.00	134	.186	.327	0	.000	-0	1	1	-0	0.0
1994 NY-N	3	2	.600	37	0	0	0	2	47^1	34	4	13	48	9.5	2.66	157	.200	.269	0	.000	-0	8	8	-0	0.7
1995 NY-N	1	2	.333	12	0	0	0	0	16	18	3	6	14	13.5	7.88	51	.273	.333	0	—	0	-7	-7	-0	-1.1
NY-A	0	0	—	11	0	0	0	0	17^1	19	1	9	11	15.6	2.08	222	.279	.380	0	—	0	5	5	0	0.1
1997 Sea-A	0	1	.000	16	0	0	0	0	18^1	19	3	17	18	17.7	5.40	83	.275	.419	0	.000	-0	-2	-2	-0	-0.1
Total 5	5	6	.455	93	1	0	0	3	129	122	13	67	113	13.7	4.67	91	.248	.347	0	.000	-1	-5	-6	-0	-1.5

● **RAVELO MANZANILLO** Manzanillo, Ravelo (Adams) b: 10/17/63, San Pedro De Macoris, D.R. BL/TL, 6', 210 lbs. Deb: 9/25/88 F

YEAR TM/L	W	L	PCT	G	GS	CG	SH	SV	IP	H	HR	BB	SO	RAT	ERA	ERA+	OAV	OOB	BH	AVG	PB	PR	/A	PD	TPI
1988 Chi-A	0	1	.000	2	2	0	0	0	9^1	7	1	12	10	19.3	5.79	69	.212	.435	0	—	0	-2	-2	0	-0.2
1994 Pit-N	4	2	.667	46	0	0	0	1	50	45	4	42	39	16.2	4.14	104	.245	.393	2	.667	1	0	1	0	0.2
1995 Pit-N	0	0	—	5	0	0	0	0	3^2	3	0	2	1	14.7	4.91	88	.231	.375	0	.000	-0	-0	-0	0	0.0
Total 3	4	3	.571	53	2	0	0	1	63	55	5	56	50	16.6	4.43	96	.239	.399	2	.500	1	-2	-1	0	0.0

● **ROLLA MAPEL** Mapel, Rolla Hamilton "Lefty" b: 3/9/1890, Lees Summit, Mo. d: 4/6/66, San Diego, Cal. BL/TL, 5'11.5", 165 lbs. Deb: 8/31/19

YEAR TM/L	W	L	PCT	G	GS	CG	SH	SV	IP	H	HR	BB	SO	RAT	ERA	ERA+	OAV	OOB	BH	AVG	PB	PR	/A	PD	TPI
1919 StL-A	0	3	.000	4	3	2	0	0	20	17	0	17	2	16.6	4.50	74	.262	.435	1	.167	-0	-3	-3	1	-0.3

● **PAUL MARAK** Marak, Paul Patrick b: 8/2/65, Lakenheath, England BR/TR, 6'2", 175 lbs. Deb: 9/1/90

YEAR TM/L	W	L	PCT	G	GS	CG	SH	SV	IP	H	HR	BB	SO	RAT	ERA	ERA+	OAV	OOB	BH	AVG	PB	PR	/A	PD	TPI
1990 Atl-N	1	2	.333	7	7	1	1	0	39	39	2	19	15	14.1	3.69	109	.267	.363	1	.091	-0	0	1	1	0.2

● **GEORGES MARANDA** Maranda, Georges Henri b: 1/15/32, Levis, Que., Can. BR/TR, 6'2", 195 lbs. Deb: 4/26/60

YEAR TM/L	W	L	PCT	G	GS	CG	SH	SV	IP	H	HR	BB	SO	RAT	ERA	ERA+	OAV	OOB	BH	AVG	PB	PR	/A	PD	TPI
1960 SF-N	1	4	.200	17	4	0	0	0	50^2	50	6	30	28	14.2	4.62	75	.254	.352	2	.167	-0	-5	-6	2	-0.4
1962 Min-A	1	3	.250	32	4	0	0	0	72^2	69	11	35	36	13.4	4.46	92	.252	.345	4	.250	1	-4	-3	1	0.0
Total 2	2	7	.222	49	8	0	0	0	123^1	119	17	65	64	13.7	4.52	85	.253	.348	6	.214	1	-9	-10	2	-0.4

● **FIRPO MARBERRY** Marberry, Fredrick b: 11/30/1898, Streetman, Tex. d: 6/30/76, Mexia, Tex. BR/TR, 6'1", 190 lbs. Deb: 8/11/23 U

YEAR TM/L	W	L	PCT	G	GS	CG	SH	SV	IP	H	HR	BB	SO	RAT	ERA	ERA+	OAV	OOB	BH	AVG	PB	PR	/A	PD	TPI
1923 Was-A	4	0	1.000	11	4	2	0	0	44^2	42	1	17	18	12.5	2.82	133	.258	.339	2	.143	-1	6	5	-0	0.3
1924 *Was-A	11	12	.478	**50**	14	6	0	**15**	195^1	190	3	70	68	12.4	3.09	131	.262	.335	8	.136	-4	25	21	-1	2.0
1925 *Was-A	9	5	.643	**55**	0	0	0	**15**	93^1	84	4	45	53	12.8	3.47	122	.246	.341	5	.263	1	**10**	**8**	1	1.5
1926 Was-A	12	7	.632	**64**	5	3	0	**22**	138	120	4	66	43	12.3	3.00	129	.243	.336	6	.176	-1	16	13	-1	1.9
1927 Was-A	10	7	.588	56	10	2	0	9	155^1	177	4	68	74	14.4	4.64	88	.296	.371	5	.122	-3	-9	-10	-1	-1.5
1928 Was-A	13	13	.500	**48**	11	7	1	3	161^1	160	4	42	76	11.4	3.85	104	.268	.319	5	.109	-4	3	3	-1	-0.1
1929 Was-A	19	12	.613	**49**	26	16	0	**11**	250^1	233	6	69	121	**11.1**	3.06	139	.252	**.308**	19	.235	2	33	33	-2	3.8
1930 Was-A	15	5	.750	33	22	9	2	1	185	190	15	53	56	11.8	4.09	113	.270	.321	24	.329	5	12	11	-1	1.3
1931 Was-A	16	4	.800	45	25	11	1	7	219	211	13	63	88	11.4	3.45	124	.252	.307	19	.232	1	23	20	-2	1.7
1932 Was-A	8	4	.667	**54**	15	8	1	**13**	197^2	202	13	72	66	12.6	4.01	108	.268	.333	11	.167	-2	10	7	1	0.4
1933 Det-A	16	11	.593	37	32	15	1	2	238^1	232	13	61	84	**11.1**	3.29	131	.254	**.302**	11	.122	-5	26	27	-3	2.0
1934 *Det-A	15	5	.750	38	19	6	1	3	155^2	174	12	48	64	12.8	4.57	96	.276	.327	12	.218	2	-1	-3	-2	-0.3
1935 Det-A	0	1	.000	5	2	1	0	0	19	22	2	9	7	14.7	4.26	98	.289	.365	1	.200	0	0	-0	-0	0.0
1936 NY-N	0	0	—	1	0	0	0	0	0^1	1	0	0	0	27.0	0.00	—	.500	.500	0	.000	-0	0	0	-0	0.0
Was-A	0	2	.000	5	1	0	0	0	14	11	2	3	4	9.6	3.86	124	.208	.263	0	.000	-0	2	1	-0	0.1
Total 14	148	88	.627	551	186	86	7	101	2067^1	2049	96	686	822	12.1	3.63	116	.262	.325	128	.192	-8	156	136	-12	13.1

● **WALT MARBET** Marbet, Walter William b: 9/13/1890, Plymouth Co., Ia. d: 9/24/56, Hohenwald, Tenn. BR/TR, 6'1", 175 lbs. Deb: 6/17/13

YEAR TM/L	W	L	PCT	G	GS	CG	SH	SV	IP	H	HR	BB	SO	RAT	ERA	ERA+	OAV	OOB	BH	AVG	PB	PR	/A	PD	TPI
1913 StL-N	0	1	.000	3	1	0	0	0	3^1	9	0	4	1	35.1	16.20	20	.500	.591	0	—	0	-5	-5	-0	-1.1

● **PHIL MARCHILDON** Marchildon, Philip Joseph "Babe"
b: 10/25/13, Penetanguishene, Ont., Canada d: 1/10/97, Toronot, Ont., Can. BR/TR, 5'11", 175 lbs. Deb: 9/22/40

YEAR TM/L	W	L	PCT	G	GS	CG	SH	SV	IP	H	HR	BB	SO	RAT	ERA	ERA+	OAV	OOB	BH	AVG	PB	PR	/A	PD	TPI
1940 Phi-A	0	2	.000	2	2	1	0	0	10	12	1	8	4	18.0	7.20	62	.286	.400	0	.000	-0	-3	-3	0	-0.5
1941 Phi-A	10	15	.400	30	27	14	1	0	204^1	188	15	118	74	13.6	3.57	117	.245	.348	11	.167	1	13	14	-3	1.3
1942 Phi-A	17	14	.548	38	31	18	1	1	244	215	14	140	110	13.2	4.20	90	.235	.339	20	.238	3	-15	-12	-3	-1.3
1945 Phi-A	0	1	.000	3	2	0	0	0	9	5	0	11	2	16.0	4.00	86	.179	.410	1	.500	1	-1	-1	0	0.0
1946 Phi-A	13	16	.448	36	29	16	1	1	226^2	197	14	114	95	12.5	3.49	101	.237	.332	5	.067	-6	0	1	-2	-0.6
1947 Phi-A	19	9	.679	35	35	21	2	0	276^2	228	15	141	128	12.2	3.22	118	.224	.323	15	.153	-2	15	18	-3	1.3

YEAR	TM/L	W	L	PCT	G	GS	CG	SH	SV	IP	H	HR	BB	SO	RAT	ERA	ERA+	OAV	OOB	BH	AVG	PB	PR	/A	PD	TPI
1948	Phi-A	9	15	.375	33	30	12	1	0	226^1	214	19	131	66	13.9	4.53	95	.251	.353	5	.069	-5	-6	-6	-1	-1.2
1949	Phi-A	0	3	.000	7	6	0	0	0	16	24	3	19	2	24.8	11.81	35	.358	.506	1	.167	-0	-14	-14	-0	-2.0
1950	Bos-A	0	0	—	1	0	0	0	0	1^1	1	0	2	0	20.3	6.75	73	.200	.429	0	—	0	-0	-0	-0	0.0
Total	9	68	75	.476	185	162	82	6	2	1214^1	1084	81	684	481	13.3	3.93	100	.240	.342	58	.143	-10	-10	-1	-11	-3.0
● JOHNNY MARCUM	Marcum, John Alfred "Footsie" b: 9/9/09, Campbellsburg, Ky. d: 9/10/84, Louisville, Ky. BL/TR, 5'11", 197 lbs. Deb: 9/7/33 ◆																									
1933	Phi-A	3	2	.600	5	5	4	2	0	37	28	0	20	14	11.7	1.95	220	.200	.300	2	.167	0	10	10	0	1.3
1934	Phi-A	14	11	.560	37	31	17	2	0	232	257	13	88	92	13.5	4.50	97	.280	.346	30	.268	6	-0	-3	-0	0.2
1935	Phi-A	17	12	.586	39	27	19	2	3	242^2	256	9	83	99	12.6	4.08	111	.268	.328	37	.311	9	10	13	-3	1.9
1936	Bos-A	8	13	.381	31	23	9	1	1	174	194	14	52	57	12.7	4.81	110	.281	.332	18	.205	1	4	10	0	1.0
1937	Bos-A	13	11	.542	37	23	9	1	3	183^2	230	17	47	59	13.7	4.85	98	.306	.348	23	.267	5	-5	-2	1	0.3
1938	Bos-A	5	6	.455	15	11	7	0	0	92^1	113	11	25	25	13.5	4.09	120	.298	.342	5	.135	-1	7	9	-1	0.7
1939	StL-A	2	5	.286	12	6	2	0	0	47^2	66	12	10	14	14.5	7.74	63	.332	.367	10	.455	3	-17	-15	-0	-1.5
	Chi-A	3	3	.500	19	6	2	0	0	90	125	15	19	32	14.4	6.00	79	.326	.357	16	.281	2	-14	-13	-1	-0.5
	Yr	5	8	.385	31	12	4	0	0	137^2	191	27	29	46	14.4	6.60	72	.327	.359	26	.329	6	-30	-28	-1	-2.0
Total	7	65	63	.508	195	132	69	8	7	1099^1	1269	91	344	392	13.3	4.66	101	.287	.340	141	.265	25	-4	7	-4	3.4
● LEO MARENTETTE	Marentette, Leo John b: 2/18/41, Detroit, Mich. BR/TR, 6'2", 200 lbs. Deb: 9/26/65																									
1965	Det-A	0	0	—	2	0	0	0	0	3	1	0	1	3	6.0	0.00	—	.111	.200	0	—	0	1	1	0	0.0
1969	Mon-N	0	0	—	3	0	0	0	0	5^1	9	1	1	4	16.9	6.75	54	.391	.417	0	.000	-0	-2	-2	0	0.0
Total	2	0	0	—	5	0	0	0	0	8^1	10	1	2	7	13.0	4.32	83	.313	.353	0	.000	-0	-1	-1	0	0.0
● JOE MARGONERI	Margoneri, Joseph Emanuel b: 1/13/30, Somerset, Pa. BL/TL, 6', 185 lbs. Deb: 4/25/56																									
1956	NY-N	6	6	.500	23	13	2	0	0	91^2	88	12	49	49	13.5	3.93	96	.254	.346	3	.103	-1	-2	-1	-0	-0.3
1957	NY-N	1	1	.500	13	2	1	0	0	34^1	44	1	21	18	17.3	5.24	75	.314	.407	0	.000	-1	-5	-5	-0	-0.4
Total	2	7	7	.500	36	15	3	0	0	126	132	13	70	67	14.5	4.29	89	.271	.364	3	.081	-2	-7	-6	-1	-0.7
● JUAN MARICHAL	Marichal, Juan Antonio (Sanchez) "Manito" b: 10/20/37, Laguna Verde, D.R. BR/TR, 6', 185 lbs. Deb: 7/19/60 H																									
1960	SF-N	6	2	.750	11	11	6	1	0	81^1	59	5	28	58	9.6	2.66	131	.200	.269	4	.129	0	10	7	0	0.7
1961	SF-N	13	10	.565	29	27	9	3	0	185	183	24	48	124	11.3	3.89	98	.257	.306	7	.119	-2	3	-2	-1	-0.5
1962	*SF-N★	18	11	.621	37	36	18	3	1	262^2	233	34	90	153	11.2	3.36	113	.234	.300	21	.236	4	17	13	-1	1.6
1963	SF-N☆	**25**	8	.758	41	40	18	5	0	**321^1**	259	27	61	248	9.0	2.41	133	.216	.256	20	.179	3	31	28	-3	2.8
1964	SF-N★	21	8	.724	33	33	**22**	4	0	269	241	18	52	206	9.8	2.48	144	.236	.273	14	.144	-1	32	33	1	3.4
1965	SF-N★	22	13	.629	39	37	24	**10**	1	295^1	224	27	46	240	8.3	2.13	**169**	.205	.240	17	.173	1	46	**48**	-0	**6.0**
1966	SF-N★	25	6	**.806**	37	36	25	4	0	307^1	228	32	36	222	**7.9**	2.23	165	**.202**	**.230**	28	.250	6	47	49	0	**5.8**
1967	SF-N★	14	10	.583	26	26	18	2	0	202^1	195	20	42	166	10.6	2.76	119	.249	.288	14	.177	3	14	12	-2	1.5
1968	SF-N★	**26**	9	.743	38	38	**30**	5	0	**326**	295	21	46	218	9.6	2.43	121	.238	.269	20	.163	1	20	19	3	2.7
1969	SF-N☆	21	11	.656	37	36	27	**8**	0	299^2	244	15	54	205	**9.1**	**2.10**	**167**	.222	.263	15	.138	-1	**50**	47	4	5.4
1970	SF-N	12	10	.545	34	33	14	1	0	242^2	269	28	48	123	11.8	4.12	97	.277	.312	5	.059	-6	-2	-4	2	-0.7
1971	*SF-N★	18	11	.621	37	37	18	4	0	279	244	27	56	159	9.8	2.94	116	.233	.274	14	.133	0	16	14	3	1.8
1972	SF-N	6	16	.273	25	24	6	0	0	165	176	15	46	72	12.3	3.71	94	.277	.329	10	.196	1	-5	-4	0	-0.4
1973	SF-N	11	15	.423	34	32	9	2	0	207^1	231	22	37	87	11.7	3.82	100	.277	.309	13	.188	1	-4	-0	4	0.5
1974	Bos-A	5	1	.833	11	9	0	0	0	57^1	61	3	14	21	12.1	4.87	79	.270	.318	0	—	0	-8	-7	-0	-0.9
1975	LA-N	0	1	.000	2	2	0	0	0	6	11	2	5	1	24.0	13.50	25	.407	.500	0	.000	-0	-7	-7	0	-0.8
Total	16	243	142	.631	471	457	244	52	2	3507^1	3153	320	709	2303	10.0	2.89	122	.237	.278	202	.165	10	262	247	9	28.9
● DAN MARION	Marion, Donald G. "Rube" b: 7/31/1890, Cleveland, Ohio d: 1/18/33, Milwaukee, Wis. BR/TR, 6'1", 187 lbs. Deb: 4/23/14																									
1914	Bro-F	3	2	.600	17	9	4	0	0	89^1	97	1	38	41	14.2	3.93	73	.281	.362	7	.194	-2	-10	-10	-1	-0.8
1915	Bro-F	12	9	.571	35	25	15	2	0	208^1	193	1	64	46	11.2	3.20	85	.248	.308	13	.176	-2	-11	-11	-1	-1.3
Total	2	15	11	.577	52	34	19	2	0	297^2	290	2	102	87	12.1	3.42	81	.258	.325	20	.182	-3	-21	-22	-2	-2.1
● DUKE MARKELL	Markell, Harry Duquesne (b: Harry Duquesne Makowsky) b: 8/17/23, Paris, France d: 6/14/84, Ft.Lauderdale, Fla. BR/TR, 6'1.5", 209 lbs. Deb: 9/6/51																									
1951	StL-A	1	1	.500	5	2	1	0	0	21^1	25	3	20	10	19.0	6.33	69	.298	.433	1	.167	-0	-5	-5	-1	-0.4
● CLIFF MARKLE	Markle, Clifford Monroe b: 5/3/1894, Dravosburg, Pa. d: 5/24/74, Temple City, Cal. BR/TR, 5'9", 163 lbs. Deb: 9/18/15																									
1915	NY-A	2	0	1.000	3	2	2	0	0	23	15	1	6	12	8.2	0.39	750	.185	.241	0	.000	0	7	6	-1	0.5
1916	NY-A	4	3	.571	11	7	3	1	0	45^2	41	0	31	14	15.0	4.53	64	.256	.390	0	.000	-1	-9	-8	-0	-1.4
1921	Cin-N	2	6	.250	10	6	5	0	0	67	75	0	20	23	12.8	3.76	95	.291	.342	3	.125	-2	0	-1	-1	-0.4
1922	Cin-N	4	5	.444	25	3	2	1	0	75^2	75	3	33	34	12.8	3.81	105	.268	.345	3	.150	-0	2	2	-0	0.1
1924	NY-A	0	3	.000	7	3	0	0	0	23^1	29	5	20	7	18.9	8.87	47	.333	.458	0	.000	-1	-12	-12	-1	-1.4
Total	5	12	17	.414	56	21	12	2	0	234^2	235	9	110	90	13.4	4.10	87	.271	.356	6	.087	-5	-12	-14	-3	-2.6
● DICK MARLOWE	Marlowe, Richard Burton b: 6/27/29, Hickory, N.C. d: 12/30/68, Toledo, Ohio BR/TR, 6'2", 170 lbs. Deb: 9/19/51																									
1951	Det-A	0	1	.000	2	1	0	0	0	1^2	5	0	2	1	37.8	32.40	13	.500	.583	0	—	0	-5	-5	-0	-1.8
1952	Det-A	0	2	.000	4	1	0	0	0	11	21	1	3	3	19.6	7.36	52	.420	.453	0	.000	-0	-5	-4	-0	-0.7
1953	Det-A	6	7	.462	42	11	2	0	0	119^2	152	13	42	52	14.7	5.26	77	.319	.377	7	.219	-0	-17	-16	-1	-1.6
1954	Det-A	5	4	.556	38	2	0	0	2	84	76	11	40	39	12.4	4.18	88	.244	.330	3	.167	0	-4	-5	-1	-0.5
1955	Det-A	1	0	1.000	4	1	1	0	1	15	12	1	4	9	9.6	1.80	213	.218	.271	0	.000	-0	4	3	-0	0.2
1956	Det-A	1	1	.500	7	1	0	0	0	11	12	1	9	4	17.2	5.73	72	.279	.404	0	.000	-0	-2	-2	0	-0.3
	Chi-A	0	0	—	1	0	0	0	0	1	2	1	1	0	27.0	9.00	46	.500	.600	0	—	0	-1	-1	-0	0.0
	Yr	1	1	.500	8	1	0	0	0	12	14	2	10	4	18.0	6.00	69	.298	.421	0	.000	-0	-2	-3	-0	-0.3
Total	6	13	15	.464	98	17	3	0	3	243^1	280	28	101	108	14.2	4.99	78	.295	.364	10	.175	-1	-30	-29	-2	-4.7
● LOU MARONE	Marone, Louis Stephen b: 12/3/45, San Diego, Cal. BR/TL, 5'11", 185 lbs. Deb: 5/30/69																									
1969	Pit-N	1	1	.500	29	0	0	0	0	35^1	24	2	13	25	9.9	2.55	137	.195	.283	0	—	0	4	4	-1	0.1
1970	Pit-N	0	0	—	1	0	0	0	0	2^1	2	1	0	0	7.7	3.86	101	.222	.222	0	—	0	0	0	-0	0.0
Total	2	1	1	.500	30	0	0	0	0	37^2	26	3	13	25	9.8	2.63	134	.197	.279	0	—	0	4	4	-1	0.1
● RUBE MARQUARD	Marquard, Richard William b: 10/9/1886, Cleveland, Ohio d: 6/1/80, Baltimore, Md. BB/TL, 6'3", 180 lbs. Deb: 9/25/08 H																									
1908	NY-N	0	1	.000	1	1	0	0	0	5	6	0	2	2	16.2	3.60	67	.316	.409	0	.000	-0	-1	-1	-0	-0.2
1909	NY-N	5	13	.278	29	21	8	0	1	173	155	2	73	109	12.3	2.60	98	.248	.335	8	.148	-1	-0	-1	-0	-0.3
1910	NY-N	4	4	.500	13	8	2	0	0	70^2	65	2	40	52	13.9	4.46	67	.254	.363	3	.111	-2	-11	-12	-0	-1.4
1911	*NY-N	24	7	**.774**	45	33	22	5	3	277^2	221	9	106	**237**	10.7	2.50	135	.219	.296	17	.163	-1	28	27	-4	2.3
1912	*NY-N	**26**	11	.703	43	38	22	1	1	294^2	286	9	80	175	11.3	2.57	132	.255	.306	21	.219	2	28	27	-3	2.9
1913	*NY-N	23	10	.697	42	33	20	4	3	288	248	10	49	151	9.4	2.50	125	.237	.273	23	.219	2	23	20	-6	1.8
1914	NY-N	12	22	.353	39	33	15	4	2	268	261	9	47	92	10.4	3.06	87	.262	.297	15	.179	-1	8	12	1	1.6
1915	NY-N	9	8	.529	27	21	10	2	2	169	178	8	33	79	11.3	3.73	69	.272	.308	6	.109	-3	-18	-22	-0	-2.4
	Bro-N	2	2	.500	6	3	0	0	1	24^2	29	0	5	13	12.4	6.20	45	.276	.309	1	.125	-0	-9	-9	-0	-1.5
	Yr	11	10	.524	33	24	10	2	3	193^2	207	8	38	92	11.4	4.04	64	.272	.307	7	.111	-3	-28	-31	-0	-3.9
1916	*Bro-N	13	6	.684	36	21	15	2	5	205	169	2	38	107	9.1	1.58	170	.229	.267	9	.143	-1	24	25	-4	2.1
1917	Bro-N	19	12	.613	37	29	14	2	0	232^2	200	5	60	117	10.1	2.55	110	.232	.282	15	.200	0	4	6	-4	0.4
1918	Bro-N	9	18	.333	34	29	19	4	0	239	231	7	59	89	11.0	2.64	106	.260	.307	13	.171	-2	3	4	-2	0.0
1919	Bro-N	3	3	.500	8	7	3	0	0	59	54	1	10	29	9.8	2.29	130	.244	.277	6	.261	1	4	4	-1	0.4
1920	*Bro-N	10	7	.588	28	26	10	1	0	189^2	181	5	35	89	10.3	3.23	99	.251	.287	10	.169	-1	-2	-0	-4	-0.6
1921	Cin-N	17	14	.548	39	36	18	2	0	265^2	291	8	50	88	11.8	3.39	106	.285	.323	19	.200	-1	12	6	-3	0.1
1922	Bos-N	11	15	.423	39	25	7	0	1	198	255	12	66	57	14.6	5.09	79	.322	.374	14	.222	-1	-22	-24	1	-2.6
1923	Bos-N	11	14	.440	38	29	11	3	0	239	265	10	65	78	12.5	3.73	107	.288	.337	12	.140	-6	7	7	0	0.0
1924	Bos-N	1	2	.333	6	6	1	0	0	36	33	3	13	10	11.8	3.00	127	.254	.326	3	.273	0	3	3	-0	0.3
1925	Bos-N	2	8	.200	26	8	0	0	0	72	105	5	27	19	16.5	5.75	70	.341	.394	3	.136	-1	-12	-14	-2	-1.9
Total	18	201	177	.532	536	407	197	30	19	3306^2	3233	107	858	1593	11.2	3.08	103	.260	.310	198	.179	-17	53	36	-31	-2.2

● ISIDRO MARQUEZ
Marquez, Isidro (Espinoza) b: 5/15/65, Navojoa, Mexico BR/TR, 6'3", 190 lbs. Deb: 4/26/95

YEAR	TM/L	W	L	PCT	G	GS	CG	SH	SV	IP	H	HR	BB	SO	RAT	ERA	ERA+	OAV	OOB	BH	AVG	PB	PR	/A	PD	TPI
1995	Chi-A	0	1	.000	7	0	0	0	0	6^2	9	3	2	8	14.9	6.75	66	.321	.367	0	—	0	-2	-2	-0	-0.1

● JIM MARQUIS
Marquis, James Milburn b: 11/18/1900, Yoakum, Tex. d: 8/5/92, Jackson, Cal. BR/TR, 5'11", 174 lbs. Deb: 8/8/25

YEAR	TM/L	W	L	PCT	G	GS	CG	SH	SV	IP	H	HR	BB	SO	RAT	ERA	ERA+	OAV	OOB	BH	AVG	PB	PR	/A	PD	TPI
1925	NY-A	0	0	—	2	0	0	0	0	7^1	12	1	6	0	22.1	9.82	43	.414	.514	0	.000	-0	-4	-5	0	0.0

● CONNIE MARRERO
Marrero, Conrado Eugenio (Ramos) b: 4/25/11, Las Villas, Cuba BR/TR, 5'7", 158 lbs. Deb: 4/21/50

YEAR	TM/L	W	L	PCT	G	GS	CG	SH	SV	IP	H	HR	BB	SO	RAT	ERA	ERA+	OAV	OOB	BH	AVG	PB	PR	/A	PD	TPI
1950	Was-A	6	10	.375	27	19	8	1	1	152	159	17	55	63	12.9	4.50	100	.269	.335	6	.122	1	1	0	-3	-0.1
1951	Was-A☆	11	9	.550	25	25	16	2	0	187	198	8	71	66	13.1	3.90	105	.268	.335	10	.164	-2	5	4	-2	0.1
1952	Was-A	11	8	.579	22	22	16	2	0	184^1	175	9	53	77	11.3	2.88	123	.249	.305	5	.079	-5	16	14	-3	0.5
1953	Was-A	8	7	.533	22	20	10	2	2	145^2	130	14	48	65	11.3	3.03	129	.241	.309	6	.125	-2	16	14	-1	1.1
1954	Was-A	3	6	.333	22	8	1	0	0	66^1	74	12	22	26	13.0	4.75	75	.287	.343	0	.000	-1	-8	-9	-1	-1.3
Total	5	39	40	.494	118	94	51	7	3	735^1	736	60	249	297	12.3	3.67	108	.260	.323	27	.114	-11	30	23	-10	0.0

● BUCK MARROW
Marrow, Charles Kennon b: 8/29/09, Tarboro, N.C. d: 11/21/82, Newport News, Va. BR/TR, 6'4", 200 lbs. Deb: 7/3/32

YEAR	TM/L	W	L	PCT	G	GS	CG	SH	SV	IP	H	HR	BB	SO	RAT	ERA	ERA+	OAV	OOB	BH	AVG	PB	PR	/A	PD	TPI
1932	Det-A	2	5	.286	18	7	2	0	1	63^2	70	6	29	31	14.8	4.81	98	.278	.366	3	.158	-0	-2	-1	1	0.0
1937	Bro-N	1	2	.333	6	3	1	0	0	16^1	19	2	9	2	15.4	6.61	61	.284	.368	0	.000	-1	-5	-5	0	-0.8
1938	Bro-N	0	1	.000	15	0	0	0	0	19^2	23	1	11	6	16.9	4.58	85	.291	.398	0	.000	-0	-2	-1	0	-0.1
Total	3	3	8	.273	39	10	3	0	1	99^2	112	9	49	39	15.4	5.06	88	.281	.373	3	.120	-1	-9	-7	1	-0.9

● ED MARS
Mars, Edward M. b: 12/4/1866, Chicago, Ill. d: 12/9/41, Chicago, Ill. 5'9", 166 lbs. Deb: 8/12/1890

YEAR	TM/L	W	L	PCT	G	GS	CG	SH	SV	IP	H	HR	BB	SO	RAT	ERA	ERA+	OAV	OOB	BH	AVG	PB	PR	/A	PD	TPI
1890	Syr-a	9	5	.643	16	14	14	0	0	121^1	132	2	49	59	13.8	4.67	76	.269	.341	14	.275	4	-11	-15	1	-1.0

● CUDDLES MARSHALL
Marshall, Clarence Westly b: 4/28/25, Bellingham, Wash. BR/TR, 6'3", 200 lbs. Deb: 4/24/46

YEAR	TM/L	W	L	PCT	G	GS	CG	SH	SV	IP	H	HR	BB	SO	RAT	ERA	ERA+	OAV	OOB	BH	AVG	PB	PR	/A	PD	TPI
1946	NY-A	3	4	.429	23	11	1	0	0	81	96	4	56	32	16.9	5.33	65	.308	.413	4	.143	-1	-16	-17	1	-1.3
1948	NY-A	0	0	—	1	0	0	0	0	1	0	0	3	0	27.0	0.00	—	.000	.500	0	—	0	0	0	-0	0.0
1949	NY-A	3	0	1.000	21	2	0	0	3	49^1	48	3	48	13	17.9	5.11	79	.259	.417	1	.111	-0	-5	-6	1	-0.4
1950	StL-A	1	3	.250	28	2	0	0	1	53^2	72	1	51	24	20.8	7.88	63	.321	.449	4	.333	0	-20	-17	-1	-1.2
Total	4	7	7	.500	73	15	1	0	4	185	216	8	158	69	18.3	5.98	67	.298	.426	9	.184	-1	-41	-40	0	-2.9

● MIKE MARSHALL
Marshall, Michael Grant b: 1/15/43, Adrian, Mich. BR/TR, 5'10", 180 lbs. Deb: 5/31/67

YEAR	TM/L	W	L	PCT	G	GS	CG	SH	SV	IP	H	HR	BB	SO	RAT	ERA	ERA+	OAV	OOB	BH	AVG	PB	PR	/A	PD	TPI
1967	Det-A	1	3	.250	37	0	0	0	10	59	51	6	20	41	11.1	1.98	165	.233	.303	2	.222	0	8	8	1	1.0
1969	Sea-A	3	10	.231	20	14	3	1	0	87^2	99	8	35	47	14.0	5.13	71	.281	.350	7	.259	3	-15	-15	3	-1.4
1970	Hou-N	0	1	.000	4	0	0	0	0	5^1	8	0	4	5	21.9	8.44	46	.400	.520	0	—	0	-3	-3	1	-0.4
	Mon-N	3	7	.300	24	5	0	0	3	64^2	56	4	29	38	11.8	3.48	118	.225	.306	1	.091	0	4	5	2	0.9
	Yr	3	8	.273	28	5	0	0	3	70	64	4	33	43	12.5	3.86	106	.237	.320	1	.091	0	1	2	2	0.5
1971	Mon-N	5	8	.385	66	0	0	0	23	111^1	100	9	50	85	12.4	4.28	82	.247	.336	3	.188	0	-10	-9	3	-1.1
1972	Mon-N	14	8	.636	**65**	0	0	0	18	116	82	3	47	95	10.2	1.78	199	.202	.289	3	.136	0	**22**	**23**	0	5.3
1973	Mon-N	14	11	.560	**92**	0	0	0	**31**	179	163	10	75	124	12.2	2.66	143	.252	.333	8	.242	1	20	**23**	3	4.4
1974	*LA-N★	15	12	.556	**106**	0	0	0	**21**	208^1	191	9	56	143	10.7	2.42	141	.247	.299	8	.235	1	**28**	**23**	1	3.5
1975	LA-N☆	9	14	.391	57	0	0	0	13	109^1	98	8	39	64	11.6	3.29	103	.242	.315	1	.067	-1	4	1	2	0.4
1976	LA-N	4	3	.571	30	0	0	0	8	62^2	64	2	25	39	12.9	4.45	76	.270	.342	0	.000	0	-7	-7	2	-0.8
	Atl-N	2	1	.667	24	0	0	0	6	36^2	35	4	14	17	12.3	3.19	119	.259	.333	1	.167	0	1	2	0	0.4
	Yr	6	4	.600	54	0	0	0	14	99^1	99	6	39	56	12.6	3.99	89	.264	.335	1	.091	1	-5	-5	2	-0.4
1977	Atl-N	1	0	1.000	4	0	0	0	0	6	12	1	2	6	21.0	9.00	49	.400	.438	1	1.000	0	-3	-3	-0	-0.4
	Tex-A	2	2	.500	12	4	0	0	1	35^2	42	0	13	18	14.4	4.04	101	.304	.373	0	—	0	0	0	0	0.0
1978	Min-A	10	12	.455	54	0	0	0	21	99	80	3	37	56	10.7	2.45	156	.225	.300	0	—	0	14	15	1	4.0
1979	Min-A	10	15	.400	**90**	1	0	0	**32**	142^2	132	8	48	81	11.6	2.65	165	.254	.322	0	—	0	25	27	3	5.7
1980	Min-A	1	3	.250	18	0	0	0	1	32^1	42	2	12	13	15.6	6.12	71	.323	.389	0	—	0	-8	-6	1	-1.1
1981	NY-N	3	2	.600	20	0	0	0	0	31	26	2	8	8	9.9	2.61	133	.224	.274	0	—	0	3	3	-0	0.5
Total	14	97	112	.464	723	24	3	1	188	1386^2	1281	79	514	880	11.9	3.14	118	.249	.321	35	.196	6	84	87	20	20.9

● RUBE MARSHALL
Marshall, Roy De Verne "Cy" b: 1/19/1890, Salineville, Ohio d: 6/11/80, Dover, Ohio BR/TR, 5'11", 170 lbs. Deb: 9/28/12

YEAR	TM/L	W	L	PCT	G	GS	CG	SH	SV	IP	H	HR	BB	SO	RAT	ERA	ERA+	OAV	OOB	BH	AVG	PB	PR	/A	PD	TPI
1912	Phi-N	0	1	.000	2	1	0	0	0	3	12	0	1	2	39.0	21.00	17	.632	.650	0	—	0	-6	-6	0	-1.2
1913	Phi-N	0	1	.000	14	1	0	0	1	45^1	54	2	22	18	15.3	4.57	73	.297	.376	1	.091	-1	-7	-6	0	-0.2
1914	Phi-N	6	7	.462	27	17	7	0	1	134^1	144	2	50	49	13.3	3.75	78	.279	.349	6	.140	-2	-14	-12	1	-1.3
1915	Buf-F	2	1	.667	21	4	2	0	0	59^1	62	1	33	21	14.7	3.94	71	.281	.379	5	.294	1	-8	-8	-1	-0.4
Total	4	8	10	.444	64	23	9	0	2	242	272	5	106	90	14.4	4.17	72	.290	.367	12	.169	-2	-35	-32	-0	-3.1

● PHONNEY MARTIN
Martin, Alphonse Case b: 8/4/1845, New York, N.Y. d: 5/24/33, Hollis, N.Y. 5'7", 148 lbs. Deb: 4/26/1872 ♦

YEAR	TM/L	W	L	PCT	G	GS	CG	SH	SV	IP	H	HR	BB	SO	RAT	ERA	ERA+	OAV	OOB	BH	AVG	PB	PR	/A	PD	TPI
1872	Tro-n	1	2	.333	8	3	0	0	0	37^1	70	0	2	1	17.4	4.82	75	.350	.356	36	.308	1	-5	-5		-0.3
	Eck-n	2	7	.222	10	9	9	0	0	85	144	1	4	2	15.7	4.24	80	.321	.327	12	.154	-3	-6	-8		-0.6
	Yr	3	9	.250	18	12	9	0	0	122^1	214	1	6	3	16.2	4.41	78	.330	.336	48	.246	-2	-11	-13		-0.9
1873	Mut-n	0	1	.000	6	1	1	0	0	34	50	0	7	1	15.1	3.44	92	.294	.322	31	.221	-0	-1	-1		-0.1
Total	2 n	3	10	.231	24	13	10	0	0	156^1	264	1	13	4	15.9	4.20	75	.322	.333	79	.236	-3	-17	-18		-1.0

● BARNEY MARTIN
Martin, Barnes Robertson b: 3/3/23, Columbia, S.C. BR/TR, 5'11", 170 lbs. Deb: 4/22/53 F

YEAR	TM/L	W	L	PCT	G	GS	CG	SH	SV	IP	H	HR	BB	SO	RAT	ERA	ERA+	OAV	OOB	BH	AVG	PB	PR	/A	PD	TPI
1953	Cin-N	0	0	—	1	0	0	0	0	2	3	0	1	1	18.0	9.00	48	.333	.400	0	—	0	-1	-1	-0	0.0

● RENIE MARTIN
Martin, Donald Renie b: 8/30/55, Dover, Del. BR/TR, 6'4", 190 lbs. Deb: 5/9/79

YEAR	TM/L	W	L	PCT	G	GS	CG	SH	SV	IP	H	HR	BB	SO	RAT	ERA	ERA+	OAV	OOB	BH	AVG	PB	PR	/A	PD	TPI
1979	KC-A	0	3	.000	25	0	0	0	5	34^2	32	1	14	25	12.2	5.19	82	.248	.326	0	—	0	-4	-4	1	-0.4
1980	*KC-A	10	10	.500	32	20	2	0	2	137^1	133	18	70	68	13.4	4.39	92	.255	.345	0	—	0	-5	-5	-0	-0.8
1981	*KC-A	4	5	.444	29	0	0	0	4	61^2	55	2	29	25	12.3	2.77	130	.244	.331	0	—	0	6	6	1	1.0
1982	SF-N	7	10	.412	29	25	1	0	0	141^1	148	14	64	63	13.5	4.65	77	.274	.350	13	.265	3	-16	-17	1	-1.4
1983	SF-N	2	4	.333	37	6	0	0	1	94^1	95	11	51	43	14.2	4.20	84	.268	.365	9	.346	4	-6	-7	1	0.2
1984	SF-N	1	1	.500	12	0	0	0	0	23^1	29	2	16	8	17.4	3.86	91	.305	.405	3	.500	1	-1	-1	1	0.1
	Phi-N	0	2	.000	9	0	0	0	0	15^2	17	2	12	5	16.7	4.60	79	.274	.392	0	.000	-0	-2	-2	1	-0.1
	Yr	1	3	.250	21	0	0	0	0	39	46	4	28	13	17.1	4.15	86	.293	.400	3	.375	1	-2	-3	2	0.0
Total	6	24	35	.407	173	51	3	0	12	508^1	509	50	256	237	13.6	4.27	88	.264	.352	25	.301	8	-28	-29	5	-1.4

● SPEED MARTIN
Martin, Elwood Good b: 9/15/1893, Wawawai, Wash. d: 6/14/83, Lemon Grove, Cal. BR/TR, 6', 165 lbs. Deb: 7/5/17

YEAR	TM/L	W	L	PCT	G	GS	CG	SH	SV	IP	H	HR	BB	SO	RAT	ERA	ERA+	OAV	OOB	BH	AVG	PB	PR	/A	PD	TPI
1917	StL-A	0	2	.000	9	2	0	0	0	15^2	20	0	5	5	14.4	5.74	45	.339	.391	0	.000	-0	-5	-5	1	-0.6
1918	Chi-N	5	2	.714	9	5	4	1	1	53^2	47	0	14	16	10.4	1.84	151	.246	.301	3	.188	-0	5	6	1	0.9
1919	Chi-N	8	8	.500	35	14	7	2	2	163^2	158	2	52	54	11.8	2.47	117	.259	.321	8	.182	-1	8	7	2	0.8
1920	Chi-N	4	15	.211	35	13	6	0	2	136	165	2	50	44	14.3	4.83	66	.305	.365	7	.159	-0	-26	-25	1	-3.1
1921	Chi-N	11	15	.423	37	28	13	1	1	217^1	245	12	68	86	13.0	4.35	88	.298	.353	17	.233	1	-14	-13	2	-1.0
1922	Chi-N	1	0	1.000	1	1	0	0	0	6	10	0	2	2	18.0	7.50	56	.385	.429	0	.000	0	-2	-2	-0	-0.3
Total	6	29	42	.408	126	63	30	4	6	592^1	645	16	191	207	12.8	3.78	87	.287	.344	35	.194	-0	-33	-32	7	-3.3

● FRED MARTIN
Martin, Fred Turner b: 6/27/15, Williams, Okla. d: 6/11/79, Chicago, Ill. BR/TR, 6'1", 185 lbs. Deb: 4/21/46 C

YEAR	TM/L	W	L	PCT	G	GS	CG	SH	SV	IP	H	HR	BB	SO	RAT	ERA	ERA+	OAV	OOB	BH	AVG	PB	PR	/A	PD	TPI
1946	StL-N	2	1	.667	6	3	2	0	0	28^2	29	0	8	19	11.6	4.08	85	.254	.303	3	.273	0	-2	-2	0	-0.1
1949	StL-N	6	0	1.000	21	5	3	0	0	70	65	3	20	30	10.9	2.44	170	.243	.295	6	.300	1	12	13	0	1.1
1950	StL-N	4	2	.667	30	2	0	0	0	63^1	87	4	30	19	16.8	5.12	84	.331	.401	4	.267	1	-7	-6	1	-0.3
Total	3	12	3	.800	57	10	5	0	0	162	181	7	58	68	13.3	3.78	108	.281	.341	13	.283	2	3	6	1	0.7

● DOC MARTIN
Martin, Harold Winthrop b: 9/23/1887, Roxbury, Mass. d: 4/14/35, Milton, Mass. BR/TR, 5'11", 165 lbs. Deb: 10/7/08

YEAR	TM/L	W	L	PCT	G	GS	CG	SH	SV	IP	H	HR	BB	SO	RAT	ERA	ERA+	OAV	OOB	BH	AVG	PB	PR	/A	PD	TPI
1908	Phi-A	0	1	.000	1	1	0	0	0	2	2	0	3	2	27.0	13.50	19	.286	.545	0	.000	-0	-2	-2	-0	-0.8
1911	Phi-A	1	1	.500	11	3	1	0	0	38	40	1	17	21	14.7	4.50	70	.272	.367	3	.214	0	-5	-6	0	-0.2
1912	Phi-A	0	0	—	2	0	0	0	0	4^1	5	0	5	4	22.8	10.38	30	.333	.524	0	.000	-1	-3	-4	0	0.0
Total	3	1	2	.333	14	4	1	0	0	44^1	47	1	25	27	16.0	5.48	57	.278	.393	3	.167	-0	-11	-12	1	-1.0

● **PEPPER MARTIN** Martin, John Leonard Roosevelt "The Wild Horse Of The Osage" b: 2/29/04, Temple, Okla. d: 3/5/65, McAlester, Okla. BR/TR, 5'8", 170 lbs. Deb: 4/16/28 C♦

YEAR TM/L	W	L	PCT	G	GS	CG	SH	SV	IP	H	HR	BB	SO	RAT	ERA	ERA+	OAV	OOB	BH	AVG	PB	PR	/A	PD	TPI
1934 *StL-N★	0	0	—	1	0	0	0	0	2	1	0	0	0	4.5	4.50	94	.167	.167	131	.289	0	-0	-0	0	0.0
1936 StL-N	0	0	—	1	0	0	0	0	2	1	0	2	0	13.5	0.00	—	.200	.429	177	.309	1	1	1	-0	0.0
Total 2	0	0	—	2	0	0	0	0	4	2	0	2	0	9.0	2.25	181	.182	.308	1227	.298	1	1	1	0	0.0

● **JOHN MARTIN** Martin, John Robert b: 4/11/56, Wyandotte, Mich. BB/TL, 6', 190 lbs. Deb: 8/27/80

YEAR TM/L	W	L	PCT	G	GS	CG	SH	SV	IP	H	HR	BB	SO	RAT	ERA	ERA+	OAV	OOB	BH	AVG	PB	PR	/A	PD	TPI
1980 StL-N	2	3	.400	9	5	1	0	0	42	39	1	9	23	10.3	4.29	86	.247	.287	3	.273	1	-3	-3	-1	-0.3
1981 StL-N	8	5	.615	17	15	4	0	0	102^2	85	10	26	36	9.9	3.42	104	.228	.283	7	.212	2	1	2	0	0.4
1982 StL-N	4	5	.444	24	7	0	0	0	66	56	6	30	21	11.7	4.23	86	.230	.314	1	.091	-0	-5	-4	-1	-0.7
1983 StL-N	3	1	.750	26	5	0	0	0	66^1	60	6	26	29	11.9	3.53	103	.242	.319	4	.222	1	1	1	1	0.2
Det-A	0	0	—	15	0	0	0	1	13^1	15	2	4	11	12.8	7.43	53	.294	.345	0	—	0	-5	-5	0	-0.1
Total 4	17	14	.548	91	32	5	0	1	290^1	255	25	95	120	11.0	3.94	92	.238	.302	15	.205	3	-11	-10	-1	-0.5

● **MORRIE MARTIN** Martin, Morris Webster "Lefty" b: 9/3/22, Dixon, Mo. BL/TL, 6', 180 lbs. Deb: 4/25/49

YEAR TM/L	W	L	PCT	G	GS	CG	SH	SV	IP	H	HR	BB	SO	RAT	ERA	ERA+	OAV	OOB	BH	AVG	PB	PR	/A	PD	TPI
1949 Bro-N	1	3	.250	10	4	0	0	0	30^2	39	5	15	15	16.4	7.04	58	.320	.403	2	.200	-0	-10	-10	0	-1.1
1951 Phi-A	11	4	.733	35	13	3	1	0	138	139	13	63	35	13.5	3.78	113	.259	.343	11	.220	-1	5	8	2	0.8
1952 Phi-A	0	2	.000	5	5	0	0	0	25^1	32	1	15	13	17.4	6.39	62	.302	.398	1	.111	-1	-8	-7	-0	-0.6
1953 Phi-A	10	12	.455	58	11	2	0	7	156^1	158	12	59	64	13.0	4.43	97	.262	.336	4	.095	-4	-8	-3	-0	-0.7
1954 Phi-A	2	4	.333	13	6	2	0	0	52^2	57	9	19	24	13.3	5.47	71	.278	.345	4	.235	0	-10	-9	-0	-0.9
Chi-A	5	4	.556	35	2	1	0	5	70	52	5	24	31	9.9	2.06	182	.210	.282	2	.133	-0	13	13	-1	1.7
Yr	7	8	.467	48	8	3	0	5	122^2	109	14	43	55	11.2	3.52	108	.237	.304	6	.188	-0	3	4	-1	0.8
1955 Chi-A	2	3	.400	37	0	0	0	2	52	50	4	20	22	12.5	3.63	109	.259	.335	3	.300	0	2	2	1	0.3
1956 Chi-A	1	0	1.000	10	0	0	0	0	18^1	21	1	7	9	13.7	4.91	84	.292	.354	1	.200	0	-2	-2	0	-0.1
Bal-A	1	1	.500	9	0	0	0	0	5	10	1	2	3	23.4	10.80	36	.400	.464	0	—	0	-4	-4	-0	-1.3
Yr	2	1	.667	19	0	0	0	0	23^1	31	2	9	12	15.8	6.17	66	.316	.380	1	.200	0	-5	-5	0	-1.4
1957 StL-N	0	0	—	4	1	0	0	0	10^2	5	0	4	7	8.4	2.53	157	.143	.250	0	.000	-0	2	2	0	0.0
1958 StL-N	3	1	.750	17	0	0	0	0	24^2	19	3	12	16	12.0	4.74	87	.211	.317	0	.000	-1	-2	-2	-0	-0.3
Cle-A	2	0	1.000	14	0	0	0	1	18^2	20	0	8	5	13.5	2.41	151	.294	.368	0	—	0	3	3	-0	0.3
1959 Chi-N	0	0	—	3	0	0	0	0	2^1	5	2	1	1	27.0	19.29	20	.455	.538	0	—	0	-4	-4	0	0.0
Total 10	38	34	.528	250	42	8	1	15	604^2	607	56	249	245	13.1	4.29	95	.262	.341	28	.170	-6	-23	-13	1	-1.9

● **PAT MARTIN** Martin, Patrick Francis b: 4/13/1892, Brooklyn, N.Y. d: 2/4/49, Brooklyn, N.Y. BL/TL, 5'11.5", 170 lbs. Deb: 9/20/19

YEAR TM/L	W	L	PCT	G	GS	CG	SH	SV	IP	H	HR	BB	SO	RAT	ERA	ERA+	OAV	OOB	BH	AVG	PB	PR	/A	PD	TPI
1919 Phi-A	0	2	.000	2	2	1	0	0	11	11	0	8	6	15.5	4.09	84	.256	.373	0	.000	-0	-1	-1	-0	-0.2
1920 Phi-A	1	4	.200	8	5	2	0	0	32^1	48	2	25	14	21.4	6.12	66	.364	.478	4	.400	1	-8	-8	-1	-0.9
Total 2	1	6	.143	10	7	3	0	0	43^1	59	2	33	20	19.9	5.61	69	.337	.453	4	.308	1	-9	-8	-1	-1.1

● **PAUL MARTIN** Martin, Paul Charles b: 3/10/32, Brownstown, Pa. BR/TR, 6'6", 235 lbs. Deb: 7/2/55

YEAR TM/L	W	L	PCT	G	GS	CG	SH	SV	IP	H	HR	BB	SO	RAT	ERA	ERA+	OAV	OOB	BH	AVG	PB	PR	/A	PD	TPI
1955 Pit-N	0	1	.000	7	1	0	0	0	7	13	0	17	3	39.9	14.14	29	.464	.674	0	—	0	-8	-8	-0	-0.9

● **RAY MARTIN** Martin, Raymond Joseph b: 3/13/25, Norwood, Mass. BR/TR, 6'2", 177 lbs. Deb: 8/15/43

YEAR TM/L	W	L	PCT	G	GS	CG	SH	SV	IP	H	HR	BB	SO	RAT	ERA	ERA+	OAV	OOB	BH	AVG	PB	PR	/A	PD	TPI
1943 Bos-N	0	0	—	2	0	0	0	0	3^1	3	0	1	1	10.8	8.10	42	.231	.286	0	.000	-0	-2	-2	0	0.0
1947 Bos-N	1	0	1.000	1	1	1	0	0	9	7	0	4	2	11.0	1.00	389	.212	.297	0	.000	-0	3	3	0	0.4
1948 Bos-N	0	0	—	2	0	0	0	0	2^1	0	0	1	0	3.9	0.00	—	.000	.125	0	—	0	1	1	-0	0.0
Total 3	1	0	1.000	5	1	1	0	0	14^2	10	0	6	3	9.8	2.45	154	.189	.271	0	.000	-0	2	2	1	0.4

● **TOM MARTIN** Martin, Thomas Edgar b: 5/21/70, Charleston, S.C. BL/TL, 6'1", 185 lbs. Deb: 4/2/97

YEAR TM/L	W	L	PCT	G	GS	CG	SH	SV	IP	H	HR	BB	SO	RAT	ERA	ERA+	OAV	OOB	BH	AVG	PB	PR	/A	PD	TPI
1997 *Hou-N	5	3	.625	55	0	0	0	2	56	52	2	23	36	12.2	2.09	191	.254	.332	0	.000	-0	13	12	-0	1.5
1998 Cle-A	1	1	.500	14	0	0	0	0	14^2	29	3	12	9	25.2	12.89	37	.408	.494	0	—	0	-13	-13	0	-1.5
Total 2	6	4	.600	69	0	0	0	2	70^2	81	5	35	45	14.9	4.33	96	.293	.375	0	.000	-0	-0	-1	-0	0.0

● **JOE MARTINA** Martina, Joseph John "Oyster Joe" b: 7/8/1889, New Orleans, La. d: 3/22/62, New Orleans, La. BR/TR, 6', 183 lbs. Deb: 4/19/24

YEAR TM/L	W	L	PCT	G	GS	CG	SH	SV	IP	H	HR	BB	SO	RAT	ERA	ERA+	OAV	OOB	BH	AVG	PB	PR	/A	PD	TPI
1924 *Was-A	6	8	.429	24	14	8	0	0	125^1	129	7	56	57	13.7	4.67	86	.271	.355	14	.326	3	-6	-9	-2	-0.7

● **ALFREDO MARTINEZ** Martinez, Alfredo b: 3/15/57, Los Angeles, Cal. BR/TR, 6'3", 185 lbs. Deb: 4/20/80

YEAR TM/L	W	L	PCT	G	GS	CG	SH	SV	IP	H	HR	BB	SO	RAT	ERA	ERA+	OAV	OOB	BH	AVG	PB	PR	/A	PD	TPI
1980 Cal-A	7	9	.438	30	23	4	1	0	149^1	150	14	59	57	12.7	4.52	87	.259	.328	0	—	0	-8	-10	-2	-1.0
1981 Cal-A	0	0	—	2	0	0	0	0	6	5	1	3	4	12.0	3.00	122	.227	.320	0	—	0	0	0	0	0.0
Total 2	7	9	.438	32	23	4	1	0	155^1	155	15	62	61	12.6	4.46	88	.257	.328	0	—	0	-8	-9	-2	-1.0

● **DAVE MARTINEZ** Martinez, David b: 9/26/64, New York, N.Y. BL/TL, 5'10", 175 lbs. Deb: 6/15/86 ♦

YEAR TM/L	W	L	PCT	G	GS	CG	SH	SV	IP	H	HR	BB	SO	RAT	ERA	ERA+	OAV	OOB	BH	AVG	PB	PR	/A	PD	TPI
1990 Mon-N	0	0	—	1	0	0	0	0	0^1	2	0	2	0	108.0	54.00	7	.667	.800	109	.279	0	-2	-2	0	0.0
1995 Chi-A	0	0	—	1	0	0	0	0	1	0	0	2	0	18.0	0.00	—	.000	.400	93	.307	0	1	0	0	0.0
Total 2	0	0	—	2	0	0	0	0	1^1	2	0	4	0	40.5	13.50	32	.333	.600	1260	.275	1	-1	-1	0	0.0

● **TIPPY MARTINEZ** Martinez, Felix Anthony b: 5/31/50, LaJunta, Colo. BL/TL, 5'10", 180 lbs. Deb: 8/9/74

YEAR TM/L	W	L	PCT	G	GS	CG	SH	SV	IP	H	HR	BB	SO	RAT	ERA	ERA+	OAV	OOB	BH	AVG	PB	PR	/A	PD	TPI
1974 NY-A	0	0	—	10	0	0	0	0	12^2	14	0	9	10	17.1	4.26	83	.286	.407	0	—	0	-1	-1	-0	0.1
1975 NY-A	1	2	.333	23	2	0	0	8	37	27	2	32	20	14.6	2.68	137	.208	.368	0	—	0	5	4	-1	0.4
1976 NY-A	2	0	1.000	11	0	0	0	2	28	18	1	14	14	10.3	1.93	177	.191	.296	0	—	0	5	5	1	0.5
Bal-A	3	1	.750	28	0	0	0	8	41^2	32	0	28	31	13.2	2.59	126	.222	.353	0	—	0	4	3	1	0.6
Yr	5	1	.833	39	0	0	0	10	69^2	50	1	42	45	12.0	2.33	143	.210	.331	0	—	0	9	8	2	1.1
1977 Bal-A	5	1	.833	41	0	0	0	9	50	47	2	27	29	13.3	2.70	140	.266	.363	0	—	0	8	6	1	1.2
1978 Bal-A	3	3	.500	42	0	0	0	5	69	77	4	40	57	15.4	4.83	72	.281	.375	0	—	0	-8	-10	1	-0.4
1979 *Bal-A	10	3	.769	39	0	0	0	3	78	59	0	31	61	10.5	2.88	139	.210	.291	0	—	0	12	10	1	1.9
1980 Bal-A	4	4	.500	53	0	0	0	10	80^2	69	5	34	68	11.6	3.01	131	.240	.322	0	—	0	9	8	2	1.1
1981 Bal-A	3	3	.500	37	0	0	0	11	59	48	4	32	50	12.2	2.90	125	.231	.333	0	—	0	5	5	1	0.7
1982 Bal-A	8	8	.500	76	0	0	0	16	95	81	6	37	78	11.3	3.41	118	.240	.317	0	—	0	7	7	-0	1.3
1983 *Bal-A☆	9	3	.750	65	0	0	0	21	103^1	76	10	37	81	9.8	2.35	168	.211	.284	0	—	0	20	18	2	3.0
1984 Bal-A	4	9	.308	55	0	0	0	17	89^2	88	9	51	72	14.0	3.91	99	.260	.356	0	—	0	1	-0	0	-0.1
1985 Bal-A	3	3	.500	49	0	0	0	4	70	70	8	37	47	13.8	5.40	75	.261	.351	0	—	0	-10	-11	1	-0.8
1986 Bal-A	0	2	.000	14	0	0	0	1	16	18	1	12	11	16.9	5.63	73	.295	.411	0	—	0	-3	-3	0	-0.3
1988 Min-A	0	0	—	3	0	0	0	0	4	8	1	4	3	29.3	18.00	23	.471	.591	0	—	0	-6	-6	-0	0.0
Total 14	55	42	.567	546	2	0	0	115	834	732	53	425	632	12.6	3.45	111	.242	.337	0	—	0	47	35	9	9.2

● **JAVIER MARTINEZ** Martinez, Javier Antonio b: 2/5/77, Bayamon, P.R. BR/TR, 6'2", 210 lbs. Deb: 4/2/98

YEAR TM/L	W	L	PCT	G	GS	CG	SH	SV	IP	H	HR	BB	SO	RAT	ERA	ERA+	OAV	OOB	BH	AVG	PB	PR	/A	PD	TPI
1998 Pit-N	0	1	.000	37	0	0	0	0	41	39	5	34	42	16.9	4.83	90	.248	.395	0	.000	-0	-3	-2	-1	-0.2

● **BUCK MARTINEZ** Martinez, John Albert b: 11/7/48, Redding, Cal. BR/TR, 5'10", 190 lbs. Deb: 6/18/69 ♦

YEAR TM/L	W	L	PCT	G	GS	CG	SH	SV	IP	H	HR	BB	SO	RAT	ERA	ERA+	OAV	OOB	BH	AVG	PB	PR	/A	PD	TPI
1979 Mil-A	0	0	—	1	0	0	0	0	1	1	0	1	0	18.0	9.00	46	.250	.400	53	.270	0	-1	-1	0	0.0

● **DENNIS MARTINEZ** Martinez, Jose Dennis (Emilia) "El Presidente" b: 5/14/55, Granada, Nicaragua BR/TR, 6'1", 185 lbs. Deb: 9/14/76

YEAR TM/L	W	L	PCT	G	GS	CG	SH	SV	IP	H	HR	BB	SO	RAT	ERA	ERA+	OAV	OOB	BH	AVG	PB	PR	/A	PD	TPI
1976 Bal-A	1	2	.333	4	2	1	0	0	27^2	23	1	8	18	10.1	2.60	126	.237	.295	0	—	0	3	2	0	0.5
1977 Bal-A	14	7	.667	42	13	5	0	4	166^2	157	10	64	107	12.4	4.10	92	.253	.330	0	—	0	-1	-6	0	-0.6
1978 Bal-A	16	11	.593	40	38	15	2	0	276^1	257	20	93	142	11.5	3.52	99	.250	.314	0	—	0	8	-1	4	0.5
1979 *Bal-A	15	16	.484	40	39	**18**	3	0	**292^1**	279	28	78	132	11.0	3.66	109	.253	.303	0	—	0	18	11	3	1.5
1980 Bal-A	6	4	.600	25	12	2	0	1	99^2	103	12	44	42	13.5	3.97	100	.272	.351	0	—	0	1	-0	0	0.0
1981 Bal-A	**14**	5	.737	25	24	9	2	0	179	173	10	62	88	11.9	3.32	109	.254	.318	0	—	0	7	6	4	1.1
1982 Bal-A	16	12	.571	40	39	10	2	0	252	262	30	87	111	12.7	4.21	96	.267	.331	0	—	0	-4	-5	0	-0.5
1983 Bal-A	7	16	.304	32	25	4	0	0	153	209	21	45	71	15.1	5.53	71	.330	.376	0	—	0	-25	-27	5	-2.9
1984 Bal-A	6	9	.400	34	20	2	0	0	141^2	145	26	37	77	11.9	5.02	77	.263	.315	0	—	0	-16	-18	1	-1.5
1985 Bal-A	13	11	.542	33	31	3	1	0	180	203	29	63	68	13.8	5.15	78	.288	.353	0	—	0	-20	-22	0	-2.5
1986 Bal-A	0	0	—	4	0	0	0	0	6^2	11	0	2	2	17.6	6.75	61	.367	.406	0	—	0	-2	-2	0	0.1
Mon-N	3	6	.333	19	15	1	1	0	98	103	11	28	63	12.3	4.59	80	.274	.329	3	.100	-0	-10	-10	1	-0.8

YEAR	TM/L	W	L	PCT	G	GS	CG	SH	SV	IP	H	HR	BB	SO	RAT	ERA	ERA+	OAV	OOB	BH	AVG	PB	PR	/A	PD	TPI
1987	Mon-N	11	4	.733	22	22	2	1	0	144^2	133	9	40	84	11.1	3.30	127	.244	.302	3	.065	-2	13	15	0	1.2
1988	Mon-N	15	13	.536	34	34	9	2	0	235^1	215	21	55	120	10.6	2.72	132	.239	.287	15	.192	2	19	23	0	3.0
1989	Mon-N	16	7	.696	34	33	5	2	0	232	227	21	49	142	11.0	3.18	111	.257	.301	9	.125	-1	8	9	3	1.1
1990	Mon-N★	10	11	.476	32	32	7	2	0	226	191	16	49	156	9.8	2.95	124	.228	.275	7	.103	-2	21	18	1	1.5
1991	Mon-N★	14	11	.560	31	31	**9**	**5**	0	222	187	9	62	123	10.3	**2.39**	151	.226	.283	11	.153	1	**32**	30	4	3.9
1992	Mon-N★	16	11	.593	32	32	6	0	0	226^1	172	12	60	147	9.6	2.47	141	.211	.273	14	.189	1	26	25	3	3.5
1993	Mon-N	15	9	.625	35	34	2	0	1	224^2	211	27	64	138	11.5	3.85	108	.246	.307	11	.159	-0	5	8	3	1.1
1994	Cle-A	11	6	.647	24	24	7	3	0	176^2	166	14	44	92	11.1	3.52	134	.247	.301	0	—	0	25	24	2	2.1
1995	*Cle-A★	12	5	.706	28	28	3	2	0	187	174	17	46	99	11.2	3.08	152	.247	.304	0	—	0	34	34	4	3.0
1996	Cle-A	9	6	.600	20	20	1	1	0	112	122	12	37	48	12.9	4.50	109	.278	.337	0	—	0	6	5	2	0.8
1997	Sea-A	1	5	.167	9	9	0	0	0	49	65	8	29	17	18.6	7.71	58	.327	.430	0	—	0	-17	-18	-0	-1.7
1998	*Atl-N	4	6	.400	53	5	1	1	2	91	109	8	19	62	13.0	4.45	95	.295	.335	1	.091	-0	-2	-2	1	-0.2
Total	23	245	193	.559	692	562	122	30	8	3999^2	3897	372	1165	2149	11.7	3.70	106	.256	.314	74	.142	-3	128	99	43	14.2

● JOSE MARTINEZ
Martinez, Jose Miguel (Martinez) b: 4/1/71, Guayubin, D.R. BR/TR, 6'2", 180 lbs. Deb: 5/10/94

YEAR	TM/L	W	L	PCT	G	GS	CG	SH	SV	IP	H	HR	BB	SO	RAT	ERA	ERA+	OAV	OOB	BH	AVG	PB	PR	/A	PD	TPI
1994	SD-N	0	2	.000	4	1	0	0	0	12	18	2	5	7	17.3	6.75	61	.375	.434	0	.000	-0	-3	-4	0	-0.5

● MARTY MARTINEZ
Martinez, Orlando (Oliva) b: 8/23/41, Havana, Cuba BB/TR, 6'1", 175 lbs. Deb: 5/2/62 MC♦

YEAR	TM/L	W	L	PCT	G	GS	CG	SH	SV	IP	H	HR	BB	SO	RAT	ERA	ERA+	OAV	OOB	BH	AVG	PB	PR	/A	PD	TPI
1969	Hou-N	0	0	—	1	0	0	0	0	0^2	1	1	0	0	13.5	13.50	26	.333	.333	61	.308	0	-1	-1	-0	0.0

● PEDRO MARTINEZ
Martinez, Pedro (Aquino) b: 11/29/68, Villa Mella, D.R. BL/TL, 6'2", 185 lbs. Deb: 6/29/93

YEAR	TM/L	W	L	PCT	G	GS	CG	SH	SV	IP	H	HR	BB	SO	RAT	ERA	ERA+	OAV	OOB	BH	AVG	PB	PR	/A	PD	TPI
1993	SD-N	3	1	.750	32	0	0	0	0	37	23	4	13	32	9.0	2.43	170	.172	.250	0	.000	-0	7	7	-0	0.6
1994	SD-N	3	2	.600	48	1	0	0	3	68^1	52	4	49	52	13.4	2.90	142	.210	.342	0	.000	-1	10	9	1	0.7
1995	Hou-N	0	0	—	25	0	0	0	0	20^2	29	3	16	17	20.5	7.40	52	.330	.443	0	—	0	-7	-8	0	0.0
1996	NY-N	0	0	—	5	0	0	0	0	7	8	1	7	6	19.3	6.43	62	.296	.441	0	—	0	-2	-2	0	0.0
	Cin-N	0	0	—	4	0	0	0	0	3	5	1	1	3	18.0	6.00	70	.357	.400	0	—	0	-1	-1	-0	0.0
	Yr	0	0	—	9	0	0	0	0	10	13	2	8	9	18.9	6.30	65	.310	.420	0	—	0	-2	-2	-0	0.0
1997	Cin-N	1	1	.500	8	0	0	0	0	6^2	8	1	7	4	21.6	9.45	45	.286	.444	0	—	0	-4	-4	-0	-1.0
Total	5	7	4	.636	122	1	0	0	3	142^2	125	14	93	114	14.1	3.97	103	.232	.350	0	.000	-1	3	2	1	0.3

● PEDRO MARTINEZ
Martinez, Pedro Jaime (b: Pedro Jaime (Martinez)) b: 7/25/71, Manoguayabo, D.R. BR/TR, 5'11", 170 lbs. Deb: 9/24/92 F♦

YEAR	TM/L	W	L	PCT	G	GS	CG	SH	SV	IP	H	HR	BB	SO	RAT	ERA	ERA+	OAV	OOB	BH	AVG	PB	PR	/A	PD	TPI
1992	LA-N	0	1	.000	2	1	0	0	0	8	6	0	1	8	7.9	2.25	153	.200	.226	0	.000	-0	1	1	-0	0.1
1993	LA-N	10	5	.667	65	2	0	0	2	107	76	5	57	119	11.5	2.61	146	.201	.312	0	.000	-0	17	14	-2	1.7
1994	Mon-N	11	5	.688	24	23	1	1	1	144^2	115	11	45	142	10.6	3.42	123	.220	.295	4	.091	-1	13	13	-1	1.1
1995	Mon-N	14	10	.583	30	30	2	2	0	194^2	158	21	66	174	10.9	3.51	122	.227	.304	7	.111	-3	14	17	-0	1.6
1996	Mon-N★	13	10	.565	33	33	4	1	0	216^2	189	19	70	222	10.9	3.70	117	.232	.296	6	.094	-2	12	15	-2	1.0
1997	Mon-N★	17	8	.680	31	31	**13**	4	0	241^1	158	16	67	305	**8.7**	**1.90**	**220**	**.184**	**.250**	8	.116	-1	**62**	**61**	1	**6.3**
1998	*Bos-A☆	19	7	.731	33	33	3	2	0	233^2	188	26	67	251	10.1	2.89	160	.217	.280	0	.000	-1	46	45	-2	4.3
Total	7	84	46	.646	218	153	23	10	3	1146	890	98	373	1221	10.3	2.98	144	.214	.285	31	.114	-8	165	166	-7	16.1

● RAMON MARTINEZ
Martinez, Ramon Jaime (b: Ramon Jaime (Martinez)) b: 3/22/68, Santo Domingo, D.R. Deb: N/A.

YEAR	TM/L	W	L	PCT	G	GS	CG	SH	SV	IP	H	HR	BB	SO	RAT	ERA	ERA+	OAV	OOB	BH	AVG	PB	PR	/A	PD	TPI
1988	LA-N	1	3	.250	9	6	0	0	0	35^2	27	0	22	23	12.4	3.79	88	.216	.333	0	.000	-1	-1	-2	-0	-0.3
1989	LA-N	6	4	.600	15	15	2	2	0	98^2	79	11	41	89	11.4	3.19	107	.219	.308	6	.162	0	3	2	1	0.4
1990	LA-N★	20	6	.769	33	33	**12**	3	0	234^1	191	22	67	223	10.1	2.92	125	.220	.279	10	.125	-2	23	19	0	1.9
1991	LA-N	17	13	.567	33	33	6	4	0	220^1	190	18	69	150	10.9	3.27	110	.229	.294	9	.117	-1	10	8	-1	0.8
1992	LA-N	8	11	.421	25	25	1	1	0	150^2	141	11	69	101	12.8	4.00	86	.245	.331	6	.120	-1	-8	-9	-1	-1.4
1993	LA-N	10	12	.455	32	32	4	3	0	211^2	202	15	104	127	13.2	3.44	111	.255	.344	9	.129	-2	14	9	2	0.8
1994	LA-N	12	7	.632	24	24	4	**3**	0	170	160	18	56	119	11.8	3.97	99	.249	.315	18	.273	5	5	-1	-1	0.2
1995	*LA-N	17	7	.708	30	30	4	2	0	206^1	176	19	81	138	11.4	3.66	103	.231	.309	11	.172	1	12	3	-0	0.4
1996	LA-N	15	6	.714	28	27	2	2	0	168^2	153	12	86	133	13.2	3.42	113	.245	.344	7	.119	-2	15	8	1	0.8
1997	LA-N	10	5	.667	22	22	1	0	0	133^2	123	14	68	120	13.3	3.64	106	.243	.339	8	.190	1	8	3	1	0.5
1998	LA-N	7	3	.700	15	15	1	0	0	101^2	76	8	41	91	10.6	2.83	138	.206	.291	6	.176	1	16	12	1	1.3
Total	11	123	77	.615	266	262	37	20	0	1731^2	1518	148	704	1314	11.8	3.45	108	.235	.316	90	.154	0	96	54	2	5.4

● ROGELIO MARTINEZ
Martinez, Rogelio (Ulloa) "Limonar" b: 11/5/18, Cidra, Cuba BR/TR, 6', 180 lbs. Deb: 7/13/50

YEAR	TM/L	W	L	PCT	G	GS	CG	SH	SV	IP	H	HR	BB	SO	RAT	ERA	ERA+	OAV	OOB	BH	AVG	PB	PR	/A	PD	TPI
1950	Was-A	0	1	.000	2	1	0	0	0	1^1	4	0	2	0	40.5	27.00	17	.500	.600	0	—	0	-3	-3	-0	-1.5

● SILVIO MARTINEZ
Martinez, Silvio Ramon (Cabrera) b: 8/19/55, Santiago, D.R. BR/TR, 5'10", 170 lbs. Deb: 4/9/77

YEAR	TM/L	W	L	PCT	G	GS	CG	SH	SV	IP	H	HR	BB	SO	RAT	ERA	ERA+	OAV	OOB	BH	AVG	PB	PR	/A	PD	TPI
1977	Chi-A	0	1	.000	10	0	0	0	1	21	28	4	12	10	17.1	5.57	73	.337	.421	0	—	0	-4	-3	0	-0.2
1978	StL-N	9	8	.529	22	22	5	2	0	138^1	114	11	71	45	12.2	3.64	96	.228	.326	8	.170	0	-1	-2	-1	-0.4
1979	StL-N	15	8	.652	32	29	7	2	0	206^2	204	14	67	102	11.8	3.27	115	.259	.317	8	.129	-2	11	11	-3	0.7
1980	StL-N	5	10	.333	25	20	2	0	0	119^2	127	8	48	39	13.3	4.81	77	.273	.343	3	.086	-2	-16	-15	-2	-2.1
1981	StL-N	2	5	.286	18	16	0	0	0	97	95	4	39	34	12.5	3.99	89	.260	.333	7	.200	1	-5	-5	-1	-0.3
Total	5	31	32	.492	107	87	14	4	1	582^2	568	41	237	230	12.5	3.88	95	.258	.331	26	.145	-3	-15	-14	-7	-2.3

● WEDO MARTINI
Martini, Guido Joe "Southern" b: 7/1/13, Birmingham, Ala. d: 10/28/70, Philadelphia, Pa. BR/TR, 5'10", 165 lbs. Deb: 7/28/35

YEAR	TM/L	W	L	PCT	G	GS	CG	SH	SV	IP	H	HR	BB	SO	RAT	ERA	ERA+	OAV	OOB	BH	AVG	PB	PR	/A	PD	TPI
1935	Phi-A	0	2	.000	3	2	0	0	0	6^1	8	0	11	1	27.0	17.05	27	.333	.543	0	.000	-0	-9	-9	1	-1.7

● JOE MARTY
Marty, Joseph Anton b: 9/1/13, Sacramento, Cal. d: 10/4/84, Sacramento, Cal. BR/TR, 6', 182 lbs. Deb: 4/22/37 ♦

YEAR	TM/L	W	L	PCT	G	GS	CG	SH	SV	IP	H	HR	BB	SO	RAT	ERA	ERA+	OAV	OOB	BH	AVG	PB	PR	/A	PD	TPI
1939	Phi-N	0	0	—	1	0	0	0	0	4	2	0	3	1	11.3	4.50	89	.154	.313	76	.254	0	-0	-0	-0	0.0

● RANDY MARTZ
Martz, Randy Carl b: 5/28/56, Harrisburg, Pa. BL/TR, 6'4", 210 lbs. Deb: 9/6/80

YEAR	TM/L	W	L	PCT	G	GS	CG	SH	SV	IP	H	HR	BB	SO	RAT	ERA	ERA+	OAV	OOB	BH	AVG	PB	PR	/A	PD	TPI
1980	Chi-N	1	2	.333	6	6	0	0	0	30^1	28	1	11	5	11.6	2.08	188	.241	.307	1	.111	-1	5	6	1	0.6
1981	Chi-N	5	7	.417	33	14	1	0	6	107^2	103	6	49	32	12.8	3.68	100	.256	.338	6	.214	1	-2	0	0	0.1
1982	Chi-N	11	10	.524	28	24	1	0	1	147^2	157	17	36	40	11.9	4.21	89	.272	.318	6	.143	1	-10	-8	1	-0.8
1983	Chi-A	0	0	—	1	1	0	0	0	5	4	0	4	1	14.4	3.60	116	.211	.348	0	—	0	0	0	-0	-0.1
Total	4	17	19	.472	68	45	2	0	7	290^2	292	24	100	78	12.3	3.78	99	.262	.325	13	.165	1	-7	-1	1	-0.2

● DEL MASON
Mason, Adelbert William b: 10/29/1883, Newfane, N.Y. d: 12/31/62, Winter Park, Fla. BR/TR, 6', 160 lbs. Deb: 4/23/04

YEAR	TM/L	W	L	PCT	G	GS	CG	SH	SV	IP	H	HR	BB	SO	RAT	ERA	ERA+	OAV	OOB	BH	AVG	PB	PR	/A	PD	TPI
1904	Was-A	0	3	.000	5	3	2	0	0	33	45	1	13	16	16.4	6.00	44	.326	.392	0	.000	-2	-12	-12	-1	-1.2
1906	Cin-N	0	1	.000	2	1	1	0	0	12	10	1	6	4	12.8	4.50	61	.250	.362	0	.000	-1	-2	-2	-0	-0.3
1907	Cin-N	5	12	.294	25	17	13	1	0	146	144	2	55	45	12.6	3.14	83	.277	.353	8	.182	-0	-11	-9	1	-1.0
Total	3	5	16	.238	32	21	16	1	0	191	199	4	74	65	13.3	3.72	70	.286	.362	8	.125	-3	-26	-23	0	-2.5

● CHARLIE MASON
Mason, Charles E. b: 6/25/1853, New Orleans, La. d: 10/21/36, Philadelphia, Pa. BR/TR, 175 lbs. Deb: 4/26/1875 M♦

YEAR	TM/L	W	L	PCT	G	GS	CG	SH	SV	IP	H	HR	BB	SO	RAT	ERA	ERA+	OAV	OOB	BH	AVG	PB	PR	/A	PD	TPI
1875	Was-n	0	0	—	1	0	0	0	0	2	3	0	1	0	18.0	4.50	53	.300	.364	3	.091	-0	-1	-0		0.0

● ERNIE MASON
Mason, Ernest b: New Orleans, La. d: 7/30/04, Covington, La. Deb: 7/17/1894

YEAR	TM/L	W	L	PCT	G	GS	CG	SH	SV	IP	H	HR	BB	SO	RAT	ERA	ERA+	OAV	OOB	BH	AVG	PB	PR	/A	PD	TPI
1894	StL-N	0	3	.000	4	2	2	0	0	22^2	34	1	10	3	17.5	7.15	76	.343	.404	3	.250	-0	-5	-4	-1	-0.4

● HANK MASON
Mason, Henry b: 6/19/31, Marshall, Mo. BR/TR, 6', 185 lbs. Deb: 9/12/58

YEAR	TM/L	W	L	PCT	G	GS	CG	SH	SV	IP	H	HR	BB	SO	RAT	ERA	ERA+	OAV	OOB	BH	AVG	PB	PR	/A	PD	TPI
1958	Phi-N	0	0	—	1	0	0	0	0	5	7	0	2	3	18.0	10.80	37	.368	.455	0	.000	-0	-4	-4	-0	0.0
1960	Phi-N	0	0	—	3	0	0	0	0	5^2	9	1	5	3	22.2	9.53	41	.375	.483	0	.000	-0	-4	-4	-0	0.0
Total	2	0	0	—	4	0	0	0	0	10^2	16	1	7	6	20.3	10.13	39	.372	.471	0	.000	-0	-7	-7	-0	0.0

● MIKE MASON
Mason, Michael Paul b: 11/21/58, Faribault, Minn. BL/TL, 6'2", 205 lbs. Deb: 9/13/82

YEAR	TM/L	W	L	PCT	G	GS	CG	SH	SV	IP	H	HR	BB	SO	RAT	ERA	ERA+	OAV	OOB	BH	AVG	PB	PR	/A	PD	TPI
1982	Tex-A	1	2	.333	4	4	0	0	0	23	21	3	9	8	11.7	5.09	76	.244	.316	0	—	0	-3	-3	0	-0.2
1983	Tex-A	0	2	.000	5	0	0	0	0	10^2	10	0	6	9	14.3	5.91	68	.244	.354	0	—	0	-2	-2	0	-0.3
1984	Tex-A	9	13	.409	36	24	4	0	0	184^1	159	18	51	113	10.4	3.61	115	.233	.288	0	—	0	8	11	-1	1.0
1985	Tex-A	8	15	.348	38	30	1	1	0	179	212	22	73	92	14.5	4.83	88	.299	.366	0	—	0	-14	-12	-0	-1.4
1986	Tex-A	7	3	.700	27	22	2	1	0	135	135	11	56	85	12.7	4.33	99	.257	.329	0	—	0	-2	-0	0	-0.1
1987	Tex-A	0	2	.000	8	6	0	0	0	29	37	6	22	21	19.6	5.59	80	.322	.447	0	—	0	-4	-4	0	-0.2
	Chi-N	4	1	.800	17	4	0	0	0	38	43	4	23	28	15.9	5.68	75	.303	.404	2	.222	0	-7	-6	-0	-0.7

YEAR	TM/L	W	L	PCT	G	GS	CG	SH	SV	IP	H	HR	BB	SO	RAT	ERA	ERA+	OAV	OOB	BH	AVG	PB	PR	/A	PD	TPI
1988	Min-A	0	1	.000	5	0	0	0	0	6^2	8	1	9	7	23.0	10.80	38	.286	.459	0	—	0	-5	-5	-0	-0.7
Total	7	29	39	.426	140	90	7	2	0	605^2	625	65	249	363	13.2	4.53	93	.268	.342	2	.222	0	-28	-21	-1	-2.6

● ROGER MASON

Mason, Roger Le Roy b: 9/18/58, Bellaire, Mich. BR/TR, 6′6″, 220 lbs. Deb: 9/4/84

YEAR	TM/L	W	L	PCT	G	GS	CG	SH	SV	IP	H	HR	BB	SO	RAT	ERA	ERA+	OAV	OOB	BH	AVG	PB	PR	/A	PD	TPI
1984	Det-A	1	1	.500	5	2	0	0	1	22	23	1	10	15	13.5	4.50	87	.271	.347	0	—	0	-1	-1	0	-0.1
1985	SF-N	1	3	.250	5	5	1	1	0	29^2	28	1	11	26	11.8	2.12	162	.243	.310	1	.091	-0	5	4	-0	0.5
1986	SF-N	3	4	.429	11	11	1	0	0	60	56	5	30	43	13.4	4.80	73	.250	.346	1	.048	-2	-7	-9	-1	-1.1
1987	SF-N	1	1	.500	5	5	0	0	0	26	30	4	10	18	13.8	4.50	85	.303	.367	1	.125	0	-1	-2	0	-0.1
1989	Hou-N	0	0	—	2	0	0	0	0	1^1	2	0	2	3	27.0	20.25	17	.333	.500	0	—	0	-2	-2	0	0.0
1991	*Pit-N	3	2	.600	24	0	0	0	3	29^2	21	2	6	21	8.5	3.03	118	.200	.250	0	—	0	2	2	0	0.4
1992	*Pit-N	5	7	.417	65	0	0	0	8	88	80	11	33	56	12.0	4.09	84	.246	.323	0	.000	-1	-6	-6	-1	-1.2
1993	SD-N	0	7	.000	34	0	0	0	0	50	43	1	18	39	11.3	3.24	128	.242	.318	0	.000	-0	4	5	-0	0.6
	*Phi-N	5	5	.500	34	0	0	0	0	49^2	47	9	16	32	11.4	4.89	81	.246	.304	1	.333	0	-5	-5	-1	-1.0
	Yr	5	12	.294	68	0	0	0	0	99^2	90	10	34	71	11.2	4.06	100	.241	.304	1	.167	-0	-0	-0	-2	-0.4
1994	Phi-N	1	1	.500	6	0	0	0	0	8^2	11	2	5	7	16.6	5.19	83	.306	.390	0	—	0	-1	-1	-0	-0.2
	NY-N	2	4	.333	41	0	0	0	1	51^1	44	6	20	26	11.6	3.51	119	.232	.311	0	—	0	4	4	-1	0.3
	Yr	3	5	.375	47	0	0	0	1	60	55	8	25	33	12.3	3.75	112	.243	.324	0	—	0	3	3	-1	0.1
Total	9	22	35	.386	232	23	2	1	13	416^1	385	42	161	286	12.1	4.02	94	.248	.323	4	.071	-2	-8	-12	-5	-1.9

● WALT MASTERS

Masters, Walter Thomas b: 3/28/07, Pen Argyl, Pa. d: 7/10/92, Ottawa, Ont., Can. BR/TR, 5′10.5″, 180 lbs. Deb: 7/9/31

YEAR	TM/L	W	L	PCT	G	GS	CG	SH	SV	IP	H	HR	BB	SO	RAT	ERA	ERA+	OAV	OOB	BH	AVG	PB	PR	/A	PD	TPI
1931	Was-A	0	0	—	3	0	0	0	1	9	7	0	4	1	11.0	2.00	215	.226	.314	0	.000	-0	2	2	1	0.1
1937	Phi-N	0	0	—	1	0	0	0	0	1	5	0	1	0	54.0	36.00	12	.714	.750	0	—	0	-4	-4	-0	0.0
1939	Phi-A	0	0	—	4	0	0	0	0	11	15	0	8	2	18.8	6.55	72	.306	.404	0	.000	-0	-2	-2	0	0.0
Total	3	0	0	—	8	0	0	0	1	21	27	0	13	3	17.1	6.00	75	.310	.400	0	.000	-1	-4	-3	1	0.1

● PAUL MASTERSON

Masterson, Paul Nicholas "Lefty" (b: Paul Nicholas Nastasowski)
b: 10/16/15, Chicago, Ill. d: 11/27/97, Chicago, Ill. BL/TL, 5′11″, 165 lbs. Deb: 9/15/40

YEAR	TM/L	W	L	PCT	G	GS	CG	SH	SV	IP	H	HR	BB	SO	RAT	ERA	ERA+	OAV	OOB	BH	AVG	PB	PR	/A	PD	TPI
1940	Phi-N	0	0	—	2	0	0	0	0	5	5	0	2	3	12.6	7.20	54	.263	.333	0	.000	-0	-2	-2	0	0.0
1941	Phi-N	1	0	1.000	2	1	1	0	0	11^1	11	0	6	8	13.5	4.76	78	.250	.340	0	.000	-1	-1	-1	0	-0.2
1942	Phi-N	0	0	—	4	0	0	0	0	8^1	10	1	5	3	16.2	6.48	51	.303	.395	0	—	0	-3	-3	0	0.0
Total	3	1	0	1.000	8	1	1	0	0	24^2	26	1	13	14	14.2	5.84	62	.271	.358	0	.000	-1	-6	-6	0	-0.2

● WALT MASTERSON

Masterson, Walter Edward b: 6/22/20, Philadelphia, Pa. BR/TR, 6′2″, 189 lbs. Deb: 5/8/39

YEAR	TM/L	W	L	PCT	G	GS	CG	SH	SV	IP	H	HR	BB	SO	RAT	ERA	ERA+	OAV	OOB	BH	AVG	PB	PR	/A	PD	TPI
1939	Was-A	2	2	.500	24	5	1	0	0	58^1	66	2	48	12	17.9	5.55	78	.293	.422	2	.154	-0	-6	-8	-1	-0.5
1940	Was-A	3	13	.188	31	19	3	0	2	130^1	128	6	88	68	15.1	4.90	85	.257	.371	7	.184	0	-8	-11	-1	-1.2
1941	Was-A	4	3	.571	34	6	1	0	3	78^1	101	3	53	40	17.8	5.97	68	.321	.420	2	.105	-1	-16	-17	1	-1.5
1942	Was-A	5	9	.357	25	15	8	4	2	142^2	138	6	54	63	12.2	3.34	109	.251	.321	7	.156	-0	5	5	-2	0.2
1945	Was-A	1	2	.333	4	2	1	1	0	25	21	1	10	14	11.2	1.08	287	.228	.304	1	.111	-1	6	6	0	0.6
1946	Was-A	5	6	.455	29	9	2	0	1	91^1	105	8	67	61	17.2	6.01	56	.295	.411	2	.080	-1	-25	-27	0	-3.1
1947	Was-A★	12	16	.429	35	31	14	4	1	253	215	11	97	135	11.2	3.13	119	.234	.309	11	.133	-3	16	17	3	1.8
1948	Was-A★	8	15	.348	33	27	9	2	2	188	171	12	122	72	14.2	3.83	113	.247	.363	11	.193	-0	10	11	-2	1.0
1949	Was-A	3	2	.600	10	7	3	0	0	53	42	4	21	17	11.2	3.23	132	.216	.303	1	.056	-1	6	6	1	0.5
	Bos-A	3	4	.429	18	5	1	0	4	55	58	2	35	19	15.2	4.25	102	.283	.387	2	.118	-0	-0	1	-1	-0.1
	Yr	6	6	.500	28	12	4	0	4	108	100	6	56	36	13.0	3.75	115	.249	.341	3	.086	-2	5	7	-0	0.4
1950	Bos-A	8	6	.571	33	15	6	0	1	129^1	145	15	82	60	15.9	5.64	87	.287	.387	6	.136	-3	-15	-11	1	-1.1
1951	Bos-A	3	0	1.000	30	1	0	0	2	59^1	53	1	32	39	12.9	3.34	134	.228	.322	2	.182	-1	5	7	0	0.3
1952	Bos-A	1	1	.500	5	1	0	0	0	9^1	18	1	11	3	28.0	11.57	34	.400	.518	0	.000	0	-8	-8	0	-1.4
	Was-A	9	8	.529	24	21	11	0	2	160^2	153	11	72	89	12.8	3.70	96	.253	.336	6	.120	-1	-0	-2	1	-0.3
	Yr	10	9	.526	29	22	11	0	2	170	171	12	83	92	13.6	4.13	87	.263	.350	6	.115	-1	-9	-10	1	-1.7
1953	Was-A	10	12	.455	29	20	10	4	0	166^1	145	16	62	95	11.4	3.63	107	.232	.304	7	.137	-1	7	5	0	0.5
1956	Det-A	1	1	.500	35	0	0	0	0	49^2	54	2	32	28	15.8	4.17	99	.289	.395	1	.250	0	-0	-0	-0	-0.1
Total	14	78	100	.438	399	184	70	15	20	1649^2	1613	101	886	815	13.8	4.15	96	.258	.353	68	.140	-14	-24	-27	0	-4.4

● LEN MATARAZZO

Matarazzo, Leonard b: 9/12/28, New Castle, Pa. BR/TR, 6′4″, 195 lbs. Deb: 9/6/52

YEAR	TM/L	W	L	PCT	G	GS	CG	SH	SV	IP	H	HR	BB	SO	RAT	ERA	ERA+	OAV	OOB	BH	AVG	PB	PR	/A	PD	TPI
1952	Phi-A	0	0	—	1	0	0	0	0	1	1	0	1	0	18.0	0.00	—	.250	.400	0	—	0	0	0	-0	0.0

● GREG MATHEWS

Mathews, Gregory Inman b: 5/17/62, Harbor City, Cal. BR/TL, 6′2″, 180 lbs. Deb: 6/3/86

YEAR	TM/L	W	L	PCT	G	GS	CG	SH	SV	IP	H	HR	BB	SO	RAT	ERA	ERA+	OAV	OOB	BH	AVG	PB	PR	/A	PD	TPI
1986	StL-N	11	8	.579	23	22	1	0	0	145^1	139	15	44	67	11.5	3.65	100	.259	.317	2	.047	-3	1	-0	-2	-0.5
1987	*StL-N	11	11	.500	32	32	2	1	0	197^2	184	17	71	108	11.6	3.73	111	.249	.314	13	.191	1	8	9	-1	0.9
1988	StL-N	4	6	.400	13	13	1	0	0	68	61	4	33	31	12.7	4.24	82	.247	.340	4	.174	0	-6	-6	0	-0.8
1990	StL-N	0	5	.000	11	10	0	0	0	50^2	53	2	30	18	15.1	5.33	72	.277	.381	3	.214	1	-9	-9	1	-0.5
1992	Phi-N	2	3	.400	14	7	0	0	0	52^1	54	7	24	27	13.6	5.16	68	.270	.351	0	.000	-1	-10	-10	-1	-1.0
Total	5	28	33	.459	93	84	4	1	0	514	491	45	202	251	12.3	4.08	94	.256	.330	22	.136	-1	-16	-15	-3	-1.9

● BOBBY MATHEWS

Mathews, Robert T. b: 11/21/1851, Baltimore, Md. d: 4/17/1898, Baltimore, Md. BR/TR, 5′5.5″, 140 lbs. Deb: 5/4/1871 U♦

YEAR	TM/L	W	L	PCT	G	GS	CG	SH	SV	IP	H	HR	BB	SO	RAT	ERA	ERA+	OAV	OOB	BH	AVG	PB	PR	/A	PD	TPI
1871	Kek-n	6	11	.353	19	19	19	**1**	0	169	261	5	21	17	15.0	5.17	88	.305	.322	24	.270	-3	-18	-11		-0.8
1872	Bal-n	25	18	.581	49	47	39	0	0	406	480	3	52	**55**	11.8	3.19	115	.257	.277	50	.224	-8	20	21		0.5
1873	Mut-n	29	23	.558	52	52	47	2	0	443	489	5	62	**75**	11.2	2.56	123	.251	.274	43	.193	-2	34	30		1.8
1874	Mut-n	42	22	.656	65	65	62	**4**	0	578	652	3	41	**101**	10.8	1.90	118	.261	.273	72	.242	-2	18	22		1.5
1875	Mut-n	29	38	.433	70	70	**69**	3	0	**625^2**	711	4	20	75	10.5	2.49	94	.260	.265	48	.182	-10	-18	-11		-2.3
1876	NY-N	21	34	.382	56	56	55	2	0	516	693	8	24	37	12.5	2.86	75	.301	.308	40	.183	-10	-32	-41	-3	-4.3
1877	Cin-N	3	12	.200	15	15	13	0	0	129^1	208	0	17	9	15.7	4.04	66	.339	.357	10	.169	-3	-18	-20	-1	-2.1
1879	Pro-N	12	6	.667	27	25	15	1	**1**	189	194	4	26	90	10.5	2.29	103	.258	.282	35	.202	-0	4	1	0	0.1
1881	Pro-N	4	8	.333	14	14	10	1	0	102^1	121	2	21	28	12.5	3.17	84	.268	.300	11	.193	-2	-4	-6	-1	-0.7
	Bos-N	1	0	1.000	5	1	1	0	2	23	22	0	11	5	12.9	2.35	113	.239	.320	12	.169	-1	1	1	-0	0.0
	Yr	5	8	.385	19	15	11	1	**2**	125^1	143	2	32	33	12.6	3.02	88	.263	.304	23	.180	-3	-3	-5	-2	-0.7
1882	Bos-N	19	15	.559	34	32	31	0	0	285	278	5	22	153	9.5	2.87	100	.232	.246	38	.225	-2	1	-0	-4	-0.6
1883	Phi-a	30	13	.698	44	44	41	1	0	381	396	11	31	203	10.1	2.46	141	.251	.265	31	.186	-7	36	43	-1	3.2
1884	Phi-a	30	18	.625	49	49	48	3	0	430^2	401	10	49	286	9.7	3.32	102	.232	.258	34	.185	-5	-4	3	-2	-0.4
1885	Phi-a	30	17	.638	48	48	46	2	0	422^1	394	3	57	286	10.0	2.43	142	.233	.267	30	.168	-7	38	47	0	3.8
1886	Phi-a	13	9	.591	24	24	22	0	0	197^2	226	3	53	93	13.3	3.96	88	.267	.320	21	.239	-0	-11	-10	0	-0.9
1887	Phi-a	3	4	.429	7	7	7	0	0	58	75	4	25	9	16.0	6.67	64	.298	.368	5	.200	-0	-15	-15	0	-1.3
Total	5 n	131	112	.539	255	253	236	10	0	2221^2	2593	20	196	323	11.3	2.68	108	.261	.276	237	.216	-25	36	52		0.7
Total	10	166	136	.550	323	315	289	10	3	2734^1	3008	50	336	1199	11.2	3.00	100	.261	.285	267	.192	-37	-3	-3	-11	-3.2

● TERRY MATHEWS

Mathews, Terry Alan b: 10/5/64, Alexandria, La. BL/TR, 6′2″, 225 lbs. Deb: 6/21/91

YEAR	TM/L	W	L	PCT	G	GS	CG	SH	SV	IP	H	HR	BB	SO	RAT	ERA	ERA+	OAV	OOB	BH	AVG	PB	PR	/A	PD	TPI
1991	Tex-A	4	0	1.000	34	2	0	0	1	57^1	54	5	18	51	11.5	3.61	112	.251	.312	0	—	0	3	3	0	0.2
1992	Tex-A	2	4	.333	40	0	0	0	0	42^1	48	4	31	26	17.0	5.95	64	.294	.410	0	—	0	-9	-10	0	-1.3
1994	Fla-N	2	1	.667	24	2	0	0	0	43	45	4	9	21	11.5	3.35	130	.268	.309	3	.500	1	4	5	0	0.5
1995	Fla-N	4	4	.500	57	0	0	0	3	82^2	70	9	27	72	10.7	3.38	125	.235	.301	6	.462	3	7	8	-0	0.9
1996	Fla-N	2	4	.333	57	0	0	0	4	55	59	7	27	49	14.2	4.91	83	.273	.357	0	.000	-0	-4	-5	0	-0.6
	*Bal-A	2	2	.500	14	0	0	0	0	18^2	20	3	7	13	13.0	3.38	146	.282	.346	0	—	0	3	3	-0	0.6
1997	*Bal-A	4	4	.500	57	0	0	0	1	63^1	63	8	36	39	14.1	4.41	100	.267	.364	0	—	0	1	-0	0	0.2
1998	Bal-A	0	1	.000	17	0	0	0	0	20^1	26	6	8	10	15.0	6.20	73	.342	.405	0	—	0	-4	-4	1	-0.1
Total	7	20	20	.500	300	4	0	0	9	382^2	385	46	163	281	13.0	4.23	100	.267	.343	9	.391	3	2	-1	1	0.4

● T. J. MATHEWS

Mathews, Timothy Jay b: 1/9/70, Belleville, Ill. BR/TR, 6′2″, 200 lbs. Deb: 7/28/95 F

YEAR	TM/L	W	L	PCT	G	GS	CG	SH	SV	IP	H	HR	BB	SO	RAT	ERA	ERA+	OAV	OOB	BH	AVG	PB	PR	/A	PD	TPI
1995	StL-N	1	1	.500	23	0	0	0	2	29^2	21	1	11	28	9.7	1.52	276	.200	.276	0	.000	-0	9	9	1	0.7
1996	*StL-N	2	6	.250	67	0	0	0	6	83^2	62	8	32	80	10.3	3.01	139	.203	.282	0	.000	-0	11	11	-2	0.9
1997	StL-N	4	4	.500	40	0	0	0	0	46	41	4	18	46	11.7	2.15	193	.238	.314	0	.000	-0	10	10	-0	1.6
	Oak-A	6	2	.750	24	0	0	0	3	28^2	34	5	12	24	14.8	4.40	103	.293	.364	0	—	0	1	0	-0	0.2

YEAR	TM/L	W	L	PCT	G	GS	CG	SH	SV	IP	H	HR	BB	SO	RAT	ERA	ERA+	OAV	OOB	BH	AVG	PB	PR	/A	PD	TPI
1998	Oak-A	7	4	.636	66	0	0	0	1	72^2	71	6	29	53	12.9	4.58	99	.258	.338	0	—	0	1	-0	-1	0.0
Total	4	20	17	.541	220	0	0	0	12	260^2	229	24	102	231	11.7	3.28	132	.235	.313	0	.000	-1	31	30	-2	3.4

● CHRISTY MATHEWSON Mathewson, Christopher "Matty" or "Big Six"
b: 8/12/1880, Factoryville, Pa. d: 10/7/25, Saranac Lake, N.Y. BR/TR, 6'1.5", 195 lbs. Deb: 7/17/00 FMCH

YEAR	TM/L	W	L	PCT	G	GS	CG	SH	SV	IP	H	HR	BB	SO	RAT	ERA	ERA+	OAV	OOB	BH	AVG	PB	PR	/A	PD	TPI
1900	NY-N	0	3	.000	6	1	1	0	0	33^2	37	1	20	15	16.3	5.08	71	.278	.389	2	.182	0	-5	-5	0	-0.3
1901	NY-N	20	17	.541	40	38	36	5	0	336	288	3	97	221	10.7	2.41	137	.230	.292	28	.215	-1	34	33	8	4.1
1902	NY-N	14	17	.452	34	32	29	**8**	0	276^2	241	3	73	159	10.5	2.11	133	.234	.292	26	.205	2	20	21	4	3.0
1903	NY-N	30	13	.698	45	42	37	3	2	366^1	321	4	100	**267**	10.6	2.26	148	.231	.287	28	.226	3	**41**	44	2	**5.3**
1904	NY-N	33	12	.733	48	46	33	4	1	367^2	306	7	78	**212**	9.5	2.03	134	.226	.270	30	.226	6	29	28	6	4.7
1905	*NY-N	**31**	9	.775	43	37	32	**8**	3	338^2	252	4	64	**206**	**8.4**	**1.28**	**230**	.205	**.245**	30	.236	10	**65**	**62**	6	**9.7**
1906	NY-N	22	12	.647	38	35	22	6	1	266^2	262	3	77	128	11.5	2.97	88	.259	.313	24	.264	7	-10	-11	4	-0.2
1907	NY-N	**24**	12	.667	41	36	31	**8**	2	315	250	5	53	**178**	**8.7**	2.00	124	.212	**.247**	20	.187	3	17	17	1	2.5
1908	NY-N	**37**	11	.771	**56**	44	**34**	**11**	**5**	**390^2**	285	5	42	**259**	**7.6**	**1.43**	**169**	.200	**.225**	20	.155	1	**41**	**43**	10	**7.3**
1909	NY-N	25	6	**.806**	37	33	26	8	2	275^1	192	2	36	149	**7.5**	**1.14**	**223**	.200	**.228**	25	.263	7	44	43	6	**7.0**
1910	NY-N	**27**	9	.750	38	35	**27**	2	0	318^1	292	5	60	184	10.0	1.89	157	.248	.286	25	.234	7	**40**	**38**	7	**6.0**
1911	*NY-N	26	13	.667	45	37	29	5	3	307	303	5	38	141	10.0	**1.99**	**169**	.259	.283	22	.196	0	**48**	**47**	7	**6.7**
1912	*NY-N	23	12	.657	43	34	27	0	4	310	311	5	34	134	10.1	2.12	159	.260	**.281**	29	.264	5	**44**	**43**	0	5.2
1913	*NY-N	25	11	.694	40	35	25	4	2	306	291	8	21	93	**9.2**	**2.06**	**152**	.252	**.266**	19	.184	-0	**39**	**36**	4	**4.6**
1914	NY-N	24	13	.649	41	35	29	5	2	312	314	16	23	80	9.8	3.00	88	.263	.278	23	.219	6	-7	-12	2	-0.6
1915	NY-N	8	14	.364	27	24	11	1	0	186	199	9	20	57	10.6	3.58	72	.277	.298	8	.157	3	-17	-21	1	-2.1
1916	NY-N	3	4	.429	12	6	4	1	2	65^2	59	3	7	16	9.0	2.33	104	.243	.264	0	.000	-1	2	1	2	0.2
	Cin-N	1	0	1.000	1	1	1	0	0	9	15	1	1	3	16.0	8.00	32	.366	.381	3	.600	1	-5	-5	0	-0.3
	Yr	4	4	.500	13	7	5	1	2	74^2	74	4	8	19	9.9	3.01	81	.261	.281	3	.136	1	-3	-5	2	-0.1
Total	17	373	188	.665	635	551	434	79	29	4780^2	4218	89	844	2502	9.6	2.13	136	.236	.273	362	.215	59	420	403	68	62.8

● HENRY MATHEWSON Mathewson, Henry b: 12/24/1886, Factoryville, Pa. d: 7/1/17, Factoryville, Pa. BR/TR, 6'3", 175 lbs. Deb: 9/28/06 F

YEAR	TM/L	W	L	PCT	G	GS	CG	SH	SV	IP	H	HR	BB	SO	RAT	ERA	ERA+	OAV	OOB	BH	AVG	PB	PR	/A	PD	TPI
1906	NY-N	0	1	.000	2	1	1	0	1	10	7	0	14	2	19.8	5.40	48	.194	.431	0	.000	-0	-3	-3	0	-0.3
1907	NY-N	0	0	—	1	0	0	0	1	1	1	0	0	0	9.0	0.00	—	.250	.250	0	—	0	0	0	-0	0.1
Total	2	0	1	.000	3	1	1	0	2	11	8	0	14	2	18.8	4.91	53	.200	.418	0	.000	-0	-3	-3	0	-0.2

● CARL MATHIAS Mathias, Carl Lynwood "Stubby" b: 6/13/36, Bechtelsville, Pa BB/TL, 5'11", 195 lbs. Deb: 7/31/60

YEAR	TM/L	W	L	PCT	G	GS	CG	SH	SV	IP	H	HR	BB	SO	RAT	ERA	ERA+	OAV	OOB	BH	AVG	PB	PR	/A	PD	TPI
1960	Cle-A	0	1	.000	7	0	0	0	0	15^1	14	2	8	13	12.9	3.52	106	.233	.324	0	.000	-0	1	0	0	0.0
1961	Was-A	0	1	.000	4	3	0	0	0	13^2	22	3	4	7	17.8	11.20	36	.361	.409	1	.200	-0	-11	-11	-0	-0.7
Total	2	0	2	.000	11	3	0	0	0	29	36	5	12	20	15.2	7.14	54	.298	.366	1	.167	-0	-10	-11	0	-0.7

● RON MATHIS Mathis, Ronald Vance b: 9/25/58, Kansas City, Mo. BR/TR, 6', 175 lbs. Deb: 4/13/85

YEAR	TM/L	W	L	PCT	G	GS	CG	SH	SV	IP	H	HR	BB	SO	RAT	ERA	ERA+	OAV	OOB	BH	AVG	PB	PR	/A	PD	TPI
1985	Hou-N	3	5	.375	23	8	0	0	1	70	83	7	27	34	14.3	6.04	57	.293	.357	1	.071	-1	-19	-20	-0	-2.2
1987	Hou-N	0	1	.000	8	0	0	0	0	12	10	2	11	8	15.8	5.25	75	.233	.389	0	.000	-0	-2	-2	0	-0.1
Total	2	3	6	.333	31	8	0	0	1	82	93	9	38	42	14.5	5.93	60	.285	.362	1	.063	-1	-21	-22	-0	-2.3

● JON MATLACK Matlack, Jonathan Trumpbour b: 1/19/50, West Chester, Pa. BL/TL, 6'3", 205 lbs. Deb: 7/11/71 C

YEAR	TM/L	W	L	PCT	G	GS	CG	SH	SV	IP	H	HR	BB	SO	RAT	ERA	ERA+	OAV	OOB	BH	AVG	PB	PR	/A	PD	TPI
1971	NY-N	0	3	.000	7	6	0	0	0	37	31	2	15	24	11.2	4.14	82	.228	.305	3	.273	1	-3	-3	-1	-0.2
1972	NY-N	15	10	.600	34	32	8	4	0	244	215	14	71	169	10.6	2.32	145	.234	.291	10	.128	1	31	28	-1	2.9
1973	*NY-N	14	16	.467	34	34	14	3	0	242	210	16	99	205	11.6	3.20	113	.236	.314	9	.138	2	12	11	1	1.6
1974	NY-N★	13	15	.464	34	34	14	**7**	0	265^1	221	8	76	195	10.2	2.41	148	.226	.285	8	.101	-4	36	34	-0	3.1
1975	NY-N★	16	12	.571	33	32	8	3	0	228^2	224	15	58	154	11.1	3.38	102	.254	.300	7	.100	0	6	2	-2	0.0
1976	NY-N☆	17	10	.630	35	35	16	**6**	0	262	236	18	57	153	10.2	2.95	112	.242	.286	17	.193	4	16	10	-1	1.3
1977	NY-N	7	15	.318	26	26	5	3	0	169	175	19	43	123	11.7	4.21	89	.273	.321	3	.060	-2	-6	-9	0	-1.2
1978	Tex-A	15	13	.536	35	33	18	2	1	270	252	14	51	157	10.2	2.27	165	.245	.284	0	—	0	45	44	0	4.7
1979	Tex-A	5	4	.556	13	13	2	0	0	85	98	9	15	35	12.1	4.13	100	.293	.325	0	—	0	1	0	0	0.1
1980	Tex-A	10	10	.500	35	34	8	1	1	234^2	265	17	48	142	12.0	3.68	106	.287	.323	0	—	0	9	6	-3	0.1
1981	Tex-A	4	7	.364	17	16	1	1	0	104^1	101	8	41	43	12.3	4.14	84	.258	.330	0	—	0	-6	-8	-0	-0.7
1982	Tex-A	7	7	.500	33	14	1	0	1	147^2	158	14	37	78	12.0	3.53	109	.275	.321	0	—	0	9	6	0	0.7
1983	Tex-A	2	4	.333	25	9	2	0	0	73^1	90	7	27	38	14.7	4.66	86	.307	.372	0	—	0	-5	-5	1	-0.3
Total	13	125	126	.498	361	318	97	30	3	2363	2276	161	638	1516	11.2	3.18	114	.254	.305	57	.129	2	145	115	-5	12.1

● AL MATTERN Mattern, Alonzo Albert b: 6/16/1883, W.Rush, N.Y. d: 11/6/58, West Rush, N.Y. BL/TR, 5'10", 165 lbs. Deb: 9/16/08

YEAR	TM/L	W	L	PCT	G	GS	CG	SH	SV	IP	H	HR	BB	SO	RAT	ERA	ERA+	OAV	OOB	BH	AVG	PB	PR	/A	PD	TPI
1908	Bos-N	1	2	.333	5	3	1	1	0	30^1	30	0	6	8	10.7	2.08	116	.265	.303	1	.125	-0	1	1	-0	0.0
1909	Bos-N	15	21	.417	47	32	24	2	3	316^1	322	4	108	98	12.3	2.85	99	.268	.330	17	.168	-1	-9	-1	3	0.1
1910	Bos-N	16	19	.457	**51**	37	17	**6**	1	305	288	5	121	94	12.2	2.98	112	.257	.332	16	.163	-4	2	12	1	0.9
1911	Bos-N	4	15	.211	33	21	11	0	0	186^1	228	13	63	51	14.1	4.97	77	.320	.376	11	.175	-2	-33	-24	2	-2.1
1912	Bos-N	0	1	.000	2	1	0	0	0	6^1	10	0	1	3	15.6	7.11	50	.313	.333	0	.000	-0	-3	-2	0	-0.3
Total	5	36	58	.383	138	94	53	9	4	844^1	878	22	299	254	12.7	3.37	95	.276	.340	45	.165	-8	-41	-15	5	-1.4

● C. V. MATTESON Matteson, Clifford Virgil b: 11/1861, Ohio d: 12/18/31, Seville, Ohio Deb: 6/13/1884 ♦

YEAR	TM/L	W	L	PCT	G	GS	CG	SH	SV	IP	H	HR	BB	SO	RAT	ERA	ERA+	OAV	OOB	BH	AVG	PB	PR	/A	PD	TPI
1884	StL-U	1	0	1.000	1	1	0	0	0	6	9	1	3	3	18.0	9.00	27	.321	.387	0	.000	-1	-4	-4	-0	-0.5

● EDDIE MATTESON Matteson, Henry Edson "Matty" b: 9/7/1884, Guys Mills, Pa. d: 9/1/43, Westfield, N.Y. BR/TR, 5'10.5", 160 lbs. Deb: 5/30/14

YEAR	TM/L	W	L	PCT	G	GS	CG	SH	SV	IP	H	HR	BB	SO	RAT	ERA	ERA+	OAV	OOB	BH	AVG	PB	PR	/A	PD	TPI
1914	Phi-N	3	2	.600	15	3	2	0	0	58	58	1	23	28	12.7	3.10	95	.278	.352	4	.182	-0	-2	-1	-2	-0.3
1918	Was-A	5	3	.625	14	6	2	0	0	67^2	57	2	15	17	9.7	1.73	158	.238	.286	2	.105	-2	8	8	-1	0.6
Total	2	8	5	.615	29	9	4	0	0	125^2	115	3	38	45	11.1	2.36	120	.257	.318	6	.146	-2	6	6	-3	0.3

● JOE MATTHEWS Matthews, John Joseph "Lefty" b: 9/29/1898, Baltimore, Md. d: 2/8/68, Hagerstown, Md. BB/TL, 6', 170 lbs. Deb: 9/18/22

YEAR	TM/L	W	L	PCT	G	GS	CG	SH	SV	IP	H	HR	BB	SO	RAT	ERA	ERA+	OAV	OOB	BH	AVG	PB	PR	/A	PD	TPI
1922	Bos-N	0	1	.000	3	1	0	0	0	10	5	1	6	0	10.8	3.60	111	.143	.286	0	.000	-0	1	0	-0	0.0

● WILLIAM MATTHEWS Matthews, William Calvin b: 1/12/1878, Mahanoy City, Pa. d: 1/23/46, Mt.Carbon, Pa. TR , Deb: 8/28/09

YEAR	TM/L	W	L	PCT	G	GS	CG	SH	SV	IP	H	HR	BB	SO	RAT	ERA	ERA+	OAV	OOB	BH	AVG	PB	PR	/A	PD	TPI
1909	Bos-A	0	0	—	5	1	0	0	0	16^2	16	1	10	6	14.0	3.24	77	.271	.377	0	.000	-1	-1	-1	-0	-0.2

● DALE MATTHEWSON Matthewson, Dale Wesley b: 5/15/23, Catasauqua, Pa. d: 2/20/84, Blairsville, Ga. BR/TR, 5'11.5", 145 lbs. Deb: 7/3/43

YEAR	TM/L	W	L	PCT	G	GS	CG	SH	SV	IP	H	HR	BB	SO	RAT	ERA	ERA+	OAV	OOB	BH	AVG	PB	PR	/A	PD	TPI
1943	Phi-N	0	3	.000	11	1	0	0	0	26	26	1	8	8	11.8	4.85	70	.271	.327	0	.000	-0	-4	-4	-0	-0.5
1944	Phi-N	0	0	—	17	1	0	0	0	32	27	1	16	8	12.1	3.94	92	.237	.331	1	.333	0	-1	-1	-0	0.0
Total	2	0	3	.000	28	2	0	0	0	58	53	2	24	16	11.9	4.34	81	.252	.329	1	.200	-0	-5	-5	-0	-0.5

● MIKE MATTIMORE Mattimore, Michael Joseph b: 1859, Renovo, Pa. d: 4/28/31, Butte, Mont. BL/TL, 5'8.5", 160 lbs. Deb: 5/3/1887 ♦

YEAR	TM/L	W	L	PCT	G	GS	CG	SH	SV	IP	H	HR	BB	SO	RAT	ERA	ERA+	OAV	OOB	BH	AVG	PB	PR	/A	PD	TPI
1887	NY-N	3	3	.500	7	7	6	1	0	57^1	47	2	28	12	12.4	2.35	160	.218	.319	8	.250	-0	11	9	-1	0.6
1888	Phi-a	15	10	.600	26	24	24	4	0	221	221	6	65	80	12.2	3.38	88	.251	.312	38	.268	7	-8	-10	4	0.0
1889	Phi-a	2	1	.667	5	1	1	0	1	31	43	0	13	6	16.5	5.81	65	.319	.383	17	.233	1	-7	-7	-0	-0.5
	KC-a	0	0	—	1	0	0	0	0	3	3	1	2	1	15.0	3.00	139	.250	.357	12	.160	-0	0	0	-0	0.0
	Yr	2	1	.667	6	1	1	0	1	34	46	1	15	7	16.1	5.56	69	.311	.374	29	.196	1	-6	-7	-0	-0.5
1890	Bro-a	6	13	.316	19	19	19	0	0	178^1	201	3	76	33	14.6	4.54	86	.276	.355	17	.132	-3	-13	-13	-0	-1.3
Total	4	26	27	.491	58	51	50	5	1	490^2	515	12	184	132	13.4	3.83	90	.261	.334	92	.204	5	-17	-20	2	-1.2

● EARL MATTINGLY Mattingly, Laurence Earl b: 11/4/04, Newport, Md. d: 9/8/93, Brookeville, Md. BR/TR, 5'10.5", 164 lbs. Deb: 4/15/31

YEAR	TM/L	W	L	PCT	G	GS	CG	SH	SV	IP	H	HR	BB	SO	RAT	ERA	ERA+	OAV	OOB	BH	AVG	PB	PR	/A	PD	TPI
1931	Bro-N	0	1	.000	8	0	0	0	0	14^1	15	0	10	6	17.0	2.51	152	.268	.397	0	.000	-0	2	2	1	0.1

● RICK MATULA Matula, Richard Carlton b: 11/22/53, Wharton, Tex. BR/TR, 6', 190 lbs. Deb: 4/8/79

YEAR	TM/L	W	L	PCT	G	GS	CG	SH	SV	IP	H	HR	BB	SO	RAT	ERA	ERA+	OAV	OOB	BH	AVG	PB	PR	/A	PD	TPI
1979	Atl-N	8	10	.444	28	28	1	0	0	171^1	193	14	64	67	13.7	4.15	98	.286	.350	5	.094	-3	-8	-2	1	-0.4
1980	Atl-N	11	13	.458	33	30	3	1	0	176^2	195	17	60	62	13.0	4.58	82	.286	.343	6	.105	-3	-19	-17	1	-2.2
1981	Atl-N	0	0	—	5	0	0	0	0	7	8	1	2	0	12.9	6.43	56	.286	.333	0	.000	-0	-2	-2	0	0.0
Total	3	19	23	.452	66	58	4	1	0	355	396	32	126	129	13.3	4.41	88	.286	.347	11	.099	-6	-30	-21	2	-2.6

YEAR	TM/L	W	L	PCT	G	GS	CG	SH	SV	IP	H	HR	BB	SO	RAT	ERA	ERA+	OAV	OOB	BH	AVG	PB	PR	/A	PD	TPI
● **HARRY MATUZAK**	Matuzak, Harry George "Matty" b: 1/27/10, Omer, Mich. d: 11/16/78, Fairhope, Ala. BR/TR, 5'11.5", 185 lbs. Deb: 4/19/34																									
1934	Phi-A	0	3	.000	11	0	0	0	0	24	28	2	10	9	14.6	4.88	90	.292	.364	1	.167	0	-1	-1	0	-0.1
1936	Phi-A	0	1	.000	6	1	0	0	0	15	21	0	4	8	15.0	7.20	71	.318	.357	0	.000	-0	-4	-3	-0	-0.2
Total	2	0	4	.000	17	1	0	0	0	39	49	2	14	17	14.8	5.77	81	.302	.362	1	.111	-0	-5	-5	0	-0.3
● **HAL MAUCK**	Mauck, Alfred Maris b: 3/6/1869, Princeton, Ind. d: 4/27/21, Princeton, Ind. BR/TR, 5'11", 185 lbs. Deb: 4/29/1893																									
1893	Chi-N	8	10	.444	23	18	12	1	0	143	168	2	60	23	14.9	4.41	105	.284	.359	9	.148	-5	4	4	-1	-0.2
● **AL MAUL**	Maul, Albert Joseph "Smiling Al" b: 10/9/1865, Philadelphia, Pa. d: 5/3/58, Philadelphia, Pa. BR/TR, 6', 175 lbs. Deb: 6/20/1884 ◆																									
1884	Phi-U	0	1	.000	1	1	1	0	0	8	10	0	1	7	12.4	4.50	52	.286	.306	0	.000	-1	-2	-2	-0	-0.3
1887	Phi-N	4	2	.667	7	5	4	0	0	50^{1}	72	2	15	18	15.9	5.54	76	.326	.374	17	.304	3	-8	-7	0	-0.5
1888	Pit-N	0	2	.000	3	1	1	0	0	17	26	0	5	12	16.4	6.35	42	.342	.383	54	.208	1	-7	-7	0	-0.6
1889	Pit-N	1	4	.200	6	4	4	0	0	42	64	3	28	11	19.9	9.86	38	.340	.429	71	.276	2	-27	-29	1	-2.0
1890	Pit-P	16	12	.571	30	28	26	2	0	246^{2}	258	13	104	81	13.6	3.79	103	.257	.335	42	.259	7	12	3	5	1.2
1891	Pit-N	1	2	.333	8	3	3	0	1	39	44	0	16	13	14.5	2.31	142	.273	.350	28	.188	1	5	4	-0	0.3
1893	Was-N	12	21	.364	37	33	29	1	0	297	355	17	144	72	15.7	5.30	87	.288	.370	34	.254	10	-21	-22	0	-1.0
1894	Was-N	11	15	.423	28	26	21	0	0	201^{2}	272	12	73	34	15.8	5.98	88	.319	.379	30	.242	3	-15	-16	2	-1.1
1895	Was-N	10	5	.667	16	16	14	0	0	135^{2}	136	5	37	34	11.7	**2.45**	**196**	.257	.309	18	.250	1	35	35	1	3.3
1896	Was-N	5	2	.714	8	8	7	0	0	62	75	0	20	18	14.4	3.63	121	.296	.357	8	.286	2	5	5	-1	0.5
1897	Was-N	0	1	.000	1	1	0	0	0	2	4	0	1	0	22.5	9.00	48	.400	.455	0	.000	-0	-1	-1	0	-0.3
	Bal-N	0	0	—	2	2	0	0	0	7^{2}	9	0	8	2	24.7	7.04	59	.290	.488	1	.333	0	-2	-2	-0	0.0
	Yr	0	1	.000	3	3	0	0	0	9^{2}	13	0	9	2	24.2	7.45	56	.317	.481	1	.250	-0	-3	-3	-0	-0.3
1898	Bal-N	20	7	.741	28	28	26	1	0	239^{2}	207	3	49	31	9.8	2.10	170	.231	.274	19	.204	4	40	39	-5	3.9
1899	Bro-N	2	0	1.000	4	4	2	0	0	26	35	1	6	2	14.9	4.50	87	.321	.368	3	.273	0	-2	-2	0	-0.1
1900	Phi-N	2	3	.400	5	4	3	0	0	38	53	2	3	6	13.7	6.16	59	.329	.349	3	.200	0	-10	-11	0	-1.0
1901	NY-N	0	3	.000	3	3	2	0	0	19	39	1	8	5	23.2	11.37	29	.419	.476	3	.375	1	-17	-17	0	-1.7
Total	15	84	80	.512	187	167	143	4	1	1431^{2}	1659	59	518	346	14.1	4.43	96	.284	.349	331	.241	32	-15	-29	4	0.6
● **ERNIE MAUN**	Maun, Ernest Gerald b: 2/3/01, Clearwater, Kan. d: 1/1/87, Corpus Christi, Tex. BR/TR, 6', 165 lbs. Deb: 5/16/24																									
1924	NY-N	2	1	.667	22	0	0	0	1	35	46	2	10	5	14.7	5.91	62	.326	.375	2	.667	1	-8	-9	-1	-0.7
1926	Phi-N	1	4	.200	14	5	0	0	0	37^{2}	57	4	18	9	18.2	6.45	64	.339	.406	3	.250	-0	-11	-10	-0	-1.1
Total	2	3	5	.375	36	5	0	0	1	72^{2}	103	6	28	14	16.5	6.19	63	.333	.392	5	.333	1	-19	-18	-1	-1.8
● **DICK MAUNEY**	Mauney, Richard b: 1/26/20, Concord, N.C. d: 2/6/70, Albemarle, N.C. BR/TR, 5'11.5", 164 lbs. Deb: 6/13/45																									
1945	Phi-N	6	10	.375	20	16	6	2	1	122^{2}	127	7	27	35	11.4	3.08	124	.268	.310	6	.146	-0	10	10	1	1.3
1946	Phi-N	6	4	.600	24	7	3	1	2	90	98	4	18	31	11.9	2.70	127	.279	.320	4	.167	-1	7	7	0	0.8
1947	Phi-N	0	0	—	9	1	0	0	1	16^{1}	15	1	7	6	12.7	3.86	104	.288	.383	0	.000	-0	0	0	1	0.1
Total	3	12	14	.462	53	24	9	3	4	229	240	12	52	72	11.7	2.99	123	.274	.319	10	.149	-1	17	18	2	2.2
● **HARRY MAUPIN**	Maupin, Harry Carr b: 7/11/1872, Wellsville, Mo. d: 8/25/52, Parsons, Kan. 5'7", 150 lbs. Deb: 10/5/1898																									
1898	StL-N	0	2	.000	2	2	2	0	0	18	22	0	3	3	14.0	5.50	69	.297	.350	3	.429	1	-4	-3	-1	-0.3
1899	Cle-N	0	3	.000	5	3	2	0	0	25	55	0	7	3	22.7	12.60	29	.437	.470	0	.000	-2	-24	-25	-1	-2.2
Total	2	0	5	.000	7	5	4	0	0	43	77	0	10	6	19.0	9.63	39	.385	.425	3	.176	-1	-28	-28	-2	-2.5
● **RALPH MAURIELLO**	Mauriello, Ralph "Tami" b: 8/25/34, Brooklyn, N.Y. BR/TR, 6'3", 195 lbs. Deb: 9/13/58																									
1958	LA-N	1	1	.500	3	2	0	0	0	11^{2}	10	1	8	11	13.9	4.63	89	.238	.360	0	.000	-1	-1	-1	-0	-0.2
● **TIM MAUSER**	Mauser, Timothy Edward b: 10/4/66, Fort Worth, Tex. BR/TR, 6', 185 lbs. Deb: 7/7/91																									
1991	Phi-N	0	0	—	3	0	0	0	0	10^{2}	18	3	3	6	17.7	7.59	48	.367	.404	0	.000	-0	-5	-5	-0	-0.1
1993	Phi-N	0	0	—	8	0	0	0	0	16^{1}	15	1	7	14	12.7	4.96	80	.238	.324	0	.000	-0	-2	-2	1	0.0
	SD-N	0	1	.000	28	0	0	0	0	37^{2}	36	5	17	32	12.7	3.58	115	.248	.327	0	.000	-0	2	2	0	0.1
	Yr	0	1	.000	36	0	0	0	0	54	51	6	24	46	12.5	4.00	102	.244	.322	0	.000	-0	0	0	1	0.1
1994	SD-N	2	4	.333	35	0	0	0	2	49	50	3	19	32	12.9	3.49	118	.269	.340	1	.250	0	4	3	-0	0.4
1995	SD-N	0	1	.000	5	0	0	0	0	5^{2}	4	0	9	9	20.6	9.53	42	.190	.433	0	.000	-0	-3	-3	-0	-0.5
Total	4	2	6	.250	79	0	0	0	2	119^{1}	123	12	55	93	13.6	4.37	93	.265	.345	1	.071	-0	-4	-4	1	-0.1
● **BRIAN MAXCY**	Maxcy, David Brian b: 5/4/71, Amory, Miss. BR/TR, 6'1", 170 lbs. Deb: 5/27/95																									
1995	Det-A	4	5	.444	41	0	0	0	0	52^{1}	61	6	31	20	16.2	6.88	69	.293	.390	0	—	0	-13	-12	1	-1.6
1996	Det-A	0	0	—	2	0	0	0	0	3^{1}	8	2	2	1	27.0	13.50	37	.471	.526	0	—	0	-3	-3	0	0.0
Total	2	4	5	.444	43	0	0	0	0	55^{2}	69	8	33	21	16.8	7.28	66	.307	.400	0	—	0	-16	-15	2	-1.6
● **LARRY MAXIE**	Maxie, Larry Hans b: 10/10/40, Upland, Cal. BR/TR, 6'4", 220 lbs. Deb: 8/30/69																									
1969	Atl-N	0	0	—	2	0	0	0	0	3	1	0	1	1	9.0	3.00	120	.111	.273	0	—	0	0	0	0	0.0
● **BERT MAXWELL**	Maxwell, James Albert b: 10/17/1886, Texarkana, Ark. d: 12/10/61, Brady, Tex. BB/TR, 6', 180 lbs. Deb: 9/12/06																									
1906	Pit-N	0	1	.000	1	1	0	0	0	8	8	0	2	1	11.3	5.63	48	.286	.333	0	.000	-0	-3	-3	0	-0.3
1908	Phi-A	0	0	—	4	0	0	0	0	13	23	0	9	7	23.5	11.08	23	.348	.442	0	.000	-1	-13	-12	-0	-0.1
1911	NY-N	1	2	.333	4	3	3	0	0	31	37	0	7	8	13.4	2.90	116	.311	.359	1	.111	-0	2	2	1	0.2
1914	Bro-F	3	4	.429	12	8	6	1	1	71^{1}	76	0	24	19	12.7	3.28	88	.276	.337	2	.087	-2	-3	-3	1	-0.5
Total	4	4	7	.364	21	12	9	1	1	123^{1}	144	0	42	35	13.9	4.16	71	.295	.357	3	.075	-3	-17	-16	1	-0.7
● **DARRELL MAY**	May, Darrell Kevin b: 6/13/72, San Bernardino, Cal. BL/TL, 6'2", 170 lbs. Deb: 9/10/95																									
1995	Atl-N	0	0	—	2	0	0	0	0	4	10	0	0	1	22.5	11.25	38	.500	.500	0	—	0	-3	-3	0	0.0
1996	Pit-N	0	1	.000	5	2	0	0	0	8^{2}	15	5	4	5	20.8	9.35	47	.357	.426	1	.333	0	-5	-5	0	-0.4
	Cal-A	0	0	—	5	0	0	0	0	2^{2}	3	1	2	1	16.9	10.13	49	.333	.455	0	—	0	-2	-2	-0	0.0
1997	Ana-A	2	1	.667	29	2	0	0	0	51^{2}	56	6	25	42	14.1	5.23	87	.277	.357	0	.000	-0	-4	-4	-0	-0.2
Total	3	2	2	.500	41	4	0	0	0	67	84	12	31	49	15.6	6.31	72	.308	.380	1	.200	0	-13	-13	-0	-0.6
● **JAKIE MAY**	May, Frank Spruiell b: 11/25/1895, Youngsville, N.C. d: 6/3/70, Wendell, N.C. BR/TL, 5'8", 178 lbs. Deb: 6/26/17																									
1917	StL-N	0	0	—	15	1	0	0	0	29^{1}	29	0	11	18	13.2	3.38	80	.302	.391	0	.000	-1	-2	-2	2	0.1
1918	StL-N	5	6	.455	29	15	6	0	0	152^{2}	149	2	69	61	13.6	3.83	71	.264	.358	3	.067	-1	-18	-19	-2	-1.7
1919	StL-N	3	12	.200	28	19	8	1	0	125^{2}	99	1	87	58	14.3	3.22	87	.230	.377	6	.162	-1	-4	-6	-1	-1.0
1920	StL-N	1	4	.200	16	5	3	0	0	70^{2}	65	0	37	33	13.9	3.06	98	.251	.360	5	.227	1	1	-1	-2	-0.1
1921	StL-N	1	3	.250	5	5	1	0	0	21	29	0	12	5	17.6	4.71	78	.333	.414	2	.333	1	-2	-2	-1	-0.4
1924	Cin-N	3	3	.500	38	3	2	0	**6**	99	104	2	29	59	12.6	3.00	126	.276	.337	3	.111	-2	10	8	-0	0.4
1925	Cin-N	8	9	.471	36	12	7	1	2	137^{1}	146	3	45	74	13.0	3.87	106	.272	.337	8	.186	0	6	4	0	0.4
1926	Cin-N	13	9	.591	45	15	9	1	3	167^{2}	175	4	44	103	12.1	3.22	115	.276	.329	7	.140	-1	11	9	-1	0.8
1927	Cin-N	15	12	.556	44	28	17	2	1	235^{2}	242	4	70	121	12.4	3.51	108	.274	.337	14	.184	0	11	7	1	0.8
1928	Cin-N	3	5	.375	21	11	1	1	1	79^{1}	99	1	35	39	15.3	4.42	89	.315	.386	8	.296	1	-4	-4	-1	-0.3
1929	Cin-N	10	14	.417	41	24	10	0	3	199	219	7	75	92	13.5	4.61	99	.285	.352	13	.203	-1	2	-1	-0	-0.2
1930	Cin-N	3	11	.214	26	18	5	1	0	112^{1}	147	6	44	44	15.5	5.77	84	.320	.383	5	.128	-1	-10	-12	0	-1.2
1931	Chi-N	5	5	.500	31	4	1	0	2	79	81	2	43	38	14.5	3.87	100	.275	.372	5	.227	1	-0	-0	0	0.1
1932	*Chi-N	2	2	.500	35	0	0	0	1	53^{2}	61	3	19	20	13.8	4.36	86	.281	.345	1	.125	-0	-3	-4	-0	-0.3
Total	14	72	95	.431	410	160	70	7	19	1562^{1}	1645	35	617	765	13.5	3.88	97	.278	.355	80	.171	-4	-3	-23	-6	-2.6
● **RUDY MAY**	May, Rudolph b: 7/18/44, Coffeyville, Kan. BL/TL, 6'3", 207 lbs. Deb: 4/18/65																									
1965	Cal-A	4	9	.308	30	19	2	1	0	124	111	7	78	76	14.0	3.92	87	.245	.361	6	.200	3	-6	-7	-2	-0.6
1969	Cal-A	10	13	.435	43	25	4	0	2	180^{1}	142	20	66	133	10.5	3.44	101	.220	.296	4	.082	-2	4	1	-1	-0.1
1970	Cal-A	7	13	.350	38	34	2	2	0	208^{2}	190	20	81	164	11.8	4.01	90	.245	.319	6	.087	-2	-7	-9	0	-1.1
1971	Cal-A	11	12	.478	32	31	7	2	0	208^{1}	160	12	87	156	10.8	3.02	107	.213	.297	10	.147	0	10	5	-1	0.5
1972	Cal-A	12	11	.522	35	30	10	3	1	205^{1}	162	15	82	169	10.7	2.94	99	.215	.293	7	.113	-1	3	-1	-2	-0.4
1973	Cal-A	7	17	.292	34	28	10	4	0	185	177	20	80	134	12.6	4.38	81	.254	.333	0	—	0	-12	-17	2	-1.8

YEAR	TM/L	W	L	PCT	G	GS	CG	SH	SV	IP	H	HR	BB	SO	RAT	ERA	ERA+	OAV	OOB	BH	AVG	PB	PR	/A	PD	TPI
1974	Cal-A	0	1	.000	18	3	0	0	2	27	29	2	10	12	13.3	7.00	49	.274	.342	0	—	0	-10	-11	1	-0.1
	NY-A	8	4	.667	17	15	8	2	0	114^1	75	5	48	90	10.0	2.28	154	.188	.282	0	—	0	17	16	-2	1.6
	Yr	8	5	.615	35	18	8	2	2	141^1	104	7	58	102	10.6	3.18	110	.204	.291	0	—	0	7	5	-0	1.5
1975	NY-A	14	12	.538	32	31	13	1	0	212	179	9	99	145	11.9	3.06	120	.231	.320	0	—	0	17	15	-1	1.7
1976	NY-A	4	3	.571	11	11	2	1	0	68	49	5	28	38	10.3	3.57	96	.206	.292	0	—	0	-0	-1	0	-0.1
	Bal-A	11	7	.611	24	21	5	1	0	152^1	156	11	42	71	11.7	3.78	87	.267	.316	0	—	0	-4	-9	-1	-1.0
	Yr	15	10	.600	35	32	7	2	0	220^1	205	16	70	109	11.2	3.72	89	.249	.308	0	—	0	-5	-10	-1	-1.1
1977	Bal-A	18	14	.563	37	37	11	4	0	251^2	243	25	78	105	11.7	3.61	105	.255	.315	0	—	0	13	5	-3	0.6
1978	Mon-N	8	10	.444	27	23	4	1	0	144	141	15	42	87	11.8	3.88	91	.255	.315	6	.143	0	-5	-6	-2	-0.8
1979	Mon-N	10	3	.769	33	7	2	1	0	93^2	88	4	31	67	11.8	2.31	159	.255	.324	3	.143	-0	15	14	1	1.9
1980	*NY-A	15	5	.750	41	17	3	1	3	175^1	144	14	39	133	**9.4**	**2.46**	**159**	.224	**.268**	0	—	0	31	28	0	3.2
1981	*NY-A	6	11	.353	27	22	4	0	1	147^2	137	10	41	79	11.0	4.14	86	.246	.300	0	—	0	-8	-9	1	-0.9
1982	NY-A	6	6	.500	41	6	0	0	3	106	109	4	14	85	10.5	2.89	138	.267	.292	0	—	0	14	13	1	1.5
1983	NY-A	1	5	.167	15	0	0	0	0	18^1	22	1	12	16	17.2	6.87	57	.293	.398	0	—	0	-6	-6	0	-1.6
Total	16	152	156	.494	535	360	87	24	12	2622	2314	199	958	1760	11.4	3.46	102	.238	.310	42	.123	-2	64	21	-7	2.5

● SCOTT MAY May, Scott Francis b: 11/11/61, West Bend, Wis. BR/TR, 6′1″, 185 lbs. Deb: 9/2/88

YEAR	TM/L	W	L	PCT	G	GS	CG	SH	SV	IP	H	HR	BB	SO	RAT	ERA	ERA+	OAV	OOB	BH	AVG	PB	PR	/A	PD	TPI
1988	Tex-A	0	0	—	3	1	0	0	0	7^1	8	3	4	4	14.7	8.59	48	.296	.387	0	—	0	-4	-4	0	-0.2
1991	Chi-N	0	0	—	2	0	0	0	0	2	6	0	1	1	31.5	18.00	22	.545	.583	0	—	0	-3	-3	-0	0.0
Total	2	0	0	—	5	1	0	0	0	9^1	14	3	5	5	18.3	10.61	38	.368	.442	0	—	0	-7	-7	-0	-0.2

● BUCKSHOT MAY May, William Herbert b: 12/13/1899, Bakersfield, Cal. d: 3/15/84, Bakersfield, Cal. BR/TR, 6′2″, 169 lbs. Deb: 5/9/24

YEAR	TM/L	W	L	PCT	G	GS	CG	SH	SV	IP	H	HR	BB	SO	RAT	ERA	ERA+	OAV	OOB	BH	AVG	PB	PR	/A	PD	TPI
1924	Pit-N	0	0	—	1	0	0	0	0	1	2	0	0	1	18.0	0.00	—	.500	.500	0	—	0	0	0	0	0.0

● ED MAYER Mayer, Edwin David b: 11/30/31, San Francisco, Cal BL/TL, 6′2″, 185 lbs. Deb: 9/15/57

YEAR	TM/L	W	L	PCT	G	GS	CG	SH	SV	IP	H	HR	BB	SO	RAT	ERA	ERA+	OAV	OOB	BH	AVG	PB	PR	/A	PD	TPI
1957	Chi-N	0	0	—	3	1	0	0	0	7^2	8	2	2	3	12.9	5.87	66	.258	.324	1	.500	0	-2	-2	0	0.1
1958	Chi-N	2	2	.500	19	0	0	0	1	23^2	15	0	16	14	12.9	3.80	103	.190	.347	1	.200	-0	0	0	-0	0.0
Total	2	2	2	.500	22	1	0	0	1	31^1	23	2	18	17	12.9	4.31	91	.209	.341	2	.286	0	-1	-1	0	0.1

● ERSKINE MAYER Mayer, Erskine John (b: James Erskine) b: 1/16/1889, Atlanta, Ga. d: 3/10/57, Los Angeles, Cal. BR/TR, 6′, 168 lbs. Deb: 9/4/12 F

YEAR	TM/L	W	L	PCT	G	GS	CG	SH	SV	IP	H	HR	BB	SO	RAT	ERA	ERA+	OAV	OOB	BH	AVG	PB	PR	/A	PD	TPI
1912	Phi-N	0	1	.000	7	1	0	0	0	21^1	27	1	7	5	14.8	6.33	57	.318	.376	0	.000	-0	-7	-6	0	-0.3
1913	Phi-N	9	9	.500	39	19	7	2	1	170^2	172	6	46	51	12.0	3.11	107	.272	.330	6	.120	-2	2	4	0	0.2
1914	Phi-N	21	19	.525	48	38	24	4	2	321	308	8	91	116	11.6	2.58	114	.256	.315	21	.194	2	8	13	4	2.3
1915	*Phi-N	21	15	.583	43	33	20	2	2	274^2	240	9	59	114	10.3	2.36	116	.243	.295	21	.239	5	12	12	1	2.2
1916	Phi-N	7	7	.500	28	16	7	2	0	140	148	7	33	62	11.9	3.15	84	.281	.328	5	.132	-1	-8	-8	3	-0.5
1917	Phi-N	11	6	.647	28	18	11	1	0	160	160	6	33	64	11.1	2.76	102	.268	.310	10	.196	-0	-1	1	-0	0.0
1918	Phi-N	7	4	.636	13	13	7	0	0	104	108	2	26	16	11.9	3.12	96	.276	.328	8	.216	1	-4	-1	-0	-0.1
	Pit-N	9	3	.750	15	14	11	1	0	123^1	122	1	27	25	11.2	2.26	127	.268	.314	7	.167	2	7	8	-2	0.8
	Yr	16	7	.696	28	27	18	1	0	227^1	230	3	53	41	11.4	2.65	110	.270	.316	15	.190	2	3	7	-2	0.7
1919	Pit-N	5	3	.625	18	10	6	0	1	88^1	100	2	12	20	11.6	4.48	67	.267	.294	6	.207	0	-15	-14	-1	-1.4
	*Chi-A	1	3	.250	6	2	0	0	0	23^2	30	1	11	9	15.6	8.37	38	.316	.387	0	.000	-1	-14	-14	-0	-1.9
Total	8	91	70	.565	245	164	93	12	6	1427	1415	43	345	482	11.4	2.96	99	.264	.316	84	.185	5	-21	-6	4	1.3

● SAM MAYER Mayer, Samuel Frankel (b: Samuel Frankel Erskine) b: 2/28/1893, Atlanta, Ga. d: 7/1/62, Atlanta, Ga. BR/TL, 5′10″, 164 lbs. Deb: 9/14/15 F♦

YEAR	TM/L	W	L	PCT	G	GS	CG	SH	SV	IP	H	HR	BB	SO	RAT	ERA	ERA+	OAV	OOB	BH	AVG	PB	PR	/A	PD	TPI
1915	Was-A	0	0	—	1	0	0	0	0	0	0	0	2	0	—	—	—	—	1.000	7	.241	0	0	0	0	0.0

● AL MAYS Mays, Albert C. b: 5/17/1865, Canal Dover, Ohio d: 5/7/05, Parkersburg, W.Va. BR , Deb: 5/10/1885

YEAR	TM/L	W	L	PCT	G	GS	CG	SH	SV	IP	H	HR	BB	SO	RAT	ERA	ERA+	OAV	OOB	BH	AVG	PB	PR	/A	PD	TPI
1885	Lou-a	6	11	.353	17	17	17	0	0	150	129	3	43	61	10.8	2.76	117	.219	.282	13	.213	0	8	8	-0	0.7
1886	NY-a	11	27	.289	41	40	39	1	0	350	330	7	140	163	12.4	3.39	101	.240	.317	16	.119	-9	2	1	-1	-0.8
1887	NY-a	17	34	.333	52	52	50	0	0	441^1	551	11	136	124	14.4	4.73	90	.298	.353	45	.204	-1	-21	-24	6	-1.5
1888	Bro-a	9	9	.500	18	18	17	1	0	160^2	150	1	32	67	10.8	2.80	107	.238	.287	5	.079	-4	5	3	2	0.1
1889	Col-a	10	7	.588	21	19	13	1	0	140	167	4	56	52	14.6	4.82	75	.287	.354	7	.130	-1	-15	-19	1	-1.7
1890	Col-a	0	1	.000	1	1	1	0	0	9	14	0	8	2	23.0	8.00	45	.341	.460	0	.000	-0	-4	-4	-1	-0.4
Total	6	53	89	.373	150	147	137	3	0	1251	1341	26	415	469	13.1	3.91	94	.265	.328	86	.160	-16	-26	-35	7	-3.6

● CARL MAYS Mays, Carl William "Sub" b: 11/12/1891, Liberty, Ky. d: 4/4/71, ElCajon, Cal. BL/TR, 5′11.5″, 195 lbs. Deb: 4/15/15

YEAR	TM/L	W	L	PCT	G	GS	CG	SH	SV	IP	H	HR	BB	SO	RAT	ERA	ERA+	OAV	OOB	BH	AVG	PB	PR	/A	PD	TPI
1915	Bos-A	6	5	.545	38	6	2	0	**7**	131^2	119	0	21	65	9.9	2.60	107	.244	.282	9	.237	2	5	3	2	0.6
1916	*Bos-A	18	13	.581	44	24	14	2	3	245	208	3	74	76	10.7	2.39	116	.234	.299	18	.234	7	12	10	9	3.2
1917	Bos-A	22	9	.710	35	33	27	2	0	289	230	1	74	91	9.9	1.74	148	.221	.282	27	.252	6	30	27	8	4.8
1918	*Bos-A	21	13	.618	35	33	**30**	**8**	0	293^1	230	2	81	114	9.9	2.21	121	.221	.284	30	.288	10	19	15	9	4.1
1919	Bos-A	5	11	.313	21	16	14	2	2	146	131	3	40	53	10.8	2.47	123	.247	.306	8	.151	-2	12	9	3	1.1
	NY-A	9	3	.750	13	13	12	1	0	120	96	2	37	54	10.4	1.65	193	.216	.283	14	.311	3	21	21	1	2.7
	Yr	14	14	.500	34	29	26	3	2	266	227	5	77	107	10.5	2.10	148	.231	.291	22	.224	1	33	30	4	3.8
1920	NY-A	26	11	.703	45	37	26	**6**	2	312	310	13	84	92	11.6	3.06	125	.263	.316	26	.239	2	26	26	6	3.7
1921	*NY-A	**27**	9	**.750**	**49**	38	30	1	**7**	**336^2**	332	11	76	70	11.1	3.05	139	.257	.303	49	.343	12	46	44	3	5.8
1922	*NY-A	13	14	.481	34	29	21	1	2	240	257	12	50	41	11.8	3.60	111	.285	.327	23	.250	1	12	11	6	1.8
1923	NY-A	5	2	.714	23	7	2	0	0	81^1	119	8	32	16	17.2	6.20	64	.357	.420	4	.148	1	-20	-20	3	-1.2
1924	Cin-N	20	9	.690	37	27	15	2	0	226	238	3	36	63	11.1	3.15	120	.270	.302	24	.289	7	18	16	8	3.4
1925	Cin-N	3	5	.375	12	5	3	0	2	51^2	60	0	13	10	13.1	3.31	124	.294	.342	4	.250	1	6	5	1	0.8
1926	Cin-N	19	12	.613	39	33	**24**	3	1	281	286	3	53	58	11.0	3.14	118	.269	.306	22	.224	2	21	17	10	3.1
1927	Cin-N	3	7	.300	14	9	6	0	0	82	89	1	10	17	11.0	3.51	108	.276	.300	13	.406	5	4	2	4	1.3
1928	Cin-N	4	1	.800	14	6	4	1	1	62^2	67	3	22	10	12.8	3.88	102	.275	.335	8	.296	1	1	1	0	0.2
1929	NY-N	7	2	.778	37	8	1	0	4	123	140	8	31	32	12.7	4.32	106	.287	.333	12	.353	4	5	4	2	0.8
Total	15	208	126	.623	490	324	231	29	31	3021^1	2912	73	734	862	11.1	2.92	119	.257	.307	291	.268	64	217	189	74	36.2

● MATT MAYSEY Maysey, Matthew Samuel b: 1/8/67, Hamilton, Ont., Canada BR/TR, 6′4″, 225 lbs. Deb: 7/8/92

YEAR	TM/L	W	L	PCT	G	GS	CG	SH	SV	IP	H	HR	BB	SO	RAT	ERA	ERA+	OAV	OOB	BH	AVG	PB	PR	/A	PD	TPI
1992	Mon-N	0	0	—	2	0	0	0	0	2^1	4	1	0	1	19.3	3.86	90	.364	.417	0	—	0	-0	-0	-0	0.0
1993	Mil-A	1	2	.333	23	0	0	0	1	22	28	4	13	10	17.2	5.73	74	.322	.416	1	1.000	0	-3	-4	-1	-0.5
Total	2	1	2	.333	25	0	0	0	1	24^1	32	5	13	11	17.4	5.55	75	.327	.416	1	1.000	0	-4	-4	-1	-0.5

● JACK McADAMS McAdams, George D. b: 12/17/1886, Benton, Ark. d: 5/21/37, San Francisco, Cal BR/TR, 6′1.5″, 170 lbs. Deb: 7/22/11

YEAR	TM/L	W	L	PCT	G	GS	CG	SH	SV	IP	H	HR	BB	SO	RAT	ERA	ERA+	OAV	OOB	BH	AVG	PB	PR	/A	PD	TPI
1911	StL-N	0	0	—	6	0	0	0	0	9^2	7	0	5	4	13.0	3.72	91	.226	.368	0	.000	-0	-0	-0	0	0.0

● BILL McAFEE McAfee, William Fort b: 9/7/07, Smithville, Ga. d: 7/8/58, Culpeper, Va. BR/TR, 6′2″, 186 lbs. Deb: 5/12/30

YEAR	TM/L	W	L	PCT	G	GS	CG	SH	SV	IP	H	HR	BB	SO	RAT	ERA	ERA+	OAV	OOB	BH	AVG	PB	PR	/A	PD	TPI
1930	Chi-N	0	0	—	2	0	0	0	0	1	3	0	2	0	45.0	0.00	—	.375	.500	0	—	0	1	1	-0	0.0
1931	Bos-N	0	1	.000	18	1	0	0	0	29^2	39	2	10	9	14.9	6.37	59	.333	.386	0	.000	-0	-8	-9	0	-0.3
1932	Was-A	6	1	.857	8	5	2	0	0	41^1	47	3	22	10	15.0	3.92	110	.287	.371	2	.111	-2	3	2	1	0.2
1933	Was-A	3	2	.600	27	1	0	0	5	53	64	3	21	14	14.6	6.62	63	.296	.361	4	.267	2	-14	-14	0	-1.2
1934	StL-A	1	0	1.000	28	0	0	0	0	61^2	84	4	26	11	16.5	5.84	86	.332	.401	3	.188	-0	-9	-6	-1	-0.2
Total	5	10	4	.714	83	7	2	0	5	186^2	237	12	81	44	15.5	5.69	78	.313	.382	9	.173	0	-28	-26	1	-1.5

● JIMMY McALEER McAleer, James Robert "Loafer" b: 7/10/1864, Youngstown, Ohio d: 4/29/31, Youngstown, Ohio BR/TR, 6′, 175 lbs. Deb: 4/24/1889 M♦

YEAR	TM/L	W	L	PCT	G	GS	CG	SH	SV	IP	H	HR	BB	SO	RAT	ERA	ERA+	OAV	OOB	BH	AVG	PB	PR	/A	PD	TPI
1901	Cle-A	0	0	—	1	0	0	0	0	0^1	2	0	3	0	135.0	0.00	—	.667	.833	1	.143	-0	0	0	0	0.0

● JACK McALEESE McAleese, John James b: 1877, Sharon, Pa. d: 11/15/50, New York, N.Y. BR/TR, 5′8″, Deb: 8/10/01 ♦

YEAR	TM/L	W	L	PCT	G	GS	CG	SH	SV	IP	H	HR	BB	SO	RAT	ERA	ERA+	OAV	OOB	BH	AVG	PB	PR	/A	PD	TPI
1901	Chi-A	0	0	—	1	0	0	0	0	3	7	0	1	1	24.0	9.00	39	.438	.471	0	.000	-0	-2	-2	0	0.0

● SPORT McALLISTER McAllister, Lewis William b: 7/23/1874, Austin, Miss. d: 7/17/62, Wyandotte, Mich. BB/TR, 5′11″, 180 lbs. Deb: 8/7/1896 ♦

YEAR	TM/L	W	L	PCT	G	GS	CG	SH	SV	IP	H	HR	BB	SO	RAT	ERA	ERA+	OAV	OOB	BH	AVG	PB	PR	/A	PD	TPI
1896	Cle-N	0	0	—	1	0	0	0	0	4	9	0	2	0	24.8	6.75	67	.450	.500	6	.222	-0	-1	-1	0	0.0
1897	Cle-N	1	2	.333	4	3	3	0	0	28	29	3	9	10	12.2	4.50	100	.266	.322	30	.219	-0	-1	-0	1	0.0
1898	Cle-N	3	4	.429	9	7	6	0	0	65^1	73	2	23	9	13.6	4.55	80	.281	.346	13	.228	1	-7	-7	-1	-0.6

YEAR	TM/L	W	L	PCT	G	GS	CG	SH	SV	IP	H	HR	BB	SO	RAT	ERA	ERA+	OAV	OOB	BH	AVG	PB	PR	/A	PD	TPI
1899	Cle-N	0	1	.000	3	1	1	0	0	16	29	0	10	2	24.2	9.56	39	.387	.483	99	.237	0	-10	-10	-0	-0.5
Total	4	4	7	.364	17	11	10	0	0	113^1	140	5	44	21	15.2	5.32	73	.302	.371	358	.247	1	-19	-18	0	-1.1

● ERNIE McANALLY McAnally, Ernest Lee b: 8/15/46, Pittsburg, Tex. BR/TR, 6'1", 190 lbs. Deb: 4/11/71

YEAR	TM/L	W	L	PCT	G	GS	CG	SH	SV	IP	H	HR	BB	SO	RAT	ERA	ERA+	OAV	OOB	BH	AVG	PB	PR	/A	PD	TPI
1971	Mon-N	11	12	.478	31	25	8	2	0	177^2	150	9	87	98	12.4	3.90	90	.228	.326	7	.117	-2	-9	-7	0	-1.1
1972	Mon-N	6	15	.286	29	27	4	2	0	170	165	13	71	102	12.7	3.81	93	.259	.337	6	.113	-2	-7	-5	3	-0.5
1973	Mon-N	7	9	.438	27	24	4	0	0	147	158	13	54	72	13.2	4.04	94	.274	.340	9	.184	-1	-6	-4	-0	-0.5
1974	Mon-N	6	13	.316	25	21	5	2	0	128^2	126	10	56	79	13.0	4.48	86	.256	.336	5	.119	-2	-12	-9	1	-1.4
Total	4	30	49	.380	112	97	21	6	0	623^1	599	45	268	351	12.8	4.03	91	.253	.334	27	.132	-6	-34	-25	3	-3.5

● JAMIE McANDREW McAndrew, James Brian b: 9/2/67, Williamsport, Pa. BR/TR, 6'2", 190 lbs. Deb: 7/17/95 F

YEAR	TM/L	W	L	PCT	G	GS	CG	SH	SV	IP	H	HR	BB	SO	RAT	ERA	ERA+	OAV	OOB	BH	AVG	PB	PR	/A	PD	TPI
1995	Mil-A	2	3	.400	10	4	0	0	0	36^1	37	2	12	19	12.4	4.71	106	.266	.329	0	—	0	0	1	-1	-0.2
1997	Mil-A	1	1	.500	5	4	0	0	0	19^1	24	1	23	8	22.8	8.38	55	.304	.471	0	—	0	-8	-8	-0	-0.7
Total	2	3	4	.429	15	8	0	0	0	55^2	61	3	35	27	16.0	5.98	81	.280	.387	0	—	0	-8	-7	-1	-0.9

● JIM McANDREW McAndrew, James Clement b: 1/11/44, Lost Nation, Iowa BR/TR, 6'2", 185 lbs. Deb: 7/21/68 F

YEAR	TM/L	W	L	PCT	G	GS	CG	SH	SV	IP	H	HR	BB	SO	RAT	ERA	ERA+	OAV	OOB	BH	AVG	PB	PR	/A	PD	TPI
1968	NY-N	4	7	.364	12	12	2	1	0	79	66	5	17	46	9.9	2.28	133	.230	.282	1	.045	-1	6	7	-1	0.8
1969	NY-N	6	7	.462	27	21	4	2	0	135	112	12	44	90	10.5	3.47	105	.225	.291	5	.135	0	2	3	-1	0.1
1970	NY-N	10	14	.417	32	27	9	3	2	184^1	166	18	38	111	10.1	3.56	113	.239	.281	8	.148	1	10	9	-2	1.0
1971	NY-N	2	5	.286	24	10	0	0	0	90^1	78	10	32	42	11.1	4.38	78	.227	.294	1	.043	-1	-9	-10	1	-0.8
1972	NY-N	11	8	.579	28	23	4	0	1	160^2	133	12	38	81	9.9	2.80	120	.225	.278	2	.047	-2	12	10	-1	0.8
1973	NY-N	3	8	.273	23	12	0	0	1	80^1	109	9	31	38	16.0	5.38	67	.330	.393	2	.133	2	-15	-16	-1	-1.9
1974	SD-N	1	4	.200	15	5	1	0	0	41^2	48	7	13	16	13.2	5.62	63	.284	.335	1	.143	0	-9	-10	-1	-1.1
Total	7	37	53	.411	161	110	20	6	4	771^1	712	73	213	424	11.0	3.65	98	.245	.300	20	.100	-3	-4	-6	-6	-1.1

● DIXIE McARTHUR McArthur, Oland Alexander b: 2/1/1892, Vernon, Ala. d: 5/31/86, West Point, Miss. BR/TR, 6'1", 185 lbs. Deb: 7/10/14

YEAR	TM/L	W	L	PCT	G	GS	CG	SH	SV	IP	H	HR	BB	SO	RAT	ERA	ERA+	OAV	OOB	BH	AVG	PB	PR	/A	PD	TPI
1914	Pit-N	0	0	—	1	0	0	0	0	1	1	0	0	1	9.0	0.00	—	.250	.250	0	—	0	0	0	0	0.0

● WICKEY McAVOY McAvoy, James Eugene b: 10/22/1894, Rochester, N.Y. d: 7/6/73, Rochester, N.Y. BR/TR, 5'11", 172 lbs. Deb: 9/29/13 ♦

YEAR	TM/L	W	L	PCT	G	GS	CG	SH	SV	IP	H	HR	BB	SO	RAT	ERA	ERA+	OAV	OOB	BH	AVG	PB	PR	/A	PD	TPI
1918	Phi-A	0	0	—	1	0	0	0	0	0^2	1	1	0	0	13.5	13.50	22	.500	.500	66	.244	0	-1	-1	0	0.0

● TOM McAVOY McAvoy, Thomas John b: 8/12/36, Brooklyn, N.Y. BL/TL, 6'3", 200 lbs. Deb: 9/27/59

YEAR	TM/L	W	L	PCT	G	GS	CG	SH	SV	IP	H	HR	BB	SO	RAT	ERA	ERA+	OAV	OOB	BH	AVG	PB	PR	/A	PD	TPI
1959	Was-A	0	0	—	1	0	0	0	0	2^2	1	0	2	0	10.1	0.00	—	.125	.300	0	.000	-0	1	1	0	0.0

● AL McBEAN McBean, Alvin O'Neal b: 5/15/38, Charlotte Amalie, V.I. BR/TR, 6', 180 lbs. Deb: 7/2/61

YEAR	TM/L	W	L	PCT	G	GS	CG	SH	SV	IP	H	HR	BB	SO	RAT	ERA	ERA+	OAV	OOB	BH	AVG	PB	PR	/A	PD	TPI
1961	Pit-N	3	2	.600	27	2	0	0	0	74^1	72	4	42	49	14.3	3.75	106	.263	.369	4	.267	1	2	2	2	0.5
1962	Pit-N	15	10	.600	33	29	6	2	0	189^2	212	11	65	119	13.5	3.70	106	.285	.348	14	.209	2	5	5	0	0.8
1963	Pit-N	13	3	.813	55	7	2	1	11	122^1	100	5	39	74	10.4	2.57	128	.222	.287	6	.194	2	10	10	2	1.8
1964	Pit-N	8	3	.727	58	0	0	0	22	89^2	76	4	17	41	9.7	1.91	184	.234	.280	1	.083	-1	**16**	**16**	4	3.3
1965	Pit-N	6	6	.500	62	1	0	0	18	114	111	5	42	54	12.3	2.29	153	.260	.331	6	.222	1	16	15	1	2.4
1966	Pit-N	4	3	.571	47	0	0	0	3	86^2	95	9	24	54	12.6	3.22	111	.280	.332	1	.100	-1	4	3	1	0.3
1967	Pit-N	7	4	.636	51	8	5	0	4	131	118	6	43	54	11.1	2.54	132	.248	.312	6	.207	2	12	12	0	1.4
1968	Pit-N	9	12	.429	36	28	9	2	0	198^1	204	10	63	100	12.3	3.58	82	.269	.330	13	.194	2	-13	-15	4	-0.9
1969	SD-N	0	1	.000	1	1	0	0	0	7	10	1	2	1	15.4	5.14	69	.345	.387	1	.500	0	-1	-1	-0	-0.1
	LA-N	2	6	.250	31	0	0	0	4	48^1	46	6	21	26	12.8	3.91	85	.258	.343	0	.000	0	-2	-3	-1	-0.7
	Yr	2	7	.222	32	1	0	0	4	55^1	56	7	23	27	13.2	4.07	82	.271	.349	1	.200	0	-3	-4	-1	-0.8
1970	LA-N	0	0	—	1	0	0	0	0	1	1	0	0	0	9.0	0.00	—	.333	.333	0	—	0	0	0	-0	0.0
	Pit-N	0	0	—	7	0	0	0	1	10	13	2	7	3	18.0	8.10	48	.317	.417	0	.000	-0	-5	-5	0	-0.1
	Yr	0	0	—	8	0	0	0	1	11	14	2	7	3	17.2	7.36	53	.318	.412	0	.000	-0	-4	-4	0	-0.1
Total	10	67	50	.573	409	76	22	5	63	1072^1	1058	63	365	575	12.2	3.13	111	.262	.327	52	.197	9	45	40	13	8.7

● PRYOR McBEE McBee, Pryor Edward "Lefty" b: 6/20/01, Blanco, Okla. d: 4/19/63, Roseville, Cal. BR/TL, 6'1", 190 lbs. Deb: 5/22/26

YEAR	TM/L	W	L	PCT	G	GS	CG	SH	SV	IP	H	HR	BB	SO	RAT	ERA	ERA+	OAV	OOB	BH	AVG	PB	PR	/A	PD	TPI
1926	Chi-A	0	0	—	1	0	0	0	0	1^1	1	0	3	1	27.0	6.75	57	.250	.571	0	—	0	-0	-0	0	0.0

● DICK McBRIDE McBride, James Dickson b: 1845, Philadelphia, Pa. d: 10/10/16, Philadelphia, Pa. TR, 5'9", 150 lbs. Deb: 5/20/1871 M

YEAR	TM/L	W	L	PCT	G	GS	CG	SH	SV	IP	H	HR	BB	SO	RAT	ERA	ERA+	OAV	OOB	BH	AVG	PB	PR	/A	PD	TPI
1871	Ath-n	18	5	**.783**	25	25	25	0	0	222	285	3	40	15	13.2	4.58	88	.280	.307	31	.235	-4	-9	-14		-1.1
1872	Ath-n	30	14	.682	47	47	47	1	0	419^1	508	3	26	44	11.5	2.85	124	.265	.275	74	.287	5	37	32		2.7
1873	Ath-n	24	19	.558	46	46	38	**3**	0	382^2	453	3	47	25	11.8	3.32	103	.263	.282	71	.281	3	-3	4		0.4
1874	Ath-n	33	22	.600	55	55	55	0	0	487	514	6	32	37	**10.1**	**1.64**	**140**	**.240**	**.251**	57	.217	-7	**29**	**36**		1.8
1875	Ath-n	44	14	.759	60	60	59	6	0	538	607	4	24	27	10.6	2.33	103	.267	.275	73	.270	3	-6	4		-0.2
1876	Bos-N	0	4	.000	4	4	3	0	0	33	53	1	5	2	15.8	2.73	83	.353	.374	3	.188	-1	-2	-2	-0	-0.3
Total	5 n	149	74	.668	233	233	224	10	0	2049	2367	19	169	148	11.1	2.70	111	.261	.274	306	.260	-0	48	69		3.6

● KEN McBRIDE McBride, Kenneth Faye b: 8/12/35, Huntsville, Ala. BR/TR, 6', 195 lbs. Deb: 8/4/59 C

YEAR	TM/L	W	L	PCT	G	GS	CG	SH	SV	IP	H	HR	BB	SO	RAT	ERA	ERA+	OAV	OOB	BH	AVG	PB	PR	/A	PD	TPI
1959	Chi-A	0	1	.000	11	2	0	0	1	22^2	20	1	17	12	14.7	3.18	118	.230	.356	1	.167	-0	2	1	1	0.1
1960	Chi-A	0	1	.000	5	0	0	0	0	4^2	6	0	3	4	19.3	3.86	98	.333	.455	0	—	0	0	-0	-0	0.0
1961	LA-A☆	12	15	.444	38	36	11	1	1	241^2	229	28	102	180	12.6	3.65	124	.252	.332	7	.084	-5	10	23	4	2.3
1962	LA-A†	11	5	.688	24	23	6	4	0	149^1	136	9	70	83	13.0	3.50	110	.249	.344	9	.164	0	8	6	5	1.1
1963	LA-A★	13	12	.520	36	36	11	2	0	251	198	22	82	147	10.5	3.26	105	.218	.293	15	.172	2	10	5	3	0.9
1964	LA-A	4	13	.235	29	21	0	0	1	116^1	104	14	75	66	15.1	5.26	62	.239	.370	6	.214	3	-21	-26	3	-2.8
1965	Cal-A	0	3	.000	8	4	0	0	0	22	24	1	14	11	16.4	6.14	55	.270	.381	0	.000	-0	-7	-7	-0	-0.9
Total	7	40	50	.444	151	122	28	7	3	807^2	717	75	363	503	12.6	3.79	101	.240	.332	38	.144	-0	2	2	15	0.7

● PETE McBRIDE McBride, Peter William b: 7/9/1875, Adams, Mass. d: 7/3/44, N.Adams, Mass. BR/TR, 5'10", 170 lbs. Deb: 9/20/1898

YEAR	TM/L	W	L	PCT	G	GS	CG	SH	SV	IP	H	HR	BB	SO	RAT	ERA	ERA+	OAV	OOB	BH	AVG	PB	PR	/A	PD	TPI
1898	Cle-N	0	1	.000	1	1	1	0	0	7	9	0	4	6	18.0	6.43	56	.310	.412	2	1.000	2	-2	-2	-0	-0.1
1899	StL-N	2	4	.333	11	6	4	0	0	64	65	4	40	26	15.3	4.08	98	.263	.375	5	.185	0	-2	-1	-1	-0.1
Total	2	2	5	.286	12	7	5	0	0	71	74	4	44	32	15.6	4.31	92	.268	.378	7	.241	2	-4	-3	-1	-0.2

● RALPH McCABE McCabe, Ralph Herbert "Mack" b: 10/21/18, Napanee, Ont., Can. d: 5/3/74, Windsor, Ont., Can. BR/TR, 6'4", 195 lbs. Deb: 9/18/46

YEAR	TM/L	W	L	PCT	G	GS	CG	SH	SV	IP	H	HR	BB	SO	RAT	ERA	ERA+	OAV	OOB	BH	AVG	PB	PR	/A	PD	TPI
1946	Cle-A	0	1	.000	1	1	0	0	0	4	5	3	2	3	18.0	11.25	29	.313	.421	0	.000	-0	-3	-4	0	-0.6

● DICK McCABE McCabe, Richard James b: 2/21/1896, Mamaroneck, N.Y. d: 4/11/50, Buffalo, N.Y. BR/TR, 5'10.5", 159 lbs. Deb: 5/30/18

YEAR	TM/L	W	L	PCT	G	GS	CG	SH	SV	IP	H	HR	BB	SO	RAT	ERA	ERA+	OAV	OOB	BH	AVG	PB	PR	/A	PD	TPI
1918	Bos-A	0	1	.000	3	1	0	0	0	9^2	13	0	2	3	14.0	2.79	96	.351	.385	0	.000	-0	-0	-0	0	0.0
1922	Chi-A	1	0	1.000	3	0	0	0	0	3^1	4	0	0	1	10.8	5.40	75	.308	.308	0	—	0	-1	-0	-0	-0.1
Total	2	1	1	.500	6	1	0	0	0	13	17	0	2	4	13.2	3.46	88	.340	.365	0	.000	-0	-1	-1	-0	-0.1

● TIM McCABE McCabe, Timothy J. b: 10/19/1894, Ironton, Mo. d: 4/12/77, Ironton, Mo. BR/TR, 6', 190 lbs. Deb: 8/16/15

YEAR	TM/L	W	L	PCT	G	GS	CG	SH	SV	IP	H	HR	BB	SO	RAT	ERA	ERA+	OAV	OOB	BH	AVG	PB	PR	/A	PD	TPI
1915	StL-A	3	1	.750	7	4	4	1	0	41^2	25	1	9	17	7.6	1.30	221	.177	.232	1	.067	-1	8	7	-1	0.5
1916	StL-A	2	0	1.000	13	0	0	0	0	25^2	29	0	7	7	13.3	3.16	87	.282	.339	0	.000	-0	-1	-1	1	0.0
1917	StL-A	0	0	—	1	0	0	0	0	2^1	4	1	4	2	30.9	23.14	11	.400	.571	0	—	0	-5	-5	0	0.0
1918	StL-A	0	0	—	1	0	0	0	0	1^1	2	0	1	0	20.3	13.50	20	.333	.429	0	—	0	-2	-2	-0	0.0
Total	4	5	1	.833	22	4	4	1	0	71	60	2	21	26	10.6	2.92	96	.231	.296	1	.053	-1	-0	-1	1	0.5

● HARRY McCAFFERY McCaffery, Harry Charles b: 11/25/1858, St.Louis, Mo. d: 4/19/28, St.Louis, Mo. BR/TR, 5'10.5", 185 lbs. Deb: 6/15/1882 U♦

YEAR	TM/L	W	L	PCT	G	GS	CG	SH	SV	IP	H	HR	BB	SO	RAT	ERA	ERA+	OAV	OOB	BH	AVG	PB	PR	/A	PD	TPI
1885	Cin-a	1	0	1.000	1	1	1	0	0	9	13	1	2	2	17.0	6.00	54	.342	.405	0	.000	-1	-3	-3	-0	-0.3

● BILL McCAHAN McCahan, William Glenn b: 6/7/21, Philadelphia, Pa. d: 7/3/86, Fort Worth, Tex. BR/TR, 5'11", 200 lbs. Deb: 9/15/46

YEAR	TM/L	W	L	PCT	G	GS	CG	SH	SV	IP	H	HR	BB	SO	RAT	ERA	ERA+	OAV	OOB	BH	AVG	PB	PR	/A	PD	TPI
1946	Phi-A	1	1	.500	4	2	2	1	0	18	16	0	9	6	12.5	1.00	355	.246	.338	2	.400	1	5	5	0	0.7
1947	Phi-A	10	5	.667	29	19	10	1	0	165^1	160	7	62	47	12.1	3.32	115	.252	.318	9	.164	-1	7	9	1	0.8
1948	Phi-A	4	7	.364	17	15	5	0	0	86^2	98	8	65	20	16.9	5.71	75	.284	.398	8	.258	1	-14	-14	-1	-1.5
1949	Phi-A	1	1	.500	7	4	0	0	0	20^2	23	0	9	3	13.9	2.61	157	.291	.364	1	.200	-0	4	3	-0	0.2
Total	4	16	14	.533	57	40	17	2	0	290^2	297	15	145	76	13.7	3.84	103	.264	.348	20	.208	1	2	4	-1	0.2

YEAR	TM/L	W	L	PCT	G	GS	CG	SH	SV	IP	H	HR	BB	SO	RAT	ERA	ERA+	OAV	OOB	BH	AVG	PB	PR	/A	PD	TPI
● WINDY McCALL	McCall, John William b: 7/18/25, San Francisco, Cal. BL/TL, 6′, 180 lbs. Deb: 4/25/48																									
1948	Bos-A	0	1	.000	1	1	0	0	0	1^1	6	1	1	0	47.3	20.25	22	.600	.636	0	—	0	-2	-2	0	-0.9
1949	Bos-A	0	0	—	5	0	0	0	0	9^1	13	2	10	8	22.2	11.57	38	.333	.469	2	.667	1	-8	-7	-0	0.0
1950	Pit-N	0	0	—	2	0	0	0	0	6^2	12	2	4	5	21.6	9.45	46	.387	.457	0	.000	0	-4	-4	0	0.0
1954	NY-N	2	5	.286	33	4	0	0	2	61	50	5	29	38	12.1	3.25	124	.219	.315	0	.000	-1	6	5	-1	0.3
1955	NY-N	6	5	.545	42	6	4	0	3	95	86	8	37	50	12.2	3.69	109	.244	.326	2	.118	-1	4	3	1	0.4
1956	NY-N	3	4	.429	46	4	0	0	7	77^1	74	7	20	41	11.1	3.61	105	.252	.302	3	.200	-0	1	1	-2	0.0
1957	NY-N	0	0	—	5	0	0	0	0	3	8	1	2	2	33.0	15.00	26	.533	.611	0	—	0	-4	-4	-0	0.0
Total	7	11	15	.423	134	15	4	0	12	253^2	249	26	103	144	12.9	4.22	94	.257	.335	7	.146	-1	-7	-7	-3	-0.2
● LARRY McCALL	McCall, Larry Stephen b: 9/8/52, Asheville, N.C. BL/TR, 6′2″, 195 lbs. Deb: 9/10/77																									
1977	NY-A	0	1	.000	2	0	0	0	0	6	12	1	1	0	19.5	7.50	53	.375	.394	0	—	0	-2	-2	-0	-0.3
1978	NY-A	1	1	.500	5	1	0	0	0	16	20	2	6	7	15.2	5.63	64	.323	.391	0	—	0	-3	-4	0	-0.2
1979	Tex-A	1	0	1.000	2	1	0	0	0	8^1	7	0	3	3	10.8	2.16	192	.226	.294	0	—	0	2	2	0	0.3
Total	3	2	2	.500	9	2	0	0	0	30^1	39	3	10	10	14.8	5.04	76	.312	.368	0	—	0	-4	-4	0	-0.2
● DUTCH McCALL	McCall, Robert Leonard b: 12/27/20, Columbia, Tenn. d: 1/7/96, Little Rock, Ark. BL/TL, 6′1″, 184 lbs. Deb: 4/27/48																									
1948	Chi-N	4	13	.235	30	20	5	0	0	151^1	158	14	85	89	14.5	4.82	81	.268	.361	9	.170	1	-14	-15	1	-1.3
● RANDY McCAMENT	McCament, Larry Randall b: 7/29/62, Albuquerque, N.Mex. BR/TR, 6′3″, 195 lbs. Deb: 6/28/89																									
1989	SF-N	1	1	.500	25	0	0	0	0	36^2	32	4	23	12	13.7	3.93	86	.241	.357	1	.333	0	-2	-2	0	0.0
1990	SF-N	0	0	—	3	0	0	0	0	6	8	0	5	5	19.5	3.00	121	.333	.448	0	.000	-0	1	0	-0	0.0
Total	2	1	1	.500	28	0	0	0	0	42^2	40	4	28	17	14.6	3.80	90	.255	.371	1	.250	0	-1	-2	0	0.0
● GENE McCANN	McCann, Henry Eugene "Mike" b: 6/13/1876, Baltimore, Md. d: 4/26/43, New York, N.Y. TR, 5′10″, Deb: 4/19/01																									
1901	Bro-N	2	3	.400	6	5	3	0	0	34	34	1	16	9	14.3	3.44	97	.260	.358	0	.000	-1	-0	-0	0	-0.1
1902	Bro-N	1	2	.333	3	3	3	0	0	30	32	0	12	9	13.2	2.40	115	.274	.341	1	.083	-1	1	1	1	0.1
Total	2	3	5	.375	9	8	6	0	0	64	66	1	28	18	13.8	2.95	104	.266	.350	1	.045	-2	1	1	1	0.0
● ARCH McCARTHY	McCarthy, Archibald Joseph b: Ypsilanti, Mich. TR, 6′, 160 lbs. Deb: 8/14/02																									
1902	Det-A	2	7	.222	10	8	8	0	0	72	90	2	31	10	15.6	6.13	60	.306	.380	2	.071	-3	-20	-20	-2	-2.3
● GREG McCARTHY	McCarthy, Gregory O'Neil b: 10/30/68, Norwalk, Conn. BL/TL, 6′2″, 195 lbs. Deb: 8/28/96																									
1996	Sea-A	0	0	—	10	0	0	0	0	9^2	8	0	4	7	14.9	1.86	266	.229	.372	0	—	0	3	3	0	0.0
1997	Sea-A	1	1	.500	37	0	0	0	0	29^2	26	4	16	34	13.0	5.46	82	.230	.331	0	—	0	-3	-3	0	-0.1
1998	Sea-A	1	2	.333	29	0	0	0	0	23^1	18	6	17	25	14.7	5.01	92	.214	.365	0	—	0	-1	-1	1	0.0
Total	3	2	3	.400	76	0	0	0	0	62^2	52	10	37	66	13.9	4.74	97	.224	.350	0	—	0	-1	-1	1	-0.1
● JOHNNY McCARTHY	McCarthy, John Joseph b: 1/7/10, Chicago, Ill. d: 9/13/73, Mundelein, Ill. BL/TL, 6′1.5″, 185 lbs. Deb: 9/2/34 ♦																									
1939	NY-N	0	0	—	1	0	0	0	0	5	8	1	2	0	18.0	7.20	55	.364	.417	21	.262	0	-2	-2	0	0.0
● TOMMY McCARTHY	McCarthy, Thomas Francis Michael b: 7/24/1863, Boston, Mass. d: 8/5/22, Boston, Mass. BR/TR, 5′7″, 170 lbs. Deb: 7/10/1884 MH♦																									
1884	Bos-U	0	7	.000	7	6	5	0	0	56	73	2	14	18	14.0	4.82	49	.296	.333	45	.215	-2	-15	-15	1	-1.4
1886	Phi-N	0	0	—	1	0	0	0	0	1	0	0	1	1	9.0	0.00	—	.000	.250	5	.185	0	0	0	0	0.0
1888	*StL-a	0	0	—	2	0	0	0	0	4^1	3	1	2	1	10.4	4.15	79	.188	.278	140	.274	0	-1	-0	-0	0.0
1889	StL-a	0	0	—	1	0	0	0	0	5	4	0	6	1	18.0	7.20	59	.211	.400	176	.291	0	-2	-2	-0	0.0
1891	StL-a	0	0	—	1	0	0	0	0	1	2	0	0	0	18.0	9.00	47	.400	.400	179	.310	0	-1	-1	-0	0.0
1894	Bos-N	0	0	—	1	0	0	0	0	2	1	0	3	0	18.0	4.50	126	.143	.400	188	.349	0	0	0	-0	0.0
Total	6	0	7	.000	13	6	5	0	0	69^1	83	3	26	21	14.1	4.93	54	.279	.337	1496	.292	-1	-17	-17	1	-1.4
● TOM McCARTHY	McCarthy, Thomas Michael b: 6/18/61, Lundstahl, W.Ger. BR/TR, 6′, 180 lbs. Deb: 7/5/85																									
1985	Bos-A	0	0	—	3	0	0	0	0	5	7	1	4	2	19.8	10.80	40	.350	.458	0	—	0	-4	-4	-0	-0.1
1988	Chi-A	2	0	1.000	6	0	0	0	1	13	9	0	2	5	9.0	1.38	287	.191	.255	0	—	0	4	4	0	0.7
1989	Chi-A	1	2	.333	31	0	0	0	0	66^2	72	8	20	27	12.7	3.51	108	.280	.337	0	—	0	3	2	1	0.2
Total	3	3	2	.600	40	0	0	0	1	84^2	88	9	26	34	12.5	3.61	107	.272	.333	0	—	0	3	2	1	0.8
● TOM McCARTHY	McCarthy, Thomas Patrick b: 5/22/1884, Ft.Wayne, Ind. d: 3/28/33, Mishawaka, Ind. TR, 5′7″, 170 lbs. Deb: 5/10/08																									
1908	Cin-N	0	1	.000	1	1	0	0	0	3^2	6	0	3	3	22.1	9.82	23	.300	.391	0	.000	-0	-3	-3	0	-0.6
	Pit-N	0	0	—	2	1	0	0	0	6	3	0	6	1	13.5	0.00	—	.176	.391	0	.000	-0	2	2	1	0.0
	Bos-N	7	3	.700	14	11	7	2	0	94	77	0	28	27	10.1	1.63	148	.235	.298	6	.171	0	8	8	0	1.0
	Yr	7	4	.636	17	13	7	2	0	103^2	86	0	37	31	10.8	1.82	132	.236	.308	6	.146	-1	6	7	1	0.4
1909	Bos-N	0	5	.000	8	7	3	0	0	46^1	47	3	28	11	15.0	3.50	81	.272	.379	2	.125	-0	-5	-3	0	-0.4
Total	2	7	9	.438	25	20	10	2	0	150	133	3	65	42	12.1	2.34	108	.248	.332	8	.140	-1	2	3	1	-0.0
● BILL McCARTHY	McCarthy, William Thomas b: 4/11/1882, Ashland, Mass. d: 5/29/39, Boston, Mass. BR/TR, 5′11″, 180 lbs. Deb: 4/21/06																									
1906	Bos-N	0	0	—	1	0	0	0	0	2	2	0	3	0	22.5	9.00	30	.182	.357	0	.000	-0	-1	-1	-0	0.0
● JOHN McCARTY	McCarty, John A. b: St.Louis, Mo. TR, Deb: 4/18/1889																									
1889	KC-a	8	6	.571	15	14	13	0	0	119^2	147	4	61	36	16.1	3.91	107	.293	.376	18	.228	-2	-1	4	-0	0.2
● KIRK McCASKILL	McCaskill, Kirk Edward b: 4/9/61, Kapuskasing, Ont., Canada BR/TR, 6′1″, 196 lbs. Deb: 5/1/85																									
1985	Cal-A	12	12	.500	30	29	6	1	0	189^2	189	23	64	102	12.2	4.70	87	.258	.321	0	—	0	-12	-12	-0	-1.4
1986	*Cal-A	17	10	.630	34	33	10	2	0	246^1	207	19	92	202	11.1	3.36	122	.229	.303	0	—	0	22	20	-0	2.2
1987	Cal-A	4	6	.400	14	13	1	1	0	74^2	84	14	34	56	14.5	5.67	76	.286	.364	0	—	0	-10	-11	1	-1.2
1988	Cal-A	8	6	.571	23	23	4	2	0	146^1	155	9	61	98	13.3	4.31	90	.274	.346	0	—	0	-6	-7	0	-0.4
1989	Cal-A	15	10	.600	32	32	6	4	0	212	202	16	59	107	11.2	2.93	130	.254	.308	0	—	0	22	21	2	2.6
1990	Cal-A	12	11	.522	29	29	2	1	0	174^1	161	9	72	78	12.1	3.25	117	.244	.320	0	—	0	13	11	2	1.5
1991	Cal-A	10	19	.345	30	30	1	0	0	177^2	193	19	66	71	13.3	4.26	96	.283	.349	0	—	0	-3	-3	1	-0.4
1992	Chi-A	12	13	.480	34	34	0	0	0	209	193	11	95	109	12.7	4.18	92	.242	.328	0	—	0	-6	-7	2	-0.6
1993	*Chi-A	4	8	.333	30	14	0	0	2	113^2	144	12	36	65	14.3	5.23	80	.313	.364	0	—	0	-11	-13	2	-1.0
1994	Chi-A	1	4	.200	40	0	0	0	3	52^2	51	6	22	37	12.5	3.42	137	.252	.326	0	—	0	8	7	0	0.7
1995	Chi-A	6	4	.600	55	1	0	0	2	81	97	10	33	50	15.0	4.89	91	.302	.376	0	—	0	-2	-4	0	-0.4
1996	Chi-A	5	5	.500	29	4	0	0	0	51^2	72	6	31	28	18.3	6.97	68	.344	.434	0	—	0	-11	-13	1	-1.7
Total	12	106	108	.495	380	242	30	11	7	1729	1748	154	665	1003	12.7	4.12	99	.264	.334	0	—	0	5	-11	9	-0.1
● STEVE McCATTY	McCatty, Steven Earl b: 3/20/54, Detroit, Mich. BR/TR, 6′3″, 205 lbs. Deb: 9/17/77																									
1977	Oak-A	0	0	—	4	2	0	0	0	14^1	16	1	7	9	15.1	5.02	80	.276	.364	0	—	0	-2	-2	-1	0.0
1978	Oak-A	0	0	—	9	0	0	0	0	20	26	1	9	10	15.7	4.50	81	.310	.376	0	—	0	-2	-2	-0	0.3
1979	Oak-A	11	12	.478	31	23	8	0	0	185^2	207	17	80	87	14.4	4.22	96	.284	.363	0	—	0	-0	-4	-2	-0.2
1980	Oak-A	14	14	.500	33	31	11	1	0	221^2	202	27	99	114	12.5	3.86	98	.240	.325	0	—	0	4	-2	-1	0.1
1981	*Oak-A	**14**	7	.667	22	22	16	**4**	0	185^2	140	12	61	91	9.8	**2.33**	149	**.211**	.279	0	—	0	**27**	**24**	-1	2.8
1982	Oak-A	6	3	.667	21	20	2	0	0	128^2	124	16	70	66	13.8	3.99	98	.255	.354	0	—	0	1	-1	-1	-0.1
1983	Oak-A	6	9	.400	38	24	3	2	5	167	156	16	82	65	12.9	3.99	97	.247	.334	0	—	0	1	-2	-2	-0.4
1984	Oak-A	8	14	.364	33	30	4	0	0	179^2	206	24	71	63	13.9	4.76	79	.289	.355	0	—	0	-15	-20	-2	-1.9
1985	Oak-A	4	4	.500	30	9	1	0	0	85^2	95	10	41	36	14.7	5.57	69	.286	.371	0	—	0	-14	-16	0	-1.2
Total	9	63	63	.500	221	161	45	7	5	1188^1	1172	124	520	541	13.0	3.99	95	.258	.339	0	—	0	2	-26	-9	-0.6
● AL McCAULEY	McCauley, Allen A. b: 3/4/1863, Indianapolis, Ind. d: 8/24/17, Wayne Twnshp., Ind BL/TL, 6′, 180 lbs. Deb: 6/21/1884 ♦																									
1884	Ind-a	2	7	.222	10	9	9	0	0	76	87	2	25	34	13.3	5.09	65	.261	.313	10	.189	2	-16	-15	2	-1.1
● JOE McCLAIN	McClain, Joseph Fred b: 5/5/33, Johnson City, Tenn. BR/TR, 6′, 183 lbs. Deb: 4/14/61																									
1961	Was-A	8	18	.308	33	29	7	2	1	212	221	22	48	76	11.6	3.86	104	.270	.313	14	.206	1	4	4	-3	0.3

YEAR	TM/L	W	L	PCT	G	GS	CG	SH	SV	IP	H	HR	BB	SO	RAT	ERA	ERA+	OAV	OOB	BH	AVG	PB	PR	/A	PD	TPI
1962	Was-A	0	4	.000	10	4	0	0	0	24	33	8	11	6	17.3	9.38	43	.327	.404	1	.143	-0	-14	-14	0	-1.9
Total	2	8	22	.267	43	33	7	2	1	236	254	30	59	82	12.2	4.42	91	.276	.324	15	.200	1	-11	-11	-3	-1.6
● **PAUL McCLELLAN**	McClellan, Paul William b: 2/3/66, San Mateo, Cal. BR/TR, 6'2", 180 lbs. Deb: 9/2/90																									
1990	SF-N	0	1	.000	4	1	0	0	0	7^2	14	3	6	2	24.7	11.74	31	.389	.488	1	.500	0	-7	-7	0	-0.7
1991	SF-N	3	6	.333	13	12	1	0	0	71	68	12	25	44	11.9	4.56	78	.252	.318	3	.143	-0	-7	-8	-1	-1.0
Total	2	3	7	.300	17	13	1	0	0	78^2	82	15	31	46	13.2	5.26	68	.268	.339	4	.174	0	-14	-15	-1	-1.7
● **JIM McCLOSKEY**	McCloskey, James Ellwood "Irish" b: 5/26/10, Danville, Pa. d: 8/18/71, Jersey City, N.J. BL/TL, 5'9.5", 180 lbs. Deb: 4/21/36																									
1936	Bos-N	0	0	—	4	1	0	0	0	8	14	1	3	2	20.3	11.25	34	.378	.439	0	.000	-0	-6	-7	0	0.0
● **JOHN McCLOSKEY**	McCloskey, James John b: 8/20/1882, Wyoming, Pa. d: 6/5/19, Wilkes-Barre, Pa. Deb: 5/3/06																									
1906	Phi-N	3	2	.600	9	4	3	0	0	41	46	2	9	6	12.3	2.85	92	.280	.322	3	.200	0	-1	-1	-1	-0.2
1907	Phi-N	0	0	—	3	0	0	0	0	9	15	0	6	3	22.0	7.00	35	.417	.512	0	.000	-0	-5	-5	0	0.0
Total	2	3	2	.600	12	4	3	0	0	50	61	2	15	9	14.0	3.60	72	.305	.359	3	.158	-0	-6	-6	-1	-0.2
● **BOB McCLURE**	McClure, Robert Craig b: 4/29/52, Oakland, Cal. BR/TL, 5'11", 170 lbs. Deb: 8/13/75 C																									
1975	KC-A	1	0	1.000	12	0	0	0	1	15^1	4	0	14	15	10.6	0.00	—	.077	.273	0	—	0	6	7	-0	0.5
1976	KC-A	0	0	—	8	0	0	0	0	4	3	0	8	3	24.8	9.00	39	.214	.500	0	—	0	-2	-2	-0	-0.1
1977	Mil-A	2	1	.667	68	0	0	0	6	71^1	64	2	34	57	12.5	2.52	161	.249	.339	0	—	0	12	12	2	0.9
1978	Mil-A	2	6	.250	44	0	0	0	9	65	53	8	30	47	12.3	3.74	101	.223	.325	0	—	0	0	0	1	0.0
1979	Mil-A	5	2	.714	36	0	0	0	5	51	53	6	24	37	14.1	3.88	107	.269	.357	0	—	0	2	2	-0	0.2
1980	Mil-A	5	8	.385	52	5	2	1	10	90^2	83	6	37	47	12.1	3.08	126	.241	.318	0	—	0	10	8	-1	1.4
1981	*Mil-A	0	0	—	4	0	0	0	0	7^2	7	1	4	6	12.9	3.52	97	.233	.324	0	—	0	0	-0	-0	0.2
1982	*Mil-A	12	7	.632	34	26	5	0	0	172^2	160	21	74	99	12.4	4.22	90	.248	.329	0	—	0	-3	-8	-1	-0.8
1983	Mil-A	9	9	.500	24	23	4	0	0	142	152	11	68	68	14.3	4.50	83	.277	.362	0	—	0	-7	-12	-1	-1.4
1984	Mil-A	4	8	.333	39	18	1	0	1	139^2	154	9	52	68	13.4	4.38	88	.282	.347	0	—	0	-6	-8	-0	-0.4
1985	Mil-A	4	1	.800	38	1	0	0	3	85^2	91	10	30	57	13.0	4.31	97	.274	.340	0	—	0	-2	-1	-0	-0.1
1986	Mil-A	2	1	.667	13	0	0	0	0	16^1	18	2	10	11	15.4	3.86	112	.286	.384	0	—	0	1	1	-0	-0.2
	Mon-N	2	5	.286	52	0	0	0	6	62^2	53	2	23	42	11.1	3.02	122	.232	.306	1	.250	0	5	5	0	0.6
1987	Mon-N	6	1	.857	52	0	0	0	5	52^1	47	8	20	33	11.5	3.44	122	.241	.312	0	.000	-0	4	4	0	0.6
1988	Mon-N	1	3	.250	19	0	0	0	2	19	23	3	6	12	14.2	6.16	58	.307	.366	0	.000	-0	-6	-5	0	-1.2
	NY-N	1	0	1.000	14	0	0	0	1	11	12	1	2	7	12.3	4.09	79	.279	.326	0	—	0	-1	-1	-0	-0.1
	Yr	2	3	.400	33	0	0	0	3	30	35	4	8	19	13.2	5.40	64	.289	.338	0	.000	-0	-7	-6	-0	-1.3
1989	Cal-A	6	1	.857	48	0	0	0	3	52^1	39	2	15	36	9.5	1.55	246	.212	.275	0	—	0	14	13	-1	1.7
1990	Cal-A	2	0	1.000	11	0	0	0	0	7	7	0	3	6	12.9	6.43	59	.269	.345	0	—	0	-2	-2	0	-0.5
1991	Cal-A	0	0	—	13	0	0	0	0	9^2	13	3	5	5	17.7	9.31	44	.317	.404	0	—	0	-6	-6	0	0.0
	StL-N	1	1	.500	32	0	0	0	0	23	24	1	8	15	12.9	3.13	119	.282	.351	1	1.000	0	1	1	-0	0.2
1992	StL-N	2	2	.500	71	0	0	0	0	54	52	6	25	24	13.2	3.17	107	.261	.350	0	—	0	2	1	-0	0.1
1993	Fla-N	1	1	.500	14	0	0	0	0	6^1	13	2	5	6	25.6	7.11	61	.419	.500	0	—	0	-2	-2	0	-0.5
Total	19	68	57	.544	698	73	12	1	52	1158^2	1125	104	497	701	12.9	3.81	101	.257	.338	2	.222	0	21	6	-4	1.1
● **HARRY McCLUSKEY**	McCluskey, Harry Robert b: 3/29/1892, Clay Center, Ohio d: 6/7/62, Toledo, Ohio BL/TL, 5'11.5", 173 lbs. Deb: 7/29/15																									
1915	Cin-N	0	0	—	3	0	0	0	0	5	4	0	0	2	7.2	5.40	53	.182	.182	0	.000	-0	-1	-1	-0	-0.1
● **ALEX McCOLL**	McColl, Alexander Boyd "Red" b: 3/29/1894, Eagleville, Ohio d: 2/6/91, Kingsville, Ohio BB/TR, 6'1", 178 lbs. Deb: 8/27/33																									
1933	*Was-A	1	0	1.000	4	1	1	0	0	17	13	0	7	5	10.6	2.65	158	.210	.290	2	.333	1	3	3	-0	0.2
1934	Was-A	3	4	.429	42	2	1	0	1	112	129	6	36	29	13.3	3.86	112	.291	.345	3	.097	-2	8	6	2	0.3
Total	2	4	4	.500	46	3	2	0	1	129	142	6	43	34	13.0	3.70	116	.281	.338	5	.135	-1	11	9	2	0.5
● **RALPH McCONNAUGHEY**	McConnaughey, Ralph James b: 8/5/1889, Vandergrift, Pa. d: 6/4/66, Detroit, Mich. BR/TR, 5'8.5", 166 lbs. Deb: 7/8/14																									
1914	Ind-F	0	2	.000	7	2	1	0	0	26	23	3	16	7	13.8	4.85	64	.245	.360	1	.125	-0	-6	-5	-0	-0.4
● **GEORGE McCONNELL**	McConnell, George Neely "Slats" b: 9/16/1877, Shelbyville, Tenn d: 5/10/64, Chattanooga, Tenn. BR/TR, 6'3", 190 lbs. Deb: 4/13/09 ♦																									
1909	NY-A	0	1	.000	2	1	0	0	0	4	3	0	3	4	13.5	2.25	112	.231	.375	9	.209	0	0	0	1	0.1
1912	NY-A	8	12	.400	23	20	19	0	0	176^2	172	3	52	91	11.6	2.75	131	.269	.328	27	.297	3	11	17	5	2.9
1913	NY-A	4	15	.211	35	20	8	0	3	180	162	2	60	72	11.4	3.20	94	.245	.314	12	.179	-1	-5	-4	5	-0.1
1914	Chi-N	0	1	.000	1	1	0	0	0	7	3	0	3	3	7.7	1.29	216	.125	.222	0	.000	-0	1	1	0	0.2
1915	Chi-F	**25**	10	**.714**	44	35	23	4	1	303	262	8	89	151	10.7	2.20	114	.232	.292	31	.248	4	18	11	3	2.0
1916	Chi-N	4	12	.250	28	21	8	1	0	171^1	137	8	35	82	9.3	2.57	113	.223	.271	9	.158	-2	1	6	2	0.6
Total	6	41	51	.446	133	98	58	5	4	842	739	21	242	403	10.7	2.60	112	.240	.300	88	.229	4	26	30	15	5.7
● **BILLY McCOOL**	McCool, William John b: 7/14/44, Batesville, Ind. BR/TL, 6'2", 203 lbs. Deb: 4/24/64																									
1964	Cin-N	6	5	.545	40	3	0	0	7	89^1	66	3	29	87	9.7	2.42	150	.206	.274	0	.000	-2	11	12	-2	1.3
1965	Cin-N	9	10	.474	62	2	0	0	21	105^1	93	9	47	120	12.3	4.27	88	.237	.324	1	.037	-2	-9	-6	-0	-1.5
1966	Cin-N☆	8	8	.500	57	0	0	0	18	105^1	76	5	41	104	10.3	2.48	157	.205	.290	3	.167	-0	13	17	2	3.4
1967	Cin-N	3	7	.300	31	11	0	0	2	97^1	92	8	56	83	14.1	3.42	110	.246	.352	2	.077	-1	-1	4	-1	0.2
1968	Cin-N	3	4	.429	30	4	0	0	2	50^2	59	4	41	30	17.8	4.97	64	.294	.413	1	.125	-0	-11	-10	-1	-1.6
1969	SD-N	3	5	.375	54	0	0	0	7	58^2	59	2	42	35	16.4	4.30	82	.266	.396	0	.000	-0	-5	-5	-0	-0.8
1970	StL-N	0	3	.000	18	0	0	0	1	21^2	20	0	16	12	15.0	6.23	66	.250	.375	0	.000	-0	-5	-5	0	-0.7
Total	7	32	42	.432	292	20	0	0	58	528^1	465	31	272	471	12.9	3.59	103	.237	.336	7	.069	-6	-6	6	-1	0.3
● **JIM McCORMICK**	McCormick, James b: 11/3/1856, Glasgow, Scotland d: 3/10/18, Paterson, N.J. BR/TR, 5'10.5", 215 lbs. Deb: 5/20/1878 M																									
1878	Ind-N	5	8	.385	14	14	12	1	0	117	128	0	15	36	11.0	1.69	120	.269	.292	8	.143	-3	8	4	2	0.3
1879	Cle-N	20	40	.333	62	60	59	3	0	546^1	582	4	74	197	10.8	2.42	103	.259	.282	62	.220	-1	4	5	4	0.7
1880	Cle-N	**45**	28	.616	**74**	74	**72**	7	0	**657^2**	585	2	75	260	9.0	1.85	127	.226	.247	71	.246	1	38	**37**	1	**4.0**
1881	Cle-N	26	30	.464	59	58	**57**	2	0	526	484	4	84	178	9.7	2.45	107	.235	.265	79	.256	6	19	10	-3	1.2
1882	Cle-N	**36**	30	.545	**68**	67	**65**	4	0	**595^2**	550	14	103	200	9.9	2.37	118	.238	.271	57	.218	-4	35	28	-2	2.0
1883	Cle-N	28	12	**.700**	43	41	36	1	1	342	316	1	65	145	10.0	**1.84**	**171**	.233	.268	37	.236	-1	49	50	7	5.4
1884	Cle-N	19	22	.463	42	41	39	3	0	359	357	17	75	182	10.8	2.86	110	.247	.285	50	.263	2	5	12	0	1.3
	Cin-U	21	3	**.875**	24	24	24	**7**	0	210	151	3	14	161	**7.1**	**1.54**	**166**	**.188**	**.202**	27	.245	-6	21	**24**	2	1.8
1885	Pro-N	1	3	.250	4	4	4	0	0	37	34	1	20	8	13.1	2.43	110	.234	.327	3	.214	0	2	1	3	0.4
	*Chi-N	20	4	.833	24	24	24	3	0	215	187	8	40	88	9.5	2.43	124	.224	.260	23	.223	0	9	14	3	1.5
	Yr	21	7	.750	28	28	28	3	0	252	221	9	60	96	10.0	2.43	122	.226	.271	26	.222	1	11	15	5	1.9
1886	*Chi-N	31	11	.738	42	42	38	2	0	347^2	341	18	100	172	11.4	2.82	128	.253	.304	41	.236	2	19	31	2	3.3
1887	Pit-N	13	23	.361	36	36	36	0	0	322^1	377	12	84	77	13.2	4.30	90	.285	.331	33	.213	0	-8	-15	5	0.0
Total	10	265	214	.553	492	485	466	33	1	4275^2	4092	84	749	1704	10.2	2.43	117	.242	.274	491	.236	-4	202	200	22	21.0
● **JERRY McCORMICK**	McCormick, John b: Philadelphia, Pa. d: 9/19/05, Philadelphia, Pa. Deb: 5/1/1883 ♦																									
1884	Phi-U	0	0	—	1	0	0	0	0	2	5	1	0	3	22.5	9.00	26	.455	.455	84	.285	-0	-1	-1	-0	0.0
● **MIKE McCORMICK**	McCormick, Michael Francis b: 9/29/38, Pasadena, Cal. BL/TL, 6'2", 195 lbs. Deb: 9/3/56																									
1956	NY-N	0	1	.000	3	2	0	0	0	6^2	7	1	10	4	23.0	9.45	40	.269	.472	0	.000	-0	-4	-4	-0	-0.5
1957	NY-N	3	1	.750	24	5	1	0	0	74^2	79	7	32	50	13.7	4.10	96	.280	.360	6	.273	1	-2	-1	-1	0.0
1958	SF-N	11	8	.579	42	28	8	2	1	178^1	192	19	60	82	12.9	4.59	83	.276	.336	12	.222	1	-13	-15	2	-1.2
1959	SF-N	12	16	.429	47	31	7	3	4	225^2	213	24	86	151	12.0	3.99	96	.248	.317	7	.106	-2	-1	-4	1	-0.6
1960	SF-N★	15	12	.556	40	34	15	4	3	253	228	15	65	154	10.5	**2.70**	129	.241	.291	16	.182	1	**30**	22	3	2.7
1961	SF-N★	13	16	.448	40	35	13	3	0	250	235	33	75	163	11.2	3.20	119	.249	.306	15	.188	1	23	17	-2	1.7
1962	SF-N	5	5	.500	28	15	1	0	0	98^2	112	18	45	42	14.4	5.38	71	.286	.361	3	.107	0	-16	-17	-1	-1.6
1963	Bal-A	6	8	.429	25	21	2	0	0	136	132	18	66	75	13.1	4.30	81	.256	.340	8	.174	1	-10	-13	-0	-1.2
1964	Bal-A	0	2	.000	4	2	0	0	0	17^1	21	1	8	13	15.1	5.19	69	.288	.358	1	.167	-0	-3	-3	-0	-0.3

YEAR	TM/L	W	L	PCT	G	GS	CG	SH	SV	IP	H	HR	BB	SO	RAT	ERA	ERA+	OAV	OOB	BH	AVG	PB	PR	/A	PD	TPI
1965	Was-A	8	8	.500	44	21	3	1	1	158	158	17	36	88	11.1	3.36	103	.260	.301	3	.073	-1	2	2	-1	0.0
1966	Was-A	11	14	.440	41	32	8	3	0	216	193	23	51	101	10.3	3.46	100	.236	.282	14	.212	3	-1	0	-1	0.3
1967	SF-N	**22**	10	.688	40	35	14	5	0	262^1	220	25	81	150	10.5	2.85	115	.226	.289	10	.119	0	15	13	-2	1.3
1968	SF-N	12	14	.462	38	28	9	2	1	198^1	196	17	49	121	11.2	3.58	82	.254	.300	6	.103	1	-13	-14	-2	-2.0
1969	SF-N	11	9	.550	32	28	9	0	0	196^2	175	20	77	76	11.6	3.34	105	.237	.310	9	.136	1	6	3	-1	0.3
1970	SF-N	3	4	.429	23	11	1	0	2	78^1	80	15	36	37	13.7	6.20	64	.262	.346	4	.160	0	-19	-19	1	-1.5
	NY-A	2	0	1.000	9	4	0	0	0	20^2	26	2	13	12	17.0	6.10	58	.295	.386	1	.200	0	-5	-6	-1	-0.6
1971	KC-A	0	0	—	4	1	0	0	0	9^2	14	0	5	2	17.7	9.31	37	.350	.422	0	.000	-0	-6	-6	1	0.1
Total	16	134	128	.511	484	333	91	23	12	2380^1	2281	255	795	1321	11.7	3.73	95	.251	.313	115	.156	9	-18	-46	-5	-3.1

● **HARRY McCORMICK** McCormick, Patrick Henry b: 10/25/1855, Syracuse, N.Y. d: 8/8/1889, Syracuse, N.Y. BR/TR, 5′9″, 155 lbs. Deb: 5/1/1879

YEAR	TM/L	W	L	PCT	G	GS	CG	SH	SV	IP	H	HR	BB	SO	RAT	ERA	ERA+	OAV	OOB	BH	AVG	PB	PR	/A	PD	TPI
1879	Syr-N	18	33	.353	54	54	49	5	0	457^1	517	3	31	96	10.8	2.99	79	.266	.277	51	.222	-0	-25	-32	-7	-3.4
1881	Wor-N	1	8	.111	9	9	9	1	0	78^1	89	1	15	7	11.9	3.56	85	.275	.307	6	.133	-2	-7	-5	-1	-0.7
1882	Cin-a	14	11	.560	25	25	24	3	0	219^2	177	4	42	33	9.0	1.52	174	.206	.243	12	.129	-5	29	27	0	2.1
1883	Cin-a	8	6	.571	15	15	14	1	0	128^2	139	1	27	21	11.6	2.87	113	.258	.294	17	.309	4	6	5	1	0.8
Total	4	41	58	.414	103	103	96	10	0	884	922	9	115	157	10.6	2.66	98	.252	.274	86	.203	-4	3	-4	-7	-1.2

● **BILL McCORRY** McCorry, William Charles b: 7/9/1887, Saranac Lake, N.Y. d: 3/22/73, Augusta, Ga. BL/TR, 5′9″, 157 lbs. Deb: 9/17/09

YEAR	TM/L	W	L	PCT	G	GS	CG	SH	SV	IP	H	HR	BB	SO	RAT	ERA	ERA+	OAV	OOB	BH	AVG	PB	PR	/A	PD	TPI
1909	StL-A	0	2	.000	2	2	2	0	0	15	29	1	6	10	21.0	9.00	27	.397	.443	0	.000	-0	-11	-11	-1	-1.1

● **LES McCRABB** McCrabb, Lester William "Buster" b: 11/4/14, Wakefield, Pa. BR/TR, 5′11″, 175 lbs. Deb: 9/7/39 C

YEAR	TM/L	W	L	PCT	G	GS	CG	SH	SV	IP	H	HR	BB	SO	RAT	ERA	ERA+	OAV	OOB	BH	AVG	PB	PR	/A	PD	TPI
1939	Phi-A	1	2	.333	5	4	2	0	0	35^2	42	4	10	11	13.4	4.04	117	.290	.340	0	.000	-2	2	3	-0	0.0
1940	Phi-A	0	0	—	4	0	0	0	0	11^2	19	2	2	4	17.0	6.94	64	.365	.400	1	.250	0	-3	-3	0	0.0
1941	Phi-A	9	13	.409	26	23	11	1	2	157^1	188	16	49	40	13.7	5.49	76	.293	.346	8	.143	-2	-24	-23	-2	-3.0
1942	Phi-A	0	0	—	1	0	0	0	0	4	14	2	2	0	38.3	31.50	12	.560	.607	0	.000	-0	-12	-12	0	0.0
1950	Phi-A	0	0	—	2	0	0	0	0	1^1	7	0	0	2	47.3	27.00	17	.636	.636	0	—	0	-3	-3	0	0.0
Total	5	10	15	.400	38	27	13	1	2	210	270	24	63	57	14.5	5.96	72	.309	.359	9	.122	-4	-40	-39	-1	-3.0

● **ED McCREERY** McCreery, Esley Porterfield "Big Ed" b: 12/24/1889, Cripple Creek, Colo. d: 10/19/60, Sacramento, Cal. BR/TR, 6′, 190 lbs. Deb: 8/16/14

YEAR	TM/L	W	L	PCT	G	GS	CG	SH	SV	IP	H	HR	BB	SO	RAT	ERA	ERA+	OAV	OOB	BH	AVG	PB	PR	/A	PD	TPI
1914	Det-A	1	0	1.000	3	1	0	0	0	4	6	0	3	4	20.3	11.25	25	.316	.409	0	.000	-0	-4	-4	0	-0.8

● **TOM McCREERY** McCreery, Thomas Livingston b: 10/19/1874, Beaver, Pa. d: 7/3/41, Beaver, Pa. BB/TR, 5′11″, 180 lbs. Deb: 6/8/1895 ♦

YEAR	TM/L	W	L	PCT	G	GS	CG	SH	SV	IP	H	HR	BB	SO	RAT	ERA	ERA+	OAV	OOB	BH	AVG	PB	PR	/A	PD	TPI
1895	Lou-N	3	1	.750	8	4	3	1	1	48^2	51	0	38	14	17.4	5.36	86	.266	.400	35	.324	1	-3	-4	1	0.0
1896	Lou-N	0	1	.000	1	1	0	0	0	1	4	1	5	0	81.0	36.00	12	.571	.750	155	.351	0	-4	-4	0	-1.4
1900	Pit-N	0	0	—	1	0	0	0	0	3	3	2	1	0	12.0	12.00	30	.250	.308	29	.220	0	-3	-3	0	0.0
Total	3	3	2	.600	10	5	3	1	1	52^2	58	3	44	14	18.3	6.32	72	.275	.412	855	.290	2	-9	-10	1	-1.4

● **LANCE McCULLERS** McCullers, Lance Graye b: 3/8/64, Tampa, Fla. BB/TR, 6′1″, 218 lbs. Deb: 8/12/85

YEAR	TM/L	W	L	PCT	G	GS	CG	SH	SV	IP	H	HR	BB	SO	RAT	ERA	ERA+	OAV	OOB	BH	AVG	PB	PR	/A	PD	TPI
1985	SD-N	0	2	.000	21	0	0	0	5	35	23	3	16	27	10.3	2.31	153	.195	.296	0	.000	-0	5	5	0	0.4
1986	SD-N	10	10	.500	70	7	0	0	5	136	103	12	58	92	10.9	2.78	131	.216	.306	2	.091	0	14	13	-1	1.9
1987	SD-N	8	10	.444	78	0	0	0	16	123^1	115	11	59	126	12.8	3.72	106	.244	.331	1	.071	-1	5	3	1	0.5
1988	SD-N	3	6	.333	60	0	0	0	10	97^2	70	8	55	81	11.5	2.49	136	.205	.315	2	.250	1	10	10	0	1.2
1989	NY-A	4	3	.571	52	1	0	0	3	84^2	83	9	37	82	13.1	4.57	85	.255	.337	0	—	0	-6	-7	-0	-0.5
1990	NY-A	1	0	1.000	11	0	0	0	0	15	14	2	6	11	12.0	3.60	110	.241	.313	0	—	0	1	1	0	0.0
	Det-A	1	0	1.000	9	1	0	0	0	29^2	18	2	13	20	9.4	2.73	145	.170	.261	0	—	0	4	4	-1	0.1
	Yr	2	0	1.000	20	1	0	0	0	44^2	32	4	19	31	10.3	3.02	131	.194	.277	0	—	0	4	5	-1	0.1
1992	Tex-A	1	0	1.000	5	0	0	0	0	5	1	0	8	3	16.2	5.40	70	.067	.391	0	—	0	-1	-1	0	0.0
Total	7	28	31	.475	306	9	0	0	39	526^1	427	47	252	442	11.8	3.25	115	.223	.317	5	.104	0	32	28	-1	3.6

● **CHARLIE McCULLOUGH** McCullough, Charles F. b: 1867, Dublin, Ireland TR, 6′1″, 185 lbs. Deb: 4/23/1890

YEAR	TM/L	W	L	PCT	G	GS	CG	SH	SV	IP	H	HR	BB	SO	RAT	ERA	ERA+	OAV	OOB	BH	AVG	PB	PR	/A	PD	TPI
1890	Bro-a	4	21	.160	26	25	24	0	0	215^2	247	5	102	61	15.2	4.59	85	.279	.364	2	.023	-12	-17	-17	-2	-2.7
	Syr-a	1	2	.333	3	3	3	0	0	26	29	1	14	8	14.9	7.27	49	.274	.358	1	.111	0	-10	-11	-0	-0.9
	Yr	5	23	.179	29	28	27	0	0	241^2	276	6	116	69	14.6	4.88	79	.274	.349	3	.032	-12	-27	-27	-3	-3.6

● **PAUL McCULLOUGH** McCullough, Paul Willard b: 7/28/1898, New Castle, Pa. d: 11/7/70, New Castle, Pa. BR/TR, 5′9.5″, 190 lbs. Deb: 7/2/29

YEAR	TM/L	W	L	PCT	G	GS	CG	SH	SV	IP	H	HR	BB	SO	RAT	ERA	ERA+	OAV	OOB	BH	AVG	PB	PR	/A	PD	TPI
1929	Was-A	0	0	—	3	0	0	0	0	7^1	7	1	2	3	11.0	8.59	49	.250	.300	0	.000	-0	-4	-4	-0	0.0

● **PHIL McCULLOUGH** McCullough, Pinson Lamar b: 7/22/17, Stockbridge, Ga. BR/TR, 6′4″, 204 lbs. Deb: 4/22/42

YEAR	TM/L	W	L	PCT	G	GS	CG	SH	SV	IP	H	HR	BB	SO	RAT	ERA	ERA+	OAV	OOB	BH	AVG	PB	PR	/A	PD	TPI
1942	Was-A	0	0	—	1	0	0	0	0	3	5	0	2	2	21.0	6.00	61	.333	.412	0	.000	-0	-1	-1	0	0.0

● **JEFF McCURRY** McCurry, Jeffrey Dee b: 1/21/70, Tokyo, Japan BR/TR, 6′7″, 210 lbs. Deb: 5/6/95

YEAR	TM/L	W	L	PCT	G	GS	CG	SH	SV	IP	H	HR	BB	SO	RAT	ERA	ERA+	OAV	OOB	BH	AVG	PB	PR	/A	PD	TPI
1995	Pit-N	1	4	.200	55	0	0	0	1	61	82	9	30	27	17.3	5.02	86	.337	.421	0	.000	-0	-6	-5	0	-0.4
1996	Det-A	0	0	—	2	0	0	0	0	3^1	9	3	2	0	29.7	24.30	21	.474	.524	0	—	0	-7	-7	1	0.1
1997	Col-N	1	4	.200	33	0	0	0	0	40^2	43	7	20	19	13.9	4.43	117	.277	.360	0	.000	-0	-1	3	-0	0.3
1998	Pit-N	1	3	.250	16	0	0	0	0	19^1	24	4	9	11	15.8	6.52	66	.324	.405	0	—	0	-5	-5	0	-0.8
Total	4	3	11	.214	106	0	0	0	1	124^1	158	23	61	57	16.3	5.57	83	.322	.403	0	.000	-0	-19	-13	1	-0.8

● **LINDY McDANIEL** McDaniel, Lyndall Dale b: 12/13/35, Hollis, Okla. BR/TR, 6′3″, 195 lbs. Deb: 9/2/55 F

YEAR	TM/L	W	L	PCT	G	GS	CG	SH	SV	IP	H	HR	BB	SO	RAT	ERA	ERA+	OAV	OOB	BH	AVG	PB	PR	/A	PD	TPI
1955	StL-N	0	0	—	4	2	0	0	0	19	22	4	7	7	13.7	4.74	86	.293	.354	1	.200	-0	-1	-1	0	0.0
1956	StL-N	7	6	.538	39	7	1	0	0	116^1	121	7	42	59	12.6	3.40	111	.273	.335	7	.219	2	5	5	1	0.8
1957	StL-N	15	9	.625	30	26	10	1	0	191	196	13	53	75	11.9	3.49	114	.266	.317	19	.257	4	8	10	-0	1.6
1958	StL-N	5	7	.417	26	17	2	1	0	108^2	139	17	31	47	14.2	5.80	71	.305	.352	2	.067	-3	-22	-20	1	-2.1
1959	StL-N	14	12	.538	62	7	1	0	**15**	132	144	11	41	86	12.7	3.82	111	.283	.338	1	.034	-2	2	6	2	1.3
1960	StL-N★	12	4	.750	65	2	1	0	**26**	116^1	85	8	24	105	8.5	2.09	196	.207	.253	6	.231	1	**22**	**26**	1	**5.0**
1961	StL-N	10	6	.625	55	0	0	0	9	94^1	117	11	31	65	14.3	4.87	90	.305	.361	4	.235	-0	-9	-5	1	-0.7
1962	StL-N	3	10	.231	55	2	0	0	14	107	96	12	29	79	10.6	4.12	104	.239	.292	2	.095	-1	-2	2	2	0.4
1963	Chi-N	13	7	.650	57	0	0	0	**22**	88	82	9	27	75	11.1	2.86	123	.251	.308	2	.091	-0	4	6	0	1.8
1964	Chi-N	1	7	.125	63	0	0	0	15	95	104	4	23	71	12.1	3.88	96	.276	.319	2	.125	-1	-4	-2	0	-0.3
1965	Chi-N	5	6	.455	71	0	0	0	2	128^2	115	12	47	92	11.3	2.59	142	.241	.309	0	.000	-1	14	16	2	1.5
1966	SF-N	10	5	.667	64	0	0	0	6	121^2	103	5	35	93	10.2	2.66	138	.228	.284	2	.091	-1	13	14	1	1.7
1967	SF-N	2	6	.250	41	3	0	0	3	72^2	69	5	24	48	11.8	3.72	88	.248	.313	1	.091	-1	-3	-3	2	-0.3
1968	SF-N	0	0	—	12	0	0	0	0	19^1	30	2	5	9	16.3	7.45	40	.357	.393	0	.000	-0	-10	-10	0	0.0
	NY-A	4	1	.800	24	0	0	0	10	51^1	30	5	12	43	7.5	1.75	165	.166	.222	0	.000	-1	7	7	2	1.1
1969	NY-A	5	6	.455	51	0	0	0	5	83^2	84	4	23	60	11.5	3.55	98	.261	.310	0	.000	-1	1	-1	1	0.0
1970	NY-A	9	5	.643	62	0	0	0	29	111^2	88	7	23	81	8.9	2.01	174	.217	.259	4	.167	0	21	19	1	3.3
1971	NY-A	5	10	.333	44	0	0	0	4	69^2	82	12	24	39	13.7	5.04	64	.296	.352	1	.111	-0	-12	-14	0	-3.0
1972	NY-A	3	1	.750	37	0	0	0	0	68	54	4	25	47	10.5	2.25	131	.217	.288	2	.286	1	6	5	1	0.6
1973	NY-A	12	6	.667	47	3	1	0	10	160^1	148	11	49	93	11.1	2.86	128	.250	.309	0	.000	-0	17	14	3	2.0
1974	KC-A	1	4	.200	38	5	2	0	1	106^2	109	6	24	47	11.2	3.46	110	.265	.306	0	—	0	2	4	1	0.2
1975	KC-A	5	1	.833	40	0	0	0	1	78	81	3	24	40	12.1	4.15	93	.273	.327	0	—	0	-3	-3	-0	-0.3
Total	21	141	119	.542	987	74	18	2	172	2139^1	2099	172	623	1361	11.5	3.45	109	.258	.312	56	.148	-4	55	74	23	14.6

● **VON McDANIEL** McDaniel, Max Von b: 4/18/39, Hollis, Okla. d: 8/20/95, Lawton, Okla. BR/TR, 6′2.5″, 180 lbs. Deb: 6/13/57 F

YEAR	TM/L	W	L	PCT	G	GS	CG	SH	SV	IP	H	HR	BB	SO	RAT	ERA	ERA+	OAV	OOB	BH	AVG	PB	PR	/A	PD	TPI
1957	StL-N	7	5	.583	17	13	4	2	0	86^2	71	7	31	45	10.7	3.22	123	.225	.296	0	.000	-3	6	7	-1	0.5
1958	StL-N	0	0	—	2	1	0	0	0	2	5	0	5	0	45.0	13.50	31	.500	.667	0	—	0	-2	-2	-0	0.0
Total	2	7	5	.583	19	14	4	2	0	88^2	76	7	36	45	11.5	3.45	115	.233	.311	0	.000	-3	4	5	-1	0.5

● **JOE McDERMOTT** McDermott, Joseph Deb: 5/4/1871 ♦

YEAR	TM/L	W	L	PCT	G	GS	CG	SH	SV	IP	H	HR	BB	SO	RAT	ERA	ERA+	OAV	OOB	BH	AVG	PB	PR	/A	PD	TPI
1872	Eck-n	0	7	.000	7	7	7	0	0	63	143	3	12	1	22.1	8.14	42	.377	.396	9	.281	2	-32	-33		-2.0

● **MICKEY McDERMOTT** McDermott, Maurice Joseph "Maury" b: 8/29/28, Poughkeepsie, N.Y. BL/TL, 6′2″, 170 lbs. Deb: 4/24/48 C♦

YEAR	TM/L	W	L	PCT	G	GS	CG	SH	SV	IP	H	HR	BB	SO	RAT	ERA	ERA+	OAV	OOB	BH	AVG	PB	PR	/A	PD	TPI
1948	Bos-A	0	0	—	7	0	0	0	0	23^1	16	2	35	17	20.1	6.17	71	.208	.460	3	.375	1	-5	-5	1	0.2

YEAR	TM/L	W	L	PCT	G	GS	CG	SH	SV	IP	H	HR	BB	SO	RAT	ERA	ERA+	OAV	OOB	BH	AVG	PB	PR	/A	PD	TPI
1949	Bos-A	5	4	.556	12	12	6	2	0	80	63	5	52	50	13.3	4.05	108	.220	.345	7	.212	1	1	3	-0	0.3
1950	Bos-A	7	3	.700	38	15	4	0	5	130	119	8	124	96	17.0	5.19	94	.249	.406	16	.364	6	-9	-4	1	0.3
1951	Bos-A	8	8	.500	34	19	9	1	3	172	141	10	92	127	12.5	3.35	133	.226	.330	18	.273	2	15	21	1	2.2
1952	Bos-A	10	9	.526	30	21	7	2	0	162	139	14	92	117	13.0	3.72	106	.234	.340	14	.226	3	-1	4	-0	0.7
1953	Bos-A	18	10	.643	32	30	8	4	0	206^1	169	9	109	92	12.2	3.01	140	.224	.323	28	.301	7	23	27	1	4.4
1954	Was-A	7	15	.318	30	26	11	1	1	196^1	172	8	110	95	13.1	3.44	103	.239	.342	19	.200	3	6	3	1	0.6
1955	Was-A	10	10	.500	31	20	8	1	1	156	140	9	100	78	14.4	3.75	102	.243	.364	25	.263	7	4	1	0	1.0
1956	*NY-A	2	6	.250	23	9	1	0	0	87	85	10	47	38	13.7	4.24	91	.261	.354	11	.212	3	-1	-4	-0	-0.1
1957	KC-A	1	4	.200	29	4	0	0	0	69	68	9	50	29	15.4	5.48	72	.266	.386	12	.245	3	-13	-12	1	0.0
1958	Det-A	0	0	—	2	0	0	0	0	2	6	0	2	0	36.0	9.00	45	.500	.571	1	.333	0	-1	-1	-0	0.0
1961	StL-N	1	0	1.000	19	0	0	0	4	27	29	3	15	15	14.7	3.67	120	.271	.361	1	.071	-1	1	2	-0	0.0
	KC-A	0	0	—	4	0	0	0	0	5^2	14	0	10	3	38.1	14.29	29	.452	.585	1	.200	1	-6	-6	-0	0.0
Total	12	69	69	.500	291	156	54	11	14	1316^2	1161	87	838	757	13.9	3.91	105	.240	.355	156	.252	36	14	29	4	9.6

● MIKE McDERMOTT McDermott, Michael H. b: 5/6/1864, Fall River, Mass. d: 5/7/47, Fall River, Mass. 5'10", 152 lbs. Deb: 9/2/1889

YEAR	TM/L	W	L	PCT	G	GS	CG	SH	SV	IP	H	HR	BB	SO	RAT	ERA	ERA+	OAV	OOB	BH	AVG	PB	PR	/A	PD	TPI
1889	Lou-a	1	8	.111	9	9	9	0	0	84^1	108	4	34	22	15.4	4.16	92	.302	.365	6	.182	-1	-3	-3	-0	-0.3

● MIKE McDERMOTT McDermott, Michael Joseph b: 9/7/1862, St.Louis, Mo. d: 6/30/43, St.Louis, Mo. TR, 5'8", 145 lbs. Deb: 4/20/1895

YEAR	TM/L	W	L	PCT	G	GS	CG	SH	SV	IP	H	HR	BB	SO	RAT	ERA	ERA+	OAV	OOB	BH	AVG	PB	PR	/A	PD	TPI
1895	Lou-N	4	19	.174	33	26	18	0	0	207^1	258	8	103	42	16.1	5.99	77	.300	.382	13	.159	-2	-28	-31	1	-2.5
1896	Lou-N	2	7	.222	12	10	4	1	0	65	87	4	44	12	19.0	7.34	59	.318	.423	8	.296	1	-21	-22	1	-2.0
1897	Cle-N	4	5	.444	9	7	4	0	0	62	75	2	25	12	15.0	4.50	100	.296	.367	8	.320	1	-1	-0	1	0.2
	StL-N	1	2	.333	4	4	1	0	0	21^1	23	2	19	3	17.7	9.28	47	.274	.408	2	.222	-0	-12	-12	1	-1.1
	Yr	5	7	.417	13	11	5	0	0	83^1	98	4	44	15	15.3	5.72	78	.288	.370	10	.294	1	-13	-12	2	-0.9
Total	3	11	33	.250	58	47	27	1	0	355^2	443	16	191	69	16.5	6.17	74	.301	.389	31	.217	0	-62	-64	4	-5.4

● DANNY McDEVITT McDevitt, Daniel Eugene b: 11/18/32, New York, N.Y. BL/TL, 5'10", 175 lbs. Deb: 6/17/57

YEAR	TM/L	W	L	PCT	G	GS	CG	SH	SV	IP	H	HR	BB	SO	RAT	ERA	ERA+	OAV	OOB	BH	AVG	PB	PR	/A	PD	TPI
1957	Bro-N	7	4	.636	22	17	5	2	0	119	105	5	72	90	13.8	3.25	128	.238	.353	6	.154	-0	8	12	2	1.2
1958	LA-N	2	6	.250	13	10	2	0	0	48^1	71	6	31	26	19.0	7.45	55	.355	.442	2	.133	-0	-19	-18	-1	-2.5
1959	LA-N	10	8	.556	39	22	6	2	4	145	149	16	51	106	13.3	3.97	106	.263	.339	5	.109	-2	-0	4	0	0.3
1960	LA-N	0	4	.000	24	7	0	0	0	53	51	7	42	30	16.8	4.25	93	.260	.406	2	.200	0	-3	-2	-0	-0.1
1961	NY-A	1	2	.333	8	2	0	0	1	13	18	2	8	8	18.7	7.62	49	.353	.450	0	.000	-0	-5	-6	0	-1.1
	Min-A	1	0	1.000	16	1	0	0	0	26^2	20	1	19	15	14.5	2.36	179	.213	.368	0	.000	-0	5	6	0	0.2
	Yr	2	2	.500	24	3	0	0	1	39^2	38	3	27	23	15.7	4.08	100	.259	.388	0	.000	-0	-0	-0	0	-0.9
1962	KC-A	0	3	.000	33	1	0	0	2	51	47	5	41	28	15.7	5.82	73	.250	.387	2	.222	0	-11	-9	1	-0.5
Total	6	21	27	.438	155	60	13	4	7	456	461	42	264	303	14.9	4.40	94	.265	.372	17	.138	-3	-25	-13	2	-2.5

● ALLEN McDILL McDill, Allen Gabriel b: 8/23/71, Greenville, Miss. BL/TL, 6', 155 lbs. Deb: 5/15/97

YEAR	TM/L	W	L	PCT	G	GS	CG	SH	SV	IP	H	HR	BB	SO	RAT	ERA	ERA+	OAV	OOB	BH	AVG	PB	PR	/A	PD	TPI
1997	KC-A	0	0	—	3	0	0	0	0	4	3	1	8	2	27.0	13.50	35	.214	.522	0	—	0	-4	-4	0	-0.1
1998	KC-A	0	0	—	7	0	0	0	0	6	9	3	2	3	16.5	10.50	47	.333	.379	0	—	0	-4	-4	0	-0.4
Total	2	0	0	—	10	0	0	0	0	10	12	4	10	5	20.7	11.70	41	.293	.442	0	—	0	-8	-8	0	-0.5

● HANK McDONALD McDonald, Henry Monroe b: 1/16/11, Santa Monica, Cal. d: 10/17/82, Hemet, Cal. BR/TR, 6'3", 200 lbs. Deb: 4/16/31

YEAR	TM/L	W	L	PCT	G	GS	CG	SH	SV	IP	H	HR	BB	SO	RAT	ERA	ERA+	OAV	OOB	BH	AVG	PB	PR	/A	PD	TPI
1931	Phi-A	2	4	.333	19	10	1	1	0	70^1	62	3	41	23	13.3	3.71	121	.239	.346	2	.095	-1	5	6	-1	0.3
1933	Phi-A	1	1	.500	4	1	0	0	0	12^1	14	0	4	1	13.1	5.11	84	.264	.316	0	.000	-0	-1	-1	-0	-0.2
	StL-A	0	4	.000	25	5	0	0	0	58^1	83	6	34	22	18.5	8.64	54	.332	.418	2	.143	-1	-28	-26	-0	-1.6
	Yr	1	5	.167	29	6	0	0	0	70^2	97	6	38	23	17.6	8.02	57	.320	.401	2	.111	-1	-29	-27	-0	-1.8
Total	2	3	9	.250	48	16	1	1	0	141	159	9	79	46	15.4	5.87	77	.283	.375	4	.103	-2	-24	-21	-1	-1.5

● JIM McDONALD McDonald, Jimmie Le Roy "Hot Rod" b: 5/17/27, Grants Pass, Ore. BR/TR, 5'10.5", 185 lbs. Deb: 7/27/50

YEAR	TM/L	W	L	PCT	G	GS	CG	SH	SV	IP	H	HR	BB	SO	RAT	ERA	ERA+	OAV	OOB	BH	AVG	PB	PR	/A	PD	TPI
1950	Bos-A	1	0	1.000	9	0	0	0	0	19	23	1	10	5	16.1	3.79	129	.329	.420	1	.333	1	2	2	1	0.3
1951	StL-A	4	7	.364	16	11	5	0	1	84	84	5	46	28	14.1	4.07	108	.260	.356	6	.207	-0	0	3	1	0.4
1952	NY-A	3	4	.429	26	5	1	0	0	69^1	71	1	40	20	14.7	3.50	95	.268	.368	6	.316	3	1	-1	3	0.5
1953	*NY-A	9	7	.563	27	18	6	2	0	129^2	128	4	39	43	11.7	3.82	97	.260	.316	4	.098	-3	3	-2	2	-0.3
1954	NY-A	4	1	.800	16	10	3	1	0	71	54	3	45	20	12.7	3.17	108	.213	.334	4	.211	2	4	2	1	0.4
1955	Bal-A	3	5	.375	21	8	0	0	0	51^2	76	5	30	20	18.5	7.14	53	.345	.424	2	.182	1	-18	-19	1	-2.3
1956	Chi-A	0	2	.000	8	3	0	0	0	18^2	29	2	7	10	17.8	8.68	47	.377	.435	0	.000	-0	-9	-9	-0	-0.9
1957	Chi-A	0	1	.000	10	0	0	0	0	22^1	18	2	10	12	11.3	2.01	185	.234	.322	0	.000	0	4	4	-0	0.2
1958	Chi-A	0	0	—	3	0	0	0	0	2^1	6	1	4	0	38.6	19.29	19	.429	.556	0	—	0	-4	-4	0	0.0
Total	9	24	27	.471	136	55	15	3	1	468	489	24	231	158	14.0	4.27	89	.273	.359	23	.180	4	-17	-25	8	-1.7

● JOHN McDONALD McDonald, John Joseph (b: John Joseph McDonnell) b: 1/27/1883, Throop, Pa. d: 4/9/50, Roselle, N.J. BR/TR, 6'1", 170 lbs. Deb: 9/3/07

YEAR	TM/L	W	L	PCT	G	GS	CG	SH	SV	IP	H	HR	BB	SO	RAT	ERA	ERA+	OAV	OOB	BH	AVG	PB	PR	/A	PD	TPI
1907	Was-A	0	0	—	1	0	0	0	0	6	12	0	2	3	21.0	9.00	27	.414	.452	1	.333	1	-4	-4	-0	0.1

● BEN McDONALD McDonald, Larry Benard b: 11/24/67, Baton Rouge, La. BR/TR, 6'7", 213 lbs. Deb: 9/6/89

YEAR	TM/L	W	L	PCT	G	GS	CG	SH	SV	IP	H	HR	BB	SO	RAT	ERA	ERA+	OAV	OOB	BH	AVG	PB	PR	/A	PD	TPI
1989	Bal-A	1	0	1.000	6	0	0	0	0	7^1	8	2	4	3	14.7	8.59	44	.286	.375	0	—	0	-4	-4	0	-0.4
1990	Bal-A	8	5	.615	21	15	3	2	0	118^2	88	9	35	65	9.3	2.43	156	.205	.265	0	—	0	20	18	0	1.9
1991	Bal-A	6	8	.429	21	21	1	0	0	126^1	126	16	43	85	12.1	4.84	82	.261	.323	0	—	0	-11	-13	-1	-1.3
1992	Bal-A	13	13	.500	35	35	4	2	0	227	213	32	74	158	11.7	4.24	95	.247	.313	0	—	0	-8	-6	1	-0.5
1993	Bal-A	13	14	.481	34	34	7	1	0	220^1	185	17	86	171	11.3	3.39	132	.228	.306	0	—	0	23	26	3	3.1
1994	Bal-A	14	7	.667	24	24	5	1	0	157^1	151	14	54	94	11.8	4.06	123	.255	.319	0	—	0	13	17	1	1.9
1995	Bal-A	3	6	.333	14	13	1	0	0	80	67	10	38	62	12.1	4.16	114	.224	.318	0	—	0	5	5	1	0.5
1996	Mil-A	12	10	.545	35	35	2	0	0	221^1	228	25	67	146	12.2	3.90	133	.264	.322	0	—	0	27	32	-0	2.5
1997	Mil-A	8	7	.533	21	21	1	0	0	133	120	13	36	110	10.9	4.06	114	.237	.294	0	.000	-0	7	8	0	0.8
Total	9	78	70	.527	211	198	24	6	0	1291^1	1186	138	437	894	11.5	3.91	115	.243	.310	0	.000	-0	72	83	4	8.5

● McDOOLAN McDoolan Deb: 4/14/1873

YEAR	TM/L	W	L	PCT	G	GS	CG	SH	SV	IP	H	HR	BB	SO	RAT	ERA	ERA+	OAV	OOB	BH	AVG	PB	PR	/A	PD	TPI
1873	Mar-n	0	1	.000	1	1	1	0	0	9	18	0	0	0	18.0	3.00	108	.305	.305	0	.000	-1	0	0		0.0

● SANDY McDOUGAL McDougal, John Auchanbolt b: 5/21/1874, Buffalo, N.Y. d: 10/2/10, Buffalo, N.Y. BR/TR, 5'10", 155 lbs. Deb: 6/12/1895

YEAR	TM/L	W	L	PCT	G	GS	CG	SH	SV	IP	H	HR	BB	SO	RAT	ERA	ERA+	OAV	OOB	BH	AVG	PB	PR	/A	PD	TPI
1895	Bro-N	0	0	—	1	0	0	0	1	3	3	0	5	2	24.0	12.00	37	.250	.471	0	.000	-0	-2	-3	-0	-0.2
1905	StL-N	1	4	.200	5	5	5	0	0	44^2	50	0	12	10	12.5	3.43	87	.301	.348	2	.133	-1	-2	-2	3	0.0
Total	2	1	4	.200	6	5	5	0	1	47^2	53	0	17	12	13.2	3.97	78	.298	.359	2	.125	-1	-5	-5	3	-0.2

● DEWEY McDOUGAL McDougal, John H. b: 9/19/1871, Aledo, Ill. d: 4/28/36, Galesburg, Ill. TR, 170 lbs. Deb: 4/24/1895

YEAR	TM/L	W	L	PCT	G	GS	CG	SH	SV	IP	H	HR	BB	SO	RAT	ERA	ERA+	OAV	OOB	BH	AVG	PB	PR	/A	PD	TPI
1895	StL-N	3	10	.231	18	14	10	0	0	114^2	187	11	46	23	19.1	8.32	58	.360	.423	6	.146	-2	-45	-44	-1	-3.6
1896	StL-N	0	1	.000	3	1	0	0	0	10	13	2	4	0	16.2	8.10	54	.310	.383	0	.000	-1	-4	-4	1	-0.3
Total	2	3	11	.214	21	15	10	0	0	124^2	200	13	50	23	18.8	8.30	58	.357	.420	6	.136	-3	-49	-49	-1	-3.9

● JACK McDOWELL McDowell, Jack Burns b: 1/16/66, Van Nuyo, Cal. BR/TR, 6'5", 180 lbs. Deb: 9/15/87

YEAR	TM/L	W	L	PCT	G	GS	CG	SH	SV	IP	H	HR	BB	SO	RAT	ERA	ERA+	OAV	OOB	BH	AVG	PB	PR	/A	PD	TPI
1987	Chi-A	3	0	1.000	4	4	0	0	0	28	16	1	6	15	7.7	1.93	237	.168	.233	0	—	0	8	8	0	0.9
1988	Chi-A	5	10	.333	26	26	1	0	0	158^2	147	12	68	84	12.6	3.97	100	.245	.329	0	—	0	-0	-0	-1	-0.1
1990	Chi-A	14	9	.609	33	33	4	0	0	205	189	20	77	165	12.0	3.82	100	.244	.317	0	—	0	2	0	-0	0.0
1991	Chi-A★	17	10	.630	35	35	**15**	3	0	253^2	212	19	82	191	10.6	3.41	117	.228	.293	0	—	0	19	16	0	1.6
1992	Chi-A★	20	10	.667	34	34	**13**	1	0	260^2	247	21	75	178	11.4	3.18	122	.251	.309	0	—	0	22	20	-1	2.1
1993	*Chi-A★	**22**	10	.688	34	34	10	**4**	0	256^2	261	20	69	158	11.7	3.37	124	.266	.316	0	—	0	27	23	2	3.0
1994	Chi-A	10	9	.526	25	25	6	2	0	181	186	12	42	127	11.6	3.73	125	.266	.312	0	—	0	22	19	-0	1.7
1995	*NY-A	15	10	.600	30	30	**8**	2	0	217^2	211	25	78	157	12.2	3.93	117	.254	.322	0	—	0	19	17	0	1.7
1996	*Cle-A	13	9	.591	30	30	5	1	0	192	214	22	67	141	13.4	5.11	96	.282	.343	0	—	0	-3	-5	1	-0.3
1997	Cle-A	3	3	.500	8	6	0	0	0	40^2	44	6	18	38	13.9	5.09	92	.282	.360	0	—	0	-2	-2	0	-0.2
1998	Ana-A	5	3	.625	14	14	0	0	0	76	96	11	19	45	13.7	5.09	92	.311	.353	0	—	0	-4	-3	0	-0.3
Total	11	127	83	.605	273	271	62	13	0	1870	1823	169	601	1299	11.9	3.81	112	.256	.318	0	—	0	110	93	2	10.1

● ROGER McDOWELL

McDowell, Roger Alan b: 12/21/60, Cincinnati, Ohio BR/TR, 6'1", 182 lbs. Deb: 4/11/85

YEAR	TM/L	W	L	PCT	G	GS	CG	SH	SV	IP	H	HR	BB	SO	RAT	ERA	ERA+	OAV	OOB	BH	AVG	PB	PR	/A	PD	TPI
1985	NY-N	6	5	.545	62	2	0	0	17	127^{1}	108	9	37	70	10.3	2.83	122	.230	.287	3	.158	0	11	9	2	1.2
1986	*NY-N	14	9	.609	75	0	0	0	22	128	107	4	42	65	10.7	3.02	117	.228	.296	5	.278	1	10	7	3	1.9
1987	NY-N	7	5	.583	56	0	0	0	25	88^{2}	95	7	28	32	12.7	4.16	91	.276	.334	3	.231	1	-1	-4	1	-0.4
1988	*NY-N	5	5	.500	62	0	0	0	16	89	80	1	31	46	11.5	2.63	122	.238	.308	3	.333	2	8	6	2	1.2
1989	NY-N	1	5	.167	25	0	0	0	4	35^{1}	34	1	16	15	13.2	3.31	99	.254	.342	1	.500	0	1	-0	2	0.2
	Phi-N	3	3	.500	44	0	0	0	19	56^{2}	45	2	22	32	10.8	1.11	319	.220	.298	0	.000	-0	15	15	1	2.8
	Yr	4	8	.333	69	0	0	0	23	92	79	3	38	47	11.5	1.96	176	.231	.310	1	.333	0	16	15	3	3.0
1990	Phi-N	6	8	.429	72	0	0	0	22	86^{1}	92	2	35	39	13.4	3.86	99	.286	.359	0	.000	-0	-1	-0	1	0.0
1991	Phi-N	3	6	.333	38	0	0	0	3	59	61	1	32	28	14.5	3.20	114	.266	.361	0	.000	-0	3	3	2	0.6
	LA-N	6	3	.667	33	0	0	0	7	42^{1}	39	3	16	22	11.7	2.55	141	.257	.327	0	—	0	5	5	1	1.1
	Yr	9	9	.500	71	0	0	0	10	101^{1}	100	4	48	50	13.1	2.93	124	.260	.343	0	.000	-0	8	8	2	1.7
1992	LA-N	6	10	.375	65	0	0	0	14	83^{2}	103	3	42	50	15.7	4.09	84	.306	.384	0	.000	1	-5	-6	2	-1.0
1993	LA-N	5	3	.625	54	0	0	0	2	68	76	2	30	27	14.3	2.25	170	.288	.365	1	.500	0	14	12	3	1.7
1994	LA-N	0	3	.000	32	0	0	0	0	41^{1}	50	3	22	29	15.9	5.23	75	.303	.388	0	.000	-0	-5	-6	0	-0.4
1995	Tex-A	7	4	.636	64	0	0	0	4	85	86	5	34	49	13.3	4.02	120	.277	.359	0	—	0	7	8	2	1.1
1996	Bal-A	1	1	.500	41	0	0	0	4	59^{1}	69	7	23	20	14.3	4.25	116	.296	.364	0	—	0	5	4	2	0.4
Total	12	70	70	.500	723	2	0	0	159	1050	1045	50	410	524	12.7	3.30	114	.263	.336	16	.222	6	66	52	23	10.4

● SAM McDOWELL

McDowell, Samuel Edward Thomas "Sudden Sam" b: 9/21/42, Pittsburgh, Pa. BL/TL, 6'5", 218 lbs. Deb: 9/15/61

YEAR	TM/L	W	L	PCT	G	GS	CG	SH	SV	IP	H	HR	BB	SO	RAT	ERA	ERA+	OAV	OOB	BH	AVG	PB	PR	/A	PD	TPI
1961	Cle-A	0	0	—	1	1	0	0	0	6^{1}	3	0	5	5	11.4	0.00	—	.136	.296	0	.000	-0	3	3	0	0.0
1962	Cle-A	3	7	.300	25	13	0	0	1	87^{2}	81	9	70	70	15.9	6.06	64	.243	.381	4	.154	-1	-20	-21	-0	-2.2
1963	Cle-A	3	5	.375	14	12	3	1	0	65	63	6	44	63	14.8	4.85	75	.256	.369	4	.211	0	-9	-9	-0	-1.0
1964	Cle-A	11	6	.647	31	24	6	2	1	173^{1}	148	8	100	177	13.0	2.70	133	.229	.336	8	.143	0	18	17	-1	1.6
1965	Cle-A★	17	11	.607	42	35	14	3	4	273	178	9	132	**325**	10.4	**2.18**	**160**	**.185**	.287	12	.126	-3	**39**	**40**	1	4.1
1966	Cle-A†	9	8	.529	35	28	8	**5**	3	194^{1}	130	12	102	**225**	11.0	2.87	120	**.188**	.298	12	.200	1	12	12	1	1.4
1967	Cle-A	13	15	.464	37	37	10	1	0	236^{1}	201	21	123	236	12.6	3.85	85	.233	.333	15	.183	1	-16	-15	-1	-1.7
1968	Cle-A★	15	14	.517	38	37	11	3	0	269	181	13	110	**283**	10.1	1.81	164	.189	.279	13	.153	0	35	34	-1	4.0
1969	Cle-A★	18	14	.563	39	38	18	4	1	285	222	13	102	**279**	10.5	2.94	128	.213	.288	16	.174	-1	22	26	-0	2.8
1970	Cle-A★	20	12	.625	39	39	19	1	0	**305**	236	25	131	**304**	11.0	2.92	136	.213	.300	13	.124	-3	27	**35**	-2	3.0
1971	Cle-A†	13	17	.433	35	31	8	2	1	214^{2}	160	22	153	192	13.2	3.40	113	.207	.340	13	.178	-1	2	10	-2	1.1
1972	SF-N	10	8	.556	28	25	4	0	0	164^{1}	155	12	86	122	13.5	4.33	81	.253	.350	7	.119	-1	-16	-15	-0	-1.7
1973	SF-N	1	2	.333	18	3	0	0	3	40	45	4	29	35	16.6	4.50	85	.285	.396	2	.167	-0	-4	-3	0	-0.3
	NY-A	5	8	.385	16	15	2	1	0	95^{2}	73	4	64	75	12.9	3.95	93	.212	.335	0	—	0	-1	-3	0	-0.3
1974	NY-A	1	6	.143	13	7	0	0	0	48	42	6	41	33	15.6	4.69	75	.236	.379	0	—	0	-6	-6	-1	-0.9
1975	Pit-N	2	1	.667	14	1	0	0	0	34^{2}	30	0	20	29	13.0	2.86	124	.242	.347	0	.000	-1	3	3	0	0.1
Total	15	141	134	.513	425	346	103	23	14	2492^{1}	1948	164	1312	2453	12.0	3.17	112	.215	.318	119	.154	-8	88	107	-5	10.0

● CHUCK McELROY

McElroy, Charles Dwayne b: 10/1/67, Port Arthur, Tex. BL/TL, 6', 195 lbs. Deb: 9/4/89

YEAR	TM/L	W	L	PCT	G	GS	CG	SH	SV	IP	H	HR	BB	SO	RAT	ERA	ERA+	OAV	OOB	BH	AVG	PB	PR	/A	PD	TPI
1989	Phi-N	0	0	—	11	0	0	0	0	10^{1}	12	1	4	8	13.9	1.74	203	.286	.348	0	—	0	2	2	-0	0.0
1990	Phi-N	0	1	.000	16	0	0	0	0	14	24	0	10	16	21.9	7.71	50	.369	.453	0	—	0	-6	-6	-0	-0.4
1991	Chi-N	6	2	.750	71	0	0	0	3	101^{1}	73	7	57	92	11.5	1.95	199	.210	.322	3	.300	1	**19**	**22**	1	1.8
1992	Chi-N	4	7	.364	72	0	0	0	6	83^{2}	73	5	51	83	13.3	3.55	101	.237	.345	4	.667	3	-0	0	-1	0.3
1993	Chi-N	2	2	.500	49	0	0	0	0	47^{1}	51	4	25	31	14.6	4.56	87	.280	.370	0	.000	-1	-3	-3	-0	-0.3
1994	Cin-N	1	2	.333	52	0	0	0	5	57^{2}	52	3	15	38	10.5	2.34	177	.244	.294	1	.167	-0	12	11	-1	0.6
1995	Cin-N	3	4	.429	44	0	0	0	0	40^{1}	46	5	15	27	13.8	6.02	68	.291	.356	0	.000	-0	-8	-9	-0	-1.4
1996	Cin-N	2	0	1.000	12	0	0	0	0	12^{1}	13	2	10	13	16.8	6.57	64	.265	.390	0	.000	-0	-3	-3	-0	-0.5
	Cal-A	5	1	.833	40	0	0	0	0	36^{2}	32	2	13	32	11.5	2.95	170	.239	.315	0	—	0	8	8	1	1.3
1997	Ana-A	0	0	—	13	0	0	0	0	15^{2}	17	2	3	18	11.5	3.45	133	.270	.303	0	—	0	2	2	-0	0.0
	Chi-A	1	3	.250	48	0	0	0	1	59^{1}	56	3	19	44	11.7	3.94	111	.247	.310	0	—	0	4	3	1	0.2
	Yr	1	3	.250	61	0	0	0	1	75	73	5	22	62	11.6	3.84	115	.252	.309	0	—	0	6	5	0	0.2
1998	Col-N	6	4	.600	78	0	0	0	2	68^{1}	68	3	24	61	12.1	2.90	175	.268	.331	1	.200	-0	10	16	-1	2.2
Total	10	30	26	.536	506	0	0	0	17	547	517	37	246	463	12.7	3.46	121	.253	.335	9	.237	2	37	45	-1	3.8

● JIM McELROY

McElroy, James D. b: 11/5/1862, Napa Co., Cal. d: 7/24/1889, Needles, Cal. 5'10", 170 lbs. Deb: 5/26/1884

YEAR	TM/L	W	L	PCT	G	GS	CG	SH	SV	IP	H	HR	BB	SO	RAT	ERA	ERA+	OAV	OOB	BH	AVG	PB	PR	/A	PD	TPI
1884	Phi-N	1	12	.077	13	13	13	0	0	111	115	1	54	45	13.7	4.86	61	.254	.333	7	.146	-3	-23	-23	-0	-2.3
	Wil-U	0	1	.000	1	1	0	0	0	5	10	0	0	3	18.0	10.80	25	.385	.385	0	.000	-0	-5	-5	0	-0.6
Total	1	1	13	.071	14	14	13	0	0	116	125	1	54	48	13.9	5.12	58	.261	.336	7	.140	-4	-28	-28	0	-2.9

● WILL McENANEY

McEnaney, William Henry b: 2/14/52, Springfield, Ohio BL/TL, 6', 180 lbs. Deb: 7/3/74

YEAR	TM/L	W	L	PCT	G	GS	CG	SH	SV	IP	H	HR	BB	SO	RAT	ERA	ERA+	OAV	OOB	BH	AVG	PB	PR	/A	PD	TPI
1974	Cin-N	2	1	.667	24	0	0	0	2	27	24	4	9	13	11.0	4.33	80	.250	.314	0	—	0	-2	-3	-1	-0.4
1975	*Cin-N	5	2	.714	70	0	0	0	15	91	92	6	23	48	11.6	2.47	145	.264	.314	0	.000	-2	12	11	-1	1.0
1976	*Cin-N	2	6	.250	55	0	0	0	7	72^{1}	97	3	23	28	15.1	4.85	72	.323	.373	1	.167	1	-11	-11	0	-1.3
1977	Mon-N	3	5	.375	69	0	0	0	3	86^{2}	92	6	22	38	12.0	3.95	96	.271	.319	0	.000	-1	-0	-1	-0	-0.2
1978	Pit-N	0	0	—	6	0	0	0	0	8^{2}	15	3	2	6	18.7	10.38	36	.395	.439	0	—	0	-7	-6	0	0.0
1979	StL-N	0	3	.000	45	0	0	0	2	64	60	3	16	15	11.0	2.95	127	.251	.304	0	.000	-0	6	6	2	0.4
Total	6	12	17	.414	269	0	0	0	29	349^{2}	380	25	95	148	12.4	3.76	97	.279	.330	1	.032	-2	-3	-4	-1	-0.5

● LOU McEVOY

McEvoy, Louis Anthony b: 5/30/02, Williamsburg, Kan. d: 12/17/53, Webster Groves, Mo BR/TR, 6'2.5", 203 lbs. Deb: 4/28/30

YEAR	TM/L	W	L	PCT	G	GS	CG	SH	SV	IP	H	HR	BB	SO	RAT	ERA	ERA+	OAV	OOB	BH	AVG	PB	PR	/A	PD	TPI
1930	NY-A	1	3	.250	28	1	0	0	3	52^{1}	64	4	29	14	16.3	6.71	64	.288	.375	2	.125	-1	-12	-14	-1	-1.2
1931	NY-A	0	0	—	6	0	0	0	1	12^{1}	19	1	12	3	23.4	12.41	32	.358	.485	0	.000	-1	-11	-12	0	-0.2
Total	2	1	3	.250	34	1	0	0	4	64^{2}	83	5	41	17	17.7	7.79	54	.302	.398	2	.100	-2	-23	-26	-1	-1.4

● BARNEY McFADDEN

McFadden, Bernard Joseph b: 2/22/1874, Eckley, Pa. d: 4/28/24, Mauch Chunk, Pa. BR/TR, 6'1", 195 lbs. Deb: 4/24/01

YEAR	TM/L	W	L	PCT	G	GS	CG	SH	SV	IP	H	HR	BB	SO	RAT	ERA	ERA+	OAV	OOB	BH	AVG	PB	PR	/A	PD	TPI
1901	Cin-N	3	4	.429	8	5	4	0	0	46	54	2	40	11	19.6	6.07	53	.290	.431	3	.150	-1	-14	-15	1	-1.8
1902	Phi-N	0	1	.000	1	1	1	0	0	9	14	0	7	3	21.0	8.00	35	.350	.447	0	.000	-0	-5	-5	0	-0.5
Total	2	3	5	.375	9	6	5	0	0	55	68	2	47	14	19.8	6.38	49	.301	.434	3	.130	-2	-19	-20	1	-2.3

● DAN McFARLAN

McFarlan, Anderson Daniel b: 11/1/1873, Gainesville, Tex. d: 9/23/24, Louisville, Ky. Deb: 9/2/1895 F

YEAR	TM/L	W	L	PCT	G	GS	CG	SH	SV	IP	H	HR	BB	SO	RAT	ERA	ERA+	OAV	OOB	BH	AVG	PB	PR	/A	PD	TPI
1895	Lou-N	0	7	.000	7	7	6	0	0	46	80	4	15	10	19.6	6.65	70	.376	.429	5	.238	-1	-10	-10	1	-1.1
1899	Bro-N	0	0	—	1	0	0	0	0	6	6	1	3	0	13.5	1.50	261	.261	.346	0	.000	-0	2	2	0	0.0
	Was-N	8	18	.308	32	28	22	1	0	211^{2}	268	5	64	41	14.6	4.76	82	.308	.363	16	.186	-0	-21	-20	-1	-2.0
	Yr	8	18	.308	33	28	22	1	0	217^{2}	274	6	67	41	14.6	4.67	84	.307	.363	16	.182	-1	-20	-18	-0	-2.0
Total	2	8	25	.242	40	35	28	1	0	263^{2}	354	10	82	51	15.4	5.02	81	.320	.375	21	.193	-1	-29	-29	1	-3.1

● CHAPPIE McFARLAND

McFarland, Charles A. b: 3/13/1875, White Hall, Ill. d: 12/14/24, Houston, Tex. TR , 6'1", Deb: 9/15/02 F

YEAR	TM/L	W	L	PCT	G	GS	CG	SH	SV	IP	H	HR	BB	SO	RAT	ERA	ERA+	OAV	OOB	BH	AVG	PB	PR	/A	PD	TPI
1902	StL-N	0	1	.000	2	1	1	0	0	11	11	1	3	3	11.5	5.73	48	.262	.311	0	.000	-1	-4	-4	0	-0.3
1903	StL-N	9	19	.321	28	26	25	1	0	229	253	2	48	76	12.1	3.07	106	.284	.325	8	.108	-4	5	5	2	0.4
1904	StL-N	14	18	.438	32	31	28	1	0	269^{1}	266	7	56	111	10.9	3.21	84	.248	.288	13	.131	-2	-14	-15	7	-1.3
1905	StL-N	8	18	.308	31	28	22	3	1	250^{1}	281	3	65	85	12.7	3.81	78	.284	.332	14	.165	1	-22	-23	1	-2.0
1906	StL-N	2	1	.667	6	4	2	0	1	37^{1}	33	1	8	16	9.9	1.93	136	.219	.258	2	.133	-1	3	3	1	0.3
	Pit-N	1	3	.250	6	5	2	1	0	35^{1}	39	0	7	11	12.2	2.55	105	.298	.343	5	.385	1	0	0	0	0.2
	Bro-N	0	1	.000	1	1	1	0	0	9	10	1	5	5	15.0	8.00	32	.286	.375	0	.000	-0	-5	-5	-0	-0.5
	Yr	3	5	.375	13	10	5	1	1	81^{2}	82	2	20	32	11.2	2.87	92	.257	.301	7	.226	0	-2	-2	1	0.0
Total	5	34	61	.358	106	96	81	6	2	841^{1}	893	15	192	307	11.8	3.35	87	.270	.313	42	.143	-6	-37	-39	11	-3.2

● CHRIS McFARLAND

McFarland, Christopher b: 8/17/1861, Fall River, Mass. d: 5/24/18, New Bedford, Mass. 5'9", 170 lbs. Deb: 4/19/1884 ♦

YEAR	TM/L	W	L	PCT	G	GS	CG	SH	SV	IP	H	HR	BB	SO	RAT	ERA	ERA+	OAV	OOB	BH	AVG	PB	PR	/A	PD	TPI
1884	Bal-U	0	1	.000	1	1	0	0	0	3	9	1	1	3	30.0	15.00	18	.500	.526	3	.214	-0	-4	-4	-0	-0.8

● MONTE McFARLAND

McFarland, Lamont Amos b: 11/7/1872, White Hall, Ill. d: 11/15/13, Peoria, Ill. Deb: 9/14/1895 F

YEAR	TM/L	W	L	PCT	G	GS	CG	SH	SV	IP	H	HR	BB	SO	RAT	ERA	ERA+	OAV	OOB	BH	AVG	PB	PR	/A	PD	TPI
1895	Chi-N	2	0	1.000	2	2	2	0	0	14	21	0	5	5	16.7	5.14	99	.339	.388	1	.143	-1	-1	-0	0	-0.1

YEAR	TM/L	W	L	PCT	G	GS	CG	SH	SV	IP	H	HR	BB	SO	RAT	ERA	ERA+	OAV	OOB	BH	AVG	PB	PR	/A	PD	TPI
1896	Chi-N	0	4	.000	4	3	2	0	0	25	32	0	21	3	19.8	7.20	63	.308	.433	0	.000	-2	-8	-7	0	-1.0
Total	2	2	4	.333	6	5	4	0	0	39	53	0	26	8	18.7	6.46	73	.319	.418	1	.053	-3	-8	-7	1	-1.1

● JACK McFETRIDGE McFetridge, John Reed b: 8/25/1869, Philadelphia, Pa. d: 1/10/17, Philadelphia, Pa. 6', 175 lbs. Deb: 6/7/1890

YEAR	TM/L	W	L	PCT	G	GS	CG	SH	SV	IP	H	HR	BB	SO	RAT	ERA	ERA+	OAV	OOB	BH	AVG	PB	PR	/A	PD	TPI
1890	Phi-N	1	0	1.000	1	1	1	0	0	9	5	0	2	4	7.0	1.00	366	.156	.206	3	.750	1	3	3	-0	0.4
1903	Phi-N	1	11	.083	14	13	11	0	0	103	120	2	49	31	15.0	4.89	67	.299	.379	6	.176	0	-19	-19	-1	-1.8
Total	2	2	11	.154	15	14	12	0	0	112	125	2	51	35	14.4	4.58	72	.288	.367	9	.237	2	-16	-16	-1	-1.4

● ANDY McGAFFIGAN McGaffigan, Andrew Joseph b: 10/25/56, W.Palm Beach, Fla. BR/TR, 6'3", 195 lbs. Deb: 9/22/81

YEAR	TM/L	W	L	PCT	G	GS	CG	SH	SV	IP	H	HR	BB	SO	RAT	ERA	ERA+	OAV	OOB	BH	AVG	PB	PR	/A	PD	TPI
1981	NY-A	0	0	—	2	0	0	0	0	7	5	1	3	2	10.3	2.57	139	.200	.286	0	—	0	1	1	-0	0.0
1982	SF-N	1	0	1.000	4	0	0	0	0	8	5	0	1	4	7.9	0.00	—	.179	.233	0	.000	-0	3	3	-0	0.4
1983	SF-N	3	9	.250	43	16	0	0	2	134^1	131	17	39	93	11.5	4.29	82	.255	.309	2	.067	-1	-10	-11	-3	-1.5
1984	Mon-N	3	4	.429	21	3	0	0	1	46	37	2	15	39	10.2	2.54	135	.220	.284	0	.000	-1	5	4	-0	0.6
	Cin-N	0	2	.000	9	3	0	0	0	23	23	2	8	18	12.1	5.48	69	.261	.323	0	.000	-0	-5	-4	-1	-0.4
	Yr	3	6	.333	30	6	0	0	1	69	60	4	23	57	10.8	3.52	101	.233	.296	0	.000	-1	1	0	-1	0.2
1985	Cin-N	3	3	.500	15	15	2	0	0	94^1	88	4	30	83	11.4	3.72	102	.247	.309	1	.034	-2	-1	1	0	-0.1
1986	Mon-N	10	5	.667	48	14	1	1	2	142^2	114	9	55	104	10.8	2.65	139	.223	.301	2	.061	-2	17	17	-2	1.3
1987	Mon-N	5	2	.714	69	0	0	0	12	120^1	105	5	42	100	11.2	2.39	176	.235	.305	0	.000	-1	23	24	-0	1.6
1988	Mon-N	6	0	1.000	63	0	0	0	4	91^1	81	4	37	71	11.8	2.76	130	.233	.311	0	.000	-0	7	8	-1	0.5
1989	Mon-N	3	5	.375	57	0	0	0	2	75	85	3	30	40	14.2	4.68	75	.293	.365	1	1.000	-0	-10	-10	-1	-1.1
1990	SF-N	0	0	—	4	0	0	0	0	4^2	10	2	4	4	27.0	17.36	21	.455	.538	0	—	0	-7	-7	-0	0.0
	KC-A	4	3	.571	24	11	0	0	1	78^2	75	6	28	49	12.0	3.09	124	.248	.315	0	—	0	7	6	-1	0.5
1991	KC-A	0	0	—	4	0	0	0	0	8	14	0	2	3	18.0	4.50	92	.389	.421	0	—	0	-0	-0	-0	0.0
Total	11	38	33	.535	363	62	3	1	24	833^1	773	55	294	610	11.7	3.38	110	.247	.314	6	.048	-7	30	32	-10	1.8

● JACK McGEACHY McGeachy, John Charles b: 5/23/1864, Clinton, Mass. d: 4/5/30, Cambridge, Mass. BR/TR, 5'8", 165 lbs. Deb: 6/17/1886 ♦

YEAR	TM/L	W	L	PCT	G	GS	CG	SH	SV	IP	H	HR	BB	SO	RAT	ERA	ERA+	OAV	OOB	BH	AVG	PB	PR	/A	PD	TPI
1887	Ind-N	0	1	.000	1	0	0	0	0	6^1	13	2	4	3	24.2	11.37	36	.351	.415	109	.269	0	-5	-5	0	-0.5
1888	Ind-N	0	0	—	1	0	0	0	0	5	5	1	3	0	14.4	7.20	41	.238	.333	99	.219	0	-2	-2	-0	0.0
1889	Ind-N	0	0	—	3	0	0	0	0	4^2	7	2	6	3	25.1	11.57	36	.333	.481	142	.267	0	-4	-4	-0	0.0
Total	3	0	1	.000	5	0	0	0	0	16	25	5	13	6	21.4	10.13	37	.316	.413	604	.245	0	-11	-11	-0	-0.5

● BILL McGEE McGee, William Henry "Fiddler Bill" b: 11/16/09, Batchtown, Ill. d: 2/11/87, St.Louis, Mo. BR/TR, 6'1", 215 lbs. Deb: 9/29/35

YEAR	TM/L	W	L	PCT	G	GS	CG	SH	SV	IP	H	HR	BB	SO	RAT	ERA	ERA+	OAV	OOB	BH	AVG	PB	PR	/A	PD	TPI
1935	StL-N	1	0	1.000	1	1	1	0	0	9	3	0	1	2	4.0	1.00	410	.103	.133	1	.333	0	3	3	-0	0.3
1936	StL-N	1	1	.500	7	2	0	0	0	16	23	3	4	8	15.2	7.88	50	.359	.397	1	.250	0	-7	-7	0	-0.7
1937	StL-N	1	0	1.000	4	1	1	0	0	14	13	1	4	9	11.6	2.57	155	.255	.321	1	.200	-0	2	2	0	0.2
1938	StL-N	7	12	.368	47	25	10	1	5	216	216	4	78	104	12.3	3.21	123	.257	.321	14	.209	1	14	18	-0	1.6
1939	StL-N	12	5	.706	43	17	5	4	0	156	155	14	59	56	12.3	3.81	108	.261	.328	8	.145	-2	2	5	0	0.3
1940	StL-N	16	10	.615	38	31	11	3	0	218	222	13	96	78	13.2	3.80	105	.263	.340	13	.178	-1	1	5	-3	0.1
1941	StL-N	0	1	.000	4	3	0	0	0	14	17	1	13	2	19.9	5.14	73	.298	.437	0	.000	-1	-2	-2	-0	-0.2
	NY-N	2	9	.182	22	14	1	0	0	106	117	9	54	41	14.5	4.92	75	.285	.368	5	.161	-1	-15	-14	-2	-1.6
	Yr	2	10	.167	26	17	1	0	0	120	134	10	67	43	15.1	4.95	75	.286	.375	5	.143	-2	-18	-17	-2	-1.8
1942	NY-N	6	3	.667	31	8	2	1	1	104	95	8	46	40	12.3	2.94	114	.244	.326	3	.103	-2	4	5	-1	0.1
Total	8	46	41	.529	197	102	31	9	6	853	861	53	355	340	12.9	3.74	104	.263	.336	46	.170	-6	2	14	-5	0.1

● CONNY McGEEHAN McGeehan, Cornelius Bernard b: 8/25/1882, Drifton, Pa. d: 7/4/07, Hazleton, Pa. Deb: 7/15/03 F

YEAR	TM/L	W	L	PCT	G	GS	CG	SH	SV	IP	H	HR	BB	SO	RAT	ERA	ERA+	OAV	OOB	BH	AVG	PB	PR	/A	PD	TPI
1903	Phi-A	1	0	1.000	3	0	0	0	0	10	9	0	1	4	9.9	4.50	68	.237	.275	0	.000	-1	-2	-2	0	-0.2

● KEVIN McGEHEE McGehee, George Kevin b: 1/18/69, Alexandria, La. BR/TR, 6', 190 lbs. Deb: 8/23/93

YEAR	TM/L	W	L	PCT	G	GS	CG	SH	SV	IP	H	HR	BB	SO	RAT	ERA	ERA+	OAV	OOB	BH	AVG	PB	PR	/A	PD	TPI
1993	Bal-A	0	0	—	5	0	0	0	0	16^2	18	5	7	7	14.6	5.94	75	.281	.370	0	—	0	-3	-3	0	-0.2

● PAT McGEHEE McGehee, Patrick Henry b: 7/2/1888, Meadville, Miss. d: 12/30/46, Paducah, Ky. BL/TR, 6'2.5", 180 lbs. Deb: 8/23/12

YEAR	TM/L	W	L	PCT	G	GS	CG	SH	SV	IP	H	HR	BB	SO	RAT	ERA	ERA+	OAV	OOB	BH	AVG	PB	PR	/A	PD	TPI
1912	Det-A	0	0	—	1	1	0	0	0	0	1	0	1	0	—	—	—	1.000	1.000	0	—	0	0	0	0	0.0

● RANDY McGILBERRY McGilberry, Randall Kent b: 10/29/53, Mobile, Ala. BB/TR, 6'1", 195 lbs. Deb: 9/6/77

YEAR	TM/L	W	L	PCT	G	GS	CG	SH	SV	IP	H	HR	BB	SO	RAT	ERA	ERA+	OAV	OOB	BH	AVG	PB	PR	/A	PD	TPI
1977	KC-A	0	1	.000	3	0	0	0	0	7	7	1	1	1	10.3	5.14	78	.280	.308	0	—	0	-1	-1	0	-0.1
1978	KC-A	0	1	.000	18	0	0	0	0	25^2	27	2	18	12	15.8	4.21	91	.276	.388	0	—	0	-1	-1	0	-0.2
Total	2	0	2	.000	21	0	0	0	0	32^2	34	3	19	13	14.6	4.41	88	.276	.373	0	—	0	-2	-2	0	-0.3

● BILL McGILL McGill, William John "Parson" b: 6/29/1880, Galva, Kan. d: 8/7/59, Alva, Okla. BR/TR, 6'2", Deb: 9/16/07

YEAR	TM/L	W	L	PCT	G	GS	CG	SH	SV	IP	H	HR	BB	SO	RAT	ERA	ERA+	OAV	OOB	BH	AVG	PB	PR	/A	PD	TPI
1907	StL-A	1	0	1.000	2	2	1	0	0	18^1	22	0	2	8	11.8	3.44	73	.301	.320	0	.000	-1	-2	-2	-0	-0.2

● WILLIE McGILL McGill, William Vaness "Kid" b: 11/10/1873, Atlanta, Ga. d: 8/29/44, Indianapolis, Ind. TL, 5'6.5", 170 lbs. Deb: 5/8/1890

YEAR	TM/L	W	L	PCT	G	GS	CG	SH	SV	IP	H	HR	BB	SO	RAT	ERA	ERA+	OAV	OOB	BH	AVG	PB	PR	/A	PD	TPI
1890	Cle-P	11	9	.550	24	20	19	0	0	183^2	222	5	96	82	16.2	4.12	97	.286	.373	10	.147	2	2	-3	1	0.1
1891	Cin-a	2	5	.286	8	8	6	0	0	65	69	1	37	19	15.1	4.98	83	.263	.361	2	.100	-0	-9	-6	-1	-0.6
	StL-a	19	10	.655	35	31	22	1	1	249	225	10	131	154	13.4	2.93	144	.233	.333	14	.161	1	22	35	-4	3.0
	Yr	21	15	.583	43	39	28	1	1	314	294	11	168	173	13.6	3.35	125	.239	.337	16	.150	1	13	29	-5	2.4
1892	Cin-N	1	1	.500	3	3	1	0	0	17	18	0	5	7	12.2	5.29	62	.261	.311	2	.286	0	-4	-4	0	-0.3
1893	Chi-N	17	18	.486	39	34	26	1	0	302^2	311	6	181	91	15.0	4.61	101	.258	.361	29	.234	2	2	1	-5	-0.1
1894	Chi-N	7	19	.269	27	23	22	0	0	208	272	2	117	58	17.3	5.84	96	.312	.400	20	.244	0	-12	-5	-2	-0.6
1895	Phi-N	10	8	.556	20	20	13	0	0	146	177	2	81	70	16.2	5.55	86	.295	.382	14	.222	-0	-12	-12	0	-1.1
1896	Phi-N	5	4	.556	12	11	7	0	0	79^2	87	0	53	29	16.3	5.31	81	.275	.386	6	.207	-0	-8	-9	0	-0.7
Total	7	72	74	.493	168	150	116	2	1	1251	1381	26	701	510	15.4	4.59	100	.273	.368	97	.202	5	-19	-1	-11	-0.3

● JOHN McGILLEN McGillen, John Joseph b: 8/6/17, Eddystone, Pa. d: 8/11/87, Upland, Pa. BL/TL, 6'1", 175 lbs. Deb: 4/20/44

YEAR	TM/L	W	L	PCT	G	GS	CG	SH	SV	IP	H	HR	BB	SO	RAT	ERA	ERA+	OAV	OOB	BH	AVG	PB	PR	/A	PD	TPI
1944	Phi-A	0	0	—	2	0	0	0	0	1	1	0	2	0	27.0	18.00	19	.333	.600	0	—	0	-2	-2	-0	0.0

● JIM McGINLEY McGinley, James William b: 10/2/1878, Groveland, Mass. d: 9/20/61, Haverhill, Mass. BR/TR, 5'9.5", 165 lbs. Deb: 9/22/04

YEAR	TM/L	W	L	PCT	G	GS	CG	SH	SV	IP	H	HR	BB	SO	RAT	ERA	ERA+	OAV	OOB	BH	AVG	PB	PR	/A	PD	TPI
1904	StL-N	2	1	.667	3	3	3	0	0	27	28	0	6	6	12.3	2.00	135	.267	.325	1	.091	-1	2	2	-1	0.0
1905	StL-N	0	1	.000	1	1	0	0	0	3	5	1	2	0	21.0	15.00	20	.333	.412	1	1.000	0	-4	-4	-0	-0.8
Total	2	2	2	.500	4	4	3	0	0	30	33	1	8	6	13.2	3.30	83	.275	.336	2	.167	-0	-2	-2	-2	-0.8

● DAN McGINN McGinn, Daniel Michael b: 11/29/43, Omaha, Neb. BL/TL, 6', 190 lbs. Deb: 9/3/68

YEAR	TM/L	W	L	PCT	G	GS	CG	SH	SV	IP	H	HR	BB	SO	RAT	ERA	ERA+	OAV	OOB	BH	AVG	PB	PR	/A	PD	TPI
1968	Cin-N	0	1	.000	14	0	0	0	0	12	13	1	11	16	18.8	5.25	60	.271	.417	0	.000	-0	-3	-3	0	-0.2
1969	Mon-N	7	10	.412	74	1	0	0	6	132^1	123	8	65	112	13.1	3.94	93	.245	.337	5	.172	1	-5	-4	1	-0.3
1970	Mon-N	7	10	.412	52	19	3	2	0	130^2	154	13	78	83	16.5	5.44	76	.296	.395	4	.114	-2	-20	-19	2	-2.2
1971	Mon-N	1	4	.200	28	6	1	0	0	71	74	7	42	40	14.8	5.96	59	.274	.374	4	.235	0	-20	-19	1	-1.1
1972	Chi-N	0	5	.000	42	2	0	0	4	62^2	78	5	29	42	15.9	5.89	65	.301	.380	2	.250	1	-17	-14	-1	-1.3
Total	5	15	30	.333	210	28	4	2	10	408^2	442	34	225	293	15.1	5.11	74	.276	.372	15	.165	-0	-65	-59	3	-5.1

● GUS McGINNIS McGinnis, August b: 1870, Painesville, Ohio TL, 5'11", 168 lbs. Deb: 4/27/1893

YEAR	TM/L	W	L	PCT	G	GS	CG	SH	SV	IP	H	HR	BB	SO	RAT	ERA	ERA+	OAV	OOB	BH	AVG	PB	PR	/A	PD	TPI
1893	Chi-N	2	5	.286	13	5	3	0	0	67^1	85	2	31	13	15.9	5.35	87	.299	.374	6	.240	2	-5	-5	0	-0.2
	Phi-N	1	3	.250	5	4	4	1	0	37^1	39	0	17	12	14.0	4.34	105	.262	.345	3	.200	-1	1	1	0	0.1
	Yr	3	8	.273	18	9	7	1	0	104^2	124	2	48	25	15.0	4.99	92	.284	.358	9	.225	1	-4	-4	1	-0.1

● JUMBO McGINNIS McGinnis, George Washington b: 2/22/1864, Alton, Mo. d: 5/18/34, St.Louis, Mo. 5'10", 197 lbs. Deb: 5/2/1882

YEAR	TM/L	W	L	PCT	G	GS	CG	SH	SV	IP	H	HR	BB	SO	RAT	ERA	ERA+	OAV	OOB	BH	AVG	PB	PR	/A	PD	TPI
1882	StL-a	25	18	.581	45	45	43	3	0	388^1	391	2	53	134	10.3	2.60	108	.245	.269	44	.217	1	4	9	-5	0.5
1883	StL-a	28	16	.636	45	45	41	**6**	0	382^2	325	3	69	128	9.3	2.33	150	.215	.249	36	.200	-6	41	49	1	4.2
1884	StL-a	24	16	.600	40	40	39	5	0	354^1	331	4	35	141	9.6	2.84	115	.233	.258	34	.233	3	16	16	-1	1.6
1885	StL-a	6	6	.500	13	13	12	3	0	112	98	1	19	41	9.9	3.38	97	.225	.267	11	.220	0	-2	-1	-1	-0.3
1886	StL-a	5	5	.500	10	10	10	1	0	87^2	107	2	27	30	14.5	3.80	91	.288	.347	7	.189	-1	-3	-3	0	-0.4
	Bal-a	11	13	.458	26	25	24	0	0	209^1	235	6	48	70	12.8	3.48	98	.280	.329	16	.188	-1	-1	-1	-0	-0.2
	Yr	16	18	.471	36	35	34	1	0	297	342	8	75	100	13.1	3.58	96	.281	.330	23	.189	-2	-4	-5	-0	-0.6

YEAR	TM/L	W	L	PCT	G	GS	CG	SH	SV	IP	H	HR	BB	SO	RAT	ERA	ERA+	OAV	OOB	BH	AVG	PB	PR	/A	PD	TPI
1887	Cin-a	3	5	.375	8	8	8	0	0	69^1	85	3	43	18	17.7	5.45	80	.296	.402	6	.194	-0	-9	-9	-0	-0.7
Total	6	102	79	.564	187	186	177	18	0	1603^2	1572	21	294	562	10.7	2.95	112	.243	.281	154	.210	-5	47	61	-7	4.7

● JOE McGINNITY

McGinnity, Joseph Jerome "Iron Man" (b: Joseph Jerome McGinty) b: 3/19/1871, Rock Island, Ill. d: 11/14/29, Brooklyn, N.Y. BR/TR, 5'11", 206 lbs. Deb: 4/18/1899 CH

YEAR	TM/L	W	L	PCT	G	GS	CG	SH	SV	IP	H	HR	BB	SO	RAT	ERA	ERA+	OAV	OOB	BH	AVG	PB	PR	/A	PD	TPI
1899	Bal-N	**28**	16	.636	48	41	38	4	2	366^1	358	3	93	74	11.7	2.68	148	.256	.314	28	.193	-5	48	52	1	5.0
1900	*Bro-N	**28**	8	**.778**	44	37	32	1	0	**343**	350	5	113	93	13.2	2.94	131	.264	.340	28	.193	-5	29	34	-2	2.3
1901	Bal-A	26	20	.565	**48**	43	**39**	1	1	**382**	412	7	96	75	12.5	3.56	109	.272	.324	31	.209	-4	5	13	-1	0.8
1902	Bal-A	13	10	.565	25	23	19	0	0	198^2	219	3	46	39	12.4	3.44	110	.280	.327	25	.287	4	3	7	-2	1.0
	NY-N	8	8	.500	19	16	16	1	0	153	122	1	32	67	9.6	2.06	136	.219	.273	8	.121	-4	12	13	1	0.9
1903	NY-N	**31**	20	.608	**55**	48	**44**	3	2	**434**	391	4	109	171	10.8	2.43	138	.236	.291	34	.206	-2	41	**44**	-4	4.0
1904	NY-N	**35**	8	**.814**	**51**	44	38	**9**	**5**	**408**	307	8	86	144	9.0	**1.61**	**169**	.206	.256	25	.176	-1	**51**	**51**	3	**5.6**
1905	*NY-N	21	15	.583	**46**	38	26	2	3	320^1	289	6	71	125	10.5	2.87	102	.240	.290	28	.233	6	5	2	2	1.0
1906	NY-N	**27**	12	.692	**45**	37	32	3	2	339^2	316	1	71	105	10.4	2.25	116	.246	.289	15	.130	-3	14	14	1	1.3
1907	NY-N	18	18	.500	**47**	34	23	3	**4**	310^1	320	6	58	120	11.4	3.16	78	.266	.308	18	.175	0	-24	-24	2	-2.6
1908	NY-N	11	7	.611	37	20	7	5	**5**	186	192	8	37	55	11.4	2.27	106	.267	.310	11	.180	-0	2	3	-1	0.2
Total	10	246	142	.634	465	381	314	32	24	3441^1	3276	52	812	1068	11.2	2.66	120	.249	.302	251	.194	-14	186	207	-0	19.5

● LYNN McGLOTHEN

McGlothen, Lynn Everatt b: 3/27/50, Monroe, La. d: 8/14/84, Dubach, La. BL/TR, 6'2", 195 lbs. Deb: 6/25/72

YEAR	TM/L	W	L	PCT	G	GS	CG	SH	SV	IP	H	HR	BB	SO	RAT	ERA	ERA+	OAV	OOB	BH	AVG	PB	PR	/A	PD	TPI
1972	Bos-A	8	7	.533	22	22	4	1	0	145	135	9	59	112	12.5	3.41	94	.247	.328	10	.189	1	-6	-3	3	0.1
1973	Bos-A	1	2	.333	6	3	0	0	0	23	39	6	8	16	18.8	8.22	49	.386	.436	0	—	0	-11	-11	-0	-1.2
1974	StL-N★	16	12	.571	31	31	8	3	0	237^1	212	12	89	142	11.5	2.69	133	.241	.312	15	.181	-1	24	23	1	2.7
1975	StL-N	15	13	.536	35	34	9	2	0	239	231	21	97	146	12.5	3.92	96	.254	.329	7	.087	-5	-8	-4	-2	-1.2
1976	StL-N	13	15	.464	33	32	10	4	0	205	209	10	68	106	12.3	3.91	90	.268	.330	15	.211	2	-9	-8	-2	-1.0
1977	SF-N	2	9	.182	21	15	2	0	0	80	94	9	52	42	16.5	5.62	69	.299	.401	2	.105	-1	-15	-15	-2	-2.0
1978	SF-N	0	0	—	5	1	0	0	0	12^2	15	0	4	9	13.5	4.97	69	.313	.365	0	.000	-0	-2	-2	-0	0.0
	Chi-N	5	3	.625	49	1	0	0	0	80	77	7	39	60	13.0	3.04	133	.257	.342	3	.231	1	5	9	-2	0.7
	Yr	5	3	.625	54	2	0	0	0	92^2	92	7	43	69	13.1	3.30	120	.264	.344	3	.188	0	3	7	-2	0.7
1979	Chi-N	13	14	.481	42	29	6	1	2	212	236	27	55	147	12.5	4.12	100	.283	.330	16	.225	1	-9	-0	-2	-0.1
1980	Chi-N	12	14	.462	39	27	2	2	0	182^1	211	24	64	119	13.6	4.79	82	.293	.352	10	.196	2	-24	-18	-2	-2.4
1981	Chi-N	1	4	.200	20	6	0	0	0	54^2	71	1	28	26	16.5	4.77	77	.317	.395	1	.083	-1	-8	-7	1	-0.6
	Chi-A	0	0	—	11	0	0	0	0	21^2	14	0	7	12	9.1	4.15	86	.189	.268	0	—	0	-1	-1	-0	0.0
1982	NY-A	0	0	—	4	0	0	0	0	5	9	1	2	2	19.8	10.80	37	.375	.423	0	—	0	-4	-4	0	0.0
Total	11	86	93	.480	318	201	41	13	2	1497^2	1553	127	572	939	12.9	3.98	94	.270	.339	79	.173	-1	-68	-42	-7	-5.0

● PAT McGLOTHIN

McGlothin, Ezra Mac b: 10/20/20, Coalfield, Tenn. BL/TR, 6'3.5", 180 lbs. Deb: 4/25/49

YEAR	TM/L	W	L	PCT	G	GS	CG	SH	SV	IP	H	HR	BB	SO	RAT	ERA	ERA+	OAV	OOB	BH	AVG	PB	PR	/A	PD	TPI
1949	Bro-N	1	1	.500	7	0	0	0	0	15^2	13	2	5	11	10.3	4.60	89	.224	.286	0	.000	-0	-1	-1	1	-0.1
1950	Bro-N	0	0	—	1	0	0	0	0	2	5	0	1	2	27.0	13.50	30	.455	.500	0	—	0	-2	-2	-0	0.0
Total	2	1	1	.500	8	0	0	0	0	17^2	18	2	6	13	12.2	5.60	73	.261	.320	0	.000	-0	-3	-3	1	-0.1

● JIM McGLOTHLIN

McGlothlin, James Milton "Red" b: 10/6/43, Los Angeles, Cal. d: 12/23/75, Union, Ky. BR/TR, 6'1", 185 lbs. Deb: 9/20/65

YEAR	TM/L	W	L	PCT	G	GS	CG	SH	SV	IP	H	HR	BB	SO	RAT	ERA	ERA+	OAV	OOB	BH	AVG	PB	PR	/A	PD	TPI
1965	Cal-A	0	3	.000	3	3	1	0	0	18	18	1	7	9	12.5	3.50	97	.261	.329	0	.000	-1	-0	-0	-0	-0.1
1966	Cal-A	3	1	.750	19	11	0	0	0	67^2	79	9	19	41	13.2	4.52	74	.292	.340	1	.059	-0	-8	-9	-0	-0.5
1967	Cal-A★	12	8	.600	32	29	9	**6**	0	197^1	163	13	56	137	10.2	2.96	106	.226	.286	8	.140	-0	6	4	1	0.5
1968	Cal-A	10	15	.400	40	32	8	0	3	208^1	187	19	60	135	11.0	3.54	82	.244	.305	7	.111	-1	-13	-15	2	-1.8
1969	Cal-A	8	16	.333	37	35	4	1	0	201	188	19	58	96	11.2	3.18	110	.249	.307	7	.121	-1	10	7	2	0.9
1970	*Cin-N	14	10	.583	35	34	5	3	0	210^2	192	19	86	97	12.0	3.59	112	.245	.322	8	.121	1	11	10	5	1.7
1971	Cin-N	8	12	.400	30	26	6	0	0	170^2	151	15	47	93	10.7	3.22	104	.243	.301	7	.137	1	5	3	1	0.5
1972	*Cin-N	9	8	.529	31	21	3	1	0	145	165	15	49	69	13.3	3.91	82	.287	.343	8	.174	3	-7	-11	-0	-1.0
1973	Cin-N	3	3	.500	24	9	0	0	0	63^1	91	13	23	18	16.2	6.68	51	.340	.392	2	.125	0	-21	-23	1	-1.8
	Chi-A	0	1	.000	5	1	0	0	0	18^1	13	2	13	14	12.8	3.93	101	.203	.338	0	—	0	-0	0	0	0.0
Total	9	67	77	.465	256	201	36	11	3	1300^1	1247	125	418	709	11.7	3.61	93	.255	.317	48	.126	2	-19	-34	11	-1.6

● STONEY McGLYNN

McGlynn, Ulysses Simpson Grant b: 5/26/1872, Lancaster, Pa. d: 8/26/41, Manitowoc, Wis. BR/TR, 5'11", 185 lbs. Deb: 9/20/06

YEAR	TM/L	W	L	PCT	G	GS	CG	SH	SV	IP	H	HR	BB	SO	RAT	ERA	ERA+	OAV	OOB	BH	AVG	PB	PR	/A	PD	TPI
1906	StL-N	2	2	.500	6	6	6	0	0	48	43	0	15	25	11.1	2.44	108	.249	.312	1	.059	-1	1	1	2	0.2
1907	StL-N	14	25	.359	45	39	**33**	3	1	**352^1**	329	6	112	109	11.4	2.91	86	.251	.312	25	.200	3	-17	-16	-1	-1.6
1908	StL-N	1	6	.143	16	6	4	0	1	75^2	76	0	17	23	11.3	3.45	68	.256	.301	2	.077	-1	-9	-9	1	-0.9
Total	3	17	33	.340	67	51	43	3	2	476	448	6	144	157	11.3	2.95	85	.252	.310	28	.167	0	-25	-24	2	-2.3

● MICKEY McGOWAN

McGowan, Tullis Earl b: 11/26/21, Dothan, Ala. BL/TL, 6'2", 200 lbs. Deb: 4/22/48

YEAR	TM/L	W	L	PCT	G	GS	CG	SH	SV	IP	H	HR	BB	SO	RAT	ERA	ERA+	OAV	OOB	BH	AVG	PB	PR	/A	PD	TPI
1948	NY-N	0	0	—	3	0	0	0	0	3^2	3	1	4	2	17.2	7.36	53	.231	.412	0	.000	-0	-1	-1	0	0.0

● HOWARD McGRANER

McGraner, Howard "Muck" b: 9/11/1889, Hamley Run, Ohio d: 10/22/52, Zaleski, Ohio BL/TL, 5'7", 155 lbs. Deb: 9/12/12

YEAR	TM/L	W	L	PCT	G	GS	CG	SH	SV	IP	H	HR	BB	SO	RAT	ERA	ERA+	OAV	OOB	BH	AVG	PB	PR	/A	PD	TPI
1912	Cin-N	1	0	1.000	4	0	0	0	0	19	22	2	7	5	14.2	7.11	47	.293	.361	2	.250	1	-8	-8	1	-0.2

● TOM McGRAW

McGraw, Thomas Virgil b: 12/8/67, Portland, Ore. BL/TL, 6'2", 195 lbs. Deb: 5/7/97

YEAR	TM/L	W	L	PCT	G	GS	CG	SH	SV	IP	H	HR	BB	SO	RAT	ERA	ERA+	OAV	OOB	BH	AVG	PB	PR	/A	PD	TPI
1997	StL-N	0	0	—	2	0	0	0	0	1^2	2	0	1	0	16.2	0.00	—	.333	.429	0	—	0	1	1	0	0.0

● TUG McGRAW

McGraw, Frank Edwin b: 8/30/44, Martinez, Cal. BR/TL, 6', 185 lbs. Deb: 4/18/65

YEAR	TM/L	W	L	PCT	G	GS	CG	SH	SV	IP	H	HR	BB	SO	RAT	ERA	ERA+	OAV	OOB	BH	AVG	PB	PR	/A	PD	TPI
1965	NY-N	2	7	.222	37	9	2	0	1	97^2	88	8	48	57	12.8	3.32	106	.249	.344	3	.130	-1	2	2	-1	0.1
1966	NY-N	2	9	.182	15	12	1	0	0	62^1	72	11	25	34	14.0	5.34	68	.294	.359	4	.235	1	-12	-12	-0	-1.8
1967	NY-N	0	3	.000	4	4	0	0	0	17^1	13	3	13	18	13.5	7.79	44	.206	.342	1	.250	0	-9	-8	0	-1.1
1969	*NY-N	9	3	.750	42	4	1	0	12	100^1	89	6	47	92	12.2	2.24	163	.243	.329	4	.167	0	**15**	**16**	1	2.4
1970	NY-N	4	6	.400	57	0	0	0	10	90^2	77	6	49	81	12.6	3.28	123	.231	.332	4	.308	1	8	8	1	1.2
1971	NY-N	11	4	.733	51	1	0	0	8	111	73	4	41	109	9.5	1.70	200	.189	.271	4	.222	2	**22**	**21**	-1	3.4
1972	NY-N★	8	6	.571	54	0	0	0	27	106	71	3	40	92	9.7	1.70	198	.197	.282	2	.100	-0	21	20	-0	3.8
1973	*NY-N	5	6	.455	60	2	0	0	25	118^2	106	11	55	81	12.4	3.87	93	.243	.331	4	.167	1	-3	-3	0	-0.3
1974	NY-N	6	11	.353	41	4	1	1	3	88^2	96	12	32	54	13.0	4.16	86	.279	.340	1	.071	-0	-5	-6	-1	-1.2
1975	Phi-N☆	9	6	.600	56	0	0	0	14	102^2	84	6	36	55	10.8	2.98	125	.226	.299	2	.154	-0	7	9	-0	1.4
1976	*Phi-N	7	6	.538	58	0	0	0	11	97^1	81	4	42	76	11.4	2.50	142	.226	.307	1	.143	0	11	11	-1	1.7
1977	*Phi-N	7	3	.700	45	0	0	0	9	79	62	6	24	58	9.9	2.62	153	.221	.284	4	.400	2	11	12	0	1.9
1978	*Phi-N	8	7	.533	55	1	0	0	9	89^2	82	6	23	63	10.5	3.21	111	.245	.293	0	.000	-0	4	4	0	0.6
1979	Phi-N	4	3	.571	65	1	0	0	16	83^2	83	9	29	57	12.3	5.16	74	.259	.324	1	.167	-0	-13	-12	-1	-1.6
1980	*Phi-N	5	4	.556	57	0	0	0	20	92^1	62	3	23	75	8.5	1.46	259	.194	.253	2	.250	0	**22**	24	0	3.5
1981	*Phi-N	2	4	.333	34	0	0	0	10	44	35	2	14	26	10.0	2.66	136	.219	.282	0	.000	-0	4	5	-1	0.8
1982	Phi-N	3	3	.500	34	0	0	0	5	39^2	50	3	12	25	14.3	4.31	85	.305	.356	0	.000	-0	-3	-3	0	-0.4
1983	Phi-N	2	1	.667	34	1	0	0	0	55^2	58	4	19	30	12.4	3.56	100	.271	.330	1	.333	0	0	0	0	0.0
1984	Phi-N	2	0	1.000	25	0	0	0	0	38	36	1	10	26	10.9	3.79	96	.245	.293	1	.333	0	-1	-1	0	0.0
Total	19	96	92	.511	824	39	5	1	180	1514^2	1318	108	582	1109	11.4	3.14	116	.237	.312	39	.182	5	81	85	-1	14.4

● JOHN McGRAW

McGraw, John (b: Roy Elmer Hoar) b: 12/8/1890, Intercourse, Pa. d: 4/27/67, Torrance, Cal. BR/TR, 5'9", 160 lbs. Deb: 7/29/14

YEAR	TM/L	W	L	PCT	G	GS	CG	SH	SV	IP	H	HR	BB	SO	RAT	ERA	ERA+	OAV	OOB	BH	AVG	PB	PR	/A	PD	TPI
1914	Bro-F	0	0	—	1	0	0	0	0	2	0	0	0	2	4.5	0.00	—	.000	.143	0	—	0	1	1	-0	0.0

● BOB McGRAW

McGraw, Robert Emmett b: 4/10/1895, LaVeta, Colo. d: 6/2/78, Boise, Idaho BR/TR, 6'2", 160 lbs. Deb: 9/25/17

YEAR	TM/L	W	L	PCT	G	GS	CG	SH	SV	IP	H	HR	BB	SO	RAT	ERA	ERA+	OAV	OOB	BH	AVG	PB	PR	/A	PD	TPI
1917	NY-A	0	1	.000	2	2	1	0	0	11	9	0	3	3	9.8	0.82	328	.257	.316	0	.000	-0	2	2	-0	0.1
1918	NY-A	0	1	.000	1	1	0	0	0	0	0	0	4	0	—	∞	—	—	1.000	0	—	0	-4	-4	0	-0.4
1919	NY-A	1	0	1.000	6	0	0	0	0	16^1	11	1	10	3	12.1	3.31	97	.216	.355	0	.000	-0	-0	-0	-0	0.0
	Bos-A	0	2	.000	10	1	0	0	0	26^2	33	0	17	6	17.9	6.75	45	.347	.461	1	.100	-1	-10	-11	-1	-0.9
	Yr	1	2	.333	16	1	0	0	0	43	44	1	27	9	15.5	5.44	57	.299	.418	1	.077	-1	-11	-11	-1	-0.9
1920	NY-A	0	0	—	15	0	0	0	0	27	24	1	20	11	15.0	4.67	82	.240	.372	0	.000	-1	-3	-3	-1	-0.2
1925	Bro-N	0	2	.000	2	2	2	0	0	19^2	14	0	13	3	12.4	3.20	130	.222	.355	1	.167	-0	2	2	-1	0.1
1926	Bro-N	9	13	.409	33	21	10	0	1	174^1	197	12	67	49	13.7	4.59	83	.292	.358	8	.145	-2	-15	-15	-1	-1.9

YEAR TM/L	W	L	PCT	G	GS	CG	SH	SV	IP	H	HR	BB	SO	RAT	ERA	ERA+	OAV	OOB	BH	AVG	PB	PR	/A	PD	TPI
1927 Bro-N	0	1	.000	1	1	0	0	0	4	5	1	2	2	15.8	9.00	44	.313	.389	0	.000	-0	-2	-2	0	-0.4
StL-N	4	5	.444	18	12	4	1	0	94	121	3	30	37	14.5	5.07	78	.323	.373	6	.182	1	-12	-12	1	-0.8
Yr	4	6	.400	19	13	4	1	0	98	126	4	32	39	14.5	5.23	75	.322	.374	6	.176	1	-14	-14	1	-1.2
1928 Phi-N	7	8	.467	39	3	0	0	1	120	148	7	56	28	15.5	5.18	83	.317	.392	4	.111	-2	-16	-12	-1	-1.6
1929 Phi-N	5	5	.500	41	4	0	0	4	86^{1}	113	6	43	22	16.5	5.73	91	.324	.401	4	.200	0	-10	-5	1	-0.4
Total 9	26	38	.406	168	47	17	1	6	579^{1}	675	31	265	164	14.8	5.00	81	.303	.380	24	.138	-6	-67	-60	-2	-6.4
● SCOTT McGREGOR	McGregor, Scott Houston b: 1/18/54, Inglewood, Cal. BB/TL, 6'1", 190 lbs. Deb: 9/19/76																								
1976 Bal-A	0	1	.000	3	2	0	0	0	14^{2}	17	0	5	6	13.5	3.68	89	.293	.349	0	—	0	-0	-1	0	0.0
1977 Bal-A	3	5	.375	29	5	1	0	4	114	119	8	30	55	12.3	4.42	86	.275	.333	0	—	0	-5	-8	-1	-0.7
1978 Bal-A	15	13	.536	35	32	13	4	1	233	217	19	47	94	10.2	3.32	105	.248	.287	0	—	0	11	4	0	1.0
1979 *Bal-A	13	6	.684	27	23	7	2	0	174^{2}	165	19	23	81	**9.8**	3.35	120	.248	**.275**	0	—	0	17	13	-1	1.4
1980 Bal-A	20	8	.714	36	36	12	4	0	252	254	16	58	119	11.2	3.32	119	.265	.308	0	—	0	20	18	-3	1.5
1981 Bal-A☆	13	5	.722	24	22	8	3	0	160	167	13	40	82	11.6	3.26	111	.273	.318	0	—	0	7	6	1	0.8
1982 Bal-A	14	12	.538	37	37	7	1	0	226^{1}	238	31	52	84	11.6	4.61	87	.267	.308	0	—	0	-14	-15	-1	-1.6
1983 *Bal-A	18	7	.720	36	36	12	2	0	260	271	24	45	86	11.0	3.18	124	.269	.301	0	—	0	25	22	-1	1.9
1984 Bal-A	15	12	.556	30	30	10	3	0	196^{1}	216	18	54	67	12.6	3.94	98	.280	.331	0	—	0	1	-2	2	0.1
1985 Bal-A	14	14	.500	35	34	8	1	0	204	226	34	65	86	12.9	4.81	84	.283	.337	0	—	0	-15	-18	-1	-2.0
1986 Bal-A	11	15	.423	34	33	4	2	0	203	216	35	57	95	12.2	4.52	91	.270	.321	0	—	0	-8	-9	-1	-0.9
1987 Bal-A	2	7	.222	26	15	1	1	0	85^{1}	112	15	35	39	15.8	6.64	66	.326	.393	0	—	0	-21	-21	3	-1.5
1988 Bal-A	0	3	.000	4	4	0	0	0	17^{1}	27	3	7	10	17.7	8.83	44	.370	.425	0	—	0	-9	-9	1	-1.1
Total 13	138	108	.561	356	309	83	23	5	2140^{2}	2245	235	518	904	11.7	3.99	98	.271	.316	0	—	0	10	-19	-2	-1.1
● SLIM McGREW	McGrew, Walter Howard b: 8/5/1899, Yoakum, Tex. d: 8/21/67, Houston, Tex. BR/TR, 6'7.5", 235 lbs. Deb: 4/18/22																								
1922 Was-A	0	0	—	1	0	0	0	0	1^{2}	4	0	2	1	32.4	10.80	36	.500	.600	0	.000	-0	-1	-1	0	0.0
1923 Was-A	0	0	—	3	0	0	0	0	5	11	0	3	1	25.2	12.60	30	.440	.500	0	.000	-0	-5	-5	0	0.0
1924 Was-A	0	1	.000	6	2	0	0	0	23^{1}	25	1	12	8	14.3	5.01	80	.281	.366	0	.000	-1	-2	-3	-1	-0.3
Total 3	0	1	.000	10	2	0	0	0	30	40	1	17	10	17.1	6.60	60	.328	.410	0	.000	-2	-8	-9	0	-0.3
● McGUIRE	McGuire Deb: 6/16/1894																								
1894 Cin-N	0	0	—	1	0	0	0	0	6	15	0	5	1	30.0	10.50	53	.469	.541	1	.250	-0	-3	-3	0	0.0
● DEACON McGUIRE	McGuire, James Thomas b: 11/18/1863, Youngstown, Ohio d: 10/31/36, Duck Lake, Mich. BR/TR, 6'1", 185 lbs. Deb: 6/21/1884 MC♦																								
1890 Roc-a	0	0	—	1	0	0	0	0	4	10	0	1	1	24.8	6.75	53	.455	.478	99	.299	0	-1	-1	0	0.0
● TOM McGUIRE	McGuire, Thomas Patrick "Elmer" b: 2/1/1892, Chicago, Ill. d: 12/7/59, Phoenix, Ariz. BR/TR, 6', 175 lbs. Deb: 4/18/14																								
1914 Chi-F	5	6	.455	24	12	7	0	0	131^{1}	143	7	57	37	14.0	3.70	72	.288	.366	19	.271	4	-12	-15	0	-0.6
1919 Chi-A	0	0	—	1	0	0	0	0	3	5	0	3	0	24.0	9.00	35	.500	.615	0	.000	-0	-2	-2	0	0.0
Total 2	5	6	.455	25	12	7	0	0	134^{1}	148	7	60	37	14.2	3.82	70	.292	.371	19	.268	3	-14	-17	1	-0.6
● BILL McGUNNIGLE	McGunnigle, William Henry "Gunner" b: 1/1/1855, Boston, Mass. d: 3/9/1899, Brockton, Mass. BR/TR, 5'9", 155 lbs. Deb: 5/2/1879 M♦																								
1879 Buf-N	9	5	.643	14	13	13	2	0	120	113	0	16	62	9.7	2.63	99	**.235**	.260	30	.175	-2	-2	-0	1	-0.1
1880 Buf-N	2	3	.400	5	5	4	1	0	37	43	0	8	3	12.4	3.41	72	.279	.315	4	.182	-1	-4	-4	-1	-0.6
Total 2	11	8	.579	19	18	17	3	0	157	156	0	24	65	10.3	2.81	92	.246	.274	35	.173	-3	-6	-4	0	-0.7
● MARTY McHALE	McHale, Martin Joseph b: 10/30/1888, Stoneham, Mass. d: 5/7/79, Hempstead, N.Y. BR/TR, 5'11.5", 174 lbs. Deb: 9/28/10																								
1910 Bos-A	0	2	.000	2	2	1	0	0	13^{2}	15	0	6	14	14.5	4.61	55	.259	.338	0	.000	-1	-3	-3	-0	-0.5
1911 Bos-A	0	0	—	4	1	0	0	0	9^{1}	19	1	3	3	22.2	9.64	34	.475	.523	0	.000	-0	-7	-7	0	0.0
1913 NY-A	2	4	.333	7	6	4	1	0	48^{2}	49	1	10	11	11.1	2.96	101	.266	.308	0	.000	-1	-0	0	-1	-0.2
1914 NY-A	6	16	.273	31	23	12	0	1	191	195	3	33	75	10.9	2.97	93	.268	.303	12	.200	2	-5	-4	-3	-0.7
1915 NY-A	3	7	.300	13	11	6	0	0	78^{1}	86	1	19	25	12.1	4.25	69	.277	.318	3	.143	1	-11	-11	0	-1.3
1916 Bos-A	0	1	.000	2	1	0	0	0	6	7	0	4	1	18.0	3.00	92	.280	.400	0	—	0	-0	-0	0	0.1
Cle-A	0	0	—	5	0	0	0	0	11^{1}	10	1	6	2	12.7	5.56	54	.270	.372	0	.000	-0	-3	-3	-0	-0.1
Yr	0	1	.000	7	1	0	0	0	17^{1}	17	1	10	3	14.0	4.67	63	.270	.370	0	.000	0	-4	-3	0	0.0
Total 6	11	30	.268	64	44	23	1	1	358^{1}	381	7	81	131	11.8	3.57	80	.275	.319	15	.140	-0	-30	-29	-4	-2.7
● VANCE McILREE	McIlree, Vance Elmer b: 10/14/1897, Riverside, Iowa d: 5/6/59, Kansas City, Mo. BR/TR, 6', 160 lbs. Deb: 9/13/21																								
1921 Was-A	0	0	—	1	0	0	0	0	1	1	0	0	0	9.0	9.00	46	.200	.200	0	—	0	-1	-1	-0	0.0
● IRISH McILVEEN	McIlveen, Henry Cooke b: 7/27/1880, Belfast, Ireland d: 10/18/60, Lorain, Ohio BL/TL, 5'11.5", 180 lbs. Deb: 7/10/06 ♦																								
1906 Pit-N	0	1	.000	2	1	0	0	0	7	10	1	2	3	15.4	7.71	35	.357	.400	2	.400	1	-4	-4	0	-0.4
● STOVER McILWAIN	McIlwain, Stover William "Smokey" (b: William Stover McIlwain) b: 9/22/39, Savannah, Ga. d: 1/15/66, Buffalo, N.Y. BR/TR, 6'2", 195 lbs. Deb: 9/25/57																								
1957 Chi-A	0	0	—	1	0	0	0	0	1	2	0	1	0	27.0	0.00	—	.500	.600	0	—	0	0	0	-0	0.0
1958 Chi-A	0	0	—	1	1	0	0	0	4	4	1	0	4	9.0	2.25	162	.250	.250	0	.000	-0	1	1	0	0.0
Total 2	0	0	—	2	1	0	0	0	5	6	1	1	4	12.6	1.80	203	.300	.333	0	.000	-0	1	1	-0	0.0
● HARRY McINTIRE	McIntire, John Reid b: 1/11/1879, Dayton, Ohio d: 1/9/49, Daytona Beach, Fla. BR/TR, 5'11", 180 lbs. Deb: 4/14/05																								
1905 Bro-N	8	25	.242	40	35	29	1	1	308^{2}	340	6	101	135	13.4	3.70	78	.285	.351	34	.246	7	-24	-28	-3	-2.3
1906 Bro-N	13	21	.382	39	31	25	4	3	276	254	2	89	121	11.6	2.97	85	.247	.316	18	.175	1	-10	-14	-1	-1.6
1907 Bro-N	7	15	.318	28	22	19	3	0	199^{2}	178	6	79	49	11.9	2.39	98	.248	.329	15	.217	5	2	-1	-1	0.4
1908 Bro-N	11	20	.355	40	35	26	4	2	288	259	5	90	108	11.5	2.69	87	.252	.324	20	.200	2	-10	-11	-2	-1.2
1909 Bro-N	7	17	.292	32	26	20	2	1	228	200	5	91	84	12.3	3.63	71	.246	.337	13	.171	1	-26	-26	-0	-2.6
1910 *Chi-N	13	9	.591	28	19	10	2	0	176	152	5	50	65	10.8	3.07	94	.240	.305	17	.258	3	-1	-4	-1	-0.1
1911 Chi-N	11	7	.611	25	17	9	1	0	149	147	5	33	56	11.1	4.11	81	.257	.302	14	.264	4	-12	-13	-0	-1.0
1912 Chi-N	1	2	.333	4	3	2	0	0	23^{2}	22	0	6	8	10.6	3.80	87	.256	.304	3	.300	1	-1	-1	-0	0.0
1913 Cin-N	0	1	.000	1	0	0	0	0	1	3	0	0	0	27.0	27.00	12	.600	.600	0	—	0	-3	-3	-0	-1.3
Total 9	71	117	.378	237	188	140	17	7	1650	1555	34	539	626	11.9	3.22	83	.256	.326	134	.218	24	-85	-100	-7	-9.7
● JOE McINTOSH	McIntosh, Joseph Anthony b: 8/4/51, Billings, Mont. BB/TR, 6'2", 185 lbs. Deb: 4/5/74																								
1974 SD-N	0	4	.000	10	5	0	0	0	37^{1}	36	3	17	22	13.0	3.62	98	.250	.333	0	.000	-1	0	-0	-0	-0.2
1975 SD-N	8	15	.348	37	28	4	1	0	183	195	14	60	71	12.6	3.69	94	.273	.332	9	.188	2	-1	-4	-0	-0.3
Total 2	8	19	.296	47	33	4	1	0	220^{1}	231	17	77	93	12.7	3.68	95	.270	.332	9	.155	1	-1	-5	-1	-0.5
● FRANK McINTYRE	McIntyre, Frank W. b: 7/12/1859, Walled Lake, Mich. d: 7/8/1887, Detroit, Mich. Deb: 5/16/1883																								
1883 Col-a	1	1	.500	2	2	2	0	0	19	20	0	7	6	12.8	5.21	59	.253	.314	0	.000	-0	-4	-5	-1	-0.4
● DOC McJAMES	McJames, James McCutchen (b: James Mc Cutchen James) b: 8/27/1873, Williamsburg, S.C. d: 9/23/01, Charleston, S.C. TR , Deb: 9/24/1895																								
1895 Was-N	1	1	.500	2	2	2	0	0	17	17	0	16	9	17.5	1.59	302	.258	.402	1	.143	-1	6	6	0	0.5
1896 Was-N	12	20	.375	37	33	29	0	1	280^{1}	310	2	135	103	14.5	4.27	103	.278	.359	18	.162	-9	3	4	-0	-0.4
1897 Was-N	15	23	.395	44	39	33	**3**	2	323^{2}	361	7	137	**156**	14.4	3.61	120	.280	.358	21	.169	-7	25	26	0	1.8
1898 Bal-N	27	15	.643	45	42	40	2	0	374	327	5	113	178	10.9	2.36	152	.234	.296	27	.181	-4	52	51	-3	4.3
1899 Bro-N	19	15	.559	37	34	27	1	1	275^{1}	295	4	122	105	14.0	3.50	112	.274	.353	19	.170	-5	11	13	3	1.1
1901 Bro-N	5	6	.455	13	12	6	0	0	91	104	1	40	42	14.9	4.75	71	.285	.367	1	.029	-4	-14	-14	-2	-1.9
Total 6	79	80	.497	178	162	137	6	4	1361^{1}	1414	19	563	593	13.4	3.43	117	.266	.343	87	.162	-30	83	86	-1	5.4
● ARCHIE McKAIN	McKain, Archie Richard "Happy" b: 5/12/11, Delphos, Kan. d: 5/21/85, Salina, Kan. BB/TL, 5'10", 175 lbs. Deb: 4/25/37																								
1937 Bos-A	8	8	.500	36	18	3	0	2	137	152	7	64	66	14.2	4.66	102	.273	.348	13	.265	3	-1	1	0	0.4
1938 Bos-A	5	4	.556	37	5	1	0	6	99^{2}	119	6	44	27	14.9	4.52	109	.297	.369	2	.065	-2	3	**5**	2	0.3
1939 Det-A	5	6	.455	32	11	4	1	4	129^{2}	120	6	54	49	12.1	3.68	133	.247	.322	9	.220	4	14	17	-2	1.6
1940 *Det-A	5	0	1.000	27	0	0	0	3	51	48	2	25	24	12.9	2.82	168	.247	.333	1	.143	0	9	11	1	1.2
1941 Det-A	2	1	.667	15	0	0	0	0	43	58	3	11	14	14.4	5.02	90	.330	.369	0	.000	-1	-4	-2	2	0.0

YEAR	TM/L	W	L	PCT	G	GS	CG	SH	SV	IP	H	HR	BB	SO	RAT	ERA	ERA+	OAV	OOB	BH	AVG	PB	PR	/A	PD	TPI
	StL-A	0	1	.000	8	0	0	0	1	10	16	2	4	2	18.9	8.10	53	.364	.429	0	.000	-0	-4	-4	1	-0.4
	Yr	2	2	.500	23	0	0	0	1	53	74	5	15	16	15.3	5.60	80	.336	.381	0	.000	-1	-9	-7	3	-0.4
1943	StL-A	1	1	.500	10	0	0	0	0	16	16	0	6	6	12.4	3.94	84	.242	.306	0	.000	-0	-1	-1	0	-0.1
Total	6	26	21	.553	165	34	8	1	16	486^1	529	26	208	188	13.7	4.26	112	.275	.347	25	.176	3	15	27	4	3.0

● HAL McKAIN
McKain, Harold Le Roy b: 7/10/06, Logan, Iowa d: 1/24/70, Sacramento, Cal. BL/TR, 5'11", 185 lbs. Deb: 9/22/27

YEAR	TM/L	W	L	PCT	G	GS	CG	SH	SV	IP	H	HR	BB	SO	RAT	ERA	ERA+	OAV	OOB	BH	AVG	PB	PR	/A	PD	TPI
1927	Cle-A	0	1	.000	2	1	0	0	0	11	18	0	4	5	18.0	4.09	103	.391	.440	0	.000	-1	0	0	0	0.0
1929	Chi-A	6	9	.400	34	10	4	1	1	158	158	10	85	33	14.4	3.65	117	.275	.378	10	.227	1	11	11	1	1.5
1930	Chi-A	6	4	.600	32	5	0	0	5	89	108	0	42	52	15.5	5.56	83	.299	.377	13	.419	7	-9	-9	1	-0.2
1931	Chi-A	6	9	.400	27	8	3	0	0	112	134	10	57	39	15.6	5.71	75	.295	.377	5	.119	-1	-16	-18	2	-1.9
1932	Chi-A	0	0	—	8	0	0	0	0	11^1	17	1	5	7	17.5	11.12	39	.340	.400	0	.000	-0	-8	-9	0	0.0
Total	5	18	23	.439	103	24	7	1	6	381^1	435	21	193	136	15.2	4.93	88	.293	.380	28	.230	8	-23	-24	7	-0.6

● REEVE McKAY
McKay, Reeve Stewart "Rip" b: 11/16/1881, Morgan, Tex. d: 1/18/46, Dallas, Tex. TR, 6'1.5", 168 lbs. Deb: 10/2/15

YEAR	TM/L	W	L	PCT	G	GS	CG	SH	SV	IP	H	HR	BB	SO	RAT	ERA	ERA+	OAV	OOB	BH	AVG	PB	PR	/A	PD	TPI
1915	StL-A	0	0	—	1	0	0	0	0	1	1	0	0	0	9.0	9.00	32	.500	.500	0	—	0	-1	-1	0	0.0

● JIM McKEE
McKee, James Marion b: 2/1/47, Columbus, Ohio BR/TR, 6'7", 215 lbs. Deb: 9/15/72

YEAR	TM/L	W	L	PCT	G	GS	CG	SH	SV	IP	H	HR	BB	SO	RAT	ERA	ERA+	OAV	OOB	BH	AVG	PB	PR	/A	PD	TPI
1972	Pit-N	1	0	1.000	2	0	0	0	0	5	2	0	1	4	5.4	0.00	—	.125	.176	0	—	0	2	2	-0	0.4
1973	Pit-N	0	1	.000	15	1	0	0	0	27	31	2	17	13	16.3	5.67	62	.287	.389	0	.000	-0	-6	-6	-0	-0.3
Total	2	1	1	.500	17	1	0	0	0	32	33	2	18	17	14.6	4.78	73	.266	.364	0	.000	-0	-4	-5	-1	0.1

● ROGERS McKEE
McKee, Rogers Hornsby b: 9/16/26, Shelby, N.C. BL/TL, 6'1", 160 lbs. Deb: 8/18/43

YEAR	TM/L	W	L	PCT	G	GS	CG	SH	SV	IP	H	HR	BB	SO	RAT	ERA	ERA+	OAV	OOB	BH	AVG	PB	PR	/A	PD	TPI
1943	Phi-N	1	0	1.000	4	1	1	0	0	13^1	12	0	5	1	11.5	6.08	56	.226	.293	1	.200	0	-4	-4	0	-0.2
1944	Phi-N	0	0	—	1	0	0	0	0	2	2	1	1	0	13.5	4.50	80	.250	.333	0	—	0	0	0	0	0.0
Total	2	1	0	1.000	5	1	1	0	0	15^1	14	1	6	1	11.7	5.87	58	.230	.299	1	.200	0	-4	-4	0	-0.2

● TIM McKEITHAN
McKeithan, Emmett James b: 11/2/06, Lawndale, N.C. d: 8/20/69, Forest City, N.C. BR/TR, 6'2", 182 lbs. Deb: 7/21/32

YEAR	TM/L	W	L	PCT	G	GS	CG	SH	SV	IP	H	HR	BB	SO	RAT	ERA	ERA+	OAV	OOB	BH	AVG	PB	PR	/A	PD	TPI
1932	Phi-A	0	1	.000	4	2	0	0	0	12^2	18	0	5	0	16.3	7.11	64	.340	.397	0	.000	0	-4	-4	0	-0.2
1933	Phi-A	1	0	1.000	3	1	0	0	0	9	10	0	4	3	14.0	4.00	107	.278	.350	1	.333	0	0	0	0	0.1
1934	Phi-A	0	0	—	3	0	0	0	0	4	7	2	5	0	27.0	15.75	28	.389	.522	0	.000	-0	-5	-5	-0	0.0
Total	3	1	1	.500	10	3	0	0	0	25^2	35	2	14	3	17.2	7.36	60	.327	.405	1	.143	0	-8	-8	0	-0.1

● RUSS McKELVY
McKelvy, Russell Errett b: 9/8/1854, Swissvale, Pa. d: 10/19/15, Omaha, Neb. BR/TR, Deb: 5/1/1878 ♦

YEAR	TM/L	W	L	PCT	G	GS	CG	SH	SV	IP	H	HR	BB	SO	RAT	ERA	ERA+	OAV	OOB	BH	AVG	PB	PR	/A	PD	TPI
1878	Ind-N	0	2	.000	4	1	1	0	0	25	38	1	3	3	14.8	2.16	94	.322	.339	57	.225	0	0	-0	1	0.1

● KIT McKENNA
McKenna, James William b: 2/10/1873, Lynchburg, Va. d: 3/31/41, Lynchburg, Va. TR, Deb: 7/7/1898

YEAR	TM/L	W	L	PCT	G	GS	CG	SH	SV	IP	H	HR	BB	SO	RAT	ERA	ERA+	OAV	OOB	BH	AVG	PB	PR	/A	PD	TPI
1898	Bro-N	2	6	.250	14	9	7	0	0	100^2	118	4	57	27	17.2	5.63	64	.290	.399	9	.225	0	-23	-23	2	-1.3
1899	Bal-N	2	3	.400	8	4	4	0	1	45	66	1	19	7	17.6	4.60	86	.340	.407	1	.059	-1	-4	-3	-0	-0.4
Total	2	4	9	.308	22	13	11	0	1	145^2	184	5	76	34	17.3	5.31	70	.306	.402	10	.175	-0	-26	-26	1	-1.7

● LIMB McKENRY
McKenry, Frank Gordon "Big Pete" b: 8/13/1888, Piney Flats, Tenn. d: 11/1/56, Fresno, Cal. BR/TR, 6'4", 205 lbs. Deb: 8/27/15

YEAR	TM/L	W	L	PCT	G	GS	CG	SH	SV	IP	H	HR	BB	SO	RAT	ERA	ERA+	OAV	OOB	BH	AVG	PB	PR	/A	PD	TPI
1915	Cin-N	5	5	.500	21	11	5	0	0	110^1	94	2	39	37	11.1	2.94	97	.238	.311	5	.152	0	-2	-1	1	0.1
1916	Cin-N	1	1	.500	6	1	0	0	0	14^2	14	0	8	2	14.7	4.30	60	.259	.375	2	.400	2	-3	-3	-0	-0.2
Total	2	6	6	.500	27	12	5	0	0	125	108	2	47	39	11.5	3.10	91	.241	.319	7	.184	2	-5	-4	1	-0.1

● JOEL McKEON
McKeon, Joel Jacob b: 2/25/63, Covington, Ky. BL/TL, 6', 185 lbs. Deb: 5/6/86

YEAR	TM/L	W	L	PCT	G	GS	CG	SH	SV	IP	H	HR	BB	SO	RAT	ERA	ERA+	OAV	OOB	BH	AVG	PB	PR	/A	PD	TPI
1986	Chi-A	3	1	.750	30	0	0	0	1	33	18	2	17	18	9.5	2.45	176	.165	.278	0	—	0	6	7	-1	0.7
1987	Chi-A	1	2	.333	13	0	0	0	0	21	27	8	15	14	18.0	9.43	49	.318	.420	0	—	0	-12	-11	-0	-1.5
Total	2	4	3	.571	43	0	0	0	1	54	45	10	32	32	12.8	5.17	85	.232	.341	0	—	0	-5	-5	-1	-0.8

● LARRY McKEON
McKeon, Lawrence G. b: 3/25/1866, New York d: 7/18/15, Indianapolis, Ind 5'10", 168 lbs. Deb: 5/1/1884

YEAR	TM/L	W	L	PCT	G	GS	CG	SH	SV	IP	H	HR	BB	SO	RAT	ERA	ERA+	OAV	OOB	BH	AVG	PB	PR	/A	PD	TPI
1884	Ind-a	18	41	.305	61	60	59	2	0	512	488	20	94	308	10.5	3.50	94	.235	.275	53	.212	-3	-14	-12	8	-0.7
1885	Cin-a	20	13	.606	33	33	32	2	0	290	273	5	50	117	10.4	2.86	114	.241	.281	20	.165	-5	13	13	-0	0.7
1886	Cin-a	8	8	.500	19	19	16	0	0	156	174	6	54	46	13.3	5.08	69	.276	.336	19	.253	1	-28	-27	1	-1.9
	KC-N	0	2	.000	3	3	3	0	0	21	44	0	8	3	22.3	10.71	35	.411	.452	0	.000	-1	-17	-16	0	-1.1
Total	3	46	64	.418	116	115	110	4	0	979	979	31	206	474	11.2	3.71	90	.248	.291	92	.202	-9	-47	-42	8	-3.0

● DENNY McLAIN
McLain, Dennis Dale b: 3/29/44, Chicago, Ill. BR/TR, 6'1", 185 lbs. Deb: 9/21/63

YEAR	TM/L	W	L	PCT	G	GS	CG	SH	SV	IP	H	HR	BB	SO	RAT	ERA	ERA+	OAV	OOB	BH	AVG	PB	PR	/A	PD	TPI
1963	Det-A	2	1	.667	3	3	2	0	0	21	20	2	16	22	15.4	4.29	87	.253	.379	1	.200	1	-2	-1	1	0.0
1964	Det-A	4	5	.444	19	16	3	0	0	100	84	16	37	70	11.0	4.05	90	.225	.297	5	.135	-1	-5	-4	-2	-0.7
1965	Det-A	16	6	.727	33	29	13	4	1	220^1	174	25	62	192	9.7	2.61	133	.216	.273	4	.054	-4	21	21	-0	1.7
1966	Det-A★	20	14	.588	38	38	14	4	0	264^1	205	42	104	192	10.6	3.92	89	.214	.294	17	.183	2	-14	-13	-1	-1.5
1967	Det-A	17	16	.515	37	37	10	3	0	235	209	35	73	161	10.9	3.79	86	.237	.297	10	.118	-3	-15	-14	-2	-2.4
1968	*Det-A★	**31**	6	**.838**	41	41	**28**	6	0	**336**	241	31	63	280	8.3	1.96	154	.200	.243	18	.162	0	38	**39**	1	**4.9**
1969	Det-A★	**24**	9	.727	42	41	23	**9**	0	**325**	288	25	67	181	9.9	2.80	133	.237	.279	17	.160	-1	30	34	-5	2.7
1970	Det-A	3	5	.375	14	14	1	0	0	91^1	100	19	28	52	12.9	4.63	80	.273	.330	2	.065	-2	-9	-9	0	-0.9
1971	Was-A	10	22	.313	33	32	9	3	0	216^2	233	31	72	103	12.8	4.28	77	.281	.341	6	.103	-1	-20	-23	-1	-3.3
1972	Oak-A	1	2	.333	5	5	0	0	0	22^1	32	4	8	8	16.1	6.04	47	.323	.374	0	.000	-0	-7	-8	0	-1.0
	Atl-N	3	5	.375	15	8	2	0	1	54	60	12	18	21	13.2	6.50	58	.279	.338	2	.167	0	-18	-16	-1	-2.3
Total	10	131	91	.590	280	264	105	29	2	1886	1646	242	548	1282	10.6	3.39	101	.234	.292	82	.133	-9	-1	5	-10	-2.8

● BARNEY McLAUGHLIN
McLaughlin, Bernard b: 1857, Ireland d: 2/13/21, Lowell, Mass. BR/TR, Deb: 8/2/1884 F♦

YEAR	TM/L	W	L	PCT	G	GS	CG	SH	SV	IP	H	HR	BB	SO	RAT	ERA	ERA+	OAV	OOB	BH	AVG	PB	PR	/A	PD	TPI
1884	KC-U	1	3	.250	7	4	4	0	0	48^2	62	2	15	14	14.2	5.36	42	.291	.338	37	.228	-1	-16	-17	0	-1.0

● BYRON McLAUGHLIN
McLaughlin, Byron Scott b: 9/29/55, Van Nuys, Cal. BR/TR, 6'1", 185 lbs. Deb: 9/18/77

YEAR	TM/L	W	L	PCT	G	GS	CG	SH	SV	IP	H	HR	BB	SO	RAT	ERA	ERA+	OAV	OOB	BH	AVG	PB	PR	/A	PD	TPI
1977	Sea-A	0	0	—	1	0	0	0	0	1^1	5	1	0	1	33.8	27.00	15	.625	.625	0	—	0	-3	-3	0	0.0
1978	Sea-A	4	8	.333	20	17	4	0	0	107	97	15	39	87	11.9	4.37	87	.238	.314	0	—	0	-7	-7	-2	-0.8
1979	Sea-A	7	7	.500	47	7	1	0	14	123^2	114	13	60	74	12.8	4.22	103	.251	.340	0	—	0	-0	2	-2	0.0
1980	Sea-A	3	6	.333	45	4	0	0	2	90^2	124	15	50	41	17.5	6.85	60	.331	.412	0	—	0	-28	-27	-2	-2.7
1983	Cal-A	2	4	.333	16	7	0	0	0	55^2	63	3	22	45	14.1	5.17	78	.286	.357	0	—	0	-7	-7	-0	-0.7
Total	5	16	25	.390	129	35	5	0	16	378^1	403	47	171	248	13.9	5.11	80	.275	.356	0	—	0	-46	-43	-5	-4.2

● FRANK McLAUGHLIN
McLaughlin, Francis Edward b: 6/19/1856, Lowell, Mass. d: 4/5/17, Lowell, Mass. BR/TR, 5'9", 160 lbs. Deb: 8/9/1882 F♦

YEAR	TM/L	W	L	PCT	G	GS	CG	SH	SV	IP	H	HR	BB	SO	RAT	ERA	ERA+	OAV	OOB	BH	AVG	PB	PR	/A	PD	TPI
1883	Pit-a	0	0	—	2	0	0	0	0	9	14	0	3	1	17.0	13.00	25	.333	.378	25	.219	0	-10	-10	-0	0.0
1884	KC-U	0	0	—	2	1	0	0	0	10	15	0	2	3	15.3	5.40	41	.326	.354	28	.228	-0	-3	-4	-1	0.0
Total	2	0	0	—	4	1	0	0	0	19	29	0	5	4	16.1	9.00	30	.330	.366	97	.228	-0	-13	-13	-1	0.0

● JIM McLAUGHLIN
McLaughlin, James Thomas b: 11/18/1860, Cleveland, Ohio d: 11/16/1895, Cleveland, Ohio BL/TL, 157 lbs. Deb: 5/30/1884

YEAR	TM/L	W	L	PCT	G	GS	CG	SH	SV	IP	H	HR	BB	SO	RAT	ERA	ERA+	OAV	OOB	BH	AVG	PB	PR	/A	PD	TPI
1884	Bal-a	1	2	.333	3	2	2	0	0	22	27	2	11	8	15.5	3.68	94	.300	.376	5	.227	0	-1	-1	0	0.0

● JOEY McLAUGHLIN
McLaughlin, Joey Richard b: 7/11/56, Tulsa, Okla. BR/TR, 6'2", 205 lbs. Deb: 6/11/77

YEAR	TM/L	W	L	PCT	G	GS	CG	SH	SV	IP	H	HR	BB	SO	RAT	ERA	ERA+	OAV	OOB	BH	AVG	PB	PR	/A	PD	TPI
1977	Atl-N	0	0	—	3	2	0	0	0	6	10	3	1	0	19.5	15.00	30	.385	.448	0	.000	-0	-7	-7	0	0.0
1979	Atl-N	5	3	.625	37	0	0	0	5	69	54	3	34	40	11.6	2.48	163	.224	.322	2	.182	0	10	12	-1	1.5
1980	Tor-A	6	9	.400	55	10	0	0	4	135^2	159	16	53	70	14.3	4.51	95	.302	.370	0	—	0	-7	-3	-0	-0.6
1981	Tor-A	1	5	.167	40	0	0	0	10	60	55	2	21	38	11.4	2.85	138	.249	.314	0	—	0	5	7	-0	0.8
1982	Tor-A	8	6	.571	44	0	0	0	8	70	54	7	30	49	10.9	3.21	139	.212	.297	0	—	0	7	10	1	1.9
1983	Tor-A	7	4	.636	50	0	0	0	9	64^2	63	11	37	47	13.9	4.45	97	.259	.357	0	—	0	-3	-1	0	-0.2
1984	Tor-A	0	0	—	6	0	0	0	0	10^2	12	0	7	3	16.0	2.53	162	.286	.388	0	—	0	2	2	-0	0.2
	Tex-A	2	1	.667	15	0	0	0	0	32^2	33	4	13	21	12.7	4.41	94	.260	.329	0	—	0	-2	-1	-0	-0.4
	Yr	2	1	.667	21	0	0	0	0	43^1	45	4	20	24	13.5	3.95	105	.265	.342	0	—	0	0	1	-0	-0.6
Total	7	29	28	.509	250	12	0	0	36	448^2	440	46	198	268	12.9	3.85	110	.262	.341	2	.167	-0	5	19	-0	2.8

● JUD McLAUGHLIN McLaughlin, Justin Theodore b: 3/24/12, Brighton, Mass. d: 9/27/64, Cambridge, Mass. BL/TL, 5'11", 155 lbs. Deb: 6/23/31

YEAR	TM/L	W	L	PCT	G	GS	CG	SH	SV	IP	H	HR	BB	SO	RAT	ERA	ERA+	OAV	OOB	BH	AVG	PB	PR	/A	PD	TPI
1931	Bos-A	0	0	—	9	0	0	0	0	12	23	1	8	3	23.3	12.00	36	.397	.470	0	—	0	-10	-10	0	0.0
1932	Bos-A	0	0	—	1	0	0	0	0	3	5	0	4	0	27.0	15.00	30	.385	.529	0	.000	-0	-4	-4	0	0.0
1933	Bos-A	0	0	—	6	0	0	0	0	8^{2}	14	1	5	1	19.7	6.23	70	.359	.432	0	—	0	-2	-2	-0	0.0
Total	3	0	0	—	16	0	0	0	0	23^{2}	42	2	17	4	22.4	10.27	42	.382	.465	0	.000	-0	-16	-16	0	0.0

● BO McLAUGHLIN McLaughlin, Michael Duane b: 10/23/53, Oakland, Cal. BR/TR, 6'5", 210 lbs. Deb: 7/20/76

YEAR	TM/L	W	L	PCT	G	GS	CG	SH	SV	IP	H	HR	BB	SO	RAT	ERA	ERA+	OAV	OOB	BH	AVG	PB	PR	/A	PD	TPI
1976	Hou-N	4	5	.444	17	11	4	2	1	79	71	6	17	32	10.3	2.85	112	.244	.290	0	.000	-1	6	3	0	0.2
1977	Hou-N	4	7	.364	46	6	0	0	5	84^{2}	81	6	34	59	12.9	4.25	84	.260	.344	0	.000	-1	-3	-6	1	-0.8
1978	Hou-N	0	1	.000	12	1	0	0	2	23^{1}	30	2	16	10	18.5	5.01	66	.313	.421	0	.000	-0	-4	-4	-0	-0.3
1979	Hou-N	1	2	.333	12	0	0	0	0	16^{1}	22	2	4	12	14.3	5.51	64	.314	.351	0	.000	-0	-3	-4	-0	-0.6
	Atl-N	1	1	.500	37	1	0	0	0	49^{2}	63	2	16	45	14.7	4.89	83	.303	.358	0	.000	-1	-6	-5	-1	-0.3
	Yr	2	3	.400	49	1	0	0	0	66	85	4	20	57	14.6	5.05	78	.305	.355	0	.000	-1	-10	-8	-1	-0.9
1981	Oak-A	0	0	—	11	0	0	0	1	11^{2}	17	1	9	3	20.8	11.57	30	.333	.443	0	—	0	-10	-10	-0	-0.1
1982	Oak-A	0	4	.000	21	2	1	0	0	48^{1}	51	3	27	27	14.7	4.84	81	.267	.361	0	—	0	-4	-5	0	-0.2
Total	6	10	20	.333	156	21	5	2	9	313	335	22	123	188	13.6	4.49	80	.275	.348	0	.000	-3	-25	-32	0	-2.1

● PAT McLAUGHLIN McLaughlin, Patrick Elmer b: 8/17/10, Taylor, Tex. BR/TR, 6'2", 175 lbs. Deb: 4/25/37

YEAR	TM/L	W	L	PCT	G	GS	CG	SH	SV	IP	H	HR	BB	SO	RAT	ERA	ERA+	OAV	OOB	BH	AVG	PB	PR	/A	PD	TPI
1937	Det-A	0	2	.000	10	3	0	0	0	32^{2}	39	3	16	8	15.2	6.34	74	.291	.367	1	.100	-1	-6	-6	-1	-0.4
1940	Phi-A	0	0	—	1	0	0	0	0	1^{2}	4	1	1	0	27.0	16.20	27	.444	.500	0	—	0	-2	-2	0	0.0
1945	Det-A	0	0	—	1	0	0	0	0	1	2	0	0	0	18.0	9.00	39	.400	.400	0	—	0	-1	-1	-0	0.0
Total	3	0	2	.000	12	3	0	0	0	35^{1}	45	4	17	8	15.8	6.88	67	.304	.376	1	.100	-1	-9	-9	-1	-0.4

● WARREN McLAUGHLIN McLaughlin, Warren A. b: 1/22/1876, N.Plainfield, N.J. d: 10/22/23, Plainfield, N.J. TL , Deb: 7/7/00

YEAR	TM/L	W	L	PCT	G	GS	CG	SH	SV	IP	H	HR	BB	SO	RAT	ERA	ERA+	OAV	OOB	BH	AVG	PB	PR	/A	PD	TPI
1900	Phi-N	0	0	—	1	0	0	0	0	6	4	0	6	1	15.0	4.50	80	.190	.370	1	.500	1	-1	-1	0	0.1
1902	Pit-N	3	0	1.000	3	3	3	0	0	26	27	0	9	13	12.8	2.77	99	.267	.333	4	.364	1	0	-0	-1	0.0
1903	Phi-N	0	3	.000	3	2	2	0	0	23	38	0	11	3	19.6	7.04	46	.376	.442	2	.200	0	-10	-10	-1	-1.0
Total	3	3	3	.500	7	5	5	0	0	55	69	0	26	17	15.9	4.75	64	.309	.386	7	.304	2	-10	-10	-2	-0.9

● AL McLEAN McLean, Albert Eldon "Elrod" b: 9/20/12, Chicago, Ill. d: 9/29/90, Asheboro, N.C. BR/TR, 6', 175 lbs. Deb: 7/16/35

YEAR	TM/L	W	L	PCT	G	GS	CG	SH	SV	IP	H	HR	BB	SO	RAT	ERA	ERA+	OAV	OOB	BH	AVG	PB	PR	/A	PD	TPI
1935	Was-A	0	0	—	4	0	0	0	0	8^{2}	12	0	5	3	17.7	7.27	59	.324	.405	0	.000	-0	-3	-3	-0	-0.1

● WAYNE McLELAND McLeland, Wayne Gaffney "Nubbin" b: 8/29/24, Milton, Iowa BR/TR, 6', 180 lbs. Deb: 4/20/51

YEAR	TM/L	W	L	PCT	G	GS	CG	SH	SV	IP	H	HR	BB	SO	RAT	ERA	ERA+	OAV	OOB	BH	AVG	PB	PR	/A	PD	TPI
1951	Det-A	0	1	.000	6	1	0	0	0	11	20	1	4	0	20.5	8.18	51	.400	.455	0	.000	-0	-5	-5	0	-0.4
1952	Det-A	0	0	—	4	0	0	0	0	2^{2}	4	0	6	0	33.8	10.13	38	.444	.667	0	—	0	-2	-2	-0	0.0
Total	2	0	1	.000	10	1	0	0	0	13^{2}	24	1	10	0	23.0	8.56	48	.407	.500	0	.000	-0	-7	-7	0	-0.4

● CAL McLISH McLish, Calvin Coolidge Julius Caesar Tuskahoma "Buster" b: 12/1/25, Anadarko, Okla. BB/TR, 6'1", 200 lbs. Deb: 5/13/44 C

YEAR	TM/L	W	L	PCT	G	GS	CG	SH	SV	IP	H	HR	BB	SO	RAT	ERA	ERA+	OAV	OOB	BH	AVG	PB	PR	/A	PD	TPI
1944	Bro-N	3	10	.231	23	13	3	0	0	84	110	10	48	24	17.0	7.82	45	.321	.406	7	.219	0	-39	-40	-2	-5.1
1946	Bro-N	0	0	—	1	0	0	0	0	0	1	0	0	0	—	∞	—	1.000	1.000	0	—	0	-2	-2	0	-0.2
1947	Pit-N	0	0	—	1	0	0	0	0	1	2	0	0	0	27.0	18.00	23	.400	.500	0	—	0	-2	-2	0	0.0
1948	Pit-N	0	0	—	2	1	0	0	0	5	8	0	2	1	18.0	9.00	45	.400	.455	0	.000	-0	-3	-3	0	0.0
1949	Chi-N	1	1	.500	8	2	0	0	0	23	31	5	12	6	16.8	5.87	69	.341	.417	3	.333	2	-5	-5	1	-0.2
1951	Chi-N	4	10	.286	30	17	5	1	0	145^{2}	159	16	52	46	13.2	4.45	92	.283	.347	5	.119	-1	-8	-6	-0	-0.6
1956	Cle-A	2	4	.333	37	2	0	0	1	61^{2}	67	5	32	27	14.4	4.96	85	.282	.367	1	.111	1	-6	-5	1	-0.2
1957	Cle-A	9	7	.563	42	7	2	0	1	144^{1}	118	11	67	88	11.7	2.74	135	.220	.309	8	.186	3	17	16	1	2.1
1958	Cle-A	16	8	.667	39	30	13	0	1	225^{2}	214	25	70	97	11.4	2.99	122	.251	.309	6	.094	-1	19	16	0	1.6
1959	Cle-A★	19	8	.704	35	32	13	0	1	235^{1}	253	26	72	113	12.6	3.63	101	.270	.326	14	.189	1	6	1	3	0.6
1960	Cin-N	4	14	.222	37	21	2	1	0	151^{1}	170	16	48	56	13.4	4.16	92	.287	.348	2	.049	-3	-7	-6	1	-0.9
1961	Chi-A	10	13	.435	31	27	4	0	1	162^{1}	178	21	47	80	12.5	4.38	89	.280	.330	9	.167	-1	-6	-8	2	-1.0
1962	Phi-N	11	5	.688	32	24	5	1	1	154^{2}	184	15	45	71	13.4	4.25	91	.293	.343	4	.078	-2	-5	-6	-1	-0.8
1963	Phi-N	13	11	.542	32	32	10	2	0	209^{2}	184	14	56	98	10.5	3.26	99	.239	.294	14	.203	4	1	-1	2	0.5
1964	Phi-N	0	1	.000	2	1	0	0	0	5^{1}	6	0	1	6	11.8	3.38	103	.261	.292	0	.000	0	0	0	0	0.0
Total	15	92	92	.500	352	209	57	5	6	1609	1685	164	552	713	12.7	4.01	93	.270	.332	73	.149	4	-39	-50	9	-4.2

● SAM McMACKIN McMackin, Samuel b: 1872, Cleveland, Ohio d: 2/11/03, Columbus, Ohio BR/TL, Deb: 9/4/02

YEAR	TM/L	W	L	PCT	G	GS	CG	SH	SV	IP	H	HR	BB	SO	RAT	ERA	ERA+	OAV	OOB	BH	AVG	PB	PR	/A	PD	TPI
1902	Chi-A	0	0	—	1	0	0	0	0	3	1	0	0	2	3.0	0.00	—	.100	.100	0	.000	-0	1	1	0	0.0
	Det-A	0	1	.000	1	1	1	0	0	8^{1}	9	0	4	2	15.1	3.24	113	.273	.368	2	.500	1	0	0	0	0.1
	Yr	0	1	.000	2	1	1	0	0	11^{1}	10	0	4	4	11.9	2.38	150	.233	.313	2	.400	0	2	2	1	0.1

● JACK McMAHAN McMahan, Jack Wally b: 7/22/32, Hot Springs, Ark. BR/TL, 6', 175 lbs. Deb: 4/18/56

YEAR	TM/L	W	L	PCT	G	GS	CG	SH	SV	IP	H	HR	BB	SO	RAT	ERA	ERA+	OAV	OOB	BH	AVG	PB	PR	/A	PD	TPI
1956	Pit-N	0	0	—	11	0	0	0	0	13^{1}	18	1	9	9	18.2	6.08	62	.340	.435	0	.000	-0	-3	-3	0	0.0
	KC-A	0	5	.000	23	9	0	0	0	61^{2}	69	7	31	13	14.9	4.82	90	.290	.376	0	.000	-2	-5	-3	0	-0.5
Total	1	0	5	.000	34	9	0	0	0	75	87	8	40	22	15.5	5.04	84	.299	.387	0	.000	-2	-8	-7	0	-0.5

● DON McMAHON McMahon, Donald John b: 1/4/30, Brooklyn, N.Y. d: 7/22/87, Los Angeles, Cal. BR/TR, 6'2", 222 lbs. Deb: 6/30/57 C

YEAR	TM/L	W	L	PCT	G	GS	CG	SH	SV	IP	H	HR	BB	SO	RAT	ERA	ERA+	OAV	OOB	BH	AVG	PB	PR	/A	PD	TPI
1957	*Mil-N	2	3	.400	32	0	0	0	9	46^{2}	33	0	29	46	12.0	1.54	227	.196	.315	2	.250	1	12	10	-0	1.6
1958	*Mil-N☆	7	2	.778	38	0	0	0	8	58^{2}	50	4	29	37	12.4	3.68	96	.235	.332	1	.111	0	2	-1	-0	-0.2
1959	Mil-N	5	3	.625	60	0	0	0	**15**	80^{2}	81	5	37	55	13.3	2.57	138	.259	.339	2	.222	1	12	9	-1	1.1
1960	Mil-N	3	6	.333	48	0	0	0	10	63^{2}	66	9	32	50	14.1	5.94	58	.263	.351	0	.000	-1	-15	-18	0	-3.0
1961	Mil-N	6	4	.600	53	0	0	0	8	92	84	4	51	55	13.4	2.84	132	.249	.351	3	.188	0	12	9	1	1.2
1962	Mil-N	0	1	.000	2	0	0	0	0	3	3	1	0	3	9.0	6.00	63	.250	.250	0	—	0	-1	-1	-0	-0.2
	Hou-N	5	5	.500	51	0	0	0	8	76^{2}	53	4	33	69	10.2	1.53	245	.201	.292	1	.083	-1	21	19	-0	2.6
	Yr	5	6	.455	53	0	0	0	8	79^{2}	56	5	33	72	10.2	1.69	221	.203	.290	1	.083	-1	20	18	-0	2.4
1963	Hou-N	1	5	.167	49	2	0	0	5	80	83	10	26	51	12.3	4.05	78	.270	.327	1	.083	0	-7	-8	-0	-0.7
1964	Cle-A	6	4	.600	70	0	0	0	16	101	67	7	52	92	10.8	2.41	150	.189	.297	2	.143	-0	14	13	-1	1.6
1965	Cle-A	3	3	.500	58	0	0	0	11	85	79	8	37	60	12.4	3.28	106	.248	.329	2	.222	0	2	2	1	0.3
1966	Cle-A	1	1	.500	12	0	0	0	1	12^{1}	8	1	6	5	10.2	2.92	118	.190	.292	0	.000	-0	1	1	-0	0.1
	Bos-A	8	7	.533	49	0	0	0	9	78	65	7	38	57	12.2	2.65	143	.232	.330	1	.091	-0	7	10	-1	2.1
	Yr	9	8	.529	61	0	0	0	10	90^{1}	73	8	44	62	12.0	2.69	140	.226	.324	1	.077	-0	7	11	-1	2.2
1967	Bos-A	1	2	.333	11	0	0	0	2	17^{2}	14	4	13	10	13.8	3.57	98	.215	.346	0	.000	-0	-1	-0	-0	0.0
	Chi-A	5	0	1.000	52	0	0	0	3	91^{2}	54	5	27	74	8.5	1.67	186	.173	.252	2	.182	0	16	15	-0	0.9
	Yr	6	2	.750	63	0	0	0	5	109^{1}	68	9	40	84	9.4	1.98	160	.180	.270	2	.154	-0	15	14	-0	0.9
1968	Chi-A	2	1	.667	25	0	0	0	0	46	31	2	20	32	10.6	1.96	155	.190	.290	1	.333	0	5	5	-1	0.3
	*Det-A	3	1	.750	20	0	0	0	1	35^{2}	22	2	10	33	8.1	2.02	149	.180	.242	0	.000	-0	4	4	-0	0.4
	Yr	5	2	.714	45	0	0	0	1	81^{2}	53	4	30	65	9.1	1.98	152	.183	.259	1	.143	-0	9	9	-1	0.7
1969	Det-A	3	5	.375	34	0	0	0	11	37	25	2	18	38	10.7	3.89	96	.192	.295	0	.000	-1	-1	-1	0	-0.2
	SF-N	3	1	.750	13	0	0	0	2	23^{2}	13	1	9	21	8.4	3.04	115	.157	.239	1	.333	0	1	1	0	0.3
1970	SF-N	9	5	.643	61	0	0	0	19	94^{1}	70	9	45	74	11.2	2.96	134	.202	.297	2	.143	0	11	11	-1	1.9
1971	*SF-N	10	6	.625	61	0	0	0	4	82	73	9	37	71	12.8	4.06	84	.242	.338	0	.000	-1	-5	-6	1	-1.2
1972	SF-N	3	3	.500	44	0	0	0	5	63	46	8	21	45	9.7	3.71	94	.206	.278	1	.250	0	-2	-2	-0	-0.2
1973	SF-N	4	0	1.000	22	0	0	0	6	30^{1}	21	1	7	20	8.3	1.48	257	.189	.237	1	1.000	0	7	8	0	1.4
1974	SF-N	0	0	—	9	0	0	0	0	11^{2}	13	2	2	5	11.6	3.09	123	.283	.313	0	—	0	1	1	-0	0.0
Total	18	90	68	.570	874	2	0	0	153	1310^{2}	1054	105	579	1003	11.4	2.96	119	.221	.310	23	.137	-1	96	83	-1	10.1

● DOC McMAHON McMahon, Henry John b: 12/19/1886, Woburn, Mass. d: 12/11/29, Woburn, Mass. Deb: 10/6/08

YEAR	TM/L	W	L	PCT	G	GS	CG	SH	SV	IP	H	HR	BB	SO	RAT	ERA	ERA+	OAV	OOB	BH	AVG	PB	PR	/A	PD	TPI
1908	Bos-A	1	0	1.000	1	1	1	0	0	9	14	0	0	3	14.0	3.00	82	.350	.350	2	.400	1	-1	-1	-0	0.0

● SADIE McMAHON McMahon, John Joseph b: 9/19/1867, Wilmington, Del. d: 2/20/54, Wilmington, Del BR/TR, 5'9.5", 165 lbs. Deb: 7/5/1889

YEAR	TM/L	W	L	PCT	G	GS	CG	SH	SV	IP	H	HR	BB	SO	RAT	ERA	ERA+	OAV	OOB	BH	AVG	PB	PR	/A	PD	TPI
1889	Phi-a	14	12	.538	28	27	27	2	0	242	230	5	102	117	12.9	3.53	107	.243	.325	16	.154	-6	8	7	4	0.4
1890	Phi-a	29	18	.617	48	46	44	0	1	410	414	5	133	225	12.4	3.34	115	.254	.318	40	.229	3	24	23	9	3.2

YEAR	TM/L	W	L	PCT	G	GS	CG	SH	SV	IP	H	HR	BB	SO	RAT	ERA	ERA+	OAV	OOB	BH	AVG	PB	PR	/A	PD	TPI
	Bal-a	7	3	.700	12	11	11	1	0	99	84	1	33	66	11.2	3.00	135	.223	.296	4	.103	-4	10	12	2	0.8
	Yr	**36**	21	.632	**60**	57	**55**	1	1	**509**	498	6	166	**291**	11.8	3.27	118	.246	.305	44	.206	-1	34	34	11	4.0
1891	Bal-a	**35**	24	.593	61	58	**53**	**5**	1	**503**	493	13	149	219	11.8	2.81	133	.248	.306	43	.205	-3	51	52	5	5.0
1892	Bal-N	19	25	.432	48	46	44	2	1	397	430	9	145	118	13.2	3.24	106	.265	.329	25	.141	-9	2	8	0	0.0
1893	Bal-N	23	18	.561	43	40	35	0	1	346^1	378	6	156	79	14.1	4.37	109	.269	.346	36	.243	-3	12	15	-1	1.0
1894	Bal-N	25	8	.758	35	33	26	0	0	275^2	317	7	111	60	14.3	4.21	130	.285	.355	36	.286	0	34	38	3	3.5
1895	*Bal-N	10	4	.714	15	15	15	**4**	0	122^1	110	1	32	37	10.7	2.94	162	.237	.291	16	.314	1	25	25	-1	2.2
1896	Bal-N	11	9	.550	22	22	19	0	0	175^2	195	4	55	33	13.0	3.48	123	.279	.334	9	.123	-7	17	16	0	0.7
1897	Bro-N	0	6	.000	9	7	5	0	0	63	75	1	29	13	15.3	5.86	70	.293	.372	5	.200	-1	-11	-12	0	-0.9
Total	9	173	127	.577	321	305	279	14	4	2634	2726	52	945	967	12.9	3.51	118	.260	.326	230	.204	-28	172	182	21	15.9

● **JOHN McMAKIN** McMakin, John Weaver "Spartanburg John" b: 3/6/1878, Spartanburg, S.C. d: 9/25/56, Lyman, S.C. BR/TL, 5'11", 165 lbs. Deb: 4/19/02

YEAR	TM/L	W	L	PCT	G	GS	CG	SH	SV	IP	H	HR	BB	SO	RAT	ERA	ERA+	OAV	OOB	BH	AVG	PB	PR	/A	PD	TPI
1902	Bro-N	2	2	.500	4	4	4	0	0	32	34	0	11	6	13.2	3.09	89	.272	.341	2	.182	1	-1	-1	-0	-0.1

● **JOE McMANUS** McManus, Joab Logan b: 9/7/1887, Palmyra, Ill. d: 12/23/55, Beckley, W.Va. BR/TR, 5'11", 180 lbs. Deb: 4/12/13

YEAR	TM/L	W	L	PCT	G	GS	CG	SH	SV	IP	H	HR	BB	SO	RAT	ERA	ERA+	OAV	OOB	BH	AVG	PB	PR	/A	PD	TPI
1913	Cin-N	0	0	—	1	0	0	0	0	2	3	0	4	1	31.5	18.00	18	.375	.583	0	—	0	-3	-3	0	0.0

● **PAT McMANUS** McManus, Patrick b: Ireland d: 10/6/17, Brooklyn, N.Y. Deb: 5/22/1879

YEAR	TM/L	W	L	PCT	G	GS	CG	SH	SV	IP	H	HR	BB	SO	RAT	ERA	ERA+	OAV	OOB	BH	AVG	PB	PR	/A	PD	TPI
1879	Tro-N	0	2	.000	2	2	2	0	0	21	24	1	1	6	10.7	3.00	83	.258	.266	1	.125	-1	-1	-1	0	-0.1

● **GREG McMICHAEL** McMichael, Gregory Winston b: 12/1/66, Knoxville, Tenn. BR/TR, 6'3", 215 lbs. Deb: 4/12/93

YEAR	TM/L	W	L	PCT	G	GS	CG	SH	SV	IP	H	HR	BB	SO	RAT	ERA	ERA+	OAV	OOB	BH	AVG	PB	PR	/A	PD	TPI
1993	*Atl-N	2	3	.400	74	0	0	0	19	91^2	68	3	29	89	9.5	2.06	195	.206	.270	0	.000	-0	20	20	2	1.8
1994	Atl-N	4	6	.400	51	0	0	0	21	58^2	66	1	19	47	13.0	3.84	111	.280	.333	0	.000	-0	2	3	-1	0.5
1995	*Atl-N	7	2	.778	67	0	0	0	2	80^2	64	8	32	74	10.7	2.79	153	.213	.289	0	.000	-0	12	13	-1	1.2
1996	*Atl-N	5	3	.625	73	0	0	0	2	86^2	84	4	27	78	11.6	3.22	137	.253	.311	0	—	0	10	11	1	1.1
1997	NY-N	7	10	.412	73	0	0	0	7	87^2	73	8	27	81	10.5	2.98	135	.233	.298	2	.667	1	12	10	1	2.1
1998	NY-N	1	2	.333	22	0	0	0	0	22^2	23	1	14	22	15.1	3.97	105	.271	.380	0	—	0	1	0	1	0.1
	LA-N	0	1	.000	12	0	0	0	1	14^1	17	1	6	11	15.1	4.40	89	.309	.387	0	—	0	-0	-1	1	0.0
	NY-N	4	1	.800	30	0	0	0	1	31	41	7	15	22	16.8	4.06	103	.318	.397	0	.000	-0	1	0	-1	0.0
	Yr	5	4	.556	64	0	0	0	2	68	81	9	35	55	15.6	4.10	100	.298	.382	0	.000	-0	1	0	1	0.1
Total	6	30	28	.517	402	0	0	0	53	473^1	436	33	169	424	11.6	3.08	135	.245	.313	2	.133	-0	58	57	2	6.8

● **GEORGE McMULLEN** McMullen, George b: California Deb: 7/2/1887

YEAR	TM/L	W	L	PCT	G	GS	CG	SH	SV	IP	H	HR	BB	SO	RAT	ERA	ERA+	OAV	OOB	BH	AVG	PB	PR	/A	PD	TPI
1887	NY-a	2	1	.667	3	3	2	0	0	21	25	2	19	2	18.9	7.71	55	.269	.393	1	.083	-2	-8	-8	0	-0.8

● **JOHN McMULLIN** McMullin, John F. "Lefty" b: 1848, Philadelphia, Pa. d: 4/11/1881, Philadelphia, Pa. BR/TL, 5'9", 160 lbs. Deb: 5/9/1871 ♦

YEAR	TM/L	W	L	PCT	G	GS	CG	SH	SV	IP	H	HR	BB	SO	RAT	ERA	ERA+	OAV	OOB	BH	AVG	PB	PR	/A	PD	TPI
1871	Tro-n	12	15	.444	29	29	28	0	0	249	430	4	75	12	18.3	5.53	76	.342	.379	38	.279	1	-36	-36		-2.0
1872	Mut-n	1	0	1.000	3	1	1	0	1	15	18	0	2	1	12.0	3.60	94	.247	.267	61	.257	0	0	-0		0.0
1873	Ath-n	1	0	1.000	1	1	1	0	0	8	10	0	1	2	12.4	2.25	152	.303	.324	62	.273	0	1	1		0.1
1875	Phi-n	0	0	—	4	0	0	0	0	11^1	32	0	1	0	26.2	7.94	29	.464	.471	57	.257	1	-7	-7		0.0
Total	4 n	14	15	.483	37	31	30	0	1	283^1	490	4	79	15	18.1	5.43	42	.342	.376	308	.285	2	-101	-99		-1.9

● **CRAIG McMURTRY** McMurtry, Joe Craig b: 11/5/59, Troy, Tex. BR/TR, 6'5", 195 lbs. Deb: 4/10/83

YEAR	TM/L	W	L	PCT	G	GS	CG	SH	SV	IP	H	HR	BB	SO	RAT	ERA	ERA+	OAV	OOB	BH	AVG	PB	PR	/A	PD	TPI
1983	Atl-N	15	9	.625	36	35	6	3	0	224^2	204	13	88	105	11.7	3.08	126	.243	.315	6	.086	-4	14	20	3	2.0
1984	Atl-N	9	17	.346	37	30	0	0	0	183^1	184	16	102	99	14.1	4.32	89	.268	.363	6	.115	-1	-15	-10	4	-1.0
1985	Atl-N	0	3	.000	17	6	0	0	1	45	56	6	27	28	16.8	6.60	58	.306	.398	1	.071	-1	-15	-14	1	-0.9
1986	Atl-N	1	6	.143	37	5	0	0	0	79^2	82	7	43	50	14.3	4.74	84	.265	.359	2	.125	-0	-9	-7	0	-0.6
1988	Tex-A	3	3	.500	32	0	0	0	3	60	37	5	24	35	9.3	2.25	181	.180	.270	0	—	0	11	12	1	1.3
1989	Tex-A	0	0	—	19	0	0	0	0	23	29	3	13	14	17.2	7.43	53	.312	.407	0	—	0	-9	-9	0	0.0
1990	Tex-A	0	3	.000	23	3	0	0	0	41^2	43	4	30	14	16.0	4.32	91	.281	.402	0	—	0	-2	-2	1	-0.1
1995	Hou-N	0	1	.000	11	0	0	0	0	10^1	15	0	9	4	21.8	7.84	49	.357	.481	0	.000	-0	-4	-5	0	-0.4
Total	8	28	42	.400	212	79	6	3	4	667^2	650	54	336	349	13.4	4.08	96	.259	.348	15	.098	-6	-29	-13	10	0.3

● **EDGAR McNABB** McNabb, Edgar J. "Texas" b: 10/24/1865, Coshocton, Ohio d: 2/28/1894, Pittsburgh, Pa. BR/TR, 5'11.5", 170 lbs. Deb: 5/12/1893

YEAR	TM/L	W	L	PCT	G	GS	CG	SH	SV	IP	H	HR	BB	SO	RAT	ERA	ERA+	OAV	OOB	BH	AVG	PB	PR	/A	PD	TPI
1893	Bal-N	8	7	.533	21	14	12	0	0	142	167	5	53	18	14.5	4.12	115	.284	.352	13	.194	-2	9	10	0	0.6

● **DAVE McNALLY** McNally, David Arthur b: 10/31/42, Billings, Mont. BR/TL, 5'11", 190 lbs. Deb: 9/26/62

YEAR	TM/L	W	L	PCT	G	GS	CG	SH	SV	IP	H	HR	BB	SO	RAT	ERA	ERA+	OAV	OOB	BH	AVG	PB	PR	/A	PD	TPI
1962	Bal-A	1	0	1.000	1	1	1	1	0	9	2	0	3	4	5.0	0.00	—	.071	.161	0	.000	-0	4	4	0	0.4
1963	Bal-A	7	8	.467	29	20	2	0	1	125^2	133	9	55	78	13.8	4.58	76	.276	.356	2	.053	-2	-13	-15	-1	-2.0
1964	Bal-A	9	11	.450	30	23	5	3	0	159^1	157	15	51	88	12.3	3.67	97	.260	.327	7	.137	0	-1	-2	0	-0.2
1965	Bal-A	11	6	.647	35	29	6	2	0	198^2	163	15	73	116	11.0	2.85	122	.222	.298	6	.092	-3	13	14	0	0.9
1966	*Bal-A	13	6	.684	34	33	5	1	0	213	212	22	64	158	11.8	3.17	105	.256	.313	15	.195	3	6	4	0	0.6
1967	Bal-A	7	7	.500	24	22	3	1	0	119	134	13	39	70	13.2	4.54	69	.295	.354	6	.158	0	-17	-18	-2	-2.2
1968	Bal-A	22	10	.688	35	35	18	5	0	273	175	24	55	202	**7.9**	1.95	150	.182	.234	11	.128	4	31	30	-3	3.9
1969	*Bal-A★	20	7	.741	41	40	11	4	0	268^2	232	21	84	166	10.8	3.22	111	.234	.297	8	.085	-2	12	10	-4	0.4
1970	*Bal-A☆	**24**	9	.727	40	40	16	1	0	296	277	29	78	185	11.0	3.22	113	.250	.304	14	.133	4	16	14	-2	1.6
1971	*Bal-A	21	5	**.808**	30	30	11	1	0	224^1	188	24	58	91	10.1	2.89	116	.229	.284	12	.162	3	14	12	-0	1.6
1972	Bal-A★	13	17	.433	36	36	12	6	0	241	220	15	68	120	10.8	2.95	104	.247	.302	12	.152	2	3	3	1	0.7
1973	*Bal-A	17	17	.500	38	38	17	4	0	266	247	16	81	87	11.3	3.21	116	.251	.312	0	—	0	18	15	1	2.0
1974	*Bal-A	16	10	.615	39	37	13	4	1	259	260	19	81	111	12.1	3.58	96	.270	.331	0	—	0	1	-4	2	-0.1
1975	Mon-N	3	6	.333	12	12	0	0	0	77^1	88	8	36	36	14.9	5.24	73	.280	.362	4	.190	2	-14	-12	-1	-1.1
Total	14	184	119	.607	424	396	120	33	2	2730	2488	230	826	1512	11.2	3.24	106	.245	.306	97	.133	10	74	54	-8	6.5

● **TIM McNAMARA** McNamara, Timothy Augustine b: 11/20/1898, Millville, Mass. d: 11/5/94, N.Smithfield, R.I. BR/TR, 5'11", 170 lbs. Deb: 4/27/22

YEAR	TM/L	W	L	PCT	G	GS	CG	SH	SV	IP	H	HR	BB	SO	RAT	ERA	ERA+	OAV	OOB	BH	AVG	PB	PR	/A	PD	TPI
1922	Bos-N	3	4	.429	24	5	4	2	0	70^2	55	2	26	16	10.4	2.42	165	.225	.303	2	.118	-1	**13**	**12**	-0	1.0
1923	Bos-N	3	13	.188	32	16	3	0	0	139^1	185	8	29	32	14.1	4.91	81	.320	.357	7	.179	1	-14	-14	-2	-1.5
1924	Bos-N	8	12	.400	35	21	6	2	0	179	242	9	31	35	13.9	5.18	74	.334	.364	6	.140	-1	-26	-27	1	-2.6
1925	Bos-N	0	0	—	1	0	0	0	0	0^2	6	0	2	1	108.0	81.00	5	.857	.889	0	—	0	-6	-6	0	0.0
1926	NY-N	0	0	—	6	0	0	0	0	6	7	0	4	4	16.5	9.00	42	.304	.407	0	—	0	-3	-3	0	0.0
Total	5	14	29	.326	98	42	13	4	0	395^2	495	19	92	88	13.6	4.78	82	.314	.355	15	.152	-1	-36	-38	-2	-3.1

● **GORDON McNAUGHTON** McNaughton, Gordon Joseph b: 7/31/10, Chicago, Ill. d: 8/6/42, Chicago, Ill. BR/TR, 6'1", 190 lbs. Deb: 8/13/32

YEAR	TM/L	W	L	PCT	G	GS	CG	SH	SV	IP	H	HR	BB	SO	RAT	ERA	ERA+	OAV	OOB	BH	AVG	PB	PR	/A	PD	TPI
1932	Bos-A	0	1	.000	6	2	0	0	0	21	21	1	22	6	19.7	6.43	70	.259	.434	2	.250	0	-5	-5	1	-0.1

● **HARRY McNEAL** McNeal, John Harley b: 8/13/1878, Iberia, Ohio d: 1/11/45, Cleveland, Ohio BL/TR, 6'2", 175 lbs. Deb: 8/5/01

YEAR	TM/L	W	L	PCT	G	GS	CG	SH	SV	IP	H	HR	BB	SO	RAT	ERA	ERA+	OAV	OOB	BH	AVG	PB	PR	/A	PD	TPI
1901	Cle-A	5	5	.500	12	10	9	0	0	85^1	120	4	30	15	16.7	4.43	80	.328	.391	6	.162	-2	-7	-8	-2	-1.1

● **ED McNICHOL** McNichol, Edwin Briggs b: 1/10/1879, Martins Ferry, O. d: 11/1/52, Salineville, O. BR/TR, 5'5", 170 lbs. Deb: 7/9/04

YEAR	TM/L	W	L	PCT	G	GS	CG	SH	SV	IP	H	HR	BB	SO	RAT	ERA	ERA+	OAV	OOB	BH	AVG	PB	PR	/A	PD	TPI
1904	Bos-N	2	12	.143	17	15	12	1	0	122	120	3	74	39	14.7	4.28	64	.262	.371	4	.093	-4	-21	-21	-2	-2.6

● **FRANK McPARTLIN** McPartlin, Frank b: 2/16/1872, Hoosick Falls, N.Y d: 11/13/43, New York, N.Y. TR, 6', 180 lbs. Deb: 8/22/1899

YEAR	TM/L	W	L	PCT	G	GS	CG	SH	SV	IP	H	HR	BB	SO	RAT	ERA	ERA+	OAV	OOB	BH	AVG	PB	PR	/A	PD	TPI
1899	NY-N	0	0	—	1	0	0	0	0	4	4	0	3	2	20.3	4.50	83	.267	.450	0	.000	-0	-0	-0	0	0.0

● **JOHN McPHERSON** McPherson, John Jacob b: 3/9/1869, Easton, Pa. d: 9/30/41, Easton, Pa. TR, Deb: 7/12/01

YEAR	TM/L	W	L	PCT	G	GS	CG	SH	SV	IP	H	HR	BB	SO	RAT	ERA	ERA+	OAV	OOB	BH	AVG	PB	PR	/A	PD	TPI
1901	Phi-A	0	1	.000	1	1	0	0	0	4	7	0	4	0	27.0	11.25	34	.368	.500	0	.000	-0	-3	-3	0	-0.5
1904	Phi-N	1	12	.077	15	12	11	1	0	128	130	1	46	32	12.8	3.66	73	.264	.334	3	.064	-4	-13	-14	0	-1.6
Total	2	1	13	.071	16	13	11	1	0	132	137	1	50	32	13.2	3.89	70	.268	.341	3	.063	-4	-16	-17	1	-2.1

● **HERB McQUAID** McQuaid, Herbert George b: 3/29/1899, San Francisco, Cal d: 4/4/66, Richmond, Cal. BR/TR, 6'2", 185 lbs. Deb: 6/22/23

YEAR	TM/L	W	L	PCT	G	GS	CG	SH	SV	IP	H	HR	BB	SO	RAT	ERA	ERA+	OAV	OOB	BH	AVG	PB	PR	/A	PD	TPI
1923	Cin-N	1	0	1.000	12	1	0	0	0	34^1	31	0	10	9	11.5	2.36	164	.238	.308	0	.000	-1	6	6	1	0.1
1926	NY-A	1	0	1.000	17	1	0	0	0	38^1	48	5	13	6	14.8	6.10	63	.329	.391	0	.000	-1	-9	-10	0	-0.3
Total	2	2	0	1.000	29	2	0	0	0	72^2	79	5	23	15	13.3	4.33	89	.286	.352	0	.000	-2	-3	-4	1	-0.2

YEAR TM/L	W	L	PCT	G	GS	CG	SH	SV	IP	H	HR	BB	SO	RAT	ERA	ERA+	OAV	OOB	BH	AVG	PB	PR	/A	PD	TPI
● **MIKE McQUEEN**	McQueen, Michael Robert b: 8/30/50, Oklahoma City, Okla BL/TL, 5'11", 190 lbs. Deb: 10/2/69																								
1969 Atl-N	0	0	—	1	1	0	0	0	3	2	0	3	3	15.0	3.00	120	.182	.357	0	—	0	0	0	-0	0.0
1970 Atl-N	1	5	.167	22	8	1	0	1	66	67	10	31	54	13.5	5.59	77	.266	.349	6	.300	2	-11	-10	-1	-0.7
1971 Atl-N	4	1	.800	17	3	0	0	1	56	47	7	23	38	11.6	3.54	105	.228	.312	4	.211	0	-0	1	-1	0.0
1972 Atl-N	0	5	.000	23	7	1	0	1	78^1	79	11	44	40	14.2	4.60	82	.260	.355	2	.087	-2	-10	-7	-1	-0.7
1974 Cin-N	0	0	—	10	0	0	0	0	15	17	4	11	5	16.8	5.40	65	.288	.400	1	1.000	0	-3	-3	-1	0.0
Total 5	5	11	.313	73	19	2	0	3	218^1	212	32	112	140	13.5	4.66	84	.255	.346	13	.206	1	-24	-18	-4	-1.4
● **GEORGE McQUILLAN**	McQuillan, George Watt b: 5/1/1885, Brooklyn, N.Y. d: 3/30/40, Columbus, Ohio BR/TR, 5'11.5", 175 lbs. Deb: 5/8/07																								
1907 Phi-N	4	0	1.000	6	5	5	3	0	41	21	0	11	28	7.2	0.66	368	.158	.228	4	.364	3	8	8	-2	1.1
1908 Phi-N	23	17	.575	48	42	32	7	2	359^2	263	1	91	114	9.0	1.53	159	.207	.263	18	.151	-1	33	36	-3	3.9
1909 Phi-N	13	16	.448	41	28	16	4	2	247^2	202	5	54	96	9.3	2.14	121	.226	.271	9	.118	-3	12	12	-2	0.8
1910 Phi-N	9	6	.600	24	17	13	3	1	152^1	109	2	50	71	9.6	**1.60**	196	.204	.276	7	.149	-1	24	26	-0	2.4
1911 Cin-N	2	6	.250	19	5	2	0	0	77	92	2	31	28	14.8	4.68	71	.308	.380	2	.091	-1	-11	-12	-1	-1.3
1913 Pit-N	8	6	.571	25	16	7	0	1	141^2	144	1	35	59	11.4	3.43	88	.273	.319	4	.103	-1	-4	-6	-1	-0.8
1914 Pit-N	13	17	.433	45	28	15	0	4	259^1	248	8	60	96	11.0	2.98	89	.261	.310	5	.068	-4	-6	-10	0	-1.5
1915 Pit-N	8	10	.444	30	20	9	0	1	149	160	1	39	56	12.1	2.84	96	.284	.332	4	.091	-3	-1	-2	0	-0.5
Phi-N	4	3	.571	9	8	5	0	0	63^2	60	1	11	13	10.2	2.12	129	.247	.282	1	.043	-2	4	4	-1	0.2
Yr	12	13	.480	39	28	14	0	1	212^2	220	2	50	69	11.5	2.62	104	.272	.315	5	.075	-5	3	3	-1	-0.3
1916 Phi-N	1	7	.125	21	3	1	0	2	62	58	2	15	22	11.0	2.76	96	.251	.305	1	.091	-1	-1	-1	-0	-0.2
1918 Cle-A	0	1	.000	5	1	0	0	1	23	25	0	4	7	11.3	2.35	128	.284	.315	0	.000	-0	1	2	0	0.1
Total 10	85	89	.489	273	173	105	17	14	1576^1	1382	23	401	590	10.4	2.38	114	.241	.294	55	.117	-14	62	59	-9	4.2
● **HUGH McQUILLAN**	McQuillan, Hugh A. "Handsome Hugh" b: 9/15/1897, New York, N.Y. d: 8/26/47, New York, N.Y. BR/TR, 6', 170 lbs. Deb: 7/26/18																								
1918 Bos-N	1	0	1.000	1	1	1	0	0	9	7	0	5	1	12.0	3.00	90	.219	.324	1	.250	0	-0	-0	0	0.0
1919 Bos-N	2	3	.400	16	7	2	0	1	60	66	3	14	13	12.2	3.45	83	.288	.332	4	.222	0	-4	-4	-1	-0.4
1920 Bos-N	11	15	.423	38	26	17	1	5	225^2	230	3	70	53	12.0	3.55	86	.273	.330	19	.257	6	-10	-13	2	-0.6
1921 Bos-N	13	17	.433	45	31	13	2	5	250	284	9	90	94	13.5	4.00	91	.291	.352	18	.205	1	-6	-10	0	-0.9
1922 Bos-N	5	10	.333	28	17	7	0	0	136	154	3	56	33	14.0	4.24	94	.299	.369	7	.167	-1	-2	-4	1	-0.4
*NY-N	6	5	.545	15	13	5	0	1	94^1	111	7	34	24	13.8	3.82	105	.301	.360	7	.189	-1	3	2	-1	0.0
Yr	11	15	.423	43	30	12	0	1	230^1	265	10	90	57	13.9	4.06	98	.299	.364	14	.177	-2	1	-2	-0	-0.4
1923 *NY-N	15	14	.517	38	32	15	5	0	229^2	224	12	66	75	11.6	3.41	112	.259	.315	14	.171	-2	15	11	-1	0.8
1924 *NY-N	14	8	.636	27	23	14	1	3	184	179	8	43	49	11.0	2.69	136	.259	.304	14	.209	-1	24	20	-2	2.0
1925 NY-N	2	3	.400	14	11	2	0	1	70	95	9	23	23	15.3	6.04	67	.343	.395	3	.143	-1	-14	-16	1	-0.9
1926 NY-N	11	10	.524	33	22	12	1	0	167	171	7	42	47	11.5	3.72	101	.271	.318	7	.132	-3	2	1	2	0.0
1927 NY-N	5	4	.556	11	9	5	0	0	58	73	4	22	17	14.9	4.50	86	.309	.371	4	.211	1	-4	-4	0	-0.5
Bos-N	3	5	.375	13	12	2	0	0	78	109	2	24	17	15.6	5.54	67	.332	.381	5	.227	0	-14	-16	0	-1.3
Yr	8	9	.471	24	21	7	0	0	136	182	6	46	34	15.2	5.10	74	.322	.375	9	.220	1	-18	-20	1	-1.8
Total 10	88	94	.484	279	204	95	10	16	1561^2	1703	67	489	446	12.7	3.83	95	.284	.340	103	.195	0	-10	-32	1	-2.2
● **NORM McRAE**	McRae, Norman b: 9/26/47, Elizabeth, N.J. BR/TR, 6'1", 195 lbs. Deb: 9/13/69																								
1969 Det-A	0	0	—	3	0	0	0	0	3	2	0	1	3	9.0	6.00	62	.200	.273	0	—	0	-1	-1	-0	0.0
1970 Det-A	0	0	—	19	0	0	0	0	31^1	26	1	25	16	14.9	2.87	130	.226	.369	0	.000	-0	3	3	1	0.0
Total 2	0	0	—	22	0	0	0	0	34^1	28	1	26	19	14.4	3.15	118	.224	.362	0	.000	-0	2	2	0	0.0
● **TRICK McSORLEY**	McSorley, John Bernard b: 12/6/1852, St.Louis, Mo. d: 2/9/36, St.Louis, Mo. BR/TR, 5'4", 142 lbs. Deb: 5/6/1875 ♦																								
1884 Tol-a	0	0	—	1	0	0	0	0	2	5	0	0	1	22.5	4.50	76	.556	.556	17	.250	0	-0	-0	-0	0.0
● **BILL McTIGUE**	McTigue, William Patrick "Rebel" b: 1/3/1891, Nashville, Tenn. d: 5/8/20, Nashville, Tenn. BL/TL, 6'1.5", 175 lbs. Deb: 5/2/11 ♦																								
1911 Bos-N	0	5	.000	14	8	0	0	0	37	37	3	49	23	21.4	7.05	54	.280	.481	1	.083	-1	-15	-13	-1	-1.7
1912 Bos-N	2	0	1.000	10	1	1	0	0	34^2	39	0	18	17	14.8	5.45	66	.289	.373	1	.077	-1	-8	-7	1	-0.4
1916 Det-A	0	0	—	3	0	0	0	0	5^1	5	0	5	1	16.9	5.06	57	.278	.435	0	.000	-0	-1	-1	0	0.0
Total 3	2	5	.286	27	9	1	0	0	77	81	3	72	41	18.1	6.19	59	.284	.432	2	.077	-2	-24	-22	0	-2.1
● **CAL McVEY**	McVey, Calvin Alexander b: 8/30/1850, Montrose, Iowa d: 8/20/26, San Francisco, Cal BR/TR, 5'9", 170 lbs. Deb: 5/5/1871 M♦																								
1875 Bos-n	1	0	1.000	3	2	0	0	1	11	15	0	1	1	13.1	4.91	44	.294	.308	138	.355	2	-3	-3		-0.2
1876 Chi-N	5	2	.714	11	6	5	0	2	59^1	57	0	2	9	8.9	1.52	161	.235	.241	107	.347	3	5	6	0	0.8
1877 Chi-N	4	8	.333	17	10	6	0	**2**	92	129	2	11	20	13.7	4.50	66	.301	.319	98	.368	6	-17	-16	-1	-1.4
1879 Cin-N	0	2	.000	3	1	1	0	0	14	34	1	2	7	23.1	8.36	28	.453	.468	105	.297	1	-9	-9	0	-0.9
Total 3	9	12	.429	31	17	12	0	4	165^1	220	3	15	36	12.8	3.76	73	.295	.309	393	.328	10	-21	-19	-1	-1.5
● **DOUG McWEENY**	McWeeny, Douglas Lawrence "Buzz" b: 8/17/1896, Chicago, Ill. d: 1/1/53, Melrose Park, Ill. BR/TR, 6'2", 190 lbs. Deb: 4/24/21																								
1921 Chi-A	3	6	.333	27	8	3	0	2	97^2	127	7	45	46	15.8	6.08	70	.325	.394	1	.032	-4	-20	-20	-1	-2.0
1922 Chi-A	0	1	.000	4	1	0	0	0	10^2	13	0	7	5	16.9	5.91	69	.325	.426	0	.000	0	-2	-2	-0	-0.2
1924 Chi-A	1	3	.250	13	5	2	0	0	43^1	47	2	17	18	13.7	4.57	90	.294	.369	0	.000	-0	-2	-2	3	0.1
1926 Bro-N	11	13	.458	42	24	10	1	1	216^1	213	6	84	96	12.7	3.04	126	.258	.333	7	.109	-4	19	19	-1	1.4
1927 Bro-N	4	8	.333	34	22	6	0	1	164^1	167	13	70	73	13.4	3.56	111	.266	.347	2	.043	-4	7	7	1	0.2
1928 Bro-N	14	14	.500	42	32	12	**4**	1	244	218	11	114	79	12.4	3.17	125	.235	.322	14	.173	-1	22	22	3	2.5
1929 Bro-N	4	10	.286	36	24	4	0	1	146	167	17	93	59	16.2	6.10	76	.288	.390	5	.104	-2	-22	-24	-2	-2.2
1930 Cin-N	0	2	.000	8	2	0	0	0	25^2	28	0	20	10	16.8	7.36	66	.283	.403	1	.143	-0	-7	-7	0	-0.4
Total 8	37	57	.394	206	118	37	5	6	948	980	56	450	386	13.8	4.17	98	.269	.353	30	.104	-16	-5	-7	2	-0.6
● **LARRY McWILLIAMS**	McWilliams, Larry Dean b: 2/10/54, Wichita, Kan. BL/TL, 6'5", 180 lbs. Deb: 7/17/78																								
1978 Atl-N	9	3	.750	15	15	3	1	0	99^1	84	11	35	42	11.0	2.81	144	.224	.294	2	.063	-2	8	14	1	1.6
1979 Atl-N	3	2	.600	13	13	1	0	0	66^1	69	4	22	32	12.9	5.56	73	.272	.339	5	.208	1	-13	-11	1	-0.5
1980 Atl-N	9	14	.391	30	30	4	1	0	163^2	188	27	39	77	12.9	4.95	76	.285	.332	8	.157	-0	-25	-22	-0	-2.8
1981 Atl-N	2	1	.667	6	5	2	1	0	37^2	31	2	8	23	9.3	3.11	115	.230	.273	1	.100	-0	2	2	1	0.2
1982 Atl-N	2	3	.400	27	2	0	0	0	37^2	52	3	20	24	17.7	6.21	60	.327	.409	1	.167	0	-11	-10	2	-1.1
Pit-N	6	5	.545	19	18	2	2	1	121^2	106	9	24	94	9.9	3.11	119	.232	.276	6	.188	-0	7	8	2	0.9
Yr	8	8	.500	46	20	2	2	1	159^1	158	12	44	118	11.6	3.84	97	.255	.309	7	.184	-0	-4	-2	4	-0.2
1983 Pit-N	15	8	.652	35	35	8	4	0	238	205	19	87	199	11.2	3.25	114	.230	.300	9	.114	-3	10	12	1	0.9
1984 Pit-N	12	11	.522	34	32	7	2	1	227^1	226	18	78	149	12.1	2.93	123	.263	.326	9	.122	-3	17	17	0	1.3
1985 Pit-N	7	9	.438	30	19	2	0	0	126^1	139	9	62	52	14.8	4.70	76	.283	.371	5	.125	-1	-16	-16	-0	-1.9
1986 Pit-N	3	11	.214	49	15	0	0	0	122^1	129	16	49	80	13.6	5.15	74	.268	.345	4	.138	0	-19	-18	-0	-1.9
1987 Atl-N	0	1	.000	9	2	0	0	0	20^1	25	2	7	13	15.0	5.75	76	.301	.370	1	.200	0	-4	-3	-0	-0.1
1988 StL-N	6	9	.400	42	17	2	1	1	136	130	10	45	70	11.8	3.90	89	.253	.319	6	.162	1	-7	-6	-0	-0.6
1989 Phi-N	2	11	.154	40	16	2	1	0	120^2	123	3	49	54	13.1	4.10	86	.265	.340	3	.111	-1	-8	-7	1	-0.8
KC-A	2	2	.500	8	5	1	0	0	32^2	31	2	8	24	11.6	4.13	93	.254	.316	0	—	0	-1	-1	-0	-0.1
1990 KC-A	0	0	—	13	0	0	0	0	8^1	10	2	9	7	21.6	9.72	39	.313	.476	0	—	0	-5	-5	0	0.1
Total 13	78	90	.464	370	224	34	13	3	1558^1	1548	137	542	940	12.4	3.99	93	.259	.326	60	.135	-8	-66	-48	8	-4.8
● **RUSTY MEACHAM**	Meacham, Russell Loren b: 1/27/68, Stuart, Fla. BR/TR, 6'2", 175 lbs. Deb: 6/29/91																								
1991 Det-A	2	1	.667	10	4	0	0	0	27^2	35	4	11	14	15.0	5.20	80	.315	.377	0	—	0	-3	-3	0	-0.4
1992 KC-A	10	4	.714	64	0	0	0	2	101^2	88	5	21	64	9.7	2.74	148	.233	.275	0	—	0	13	15	2	2.0
1993 KC-A	2	2	.500	15	0	0	0	0	21	31	2	5	13	16.7	5.57	82	.326	.379	0	—	0	-3	-2	0	-0.6
1994 KC-A	3	3	.500	36	0	0	0	4	50^2	51	7	12	36	11.5	3.73	134	.263	.313	0	—	0	6	7	0	0.6
1995 KC-A	4	3	.571	49	0	0	0	2	59^2	72	6	19	30	13.9	4.98	96	.304	.358	0	—	0	-2	-1	0	-0.2
1996 Sea-A	1	1	.500	15	5	0	0	1	42^1	57	9	13	25	15.7	5.74	86	.328	.387	0	—	0	-4	-4	-1	-0.2
Total 6	22	14	.611	189	9	0	0	9	303	334	33	81	182	12.7	4.19	108	.281	.333	0	—	0	8	11	3	1.2

YEAR	TM/L	W	L	PCT	G	GS	CG	SH	SV	IP	H	HR	BB	SO	RAT	ERA	ERA+	OAV	OOB	BH	AVG	PB	PR	/A	PD	TPI
● **JOHNNY MEADOR**	Meador, John Davis b: 12/4/1892, Madison, N.C. d: 4/11/70, Winston-Salem, N.C BR/TR, 5′10.5″, 165 lbs. Deb: 4/24/20																									
1920	Pit-N	0	2	.000	12	2	0	0	0	36^1	48	1	7	5	13.6	4.21	76	.340	.372	1	.167	-0	-4	-4	1	-0.2
● **LEE MEADOWS**	Meadows, Henry Lee "Specs" b: 7/12/1894, Oxford, N.C. d: 1/29/63, Daytona Beach, Fla BL/TR, 6′, 190 lbs. Deb: 4/19/15																									
1915	StL-N	13	11	.542	39	26	14	1	0	244	232	5	88	104	12.0	2.99	93	.259	.329	8	.096	-4	-6	-5	-3	-1.2
1916	StL-N	12	23	.343	**51**	36	11	1	2	289	261	3	119	120	12.3	2.58	102	.247	.332	15	.158	-1	1	2	1	0.2
1917	StL-N	15	9	.625	43	37	18	4	2	265^2	253	5	90	100	11.8	3.08	87	.262	.328	9	.101	-6	-11	-12	-3	-2.0
1918	StL-N	8	14	.364	30	23	12	0	1	165^1	176	1	56	49	13.2	3.59	75	.280	.348	7	.127	-2	-15	-16	-2	-2.5
1919	StL-N	4	10	.286	22	12	3	1	0	92	100	3	30	28	12.9	3.03	92	.292	.352	3	.103	-2	-1	-2	3	-0.3
	Phi-N	8	10	.444	18	17	15	3	0	158^1	128	2	49	88	10.5	2.33	138	.229	.300	6	.118	-3	10	16	-1	1.4
	Yr	12	20	.375	40	29	18	4	0	250^1	228	5	79	116	11.3	2.59	118	.252	.317	9	.112	-5	9	13	2	1.1
1920	Phi-N	16	14	.533	35	33	19	3	0	247	249	5	90	95	12.6	2.84	120	.270	.341	14	.171	-3	8	16	0	1.6
1921	Phi-N	11	16	.407	28	27	15	2	0	194^1	226	10	62	52	13.5	4.31	98	.288	.343	13	.210	2	-11	-2	4	0.4
1922	Phi-N	12	18	.400	33	33	19	2	0	237	264	8	71	62	13.1	4.03	116	.288	.346	27	.314	3	2	17	3	2.6
1923	Phi-N	1	3	.250	8	5	0	0	1	19^2	40	0	15	10	25.2	13.27	35	.430	.509	4	.400	2	-20	-19	0	-2.8
	Pit-N	16	10	.615	31	25	17	1	0	227	250	3	44	66	11.7	3.01	133	.284	.319	22	.250	3	25	25	2	3.1
	Yr	17	13	.567	39	30	17	1	1	246^2	290	3	59	76	12.8	3.83	106	.298	.339	26	.265	5	5	6	2	0.3
1924	Pit-N	13	12	.520	36	30	15	3	0	229^1	240	7	51	61	11.6	3.26	118	.278	.322	16	.195	-1	16	15	-1	1.2
1925	*Pit-N	19	10	.655	35	31	20	1	1	255^1	272	11	67	87	12.2	3.67	122	.273	.323	17	.175	-1	17	23	1	2.2
1926	Pit-N	**20**	9	.690	36	31	15	1	0	226^2	254	10	52	54	12.3	3.97	99	.287	.329	20	.227	-1	-4	-1	3	0.1
1927	*Pit-N	19	10	.655	40	38	**25**	2	0	299^1	315	11	66	84	11.7	3.40	121	.273	.317	18	.157	-5	17	24	-1	1.5
1928	Pit-N	1	1	.500	4	2	1	0	0	10	18	0	5	3	20.7	8.10	50	.383	.442	2	.500	1	-5	-4	-0	-0.7
1929	Pit-N	0	0	—	1	0	0	0	0	0^2	2	0	1	0	40.5	13.50	35	.500	.600	0	.000	-0	-1	-1	-0	0.0
Total	15	188	180	.511	490	406	219	25	7	3160^2	3280	84	956	1063	12.3	3.37	106	.274	.332	201	.180	-19	22	71	6	4.8
● **BRIAN MEADOWS**	Meadows, Matthew Brian b: 11/21/75, Montgomery, Ala. BR/TR, 6′4″, 210 lbs. Deb: 4/4/98																									
1998	Fla-N	11	13	.458	31	31	1	0	0	174^1	222	20	46	88	14.0	5.21	78	.315	.359	7	.130	-1	-19	-22	-1	-2.6
● **RUFUS MEADOWS**	Meadows, Rufus Rivers b: 8/25/07, Chase City, Va. d: 5/10/70, Wichita, Kan. BL/TL, 5′11″, 175 lbs. Deb: 4/23/26																									
1926	Cin-N	0	0	—	1	0	0	0	0	0^1	0	0	0	0	0.0	0.00	—	.000	.000	0	.000	-0	0	0	0	0.0
● **DAVE MEADS**	Meads, David Donald b: 1/7/64, Montclair, N.J. BL/TL, 6′ ", 175 lbs. Deb: 4/13/87																									
1987	Hou-N	5	3	.625	45	0	0	0	0	48^2	60	8	16	32	14.2	5.55	71	.321	.377	1	.333	1	-8	-9	-1	-1.3
1988	Hou-N	3	1	.750	22	2	0	0	0	39^2	37	4	14	27	11.6	3.18	105	.240	.304	1	.250	1	1	1	-0	0.1
Total	2	8	4	.667	67	2	0	0	0	88^1	97	12	30	59	13.0	4.48	81	.284	.344	2	.286	1	-7	-8	-1	-1.2
● **GEORGE MEAKIM**	Meakim, George Clinton b: 7/11/1865, Brooklyn, N.Y. d: 2/17/23, Queens, N.Y. BR/TR, 5′7.5″, 154 lbs. Deb: 5/2/1890																									
1890	*Lou-a	12	7	.632	28	21	16	3	1	192	173	4	63	123	11.3	2.91	132	.233	.298	11	.153	-2	21	20	-1	1.4
1891	Phi-a	1	4	.200	6	6	4	0	0	35	51	1	22	13	19.0	6.94	55	.329	.416	3	.200	0	-13	-12	2	-1.1
1892	Chi-N	0	1	.000	1	1	1	0	0	9	18	0	2	0	20.0	11.00	30	.400	.426	2	.400	0	-8	-8	-0	-0.5
	Cin-N	1	1	.500	3	3	1	0	0	13^2	19	1	9	4	19.8	8.56	38	.317	.423	0	.000	-1	-8	-8	0	-0.9
	Yr	1	2	.333	4	4	2	0	0	22^2	37	1	11	4	19.9	9.53	35	.352	.424	2	.200	-0	-16	-16	-0	-1.4
1895	Lou-N	1	0	1.000	1	1	1	0	0	7	7	0	4	2	14.1	2.57	180	.259	.355	1	.333	0	2	2	0	0.2
Total	4	15	13	.536	39	32	23	3	1	256^2	268	6	100	142	13.2	4.03	95	.260	.331	17	.170	-2	-6	-6	1	-0.9
● **JIM MECIR**	Mecir, James Jason b: 5/16/70, Bayside, N.Y. BB/TR, 6′1″, 195 lbs. Deb: 9/4/95																									
1995	Sea-A	0	0	—	2	0	0	0	0	4^2	5	0	2	3	13.5	0.00	—	.263	.333	0	—	0	2	2	-0	-0.1
1996	NY-A	1	1	.500	26	0	0	0	0	40^1	42	6	23	38	14.5	5.13	96	.275	.369	0	—	0	-1	-1	2	0.1
1997	NY-A	0	4	.000	25	0	0	0	0	33^2	36	5	10	25	12.8	5.88	76	.279	.340	0	—	0	-5	-5	-0	-0.5
1998	TB-A	7	2	.778	68	0	0	0	0	84	68	6	33	77	11.1	3.11	158	.225	.308	0	.000	-0	14	17	2	1.7
Total	4	8	7	.533	121	0	0	0	0	162^2	151	17	68	143	12.4	4.09	118	.250	.331	0	.000	-0	11	13	3	1.2
● **DOC MEDICH**	Medich, George Francis b: 12/9/48, Aliquippa, Pa. BR/TR, 6′5″, 227 lbs. Deb: 9/5/72																									
1972	NY-A	0	0	—	1	1	0	0	0	0	2	0	2	0	—	∞	—	1.000	1.000	0	—	0	-2	-2	0	-0.2
1973	NY-A	14	9	.609	34	32	11	3	0	235	217	20	74	145	11.3	2.95	124	.241	.300	0	—	0	23	19	-2	1.7
1974	NY-A	19	15	.559	38	38	17	4	0	279^2	275	24	91	154	12.0	3.60	98	.259	.323	0	—	0	0	-2	-1	-0.3
1975	NY-A	16	16	.500	38	37	15	2	0	272^1	271	25	72	132	11.4	3.50	105	.264	.313	0	—	0	8	5	-3	0.4
1976	Pit-N	8	11	.421	29	26	3	0	0	179	193	10	48	86	12.2	3.52	99	.281	.330	5	.096	-2	-0	-1	1	-0.1
1977	Oak-A	10	6	.625	26	25	1	0	0	147^2	155	19	49	74	12.6	4.69	86	.265	.325	0	—	0	-10	-11	-1	-1.0
	Sea-A	2	0	1.000	3	3	1	0	0	22^1	26	1	4	3	12.9	3.63	113	.286	.330	0	—	0	1	1	-1	0.1
	Yr	12	6	.667	29	28	2	0	0	170	181	20	53	77	12.5	4.55	89	.265	.319	0	—	0	-9	-10	-2	-0.9
	NY-N	0	1	.000	1	1	0	0	0	7	6	0	1	3	9.0	3.86	97	.261	.292	0	.000	-0	0	-0	-0	-0.1
1978	Tex-A	9	8	.529	28	22	6	2	2	171	166	10	52	71	11.6	3.74	100	.255	.313	0	—	0	0	0	1	0.1
1979	Tex-A	10	7	.588	29	19	4	1	0	149	156	9	49	58	12.6	4.17	100	.269	.330	0	—	0	1	-0	1	0.2
1980	Tex-A	14	11	.560	34	32	6	0	0	204^1	230	13	56	91	12.7	3.92	99	.285	.334	0	—	0	3	-1	-1	-0.2
1981	Tex-A	10	6	.625	20	20	4	**4**	0	143^1	136	8	33	65	10.7	3.08	113	.252	.297	0	—	0	9	6	1	1.1
1982	Tex-A	7	11	.389	21	21	2	0	0	122^2	146	8	61	37	15.4	5.06	76	.307	.390	0	—	0	-13	-16	0	-1.7
	*Mil-A	5	4	.556	10	10	1	0	0	63	57	4	32	36	12.9	5.00	76	.242	.335	0	—	0	-6	-9	-1	-0.6
	Yr	12	15	.444	31	31	3	0	0	185^2	203	12	93	73	14.4	5.04	76	.281	.364	0	—	0	-20	-25	-0	-2.3
Total	11	124	105	.541	312	287	71	16	2	1996^1	2036	151	624	955	12.1	3.78	99	.266	.324	5	.093	-2	13	-10	-5	-0.6
● **RAFAEL MEDINA**	Medina, Rafael Eduardo b: 2/15/75, Panama City, Panama BR/TR, 6′3″, 194 lbs. Deb: 4/2/98																									
1998	Fla-N	2	6	.250	12	12	0	0	0	67^1	76	8	52	49	17.5	6.01	68	.289	.412	1	.053	-2	-13	-14	-1	-1.6
● **IRV MEDLINGER**	Medlinger, Irving John b: 6/18/27, Chicago, Ill. d: 9/3/75, Wheeling, Ill. BL/TL, 5′11″, 185 lbs. Deb: 4/20/49																									
1949	StL-A	0	0	—	3	0	0	0	0	4	11	1	3	4	31.5	27.00	17	.478	.538	0	—	0	-10	-10	-0	0.0
1951	StL-A	0	0	—	6	0	0	0	0	9^2	10	1	12	5	20.5	8.38	52	.270	.449	0	—	0	-5	-4	-0	0.0
Total	2	0	0	—	9	0	0	0	0	13^2	21	2	15	9	23.7	13.83	32	.350	.480	0	—	0	-15	-14	-0	0.0
● **SCOTT MEDVIN**	Medvin, Scott Howard b: 9/16/61, North Olmsted, O. BR/TR, 6′1″, 195 lbs. Deb: 5/11/88																									
1988	Pit-N	3	0	1.000	17	0	0	0	0	27^2	23	1	9	16	10.7	4.88	70	.230	.300	0	.000	-0	-4	-5	0	-0.5
1989	Pit-N	0	1	.000	6	0	0	0	0	6^1	6	0	5	4	15.6	5.68	59	.240	.367	0	—	0	-2	-2	0	-0.2
1990	Sea-A	0	1	.000	5	0	0	0	0	4^1	7	0	2	1	20.8	6.23	64	.368	.455	0	—	0	-1	-1	0	-0.2
Total	3	3	2	.600	28	0	0	0	0	38^1	36	1	16	21	12.7	5.17	67	.250	.333	0	.000	-0	-7	-7	1	-0.9
● **PETE MEEGAN**	Meegan, Peter J. "Steady Pete" b: 11/13/1863, San Francisco, Cal d: 3/15/05, San Francisco, Cal Deb: 8/12/1884																									
1884	Ric-a	7	12	.368	22	22	22	1	0	179	177	7	29	106	11.1	4.32	77	.246	.288	12	.160	-2	-21	-20	2	-1.7
1885	Pit-a	7	8	.467	18	16	14	1	0	146	146	1	38	58	12.0	3.39	95	.247	.303	13	.194	-1	-2	-3	-1	-0.4
Total	2	14	20	.412	40	38	36	2	0	325	323	8	67	164	11.5	3.90	84	.246	.295	25	.176	-3	-24	-23	1	-2.1
● **BILL MEEHAN**	Meehan, William Thomas b: 9/4/1889, Osceola Mills, Pa. d: 10/8/82, Douglas, Wyo. BR/TR, 5′9″, 155 lbs. Deb: 9/17/15																									
1915	Phi-A	0	1	.000	1	1	0	0	0	4	7	0	3	4	22.5	11.25	26	.389	.476	1	1.000	0	-4	-4	0	-0.6
● **ROY MEEKER**	Meeker, Charles Roy b: 9/15/1900, Lead Mine, Mo. d: 3/25/29, Orlando, Fla. BL/TL, 5′9″, 175 lbs. Deb: 9/22/23																									
1923	Phi-A	3	0	1.000	5	2	2	0	0	25	24	0	13	12	13.3	3.60	114	.253	.343	1	.111	-1	1	1	-0	0.1
1924	Phi-A	5	12	.294	30	14	5	1	0	146	166	7	81	37	15.5	4.68	91	.288	.381	11	.229	-0	-7	-6	-1	-0.8
1926	Cin-N	0	2	.000	7	1	1	0	0	21	24	1	9	5	14.1	6.43	57	.324	.398	0	.000	-1	-6	-6	0	-0.6
Total	3	8	14	.364	42	17	8	1	0	192	214	8	103	54	15.1	4.73	89	.287	.377	12	.190	-2	-12	-11	-1	-1.3
● **JOUETT MEEKIN**	Meekin, George Jouett b: 2/21/1867, New Albany, Ind. d: 12/14/44, New Albany, Ind. BR/TR, 6′1″, 180 lbs. Deb: 6/13/1891																									
1891	Lou-a	10	16	.385	29	26	25	2	0	228	227	2	113	144	13.7	4.30	85	.251	.338	21	.216	4	-15	-16	-2	-1.2
1892	Lou-N	7	10	.412	19	18	17	0	0	156^1	168	3	78	67	14.5	4.03	76	.264	.350	5	.078	-5	-13	-17	0	-1.9

YEAR	TM/L	W	L	PCT	G	GS	CG	SH	SV	IP	H	HR	BB	SO	RAT	ERA	ERA+	OAV	OOB	BH	AVG	PB	PR	/A	PD	TPI
	Was-N	3	10	.231	14	14	13	1	0	112	112	2	48	58	13.2	3.46	94	.250	.328	6	.133	-1	-2	-3	0	-0.3
	Yr	10	20	.333	33	32	30	1	0	268^1	280	5	126	125	13.8	3.79	83	.257	.336	11	.101	-5	-15	-19	0	-2.2
1893	Was-N	10	15	.400	31	28	24	1	0	245	289	6	140	91	16.0	4.96	93	.285	.376	29	.257	3	-8	-9	1	-0.4
1894	*NY-N	33	9	**.786**	52	48	40	1	2	409	404	13	171	133	12.9	3.70	142	.255	.332	48	.282	7	74	70	-3	5.5
1895	NY-N	16	11	.593	29	29	24	1	0	225^2	296	10	73	76	15.1	5.30	88	.312	.366	28	.292	4	-13	-17	-1	-1.2
1896	NY-N	26	14	.650	42	41	34	0	0	334^1	378	8	127	110	14.0	3.82	110	.283	.351	43	.299	12	20	14	-3	2.1
1897	NY-N	20	11	.645	37	34	30	2	0	303^2	328	9	99	83	12.9	3.76	110	.273	.333	41	.299	6	19	13	-3	1.3
1898	NY-N	16	18	.471	38	37	34	1	0	320	329	9	108	82	12.6	3.77	92	.264	.328	27	.209	1	-6	-10	-5	-1.3
1899	NY-N	5	11	.313	18	18	16	0	0	148^1	169	4	70	30	15.0	4.37	86	.286	.369	12	.207	1	-8	-10	-3	-1.1
	Bos-N	7	6	.538	13	13	12	0	0	108	111	0	23	23	11.3	2.83	147	.266	.307	7	.171	-1	12	16	-2	1.3
	Yr	12	17	.414	31	31	28	0	0	256^1	280	4	93	53	13.2	3.72	105	.275	.337	19	.192	-1	4	6	-5	0.2
1900	Pit-N	0	2	.000	2	2	1	0	0	13	20	1	8	3	20.1	6.92	52	.351	.439	0	.000	-1	-5	-5	-1	-0.6
Total	10	153	133	.535	324	308	270	9	2	2603^1	2831	67	1058	900	13.8	4.07	102	.273	.345	267	.243	29	55	27	-22	2.2

● **PHIL MEELER** Meeler, Charles Phillip b: 7/3/48, South Boston, Va. BR/TR, 6'5", 215 lbs. Deb: 5/10/72

YEAR	TM/L	W	L	PCT	G	GS	CG	SH	SV	IP	H	HR	BB	SO	RAT	ERA	ERA+	OAV	OOB	BH	AVG	PB	PR	/A	PD	TPI
1972	Det-A	0	1	.000	7	0	0	0	0	8^1	10	0	7	5	18.4	4.32	73	.303	.425	0	.000	-0	-1	-1	-0	-0.2

● **RUSS MEERS** Meers, Russell Harlan "Babe" b: 11/28/18, Tilton, Ill. d: 11/16/94, Lancaster, Pa. BL/TL, 5'10", 170 lbs. Deb: 9/28/41

YEAR	TM/L	W	L	PCT	G	GS	CG	SH	SV	IP	H	HR	BB	SO	RAT	ERA	ERA+	OAV	OOB	BH	AVG	PB	PR	/A	PD	TPI
1941	Chi-N	0	1	.000	1	1	0	0	0	8	5	0	0	5	6.8	1.13	312	.172	.200	0	.000	-0	2	2	-0	0.2
1946	Chi-N	1	2	.333	7	2	0	0	0	11^1	10	0	10	2	15.9	3.18	104	.238	.385	1	1.000	0	0	0	0	0.1
1947	Chi-N	2	0	1.000	35	1	0	0	0	64^1	61	5	38	28	14.1	4.48	88	.263	.371	2	.143	-1	-3	-4	-0	-0.2
Total	3	3	3	.500	43	4	0	0	0	83^2	76	5	48	35	13.7	3.98	96	.251	.359	3	.176	-0	-0	-1	-0	0.1

● **HEINIE MEINE** Meine, Henry William "The Count Of Luxemburg" b: 5/1/1896, St.Louis, Mo. d: 3/18/68, St.Louis, Mo. BR/TR, 5'11", 180 lbs. Deb: 8/16/22

YEAR	TM/L	W	L	PCT	G	GS	CG	SH	SV	IP	H	HR	BB	SO	RAT	ERA	ERA+	OAV	OOB	BH	AVG	PB	PR	/A	PD	TPI
1922	StL-A	0	0	—	1	0	0	0	0	4	5	1	2	0	15.8	4.50	92	.313	.389	0	.000	-0	-0	-0	0	0.0
1929	Pit-N	7	6	.538	22	13	7	1	0	108	120	4	34	19	13.4	4.50	106	.291	.355	4	.103	-2	3	3	-2	0.0
1930	Pit-N	6	8	.429	20	16	4	0	1	117^1	168	6	44	18	16.6	6.14	81	.346	.406	5	.122	-3	-15	-15	3	-1.4
1931	Pit-N	**19**	13	.594	36	35	22	3	0	**284**	278	8	87	58	11.8	2.98	129	.254	.313	14	.146	-2	28	27	-0	2.6
1932	Pit-N	12	9	.571	28	25	13	1	1	172^1	193	6	45	32	12.6	3.86	99	.278	.324	10	.164	-2	0	-1	-1	-0.4
1933	Pit-N	15	8	.652	32	29	12	2	0	207^1	227	10	50	50	12.1	3.65	91	.278	.321	13	.173	-1	-7	-8	-3	-1.2
1934	Pit-N	7	6	.538	26	14	2	0	0	106^1	134	12	25	22	13.5	4.32	95	.306	.345	3	.107	-1	-3	-2	-1	-0.5
Total	7	66	50	.569	165	132	60	7	3	999^1	1125	47	287	199	12.9	3.95	101	.284	.337	49	.144	-12	5	4	-4	-0.9

● **FRANK MEINKE** Meinke, Frank Louis b: 10/18/1863, Chicago, Ill. d: 11/8/31, Chicago, Ill. BR , 5'10.5", 172 lbs. Deb: 5/1/1884 F♦

YEAR	TM/L	W	L	PCT	G	GS	CG	SH	SV	IP	H	HR	BB	SO	RAT	ERA	ERA+	OAV	OOB	BH	AVG	PB	PR	/A	PD	TPI
1884	Det-N	8	23	.258	35	31	31	1	0	289	341	10	63	124	12.6	3.18	91	.275	.310	56	.164	-3	-6	-9	-2	-1.1
1885	Det-N	0	1	.000	1	1	0	0	0	5	13	0	4	0	30.6	3.60	79	.433	.500	0	.000	-0	-0	-0	0	-0.1
Total	2	8	24	.250	36	32	31	1	0	294	354	10	67	124	12.9	3.18	91	.279	.315	56	.163	-3	-7	-9	-2	-1.2

● **SAM MEJIAS** Mejias, Samuel Elias b: 5/9/52, Santiago, D.R. BR/TR, 6', 170 lbs. Deb: 9/6/76 C♦

YEAR	TM/L	W	L	PCT	G	GS	CG	SH	SV	IP	H	HR	BB	SO	RAT	ERA	ERA+	OAV	OOB	BH	AVG	PB	PR	/A	PD	TPI
1978	Mon-N	0	0	—	1	0	0	0	0	1	0	0	0	0	9.0	0.00	—	.000	.250	13	.232	0	0	0	0	0.0

● **JOSE MELENDEZ** Melendez, Jose Luis (Garcia) b: 9/2/65, Naguabo, P.R. BR/TR, 6'2", 175 lbs. Deb: 9/11/90

YEAR	TM/L	W	L	PCT	G	GS	CG	SH	SV	IP	H	HR	BB	SO	RAT	ERA	ERA+	OAV	OOB	BH	AVG	PB	PR	/A	PD	TPI
1990	Sea-A	0	0	—	3	0	0	0	0	5^1	8	2	3	7	20.3	11.81	33	.333	.429	0	—	0	-5	-5	-0	0.0
1991	SD-N	8	5	.615	31	9	0	0	3	93^2	77	11	24	60	9.8	3.27	116	.221	.273	2	.100	-0	4	6	-1	0.6
1992	SD-N	6	7	.462	56	3	0	0	0	89^1	82	9	20	82	10.6	2.92	122	.249	.298	0	.000	-0	6	7	-1	0.8
1993	Bos-A	2	1	.667	9	0	0	0	0	16	10	2	5	14	8.4	2.25	205	.179	.246	0	—	0	4	4	0	0.5
1994	Bos-A	0	1	.000	10	0	0	0	0	16^1	20	3	8	9	16.5	6.06	83	.323	.417	0	—	0	-2	-2	0	-0.2
Total	5	16	14	.533	109	12	0	0	3	220^2	197	27	60	172	10.8	3.47	111	.241	.298	2	.080	-1	7	10	-2	1.7

● **STEVE MELTER** Melter, Stephen Blazius b: 1/2/1886, Cherokee, Iowa d: 1/28/62, Mishawaka, Ind. BR/TR, 6'2", 180 lbs. Deb: 6/27/09

YEAR	TM/L	W	L	PCT	G	GS	CG	SH	SV	IP	H	HR	BB	SO	RAT	ERA	ERA+	OAV	OOB	BH	AVG	PB	PR	/A	PD	TPI
1909	StL-N	0	1	.000	23	1	0	0	3	64^1	79	1	20	24	14.1	3.50	72	.322	.378	2	.133	-0	-6	-7	1	-0.1

● **CLIFF MELTON** Melton, Clifford George "Mickey Mouse" or "Mountain Music"
b: 1/3/12, Brevard, N.C. d: 7/28/86, Baltimore, Md. BL/TL, 6'5.5", 203 lbs. Deb: 4/25/37

YEAR	TM/L	W	L	PCT	G	GS	CG	SH	SV	IP	H	HR	BB	SO	RAT	ERA	ERA+	OAV	OOB	BH	AVG	PB	PR	/A	PD	TPI
1937	*NY-N	20	9	.690	46	27	14	2	**7**	248	216	9	55	142	10.1	2.61	149	.233	.280	10	.122	-5	36	**35**	4	3.9
1938	NY-N	14	14	.500	36	31	10	1	0	243	266	19	61	101	12.1	3.89	97	.276	.319	14	.175	-1	-3	-3	2	-0.3
1939	NY-N	12	15	.444	41	23	9	2	5	207^1	214	7	65	95	12.3	3.56	110	.269	.327	12	.182	-1	8	8	1	1.0
1940	NY-N	10	11	.476	37	21	4	1	2	166^2	185	9	68	91	13.8	4.91	79	.285	.355	12	.222	2	-20	-19	2	-1.9
1941	NY-N	8	11	.421	42	22	9	3	1	194^1	181	14	61	100	11.3	3.01	123	.246	.305	7	.115	-3	13	15	4	1.4
1942	NY-N†	11	5	.688	23	17	12	2	1	143^2	122	9	33	61	9.8	2.63	128	.229	.276	11	.234	2	11	12	3	1.8
1943	NY-N	9	13	.409	34	28	6	2	0	186^1	184	7	69	55	12.4	3.19	108	.257	.325	8	.148	0	4	5	3	1.0
1944	NY-N	2	2	.500	13	10	1	0	0	64^1	78	5	19	15	13.7	4.06	90	.294	.344	3	.120	-2	-3	-3	1	-0.2
Total	8	86	80	.518	272	179	65	13	16	1453^2	1446	79	431	660	11.8	3.42	109	.259	.314	77	.164	-9	47	50	20	6.7

● **RUBE MELTON** Melton, Reuben Franklin b: 2/27/17, Cramerton, N.C. d: 9/11/71, Greer, S.C. BR/TR, 6'5", 205 lbs. Deb: 4/17/41

YEAR	TM/L	W	L	PCT	G	GS	CG	SH	SV	IP	H	HR	BB	SO	RAT	ERA	ERA+	OAV	OOB	BH	AVG	PB	PR	/A	PD	TPI
1941	Phi-N	1	5	.167	25	5	2	0	0	83^2	81	7	47	57	13.8	4.73	78	.258	.355	2	.105	-1	-10	-10	-1	-0.9
1942	Phi-N	9	20	.310	42	29	10	1	4	209^1	180	7	114	107	12.8	3.70	89	.234	.335	8	.123	-1	-9	-9	-2	-1.5
1943	Bro-N	5	8	.385	30	17	4	2	0	119^1	106	3	79	63	14.3	3.92	86	.243	.365	4	.105	-2	-7	-7	-1	-1.2
1944	Bro-N	9	13	.409	37	23	6	1	0	187^1	178	1	96	91	13.3	3.46	103	.254	.345	7	.123	-3	3	2	0	0.0
1946	Bro-N	6	3	.667	24	12	3	2	1	99^2	72	3	52	44	11.5	1.99	170	.206	.314	3	.107	-2	16	15	-0	1.2
1947	Bro-N	0	1	.000	4	1	0	0	0	4^2	7	1	7	1	27.0	13.50	31	.350	.519	1	1.000	0	-5	-5	-0	-0.8
Total	6	30	50	.375	162	87	25	6	5	704	624	22	395	363	13.2	3.62	95	.241	.344	25	.120	-9	-12	-14	-5	-3.2

● **MARIO MENDOZA** Mendoza, Mario (Aizpuru) b: 12/26/50, Chihuahua, Mex. BR/TR, 5'11", 187 lbs. Deb: 4/26/74 ♦

YEAR	TM/L	W	L	PCT	G	GS	CG	SH	SV	IP	H	HR	BB	SO	RAT	ERA	ERA+	OAV	OOB	BH	AVG	PB	PR	/A	PD	TPI
1977	Pit-N	0	0	—	1	0	0	0	0	2	3	1	2	0	22.5	13.50	30	.375	.500	16	.198	0	-2	-2	0	0.0

● **MIKE MENDOZA** Mendoza, Michael Joseph b: 11/26/55, Inglewood, Cal. BR/TR, 6'5", 215 lbs. Deb: 9/7/79 ♦

YEAR	TM/L	W	L	PCT	G	GS	CG	SH	SV	IP	H	HR	BB	SO	RAT	ERA	ERA+	OAV	OOB	BH	AVG	PB	PR	/A	PD	TPI
1979	Hou-N	0	0	—	1	0	0	0	0	1	0	0	0	0	0.0	0.00	—	.000	.000	0	—	0	0	0	0	0.0

● **RAMIRO MENDOZA** Mendoza, Ramiro b: 6/15/72, Los Santos, Panama BR/TR, 6'2", 154 lbs. Deb: 5/25/96

YEAR	TM/L	W	L	PCT	G	GS	CG	SH	SV	IP	H	HR	BB	SO	RAT	ERA	ERA+	OAV	OOB	BH	AVG	PB	PR	/A	PD	TPI
1996	NY-A	4	5	.444	12	11	0	0	0	53	80	5	10	34	16.0	6.79	73	.343	.381	0	—	0	-11	-11	1	-1.4
1997	*NY-A	8	6	.571	39	15	0	0	2	133^2	157	15	28	82	12.8	4.24	105	.292	.333	0	—	0	5	3	2	0.5
1998	*NY-A	10	2	.833	41	14	1	1	1	130^1	131	9	30	56	11.7	3.25	137	.264	.318	0	—	0	20	17	1	1.5
Total	3	22	13	.629	92	40	1	1	3	317	368	29	68	172	12.9	4.26	106	.291	.336	0	—	0	14	9	4	0.6

● **JOCK MENEFEE** Menefee, John b: 1/15/1868, Rowlesburg, W.Va. d: 3/11/53, Belle Vernon, Pa. BR/TR, 6', 165 lbs. Deb: 8/17/1892 ♦

YEAR	TM/L	W	L	PCT	G	GS	CG	SH	SV	IP	H	HR	BB	SO	RAT	ERA	ERA+	OAV	OOB	BH	AVG	PB	PR	/A	PD	TPI
1892	Pit-N	0	0	—	1	0	0	0	0	4	10	0	2	0	27.0	11.25	29	.455	.500	0	.000	-0	-4	-4	0	0.0
1893	Lou-N	8	7	.533	15	15	14	1	0	129^1	150	3	40	30	13.4	4.24	104	.281	.335	20	.274	4	6	2	2	0.7
1894	Lou-N	8	17	.320	28	24	20	1	0	211^2	258	3	50	43	13.5	4.29	119	.297	.342	13	.165	-6	24	19	2	1.3
	Pit-N	5	8	.385	13	13	13	0	0	111^2	159	4	39	33	16.1	5.40	97	.331	.383	12	.255	0	-1	-2	2	0.0
	Yr	13	25	.342	41	37	33	1	0	323^1	417	7	89	76	14.1	4.68	110	.307	.351	25	.198	-5	23	17	4	1.3
1895	Pit-N	0	1	.000	2	1	0	0	0	1^2	2	0	7	0	54.0	16.20	28	.286	.667	0	—	0	-2	-2	0	-0.8
1898	NY-N	0	1	.000	1	1	1	0	0	9^1	11	0	2	3	14.5	4.82	72	.289	.357	0	.000	-1	-1	-1	0	-0.2
1900	Chi-N	9	4	.692	16	13	11	0	0	117	140	1	35	30	14.2	3.85	94	.296	.357	5	.109	-3	-2	-3	-2	-0.7
1901	Chi-N	8	12	.400	21	20	19	0	0	182^1	201	4	34	55	11.9	3.80	85	.278	.315	39	.257	4	-10	-11	-1	-0.6
1902	Chi-N	12	10	.545	22	21	20	4	0	197^1	201	1	26	60	10.6	2.42	112	.264	.293	50	.231	3	8	6	-1	0.9
1903	Chi-N	8	10	.444	20	17	13	1	0	147	157	3	38	39	12.3	3.00	105	.275	.327	13	.203	1	4	2	3	0.6
Total	9	58	70	.453	139	125	111	7	0	1111^1	1289	19	273	293	13.0	3.81	101	.288	.335	152	.222	2	23	6	6	1.2

● **TONY MENENDEZ** Menendez, Antonio Gustavo (Remon) b: 2/20/65, Havana, Cuba BR/TR, 6'2", 190 lbs. Deb: 6/22/92

YEAR	TM/L	W	L	PCT	G	GS	CG	SH	SV	IP	H	HR	BB	SO	RAT	ERA	ERA+	OAV	OOB	BH	AVG	PB	PR	/A	PD	TPI
1992	Cin-N	1	0	1.000	3	0	0	0	0	4^2	1	1	0	5	1.9	1.93	187	.067	.067	0	—	0	1	1	-0	0.2
1993	Pit-N	2	0	1.000	14	0	0	0	0	21	20	4	4	13	10.7	3.00	135	.256	.301	0	.000	-0	2	2	-0	0.2

YEAR	TM/L	W	L	PCT	G	GS	CG	SH	SV	IP	H	HR	BB	SO	RAT	ERA	ERA+	OAV	OOB	BH	AVG	PB	PR	/A	PD	TPI
1994	SF-N	0	1	.000	6	0	0	0	0	3^1	8	2	2	2	27.0	21.60	19	.471	.526	0	—	0	-6	-7	-0	-1.5
Total	3	3	1	.750	23	0	0	0	0	29	29	7	6	20	11.2	4.97	80	.264	.308	0	.000	-0	-3	-3	-1	-1.1
● PAUL MENHART	Menhart, Paul Gerard b: 3/25/69, St.Louis, Mo. BR/TR, 6'2", 190 lbs. Deb: 4/27/95																									
1995	Tor-A	1	4	.200	21	9	1	0	0	78^2	72	9	47	50	14.3	4.92	96	.248	.364	0	—	0	-2	-2	-0	-0.1
1996	Sea-A	2	2	.500	11	6	0	0	0	42	55	9	25	18	17.6	7.29	68	.327	.421	0	—	0	-11	-11	1	-0.8
1997	SD-N	2	3	.400	9	8	0	0	0	44	42	6	13	22	11.3	4.70	82	.256	.311	0	.000	-1	-2	-4	-0	-0.5
Total	3	5	9	.357	41	23	1	0	0	164^2	169	24	85	90	14.3	5.47	83	.272	.366	0	.000	-1	-15	-17	0	-1.4
● MIKE MEOLA	Meola, Emile Michael b: 10/19/05, New York, N.Y. d: 9/1/76, Fair Lawn, N.J. BR/TR, 5'11", 175 lbs. Deb: 4/24/33																									
1933	Bos-A	0	0	—	3	0	0	0	0	2^1	5	0	2	1	27.0	23.14	19	.417	.500	0	—	0	-5	-5	-0	0.0
1936	StL-A	0	1	.000	9	0	0	0	0	19^1	29	0	13	6	20.0	9.31	58	.358	.453	1	.500	1	-9	-8	0	-0.3
	Bos-A	0	2	.000	6	3	1	0	1	21^1	29	0	10	8	16.9	5.48	97	.326	.400	1	.143	-0	-1	-0	1	0.0
	Yr	0	3	.000	15	3	1	0	1	40^2	58	0	23	14	18.1	7.30	73	.339	.421	2	.222	0	-10	-9	1	-0.3
Total	2	0	3	.000	18	3	1	0	1	43	63	0	25	15	18.8	8.16	65	.346	.431	2	.222	0	-15	-14	1	-0.3
● JOSE MERCEDES	Mercedes, Jose Miguel (Santana) b: 3/5/71, ElSeibo, D.R. BR/TR, 6'1", 180 lbs. Deb: 5/31/94																									
1994	Mil-A	2	0	1.000	19	0	0	0	0	31	22	4	16	11	11.6	2.32	217	.216	.333	0	—	0	9	9	-1	0.4
1995	Mil-A	0	1	.000	5	0	0	0	0	7^1	12	1	8	6	24.5	9.82	51	.375	.500	0	—	0	-4	-4	-0	-0.5
1996	Mil-A	0	2	.000	11	0	0	0	0	16^2	20	6	5	6	13.5	9.18	56	.294	.342	0	—	0	-8	-7	-0	-0.7
1997	Mil-A	7	10	.412	29	23	2	1	0	159	146	24	53	80	11.5	3.79	122	.248	.316	0	.000	-0	14	14	-2	1.2
1998	Mil-N	2	2	.500	7	5	0	0	0	32	42	5	9	11	14.6	6.75	64	.316	.364	1	.091	-0	-9	-9	-1	-1.0
Total	5	11	15	.423	71	28	2	1	0	246	242	40	91	114	12.5	4.54	103	.262	.334	1	.077	-1	1	4	-3	-0.6
● WIN MERCER	Mercer, George Barclay b: 6/20/1874, Chester, W.Va. d: 1/12/03, San Francisco, Cal BR/TR, 5'7", 140 lbs. Deb: 4/21/1894 ♦																									
1894	Was-N	17	23	.425	50	39	30	0	3	339^1	445	9	126	72	15.5	3.85	137	.313	.375	48	.291	3	56	54	2	5.0
1895	Was-N	13	23	.361	43	38	32	0	2	311	430	17	96	84	15.7	4.46	108	.323	.376	50	.255	0	11	12	-1	1.0
1896	Was-N	25	18	.581	46	45	38	2	0	366^1	456	10	117	94	14.6	4.13	107	.302	.360	38	.244	0	10	11	1	1.2
1897	Was-N	21	20	.512	**47**	43	35	**3**	**3**	342	403	5	104	91	14.1	3.18	136	.291	.353	44	.317	8	43	44	-1	5.0
1898	Was-N	12	18	.400	33	30	24	0	0	233^2	309	3	71	52	15.3	4.81	76	.316	.373	80	.321	8	-31	-30	-1	-2.5
1899	Was-N	7	14	.333	23	21	21	0	0	186	234	2	53	28	14.2	4.60	85	.307	.356	112	.299	5	-15	-14	3	-0.5
1900	NY-N	13	17	.433	33	29	26	1	0	242^2	303	5	58	39	14.1	3.86	94	.305	.355	73	.294	7	-4	-7	2	0.1
1901	Was-A	9	13	.409	24	22	19	1	1	179^2	217	8	50	31	13.9	4.56	80	.295	.348	42	.300	6	-18	-18	1	-1.1
1902	Det-A	15	18	.455	35	33	28	4	1	281^2	282	5	80	40	11.9	3.04	120	.261	.318	18	.180	-2	17	19	4	2.1
Total	9	132	164	.446	334	300	253	11	10	2482^1	3079	64	755	531	14.4	3.98	107	.302	.358	505	.286	35	68	72	9	10.3
● JACK MERCER	Mercer, Harry Vernon b: 3/10/1889, Zanesville, Ohio d: 6/25/45, Dayton, Ohio Deb: 8/2/10																									
1910	Pit-N	0	0	—	1	0	0	0	0	1	0	0	2	1	18.0	0.00	—	.000	.500	0	—	0	0	0	0	0.0
● MARK MERCER	Mercer, Mark Kenneth b: 5/22/54, Fort Bragg, N.C. BL/TL, 6'5", 220 lbs. Deb: 9/1/81																									
1981	Tex-A	0	1	.000	7	0	0	0	2	7^2	7	1	7	8	16.4	4.70	74	.241	.389	0	—	0	-1	-1	0	0.0
● KENT MERCKER	Mercker, Kent Franklin b: 2/1/68, Indianapolis, Ind. BL/TL, 6'2", 195 lbs. Deb: 9/22/89																									
1989	Atl-N	0	0	—	2	1	0	0	0	4^1	8	0	6	4	29.1	12.46	29	.400	.538	0	.000	-0	-4	-4	-0	0.0
1990	Atl-N	4	7	.364	36	0	0	0	7	48^1	43	6	24	39	12.8	3.17	127	.236	.332	0	.000	-0	3	5	-1	1.0
1991	*Atl-N	5	3	.625	50	4	0	0	6	73^1	56	5	35	62	11.3	2.58	151	.211	.305	1	.100	-0	9	11	-1	1.2
1992	*Atl-N	3	2	.600	53	0	0	0	6	68^1	51	4	35	49	11.7	3.42	107	.207	.313	0	.000	-0	1	2	-2	-0.1
1993	*Atl-N	3	1	.750	43	6	0	0	0	66	52	2	36	59	12.3	2.86	140	.212	.318	0	.000	-1	9	8	-1	0.2
1994	Atl-N	9	4	.692	20	17	2	1	0	112^1	90	16	45	111	10.8	3.45	123	.220	.297	2	.054	-2	10	10	0	0.8
1995	*Atl-N	7	8	.467	29	26	0	0	0	143	140	16	61	102	12.8	4.15	103	.258	.336	5	.104	-2	0	2	0	0.0
1996	Bal-A	3	6	.333	14	12	0	0	0	58	73	12	35	22	17.2	7.76	63	.307	.402	0	—	0	-18	-18	-1	-2.2
	Cle-A	1	0	1.000	10	0	0	0	0	11^2	10	1	3	7	10.0	3.09	158	.244	.295	0	—	0	2	2	-0	0.2
	Yr	4	6	.400	24	12	0	0	0	69^2	83	13	38	29	15.6	6.98	70	.290	.373	0	—	0	-15	-16	-1	-2.0
1997	Cin-N	8	11	.421	28	25	0	0	0	144^2	135	16	62	75	12.4	3.92	109	.250	.329	7	.156	1	5	6	0	0.8
1998	StL-N	11	11	.500	30	29	0	0	0	161^2	199	11	53	72	14.2	5.07	83	.310	.366	8	.148	1	-15	-16	-1	-1.9
Total	10	54	53	.505	315	120	2	1	19	891^2	857	89	395	602	12.8	4.12	102	.254	.336	23	.106	-5	1	7	-7	0.0
● SPIKE MERENA	Merena, John Joseph b: 11/18/09, Paterson, N.J. d: 3/9/77, Bridgeport, Conn. BL/TL, 6', 185 lbs. Deb: 9/16/34																									
1934	Bos-A	1	2	.333	4	3	2	1	0	24^2	20	2	16	7	13.5	2.92	165	.222	.346	1	.143	-0	4	5	-1	0.5
● RON MERIDITH	Meridith, Ronald Knox b: 11/26/56, San Pedro, Cal. BL/TL, 6', 175 lbs. Deb: 9/16/84																									
1984	Chi-N	0	0	—	3	0	0	0	0	5^1	6	1	2	4	13.5	3.38	116	.273	.333	0	—	0	0	0	-0	0.0
1985	Chi-N	3	2	.600	32	0	0	0	1	46^1	53	3	24	23	15.2	4.47	89	.301	.388	1	.250	0	-5	-2	0	-0.2
1986	Tex-A	1	0	1.000	5	0	0	0	0	3	2	0	1	2	9.0	3.00	143	.286	.375	0	—	0	0	0	0	0.1
1987	Tex-A	1	0	1.000	11	0	0	0	0	20^2	25	7	12	17	16.1	6.10	73	.298	.385	0	—	0	-4	-4	0	-0.1
Total	4	5	2	.714	51	0	0	0	1	75^1	86	11	39	46	15.1	4.78	87	.298	.383	1	.250	0	-8	-5	1	-0.2
● BRETT MERRIMAN	Merriman, Brett Alan b: 7/15/66, Jacksonville, Ill. BR/TR, 6'2", 180 lbs. Deb: 4/8/93																									
1993	Min-A	1	1	.500	19	0	0	0	0	27	36	3	23	14	20.7	9.67	45	.343	.473	0	—	0	-16	-16	0	-1.0
1994	Min-A	0	1	.000	15	0	0	0	0	17	18	0	14	10	19.1	6.35	77	.269	.424	0	—	0	-3	-3	-0	-0.2
Total	2	1	2	.333	34	0	0	0	0	44	54	3	37	24	20.0	8.39	54	.314	.454	0	—	0	-19	-19	-0	-1.2
● GEORGE MERRITT	Merritt, George Washington b: 4/14/1880, Paterson, N.J. d: 2/21/38, Memphis, Tenn. TR, 6', 160 lbs. Deb: 9/6/01 ♦																									
1901	Pit-N	3	0	1.000	3	3	3	0	0	24	28	0	5	5	13.1	4.88	67	.289	.337	3	.273	1	-4	-4	-0	-0.3
1903	Pit-N	0	0	—	1	0	0	0	0	4	4	0	1	2	11.3	2.25	144	.267	.313	4	.148	0	0	0	-0	0.0
Total	2	3	0	1.000	4	3	3	0	0	28	32	0	6	7	12.9	4.50	73	.286	.333	10	.213	1	-4	-4	-0	-0.3
● JIM MERRITT	Merritt, James Joseph b: 12/9/43, Altadena, Cal. BL/TL, 6'2", 180 lbs. Deb: 8/2/65																									
1965	*Min-A	5	4	.556	16	9	1	0	2	76^2	68	11	20	61	10.3	3.17	112	.239	.289	3	.136	0	2	3	-0	0.4
1966	Min-A	7	14	.333	31	18	5	1	3	144	112	17	33	124	9.1	3.38	107	.212	.258	4	.103	-1	1	4	-0	0.4
1967	Min-A	13	7	.650	37	28	11	4	0	227^2	196	21	30	161	9.2	2.53	137	.230	.262	10	.135	0	18	24	-2	2.0
1968	Min-A	12	16	.429	38	34	11	1	1	238^1	207	21	52	181	10.0	3.25	95	.232	.279	10	.141	0	-7	-4	1	-0.5
1969	Cin-N	17	9	.654	42	36	8	1	0	251	269	33	61	144	12.0	4.37	86	.273	.318	11	.143	0	-22	-17	-3	-1.9
1970	*Cin-N★	20	12	.625	35	35	12	1	0	234	248	21	53	136	11.6	4.08	99	.270	.311	14	.169	3	-1	-1	-2	-0.1
1971	Cin-N	1	11	.083	28	11	0	0	0	107	115	14	31	38	12.5	4.37	77	.279	.334	4	.138	0	-11	-12	-2	-1.4
1972	Cin-N	1	0	1.000	4	1	0	0	0	8	13	1	2	4	16.9	4.50	71	.361	.395	0	.000	-0	-1	-1	-0	-0.2
1973	Tex-A	5	13	.278	35	19	8	1	1	160	191	18	34	65	12.7	4.05	92	.296	.332	0	—	0	-4	-6	-1	-0.5
1974	Tex-A	0	0	—	26	1	0	0	0	32^2	46	3	6	18	14.3	4.13	86	.329	.356	0	—	0	-2	-2	-1	0.0
1975	Tex-A	0	0	—	5	0	0	0	0	3^2	3	0	0	0	9.8	0.00	—	.214	.267	0	—	0	2	2	-0	0.0
Total	11	81	86	.485	297	192	56	9	7	1483	1468	160	322	932	11.0	3.65	98	.257	.300	56	.141	3	-25	-11	-10	-1.8
● LLOYD MERRITT	Merritt, Lloyd Wesley b: 4/8/33, St.Louis, Mo. BR/TR, 6', 189 lbs. Deb: 4/22/57																									
1957	StL-N	1	2	.333	44	0	0	0	7	65^1	60	7	28	35	12.7	3.31	120	.251	.339	0	.000	-0	4	5	0	0.3
● SAM MERTES	Mertes, Samuel Blair "Sandow" b: 8/6/1872, San Francisco, Cal. d: 3/11/45, San Francisco, Cal. BR/TR, 6', 225 lbs. Deb: 6/30/1896 ♦																									
1902	Chi-A	1	0	1.000	1	0	0	0	0	8	6	0	0	0	6.8	1.13	301	.207	.207	140	.282	0	2	2	-1	0.2
● JIM MERTZ	Mertz, James Verlin b: 8/10/16, Lima, Ohio BR/TR, 5'10.5", 170 lbs. Deb: 5/1/43																									
1943	Was-A	5	7	.417	33	10	2	0	3	116^2	109	7	58	53	12.9	4.63	69	.251	.339	7	.184	0	-17	-18	0	-1.8
● JOSE MESA	Mesa, Jose Ramon Nova (b: Jose Ramon Nova (Mesa)) b: 5/22/66, Pueblo Viejo, D.R. BR/TR, 6'3", 225 lbs. Deb: 9/10/87																									
1987	Bal-A	1	3	.250	6	5	0	0	0	31^1	38	7	15	17	15.2	6.03	73	.297	.371	0	—	0	-5	-6	-1	-0.7
1990	Bal-A	3	2	.600	7	7	0	0	0	46^2	37	2	27	24	12.5	3.86	98	.218	.328	0	—	0	0	-0	-0	0.1

YEAR	TM/L	W	L	PCT	G	GS	CG	SH	SV	IP	H	HR	BB	SO	RAT	ERA	ERA+	OAV	OOB	BH	AVG	PB	PR	/A	PD	TPI
1991	Bal-A	6	11	.353	23	23	2	1	0	123^2	151	11	62	64	15.7	5.97	66	.307	.388	0	—	0	-26	-28	1	-3.1
1992	Bal-A	3	8	.273	13	12	0	0	0	67^2	77	9	27	22	14.1	5.19	78	.287	.357	0	—	0	-9	-9	0	-1.2
	Cle-A	4	4	.500	15	15	1	1	0	93	92	5	43	40	13.3	4.16	94	.262	.346	0	—	0	-2	-3	-1	-0.2
	Yr	7	12	.368	28	27	1	1	0	160^2	169	14	70	62	13.5	4.59	86	.271	.346	0	—	0	-12	-11	-0	-1.4
1993	Cle-A	10	12	.455	34	33	3	0	0	208^2	232	21	62	118	13.0	4.92	88	.286	.342	0	—	0	-14	-14	-0	-1.3
1994	Cle-A	7	5	.583	51	0	0	0	2	73	71	3	26	63	12.3	3.82	123	.254	.325	0	—	0	8	7	0	1.1
1995	*Cle-A★	3	0	1.000	62	0	0	0	**46**	64	49	3	17	58	9.3	1.13	417	.216	.270	0	—	0	**26**	**25**	1	4.3
1996	*Cle-A☆	2	7	.222	69	0	0	0	39	72^1	69	6	28	64	12.4	3.73	131	.257	.333	0	—	0	10	9	-1	1.7
1997	*Cle-A	4	4	.500	66	0	0	0	16	82^1	83	7	28	69	12.5	2.40	195	.259	.324	0	—	0	20	21	-0	2.4
1998	Cle-A	3	4	.429	44	0	0	0	1	54	61	7	20	35	14.2	5.17	92	.282	.354	0	—	0	-3	-2	1	-0.3
	SF-N	5	3	.625	32	0	0	0	0	30^2	30	1	18	28	14.1	3.52	115	.256	.356	0	—	0	2	2	-1	0.4
Total	10	51	63	.447	422	95	6	2	104	947^1	990	82	373	602	13.2	4.30	101	.271	.344	0	—	0	6	3	-2	3.2

● BUD MESSENGER
Messenger, Andrew Warren b: 2/1/1898, Grand Blanc, Mich. d: 11/4/71, Lansing, Mich. BR/TR, 6', 175 lbs. Deb: 7/31/24

YEAR	TM/L	W	L	PCT	G	GS	CG	SH	SV	IP	H	HR	BB	SO	RAT	ERA	ERA+	OAV	OOB	BH	AVG	PB	PR	/A	PD	TPI
1924	Cle-A	2	0	1.000	5	2	1	0	0	25	28	4	14	4	15.1	4.32	99	.283	.372	1	.125	-0	-0	-0	-0	-0.1

● ANDY MESSERSMITH
Messersmith, John Alexander b: 8/6/45, Toms River, N.J. BR/TR, 6'1", 200 lbs. Deb: 7/4/68

YEAR	TM/L	W	L	PCT	G	GS	CG	SH	SV	IP	H	HR	BB	SO	RAT	ERA	ERA+	OAV	OOB	BH	AVG	PB	PR	/A	PD	TPI
1968	Cal-A	4	2	.667	28	5	2	1	4	81^1	44	3	35	74	8.9	2.21	132	.157	.253	2	.100	-1	7	6	0	0.5
1969	Cal-A	16	11	.593	40	33	10	2	2	250	169	17	100	211	9.9	2.52	138	**.190**	.276	12	.156	2	31	27	-1	3.0
1970	Cal-A	11	10	.524	37	26	6	1	5	194^2	144	21	78	162	10.5	3.01	120	**.205**	.290	11	.157	0	15	13	-1	1.4
1971	Cal-A☆	20	13	.606	38	38	14	4	0	276^2	224	16	121	179	11.5	2.99	108	.218	.304	16	.172	4	14	8	1	1.4
1972	Cal-A	8	11	.421	25	21	10	3	2	169^2	125	5	68	142	10.3	2.81	104	.207	.290	10	.189	2	5	2	0	0.5
1973	LA-N	14	10	.583	33	33	10	3	0	249^2	196	24	77	177	10.1	2.70	127	.214	.279	15	.169	2	27	20	-0	2.0
1974	*LA-N★	**20**	6	**.769**	39	39	13	3	0	292^1	227	24	94	221	**10.0**	2.59	132	.212	**.278**	23	.240	9	34	26	0	3.4
1975	LA-N☆	19	14	.576	42	40	**19**	**7**	1	**321^2**	244	22	96	213	9.7	2.29	148	**.213**	.276	17	.157	2	**47**	**40**	-2	4.1
1976	Atl-N†	11	11	.500	29	28	12	3	1	207^1	166	14	74	135	10.5	3.04	125	.219	.290	12	.179	0	11	17	1	2.0
1977	Atl-N	5	4	.556	16	16	1	0	0	102^1	101	12	39	69	12.5	4.40	101	.256	.326	4	.118	-0	-6	1	-0	0.0
1978	NY-A	0	3	.000	6	5	0	0	0	22^1	24	7	15	16	16.1	5.64	64	.267	.377	0	—	0	-5	-5	-0	-0.4
1979	LA-N	2	4	.333	11	11	1	0	0	62^1	55	9	34	26	12.9	4.91	74	.244	.344	2	.091	-1	-8	-9	0	-0.8
Total	12	130	99	.568	344	295	98	27	15	2230^1	1719	174	831	1625	10.5	2.86	121	.212	.289	124	.170	20	172	145	-1	17.1

● TOM METCALF
Metcalf, Thomas John b: 7/16/40, Amherst, Wis. BR/TR, 6'2.5", 174 lbs. Deb: 8/4/63

YEAR	TM/L	W	L	PCT	G	GS	CG	SH	SV	IP	H	HR	BB	SO	RAT	ERA	ERA+	OAV	OOB	BH	AVG	PB	PR	/A	PD	TPI
1963	NY-A	1	0	1.000	8	0	0	0	0	13	12	1	3	3	10.4	2.77	127	.250	.294	0	—	0	1	1	-0	0.1

● DEWEY METIVIER
Metivier, George Dewey b: 5/6/1898, Cambridge, Mass. d: 3/2/47, Cambridge, Mass. BL/TR, 5'11", 175 lbs. Deb: 9/15/22

YEAR	TM/L	W	L	PCT	G	GS	CG	SH	SV	IP	H	HR	BB	SO	RAT	ERA	ERA+	OAV	OOB	BH	AVG	PB	PR	/A	PD	TPI
1922	Cle-A	2	0	1.000	2	2	2	0	0	18	18	1	3	1	11.0	4.50	89	.265	.306	1	.167	-0	-1	-1	-1	-0.1
1923	Cle-A	4	2	.667	26	5	1	0	1	73^1	111	1	38	9	19.0	6.50	61	.368	.448	3	.150	-0	-21	-21	0	-1.5
1924	Cle-A	1	5	.167	26	6	1	0	3	76^1	110	3	34	14	17.0	5.31	81	.358	.422	3	.125	-2	-9	-9	-1	-0.9
Total	3	7	7	.500	54	13	4	0	4	167^2	239	5	75	24	17.2	5.74	72	.353	.423	7	.140	-2	-31	-30	-1	-2.5

● BUTCH METZGER
Metzger, Clarence Edward b: 5/23/52, Lafayette, Ind. BR/TR, 6'1", 185 lbs. Deb: 9/8/74

YEAR	TM/L	W	L	PCT	G	GS	CG	SH	SV	IP	H	HR	BB	SO	RAT	ERA	ERA+	OAV	OOB	BH	AVG	PB	PR	/A	PD	TPI
1974	SF-N	1	0	1.000	10	0	0	0	0	12^2	11	0	12	5	16.3	3.55	107	.239	.397	0	—	0	0	0	-0	0.0
1975	SD-N	1	0	1.000	4	0	0	0	0	4^2	6	1	4	6	19.3	7.71	45	.316	.435	0	—	0	-2	-2	0	-0.4
1976	SD-N	11	4	.733	77	0	0	0	16	123^1	119	5	52	89	12.7	2.92	112	.258	.337	0	.000	-0	8	5	-0	0.7
1977	SD-N	0	0	—	17	1	0	0	0	22^2	27	5	12	6	15.9	5.56	64	.307	.396	0	.000	-0	-4	-5	-0	-0.1
	StL-N	4	2	.667	58	0	0	0	7	92^2	78	8	38	48	11.4	3.11	124	.228	.307	0	.000	-0	8	8	-1	0.4
	Yr	4	2	.667	75	1	0	0	7	115^1	105	13	50	54	12.2	3.59	105	.242	.322	0	.000	-1	4	3	-1	0.3
1978	NY-N	1	3	.250	25	0	0	0	0	37^1	48	4	22	21	17.1	6.51	54	.324	.415	0	—	0	-12	-13	-1	-1.3
Total	5	18	9	.667	191	1	0	0	23	293^1	289	23	140	175	13.3	3.74	94	.262	.348	0	.000	-1	-2	-7	-2	-0.7

● BRIAN MEYER
Meyer, Brian Scott b: 1/29/63, Camden, N.J. BR/TR, 6', 190 lbs. Deb: 9/3/88

YEAR	TM/L	W	L	PCT	G	GS	CG	SH	SV	IP	H	HR	BB	SO	RAT	ERA	ERA+	OAV	OOB	BH	AVG	PB	PR	/A	PD	TPI
1988	Hou-N	0	0	—	8	0	0	0	0	12^1	9	2	4	10	9.5	1.46	227	.225	.295	0	—	0	3	3	1	0.1
1989	Hou-N	0	1	.000	12	0	0	0	1	18	16	0	13	13	15.0	4.50	75	.239	.370	0	—	0	-2	-2	0	-0.1
1990	Hou-N	0	4	.000	14	0	0	0	1	20^1	16	3	6	6	9.7	2.21	168	.211	.268	0	.000	-0	4	3	1	0.7
Total	3	0	5	.000	34	0	0	0	2	50^2	41	5	23	29	11.5	2.84	123	.224	.314	0	.000	-0	4	4	1	0.7

● JACK MEYER
Meyer, John Robert b: 3/23/32, Philadelphia, Pa. d: 3/9/67, Philadelphia, Pa. BR/TR, 6'1", 175 lbs. Deb: 4/16/55

YEAR	TM/L	W	L	PCT	G	GS	CG	SH	SV	IP	H	HR	BB	SO	RAT	ERA	ERA+	OAV	OOB	BH	AVG	PB	PR	/A	PD	TPI
1955	Phi-N	6	11	.353	50	5	0	0	**16**	110^1	75	14	66	97	11.7	3.43	116	.190	.310	2	.100	0	8	7	-1	1.1
1956	Phi-N	7	11	.389	41	7	2	0	2	96	86	8	51	66	13.2	4.41	84	.242	.343	4	.200	1	-7	-7	0	-1.1
1957	Phi-N	0	2	.000	19	2	0	0	0	37^2	44	7	28	34	17.4	5.73	66	.297	.412	1	.167	0	-8	-8	0	-0.3
1958	Phi-N	3	6	.333	37	5	1	0	2	90^1	77	8	33	87	11.1	3.59	110	.232	.303	5	.278	1	4	4	-1	0.3
1959	Phi-N	5	3	.625	47	1	1	0	1	93^2	76	9	53	71	12.5	3.36	122	.222	.328	1	.071	-1	6	8	0	0.5
1960	Phi-N	3	1	.750	7	4	0	0	0	25	25	2	11	18	13.0	4.32	90	.272	.350	1	.125	-0	-2	-1	-0	-0.2
1961	Phi-N	0	0	—	1	0	0	0	0	2	2	1	2	2	18.0	9.00	45	.286	.444	0	—	0	-1	-1	-0	0.0
Total	7	24	34	.414	202	24	4	0	21	455	385	49	244	375	12.6	3.92	100	.230	.332	14	.163	1	0	0	-1	0.3

● BOB MEYER
Meyer, Robert Bernard b: 8/4/39, Toledo, Ohio BR/TL, 6'2", 185 lbs. Deb: 4/20/64

YEAR	TM/L	W	L	PCT	G	GS	CG	SH	SV	IP	H	HR	BB	SO	RAT	ERA	ERA+	OAV	OOB	BH	AVG	PB	PR	/A	PD	TPI
1964	NY-A	0	3	.000	7	1	0	0	0	18^1	16	1	12	12	13.7	4.91	74	.235	.350	0	.000	-0	-3	-3	1	-0.4
	LA-A	1	1	.500	6	5	0	0	0	18	25	2	13	13	19.5	5.00	66	.333	.438	0	.000	-1	-3	-3	0	-0.4
	KC-A	1	4	.200	9	7	2	0	0	42	37	2	33	30	15.0	3.86	99	.248	.385	0	.000	-1	-1	-0	-1	-0.2
	Yr	2	8	.200	22	13	2	0	0	78^1	78	5	58	55	15.6	4.37	84	.266	.387	0	.000	-2	-6	-6	-0	-1.0
1969	Sea-A	0	3	.000	6	5	1	0	0	32^2	30	4	10	17	11.6	3.31	110	.252	.321	1	.091	-1	1	1	-1	-0.1
1970	Mil-A	0	1	.000	10	0	0	0	0	18^1	24	3	12	20	17.7	6.38	59	.329	.424	1	.333	0	-5	-5	0	-0.2
Total	3	2	12	.143	38	18	3	0	0	129^1	132	12	80	92	15.0	4.38	84	.273	.379	2	.057	-3	-11	-10	-1	-1.3

● RUSS MEYER
Meyer, Russell Charles "Rowdy" or "The Mad Monk" b: 10/25/23, Peru, Ill. d: 11/16/98, Oglesby, Ill. BB/TR, 6'1", 185 lbs. Deb: 9/13/46 C

YEAR	TM/L	W	L	PCT	G	GS	CG	SH	SV	IP	H	HR	BB	SO	RAT	ERA	ERA+	OAV	OOB	BH	AVG	PB	PR	/A	PD	TPI
1946	Chi-N	0	0	—	4	1	0	0	1	17	21	2	10	10	16.4	3.18	104	.309	.397	1	.200	0	0	0	0	0.0
1947	Chi-N	3	2	.600	23	2	1	0	0	45	43	4	14	22	11.6	3.40	116	.257	.319	3	.250	0	3	3	-0	0.3
1948	Chi-N	10	10	.500	29	26	8	3	0	164^2	157	8	77	89	12.8	3.66	107	.254	.338	6	.107	-3	5	4	-0	0.2
1949	Phi-N	17	8	.680	37	28	14	2	1	213	199	14	70	78	11.4	3.08	128	.250	.311	10	.143	-1	23	20	-2	1.9
1950	*Phi-N	9	11	.450	32	25	3	0	1	159^2	193	21	67	74	14.8	5.30	76	.304	.373	7	.140	-1	-21	-22	1	-2.4
1951	Phi-N	8	9	.471	28	24	7	2	0	168	172	13	55	65	12.3	3.48	111	.263	.322	5	.104	-2	9	7	-3	0.2
1952	Phi-N	13	14	.481	37	32	14	1	1	232^1	235	10	65	92	11.7	3.14	116	.260	.311	7	.089	-2	15	13	-2	1.0
1953	*Bro-N	15	5	.750	34	32	10	2	0	191^1	201	25	63	106	12.5	4.56	93	.269	.327	11	.147	-2	-6	-6	-0	-0.8
1954	Bro-N	11	6	.647	36	28	6	2	0	180^1	193	17	49	70	12.2	3.99	102	.275	.324	2	.043	-3	2	2	-2	-0.4
1955	*Bro-N	6	2	.750	18	11	2	1	0	73	86	8	31	26	14.4	5.42	75	.300	.368	1	.037	-3	-11	-11	1	-1.2
1956	Chi-N	1	6	.143	20	9	0	0	0	57	71	11	26	28	15.6	6.32	60	.313	.388	1	.083	-1	-16	-16	2	-1.6
	Cin-N	0	0	—	1	0	0	0	0	1	1	0	0	1	9.0	0.00	—	.250	.250	0	—	0	0	0	0	0.0
	Yr	1	6	.143	21	9	0	0	0	58	72	11	26	29	15.2	6.21	61	.305	.374	1	.083	-1	-16	-16	2	-1.6
1957	Bos-A	0	0	—	2	1	0	0	0	5	10	0	3	1	23.4	5.40	74	.417	.481	1	1.000	0	-1	-1	1	0.1
1959	KC-A	1	0	1.000	18	0	0	0	1	24	24	3	11	10	13.5	4.50	89	.261	.346	0	.000	-0	-2	-1	-0	-0.1
Total	13	94	73	.563	319	219	65	13	5	1531^1	1606	136	541	672	12.7	3.99	99	.271	.334	55	.114	-18	2	-8	-5	-2.8

● LEVI MEYERLE
Meyerle, Levi Samuel "Long Levi" b: 7/1845, Philadelphia, Pa. d: 11/4/21, Philadelphia, Pa. BR/TR, 6'1", 177 lbs. Deb: 5/20/1871 ♦

YEAR	TM/L	W	L	PCT	G	GS	CG	SH	SV	IP	H	HR	BB	SO	RAT	ERA	ERA+	OAV	OOB	BH	AVG	PB	PR	/A	PD	TPI
1871	Ath-n	0	0	—	1	0	0	0	0	1	1	0	2	0	27.0	9.00	45	.250	.500	64	.492	1	-1	-1		0.0
1876	Phi-N	0	2	.000	2	2	2	0	0	18	28	0	1	0	14.5	5.00	48	.337	.345	87	.340	1	-5	-5	-0	-0.4

● DAN MICELI
Miceli, Daniel b: 9/9/70, Newark, N.J. BR/TR, 6', 207 lbs. Deb: 9/9/93

YEAR	TM/L	W	L	PCT	G	GS	CG	SH	SV	IP	H	HR	BB	SO	RAT	ERA	ERA+	OAV	OOB	BH	AVG	PB	PR	/A	PD	TPI
1993	Pit-N	0	0	—	9	0	0	0	0	5^1	6	0	3	4	15.2	5.06	80	.273	.360	0	—	0	-1	-1	-0	0.0
1994	Pit-N	2	1	.667	28	0	0	0	2	27^1	28	5	11	27	13.5	5.93	73	.267	.347	0	.000	-0	-5	-5	0	-0.5
1995	Pit-N	4	4	.500	58	0	0	0	21	58	61	7	28	56	14.4	4.66	92	.270	.360	0	.000	-0	-3	-2	-1	-0.5
1996	Pit-N	2	10	.167	44	9	0	0	1	85^2	99	15	45	66	15.4	5.78	75	.291	.379	0	.000	-1	-15	-14	-2	-2.0

YEAR	TM/L	W	L	PCT	G	GS	CG	SH	SV	IP	H	HR	BB	SO	RAT	ERA	ERA+	OAV	OOB	BH	AVG	PB	PR	/A	PD	TPI
1997	Det-A	3	2	.600	71	0	0	0	3	82^2	77	13	38	79	12.6	5.01	91	.248	.332	0	—	0	-4	-4	-1	-0.3
1998	*SD-N	10	5	.667	67	0	0	0	2	72^2	64	6	27	70	11.4	3.22	119	.238	.310	1	1.000	1	8	5	-1	0.9
Total	6	21	22	.488	277	9	0	0	29	331^2	335	46	152	302	13.5	4.83	89	.263	.347	1	.056	-1	-20	-20	-5	-2.4

● GENE MICHAEL

Michael, Eugene Richard "Stick" b: 6/2/38, Kent, Ohio BB/TR, 6'2", 183 lbs. Deb: 7/15/66 MC◆

YEAR	TM/L	W	L	PCT	G	GS	CG	SH	SV	IP	H	HR	BB	SO	RAT	ERA	ERA+	OAV	OOB	BH	AVG	PB	PR	/A	PD	TPI
1968	NY-A	0	0	—	1	0	0	0	0	3	5	0	0	3	18.0	0.00	—	.357	.400	23	.198	0	1	1	0	0.0

● JOHN MICHAELS

Michaels, John Joseph b: 7/10/07, Bridgeport, Conn. d: 11/18/96, Sebring, Fla. BL/TL, 5'10.5", 154 lbs. Deb: 4/16/32

YEAR	TM/L	W	L	PCT	G	GS	CG	SH	SV	IP	H	HR	BB	SO	RAT	ERA	ERA+	OAV	OOB	BH	AVG	PB	PR	/A	PD	TPI
1932	Bos-A	1	6	.143	28	8	2	0	0	80^2	101	4	27	16	14.6	5.13	88	.304	.362	3	.143	-1	-6	-6	1	-0.4

● JOHN MICHAELSON

Michaelson, John August "Mike" b: 8/12/1893, Tivalkoski, Finland d: 4/16/68, Woodruff, Wis. BR/TR, 5'9", 165 lbs. Deb: 8/28/21

YEAR	TM/L	W	L	PCT	G	GS	CG	SH	SV	IP	H	HR	BB	SO	RAT	ERA	ERA+	OAV	OOB	BH	AVG	PB	PR	/A	PD	TPI
1921	Chi-A	0	0	—	2	0	0	0	0	2^2	4	0	1	1	16.9	10.13	42	.400	.455	0	—	0	-2	-2	-0	0.0

● CHRIS MICHALAK

Michalak, Christian Matthew b: 1/4/71, Joliet, Ill. BL/TL, 6'2", 195 lbs. Deb: 8/22/98

YEAR	TM/L	W	L	PCT	G	GS	CG	SH	SV	IP	H	HR	BB	SO	RAT	ERA	ERA+	OAV	OOB	BH	AVG	PB	PR	/A	PD	TPI
1998	Ari-N	0	0	—	5	0	0	0	0	5^1	9	1	4	5	21.9	11.81	36	.375	.464	0	—	0	-4	-4	-0	0.0

● GLENN MICKENS

Mickens, Glenn Roger b: 7/26/30, Wilmar, Cal. BR/TR, 6', 175 lbs. Deb: 7/19/53

YEAR	TM/L	W	L	PCT	G	GS	CG	SH	SV	IP	H	HR	BB	SO	RAT	ERA	ERA+	OAV	OOB	BH	AVG	PB	PR	/A	PD	TPI
1953	Bro-N	0	1	.000	4	2	0	0	0	6^1	11	2	4	5	21.3	11.37	37	.393	.469	0	.000	-0	-5	-5	0	-0.6

● JIM MIDDLETON

Middleton, James Blaine "Rifle Jim" b: 5/28/1889, Argos, Ind. d: 1/12/74, Argos, Ind. BR/TR, 5'11.5", 165 lbs. Deb: 4/18/17

YEAR	TM/L	W	L	PCT	G	GS	CG	SH	SV	IP	H	HR	BB	SO	RAT	ERA	ERA+	OAV	OOB	BH	AVG	PB	PR	/A	PD	TPI
1917	NY-N	1	1	.500	13	0	0	0	1	36	35	1	8	9	11.0	2.75	93	.255	.301	0	.000	-1	-0	-1	1	-0.1
1921	Det-A	6	11	.353	38	10	2	0	7	121^2	149	5	44	31	14.4	5.03	85	.302	.361	5	.147	-2	-10	-10	1	-1.4
Total	2	7	12	.368	51	10	2	0	8	157^2	184	6	52	40	13.6	4.51	86	.292	.348	5	.119	-3	-10	-11	2	-1.5

● JOHN MIDDLETON

Middleton, John Wayne "Lefty" b: 4/11/1900, Mt.Calm, Tex. d: 11/3/86, Amarillo, Tex. BL/TL, 6'1", 185 lbs. Deb: 9/6/22

YEAR	TM/L	W	L	PCT	G	GS	CG	SH	SV	IP	H	HR	BB	SO	RAT	ERA	ERA+	OAV	OOB	BH	AVG	PB	PR	/A	PD	TPI
1922	Cle-A	0	1	.000	2	1	0	0	0	7^1	8	1	6	2	17.2	7.36	54	.286	.412	1	.333	0	-3	-3	0	-0.3

● DICK MIDKIFF

Midkiff, Richard b: 9/28/14, Gonzales, Tex. d: 10/30/56, Temple, Tex. BR/TR, 6'2", 185 lbs. Deb: 4/24/38

YEAR	TM/L	W	L	PCT	G	GS	CG	SH	SV	IP	H	HR	BB	SO	RAT	ERA	ERA+	OAV	OOB	BH	AVG	PB	PR	/A	PD	TPI
1938	Bos-A	1	1	.500	13	2	0	0	0	35^1	43	5	21	10	16.3	5.09	97	.305	.395	2	.200	0	-1	-1	0	0.0

● GARY MIELKE

Mielke, Gary Roger b: 1/28/63, St.James, Minn. BR/TR, 6'3", 185 lbs. Deb: 8/19/87

YEAR	TM/L	W	L	PCT	G	GS	CG	SH	SV	IP	H	HR	BB	SO	RAT	ERA	ERA+	OAV	OOB	BH	AVG	PB	PR	/A	PD	TPI
1987	Tex-A	0	0	—	3	0	0	0	0	3	3	2	1	3	12.0	6.00	75	.250	.308	0	—	0	-1	-1	-0	0.0
1989	Tex-A	1	0	1.000	43	0	0	0	1	49^2	52	4	25	26	14.3	3.26	122	.280	.371	0	—	0	3	4	-0	0.0
1990	Tex-A	0	3	.000	33	0	0	0	0	41	42	4	15	13	13.0	3.73	105	.271	.343	0	—	0	1	1	0	0.1
Total	3	1	3	.250	79	0	0	0	1	93^2	97	10	41	42	13.6	3.56	111	.275	.357	0	—	0	4	4	-0	0.1

● PETE MIKKELSEN

Mikkelsen, Peter James b: 10/25/39, Staten Island, N.Y. BR/TR, 6'2", 220 lbs. Deb: 4/17/64

YEAR	TM/L	W	L	PCT	G	GS	CG	SH	SV	IP	H	HR	BB	SO	RAT	ERA	ERA+	OAV	OOB	BH	AVG	PB	PR	/A	PD	TPI
1964	*NY-A	7	4	.636	50	0	0	0	12	86	79	3	41	63	13.0	3.56	102	.247	.340	1	.063	-1	1	1	1	0.1
1965	NY-A	4	9	.308	41	3	0	0	1	82^1	78	10	36	69	12.8	3.28	104	.249	.332	1	.100	-0	2	1	1	0.3
1966	Pit-N	9	8	.529	71	0	0	0	14	126	106	8	51	76	11.6	3.07	116	.234	.318	3	.150	-0	7	7	-0	1.0
1967	Pit-N	1	2	.333	32	0	0	0	2	56^1	50	7	19	30	11.5	4.31	78	.237	.309	0	.000	-0	-6	-6	-1	-0.5
	Chi-N	0	0	—	7	0	0	0	0	7	9	1	5	0	19.3	6.43	55	.333	.455	0	—	0	-2	-2	-0	0.0
	Yr	1	2	.333	39	0	0	0	2	63^1	59	8	24	30	11.9	4.55	74	.244	.315	0	.000	-0	-8	-8	-1	-0.5
1968	Chi-N	0	0	—	3	0	0	0	0	4^2	7	3	1	5	15.4	7.71	41	.350	.381	1	1.000	0	-2	-2	0	0.1
	StL-N	0	0	—	5	0	0	0	0	16	10	0	7	8	9.6	1.13	257	.179	.270	0	.000	-0	3	3	-1	-0.1
	Yr	0	0	—	8	0	0	0	0	20^2	17	3	8	13	10.9	2.61	113	.224	.298	1	.250	0	1	1	-0	0.0
1969	LA-N	7	5	.583	48	0	0	0	4	81^1	57	9	30	51	10.1	2.77	120	.193	.277	1	.167	-0	7	5	1	0.8
1970	LA-N	4	2	.667	33	0	0	0	6	62	48	5	20	47	10.5	2.76	139	.211	.287	2	.333	1	9	7	0	0.9
1971	LA-N	8	5	.615	41	0	0	0	5	74	67	10	17	46	10.3	3.65	89	.242	.288	2	.200	0	-2	-3	1	-0.5
1972	LA-N	5	5	.500	33	0	0	0	5	57^2	65	3	23	41	14.5	4.06	82	.283	.360	2	.000	-0	-4	-5	-0	-0.9
Total	9	45	40	.529	364	3	0	0	49	653^1	576	59	250	436	11.8	3.38	102	.237	.316	11	.133	-2	13	6	2	1.2

● HANK MIKLOS

Miklos, John Joseph b: 11/27/10, Chicago, Ill. BL/TL, 5'11", 175 lbs. Deb: 4/23/44

YEAR	TM/L	W	L	PCT	G	GS	CG	SH	SV	IP	H	HR	BB	SO	RAT	ERA	ERA+	OAV	OOB	BH	AVG	PB	PR	/A	PD	TPI
1944	Chi-N	0	0	—	2	0	0	0	0	7	9	1	3	0	15.4	7.71	46	.333	.400	0	.000	-0	-3	-3	1	0.0

● BOB MILACKI

Milacki, Robert b: 7/28/64, Trenton, N.J. BR/TR, 6'4", 234 lbs. Deb: 9/18/88

YEAR	TM/L	W	L	PCT	G	GS	CG	SH	SV	IP	H	HR	BB	SO	RAT	ERA	ERA+	OAV	OOB	BH	AVG	PB	PR	/A	PD	TPI
1988	Bal-A	2	0	1.000	3	3	1	1	0	25	9	1	9	18	6.5	0.72	542	.110	.198	0	—	0	9	9	0	0.9
1989	Bal-A	14	12	.538	37	36	3	2	0	243	233	21	88	113	12.0	3.74	101	.254	.320	0	—	0	4	1	-0	0.2
1990	Bal-A	5	8	.385	27	24	1	1	0	135^1	143	18	61	60	13.6	4.46	85	.273	.349	0	—	0	-8	-10	1	-0.8
1991	Bal-A	10	9	.526	31	26	3	1	0	184	175	17	53	108	11.2	4.01	99	.253	.307	0	—	0	2	-1	1	0.1
1992	Bal-A	6	8	.429	23	20	0	0	1	115^2	140	16	44	51	14.5	5.84	69	.296	.358	0	—	0	-24	-23	-1	-2.5
1993	Cle-A	1	1	.500	5	2	0	0	0	16	19	3	11	7	16.9	3.38	128	.302	.405	0	—	0	2	2	0	0.2
1994	KC-A	0	5	.000	10	10	0	0	0	55^2	68	6	20	17	14.4	6.14	81	.298	.357	0	—	0	-8	-7	1	-0.5
1996	Sea-A	1	4	.200	7	4	0	0	0	21	30	3	15	13	19.3	6.86	72	.330	.425	0	—	0	-4	-4	-0	-0.8
Total	8	39	47	.453	143	125	8	5	1	795^2	817	85	301	387	12.7	4.38	91	.266	.333	0	—	0	-29	-34	2	-3.2

● MIKE MILCHIN

Milchin, Michael Wayne b: 2/28/68, Knoxville, Tenn. BL/TL, 6'3", 190 lbs. Deb: 5/14/96

YEAR	TM/L	W	L	PCT	G	GS	CG	SH	SV	IP	H	HR	BB	SO	RAT	ERA	ERA+	OAV	OOB	BH	AVG	PB	PR	/A	PD	TPI
1996	Min-A	2	1	.667	26	0	0	0	0	21^2	31	6	12	19	17.9	8.31	62	.341	.417	0	—	0	-8	-8	0	-0.9
	Bal-A	1	0	1.000	13	0	0	0	0	11	13	0	5	10	14.7	5.73	86	.325	.400	0	—	0	-1	-1	0	0.0
	Yr	3	1	.750	39	0	0	0	0	32^2	44	6	17	29	16.8	7.44	68	.336	.412	0	—	0	-9	-9	0	-0.9

● CARL MILES

Miles, Carl Thomas b: 3/22/18, Trenton, Mo. BB/TL, 5'11", 178 lbs. Deb: 6/8/40

YEAR	TM/L	W	L	PCT	G	GS	CG	SH	SV	IP	H	HR	BB	SO	RAT	ERA	ERA+	OAV	OOB	BH	AVG	PB	PR	/A	PD	TPI
1940	Phi-A	0	0	—	2	0	0	0	0	8	9	2	8	6	19.1	13.50	33	.281	.425	3	.750	2	-8	-8	-0	0.2

● JIM MILES

Miles, James Charlie b: 8/8/43, Grenada, Miss. BR/TR, 6'2", 210 lbs. Deb: 9/7/68

YEAR	TM/L	W	L	PCT	G	GS	CG	SH	SV	IP	H	HR	BB	SO	RAT	ERA	ERA+	OAV	OOB	BH	AVG	PB	PR	/A	PD	TPI
1968	Was-A	0	0	—	3	0	0	0	0	4^1	8	0	2	5	20.8	12.46	23	.421	.476	0	—	0	-5	-5	-0	0.0
1969	Was-A	0	1	.000	10	1	0	0	0	20^1	19	2	15	15	16.8	6.20	56	.257	.409	1	.333	0	-6	-6	1	-0.2
Total	2	0	1	.000	13	1	0	0	0	24^2	27	2	17	20	17.5	7.30	46	.290	.421	1	.333	0	-10	-11	1	-0.2

● SAM MILITELLO

Militello, Sam Salvatore b: 11/26/69, Tampa, Fla. BR/TR, 6'3", 200 lbs. Deb: 8/9/92

YEAR	TM/L	W	L	PCT	G	GS	CG	SH	SV	IP	H	HR	BB	SO	RAT	ERA	ERA+	OAV	OOB	BH	AVG	PB	PR	/A	PD	TPI
1992	NY-A	3	3	.500	9	9	0	0	0	60	43	6	32	42	11.6	3.45	113	.195	.302	0	—	0	3	3	-1	0.2
1993	NY-A	1	1	.500	3	2	0	0	0	9^1	10	1	7	5	18.3	6.75	62	.270	.413	0	—	0	-3	-3	0	-0.4
Total	2	4	4	.500	12	11	0	0	0	69^1	53	7	39	47	12.5	3.89	101	.205	.319	0	—	0	1	0	-1	-0.2

● JOHNNY MILJUS

Miljus, John Kenneth "Jovo" or "Big Serb"
b: 6/30/1895, Pittsburgh, Pa. d: 2/11/76, Fort Harrison, Mont. BR/TR, 6'1", 178 lbs. Deb: 10/2/15

YEAR	TM/L	W	L	PCT	G	GS	CG	SH	SV	IP	H	HR	BB	SO	RAT	ERA	ERA+	OAV	OOB	BH	AVG	PB	PR	/A	PD	TPI
1915	Pit-F	0	0	—	1	0	0	0	0	1	1	0	0	1	9.0	0.00	—	.250	.250	0	—	0	0	0	0	0.0
1917	Bro-N	0	1	.000	4	1	1	0	0	15	14	0	8	9	15.0	0.60	466	.250	.373	0	.000	-1	4	4	-0	0.1
1920	Bro-N	1	0	1.000	9	0	0	0	0	23^1	24	2	4	9	10.8	3.09	104	.267	.298	2	.333	1	0	0	1	0.2
1921	Bro-N	6	3	.667	28	9	3	0	1	93^2	115	1	27	37	13.8	4.23	92	.312	.362	5	.167	-2	-5	-4	2	-0.3
1927	*Pit-N	8	3	.727	19	6	3	2	0	75^2	62	0	17	24	9.4	1.90	216	.228	.273	5	.179	-1	17	19	2	2.6
1928	Pit-N	5	7	.417	21	10	3	0	1	69^2	90	2	33	26	16.3	5.30	77	.313	.389	8	.308	1	-10	-10	-0	-1.3
	Cle-A	1	4	.200	11	4	1	0	1	50^2	46	1	20	19	11.7	2.66	156	.243	.316	3	.200	-0	8	8	-0	0.7
1929	Cle-A	8	8	.500	34	15	4	0	2	128^1	174	10	64	42	16.9	5.19	86	.331	.406	11	.256	1	-13	-11	0	-1.0
Total	7	29	26	.527	127	45	15	2	5	457^1	526	16	173	166	14.0	3.92	104	.293	.359	34	.222	0	7	4	1	1.0

● DYAR MILLER

Miller, Dyar K b: 5/29/46, Batesville, Ind. BR/TR, 6'1", 195 lbs. Deb: 6/9/75 C

YEAR	TM/L	W	L	PCT	G	GS	CG	SH	SV	IP	H	HR	BB	SO	RAT	ERA	ERA+	OAV	OOB	BH	AVG	PB	PR	/A	PD	TPI
1975	Bal-A	6	3	.667	30	0	0	0	8	46^1	32	3	16	33	9.3	2.72	129	.199	.271	0	—	0	5	4	0	1.1
1976	Bal-A	2	4	.333	49	0	0	0	7	88^2	79	5	36	37	11.8	2.94	111	.246	.324	0	—	0	6	3	-1	0.2
1977	Bal-A	2	2	.500	12	0	0	0	1	22^1	25	6	10	9	14.1	5.64	67	.278	.350	0	—	0	-4	-5	-0	-0.6
	Cal-A	4	4	.500	41	0	0	0	4	92^1	81	10	30	49	10.8	3.02	129	.242	.304	0	—	0	11	9	-1	0.8
	Yr	6	6	.500	53	0	0	0	5	114^2	106	16	40	58	11.5	3.53	110	.249	.314	0	—	0	7	5	-1	0.2
1978	Cal-A	6	2	.750	41	0	0	0	1	84^2	85	3	41	34	13.9	2.66	136	.264	.356	0	—	0	10	9	-2	0.7

YEAR	TM/L	W	L	PCT	G	GS	CG	SH	SV	IP	H	HR	BB	SO	RAT	ERA	ERA+	OAV	OOB	BH	AVG	PB	PR	/A	PD	TPI
1979	Cal-A	1	0	1.000	14	1	0	0	0	35^{1}	44	2	13	16	15.0	3.31	123	.319	.386	0	—	0	4	3	-1	0.2
	Tor-A	0	0	—	10	0	0	0	0	15^{1}	27	3	5	7	18.8	10.57	41	.391	.432	0	—	0	-11	-11	-0	-0.1
	Yr	1	0	1.000	24	1	0	0	0	50^{2}	71	5	18	23	15.8	5.51	75	.333	.385	0	—	0	-7	-8	-1	0.1
1980	NY-N	1	2	.333	31	0	0	0	1	42	37	1	11	28	10.3	1.93	184	.242	.293	0	.000	-0	8	8	-1	0.5
1981	NY-N	1	0	1.000	23	0	0	0	0	38^{1}	49	2	15	22	15.3	3.29	106	.327	.392	1	.333	0	1	1	-1	0.0
Total	7	23	17	.575	251	1	0	0	22	465^{1}	459	35	177	235	12.5	3.23	113	.264	.335	1	.250	0	30	22	-7	2.8

● ELMER MILLER Miller, Elmer Joseph “Lefty” b: 4/17/03, Detroit, Mich. d: 1/8/87, Corona, Cal. BL/TL, 5'11", 189 lbs. Deb: 6/21/29 ♦

1929	Phi-N	0	1	.000	8	2	0	0	0	11^{1}	12	1	21	5	28.6	11.12	47	.279	.537	9	.237	0	-8	-7	-0	-0.5

● FRANK MILLER Miller, Frank Lee “Bullet” b: 5/13/1886, Allegan, Mich. d: 2/19/74, Allegan, Mich. BR/TR, 6', 188 lbs. Deb: 7/12/13

1913	Chi-A	0	1	.000	1	1	0	0	0	1^{2}	4	0	3	2	37.8	27.00	11	.571	.700	0	—	0	-4	-4	0	-1.3
1916	Pit-N	7	10	.412	30	20	10	2	1	173	135	4	49	88	9.9	2.29	117	.226	.292	7	.137	-1	6	8	-1	0.6
1917	Pit-N	10	19	.345	38	28	14	5	1	224	216	1	60	92	11.3	3.13	91	.251	.304	9	.118	-4	-11	-7	1	-1.4
1918	Pit-N	11	8	.579	23	23	14	2	0	170^{1}	152	1	37	47	10.4	2.38	121	.250	.301	6	.105	-3	7	9	-0	0.7
1919	Pit-N	13	12	.520	32	26	16	3	0	201^{2}	170	6	34	59	9.3	3.03	99	.234	.272	7	.106	-5	-3	-0	1	-0.5
1922	Bos-N	11	13	.458	31	23	14	2	1	200	213	7	60	65	12.4	3.51	114	.279	.333	8	.118	-5	13	11	1	0.8
1923	Bos-N	0	3	.000	8	6	0	0	1	39^{1}	54	2	11	6	15.6	4.58	87	.335	.389	1	.143	-0	-3	-3	-1	-0.3
Total	7	52	66	.441	163	127	68	14	4	1010	944	21	254	359	10.9	3.01	104	.253	.306	38	.117	-18	7	14	1	-1.4

● FRED MILLER Miller, Frederick Holman “Speedy” b: 6/28/1886, Fairfield, Ind. d: 5/2/53, Brookville, Ind. BL/TL, 6'2", 190 lbs. Deb: 7/8/10

1910	Bro-N	1	1	.500	6	2	0	0	0	21	25	1	13	2	17.6	4.71	64	.309	.423	2	.250	0	-4	-4	0	-0.3

● BERT MILLER Miller, Herbert A. b: 10/26/1875, Riley, Mich. d: 6/14/37, Flint, Mich. Deb: 7/15/1897

1897	Lou-N	0	1	.000	4	1	1	0	0	17	32	0	3	3	18.5	7.94	54	.395	.417	1	.167	-1	-7	-7	0	-0.3

● OX MILLER Miller, John Anthony b: 5/4/15, Gause, Tex. BR/TR, 6'1", 190 lbs. Deb: 8/7/43

1943	Was-A	0	0	—	3	0	0	0	0	6	10	1	5	1	22.5	10.50	31	.370	.469	0	.000	-0	-5	-5	1	0.0
	StL-A	0	0	—	2	0	0	0	0	6	7	2	3	3	18.0	12.00	28	.304	.429	0	.000	-0	-6	-6	1	0.0
	Yr	0	0	—	5	0	0	0	0	12	17	3	8	4	20.3	11.25	29	.340	.450	0	.000	-0	-11	-11	1	0.0
1945	StL-A	2	1	.667	4	3	3	0	0	28^{1}	23	2	5	4	8.9	1.59	222	.219	.255	2	.182	-0	6	6	-1	0.5
1946	StL-A	1	3	.250	11	3	0	0	1	35^{1}	52	5	15	12	17.1	6.88	54	.338	.396	2	.286	1	-13	-12	1	-1.2
1947	Chi-N	1	2	.333	4	4	1	0	0	16	31	2	5	7	20.3	10.13	39	.397	.434	3	.429	2	-11	-11	-0	-1.4
Total	4	4	6	.400	24	10	4	0	1	91^{2}	123	12	33	27	15.5	6.38	57	.318	.374	7	.259	2	-29	-28	0	-2.1

● JOHN MILLER Miller, John Ernest b: 5/30/41, Baltimore, Md. BR/TR, 6'2", 210 lbs. Deb: 9/22/62

1962	Bal-A	1	1	.500	2	1	0	0	0	10	2	0	5	4	6.3	0.90	411	.065	.194	0	.000	-0	3	3	0	0.7
1963	Bal-A	1	1	.500	3	2	0	0	0	17	12	0	14	16	13.8	3.18	109	.194	.342	0	.000	-1	1	1	-0	0.0
1965	Bal-A	6	4	.600	16	16	1	0	0	93^{1}	75	4	58	71	12.9	3.18	109	.223	.338	3	.100	-1	3	3	0	0.3
1966	Bal-A	4	8	.333	23	16	0	0	0	100^{2}	92	15	58	81	13.4	4.74	70	.241	.342	4	.118	-1	-15	-16	1	-1.8
1967	Bal-A	0	0	—	2	0	0	0	0	6	7	1	3	6	18.0	7.50	42	.304	.429	0	—	0	-3	-3	0	0.0
Total	5	12	14	.462	46	35	1	0	0	227	188	20	138	178	13.0	3.89	88	.225	.337	7	.096	-3	-10	-12	1	-0.8

● CYCLONE MILLER Miller, Joseph H. b: 9/24/1859, Springfield, Mass d: 10/13/16, New London, Conn. TL, 5'9.5", 165 lbs. Deb: 7/11/1884

1884	CP-U	1	0	1.000	1	1	1	0	0	9	4	0	0	13	4.0	1.00	244	.125	.125	1	.250	-0	1	1	1	0.2
	Pro-N	3	2	.600	6	5	2	0	0	34^{2}	36	0	11	12	12.2	2.08	137	.259	.313	1	.043	-3	3	3	-1	0.1
	Phi-N	0	1	.000	1	1	1	0	0	9	17	5	6	1	23.0	10.00	30	.386	.460	0	.000	-1	-7	-7	0	-0.5
	Yr	3	3	.500	7	6	3	0	0	43^{2}	53	5	17	13	14.4	3.71	78	.290	.350	1	.037	-4	-4	-4	-1	-0.4
1886	Phi-a	10	8	.556	19	19	19	1	0	169^{2}	158	6	59	99	11.7	2.97	118	.239	.305	9	.136	-1	9	10	1	0.9
Total	2	14	11	.560	27	26	23	1	0	222^{1}	215	11	76	125	11.9	3.04	110	.245	.308	11	.113	-5	7	7	1	0.7

● WHITEY MILLER Miller, Kenneth Albert b: 5/2/15, St.Louis, Mo. d: 4/3/91, St.Louis, Mo. BR/TR, 6'1", 195 lbs. Deb: 9/15/44

1944	NY-N	0	1	.000	4	0	0	0	0	5	1	0	4	2	9.0	0.00	—	.059	.238	0	.000	-0	2	2	0	0.4

● KURT MILLER Miller, Kurt Everett b: 8/24/72, Tucson, Ariz. BR/TR, 6'5", 205 lbs. Deb: 6/11/94

1994	Fla-N	1	3	.250	4	4	0	0	0	20	26	3	7	11	15.7	8.10	54	.317	.385	1	.167	-0	-9	-8	1	-1.2
1996	Fla-N	1	3	.250	26	5	0	0	0	46^{1}	57	5	33	30	17.9	6.80	60	.313	.424	3	.375	1	-13	-14	0	-0.9
1997	Fla-N	0	1	.000	7	0	0	0	0	7^{1}	12	2	7	7	24.5	9.82	41	.364	.488	0	—	0	-5	-5	-0	-0.6
1998	Chi-N	0	0	—	3	0	0	0	0	4	3	0	0	6	6.8	0.00	—	.200	.200	0	—	0	2	2	-0	0.0
Total	4	2	7	.222	40	9	0	0	0	77^{2}	98	10	47	54	17.4	7.07	59	.314	.412	4	.286	1	-25	-25	1	-2.7

● LARRY MILLER Miller, Larry Don b: 6/19/37, Topeka, Kan. BL/TL, 6', 195 lbs. Deb: 6/21/64

1964	LA-N	4	8	.333	16	14	1	0	0	79^{2}	87	1	28	50	13.2	4.18	78	.275	.338	7	.269	2	-6	-8	-1	-1.0
1965	NY-N	1	4	.200	28	5	0	0	0	57^{1}	66	6	25	36	14.4	5.02	70	.289	.362	2	.182	0	-9	-10	-0	-0.8
1966	NY-N	0	2	.000	4	1	0	0	0	8^{1}	9	3	4	7	14.0	7.56	48	.273	.351	1	.500	0	-4	-4	-0	-0.7
Total	3	5	14	.263	48	20	1	0	0	145^{1}	162	10	57	93	13.7	4.71	72	.281	.349	10	.256	2	-19	-21	-1	-2.5

● RED MILLER Miller, Leo Alphonso b: 2/11/1897, Philadelphia, Pa. d: 10/20/73, Orlando, Fla. BR/TR, 5'11", 195 lbs. Deb: 4/13/23

1923	Phi-N	0	0	—	1	0	0	0	0	1^{2}	6	0	1	0	37.8	32.40	14	.545	.583	0	.000	-0	-5	-5	-0	0.0

● PAUL MILLER Miller, Paul Robert b: 4/27/65, Burlington, Wis. BR/TR, 6'5", 215 lbs. Deb: 7/30/91

1991	Pit-N	0	0	—	1	1	0	0	0	5	4	0	3	2	12.6	5.40	66	.222	.333	0	.000	-0	-1	-1	-0	-0.1
1992	Pit-N	1	0	1.000	6	0	0	0	0	11^{1}	11	0	1	5	9.5	2.38	144	.256	.273	0	.000	-0	1	1	-0	0.1
1993	Pit-N	0	0	—	3	2	0	0	0	10	15	2	2	2	15.3	5.40	75	.349	.378	0	.000	-0	-2	-2	-0	-0.1
Total	3	1	0	1.000	10	3	0	0	0	26^{1}	30	2	6	9	12.3	4.10	90	.288	.327	0	.000	-1	-1	-1	-1	-0.1

● RALPH MILLER Miller, Ralph Darwin b: 3/15/1873, Cincinnati, Ohio d: 5/8/73, Cincinnati, Ohio BR/TR, 5'11", 170 lbs. Deb: 5/4/1898

1898	Bro-N	4	14	.222	23	21	16	0	0	151^{2}	161	4	86	43	15.4	5.34	67	.270	.374	12	.194	-1	-29	-30	3	-2.6
1899	Bal-N	1	3	.250	6	4	3	0	0	37	44	0	14	3	15.1	4.38	91	.295	.371	2	.182	1	-2	-2	-1	-0.1
Total	2	5	17	.227	29	25	19	0	0	188^{2}	205	4	100	46	15.4	5.15	71	.275	.374	14	.192	1	-31	-31	2	-2.7

● RALPH MILLER Miller, Ralph Henry “Moose” or “Lefty”
b: 1/14/1899, Vinton, Iowa d: 2/18/67, White Bear Lake, Minn. BR/TL, 6'1.5", 190 lbs. Deb: 9/16/21 F

1921	Was-A	0	0	—	1	0	0	0	0	1	0	0	0	0	0.0	0.00	—	.000	.000	0	—	0	0	0	-0	0.0

● RANDY MILLER Miller, Randall Scott b: 3/18/53, Oxnard, Cal. BR/TR, 6'1", 180 lbs. Deb: 9/7/77

1977	Bal-A	0	0	—	1	0	0	0	0	0^{2}	4	0	0	0	54.0	40.50	9	.800	.800	0	—	0	-3	-3	-0	0.0
1978	Mon-N	0	1	.000	5	0	0	0	0	7	11	1	3	6	18.0	10.29	34	.393	.452	0	.000	-0	-5	-5	0	-0.7
Total	2	0	1	.000	6	0	0	0	0	7^{2}	15	1	3	6	21.1	12.91	27	.455	.500	0	.000	-0	-8	-8	0	-0.7

● BOB MILLER Miller, Robert Gerald b: 7/15/35, Berwyn, Ill. BR/TL, 6'1", 185 lbs. Deb: 6/25/53

1953	Det-A	1	2	.333	13	1	0	0	0	36^{1}	43	2	21	9	16.1	5.94	68	.289	.380	1	.125	-1	-8	-8	0	-0.6
1954	Det-A	1	1	.500	32	1	0	0	1	69^{2}	62	1	26	27	11.4	2.45	150	.244	.314	2	.133	-0	10	10	1	0.2
1955	Det-A	2	1	.667	7	3	1	0	0	25^{1}	26	4	12	11	13.5	2.49	154	.263	.342	2	.222	0	4	4	-0	0.4
1956	Det-A	0	2	.000	11	3	0	0	0	31^{2}	37	5	22	16	16.8	5.68	72	.308	.415	1	.143	0	-5	-6	-1	-0.3
1962	Cin-N	0	0	—	6	0	0	0	0	5^{1}	14	1	3	4	32.1	21.94	18	.538	.613	0	.000	-0	-11	-11	0	0.0
	NY-N	2	2	.500	17	0	0	0	1	20^{1}	24	2	8	8	14.6	7.08	59	.312	.384	0	.000	-0	-7	-7	0	-1.2
	Yr	2	2	.500	23	0	0	0	1	25^{2}	38	3	11	12	17.5	10.17	41	.355	.420	0	.000	-0	-18	-17	0	-1.2
Total	5	6	8	.429	86	8	1	0	2	188^{2}	206	15	92	75	14.4	4.72	83	.284	.368	6	.146	-1	-17	-17	-1	-1.5

● BOB MILLER Miller, Robert John b: 6/16/26, Detroit, Mich. BR/TR, 6'3", 190 lbs. Deb: 9/16/49

1949	Phi-N	0	0	—	3	0	0	0	0	2^{2}	2	0	2	0	13.5	0.00	—	.200	.333	0	—	0	1	1	0	0.0
1950	*Phi-N	11	6	.647	35	22	7	2	1	174	190	9	57	44	13.0	3.57	113	.277	.337	11	.180	-1	11	9	2	0.9

YEAR	TM/L	W	L	PCT	G	GS	CG	SH	SV	IP	H	HR	BB	SO	RAT	ERA	ERA+	OAV	OOB	BH	AVG	PB	PR	/A	PD	TPI
1951	Phi-N	2	1	.667	17	3	0	0	0	34^1	47	2	18	10	17.3	6.82	56	.331	.410	3	.429	1	-11	-11	-1	-0.9
1952	Phi-N	0	1	.000	3	1	0	0	0	9	13	2	1	2	14.0	6.00	61	.351	.368	0	.000	-0	-2	-2	0	-0.2
1953	Phi-N	8	9	.471	35	20	8	3	2	157^1	169	14	42	63	12.2	4.00	105	.271	.319	10	.182	-1	5	4	-1	0.2
1954	Phi-N	7	9	.438	30	16	5	0	0	150	176	14	39	42	13.1	4.56	89	.300	.347	8	.160	0	-8	-9	-1	-0.7
1955	Phi-N	8	4	.667	40	0	0	0	1	89^2	80	6	28	28	10.9	2.41	165	.242	.304	5	.278	1	16	16	0	2.0
1956	Phi-N	3	6	.333	49	6	3	1	5	122^1	115	14	34	53	11.2	3.24	115	.248	.303	2	.091	-1	7	7	-0	0.4
1957	Phi-N	2	5	.286	32	1	0	0	6	60^1	61	4	17	12	11.8	2.69	142	.265	.319	2	.250	2	8	8	-1	1.1
1958	Phi-N	1	1	.500	17	0	0	0	0	22^1	36	7	9	9	18.1	11.69	34	.360	.413	0	.000	-0	-19	-19	-0	-1.5
Total	10	42	42	.500	261	69	23	6	15	822	889	72	247	263	12.6	3.96	101	.277	.332	41	.184	1	8	2	1	1.3

● BOB MILLER

Miller, Robert Lane (b: Robert Lane Gemeinweiser)
b: 2/18/39, St.Louis, Mo. d: 8/6/93, Rancho Bernardo, Cal. BR/TR, 6'1", 182 lbs. Deb: 6/26/57 C

YEAR	TM/L	W	L	PCT	G	GS	CG	SH	SV	IP	H	HR	BB	SO	RAT	ERA	ERA+	OAV	OOB	BH	AVG	PB	PR	/A	PD	TPI
1957	StL-N	0	0	—	5	0	0	0	0	9	13	2	5	7	18.0	7.00	57	.325	.400	0	—	0	-3	-3	0	0.0
1959	StL-N	4	3	.571	11	10	3	0	0	70^2	66	2	21	43	11.2	3.31	128	.248	.306	5	.208	0	5	7	1	0.8
1960	StL-N	4	3	.571	15	7	0	0	0	52^2	53	2	17	33	12.1	3.42	120	.262	.323	2	.143	-1	2	4	0	0.5
1961	StL-N	1	3	.250	34	5	0	0	3	74^1	82	6	46	39	15.5	4.24	104	.290	.389	5	.357	2	-2	1	0	0.3
1962	NY-N	1	12	.077	33	21	1	0	0	143^2	146	20	62	91	13.4	4.89	86	.259	.339	5	.122	-1	-15	-11	2	-0.8
1963	LA-N	10	8	.556	42	23	2	0	1	187	171	7	65	125	11.5	2.89	105	.244	.311	4	.070	-3	8	3	5	0.5
1964	LA-N	7	7	.500	**74**	2	0	0	9	137^2	115	1	63	94	11.8	2.62	124	.226	.314	3	.158	1	14	10	2	1.4
1965	*LA-N	6	7	.462	61	1	0	0	9	103	82	9	26	77	9.7	2.97	110	.225	.282	0	.000	-1	7	5	2	0.5
1966	*LA-N	4	2	.667	46	0	0	0	5	84^1	70	5	29	58	10.7	2.77	119	.230	.299	1	.077	-1	8	5	-1	0.2
1967	LA-N	2	9	.182	52	4	0	0	0	85^2	88	9	27	32	12.4	4.31	72	.273	.335	1	.125	-0	-9	-12	1	-1.4
1968	Min-A	0	3	.000	45	0	0	0	2	72^1	65	1	24	41	11.7	2.74	113	.239	.312	1	.143	-0	2	3	1	0.2
1969	*Min-A	5	5	.500	48	11	1	0	3	119^1	118	9	32	57	11.3	3.02	121	.264	.313	0	.000	-3	8	8	1	0.5
1970	Cle-A	2	2	.500	15	2	0	0	1	28	35	1	15	15	16.1	4.18	95	.310	.391	1	.200	0	-1	-1	-1	-0.2
	Chi-A	4	6	.400	15	12	0	0	0	70	88	11	33	36	16.1	5.01	78	.315	.396	4	.174	0	-10	-9	2	-0.9
	Yr	6	8	.429	30	14	0	0	1	98	123	12	48	51	16.1	4.78	82	.313	.393	5	.179	1	-12	-9	1	-1.1
	Chi-N	0	0	—	7	1	0	0	2	9	6	3	6	4	12.0	5.00	90	.194	.324	0	—	0	-1	-0	0	0.0
1971	Chi-N	0	0	—	2	0	0	0	0	7	10	0	1	2	14.1	5.14	76	.357	.379	0	.000	-0	-1	-1	0	0.0
	SD-N	7	3	.700	38	0	0	0	7	63^2	53	0	26	36	11.3	1.41	233	.227	.308	0	.000	-1	15	13	1	2.4
	*Pit-N	1	2	.333	16	0	0	0	3	28	20	1	13	13	10.6	1.29	263	.200	.292	0	.000	0	7	7	0	0.9
	Yr	8	5	.615	56	0	0	0	10	98^2	83	1	40	51	11.2	1.64	205	.229	.305	0	.000	-1	20	19	2	3.3
1972	*Pit-N	5	2	.714	36	0	0	0	3	54^1	54	3	24	18	13.1	2.65	125	.263	.343	0	.000	-0	5	4	-0	0.5
1973	SD-N	0	0	—	18	0	0	0	0	30^2	29	4	12	15	12.0	4.11	84	.244	.313	0	.000	-0	-2	-2	-1	-0.1
	NY-N	0	0	—	1	0	0	0	0	1	0	0	0	1	0.0	0.00	—	.000	.000	0	—	0	0	0	0	0.0
	Yr	0	0	—	19	0	0	0	0	31^2	29	4	12	16	11.7	3.98	87	.236	.304	0	.000	-0	-1	-2	-1	-0.1
	Det-A	4	2	.667	22	0	0	0	1	42	34	3	22	23	12.0	3.43	119	.230	.329	0	—	0	2	3	0	0.0
1974	NY-N	2	2	.500	58	0	0	0	2	78	89	2	39	35	14.9	3.58	100	.296	.378	1	.111	-0	0	-0	0	0.0
Total	17	69	81	.460	694	99	7	0	51	1551^1	1487	101	608	895	12.3	3.37	105	.255	.328	33	.110	-8	38	31	18	5.3

● BOB MILLER

Miller, Robert W. b: 1862, d: 5/23/31, Newark, N.J. Deb: 8/30/1890

YEAR	TM/L	W	L	PCT	G	GS	CG	SH	SV	IP	H	HR	BB	SO	RAT	ERA	ERA+	OAV	OOB	BH	AVG	PB	PR	/A	PD	TPI
1890	Roc-a	3	7	.300	13	12	11	0	1	92^1	89	2	26	20	11.5	4.29	83	.246	.302	6	.150	-1	-4	-7	0	-0.7
1891	Was-a	2	5	.286	7	7	3	0	0	42	53	3	24	13	17.8	4.29	87	.298	.399	2	.111	-2	-3	-3	-1	-0.4
Total	2	5	12	.294	20	19	14	0	1	134^1	142	5	50	33	13.5	4.29	84	.263	.336	8	.138	-3	-7	-10	1	-1.1

● ROGER MILLER

Miller, Roger Wesley b: 8/1/54, Connellsville, Pa. d: 4/26/93, Mill Run, Pa. BR/TR, 6'3", 200 lbs. Deb: 9/8/74

YEAR	TM/L	W	L	PCT	G	GS	CG	SH	SV	IP	H	HR	BB	SO	RAT	ERA	ERA+	OAV	OOB	BH	AVG	PB	PR	/A	PD	TPI
1974	Mil-A	0	0	—	2	0	0	0	0	2^1	3	1	0	2	15.4	11.57	31	.300	.364	0	—	0	-2	-2	-0	0.0

● RONNIE MILLER

Miller, Roland Arthur b: 8/28/18, Mason City, Iowa d: 1/6/98, Ferguson, Mo. BB/TR, 5'11", 167 lbs. Deb: 9/10/41

YEAR	TM/L	W	L	PCT	G	GS	CG	SH	SV	IP	H	HR	BB	SO	RAT	ERA	ERA+	OAV	OOB	BH	AVG	PB	PR	/A	PD	TPI
1941	Was-A	0	0	—	1	0	0	0	0	2	2	0	1	0	13.5	4.50	90	.333	.429	0	—	0	-0	-0	-0	0.0

● ROSCOE MILLER

Miller, Roscoe Clyde "Roxy" or "Rubberlegs"
b: 12/2/1876, Greenville, Ind. d: 4/18/13, Corydon, Ind. BR/TR, 6'2", 190 lbs. Deb: 4/25/01

YEAR	TM/L	W	L	PCT	G	GS	CG	SH	SV	IP	H	HR	BB	SO	RAT	ERA	ERA+	OAV	OOB	BH	AVG	PB	PR	/A	PD	TPI
1901	Det-A	23	13	.639	38	36	35	3	1	332	339	1	98	79	12.2	2.95	130	.261	.320	27	.208	0	26	33	4	3.5
1902	Det-A	6	12	.333	20	18	15	1	1	148^2	158	3	57	39	13.6	3.69	99	.273	.347	11	.183	-2	-2	-1	1	-0.2
	NY-N	1	8	.111	10	9	7	0	0	72^2	77	1	11	15	11.5	4.58	61	.271	.310	1	.048	-2	-15	-14	-1	-1.8
1903	NY-N	2	5	.286	15	8	6	0	**3**	85	101	1	24	30	13.3	4.13	81	.302	.351	5	.161	-1	-8	-7	-1	-0.7
1904	Pit-N	7	7	.500	19	17	11	2	0	134^1	133	4	39	35	11.8	3.35	82	.256	.313	2	.043	-4	-9	-9	-1	-1.4
Total	4	39	45	.464	102	88	74	6	5	772^2	808	10	229	198	12.5	3.45	100	.268	.326	46	.160	-8	-7	1	2	-0.6

● RUSS MILLER

Miller, Russell Lewis b: 3/25/1900, Etna, Ohio d: 4/30/62, Bucyrus, Ohio BR/TR, 5'11", 165 lbs. Deb: 9/24/27 F

YEAR	TM/L	W	L	PCT	G	GS	CG	SH	SV	IP	H	HR	BB	SO	RAT	ERA	ERA+	OAV	OOB	BH	AVG	PB	PR	/A	PD	TPI
1927	Phi-N	1	1	.500	2	2	1	0	0	15^1	21	2	3	4	14.7	5.28	78	.339	.379	1	.333	0	-2	-2	-0	-0.2
1928	Phi-N	0	12	.000	33	12	1	0	1	108	137	14	34	19	14.3	5.42	79	.315	.365	4	.148	-1	-17	-14	0	-1.4
Total	2	1	13	.071	35	14	2	0	1	123^1	158	16	37	23	14.3	5.40	79	.318	.366	5	.167	-1	-19	-16	0	-1.6

● STU MILLER

Miller, Stuart Leonard b: 12/26/27, Northampton, Mass. BR/TR, 5'11.5", 165 lbs. Deb: 8/12/52

YEAR	TM/L	W	L	PCT	G	GS	CG	SH	SV	IP	H	HR	BB	SO	RAT	ERA	ERA+	OAV	OOB	BH	AVG	PB	PR	/A	PD	TPI
1952	StL-N	6	3	.667	12	11	6	2	0	88	63	3	26	64	9.3	2.05	182	.197	.262	3	.120	-1	16	16	3	1.8
1953	StL-N	7	8	.467	40	18	8	2	4	137^2	161	19	47	79	13.7	5.56	77	.293	.351	8	.186	1	-19	-20	5	-1.5
1954	StL-N	2	3	.400	19	4	0	0	2	46^2	55	5	29	22	16.8	5.79	71	.307	.412	4	.308	1	-9	-9	2	-0.6
1956	StL-N	0	1	.000	3	0	0	0	1	7^1	12	3	5	5	20.9	4.91	77	.387	.472	0	.000	-0	-1	-1	0	-0.1
	Phi-N	5	8	.385	24	15	2	0	0	106^2	109	16	51	55	13.8	4.47	83	.263	.349	4	.160	2	-8	-9	0	-0.7
	Yr	5	9	.357	27	15	2	0	1	114	121	19	56	60	14.3	4.50	83	.271	.357	4	.154	2	-9	-10	0	-0.8
1957	NY-N	7	9	.438	38	13	0	0	1	124	110	15	45	60	11.5	3.63	108	.242	.315	2	.057	-3	3	4	2	0.3
1958	SF-N	6	9	.400	41	20	4	1	0	182	160	16	49	119	10.4	**2.47**	**154**	.233	**.286**	6	.120	-0	30	27	1	2.2
1959	SF-N	8	7	.533	59	9	2	0	8	167^2	164	15	57	95	12.1	2.84	134	.260	.326	2	.044	-3	**21**	18	3	1.7
1960	SF-N	7	6	.538	47	3	2	0	2	101^2	100	9	31	65	11.9	3.90	89	.256	.315	5	.200	1	-2	-5	2	-0.3
1961	SF-N★	14	5	.737	63	0	0	0	**17**	122	95	4	37	89	9.8	2.66	143	.215	.277	4	.200	2	**19**	16	2	3.1
1962	*SF-N	5	8	.385	59	0	0	0	19	107	107	8	42	78	12.7	4.12	92	.268	.341	2	.125	-0	-2	-4	0	-0.6
1963	Bal-A	5	8	.385	**71**	0	0	0	**27**	112^1	93	5	53	114	11.9	2.24	155	.232	.326	5	.313	2	17	15	2	3.0
1964	Bal-A	7	7	.500	66	0	0	0	23	97	77	7	34	87	10.6	3.06	117	.222	.297	1	.111	-0	6	5	1	1.1
1965	Bal-A	14	7	.667	67	0	0	0	24	119^1	87	5	32	104	9.1	1.89	184	.207	.265	1	.063	-1	21	21	1	**4.7**
1966	Bal-A	9	4	.692	51	0	0	0	18	92	65	5	22	67	8.9	2.25	148	.201	.260	2	.105	-1	12	11	-1	1.8
1967	Bal-A	3	10	.231	42	0	0	0	8	81^1	63	5	36	60	11.1	2.55	124	.220	.309	0	.000	-1	6	5	-0	0.8
1968	Atl-N	0	0	—	2	0	0	0	0	1^1	1	0	4	1	33.8	27.00	11	.500	.833	0	—	0	-4	-4	0	0.0
Total	16	105	103	.505	704	93	24	5	154	1694	1522	140	600	1164	11.5	3.24	115	.242	.312	49	.133	-2	107	89	22	16.7

● TRAVIS MILLER

Miller, Travis Eugene b: 11/2/72, Dayton, Ohio BR/TL, 6'3", 205 lbs. Deb: 8/25/96

YEAR	TM/L	W	L	PCT	G	GS	CG	SH	SV	IP	H	HR	BB	SO	RAT	ERA	ERA+	OAV	OOB	BH	AVG	PB	PR	/A	PD	TPI
1996	Min-A	1	2	.333	7	7	0	0	0	26^1	45	7	9	15	18.5	9.23	55	.388	.432	0	—	0	-12	-12	-1	-1.1
1997	Min-A	1	5	.167	13	7	0	0	0	48^1	64	8	23	26	16.4	7.63	61	.320	.393	0	—	0	-16	-16	0	-1.6
1998	Min-A	0	2	.000	14	0	0	0	0	23^1	25	0	11	23	13.9	3.86	122	.272	.350	0	—	0	2	2	-0	0.1
Total	3	2	9	.182	34	14	0	0	0	98	134	15	43	64	16.3	7.16	67	.328	.394	0	—	0	-27	-26	-0	-2.6

● TREVER MILLER

Miller, Trever Douglas b: 5/29/73, Louisville, Ky. BR/TL, 6'3", 175 lbs. Deb: 9/4/96

YEAR	TM/L	W	L	PCT	G	GS	CG	SH	SV	IP	H	HR	BB	SO	RAT	ERA	ERA+	OAV	OOB	BH	AVG	PB	PR	/A	PD	TPI
1996	Det-A	0	4	.000	5	4	0	0	0	16^2	28	3	9	8	21.1	9.18	55	.384	.464	0	—	0	-8	-8	0	-1.3
1998	*Hou-N	2	0	1.000	37	1	0	0	1	53^1	57	4	20	30	13.2	3.04	134	.266	.332	1	.333	1	7	6	-0	0.2
Total	2	2	4	.333	42	5	0	0	1	70	85	7	29	38	15.0	4.50	95	.296	.367	1	.333	1	-1	-2	-0	-1.1

● JAKE MILLER

Miller, Walter b: 2/28/1898, Wagram, Ohio d: 8/20/75, Venice, Fla. BL/TL, 6'2", 170 lbs. Deb: 9/11/24 F

YEAR	TM/L	W	L	PCT	G	GS	CG	SH	SV	IP	H	HR	BB	SO	RAT	ERA	ERA+	OAV	OOB	BH	AVG	PB	PR	/A	PD	TPI
1924	Cle-A	0	1	.000	2	2	1	0	0	12	13	0	5	4	13.5	3.00	142	.265	.333	0	.000	-1	2	2	0	0.0
1925	Cle-A	10	13	.435	32	22	13	0	2	190^1	207	4	62	51	13.1	3.31	133	.279	.340	13	.183	-3	23	23	0	2.2
1926	Cle-A	7	4	.636	18	11	5	3	1	82^2	99	1	18	24	13.0	3.27	124	.307	.348	2	.083	-2	7	7	-1	0.6
1927	Cle-A	10	8	.556	34	23	11	0	0	185^1	189	4	48	53	11.8	3.21	131	.271	.324	8	.138	-4	19	21	1	1.4

YEAR	TM/L	W	L	PCT	G	GS	CG	SH	SV	IP	H	HR	BB	SO	RAT	ERA	ERA+	OAV	OOB	BH	AVG	PB	PR	/A	PD	TPI
1928	Cle-A	8	9	.471	25	24	8	0	0	158	203	6	43	37	14.3	4.44	93	.332	.381	7	.135	-4	-7	-5	1	-0.8
1929	Cle-A	14	12	.538	29	29	14	2	0	206	227	7	60	58	12.8	3.58	124	.279	.334	15	.200	-3	15	20	1	2.0
1930	Cle-A	4	4	.500	24	9	1	0	0	88^{1}	147	6	38	31	19.3	7.13	68	.373	.433	10	.303	1	-24	-23	2	-1.4
1931	Cle-A	2	1	.667	10	5	1	1	0	41^{1}	45	2	19	17	13.9	4.35	106	.273	.348	1	.077	-1	0	1	1	0.0
1933	Chi-A	5	6	.455	26	14	4	2	0	105^{2}	130	3	47	30	15.6	5.62	75	.297	.373	7	.189	-1	-16	-16	1	-1.4
Total	9	60	58	.508	200	139	58	8	3	1069^{2}	1260	33	340	305	13.8	4.09	106	.298	.355	63	.171	-19	19	30	6	2.6
● **WALT MILLER**	Miller, Walter W. b: 10/19/1884, Spiceland, Ind. d: 3/1/56, Marion, Ind. BR/TR, 5'11.5", 180 lbs. Deb: 9/20/11																									
1911	Bro-N	0	1	.000	3	2	0	0	0	11	16	0	6	0	18.8	6.55	51	.356	.442	0	.000	-1	-4	-4	-0	-0.4
● **BILL MILLER**	Miller, William Francis "Wild Bill" b: 4/12/10, Hannibal, Mo. d: 2/26/82, Hannibal, Mo. BR/TR, 6', 180 lbs. Deb: 10/2/37																									
1937	StL-A	0	1	.000	1	1	0	0	0	4	7	1	4	1	27.0	13.50	36	.389	.522	0	.000	-0	-4	-4	0	-0.6
● **BILL MILLER**	Miller, William Paul "Lefty" or "Hooks" b: 7/26/27, Minersville, Pa. BL/TL, 6', 175 lbs. Deb: 4/20/52																									
1952	NY-A	4	6	.400	21	13	5	2	0	88	78	4	49	45	13.2	3.48	96	.241	.345	6	.214	1	2	-2	-0	-0.1
1953	NY-A	2	1	.667	13	3	0	0	1	34	46	3	19	17	17.5	4.76	77	.324	.407	2	.200	0	-3	-4	1	-0.3
1954	NY-A	0	1	.000	2	1	0	0	0	5^{2}	9	0	1	6	15.9	6.35	54	.375	.400	0	.000	-0	-2	-2	-0	-0.3
1955	Bal-A	0	1	.000	5	1	0	0	0	4	3	0	10	4	29.3	13.50	28	.200	.520	1	1.000	0	-4	-4	0	-0.8
Total	4	6	9	.400	41	18	5	2	1	131^{2}	136	7	79	72	14.9	4.24	81	.270	.372	9	.225	1	-7	-12	0	-1.5
● **JOHN MILLIGAN**	Milligan, John Alexander b: 1/22/04, Schuylerville, N.Y. d: 5/15/72, Fort Pierce, Fla. BR/TL, 5'10", 172 lbs. Deb: 8/11/28																									
1928	Phi-N	2	5	.286	13	7	3	0	0	68	69	2	32	22	13.5	4.37	98	.274	.358	1	.050	-2	-3	-1	1	-0.2
1929	Phi-N	0	1	.000	8	3	0	0	0	9^{2}	29	0	10	2	38.2	16.76	31	.527	.612	1	.333	0	-13	-12	0	-1.0
1930	Phi-N	1	2	.333	9	2	1	0	0	28^{1}	26	0	21	7	15.6	3.18	172	.255	.392	1	.111	-1	6	7	1	0.7
1931	Phi-N	0	0	—	3	0	0	0	0	8	11	0	4	6	18.0	3.38	126	.324	.410	0	.000	-0	0	1	-0	-0.1
1934	Was-A	0	0	—	2	0	0	0	0	2^{2}	6	0	0	1	20.3	10.13	43	.500	.500	0	—	0	-2	-2	0	0.0
Total	5	3	8	.273	35	12	4	0	0	116^{2}	141	2	67	38	16.5	5.17	90	.310	.405	3	.088	-3	-11	-7	2	-0.6
● **BILLY MILLIGAN**	Milligan, William Joseph b: 8/19/1878, Buffalo, N.Y. d: 10/14/28, Buffalo, N.Y. BR/TL, 5'7", Deb: 4/30/01																									
1901	Phi-A	0	3	.000	6	3	2	0	0	33	43	1	14	5	16.1	4.36	86	.312	.383	5	.333	2	-3	-2	-0	0.0
1904	NY-N	0	1	.000	5	1	1	0	2	25	36	2	4	6	14.8	5.40	51	.310	.339	1	.111	0	-7	-7	-0	-0.4
Total	2	0	4	.000	11	4	3	0	2	58	79	3	18	11	15.5	4.81	69	.311	.364	6	.250	2	-10	-10	-1	-0.4
● **BOB MILLIKEN**	Milliken, Robert Fogle "Bobo" b: 8/25/26, Majorsville, W.Va. BR/TR, 6', 195 lbs. Deb: 4/22/53 C																									
1953	*Bro-N	8	4	.667	37	10	3	0	2	117^{2}	94	13	42	65	10.4	3.37	127	.214	.283	4	.118	-1	12	12	-2	0.8
1954	Bro-N	5	2	.714	24	3	0	0	2	62^{2}	58	12	18	25	11.2	4.02	102	.246	.305	3	.176	-0	0	0	-1	-0.1
Total	2	13	6	.684	61	13	3	0	4	180^{1}	152	25	60	90	10.7	3.59	117	.225	.290	7	.137	-2	12	12	-3	0.7
● **ALAN MILLS**	Mills, Alan Bernard b: 10/18/66, Lakeland, Fla. BR/TR, 6'1", 192 lbs. Deb: 4/14/90																									
1990	NY-A	1	5	.167	36	0	0	0	0	41^{2}	48	4	33	24	17.7	4.10	97	.298	.421	0	—	0	-1	-1	1	0.0
1991	NY-A	1	1	.500	6	2	0	0	0	16^{1}	16	1	8	11	13.2	4.41	94	.254	.338	0	—	0	-1	-0	1	0.0
1992	Bal-A	10	4	.714	35	3	0	0	2	103^{1}	78	5	54	60	11.6	2.61	154	.215	.319	0	—	0	15	16	1	2.1
1993	Bal-A	5	4	.556	45	0	0	0	4	100^{1}	80	14	51	68	12.1	3.23	138	.225	.328	0	—	0	12	14	-0	1.1
1994	Bal-A	3	3	.500	47	0	0	0	2	45^{1}	43	7	24	44	13.7	5.16	97	.251	.350	0	—	0	-2	-1	-1	-0.2
1995	Bal-A	3	0	1.000	21	0	0	0	0	23	30	4	18	16	19.6	7.43	64	.309	.427	0	—	0	-7	-7	-1	-0.8
1996	*Bal-A	3	2	.600	49	0	0	0	3	54^{2}	40	10	35	50	12.5	4.28	115	.208	.333	0	—	0	4	4	0	0.4
1997	*Bal-A	2	3	.400	39	0	0	0	0	38^{2}	41	5	33	32	17.5	4.89	97	.268	.401	0	—	0	-1	-2	-0	-0.2
1998	Bal-A	3	4	.429	72	0	0	0	2	77	55	8	50	57	12.4	3.74	121	.203	.329	0	—	0	8	7	0	0.6
Total	9	31	26	.544	350	5	0	0	13	500^{1}	431	58	306	362	13.5	3.90	114	.236	.350	0	—	0	28	30	1	3.0
● **ART MILLS**	Mills, Arthur Grant b: 3/2/03, Utica, N.Y. d: 7/23/75, Utica, N.Y. BR/TR, 5'10", 155 lbs. Deb: 4/16/27 FC																									
1927	Bos-N	0	1	.000	15	1	0	0	0	37^{2}	41	1	18	7	14.8	3.82	97	.287	.378	0	.000	-1	0	-0	1	0.0
1928	Bos-N	0	0	—	4	0	0	0	0	7^{2}	17	3	8	0	31.7	12.91	30	.472	.587	0	.000	-0	-8	-8	-0	0.0
Total	2	0	1	.000	19	1	0	0	0	45^{1}	58	4	26	7	17.7	5.36	70	.324	.424	0	.000	-1	-7	-8	1	0.0
● **LEFTY MILLS**	Mills, Howard Robinson b: 5/12/10, Dedham, Mass. d: 9/23/82, Riverside, Cal. BL/TL, 6'1", 187 lbs. Deb: 6/10/34																									
1934	StL-A	0	0	—	4	0	0	0	0	8^{2}	10	0	11	2	21.8	4.15	120	.303	.477	1	.333	0	0	1	-0	0.0
1937	StL-A	1	1	.500	2	2	1	0	0	12^{2}	16	1	10	10	18.5	6.39	75	.286	.394	0	.000	-1	-2	-2	0	-0.3
1938	StL-A	10	12	.455	30	27	15	1	0	210^{1}	216	16	116	134	14.5	5.31	94	.262	.358	6	.091	-3	-12	-8	-2	-1.1
1939	StL-A	4	11	.267	34	14	4	0	2	144^{1}	147	16	113	103	16.7	6.55	74	.264	.395	11	.234	1	-31	-27	-1	-2.3
1940	StL-A	0	6	.000	26	5	1	0	0	59	64	7	52	18	18.2	7.78	59	.275	.413	2	.154	-0	-22	-21	0	-1.7
Total	5	15	30	.333	96	48	21	1	2	435	453	40	302	267	16.0	6.06	81	.266	.382	20	.149	-3	-67	-57	-3	-5.4
● **DICK MILLS**	Mills, Richard Alan b: 1/29/45, Boston, Mass. BR/TR, 6'3", 195 lbs. Deb: 9/7/70																									
1970	Bos-A	0	0	—	2	0	0	0	0	3^{2}	6	0	3	3	24.5	2.45	161	.353	.476	0	—	0	1	1	0	0.0
● **WILLIE MILLS**	Mills, William Grant "Wee Willie" b: 8/15/1877, Schenevus, N.Y. d: 7/5/14, Norwood, N.Y. BR/TR, 5'7", 150 lbs. Deb: 7/13/01 F																									
1901	NY-N	0	2	.000	2	2	2	0	0	16	21	2	4	3	14.6	8.44	39	.313	.361	1	.167	0	-9	-9	-0	-0.8
● **KEVIN MILLWOOD**	Millwood, Kevin Austin b: 12/24/74, Gastonia, N.C. BR/TR, 6'4", 205 lbs. Deb: 7/14/97																									
1997	Atl-N	5	3	.625	12	8	0	0	0	51^{1}	55	1	21	42	13.7	4.03	104	.281	.356	0	.000	-1	1	1	-0	0.0
1998	Atl-N	17	8	.680	31	29	3	1	0	174^{1}	175	18	56	163	12.1	4.08	104	.258	.318	4	.080	-1	3	3	-1	0.1
Total	2	22	11	.667	43	37	3	1	0	225^{2}	230	19	77	205	12.4	4.07	104	.263	.326	4	.065	-2	4	4	-2	0.1
● **AL MILNAR**	Milnar, Albert Joseph "Happy" (b: Albert Joseph Mlinar) b: 12/26/13, Cleveland, Ohio BL/TL, 6'2", 195 lbs. Deb: 4/30/36																									
1936	Cle-A	1	2	.333	4	3	1	0	0	22	26	0	18	9	18.0	7.36	68	.286	.404	3	.300	0	-6	-6	0	-0.5
1938	Cle-A	3	1	.750	23	5	2	0	1	68^{1}	90	5	26	29	15.3	5.00	93	.320	.378	4	.154	-0	-2	-3	0	-0.1
1939	Cle-A	14	12	.538	37	26	12	2	3	209	212	11	99	76	13.4	3.79	116	.264	.345	20	.253	4	19	14	0	1.9
1940	Cle-A☆	18	10	.643	37	33	15	**4**	3	242^{1}	242	14	99	99	12.7	3.27	129	.257	.328	17	.181	-1	30	26	-5	2.1
1941	Cle-A	12	19	.387	35	30	9	1	0	229^{1}	236	9	116	82	13.9	4.36	90	.266	.352	14	.171	2	-5	-11	-3	-1.3
1942	Cle-A	6	8	.429	28	19	8	2	0	157	146	3	85	35	13.5	4.13	84	.251	.350	12	.171	2	-8	-12	1	-0.7
1943	Cle-A	1	3	.250	16	6	0	0	0	39	51	0	35	12	20.1	8.08	38	.329	.455	4	.211	0	-21	-22	0	-2.0
	StL-A	1	2	.333	3	2	1	0	0	14^{2}	23	0	9	7	19.6	5.52	60	.354	.432	2	.333	1	-4	-4	0	-0.5
	Yr	2	5	.286	19	8	1	0	0	53^{2}	74	0	44	19	19.8	7.38	43	.335	.445	6	.240	1	-24	-25	0	-2.5
1946	StL-A	1	1	.500	4	2	1	1	0	14^{2}	15	1	6	1	12.9	2.45	152	.278	.350	3	.750	1	2	2	-0	0.4
	Phi-N	0	0	—	1	1	0	0	0	0	2	0	2	0	—	∞	—	1.000	1.000	0	—	0	-4	-4	0	-0.3
Total	8	57	58	.496	188	127	49	10	7	996^{1}	1043	43	495	350	14.0	4.22	96	.270	.354	79	.203	9	2	-18	-6	-1.0
● **GEORGE MILSTEAD**	Milstead, George Earl "Cowboy" b: 6/26/03, Cleburne, Tex. d: 8/9/77, Cleburne, Tex. BL/TL, 5'10", 144 lbs. Deb: 6/27/24																									
1924	Chi-N	1	1	.500	13	2	1	0	0	29^{2}	41	3	13	6	16.7	6.07	64	.328	.396	1	.167	0	-7	-7	0	-0.4
1925	Chi-N	1	1	.500	5	3	1	0	0	21	26	0	8	7	14.6	3.00	144	.310	.370	0	.000	-1	3	3	0	0.2
1926	Chi-N	1	5	.167	18	4	0	0	2	55^{1}	63	0	24	14	14.3	3.58	107	.309	.384	1	.053	-2	2	2	2	0.2
Total	3	3	7	.300	36	9	2	0	2	106	130	3	45	27	15.0	4.16	95	.315	.385	2	.063	-3	-3	-2	3	0.0
● **ERIC MILTON**	Milton, Eric Robert b: 8/4/75, State College, Pa. BL/TL, 6'3", 200 lbs. Deb: 4/5/98																									
1998	Min-A	8	14	.364	32	32	1	0	0	172^{1}	195	25	70	107	13.9	5.64	83	.282	.349	4	.444	1	-19	-18	-1	-1.9
● **LARRY MILTON**	Milton, Samuel Lawrence "Tug" b: 5/4/1879, Owensboro, Ky. d: 5/16/42, Hannibal, Mo. TR, Deb: 5/7/03																									
1903	StL-N	0	0	—	1	0	0	0	0	4	3	0	1	0	9.0	2.25	145	.200	.250	1	.500	0	0	0	0	0.1
● **MIKE MIMBS**	Mimbs, Michael Randall b: 2/13/69, Macon, Ga. BL/TL, 6'2", 180 lbs. Deb: 5/6/95																									
1995	Phi-N	9	7	.563	35	19	2	1	1	136^{2}	127	10	75	93	13.7	4.15	102	.250	.353	5	.143	-1	0	1	1	0.1
1996	Phi-N	3	9	.250	21	17	0	0	0	99^{1}	116	13	41	56	14.4	5.53	78	.294	.364	4	.121	-1	-14	-13	-1	-1.6

YEAR	TM/L	W	L	PCT	G	GS	CG	SH	SV	IP	H	HR	BB	SO	RAT	ERA	ERA+	OAV	OOB	BH	AVG	PB	PR	/A	PD	TPI
1997	Phi-N	0	3	.000	17	1	0	0	0	28^{2}	31	6	27	29	19.2	7.53	56	.272	.424	0	.000	-0	-11	-10	-1	-1.0
Total	3	12	19	.387	73	37	2	1	1	264^{2}	274	29	143	178	14.6	5.03	85	.270	.366	9	.129	-2	-25	-23	-1	-2.5
● **COTTON MINAHAN**	Minahan, Edmund Joseph b: 12/10/1882, Springfield, Ohio d: 5/20/58, E.Orange, N.J. BR/TR, 6', 190 lbs. Deb: 4/21/07																									
1907	Cin-N	0	2	.000	2	2	1	0	0	14	12	0	13	4	16.7	1.29	202	.261	.433	0	.000	-1	2	2	-1	0.2
● **RUDY MINARCIN**	Minarcin, Rudy Anthony "Buster" b: 3/25/30, N.Vandergrift, Pa. BR/TR, 6', 195 lbs. Deb: 4/11/55																									
1955	Cin-N	5	9	.357	41	12	3	1	1	115^{2}	116	17	51	45	13.2	4.90	86	.261	.341	5	.179	-1	-11	-9	2	-0.8
1956	Bos-A	1	0	1.000	3	1	0	0	0	9^{2}	9	2	8	5	16.8	2.79	165	.250	.400	1	.500	1	1	2	0	0.3
1957	Bos-A	0	0	—	26	0	0	0	2	44^{2}	44	5	30	20	15.1	4.43	90	.267	.383	0	.000	0	-3	-2	-0	0.0
Total	3	6	9	.400	70	13	3	1	3	170	169	24	89	70	13.9	4.66	90	.262	.356	6	.188	0	-13	-9	2	-0.5
● **NATE MINCHEY**	Minchey, Nathan Derek b: 8/31/69, Austin, Tex. BR/TR, 6'8", 225 lbs. Deb: 9/12/93																									
1993	Bos-A	1	2	.333	5	5	1	0	0	33	35	5	8	18	11.7	3.55	130	.265	.307	0	—	0	3	4	-1	0.2
1994	Bos-A	2	3	.400	6	5	0	0	0	23	44	1	14	15	22.7	8.61	58	.427	.496	0	—	0	-10	-9	0	-1.5
1996	Bos-A	0	2	.000	2	2	0	0	0	6	16	1	5	4	31.5	15.00	34	.533	.600	0	—	0	-7	-7	0	-1.4
1997	Col-N	0	0	—	2	0	0	0	0	2	5	0	1	1	27.0	13.50	38	.556	.600	0	—	0	-2	-2	0	0.0
Total	4	3	7	.300	15	12	1	0	0	64	100	7	28	38	18.0	6.75	72	.365	.424	0	—	0	-16	-14	-0	-2.7
● **RAY MINER**	Miner, Raymond Theadore "Lefty" b: 4/4/1897, Glens Falls, N.Y. d: 9/15/63, Glenridge, N.Y. BR/TL, 5'11", 160 lbs. Deb: 9/15/21																									
1921	Phi-A	0	0	—	1	0	0	0	0	1	2	0	3	0	45.0	36.00	12	.400	.625	0	—	0	-4	-4	-0	0.0
● **CRAIG MINETTO**	Minetto, Craig Stephen b: 4/25/54, Stockton, Cal. BL/TL, 6', 185 lbs. Deb: 7/4/78																									
1978	Oak-A	0	0	—	4	1	0	0	0	12	13	1	7	3	16.5	3.75	97	.283	.400	0	—	0	0	-0	-0	0.0
1979	Oak-A	1	5	.167	36	13	0	0	0	118^{1}	131	16	58	64	14.6	5.55	73	.282	.365	0	—	0	-18	-20	-2	-0.7
1980	Oak-A	0	2	.000	7	1	0	0	1	8	11	2	3	5	15.8	7.88	48	.324	.378	0	—	0	-3	-4	-0	-0.5
1981	Oak-A	0	0	—	8	0	0	0	0	6^{2}	7	0	4	4	16.2	2.70	129	.280	.400	0	—	0	1	1	-0	0.2
Total	4	1	7	.125	55	15	0	0	1	145	162	19	72	76	14.9	5.40	73	.284	.370	0	—	0	-20	-23	-2	-1.0
● **STEVE MINGORI**	Mingori, Stephen Bernard b: 2/29/44, Kansas City, Mo. BL/TL, 5'10", 170 lbs. Deb: 8/5/70																									
1970	Cle-A	1	0	1.000	21	0	0	0	1	20^{1}	17	2	12	16	13.3	2.66	149	.227	.341	0	.000	-0	2	3	0	0.2
1971	Cle-A	1	2	.333	54	0	0	0	4	56^{2}	31	2	24	45	8.9	1.43	268	.166	.264	1	.500	0	13	15	1	1.2
1972	Cle-A	0	6	.000	41	0	0	0	10	57	67	4	36	47	16.6	3.95	81	.293	.393	1	.125	-0	-6	-5	1	-0.7
1973	Cle-A	0	0	—	5	0	0	0	0	11^{2}	10	3	10	4	15.4	6.17	64	.233	.377	0	—	0	-3	-3	1	0.0
	KC-A	3	3	.500	19	1	0	0	1	56^{1}	59	6	23	46	13.6	3.04	135	.267	.344	0	—	0	5	7	-0	0.2
	Yr	3	3	.500	24	1	0	0	1	68	69	9	33	50	13.9	3.57	114	.261	.350	0	—	0	2	4	1	0.2
1974	KC-A	2	3	.400	36	0	0	0	2	67^{1}	53	4	23	43	10.4	2.81	136	.212	.284	0	—	0	6	8	2	0.6
1975	KC-A	0	3	.000	36	0	0	0	2	50^{1}	42	2	20	25	11.3	2.50	154	.226	.304	0	.000	-0	7	8	0	0.5
1976	*KC-A	5	5	.500	55	0	0	0	10	85^{1}	73	3	25	38	10.7	2.32	151	.238	.301	0	—	0	11	11	3	1.9
1977	*KC-A	2	4	.333	43	0	0	0	4	64	59	4	19	19	11.1	3.09	130	.254	.313	0	—	0	7	7	1	0.7
1978	*KC-A	1	4	.200	45	0	0	0	7	69	64	5	16	28	10.8	2.74	140	.242	.292	0	—	0	8	8	0	0.8
1979	KC-A	3	3	.500	30	1	0	0	1	46^{2}	69	10	17	18	16.8	5.79	74	.348	.403	0	—	0	-8	-8	-1	-1.1
Total	10	18	33	.353	385	2	0	0	42	584^{2}	544	45	225	329	12.1	3.03	126	.248	.323	2	.167	-0	43	51	7	4.3
● **PAUL MINNER**	Minner, Paul Edison "Lefty" b: 7/30/23, New Wilmington, Pa. BL/TL, 6'5", 210 lbs. Deb: 9/12/46																									
1946	Bro-N	0	1	.000	3	0	0	0	0	4	6	1	3	3	20.3	6.75	50	.333	.429	0	—	0	-1	-1	-0	-0.4
1948	Bro-N	4	3	.571	28	2	0	0	1	62^{2}	61	5	26	23	12.5	2.44	164	.257	.331	4	.190	1	11	11	0	1.3
1949	*Bro-N	3	1	.750	27	1	0	0	2	47^{1}	49	7	18	17	12.9	3.80	108	.272	.342	3	.214	-0	1	2	0	0.2
1950	Chi-N	8	13	.381	39	24	9	1	4	190^{1}	217	18	72	99	13.7	4.11	102	.287	.350	14	.215	2	1	2	3	0.7
1951	Chi-N	6	17	.261	33	28	14	3	1	201^{2}	219	20	64	68	12.6	3.79	108	.277	.331	18	.254	5	4	7	3	1.6
1952	Chi-N	14	9	.609	28	27	12	2	0	180^{2}	180	13	54	61	11.7	3.74	103	.258	.312	15	.234	6	-0	2	2	1.1
1953	Chi-N	12	15	.444	31	27	9	2	1	201	227	15	40	64	12.1	4.21	106	.283	.320	15	.221	2	2	5	4	1.2
1954	Chi-N	11	11	.500	32	29	12	0	1	218	236	19	50	79	11.8	3.96	106	.280	.321	13	.171	3	3	6	1	1.0
1955	Chi-N	9	9	.500	22	22	7	1	0	157^{2}	173	15	47	53	12.6	3.48	117	.283	.335	13	.232	2	10	11	2	1.5
1956	Chi-N	2	5	.286	10	9	1	0	0	47	60	9	19	14	15.5	6.89	55	.324	.393	3	.250	2	-16	-16	0	-1.8
Total	10	69	84	.451	253	169	64	9	10	1310^{1}	1428	122	393	481	12.6	3.94	105	.279	.332	98	.219	22	12	27	15	6.4
● **DON MINNICK**	Minnick, Donald Athey b: 4/14/31, Lynchburg, Va. BR/TR, 6'3", 195 lbs. Deb: 9/23/57																									
1957	Was-A	0	1	.000	2	1	0	0	0	9^{1}	14	1	2	7	15.4	4.82	81	.341	.372	0	.000	-0	-1	-1	-0	-0.1
● **BLAS MINOR**	Minor, Blas b: 3/20/66, Merced, Cal. BR/TR, 6'3", 203 lbs. Deb: 7/28/92																									
1992	Pit-N	0	0	—	1	0	0	0	0	2	3	0	0	0	13.5	4.50	76	.333	.333	0	—	0	-0	-0	0	0.0
1993	Pit-N	8	6	.571	65	0	0	0	2	94^{1}	94	8	26	84	11.8	4.10	99	.263	.320	2	.200	1	-1	-1	1	0.1
1994	Pit-N	0	1	.000	17	0	0	0	1	19	27	4	9	17	17.5	8.05	54	.351	.425	0	—	0	-8	-8	-0	-0.4
1995	NY-N	4	2	.667	35	0	0	0	1	46^{2}	44	6	13	43	11.2	3.66	110	.253	.309	0	.000	-0	3	2	0	0.2
1996	NY-N	0	0	—	17	0	0	0	0	25^{2}	23	4	6	20	10.2	3.51	114	.237	.282	0	.000	-0	2	1	0	0.0
	Sea-A	0	1	.000	11	0	0	0	0	25^{1}	27	6	11	14	13.5	4.97	99	.276	.349	0	—	0	0	-0	-0	0.0
1997	Hou-N	1	0	1.000	11	0	0	0	1	12	13	1	5	6	14.3	4.50	89	.277	.358	0	—	0	-0	-1	0	-0.1
Total	6	13	10	.565	157	0	0	0	5	225	231	29	70	184	12.3	4.40	95	.269	.329	2	.154	0	-5	-6	1	-0.2
● **JIM MINSHALL**	Minshall, James Edward b: 7/4/47, Covington, Ky. BR/TR, 6'6", 215 lbs. Deb: 9/14/74																									
1974	Pit-N	0	1	.000	5	0	0	0	0	4^{1}	1	0	2	3	6.2	0.00	—	.083	.214	0	—	0	2	2	-0	0.4
1975	Pit-N	0	0	—	1	0	0	0	0	1	0	0	2	2	18.0	0.00	—	.000	.400	0	—	0	0	0	0	0.0
Total	2	0	1	.000	6	0	0	0	0	5^{1}	1	0	4	5	8.4	0.00	—	.067	.263	0	—	0	2	2	-0	0.4
● **GREG MINTON**	Minton, Gregory Brian b: 7/29/51, Lubbock, Tex. BB/TR, 6'2", 190 lbs. Deb: 9/7/75																									
1975	SF-N	1	1	.500	4	2	0	0	0	17	19	1	11	6	16.4	6.88	55	.288	.397	0	.000	-1	-6	-6	1	-0.6
1976	SF-N	0	3	.000	10	2	0	0	0	25^{2}	32	0	12	7	15.8	4.91	74	.317	.395	1	.200	-0	-4	-4	-0	-0.4
1977	SF-N	1	1	.500	2	2	0	0	0	14	14	0	4	5	11.6	4.50	87	.264	.316	1	.333	1	-1	-1	0	0.0
1978	SF-N	0	1	.000	11	0	0	0	0	15^{2}	22	3	8	6	17.8	8.04	43	.338	.419	0	.000	-0	-8	-8	0	-0.5
1979	SF-N	4	3	.571	46	0	0	0	4	79^{2}	59	0	27	33	9.9	1.81	193	.215	.289	0	.000	-0	17	15	2	1.6
1980	SF-N	4	6	.400	68	0	0	0	19	91^{1}	81	0	34	42	11.3	2.46	144	.243	.313	1	.125	-0	12	11	2	1.8
1981	SF-N	4	5	.444	55	0	0	0	21	84^{1}	84	0	36	29	12.8	2.88	119	.267	.342	0	.000	-1	6	5	3	1.0
1982	SF-N★	10	4	.714	78	0	0	0	30	123	108	5	42	58	11.1	1.83	196	.244	.313	3	.176	0	**24**	**24**	1	**3.9**
1983	SF-N	7	11	.389	73	0	0	0	22	106^{2}	117	6	47	38	13.8	3.54	100	.283	.356	6	.545	4	1	-0	-0	0.4
1984	SF-N	4	9	.308	74	1	0	0	19	124^{1}	130	6	57	48	13.5	3.76	93	.267	.344	1	.048	-1	-2	-4	2	-0.4
1985	SF-N	5	4	.556	68	0	0	0	4	96^{2}	98	6	54	37	14.2	3.54	97	.272	.367	0	.000	-1	1	-1	2	0.1
1986	SF-N	4	4	.500	48	0	0	0	5	68^{2}	63	4	34	34	12.8	3.93	90	.251	.343	2	.400	2	-2	-3	2	0.0
1987	SF-N	1	0	1.000	15	0	0	0	1	23^{1}	30	2	10	9	15.8	3.47	111	.323	.394	0	.000	-0	2	1	0	0.0
	Cal-A	5	4	.556	41	0	0	0	10	76	71	4	29	35	12.0	3.08	140	.257	.330	0	—	0	12	10	2	1.6
1988	Cal-A	4	5	.444	44	0	0	0	7	79	67	1	34	46	11.8	2.85	135	.233	.320	0	—	0	10	9	2	1.3
1989	Cal-A	4	3	.571	62	0	0	0	8	90	76	4	37	42	11.5	2.20	173	.230	.311	0	—	0	17	16	2	1.7
1990	Cal-A	1	1	.500	11	0	0	0	0	15^{1}	11	1	7	4	11.2	2.35	163	.212	.317	0	—	0	3	3	0	0.4
Total	16	59	65	.476	710	7	0	0	150	1130^{2}	1082	43	483	479	12.6	3.10	117	.257	.336	15	.146	2	80	68	19	11.9
● **STEVE MINTZ**	Mintz, Stephen Wayne b: 11/24/68, Wilmington, N.C. BL/TR, 5'11", 190 lbs. Deb: 5/18/95																									
1995	SF-N	1	2	.333	14	0	0	0	0	19^{1}	26	4	12	7	18.6	7.45	55	.329	.430	0	.000	-0	-7	-7	-0	-1.0
● **GINO MINUTELLI**	Minutelli, Gino Michael b: 5/23/64, Wilmington, Del. BL/TL, 6', 180 lbs. Deb: 9/18/90																									
1990	Cin-N	0	0	—	2	0	0	0	0	1	0	0	2	0	27.0	9.00	44	.000	.500	0	—	0	-1	-1	0	0.0
1991	Cin-N	0	2	.000	16	3	0	0	0	25^{1}	30	5	18	21	17.1	6.04	63	.288	.393	0	.000	-0	-7	-6	0	-0.5

YEAR	TM/L	W	L	PCT	G	GS	CG	SH	SV	IP	H	HR	BB	SO	RAT	ERA	ERA+	OAV	OOB	BH	AVG	PB	PR	/A	PD	TPI
1993	SF-N	0	1	.000	9	0	0	0	0	14^1	7	2	15	10	13.8	3.77	104	.152	.361	0	.000	-0	0	0	-0	-0.1
Total	3	0	3	.000	27	3	0	0	0	40^2	37	7	35	31	16.2	5.31	72	.242	.386	0	.000	-1	-7	-7	0	-0.6

● **PAUL MIRABELLA** Mirabella, Paul Thomas b: 3/20/54, Belleville, N.J. BL/TL, 6′2″, 196 lbs. Deb: 7/28/78

YEAR	TM/L	W	L	PCT	G	GS	CG	SH	SV	IP	H	HR	BB	SO	RAT	ERA	ERA+	OAV	OOB	BH	AVG	PB	PR	/A	PD	TPI
1978	Tex-A	3	2	.600	10	4	0	0	1	28	30	2	17	23	15.1	5.79	65	.286	.385	0	—	0	-6	-6	-0	-1.1
1979	NY-A	0	4	.000	10	1	0	0	0	14^1	16	3	10	4	17.0	8.79	46	.276	.391	0	—	0	-7	-8	-0	-1.6
1980	Tor-A	5	12	.294	33	22	3	1	0	130^2	151	11	66	53	15.2	4.34	99	.294	.378	0	—	0	-4	-1	0	-0.1
1981	Tor-A	0	0	—	8	1	0	0	0	14^2	20	2	7	9	17.2	7.36	53	.313	.389	0	—	0	-6	-6	-0	-0.3
1982	Tex-A	1	1	.500	40	0	0	0	3	50^2	46	4	22	29	12.4	4.80	81	.241	.326	0	—	0	-4	-5	-0	0.0
1983	Bal-A	0	0	—	3	2	0	0	0	9^2	9	1	7	4	14.9	5.59	71	.243	.364	0	—	0	-2	-2	-0	0.0
1984	Sea-A	2	5	.286	52	1	0	0	3	68	74	6	32	41	14.2	4.37	91	.282	.363	0	—	0	-3	-3	1	-0.2
1985	Sea-A	0	0	—	10	0	0	0	0	13^2	9	0	4	8	9.9	1.32	320	.188	.278	0	—	0	4	4	-0	0.0
1986	Sea-A	0	0	—	8	0	0	0	0	6^1	13	1	3	6	22.7	8.53	50	.419	.471	0	—	0	-3	-3	0	0.0
1987	Mil-A	2	1	.667	29	0	0	0	2	29^1	30	0	16	14	14.1	4.91	93	.268	.359	0	—	0	-1	-1	1	-0.1
1988	Mil-A	2	2	.500	38	0	0	0	4	60	44	3	21	33	9.8	1.65	241	.204	.274	0	—	0	15	16	1	1.2
1989	Mil-A	0	0	—	13	0	0	0	0	15^1	18	1	7	6	15.3	7.63	50	.290	.371	0	—	0	-6	-6	0	0.1
1990	Mil-A	4	2	.667	44	2	0	0	0	59	66	9	27	28	14.5	3.97	98	.281	.360	0	—	0	-0	-1	-0	0.0
Total	13	19	29	.396	298	33	3	1	13	499^2	526	43	239	258	14.0	4.45	91	.272	.356	0	—	0	-24	-21	0	-2.1

● **ANGEL MIRANDA** Miranda, Angel Luis (Andujar) b: 11/9/69, Arecibo, P.R. BL/TL, 6′1″, 195 lbs. Deb: 6/5/93

YEAR	TM/L	W	L	PCT	G	GS	CG	SH	SV	IP	H	HR	BB	SO	RAT	ERA	ERA+	OAV	OOB	BH	AVG	PB	PR	/A	PD	TPI
1993	Mil-A	4	5	.444	22	17	2	0	0	120	100	12	52	88	11.6	3.30	129	.226	.310	0	—	0	14	13	-1	0.8
1994	Mil-A	2	5	.286	8	8	1	0	0	46	39	8	27	24	12.9	5.28	95	.234	.340	0	—	0	-2	-1	-1	-0.2
1995	Mil-A	4	5	.444	30	10	0	0	1	74	83	8	49	45	16.1	5.23	95	.291	.395	0	—	0	-4	-2	-0	-0.2
1996	Mil-A	7	6	.538	46	12	0	0	1	109^1	116	12	69	78	15.4	4.94	105	.277	.382	0	—	0	1	3	-1	0.0
1997	Mil-A	0	0	—	10	0	0	0	0	14	17	1	9	8	18.6	3.86	120	.309	.433	0	—	0	1	1	0	0.0
Total	5	17	21	.447	116	47	3	0	2	363^1	355	41	206	243	14.1	4.46	107	.260	.359	0	—	0	9	13	-3	0.4

● **MIKE MISURACA** Misuraca, Michael William b: 8/21/68, Long Beach, Cal. BR/TR, 6′, 190 lbs. Deb: 7/27/97

YEAR	TM/L	W	L	PCT	G	GS	CG	SH	SV	IP	H	HR	BB	SO	RAT	ERA	ERA+	OAV	OOB	BH	AVG	PB	PR	/A	PD	TPI
1997	Mil-A	0	0	—	5	0	0	0	0	10^1	15	5	7	10	19.2	11.32	41	.333	.423	0	—	0	-8	-8	-0	0.0

● **ROY MITCHELL** Mitchell, Albert Roy b: 4/19/1885, Belton, Tex. d: 9/8/59, Temple, Tex. BR/TR, 5′9.5″, 170 lbs. Deb: 9/10/10

YEAR	TM/L	W	L	PCT	G	GS	CG	SH	SV	IP	H	HR	BB	SO	RAT	ERA	ERA+	OAV	OOB	BH	AVG	PB	PR	/A	PD	TPI
1910	StL-A	4	2	.667	6	6	6	0	0	52	43	0	12	23	9.9	2.60	95	.244	.300	4	.211	0	-0	-1	1	0.0
1911	StL-A	4	8	.333	28	12	8	1	0	133^1	134	4	45	40	12.5	3.85	88	.273	.341	11	.224	1	-7	-7	-0	-0.4
1912	StL-A	3	4	.429	13	7	5	0	0	62	81	2	17	22	14.8	4.65	71	.323	.375	6	.316	3	-9	-9	-1	-0.7
1913	StL-A	13	16	.448	33	27	21	4	1	245^1	265	6	47	59	11.6	3.01	97	.280	.318	13	.148	-1	-2	-2	-1	-0.5
1914	StL-A	4	5	.444	28	9	4	0	**4**	103^1	134	1	38	38	15.5	4.35	62	.320	.384	7	.206	1	-19	-19	0	-1.6
1918	Chi-A	0	1	.000	2	2	0	0	0	12	18	1	4	3	16.5	7.50	36	.346	.393	0	.000	-0	-6	-6	0	-0.5
	Cin-N	4	0	1.000	5	3	3	2	0	36^1	27	0	5	9	7.9	0.74	359	.208	.237	3	.214	0	8	8	-0	1.0
1919	Cin-N	0	1	.000	7	1	0	0	0	31	32	0	9	10	11.9	2.32	119	.276	.328	0	.000	-2	2	2	1	0.0
Total	7	32	37	.464	122	67	47	7	5	675^1	734	14	177	204	12.4	3.42	86	.284	.336	44	.187	3	-34	-35	-1	-2.7

● **CHARLIE MITCHELL** Mitchell, Charles Ross b: 6/24/62, Dickson, Tenn. BR/TR, 6′3″, 170 lbs. Deb: 8/9/84 F

YEAR	TM/L	W	L	PCT	G	GS	CG	SH	SV	IP	H	HR	BB	SO	RAT	ERA	ERA+	OAV	OOB	BH	AVG	PB	PR	/A	PD	TPI
1984	Bos-A	0	0	—	10	0	0	0	0	16^1	14	1	6	7	12.1	2.76	151	.226	.314	0	—	0	2	3	0	-0.1
1985	Bos-A	0	0	—	2	0	0	0	0	1^2	5	1	0	2	27.0	16.20	26	.500	.500	0	—	0	-2	-2	0	0.0
Total	2	0	0	—	12	0	0	0	0	18	19	2	6	9	13.5	4.00	104	.264	.338	0	—	0	0	0	0	-0.1

● **CLARENCE MITCHELL** Mitchell, Clarence Elmer b: 2/22/1891, Franklin, Neb. d: 11/6/63, Grand Island, Neb. BL/TL, 5′11.5″, 190 lbs. Deb: 6/2/11 C♦

YEAR	TM/L	W	L	PCT	G	GS	CG	SH	SV	IP	H	HR	BB	SO	RAT	ERA	ERA+	OAV	OOB	BH	AVG	PB	PR	/A	PD	TPI
1911	Det-A	1	0	1.000	5	1	0	0	0	14^1	20	1	7	4	17.0	8.16	42	.351	.422	2	.500	1	-8	-7	-1	-0.4
1916	Cin-N	11	10	.524	29	24	17	1	0	194^2	211	4	45	52	12.3	3.14	83	.285	.334	28	.239	2	-11	-12	1	-0.8
1917	Cin-N	9	15	.375	32	20	10	2	1	159^1	166	4	34	37	11.4	3.22	81	.268	.308	25	.278	4	-9	-11	0	-1.2
1918	Bro-N	0	1	.000	1	1	0	0	0	0^1	4	0	0	0	108.0	108.00	3	1.000	1.000	6	.250	0	-4	-4	0	-3.0
1919	Bro-N	7	5	.583	23	11	9	0	0	108^2	123	0	23	43	12.1	3.06	97	.297	.334	18	.367	6	-2	-1	1	0.7
1920	*Bro-N	5	2	.714	19	7	3	1	1	78^2	85	1	23	18	12.4	3.09	104	.288	.340	25	.234	1	0	1	1	0.4
1921	Bro-N	11	9	.550	37	18	13	**3**	2	190	206	7	46	39	12.2	2.89	135	.280	.327	24	.264	3	19	21	3	2.8
1922	Bro-N	0	3	.000	5	3	0	0	0	12^2	28	0	7	1	25.6	14.21	29	.467	.529	45	.290	2	-14	-14	1	-2.2
1923	Phi-N	9	10	.474	29	19	8	1	0	139^1	170	8	46	41	14.2	4.72	98	.299	.355	21	.269	3	-11	-2	-3	-0.2
1924	Phi-N	6	13	.316	30	26	9	1	1	165	223	10	58	36	15.7	5.62	79	.321	.379	26	.255	-1	-32	-21	3	-1.9
1925	Phi-N	10	17	.370	32	26	12	1	1	199^1	245	23	51	46	13.6	5.28	90	.302	.347	18	.196	-2	-22	-11	4	-1.0
1926	Phi-N	9	14	.391	28	25	12	0	1	178^2	232	7	55	52	14.7	4.58	90	.318	.369	19	.244	1	-15	-9	4	-0.4
1927	Phi-N	6	3	.667	13	12	8	1	0	94^2	99	7	28	17	12.3	4.09	101	.271	.327	10	.238	2	-2	0	1	0.3
1928	Phi-N	0	0	—	3	0	0	0	0	5^2	13	0	2	0	23.8	9.53	45	.542	.577	1	.250	0	-3	-3	0	0.0
	*StL-N	8	9	.471	19	18	9	1	0	150	149	8	38	31	11.4	3.30	121	.265	.315	7	.125	-3	12	12	2	1.1
	Yr	8	9	.471	22	18	9	1	0	155^2	162	8	40	31	11.9	3.53	114	.276	.326	8	.133	-3	8	8	3	1.1
1929	StL-N	8	11	.421	25	22	16	0	0	173	221	13	60	39	14.9	4.27	109	.320	.379	18	.273	4	9	8	-1	0.9
1930	StL-N	1	0	1.000	1	1	0	0	0	3	5	0	2	1	21.0	6.00	84	.357	.438	1	.500	0	-0	-0	-0	-0.1
	NY-N	10	3	.769	24	16	5	0	0	129	151	10	36	40	13.1	3.98	119	.298	.346	12	.255	0	14	11	2	1.1
	Yr	11	3	.786	25	17	5	0	0	132	156	10	38	41	13.3	4.02	118	.300	.349	13	.265	1	14	11	2	1.0
1931	NY-N	13	11	.542	27	25	13	0	0	190^1	221	12	52	39	13.1	4.07	91	.285	.332	16	.219	2	-4	-8	-2	-0.9
1932	NY-N	1	3	.250	8	3	1	0	2	30^1	41	1	11	7	15.7	4.15	89	.325	.384	2	.200	0	-1	-1	-1	-0.3
Total	18	125	139	.473	390	278	145	12	9	2217	2613	116	624	543	13.4	4.12	95	.297	.347	324	.252	26	-86	-54	17	-5.1

● **CRAIG MITCHELL** Mitchell, Craig Seton b: 4/14/54, Santa Rosa, Cal. BR/TR, 6′3″, 180 lbs. Deb: 9/25/75

YEAR	TM/L	W	L	PCT	G	GS	CG	SH	SV	IP	H	HR	BB	SO	RAT	ERA	ERA+	OAV	OOB	BH	AVG	PB	PR	/A	PD	TPI
1975	Oak-A	0	1	.000	1	1	0	0	0	3^2	6	0	2	2	19.6	12.27	30	.375	.444	0	—	0	-3	-4	0	-0.6
1976	Oak-A	0	0	—	1	0	0	0	0	3^1	3	0	0	0	8.1	2.70	124	.231	.231	0	—	0	0	0	0	0.0
1977	Oak-A	0	1	.000	3	1	0	0	0	5^2	9	1	2	1	17.5	7.94	51	.346	.393	0	—	0	-2	-2	-0	-0.3
Total	3	0	2	.000	5	2	0	0	0	12^2	18	1	4	3	15.6	7.82	48	.327	.373	0	—	0	-6	-6	0	-0.9

● **FRED MITCHELL** Mitchell, Frederick Francis (b: Frederick Francis Yapp)
b: 6/5/1878, Cambridge, Mass. d: 10/13/70, Newton, Mass. BR/TR, 5′9.5″, 185 lbs. Deb: 4/27/01 MC♦

YEAR	TM/L	W	L	PCT	G	GS	CG	SH	SV	IP	H	HR	BB	SO	RAT	ERA	ERA+	OAV	OOB	BH	AVG	PB	PR	/A	PD	TPI
1901	Bos-A	6	6	.500	17	13	10	0	0	108^2	115	2	51	34	14.7	3.81	93	.268	.360	7	.159	-1	-2	-3	0	-0.4
1902	Bos-A	0	1	.000	1	0	0	0	0	4	8	1	5	2	29.3	11.25	32	.421	.542	0	.000	-0	-3	-3	0	-0.5
	Phi-A	5	8	.385	18	14	9	0	1	107^2	120	4	59	22	15.6	3.59	102	.282	.380	9	.188	-1	-0	1	2	0.2
	Yr	5	9	.357	19	14	9	0	1	111^2	128	5	64	24	16.1	3.87	95	.288	.388	9	.184	-1	-4	-3	3	-0.3
1903	Phi-N	11	16	.407	28	28	24	1	0	227	250	4	102	69	14.7	4.48	73	.284	.370	19	.200	-1	-31	-30	-3	-3.3
1904	Phi-N	4	7	.364	13	13	11	0	0	108^2	133	3	25	29	13.7	3.40	79	.306	.353	17	.207	1	-8	-9	3	-0.4
	Bro-N	2	5	.286	8	8	8	1	0	66	73	0	23	16	13.5	3.82	72	.291	.357	7	.292	2	-8	-8	1	-0.4
	Yr	6	12	.333	21	21	19	1	0	174^2	206	3	48	45	13.2	3.56	76	.297	.345	24	.226	4	-16	-17	4	-0.8
1905	Bro-N	3	7	.300	12	10	9	0	0	96^1	107	2	38	44	14.0	4.76	61	.285	.358	15	.190	0	-19	-20	1	-1.7
Total	5	31	50	.383	97	86	71	2	1	718^1	806	16	303	216	14.6	4.10	78	.286	.366	120	.210	1	-71	-73	5	-6.5

● **JOHN MITCHELL** Mitchell, John Kyle b: 8/11/65, Dickson, Tenn. BR/TR, 6′2″, 195 lbs. Deb: 9/8/86 F

YEAR	TM/L	W	L	PCT	G	GS	CG	SH	SV	IP	H	HR	BB	SO	RAT	ERA	ERA+	OAV	OOB	BH	AVG	PB	PR	/A	PD	TPI
1986	NY-N	0	1	.000	4	1	0	0	0	10	10	1	4	2	12.6	3.60	98	.278	.350	0	.000	-0	0	-0	0	0.0
1987	NY-N	3	6	.333	20	19	1	0	0	111^2	124	6	36	57	13.1	4.11	92	.279	.336	4	.114	-1	-0	-4	1	-0.3
1988	NY-N	0	0	—	1	0	0	0	0	1	2	0	1	1	27.0	0.00	—	.500	.600	0	.000	-0	0	0	0	0.0
1989	NY-N	0	1	.000	2	0	0	0	0	3	3	0	4	4	21.0	6.00	54	.231	.412	0	—	0	-1	-1	-0	-0.3
1990	Bal-A	6	6	.500	24	17	0	0	0	114^1	133	7	48	43	14.5	4.64	82	.300	.372	0	—	0	-9	-11	1	-0.8
Total	5	9	14	.391	51	37	1	0	0	240	272	14	93	107	13.9	4.35	87	.289	.356	4	.105	-1	-10	-16	2	-1.4

● **LARRY MITCHELL** Mitchell, Larry Paul b: 10/16/71, Flint, Mich. BR/TR, 6′1″, 200 lbs. Deb: 8/11/96

YEAR	TM/L	W	L	PCT	G	GS	CG	SH	SV	IP	H	HR	BB	SO	RAT	ERA	ERA+	OAV	OOB	BH	AVG	PB	PR	/A	PD	TPI
1996	Phi-N	0	0	—	7	0	0	0	0	12	14	1	5	7	14.3	4.50	96	.311	.380	0	.000	-0	-0	-0	-0	-0.1

YEAR	TM/L	W	L	PCT	G	GS	CG	SH	SV	IP	H	HR	BB	SO	RAT	ERA	ERA+	OAV	OOB	BH	AVG	PB	PR	/A	PD	TPI
● MONROE MITCHELL	Mitchell, Monroe Barr b: 9/11/01, Starkville, Miss. d: 9/4/76, Valdosta, Ga. BR/TL, 6′1.5″, 170 lbs. Deb: 7/11/23																									
1923	Was-A	2	4	.333	10	6	3	1	2	41^{2}	57	0	22	8	17.3	6.48	58	.350	.430	3	.250	1	-12	-13	-1	-1.6
● PAUL MITCHELL	Mitchell, Paul Michael b: 8/19/49, Worcester, Mass. BR/TR, 6′1″, 195 lbs. Deb: 7/1/75																									
1975	Bal-A	3	0	1.000	11	4	1	0	0	57	41	8	19	31	9.5	3.63	97	.204	.273	0	—	0	1	-1	-1	-0.1
1976	Oak-A	9	7	.563	26	26	4	1	0	142	169	15	30	67	12.7	4.25	79	.294	.331	0	—	0	-11	-14	-1	-1.6
1977	Oak-A	0	3	.000	5	3	0	0	0	13^{2}	21	3	7	5	18.4	10.54	38	.339	.406	0	—	0	-10	-10	0	-1.6
	Sea-A	3	3	.500	9	9	0	0	0	39^{2}	50	7	16	20	15.2	4.99	82	.311	.376	0	—	0	-4	-4	0	-0.4
	Yr	3	6	.333	14	12	0	0	0	53^{1}	71	10	23	25	16.0	6.41	64	.318	.385	0	—	0	-14	-14	1	-2.0
1978	Sea-A	8	14	.364	29	29	4	2	0	168	173	21	79	75	13.6	4.18	91	.270	.352	0	—	0	-8	-7	-1	-0.9
1979	Sea-A	1	4	.200	10	6	1	0	0	36^{2}	46	4	15	18	15.0	4.42	99	.309	.372	0	—	0	-1	-0	-0	-0.1
	Mil-A	3	3	.500	18	8	0	0	0	75	81	11	10	32	11.3	5.76	72	.276	.307	0	—	0	-13	-13	-1	-1.0
	Yr	4	7	.364	28	14	1	0	0	111^{2}	127	15	25	50	12.5	5.32	79	.287	.329	0	—	0	-14	-14	-1	-1.1
1980	Mil-A	5	5	.500	17	11	1	1	1	89^{1}	92	7	15	29	10.9	3.53	110	.267	.300	0	—	0	5	3	0	0.4
Total	6	32	39	.451	125	96	11	4	1	621^{1}	673	76	191	277	12.6	4.45	85	.278	.332	0	—	0	-41	-46	-3	-5.3
● BOBBY MITCHELL	Mitchell, Robert McKasha b: 2/6/1856, Cincinnati, Ohio d: 5/1/33, Springfield, Ohio BL/TL, 5′5″, 135 lbs. Deb: 9/6/1877 ♦																									
1877	Cin-N	6	5	.545	12	12	11	1	0	100	123	0	11	41	12.1	3.51	75	.281	.299	10	.204	-0	-8	-10	-0	-0.8
1878	Cin-N	7	2	.778	9	9	9	1	0	80	69	1	18	51	9.8	2.14	100	**.223**	.265	12	.245	1	2	-0	0	0.1
1879	Cle-N	7	15	.318	23	22	20	0	0	194^{2}	236	0	42	90	12.9	3.28	76	.283	.317	16	.147	-4	-17	-17	-4	-2.2
1882	StL-a	0	1	.000	1	1	0	0	0	7	12	0	2	2	18.0	7.71	36	.353	.389	0	.000	-1	-4	-4	-0	-0.4
Total	4	20	23	.465	45	44	40	2	0	381^{2}	440	1	73	184	12.1	3.18	77	.272	.304	38	.180	-5	-27	-30	-4	-3.3
● WILLIE MITCHELL	Mitchell, William b: 12/1/1889, Pleasant Grove, Miss. d: 11/23/73, Sardis, Miss. BR/TL, 6′, 176 lbs. Deb: 9/22/09																									
1909	Cle-A	1	2	.333	3	3	3	0	0	23	18	0	10	8	12.5	1.57	163	.225	.340	2	.286	1	2	3	0	0.5
1910	Cle-A	12	8	.600	35	18	11	1	0	183^{2}	155	2	55	102	11.0	2.60	100	.236	.310	10	.159	-3	-2	-0	-2	-0.6
1911	Cle-A	7	14	.333	30	22	9	0	0	177^{1}	190	1	60	78	13.3	3.76	91	.284	.354	7	.109	-5	-8	-7	-1	-1.3
1912	Cle-A	5	8	.385	29	15	8	0	1	163^{2}	149	0	56	94	11.7	2.80	121	.240	.309	6	.113	-4	9	11	-3	0.1
1913	Cle-A	14	8	.636	35	22	14	4	0	217	153	1	88	141	10.3	1.91	159	.199	.288	10	.143	-2	25	27	-3	2.2
1914	Cle-A	11	17	.393	39	32	16	3	1	257	228	3	124	179	12.6	3.19	91	.238	.330	7	.086	-3	-13	-9	-5	-1.9
1915	Cle-A	11	14	.440	36	30	12	1	1	236	210	1	84	149	11.3	2.82	108	.241	.309	10	.127	-5	3	6	-4	-0.3
1916	Cle-A	2	5	.286	12	6	1	0	1	43^{2}	55	1	19	24	15.3	5.15	58	.309	.376	0	.000	-1	-11	-10	-1	-1.8
	Det-A	7	5	.583	23	17	7	2	0	127^{2}	119	1	48	60	12.1	3.31	86	.253	.329	9	.250	2	-7	-6	-3	-0.7
	Yr	9	10	.474	35	23	8	2	1	171^{1}	174	2	67	84	12.9	3.78	77	.269	.342	9	.191	1	-18	-17	-4	-2.5
1917	Det-A	12	8	.600	30	22	12	5	0	185^{1}	172	2	46	80	11.2	2.19	121	.250	.309	7	.119	-3	10	9	-2	0.4
1918	Det-A	0	1	.000	1	1	0	0	0	4	3	0	5	2	18.0	9.00	30	.200	.400	0	.000	-0	-3	-3	0	-0.5
1919	Det-A	1	2	.333	3	2	0	0	0	13^{2}	12	2	10	4	15.1	5.27	61	.255	.397	1	.200	0	-3	-3	0	-0.6
Total	11	83	92	.474	276	190	93	16	4	1632	1464	14	605	921	11.8	2.88	103	.243	.320	69	.130	-24	3	18	-23	-4.5
● VINEGAR BEND MIZELL	Mizell, Wilmer David b: 8/13/30, Leakesville, Miss. BR/TL, 6′3.5″, 205 lbs. Deb: 4/22/52																									
1952	StL-N	10	8	.556	30	30	7	2	0	190	171	12	103	146	13.0	3.65	102	.237	.333	3	.044	-5	2	1	-2	-0.6
1953	StL-N	13	11	.542	33	33	10	1	0	224^{1}	193	12	114	173	12.5	3.49	122	.227	.321	7	.084	-4	20	19	-0	1.4
1956	StL-N	14	14	.500	33	33	11	3	0	208^{2}	172	20	92	153	11.7	3.62	104	.222	.310	8	.107	-3	3	4	0	0.2
1957	StL-N	8	10	.444	33	21	7	2	0	149^{1}	136	18	51	87	11.3	3.74	106	.241	.305	4	.089	-2	2	4	1	0.3
1958	StL-N	10	14	.417	30	29	8	2	0	189^{2}	178	17	91	80	12.9	3.42	121	.252	.339	7	.115	-3	11	15	-1	1.4
1959	StL-N†	13	10	.565	31	30	8	1	0	201^{1}	196	21	89	108	13.1	4.20	101	.252	.334	14	.187	1	-6	1	-2	-0.1
1960	StL-N	1	3	.250	9	9	0	0	0	55^{1}	64	7	28	42	15.0	4.55	90	.291	.371	2	.111	-1	-5	-3	0	-0.2
	*Pit-N	13	5	.722	23	23	8	3	0	155^{2}	141	7	46	71	11.0	3.12	120	.247	.306	7	.137	-1	11	11	-3	0.8
	Yr	14	8	.636	32	32	8	3	0	211	205	14	74	113	12.0	3.50	110	.259	.325	9	.130	-1	6	8	-2	0.6
1961	Pit-N	7	10	.412	25	17	2	1	0	100	120	16	31	37	13.6	5.04	79	.299	.350	3	.130	-1	-11	-12	-3	-2.0
1962	Pit-N	1	1	.500	4	3	0	0	0	16^{1}	15	3	10	6	14.3	4.96	79	.254	.371	0	.000	-0	-2	-2	0	-0.2
	NY-N	0	2	.000	17	2	0	0	0	38	48	10	25	15	17.5	7.34	57	.324	.425	2	.250	0	-14	-13	-1	-0.7
	Yr	1	3	.250	21	5	0	0	0	54^{1}	63	13	35	21	16.4	6.63	62	.301	.404	2	.143	-0	-16	-15	-0	-0.9
Total	9	90	88	.506	268	230	61	15	0	1528^{2}	1434	143	680	918	12.6	3.85	104	.247	.329	57	.111	-19	12	25	-9	0.3
● DAVE MLICKI	Mlicki, David John b: 6/8/68, Cleveland, Ohio BR/TR, 6′4″, 190 lbs. Deb: 9/12/92																									
1992	Cle-A	0	2	.000	4	4	0	0	0	21^{2}	23	3	16	16	16.6	4.98	78	.280	.404	0	—	0	-3	-3	1	-0.1
1993	Cle-A	0	0	—	3	3	0	0	0	13^{1}	11	2	6	7	12.8	3.38	128	.220	.328	0	—	0	1	1	-0	0.0
1995	NY-N	9	7	.563	29	25	0	0	0	160^{2}	160	23	54	123	12.2	4.26	95	.256	.319	2	.051	-1	-1	-4	-1	-0.5
1996	NY-N	6	7	.462	51	2	0	0	1	90	95	9	33	83	13.4	3.30	121	.277	.351	1	.100	-0	9	7	-1	0.8
1997	NY-N	8	12	.400	32	32	1	1	0	193^{2}	194	21	76	157	12.8	4.00	101	.259	.332	9	.188	2	4	1	-2	0.1
1998	NY-N	1	4	.200	10	10	1	0	0	57	68	8	25	39	15.5	5.68	73	.297	.378	3	.188	1	-9	-10	0	-0.7
	LA-N	7	3	.700	20	20	2	1	0	124^{1}	120	15	38	78	11.6	4.05	96	.253	.311	2	.059	-2	2	-2	-0	-0.3
	Yr	8	7	.533	30	30	3	1	0	181^{1}	188	23	63	117	12.6	4.57	87	.264	.326	5	.100	-1	-7	-12	0	-1.0
Total	6	31	35	.470	149	96	4	2	1	660^{2}	671	81	248	503	12.9	4.14	97	.263	.334	17	.116	0	4	-9	-4	-0.7
● KEVIN MMAHAT	Mmahat, Kevin Paul b: 11/9/64, Memphis, Tenn. BL/TL, 6′5″, 220 lbs. Deb: 9/9/89																									
1989	NY-A	0	2	.000	4	2	0	0	0	7^{2}	13	2	8	3	25.8	12.91	30	.406	.537	0	—	0	-8	-8	-0	-1.5
● MIKE MODAK	Modak, Michael b: 5/18/22, Campbell, Ohio d: 12/12/95, Lakeland, Fla. BR/TR, 5′10.5″, 195 lbs. Deb: 7/4/45																									
1945	Cin-N	1	2	.333	20	3	1	1	1	42^{1}	52	0	23	7	15.9	5.74	65	.308	.391	1	.100	-1	-9	-9	-1	-0.8
● BRIAN MOEHLER	Moehler, Brian Merritt b: 12/31/71, Rockingham, N.C. BR/TR, 6′3″, 195 lbs. Deb: 9/22/96																									
1996	Det-A	0	1	.000	2	2	0	0	0	10^{1}	11	1	8	2	16.5	4.35	116	.262	.380	0	—	0	1	1	-0	0.0
1997	Det-A	11	12	.478	31	31	2	1	0	175^{1}	198	22	61	97	13.6	4.67	98	.285	.347	0	.000	-0	-2	-2	0	-0.2
1998	Det-A	14	13	.519	33	33	4	3	0	221^{1}	220	30	56	123	11.3	3.90	121	.259	.307	0	.000	-0	18	20	0	2.1
Total	3	25	26	.490	66	66	6	4	0	407	429	53	125	222	12.4	4.25	110	.271	.327	0	.000	-1	17	19	0	1.9
● DENNIS MOELLER	Moeller, Dennis Michael b: 9/15/67, Tarzana, Cal. BR/TL, 6′2″, 195 lbs. Deb: 7/28/92																									
1992	KC-A	0	3	.000	5	4	0	0	0	18	24	5	11	6	17.5	7.00	58	.333	.422	0	—	0	-6	-6	0	-0.9
1993	Pit-N	1	0	1.000	10	0	0	0	0	16^{1}	26	2	7	13	18.7	9.92	41	.356	.420	0	—	0	-11	-11	0	-0.6
Total	2	1	3	.250	15	4	0	0	0	34^{1}	50	7	18	19	18.1	8.39	48	.345	.421	0	—	0	-17	-17	1	-1.5
● JOE MOELLER	Moeller, Joseph Douglas b: 2/15/43, Blue Island, Ill. BR/TR, 6′5″, 208 lbs. Deb: 4/12/62																									
1962	LA-N	6	5	.545	19	15	1	0	1	85^{2}	87	10	58	46	15.2	5.25	69	.266	.377	7	.212	1	-12	-15	1	-1.6
1964	LA-N	7	13	.350	27	24	1	0	0	145^{1}	153	14	31	97	11.6	4.21	77	.265	.307	3	.067	-2	-11	-16	-0	-2.2
1966	*LA-N	2	4	.333	29	8	0	0	0	78^{2}	73	4	14	31	10.3	2.52	131	.244	.285	2	.167	1	10	7	1	0.7
1967	LA-N	0	0	—	6	0	0	0	0	5	9	1	3	2	21.6	9.00	34	.409	.480	0	—	0	-3	-3	0	0.0
1968	LA-N	1	1	.500	3	3	0	0	0	16	17	1	2	11	11.3	5.06	55	.270	.303	0	.000	-1	-4	-4	0	-0.5
1969	LA-N	1	0	1.000	23	4	0	0	1	51^{1}	54	4	13	25	11.7	3.33	100	.278	.324	2	.200	0	1	-0	1	0.1
1970	LA-N	7	9	.438	31	19	2	1	4	135^{1}	131	16	43	63	11.6	3.92	98	.248	.306	6	.154	0	2	-1	-2	-0.3
1971	LA-N	2	4	.333	28	1	0	0	1	66^{1}	72	5	12	32	11.4	3.80	85	.279	.311	0	.000	-0	-2	-4	1	-0.4
Total	8	26	36	.419	166	74	4	1	7	583^{2}	596	55	176	307	12.0	4.01	86	.263	.318	20	.129	-2	-20	-37	2	-4.2
● RON MOELLER	Moeller, Ronald Ralph "The Kid" b: 10/13/38, Cincinnati, Ohio BL/TL, 6′, 180 lbs. Deb: 9/8/56																									
1956	Bal-A	0	1	.000	4	1	0	0	0	8^{2}	10	0	3	2	13.5	4.15	94	.286	.342	0	.000	-0	0	-0	-0	-0.1
1958	Bal-A	0	0	—	4	0	0	0	0	4^{1}	6	0	3	3	18.7	4.15	87	.333	.429	0	—	0	-0	-0	0	0.0
1961	LA-A	4	8	.333	33	18	1	1	0	112^{2}	122	15	83	87	16.5	5.83	77	.275	.392	6	.207	2	-23	-17	1	-1.3
1963	LA-A	0	0	—	3	0	0	0	0	2^{2}	5	1	1	2	20.3	6.75	51	.385	.429	0	—	0	-1	-1	0	0.0
	Was-A	2	0	1.000	8	3	0	0	0	24^{1}	31	4	10	10	15.5	6.29	59	.316	.385	2	.222	0	-7	-7	-1	-0.6

YEAR	TM/L	W	L	PCT	G	GS	CG	SH	SV	IP	H	HR	BB	SO	RAT	ERA	ERA+	OAV	OOB	BH	AVG	PB	PR	/A	PD	TPI
	Yr	2	0	1.000	11	3	0	0	0	27	36	5	11	12	16.0	6.33	58	.324	.390	2	.222	0	-8	-8	-1	-0.6
Total	4	6	9	.400	52	22	1	1	0	152^2	174	20	100	104	16.3	5.78	74	.287	.390	8	.205	2	-31	-25	0	-2.0

● SAM MOFFETT Moffett, Samuel R. b: 3/14/1857, Wheeling, W.Va. d: 5/5/07, Butte, Mont. BR/TR, 6′, 175 lbs. Deb: 5/15/1884 F♦

1884	Cle-N	3	19	.136	24	22	21	0	0	197^2	236	9	58	84	13.4	3.87	81	.284	.330	47	.184	-3	-20	-16	2	-1.4
1887	Ind-N	1	5	.167	6	6	6	0	0	50	47	1	23	3	13.3	3.78	110	.242	.335	5	.122	-2	2	2	-0	-0.1
1888	Ind-N	2	5	.286	7	7	6	1	0	56	62	3	17	7	13.0	4.66	64	.278	.335	4	.114	-1	-11	-11	-2	-1.3
Total	3	6	29	.171	37	35	33	1	0	303^2	345	13	98	94	13.3	4.00	82	.276	.332	56	.169	-6	-29	-24	-0	-2.8

● RANDY MOFFITT Moffitt, Randall James b: 10/13/48, Long Beach, Cal. BR/TR, 6′3″, 190 lbs. Deb: 6/11/72

1972	SF-N	1	5	.167	40	0	0	0	4	70^2	72	5	30	37	13.2	3.69	94	.266	.343	0	.000	-1	-2	-2	0	-0.2
1973	SF-N	4	4	.500	60	0	0	0	14	100^1	86	9	31	65	10.6	2.42	158	.225	.285	1	.059	-1	14	16	-1	1.4
1974	SF-N	5	7	.417	61	1	0	0	15	102	99	9	29	49	11.5	4.50	84	.256	.311	5	.313	2	-10	-8	1	-0.9
1975	SF-N	4	5	.444	55	0	0	0	11	74	73	6	32	39	13.1	3.89	98	.257	.339	3	.214	1	-2	-1	-0	-0.1
1976	SF-N	6	6	.500	58	0	0	0	14	103	92	6	35	50	11.2	2.27	160	.238	.303	2	.143	-0	14	16	-0	2.2
1977	SF-N	4	9	.308	64	0	0	0	11	87^2	91	4	39	68	13.7	3.59	109	.273	.355	0	.000	-0	3	3	1	0.5
1978	SF-N	8	4	.667	70	0	0	0	12	81^2	79	5	33	52	12.7	3.31	104	.258	.336	1	.143	0	2	1	-1	0.1
1979	SF-N	2	5	.286	28	0	0	0	2	35	53	5	14	16	17.7	7.71	45	.356	.418	0	.000	-0	-15	-16	-0	-3.1
1980	SF-N	1	1	.500	13	0	0	0	0	16^2	18	2	4	10	12.4	4.86	73	.281	.333	0	.000	-0	-2	-2	0	-0.3
1981	SF-N	0	0	—	10	0	0	0	0	11^1	15	2	2	11	13.5	7.94	43	.313	.340	0	—	0	-6	-6	-0	0.0
1982	Hou-N	2	4	.333	30	0	0	0	3	41^2	36	3	13	20	11.7	3.02	110	.228	.307	0	.000	-0	3	1	-1	0.1
1983	Tor-A	6	2	.750	45	0	0	0	10	57^1	52	5	24	38	12.1	3.77	114	.243	.322	0	—	0	2	3	0	0.4
Total	12	43	52	.453	534	1	0	0	96	781^1	766	61	286	455	12.4	3.65	102	.257	.327	12	.140	-1	0	5	-3	0.1

● HERB MOFORD Moford, Herbert b: 8/6/28, Brooksville, Ky. BR/TR, 6′1″, 175 lbs. Deb: 4/12/55

1955	StL-N	1	1	.500	14	1	0	0	2	24	29	5	15	8	16.9	7.88	52	.299	.398	0	.000	-0	-10	-10	1	-0.9
1958	Det-A	4	9	.308	25	11	6	0	1	109^2	83	10	42	58	11.0	3.61	112	.214	.305	1	.027	-4	2	5	1	0.3
1959	Bos-A	0	2	.000	4	2	0	0	0	8^2	10	3	6	7	16.6	11.42	36	.286	.390	0	.000	-0	-7	-7	0	-1.3
1962	NY-N	0	1	.000	7	0	0	0	0	15	21	3	1	5	13.2	7.20	58	.318	.328	1	.250	0	-5	-5	-0	-0.3
Total	4	5	13	.278	50	14	6	0	3	157^1	143	21	64	78	12.4	5.03	81	.244	.329	2	.045	-4	-21	-17	2	-2.2

● GEORGE MOGRIDGE Mogridge, George Anthony b: 2/18/1889, Rochester, N.Y. d: 3/4/62, Rochester, N.Y. BL/TL, 6′2″, 165 lbs. Deb: 8/17/11

1911	Chi-A	0	2	.000	4	1	0	0	0	12^2	12	1	1	5	9.2	4.97	65	.255	.271	2	.400	0	-2	-2	-0	-0.3
1912	Chi-A	3	4	.429	17	8	2	0	3	64^2	69	2	15	31	11.8	4.04	79	.264	.307	2	.125	-0	-5	-6	-1	-0.7
1915	NY-A	2	3	.400	6	5	3	1	0	41	33	0	11	11	10.3	1.76	167	.219	.285	1	.083	-1	5	5	-1	0.6
1916	NY-A	6	12	.333	30	21	10	2	0	194^2	174	3	45	66	10.4	2.31	125	.252	.305	14	.212	1	11	13	1	1.4
1917	NY-A	9	11	.450	29	25	15	1	0	196^1	185	5	39	46	10.7	2.98	90	.255	.301	11	.159	-1	-7	-6	1	-0.7
1918	NY-A	16	13	.552	**45**	19	13	1	**7**	239^1	232	6	43	62	10.6	2.18	130	.263	.304	15	.190	-0	16	17	3	2.5
1919	NY-A	10	9	.526	35	18	13	3	0	169	159	6	46	58	11.3	2.77	115	.250	.307	6	.125	-1	9	8	1	0.8
1920	NY-A	5	9	.357	26	15	7	0	1	125^1	146	4	36	35	13.3	4.31	89	.287	.338	7	.167	-1	-7	-7	1	-0.7
1921	Was-A	18	14	.563	38	36	21	4	0	288	301	12	66	101	11.7	3.00	137	.269	.313	15	.153	-5	41	36	2	3.0
1922	Was-A	18	13	.581	34	32	18	3	0	251^2	300	12	72	61	13.7	3.58	108	.304	.358	21	.244	4	13	8	-1	1.2
1923	Was-A	13	13	.500	33	30	17	3	1	211	228	10	56	62	12.2	3.11	121	.285	.334	17	.227	1	20	15	1	2.0
1924	*Was-A	16	11	.593	30	30	13	2	0	213	217	2	61	48	12.0	3.76	107	.270	.327	13	.176	-2	11	7	0	0.5
1925	Was-A	3	4	.429	10	8	3	0	0	53	58	2	18	12	13.6	4.08	104	.291	.362	2	.105	-2	2	1	-0	-0.1
	StL-A	1	1	.500	2	2	1	0	0	15^1	17	2	5	8	13.5	5.87	80	.279	.343	0	.000	-0	-3	-2	0	-0.2
	Yr	4	5	.444	12	10	4	0	0	68^1	75	4	23	20	13.0	4.48	97	.284	.344	2	.087	-2	-1	-1	0	-0.3
1926	Bos-N	6	10	.375	39	10	2	0	3	142	173	6	36	46	13.4	4.50	79	.311	.356	8	.174	-1	-11	-15	2	-1.4
1927	Bos-N	6	4	.600	20	1	0	0	5	48^2	48	4	15	26	12.0	3.70	100	.257	.319	3	.200	-0	1	0	1	0.1
Total	15	132	133	.498	398	261	138	20	20	2265^2	2352	77	565	678	11.9	3.23	109	.273	.323	137	.182	-8	95	75	11	8.0

● GEORGE MOHART Mohart, George Benjamin b: 3/6/1892, Buffalo, N.Y. d: 10/2/70, Silver Creek, N.Y. BR/TR, 5′9″, 165 lbs. Deb: 4/15/20

1920	Bro-N	0	1	.000	13	1	0	0	0	35^2	33	0	7	13	10.9	1.77	181	.250	.303	1	.125	-0	5	6	1	0.2
1921	Bro-N	0	0	—	2	0	0	0	0	7	8	0	1	1	12.9	3.86	101	.296	.345	1	.500	0	-0	0	-0	0.0
Total	2	0	1	.000	15	1	0	0	0	42^2	41	0	8	14	11.2	2.11	157	.258	.310	2	.200	0	5	6	1	0.2

● MIKE MOHLER Mohler, Michael Ross b: 7/26/68, Dayton, Ohio BR/TL, 6′2″, 195 lbs. Deb: 4/7/93

1993	Oak-A	1	6	.143	42	9	0	0	0	64^1	57	10	44	42	14.4	5.60	73	.241	.364	0	—	0	-9	-11	0	-1.0
1994	Oak-A	0	1	.000	1	1	0	0	0	2^1	2	1	2	4	15.4	7.71	57	.167	.286	0	—	0	-1	-1	0	-0.1
1995	Oak-A	1	1	.500	28	0	0	0	1	23^2	16	0	18	15	12.9	3.04	147	.198	.343	0	—	0	4	4	-0	0.3
1996	Oak-A	6	3	.667	72	0	0	0	7	81	79	9	41	64	13.4	3.67	134	.263	.354	0	—	0	12	11	1	1.3
1997	Oak-A	1	10	.091	62	10	0	0	1	101^2	116	11	54	66	15.7	5.13	88	.301	.397	0	—	0	-6	-7	1	-0.6
1998	Oak-A	3	3	.500	57	0	0	0	0	61	70	6	26	42	14.8	5.16	88	.289	.368	0	—	0	-4	-4	-1	-0.4
Total	6	12	24	.333	262	20	0	0	9	334	340	37	185	233	14.5	4.74	96	.270	.370	0	—	0	-4	-8	1	-0.5

● DALE MOHORCIC Mohorcic, Dale Robert b: 1/25/56, Cleveland, Ohio BR/TR, 6′3″, 220 lbs. Deb: 5/31/86

1986	Tex-A	2	4	.333	58	0	0	0	7	79	86	5	15	29	11.6	2.51	172	.279	.315	0	—	0	15	16	0	1.4
1987	Tex-A	7	6	.538	74	0	0	0	16	99^1	88	11	19	48	9.9	2.99	150	.244	.286	0	—	0	16	16	2	2.6
1988	Tex-A	2	6	.250	43	0	0	0	5	52	62	6	20	25	15.1	4.85	84	.295	.370	0	—	0	-5	-4	0	-0.7
	NY-A	2	2	.500	13	0	0	0	1	22^2	21	1	9	19	13.1	2.78	142	.239	.330	0	—	0	3	3	-1	0.5
	Yr	4	8	.333	56	0	0	0	6	74^2	83	7	29	44	13.9	4.22	96	.269	.338	0	—	0	-2	-2	-0	-0.2
1989	NY-A	2	1	.667	32	0	0	0	2	57^2	65	8	18	24	13.9	4.99	77	.286	.355	0	—	0	-7	-7	1	-0.3
1990	Mon-N	1	2	.333	34	0	0	0	2	53	56	6	18	29	13.2	3.23	113	.286	.358	1	.125	-0	3	2	0	0.2
Total	5	16	21	.432	254	0	0	0	33	363^2	378	37	99	174	12.3	3.49	118	.272	.330	1	.125	-0	25	26	3	3.7

● BILL MOISAN Moisan, William Joseph b: 7/30/25, Bradford, Mass. BL/TR, 6′1″, 170 lbs. Deb: 9/17/53

1953	Chi-N	0	0	—	3	0	0	0	0	5	5	0	2	1	14.4	5.40	82	.278	.381	0	—	0	-1	-1	0	0.0

● CARLTON MOLESWORTH Molesworth, Carlton b: 2/15/1876, Frederick, Md. d: 7/25/61, Frederick, Md. BL/TL, 5′6″, 200 lbs. Deb: 9/14/1895

1895	Was-N	0	2	.000	4	3	1	0	0	16	33	1	15	7	29.3	14.63	33	.418	.531	1	.143	-1	-17	-17	-0	-1.4

● RICHIE MOLONEY Moloney, Richard Henry b: 6/7/50, Brookline, Mass. BR/TR, 6′3″, 185 lbs. Deb: 9/20/70

1970	Chi-A	0	0	—	1	0	0	0	0	1	2	0	0	1	18.0	0.00	—	.400	.400	0	—	0	0	0	0	0.0

● VINCE MOLYNEAUX Molyneaux, Vincent Leo b: 8/17/1888, Lewiston, N.Y. d: 5/4/50, Stamford, Conn. BR/TR, 6′, 180 lbs. Deb: 7/5/17

1917	StL-A	0	0	—	7	0	0	0	0	22	18	0	20	4	15.5	4.91	53	.237	.396	0	.000	-1	-5	-6	0	0.0
1918	Bos-A	1	0	1.000	6	0	0	0	0	10^2	3	0	8	1	9.3	3.38	80	.086	.256	0	.000	-0	-1	-1	0	-0.1
Total	2	1	0	1.000	13	0	0	0	0	32^2	21	0	28	5	13.5	4.41	60	.189	.353	0	.000	-1	-6	-6	1	-0.1

● RINTY MONAHAN Monahan, Edward Francis b: 4/28/28, Brooklyn, N.Y. BR/TR, 6′1.5″, 195 lbs. Deb: 8/9/53

1953	Phi-A	0	0	—	4	0	0	0	0	10^2	11	0	7	2	15.2	4.22	102	.275	.383	0	.000	-0	-0	0	-0	-0.1

● BILL MONBOUQUETTE Monbouquette, William Charles b: 8/11/36, Medford, Mass. BR/TR, 5′11″, 195 lbs. Deb: 7/18/58 C

1958	Bos-A	3	4	.429	10	8	3	0	0	54^1	52	4	20	30	11.9	3.31	121	.251	.317	3	.176	-1	3	4	-1	0.4
1959	Bos-A	7	7	.500	34	17	4	0	0	151^2	165	15	33	87	11.9	4.15	98	.285	.327	3	.065	-4	-5	-2	-0	-0.5
1960	Bos-A★	14	11	.560	35	30	12	3	0	215	217	18	68	134	12.0	3.64	111	.263	.320	6	.092	-3	6	10	-0	0.7
1961	Bos-A	14	14	.500	32	32	12	1	0	236^1	233	24	100	161	12.7	3.39	123	.254	.327	9	.130	-1	17	20	-1	2.1
1962	Bos-A☆	15	13	.536	35	35	11	4	0	235^1	227	22	65	153	11.3	3.33	124	.251	.303	7	.096	-3	17	21	-4	1.6
1963	Bos-A☆	20	10	.667	37	36	13	1	0	266^2	258	31	42	174	10.1	3.81	99	.250	.280	10	.114	-3	-5	-1	1	-0.4
1964	Bos-A	13	14	.481	36	35	7	5	1	234	258	34	40	120	11.5	4.04	95	.277	.308	6	.083	-2	-11	-5	0	-0.7
1965	Bos-A	10	18	.357	35	35	10	2	0	228^2	239	32	40	110	11.0	3.70	101	.269	.301	4	.059	-3	-6	1	0	-0.2
1966	Det-A	7	8	.467	30	14	2	1	0	102^2	120	14	22	61	12.7	4.73	74	.293	.333	4	.154	-0	-15	-14	-1	-2.0

YEAR	TM/L	W	L	PCT	G	GS	CG	SH	SV	IP	H	HR	BB	SO	RAT	ERA	ERA+	OAV	OOB	BH	AVG	PB	PR	/A	PD	TPI
1967	Det-A	0	0	—	2	0	0	0	0	2	1	0	0	2	4.5	0.00	—	.143	.143	0	—	0	1	1	0	0.0
	NY-A	6	5	.545	33	10	2	1	1	133^1	122	6	17	53	9.7	2.36	132	.246	.277	5	.156	-0	13	11	-1	0.9
	Yr	6	5	.545	35	10	2	1	1	135^1	123	6	17	55	9.6	2.33	134	.245	.275	5	.156	-0	14	12	-1	0.9
1968	NY-A	5	7	.417	17	11	2	0	0	89^1	92	7	13	32	10.9	4.43	65	.264	.296	3	.115	0	-14	-15	1	-1.9
	SF-N	0	1	.000	7	0	0	0	1	12^1	11	4	2	5	9.5	3.65	81	.239	.271	0	—	0	-1	-1	0	-0.1
Total	11	114	112	.504	343	263	78	18	3	1961^2	1995	211	462	1122	11.4	3.68	104	.263	.307	60	.103	-20	-2	29	-6	-0.1

● **SID MONGE** Monge, Isidro Pedroza b: 4/11/51, Agua Prieta, Mexico BB/TL, 6′2″, 195 lbs. Deb: 9/12/75

YEAR	TM/L	W	L	PCT	G	GS	CG	SH	SV	IP	H	HR	BB	SO	RAT	ERA	ERA+	OAV	OOB	BH	AVG	PB	PR	/A	PD	TPI
1975	Cal-A	0	2	.000	4	2	2	0	0	23^2	22	3	10	17	12.5	4.18	85	.242	.324	0	—	0	-1	-2	-0	0.2
1976	Cal-A	6	7	.462	32	13	2	0	0	117^2	108	10	49	53	12.1	3.37	99	.248	.326	0	—	0	2	-1	-1	0.2
1977	Cal-A	0	1	.000	4	0	0	0	1	12^1	14	2	6	4	14.6	2.92	134	.304	.385	0	—	0	2	1	0	0.5
	Cle-A	1	2	.333	33	0	0	0	3	39	47	6	27	25	17.1	6.23	63	.309	.413	0	—	0	-9	-10	-1	-0.7
	Yr	1	3	.250	37	0	0	0	4	51^1	61	8	33	29	16.5	5.44	72	.307	.405	0	—	0	-8	-9	-1	-0.2
1978	Cle-A	4	3	.571	48	2	0	0	6	84^2	71	4	51	54	13.0	2.76	135	.225	.332	0	—	0	9	9	-0	0.9
1979	Cle-A☆	12	10	.545	76	0	0	0	19	131	96	9	64	108	11.1	2.40	177	.209	.307	0	—	0	26	27	-0	5.0
1980	Cle-A	3	5	.375	67	0	0	0	14	94^1	80	12	40	61	11.7	3.53	115	.227	.311	0	—	0	5	6	-2	0.5
1981	Cle-A	3	5	.375	31	0	0	0	4	58	58	9	21	41	12.3	4.34	83	.266	.331	0	—	0	-4	-5	-1	-0.7
1982	Phi-N	7	1	.875	47	0	0	0	2	72	70	8	22	43	11.8	3.75	98	.256	.316	1	.111	-0	-1	-1	1	0.0
1983	Phi-N	3	0	1.000	14	0	0	0	0	11^2	20	4	6	7	20.1	6.94	51	.377	.441	0	.000	-0	-4	-4	-0	-1.0
	SD-N	7	3	.700	47	0	0	0	7	68^2	65	4	31	32	12.7	3.15	111	.257	.340	1	.100	-0	4	3	-0	0.3
	Yr	10	3	.769	61	0	0	0	7	80^1	85	8	37	39	13.8	3.70	95	.277	.357	1	.091	-1	-1	-2	-1	-0.7
1984	SD-N	2	1	.667	13	0	0	0	0	15	17	3	17	7	20.4	4.80	74	.293	.453	0	.000	-0	-2	-2	-0	-0.4
	Det-A	1	0	1.000	19	0	0	0	0	36	40	5	12	19	13.5	4.25	92	.282	.346	0	—	0	-1	-1	-1	-0.1
Total	10	49	40	.551	435	17	4	0	56	764	708	79	356	471	12.7	3.53	107	.248	.334	2	.095	-1	25	20	-6	4.7

● **ED MONROE** Monroe, Edward Oliver "Peck" b: 2/22/1895, Louisville, Ky. d: 4/29/69, Louisville, Ky. BR/TR, 6′5″, 187 lbs. Deb: 5/29/17

YEAR	TM/L	W	L	PCT	G	GS	CG	SH	SV	IP	H	HR	BB	SO	RAT	ERA	ERA+	OAV	OOB	BH	AVG	PB	PR	/A	PD	TPI
1917	NY-A	1	0	1.000	9	1	1	0	1	28^2	35	1	6	12	13.5	3.45	78	.310	.355	2	.167	-0	-3	-2	-0	-0.1
1918	NY-A	0	0	—	1	0	0	0	0	2	1	0	2	1	13.5	4.50	63	.143	.333	0	—	0	-0	-0	0	0.0
Total	2	1	0	1.000	10	1	1	0	1	30^2	36	1	8	13	13.5	3.52	77	.300	.354	2	.167	-0	-3	-3	0	-0.1

● **LARRY MONROE** Monroe, Lawrence James b: 6/20/56, Detroit, Mich. BR/TR, 6′4″, 200 lbs. Deb: 8/23/76

YEAR	TM/L	W	L	PCT	G	GS	CG	SH	SV	IP	H	HR	BB	SO	RAT	ERA	ERA+	OAV	OOB	BH	AVG	PB	PR	/A	PD	TPI
1976	Chi-A	0	1	.000	8	2	0	0	0	21^2	23	0	13	9	15.0	4.15	86	.284	.383	0	—	0	-2	-1	-0	-0.1

● **ZACH MONROE** Monroe, Zachary Charles b: 7/8/31, Peoria, Ill. BR/TR, 6′, 198 lbs. Deb: 6/27/58

YEAR	TM/L	W	L	PCT	G	GS	CG	SH	SV	IP	H	HR	BB	SO	RAT	ERA	ERA+	OAV	OOB	BH	AVG	PB	PR	/A	PD	TPI
1958	*NY-A	4	2	.667	21	6	1	0	1	58	57	8	27	18	13.0	3.26	108	.263	.344	2	.118	-1	3	2	0	0.1
1959	NY-A	0	0	—	3	0	0	0	0	3^1	3	2	2	1	13.5	5.40	67	.231	.333	0	—	0	-1	-1	0	0.0
Total	2	4	2	.667	24	6	1	0	1	61^1	60	10	29	19	13.1	3.38	105	.261	.344	2	.118	-1	3	1	1	0.1

● **JOHN MONTAGUE** Montague, John Evans b: 9/12/47, Newport News, Va. BR/TR, 6′2″, 213 lbs. Deb: 9/9/73

YEAR	TM/L	W	L	PCT	G	GS	CG	SH	SV	IP	H	HR	BB	SO	RAT	ERA	ERA+	OAV	OOB	BH	AVG	PB	PR	/A	PD	TPI
1973	Mon-N	0	0	—	4	0	0	0	0	7^2	8	0	2	7	12.9	3.52	108	.286	.355	0	.000	-0	0	0	-0	0.0
1974	Mon-N	3	4	.429	46	1	0	0	3	82^2	73	5	38	43	12.5	3.16	122	.241	.333	1	.100	-0	4	6	-2	0.4
1975	Mon-N	0	1	.000	12	0	0	0	2	17^2	23	4	6	9	15.8	5.60	68	.324	.392	0	.000	-0	-4	-3	-0	-0.3
	Phi-N	0	0	—	3	0	0	0	0	5	8	1	4	1	21.6	9.00	41	.400	.500	0	—	0	-3	-3	0	0.0
	Yr	0	1	.000	15	0	0	0	2	22^2	31	5	10	10	16.3	6.35	60	.326	.390	0	.000	-0	-7	-6	0	-0.3
1977	Sea-A	8	12	.400	47	15	2	0	4	182^1	193	20	75	98	13.4	4.29	96	.272	.345	0	—	0	-5	-4	1	-0.2
1978	Sea-A	1	3	.250	19	0	0	0	2	43^2	52	2	24	14	15.7	6.18	62	.308	.394	0	—	0	-12	-12	-1	-1.1
1979	Sea-A	6	4	.600	41	1	0	0	1	116^1	125	14	47	60	13.5	5.57	78	.284	.356	0	—	0	-18	-16	1	-1.2
	*Cal-A	2	0	1.000	14	0	0	0	6	17^2	16	3	9	6	12.7	5.09	80	.242	.333	0	—	0	-2	-2	-1	-0.3
	Yr	8	4	.667	55	1	0	0	7	134	141	17	56	66	13.2	5.51	78	.273	.344	0	—	0	-19	-18	-0	-1.5
1980	Cal-A	4	2	.667	37	0	0	0	3	73^2	97	8	21	22	14.5	5.13	77	.324	.371	0	—	0	-9	-10	0	-0.7
Total	7	24	26	.480	223	17	2	0	21	546^2	595	57	226	260	13.7	4.76	85	.283	.356	1	.083	-0	-47	-42	-1	-3.4

● **RAFAEL MONTALVO** Montalvo, Rafael Edgardo (Torres) b: 3/31/64, Rio Piedras, P.R. BR/TR, 6′, 185 lbs. Deb: 4/13/86

YEAR	TM/L	W	L	PCT	G	GS	CG	SH	SV	IP	H	HR	BB	SO	RAT	ERA	ERA+	OAV	OOB	BH	AVG	PB	PR	/A	PD	TPI
1986	Hou-N	0	0	—	1	0	0	0	0	1	1	0	2	0	27.0	9.00	40	.250	.500	0	—	0	-1	-1	0	0.0

● **AURELIO MONTEAGUDO** Monteagudo, Aurelio Faustino (Cintra) b: 11/19/43, Caibarien, Cuba d: 11/10/90, Saltillo, Mexico BR/TR, 5′11″, 185 lbs. Deb: 9/1/63 F

YEAR	TM/L	W	L	PCT	G	GS	CG	SH	SV	IP	H	HR	BB	SO	RAT	ERA	ERA+	OAV	OOB	BH	AVG	PB	PR	/A	PD	TPI
1963	KC-A	0	0	—	4	0	0	0	0	7	4	0	3	3	9.0	2.57	152	.182	.280	0	—	0	1	1	0	0.0
1964	KC-A	0	4	.000	11	6	0	0	0	31^1	40	11	10	14	14.6	8.90	43	.317	.372	2	.286	1	-18	-18	-0	-1.9
1965	KC-A	0	0	—	4	0	0	0	0	7	5	1	4	5	11.6	3.86	90	.185	.290	0	—	0	-0	-0	-0	0.0
1966	KC-A	0	0	—	6	0	0	0	0	12^2	12	0	7	3	13.5	2.84	120	.261	.358	0	—	0	1	1	-0	0.0
	Hou-N	0	0	—	10	0	0	0	1	15^1	14	1	11	7	14.7	4.70	73	.241	.362	0	.000	-0	-2	-2	-0	-0.1
1967	Chi-A	0	1	.000	1	1	0	0	0	1^1	4	1	2	0	40.5	20.25	15	.500	.600	0	—	0	-3	-3	-0	-1.0
1970	KC-A	1	1	.500	21	0	0	0	0	27^1	20	2	9	18	9.9	2.96	126	.200	.273	0	.000	-0	2	2	-1	0.1
1973	Cal-A	2	1	.667	15	0	0	0	3	30	23	2	16	8	12.9	4.20	84	.215	.339	0	—	0	-1	-2	0	0.3
Total	7	3	7	.300	72	7	0	0	4	132	122	18	62	58	13.0	5.05	72	.247	.338	2	.200	1	-20	-21	-1	-2.6

● **RENE MONTEAGUDO** Monteagudo, Rene (Miranda) b: 3/12/16, Havana, Cuba d: 9/14/73, Hialeah, Fla. BL/TL, 5′7″, 165 lbs. Deb: 9/6/38 F♦

YEAR	TM/L	W	L	PCT	G	GS	CG	SH	SV	IP	H	HR	BB	SO	RAT	ERA	ERA+	OAV	OOB	BH	AVG	PB	PR	/A	PD	TPI
1938	Was-A	1	1	.500	5	3	2	0	0	22	26	3	15	13	16.8	5.73	79	.286	.387	3	.500	1	-2	-3	-1	-0.2
1940	Was-A	2	6	.250	27	8	3	0	2	100^2	128	7	52	64	16.4	6.08	69	.316	.398	6	.182	0	-19	-21	-1	-1.6
1945	Phi-N	0	0	—	14	0	0	0	0	45^2	67	1	28	16	19.1	7.49	51	.347	.435	58	.301	2	-19	-19	-1	0.2
Total	3	3	7	.300	46	11	5	0	2	168^1	221	11	95	93	17.2	6.42	64	.321	.407	78	.289	4	-40	-43	-3	-1.6

● **JOHN MONTEFUSCO** Montefusco, John Joseph "Count" b: 5/25/50, Long Branch, N.J. BR/TR, 6′1″, 180 lbs. Deb: 9/3/74

YEAR	TM/L	W	L	PCT	G	GS	CG	SH	SV	IP	H	HR	BB	SO	RAT	ERA	ERA+	OAV	OOB	BH	AVG	PB	PR	/A	PD	TPI
1974	SF-N	3	2	.600	7	5	1	1	0	39^1	41	3	19	34	13.7	4.81	79	.256	.335	4	.286	3	-5	-4	-0	-0.3
1975	SF-N	15	9	.625	35	34	10	4	0	243^2	210	11	86	215	11.2	2.88	132	.233	.305	7	.087	-2	20	25	-1	2.0
1976	SF-N★	16	14	.533	37	36	11	**6**	0	253^1	224	11	74	172	10.7	2.84	128	.238	.296	8	.103	-2	19	22	-4	2.0
1977	SF-N	7	12	.368	26	25	4	0	0	157^1	170	10	46	110	12.5	3.49	112	.273	.326	6	.122	-1	7	7	-2	0.5
1978	SF-N	11	9	.550	36	36	3	0	0	238^2	233	25	68	177	11.5	3.81	91	.255	.310	4	.057	-3	-6	-10	-2	-1.2
1979	SF-N	3	8	.273	22	22	0	0	0	137	145	15	51	76	13.0	3.94	89	.279	.346	7	.167	2	-3	-7	0	-0.4
1980	SF-N	4	8	.333	22	17	1	0	0	113^1	120	15	39	85	12.8	4.37	81	.265	.327	1	.033	-2	-10	-10	-1	-1.4
1981	Atl-N	2	3	.400	26	9	0	0	1	77^1	75	9	27	34	11.9	3.49	103	.260	.324	1	.067	-1	-0	1	0	0.0
1982	SD-N	10	11	.476	32	32	1	0	0	184^1	177	17	41	83	10.8	4.00	86	.251	.295	5	.086	-2	-8	-12	-1	-1.5
1983	SD-N	9	4	.692	31	10	1	0	4	95^1	94	6	32	52	12.0	3.30	105	.265	.327	1	.053	-1	3	2	-1	0.1
	NY-A	5	0	1.000	6	6	0	0	0	38	39	3	10	15	11.8	3.32	117	.271	.323	0	—	0	3	2	-1	0.3
1984	NY-A	5	3	.625	11	11	0	0	0	55^1	55	5	13	23	11.2	3.58	106	.253	.299	0	—	0	3	1	-1	0.1
1985	NY-A	0	0	—	3	1	0	0	0	7	12	3	2	2	18.0	10.29	39	.387	.424	0	—	0	-5	-5	0	0.2
1986	NY-A	0	0	—	4	0	0	0	0	12^1	9	2	5	3	10.2	2.19	187	.200	.280	0	—	0	3	3	0	0.1
Total	13	90	83	.520	298	244	32	11	5	1652^1	1604	135	513	1081	11.7	3.54	102	.255	.314	44	.097	-10	20	16	-12	0.5

● **MANNY MONTEJO** Montejo, Manuel (Bofill) b: 10/16/35, Caibarien, Cuba BR/TR, 5′11″, 150 lbs. Deb: 7/25/61

YEAR	TM/L	W	L	PCT	G	GS	CG	SH	SV	IP	H	HR	BB	SO	RAT	ERA	ERA+	OAV	OOB	BH	AVG	PB	PR	/A	PD	TPI
1961	Det-A	0	0	—	12	0	0	0	0	16^1	13	2	6	15	11.6	3.86	106	.217	.309	0	—	0	0	0	-1	-0.1

● **RICH MONTELEONE** Monteleone, Richard b: 3/22/63, Tampa, Fla. BR/TR, 6′2″, 234 lbs. Deb: 4/15/87

YEAR	TM/L	W	L	PCT	G	GS	CG	SH	SV	IP	H	HR	BB	SO	RAT	ERA	ERA+	OAV	OOB	BH	AVG	PB	PR	/A	PD	TPI
1987	Sea-A	0	0	—	3	0	0	0	0	7	10	2	4	2	19.3	6.43	73	.345	.441	0	—	0	-2	-1	0	-0.3
1988	Cal-A	0	0	—	3	0	0	0	0	4^1	4	0	1	3	12.5	0.00	—	.222	.300	0	—	0	2	2	0	0.2
1989	Cal-A	2	2	.500	24	0	0	0	0	39^2	39	3	13	27	12.0	3.18	120	.255	.317	0	—	0	3	3	1	0.5
1990	NY-A	0	1	.000	5	0	0	0	0	7^1	8	0	2	8	12.3	6.14	65	.276	.323	0	—	0	-2	-2	0	-0.2
1991	NY-A	3	1	.750	26	0	0	0	0	47	42	5	19	34	11.7	3.64	114	.236	.310	0	—	0	2	3	1	0.2
1992	NY-A	7	3	.700	47	0	0	0	0	92^2	82	7	27	62	10.6	3.30	119	.235	.290	0	—	0	7	6	-1	0.6
1993	NY-A	7	4	.636	42	0	0	0	0	85^2	85	14	35	50	12.6	4.94	84	.262	.333	0	—	0	-6	-7	0	-0.5
1994	SF-N	4	3	.571	39	0	0	0	0	45^1	43	6	13	16	11.1	3.18	126	.253	.306	0	.000	-0	5	4	-1	0.4

YEAR	TM/L	W	L	PCT	G	GS	CG	SH	SV	IP	H	HR	BB	SO	RAT	ERA	ERA+	OAV	OOB	BH	AVG	PB	PR	/A	PD	TPI
1995	Cal-A	1	0	1.000	9	0	0	0	0	9	8	1	3	5	11.0	2.00	235	.267	.333	0	—	0	3	3	-0	0.3
1996	Cal-A	0	3	.000	12	0	0	0	0	15^{1}	23	5	2	5	15.3	5.87	85	.348	.377	0	—	0	-1	-1	-1	-0.3
Total	10	24	17	.585	210	0	0	0	0	353^{1}	344	43	119	212	11.9	3.87	106	.255	.318	0	.000	-0	11	8	-1	0.9
● JEFF MONTGOMERY Montgomery, Jeffrey Thomas b: 1/7/62, Wellston, Ohio BR/TR, 5'11", 180 lbs. Deb: 8/1/87																										
1987	Cin-N	2	2	.500	14	1	0	0	0	19^{1}	25	2	9	13	15.8	6.52	65	.313	.382	0	.000	-0	-5	-5	0	-0.9
1988	KC-A	7	2	.778	45	0	0	0	1	62^{2}	54	6	30	47	12.4	3.45	116	.231	.323	0	—	0	4	4	0	0.5
1989	KC-A	7	3	.700	63	0	0	0	18	92	66	3	25	94	9.1	1.37	281	.198	.258	0	—	0	**26**	**25**	-1	3.5
1990	KC-A	6	5	.545	73	0	0	0	24	94^{1}	81	6	34	94	11.4	2.39	161	.227	.303	0	—	0	16	15	0	2.4
1991	KC-A	4	4	.500	67	0	0	0	33	90	83	6	28	77	11.3	2.90	142	.246	.307	0	—	0	12	12	-0	1.7
1992	KC-A★	1	6	.143	65	0	0	0	39	82^{2}	61	5	27	69	9.9	2.18	186	.205	.278	0	—	0	16	17	2	2.7
1993	KC-A★	7	5	.583	69	0	0	0	**45**	87^{1}	65	3	23	66	9.3	2.27	202	.206	.264	0	—	0	**20**	**22**	1	4.3
1994	KC-A	2	3	.400	42	0	0	0	27	44^{2}	48	5	15	50	12.9	4.03	124	.276	.337	0	—	0	4	5	-1	0.7
1995	KC-A	2	3	.400	54	0	0	0	31	65^{2}	60	7	25	49	11.9	3.43	140	.252	.328	0	—	0	9	10	0	1.4
1996	KC-A☆	4	6	.400	48	0	0	0	24	63^{1}	59	14	19	45	11.5	4.26	117	.251	.315	0	—	0	5	5	1	1.2
1997	KC-A	1	4	.200	55	0	0	0	14	59^{1}	53	9	18	48	10.8	3.49	135	.240	.297	0	—	0	7	8	0	0.8
1998	KC-A	2	5	.286	56	0	0	0	36	56	58	8	22	54	13.2	4.98	98	.264	.336	0	—	0	-2	-0	-0	-0.2
Total	12	45	48	.484	651	1	0	0	292	817^{1}	713	74	275	706	11.1	3.05	143	.234	.303	0	.000	-0	111	118	3	18.1
● MONTY MONTGOMERY Montgomery, Monty Bryson b: 9/1/46, Albemarle, N.C. BR/TR, 6'3", 200 lbs. Deb: 9/14/71																										
1971	KC-A	3	0	1.000	3	2	0	0	0	21^{1}	16	0	3	12	8.0	2.11	163	.205	.235	0	.000	-0	3	3	0	0.4
1972	KC-A	3	3	.500	9	8	1	1	0	56^{1}	55	2	17	24	11.5	3.04	100	.263	.319	3	.176	1	0	-0	-0	0.0
Total	2	6	3	.667	12	10	1	1	0	77^{2}	71	2	20	36	10.5	2.78	113	.247	.296	3	.125	0	3	3	-0	0.4
● STEVE MONTGOMERY Montgomery, Steven Lewis b: 12/25/70, Westminster, Cal. BR/TR, 6'4", 210 lbs. Deb: 4/3/96																										
1996	Oak-A	1	0	1.000	8	0	0	0	0	13^{2}	18	5	13	8	20.4	9.22	53	.310	.437	0	—	0	-6	-7	-1	-0.2
1997	Oak-A	0	1	.000	4	0	0	0	0	6^{1}	10	2	8	1	25.6	9.95	45	.385	.529	0	—	0	-4	-4	-0	-0.4
Total	2	1	1	.500	12	0	0	0	0	20	28	7	21	9	22.0	9.45	51	.333	.467	0	—	0	-10	-10	-1	-0.6
● RAMON MONZANT Monzant, Ramon Segundo (Espina) b: 1/4/33, Maracaibo, Venez. BR/TR, 6', 165 lbs. Deb: 7/2/54																										
1954	NY-N	0	0	—	6	1	0	0	0	7^{2}	8	0	11	5	22.3	4.70	86	.276	.475	0	.000	-0	-1	-1	-0	-0.1
1955	NY-N	4	8	.333	28	12	3	0	0	94^{2}	98	11	43	54	13.7	3.99	101	.278	.361	3	.125	-1	0	0	-1	-0.2
1956	NY-N	1	0	1.000	4	1	1	0	0	13	8	4	7	11	10.4	4.15	91	.170	.278	0	.000	-1	-1	-1	-0	-0.1
1957	NY-N	3	2	.600	24	2	0	0	0	49^{2}	55	6	16	37	13.2	3.99	99	.286	.348	3	.300	1	-1	-0	-1	-0.1
1958	SF-N	8	11	.421	43	16	4	1	1	150^{2}	160	21	57	93	13.3	4.72	81	.273	.344	8	.163	-1	-13	-15	1	-1.7
1960	SF-N	0	0	—	1	0	0	0	0	1	1	1	0	1	9.0	9.00	39	.250	.250	0	—	0	-1	-1	0	0.0
Total	6	16	21	.432	106	32	8	1	1	316^{2}	330	43	134	201	13.5	4.38	89	.273	.350	14	.157	-2	-15	-17	-1	-2.2
● ERIC MOODY Moody, Eric Lane b: 1/6/71, Greenville, S.C. BR/TR, 6'6", 185 lbs. Deb: 8/3/97																										
1997	Tex-A	0	1	.000	10	1	0	0	0	19	26	4	2	12	13.3	4.26	112	.329	.346	0	—	0	1	1	-0	-0.3
● LEO MOON Moon, Leo "Lefty" b: 6/22/1899, Bellemont, N.C. d: 8/25/70, New Orleans, La. BR/TL, 5'11", 165 lbs. Deb: 7/9/32																										
1932	Cle-A	0	0	—	1	0	0	0	0	5^{2}	11	0	7	1	28.6	11.12	43	.379	.500	1	.500	0	-4	-4	0	0.0
● JIM MOONEY Mooney, Jim Irving b: 9/4/06, Mooresburg, Tenn. d: 4/27/79, Johnson City, Tenn BR/TL, 5'11", 168 lbs. Deb: 8/14/31																										
1931	NY-N	7	1	.875	10	8	6	2	0	71^{2}	71	1	16	38	11.1	2.01	184	.262	.306	4	.160	-1	15	13	-1	1.2
1932	NY-N	6	10	.375	29	18	4	1	0	124^{2}	154	18	42	37	14.1	5.05	73	.299	.352	5	.122	-2	-16	-19	-2	-2.3
1933	StL-N	2	5	.286	21	8	2	0	1	77^{1}	87	1	26	14	13.2	3.72	93	.296	.353	1	.050	-2	-3	-2	1	-0.3
1934	*StL-N	2	4	.333	32	7	1	0	1	82^{1}	114	3	49	27	18.3	5.47	77	.326	.414	1	.053	-2	-13	-11	-1	-1.1
Total	4	17	20	.459	92	41	13	3	2	356	426	23	133	116	14.3	4.25	89	.298	.360	11	.105	-7	-18	-19	-3	-2.5
● BILL MOONEYHAM Mooneyham, William Craig b: 8/16/60, Livermore, Cal. BR/TR, 6', 175 lbs. Deb: 4/19/86																										
1986	Oak-A	4	5	.444	45	6	0	0	2	99^{2}	103	4	67	75	15.6	4.52	86	.270	.384	0	—	0	-4	-7	1	-0.1
● BALOR MOORE Moore, Balor Lilbon b: 1/25/51, Smithville, Tex. BL/TL, 6'2", 184 lbs. Deb: 5/21/70																										
1970	Mon-N	0	2	.000	6	2	0	0	0	9^{2}	14	0	8	6	20.5	7.45	55	.368	.478	1	.333	0	-4	-4	0	-0.6
1972	Mon-N	9	9	.500	22	22	6	3	0	147^{2}	122	15	59	161	11.3	3.47	102	.226	.307	8	.145	-0	-0	1	0	0.1
1973	Mon-N	7	16	.304	35	32	3	1	0	176^{1}	151	18	109	151	13.4	4.49	85	.233	.346	3	.057	-3	-16	-13	-1	-2.0
1974	Mon-N	0	2	.000	8	2	0	0	0	13^{2}	13	1	15	16	18.4	3.95	97	.245	.412	0	.000	-0	-1	-0	-0	-0.1
1977	Cal-A	0	2	.000	7	3	0	0	0	22^{2}	28	7	10	14	16.3	3.97	99	.298	.383	0	—	0	0	-0	-1	0.0
1978	Tor-A	6	9	.400	37	18	2	0	0	144^{1}	165	16	54	75	14.1	4.93	80	.294	.363	0	—	0	-19	-16	1	-1.4
1979	Tor-A	5	7	.417	34	16	5	0	0	139^{1}	135	17	79	51	14.3	4.84	90	.262	.369	0	—	0	-10	-8	-1	-0.7
1980	Tor-A	1	1	.500	31	3	0	0	1	64^{2}	76	6	31	22	15.4	5.29	81	.309	.395	0	—	0	-9	-7	-0	-0.3
Total	8	28	48	.368	180	98	16	4	1	718^{1}	704	80	365	496	13.8	4.52	87	.261	.355	12	.106	-3	-58	-47	-1	-5.0
● BRAD MOORE Moore, Bradley Alan b: 6/21/64, Loveland, Colo. BR/TR, 6'1", 185 lbs. Deb: 6/14/88																										
1988	Phi-N	0	0	—	5	0	0	0	0	5^{2}	4	0	4	2	12.7	0.00	—	.267	.421	0	—	0	2	2	0	0.0
1990	Phi-N	0	0	—	3	0	0	0	0	2^{2}	4	0	2	1	20.3	3.38	113	.400	.500	0	—	0	0	0	0	0.0
Total	2	0	0	—	8	0	0	0	0	8^{1}	8	0	6	3	15.1	1.08	338	.320	.452	0	—	0	2	2	0	0.0
● CARLOS MOORE Moore, Carlos Whitman b: 8/13/06, Clinton, Tenn. d: 7/2/58, New Orleans, La. BR/TR, 6'1.5", 180 lbs. Deb: 5/4/30																										
1930	Was-A	0	0	—	4	0	0	0	0	11^{2}	9	0	4	2	10.0	2.31	199	.225	.295	0	.000	-1	3	3	-0	-0.1
● DEE MOORE Moore, D C b: 4/6/14, Hedley, Tex. d: 7/2/97, Williston, N.Dak. BR/TR, 5'11", 190 lbs. Deb: 9/12/36 ♦																										
1936	Cin-N	0	0	—	2	1	0	0	0	7	3	0	2	3	6.4	0.00	—	.120	.185	4	.400	1	3	3	0	0.1
● DONNIE MOORE Moore, Donnie Ray b: 2/13/54, Lubbock, Tex. d: 7/18/89, Anaheim, Cal. BL/TR, 6', 185 lbs. Deb: 9/14/75																										
1975	Chi-N	0	0	—	4	1	0	0	0	8^{2}	12	1	4	8	16.6	4.15	92	.316	.381	0	.000	-0	-1	-0	-0	0.0
1977	Chi-N	4	2	.667	27	1	0	0	0	48^{2}	51	1	18	34	12.8	4.07	108	.285	.350	3	.300	1	-1	2	1	0.4
1978	Chi-N	9	7	.563	71	1	0	0	4	103	117	7	31	50	13.1	4.11	98	.287	.340	4	.267	1	-6	-1	0	0.0
1979	Chi-N	1	4	.200	39	1	0	0	1	73	95	8	25	43	15.0	5.18	79	.321	.378	2	.154	0	-12	-9	1	-0.5
1980	StL-N	1	1	.500	11	0	0	0	0	21^{2}	25	1	5	10	12.9	6.23	59	.298	.344	3	.750	2	-6	-6	-1	-0.4
1981	Mil-A	0	0	—	3	0	0	0	0	4	4	0	4	2	18.0	6.75	51	.286	.444	0	—	0	-1	-1	0	0.1
1982	*Atl-N	3	1	.750	16	0	0	0	1	27^{2}	32	1	7	17	13.3	4.23	88	.294	.347	0	.000	-0	-2	-2	0	-0.2
1983	Atl-N	2	3	.400	43	0	0	0	6	68^{2}	72	6	10	41	10.7	3.67	106	.279	.306	4	.500	1	-0	2	-1	0.2
1984	Atl-N	4	5	.444	47	0	0	0	16	64^{1}	63	3	18	47	11.5	2.94	131	.258	.312	0	.000	-0	5	7	0	1.2
1985	Cal-A★	8	8	.500	65	0	0	0	31	103	91	9	21	72	9.8	1.92	214	.237	.277	0	—	0	**25**	25	-1	5.1
1986	*Cal-A	4	5	.444	49	0	0	0	21	72^{2}	00	10	22	53	10.2	2.97	138	.228	.288	0	—	0	10	9	-1	1.5
1987	Cal-A	2	2	.500	14	0	0	0	5	26^{2}	28	2	13	17	13.8	2.70	159	.259	.339	0	—	0	5	5	-1	0.8
1988	Cal-A	5	2	.714	27	0	0	0	4	33	48	4	8	22	15.3	4.91	79	.343	.378	0	—	0	-3	-4	0	-0.6
Total	13	43	40	.518	416	4	0	0	89	655	698	53	186	416	12.3	3.67	110	.276	.328	16	.281	5	12	27	-1	7.6
● EARL MOORE Moore, Earl Alonzo "Big Ebbie" or "Crossfire" b: 7/29/1879, Pickerington, O. d: 11/28/61, Columbus, Ohio BR/TR, 6', 195 lbs. Deb: 4/25/01																										
1901	Cle-A	16	14	.533	31	30	28	4	0	251^{1}	234	4	107	99	12.5	2.90	122	.244	.325	16	.162	-5	21	18	-4	0.9
1902	Cle-A	17	18	.486	36	34	29	4	1	293	304	8	101	84	12.7	2.95	117	.268	.331	24	.212	-0	20	16	-1	1.5
1903	Cle-A	20	8	.714	29	27	27	3	0	247^{2}	196	0	62	148	9.6	**1.74**	**164**	**.217**	.271	8	.092	-5	**34**	31	-3	2.5
1904	Cle-A	12	11	.522	26	24	22	1	0	227^{2}	186	2	61	139	10.2	2.25	113	.224	.285	12	.140	-2	9	7	-7	-0.3
1905	Cle-A	15	15	.500	31	30	28	3	0	269	232	6	92	131	11.4	2.64	99	.234	.311	10	.104	-4	0	-0	-2	-0.8
1906	Cle-A	1	1	.500	5	4	2	0	0	29^{2}	27	1	18	8	14.3	3.94	66	.245	.362	0	.000	-1	-4	-4	-1	-0.5
1907	Cle-A	1	1	.500	3	2	1	0	0	19^{1}	18	0	8	7	12.6	4.66	54	.250	.333	0	.000	-1	-5	-5	0	-0.5
	NY-A	2	6	.250	12	9	3	0	1	64	72	1	30	28	14.9	3.94	71	.286	.371	6	.273	1	-10	-8	-0	-0.9
	Yr	3	7	.300	15	11	4	0	1	83^{1}	90	1	38	35	14.3	4.10	66	.277	.360	6	.207	0	-14	-13	-0	-1.4

YEAR	TM/L	W	L	PCT	G	GS	CG	SH	SV	IP	H	HR	BB	SO	RAT	ERA	ERA+	OAV	OOB	BH	AVG	PB	PR	/A	PD	TPI
1908	Phi-N	2	1	.667	3	3	3	1	0	26	20	0	8	16	10.4	0.00	—	.217	.294	2	.222	0	7	7	-1	1.0
1909	Phi-N	18	12	.600	38	34	24	4	0	299^2	238	7	108	173	10.7	2.10	124	.210	.283	9	.094	-4	17	17	-5	0.6
1910	Phi-N	22	15	.595	46	35	18	**6**	0	283	228	5	121	**185**	11.4	2.58	121	.228	.318	20	.230	2	14	17	-4	2.0
1911	Phi-N	15	19	.441	42	36	21	5	1	308^1	265	11	164	174	12.9	2.63	131	.240	.345	11	.109	-6	27	28	-3	2.0
1912	Phi-N	9	14	.391	31	24	10	1	0	182^1	186	3	77	79	13.3	3.31	110	.275	.355	6	.107	-4	2	7	-2	0.1
1913	Phi-N	1	3	.250	12	5	0	0	1	52	50	3	40	24	15.8	5.02	66	.254	.382	0	.000	-2	-10	-10	1	-0.9
	Chi-N	1	1	.500	7	2	0	0	0	28^1	34	3	12	12	14.6	4.45	71	.321	.390	1	.125	-0	-4	-4	1	-0.2
	Yr	2	4	.333	19	7	0	0	1	80^1	84	6	52	36	15.2	4.82	68	.276	.382	1	.042	-2	-14	-14	2	-1.1
1914	Buf-F	11	15	.423	36	27	14	2	2	194^2	184	3	99	96	13.5	4.30	69	.263	.362	9	.161	-2	-31	-29	-2	-3.9
Total	14	163	154	.514	388	326	230	34	6	2776	2474	57	1108	1403	12.0	2.78	110	.241	.321	134	.141	-34	87	88	-33	2.6

● EUEL MOORE

Moore, Euel Walton "Chief" b: 5/27/08, Reagan, Okla. d: 2/12/89, Tishomingo, Okla. BR/TR, 6'2", 185 lbs. Deb: 7/8/34

YEAR	TM/L	W	L	PCT	G	GS	CG	SH	SV	IP	H	HR	BB	SO	RAT	ERA	ERA+	OAV	OOB	BH	AVG	PB	PR	/A	PD	TPI
1934	Phi-N	5	7	.417	20	16	3	0	1	122^1	145	9	41	38	13.7	4.05	117	.288	.342	5	.109	-4	0	9	-1	0.3
1935	Phi-N	1	6	.143	15	8	1	0	1	40^1	63	5	20	15	19.0	7.81	58	.354	.425	6	.400	1	-17	-15	0	-2.0
	NY-N	1	0	1.000	6	0	0	0	0	8	9	0	4	3	14.6	5.63	69	.281	.361	0	.000	-0	-1	-2	0	-0.2
	Yr	2	6	.250	21	8	1	0	1	48^1	72	5	24	18	17.9	7.45	59	.340	.407	6	.353	1	-18	-16	0	-2.2
1936	Phi-N	2	3	.400	20	5	1	0	1	54^1	76	4	12	19	14.7	6.96	65	.311	.346	4	.222	-0	-18	-15	-1	-1.3
Total	3	9	16	.360	61	29	5	0	3	225	293	18	77	75	14.9	5.48	84	.306	.360	15	.185	-3	-36	-22	-3	-3.2

● GENE MOORE

Moore, Eugene Sr. "Blue Goose" b: 11/9/1885, Lancaster, Tex. d: 8/31/38, Dallas, Tex. BL/TL, 6'2", 185 lbs. Deb: 9/28/09 F

YEAR	TM/L	W	L	PCT	G	GS	CG	SH	SV	IP	H	HR	BB	SO	RAT	ERA	ERA+	OAV	OOB	BH	AVG	PB	PR	/A	PD	TPI
1909	Pit-N	0	0	—	1	0	0	0	0	2	4	0	3	2	31.5	18.00	15	.364	.500	0	.000	-0	-3	-3	-0	0.0
1910	Pit-N	2	1	.667	4	1	0	0	0	17^1	19	1	7	9	13.5	3.12	99	.268	.333	0	.000	-1	-0	-0	0	-0.1
1912	Cin-N	0	1	.000	5	2	0	0	1	14^2	17	0	11	6	18.4	4.91	68	.304	.435	0	.000	-1	-2	-3	-0	-0.3
Total	3	2	2	.500	10	3	0	0	1	34	40	1	21	17	16.7	4.76	67	.290	.391	0	.000	-2	-6	-6	0	-0.4

● GEORGE MOORE

Moore, George b: Ohio BB/TR, 6'4", 200 lbs. Deb: 6/14/05

YEAR	TM/L	W	L	PCT	G	GS	CG	SH	SV	IP	H	HR	BB	SO	RAT	ERA	ERA+	OAV	OOB	BH	AVG	PB	PR	/A	PD	TPI
1905	Pit-N	0	0	—	1	0	0	0	0	3	2	0	0	1	6.0	0.00	—	.200	.200	0	.000	-0	1	1	-0	0.0

● JIM MOORE

Moore, James Stanford b: 12/14/03, Prescott, Ark. d: 5/19/73, Seattle, Wash. BR/TR, 6', 165 lbs. Deb: 9/21/28

YEAR	TM/L	W	L	PCT	G	GS	CG	SH	SV	IP	H	HR	BB	SO	RAT	ERA	ERA+	OAV	OOB	BH	AVG	PB	PR	/A	PD	TPI
1928	Cle-A	0	1	.000	1	1	1	0	0	9	5	0	5	1	10.0	2.00	207	.161	.278	0	.000	-0	2	2	-0	0.1
1929	Cle-A	0	0	—	2	0	0	0	0	5^2	6	1	4	0	15.9	9.53	47	.273	.385	0	.000	-0	-3	-3	0	0.0
1930	Chi-A	2	1	.667	9	5	2	0	1	40	42	0	12	11	12.1	3.60	128	.268	.320	3	.231	-0	5	5	-0	0.3
1931	Chi-A	0	2	.000	33	4	0	0	0	83^2	93	3	27	15	13.0	4.95	86	.282	.338	1	.063	-1	-5	-6	1	-0.2
1932	Chi-A	0	0	—	1	0	0	0	0	1	1	0	1	2	18.0	0.00	—	.250	.400	0	.000	-0	0	0	0	0.0
Total	5	2	4	.333	46	10	3	0	1	139^1	147	4	49	29	12.7	4.52	97	.270	.332	4	.114	-2	-1	-2	1	0.2

● WHITEY MOORE

Moore, Lloyd Albert b: 6/10/12, Tuscarawas, Ohio d: 12/10/87, Uhrichsville, O. BR/TR, 6'1", 195 lbs. Deb: 9/27/36

YEAR	TM/L	W	L	PCT	G	GS	CG	SH	SV	IP	H	HR	BB	SO	RAT	ERA	ERA+	OAV	OOB	BH	AVG	PB	PR	/A	PD	TPI
1936	Cin-N	1	0	1.000	1	0	0	0	0	5	3	0	3	4	10.8	5.40	71	.167	.286	0	.000	-0	-1	-1	-0	-0.2
1937	Cin-N	0	3	.000	13	6	0	0	0	38^2	32	1	39	27	17.5	4.89	76	.239	.424	0	.000	-1	-4	-5	-0	-0.5
1938	Cin-N	6	4	.600	19	11	3	1	0	90^1	66	4	42	38	11.1	3.49	105	.205	.302	2	.077	-2	3	2	-1	-0.2
1939	*Cin-N	13	12	.520	42	24	9	2	3	187^2	177	10	95	81	13.3	3.45	111	.254	.348	6	.098	-4	10	8	-1	0.5
1940	*Cin-N	8	8	.500	25	15	5	1	1	116^2	100	8	56	60	12.6	3.63	104	.231	.329	5	.128	-1	3	2	-3	-0.2
1941	Cin-N	2	1	.667	23	4	1	0	0	61^2	62	2	45	17	16.1	4.38	82	.256	.379	3	.167	-1	-5	-5	-1	-0.4
1942	Cin-N	0	0	—	1	0	0	0	0	1	0	0	1	0	9.0	0.00	—	.000	.250	0	—	0	0	0	-0	0.0
	StL-N	0	1	.000	9	0	0	0	0	12^1	10	0	11	1	16.1	4.38	78	.217	.379	0	.000	-0	-1	-1	-1	-0.2
	Yr	0	1	.000	10	0	0	0	0	13^1	10	0	12	1	15.5	4.05	84	.204	.371	0	.000	-0	-1	-1	-1	-0.2
Total	7	30	29	.508	133	60	18	4	4	513^1	450	25	292	228	13.4	3.75	100	.237	.346	16	.103	-10	4	-0	-7	-1.2

● MARCUS MOORE

Moore, Marcus Braymont b: 11/2/70, Oakland, Cal. BB/TR, 6'5", 195 lbs. Deb: 7/8/93

YEAR	TM/L	W	L	PCT	G	GS	CG	SH	SV	IP	H	HR	BB	SO	RAT	ERA	ERA+	OAV	OOB	BH	AVG	PB	PR	/A	PD	TPI
1993	Col-N	3	1	.750	27	0	0	0	0	26^1	30	4	20	13	17.4	6.84	70	.291	.411	0	.000	-0	-8	-6	-1	-0.9
1994	Col-N	1	1	.500	29	0	0	0	0	33^2	33	4	21	33	15.8	6.15	81	.252	.376	0	.000	-0	-7	-4	-0	-0.3
1996	Cin-N	3	3	.500	23	0	0	0	2	26^1	26	3	22	27	17.1	5.81	73	.263	.407	1	.333	1	-5	-5	-1	-1.0
Total	3	7	5	.583	79	0	0	0	2	86^1	89	11	63	73	16.7	6.25	75	.267	.396	1	.200	0	-20	-15	-2	-2.2

● MIKE MOORE

Moore, Michael Wayne b: 11/26/59, Eakly, Okla. BR/TR, 6'4", 205 lbs. Deb: 4/11/82

YEAR	TM/L	W	L	PCT	G	GS	CG	SH	SV	IP	H	HR	BB	SO	RAT	ERA	ERA+	OAV	OOB	BH	AVG	PB	PR	/A	PD	TPI
1982	Sea-A	7	14	.333	28	27	1	1	0	144^1	159	21	79	73	15.0	5.36	79	.285	.376	0	—	0	-21	-18	1	-2.2
1983	Sea-A	6	8	.429	22	21	3	2	0	128	130	10	60	108	13.6	4.71	90	.267	.352	0	—	0	-9	-6	2	-0.5
1984	Sea-A	7	17	.292	34	33	6	0	0	212	236	16	85	158	13.8	4.97	80	.282	.352	0	—	0	-23	-23	3	-2.0
1985	Sea-A	17	10	.630	35	34	14	2	0	247	230	18	70	155	11.1	3.46	122	.247	.302	0	—	0	19	21	2	2.3
1986	Sea-A	11	13	.458	38	37	11	1	1	266	279	28	94	146	13.0	4.30	99	.273	.341	0	—	0	-4	-2	-1	-0.2
1987	Sea-A	9	19	.321	33	33	12	0	0	231	268	29	84	115	13.7	4.71	100	.292	.351	0	.000	-0	-7	0	1	0.1
1988	Sea-A	9	15	.375	37	32	9	3	1	228^2	196	24	63	182	10.3	3.78	110	.232	.287	0	—	0	5	10	1	0.7
1989	*Oak-A★	19	11	.633	35	35	6	3	0	241^2	193	14	83	172	10.4	2.61	141	.219	.288	0	—	0	34	29	2	4.0
1990	*Oak-A	13	15	.464	33	33	3	0	0	199^1	204	14	84	73	13.1	4.65	80	.267	.342	0	—	0	-16	-21	1	-2.2
1991	Oak-A	17	8	.680	33	33	3	1	0	210	176	11	105	153	12.3	2.96	130	.229	.326	0	—	0	27	20	2	2.5
1992	*Oak-A	17	12	.586	36	36	2	0	0	223	229	20	103	117	13.7	4.12	91	.268	.353	0	—	0	-4	-9	-1	-0.8
1993	Det-A	13	9	.591	36	36	4	3	0	213^2	227	35	89	89	13.4	5.22	82	.271	.343	0	—	0	-21	-22	4	-1.5
1994	Det-A	11	10	.524	25	25	4	0	0	154^1	152	27	89	62	14.2	5.42	89	.263	.364	0	—	0	-11	-10	3	-0.9
1995	Det-A	5	15	.250	25	25	1	0	0	132^2	179	24	68	64	16.9	7.53	63	.323	.399	0	—	0	-42	-41	1	-4.6
Total	14	161	176	.478	450	440	79	16	2	2831^2	2858	291	1156	1667	12.9	4.39	95	.264	.338	0	.000	-0	-73	-74	22	-5.3

● RAY MOORE

Moore, Raymond Leroy "Farmer" b: 6/1/26, Meadows, Md. d: 3/2/95, Clinton, Md. BR/TR, 6'1", 205 lbs. Deb: 8/1/52

YEAR	TM/L	W	L	PCT	G	GS	CG	SH	SV	IP	H	HR	BB	SO	RAT	ERA	ERA+	OAV	OOB	BH	AVG	PB	PR	/A	PD	TPI
1952	Bro-N	1	2	.333	14	2	0	0	0	28^1	29	3	26	11	18.1	4.76	76	.274	.425	0	.000	-0	-3	-4	-0	-0.4
1953	Bro-N	0	1	.000	1	1	1	0	0	8	6	1	4	4	11.3	3.38	126	.214	.313	0	.000	-0	1	1	-0	0.0
1955	Bal-A	10	10	.500	46	14	3	1	6	151^2	128	14	80	80	12.6	3.92	97	.229	.329	6	.136	-2	1	-2	-2	-0.5
1956	Bal-A	12	7	.632	32	27	9	1	0	185	161	12	99	105	12.7	4.18	94	.238	.336	19	.271	6	-1	-5	-2	-0.1
1957	Bal-A	11	13	.458	34	32	7	1	0	227^1	196	17	112	117	12.3	3.72	97	.236	.328	18	.214	4	2	-3	-2	-0.2
1958	Chi-A	9	7	.563	32	20	4	2	2	136^2	107	10	70	73	11.7	3.82	95	.220	.318	9	.205	2	-1	-3	-1	-0.2
1959	*Chi-A	3	6	.333	29	8	0	0	0	89^2	86	10	46	49	13.3	4.12	91	.261	.354	2	.087	-1	-3	-4	-1	-0.5
1960	Chi-A	1	1	.500	14	0	0	0	0	20^2	19	5	11	3	13.1	5.66	67	.253	.349	0	.000	-0	-4	-4	-0	-0.4
	Was-A	3	2	.600	37	0	0	0	13	65^2	49	5	27	29	10.6	2.88	135	.213	.298	1	.071	-1	7	7	-2	0.6
	Yr	4	3	.571	51	0	0	0	13	86^1	68	10	38	32	11.2	3.54	109	.222	.310	1	.063	-1	3	3	-2	0.2
1961	Min-A	4	4	.500	46	0	0	0	14	56^1	49	8	38	45	14.1	3.67	115	.233	.353	0	.000	0	2	4	-0	0.6
1962	Min-A	8	3	.727	49	0	0	0	9	64^2	55	8	30	58	12.1	4.73	86	.231	.322	0	.000	-1	-5	-5	-1	-1.0
1963	Min-A	1	3	.250	31	1	0	0	2	38^2	50	8	17	38	15.8	6.98	52	.309	.378	1	.333	0	-14	-14	0	-1.5
Total	11	63	59	.516	365	105	24	5	46	1072^2	935	101	560	612	12.7	4.06	93	.238	.335	56	.187	6	-18	-32	-10	-3.6

● BARRY MOORE

Moore, Robert Barry b: 4/3/43, Statesville, N.C. BL/TL, 6'1", 190 lbs. Deb: 5/29/65

YEAR	TM/L	W	L	PCT	G	GS	CG	SH	SV	IP	H	HR	BB	SO	RAT	ERA	ERA+	OAV	OOB	BH	AVG	PB	PR	/A	PD	TPI
1965	Was-A	0	0	—	1	0	0	0	0	1	1	0	1	0	18.0	0.00	—	.333	.500	0	—	0	0	0	-0	0.0
1966	Was-A	3	3	.500	12	11	1	0	0	62^1	55	3	39	28	13.7	3.75	92	.240	.353	2	.105	-1	-2	-2	0	-0.3
1967	Was-A	7	11	.389	27	26	3	1	0	143^2	127	15	71	74	12.6	3.76	84	.240	.333	6	.130	-0	-8	-10	1	-1.1
1968	Was-A	4	6	.400	32	18	0	0	3	117^2	116	8	42	56	12.2	3.37	87	.261	.327	3	.097	-1	-5	-6	1	-0.6
1969	Was-A	9	8	.529	31	25	4	0	0	134	123	12	67	51	12.9	4.30	81	.246	.338	9	.209	2	-10	-12	-2	-1.5
1970	Cle-A	3	5	.375	13	12	0	0	0	70^1	70	8	46	35	15.0	4.22	94	.262	.373	2	.095	-1	-4	-2	1	-0.3
	Chi-A	0	4	.000	24	7	0	0	0	70^2	85	12	34	34	16.2	6.37	61	.302	.393	5	.263	1	-21	-19	1	-0.8
	Yr	3	9	.250	37	19	0	0	0	141	155	20	80	69	15.5	5.30	74	.281	.380	7	.175	-0	-25	-21	1	-1.1
Total	6	26	37	.413	140	99	8	1	3	599^2	577	58	300	278	13.4	4.16	82	.256	.348	27	.151	-1	-50	-51	2	-4.6

● BOBBY MOORE

Moore, Robert Devell b: 11/8/58, Sweetwater, La. BR/TR, 6'4", 200 lbs. Deb: 9/11/85

YEAR	TM/L	W	L	PCT	G	GS	CG	SH	SV	IP	H	HR	BB	SO	RAT	ERA	ERA+	OAV	OOB	BH	AVG	PB	PR	/A	PD	TPI
1985	SF-N	0	0	—	11	0	0	0	0	16^2	18	1	10	10	15.1	3.24	106	.269	.364	0	.000	-0	1	0	-1	-0.1

YEAR	TM/L	W	L	PCT	G	GS	CG	SH	SV	IP	H	HR	BB	SO	RAT	ERA	ERA+	OAV	OOB	BH	AVG	PB	PR	/A	PD	TPI
● ROY MOORE Moore, Roy Daniel b: 10/26/1898, Austin, Tex. d: 4/5/51, Seattle, Wash. BB/TL, 6′, 185 lbs. Deb: 4/15/20																										
1920	Phi-A	1	13	.071	24	14	5	0	0	132^2	161	6	64	45	15.5	4.68	86	.314	.393	10	.200	-1	-13	-10	2	-0.9
1921	Phi-A	10	10	.500	29	26	12	0	0	191^2	206	4	122	64	15.6	4.51	99	.280	.385	19	.257	3	-5	-1	2	0.5
1922	Phi-A	0	3	.000	15	6	0	0	0	50^2	65	1	32	29	17.8	7.64	56	.319	.418	5	.263	1	-20	-19	-0	-0.9
	Det-A	0	0	—	9	0	0	0	2	19^2	29	0	10	9	20.1	5.95	65	.367	.468	3	.429	1	-4	-5	0	0.0
	Yr	0	3	.000	24	6	0	0	2	70^1	94	1	42	38	18.0	7.17	58	.329	.423	8	.308	2	-24	-24	-0	-0.9
1923	Det-A	0	0	—	3	0	0	0	1	12	15	0	11	7	19.5	3.00	129	.288	.413	0	.000	-0	1	1	1	0.0
Total	4	11	26	.297	80	46	17	0	3	406^2	476	11	239	154	16.2	4.98	85	.300	.397	37	.239	4	-41	-33	4	-1.3
● TERRY MOORE Moore, Terry Bluford b: 5/27/12, Vernon, Ala. d: 3/29/95, Collinsville, Ill. BR/TR, 5′11″, 195 lbs. Deb: 4/16/35 MC♦																										
1939	StL-N★	0	0	—	1	0	0	0	0	1	0	0	0	1	0.0	0.00	—	.000	.000	123	.295	0	0	0	0	0.0
● TOMMY MOORE Moore, Tommy Joe b: 7/7/48, Lynwood, Cal. BR/TR, 5′11″, 175 lbs. Deb: 9/15/72																										
1972	NY-N	0	0	—	3	1	0	0	0	12^1	12	1	1	5	9.5	2.92	115	.273	.289	1	.333	0	1	1	0	0.0
1973	NY-N	0	1	.000	3	1	0	0	0	3^1	6	1	3	1	24.3	10.80	33	.400	.500	0	—	0	-3	-3	-0	-0.7
1975	StL-N	0	0	—	10	0	0	0	0	18^2	15	2	12	6	13.0	3.86	97	.203	.314	1	.500	0	-0	-0	0	0.1
	Tex-A	0	2	.000	12	0	0	0	0	21	31	1	12	15	18.9	8.14	46	.352	.436	0	—	0	-10	-10	0	-0.8
1977	Sea-A	2	1	.667	14	1	0	0	0	33	36	1	21	13	16.4	4.91	84	.281	.395	0	—	0	-3	-3	-1	-0.3
Total	4	2	4	.333	42	3	0	0	0	88^1	100	6	49	40	15.6	5.40	71	.287	.381	2	.400	1	-16	-15	-0	-1.7
● TREY MOORE Moore, Warren Neal b: 10/2/72, Houston, Tex. BL/TL, 6′1″, 200 lbs. Deb: 4/5/98																										
1998	Mon-N	2	5	.286	13	11	0	0	0	61	78	5	17	35	14.2	5.02	82	.306	.352	4	.235	1	-5	-6	0	-0.5
● CY MOORE Moore, William Austin b: 2/7/05, Elberton, Ga. d: 3/28/72, Augusta, Ga. BR/TR, 6′1″, 178 lbs. Deb: 6/7/29																										
1929	Bro-N	3	3	.500	32	4	0	0	2	68	87	3	31	17	15.6	5.56	83	.320	.389	3	.188	-0	-6	-7	-1	-0.7
1930	Bro-N	0	0	—	1	0	0	0	0	0	2	0	0	0	—	—	—	1.000	1.000	0	—	0	0	0	0	0.0
1931	Bro-N	1	2	.333	23	1	1	0	0	61^2	62	5	13	35	11.5	3.79	100	.262	.311	2	.154	-1	0	0	0	-0.1
1932	Bro-N	0	3	.000	20	2	0	0	0	48^2	56	3	17	21	13.7	4.81	79	.293	.354	3	.214	0	-5	-5	0	-0.2
1933	Phi-N	8	9	.471	36	18	9	3	1	161^1	177	7	42	53	12.4	3.74	102	.279	.326	3	.063	-4	-7	1	0	-0.3
1934	Phi-N	4	9	.308	35	15	3	0	0	126^2	163	11	65	55	16.3	6.47	73	.309	.387	6	.143	-3	-34	-25	-1	-2.5
Total	6	16	26	.381	147	40	13	3	3	466^1	547	29	168	181	14.0	4.86	86	.293	.355	17	.128	-8	-52	-34	-2	-3.8
● BILL MOORE Moore, William Christopher b: 9/3/02, Corning, N.Y. d: 1/24/84, Corning, N.Y. BR/TR, 6′3″, 195 lbs. Deb: 4/15/25																										
1925	Det-A	0	0	—	1	0	0	0	0	0	0	0	3	0	—	∞	—	—	1.000	0	—	0	-2	-2	0	-0.2
● WILCY MOORE Moore, William Wilcy "Cy" b: 5/20/1897, Bonita, Tex. d: 3/29/63, Hollis, Okla. BR/TR, 6′, 195 lbs. Deb: 4/14/27																										
1927	*NY-A	19	7	.731	50	12	6	1	**13**	213	185	3	59	75	**10.4**	**2.28**	**169**	**.234**	**.289**	6	.080	-7	44	37	8	4.8
1928	NY-A	4	4	.500	35	2	0	0	2	60^1	71	4	31	18	15.2	4.18	90	.286	.366	2	.143	-1	-1	-3	1	-0.3
1929	NY-A	6	4	.600	41	0	0	0	8	61	64	4	19	21	12.2	4.13	93	.268	.322	1	.067	-2	**1**	-2	2	-0.3
1931	Bos-A	11	13	.458	53	15	8	1	**10**	185^1	195	7	55	37	12.2	3.88	111	.269	.322	9	.161	-3	10	9	6	1.3
1932	Bos-A	4	10	.286	37	2	0	0	4	84^1	98	5	42	28	15.0	5.23	86	.284	.363	1	.045	-2	-7	-7	3	-1.0
	*NY-A	2	0	1.000	10	1	0	0	4	25	27	1	6	8	11.9	2.52	162	.273	.314	0	.000	-1	5	4	-0	0.3
	Yr	6	10	.375	47	3	0	0	8	109^1	125	6	48	36	14.2	4.61	95	.281	.351	1	.033	-4	-2	-3	3	-0.7
1933	NY-A	5	6	.455	35	0	0	0	8	62	92	1	20	17	16.3	5.52	70	.333	.378	2	.133	-1	-9	-11	0	-2.0
Total	6	51	44	.537	261	32	14	2	49	691	732	25	232	204	12.6	3.70	110	.269	.327	21	.102	-17	44	27	20	2.8
● BOB MOORHEAD Moorhead, Charles Robert b: 1/23/38, Chambersburg, Pa. d: 12/3/86, Lemoyne, Pa. BR/TR, 6′1″, 208 lbs. Deb: 4/11/62																										
1962	NY-N	0	2	.000	38	7	0	0	0	105^1	118	13	42	63	14.0	4.53	92	.289	.361	1	.045	-1	-7	-4	2	0.1
1965	NY-N	0	1	.000	9	0	0	0	0	14^1	16	0	5	5	13.2	4.40	80	.271	.328	0	—	0	-1	-1	0	-0.1
Total	2	0	3	.000	47	7	0	0	0	119^2	134	13	47	68	13.9	4.51	91	.287	.357	1	.045	-1	-8	-5	3	0.0
● BOB MOOSE Moose, Robert Ralph b: 10/9/47, Export, Pa. d: 10/9/76, Martins Ferry, Ohio BR/TR, 6′, 200 lbs. Deb: 9/19/67																										
1967	Pit-N	1	0	1.000	2	2	1	0	0	14^2	14	1	4	7	11.7	3.68	91	.259	.322	2	.333	1	-1	-1	-0	0.1
1968	Pit-N	8	12	.400	38	22	3	3	3	171^1	136	5	41	126	9.5	2.73	107	.218	.269	5	.093	-2	5	4	2	0.5
1969	Pit-N	14	3	.824	44	19	6	1	4	170	149	9	62	165	11.4	2.91	120	.231	.303	4	.075	-1	13	11	1	1.0
1970	*Pit-N	11	10	.524	28	27	9	2	0	189^2	186	14	64	119	12.0	3.99	98	.262	.326	12	.182	3	1	-2	-1	-0.1
1971	*Pit-N	11	7	.611	30	18	3	1	1	140	169	12	35	68	13.2	4.11	82	.301	.344	4	.103	-1	-10	-11	0	-1.4
1972	*Pit-N	13	10	.565	31	30	6	3	1	226	213	11	47	144	10.5	2.91	114	.248	.290	12	.169	3	14	10	1	1.4
1973	Pit-N	12	13	.480	33	29	6	3	0	201^1	219	11	70	111	13.1	3.53	100	.280	.342	9	.134	-0	3	-0	2	0.1
1974	Pit-N	1	5	.167	7	6	0	0	0	35^2	59	4	7	15	17.2	7.57	45	.386	.420	2	.182	0	-16	-16	2	-2.0
1975	Pit-N	2	2	.500	23	5	1	0	0	67^2	63	4	25	34	12.0	3.72	95	.246	.318	3	.167	0	-1	-1	2	0.1
1976	Pit-N	3	9	.250	53	2	0	0	10	88	100	4	32	38	13.9	3.68	95	.294	.362	3	.250	2	-2	-2	-0	-0.1
Total	10	76	71	.517	289	160	35	13	19	1304^1	1308	75	387	827	11.9	3.50	98	.262	.319	56	.141	4	7	-9	8	-0.4
● JAKE MOOTY Mooty, J T b: 4/13/13, Mislap, Tex. d: 4/20/70, Fort Worth, Tex. BR/TR, 5′10.5″, 170 lbs. Deb: 9/9/36																										
1936	Cin-N	0	0	—	8	0	0	0	1	13^2	10	0	4	11	9.2	3.95	97	.204	.264	0	.000	-0	0	-0	-0	-0.1
1937	Cin-N	0	3	.000	14	2	0	0	1	39	54	2	22	11	17.5	8.31	45	.327	.406	0	.000	-1	-19	-20	-0	-1.5
1940	Chi-N	6	6	.500	20	12	6	0	1	114	101	11	49	42	11.9	2.92	128	.243	.325	10	.263	2	12	10	-2	1.0
1941	Chi-N	8	9	.471	33	14	7	1	4	153^1	143	9	56	45	11.8	3.35	105	.251	.320	10	.200	1	5	3	1	0.5
1942	Chi-N	2	5	.286	19	10	1	0	1	84^1	89	11	44	28	14.2	4.70	68	.265	.350	6	.214	0	-13	-14	0	-1.1
1943	Chi-N	0	0	—	2	0	0	0	0	1	2	0	1	1	27.0	0.00	—	.400	.500	0	—	0	0	0	0	0.0
1944	Det-A	0	0	—	15	0	0	0	0	28^1	35	0	18	7	17.2	4.45	80	.310	.409	1	.143	-0	-3	-3	-0	-0.1
Total	7	16	23	.410	111	38	14	1	8	433^2	434	33	194	145	13.1	4.03	88	.263	.341	27	.205	1	-18	-23	-1	-1.3
● HIKER MORAN Moran, Albert Thomas b: 1/1/12, Rochester, N.Y. d: 1/7/98, Saratoga Springs, N.Y. BR/TR, 6′4.5″, 185 lbs. Deb: 9/29/38																										
1938	Bos-N	0	0	—	1	0	0	0	0	3	1	0	1	0	6.0	0.00	—	.111	.200	0	.000	-0	1	1	-0	0.0
1939	Bos-N	1	1	.500	6	2	1	0	0	20	21	3	11	4	14.4	4.50	82	.276	.368	1	.200	1	-1	-2	-0	-0.1
Total	2	1	1	.500	7	2	1	0	0	23	22	3	12	4	13.3	3.91	94	.259	.351	1	.167	0	-0	-1	-1	-0.1
● BILL MORAN Moran, Carl William "Bugs" b: 9/26/50, Portsmouth, Va. BR/TR, 6′4″, 210 lbs. Deb: 4/12/74																										
1974	Chi-A	1	3	.250	15	5	0	0	0	46^1	57	5	23	17	16.7	4.66	80	.302	.394	0	—	0	-5	-5	-1	-0.5
● CHARLIE MORAN Moran, Charles Barthell "Uncle Charlie" b: 2/22/1878, Nashville, Tenn. d: 6/14/49, Horse Cave, Ky. BR/TR, 5′8″, 180 lbs. Deb: 9/9/03 U♦																										
1903	StL-N	0	1	.000	3	2	2	0	0	24	30	0	19	7	18.8	5.25	62	.297	.413	6	.429	1	-5	-5	-1	-0.1
● HARRY MORAN Moran, Harry Edwin b: 4/2/1889, Slater, W.Va. d: 11/28/62, Beckley, W.Va. BL/TL, 6′1″, 165 lbs. Deb: 6/23/12																										
1912	Det-A	0	1	.000	5	2	1	0	0	14^2	19	1	12	3	20.3	4.91	66	.339	.471	1	.200	-0	-3	-3	-0	-0.2
1914	Buf-F	10	7	.588	34	16	7	2	2	154	159	7	53	73	13.0	4.27	69	.276	.348	10	.196	-0	-24	-22	-1	-2.4
1915	New-F	13	9	.591	34	23	13	2	0	205^2	193	2	66	87	12.1	2.54	101	.262	.337	11	.180	-1	4	1	1	0.2
Total	3	23	17	.575	73	41	21	4	2	374^1	371	10	131	163	12.8	3.34	82	.271	.348	22	.188	-1	-22	-25	-0	-2.4
● SAM MORAN Moran, Samuel b: 9/16/1870, Rochester, N.Y. d: 8/27/1897, Rochester, N.Y. TL , 160 lbs. Deb: 8/28/1895																										
1895	Pit-N	2	4	.333	10	6	6	0	0	62^2	78	2	51	19	19.0	7.47	61	.300	.420	4	.154	-1	-19	-21	0	-1.4
● FORREST MORE More, Forrest b: 9/30/1883, Hayden, Ind. d: 8/17/68, Columbus, Ind. BR/TR, 6′, 180 lbs. Deb: 4/15/09																										
1909	StL-N	1	5	.167	15	2	1	0	0	50	48	0	20	17	12.8	5.04	50	.258	.340	2	.154	1	-14	-14	1	-1.4
	Bos-N	1	5	.167	10	4	3	0	0	48^2	47	0	20	10	13.1	4.44	64	.270	.359	1	.067	-1	-10	-9	0	-1.1
	Yr	2	10	.167	25	6	4	0	0	98^2	95	0	40	27	12.7	4.74	56	.262	.342	3	.107	-1	-24	-23	1	-2.5
● DAVE MOREHEAD Morehead, David Michael "Moe" b: 9/5/42, San Diego, Cal. BR/TR, 6′1″, 185 lbs. Deb: 4/13/63																										
1963	Bos-A	10	13	.435	29	29	6	1	0	174^2	137	20	99	136	12.2	3.81	99	.211	.316	6	.105	-3	-4	-1	1	-0.3
1964	Bos-A	8	15	.348	32	30	3	1	0	166^2	156	14	112	139	14.7	4.97	78	.248	.365	5	.093	-2	-25	-21	-1	-2.9
1965	Bos-A	10	18	.357	34	33	5	2	0	192^2	157	18	113	163	12.8	4.06	92	.217	.326	8	.131	0	-13	-7	-2	-1.2

YEAR	TM/L	W	L	PCT	G	GS	CG	SH	SV	IP	H	HR	BB	SO	RAT	ERA	ERA+	OAV	OOB	BH	AVG	PB	PR	/A	PD	TPI
1966	Bos-A	1	2	.333	12	5	0	0	0	28	31	7	7	20	12.2	5.46	70	.274	.317	3	.500	1	-6	-5	-0	-0.5
1967	*Bos-A	5	4	.556	10	9	1	1	0	47^2	48	0	22	40	13.6	4.34	80	.264	.350	1	.083	-0	-6	-5	-1	-0.9
1968	Bos-A	1	4	.200	11	9	3	1	0	55	52	3	20	28	12.1	2.45	129	.249	.320	2	.125	-0	3	4	-1	0.2
1969	KC-A	2	3	.400	21	2	0	0	0	33	28	7	28	32	15.3	5.73	64	.239	.386	0	.000	0	-8	-7	-0	-1.1
1970	KC-A	3	5	.375	28	17	1	0	1	121^2	121	9	62	69	13.6	3.62	103	.261	.349	6	.167	-0	1	2	-2	-0.1
Total	8	40	64	.385	177	134	19	6	1	819^1	730	78	463	627	13.2	4.15	90	.237	.338	31	.127	-5	-57	-39	-7	-6.8

● SETH MOREHEAD Morehead, Seth Marvin "Moe" b: 8/15/34, Houston, Tex. BL/TL, 6'0.5", 195 lbs. Deb: 4/27/57

YEAR	TM/L	W	L	PCT	G	GS	CG	SH	SV	IP	H	HR	BB	SO	RAT	ERA	ERA+	OAV	OOB	BH	AVG	PB	PR	/A	PD	TPI
1957	Phi-N	1	1	.500	34	1	1	0	1	58^2	57	1	20	36	12.1	3.68	103	.254	.321	0	.000	-1	1	1	-1	-0.1
1958	Phi-N	1	6	.143	27	11	0	0	0	92^1	121	8	26	54	14.4	5.85	68	.319	.365	4	.182	0	-19	-19	-2	-1.4
1959	Phi-N	0	2	.000	3	3	0	0	0	10	15	3	3	8	17.1	9.90	41	.333	.388	0	.000	-0	-7	-6	0	-1.0
	Chi-N	0	1	.000	11	2	0	0	0	18^2	25	1	8	9	15.9	4.82	82	.313	.375	1	.500	1	-2	-2	-1	-0.1
	Yr	0	3	.000	14	5	0	0	0	28^2	40	4	11	17	16.0	6.59	61	.317	.372	1	.200	0	-8	-8	-1	-1.1
1960	Chi-N	2	9	.182	45	7	2	0	4	123^1	123	17	46	64	12.5	3.94	96	.258	.326	4	.138	-1	-2	-2	-0	-0.3
1961	Mil-N	1	0	1.000	12	0	0	0	0	15^1	16	4	7	13	14.1	6.46	58	.271	.358	0	—	0	-4	-5	-0	-0.3
Total	5	5	19	.208	132	24	3	0	5	318^1	357	34	110	184	13.4	4.81	80	.282	.343	9	.145	-1	-33	-34	-4	-3.2

● RAMON MOREL Morel, Ramon Rafael b: 8/15/74, Villa Gonzalez, D.R. BR/TR, 6'2", 175 lbs. Deb: 7/6/95

YEAR	TM/L	W	L	PCT	G	GS	CG	SH	SV	IP	H	HR	BB	SO	RAT	ERA	ERA+	OAV	OOB	BH	AVG	PB	PR	/A	PD	TPI
1995	Pit-N	0	1	.000	5	0	0	0	0	6^1	6	0	2	3	11.4	2.84	151	.300	.364	0	—	0	1	1	0	0.2
1996	Pit-N	2	1	.667	29	0	0	0	0	42	57	4	19	22	16.5	5.36	81	.324	.393	0	.000	-0	-5	-5	-1	-0.4
1997	Pit-N	0	0	—	5	0	0	0	0	7^2	11	2	4	4	17.6	4.70	91	.344	.417	0	—	0	-0	-0	0	0.0
	Chi-N	0	0	—	3	0	0	0	0	3^2	3	1	3	3	14.7	4.91	88	.214	.353	0	—	0	-0	-0	-0	0.0
	Yr	0	0	—	8	0	0	0	0	11^1	14	3	7	7	16.7	4.76	90	.304	.396	0	—	0	-1	-1	0	0.0
Total	3	2	2	.500	42	0	0	0	0	59^2	77	7	28	32	16.0	4.98	87	.318	.391	0	.000	-0	-5	-4	-0	-0.2

● LEW MOREN Moren, Lewis Howard "Hicks" b: 8/4/1883, Pittsburgh, Pa. d: 11/2/66, Pittsburgh, Pa. BR/TR, 5'11", 150 lbs. Deb: 9/21/03

YEAR	TM/L	W	L	PCT	G	GS	CG	SH	SV	IP	H	HR	BB	SO	RAT	ERA	ERA+	OAV	OOB	BH	AVG	PB	PR	/A	PD	TPI
1903	Pit-N	0	1	.000	1	1	1	0	0	6	9	0	2	2	18.0	9.00	36	.346	.414	0	.000	-0	-4	-4	-0	-0.5
1904	Pit-N	0	0	—	1	0	0	0	0	4	7	1	4	0	27.0	9.00	30	.412	.545	0	.000	-0	-3	-3	0	0.0
1907	Phi-N	11	18	.379	37	31	21	3	1	255	202	3	101	98	11.0	2.54	95	.226	.311	6	.081	-2	-2	-3	-0	-0.7
1908	Phi-N	8	9	.471	28	16	9	4	0	154	146	1	49	72	11.5	2.92	83	.258	.320	12	.245	2	-10	-8	0	-0.8
1909	Phi-N	16	15	.516	40	31	19	2	1	257^2	226	6	93	110	11.3	2.65	98	.239	.309	10	.111	-3	-2	-2	-5	-1.1
1910	Phi-N	13	14	.481	34	26	12	1	1	205^1	207	6	82	74	13.1	3.55	88	.269	.347	11	.149	-1	-12	-10	-0	-1.4
Total	6	48	57	.457	141	105	62	10	3	882	797	17	331	356	11.8	2.95	90	.248	.323	39	.134	-5	-32	-30	-5	-4.5

● ANGEL MORENO Moreno, Angel (Veneroso) b: 6/6/55, LaMendosa Soledad, Mex. BL/TL, 5'9", 165 lbs. Deb: 8/15/81

YEAR	TM/L	W	L	PCT	G	GS	CG	SH	SV	IP	H	HR	BB	SO	RAT	ERA	ERA+	OAV	OOB	BH	AVG	PB	PR	/A	PD	TPI
1981	Cal-A	1	3	.250	8	4	1	0	0	31^1	27	2	14	12	11.8	2.87	127	.233	.315	0	—	0	3	3	-0	0.3
1982	Cal-A	3	7	.300	13	8	2	0	1	49^1	55	7	23	22	14.4	4.74	85	.288	.367	0	—	0	-4	-4	-0	-0.7
Total	2	4	10	.286	21	12	3	0	1	80^2	82	9	37	34	13.4	4.02	97	.267	.348	0	—	0	-1	-1	-0	-0.4

● JULIO MORENO Moreno, Julio (Gonzalez) b: 1/28/21, Guines, Cuba d: 1/2/87, Miami, Fla. BR/TR, 5'8", 165 lbs. Deb: 9/8/50

YEAR	TM/L	W	L	PCT	G	GS	CG	SH	SV	IP	H	HR	BB	SO	RAT	ERA	ERA+	OAV	OOB	BH	AVG	PB	PR	/A	PD	TPI
1950	Was-A	1	1	.500	4	3	1	0	0	21^1	22	1	12	7	14.8	4.64	97	.268	.368	1	.125	-1	-0	-0	0	-0.1
1951	Was-A	5	11	.313	31	18	5	0	2	132^2	132	18	80	37	14.4	4.88	84	.256	.357	7	.175	-1	-11	-12	0	-1.4
1952	Was-A	9	9	.500	26	22	7	0	0	147^1	154	10	52	62	12.9	3.97	90	.270	.337	6	.122	-2	-5	-7	-1	-1.1
1953	Was-A	3	1	.750	12	2	1	0	0	35^1	41	2	13	13	13.8	2.80	139	.291	.351	0	.000	-1	5	4	-0	0.3
Total	4	18	22	.450	73	45	14	0	2	336^2	349	31	157	119	13.7	4.25	91	.267	.349	14	.132	-5	-12	-15	-1	-2.3

● ROGER MORET Moret, Rogelio (Torres) b: 9/16/49, Guayama, P.R. BB/TL, 6'4", 175 lbs. Deb: 9/13/70

YEAR	TM/L	W	L	PCT	G	GS	CG	SH	SV	IP	H	HR	BB	SO	RAT	ERA	ERA+	OAV	OOB	BH	AVG	PB	PR	/A	PD	TPI
1970	Bos-A	1	0	1.000	3	1	0	0	0	8^1	7	0	4	2	11.9	3.24	122	.226	.314	0	.000	-0	0	1	-0	0.0
1971	Bos-A	4	3	.571	13	7	4	1	0	71	50	5	40	47	11.7	2.92	127	.205	.322	2	.087	-1	4	6	-0	0.5
1972	Bos-A	0	0	—	3	0	0	0	0	5	5	0	6	4	19.8	3.60	89	.263	.440	0	.000	-0	-0	-0	-0	0.0
1973	Bos-A	13	2	.867	30	15	5	2	3	156^1	138	19	67	90	12.0	3.17	127	.238	.320	0	—	0	11	15	-0	1.4
1974	Bos-A	9	10	.474	31	21	10	1	2	173^1	158	15	79	111	12.4	3.74	103	.243	.327	0	—	0	-2	2	-2	-0.2
1975	*Bos-A	14	3	.824	36	16	4	1	1	145	132	8	76	80	13.0	3.60	113	.248	.344	0	—	0	3	8	-1	0.7
1976	Atl-N	3	5	.375	27	12	1	0	1	77^1	84	7	27	30	13.0	5.00	76	.280	.341	3	.130	-1	-13	-10	-0	-1.2
1977	Tex-A	3	3	.500	18	8	0	0	4	72^1	59	6	38	39	12.1	3.73	109	.220	.317	0	—	0	3	3	-1	0.1
1978	Tex-A	0	1	.000	7	2	0	0	1	14^2	23	1	2	5	16.0	4.91	76	.390	.419	0	—	0	-2	-2	-0	-0.2
Total	9	47	27	.635	168	82	24	5	12	723^1	656	61	339	408	12.5	3.66	107	.245	.332	5	.100	-2	4	22	-6	1.1

● DAVE MOREY Morey, David Beale b: 2/25/1889, Malden, Mass. d: 1/4/86, Oak Bluffs, Mass. BL/TR, 6', 185 lbs. Deb: 7/4/13

YEAR	TM/L	W	L	PCT	G	GS	CG	SH	SV	IP	H	HR	BB	SO	RAT	ERA	ERA+	OAV	OOB	BH	AVG	PB	PR	/A	PD	TPI
1913	Phi-A	0	0	—	2	0	0	0	0	4	2	0	2	1	11.3	4.50	61	.182	.357	0	.000	-0	-1	-1	0	0.0

● CY MORGAN Morgan, Cyril Arlon b: 11/11/1895, Lakeville, Mass. d: 9/11/46, Lakeville, Mass. BR/TR, 6', 170 lbs. Deb: 6/8/21

YEAR	TM/L	W	L	PCT	G	GS	CG	SH	SV	IP	H	HR	BB	SO	RAT	ERA	ERA+	OAV	OOB	BH	AVG	PB	PR	/A	PD	TPI
1921	Bos-N	1	1	.500	17	0	0	0	1	30^1	37	0	17	8	16.3	6.53	56	.314	.404	0	.000	-1	-9	-10	1	-0.6
1922	Bos-N	0	0	—	2	0	0	0	0	1^1	8	0	2	0	67.5	27.00	15	.667	.714	0	—	0	-3	-3	-0	0.0
Total	2	1	1	.500	19	0	0	0	1	31^2	45	0	19	8	18.5	7.39	50	.346	.433	0	.000	-1	-13	-13	1	-0.6

● CY MORGAN Morgan, Harry Richard b: 11/10/1878, Pomeroy, Ohio d: 6/28/62, Wheeling, W.Va. BR/TR, 6', 175 lbs. Deb: 9/18/03

YEAR	TM/L	W	L	PCT	G	GS	CG	SH	SV	IP	H	HR	BB	SO	RAT	ERA	ERA+	OAV	OOB	BH	AVG	PB	PR	/A	PD	TPI
1903	StL-A	0	2	.000	2	1	1	0	0	13	12	0	6	6	13.8	4.15	70	.245	.351	1	.250	0	-2	-2	-0	-0.3
1904	StL-A	0	2	.000	8	3	2	0	0	51	51	3	10	24	11.1	3.71	67	.262	.304	1	.056	-2	-6	-7	1	-0.4
1905	StL-A	2	5	.286	13	8	5	1	0	77^1	82	1	37	44	14.9	3.61	71	.273	.370	8	.258	2	-8	-9	2	-0.4
1907	StL-A	2	5	.286	10	6	4	0	0	55	77	3	17	14	15.7	6.05	42	.333	.384	2	.100	-1	-21	-22	1	-2.4
	Bos-A	6	6	.500	16	13	9	2	0	114^1	77	1	34	50	9.0	1.97	131	.193	.262	2	.057	-4	7	8	-1	0.3
	Yr	8	11	.421	26	19	13	2	0	169^1	154	4	51	64	11.1	3.30	78	.244	.304	4	.073	-5	-14	-14	1	-2.1
1908	Bos-A	14	13	.519	30	26	17	2	1	205	166	7	90	99	11.7	2.46	100	.226	.319	8	.127	-3	-1	0	1	-0.3
1909	Bos-A	2	6	.250	12	10	5	0	1	64^2	52	0	31	30	12.4	2.37	106	.240	.350	1	.050	-2	1	1	2	0.2
	Phi-A	16	11	.593	28	26	21	5	0	228^2	152	3	71	81	9.4	1.65	146	.191	.271	8	.108	-3	21	19	-2	1.8
	Yr	18	17	.514	40	36	26	5	1	293^1	204	3	102	111	9.9	1.81	134	**.200**	.283	9	.096	-4	22	20	1	2.0
1910	Phi-A	18	12	.600	36	34	23	3	0	290^2	214	0	117	134	10.8	1.55	153	.216	.310	14	.141	-4	31	27	1	2.5
1911	Phi-A	15	7	.682	38	30	15	2	1	249^2	217	0	113	136	12.7	2.70	117	.243	.341	15	.160	-5	18	13	3	0.8
1912	Phi-A	3	8	.273	16	14	5	0	0	93^2	75	0	51	47	12.6	3.75	82	.226	.338	1	.033	-3	-4	-7	2	-0.8
1913	Cin-N	0	1	.000	1	1	0	0	0	2^1	5	0	1	2	27.0	15.43	21	.500	.583	0	.000	-0	-3	-3	0	-0.8
Total	10	78	78	.500	210	172	107	15	3	1445^1	1180	18	578	667	11.5	2.51	105	.229	.318	61	.125	-25	32	19	12	0.2

● BILL MORGAN Morgan, Henry William b: 10/1857, Washington, D.C. Deb: 5/4/1875 ◆

YEAR	TM/L	W	L	PCT	G	GS	CG	SH	SV	IP	H	HR	BB	SO	RAT	ERA	ERA+	OAV	OOB	BH	AVG	PB	PR	/A	PD	TPI
1875	RS-n	1	3	.250	7	4	4	1	0	42	40	0	1	7	8.8	1.29	170	.212	.216	18	.261	1	4	4		0.4

● MIKE MORGAN Morgan, Michael Thomas b: 10/8/59, Tulare, Cal. BR/TR, 6'2", 215 lbs. Deb: 6/11/78

YEAR	TM/L	W	L	PCT	G	GS	CG	SH	SV	IP	H	HR	BB	SO	RAT	ERA	ERA+	OAV	OOB	BH	AVG	PB	PR	/A	PD	TPI
1978	Oak-A	0	3	.000	3	3	1	0	0	12^1	19	1	8	0	19.7	7.30	50	.373	.458	0	—	0	-5	-5	1	-0.8
1979	Oak-A	2	10	.167	13	13	2	0	0	77^1	102	7	50	17	18.0	5.94	68	.332	.431	0	—	0	-15	-16	1	-1.7
1982	NY-A	7	11	.389	30	23	2	0	0	150^1	167	15	67	71	14.1	4.37	91	.285	.360	0	—	0	-5	-6	1	-0.6
1983	Tor-A	0	3	.000	16	4	0	0	0	45^1	48	6	21	22	13.7	5.16	83	.273	.350	0	—	0	-6	-4	1	-0.3
1985	Sea-A	1	1	.500	2	2	0	0	0	6	11	2	5	2	24.0	12.00	35	.393	.485	0	—	0	-5	-5	0	-1.1
1986	Sea-A	11	17	.393	37	33	9	1	1	216^1	243	24	86	116	13.9	4.53	94	.286	.354	0	—	0	-9	-7	-0	-0.9
1987	Sea-A	12	17	.414	34	31	8	2	0	207	245	25	53	85	13.2	4.65	101	.296	.342	0	—	0	-5	2	1	0.3
1988	Bal-A	1	6	.143	22	10	2	0	1	71^1	70	6	23	29	11.9	5.43	72	.255	.315	0	—	0	-12	-12	0	-0.8
1989	LA-N	8	11	.421	40	19	0	0	0	152^2	130	6	33	72	9.7	2.53	135	.234	.280	3	.083	-2	16	15	4	2.1
1990	LA-N	11	15	.423	33	33	6	**4**	0	211	216	19	60	106	12.0	3.75	97	.266	.321	8	.113	-2	1	-2	3	-0.1
1991	LA-N★	14	10	.583	34	33	5	1	1	236^1	197	12	61	140	9.9	2.78	129	.226	.279	7	.092	-3	24	21	2	2.0
1992	Chi-N	16	8	.667	34	34	6	1	0	240	203	14	79	123	10.7	2.55	141	.234	.300	8	.108	-2	25	28	2	2.8
1993	Chi-N	10	15	.400	32	32	1	1	0	207^2	206	15	74	111	12.4	4.03	99	.262	.331	4	.061	-4	0	-1	0	-0.4
1994	Chi-N	2	10	.167	15	15	1	0	0	80^2	111	12	35	57	16.7	6.69	62	.338	.409	3	.125	-1	-22	-23	-1	-2.9
1995	Chi-N	2	1	.667	4	4	0	0	0	24^2	19	2	9	15	10.6	2.19	187	.216	.296	1	.143	-0	5	5	1	0.7

YEAR	TM/L	W	L	PCT	G	GS	CG	SH	SV	IP	H	HR	BB	SO	RAT	ERA	ERA+	OAV	OOB	BH	AVG	PB	PR	/A	PD	TPI
	StL-N	5	6	.455	17	17	1	0	0	106^2	114	10	25	46	12.2	3.88	108	.283	.333	1	.032	-2	4	4	2	0.3
	Yr	7	7	.500	21	21	1	0	0	131^1	133	12	34	61	11.8	3.56	117	.270	.324	2	.053	-2	9	9	2	1.0
1996	StL-N	4	8	.333	18	18	0	0	0	103	118	14	40	55	13.8	5.24	80	.294	.358	2	.061	-3	-12	-12	-1	-1.5
	Cin-N	2	3	.400	5	5	0	0	0	27^1	28	2	7	19	11.9	2.30	183	.267	.319	0	.000	-1	6	6	-0	0.9
	Yr	6	11	.353	23	23	0	0	0	130^1	146	16	47	74	13.4	4.63	91	.285	.346	2	.050	-3	-6	-6	-1	-0.6
1997	Cin-N	9	12	.429	31	30	1	0	0	162	165	13	49	103	12.3	4.78	89	.266	.328	4	.091	-2	-10	-9	-0	-1.2
1998	Min-A	4	2	.667	18	17	0	0	0	98	108	13	24	50	12.8	3.49	134	.286	.340	1	.500	0	13	13	1	0.8
	*Chi-N	0	1	.000	5	5	0	0	0	22^2	30	8	15	10	18.3	7.15	61	.323	.422	4	.667	2	-7	-7	1	0.0
Total	18	121	170	.416	443	381	45	10	3	2458^2	2550	226	824	1249	12.6	4.07	98	.271	.334	46	.096	-19	-18	-18	17	-2.4

● TOM MORGAN Morgan, Tom Stephen "Plowboy" b: 5/20/30, ElMonte, Cal. d: 1/13/87, Anaheim, Cal. BR/TR, 6'2", 195 lbs. Deb: 4/20/51 C

YEAR	TM/L	W	L	PCT	G	GS	CG	SH	SV	IP	H	HR	BB	SO	RAT	ERA	ERA+	OAV	OOB	BH	AVG	PB	PR	/A	PD	TPI
1951	*NY-A	9	3	.750	27	16	4	2	2	124^2	119	11	36	57	11.4	3.68	104	.253	.310	12	.273	2	6	2	2	0.5
1952	NY-A	5	4	.556	16	12	2	1	2	93^2	86	8	33	35	11.8	3.07	108	.252	.325	6	.182	1	6	3	3	0.6
1954	NY-A	11	5	.688	32	17	7	4	1	143	149	8	40	34	12.2	3.34	103	.274	.330	7	.143	0	6	2	3	0.4
1955	*NY-A	7	3	.700	40	1	0	0	10	72	72	3	24	17	12.6	3.25	115	.267	.338	4	.222	0	6	4	2	0.9
1956	*NY-A	6	7	.462	41	0	0	0	11	71^1	74	2	27	20	13.1	4.16	93	.284	.357	2	.154	-0	-0	-2	1	-0.4
1957	KC-A	9	7	.563	46	13	5	0	7	143^2	160	19	61	32	14.0	4.64	85	.299	.373	3	.091	-2	-14	-11	4	-1.1
1958	Det-A	2	5	.286	39	1	0	0	1	62^2	70	7	4	32	10.8	3.16	128	.286	.300	2	.200	-0	4	6	-0	0.6
1959	Det-A	1	4	.200	46	1	0	0	9	92^2	94	11	18	39	11.5	3.98	102	.265	.311	9	.391	4	-1	1	-0	0.4
1960	Det-A	3	2	.600	22	0	0	0	1	29	33	6	10	12	13.3	4.66	85	.295	.352	0	—	0	-3	-2	0	-0.3
	Was-A	1	3	.250	14	0	0	0	0	24	36	6	5	11	15.8	3.75	104	.343	.378	0	.000	-1	0	0	-0	0.0
	Yr	4	5	.444	36	0	0	0	1	53	69	12	15	23	14.4	4.25	92	.315	.362	0	.000	-1	-2	-2	0	-0.3
1961	LA-A	8	2	.800	59	0	0	0	10	91^2	74	7	17	39	9.4	2.36	191	.224	.272	1	.083	-1	17	**22**	1	2.7
1962	LA-A	5	2	.714	48	0	0	0	9	58^2	53	6	19	29	11.2	2.91	132	.247	.311	0	.000	-1	7	6	-1	0.7
1963	LA-A	0	0	—	13	0	0	0	1	16^1	20	1	6	7	16.0	5.51	62	.313	.397	0	.000	-0	-3	-4	-0	-0.1
Total	12	67	47	.588	443	61	18	7	64	1023^1	1040	95	300	364	12.1	3.61	106	.270	.329	46	.186	3	32	26	13	4.9

● GENE MORIARITY Moriarity, Eugene John b: 1/5/1865, Holyoke, Mass. BL/TL, 5'8", 130 lbs. Deb: 6/18/1884 ♦

YEAR	TM/L	W	L	PCT	G	GS	CG	SH	SV	IP	H	HR	BB	SO	RAT	ERA	ERA+	OAV	OOB	BH	AVG	PB	PR	/A	PD	TPI
1884	Ind-a	0	2	.000	2	2	2	0	0	13^2	16	0	7	4	15.8	5.27	62	.267	.353	8	.216	0	-3	-3	0	-0.3
1885	Det-N	0	0	—	1	0	0	0	0	2	3	0	1	1	18.0	9.00	32	.300	.364	1	.026	-0	-1	-1	-0	0.0
Total	2	0	2	.000	3	2	2	0	0	15^2	19	0	8	5	16.1	5.74	56	.271	.354	41	.152	-0	-4	-4	0	-0.3

● JOHN MORLAN Morlan, John Glen b: 11/22/47, Columbus, Ohio BR/TR, 6', 178 lbs. Deb: 7/20/73

YEAR	TM/L	W	L	PCT	G	GS	CG	SH	SV	IP	H	HR	BB	SO	RAT	ERA	ERA+	OAV	OOB	BH	AVG	PB	PR	/A	PD	TPI
1973	Pit-N	2	2	.500	10	7	1	0	0	41	42	4	23	23	14.3	3.95	89	.276	.371	2	.182	1	-1	-2	-1	-0.2
1974	Pit-N	0	3	.000	39	0	0	0	0	65	54	2	48	38	14.5	4.29	80	.227	.363	0	.000	-1	-5	-6	-1	-0.4
Total	2	2	5	.286	49	7	1	0	0	106	96	6	71	61	14.4	4.16	83	.246	.366	2	.111	0	-6	-8	-1	-0.6

● ALVIN MORMAN Morman, Alvin b: 1/6/69, Rockingham, N.C. BL/TL, 6'3", 210 lbs. Deb: 4/2/96

YEAR	TM/L	W	L	PCT	G	GS	CG	SH	SV	IP	H	HR	BB	SO	RAT	ERA	ERA+	OAV	OOB	BH	AVG	PB	PR	/A	PD	TPI
1996	Hou-N	4	1	.800	53	0	0	0	0	42	43	8	24	31	14.4	4.93	78	.261	.354	0	—	0	-3	-5	0	-0.5
1997	*Cle-A	0	0	—	34	0	0	0	2	18^1	19	2	14	13	16.7	5.89	80	.268	.395	0	.000	-0	-3	-2	-0	-0.1
1998	Cle-A	0	1	.000	31	0	0	0	0	22	25	1	11	16	14.7	5.32	90	.298	.379	0	—	0	-2	-1	0	0.0
	SF-N	0	1	.000	9	0	0	0	0	7	8	4	3	7	14.1	5.14	79	.276	.344	0	—	0	-1	-1	0	-0.1
Total	3	4	3	.571	127	0	0	0	2	89^1	95	15	52	67	14.9	5.24	81	.272	.368	0	.000	-0	-8	-10	0	-0.7

● DAN MOROGIELLO Morogiello, Daniel Joseph b: 3/26/55, Brooklyn, N.Y. BL/TL, 6'1", 200 lbs. Deb: 5/20/83

YEAR	TM/L	W	L	PCT	G	GS	CG	SH	SV	IP	H	HR	BB	SO	RAT	ERA	ERA+	OAV	OOB	BH	AVG	PB	PR	/A	PD	TPI
1983	Bal-A	0	1	.000	22	0	0	0	1	37^2	39	1	10	15	11.9	2.39	165	.265	.316	0	—	0	7	7	-1	0.1

● JIM MORONEY Moroney, James Francis b: 12/4/1883, Boston, Mass. d: 2/26/29, Philadelphia, Pa. BL/TL, 6'1", 175 lbs. Deb: 4/24/06

YEAR	TM/L	W	L	PCT	G	GS	CG	SH	SV	IP	H	HR	BB	SO	RAT	ERA	ERA+	OAV	OOB	BH	AVG	PB	PR	/A	PD	TPI
1906	Bos-N	0	3	.000	3	3	3	0	0	27	28	1	12	11	15.3	5.33	50	.259	.365	1	.100	-1	-8	-8	0	-0.8
1910	Phi-N	1	2	.333	12	2	1	0	1	42	43	1	11	13	12.4	2.14	146	.295	.360	0	.000	-1	4	5	-0	0.2
1912	Chi-N	1	1	.500	10	3	1	0	1	23^2	25	0	17	5	17.5	4.56	73	.316	.460	3	.500	-1	-3	-3	-0	-0.2
Total	3	2	6	.250	25	8	5	0	2	92^2	96	2	40	29	14.6	3.69	83	.288	.388	4	.154	-1	-7	-7	-1	-0.8

● BILL MORRELL Morrell, Willard Blackmer b: 4/9/1893, Hyde Park, Mass. d: 8/5/75, Birmingham, Ala. BR/TR, 6', 172 lbs. Deb: 4/20/26

YEAR	TM/L	W	L	PCT	G	GS	CG	SH	SV	IP	H	HR	BB	SO	RAT	ERA	ERA+	OAV	OOB	BH	AVG	PB	PR	/A	PD	TPI
1926	Was-A	3	3	.500	26	2	1	0	1	69^2	83	5	29	16	14.7	5.30	73	.311	.383	4	.235	1	-10	-11	-1	-0.9
1930	NY-N	0	0	—	2	0	0	0	0	8	6	0	1	3	7.9	1.13	421	.214	.241	0	.000	-0	3	3	0	0.0
1931	NY-N	5	3	.625	20	7	2	0	1	66	83	4	27	16	15.0	4.36	85	.306	.369	2	.111	-0	-4	-5	-0	-0.6
Total	3	8	6	.571	48	9	3	0	2	143^2	172	9	57	35	14.5	4.64	83	.304	.370	6	.162	-0	-10	-13	-1	-1.5

● JOHN MORRILL Morrill, John Francis "Honest John" b: 2/19/1855, Boston, Mass. d: 4/2/32, Brookline, Mass. BR/TR, 5'10.5", 155 lbs. Deb: 4/24/1876 M♦

YEAR	TM/L	W	L	PCT	G	GS	CG	SH	SV	IP	H	HR	BB	SO	RAT	ERA	ERA+	OAV	OOB	BH	AVG	PB	PR	/A	PD	TPI
1880	Bos-N	0	0	—	3	0	0	0	0	10^2	9	0	1	0	8.4	0.84	269	.273	.294	81	.237	0	2	2	0	0.0
1881	Bos-N	0	1	.000	3	0	0	0	1	5^2	9	0	1	0	15.9	6.35	42	.333	.357	90	.289	1	-2	-2	-0	-0.4
1882	Bos-N	0	0	—	1	0	0	0	0	2	3	0	0	2	13.5	0.00	—	.375	.375	101	.289	0	1	1	0	0.0
1883	Bos-N	1	0	1.000	2	1	1	0	0	13	15	0	4	5	13.2	2.77	112	.268	.317	129	.319	1	1	0	-0	0.1
1884	Bos-N	0	1	.000	7	1	1	0	**2**	23	34	0	6	13	15.7	7.43	39	.315	.351	114	.260	1	-11	-12	0	-0.5
1886	Bos-N	0	0	—	1	0	0	0	0	4	5	0	0	2	11.3	0.00	—	.313	.313	106	.247	0	1	1	0	0.0
1889	Was-N	0	0	—	1	0	0	0	0	0^1	0	0	0	0	0.0	0.00	—	.000	.000	27	.185	0	0	0	0	0.0
Total	7	1	2	.333	18	2	2	0	3	58^2	75	0	12	22	13.3	4.30	66	.301	.333	1275	.260	4	-9	-10	0	-0.8

● DANNY MORRIS Morris, Danny Walker b: 6/11/46, Greenville, Ky. BR/TR, 6'1", 200 lbs. Deb: 9/10/68

YEAR	TM/L	W	L	PCT	G	GS	CG	SH	SV	IP	H	HR	BB	SO	RAT	ERA	ERA+	OAV	OOB	BH	AVG	PB	PR	/A	PD	TPI
1968	Min-A	0	1	.000	3	2	0	0	0	10^2	11	0	4	6	12.7	1.69	183	.262	.326	0	.000	-0	2	2	0	0.1
1969	Min-A	0	1	.000	3	1	0	0	0	5^1	5	1	4	1	15.2	5.06	72	.238	.360	0	—	0	-1	-1	0	-0.1
Total	2	0	2	.000	6	3	0	0	0	16	16	1	8	7	13.5	2.81	117	.254	.338	0	.000	-0	1	1	0	0.0

● E. MORRIS Morris, E. b: Trenton, N.J. Deb: 9/11/1884 ♦

YEAR	TM/L	W	L	PCT	G	GS	CG	SH	SV	IP	H	HR	BB	SO	RAT	ERA	ERA+	OAV	OOB	BH	AVG	PB	PR	/A	PD	TPI
1884	Bal-U	0	0	—	1	0	0	0	0	1	2	0	2	0	36.0	9.00	30	.400	.571	0	.000	-1	-1	-1	-0	0.0

● ED MORRIS Morris, Edward "Cannonball" b: 9/29/1862, Brooklyn, N.Y. d: 4/12/37, Pittsburgh, Pa. BB/TL, 5'7", 165 lbs. Deb: 5/1/1884

YEAR	TM/L	W	L	PCT	G	GS	CG	SH	SV	IP	H	HR	BB	SO	RAT	ERA	ERA+	OAV	OOB	BH	AVG	PB	PR	/A	PD	TPI
1884	Col-a	34	13	**.723**	52	52	47	3	0	429^2	335	3	51	302	8.4	2.18	139	.204	.234	37	.186	2	51	41	2	4.2
1885	Pit-a	39	24	.619	**63**	63	**63**	**7**	0	**581**	459	5	101	**298**	**8.9**	2.35	137	**.208**	**.247**	44	.186	-5	58	56	-1	4.5
1886	Pit-a	**41**	20	.672	64	63	63	**12**	**1**	555^1	455	5	118	326	**9.4**	2.45	138	.214	**.258**	38	.167	-7	62	58	-1	4.4
1887	Pit-N	14	22	.389	38	38	37	1	0	317^2	375	13	71	91	12.9	4.31	90	.286	.326	25	.198	-4	-8	-15	-2	-1.8
1888	Pit-N	29	23	.558	**55**	55	**54**	5	0	480	470	7	74	135	10.4	2.31	116	.245	.276	19	.101	-11	29	19	1	0.7
1889	Pit-N	6	13	.316	21	21	18	0	0	170	196	4	48	40	13.2	4.13	91	.280	.332	7	.097	-5	-2	-7	-2	-1.2
1890	Pit-P	8	7	.533	18	15	15	1	0	144^1	178	5	35	25	13.5	4.86	80	.290	.332	9	.143	-4	-10	-15	-3	-1.6
Total	7	171	122	.584	311	307	297	29	1	2678	2468	42	498	1217	10.2	2.82	116	.235	.273	179	.161	-35	179	137	-5	9.2

● JACK MORRIS Morris, John Scott b: 5/16/55, St.Paul, Minn. BR/TR, 6'3", 200 lbs. Deb: 7/26/77

YEAR	TM/L	W	L	PCT	G	GS	CG	SH	SV	IP	H	HR	BB	SO	RAT	ERA	ERA+	OAV	OOB	BH	AVG	PB	PR	/A	PD	TPI
1977	Det-A	1	1	.500	7	6	1	0	0	45^2	38	4	23	28	12.0	3.74	114	.235	.330	0	—	0	2	3	0	0.0
1978	Det-A	3	5	.375	28	7	0	0	0	106	107	8	49	48	13.5	4.33	89	.268	.352	0	—	0	-7	-5	-0	-0.5
1979	Det-A	17	7	.708	27	27	9	1	0	197^2	179	19	59	113	11.0	3.28	132	.244	.304	0	—	0	21	23	-1	2.5
1980	Det-A	16	15	.516	36	36	11	2	0	250	252	20	87	112	12.3	4.18	98	.262	.326	0	—	0	-4	-2	3	0.1
1981	Det-A★	**14**	7	.667	25	25	15	1	0	198	153	14	78	97	10.6	3.05	124	.218	.298	0	—	0	13	16	-0	1.6
1982	Det-A	17	16	.515	37	37	17	3	0	266^1	247	37	96	135	11.6	4.06	100	.247	.312	0	—	0	1	0	-0	0.0
1983	Det-A	20	13	.606	37	37	20	1	0	**293^2**	257	30	83	**232**	10.5	3.34	117	.233	.289	0	—	0	24	19	-1	1.8
1984	*Det-A★	19	11	.633	35	35	9	1	0	240^1	221	20	87	148	11.6	3.60	109	.241	.308	0	—	0	11	9	2	1.2
1985	Det-A★	16	11	.593	35	35	13	4	0	257	212	21	110	191	11.5	3.33	122	.225	.309	0	—	0	23	21	-1	2.0
1986	Det-A	21	8	.724	35	35	15	**6**	0	267	229	40	82	223	10.5	3.27	126	.229	.287	0	—	0	27	25	0	2.6
1987	*Det-A★	18	11	.621	34	34	13	0	0	266	227	39	93	208	10.9	3.38	125	.228	.294	0	.000	-0	32	25	-2	2.2
1988	Det-A	15	13	.536	34	34	10	2	0	235	225	20	83	168	11.9	3.94	97	.251	.318	0	—	0	1	-3	0	-0.3
1989	Det-A	6	14	.300	24	24	10	0	0	170^1	189	23	59	115	13.2	4.86	79	.283	.342	0	—	0	-19	-20	1	-2.0
1990	Det-A	15	18	.455	36	36	**11**	3	0	249^2	231	26	97	162	12.0	4.51	88	.242	.316	0	—	0	-17	-15	-1	-1.9

YEAR	TM/L	W	L	PCT	G	GS	CG	SH	SV	IP	H	HR	BB	SO	RAT	ERA	ERA+	OAV	OOB	BH	AVG	PB	PR	/A	PD	TPI
1991	*Min-A★	18	12	.600	35	35	10	2	0	246^{2}	226	18	92	163	11.8	3.43	124	.245	.317	0	—	0	18	23	-1	2.5
1992	*Tor-A	**21**	6	.778	34	34	6	1	0	240^{2}	222	18	80	132	11.7	4.04	101	.246	.314	0	—	0	-3	1	-1	0.0
1993	Tor-A	7	12	.368	27	27	4	1	0	152^{2}	189	18	65	103	15.2	6.19	70	.302	.371	0	—	0	-32	-32	-2	-3.5
1994	Cle-A	10	6	.625	23	23	1	0	0	141^{1}	163	14	67	100	14.9	5.60	84	.292	.371	0	—	0	-13	-14	0	-1.3
Total	18	254	186	.577	549	527	175	28	0	3824	3567	389	1390	2478	11.8	3.90	104	.247	.316	0	.000	-0	78	74	-4	7.0

● JOHN MORRIS Morris, John Wallace b: 8/23/41, Lewes, Del. BR/TL, 6'1", 198 lbs. Deb: 7/19/66

YEAR	TM/L	W	L	PCT	G	GS	CG	SH	SV	IP	H	HR	BB	SO	RAT	ERA	ERA+	OAV	OOB	BH	AVG	PB	PR	/A	PD	TPI
1966	Phi-N	1	1	.500	13	0	0	0	0	13^{2}	15	2	3	8	12.5	5.27	68	.278	.328	0	—	0	-3	-3	0	-0.3
1968	Bal-A	2	0	1.000	19	0	0	0	0	31^{2}	19	4	17	22	11.4	2.56	114	.173	.305	0	.000	-1	1	1	0	0.0
1969	Sea-A	0	0	—	6	0	0	0	0	12^{2}	16	2	8	8	17.1	6.39	57	.308	.400	1	1.000	1	-4	-4	1	0.2
1970	Mil-A	4	3	.571	20	9	2	0	0	73^{1}	70	4	22	40	11.5	3.93	96	.253	.312	3	.176	0	-2	-1	1	0.0
1971	Mil-A	2	2	.500	43	1	0	0	1	67^{2}	69	4	27	42	12.9	3.72	93	.270	.342	1	.200	0	-2	-2	1	0.0
1972	SF-N	0	0	—	7	0	0	0	0	6^{1}	9	2	2	5	15.6	4.26	82	.310	.355	0	—	0	-1	-1	0	0.0
1973	SF-N	1	0	1.000	7	0	0	0	0	6^{1}	12	0	3	3	21.3	8.53	45	.429	.484	0	.000	-0	-3	-3	0	-0.5
1974	SF-N	1	1	.500	17	0	0	0	1	20^{2}	17	1	4	9	9.1	3.05	125	.215	.253	1	1.000	0	1	2	-1	0.2
Total	8	11	7	.611	132	10	2	0	2	232^{1}	227	19	86	137	12.4	3.95	90	.256	.328	6	.194	1	-11	-10	3	-0.4

● BUGS MORRIS Morris, Joseph Harley (a.k.a. Joseph Harley Bennett In 1918) b: 4/19/1892, Weir City, Kan. d: 11/21/57, Noel, Mo. BR/TR, 5'9.5", 163 lbs. Deb: 7/20/18

YEAR	TM/L	W	L	PCT	G	GS	CG	SH	SV	IP	H	HR	BB	SO	RAT	ERA	ERA+	OAV	OOB	BH	AVG	PB	PR	/A	PD	TPI
1918	StL-A	0	2	.000	4	2	0	0	0	10^{1}	12	1	7	0	16.5	3.48	79	.308	.413	1	.250	0	-1	-1	0	-0.1
1921	Chi-A	0	3	.000	3	2	1	0	0	17^{2}	19	1	16	2	17.8	6.11	69	.297	.438	2	.333	0	-4	-4	1	-0.4
	StL-A	0	0	—	3	1	0	0	0	5^{2}	11	1	6	3	30.2	14.29	31	.407	.543	1	1.000	0	-6	-6	-0	0.0
	Yr	0	3	.000	6	3	1	0	0	23^{1}	30	2	22	5	20.8	8.10	53	.330	.470	3	.429	1	-10	-10	0	-0.4
Total	2	0	5	.000	10	5	1	0	0	33^{2}	42	3	29	5	19.5	6.68	57	.323	.453	4	.364	1	-11	-11	1	-0.5

● MATT MORRIS Morris, Matthew Christian b: 8/9/74, Middletown, N.Y. BR/TR, 6'5", 210 lbs. Deb: 4/4/97

YEAR	TM/L	W	L	PCT	G	GS	CG	SH	SV	IP	H	HR	BB	SO	RAT	ERA	ERA+	OAV	OOB	BH	AVG	PB	PR	/A	PD	TPI
1997	StL-N	12	9	.571	33	33	3	0	0	217	208	12	69	149	11.8	3.19	130	.258	.322	15	.205	3	24	23	-2	2.1
1998	StL-N	7	5	.583	17	17	2	1	0	113^{2}	101	8	42	79	11.6	2.53	165	.243	.317	2	.069	-0	21	21	0	2.1
Total	2	19	14	.576	50	50	5	1	0	330^{2}	309	20	111	228	11.7	2.97	140	.253	.320	17	.167	3	46	44	-2	4.2

● ED MORRIS Morris, Walter Edward "Big Ed" b: 12/7/1899, Foshee, Ala. d: 3/3/32, Century, Fla. BR/TR, 6'2", 185 lbs. Deb: 8/5/22

YEAR	TM/L	W	L	PCT	G	GS	CG	SH	SV	IP	H	HR	BB	SO	RAT	ERA	ERA+	OAV	OOB	BH	AVG	PB	PR	/A	PD	TPI
1922	Chi-N	0	0	—	5	0	0	0	0	12	22	1	6	5	21.0	8.25	51	.386	.444	1	.250	-0	-6	-5	-0	0.0
1928	Bos-A	19	15	.559	47	29	20	0	5	257^{2}	255	7	80	104	11.9	3.53	117	.264	.323	14	.154	-4	15	17	-2	1.5
1929	Bos-A	14	14	.500	33	26	17	2	1	208^{1}	227	7	95	73	14.0	4.45	96	.282	.360	16	.232	2	-5	-4	-2	-0.4
1930	Bos-A	4	9	.308	18	9	3	0	0	65^{1}	67	1	38	28	14.5	4.13	112	.260	.355	6	.316	2	4	3	-0	0.7
1931	Bos-A	5	7	.417	37	14	3	0	0	130^{2}	131	4	74	46	14.5	4.75	91	.260	.361	6	.158	-2	-5	-6	0	-0.6
Total	5	42	45	.483	140	78	43	2	6	674	702	20	293	256	13.4	4.19	101	.271	.348	43	.195	-1	3	4	-4	1.2

● BILL MORRISETTE Morrisette, William Lee b: 1/17/1893, Baltimore, Md. d: 3/25/66, Virginia Beach, Va BR/TR, 6', 176 lbs. Deb: 9/19/15

YEAR	TM/L	W	L	PCT	G	GS	CG	SH	SV	IP	H	HR	BB	SO	RAT	ERA	ERA+	OAV	OOB	BH	AVG	PB	PR	/A	PD	TPI
1915	Phi-A	2	0	1.000	4	1	1	0	0	20	15	0	5	11	9.0	1.35	217	.195	.244	2	.286	0	4	4	0	0.4
1916	Phi-A	0	0	—	1	0	0	0	0	4	6	0	5	2	24.8	6.75	42	.429	.579	0	.000	0	-2	-2	1	0.1
1920	Det-A	1	1	.500	8	3	1	0	0	27	25	0	19	15	15.7	4.33	86	.245	.379	0	.000	-1	-2	-2	-0	-0.3
Total	3	3	1	.750	13	4	2	0	0	51	46	0	29	28	13.8	3.35	100	.238	.347	2	.125	-1	0	-0	0	0.2

● JIM MORRISON Morrison, James Forrest b: 9/23/52, Pensacola, Fla. BR/TR, 5'11", 182 lbs. Deb: 9/18/77 ♦

YEAR	TM/L	W	L	PCT	G	GS	CG	SH	SV	IP	H	HR	BB	SO	RAT	ERA	ERA+	OAV	OOB	BH	AVG	PB	PR	/A	PD	TPI
1988	Atl-N	0	0	—	3	0	0	0	0	3^{2}	3	0	2	1	12.3	0.00	—	.214	.313	14	.152	0	1	1	-0	0.0

● JOHNNY MORRISON Morrison, John Dewey "Jughandle Johnny" b: 10/22/1895, Pellville, Ky. d: 3/20/66, Louisville, Ky. BR/TR, 5'11", 188 lbs. Deb: 9/28/20 F

YEAR	TM/L	W	L	PCT	G	GS	CG	SH	SV	IP	H	HR	BB	SO	RAT	ERA	ERA+	OAV	OOB	BH	AVG	PB	PR	/A	PD	TPI
1920	Pit-N	1	0	1.000	2	1	1	1	0	7	4	0	1	3	6.4	0.00	—	.167	.200	0	.000	-0	2	3	0	0.3
1921	Pit-N	9	7	.563	21	17	11	**3**	0	144	131	3	33	52	10.3	2.88	133	.258	.305	5	.119	-1	15	15	-0	1.4
1922	Pit-N	17	11	.607	45	33	20	**5**	1	286^{1}	315	10	87	104	12.8	3.43	119	.286	.341	20	.198	-2	21	21	0	1.5
1923	Pit-N	25	13	.658	42	37	27	2	2	301^{2}	287	6	110	114	12.0	3.49	115	.253	.321	21	.183	-3	17	17	-0	1.6
1924	Pit-N	11	16	.407	**41**	25	10	0	2	237^{2}	213	7	73	85	11.0	3.75	102	.245	.307	13	.169	-2	3	2	-2	-0.2
1925	*Pit-N	17	14	.548	**44**	26	10	0	**4**	211	245	12	60	60	13.3	3.88	115	.291	.343	13	.178	-2	9	14	-2	1.3
1926	Pit-N	6	8	.429	26	13	6	2	2	122^{1}	119	2	44	39	12.1	3.38	116	.267	.335	3	.077	-4	6	7	-2	0.2
1927	Pit-N	3	2	.600	21	2	1	0	3	53^{2}	63	2	21	21	14.1	4.19	98	.304	.368	2	.154	-0	-2	-0	-1	-0.2
1929	Bro-N	13	7	.650	39	10	4	0	**8**	136^{2}	150	11	61	57	14.1	4.48	103	.279	.355	7	.163	-2	4	2	-3	-0.2
1930	Bro-N	1	2	.333	16	0	0	0	1	34^{2}	47	4	16	11	16.4	5.45	90	.346	.414	0	.000	-1	-2	-2	-0	-0.2
Total	10	103	80	.563	297	164	90	13	23	1535	1574	57	506	546	12.4	3.65	113	.271	.332	84	.164	-18	74	79	-12	5.5

● MIKE MORRISON Morrison, Michael b: 2/6/1867, Erie, Pa. d: 6/16/55, Erie, Pa. BR/TR, 5'8.5", 156 lbs. Deb: 4/19/1887

YEAR	TM/L	W	L	PCT	G	GS	CG	SH	SV	IP	H	HR	BB	SO	RAT	ERA	ERA+	OAV	OOB	BH	AVG	PB	PR	/A	PD	TPI
1887	Cle-a	12	25	.324	40	40	35	0	0	316^{2}	385	13	205	158	17.4	4.92	88	.294	.398	27	.191	-4	-22	-20	10	-1.2
1888	Cle-a	1	3	.250	4	4	4	0	0	35	40	3	19	14	15.4	5.40	57	.278	.366	4	.235	-0	-9	-9	0	-0.8
1890	Syr-a	6	9	.400	17	14	13	1	0	127	131	4	81	69	15.9	5.88	60	.258	.374	29	.242	3	-28	-33	2	-2.5
	Bal-a	1	2	.333	4	4	3	0	0	26	15	0	20	13	12.8	3.81	107	.163	.325	1	.111	-1	0	1	1	0.1
	Yr	7	11	.389	21	18	16	1	0	153	146	4	101	82	14.6	5.53	66	.239	.348	30	.233	3	-28	-32	3	-2.4
Total	3	20	39	.339	65	62	55	1	0	504^{2}	571	20	325	254	16.7	5.14	78	.278	.387	61	.213	-2	-59	-62	12	-4.4

● PHIL MORRISON Morrison, Philip Melvin b: 10/18/1894, Rockport, Ind. d: 1/18/55, Lexington, Ky. BB/TR, 6'2", 190 lbs. Deb: 9/30/21 F

YEAR	TM/L	W	L	PCT	G	GS	CG	SH	SV	IP	H	HR	BB	SO	RAT	ERA	ERA+	OAV	OOB	BH	AVG	PB	PR	/A	PD	TPI
1921	Pit-N	0	0	—	1	0	0	0	0	0^{2}	1	0	0	1	13.5	0.00	—	.333	.333	0	—	0	0	0	0	0.0

● HANK MORRISON Morrison, Stephen Henry b: 5/22/1866, Olneyville, R.I. d: 9/30/27, Attleboro, Mass. BR/TR, 5'10", 180 lbs. Deb: 5/28/1887

YEAR	TM/L	W	L	PCT	G	GS	CG	SH	SV	IP	H	HR	BB	SO	RAT	ERA	ERA+	OAV	OOB	BH	AVG	PB	PR	/A	PD	TPI
1887	Ind-N	3	4	.429	7	7	5	0	0	57	79	2	27	13	16.9	7.58	55	.307	.375	3	.115	-2	-22	-22	-1	-2.0

● GUY MORRISON Morrison, Walter Guy b: 8/29/1895, Hinton, W.Va. d: 8/14/34, Grand Rapids, Mich BR/TR, 5'11", 185 lbs. Deb: 8/31/27

YEAR	TM/L	W	L	PCT	G	GS	CG	SH	SV	IP	H	HR	BB	SO	RAT	ERA	ERA+	OAV	OOB	BH	AVG	PB	PR	/A	PD	TPI
1927	Bos-N	1	2	.333	11	3	1	0	0	34^{1}	40	1	15	6	14.4	4.46	83	.296	.367	1	.125	1	-2	-3	1	0.0
1928	Bos-N	0	0	—	1	0	0	0	0	3	4	1	3	0	21.0	12.00	33	.308	.438	0	—	0	-3	-3	0	0.0
Total	2	1	2	.333	12	3	1	0	0	37^{1}	44	2	18	6	14.9	5.06	74	.297	.373	1	.125	1	-5	-6	1	0.0

● FRANK MORRISSEY Morrissey, Michael Joseph "Deacon" b: 5/5/1876, Baltimore, Md. d: 2/22/39, Baltimore, Md. TR , 5'4", 140 lbs. Deb: 7/13/01

YEAR	TM/L	W	L	PCT	G	GS	CG	SH	SV	IP	H	HR	BB	SO	RAT	ERA	ERA+	OAV	OOB	BH	AVG	PB	PR	/A	PD	TPI
1901	Bos-A	0	0	—	1	0	0	0	0	4^{1}	5	0	2	1	18.7	2.08	170	.278	.409	0	.000	-1	1	1	0	0.0
1902	Chi-N	1	3	.250	5	5	5	0	0	40	40	0	8	13	11.2	2.25	120	.260	.305	2	.091	-1	2	2	0	0.1
Total	2	1	3	.250	6	5	5	0	0	44^{1}	45	0	10	14	12.0	2.23	125	.262	.317	2	.080	-1	3	3	1	0.1

● CARL MORTON Morton, Carl Wendle b: 1/18/44, Kansas City, Mo. d: 4/12/83, Tulsa, Okla. BR/TR, 6', 200 lbs. Deb: 4/11/69

YEAR	TM/L	W	L	PCT	G	GS	CG	SH	SV	IP	H	HR	BB	SO	RAT	ERA	ERA+	OAV	OOB	BH	AVG	PB	PR	/A	PD	TPI
1969	Mon-N	0	3	.000	8	5	0	0	0	29^{1}	29	2	18	16	15.0	4.60	80	.264	.377	0	.000	-0	-3	-3	1	-0.3
1970	Mon-N	18	11	.621	43	37	10	4	0	284^{2}	281	27	125	154	13.0	3.60	114	.262	.341	15	.161	2	14	16	1	1.8
1971	Mon-N	10	18	.357	36	35	9	0	1	213^{2}	252	22	83	84	14.3	4.80	73	.295	.360	14	.182	2	-32	-30	2	-3.2
1972	Mon-N	7	13	.350	27	27	3	1	0	172	170	16	53	51	11.8	3.92	90	.258	.316	7	.135	1	-9	-7	1	-0.6
1973	Atl-N	15	10	.600	38	37	10	4	0	256^{1}	254	18	70	112	11.5	3.41	115	.259	.311	17	.181	4	7	15	0	1.8
1974	Atl-N	16	12	.571	38	38	7	1	0	274^{2}	293	10	89	113	12.6	3.15	120	.277	.334	10	.112	-4	14	19	-1	1.4
1975	Atl-N	17	16	.515	39	39	11	2	0	277^{2}	302	19	82	78	12.5	3.50	108	.278	.330	15	.160	-1	4	8	0	0.9
1976	Atl-N	4	9	.308	26	24	1	1	0	140^{1}	172	6	45	42	14.2	4.17	91	.306	.362	8	.178	-0	-10	-6	2	-0.3
Total	8	87	92	.486	255	242	51	13	1	1648^{2}	1753	120	565	650	12.8	3.73	102	.275	.336	86	.156	3	-15	13	6	1.5

● CHARLIE MORTON Morton, Charles Hazen b: 10/12/1854, Kingsville, Ohio d: 12/9/21, Massillon, Ohio BR/TR, 150 lbs. Deb: 5/2/1882 MU♦

YEAR	TM/L	W	L	PCT	G	GS	CG	SH	SV	IP	H	HR	BB	SO	RAT	ERA	ERA+	OAV	OOB	BH	AVG	PB	PR	/A	PD	TPI
1884	Tol-a	0	1	.000	3	1	1	0	0	23^{1}	18	0	5	7	9.3	3.09	111	.209	.261	18	.162	-0	0	1	-1	-0.1

● GUY MORTON Morton, Guy Sr. "The Alabama Blossom" b: 6/1/1893, Vernon, Ala. d: 10/18/34, Sheffield, Ala. BR/TR, 6'1", 175 lbs. Deb: 6/20/14 F

YEAR	TM/L	W	L	PCT	G	GS	CG	SH	SV	IP	H	HR	BB	SO	RAT	ERA	ERA+	OAV	OOB	BH	AVG	PB	PR	/A	PD	TPI
1914	Cle-A	1	13	.071	25	13	5	0	1	128	116	1	55	80	12.2	3.02	95	.257	.341	1	.029	-4	-4	-2	-1	-0.8
1915	Cle-A	16	15	.516	34	27	15	6	1	240	189	5	60	134	9.4	2.14	143	.216	.268	12	.146	-4	21	24	-0	2.6
1916	Cle-A	12	6	.667	27	18	9	0	0	149^{2}	139	1	42	88	11.1	2.89	104	.246	.302	12	.211	-1	-1	2	-1	0.1

YEAR	TM/L	W	L	PCT	G	GS	CG	SH	SV	IP	H	HR	BB	SO	RAT	ERA	ERA+	OAV	OOB	BH	AVG	PB	PR	/A	PD	TPI
1917	Cle-A	10	10	.500	35	18	6	1	2	161	158	3	59	62	12.2	2.74	103	.266	.335	4	.085	-4	-1	2	-2	-0.5
1918	Cle-A	14	8	.636	30	28	13	1	0	214^2	189	1	77	123	11.3	2.64	114	.240	.310	12	.156	-1	3	9	-1	0.6
1919	Cle-A	9	9	.500	26	20	9	3	0	147^1	128	3	47	64	10.7	2.81	119	.233	.293	9	.161	-2	7	9	-1	0.7
1920	Cle-A	8	6	.571	29	17	6	1	1	137	140	2	57	72	13.0	4.47	85	.270	.344	10	.217	-1	-10	-10	-2	-1.3
1921	Cle-A	8	3	.727	30	7	3	2	0	107^2	98	1	32	45	11.0	2.76	155	.244	.303	6	.171	-2	18	18	-2	1.2
1922	Cle-A	14	9	.609	38	23	13	3	0	202^2	218	7	85	102	13.6	4.00	100	.277	.351	13	.191	-2	1	0	3	0.2
1923	Cle-A	6	6	.500	33	14	3	2	1	129^1	133	3	56	54	13.3	4.24	93	.276	.354	7	.159	-2	-4	-4	-1	-0.6
1924	Cle-A	0	1	.000	10	0	0	0	0	12^1	12	0	13	6	18.2	6.57	65	.250	.410	0	.000	-0	-3	-3	-0	-0.3
Total	11	98	86	.533	317	185	82	19	6	1629^2	1520	27	583	830	11.7	3.13	108	.251	.319	86	.157	-24	27	48	-7	1.9
● KEVIN MORTON	Morton, Kevin Joseph b: 8/3/68, Norwalk, Conn. BR/TL, 6'2", 185 lbs. Deb: 7/5/91																									
1991	Bos-A	6	5	.545	16	15	1	0	0	86^1	93	9	40	45	14.0	4.59	94	.284	.363	0	—	0	-5	-3	1	-0.2
● SPARROW MORTON	Morton, William P. TL, Deb: 7/15/1884																									
1884	Phi-N	0	2	.000	2	2	2	0	0	17	16	0	11	5	14.3	5.29	56	.222	.325	3	.375	1	-4	-4	-0	-0.3
● EARL MOSELEY	Moseley, Earl Victor "Vic" b: 9/7/1884, Middleburg, Ohio d: 7/1/63, Alliance, Ohio BR/TR, 5'9.5", 168 lbs. Deb: 6/17/13																									
1913	Bos-A	8	5	.615	24	15	7	3	0	120^2	105	1	49	62	11.5	3.13	94	.245	.322	3	.081	-2	-3	-3	1	-0.4
1914	Ind-F	19	18	.514	43	38	29	4	1	316^2	303	5	123	205	12.2	3.47	90	.258	.330	12	.110	-8	-20	-12	-0	-2.2
1915	New-F	15	15	.500	38	32	22	5	1	268	222	2	99	142	10.8	**1.91**	134	.229	.302	13	.148	-4	**24**	19	-4	1.3
1916	Cin-N	7	10	.412	31	15	7	0	1	150^1	145	5	69	60	12.8	3.89	67	.257	.338	4	.087	-2	-21	-22	-2	-2.8
Total	4	49	48	.505	136	100	65	12	3	855^2	775	13	340	469	11.8	3.01	94	.247	.322	32	.114	-17	-20	-18	-5	-4.1
● WALTER MOSER	Moser, Walter Fredrick b: 2/27/1881, Concord, N.C. d: 12/10/46, Philadelphia, Pa. BR/TR, 5'9", 170 lbs. Deb: 9/3/06																									
1906	Phi-N	0	4	.000	6	4	4	0	0	42^2	49	0	15	17	13.7	3.59	73	.295	.357	0	.000	-2	-5	-5	-1	-0.7
1911	Bos-A	0	1	.000	6	3	1	0	0	24^2	37	0	11	11	17.9	4.01	82	.366	.434	0	.000	-1	-2	-2	0	-0.2
	StL-A	0	2	.000	2	2	0	0	0	3^1	11	0	4	2	40.5	21.60	16	.478	.556	1	1.000	0	-7	-7	0	-2.1
	Yr	0	3	.000	8	5	1	0	0	28	48	0	15	13	20.3	6.11	54	.384	.450	1	.125	-1	-9	-9	0	-2.3
Total	2	0	7	.000	14	9	5	0	0	70^2	97	0	30	30	16.4	4.58	63	.334	.401	1	.045	-2	-13	-13	-1	-3.0
● JOHN MOSES	Moses, John William b: 8/9/57, Los Angeles, Cal. BB/TL, 5'10", 170 lbs. Deb: 8/23/82 ◆																									
1989	Min-A	0	0	—	1	0	0	0	0	1	0	0	1	0	9.0	0.00	—	.000	.333	68	.281	0	0	0	0	0.0
1990	Min-A	0	0	—	2	0	0	0	0	2	5	0	2	0	31.5	13.50	31	.455	.538	38	.221	0	-2	-2	-0	0.0
Total	2	0	0	—	3	0	0	0	0	3	5	0	3	0	24.0	9.00	46	.385	.500	438	.254	0	-2	-2	-0	0.0
● PAUL MOSKAU	Moskau, Paul Richard b: 12/20/53, St.Joseph, Mo. BR/TR, 6'2", 210 lbs. Deb: 6/21/77																									
1977	Cin-N	6	6	.500	20	19	2	2	0	108	116	10	40	71	13.1	4.00	98	.278	.342	7	.184	2	-1	-1	1	0.1
1978	Cin-N	6	4	.600	26	25	2	1	1	145	139	17	57	88	12.4	3.97	89	.255	.329	10	.204	4	-6	-7	-2	-0.3
1979	Cin-N	5	4	.556	21	15	1	0	0	106^1	107	9	51	58	13.4	3.89	96	.263	.345	3	.081	-2	-2	-2	1	-0.3
1980	Cin-N	9	7	.563	33	19	2	1	2	152^2	147	13	41	94	11.1	4.01	89	.257	.308	7	.159	-0	-7	-7	0	-0.8
1981	Cin-N	2	1	.667	27	1	0	0	2	54^2	54	4	32	32	14.3	4.94	72	.258	.360	0	.000	-0	-9	-8	1	-0.5
1982	Pit-N	1	3	.250	13	5	0	0	0	35	43	7	8	15	13.1	4.37	85	.303	.340	1	.091	-1	-3	-3	-0	-0.4
1983	Chi-N	3	2	.600	8	8	0	0	0	32	44	7	14	16	16.3	6.75	56	.331	.395	2	.182	0	-11	-11	-0	-1.4
Total	7	32	27	.542	148	92	7	4	5	633^2	650	67	243	374	12.8	4.22	87	.268	.336	30	.153	2	-39	-39	-0	-3.6
● JIM MOSOLF	Mosolf, James Frederick b: 8/21/05, Puyallup, Wash. d: 12/28/79, Dallas, Ore. BL/TR, 5'10", 186 lbs. Deb: 9/9/29 ◆																									
1930	Pit-N	0	0	—	1	0	0	0	0	0^1	1	0	0	1	27.0	27.00	18	.500	.500	17	.333	0	-1	-1	0	0.0
● MAL MOSS	Moss, Charles Malcolm b: 4/18/05, Sullivan, Ind. d: 2/5/83, Savannah, Ga. BR/TL, 6', 175 lbs. Deb: 4/29/30																									
1930	Chi-N	0	0	—	12	1	0	0	1	18^2	18	0	14	4	15.4	6.27	78	.254	.376	3	.273	0	-3	-3	0	0.0
● RAY MOSS	Moss, Raymond Earl b: 12/5/01, Chattanooga, Tenn. d: 8/9/98, Chattanooga, Tenn. BR/TR, 6'1", 185 lbs. Deb: 4/17/26																									
1926	Bro-N	0	0	—	1	0	0	0	0	1	3	0	0	0	27.0	9.00	42	.600	.600	0	.000	-0	-1	-1	-0	0.0
1927	Bro-N	1	0	1.000	1	1	0	0	0	8^1	11	0	1	1	13.0	3.24	122	.333	.353	1	.333	1	1	1	-0	0.1
1928	Bro-N	0	3	.000	22	5	1	1	1	60^1	62	5	35	5	14.5	4.92	81	.279	.377	8	.320	2	-6	-6	-0	-0.1
1929	Bro-N	11	6	.647	39	20	7	2	0	182	214	9	81	59	14.9	5.04	92	.296	.373	5	.076	-5	-7	-9	-2	-1.3
1930	Bro-N	9	6	.600	36	11	5	0	1	118^1	127	13	55	30	14.1	5.10	96	.270	.352	6	.154	-2	-2	-2	-2	-0.6
1931	Bro-N	0	0	—	1	0	0	0	0	1	1	0	1	0	18.0	0.00	—	.333	.500	0	—	0	0	0	0	0.0
	Bos-N	1	3	.250	12	5	0	0	0	45	56	2	16	14	14.4	4.60	82	.306	.362	2	.133	-1	-4	-4	-0	-0.4
	Yr	1	3	.250	13	5	0	0	0	46	57	2	17	14	14.5	4.50	84	.306	.365	2	.133	-1	-3	-4	0	-0.4
Total	6	22	18	.550	112	42	13	3	2	416	474	29	189	109	14.6	4.95	91	.289	.367	22	.148	-5	-18	-21	-4	-2.3
● DON MOSSI	Mossi, Donald Louis "The Sphinx" b: 1/11/29, St.Helena, Cal. BL/TL, 6'1", 195 lbs. Deb: 4/17/54																									
1954	*Cle-A	6	1	.857	40	5	2	0	7	93	56	5	39	55	9.3	1.94	190	.176	.268	3	.158	0	**18**	**18**	-1	1.5
1955	Cle-A	4	3	.571	57	1	0	0	9	81^2	81	4	18	69	11.0	2.42	164	.253	.295	1	.111	0	14	14	2	1.7
1956	Cle-A	6	5	.545	48	3	0	0	11	87^2	79	6	33	59	11.6	3.59	117	.240	.311	3	.150	0	6	6	0	0.8
1957	Cle-A★	11	10	.524	36	22	6	1	2	159	165	16	57	97	12.7	4.13	90	.265	.329	12	.218	2	-6	-7	-1	-0.8
1958	Cle-A	7	8	.467	43	5	0	0	3	101^2	106	6	30	55	12.4	3.90	94	.269	.327	3	.115	-2	-1	-3	0	-0.5
1959	Det-A	17	9	.654	34	30	15	3	0	228	210	20	49	125	10.3	3.36	121	.243	.286	13	.169	0	13	18	0	2.0
1960	Det-A	9	8	.529	23	22	9	2	0	158^1	158	17	32	69	10.9	3.47	114	.258	.296	5	.116	-0	7	9	-1	0.8
1961	Det-A	15	7	.682	35	34	12	1	1	240^1	237	29	47	137	10.6	2.96	139	.258	.294	13	.165	1	28	**30**	0	2.7
1962	Det-A	11	13	.458	35	27	8	1	1	180^1	195	24	36	121	11.6	4.19	97	.270	.305	9	.164	1	-4	-2	-2	-0.3
1963	Det-A	7	7	.500	24	16	3	0	2	122^2	110	20	17	68	9.6	3.74	100	.236	.269	8	.205	2	-2	0	-0	0.2
1964	Chi-A	3	1	.750	34	0	0	0	7	40	37	9	7	36	10.1	2.93	118	.240	.278	1	.167	-0	3	2	-0	0.3
1965	KC-A	5	8	.385	51	0	0	0	7	55^1	59	0	20	41	12.8	3.74	93	.278	.341	0	.000	-1	-2	-2	-0	-0.5
Total	12	101	80	.558	460	165	55	8	50	1548	1493	156	385	932	11.0	3.43	114	.252	.299	71	.163	4	74	83	-2	7.9
● EARL MOSSOR	Mossor, Earl Dalton b: 7/21/25, Forbus, Tenn. d: 12/29/88, Batavia, Ohio BL/TR, 6'1", 175 lbs. Deb: 4/30/51																									
1951	Bro-N	0	0	—	3	0	0	0	0	1^2	2	1	7	1	48.6	32.40	12	.333	.692	1	1.000	0	-5	-5	-0	0.0
● GLEN MOULDER	Moulder, Glen Hubert b: 9/28/17, Cleveland, Okla. d: 11/27/94, Decatur, Ga. BR/TR, 6', 180 lbs. Deb: 4/28/46																									
1946	Bro-N	0	0	—	1	0	0	0	0	2	2	1	1	1	13.5	4.50	75	.286	.375	0	—	0	-0	-0	-0	0.0
1947	StL-A	4	2	.667	32	2	0	0	2	73	78	4	43	23	14.9	3.82	101	.283	.379	4	.235	-0	-1	0	1	0.1
1948	Chi-A	3	6	.333	33	9	0	0	2	85^2	108	8	54	26	17.1	6.41	66	.316	.411	6	.300	2	-20	-20	-0	-1.8
Total	3	7	8	.467	66	11	0	0	4	160^2	188	13	98	50	16.1	5.21	78	.301	.396	10	.270	1	-21	-20	1	-1.7
● FRANK MOUNTAIN	Mountain, Frank Henry b: 5/17/1860, Ft.Edward, N.Y. d: 11/19/39, Schenectady, N.Y. BR/TR, 5'11", 185 lbs. Deb: 7/19/1880 ◆																									
1880	Tro-N	1	1	.500	2	2	2	0	0	17	23	0	6	2	15.4	5.29	48	.307	.358	2	.222	-0	-6	-5	0	-0.5
1881	Det-N	3	4	.429	7	7	7	0	0	60	80	2	18	13	14.7	5.25	56	.292	.336	4	.160	-0	-17	-16	-1	-1.5
1882	Wor-N	0	5	.000	5	5	5	0	0	42	47	0	11	5	12.4	3.00	104	.255	.297	1	.063	-2	-0	1	-1	-0.2
	Phi-a	2	6	.250	8	8	8	0	0	69	72	1	11	15	10.8	3.91	76	.251	.279	12	.333	2	-9	-7	1	-0.3
	Wor-N	2	11	.154	13	13	11	0	0	102	138	4	24	24	14.3	3.97	78	.299	.334	19	.271	2	-12	-10	-1	-0.9
1883	Col-a	26	33	.441	59	59	57	4	0	503	546	8	123	159	12.0	3.60	86	.259	.300	60	.217	7	-16	-29	1	-1.9
1884	Col-a	23	17	.575	42	41	40	5	**1**	360^2	289	7	78	156	9.4	2.45	124	.209	.257	50	.238	9	32	23	4	3.5
1885	Pit-a	1	4	.200	5	5	5	0	0	46	56	1	24	7	16.0	4.30	75	.320	.408	2	.100	-1	-5	-6	0	-0.5
1886	Pit-a	0	2	.000	2	2	2	0	0	16	22	0	14	2	23.1	7.88	43	.319	.466	8	.145	0	-8	-8	0	-0.7
Total	7	58	83	.411	143	142	137	9	1	1215^2	1273	23	309	383	11.8	3.47	88	.254	.299	158	.220	16	-41	-54	4	-3.0
● BILL MOUNTJOY	Mountjoy, William Henry "Medicine Bill" b: 12/11/1858, London, Ontario, Canada d: 5/19/1894, London, Ont., Can. BL/TR, 5'6", 150 lbs. Deb: 9/29/1883																									
1883	Cin-a	0	1	.000	1	1	1	0	0	8	9	0	2	3	12.4	2.25	144	.265	.306	0	.000	-1	1	1	-0	0.0
1884	Cin-a	19	12	.613	33	33	32	3	0	289	274	5	43	96	10.4	2.93	114	.238	.275	18	.151	-3	10	13	-0	0.8
1885	Cin-a	10	7	.588	17	17	17	1	0	153^2	149	5	52	50	12.2	3.16	103	.247	.314	10	.167	0	1	2	-1	0.1

YEAR	TM/L	W	L	PCT	G	GS	CG	SH	SV	IP	H	HR	BB	SO	RAT	ERA	ERA+	OAV	OOB	BH	AVG	PB	PR	/A	PD	TPI
	Bal-a	2	4	.333	6	6	6	1	0	53	72	1	13	15	15.1	5.43	60	.316	.363	1	.056	-0	-13	-13	1	-1.0
	Yr	12	11	.522	23	23	23	2	0	206^2	221	6	65	65	12.6	3.75	87	.264	.320	11	.141	0	-11	-11	-0	-0.9
Total	3	31	24	.564	57	57	56	5	0	503^2	504	11	110	164	11.5	3.25	102	.250	.297	29	.145	-4	-0	3	-1	-0.1

● ED MOYER Moyer, Charles Edward b: 8/15/1885, Andover, Ohio d: 11/18/62, Jacksonville, Fla. Deb: 7/20/10

YEAR	TM/L	W	L	PCT	G	GS	CG	SH	SV	IP	H	HR	BB	SO	RAT	ERA	ERA+	OAV	OOB	BH	AVG	PB	PR	/A	PD	TPI
1910	Was-A	0	3	.000	6	3	2	0	0	25	22	1	13	3	13.7	3.24	77	.253	.369	1	.125	-1	-2	-2	1	-0.2

● JAMIE MOYER Moyer, Jamie b: 11/18/62, Sellersville, Pa. BL/TL, 6', 170 lbs. Deb: 6/16/86

YEAR	TM/L	W	L	PCT	G	GS	CG	SH	SV	IP	H	HR	BB	SO	RAT	ERA	ERA+	OAV	OOB	BH	AVG	PB	PR	/A	PD	TPI
1986	Chi-N	7	4	.636	16	16	1	1	0	87^1	107	10	42	45	15.7	5.05	80	.311	.391	2	.091	-0	-13	-10	1	-1.0
1987	Chi-N	12	15	.444	35	33	1	0	0	201	210	28	97	147	14.0	5.10	84	.271	.355	14	.230	3	-23	-19	2	-1.7
1988	Chi-N	9	15	.375	34	30	3	1	0	202	212	20	55	121	12.1	3.48	104	.272	.324	5	.083	-2	-1	3	3	0.4
1989	Tex-A	4	9	.308	15	15	1	0	0	76	84	10	33	44	14.1	4.86	82	.283	.358	0	—	0	-8	-8	1	-1.1
1990	Tex-A	2	6	.250	33	10	1	0	0	102^1	115	6	39	58	13.9	4.66	84	.290	.360	0	—	0	-9	-8	0	-0.6
1991	StL-N	0	5	.000	8	7	0	0	0	31^1	38	5	16	20	15.8	5.74	65	.319	.404	0	.000	-1	-7	-7	-0	-1.0
1993	Bal-A	12	9	.571	25	25	3	1	0	152	154	11	38	90	11.7	3.43	130	.265	.316	0	—	0	15	18	1	2.0
1994	Bal-A	5	7	.417	23	23	0	0	0	149	158	23	38	87	12.0	4.77	105	.271	.317	0	—	0	0	4	-0	-0.1
1995	Bal-A	8	6	.571	27	18	0	0	0	115^2	117	18	30	65	11.7	5.21	91	.265	.316	0	—	0	-6	-6	1	-0.5
1996	Bos-A	7	1	.875	23	10	0	0	0	90	111	14	27	50	13.9	4.50	113	.300	.349	0	—	0	5	6	0	0.4
	Sea-A	6	2	.750	11	11	0	0	0	70^2	66	9	19	29	11.0	3.31	149	.243	.295	0	—	0	13	13	-1	1.2
	Yr	13	3	.813	34	21	0	0	0	160^2	177	23	46	79	12.5	3.98	126	.274	.323	0	—	0	18	19	-0	1.6
1997	*Sea-A	17	5	.773	30	30	2	0	0	188^2	187	21	43	113	11.3	3.86	116	.256	.304	1	.333	0	15	13	2	1.6
1998	Sea-A	15	9	.625	34	34	4	3	0	234^1	234	23	42	158	11.0	3.53	131	.256	.296	0	.000	-0	29	29	0	2.6
Total	12	104	93	.528	314	262	16	6	0	1700^1	1793	198	519	1027	12.5	4.25	104	.271	.329	22	.141	1	10	29	11	2.2

● RON MROZINSKI Mrozinski, Ronald Frank b: 9/16/30, White Haven, Pa. BR/TL, 5'11", 160 lbs. Deb: 6/20/54

YEAR	TM/L	W	L	PCT	G	GS	CG	SH	SV	IP	H	HR	BB	SO	RAT	ERA	ERA+	OAV	OOB	BH	AVG	PB	PR	/A	PD	TPI
1954	Phi-N	1	1	.500	15	4	1	0	0	48	49	10	25	26	13.9	4.50	90	.261	.347	1	.083	-1	-2	-2	-1	-0.3
1955	Phi-N	0	2	.000	22	1	0	0	1	34^1	38	2	19	18	16.0	6.55	61	.299	.407	0	.000	-1	-10	-10	-0	-0.6
Total	2	1	3	.250	37	5	1	0	1	82^1	87	12	44	44	14.8	5.36	75	.276	.372	1	.063	-2	-12	-12	-1	-0.9

● PHIL MUDROCK Mudrock, Philip Ray b: 6/12/37, Louisville, Colo. BR/TR, 6'1", 190 lbs. Deb: 4/19/63

YEAR	TM/L	W	L	PCT	G	GS	CG	SH	SV	IP	H	HR	BB	SO	RAT	ERA	ERA+	OAV	OOB	BH	AVG	PB	PR	/A	PD	TPI
1963	Chi-N	0	0	—	1	0	0	0	0	1	2	0	0	0	18.0	9.00	39	.400	.400	0	—	0	-1	-1	-0	0.0

● GORDIE MUELLER Mueller, Joseph Gordon b: 12/10/22, Baltimore, Md. BR/TR, 6'4", 200 lbs. Deb: 4/19/50

YEAR	TM/L	W	L	PCT	G	GS	CG	SH	SV	IP	H	HR	BB	SO	RAT	ERA	ERA+	OAV	OOB	BH	AVG	PB	PR	/A	PD	TPI
1950	Bos-A	0	0	—	8	0	0	0	0	7	11	1	13	1	30.9	10.29	48	.344	.533	0	.000	-0	-4	-4	0	0.0

● LES MUELLER Mueller, Leslie Clyde b: 3/4/19, Belleville, Ill. BR/TR, 6'3", 190 lbs. Deb: 8/15/41

YEAR	TM/L	W	L	PCT	G	GS	CG	SH	SV	IP	H	HR	BB	SO	RAT	ERA	ERA+	OAV	OOB	BH	AVG	PB	PR	/A	PD	TPI
1941	Det-A	0	0	—	4	0	0	0	0	13	9	1	10	8	13.2	4.85	94	.205	.352	0	.000	-0	-1	-0	0	0.0
1945	*Det-A	6	8	.429	26	18	6	2	1	134^2	117	8	58	42	11.8	3.68	96	.234	.316	8	.182	0	-5	-2	-2	-0.4
Total	2	6	8	.429	30	18	6	2	1	147^2	126	9	68	50	11.9	3.78	95	.231	.319	8	.170	0	-6	-3	-2	-0.4

● WILLIE MUELLER Mueller, Willard Lawrence b: 8/30/56, West Bend, Wis. BR/TR, 6'4", 220 lbs. Deb: 8/12/78

YEAR	TM/L	W	L	PCT	G	GS	CG	SH	SV	IP	H	HR	BB	SO	RAT	ERA	ERA+	OAV	OOB	BH	AVG	PB	PR	/A	PD	TPI
1978	Mil-A	1	0	1.000	5	0	0	0	0	12^2	16	1	6	6	15.6	6.39	59	.291	.361	0	—	0	-4	-4	0	-0.3
1981	Mil-A	0	0	—	1	0	0	0	0	2	4	0	0	1	18.0	4.50	76	.400	.400	0	—	0	-0	-0	0	0.1
Total	2	1	0	1.000	6	0	0	0	0	14^2	20	1	6	7	16.0	6.14	60	.308	.366	0	—	0	-4	-4	0	-0.2

● BILLY MUFFETT Muffett, Billy Arnold "Muff" b: 9/21/30, Hammond, Ind. BR/TR, 6'1", 198 lbs. Deb: 8/3/57 C

YEAR	TM/L	W	L	PCT	G	GS	CG	SH	SV	IP	H	HR	BB	SO	RAT	ERA	ERA+	OAV	OOB	BH	AVG	PB	PR	/A	PD	TPI
1957	StL-N	3	2	.600	23	0	0	0	8	44	35	1	13	21	9.8	2.25	176	.222	.281	0	.000	-1	8	8	-1	1.1
1958	StL-N	4	6	.400	35	6	1	0	5	84	107	11	42	41	16.5	4.93	84	.316	.399	4	.200	0	-9	-7	-1	-0.9
1959	SF-N	0	0	—	5	0	0	0	0	6^2	11	2	3	3	18.9	5.40	71	.407	.467	0	—	0	-1	-1	-0	0.0
1960	Bos-A	6	4	.600	23	14	4	1	0	125	116	6	36	75	11.3	3.24	125	.242	.301	11	.268	2	9	11	-0	1.1
1961	Bos-A	3	11	.214	38	11	2	0	2	112^2	130	18	36	47	13.4	5.67	73	.291	.346	5	.217	2	-21	-19	-0	-2.0
1962	Bos-A	0	0	—	1	1	0	0	0	4	8	0	2	1	22.5	9.00	46	.471	.526	0	.000	-0	-2	-2	-0	0.0
Total	6	16	23	.410	125	32	7	1	15	376^1	407	38	132	188	13.2	4.33	94	.277	.342	20	.217	3	-16	-10	-2	-0.7

● JOE MUICH Muich, Ignatius Andrew b: 11/23/03, St.Louis, Mo. d: 7/2/93, St.Louis, Mo. BR/TR, 6'2", 175 lbs. Deb: 9/4/24

YEAR	TM/L	W	L	PCT	G	GS	CG	SH	SV	IP	H	HR	BB	SO	RAT	ERA	ERA+	OAV	OOB	BH	AVG	PB	PR	/A	PD	TPI
1924	Bos-N	0	0	—	3	0	0	0	0	9	19	1	5	1	24.0	11.00	35	.432	.490	0	.000	-1	-7	-7	-0	-0.1

● JOE MUIR Muir, Joseph Allen b: 11/26/22, Oriole, Md. d: 6/25/80, Baltimore, Md. BL/TL, 6'1", 172 lbs. Deb: 4/21/51

YEAR	TM/L	W	L	PCT	G	GS	CG	SH	SV	IP	H	HR	BB	SO	RAT	ERA	ERA+	OAV	OOB	BH	AVG	PB	PR	/A	PD	TPI
1951	Pit-N	0	2	.000	9	1	0	0	0	16^1	11	2	7	5	9.9	2.76	153	.180	.265	0	.000	-0	2	3	1	0.4
1952	Pit-N	2	3	.400	12	5	1	0	0	35^2	42	3	18	17	15.1	6.31	63	.288	.366	1	.111	-0	-10	-9	-0	-1.2
Total	2	2	5	.286	21	6	1	0	0	52	53	5	25	22	13.5	5.19	78	.256	.336	1	.100	-0	-8	-7	1	-0.8

● HUGH MULCAHY Mulcahy, Hugh Noyes "Losing Pitcher" b: 9/9/13, Brighton, Mass. BR/TR, 6'2", 190 lbs. Deb: 7/24/35 C

YEAR	TM/L	W	L	PCT	G	GS	CG	SH	SV	IP	H	HR	BB	SO	RAT	ERA	ERA+	OAV	OOB	BH	AVG	PB	PR	/A	PD	TPI
1935	Phi-N	1	5	.167	18	5	0	0	1	52^2	62	2	25	11	15.7	4.78	95	.295	.383	0	.000	-2	-4	-1	1	-0.3
1936	Phi-N	1	1	.500	3	2	2	0	0	22^2	20	0	12	2	13.5	3.18	143	.238	.347	2	.250	0	2	3	0	0.3
1937	Phi-N	8	18	.308	**56**	26	9	1	3	215^2	256	17	97	54	15.0	5.13	84	.296	.372	11	.151	-3	-29	-19	3	-2.0
1938	Phi-N	10	20	.333	46	34	15	0	1	267^1	294	14	120	90	14.1	4.61	84	.278	.354	16	.170	-2	-24	-22	1	-2.3
1939	Phi-N	9	16	.360	38	32	14	1	4	225^2	246	19	93	59	14.0	4.99	80	.282	.359	12	.158	-3	-27	-25	0	-2.7
1940	Phi-N☆	13	22	.371	36	36	21	3	0	280	283	12	91	82	12.1	3.60	108	.261	.320	19	.202	1	8	9	3	1.5
1945	Phi-N	1	3	.250	5	4	1	0	0	28^1	33	1	9	2	13.3	3.81	101	.295	.347	0	.000	-1	-0	0	1	0.0
1946	Phi-N	2	4	.333	16	5	1	0	0	62^2	69	3	33	12	15.4	4.45	77	.295	.393	3	.188	1	-7	-7	1	-0.4
1947	Pit-N	0	0	—	2	1	0	0	0	6^2	8	1	7	2	20.3	4.05	104	.333	.484	1	.333	0	0	0	1	0.1
Total	9	45	89	.336	220	145	63	5	9	1161^2	1271	69	487	314	13.9	4.49	89	.280	.355	64	.165	-9	-82	-61	11	-5.8

● TERRY MULHOLLAND Mulholland, Terence John b: 3/9/63, Uniontown, Pa. BR/TL, 6'3", 206 lbs. Deb: 6/8/86

YEAR	TM/L	W	L	PCT	G	GS	CG	SH	SV	IP	H	HR	BB	SO	RAT	ERA	ERA+	OAV	OOB	BH	AVG	PB	PR	/A	PD	TPI
1986	SF-N	1	7	.125	15	10	0	0	0	54^2	51	3	35	27	14.3	4.94	71	.251	.364	1	.053	-1	-7	-9	-1	-1.3
1988	SF-N	2	1	.667	9	6	2	1	0	46	50	3	7	18	11.3	3.72	88	.281	.312	0	.000	-1	-1	-2	0	-0.2
1989	SF-N	0	0	—	5	1	0	0	0	11	15	0	4	6	15.5	4.09	82	.319	.373	0	.000	-0	-1	-1	0	0.0
	Phi-N	4	7	.364	20	17	2	1	0	104^1	122	8	32	60	13.6	5.00	71	.292	.348	2	.059	-2	-17	-17	1	-1.8
	Yr	4	7	.364	25	18	2	1	0	115^1	137	8	36	66	13.8	4.92	72	.295	.350	2	.056	-2	-18	-18	1	-1.8
1990	Phi-N	9	10	.474	33	26	6	1	0	180^2	172	15	42	75	10.8	3.34	115	.252	.297	6	.097	-2	9	10	-3	0.4
1991	Phi-N	16	13	.552	34	34	8	3	0	232	231	15	49	142	11.0	3.61	102	.260	.301	7	.087	-4	2	1	-2	-0.4
1992	Phi-N	13	11	.542	32	32	**12**	2	0	229	227	14	46	125	10.8	3.81	92	.261	.300	8	.096	-2	-8	-8	1	-1.0
1993	*Phi-N★	12	9	.571	29	28	7	2	0	191	177	20	40	116	10.4	3.25	122	.241	.283	4	.065	-4	17	15	-1	1.0
1994	NY-A	6	7	.462	24	19	2	0	0	120^2	150	24	37	72	14.2	6.49	70	.303	.355	0	—	0	-23	-26	-1	-2.0
1995	SF-N	5	13	.278	29	24	2	0	0	149	190	25	38	65	14.0	5.80	70	.313	.357	5	.102	-0	-27	-28	-1	-3.0
1996	Phi-N	8	7	.533	21	21	3	0	0	133^1	157	17	21	52	12.2	4.66	92	.293	.323	8	.178	1	-7	-5	-2	-0.6
	Sea-A	5	4	.556	12	12	0	0	0	69^1	75	5	28	34	13.6	4.67	106	.286	.360	0	—	0	2	2	-1	0.2
1997	Chi-N	6	12	.333	25	25	1	0	0	157	162	20	45	74	12.4	4.07	106	.271	.331	8	.163	-0	2	4	2	0.6
	SF-N	0	1	.000	15	2	0	0	0	29^2	28	4	6	25	10.9	5.16	80	.248	.298	1	.167	0	-3	-3	0	0.0
	Yr	6	13	.316	40	27	1	0	0	186^2	190	24	51	99	11.7	4.24	101	.263	.313	9	.164	0	-1	1	2	0.6
1998	*Chi-N	6	5	.545	70	6	0	0	3	112	100	7	39	72	11.5	2.89	151	.235	.306	5	.294	2	17	18	-2	1.7
Total	12	93	107	.465	373	263	45	10	3	1819^2	1907	180	469	963	12.0	4.20	94	.270	.320	55	.105	-15	-45	-49	-7	-6.4

● TONY MULLANE Mullane, Anthony John "Count" or "The Apollo Of The Box"
b: 1/20/1859, Cork, Ireland d: 4/25/44, Chicago, Ill. BB/TR, 5'10.5", 165 lbs. Deb: 8/27/1881 ♦

YEAR	TM/L	W	L	PCT	G	GS	CG	SH	SV	IP	H	HR	BB	SO	RAT	ERA	ERA+	OAV	OOB	BH	AVG	PB	PR	/A	PD	TPI
1881	Det-N	1	4	.200	5	5	5	0	0	44	55	2	17	7	14.7	4.91	59	.302	.362	5	.263	-0	-10	-10	0	-0.9
1882	Lou-a	30	24	.556	**55**	55	51	5	0	460^1	418	4	78	**170**	9.7	1.88	132	.226	.257	78	.257	11	41	31	11	5.1
1883	StL-a	35	15	**.700**	53	49	49	3	**1**	460^2	372	3	74	191	8.7	2.19	**159**	.207	.238	69	.225	1	57	66	1	6.2
1884	Tol-a	36	26	.581	67	65	64	**7**	0	567	481	5	89	325	9.6	2.52	135	.214	.255	97	.276	15	46	56	10	7.7
1886	Cin-a	33	27	.550	63	56	55	1	0	529^2	501	11	166	250	11.6	3.70	95	.242	.303	73	.225	2	-15	-11	2	-0.6
1887	Cin-a	31	17	.646	48	48	47	**6**	0	416^1	414	11	121	97	12.3	3.24	134	.257	.322	44	.221	2	49	51	-1	4.5

YEAR	TM/L	W	L	PCT	G	GS	CG	SH	SV	IP	H	HR	BB	SO	RAT	ERA	ERA+	OAV	OOB	BH	AVG	PB	PR	/A	PD	TPI
1888	Cin-a	26	16	.619	44	42	41	4	**1**	380^1	341	9	75	186	10.5	2.84	112	.231	.282	44	.251	5	9	14	-0	1.8
1889	Cin-a	11	9	.550	33	24	17	0	**5**	220	218	4	89	112	13.1	2.99	131	.251	.329	58	.296	9	21	22	-1	2.2
1890	Cin-N	12	10	.545	25	21	21	0	1	209	175	7	96	91	12.0	2.24	159	.220	.311	79	.276	7	31	31	0	3.4
1891	Cin-N	23	26	.469	51	47	42	1	0	426^1	390	15	187	124	12.6	3.23	104	.234	.318	31	.148	-5	6	7	1	0.3
1892	Cin-N	21	13	.618	37	34	30	3	1	295	222	12	127	109	11.0	2.59	126	**.201**	.290	20	.169	-1	23	22	6	2.7
1893	Cin-N	6	6	.500	15	13	11	0	1	122^1	130	4	65	24	15.0	4.41	108	.264	.360	15	.288	3	3	5	0	0.6
	Bal-N	12	16	.429	34	26	23	0	1	244^2	277	4	124	71	15.0	4.45	107	.277	.360	26	.228	-3	6	8	3	0.7
	Yr	18	22	.450	49	39	34	0	**2**	367	407	8	189	95	14.8	4.44	107	.271	.355	41	.247	-0	9	13	3	1.3
1894	Bal-N	6	9	.400	21	15	9	0	4	122^2	155	4	90	43	18.5	6.31	87	.305	.417	21	.396	5	-13	-12	-1	-0.7
	Cle-N	1	2	.333	4	4	3	0	0	33	46	3	10	3	15.3	7.64	72	.326	.371	1	.077	-1	-8	-8	2	-0.4
	Yr	7	11	.389	25	19	12	0	**4**	155^2	201	7	100	46	17.4	6.59	83	.306	.398	22	.333	4	-22	-20	1	-1.1
Total	13	284	220	.563	555	504	468	30	15	4531^1	4195	98	1408	1803	11.5	3.05	118	.236	.298	661	.243	50	245	270	33	32.6

● JOE MULLIGAN

Mulligan, Joseph Ignatius "Big Joe" b: 7/31/13, Weymouth, Mass. d: 6/5/86, W.Roxbury, Mass. BR/TR, 6'4", 210 lbs. Deb: 6/28/34

YEAR	TM/L	W	L	PCT	G	GS	CG	SH	SV	IP	H	HR	BB	SO	RAT	ERA	ERA+	OAV	OOB	BH	AVG	PB	PR	/A	PD	TPI
1934	Bos-A	1	0	1.000	14	2	1	0	0	44^2	46	1	27	13	15.1	3.63	132	.279	.387	0	.000	-1	4	6	0	0.0

● DICK MULLIGAN

Mulligan, Richard Charles b: 3/18/18, Swoyersville, Pa. d: 12/15/92, Victoria, Tex. BL/TL, 6', 167 lbs. Deb: 9/24/41

YEAR	TM/L	W	L	PCT	G	GS	CG	SH	SV	IP	H	HR	BB	SO	RAT	ERA	ERA+	OAV	OOB	BH	AVG	PB	PR	/A	PD	TPI
1941	Was-A	0	1	.000	1	1	1	0	0	9	11	0	2	2	13.0	5.00	81	.306	.342	0	.000	-0	-1	-1	0	-0.1
1946	Phi-N	2	2	.500	19	5	1	0	1	54^2	61	0	27	16	15.1	4.77	72	.289	.380	0	.000	-1	-8	-8	0	-0.7
	Bos-N	1	0	1.000	4	0	0	0	0	15^1	6	1	9	4	8.8	2.35	146	.122	.259	0	.000	0	2	2	-0	0.1
	Yr	3	2	.600	23	5	1	0	1	70	67	1	36	20	13.2	4.24	81	.254	.343	0	.000	-1	-6	-6	-0	-0.6
1947	Bos-N	0	0	—	1	0	0	0	0	2	4	0	1	1	22.5	9.00	43	.400	.455	0	—	0	-1	-1	-0	0.0
Total	3	3	3	.500	25	6	2	0	1	81	82	1	39	23	13.9	4.44	79	.268	.358	0	.000	-1	-8	-8	-0	-0.7

● GEORGE MULLIN

Mullin, George Joseph "Wabash George" b: 7/4/1880, Toledo, Ohio d: 1/7/44, Wabash, Ind. BR/TR, 5'11", 188 lbs. Deb: 5/4/02 ♦

YEAR	TM/L	W	L	PCT	G	GS	CG	SH	SV	IP	H	HR	BB	SO	RAT	ERA	ERA+	OAV	OOB	BH	AVG	PB	PR	/A	PD	TPI
1902	Det-A	13	16	.448	35	30	25	0	0	260	282	4	95	78	13.3	3.67	99	.277	.343	39	.325	9	-3	-1	2	1.1
1903	Det-A	19	15	.559	41	36	31	6	**2**	320^2	284	4	106	170	11.2	2.25	130	.237	.303	35	.278	8	26	24	5	4.1
1904	Det-A	17	23	.425	45	44	42	7	0	382^1	345	1	131	161	11.4	2.40	106	.242	.310	45	.290	11	8	6	8	3.2
1905	Det-A	21	21	.500	44	41	**35**	1	0	**347^2**	303	4	138	168	11.6	2.51	109	.236	.314	35	.259	6	6	9	7	2.6
1906	Det-A	21	18	.538	40	40	35	2	0	330	315	3	108	123	11.9	2.78	99	.254	.322	32	.225	3	-3	-1	3	0.7
1907	*Det-A	20	20	.500	46	42	35	5	3	357^1	346	1	106	146	11.8	2.59	100	.256	.318	34	.217	3	-2	0	4	1.0
1908	*Det-A	17	13	.567	39	30	26	1	0	290^2	301	1	71	121	11.7	3.10	78	.271	.319	32	.256	8	-23	-22	3	-1.1
1909	*Det-A	**29**	8	**.784**	40	35	29	3	1	303^2	258	1	78	124	10.2	2.22	113	.234	.289	27	.214	5	9	10	1	2.0
1910	Det-A	21	12	.636	38	32	27	5	0	289	260	7	102	98	11.7	2.87	92	.254	.330	33	.256	6	-11	-8	1	-0.1
1911	Det-A	18	10	.643	30	29	25	2	0	234^1	245	7	61	87	12.2	3.07	113	.276	.331	28	.286	8	7	10	-2	1.6
1912	Det-A	12	17	.414	30	29	22	2	0	226	214	3	92	88	12.5	3.54	92	.255	.335	25	.278	9	-6	-7	0	0.2
1913	Det-A	1	6	.143	7	7	4	0	0	52^1	53	1	18	16	12.6	2.75	106	.268	.335	7	.350	3	1	1	1	0.5
	Was-A	3	5	.375	11	9	3	0	0	57^1	69	1	25	14	15.5	5.02	59	.283	.361	4	.190	0	-13	-13	1	-1.5
	Yr	4	11	.267	18	16	7	0	0	109^2	122	2	43	30	14.0	3.94	75	.275	.346	11	.268	3	-12	-12	1	-1.0
1914	Ind-F	14	10	.583	36	20	11	1	2	203	202	4	91	74	13.4	2.70	115	.261	.346	24	.312	8	4	9	-4	1.5
1915	New-F	2	2	.500	5	4	3	0	0	32^1	41	0	16	14	15.9	5.85	44	.318	.393	1	.100	-0	-11	-12	-1	-1.3
Total	14	228	196	.538	487	428	353	35	8	3686^2	3518	42	1238	1482	11.9	2.82	101	.255	.322	401	.262	87	-12	7	28	14.5

● GREG MULLINS

Mullins, Gregory E. b: 12/13/71, Palatka, Fla. BL/TL, 5'10", 160 lbs. Deb: 9/18/98

YEAR	TM/L	W	L	PCT	G	GS	CG	SH	SV	IP	H	HR	BB	SO	RAT	ERA	ERA+	OAV	OOB	BH	AVG	PB	PR	/A	PD	TPI
1998	Mil-N	0	0	—	2	0	0	0	0	1	1	0	0	1	18.0	0.00	—	.250	.400	0	—	0	0	0	0	0.0

● DOMINIC MULRENAN

Mulrenan, Dominic Joseph b: 12/18/1893, Woburn, Mass. d: 7/27/64, Melrose, Mass. BR/TR, 5'11", 170 lbs. Deb: 4/24/21

YEAR	TM/L	W	L	PCT	G	GS	CG	SH	SV	IP	H	HR	BB	SO	RAT	ERA	ERA+	OAV	OOB	BH	AVG	PB	PR	/A	PD	TPI
1921	Chi-A	2	8	.200	12	10	3	0	0	56	84	2	36	10	19.6	7.23	59	.359	.449	3	.150	-1	-18	-19	0	-2.6

● FRANK MULRONEY

Mulroney, Francis Joseph b: 4/8/03, Mallard, Iowa d: 11/11/85, Aberdeen, Wash. BR/TR, 6', 170 lbs. Deb: 4/15/30

YEAR	TM/L	W	L	PCT	G	GS	CG	SH	SV	IP	H	HR	BB	SO	RAT	ERA	ERA+	OAV	OOB	BH	AVG	PB	PR	/A	PD	TPI
1930	Bos-A	0	1	.000	2	0	0	0	0	3	3	0	0	2	9.0	3.00	154	.273	.273	0	—	0	1	1	0	0.2

● BOB MUNCRIEF

Muncrief, Robert Cleveland b: 1/28/16, Madill, Okla. d: 2/6/96, Duncanville, Tex. BR/TR, 6'2", 190 lbs. Deb: 9/30/37

YEAR	TM/L	W	L	PCT	G	GS	CG	SH	SV	IP	H	HR	BB	SO	RAT	ERA	ERA+	OAV	OOB	BH	AVG	PB	PR	/A	PD	TPI
1937	StL-A	0	0	—	1	1	0	0	0	2	3	1	2	0	22.5	4.50	107	.300	.417	0	—	0	0	0	-0	0.0
1939	StL-A	0	0	—	2	0	0	0	0	3	7	1	3	1	30.0	15.00	32	.500	.588	0	—	0	-3	-3	-0	0.0
1941	StL-A	13	9	.591	36	24	12	2	1	214^1	221	18	53	67	11.7	3.65	118	.266	.314	18	.237	2	12	15	-1	1.5
1942	StL-A	6	8	.429	24	18	7	1	0	134^1	149	11	31	39	12.1	3.89	95	.280	.319	5	.111	-1	-3	-3	-0	-0.4
1943	StL-A	13	12	.520	35	27	12	3	1	205	211	13	48	80	11.5	2.81	118	.264	.307	10	.152	-2	11	12	-3	0.9
1944	*StL-A★	13	8	.619	33	27	12	3	1	219^1	216	11	50	88	11.0	3.08	117	.258	.302	18	.231	1	9	13	-1	1.3
1945	StL-A	13	4	.765	27	15	10	0	1	145^2	132	8	44	54	11.0	2.72	130	.239	.297	3	.067	-4	10	13	-1	0.9
1946	StL-A	3	12	.200	29	14	4	1	0	115^1	149	6	31	49	14.0	4.99	75	.314	.356	1	.031	-3	-19	-16	-1	-2.4
1947	StL-A	8	14	.364	31	23	7	0	0	176^1	210	14	51	74	13.4	4.90	79	.299	.348	6	.105	-3	-23	-20	0	-2.5
1948	*Cle-A	5	4	.556	21	9	1	1	0	72^1	76	8	31	24	13.3	3.98	102	.279	.353	2	.111	-1	2	1	-0	-0.1
1949	Pit-N	1	5	.167	13	4	1	0	3	35^2	44	8	13	11	14.4	6.31	67	.310	.368	1	.143	-0	-9	-8	1	-1.3
	Chi-N	5	6	.455	34	3	1	0	2	75	80	9	31	36	13.4	4.56	88	.276	.348	4	.286	1	-4	-4	-0	-0.5
	Yr	6	11	.353	47	7	2	0	5	110^2	124	17	44	47	13.7	5.12	80	.287	.354	5	.238	1	-13	-13	1	-1.8
1951	NY-A	0	0	—	2	0	0	0	0	3	5	0	4	2	27.0	9.00	43	.417	.563	0	—	0	-2	-2	0	0.0
Total	12	80	82	.494	288	165	67	11	9	1401^1	1503	108	392	525	12.3	3.80	100	.275	.325	68	.155	-10	-20	-3	-7	-2.6

● RED MUNGER

Munger, George David b: 10/4/18, Houston, Tex. d: 7/23/96, Houston, Tex. BR/TR, 6'2", 200 lbs. Deb: 5/1/43

YEAR	TM/L	W	L	PCT	G	GS	CG	SH	SV	IP	H	HR	BB	SO	RAT	ERA	ERA+	OAV	OOB	BH	AVG	PB	PR	/A	PD	TPI
1943	StL-N	9	5	.643	32	9	5	0	2	93^1	101	2	42	45	13.8	3.95	85	.281	.357	6	.214	1	-6	-6	1	-0.7
1944	StL-N†	11	3	.786	21	12	7	2	2	121	92	2	41	55	10.0	1.34	263	.212	.284	5	.114	-3	31	29	3	3.6
1946	*StL-N	2	2	.500	10	7	2	0	1	48^2	47	0	12	28	10.9	3.33	104	.255	.301	4	.250	1	0	1	2	0.3
1947	StL-N☆	16	5	.762	40	31	13	6	3	224^1	218	12	76	123	11.9	3.37	123	.255	.318	15	.185	1	17	19	3	2.0
1948	StL-N	10	11	.476	39	25	7	2	0	166	179	13	74	72	13.8	4.50	91	.272	.347	8	.160	0	-10	-8	2	-0.7
1949	StL-N★	15	8	.652	35	28	12	2	2	188^1	179	13	87	82	12.8	3.87	108	.255	.339	17	.258	4	4	6	1	1.1
1950	StL-N	7	8	.467	32	20	5	1	0	154^2	158	15	70	61	13.4	3.90	110	.262	.342	7	.137	-2	4	7	0	0.4
1951	StL-N	4	6	.400	23	11	3	0	0	94^2	106	13	46	44	14.5	5.32	74	.286	.365	5	.172	-0	-14	-14	2	-1.2
1952	StL-N	0	1	.000	1	1	0	0	0	4^1	7	2	1	1	18.7	12.46	30	.389	.450	0	.000	-0	-4	-4	0	-0.6
	Pit-N	0	3	.000	5	4	0	0	0	26^1	30	6	10	8	13.7	7.18	56	.283	.345	0	.000	-1	-10	-9	1	-0.9
	Yr	0	4	.000	6	5	0	0	0	30^2	37	8	11	9	14.1	7.92	50	.296	.353	0	.000	-1	-14	-14	1	-1.5
1956	Pit-N	3	4	.429	35	13	0	0	2	107	126	8	41	45	14.0	4.04	93	.299	.361	3	.107	-0	-3	-3	-1	-0.3
Total	10	77	56	.579	273	161	54	13	12	1228^2	1243	86	500	564	12.8	3.83	103	.264	.336	70	.174	0	8	17	13	3.0

● VAN MUNGO

Mungo, Van Lingle b: 6/8/11, Pageland, S.C. d: 2/12/85, Pageland, S.C. BR/TR, 6'2", 185 lbs. Deb: 9/7/31 C

YEAR	TM/L	W	L	PCT	G	GS	CG	SH	SV	IP	H	HR	BB	SO	RAT	ERA	ERA+	OAV	OOB	BH	AVG	PB	PR	/A	PD	TPI
1931	Bro-N	3	1	.750	5	4	2	1	0	31	27	0	13	12	11.9	2.32	164	.241	.325	3	.250	1	5	5	-1	0.7
1932	Bro-N	13	11	.542	39	33	11	1	2	223^1	224	9	115	107	13.9	4.43	86	.260	.351	16	.203	0	-14	-15	2	-1.3
1933	Bro-N	16	15	.516	41	28	18	3	0	248	223	7	84	110	11.1	2.72	118	.236	.298	15	.179	-0	17	14	1	1.8
1934	Bro-N★	18	16	.529	45	38	22	3	3	**315^1**	300	15	104	184	11.6	3.37	116	.249	.310	30	.248	4	24	19	2	2.5
1935	Bro-N	16	10	.615	37	26	18	**4**	2	214^1	205	13	90	143	12.5	3.65	109	.252	.328	26	.289	5	9	8	1	1.4
1936	Bro-N☆	18	19	.486	45	37	22	2	3	311^2	275	8	118	**238**	11.4	3.35	123	**.234**	.305	22	.179	-4	23	27	2	2.8
1937	Bro-N★	9	11	.450	25	21	14	0	3	161	136	3	56	122	10.9	2.91	139	**.229**	.298	16	.250	2	18	20	3	3.0
1938	Bro-N	4	11	.267	24	18	6	2	0	133^1	133	11	72	72	14.0	3.92	100	.259	.353	9	.191	1	-2	-0	1	0.2
1939	Bro-N	4	5	.444	14	10	1	0	0	77^1	70	7	33	34	12.3	3.26	124	.239	.322	10	.345	2	6	7	-1	1.0
1940	Bro-N	1	0	1.000	7	0	0	0	1	22	24	1	10	9	13.9	2.45	163	.282	.358	0	.000	-1	3	4	-0	0.1
1941	Bro-N	0	0	—	2	0	0	0	0	2	1	0	2	0	13.5	4.50	81	.143	.333	0	—	0	-0	-0	0	0.0
1942	NY-N	1	2	.333	9	5	0	0	0	36^1	38	4	21	27	14.6	5.94	57	.273	.369	3	.214	-0	-11	-10	0	-0.8
1943	NY-N	3	7	.300	45	13	2	2	2	154^1	140	7	79	83	13.1	3.91	88	.243	.341	7	.159	-1	-9	-8	1	-0.5
1945	NY-N†	14	7	.667	26	26	7	2	0	183	161	4	71	101	11.6	3.20	122	.238	.314	17	.233	4	12	15	-0	1.9
Total	14	120	115	.511	364	259	123	20	16	2113	1957	89	868	1242	12.2	3.47	110	.245	.321	174	.221	13	83	83	11	12.8

YEAR	TM/L	W	L	PCT	G	GS	CG	SH	SV	IP	H	HR	BB	SO	RAT	ERA	ERA+	OAV	OOB	BH	AVG	PB	PR	/A	PD	TPI
● MANNY MUNIZ Muniz, Manuel (Rodriguez) b: 12/31/47, Caguas, P.R. BR/TR, 5'11", 190 lbs. Deb: 9/3/71																										
1971	Phi-N	0	1	.000	5	0	0	0	0	10^1	9	2	8	6	14.8	6.97	51	.225	.354	0	.000	-0	-4	-4	-0	-0.4
● SCOTT MUNNINGHOFF Munninghoff, Scott Andrew b: 12/5/58, Cincinnati, Ohio BR/TR, 6', 175 lbs. Deb: 4/13/80																										
1980	Phi-N	0	0	—	4	0	0	0	0	6	8	0	5	2	19.5	4.50	84	.320	.433	1	1.000	1	-1	-0	0	0.1
● LES MUNNS Munns, Leslie Ernest "Big Ed" or "Nemo" b: 12/1/08, Fort Bragg, Cal. d: 2/28/97, Cedar Rapids, Ia. BR/TR, 6'5", 212 lbs. Deb: 4/22/34																										
1934	Bro-N	3	7	.300	33	9	4	0	0	99^1	106	7	60	41	15.0	4.71	83	.280	.378	7	.241	2	-7	-9	2	-0.4
1935	Bro-N	1	3	.250	21	5	0	0	1	58^1	74	5	33	13	17.1	5.55	72	.319	.413	3	.188	-0	-10	-10	-2	-0.8
1936	StL-N	0	3	.000	7	1	0	0	1	24	23	2	12	4	13.1	3.00	131	.240	.324	1	.111	-1	3	3	1	0.3
Total	3	4	13	.235	61	15	4	0	2	181^2	203	14	105	58	15.5	4.76	83	.287	.382	11	.204	1	-14	-17	1	-0.9
● OSCAR MUNOZ Munoz, Juan Oscar b: 9/25/69, Hialeah, Fla. BR/TR, 6'3", 222 lbs. Deb: 8/6/95																										
1995	Min-A	2	1	.667	10	3	0	0	0	35^1	40	6	17	25	14.8	5.60	85	.276	.356	0	—	0	-3	-3	-0	-0.3
● MIKE MUNOZ Munoz, Michael Anthony b: 7/12/65, Baldwin Park, Cal. BL/TL, 6'2", 200 lbs. Deb: 9/6/89																										
1989	LA-N	0	0	—	3	0	0	0	0	2^2	5	1	2	3	23.6	16.88	20	.417	.500	0	—	0	-4	-4	0	0.0
1990	LA-N	0	1	.000	8	0	0	0	0	5^2	6	0	3	2	14.3	3.18	115	.300	.391	0	.000	-0	0	0	-0	0.0
1991	Det-A	0	0	—	6	0	0	0	0	9^1	14	0	5	3	18.3	9.64	43	.350	.422	0	—	0	-6	-6	0	0.0
1992	Det-A	1	2	.333	65	0	0	0	2	48	44	3	25	23	12.9	3.00	132	.246	.338	0	—	0	5	5	2	0.5
1993	Det-A	0	1	.000	8	0	0	0	0	3	4	1	6	1	30.0	6.00	71	.308	.526	0	—	0	-1	-1	0	-0.1
	Col-N	2	1	.667	21	0	0	0	0	18	21	1	9	16	15.0	4.50	106	.309	.390	0	—	0	-1	1	0	0.1
1994	Col-N	4	2	.667	57	0	0	0	1	45^2	37	3	31	32	13.4	3.74	133	.223	.345	0	—	0	2	6	2	0.9
1995	*Col-N	2	4	.333	64	0	0	0	2	43^2	54	9	27	37	16.9	7.42	73	.307	.402	1	.500	1	-16	-10	1	-1.1
1996	Col-N	2	2	.500	54	0	0	0	0	44^2	55	4	16	45	14.5	6.65	78	.302	.362	0	.000	-0	-12	-7	1	-0.4
1997	Col-N	3	3	.500	64	0	0	0	2	45^2	52	4	13	26	12.8	4.53	114	.294	.342	0	.000	0	-2	3	-0	0.4
1998	Col-N	2	2	.500	40	0	0	0	3	41^1	53	2	16	24	15.2	5.66	89	.312	.374	0	.000	-0	-7	-3	0	-0.3
Total	10	16	18	.471	390	0	0	0	10	307^2	345	28	153	212	14.7	5.29	92	.287	.369	1	.143	1	-39	-15	6	-0.0
● BOBBY MUNOZ Munoz, Roberto (Sbert) b: 3/3/68, Rio Piedras, P.R. BR/TR, 6'7", 252 lbs. Deb: 5/29/93																										
1993	NY-A	3	3	.500	38	0	0	0	0	45^2	48	1	26	33	14.6	5.32	78	.270	.363	0	—	0	-5	-6	-0	-0.5
1994	Phi-N	7	5	.583	21	14	1	0	1	104^1	101	8	35	59	11.8	2.67	160	.252	.314	7	.206	1	18	19	1	2.3
1995	Phi-N	0	2	.000	3	3	0	0	0	15^2	15	2	9	6	15.5	5.74	74	.268	.397	0	.000	-1	-3	-3	-0	-0.3
1996	Phi-N	0	3	.000	6	6	0	0	0	25^1	42	5	7	8	17.8	7.82	55	.375	.417	1	.143	0	-10	-10	-0	-1.0
1997	Phi-N	1	5	.167	8	7	0	0	0	33^1	47	4	15	20	17.3	8.91	48	.338	.410	3	.300	1	-17	-17	0	-2.3
1998	Bal-A	0	0	—	9	1	0	0	0	12	18	4	6	6	18.8	9.75	46	.383	.463	0	—	0	-7	-7	0	0.0
Total	6	11	18	.379	85	31	1	0	1	236^1	271	24	98	132	14.4	5.18	82	.290	.363	11	.196	2	-24	-24	0	-1.8
● STEVE MURA Mura, Stephen Andrew b: 2/12/55, New Orleans, La. BR/TR, 6'2", 190 lbs. Deb: 9/5/78																										
1978	SD-N	0	2	.000	5	2	0	0	0	7^2	15	1	5	5	23.5	11.74	28	.441	.513	0	.000	-0	-7	-7	-0	-1.5
1979	SD-N	4	4	.500	38	5	0	0	2	73	57	6	37	59	11.7	3.08	114	.217	.316	0	.000	-1	5	4	-0	0.2
1980	SD-N	8	7	.533	37	23	3	1	2	168^2	149	9	86	109	12.7	3.68	93	.246	.343	7	.137	-0	-2	-5	0	-0.4
1981	SD-N	5	14	.263	23	22	2	0	0	138^2	156	10	50	70	13.4	4.28	76	.285	.344	6	.136	-0	-12	-16	1	-1.9
1982	StL-N	12	11	.522	35	30	7	1	0	184^1	196	16	80	84	13.5	4.05	89	.278	.352	3	.057	-4	-9	-9	-1	-1.5
1983	Chi-A	0	0	—	6	0	0	0	0	12^1	13	1	6	4	13.9	4.38	96	.260	.339	0	—	0	-0	-0	-0	-0.2
1985	Oak-A	1	1	.500	23	1	0	0	1	48	41	3	25	29	12.4	4.13	93	.225	.319	0	—	0	0	-1	-0	0.3
Total	7	30	39	.435	167	83	12	2	5	632^2	627	46	289	360	13.1	4.00	88	.263	.343	16	.101	-5	-25	-35	-1	-5.0
● MASANORI MURAKAMI Murakami, Masanori b: 5/6/44, Otsuki, Japan BL/TL, 6', 180 lbs. Deb: 9/1/64																										
1964	SF-N	1	0	1.000	9	0	0	0	1	15	8	1	1	15	5.4	1.80	198	.163	.180	0	.000	-0	3	3	-1	0.1
1965	SF-N	4	1	.800	45	1	0	0	8	74^1	57	9	22	85	9.9	3.75	96	.205	.271	2	.154	-0	-2	-1	-2	-0.3
Total	2	5	1	.833	54	1	0	0	9	89^1	65	10	23	100	9.2	3.43	105	.199	.258	2	.125	-1	1	2	-2	-0.2
● TIM MURCHISON Murchison, Thomas Malcolm b: 10/8/1896, Liberty, N.C. d: 10/20/62, Liberty, N.C. BR/TL, 6', 185 lbs. Deb: 6/21/17																										
1917	StL-N	0	0	—	1	0	0	0	0	1	0	0	2	2	18.0	0.00	—	.000	.400	0	—	0	0	0	0	0.0
1920	Cle-A	0	0	—	2	0	0	0	0	5	3	0	4	0	12.6	0.00	—	.200	.368	0	.000	-0	2	2	1	0.0
Total	2	0	0	—	3	0	0	0	0	6	3	0	6	2	13.5	0.00	—	.167	.375	0	.000	-0	2	2	1	0.0
● RED MURFF Murff, John Robert b: 4/1/21, Burlington, Tex. BR/TR, 6'3", 195 lbs. Deb: 4/21/56																										
1956	Mil-N	0	0	—	14	1	0	0	1	24^1	25	3	7	18	11.8	4.44	78	.272	.323	1	.200	0	-2	-3	0	0.0
1957	Mil-N	2	2	.500	12	1	0	0	2	26	31	3	11	13	14.5	4.85	72	.301	.368	0	.000	-1	-3	-4	0	-0.6
Total	2	2	2	.500	26	2	0	0	3	50^1	56	6	18	31	13.2	4.65	75	.287	.347	1	.091	-1	-5	-7	1	-0.6
● CON MURPHY Murphy, Cornelius B. "Monk" or "Razzle Dazzle" b: 10/15/1863, Worcester, Mass. d: 8/1/14, Worcester, Mass. TR , 5'9", 130 lbs. Deb: 9/11/1884																										
1884	Phi-N	0	3	.000	3	3	3	0	0	26	37	1	6	10	14.9	6.58	45	.319	.352	0	.000	-1	-10	-10	0	-0.9
1890	Bro-P	4	10	.286	20	14	11	0	2	139	168	2	82	29	16.6	4.79	93	.286	.379	15	.217	-1	-9	-5	-1	-0.5
Total	2	4	13	.235	23	17	14	0	2	165	205	3	88	39	16.3	5.07	83	.292	.375	15	.190	-3	-19	-16	-0	-1.4
● DANNY MURPHY Murphy, Daniel Francis b: 8/23/42, Beverly, Mass. BL/TR, 5'11", 185 lbs. Deb: 6/18/60 ♦																										
1969	Chi-A	2	1	.667	17	0	0	0	4	31^1	28	2	10	16	11.5	2.01	192	.252	.325	0	.000	0	6	6	-0	0.8
1970	Chi-A	2	3	.400	51	0	0	0	5	80^2	82	11	49	42	15.1	5.69	68	.273	.382	2	.333	2	-18	-16	-1	-1.0
Total	2	4	4	.500	68	0	0	0	9	112	110	13	59	58	14.1	4.66	83	.268	.368	23	.177	2	-12	-10	-1	-0.2
● DAN MURPHY Murphy, Daniel Lee b: 9/18/64, Artesia, Cal. BR/TR, 6'2", 195 lbs. Deb: 8/10/89																										
1989	SD-N	0	0	—	7	0	0	0	0	6^1	6	1	4	1	14.2	5.68	61	.231	.333	0	—	0	-2	-2	-0	0.0
● ED MURPHY Murphy, Edward J. b: 1/22/1877, Auburn, N.Y. d: 1/29/35, Weedsport, N.Y. TR , 6'1", 186 lbs. Deb: 4/23/1898																										
1898	Phi-N	1	2	.333	7	3	2	0	0	30	41	3	10	8	15.6	5.10	67	.323	.377	5	.357	1	-5	-6	1	-0.3
1901	StL-N	10	9	.526	23	21	16	0	0	165	201	5	32	42	12.8	4.20	76	.298	.331	16	.250	3	-16	-19	2	-1.4
1902	StL-N	10	6	.625	23	17	12	1	1	164	187	7	31	37	12.1	3.02	91	.286	.321	16	.262	1	-4	-5	2	-0.2
1903	StL-N	4	8	.333	15	12	9	0	0	106	108	2	38	16	12.9	3.31	99	.262	.333	13	.203	-1	-0	-1	0	-0.1
Total	4	25	25	.500	68	53	39	1	1	465	537	17	111	103	12.7	3.64	84	.288	.331	50	.246	5	-26	-30	5	-2.0
● JOHN MURPHY Murphy, John Henry 5'11", 165 lbs. Deb: 4/17/1884																										
1884	Wil-U	0	6	.000	7	6	5	0	0	48	52	3	2	27	10.1	3.00	89	.259	.266	2	.065	-4	-3	-2	-1	-0.5
	Alt-U	5	6	.455	14	10	10	0	0	111^2	141	3	9	46	12.1	3.87	69	.289	.302	14	.149	-7	-18	-15	1	-1.5
	Yr	5	12	.294	21	16	15	0	0	159^2	193	6	11	73	11.5	3.61	74	.280	.291	16	.128	-11	-21	-17	0	-2.0
● JOHNNY MURPHY Murphy, John Joseph "Grandma" "Fireman" Or "Fordham Johnny" b: 7/14/08, New York, N.Y. d: 1/14/70, New York, N.Y. BR/TR, 6'2", 190 lbs. Deb: 5/19/32																										
1932	NY-A	0	0	—	2	0	0	0	0	3^1	7	0	3	2	27.0	16.20	25	.438	.526	1	1.000	1	-4	-4	0	0.1
1934	NY-A	14	10	.583	40	20	10	0	4	207^2	193	11	76	70	11.7	3.12	130	.250	.317	7	.099	-3	32	22	1	2.1
1935	NY-A	10	5	.667	40	8	4	0	5	117	110	7	55	28	12.7	4.08	99	.243	.325	5	.156	2	5	-0	-1	0.1
1936	*NY-A	9	3	.750	27	5	2	0	5	88	90	5	36	34	13.0	3.38	138	.262	.334	13	.361	4	16	13	1	2.0
1937	*NY-A☆	13	4	.765	39	4	0	0	10	110	121	7	50	36	14.1	4.17	107	.277	.352	8	.229	2	5	3	4	1.0
1938	*NY-A☆	8	2	.800	32	2	1	0	**11**	91^1	90	5	41	43	13.0	4.24	107	.256	.336	2	.063	-3	**6**	3	1	0.2
1939	*NY-A☆	3	6	.333	38	0	0	0	**19**	61^1	57	2	28	30	12.5	4.40	99	.252	.335	2	.182	1	1	-0	1	0.0
1940	NY-A	8	4	.667	35	1	0	0	9	63^1	58	5	15	23	10.4	3.69	109	.247	.292	1	.077	0	5	2	1	0.5
1941	*NY-A	8	3	.727	35	0	0	0	**15**	77^1	68	1	40	29	12.6	1.98	199	.237	.330	1	.056	-1	**19**	**17**	-1	2.7
1942	NY-A	4	10	.286	31	0	0	0	**11**	58	66	2	23	24	14.1	3.41	101	.293	.364	2	.154	0	2	0	0	0.1
1943	*NY-A	12	4	.750	37	0	0	0	8	68	44	2	30	31	9.8	2.51	128	.183	.273	1	.053	-2	6	5	-0	1.1
1946	NY-A	4	2	.667	27	0	0	0	7	45	40	4	19	19	11.8	3.40	102	.240	.317	0	.000	-0	1	0	1	0.1

YEAR	TM/L	W	L	PCT	G	GS	CG	SH	SV	IP	H	HR	BB	SO	RAT	ERA	ERA+	OAV	OOB	BH	AVG	PB	PR	/A	PD	TPI
1947	Bos-A	0	0	—	32	0	0	0	3	54^2	41	1	28	9	11.4	2.80	139	.206	.304	3	.273	1	6	7	0	0.2
Total	13	93	53	.637	415	40	17	0	107	1045	985	52	444	378	12.4	3.50	117	.249	.326	46	.154	-0	98	68	8	10.2

● JOE MURPHY

Murphy, Joseph Akin b: 9/7/1866, St.Louis, Mo. d: 3/28/51, Coral Gables, Fla. 5'11", 160 lbs. Deb: 4/28/1886

YEAR	TM/L	W	L	PCT	G	GS	CG	SH	SV	IP	H	HR	BB	SO	RAT	ERA	ERA+	OAV	OOB	BH	AVG	PB	PR	/A	PD	TPI
1886	Cin-a	2	3	.400	5	5	5	0	0	46	50	0	21	11	14.1	4.89	72	.256	.332	0	.000	-3	-7	-7	-1	-0.9
	StL-N	0	4	.000	4	4	3	0	0	33	45	3	16	11	16.6	8.18	39	.319	.389	3	.214	0	-18	-18	-0	-1.5
	StL-a	1	0	1.000	1	1	1	0	0	7	5	0	3	3	10.3	3.86	89	.179	.258	0	.000	-1	-0	-0	-0	-0.1
1887	StL-a	1	0	1.000	1	1	1	0	0	9	13	0	4	5	17.0	5.00	91	.317	.378	1	.167	-1	-1	-0	0	-0.1
Total	2	4	7	.364	11	11	10	0	0	95	113	3	44	30	15.0	5.97	59	.279	.351	4	.098	-4	-26	-26	-2	-2.6

● ROB MURPHY

Murphy, Robert Albert b: 5/26/60, Miami, Fla. BL/TL, 6'2", 215 lbs. Deb: 9/13/85

YEAR	TM/L	W	L	PCT	G	GS	CG	SH	SV	IP	H	HR	BB	SO	RAT	ERA	ERA+	OAV	OOB	BH	AVG	PB	PR	/A	PD	TPI
1985	Cin-N	0	0	—	2	0	0	0	0	3	2	1	2	1	12.0	6.00	63	.200	.333	0	—	0	-1	-1	-0	0.0
1986	Cin-N	6	0	1.000	34	0	0	0	1	50^1	26	0	21	36	8.4	0.72	541	.155	.249	0	.000	-0	17	18	0	2.1
1987	Cin-N	8	5	.615	87	0	0	0	3	100^2	91	7	32	99	11.0	3.04	140	.239	.299	1	.200	0	12	13	0	1.7
1988	Cin-N	0	6	.000	**76**	0	0	0	3	84^2	69	1	38	74	11.5	3.08	116	.229	.318	0	—	0	3	5	1	0.4
1989	Bos-A	5	7	.417	74	0	0	0	9	105	97	7	41	107	11.9	2.74	149	.251	.325	0	—	0	13	16	1	1.8
1990	*Bos-A	0	6	.000	68	0	0	0	7	57	85	10	32	54	18.6	6.32	65	.348	.426	0	—	0	-15	-14	0	-1.6
1991	Sea-A	0	1	.000	57	0	0	0	4	48	47	4	19	34	12.6	3.00	137	.250	.322	0	—	0	6	6	0	0.2
1992	Hou-N	3	1	.750	59	0	0	0	0	55^2	56	2	21	42	12.4	4.04	83	.260	.326	0	.000	-0	-3	-4	1	-0.2
1993	StL-N	5	7	.417	73	0	0	0	1	64^2	73	8	20	41	13.1	4.87	81	.290	.344	1	.500	0	-6	-7	-0	-1.1
1994	StL-N	4	3	.571	50	0	0	0	2	40^1	35	7	13	25	10.7	3.79	109	.230	.291	0	—	0	2	2	-0	0.3
	NY-A	0	0	—	3	0	0	0	0	1^2	3	2	0	0	16.2	16.20	28	.375	.375	0	—	0	-2	-2	0	0.1
1995	LA-N	0	1	.000	6	0	0	0	0	5	6	2	3	2	16.2	12.60	30	.300	.391	1	1.000	1	-5	-5	0	-0.8
	Fla-N	1	1	.500	8	0	0	0	0	7^1	8	1	5	5	16.0	9.82	43	.286	.394	0	—	0	-5	-5	0	-1.0
	Yr	1	2	.333	14	0	0	0	0	12^1	14	3	8	7	16.1	10.95	37	.292	.393	1	1.000	1	-9	-9	0	-1.8
Total	11	32	38	.457	597	0	0	0	30	623^1	598	54	247	520	12.3	3.64	109	.254	.326	3	.250	1	16	22	2	1.9

● BOB MURPHY

Murphy, Robert J. b: 12/26/1866, Dutchess Co., N.Y. Deb: 5/27/1890

YEAR	TM/L	W	L	PCT	G	GS	CG	SH	SV	IP	H	HR	BB	SO	RAT	ERA	ERA+	OAV	OOB	BH	AVG	PB	PR	/A	PD	TPI
1890	NY-N	1	0	1.000	3	2	1	0	0	18	23	0	10	8	16.5	5.50	64	.303	.384	1	.111	-1	-4	-4	-0	-0.3
	Bro-a	3	9	.250	12	12	10	0	0	96	121	6	46	26	16.1	5.72	68	.299	.377	9	.180	0	-20	-19	2	-1.6
Total	1	4	9	.308	15	14	11	0	0	114	144	6	56	34	16.2	5.68	67	.299	.378	10	.169	-1	-24	-23	2	-1.9

● TOM MURPHY

Murphy, Thomas Andrew b: 12/30/45, Cleveland, Ohio BR/TR, 6'3", 185 lbs. Deb: 6/13/68

YEAR	TM/L	W	L	PCT	G	GS	CG	SH	SV	IP	H	HR	BB	SO	RAT	ERA	ERA+	OAV	OOB	BH	AVG	PB	PR	/A	PD	TPI
1968	Cal-A	5	6	.455	15	15	3	0	0	99^1	67	5	28	56	9.1	2.17	134	.191	.261	0	.000	-3	9	8	-1	0.5
1969	Cal-A	10	16	.385	36	35	4	0	0	215^2	213	12	69	100	12.6	4.21	83	.260	.333	10	.141	-0	-14	-18	1	-1.9
1970	Cal-A	16	13	.552	39	38	5	2	0	227	223	32	81	99	12.3	4.24	85	.261	.330	14	.184	3	-13	-16	-1	-1.7
1971	Cal-A	6	17	.261	37	36	7	0	0	243^1	228	24	82	89	11.8	3.77	86	.256	.325	13	.173	1	-8	-14	1	-1.0
1972	Cal-A	0	0	—	6	0	0	0	0	10	13	0	8	2	18.9	5.40	54	.342	.457	0	.000	-0	-3	-3	1	0.1
	KC-A	4	4	.500	18	9	1	1	1	70^1	77	3	16	34	12.7	3.07	99	.287	.341	0	.000	-1	-0	-0	1	-0.1
	Yr	4	4	.500	24	9	1	1	1	80^1	90	3	24	36	13.4	3.36	90	.293	.356	0	.000	-1	-3	-3	1	0.0
1973	StL-N	3	7	.300	19	13	2	0	0	88^2	89	5	22	42	11.6	3.76	97	.269	.320	4	.174	0	-1	-1	1	0.0
1974	Mil-A	10	10	.500	70	0	0	0	20	123	97	6	51	47	11.0	1.90	190	.224	.309	1	.500	0	23	23	2	**4.9**
1975	Mil-A	1	9	.100	52	0	0	0	20	72^1	85	5	27	32	14.6	4.60	83	.295	.366	0	—	0	-7	-6	0	-1.2
1976	Mil-A	0	1	.000	15	0	0	0	1	18^1	25	2	9	7	17.7	7.36	47	.313	.396	0	—	0	-8	-8	0	-0.3
	Bos-A	4	5	.444	37	0	0	0	8	81	91	5	25	32	13.1	3.44	114	.290	.346	0	—	0	1	4	-0	-0.4
	Yr	4	6	.400	52	0	0	0	9	99^1	116	7	34	39	13.8	4.17	92	.293	.352	0	—	0	-7	-4	0	-0.7
1977	Bos-A	0	1	.000	16	0	0	0	0	30^2	44	6	12	13	16.4	6.75	67	.338	.394	0	—	0	-9	-8	0	-1.0
	Tor-A	2	1	.667	19	1	0	0	2	52	63	6	18	26	14.2	3.63	115	.304	.363	0	—	0	2	3	-0	0.1
	Yr	2	2	.500	35	1	0	0	2	82^2	107	12	30	39	15.0	4.79	90	.317	.374	0	—	0	-7	-4	0	-0.9
1978	Tor-A	6	9	.400	50	0	0	0	7	94	87	11	37	36	11.9	3.93	100	.256	.329	0	—	0	-2	-0	2	0.2
1979	Tor-A	1	2	.333	10	0	0	0	0	18^1	23	1	8	6	15.2	5.40	80	.311	.378	0	—	0	-2	-2	1	-0.3
Total	12	68	101	.402	439	147	22	3	59	1444	1425	123	493	621	12.3	3.78	94	.263	.332	42	.145	0	-32	-38	7	-2.1

● WALTER MURPHY

Murphy, Walter Joseph b: 9/27/07, New York, N.Y. d: 3/23/76, Houston, Tex. BR/TR, 6'1.5", 180 lbs. Deb: 4/19/31

YEAR	TM/L	W	L	PCT	G	GS	CG	SH	SV	IP	H	HR	BB	SO	RAT	ERA	ERA+	OAV	OOB	BH	AVG	PB	PR	/A	PD	TPI
1931	Bos-A	0	0	—	2	0	0	0	0	2	4	0	1	0	22.5	9.00	48	.444	.500	0	—	0	-1	-1	-0	0.0

● AMBY MURRAY

Murray, Ambrose Joseph b: 6/4/13, Fall River, Mass. d: 2/6/97, Port Salerno, Fla. BL/TL, 5'7", 150 lbs. Deb: 7/5/36

YEAR	TM/L	W	L	PCT	G	GS	CG	SH	SV	IP	H	HR	BB	SO	RAT	ERA	ERA+	OAV	OOB	BH	AVG	PB	PR	/A	PD	TPI
1936	Bos-N	0	0	—	4	1	0	0	0	11	15	1	3	2	14.7	4.09	94	.319	.360	1	.250	0	-0	-0	0	0.0

● DALE MURRAY

Murray, Dale Albert b: 2/2/50, Cuero, Tex. BR/TR, 6'4", 205 lbs. Deb: 7/7/74

YEAR	TM/L	W	L	PCT	G	GS	CG	SH	SV	IP	H	HR	BB	SO	RAT	ERA	ERA+	OAV	OOB	BH	AVG	PB	PR	/A	PD	TPI
1974	Mon-N	1	1	.500	32	0	0	0	10	69^2	46	1	23	31	8.9	1.03	371	.187	.257	0	.000	-1	20	22	0	1.3
1975	Mon-N	15	8	.652	63	0	0	0	9	111^1	134	0	39	43	14.2	3.96	97	.305	.365	3	.214	1	-4	-2	3	0.0
1976	Mon-N	4	9	.308	**81**	0	0	0	13	113^1	117	1	37	35	12.2	3.26	114	.277	.336	0	.000	-1	3	6	4	1.2
1977	Cin-N	7	2	.778	61	1	0	0	4	102	125	13	46	42	15.3	4.94	80	.314	.388	2	.167	-0	-12	-11	0	-1.0
1978	Cin-N	1	1	.500	15	0	0	0	2	32^2	34	1	17	25	14.3	4.13	86	.272	.364	0	.000	-0	-2	-2	1	-0.1
	NY-N	8	5	.615	53	0	0	0	5	86^1	85	4	36	37	12.8	3.65	96	.266	.345	0	.000	-0	-1	-2	2	-0.1
	Yr	9	6	.600	68	0	0	0	7	119	119	5	53	62	13.2	3.78	93	.266	.346	0	.000	-1	-3	-4	2	-0.2
1979	NY-N	4	8	.333	58	0	0	0	4	97	105	6	52	37	14.6	4.82	75	.287	.376	0	.000	-0	-12	-13	1	-1.5
	Mon-N	1	2	.333	9	0	0	0	1	13^1	14	1	3	4	11.5	2.70	136	.292	.333	0	.000	-0	2	1	0	0.3
	Yr	5	10	.333	67	0	0	0	5	110^1	119	7	55	41	14.2	4.57	80	.285	.369	0	.000	-1	-10	-11	0	-1.2
1980	Mon-N	0	1	.000	16	0	0	0	0	29^1	39	3	12	16	15.6	6.14	58	.315	.375	0	.000	-0	-8	-8	-1	-0.4
1981	Tor-A	1	0	1.000	11	0	0	0	0	15^1	12	0	5	12	10.0	1.17	336	.211	.274	0	—	0	4	5	1	0.0
1982	Tor-A	8	7	.533	56	0	0	0	11	111	115	3	32	60	12.2	3.16	142	.268	.323	0	—	0	11	16	3	2.0
1983	NY-A	2	4	.333	40	0	0	0	1	94^1	113	5	22	45	13.0	4.48	87	.297	.337	0	—	0	-4	-6	0	-0.1
1984	NY-A	1	2	.333	19	0	0	0	0	23^2	30	2	5	13	14.1	4.94	77	.306	.352	0	—	0	-3	-3	-0	-0.1
1985	NY-A	0	0	—	3	0	0	0	0	2	4	0	0	0	18.0	13.50	30	.400	.400	0	—	0	-2	-2	-0	0.2
	Tex-A	0	0	—	1	0	0	0	0	1	3	0	0	0	27.0	18.00	23	.750	.750	0	—	0	-2	-2	0	-0.1
	Yr	0	0	—	4	0	0	0	0	3	7	0	0	0	21.0	15.00	27	.500	.500	0	—	0	-4	-4	0	0.1
Total	12	53	50	.515	518	1	0	0	60	902^1	976	40	329	400	13.2	3.85	100	.282	.346	5	.077	-3	-9	-1	13	1.6

● GEORGE MURRAY

Murray, George King "Smiler" b: 9/23/1898, Charlotte, N.C. d: 10/18/55, Memphis, Tenn. BR/TR, 6'2", 200 lbs. Deb: 5/8/22

YEAR	TM/L	W	L	PCT	G	GS	CG	SH	SV	IP	H	HR	BB	SO	RAT	ERA	ERA+	OAV	OOB	BH	AVG	PB	PR	/A	PD	TPI
1922	NY-A	3	2	.600	22	2	0	0	0	56^2	53	0	26	14	12.7	3.97	101	.255	.340	5	.278	2	**0**	**0**	-0	0.2
1923	Bos-A	7	11	.389	39	18	5	0	0	177^2	190	9	87	40	14.4	4.91	84	.291	.380	9	.164	-3	-18	-16	-2	-1.8
1924	Bos-A	2	9	.182	28	7	0	0	0	80^1	97	6	32	27	15.2	6.72	65	.307	.383	4	.182	-1	-22	-21	0	-2.4
1926	Was-A	6	3	.667	12	12	5	0	0	81^1	89	1	37	28	14.6	5.64	69	.287	.374	5	.139	-2	-15	-16	-1	-1.7
1927	Was-A	1	1	.500	7	3	0	0	0	18	18	1	15	5	17.5	7.00	58	.265	.412	1	.167	-0	-6	-6	-1	-0.6
1933	Chi-A	0	0	—	2	0	0	0	0	2^1	3	0	2	0	19.3	7.71	55	.375	.500	0	—	0	-1	-1	0	0.0
Total	6	19	26	.422	110	42	10	0	0	416^1	450	17	199	114	14.5	5.38	76	.288	.376	24	.175	-4	-61	-59	-3	-6.3

● HEATH MURRAY

Murray, Heath Robertson b: 4/19/73, Troy, O. BL/TL, 6'4", 205 lbs. Deb: 5/24/97

YEAR	TM/L	W	L	PCT	G	GS	CG	SH	SV	IP	H	HR	BB	SO	RAT	ERA	ERA+	OAV	OOB	BH	AVG	PB	PR	/A	PD	TPI
1997	SD-N	1	2	.333	17	3	0	0	0	33^1	50	3	21	16	20.3	6.75	57	.376	.475	0	.000	-1	-9	-11	-1	-0.9

● JIM MURRAY

Murray, James Francis "Big Jim" b: 12/31/1900, Scranton, Pa. d: 7/15/73, New York, N.Y. BB/TL, 6'2", 210 lbs. Deb: 7/3/22

YEAR	TM/L	W	L	PCT	G	GS	CG	SH	SV	IP	H	HR	BB	SO	RAT	ERA	ERA+	OAV	OOB	BH	AVG	PB	PR	/A	PD	TPI
1922	Bro-N	0	0	—	4	0	0	0	1	6	8	0	3	3	16.5	4.50	90	.320	.393	1	.500	0	-0	-0	-0	0.0

● JOE MURRAY

Murray, Joseph Ambrose b: 11/11/20, Wilkes-Barre, Pa. BL/TL, 6', 165 lbs. Deb: 8/17/50

YEAR	TM/L	W	L	PCT	G	GS	CG	SH	SV	IP	H	HR	BB	SO	RAT	ERA	ERA+	OAV	OOB	BH	AVG	PB	PR	/A	PD	TPI
1950	Phi-A	0	3	.000	8	2	0	0	0	30	34	1	21	8	16.5	5.70	80	.283	.390	0	.000	-2	-4	-4	1	-0.4

● MATT MURRAY

Murray, Matthew Michael b: 9/26/70, Boston, Mass. BL/TR, 6'6", 240 lbs. Deb: 8/12/95

YEAR	TM/L	W	L	PCT	G	GS	CG	SH	SV	IP	H	HR	BB	SO	RAT	ERA	ERA+	OAV	OOB	BH	AVG	PB	PR	/A	PD	TPI
1995	Atl-N	0	2	.000	4	1	0	0	0	10^2	10	3	5	3	13.5	6.75	63	.256	.356	1	.500	0	-3	-3	0	-0.4
	Bos-A	0	1	.000	2	1	0	0	0	3^1	11	1	3	1	37.8	18.90	26	.524	.583	0	—	0	-5	-5	0	-1.1
Total	1	0	3	.000	6	2	0	0	0	14	21	4	8	4	19.3	9.64	46	.350	.435	1	.500	0	-8	-8	1	-1.5

YEAR	TM/L	W	L	PCT	G	GS	CG	SH	SV	IP	H	HR	BB	SO	RAT	ERA	ERA+	OAV	OOB	BH	AVG	PB	PR	/A	PD	TPI
● **PAT MURRAY**	Murray, Patrick Joseph b: 7/18/1897, Scottsville, N.Y. d: 11/5/83, Rochester, N.Y. BR/TL, 6', 175 lbs. Deb: 7/1/19																									
1919	Phi-N	0	2	.000	8	2	1	0	0	34^1	50	0	12	11	17.3	6.29	51	.347	.412	0	.000	-1	-13	-12	-0	-0.8
● **DENNIS MUSGRAVES**	Musgraves, Dennis Eugene b: 12/25/43, Indianapolis, Ind. BR/TR, 6'4", 188 lbs. Deb: 7/9/65																									
1965	NY-N	0	0	—	5	1	0	0	0	16	11	0	7	11	11.3	0.56	627	.200	.313	0	.000	-0	5	5	-0	0.0
● **STAN MUSIAL**	Musial, Stanley Frank "Stan The Man" b: 11/21/20, Donora, Pa. BL/TL, 6', 175 lbs. Deb: 9/17/41 H♦																									
1952	StL-N★	0	0	—	1	0	0	0	0	0	0	0	0	0	—	—	—	.000	.000	194	.336	1	0	0	0	0.0
● **JEFF MUSSELMAN**	Musselman, Jeffrey Joseph b: 6/21/63, Doylestown, Pa. BL/TL, 6', 180 lbs. Deb: 9/2/86																									
1986	Tor-A	0	0	—	6	0	0	0	0	5^1	8	1	5	4	21.9	10.13	42	.333	.448	0	—	0	-4	-4	0	-0.1
1987	Tor-A	12	5	.706	68	1	0	0	3	89	75	7	54	54	13.3	4.15	108	.237	.354	0	—	0	3	3	1	0.5
1988	Tor-A	8	5	.615	15	15	0	0	0	85	80	4	30	39	12.0	3.18	124	.252	.322	0	—	0	7	7	-1	0.9
1989	Tor-A	0	1	.000	5	3	0	0	0	11	19	2	9	3	22.9	10.64	35	.404	.500	0	—	0	-8	-8	-0	-0.6
	NY-N	3	2	.600	20	0	0	0	0	26^1	27	1	14	11	14.0	3.08	106	.267	.357	0	—	0	1	1	2	0.3
1990	NY-N	0	2	.000	28	0	0	0	0	32	40	3	11	14	14.6	5.63	67	.310	.369	0	.000	-0	-7	-7	0	-0.4
Total	5	23	15	.605	142	19	0	0	3	248^2	249	18	123	125	13.7	4.31	94	.266	.356	0	.000	0	-7	-8	2	0.6
● **RON MUSSELMAN**	Musselman, Ralph Ronald b: 11/11/54, Wilmington, N.C. BR/TR, 6'2", 185 lbs. Deb: 8/18/82																									
1982	Sea-A	1	0	1.000	12	0	0	0	0	15^2	18	2	6	9	14.4	3.45	123	.300	.373	0	—	0	1	1	0	-0.1
1984	Tor-A	0	2	.000	11	0	0	0	1	21^1	18	2	10	9	11.8	2.11	194	.225	.311	0	—	0	4	5	-0	0.1
1985	Tor-A	3	0	1.000	25	4	0	0	0	52^1	59	2	24	29	14.3	4.47	94	.284	.358	0	—	0	-2	-2	-1	-0.4
Total	3	4	2	.667	48	4	0	0	1	89^1	95	6	40	47	13.7	3.73	112	.273	.350	0	—	0	4	5	-1	-0.4
● **PAUL MUSSER**	Musser, Paul b: 6/24/1889, Millheim, Pa. d: 7/7/73, State College, Pa. BR/TR, 6', 175 lbs. Deb: 6/6/12																									
1912	Was-A	0	0	—	7	2	0	0	2	20^2	16	0	16	10	14.8	2.61	128	.225	.382	0	.000	-1	2	2	0	-0.1
1919	Bos-A	0	2	.000	5	4	1	0	0	19^2	26	0	8	14	15.6	4.12	73	.342	.405	0	.000	-1	-2	-2	-0	-0.4
Total	2	0	2	.000	12	6	1	0	2	40^1	42	0	24	24	15.2	3.35	95	.286	.393	0	.000	-2	-0	-1	0	-0.5
● **BARNEY MUSSILL**	Mussill, Bernard James b: 10/1/19, Bower Hill, Pa. BR/TL, 6'1", 200 lbs. Deb: 4/20/44																									
1944	Phi-N	0	1	.000	16	0	0	0	0	19^1	20	1	13	5	15.4	6.05	60	.267	.375	0	.000	-0	-5	-5	-0	-0.3
● **MIKE MUSSINA**	Mussina, Michael Cole b: 12/8/68, Williamsport, Pa. BR/TR, 6'2", 185 lbs. Deb: 8/4/91																									
1991	Bal-A	4	5	.444	12	12	2	0	0	87^2	77	7	21	52	10.2	2.87	137	.239	.288	0	—	0	12	10	-0	1.1
1992	Bal-A★	18	5	**.783**	32	32	8	4	0	241	212	16	48	130	**9.8**	2.54	158	.239	**.279**	0	—	0	37	40	-0	3.5
1993	Bal-A☆	14	6	.700	25	25	3	2	0	167^2	163	20	44	117	11.3	4.46	100	.256	.307	0	—	0	-3	0	-0	-0.2
1994	Bal-A★	16	5	.762	24	24	3	0	0	176^1	163	19	42	99	10.5	3.06	163	.248	.294	0	—	0	34	38	1	3.9
1995	Bal-A	**19**	9	.679	32	32	7	**4**	0	221^2	187	24	50	158	9.7	3.29	144	.226	.271	0	—	0	35	36	-1	3.9
1996	*Bal-A	19	11	.633	36	36	4	1	0	243^1	264	31	69	204	12.4	4.81	102	.275	.326	0	—	0	5	3	1	0.4
1997	*Bal-A☆	15	8	.652	33	33	4	1	0	224^2	197	27	54	218	10.2	3.20	137	.234	.282	1	.250	0	34	30	0	2.8
1998	Bal-A	13	10	.565	29	29	4	2	0	206^1	189	22	41	175	10.2	3.49	130	.242	.283	0	.000	-0	27	24	2	2.6
Total	8	118	59	.667	223	223	35	14	0	1568^2	1452	166	369	1153	10.6	3.50	130	.246	.292	1	.167	-0	181	181	3	18.0
● **ALEX MUSTAIKIS**	Mustaikis, Alexander Dominick b: 3/26/09, Chelsea, Mass. d: 1/17/70, Scranton, Pa. BR/TR, 6'3", 180 lbs. Deb: 7/7/40																									
1940	Bos-A	0	1	.000	6	1	0	0	0	15	15	1	15	6	18.0	9.00	50	.254	.405	2	.333	1	-8	-8	1	-0.3
● **JEFF MUTIS**	Mutis, Jeffrey Thomas b: 12/20/66, Allentown, Pa. BL/TL, 6'2", 185 lbs. Deb: 6/15/91																									
1991	Cle-A	0	3	.000	3	3	0	0	0	12^1	23	1	7	6	21.9	11.68	36	.397	.462	0	—	0	-10	-10	-0	-1.7
1992	Cle-A	0	2	.000	3	2	0	0	0	11^1	24	4	6	8	23.8	9.53	41	.429	.484	0	—	0	-7	-7	0	-0.9
1993	Cle-A	3	6	.333	17	13	1	1	0	81	93	14	33	29	14.8	5.78	75	.289	.367	0	—	0	-13	-13	1	-1.1
1994	Fla-N	1	0	1.000	35	0	0	0	0	38^1	51	6	15	30	15.7	5.40	81	.331	.394	0	.000	-0	-5	-4	0	-0.1
Total	4	4	11	.267	58	18	1	1	0	143	191	25	61	73	16.4	6.48	66	.324	.395	0	.000	-0	-36	-35	1	-3.8
● **ELMER MYERS**	Myers, Elmer Glenn b: 3/2/1894, York Springs, Pa. d: 7/29/76, Collingswood, N.J. BR/TR, 6'2", 185 lbs. Deb: 10/6/15																									
1915	Phi-A	1	0	1.000	1	1	1	1	0	9	2	0	5	12	7.0	0.00	—	.074	.219	0	.000	-0	3	3	-0	0.2
1916	Phi-A	14	23	.378	44	35	31	2	1	315	280	7	168	182	13.2	3.66	78	.248	.353	27	.214	2	-29	-28	5	-2.3
1917	Phi-A	9	16	.360	38	23	13	2	3	201^2	221	2	79	88	13.6	4.42	62	.283	.353	18	.247	2	-39	-37	1	-4.1
1918	Phi-A	4	8	.333	18	15	5	1	1	95^1	101	4	42	17	13.9	4.63	63	.283	.365	5	.143	-2	-20	-18	2	-2.2
1919	Cle-A	8	7	.533	23	15	6	1	1	134^2	134	3	43	38	12.5	3.74	89	.264	.334	11	.239	2	-8	-6	1	-0.3
1920	Cle-A	2	4	.333	16	7	2	0	1	71^2	93	1	23	16	15.1	4.77	80	.316	.374	6	.240	0	-8	-8	0	-0.6
	Bos-A	9	1	.900	12	10	9	1	0	97	90	1	24	34	10.8	2.13	171	.249	.299	12	.316	3	18	16	-1	1.8
	Yr	11	5	.688	28	17	11	1	1	168^2	183	2	47	50	12.4	3.25	114	.277	.327	18	.286	3	10	9	-1	1.2
1921	Bos-A	8	12	.400	30	20	11	0	0	172	217	11	53	40	14.7	4.87	87	.315	.373	14	.215	-2	-11	-12	0	-1.3
1922	Bos-A	0	1	.000	3	1	0	0	0	5^2	10	1	3	1	23.8	17.47	24	.370	.469	0	.000	-0	-8	-8	0	-1.1
Total	8	55	72	.433	185	127	78	8	7	1102	1148	30	440	428	13.4	4.06	80	.275	.352	93	.226	4	-102	-97	8	-9.9
● **HENRY MYERS**	Myers, Henry C. b: 5/1858, Philadelphia, Pa. d: 4/18/1895, Philadelphia, Pa. BR/TR, 5'9", 159 lbs. Deb: 8/20/1881 M♦																									
1882	Bal-a	0	2	.000	6	2	1	0	0	26	30	2	4	7	11.8	6.58	42	.270	.296	53	.180	-1	-11	-11	-0	-0.7
● **JIMMY MYERS**	Myers, James Xavier b: 4/28/69, Oklahoma City, Okla. BR/TR, 6'1", 190 lbs. Deb: 4/6/96																									
1996	Bal-A	0	0	—	11	0	0	0	0	14	18	4	3	6	13.5	7.07	70	.305	.339	0	—	0	-3	-3	-0	0.0
● **JOSEPH MYERS**	Myers, Joseph William b: 3/18/1882, Wilmington, Del. d: 2/11/56, Delaware City, Del. BR/TR, 5'10.5", 205 lbs. Deb: 10/7/05																									
1905	Phi-A	0	0	—	1	1	1	0	0	5	3	0	3	5	12.6	3.60	74	.176	.333	0	.000	-0	-1	-1	-0	0.0
● **MIKE MYERS**	Myers, Michael Stanley b: 6/26/69, Cook County, Ill. BL/TL, 6'3", 200 lbs. Deb: 4/25/95																									
1995	Fla-N	0	0	—	2	0	0	0	0	2	1	0	3	0	18.0	0.00	—	.167	.444	0	—	0	1	1	-0	0.0
	Det-A	1	0	1.000	11	0	0	0	0	6^1	10	1	4	4	22.7	9.95	48	.385	.500	0	—	0	-4	-4	0	-0.4
1996	Det-A	1	5	.167	**83**	0	0	0	6	64^2	70	6	34	69	15.0	5.01	101	.272	.366	0	—	0	-0	0	2	0.2
1997	Det-A	0	4	.000	**88**	0	0	0	2	53^2	58	12	25	50	14.3	5.70	80	.274	.356	0	—	0	-7	-7	0	-0.4
1998	Mil-N	2	2	.500	70	0	0	0	1	50	44	5	22	40	13.0	2.70	159	.249	.351	0	—	0	9	9	1	0.8
Total	4	4	11	.267	254	0	0	0	9	176^2	183	24	88	163	14.5	4.69	100	.270	.365	0	—	0	-1	-0	3	0.2
● **RANDY MYERS**	Myers, Randall Kirk b: 9/19/62, Vancouver, Wash. BL/TL, 6'1", 215 lbs. Deb: 10/6/85																									
1985	NY-N	0	0	—	1	0	0	0	0	2	0	0	1	2	4.5	0.00	—	.000	.143	0	—	0	1	1	0	0.0
1986	NY-N	0	0	—	10	0	0	0	0	10^2	11	1	9	13	17.7	4.22	84	.256	.396	0	—	0	-1	-1	0	0.0
1987	NY-N	3	6	.333	54	0	0	0	6	75	61	6	30	92	10.9	3.96	95	.225	.302	2	.286	1	1	-2	0	-0.1
1988	*NY-N	7	3	.700	55	0	0	0	26	68	45	5	17	69	8.5	1.72	187	.190	.250	1	.250	1	13	11	-1	2.5
1989	NY-N	7	4	.636	65	0	0	0	24	84^1	62	4	40	88	10.9	2.35	139	.206	.299	0	.000	-1	11	9	0	1.5
1990	*Cin-N★	4	6	.400	66	0	0	0	31	86^2	59	6	38	98	10.4	2.08	190	.193	.288	1	.250	0	17	18	0	3.3
1991	Cin-N	6	13	.316	58	12	1	0	6	132	116	8	80	108	13.4	3.55	107	.242	.351	5	.172	0	2	4	-1	0.4
1992	SD-N	3	6	.333	66	0	0	0	38	79^2	84	7	34	66	13.4	4.29	83	.279	.354	1	.143	-0	-7	-6	-0	-1.3
1993	Chi-N	2	4	.333	73	0	0	0	**53**	75^1	65	7	26	86	11.0	3.11	128	.230	.297	1	.500	1	8	7	-1	1.5
1994	Chi-N★	1	5	.167	38	0	0	0	21	40^1	40	3	16	32	12.5	3.79	109	.260	.329	0	.000	-0	2	2	-1	0.3
1995	Chi-N★	1	2	.333	57	0	0	0	**38**	55^2	49	7	28	59	12.4	3.88	106	.237	.328	0	—	0	2	1	0	0.3
1996	*Bal-A	4	4	.500	62	0	0	0	31	58^2	60	7	29	74	13.8	3.53	139	.265	.352	0	—	0	10	9	-1	1.9
1997	*Bal-A★	2	3	.400	61	0	0	0	**45**	59^2	47	2	22	56	10.4	1.51	292	.217	.289	0	—	0	20	19	-1	3.9
1998	Tor-A	3	4	.429	41	0	0	0	28	42^1	44	4	19	32	13.8	4.46	104	.265	.348	0	.000	-0	1	1	-1	0.1
	*SD-N	1	3	.250	21	0	0	0	0	14^1	15	2	7	9	13.8	6.28	61	.273	.355	0	—	0	-3	-4	-0	-1.0
Total	14	44	63	.411	728	12	1	0	347	884^2	758	69	396	884	11.9	3.19	122	.233	.318	11	.183	2	75	69	-5	13.3
● **RODNEY MYERS**	Myers, Rodney Luther b: 6/26/69, Rockford, Ill. BR/TR, 6'1", 200 lbs. Deb: 4/3/96																									
1996	Chi-N	2	1	.667	45	0	0	0	0	67^1	61	6	38	50	13.6	4.68	93	.243	.349	0	.000	-1	-3	-3	-1	-0.2

YEAR	TM/L	W	L	PCT	G	GS	CG	SH	SV	IP	H	HR	BB	SO	RAT	ERA	ERA+	OAV	OOB	BH	AVG	PB	PR	/A	PD	TPI
1997	Chi-N	0	0	—	5	1	0	0	0	9	12	1	7	6	20.0	6.00	72	.333	.455	0	—	0	-2	-2	-0	0.0
1998	Chi-N	0	0	—	12	0	0	0	0	18	26	3	6	15	16.0	7.00	62	.342	.390	0	.000	-0	-6	-5	-0	0.0
Total	3	2	1	.667	62	1	0	0	0	94^1	99	10	51	71	14.7	5.25	83	.273	.368	0	.000	-1	-11	-10	-1	-0.2

● BOB MYRICK Myrick, Robert Howard b: 10/1/52, Hattiesburg, Miss. BR/TL, 6'1", 195 lbs. Deb: 5/28/76

YEAR	TM/L	W	L	PCT	G	GS	CG	SH	SV	IP	H	HR	BB	SO	RAT	ERA	ERA+	OAV	OOB	BH	AVG	PB	PR	/A	PD	TPI
1976	NY-N	1	1	.500	21	1	0	0	0	27^2	34	2	13	11	15.3	3.25	101	.306	.379	0	.000	-0	1	0	0	0.0
1977	NY-N	2	2	.500	44	4	0	0	2	87^1	86	5	33	49	12.4	3.61	104	.265	.334	2	.182	-0	3	1	0	0.1
1978	NY-N	0	3	.000	17	0	0	0	0	24^2	18	3	13	13	11.3	3.28	106	.207	.310	0	.000	-0	1	1	0	0.1
Total	3	3	6	.333	82	5	0	0	2	139^2	138	10	59	73	12.8	3.48	104	.264	.340	2	.125	-1	4	2	1	0.2

● CHRIS NABHOLZ Nabholz, Christopher William b: 1/5/67, Harrisburg, Pa. BL/TL, 6'5", 212 lbs. Deb: 6/11/90

YEAR	TM/L	W	L	PCT	G	GS	CG	SH	SV	IP	H	HR	BB	SO	RAT	ERA	ERA+	OAV	OOB	BH	AVG	PB	PR	/A	PD	TPI
1990	Mon-N	6	2	.750	11	11	1	1	0	70	43	6	32	53	9.9	2.83	129	.176	.276	0	.000	-2	7	6	-0	0.5
1991	Mon-N	8	7	.533	24	24	1	0	0	153^2	134	5	57	99	11.3	3.63	100	.237	.309	6	.115	-1	1	-0	1	0.0
1992	Mon-N	11	12	.478	32	32	1	1	0	195	176	11	74	130	11.8	3.32	104	.244	.318	8	.123	-1	4	3	3	0.6
1993	Mon-N	9	8	.529	26	21	1	0	0	116^2	100	9	63	74	13.2	4.09	102	.236	.346	5	.128	-1	1	1	0	0.0
1994	Cle-A	0	1	.000	6	4	0	0	0	11	23	1	9	5	27.0	11.45	41	.418	.508	0	—	0	-8	-8	0	-0.6
	Bos-A	3	4	.429	8	8	0	0	0	42	44	5	29	23	16.1	6.64	76	.282	.401	0	—	0	-9	-8	0	-1.0
	Yr	3	5	.375	14	12	0	0	0	53	67	6	38	28	18.2	7.64	65	.315	.423	0	—	0	-17	-16	0	-1.6
1995	Chi-N	0	1	.000	34	0	0	0	0	23^1	22	4	14	21	13.9	5.40	76	.253	.356	0	.000	-0	-3	-3	0	-0.1
Total	6	37	35	.514	141	100	4	2	0	611^2	542	41	278	405	12.4	3.94	97	.240	.329	19	.107	-5	-8	-9	4	-0.6

● JACK NABORS Nabors, Herman John b: 11/19/1887, Montevallo, Ala. d: 11/20/23, Wilton, Ala. BR/TR, 6'3", 185 lbs. Deb: 8/9/15

YEAR	TM/L	W	L	PCT	G	GS	CG	SH	SV	IP	H	HR	BB	SO	RAT	ERA	ERA+	OAV	OOB	BH	AVG	PB	PR	/A	PD	TPI
1915	Phi-A	0	5	.000	10	7	2	0	0	54	58	1	35	18	16.3	5.50	53	.304	.424	2	.125	-1	-15	-15	-0	-1.4
1916	Phi-A	1	20	.048	40	30	11	0	1	212^2	206	2	95	74	12.9	3.47	82	.266	.349	7	.101	-4	-15	-14	-2	-2.1
1917	Phi-A	0	0	—	2	0	0	0	0	3	2	0	1	2	9.0	3.00	92	.200	.273	0	—	0	-0	-0	0	0.0
Total	3	1	25	.038	52	37	13	0	1	269^2	266	3	131	94	13.5	3.87	74	.273	.364	9	.106	-6	-31	-30	-2	-3.5

● BILL NAGEL Nagel, William Taylor b: 8/19/15, Memphis, Tenn. d: 10/8/81, Freehold, N.J. BR/TR, 6'1", 190 lbs. Deb: 4/20/39 ♦

YEAR	TM/L	W	L	PCT	G	GS	CG	SH	SV	IP	H	HR	BB	SO	RAT	ERA	ERA+	OAV	OOB	BH	AVG	PB	PR	/A	PD	TPI
1939	Phi-A	0	0	—	1	0	0	0	0	3	7	1	1	0	24.0	12.00	39	.438	.471	86	.252	0	-2	-2	-0	0.0

● JUDGE NAGLE Nagle, Walter Harold "Lucky" b: 3/10/1880, Santa Rosa, Cal. d: 5/26/71, Santa Rosa, Cal. BR/TR, 6', 176 lbs. Deb: 4/26/11

YEAR	TM/L	W	L	PCT	G	GS	CG	SH	SV	IP	H	HR	BB	SO	RAT	ERA	ERA+	OAV	OOB	BH	AVG	PB	PR	/A	PD	TPI
1911	Pit-N	4	2	.667	8	3	1	0	1	27^1	33	3	6	11	13.2	3.62	95	.324	.367	1	.143	-0	-1	-1	0	-0.1
	Bos-A	1	1	.500	5	1	0	0	0	27	27	2	6	12	11.0	3.33	98	.262	.303	1	.100	-1	0	-0	-1	-0.2
Total	1	5	3	.625	13	4	1	0	1	54^1	60	5	12	23	12.1	3.48	97	.293	.335	2	.118	-1	-1	-1	-1	-0.3

● CHARLES NAGY Nagy, Charles Harrison b: 5/5/67, Bridgeport, Conn. BL/TR, 6'3", 200 lbs. Deb: 6/29/90

YEAR	TM/L	W	L	PCT	G	GS	CG	SH	SV	IP	H	HR	BB	SO	RAT	ERA	ERA+	OAV	OOB	BH	AVG	PB	PR	/A	PD	TPI
1990	Cle-A	2	4	.333	9	8	0	0	0	45^2	58	7	21	26	15.8	5.91	66	.315	.388	0	—	0	-10	-10	1	-1.1
1991	Cle-A	10	15	.400	33	33	6	1	0	211^1	228	15	66	109	12.8	4.13	101	.275	.333	0	—	0	-1	1	-1	-0.1
1992	Cle-A★	17	10	.630	33	33	10	3	0	252	245	11	57	169	10.9	2.96	132	.260	.303	0	—	0	27	26	3	3.1
1993	Cle-A	2	6	.250	9	9	1	0	0	48^2	66	6	13	30	15.0	6.29	69	.322	.368	0	—	0	-11	-11	2	-1.2
1994	Cle-A	10	8	.556	23	23	3	0	0	169^1	175	15	48	108	12.1	3.45	137	.265	.320	0	—	0	25	24	1	2.2
1995	*Cle-A	16	6	.727	29	29	2	1	0	178	194	20	61	139	13.2	4.55	103	.278	.342	0	—	0	3	3	3	0.5
1996	*Cle-A★	17	5	**.773**	32	32	5	0	0	222	217	21	61	167	11.4	3.41	144	.255	.307	0	—	0	39	37	3	3.5
1997	*Cle-A	15	11	.577	34	34	1	1	0	227	253	27	77	149	13.4	4.28	109	.282	.344	1	.200	0	7	10	3	1.3
1998	*Cle-A	15	10	.600	33	33	2	0	0	210^1	250	34	66	120	13.9	5.22	92	.297	.355	0	.000	-1	-13	-10	4	-0.7
Total	9	104	75	.581	235	234	30	6	0	1564^1	1686	156	470	1017	12.6	4.10	110	.276	.332	1	.100	-0	67	69	18	7.5

● MIKE NAGY Nagy, Michael Timothy b: 3/25/48, Bronx, N.Y. BR/TR, 6'3", 200 lbs. Deb: 4/21/69

YEAR	TM/L	W	L	PCT	G	GS	CG	SH	SV	IP	H	HR	BB	SO	RAT	ERA	ERA+	OAV	OOB	BH	AVG	PB	PR	/A	PD	TPI
1969	Bos-A	12	2	.857	33	28	7	1	0	196^2	183	10	106	84	13.7	3.11	122	.245	.347	5	.077	-2	11	15	0	0.8
1970	Bos-A	6	5	.545	23	20	4	0	0	128^2	138	16	64	56	14.3	4.48	88	.275	.359	11	.250	2	-11	-7	-1	-0.5
1971	Bos-A	1	3	.250	12	7	0	0	0	38	46	4	20	9	15.6	6.63	56	.315	.398	1	.083	-1	-13	-12	-0	-1.3
1972	Bos-A	0	0	—	1	0	0	0	0	2	3	0	0	2	18.0	9.00	36	.375	.444	0	—	0	-1	-1	-0	0.0
1973	StL-N	0	2	.000	9	7	0	0	0	40^2	44	4	15	14	13.3	4.20	87	.282	.349	1	.091	-1	-2	-3	-0	-0.2
1974	Hou-N	1	1	.500	9	0	0	0	0	12^2	17	3	5	5	16.3	8.53	41	.309	.377	0	.000	-0	-7	-7	-0	-1.0
Total	6	20	13	.606	87	62	11	1	0	418^2	431	37	210	170	14.1	4.15	92	.267	.357	18	.135	-2	-24	-16	-1	-2.2

● STEVE NAGY Nagy, Stephen b: 5/28/19, Franklin, N.J. BL/TL, 5'10", 170 lbs. Deb: 4/20/47

YEAR	TM/L	W	L	PCT	G	GS	CG	SH	SV	IP	H	HR	BB	SO	RAT	ERA	ERA+	OAV	OOB	BH	AVG	PB	PR	/A	PD	TPI
1947	Pit-N	1	3	.250	6	1	0	0	0	14	18	1	9	4	17.4	5.79	73	.310	.403	1	.250	0	-3	-2	0	-0.6
1950	Was-A	2	5	.286	9	9	2	0	0	53^1	69	5	29	17	16.5	6.58	68	.307	.386	5	.227	2	-12	-12	-0	-1.1
Total	2	3	8	.273	15	10	2	0	0	67^1	87	6	38	21	16.7	6.42	69	.307	.389	6	.231	2	-15	-15	-0	-1.7

● SAM NAHEM Nahem, Samuel Ralph "Subway Sam" b: 10/19/15, New York, N.Y. BR/TR, 6'1.5", 190 lbs. Deb: 10/2/38

YEAR	TM/L	W	L	PCT	G	GS	CG	SH	SV	IP	H	HR	BB	SO	RAT	ERA	ERA+	OAV	OOB	BH	AVG	PB	PR	/A	PD	TPI
1938	Bro-N	1	0	1.000	1	1	1	0	0	9	6	0	4	2	10.0	3.00	130	.194	.286	2	.400	0	1	1	-0	0.1
1941	StL-N	5	2	.714	26	8	2	0	1	81^2	76	2	38	31	12.8	2.98	126	.243	.329	4	.174	-1	6	7	1	0.6
1942	Phi-N	1	3	.250	35	2	0	0	0	74^2	72	2	40	38	13.7	4.94	67	.254	.350	2	.100	-1	-13	-14	1	-0.7
1948	Phi-N	3	3	.500	28	1	0	0	0	59	68	4	45	30	17.7	7.02	56	.288	.408	2	.154	-0	-20	-20	-1	-1.9
Total	4	10	8	.556	90	12	3	0	1	224^1	222	8	127	101	14.3	4.69	78	.257	.357	10	.164	-2	-27	-26	1	-1.9

● PETE NAKTENIS Naktenis, Peter Ernest b: 6/12/14, Aberdeen, Wash. BL/TL, 6'1", 185 lbs. Deb: 6/13/36

YEAR	TM/L	W	L	PCT	G	GS	CG	SH	SV	IP	H	HR	BB	SO	RAT	ERA	ERA+	OAV	OOB	BH	AVG	PB	PR	/A	PD	TPI
1936	Phi-A	0	1	.000	7	1	0	0	0	18^2	24	2	27	18	25.6	12.54	41	.324	.515	1	.200	-0	-16	-15	-1	-0.7
1939	Cin-N	0	0	—	3	0	0	0	0	4	2	0	0	1	9.0	2.25	170	.154	.267	0	—	0	1	1	0	0.0
Total	2	0	1	.000	10	1	0	0	0	22^2	26	2	27	19	22.6	10.72	45	.299	.483	1	.200	-0	-15	-15	-0	-0.7

● BUDDY NAPIER Napier, Skelton Le Roy b: 12/18/1889, Byromville, Ga. d: 3/29/68, Hutchins, Tex. BR/TR, 5'11", 165 lbs. Deb: 8/14/12

YEAR	TM/L	W	L	PCT	G	GS	CG	SH	SV	IP	H	HR	BB	SO	RAT	ERA	ERA+	OAV	OOB	BH	AVG	PB	PR	/A	PD	TPI
1912	StL-A	1	2	.333	7	2	0	0	0	25^1	33	0	5	10	14.6	4.97	67	.317	.366	0	.000	-1	-5	-5	-0	-0.6
1918	Chi-N	0	0	—	1	0	0	0	0	6^2	10	0	4	2	18.9	5.40	52	.357	.438	1	.333	0	-2	-2	-0	0.0
1920	Cin-N	4	2	.667	9	5	5	1	0	49	47	0	7	17	10.1	1.29	236	.254	.285	3	.214	1	10	10	0	1.3
1921	Cin-N	0	2	.000	22	6	1	0	1	56^2	72	2	13	14	13.5	5.56	64	.329	.366	2	.143	1	-11	-12	1	-0.2
Total	4	5	6	.455	39	13	6	1	1	137^2	162	2	29	43	12.7	3.92	84	.302	.343	6	.158	1	-8	-9	1	0.5

● CHOLLY NARANJO Naranjo, Lazaro Ramon Gonzalo "Gonzalo" b: 11/25/34, Havana, Cuba BL/TR, 5'11.5", 165 lbs. Deb: 7/8/56

YEAR	TM/L	W	L	PCT	G	GS	CG	SH	SV	IP	H	HR	BB	SO	RAT	ERA	ERA+	OAV	OOB	BH	AVG	PB	PR	/A	PD	TPI
1956	Pit-N	1	2	.333	17	3	0	0	0	34^1	37	7	17	26	14.4	4.46	85	.282	.369	1	.143	0	-3	-3	1	-0.1

● RAY NARLESKI Narleski, Raymond Edmond b: 11/25/28, Camden, N.J. BR/TR, 6'1", 175 lbs. Deb: 4/17/54 F

YEAR	TM/L	W	L	PCT	G	GS	CG	SH	SV	IP	H	HR	BB	SO	RAT	ERA	ERA+	OAV	OOB	BH	AVG	PB	PR	/A	PD	TPI
1954	*Cle-A	3	3	.500	42	2	1	0	13	89	59	8	44	52	10.6	2.22	165	.189	.293	0	.000	-2	15	14	-1	1.1
1955	Cle-A	9	1	.900	**60**	1	1	0	**19**	111^2	91	11	52	94	11.5	3.71	108	.220	.308	7	.292	1	3	3	-2	0.3
1956	Cle-A†	3	2	.600	32	0	0	0	4	59^1	36	5	19	42	8.5	1.52	277	.170	.241	2	.250	0	**17**	**18**	-1	1.6
1957	Cle-A	11	5	.688	46	15	7	1	16	154^1	136	14	70	93	12.2	3.09	120	.235	.322	4	.093	-2	12	11	-4	0.7
1958	Cle-A★	13	10	.565	44	24	7	0	1	183^1	179	21	91	102	13.4	4.07	90	.255	.343	11	.204	1	-6	-9	-3	-1.2
1959	Det-A	4	12	.250	42	10	1	0	5	104^1	105	21	59	71	14.2	5.78	70	.254	.348	2	.095	-1	-22	-20	-2	-3.2
Total	6	43	33	.566	266	52	17	1	58	702	606	80	335	454	12.2	3.60	106	.230	.320	26	.157	-2	19	18	-12	-0.7

● BUSTER NARUM Narum, Leslie Ferdinand b: 11/16/40, Philadelphia, Pa. BR/TR, 6'1", 200 lbs. Deb: 4/14/63

YEAR	TM/L	W	L	PCT	G	GS	CG	SH	SV	IP	H	HR	BB	SO	RAT	ERA	ERA+	OAV	OOB	BH	AVG	PB	PR	/A	PD	TPI
1963	Bal-A	0	0	—	7	0	0	0	0	9	8	0	5	5	13.0	3.00	116	.242	.342	1	1.000	1	1	0	0	0.2
1964	Was-A	9	15	.375	38	32	7	2	0	199	195	31	73	121	12.3	4.30	86	.259	.328	4	.061	-5	-15	-13	-3	-2.2
1965	Was-A	4	12	.250	46	24	2	0	0	173^2	176	16	91	86	14.2	4.46	78	.267	.361	2	.043	-2	-19	-19	2	-1.6
1966	Was-A	0	0	—	3	0	0	0	0	3^1	11	2	4	0	40.5	21.60	16	.579	.652	0	—	0	-7	-7	-0	0.0
1967	Was-A	1	0	1.000	2	2	0	0	0	11^2	8	1	4	8	9.3	3.09	103	.195	.267	0	.000	-1	0	0	-0	-0.1
Total	5	14	27	.341	96	58	9	2	0	396^2	398	50	177	220	13.3	4.45	80	.264	.346	7	.059	-6	-40	-38	-1	-3.7

● JIM NASH Nash, James Edwin b: 2/9/45, Hawthorne, Nev. BR/TR, 6'5", 230 lbs. Deb: 7/3/66

YEAR	TM/L	W	L	PCT	G	GS	CG	SH	SV	IP	H	HR	BB	SO	RAT	ERA	ERA+	OAV	OOB	BH	AVG	PB	PR	/A	PD	TPI
1966	KC-A	12	1	.923	18	17	5	0	1	127	95	6	47	98	10.1	2.06	165	.204	.277	5	.102	-2	19	19	-3	1.5
1967	KC-A	12	17	.414	37	34	8	2	0	222^1	200	21	87	186	11.8	3.76	85	.242	.317	7	.100	-2	-13	-14	-2	-2.2

YEAR	TM/L	W	L	PCT	G	GS	CG	SH	SV	IP	H	HR	BB	SO	RAT	ERA	ERA+	OAV	OOB	BH	AVG	PB	PR	/A	PD	TPI
1968	Oak-A	13	13	.500	34	33	12	6	0	228^2	185	18	55	169	9.6	2.28	123	.219	.270	5	.068	-2	18	14	-3	1.1
1969	Oak-A	8	8	.500	26	19	3	1	0	115^1	112	17	30	75	11.2	3.67	94	.247	.296	4	.111	-1	-1	-3	-1	-0.5
1970	Atl-N	13	9	.591	34	33	6	2	0	212^1	211	22	90	153	13.0	4.07	105	.257	.334	7	.087	-3	-1	5	0	0.2
1971	Atl-N	9	7	.563	32	19	2	0	2	133	166	17	50	65	14.6	4.94	75	.314	.374	7	.149	-1	-22	-18	-1	-2.3
1972	Atl-N	1	1	.500	11	4	0	0	1	31^1	35	2	25	10	17.2	5.46	69	.307	.432	2	.222	0	-7	-6	-0	-0.4
	Phi-N	0	8	.000	9	8	0	0	0	37^1	46	5	17	15	15.9	6.27	57	.311	.393	1	.100	-0	-12	-11	0	-2.0
	Yr	1	9	.100	20	12	0	0	1	68^2	81	7	42	25	16.5	5.90	62	.305	.405	3	.158	-0	-19	-17	-0	-2.4
Total	7	68	64	.515	201	167	36	11	4	1107^1	1050	108	401	771	11.9	3.58	96	.250	.318	38	.101	-11	-18	-16	-10	-4.6

● BILLY NASH

Nash, William Mitchell b: 6/24/1865, Richmond, Va. d: 11/15/29, E.Orange, N.J. BR/TR, 5'8.5", 167 lbs. Deb: 8/5/1884 MU ♦

YEAR	TM/L	W	L	PCT	G	GS	CG	SH	SV	IP	H	HR	BB	SO	RAT	ERA	ERA+	OAV	OOB	BH	AVG	PB	PR	/A	PD	TPI
1889	Bos-N	0	0	—	1	0	0	0	0	1	0	0	1	0	9.0	0.00	—	.000	.250	132	.274	0	0	0	-0	0.0
1890	Bos-P	0	0	—	1	0	0	0	0	0^1	1	0	0	0	27.0	0.00	—	.500	.500	130	.266	0	0	0	-0	0.0
Total	2	0	0	—	2	0	0	0	0	1^1	1	0	1	0	13.5	0.00	—	.200	.333	1606	.275	1	1	1	-0	0.0

● PHILIP NASTU

Nastu, Philip b: 3/8/55, Bridgeport, Conn. BL/TL, 6'2", 180 lbs. Deb: 9/15/78

YEAR	TM/L	W	L	PCT	G	GS	CG	SH	SV	IP	H	HR	BB	SO	RAT	ERA	ERA+	OAV	OOB	BH	AVG	PB	PR	/A	PD	TPI
1978	SF-N	0	1	.000	3	1	0	0	0	8	8	1	2	5	11.3	5.63	61	.258	.303	0	.000	-0	-2	-2	-0	-0.2
1979	SF-N	3	4	.429	25	14	1	0	0	100	105	14	41	47	13.3	4.32	81	.272	.345	1	.042	-1	-7	-9	0	-0.7
1980	SF-N	0	0	—	6	0	0	0	0	6	10	1	5	1	22.5	6.00	59	.357	.455	0	—	0	-2	-2	0	0.0
Total	3	3	5	.375	34	15	1	0	0	114	123	16	48	53	13.7	4.50	78	.276	.349	1	.040	-1	-10	-13	0	-0.9

● DAN NAULTY

Naulty, Daniel Donovan b: 1/6/70, Los Angeles, Cal. BR/TR, 6'6", 210 lbs. Deb: 4/2/96

YEAR	TM/L	W	L	PCT	G	GS	CG	SH	SV	IP	H	HR	BB	SO	RAT	ERA	ERA+	OAV	OOB	BH	AVG	PB	PR	/A	PD	TPI
1996	Min-A	3	2	.600	49	0	0	0	4	57	43	5	35	56	12.3	3.79	135	.207	.321	0	—	0	8	8	0	0.6
1997	Min-A	1	1	.500	29	0	0	0	1	30^2	29	8	10	23	11.4	5.87	79	.254	.315	0	—	0	-4	-4	-1	-0.3
1998	Min-A	0	2	.000	19	0	0	0	0	23^2	25	3	10	15	13.3	4.94	95	.269	.340	0	—	0	-1	-1	-1	-0.1
Total	3	4	5	.444	97	0	0	0	5	111^1	97	16	55	94	12.3	4.61	106	.234	.323	0	—	0	2	4	-1	0.2

● JAIME NAVARRO

Navarro, Jaime (Cintron) b: 3/27/67, Bayamon, P.R. BR/TR, 6'4", 210 lbs. Deb: 6/20/89 F

YEAR	TM/L	W	L	PCT	G	GS	CG	SH	SV	IP	H	HR	BB	SO	RAT	ERA	ERA+	OAV	OOB	BH	AVG	PB	PR	/A	PD	TPI
1989	Mil-A	7	8	.467	19	17	1	0	0	109^2	119	6	32	56	12.5	3.12	123	.277	.328	0	—	0	9	9	-0	1.1
1990	Mil-A	8	7	.533	32	22	3	0	1	149^1	176	11	41	75	13.3	4.46	87	.293	.343	0	—	0	-9	-10	-0	-0.9
1991	Mil-A	15	12	.556	34	34	10	2	0	234	237	18	73	114	12.2	3.92	101	.261	.320	0	—	0	4	1	-1	0.0
1992	Mil-A	17	11	.607	34	34	5	3	0	246	224	14	64	100	10.8	3.33	115	.246	.299	0	—	0	17	14	-3	1.2
1993	Mil-A	11	12	.478	35	34	5	1	0	214^1	254	21	73	114	14.2	5.33	80	.300	.363	0	—	0	-24	-26	-2	-2.5
1994	Mil-A	4	9	.308	29	10	0	0	0	89^2	115	10	35	65	15.5	6.62	76	.314	.380	0	—	0	-18	-16	-1	-2.1
1995	Chi-N	14	6	.700	29	29	1	1	0	200^1	194	19	56	128	11.4	3.28	125	.251	.304	12	.185	2	20	18	-3	1.5
1996	Chi-N	15	12	.556	35	35	4	1	0	236^2	244	25	72	158	12.4	3.92	111	.269	.329	10	.130	-2	8	11	-3	0.6
1997	Chi-A	9	14	.391	33	33	2	0	0	209^2	267	22	73	142	14.7	5.79	76	.309	.365	0	.000	-0	-29	-33	-3	-3.2
1998	Chi-A	8	16	.333	37	27	1	0	1	172^2	223	30	77	71	16.0	6.36	72	.315	.388	0	.000	-0	-33	-35	-2	-4.0
Total	10	108	107	.502	317	275	32	8	2	1862^1	2053	176	596	1023	13.1	4.50	93	.281	.339	22	.153	-1	-55	-66	-18	-8.3

● JULIO NAVARRO

Navarro, Julio (Ventura) "Whiplash" b: 1/9/36, Vieques, P.R. BR/TR, 5'11", 190 lbs. Deb: 9/3/62 F

YEAR	TM/L	W	L	PCT	G	GS	CG	SH	SV	IP	H	HR	BB	SO	RAT	ERA	ERA+	OAV	OOB	BH	AVG	PB	PR	/A	PD	TPI
1962	LA-A	1	1	.500	9	0	0	0	0	15^1	20	2	4	11	14.1	4.70	82	.317	.358	1	.500	0	-1	-1	-0	-0.1
1963	LA-A	4	5	.444	57	0	0	0	12	90^1	75	7	32	53	10.9	2.89	119	.228	.300	3	.200	1	7	5	1	0.9
1964	LA-A	0	0	—	5	0	0	0	1	9^1	5	0	5	8	11.6	1.93	170	.167	.324	0	.000	-0	2	1	0	0.0
	Det-A	2	1	.667	26	0	0	0	2	41	40	9	16	36	12.7	3.95	93	.250	.326	0	.000	-1	-1	-1	-0	-0.2
	Yr	2	1	.667	31	0	0	0	3	50^1	45	9	21	44	12.2	3.58	100	.234	.316	0	.000	-1	0	0	0	-0.2
1965	Det-A	0	2	.000	15	1	0	0	1	30	25	5	12	22	11.1	4.20	83	.238	.316	0	.000	-0	-2	-2	0	-0.2
1966	Det-A	0	0	—	1	0	0	0	0	0	2	2	0	0	—	∞	—	1.000	1.000	0	—	0	-3	-3	0	-0.3
1970	Atl-N	0	0	—	17	0	0	0	1	26^1	24	7	1	21	8.9	4.10	105	.233	.248	1	.167	-0	-0	1	0	0.0
Total	6	7	9	.438	130	1	0	0	17	212^1	191	32	70	151	11.4	3.65	99	.241	.309	5	.147	-0	1	-1	1	0.1

● EARL NAYLOR

Naylor, Earl Eugene b: 5/19/19, Kansas City, Mo. d: 1/16/90, Winter Haven, Fla. BR/TR, 6', 190 lbs. Deb: 4/15/42 ♦

YEAR	TM/L	W	L	PCT	G	GS	CG	SH	SV	IP	H	HR	BB	SO	RAT	ERA	ERA+	OAV	OOB	BH	AVG	PB	PR	/A	PD	TPI
1942	Phi-N	0	5	.000	20	4	1	0	0	60^1	68	5	29	19	14.5	6.12	54	.286	.363	33	.196	1	-19	-19	-0	-1.4

● ROLLIE NAYLOR

Naylor, Roleine Cecil b: 2/4/1892, Krum, Tex. d: 6/18/66, Fort Worth, Tex. BR/TR, 6'1.5", 180 lbs. Deb: 9/14/17

YEAR	TM/L	W	L	PCT	G	GS	CG	SH	SV	IP	H	HR	BB	SO	RAT	ERA	ERA+	OAV	OOB	BH	AVG	PB	PR	/A	PD	TPI
1917	Phi-A	2	2	.500	5	5	3	0	0	33	30	1	11	11	11.5	1.64	168	.265	.336	1	.091	-1	4	4	1	0.6
1919	Phi-A	5	18	.217	31	23	17	0	0	204^2	210	2	64	68	12.2	3.34	103	.280	.339	12	.169	-2	-3	2	-0	-0.1
1920	Phi-A	10	23	.303	42	36	20	0	0	251^1	306	7	86	90	14.3	3.47	116	.312	.371	14	.163	-6	9	15	2	1.4
1921	Phi-A	3	13	.188	32	19	6	0	0	169^1	214	10	55	39	14.5	4.84	92	.315	.369	6	.115	-4	-10	-7	-2	-1.1
1922	Phi-A	10	15	.400	35	26	11	0	0	171^1	212	7	51	37	14.0	4.73	90	.309	.359	11	.200	1	-13	-9	1	-1.0
1923	Phi-A	12	7	.632	26	20	9	2	0	143	149	5	59	27	13.1	3.46	119	.273	.344	11	.244	1	8	10	-2	1.2
1924	Phi-A	0	5	.000	10	7	1	0	0	38^1	53	2	20	10	17.1	6.34	68	.333	.408	3	.375	1	-9	-9	0	-0.8
Total	7	42	83	.336	181	136	67	2	0	1011	1174	34	346	282	13.7	3.93	102	.300	.359	58	.177	-11	-14	7	1	0.2

● MIKE NAYMICK

Naymick, Michael John b: 9/6/17, Berlin, Pa. BR/TR, 6'8", 225 lbs. Deb: 9/24/39

YEAR	TM/L	W	L	PCT	G	GS	CG	SH	SV	IP	H	HR	BB	SO	RAT	ERA	ERA+	OAV	OOB	BH	AVG	PB	PR	/A	PD	TPI
1939	Cle-A	0	1	.000	2	1	1	0	0	4^2	3	0	5	3	15.4	1.93	228	.188	.381	0	.000	-0	1	1	-0	0.2
1940	Cle-A	1	2	.333	13	4	0	0	0	30	36	1	17	15	16.8	5.10	83	.290	.389	1	.167	-0	-2	-3	1	-0.2
1943	Cle-A	4	4	.500	29	4	0	0	2	62^2	32	3	47	41	11.8	2.30	135	.160	.328	3	.188	-0	7	6	1	0.8
1944	Cle-A	0	0	—	7	0	0	0	0	13	16	1	10	4	18.0	9.69	34	.314	.426	0	.000	-0	-9	-9	0	-1.0
	StL-N	0	0	—	1	0	0	0	0	2	2	0	1	1	13.5	4.50	78	.333	.429	0	—	0	-0	-0	0	0.0
Total	4	5	7	.417	52	9	1	0	2	112^1	89	5	80	64	14.0	3.93	89	.224	.362	4	.154	-1	-3	-6	1	0.8

● DENNY NEAGLE

Neagle, Dennis Edward b: 9/13/68, Gambrills, Md. BL/TL, 6'2", 217 lbs. Deb: 7/27/91

YEAR	TM/L	W	L	PCT	G	GS	CG	SH	SV	IP	H	HR	BB	SO	RAT	ERA	ERA+	OAV	OOB	BH	AVG	PB	PR	/A	PD	TPI
1991	Min-A	0	1	.000	7	3	0	0	0	20	28	3	7	14	15.7	4.05	105	.329	.380	0	—	0	0	0	-0	-0.1
1992	*Pit-N	4	6	.400	55	6	0	0	2	86^1	81	9	43	77	13.1	4.48	77	.247	.338	0	.000	-1	-9	-10	-0	-1.4
1993	Pit-N	3	5	.375	50	7	0	0	1	81^1	82	10	37	73	13.5	5.31	76	.258	.341	0	.000	-2	-11	-11	-1	-1.3
1994	Pit-N	9	10	.474	24	24	2	0	0	137	135	18	49	122	12.3	5.12	84	.259	.326	8	.190	1	-14	-12	0	-1.4
1995	Pit-N★	13	8	.619	31	31	5	1	0	**209^2**	221	20	45	150	11.5	3.43	125	.273	.314	9	.122	-0	17	20	1	1.9
1996	Pit-N	14	6	.700	27	27	1	0	0	182^2	186	21	34	131	11.0	3.05	143	.267	.304	10	.182	0	24	26	-0	2.6
	*Atl-N	2	3	.400	6	6	1	0	0	38^2	40	5	14	18	12.6	5.59	79	.268	.331	2	.143	-0	-6	-5	-1	-0.6
	Yr	16	9	.640	33	33	2	0	0	221^1	226	26	48	149	11.1	3.50	125	.266	.305	12	.174	-0	18	21	-1	2.0
1997	*Atl-N☆	**20**	5	.800	34	34	4	4	0	233^1	204	18	49	172	10.0	2.97	141	.233	.279	11	.153	1	32	31	-0	3.2
1998	*Atl-N	16	11	.593	32	31	5	2	0	210^1	196	25	60	165	11.2	3.55	119	.250	.308	11	.175	1	16	16	-3	1.7
Total	8	81	55	.596	266	169	18	7	3	1199^1	1173	129	338	922	11.5	3.78	111	.257	.312	51	.148	-0	48	55	-5	4.6

● JACK NEAGLE

Neagle, John Henry b: 1/2/1858, Syracuse, N.Y. d: 9/20/04, Syracuse, N.Y. BR/TR, 5'6", 155 lbs. Deb: 7/8/1879 ♦

YEAR	TM/L	W	L	PCT	G	GS	CG	SH	SV	IP	H	HR	BB	SO	RAT	ERA	ERA+	OAV	OOB	BH	AVG	PB	PR	/A	PD	TPI
1879	Cin-N	0	1	.000	2	2	1	0	0	13	13	0	5	4	12.5	3.46	67	.241	.305	2	.167	-0	-1	-2	-0	-0.2
1883	Phi-N	1	7	.125	8	7	6	0	0	61^1	88	0	21	13	16.0	6.90	45	.315	.363	12	.164	-2	-26	-26	-1	-2.5
	Bal-a	1	4	.200	6	5	4	0	0	46	48	1	20	9	13.3	4.89	71	.251	.322	10	.286	1	-8	-7	-0	-0.5
	Pit-a	3	12	.200	16	16	12	0	0	114	156	9	25	41	14.3	5.84	55	.306	.338	19	.188	-1	-32	-33	-1	-3.3
	Yr	4	16	.200	22	21	16	0	0	160	204	10	45	50	14.0	5.57	59	.291	.334	29	.213	-0	-40	-41	-1	-3.8
1884	Pit-a	11	26	.297	38	38	37	2	0	326	354	6	70	85	12.2	3.73	90	.255	.300	22	.149	-6	-17	-13	-3	-1.9
Total	3	16	50	.242	70	68	60	2	0	560^1	659	16	141	152	13.1	4.59	72	.272	.317	65	.176	-8	-85	-81	-5	-8.4

● JOE NEALE

Neale, Joseph Hunt b: 5/7/1866, Wadsworth, Ohio d: 12/30/13, Akron, Ohio BR/TR, 5'8", 153 lbs. Deb: 6/21/1886 ♦

YEAR	TM/L	W	L	PCT	G	GS	CG	SH	SV	IP	H	HR	BB	SO	RAT	ERA	ERA+	OAV	OOB	BH	AVG	PB	PR	/A	PD	TPI
1886	Lou-a	0	1	.000	1	1	0	0	0	7	11	0	7	0	24.4	7.71	47	.393	.528	0	.000	-0	-3	-3	1	-0.3
1887	Lou-a	1	4	.200	5	4	4	0	0	41^1	60	4	15	11	16.8	6.97	63	.326	.383	1	.053	-2	-12	-12	0	-1.1
1890	StL-a	5	3	.625	10	9	8	0	0	69	53	4	15	23	9.4	3.39	127	.206	.261	2	.067	-3	4	7	-2	0.3
1891	StL-a	6	4	.600	15	11	9	1	1	110^1	109	4	36	24	12.4	4.24	99	.249	.317	6	.118	-3	-6	-0	2	-0.2
Total	4	12	12	.500	31	25	21	1	1	227^2	233	12	73	58	12.7	4.59	93	.257	.322	9	.086	-9	-18	-8	1	-1.3

● RON NECCIAI

Necciai, Ronald Andrew b: 6/18/32, Gallatin, Pa. BR/TR, 6'5", 185 lbs. Deb: 8/10/52

YEAR	TM/L	W	L	PCT	G	GS	CG	SH	SV	IP	H	HR	BB	SO	RAT	ERA	ERA+	OAV	OOB	BH	AVG	PB	PR	/A	PD	TPI
1952	Pit-N	1	6	.143	12	9	0	0	0	54^2	63	5	32	31	15.8	7.08	56	.296	.390	1	.059	-1	-20	-19	-0	-2.2

YEAR	TM/L	W	L	PCT	G	GS	CG	SH	SV	IP	H	HR	BB	SO	RAT	ERA	ERA+	OAV	OOB	BH	AVG	PB	PR	/A	PD	TPI
● RON NEGRAY	Negray, Ronald Alvin b: 2/26/30, Akron, Ohio BR/TR, 6'1", 185 lbs. Deb: 9/14/52																									
1952	Bro-N	0	0	—	4	1	0	0	0	13	15	0	5	5	13.8	3.46	105	.294	.357	0	.000	-0	0	0	-0	0.0
1955	Phi-N	4	3	.571	19	10	2	0	0	71^2	71	13	21	30	11.6	3.52	113	.257	.310	0	.000	-3	4	4	-0	0.0
1956	Phi-N	2	3	.400	39	4	0	0	3	66^2	72	6	24	44	13.1	4.18	89	.280	.344	3	.429	1	-3	-3	0	-0.1
1958	LA-N	0	0	—	4	0	0	0	0	11^1	12	4	7	2	15.1	7.15	57	.279	.380	0	.000	-0	-4	-4	-0	0.0
Total	4	6	6	.500	66	15	2	0	3	162^2	170	23	57	81	12.6	4.04	95	.271	.333	3	.086	-3	-3	-3	-1	-0.1
● JIM NEHER	Neher, James Gilmore b: 2/5/1889, Rochester, N.Y. d: 11/11/51, Buffalo, N.Y. BR/TR, 5'11", 185 lbs. Deb: 9/10/12																									
1912	Cle-A	0	0	—	1	0	0	0	0	1	0	0	0	0	0.0	0.00	—	.000	.000	0	—	0	0	0	-0	0.0
● ART NEHF	Nehf, Arthur Neukom b: 7/31/1892, Terre Haute, Ind. d: 12/18/60, Phoenix, Ariz. BL/TL, 5'9.5", 176 lbs. Deb: 8/13/15																									
1915	Bos-N	5	4	.556	12	10	6	4	0	78^1	60	0	21	39	9.7	2.53	103	.214	.276	4	.143	-1	2	1	0	0.0
1916	Bos-N	7	5	.583	22	13	6	1	0	121	110	1	20	36	9.9	2.01	124	.244	.281	5	.125	-0	8	6	-1	0.5
1917	Bos-N	17	8	.680	38	23	17	5	0	233^1	197	4	39	101	9.3	2.16	118	.231	.268	12	.171	5	14	10	-0	1.7
1918	Bos-N	15	15	.500	32	31	**28**	2	0	284^1	274	2	76	96	11.3	2.69	100	.259	.312	16	.168	1	2	-0	3	0.6
1919	Bos-N	8	9	.471	22	19	13	1	0	168^2	151	6	40	53	10.5	3.09	92	.242	.294	13	.206	2	-3	-4	1	-0.1
	NY-N	9	2	.818	13	12	9	2	0	102	70	2	19	24	8.0	1.50	187	.196	.240	8	.229	3	16	15	-1	2.0
	Yr	17	11	.607	35	31	22	3	0	270^2	221	8	59	77	9.4	2.49	114	.224	.269	21	.214	5	13	10	0	1.9
1920	NY-N	21	12	.636	40	33	22	4	0	280^2	273	8	45	79	10.2	3.08	97	.260	.291	26	.268	5	2	-3	3	0.5
1921	*NY-N	20	10	.667	41	34	18	2	1	260^2	266	18	55	67	11.2	3.63	101	.271	.311	18	.202	0	5	1	3	0.4
1922	*NY-N	19	13	.594	37	35	20	2	1	268^1	286	15	64	60	11.9	3.29	122	.276	.321	25	.255	4	24	21	1	2.5
1923	*NY-N	13	10	.565	34	27	7	1	2	196	219	14	49	50	12.4	4.50	85	.281	.326	12	.190	1	-11	-15	1	-1.3
1924	*NY-N	14	4	.778	30	20	11	0	2	171^2	167	14	42	72	11.1	3.62	101	.254	.301	13	.228	6	5	1	2	0.9
1925	NY-N	11	9	.550	29	20	8	1	1	155	193	7	50	63	14.2	3.77	107	.308	.360	11	.216	1	9	5	2	0.8
1926	NY-N	0	0	—	2	0	0	0	0	1^2	2	0	1	0	16.2	10.80	35	.286	.375	0	.000	-0	-1	-1	0	0.0
	Cin-N	0	1	.000	7	1	0	0	0	17	25	0	5	4	16.4	3.71	100	.379	.431	1	.200	-0	0	-0	1	0.0
	Yr	0	1	.000	9	1	0	0	0	18^2	27	0	6	4	16.4	4.34	85	.370	.425	1	.167	-0	-1	-1	1	0.0
1927	Cin-N	3	5	.375	21	5	1	0	4	45^1	59	2	14	21	14.5	5.56	68	.319	.367	1	.077	-1	-8	-9	1	-1.5
	Chi-N	1	1	.500	8	2	2	1	1	26^1	25	0	9	12	11.6	1.37	283	.260	.324	3	.429	1	7	7	-0	0.7
	Yr	4	6	.400	29	7	3	1	5	71^2	84	2	23	33	13.4	4.02	95	.299	.352	4	.200	0	-1	-2	1	-0.8
1928	Chi-N	13	7	.650	31	21	10	2	0	176^2	190	3	52	40	12.4	2.65	145	.281	.334	11	.190	2	26	24	1	2.8
1929	*Chi-N	8	5	.615	32	15	4	0	1	120^2	148	11	39	27	14.1	5.59	83	.310	.365	13	.289	4	-12	-13	1	-0.8
Total	15	184	120	.605	451	321	182	28	13	2707^2	2715	107	640	844	11.3	3.20	105	.265	.310	192	.210	34	85	45	17	9.7
● GARY NEIBAUER	Neibauer, Gary Wayne b: 10/29/44, Billings, Mont. BR/TR, 6'3", 200 lbs. Deb: 4/12/69																									
1969	*Atl-N	1	2	.333	29	0	0	0	0	57^2	42	9	31	42	11.5	3.90	92	.204	.311	0	.000	-1	-2	-2	-0	-0.2
1970	Atl-N	0	3	.000	7	0	0	0	0	12^2	11	0	8	9	13.5	4.97	86	.239	.352	0	.000	-0	-1	-1	-0	-0.2
1971	Atl-N	1	0	1.000	6	1	0	0	1	21	14	3	9	6	10.3	2.14	173	.187	.282	0	.000	-1	3	4	0	0.2
1972	Atl-N	0	0	—	8	0	0	0	0	17^1	27	6	6	8	17.7	7.27	52	.360	.415	0	.000	-0	-7	-7	-0	-0.1
	Phi-N	0	2	.000	9	2	0	0	0	18^2	17	1	14	7	15.4	5.30	68	.239	.372	1	.250	0	-4	-4	-0	-0.4
	Yr	0	2	.000	17	2	0	0	0	36	44	7	20	15	16.3	6.25	59	.297	.385	1	.125	-0	-11	-10	-1	-0.5
1973	Atl-N	2	1	.667	16	1	0	0	0	21^1	24	3	19	9	19.0	7.17	55	.282	.425	1	.250	1	-8	-8	-1	-0.9
Total	5	4	8	.333	75	4	0	0	1	148^2	135	22	87	81	13.8	4.78	78	.242	.350	2	.069	-1	-20	-17	-2	-1.6
● JIM NEIDLINGER	Neidlinger, James Llewellyn b: 9/24/64, Vallejo, Cal. BB/TR, 6'4", 180 lbs. Deb: 8/1/90																									
1990	LA-N	5	3	.625	12	12	0	0	0	74	67	4	15	46	10.1	3.28	111	.241	.282	3	.120	-0	4	3	-1	0.2
● AL NEIGER	Neiger, Alvin Edward b: 3/26/39, Wilmington, Del. BL/TL, 6', 195 lbs. Deb: 7/30/60																									
1960	Phi-N	0	0	—	6	0	0	0	0	12^2	16	2	4	3	15.6	5.68	68	.340	.415	1	.500	0	-3	-3	-0	0.0
● ERNIE NEITZKE	Neitzke, Ernest Fredrich b: 11/13/1894, Toledo, Ohio d: 4/27/77, Sylvania, Ohio BR/TR, 5'10", 180 lbs. Deb: 6/2/21 ♦																									
1921	Bos-A	0	0	—	2	0	0	0	0	7^1	8	0	4	1	14.7	6.14	69	.333	.429	6	.240	0	-2	-2	0	0.0
● BOTS NEKOLA	Nekola, Francis Joseph b: 12/10/06, New York, N.Y. d: 3/11/87, Rockville, Md. BL/TL, 5'11.5", 175 lbs. Deb: 7/19/29																									
1929	NY-A	0	0	—	9	1	0	0	0	18^2	21	0	15	2	17.4	4.34	89	.296	.419	2	.500	1	-0	-1	1	0.2
1933	Det-A	0	0	—	2	0	0	0	0	1^1	4	1	1	0	33.8	27.00	16	.500	.556	0	—	0	-3	-3	-0	0.0
Total	2	0	0	—	11	1	0	0	0	20	25	1	16	2	18.4	5.85	66	.316	.432	2	.500	1	-4	-4	1	0.2
● RED NELSON	Nelson, Albert Francis (b: Albert W. Horazdovsky) b: 5/19/1886, Cleveland, Ohio d: 10/26/56, St.Petersburg, Fla BR/TR, 5'11", 190 lbs. Deb: 9/9/10																									
1910	StL-A	5	1	.833	7	6	6	1	0	60	57	0	14	30	11.3	2.55	97	.261	.318	6	.261	2	-0	-1	4	0.6
1911	StL-A	3	9	.250	16	13	6	0	0	81^1	103	1	44	24	17.1	5.22	65	.324	.417	3	.111	-2	-17	-17	-1	-2.3
1912	StL-A	0	2	.000	8	3	0	0	1	18	21	0	13	9	17.0	7.00	47	.318	.430	1	.333	1	-7	-7	-1	-0.8
	Phi-N	2	0	1.000	4	2	1	0	0	19^1	25	2	6	2	15.4	3.72	97	.305	.367	1	.100	-1	-1	-0	-0	-0.1
1913	Phi-N	0	0	—	2	0	0	0	0	8^1	9	0	4	3	14.0	2.16	154	.290	.371	1	.333	0	1	1	0	0.1
	Cin-N	0	0	—	2	0	0	0	0	1^2	6	1	4	0	59.4	37.80	9	.667	.786	0	—	0	-6	-6	-0	0.0
	Yr	0	0	—	4	0	0	0	0	10	15	1	8	3	21.6	8.10	41	.375	.490	1	.333	0	-5	-5	0	0.1
Total	4	10	12	.455	39	24	13	1	1	188^1	221	4	85	68	15.3	4.54	68	.305	.389	12	.182	0	-31	-30	2	-2.5
● ANDY NELSON	Nelson, Andrew "Peaches" TL , Deb: 5/26/08																									
1908	Chi-A	0	0	—	2	1	0	0	0	9	11	0	4	1	16.0	2.00	116	.282	.364	0	.000	0	0	0	-1	-0.1
● EMMETT NELSON	Nelson, George Emmett "Ramrod" b: 2/26/05, Viborg, S.Dak. d: 8/25/67, Sioux Falls, S.D. BR/TR, 6'3", 180 lbs. Deb: 6/24/35																									
1935	Cin-N	4	4	.500	19	7	3	1	1	60^1	70	2	23	14	14.2	4.33	92	.295	.363	2	.133	-1	-2	-2	1	-0.3
1936	Cin-N	1	0	1.000	6	1	0	0	0	17	24	1	4	3	15.4	3.18	120	.333	.377	1	.167	-0	2	1	-0	0.0
Total	2	5	4	.556	25	8	3	1	1	77^1	94	3	27	17	14.4	4.07	97	.304	.366	3	.143	-1	-0	-1	1	-0.3
● JIM NELSON	Nelson, James Lorin b: 7/4/47, Birmingham, Ala. BR/TR, 6', 180 lbs. Deb: 5/30/70																									
1970	Pit-N	4	2	.667	15	10	1	1	0	68^1	64	5	38	42	13.8	3.42	114	.255	.360	4	.200	0	5	4	-1	0.2
1971	Pit-N	2	2	.500	17	2	0	0	0	34^2	27	0	26	11	15.1	2.34	145	.225	.384	3	.500	2	4	4	-0	0.6
Total	2	6	4	.600	32	12	1	1	0	103	91	5	64	53	14.2	3.06	122	.245	.368	7	.269	2	9	8	-1	0.8
● JEFF NELSON	Nelson, Jeffrey Allan b: 11/17/66, Baltimore, Md. BR/TR, 6'8", 235 lbs. Deb: 4/16/92																									
1992	Sea-A	1	7	.125	66	0	0	0	6	81	71	7	44	46	13.4	3.44	115	.245	.356	0	—	0	4	5	0	0.5
1993	Sea-A	5	3	.625	71	0	0	0	1	60	57	5	34	61	14.9	4.35	101	.258	.376	0	—	0	-0	0	1	0.1
1994	Sea-A	0	0	—	28	0	0	0	0	42^1	35	3	20	44	13.4	2.76	177	.226	.344	0	—	0	10	10	-0	-0.1
1995	*Sea-A	7	3	.700	62	0	0	0	2	78^2	58	4	27	96	10.4	2.17	218	.209	.294	0	—	0	22	22	0	2.5
1996	*NY-A	4	4	.500	73	0	0	0	2	74^1	75	6	36	91	13.7	4.36	113	.262	.349	0	—	0	5	5	2	0.6
1997	*NY-A	3	7	.300	77	0	0	0	2	78^2	53	7	37	81	10.8	2.86	155	.191	.296	0	—	0	15	14	2	1.7
1998	*NY-A	5	3	.625	45	0	0	0	3	40^1	44	1	22	35	16.5	3.79	117	.278	.394	0	.000	-0	4	3	1	0.6
Total	7	25	27	.481	422	0	0	0	16	455^1	393	33	220	454	12.9	3.36	135	.236	.340	0	.000	-0	60	59	5	5.9
● LUKE NELSON	Nelson, Luther Martin b: 12/4/1893, Cable, Ill. d: 11/14/85, Moline, Ill. BR/TR, 6', 180 lbs. Deb: 5/25/19																									
1919	NY-A	3	0	1.000	9	1	0	0	0	24^1	22	1	11	11	12.6	2.96	108	.244	.333	1	.143	-0	1	1	-0	0.0
● LYNN NELSON	Nelson, Lynn Bernard "Line Drive" b: 2/24/05, Sheldon, N.Dak. d: 2/15/55, Kansas City, Mo. BL/TR, 5'10.5", 170 lbs. Deb: 4/18/30 ♦																									
1930	Chi-N	3	2	.600	37	3	0	0	0	81^1	97	10	28	29	14.5	5.09	96	.300	.367	4	.222	0	-1	-2	1	0.1
1933	Chi-N	5	5	.500	24	3	3	0	1	75^2	65	2	30	20	11.3	3.21	102	.232	.306	5	.238	2	1	1	1	0.3
1934	Chi-N	0	1	.000	2	1	0	0	0	1	4	1	1	0	45.0	36.00	11	.667	.714	0	—	0	-4	-4	-0	-1.9
1937	Phi-A	4	9	.308	30	4	1	0	2	116	140	12	51	49	15.0	5.90	80	.300	.371	40	.354	6	-16	-15	-2	-0.5
1938	Phi-A	10	11	.476	32	23	13	0	2	191	215	29	79	75	14.1	5.65	85	.277	.347	31	.277	4	-18	-17	-0	-1.1
1939	Phi-A	10	13	.435	35	24	12	2	1	197^2	233	27	64	75	13.7	4.78	98	.292	.347	15	.188	-2	-4	-2	-1	-0.4

YEAR	TM/L	W	L	PCT	G	GS	CG	SH	SV	IP	H	HR	BB	SO	RAT	ERA	ERA+	OAV	OOB	BH	AVG	PB	PR	/A	PD	TPI
1940	Det-A	1	1	.500	6	2	0	0	0	14	23	5	9	7	20.6	10.93	44	.371	.451	8	.348	2	-10	-10	0	-0.9
Total	7	33	42	.440	166	60	29	2	6	676^{2}	777	86	262	255	14.0	5.25	88	.287	.353	103	.281	13	-52	-49	-1	-4.4
● MEL NELSON	Nelson, Melvin Frederick b: 5/30/36, San Diego, Cal. BR/TL, 6′, 185 lbs. Deb: 9/27/60																									
1960	StL-N	0	1	.000	2	1	0	0	0	8	7	1	2	7	10.1	3.38	121	.226	.273	1	.500	0	0	1	-0	0.1
1963	LA-A	2	3	.400	36	3	0	0	1	52^{2}	55	7	32	41	15.2	5.30	65	.263	.366	1	.091	-1	-10	-11	1	-1.0
1965	Min-A	0	4	.000	28	3	0	0	3	54^{2}	57	7	23	31	13.5	4.12	86	.261	.337	1	.111	-0	-4	-3	-0	-0.4
1967	Min-A	0	0	—	1	0	0	0	0	0^{1}	3	1	0	0	81.0	54.00	6	.750	.750	0	—	0	-2	-2	0	0.0
1968	*StL-N	2	1	.667	18	4	1	0	1	52^{2}	49	3	9	16	9.9	2.91	100	.254	.287	2	.167	0	0	-0	-0	0.0
1969	StL-N	0	1	.000	8	0	0	0	0	5^{1}	13	0	3	3	27.0	11.81	30	.520	.571	0	—	0	-5	-5	-0	-0.8
Total	6	4	10	.286	93	11	1	0	5	173^{2}	184	19	69	98	13.3	4.40	76	.271	.341	5	.147	-1	-20	-21	0	-2.1
● ROGER NELSON	Nelson, Roger Eugene "Spider" b: 6/7/44, Altadena, Cal. BR/TR, 6′3″, 205 lbs. Deb: 9/9/67																									
1967	Chi-A	0	1	.000	5	0	0	0	0	7	4	1	0	4	7.7	1.29	241	.182	.250	0	—	0	2	1	0	0.2
1968	Bal-A	4	3	.571	19	6	0	0	1	71	49	3	26	70	9.6	2.41	121	.192	.270	1	.063	-0	5	4	-0	0.4
1969	KC-A	7	13	.350	29	29	8	1	0	193^{1}	170	12	65	82	11.2	3.31	112	.243	.313	8	.138	-1	7	8	-1	0.6
1970	KC-A	0	2	.000	4	2	0	0	0	9	18	3	0	3	19.0	10.00	37	.419	.432	0	—	0	-6	-6	0	-1.1
1971	KC-A	0	1	.000	13	1	0	0	0	34	35	1	5	29	10.6	5.29	65	.269	.296	2	.333	1	-7	-7	1	0.0
1972	KC-A	11	6	.647	34	19	10	6	3	173^{1}	120	13	31	120	**7.9**	2.08	146	.196	**.236**	5	.093	-2	19	18	1	1.9
1973	*Cin-N	3	2	.600	14	8	1	0	0	54^{2}	49	4	24	17	12.5	3.46	98	.246	.336	2	.111	-1	1	-0	1	0.0
1974	Cin-N	4	4	.500	14	12	1	0	1	85^{1}	67	7	35	42	10.9	3.38	103	.213	.293	5	.179	0	2	1	-1	0.0
1976	KC-A	0	0	—	3	0	0	0	0	8^{2}	4	0	4	4	10.4	2.08	169	.138	.286	0	—	0	1	1	0	0.0
Total	9	29	32	.475	135	77	20	7	5	636^{1}	516	44	190	371	10.2	3.06	110	.224	.288	23	.128	-3	23	21	2	2.0
● GENE NELSON	Nelson, Wayland Eugene b: 12/3/60, Tampa, Fla. BR/TR, 6′, 174 lbs. Deb: 5/4/81																									
1981	NY-A	3	1	.750	8	7	0	0	0	39^{1}	40	5	23	16	14.6	4.81	74	.261	.362	0	—	0	-5	-5	-0	-0.5
1982	Sea-A	6	9	.400	22	19	2	1	0	122^{2}	133	16	60	71	14.3	4.62	92	.279	.362	0	—	0	-7	-5	1	-0.5
1983	Sea-A	0	3	.000	10	5	1	0	0	32	38	6	21	11	16.9	7.88	54	.295	.397	0	—	0	-14	-13	1	-1.1
1984	Chi-A	3	5	.375	20	9	2	0	1	74^{2}	72	9	17	36	10.8	4.46	93	.254	.299	0	—	0	-4	-3	0	-0.2
1985	Chi-A	10	10	.500	46	18	1	0	2	145^{2}	144	23	67	101	13.5	4.26	101	.258	.345	0	.000	-0	-2	1	0	0.1
1986	Chi-A	6	6	.500	54	1	0	0	6	114^{2}	118	7	41	70	12.7	3.85	112	.271	.338	0	—	0	4	6	1	0.7
1987	Oak-A	6	5	.545	54	6	0	0	3	123^{2}	120	12	35	94	11.6	3.93	105	.249	.307	0	—	0	7	3	-1	0.1
1988	*Oak-A	9	6	.600	54	1	0	0	3	111^{2}	93	9	38	67	10.8	3.06	123	.228	.298	0	—	0	11	9	-1	1.1
1989	*Oak-A	3	5	.375	50	0	0	0	3	80	60	5	30	70	10.3	3.26	113	.203	.280	0	—	0	6	4	-1	0.2
1990	*Oak-A	3	3	.500	51	0	0	0	5	74^{2}	55	5	17	38	9.0	1.57	237	.208	.263	0	—	0	19	18	-1	1.5
1991	Oak-A	1	5	.167	44	0	0	0	0	48^{2}	60	12	23	23	15.9	6.84	56	.306	.387	0	—	0	-15	-16	-1	-1.8
1992	Oak-A	3	1	.750	28	2	0	0	0	51^{2}	68	5	22	23	15.7	6.45	58	.335	.400	0	—	0	-14	-16	-1	-1.1
1993	Cal-A	0	5	.000	46	0	0	0	4	52^{2}	50	3	23	31	12.8	3.08	146	.251	.335	0	—	0	7	8	0	0.6
	Tex-A	0	0	—	6	0	0	0	1	8	10	0	1	4	12.4	3.38	123	.303	.324	0	—	0	1	1	-0	0.2
	Yr	0	5	.000	52	0	0	0	5	60^{2}	60	3	24	35	12.5	3.12	143	.252	.321	0	—	0	8	9	0	0.8
Total	13	53	64	.453	493	68	6	1	28	1080	1061	117	418	655	12.6	4.13	98	.258	.331	0	.000	-0	-5	-9	-3	-0.7
● BILL NELSON	Nelson, William F. b: 9/28/1863, Terre Haute, Ind. d: 6/23/41, Terre Haute, Ind. TR, Deb: 9/3/1884																									
1884	Pit-a	1	2	.333	3	3	3	0	0	26	26	1	8	6	13.2	4.50	75	.252	.330	2	.167	-1	-4	-3	-0	-0.4
● ROBB NEN	Nen, Robert Allen b: 11/28/69, San Pedro, Cal. BR/TR, 6′4″, 200 lbs. Deb: 4/10/93 F																									
1993	Tex-A	1	1	.500	9	3	0	0	0	22^{2}	28	1	26	12	21.4	6.35	65	.326	.482	0	—	0	-5	-6	0	-0.2
	Fla-N	1	0	1.000	15	1	0	0	0	33^{1}	35	5	20	27	14.9	7.02	62	.255	.350	0	.000	-0	-11	-10	-0	-0.3
1994	Fla-N	5	5	.500	44	0	0	0	15	58	46	6	17	60	9.8	2.95	148	.222	.281	0	.000	-0	8	9	-0	1.8
1995	Fla-N	0	7	.000	62	0	0	0	23	65^{2}	62	6	23	68	11.8	3.29	128	.244	.309	0	—	0	6	7	0	1.1
1996	Fla-N	5	1	.833	75	0	0	0	35	83	67	2	21	92	9.7	1.95	208	.225	.278	0	.000	-0	**21**	20	-0	2.7
1997	*Fla-N	9	3	.750	73	0	0	0	35	74	72	7	40	81	13.6	3.89	103	.250	.341	0	—	0	3	1	0	0.3
1998	SF-N★	7	7	.500	78	0	0	0	40	88^{2}	59	4	25	110	8.6	1.52	267	.180	.241	0	.000	-0	**27**	**25**	-0	5.6
Total	6	28	24	.538	356	4	0	0	148	425^{1}	369	31	172	450	11.5	3.17	131	.231	.307	0	.000	-1	49	46	-0	11.0
● HAL NEUBAUER	Neubauer, Harold Charles b: 5/13/02, Hoboken, N.J. d: 9/9/49, Providence, R.I. BR/TR, 6′0.5″, 185 lbs. Deb: 6/12/25																									
1925	Bos-A	1	0	1.000	7	0	0	0	0	10^{1}	17	2	11	4	24.4	12.19	37	.378	.500	0	—	0	-9	-9	0	-0.7
● TEX NEUER	Neuer, John S. b: 6/8/1877, Fremont, Ohio d: 1/14/66, Northumberland, Pa TL, Deb: 8/28/07																									
1907	NY-A	4	2	.667	7	6	6	3	0	54	40	1	19	22	9.8	2.17	129	.208	.280	2	.095	-2	2	4	-1	0.1
● DAN NEUMEIER	Neumeier, Daniel George b: 3/9/48, Shawano, Wis. BR/TR, 6′5″, 205 lbs. Deb: 9/8/72																									
1972	Chi-A	0	0	—	3	0	0	0	0	3^{1}	2	0	3	0	15.0	9.00	35	.200	.385	0	.000	-0	-2	-2	-0	0.0
● ERNIE NEVEL	Nevel, Ernie Wyre b: 8/17/18, Charleston, Mo. d: 7/10/88, Springfield, Mo. BR/TR, 6′1″, 200 lbs. Deb: 9/26/50																									
1950	NY-A	0	1	.000	3	1	0	0	0	6^{1}	10	0	6	3	22.7	9.95	43	.345	.457	0	.000	-0	-4	-4	0	-0.5
1951	NY-A	0	0	—	1	0	0	0	1	4	1	0	1	1	4.5	0.00	—	.083	.154	0	.000	-0	2	2	-0	0.1
1953	Cin-N	0	0	—	10	0	0	0	0	10^{1}	16	0	1	5	14.8	6.10	71	.390	.405	0	—	0	-2	-2	0	0.0
Total	3	0	1	.000	14	1	0	0	1	20^{2}	27	0	8	9	15.2	6.10	69	.329	.389	0	.000	-0	-4	-4	0	-0.4
● ERNIE NEVERS	Nevers, Ernest Alonzo b: 6/11/02, Willow River, Minn. d: 5/3/76, San Rafael, Cal. BR/TR, 6′, 205 lbs. Deb: 4/26/26																									
1926	StL-A	2	4	.333	11	7	4	0	0	74^{2}	82	4	24	16	12.9	4.46	96	.290	.347	5	.185	-1	-4	-1	2	0.0
1927	StL-A	3	8	.273	27	5	2	0	2	94^{2}	105	8	35	22	13.5	4.94	88	.311	.379	7	.219	-1	-8	-6	1	-0.6
1928	StL-A	1	0	1.000	6	0	0	0	0	9	9	1	2	1	11.0	3.00	140	.281	.324	0	.000	-0	1	1	0	0.1
Total	3	6	12	.333	44	12	6	0	2	178^{1}	196	13	61	39	13.1	4.64	93	.300	.363	12	.200	-2	-11	-6	3	-0.5
● DON NEWCOMBE	Newcombe, Donald "Newk" b: 6/14/26, Madison, N.J. BL/TR, 6′4″, 225 lbs. Deb: 5/20/49 ♦																									
1949	*Bro-N★	17	8	.680	38	31	19	**5**	1	244^{1}	223	17	73	149	11.0	3.17	129	.243	.301	22	.229	3	24	25	1	2.8
1950	Bro-N★	19	11	.633	40	35	20	4	3	267^{1}	258	22	75	130	11.3	3.70	111	.254	.306	24	.247	7	13	12	-0	1.8
1951	Bro-N★	20	9	.690	40	36	18	3	0	272	235	19	91	**164**	11.0	3.28	120	.230	.297	23	.223	5	21	20	1	2.5
1954	Bro-N	9	8	.529	29	25	6	0	0	144^{1}	158	24	49	82	13.2	4.55	90	.274	.337	15	.319	4	-8	-8	-1	-0.5
1955	*Bro-N★	20	5	**.800**	34	31	17	1	0	233^{2}	222	35	38	143	**10.1**	3.20	127	.249	.280	42	.359	20	22	22	-2	**4.2**
1956	*Bro-N	**27**	7	**.794**	38	36	18	5	0	268	219	33	46	139	**9.0**	3.06	130	**.221**	**.257**	26	.234	8	21	**27**	0	**4.3**
1957	Bro-N	11	12	.478	28	28	12	4	0	198^{2}	199	28	33	90	10.6	3.49	119	.258	.290	17	.230	5	9	15	1	2.2
1958	LA-N	0	6	.000	11	8	1	0	0	34^{1}	53	11	8	16	16.0	7.86	52	.346	.379	5	.417	2	-15	-14	0	-1.9
	Cin-N	7	7	.500	20	18	7	0	1	133^{1}	159	20	28	53	12.7	3.85	108	.298	.335	21	.350	8	2	4	-2	1.1
	Yr	7	13	.350	31	26	8	0	1	167^{2}	212	31	36	69	13.4	4.67	89	.309	.344	26	.361	10	-13	-10	-2	-0.8
1959	Cin-N	13	8	.619	30	29	17	2	1	222	216	25	27	100	10.1	3.16	128	.253	.280	32	.305	15	19	22	-1	**3.5**
1960	Cin-N	4	6	.400	16	15	1	0	0	82^{2}	99	12	14	36	12.6	4.57	84	.304	.338	5	.139	-0	-7	-7	-1	-0.9
	Cle-A	2	3	.400	20	2	0	0	1	54	61	6	8	27	11.5	4.33	86	.289	.315	6	.300	2	-3	-4	-1	-0.2
Total	10	149	90	.623	344	294	136	24	7	2154^{2}	2102	252	490	1129	11.0	3.56	114	.254	.299	238	.271	79	97	116	-6	18.9
● TOM NEWELL	Newell, Thomas Dean b: 5/17/63, Monrovia, Cal. BR/TR, 6′1″, 185 lbs. Deb: 9/9/87																									
1987	Phi-N	0	0	—	2	0	0	0	0	1	4	1	3	1	63.0	36.00	12	.571	.700	0	—	0	-4	-4	0	0.0
● DON NEWHAUSER	Newhauser, Donald Louis b: 11/7/47, Miami, Fla. BR/TR, 6′4″, 200 lbs. Deb: 6/15/72																									
1972	Bos-A	4	2	.667	31	0	0	0	4	37	30	2	25	27	13.9	2.43	132	.226	.356	0	.000	-0	3	3	-0	0.6
1973	Bos-A	0	0	—	9	0	0	0	1	12	9	0	13	8	17.3	0.00	—	.205	.397	0	—	0	5	5	-0	-0.4
1974	Bos-A	0	1	.000	2	0	0	0	0	3^{2}	5	0	4	2	22.1	9.82	39	.357	.500	0	—	0	-3	-2	0	-0.6
Total	3	4	3	.571	42	0	0	0	5	52^{2}	44	2	42	37	15.2	2.39	144	.230	.377	0	.000	-0	5	6	-0	-0.4

YEAR	TM/L	W	L	PCT	G	GS	CG	SH	SV	IP	H	HR	BB	SO	RAT	ERA	ERA+	OAV	OOB	BH	AVG	PB	PR	/A	PD	TPI
● **HAL NEWHOUSER**	Newhouser, Harold "Prince Hal" b: 5/20/21, Detroit, Mich. d: 11/10/98, Bloomfield Hills, Mich. BL/TL, 6'2", 192 lbs. Deb: 9/29/39 H																									
1939	Det-A	0	1	.000	1	1	1	0	0	5	3	0	4	4	12.6	5.40	91	.188	.350	0	.000	-0	-0	-0	0	-0.1
1940	Det-A	9	9	.500	28	20	7	0	0	133^1	149	12	76	89	15.3	4.86	98	.282	.374	8	.200	-1	-7	-2	2	-0.1
1941	Det-A	9	11	.450	33	27	5	1	0	173	166	6	137	106	15.8	4.79	95	.249	.378	9	.150	-2	-12	-5	2	-0.5
1942	Det-A☆	8	14	.364	38	23	11	1	5	183^2	137	4	114	103	12.4	2.45	161	**.207**	.325	8	.154	-1	25	31	2	4.0
1943	Det-A★	8	17	.320	37	25	10	1	1	195^2	163	3	111	144	12.6	3.04	116	.224	.327	12	.185	-1	6	11	3	1.6
1944	Det-A★	**29**	9	.763	47	34	25	6	2	312^1	264	6	102	**187**	10.6	2.22	161	.230	.293	29	.242	3	42	47	1	6.5
1945	*Det-A†	**25**	9	**.735**	40	36	**29**	**8**	2	**313^1**	239	5	110	**212**	10.0	**1.81**	**194**	**.211**	.281	28	.257	4	**54**	**59**	3	**7.8**
1946	Det-A★	**26**	9	.743	37	34	29	6	1	292^2	215	10	98	275	**9.7**	**1.94**	**189**	**.201**	**.269**	13	.126	-1	51	**56**	2	**7.1**
1947	Det-A★	17	17	.500	40	36	**24**	3	2	285	268	9	110	176	12.0	2.87	131	.249	.320	19	.198	2	26	**28**	3	**3.9**
1948	Det-A★	**21**	12	.636	39	35	19	2	1	272^1	249	10	99	143	11.5	3.01	145	.242	.309	19	.207	1	39	41	2	4.9
1949	Det-A	18	11	.621	38	35	22	3	1	292	277	19	111	144	12.0	3.36	124	.251	.319	18	.198	2	27	26	3	2.7
1950	Det-A	15	13	.536	35	30	15	1	3	213^2	232	23	81	87	13.4	4.34	108	.279	.346	13	.176	-2	6	8	-0	0.8
1951	Det-A	6	6	.500	15	14	7	1	0	96^1	98	10	19	37	11.2	3.92	106	.268	.310	9	.310	2	2	3	1	0.6
1952	Det-A	9	9	.500	25	19	8	0	0	154	148	13	47	57	11.4	3.74	102	.254	.310	10	.217	3	-1	1	1	0.5
1953	Det-A	0	1	.000	7	4	0	0	1	21^2	31	4	8	6	17.0	7.06	58	.348	.414	4	.500	2	-7	-7	0	-0.2
1954	*Cle-A	7	2	.778	26	1	0	0	7	46^2	34	3	18	25	10.0	2.51	147	.209	.287	2	.154	-0	6	6	-0	1.3
1955	Cle-A	0	0	—	2	0	0	0	0	2^1	1	0	4	1	19.3	0.00	—	.125	.417	0	—	0	1	1	-0	0.0
Total	17	207	150	.580	488	374	212	33	26	2993	2674	137	1249	1796	11.9	3.06	130	.239	.316	201	.201	12	257	305	22	40.8
● **FLOYD NEWKIRK**	Newkirk, Floyd Elmo "Three-Finger" b: 7/16/08, Norris City, Ill. d: 4/15/76, Clayton, Mo. BR/TR, 5'11", 178 lbs. Deb: 8/21/34 F																									
1934	NY-A	0	0	—	1	0	0	0	0	1	1	0	1	0	18.0	0.00	—	.333	.500	0	—	0	0	0	0	0.0
● **JOEL NEWKIRK**	Newkirk, Joel Inez "Sailor" b: 5/1/1896, Kyana, Ind. d: 1/22/66, Eldorado, Ill. BR/TR, 6', 180 lbs. Deb: 8/20/19 F																									
1919	Chi-N	0	0	—	1	0	0	0	0	2	2	0	3	1	27.0	13.50	21	.286	.545	0	.000	-0	-2	-2	0	0.0
1920	Chi-N	0	1	.000	2	1	0	0	0	6^2	8	1	6	2	18.9	5.40	59	.333	.467	0	.000	-0	-2	-2	-1	-0.3
Total	2	0	1	.000	3	1	0	0	0	8^2	10	1	9	3	20.8	7.27	43	.323	.488	0	.000	-1	-4	-4	-0	-0.3
● **MAURY NEWLIN**	Newlin, Maurice Milton b: 6/22/14, Bloomingdale, Ind d: 8/14/78, Houston, Tex. BR/TR, 6', 176 lbs. Deb: 9/20/40																									
1940	StL-A	1	0	1.000	1	1	0	0	0	6	4	1	2	3	9.0	6.00	76	.190	.261	1	.500	0	-1	-1	-0	-0.1
1941	StL-A	0	2	.000	14	0	0	0	1	27^2	43	4	12	10	17.9	6.51	66	.361	.420	0	.000	-1	-7	-7	1	-0.5
Total	2	1	2	.333	15	1	0	0	1	33^2	47	5	14	13	16.3	6.42	68	.336	.396	1	.125	-1	-8	-8	0	-0.6
● **FRED NEWMAN**	Newman, Frederick William b: 2/21/42, Boston, Mass. d: 6/24/87, Framingham, Mass. BR/TR, 6'3", 190 lbs. Deb: 9/16/62																									
1962	LA-A	0	1	.000	4	1	0	0	0	6^1	11	0	3	4	19.9	9.95	39	.393	.452	0	.000	-0	-4	-4	-0	-0.6
1963	LA-A	1	5	.167	12	8	0	0	0	44	56	6	15	16	14.9	5.32	64	.316	.376	4	.250	1	-8	-9	-0	-1.1
1964	LA-A	13	10	.565	32	28	7	2	0	190	177	9	39	83	10.6	2.75	120	.246	.291	11	.180	2	19	11	4	2.1
1965	Cal-A	14	16	.467	36	36	10	2	0	260^2	225	15	64	109	10.0	2.93	116	.234	.282	7	.095	-0	15	13	8	2.4
1966	Cal-A	4	7	.364	21	19	1	0	0	102^2	112	7	31	42	13.1	4.73	71	.289	.351	6	.200	1	-15	-16	1	-1.4
1967	Cal-A	1	0	1.000	3	1	0	0	0	6^1	8	1	2	0	15.6	1.42	221	.320	.393	0	.000	-0	1	1	-0	0.2
Total	6	33	39	.458	108	93	18	4	0	610	589	38	154	254	11.2	3.41	99	.256	.308	28	.153	3	8	-3	12	1.6
● **JEFF NEWMAN**	Newman, Jeffrey Lynn b: 9/11/48, Fort Worth, Tex. BR/TR, 6'2", 218 lbs. Deb: 6/30/76 MC♦																									
1977	Oak-A	0	0	—	1	0	0	0	0	1	1	0	0	0	18.0	0.00	—	.250	.400	36	.222	0	0	0	0	0.0
● **RAY NEWMAN**	Newman, Raymond Francis b: 6/20/45, Evansville, Ind. BL/TL, 6'5", 205 lbs. Deb: 5/16/71																									
1971	Chi-N	1	2	.333	30	0	0	0	2	38^1	30	4	17	35	11.0	3.52	112	.219	.305	0	.000	-1	-0	2	0	0.1
1972	Mil-A	0	0	—	4	0	0	0	1	7	4	0	2	1	7.7	0.00	—	.182	.250	1	1.000	0	2	2	0	0.2
1973	Mil-A	2	1	.667	11	0	0	0	1	18^1	19	2	5	10	11.8	2.95	128	.260	.308	0	—	0	2	2	1	0.5
Total	3	3	3	.500	45	0	0	0	4	63^2	53	6	24	46	10.9	2.97	128	.228	.301	1	.143	-0	4	6	1	0.8
● **BOBO NEWSOM**	Newsom, Louis Norman "Buck" b: 8/11/07, Hartsville, S.C. d: 12/7/62, Orlando, Fla. BR/TR, 6'2", 220 lbs. Deb: 9/11/29																									
1929	Bro-N	0	3	.000	3	2	0	0	0	9^1	15	0	5	6	19.3	10.61	44	.375	.444	0	.000	-0	-6	-6	0	-1.3
1930	Bro-N	0	0	—	2	0	0	0	0	3	2	0	2	1	12.0	0.00	—	.167	.286	0	—	0	2	2	-0	0.0
1932	Chi-N	0	0	—	1	0	0	0	0	1	1	0	0	0	9.0	0.00	—	.333	.333	0	—	0	0	0	0	0.0
1934	StL-A	16	20	.444	47	32	15	2	5	262^1	259	15	149	135	14.0	4.01	124	.261	.358	17	.183	-3	14	29	0	3.2
1935	StL-A	0	6	.000	7	6	1	0	1	42^2	54	2	13	22	14.1	4.85	99	.303	.351	1	.091	-1	-2	-0	0	-0.1
	Was-A	11	12	.478	28	23	17	2	2	198^1	222	9	84	65	14.1	4.45	97	.288	.361	22	.301	4	0	-3	-3	-0.1
	Yr	11	18	.379	35	29	18	2	3	241	276	11	97	87	14.1	4.52	97	.291	.359	23	.274	3	-2	-3	-2	-0.2
1936	Was-A	17	15	.531	43	38	24	4	2	285^2	294	13	146	156	14.0	4.32	111	.268	.355	23	.213	0	23	15	1	1.4
1937	Was-A	3	4	.429	11	10	3	0	0	67^2	76	4	48	39	16.9	5.85	76	.287	.402	3	.120	-1	-9	-11	0	-0.9
	Bos-A	13	10	.565	30	27	14	1	0	207^2	193	14	119	127	13.7	4.46	106	.243	.344	19	.253	2	4	6	-2	0.6
	Yr	16	14	.533	41	37	17	1	0	275^1	269	18	167	166	14.3	4.81	97	.253	.356	22	.220	1	-6	-4	-1	-0.3
1938	StL-A☆	20	16	.556	44	40	**31**	0	1	**329^2**	334	30	192	226	14.5	5.08	98	.265	.364	31	.250	1	-11	-4	-3	-0.4
1939	StL-A	3	1	.750	6	6	3	0	0	45^2	50	5	22	28	14.4	4.73	103	.266	.346	4	.222	-0	-1	1	0	0.0
	Det-A☆	17	10	.630	35	31	21	3	2	246	222	14	104	164	12.0	3.37	145	.238	.316	18	.186	-4	34	42	-1	3.6
	Yr	20	11	.645	41	37	**24**	3	2	291^2	272	19	126	192	12.3	3.58	136	.243	.320	22	.191	-4	34	42	-1	3.6
1940	*Det-A★	21	5	.808	36	34	20	3	0	264	235	19	100	164	11.5	2.83	**168**	.238	.310	23	.215	-1	46	56	-3	4.6
1941	Det-A	12	20	.375	43	36	12	2	2	250^1	265	15	118	175	13.9	4.60	99	.264	.343	9	.102	-6	-13	-2	-2	-0.9
1942	Was-A	11	17	.393	30	29	15	2	0	213^2	236	5	92	**113**	13.9	4.93	74	.280	.353	12	.160	-2	-30	-30	-3	-3.8
	Bro-N	2	2	.500	6	5	2	1	0	32	28	1	14	21	12.1	3.38	97	.235	.321	0	.000	-1	-0	-0	-1	-0.3
1943	Bro-N	9	4	.692	22	12	6	1	1	125	113	4	57	75	12.4	3.02	111	.244	.329	11	.250	1	5	5	0	0.6
	StL-A	1	6	.143	10	9	0	0	0	52^1	69	7	35	37	18.1	7.39	45	.318	.415	5	.333	1	-24	-24	-1	-2.6
	Was-A	3	3	.500	6	6	2	0	0	40	38	1	21	11	13.7	3.82	84	.247	.345	2	.133	-1	-2	-3	-1	-0.6
	Yr	4	9	.308	16	15	2	0	0	92^1	107	8	56	48	16.1	5.85	56	.288	.384	7	.233	0	-26	-26	-2	-3.2
1944	Phi-A★	13	15	.464	37	33	18	2	1	265	243	11	82	142	11.2	2.82	123	.244	.304	10	.114	-6	18	19	-1	1.3
1945	Phi-A	8	20	.286	36	34	16	3	0	257^1	255	12	103	127	12.6	3.29	104	.260	.332	14	.163	-4	2	4	-4	-0.4
1946	Phi-A	3	5	.375	10	9	3	1	0	58^2	61	2	30	32	14.7	3.38	105	.266	.364	2	.105	-1	1	1	-1	0.0
	Was-A	11	8	.579	24	22	14	2	1	178	163	5	60	82	11.4	2.78	120	.242	.306	10	.161	-2	14	11	-3	0.6
	Yr	14	13	.519	34	31	17	3	1	236^2	224	7	90	114	12.0	2.93	116	.247	.316	12	.148	-3	15	12	-4	0.6
1947	Was-A	4	6	.400	14	13	1	0	0	83^2	99	2	37	40	14.7	4.09	91	.296	.368	7	.241	1	-4	-3	-2	-0.5
	*NY-A	7	5	.583	17	15	6	2	0	115^2	109	8	30	42	11.0	2.80	126	.250	.301	4	.095	-3	12	9	-2	0.4
	Yr	11	11	.500	31	28	7	2	0	199^1	208	10	67	82	12.5	3.34	108	.270	.330	11	.155	-3	8	6	-3	-0.1
1948	NY-N	0	4	.000	11	4	0	0	0	25^2	35	1	13	9	16.8	4.21	94	.330	.403	3	.429	1	-1	-1	-0	-0.1
1952	Was-A	1	1	.500	10	0	0	0	2	12^2	16	2	9	5	17.8	4.97	72	.302	.403	0	.000	-0	-2	-2	0	-0.4
	Phi-A	3	3	.500	14	5	1	0	1	47^2	38	2	23	22	11.9	3.59	110	.220	.318	2	.133	-1	0	2	0	0.2
	Yr	4	4	.500	24	5	1	0	3	60^1	54	4	32	27	13.1	3.88	100	.239	.338	2	.118	-1	-1	-0	1	-0.2
1953	Phi-A	2	1	.667	17	2	1	0	0	38^2	44	3	24	16	17.0	4.89	88	.282	.395	1	.167	-0	-4	-3	0	-0.2
Total	20	211	222	.487	600	483	246	31	21	3759^1	3769	206	1732	2082	13.3	3.98	107	.261	.342	253	.189	-26	67	109	-29	3.9
● **DICK NEWSOME**	Newsome, Heber Hampton b: 12/13/09, Ahoskie, N.C. d: 12/15/65, Ahoskie, N.C. BR/TR, 6', 185 lbs. Deb: 4/25/41																									
1941	Bos-A	19	10	.655	36	29	17	2	0	213^2	235	13	79	58	13.5	4.13	101	.277	.344	19	.244	3	0	1	3	0.7
1942	Bos-A	8	10	.444	24	23	11	0	0	158	174	11	67	40	13.7	5.01	74	.278	.348	13	.236	2	-24	-23	1	-2.0
1943	Bos-A	8	13	.381	25	22	8	2	0	154^1	166	8	68	40	13.9	4.49	74	.274	.352	7	.146	-1	-20	-20	-2	-2.8
Total	3	35	33	.515	85	74	36	4	0	526	575	32	214	138	13.7	4.50	84	.276	.347	39	.215	3	-44	-42	2	-4.1
● **DOC NEWTON**	Newton, Eustace James b: 10/26/1877, Indianapolis, Ind. d: 5/14/31, Memphis, Tenn. BL/TL, 6', 185 lbs. Deb: 4/27/00																									
1900	Cin-N	9	15	.375	35	27	22	1	0	234^2	255	4	100	88	14.1	4.14	89	.276	.355	17	.198	-1	-12	-12	-2	-1.3
1901	Cin-N	4	13	.235	20	18	17	0	0	168^1	190	6	59	65	14.1	4.12	78	.282	.353	9	.130	-4	-15	-17	1	-1.8
	Bro-N	6	5	.545	13	12	9	0	0	105	110	1	30	45	12.6	2.83	119	.268	.328	9	.220	1	6	6	-0	0.6
	Yr	10	18	.357	33	30	26	0	0	273^1	300	7	89	110	13.0	3.62	90	.273	.332	18	.164	-4	-9	-11	1	-1.2

YEAR	TM/L	W	L	PCT	G	GS	CG	SH	SV	IP	H	HR	BB	SO	RAT	ERA	ERA+	OAV	OOB	BH	AVG	PB	PR	/A	PD	TPI
1902	Bro-N	15	14	.517	31	28	26	4	2	264^1	208	2	87	107	10.4	2.42	114	**.217**	.289	19	.174	-1	11	10	-2	0.8
1905	NY-A	2	2	.500	11	7	2	0	0	59^2	61	1	24	15	13.1	2.11	139	.266	.341	3	.136	-1	4	5	-1	0.1
1906	NY-A	7	5	.583	21	15	6	2	0	125	118	3	33	52	11.4	3.17	94	.252	.311	9	.220	-0	-7	-3	2	-0.1
1907	NY-A	7	10	.412	19	15	10	0	0	133	132	0	31	70	11.5	3.18	88	.261	.313	4	.108	-1	-9	-6	1	-0.8
1908	NY-A	4	5	.444	23	13	6	1	1	88^1	78	0	41	49	12.8	2.95	84	.242	.341	4	.160	-0	-6	-5	0	-0.5
1909	NY-A	0	3	.000	4	4	1	0	0	22^1	27	0	11	11	16.5	2.82	90	.300	.394	1	.167	0	-1	-1	1	0.0
Total	8	54	72	.429	177	139	99	8	3	1200^2	1179	17	416	502	12.5	3.22	95	.257	.329	75	.172	-9	-29	-20	-2	-3.0

KID NICHOLS Nichols, Charles Augustus b: 9/14/1869, Madison, Wis. d: 4/11/53, Kansas City, Mo. BB/TR, 5′10.5″, 175 lbs. Deb: 4/23/1890 MH

YEAR	TM/L	W	L	PCT	G	GS	CG	SH	SV	IP	H	HR	BB	SO	RAT	ERA	ERA+	OAV	OOB	BH	AVG	PB	PR	/A	PD	TPI
1890	Bos-N	27	19	.587	48	47	47	**7**	0	424	374	8	112	222	10.5	2.23	168	.229	.284	43	.247	1	63	**72**	0	6.7
1891	Bos-N	30	17	.638	52	48	45	5	**3**	425^1	413	15	103	240	11.3	2.39	**153**	.245	.295	36	.197	-3	**45**	**60**	6	**5.8**
1892	*Bos-N	35	16	.686	53	51	49	5	0	453	404	15	121	192	10.6	2.84	124	.229	.282	39	.198	1	22	34	-1	3.2
1893	Bos-N	34	14	.708	52	44	43	1	1	425	426	15	118	94	11.8	3.52	140	.253	.308	39	.220	-2	54	67	-2	5.5
1894	Bos-N	32	13	.711	50	46	40	**3**	0	407	488	23	121	113	13.7	4.75	120	.294	.345	50	.294	3	26	42	0	3.5
1895	Bos-N	26	16	.619	47	42	42	1	**3**	379^2	417	15	86	140	12.0	3.41	149	.275	.316	37	.236	-4	58	**71**	-0	5.7
1896	Bos-N	**30**	14	.682	49	43	37	3	1	372^1	387	14	101	102	12.0	2.83	161	.266	.316	28	.190	-3	**63**	**71**	2	**6.6**
1897	*Bos-N	**31**	11	.738	46	40	37	2	**3**	**368**	362	9	68	127	**10.6**	2.64	**169**	.255	**.291**	39	.265	4	**68**	**75**	-2	**7.3**
1898	Bos-N	**31**	12	.721	**50**	42	40	5	**4**	388	316	7	85	138	**9.6**	2.13	173	**.221**	**.272**	38	.241	3	**64**	**67**	-2	**6.9**
1899	Bos-N	21	19	.525	42	37	37	4	1	343^1	326	11	82	108	10.9	2.99	139	.250	.298	26	.191	-5	33	45	-1	3.9
1900	Bos-N	13	16	.448	29	27	25	**4**	0	231^1	215	11	72	53	11.6	3.07	134	.246	.311	18	.200	-2	16	27	-1	2.6
1901	Bos-N	19	16	.543	38	34	33	4	0	321	306	8	90	143	11.4	3.22	112	.250	.306	46	.282	9	4	14	-1	2.3
1904	StL-N	21	13	.618	36	35	35	3	1	317	268	3	50	134	9.2	2.02	134	.222	.256	17	.156	-1	25	24	-1	2.4
1905	StL-N	1	5	.167	7	7	5	0	0	51^2	64	1	18	16	14.3	5.40	55	.296	.350	5	.227	0	-14	-14	-1	-1.4
	Phi-N	10	6	.625	17	16	15	1	0	138^2	129	1	28	50	10.4	2.27	129	.250	.294	10	.189	0	11	10	-4	0.7
	Yr	11	11	.500	24	23	20	1	0	190^1	193	2	46	66	11.5	3.12	94	.264	.311	15	.200	0	-2	-4	-5	-0.7
1906	Phi-N	0	1	.000	4	2	1	0	0	11	17	0	13	1	26.2	9.82	27	.386	.542	0	.000	-0	-9	-9	-1	-0.8
Total	15	361	208	.634	620	561	531	48	17	5056^1	4912	156	1268	1873	11.2	2.95	139	.250	.300	471	.226	-0	531	653	-9	60.9

CHET NICHOLS Nichols, Chester Raymond Jr. b: 2/22/31, Pawtucket, R.I. d: 3/27/95, Lincoln, R.I. BB/TL, 6′1.5″, 195 lbs. Deb: 4/19/51 F

YEAR	TM/L	W	L	PCT	G	GS	CG	SH	SV	IP	H	HR	BB	SO	RAT	ERA	ERA+	OAV	OOB	BH	AVG	PB	PR	/A	PD	TPI
1951	Bos-N	11	8	.579	33	19	12	3	2	156	142	4	69	71	12.2	**2.88**	127	.246	.327	7	.137	-2	19	14	2	1.5
1954	Mil-N	9	11	.450	35	20	5	1	1	122^1	132	5	65	55	14.8	4.41	84	.286	.379	3	.086	-3	-5	-9	1	-1.5
1955	Mil-N	9	8	.529	34	21	6	0	1	144	139	20	67	44	12.9	4.00	94	.253	.335	8	.154	-2	1	-4	2	-0.5
1956	Mil-N	0	1	.000	2	0	0	0	0	4	9	1	3	2	27.0	6.75	51	.563	.632	0	.000	-0	-1	-1	0	-0.3
1960	Bos-A	0	2	.000	6	1	0	0	0	12^2	12	0	4	11	11.4	4.26	95	.240	.296	0	.000	-0	-1	-0	0	0.0
1961	Bos-A	3	2	.600	26	2	0	0	3	51^2	40	3	26	20	11.5	2.09	199	.221	.319	1	.111	-0	11	12	3	1.5
1962	Bos-A	1	1	.500	29	1	0	0	3	57	61	3	22	33	13.1	3.00	138	.276	.342	0	.000	-1	6	7	1	0.4
1963	Bos-A	1	3	.250	21	7	0	0	0	52^2	61	8	24	27	14.5	4.78	79	.298	.371	3	.231	0	-7	-6	-0	-0.4
1964	Cin-N	0	0	—	3	0	0	0	0	3	4	1	0	3	12.0	6.00	60	.308	.308	0	—	0	-1	-1	-0	0.0
Total	9	34	36	.486	189	71	23	4	10	603^1	600	45	280	266	13.2	3.64	105	.264	.346	22	.127	-8	22	11	8	0.7

CHET NICHOLS Nichols, Chester Raymond Sr. "Nick" b: 7/3/1897, Woonsocket, R.I. d: 7/11/82, Pawtucket, R.I. BR/TR, 5′11″, 160 lbs. Deb: 7/30/26 F

YEAR	TM/L	W	L	PCT	G	GS	CG	SH	SV	IP	H	HR	BB	SO	RAT	ERA	ERA+	OAV	OOB	BH	AVG	PB	PR	/A	PD	TPI
1926	Pit-N	0	0	—	3	0	0	0	0	7^2	13	0	5	2	21.1	8.22	48	.342	.419	1	.333	0	-4	-4	0	0.0
1927	Pit-N	0	3	.000	8	0	0	0	0	27^2	34	1	17	9	16.9	5.86	70	.309	.406	1	.111	-0	-6	-5	-0	-0.6
1928	NY-N	0	0	—	3	0	0	0	0	2^2	11	0	3	1	50.6	23.63	17	.611	.682	0	—	0	-6	-6	0	0.0
1930	Phi-N	1	2	.333	16	5	1	0	0	59^2	76	8	16	15	14.2	6.79	80	.306	.353	6	.300	0	-12	-9	1	-0.2
1931	Phi-N	0	1	.000	3	0	0	0	0	5^2	10	0	1	1	17.5	9.53	45	.435	.458	0	.000	-0	-4	-3	0	-0.5
1932	Phi-N	0	2	.000	11	0	0	0	1	19^1	23	2	14	5	17.2	6.98	63	.299	.407	0	.000	-1	-7	-6	0	-0.6
Total	6	1	8	.111	44	5	1	0	1	122^2	167	11	56	33	16.7	7.19	67	.325	.395	8	.211	-1	-38	-33	1	-1.9

DOLAN NICHOLS Nichols, Dolan Levon "Nick" b: 2/28/30, Tishomingo, Miss. d: 11/20/89, Tupelo, Miss. BR/TR, 6′, 195 lbs. Deb: 4/15/58

YEAR	TM/L	W	L	PCT	G	GS	CG	SH	SV	IP	H	HR	BB	SO	RAT	ERA	ERA+	OAV	OOB	BH	AVG	PB	PR	/A	PD	TPI
1958	Chi-N	0	4	.000	24	0	0	0	1	41^1	46	1	16	9	13.7	5.01	78	.295	.364	0	.000	-1	-5	-5	1	-0.4

TRICKY NICHOLS Nichols, Frederick C. b: 7/26/1850, Bridgeport, Conn. d: 8/22/1897, Bridgeport, Conn. BR/TR, 5′7.5″, 150 lbs. Deb: 4/21/1875

YEAR	TM/L	W	L	PCT	G	GS	CG	SH	SV	IP	H	HR	BB	SO	RAT	ERA	ERA+	OAV	OOB	BH	AVG	PB	PR	/A	PD	TPI
1875	NH-n	4	29	.121	34	33	30	0	0	288	321	2	9	48	10.3	2.38	87	.242	.248	23	.193	-2	-5	-10		-0.2
1876	Bos-N	1	0	1.000	1	1	1	0	0	9	7	0	0	0	7.0	1.00	226	.200	.200	0	.000	-1	1	1	0	0.1
1877	StL-N	18	23	.439	42	39	35	1	0	350	376	2	53	80	11.0	2.60	100	.263	.289	31	.167	-6	8	0	-0	-0.6
1878	Pro-N	4	7	.364	11	10	10	0	0	98	157	0	8	21	15.2	4.22	52	.344	.356	9	.184	-0	-21	-22	2	-1.8
1880	Wor-N	0	2	.000	2	2	2	0	0	17^2	29	0	4	4	16.8	4.08	64	.358	.388	0	.000	-1	-3	-3	-1	-0.4
1882	Bal-a	1	12	.077	16	13	12	0	0	118^1	155	2	17	21	13.1	5.02	55	.296	.319	15	.158	-2	-31	-30	-2	-2.7
Total	5	24	44	.353	72	65	60	1	0	593	724	4	82	126	12.2	3.37	76	.287	.309	55	.161	-10	-45	-53	-1	-5.4

ROD NICHOLS Nichols, Rodney Lea b: 12/29/64, Burlington, Iowa BR/TR, 6′2″, 200 lbs. Deb: 7/30/88

YEAR	TM/L	W	L	PCT	G	GS	CG	SH	SV	IP	H	HR	BB	SO	RAT	ERA	ERA+	OAV	OOB	BH	AVG	PB	PR	/A	PD	TPI
1988	Cle-A	1	7	.125	11	10	3	0	0	69^1	73	5	23	31	12.7	5.06	81	.272	.334	0	—	0	-8	-7	-0	-0.8
1989	Cle-A	4	6	.400	15	11	0	0	0	71^2	81	9	24	42	13.4	4.40	90	.285	.345	0	—	0	-4	-3	-0	-0.6
1990	Cle-A	0	3	.000	4	2	0	0	0	16	24	5	6	3	18.0	7.88	50	.343	.410	0	—	0	-7	-7	0	-1.0
1991	Cle-A	2	11	.154	31	16	3	1	1	137^1	145	6	30	76	11.9	3.54	117	.273	.319	0	—	0	8	9	-1	0.7
1992	Cle-A	4	3	.571	30	9	0	0	0	105^1	114	13	31	56	12.6	4.53	86	.273	.327	0	—	0	-7	-7	-0	-0.4
1993	LA-N	0	1	.000	4	0	0	0	0	6^1	9	1	2	3	15.6	5.68	67	.360	.407	0	—	0	-1	-1	0	-0.1
1995	Atl-N	0	0	—	5	0	0	0	0	6^2	14	3	5	3	25.7	5.40	79	.424	.500	0	—	0	-1	-1	0	0.0
Total	7	11	31	.262	100	48	6	1	1	412^2	460	42	121	214	13.0	4.43	91	.282	.337	0	—	0	-20	-18	-1	-2.2

FRANK NICHOLSON Nicholson, Frank Collins b: 8/29/1889, Berlin, Pa. d: 11/10/72, Jersey Shore, Pa. BR/TR, 6′2″, 175 lbs. Deb: 9/6/12

YEAR	TM/L	W	L	PCT	G	GS	CG	SH	SV	IP	H	HR	BB	SO	RAT	ERA	ERA+	OAV	OOB	BH	AVG	PB	PR	/A	PD	TPI
1912	Phi-N	0	0	—	2	0	0	0	0	4	8	1	2	1	22.5	6.75	54	.471	.526	0	—	0	-1	-1	0	0.0

CHRIS NICHTING Nichting, Christopher Thomas b: 5/13/66, Cincinnati, Ohio BR/TR, 6′1″, 205 lbs. Deb: 5/15/95

YEAR	TM/L	W	L	PCT	G	GS	CG	SH	SV	IP	H	HR	BB	SO	RAT	ERA	ERA+	OAV	OOB	BH	AVG	PB	PR	/A	PD	TPI
1995	Tex-A	0	0	—	13	0	0	0	0	24^1	36	1	13	6	18.5	7.03	69	.343	.420	0	—	0	-6	-6	1	0.1

GEORGE NICOL Nicol, George Edward b: 10/17/1870, Barry, Ill. d: 8/10/24, Milwaukee, Wis. TL , 5′7″, 155 lbs. Deb: 9/23/1890 ♦

YEAR	TM/L	W	L	PCT	G	GS	CG	SH	SV	IP	H	HR	BB	SO	RAT	ERA	ERA+	OAV	OOB	BH	AVG	PB	PR	/A	PD	TPI
1890	StL-a	2	1	.667	3	3	2	0	0	17	11	1	19	16	16.9	4.76	91	.180	.390	2	.286	1	-2	-1	-0	0.0
1891	Chi-N	0	1	.000	3	2	0	0	0	11	14	0	10	12	20.5	4.91	68	.298	.431	2	.333	1	-2	-2	-1	-0.1
1894	Pit-N	3	4	.429	8	5	3	0	0	44^1	57	2	33	11	19.3	6.50	81	.308	.426	9	.450	2	-6	-6	-1	-0.6
	Lou-N	0	1	.000	1	1	1	0	0	9	19	2	5	3	25.0	15.00	34	.422	.490	38	.352	0	-10	-10	0	-0.6
	Yr	3	5	.375	9	6	4	0	0	53^1	76	4	38	14	19.4	7.93	66	.323	.420	47	.367	2	-15	-16	-1	-1.2
Total	3	5	7	.417	15	11	6	0	0	81^1	101	5	67	42	19.6	6.86	70	.299	.428	51	.362	5	-19	-19	-2	-1.3

DAVID NIED Nied, David Glen b: 12/22/68, Dallas, Texas BR/TR, 6′2″, 188 lbs. Deb: 9/1/92

YEAR	TM/L	W	L	PCT	G	GS	CG	SH	SV	IP	H	HR	BB	SO	RAT	ERA	ERA+	OAV	OOB	BH	AVG	PB	PR	/A	PD	TPI
1992	Atl-N	3	0	1.000	6	2	0	0	0	23	10	0	5	19	5.9	1.17	312	.130	.183	2	.286	0	6	6	-0	0.9
1993	Col-N	5	9	.357	16	16	1	0	0	87	99	8	42	46	14.7	5.17	92	.296	.376	4	.174	0	-11	-4	1	-0.5
1994	Col-N	9	7	.563	22	22	2	1	0	122	137	15	47	74	13.9	4.80	104	.287	.356	4	.100	-2	-8	2	-2	-0.1
1995	Col-N	0	0	—	2	0	0	0	0	4^1	11	2	3	3	29.1	20.77	26	.458	.519	0	—	0	-8	-7	-0	0.0
1996	Col-N	0	2	.000	6	1	0	0	0	5^1	5	1	8	4	21.9	13.50	39	.250	.464	0	.000	-0	-6	-5	-0	-1.4
Total	5	17	18	.486	52	41	3	1	0	241^2	262	26	105	146	13.9	5.06	94	.281	.357	10	.141	-2	-26	-8	-2	-1.1

TOM NIEDENFUER Niedenfuer, Thomas Edward b: 8/13/59, St.Louis Park, Minn. BR/TR, 6′5″, 225 lbs. Deb: 8/15/81

YEAR	TM/L	W	L	PCT	G	GS	CG	SH	SV	IP	H	HR	BB	SO	RAT	ERA	ERA+	OAV	OOB	BH	AVG	PB	PR	/A	PD	TPI
1981	*LA-N	3	1	.750	17	0	0	0	2	26	25	1	6	12	11.1	3.81	87	.258	.308	0	—	0	-1	-1	-0	-0.3
1982	LA-N	3	4	.429	55	0	0	0	9	69^2	71	3	25	60	12.7	2.71	128	.269	.337	0	.000	-0	7	6	-1	0.6
1983	*LA-N	8	3	.727	66	0	0	0	11	94^2	55	6	29	66	8.1	1.90	189	.170	.240	0	.000	-0	18	18	-1	2.2
1984	LA-N	2	5	.286	33	0	0	0	11	47^1	39	3	23	45	12.2	2.47	143	.227	.325	0	.000	-0	6	6	-0	1.0
1985	*LA-N	7	9	.438	64	0	0	0	19	106^1	86	6	24	102	9.4	2.71	128	.223	.270	1	.111	-0	10	9	-1	1.5
1986	LA-N	6	6	.500	60	0	0	0	11	80	86	11	29	55	13.0	3.71	93	.280	.344	2	.500	1	0	-2	0	-0.3
1987	LA-N	1	0	1.000	15	0	0	0	1	16^1	13	1	9	10	12.7	2.76	144	.220	.333	0	—	0	2	2	0	0.2
	Bal-A	3	5	.375	45	0	0	0	13	52^1	55	11	22	37	13.4	4.99	88	.266	.339	0	—	0	-3	-3	-1	-0.7

YEAR	TM/L	W	L	PCT	G	GS	CG	SH	SV	IP	H	HR	BB	SO	RAT	ERA	ERA+	OAV	OOB	BH	AVG	PB	PR	/A	PD	TPI
1988	Bal-A	3	4	.429	52	0	0	0	18	59	59	8	19	40	12.2	3.51	111	.259	.321	0	—	0	3	3	-1	0.4
1989	Sea-A	0	3	.000	25	0	0	0	0	36^1	46	7	15	15	15.4	6.69	60	.309	.376	0	—	0	-11	-11	0	-1.0
1990	StL-N	0	6	.000	52	0	0	0	2	65	66	3	25	32	12.6	3.46	110	.269	.337	0	.000	-0	2	3	-1	0.1
Total	10	36	46	.439	484	0	0	0	97	653	601	60	226	474	11.6	3.29	112	.247	.314	3	.115	-1	34	28	-5	3.7

● DICK NIEHAUS

Niehaus, Richard J. b: 10/24/1892, Covington, Ky. d: 3/12/57, Atlanta, Ga. BL/TL, 5′11″, 165 lbs. Deb: 9/9/13

YEAR	TM/L	W	L	PCT	G	GS	CG	SH	SV	IP	H	HR	BB	SO	RAT	ERA	ERA+	OAV	OOB	BH	AVG	PB	PR	/A	PD	TPI
1913	StL-N	0	2	.000	3	3	2	0	0	24	20	1	13	4	12.4	4.13	78	.241	.344	2	.286	1	-2	-2	0	-0.1
1914	StL-N	1	0	1.000	8	1	1	0	0	17^1	18	1	8	6	13.5	3.12	90	.269	.347	1	.250	1	-1	-1	-1	0.0
1915	StL-N	2	1	.667	15	2	0	0	0	45^1	48	2	22	21	14.1	3.97	70	.281	.366	1	.071	-1	-6	-6	0	-0.4
1920	Cle-A	1	2	.333	19	3	0	0	2	40	42	0	16	12	13.3	3.60	106	.269	.341	4	.444	2	1	1	-1	0.1
Total	4	4	5	.444	45	9	3	0	2	126^2	128	4	59	43	13.4	3.77	85	.268	.351	8	.235	2	-8	-8	-1	-0.4

● JOE NIEKRO

Niekro, Joseph Franklin b: 11/7/44, Martins Ferry, Ohio BR/TR, 6′1″, 190 lbs. Deb: 4/16/67 F

YEAR	TM/L	W	L	PCT	G	GS	CG	SH	SV	IP	H	HR	BB	SO	RAT	ERA	ERA+	OAV	OOB	BH	AVG	PB	PR	/A	PD	TPI
1967	Chi-N	10	7	.588	36	22	7	2	0	169^2	171	15	32	77	10.9	3.34	106	.257	.293	9	.196	1	1	4	-1	0.4
1968	Chi-N	14	10	.583	34	29	2	1	2	177	204	18	59	65	13.5	4.32	73	.294	.351	6	.100	-2	-26	-23	0	-3.2
1969	Chi-N	0	1	.000	4	3	0	0	0	19^1	24	3	6	7	14.0	3.72	108	.304	.353	1	.200	0	-0	1	1	0.1
	SD-N	8	17	.320	37	31	8	3	0	202	213	15	45	55	11.5	3.70	96	.273	.312	6	.118	0	-2	-4	-1	-0.5
	Yr	8	18	.308	41	34	8	3	0	221^1	237	18	51	62	11.7	3.70	97	.275	.316	7	.125	0	-3	-3	-1	-0.4
1970	Det-A	12	13	.480	38	34	6	2	0	213	221	28	72	101	12.5	4.06	92	.266	.327	13	.197	4	-8	-8	1	-0.4
1971	Det-A	6	7	.462	31	15	0	0	1	122^1	136	13	49	43	13.8	4.49	80	.283	.352	4	.133	-0	-14	-12	1	-1.2
1972	*Det-A	3	2	.600	18	7	1	0	1	47	62	3	8	24	13.6	3.83	82	.330	.360	3	.250	1	-4	-4	-0	-0.3
1973	Atl-N	2	4	.333	20	0	0	0	3	24	23	2	11	12	12.8	4.13	95	.277	.362	1	.333	0	-1	-1	1	-0.1
1974	Atl-N	3	2	.600	27	2	0	0	0	43	36	5	18	31	11.7	3.56	106	.237	.326	0	.000	-1	0	1	1	0.1
1975	Hou-N	6	4	.600	40	4	1	1	4	88	79	3	39	54	12.3	3.07	110	.240	.324	3	.214	1	5	3	0	0.5
1976	Hou-N	4	8	.333	36	13	0	0	0	118	107	8	56	77	12.5	3.36	95	.238	.324	5	.185	2	2	-2	-1	0.0
1977	Hou-N	13	8	.619	44	14	9	2	5	180^2	155	14	64	101	11.0	3.04	117	.237	.306	7	.140	-1	17	11	1	1.2
1978	Hou-N	14	14	.500	35	29	10	1	0	202^2	190	13	73	97	12.1	3.86	86	.248	.321	9	.138	-1	-6	-13	-1	-1.8
1979	Hou-N☆	**21**	11	.656	38	38	11	**5**	0	263^2	221	17	107	119	11.4	3.00	117	.228	.309	10	.120	-2	21	15	0	1.5
1980	*Hou-N	20	12	.625	37	36	11	2	0	256	268	12	79	127	12.3	3.55	93	.270	.326	22	.275	8	1	-8	-1	-0.1
1981	*Hou-N	9	9	.500	24	24	5	2	0	166	150	8	47	77	10.7	2.82	117	.243	.297	9	.176	1	12	9	-1	0.9
1982	Hou-N	17	12	.586	35	35	16	5	0	270	224	12	64	130	9.8	2.47	134	.229	.279	8	.090	-4	34	25	0	2.3
1983	Hou-N	15	14	.517	38	38	9	1	0	263^2	238	15	101	152	11.7	3.48	98	.241	.313	8	.094	-3	4	-2	-2	-0.8
1984	Hou-N	16	12	.571	38	38	6	1	0	248^1	223	16	89	127	11.5	3.04	109	.241	.310	11	.133	-2	15	8	1	0.7
1985	Hou-N	9	12	.429	32	32	4	1	0	213	197	21	99	117	12.7	3.72	93	.247	.333	17	.250	4	-3	-6	0	-0.2
	NY-A	2	1	.667	3	3	0	0	0	12^1	14	3	8	4	16.1	5.84	69	.280	.379	0	—	0	-2	-3	0	-0.5
1986	NY-A	9	10	.474	25	25	0	0	0	125^2	139	15	63	59	14.5	4.87	84	.275	.356	0	—	0	-10	-11	-1	-1.5
1987	NY-A	3	4	.429	8	8	1	0	0	50^2	40	4	19	30	11.2	3.55	123	.215	.301	0	—	0	5	5	-0	0.5
	*Min-A	4	9	.308	19	18	0	0	0	96^1	115	11	45	54	15.5	6.26	74	.296	.378	0	—	0	-19	-18	-1	-2.0
	Yr	7	13	.350	27	26	1	0	0	147	155	15	64	84	13.8	5.33	85	.268	.347	0	—	0	-14	-13	-1	-1.5
1988	Min-A	1	1	.500	5	2	0	0	0	11^2	16	2	9	7	19.3	10.03	41	.320	.424	0	—	0	-8	-8	1	-1.0
Total	22	221	204	.520	702	500	107	29	16	3584	3466	276	1262	1747	12.0	3.59	97	.255	.321	152	.156	6	14	-38	-3	-5.4

● PHIL NIEKRO

Niekro, Philip Henry b: 4/1/39, Blaine, Ohio BR/TR, 6′1″, 180 lbs. Deb: 4/15/64 FH

YEAR	TM/L	W	L	PCT	G	GS	CG	SH	SV	IP	H	HR	BB	SO	RAT	ERA	ERA+	OAV	OOB	BH	AVG	PB	PR	/A	PD	TPI
1964	Mil-N	0	0	—	10	0	0	0	0	15	15	1	7	8	13.8	4.80	73	.273	.365	0	—	0	-2	-2	-0	0.0
1965	Mil-N	2	3	.400	41	1	0	0	6	74^2	73	5	26	49	12.3	2.89	122	.258	.327	1	.100	-0	5	5	1	0.5
1966	Atl-N	4	3	.571	28	0	0	0	2	50^1	48	4	23	17	13.1	4.11	88	.249	.335	0	.000	-1	-3	-3	2	-0.3
1967	Atl-N	11	9	.550	46	20	10	1	9	207	164	9	55	129	9.8	**1.87**	**178**	.218	.277	7	.123	-0	35	33	1	3.8
1968	Atl-N	14	12	.538	37	34	15	5	2	257	228	16	45	140	9.7	2.59	116	.239	.277	8	.104	-1	11	11	3	1.5
1969	*Atl-N★	23	13	.639	40	35	21	4	1	284^1	235	21	57	193	9.4	2.56	141	.221	.264	20	.211	3	33	33	2	4.8
1970	Atl-N	12	18	.400	34	32	10	3	0	229^2	222	40	68	168	11.6	4.27	100	.248	.305	12	.152	-1	-6	0	2	0.1
1971	Atl-N	15	14	.517	42	36	18	4	2	268^2	248	27	70	173	10.8	2.98	124	.245	.296	14	.152	-2	14	22	2	2.3
1972	Atl-N	16	12	.571	38	36	17	1	0	282^1	254	22	53	164	9.9	3.06	124	.236	.275	18	.194	1	12	23	1	2.5
1973	Atl-N	13	10	.565	42	30	9	1	4	245	214	21	89	131	11.3	3.31	119	.234	.306	10	.122	-1	10	17	2	1.7
1974	Atl-N	**20**	13	.606	41	39	**18**	6	1	**302^1**	249	19	88	195	10.2	2.38	159	.225	.286	20	.192	-0	**42**	**47**	0	**5.2**
1975	Atl-N☆	15	15	.500	39	37	13	1	0	275^2	285	29	72	144	12.0	3.20	118	.269	.322	17	.172	-0	13	18	1	1.9
1976	Atl-N	17	11	.607	38	37	10	2	0	270^2	249	18	101	173	11.9	3.29	115	.242	.315	18	.191	1	6	15	1	1.7
1977	Atl-N	16	20	.444	44	43	**20**	2	0	**330^1**	315	26	164	**262**	13.3	4.03	110	.255	.346	19	.174	-3	-5	15	2	1.4
1978	Atl-N★	19	18	.514	44	42	**22**	4	1	**334^1**	295	16	102	248	11.0	2.88	141	.235	.299	27	.225	2	26	**43**	4	**5.7**
1979	Atl-N	**21**	20	.512	44	44	**23**	1	0	**342**	311	41	113	208	11.4	3.39	119	.241	.307	24	.195	1	13	25	3	3.4
1980	Atl-N	15	18	.455	40	38	11	3	1	275	256	30	85	176	11.3	3.63	103	.249	.308	12	.133	-2	-1	3	1	0.2
1981	Atl-N	7	7	.500	22	22	3	3	0	139^1	120	6	56	62	11.4	3.10	115	.233	.310	4	.077	-4	6	7	0	0.3
1982	*Atl-N☆	17	4	**.810**	35	35	4	2	0	234^1	225	23	73	144	11.6	3.61	103	.255	.314	17	.195	2	-0	3	1	0.6
1983	Atl-N	11	10	.524	34	33	2	0	0	201^2	212	18	105	128	14.2	3.97	98	.276	.364	12	.185	0	-8	-2	0	-0.2
1984	NY-A☆	16	8	.667	32	31	5	1	0	215^2	219	15	76	136	12.4	3.09	123	.267	.331	0	—	0	22	17	2	2.0
1985	NY-A	16	12	.571	33	33	7	1	0	220	203	29	120	149	13.3	4.09	98	.245	.342	0	—	0	1	-2	-2	-0.4
1986	Cle-A	11	11	.500	34	32	5	0	0	210^1	241	24	95	81	14.6	4.32	96	.287	.363	0	—	0	-3	-4	-1	-0.4
1987	Tor-A	0	2	.000	3	3	0	0	0	12	15	4	7	7	16.5	8.25	54	.306	.393	0	—	0	-5	-5	-0	-0.7
	Cle-A	7	11	.389	22	22	2	0	0	123^2	142	18	53	57	14.5	5.89	77	.286	.359	0	—	0	-20	-19	0	-2.2
	Yr	7	13	.350	25	25	2	0	0	135^2	157	22	60	64	14.7	6.10	74	.288	.362	0	—	0	-25	-24	-0	-2.9
	Atl-N	0	0	—	1	1	0	0	0	3	6	0	6	0	36.0	15.00	29	.429	.600	0	.000	-0	-4	-4	-0	0.0
Total	24	318	274	.537	864	716	245	45	29	5404^1	5044	482	1809	3342	11.6	3.35	115	.247	.312	260	.169	-6	192	299	28	35.4

● JERRY NIELSEN

Nielsen, Gerald Arthur b: 8/5/66, Sacramento, Cal. BL/TL, 6′3″, 185 lbs. Deb: 7/12/92

YEAR	TM/L	W	L	PCT	G	GS	CG	SH	SV	IP	H	HR	BB	SO	RAT	ERA	ERA+	OAV	OOB	BH	AVG	PB	PR	/A	PD	TPI
1992	NY-A	1	0	1.000	20	0	0	0	0	19^2	17	1	18	12	16.0	4.58	86	.243	.398	0	—	0	-1	-1	0	0.0
1993	Cal-A	0	0	—	10	0	0	0	0	12^1	18	1	4	8	16.8	8.03	56	.340	.397	0	—	0	-5	-5	-0	0.0
Total	2	1	0	1.000	30	0	0	0	0	32	35	2	22	20	16.3	5.91	70	.285	.397	0	—	0	-6	-6	0	0.0

● SCOTT NIELSEN

Nielsen, Jeffrey Scott b: 12/18/58, Salt Lake City, Ut. BR/TR, 6′1″, 190 lbs. Deb: 7/7/86

YEAR	TM/L	W	L	PCT	G	GS	CG	SH	SV	IP	H	HR	BB	SO	RAT	ERA	ERA+	OAV	OOB	BH	AVG	PB	PR	/A	PD	TPI
1986	NY-A	4	4	.500	10	9	2	2	0	56	66	12	12	20	12.9	4.02	102	.299	.340	0	—	0	1	0	-1	0.0
1987	Chi-A	3	5	.375	19	7	1	1	2	66^1	83	9	25	23	14.8	6.24	73	.307	.368	0	—	0	-13	-12	-1	-1.3
1988	NY-A	1	2	.333	7	2	0	0	0	19^2	27	5	13	4	18.3	6.86	57	.333	.426	0	—	0	-6	-6	0	-0.8
1989	NY-A	1	0	1.000	2	0	0	0	0	0^2	2	0	1	0	40.5	13.50	29	.500	.600	0	—	0	-1	-1	0	-0.7
Total	4	9	11	.450	38	18	3	3	2	142^2	178	26	51	47	14.6	5.49	78	.309	.368	0	—	0	-19	-19	-1	-2.8

● RANDY NIEMANN

Niemann, Randal Harold b: 11/15/55, Scotia, Cal. BL/TL, 6′4″, 200 lbs. Deb: 5/20/79 C

YEAR	TM/L	W	L	PCT	G	GS	CG	SH	SV	IP	H	HR	BB	SO	RAT	ERA	ERA+	OAV	OOB	BH	AVG	PB	PR	/A	PD	TPI
1979	Hou-N	3	2	.600	26	7	3	2	1	67	68	1	22	24	12.2	3.76	93	.272	.333	2	.133	-0	-0	-2	-1	-0.2
1980	Hou-N	0	1	.000	22	1	0	0	1	33	40	2	12	18	14.2	5.45	60	.299	.356	2	.333	1	-7	-8	1	-0.1
1982	Pit-N	1	1	.500	20	0	0	0	1	35^1	34	1	17	26	13.5	5.09	73	.254	.346	2	1.000	1	-6	-5	1	-0.2
1983	Pit-N	0	1	.000	8	1	0	0	0	13^2	20	2	7	8	18.4	9.22	40	.357	.438	0	.000	-0	-8	-8	0	-0.5
1984	Chi-A	0	0	—	5	0	0	0	0	5^1	5	0	5	5	16.9	1.69	246	.263	.417	0	—	0	1	1	0	0.0
1985	NY-N	0	0	—	4	0	0	0	0	4^2	5	0	0	2	9.6	0.00	—	.278	.278	0	—	0	2	2	0	0.0
1986	NY-N	2	3	.400	31	1	0	0	0	35^2	44	2	12	18	14.1	3.79	93	.308	.361	2	.333	1	-0	-1	1	0.0
1987	Min-A	1	0	1.000	6	0	0	0	0	5^1	3	0	7	1	20.3	8.44	55	.158	.429	0	—	0	-2	-2	0	-0.4
Total	8	7	8	.467	122	10	3	2	3	200	219	8	82	102	13.8	4.64	77	.283	.357	8	.267	2	-21	-24	2	-1.4

● JACK NIEMES

Niemes, Jacob Leland b: 10/19/19, Cincinnati, Ohio d: 3/4/66, Hamilton, Ohio BR/TL, 6′1″, 180 lbs. Deb: 5/30/43

YEAR	TM/L	W	L	PCT	G	GS	CG	SH	SV	IP	H	HR	BB	SO	RAT	ERA	ERA+	OAV	OOB	BH	AVG	PB	PR	/A	PD	TPI
1943	Cin-N	0	0	—	3	0	0	0	0	3	5	0	2	1	21.0	6.00	55	.385	.467	0	—	0	-1	-1	-0	0.0

● CHUCK NIESON

Nieson, Charles Bassett b: 9/24/42, Hanford, Cal. BR/TR, 6′2″, 185 lbs. Deb: 9/18/64

YEAR	TM/L	W	L	PCT	G	GS	CG	SH	SV	IP	H	HR	BB	SO	RAT	ERA	ERA+	OAV	OOB	BH	AVG	PB	PR	/A	PD	TPI
1964	Min-A	0	0	—	2	0	0	0	0	2	1	1	1	5	9.0	4.50	79	.143	.250	0	—	0	-0	-0	0	0.0

YEAR	TM/L	W	L	PCT	G	GS	CG	SH	SV	IP	H	HR	BB	SO	RAT	ERA	ERA+	OAV	OOB	BH	AVG	PB	PR	/A	PD	TPI
● **JUAN NIEVES**	Nieves, Juan Manuel (Cruz) b: 1/5/65, Las Lomas, P.R. BL/TL, 6'3", 175 lbs. Deb: 4/10/86																									
1986	Mil-A	11	12	.478	35	33	4	3	0	184^2	224	17	77	116	14.7	4.92	88	.299	.366	0	—	0	-15	-12	-2	-1.6
1987	Mil-A	14	8	.636	34	33	3	1	0	195^2	199	24	100	163	13.8	4.88	94	.264	.351	0	—	0	-9	-7	-1	-0.8
1988	Mil-A	7	5	.583	25	15	1	1	1	110^1	84	13	50	73	11.0	4.08	98	.208	.297	0	—	0	-1	-1	-0	-0.2
Total	3	32	25	.561	94	81	8	5	1	490^2	507	54	227	352	13.5	4.71	92	.266	.345	0	—	0	-26	-20	-4	-2.6
● **JOHNNY NIGGELING**	Niggeling, John Arnold b: 7/10/03, Remsen, Iowa d: 9/16/63, LeMars, Iowa BR/TR, 6', 170 lbs. Deb: 4/30/38																									
1938	Bos-N	1	0	1.000	2	0	0	0	0	2	4	0	1	1	22.5	9.00	38	.400	.455	0	—	0	-1	-1	-0	-0.5
1939	Cin-N	2	1	.667	10	5	2	1	0	40^1	51	2	13	20	14.7	5.80	66	.309	.367	2	.154	-0	-8	-9	-0	-0.6
1940	StL-A	7	11	.389	28	20	10	0	0	153^2	148	9	69	82	13.0	4.45	103	.250	.333	9	.176	-1	-1	2	-0	0.1
1941	StL-A	7	9	.438	24	20	13	1	0	168^1	168	17	63	68	12.4	3.80	113	.255	.320	10	.167	-1	7	9	-1	0.5
1942	StL-A	15	11	.577	28	27	16	3	0	206^1	173	10	93	107	12.1	2.66	139	.226	.319	10	.139	-2	23	24	-2	2.5
1943	StL-A	6	8	.429	20	20	7	0	0	150^1	122	7	57	73	11.1	3.17	105	.220	.299	3	.061	-4	2	3	-0	-0.3
	Was-A	4	2	.667	6	6	5	3	0	51	27	0	17	24	7.8	0.88	363	.153	.227	5	.278	1	14	13	0	2.0
	Yr	10	10	.500	26	26	12	3	0	201^1	149	7	74	97	10.0	2.59	127	.202	.275	8	.119	-3	16	16	0	1.7
1944	Was-A	10	8	.556	24	24	14	2	0	206	164	5	88	121	11.2	2.32	141	.221	.307	9	.130	-2	25	21	-1	1.5
1945	Was-A	7	12	.368	26	25	8	2	0	176^2	161	7	73	90	12.1	3.16	98	.240	.318	7	.119	-4	4	-1	-2	-0.7
1946	Was-A	3	2	.600	8	6	3	0	0	38	39	1	21	10	14.4	4.03	83	.265	.361	2	.182	0	-2	-3	-0	-0.3
	Bos-N	2	5	.286	8	8	3	0	0	58	54	2	21	24	11.8	3.26	105	.243	.311	2	.111	-1	1	1	0	0.0
Total	9	64	69	.481	184	161	81	12	0	1250^2	1111	60	516	620	12.0	3.22	113	.236	.316	59	.140	-14	63	58	-7	4.2
● **AL NIPPER**	Nipper, Albert Samuel b: 4/2/59, San Diego, Cal. BR/TR, 6', 194 lbs. Deb: 9/6/83 C																									
1983	Bos-A	1	1	.500	3	2	1	0	0	16	17	0	7	5	14.1	2.25	193	.293	.379	0	—	0	3	4	-0	0.2
1984	Bos-A	11	6	.647	29	24	6	0	0	182^2	183	18	52	84	11.9	3.89	107	.257	.313	0	—	0	2	5	3	0.7
1985	Bos-A	9	12	.429	25	25	5	0	0	162	157	14	82	85	13.8	4.06	106	.256	.352	0	—	0	2	4	2	0.7
1986	*Bos-A	10	12	.455	26	26	3	0	0	159	186	24	47	79	13.4	5.38	77	.290	.342	0	—	0	-21	-21	3	-2.2
1987	Bos-A	11	12	.478	30	30	6	0	0	174	196	30	62	89	13.7	5.43	84	.284	.349	0	—	0	-19	-17	1	-1.8
1988	Chi-N	2	4	.333	22	12	0	0	1	80	72	9	34	27	12.3	3.04	119	.238	.322	2	.087	-1	4	5	-2	0.1
1990	Cle-A	2	3	.400	9	5	0	0	0	24	35	2	19	12	21.0	6.75	58	.354	.467	0	—	0	-8	-8	-0	-1.3
Total	7	46	50	.479	144	124	21	0	1	797^2	846	97	303	381	13.3	4.52	93	.271	.342	2	.087	-1	-37	-28	7	-3.6
● **MERLIN NIPPERT**	Nippert, Merlin Lee b: 9/1/38, Mangum, Okla. BR/TR, 6'1", 175 lbs. Deb: 9/12/62																									
1962	Bos-A	0	0	—	4	0	0	0	0	6	4	1	4	3	12.0	4.50	92	.200	.333	0	—	0	-0	-0	-0	0.0
● **RON NISCHWITZ**	Nischwitz, Ronald Lee b: 7/1/37, Dayton, Ohio BB/TL, 6'3", 205 lbs. Deb: 9/4/61																									
1961	Det-A	0	1	.000	6	1	0	0	0	11^1	13	2	8	8	16.7	5.56	74	.295	.404	0	.000	-0	-2	-2	-0	-0.2
1962	Det-A	4	5	.444	48	0	0	0	4	64^2	73	5	26	28	13.9	3.90	104	.285	.353	5	.417	2	1	1	0	0.4
1963	Cle-A	0	2	.000	14	0	0	0	1	16^2	17	3	8	10	13.5	6.48	56	.262	.342	0	.000	-0	-5	-5	0	-0.7
1965	Det-A	1	0	1.000	20	0	0	0	1	22^2	21	2	6	12	10.7	2.78	125	.259	.310	0	.000	-0	2	2	-0	0.0
Total	4	5	8	.385	88	1	0	0	6	115^1	124	12	48	58	13.5	4.21	92	.278	.349	5	.278	1	-5	-4	0	-0.5
● **OTHO NITCHOLAS**	Nitcholas, Otho James b: 9/13/08, McKinney, Tex. d: 9/11/86, McKinney, Tex. BR/TR, 6', 190 lbs. Deb: 4/18/45																									
1945	Bro-N	1	0	1.000	7	0	0	0	0	18^2	19	4	1	4	9.6	5.30	71	.257	.267	1	.250	0	-3	-3	-0	-0.2
● **C. J. NITKOWSKI**	Nitkowski, Christopher John b: 3/9/73, Suffern, N.Y. BL/TL, 6'2", 185 lbs. Deb: 6/3/95																									
1995	Cin-N	1	3	.250	9	7	0	0	0	32^1	41	4	15	18	16.1	6.12	67	.306	.384	2	.200	0	-7	-7	-1	-0.8
	Det-A	1	4	.200	11	11	0	0	0	39^1	53	7	20	13	17.4	7.09	67	.335	.420	0	—	0	-10	-10	-0	-1.0
1996	Det-A	2	3	.400	11	8	0	0	0	45^2	62	7	38	36	21.1	8.08	63	.332	.461	0	—	0	-16	-15	-0	-1.3
1998	Hou-N	3	3	.500	43	0	0	0	3	59^2	49	4	23	44	11.8	3.77	108	.228	.320	0	.000	-0	3	2	0	0.2
Total	3	7	13	.350	74	26	0	0	3	177	205	22	96	111	16.2	6.05	74	.295	.395	2	.143	-0	-30	-31	-1	-2.9
● **WILLARD NIXON**	Nixon, Willard Lee b: 6/17/28, Taylorsville, Ga. BL/TR, 6'2", 195 lbs. Deb: 7/7/50																									
1950	Bos-A	8	6	.571	22	15	2	0	2	101^1	126	8	58	57	16.5	6.04	81	.310	.398	5	.139	-1	-16	-13	-0	-1.6
1951	Bos-A	7	4	.636	33	14	2	1	1	125	136	12	56	70	14.3	4.90	91	.285	.368	13	.289	3	-11	-6	-0	-0.2
1952	Bos-A	5	4	.556	23	13	5	0	0	103^2	115	12	61	50	15.6	4.86	81	.290	.390	11	.208	1	-14	-11	1	-0.7
1953	Bos-A	4	8	.333	23	15	5	1	0	116^2	114	6	59	57	13.4	3.93	107	.254	.343	8	.190	0	1	4	-0	0.3
1954	Bos-A	11	12	.478	31	30	8	2	0	199^2	182	16	87	102	12.5	4.06	101	.248	.335	18	.265	5	-7	1	1	0.7
1955	Bos-A	12	10	.545	31	31	7	3	0	208	207	10	85	95	12.8	4.07	105	.259	.333	18	.261	5	-2	5	2	1.2
1956	Bos-A	9	8	.529	23	22	9	1	0	145^1	142	9	57	74	12.8	4.21	110	.255	.333	11	.204	-1	-1	7	2	0.8
1957	Bos-A	12	13	.480	29	29	11	1	0	191	207	10	56	96	12.7	3.68	108	.280	.337	22	.293	5	2	7	-1	1.2
1958	Bos-A	1	7	.125	10	8	2	0	0	43^1	48	7	11	15	12.3	6.02	67	.281	.324	5	.294	1	-11	-10	0	-1.5
Total	9	69	72	.489	225	177	51	9	3	1234	1277	90	530	616	13.5	4.39	97	.270	.349	111	.242	17	-59	-16	5	0.2
● **JUNIOR NOBOA**	Noboa, Milciades Arturo (Diaz) b: 11/10/64, Azua, D.R. BR/TR, 5'10", 160 lbs. Deb: 8/22/84 ♦																									
1990	Mon-N	0	0	—	1	0	0	0	0	0^2	0	0	1	0	13.5	0.00	—	.000	.500	42	.266	0	0	0	0	0.0
● **THE ONLY NOLAN**	Nolan, Edward Sylvester b: 11/7/1857, Paterson, N.J. d: 5/18/13, Paterson, N.J. BL/TR, 5'8", 171 lbs. Deb: 5/1/1878																									
1878	Ind-N	13	22	.371	38	38	37	1	0	347	357	1	56	125	10.7	2.57	79	.253	.281	37	.243	6	-10	-21	2	-1.0
1881	Cle-N	8	14	.364	22	21	20	0	0	180	183	3	38	54	11.1	3.05	86	.251	.288	41	.244	1	-6	-9	-1	-0.9
1883	Pit-a	0	7	.000	7	7	6	0	0	55	81	0	10	23	14.9	4.25	75	.321	.347	8	.308	2	-6	-6	-0	-0.5
1884	Wil-U	1	4	.200	5	5	5	0	0	40	44	1	7	52	11.5	2.93	91	.262	.291	9	.273	-0	-2	-1	1	0.0
1885	Phi-N	1	5	.167	7	7	6	0	0	54	55	1	24	20	13.2	4.17	67	.256	.331	2	.077	-2	-8	-8	-1	-0.9
Total	5	23	52	.307	79	78	74	1	0	676	720	6	135	274	11.4	2.98	80	.259	.294	97	.240	7	-32	-46	1	-3.3
● **GARY NOLAN**	Nolan, Gary Lynn b: 5/27/48, Herlong, Cal. BR/TR, 6'2.5", 197 lbs. Deb: 4/15/67																									
1967	Cin-N	14	8	.636	33	32	8	5	0	226^2	193	18	62	206	10.3	2.58	145	.228	.284	7	.104	-1	20	29	-1	2.6
1968	Cin-N	9	4	.692	23	22	4	2	0	150	105	10	49	111	9.4	2.40	132	.196	.267	6	.130	2	10	13	-2	1.2
1969	Cin-N	8	8	.500	16	15	2	1	0	108^2	102	11	40	83	11.8	3.56	106	.247	.313	8	.229	3	0	2	-2	0.5
1970	*Cin-N	18	7	.720	37	37	4	2	0	250^2	226	25	96	181	11.6	3.27	123	.240	.311	13	.159	1	22	21	-1	1.9
1971	Cin-N	12	15	.444	35	35	9	0	0	244^2	208	12	59	146	9.9	3.16	106	.227	.275	11	.147	-1	8	5	1	0.5
1972	*Cin-N†	15	5	**.750**	25	25	6	2	0	176	147	13	30	90	9.1	1.99	161	.227	.262	7	.117	-1	29	24	-1	2.6
1973	Cin-N	0	1	.000	2	2	0	0	0	10^1	6	1	7	3	11.3	3.48	98	.167	.302	0	.000	0	0	-0	-0	0.0
1975	*Cin-N	15	9	.625	32	32	5	1	0	210^2	202	18	29	74	9.9	3.16	114	.251	.278	12	.176	2	11	10	-2	1.1
1976	*Cin-N	15	9	.625	34	34	7	1	0	239^1	232	28	27	113	9.8	3.46	101	.254	.276	8	.101	-3	1	1	-4	-0.6
1977	Cin-N	4	1	.800	8	8	0	0	0	39^1	53	5	12	28	14.9	4.81	82	.321	.367	1	.067	-1	-4	-4	-0	-0.6
	Cal-A	0	3	.000	5	5	0	0	0	18^1	31	5	2	4	16.2	8.84	44	.365	.379	0	—	0	-10	-10	-0	-1.3
Total	10	110	70	.611	250	247	45	14	0	1674^2	1505	146	413	1039	10.4	3.08	116	.239	.287	73	.138	0	87	93	-12	7.9
● **DICK NOLD**	Nold, Richard Louis b: 5/4/43, San Francisco, Cal. BR/TR, 6'2", 190 lbs. Deb: 8/19/67																									
1967	Was-A	0	2	.000	7	3	0	0	0	20^1	19	1	13	10	14.2	4.87	65	.241	.348	0	.000	-0	-4	-4	-0	-0.4
● **DICKIE NOLES**	Noles, Dickie Ray b: 11/19/56, Charlotte, N.C. BR/TR, 6'2", 190 lbs. Deb: 7/5/79																									
1979	Phi-N	3	4	.429	14	14	0	0	0	90	80	6	38	42	12.0	3.80	101	.246	.329	3	.100	-1	-1	0	1	0.0
1980	*Phi-N	1	4	.200	48	3	0	0	6	81	80	5	42	57	13.7	3.89	97	.254	.344	4	.308	1	-3	-1	-0	0.0
1981	*Phi-N	2	2	.500	13	8	0	0	0	58^1	57	2	23	34	12.8	4.17	87	.260	.339	2	.105	-1	-4	-4	-1	-0.5
1982	Chi-N	10	13	.435	31	30	2	2	0	171	180	11	61	85	12.9	4.42	84	.274	.340	6	.107	-2	-16	-13	-0	-1.8
1983	Chi-N	5	10	.333	24	18	1	1	0	116^1	133	9	37	59	13.2	4.72	80	.287	.341	9	.237	1	-14	-12	-0	-1.3
1984	Chi-N	2	2	.500	21	1	0	0	0	50^2	60	4	16	14	13.7	5.15	76	.305	.360	0	.000	-1	-9	-7	-1	-0.7
	Tex-A	2	3	.400	18	6	0	0	0	57^2	60	6	30	39	14.8	5.15	80	.262	.360	0	—	0	-7	-6	-1	-0.7
1985	Tex-A	4	8	.333	28	13	0	0	1	110^1	129	11	33	59	13.7	5.06	84	.289	.346	0	—	0	-11	-10	1	-0.9
1986	Cle-A	3	2	.600	32	0	0	0	0	54^2	56	9	30	32	15.0	5.10	81	.269	.374	0	—	0	-6	-6	0	-0.4
1987	Chi-N	4	2	.667	41	1	0	0	2	64^1	59	1	27	33	12.7	3.50	122	.239	.326	0	.000	-1	4	6	1	0.5

YEAR	TM/L	W	L	PCT	G	GS	CG	SH	SV	IP	H	HR	BB	SO	RAT	ERA	ERA+	OAV	OOB	BH	AVG	PB	PR	/A	PD	TPI
	Det-A	0	0	—	4	0	0	0	2	2	2	0	1	0	13.5	4.50	94	.250	.333	0	—	0	-0	-0	0	0.3
1988	Bal-A	0	2	.000	2	2	0	0	0	3^1	11	2	0	1	32.4	24.30	16	.500	.522	0	—	0	-8	-8	-0	-2.2
1990	Phi-N	0	1	.000	1	0	0	0	0	0^1	2	0	0	0	54.0	27.00	14	.667	.667	0	—	0	-1	-1	0	-1.2
Total	11	36	53	.404	277	96	3	3	11	860	909	66	338	455	13.4	4.56	86	.272	.345	24	.136	-3	-75	-61	-2	-8.9
● ERIC NOLTE	Nolte, Eric Carl b: 4/28/64, Canoga Park, Cal. BL/TL, 6'3", 205 lbs. Deb: 8/1/87																									
1987	SD-N	2	6	.250	12	12	1	0	0	67^1	57	6	36	44	12.7	3.21	123	.226	.328	2	.095	-1	7	6	-1	0.5
1988	SD-N	0	0	—	2	0	0	0	0	3	3	1	2	1	15.0	6.00	57	.273	.385	0	—	0	-1	-1	-0	0.0
1989	SD-N	0	0	—	3	1	0	0	0	9	15	1	7	8	22.0	11.00	32	.375	.468	0	.000	-0	-8	-8	0	0.0
1991	SD-N	3	2	.600	6	6	0	0	0	22	37	6	10	15	19.2	11.05	34	.378	.435	1	.111	-0	-18	-18	-0	-2.9
	Tex-A	0	0	—	3	0	0	0	0	2^2	3	0	3	1	20.3	3.38	119	.273	.429	0	—	0	0	0	-0	0.1
Total	4	5	8	.385	26	19	1	0	0	104	115	14	58	69	15.1	5.63	69	.279	.371	3	.094	-1	-20	-20	-1	-2.3
● HIDEO NOMO	Nomo, Hideo b: 8/31/68, Osaka, Japan BR/TR, 6'2", 210 lbs. Deb: 5/2/95																									
1995	*LA-N★	13	6	.684	28	28	4	**3**	0	191^1	124	14	78	**236**	9.7	2.54	149	**.182**	.271	6	.091	-4	35	27	-2	1.8
1996	*LA-N	16	11	.593	33	33	3	2	0	228^1	180	23	85	234	10.5	3.19	121	.218	.292	10	.133	-0	26	17	-1	1.7
1997	LA-N	14	12	.538	33	33	1	0	0	207^1	193	23	92	233	12.8	4.25	91	.243	.328	11	.159	2	-1	-9	-3	-1.1
1998	LA-N	2	7	.222	12	12	2	0	0	67^2	57	8	38	73	13.0	5.05	77	.228	.337	1	.050	-1	-6	-9	-1	-1.1
	NY-N	4	5	.444	17	16	1	0	0	89^2	73	11	56	94	13.0	4.82	86	.224	.339	8	.267	2	-6	-6	0	-0.4
	Yr	6	12	.333	29	28	3	0	0	157^1	130	19	94	167	12.9	4.92	82	.224	.333	9	.180	1	-12	-15	-1	-1.5
Total	4	49	41	.544	123	122	11	5	0	784^1	627	79	349	870	11.4	3.66	106	.218	.307	36	.138	-1	47	19	-7	0.9
● JERRY NOPS	Nops, Jeremiah H. b: 6/23/1875, Toledo, Ohio d: 3/26/37, Camden, N.J. BL/TL, 5'8.5", 168 lbs. Deb: 9/7/1896																									
1896	Phi-N	1	0	1.000	1	1	1	0	0	7	11	0	1	1	15.4	5.14	84	.355	.375	0	.000	-1	-1	-1	-0	-0.2
	Bal-N	2	1	.667	3	3	3	0	0	22	29	0	2	8	12.7	6.14	70	.315	.330	1	.111	-1	-4	-5	-0	-0.5
	Yr	3	1	.750	4	4	4	0	0	29	40	0	3	9	13.3	5.90	73	.325	.341	1	.077	-2	-5	-5	-0	-0.7
1897	*Bal-N	20	6	.769	30	25	23	1	0	220^2	235	5	52	69	12.1	2.81	148	.271	.319	18	.196	-3	37	33	-2	2.7
1898	Bal-N	16	9	.640	33	29	23	2	0	235	241	5	78	91	12.8	3.56	101	.263	.332	20	.220	2	1	0	-4	-0.2
1899	Bal-N	17	11	.607	33	33	26	2	0	259	296	1	71	60	13.1	4.03	98	.287	.339	29	.276	1	-5	-2	-3	-0.3
1900	Bro-N	4	4	.500	9	8	6	1	0	68	79	1	18	22	13.1	3.84	100	.289	.338	4	.160	-1	-1	0	-1	-0.2
1901	Bal-A	12	10	.545	27	23	17	1	1	176^2	192	5	59	43	13.4	4.08	95	.274	.341	13	.220	-0	-8	-4	-4	-0.8
Total	6	72	41	.637	136	122	99	7	1	988^1	1083	17	281	294	12.9	3.70	106	.277	.333	85	.221	-2	19	23	-15	0.5
● WAYNE NORDHAGEN	Nordhagen, Wayne Oren b: 7/4/48, Thief River Falls, Minn. BR/TR, 6'2", 205 lbs. Deb: 7/16/76 ♦																									
1979	Chi-A	0	0	—	2	0	0	0	0	2	2	0	1	2	13.5	9.00	47	.286	.375	54	.280	1	-1	-1	-0	0.0
● JOHN NORIEGA	Noriega, John Alan b: 12/20/43, Ogden, Utah BR/TR, 6'4", 185 lbs. Deb: 5/1/69																									
1969	Cin-N	0	0	—	5	0	0	0	0	7^2	12	1	3	4	17.6	5.87	64	.400	.455	0	—	0	-2	-2	-0	0.0
1970	Cin-N	0	0	—	8	0	0	0	0	18	25	0	10	6	18.5	8.00	50	.333	.425	1	.250	0	-8	-8	1	0.1
Total	2	0	0	—	13	0	0	0	0	25^2	37	1	13	10	18.2	7.36	54	.352	.433	1	.250	0	-10	-10	1	0.1
● FRED NORMAN	Norman, Fredie Hubert b: 8/20/42, San Antonio, Tex. BB/TL, 5'8", 160 lbs. Deb: 9/21/62																									
1962	KC-A	0	0	—	2	0	0	0	0	4	4	0	1	2	11.3	2.25	188	.250	.294	0	—	0	1	1	-0	0.0
1963	KC-A	0	1	.000	2	2	0	0	0	6^1	9	1	7	6	22.7	11.37	34	.346	.485	0	.000	-0	-5	-5	0	-0.7
1964	Chi-N	0	4	.000	8	5	0	0	0	31^2	34	9	21	20	15.9	6.54	57	.279	.389	1	.091	-1	-11	-10	-0	-1.2
1966	Chi-N	0	0	—	2	0	0	0	0	4	5	0	2	6	15.8	4.50	82	.313	.389	0	—	0	-0	-0	-0	0.0
1967	Chi-N	0	0	—	1	0	0	0	0	1	0	0	0	3	0.0	0.00	—	.000	.000	0	—	0	0	0	0	0.0
1970	LA-N	2	0	1.000	30	0	0	0	1	62	65	8	33	47	14.5	5.23	73	.273	.366	1	.143	0	-8	-10	-1	-0.3
	StL-N	0	0	—	1	0	0	0	0	1	1	0	0	0	9.0	0.00	—	.333	.333	0	—	0	0	0	0	0.0
	Yr	2	0	1.000	31	0	0	0	1	63	66	8	33	47	14.1	5.14	75	.269	.356	1	.143	0	-8	-9	-1	-0.3
1971	StL-N	0	0	—	4	0	0	0	0	3^2	7	1	7	4	34.4	12.27	29	.438	.609	0	—	0	-4	-4	-0	0.0
	SD-N	3	12	.200	20	18	5	0	0	127^1	114	7	56	77	12.2	3.32	99	.240	.323	9	.237	2	2	-0	-1	0.1
	Yr	3	12	.200	24	18	5	0	0	131	121	8	63	81	12.8	3.57	92	.246	.334	9	.237	2	-2	-4	-1	0.1
1972	SD-N	9	11	.450	42	28	10	6	2	211^2	195	18	88	167	12.1	3.44	95	.244	.321	8	.125	1	0	-4	-1	-0.3
1973	SD-N	1	7	.125	12	11	1	0	0	74	72	9	29	49	12.4	4.26	82	.262	.334	3	.136	-0	-5	-6	1	-0.6
	*Cin-N	12	6	.667	24	24	7	3	0	166^1	136	18	72	112	11.3	3.30	103	.224	.307	3	.052	-4	7	2	-1	-0.3
	Yr	13	13	.500	36	35	8	3	0	240^1	208	27	101	161	11.6	3.60	95	.235	.314	6	.075	-4	2	-5	-0	-0.9
1974	Cin-N	13	12	.520	35	26	8	2	0	186^1	170	15	68	141	11.6	3.14	111	.241	.309	8	.131	-2	10	7	-3	0.4
1975	*Cin-N	12	4	.750	34	26	2	0	0	188	163	23	84	119	11.8	3.73	96	.235	.318	7	.117	-2	-2	-3	-2	-0.6
1976	*Cin-N	12	7	.632	33	24	8	3	0	180^1	153	10	70	126	11.3	3.09	113	.231	.308	7	.140	-1	8	8	-3	0.4
1977	Cin-N	14	13	.519	35	34	8	1	0	221^1	200	28	98	160	12.2	3.38	116	.241	.324	8	.110	-2	13	14	-0	1.2
1978	Cin-N	11	9	.550	36	31	0	0	1	177^1	173	19	82	111	13.1	3.70	96	.255	.338	7	.140	-1	-3	-3	-1	-0.5
1979	*Cin-N	11	13	.458	34	31	5	0	0	195^1	193	14	57	95	11.5	3.64	103	.258	.311	9	.153	0	2	2	-2	0.1
1980	Mon-N	4	4	.500	48	8	2	0	4	98	96	8	40	58	12.8	4.13	86	.259	.337	1	.050	-2	-6	-6	-1	-0.9
Total	16	104	103	.502	403	268	56	15	8	1939^2	1790	188	815	1303	12.2	3.64	98	.246	.324	72	.125	-11	-0	-17	-15	-3.2
● MIKE NORRIS	Norris, Michael Kelvin b: 3/19/55, San Francisco, Cal. BR/TR, 6'2", 175 lbs. Deb: 4/10/75																									
1975	Oak-A	1	0	1.000	4	3	1	1	0	16^2	6	0	8	5	7.6	0.00	—	.107	.219	0	—	0	7	7	0	0.4
1976	Oak-A	4	5	.444	24	19	1	1	0	96	91	10	56	44	14.0	4.78	70	.250	.353	0	—	0	-13	-15	3	-1.0
1977	Oak-A	2	7	.222	16	12	1	1	0	77^1	77	14	31	35	13.0	4.77	84	.260	.338	0	.000	-0	-6	-6	1	-0.6
1978	Oak-A	0	5	.000	14	5	1	0	0	49	46	2	35	36	15.4	5.51	66	.249	.377	0	—	0	-10	-10	-0	-0.8
1979	Oak-A	5	8	.385	29	18	3	0	0	146^1	146	11	94	96	15.3	4.80	84	.265	.381	0	—	0	-9	-12	-1	-0.8
1980	Oak-A	22	9	.710	33	33	24	1	0	284^1	215	18	83	180	9.6	2.53	149	**.209**	.272	0	—	0	**47**	**39**	3	**4.7**
1981	*Oak-A★	12	9	.571	23	23	12	2	0	172^2	145	17	63	78	11.4	3.75	93	.228	.308	0	—	0	-2	-5	-0	-0.6
1982	Oak-A	7	11	.389	28	28	7	1	0	166^1	154	25	84	83	13.2	4.76	82	.242	.336	0	—	0	-13	-16	1	-1.4
1983	Oak-A	4	5	.444	16	16	2	0	0	88^2	68	11	36	63	10.9	3.76	103	.213	.299	0	—	0	3	1	-2	0.1
1990	Oak-A	1	0	1.000	14	0	0	0	0	27	24	0	9	16	11.7	3.00	124	.242	.318	0	—	0	3	2	0	0.2
Total	10	58	59	.496	201	157	52	7	0	1124^1	972	108	499	636	12.1	3.89	97	.233	.322	0	.000	-0	7	-16	5	0.2
● LOU NORTH	North, Louis Alexander b: 6/15/1891, Elgin, Ill. d: 5/15/74, Shelton, Conn. BR/TR, 5'11", 175 lbs. Deb: 8/22/13																									
1913	Det-A	0	1	.000	1	1	0	0	0	6	10	1	9	3	28.5	15.00	19	.357	.514	0	.000	-0	-8	-8	-0	-0.8
1917	StL-N	0	0	—	5	0	0	0	0	11^1	14	1	4	4	14.3	3.97	68	.350	.409	0	.000	-0	-2	-2	0	0.0
1920	StL-N	3	2	.600	24	6	3	0	1	88	90	3	32	37	12.7	3.27	91	.278	.346	7	.226	0	-1	-3	-1	-0.3
1921	StL-N	4	4	.500	40	0	0	0	**7**	86^1	81	5	32	28	11.9	3.54	103	.256	.327	3	.158	-1	**2**	**1**	-2	-0.2
1922	StL-N	10	3	.769	**53**	10	4	0	4	149^2	164	4	64	84	14.1	4.45	87	.283	.361	11	.234	2	-6	-10	4	-0.2
1923	StL-N	3	4	.429	34	3	0	0	1	71^2	90	8	31	24	15.6	5.15	76	.308	.380	4	.182	-1	-9	-10	1	-0.9
1924	StL-N	0	0	—	6	1	0	0	0	14^2	15	1	9	8	14.7	6.75	56	.273	.375	1	.250	-0	-5	-5	-0	0.0
	Bos-N	1	2	.333	9	4	1	0	0	35^1	45	1	19	11	16.3	5.35	71	.321	.403	1	.111	-1	-6	-6	-1	-0.6
	Yr	1	2	.333	15	5	1	0	0	50	60	2	28	19	15.8	5.76	66	.308	.395	2	.154	-1	-11	-11	-1	-0.6
Total	7	21	16	.568	172	25	8	0	13	463	509	24	200	199	14.0	4.43	82	.287	.363	27	.197	-1	-34	-42	0	-3.0
● JAKE NORTHROP	Northrop, George Howard "Jerky" b: 3/5/1888, Monroeton, Pa. d: 11/16/45, Monroeton, Pa. BL/TR, 5'11", 170 lbs. Deb: 7/29/18																									
1918	Bos-N	5	1	.833	7	4	4	1	0	40	26	0	3	4	6.5	1.35	199	.183	.200	2	.154	-1	6	6	0	0.9
1919	Bos-N	1	5	.167	11	3	2	0	0	37^1	43	2	10	9	13.0	4.58	62	.301	.351	4	.500	3	-7	-7	1	-0.7
Total	2	6	6	.500	18	7	6	1	0	77^1	69	2	13	13	9.7	2.91	95	.242	.278	6	.286	2	-1	-1	1	0.2
● EFFIE NORTON	Norton, Elisha Strong "Leiter" b: 8/17/1873, Conneaut, Ohio d: 3/5/50, Aspinwall, Pa. BR/TR, Deb: 8/8/1896																									
1896	Was-N	3	1	.750	8	5	2	0	0	44	49	2	14	13	14.1	3.07	144	.280	.354	4	.211	-0	6	7	-0	0.4
1897	Was-N	2	1	.667	4	2	1	0	0	17	31	0	11	3	22.2	6.88	63	.387	.462	5	.278	1	-5	-5	-0	-0.6
Total	2	5	2	.714	12	7	3	0	0	61	80	2	25	16	16.4	4.13	106	.314	.388	9	.243	0	1	2	-1	-0.2

YEAR	TM/L	W	L	PCT	G	GS	CG	SH	SV	IP	H	HR	BB	SO	RAT	ERA	ERA+	OAV	OOB	BH	AVG	PB	PR	/A	PD	TPI
● TOM NORTON	Norton, Thomas John b: 4/26/50, Elyria, Ohio BR/TR, 6′1″, 200 lbs. Deb: 4/18/72																									
1972	Min-A	0	1	.000	21	0	0	0	0	32^1	31	1	14	22	12.8	2.78	115	.252	.333	0	—	0	1	2	1	0.2
● RANDY NOSEK	Nosek, Randall William b: 1/8/67, Omaha, Neb. BR/TR, 6′4″, 215 lbs. Deb: 5/27/89																									
1989	Det-A	0	2	.000	2	2	0	0	0	5^1	7	2	10	4	28.7	13.50	28	.333	.548	0	—	0	-6	-6	-0	-1.3
1990	Det-A	1	1	.500	3	2	0	0	0	7	7	1	9	3	20.6	7.71	51	.280	.471	0	—	0	-3	-3	-0	-0.7
Total	2	1	3	.250	5	4	0	0	0	12^1	14	3	19	7	24.1	10.22	38	.304	.508	0	—	0	-9	-9	-0	-2.0
● DON NOTTEBART	Nottebart, Donald Edward b: 1/23/36, West Newton, Mass. BR/TR, 6′1″, 190 lbs. Deb: 7/1/60																									
1960	Mil-N	1	0	1.000	5	1	0	0	1	15^1	14	0	15	8	17.0	4.11	83	.233	.387	0	.000	-1	-1	-1	1	-0.1
1961	Mil-N	6	7	.462	38	11	2	0	3	126^1	117	11	48	66	11.9	4.06	92	.251	.323	7	.184	0	-0	-4	2	-0.2
1962	Mil-N	2	2	.500	39	0	0	0	2	64	64	4	20	36	12.4	3.23	117	.258	.324	2	.333	1	5	4	2	0.5
1963	Hou-N	11	8	.579	31	27	9	2	0	193	170	10	39	118	9.8	3.17	99	.234	.275	11	.167	0	3	-0	-0	0.0
1964	Hou-N	6	11	.353	28	24	2	0	0	157	165	12	37	90	11.6	3.90	88	.275	.319	3	.064	-2	-6	-8	4	-0.7
1965	Hou-N	4	15	.211	29	25	3	0	0	158	166	14	55	77	12.9	4.67	72	.273	.338	5	.104	-1	-20	-23	2	-2.4
1966	Cin-N	5	4	.556	59	1	0	0	11	111^1	97	11	43	69	11.5	3.07	127	.235	.311	4	.167	-0	7	10	1	1.1
1967	Cin-N	0	3	.000	47	0	0	0	4	79^1	75	4	19	48	10.9	1.93	194	.253	.303	0	.000	-0	13	16	1	0.8
1969	NY-A	0	0	—	4	0	0	0	0	6	6	1	0	5	10.5	4.50	77	.261	.292	0	—	0	-1	-1	0	0.0
	Chi-N	1	1	.500	16	0	0	0	0	18	28	2	7	8	17.5	7.00	58	.350	.402	0	.000	0	-7	-6	0	-0.6
Total	9	36	51	.414	296	89	16	2	21	928^1	902	69	283	525	11.7	3.65	96	.256	.315	32	.134	-3	-8	-13	11	-1.6
● CHET NOURSE	Nourse, Chester Linwood b: 8/7/1887, Ipswich, Mass. d: 4/20/58, Clearwater, Fla. BR/TR, 6′3″, 185 lbs. Deb: 7/27/09																									
1909	Bos-A	0	0	—	3	0	0	0	0	5	5	0	5	3	18.0	7.20	35	.263	.417	0	.000	-0	-3	-3	0	0.0
● RAFAEL NOVOA	Novoa, Rafael Angel b: 10/26/67, New York, N.Y. BL/TL, 6′, 180 lbs. Deb: 7/31/90																									
1990	SF-N	0	1	.000	7	2	0	0	1	18^2	21	3	13	14	16.4	6.75	54	.284	.391	1	.200	0	-6	-6	-1	-0.4
1993	Mil-A	0	3	.000	15	7	2	0	0	56	58	7	22	17	13.5	4.50	94	.267	.346	0	—	0	-1	-2	-1	-0.1
Total	2	0	4	.000	22	9	2	0	1	74^2	79	10	35	31	14.2	5.06	81	.271	.358	1	.200	0	-7	-8	-1	-0.5
● WIN NOYES	Noyes, Winfield Charles b: 6/16/1889, Pleasanton, Neb. d: 4/8/69, Cashmere, Wash. BR/TR, 6′, 180 lbs. Deb: 5/19/13																									
1913	Bos-N	0	0	—	11	0	0	0	0	20^2	22	1	6	5	13.9	4.79	69	.289	.372	1	.250	0	-4	-3	0	0.0
1917	Phi-A	10	10	.500	27	22	11	1	1	171	156	5	77	64	12.5	2.95	93	.258	.345	6	.115	-2	-5	-4	-1	-0.8
1919	Phi-A	1	5	.167	10	6	3	0	0	49	66	1	15	20	15.1	5.69	60	.332	.381	2	.125	-1	-13	-12	0	-1.4
	Chi-A	0	0	—	1	1	0	0	0	6	10	0	0	4	15.0	7.50	42	.385	.385	1	.500	0	-3	-3	-0	0.0
	Yr	1	5	.167	11	7	3	0	0	55	76	1	15	24	14.9	5.89	58	.336	.378	3	.167	-1	-16	-15	0	-1.4
Total	3	11	15	.423	49	29	14	1	1	246^2	254	7	98	93	13.2	3.76	78	.280	.356	10	.135	-3	-25	-22	-1	-2.2
● EDWIN NUNEZ	Nunez, Edwin (Martinez) b: 5/27/63, Humacao, P.R. BR/TR, 6′5″, 237 lbs. Deb: 4/7/82																									
1982	Sea-A	1	2	.333	8	5	0	0	0	35^1	36	7	16	27	13.2	4.58	92	.269	.347	0	—	0	-2	-1	0	-0.1
1983	Sea-A	0	4	.000	14	5	0	0	0	37	40	3	22	35	15.8	4.38	97	.278	.385	0	—	0	-1	-0	0	-0.1
1984	Sea-A	2	2	.500	37	0	0	0	7	67^2	55	8	21	57	10.5	3.19	125	.218	.286	0	—	0	6	6	-1	0.4
1985	Sea-A	7	3	.700	70	0	0	0	16	90^1	79	13	34	58	11.3	3.09	136	.234	.305	0	—	0	11	11	0	1.5
1986	Sea-A	1	2	.333	14	1	0	0	0	21^2	25	5	5	17	12.5	5.82	73	.284	.323	0	—	0	-4	-4	-0	-0.5
1987	Sea-A	3	4	.429	48	0	0	0	12	47^1	45	7	18	34	12.2	3.80	124	.262	.335	0	—	0	3	5	-0	0.5
1988	Sea-A	1	4	.200	14	3	0	0	0	29^1	45	4	14	19	18.7	7.98	52	.366	.439	0	—	0	-13	-12	1	-1.9
	NY-N	1	0	1.000	10	0	0	0	0	14	21	1	3	8	15.4	4.50	72	.339	.369	0	—	0	-2	-2	-0	-0.2
1989	Det-A	3	4	.429	27	0	0	0	1	54	49	6	36	41	14.2	4.17	92	.254	.371	0	—	0	-2	-2	1	-0.1
1990	Det-A	3	1	.750	42	0	0	0	6	80^1	65	4	37	66	11.7	2.24	177	.218	.309	0	—	0	15	15	-1	0.8
1991	Mil-A	2	1	.667	23	0	0	0	8	25^1	28	6	13	24	14.6	6.04	66	.277	.360	0	—	0	-5	-6	-0	-0.8
1992	Mil-A	1	1	.500	10	0	0	0	0	13^2	12	1	6	10	11.9	2.63	146	.231	.310	0	—	0	2	2	-0	0.3
	Tex-A	0	2	.000	39	0	0	0	3	45^2	51	5	16	39	13.6	5.52	69	.279	.343	0	—	0	-8	-9	-1	-0.3
	Yr	1	3	.250	49	0	0	0	3	59^1	63	6	22	49	13.2	4.85	78	.268	.336	0	—	0	-6	-7	-1	0.0
1993	Oak-A	3	6	.333	56	0	0	0	1	75^2	89	2	29	58	14.7	3.81	107	.298	.371	0	—	0	4	2	-0	0.4
1994	Oak-A	0	0	—	15	0	0	0	0	15	26	2	10	15	21.6	12.00	37	.382	.462	0	—	0	-12	-13	0	0.1
Total	13	28	36	.438	427	14	0	0	54	652^1	666	74	280	508	13.3	4.19	97	.266	.344	0	—	0	-8	-8	-1	0.0
● JOSE NUNEZ	Nunez, Jose (Jimenez) b: 1/13/64, Jarabacoa, D.R. BR/TR, 6′3″, 175 lbs. Deb: 4/9/87																									
1987	Tor-A	5	2	.714	37	9	0	0	0	97	91	12	58	99	13.8	5.01	90	.256	.360	0	—	0	-6	-6	-1	-0.4
1988	Tor-A	0	1	.000	13	2	0	0	0	29^1	28	3	17	18	14.1	3.07	128	.259	.365	0	—	0	3	3	0	0.1
1989	Tor-A	0	0	—	6	1	0	0	0	10^2	8	0	2	14	8.4	2.53	149	.200	.238	0	—	0	2	1	-0	0.0
1990	Chi-N	4	7	.364	21	10	0	0	0	60^2	61	5	34	40	14.1	6.53	62	.270	.365	0	.000	-1	-18	-17	0	-2.6
Total	4	9	10	.474	77	22	0	0	0	197^2	188	20	111	171	13.7	5.05	84	.258	.356	0	.000	-1	-20	-18	-1	-2.9
● VLADIMIR NUNEZ	Nunez, Vladimir b: 3/15/75, Havana, Cuba BR/TR, 6′4″, 235 lbs. Deb: 9/11/98																									
1998	Ari-N	0	0	—	4	0	0	0	0	5^1	7	0	2	2	15.2	10.13	43	.318	.375	0	—	0	-3	-3	-0	0.0
● HOWIE NUNN	Nunn, Howard Ralph b: 10/18/35, Westfield, N.C. BR/TR, 6′, 173 lbs. Deb: 4/11/59																									
1959	StL-N	2	2	.500	16	0	0	0	0	21^1	23	3	15	20	16.0	7.59	56	.291	.404	0	.000	-0	-9	-8	1	-1.2
1961	Cin-N	2	1	.667	24	0	0	0	0	37^2	35	0	24	26	14.3	3.58	113	.252	.366	2	.250	0	2	2	-0	0.1
1962	Cin-N	0	0	—	6	0	0	0	0	9^2	15	0	3	4	16.8	5.59	72	.375	.419	0	.000	-0	-2	-2	0	0.0
Total	3	4	3	.571	46	0	0	0	0	68^2	73	3	42	50	15.2	5.11	80	.283	.385	2	.200	-0	-9	-8	1	-1.1
● JOE NUXHALL	Nuxhall, Joseph Henry b: 7/30/28, Hamilton, Ohio BL/TL, 6′3″, 219 lbs. Deb: 6/10/44																									
1944	Cin-N	0	0	—	1	0	0	0	0	0^2	2	0	5	0	94.5	67.50	5	.500	.778	0	—	0	-5	-5	-0	0.0
1952	Cin-N	1	4	.200	37	5	2	0	1	92^1	83	4	42	52	12.5	3.22	117	.246	.334	2	.087	-1	5	6	2	0.3
1953	Cin-N	9	11	.450	30	17	5	1	2	141^2	136	13	69	52	13.5	4.32	101	.252	.345	16	.327	7	-1	1	-2	0.6
1954	Cin-N	12	5	.706	35	14	5	1	0	166^2	188	11	59	85	13.7	3.89	108	.292	.357	9	.173	4	3	6	0	0.9
1955	Cin-N★	17	12	.586	50	33	14	**5**	3	257	240	25	78	98	11.3	3.47	122	.249	.309	17	.198	4	16	22	-2	2.5
1956	Cin-N☆	13	11	.542	44	32	10	2	3	200^2	196	18	87	120	13.0	3.72	107	.257	.338	11	.186	3	1	6	-1	0.9
1957	Cin-N	10	10	.500	39	28	6	2	1	174^1	192	24	53	99	13.0	4.75	87	.275	.332	14	.237	3	-17	-12	-2	-1.2
1958	Cin-N	12	11	.522	36	26	5	0	0	175^2	169	15	63	111	11.9	3.79	109	.257	.323	13	.210	0	3	7	-0	0.7
1959	Cin-N	9	9	.500	28	21	6	1	1	131^2	155	10	35	75	13.1	4.24	96	.292	.337	11	.250	3	-4	-3	-1	-0.1
1960	Cin-N	1	8	.111	38	6	0	0	0	112	130	8	27	72	12.9	4.42	86	.297	.344	2	.077	-1	-8	-7	2	-0.5
1961	KC-A	5	8	.385	37	13	1	0	1	128	135	12	65	81	14.3	5.34	78	.268	.355	19	.292	7	-19	-17	-1	-0.9
1962	LA-A	0	0	—	5	0	0	0	0	5^1	7	0	5	2	21.9	10.13	38	.304	.448	0	—	0	-4	-4	0	0.0
	Cin-N	5	0	1.000	12	9	1	0	1	66	59	4	25	57	11.6	2.45	164	.240	.313	7	.269	3	11	12	-0	1.1
1963	Cin-N	15	8	.652	35	29	14	2	2	217^1	194	14	39	169	9.9	2.61	128	.237	.277	12	.158	0	16	18	-1	1.8
1964	Cin-N	9	8	.529	32	22	7	4	2	154^2	146	19	51	111	11.8	4.07	89	.250	.317	7	.130	-1	-9	-8	-2	-1.1
1965	Cin-N	11	4	.733	32	16	5	1	2	148^2	142	18	31	117	10.7	3.45	109	.252	.295	8	.178	1	1	5	-3	0.3
1966	Cin-N	6	8	.429	35	16	2	1	0	130	136	14	42	71	12.9	4.50	87	.270	.338	4	.100	-2	-13	-9	-1	-1.2
Total	16	135	117	.536	526	287	83	20	19	2302^2	2310	209	776	1372	12.3	3.90	102	.262	.327	152	.198	28	-21	17	-12	4.1
● RICH NYE	Nye, Richard Raymond b: 8/4/44, Oakland, Cal. BL/TL, 6′4″, 185 lbs. Deb: 9/16/66																									
1966	Chi-N	0	2	.000	3	2	0	0	0	17	16	1	7	9	12.2	2.12	174	.254	.329	1	.250	0	3	3	-1	0.3
1967	Chi-N	13	10	.565	35	30	7	0	0	205	179	15	52	119	10.2	3.20	111	.234	.284	16	.213	3	4	8	-0	1.2
1968	Chi-N	7	12	.368	27	20	6	1	1	132^2	145	16	34	74	12.2	3.80	83	.276	.321	8	.182	-0	-12	-9	-0	-1.4
1969	Chi-N	3	5	.375	34	5	1	0	3	68^2	72	13	21	39	12.3	5.11	79	.271	.326	1	.063	-1	-12	-8	-1	-1.2
1970	StL-N	0	0	—	6	0	0	0	0	8	13	2	6	5	21.4	4.50	91	.371	.463	1	.500	1	-0	-0	0	0.1
	Mon-N	3	2	.600	8	6	2	0	0	46^1	47	3	20	21	13.0	4.08	101	.260	.333	3	.176	0	-0	0	0	0.0
	Yr	3	2	.600	14	6	2	0	0	54^1	60	5	26	26	14.2	4.14	99	.276	.354	4	.211	1	-1	-0	0	0.1
Total	5	26	31	.456	113	63	16	1	4	477^2	472	50	140	267	11.6	3.71	96	.257	.311	30	.190	2	-17	-7	-2	-1.0

YEAR TM/L	W	L	PCT	G	GS	CG	SH	SV	IP	H	HR	BB	SO	RAT	ERA	ERA+	OAV	OOB	BH	AVG	PB	PR	/A	PD	TPI
● RYAN NYE Nye, Ryan Craig b: 6/24/73, Biloxi, Miss. BR/TR, 6'2", 195 lbs. Deb: 6/7/97																									
1997 Phi-N	0	2	.000	4	2	0	0	0	12	20	2	9	7	23.3	8.25	51	.392	.500	0	.000	-0	-5	-5	0	-0.7
1998 Phi-N	0	0	—	1	0	0	0	0	1	3	1	0	3	27.0	27.00	16	.500	.500	0	—	0	-3	-3	0	0.0
Total 2	0	2	.000	5	2	0	0	0	13	23	3	9	10	23.5	9.69	44	.404	.500	0	.000	-0	-8	-8	0	-0.7
● JERRY NYMAN Nyman, Gerald Smith b: 11/23/42, Logan, Utah BL/TL, 5'10", 165 lbs. Deb: 8/24/68																									
1968 Chi-A	2	1	.667	8	7	1	1	0	40^1	38	1	16	27	12.0	2.01	151	.247	.318	2	.154	-0	4	5	-0	0.3
1969 Chi-A	4	4	.500	20	10	2	1	0	64^2	58	7	39	40	13.5	5.29	73	.244	.350	1	.050	-1	-12	-10	-1	-1.3
1970 SD-N	0	2	.000	2	2	0	0	0	5^1	8	1	2	2	16.9	15.19	26	.364	.417	0	—	0	-7	-7	-0	-1.5
Total 3	6	7	.462	30	19	3	2	0	110^1	104	9	57	69	13.1	4.57	78	.251	.342	3	.091	-1	-14	-12	-1	-2.5
● PRINCE OANA Oana, Henry Kauhane b: 1/22/08, Waipahu, Hawaii d: 6/19/76, Austin, Tex. BR/TR, 6'2", 193 lbs. Deb: 4/22/34 ♦																									
1943 Det-A	3	2	.600	10	0	0	0	0	34	34	4	19	15	14.6	4.50	78	.262	.364	10	.385	4	-5	-4	-0	-0.1
1945 Det-A	0	0	—	3	1	0	0	1	11^1	3	0	7	3	7.9	1.59	221	.086	.238	1	.200	-0	2	2	-0	0.0
Total 2	3	2	.600	13	1	0	0	1	45^1	37	4	26	18	12.9	3.77	93	.224	.337	16	.308	4	-2	-1	-1	-0.1
● HENRY OBERBECK Oberbeck, Henry A. b: 5/17/1858, Missouri d: 8/26/21, St.Louis, Mo. Deb: 5/7/1883 ♦																									
1884 Bal-U	0	0	—	2	1	0	0	0	6	9	0	2	1	16.5	3.00	89	.321	.367	23	.184	-1	-0	-0	-0	-0.1
KC-U	0	5	.000	6	4	3	0	0	29^2	47	0	3	6	15.2	5.76	39	.338	.352	17	.189	-1	-11	-12	-1	-1.5
Yr	0	5	.000	8	5	3	0	0	35^2	56	0	5	7	15.4	5.30	44	.335	.355	40	.186	-2	-11	-12	-1	-1.6
● DOC OBERLANDER Oberlander, Hartman Louis b: 5/12/1864, Waukegan, Ill. d: 11/14/22, Pryor, Montana TL, Deb: 5/16/1888																									
1888 Cle-a	1	2	.333	3	3	3	0	0	25^2	27	2	18	23	16.1	5.26	59	.260	.374	3	.214	0	-6	-6	-0	-0.5
● FRANK OBERLIN Oberlin, Frank Rufus "Flossie" b: 3/29/1876, Elsie, Mich. d: 1/6/52, Ashley, Ind. BR/TR, 6'1", 165 lbs. Deb: 9/20/06																									
1906 Bos-A	1	3	.250	4	4	4	0	0	34	38	0	13	13	14.0	3.18	87	.286	.358	2	.154	-0	-2	-2	1	-0.1
1907 Bos-A	1	5	.167	12	4	2	0	0	46	48	2	24	18	14.5	4.30	60	.271	.365	2	.154	-0	-9	-9	-1	-1.1
Was-A	2	6	.250	11	8	3	0	0	48^2	57	0	12	18	13.1	4.62	52	.294	.341	1	.056	-2	-11	-12	-1	-2.0
Yr	3	11	.214	23	12	5	0	0	94^2	105	2	36	36	13.6	4.47	56	.282	.348	3	.097	-2	-20	-21	-2	-3.1
1909 Was-A	1	4	.200	9	4	1	0	0	41	41	1	16	13	13.8	3.73	65	.266	.358	2	.143	-1	-6	-6	-1	-0.9
1910 Was-A	0	6	.000	8	6	6	0	0	57^1	52	0	23	18	12.1	2.98	84	.259	.341	1	.053	-2	-3	-3	-1	-0.6
Total 4	5	24	.172	44	26	16	0	0	227	236	3	88	80	13.4	3.77	67	.275	.352	8	.104	-4	-31	-31	-3	-4.7
● DAN O'BRIEN O'Brien, Daniel Jogues b: 4/22/54, St.Petersburg, Fla. BR/TR, 6'4", 215 lbs. Deb: 9/4/78																									
1978 StL-N	0	2	.000	7	2	0	0	0	18	22	1	8	12	16.0	4.50	78	.301	.386	0	.000	-0	-2	-2	-0	-0.3
1979 StL-N	1	1	.500	6	0	0	0	0	11	21	0	3	5	19.6	8.18	46	.420	.453	0	.000	-0	-5	-5	-0	-0.9
Total 2	1	3	.250	13	2	0	0	0	29	43	1	11	17	17.4	5.90	61	.350	.412	0	.000	-1	-7	-7	-1	-1.2
● EDDIE O'BRIEN O'Brien, Edward Joseph b: 12/11/30, S.Amboy, N.J. BR/TR, 5'9", 165 lbs. Deb: 4/25/53 FC♦																									
1956 Pit-N	0	0	—	1	0	0	0	0	2	1	0	0	0	9.0	0.00	—	.167	.286	14	.264	0	1	1	-0	0.0
1957 Pit-N	1	0	1.000	3	1	1	0	0	12^1	11	2	3	10	10.2	2.19	173	.229	.275	0	.000	-1	2	2	0	0.1
1958 Pit-N	0	0	—	1	0	0	0	0	2	4	1	1	1	22.5	13.50	29	.444	.500	0	—	0	-2	-2	-0	0.0
Total 3	1	0	1.000	5	1	1	0	0	16^1	16	3	4	11	11.6	3.31	115	.254	.309	131	.236	-0	1	1	-0	0.1
● DARBY O'BRIEN O'Brien, John F. b: 4/15/1867, Troy, N.Y. d: 3/11/1892, W.Troy, N.Y. BR/TR, 5'10", 165 lbs. Deb: 6/23/1888																									
1888 Cle-a	11	19	.367	30	30	30	1	0	259	245	5	99	135	12.4	3.30	94	.241	.315	20	.183	-3	-7	-6	2	-0.7
1889 Cle-N	22	17	.564	41	41	39	1	0	346^2	345	9	167	122	13.9	4.15	97	.251	.343	35	.250	4	-5	-5	2	0.1
1890 Cle-P	8	16	.333	25	25	22	0	0	206^1	229	9	93	54	14.9	3.40	117	.269	.354	15	.156	-6	19	13	-1	0.5
1891 Bos-a	18	13	.581	40	30	22	0	**2**	268^2	300	13	127	87	15.0	3.65	96	.273	.359	30	.234	1	2	-5	-3	-0.7
Total 4	59	65	.476	136	126	113	2	2	1080^2	1119	36	486	398	14.0	3.68	100	.258	.343	100	.211	-4	9	-2	0	-0.8
● JOHNNY O'BRIEN O'Brien, John Thomas b: 12/11/30, S.Amboy, N.J. BR/TR, 5'9", 170 lbs. Deb: 4/19/53 F♦																									
1956 Pit-N	1	0	1.000	8	0	0	0	0	19	8	2	9	9	9.0	2.84	133	.133	.268	18	.173	-0	2	2	-1	0.0
1957 Pit-N	0	3	.000	16	1	0	0	0	40	46	7	24	19	16.0	6.07	62	.293	.390	11	.314	2	-10	-10	-1	-0.5
1958 StL-N	0	0	—	1	0	0	0	0	2	7	0	2	2	40.5	22.50	18	.538	.600	0	.000	0	-4	-4	-0	0.0
Total 3	1	3	.250	25	1	0	0	0	61	61	9	35	30	14.6	5.61	68	.265	.369	204	.250	2	-12	-12	-2	-0.5
● BOB O'BRIEN O'Brien, Robert Allen b: 4/23/49, Pittsburgh, Pa. BL/TL, 5'10", 170 lbs. Deb: 4/11/71																									
1971 LA-N	2	2	.500	14	4	1	1	0	42	42	4	13	15	12.0	3.00	108	.262	.322	1	.111	-0	2	1	-1	0.0
● TOM O'BRIEN O'Brien, Thomas H. b: 6/22/1860, Salem, Mass. d: 4/21/21, Worcester, Mass. BR/TR, 6'1", 185 lbs. Deb: 6/14/1882 ♦																									
1887 NY-a	0	0	—	1	0	0	0	0	3^2	4	0	5	0	22.1	7.36	58	.211	.375	25	.194	-0	-1	-1	-0	0.0
● BUCK O'BRIEN O'Brien, Thomas Joseph b: 5/9/1882, Brockton, Mass. d: 7/25/59, Boston, Mass. BR/TR, 5'10", 188 lbs. Deb: 9/9/11																									
1911 Bos-A	5	1	.833	6	5	5	2	0	47^2	30	0	21	31	9.8	0.38	868	.180	.275	2	.125	-1	16	15	1	2.0
1912 *Bos-A	20	13	.606	37	34	25	2	0	275^2	237	3	90	115	11.0	2.58	132	.237	.306	13	.138	-5	23	25	0	2.4
1913 Bos-A	4	9	.308	15	12	6	0	0	90^1	103	0	35	54	13.7	3.69	80	.305	.370	5	.167	0	-8	-7	1	-0.9
Chi-A	0	2	.000	6	3	0	0	0	18^1	21	0	13	4	16.7	3.93	74	.318	.430	0	.000	-0	-2	-2	-0	-0.3
Yr	4	11	.267	21	15	6	0	0	108^2	124	0	48	58	14.2	3.73	79	.307	.381	5	.152	-0	-10	-10	0	-1.2
Total 3	29	25	.537	64	54	36	4	0	432	391	3	159	204	11.7	2.63	125	.249	.322	20	.140	-6	29	31	1	3.2
● DARBY O'BRIEN O'Brien, William D. b: 9/1/1863, Peoria, Ill. d: 6/15/1893, Peoria, Ill. BR/TR, 6'1", 186 lbs. Deb: 4/16/1887 ♦																									
1887 NY-a	0	0	—	1	0	0	0	0	1	1	0	1	0	18.0	0.00	—	.333	.500	157	.301	0	0	0	-0	0.0
● BILLY O'BRIEN O'Brien, William Smith b: 3/14/1860, Albany, N.Y. d: 5/26/11, Kansas City, Mo. BR, 6', 185 lbs. Deb: 9/27/1884 ♦																									
1884 StP-U	1	0	1.000	2	0	0	0	0	10	8	0	3	7	9.9	1.80	74	.205	.262	7	.233	-0	1	-1	0	0.0
● WALTER OCKEY Ockey, Walter Andrew "Footie" (b: Walter Andrew Okpych) b: 1/4/20, New York, N.Y. d: 12/4/71, Staten Island, N.Y. BR/TR, 6', 175 lbs. Deb: 5/3/44																									
1944 NY-N	0	0	—	2	0	0	0	0	2^2	2	1	2	1	13.5	3.38	109	.200	.333	0	—	0	0	0	0	0.0
● PAT O'CONNELL O'Connell, Patrick H. b: 6/10/1861, Bangor, Me. d: 1/24/43, Lewiston, Maine BR/TR, 5'10", 175 lbs. Deb: 7/22/1886 ♦																									
1886 Bal-a	0	0	—	1	0	0	0	0	3	4	0	2	1	18.0	6.00	57	.333	.429	30	.181	-0	-1	-1	-0	0.0
● ANDY O'CONNOR O'Connor, Andrew James b: 9/14/1884, Roxbury, Mass. d: 9/26/80, Norwood, Mass. BR/TR, 6', 160 lbs. Deb: 10/6/08																									
1908 NY-A	0	1	.000	1	1	1	0	0	8	15	0	7	5	28.1	10.13	24	.429	.556	0	.000	-0	-7	-7	-0	-0.6
● FRANK O'CONNOR O'Connor, Frank Henry b: 9/15/1870, Keeseville, N.Y. d: 12/26/13, Brattleboro, Vt. BL/TL, 6', 185 lbs. Deb: 8/3/1893																									
1893 Phi-N	0	0	—	3	1	0	0	1	4	2	0	9	0	24.8	11.25	41	.143	.478	2	1.000	2	-3	-3	0	0.0
● JACK O'CONNOR O'Connor, Jack William b: 6/2/58, Twentynine Palms, Cal. BL/TL, 6'3", 215 lbs. Deb: 4/9/81																									
1981 Min-A	3	2	.600	28	0	0	0	0	35^1	46	3	30	16	19.9	5.86	67	.336	.462	0	—	0	-9	-8	1	-0.9
1982 Min-A	8	9	.471	23	19	6	1	0	126	122	13	57	56	12.9	4.29	99	.255	.337	0	—	0	-3	-1	-3	-0.4
1983 Min-A	2	3	.400	27	8	0	0	0	83	107	13	36	56	15.5	5.86	73	.315	.380	0	—	0	-17	-15	-1	-1.1
1984 Min-A	0	0	—	2	0	0	0	0	4^2	1	1	4	0	9.6	1.93	218	.067	.263	0	—	0	1	1	-0	-0.3
1985 Mon-N	0	2	.000	20	1	0	0	0	23^2	21	1	13	16	12.9	4.94	69	.239	.337	0	—	0	-4	-4	-1	-0.4
1987 Bal-A	1	1	.500	29	0	0	0	2	46	46	5	23	33	13.5	4.30	102	.263	.348	0	—	0	1	0	-1	0.2
Total 6	14	17	.452	129	28	6	1	2	318^2	343	36	163	177	14.4	4.89	85	.278	.364	0	—	0	-30	-25	-5	-2.9
● HANK O'DAY O'Day, Henry Francis b: 7/8/1862, Chicago, Ill. d: 7/2/35, Chicago, Ill. TR, 6', 180 lbs. Deb: 5/2/1884 MU																									
1884 Tol-a	9	28	.243	41	40	35	2	**1**	326^2	335	6	66	163	11.5	3.75	91	.252	.297	51	.211	-1	-18	-12	4	-0.9
1885 Pit-a	5	7	.417	12	12	10	0	0	103	110	4	16	36	11.6	3.67	88	.258	.296	12	.245	1	-5	-5	0	-0.3
1886 Was-N	2	2	.500	6	6	6	0	0	49	41	1	17	47	10.7	1.65	199	.219	.284	1	.053	-2	9	9	1	0.5
1887 Was-N	8	20	.286	30	30	29	0	0	254^2	255	15	109	86	13.2	4.17	97	.254	.332	23	.198	-3	-3	-3	1	-0.5

YEAR	TM/L	W	L	PCT	G	GS	CG	SH	SV	IP	H	HR	BB	SO	RAT	ERA	ERA+	OAV	OOB	BH	AVG	PB	PR	/A	PD	TPI
1888	Was-N	16	29	.356	46	46	46	2	0	403	359	19	117	186	11.0	3.10	90	.232	.293	23	.139	-7	-11	-13	-3	-2.2
1889	Was-N	2	10	.167	13	13	11	0	0	108	117	7	57	23	15.0	4.33	91	.268	.360	8	.182	-1	-4	-5	0	-0.4
	*NY-N	9	1	.900	10	10	8	0	0	78	83	2	35	28	14.4	4.27	92	.264	.351	3	.097	-1	-2	-3	-1	-0.4
	Yr	11	11	.500	23	23	19	0	0	186	200	9	92	51	14.5	4.31	92	.264	.349	11	.147	-2	-6	-8	-0	-0.8
1890	NY-P	22	13	.629	43	35	32	1	**3**	329	355	11	161	94	14.6	4.21	108	.264	.350	34	.227	-3	1	12	-4	0.4
Total	7	73	110	.399	201	192	177	5	4	1651^{1}	1655	65	578	663	12.6	3.74	97	.251	.319	155	.190	-17	-33	-22	-0	-3.8

● PAUL O'DEA O'Dea, Paul "Lefty" b: 7/3/20, Cleveland, Ohio d: 12/11/78, Cleveland, Ohio BL/TL, 6', 200 lbs. Deb: 4/19/44 ♦

YEAR	TM/L	W	L	PCT	G	GS	CG	SH	SV	IP	H	HR	BB	SO	RAT	ERA	ERA+	OAV	OOB	BH	AVG	PB	PR	/A	PD	TPI
1944	Cle-A	0	0	—	3	0	0	0	0	4^{1}	5	0	6	0	22.8	2.08	159	.333	.524	55	.318	1	1	1	-0	0.0
1945	Cle-A	0	0	—	1	0	0	0	0	2	4	0	2	0	27.0	13.50	24	.400	.500	52	.235	0	-2	-2	0	0.0
Total	2	0	0	—	4	0	0	0	0	6^{1}	9	0	8	0	24.2	5.68	58	.360	.515	107	.272	1	-2	-2	-0	0.0

● BILLY O'DELL O'Dell, William Oliver b: 2/10/32, Whitmire, S.C. BB/TL, 5'11", 170 lbs. Deb: 6/20/54

YEAR	TM/L	W	L	PCT	G	GS	CG	SH	SV	IP	H	HR	BB	SO	RAT	ERA	ERA+	OAV	OOB	BH	AVG	PB	PR	/A	PD	TPI
1954	Bal-A	1	1	.500	7	2	1	0	0	16^{1}	15	0	5	6	11.0	2.76	130	.242	.299	0	.000	-0	2	1	0	0.2
1956	Bal-A	0	0	—	4	1	0	0	0	8	6	0	6	6	13.5	1.13	349	.222	.364	0	.000	-0	3	2	-0	0.0
1957	Bal-A	4	10	.286	35	15	2	1	4	140^{1}	107	12	39	97	9.7	2.69	133	.212	.276	5	.147	-1	17	14	-2	1.1
1958	Bal-A★	14	11	.560	41	25	12	3	8	221^{1}	201	13	51	137	10.4	2.97	121	.241	.288	8	.111	-1	20	15	-0	1.7
1959	Bal-A★	10	12	.455	38	24	6	2	1	199^{1}	163	18	67	88	10.4	2.93	129	.220	.286	5	.083	-3	21	19	1	1.8
1960	SF-N	8	13	.381	43	24	6	1	2	202^{2}	198	16	72	145	12.1	3.20	109	.252	.317	6	.107	1	13	6	-1	0.5
1961	SF-N	7	5	.583	46	14	4	1	2	130^{1}	132	10	33	110	11.5	3.59	106	.260	.306	4	.103	-2	6	3	-1	0.0
1962	*SF-N	19	14	.576	43	39	20	2	0	280^{2}	282	18	66	195	11.4	3.53	108	.258	.304	12	.133	-1	13	8	-2	0.5
1963	SF-N	14	10	.583	36	33	10	3	1	222^{1}	218	14	70	116	11.9	3.16	101	.253	.314	16	.205	4	3	1	-4	0.0
1964	SF-N	8	7	.533	36	8	1	0	2	85	82	10	35	54	12.8	5.40	66	.252	.332	0	.000	-2	-18	-17	-1	-3.2
1965	Mil-N	10	6	.625	62	1	0	0	18	111^{1}	87	10	30	78	9.6	2.18	161	.215	.272	4	.174	1	17	17	-0	3.0
1966	Atl-N	2	3	.400	24	0	0	0	6	41^{1}	44	3	18	20	13.9	2.40	152	.272	.352	2	.250	0	6	6	-0	0.8
	Pit-N	3	2	.600	37	2	0	0	4	71^{1}	74	3	23	47	12.7	2.78	129	.275	.341	1	.063	-1	7	6	-1	0.3
	Yr	5	5	.500	61	2	0	0	10	112^{2}	118	6	41	67	13.0	2.64	136	.273	.341	3	.125	-1	12	12	-1	1.1
1967	Pit-N	5	6	.455	27	11	1	0	0	86^{2}	88	10	41	34	13.7	5.82	58	.265	.351	3	.115	-0	-24	-24	-1	-2.9
Total	13	105	100	.512	479	199	63	13	48	1817	1697	137	556	1133	11.4	3.29	109	.246	.306	66	.125	-7	85	59	-12	3.8

● TED ODENWALD Odenwald, Theodore Joseph "Lefty" b: 1/4/02, Hudson, Wis. d: 10/23/65, Shakopee, Minn. BR/TL, 5'10", 147 lbs. Deb: 4/13/21

YEAR	TM/L	W	L	PCT	G	GS	CG	SH	SV	IP	H	HR	BB	SO	RAT	ERA	ERA+	OAV	OOB	BH	AVG	PB	PR	/A	PD	TPI
1921	Cle-A	1	0	1.000	10	0	0	0	0	17^{1}	16	0	6	4	11.9	1.56	274	.262	.338	0	.000	-1	5	5	0	0.2
1922	Cle-A	0	0	—	1	0	0	0	0	1^{1}	6	0	2	2	54.0	40.50	10	.600	.667	0	—	0	-5	-5	0	0.0
Total	2	1	0	1.000	11	0	0	0	0	18^{2}	22	0	8	6	14.9	4.34	98	.310	.387	0	.000	-1	-0	-0	0	0.2

● DAVE ODOM Odom, David Everett "Blimp" or "Porky" b: 6/5/18, Dinuba, Cal. d: 11/19/87, Myrtle Beach, S.C. BR/TR, 6'1", 220 lbs. Deb: 5/31/43

YEAR	TM/L	W	L	PCT	G	GS	CG	SH	SV	IP	H	HR	BB	SO	RAT	ERA	ERA+	OAV	OOB	BH	AVG	PB	PR	/A	PD	TPI
1943	Bos-N	0	3	.000	22	3	1	0	2	54^{2}	54	3	30	17	14.5	5.27	65	.269	.374	0	.000	-2	-11	-11	-1	-1.0

● BLUE MOON ODOM Odom, Johnny Lee b: 5/29/45, Macon, Ga. BR/TR, 6', 185 lbs. Deb: 9/5/64 ♦

YEAR	TM/L	W	L	PCT	G	GS	CG	SH	SV	IP	H	HR	BB	SO	RAT	ERA	ERA+	OAV	OOB	BH	AVG	PB	PR	/A	PD	TPI
1964	KC-A	1	2	.333	5	5	1	1	0	17	29	5	11	10	21.2	10.06	38	.363	.440	0	.000	-0	-12	-12	0	-1.7
1965	KC-A	0	0	—	1	0	0	0	0	1	2	0	2	0	36.0	9.00	39	.400	.571	0	—	0	-1	-1	0	0.0
1966	KC-A	5	5	.500	14	14	4	2	0	90^{1}	70	1	53	47	12.5	2.49	136	.215	.328	3	.097	-1	9	9	2	1.1
1967	KC-A	3	8	.273	29	17	0	0	0	103^{2}	94	9	68	67	14.3	5.04	63	.243	.360	8	.286	2	-21	-21	0	-1.9
1968	Oak-A★	16	10	.615	32	31	9	4	0	231^{1}	179	9	98	143	11.0	2.45	115	.216	.304	17	.218	6	14	9	1	2.0
1969	Oak-A★	15	6	.714	32	32	10	3	0	231^{1}	179	15	112	150	11.6	2.92	118	.215	.312	21	.266	11	18	13	1	2.5
1970	Oak-A	9	8	.529	29	29	4	1	0	156^{1}	128	14	100	88	13.6	3.80	93	.227	.351	13	.241	6	-1	-5	2	0.5
1971	Oak-A	10	12	.455	25	25	3	1	0	140^{2}	147	13	71	69	13.9	4.29	78	.271	.355	8	.160	1	-13	-15	-1	-2.1
1972	*Oak-A	15	6	.714	31	30	4	2	0	194^{1}	164	10	87	86	11.8	2.50	114	.234	.321	8	.121	0	12	7	0	0.8
1973	*Oak-A	5	12	.294	30	24	3	0	0	150^{1}	153	14	67	83	13.3	4.49	79	.263	.341	0	.000	-0	-11	-16	-1	-1.8
1974	*Oak-A	1	5	.167	34	5	1	0	1	87^{1}	85	4	52	52	14.4	3.81	87	.267	.375	0	—	0	-2	-5	1	-0.3
1975	Oak-A	0	2	.000	7	2	0	0	0	11	19	1	11	4	25.4	12.27	30	.422	.544	0	—	0	-10	-11	0	-1.6
	Cle-A	1	0	1.000	3	1	1	1	0	10^{1}	4	1	8	10	10.5	2.61	145	.118	.286	0	—	0	1	1	-0	0.1
	Yr	1	2	.333	10	3	1	1	0	21^{1}	23	2	19	14	17.7	7.59	49	.284	.420	0	—	0	-9	-9	-0	-1.5
	Atl-N	1	7	.125	15	10	0	0	0	56	78	5	28	30	17.0	7.07	53	.342	.414	1	.077	-1	-21	-21	0	-2.5
1976	Chi-A	2	2	.500	8	4	0	0	0	28	31	2	20	18	16.7	5.79	62	.282	.397	0	—	0	-7	-7	-1	-0.9
Total	13	84	85	.497	295	229	40	15	1	1509	1362	103	788	857	13.0	3.70	89	.244	.341	79	.195	26	-45	-71	5	-5.8

● GEORGE O'DONNELL O'Donnell, George Dana b: 5/27/29, Winchester, Ill. BR/TR, 6'3", 175 lbs. Deb: 4/18/54

YEAR	TM/L	W	L	PCT	G	GS	CG	SH	SV	IP	H	HR	BB	SO	RAT	ERA	ERA+	OAV	OOB	BH	AVG	PB	PR	/A	PD	TPI
1954	Pit-N	3	9	.250	21	10	3	0	1	87^{1}	105	4	21	8	13.2	4.53	92	.315	.360	2	.087	-1	-4	-3	1	-0.4

● JOHN O'DONOGHUE O'Donoghue, John Eugene b: 10/7/39, Kansas City, Mo. BR/TL, 6'3", 210 lbs. Deb: 9/29/63 F

YEAR	TM/L	W	L	PCT	G	GS	CG	SH	SV	IP	H	HR	BB	SO	RAT	ERA	ERA+	OAV	OOB	BH	AVG	PB	PR	/A	PD	TPI
1963	KC-A	0	1	.000	1	1	0	0	0	6	6	0	2	1	12.0	1.50	260	.286	.348	0	.000	-0	1	2	-0	0.2
1964	KC-A	10	14	.417	39	32	2	1	0	173^{2}	202	24	65	79	14.0	4.92	78	.286	.349	13	.236	2	-25	-21	-1	-2.6
1965	KC-A☆	9	18	.333	34	30	4	1	0	177^{2}	183	15	66	82	12.7	3.95	88	.267	.332	12	.218	3	-10	-9	0	-1.0
1966	Cle-A	6	8	.429	32	13	2	0	0	108	109	13	23	49	11.2	3.83	90	.264	.306	5	.152	-0	-5	-5	1	-0.5
1967	Cle-A	8	9	.471	33	17	5	2	2	130^{2}	120	10	33	81	10.7	3.24	101	.247	.298	4	.100	-0	-0	0	3	0.4
1968	Bal-A	0	0	—	16	0	0	0	2	22	34	2	7	11	16.8	6.14	48	.374	.418	0	.000	-0	-8	-8	0	-0.2
1969	Sea-A	2	2	.500	55	0	0	0	6	70	58	5	37	48	12.6	2.96	123	.230	.336	1	.077	-1	5	5	-0	0.3
1970	Mil-A	2	0	1.000	25	0	0	0	0	23^{1}	29	4	9	13	14.7	5.01	76	.299	.358	0	.000	-0	-3	-3	1	-0.2
	Mon-N	2	3	.400	9	3	0	0	0	22^{1}	20	2	11	6	13.3	5.24	78	.263	.371	0	.000	-0	-3	-3	0	-0.6
1971	Mon-N	0	0	—	13	0	0	0	0	17^{1}	19	3	7	7	13.5	4.67	75	.271	.338	0	—	0	-2	-2	-0	0.0
Total	9	39	55	.415	257	96	13	4	10	751	780	78	260	377	12.6	4.07	87	.269	.332	35	.170	2	-49	-44	4	-4.2

● JOHN O'DONOGHUE O'Donoghue, John Preston b: 5/26/69, Wilmington, Del. BL/TL, 6'6", 198 lbs. Deb: 6/27/93 F

YEAR	TM/L	W	L	PCT	G	GS	CG	SH	SV	IP	H	HR	BB	SO	RAT	ERA	ERA+	OAV	OOB	BH	AVG	PB	PR	/A	PD	TPI
1993	Bal-A	0	1	.000	11	1	0	0	0	19^{2}	22	4	10	16	15.1	4.58	98	.278	.367	0	—	0	-1	-0	-0	-0.2

● LEFTY O'DOUL O'Doul, Francis Joseph b: 3/4/1897, San Francisco, Cal. d: 12/7/69, San Francisco, Cal. BL/TL, 6', 180 lbs. Deb: 4/29/19 ♦

YEAR	TM/L	W	L	PCT	G	GS	CG	SH	SV	IP	H	HR	BB	SO	RAT	ERA	ERA+	OAV	OOB	BH	AVG	PB	PR	/A	PD	TPI
1919	NY-A	0	0	—	3	0	0	0	0	5	7	0	4	2	19.8	3.60	89	.304	.407	4	.250	0	-0	-0	-0	0.0
1920	NY-A	0	0	—	2	0	0	0	0	3^{2}	4	0	2	2	17.2	4.91	78	.286	.412	2	.167	-0	-0	-0	-0	0.0
1922	NY-A	0	0	—	6	0	0	0	0	16	24	0	12	5	20.3	3.38	119	.353	.450	3	.333	1	1	1	0	0.1
1923	Bos-A	1	1	.500	23	1	0	0	0	53	69	2	31	10	17.7	5.43	76	.337	.433	5	.143	-1	-9	-8	1	-0.3
Total	4	1	1	.500	34	1	0	0	0	77^{2}	104	2	49	19	18.3	4.87	83	.335	.434	1140	.349	-1	-8	-7	1	-0.2

● BRYAN OELKERS Oelkers, Bryan Alois b: 3/11/61, Zaragoza, Spain BL/TL, 6'3", 192 lbs. Deb: 4/9/83

YEAR	TM/L	W	L	PCT	G	GS	CG	SH	SV	IP	H	HR	BB	SO	RAT	ERA	ERA+	OAV	OOB	BH	AVG	PB	PR	/A	PD	TPI
1983	Min-A	0	5	.000	10	8	0	0	0	34^{1}	56	7	17	13	19.1	8.65	49	.376	.440	0	—	0	-18	-17	-1	-2.2
1986	Cle-A	3	3	.500	35	4	0	0	1	69	70	13	40	33	15.1	4.70	88	.262	.371	0	—	0	-4	-4	-1	-0.3
Total	2	3	8	.273	45	12	0	0	1	103^{1}	126	20	57	46	16.5	6.01	70	.303	.395	0	—	0	-21	-21	-2	-2.5

● JOE OESCHGER Oeschger, Joseph Carl b: 5/24/1892, Chicago, Ill. d: 7/28/86, Rohnert Park, Cal BR/TR, 6' ", 190 lbs. Deb: 4/21/14

YEAR	TM/L	W	L	PCT	G	GS	CG	SH	SV	IP	H	HR	BB	SO	RAT	ERA	ERA+	OAV	OOB	BH	AVG	PB	PR	/A	PD	TPI
1914	Phi-N	4	8	.333	32	12	5	0	1	124	129	5	54	47	14.0	3.77	78	.279	.366	3	.075	-4	-14	-11	-1	-1.6
1915	Phi-N	1	0	1.000	6	1	1	0	0	23^{2}	21	1	9	8	11.4	3.42	80	.247	.319	0	.000	-1	-2	-2	-0	-0.2
1916	Phi-N	1	0	1.000	14	0	0	0	0	30^{1}	18	2	14	17	9.8	2.37	112	.184	.292	0	.000	-1	1	1	1	0.0
1917	Phi-N	15	14	.517	42	30	18	5	1	262	241	7	72	123	11.0	2.75	102	.249	.305	10	.114	-4	-1	2	-3	-0.6
1918	Phi-N	6	18	.250	30	23	13	2	**3**	184	159	3	83	60	12.2	3.03	99	.238	.328	5	.083	-4	-6	-1	-2	-0.7
1919	Phi-N	0	1	.000	5	4	2	0	0	38	52	1	16	5	16.6	5.92	54	.340	.409	0	.000	-2	-13	-11	-0	-0.5
	NY-N	0	1	.000	5	1	0	0	0	8	12	0	2	3	15.8	4.50	62	.400	.438	0	.000	-0	-1	-2	0	-0.2
	Bos-N	4	2	.667	7	7	4	1	0	56^{2}	63	0	21	16	13.5	2.54	112	.300	.366	2	.091	-1	2	2	-1	-0.1
	Yr	4	4	.500	17	12	6	1	0	102^{2}	127	1	39	24	14.6	3.94	76	.322	.384	2	.053	-4	-12	-11	-2	-0.8
1920	Bos-N	15	13	.536	38	30	20	5	0	299	294	10	99	80	12.1	3.46	88	.265	.329	18	.178	-3	-11	-14	-3	-1.8
1921	Bos-N	20	14	.588	46	36	19	**3**	0	299	303	11	97	68	12.5	3.52	104	.274	.341	28	.255	2	9	4	2	0.9
1922	Bos-N	6	21	.222	46	23	10	1	1	195^{2}	234	8	81	51	14.9	5.06	79	.303	.375	12	.190	-0	-21	-23	1	-2.6
1923	Bos-N	5	15	.250	44	19	6	1	2	166^{1}	227	4	54	33	15.5	5.68	70	.330	.383	12	.231	-0	-31	-31	0	-3.2

YEAR	TM/L	W	L	PCT	G	GS	CG	SH	SV	IP	H	HR	BB	SO	RAT	ERA	ERA+	OAV	OOB	BH	AVG	PB	PR	/A	PD	TPI
1924	NY-N	2	0	1.000	10	2	0	0	0	29	35	1	14	10	15.2	3.10	118	.287	.360	3	.429	1	2	2	-1	0.1
	Phi-N	2	7	.222	19	8	0	0	0	65^1	88	6	16	8	14.7	4.41	101	.333	.378	5	.250	-1	-4	0	-0	0.0
	Yr	4	7	.364	29	10	0	0	0	94^1	123	7	30	18	14.9	4.01	105	.319	.372	8	.296	0	-1	2	-1	0.1
1925	Bro-N	1	2	.333	21	3	1	0	0	37	60	2	19	6	19.5	6.08	69	.382	.452	1	.125	-0	-7	-8	-0	-0.6
Total	12	82	116	.414	365	199	99	18	8	1818	1936	61	651	535	13.1	3.81	88	.281	.349	99	.165	-18	-96	-89	-8	-11.1

● JACK OGDEN

Ogden, John Mahlon b: 11/5/1897, Ogden, Pa. d: 11/9/77, Philadelphia, Pa. BR/TR, 6', 190 lbs. Deb: 6/22/18 F

YEAR	TM/L	W	L	PCT	G	GS	CG	SH	SV	IP	H	HR	BB	SO	RAT	ERA	ERA+	OAV	OOB	BH	AVG	PB	PR	/A	PD	TPI
1918	NY-N	0	0	—	5	0	0	0	0	8^2	8	0	3	1	13.5	3.12	84	.296	.406	0	.000	-0	-0	-0	-0	-0.1
1928	StL-A	15	16	.484	38	31	18	1	2	242^2	257	23	80	67	12.5	4.15	101	.274	.331	17	.200	-1	-3	1	-4	-0.3
1929	StL-A	4	8	.333	34	14	7	0	0	131^1	154	8	44	32	13.6	4.93	90	.301	.357	11	.244	0	-10	-7	0	-0.5
1931	Cin-N	4	8	.333	22	9	3	1	1	89	79	3	32	24	11.2	2.93	127	.242	.310	4	.148	-1	9	8	-1	0.8
1932	Cin-N	2	2	.500	24	3	1	0	0	57	72	5	22	20	14.8	5.21	74	.310	.370	2	.167	0	-8	-9	1	-0.5
Total	5	25	34	.424	123	57	29	2	3	528^2	570	39	181	144	12.8	4.24	97	.280	.340	34	.200	-1	-13	-8	-4	-0.6

● CURLY OGDEN

Ogden, Warren Harvey b: 1/24/01, Ogden, Pa. d: 8/6/64, Upland, Pa. BR/TR, 6'1.5", 180 lbs. Deb: 7/18/22 F

YEAR	TM/L	W	L	PCT	G	GS	CG	SH	SV	IP	H	HR	BB	SO	RAT	ERA	ERA+	OAV	OOB	BH	AVG	PB	PR	/A	PD	TPI
1922	Phi-A	1	4	.200	15	6	4	0	0	72^1	59	4	33	20	12.1	3.11	137	.237	.338	7	.241	-0	8	9	-0	0.5
1923	Phi-A	1	2	.333	18	2	0	0	0	46^1	63	2	32	14	19.0	5.63	73	.330	.434	5	.294	1	-8	-8	0	-0.4
1924	Phi-A	0	3	.000	5	1	0	0	0	12^2	14	1	7	4	15.6	4.97	86	.275	.373	0	.000	-1	-1	-1	-0	-0.3
	*Was-A	9	5	.643	16	16	9	3	0	108	83	3	51	23	11.3	2.58	156	.221	.317	13	.277	2	20	17	-0	2.2
	Yr	9	8	.529	21	17	9	3	0	120^2	97	4	58	27	11.7	2.83	143	.227	.322	13	.260	1	19	16	-1	1.9
1925	Was-A	3	1	.750	17	4	2	1	0	42	45	1	18	6	13.9	4.50	94	.288	.369	3	.250	-0	-0	-1	-0	-0.1
1926	Was-A	4	4	.500	22	9	4	0	0	96^1	114	2	45	21	15.3	4.30	90	.305	.387	5	.185	-1	-3	-5	-1	-0.5
Total	5	18	19	.486	93	38	19	4	0	377^2	378	13	186	88	13.9	3.79	108	.271	.364	33	.244	1	14	12	-2	1.4

● CHAD OGEA

Ogea, Chad Wayne b: 11/9/70, Lake Charles, La. BR/TR, 6'2", 200 lbs. Deb: 5/3/94

YEAR	TM/L	W	L	PCT	G	GS	CG	SH	SV	IP	H	HR	BB	SO	RAT	ERA	ERA+	OAV	OOB	BH	AVG	PB	PR	/A	PD	TPI
1994	Cle-A	0	1	.000	4	1	0	0	0	16^1	21	2	10	11	17.6	6.06	78	.304	.400	0	—	0	-2	-2	-0	-0.1
1995	*Cle-A	8	3	.727	20	14	1	0	0	106^1	95	11	29	57	10.6	3.05	154	.233	.286	0	—	0	20	19	-1	1.7
1996	*Cle-A	10	6	.625	29	21	1	1	0	146^2	151	22	42	101	12.1	4.79	102	.266	.322	0	—	0	3	2	-1	0.1
1997	*Cle-A	8	9	.471	21	21	1	0	0	126^1	139	13	47	80	13.6	4.99	94	.283	.351	0	.000	-0	-6	-4	-0	-0.5
1998	*Cle-A	5	4	.556	19	9	0	0	0	69	74	9	25	43	13.8	5.61	85	.273	.350	0	—	0	-7	-6	-0	-1.0
Total	5	31	23	.574	93	66	3	1	0	464^2	480	57	153	292	12.6	4.61	103	.266	.330	0	.000	-0	7	8	-3	-0.2

● JOE OGRODOWSKI

Ogrodowski, Joseph Anthony b: 11/20/06, Hoytville, Pa. d: 6/24/59, Elmira, N.Y. BR/TR, 5'11", 165 lbs. Deb: 4/27/25

YEAR	TM/L	W	L	PCT	G	GS	CG	SH	SV	IP	H	HR	BB	SO	RAT	ERA	ERA+	OAV	OOB	BH	AVG	PB	PR	/A	PD	TPI
1925	Bos-N	0	0	—	1	0	0	0	0	1	6	0	3	0	81.0	54.00	7	.600	.692	0	—	0	-6	-6	-0	0.0

● BILL O'HARA

O'Hara, William Alexander b: 8/14/1883, Toronto, Ont., Can. d: 6/15/31, Jersey City, N.J. BL/TR, 5'10", Deb: 4/15/09 ♦

YEAR	TM/L	W	L	PCT	G	GS	CG	SH	SV	IP	H	HR	BB	SO	RAT	ERA	ERA+	OAV	OOB	BH	AVG	PB	PR	/A	PD	TPI
1910	StL-N	0	0	—	1	0	0	0	0	1	0	0	0	0	0.0	0.00	—	.000	.000	3	.150	-0	0	0	-0	0.0

● JOE OHL

Ohl, Joseph Earl (b: Joseph Earl Von Ohl) b: 1/10/1888, Jobstown, N.J. d: 12/18/51, Camden, N.J. BL/TL, Deb: 7/29/09

YEAR	TM/L	W	L	PCT	G	GS	CG	SH	SV	IP	H	HR	BB	SO	RAT	ERA	ERA+	OAV	OOB	BH	AVG	PB	PR	/A	PD	TPI
1909	Was-A	0	0	—	4	0	0	0	0	8^2	7	0	1	2	9.3	2.08	117	.194	.237	0	.000	-0	0	0	-0	0.0

● KIRT OJALA

Ojala, Kirt Stanley b: 12/24/68, Kalamazoo, Mich. BL/TL, 6'2", 200 lbs. Deb: 8/18/97

YEAR	TM/L	W	L	PCT	G	GS	CG	SH	SV	IP	H	HR	BB	SO	RAT	ERA	ERA+	OAV	OOB	BH	AVG	PB	PR	/A	PD	TPI
1997	Fla-N	1	2	.333	7	5	0	0	0	28^2	28	4	18	19	14.4	3.14	128	.252	.357	0	.000	-1	3	3	0	0.2
1998	Fla-N	2	7	.222	41	13	1	0	0	125	128	14	59	75	13.8	4.25	96	.267	.352	4	.154	1	-0	-2	1	0.1
Total	2	3	9	.250	48	18	1	0	0	153^2	156	18	77	94	13.9	4.04	101	.264	.353	4	.121	0	3	1	2	0.3

● BOB OJEDA

Ojeda, Robert Michael b: 12/17/57, Los Angeles, Cal. BL/TL, 6'1", 190 lbs. Deb: 7/13/80

YEAR	TM/L	W	L	PCT	G	GS	CG	SH	SV	IP	H	HR	BB	SO	RAT	ERA	ERA+	OAV	OOB	BH	AVG	PB	PR	/A	PD	TPI
1980	Bos-A	1	1	.500	7	7	0	0	0	26	39	2	14	12	18.3	6.92	61	.361	.434	0	—	0	-8	-8	-0	-0.9
1981	Bos-A	6	2	.750	10	10	2	0	0	66^1	50	6	25	28	10.4	3.12	124	.212	.293	0	—	0	4	6	-0	0.3
1982	Bos-A	4	6	.400	22	14	0	0	0	78^1	95	13	29	52	14.4	5.63	76	.296	.356	0	—	0	-14	-12	-1	-1.8
1983	Bos-A	12	7	.632	29	28	5	0	0	173^2	173	15	73	94	12.9	4.04	108	.265	.342	0	—	0	0	6	0	0.2
1984	Bos-A	12	12	.500	33	32	8	**5**	0	216^2	211	17	96	137	12.8	3.99	104	.259	.338	0	—	0	0	4	1	0.2
1985	Bos-A	9	11	.450	39	22	5	0	1	157^2	166	11	48	102	12.3	4.00	107	.273	.328	0	—	0	3	5	0	0.4
1986	*NY-N	18	5	**.783**	32	30	7	2	0	217^1	185	15	52	148	9.9	2.57	138	.230	.279	8	.113	-2	28	23	1	2.2
1987	NY-N	3	5	.375	10	7	0	0	0	46^1	45	5	10	21	10.7	3.88	97	.253	.293	1	.071	-0	1	-1	0	-0.1
1988	NY-N	10	13	.435	29	29	5	5	0	190^1	158	6	33	133	9.2	2.88	112	.225	.264	10	.164	1	12	7	2	1.1
1989	NY-N	13	11	.542	31	31	5	2	0	192	179	16	78	95	12.1	3.47	94	.245	.319	7	.106	-2	1	-4	2	-0.5
1990	NY-N	7	6	.538	38	12	0	0	0	118	123	10	40	62	12.6	3.66	102	.272	.334	4	.133	-0	2	1	3	0.3
1991	LA-N	12	9	.571	31	31	2	1	0	189^1	181	15	70	120	12.1	3.18	113	.257	.326	9	.161	1	11	9	1	1.2
1992	LA-N	6	9	.400	29	29	2	1	0	166^1	169	8	81	94	13.6	3.63	95	.268	.352	5	.102	-1	-2	-3	2	-0.2
1993	Cle-A	2	1	.667	9	7	0	0	0	43	48	5	21	27	14.4	4.40	98	.289	.369	0	—	0	-0	-0	1	0.1
1994	NY-A	0	0	—	2	2	0	0	0	3	11	1	6	3	51.0	24.00	19	.611	.708	0	—	0	-6	-6	0	0.1
Total	15	115	98	.540	351	291	41	16	1	1884^1	1833	145	676	1128	12.1	3.65	103	.257	.323	44	.127	-4	30	24	10	2.6

● FRANK OKRIE

Okrie, Frank Anthony "Lefty" b: 10/28/1896, Detroit, Mich. d: 10/16/59, Detroit, Mich. BL/TL, 5'11", 175 lbs. Deb: 4/20/20 F

YEAR	TM/L	W	L	PCT	G	GS	CG	SH	SV	IP	H	HR	BB	SO	RAT	ERA	ERA+	OAV	OOB	BH	AVG	PB	PR	/A	PD	TPI
1920	Det-A	1	2	.333	21	1	1	0	0	41	44	2	18	9	14.7	5.27	71	.295	.390	1	.200	-0	-7	-7	6	0.1

● RED OLDHAM

Oldham, John Cyrus b: 7/15/1893, Zion, Md. d: 1/28/61, Costa Mesa, Cal. BB/TL, 6' ", 176 lbs. Deb: 8/19/14

YEAR	TM/L	W	L	PCT	G	GS	CG	SH	SV	IP	H	HR	BB	SO	RAT	ERA	ERA+	OAV	OOB	BH	AVG	PB	PR	/A	PD	TPI
1914	Det-A	2	4	.333	9	7	3	0	0	45^1	42	1	8	23	10.5	3.38	83	.243	.288	4	.267	1	-3	-3	-1	-0.4
1915	Det-A	3	0	1.000	17	2	1	0	4	57^2	52	1	17	17	11.4	2.81	108	.243	.311	2	.143	-0	1	1	-1	0.0
1920	Det-A	8	13	.381	39	22	10	1	1	215^1	248	5	91	62	14.4	3.85	97	.302	.376	12	.174	-1	-1	-3	4	0.0
1921	Det-A	11	14	.440	40	28	12	1	1	229^1	258	11	81	67	13.5	4.24	101	.288	.351	19	.224	2	1	1	1	0.4
1922	Det-A	10	13	.435	43	28	9	0	3	212	256	14	59	72	13.8	4.67	83	.305	.358	19	.260	4	-15	-19	1	-1.3
1925	*Pit-N	3	2	.600	11	4	3	0	1	53	66	2	18	10	14.6	3.91	114	.313	.372	6	.333	2	2	3	0	0.5
1926	Pit-N	2	2	.500	17	2	0	0	2	41^2	56	1	18	16	16.2	5.62	70	.359	.429	2	.222	0	-8	-8	0	-0.7
Total	7	39	48	.448	176	93	38	2	12	854^1	978	35	292	267	13.7	4.15	93	.295	.358	64	.226	9	-23	-26	4	-1.5

● STEVE OLIN

Olin, Steven Robert b: 10/4/65, Portland, Ore. d: 3/22/93, Little Lake Nellie, Fla. BR/TR, 6'3", 185 lbs. Deb: 7/29/89

YEAR	TM/L	W	L	PCT	G	GS	CG	SH	SV	IP	H	HR	BB	SO	RAT	ERA	ERA+	OAV	OOB	BH	AVG	PB	PR	/A	PD	TPI
1989	Cle-A	1	4	.200	25	0	0	0	1	36	35	1	14	24	12.3	3.75	106	.255	.325	0	—	0	1	1	0	0.1
1990	Cle-A	4	4	.500	50	1	0	0	1	92^1	96	3	26	64	12.5	3.41	115	.270	.331	0	—	0	5	5	2	0.7
1991	Cle-A	3	6	.333	48	0	0	0	17	56^1	61	2	23	38	13.6	3.36	124	.274	.344	0	—	0	5	5	0	1.0
1992	Cle-A	8	5	.615	72	0	0	0	29	88^1	80	8	27	47	11.3	2.34	167	.248	.314	0	—	0	16	15	1	3.2
Total	4	16	19	.457	195	1	0	0	48	273	272	14	90	173	12.3	3.10	128	.262	.328	0	—	0	26	26	3	5.0

● OMAR OLIVARES

Olivares, Omar (Palqu) b: 7/6/67, Mayaguez, P.R. BR/TR, 6'1", 193 lbs. Deb: 8/18/90 F

YEAR	TM/L	W	L	PCT	G	GS	CG	SH	SV	IP	H	HR	BB	SO	RAT	ERA	ERA+	OAV	OOB	BH	AVG	PB	PR	/A	PD	TPI
1990	StL-N	1	1	.500	9	6	0	0	0	49^1	45	2	17	20	11.7	2.92	131	.249	.320	3	.176	1	5	5	1	0.4
1991	StL-N	11	7	.611	28	24	0	0	1	167^1	148	13	61	91	11.5	3.71	100	.243	.317	12	.226	3	-1	0	2	0.5
1992	StL-N	9	9	.500	32	30	1	0	0	197	189	20	63	124	11.7	3.84	88	.257	.319	16	.235	4	-7	-10	3	-0.1
1993	StL-N	5	3	.625	58	9	0	0	1	118^2	134	10	54	63	14.9	4.17	95	.288	.372	7	.269	2	-2	-3	4	0.4
1994	StL-N	3	4	.429	14	12	1	0	1	73^2	84	10	37	26	15.3	5.74	72	.294	.382	6	.214	2	-13	-13	1	-0.9
1995	Col-N	1	3	.250	11	6	0	0	0	31^2	44	4	21	15	19.0	7.39	73	.349	.450	1	.143	0	-11	-7	0	-0.7
	Phi-N	0	1	.000	5	0	0	0	0	10	11	1	2	7	12.6	5.40	78	.282	.333	1	.500	1	-1	-1	0	0.0
	Yr	1	4	.200	16	6	0	0	0	41^2	55	5	23	22	17.1	6.91	74	.327	.411	2	.222	1	-13	-8	1	-0.7
1996	Det-A	7	11	.389	25	25	4	0	0	160	169	16	75	81	14.2	4.89	103	.275	.362	0	—	0	2	3	0	0.3
1997	Det-A	5	6	.455	19	19	3	2	0	115	110	8	53	74	13.5	4.70	98	.253	.347	2	.667	1	-2	-1	1	0.1
	Sea-A	1	4	.200	13	12	0	0	0	62^1	81	10	28	29	16.3	5.49	82	.315	.391	1	.500	0	-6	-7	-1	-0.5
	Yr	6	10	.375	32	31	3	2	0	177^1	191	18	81	103	14.0	4.97	91	.271	.350	3	.600	2	-8	-8	0	-0.4
1998	Ana-A	9	9	.500	37	26	1	0	0	183	189	19	91	112	14.0	4.03	116	.270	.358	0	.000	0	12	13	3	1.5
Total	9	52	58	.473	251	169	10	2	3	1168	1204	113	502	642	13.6	4.39	96	.271	.352	49	.236	15	-24	-22	14	1.0

● DARREN OLIVER

Oliver, Darren Christopher b: 10/6/70, Rio Linda, Cal. BR/TL, 6'2", 200 lbs. Deb: 9/1/93 F

YEAR	TM/L	W	L	PCT	G	GS	CG	SH	SV	IP	H	HR	BB	SO	RAT	ERA	ERA+	OAV	OOB	BH	AVG	PB	PR	/A	PD	TPI
1993	Tex-A	0	0	—	2	0	0	0	0	3^1	2	1	1	4	8.1	2.70	154	.154	.214	0	—	0	1	1	0	0.3

YEAR	TM/L	W	L	PCT	G	GS	CG	SH	SV	IP	H	HR	BB	SO	RAT	ERA	ERA+	OAV	OOB	BH	AVG	PB	PR	/A	PD	TPI
1994	Tex-A	4	0	1.000	43	0	0	0	2	50	40	4	35	50	14.6	3.42	141	.223	.368	0	—	0	8	8	2	0.8
1995	Tex-A	4	2	.667	17	7	0	0	0	49	47	3	32	39	14.7	4.22	114	.257	.370	0	—	0	3	3	1	0.2
1996	*Tex-A	14	6	.700	30	30	1	1	0	173^2	190	20	76	112	14.3	4.66	112	.279	.359	0	—	0	6	11	-1	0.7
1997	Tex-A	13	12	.520	32	32	3	1	0	201^1	213	29	82	104	13.7	4.20	114	.271	.348	1	.500	1	8	13	-2	1.3
1998	Tex-A	6	7	.462	19	19	2	0	0	103^1	140	11	43	58	16.8	6.53	74	.325	.399	1	.167	0	-22	-19	-0	-2.0
	StL-N	4	4	.500	10	10	0	0	0	57	64	7	23	29	13.7	4.26	98	.283	.349	2	.087	-1	-0	-1	0	-0.1
Total	6	45	31	.592	153	98	6	2	2	637^2	696	75	292	396	14.5	4.64	105	.278	.362	4	.129	0	3	16	1	1.2

● FRANCISCO OLIVERAS Oliveras, Francisco Javier (Noa) b: 1/31/63, Santurce, P.R. BR/TR, 5'10", 170 lbs. Deb: 5/3/89

YEAR	TM/L	W	L	PCT	G	GS	CG	SH	SV	IP	H	HR	BB	SO	RAT	ERA	ERA+	OAV	OOB	BH	AVG	PB	PR	/A	PD	TPI
1989	Min-A	3	4	.429	12	8	1	0	0	55^2	64	8	15	24	12.9	4.53	91	.288	.336	0	—	0	-4	-2	-1	-0.4
1990	SF-N	2	2	.500	33	2	0	0	2	55^1	47	5	21	41	11.4	2.77	132	.230	.308	0	.000	-1	6	5	-1	0.3
1991	SF-N	6	6	.500	55	1	0	0	3	79^1	69	12	22	48	10.4	3.86	93	.242	.299	2	.200	0	-2	-2	-0	-0.4
1992	SF-N	0	3	.000	16	7	0	0	0	44^2	41	11	10	17	10.5	3.63	91	.250	.297	1	.143	0	-1	-2	-0	-0.1
Total	4	11	15	.423	116	18	1	0	5	235	221	36	68	130	11.3	3.71	99	.253	.310	3	.136	-0	0	-1	-2	-0.6

● DIOMEDES OLIVO Olivo, Diomedes Antonio (Maldonado) b: 1/22/19, Guayubin, D.R. d: 2/15/77, Santo Domingo, D.R. BL/TL, 6'1", 195 lbs. Deb: 9/5/60 F

YEAR	TM/L	W	L	PCT	G	GS	CG	SH	SV	IP	H	HR	BB	SO	RAT	ERA	ERA+	OAV	OOB	BH	AVG	PB	PR	/A	PD	TPI
1960	Pit-N	0	0	—	4	0	0	0	0	9^2	8	1	5	10	12.1	2.79	134	.216	.310	0	.000	-0	1	1	-0	0.0
1962	Pit-N	5	1	.833	62	1	0	0	7	84^1	88	5	25	66	12.1	2.77	142	.277	.329	3	.188	1	11	11	-1	0.9
1963	StL-N	0	5	.000	19	0	0	0	0	13^1	16	1	9	9	17.6	5.40	66	.296	.406	0	—	0	-3	-3	0	-0.9
Total	3	5	6	.455	85	1	0	0	7	107^1	112	7	39	85	12.7	3.10	125	.274	.339	3	.176	0	9	9	-0	0.0

● CHI-CHI OLIVO Olivo, Federico Emilio (Maldonado) b: 3/18/28, Guayubin, D.R. d: 2/3/77, Guayubin, D.R. BR/TR, 6'2", 215 lbs. Deb: 6/5/61 F

YEAR	TM/L	W	L	PCT	G	GS	CG	SH	SV	IP	H	HR	BB	SO	RAT	ERA	ERA+	OAV	OOB	BH	AVG	PB	PR	/A	PD	TPI
1961	Mil-N	0	0	—	3	0	0	0	0	2	3	1	5	1	36.0	18.00	21	.500	.727	0	—	0	-3	-3	-0	0.0
1964	Mil-N	2	1	.667	38	0	0	0	5	60	55	7	21	45	11.4	3.75	94	.247	.311	1	.250	0	-1	-2	1	0.0
1965	Mil-N	0	1	.000	8	0	0	0	0	13	12	1	5	11	11.8	1.38	254	.267	.340	0	—	0	3	3	-0	0.2
1966	Atl-N	5	4	.556	47	0	0	0	7	66	59	4	19	41	10.8	4.23	86	.240	.297	1	.111	-0	-5	-4	-1	-0.8
Total	4	7	6	.538	96	0	0	0	12	141	129	13	50	98	11.5	3.96	90	.248	.315	2	.154	-0	-6	-6	-1	-0.6

● JIM OLLOM Ollom, James Donald b: 7/8/45, Snohomish, Wash. BR/TL, 6'4", 210 lbs. Deb: 9/3/66

YEAR	TM/L	W	L	PCT	G	GS	CG	SH	SV	IP	H	HR	BB	SO	RAT	ERA	ERA+	OAV	OOB	BH	AVG	PB	PR	/A	PD	TPI
1966	Min-A	0	0	—	3	1	0	0	0	10	6	1	1	11	7.2	3.60	100	.167	.211	0	.000	-0	-0	-0	-0	0.0
1967	Min-A	0	1	.000	21	2	0	0	0	35	33	4	11	17	12.3	5.40	64	.258	.336	1	.200	0	-8	-8	-0	-0.2
Total	2	0	1	.000	24	3	0	0	0	45	39	5	12	28	11.2	5.00	70	.238	.309	1	.143	-0	-9	-8	-0	-0.2

● FRED OLMSTEAD Olmstead, Frederic William b: 7/3/1881, Grand Rapids, Mich. d: 10/22/36, Muskogee, Okla. BR/TR, 5'11", 170 lbs. Deb: 7/2/08

YEAR	TM/L	W	L	PCT	G	GS	CG	SH	SV	IP	H	HR	BB	SO	RAT	ERA	ERA+	OAV	OOB	BH	AVG	PB	PR	/A	PD	TPI
1908	Chi-A	0	0	—	1	0	0	0	0	2	6	0	1	1	31.5	13.50	17	.600	.636	0	.000	1	-2	-2	-0	0.0
1909	Chi-A	3	2	.600	8	6	5	0	0	54^2	52	1	12	21	10.7	1.81	129	.277	.323	2	.095	-1	4	3	-0	0.2
1910	Chi-A	10	12	.455	32	20	14	4	0	184^1	174	1	50	68	11.1	1.95	123	.260	.316	10	.154	-2	12	9	1	0.9
1911	Chi-A	6	6	.500	25	11	7	1	2	117^2	146	3	30	45	13.9	4.21	77	.309	.358	7	.189	-0	-11	-13	-1	-1.3
Total	4	19	20	.487	66	37	26	5	2	358^2	378	5	93	135	12.1	2.74	97	.283	.334	19	.153	-3	2	-3	-0	-0.2

● AL OLMSTED Olmsted, Alan Ray b: 3/18/57, St.Louis, Mo. BR/TL, 6'2", 195 lbs. Deb: 9/12/80

YEAR	TM/L	W	L	PCT	G	GS	CG	SH	SV	IP	H	HR	BB	SO	RAT	ERA	ERA+	OAV	OOB	BH	AVG	PB	PR	/A	PD	TPI
1980	StL-N	1	1	.500	5	5	0	0	0	34^2	32	2	14	14	12.2	2.86	129	.244	.322	2	.182	-0	3	3	1	0.2

● HANK OLMSTED Olmsted, Henry Theodore b: 1/12/1879, Sac Bay, Mich. d: 1/6/69, Bradenton, Fla. BR/TR, 5'8.5", 147 lbs. Deb: 7/15/05

YEAR	TM/L	W	L	PCT	G	GS	CG	SH	SV	IP	H	HR	BB	SO	RAT	ERA	ERA+	OAV	OOB	BH	AVG	PB	PR	/A	PD	TPI
1905	Bos-A	1	2	.333	3	3	3	0	0	25	18	0	12	6	10.8	3.24	83	.205	.300	1	.125	-0	-2	-2	-1	-0.3

● OLE OLSEN Olsen, Arthur b: 9/12/1894, S.Norwalk, Conn. d: 9/12/80, Norwalk, Conn. BR/TR, 5'10", 163 lbs. Deb: 4/12/22

YEAR	TM/L	W	L	PCT	G	GS	CG	SH	SV	IP	H	HR	BB	SO	RAT	ERA	ERA+	OAV	OOB	BH	AVG	PB	PR	/A	PD	TPI
1922	Det-A	7	6	.538	37	15	5	0	3	137	147	8	40	52	13.2	4.53	86	.281	.348	7	.179	-1	-7	-10	1	-0.9
1923	Det-A	1	1	.500	17	2	1	0	0	41^1	42	1	17	12	13.9	6.31	61	.290	.383	1	.125	-1	-11	-11	-1	-0.6
Total	2	8	7	.533	54	17	6	0	3	178^1	189	9	57	64	13.4	4.95	78	.283	.356	8	.170	-2	-18	-21	-0	-1.5

● VERN OLSEN Olsen, Vern Jarl b: 3/16/18, Hillsboro, Ore. d: 7/13/89, Maywood, Ill. BR/TL, 6'0.5", 175 lbs. Deb: 9/8/39

YEAR	TM/L	W	L	PCT	G	GS	CG	SH	SV	IP	H	HR	BB	SO	RAT	ERA	ERA+	OAV	OOB	BH	AVG	PB	PR	/A	PD	TPI
1939	Chi-N	1	0	1.000	4	0	0	0	0	7^2	2	0	7	3	10.6	0.00	—	.087	.300	0	.000	0	3	3	-0	0.5
1940	Chi-N	13	9	.591	34	20	9	4	0	172^2	172	5	62	71	12.3	2.97	126	.260	.325	15	.263	3	17	15	4	2.6
1941	Chi-N	10	8	.556	37	23	10	2	1	185^2	202	7	59	73	12.7	3.15	111	.276	.331	15	.238	3	10	7	2	1.3
1942	Chi-N	6	9	.400	32	17	4	1	1	140^1	161	6	55	46	13.9	4.49	71	.283	.347	9	.188	1	-18	-20	1	-1.8
1946	Chi-N	0	0	—	5	0	0	0	0	9^2	10	0	9	8	17.7	2.79	119	.294	.442	0	—	0	1	1	0	0.0
Total	5	30	26	.536	112	60	23	7	2	516	547	18	192	201	13.0	3.40	103	.271	.335	39	.231	8	12	6	7	2.6

● GREGG OLSON Olson, Greggory William b: 10/11/66, Scribner, Neb. BR/TR, 6'4", 206 lbs. Deb: 9/2/88

YEAR	TM/L	W	L	PCT	G	GS	CG	SH	SV	IP	H	HR	BB	SO	RAT	ERA	ERA+	OAV	OOB	BH	AVG	PB	PR	/A	PD	TPI
1988	Bal-A	1	1	.500	10	0	0	0	0	11	10	1	10	9	16.4	3.27	119	.244	.392	0	—	0	1	1	0	0.4
1989	Bal-A	5	2	.714	64	0	0	0	27	85	57	1	46	90	11.0	1.69	224	.188	.296	0	—	0	21	20	0	2.7
1990	Bal-A☆	6	5	.545	64	0	0	0	37	74^1	57	3	31	74	11.0	2.42	157	.213	.301	0	—	0	12	11	-1	2.6
1991	Bal-A	4	6	.400	72	0	0	0	31	73^2	74	1	29	72	12.7	3.18	124	.261	.332	0	—	0	8	6	0	1.5
1992	Bal-A	1	5	.167	60	0	0	0	36	61^1	46	3	24	58	10.3	2.05	196	.211	.289	0	—	0	13	13	1	2.5
1993	Bal-A	0	2	.000	50	0	0	0	29	45	37	1	18	44	11.0	1.60	279	.223	.299	0	.000	-0	14	14	0	2.2
1994	Atl-N	0	2	.000	16	0	0	0	1	14^2	19	1	13	10	20.3	9.20	46	.317	.446	0	.000	-0	-8	-8	-1	-1.1
1995	Cle-A	0	0	—	3	0	0	0	0	2^2	5	1	2	0	23.6	13.50	35	.417	.500	0	—	0	-3	-3	-0	-0.1
	KC-A	3	3	.500	20	0	0	0	3	30^1	23	3	17	21	11.9	3.26	147	.215	.323	0	—	0	5	5	0	0.9
	Yr	3	3	.500	23	0	0	0	3	33	28	4	19	21	12.8	4.09	117	.235	.341	0	—	0	2	3	0	0.8
1996	Det-A	3	0	1.000	43	0	0	0	8	43	43	6	28	29	15.1	5.02	101	.259	.369	0	—	0	-0	0	-1	0.0
	Hou-N	1	0	1.000	9	0	0	0	0	9^1	12	1	7	8	18.3	4.82	80	.308	.413	0	—	0	-1	-1	0	-0.1
1997	Min-A	0	0	—	11	0	0	0	0	8^1	19	0	11	6	32.4	18.36	25	.432	.545	0	—	0	-13	-13	0	0.0
	KC-A	4	3	.571	34	0	0	0	1	41^2	39	3	17	28	12.3	3.02	156	.260	.339	0	—	0	7	8	-0	1.1
	Yr	4	3	.571	45	0	0	0	1	50	58	3	28	34	15.7	5.58	84	.299	.390	0	—	0	-6	-5	-0	1.1
1998	Ari-N	3	4	.429	64	0	0	0	30	68^2	56	4	25	55	10.7	3.01	143	.223	.296	1	.500	1	9	10	-1	1.7
Total	11	31	33	.484	520	0	0	0	203	569	497	29	278	504	12.4	3.18	132	.236	.327	1	.250	1	65	64	-0	14.3

● TED OLSON Olson, Theodore Otto b: 8/27/12, Quincy, Mass. d: 12/9/80, Weymouth, Mass. BR/TR, 6'2.5", 185 lbs. Deb: 6/21/36

YEAR	TM/L	W	L	PCT	G	GS	CG	SH	SV	IP	H	HR	BB	SO	RAT	ERA	ERA+	OAV	OOB	BH	AVG	PB	PR	/A	PD	TPI
1936	Bos-A	1	1	.500	5	3	1	0	0	18^1	24	3	8	5	15.7	7.36	72	.324	.390	1	.143	-0	-5	-4	0	-0.4
1937	Bos-A	0	0	—	11	0	0	0	0	32^1	42	4	15	11	15.9	7.24	66	.318	.388	3	.300	1	-9	-9	1	0.2
1938	Bos-A	0	0	—	2	0	0	0	0	7	9	0	2	2	14.1	6.43	77	.310	.355	0	.000	-0	-1	-1	-0	0.0
Total	3	1	1	.500	18	3	1	0	0	57^2	75	7	25	18	15.6	7.18	69	.319	.385	4	.222	1	-15	-14	1	-0.2

● ED OLWINE Olwine, Edward R. b: 5/28/58, Greenville, Ohio BL/TL, 6'2", 165 lbs. Deb: 6/2/86

YEAR	TM/L	W	L	PCT	G	GS	CG	SH	SV	IP	H	HR	BB	SO	RAT	ERA	ERA+	OAV	OOB	BH	AVG	PB	PR	/A	PD	TPI
1986	Atl-N	0	0	—	37	0	0	0	1	47^2	35	5	17	37	10.0	3.40	117	.207	.283	1	.333	1	2	3	-0	0.0
1987	Atl-N	0	1	.000	27	0	0	0	1	23^1	25	4	8	12	13.1	5.01	87	.269	.333	0	—	0	-2	-2	-0	-0.1
1988	Atl-N	0	0	—	16	0	0	0	1	18^2	22	4	4	5	13.0	6.75	54	.286	.329	0	—	0	-7	-6	-1	-0.1
Total	3	0	1	.000	80	0	0	0	3	89^2	82	13	29	54	11.4	4.52	89	.242	.307	1	.333	1	-8	-5	-1	-0.2

● SKINNY O'NEAL O'Neal, Oran Herbert b: 5/2/1899, Gatewood, Mo. d: 6/2/81, Springfield, Mo. BR/TR, 5'11", 160 lbs. Deb: 4/18/25

YEAR	TM/L	W	L	PCT	G	GS	CG	SH	SV	IP	H	HR	BB	SO	RAT	ERA	ERA+	OAV	OOB	BH	AVG	PB	PR	/A	PD	TPI
1925	Phi-N	0	0	—	11	1	0	0	0	20^1	35	2	12	6	20.8	9.30	51	.407	.480	1	.167	-0	-11	-10	-0	0.0
1927	Phi-N	0	0	—	2	0	0	0	0	5	9	0	2	2	19.8	9.00	46	.409	.458	0	.000	-0	-3	-3	1	0.0
Total	2	0	0	—	13	1	0	0	0	25^1	44	2	14	8	20.6	9.24	50	.407	.475	1	.143	-0	-14	-13	0	0.0

● RANDY O'NEAL O'Neal, Randall Jeffrey b: 8/30/60, Ashland, Ky. BR/TR, 6'2", 195 lbs. Deb: 9/12/84

YEAR	TM/L	W	L	PCT	G	GS	CG	SH	SV	IP	H	HR	BB	SO	RAT	ERA	ERA+	OAV	OOB	BH	AVG	PB	PR	/A	PD	TPI
1984	Det-A	2	1	.667	4	3	0	0	0	18^2	16	0	6	12	10.6	3.38	116	.222	.282	0	—	0	1	1	-0	0.1
1985	Det-A	5	5	.500	28	12	1	0	1	94^1	82	8	36	52	11.4	3.24	126	.240	.316	0	—	0	9	9	1	0.9
1986	Det-A	3	7	.300	37	11	1	0	2	122^2	121	13	44	68	12.3	4.33	95	.260	.327	0	—	0	-2	-3	1	-0.1
1987	Atl-N	4	2	.667	16	10	0	0	0	61	79	12	24	33	15.5	5.61	78	.316	.380	2	.105	-1	-10	-9	1	-0.7
	StL-N	0	0	—	1	1	0	0	0	5	2	0	2	4	7.2	1.80	231	.111	.200	1	1.000	1	1	1	0	0.1
	Yr	4	2	.667	17	11	0	0	0	66	81	12	26	37	14.6	5.32	81	.298	.359	3	.150	-0	-9	-7	1	-0.6

YEAR	TM/L	W	L	PCT	G	GS	CG	SH	SV	IP	H	HR	BB	SO	RAT	ERA	ERA+	OAV	OOB	BH	AVG	PB	PR	/A	PD	TPI
1988	StL-N	2	3	.400	10	8	0	0	0	53	57	7	10	20	11.7	4.58	76	.274	.314	0	.000	-2	-7	-7	1	-0.7
1989	Phi-N	0	1	.000	20	1	0	0	0	39	46	5	9	29	12.7	6.23	57	.301	.340	0	.000	-1	-12	-12	1	-0.3
1990	SF-N	1	0	1.000	26	0	0	0	0	47	58	3	18	30	14.6	3.83	95	.314	.374	1	.167	-0	-0	-1	0	0.0
Total	7	17	19	.472	142	46	2	0	3	440^2	461	48	149	248	12.6	4.35	91	.272	.334	4	.080	-3	-19	-19	5	-0.7
● ED O'NEIL	O'Neil, Edward J. b: 3/11/1859, Fall River, Mass. d: 9/30/1892, Fall River, Mass. TR , 5'11", 180 lbs. Deb: 6/20/1890																									
1890	Tol-a	0	2	.000	2	2	2	0	0	16	27	0	13	2	22.5	7.88	50	.365	.460	0	.000	-2	-7	-7	0	-0.7
	Phi-a	0	6	.000	6	6	6	0	0	52	84	0	32	17	21.3	9.69	40	.353	.444	5	.161	-1	-34	-34	1	-2.5
	Yr	0	8	.000	8	8	8	0	0	68	111	0	45	19	21.6	9.26	42	.356	.448	5	.125	-2	-41	-41	1	-3.2
● J. O'NEILL	O'Neill, J. b: Brooklyn, N.Y. Deb: 8/20/1875																									
1875	Atl-n	0	4	.000	5	4	3	0	0	34	59	3	0	0	15.6	5.03	41	.343	.343	2	.077	-2	-11	-11		-1.0
● TIP O'NEILL	O'Neill, James Edward b: 5/25/1858, Woodstock, Ont., Canada d: 12/31/15, Montreal, Que., Can BR/TR, 6'1.5", 167 lbs. Deb: 5/5/1883 ♦																									
1883	NY-N	5	12	.294	19	19	15	0	0	148	182	5	64	55	15.0	4.07	76	.289	.354	15	.197	-1	-15	-16	-1	-1.6
1884	StL-a	11	4	.733	17	14	14	0	0	141	125	3	51	36	11.5	2.68	122	.219	.288	82	.276	5	9	9	0	1.2
Total	2	16	16	.500	36	33	29	0	0	289	307	8	115	91	13.3	3.39	94	.256	.323	1386	.326	3	-6	-7	-1	-0.4
● HARRY O'NEILL	O'Neill, Joseph Henry b: 2/20/1897, Ridgetown, Ont., Canada d: 9/5/69, Ridgetown, Ont., Can. BR/TR, 6', 180 lbs. Deb: 9/15/22																									
1922	Phi-A	0	0	—	1	0	0	0	0	3	2	0	1	0	12.0	3.00	142	.200	.333	0	.000	-0	0	0	0	0.0
1923	Phi-A	0	0	—	3	0	0	0	0	2	1	0	3	2	18.0	0.00	—	.167	.444	0	—	0	1	1	-0	0.0
Total	2	0	0	—	4	0	0	0	0	5	3	0	4	2	14.4	1.80	233	.188	.381	0	.000	-0	1	1	0	0.0
● MIKE O'NEILL	O'Neill, Michael Joyce (a.k.a. Michael Joyce In 1901) b: 9/7/1877, Maam, Ireland d: 8/12/59, Scranton, Pa. BL/TL, 5'11", 185 lbs. Deb: 9/20/01 F♦																									
1901	StL-N	2	2	.500	5	4	4	1	0	41	29	2	10	16	9.7	1.32	242	.197	.272	6	.400	3	9	8	-1	1.0
1902	StL-N	16	15	.516	36	32	29	2	2	288^1	297	3	66	105	11.7	2.90	94	.266	.314	43	.319	9	-4	-5	0	0.8
1903	StL-N	4	13	.235	19	17	12	0	0	145	184	2	43	39	14.5	3.79	86	.304	.356	25	.227	2	-8	-8	-0	-0.6
1904	StL-N	10	14	.417	25	24	23	1	0	220	229	1	50	68	11.5	2.09	129	.262	.304	21	.231	5	16	15	1	2.4
Total	4	32	44	.421	85	77	68	4	2	694^1	739	8	169	228	12.1	2.73	105	.269	.318	97	.255	19	13	10	-0	3.6
● PAUL O'NEILL	O'Neill, Paul Andrew b: 2/25/63, Columbus, Ohio BL/TL, 6'4", 215 lbs. Deb: 9/3/85 ♦																									
1987	Cin-N	0	0	—	1	0	0	0	0	2	2	1	4	2	27.0	13.50	31	.286	.545	41	.256	0	-2	-2	-0	0.0
● EMMETT O'NEILL	O'Neill, Robert Emmett "Pinky" b: 1/13/18, San Mateo, Cal. d: 10/11/93, Sparks, Nevada BR/TR, 6'2.5", 180 lbs. Deb: 8/3/43																									
1943	Bos-A	1	4	.200	11	5	1	0	0	57^2	56	3	46	20	16.1	4.53	73	.256	.387	3	.188	1	-8	-8	0	-0.6
1944	Bos-A	6	11	.353	28	22	8	1	0	151^2	154	6	89	68	14.5	4.63	73	.265	.365	10	.182	-0	-20	-21	-2	-2.3
1945	Bos-A	8	11	.421	24	22	10	1	0	141^2	134	5	117	55	16.3	5.15	66	.258	.399	9	.180	2	-28	-27	1	-3.1
1946	Chi-N	0	0	—	1	0	0	0	0	1	0	0	3	1	27.0	0.00	—	.000	.500	0	—	0	0	0	0	0.0
	Chi-A	0	0	—	2	0	0	0	0	3^2	4	0	5	0	22.1	0.00	—	.333	.529	0	.000	-0	1	1	0	0.0
Total	4	15	26	.366	66	49	19	2	0	355^2	348	14	260	144	15.6	4.76	71	.261	.385	22	.180	2	-54	-54	-2	-6.0
● STEVE ONTIVEROS	Ontiveros, Steven b: 3/5/61, Tularosa, N.Mex. BR/TR, 6', 190 lbs. Deb: 6/14/85																									
1985	Oak-A	1	3	.250	39	0	0	0	8	74^2	45	4	19	36	8.0	1.93	200	.174	.236	0	—	0	18	16	1	1.2
1986	Oak-A	2	2	.500	46	0	0	0	10	72^2	72	10	25	54	12.1	4.71	82	.265	.329	0	—	0	-4	-7	0	-0.5
1987	Oak-A	10	8	.556	35	22	2	1	1	150^2	141	19	50	97	11.6	4.00	103	.242	.306	0	—	0	8	2	2	0.5
1988	Oak-A	3	4	.429	10	10	0	0	0	54^2	57	4	21	30	12.8	4.61	82	.265	.331	0	—	0	-4	-5	1	-0.5
1989	Phi-N	2	1	.667	6	5	0	0	0	30^2	34	2	15	12	14.4	3.82	93	.288	.368	1	.083	-0	-1	-1	1	0.0
1990	Phi-N	0	0	—	5	0	0	0	0	10	9	1	3	6	10.8	2.70	142	.225	.279	0	—	0	1	1	1	0.0
1993	Sea-A	0	2	.000	14	0	0	0	0	18	18	0	6	13	12.0	1.00	440	.277	.338	0	—	0	7	7	-0	0.6
1994	Oak-A	6	4	.600	27	13	2	0	0	115^1	93	7	26	56	**9.8**	**2.65**	167	.217	**.272**	0	—	0	28	23	2	2.4
1995	Oak-A★	9	6	.600	22	22	2	1	0	129^2	144	12	38	77	12.9	4.37	102	.283	.338	0	—	0	5	1	3	0.8
Total	9	33	30	.524	204	72	6	2	19	656^1	613	59	203	381	11.4	3.62	114	.246	.308	1	.083	-0	57	38	11	4.5
● JOSE OQUENDO	Oquendo, Jose Manuel (Contreras) b: 7/4/63, Rio Piedras, P.R. BB/TR, 5'10", 160 lbs. Deb: 5/2/83 ♦																									
1987	*StL-N	0	0	—	1	0	0	0	0	1	4	0	1	0	54.0	27.00	15	.571	.667	71	.286	0	-3	-3	-0	0.0
1988	StL-N	0	1	.000	1	0	0	0	0	4	4	0	6	1	22.5	4.50	77	.267	.476	125	.277	0	-0	-0	-0	-0.1
1991	StL-N	0	0	—	1	0	0	0	0	1	2	0	2	1	36.0	27.00	14	.400	.571	88	.240	0	-3	-3	0	0.0
Total	3	0	1	.000	3	0	0	0	0	6	10	0	9	2	30.0	12.00	30	.370	.541	821	.256	1	-6	-6	-0	-0.1
● MIKE OQUIST	Oquist, Michael Lee b: 5/30/68, LaJunta, Colo. BR/TR, 6'2", 170 lbs. Deb: 8/14/93																									
1993	Bal-A	0	0	—	5	0	0	0	0	11^2	12	0	4	8	12.3	3.86	116	.261	.320	0	—	0	1	1	-0	-0.3
1994	Bal-A	3	3	.500	15	9	0	0	0	58^1	75	7	30	39	17.1	6.17	81	.319	.410	0	—	0	-9	-8	0	-0.9
1995	Bal-A	2	1	.667	27	0	0	0	0	54	51	6	41	27	15.7	4.17	114	.246	.376	0	—	0	3	4	-0	0.0
1996	SD-N	0	0	—	8	0	0	0	0	7^2	6	0	4	4	11.7	2.35	169	.231	.333	0	—	0	2	1	-0	0.0
1997	Oak-A	4	6	.400	19	17	1	0	0	107^2	111	15	43	72	13.4	5.02	90	.266	.343	1	.250	0	-5	-6	-1	-0.5
1998	Oak-A	7	11	.389	31	29	0	0	0	175	210	27	57	112	14.0	6.22	73	.298	.355	0	.000	-0	-31	-32	-2	-2.9
Total	6	16	21	.432	105	55	1	0	0	414^1	465	55	179	262	14.4	5.50	84	.284	.362	1	.200	0	-39	-40	-3	-4.6
● DON O'RILEY	O'Riley, Donald Lee b: 3/12/45, Topeka, Kan. d: 5/2/97, Kansas City, Mo. BR/TR, 6'3", 205 lbs. Deb: 6/20/69																									
1969	KC-A	1	1	.500	18	0	0	0	1	23^1	32	0	15	10	18.1	6.94	53	.311	.398	0	.000	-0	-9	-8	-0	-0.8
1970	KC-A	0	0	—	9	2	0	0	0	23^1	26	5	9	13	13.9	5.40	69	.277	.346	0	.000	-0	-4	-4	-0	-0.1
Total	2	1	1	.500	27	2	0	0	1	46^2	58	5	24	23	16.0	6.17	60	.294	.374	0	.000	-1	-13	-13	-1	-0.9
● JESSE OROSCO	Orosco, Jesse Russell b: 4/21/57, Santa Barbara, Cal. BR/TL, 6'2", 185 lbs. Deb: 4/5/79																									
1979	NY-N	1	2	.333	18	2	0	0	0	35	33	4	22	22	14.7	4.89	74	.260	.377	0	.000	-1	-4	-5	1	-0.4
1981	NY-N	0	1	.000	8	0	0	0	1	17^1	13	2	6	18	9.9	1.56	224	.213	.284	0	.000	-0	4	4	0	0.2
1982	NY-N	4	10	.286	54	2	0	0	4	109^1	92	7	40	89	11.0	2.72	134	.230	.303	2	.143	-0	11	11	0	1.4
1983	NY-N★	13	7	.650	62	0	0	0	17	110	76	3	38	84	9.4	1.47	246	.197	.271	4	.333	1	**26**	**26**	1	**5.8**
1984	NY-N☆	10	6	.625	60	0	0	0	31	87	58	7	34	85	9.7	2.59	137	.185	.269	1	.250	1	10	9	-0	2.4
1985	NY-N	8	6	.571	54	0	0	0	17	79	66	6	34	68	11.4	2.73	126	.224	.304	3	.429	1	8	6	-1	1.4
1986	*NY-N	8	6	.571	58	0	0	0	21	81	64	6	35	62	11.3	2.33	151	.217	.306	0	.000	0	12	11	-1	2.3
1987	NY-N	3	9	.250	58	0	0	0	16	77	78	5	31	78	13.0	4.44	85	.266	.340	0	.000	-1	-3	-6	-0	-1.1
1988	*LA-N	3	2	.600	55	0	0	0	9	53	41	4	30	43	12.4	2.72	123	.215	.327	0	.000	-0	4	4	0	0.5
1989	Cle-A	3	4	.429	69	0	0	0	3	78	54	7	26	79	9.5	2.08	191	.198	.272	0	—	0	16	16	1	1.6
1990	Cle-A	5	4	.556	55	0	0	0	2	64^2	58	9	38	55	13.4	3.90	101	.239	.342	0	—	0	0	0	1	0.1
1991	Cle-A	2	0	1.000	47	0	0	0	0	45^2	52	4	15	36	13.4	3.74	111	.286	.343	0	—	0	2	2	-1	0.0
1992	Mil-A	3	1	.750	59	0	0	0	1	39	33	5	13	40	10.8	3.23	119	.232	.301	0	—	0	3	3	-0	0.4
1993	Mil-A	3	5	.375	57	0	0	0	8	56^2	47	2	17	67	10.6	3.18	134	.224	.291	0	.000	-0	7	7	3	1.2
1994	Mil-A	3	1	.750	40	0	0	0	0	39	32	4	26	36	13.8	5.08	99	.222	.349	0	—	0	-1	-0	-0	-0.3
1995	Bal-A	2	4	.333	**65**	0	0	0	3	49^2	28	4	27	58	10.1	3.26	146	.169	.289	0	—	0	8	8	1	0.9
1996	*Bal-A	3	1	.750	66	0	0	0	0	55^2	42	5	28	52	11.6	3.40	145	.207	.309	0	—	0	10	9	0	0.6
1997	*Bal-A	6	3	.667	71	0	0	0	0	50^1	29	6	30	46	10.5	2.32	189	.169	.292	0	—	0	13	12	0	1.8
1998	Bal-A	4	1	.800	69	0	0	0	7	56^2	46	6	28	50	11.9	3.18	142	.221	.316	0	—	0	9	8	-1	0.9
Total	19	84	73	.535	1025	4	0	0	140	1184	942	96	518	1068	11.3	2.96	132	.219	.307	10	.169	2	133	126	4	19.7
● O'ROURKE	O'Rourke Deb: 7/9/1872																									
1872	Eck-n	0	1	.000	1	1	1	0	0	9	16	0	2	0	18.0	8.00	42	.327	.353	0	.000	-1	-4	-5		-0.4
● JIM O'ROURKE	O'Rourke, James Henry "Orator Jim" b: 9/1/1850, Bridgeport, Conn. d: 1/8/19, Bridgeport, Conn. BR/TR, 5'8", 185 lbs. Deb: 4/26/1872 FMUH♦																									
1883	Buf-N	0	0	—	2	0	0	0	1	7	10	0	1	1	14.1	6.43	49	.357	.379	143	.328	1	-3	-3	-0	-0.1
1884	Buf-N	0	1	.000	4	0	0	0	1	12^2	7	0	1	3	5.7	2.84	111	.175	.195	162	.347	2	0	0	-0	0.1
Total	2	0	1	.000	6	0	0	0	2	19^2	17	0	2	4	8.7	4.12	77	.250	.271	2304	.310	2	-2	-2	-1	0.0

YEAR	TM/L	W	L	PCT	G	GS	CG	SH	SV	IP	H	HR	BB	SO	RAT	ERA	ERA+	OAV	OOB	BH	AVG	PB	PR	/A	PD	TPI
● **MIKE O'ROURKE** O'Rourke, Michael J. Deb: 9/1/1890																										
1890	Bal-a	1	2	.333	5	5	5	0	0	41	45	0	10	8	12.7	3.95	103	.271	.324	3	.115	-1	-0	0	1	0.0
● **DAVE ORR** Orr, David L. b: 9/29/1859, New York, N.Y. d: 6/2/15, Richmond Hill, N.Y. BR/TR, 5'11", 250 lbs. Deb: 5/17/1883 M♦																										
1885	NY-a	0	0	—	3	0	0	0	0	10	11	2	5	1	14.4	7.20	41	.229	.302	152	.342	2	-4	-5	-0	0.0
● **JOE ORRELL** Orrell, Forrest Gordon b: 10/6/17, National City, Cal. d: 1/12/93, Chula Vista, Cal. BR/TR, 6'4", 210 lbs. Deb: 8/12/43																										
1943	Det-A	0	0	—	10	0	0	0	1	19^1	18	0	11	2	14.4	3.72	95	.257	.373	1	.250	0	-1	-0	-0	0.0
1944	Det-A	2	1	.667	10	2	0	0	0	22^1	26	0	11	10	15.3	2.42	147	.286	.369	1	.250	0	3	3	1	0.5
1945	Det-A	2	3	.400	12	5	1	0	0	48	46	1	24	14	13.5	3.00	117	.260	.355	2	.133	-1	2	3	-0	0.1
Total	3	4	4	.500	32	7	1	0	1	89^2	90	1	46	26	14.2	3.01	117	.266	.362	4	.174	-1	4	5	0	0.6
● **PHIL ORTEGA** Ortega, Filomeno Coronado "Kemo" b: 10/7/39, Gilbert, Ariz. BR/TR, 6'2", 175 lbs. Deb: 9/10/60																										
1960	LA-N	0	0	—	3	1	0	0	0	6^1	12	1	5	4	24.2	17.05	23	.400	.486	0	.000	-0	-9	-9	0	0.0
1961	LA-N	0	2	.000	4	2	1	0	0	13	10	6	2	15	8.3	5.54	78	.208	.240	1	.250	0	-2	-2	-0	-0.2
1962	LA-N	0	2	.000	24	3	0	0	1	53^2	60	8	39	30	17.1	6.88	53	.276	.394	0	.000	-1	-17	-19	-1	-0.9
1963	LA-N	0	0	—	1	0	0	0	0	1	2	1	0	1	18.0	18.00	17	.400	.400	0	—	0	-2	-2	0	0.0
1964	LA-N	7	9	.438	34	25	4	3	1	157^1	149	22	56	107	12.1	4.00	81	.249	.320	6	.136	-0	-8	-13	-2	-1.6
1965	Was-A	12	15	.444	35	29	4	2	0	179^2	176	33	97	88	13.9	5.11	68	.262	.359	11	.208	4	-33	-33	-1	-4.1
1966	Was-A	12	12	.500	33	31	5	1	0	197^1	158	29	53	121	9.9	3.92	88	.218	.276	3	.056	-2	-11	-10	-1	-1.5
1967	Was-A	10	10	.500	34	34	5	2	0	219^2	189	16	57	122	10.3	3.03	104	.231	.286	4	.061	-3	5	3	-1	-0.1
1968	Was-A	5	12	.294	31	16	1	1	0	115^2	115	12	62	57	14.2	4.98	59	.263	.361	4	.167	1	-26	-27	-0	-3.6
1969	Cal-A	0	0	—	5	0	0	0	0	8	13	3	7	4	22.5	10.13	34	.333	.435	0	—	0	-6	-6	0	0.0
Total	10	46	62	.426	204	141	20	9	2	951^2	884	131	378	549	12.2	4.43	75	.246	.323	29	.115	-1	-109	-117	-6	-12.0
● **AL ORTH** Orth, Albert Lewis "Smiling Al" or "The Curveless Wonder" b: 9/5/1872, Tipton, Ind. d: 10/8/48, Lynchburg, Va. BL/TR, 6', 200 lbs. Deb: 8/15/1895 U♦																										
1895	Phi-N	8	1	.889	11	10	9	0	1	88	103	0	22	25	13.0	3.89	123	.288	.332	16	.356	4	9	9	-2	0.9
1896	Phi-N	15	10	.600	25	23	19	0	0	196	244	10	46	23	13.5	4.41	98	.302	.342	21	.256	3	-1	-2	1	0.1
1897	Phi-N	14	19	.424	36	34	29	2	0	282^1	349	12	82	64	13.9	4.62	91	.301	.350	50	.329	7	-10	-13	1	-0.4
1898	Phi-N	15	13	.536	32	28	25	1	0	250	290	2	53	52	12.6	3.02	114	.288	.329	36	.293	8	16	11	0	2.0
1899	Phi-N	14	3	.824	21	15	13	3	1	144^2	149	0	19	35	10.6	**2.49**	148	.266	.294	13	.210	1	22	19	-4	1.6
1900	Phi-N	14	14	.500	33	30	24	2	1	262	302	4	60	68	12.9	3.78	96	.288	.335	40	.310	7	-2	-5	1	0.3
1901	Phi-N	20	12	.625	35	33	30	**6**	1	281^2	250	3	32	92	**9.3**	2.27	150	.237	**.264**	36	.281	5	33	35	3	**4.8**
1902	Was-A	19	18	.514	38	37	36	1	0	324	367	18	40	76	11.6	3.97	93	.286	.312	38	.217	1	-14	-10	1	-0.6
1903	Was-A	10	22	.313	36	32	30	2	**2**	279^2	326	8	62	88	12.7	4.34	72	.290	.331	49	.302	9	-43	-38	-0	-2.8
1904	Was-A	3	4	.429	10	7	7	0	0	73^2	88	2	15	23	13.0	4.76	56	.297	.338	22	.216	0	-18	-17	0	-1.4
	NY-A	11	6	.647	20	18	11	2	0	137^2	122	0	19	47	9.4	2.68	101	.238	.270	19	.297	3	-1	0	1	0.5
	Yr	14	10	.583	30	25	18	2	0	211^1	210	2	34	70	10.5	3.41	79	.259	.291	41	.247	3	-19	-17	1	-0.9
1905	NY-A	18	16	.529	40	37	26	6	0	305^1	273	8	61	121	10.1	2.86	103	.241	.284	24	.183	-1	-7	3	-0	0.1
1906	NY-A	**27**	17	.614	45	39	**36**	3	0	**338^2**	317	2	66	133	10.2	2.34	127	.251	.289	37	.274	6	13	24	-1	**3.7**
1907	NY-A	14	21	.400	36	33	21	2	0	248^2	244	2	53	78	11.0	2.61	107	.259	.303	34	.324	7	-2	5	2	1.9
1908	NY-A	2	13	.133	21	17	8	1	0	139^1	134	4	30	22	10.9	3.42	72	.255	.300	20	.290	5	-16	-15	-1	-1.1
1909	NY-A	0	0	—	1	1	0	0	0	3	6	0	1	1	21.0	12.00	21	.429	.467	9	.265	0	-3	-3	-0	0.0
Total	15	204	189	.519	440	394	324	31	6	3354^2	3564	75	661	948	11.6	3.37	101	.272	.311	464	.273	63	-24	15	2	9.6
● **BABY ORTIZ** Ortiz, Oliverio (Nunez) b: 12/5/19, Camaguey, Cuba d: 3/27/84, Central Senado, Camaguey, Cuba BR/TR, 6', 190 lbs. Deb: 9/23/44 F																										
1944	Was-A	0	2	.000	2	2	1	0	0	13	13	0	6	4	13.2	6.23	52	.255	.333	1	.167	-0	-4	-4	-1	-0.6
● **RUSS ORTIZ** Ortiz, Russell Reid b: 6/5/74, Van Nuys, Cal. BR/TR, 6'1", 200 lbs. Deb: 4/2/98																										
1998	SF-N	4	4	.500	22	13	0	0	0	88^1	90	11	46	75	14.3	4.99	81	.269	.364	7	.280	3	-7	-9	1	-0.4
● **OSSIE ORWOLL** Orwoll, Oswald Christian b: 11/17/1900, Portland, Ore. d: 5/8/67, Decorah, Iowa BL/TL, 6', 174 lbs. Deb: 4/13/28 ♦																										
1928	Phi-A	6	5	.545	27	8	3	0	2	106	110	7	50	53	13.8	4.58	87	.274	.358	52	.306	7	-6	-7	-0	-0.3
1929	Phi-A	0	2	.000	12	0	0	0	1	30	32	6	6	12	11.4	4.80	88	.278	.314	13	.255	1	-2	-2	-0	-0.1
Total	2	6	7	.462	39	8	3	0	3	136	142	13	56	65	13.2	4.63	88	.275	.348	65	.294	7	-8	-9	-1	-0.4
● **OZZIE OSBORN** Osborn, Danny Leon b: 6/19/46, Springfield, Mo. BR/TR, 6'2", 195 lbs. Deb: 4/26/75																										
1975	Chi-A	3	0	1.000	24	0	0	0	0	58	57	2	37	38	14.9	4.50	86	.265	.378	0	—	0	-5	-4	-1	-0.4
● **BOB OSBORN** Osborn, John Bode b: 4/17/03, San Diego, Tex. d: 4/19/60, Paris, Ark. BR/TR, 6'1", 175 lbs. Deb: 9/16/25																										
1925	Chi-N	0	0	—	1	0	0	0	0	2	6	0	0	0	27.0	0.00	—	.600	.600	0	—	0	1	1	0	0.0
1926	Chi-N	6	5	.545	31	15	6	0	1	136^1	157	3	58	43	14.2	3.63	106	.301	.371	6	.146	-3	3	3	2	0.2
1927	Chi-N	5	5	.500	24	12	2	0	0	107^2	125	2	48	45	14.5	4.18	92	.294	.367	8	.205	-0	-3	-4	-1	-0.4
1929	Chi-N	0	0	—	3	1	0	0	0	9	8	0	2	1	10.0	3.00	154	.242	.286	1	.250	0	2	2	-0	0.0
1930	Chi-N	10	6	.625	35	13	3	0	1	126^2	147	9	53	42	14.3	4.97	98	.300	.369	4	.095	-5	-0	-1	2	-0.4
1931	Pit-N	6	1	.857	27	2	0	0	0	64^2	85	3	20	9	14.8	5.01	77	.316	.366	3	.167	-0	-8	-8	-1	-0.9
Total	6	27	17	.614	121	43	11	0	2	446^1	528	17	181	140	14.4	4.32	97	.302	.368	22	.153	-8	-6	-7	2	-1.5
● **DONOVAN OSBORNE** Osborne, Donovan Alan b: 6/21/69, Roseville, Cal. BB/TL, 6'2", 195 lbs. Deb: 4/9/92																										
1992	StL-N	11	9	.550	34	29	0	0	0	179	193	14	38	104	11.7	3.77	90	.275	.314	7	.121	-1	-5	-8	-3	-1.2
1993	StL-N	10	7	.588	26	26	1	0	0	155^2	153	18	47	83	12.0	3.76	105	.257	.319	10	.204	2	5	4	0	0.5
1995	StL-N	4	6	.400	19	19	0	0	0	113^1	112	17	34	82	11.8	3.81	110	.260	.318	5	.161	2	5	5	-0	0.5
1996	*StL-N	13	9	.591	30	30	2	1	0	198^2	191	22	57	134	11.3	3.53	118	.254	.307	13	.220	4	15	14	-2	1.6
1997	StL-N	3	7	.300	14	14	0	0	0	80^1	84	10	23	51	12.1	4.93	84	.274	.326	5	.208	1	-7	-7	-0	-0.7
1998	StL-N	5	4	.556	14	14	1	1	0	83^2	84	11	22	60	11.5	4.09	102	.256	.305	1	.040	-1	1	1	-1	-0.1
Total	6	46	42	.523	137	132	4	2	0	810^2	817	92	221	514	11.7	3.86	102	.262	.314	41	.167	6	14	9	-6	0.6
● **TINY OSBORNE** Osborne, Earnest Preston b: 4/9/1893, Porterdale, Ga. d: 1/5/69, Atlanta, Ga. BL/TR, 6'4.5", 215 lbs. Deb: 4/15/22 F																										
1922	Chi-N	9	5	.643	41	14	7	1	3	184	183	7	95	81	14.2	4.50	93	.271	.370	9	.134	-4	-8	-6	-3	-1.0
1923	Chi-N	8	15	.348	37	25	8	1	1	179^2	174	14	89	69	13.3	4.56	88	.255	.342	12	.200	-1	-11	-11	-1	-1.4
1924	Chi-N	0	0	—	2	0	0	0	1	3	3	0	2	2	15.0	3.00	130	.300	.417	0	—	0	0	0	0	0.0
	Bro-N	6	5	.545	21	13	6	0	0	104^1	123	1	54	52	15.6	5.09	74	.298	.384	9	.250	1	-14	-16	-1	-1.4
	Yr	6	5	.545	23	13	6	0	1	107^1	126	1	56	54	15.6	5.03	75	.298	.385	9	.250	1	-14	-15	-1	-1.4
1925	Bro-N	8	15	.348	41	22	10	0	1	175	210	9	75	59	14.9	4.94	85	.304	.375	14	.246	1	-13	-15	-2	-1.6
Total	4	31	40	.437	142	74	31	2	6	646	693	31	315	263	14.3	4.72	86	.280	.367	44	.200	-3	-46	-47	-6	-5.4
● **FRED OSBORNE** Osborne, Frederick W. b: Hampton, Iowa TL, Deb: 7/14/1890 ♦																										
1890	Pit-N	0	5	.000	8	5	5	0	0	58	82	6	45	14	20.8	8.38	39	.323	.438	40	.238	1	-31	-33	-0	-2.0
● **WAYNE OSBORNE** Osborne, Wayne Harold "Ossie" or "Fish Hook" b: 10/11/12, Watsonville, Cal. d: 3/13/87, Vancouver, Wash. BL/TR, 6'2.5", 172 lbs. Deb: 4/18/35																										
1935	Pit-N	0	0	—	2	0	0	0	0	1^1	1	0	0	1	6.8	6.75	61	.250	.250	0	—	0	-0	-0	0	0.0
1936	Bos-N	1	1	.500	5	3	0	0	0	20	31	1	9	8	18.0	5.85	66	.352	.412	2	.250	0	-4	-4	0	-0.4
Total	2	1	1	.500	7	3	0	0	0	21^1	32	1	9	9	17.3	5.91	65	.348	.406	2	.250	0	-4	-5	0	-0.4
● **PAT OSBURN** Osburn, Larry Patrick b: 5/4/49, Murray, Ky. BL/TL, 6'4", 195 lbs. Deb: 4/13/74																										
1974	Cin-N	0	0	—	6	0	0	0	0	9	11	2	4	4	15.0	8.00	44	.297	.366	0	.000	-0	-4	-5	0	0.0
1975	Mil-A	0	1	.000	6	1	0	0	0	11^2	19	2	9	1	23.1	5.40	71	.404	.517	0	—	0	-2	-2	0	-0.2
Total	2	0	1	.000	12	1	0	0	0	20^2	30	4	13	5	19.6	6.53	56	.357	.455	0	.000	-0	-6	-7	1	-0.2
● **CHARLIE OSGOOD** Osgood, Charles Benjamin b: 11/23/26, Somerville, Mass. BR/TR, 5'10", 180 lbs. Deb: 6/18/44																										
1944	Bro-N	0	0	—	1	0	0	0	0	3	2	0	3	0	18.0	3.00	118	.222	.462	0	—	0	0	0	-0	0.0

YEAR	TM/L	W	L	PCT	G	GS	CG	SH	SV	IP	H	HR	BB	SO	RAT	ERA	ERA+	OAV	OOB	BH	AVG	PB	PR	/A	PD	TPI
● **DAN OSINSKI**	Osinski, Daniel b: 11/17/33, Chicago, Ill. BR/TR, 6'2", 195 lbs. Deb: 4/11/62																									
1962	KC-A	0	0	—	4	0	0	0	0	4^{2}	8	1	8	4	30.9	17.36	24	.381	.552	0	—	0	-7	-7	0	0.0
	LA-A	6	4	.600	33	0	0	0	4	54^{1}	45	3	30	44	12.4	2.82	137	.223	.323	0	.000	-1	7	6	0	1.1
	Yr	6	4	.600	37	0	0	0	4	59	53	4	38	48	13.9	3.97	98	.237	.347	0	.000	-1	0	-1	0	1.1
1963	LA-A	8	8	.500	47	16	4	1	0	159^{1}	145	15	80	100	12.8	3.28	105	.242	.333	5	.111	-2	6	3	-1	-0.1
1964	LA-A	3	3	.500	47	4	1	1	2	93	87	8	39	88	12.4	3.48	94	.244	.322	1	.056	-1	1	-2	1	-0.1
1965	Mil-N	0	3	.000	61	0	0	0	6	83	81	4	40	54	13.2	2.82	125	.261	.348	1	.167	-0	7	6	-0	0.3
1966	Bos-A	4	3	.571	44	1	0	0	2	67^{1}	68	8	28	44	13.0	3.61	105	.274	.350	2	.333	0	-1	1	-1	0.1
1967	*Bos-A	3	1	.750	34	0	0	0	2	63^{2}	61	5	14	38	10.6	2.54	137	.243	.283	3	.333	1	5	7	-0	0.5
1969	Chi-A	5	5	.500	51	0	0	0	2	60^{2}	56	3	23	27	11.7	3.56	108	.251	.321	0	.000	-0	0	2	2	0.5
1970	Hou-N	0	1	.000	3	0	0	0	0	3^{2}	5	0	2	1	17.2	9.82	39	.357	.438	0	—	0	-2	-2	-0	-0.5
Total	8	29	28	.509	324	21	5	2	18	589^{2}	556	47	264	400	12.6	3.34	107	.250	.331	12	.122	-3	16	15	1	1.8
● **CLAUDE OSTEEN**	Osteen, Claude Wilson b: 8/9/39, Caney Spring, Tenn. BL/TL, 5'11", 173 lbs. Deb: 7/6/57 C																									
1957	Cin-N	0	0	—	3	0	0	0	0	4	4	0	3	3	15.8	2.25	183	.250	.368	0	.000	-0	1	1	-0	0.0
1959	Cin-N	0	0	—	2	0	0	0	0	7^{2}	11	1	9	3	23.5	7.04	58	.333	.476	0	.000	-0	-3	-3	-0	0.0
1960	Cin-N	0	1	.000	20	3	0	0	0	48^{1}	53	5	30	15	15.6	5.03	76	.293	.396	1	.083	-1	-7	-6	0	-0.2
1961	Cin-N	0	0	—	1	0	0	0	0	0^{1}	0	0	0	0	0.0	0.00	—	.000	.000	0	—	0	0	0	0	0.0
	Was-A	1	1	.500	3	3	0	0	0	18^{1}	14	3	9	14	11.8	4.91	82	.219	.324	1	.143	-0	-2	-2	-0	-0.2
1962	Was-A	8	13	.381	28	22	7	2	1	150^{1}	140	12	47	59	11.4	3.65	111	.246	.309	10	.208	1	5	6	0	1.0
1963	Was-A	9	14	.391	40	29	8	2	0	212^{1}	222	23	60	109	12.0	3.35	111	.270	.320	12	.171	1	7	9	-1	0.8
1964	Was-A	15	13	.536	37	36	13	0	0	257	256	20	64	133	11.3	3.33	111	.259	.306	14	.156	1	8	11	2	1.5
1965	*LA-N	15	15	.500	40	40	9	1	0	287	253	19	78	162	10.5	2.79	117	.236	.290	12	.121	-1	24	15	6	2.0
1966	*LA-N	17	14	.548	39	38	8	3	0	240^{1}	238	6	65	137	11.4	2.85	116	.261	.312	16	.211	6	20	12	1	2.2
1967	LA-N☆	17	17	.500	39	39	14	5	0	288^{1}	298	19	52	152	11.0	3.22	96	.270	.304	18	.178	6	5	-4	-0	0.2
1968	LA-N	12	18	.400	39	36	5	3	0	253^{2}	267	14	54	119	11.6	3.09	90	.275	.316	15	.179	2	-3	-9	1	-0.7
1969	LA-N	20	15	.571	41	41	16	7	0	321	293	17	74	183	10.5	2.66	125	.245	.293	24	.216	6	33	24	3	3.5
1970	LA-N★	16	14	.533	37	37	11	4	0	258^{2}	280	24	52	114	11.7	3.83	100	.276	.313	19	.204	5	6	0	-1	0.4
1971	LA-N	14	11	.560	38	38	11	4	0	259	262	25	63	109	11.4	3.51	92	.266	.312	16	.186	2	-1	-8	6	0.1
1972	LA-N	20	11	.645	33	33	14	4	0	252	232	16	69	100	10.9	2.64	126	.245	.299	24	.273	10	23	19	-0	3.5
1973	LA-N★	16	11	.593	33	33	12	3	0	236^{2}	227	20	61	86	11.0	3.31	104	.258	.307	12	.154	-1	9	3	2	0.5
1974	Hou-N	9	9	.500	23	21	7	2	0	138^{1}	158	8	47	45	13.5	3.71	93	.292	.351	13	.283	3	-1	-4	0	-0.1
	StL-N	0	2	.000	8	2	0	0	0	22^{2}	26	1	11	6	14.7	4.37	82	.286	.363	0	.000	-1	-2	-2	0	-0.2
	Yr	9	11	.450	31	23	7	2	0	161	184	9	58	51	13.5	3.80	92	.288	.347	13	.245	3	-3	-6	0	-0.3
1975	Chi-A	7	16	.304	37	37	5	0	0	204^{1}	237	16	92	63	14.6	4.36	89	.294	.367	0	—	0	-13	-11	1	-1.1
Total	18	196	195	.501	541	488	140	40	1	3460^{1}	3471	249	940	1612	11.6	3.30	104	.263	.314	207	.188	38	110	50	20	13.2
● **DARRELL OSTEEN**	Osteen, Milton Darrell b: 2/14/43, Oklahoma City, Okla. BR/TR, 6'1", 170 lbs. Deb: 9/2/65																									
1965	Cin-N	0	0	—	3	0	0	0	0	3	2	0	4	1	18.0	0.00	—	.200	.429	0	—	0	1	1	0	0.0
1966	Cin-N	0	2	.000	13	0	0	0	1	15	26	3	9	17	21.0	12.00	33	.371	.443	1	.500	0	-14	-13	-0	-1.8
1967	Cin-N	0	2	.000	10	0	0	0	2	14^{1}	10	1	13	13	16.3	6.28	60	.196	.388	0	.000	-0	-5	-4	0	-0.6
1970	Oak-A	1	0	1.000	3	1	0	0	0	5^{2}	9	0	3	3	19.1	6.35	56	.346	.414	0	.000	-0	-2	-2	-0	-0.3
Total	4	1	4	.200	29	1	0	0	3	38	47	4	29	34	18.7	8.05	47	.299	.418	1	.200	-0	-19	-18	-0	-2.7
● **FRED OSTENDORF**	Ostendorf, Frederick K. b: 8/5/1890, Baltimore, Md. d: 3/2/65, Kecoughtan, Va. BL/TL, 6'0.5", 169 lbs. Deb: 7/16/14																									
1914	Ind-F	0	0	—	1	0	0	0	0	2	5	0	2	0	36.0	22.50	14	.500	.615	0	.000	-0	-4	-4	0	0.0
● **BILL OSTER**	Oster, William Charles b: 1/2/33, New York, N.Y. BL/TL, 6'3", 198 lbs. Deb: 8/23/54																									
1954	Phi-A	0	1	.000	8	1	0	0	0	15^{2}	19	2	12	5	17.8	6.32	62	.311	.425	1	.333	0	-5	-4	-0	-0.2
● **FRITZ OSTERMUELLER**	Ostermueller, Frederick Raymond b: 9/15/07, Quincy, Ill. d: 12/17/57, Quincy, Ill. BL/TL, 5'11", 175 lbs. Deb: 4/21/34																									
1934	Bos-A	10	13	.435	33	23	10	0	3	198^{2}	200	7	99	75	13.6	3.49	138	.262	.348	13	.167	-2	22	29	3	3.1
1935	Bos-A	7	8	.467	22	19	10	0	1	137^{2}	135	0	78	41	14.1	3.92	121	.257	.356	14	.286	1	8	13	-0	1.3
1936	Bos-A	10	16	.385	43	23	7	1	2	180^{2}	210	8	84	90	14.8	4.88	109	.288	.364	15	.234	0	3	9	3	1.3
1937	Bos-A	3	7	.300	25	7	2	0	1	86^{2}	101	2	44	29	15.2	4.98	95	.286	.367	11	.333	3	-4	-2	0	0.0
1938	Bos-A	13	5	.722	31	18	10	1	2	176^{2}	199	15	58	46	13.2	4.58	108	.275	.331	16	.216	2	4	7	-0	0.7
1939	Bos-A	11	7	.611	34	20	8	0	4	159^{1}	173	6	58	61	13.2	4.24	112	.277	.341	9	.161	-2	7	9	-1	0.7
1940	Bos-A	5	9	.357	31	16	5	0	0	143^{2}	166	7	70	80	14.8	4.95	91	.284	.361	17	.315	4	-9	-7	-1	-0.4
1941	StL-A	0	3	.000	15	2	0	0	0	46	45	3	23	20	13.3	4.50	96	.257	.343	3	.214	0	-2	-1	0	0.0
1942	StL-A	3	1	.750	10	4	2	0	0	43^{2}	46	4	17	21	13.0	3.71	100	.266	.332	3	.188	-0	-0	-0	-1	-0.1
1943	StL-A	0	2	.000	11	3	0	0	0	28^{2}	36	1	13	4	15.4	5.02	66	.321	.392	2	.286	0	-5	-5	0	-0.3
	Bro-N	1	1	.500	7	1	0	0	0	27^{1}	21	0	12	15	10.9	3.29	102	.212	.297	0	.000	-1	0	0	-0	-0.2
1944	Bro-N	2	1	.667	10	4	3	0	1	41^{2}	46	3	12	17	12.5	3.24	110	.267	.315	2	.154	-0	2	1	-0	0.0
	Pit-N	11	7	.611	28	24	14	1	1	204^{2}	201	7	65	80	11.7	2.73	136	.260	.318	20	.250	2	20	23	-1	2.0
	Yr	13	8	.619	38	28	17	1	2	246^{1}	247	10	77	97	11.9	2.81	131	.261	.317	22	.237	2	22	24	-1	2.0
1945	Pit-N	5	4	.556	14	11	4	1	0	80^{2}	74	6	37	29	12.6	4.57	86	.236	.321	9	.321	2	-7	-6	0	-0.3
1946	Pit-N	13	10	.565	27	25	16	2	0	193^{1}	193	5	56	57	11.7	2.84	124	.263	.318	21	.328	6	12	15	-2	2.3
1947	Pit-N	12	10	.545	26	24	12	3	0	183	181	18	68	66	12.3	3.84	110	.254	.320	12	.188	1	5	8	1	0.7
1948	Pit-N	8	11	.421	23	22	10	2	0	134^{1}	143	13	41	43	12.4	4.42	92	.262	.315	8	.182	-0	-7	-5	-1	-0.8
Total	15	114	115	.498	390	246	113	11	15	2066^{2}	2170	105	835	774	13.2	3.99	109	.268	.337	175	.234	16	49	85	-3	10.0
● **JOE OSTROWSKI**	Ostrowski, Joseph Paul "Professor" or "Specs" b: 11/15/16, W.Wyoming, Pa. BL/TL, 6', 180 lbs. Deb: 7/18/48																									
1948	StL-A	4	6	.400	26	9	3	0	3	78^{1}	108	6	17	20	14.4	5.97	76	.333	.367	4	.222	1	-15	-12	2	-1.2
1949	StL-A	8	8	.500	40	13	4	0	2	141	185	16	27	34	13.5	4.79	95	.307	.337	7	.189	2	-9	-4	-1	-0.3
1950	StL-A	2	4	.333	9	7	2	0	0	57^{1}	57	2	7	15	10.0	2.51	197	.251	.274	4	.222	1	13	16	-1	1.6
	NY-A	1	1	.500	21	4	1	0	3	43^{2}	50	11	15	15	13.4	5.15	83	.294	.351	1	.111	-0	-3	-4	0	-0.2
	Yr	3	5	.375	30	11	3	0	3	101	107	13	22	30	11.5	3.65	128	.270	.308	5	.185	1	10	11	-1	1.4
1951	*NY-A	6	4	.600	34	3	2	0	5	95^{1}	103	4	18	30	11.5	3.49	110	.279	.314	3	.107	-2	7	4	-1	0.1
1952	NY-A	2	2	.500	20	1	0	0	2	40	56	5	14	17	16.0	5.62	59	.327	.382	0	.000	-1	-9	-10	-1	-1.2
Total	5	23	25	.479	150	37	12	0	15	455^{2}	559	44	98	131	13.0	4.54	95	.300	.336	19	.161	1	-16	-12	-1	-1.2
● **AL OSUNA**	Osuna, Alfonso b: 8/10/65, Inglewood, Cal. BR/TL, 6'3", 200 lbs. Deb: 9/2/90																									
1990	Hou-N	2	0	1.000	12	0	0	0	0	11^{1}	10	1	6	6	15.1	4.76	78	.270	.413	0	—	0	-1	-1	-0	-0.2
1991	Hou-N	7	6	.538	71	0	0	0	12	81^{2}	59	5	46	68	11.9	3.42	103	.201	.316	0	.000	-0	2	1	-0	0.1
1992	Hou-N	6	3	.667	66	0	0	0	0	61^{2}	52	8	38	37	13.3	4.23	79	.236	.351	0	—	0	-5	-6	0	-0.8
1993	Hou-N	1	1	.500	44	0	0	0	2	25^{1}	17	3	13	21	11.0	3.20	121	.200	.313	0	—	0	2	2	-1	0.1
1994	LA-N	2	0	1.000	15	0	0	0	0	8^{2}	13	0	4	7	17.7	6.23	63	.333	.395	0	—	0	-2	-2	-0	-0.5
1996	SD-N	0	0	—	10	0	0	0	0	4	5	0	2	4	18.0	2.25	176	.313	.421	0	.000	-0	1	1	0	0.0
Total	6	18	10	.643	218	0	0	0	14	192^{2}	156	17	109	143	12.8	3.83	93	.226	.339	0	.000	-0	-2	-6	-1	-1.3
● **ANTONIO OSUNA**	Osuna, Antonio Pedro b: 4/12/73, Sinaloa, Mexico BR/TR, 5'11", 160 lbs. Deb: 4/25/95																									
1995	*LA-N	2	4	.333	39	0	0	0	0	44^{2}	39	5	20	46	12.1	4.43	86	.241	.328	0	.000	-0	-1	-3	0	-0.4
1996	*LA-N	9	6	.600	73	0	0	0	4	84	65	6	32	85	10.6	3.00	129	.220	.300	0	.000	0	11	8	0	1.4
1997	LA-N	3	4	.429	48	0	0	0	0	61^{2}	46	6	19	68	9.6	2.19	176	.209	.275	1	.500	0	14	11	1	1.3
1998	LA-N	7	1	.875	54	0	0	0	6	64^{2}	50	8	32	72	11.7	3.06	127	.214	.313	0	.000	-0	8	6	0	0.7
Total	4	21	15	.583	214	0	0	0	10	255	200	25	103	271	10.9	3.07	126	.219	.303	1	.143	0	32	22	1	3.0
● **BILL OTEY**	Otey, William Tilford "Steamboat Bill" b: 12/16/1886, Dayton, Ohio d: 4/23/31, Dayton, Ohio BL/TL, 6'2", 181 lbs. Deb: 9/27/07																									
1907	Pit-N	0	1	.000	3	2	1	0	0	16^{1}	23	1	4	5	15.4	4.41	55	.319	.364	1	.250	0	-4	-4	-0	-0.3
1910	Was-A	0	1	.000	9	1	1	0	0	34^{2}	40	1	6	12	12.2	3.38	74	.301	.336	5	.385	2	-3	-3	-1	0.0

YEAR	TM/L	W	L	PCT	G	GS	CG	SH	SV	IP	H	HR	BB	SO	RAT	ERA	ERA+	OAV	OOB	BH	AVG	PB	PR	/A	PD	TPI
1911	Was-A	1	3	.250	12	2	0	0	0	49^{2}	68	2	15	16	15.6	6.34	52	.333	.387	1	.059	-2	-17	-17	1	-1.2
Total	3	1	5	.167	24	5	2	0	0	100^{2}	131	4	25	33	14.4	5.01	57	.320	.367	7	.206	0	-23	-24	-1	-1.5

● HARRY OTIS

Otis, Harry George "Cannonball" b: 10/5/1886, W.New York, N.J. d: 1/29/76, Teaneck, N.J. BR/TL, 6' ", 180 lbs. Deb: 9/5/09

YEAR	TM/L	W	L	PCT	G	GS	CG	SH	SV	IP	H	HR	BB	SO	RAT	ERA	ERA+	OAV	OOB	BH	AVG	PB	PR	/A	PD	TPI
1909	Cle-A	2	2	.500	5	3	0	0	0	26^{1}	26	0	18	6	16.1	1.37	187	.283	.416	1	.111	-0	3	3	-0	0.5

● DENNIS O'TOOLE

O'Toole, Dennis Joseph b: 3/13/49, Chicago, Ill. BR/TR, 6'3", 195 lbs. Deb: 9/8/69 F

YEAR	TM/L	W	L	PCT	G	GS	CG	SH	SV	IP	H	HR	BB	SO	RAT	ERA	ERA+	OAV	OOB	BH	AVG	PB	PR	/A	PD	TPI
1969	Chi-A	0	0	—	2	0	0	0	0	4	5	0	2	4	15.8	6.75	57	.333	.412	0	—	0	-1	-1	-0	0.0
1970	Chi-A	0	0	—	3	0	0	0	0	3^{1}	5	0	2	3	18.9	2.70	144	.357	.438	0	—	0	0	0	-0	0.0
1971	Chi-A	0	0	—	1	0	0	0	0	2	0	0	1	2	4.5	0.00	—	.000	.143	0	—	0	1	1	-0	0.0
1972	Chi-A	0	0	—	3	0	0	0	0	5	10	0	2	5	21.6	5.40	58	.417	.462	0	—	0	-1	-1	0	0.0
1973	Chi-A	0	0	—	6	0	0	0	0	16	23	3	3	8	14.6	5.63	70	.329	.356	0	—	0	-3	-3	0	-0.2
Total	5	0	0	—	15	0	0	0	0	30^{1}	43	3	10	22	15.7	5.04	75	.333	.381	0	—	0	-5	-4	-0	-0.2

● JIM O'TOOLE

O'Toole, James Jerome b: 1/10/37, Chicago, Ill. BB/TL, 6', 198 lbs. Deb: 9/26/58 F

YEAR	TM/L	W	L	PCT	G	GS	CG	SH	SV	IP	H	HR	BB	SO	RAT	ERA	ERA+	OAV	OOB	BH	AVG	PB	PR	/A	PD	TPI
1958	Cin-N	0	1	.000	1	1	0	0	0	7	4	0	5	4	11.6	1.29	322	.154	.290	0	.000	-0	2	2	-0	0.3
1959	Cin-N	5	8	.385	28	19	3	1	0	129^{1}	144	14	73	68	15.4	5.15	79	.287	.382	5	.135	-0	-17	-16	1	-1.4
1960	Cin-N	12	12	.500	34	31	7	2	1	196^{1}	198	14	66	124	12.3	3.80	100	.263	.325	7	.106	-3	-1	0	-3	-0.6
1961	*Cin-N	19	9	.679	39	35	11	3	2	252^{2}	229	16	93	178	11.6	3.10	131	.240	.310	16	.172	-1	26	27	-0	2.7
1962	Cin-N	16	13	.552	36	34	11	3	0	251^{2}	222	20	87	170	11.2	3.50	115	.238	.307	10	.110	-5	12	15	-2	0.8
1963	Cin-N★	17	14	.548	33	32	12	5	0	234^{1}	208	13	57	146	10.3	2.88	116	.239	.288	11	.149	-1	11	12	-3	1.2
1964	Cin-N	17	7	.708	30	30	9	3	0	220	194	8	51	145	10.0	2.66	136	.235	.279	7	.100	-1	21	23	-2	2.2
1965	Cin-N	3	10	.231	29	22	2	0	1	127^{2}	154	14	47	71	14.4	5.92	63	.294	.355	4	.089	-2	-34	-31	-2	-3.2
1966	Cin-N	5	7	.417	25	24	2	0	0	142	139	16	49	96	12.1	3.55	110	.254	.318	6	.128	-2	1	6	-1	0.2
1967	Chi-A	4	3	.571	15	10	1	1	0	54^{1}	53	4	18	37	11.9	2.82	110	.251	.313	1	.077	-1	3	2	-1	0.1
Total	10	98	84	.538	270	238	58	18	4	1615^{1}	1545	119	546	1039	11.8	3.57	106	.251	.315	67	.125	-15	24	40	-12	2.3

● MARTY O'TOOLE

O'Toole, Martin James b: 11/27/1888, Wm.Penn, Pa. d: 2/18/49, Aberdeen, Wash. BR/TR, 5'11", 175 lbs. Deb: 9/21/08

YEAR	TM/L	W	L	PCT	G	GS	CG	SH	SV	IP	H	HR	BB	SO	RAT	ERA	ERA+	OAV	OOB	BH	AVG	PB	PR	/A	PD	TPI
1908	Cin-N	1	0	1.000	3	2	1	0	0	15	15	0	7	5	13.2	2.40	96	.273	.355	1	.200	-0	-0	-0	-0	0.0
1911	Pit-N	3	2	.600	5	5	3	0	0	38	28	1	20	34	11.4	2.37	145	.215	.320	5	.357	2	4	5	0	0.8
1912	Pit-N	15	17	.469	37	36	17	**6**	0	275^{1}	237	4	159	150	13.0	2.71	120	.241	.348	22	.222	2	21	17	1	2.0
1913	Pit-N	6	8	.429	26	16	7	0	1	144^{2}	148	3	55	58	12.8	3.30	92	.271	.341	7	.132	-2	-1	-4	-0	-0.7
1914	Pit-N	1	8	.111	19	9	1	0	1	92^{1}	92	3	47	36	13.5	4.68	57	.270	.358	5	.167	0	-19	-21	-1	-2.0
	NY-N	1	1	.500	10	5	2	0	0	34	34	0	12	13	12.2	4.24	63	.262	.324	3	.300	1	-5	-6	-0	-0.3
	Yr	2	9	.182	29	14	3	0	1	126^{1}	126	3	59	49	13.2	4.56	58	.268	.349	8	.200	1	-25	-27	-1	-2.3
Total	5	27	36	.429	100	73	31	6	2	599^{1}	554	11	300	296	12.9	3.21	95	.254	.345	43	.204	2	-1	-10	-0	-0.2

● JIM OTTEN

Otten, James Edward b: 7/1/51, Lewistown, Mont. BR/TR, 6'2", 195 lbs. Deb: 7/31/74

YEAR	TM/L	W	L	PCT	G	GS	CG	SH	SV	IP	H	HR	BB	SO	RAT	ERA	ERA+	OAV	OOB	BH	AVG	PB	PR	/A	PD	TPI
1974	Chi-A	0	1	.000	5	1	0	0	0	16^{1}	22	0	12	11	19.3	5.51	68	.324	.432	0	—	0	-3	-3	-0	-0.4
1975	Chi-A	0	0	—	2	0	0	0	0	5^{1}	4	1	7	3	18.6	6.75	57	.235	.458	0	—	0	-2	-2	0	-0.1
1976	Chi-A	0	0	—	2	0	0	0	0	6	9	0	2	3	16.5	4.50	79	.333	.379	0	—	0	-1	-1	-0	-0.1
1980	StL-N	0	5	.000	31	4	0	0	0	55^{1}	71	3	26	38	16.1	5.53	67	.323	.399	1	.200	-0	-12	-11	1	-0.9
1981	StL-N	1	0	1.000	24	0	0	0	0	35^{2}	44	3	20	20	16.1	5.30	67	.321	.408	0	.000	-0	-7	-7	-1	-0.3
Total	5	1	6	.143	64	5	0	0	0	118^{2}	150	7	67	75	16.7	5.46	67	.320	.408	1	.143	-0	-25	-24	-1	-1.8

● DAVE OTTO

Otto, David Alan b: 11/12/64, Chicago, Ill. BL/TL, 6'7", 210 lbs. Deb: 9/8/87

YEAR	TM/L	W	L	PCT	G	GS	CG	SH	SV	IP	H	HR	BB	SO	RAT	ERA	ERA+	OAV	OOB	BH	AVG	PB	PR	/A	PD	TPI
1987	Oak-A	0	0	—	3	0	0	0	0	6	7	1	1	3	12.0	9.00	46	.304	.333	0	—	0	-3	-3	-0	0.0
1988	Oak-A	0	0	—	3	2	0	0	0	10	9	0	6	7	13.5	1.80	210	.243	.349	0	—	0	2	2	0	0.2
1989	Oak-A	0	0	—	1	1	0	0	0	6^{2}	6	0	2	4	10.8	2.70	136	.261	.320	0	—	0	1	1	-0	0.0
1990	Oak-A	0	0	—	2	0	0	0	0	2^{1}	3	0	3	2	23.1	7.71	48	.300	.462	0	—	0	-1	-1	0	0.1
1991	Cle-A	2	8	.200	18	14	1	0	0	100	108	7	27	47	12.5	4.23	98	.283	.337	0	—	0	-2	-1	-0	-0.1
1992	Cle-A	5	9	.357	18	16	0	0	0	80^{1}	110	12	33	32	16.1	7.06	55	.333	.396	0	—	0	-28	-28	0	-3.9
1993	Pit-N	3	4	.429	28	8	0	0	0	68	85	9	28	30	15.4	5.03	81	.317	.388	4	.222	1	-7	-7	1	-0.5
1994	Chi-N	0	1	.000	36	0	0	0	0	45	49	4	22	19	14.4	3.80	109	.283	.367	0	.000	-0	2	2	-1	-0.1
Total	8	10	22	.313	109	41	1	0	0	318^{1}	377	33	122	144	14.4	5.06	80	.303	.369	4	.200	1	-35	-36	0	-4.3

● ORVAL OVERALL

Overall, Orval b: 2/2/1881, Farmersville, Cal. d: 7/14/47, Fresno, Cal. BB/TR, 6'2", 214 lbs. Deb: 4/16/05

YEAR	TM/L	W	L	PCT	G	GS	CG	SH	SV	IP	H	HR	BB	SO	RAT	ERA	ERA+	OAV	OOB	BH	AVG	PB	PR	/A	PD	TPI
1905	Cin-N	18	23	.439	42	39	32	2	0	318	290	4	147	173	12.8	2.86	116	.252	.343	17	.145	-2	5	16	-1	1.5
1906	Cin-N	4	5	.444	13	10	6	0	0	82^{1}	77	1	46	33	13.9	4.26	65	.253	.359	6	.194	0	-15	-14	-1	-1.5
	*Chi-N	12	3	.800	18	14	13	2	1	144	116	1	51	94	10.7	1.88	141	.217	.290	9	.170	-1	12	12	0	1.2
	Yr	16	8	.667	31	24	19	2	1	226^{1}	193	2	97	127	11.7	2.74	98	.229	.311	15	.179	-1	-3	-2	-1	-0.3
1907	*Chi-N	23	7	.767	36	30	26	**8**	3	268^{1}	201	3	69	141	9.4	1.68	149	.208	.268	20	.213	3	24	24	2	3.5
1908	*Chi-N	15	11	.577	37	27	16	4	4	225	165	3	78	167	9.8	1.92	123	.208	.280	9	.129	-0	11	11	-1	1.1
1909	Chi-N	20	11	.645	38	32	23	**9**	3	285	204	1	80	**205**	9.2	1.42	179	**.198**	.262	22	.229	8	37	35	0	5.1
1910	*Chi-N	12	6	.667	23	21	11	4	1	144^{2}	106	2	54	92	10.0	2.68	108	.212	.291	5	.122	-1	6	3	1	0.5
1913	Chi-N	4	5	.444	11	9	6	1	0	68	73	1	26	30	13.2	3.31	96	.284	.352	6	.250	2	-1	-1	1	0.2
Total	7	108	71	.603	218	182	133	30	12	1535^{1}	1232	16	551	935	10.7	2.23	123	.223	.298	94	.179	9	79	86	1	11.6

● STUBBY OVERMIRE

Overmire, Frank W. b: 5/16/19, Moline, Mich. d: 3/3/77, Lakeland, Fla. BR/TL, 5'7", 170 lbs. Deb: 4/25/43 C

YEAR	TM/L	W	L	PCT	G	GS	CG	SH	SV	IP	H	HR	BB	SO	RAT	ERA	ERA+	OAV	OOB	BH	AVG	PB	PR	/A	PD	TPI
1943	Det-A	7	6	.538	29	18	8	3	1	147	135	5	38	48	10.7	3.18	111	.243	.293	7	.167	0	2	6	-1	0.4
1944	Det-A	11	11	.500	32	28	11	3	1	199^{2}	214	2	41	57	11.6	3.07	116	.271	.309	11	.175	1	8	11	2	1.4
1945	*Det-A	9	9	.500	31	22	9	0	4	162^{1}	189	6	42	36	13.0	3.88	91	.294	.341	10	.189	0	-9	-7	0	-0.7
1946	Det-A	5	7	.417	24	13	3	0	1	97^{1}	106	6	29	34	12.5	4.62	79	.274	.325	5	.152	-1	-12	-10	1	-1.2
1947	Det-A	11	5	.688	28	17	7	3	0	140^{2}	142	9	44	33	12.0	3.77	100	.259	.315	7	.149	-1	-1	-0	-0	-0.1
1948	Det-A	3	4	.429	37	4	0	0	3	66^{1}	89	5	31	14	16.3	5.97	73	.326	.395	1	.071	-1	-12	-12	1	-1.2
1949	Det-A	1	3	.250	14	1	0	0	0	17^{1}	29	2	9	3	20.3	9.87	42	.377	.448	1	.333	0	-11	-11	0	-2.0
1950	StL-A	9	12	.429	31	19	8	2	0	161	200	11	45	39	13.8	4.19	118	.298	.343	8	.167	1	7	14	-2	1.4
1951	StL-A	1	6	.143	8	7	3	0	0	53^{1}	61	5	21	13	13.8	3.54	124	.281	.345	1	.071	-1	3	5	-1	0.4
	NY-A	1	1	.500	15	4	1	0	0	44^{2}	50	2	18	14	14.1	4.63	83	.287	.361	1	.143	0	-3	-4	0	-0.1
	Yr	2	7	.222	23	11	4	0	0	98	111	7	39	27	14.0	4.04	102	.284	.352	2	.095	-0	1	1	-1	0.3
1952	StL-A	0	3	.000	17	4	0	0	0	41	44	3	7	10	11.2	3.73	105	.270	.300	2	.182	-0	-0	1	1	0.1
Total	10	58	67	.464	266	137	50	11	10	1130^{2}	1259	56	325	301	12.7	3.96	98	.280	.330	54	.161	-1	-28	-8	1	-1.6

● MIKE OVERY

Overy, Harry Michael b: 1/27/51, Clinton, Ill. BR/TR, 6'2", 190 lbs. Deb: 8/14/76

YEAR	TM/L	W	L	PCT	G	GS	CG	SH	SV	IP	H	HR	BB	SO	RAT	ERA	ERA+	OAV	OOB	BH	AVG	PB	PR	/A	PD	TPI
1976	Cal-A	0	2	.000	5	0	0	0	0	7^{1}	6	1	3	8	12.3	6.14	54	.214	.313	0	—	0	-2	-2	0	-0.1

● ERNIE OVITZ

Ovitz, Ernest Gayhart b: 10/7/1885, Mineral Point, Wis. d: 9/11/80, Green Bay, Wis. BR/TR, 5'8.5", 156 lbs. Deb: 6/22/11

YEAR	TM/L	W	L	PCT	G	GS	CG	SH	SV	IP	H	HR	BB	SO	RAT	ERA	ERA+	OAV	OOB	BH	AVG	PB	PR	/A	PD	TPI
1911	Chi-N	0	0	—	1	0	0	0	0	2	3	0	3	0	27.0	4.50	74	.375	.545	0	—	0	-0	-0	-0	0.0

● BOB OWCHINKO

Owchinko, Robert Dennis b: 1/1/55, Detroit, Mich. BL/TL, 6'2", 195 lbs. Deb: 9/25/76

YEAR	TM/L	W	L	PCT	G	GS	CG	SH	SV	IP	H	HR	BB	SO	RAT	ERA	ERA+	OAV	OOB	BH	AVG	PB	PR	/A	PD	TPI
1976	SD-N	0	2	.000	2	2	0	0	0	4^{1}	11	0	3	4	29.1	16.62	20	.478	.538	0	.000	-0	-6	-6	0	-1.7
1977	SD-N	9	12	.429	30	28	3	2	0	170	191	20	67	101	13.7	4.45	80	.287	.352	4	.082	-2	-10	-17	-2	-2.2
1978	SD-N	10	13	.435	36	33	4	1	0	202^{1}	198	14	78	94	12.3	3.56	93	.263	.333	11	.175	1	0	-5	-1	-0.5
1979	SD-N	6	12	.333	42	20	2	0	0	149^{1}	144	16	55	66	12.1	3.74	94	.259	.328	4	.121	-0	-0	-3	-0	-0.5
1980	Cle-A	2	9	.182	29	14	1	1	0	114^{1}	138	13	47	66	14.7	5.27	77	.301	.368	0	—	0	-16	-15	-0	-1.3
1981	*Oak-A	4	3	.571	29	0	0	0	2	39^{1}	34	2	19	26	12.4	3.20	109	.245	.340	0	—	0	2	1	-0	0.3
1982	Oak-A	2	4	.333	54	0	0	0	3	102	111	11	52	67	14.4	5.21	75	.275	.358	0	—	0	-13	-15	-1	-0.7
1983	Pit-N	0	0	—	1	0	0	0	0	0	2	1	0	0	—	∞	—	1.000	1.000	0	—	0	-1	-1	0	-0.1
1984	Cin-N	3	5	.375	49	4	0	0	2	94	91	10	39	60	12.4	4.12	92	.253	.327	2	.167	1	-6	-4	-1	-0.3
1986	Mon-N	1	0	1.000	3	3	0	0	0	15	17	1	3	6	12.0	3.60	103	.288	.323	1	.200	0	0	0	-0	0.0
Total	10	37	60	.381	275	104	10	4	7	890^{2}	937	88	363	490	13.2	4.28	85	.274	.345	22	.135	-0	-49	-66	-5	-7.0

● FRANK OWEN Owen, Frank Malcolm "Yip" b: 12/23/1879, Ypsilanti, Mich. d: 11/24/42, Dearborn, Mich. BB/TR, 5'11", 160 lbs. Deb: 4/29/01

YEAR	TM/L	W	L	PCT	G	GS	CG	SH	SV	IP	H	HR	BB	SO	RAT	ERA	ERA+	OAV	OOB	BH	AVG	PB	PR	/A	PD	TPI
1901	Det-A	1	3	.250	8	5	3	0	0	56	70	1	30	17	16.7	4.34	89	.302	.391	1	.050	-2	-4	-3	2	-0.2
1903	Chi-A	8	12	.400	26	20	15	1	1	167^1	167	1	44	66	11.7	3.50	80	.259	.314	7	.123	-1	-10	-13	4	-1.2
1904	Chi-A	21	15	.583	37	36	34	4	1	315	243	2	61	103	9.0	1.94	126	.214	.261	23	.215	5	23	18	6	3.5
1905	Chi-A	21	13	.618	42	38	32	3	0	334	276	6	56	125	9.2	2.10	117	.227	.266	18	.145	-4	21	14	3	1.3
1906	*Chi-A	22	13	.629	42	36	27	7	0	293	289	4	54	66	10.7	2.33	109	.261	.298	14	.136	-2	12	7	4	1.0
1907	Chi-A	2	3	.400	11	4	2	0	0	47	43	1	13	15	10.7	2.49	96	.246	.298	4	.250	0	0	-0	1	0.0
1908	Chi-A	6	7	.462	25	14	5	1	0	140	142	2	37	48	11.7	3.41	68	.260	.310	9	.180	1	-16	-17	2	-1.3
1909	Chi-A	1	1	.500	3	2	1	0	0	16	19	0	3	3	12.9	4.50	52	.279	.319	1	.167	-0	-4	-4	-0	-0.5
Total	8	82	67	.550	194	155	119	16	2	1368^1	1249	17	298	443	10.4	2.55	100	.244	.290	77	.159	-3	22	0	22	2.6

● JIM OWENS Owens, James Philip "Bear" b: 1/16/34, Gifford, Pa. BR/TR, 5'11", 190 lbs. Deb: 4/19/55 C

YEAR	TM/L	W	L	PCT	G	GS	CG	SH	SV	IP	H	HR	BB	SO	RAT	ERA	ERA+	OAV	OOB	BH	AVG	PB	PR	/A	PD	TPI
1955	Phi-N	0	2	.000	3	2	0	0	0	8^2	13	2	7	6	20.8	8.31	48	.382	.488	0	.000	-0	-4	-4	-0	-0.8
1956	Phi-N	0	4	.000	10	5	0	0	0	29^2	35	3	22	22	17.9	7.28	51	.313	.434	1	.167	0	-12	-12	0	-1.3
1958	Phi-N	1	0	1.000	1	1	0	0	0	7	4	1	5	3	11.6	2.57	154	.154	.290	0	.000	0	1	1	-0	0.1
1959	Phi-N	12	12	.500	31	30	11	1	1	221^1	203	14	73	135	11.4	3.21	128	.244	.308	9	.120	-1	18	22	-0	2.1
1960	Phi-N	4	14	.222	31	22	6	0	0	150	182	21	64	83	14.8	5.04	77	.299	.367	3	.068	-3	-21	-19	-1	-2.5
1961	Phi-N	5	10	.333	20	17	3	0	0	106^2	119	8	32	38	12.7	4.47	91	.287	.339	2	.074	-1	-5	-5	-2	-0.9
1962	Phi-N	2	4	.333	23	12	1	0	0	69^2	90	12	33	21	15.9	6.33	61	.318	.389	2	.143	0	-18	-19	-1	-1.6
1963	Cin-N	0	2	.000	19	3	0	0	4	42^1	42	6	24	29	14.0	5.31	63	.259	.355	1	.125	0	-10	-9	1	-0.6
1964	Hou-N	8	7	.533	48	11	0	0	6	118	115	7	32	88	11.2	3.28	104	.262	.312	3	.103	-1	3	2	-1	0.0
1965	Hou-N	6	5	.545	50	0	0	0	8	71^1	64	4	29	53	11.7	3.28	102	.238	.312	1	.125	-0	2	1	-0	0.0
1966	Hou-N	4	7	.364	40	0	0	0	2	50	53	5	17	32	12.8	4.68	73	.273	.335	0	.000	-0	-6	-7	1	-1.5
1967	Hou-N	0	1	.000	10	0	0	0	0	10^2	12	1	2	6	11.8	4.22	78	.308	.341	0	—	0	-1	-1	-0	-0.1
Total	12	42	68	.382	286	103	21	1	21	885^1	932	84	340	516	13.0	4.31	88	.273	.340	22	.101	-7	-53	-51	-5	-7.1

● RICK OWNBEY Ownbey, Richard Wayne b: 10/20/57, Corona, Cal. BR/TR, 6'3", 185 lbs. Deb: 8/17/82

YEAR	TM/L	W	L	PCT	G	GS	CG	SH	SV	IP	H	HR	BB	SO	RAT	ERA	ERA+	OAV	OOB	BH	AVG	PB	PR	/A	PD	TPI
1982	NY-N	1	2	.333	8	8	2	0	0	50^1	44	3	43	28	15.6	3.75	97	.242	.387	3	.200	1	-1	-1	-1	0.0
1983	NY-N	1	3	.250	10	4	0	0	0	34^2	31	4	21	19	13.8	4.67	78	.240	.351	1	.111	-0	-4	-4	0	-0.5
1984	StL-N	0	3	.000	4	4	0	0	0	19	23	1	8	11	14.7	4.74	73	.303	.369	0	.000	-0	-2	-3	-0	-0.5
1986	StL-N	1	3	.250	17	3	0	0	0	42^2	47	4	19	25	14.3	3.80	96	.294	.376	0	.000	-1	-0	-1	-1	-0.2
Total	4	3	11	.214	39	19	2	0	0	146^2	145	12	91	83	14.7	4.11	88	.265	.373	4	.114	-1	-8	-8	-2	-1.2

● DOC OZMER Ozmer, Horace Robert b: 5/25/01, Atlanta, Ga. d: 12/28/70, Atlanta, Ga. BR/TR, 5'10.5", 185 lbs. Deb: 5/11/23

YEAR	TM/L	W	L	PCT	G	GS	CG	SH	SV	IP	H	HR	BB	SO	RAT	ERA	ERA+	OAV	OOB	BH	AVG	PB	PR	/A	PD	TPI
1923	Phi-A	0	0	—	1	0	0	0	0	2	1	0	1	1	9.0	4.50	91	.167	.286	0	—	0	-0	-0	0	0.0

● CHARLIE PABOR Pabor, Charles Henry b: 9/24/1846, New York, N.Y. d: 4/23/13, New Haven, Conn. BL/TL, 5'8", 155 lbs. Deb: 5/4/1871 M♦

YEAR	TM/L	W	L	PCT	G	GS	CG	SH	SV	IP	H	HR	BB	SO	RAT	ERA	ERA+	OAV	OOB	BH	AVG	PB	PR	/A	PD	TPI
1871	Cle-n	0	2	.000	7	1	1	0	0	29^1	50	4	6	0	17.2	6.75	61	.325	.350	42	.296	0	-8	-9		-0.3
1872	Cle-n	1	1	.500	2	2	2	0	0	18	20	0	3	0	11.5	4.00	89	.247	.274	19	.207	-0	-1	-1		-0.1
1875	Atl-n	0	1	.000	1	1	0	0	0	4	11	0	1	0	27.0	9.00	23	.407	.429	36	.235	0	-3	-3		-0.5
Total	3 n	1	4	.200	10	4	3	0	0	51^1	81	4	10	0	16.0	5.96	35	.309	.335	204	.285	-0	-21	-22		-0.9

● JOHN PACELLA Pacella, John Lewis b: 9/15/56, Brooklyn, N.Y. BR/TR, 6'3", 195 lbs. Deb: 9/15/77

YEAR	TM/L	W	L	PCT	G	GS	CG	SH	SV	IP	H	HR	BB	SO	RAT	ERA	ERA+	OAV	OOB	BH	AVG	PB	PR	/A	PD	TPI
1977	NY-N	0	0	—	3	0	0	0	0	4	2	0	2	1	9.0	0.00	—	.133	.235	0	—	0	2	2	-0	0.0
1979	NY-N	0	2	.000	4	3	0	0	0	16^1	16	0	4	12	11.0	4.41	83	.246	.290	0	.000	-0	-1	-1	-0	-0.2
1980	NY-N	3	4	.429	32	15	0	0	0	84	89	5	59	68	16.1	5.14	69	.280	.396	2	.100	-1	-14	-15	-0	-1.3
1982	NY-A	0	1	.000	3	1	0	0	0	10	13	0	9	2	20.7	7.20	55	.342	.479	0	—	0	-3	-4	-0	-0.2
	Min-A	1	2	.333	21	1	0	0	2	51^2	61	14	37	20	17.1	7.32	58	.299	.407	0	—	0	-19	-18	-1	-1.3
	Yr	1	3	.250	24	2	0	0	2	61^2	74	14	46	22	17.5	7.30	58	.301	.411	0	—	0	-22	-21	-2	-1.5
1984	Bal-A	0	1	.000	6	1	0	0	0	14^2	15	2	9	8	14.7	6.75	57	.268	.369	0	—	0	-4	-5	-0	-0.2
1986	Det-A	0	0	—	5	0	0	0	1	11	10	0	13	5	18.8	4.09	101	.294	.489	0	—	0	0	0	1	0.1
Total	6	4	10	.286	74	21	0	0	3	191^2	206	21	133	116	16.1	5.73	67	.282	.395	2	.083	-1	-40	-41	-2	-3.1

● ALEX PACHECO Pacheco, Alexander Melchor (Lara) b: 7/19/73, Caracas, Venez. BR/TR, 6'3", 200 lbs. Deb: 4/17/96

YEAR	TM/L	W	L	PCT	G	GS	CG	SH	SV	IP	H	HR	BB	SO	RAT	ERA	ERA+	OAV	OOB	BH	AVG	PB	PR	/A	PD	TPI
1996	Mon-N	0	0	—	5	0	0	0	0	5^2	8	2	1	7	14.3	11.12	39	.320	.346	0	—	0	-4	-4	-0	0.0

● PAT PACILLO Pacillo, Patrick Michael b: 7/23/63, Jersey City, N.J. BR/TR, 6'2", 205 lbs. Deb: 5/23/87

YEAR	TM/L	W	L	PCT	G	GS	CG	SH	SV	IP	H	HR	BB	SO	RAT	ERA	ERA+	OAV	OOB	BH	AVG	PB	PR	/A	PD	TPI
1987	Cin-N	3	3	.500	12	7	0	0	0	39^2	41	7	19	23	13.8	6.13	69	.270	.355	1	.091	-0	-9	-8	-0	-1.1
1988	Cin-N	1	0	1.000	6	0	0	0	0	10^2	14	2	4	11	15.2	5.06	71	.318	.375	0	.000	-0	-2	-2	-0	-0.2
Total	2	4	3	.571	18	7	0	0	0	50^1	55	9	23	34	14.1	5.90	70	.281	.359	1	.083	-0	-11	-10	-1	-1.3

● GENE PACKARD Packard, Eugene Milo b: 7/13/1887, Colorado Springs, Colorado d: 5/18/59, Riverside, Cal. BL/TL, 5'10", 155 lbs. Deb: 9/27/12

YEAR	TM/L	W	L	PCT	G	GS	CG	SH	SV	IP	H	HR	BB	SO	RAT	ERA	ERA+	OAV	OOB	BH	AVG	PB	PR	/A	PD	TPI
1912	Cin-N	1	0	1.000	1	1	1	0	0	9	7	0	4	2	11.0	3.00	112	.206	.289	1	.250	1	0	0	0	0.1
1913	Cin-N	7	11	.389	39	21	9	2	0	190^2	208	2	64	73	13.2	2.97	109	.286	.350	11	.180	-0	5	6	-1	0.4
1914	KC-F	20	14	.588	42	34	24	4	5	302	282	5	88	154	11.1	2.89	96	.246	.301	28	.241	2	-0	-4	9	0.7
1915	KC-F	20	12	.625	42	31	21	5	2	281^2	250	3	74	108	10.6	2.68	98	.242	.298	22	.232	2	1	-2	7	0.7
1916	Chi-N	10	6	.625	37	16	5	2	5	155^1	154	4	38	36	11.3	2.78	105	.256	.304	7	.130	-1	-3	2	5	0.7
1917	Chi-N	0	0	—	2	0	0	0	0	1^2	3	1	0	1	16.2	10.80	27	.375	.375	0	—	0	-1	-1	0	0.0
	StL-N	9	6	.600	34	11	6	0	2	153^1	138	4	25	44	9.7	2.47	109	.246	.281	15	.288	3	4	4	-1	0.7
	Yr	9	6	.600	36	11	6	0	2	155	141	5	25	45	9.8	2.55	105	.247	.283	15	.288	3	3	2	-0	0.7
1918	StL-N	12	12	.500	30	23	10	1	2	182^1	184	6	33	46	11.0	3.50	77	.266	.304	12	.174	-1	-15	-16	-1	-2.3
1919	Phi-N	6	8	.429	21	16	10	1	1	134^1	167	3	30	24	13.5	4.15	78	.321	.363	7	.137	-2	-19	-14	-0	-1.6
Total	8	85	69	.552	248	153	86	15	17	1410^1	1393	28	356	488	11.4	3.01	95	.262	.312	103	.205	4	-27	-25	17	-0.6

● JOE PACTWA Pactwa, Joseph Martin b: 6/2/48, Hammond, Ind. BL/TL, 5'11", 185 lbs. Deb: 9/15/75

YEAR	TM/L	W	L	PCT	G	GS	CG	SH	SV	IP	H	HR	BB	SO	RAT	ERA	ERA+	OAV	OOB	BH	AVG	PB	PR	/A	PD	TPI
1975	Cal-A	1	0	1.000	4	3	0	0	0	16^1	23	0	10	3	18.2	3.86	92	.343	.429	0	—	0	-0	-1	-0	0.4

● DAVE PAGAN Pagan, David Percy b: 9/15/49, Nipawin, Sask., Canada BR/TR, 6'2", 175 lbs. Deb: 7/1/73

YEAR	TM/L	W	L	PCT	G	GS	CG	SH	SV	IP	H	HR	BB	SO	RAT	ERA	ERA+	OAV	OOB	BH	AVG	PB	PR	/A	PD	TPI
1973	NY-A	0	0	—	4	1	0	0	0	12^2	16	1	1	9	12.1	2.84	129	.320	.333	0	—	0	1	1	0	0.3
1974	NY-A	1	3	.250	16	6	1	0	0	49^1	49	1	28	39	14.0	5.11	69	.265	.362	0	—	0	-8	-9	-0	-0.7
1975	NY-A	0	0	—	13	0	0	0	1	31	30	2	13	18	13.1	4.06	91	.256	.341	0	—	0	-1	-1	-1	0.0
1976	NY-A	1	1	.500	7	2	1	0	0	23^2	18	0	4	13	8.4	2.28	150	.222	.259	0	—	0	3	3	-1	0.3
	Bal-A	1	4	.200	20	5	0	0	1	46^2	54	2	23	34	15.0	5.98	55	.298	.380	0	—	0	-13	-14	-1	-1.1
	Yr	2	5	.286	27	7	1	0	1	70^1	72	2	27	47	12.8	4.73	70	.273	.342	0	—	0	-9	-11	-2	-0.8
1977	Sea-A	1	1	.500	24	4	1	1	2	66	86	3	26	30	15.5	6.14	67	.323	.388	0	—	0	-15	-15	-0	-0.5
	Pit-N	0	0	—	1	0	0	0	0	3	1	0	0	4	3.0	0.00	—	.100	.100	0	—	0	1	1	0	0.0
Total	5	4	9	.308	85	18	3	1	4	232^1	254	9	95	147	13.7	4.96	74	.285	.358	0	—	0	-31	-34	-2	-1.7

● JOE PAGE Page, Joseph Francis "Fireman" b: 10/28/17, Cherry Valley, Pa. d: 4/21/80, Latrobe, Pa. BL/TL, 6'2", 205 lbs. Deb: 4/19/44

YEAR	TM/L	W	L	PCT	G	GS	CG	SH	SV	IP	H	HR	BB	SO	RAT	ERA	ERA+	OAV	OOB	BH	AVG	PB	PR	/A	PD	TPI
1944	NY-A☆	5	7	.417	19	16	4	0	0	102^2	100	3	52	63	13.6	4.56	76	.258	.351	5	.156	-0	-13	-12	-1	-1.4
1945	NY-A	6	3	.667	20	9	4	0	0	102	95	1	46	50	12.4	2.82	123	.246	.326	9	.250	1	6	7	-2	0.5
1946	NY-A	9	8	.529	31	17	6	1	3	136	126	7	72	77	13.4	3.57	97	.252	.351	7	.163	-0	-1	-2	-1	-0.3
1947	*NY-A★	14	8	.636	56	2	0	0	**17**	141^1	105	5	72	116	11.3	2.48	142	.208	.308	10	.217	1	**19**	**17**	-1	3.0
1948	NY-A☆	7	8	.467	**55**	1	0	0	16	107^2	116	6	66	77	15.3	4.26	96	.275	.374	7	.292	3	0	-2	-1	-0.1
1949	*NY-A	13	8	.619	**60**	0	0	0	**27**	135^1	103	8	75	99	12.2	2.59	156	.215	.328	7	.175	-1	**24**	**22**	-2	3.8
1950	NY-A	3	7	.300	37	0	0	0	13	55^1	66	8	31	33	15.8	5.04	85	.295	.380	2	.250	1	-3	-5	-1	-0.9
1954	Pit-N	0	0	—	7	0	0	0	0	9^2	16	4	7	4	22.3	11.17	37	.364	.462	0	—	0	-8	-8	0	0.0
Total	8	57	49	.538	285	45	14	1	76	790	727	42	421	519	13.2	3.53	106	.247	.344	47	.205	5	25	18	-7	4.6

● PHIL PAGE Page, Philippe Rausac b: 8/23/05, Springfield, Mass. d: 7/27/58, Springfield, Mass BR/TL, 6'2", 175 lbs. Deb: 9/18/28 C

YEAR	TM/L	W	L	PCT	G	GS	CG	SH	SV	IP	H	HR	BB	SO	RAT	ERA	ERA+	OAV	OOB	BH	AVG	PB	PR	/A	PD	TPI
1928	Det-A	2	0	1.000	3	2	2	0	0	22	21	1	10	3	12.7	2.45	167	.256	.337	2	.222	-0	4	4	1	0.4
1929	Det-A	0	2	.000	10	4	1	0	0	25^1	29	1	19	6	17.4	8.17	53	.296	.415	1	.125	-1	-11	-11	-1	-0.8

YEAR	TM/L	W	L	PCT	G	GS	CG	SH	SV	IP	H	HR	BB	SO	RAT	ERA	ERA+	OAV	OOB	BH	AVG	PB	PR	/A	PD	TPI
1930	Det-A	0	1	.000	12	0	0	0	0	12	23	1	9	2	24.0	9.75	49	.434	.516	0	—	0	-7	-7	0	-0.4
1934	Bro-N	1	0	1.000	6	0	0	0	0	10	13	1	6	4	17.1	5.40	72	.342	.432	0	.000	-0	-1	-2	1	-0.1
Total	4	3	3	.500	31	6	3	0	0	69^1	86	4	44	15	17.0	6.23	68	.317	.415	3	.167	-1	-15	-15	1	-0.9
● **SAM PAGE**	Page, Samuel Walter b: 2/11/16, Woodruff, S.C. BL/TR, 6', 172 lbs. Deb: 9/11/39																									
1939	Phi-A	0	3	.000	4	3	1	0	0	22	34	1	15	11	20.0	6.95	68	.343	.430	3	.429	1	-6	-5	1	-0.4
● **VANCE PAGE**	Page, Vance Linwood b: 9/15/05, Elm City, N.C. d: 7/14/51, Wilson, N.C. BR/TR, 6', 180 lbs. Deb: 8/6/38																									
1938	*Chi-N	5	4	.556	13	9	3	0	1	68	90	4	13	18	13.6	3.84	100	.323	.353	4	.154	-1	-0	-0	3	0.1
1939	Chi-N	7	7	.500	27	17	8	1	1	139^1	169	8	37	43	13.4	3.88	102	.298	.342	12	.255	3	1	1	1	0.4
1940	Chi-N	1	3	.250	30	1	0	0	2	59	65	1	26	22	13.9	4.42	85	.271	.342	4	.308	2	-4	-4	0	-0.1
1941	Chi-N	2	2	.500	25	3	1	0	1	48^1	48	2	30	17	14.9	4.28	82	.254	.362	2	.286	1	-3	-4	0	-0.2
Total	4	15	16	.484	95	30	12	1	5	314^2	372	15	106	100	13.8	4.03	95	.292	.348	22	.237	4	-7	-8	4	0.2
● **PAT PAIGE**	Paige, George Lynn "Piggy" b: 5/5/1882, Paw Paw, Mich. d: 6/8/39, Berlin, Wis. BL/TR, 5'10", 175 lbs. Deb: 5/20/11																									
1911	Cle-A	1	0	1.000	2	1	1	0	0	16	21	0	7	6	15.8	4.50	76	.339	.406	1	.143	-0	-2	-2	1	-0.1
● **SATCHEL PAIGE**	Paige, Leroy Robert b: 7/7/06, Mobile, Ala. d: 6/8/82, Kansas City, Mo. BR/TR, 6'3.5", 180 lbs. Deb: 7/9/48 CH																									
1948	*Cle-A	6	1	.857	21	7	3	2	1	72^2	61	2	22	43	10.4	2.48	164	.228	.290	2	.087	-2	15	13	-0	0.9
1949	Cle-A	4	7	.364	31	5	1	0	5	83	70	4	33	54	11.3	3.04	131	.230	.308	1	.063	-1	11	9	-1	1.0
1951	StL-A	3	4	.429	23	3	0	0	5	62	67	6	29	48	14.1	4.79	92	.276	.355	2	.125	-2	-5	-3	-1	-0.6
1952	StL-A☆	12	10	.545	46	6	3	2	10	138	116	5	57	91	11.5	3.07	128	.226	.307	5	.128	-2	9	13	0	2.0
1953	StL-A★	3	9	.250	57	4	0	0	11	117^1	114	12	39	51	11.8	3.53	119	.257	.319	2	.069	-3	6	9	-2	0.5
1965	KC-A	0	0	—	1	1	0	0	0	3	1	0	0	1	3.0	0.00	—	.100	.100	0	.000	-0	1	1	-0	0.0
Total	6	28	31	.475	179	26	7	4	32	476	429	29	180	288	11.6	3.29	124	.241	.313	12	.097	-10	37	42	-3	3.8
● **PHIL PAINE**	Paine, Phillips Steere "Flip" b: 6/8/30, Chepachet, R.I. d: 2/19/78, Lebanon, Pa. BR/TR, 6'2", 181 lbs. Deb: 7/14/51																									
1951	Bos-N	2	0	1.000	21	0	0	0	0	35^1	36	2	20	17	15.3	3.06	120	.271	.382	0	.000	-1	4	2	-0	0.0
1954	Mil-N	1	0	1.000	11	0	0	0	0	14	14	1	12	11	17.4	3.86	97	.292	.443	0	—	0	0	-0	-0	-0.1
1955	Mil-N	2	0	1.000	15	0	0	0	0	25^1	20	2	14	26	12.1	2.49	151	.225	.330	1	.333	0	4	4	0	0.3
1956	Mil-N	0	0	—	1	0	0	0	0	0	3	0	0	0	—	∞	—	1.000	1.000	0	—	0	-2	-2	0	-0.2
1957	Mil-N	0	0	—	1	0	0	0	0	2	1	0	3	2	18.0	0.00	—	.143	.400	0	—	0	1	1	0	0.0
1958	StL-N	5	1	.833	46	0	0	0	1	73^1	70	7	31	45	13.0	3.56	116	.256	.343	2	.286	0	3	5	0	0.4
Total	6	10	1	.909	95	0	0	0	1	150	144	12	80	101	14.0	3.36	116	.260	.364	3	.214	-0	10	9	-0	0.4
● **LANCE PAINTER**	Painter, Lance Telford b: 7/21/67, Bedford, England BL/TL, 6'1", 195 lbs. Deb: 5/19/93																									
1993	Col-N	2	2	.500	10	6	1	0	0	39	52	5	9	16	14.1	6.00	79	.333	.370	3	.300	1	-8	-5	0	-0.3
1994	Col-N	4	6	.400	15	14	0	0	0	73^2	91	9	26	41	14.4	6.11	81	.302	.360	3	.143	-1	-16	-9	0	-1.1
1995	*Col-N	3	0	1.000	33	1	0	0	1	45^1	55	9	10	36	13.3	4.37	123	.296	.338	1	.111	-0	-1	5	0	0.3
1996	Col-N	4	2	.667	34	1	0	0	0	50^2	56	12	25	48	14.9	5.86	89	.280	.368	2	.133	-1	-9	-4	-0	-0.5
1997	StL-N	1	1	.500	14	0	0	0	0	17	13	1	8	11	11.1	4.76	87	.213	.304	0	.000	-0	-1	-1	1	-0.1
1998	StL-N	4	0	1.000	65	0	0	0	1	47^1	42	5	28	39	14.1	3.99	105	.249	.368	1	1.000	0	1	1	2	0.3
Total	6	18	11	.621	171	22	1	0	2	273	309	41	106	191	14.0	5.31	92	.288	.357	10	.175	-0	-34	-13	2	-1.4
● **VICENTE PALACIOS**	Palacios, Vicente (Diaz) b: 7/19/63, Veracruz, Mex. BR/TR, 6'3", 195 lbs. Deb: 9/4/87																									
1987	Pit-N	2	1	.667	6	4	0	0	0	29^1	27	1	9	13	11.4	4.30	96	.250	.314	1	.111	-0	-1	-1	-1	-0.2
1988	Pit-N	1	2	.333	7	3	0	0	0	24^1	28	3	15	15	15.9	6.66	51	.295	.391	0	.000	-0	-9	-9	0	-1.0
1990	Pit-N	0	0	—	7	0	0	0	3	15	4	0	2	8	3.6	0.00	—	.083	.120	0	.000	-0	6	6	-0	0.2
1991	Pit-N	6	3	.667	36	7	1	1	3	81^2	69	12	38	64	11.9	3.75	95	.228	.316	1	.071	-1	-1	-2	-1	-0.3
1992	Pit-N	3	2	.600	20	8	0	0	0	53	56	1	27	33	14.1	4.25	81	.280	.366	1	.071	-1	-4	-5	-0	-0.5
1994	StL-N	3	8	.273	31	17	1	1	1	117^2	104	16	43	95	11.5	4.44	94	.245	.319	0	.000	-4	-3	-4	-0	-0.7
1995	StL-N	2	3	.400	20	5	0	0	0	40^1	48	7	19	34	15.4	5.80	72	.300	.381	1	.167	-0	-7	-7	-0	-0.8
Total	7	17	19	.472	127	44	2	2	7	361^1	336	40	153	262	12.4	4.36	88	.251	.331	4	.045	-6	-18	-21	-2	-3.3
● **MIKE PALAGYI**	Palagyi, Michael Raymond b: 7/4/17, Conneaut, Ohio BR/TR, 6'2", 185 lbs. Deb: 8/18/39																									
1939	Was-A	0	0	—	1	0	0	0	0	0	0	0	3	0	—	∞	—	—	1.000	0	—	0	-3	-3	0	-0.2
● **ERV PALICA**	Palica, Ervin Martin (b: Ervin Martin Pavliecivich) b: 2/9/28, Lomita, Cal. d: 5/29/82, Huntington Beach, Cal. BR/TR, 6'1.5", 180 lbs. Deb: 4/21/45 ♦																									
1947	Bro-N	0	1	.000	3	0	0	0	0	3	2	0	2	1	15.0	3.00	138	.182	.357	0	—	0	0	0	-0	0.1
1948	Bro-N	6	6	.500	41	10	3	0	3	125^1	111	13	58	74	12.4	4.45	90	.239	.327	5	.128	0	-7	-6	-1	-0.7
1949	*Bro-N	8	9	.471	49	1	0	0	6	97	93	6	49	44	13.3	3.62	113	.261	.352	3	.158	0	5	5	-0	0.9
1950	Bro-N	13	8	.619	43	19	10	2	1	201^1	176	13	98	131	12.3	3.58	115	.237	.327	15	.221	2	13	12	-4	0.9
1951	Bro-N	2	6	.250	19	8	0	0	0	53	55	10	20	15	12.7	4.75	83	.259	.323	2	.154	0	-5	-5	1	-0.6
1953	Bro-N	0	0	—	4	0	0	0	0	6	10	1	8	3	27.0	12.00	36	.370	.514	1	1.000	0	-5	-5	0	0.1
1954	Bro-N	3	3	.500	25	3	0	0	0	67^2	77	9	31	25	14.5	5.32	77	.285	.361	4	.250	1	-9	-9	-2	-0.8
1955	Bal-A	5	11	.313	33	25	5	1	0	169^2	165	10	83	68	13.3	4.14	92	.260	.348	13	.236	2	-3	-6	-1	-0.3
1956	Bal-A	4	11	.267	29	14	2	0	0	116^1	117	10	50	62	13.0	4.49	87	.264	.339	5	.156	-2	-4	-7	-0	-1.0
Total	9	41	55	.427	246	80	20	3	10	839^1	806	72	399	423	13.0	4.22	94	.255	.340	48	.198	5	-16	-22	-7	-1.4
● **DONN PALL**	Pall, Donn Steven b: 1/11/62, Chicago, Ill. BR/TR, 6'1", 183 lbs. Deb: 8/1/88																									
1988	Chi-A	0	2	.000	17	0	0	0	0	28^2	39	1	8	16	14.8	3.45	115	.328	.370	0	—	0	2	2	1	0.2
1989	Chi-A	4	5	.444	53	0	0	0	6	87	90	9	19	58	12.1	3.31	115	.270	.325	0	—	0	6	5	-1	0.4
1990	Chi-A	3	5	.375	56	0	0	0	2	76	63	7	24	39	10.8	3.32	115	.232	.303	0	—	0	5	4	-0	0.4
1991	Chi-A	7	2	.778	51	0	0	0	0	71	59	7	20	40	10.4	2.41	165	.231	.295	0	—	0	13	12	-1	1.5
1992	Chi-A	5	2	.714	39	0	0	0	1	73	79	9	27	27	13.3	4.93	78	.272	.339	0	—	0	-8	-9	-1	-0.8
1993	Chi-A	2	3	.400	39	0	0	0	1	58^2	62	5	11	29	11.5	3.22	130	.268	.307	0	—	0	7	6	0	0.6
	Phi-N	1	0	1.000	8	0	0	0	0	17^2	15	1	3	11	9.2	2.55	156	.231	.265	0	—	0	3	3	-0	0.1
1994	NY-A	1	2	.333	26	0	0	0	0	35	43	3	9	21	13.6	3.60	127	.295	.340	0	—	0	5	4	0	0.4
	Chi-N	0	0	—	2	0	0	0	0	4	8	1	1	2	20.3	4.50	92	.444	.474	0	—	0	-0	-0	-0	0.0
1996	Fla-N	1	1	.500	12	0	0	0	0	18^2	16	3	9	9	12.1	5.79	70	.232	.321	0	.000	0	-3	-4	-0	-0.4
1997	Fla-N	0	0	—	2	0	0	0	0	2^1	3	1	1	0	15.4	3.86	104	.300	.364	0	.000	-0	0	0	-0	0.0
1998	Fla-N	0	1	.000	23	0	0	0	0	33^1	42	5	7	26	13.5	5.13	80	.326	.365	0	.000	-0	-3	-4	0	-0.1
Total	10	24	23	.511	328	0	0	0	10	505^1	519	52	139	278	12.1	3.63	110	.268	.324	0	.000	-0	26	20	-2	2.3
● **MIKE PALM**	Palm, Richard Paul b: 2/13/25, Boston, Mass. BR/TR, 6'3.5", 190 lbs. Deb: 7/11/48																									
1948	Bos-A	0	0	—	3	0	0	0	0	3	6	0	5	1	33.0	6.00	73	.400	.550	0	.000	-0	-1	-1	-0	-0.1
● **PALMER**	Palmer b: St.Louis, Mo. Deb: 5/28/1885																									
1885	StL-N	0	4	.000	4	4	4	0	0	34	46	2	20	9	17.5	3.44	80	.311	.393	1	.091	-0	-2	-3	-1	-0.4
● **DAVID PALMER**	Palmer, David William b: 10/19/57, Glens Falls, N.Y. BR/TR, 6'1", 205 lbs. Deb: 9/9/78																									
1978	Mon-N	0	1	.000	5	1	0	0	0	9^2	9	1	2	7	10.2	2.79	126	.243	.282	0	.000	-0	1	1	1	0.1
1979	Mon-N	10	2	.833	36	11	2	1	2	122^2	110	10	30	72	10.4	2.64	139	.237	.286	1	.032	-3	15	14	-0	1.0
1980	Mon-N	8	6	.571	24	19	3	1	0	129^2	124	11	30	73	10.8	2.98	119	.255	.301	9	.200	1	9	8	1	1.1
1982	Mon-N	6	4	.600	13	13	1	0	0	73^2	60	3	36	46	12.0	3.18	115	.224	.320	1	.042	-2	3	4	0	0.3
1984	Mon-N	7	3	.700	20	19	1	1	0	105^1	101	5	44	66	12.4	3.84	89	.256	.331	5	.152	1	-3	-5	1	-0.3
1985	Mon-N	7	10	.412	24	23	0	0	0	135^2	128	5	67	106	13.1	3.71	91	.250	.341	4	.111	-1	-2	-5	2	-0.5
1986	Atl-N	11	10	.524	35	35	2	0	0	209^2	181	17	102	170	12.4	3.65	109	.234	.327	12	.182	1	2	8	2	1.1
1987	Atl-N	8	11	.421	28	28	0	0	0	152^1	169	17	64	111	14.2	4.90	89	.281	.357	6	.125	-0	-14	-9	1	-1.0
1988	Phi-N	7	9	.438	22	22	1	1	0	129	129	8	48	85	12.3	4.47	80	.261	.327	10	.256	5	-15	-13	-1	-1.1

YEAR	TM/L	W	L	PCT	G	GS	CG	SH	SV	IP	H	HR	BB	SO	RAT	ERA	ERA+	OAV	OOB	BH	AVG	PB	PR	/A	PD	TPI
1989	Det-A	0	3	.000	5	5	0	0	0	17^1	25	1	11	12	18.7	7.79	49	.342	.429	0	—	0	-8	-8	-0	-1.0
Total	10	64	59	.520	212	176	10	4	2	1085	1036	78	434	748	12.4	3.78	99	.252	.327	48	.149	2	-11	-6	5	-0.3
● **JIM PALMER** Palmer, James Alvin b: 10/15/45, New York, N.Y. BR/TR, 6'3", 196 lbs. Deb: 4/17/65 H																										
1965	Bal-A	5	4	.556	27	6	0	0	1	92	75	6	56	75	13.0	3.72	93	.229	.345	5	.192	1	-3	-3	0	-0.1
1966	*Bal-A	15	10	.600	30	30	6	0	0	208^1	176	21	91	147	11.5	3.46	96	.231	.313	7	.096	-2	-0	-3	-1	-0.6
1967	Bal-A	3	1	.750	9	9	2	1	0	49	34	6	20	23	9.9	2.94	107	.199	.283	1	.077	0	2	1	0	0.1
1969	*Bal-A	16	4	**.800**	26	23	11	6	0	181	131	11	64	123	9.7	2.34	152	.200	.272	13	.203	2	26	25	-4	2.6
1970	*Bal-A★	20	10	.667	39	39	17	**5**	0	**305**	263	21	100	199	10.7	2.71	134	.231	.294	17	.150	-1	**34**	32	-0	2.8
1971	*Bal-A★	20	9	.690	37	37	20	3	0	282	231	19	106	184	10.9	2.68	125	.221	.295	20	.196	2	24	21	0	2.4
1972	Bal-A★	21	10	.677	36	36	18	3	0	274^1	219	21	70	184	9.5	2.07	149	.217	.269	22	.224	4	30	31	-1	4.2
1973	*Bal-A	22	9	.710	38	37	19	6	1	296^1	225	16	113	158	10.4	**2.40**	156	.211	.289	0	—	0	47	44	-1	4.5
1974	*Bal-A	7	12	.368	26	26	5	2	0	178^2	176	12	69	84	12.5	3.27	105	.257	.328	0	—	0	7	4	2	0.5
1975	Bal-A☆	**23**	11	.676	39	38	25	**10**	1	323	253	20	80	193	9.3	**2.09**	**168**	.216	.267	0	—	0	**61**	**51**	2	**6.1**
1976	Bal-A	**22**	13	.629	40	40	23	6	0	**315**	255	20	84	159	9.9	2.51	130	.224	.282	0	—	0	35	27	1	3.6
1977	Bal-A★	**20**	11	.645	39	39	**22**	3	0	**319**	263	24	99	193	10.3	2.91	130	.229	.292	0	—	0	41	31	0	3.3
1978	Bal-A★	21	12	.636	38	38	19	6	0	**296**	246	19	97	138	10.5	2.46	142	.227	.291	0	—	0	43	34	1	4.3
1979	*Bal-A	10	6	.625	23	22	7	0	0	155^2	144	12	43	67	10.8	3.30	122	.246	.297	0	—	0	16	12	-0	1.4
1980	Bal-A	16	10	.615	34	33	4	0	0	224	238	26	74	109	12.7	3.98	99	.275	.334	0	—	0	1	-1	1	0.1
1981	Bal-A	7	8	.467	22	22	5	0	0	127^1	117	14	46	35	11.7	3.75	97	.247	.316	0	—	0	-1	-2	1	-0.1
1982	Bal-A	15	5	**.750**	36	32	8	2	1	227	195	22	63	103	**10.4**	3.13	129	.231	**.287**	0	—	0	24	23	1	2.0
1983	*Bal-A	5	4	.556	14	11	0	0	0	76^2	86	11	19	34	12.3	4.23	94	.281	.323	0	—	0	-1	-2	-1	-0.3
1984	Bal-A	0	3	.000	5	3	0	0	0	17^2	22	2	17	4	19.9	9.17	42	.319	.453	0	—	0	-10	-10	0	-1.3
Total	19	268	152	.638	558	521	211	53	4	3948	3349	303	1311	2212	10.7	2.86	125	.230	.296	85	.174	7	374	315	3	35.5
● **LOWELL PALMER** Palmer, Lowell Raymond b: 8/18/47, Sacramento, Cal. BR/TR, 6'1", 190 lbs. Deb: 6/21/69																										
1969	Phi-N	2	8	.200	26	9	1	1	0	90	91	12	47	68	14.4	5.20	68	.264	.362	3	.136	1	-16	-17	-0	-1.6
1970	Phi-N	1	2	.333	38	5	0	0	0	102	98	15	55	85	13.9	5.47	73	.255	.355	4	.148	1	-16	-17	-1	-0.4
1971	Phi-N	0	0	—	3	1	0	0	0	15	13	3	13	6	18.0	6.00	59	.236	.417	1	.200	-0	-4	-4	-0	0.0
1972	StL-N	0	3	.000	16	2	0	0	0	34^2	30	2	26	25	14.8	3.89	87	.244	.380	0	.000	-1	-2	-2	0	-0.2
	Cle-A	0	0	—	1	0	0	0	0	2	2	0	2	3	18.0	4.50	71	.222	.364	0	—	0	-0	-0	-0	0.0
1974	SD-N	2	5	.286	22	8	1	0	0	73	68	9	59	52	16.5	5.67	63	.256	.404	2	.087	-1	-17	-17	-1	-1.6
Total	5	5	18	.217	106	25	2	1	0	316^2	302	41	202	239	15.0	5.29	69	.255	.374	10	.122	-0	-55	-57	-1	-3.8
● **EMILIO PALMERO** Palmero, Emilio Antonio "Pal" b: 6/13/1895, Guanabacoa, Cuba d: 7/15/70, Toledo, Ohio BL/TL, 5'11", 157 lbs. Deb: 9/21/15																										
1915	NY-N	0	2	.000	3	2	1	0	0	11^2	10	0	9	8	17.0	3.09	83	.233	.400	1	.250	0	-0	-1	0	-0.1
1916	NY-N	0	3	.000	4	2	0	0	0	15^2	17	2	8	8	14.9	8.04	30	.288	.382	0	.000	-0	-9	-10	1	-1.5
1921	StL-A	4	7	.364	24	9	4	0	0	90	109	1	49	26	16.4	5.00	90	.319	.413	8	.216	1	-7	-5	1	-0.4
1926	Was-A	2	2	.500	7	3	0	0	0	17	22	1	15	6	20.1	4.76	81	.344	.475	1	.333	0	-1	-2	-0	-0.3
1928	Bos-N	0	1	.000	3	1	0	0	0	6^2	14	0	2	0	21.6	5.40	72	.452	.485	0	.000	-0	-1	-1	-0	-0.2
Total	5	6	15	.286	41	17	5	0	0	141	172	4	83	48	17.0	5.17	77	.319	.420	10	.208	1	-19	-19	2	-2.5
● **ED PALMQUIST** Palmquist, Edwin Lee b: 6/10/33, Los Angeles, Cal. BR/TR, 6'3", 195 lbs. Deb: 6/10/60																										
1960	LA-N	0	1	.000	22	0	0	0	0	39	34	6	16	23	11.8	2.54	156	.243	.325	0	.000	-1	5	6	0	0.1
1961	LA-N	0	1	.000	5	0	0	0	1	8^2	10	0	7	5	19.7	6.23	70	.333	.487	0	—	0	-2	-2	-0	-0.2
	Min-A	1	1	.500	9	2	0	0	0	21	33	7	13	13	21.0	9.43	45	.359	.454	0	.000	-0	-13	-12	0	-1.0
Total	2	1	3	.250	36	2	0	0	1	68^2	77	13	36	41	15.6	5.11	80	.294	.391	0	.000	-1	-9	-8	0	-1.1
● **JOSE PANIAGUA** Paniagua, Jose Luis (Sanchez) b: 8/20/73, San Jose De Ocoa, D.R. BR/TR, 6'2", 185 lbs. Deb: 4/4/96																										
1996	Mon-N	2	4	.333	13	11	0	0	0	51	55	7	23	27	14.3	3.53	122	.282	.367	0	.000	-1	4	4	0	0.4
1997	Mon-N	1	2	.333	9	3	0	0	0	18	29	2	16	8	24.5	12.00	35	.372	.500	0	.000	-1	-16	-16	-0	-2.1
1998	Sea-A	2	0	1.000	18	0	0	0	1	22	15	3	5	16	9.4	2.05	226	.200	.277	0	—	0	6	6	1	0.6
Total	3	5	6	.455	40	14	0	0	1	91	99	12	44	51	15.1	4.85	90	.284	.381	0	.000	-1	-5	-5	1	-1.1
● **JIM PANTHER** Panther, James Edward b: 3/1/45, Burlington, Iowa BR/TR, 6'1", 190 lbs. Deb: 4/5/71																										
1971	Oak-A	0	1	.000	4	0	0	0	0	5^2	10	1	5	4	23.8	11.12	30	.385	.484	0	.000	-0	-5	-5	0	-0.8
1972	Tex-A	5	9	.357	58	4	0	0	0	93^2	101	8	46	44	14.6	4.13	73	.277	.365	1	.125	0	-11	-12	0	-1.7
1973	Atl-N	2	3	.400	23	0	0	0	0	30^2	45	3	9	8	15.8	7.63	52	.363	.406	0	—	0	-14	-13	-1	-1.9
Total	3	7	13	.350	85	4	0	0	0	130	156	12	60	56	15.3	5.26	61	.303	.381	1	.111	-0	-30	-29	-1	-4.4
● **JOHN PAPA** Papa, John Paul b: 12/5/40, Bridgeport, Conn. BR/TR, 5'11", 190 lbs. Deb: 4/11/61																										
1961	Bal-A	0	0	—	2	0	0	0	0	1	2	1	3	3	45.0	18.00	21	.400	.625	0	—	0	-2	-2	0	0.0
1962	Bal-A	0	0	—	1	0	0	0	0	1	3	0	1	0	36.0	27.00	14	.600	.667	0	—	0	-3	-3	-0	0.0
Total	2	0	0	—	3	0	0	0	0	2	5	1	4	3	40.5	22.50	17	.500	.643	0	—	0	-4	-4	-0	0.0
● **AL PAPAI** Papai, Alfred Thomas b: 5/7/17, Divernon, Ill. d: 9/7/95, Springfield, Ill. BR/TR, 6'3", 185 lbs. Deb: 4/24/48																										
1948	StL-N	0	1	.000	10	0	0	0	0	16	14	3	7	8	11.8	5.06	81	.241	.323	0	.000	-0	-2	-2	0	-0.1
1949	StL-A	4	11	.267	42	15	6	0	2	142^1	175	8	81	31	16.3	5.06	90	.298	.384	3	.079	-2	-14	-8	3	-0.7
1950	Bos-A	4	2	.667	16	3	2	0	2	50^2	61	5	28	19	15.8	6.75	73	.293	.377	3	.176	-0	-12	-10	-1	-1.1
	StL-N	1	0	1.000	13	0	0	0	0	19	21	0	14	7	16.6	5.21	82	.300	.417	0	.000	-0	-2	-2	0	-0.1
1955	Chi-A	0	0	—	7	0	0	0	0	11^2	10	1	8	5	13.9	3.86	102	.244	.367	0	.000	-0	0	0	1	0.1
Total	4	9	14	.391	88	18	8	0	4	239^2	281	17	138	70	15.8	5.37	84	.291	.381	6	.097	-3	-30	-22	4	-1.9
● **LARRY PAPE** Pape, Laurence Albert b: 7/21/1883, Norwood, Ohio d: 7/21/18, Swissvale, Pa. BR/TR, 5'11", 175 lbs. Deb: 7/6/09																										
1909	Bos-A	2	0	1.000	11	3	2	1	2	57^1	46	0	12	18	9.9	2.04	123	.221	.280	3	.143	-1	3	3	-3	-0.2
1911	Bos-A	10	8	.556	27	19	10	1	0	176^1	167	3	63	49	11.9	2.45	134	.264	.335	13	.203	-1	18	16	5	1.8
1912	Bos-A	1	1	.500	13	2	1	0	1	48^2	74	0	16	17	17.0	4.99	68	.366	.418	4	.235	1	-9	-9	0	-0.3
Total	3	13	9	.591	51	24	13	2	3	282^1	287	3	91	84	12.4	2.81	112	.275	.340	20	.196	-1	11	11	2	1.3
● **FRANK PAPISH** Papish, Frank Richard "Pap" b: 10/21/17, Pueblo, Colo. d: 8/30/65, Pueblo, Colo. BR/TL, 6'2", 192 lbs. Deb: 5/8/45																										
1945	Chi-A	4	4	.500	19	5	3	0	1	84^1	75	3	40	45	12.3	3.74	89	.241	.328	6	.231	1	-3	-4	1	-0.1
1946	Chi-A	7	5	.583	31	15	6	2	0	138	122	7	63	66	12.1	2.74	125	.243	.328	8	.186	-0	12	10	0	0.9
1947	Chi-A	12	12	.500	38	26	6	1	3	199	185	6	98	79	12.9	3.26	112	.245	.333	5	.086	-5	10	9	-1	0.4
1948	Chi-A	2	8	.200	32	14	2	0	4	95^1	97	7	75	41	16.5	5.00	85	.265	.394	5	.185	-1	-8	-8	-1	-0.9
1949	Cle-A	1	0	1.000	25	3	1	0	1	62	54	2	39	23	13.5	3.19	125	.240	.352	1	.125	0	7	5	0	0.1
1950	Pit-N	0	0	—	4	1	0	0	0	2^1	8	1	4	1	46.3	27.00	16	.533	.632	0	—	0	-6	-6	0	0.0
Total	6	26	29	.473	149	64	18	3	9	581	541	26	319	255	13.4	3.58	103	.249	.346	25	.154	-5	12	7	0	0.4
● **JOHN PAPPALAU** Pappalau, John Joseph b: 4/3/1875, Albany, N.Y. d: 5/12/44, Albany, N.Y. BR/TR, 6', 175 lbs. Deb: 6/9/1897																										
1897	Cle-N	0	1	.000	2	1	1	0	0	12	22	0	6	3	22.5	10.50	43	.393	.469	0	.000	-0	-8	-8	0	-0.5
● **MILT PAPPAS** Pappas, Milton Stephen "Gimpy" (b: Miltiades Stergios Papastegios) b: 5/11/39, Detroit, Mich. BR/TR, 6'3", 190 lbs. Deb: 8/10/57																										
1957	Bal-A	0	0	—	4	0	0	0	0	9	6	0	3	3	9.0	1.00	359	.200	.273	0	.000	-0	3	3	0	0.0
1958	Bal-A	10	10	.500	31	21	3	0	0	135^1	135	8	48	72	12.3	4.06	89	.262	.327	6	.143	-0	-4	-7	1	-0.8
1959	Bal-A	15	9	.625	33	27	15	4	3	209^1	175	8	75	120	10.9	3.27	116	.226	.298	11	.139	-3	14	12	-1	0.9
1960	Bal-A	15	11	.577	30	27	11	3	0	205^2	184	15	83	126	11.9	3.37	113	.243	.323	3	.043	-5	12	10	1	0.7
1961	Bal-A	13	9	.591	26	23	11	4	1	177^2	134	16	78	89	11.1	3.04	127	.208	.301	9	.136	1	19	16	2	2.2
1962	Bal-A★	12	10	.545	35	32	9	1	0	205^1	200	31	75	130	12.1	4.03	92	.257	.324	6	.087	-0	-1	-8	2	-0.6
1963	Bal-A	16	9	.640	34	32	11	4	0	216^2	186	21	69	120	10.8	3.03	115	.233	.298	9	.127	-0	14	11	3	1.4
1964	Bal-A	16	7	.696	37	36	13	7	0	251^2	225	21	48	157	10.0	2.97	120	.239	.281	12	.129	-2	18	17	-1	1.2
1965	Bal-A★	13	9	.591	34	34	9	3	0	221^1	192	22	52	127	10.0	2.60	133	.233	.281	5	.071	-3	21	21	-3	1.3
1966	Cin-N	12	11	.522	33	32	6	2	0	209^2	224	23	39	133	11.4	4.29	91	.275	.310	8	.107	-2	-16	-9	0	-1.1

YEAR	TM/L	W	L	PCT	G	GS	CG	SH	SV	IP	H	HR	BB	SO	RAT	ERA	ERA+	OAV	OOB	BH	AVG	PB	PR	/A	PD	TPI
1967	Cin-N	16	13	.552	34	32	5	3	0	217^2	218	19	38	129	10.8	3.35	112	.259	.295	7	.097	-2	1	10	0	1.0
1968	Cin-N	2	5	.286	15	11	0	0	0	62^2	70	9	10	43	11.8	5.60	56	.275	.307	1	.063	-1	-18	-17	-0	-1.9
	Atl-N	10	8	.556	22	19	3	1	0	121^1	111	8	22	75	10.1	2.37	126	.246	.285	6	.162	2	8	8	-1	1.5
	Yr	12	13	.480	37	30	3	1	0	184	181	17	32	118	10.6	3.47	88	.255	.290	7	.132	1	-10	-9	-1	-0.4
1969	*Atl-N	6	10	.375	26	24	1	0	0	144	149	14	44	72	12.3	3.63	99	.267	.325	7	.156	3	-0	-0	-0	0.2
1970	Atl-N	2	2	.500	11	3	1	0	0	35^2	44	6	7	25	13.4	6.06	71	.293	.333	0	.000	-1	-8	-7	0	-0.8
	Chi-N	10	8	.556	21	20	6	2	0	144^2	135	14	36	80	10.6	2.68	168	.248	.294	12	.240	4	22	29	-1	4.0
	Yr	12	10	.545	32	23	7	2	0	180^1	179	20	43	105	11.1	3.34	133	.256	.300	12	.200	3	14	22	-1	3.2
1971	Chi-N	17	14	.548	35	35	14	**5**	0	261^1	279	25	62	99	11.9	3.51	112	.274	.319	14	.154	-1	-1	12	-2	1.1
1972	Chi-N	17	7	.708	29	28	10	3	0	195	187	18	29	80	10.3	2.77	138	.251	.287	13	.191	1	15	23	0	3.1
1973	Chi-N	7	12	.368	30	29	1	1	0	162	192	20	40	48	13.1	4.28	92	.299	.344	3	.063	-3	-11	-6	-1	-1.0
Total	17	209	164	.560	520	465	129	43	4	3186	3046	298	858	1728	11.2	3.40	110	.252	.306	132	.123	-14	86	120	0	12.4

● CHAN HO PARK Park, Chan Ho b: 6/30/73, Kongju, South Korea BR/TR, 6′2″, 185 lbs. Deb: 4/8/94

YEAR	TM/L	W	L	PCT	G	GS	CG	SH	SV	IP	H	HR	BB	SO	RAT	ERA	ERA+	OAV	OOB	BH	AVG	PB	PR	/A	PD	TPI
1994	LA-N	0	0	—	2	0	0	0	0	4	5	1	5	6	24.8	11.25	35	.294	.478	0	—	0	-3	-3	-0	0.0
1995	LA-N	0	0	—	2	1	0	0	0	4	2	1	2	7	9.0	4.50	84	.143	.250	0	.000	-0	-0	-0	-0	0.0
1996	LA-N	5	5	.500	48	10	0	0	0	108^2	82	7	71	119	13.0	3.64	106	.209	.335	1	.053	-1	7	3	2	0.3
1997	LA-N	14	8	.636	32	29	2	0	0	192	149	24	70	166	10.6	3.38	114	.213	.292	9	.176	3	18	10	-0	1.3
1998	LA-N	15	9	.625	34	34	2	0	0	220^2	199	16	97	191	12.5	3.71	105	.244	.332	14	.194	3	13	5	1	0.8
Total	5	34	22	.607	118	74	4	0	0	529^1	437	49	245	489	12.0	3.64	106	.225	.319	24	.168	4	34	14	3	2.4

● JIM PARK Park, James b: 11/10/1892, Richmond, Ky. d: 12/17/70, Lexington, Ky. BR/TR, 6′2″, 175 lbs. Deb: 9/7/15

YEAR	TM/L	W	L	PCT	G	GS	CG	SH	SV	IP	H	HR	BB	SO	RAT	ERA	ERA+	OAV	OOB	BH	AVG	PB	PR	/A	PD	TPI
1915	StL-A	2	0	1.000	3	3	1	0	0	22^2	18	1	9	5	10.7	1.19	240	.214	.290	4	.400	1	4	4	-1	0.5
1916	StL-A	1	4	.200	26	6	1	0	0	79	69	2	25	26	10.8	2.62	105	.244	.307	2	.100	-2	2	1	-2	-0.3
1917	StL-A	1	1	.500	13	0	0	0	0	20^1	27	1	12	9	17.3	6.64	39	.333	.419	0	.000	-0	-9	-9	0	-0.9
Total	3	4	5	.444	42	9	2	0	0	122	114	4	46	40	11.9	3.02	91	.254	.325	6	.188	-0	-3	-4	-2	-0.7

● DOC PARKER Parker, Harley Park b: 6/14/1872, Theresa, N.Y. d: 3/3/41, Chicago, Ill. BR/TR, 6′2″, 200 lbs. Deb: 7/11/1893 F

YEAR	TM/L	W	L	PCT	G	GS	CG	SH	SV	IP	H	HR	BB	SO	RAT	ERA	ERA+	OAV	OOB	BH	AVG	PB	PR	/A	PD	TPI
1893	Chi-N	0	0	—	1	0	0	0	1	2	5	0	1	0	27.0	13.50	34	.455	.500	0	.000	-0	-2	-2	-0	-0.2
1895	Chi-N	4	2	.667	7	6	5	1	0	51^1	65	1	9	9	13.5	3.68	138	.304	.341	7	.318	1	6	8	0	0.8
1896	Chi-N	1	5	.167	9	7	7	0	0	73	100	3	27	15	16.0	6.16	74	.323	.382	10	.278	0	-15	-13	1	-0.7
1901	Cin-N	0	1	.000	1	1	1	0	0	8	26	1	2	0	31.5	15.75	20	.531	.549	0	.000	-0	-11	-11	-0	-0.8
Total	4	5	8	.385	18	14	13	1	1	134^1	196	5	39	24	16.1	5.90	79	.336	.383	17	.274	0	-21	-18	1	-0.9

● HARRY PARKER Parker, Harry William b: 9/14/47, Highland, Ill. BR/TR, 6′3″, 190 lbs. Deb: 8/8/70

YEAR	TM/L	W	L	PCT	G	GS	CG	SH	SV	IP	H	HR	BB	SO	RAT	ERA	ERA+	OAV	OOB	BH	AVG	PB	PR	/A	PD	TPI
1970	StL-N	1	1	.500	7	4	0	0	0	22^1	24	0	15	9	15.7	3.22	128	.276	.382	2	.250	0	2	2	0	0.2
1971	StL-N	0	0	—	4	0	0	0	0	5	6	2	2	2	14.4	7.20	50	.286	.348	0	—	0	-2	-2	-0	0.0
1973	*NY-N	8	4	.667	38	9	0	0	5	96^2	79	7	36	63	11.0	3.35	108	.217	.293	4	.174	-0	3	3	-0	0.3
1974	NY-N	4	12	.250	40	16	1	0	4	131	145	10	46	58	13.3	3.92	91	.281	.343	0	.000	-4	-4	-5	-2	-1.2
1975	NY-N	2	3	.400	18	1	0	0	2	34^2	37	2	19	22	14.5	4.41	78	.272	.361	0	.000	1	-3	-4	-0	-0.5
	StL-N	0	1	.000	14	0	0	0	1	18^2	21	3	10	13	14.9	6.27	60	.288	.373	0	.000	0	-5	-5	1	-0.2
	Yr	2	4	.333	32	1	0	0	3	53^1	58	5	29	35	14.7	5.06	70	.278	.366	0	.000	1	-9	-9	0	-0.7
1976	Cle-A	0	0	—	3	0	0	0	0	7	3	0	0	5	3.9	0.00	—	.136	.136	0	—	0	3	3	0	0.0
Total	6	15	21	.417	124	30	1	0	12	315^1	315	24	128	172	12.8	3.85	94	.258	.332	6	.086	-3	-7	-8	-1	-1.4

● CLAY PARKER Parker, James Clayton b: 12/19/62, Columbia, La. BR/TR, 6′1″, 185 lbs. Deb: 9/14/87

YEAR	TM/L	W	L	PCT	G	GS	CG	SH	SV	IP	H	HR	BB	SO	RAT	ERA	ERA+	OAV	OOB	BH	AVG	PB	PR	/A	PD	TPI
1987	Sea-A	0	0	—	3	1	0	0	0	7^2	15	2	4	8	23.5	10.57	45	.405	.476	0	—	0	-5	-5	0	-0.3
1989	NY-A	4	5	.444	22	17	2	0	0	120	123	12	31	53	11.7	3.68	105	.264	.313	0	—	0	3	3	0	0.3
1990	NY-A	1	1	.500	5	2	0	0	0	22	19	5	7	20	10.6	4.50	88	.229	.289	0	—	0	-1	-1	-0	-0.2
	Det-A	2	2	.500	24	1	0	0	0	51	45	6	25	20	12.5	3.18	125	.242	.335	0	—	0	4	4	0	0.3
	Yr	3	3	.500	29	3	0	0	0	73	64	11	32	40	12.0	3.58	111	.237	.320	0	—	0	3	3	0	0.1
1992	Sea-A	0	2	.000	8	6	0	0	0	33^1	47	6	11	20	16.2	7.56	53	.338	.395	0	—	0	-13	-13	-0	-0.7
Total	4	7	10	.412	62	27	2	0	0	234	249	31	78	121	12.8	4.42	89	.273	.335	0	—	0	-13	-13	0	-0.6

● JAY PARKER Parker, Jay b: 7/8/1874, Theresa, N.Y. d: 6/8/35, Hartford, Mich. BR/TR, 5′11″, 185 lbs. Deb: 9/27/1899 F

YEAR	TM/L	W	L	PCT	G	GS	CG	SH	SV	IP	H	HR	BB	SO	RAT	ERA	ERA+	OAV	OOB	BH	AVG	PB	PR	/A	PD	TPI
1899	Pit-N	0	0	—	1	1	0	0	0	0	0	0	2	0	—	∞	—	—	1.000	0	—	0	-2	-2	0	-0.2

● ROY PARKER Parker, Roy William b: 2/29/1896, Union, Mo. d: 5/17/54, Tulsa, Okla. BR/TR, 6′3″, 200 lbs. Deb: 9/10/19

YEAR	TM/L	W	L	PCT	G	GS	CG	SH	SV	IP	H	HR	BB	SO	RAT	ERA	ERA+	OAV	OOB	BH	AVG	PB	PR	/A	PD	TPI
1919	StL-N	0	0	—	2	0	0	0	0	2	6	0	1	0	36.0	31.50	9	.333	.400	0	—	0	-6	-6	0	0.0

● SLICKER PARKS Parks, Vernon Henry b: 11/10/1895, Dallas, Mich. d: 2/21/78, Royal Oak, Mich. BR/TR, 5′10″, 158 lbs. Deb: 7/11/21

YEAR	TM/L	W	L	PCT	G	GS	CG	SH	SV	IP	H	HR	BB	SO	RAT	ERA	ERA+	OAV	OOB	BH	AVG	PB	PR	/A	PD	TPI
1921	Det-A	3	2	.600	10	1	0	0	0	25^1	33	2	16	10	17.8	5.68	75	.306	.400	1	.111	-1	-4	-4	-1	-0.8

● BILL PARKS Parks, William Robert b: 6/4/1849, Easton, Pa. d: 10/10/11, Easton, Pa. BR/TR, 5′8″, 150 lbs. Deb: 4/26/1875 M♦

YEAR	TM/L	W	L	PCT	G	GS	CG	SH	SV	IP	H	HR	BB	SO	RAT	ERA	ERA+	OAV	OOB	BH	AVG	PB	PR	/A	PD	TPI
1875	Was-n	4	8	.333	14	11	9	0	0	106^2	144	3	5	3	12.6	3.29	72	.280	.287	20	.180	-3	-13	-11		-1.1
	Phi-n	0	0	—	2	0	0	0	0	5^1	13	0	1	0	23.6	8.44	27	.419	.438	1	.167	-0	-4	-4		0.0
	Yr	4	8	.333	16	11	9	0	0	112	157	3	6	3	13.1	3.54	67	.288	.295	21	.179	-3	-16	-15		-1.1

● ROY PARMELEE Parmelee, Le Roy Earl "Tarzan" b: 4/25/07, Lambertville, Mich d: 8/31/81, Monroe, Mich. BR/TR, 6′1″, 190 lbs. Deb: 9/28/29

YEAR	TM/L	W	L	PCT	G	GS	CG	SH	SV	IP	H	HR	BB	SO	RAT	ERA	ERA+	OAV	OOB	BH	AVG	PB	PR	/A	PD	TPI
1929	NY-N	1	0	1.000	2	1	0	0	0	7	13	1	3	1	21.9	9.00	51	.481	.548	1	.500	0	-3	-3	0	-0.3
1930	NY-N	0	1	.000	11	1	0	0	0	21	18	3	26	19	18.9	9.43	50	.228	.419	1	.250	1	-10	-11	0	-0.4
1931	NY-N	2	2	.500	13	5	4	0	0	58^2	47	1	33	30	12.7	3.68	100	.223	.336	4	.200	-0	1	0	0	0.0
1932	NY-N	0	3	.000	8	3	0	0	0	25^1	25	0	14	23	14.6	3.91	95	.250	.353	2	.400	1	-0	-1	0	0.1
1933	NY-N	13	8	.619	32	32	14	3	0	218^1	191	9	77	132	11.6	3.17	101	.232	.309	19	.235	4	4	1	0	0.5
1934	NY-N	10	6	.625	22	21	7	2	0	152^2	134	6	60	83	11.8	3.42	113	**.238**	.318	11	.200	2	11	8	2	1.1
1935	NY-N	14	10	.583	34	31	13	0	0	226	214	20	97	79	12.7	4.22	91	.249	.332	18	.209	3	-5	-9	2	-0.4
1936	StL-N	11	11	.500	37	28	9	0	2	221	226	13	107	79	14.0	4.56	86	.270	.360	15	.197	-0	-13	-15	-1	-1.4
1937	Chi-N	7	8	.467	33	18	8	0	0	145^2	165	13	79	55	15.5	5.13	78	.286	.379	9	.173	0	-20	-19	1	-1.6
1939	Phi-A	1	6	.143	14	5	0	0	1	44^2	42	2	35	13	16.1	6.45	73	.235	.369	2	.133	-1	-9	-9	0	-1.2
Total	10	59	55	.518	206	145	55	5	3	1120^1	1075	68	531	514	13.3	4.27	89	.253	.343	82	.207	9	-45	-58	5	-3.6

● MEL PARNELL Parnell, Melvin Lloyd "Dusty" b: 6/13/22, New Orleans, La. BL/TL, 6′, 180 lbs. Deb: 4/20/47

YEAR	TM/L	W	L	PCT	G	GS	CG	SH	SV	IP	H	HR	BB	SO	RAT	ERA	ERA+	OAV	OOB	BH	AVG	PB	PR	/A	PD	TPI
1947	Bos-A	2	3	.400	15	5	1	0	0	50^2	60	1	27	23	15.6	6.39	61	.296	.381	1	.056	-2	-15	-14	-1	-1.5
1948	Bos-A	15	8	.652	35	27	16	1	0	212	205	7	90	77	12.7	3.14	140	.252	.330	13	.162	-4	27	29	2	2.7
1949	Bos-A★	**25**	7	.781	39	33	**27**	4	2	**295^1**	258	8	134	122	12.1	2.77	157	.237	.324	29	.254	2	**47**	**52**	-0	5.5
1950	Bos-A	18	10	.643	40	31	21	2	3	249	244	17	106	93	12.9	3.61	136	.259	.338	19	.194	-1	27	36	5	3.9
1951	Bos-A★	18	11	.621	36	29	11	3	2	221	229	11	77	77	12.5	3.26	137	.272	.333	25	.309	4	21	30	-0	**4.1**
1952	Bos-A	12	12	.500	33	29	15	3	2	214	207	13	89	107	12.7	3.62	109	.255	.332	8	.095	-3	1	8	1	0.6
1953	Bos-A	21	8	.724	38	34	12	5	0	241	217	15	116	136	12.6	3.06	137	.239	.328	21	.223	1	25	31	-2	3.4
1954	Bos-A	3	7	.300	19	15	4	1	0	92^1	104	7	35	38	13.6	3.70	111	.287	.352	3	.088	-2	0	4	0	0.2
1955	Bos-A	2	3	.400	13	9	0	0	1	46	62	12	25	18	17.2	7.83	55	.318	.398	6	.316	1	-20	-18	0	-1.6
1956	Bos-A	7	6	.538	21	20	6	1	0	131^1	129	13	59	41	12.9	3.77	123	.256	.335	7	.152	-2	6	12	-1	0.8
Total	10	123	75	.621	289	232	113	20	10	1752^2	1715	104	758	732	12.8	3.50	125	.257	.336	132	.198	-7	119	170	3	18.1

● RUBE PARNHAM Parnham, James Arthur b: 2/1/1894, Heidelberg, Pa. d: 11/25/63, McKeesport, Pa. BR/TR, 6′3″, 185 lbs. Deb: 9/20/16

YEAR	TM/L	W	L	PCT	G	GS	CG	SH	SV	IP	H	HR	BB	SO	RAT	ERA	ERA+	OAV	OOB	BH	AVG	PB	PR	/A	PD	TPI
1916	Phi-A	2	1	.667	4	3	2	0	0	24^2	27	0	13	8	14.6	4.01	71	.300	.388	3	.273	1	-3	-3	1	-0.2
1917	Phi-A	0	1	.000	2	2	0	0	0	11	12	1	9	4	17.2	4.09	67	.316	.447	0	.000	-0	-2	-2	0	-0.2
Total	2	2	2	.500	6	5	2	0	0	35^2	39	1	22	12	15.4	4.04	70	.305	.407	3	.214	0	-5	-5	1	-0.4

● JIM PARQUE Parque, Jim Vo b: 2/8/75, Norwalk, Cal. BL/TL, 5′11″, 165 lbs. Deb: 5/26/98

YEAR	TM/L	W	L	PCT	G	GS	CG	SH	SV	IP	H	HR	BB	SO	RAT	ERA	ERA+	OAV	OOB	BH	AVG	PB	PR	/A	PD	TPI
1998	Chi-A	7	5	.583	21	21	0	0	0	113	135	14	49	77	15.1	5.10	89	.299	.375	0	.000	-0	-6	-7	0	-0.6

YEAR	TM/L	W	L	PCT	G	GS	CG	SH	SV	IP	H	HR	BB	SO	RAT	ERA	ERA+	OAV	OOB	BH	AVG	PB	PR	/A	PD	TPI
● **JOSE PARRA**	Parra, Jose Miguel b: 11/28/72, Jacagua, D.R. BR/TR, 5'11", 160 lbs. Deb: 5/7/95																									
1995	LA-N	0	0	—	8	0	0	0	0	10^1	10	2	6	7	14.8	4.35	87	.256	.370	0	—	0	-0	-1	-0	0.0
	Min-A	1	5	.167	12	12	0	0	0	61^2	83	11	22	29	15.6	7.59	63	.313	.370	0	—	0	-20	-19	-0	-1.5
1996	Min-A	5	5	.500	27	5	0	0	0	70	88	15	27	50	15.2	6.04	85	.308	.373	0	—	0	-8	-7	0	-0.8
Total	2	6	10	.375	47	17	0	0	0	142	181	28	55	86	15.3	6.59	74	.307	.372	0	—	0	-28	-27	-1	-2.3
● **JEFF PARRETT**	Parrett, Jeffrey Dale b: 8/26/61, Indianapolis, Ind. BR/TR, 6'3", 193 lbs. Deb: 4/11/86																									
1986	Mon-N	0	1	.000	12	0	0	0	0	20^1	19	3	13	21	14.2	4.87	76	.247	.356	1	.500	0	-3	-3	0	-0.1
1987	Mon-N	7	6	.538	45	0	0	0	6	62	53	8	30	56	12.0	4.21	100	.229	.318	0	.000	-1	-1	-0	0	-0.1
1988	Mon-N	12	4	.750	61	0	0	0	6	91^2	66	8	45	62	11.0	2.65	136	.214	.316	0	—	0	8	10	-1	1.7
1989	Phi-N	12	6	.667	72	0	0	0	6	105^2	90	6	44	98	11.4	2.98	119	.232	.310	0	.000	-1	6	7	-1	1.0
1990	Phi-N	4	9	.308	47	5	0	0	1	81^2	92	10	36	69	14.2	5.18	74	.293	.368	0	.000	-1	-13	-12	-0	-1.9
	Atl-N	1	1	.500	20	0	0	0	1	27	27	1	19	17	15.7	3.00	134	.281	.405	1	1.000	0	2	3	0	0.3
	Yr	5	10	.333	67	5	0	0	2	108^2	119	11	55	86	14.5	4.64	84	.289	.374	1	.091	-1	-10	-9	0	-1.6
1991	Atl-N	1	2	.333	18	0	0	0	1	21^1	31	2	12	14	18.1	6.33	61	.326	.402	0	—	0	-6	-6	1	-0.7
1992	*Oak-A	9	1	.900	66	0	0	0	0	98^1	81	7	42	78	11.4	3.02	124	.226	.311	0	—	0	10	8	-1	0.7
1993	Col-N	3	3	.500	40	6	0	0	1	73^2	78	6	45	66	15.3	5.38	89	.274	.377	1	.091	-1	-11	-5	-0	-0.5
1995	StL-N	4	7	.364	59	0	0	0	0	76^2	71	8	28	71	11.7	3.64	115	.243	.312	1	.500	0	5	5	-1	0.6
1996	StL-N	2	2	.500	33	0	0	0	0	42^1	40	2	20	42	13.0	4.25	98	.245	.332	0	.000	0	-0	-0	1	0.0
	Phi-N	1	1	.500	18	0	0	0	0	24	24	0	11	22	13.1	1.88	230	.270	.350	0	—	0	6	6	-0	0.4
	Yr	3	3	.500	51	0	0	0	0	66^1	64	2	31	64	12.9	3.39	125	.252	.333	0	.000	0	6	6	0	0.4
Total	10	56	43	.566	491	11	0	0	22	724^2	672	61	345	616	12.7	3.80	104	.249	.336	4	.105	-1	4	12	-3	1.4
● **STEVE PARRIS**	Parris, Steven Michael b: 12/17/67, Joliet, Ill. BR/TR, 6', 190 lbs. Deb: 6/21/95																									
1995	Pit-N	6	6	.500	15	15	1	1	0	82	89	12	33	61	14.2	5.38	80	.283	.363	7	.250	1	-11	-10	-0	-1.1
1996	Pit-N	0	3	.000	8	4	0	0	0	26^1	35	4	11	27	16.1	7.18	61	.321	.388	1	.167	0	-9	-8	0	-0.7
1998	Cin-N	6	5	.545	18	16	1	1	0	99	89	9	32	77	11.4	3.73	116	.236	.303	4	.138	-1	6	7	1	0.7
Total	3	12	14	.462	41	35	2	2	0	207^1	213	25	76	165	13.1	4.82	90	.266	.339	12	.190	1	-14	-11	1	-1.1
● **MIKE PARROTT**	Parrott, Michael Everett Arch b: 12/6/54, Oxnard, Cal. BR/TR, 6'4", 210 lbs. Deb: 9/5/77																									
1977	Bal-A	0	0	—	3	0	0	0	0	4^1	4	0	2	2	12.5	2.08	183	.250	.333	0	—	0	1	1	-0	0.0
1978	Sea-A	1	5	.167	27	10	0	0	1	82^1	108	8	32	41	15.6	5.14	74	.316	.379	0	—	0	-13	-12	0	-0.8
1979	Sea-A	14	12	.538	38	30	13	2	0	229^1	231	17	86	127	12.7	3.77	116	.267	.338	0	—	0	11	15	3	1.7
1980	Sea-A	1	16	.059	27	16	1	0	3	94	136	16	42	53	17.1	7.28	57	.348	.412	0	—	0	-34	-33	4	-4.8
1981	Sea-A	3	6	.333	24	12	0	0	1	85	102	3	28	43	13.9	5.08	76	.299	.354	0	—	0	-13	-12	0	-1.3
Total	5	19	39	.328	119	68	14	2	5	495	581	44	190	266	14.2	4.87	85	.297	.363	0	—	0	-48	-41	6	-5.2
● **TOM PARROTT**	Parrott, Thomas William "Tacky Tom" b: 4/10/1868, Portland, Ore. d: 1/1/32, Dundee, Ore. BR/TR, 5'10.5", 170 lbs. Deb: 6/18/1893 F◆																									
1893	Chi-N	0	3	.000	4	3	2	0	0	27	35	1	17	7	17.3	6.67	69	.304	.394	7	.259	-0	-6	-6	-1	-0.5
	Cin-N	10	7	.588	22	17	11	1	0	154	174	1	70	33	14.8	4.09	117	.276	.357	13	.191	-3	10	12	2	0.9
	Yr	10	10	.500	26	20	13	1	0	181	209	2	87	40	15.2	4.48	106	.281	.363	20	.211	-3	4	6	1	0.4
1894	Cin-N	17	19	.472	41	36	31	1	1	308^2	402	19	126	61	15.7	5.60	99	.311	.377	74	.323	8	-9	-1	3	0.7
1895	Cin-N	11	18	.379	41	31	23	0	**3**	263^1	382	8	76	57	15.8	5.47	91	.334	.378	69	.343	10	-20	-14	3	-0.2
1896	StL-N	1	1	.500	7	2	2	0	0	42	62	4	18	8	17.8	6.21	70	.339	.407	138	.291	1	-9	-9	-0	-0.3
Total	4	39	48	.448	115	89	69	2	4	795	1055	33	307	166	15.7	5.33	96	.314	.376	301	.301	16	-34	-19	6	0.6
● **JIGGS PARSON**	Parson, William Edwin b: 12/28/1885, Parker, S.Dak. d: 5/19/67, Los Angeles, Cal. BR/TR, 6'2", 180 lbs. Deb: 5/16/10																									
1910	Bos-N	0	2	.000	10	4	0	0	0	35^1	35	2	26	7	16.0	3.82	87	.278	.409	1	.083	-1	-3	-2	-0	-0.2
1911	Bos-N	0	1	.000	7	0	0	0	0	25	36	2	15	7	19.8	6.48	59	.375	.478	2	.200	-0	-9	-7	-1	-0.3
Total	2	0	3	.000	17	4	0	0	0	60^1	71	4	41	14	17.6	4.92	72	.320	.439	3	.136	-2	-12	-9	-1	-0.5
● **CHARLIE PARSONS**	Parsons, Charles James b: 7/18/1863, Cherry Flats, Pa. d: 3/24/36, Mansfield, Pa. BL/TL, 5'10", 160 lbs. Deb: 5/29/1886																									
1886	Bos-N	0	2	.000	2	2	2	0	0	16	20	0	4	5	13.5	3.94	81	.308	.348	3	.375	1	-1	-1	-1	-0.1
1887	NY-a	1	1	.500	4	4	4	0	0	34	51	0	6	5	15.4	4.50	94	.319	.347	3	.200	-1	-1	-1	0	-0.1
1890	Cle-N	0	1	.000	2	1	0	0	0	9	12	0	6	2	22.0	6.00	60	.308	.449	3	.750	1	-2	-2	0	-0.1
Total	3	1	4	.200	8	7	6	0	0	59	83	0	16	12	15.9	4.58	84	.314	.365	9	.333	2	-4	-5	-1	-0.3
● **TOM PARSONS**	Parsons, Thomas Anthony b: 9/13/39, Lakeville, Conn. BR/TR, 6'7", 210 lbs. Deb: 9/5/63																									
1963	Pit-N	0	1	.000	1	1	0	0	0	4^1	7	1	2	2	18.7	8.31	40	.368	.429	0	.000	-0	-2	-2	0	-0.4
1964	NY-N	1	2	.333	4	2	1	0	0	19^1	20	1	6	10	12.1	4.19	85	.274	.329	0	.000	-1	-1	-1	-0	-0.3
1965	NY-N	1	10	.091	35	11	1	1	1	90^2	108	17	17	58	12.4	4.67	76	.290	.321	1	.056	-1	-11	-11	1	-1.3
Total	3	2	13	.133	40	14	2	1	1	114^1	135	19	25	70	12.6	4.72	75	.291	.327	1	.037	-2	-15	-15	1	-2.0
● **BILL PARSONS**	Parsons, William Raymond b: 8/17/48, Riverside, Cal. BR/TR, 6'6", 195 lbs. Deb: 4/13/71																									
1971	Mil-A	13	17	.433	36	35	12	4	0	244^2	219	19	93	139	11.6	3.20	108	.241	.315	12	.167	3	7	7	0	1.3
1972	Mil-A	13	13	.500	33	30	10	2	0	214	194	27	68	111	11.1	3.91	77	.240	.301	11	.164	0	-20	-21	-3	-2.7
1973	Mil-A	3	6	.333	20	17	0	0	0	59^2	59	6	67	30	19.0	6.79	55	.257	.424	0	—	0	-20	-20	-0	-2.6
1974	Oak-A	0	0	—	4	0	0	0	0	2	1	0	3	2	18.0	0.00	—	.143	.400	0	—	0	1	1	-0	0.0
Total	4	29	36	.446	93	82	22	6	0	520^1	473	52	231	282	12.3	3.89	85	.242	.325	23	.165	3	-32	-33	-3	-4.0
● **STAN PARTENHEIMER**	Partenheimer, Stanwood Wendell "Party" b: 10/21/22, Chicopee Falls, Mass. d: 1/28/89, Wilson, N.C. BR/TL, 5'11", 175 lbs. Deb: 5/27/44 F																									
1944	Bos-A	0	0	—	1	1	0	0	0	1	3	0	2	0	45.0	18.00	19	.500	.625	0	.000	-0	-2	-2	-0	0.0
1945	StL-N	0	0	—	8	2	0	0	0	13^1	12	2	16	6	18.9	6.08	62	.250	.438	0	.000	-0	-3	-3	0	0.0
Total	2	0	0	—	9	3	0	0	0	14^1	15	2	18	6	20.7	6.91	54	.278	.458	0	.000	-1	-5	-5	0	0.0
● **BILL PASCHALL**	Paschall, William Herbert b: 4/22/54, Norfolk, Va. BR/TR, 6', 175 lbs. Deb: 9/20/78																									
1978	KC-A	0	1	.000	2	0	0	0	1	8	6	0	0	5	7.9	3.38	113	.207	.233	0	—	0	0	0	-0	-0.1
1979	KC-A	0	1	.000	7	0	0	0	0	13^2	18	2	5	3	16.5	6.59	65	.300	.373	0	—	0	-4	-4	-0	-0.4
1981	KC-A	0	0	—	2	0	0	0	0	2	2	0	0	1	9.0	4.50	80	.286	.286	0	—	0	-0	-0	-0	0.0
Total	3	0	2	.000	11	0	0	0	1	23^2	26	2	5	9	12.9	5.32	76	.271	.327	0	—	0	-3	-3	-1	-0.5
● **CAMILO PASCUAL**	Pascual, Camilo Alberto (Lus) b: 1/20/34, Havana, Cuba BR/TR, 5'11", 185 lbs. Deb: 4/15/54 FC																									
1954	Was-A	4	7	.364	48	4	1	0	3	119^1	126	7	61	60	14.6	4.22	84	.276	.368	4	.133	-0	-7	-9	3	-0.5
1955	Was-A	2	12	.143	43	16	1	0	3	129	158	5	70	82	16.3	6.14	62	.311	.401	7	.219	0	-31	-33	2	-3.0
1956	Was-A	6	18	.250	39	27	6	0	2	188^2	194	33	89	162	13.8	5.87	74	.261	.345	8	.138	-2	-36	-32	1	-3.6
1957	Was-A	8	17	.320	29	26	8	2	0	175^2	168	11	76	113	12.7	4.10	95	.258	.338	7	.140	-2	-6	-4	2	-0.5
1958	Was-A	8	12	.400	31	27	6	2	0	177^1	166	14	60	146	11.6	3.15	121	.248	.313	9	.158	-1	12	13	1	1.4
1959	Was-A†	17	10	.630	32	30	**17**	**6**	0	238^2	202	10	69	185	10.3	2.64	148	.226	.284	26	.302	6	32	34	5	**5.0**
1960	Was-A†	12	8	.600	26	22	8	3	2	151^2	139	11	53	143	11.5	3.03	128	.240	.306	9	.176	3	14	15	0	2.2
1961	Min-A★	15	16	.484	35	33	15	**8**	0	252^1	205	26	100	**221**	11.0	3.46	123	.217	.294	14	.165	-0	16	22	1	2.5
1962	Min-A★	20	11	.645	34	33	**18**	**5**	0	257^2	236	25	59	**206**	10.4	3.32	123	.241	.286	26	.268	8	19	22	0	3.4
1963	Min-A	21	9	.700	31	31	**18**	3	0	248^1	205	21	81	**202**	10.5	2.46	148	.224	.289	23	.250	6	32	**33**	-1	4.6
1964	Min-A★	15	12	.556	36	36	14	1	0	267^1	245	30	98	213	11.6	3.30	108	.241	.309	17	.181	4	10	8	0	1.2
1965	*Min-A	9	3	.750	27	27	5	1	0	156	126	12	63	96	11.2	3.35	106	.217	.299	12	.200	3	2	4	2	0.7
1966	Min-A	8	6	.571	21	19	2	0	0	103	113	9	30	56	12.7	4.89	73	.278	.330	8	.216	1	-17	-15	2	-1.6
1967	Was-A	12	10	.545	28	27	5	1	0	164^2	147	15	43	106	10.5	3.28	96	.237	.289	9	.176	1	-1	-2	-0	-0.1
1968	Was-A	13	12	.520	31	31	8	4	0	201	181	11	59	111	10.9	2.69	109	.239	.298	12	.185	1	7	5	1	0.9
1969	Was-A	2	5	.286	14	13	0	0	0	55^1	49	12	38	34	15.0	6.83	51	.239	.371	4	.235	0	-20	-21	-0	-2.2
	Cin-N	0	0	—	5	1	0	0	0	7^1	14	2	4	3	22.1	8.59	44	.424	.486	0	—	0	-4	-4	-0	0.0
1970	LA-N	0	0	—	10	0	0	0	0	14	12	2	5	8	11.6	2.57	149	.231	.310	0	—	0	2	2	0	0.0

YEAR	TM/L	W	L	PCT	G	GS	CG	SH	SV	IP	H	HR	BB	SO	RAT	ERA	ERA+	OAV	OOB	BH	AVG	PB	PR	/A	PD	TPI
1971	Cle-A	2	2	.500	9	1	0	0	0	23^1	17	0	11	20	11.2	3.09	124	.205	.305	3	.600	1	1	2	1	0.5
Total	18	174	170	.506	529	404	132	36	10	2930^2	2703	256	1069	2167	11.8	3.63	103	.244	.314	198	.205	29	26	38	18	10.9

● CARLOS PASCUAL Pascual, Carlos Alberto (Lus) "Little Potato" b: 3/13/31, Havana, Cuba BR/TR, 5'6", 165 lbs. Deb: 9/24/50 F

YEAR	TM/L	W	L	PCT	G	GS	CG	SH	SV	IP	H	HR	BB	SO	RAT	ERA	ERA+	OAV	OOB	BH	AVG	PB	PR	/A	PD	TPI
1950	Was-A	1	1	.500	2	2	2	0	0	17	12	0	8	3	11.1	2.12	212	.194	.296	1	.250	0	5	4	-1	0.4

● LARRY PASHNICK Pashnick, Larry John b: 4/25/56, Lincoln Park, Mich. BR/TR, 6'3", 205 lbs. Deb: 4/10/82

YEAR	TM/L	W	L	PCT	G	GS	CG	SH	SV	IP	H	HR	BB	SO	RAT	ERA	ERA+	OAV	OOB	BH	AVG	PB	PR	/A	PD	TPI
1982	Det-A	4	4	.500	28	13	1	0	0	94^1	110	17	25	19	13.0	4.01	101	.297	.343	0	—	0	1	1	-1	0.0
1983	Det-A	1	3	.250	12	6	0	0	0	37^2	48	5	18	17	16.5	5.26	74	.308	.390	0	—	0	-5	-6	1	-0.5
1984	Min-A	2	1	.667	13	1	0	0	0	38^1	38	3	11	10	12.0	3.52	119	.260	.321	0	—	0	2	3	0	0.2
Total	3	7	8	.467	53	20	1	0	0	170^1	196	25	54	46	13.5	4.17	97	.292	.350	0	—	0	-2	-2	0	-0.3

● CLAUDE PASSEAU Passeau, Claude William b: 4/9/09, Waynesboro, Miss. BR/TR, 6'3", 198 lbs. Deb: 9/29/35

YEAR	TM/L	W	L	PCT	G	GS	CG	SH	SV	IP	H	HR	BB	SO	RAT	ERA	ERA+	OAV	OOB	BH	AVG	PB	PR	/A	PD	TPI
1935	Pit-N	0	1	.000	1	1	0	0	0	3	7	0	2	1	27.0	12.00	34	.500	.563	0	.000	-0	-3	-3	0	-0.6
1936	Phi-N	11	15	.423	49	21	8	2	3	217^1	247	7	55	85	12.7	3.48	130	.280	.325	22	.282	3	13	26	1	3.3
1937	Phi-N	14	18	.438	50	34	18	1	2	**292^1**	348	16	79	135	13.3	4.34	100	.296	.343	21	.196	-0	-14	-0	0	0.0
1938	Phi-N	11	18	.379	44	33	15	0	1	239	281	8	93	100	14.4	4.52	86	.287	.354	13	.162	-2	-19	-17	3	-1.7
1939	Phi-N	2	4	.333	8	8	4	1	0	53^1	54	1	25	29	13.5	4.22	95	.263	.346	4	.200	-0	-2	-1	0	-0.2
	Chi-N	13	9	.591	34	27	13	1	3	221	215	8	48	108	10.9	3.05	129	.254	.297	12	.156	-1	21	22	1	2.0
	Yr	15	13	.536	42	35	17	2	3	274^1	269	9	73	**137**	11.4	3.28	120	.255	.306	16	.165	-2	19	20	1	1.8
1940	Chi-N	20	13	.606	46	31	20	4	5	280^2	259	8	59	124	10.3	2.50	150	.237	.278	20	.204	6	42	39	1	**5.3**
1941	Chi-N★	14	14	.500	34	30	20	3	0	231	262	10	52	80	12.3	3.35	105	.281	.320	19	.221	5	7	4	-1	0.9
1942	Chi-N★	19	14	.576	35	34	24	3	0	278^1	284	13	74	89	11.7	2.68	119	.260	.309	19	.181	1	20	16	1	2.0
1943	Chi-N☆	15	12	.556	35	31	18	1	1	257	245	10	66	93	11.0	2.91	115	.249	.299	19	.198	1	14	12	1	1.5
1944	Chi-N	15	9	.625	34	27	18	2	3	227	234	8	50	89	11.3	2.89	122	.266	.306	13	.162	-1	18	16	1	1.6
1945	*Chi-N†	17	9	.654	34	27	19	**5**	1	227	205	4	59	98	10.5	2.46	149	.238	.289	17	.187	2	34	**30**	3	**3.8**
1946	Chi-N★	9	8	.529	21	21	10	2	0	129^1	118	5	42	47	11.2	3.13	106	.237	.298	10	.204	3	4	3	1	0.7
1947	Chi-N	2	6	.250	19	6	1	1	2	63^1	97	7	24	26	17.3	6.25	63	.353	.407	0	.000	-2	-15	-16	-1	-2.1
Total	13	162	150	.519	444	331	188	26	21	2719^2	2856	105	728	1104	12.0	3.32	113	.267	.316	189	.192	13	120	128	11	16.5

● FRANK PASTORE Pastore, Frank Enrico b: 8/21/57, Alhambra, Cal. BR/TR, 6'3", 205 lbs. Deb: 4/4/79

YEAR	TM/L	W	L	PCT	G	GS	CG	SH	SV	IP	H	HR	BB	SO	RAT	ERA	ERA+	OAV	OOB	BH	AVG	PB	PR	/A	PD	TPI
1979	*Cin-N	6	7	.462	30	9	2	1	4	95^1	102	8	23	63	11.9	4.25	88	.271	.315	4	.160	-0	-5	-5	0	-0.8
1980	Cin-N	13	7	.650	27	27	9	2	0	184^2	161	13	42	110	9.9	3.27	109	.233	.277	10	.156	-1	7	6	-1	0.5
1981	Cin-N	4	9	.308	22	22	2	1	0	132	125	11	35	81	11.1	4.02	88	.247	.300	5	.114	-2	-8	-7	-2	-1.0
1982	Cin-N	8	13	.381	31	29	3	2	0	188^1	210	13	57	94	13.0	3.97	93	.286	.341	10	.172	1	-8	-6	-2	-0.7
1983	Cin-N	9	12	.429	36	29	4	1	0	184^1	207	20	64	93	13.3	4.88	78	.290	.349	11	.186	2	-26	-22	-1	-2.3
1984	Cin-N	3	8	.273	24	16	1	0	0	98^1	110	10	40	53	14.0	6.50	58	.285	.357	2	.071	-2	-32	-30	0	-3.1
1985	Cin-N	2	1	.667	17	6	1	0	0	54	60	1	16	29	12.8	3.83	99	.287	.341	2	.143	-0	-1	-0	0	0.0
1986	Min-A	3	1	.750	33	1	0	0	2	49^1	54	4	24	18	14.2	4.01	107	.283	.363	0	—	0	1	2	-1	0.0
Total	8	48	58	.453	220	139	22	7	6	986^1	1029	80	301	541	12.3	4.29	87	.270	.326	44	.151	-2	-72	-62	-5	-7.4

● JIM PASTORIUS Pastorius, James W. "Sunny Jim" b: 7/12/1881, Pittsburgh, Pa. d: 5/10/41, Pittsburgh, Pa. BL/TL, 5'9", 165 lbs. Deb: 4/15/06

YEAR	TM/L	W	L	PCT	G	GS	CG	SH	SV	IP	H	HR	BB	SO	RAT	ERA	ERA+	OAV	OOB	BH	AVG	PB	PR	/A	PD	TPI
1906	Bro-N	10	14	.417	29	24	16	3	0	211^2	225	4	69	58	12.6	3.61	70	.274	.333	10	.141	-0	-23	-26	-1	-2.9
1907	Bro-N	16	12	.571	28	26	20	4	0	222	218	2	77	70	12.2	2.35	100	.264	.331	15	.205	3	3	-0	-1	0.2
1908	Bro-N	4	20	.167	28	25	16	2	0	213^2	171	5	74	54	10.6	2.44	96	.216	.288	8	.129	-0	-2	-2	0	-0.3
1909	Bro-N	1	9	.100	12	9	5	1	0	79^2	91	4	58	23	16.9	5.76	45	.313	.429	2	.080	-1	-28	-28	1	-3.1
Total	4	31	55	.360	97	84	57	10	0	727	705	15	278	205	12.4	3.12	78	.258	.330	35	.152	1	-50	-56	-1	-6.1

● JOE PATE Pate, Joseph William b: 6/6/1892, Alice, Tex. d: 12/26/48, Fort Worth, Tex. BL/TL, 5'10", 184 lbs. Deb: 4/15/26

YEAR	TM/L	W	L	PCT	G	GS	CG	SH	SV	IP	H	HR	BB	SO	RAT	ERA	ERA+	OAV	OOB	BH	AVG	PB	PR	/A	PD	TPI
1926	Phi-A	9	0	1.000	47	2	0	0	6	113	109	3	51	24	12.9	2.71	154	.262	.345	4	.148	-0	**16**	**18**	3	1.8
1927	Phi-A	0	3	.000	32	0	0	0	6	53^2	67	3	21	14	14.9	5.20	82	.318	.382	3	.300	1	-6	-6	0	-0.3
Total	2	9	3	.750	79	2	0	0	12	166^2	176	6	72	38	13.6	3.51	120	.281	.358	7	.189	1	10	13	4	1.5

● BRONSWELL PATRICK Patrick, Bronswell Dante b: 9/16/70, Greenville, N.C. BR/TR, 6'1", 220 lbs. Deb: 5/18/98

YEAR	TM/L	W	L	PCT	G	GS	CG	SH	SV	IP	H	HR	BB	SO	RAT	ERA	ERA+	OAV	OOB	BH	AVG	PB	PR	/A	PD	TPI
1998	Mil-N	4	1	.800	32	3	0	0	0	78^2	83	9	29	49	12.8	4.69	92	.279	.343	3	.200	2	-4	-3	-1	-0.2

● CASE PATTEN Patten, Case Lyman "Casey" b: 5/7/1876, Westport, N.Y. d: 5/31/35, Rochester, N.Y. BB/TL, 6', 175 lbs. Deb: 5/4/01

YEAR	TM/L	W	L	PCT	G	GS	CG	SH	SV	IP	H	HR	BB	SO	RAT	ERA	ERA+	OAV	OOB	BH	AVG	PB	PR	/A	PD	TPI
1901	Was-A	18	10	.643	32	30	26	4	0	254^1	285	8	74	109	13.3	3.93	93	.280	.339	13	.135	-5	-7	-7	0	-1.1
1902	Was-A	18	17	.514	36	34	33	1	1	299^2	331	11	89	92	12.9	4.05	91	.281	.337	12	.096	-10	-16	-12	-1	-2.1
1903	Was-A	11	22	.333	36	34	32	0	1	300	313	11	80	133	11.9	3.60	87	.268	.317	14	.132	-6	-21	-16	1	-2.1
1904	Was-A	14	23	.378	45	39	37	2	**3**	357^2	367	2	79	150	11.7	3.07	87	.266	.315	16	.127	-5	-19	-16	1	-2.1
1905	Was-A	14	21	.400	42	36	29	2	0	309^2	300	3	86	113	11.5	3.14	84	.256	.312	16	.155	-2	-17	-17	-2	-2.3
1906	Was-A	19	16	.543	38	32	28	7	0	282^2	253	2	79	96	10.8	2.17	122	.242	.299	11	.117	-4	17	15	-1	1.3
1907	Was-A	12	16	.429	36	29	20	1	0	237^1	272	3	63	58	12.9	3.56	68	.290	.339	11	.126	-3	-27	-30	-5	-4.1
1908	Was-A	0	2	.000	4	3	1	0	0	18	25	0	6	6	15.5	3.50	65	.333	.383	1	.200	-0	-2	-2	-0	-0.3
	Bos-A	0	1	.000	1	1	0	0	0	3	8	0	1	0	27.0	15.00	16	.533	.563	0	.000	-0	-4	-4	0	-0.9
	Yr	0	3	.000	5	4	1	0	0	21	33	0	7	6	17.1	5.14	45	.367	.412	1	.167	-0	-6	-7	-0	-1.2
Total	8	106	128	.453	270	238	206	17	5	2062^1	2154	40	557	757	12.2	3.36	88	.270	.323	94	.127	-35	-97	-91	-7	-13.7

● DANNY PATTERSON Patterson, Danny Shane b: 2/17/71, San Gabriel, Cal. BR/TR, 6', 170 lbs. Deb: 7/26/96

YEAR	TM/L	W	L	PCT	G	GS	CG	SH	SV	IP	H	HR	BB	SO	RAT	ERA	ERA+	OAV	OOB	BH	AVG	PB	PR	/A	PD	TPI
1996	*Tex-A	0	0	—	7	0	0	0	0	8^2	10	0	3	5	13.5	0.00	—	.286	.342	0	—	0	5	5	0	0.0
1997	Tex-A	10	6	.625	54	0	0	0	1	71	70	3	23	69	11.8	3.42	140	.263	.322	0	—	0	9	11	-0	2.0
1998	Tex-A	2	5	.286	56	0	0	0	2	60^2	64	11	19	33	12.6	4.45	109	.274	.333	0	—	0	1	3	-0	0.2
Total	3	12	11	.522	117	0	0	0	3	140^1	144	14	45	107	12.2	3.66	132	.269	.328	0	—	0	15	18	-0	2.2

● DARYL PATTERSON Patterson, Daryl Alan b: 11/21/43, Coalinga, Cal. BL/TR, 6'4", 195 lbs. Deb: 4/10/68

YEAR	TM/L	W	L	PCT	G	GS	CG	SH	SV	IP	H	HR	BB	SO	RAT	ERA	ERA+	OAV	OOB	BH	AVG	PB	PR	/A	PD	TPI
1968	*Det-A	2	3	.400	38	1	0	0	7	68	53	3	27	49	11.1	2.12	142	.213	.300	0	.000	-1	7	7	-0	0.5
1969	Det-A	0	2	.000	18	0	0	0	0	22^1	15	2	19	12	13.7	2.82	132	.205	.370	0	.000	-0	2	2	-1	0.1
1970	Det-A	7	1	.875	43	0	0	0	2	78	81	9	39	55	14.4	4.85	77	.269	.362	0	.000	-1	-10	-10	-1	-1.2
1971	Det-A	0	1	.000	12	0	0	0	0	9^1	14	1	6	5	20.3	4.82	74	.359	.457	0	—	0	-1	-1	-0	-0.1
	Oak-A	0	0	—	4	0	0	0	0	5^2	5	2	4	2	15.9	7.94	42	.238	.385	0	.000	-0	-3	-3	-0	0.0
	Yr	0	1	.000	16	0	0	0	0	15	19	3	10	7	18.0	6.00	58	.311	.417	0	.000	-0	-4	-4	-0	-0.1
	StL-N	0	1	.000	13	2	0	0	1	26^2	20	3	15	11	11.8	4.39	82	.211	.318	0	.000	-0	-3	-2	-1	-0.2
1974	Pit-N	2	1	.667	14	0	0	0	1	21	35	3	9	8	18.9	7.29	47	.376	.431	0	.000	-1	-9	-9	0	-1.3
Total	5	11	9	.550	142	3	0	0	11	231	223	23	119	142	13.8	4.09	85	.256	.353	0	.000	-3	-17	-16	-3	-2.2

● DAVE PATTERSON Patterson, David Glenn b: 7/25/56, Springfield, Mo. BR/TR, 6', 170 lbs. Deb: 6/9/79

YEAR	TM/L	W	L	PCT	G	GS	CG	SH	SV	IP	H	HR	BB	SO	RAT	ERA	ERA+	OAV	OOB	BH	AVG	PB	PR	/A	PD	TPI
1979	LA-N	4	1	.800	36	0	0	0	6	53	62	5	22	34	14.3	5.26	69	.292	.359	1	.143	-0	-9	-10	-0	-1.1

● GIL PATTERSON Patterson, Gilbert Thomas b: 9/5/55, Philadelphia, Pa. BR/TR, 6'1", 185 lbs. Deb: 4/19/77

YEAR	TM/L	W	L	PCT	G	GS	CG	SH	SV	IP	H	HR	BB	SO	RAT	ERA	ERA+	OAV	OOB	BH	AVG	PB	PR	/A	PD	TPI
1977	NY-A	1	2	.333	10	6	0	0	1	33^1	38	3	20	29	16.5	5.40	73	.290	.396	0	—	0	-5	-5	1	-0.3

● JEFF PATTERSON Patterson, Jeffrey Simmons b: 10/1/68, Anaheim, Cal. BR/TR, 6'2", 200 lbs. Deb: 4/30/95

YEAR	TM/L	W	L	PCT	G	GS	CG	SH	SV	IP	H	HR	BB	SO	RAT	ERA	ERA+	OAV	OOB	BH	AVG	PB	PR	/A	PD	TPI
1995	NY-A	0	0	—	3	0	0	0	0	3^1	3	1	3	3	16.2	2.70	171	.231	.375	0	—	0	1	1	-0	0.0

● KEN PATTERSON Patterson, Kenneth Brian b: 7/8/64, Costa Mesa, Cal. BL/TL, 6'4", 210 lbs. Deb: 7/9/88

YEAR	TM/L	W	L	PCT	G	GS	CG	SH	SV	IP	H	HR	BB	SO	RAT	ERA	ERA+	OAV	OOB	BH	AVG	PB	PR	/A	PD	TPI
1988	Chi-A	0	2	.000	9	2	0	0	1	20^2	25	2	7	8	13.9	4.79	83	.294	.348	0	—	0	-2	-2	-0	-0.2
1989	Chi-A	6	1	.857	50	1	0	0	0	65^2	64	11	28	43	12.9	4.52	84	.257	.337	0	—	0	-5	-5	-1	-0.5
1990	Chi-A	2	1	.667	43	0	0	0	2	66^1	58	6	34	40	12.8	3.39	113	.242	.341	0	—	0	4	3	0	0.3
1991	Chi-A	3	0	1.000	43	0	0	0	1	63^2	48	5	35	32	11.9	2.83	140	.214	.323	0	—	0	9	8	-1	0.4
1992	Chi-N	2	3	.400	32	1	0	0	0	41^2	41	7	27	23	14.9	3.89	93	.268	.381	0	.000	-0	-2	-1	-0	-0.2
1993	Cal-A	1	1	.500	46	0	0	0	1	59	54	7	35	36	13.6	4.58	98	.249	.353	0	—	0	-2	-0	-0	-0.1

YEAR	TM/L	W	L	PCT	G	GS	CG	SH	SV	IP	H	HR	BB	SO	RAT	ERA	ERA+	OAV	OOB	BH	AVG	PB	PR	/A	PD	TPI
1994	Cal-A	0	0	—	1	0	0	0	0	0^2	0	0	0	1	0.0	0.00	—	.000	.000	0	—	0	0	0	0	0.0
Total	7	14	8	.636	224	4	0	0	5	317^2	290	38	166	183	13.1	3.88	102	.248	.344	0	.000	-0	3	3	-3	-0.3

● REGGIE PATTERSON Patterson, Reginald Allen b: 11/7/58, Birmingham, Ala. BR/TR, 6'4", 180 lbs. Deb: 8/13/81

YEAR	TM/L	W	L	PCT	G	GS	CG	SH	SV	IP	H	HR	BB	SO	RAT	ERA	ERA+	OAV	OOB	BH	AVG	PB	PR	/A	PD	TPI
1981	Chi-A	0	1	.000	6	1	0	0	0	7^1	14	1	6	2	24.5	13.50	26	.412	.500	0	—	0	-8	-8	0	-0.9
1983	Chi-N	1	2	.333	5	2	0	0	0	18^2	17	3	6	10	12.1	4.82	79	.246	.325	0	.000	-1	-2	-2	-0	-0.4
1984	Chi-N	0	1	.000	3	1	0	0	0	6	10	1	2	5	18.0	10.50	37	.357	.400	0	.000	-0	-5	-4	0	-0.6
1985	Chi-N	3	0	1.000	8	5	1	0	0	39	36	2	10	17	10.6	3.00	133	.250	.299	1	.100	-0	3	4	-0	0.3
Total	4	4	4	.500	22	9	1	0	0	71	77	7	24	34	13.1	5.20	75	.280	.342	1	.056	-1	-13	-10	0	-1.6

● BOB PATTERSON Patterson, Robert Chandler b: 5/16/59, Jacksonville, Fla. BR/TL, 6'2", 192 lbs. Deb: 9/2/85

YEAR	TM/L	W	L	PCT	G	GS	CG	SH	SV	IP	H	HR	BB	SO	RAT	ERA	ERA+	OAV	OOB	BH	AVG	PB	PR	/A	PD	TPI
1985	SD-N	0	0	—	3	0	0	0	0	4	13	2	3	1	36.0	24.75	14	.565	.615	0	—	0	-9	-9	-0	0.0
1986	Pit-N	2	3	.400	11	5	0	0	0	36^1	49	0	5	20	13.4	4.95	77	.322	.344	1	.125	-0	-5	-5	1	-0.5
1987	Pit-N	1	4	.200	15	7	0	0	0	43	49	5	22	27	15.1	6.70	61	.290	.375	1	.083	-1	-13	-12	-0	-1.3
1989	Pit-N	4	3	.571	12	3	0	0	1	26^2	23	3	8	20	10.5	4.05	83	.232	.290	0	.000	-0	-2	-2	-0	-0.6
1990	*Pit-N	8	5	.615	55	5	0	0	5	94^2	88	9	21	70	10.6	2.95	123	.249	.296	1	.053	-1	9	7	-0	0.8
1991	*Pit-N	4	3	.571	54	1	0	0	2	65^2	67	7	15	57	11.2	4.11	87	.267	.308	1	.250	0	-3	-4	0	-0.4
1992	*Pit-N	6	3	.667	60	0	0	0	9	64^2	59	7	23	43	11.4	2.92	118	.246	.312	2	.333	1	4	4	-1	0.7
1993	Tex-A	2	4	.333	52	0	0	0	1	52^2	59	8	11	46	12.1	4.78	87	.282	.321	0	—	0	-3	-4	0	-0.3
1994	Cal-A	2	3	.400	47	0	0	0	1	42	35	6	15	30	11.1	4.07	120	.229	.306	0	—	0	3	4	-1	0.3
1995	Cal-A	5	2	.714	62	0	0	0	0	53^1	48	6	13	41	10.5	3.04	155	.246	.297	0	—	0	10	10	-1	1.0
1996	Chi-N	3	3	.500	79	0	0	0	8	54^2	46	6	22	53	11.4	3.13	138	.229	.308	1	.333	0	7	7	-1	0.8
1997	Chi-N	1	6	.143	76	0	0	0	0	59^1	47	9	10	58	8.6	3.34	129	.222	.257	0	.000	-0	6	6	0	0.7
1998	Chi-N	1	1	.500	33	0	0	0	1	20^1	36	2	12	17	21.2	7.52	58	.391	.462	0	—	-0	-7	-7	-0	-0.7
Total	13	39	40	.494	559	21	0	0	28	617^1	619	70	180	483	11.8	4.08	98	.263	.318	7	.125	-1	-3	-6	-4	0.5

● ROY PATTERSON Patterson, Roy Lewis "Boy Wonder" b: 12/17/1876, Stoddard, Wis. d: 4/14/53, St.Croix Falls, Wis. BR/TR, 6', 185 lbs. Deb: 4/24/01

YEAR	TM/L	W	L	PCT	G	GS	CG	SH	SV	IP	H	HR	BB	SO	RAT	ERA	ERA+	OAV	OOB	BH	AVG	PB	PR	/A	PD	TPI
1901	Chi-A	20	15	.571	41	35	30	4	0	312^1	345	11	62	127	12.0	3.37	103	.277	.317	26	.222	1	10	4	0	0.4
1902	Chi-A	19	14	.576	34	30	26	2	0	268	262	5	67	61	11.1	3.06	111	.256	.304	20	.190	-2	15	10	1	1.0
1903	Chi-A	15	15	.500	34	30	26	2	1	293	275	5	69	89	10.9	2.70	104	.248	.298	11	.105	-6	8	3	2	-0.1
1904	Chi-A	9	9	.500	22	17	14	4	0	165	148	1	24	64	9.8	2.29	107	.241	.277	6	.103	-4	6	3	-1	-0.2
1905	Chi-A	4	6	.400	13	9	7	0	0	88^2	73	0	16	29	9.0	1.83	135	.226	.263	8	.267	2	8	6	1	1.0
1906	Chi-A	10	7	.588	21	18	12	3	1	142	119	1	17	45	8.9	2.09	121	.231	.261	3	.061	-5	9	7	0	0.4
1907	Chi-A	4	6	.400	19	13	4	1	0	96	105	0	18	27	11.7	2.63	91	.280	.316	3	.097	-3	-1	-2	1	-0.4
Total	7	81	72	.529	184	152	119	16	2	1365	1327	23	273	442	10.8	2.75	107	.255	.297	77	.156	-16	57	31	5	2.1

● MARTY PATTIN Pattin, Martin William b: 4/6/43, Charleston, Ill. BR/TR, 5'11", 180 lbs. Deb: 5/14/68 C

YEAR	TM/L	W	L	PCT	G	GS	CG	SH	SV	IP	H	HR	BB	SO	RAT	ERA	ERA+	OAV	OOB	BH	AVG	PB	PR	/A	PD	TPI
1968	Cal-A	4	4	.500	52	4	0	0	3	84	67	7	37	66	11.4	2.79	104	.221	.310	1	.083	-1	2	1	-1	-0.1
1969	Sea-A	7	12	.368	34	27	2	1	0	158^2	166	29	71	126	13.6	5.62	65	.268	.345	9	.155	-1	-35	-35	-1	-3.9
1970	Mil-A	14	12	.538	37	29	11	0	0	233^1	204	20	71	161	10.8	3.39	112	.235	.298	9	.129	-2	8	10	2	1.1
1971	Mil-A☆	14	14	.500	36	36	9	5	0	264^2	225	29	73	169	10.3	3.13	111	.235	.292	7	.084	-3	10	10	-1	0.7
1972	Bos-A	17	13	.567	38	35	13	4	0	253	232	19	65	168	10.9	3.24	99	.243	.297	12	.140	0	-5	-1	0	0.0
1973	Bos-A	15	15	.500	34	30	11	2	1	219^1	238	31	69	119	12.9	4.31	93	.277	.337	0	—	0	-12	-7	1	-1.2
1974	KC-A	3	7	.300	25	11	2	0	0	117^1	121	10	28	50	11.6	3.99	96	.264	.309	0	—	0	-5	-2	-1	-0.7
1975	KC-A	10	10	.500	44	15	5	1	5	177	173	13	45	89	11.2	3.25	118	.253	.302	0	—	0	10	12	-1	1.1
1976	*KC-A	8	14	.364	44	15	4	1	5	141	114	9	38	65	9.9	2.49	141	.216	.273	0	—	0	16	16	-0	2.5
1977	*KC-A	10	3	.769	31	10	4	0	0	128^1	115	16	37	55	10.8	3.58	113	.242	.300	0	—	0	7	7	-1	0.5
1978	*KC-A	3	3	.500	32	5	2	0	4	78^2	72	8	25	30	11.3	3.32	115	.248	.312	0	—	0	4	4	-2	0.0
1979	KC-A	5	2	.714	31	7	1	0	3	94^1	109	11	21	41	12.5	4.58	93	.293	.332	0	—	0	-4	-3	-1	-0.4
1980	*KC-A	4	0	1.000	37	0	0	0	4	89	97	7	23	40	12.2	3.64	111	.277	.324	0	—	0	4	4	-1	0.1
Total	13	114	109	.511	475	224	64	14	25	2038^2	1933	209	603	1179	11.4	3.62	102	.250	.309	38	.123	-7	0	16	-6	-0.3

● JIMMY PATTISON Pattison, James Wells b: 12/18/08, Bronx, N.Y. d: 2/22/91, Melbourne, Fla. BL/TL, 6', 185 lbs. Deb: 4/18/29

YEAR	TM/L	W	L	PCT	G	GS	CG	SH	SV	IP	H	HR	BB	SO	RAT	ERA	ERA+	OAV	OOB	BH	AVG	PB	PR	/A	PD	TPI
1929	Bro-N	0	1	.000	6	0	0	0	0	11^2	9	1	4	5	10.0	4.63	100	.231	.302	1	.500	0	0	-0	-0	0.0

● HARRY PATTON Patton, Harry Claude b: 6/29/1884, Gillespie, Ill. d: 6/9/30, St.Louis, Mo. Deb: 8/22/10

YEAR	TM/L	W	L	PCT	G	GS	CG	SH	SV	IP	H	HR	BB	SO	RAT	ERA	ERA+	OAV	OOB	BH	AVG	PB	PR	/A	PD	TPI
1910	StL-N	0	0	—	1	0	0	0	0	4	4	0	2	2	13.5	2.25	132	.267	.353	0	—	0	0	0	0	0.0

● MIKE PAUL Paul, Michael George b: 4/18/45, Detroit, Mich. BL/TL, 6', 183 lbs. Deb: 5/27/68 C

YEAR	TM/L	W	L	PCT	G	GS	CG	SH	SV	IP	H	HR	BB	SO	RAT	ERA	ERA+	OAV	OOB	BH	AVG	PB	PR	/A	PD	TPI
1968	Cle-A	5	8	.385	36	7	0	0	3	91^2	72	11	35	87	11.0	3.93	75	.213	.296	4	.167	0	-10	-10	-1	-1.6
1969	Cle-A	5	10	.333	47	12	0	0	2	117^1	104	12	54	98	12.3	3.61	104	.241	.328	0	.000	-3	0	2	-1	-0.1
1970	Cle-A	2	8	.200	30	15	1	0	0	88	91	13	45	70	13.9	4.81	82	.271	.357	4	.154	-1	-11	-8	-2	-1.1
1971	Cle-A	2	7	.222	17	12	1	0	0	62	78	8	14	33	14.1	5.95	64	.318	.367	1	.053	-1	-17	-15	-1	-2.1
1972	Tex-A	8	9	.471	49	20	2	1	1	161^2	149	4	52	108	11.3	2.17	139	.246	.308	8	.167	1	16	15	-1	1.7
1973	Tex-A	5	4	.556	36	10	1	0	2	87^1	104	9	36	49	14.9	4.95	75	.295	.368	0	—	0	-11	-12	1	-1.1
	Chi-N	0	1	.000	11	1	0	0	0	18^1	17	2	9	6	12.8	3.44	115	.258	.347	0	.000	-0	0	1	0	0.0
1974	Chi-N	0	1	.000	2	0	0	0	0	1^1	4	1	1	1	33.8	27.00	14	.500	.556	0	—	0	-3	-3	0	-1.6
Total	7	27	48	.360	228	77	5	1	8	627^2	619	60	246	452	12.7	3.91	89	.260	.334	17	.115	-4	-35	-30	-4	-5.9

● GENE PAULETTE Paulette, Eugene Edward b: 5/26/1891, Centralia, Ill. d: 2/8/66, Little Rock, Ark. BR/TR, 6', 150 lbs. Deb: 6/16/11 ♦

YEAR	TM/L	W	L	PCT	G	GS	CG	SH	SV	IP	H	HR	BB	SO	RAT	ERA	ERA+	OAV	OOB	BH	AVG	PB	PR	/A	PD	TPI
1918	StL-N	0	0	—	1	0	0	0	0	0^1	1	0	0	0	27.0	0.00	—	.500	.500	126	.273	0	0	0	0	0.0

● GIL PAULSEN Paulsen, Guilford Paul Hans b: 11/14/02, Graettinger, Iowa d: 4/2/94, Harlan, Iowa BR/TR, 6'2.5", 190 lbs. Deb: 10/3/25

YEAR	TM/L	W	L	PCT	G	GS	CG	SH	SV	IP	H	HR	BB	SO	RAT	ERA	ERA+	OAV	OOB	BH	AVG	PB	PR	/A	PD	TPI
1925	StL-N	0	0	—	1	0	0	0	0	2	1	0	0	1	4.5	0.00	—	.125	.125	0	—	0	1	1	0	0.0

● CARL PAVANO Pavano, Carl Anthony b: 1/8/76, New Britain, Conn. BR/TR, 6'5", 228 lbs. Deb: 5/23/98

YEAR	TM/L	W	L	PCT	G	GS	CG	SH	SV	IP	H	HR	BB	SO	RAT	ERA	ERA+	OAV	OOB	BH	AVG	PB	PR	/A	PD	TPI
1998	Mon-N	6	9	.400	24	23	0	0	0	134^2	130	18	43	83	12.1	4.21	97	.251	.318	6	.158	-0	0	-2	-1	-0.3

● DAVE PAVLAS Pavlas, David Lee b: 8/12/62, Frankfurt, W.Germany BR/TR, 6'7", 180 lbs. Deb: 8/21/90

YEAR	TM/L	W	L	PCT	G	GS	CG	SH	SV	IP	H	HR	BB	SO	RAT	ERA	ERA+	OAV	OOB	BH	AVG	PB	PR	/A	PD	TPI
1990	Chi-N	2	0	1.000	13	0	0	0	0	21^1	23	2	6	12	12.2	2.11	193	.271	.319	0	.000	0	4	5	-0	0.4
1991	Chi-N	0	0	—	1	0	0	0	0	1	3	1	0	0	27.0	18.00	22	.750	.750	0	—	0	-2	-2	-0	0.0
1995	NY-A	0	0	—	4	0	0	0	0	5^2	8	0	0	3	12.7	3.18	145	.333	.333	0	—	0	1	1	-0	0.0
1996	NY-A	0	0	—	16	0	0	0	1	23	23	0	7	18	12.1	2.35	210	.264	.326	0	—	0	7	7	0	0.1
Total	4	2	0	1.000	34	0	0	0	1	51	57	3	13	33	12.5	2.65	172	.285	.332	0	.000	0	10	11	-0	0.5

● ROGER PAVLIK Pavlik, Roger Allen b: 10/4/67, Houston, Tex. BB/TR, 6'2", 220 lbs. Deb: 5/2/92

YEAR	TM/L	W	L	PCT	G	GS	CG	SH	SV	IP	H	HR	BB	SO	RAT	ERA	ERA+	OAV	OOB	BH	AVG	PB	PR	/A	PD	TPI
1992	Tex-A	4	4	.500	13	12	1	0	0	62	66	3	34	45	15.0	4.21	90	.280	.377	0	—	0	-2	-3	-1	-0.3
1993	Tex-A	12	6	.667	26	26	2	0	0	166^1	151	18	80	131	12.8	3.41	122	.245	.336	0	—	0	17	14	1	1.6
1994	Tex-A	2	5	.286	11	11	0	0	0	50^1	61	8	30	31	17.0	7.69	63	.300	.401	0	—	0	-16	-16	0	-1.7
1995	Tex-A	10	10	.500	31	31	2	1	0	191^2	174	19	90	149	12.6	4.37	111	.243	.331	0	—	0	7	10	3	1.1
1996	*Tex-A★	15	8	.652	34	34	7	0	0	201	216	28	81	127	13.5	5.19	101	.276	.347	0	—	0	-5	1	-3	-0.2
1997	Tex-A	3	5	.375	11	11	0	0	0	57^2	59	7	31	35	14.2	4.37	110	.267	.360	0	—	0	1	3	-1	0.1
1998	Tex-A	1	1	.500	5	0	0	0	1	14	16	2	5	8	14.1	3.86	125	.286	.355	0	—	0	1	2	-0	0.2
Total	7	47	39	.547	131	125	12	1	1	743	743	85	351	526	13.5	4.58	102	.262	.348	0	—	0	4	9	-1	0.8

● JOHN PAWLOWSKI Pawlowski, John b: 9/6/63, Johnson City, N.Y. BR/TR, 6'2", 175 lbs. Deb: 9/19/87

YEAR	TM/L	W	L	PCT	G	GS	CG	SH	SV	IP	H	HR	BB	SO	RAT	ERA	ERA+	OAV	OOB	BH	AVG	PB	PR	/A	PD	TPI
1987	Chi-A	0	0	—	2	0	0	0	0	3^2	7	0	3	2	24.5	4.91	93	.438	.526	0	—	0	-0	-0	-0	-0.1
1988	Chi-A	1	0	1.000	6	0	0	0	0	14	20	2	3	10	14.8	8.36	48	.328	.359	0	—	0	-7	-7	0	-0.4
Total	2	1	0	1.000	8	0	0	0	0	17^2	27	2	6	12	16.8	7.64	54	.351	.398	0	—	0	-7	-7	-0	-0.5

● MIKE PAXTON Paxton, Michael De Wayne b: 9/3/53, Memphis, Tenn. BR/TR, 5'11", 190 lbs. Deb: 5/25/77

YEAR	TM/L	W	L	PCT	G	GS	CG	SH	SV	IP	H	HR	BB	SO	RAT	ERA	ERA+	OAV	OOB	BH	AVG	PB	PR	/A	PD	TPI
1977	Bos-A	10	5	.667	29	12	2	1	0	108	134	7	25	58	13.5	3.83	117	.311	.353	0	—	0	3	8	-0	0.2

YEAR	TM/L	W	L	PCT	G	GS	CG	SH	SV	IP	H	HR	BB	SO	RAT	ERA	ERA+	OAV	OOB	BH	AVG	PB	PR	/A	PD	TPI
1978	Cle-A	12	11	.522	33	27	5	2	1	191	179	13	63	96	11.8	3.86	97	.247	.314	0	—	0	-2	-3	-1	-0.3
1979	Cle-A	8	8	.500	33	24	3	0	0	159^2	210	14	52	70	14.9	5.92	72	.315	.366	0	—	0	-30	-30	0	-2.5
1980	Cle-A	0	0	—	4	0	0	0	0	7^2	13	4	6	6	22.3	12.91	32	.394	.487	0	—	0	-8	-8	-0	0.0
Total	4	30	24	.556	99	63	10	3	1	466^1	536	38	146	230	13.4	4.71	87	.289	.345	0	—	0	-37	-32	-2	-2.6

● GEORGE PAYNE
Payne, George Washington b: 5/23/1890, Mt.Vernon, Ky. d: 1/24/59, Bellflower, Cal. BR/TR, 5'11", 172 lbs. Deb: 5/8/20

1920	Chi-A	1	1	.500	12	0	0	0	0	29^2	39	2	9	7	14.6	5.46	69	.312	.358	1	.125	-0	-5	-6	-1	-0.5

● HARLEY PAYNE
Payne, Harley Fenwick "Lady" b: 1/9/1868, Windsor, Ont., Can. d: 12/29/35, Orwell, Ohio BB/TL, 6', 160 lbs. Deb: 4/18/1896

1896	Bro-N	14	16	.467	34	28	24	2	0	241^2	284	4	58	52	13.0	3.39	122	.290	.335	21	.214	0	26	20	3	2.2
1897	Bro-N	14	17	.452	40	38	30	1	0	280	350	8	71	86	14.1	4.63	89	.303	.353	26	.236	-0	-10	-16	1	-1.3
1898	Bro-N	1	0	1.000	1	1	1	0	0	9	11	0	3	2	14.0	4.00	90	.297	.350	3	.750	1	-0	-0	0	0.1
1899	Pit-N	1	3	.250	5	5	2	0	0	26^1	33	2	4	8	13.3	3.76	101	.306	.342	1	.100	-1	0	0	2	0.1
Total	4	30	36	.455	80	72	57	3	0	557	678	14	136	148	13.6	4.04	101	.298	.345	51	.230	0	16	3	7	1.1

● MIKE PAYNE
Payne, Michael Earl b: 11/15/61, Woonsocket, R.I. BR/TR, 5'11", 165 lbs. Deb: 8/22/84

1984	Atl-N	0	1	.000	3	1	0	0	0	5^2	7	0	3	3	15.9	6.35	61	.333	.417	0	.000	-0	-2	-2	0	-0.3

● MIKE PAZIK
Pazik, Michael Joseph b: 1/26/50, Lynn, Mass. BL/TL, 6'2", 195 lbs. Deb: 5/11/75 C

1975	Min-A	0	4	.000	5	3	0	0	0	19^2	28	5	10	8	17.4	8.24	46	.329	.400	0	—	0	-10	-10	-1	-1.6
1976	Min-A	0	0	—	5	0	0	0	0	9	13	0	4	6	18.0	7.00	51	.342	.419	0	—	0	-3	-3	-0	-0.1
1977	Min-A	1	0	1.000	3	3	0	0	0	18	18	1	6	6	12.0	2.50	159	.265	.324	0	—	0	3	3	0	0.3
Total	3	1	4	.200	13	6	0	0	0	46^2	59	6	20	20	15.4	5.79	66	.309	.377	0	—	0	-10	-10	-1	-1.4

● FRANK PEARCE
Pearce, Franklin Johnson b: 3/30/1860, Jefferson County, Ky. d: 11/13/26, Louisville, Ky. Deb: 10/4/1876

1876	Lou-N	0	0	—	1	0	0	0	0	4	5	0	1	1	13.5	4.50	60	.263	.300	0	.000	-0	-1	-1	-0	0.0

● FRANK PEARCE
Pearce, Franklin Thomas b: 8/31/05, Middletown, Ky. d: 9/3/50, Van Buren, N.Y. BR/TR, 6', 170 lbs. Deb: 4/20/33

1933	Phi-N	5	4	.556	20	7	3	1	0	82	78	5	29	18	11.7	3.62	105	.251	.315	5	.192	-1	-3	2	0	0.1
1934	Phi-N	0	2	.000	7	1	0	0	0	20	25	4	5	4	13.5	7.20	66	.301	.341	2	.667	1	-7	-6	-1	-0.5
1935	Phi-N	0	0	—	5	0	0	0	0	13	22	0	6	7	19.4	8.31	55	.361	.418	2	.500	1	-6	-5	0	0.1
Total	3	5	6	.455	32	8	3	1	0	115	125	9	40	29	12.9	4.77	85	.275	.333	9	.273	1	-16	-9	-0	-0.3

● GEORGE PEARCE
Pearce, George Thomas "Filbert" b: 1/10/1888, Aurora, Ill. d: 10/11/35, Joliet, Ill. BL/TL, 5'10.5", 175 lbs. Deb: 4/16/12

1912	Chi-N	0	0	—	3	2	0	0	0	14^2	15	0	12	9	16.6	5.52	60	.185	.290	1	.167	0	-3	-4	1	0.1
1913	Chi-N	13	5	.722	25	21	15	3	0	163^1	137	4	59	73	11.0	2.31	137	.234	.308	4	.073	-3	16	16	-0	1.3
1914	Chi-N	9	12	.429	30	17	4	0	1	141	122	3	65	78	12.1	3.51	79	.239	.327	4	.089	-3	-11	-11	2	-1.8
1915	Chi-N	13	9	.591	36	20	8	2	0	176	158	1	77	96	12.2	3.32	84	.244	.328	11	.196	1	-11	-11	-0	-1.2
1916	Chi-N	0	0	—	4	1	0	0	0	4^1	6	0	1	0	14.5	2.08	140	.300	.333	0	—	0	0	0	-0	0.0
1917	StL-N	1	1	.500	5	0	0	0	0	10^1	7	0	3	4	9.6	3.48	77	.184	.262	0	.000	-1	-1	-1	0	-0.2
Total	6	36	27	.571	103	61	27	5	1	509^2	445	8	217	260	11.9	3.11	94	.236	.318	20	.120	-6	-10	-10	2	-1.8

● JIM PEARCE
Pearce, James Madison b: 6/9/25, Zebulon, N.C. BR/TR, 6'6", 180 lbs. Deb: 9/8/49

1949	Was-A	0	1	.000	2	1	0	0	0	5^1	9	1	5	1	23.6	8.44	50	.375	.483	0	.000	-0	-3	-2	1	-0.3
1950	Was-A	2	1	.667	20	3	1	0	0	56^2	58	2	37	18	15.2	6.04	74	.270	.379	2	.154	-1	-9	-10	-0	-0.5
1953	Was-A	0	1	.000	4	1	0	0	0	9^1	15	3	6	0	20.3	7.71	51	.405	.488	0	.000	-0	-4	-4	-0	-0.4
1954	Cin-N	1	0	1.000	2	1	1	0	0	11	7	0	5	3	10.6	0.00	—	.194	.310	0	.000	-0	5	5	0	0.4
1955	Cin-N	0	1	.000	2	1	0	0	0	3^1	8	0	0	0	21.6	10.80	39	.471	.471	0	—	0	-3	-2	0	-0.6
Total	5	3	4	.429	30	7	2	0	0	85^2	97	6	53	22	16.0	5.78	76	.295	.396	2	.105	-2	-13	-13	0	-1.4

● DICKEY PEARCE
Pearce, Richard J. b: 2/29/1836, Brooklyn, N.Y. d: 10/12/08, Wareham, Mass. BR/TR, 5'3.5", 161 lbs. Deb: 5/18/1871 MU♦

1875	StL-n	0	0	—	2	0	0	0	0	5^1	10	0	0	0	16.9	3.38	60	.333	.333	77	.248	0	-1	-1		0.0

● FRANK PEARS
Pears, Frank H. b: 8/30/1866, Kentucky d: 11/29/23, St.Louis, Mo. TR, 5'9", 145 lbs. Deb: 10/6/1889 U

1889	KC-a	0	2	.000	3	2	2	0	0	22	21	2	9	5	12.7	4.91	85	.244	.323	1	.091	-1	-3	-2	-0	-0.2
1893	StL-N	0	0	—	1	0	0	0	0	4	9	0	2	0	27.0	13.50	35	.429	.500	0	.000	-0	-4	-4	0	0.0
Total	2	0	2	.000	4	2	2	0	0	26	30	2	11	5	14.9	6.23	69	.280	.358	1	.077	-2	-7	-6	0	-0.2

● ALEX PEARSON
Pearson, Alexander Franklin b: 3/9/1877, Greensboro, Pa. d: 10/30/66, Rochester, Pa. BR/TR, 5'10.5", 160 lbs. Deb: 8/1/02

1902	StL-N	2	6	.250	11	10	8	0	0	82	90	0	22	24	12.6	3.95	69	.279	.330	9	.265	0	-11	-11	-0	-0.9
1903	Cle-A	1	2	.333	4	3	2	0	0	30^1	34	1	3	12	11.3	3.56	80	.281	.304	1	.083	-1	-2	-2	0	-0.3
Total	2	3	8	.273	15	13	10	0	0	112^1	124	1	25	36	12.3	3.85	72	.279	.323	10	.217	-0	-13	-13	-0	-1.2

● IKE PEARSON
Pearson, Issac Overton b: 3/1/17, Grenada, Miss. d: 3/17/85, Sarasota, Fla. BR/TR, 6'1", 180 lbs. Deb: 6/6/39

1939	Phi-N	2	13	.133	26	13	4	0	0	125	144	15	56	29	14.8	5.76	70	.296	.374	2	.054	-3	-26	-24	1	-2.7
1940	Phi-N	3	14	.176	29	20	5	1	1	145^1	160	13	57	43	13.6	5.45	72	.275	.343	9	.205	1	-26	-25	1	-2.4
1941	Phi-N	4	14	.222	46	10	0	0	6	136	139	8	70	38	14.4	3.57	104	.266	.361	5	.125	-2	1	2	0	0.0
1942	Phi-N	1	6	.143	35	7	0	0	0	85^1	87	4	50	21	14.9	4.54	73	.271	.376	1	.043	-2	-12	-12	-0	-1.2
1946	Phi-N	1	0	1.000	5	2	1	1	0	14^1	16	1	8	6	15.7	3.77	91	.271	.368	1	.200	1	-1	-1	0	0.1
1948	Chi-A	2	3	.400	23	2	0	0	1	53	62	8	27	12	15.5	4.92	87	.292	.378	2	.200	-0	-4	-4	1	-0.3
Total	6	13	50	.206	164	54	10	2	8	559	608	49	268	149	14.5	4.83	79	.279	.363	20	.126	-6	-66	-64	2	-6.5

● MONTE PEARSON
Pearson, Montgomery Marcellus "Hoot" b: 9/2/09, Oakland, Cal. d: 1/27/78, Fresno, Cal. BR/TR, 6', 175 lbs. Deb: 4/22/32

1932	Cle-A	0	0	—	8	0	0	0	0	8	10	1	11	5	23.6	10.13	47	.323	.500	0	—	0	-5	-5	1	0.1
1933	Cle-A	10	5	.667	19	16	10	0	0	135^1	111	5	55	54	11.0	**2.33**	191	.221	.297	13	.260	1	29	32	-1	3.3
1934	Cle-A	18	13	.581	39	33	19	0	2	254^2	257	16	130	140	13.7	4.52	101	.260	.346	25	.272	6	-1	1	1	0.7
1935	Cle-A	8	13	.381	30	24	10	1	0	181^2	199	9	103	90	15.0	4.90	92	.279	.371	11	.177	-0	-9	-8	2	-0.6
1936	*NY-A☆	19	7	**.731**	33	31	15	1	1	223	191	13	135	118	13.3	3.71	125	**.233**	.343	23	.253	6	33	23	1	2.9
1937	*NY-A	9	3	.750	22	20	7	1	1	144^2	145	6	64	71	13.1	3.17	140	.261	.339	11	.216	1	23	20	-1	1.5
1938	*NY-A	16	7	.696	28	27	17	1	0	202	198	12	113	98	13.9	3.97	114	.258	.354	13	.171	1	18	13	2	1.4
1939	*NY-A	12	5	.706	22	20	8	0	0	146^1	151	9	70	76	13.7	4.49	97	.272	.354	17	.321	6	2	-2	1	0.4
1940	NY-A☆	7	5	.583	16	16	7	1	0	109^2	108	8	44	43	12.5	3.69	109	.262	.333	4	.121	-1	8	4	2	0.5
1941	Cin-N	1	3	.250	7	4	1	0	0	24^1	22	3	15	8	13.7	5.18	69	.242	.349	0	.000	-1	-4	-4	-0	-0.7
Total	10	100	61	.621	224	191	94	5	4	1429^2	1392	82	740	703	13.5	4.00	112	.256	.346	117	.228	19	95	75	8	9.5

● MARV PEASLEY
Peasley, Marvin Warren b: 7/16/1888, Jonesport, Me. d: 12/27/48, San Francisco, Cal BL/TL, 6'1", 175 lbs. Deb: 9/27/10

1910	Det-A	0	1	.000	2	1	0	0	0	10	13	0	11	4	22.5	8.10	32	.295	.446	0	.000	0	-6	-6	-0	-0.5

● GEORGE PECHINEY
Pechiney, George Adolphe "Pisch" b: 9/20/1861, Cincinnati, Ohio d: 7/14/43, Cincinnati, Ohio BR/TR, 5'9", 184 lbs. Deb: 8/4/1885

1885	Cin-a	7	4	.636	11	11	11	1	0	98	95	1	30	49	12.0	2.02	161	.247	.311	6	.150	-2	13	13	1	1.2
1886	Cin-a	15	21	.417	40	40	35	2	0	330^1	355	4	133	110	13.7	4.14	85	.266	.339	30	.208	-1	-25	-23	-3	-2.3
1887	Cle-a	1	9	.100	10	10	10	0	0	86	118	8	44	24	17.3	7.12	61	.303	.378	9	.250	-0	-27	-27	0	-2.1
Total	3	23	34	.404	61	61	56	3	0	514^1	568	13	207	183	14.0	4.23	85	.269	.341	45	.205	-3	-39	-36	-2	-3.2

● BILL PECOTA
Pecota, William Joseph b: 2/16/60, Redwood City, Cal. BR/TR, 6'2", 190 lbs. Deb: 9/19/86 ♦

1991	KC-A	0	0	—	1	0	0	0	0	2	4	0	0	0	18.0	4.50	92	.444	.444	114	.286	0	-0	-0	-0	0.0
1992	NY-N	0	0	—	1	0	0	0	0	1	1	1	0	0	9.0	9.00	39	.250	.250	61	.227	0	-1	-1	-0	0.0
Total	2	0	0	—	2	0	0	0	0	3	5	1	0	0	15.0	6.00	65	.385	.385	380	.249	0	-1	-1	-0	0.0

● STEVE PEEK
Peek, Stephen George b: 7/30/14, Springfield, Mass d: 9/20/91, Syracuse, N.Y. BB/TR, 6'2", 195 lbs. Deb: 4/16/41

1941	NY-A	4	2	.667	17	8	2	0	0	80	85	6	39	18	13.9	5.06	78	.276	.357	1	.036	-3	-8	-10	0	-0.9

YEAR	TM/L	W	L	PCT	G	GS	CG	SH	SV	IP	H	HR	BB	SO	RAT	ERA	ERA+	OAV	OOB	BH	AVG	PB	PR	/A	PD	TPI
● **RED PEERY**	Peery, George Allan b: 8/15/06, Payson, Utah d: 5/6/85, Salt Lake City, Ut. BL/TL, 5'11", 160 lbs. Deb: 9/22/27																									
1927	Pit-N	0	0	—	1	0	0	0	0	1	0	0	1	0	9.0	0.00	—	.000	.200	0	—	0	0	0	0	0.0
1929	Bos-N	0	1	.000	9	1	0	0	0	44	53	1	9	3	12.7	5.11	91	.305	.339	3	.214	1	-2	-2	-0	0.0
Total	2	0	1	.000	10	1	0	0	0	45	53	1	10	3	12.6	5.00	93	.298	.335	3	.214	1	-2	-2	0	0.0
● **HEINIE PEITZ**	Peitz, Henry Clement b: 11/28/1870, St.Louis, Mo. d: 10/23/43, Cincinnati, Ohio BR/TR, 5'11", 165 lbs. Deb: 10/15/1892 FC♦																									
1894	StL-N	0	0	—	1	0	0	0	0	3	7	0	2	0	30.0	9.00	60	.438	.526	89	.263	0	-1	-1	-0	0.0
1897	Cin-N	0	1	.000	2	1	1	0	0	8	9	0	4	0	16.9	7.88	58	.281	.395	78	.293	0	-3	-3	1	-0.2
1899	Cin-N	0	0	—	1	0	0	0	0	5	6	0	1	3	12.6	5.40	73	.300	.333	79	.272	0	-1	-1	0	0.0
Total	3	0	1	.000	4	1	1	0	0	16	22	0	7	3	18.0	7.31	62	.324	.410	1117	.271	1	-5	-5	1	-0.2
● **BARNEY PELTY**	Pelty, Barney b: 9/10/1880, Farmington, Mo. d: 5/24/39, Farmington, Mo. BR/TR, 5'9", 175 lbs. Deb: 8/20/03																									
1903	StL-A	3	3	.500	7	6	5	0	1	48^{2}	49	1	15	20	12.2	2.40	121	.261	.322	3	.150	-0	3	3	-1	0.2
1904	StL-A	15	18	.455	39	35	31	2	0	301	270	7	77	126	11.0	2.84	87	.241	.301	15	.127	-6	-8	-12	-1	-2.1
1905	StL-A	14	14	.500	31	28	27	1	0	258^{2}	222	3	68	114	10.5	2.75	93	.233	.293	15	.153	-3	-3	-6	3	-0.7
1906	StL-A	16	11	.593	34	30	25	4	2	260^{2}	189	1	59	92	9.2	1.59	163	**.206**	.267	15	.165	-3	**32**	29	4	3.3
1907	StL-A	12	21	.364	36	31	29	5	1	273	234	1	64	85	10.4	2.57	98	.234	.292	16	.168	-2	-1	-2	2	-0.2
1908	StL-A	7	4	.636	20	13	7	1	0	122	104	0	32	36	10.8	1.99	120	.241	.309	5	.119	-3	5	5	1	0.3
1909	StL-A	11	11	.500	27	23	17	5	0	199^{1}	158	2	53	88	9.8	2.30	105	.222	.281	15	.165	0	4	3	4	0.8
1910	StL-A	5	11	.313	27	19	13	3	0	165^{1}	157	3	70	48	12.8	3.48	71	.263	.348	5	.089	-4	-18	-19	4	-1.7
1911	StL-A	7	15	.318	28	22	18	1	0	197	197	4	69	59	12.3	2.97	114	.265	.331	9	.138	-3	8	9	1	0.7
1912	StL-A	1	5	.167	6	6	2	0	0	38^{2}	43	0	15	10	14.2	5.59	59	.297	.374	0	.000	-2	-10	-10	0	-1.4
	Was-A	1	4	.200	11	4	1	0	0	43^{2}	40	0	10	15	11.1	3.30	101	.250	.310	2	.222	0	0	0	-1	0.0
	Yr	2	9	.182	17	10	3	0	0	82^{1}	83	0	25	25	12.2	4.37	76	.269	.332	2	.095	-2	-10	-10	-1	-1.4
Total	10	92	117	.440	266	217	175	22	4	1908	1663	22	532	693	10.8	2.63	100	.239	.302	100	.143	-25	14	0	16	-0.8
● **ALEJANDRO PENA**	Pena, Alejandro (Vasquez) b: 6/25/59, Cambiaso, D.R. BR/TR, 6'1", 205 lbs. Deb: 9/14/81																									
1981	*LA-N	1	1	.500	14	0	0	0	2	25^{1}	18	2	11	14	10.3	2.84	117	.194	.279	0	.000	-1	2	1	0	0.1
1982	LA-N	0	2	.000	29	0	0	0	0	35^{2}	37	2	21	20	14.9	4.79	72	.272	.373	0	—	0	-5	-5	1	-0.2
1983	*LA-N	12	9	.571	34	26	4	3	1	177	152	7	51	120	10.4	2.75	131	.229	.285	6	.100	-2	17	17	2	1.9
1984	LA-N	12	6	.667	28	28	8	**4**	0	199^{1}	186	7	46	135	10.6	**2.48**	**142**	.246	.292	8	.121	-1	**24**	23	-1	1.8
1985	LA-N	0	1	.000	2	1	0	0	0	4^{1}	7	1	3	2	20.8	8.31	42	.350	.435	0	.000	-0	-2	-2	-0	-0.5
1986	LA-N	1	2	.333	24	10	0	0	1	70	74	6	30	46	13.5	4.89	71	.270	.344	3	.176	0	-9	-11	-1	-0.6
1987	LA-N	2	7	.222	37	7	0	0	11	87^{1}	82	9	37	76	12.5	3.50	113	.251	.331	1	.077	-1	6	4	-2	0.2
1988	*LA-N	6	7	.462	60	0	0	0	12	94^{1}	75	4	27	83	9.8	1.91	175	.218	.277	0	.000	-1	16	15	-0	2.3
1989	LA-N	4	3	.571	53	0	0	0	5	76	62	6	18	75	9.7	2.13	160	.220	.272	1	1.000	0	12	11	-1	1.0
1990	NY-N	3	3	.500	52	0	0	0	5	76	71	4	22	76	11.1	3.20	117	.245	.300	1	.167	0	5	5	-1	0.3
1991	NY-N	6	1	.857	44	0	0	0	4	63	63	5	19	49	11.7	2.71	134	.267	.322	0	—	0	7	6	-0	0.7
	*Atl-N	2	0	1.000	15	0	0	0	11	19^{1}	11	1	3	13	6.5	1.40	278	.167	.203	0	.000	-0	5	5	-0	1.1
	Yr	8	1	.889	59	0	0	0	15	82^{1}	74	6	22	62	10.5	2.40	154	.242	.293	0	.000	-0	12	12	-0	1.8
1992	Atl-N	1	6	.143	41	0	0	0	15	42	40	7	13	34	11.4	4.07	90	.255	.312	0	.000	-0	-3	-2	-1	-0.6
1994	Pit-N	3	2	.600	22	0	0	0	7	28^{2}	22	4	10	27	10.4	5.02	86	.206	.280	0	.000	-0	-3	-2	-1	-0.5
1995	Bos-A	1	1	.500	17	0	0	0	0	24^{1}	33	5	12	25	16.6	7.40	66	.314	.385	0	—	0	-7	-7	-0	-0.5
	Fla-N	2	0	1.000	13	0	0	0	0	18	11	2	3	21	7.0	1.50	281	.169	.206	0	.000	-0	5	5	-1	0.5
	*Atl-N	0	0	—	14	0	0	0	0	13	11	1	4	18	10.4	4.15	103	.224	.283	0	—	0	0	0	0	0.0
	Yr	2	0	1.000	27	0	0	0	0	31	22	3	7	39	8.4	2.61	162	.193	.240	0	.000	-0	5	6	-0	0.5
1996	Fla-N	0	1	.000	4	0	0	0	0	4	4	2	1	5	11.3	4.50	90	.235	.278	0	—	0	-0	-0	-0	-0.1
Total	15	56	52	.519	503	72	12	7	74	1057^{2}	959	75	331	839	11.1	3.11	117	.240	.301	20	.110	-5	70	63	-8	6.9
● **HIPOLITO PENA**	Pena, Hipolito (Concepcion) b: 1/30/64, Fantino, D.R. BL/TL, 6'3", 165 lbs. Deb: 9/1/86																									
1986	Pit-N	0	3	.000	10	1	0	0	1	8^{1}	7	3	3	6	11.9	8.64	44	.206	.289	0	—	0	-5	-4	-0	-1.5
1987	Pit-N	0	3	.000	16	1	0	0	1	25^{2}	16	2	26	16	14.7	4.56	90	.184	.372	1	.167	-0	-1	-1	-0	-0.2
1988	NY-A	1	1	.500	16	0	0	0	0	14^{1}	10	1	9	10	11.9	3.14	125	.192	.311	0	—	0	1	1	0	0.2
Total	3	1	7	.125	42	2	0	0	2	48^{1}	33	6	38	32	13.4	4.84	83	.191	.340	1	.167	-0	-5	-4	0	-1.5
● **JIM PENA**	Pena, James Patrick b: 9/17/64, Los Angeles, Cal. BL/TL, 6', 175 lbs. Deb: 7/7/92																									
1992	SF-N	1	1	.500	25	2	0	0	0	44	49	4	20	32	14.3	3.48	95	.282	.359	1	.200	0	0	-1	1	0.0
● **JOSE PENA**	Pena, Jose (Gutierrez) b: 12/3/42, Ciudad Juarez, Mex. BR/TR, 6'2", 190 lbs. Deb: 6/1/69																									
1969	Cin-N	1	1	.500	6	0	0	0	0	5	10	0	5	3	27.0	18.00	21	.400	.500	0	—	0	-8	-8	0	-2.4
1970	LA-N	4	3	.571	29	0	0	0	4	57	51	8	29	31	13.1	4.42	87	.241	.340	1	.125	0	-2	-4	1	-0.4
1971	LA-N	2	0	1.000	21	0	0	0	1	43	32	7	18	44	10.7	3.56	91	.211	.298	2	.667	1	-0	-2	-1	0.0
1972	LA-N	0	0	—	5	0	0	0	0	7^{1}	13	1	6	4	23.3	8.59	39	.371	.463	0	—	0	-4	-4	-0	0.0
Total	4	7	4	.636	61	0	0	0	5	112^{1}	106	16	58	82	13.5	4.97	72	.250	.346	3	.273	1	-15	-18	0	-2.8
● **ORLANDO PENA**	Pena, Orlando Gregorio (Quevara) b: 11/17/33, Victoria De Las Tunas, Cuba BR/TR, 5'11", 154 lbs. Deb: 8/24/58																									
1958	Cin-N	1	0	1.000	9	0	0	0	3	15	10	0	4	11	8.4	0.60	691	.185	.241	0	—	0	6	6	-0	0.6
1959	Cin-N	5	9	.357	46	8	1	0	5	136	150	26	39	76	12.5	4.76	85	.280	.329	3	.088	-0	-12	-11	-1	-1.2
1960	Cin-N	0	1	.000	4	0	0	0	0	9^{1}	8	0	3	9	10.6	2.89	132	.222	.282	0	.000	0	1	1	-0	0.1
1962	KC-A	6	4	.600	13	12	6	1	0	89^{2}	71	9	27	56	9.9	3.01	140	.213	.274	5	.161	-0	10	12	-1	1.1
1963	KC-A	12	20	.375	35	33	9	3	0	217	218	24	53	128	11.4	3.69	106	.260	.308	9	.145	0	-1	5	-2	0.5
1964	KC-A	12	14	.462	40	32	5	0	0	219^{1}	231	40	73	184	12.8	4.43	86	.268	.331	12	.160	0	-20	-15	-2	-1.8
1965	KC-A	0	6	.000	12	5	0	0	0	35^{1}	42	4	13	24	14.5	6.88	51	.302	.370	1	.111	-0	-13	-13	-0	-2.0
	Det-A	4	6	.400	30	0	0	0	4	57^{1}	54	5	20	55	11.8	2.51	138	.252	.319	2	.250	1	6	6	-1	1.1
	Yr	4	12	.250	42	5	0	0	4	92^{2}	96	9	33	79	12.6	4.18	83	.270	.333	3	.176	1	-7	-7	-1	-0.9
1966	Det-A	4	2	.667	54	0	0	0	7	108	105	16	35	79	12.1	3.08	113	.252	.317	2	.111	-1	4	5	2	0.5
1967	Det-A	0	1	.000	2	0	0	0	0	2	5	0	0	2	27.0	13.50	24	.500	.545	0	—	0	-2	-2	-0	-0.9
	Cle-A	0	3	.000	48	1	0	0	8	88^{1}	67	8	22	72	9.2	3.36	97	.208	.261	0	.000	-1	-1	-1	-0	-0.2
	Yr	0	4	.000	50	1	0	0	8	90^{1}	72	8	22	74	9.5	3.59	91	.216	.266	0	.000	-1	-4	-3	-1	-1.1
1970	Pit-N	2	1	.667	23	0	0	0	2	37^{2}	38	6	7	25	11.0	4.78	82	.268	.307	0	.000	-1	-3	-4	1	-0.3
1971	Bal-A	0	1	.000	5	0	0	0	0	14^{2}	16	0	5	4	12.9	3.07	109	.281	.339	0	.000	-0	1	0	0	0.0
1973	Bal-A	1	1	.500	11	2	0	0	1	44^{2}	36	10	8	23	9.3	4.03	93	.218	.263	0	—	0	-1	-1	-0	-0.1
	StL-N	4	4	.500	42	0	0	0	6	62	60	3	14	38	10.7	2.18	167	.251	.292	1	.143	-0	10	10	0	1.5
1974	StL-N	5	2	.714	42	0	0	0	1	45	45	0	20	23	13.2	2.60	137	.269	.351	1	.500	0	5	5	-0	0.8
	Cal-A	0	0	—	4	0	0	0	3	8	6	0	1	5	7.9	0.00	—	.214	.241	0	—	0	3	3	0	0.8
1975	Cal-A	0	2	.000	7	0	0	0	0	12^{2}	13	0	8	4	14.9	2.13	166	.283	.389	0	—	0	2	2	-1	0.7
Total	14	56	77	.421	427	93	21	4	40	1202	1175	151	352	818	11.6	3.71	102	.255	.312	36	.136	-3	-7	8	-6	1.2
● **RAMON PENA**	Pena, Ramon Arturo (Padilla) b: 5/5/62, Santiago, D.R. BR/TR, 5'10", 155 lbs. Deb: 4/27/89 F																									
1989	Det-A	0	0	—	8	0	0	0	0	18	26	0	8	12	18.0	6.00	64	.338	.414	0	—	0	-4	-4	1	0.1
● **RUSTY PENCE**	Pence, Russell William b: 3/11/1900, Marine, Ill. d: 8/11/71, Hot Springs, Ark. BR/TR, 6', 185 lbs. Deb: 5/13/21																									
1921	Chi-A	0	0	—	4	0	0	0	0	5^{1}	6	0	7	2	23.6	8.44	50	.286	.483	0	.000	-0	-2	-2	0	0.0
● **KEN PENNER**	Penner, Kenneth William b: 4/24/1896, Boonville, Ind. d: 5/28/59, Sacramento, Cal. BL/TR, 5'11.5", 170 lbs. Deb: 9/11/16																									
1916	Cle-A	1	1	.500	4	2	0	0	0	12^{2}	14	0	4	5	12.8	4.26	71	.304	.360	0	.000	-0	-2	-2	1	-0.2
1929	Chi-N	0	1	.000	5	0	0	0	0	12^{2}	14	1	6	3	14.2	2.84	162	.280	.357	1	.250	0	3	2	-0	0.2
Total	2	1	2	.333	9	2	0	0	0	25^{1}	28	1	10	8	13.5	3.55	108	.292	.358	1	.167	-0	1	1	1	0.0
● **BRAD PENNINGTON**	Pennington, Brad Lee b: 4/14/69, Salem, Ind. BL/TL, 6'5", 205 lbs. Deb: 4/17/93																									
1993	Bal-A	3	2	.600	34	0	0	0	4	33	34	7	25	39	16.6	6.55	68	.266	.394	0	—	0	-8	-8	-0	-1.3

YEAR	TM/L	W	L	PCT	G	GS	CG	SH	SV	IP	H	HR	BB	SO	RAT	ERA	ERA+	OAV	OOB	BH	AVG	PB	PR	/A	PD	TPI
1994	Bal-A	0	1	.000	8	0	0	0	0	6	9	2	8	7	25.5	12.00	42	.346	.500	0	—	0	-5	-5	-0	-0.7
1995	Bal-A	0	1	.000	8	0	0	0	0	6^2	3	1	11	10	18.9	8.10	59	.136	.424	0	—	0	-3	-2	-0	-0.3
	Cin-N	0	0	—	6	0	0	0	0	9^2	9	0	11	7	19.6	5.59	74	.273	.467	0	.000	-0	-2	-2	-0	-0.1
1996	Bos-A	0	2	.000	14	0	0	0	0	13	6	1	15	13	14.5	2.77	183	.140	.362	0	—	0	3	3	0	0.4
	Cal-A	0	0	—	8	0	0	0	0	7^1	5	1	16	7	25.8	12.27	41	.185	.488	0	—	0	-6	-6	-0	0.0
	Yr	0	2	.000	22	0	0	0	0	20^1	11	2	31	20	18.6	6.20	81	.155	.412	0	—	0	-3	-3	-0	0.4
1998	TB-A	0	0	—	1	0	0	0	0	0	1	0	3	0	—	∞	—	1.000	1.000	0	—	0	-1	-1	0	-0.2
Total	5	3	6	.333	79	0	0	0	4	75^2	67	12	89	83	18.9	7.02	66	.239	.427	0	.000	-0	-21	-20	-1	-2.2

● KEWPIE PENNINGTON

Pennington, George Louis b: 9/24/1896, New York, N.Y. d: 5/3/53, Newark, N.J. BR/TR, 5′8.5″, 168 lbs. Deb: 4/14/17

YEAR	TM/L	W	L	PCT	G	GS	CG	SH	SV	IP	H	HR	BB	SO	RAT	ERA	ERA+	OAV	OOB	BH	AVG	PB	PR	/A	PD	TPI
1917	StL-A	0	0	—	1	0	0	0	0	1	1	0	0	0	9.0	0.00	—	.250	.250	0	—	0	0	0	-0	0.0

● HERB PENNOCK

Pennock, Herbert Jefferis "The Knight Of Kennett Square"
b: 2/10/1894, Kennett Square, Pa d: 1/30/48, New York, N.Y. BB/TL, 6′, 160 lbs. Deb: 5/14/12 CH

YEAR	TM/L	W	L	PCT	G	GS	CG	SH	SV	IP	H	HR	BB	SO	RAT	ERA	ERA+	OAV	OOB	BH	AVG	PB	PR	/A	PD	TPI
1912	Phi-A	1	2	.333	17	2	1	0	2	50	48	1	30	38	14.6	4.50	68	.262	.375	2	.133	-1	-7	-8	1	-0.5
1913	Phi-A	2	1	.667	14	3	1	0	0	33^1	30	4	22	17	14.0	5.13	54	.221	.329	1	.111	-0	-8	-9	-0	-0.8
1914	*Phi-A	11	4	.733	28	14	8	3	3	151^2	136	1	65	90	12.0	2.79	94	.248	.330	12	.214	2	-1	-3	-1	-0.1
1915	Phi-A	3	6	.333	11	8	3	1	1	44	46	2	29	24	15.8	5.32	55	.266	.377	5	.278	1	-12	-12	1	-2.0
	Bos-A	0	0	—	5	1	0	0	0	14	23	0	10	7	21.2	9.64	29	.390	.478	1	.167	0	-10	-11	-1	-0.1
	Yr	3	6	.333	16	9	3	1	1	58	69	2	39	31	16.8	6.36	45	.295	.396	6	.250	1	-22	-22	-0	-2.1
1916	Bos-A	0	2	.000	9	2	0	0	1	26^2	23	0	8	12	10.8	3.04	91	.245	.311	1	.125	-0	-1	-1	-1	-0.1
1917	Bos-A	5	5	.500	24	5	4	1	1	100^2	90	2	23	35	10.4	3.31	78	.243	.292	4	.167	2	-7	-8	-0	-0.7
1919	Bos-A	16	8	.667	32	26	16	5	0	219	223	2	48	70	11.3	2.71	111	.274	.316	13	.173	1	13	8	-2	0.6
1920	Bos-A	16	13	.552	37	31	19	4	2	242^1	244	9	61	68	11.5	3.68	99	.264	.312	20	.260	4	3	-1	-3	0.1
1921	Bos-A	13	14	.481	32	31	15	1	0	222^2	268	7	59	91	13.3	4.04	105	.307	.352	18	.212	2	6	5	1	0.8
1922	Bos-A	10	17	.370	32	26	15	1	1	202	230	7	74	59	13.6	4.32	95	.297	.359	9	.138	-3	-6	-5	1	-0.7
1923	*NY-A	19	6	**.760**	35	27	21	1	3	238^1	235	11	68	93	11.5	3.13	126	.261	.314	16	.193	0	23	21	1	2.1
1924	NY-A	21	9	.700	40	34	25	4	3	286^1	302	13	64	101	11.5	2.83	147	.273	.314	16	.158	-2	45	**42**	-1	3.8
1925	NY-A	16	17	.485	47	31	21	2	2	**277**	267	11	71	88	**11.0**	2.96	144	.254	**.303**	20	.202	-3	**44**	**40**	-3	3.6
1926	*NY-A	23	11	.676	40	33	19	1	2	266^1	294	11	43	78	**11.5**	3.62	107	.282	**.313**	18	.212	3	12	7	1	1.1
1927	*NY-A	19	8	.704	34	26	18	1	2	209^2	225	5	48	51	11.8	3.00	128	.283	.325	15	.217	-0	26	20	-2	2.1
1928	NY-A	17	6	.739	28	24	18	**5**	3	211	215	2	40	53	10.9	2.56	147	.267	.302	15	.203	-1	35	28	2	2.9
1929	NY-A	9	11	.450	27	23	8	1	2	157^1	205	11	28	49	13.5	4.92	78	.318	.349	9	.176	-1	-12	-19	-1	-2.1
1930	NY-A	11	7	.611	25	19	11	1	0	156^1	194	8	20	46	12.3	4.32	100	.301	.322	11	.183	-2	6	-0	-2	-0.4
1931	NY-A	11	6	.647	25	25	12	1	0	189^1	247	7	30	65	13.2	4.28	93	.315	.342	10	.152	1	2	-7	-1	-0.5
1932	*NY-A	9	5	.643	22	21	9	1	0	146^2	191	8	38	54	14.1	4.60	89	.310	.350	8	.151	0	-2	-9	-1	-0.7
1933	NY-A	7	4	.636	23	5	2	1	4	65	96	4	21	22	16.2	5.54	70	.342	.387	5	.238	0	-9	-12	-0	-1.8
1934	Bos-A	2	0	1.000	30	2	1	0	1	62	68	2	16	16	12.2	3.05	158	.276	.321	3	.214	-0	**10**	**12**	-1	0.2
Total	22	241	162	.598	617	419	247	35	33	3571^2	3900	128	916	1227	12.2	3.60	106	.281	.328	232	.191	3	150	81	-11	6.8

● PAUL PENSON

Penson, Paul Eugene b: 7/12/31, Kansas City, Kan. BR/TR, 6′1″, 185 lbs. Deb: 4/21/54

YEAR	TM/L	W	L	PCT	G	GS	CG	SH	SV	IP	H	HR	BB	SO	RAT	ERA	ERA+	OAV	OOB	BH	AVG	PB	PR	/A	PD	TPI
1954	Phi-N	1	1	.500	5	3	0	0	0	16	14	1	14	3	15.8	4.50	90	.237	.384	0	.000	-1	-1	-1	-1	-0.2

● GENE PENTZ

Pentz, Eugene David b: 6/21/53, Johnstown, Pa. BR/TR, 6′1″, 200 lbs. Deb: 7/29/75

YEAR	TM/L	W	L	PCT	G	GS	CG	SH	SV	IP	H	HR	BB	SO	RAT	ERA	ERA+	OAV	OOB	BH	AVG	PB	PR	/A	PD	TPI
1975	Det-A	0	4	.000	13	0	0	0	0	25^1	27	0	20	21	16.7	3.20	126	.293	.420	0	—	0	2	2	-0	0.0
1976	Hou-N	3	3	.500	40	0	0	0	5	63^2	62	5	31	36	13.3	2.97	108	.259	.347	1	.200	0	4	2	1	0.3
1977	Hou-N	5	2	.714	41	4	0	0	2	87	76	8	44	51	12.5	3.83	93	.236	.330	0	.000	-2	1	-3	0	-0.4
1978	Hou-N	0	0	—	10	0	0	0	0	15	12	1	13	8	15.6	6.00	55	.214	.371	0	.000	-0	-4	-4	1	0.1
Total	4	8	9	.471	104	4	0	0	7	191	177	14	108	116	13.6	3.63	96	.250	.351	1	.053	-1	2	-3	1	0.0

● JIMMY PEOPLES

Peoples, James Elsworth b: 10/8/1863, Big Beaver, Mich. d: 8/29/20, Detroit, Mich. TR , 5′8″, 200 lbs. Deb: 5/29/1884 U♦

YEAR	TM/L	W	L	PCT	G	GS	CG	SH	SV	IP	H	HR	BB	SO	RAT	ERA	ERA+	OAV	OOB	BH	AVG	PB	PR	/A	PD	TPI
1885	Cin-a	0	2	.000	2	2	1	0	0	15	30	0	2	4	21.0	12.00	27	.390	.427	4	.182	-0	-15	-15	1	-1.2

● LAURIN PEPPER

Pepper, Hugh McLaurin b: 1/18/31, Vaughan, Miss. BR/TR, 5′11″, 190 lbs. Deb: 7/4/54

YEAR	TM/L	W	L	PCT	G	GS	CG	SH	SV	IP	H	HR	BB	SO	RAT	ERA	ERA+	OAV	OOB	BH	AVG	PB	PR	/A	PD	TPI
1954	Pit-N	1	5	.167	14	8	0	0	0	50^2	63	4	43	17	18.8	7.99	52	.315	.436	4	.235	0	-22	-21	1	-1.9
1955	Pit-N	0	1	.000	14	1	0	0	0	20	30	5	25	7	25.6	10.35	40	.370	.528	0	.000	-0	-14	-14	-0	-0.7
1956	Pit-N	1	1	.500	11	7	0	0	0	30	30	1	25	12	16.5	3.00	126	.256	.387	0	.000	-0	3	3	-1	0.0
1957	Pit-N	0	1	.000	5	1	0	0	0	9	11	1	5	4	16.0	8.00	47	.297	.381	0	—	0	-4	-4	-0	-0.4
Total	4	2	8	.200	44	17	0	0	0	109^2	134	11	98	40	19.2	7.06	57	.308	.437	4	.160	-0	-38	-37	0	-3.0

● BOB PEPPER

Pepper, Robert Ernest b: 5/3/1895, Rosston, Pa. d: 4/8/68, Ford Cliff, Pa. BR/TR, 6′2″, 178 lbs. Deb: 7/23/15

YEAR	TM/L	W	L	PCT	G	GS	CG	SH	SV	IP	H	HR	BB	SO	RAT	ERA	ERA+	OAV	OOB	BH	AVG	PB	PR	/A	PD	TPI
1915	Phi-A	0	0	—	1	0	0	0	0	5	6	0	4	0	19.8	1.80	163	.333	.478	0	.000	-0	1	1	-0	0.0

● HARRISON PEPPERS

Peppers, Harrison (b: William Harrison Pepper) b: 9/1866, Kentucky d: 11/5/03, Webb City, Mo. BL , Deb: 6/30/1894

YEAR	TM/L	W	L	PCT	G	GS	CG	SH	SV	IP	H	HR	BB	SO	RAT	ERA	ERA+	OAV	OOB	BH	AVG	PB	PR	/A	PD	TPI
1894	Lou-N	0	1	.000	2	1	0	0	0	8	10	0	4	0	15.8	6.75	75	.303	.378	0	.000	-1	-1	-1	-0	-0.2

● LUIS PERAZA

Peraza, Luis (Rios) b: 6/17/42, Rio Piedras, P.R. BR/TR, 5′11″, 185 lbs. Deb: 4/9/69

YEAR	TM/L	W	L	PCT	G	GS	CG	SH	SV	IP	H	HR	BB	SO	RAT	ERA	ERA+	OAV	OOB	BH	AVG	PB	PR	/A	PD	TPI
1969	Phi-N	0	0	—	8	0	0	0	0	9	12	1	2	7	14.0	6.00	59	.364	.400	0	.000	-0	-2	-2	-0	0.0

● OSWALDO PERAZA

Peraza, Oswald Jose b: 10/19/62, Puerto Cabello, Venez. BR/TR, 6′4″, 172 lbs. Deb: 4/4/88

YEAR	TM/L	W	L	PCT	G	GS	CG	SH	SV	IP	H	HR	BB	SO	RAT	ERA	ERA+	OAV	OOB	BH	AVG	PB	PR	/A	PD	TPI
1988	Bal-A	5	7	.417	19	15	1	0	0	86	98	10	37	61	14.3	5.55	70	.282	.355	0	—	0	-15	-16	0	-1.8

● TROY PERCIVAL

Percival, Troy Eugene b: 8/9/69, Fontana, Cal. BR/TR, 6′3″, 200 lbs. Deb: 4/26/95

YEAR	TM/L	W	L	PCT	G	GS	CG	SH	SV	IP	H	HR	BB	SO	RAT	ERA	ERA+	OAV	OOB	BH	AVG	PB	PR	/A	PD	TPI
1995	Cal-A	3	2	.600	62	0	0	0	3	74	37	6	26	94	7.8	1.95	241	.147	.229	0	—	0	23	23	-1	1.4
1996	Cal-A★	0	2	.000	62	0	0	0	36	74	38	8	31	100	8.6	2.31	216	.149	.247	0	.000	-0	22	22	-1	2.3
1997	Ana-A	5	5	.500	55	0	0	0	27	52	40	6	22	72	11.4	3.46	132	.205	.299	0	—	0	6	6	-1	1.6
1998	Ana-A★	2	7	.222	67	0	0	0	42	66^2	45	5	37	87	11.5	3.65	129	.186	.301	0	—	0	7	8	-1	1.6
Total	4	10	16	.385	246	0	0	0	108	266^2	160	25	116	353	9.7	2.77	172	.169	.267	0	.000	-0	59	59	-3	6.9

● HUB PERDUE

Perdue, Herbert Rodney "The Gallatin Squash" b: 6/7/1882, Bethpage, Tenn. d: 10/31/68, Gallatin, Tex. BR/TR, 5′10.5″, 192 lbs. Deb: 4/19/11

YEAR	TM/L	W	L	PCT	G	GS	CG	SH	SV	IP	H	HR	BB	SO	RAT	ERA	ERA+	OAV	OOB	BH	AVG	PB	PR	/A	PD	TPI
1911	Bos-N	6	10	.375	24	19	9	0	1	137^1	180	10	41	40	14.7	4.98	77	.321	.372	10	.208	-1	-24	-18	-0	-1.9
1912	Bos-N	13	16	.448	37	30	20	1	3	249	295	11	54	101	12.7	3.80	94	.303	.341	12	.138	-5	-11	-6	-4	-1.5
1913	Bos-N	16	13	.552	38	32	16	3	1	212^1	201	7	39	91	10.3	3.26	101	.249	.287	7	.104	-5	-1	0	-7	-1.1
1914	Bos-N	2	5	.286	9	9	2	0	0	51	60	5	11	13	13.1	5.82	47	.311	.357	1	.071	-0	-17	-17	0	-2.0
	StL-N	8	8	.500	22	19	12	0	1	153^1	160	3	35	43	11.7	2.82	99	.290	.338	8	.167	-1	-0	-0	-4	-0.6
	Yr	10	13	.435	31	28	14	0	1	204^1	220	8	46	56	11.9	3.57	78	.295	.340	9	.145	-1	-18	-18	-4	-2.6
1915	StL-N	6	12	.333	31	13	5	1	1	115^1	141	7	19	29	12.6	4.21	66	.311	.341	4	.111	-1	-19	-18	-0	-2.9
Total	5	51	64	.443	161	122	64	5	7	918^1	1037	43	199	317	12.3	3.85	85	.293	.334	42	.140	-13	-73	-60	-15	-10.0

● CARLOS PEREZ

Perez, Carlos Gross (b: Carlos Gross (Perez)) b: 4/14/71, Nigua, D.R. BL/TL, 6′3″, 195 lbs. Deb: 4/27/95 F

YEAR	TM/L	W	L	PCT	G	GS	CG	SH	SV	IP	H	HR	BB	SO	RAT	ERA	ERA+	OAV	OOB	BH	AVG	PB	PR	/A	PD	TPI
1995	Mon-N★	10	8	.556	28	23	2	1	0	141^1	142	18	28	106	11.1	3.69	116	.257	.299	6	.133	1	8	9	0	1.2
1997	Mon-N	12	13	.480	33	32	8	**5**	0	206^2	206	21	48	110	11.2	3.88	108	.260	.305	11	.172	2	7	7	2	1.1
1998	Mon-N	7	10	.412	23	23	3	0	0	163^1	177	12	33	82	11.7	3.75	110	.277	.315	9	.191	2	9	6	1	0.9
	LA-N	4	4	.500	11	11	4	2	0	77^2	67	9	30	46	11.2	3.24	120	.234	.307	2	.083	-0	9	6	1	0.5
	Yr	11	14	.440	34	34	7	2	0	241	244	21	63	128	11.5	3.59	113	.262	.309	11	.155	2	17	12	1	1.4
Total	3	33	35	.485	95	89	17	8	0	589	592	60	139	344	11.4	3.71	112	.261	.307	28	.156	5	32	29	3	3.7

● GEORGE PEREZ

Perez, George Thomas b: 12/29/37, San Fernando, Cal. BR/TR, 6′2.5″, 200 lbs. Deb: 4/17/58

YEAR	TM/L	W	L	PCT	G	GS	CG	SH	SV	IP	H	HR	BB	SO	RAT	ERA	ERA+	OAV	OOB	BH	AVG	PB	PR	/A	PD	TPI
1958	Pit-N	0	1	.000	4	0	0	0	1	8^1	9	1	4	2	14.0	5.40	72	.300	.382	0	.000	-0	-1	-1	-0	-0.2

● MELIDO PEREZ

Perez, Melido Turpen Gross (b: Melido Turpen Gross (Perez)) b: 2/15/66, San Cristobal, D.R. BR/TR, 6′4″, 180 lbs. Deb: 9/4/87 F

YEAR	TM/L	W	L	PCT	G	GS	CG	SH	SV	IP	H	HR	BB	SO	RAT	ERA	ERA+	OAV	OOB	BH	AVG	PB	PR	/A	PD	TPI
1987	KC-A	1	1	.500	3	3	0	0	0	10^1	18	2	5	5	20.0	7.84	58	.375	.434	0	—	0	-4	-4	-1	-0.6
1988	Chi-A	12	10	.545	32	32	3	1	0	197	186	26	72	138	11.9	3.79	105	.248	.316	0	—	0	4	4	-2	0.2

YEAR	TM/L	W	L	PCT	G	GS	CG	SH	SV	IP	H	HR	BB	SO	RAT	ERA	ERA+	OAV	OOB	BH	AVG	PB	PR	/A	PD	TPI
1989	Chi-A	11	14	.440	31	31	2	0	0	183^1	187	23	90	141	13.7	5.01	76	.264	.350	0	—	0	-23	-25	-1	-3.0
1990	Chi-A	13	14	.481	35	35	3	3	0	197	177	14	86	161	12.1	4.61	83	.241	.322	0	—	0	-16	-17	-2	-2.1
1991	Chi-A	8	7	.533	49	8	0	0	1	135^2	111	15	52	128	10.9	3.12	127	.224	.299	0	—	0	15	13	1	1.5
1992	NY-A	13	16	.448	33	33	10	1	0	247^2	212	16	93	218	11.3	2.87	136	.235	.310	0	—	0	29	29	-1	3.2
1993	NY-A	6	14	.300	25	25	0	0	0	163	173	22	64	148	13.1	5.19	80	.267	.334	0	—	0	-16	-19	-1	-1.9
1994	NY-A	9	4	.692	22	22	1	0	0	151^1	134	16	58	109	11.6	4.10	111	.238	.313	0	—	0	12	8	-0	0.6
1995	NY-A	5	5	.500	13	12	1	0	0	69^1	70	10	31	44	13.2	5.58	83	.261	.340	0	—	0	-7	-7	-1	-1.0
Total	9	78	85	.479	243	201	20	5	1	1354^2	1268	144	551	1092	12.2	4.17	97	.248	.323	0	—	0	-5	-18	-8	-3.1

● MIKE PEREZ Perez, Michael Irvin (Ortega) b: 10/19/64, Yauco, P.R. BR/TR, 6', 187 lbs. Deb: 9/5/90

YEAR	TM/L	W	L	PCT	G	GS	CG	SH	SV	IP	H	HR	BB	SO	RAT	ERA	ERA+	OAV	OOB	BH	AVG	PB	PR	/A	PD	TPI
1990	StL-N	1	0	1.000	13	0	0	0	1	13^2	12	0	3	5	9.9	3.95	97	.240	.283	0	.000	-0	-0	-0	0	0.0
1991	StL-N	0	2	.000	14	0	0	0	0	17	19	1	7	7	14.3	5.82	64	.288	.365	0	—	0	-4	-4	-0	-0.5
1992	StL-N	9	3	.750	77	0	0	0	0	93	70	4	32	46	10.0	1.84	184	.210	.281	0	.000	-0	17	16	0	2.0
1993	StL-N	7	2	.778	65	0	0	0	7	72^2	65	4	20	58	10.7	2.48	160	.243	.299	0	.000	0	13	12	0	1.6
1994	StL-N	2	3	.400	36	0	0	0	12	31	52	5	10	20	18.9	8.71	48	.391	.445	0	—	0	-15	-16	-0	-3.2
1995	Chi-N	2	6	.250	68	0	0	0	2	71^1	72	8	27	49	13.0	3.66	112	.268	.343	0	.000	0	4	4	-1	0.3
1996	Chi-N	1	0	1.000	24	0	0	0	0	27	29	2	13	22	15.0	4.67	93	.264	.357	0	.000	-0	-1	-1	-0	-0.1
1997	KC-A	2	0	1.000	16	0	0	0	0	20^1	15	2	8	17	10.6	3.54	133	.214	.304	0	—	0	2	3	0	0.2
Total	8	24	16	.600	313	0	0	0	22	346	334	26	120	224	12.2	3.56	110	.257	.327	0	.000	-0	15	13	0	0.3

● ODALIZ PEREZ Perez, Odaliz Amadol b: 6/7/78, Las Matas De Farfan, D.R. BL/TL, 6', 175 lbs. Deb: 9/1/98

YEAR	TM/L	W	L	PCT	G	GS	CG	SH	SV	IP	H	HR	BB	SO	RAT	ERA	ERA+	OAV	OOB	BH	AVG	PB	PR	/A	PD	TPI
1998	*Atl-N	0	1	.000	10	0	0	0	0	10^2	10	1	4	5	11.8	4.22	100	.244	.311	0	—	0	0	0	-0	0.0

● PASCUAL PEREZ Perez, Pascual Gross (b: Pascual Gross (Perez)) b: 5/17/57, San Cristobal, D.R. BR/TR, 6'2", 163 lbs. Deb: 5/7/80 F

YEAR	TM/L	W	L	PCT	G	GS	CG	SH	SV	IP	H	HR	BB	SO	RAT	ERA	ERA+	OAV	OOB	BH	AVG	PB	PR	/A	PD	TPI
1980	Pit-N	0	1	.000	2	2	0	0	0	12	15	0	2	7	14.3	3.75	97	.341	.396	1	.250	0	-0	-0	-0	0.0
1981	Pit-N	2	7	.222	17	13	2	0	0	86^1	92	5	34	46	13.4	3.96	91	.273	.345	3	.136	-0	-5	-4	-0	-0.4
1982	*Atl-N	4	4	.500	16	11	0	0	0	79^1	85	4	17	29	11.6	3.06	122	.276	.314	3	.167	1	5	6	0	0.7
1983	Atl-N★	15	8	.652	33	33	7	1	0	215^1	213	20	51	144	11.2	3.43	113	.260	.307	12	.160	-1	5	11	1	1.2
1984	Atl-N	14	8	.636	30	30	4	1	0	211^2	208	26	51	145	11.1	3.74	103	.260	.307	5	.076	-2	-4	3	3	0.4
1985	Atl-N	1	13	.071	22	22	0	0	0	95^1	115	10	57	57	16.3	6.14	63	.297	.389	3	.120	-0	-27	-24	-1	-3.2
1987	Mon-N	7	0	1.000	10	10	2	0	0	70^1	52	5	16	58	8.8	2.30	182	.206	.257	1	.042	-2	14	15	1	1.4
1988	Mon-N	12	8	.600	27	27	4	2	0	188	133	15	44	131	**8.8**	2.44	147	.196	**.253**	2	.037	-3	21	24	2	2.5
1989	Mon-N	9	13	.409	33	28	2	0	0	198^1	178	15	45	152	10.3	3.31	107	.237	.283	11	.204	2	4	5	0	0.8
1990	NY-A	1	2	.333	3	3	0	0	0	14	8	0	3	12	7.1	1.29	309	.163	.212	0	—	0	4	4	-0	0.9
1991	NY-A	2	4	.333	14	14	0	0	0	73^2	68	7	24	41	11.2	3.18	130	.250	.311	0	—	0	8	8	-0	0.5
Total	11	67	68	.496	207	193	21	4	0	1244^1	1167	107	344	822	11.1	3.44	110	.249	.303	41	.120	-5	25	47	6	4.8

● YORKIS PEREZ Perez, Yorkis Miguel Vargas (b: Yorkis Miguel Vargas (Perez)) b: 9/30/67, Bajos De Haina, D.R. BL/TL, 6', 180 lbs. Deb: 9/30/91

YEAR	TM/L	W	L	PCT	G	GS	CG	SH	SV	IP	H	HR	BB	SO	RAT	ERA	ERA+	OAV	OOB	BH	AVG	PB	PR	/A	PD	TPI
1991	Chi-N	1	0	1.000	3	0	0	0	0	4^1	2	0	2	3	8.3	2.08	187	.167	.286	0	—	0	1	1	0	0.2
1994	Fla-N	3	0	1.000	44	0	0	0	0	40^2	33	4	14	41	10.6	3.54	123	.220	.291	0	.000	-0	3	4	-1	0.2
1995	Fla-N	2	6	.250	69	0	0	0	1	46^2	35	6	28	47	12.5	5.21	81	.203	.322	0	.000	-0	-5	-5	-1	-0.9
1996	Fla-N	3	4	.429	64	0	0	0	0	47^2	51	2	31	47	15.7	5.29	77	.274	.381	0	.000	-0	-6	-6	0	-0.8
1997	NY-N	0	1	.000	9	0	0	0	0	8^2	15	2	4	7	19.7	8.31	49	.375	.432	0	.000	-0	-4	-4	-0	-0.4
1998	Phi-N	0	2	.000	57	0	0	0	0	52	40	3	25	42	11.3	3.81	114	.209	.301	0	.000	-0	2	3	-0	0.1
Total	6	9	13	.409	246	0	0	0	1	200	176	17	104	187	12.8	4.59	92	.234	.331	0	.000	-1	-9	-8	-1	-1.6

● MATT PERISHO Perisho, Matthew Alan b: 6/8/75, Burlington, Ia. BL/TL, 6', 175 lbs. Deb: 5/27/97

YEAR	TM/L	W	L	PCT	G	GS	CG	SH	SV	IP	H	HR	BB	SO	RAT	ERA	ERA+	OAV	OOB	BH	AVG	PB	PR	/A	PD	TPI
1997	Ana-A	0	2	.000	11	8	0	0	0	45	59	6	28	35	18.0	6.00	76	.324	.423	0	.000	-0	-7	-7	0	-0.3
1998	Tex-A	0	2	.000	2	2	0	0	0	5	15	2	8	2	45.0	27.00	18	.500	.625	0	—	0	-12	-12	-0	-2.3
Total	2	0	4	.000	13	10	0	0	0	50	74	8	36	37	20.7	8.10	57	.349	.455	0	.000	-0	-20	-19	0	-2.6

● CECIL PERKINS Perkins, Cecil Boyce b: 12/1/40, Baltimore, Md. BR/TR, 6', 175 lbs. Deb: 7/5/67

YEAR	TM/L	W	L	PCT	G	GS	CG	SH	SV	IP	H	HR	BB	SO	RAT	ERA	ERA+	OAV	OOB	BH	AVG	PB	PR	/A	PD	TPI
1967	NY-A	0	1	.000	2	1	0	0	0	5	6	1	2	1	14.4	9.00	35	.316	.381	0	.000	-0	-3	-3	0	-0.6

● CHARLIE PERKINS Perkins, Charles Sullivan "Lefty" b: 9/9/05, Ensley, Ala. d: 5/25/88, Salem, Ore. BR/TL, 6'1", 175 lbs. Deb: 5/1/30

YEAR	TM/L	W	L	PCT	G	GS	CG	SH	SV	IP	H	HR	BB	SO	RAT	ERA	ERA+	OAV	OOB	BH	AVG	PB	PR	/A	PD	TPI
1930	Phi-A	0	0	—	8	1	0	0	0	23^2	25	0	15	15	15.2	6.46	72	.313	.421	1	.125	-1	-5	-5	0	-0.1
1934	Bro-N	0	3	.000	11	2	0	0	0	24^1	37	3	14	5	19.6	8.51	46	.336	.421	2	.286	0	-12	-12	-1	-1.3
Total	2	0	3	.000	19	3	0	0	0	48	62	3	29	20	17.4	7.50	57	.326	.421	3	.200	-1	-17	-17	-1	-1.4

● JOHN PERKOVICH Perkovich, John Joseph "Perky" b: 3/10/24, Chicago, Ill. BR/TR, 5'11", 170 lbs. Deb: 5/6/50

YEAR	TM/L	W	L	PCT	G	GS	CG	SH	SV	IP	H	HR	BB	SO	RAT	ERA	ERA+	OAV	OOB	BH	AVG	PB	PR	/A	PD	TPI
1950	Chi-A	0	0	—	1	0	0	0	0	5	7	3	1	3	14.4	7.20	62	.318	.348	0	.000	-0	-1	-2	-0	0.0

● HARRY PERKOWSKI Perkowski, Harry Walter b: 9/6/22, Dante, Va. BL/TL, 6'2.5", 196 lbs. Deb: 9/13/47

YEAR	TM/L	W	L	PCT	G	GS	CG	SH	SV	IP	H	HR	BB	SO	RAT	ERA	ERA+	OAV	OOB	BH	AVG	PB	PR	/A	PD	TPI
1947	Cin-N	0	0	—	3	1	0	0	0	7^1	12	1	3	2	18.4	3.68	111	.375	.429	0	.000	0	0	0	-0	0.0
1949	Cin-N	1	1	.500	5	3	2	0	0	23^2	21	2	14	3	13.3	4.56	92	.236	.340	3	.333	1	-1	-1	-1	-0.1
1950	Cin-N	0	0	—	22	0	0	0	0	34^1	36	6	23	19	15.7	5.24	81	.286	.400	7	.318	2	-4	-4	1	0.3
1951	Cin-N	3	6	.333	35	7	1	0	1	102	96	2	46	56	12.6	2.82	144	.251	.333	1	.040	-3	13	14	1	1.0
1952	Cin-N	12	10	.545	33	24	11	1	0	194	197	9	89	86	13.4	3.80	99	.265	.347	12	.160	-0	-2	-1	1	0.0
1953	Cin-N	12	11	.522	33	25	7	2	2	193	204	26	62	70	12.5	4.52	96	.271	.327	14	.203	1	-5	-4	-0	-0.2
1954	Cin-N	2	8	.200	28	12	3	1	0	95^2	100	16	62	32	15.3	6.11	69	.276	.384	4	.160	2	-22	-20	-1	-1.9
1955	Chi-N	3	4	.429	25	4	0	0	2	47^2	53	3	25	28	14.7	5.29	77	.283	.368	2	.154	-0	-7	-6	1	-0.8
Total	8	33	40	.452	184	76	24	4	5	697^2	719	65	324	296	13.5	4.37	94	.269	.350	43	.180	1	-27	-21	2	-1.7

● JON PERLMAN Perlman, Jonathan Samuel b: 12/13/56, Dallas, Tex. BL/TR, 6'3", 185 lbs. Deb: 9/6/85

YEAR	TM/L	W	L	PCT	G	GS	CG	SH	SV	IP	H	HR	BB	SO	RAT	ERA	ERA+	OAV	OOB	BH	AVG	PB	PR	/A	PD	TPI
1985	Chi-N	1	0	1.000	6	0	0	0	0	8^2	10	3	8	4	18.7	11.42	35	.313	.450	0	.000	-0	-8	-7	0	-0.7
1987	SF-N	0	0	—	10	0	0	0	0	11^1	11	1	4	3	12.7	3.97	97	.256	.333	0	—	0	0	-0	-0	0.0
1988	Cle-A	0	2	.000	10	0	0	0	0	19^2	25	0	11	10	16.5	5.49	75	.309	.391	0	—	0	-3	-3	1	-0.3
Total	3	1	2	.333	26	0	0	0	0	39^2	46	4	23	17	15.9	6.35	63	.295	.389	0	.000	-0	-11	-10	1	-1.0

● LEN PERME Perme, Leonard John b: 11/25/17, Cleveland, Ohio BL/TL, 6', 170 lbs. Deb: 9/8/42

YEAR	TM/L	W	L	PCT	G	GS	CG	SH	SV	IP	H	HR	BB	SO	RAT	ERA	ERA+	OAV	OOB	BH	AVG	PB	PR	/A	PD	TPI
1942	Chi-A	0	1	.000	4	1	1	0	0	13	5	0	4	4	6.9	1.38	260	.119	.213	1	.333	0	3	3	-0	0.2
1946	Chi-A	0	0	—	4	0	0	0	0	4^1	6	0	7	2	27.0	8.31	41	.316	.500	0	—	0	-2	-2	0	0.0
Total	2	0	1	.000	8	1	1	0	0	17^1	11	0	11	6	11.9	3.12	114	.180	.315	1	.333	0	1	1	0	0.2

● HUB PERNOLL Pernoll, Henry Hubbard b: 3/14/1888, Grants Pass, Ore. d: 2/18/44, Grants Pass, Ore. BR/TL, 5'8", 175 lbs. Deb: 4/25/10

YEAR	TM/L	W	L	PCT	G	GS	CG	SH	SV	IP	H	HR	BB	SO	RAT	ERA	ERA+	OAV	OOB	BH	AVG	PB	PR	/A	PD	TPI
1910	Det-A	4	3	.571	11	5	4	0	0	54^2	54	1	14	25	12.0	2.96	89	.270	.333	1	.063	-2	-3	-2	3	-0.1
1912	Det-A	0	0	—	3	0	0	0	0	9	9	0	4	3	13.0	6.00	54	.265	.342	0	.000	-0	-3	-3	0	0.0
Total	2	4	3	.571	14	5	4	0	0	63^2	63	1	18	28	12.2	3.39	80	.269	.335	1	.053	-2	-5	-5	3	-0.1

● RON PERRANOSKI Perranoski, Ronald Peter (b: Ronald Peter Perzanowski) b: 4/1/36, Paterson, N.J. BL/TL, 6', 192 lbs. Deb: 4/14/61 C

YEAR	TM/L	W	L	PCT	G	GS	CG	SH	SV	IP	H	HR	BB	SO	RAT	ERA	ERA+	OAV	OOB	BH	AVG	PB	PR	/A	PD	TPI
1961	LA-N	7	5	.583	53	1	0	0	6	91^2	82	5	41	56	12.5	2.65	164	.244	.333	1	.083	-0	14	**17**	0	2.3
1962	LA-N	6	6	.500	**70**	0	0	0	20	107^1	103	1	36	68	11.7	2.85	127	.255	.316	1	.071	-1	13	9	-1	1.2
1963	*LA-N	16	3	**.842**	**69**	0	0	0	21	129	112	7	43	75	11.1	1.67	180	.231	.299	3	.125	0	**23**	19	0	3.7
1964	LA-N	5	7	.417	72	0	0	0	14	125^1	128	5	46	79	12.6	3.09	105	.263	.328	2	.105	-0	6	2	2	0.4
1965	*LA-N	6	6	.500	59	0	0	0	17	104^2	85	2	40	53	11.0	2.24	146	.226	.305	3	.158	1	15	12	-1	1.7
1966	*LA-N	6	7	.462	55	0	0	0	7	82	82	4	31	50	12.5	3.18	104	.269	.338	2	.250	1	4	1	2	0.5
1967	LA-N	6	7	.462	**70**	0	0	0	16	110	97	4	45	75	11.9	2.45	126	.240	.320	1	.100	-0	11	8	1	1.3
1968	Min-A	8	7	.533	66	0	0	0	6	87	86	5	38	65	12.8	3.10	100	.252	.327	0	.000	-1	-1	-0	-1	-0.1
1969	*Min-A	9	10	.474	75	0	0	0	**31**	119^2	85	4	52	62	10.4	2.11	173	.205	.295	2	.083	-1	20	**21**	1	**4.4**
1970	*Min-A	7	8	.467	67	0	0	0	**34**	111	108	7	42	55	12.2	2.43	153	.259	.328	1	.042	-2	16	16	-1	2.7
1971	Min-A	1	4	.200	36	0	0	0	5	42^2	60	2	28	21	19.2	6.75	53	.337	.435	0	.000	-2	-16	-15	-0	-2.1
	Det-A	0	1	.000	11	0	0	0	2	18	16	2	3	8	10.0	2.50	144	.254	.299	0	.000	-0	2	2	-0	0.1

YEAR	TM/L	W	L	PCT	G	GS	CG	SH	SV	IP	H	HR	BB	SO	RAT	ERA	ERA+	OAV	OOB	BH	AVG	PB	PR	/A	PD	TPI
	Yr	1	5	.167	47	0	0	0	7	60^2	76	4	31	29	16.0	5.49	65	.309	.388	0	.000	-1	-14	-13	-1	-2.0
1972	Det-A	0	1	.000	17	0	0	0	0	18^2	23	2	8	10	15.4	7.71	41	.307	.381	0	.000	-0	-10	-9	-1	-0.6
	LA-N	2	0	1.000	9	0	0	0	0	16^2	19	0	8	5	14.6	2.70	123	.292	.370	0	—	0	1	1	-0	0.1
1973	Cal-A	0	2	.000	8	0	0	0	0	11	11	0	7	5	15.5	4.09	87	.282	.404	0	—	0	-0	-1	0	-0.1
Total	13	79	74	.516	737	1	0	0	179	1174^2	1097	50	468	687	12.2	2.79	123	.250	.325	16	.096	-4	99	83	2	15.5

● BILL PERRIN

Perrin, William Joseph "Lefty" b: 6/23/10, New Orleans, La. d: 6/30/74, New Orleans, La. BR/TL, 5'11", 172 lbs. Deb: 9/30/34

YEAR	TM/L	W	L	PCT	G	GS	CG	SH	SV	IP	H	HR	BB	SO	RAT	ERA	ERA+	OAV	OOB	BH	AVG	PB	PR	/A	PD	TPI
1934	Cle-A	0	1	.000	1	1	0	0	0	5	13	0	2	3	28.8	14.40	32	.520	.571	0	.000	-0	-6	-5	0	-0.7

● GEORGE PERRING

Perring, George Wilson b: 8/13/1884, Sharon, Wis. d: 8/20/60, Beloit, Wis. BR/TR, 6', 190 lbs. Deb: 4/25/08 ◆

YEAR	TM/L	W	L	PCT	G	GS	CG	SH	SV	IP	H	HR	BB	SO	RAT	ERA	ERA+	OAV	OOB	BH	AVG	PB	PR	/A	PD	TPI
1914	KC-F	0	0	—	1	0	0	0	0	0^2	2	0	1	0	40.5	13.50	21	1.000	1.000	138	.278	0	-1	-1	-0	0.0

● POL PERRITT

Perritt, William Dayton b: 8/30/1892, Arcadia, La. d: 10/15/47, Shreveport, La. BR/TR, 6'2", 168 lbs. Deb: 9/7/12

YEAR	TM/L	W	L	PCT	G	GS	CG	SH	SV	IP	H	HR	BB	SO	RAT	ERA	ERA+	OAV	OOB	BH	AVG	PB	PR	/A	PD	TPI
1912	StL-N	1	1	.500	6	3	1	0	0	31	25	0	10	13	10.2	3.19	107	.243	.310	2	.222	-0	1	1	0	0.0
1913	StL-N	6	14	.300	36	21	8	0	0	175	205	9	64	64	14.2	5.25	62	.300	.367	12	.203	-1	-40	-39	1	-4.0
1914	StL-N	16	13	.552	41	32	18	3	2	286	248	7	93	115	11.2	2.36	118	.245	.318	13	.141	-2	14	14	-3	0.8
1915	NY-N	12	18	.400	35	29	16	4	0	220	226	6	59	91	12.1	2.66	96	.266	.323	11	.162	-1	2	-2	-5	-1.0
1916	NY-N	18	11	.621	40	29	17	5	2	251	243	11	56	115	11.0	2.62	93	.257	.304	7	.084	-4	0	-5	-2	-1.3
1917	*NY-N	17	7	.708	35	26	14	5	1	215	186	3	45	72	10.0	1.88	135	.237	.284	11	.157	-2	20	16	1	1.7
1918	NY-N	18	13	.581	35	31	19	6	0	233	212	5	38	60	9.7	2.74	96	.246	.278	14	.175	-1	1	-3	-3	-0.8
1919	NY-N	1	1	.500	11	3	0	0	1	19	27	0	12	2	19.4	7.11	39	.386	.488	0	.000	-1	-9	-9	0	-1.0
1920	NY-N	0	0	—	8	0	0	0	2	15	9	0	4	3	7.8	1.80	167	.167	.224	0	.000	-1	2	2	0	0.0
1921	NY-N	2	0	1.000	5	1	0	0	0	11^2	17	0	2	5	14.7	3.86	95	.321	.345	0	.000	-0	-0	-0	-1	-0.1
	Det-A	1	0	1.000	4	2	0	0	0	13	18	0	7	3	18.0	4.85	88	.383	.473	2	.400	-0	-1	-1	-0	0.0
Total	10	92	78	.541	256	177	93	23	8	1469^2	1416	41	390	543	11.4	2.89	94	.259	.315	72	.151	-13	-10	-28	-11	-5.7

● GAYLORD PERRY

Perry, Gaylord Jackson b: 9/15/38, Williamston, N.C. BR/TR, 6'4", 215 lbs. Deb: 4/14/62 FH

YEAR	TM/L	W	L	PCT	G	GS	CG	SH	SV	IP	H	HR	BB	SO	RAT	ERA	ERA+	OAV	OOB	BH	AVG	PB	PR	/A	PD	TPI
1962	SF-N	3	1	.750	13	7	1	0	0	43	54	3	14	20	14.2	5.23	73	.310	.362	3	.231	0	-6	-7	-1	-0.6
1963	SF-N	1	6	.143	31	4	0	0	2	76	84	10	29	52	13.6	4.03	79	.279	.346	4	.222	1	-6	-7	-0	-0.6
1964	SF-N	12	11	.522	44	19	5	2	5	206^1	179	16	43	155	9.9	2.75	130	.232	.278	3	.054	-3	18	19	-2	1.6
1965	SF-N	8	12	.400	47	26	6	0	1	195^2	194	21	70	170	12.4	4.19	86	.256	.324	10	.156	-0	-14	-13	3	-0.9
1966	SF-N★	21	8	.724	36	35	13	3	0	255^2	242	15	40	201	10.1	2.99	123	.247	.280	16	.186	-0	17	19	1	2.1
1967	SF-N	15	17	.469	39	37	18	3	1	293	231	20	84	230	9.8	2.61	126	.214	.274	13	.143	-1	25	22	4	2.7
1968	SF-N	16	15	.516	39	38	19	3	1	291	240	10	59	173	9.4	2.44	120	.222	.265	11	.113	-3	18	16	4	2.0
1969	SF-N	19	14	.576	40	39	26	3	0	**325^1**	290	23	91	233	10.8	2.49	141	.237	.295	14	.120	-2	40	37	3	3.9
1970	SF-N★	**23**	13	.639	41	41	23	**5**	0	**328^2**	292	27	84	214	10.5	3.20	124	.237	.290	14	.117	-4	31	28	5	3.0
1971	*SF-N	16	12	.571	37	37	14	2	0	280	255	20	67	158	10.5	2.76	123	.242	.290	10	.102	-3	22	20	0	1.6
1972	Cle-A★	**24**	16	.600	41	40	**29**	5	1	342^2	253	17	82	234	9.1	1.92	168	.205	.261	17	.155	0	**44**	**49**	2	**7.0**
1973	Cle-A	19	19	.500	41	41	**29**	7	0	344	315	34	115	238	11.4	3.38	116	.246	.311	0	—	0	17	21	1	2.3
1974	Cle-A★	21	13	.618	37	37	28	4	0	322^1	230	25	99	216	9.4	2.51	**144**	.204	.272	0	—	0	40	**39**	1	4.4
1975	Cle-A	6	9	.400	15	15	10	1	0	121^2	120	16	34	85	11.5	3.55	106	.256	.308	0	—	0	3	3	-1	0.5
	Tex-A	12	8	.600	22	22	15	4	0	184	157	12	36	148	9.6	3.03	124	.227	.268	0	—	0	15	15	-1	1.5
	Yr	18	17	.514	37	37	25	5	0	305^2	277	28	70	233	10.3	3.24	116	.238	.283	0	—	0	18	18	1	2.0
1976	Tex-A	15	14	.517	32	32	21	2	0	250^1	232	14	52	143	10.2	3.24	111	.247	.287	0	—	0	8	10	-3	0.6
1977	Tex-A	15	12	.556	34	34	13	4	0	238	239	21	56	177	11.3	3.37	121	.262	.308	0	—	0	18	19	-1	1.9
1978	SD-N	**21**	6	**.778**	37	37	5	2	0	260^2	241	9	66	154	10.7	2.73	122	.248	.298	8	.092	-3	25	17	0	1.4
1979	SD-N★	12	11	.522	32	32	10	0	0	232^2	225	12	67	140	11.4	3.06	115	.257	.313	6	.085	-2	17	12	1	1.1
1980	Tex-A	6	9	.400	24	24	6	2	0	155	159	12	46	107	12.3	3.43	114	.268	.328	0	—	0	10	8	1	1.1
	NY-A	4	4	.500	10	8	0	0	0	50^2	65	2	18	28	14.9	4.44	88	.320	.378	0	—	0	-2	-3	-0	-0.3
	Yr	10	13	.435	34	32	6	2	0	205^2	224	14	64	135	12.6	3.68	106	.278	.332	0	—	0	8	5	1	0.8
1981	Atl-N	8	9	.471	23	23	3	0	0	150^2	182	9	24	60	12.5	3.94	91	.304	.335	12	.250	3	-8	-6	-1	-0.5
1982	Sea-A	10	12	.455	32	32	6	0	0	216^2	245	27	54	116	12.6	4.40	96	.287	.332	0	—	0	-8	-4	0	-0.4
1983	Sea-A	3	10	.231	16	16	2	0	0	102	116	18	23	42	12.5	4.94	86	.286	.329	0	—	0	-10	-8	0	-0.9
	KC-A	4	4	.500	14	14	1	1	0	84^1	98	6	26	40	13.3	4.27	95	.292	.344	0	—	0	-2	-2	0	-0.1
	Yr	7	14	.333	30	30	3	1	0	186^1	214	24	49	82	12.8	4.64	90	.286	.331	0	—	0	-12	-10	1	-1.0
Total	22	314	265	.542	777	690	303	53	11	5350^1	4938	399	1379	3534	10.8	3.11	117	.245	.297	141	.131	-16	311	305	21	34.4

● SCOTT PERRY

Perry, Herbert Scott b: 4/17/1891, Denison, Tex. d: 10/27/59, Kansas City, Mo. BR/TR, 6', 175 lbs. Deb: 5/13/15

YEAR	TM/L	W	L	PCT	G	GS	CG	SH	SV	IP	H	HR	BB	SO	RAT	ERA	ERA+	OAV	OOB	BH	AVG	PB	PR	/A	PD	TPI
1915	StL-A	0	0	—	1	1	0	0	0	2	5	0	1	0	31.5	13.50	21	.455	.538	0	—	0	-2	-2	-0	0.0
1916	Chi-N	2	1	.667	4	3	2	1	0	28^1	30	0	3	10	10.5	2.54	115	.291	.311	3	.273	1	0	1	0	0.2
1917	Cin-N	0	0	—	4	1	0	0	0	13^1	17	0	8	4	17.6	6.75	39	.321	.419	0	.000	-1	-6	-6	-0	-0.1
1918	Phi-A	20	19	.513	44	36	**30**	3	2	**332^1**	295	1	111	81	11.0	1.98	148	.247	.312	15	.134	-6	30	35	2	3.9
1919	Phi-A	4	17	.190	25	21	12	0	1	183^2	193	4	72	38	13.1	3.58	96	.282	.352	8	.136	-3	-7	-3	6	0.6
1920	Phi-A	11	25	.306	42	34	20	1	1	263^2	310	14	65	79	13.0	3.62	111	.300	.345	13	.157	-4	5	12	0	1.1
1921	Phi-A	3	6	.333	12	8	5	0	1	70	77	4	24	19	13.1	4.11	108	.288	.349	1	.038	-4	1	3	1	0.0
Total	7	40	68	.370	132	104	69	5	5	893^1	927	23	284	231	12.3	3.07	113	.277	.336	40	.135	-17	21	40	9	5.2

● JIM PERRY

Perry, James Evan b: 10/30/35, Williamston, N.C. BB/TR, 6'4", 200 lbs. Deb: 4/23/59 F

YEAR	TM/L	W	L	PCT	G	GS	CG	SH	SV	IP	H	HR	BB	SO	RAT	ERA	ERA+	OAV	OOB	BH	AVG	PB	PR	/A	PD	TPI
1959	Cle-A	12	10	.545	44	13	8	2	4	153	122	10	55	79	10.5	2.65	139	.225	.298	15	.300	3	21	18	-0	2.8
1960	Cle-A	**18**	10	**.643**	41	36	10	**4**	1	261^1	257	35	91	120	12.1	3.62	103	.260	.324	22	.242	3	7	4	0	0.6
1961	Cle-A☆	10	17	.370	35	35	6	1	0	223^2	238	28	87	90	13.3	4.71	84	.273	.343	12	.164	-1	-17	-19	-0	-2.1
1962	Cle-A	12	12	.500	35	27	7	3	0	193^2	213	21	59	74	12.7	4.14	94	.285	.339	11	.183	0	-4	-6	1	-0.5
1963	Cle-A	0	0	—	5	0	0	0	0	10^1	12	0	2	7	12.2	5.23	69	.293	.326	0	.000	-0	-2	-2	-0	0.0
	Min-A	9	9	.500	35	25	5	1	1	168^1	167	17	57	65	12.1	3.74	97	.256	.318	11	.216	3	-2	-2	-1	0.0
	Yr	9	9	.500	40	25	5	1	1	178^2	179	17	59	72	12.1	3.83	95	.258	.318	11	.208	3	-4	-4	-1	0.0
1964	Min-A	6	3	.667	42	1	0	0	2	65^1	61	7	23	55	11.7	3.44	104	.245	.311	2	.154	-0	1	1	-0	0.1
1965	*Min-A	12	7	.632	36	19	4	2	0	167^2	142	18	47	88	10.3	2.63	135	.232	.290	9	.170	1	15	17	-1	1.9
1966	Min-A	11	7	.611	33	25	8	1	0	184^1	149	17	53	122	10.1	2.54	142	.222	.284	13	.220	4	18	22	-2	2.4
1967	Min-A	8	7	.533	37	11	3	2	0	130^2	123	8	50	94	12.1	3.03	114	.255	.328	8	.190	1	5	6	-1	0.7
1968	Min-A	8	6	.571	32	18	3	2	0	139	113	8	26	69	9.3	2.27	136	.219	.263	6	.143	2	11	13	1	1.7
1969	*Min-A	20	6	.769	46	36	12	3	0	261^2	244	18	66	153	11.0	2.82	129	.247	.300	16	.172	1	23	24	-2	2.2
1970	*Min-A★	**24**	12	.667	40	40	13	4	0	278^2	258	20	57	168	10.5	3.04	123	.243	.287	24	.247	5	21	21	1	3.3
1971	Min-A☆	17	17	.500	40	39	8	0	1	270	263	39	102	126	12.3	4.23	84	.259	.329	17	.185	1	-23	-20	0	-2.3
1972	Min-A	13	16	.448	35	35	5	2	0	217^2	191	14	60	85	10.7	3.35	96	.236	.295	11	.155	-1	-7	-3	-1	-0.7
1973	Det-A	14	13	.519	35	34	7	1	0	203	225	22	55	66	12.6	4.03	101	.282	.331	0	—	0	-5	1	-0	0.1
1974	Cle-A	17	12	.586	36	36	8	3	0	252	242	11	64	71	11.1	2.96	122	.254	.304	0	—	0	18	18	-1	2.0
1975	Cle-A	1	6	.143	8	6	0	0	0	37^2	46	8	18	11	15.3	6.69	57	.309	.383	0	—	0	-12	-12	0	-1.8
	Oak-A	3	4	.429	15	11	2	1	0	67^2	61	7	26	33	12.5	4.66	78	.237	.324	0	—	0	-7	-8	-1	-0.7
	Yr	4	10	.286	23	17	2	1	0	105^1	107	15	44	44	13.5	5.38	68	.264	.346	0	—	0	-19	-20	-1	-2.5
Total	17	215	174	.553	630	447	109	32	10	3285^2	3127	308	998	1576	11.5	3.45	106	.252	.312	177	.199	23	61	75	-7	9.7

● PAT PERRY

Perry, William Patrick b: 2/4/59, Taylorville, Ill. BL/TL, 6'1", 170 lbs. Deb: 9/12/85

YEAR	TM/L	W	L	PCT	G	GS	CG	SH	SV	IP	H	HR	BB	SO	RAT	ERA	ERA+	OAV	OOB	BH	AVG	PB	PR	/A	PD	TPI
1985	StL-N	1	0	1.000	6	0	0	0	0	12^1	3	0	3	6	4.4	0.00	—	.077	.143	1	.500	0	5	5	-0	0.4
1986	StL-N	2	3	.400	46	0	0	0	2	68^2	59	5	34	29	12.2	3.80	96	.239	.331	0	.000	-1	-1	-1	1	-0.1
1987	StL-N	4	2	.667	45	0	0	0	1	65^2	54	7	21	33	10.6	4.39	95	.222	.289	1	.143	-0	-2	-2	0	-0.1
	Cin-N	1	0	1.000	12	0	0	0	0	15^1	6	0	4	6	6.5	0.00	—	.122	.204	0	—	0	7	7	0	0.5
	Yr	5	2	.714	57	0	0	0	2	81	60	7	25	39	9.6	3.56	117	.203	.268	1	.143	-0	5	6	1	0.4
1988	Cin-N	2	2	.500	12	0	0	0	0	20^2	21	4	9	11	13.1	5.66	63	.262	.337	0	.000	-0	-5	-5	-0	-0.9
	Chi-N	2	2	.500	35	0	0	0	1	38	40	5	7	24	11.4	3.32	109	.270	.308	1	1.000	1	1	1	-0	0.3
	Yr	4	4	.500	47	0	0	0	1	58^2	61	9	16	35	12.0	4.14	87	.264	.315	1	.333	1	-5	-4	-0	-0.6
1989	Chi-N	0	1	.000	19	0	0	0	1	35^2	23	2	16	20	9.8	1.77	213	.187	.281	1	.167	-0	7	8	-1	0.2

YEAR	TM/L	W	L	PCT	G	GS	CG	SH	SV	IP	H	HR	BB	SO	RAT	ERA	ERA+	OAV	OOB	BH	AVG	PB	PR	/A	PD	TPI
1990	LA-N	0	0	—	7	0	0	0	0	6^2	9	0	5	2	20.3	8.10	45	.310	.429	0	.000	-0	-3	-3	-0	0.0
Total	6	12	10	.545	182	0	0	0	6	263	215	23	99	131	10.9	3.46	110	.224	.300	4	.148	0	8	10	-0	0.3
● **PARSON PERRYMAN**	Perryman, Emmett Key b: 10/24/1888, Everett Springs, Ga. d: 9/12/66, Starke, Fla. BR/TR, 6'4.5", 193 lbs. Deb: 4/14/15																									
1915	StL-A	2	4	.333	24	3	0	0	0	50^1	52	2	16	19	12.3	3.93	73	.281	.342	0	.000	-1	-6	-6	1	-0.7
● **ROBERT PERSON**	Person, Robert Alan b: 10/6/69, Lowell, Mass. BR/TR, 5'11", 180 lbs. Deb: 9/18/95																									
1995	NY-N	1	0	1.000	3	1	0	0	0	12	5	1	2	10	5.3	0.75	539	.119	.159	2	.667	1	5	4	-0	0.4
1996	NY-N	4	5	.444	27	13	0	0	0	89^2	86	16	35	76	12.3	4.52	89	.247	.319	3	.143	-0	-3	-5	-2	-0.6
1997	Tor-A	5	10	.333	23	22	0	0	0	128^1	125	19	60	99	13.3	5.61	82	.255	.342	0	.000	-0	-15	-15	-2	-1.6
1998	Tor-A	3	1	.750	27	0	0	0	6	38^1	45	9	22	31	16.2	7.04	66	.294	.390	0	—	0	-10	-10	-1	-1.2
Total	4	13	16	.448	80	36	0	0	6	268^1	261	45	119	216	13.0	5.23	84	.252	.335	5	.179	1	-24	-26	-5	-3.0
● **BILL PERTICA**	Pertica, William Andrew b: 3/5/1897, Santa Barbara, Cal. d: 12/28/67, Los Angeles, Cal. BR/TR, 5'9", 165 lbs. Deb: 8/7/18																									
1918	Bos-A	0	0	—	1	0	0	0	0	3	3	0	0	1	9.0	3.00	89	.273	.273	0	.000	-0	-0	-0	0	0.0
1921	StL-N	14	10	.583	38	31	15	2	2	208^1	212	9	70	67	12.6	3.37	109	.267	.334	10	.143	-3	10	7	-3	0.1
1922	StL-N	8	8	.500	34	15	2	0	0	117^1	153	5	65	30	17.0	5.91	65	.333	.419	6	.182	-0	-24	-27	1	-2.9
1923	StL-N	0	0	—	1	1	0	0	0	2^1	2	0	3	0	23.1	3.86	101	.250	.500	0	.000	-0	0	0	0	0.0
Total	4	22	18	.550	74	47	17	2	2	331	370	14	138	98	14.2	4.27	87	.291	.367	16	.152	-4	-14	-20	-2	-2.8
● **STAN PERZANOWSKI**	Perzanowski, Stanley b: 8/25/50, East Chicago, Ind. BB/TR, 6'2", 170 lbs. Deb: 6/20/71																									
1971	Chi-A	0	1	.000	5	0	0	0	1	6	14	1	3	5	25.5	12.00	30	.412	.459	0	.000	-0	-6	-6	-0	-1.0
1974	Chi-A	0	0	—	2	1	0	0	0	2^1	8	1	2	2	38.6	19.29	19	.533	.588	0	—	0	-4	-4	0	-0.1
1975	Tex-A	3	3	.500	12	8	1	0	0	66	59	1	25	26	12.1	3.00	125	.246	.330	0	—	0	6	6	1	0.7
1976	Tex-A	0	0	—	5	0	0	0	0	11^2	20	3	4	6	20.1	10.03	36	.385	.448	0	—	0	-8	-8	0	-0.1
1978	Min-A	2	7	.222	13	7	1	0	1	56^2	59	1	26	31	14.1	5.24	73	.276	.365	0	—	0	-9	-9	1	-1.2
Total	5	5	11	.313	37	16	2	0	2	142^2	160	7	60	70	14.6	5.11	74	.288	.369	0	.000	-0	-22	-21	2	-1.7
● **JEFF PETEREK**	Peterek, Jeffrey Allen b: 9/22/63, Michigan City, Ind. BR/TR, 6'2", 195 lbs. Deb: 8/14/89																									
1989	Mil-A	0	2	.000	7	4	0	0	0	31^1	31	3	14	16	12.9	4.02	95	.252	.328	0	—	0	-0	-1	0	0.0
● **CHRIS PETERS**	Peters, Christopher Michael b: 1/28/72, Fort Thomas, Ky. BL/TL, 6'1", 170 lbs. Deb: 7/19/96																									
1996	Pit-N	2	4	.333	16	10	0	0	0	64	72	9	25	28	13.8	5.63	77	.287	.354	4	.211	0	-10	-9	-0	-0.7
1997	Pit-N	2	2	.500	31	1	0	0	0	37^1	38	6	21	17	14.9	4.58	94	.277	.385	1	.250	0	-2	-1	0	-0.1
1998	Pit-N	8	10	.444	39	21	1	0	1	148	142	13	55	103	12.2	3.47	125	.252	.322	9	.231	1	13	14	-2	1.5
Total	3	12	16	.429	86	32	1	0	1	249^1	252	28	101	148	13.0	4.19	103	.265	.340	14	.226	2	1	4	-2	0.7
● **GARY PETERS**	Peters, Gary Charles b: 4/21/37, Grove City, Pa. BL/TL, 6'2", 200 lbs. Deb: 9/10/59																									
1959	Chi-A	0	0	—	2	0	0	0	0	1	2	0	2	1	36.0	0.00	—	.400	.571	0	—	0	0	0	0	0.0
1960	Chi-A	0	0	—	2	0	0	0	0	3^1	4	0	1	4	13.5	2.70	140	.286	.333	0	—	0	0	0	-0	0.0
1961	Chi-A	0	0	—	3	0	0	0	1	10^1	10	0	2	6	10.5	1.74	225	.270	.308	1	.333	0	3	2	1	0.2
1962	Chi-A	0	1	.000	5	0	0	0	0	6^1	8	0	1	4	14.2	5.68	69	.308	.357	0	—	0	-1	-1	0	-0.2
1963	Chi-A	19	8	.704	41	30	13	4	1	243	192	9	68	189	9.9	**2.33**	**150**	.216	.278	21	.259	9	**35**	32	-1	4.5
1964	Chi-A☆	**20**	8	.714	37	36	11	3	0	273^2	217	20	104	205	10.8	2.50	138	.219	.297	25	.208	8	34	29	0	3.9
1965	Chi-A	10	12	.455	33	30	1	0	0	176^1	181	19	63	95	12.7	3.62	88	.265	.331	13	.181	2	-3	-8	0	-0.8
1966	Chi-A	12	10	.545	30	27	11	4	0	204^2	156	11	45	129	**9.0**	**1.98**	**160**	.212	**.261**	19	.235	6	**33**	27	1	3.9
1967	Chi-A★	16	11	.593	38	36	11	3	0	260	187	15	91	215	10.0	2.28	136	**.199**	.277	21	.212	7	27	24	3	**3.7**
1968	Chi-A	4	13	.235	31	25	6	1	1	162^2	146	7	60	110	11.8	3.76	80	.242	.318	15	.208	7	-14	-13	-0	-0.7
1969	Chi-A	10	15	.400	36	32	7	3	0	218^2	238	21	78	140	13.2	4.53	85	.283	.347	12	.169	2	-22	-16	-2	-1.7
1970	Bos-A	16	11	.593	34	34	10	4	0	221^2	221	20	83	155	12.6	4.06	98	.257	.328	20	.244	6	-9	-2	-1	0.2
1971	Bos-A	14	11	.560	34	32	9	1	1	214	241	25	70	100	13.3	4.37	84	.288	.347	26	.271	8	-22	-16	-2	-1.2
1972	Bos-A	3	3	.500	33	4	0	0	1	85^1	91	10	38	67	13.9	4.32	74	.279	.360	6	.200	1	-12	-11	-1	-0.7
Total	14	124	103	.546	359	286	79	23	5	2081	1894	157	706	1420	11.5	3.25	106	.243	.311	179	.222	57	50	46	-1	11.1
● **JOHN PETERS**	Peters, John Paul b: 4/8/1850, Louisiana, Mo. d: 1/4/24, St.Louis, Mo. BR/TR, 5'7", 180 lbs. Deb: 5/23/1874 ◆																									
1876	Chi-N	0	0	—	1	0	0	0	1	1	1	0	1	0	18.0	0.00	—	.250	.400	111	.351	0	0	0	0	0.1
● **RUBE PETERS**	Peters, Oscar Casper b: 3/15/1885, Grantfork, Ill. d: 2/7/65, Pequannock, N.J. BR/TR, 6'1", 195 lbs. Deb: 4/13/12																									
1912	Chi-A	5	6	.455	28	11	4	0	0	108^2	134	2	33	39	14.3	4.14	77	.309	.366	6	.194	-1	-10	-11	4	-0.6
1914	Bro-F	2	2	.500	11	3	1	0	0	37^2	52	1	16	13	16.2	3.82	75	.335	.398	1	.091	-1	-4	-4	0	-0.5
Total	2	7	8	.467	39	14	5	0	0	146^1	186	3	49	52	14.8	4.06	77	.316	.374	7	.167	-1	-14	-15	4	-1.1
● **RAY PETERS**	Peters, Raymond James b: 8/27/46, Buffalo, N.Y. BR/TR, 6'5.5", 210 lbs. Deb: 6/4/70																									
1970	Mil-A	0	2	.000	2	2	0	0	0	2	7	0	5	1	54.0	31.50	12	.583	.706	0	—	0	-6	-6	0	-2.8
● **STEVE PETERS**	Peters, Steven Bradley b: 11/14/62, Oklahoma City, Okla BL/TL, 5'10", 170 lbs. Deb: 8/11/87																									
1987	StL-N	0	0	—	12	0	0	0	1	15	17	1	6	11	13.8	1.80	231	.298	.365	0	.000	-0	4	4	1	0.1
1988	StL-N	3	3	.500	44	0	0	0	0	45	57	8	22	30	15.8	6.40	54	.313	.387	0	.000	-0	-15	-15	-1	-1.9
Total	2	3	3	.500	56	0	0	0	1	60	74	9	28	41	15.3	5.25	69	.310	.382	0	.000	-1	-11	-11	0	-1.8
● **ADAM PETERSON**	Peterson, Adam Charles b: 12/11/65, Long Beach, Cal. BR/TR, 6'3", 190 lbs. Deb: 9/19/87																									
1987	Chi-A	0	0	—	1	1	0	0	0	4	8	1	3	1	24.8	13.50	34	.444	.524	0	—	0	-4	-4	-0	-0.1
1988	Chi-A	0	1	.000	2	2	0	0	0	6	6	0	6	5	18.0	13.50	29	.240	.387	0	—	0	-6	-6	-0	-0.8
1989	Chi-A	0	1	.000	3	2	0	0	0	5^1	13	1	2	3	25.3	15.19	25	.464	.500	0	—	0	-7	-7	-0	-1.0
1990	Chi-A	2	5	.286	20	11	2	0	0	85	90	12	26	29	12.5	4.55	84	.278	.335	0	—	0	-6	-7	-1	-0.5
1991	SD-N	3	4	.429	13	11	0	0	0	54^2	50	10	28	37	12.8	4.45	85	.242	.332	0	.000	-1	-5	-4	-0	-0.6
Total	5	5	11	.313	39	27	2	0	0	155	167	24	65	75	13.6	5.46	70	.277	.350	0	.000	-1	-28	-28	-2	-3.0
● **FRITZ PETERSON**	Peterson, Fritz Fred (b: Fred Ingels Peterson) b: 2/8/42, Chicago, Ill. BB/TL, 6', 200 lbs. Deb: 4/15/66																									
1966	NY-A	12	11	.522	34	32	11	2	0	215	196	15	40	96	10.0	3.31	101	.241	.279	15	.224	4	3	0	-0	0.4
1967	NY-A	8	14	.364	36	30	6	1	0	181^1	179	11	43	102	11.2	3.47	90	.256	.302	7	.146	1	-5	-7	1	-0.6
1968	NY-A	12	11	.522	36	27	6	2	0	212^1	187	13	29	115	9.3	2.63	110	.241	.272	5	.079	-2	8	6	4	1.0
1969	NY-A	17	16	.515	37	37	16	4	0	272	228	15	43	150	**9.1**	2.55	136	.229	.263	9	.112	-0	32	28	2	3.7
1970	NY-A★	20	11	.645	39	37	8	2	0	260^1	247	24	40	127	**10.0**	2.90	121	.248	**.280**	20	.222	5	23	18	2	2.9
1971	NY-A	15	13	.536	37	35	16	4	1	274	269	25	42	139	10.3	3.05	106	.258	.289	7	.082	-3	12	5	2	0.4
1972	NY-A	17	15	.531	35	35	12	3	0	250^1	270	17	44	100	11.5	3.24	91	.276	.310	19	.232	4	-5	-8	1	-0.5
1973	NY-A	8	15	.348	31	31	6	0	0	184^1	207	18	49	59	12.8	3.95	93	.286	.337	0	—	0	-3	-6	0	-0.7
1974	NY-A	0	0	—	3	1	0	0	0	7^2	13	1	2	5	17.6	4.70	75	.361	.395	0	—	0	-1	-1	-0	0.1
	Cle-A	9	14	.391	29	29	3	0	0	152^2	187	16	37	52	13.4	4.36	83	.305	.349	0	—	0	-13	-13	1	-1.6
	Yr	9	14	.391	32	30	3	0	0	160^1	200	17	39	57	13.6	4.38	82	.308	.351	0	—	0	-14	-14	1	-1.5
1975	Cle-A	14	8	.636	25	25	6	2	0	146^1	154	15	40	47	12.3	3.94	96	.275	.331	0	—	0	-3	-3	1	-0.3
1976	Cle-A	0	3	.000	9	9	0	0	0	47	59	3	10	19	13.2	5.55	63	.309	.343	0	—	0	-11	-11	-0	-0.6
	Tex-A	1	0	1.000	4	2	0	0	0	15	21	0	7	4	16.8	3.60	100	.344	.412	0	—	0	-0	-0	0	-0.1
	Yr	1	3	.250	13	11	0	0	0	62	80	3	17	23	14.1	5.08	69	.316	.359	0	—	0	-11	-11	0	-0.7
Total	11	133	131	.504	355	330	90	20	1	2218^1	2217	173	426	1015	10.9	3.30	101	.261	.300	82	.159	8	40	10	15	4.1
● **JIM PETERSON**	Peterson, James Niels b: 8/18/08, Philadelphia, Pa. d: 4/8/75, Palm Beach, Fla. BR/TR, 6'0.5", 200 lbs. Deb: 7/9/31																									
1931	Phi-A	0	1	.000	6	1	1	0	0	13	18	0	4	7	15.2	6.23	72	.321	.367	1	.500	1	-3	-3	-0	-0.1
1933	Phi-A	2	5	.286	32	5	0	0	0	90^2	114	6	36	18	14.9	4.96	86	.305	.366	4	.148	-1	-7	-7	2	-0.3
1937	Bro-N	0	0	—	3	0	0	0	0	5^2	8	3	2	4	15.9	7.94	51	.333	.385	0	—	0	-3	-2	1	0.1
Total	3	2	6	.250	41	6	1	0	0	109^1	140	9	42	29	15.0	5.27	82	.308	.367	5	.172	0	-12	-12	3	-0.3

● KENT PETERSON Peterson, Kent Franklin "Pete" b: 12/21/25, Goshen, Utah d: 4/27/95, Highland, Utah BR/TL, 5'10", 175 lbs. Deb: 7/15/44

YEAR	TM/L	W	L	PCT	G	GS	CG	SH	SV	IP	H	HR	BB	SO	RAT	ERA	ERA+	OAV	OOB	BH	AVG	PB	PR	/A	PD	TPI
1944	Cin-N	0	0	—	1	0	0	0	0	1	0	0	0	0	0.0	0.00	—	.000	.000	0	—	0	0	0	-0	0.0
1947	Cin-N	6	13	.316	37	17	3	1	2	152^1	156	8	62	78	13.1	4.25	96	.265	.338	3	.068	-3	-3	-3	-2	-0.8
1948	Cin-N	2	15	.118	43	17	2	0	1	137	146	10	59	64	13.9	4.60	85	.271	.350	5	.139	-2	-10	-10	0	-1.3
1949	Cin-N	4	5	.444	30	7	2	0	0	66^1	66	8	46	28	15.7	6.24	67	.261	.383	1	.056	-2	-16	-15	-1	-2.0
1950	Cin-N	0	3	.000	9	2	0	0	0	20	25	4	17	6	18.9	7.20	59	.305	.424	1	.333	0	-7	-7	0	-0.9
1951	Cin-N	1	1	.500	9	0	0	0	0	9^2	13	0	8	5	20.5	6.52	63	.317	.440	0	.000	-0	-3	-3	0	-0.5
1952	Phi-N	0	0	—	3	0	0	0	2	7	2	0	2	7	5.1	0.00	—	.091	.167	0	.000	-0	3	3	-0	0.2
1953	Phi-N	0	1	.000	15	0	0	0	0	27	26	3	21	20	16.0	6.67	63	.252	.384	0	.000	-1	-7	-7	-0	-0.3
Total	8	13	38	.255	147	43	7	1	5	420^1	434	33	215	208	14.2	4.95	82	.266	.357	10	.091	-8	-43	-42	-4	-5.6

● SID PETERSON Peterson, Sidney Herbert b: 1/31/18, Havelock, N.Dak. BR/TR, 6'3", 220 lbs. Deb: 5/4/43

YEAR	TM/L	W	L	PCT	G	GS	CG	SH	SV	IP	H	HR	BB	SO	RAT	ERA	ERA+	OAV	OOB	BH	AVG	PB	PR	/A	PD	TPI
1943	StL-A	2	0	1.000	3	0	0	0	0	10	15	0	3	0	17.1	2.70	123	.341	.396	0	.000	-0	1	1	-0	0.1

● MARK PETKOVSEK Petkovsek, Mark Joseph b: 11/18/65, Beaumont, Tex. BR/TR, 6', 185 lbs. Deb: 6/8/91

YEAR	TM/L	W	L	PCT	G	GS	CG	SH	SV	IP	H	HR	BB	SO	RAT	ERA	ERA+	OAV	OOB	BH	AVG	PB	PR	/A	PD	TPI
1991	Tex-A	0	1	.000	4	1	0	0	0	9^1	21	4	4	6	24.1	14.46	28	.438	.481	0	—	0	-11	-11	-0	-0.9
1993	Pit-N	3	0	1.000	26	0	0	0	0	32^1	43	7	9	14	14.5	6.96	58	.328	.371	0	—	0	-10	-10	1	-0.8
1995	StL-N	6	6	.500	26	21	1	1	0	137^1	136	11	35	71	11.6	4.00	105	.262	.316	3	.081	-1	3	3	-1	0.1
1996	*StL-N	11	2	.846	48	6	0	0	0	88^2	83	9	35	45	12.5	3.55	118	.251	.332	3	.188	0	7	6	0	0.9
1997	StL-N	4	7	.364	55	2	0	0	2	96	109	14	31	51	13.7	5.06	82	.292	.356	1	.091	-0	-9	-10	1	-0.9
1998	StL-N	7	4	.636	48	10	0	0	0	105^2	131	9	36	55	14.9	4.77	88	.312	.377	7	.318	2	-6	-7	-1	-0.5
Total	6	31	20	.608	207	40	1	1	2	469^1	523	54	150	242	13.4	4.72	88	.287	.349	14	.163	1	-27	-29	0	-2.1

● DAN PETRY Petry, Daniel Joseph b: 11/13/58, Palo Alto, Cal. BR/TR, 6'4", 200 lbs. Deb: 7/8/79

YEAR	TM/L	W	L	PCT	G	GS	CG	SH	SV	IP	H	HR	BB	SO	RAT	ERA	ERA+	OAV	OOB	BH	AVG	PB	PR	/A	PD	TPI
1979	Det-A	6	5	.545	15	15	2	0	0	98	90	11	33	43	11.7	3.95	110	.254	.325	0	—	0	3	4	-1	0.3
1980	Det-A	10	9	.526	27	25	4	3	0	164^2	156	9	83	88	13.1	3.94	104	.253	.342	0	—	0	2	3	2	0.4
1981	Det-A	10	9	.526	23	22	7	2	0	141	115	10	57	79	11.0	3.00	126	.224	.302	0	—	0	10	12	2	1.7
1982	Det-A	15	9	.625	35	35	8	1	0	246	220	15	100	132	11.9	3.22	126	.241	.319	0	—	0	23	23	4	2.6
1983	Det-A	19	11	.633	38	38	9	2	0	266^1	256	37	99	122	12.2	3.92	100	.256	.327	0	—	0	4	-0	3	0.3
1984	*Det-A	18	8	.692	35	35	7	2	0	233^1	231	21	66	144	11.6	3.24	121	.259	.312	0	—	0	19	18	3	2.2
1985	Det-A★	15	13	.536	34	34	8	0	0	238^2	190	24	81	109	10.3	3.36	121	.217	.285	0	—	0	21	19	0	2.1
1986	Det-A	5	10	.333	20	20	2	0	0	116	122	15	53	56	14.0	4.66	89	.268	.350	0	—	0	-6	-7	1	-0.7
1987	*Det-A	9	7	.563	30	21	0	0	0	134^2	148	22	76	93	15.6	5.61	75	.279	.379	0	—	0	-17	-21	1	-1.8
1988	Cal-A	3	9	.250	22	22	4	1	0	139^2	139	18	59	64	13.1	4.38	88	.263	.344	0	—	0	-6	-8	2	-0.3
1989	Cal-A	3	2	.600	19	4	0	0	0	51	53	8	23	21	13.6	5.47	70	.275	.355	0	—	0	-9	-9	0	-0.8
1990	Det-A	10	9	.526	32	23	1	0	0	149^2	148	14	77	73	13.6	4.45	89	.263	.353	0	—	0	-9	-8	2	-0.8
1991	Det-A	2	3	.400	17	6	0	0	0	54^2	66	9	19	18	14.0	4.94	84	.300	.356	0	—	0	-5	-5	2	-0.3
	Atl-N	0	0	—	10	0	0	0	0	24^1	29	2	14	9	16.3	5.55	70	.296	.389	1	.200	0	-5	-4	0	0.0
	Bos-A	0	0	—	13	0	0	0	1	22^1	21	3	12	12	13.7	4.43	97	.250	.351	0	—	0	-1	-0	0	-0.1
Total	13	125	104	.546	370	300	52	11	1	2080^1	1984	218	852	1063	12.5	3.95	102	.253	.330	1	.200	0	24	16	22	4.8

● JAY PETTIBONE Pettibone, Harry Jonathan b: 6/21/57, Mt.Clemens, Mich. BR/TR, 6'4", 182 lbs. Deb: 9/11/83

YEAR	TM/L	W	L	PCT	G	GS	CG	SH	SV	IP	H	HR	BB	SO	RAT	ERA	ERA+	OAV	OOB	BH	AVG	PB	PR	/A	PD	TPI
1983	Min-A	0	4	.000	4	4	1	0	0	27	28	8	8	10	12.7	5.33	80	.280	.345	0	—	0	-4	-3	0	-0.4

● PAUL PETTIT Pettit, George William Paul "Lefty" b: 11/29/31, Los Angeles, Cal. BL/TL, 6'2", 195 lbs. Deb: 5/4/51

YEAR	TM/L	W	L	PCT	G	GS	CG	SH	SV	IP	H	HR	BB	SO	RAT	ERA	ERA+	OAV	OOB	BH	AVG	PB	PR	/A	PD	TPI
1951	Pit-N	0	0	—	2	0	0	0	0	2^2	2	1	1	0	10.1	3.38	125	.200	.273	0	.000	-0	0	0	-0	0.0
1953	Pit-N	1	2	.333	10	5	0	0	0	28	33	1	20	14	17.0	7.71	58	.297	.405	2	.250	1	-11	-10	0	-0.8
Total	2	1	2	.333	12	5	0	0	0	30^2	35	2	21	14	16.4	7.34	61	.289	.394	2	.222	1	-10	-10	0	-0.8

● LEON PETTIT Pettit, Leon Arthur "Lefty" b: 6/23/02, Waynesburg, Pa. d: 11/21/74, Columbia, Tenn. BL/TL, 5'10.5", 165 lbs. Deb: 4/18/35

YEAR	TM/L	W	L	PCT	G	GS	CG	SH	SV	IP	H	HR	BB	SO	RAT	ERA	ERA+	OAV	OOB	BH	AVG	PB	PR	/A	PD	TPI
1935	Was-A	8	5	.615	41	7	1	0	3	109	129	6	58	45	15.8	4.95	87	.301	.390	2	.080	0	-6	-8	-0	-0.8
1937	Phi-N	0	1	.000	3	1	0	0	0	4	6	1	4	0	22.5	11.25	39	.353	.476	0	—	0	-3	-3	0	-0.6
Total	2	8	6	.571	44	8	1	0	3	113	135	7	62	45	16.0	5.18	84	.303	.393	2	.080	0	-9	-11	-0	-1.4

● BOB PETTIT Pettit, Robert Henry b: 7/19/1861, Williamstown, Mass. d: 11/1/10, Derby, Conn. BL/TR, 5'9", 160 lbs. Deb: 9/3/1887 ♦

YEAR	TM/L	W	L	PCT	G	GS	CG	SH	SV	IP	H	HR	BB	SO	RAT	ERA	ERA+	OAV	OOB	BH	AVG	PB	PR	/A	PD	TPI
1887	Chi-N	0	0	—	1	0	0	0	**1**	1	3	0	2	0	45.0	0.00	—	.375	.500	36	.261	0	0	0	0	0.1

● ANDY PETTITTE Pettitte, Andrew Eugene b: 6/15/72, Baton Rouge, La. BL/TL, 6'5", 235 lbs. Deb: 4/29/95

YEAR	TM/L	W	L	PCT	G	GS	CG	SH	SV	IP	H	HR	BB	SO	RAT	ERA	ERA+	OAV	OOB	BH	AVG	PB	PR	/A	PD	TPI
1995	*NY-A	12	9	.571	31	26	3	0	0	175	183	15	63	114	12.7	4.17	111	.272	.336	0	—	0	11	9	0	0.9
1996	*NY-A☆	**21**	8	.724	35	34	2	0	0	221	229	23	72	162	12.4	3.87	128	.271	.331	0	—	0	28	26	1	3.0
1997	*NY-A	18	7	.720	35	35	4	1	0	240^1	233	7	65	166	11.3	2.88	154	.256	.308	0	—	0	45	42	2	4.2
1998	*NY-A	16	11	.593	33	32	5	0	0	216^1	226	20	87	146	13.3	4.24	105	.274	.347	0	.000	-0	10	5	2	0.6
Total	4	67	35	.657	134	127	14	1	0	852^2	871	65	287	588	12.4	3.75	123	.268	.330	0	.000	-0	93	81	5	8.7

● CHARLIE PETTY Petty, Charles E. b: 6/28/1866, Nashville, Tenn. TR , Deb: 7/30/1889

YEAR	TM/L	W	L	PCT	G	GS	CG	SH	SV	IP	H	HR	BB	SO	RAT	ERA	ERA+	OAV	OOB	BH	AVG	PB	PR	/A	PD	TPI
1889	Cin-a	2	3	.400	5	5	5	0	0	44	44	3	20	10	14.3	5.52	71	.253	.350	6	.300	1	-8	-8	0	-0.6
1893	NY-N	5	2	.714	9	6	4	0	0	54	66	0	28	12	15.8	3.33	140	.292	.373	7	.318	3	8	8	-0	1.0
1894	Was-N	3	8	.273	16	12	8	0	0	103	156	4	32	14	17.2	5.59	94	.344	.399	8	.195	-2	-3	-4	-1	-0.5
	Cle-N	0	2	.000	4	3	2	0	0	27	42	4	14	4	19.7	8.67	63	.350	.431	1	.083	-2	-10	-10	-1	-0.7
	Yr	3	10	.231	20	15	10	0	0	130	198	8	46	18	17.1	6.23	85	.340	.391	9	.170	-4	-13	-13	-1	-1.2
Total	3	10	15	.400	34	26	19	0	0	228	308	11	94	40	16.6	5.41	90	.317	.388	22	.232	-0	-13	-13	-2	-0.8

● JESSE PETTY Petty, Jesse Lee "The Silver Fox" b: 11/23/1894, Orr, Okla. d: 10/23/71, St.Paul, Minn. BR/TL, 6', 195 lbs. Deb: 4/14/21

YEAR	TM/L	W	L	PCT	G	GS	CG	SH	SV	IP	H	HR	BB	SO	RAT	ERA	ERA+	OAV	OOB	BH	AVG	PB	PR	/A	PD	TPI
1921	Cle-A	0	0	—	4	0	0	0	0	9	10	0	0	0	10.0	2.00	213	.345	.345	0	.000	-0	2	2	1	0.0
1925	Bro-N	9	9	.500	28	21	7	0	0	153	188	15	47	39	13.9	4.88	86	.304	.355	7	.140	-3	-10	-12	-2	-1.5
1926	Bro-N	17	17	.500	38	33	23	1	1	275^2	246	9	79	101	10.7	2.84	135	**.240**	.296	17	.175	-3	30	30	-4	2.7
1927	Bro-N	13	18	.419	42	33	19	2	1	271^2	263	13	53	101	10.6	2.98	133	.254	.293	9	.099	-7	28	30	-3	2.1
1928	Bro-N	15	15	.500	40	31	15	2	1	234	264	18	56	74	12.5	4.04	98	.289	.334	9	.111	-5	1	-2	-4	-1.1
1929	Pit-N	11	10	.524	36	25	12	1	0	184^1	197	12	42	58	11.7	3.71	129	.277	.317	7	.104	-5	21	22	-2	1.4
1930	Pit-N	1	6	.143	10	7	0	0	1	41^1	67	8	13	16	17.9	8.27	60	.362	.410	1	.083	-1	-15	-15	-0	-2.0
	Chi-N	1	3	.250	9	3	0	0	0	39^1	51	2	6	18	13.0	2.97	164	.317	.341	3	.231	0	9	8	-0	0.7
	Yr	2	9	.182	19	10	0	0	1	80^2	118	10	19	34	15.3	5.69	87	.339	.373	4	.160	-1	-6	-7	-0	-1.3
Total	7	67	78	.462	207	153	76	6	4	1208^1	1286	77	296	407	11.9	3.68	113	.275	.320	53	.128	-25	63	63	-14	2.3

● PRETZEL PEZZULLO Pezzullo, John b: 12/10/10, Bridgeport, Conn. d: 5/16/90, Dallas, Tex. BL/TL, 5'11.5", 180 lbs. Deb: 4/18/35

YEAR	TM/L	W	L	PCT	G	GS	CG	SH	SV	IP	H	HR	BB	SO	RAT	ERA	ERA+	OAV	OOB	BH	AVG	PB	PR	/A	PD	TPI
1935	Phi-N	3	5	.375	41	7	2	0	1	84^1	115	5	45	24	17.8	6.40	71	.321	.407	6	.250	0	-22	-18	-2	-1.6
1936	Phi-N	0	0	—	1	0	0	0	0	2	1	0	6	0	31.5	4.50	101	.167	.583	0	—	0	-0	0	-0	0.0
Total	2	3	5	.375	42	7	2	0	1	86^1	116	5	51	24	18.1	6.36	71	.319	.412	6	.250	0	-22	-18	-2	-1.6

● BILL PFANN Pfann, William F. b: 6/1863, Hamilton, Ont., Can. d: 6/3/04, Hamilton, Ont., Can 6', 205 lbs. Deb: 6/16/1894

YEAR	TM/L	W	L	PCT	G	GS	CG	SH	SV	IP	H	HR	BB	SO	RAT	ERA	ERA+	OAV	OOB	BH	AVG	PB	PR	/A	PD	TPI
1894	Cin-N	0	1	.000	1	1	0	0	0	3	10	1	4	0	42.0	27.00	21	.526	.609	0	.000	-0	-7	-7	0	-1.1

● JEFF PFEFFER Pfeffer, Edward Joseph b: 3/4/1888, Seymour, Ill. d: 8/15/72, Chicago, Ill. BR/TR, 6'3", 210 lbs. Deb: 4/16/11 F

YEAR	TM/L	W	L	PCT	G	GS	CG	SH	SV	IP	H	HR	BB	SO	RAT	ERA	ERA+	OAV	OOB	BH	AVG	PB	PR	/A	PD	TPI
1911	StL-A	0	0	—	2	0	0	0	0	10	11	0	4	4	13.5	7.20	47	.297	.366	0	.000	-1	-4	-4	-0	-0.1
1913	Bro-N	0	1	.000	5	2	1	0	0	24^1	28	0	13	13	16.6	3.33	99	.311	.421	0	.000	-1	-0	-0	0	-0.1
1914	Bro-N	23	12	.657	43	34	27	3	4	315	264	9	91	135	10.3	1.97	145	.232	.293	23	.198	-1	29	31	-4	3.1
1915	Bro-N	19	14	.576	40	34	26	6	3	291^2	243	8	76	84	10.4	2.10	132	.231	.293	27	.255	5	21	22	-4	2.6
1916	*Bro-N	25	11	.694	41	36	30	6	1	328^2	274	5	63	128	9.7	1.92	140	.230	.278	34	.279	7	26	28	-5	3.6
1917	Bro-N	11	15	.423	30	30	24	3	0	266	225	4	66	115	10.4	2.23	125	.234	.294	13	.130	-4	14	17	-2	0.9
1918	Bro-N	1	0	1.000	1	1	1	1	0	9	2	0	3	1	5.0	0.00	—	.071	.161	1	.250	0	3	3	0	0.5
1919	Bro-N	17	13	.567	30	30	26	4	0	267	270	7	49	92	11.2	2.66	112	.267	.308	20	.206	1	7	9	1	1.2
1920	*Bro-N	16	9	.640	30	28	20	2	0	215	225	5	45	80	11.5	3.01	106	.273	.314	18	.243	1	3	5	-3	0.3

YEAR	TM/L	W	L	PCT	G	GS	CG	SH	SV	IP	H	HR	BB	SO	RAT	ERA	ERA+	OAV	OOB	BH	AVG	PB	PR	/A	PD	TPI
1921	Bro-N	1	5	.167	6	5	2	0	0	31^{2}	36	0	9	8	13.1	4.55	86	.310	.365	0	.000	-2	-3	-2	0	-0.5
	StL-N	9	3	.750	18	13	7	1	0	98^{2}	115	3	28	22	13.5	4.29	86	.305	.361	4	.138	-1	-6	-7	-2	-0.9
	Yr	10	8	.556	24	18	9	1	0	130^{1}	151	3	37	30	13.3	4.35	86	.306	.360	4	.100	-2	-8	-9	-1	-1.4
1922	StL-N	19	12	.613	44	32	19	1	2	261^{1}	286	12	58	83	12.2	3.58	108	.279	.324	24	.245	4	15	8	1	1.3
1923	StL-N	8	9	.471	26	18	7	1	0	152^{1}	171	8	40	32	13.0	4.02	97	.287	.341	7	.127	-4	-0	-2	-1	-0.7
1924	StL-N	4	5	.444	16	12	3	0	0	78	102	3	30	20	15.3	5.31	71	.318	.378	3	.115	-2	-12	-13	-1	-1.6
	Pit-N	5	3	.625	15	4	1	0	0	58^{2}	68	3	17	19	13.0	3.07	125	.293	.341	6	.240	-0	5	5	-1	0.5
	Yr	9	8	.529	31	16	4	0	0	136^{2}	170	6	47	39	14.3	4.35	88	.307	.361	9	.176	-3	-7	-8	-2	-1.1
Total	13	158	112	.585	347	279	194	28	10	2407^{1}	2320	67	592	836	11.3	2.77	114	.258	.311	180	.206	2	97	103	-21	10.1

● BIG JEFF PFEFFER Pfeffer, Francis Xavier b: 3/31/1882, Champaign, Ill. d: 12/19/54, Kankakee, Ill. BR/TR, 6'1", 185 lbs. Deb: 4/15/05 F

YEAR	TM/L	W	L	PCT	G	GS	CG	SH	SV	IP	H	HR	BB	SO	RAT	ERA	ERA+	OAV	OOB	BH	AVG	PB	PR	/A	PD	TPI
1905	Chi-N	4	4	.500	15	11	9	0	0	101	84	2	36	56	11.0	2.50	120	.240	.318	8	.200	1	6	5	-1	0.4
1906	Bos-N	13	22	.371	36	36	33	4	0	302^{1}	270	4	114	158	11.9	2.95	91	.246	.325	31	.196	3	-11	-9	2	-0.3
1907	Bos-N	6	8	.429	19	16	12	1	0	144	129	3	61	65	12.3	3.00	85	.253	.341	15	.250	3	-8	-7	-0	-0.4
1908	Bos-N	0	0	—	4	0	0	0	0	10	18	1	8	3	23.4	12.60	19	.383	.473	0	.000	-0	-11	-11	-0	-0.1
1910	Chi-N	1	0	1.000	13	1	1	0	0	41^{1}	43	1	16	11	13.1	3.27	88	.281	.353	3	.176	1	-1	-2	-1	0.0
1911	Bos-N	7	5	.583	26	6	4	1	2	97	116	3	57	24	16.1	4.73	81	.301	.391	9	.196	1	-14	-10	0	-1.0
Total	6	31	39	.443	113	70	59	6	2	695^{2}	660	14	292	317	12.7	3.30	87	.260	.342	66	.204	8	-40	-34	-0	-1.4

● FRED PFEFFER Pfeffer, Nathaniel Frederick "Fritz" or "Dandelion"
b: 3/17/1860, Louisville, Ky. d: 4/10/32, Chicago, Ill. BR/TR, 5'10.5", 184 lbs. Deb: 5/1/1882 M♦

YEAR	TM/L	W	L	PCT	G	GS	CG	SH	SV	IP	H	HR	BB	SO	RAT	ERA	ERA+	OAV	OOB	BH	AVG	PB	PR	/A	PD	TPI
1884	Chi-N	0	0	—	1	0	0	0	0	1	3	0	1	0	36.0	9.00	35	.333	.400	135	.289	0	-1	-1	-0	0.0
1885	*Chi-N	2	1	.667	5	2	2	0	**2**	31^{2}	26	1	8	13	9.7	2.56	118	.222	.272	113	.241	1	1	2	-0	0.1
1892	Lou-N	0	0	—	1	0	0	0	0	5	4	0	5	0	16.2	1.80	170	.211	.375	121	.257	0	1	1	0	0.0
1894	Lou-N	0	0	—	1	0	0	0	0	7	8	0	6	0	19.3	2.57	198	.286	.429	126	.308	0	2	2	-0	0.0
Total	4	2	1	.667	8	2	2	0	2	44^{2}	41	1	20	13	12.5	2.62	129	.237	.320	1671	.255	1	3	4	-1	0.1

● JACK PFIESTER Pfiester, John Albert "Jack The Giant Killer" (b: John Albert Hagenbush)
b: 5/24/1878, Cincinnati, Ohio d: 9/3/53, Loveland, Ohio BR/TL, 5'11", 180 lbs. Deb: 9/8/03

YEAR	TM/L	W	L	PCT	G	GS	CG	SH	SV	IP	H	HR	BB	SO	RAT	ERA	ERA+	OAV	OOB	BH	AVG	PB	PR	/A	PD	TPI
1903	Pit-N	0	3	.000	3	3	2	0	0	19	26	0	10	15	18.0	6.16	53	.321	.409	0	.000	-1	-6	-6	-0	-0.8
1904	Pit-N	1	1	.500	3	2	1	0	0	20	28	0	9	6	16.6	7.20	38	.318	.381	2	.286	1	-10	-10	0	-0.7
1906	*Chi-N	20	8	.714	31	29	20	4	0	250^{2}	173	3	63	153	8.9	1.51	175	.194	.258	4	.048	-7	31	32	-1	2.8
1907	*Chi-N	14	9	.609	30	22	13	3	0	195	143	1	48	90	9.0	**1.15**	**216**	.207	.263	6	.094	-3	29	29	-2	3.1
1908	*Chi-N	12	10	.545	33	29	18	3	0	252	204	1	70	117	10.2	2.00	118	.223	.287	8	.101	-4	10	10	-3	0.1
1909	Chi-N	17	6	.739	29	25	13	5	0	196^{2}	179	1	49	73	10.7	2.43	105	.240	.291	11	.169	0	4	3	3	0.6
1910	*Chi-N	6	3	.667	14	13	5	2	0	100^{1}	82	0	26	34	9.8	1.79	161	.225	.279	3	.091	-2	14	12	-0	0.7
1911	Chi-N	1	4	.200	6	5	3	0	0	33^{2}	34	0	18	15	14.4	4.01	83	.262	.360	2	.182	0	-2	-3	1	-0.3
Total	8	71	44	.617	149	128	75	17	0	1067^{1}	869	6	293	503	10.1	2.02	128	.223	.284	36	.103	-15	69	67	-3	5.5

● DAN PFISTER Pfister, Daniel Albin b: 12/20/36, Plainfield, N.J. BR/TR, 6', 187 lbs. Deb: 9/9/61

YEAR	TM/L	W	L	PCT	G	GS	CG	SH	SV	IP	H	HR	BB	SO	RAT	ERA	ERA+	OAV	OOB	BH	AVG	PB	PR	/A	PD	TPI
1961	KC-A	0	0	—	2	0	0	0	0	2^{1}	5	2	4	3	34.7	15.43	27	.417	.563	0	—	0	-3	-3	-0	0.0
1962	KC-A	4	14	.222	41	25	2	0	1	196^{1}	175	27	106	123	13.3	4.54	93	.238	.341	12	.185	-1	-12	-7	1	-0.6
1963	KC-A	1	0	1.000	3	1	0	0	0	9^{1}	8	1	3	9	11.6	1.93	202	.229	.308	0	.000	-0	2	2	0	0.2
1964	KC-A	1	5	.167	19	3	0	0	0	41^{1}	50	10	29	21	18.5	6.53	58	.311	.434	0	.000	-0	-13	-12	-0	-1.7
Total	4	6	19	.240	65	29	2	0	1	249^{1}	238	40	142	156	14.3	4.87	85	.252	.359	12	.162	-2	-27	-20	1	-2.1

● LEE PFUND Pfund, Le Roy Herbert b: 10/10/18, Oak Park, Ill. BR/TR, 6'1", 185 lbs. Deb: 4/21/45

YEAR	TM/L	W	L	PCT	G	GS	CG	SH	SV	IP	H	HR	BB	SO	RAT	ERA	ERA+	OAV	OOB	BH	AVG	PB	PR	/A	PD	TPI
1945	Bro-N	3	2	.600	15	10	2	0	0	62^{1}	69	4	35	27	15.7	5.20	72	.274	.373	4	.182	0	-10	-10	1	-0.6

● BILL PHEBUS Phebus, Raymond William b: 8/2/09, Cherryvale, Kan. d: 10/11/89, Bartow, Fla. BR/TR, 5'9", 170 lbs. Deb: 9/6/36

YEAR	TM/L	W	L	PCT	G	GS	CG	SH	SV	IP	H	HR	BB	SO	RAT	ERA	ERA+	OAV	OOB	BH	AVG	PB	PR	/A	PD	TPI
1936	Was-A	0	0	—	2	1	0	0	0	7^{1}	4	1	4	4	11.0	2.45	195	.114	.225	0	.000	0	2	2	-0	0.0
1937	Was-A	3	2	.600	6	5	4	1	1	40^{2}	33	2	24	12	13.1	2.21	200	.232	.351	0	.000	1	11	10	-1	1.2
1938	Was-A	0	0	—	5	0	0	0	1	6^{1}	9	1	7	2	22.7	11.37	40	.346	.485	0	.000	-0	-5	-5	0	-0.1
Total	3	3	2	.600	13	6	4	1	2	54^{1}	46	4	35	18	13.9	3.31	135	.227	.349	0	.000	1	8	7	-1	1.1

● RAY PHELPS Phelps, Raymond Clifford b: 12/11/03, Dunlap, Tenn. d: 7/7/71, Fort Pierce, Fla. BR/TR, 6'2", 200 lbs. Deb: 4/23/30

YEAR	TM/L	W	L	PCT	G	GS	CG	SH	SV	IP	H	HR	BB	SO	RAT	ERA	ERA+	OAV	OOB	BH	AVG	PB	PR	/A	PD	TPI
1930	Bro-N	14	7	.667	36	24	11	2	0	179^{2}	198	21	52	64	12.7	4.11	120	.280	.332	10	.147	-2	17	16	2	1.5
1931	Bro-N	7	9	.438	28	26	3	1	0	149^{1}	184	3	44	50	14.0	5.00	76	.306	.357	8	.157	-1	-19	-20	0	-1.9
1932	Bro-N	4	5	.444	20	8	4	1	0	79^{1}	101	5	27	21	14.9	5.90	65	.323	.382	2	.087	-1	-18	-18	0	-1.8
1935	Chi-A	4	8	.333	27	17	4	0	1	125	126	10	55	38	13.2	4.82	96	.262	.341	5	.122	-4	-5	-3	2	-0.4
1936	Chi-A	4	6	.400	15	4	2	0	0	68^{2}	91	9	42	17	17.7	6.03	86	.331	.423	6	.231	1	-8	-6	1	-0.6
Total	5	33	35	.485	126	79	24	4	1	602	700	48	220	190	14.0	4.93	90	.294	.358	31	.148	-8	-32	-31	5	-3.2

● DEACON PHILLIPPE Phillippe, Charles Louis b: 5/23/1872, Rural Retreat, Va. d: 3/30/52, Avalon, Pa. BR/TR, 6'0.5", 180 lbs. Deb: 4/21/1899

YEAR	TM/L	W	L	PCT	G	GS	CG	SH	SV	IP	H	HR	BB	SO	RAT	ERA	ERA+	OAV	OOB	BH	AVG	PB	PR	/A	PD	TPI
1899	Lou-N	21	17	.553	42	38	33	2	1	321	331	10	64	68	11.3	3.17	122	.266	.306	26	.203	-1	24	25	-0	2.3
1900	*Pit-N	20	13	.606	38	33	29	1	0	279	274	7	42	75	**10.4**	2.84	128	.257	**.289**	19	.181	-2	27	25	-2	2.0
1901	Pit-N	22	12	.647	37	32	30	1	2	296	274	7	38	103	9.8	2.22	147	.244	.275	26	.230	5	**36**	34	3	4.4
1902	Pit-N	20	9	.690	31	30	29	5	0	272	265	1	26	122	9.8	2.05	133	.255	.276	25	.221	3	22	21	-2	2.1
1903	*Pit-N	25	9	.735	36	33	31	4	2	289^{1}	269	4	29	123	**9.4**	2.43	133	.241	**.263**	26	.210	2	27	26	-2	2.7
1904	Pit-N	10	10	.500	21	19	17	3	1	166^{2}	183	1	26	82	11.4	3.24	85	.272	.302	8	.123	-4	-9	-9	-0	-1.4
1905	Pit-N	20	13	.606	38	33	25	5	0	279	235	0	48	133	9.5	2.19	137	.233	.274	9	.093	-4	25	25	-1	2.2
1906	Pit-N	15	10	.600	33	24	19	3	0	218^{2}	216	3	26	90	10.0	2.47	108	.252	.276	20	.244	3	4	5	-1	0.8
1907	Pit-N	14	11	.560	35	26	17	1	2	214	214	2	36	61	10.7	2.61	93	.264	.300	12	.185	1	-3	-4	-2	-0.6
1908	Pit-N	0	0	—	5	0	0	0	0	12	20	0	3	1	17.3	11.25	20	.357	.390	1	.250	0	-12	-12	-1	0.0
1909	*Pit-N	8	3	.727	22	13	7	1	0	131^{2}	121	2	14	38	9.5	2.32	117	.253	.280	3	.071	-3	4	6	-2	-0.1
1910	Pit-N	14	2	.875	31	8	5	1	4	121^{2}	111	4	9	30	9.1	2.29	135	.239	.258	9	.220	1	10	11	-3	1.2
1911	Pit-N	0	0	—	3	0	0	0	0	6	5	0	2	3	10.5	7.50	46	.238	.304	1	1.000	1	-3	-3	0	0.1
Total	13	189	109	.634	372	289	242	27	12	2607	2518	41	363	929	10.1	2.59	120	.253	.283	185	.189	2	153	150	-14	15.7

● BUZ PHILLIPS Phillips, Albert Abernathy b: 5/25/04, Newton, N.C. d: 11/6/64, Baltimore, Md. BR/TR, 5'11.5", 185 lbs. Deb: 8/5/30

YEAR	TM/L	W	L	PCT	G	GS	CG	SH	SV	IP	H	HR	BB	SO	RAT	ERA	ERA+	OAV	OOB	BH	AVG	PB	PR	/A	PD	TPI
1930	Phi-N	0	0	—	14	1	0	0	0	43^{2}	68	6	18	9	17.9	8.04	68	.354	.412	6	.462	2	-15	-12	-1	0.1

● RED PHILLIPS Phillips, Clarence Lemuel b: 11/3/08, Pauls Valley, Okla. d: 2/1/88, Wichita, Kan. BR/TR, 6'3.5", 195 lbs. Deb: 7/24/34

YEAR	TM/L	W	L	PCT	G	GS	CG	SH	SV	IP	H	HR	BB	SO	RAT	ERA	ERA+	OAV	OOB	BH	AVG	PB	PR	/A	PD	TPI
1934	Det-A	2	0	1.000	7	1	1	0	1	23^{1}	31	1	16	3	18.1	6.17	71	.316	.412	3	.250	1	-4	-5	-1	-0.3
1936	Det-A	2	4	.333	22	6	3	0	0	87^{1}	124	12	22	15	15.0	6.49	76	.332	.370	10	.303	2	-14	-15	-0	-0.7
Total	2	4	4	.500	29	7	4	0	1	110^{2}	155	13	38	18	15.7	6.42	75	.329	.379	13	.289	3	-18	-20	-1	-1.0

● JACK PHILLIPS Phillips, Jack Dorn "Stretch" b: 9/6/21, Clarence, N.Y. BR/TR, 6'4", 193 lbs. Deb: 8/22/47 ♦

YEAR	TM/L	W	L	PCT	G	GS	CG	SH	SV	IP	H	HR	BB	SO	RAT	ERA	ERA+	OAV	OOB	BH	AVG	PB	PR	/A	PD	TPI
1950	Pit-N	0	0	—	1	0	0	0	0	5	7	0	1	2	14.4	7.20	61	.333	.364	61	.293	0	-2	-2	0	0.0

● JACK PHILLIPS Phillips, John Stephen b: 5/24/19, St.Louis, Mo. d: 6/16/58, St.Louis, Mo. BR/TR, 6'1", 185 lbs. Deb: 7/13/45 ♦

YEAR	TM/L	W	L	PCT	G	GS	CG	SH	SV	IP	H	HR	BB	SO	RAT	ERA	ERA+	OAV	OOB	BH	AVG	PB	PR	/A	PD	TPI
1945	NY-N	0	0	—	1	0	0	0	0	4^{1}	5	1	5	0	22.8	10.38	38	.313	.500	1	.500	0	-3	-3	-0	0.0

● ED PHILLIPS Phillips, Norman Edwin b: 9/20/44, Ardmore, Okla. BR/TR, 6'1", 190 lbs. Deb: 4/9/70

YEAR	TM/L	W	L	PCT	G	GS	CG	SH	SV	IP	H	HR	BB	SO	RAT	ERA	ERA+	OAV	OOB	BH	AVG	PB	PR	/A	PD	TPI
1970	Bos-A	0	2	.000	18	0	0	0	0	23^{2}	29	4	10	23	15.6	5.32	74	.312	.390	0	.000	-0	-4	-4	-1	-0.4

● TOM PHILLIPS Phillips, Thomas Gerald b: 4/5/1889, Philipsburg, Pa. d: 4/12/29, Philipsburg, Pa. BR/TR, 6'2", 190 lbs. Deb: 9/13/15

YEAR	TM/L	W	L	PCT	G	GS	CG	SH	SV	IP	H	HR	BB	SO	RAT	ERA	ERA+	OAV	OOB	BH	AVG	PB	PR	/A	PD	TPI
1915	StL-A	1	3	.250	5	4	1	0	0	27^{1}	28	0	12	5	13.8	2.96	97	.283	.372	1	.111	-1	-0	-0	-1	-0.2
1919	Cle-A	3	2	.600	22	3	1	0	0	55	55	2	34	18	15.1	2.95	114	.272	.385	4	.364	1	**2**	**2**	-1	0.2
1921	Was-A	1	0	1.000	1	1	1	0	0	9	9	0	3	2	12.0	2.00	206	.290	.353	0	.000	-1	2	2	-0	0.1
1922	Was-A	3	7	.300	17	7	2	1	0	70	72	2	22	19	12.6	4.89	79	.273	.338	3	.150	-1	-7	-8	-1	-1.1
Total	4	8	12	.400	45	15	5	1	0	161^{1}	164	4	71	44	13.6	3.74	95	.275	.361	8	.186	-1	-3	-3	-3	-1.0

● BILL PHILLIPS Phillips, William Corcoran "Whoa Bill" or "Silver Bill"
b: 11/9/1868, Allenport, Pa. d: 10/25/41, Charleroi, Pa. BR/TR, 5'11", 180 lbs. Deb: 8/11/1890 M

YEAR	TM/L	W	L	PCT	G	GS	CG	SH	SV	IP	H	HR	BB	SO	RAT	ERA	ERA+	OAV	OOB	BH	AVG	PB	PR	/A	PD	TPI
1890	Pit-N	1	9	.100	10	10	9	0	0	82	123	8	29	25	16.8	7.57	44	.336	.386	11	.239	1	-36	-39	0	-3.2
1895	Cin-N	6	7	.462	18	9	6	0	2	109	126	6	44	15	14.6	6.03	83	.285	.359	15	.313	2	-15	-13	1	-1.0
1899	Cin-N	17	9	.654	33	27	18	1	1	227^{2}	234	3	71	43	12.6	3.32	118	.265	.330	12	.130	-5	14	15	-0	0.9
1900	Cin-N	9	11	.450	29	24	17	3	0	208^{1}	229	5	67	51	13.3	4.28	86	.279	.343	13	.165	-4	-13	-14	6	-0.9
1901	Cin-N	14	18	.438	37	36	29	1	0	281^{1}	364	7	67	109	14.2	4.64	69	.311	.354	22	.202	2	-41	-45	5	-3.6
1902	Cin-N	16	16	.500	33	33	30	0	0	269	267	3	55	85	11.1	2.51	119	.259	.302	39	.342	10	8	15	3	3.1
1903	Cin-N	7	6	.538	16	13	11	1	0	118^{1}	134	0	30	46	13.0	3.35	106	.279	.330	10	.175	-1	-1	3	2	0.3
Total	7	70	76	.479	176	152	120	6	3	1295^{2}	1477	32	363	374	13.2	4.09	87	.284	.338	122	.224	4	-85	-77	16	-4.4

● TAYLOR PHILLIPS Phillips, William Taylor "Tay" b: 6/18/33, Atlanta, Ga. BL/TL, 5'11", 185 lbs. Deb: 6/8/56

YEAR	TM/L	W	L	PCT	G	GS	CG	SH	SV	IP	H	HR	BB	SO	RAT	ERA	ERA+	OAV	OOB	BH	AVG	PB	PR	/A	PD	TPI
1956	Mil-N	5	3	.625	23	6	3	0	2	87^{2}	69	6	33	36	11.2	2.26	153	.223	.311	0	.000	-2	15	12	2	1.1
1957	Mil-N	3	2	.600	27	6	0	0	2	73	82	3	40	36	15.2	5.55	63	.300	.392	2	.100	-1	-14	-17	0	-1.2
1958	Chi-N	7	10	.412	39	27	5	1	1	170^{1}	178	22	79	102	13.9	4.76	82	.266	.349	3	.056	-4	-15	-16	1	-1.7
1959	Chi-N	0	2	.000	7	2	0	0	0	16^{2}	22	3	11	5	18.9	7.56	52	.319	.427	0	.000	-0	-7	-7	0	-0.7
	Phi-N	1	4	.200	32	3	1	0	1	63	72	4	31	35	15.3	5.00	82	.303	.392	1	.091	-1	-7	-6	0	-0.5
	Yr	1	6	.143	39	5	1	0	1	79^{2}	94	7	42	40	15.8	5.54	74	.303	.393	1	.067	-1	-14	-13	1	-1.2
1960	Phi-N	0	1	.000	10	1	0	0	0	14	21	2	4	6	16.7	8.36	46	.356	.406	0	.000	-0	-7	-7	-0	-0.5
1963	Chi-A	0	0	—	9	0	0	0	0	14	16	2	13	13	19.3	10.29	34	.302	.448	0	.000	-0	-10	-11	0	0.0
Total	6	16	22	.421	147	45	9	1	6	438^{2}	460	42	211	233	14.2	4.82	78	.275	.364	6	.053	-9	-46	-51	4	-3.5

● TOM PHOEBUS Phoebus, Thomas Harold b: 4/7/42, Baltimore, Md. BR/TR, 5'8", 185 lbs. Deb: 9/15/66

YEAR	TM/L	W	L	PCT	G	GS	CG	SH	SV	IP	H	HR	BB	SO	RAT	ERA	ERA+	OAV	OOB	BH	AVG	PB	PR	/A	PD	TPI
1966	Bal-A	2	1	.667	3	3	2	2	0	22	16	0	6	17	9.0	1.23	271	.213	.272	1	.167	0	5	5	-0	0.8
1967	Bal-A	14	9	.609	33	33	7	4	0	208	177	16	114	179	12.6	3.33	95	.227	.326	11	.145	1	-2	-4	-2	-0.6
1968	Bal-A	15	15	.500	36	36	9	3	0	240^{2}	186	10	105	193	11.0	2.62	112	.212	.299	15	.183	3	10	8	-0	1.4
1969	Bal-A	14	7	.667	35	33	6	2	0	202	180	23	87	117	12.1	3.52	101	.241	.324	15	.200	2	2	1	-1	0.1
1970	*Bal-A	5	5	.500	27	21	3	0	0	135	106	11	62	72	11.6	3.07	119	.219	.315	7	.163	-0	10	9	0	0.6
1971	SD-N	3	11	.214	29	21	2	0	0	133^{1}	144	14	64	80	14.2	4.45	74	.280	.363	6	.167	1	-15	-17	-1	-1.6
1972	SD-N	0	1	.000	1	1	0	0	0	5^{2}	3	2	6	8	14.3	7.94	41	.150	.346	0	.000	-0	-3	-3	0	-0.4
	Chi-N	3	3	.500	37	1	0	0	6	83^{1}	76	9	45	59	13.3	3.78	101	.247	.346	2	.133	-1	-3	0	1	0.0
	Yr	3	4	.429	38	2	0	0	6	89	79	11	51	67	13.3	4.04	93	.241	.346	2	.118	-1	-6	-3	1	-0.4
Total	7	56	52	.519	201	149	29	11	6	1030	888	85	489	725	12.2	3.33	100	.233	.324	57	.170	6	4	-1	-3	0.3

● STEVE PHOENIX Phoenix, Steven Robert b: 1/31/68, Phoenix, Ariz. BR/TR, 6'2", 175 lbs. Deb: 7/30/94

YEAR	TM/L	W	L	PCT	G	GS	CG	SH	SV	IP	H	HR	BB	SO	RAT	ERA	ERA+	OAV	OOB	BH	AVG	PB	PR	/A	PD	TPI
1994	Oak-A	0	0	—	2	0	0	0	0	4^{1}	4	0	2	3	12.5	6.23	71	.235	.316	0	—	0	-1	-1	-0	0.7
1995	Oak-A	0	0	—	1	0	0	0	0	1^{2}	3	1	3	3	32.4	32.40	14	.429	.600	0	—	0	-5	-5	0	0.6
Total	2	0	0	—	3	0	0	0	0	6	7	1	5	6	18.0	13.50	33	.292	.414	0	—	0	-6	-6	-0	1.3

● BILL PHYLE Phyle, William Joseph b: 6/25/1875, Duluth, Minn. d: 8/6/53, Los Angeles, Cal. TR , Deb: 9/17/1898 ♦

YEAR	TM/L	W	L	PCT	G	GS	CG	SH	SV	IP	H	HR	BB	SO	RAT	ERA	ERA+	OAV	OOB	BH	AVG	PB	PR	/A	PD	TPI
1898	Chi-N	2	1	.667	3	3	3	2	0	23	24	0	6	4	12.5	0.78	458	.267	.327	1	.111	-0	7	7	-1	0.8
1899	Chi-N	1	8	.111	10	9	9	0	1	83^{2}	92	2	29	10	13.4	4.20	89	.279	.344	6	.176	-2	-3	-4	1	-0.5
1901	NY-N	7	10	.412	24	19	16	0	1	168^{2}	208	2	54	62	14.3	4.27	77	.301	.356	12	.182	-1	-18	-18	1	-1.5
Total	3	10	19	.345	37	31	28	2	2	275^{1}	324	4	89	76	13.9	3.96	88	.291	.350	32	.176	-4	-14	-15	2	-1.2

● DOUG PIATT Piatt, Douglas William b: 9/26/65, Beaver, Pa. BL/TR, 6'1", 185 lbs. Deb: 6/11/91

YEAR	TM/L	W	L	PCT	G	GS	CG	SH	SV	IP	H	HR	BB	SO	RAT	ERA	ERA+	OAV	OOB	BH	AVG	PB	PR	/A	PD	TPI
1991	Mon-N	0	0	—	21	0	0	0	0	34^{2}	29	3	17	29	11.9	2.60	139	.230	.322	0	.000	-0	4	4	0	0.0

● WILEY PIATT Piatt, Wiley Harold "Iron Man" b: 7/13/1874, Blue Creek, Ohio d: 9/20/46, Cincinnati, Ohio BL/TL, 5'10", 175 lbs. Deb: 4/22/1898

YEAR	TM/L	W	L	PCT	G	GS	CG	SH	SV	IP	H	HR	BB	SO	RAT	ERA	ERA+	OAV	OOB	BH	AVG	PB	PR	/A	PD	TPI
1898	Phi-N	24	14	.632	39	37	33	**6**	0	306	285	2	97	121	11.8	3.18	108	.245	.314	32	.262	4	15	9	-2	1.1
1899	Phi-N	23	15	.605	39	38	31	2	0	305	323	6	86	89	12.7	3.45	107	.271	.332	33	.270	4	14	8	-5	0.8
1900	Phi-N	9	10	.474	22	20	16	1	0	160^{2}	194	5	71	47	15.7	4.71	77	.298	.380	17	.250	2	-18	-19	-3	-1.9
1901	Phi-A	5	12	.294	18	16	15	0	1	140	176	4	60	45	15.4	4.63	82	.303	.372	13	.224	0	-15	-13	-4	-1.6
	Chi-A	4	2	.667	7	6	4	1	0	51^{2}	42	2	14	19	10.5	2.79	125	.220	.287	2	.118	-1	5	4	-1	0.2
	Yr	9	14	.391	25	22	19	1	1	191^{2}	218	6	74	64	13.9	4.13	89	.282	.347	15	.200	-1	-10	-9	-5	-1.4
1902	Chi-A	12	12	.500	32	30	22	2	0	246	263	3	66	96	12.4	3.51	96	.274	.327	17	.200	2	2	-3	-3	-0.4
1903	Bos-N	9	14	.391	25	23	18	0	0	181	198	5	61	100	13.1	3.18	101	.280	.340	16	.225	2	2	1	-3	0.0
Total	6	86	79	.521	182	170	139	12	1	1390^{1}	1481	27	455	517	13.0	3.61	97	.272	.337	130	.239	13	4	-15	-20	-1.8

● HIPOLITO PICHARDO Pichardo, Hipolito Antonio (Balbina) b: 8/22/69, Jicome Esperanza, D.R. BR/TR, 6'1", 185 lbs. Deb: 4/21/92

YEAR	TM/L	W	L	PCT	G	GS	CG	SH	SV	IP	H	HR	BB	SO	RAT	ERA	ERA+	OAV	OOB	BH	AVG	PB	PR	/A	PD	TPI
1992	KC-A	9	6	.600	31	24	1	1	0	143^{2}	148	9	49	59	12.5	3.95	103	.267	.330	0	—	0	-0	2	0	0.0
1993	KC-A	7	8	.467	30	25	2	0	0	165	183	10	53	70	13.2	4.04	113	.282	.341	0	—	0	5	10	2	0.5
1994	KC-A	5	3	.625	45	0	0	0	3	67^{2}	82	4	24	36	15.0	4.92	102	.308	.380	0	—	0	-1	1	0	-0.1
1995	KC-A	8	4	.667	44	0	0	0	1	64	66	4	30	43	14.1	4.36	110	.265	.353	0	.000	-0	3	3	1	0.5
1996	KC-A	3	5	.375	57	0	0	0	3	68	74	5	26	43	13.5	5.43	92	.284	.353	0	—	0	-3	-3	1	-0.2
1997	KC-A	3	5	.375	47	0	0	0	11	49	51	7	24	34	14.0	4.22	111	.271	.357	0	—	0	2	3	2	0.5
1998	KC-A	7	8	.467	27	18	0	0	1	112^{1}	126	11	43	55	13.9	5.13	96	.280	.348	0	.000	-0	-6	-3	1	-0.2
Total	7	42	39	.519	281	67	3	1	19	669^{2}	730	50	249	340	13.5	4.48	104	.279	.348	0	.000	-0	-1	12	7	1.0

● RON PICHE Piche, Ronald Jacques b: 5/22/35, Verdun, Que., Canada BR/TR, 5'11", 165 lbs. Deb: 5/30/60 C

YEAR	TM/L	W	L	PCT	G	GS	CG	SH	SV	IP	H	HR	BB	SO	RAT	ERA	ERA+	OAV	OOB	BH	AVG	PB	PR	/A	PD	TPI
1960	Mil-N	3	5	.375	37	0	0	0	9	48	48	3	23	38	13.9	3.56	96	.258	.349	0	.000	-0	1	-1	-1	-0.2
1961	Mil-N	2	2	.500	12	1	1	0	1	23^{1}	20	1	16	16	13.9	3.47	108	.238	.360	0	.000	-1	1	1	0	0.1
1962	Mil-N	3	2	.600	14	8	2	0	0	52	54	6	29	28	14.9	4.85	78	.273	.374	1	.056	-1	-5	-6	1	-0.6
1963	Mil-N	1	1	.500	37	1	0	0	0	53	53	4	25	40	13.2	3.40	95	.256	.336	0	.000	-1	-1	-1	1	0.0
1965	Cal-A	0	3	.000	14	1	0	0	0	19^{2}	20	5	12	14	14.6	6.86	50	.267	.368	0	.000	-0	-7	-8	0	-1.1
1966	StL-N	1	3	.250	20	0	0	0	2	25^{1}	21	4	18	21	14.2	4.26	84	.214	.342	0	.000	-0	-2	-2	-0	-0.4
Total	6	10	16	.385	134	11	3	0	12	221^{1}	216	23	123	157	14.1	4.19	84	.255	.354	1	.024	-3	-13	-16	1	-2.2

● RICKY PICKETT Pickett, Cecil Lee b: 1/19/70, Fort Worth, Tex. BL/TL, 6'1", 220 lbs. Deb: 4/28/98

YEAR	TM/L	W	L	PCT	G	GS	CG	SH	SV	IP	H	HR	BB	SO	RAT	ERA	ERA+	OAV	OOB	BH	AVG	PB	PR	/A	PD	TPI
1998	Ari-N	0	0	—	2	0	0	0	0	0^{2}	3	0	4	2	94.5	81.00	5	.600	.778	0	—	0	-6	-6	0	0.0

● CHARLIE PICKETT Pickett, Charles Albert b: 3/1/1883, Delaware, Ohio d: 5/20/69, Springfield, Ohio BR/TR, 6'1", 175 lbs. Deb: 6/21/10

YEAR	TM/L	W	L	PCT	G	GS	CG	SH	SV	IP	H	HR	BB	SO	RAT	ERA	ERA+	OAV	OOB	BH	AVG	PB	PR	/A	PD	TPI
1910	StL-N	0	0	—	2	0	0	0	0	6	7	0	2	2	13.5	1.50	199	.280	.333	0	—	0	1	1	-0	0.0

● CLARENCE PICKREL Pickrel, Clarence Douglas b: 3/28/11, Gretna, Va. d: 11/4/83, Rocky Mount, Va. BR/TR, 6'1", 180 lbs. Deb: 4/22/33

YEAR	TM/L	W	L	PCT	G	GS	CG	SH	SV	IP	H	HR	BB	SO	RAT	ERA	ERA+	OAV	OOB	BH	AVG	PB	PR	/A	PD	TPI
1933	Phi-N	1	0	1.000	9	0	0	0	0	13^{2}	20	0	3	6	15.8	3.95	97	.357	.400	0	.000	-0	-1	-0	-1	-0.1
1934	Bos-N	0	0	—	10	1	0	0	0	16	24	0	7	9	17.4	5.06	76	.333	.392	0	.000	-0	-2	-2	-1	-0.1
Total	2	1	0	1.000	19	1	0	0	0	29^{2}	44	0	10	15	16.7	4.55	85	.344	.396	0	.000	-0	-3	-2	-1	-0.2

● JEFF PICO Pico, Jeffrey Mark b: 2/12/66, Antioch, Cal. BR/TR, 6'1", 190 lbs. Deb: 5/31/88

YEAR	TM/L	W	L	PCT	G	GS	CG	SH	SV	IP	H	HR	BB	SO	RAT	ERA	ERA+	OAV	OOB	BH	AVG	PB	PR	/A	PD	TPI
1988	Chi-N	6	7	.462	29	13	3	2	1	112^{2}	108	6	37	57	11.6	4.15	87	.252	.312	5	.147	-0	-9	-7	-0	-0.8
1989	Chi-N	3	1	.750	53	5	0	0	2	90^{2}	99	8	31	38	12.9	3.77	100	.278	.336	1	.100	-1	-3	-0	1	0.1
1990	Chi-N	4	4	.500	31	8	0	0	2	92	120	7	37	37	15.5	4.79	85	.321	.383	6	.273	2	-10	-7	1	-0.3
Total	3	13	12	.520	113	26	3	2	5	295^{1}	327	21	105	132	13.2	4.24	90	.282	.343	12	.182	1	-22	-14	2	-1.0

● MARIO PICONE Picone, Mario Peter "Babe" b: 7/5/26, Brooklyn, N.Y. BR/TR, 5'11", 180 lbs. Deb: 9/27/47

YEAR	TM/L	W	L	PCT	G	GS	CG	SH	SV	IP	H	HR	BB	SO	RAT	ERA	ERA+	OAV	OOB	BH	AVG	PB	PR	/A	PD	TPI
1947	NY-N	0	0	—	2	1	0	0	0	7	10	1	2	1	15.4	7.71	53	.345	.387	1	.500	1	-3	-3	0	0.1
1952	NY-N	0	1	.000	2	1	0	0	0	9	11	2	5	3	16.0	7.00	53	.306	.390	0	.000	-0	-3	-3	0	-0.3
1954	NY-N	0	0	—	5	0	0	0	0	13^{2}	13	1	11	6	15.8	5.27	77	.283	.421	0	.000	0	-2	-2	-0	0.0
	Cin-N	0	1	.000	4	1	0	0	0	10^{1}	9	3	7	1	13.9	6.10	69	.243	.364	0	.000	0	-2	-2	0	-0.1
	Yr	0	1	.000	9	1	0	0	0	24	22	4	18	7	15.0	5.63	73	.265	.396	0	.000	0	-4	-4	0	-0.1
Total	3	0	2	.000	13	3	0	0	0	40	43	7	25	11	15.3	6.30	64	.291	.393	1	.167	1	-10	-10	1	-0.3

YEAR	TM/L	W	L	PCT	G	GS	CG	SH	SV	IP	H	HR	BB	SO	RAT	ERA	ERA+	OAV	OOB	BH	AVG	PB	PR	/A	PD	TPI
● AL PIECHOTA	Piechota, Aloysius Edward "Pie" b: 1/19/14, Chicago, Ill. d: 6/13/96, Chicago, Ill. BR/TR, 6', 195 lbs. Deb: 5/7/40																									
1940	Bos-N	2	5	.286	21	8	2	0	0	61	68	6	41	18	16.1	5.75	65	.278	.381	4	.200	1	-13	-14	-0	-1.3
1941	Bos-N	0	0	—	1	0	0	0	0	1	0	0	1	0	9.0	0.00	—	.000	.250	0	—	0	0	0	-0	0.0
Total	2	2	5	.286	22	8	2	0	0	62	68	6	42	18	16.0	5.66	66	.274	.379	4	.200	1	-13	-13	-0	-1.3
● CY PIEH	Pieh, Edwin John b: 9/29/1886, Waunakee, Wis. d: 9/12/45, Jacksonville, Fla BR/TR, 6'2", 190 lbs. Deb: 9/6/13																									
1913	NY-A	1	0	1.000	4	0	0	0	0	10^1	10	0	7	6	14.8	4.35	69	.250	.362	1	.250	0	-2	-2	1	0.0
1914	NY-A	3	4	.429	18	4	1	0	0	62^1	68	6	29	24	14.0	5.05	55	.289	.367	2	.118	-0	-16	-16	-1	-1.8
1915	NY-A	4	5	.444	21	8	3	2	0	94	78	2	39	46	11.7	2.87	102	.234	.324	2	.067	-3	1	1	0	-0.3
Total	3	8	9	.471	43	12	4	2	0	166^2	156	8	75	76	12.7	3.78	76	.257	.343	5	.098	-3	-17	-17	-0	-2.1
● ED PIERCE	Pierce, Edward John b: 10/6/68, Arcadia, Cal. BL/TL, 6'1", 185 lbs. Deb: 9/6/92																									
1992	KC-A	0	0	—	2	1	0	0	0	5^1	9	1	4	3	21.9	3.38	120	.429	.520	0	—	0	0	0	0	-0.2
● JEFF PIERCE	Pierce, Jeffrey Charles b: 6/7/69, Poughkeepsie, N.Y. BR/TR, 6'1", 190 lbs. Deb: 4/26/95																									
1995	Bos-A	0	3	.000	12	0	0	0	0	15	16	0	14	12	18.0	6.60	74	.286	.429	0	—	0	-3	-3	-0	-0.5
● RAY PIERCE	Pierce, Raymond Lester "Lefty" b: 6/6/1897, Emporia, Kan. d: 5/4/63, Denver, Colo. BL/TL, 5'7", 156 lbs. Deb: 5/12/24																									
1924	Chi-N	0	0	—	6	0	0	0	0	7^1	7	2	4	2	13.5	7.36	53	.269	.367	0	—	0	-3	-3	-0	0.0
1925	Phi-N	5	4	.556	23	8	4	0	0	90	134	7	24	18	15.9	5.50	87	.356	.397	5	.179	-0	-12	-7	0	-0.6
1926	Phi-N	2	7	.222	37	7	1	0	0	84^2	128	3	35	18	17.4	5.63	74	.348	.406	3	.125	-2	-17	-14	-1	-1.5
Total	3	7	11	.389	66	15	5	0	0	182	269	12	63	38	16.5	5.64	79	.349	.400	8	.154	-2	-32	-24	-1	-2.1
● TONY PIERCE	Pierce, Tony Michael b: 1/29/46, Brunswick, Ga. BR/TL, 6'1", 190 lbs. Deb: 4/14/67																									
1967	KC-A	3	4	.429	49	6	0	0	7	97^2	79	6	30	61	10.5	3.04	105	.221	.290	0	.000	-2	2	2	-1	-0.2
1968	Oak-A	1	2	.333	17	3	0	0	1	32^2	39	3	10	16	13.8	3.86	73	.295	.350	0	.000	-1	-3	-4	1	-0.4
Total	2	4	6	.400	66	9	0	0	8	130^1	118	9	40	77	11.3	3.25	95	.241	.306	0	.000	-3	-1	-2	-1	-0.6
● BILLY PIERCE	Pierce, Walter William b: 4/2/27, Detroit, Mich. BL/TL, 5'10", 160 lbs. Deb: 6/1/45																									
1945	Det-A	0	0	—	5	0	0	0	0	10	6	1	10	10	15.3	1.80	195	.182	.386	0	.000	-0	2	2	0	0.0
1948	Det-A	3	0	1.000	22	5	0	0	0	55^1	47	5	51	36	16.1	6.34	69	.234	.391	5	.294	2	-13	-12	0	-0.4
1949	Chi-A	7	15	.318	32	26	8	0	0	171^2	145	11	112	95	13.5	3.88	108	.228	.344	9	.176	-1	6	6	1	0.7
1950	Chi-A	12	16	.429	33	29	15	1	1	219^1	189	11	137	118	13.5	3.98	113	.228	.339	20	.260	4	15	12	-2	1.6
1951	Chi-A	15	14	.517	37	28	18	1	2	240^1	237	14	73	113	11.6	3.03	133	.258	.313	16	.203	-0	29	27	-1	2.9
1952	Chi-A	15	12	.556	33	32	14	4	1	255^1	214	12	79	144	10.4	2.57	142	.227	.289	17	.187	0	31	31	0	3.2
1953	Chi-A★	18	12	.600	40	33	19	7	3	271^1	216	20	102	**186**	10.6	2.72	148	**.218**	.292	11	.126	-4	**38**	**39**	-2	3.5
1954	Chi-A	9	10	.474	36	26	12	4	3	188^2	179	15	86	148	12.8	3.48	107	.249	.332	11	.193	0	5	5	-2	0.3
1955	Chi-A★	15	10	.600	33	26	16	6	1	205^2	162	16	64	157	**10.0**	**1.97**	**200**	.213	**.277**	12	.171	-1	**45**	**45**	-1	**5.3**
1956	Chi-A★	20	9	.690	35	33	**21**	1	1	276^1	261	24	100	192	11.9	3.32	123	.249	.316	16	.157	-4	26	24	-3	1.5
1957	Chi-A★	**20**	12	.625	37	34	**16**	4	2	257	228	18	71	171	10.5	3.26	115	.234	.287	17	.172	-2	15	14	0	1.4
1958	Chi-A☆	17	11	.607	35	32	**19**	3	2	245	204	33	66	144	10.0	2.68	136	.227	.280	17	.205	2	30	26	-3	2.8
1959	*Chi-A☆	14	15	.483	34	33	12	2	0	224	217	26	62	114	11.3	3.62	104	.253	.306	13	.191	3	6	4	0	0.7
1960	Chi-A	14	7	.667	32	30	8	1	0	196^1	201	24	46	108	11.3	3.62	104	.266	.308	12	.179	1	5	3	-1	0.3
1961	Chi-A☆	10	9	.526	39	28	5	1	3	180	190	17	54	106	12.3	3.80	103	.275	.328	8	.143	-2	4	2	-0	0.0
1962	*SF-N	16	6	.727	30	23	7	2	1	162^1	147	19	35	76	10.3	3.49	109	.239	.284	12	.214	2	8	5	-1	0.7
1963	SF-N	3	11	.214	38	13	3	1	8	99	106	12	20	52	11.5	4.27	75	.272	.309	4	.129	-0	-11	-12	0	-1.8
1964	SF-N	3	0	1.000	34	1	0	0	4	49	40	6	10	29	9.2	2.20	162	.222	.263	3	.333	1	7	7	-1	0.6
Total	18	211	169	.555	585	432	193	38	32	3306^2	2989	284	1178	1999	11.4	3.27	119	.240	.307	203	.184	0	250	229	-15	23.3
● BILL PIERCY	Piercy, William Benton "Wild Bill" b: 5/2/1896, ElMonte, Cal. d: 8/28/51, Long Beach, Cal. BR/TR, 6'1", 185 lbs. Deb: 10/3/17																									
1917	NY-A	0	1	.000	1	1	1	0	0	9	9	0	2	4	11.0	3.00	90	.257	.297	0	.000	0	-0	-0	-0	0.0
1921	*NY-A	5	4	.556	14	10	5	1	0	81^2	82	4	28	35	12.9	2.98	142	.263	.337	6	.214	0	12	11	-0	1.1
1922	Bos-A	3	9	.250	29	12	7	1	0	121^1	140	2	62	24	15.4	4.67	88	.304	.394	5	.147	-1	-8	-8	2	-0.6
1923	Bos-A	8	17	.320	30	24	11	0	0	187^1	193	5	73	51	13.5	3.41	121	.277	.357	7	.132	-3	12	15	3	1.8
1924	Bos-A	5	7	.417	23	18	3	0	0	121	156	4	66	20	17.3	5.95	73	.335	.429	6	.154	-2	-23	-21	1	-1.8
1926	Chi-N	6	5	.545	19	5	1	0	0	90^1	96	1	37	31	13.8	4.48	86	.280	.360	9	.257	1	-7	-6	0	-0.6
Total	6	27	43	.386	116	70	28	2	0	610^2	676	16	268	165	14.5	4.26	97	.292	.376	33	.173	-5	-15	-10	7	-0.1
● MARINO PIERETTI	Pieretti, Marino Paul "Chick" b: 9/23/20, Lucca, Italy d: 1/30/81, San Francisco, Cal. BR/TR, 5'7", 158 lbs. Deb: 4/19/45																									
1945	Was-A	14	13	.519	44	27	14	3	2	233^1	235	3	91	66	12.6	3.32	94	.257	.325	18	.222	2	1	-6	1	-0.3
1946	Was-A	2	2	.500	30	2	1	0	0	62	70	9	40	20	16.3	5.95	56	.292	.397	3	.214	0	-17	-18	1	-1.0
1947	Was-A	2	4	.333	23	10	2	1	0	83^1	97	3	47	32	15.8	4.21	88	.287	.377	6	.231	-0	-5	-5	-0	-0.3
1948	Was-A	0	2	.000	8	1	0	0	0	11^2	18	1	7	6	19.3	10.80	40	.375	.455	0	.000	-0	-8	-8	-0	-1.2
	Chi-A	8	10	.444	21	18	4	0	1	120	117	6	52	28	12.7	4.95	86	.262	.339	7	.179	-1	-9	-9	1	-1.2
	Yr	8	12	.400	29	19	4	0	1	131^2	135	7	59	34	13.3	5.47	78	.273	.351	7	.171	-1	-17	-18	1	-2.4
1949	Chi-A	4	6	.400	39	9	0	0	4	116	131	10	54	25	14.4	5.51	76	.289	.364	9	.237	1	-17	-17	2	-1.2
1950	Cle-A	0	1	.000	29	1	0	0	1	47^1	45	2	30	11	14.3	4.18	104	.253	.361	2	.286	0	2	1	1	0.1
Total	6	30	38	.441	194	68	21	4	8	673^2	713	34	321	188	13.9	4.53	81	.272	.353	45	.217	2	-52	-63	5	-5.1
● AL PIEROTTI	Pierotti, Albert Felix b: 10/24/1895, Boston, Mass. d: 2/12/64, Everett, Mass. BR/TR, 5'10.5", 195 lbs. Deb: 8/9/20																									
1920	Bos-N	1	1	.500	6	2	2	0	0	25	23	2	9	12	11.5	2.88	106	.250	.317	2	.250	0	1	0	-0	0.0
1921	Bos-N	0	1	.000	2	0	0	0	0	1^2	3	0	3	1	32.4	21.60	17	.375	.545	0	.000	-0	-3	-3	0	-1.3
Total	2	1	2	.333	8	2	2	0	0	26^2	26	2	12	13	12.8	4.05	76	.260	.339	2	.222	-0	-3	-3	-0	-1.3
● BILL PIERRO	Pierro, William Leonard "Wild Bill" b: 4/15/26, Brooklyn, N.Y. BR/TR, 6'1", 155 lbs. Deb: 7/17/50																									
1950	Pit-N	0	2	.000	12	3	0	0	0	29	33	2	28	13	19.6	10.55	42	.289	.438	2	.222	-0	-21	-20	-1	-1.2
● DAVE PIERSON	Pierson, David P. b: 8/20/1855, Newark, N.J. d: 11/11/22, Trenton, N.J. BR/TR, 5'7", 142 lbs. Deb: 4/25/1876 F♦																									
1876	Cin-N	0	1	.000	1	1	0	0	0	0	2	1	0	0	—	∞	—	1.000	1.000	55	.236	-0	-2	-2	0	-0.2
● WILLIAM PIERSON	Pierson, William Morris b: 6/14/1899, Atlantic City, N.J. d: 2/20/59, Atlantic City, N.J BL/TL, 6'2", 180 lbs. Deb: 7/4/18																									
1918	Phi-A	0	1	.000	8	1	0	0	0	21^2	20	0	20	6	17.4	3.32	88	.286	.457	1	.250	-0	-1	-1	-1	-0.2
1919	Phi-A	0	0	—	2	1	0	0	0	7^2	9	0	8	4	20.0	3.52	97	.333	.486	1	.333	0	-0	-0	0	0.1
1924	Phi-A	0	0	—	1	0	0	0	0	2^2	3	0	3	0	20.3	3.38	127	.300	.462	0	—	0	0	0	0	0.0
Total	3	0	1	.000	11	2	0	0	0	32	32	0	31	10	18.3	3.38	94	.299	.464	2	.286	0	-1	-1	-1	-0.1
● GEORGE PIKTUZIS	Piktuzis, George Richard b: 1/3/32, Chicago, Ill. d: 11/28/93, Long Beach, Cal. BR/TL, 6'2", 200 lbs. Deb: 4/25/56																									
1956	Chi-N	0	0	—	2	0	0	0	0	5	6	1	2	3	14.4	7.20	52	.333	.400	0	—	0	-2	-2	-0	0.0
● DUANE PILLETTE	Pillette, Duane Xavier "Dee" b: 7/24/22, Detroit, Mich. BR/TR, 6'3", 205 lbs. Deb: 7/19/49 F																									
1949	NY-A	2	4	.333	12	3	2	0	0	37^1	43	6	19	9	14.9	4.34	93	.299	.380	0	.000	-1	-1	-1	1	-0.2
1950	NY-A	0	0	—	4	0	0	0	0	7	9	0	3	4	15.4	1.29	334	.321	.387	0	—	0	3	2	-0	0.0
	StL-A	3	5	.375	24	7	1	0	2	73^2	104	6	44	18	18.3	7.09	70	.337	.423	3	.136	-1	-21	-17	-0	-1.7
	Yr	3	5	.375	28	7	1	0	2	80^2	113	6	47	22	18.1	6.58	74	.335	.420	3	.136	-1	-18	-15	-1	-1.7
1951	StL-A	6	14	.300	35	24	6	1	0	191	205	14	115	65	15.3	4.99	88	.276	.376	8	.136	-3	-19	-13	-1	-1.6
1952	StL-A	10	13	.435	30	30	9	1	0	205^1	222	14	55	62	12.4	3.59	109	.274	.325	12	.182	0	2	7	-2	0.6
1953	StL-A	7	13	.350	31	25	5	1	0	166^2	181	16	62	58	13.2	4.48	94	.277	.341	7	.132	-1	-9	-5	-1	-0.7
1954	Bal-A	10	14	.417	25	25	11	1	0	179	158	9	67	66	11.4	3.12	115	.234	.305	7	.132	-1	12	9	3	1.4
1955	Bal-A	0	3	.000	7	5	0	0	0	20^2	31	0	14	13	19.6	6.53	58	.344	.433	1	.167	0	-6	-6	0	-0.7
1956	Phi-N	0	0	—	20	0	0	0	0	23^1	32	2	12	10	17.0	6.56	57	.330	.404	0	.000	-0	-7	-7	-0	0.0
Total	8	38	66	.365	188	119	34	4	2	904	985	67	391	305	13.9	4.40	93	.277	.352	38	.140	-7	-45	-32	-1	-2.9

YEAR TM/L	W	L	PCT	G	GS	CG	SH	SV	IP	H	HR	BB	SO	RAT	ERA	ERA+	OAV	OOB	BH	AVG	PB	PR	/A	PD	TPI
● **HERMAN PILLETTE**	Pillette, Herman Polycarp "Old Folks" b: 12/26/1895, St.Paul, Ore. d: 4/30/60, Sacramento, Cal. BR/TR, 6'2", 190 lbs. Deb: 7/30/17 F																								
1917 Cin-N	0	0	—	1	0	0	0	0	1	4	0	0	0	36.0	18.00	15	.571	.571	0	—	0	-2	-2	-0	0.0
1922 Det-A	19	12	.613	40	37	18	4	1	274^2	270	6	95	71	12.5	2.85	136	.258	.328	17	.172	-3	36	31	3	3.2
1923 Det-A	14	19	.424	47	36	14	0	1	250^1	280	7	83	64	13.3	3.85	100	.288	.347	21	.247	4	4	0	4	0.8
1924 Det-A	1	1	.500	19	3	1	0	1	37^2	46	1	14	13	15.1	4.78	86	.297	.366	4	.364	1	-2	-3	0	0.0
Total 4	34	32	.515	107	76	33	4	3	563^2	600	14	192	148	13.0	3.45	113	.275	.340	42	.215	2	36	27	7	4.0
● **SQUIZ PILLION**	Pillion, Cecil Randolph b: 4/13/1894, Hartford, Conn. d: 9/30/62, Pittsburgh, Pa. BL/TL, 6', 178 lbs. Deb: 8/20/15																								
1915 Phi-A	0	0	—	2	0	0	0	0	5^1	10	0	2	0	21.9	6.75	43	.400	.464	0	.000	-0	-2	-2	0	0.0
● **HORACIO PINA**	Pina, Horacio (Garcia) b: 3/12/45, Coahuila, Mexico BR/TR, 6'2", 177 lbs. Deb: 8/14/68																								
1968 Cle-A	1	1	.500	12	3	0	0	2	31^1	24	0	15	24	11.5	1.72	172	.218	.317	0	.000	-1	4	4	-0	0.3
1969 Cle-A	4	2	.667	31	4	0	0	1	46^2	44	6	27	32	14.7	5.21	72	.256	.373	3	.500	1	-8	-7	0	-0.8
1970 Was-A	5	3	.625	61	0	0	0	6	71	66	4	35	41	13.2	2.79	127	.250	.344	0	.000	-0	7	6	1	0.8
1971 Was-A	1	1	.500	56	0	0	0	2	57^2	47	2	31	38	12.8	3.59	92	.227	.339	0	.000	-0	-1	-2	1	0.0
1972 Tex-A	2	7	.222	60	0	0	0	15	76	61	3	43	60	13.3	3.20	94	.228	.352	1	.200	0	-1	-2	3	0.1
1973 *Oak-A	6	3	.667	47	0	0	0	8	88	58	8	34	41	10.2	2.76	128	.193	.292	0	—	0	10	8	3	1.4
1974 Chi-N	3	4	.429	34	0	0	0	4	47^1	49	4	28	32	15.0	3.99	96	.268	.371	1	.200	-0	-2	-1	1	-0.1
Cal-A	1	2	.333	11	0	0	0	0	11^2	9	1	3	6	9.3	2.31	149	.209	.261	0	—	0	2	1	1	0.8
1978 Phi-N	0	0	—	2	0	0	0	0	2^1	0	0	0	4	0.0	0.00	—	.000	.000	0	.000	-0	1	1	0	0.0
Total 8	23	23	.500	314	7	0	0	38	432	358	28	216	278	12.6	3.25	106	.231	.336	5	.185	0	12	9	9	2.5
● **ED PINKHAM**	Pinkham, Edward b: 1849, Brooklyn, N.Y. TL, 5'7", 142 lbs. Deb: 5/8/1871 ♦																								
1871 Chi-n	1	0	1.000	3	0	0	0	1	10^1	10	0	3	0	11.3	3.48	132	.208	.255	25	.263	1	**1**	**1**		0.1
● **GEORGE PINKNEY**	Pinkney, George Burton b: 1/11/1862, Orange Prairie, Ill. d: 11/10/26, Peoria, Ill. BR/TR, 5'7", 160 lbs. Deb: 8/16/1884 ♦																								
1886 Bro-a	0	0	—	1	0	0	0	0	2	2	0	0	0	9.0	4.50	78	.400	.400	156	.261	0	-0	-0	-0	0.0
● **ED PINNANCE**	Pinnance, Edward D. "Peanuts" b: 10/22/1879, Walpole Island, Ont., Canada d: 12/12/44, Walpole Island, Ontario, Canada BL/TR, 6'1", 180 lbs. Deb: 9/14/03																								
1903 Phi-A	0	0	—	2	1	0	0	1	7	5	0	2	2	9.0	2.57	119	.200	.259	0	.000	-0	0	0	-0	0.0
● **LERTON PINTO**	Pinto, William Lerton b: 4/8/1899, Chillicothe, Ohio d: 5/13/83, Oxnard, Cal. BL/TL, 6', 190 lbs. Deb: 5/23/22																								
1922 Phi-N	0	1	.000	9	0	0	0	0	24^2	31	1	14	4	16.4	5.11	91	.320	.405	1	.111	-1	-3	-1	-1	-0.1
1924 Phi-N	0	0	—	3	0	0	0	0	4	7	1	0	1	15.8	9.00	50	.467	.467	0	.000	-0	-2	-2	0	0.0
Total 2	0	1	.000	12	0	0	0	0	28^2	38	2	14	5	16.3	5.65	82	.339	.413	1	.100	-1	-5	-3	-1	-0.1
● **ED PIPGRAS**	Pipgras, Edward John b: 6/15/04, Schleswig, Iowa d: 4/13/64, Currie, Minn. BR/TR, 6'2.5", 175 lbs. Deb: 8/25/32 F																								
1932 Bro-N	0	1	.000	5	1	0	0	0	10	16	2	6	5	19.8	5.40	71	.348	.423	0	.000	-0	-2	-2	0	-0.2
● **GEORGE PIPGRAS**	Pipgras, George William b: 12/20/1899, Ida Grove, Iowa d: 10/19/86, Gainesville, Fla. BR/TR, 6'1.5", 185 lbs. Deb: 6/9/23 FU																								
1923 NY-A	1	3	.250	8	2	2	0	0	33^1	34	2	25	12	16.2	5.94	66	.276	.403	0	.000	-1	-7	-7	-0	-0.9
1924 NY-A	0	1	.000	9	1	0	0	1	15^1	20	0	18	4	24.7	9.98	42	.351	.532	1	.333	0	-10	-10	1	-0.6
1927 *NY-A	10	3	.769	29	21	9	1	0	166^1	148	2	77	81	12.2	4.11	94	.247	.334	16	.239	2	1	-5	-1	-0.3
1928 *NY-A	**24**	13	.649	46	38	22	4	3	**300^2**	314	4	103	139	12.6	3.38	111	.272	.333	18	.157	-4	22	13	-4	0.6
1929 NY-A	18	12	.600	39	33	13	3	0	225^1	229	16	95	125	13.1	4.23	91	.264	.340	12	.143	-4	0	-9	-3	-1.7
1930 NY-A	15	15	.500	44	30	15	**3**	4	221	230	9	70	111	12.5	4.11	105	.263	.324	12	.150	-2	13	5	-2	0.0
1931 NY-A	7	6	.538	36	14	6	1	3	137^2	134	8	58	59	12.7	3.79	105	.251	.327	1	.024	-6	9	3	-2	-0.5
1932 *NY-A	16	9	.640	32	27	14	2	0	219	235	15	87	111	13.5	4.19	97	.269	.340	18	.220	1	7	-3	-2	-0.4
1933 NY-A	2	2	.500	4	4	3	0	0	33	32	1	12	14	12.0	3.27	119	.252	.317	1	.091	-1	4	2	1	0.3
Bos-A	9	8	.529	22	17	9	2	1	128^1	140	5	45	56	13.1	4.07	108	.276	.337	9	.196	-1	3	4	-2	0.3
Yr	11	10	.524	26	21	12	2	1	161^1	172	6	57	70	12.9	3.90	110	.271	.333	10	.175	-1	7	7	-1	0.6
1934 Bos-A	0	0	—	2	1	0	0	0	3^1	4	1	3	0	18.9	8.10	59	.308	.438	0	.000	-0	-1	-1	0	0.0
1935 Bos-A	0	1	.000	5	1	0	0	0	5	9	3	5	2	27.0	14.40	33	.391	.517	0	—	0	-6	-5	0	-0.8
Total 11	102	73	.583	276	189	93	16	12	1488^1	1529	66	598	714	13.1	4.09	98	.266	.339	88	.163	-15	35	-14	-15	-4.0
● **COTTON PIPPEN**	Pippen, Henry Harold b: 4/2/11, Cisco, Tex. d: 2/15/81, Williams, Cal. BR/TR, 6'2", 180 lbs. Deb: 8/28/36																								
1936 StL-N	0	2	.000	6	3	0	0	0	21	37	5	8	8	20.1	7.71	51	.402	.461	1	.167	0	-9	-9	1	-0.6
1939 Phi-A	4	11	.267	25	17	5	0	1	118^2	169	13	40	33	15.9	5.99	79	.329	.378	3	.086	-2	-18	-17	2	-1.8
Det-A	0	1	.000	3	2	0	0	0	14	18	1	6	5	15.4	7.07	69	.310	.375	2	.400	0	-4	-3	-0	-0.2
Yr	4	12	.250	28	19	5	0	1	132^2	187	14	46	38	15.8	6.11	77	.326	.376	5	.125	-2	-22	-20	1	-2.0
1940 Det-A	1	2	.333	4	3	0	0	0	21^1	29	3	10	9	16.9	6.75	70	.326	.400	0	.000	-1	-6	-5	0	-0.6
Total 3	5	16	.238	38	25	5	0	1	175	253	22	64	55	16.5	6.38	73	.336	.391	6	.111	-3	-36	-34	2	-3.2
● **GERRY PIRTLE**	Pirtle, Gerald Eugene b: 12/3/47, Tulsa, Okla. BR/TR, 6'1", 185 lbs. Deb: 7/2/78																								
1978 Mon-N	0	2	.000	19	0	0	0	0	25^2	33	5	23	14	20.3	5.96	59	.314	.446	0	—	0	-7	-7	-0	-0.5
● **MARC PISCIOTTA**	Pisciotta, Marc George b: 8/7/70, Edison, N.J. BR/TR, 6'5", 240 lbs. Deb: 6/30/97																								
1997 Chi-N	3	1	.750	24	0	0	0	0	28^1	20	1	16	21	11.8	3.18	135	.200	.316	0	.000	-0	3	4	0	0.4
1998 Chi-N	1	2	.333	43	0	0	0	0	44	44	4	32	31	16.0	4.09	107	.259	.382	1	.333	0	1	1	-0	0.1
Total 2	4	3	.571	67	0	0	0	0	72^1	64	5	48	52	14.3	3.73	116	.237	.358	1	.250	0	4	5	-0	0.5
● **SKIP PITLOCK**	Pitlock, Lee Patrick Thomas b: 11/6/47, Hillside, Ill. BL/TL, 6'2", 180 lbs. Deb: 6/12/70																								
1970 SF-N	5	5	.500	18	15	1	0	0	87	92	13	48	56	14.9	4.66	85	.274	.371	2	.080	-0	-6	-7	0	-0.7
1974 Chi-A	3	3	.500	40	5	0	0	1	105^2	103	7	55	68	14.1	4.43	84	.257	.356	0	—	0	-10	-8	-1	-0.7
1975 Chi-A	0	0	—	1	0	0	0	0	0	1	0	0	0	—	—	—	1.000	1.000	0	—	0	0	0	0	-0.1
Total 3	8	8	.500	59	20	1	0	1	192^2	196	20	103	124	14.5	4.53	85	.266	.364	2	.080	-0	-15	-15	-1	-1.5
● **TOGIE PITTINGER**	Pittinger, Charles Reno b: 1/12/1872, Greencastle, Pa. d: 1/14/09, Greencastle, Pa. BL/TR, 6'2", 175 lbs. Deb: 4/26/00																								
1900 Bos-N	2	9	.182	18	13	8	0	0	114	135	7	54	27	15.6	5.13	80	.293	.377	6	.130	-4	-18	-13	-1	-1.4
1901 Bos-N	13	16	.448	34	33	27	1	0	281^1	288	7	76	129	11.9	3.01	120	.263	.316	11	.110	-8	10	19	3	1.2
1902 Bos-N	27	16	.628	46	40	36	7	0	389^1	360	4	128	174	11.7	2.52	112	.245	.313	20	.136	-8	11	13	-2	0.2
1903 Bos-N	18	22	.450	44	39	35	3	1	351^2	396	12	143	140	14.2	3.48	92	.294	.369	14	.109	-9	-8	-11	-3	-2.1
1904 Bos-N	15	21	.417	38	37	35	5	0	335^1	298	1	144	146	12.2	2.66	104	.242	.329	13	.107	-9	3	4	5	0.0
1905 Phi-N	23	14	.622	**46**	37	29	4	2	337^1	311	3	104	136	11.5	3.09	94	.247	.313	19	.156	-3	-3	-6	-3	-1.3
1906 Phi-N	8	10	.444	20	16	9	2	0	129^2	128	2	50	43	13.2	3.40	77	.252	.334	4	.091	-1	-11	-11	-1	-1.8
1907 Phi-N	9	5	.643	16	12	8	1	0	102	101	3	35	37	12.4	3.00	81	.261	.330	5	.139	-1	-6	-7	-1	-1.0
Total 8	115	113	.504	262	227	187	23	3	2040^2	2017	39	734	832	12.6	3.10	98	.260	.332	92	.124	-43	-23	-13	-3	-6.2
● **JIM PITTSLEY**	Pittsley, James Michael b: 4/3/74, DuBois, Pa. BR/TR, 6'7", 215 lbs. Deb: 5/23/95																								
1995 KC-A	0	0	—	1	1	0	0	0	3^1	7	3	1	0	21.6	13.50	35	.438	.471	0	—	0	-3	-3	-0	0.0
1997 KC-A	5	8	.385	21	21	0	0	0	112	120	15	54	52	14.5	5.46	86	.277	.365	1	.500	1	-11	-9	-2	-1.0
1998 KC-A	1	1	.500	39	2	0	0	0	68^1	88	13	37	44	16.7	6.59	75	.322	.407	0	.000	-0	-15	-13	0	-0.3
Total 3	6	9	.400	61	24	0	0	0	183^2	215	31	92	96	15.4	6.03	79	.298	.383	1	.250	0	-29	-25	-1	-1.3
● **STAN PITULA**	Pitula, Stanley b: 3/23/31, Hackensack, N.J. d: 8/15/65, Hackensack, N.J. BR/TR, 5'10", 170 lbs. Deb: 4/24/57																								
1957 Cle-A	2	2	.500	23	5	1	0	0	59^2	67	8	32	17	15.2	4.98	75	.296	.388	3	.200	0	-8	-8	-1	-0.6
● **JUAN PIZARRO**	Pizarro, Juan Ramon (Cordova) b: 2/7/37, Santurce, P.R. BL/TL, 5'11", 190 lbs. Deb: 5/4/57																								
1957 *Mil-N	5	6	.455	24	10	3	0	0	99^1	99	16	51	68	13.7	4.62	76	.261	.350	9	.250	3	-8	-12	-1	-1.0
1958 *Mil-N	6	4	.600	16	10	7	1	1	96^2	75	12	47	84	11.7	2.70	130	.212	.312	8	.250	3	13	9	1	1.2
1959 Mil-N	6	2	.750	29	14	6	2	0	133^2	117	13	70	126	13.1	3.77	94	.237	.342	5	.122	-0	3	-3	0	-0.2

YEAR	TM/L	W	L	PCT	G	GS	CG	SH	SV	IP	H	HR	BB	SO	RAT	ERA	ERA+	OAV	OOB	BH	AVG	PB	PR	/A	PD	TPI
1960	Mil-N	6	7	.462	21	17	3	0	0	114^2	105	13	72	88	14.2	4.55	75	.244	.357	11	.275	3	-10	-14	-1	-1.2
1961	Chi-A	14	7	.667	39	25	12	1	2	194^2	164	17	89	188	11.9	3.05	128	.226	.314	17	.246	5	21	19	-1	2.3
1962	Chi-A	12	14	.462	36	32	9	1	1	203^1	182	16	97	173	12.4	3.81	103	.236	.322	11	.159	-0	4	2	-2	0.0
1963	Chi-A★	16	8	.667	32	28	10	3	1	214^2	177	14	63	163	10.2	2.39	147	.224	.284	13	.178	3	30	27	-3	3.0
1964	Chi-A☆	19	9	.679	33	33	11	4	0	239	193	23	55	162	9.5	2.56	135	.219	.267	19	.211	5	28	24	-1	3.1
1965	Chi-A	6	3	.667	18	18	2	1	0	97	96	9	37	65	12.4	3.43	93	.254	.322	8	.235	3	0	-3	-0	0.1
1966	Chi-A	8	6	.571	34	9	1	0	3	88^2	91	9	39	42	13.3	3.76	84	.269	.347	4	.154	0	-3	-6	1	-0.8
1967	Pit-N	8	10	.444	50	9	1	1	9	107	99	10	52	96	12.9	3.95	85	.245	.334	7	.259	2	-7	-7	-1	-1.2
1968	Pit-N	1	1	.500	12	0	0	0	0	11	14	2	10	6	20.5	3.27	89	.311	.446	0	.000	-0	-0	-0	-0	-0.2
	Bos-A	6	8	.429	19	12	6	0	2	107^2	97	15	44	84	11.8	3.59	88	.242	.317	5	.161	1	-7	-5	2	-0.4
1969	Bos-A	0	1	.000	6	0	0	0	2	9	14	2	6	4	20.0	6.00	63	.359	.444	1	.333	0	-2	-2	0	-0.3
	Cle-A	3	3	.500	48	4	1	0	4	82^2	67	6	49	44	12.8	3.16	119	.229	.343	3	.200	0	4	6	0	0.5
	Oak-A	1	1	.500	3	0	0	0	1	7^2	3	1	3	4	7.0	2.35	146	.125	.222	1	.500	0	1	1	-0	0.3
	Yr	4	5	.444	57	4	1	0	7	99^1	84	9	58	52	12.9	3.35	112	.230	.335	5	.250	1	3	4	0	0.5
1970	Chi-N	0	0	—	12	0	0	0	1	15^2	16	2	9	14	14.9	4.60	98	.262	.366	0	.000	-0	-1	-0	0	0.0
1971	Chi-N	7	6	.538	16	14	6	3	0	101^1	78	10	40	67	10.7	3.46	114	.209	.289	6	.176	1	0	5	0	0.8
1972	Chi-N	4	5	.444	16	7	1	0	1	59^1	66	7	32	24	15.0	3.94	97	.293	.384	3	.143	-0	-3	-1	1	-0.1
1973	Chi-N	0	1	.000	2	0	0	0	0	4	6	1	1	3	18.0	11.25	35	.353	.421	0	.000	-0	-3	-3	0	-0.6
	Hou-N	2	2	.500	15	1	0	0	0	23^1	28	1	11	10	15.4	6.56	55	.301	.381	0	.000	-0	-8	-8	1	-1.1
	Yr	2	3	.400	17	1	0	0	0	27^1	34	2	12	13	15.5	7.24	51	.304	.376	0	.000	-0	-11	-11	1	-1.7
1974	*Pit-N	1	1	.500	7	2	0	0	0	24	20	2	11	7	11.6	1.88	184	.220	.304	2	.333	0	5	4	-0	0.4
Total	18	131	105	.555	488	245	79	17	28	2034^1	1807	201	888	1522	12.1	3.43	104	.237	.320	133	.202	29	55	33	-5	4.6

● GORDIE PLADSON

Pladson, Gordon Cecil b: 7/31/56, New Westminster, B.C., Canada BR/TR, 6'4", 210 lbs. Deb: 9/7/79

YEAR	TM/L	W	L	PCT	G	GS	CG	SH	SV	IP	H	HR	BB	SO	RAT	ERA	ERA+	OAV	OOB	BH	AVG	PB	PR	/A	PD	TPI
1979	Hou-N	0	0	—	4	0	0	0	0	4	9	1	2	2	24.8	4.50	78	.450	.500	0	—	0	-0	-0	-0	0.0
1980	Hou-N	0	4	.000	12	6	0	0	0	41^1	38	3	16	13	11.8	4.35	75	.244	.314	0	.000	-1	-3	-5	0	-0.5
1981	Hou-N	0	0	—	2	0	0	0	0	4	9	0	3	3	27.0	9.00	37	.429	.500	0	—	0	-2	-3	-0	0.0
1982	Hou-N	0	0	—	2	0	0	0	0	1^1	10	0	2	0	81.0	54.00	6	.769	.800	0	—	0	-7	-8	-0	0.0
Total	4	0	4	.000	20	6	0	0	0	50^2	66	4	23	18	15.8	6.04	55	.314	.382	0	.000	-1	-14	-15	-0	-0.5

● EMIL PLANETA

Planeta, Emil Joseph b: 1/31/09, Higganum, Conn. d: 2/2/63, Rocky Hill, Conn. BR/TR, 6', 190 lbs. Deb: 9/20/31

YEAR	TM/L	W	L	PCT	G	GS	CG	SH	SV	IP	H	HR	BB	SO	RAT	ERA	ERA+	OAV	OOB	BH	AVG	PB	PR	/A	PD	TPI
1931	NY-N	0	0	—	2	0	0	0	0	5^1	7	0	4	0	18.6	10.13	36	.292	.393	0	.000	-0	-4	-4	-0	0.0

● ED PLANK

Plank, Edward Arthur b: 4/9/52, Chicago, Ill. BR/TR, 6'1", 205 lbs. Deb: 9/6/78

YEAR	TM/L	W	L	PCT	G	GS	CG	SH	SV	IP	H	HR	BB	SO	RAT	ERA	ERA+	OAV	OOB	BH	AVG	PB	PR	/A	PD	TPI
1978	SF-N	0	0	—	5	0	0	0	0	6^2	6	1	2	1	10.8	4.05	85	.273	.333	0	—	0	-0	-0	-0	0.0
1979	SF-N	0	0	—	4	0	0	0	0	3^2	9	0	2	1	27.0	7.36	47	.450	.500	0	—	0	-1	-2	-0	0.0
Total	2	0	0	—	9	0	0	0	0	10^1	15	1	4	2	16.5	5.23	66	.357	.413	0	—	0	-2	-2	-1	0.0

● EDDIE PLANK

Plank, Edward Stewart "Gettysburg Eddie" b: 8/31/1875, Gettysburg, Pa. d: 2/24/26, Gettysburg, Pa. BL/TL, 5'11.5", 175 lbs. Deb: 5/13/01 H

YEAR	TM/L	W	L	PCT	G	GS	CG	SH	SV	IP	H	HR	BB	SO	RAT	ERA	ERA+	OAV	OOB	BH	AVG	PB	PR	/A	PD	TPI
1901	Phi-A	17	13	.567	33	32	28	1	0	260^2	254	2	68	90	11.4	3.31	114	.252	.304	18	.182	-3	10	13	-2	0.8
1902	Phi-A	20	15	.571	36	32	31	1	0	300	319	5	61	107	11.9	3.30	111	.273	.319	35	.292	6	9	12	-2	1.6
1903	Phi-A	23	16	.590	**43**	40	33	3	0	336	317	5	65	176	10.8	2.38	128	.249	.297	25	.187	-1	22	25	-1	2.5
1904	Phi-A	26	17	.605	44	43	37	7	0	357^1	311	2	86	201	10.5	2.17	124	.235	.292	31	.240	3	17	20	-0	2.8
1905	*Phi-A	24	12	.667	41	41	**35**	4	0	346^2	287	3	75	210	10.0	2.26	118	.227	.283	29	.230	3	15	15	-3	1.6
1906	Phi-A	19	6	**.760**	26	25	21	5	0	211^2	173	1	51	108	10.2	2.25	121	.226	.288	17	.233	2	10	11	-2	1.3
1907	Phi-A	24	16	.600	43	40	33	**8**	0	343^2	282	5	85	183	10.1	2.20	118	.226	.285	26	.211	2	13	15	-1	1.9
1908	Phi-A	14	16	.467	34	28	21	4	0	244^2	202	1	46	135	9.5	2.17	118	.224	.269	16	.180	-1	6	11	-4	0.7
1909	Phi-A	19	10	.655	34	33	24	3	0	265^1	215	1	62	132	9.7	1.76	136	.224	.277	21	.219	4	21	19	1	2.7
1910	Phi-A	16	10	.615	38	32	22	1	2	250^1	218	3	55	123	10.1	2.01	118	.237	.286	11	.128	-3	14	10	-3	0.4
1911	*Phi-A	23	8	.742	40	30	24	**6**	**4**	256^2	237	2	77	149	11.5	2.10	150	.255	.322	18	.191	-1	35	30	1	3.4
1912	Phi-A	26	6	.813	37	30	23	5	2	259^2	234	1	83	110	11.2	2.22	139	.245	.309	24	.267	4	32	25	-2	3.2
1913	*Phi-A	18	10	.643	41	30	18	7	4	242^2	211	3	57	151	10.1	2.60	106	.234	.283	8	.105	-0	9	5	-1	0.3
1914	*Phi-A	15	7	.682	34	22	12	4	3	185^1	178	2	42	110	11.0	2.87	91	.266	.315	9	.150	0	-3	-5	-3	-0.9
1915	StL-F	21	11	.656	42	31	23	6	3	268^1	212	1	54	147	**9.0**	2.08	**138**	.218	**.262**	24	.258	3	19	24	-3	**2.9**
1916	StL-A	16	15	.516	37	26	17	3	3	235^2	203	2	67	88	10.5	2.33	118	.237	.297	15	.185	-0	13	11	-4	1.1
1917	StL-A	5	6	.455	20	14	8	1	1	131	105	2	38	26	10.0	1.79	145	.225	.287	4	.105	-1	13	12	-1	0.7
Total	17	326	194	.627	623	529	410	69	23	4495^2	3958	41	1072	2246	10.5	2.35	122	.239	.293	331	.206	17	257	254	-32	27.0

● ERIK PLANTENBERG

Plantenberg, Erik John b: 10/30/68, Renton, Wash. BB/TL, 6'1", 180 lbs. Deb: 7/31/93

YEAR	TM/L	W	L	PCT	G	GS	CG	SH	SV	IP	H	HR	BB	SO	RAT	ERA	ERA+	OAV	OOB	BH	AVG	PB	PR	/A	PD	TPI
1993	Sea-A	0	0	—	20	0	0	0	1	9^2	11	0	12	3	22.3	6.52	68	.282	.462	0	—	0	-2	-2	0	0.0
1994	Sea-A	0	0	—	6	0	0	0	0	7	4	0	7	1	15.4	0.00	—	.174	.387	0	—	0	4	4	0	0.0
1997	Phi-N	0	0	—	35	0	0	0	0	25^2	25	1	12	12	13.3	4.91	86	.255	.342	0	—	0	-2	-2	-1	0.0
Total	3	0	0	—	61	0	0	0	1	42^1	40	1	31	16	15.7	4.46	98	.250	.381	0	—	0	-1	-0	-0	0.0

● BILL PLEIS

Pleis, William b: 8/5/37, St.Louis, Mo. BL/TL, 5'10", 175 lbs. Deb: 4/16/61

YEAR	TM/L	W	L	PCT	G	GS	CG	SH	SV	IP	H	HR	BB	SO	RAT	ERA	ERA+	OAV	OOB	BH	AVG	PB	PR	/A	PD	TPI
1961	Min-A	4	2	.667	37	0	0	0	2	56^1	59	4	34	32	15.5	4.95	86	.266	.373	1	.111	-1	-6	-4	-1	-0.6
1962	Min-A	2	5	.286	21	4	0	0	3	45	46	7	14	31	12.2	4.40	93	.264	.323	4	.286	1	-2	-2	-1	-0.2
1963	Min-A	6	2	.750	36	4	1	0	0	68	67	10	16	37	11.0	4.37	83	.258	.301	2	.125	0	-6	-5	-0	-0.6
1964	Min-A	4	1	.800	47	0	0	0	4	50^2	43	6	31	42	13.3	3.91	92	.232	.346	1	.250	0	-2	-2	0	-0.1
1965	*Min-A	4	4	.500	41	2	0	0	4	51^1	49	3	27	33	13.3	2.98	119	.250	.341	0	.000	-1	3	3	-0	0.4
1966	Min-A	1	2	.333	8	0	0	0	0	9^1	5	1	4	9	8.7	1.93	186	.152	.243	0	—	0	2	2	-0	0.5
Total	6	21	16	.568	190	10	1	0	13	280^2	269	31	126	184	12.9	4.07	93	.251	.334	8	.160	0	-11	-8	-3	-0.6

● DAN PLESAC

Plesac, Daniel Thomas b: 2/4/62, Gary, Ind. BL/TL, 6'5", 215 lbs. Deb: 4/11/86

YEAR	TM/L	W	L	PCT	G	GS	CG	SH	SV	IP	H	HR	BB	SO	RAT	ERA	ERA+	OAV	OOB	BH	AVG	PB	PR	/A	PD	TPI
1986	Mil-A	10	7	.588	51	0	0	0	14	91	81	5	29	75	10.9	2.97	146	.240	.301	0	—	0	12	14	-1	2.7
1987	Mil-A★	5	6	.455	57	0	0	0	23	79^1	63	8	23	89	10.1	2.61	175	.213	.276	0	—	0	16	17	0	3.2
1988	Mil-A★	1	2	.333	50	0	0	0	30	52^1	46	2	12	52	10.0	2.41	165	.234	.278	0	—	0	9	9	-0	1.4
1989	Mil-A★	3	4	.429	52	0	0	0	33	61^1	47	6	17	52	9.4	2.35	163	.213	.269	0	—	0	10	10	-0	2.1
1990	Mil-A	3	7	.300	66	0	0	0	24	69	67	5	31	65	13.2	4.43	87	.257	.342	0	—	0	-4	-4	-0	-0.8
1991	Mil-A	2	7	.222	45	10	0	0	8	92^1	92	12	39	61	13.1	4.29	93	.263	.342	0	—	0	-2	-3	-2	-0.5
1992	Mil-A	5	4	.556	44	4	0	0	1	79	64	5	35	54	11.6	2.96	130	.229	.321	0	—	0	9	8	-1	0.9
1993	Chi-N	2	1	.667	57	0	0	0	0	62^2	74	10	21	47	13.6	4.74	84	.298	.353	0	.000	-0	-5	-5	-0	-0.3
1994	Chi-N	2	3	.400	54	0	0	0	1	54^2	61	9	13	53	12.3	4.61	90	.279	.322	0	.000	-0	-2	-3	-1	-0.4
1995	Pit-N	4	4	.500	58	0	0	0	3	60^1	53	3	27	57	12.1	3.58	120	.237	.321	1	.250	0	4	5	0	0.6
1996	Pit-N	6	5	.545	73	0	0	0	11	70^1	67	4	24	76	11.6	4.09	106	.247	.308	0	.000	-1	1	2	-2	0.1
1997	Tor-A	2	4	.333	73	0	0	0	1	50^1	47	8	19	61	11.8	3.58	128	.244	.311	0	—	0	6	6	-1	0.5
1998	Tor-A	4	3	.571	78	0	0	0	4	50	41	4	16	55	10.4	3.78	123	.224	.290	0	—	0	5	5	-1	0.5
Total	13	49	57	.462	758	14	0	0	153	872^2	803	81	306	797	11.6	3.56	117	.245	.312	1	.071	-1	59	60	-9	10.0

● NORMAN PLITT

Plitt, Norman William b: 2/21/1893, York, Pa. d: 2/1/54, New York, N.Y. BR/TR, 5'11", 180 lbs. Deb: 4/26/18

YEAR	TM/L	W	L	PCT	G	GS	CG	SH	SV	IP	H	HR	BB	SO	RAT	ERA	ERA+	OAV	OOB	BH	AVG	PB	PR	/A	PD	TPI
1918	Bro-N	0	0	—	1	0	0	0	0	2	3	0	1	0	18.0	4.50	62	.429	.500	1	1.000	0	-0	-0	-0	0.0
1927	Bro-N	2	6	.250	19	8	1	0	0	62^1	73	3	36	9	15.9	4.91	81	.303	.396	4	.222	-0	-7	-7	0	-0.7
	NY-N	1	0	1.000	3	0	0	0	0	7^1	9	0	1	0	13.5	3.68	105	.310	.355	0	.000	-0	0	0	0	0.0
	Yr	3	6	.333	22	8	1	0	0	69^2	82	3	37	9	15.5	4.78	83	.303	.388	4	.211	-0	-7	-6	1	-0.7
Total	2	3	6	.333	23	8	1	0	0	71^2	85	3	38	9	15.7	4.77	82	.307	.394	5	.250	-0	-7	-7	1	-0.7

● TIM PLODINEC

Plodinec, Timothy Alfred b: 1/27/47, Aliquippa, Pa. BR/TR, 6'4", 190 lbs. Deb: 6/2/72

YEAR	TM/L	W	L	PCT	G	GS	CG	SH	SV	IP	H	HR	BB	SO	RAT	ERA	ERA+	OAV	OOB	BH	AVG	PB	PR	/A	PD	TPI
1972	StL-N	0	0	—	1	0	0	0	0	0^1	3	0	0	0	81.0	27.00	13	.750	.750	0	—	0	-1	-1	0	0.0

● ERIC PLUNK

Plunk, Eric Vaughn b: 9/3/63, Wilmington, Cal. BR/TR, 6'5", 217 lbs. Deb: 5/12/86

YEAR	TM/L	W	L	PCT	G	GS	CG	SH	SV	IP	H	HR	BB	SO	RAT	ERA	ERA+	OAV	OOB	BH	AVG	PB	PR	/A	PD	TPI
1986	Oak-A	4	7	.364	26	15	0	0	0	120^1	91	14	102	98	14.8	5.31	73	.214	.372	0	—	0	-15	-19	-2	-1.7
1987	Oak-A	4	6	.400	32	11	0	0	2	95	91	8	62	90	14.7	4.74	87	.253	.366	0	—	0	-3	-6	-1	-0.7

YEAR	TM/L	W	L	PCT	G	GS	CG	SH	SV	IP	H	HR	BB	SO	RAT	ERA	ERA+	OAV	OOB	BH	AVG	PB	PR	/A	PD	TPI
1988	*Oak-A	7	2	.778	49	0	0	0	5	78	62	6	39	79	11.8	3.00	126	.217	.313	0	—	0	8	7	-1	0.8
1989	Oak-A	1	1	.500	23	0	0	0	1	28^2	17	1	12	24	9.4	2.20	167	.172	.268	0	—	0	5	5	-0	0.5
	NY-A	7	5	.583	27	7	0	0	0	75^2	65	9	52	61	13.9	3.69	105	.237	.359	0	—	0	2	2	-2	0.1
	Yr	8	6	.571	50	7	0	0	1	104^1	82	10	64	85	12.6	3.28	116	.219	.333	0	—	0	7	6	-2	0.6
1990	NY-A	6	3	.667	47	0	0	0	0	72^2	58	6	43	67	12.8	2.72	146	.225	.340	0	—	0	10	10	2	1.3
1991	NY-A	2	5	.286	43	8	0	0	0	111^2	128	18	62	103	15.4	4.76	87	.286	.374	0	—	0	-8	-8	-2	-0.6
1992	Cle-A	9	6	.600	58	0	0	0	4	71^2	61	5	38	50	12.4	3.64	107	.229	.326	0	—	0	2	2	-0	0.5
1993	Cle-A	4	5	.444	70	0	0	0	15	71	61	5	30	77	11.5	2.79	155	.226	.303	0	—	0	12	12	-1	1.7
1994	Cle-A	7	2	.778	41	0	0	0	3	71	61	3	37	73	12.7	2.54	186	.231	.330	0	—	0	18	17	-1	1.9
1995	*Cle-A	6	2	.750	56	0	0	0	2	64	48	5	27	71	11.1	2.67	176	.211	.305	0	—	0	15	14	0	1.6
1996	*Cle-A	3	2	.600	56	0	0	0	2	77^2	56	6	34	85	10.8	2.43	201	.203	.297	0	—	0	22	21	-0	1.2
1997	*Cle-A	4	5	.444	55	0	0	0	0	65^2	62	12	36	66	13.6	4.66	101	.245	.341	0	.000	-0	-1	0	-1	-0.1
1998	Cle-A	3	1	.750	37	0	0	0	0	41	44	6	15	38	13.4	4.83	99	.282	.353	0	—	0	-1	-0	-0	-0.1
	Mil-N	1	2	.333	26	0	0	0	1	31^2	33	3	15	36	14.5	3.69	116	.270	.364	0	.000	0	2	2	-1	0.1
Total	13	68	54	.557	646	41	0	0	35	1075^2	938	107	604	1018	13.1	3.73	113	.235	.340	0	.000	0	68	59	-10	6.5

● **JEFF PLYMPTON** Plympton, Jeffrey Hunter b: 11/24/65, Framingham, Mass. BR/TR, 6′2″, 205 lbs. Deb: 6/15/91

YEAR	TM/L	W	L	PCT	G	GS	CG	SH	SV	IP	H	HR	BB	SO	RAT	ERA	ERA+	OAV	OOB	BH	AVG	PB	PR	/A	PD	TPI
1991	Bos-A	0	0	—	4	0	0	0	0	5^1	5	0	4	2	15.2	0.00	—	.263	.391	0	—	0	2	3	-0	-0.1

● **RAY POAT** Poat, Raymond Willis b: 12/19/17, Chicago, Ill. d: 4/29/90, Oak Lawn, Ill. BR/TR, 6′2″, 200 lbs. Deb: 4/15/42

YEAR	TM/L	W	L	PCT	G	GS	CG	SH	SV	IP	H	HR	BB	SO	RAT	ERA	ERA+	OAV	OOB	BH	AVG	PB	PR	/A	PD	TPI
1942	Cle-A	1	3	.250	4	4	1	1	0	18^1	24	1	9	8	16.7	5.40	64	.296	.374	0	.000	-0	-4	-4	0	-0.7
1943	Cle-A	2	5	.286	17	4	1	0	0	45	44	3	20	31	12.8	4.40	71	.259	.337	2	.154	-1	-6	-6	-0	-1.0
1944	Cle-A	4	8	.333	36	6	1	0	1	80^2	82	9	37	40	13.3	5.13	64	.265	.343	0	.000	-2	-15	-16	-0	-2.5
1947	NY-N	4	3	.571	7	7	5	0	0	60	53	8	13	25	9.9	2.55	160	.238	.280	4	.190	2	10	10	-0	1.3
1948	NY-N	11	10	.524	39	24	7	3	0	157^2	162	21	67	57	13.2	4.34	91	.262	.337	7	.125	-1	-7	-7	-2	-1.2
1949	NY-N	0	0	—	2	0	0	0	0	2^1	8	0	1	0	34.7	19.29	21	.615	.643	0	—	0	-4	-4	-0	0.0
	Pit-N	0	1	.000	11	2	0	0	0	36	52	6	15	17	16.8	6.25	67	.335	.394	1	.100	-1	-9	-8	-0	-0.3
	Yr	0	1	.000	13	2	0	0	0	38^1	60	6	16	17	17.8	7.04	59	.357	.413	1	.100	-1	-13	-12	-0	-0.3
Total	6	22	30	.423	116	47	15	4	1	400	425	48	162	178	13.3	4.55	82	.271	.340	14	.115	-3	-34	-36	-3	-4.4

● **BUD PODBIELAN** Podbielan, Clarence Anthony b: 3/6/24, Curlew, Wash. d: 10/26/82, Syracuse, N.Y. BR/TR, 6′1.5″, 170 lbs. Deb: 4/25/49

YEAR	TM/L	W	L	PCT	G	GS	CG	SH	SV	IP	H	HR	BB	SO	RAT	ERA	ERA+	OAV	OOB	BH	AVG	PB	PR	/A	PD	TPI
1949	Bro-N	0	1	.000	7	1	0	0	0	12^1	9	1	9	5	13.9	3.65	112	.205	.352	0	.000	-0	1	1	1	0.1
1950	Bro-N	5	4	.556	20	10	2	0	1	72^2	93	10	29	28	15.4	5.33	77	.307	.371	3	.107	-1	-10	-10	1	-1.1
1951	Bro-N	2	2	.500	27	5	1	0	0	79^2	67	9	36	26	11.9	3.50	112	.233	.322	7	.304	1	4	4	0	0.3
1952	Bro-N	0	0	—	3	0	0	0	0	2	4	1	3	1	31.5	18.00	20	.444	.583	0	—	0	-3	-3	-0	0.0
	Cin-N	4	5	.444	24	7	4	1	1	86^2	78	8	26	22	10.9	2.80	135	.245	.304	4	.160	0	9	9	-1	0.9
	Yr	4	5	.444	27	7	4	1	1	88^2	82	9	29	23	11.4	3.15	120	.251	.314	4	.160	0	6	6	-1	0.9
1953	Cin-N	6	16	.273	36	24	8	1	1	186^1	214	21	67	74	14.0	4.73	92	.290	.356	7	.125	-3	-9	-8	-0	-1.1
1954	Cin-N	7	10	.412	27	24	4	0	0	131	157	20	58	42	14.9	5.36	78	.300	.372	6	.143	-1	-19	-17	-2	-2.1
1955	Cin-N	1	2	.333	17	2	0	0	0	42	36	4	11	26	10.3	3.21	132	.234	.289	2	.400	1	4	5	0	0.4
1957	Cin-N	0	1	.000	5	3	1	0	0	16	18	4	4	13	12.4	6.19	66	.290	.333	0	.000	-1	-4	-4	-1	-0.3
1959	Cle-A	0	1	.000	6	0	0	0	0	12^1	17	1	2	5	13.9	5.84	63	.354	.380	0	.000	-0	-3	-3	0	-0.2
Total	9	25	42	.373	172	76	20	2	3	641	693	79	245	242	13.4	4.49	92	.279	.348	29	.154	-4	-30	-26	-2	-3.1

● **JOHNNY PODGAJNY** Podgajny, John Sigmund "Specs" b: 6/10/20, Chester, Pa. d: 3/2/71, Chester, Pa. BR/TR, 6′2″, 173 lbs. Deb: 9/15/40

YEAR	TM/L	W	L	PCT	G	GS	CG	SH	SV	IP	H	HR	BB	SO	RAT	ERA	ERA+	OAV	OOB	BH	AVG	PB	PR	/A	PD	TPI
1940	Phi-N	1	3	.250	4	4	3	0	0	35	33	0	1	12	9.0	2.83	138	.250	.261	2	.167	-0	4	4	0	0.5
1941	Phi-N	9	12	.429	34	24	8	0	0	181^1	191	8	70	53	13.2	4.62	80	.270	.339	8	.129	-3	-20	-18	1	-2.1
1942	Phi-N	6	14	.300	43	23	6	0	0	186^2	191	9	63	40	12.8	3.91	85	.268	.337	11	.183	-0	-12	-12	-1	-1.4
1943	Phi-N	4	4	.500	13	5	3	0	0	64	77	4	16	13	13.1	4.22	80	.310	.352	5	.250	1	-6	-6	1	-0.5
	Pit-N	0	4	.000	15	5	0	0	0	34^1	37	1	13	7	13.1	4.72	74	.266	.329	1	.143	-0	-5	-5	2	-0.4
	Yr	4	8	.333	28	10	3	0	0	98^1	114	5	29	20	13.1	4.39	78	.295	.344	6	.222	0	-11	-11	3	-0.9
1946	Cle-A	0	0	—	6	0	0	0	0	9	13	0	2	4	15.0	5.00	66	.302	.333	0	—	0	-1	-2	0	0.0
Total	5	20	37	.351	115	61	20	0	0	510^1	542	22	165	129	12.8	4.20	84	.273	.334	27	.168	-3	-41	-39	3	-3.9

● **JOHNNY PODRES** Podres, John Joseph b: 9/30/32, Witherbee, N.Y. BL/TL, 5′11″, 192 lbs. Deb: 4/17/53 C

YEAR	TM/L	W	L	PCT	G	GS	CG	SH	SV	IP	H	HR	BB	SO	RAT	ERA	ERA+	OAV	OOB	BH	AVG	PB	PR	/A	PD	TPI
1953	*Bro-N	9	4	.692	33	18	3	1	0	115	126	12	64	82	14.9	4.23	101	.282	.373	11	.306	2	1	0	-0	0.2
1954	Bro-N	11	7	.611	29	21	6	2	0	151^2	147	13	53	79	11.9	4.27	96	.255	.319	17	.283	5	-3	-3	-2	0.0
1955	*Bro-N	9	10	.474	27	24	5	2	0	159^1	160	15	57	114	12.5	3.95	103	.259	.326	11	.183	-0	1	2	-1	0.0
1957	Bro-N	12	9	.571	31	27	10	**6**	3	196	168	15	44	109	**9.8**	**2.66**	**156**	.230	**.274**	15	.208	1	26	33	-0	3.5
1958	LA-N☆	13	15	.464	39	31	10	2	1	210^1	208	27	78	143	12.3	3.72	110	.261	.328	9	.127	-3	5	9	-2	0.6
1959	*LA-N	14	9	.609	34	29	6	2	0	195	192	23	74	145	12.4	4.11	103	.261	.331	16	.246	3	-3	3	1	0.7
1960	LA-N★	14	12	.538	34	33	8	1	0	227^2	217	25	71	159	11.4	3.08	129	.250	.308	9	.136	-1	17	22	-2	2.1
1961	LA-N	18	5	**.783**	32	29	6	1	0	182^2	192	27	51	124	12.2	3.74	116	.271	.324	16	.232	1	6	12	-2	1.3
1962	LA-N★	15	13	.536	40	40	8	0	0	255	270	20	71	178	12.1	3.81	95	.272	.323	14	.159	1	4	-5	-4	-0.8
1963	*LA-N	14	12	.538	37	34	10	5	1	198^1	196	16	64	134	11.9	3.54	85	.257	.316	9	.141	1	-6	-11	-1	-1.4
1964	LA-N	0	2	.000	2	2	0	0	0	2^2	5	1	3	0	27.0	16.88	19	.417	.533	0	—	0	-4	-4	-0	-1.7
1965	LA-N	7	6	.538	27	22	2	1	1	134	126	17	39	63	11.2	3.43	95	.247	.303	8	.178	1	2	-2	-3	-0.4
1966	LA-N	0	0	—	1	0	0	0	0	1^2	2	0	1	1	16.2	0.00	—	.400	.500	0	—	0	1	1	0	0.0
	Det-A	4	5	.444	36	13	2	1	4	107^2	106	12	34	53	11.8	3.43	102	.259	.317	7	.233	2	0	1	-1	0.2
1967	Det-A	3	1	.750	21	8	0	0	1	63^1	58	12	11	34	9.9	3.84	85	.244	.280	2	.100	-1	-4	-4	-1	-0.4
1969	SD-N	5	6	.455	17	9	1	0	0	64^2	66	7	28	17	13.2	4.31	82	.264	.341	1	.063	-1	-5	-6	-1	-1.1
Total	15	148	116	.561	440	340	77	24	11	2265	2239	242	743	1435	12.0	3.68	105	.259	.319	145	.190	12	37	45	-17	2.8

● **JOE POETZ** Poetz, Joseph Frank "Bull Montana" b: 6/22/1900, St.Louis, Mo. d: 2/7/42, St.Louis, Mo. BR/TR, 5′10.5″, 175 lbs. Deb: 9/14/26

YEAR	TM/L	W	L	PCT	G	GS	CG	SH	SV	IP	H	HR	BB	SO	RAT	ERA	ERA+	OAV	OOB	BH	AVG	PB	PR	/A	PD	TPI
1926	NY-N	0	1	.000	2	1	0	0	0	8	5	2	8	0	15.8	3.38	111	.192	.400	0	.000	0	0	0	0	0.1

● **BOOTS POFFENBERGER** Poffenberger, Cletus Elwood b: 7/1/15, Williamsport, Md. BR/TR, 5′10″, 178 lbs. Deb: 6/11/37

YEAR	TM/L	W	L	PCT	G	GS	CG	SH	SV	IP	H	HR	BB	SO	RAT	ERA	ERA+	OAV	OOB	BH	AVG	PB	PR	/A	PD	TPI
1937	Det-A	10	5	.667	29	16	5	0	3	137^1	147	8	79	35	15.1	4.65	100	.277	.375	11	.216	-0	-1	0	1	0.1
1938	Det-A	6	7	.462	25	15	8	1	1	125	147	8	66	28	15.5	4.82	104	.297	.382	8	.182	-1	-1	2	-2	0.0
1939	Bro-N	0	0	—	3	1	0	0	0	5	7	1	4	2	19.8	5.40	75	.318	.423	0	.000	-0	-1	-1	0	0.0
Total	3	16	12	.571	57	32	13	1	4	267^1	301	17	149	65	15.4	4.75	101	.287	.379	19	.198	-2	-2	2	-0	0.1

● **TOM POHOLSKY** Poholsky, Thomas George b: 8/26/29, Detroit, Mich. BR/TR, 6′3″, 205 lbs. Deb: 4/20/50

YEAR	TM/L	W	L	PCT	G	GS	CG	SH	SV	IP	H	HR	BB	SO	RAT	ERA	ERA+	OAV	OOB	BH	AVG	PB	PR	/A	PD	TPI
1950	StL-N	0	0	—	5	1	0	0	0	14^2	16	2	3	2	11.7	3.68	117	.281	.317	0	.000	-0	1	1	-0	-0.1
1951	StL-N	7	13	.350	38	26	10	1	1	195	204	15	68	70	12.6	4.43	89	.271	.331	14	.209	0	-10	-10	1	-0.8
1954	StL-N	5	7	.417	25	13	4	0	0	106	101	11	20	55	10.6	3.06	135	.254	.296	4	.148	-1	12	12	0	1.2
1955	StL-N	9	11	.450	30	24	8	2	0	151	143	26	35	66	10.7	3.81	106	.244	.289	8	.182	-0	4	4	-1	0.4
1956	StL-N	9	14	.391	33	29	7	2	0	203	210	27	44	95	11.5	3.59	105	.268	.311	11	.159	-1	4	4	0	0.4
1957	Chi-N	1	7	.125	28	11	1	0	0	84	117	9	22	28	15.1	4.93	79	.330	.372	2	.105	-1	-10	-10	0	-0.9
Total	6	31	52	.373	159	104	30	5	1	753^2	791	90	192	316	11.9	3.93	101	.270	.317	39	.171	-3	1	2	1	0.2

● **JENNINGS POINDEXTER** Poindexter, Chester Jennings "Jinx"
b: 9/30/10, Pauls Valley, Okla. d: 3/3/83, Norman, Okla. BL/TL, 5′10″, 165 lbs. Deb: 9/15/36

YEAR	TM/L	W	L	PCT	G	GS	CG	SH	SV	IP	H	HR	BB	SO	RAT	ERA	ERA+	OAV	OOB	BH	AVG	PB	PR	/A	PD	TPI
1936	Bos-A	0	2	.000	3	3	0	0	0	10^2	13	0	16	2	24.5	6.75	79	.302	.492	0	.000	-1	-2	-2	-0	-0.3
1939	Phi-N	0	0	—	11	1	0	0	0	30^1	29	0	15	12	13.1	4.15	96	.250	.336	2	.200	-0	-1	-0	-0	0.0
Total	2	0	2	.000	14	4	0	0	0	41	42	0	31	14	16.0	4.83	90	.264	.384	2	.143	-1	-3	-2	-0	-0.3

● **LOU POLCHOW** Polchow, Louis William b: 3/14/1881, Mankato, Minn. d: 8/15/12, Good Thunder, Minn 5′9″, Deb: 9/14/02

YEAR	TM/L	W	L	PCT	G	GS	CG	SH	SV	IP	H	HR	BB	SO	RAT	ERA	ERA+	OAV	OOB	BH	AVG	PB	PR	/A	PD	TPI
1902	Cle-A	0	1	.000	1	1	1	0	0	8	9	0	4	2	14.6	5.63	61	.281	.361	0	.000	-1	-2	-2	-0	-0.2

● **DICK POLE** Pole, Richard Henry b: 10/13/50, Trout Creek, Mich. BR/TR, 6′3″, 210 lbs. Deb: 8/3/73 C

YEAR	TM/L	W	L	PCT	G	GS	CG	SH	SV	IP	H	HR	BB	SO	RAT	ERA	ERA+	OAV	OOB	BH	AVG	PB	PR	/A	PD	TPI
1973	Bos-A	3	2	.600	12	7	0	0	0	54^2	70	4	18	24	14.5	5.60	72	.318	.370	0	—	0	-11	-10	-0	-1.1

YEAR	TM/L	W	L	PCT	G	GS	CG	SH	SV	IP	H	HR	BB	SO	RAT	ERA	ERA+	OAV	OOB	BH	AVG	PB	PR	/A	PD	TPI
1974	Bos-A	1	1	.500	15	2	0	0	1	45	55	6	13	32	13.8	4.20	91	.304	.354	0	—	0	-3	-2	1	-0.1
1975	*Bos-A	4	6	.400	18	11	2	1	0	89^2	102	11	32	42	13.7	4.42	92	.290	.352	0	—	0	-6	-3	0	-0.4
1976	Bos-A	6	5	.545	31	15	1	0	0	120^2	131	8	48	49	13.5	4.33	90	.279	.348	0	.000	-0	-11	-6	-1	-0.6
1977	Sea-A	7	12	.368	25	24	3	0	0	122^1	127	16	57	51	14.0	5.15	80	.270	.356	0	—	0	-15	-14	-3	-2.1
1978	Sea-A	4	11	.267	21	18	2	0	0	98^2	122	16	41	41	15.1	6.48	59	.306	.375	0	—	0	-30	-29	-1	-3.8
Total	6	25	37	.403	122	77	8	1	1	531	607	61	209	239	14.1	5.05	79	.290	.359	0	.000	-0	-76	-63	-5	-8.1

● CLIFF POLITTE Politte, Clifford Anthony b: 2/27/74, Kirkwood, Mo. BR/TR, 5'11", 185 lbs. Deb: 4/2/98

YEAR	TM/L	W	L	PCT	G	GS	CG	SH	SV	IP	H	HR	BB	SO	RAT	ERA	ERA+	OAV	OOB	BH	AVG	PB	PR	/A	PD	TPI
1998	StL-N	2	3	.400	8	8	0	0	0	37	45	6	18	22	15.6	6.32	66	.302	.381	1	.071	-1	-9	-9	-0	-1.1

● KEN POLIVKA Polivka, Kenneth Lyle "Soup" b: 1/21/21, Chicago, Ill. d: 7/23/88, Aurora, Ill. BL/TL, 5'10.5", 175 lbs. Deb: 4/18/47

YEAR	TM/L	W	L	PCT	G	GS	CG	SH	SV	IP	H	HR	BB	SO	RAT	ERA	ERA+	OAV	OOB	BH	AVG	PB	PR	/A	PD	TPI
1947	Cin-N	0	0	—	2	0	0	0	0	3	3	0	3	1	18.0	3.00	137	.250	.400	0	—	0	0	0	-0	0.0

● HOWIE POLLET Pollet, Howard Joseph b: 6/26/21, New Orleans, La. d: 8/8/74, Houston, Tex. BL/TL, 6'1.5", 175 lbs. Deb: 8/20/41 C

YEAR	TM/L	W	L	PCT	G	GS	CG	SH	SV	IP	H	HR	BB	SO	RAT	ERA	ERA+	OAV	OOB	BH	AVG	PB	PR	/A	PD	TPI
1941	StL-N	5	2	.714	9	8	6	2	0	70	55	1	27	37	10.7	1.93	195	.212	.289	5	.179	-0	13	14	1	1.5
1942	*StL-N	7	5	.583	27	13	5	2	0	109^1	102	7	39	42	11.8	2.88	119	.242	.309	7	.226	3	5	7	-2	0.8
1943	StL-N†	8	4	.667	16	14	12	5	0	118^1	83	2	32	61	8.9	**1.75**	192	.200	.261	7	.163	-1	21	21	-2	1.9
1946	*StL-N☆	**21**	10	.677	40	32	22	4	5	**266**	228	12	86	107	10.8	**2.10**	**165**	.234	.300	14	.161	-0	**39**	**40**	1	5.1
1947	StL-N	9	11	.450	37	24	9	0	2	176^1	195	11	87	73	14.5	4.34	95	.286	.369	15	.231	2	-5	-4	0	-0.2
1948	StL-N	13	8	.619	36	26	11	0	0	186^1	216	10	67	80	13.8	4.54	90	.289	.349	8	.118	-3	-12	-9	2	-1.1
1949	StL-N★	20	9	.690	39	28	17	**5**	1	230^2	228	9	59	108	11.3	2.77	150	.256	.304	16	.195	1	33	**36**	-2	**4.2**
1950	StL-N	14	13	.519	37	30	14	2	2	232^1	228	19	68	117	11.5	3.29	130	.256	.310	12	.143	-2	22	26	0	2.6
1951	StL-N	0	3	.000	6	2	0	0	1	12^1	10	1	8	10	13.1	4.38	91	.208	.321	0	.000	1	-1	-1	0	0.0
	Pit-N	6	10	.375	21	21	4	1	0	128^2	149	24	51	47	14.1	5.04	84	.294	.360	5	.139	-0	-15	-12	-0	-1.3
	Yr	6	13	.316	27	23	4	1	1	141	159	25	59	57	14.0	4.98	84	.287	.357	5	.135	0	-16	-12	0	-1.3
1952	Pit-N	7	16	.304	31	30	9	1	0	214	217	22	71	90	12.2	4.12	97	.266	.327	13	.191	2	-9	-3	1	0.0
1953	Pit-N	1	1	.500	5	2	0	0	0	12^2	27	2	6	8	23.4	10.66	42	.482	.532	1	.333	0	-9	-9	-0	-1.1
	Chi-N	5	6	.455	25	17	2	0	1	111^1	120	6	44	45	13.3	4.12	108	.271	.338	4	.129	-1	2	4	-1	0.2
	Yr	6	7	.462	30	19	2	0	1	124	147	8	50	53	14.4	4.79	93	.295	.360	5	.147	-1	-7	-5	-1	-0.9
1954	Chi-N	8	10	.444	20	20	4	2	0	128^1	131	4	54	58	13.0	3.58	117	.263	.335	13	.277	2	7	9	-0	1.4
1955	Chi-N	4	3	.571	24	7	1	1	5	61	62	11	27	27	13.1	5.61	73	.265	.341	6	.400	3	-11	-10	1	-0.8
1956	Chi-A	3	1	.750	11	4	0	0	0	26^1	27	2	11	14	13.0	4.10	100	.252	.322	3	.375	1	0	-0	0	0.1
	Pit-N	0	4	.000	19	0	0	0	3	23^1	18	3	8	10	10.0	3.09	122	.212	.280	0	.000	0	2	2	0	0.4
Total	14	131	116	.530	403	278	116	25	20	2107^1	2096	146	745	934	12.2	3.51	113	.260	.324	129	.185	7	82	111	0	13.7

● DALE POLLEY Polley, Ezra Dale b: 8/9/65, Georgetown, Ky. BR/TL, 6', 165 lbs. Deb: 6/23/96

YEAR	TM/L	W	L	PCT	G	GS	CG	SH	SV	IP	H	HR	BB	SO	RAT	ERA	ERA+	OAV	OOB	BH	AVG	PB	PR	/A	PD	TPI
1996	NY-A	1	3	.250	32	0	0	0	0	21^2	23	5	11	14	15.4	7.89	63	.264	.366	0	—	0	-7	-7	0	-1.1

● LOU POLLI Polli, Louis Americo "Crip" b: 7/9/01, Barre, Vt. BR/TR, 5'10.5", 165 lbs. Deb: 4/18/32

YEAR	TM/L	W	L	PCT	G	GS	CG	SH	SV	IP	H	HR	BB	SO	RAT	ERA	ERA+	OAV	OOB	BH	AVG	PB	PR	/A	PD	TPI
1932	StL-A	0	0	—	5	0	0	0	0	6^2	13	0	3	5	21.6	5.40	90	.406	.457	1	.500	0	-1	-0	-0	0.0
1944	NY-N	0	2	.000	19	0	0	0	3	35^2	42	3	20	6	15.6	4.54	81	.294	.380	0	.000	-1	-4	-3	-0	-0.4
Total	2	0	2	.000	24	0	0	0	3	42^1	55	3	23	11	16.6	4.68	82	.314	.394	1	.125	-1	-4	-4	-1	-0.4

● JOHN POLONI Poloni, John Paul b: 2/28/54, Dearborn, Mich. BL/TL, 6'5", 210 lbs. Deb: 9/16/77

YEAR	TM/L	W	L	PCT	G	GS	CG	SH	SV	IP	H	HR	BB	SO	RAT	ERA	ERA+	OAV	OOB	BH	AVG	PB	PR	/A	PD	TPI
1977	Tex-A	1	0	1.000	2	1	0	0	0	7	8	1	1	5	11.6	6.43	63	.286	.310	0	—	0	-2	-2	-0	-0.3

● JOHN POMORSKI Pomorski, John Leon b: 12/30/05, Brooklyn, N.Y. d: 12/6/77, Brampton, Ont., Can. BR/TR, 6', 178 lbs. Deb: 4/17/34

YEAR	TM/L	W	L	PCT	G	GS	CG	SH	SV	IP	H	HR	BB	SO	RAT	ERA	ERA+	OAV	OOB	BH	AVG	PB	PR	/A	PD	TPI
1934	Chi-A	0	0	—	3	0	0	0	0	1^2	1	0	2	0	16.2	5.40	88	.143	.333	0	—	0	-0	-0	0	0.0

● ARLIE POND Pond, Erasmus Arlington b: 1/19/1872, Rutland, Vt. d: 9/19/30, Cebu, Philippines BR/TR, 5'10", 160 lbs. Deb: 7/4/1895

YEAR	TM/L	W	L	PCT	G	GS	CG	SH	SV	IP	H	HR	BB	SO	RAT	ERA	ERA+	OAV	OOB	BH	AVG	PB	PR	/A	PD	TPI
1895	Bal-N	0	1	.000	6	1	1	0	2	13^2	10	0	12	13	15.1	5.93	80	.200	.365	2	.333	1	-2	-2	0	-0.1
1896	Bal-N	16	8	.667	28	26	21	2	0	214^1	232	4	57	80	12.4	3.49	123	.274	.324	19	.235	0	21	19	-2	1.5
1897	Bal-N	18	9	.667	32	28	23	0	0	248	267	4	72	59	12.8	3.52	119	.273	.332	22	.244	2	22	18	-1	1.6
1898	Bal-N	1	1	.500	3	2	1	1	0	20	8	0	9	4	8.5	0.45	796	.123	.250	2	.286	1	7	7	-1	0.7
Total	4	35	19	.648	69	57	46	3	2	496	517	8	150	156	12.5	3.45	122	.266	.327	45	.245	3	48	42	-3	3.7

● ELMER PONDER Ponder, Charles Elmer b: 6/26/1893, Reed, Okla. d: 4/20/74, Albuquerque, N.Mex BR/TR, 6', 178 lbs. Deb: 9/18/17

YEAR	TM/L	W	L	PCT	G	GS	CG	SH	SV	IP	H	HR	BB	SO	RAT	ERA	ERA+	OAV	OOB	BH	AVG	PB	PR	/A	PD	TPI
1917	Pit-N	1	1	.500	3	2	1	1	0	21^1	12	0	6	11	8.0	1.69	168	.167	.241	0	.000	-1	2	3	-1	0.0
1919	Pit-N	0	5	.000	9	5	0	0	0	47^1	55	0	6	6	12.2	3.99	76	.297	.330	2	.133	-1	-6	-5	-1	-0.7
1920	Pit-N	11	15	.423	33	23	13	2	0	196	182	3	40	62	10.3	2.62	123	.246	.286	7	.119	-4	11	13	1	1.3
1921	Pit-N	2	0	1.000	8	1	1	0	0	24^2	29	1	3	3	11.7	2.19	175	.305	.327	0	.000	-2	4	5	0	0.2
	Chi-N	3	6	.333	16	11	5	0	0	89^1	117	7	17	31	13.8	4.74	81	.321	.356	4	.121	-2	-9	-9	2	-0.9
	Yr	5	6	.455	24	12	6	0	0	114	146	8	20	34	13.3	4.18	91	.317	.350	4	.093	-4	-5	-5	2	-0.7
Total	4	17	27	.386	69	42	20	3	0	378^2	395	11	72	113	11.3	3.21	105	.271	.309	13	.105	-10	3	6	0	-0.1

● SIDNEY PONSON Ponson, Sidney Alton b: 11/2/76, Noord, Aruba BR/TR, 6'1", 220 lbs. Deb: 4/19/98

YEAR	TM/L	W	L	PCT	G	GS	CG	SH	SV	IP	H	HR	BB	SO	RAT	ERA	ERA+	OAV	OOB	BH	AVG	PB	PR	/A	PD	TPI
1998	Bal-A	8	9	.471	31	20	0	0	1	135	157	19	42	85	13.5	5.27	86	.293	.348	2	.500	1	-9	-11	-1	-1.2

● ED POOLE Poole, Edward I. b: 9/7/1874, Canton, Ohio d: 3/11/19, Malvern, Ohio BR/TR, 5'10", 175 lbs. Deb: 10/6/00 ♦

YEAR	TM/L	W	L	PCT	G	GS	CG	SH	SV	IP	H	HR	BB	SO	RAT	ERA	ERA+	OAV	OOB	BH	AVG	PB	PR	/A	PD	TPI
1900	Pit-N	1	0	1.000	1	0	0	0	0	7	4	0	0	3	5.1	1.29	283	.167	.167	2	.500	1	2	2	0	0.4
1901	Pit-N	5	4	.556	12	10	8	1	0	80	78	3	30	26	12.8	3.60	91	.254	.332	16	.205	1	-2	-3	0	-0.2
1902	Pit-N	0	0	—	1	0	0	0	0	8	7	0	3	2	11.3	1.13	243	.233	.303	1	.250	0	1	1	-0	0.0
	Cin-N	12	4	.750	16	16	16	2	0	138	129	2	54	55	12.5	2.15	139	.248	.328	7	.115	-4	10	13	-0	1.0
	Yr	12	4	.750	17	16	16	2	0	146	136	2	57	57	12.4	2.10	142	.247	.326	8	.123	-4	11	14	-0	1.0
1903	Cin-N	7	13	.350	25	21	18	1	0	184	188	4	77	73	13.5	3.28	109	.270	.352	17	.243	0	-0	6	2	0.7
1904	Bro-N	8	14	.364	25	23	19	1	1	178	178	4	74	67	13.1	3.39	81	.268	.349	8	.129	-3	-13	-13	3	-1.5
Total	5	33	35	.485	80	70	61	5	1	595	584	13	238	226	12.9	3.04	103	.260	.340	51	.183	-6	-2	6	6	0.4

● JIM POOLE Poole, James Richard b: 4/28/66, Rochester, N.Y. BL/TL, 6'2", 203 lbs. Deb: 6/15/90

YEAR	TM/L	W	L	PCT	G	GS	CG	SH	SV	IP	H	HR	BB	SO	RAT	ERA	ERA+	OAV	OOB	BH	AVG	PB	PR	/A	PD	TPI
1990	LA-N	0	0	—	16	0	0	0	0	10^2	7	1	8	6	12.7	4.22	87	.184	.326	0	—	0	-1	-1	-0	0.0
1991	Tex-A	0	0	—	5	0	0	0	1	6	10	0	3	4	19.5	4.50	90	.370	.433	0	—	0	-0	-0	-0	0.1
	Bal-A	3	2	.600	24	0	0	0	0	36	19	3	9	34	7.0	2.00	198	.157	.215	0	—	0	8	8	0	1.4
	Yr	3	2	.600	29	0	0	0	1	42	29	3	12	38	8.8	2.36	168	.195	.255	0	—	0	8	7	0	1.5
1992	Bal-A	0	0	—	6	0	0	0	0	3^1	3	0	1	3	10.8	0.00	—	.231	.286	0	—	0	1	1	0	-0.1
1993	Bal-A	2	1	.667	55	0	0	0	2	50^1	30	2	21	29	9.1	2.15	208	.175	.266	0	—	0	12	13	0	0.5
1994	Bal-A	1	0	1.000	38	0	0	0	0	20^1	32	4	11	18	19.0	6.64	75	.372	.443	0	—	0	-4	-4	1	-0.3
1995	*Cle-A	3	3	.500	42	0	0	0	0	50^1	40	7	17	41	10.5	3.75	125	.217	.291	0	—	0	5	5	0	0.5
1996	Cle-A	4	0	1.000	32	0	0	0	0	26^2	29	3	14	19	14.5	3.04	161	.274	.358	0	—	0	6	5	1	0.7
	SF-N	2	1	.667	35	0	0	0	0	23^2	15	2	13	19	11.0	2.66	154	.188	.309	0	.000	-0	4	4	1	0.5
1997	SF-N	3	1	.750	63	0	0	0	0	49^1	73	6	25	26	18.6	7.11	58	.353	.432	0	—	0	-16	-16	-1	-1.2
1998	SF-N	1	3	.250	26	0	0	0	0	32^1	38	5	9	16	13.1	5.29	77	.302	.348	1	.250	0	-4	-4	0	-0.4
	*Cle-A	0	0	—	12	0	0	0	0	7	9	0	3	11	16.7	5.14	93	.300	.382	0	—	0	0	-0	0	0.0
Total	9	19	11	.633	354	0	0	0	3	316	305	33	134	226	12.7	4.04	108	.257	.336	1	.167	0	12	11	2	1.7

● TOM POORMAN Poorman, Thomas Iverson b: 10/14/1857, Lock Haven, Pa. d: 2/18/05, Lock Haven, Pa. BL/TR, 5'7", 135 lbs. Deb: 5/5/1880 ♦

YEAR	TM/L	W	L	PCT	G	GS	CG	SH	SV	IP	H	HR	BB	SO	RAT	ERA	ERA+	OAV	OOB	BH	AVG	PB	PR	/A	PD	TPI
1880	Buf-N	1	8	.111	11	9	9	0	1	85	117	3	19	13	14.4	4.13	59	.307	.340	11	.157	-3	-17	-16	1	-1.6
	Chi-N	2	0	1.000	2	1	0	0	0	15	12	0	8	0	12.0	2.40	101	.203	.299	5	.200	0	-0	0	-1	-0.1
	Yr	3	8	.273	13	10	9	0	1	100	129	3	27	13	14.0	3.87	63	.293	.334	16	.168	-3	-17	-16	0	-1.7
1884	Tol-a	0	1	.000	1	1	1	0	0	9	13	1	2	0	15.0	3.00	114	.310	.341	89	.233	0	0	0	0	0.0
1887	Phi-a	0	0	—	1	0	0	0	0	0^2	5	1	1	1	81.0	40.50	11	.714	.750	155	.265	0	-3	-3	0	0.0
Total	3	3	9	.250	15	11	10	0	1	109^2	147	5	30	14	14.5	4.02	63	.301	.341	498	.244	-2	-19	-18	0	-1.7

YEAR	TM/L	W	L	PCT	G	GS	CG	SH	SV	IP	H	HR	BB	SO	RAT	ERA	ERA+	OAV	OOB	BH	AVG	PB	PR	/A	PD	TPI
● BILL POPP	Popp, William Peter b: 6/7/1877, St.Louis, Mo. d: 9/5/09, St.Louis, Mo. TR, 5'10.5", 170 lbs. Deb: 4/19/02																									
1902	StL-N	2	6	.250	9	7	5	0	0	60^1	87	2	26	20	17.6	4.92	56	.336	.407	1	.048	-3	-14	-15	1	-1.8
● ED PORRAY	Porray, Edmund Joseph b: 12/5/1888, AtSea On Atlantic Ocean d: 7/13/54, Lackawaxen, Pa. BR/TR, 5'11", 170 lbs. Deb: 4/17/14																									
1914	Buf-F	0	1	.000	3	3	0	0	0	10^1	18	2	7	0	21.8	4.35	68	.391	.472	0	.000	-1	-2	-2	1	-0.2
● CHUCK PORTER	Porter, Charles William b: 1/12/56, Baltimore, Md. BR/TR, 6'3", 188 lbs. Deb: 9/14/81																									
1981	Mil-A	0	0	—	3	0	0	0	0	4^1	6	0	1	1	14.5	4.15	82	.316	.350	0	—	0	-0	-0	-0	0.0
1982	Mil-A	0	0	—	3	0	0	0	0	3^2	3	0	1	3	9.8	4.91	77	.250	.308	0	—	0	-0	-0	-0	0.0
1983	Mil-A	7	9	.438	25	21	6	1	0	134	162	9	38	76	13.6	4.50	83	.298	.346	0	—	0	-7	-11	0	-1.0
1984	Mil-A	6	4	.600	17	12	1	0	0	81^1	92	8	12	48	11.5	3.87	99	.284	.310	0	—	0	1	-0	0	0.0
1985	Mil-A	0	0	—	6	1	0	0	0	13^2	15	1	2	8	11.2	1.98	211	.273	.298	0	—	0	3	3	-0	0.0
Total	5	13	13	.500	54	34	7	1	0	237	278	18	54	136	12.7	4.14	92	.291	.331	0	—	0	-3	-9	-0	-1.0
● HENRY PORTER	Porter, Henry b: 6/1858, Vergennes, Vt. d: 12/30/06, Brockton, Mass. BR/TR, Deb: 9/27/1884																									
1884	Mil-U	3	3	.500	6	6	6	1	0	51	32	1	9	71	7.2	3.00	44	.168	.205	11	.275	1	-3	-9	1	-0.7
1885	Bro-a	33	21	.611	54	54	53	2	0	481^2	427	11	107	197	10.3	2.78	118	.223	.270	40	.205	-2	25	27	3	2.6
1886	Bro-a	27	19	.587	48	48	48	1	0	424	439	8	120	163	12.0	3.42	102	.252	.303	33	.179	-9	2	3	-2	-0.7
1887	Bro-a	15	24	.385	40	40	38	1	0	339^2	416	7	96	74	13.8	4.21	102	.297	.345	29	.199	-3	3	3	-2	-0.1
1888	KC-a	18	37	.327	55	54	53	4	0	474	527	16	120	145	12.7	4.16	83	.272	.321	28	.144	-13	-58	-38	4	-4.3
1889	KC-a	0	3	.000	4	4	3	0	0	23	52	0	14	9	26.2	12.52	33	.433	.496	1	.100	-1	-22	-21	0	-1.8
Total	6	96	107	.473	207	206	201	9	0	1793^1	1893	43	466	659	12.1	3.70	95	.259	.308	142	.184	-27	-53	-35	3	-5.0
● NED PORTER	Porter, Ned Swindell b: 5/6/05, Apalachicola, Fla. d: 6/30/68, Gainesville, Fla. BR/TR, 6', 173 lbs. Deb: 8/7/26																									
1926	NY-N	0	0	—	2	0	0	0	0	2	2	1	0	1	9.0	4.50	83	.250	.250	0	—	0	-0	-0	-0	0.0
1927	NY-N	0	0	—	1	0	0	0	0	2	3	0	1	0	18.0	0.00	—	.333	.400	0	—	0	1	1	-0	0.0
Total	2	0	0	—	3	0	0	0	0	4	5	1	1	1	13.5	2.25	169	.294	.333	0	—	0	1	1	-0	0.0
● ODIE PORTER	Porter, Odie Oscar b: 5/24/1877, Borden, Ind. d: 5/2/03, Borden, Ind. TL, Deb: 6/16/02																									
1902	Phi-A	0	1	.000	1	1	1	0	0	8	12	0	5	2	19.1	3.38	109	.343	.425	0	.000	-0	0	0	0	0.0
● BOB PORTERFIELD	Porterfield, Erwin Coolidge b: 8/10/23, Newport, Va. d: 4/28/80, Sealy, Tex. BR/TR, 6', 190 lbs. Deb: 8/8/48																									
1948	NY-A	5	3	.625	16	12	2	1	0	78	85	5	34	30	13.7	4.50	91	.273	.345	6	.250	0	-2	-4	-1	-0.4
1949	NY-A	2	5	.286	12	8	3	0	0	57^2	53	3	29	25	13.0	4.06	100	.251	.344	1	.053	-2	1	-0	-1	-0.2
1950	NY-A	1	1	.500	10	2	0	0	1	19^2	28	2	8	9	16.5	8.69	49	.341	.400	1	.333	1	-9	-10	-0	-0.9
1951	NY-A	0	0	—	2	0	0	0	0	3	5	0	3	2	24.0	15.00	26	.385	.500	0	—	0	-4	-4	0	0.0
	Was-A	9	8	.529	19	19	10	3	0	133^1	109	8	54	53	11.0	3.24	126	.224	.302	6	.130	-3	13	13	-0	1.1
	Yr	9	8	.529	21	19	10	3	0	136^1	114	8	57	55	11.3	3.50	117	.228	.308	6	.130	-3	9	9	-0	1.1
1952	Was-A	13	14	.481	31	29	15	3	0	231^1	222	7	85	80	12.1	2.72	131	.254	.323	15	.190	0	24	21	-3	2.2
1953	Was-A	**22**	10	.688	34	32	**24**	**9**	0	255	243	19	73	77	11.2	3.35	116	.257	.310	25	.255	8	18	15	2	2.9
1954	Was-A★	13	15	.464	32	31	**21**	2	0	244	249	14	77	82	12.1	3.32	107	.266	.324	9	.102	-3	11	6	3	0.7
1955	Was-A	10	17	.370	30	27	8	2	0	178	197	14	54	74	12.8	4.45	86	.282	.335	12	.190	1	-10	-12	-1	-1.6
1956	Bos-A	3	12	.200	25	18	4	1	0	126	127	21	64	53	13.7	5.14	90	.260	.347	14	.326	3	-14	-7	-2	-0.6
1957	Bos-A	4	4	.500	28	9	3	1	1	102^1	107	8	30	28	12.1	4.05	99	.272	.325	5	.172	-0	-3	-1	1	0.0
1958	Bos-A	0	0	—	2	0	0	0	0	4	3	1	0	1	6.8	4.50	89	.214	.214	0	—	0	-0	-0	-0	0.0
	Pit-N	4	6	.400	37	6	2	1	5	87^2	78	7	19	39	10.1	3.29	118	.241	.285	1	.050	-1	6	6	-0	0.6
1959	Pit-N	0	0	—	6	0	0	0	0	5^1	6	1	2	1	13.5	1.69	229	.286	.348	0	—	0	1	1	-0	0.0
	Chi-N	0	0	—	4	0	0	0	0	6^1	14	1	3	0	24.2	11.37	35	.424	.472	0	.000	-0	-5	-5	0	0.0
	Pit-N	1	2	.333	30	0	0	0	1	36	45	2	17	18	15.5	4.75	81	.321	.395	0	.000	-0	-3	-4	1	-0.2
	Yr	1	2	.333	40	0	0	0	1	47^2	65	4	22	19	16.4	5.29	73	.335	.403	0	.000	-0	-7	-7	1	-0.2
Total	12	87	97	.473	318	193	92	23	8	1567^2	1571	113	552	572	12.3	3.79	102	.263	.327	95	.184	4	26	16	0	3.6
● AL PORTO	Porto, Alfred "Lefty" b: 6/27/26, Heilwood, Pa. BL/TL, 5'11", 176 lbs. Deb: 4/22/48																									
1948	Phi-N	0	0	—	3	0	0	0	0	4	2	0	1	1	6.8	0.00	—	.143	.200	0	—	0	2	2	-0	0.0
● ARNIE PORTOCARRERO	Portocarrero, Arnold Mario b: 7/5/31, New York, N.Y. d: 6/21/86, Kansas City, Kan. BR/TR, 6'3", 196 lbs. Deb: 4/18/54																									
1954	Phi-A	9	18	.333	34	33	16	1	0	248	233	25	114	132	12.8	4.06	96	.249	.334	8	.107	-2	-9	-4	-4	-1.0
1955	KC-A	5	9	.357	24	20	4	1	0	111^1	109	12	67	34	14.6	4.77	88	.259	.366	4	.108	-1	-10	-7	-1	-1.0
1956	KC-A	0	1	.000	3	1	0	0	0	8	9	2	7	2	18.0	10.13	43	.300	.432	0	.000	-0	-5	-5	-0	-0.5
1957	KC-A	4	9	.308	33	17	1	0	0	114^2	103	10	34	42	11.0	3.92	101	.240	.300	3	.107	-1	-2	0	-1	-0.2
1958	Bal-A	15	11	.577	32	27	10	3	2	204^2	173	17	57	90	10.2	3.25	110	.229	.286	11	.164	0	12	8	-3	0.7
1959	Bal-A	2	7	.222	27	14	1	0	0	90	107	10	32	23	14.1	6.80	56	.294	.354	0	.000	-3	-29	-30	1	-2.8
1960	Bal-A	3	2	.600	13	5	1	0	0	40^2	44	6	9	15	11.7	4.43	86	.275	.314	0	.000	-1	-2	-3	-1	-0.5
Total	7	38	57	.400	166	117	33	5	2	817^1	778	82	320	338	12.3	4.32	89	.252	.325	26	.108	-9	-47	-42	-9	-5.3
● MARK PORTUGAL	Portugal, Mark Steven b: 10/30/62, Los Angeles, Cal. BR/TR, 6', 190 lbs. Deb: 8/14/85																									
1985	Min-A	1	3	.250	6	4	0	0	0	24^1	24	3	14	12	14.1	5.55	79	.270	.369	0	—	0	-4	-3	1	-0.4
1986	Min-A	6	10	.375	27	15	3	0	1	112^2	112	10	50	67	13.0	4.31	100	.265	.345	0	—	0	-2	-0	-0	-0.1
1987	Min-A	1	3	.250	13	7	0	0	0	44	58	13	24	28	17.0	7.77	59	.326	.409	0	—	0	-16	-15	0	-1.2
1988	Min-A	3	3	.500	26	0	0	0	3	57^2	60	11	17	31	12.2	4.53	90	.274	.329	0	—	0	-4	-3	-2	-0.6
1989	Hou-N	7	1	.875	20	15	2	1	0	108	91	7	37	86	10.8	2.75	123	.232	.302	7	.206	3	9	8	0	0.9
1990	Hou-N	11	10	.524	32	32	1	0	0	196^2	187	21	67	136	11.8	3.62	103	.250	.315	9	.136	-1	4	2	-0	0.1
1991	Hou-N	10	12	.455	32	27	1	0	1	168^1	163	19	59	120	12.0	4.49	78	.256	.321	9	.196	3	-15	-18	-1	-2.0
1992	Hou-N	6	3	.667	18	16	1	1	0	101^1	76	7	41	62	10.5	2.66	126	.213	.296	3	.107	-1	9	8	0	0.6
1993	Hou-N	18	4	**.818**	33	33	1	1	0	208	194	10	77	131	11.9	2.77	140	.248	.319	15	.231	4	29	25	1	3.0
1994	SF-N	10	8	.556	21	21	1	0	0	137^1	135	17	45	87	12.2	3.93	102	.260	.326	17	.354	8	4	1	-2	0.8
1995	SF-N	5	5	.500	17	17	1	0	0	104	106	10	34	63	12.3	4.15	98	.262	.323	3	.103	-0	0	-1	-1	-0.2
	*Cin-N	6	5	.545	14	14	0	0	0	77^2	79	7	22	33	11.9	3.82	108	.262	.317	5	.172	2	3	3	-1	0.4
	Yr	11	10	.524	31	31	1	0	0	181^2	185	17	56	96	12.0	4.01	102	.262	.318	8	.138	1	3	2	-2	0.2
1996	Cin-N	8	9	.471	27	26	1	1	0	156	146	20	42	93	11.0	3.98	106	.248	.300	8	.167	-0	4	4	-2	0.3
1997	Phi-N	0	2	.000	3	3	0	0	0	13^2	17	0	5	2	14.5	4.61	92	.321	.379	0	.000	-0	-1	-1	-0	-0.1
1998	Phi-N	10	5	.667	26	26	3	0	0	166^1	186	26	32	104	12.0	4.44	98	.283	.320	13	.260	4	-4	-1	-0	0.3
Total	14	102	83	.551	315	256	15	4	5	1676	1634	181	566	1055	12.0	3.89	101	.257	.321	89	.199	20	18	7	-6	1.8
● BILL POSEDEL	Posedel, William John "Sailor Bill" or "Barnacle Bill" b: 8/2/06, San Francisco, Cal. d: 11/28/89, Livermore, Cal. BR/TR, 5'11", 175 lbs. Deb: 4/23/38 C																									
1938	Bro-N	8	9	.471	33	17	6	1	1	140	178	14	46	49	14.5	5.66	69	.311	.365	10	.227	1	-29	-27	-1	-2.9
1939	Bos-N	15	13	.536	33	29	18	5	0	220^2	221	8	78	73	12.2	3.92	94	.268	.331	8	.110	-4	0	-5	-1	-1.1
1940	Bos-N	12	17	.414	35	32	18	0	1	233	263	16	81	86	13.3	4.13	90	.288	.346	14	.171	1	-7	-11	-0	-1.1
1941	Bos-N	4	4	.500	18	9	3	0	0	57^1	61	6	30	10	14.4	4.87	73	.279	.368	8	.320	2	-8	-8	-0	-0.8
1946	Bos-N	2	0	1.000	19	0	0	0	4	28^1	34	4	13	9	14.9	6.99	49	.304	.376	0	.000	-0	-11	-11	-0	-1.2
Total	5	41	43	.488	138	87	45	6	6	679^1	757	48	248	227	13.4	4.56	82	.286	.349	40	.176	0	-55	-63	-4	-7.1
● BOB POSER	Poser, John Falk b: 3/16/10, Columbus, Wis. BL/TR, 6', 173 lbs. Deb: 4/17/32																									
1932	Chi-A	0	0	—	1	0	0	0	0	0^2	3	0	2	1	67.5	27.00	16	.600	.714	0	.000	-0	-2	-2	0	0.0
1935	StL-A	1	1	.500	4	1	0	0	0	13^2	26	0	4	1	19.8	9.22	52	.400	.435	1	.250	0	-7	-7	-1	-0.8
Total	2	1	1	.500	5	1	0	0	0	14^1	29	0	6	2	22.0	10.05	47	.414	.461	1	.143	0	-9	-8	-1	-0.8
● LOU POSSEHL	Possehl, Louis Thomas b: 4/12/26, Chicago, Ill. d: 10/7/97, Sarasota, Fla. BR/TR, 6'2", 180 lbs. Deb: 8/25/46 F																									
1946	Phi-N	1	2	.333	4	4	0	0	0	13^2	19	0	10	4	19.8	5.93	58	.339	.448	0	.000	-0	-4	-4	0	-0.7
1947	Phi-N	0	0	—	2	0	0	0	0	4^1	5	0	0	1	12.5	4.15	96	.385	.429	0	—	0	-0	-0	0	0.1
1948	Phi-N	1	1	.500	3	2	1	0	0	14^2	17	3	4	7	12.9	4.91	80	.304	.350	1	.250	0	-2	-2	0	-0.2

YEAR	TM/L	W	L	PCT	G	GS	CG	SH	SV	IP	H	HR	BB	SO	RAT	ERA	ERA+	OAV	OOB	BH	AVG	PB	PR	/A	PD	TPI
1951	Phi-N	0	1	.000	2	1	0	0	0	6	9	0	3	6	18.0	6.00	64	.333	.400	0	.000	-0	-1	-1	0	-0.2
1952	Phi-N	0	1	.000	4	1	0	0	0	12^2	12	3	7	4	13.5	4.97	73	.235	.328	0	.000	-0	-2	-2	-0	-0.2
Total	5	2	5	.286	15	8	1	0	0	51^1	62	6	24	22	15.4	5.26	71	.305	.384	1	.100	-0	-9	-9	0	-1.2

● NELLIE POTT

Pott, Nelson Adolph "Lefty" b: 7/16/1899, Cincinnati, Ohio d: 12/3/63, Cincinnati, Ohio BL/TL, 6', 185 lbs. Deb: 4/19/22

YEAR	TM/L	W	L	PCT	G	GS	CG	SH	SV	IP	H	HR	BB	SO	RAT	ERA	ERA+	OAV	OOB	BH	AVG	PB	PR	/A	PD	TPI
1922	Cle-A	0	0	—	2	0	0	0	0	2	7	1	2	0	40.5	31.50	13	.583	.643	0	—	0	-6	-6	-0	0.0

● DYKES POTTER

Potter, Maryland Dykes b: 9/7/10, Ashland, Ky. BR/TR, 6', 185 lbs. Deb: 4/26/38 F

YEAR	TM/L	W	L	PCT	G	GS	CG	SH	SV	IP	H	HR	BB	SO	RAT	ERA	ERA+	OAV	OOB	BH	AVG	PB	PR	/A	PD	TPI
1938	Bro-N	0	0	—	2	0	0	0	0	2	4	1	0	1	18.0	4.50	87	.400	.400	0	—	0	-0	-0	-0	0.0

● NELS POTTER

Potter, Nelson Thomas "Nellie" b: 8/23/11, Mt.Morris, Ill. d: 9/30/90, Mt.Morris, Ill. BL/TR, 5'11", 180 lbs. Deb: 4/25/36

YEAR	TM/L	W	L	PCT	G	GS	CG	SH	SV	IP	H	HR	BB	SO	RAT	ERA	ERA+	OAV	OOB	BH	AVG	PB	PR	/A	PD	TPI
1936	StL-N	0	0	—	1	0	0	0	0	1	0	0	0	0	0.0	0.00	—	.000	.000	0	—	0	0	0	-0	0.0
1938	Phi-A	2	12	.143	35	9	4	0	5	111^1	139	15	49	43	15.4	6.47	75	.306	.376	10	.256	1	-21	-20	-1	-2.1
1939	Phi-A	8	12	.400	41	25	9	0	2	196^1	258	26	88	60	16.1	6.60	71	.321	.391	12	.179	-1	-43	-41	-0	-3.5
1940	Phi-A	9	14	.391	31	25	13	0	0	200^2	213	18	71	73	12.8	4.44	100	.269	.330	18	.254	2	-1	0	-0	0.2
1941	Phi-A	1	1	.500	10	3	1	0	2	23^1	35	3	16	7	19.7	9.26	45	.337	.425	1	.167	0	-13	-13	0	-1.1
	Bos-A	2	0	1.000	10	0	0	0	0	20	21	0	16	6	16.6	4.50	93	.284	.411	0	.000	-0	-1	-1	-0	-0.1
	Yr	3	1	.750	20	3	1	0	2	43^1	56	3	32	13	18.3	7.06	59	.315	.419	1	.111	0	-14	-14	-0	-1.2
1943	StL-A	10	5	.667	33	13	8	0	1	168^1	146	11	54	80	10.9	2.78	120	.235	.299	8	.145	-1	10	10	1	0.9
1944	*StL-A	19	7	.731	32	29	16	3	0	232	211	6	70	91	10.9	2.83	127	.244	.301	13	.159	-2	15	20	2	2.1
1945	StL-A	15	11	.577	32	32	21	3	0	255^1	212	10	68	129	9.9	2.47	143	.226	.279	28	.304	4	25	30	-1	3.5
1946	StL-A	8	9	.471	23	19	10	0	0	145	152	9	59	72	13.3	3.72	100	.268	.340	12	.231	2	-4	0	-1	0.2
1947	StL-A	4	10	.286	32	10	3	0	2	122^2	130	13	44	65	12.9	4.04	96	.277	.342	9	.257	3	-5	-2	1	0.2
1948	StL-A	1	1	.500	2	2	0	0	0	10^1	11	1	4	4	14.8	5.23	87	.262	.354	2	.500	1	-1	-1	1	0.0
	Phi-A	2	2	.500	8	0	0	0	1	18	17	1	5	13	11.0	4.00	107	.250	.301	1	.250	0	1	1	-0	0.1
	Yr	3	3	.500	10	2	0	0	1	28^1	28	2	9	17	11.8	4.45	99	.250	.306	3	.375	1	-0	-0	0	0.1
	*Bos-N	5	2	.714	18	7	3	0	2	85	77	4	8	47	9.0	2.33	165	.245	.264	11	.379	3	15	14	1	1.6
1949	Bos-N	6	11	.353	41	3	1	0	7	96^2	99	6	30	57	12.1	4.19	90	.265	.321	3	.130	-0	-2	-4	1	-0.7
Total	12	92	97	.487	349	177	89	6	22	1686	1721	123	582	747	12.4	3.99	99	.265	.328	128	.228	11	-23	-6	3	1.3

● SQUIRE POTTER

Potter, Robert b: 3/18/02, Flatwoods, Ky. d: 1/27/83, Ashland, Ky. BR/TR, 6'1", 185 lbs. Deb: 8/7/23 F

YEAR	TM/L	W	L	PCT	G	GS	CG	SH	SV	IP	H	HR	BB	SO	RAT	ERA	ERA+	OAV	OOB	BH	AVG	PB	PR	/A	PD	TPI
1923	Was-A	0	0	—	1	0	0	0	0	3	11	0	4	1	45.0	21.00	18	.688	.750	0	—	0	-6	-6	-0	0.0

● MIKE POTTS

Potts, Michael Larry b: 9/5/70, Langdale, Ala. BL/TL, 5'9", 179 lbs. Deb: 4/6/96

YEAR	TM/L	W	L	PCT	G	GS	CG	SH	SV	IP	H	HR	BB	SO	RAT	ERA	ERA+	OAV	OOB	BH	AVG	PB	PR	/A	PD	TPI
1996	Mil-A	1	2	.333	24	0	0	0	1	45^1	58	7	30	21	17.5	7.15	73	.319	.415	0	—	0	-11	-10	-1	-0.7

● BILL POUNDS

Pounds, Jeared Wells b: 3/11/1878, Paterson, N.J. d: 7/7/36, Paterson, N.J. BR/TR, 5'10.5", 178 lbs. Deb: 5/2/03

YEAR	TM/L	W	L	PCT	G	GS	CG	SH	SV	IP	H	HR	BB	SO	RAT	ERA	ERA+	OAV	OOB	BH	AVG	PB	PR	/A	PD	TPI
1903	Cle-A	0	0	—	1	0	0	0	0	5	8	0	0	2	14.4	10.80	26	.364	.364	1	.500	1	-4	-4	-0	0.1
	Bro-N	0	0	—	1	0	0	0	0	6	8	1	2	2	15.0	6.00	53	.348	.400	2	.667	1	-2	-2	0	0.1
Total	1	0	0	—	2	0	0	0	0	11	16	1	2	4	14.7	8.18	37	.356	.383	3	.600	1	-6	-6	0	0.2

● ABNER POWELL

Powell, Charles Abner "Ab" b: 12/15/1860, Shenandoah, Pa. d: 8/7/53, New Orleans, La. BL/TR, 5'7", 160 lbs. Deb: 8/4/1884 ♦

YEAR	TM/L	W	L	PCT	G	GS	CG	SH	SV	IP	H	HR	BB	SO	RAT	ERA	ERA+	OAV	OOB	BH	AVG	PB	PR	/A	PD	TPI
1884	Was-U	6	12	.333	18	17	14	1	0	134	135	3	19	78	10.3	3.43	70	.245	.270	54	.283	0	-15	-15	2	-1.4
1886	Bal-a	2	5	.286	7	7	7	0	0	60	66	2	26	15	14.0	5.10	67	.264	.336	7	.179	-1	-11	-11	2	-0.9
	Cin-a	0	1	.000	4	1	1	0	0	15^1	16	0	9	4	14.7	4.70	75	.271	.368	17	.230	-0	-2	-2	-0	-0.1
	Yr	2	6	.250	11	8	8	0	0	75^1	82	2	35	19	14.0	5.02	69	.265	.339	24	.212	-1	-13	-13	1	-1.0
Total	2	8	18	.308	29	25	22	1	0	209^1	217	5	54	97	11.7	4.00	69	.252	.297	78	.257	-1	-28	-29	3	-2.4

● DENNIS POWELL

Powell, Dennis Clay b: 8/13/63, Moultrie, Ga. BR/TL, 6'3", 200 lbs. Deb: 7/7/85

YEAR	TM/L	W	L	PCT	G	GS	CG	SH	SV	IP	H	HR	BB	SO	RAT	ERA	ERA+	OAV	OOB	BH	AVG	PB	PR	/A	PD	TPI
1985	LA-N	1	1	.500	16	2	0	0	1	29^1	30	7	13	19	13.5	5.22	67	.263	.344	0	.000	-0	-5	-6	0	-0.4
1986	LA-N	2	7	.222	27	6	0	0	0	65^1	65	5	25	31	12.5	4.27	81	.272	.343	3	.214	1	-4	-6	-1	-0.7
1987	Sea-A	1	3	.250	16	3	0	0	0	34^1	32	3	15	17	12.3	3.15	150	.250	.329	0	—	0	5	6	0	0.5
1988	Sea-A	1	3	.250	12	2	0	0	0	18^2	29	2	11	15	20.3	8.68	48	.363	.452	0	—	0	-10	-9	0	-1.8
1989	Sea-A	2	2	.500	43	1	0	0	2	45	49	6	21	27	14.4	5.00	81	.285	.369	0	—	0	-6	-5	1	-0.4
1990	Sea-A	0	0	—	2	0	0	0	0	3	5	0	2	0	24.0	9.00	44	.357	.471	0	—	0	-2	-2	-0	-0.1
	Mil-A	0	4	.000	9	7	0	0	0	39^1	59	0	19	23	18.1	6.86	56	.341	.409	0	—	0	-13	-13	1	-1.0
	Yr	0	4	.000	11	7	0	0	0	42^1	64	0	21	23	18.3	7.02	55	.340	.410	0	—	0	-15	-15	1	-1.1
1992	Sea-A	4	2	.667	49	0	0	0	0	57	49	5	29	35	12.8	4.58	87	.238	.340	0	—	0	-4	-4	-0	-0.4
1993	Sea-A	0	0	—	33	2	0	0	0	47^2	42	7	24	32	12.7	4.15	106	.255	.353	0	—	0	1	1	-0	-0.1
Total	8	11	22	.333	207	23	0	0	3	339^2	360	35	159	199	14.1	4.95	80	.279	.363	3	.176	1	-37	-37	1	-4.4

● GROVER POWELL

Powell, Grover David b: 10/10/40, Sayre, Pa. d: 5/21/85, Raleigh, N.C. BL/TL, 5'10", 175 lbs. Deb: 7/13/63

YEAR	TM/L	W	L	PCT	G	GS	CG	SH	SV	IP	H	HR	BB	SO	RAT	ERA	ERA+	OAV	OOB	BH	AVG	PB	PR	/A	PD	TPI
1963	NY-N	1	1	.500	20	4	1	1	0	49^2	37	2	32	39	12.7	2.72	128	.202	.324	2	.200	1	3	4	0	0.3

● JAY POWELL

Powell, James Willard b: 1/9/72, Meridian, Miss. BR/TR, 6'4", 220 lbs. Deb: 9/10/95

YEAR	TM/L	W	L	PCT	G	GS	CG	SH	SV	IP	H	HR	BB	SO	RAT	ERA	ERA+	OAV	OOB	BH	AVG	PB	PR	/A	PD	TPI
1995	Fla-N	0	0	—	9	0	0	0	0	8^1	7	0	6	4	16.2	1.08	390	.241	.405	0	—	0	3	3	0	0.0
1996	Fla-N	4	3	.571	67	0	0	0	2	71^1	71	5	36	52	14.0	4.54	90	.255	.349	0	.000	-1	-3	-4	-1	-0.5
1997	*Fla-N	7	2	.778	74	0	0	0	2	79^2	71	3	30	65	11.9	3.28	123	.242	.321	2	.500	1	8	7	1	0.9
1998	Fla-N	4	4	.500	33	0	0	0	3	36^1	36	5	22	24	14.9	4.21	97	.263	.373	0	—	0	0	-0	0	-0.1
	*Hou-N	3	3	.500	29	0	0	0	4	34	22	1	15	38	10.1	2.38	171	.182	.277	0	.000	-0	7	6	-1	1.1
	Yr	7	7	.500	62	0	0	0	7	70^1	58	6	37	62	12.3	3.33	123	.222	.321	0	.000	-0	7	6	-1	1.0
Total	4	18	12	.600	212	0	0	0	11	229^2	207	14	109	183	12.9	3.61	113	.241	.336	2	.200	0	16	12	-0	1.4

● JEREMY POWELL

Powell, Jeremy Robert b: 6/18/76, Bellflower, Cal. BR/TR, 6'5", 230 lbs. Deb: 7/23/98

YEAR	TM/L	W	L	PCT	G	GS	CG	SH	SV	IP	H	HR	BB	SO	RAT	ERA	ERA+	OAV	OOB	BH	AVG	PB	PR	/A	PD	TPI
1998	Mon-N	1	5	.167	7	6	0	0	0	25	27	5	11	14	15.1	7.92	52	.290	.389	0	.000	-1	-10	-11	-0	-2.0

● JACK POWELL

Powell, John Joseph "Red" b: 7/9/1874, Bloomington, Ill. d: 10/17/44, Chicago, Ill. BR/TR, 5'11", 195 lbs. Deb: 6/23/1897

YEAR	TM/L	W	L	PCT	G	GS	CG	SH	SV	IP	H	HR	BB	SO	RAT	ERA	ERA+	OAV	OOB	BH	AVG	PB	PR	/A	PD	TPI
1897	Cle-N	15	10	.600	27	26	24	2	0	225	245	2	62	61	12.6	3.16	142	.275	.328	20	.206	-4	29	33	-1	2.5
1898	Cle-N	23	15	.605	42	41	36	**6**	0	342	328	8	112	93	12.0	3.00	121	.251	.317	18	.132	-7	23	24	-2	1.4
1899	StL-N	23	19	.548	48	43	**40**	2	0	373	433	15	85	87	12.9	3.52	113	.290	.334	27	.201	-1	14	19	-3	1.4
1900	StL-N	17	16	.515	38	37	28	3	0	287^2	325	9	77	77	12.7	4.44	82	.284	.331	31	.284	10	-24	-26	0	-1.5
1901	StL-N	19	19	.500	**45**	37	33	2	**3**	338^1	351	14	50	133	11.0	3.54	90	.266	.299	21	.176	1	-8	-13	-5	-1.6
1902	StL-A	22	17	.564	42	39	36	3	**2**	328^1	320	12	93	137	11.6	3.21	110	.256	.312	26	.205	4	13	12	-5	1.0
1903	StL-A	15	19	.441	38	34	33	4	**2**	306^1	294	11	58	169	10.5	2.91	100	.252	.290	25	.208	2	2	0	-1	0.2
1904	NY-A	23	19	.548	47	45	38	3	0	390^1	340	15	92	202	10.2	2.44	111	.235	.286	26	.178	-3	7	12	-6	0.3
1905	NY-A	8	13	.381	37	23	13	1	1	203	214	4	57	84	12.3	3.50	84	.272	.326	12	.185	-0	-19	-13	-6	-2.0
	StL-A	2	1	.667	3	3	3	0	0	28	22	0	5	12	9.0	1.61	158	.218	.262	1	.100	-0	3	3	-1	0.2
	Yr	10	14	.417	40	26	16	1	1	231	236	4	62	96	11.6	3.27	88	.264	.313	13	.173	-1	-16	-10	-7	-1.8
1906	StL-A	13	14	.481	28	26	25	3	1	244	196	2	55	132	9.6	1.77	146	.223	.275	21	.231	3	25	22	-4	2.5
1907	StL-A	13	16	.448	32	31	27	4	1	255^2	229	4	62	96	10.4	2.68	94	.242	.292	12	.132	-3	-4	-5	-3	-1.2
1908	StL-A	16	13	.552	33	32	23	5	1	256	208	1	47	85	9.2	2.11	113	.231	.274	21	.236	3	8	8	-6	0.5
1909	StL-A	12	16	.429	34	27	18	4	3	239	221	1	42	82	10.1	2.11	115	.250	.287	14	.179	0	10	8	-4	0.6
1910	StL-A	7	11	.389	21	18	8	3	0	129^1	121	0	28	52	10.4	2.30	108	.250	.292	7	.163	-1	3	3	-3	-0.2
1911	StL-A	8	19	.296	31	27	18	1	1	207^2	224	7	44	52	11.9	3.29	102	.262	.304	12	.164	-3	1	2	-5	-0.5
1912	StL-A	9	17	.346	32	27	19	0	0	235^1	248	5	52	67	11.6	3.10	107	.276	.318	15	.183	0	6	6	-4	0.3
Total	16	245	254	.491	578	516	422	46	15	4389	4319	110	1021	1621	11.2	2.97	106	.258	.305	309	.192	-1	89	94	-58	3.9

● JACK POWELL

Powell, Reginald Bertrand b: 8/17/1891, Holcomb, Mo. d: 3/12/30, Memphis, Tenn. TR , 6'2", Deb: 6/14/13

YEAR	TM/L	W	L	PCT	G	GS	CG	SH	SV	IP	H	HR	BB	SO	RAT	ERA	ERA+	OAV	OOB	BH	AVG	PB	PR	/A	PD	TPI
1913	StL-A	0	0	—	2	0	0	0	0	2	1	0	2	0	13.5	0.00	—	.143	.333	0	—	0	1	1	1	0.0

● ROSS POWELL

Powell, Ross John b: 1/24/68, Grand Rapids, Mich. BL/TL, 6', 180 lbs. Deb: 9/5/93

YEAR	TM/L	W	L	PCT	G	GS	CG	SH	SV	IP	H	HR	BB	SO	RAT	ERA	ERA+	OAV	OOB	BH	AVG	PB	PR	/A	PD	TPI
1993	Cin-N	0	3	.000	9	1	0	0	0	16^1	13	1	6	17	10.5	4.41	91	.224	.297	0	.000	-0	-1	-1	-0	-0.1

YEAR	TM/L	W	L	PCT	G	GS	CG	SH	SV	IP	H	HR	BB	SO	RAT	ERA	ERA+	OAV	OOB	BH	AVG	PB	PR	/A	PD	TPI
1994	Hou-N	0	0	—	12	0	0	0	0	7^1	6	0	5	5	14.7	1.23	322	.240	.387	0	—	0	2	2	0	0.0
1995	Hou-N	0	0	—	15	0	0	0	0	9	16	1	11	8	27.0	11.00	35	.381	.509	0	—	0	-7	-7	0	0.0
	Pit-N	0	2	.000	12	3	0	0	0	20^2	20	5	10	12	13.9	5.23	82	.253	.352	0	.000	-0	-2	-2	0	-0.2
	Yr	0	2	.000	27	3	0	0	0	29^2	36	6	21	20	17.9	6.98	60	.295	.407	0	.000	-0	-9	-9	0	-0.2
Total	3	0	5	.000	48	4	0	0	0	53^1	55	7	32	42	15.2	5.40	76	.270	.377	0	.000	-0	-7	-8	0	-0.3

● BRIAN POWELL

Powell, William Brian b: 10/10/73, Bainbridge, Ga. BR/TR, 6'2", 205 lbs. Deb: 6/27/98

YEAR	TM/L	W	L	PCT	G	GS	CG	SH	SV	IP	H	HR	BB	SO	RAT	ERA	ERA+	OAV	OOB	BH	AVG	PB	PR	/A	PD	TPI
1998	Det-A	3	8	.273	18	16	0	0	0	83^2	101	17	36	46	15.0	6.35	74	.294	.365	0	.000	-0	-16	-15	-1	-1.7

● BILL POWELL

Powell, William Burris "Big Bill" b: 5/8/1885, Taylor County, W.Va. d: 9/28/67, E.Liverpool, Ohio BR/TR, 6'2.5", 182 lbs. Deb: 4/16/09

YEAR	TM/L	W	L	PCT	G	GS	CG	SH	SV	IP	H	HR	BB	SO	RAT	ERA	ERA+	OAV	OOB	BH	AVG	PB	PR	/A	PD	TPI
1909	Pit-N	0	1	.000	3	1	0	0	0	7^1	7	0	6	2	17.2	3.68	74	.292	.452	1	.333	0	-1	-1	0	-0.1
1910	Pit-N	4	6	.400	12	9	4	2	0	75	65	0	34	23	12.5	2.40	129	.242	.338	6	.261	1	5	6	2	1.0
1912	Chi-N	0	0	—	1	0	0	0	0	2	2	0	1	0	13.5	9.00	37	.250	.333	0	—	0	-1	-1	0	0.0
1913	Cin-N	0	1	.000	1	1	0	0	0	0^1	2	0	2	0	108.0	54.00	6	1.000	1.000	0	—	0	-2	-2	0	-2.0
Total	4	4	8	.333	17	11	4	2	0	84^2	76	0	43	25	13.3	2.87	107	.251	.355	7	.269	1	1	2	2	-1.1

● TED POWER

Power, Ted Henry b: 1/31/55, Guthrie, Okla. BR/TR, 6'4", 225 lbs. Deb: 9/9/81

YEAR	TM/L	W	L	PCT	G	GS	CG	SH	SV	IP	H	HR	BB	SO	RAT	ERA	ERA+	OAV	OOB	BH	AVG	PB	PR	/A	PD	TPI
1981	LA-N	1	3	.250	5	2	0	0	0	14^1	16	0	7	7	15.1	3.14	106	.286	.375	0	.000	-0	1	0	-1	0.0
1982	LA-N	1	1	.500	12	4	0	0	0	33^2	38	4	23	15	16.3	6.68	52	.288	.394	0	.000	-1	-12	-12	-0	-0.7
1983	Cin-N	5	6	.455	49	6	1	0	2	111	120	10	49	57	13.8	4.54	84	.286	.362	0	.000	-1	-11	-9	-2	-1.2
1984	Cin-N	9	7	.563	**78**	0	0	0	11	108^2	93	4	46	81	11.5	2.82	134	.237	.317	0	.000	-0	9	12	0	1.9
1985	Cin-N	8	6	.571	64	0	0	0	27	80	65	2	45	42	12.5	2.70	140	.227	.334	0	—	0	8	10	-2	2.1
1986	Cin-N	10	6	.625	56	10	0	0	1	129	115	13	52	95	11.7	3.70	105	.245	.322	3	.125	0	0	2	-0	0.3
1987	Cin-N	10	13	.435	34	34	2	1	0	204	213	28	71	133	12.7	4.50	94	.267	.329	7	.119	0	-10	-6	-3	-0.9
1988	KC-A	5	6	.455	22	12	2	2	0	80^1	98	7	30	44	14.7	5.94	67	.305	.370	0	—	0	-18	-17	-0	-2.1
	Det-A	1	1	.500	4	2	0	0	0	18^2	23	1	8	13	14.9	5.79	66	.307	.373	0	—	0	-4	-4	0	-0.3
	Yr	6	7	.462	26	14	2	2	0	99	121	8	38	57	14.5	5.91	67	.300	.361	0	—	0	-21	-22	-0	-2.4
1989	StL-N	7	7	.500	23	15	0	0	0	97	96	7	21	43	10.9	3.71	98	.255	.296	3	.091	-2	-2	-1	-2	-0.5
1990	*Pit-N	1	3	.250	40	0	0	0	7	51^2	50	5	17	42	11.7	3.66	99	.255	.315	1	.125	0	1	-0	-1	-0.1
1991	Cin-N	5	3	.625	68	0	0	0	3	87	87	6	31	51	12.4	3.62	105	.265	.332	0	.000	-0	1	2	-0	0.1
1992	Cle-A	3	3	.500	64	0	0	0	6	99^1	88	7	35	51	11.5	2.54	154	.248	.322	0	—	0	15	15	0	1.1
1993	Cle-A	0	2	.000	20	0	0	0	0	20	30	2	8	11	17.1	7.20	60	.333	.388	0	—	0	-6	-6	-1	-0.6
	Sea-A	2	2	.500	25	0	0	0	13	25^1	27	1	9	16	12.8	3.91	113	.287	.350	0	—	0	1	1	0	0.2
	Yr	2	4	.333	45	0	0	0	13	45^1	57	3	17	27	14.7	5.36	81	.308	.366	0	—	0	-5	-5	-1	-0.4
Total	13	68	69	.496	564	85	5	3	70	1160	1159	97	452	701	12.6	4.00	97	.264	.335	14	.089	-4	-26	-14	-11	-0.7

● JIM POWERS

Powers, James T. b: 1868, New York, N.Y. 5'10", 150 lbs. Deb: 4/18/1890

YEAR	TM/L	W	L	PCT	G	GS	CG	SH	SV	IP	H	HR	BB	SO	RAT	ERA	ERA+	OAV	OOB	BH	AVG	PB	PR	/A	PD	TPI
1890	Bro-a	1	2	.333	4	2	2	0	0	30	38	1	16	3	16.5	5.70	68	.299	.382	2	.154	-0	-6	-6	-0	-0.5

● IKE POWERS

Powers, John Lloyd b: 3/13/06, Hancock, Md. d: 12/22/68, Hancock, Md. BR/TR, 6'0.5", 188 lbs. Deb: 7/26/27

YEAR	TM/L	W	L	PCT	G	GS	CG	SH	SV	IP	H	HR	BB	SO	RAT	ERA	ERA+	OAV	OOB	BH	AVG	PB	PR	/A	PD	TPI
1927	Phi-A	1	1	.500	11	1	0	0	0	26	26	1	7	3	11.4	4.50	95	.271	.320	2	.400	1	-1	-1	0	0.0
1928	Phi-A	1	0	1.000	9	0	0	0	2	12	8	1	10	4	14.3	4.50	89	.222	.404	0	—	0	-1	-1	1	0.0
Total	2	2	1	.667	20	1	0	0	2	38	34	2	17	7	12.3	4.50	93	.258	.347	2	.400	1	-2	-1	1	0.0

● WILLIE PRALL

Prall, Wilfred Anthony b: 4/20/50, Hackensack, N.J. BL/TL, 6'3", 200 lbs. Deb: 9/3/75

YEAR	TM/L	W	L	PCT	G	GS	CG	SH	SV	IP	H	HR	BB	SO	RAT	ERA	ERA+	OAV	OOB	BH	AVG	PB	PR	/A	PD	TPI
1975	Chi-N	0	2	.000	3	3	0	0	0	14^2	21	1	8	7	17.8	8.59	45	.339	.414	0	.000	-0	-8	-8	0	-0.9

● AL PRATT

Pratt, Albert George "Uncle Al" b: 11/19/1848, Allegheny, Pa. d: 11/21/37, Pittsburgh, Pa. TR, 5'7", 140 lbs. Deb: 5/4/1871 MU

YEAR	TM/L	W	L	PCT	G	GS	CG	SH	SV	IP	H	HR	BB	SO	RAT	ERA	ERA+	OAV	OOB	BH	AVG	PB	PR	/A	PD	TPI
1871	Cle-n	10	17	.370	28	28	22	0	0	224^2	296	9	47	**34**	13.7	3.77	110	.277	.307	34	.262	2	11	9		1.0
1872	Cle-n	2	9	.182	15	12	8	0	0	105^2	150	3	14	7	14.0	5.79	61	.286	.305	18	.277	1	-25	-26		-1.6
Total	2 n	12	26	.316	43	40	30	0	0	330^1	446	12	61	41	13.8	4.41	81	.280	.306	52	.267	3	-28	-31		-0.6

● JOHN PREGENZER

Pregenzer, John Arthur b: 8/2/35, Burlington, Wis. BR/TR, 6'5", 220 lbs. Deb: 4/20/63

YEAR	TM/L	W	L	PCT	G	GS	CG	SH	SV	IP	H	HR	BB	SO	RAT	ERA	ERA+	OAV	OOB	BH	AVG	PB	PR	/A	PD	TPI
1963	SF-N	0	0	—	6	0	0	0	0	9^1	8	0	8	5	16.4	4.82	66	.242	.405	0	—	0	-2	-2	0	0.0
1964	SF-N	2	0	1.000	13	0	0	0	1	18^1	21	1	11	8	16.2	4.91	73	.296	.398	0	—	0	-3	-3	-0	-0.3
Total	2	2	0	1.000	19	0	0	0	1	27^2	29	1	19	13	16.3	4.88	70	.279	.400	0	—	0	-4	-4	-0	-0.3

● JIM PRENDERGAST

Prendergast, James Bartholomew b: 8/23/17, Brooklyn, N.Y. d: 8/23/94, Amherst, N.Y. BL/TL, 6'1", 208 lbs. Deb: 4/25/48

YEAR	TM/L	W	L	PCT	G	GS	CG	SH	SV	IP	H	HR	BB	SO	RAT	ERA	ERA+	OAV	OOB	BH	AVG	PB	PR	/A	PD	TPI
1948	Bos-N	1	1	.500	10	2	0	0	1	16^2	30	1	5	3	18.9	10.26	37	.380	.417	0	.000	-1	-12	-12	0	-1.4

● MIKE PRENDERGAST

Prendergast, Michael Thomas b: 12/15/1888, Arlington, Ill. d: 11/18/67, Omaha, Neb. BR/TR, 5'9.5", 165 lbs. Deb: 4/26/14

YEAR	TM/L	W	L	PCT	G	GS	CG	SH	SV	IP	H	HR	BB	SO	RAT	ERA	ERA+	OAV	OOB	BH	AVG	PB	PR	/A	PD	TPI
1914	Chi-F	5	9	.357	30	19	7	1	0	136	131	6	40	71	11.5	2.38	111	.255	.313	4	.108	-3	8	4	-2	0.0
1915	Chi-F	14	12	.538	42	30	16	3	0	253^2	220	6	67	95	10.3	2.48	101	.240	.295	6	.075	-9	7	1	-3	-1.1
1916	Chi-N	6	11	.353	35	10	4	2	2	152	127	5	23	56	8.9	2.31	126	.228	.260	7	.152	-2	5	10	-1	0.9
1917	Chi-N	3	6	.333	35	8	1	0	1	99^1	112	6	21	43	12.1	3.35	86	.302	.339	7	.250	1	-7	-5	-1	-0.4
1918	Phi-N	13	14	.481	33	30	20	0	1	252^1	257	6	46	41	10.8	2.89	104	.273	.308	7	.082	-8	-4	3	-2	-0.7
1919	Phi-N	0	1	.000	5	1	0	0	0	15	20	0	10	5	18.6	8.40	38	.351	.456	1	.333	0	-9	-9	0	-0.5
Total	6	41	53	.436	180	98	48	6	4	908^1	867	29	207	311	10.7	2.74	102	.258	.304	32	.115	-19	0	5	-8	-1.8

● GEORGE PRENTISS

Prentiss, George Pepper (a.k.a. George Pepper Wilson In 1901)
b: 6/10/1876, Wilmington, Del. d: 9/8/02, Wilmington, Del. BB/TR, 5'11", 175 lbs. Deb: 9/23/01

YEAR	TM/L	W	L	PCT	G	GS	CG	SH	SV	IP	H	HR	BB	SO	RAT	ERA	ERA+	OAV	OOB	BH	AVG	PB	PR	/A	PD	TPI
1901	Bos-A	1	0	1.000	2	1	1	0	0	10	7	0	6	0	11.7	1.80	196	.194	.310	1	.333	1	2	2	-0	0.2
1902	Bos-A	2	2	.500	7	4	3	0	0	41	55	0	10	9	14.3	5.27	68	.322	.359	5	.313	1	-8	-8	-0	-0.6
	Bal-A	0	1	.000	2	2	0	0	0	6^2	14	1	5	1	25.7	10.80	35	.424	.500	0	.000	-1	-5	-5	-0	-0.6
	Yr	2	3	.400	9	6	3	0	0	47^2	69	1	15	10	15.9	6.04	60	.338	.384	5	.250	-0	-13	-13	-0	-1.2
Total	2	3	3	.500	11	7	4	0	0	57^2	76	1	21	10	15.1	5.31	68	.317	.372	6	.261	1	-11	-11	-0	-1.0

● JOE PRESKO

Presko, Joseph Edward "Baby Joe" b: 10/7/28, Kansas City, Mo. BR/TR, 6', 170 lbs. Deb: 5/3/51

YEAR	TM/L	W	L	PCT	G	GS	CG	SH	SV	IP	H	HR	BB	SO	RAT	ERA	ERA+	OAV	OOB	BH	AVG	PB	PR	/A	PD	TPI
1951	StL-N	7	4	.636	15	12	5	0	2	88^2	86	9	20	38	11.0	3.45	115	.251	.296	6	.162	-1	5	5	-1	0.4
1952	StL-N	7	10	.412	28	18	5	1	0	146^2	140	15	57	63	12.1	4.05	92	.247	.317	4	.093	-2	-5	-5	-1	-0.9
1953	StL-N	6	13	.316	34	25	4	0	1	161^2	165	19	65	56	13.1	5.01	85	.261	.335	13	.220	1	-13	-14	-1	-1.4
1954	StL-N	4	9	.308	37	6	1	0	0	71^2	97	14	41	36	18.0	6.91	60	.327	.417	4	.250	0	-23	-22	-0	-3.4
1957	Det-A	1	1	.500	7	0	0	0	0	11	10	0	4	3	12.3	1.64	236	.278	.366	0	.000	-0	3	3	-0	0.4
1958	Det-A	0	0	—	7	0	0	0	2	10^2	13	0	1	6	11.8	3.38	120	.317	.333	0	—	0	0	1	-0	0.1
Total	6	25	37	.403	128	61	15	2	5	490^1	511	57	188	202	13.1	4.61	87	.267	.337	27	.173	-1	-33	-33	-4	-4.8

● TOT PRESSNELL

Pressnell, Forest Charles b: 8/8/06, Findlay, Ohio BR/TR, 5'10", 175 lbs. Deb: 4/21/38

YEAR	TM/L	W	L	PCT	G	GS	CG	SH	SV	IP	H	HR	BB	SO	RAT	ERA	ERA+	OAV	OOB	BH	AVG	PB	PR	/A	PD	TPI
1938	Bro-N	11	14	.440	43	19	6	1	3	192	209	11	56	57	12.8	3.56	110	.276	.332	9	.143	-1	5	7	-1	0.7
1939	Bro-N	9	7	.563	31	18	10	2	2	156^2	171	8	33	43	11.8	4.02	100	.273	.311	10	.196	-1	-2	0	0	-0.1
1940	Bro-N	6	5	.545	24	4	1	1	2	68^1	58	4	17	21	10.1	3.69	108	.221	.274	0	.000	-2	1	2	-1	0.0
1941	Chi-N	5	3	.625	29	1	0	0	1	70	69	2	23	27	12.3	3.09	114	.253	.320	3	.200	0	**4**	**3**	-1	0.3
1942	Chi-N	1	1	.500	27	0	0	0	4	39^1	40	5	5	9	11.4	5.49	58	.260	.305	2	.667	1	-10	-10	-0	-0.6
Total	5	32	30	.516	154	42	17	4	12	526^1	547	30	134	157	12.0	3.80	101	.264	.315	24	.161	-3	-1	3	-3	0.3

● JOE PRICE

Price, Joseph Walter b: 11/29/56, Inglewood, Cal. BR/TL, 6'4", 220 lbs. Deb: 6/14/80

YEAR	TM/L	W	L	PCT	G	GS	CG	SH	SV	IP	H	HR	BB	SO	RAT	ERA	ERA+	OAV	OOB	BH	AVG	PB	PR	/A	PD	TPI
1980	Cin-N	7	3	.700	24	13	2	0	0	111^1	95	10	37	44	10.8	3.56	101	.236	.302	5	.128	-2	1	0	-1	-0.3
1981	Cin-N	6	1	.857	41	0	0	0	4	53^2	42	3	18	41	10.1	2.52	141	.222	.290	0	.000	-0	6	6	1	0.9
1982	Cin-N	3	4	.429	59	1	0	0	3	72^2	73	7	32	71	13.5	2.85	130	.263	.347	1	.333	0	7	6	-1	0.6
1983	Cin-N	10	6	.625	21	21	5	0	0	144	118	12	46	83	10.3	2.88	132	.225	.287	4	.098	-1	12	15	-0	1.4
1984	Cin-N	7	13	.350	30	30	3	1	0	171^2	176	19	61	129	12.5	4.19	90	.261	.324	7	.146	-1	-12	-8	-3	-1.2
1985	Cin-N	2	2	.500	26	8	0	0	1	64^2	59	10	23	52	11.4	3.90	97	.242	.307	0	.000	-1	-2	-1	-1	-0.3
1986	Cin-N	1	2	.333	25	2	0	0	0	41^2	49	5	22	30	15.3	5.40	72	.293	.376	1	.143	0	-8	-7	-1	-0.6
1987	*SF-N	2	2	.500	20	0	0	0	1	35	19	5	13	42	8.5	2.57	149	.154	.241	1	.167	-0	6	5	-1	0.5

YEAR	TM/L	W	L	PCT	G	GS	CG	SH	SV	IP	H	HR	BB	SO	RAT	ERA	ERA+	OAV	OOB	BH	AVG	PB	PR	/A	PD	TPI
1988	SF-N	1	6	.143	38	3	0	0	4	61^2	59	5	27	49	12.7	3.94	83	.249	.328	0	.000	-0	-3	-5	-0	-0.6
1989	SF-N	1	1	.500	7	1	0	0	0	14	16	3	4	10	12.9	5.79	58	.314	.364	0	.000	0	-4	-4	0	-0.5
	Bos-A	2	5	.286	31	5	0	0	0	70^1	71	8	30	52	12.9	4.35	94	.262	.336	0	—	0	-4	-2	-1	-0.6
1990	Bal-A	3	4	.429	50	0	0	0	0	65^1	62	8	24	54	11.8	3.58	106	.253	.320	0	—	0	2	2	-0	0.3
Total	11	45	49	.479	372	84	10	1	13	906	839	95	337	657	11.8	3.65	102	.246	.316	19	.111	-5	0	8	-8	-0.4

● BILL PRICE Price, William b: Philadelphia, Pa. Deb: 4/27/1890

YEAR	TM/L	W	L	PCT	G	GS	CG	SH	SV	IP	H	HR	BB	SO	RAT	ERA	ERA+	OAV	OOB	BH	AVG	PB	PR	/A	PD	TPI
1890	Phi-a	1	0	1.000	1	1	1	0	0	9	6	0	7	1	14.0	2.00	192	.182	.341	1	.250	-0	2	2	0	0.2

● BOB PRIDDY Priddy, Robert Simpson b: 12/10/39, Pittsburgh, Pa. BR/TR, 6'1", 200 lbs. Deb: 9/20/62

YEAR	TM/L	W	L	PCT	G	GS	CG	SH	SV	IP	H	HR	BB	SO	RAT	ERA	ERA+	OAV	OOB	BH	AVG	PB	PR	/A	PD	TPI
1962	Pit-N	1	0	1.000	2	0	0	0	0	3	4	0	1	1	15.0	3.00	131	.308	.357	0	—	0	0	0	-0	0.1
1964	Pit-N	1	2	.333	19	0	0	0	1	34^1	35	2	15	23	13.4	3.93	89	.282	.364	0	.000	0	-2	-2	-1	-0.2
1965	SF-N	1	0	1.000	8	0	0	0	0	10^1	6	1	2	7	7.0	1.74	207	.176	.222	0	.000	-0	2	2	0	0.2
1966	SF-N	6	3	.667	38	3	0	0	1	91	88	8	28	51	11.8	3.96	93	.259	.321	3	.176	0	-4	-3	-1	-0.4
1967	Was-A	3	7	.300	46	8	1	0	4	110	98	12	33	57	10.7	3.44	92	.240	.297	4	.182	1	-3	-3	1	0.0
1968	Chi-A	3	11	.214	35	18	2	0	0	114	106	14	41	66	11.9	3.63	83	.244	.315	1	.042	-1	-8	-8	-2	-1.2
1969	Chi-A	0	0	—	4	0	0	0	0	8	10	2	2	5	13.5	4.50	86	.303	.343	0	—	0	-1	-1	0	0.0
	Cal-A	0	1	.000	15	0	0	0	0	26^1	24	4	7	15	10.6	4.78	73	.242	.292	0	.000	0	-3	-4	0	-0.1
	Yr	0	1	.000	19	0	0	0	0	34^1	34	6	9	20	11.3	4.72	76	.258	.305	0	.000	0	-4	-4	0	-0.1
	Atl-N	0	0	—	1	0	0	0	0	2	1	0	1	1	9.0	0.00	—	.143	.250	0	—	0	1	1	-0	0.0
1970	Atl-N	5	5	.500	41	0	0	0	8	73	75	9	24	32	12.6	5.42	79	.269	.333	3	.200	0	-11	-9	1	-1.2
1971	Atl-N	4	9	.308	40	0	0	0	4	64	71	8	44	36	16.3	4.22	88	.289	.399	2	.182	0	-5	-4	1	-0.7
Total	9	24	38	.387	249	29	3	0	18	536	518	60	198	294	12.2	4.00	87	.257	.327	13	.137	1	-33	-30	-2	-3.5

● EDDIE PRIEST Priest, Eddie Lee b: 4/8/74, Boaz, Ala. BR/TL, 6'1", 200 lbs. Deb: 5/27/98

YEAR	TM/L	W	L	PCT	G	GS	CG	SH	SV	IP	H	HR	BB	SO	RAT	ERA	ERA+	OAV	OOB	BH	AVG	PB	PR	/A	PD	TPI
1998	Cin-N	0	1	.000	2	2	0	0	0	6	12	2	1	1	19.5	10.50	41	.444	.464	0	.000	-0	-4	-4	-0	-0.6

● ARIEL PRIETO Prieto, Ariel b: 10/22/69, Havana, Cuba BR/TR, 6'3", 225 lbs. Deb: 7/2/95

YEAR	TM/L	W	L	PCT	G	GS	CG	SH	SV	IP	H	HR	BB	SO	RAT	ERA	ERA+	OAV	OOB	BH	AVG	PB	PR	/A	PD	TPI
1995	Oak-A	2	6	.250	14	9	1	0	0	58	57	4	32	37	14.6	4.97	90	.264	.372	0	—	0	-2	-3	-0	-0.4
1996	Oak-A	6	7	.462	21	21	2	0	0	125^2	130	9	54	75	13.7	4.15	118	.273	.356	0	—	0	12	11	0	1.0
1997	Oak-A	6	8	.429	22	22	0	0	0	125	155	16	70	90	16.6	5.04	90	.306	.396	0	—	0	-7	-7	0	-0.6
1998	Oak-A	0	1	.000	2	2	0	0	0	8^1	17	2	5	8	24.8	11.88	38	.415	.489	0	—	0	-7	-7	0	-0.6
Total	4	14	22	.389	59	54	3	0	0	317	359	31	161	210	15.3	4.85	96	.290	.379	0	—	0	-3	-6	0	-0.6

● RAY PRIM Prim, Raymond Lee "Pop" b: 12/30/06, Salitpa, Ala. d: 4/29/95, Monte Rio, Cal. BR/TL, 6', 178 lbs. Deb: 9/24/33

YEAR	TM/L	W	L	PCT	G	GS	CG	SH	SV	IP	H	HR	BB	SO	RAT	ERA	ERA+	OAV	OOB	BH	AVG	PB	PR	/A	PD	TPI
1933	Was-A	0	1	.000	2	1	0	0	0	14^1	13	0	2	6	9.4	3.14	133	.232	.259	0	.000	-1	2	2	1	0.1
1934	Was-A	0	2	.000	8	1	0	0	0	14^2	19	1	8	3	16.6	6.75	64	.339	.422	0	.000	-0	-4	-4	0	-0.4
1935	Phi-N	3	4	.429	29	6	1	0	0	73^1	110	4	15	27	15.3	5.77	79	.340	.369	2	.083	-2	-14	-10	-0	-1.1
1943	Chi-N	4	3	.571	29	5	0	0	1	60	67	2	14	27	12.2	2.55	131	.282	.321	2	.167	-0	6	5	2	0.8
1945	*Chi-N	13	8	.619	34	19	9	2	2	165^1	142	9	23	88	**9.0**	2.40	**153**	**.228**	**.256**	13	.255	3	26	23	-1	3.0
1946	Chi-N	2	3	.400	14	2	0	0	1	23^1	28	5	10	10	14.7	5.79	57	.289	.355	1	.200	0	-6	-6	1	-1.2
Total	6	22	21	.512	116	34	10	2	4	351	379	21	72	161	11.6	3.56	107	.272	.308	18	.180	-0	9	9	3	1.2

● DON PRINCE Prince, Donald Mark b: 4/5/38, Clarkton, N.C. BR/TR, 6'4", 200 lbs. Deb: 9/21/62

YEAR	TM/L	W	L	PCT	G	GS	CG	SH	SV	IP	H	HR	BB	SO	RAT	ERA	ERA+	OAV	OOB	BH	AVG	PB	PR	/A	PD	TPI
1962	Chi-N	0	0	—	1	0	0	0	0	1	0	0	1	0	18.0	0.00	—	.000	.500	0	—	0	0	0	0	0.0

● JIM PROCTOR Proctor, James Arthur b: 9/9/35, Brandywine, Md. BR/TR, 6', 165 lbs. Deb: 9/14/59

YEAR	TM/L	W	L	PCT	G	GS	CG	SH	SV	IP	H	HR	BB	SO	RAT	ERA	ERA+	OAV	OOB	BH	AVG	PB	PR	/A	PD	TPI
1959	Det-A	0	1	.000	2	1	0	0	0	2^2	8	0	3	0	37.1	16.88	24	.533	.611	0	—	0	-4	-4	0	-1.0

● RED PROCTOR Proctor, Noah Richard b: 10/27/1900, Williamsburg, Va. d: 12/17/54, Richmond, Va. BR/TR, 6'1", 165 lbs. Deb: 8/6/23

YEAR	TM/L	W	L	PCT	G	GS	CG	SH	SV	IP	H	HR	BB	SO	RAT	ERA	ERA+	OAV	OOB	BH	AVG	PB	PR	/A	PD	TPI
1923	Chi-A	0	0	—	2	0	0	0	0	4	11	0	2	0	29.3	13.50	29	.550	.591	0	—	0	-4	-4	-0	0.0

● GEORGE PROESER Proeser, George "Yatz" b: 5/30/1864, Cincinnati, Ohio d: 10/13/41, New Burlington, O. BL/TL, 5'10", 190 lbs. Deb: 9/15/1888 ♦

YEAR	TM/L	W	L	PCT	G	GS	CG	SH	SV	IP	H	HR	BB	SO	RAT	ERA	ERA+	OAV	OOB	BH	AVG	PB	PR	/A	PD	TPI
1888	Cle-a	3	4	.429	7	7	7	1	0	59	53	4	30	20	13.7	3.81	81	.231	.338	7	.304	2	-5	-5	-1	-0.4

● MIKE PROLY Proly, Michael James b: 12/15/50, Jamaica, N.Y. BR/TR, 6', 185 lbs. Deb: 4/10/76

YEAR	TM/L	W	L	PCT	G	GS	CG	SH	SV	IP	H	HR	BB	SO	RAT	ERA	ERA+	OAV	OOB	BH	AVG	PB	PR	/A	PD	TPI
1976	StL-N	1	0	1.000	14	0	0	0	0	17	21	0	6	4	14.3	3.71	95	.328	.386	0	—	0	-0	-0	0	0.0
1978	Chi-A	5	2	.714	14	6	2	0	1	65^2	63	4	12	19	10.3	2.74	139	.250	.284	0	—	0	7	8	-1	0.7
1979	Chi-A	3	8	.273	38	6	0	0	9	88^1	89	6	40	32	13.2	3.87	110	.260	.339	0	—	0	3	4	1	0.6
1980	Chi-A	5	10	.333	62	3	0	0	8	146^2	136	7	58	56	12.1	3.07	131	.253	.329	0	—	0	16	16	2	1.8
1981	Phi-N	2	1	.667	35	2	0	0	2	63	66	6	19	19	12.3	3.86	94	.282	.339	0	.000	-1	-3	-2	1	-0.1
1982	Chi-N	5	3	.625	44	1	0	0	1	82	77	5	22	24	11.1	2.30	162	.257	.312	4	.286	1	12	13	0	1.4
1983	Chi-N	1	5	.167	60	0	0	0	1	83	79	5	38	31	12.8	3.58	106	.259	.343	1	.091	-0	0	2	0	0.1
Total	7	22	29	.431	267	18	2	0	22	545^2	531	33	195	185	12.1	3.23	121	.261	.328	5	.156	-0	36	40	4	4.5

● BILL PROUGH Prough, Herschel Clinton "Clint" b: 11/28/1887, Markle, Ind. d: 12/29/36, Richmond, Ind. BR/TR, 6'3", 185 lbs. Deb: 4/27/12

YEAR	TM/L	W	L	PCT	G	GS	CG	SH	SV	IP	H	HR	BB	SO	RAT	ERA	ERA+	OAV	OOB	BH	AVG	PB	PR	/A	PD	TPI
1912	Cin-N	0	0	—	1	0	0	0	0	3	7	0	1	1	24.0	6.00	56	.538	.571	0	.000	-0	-1	-1	-0	0.0

● AUGIE PRUDHOMME Prudhomme, John Olgus b: 11/20/02, Frierson, La. d: 10/4/92, Shreveport, La. BR/TR, 6'2", 186 lbs. Deb: 4/19/29

YEAR	TM/L	W	L	PCT	G	GS	CG	SH	SV	IP	H	HR	BB	SO	RAT	ERA	ERA+	OAV	OOB	BH	AVG	PB	PR	/A	PD	TPI
1929	Det-A	1	6	.143	34	6	2	0	1	94	119	7	53	26	16.7	6.22	69	.322	.410	5	.238	1	-21	-20	1	-1.1

● HUB PRUETT Pruett, Hubert Shelby "Shucks" b: 9/1/1900, Malden, Mo. d: 1/28/82, Ladue, Mo. BL/TL, 5'10.5", 165 lbs. Deb: 4/26/22

YEAR	TM/L	W	L	PCT	G	GS	CG	SH	SV	IP	H	HR	BB	SO	RAT	ERA	ERA+	OAV	OOB	BH	AVG	PB	PR	/A	PD	TPI
1922	StL-A	7	7	.500	39	8	4	0	7	119^2	99	2	59	70	12.3	2.33	178	.235	.336	5	.147	-1	23	24	2	2.9
1923	StL-A	4	7	.364	32	8	3	0	2	104^1	109	3	64	59	15.2	4.31	97	.279	.385	3	.130	-1	-4	-2	1	-0.1
1924	StL-A	3	4	.429	33	1	0	0	0	65	64	1	42	27	15.2	4.57	99	.270	.389	3	.200	-1	-2	-0	1	0.0
1927	Phi-N	7	17	.292	31	28	12	1	1	186	238	6	89	90	16.4	6.05	68	.314	.395	13	.217	1	-44	-40	3	-3.9
1928	Phi-N	2	4	.333	13	9	4	0	0	71^1	78	2	49	35	16.4	4.54	94	.291	.406	5	.208	-0	-4	-2	0	-0.2
1930	NY-N	5	4	.556	45	8	1	0	3	135^2	152	11	63	49	14.5	4.78	99	.287	.367	5	.135	-1	3	-1	1	-0.1
1932	Bos-N	1	5	.167	18	7	4	0	0	63	76	3	30	27	16.0	5.14	73	.308	.396	2	.105	-1	-9	-10	2	-0.7
Total	7	29	48	.377	211	69	28	1	13	745	816	28	396	357	15.1	4.63	92	.286	.380	36	.170	-3	-38	-29	10	-2.1

● TEX PRUIETT Pruiett, Charles Le Roy b: 4/10/1883, Osgood, Ind. d: 3/6/53, Ventura, Cal. BL/TR, Deb: 4/26/07

YEAR	TM/L	W	L	PCT	G	GS	CG	SH	SV	IP	H	HR	BB	SO	RAT	ERA	ERA+	OAV	OOB	BH	AVG	PB	PR	/A	PD	TPI
1907	Bos-A	3	11	.214	35	17	6	2	3	173^2	166	1	59	54	12.1	3.11	83	.254	.323	8	.157	-1	-11	-10	1	-0.8
1908	Bos-A	1	7	.125	13	6	1	1	2	58^2	55	1	21	28	12.0	1.99	123	.275	.350	1	.063	-2	3	3	0	0.3
Total	2	4	18	.182	48	23	7	3	5	232^1	221	2	80	82	12.0	2.83	90	.259	.329	9	.134	-2	-8	-7	1	-0.5

● TROY PUCKETT Puckett, Troy Levi b: 12/10/1889, Winchester, Ind. d: 4/13/71, Winchester, Ind. BL/TR, 6'2", 186 lbs. Deb: 10/4/11

YEAR	TM/L	W	L	PCT	G	GS	CG	SH	SV	IP	H	HR	BB	SO	RAT	ERA	ERA+	OAV	OOB	BH	AVG	PB	PR	/A	PD	TPI
1911	Phi-N	0	0	—	1	0	0	0	0	2	4	0	2	1	31.5	13.50	26	.444	.583	0	—	0	-2	-2	0	0.0

● MIGUEL PUENTE Puente, Miguel Antonio (Aguilar) b: 5/8/48, San Luis Potosi, Mex BR/TR, 6', 160 lbs. Deb: 5/3/70

YEAR	TM/L	W	L	PCT	G	GS	CG	SH	SV	IP	H	HR	BB	SO	RAT	ERA	ERA+	OAV	OOB	BH	AVG	PB	PR	/A	PD	TPI
1970	SF-N	1	3	.250	6	4	1	0	0	18^2	25	5	11	14	17.4	8.20	48	.325	.409	0	.000	-1	-9	-9	0	-1.5

● TIM PUGH Pugh, Timothy Dean b: 1/26/67, S.Lake Tahoe, Cal. BR/TR, 6'6", 230 lbs. Deb: 9/1/92

YEAR	TM/L	W	L	PCT	G	GS	CG	SH	SV	IP	H	HR	BB	SO	RAT	ERA	ERA+	OAV	OOB	BH	AVG	PB	PR	/A	PD	TPI
1992	Cin-N	4	2	.667	7	7	0	0	0	45^1	47	2	13	18	12.1	2.58	139	.276	.332	1	.077	-0	5	5	-0	0.6
1993	Cin-N	10	15	.400	31	27	3	1	0	164^1	200	19	59	94	14.6	5.26	77	.303	.366	12	.222	2	-22	-23	-0	-2.8
1994	Cin-N	3	3	.500	10	9	1	0	0	47^2	60	5	26	24	16.8	6.04	68	.314	.405	5	.357	2	-10	-10	0	-0.9
1995	Cin-N	6	5	.545	28	12	0	0	0	98^1	100	13	32	38	12.2	3.84	107	.266	.325	4	.143	0	4	3	-1	0.2
1996	Cin-N	1	0	1.000	9	0	0	0	0	15^1	20	3	11	9	18.8	10.57	40	.317	.427	0	—	0	-11	-11	1	-0.5
	KC-A	0	1	.000	19	1	0	0	0	36^1	42	9	12	27	13.9	5.45	92	.282	.344	0	—	0	-2	-2	0	0.0
	Cin-N	0	1	.000	1	0	0	0	0	0^1	4	0	0	0	108.0	54.00	8	.800	.800	0	—	0	-2	-2	0	-1.9
1997	Det-A	1	1	.500	2	2	0	0	0	9	6	0	5	4	11.0	5.00	92	.188	.297	0	—	0	-0	-0	0	-0.1
Total	6	25	28	.472	107	58	4	1	0	416^2	479	51	158	214	14.1	4.97	83	.291	.358	22	.202	4	-39	-39	-1	-5.4

YEAR	TM/L	W	L	PCT	G	GS	CG	SH	SV	IP	H	HR	BB	SO	RAT	ERA	ERA+	OAV	OOB	BH	AVG	PB	PR	/A	PD	TPI
● **CHARLIE PULEO**	Puleo, Charles Michael b: 2/7/55, Glen Ridge, N.J. BR/TR, 6'3", 200 lbs. Deb: 9/16/81																									
1981	NY-N	0	0	—	4	1	0	0	0	13^{1}	8	0	8	8	10.8	0.00	—	.182	.308	0	.000	-0	5	5	0	0.0
1982	NY-N	9	9	.500	36	24	1	1	1	171	179	13	90	98	14.3	4.47	81	.275	.364	6	.125	-1	-17	-16	3	-1.4
1983	Cin-N	6	12	.333	27	24	0	0	0	143^{2}	145	18	91	71	15.1	4.89	78	.269	.379	5	.100	-2	-20	-17	-2	-2.2
1984	Cin-N	1	2	.333	5	4	0	0	0	22	27	2	15	6	17.2	5.73	66	.297	.396	1	.200	0	-5	-5	-1	-0.6
1986	Atl-N	1	2	.333	5	3	1	0	0	24^{1}	13	4	12	18	9.6	2.96	134	.160	.277	2	.333	0	2	3	-0	0.4
1987	Atl-N	6	8	.429	35	16	1	0	0	123^{1}	122	11	40	99	12.0	4.23	103	.262	.325	5	.179	1	-2	2	-2	0.1
1988	Atl-N	5	5	.500	53	3	0	0	1	106^{1}	101	9	47	70	12.8	3.47	106	.251	.333	3	.231	0	-0	2	-0	0.2
1989	Atl-N	1	1	.500	15	1	0	0	0	29	26	2	16	17	13.0	4.66	78	.245	.344	0	.000	-0	-4	-3	-1	-0.3
Total	8	29	39	.426	180	76	3	1	2	633	621	59	319	387	13.6	4.25	90	.261	.351	22	.144	-1	-41	-30	-2	-3.8
● **ALFONSO PULIDO**	Pulido, Alfonso (Manzo) b: 1/23/57, Veracruz, Mexico BL/TL, 5'11", 170 lbs. Deb: 9/5/83																									
1983	Pit-N	0	0	—	1	1	0	0	0	2	4	2	1	1	22.5	9.00	41	.400	.455	0	—	0	-1	-1	-0	0.0
1984	Pit-N	0	0	—	1	0	0	0	0	2	3	0	1	2	18.0	9.00	40	.333	.400	0	—	0	-1	-1	-0	0.0
1986	NY-A	1	1	.500	10	3	0	0	1	30^{2}	38	8	9	13	13.8	4.70	87	.306	.353	0	—	0	-2	-2	-0	0.0
Total	3	1	1	.500	12	4	0	0	1	34^{2}	45	10	11	16	14.5	5.19	78	.315	.364	0	—	0	-4	-4	-0	0.0
● **CARLOS PULIDO**	Pulido, Juan Carlos (Valera) b: 8/5/71, Caracas, Venez. BL/TL, 6', 195 lbs. Deb: 4/9/94																									
1994	Min-A	3	7	.300	19	14	0	0	0	84^{1}	87	17	40	32	13.7	5.98	81	.273	.356	0	—	0	-11	-10	-1	-1.1
● **BILL PULSIPHER**	Pulsipher, William Thomas b: 10/9/73, Fort Benning, Ga. BL/TL, 6'3", 210 lbs. Deb: 6/17/95																									
1995	NY-N	5	7	.417	17	17	2	0	0	126^{2}	122	11	45	81	12.2	3.98	102	.255	.324	4	.105	0	3	1	-0	0.1
1998	NY-N	0	0	—	15	1	0	0	0	14^{1}	23	2	5	13	17.6	6.91	60	.371	.418	0	.000	-0	-4	-4	1	0.0
	Mil-N	3	4	.429	11	10	0	0	0	58	63	6	26	38	14.0	4.66	92	.289	.367	3	.158	-0	-3	-2	-1	-0.3
	Yr	3	4	.429	26	11	0	0	0	72^{1}	86	8	31	51	14.7	5.10	84	.307	.378	3	.150	-1	-7	-7	0	-0.3
Total	2	8	11	.421	43	28	2	0	0	199	208	19	76	132	13.1	4.39	94	.274	.344	7	.121	-0	-4	-6	-0	-0.2
● **SPENCER PUMPELLY**	Pumpelly, Spencer Armstrong b: 4/11/1893, Owego, N.Y. d: 12/5/73, Sayre, Pa. TR, 5'11", 175 lbs. Deb: 7/11/25																									
1925	Was-A	0	0	—	1	0	0	0	0	1	1	1	1	0	18.0	9.00	47	.333	.500	0	—	0	-1	-1	-0	0.0
● **BLONDIE PURCELL**	Purcell, William Aloysius b: Paterson, N.J. BR/TR, 5'9.5", 159 lbs. Deb: 5/1/1879 M♦																									
1879	Syr-N	4	15	.211	22	17	15	0	0	179^{2}	245	1	19	28	13.2	3.76	63	.303	.319	72	.260	3	-25	-28	-3	-2.3
	Cin-N	0	2	.000	2	2	2	0	0	18	27	0	2	3	14.5	4.00	58	.355	.372	11	.220	-0	-3	-3	0	-0.3
	Yr	4	17	.190	24	19	17	0	0	197^{2}	272	1	21	31	13.3	3.78	63	.308	.324	83	.254	3	-28	-31	-2	-2.6
1880	Cin-N	3	17	.150	25	21	21	0	0	196	235	1	32	47	12.3	3.21	77	.271	.297	95	.292	4	-18	-16	-0	-1.0
1881	Buf-N	4	1	.800	9	5	5	0	0	61^{2}	62	2	9	15	10.4	2.77	100	.248	.274	33	.292	2	0	0	1	0.2
1882	Buf-N	2	1	.667	6	3	2	0	0	31	44	2	4	9	13.9	4.94	59	.338	.358	105	.276	1	-7	-7	1	-0.4
1883	Phi-N	2	6	.250	11	9	7	0	0	80	110	0	12	30	13.7	4.39	70	.306	.329	114	.268	2	-11	-12	1	-0.6
1884	Phi-N	0	0	—	1	0	0	0	0	4	3	0	0	1	6.8	2.25	133	.188	.188	108	.252	0	0	0	-0	0.0
1885	Phi-a	0	1	.000	1	0	0	0	0	6	11	0	2	3	19.5	6.00	57	.423	.464	90	.296	0	-2	-2	0	-0.2
1886	Bal-a	0	0	—	1	0	0	0	0	1	1	0	0	0	9.0	9.00	38	.200	.200	19	.224	0	-1	-1	0	0.0
1887	Bal-a	0	0	—	1	0	0	0	0	4	8	0	4	2	29.3	15.75	26	.381	.500	142	.250	0	-5	-5	-0	0.0
Total	9	15	43	.259	79	57	52	0	0	581^{1}	746	6	84	138	12.9	3.73	70	.292	.314	1217	.267	12	-72	-73	-1	-4.6
● **JOHN PURDIN**	Purdin, John Nolan b: 7/16/42, Lynx, Ohio BR/TR, 6'2", 185 lbs. Deb: 9/16/64																									
1964	LA-N	2	0	1.000	3	2	1	1	0	16	6	1	6	8	6.8	0.56	576	.115	.207	1	.200	0	5	5	-0	0.6
1965	LA-N	2	1	.667	11	2	0	0	0	22^{2}	26	8	13	16	15.5	6.75	48	.283	.371	0	.000	-0	-8	-9	-1	-1.2
1968	LA-N	2	3	.400	35	1	0	0	2	55^{2}	42	2	21	38	10.2	3.07	90	.206	.280	3	.500	1	-1	-2	-0	-0.1
1969	LA-N	0	0	—	9	0	0	0	0	16^{1}	19	7	12	6	17.1	6.06	55	.292	.403	0	.000	-0	-4	-5	0	0.0
Total	4	6	4	.600	58	5	1	1	2	110^{2}	93	18	52	68	11.8	3.90	77	.225	.312	4	.250	1	-8	-11	-1	-0.7
● **BOB PURKEY**	Purkey, Robert Thomas b: 7/14/29, Pittsburgh, Pa. BR/TR, 6'2", 195 lbs. Deb: 4/14/54																									
1954	Pit-N	3	8	.273	36	11	0	0	0	131^{1}	145	3	62	38	14.7	5.07	83	.293	.379	2	.077	-1	-15	-13	5	-0.6
1955	Pit-N	2	7	.222	14	10	2	0	1	67^{2}	77	5	25	24	13.8	5.32	77	.287	.353	6	.316	2	-10	-9	1	-0.8
1956	Pit-N	0	0	—	2	0	0	0	0	4	2	1	0	1	4.5	2.25	168	.143	.143	0	—	0	1	1	0	0.0
1957	Pit-N	11	14	.440	48	21	6	1	2	179^{2}	194	10	38	51	12.0	3.86	98	.278	.322	5	.111	-0	0	-1	-1	-0.2
1958	Cin-N☆	17	11	.607	37	34	17	3	0	250	259	25	49	70	11.2	3.60	115	.268	.306	9	.111	-2	10	15	2	1.5
1959	Cin-N	13	18	.419	38	33	9	1	1	218	241	25	43	78	12.0	4.25	95	.279	.318	11	.167	3	-7	-5	-0	-0.4
1960	Cin-N	17	11	.607	41	33	11	1	0	252^{2}	259	23	59	97	11.6	3.60	106	.265	.312	11	.133	-2	5	6	2	0.7
1961	*Cin-N★	16	12	.571	36	34	13	1	1	246^{1}	245	27	51	116	11.0	3.73	109	.255	.297	8	.100	-3	8	9	6	1.2
1962	Cin-N★	23	5	**.821**	37	37	18	2	0	288^{1}	260	28	64	141	10.6	2.81	143	.240	.291	11	.103	-2	36	**39**	3	3.6
1963	Cin-N	6	10	.375	21	21	4	1	0	137	143	12	33	55	11.7	3.55	94	.272	.318	4	.098	-1	-4	-3	1	-0.3
1964	Cin-N	11	9	.550	34	25	9	2	1	195^{2}	181	16	49	78	10.9	3.04	119	.246	.299	3	.052	-4	11	13	2	1.0
1965	StL-N	10	9	.526	32	17	3	1	2	124^{1}	148	20	33	39	13.6	5.79	66	.294	.346	1	.029	-3	-31	-27	1	-4.0
1966	Pit-N	0	1	.000	10	0	0	0	1	19^{2}	16	0	4	5	9.2	1.37	260	.235	.278	0	.000	-0	5	5	1	0.4
Total	13	129	115	.529	386	276	92	13	9	2114^{2}	2170	195	510	793	11.7	3.79	103	.266	.315	71	.110	-13	9	30	21	2.1
● **OSCAR PURNER**	Purner, Oscar E. b: 1873, Washington, D.C. Deb: 9/2/1895																									
1895	Was-N	0	0	—	1	0	0	0	0	2	4	1	3	0	31.5	9.00	53	.400	.538	0	.000	-0	-1	-1	-0	0.0
● **AMBROSE PUTTMANN**	Puttmann, Ambrose Nicholas "Putty" or "Brose" b: 9/9/1880, Cincinnati, Ohio d: 6/21/36, Jamaica, N.Y. TL, 6'4", 185 lbs. Deb: 9/4/03																									
1903	NY-A	2	0	1.000	3	2	1	0	0	19	16	0	4	8	9.9	0.95	330	.229	.280	1	.143	-0	4	5	1	0.6
1904	NY-A	2	0	1.000	9	3	2	1	0	49^{1}	40	0	17	26	10.4	2.74	99	.222	.289	5	.278	2	-1	-0	0	0.2
1905	NY-A	2	7	.222	17	9	5	1	1	86^{1}	79	2	37	39	12.6	4.27	69	.245	.332	10	.313	3	-16	-13	-0	-1.1
1906	StL-N	2	2	.500	4	4	0	0	0	18^{2}	23	2	9	12	16.4	5.30	50	.303	.391	2	.333	0	-6	-6	0	-1.0
Total	4	8	9	.471	33	18	8	2	1	173^{1}	158	4	67	85	12.1	3.58	80	.244	.322	18	.286	4	-18	-14	1	-1.3
● **JOHN PYECHA**	Pyecha, John Nicholas b: 11/25/31, Aliquippa, Pa. BR/TR, 6'5", 200 lbs. Deb: 4/24/54																									
1954	Chi-N	0	1	.000	1	0	0	0	0	2^{2}	4	1	2	2	20.3	10.13	41	.333	.429	0	.000	-0	-2	-2	-0	-0.5
● **HARLAN PYLE**	Pyle, Harlan Albert "Firpo" b: 11/29/05, Burchard, Neb. d: 1/13/93, Beatrice, Neb. BR/TR, 6'2", 180 lbs. Deb: 9/21/28																									
1928	Cin-N	0	0	—	2	1	0	0	0	1^{1}	1	0	4	1	33.8	20.25	20	.143	.455	0	.000	-0	-2	-2	0	0.0
● **SHADOW PYLE**	Pyle, Harry Thomas b: 11/29/1861, Reading, Pa. d: 12/26/08, Reading, Pa. TL, 5'8", 136 lbs. Deb: 10/15/1884																									
1884	Phi-N	0	1	.000	1	1	1	0	0	9	9	0	6	4	15.0	4.00	75	.257	.366	0	.000	-1	-1	-1	-0	-0.2
1887	Chi-N	1	3	.250	4	4	3	0	0	26^{2}	32	1	21	5	18.6	4.73	95	.291	.414	3	.188	-0	-2	-1	1	0.0
Total	2	1	4	.200	5	5	4	0	0	35^{2}	41	1	27	9	17.7	4.54	90	.283	.402	3	.150	-1	-3	-2	1	-0.2
● **EWALD PYLE**	Pyle, Herbert Ewald "Lefty" b: 8/27/10, St.Louis, Mo. BL/TL, 6'0.5", 175 lbs. Deb: 4/23/39																									
1939	StL-A	0	2	.000	6	1	0	0	0	8^{1}	17	3	11	5	30.2	12.96	38	.405	.528	0	.000	-0	-8	-7	1	-1.3
1942	StL-A	0	0	—	2	0	0	0	0	5^{1}	6	0	4	1	16.9	6.75	55	.286	.400	0	.000	-0	-2	-2	-0	-0.1
1943	Was-A	4	8	.333	18	11	2	1	1	72^{2}	70	0	45	25	14.4	4.09	78	.254	.360	2	.100	-1	-6	-7	-1	-1.3
1944	NY-N	7	10	.412	31	21	3	0	0	164	152	12	68	79	12.4	4.34	85	.241	.321	8	.157	-0	-13	-12	0	-1.2
1945	NY-N	0	0	—	6	1	0	0	0	6^{1}	16	0	4	2	28.4	17.05	23	.457	.513	0	.000	-0	-9	-9	1	0.0
	Bos-N	0	1	.000	4	2	0	0	0	13^{2}	16	1	18	10	22.4	7.24	53	.302	.479	2	.333	1	-5	-5	-0	-0.3
	Yr	0	1	.000	10	3	0	0	0	20	32	1	22	12	24.3	10.35	37	.364	.491	2	.250	0	-15	-14	0	-0.3
Total	5	11	21	.344	67	36	5	1	1	270^{1}	277	16	150	122	14.4	5.03	71	.262	.357	12	.143	-2	-44	-43	-0	-4.2
● **TOM QUALTERS**	Qualters, Thomas Francis "Money Bags" b: 4/1/35, McKeesport, Pa. BR/TR, 6'0.5", 190 lbs. Deb: 9/13/53																									
1953	Phi-N	0	0	—	1	0	0	0	0	0^{1}	4	1	1	0	162.0	162.00	3	.800	.857	0	—	0	-6	-6	0	0.0
1957	Phi-N	0	0	—	6	0	0	0	0	7^{1}	12	0	4	6	19.6	7.36	52	.400	.471	0	—	0	-3	-3	0	0.0

YEAR	TM/L	W	L	PCT	G	GS	CG	SH	SV	IP	H	HR	BB	SO	RAT	ERA	ERA+	OAV	OOB	BH	AVG	PB	PR	/A	PD	TPI
1958	Phi-N	0	0	—	1	0	0	0	0	2	2	0	1	0	13.5	4.50	88	.222	.300	0	—	0	-0	-0	-0	0.0
	Chi-A	0	0	—	26	0	0	0	0	43	45	1	20	14	13.6	4.19	87	.281	.361	0	.000	0	-2	-3	1	0.1
Total	3	0	0	—	34	0	0	0	0	52^{2}	63	2	26	20	15.4	5.64	65	.309	.390	0	.000	0	-11	-11	1	0.1

● PAUL QUANTRILL

Quantrill, Paul John b: 11/3/68, London, Ont., Canada BL/TR, 6'1", 185 lbs. Deb: 7/20/92

YEAR	TM/L	W	L	PCT	G	GS	CG	SH	SV	IP	H	HR	BB	SO	RAT	ERA	ERA+	OAV	OOB	BH	AVG	PB	PR	/A	PD	TPI
1992	Bos-A	2	3	.400	27	0	0	0	1	49^{1}	55	1	15	24	13.0	2.19	192	.288	.343	0	—	0	10	11	-0	1.1
1993	Bos-A	6	12	.333	49	14	1	1	1	138	151	13	44	66	12.8	3.91	118	.279	.335	0	—	0	6	11	-1	1.1
1994	Bos-A	1	1	.500	17	0	0	0	0	23	25	4	5	15	12.5	3.52	143	.278	.330	0	—	0	3	4	-0	0.0
	Phi-N	2	2	.500	18	1	0	0	1	30	39	3	10	13	15.6	6.00	71	.331	.397	0	.000	-0	-6	-6	0	-0.7
1995	Phi-N	11	12	.478	33	29	0	0	0	179^{1}	212	20	44	103	13.1	4.67	91	.295	.341	6	.105	-2	-10	-9	1	-1.1
1996	Tor-A	5	14	.263	38	20	0	0	0	134^{1}	172	27	51	86	15.1	5.43	92	.316	.377	0	—	0	-6	-6	1	-0.7
1997	Tor-A	6	7	.462	77	0	0	0	5	88	103	5	17	56	12.4	1.94	236	.297	.332	0	.000	-0	**26**	**26**	1	3.7
1998	Tor-A	3	4	.429	82	0	0	0	7	80	88	5	22	59	12.7	2.59	179	.285	.338	0	—	0	18	18	1	1.7
Total	7	36	55	.396	341	64	1	1	15	722	845	78	208	422	13.4	3.95	116	.295	.347	6	.098	-3	41	49	2	5.1

● BILL QUARLES

Quarles, William H. b: 1869, Petersburg, Va. d: 3/25/1897, Petersburg, Va. 6'3", Deb: 5/21/1891

YEAR	TM/L	W	L	PCT	G	GS	CG	SH	SV	IP	H	HR	BB	SO	RAT	ERA	ERA+	OAV	OOB	BH	AVG	PB	PR	/A	PD	TPI
1891	Was-a	1	1	.500	3	2	2	0	0	22	32	1	12	10	18.8	8.18	46	.330	.414	0	.000	-2	-11	-11	-0	-0.8
1893	Bos-N	2	1	.667	3	3	3	0	0	27	31	2	5	6	12.7	4.67	106	.279	.322	2	.222	0	-0	1	-0	0.0
Total	2	3	2	.600	6	5	5	0	0	49	63	3	17	16	15.4	6.24	70	.303	.367	2	.100	-2	-11	-10	-1	-0.8

● MEL QUEEN

Queen, Melvin Douglas b: 3/26/42, Johnson City, N.Y. BL/TR, 6'1", 197 lbs. Deb: 4/13/64 FMC♦

YEAR	TM/L	W	L	PCT	G	GS	CG	SH	SV	IP	H	HR	BB	SO	RAT	ERA	ERA+	OAV	OOB	BH	AVG	PB	PR	/A	PD	TPI
1966	Cin-N	0	0	—	7	0	0	0	1	7	11	0	6	9	21.9	6.43	61	.367	.472	7	.127	0	-2	-2	0	-0.1
1967	Cin-N	14	8	.636	31	24	6	2	0	195^{2}	155	17	52	154	9.8	2.76	136	.215	.273	17	.210	3	13	22	-2	2.6
1968	Cin-N	0	1	.000	5	4	0	0	0	18^{1}	25	7	6	20	15.2	5.89	54	.333	.383	1	.125	0	-6	-6	0	-0.3
1969	Cin-N	1	0	1.000	2	2	0	0	0	12	7	2	3	7	8.3	2.25	167	.163	.234	1	.167	-0	2	2	-0	0.1
1970	Cal-A	3	6	.333	34	3	0	0	9	60	58	5	28	44	13.7	4.20	86	.261	.357	4	.250	1	-3	-4	-1	-0.7
1971	Cal-A	2	2	.500	44	0	0	0	4	65^{2}	49	3	29	53	11.8	1.78	182	.212	.321	0	.000	-1	12	11	-1	0.6
1972	Cal-A	0	0	—	17	0	0	0	0	31	31	2	19	19	15.4	4.35	67	.265	.381	0	.000	0	-4	-5	-0	0.0
Total	7	20	17	.541	140	33	6	2	14	389^{2}	336	36	143	306	11.6	3.14	113	.233	.313	49	.179	3	12	18	-4	2.2

● MEL QUEEN

Queen, Melvin Joseph b: 3/4/18, Maxwell, Pa. d: 4/4/82, Fort Smith, Ark. BR/TR, 6'0.5", 204 lbs. Deb: 4/18/42 F

YEAR	TM/L	W	L	PCT	G	GS	CG	SH	SV	IP	H	HR	BB	SO	RAT	ERA	ERA+	OAV	OOB	BH	AVG	PB	PR	/A	PD	TPI
1942	NY-A	1	0	1.000	4	0	0	0	0	5^{2}	6	0	3	0	17.5	0.00	—	.300	.440	0	—	0	2	2	0	0.4
1944	NY-A	6	3	.667	10	10	4	1	0	81^{2}	68	7	34	30	11.4	3.31	105	.227	.308	6	.194	0	1	2	-2	0.0
1946	NY-A	1	1	.500	14	3	1	0	0	30^{1}	40	2	21	26	18.1	6.53	53	.315	.412	1	.143	-0	-10	-10	-0	-0.7
1947	NY-A	0	0	—	5	0	0	0	0	6^{2}	9	2	4	2	18.9	9.45	37	.321	.424	0	.000	-0	-4	-4	-0	0.0
	Pit-N	3	7	.300	14	12	2	0	0	74	70	8	51	34	14.8	4.01	105	.244	.360	2	.077	-2	0	2	-1	-0.1
1948	Pit-N	4	4	.500	25	8	0	0	1	66^{1}	82	8	40	34	17.0	6.65	61	.308	.405	1	.059	-2	-20	-19	-1	-2.2
1950	Pit-N	5	14	.263	33	21	4	1	0	120^{1}	135	18	73	76	15.7	5.98	73	.284	.381	2	.057	-3	-25	-21	-1	-3.2
1951	Pit-N	7	9	.438	39	21	4	1	0	168^{1}	149	21	99	123	13.3	4.44	95	.233	.337	5	.106	-3	-9	-4	-3	-0.9
1952	Pit-N	0	2	.000	2	2	0	0	0	3^{1}	8	2	4	3	32.4	29.70	13	.381	.480	0	—	0	-10	-10	-0	-2.6
Total	8	27	40	.403	146	77	15	3	1	556^{2}	567	68	329	328	14.7	5.09	80	.262	.362	17	.104	-10	-74	-63	-9	-9.3

● EDDIE QUICK

Quick, Edward b: 12/1881, Baltimore, Md. d: 6/19/13, Rocky Ford, Colo. TR, 5'11", Deb: 9/28/03

YEAR	TM/L	W	L	PCT	G	GS	CG	SH	SV	IP	H	HR	BB	SO	RAT	ERA	ERA+	OAV	OOB	BH	AVG	PB	PR	/A	PD	TPI
1903	NY-A	0	0	—	1	1	0	0	0	2	5	0	1	0	27.0	9.00	35	.455	.500	0	.000	-0	-1	-1	0	0.0

● TAD QUINN

Quinn, Clarence Carr b: 9/21/1882, Torrington, Conn. d: 8/6/46, Waterbury, Conn. TR, 6'1", 210 lbs. Deb: 9/27/02

YEAR	TM/L	W	L	PCT	G	GS	CG	SH	SV	IP	H	HR	BB	SO	RAT	ERA	ERA+	OAV	OOB	BH	AVG	PB	PR	/A	PD	TPI
1902	Phi-A	0	1	.000	1	1	1	0	0	8	12	1	1	3	14.6	4.50	82	.343	.361	0	.000	-0	-1	-1	-0	-0.1
1903	Phi-A	0	0	—	2	0	0	0	0	9	11	0	5	1	17.0	5.00	61	.297	.395	2	.667	1	-2	-2	1	0.2
Total	2	0	1	.000	3	1	1	0	0	17	23	1	6	4	15.9	4.76	70	.319	.380	2	.333	1	-3	-3	0	0.1

● FRANK QUINN

Quinn, Frank William b: 11/27/27, Springfield, Mass. d: 1/11/93, Boynton Beach, Fla. BR/TR, 6'2", 180 lbs. Deb: 5/29/49

YEAR	TM/L	W	L	PCT	G	GS	CG	SH	SV	IP	H	HR	BB	SO	RAT	ERA	ERA+	OAV	OOB	BH	AVG	PB	PR	/A	PD	TPI
1949	Bos-A	0	0	—	8	0	0	0	0	22	18	2	9	4	11.5	2.86	152	.222	.308	1	.167	-0	3	4	-0	0.0
1950	Bos-A	0	0	—	1	0	0	0	0	2	2	0	1	0	13.5	9.00	54	.250	.333	0	—	0	-1	-1	0	0.0
Total	2	0	0	—	9	0	0	0	0	24	20	2	10	4	11.6	3.38	131	.225	.310	1	.167	-0	2	3	0	0.0

● JACK QUINN

Quinn, John Picus (b: John Quinn Picus) b: 7/5/1883, Janesville, Pa. d: 4/17/46, Pottsville, Pa. BR/TR, 6' ", 196 lbs. Deb: 4/15/09

YEAR	TM/L	W	L	PCT	G	GS	CG	SH	SV	IP	H	HR	BB	SO	RAT	ERA	ERA+	OAV	OOB	BH	AVG	PB	PR	/A	PD	TPI
1909	NY-A	9	5	.643	23	11	8	0	1	118^{2}	110	1	24	36	10.5	1.97	128	.252	.297	7	.156	0	7	7	3	1.3
1910	NY-A	18	12	.600	35	31	20	0	0	235^{2}	214	2	58	82	10.6	2.37	112	.247	.299	19	.232	4	4	8	7	2.2
1911	NY-A	8	10	.444	40	16	7	0	2	174^{2}	203	2	41	71	12.8	3.76	96	.297	.341	10	.164	-1	-8	-3	3	-0.1
1912	NY-A	5	7	.417	18	11	7	0	0	102^{2}	139	4	23	47	14.6	5.79	62	.325	.365	8	.205	-1	-28	-25	2	-2.3
1913	Bos-N	4	3	.571	8	7	6	1	0	56^{1}	55	1	7	33	10.1	2.40	137	.261	.288	4	.200	1	5	6	2	1.1
1914	Bal-F	26	14	.650	46	42	27	4	1	342^{2}	335	3	65	164	10.7	2.60	117	.266	.307	33	.273	6	11	16	1	2.7
1915	Bal-F	9	22	.290	44	31	21	0	1	273^{2}	289	9	63	118	11.8	3.45	83	.278	.325	29	.264	3	-22	-18	3	-1.2
1918	Chi-A	5	1	.833	6	5	5	0	0	51	38	0	7	22	7.9	2.29	119	.216	.246	4	.222	1	3	3	0	0.5
1919	NY-A	15	14	.517	38	31	18	4	0	266	242	8	65	97	10.6	2.61	123	.244	.295	19	.209	1	18	17	1	2.0
1920	NY-A	18	10	.643	41	32	17	2	3	253^{1}	271	8	48	101	11.4	3.20	119	.273	.308	8	.091	-5	17	18	3	1.5
1921	*NY-A	8	7	.533	33	13	6	0	0	119	158	2	32	44	14.7	3.78	112	.327	.375	9	.220	1	7	6	1	0.8
1922	Bos-A	13	16	.448	40	32	16	4	0	256	263	9	59	67	11.4	3.48	118	.267	.311	9	.099	-5	16	18	5	1.8
1923	Bos-A	13	17	.433	42	28	16	1	7	243	302	6	53	71	13.4	3.89	106	.316	.356	18	.225	0	3	6	-1	0.6
1924	Bos-A	12	13	.480	44	25	13	2	7	228^{2}	241	10	52	64	12.0	3.27	134	.273	.322	14	.179	-4	24	28	4	2.9
1925	Bos-A	7	8	.467	19	15	8	0	0	105	140	3	26	24	14.5	4.37	104	.315	.357	3	.094	-2	0	2	2	0.2
	Phi-A	6	3	.667	18	13	4	0	0	99^{2}	119	3	16	19	12.5	3.88	120	.296	.328	3	.097	-3	6	8	1	0.5
	Yr	13	11	.542	37	28	12	0	0	204^{2}	259	6	42	43	13.4	4.13	111	.305	.340	6	.095	-5	6	11	3	0.7
1926	Phi-A	10	11	.476	31	21	8	3	1	163^{2}	191	4	36	58	12.5	3.41	122	.296	.334	8	.174	-0	11	14	1	1.7
1927	Phi-A	15	10	.600	34	26	11	3	1	201^{1}	211	8	37	43	11.3	3.26	131	.278	.315	6	.091	-7	20	22	-1	1.7
1928	Phi-A	18	7	.720	31	28	18	4	1	211^{1}	239	3	34	43	11.9	2.90	139	.286	.320	13	.165	-3	27	26	1	2.6
1929	*Phi-A	11	9	.550	35	18	7	0	2	161	182	8	39	41	12.4	3.97	107	.290	.332	8	.133	-4	5	5	0	0.1
1930	*Phi-A	9	7	.563	35	7	0	0	6	89^{2}	109	6	22	28	13.2	4.42	106	.302	.344	9	.265	1	**2**	**3**	2	0.7
1931	Bro-N	5	4	.556	39	1	0	0	**15**	64^{1}	65	1	24	25	12.6	2.66	143	.266	.335	3	.200	0	9	8	1	1.6
1932	Bro-N	3	7	.300	42	0	0	0	**8**	87^{1}	102	1	24	28	13.1	3.30	116	.296	.343	4	.200	0	**6**	**5**	0	0.7
1933	Cin-N	0	1	.000	14	0	0	0	1	15^{2}	20	0	5	3	14.4	4.02	84	.323	.373	0	.000	-0	-1	-1	1	0.0
Total	23	247	218	.531	756	444	243	28	57	3920^{1}	4238	102	860	1329	11.9	3.29	113	.280	.323	248	.184	-16	140	182	40	23.6

● WIMPY QUINN

Quinn, Wellington Hunt b: 5/12/18, Birmingham, Ala. d: 9/1/54, Santa Monica, Cal. BR/TR, 6'2", 187 lbs. Deb: 6/8/41

YEAR	TM/L	W	L	PCT	G	GS	CG	SH	SV	IP	H	HR	BB	SO	RAT	ERA	ERA+	OAV	OOB	BH	AVG	PB	PR	/A	PD	TPI
1941	Chi-N	0	0	—	3	0	0	0	0	5	3	0	3	2	10.8	7.20	49	.158	.273	1	.500	0	-2	-2	-0	0.0

● LUIS QUINTANA

Quintana, Luis Joaquin (Santos) b: 12/25/51, Vega Baja, P.R. BL/TL, 6'2", 175 lbs. Deb: 7/9/74

YEAR	TM/L	W	L	PCT	G	GS	CG	SH	SV	IP	H	HR	BB	SO	RAT	ERA	ERA+	OAV	OOB	BH	AVG	PB	PR	/A	PD	TPI
1974	Cal-A	2	1	.667	18	0	0	0	0	12^{2}	17	0	14	11	22.0	4.26	81	.327	.470	0	—	0	-1	-1	-0	0.0
1975	Cal-A	0	2	.000	4	0	0	0	0	7	13	2	6	5	24.4	6.43	55	.394	.487	0	—	0	-2	-2	-0	-0.6
Total	2	2	3	.400	22	0	0	0	0	19^{2}	30	2	20	16	22.9	5.03	69	.353	.476	0	—	0	-3	-3	-0	-0.6

● RAFAEL QUIRICO

Quirico, Rafael Octavio (Dottin) b: 9/7/69, Santo Domingo, D.R. BL/TL, 6'3", 170 lbs. Deb: 6/25/96

YEAR	TM/L	W	L	PCT	G	GS	CG	SH	SV	IP	H	HR	BB	SO	RAT	ERA	ERA+	OAV	OOB	BH	AVG	PB	PR	/A	PD	TPI
1996	Phi-N	0	1	.000	1	1	0	0	0	1^{2}	4	1	5	1	48.6	37.80	11	.444	.643	0	—	0	-6	-6	0	-1.5

● ART QUIRK

Quirk, Arthur Lincoln b: 4/11/38, Providence, R.I. BR/TL, 5'11", 170 lbs. Deb: 4/17/62

YEAR	TM/L	W	L	PCT	G	GS	CG	SH	SV	IP	H	HR	BB	SO	RAT	ERA	ERA+	OAV	OOB	BH	AVG	PB	PR	/A	PD	TPI
1962	Bal-A	2	2	.500	7	5	0	0	0	27^{1}	36	3	18	18	17.8	5.93	62	.308	.400	1	.143	0	-6	-7	1	-0.8
1963	Was-A	1	0	1.000	7	3	0	0	0	21	23	3	8	12	13.3	4.29	87	.280	.344	1	.250	0	-2	-1	-0	-0.1
Total	2	3	2	.600	14	8	0	0	0	48^{1}	59	6	26	30	15.8	5.21	71	.296	.378	2	.182	0	-7	-8	0	-0.9

● DAN QUISENBERRY

Quisenberry, Daniel Raymond b: 2/7/53, Santa Monica, Cal. d: 9/30/98, Leawood, Kan. BR/TR, 6'2", 180 lbs. Deb: 7/8/79

YEAR	TM/L	W	L	PCT	G	GS	CG	SH	SV	IP	H	HR	BB	SO	RAT	ERA	ERA+	OAV	OOB	BH	AVG	PB	PR	/A	PD	TPI
1979	KC-A	3	2	.600	32	0	0	0	5	40	42	5	7	13	11.0	3.15	135	.278	.310	0	—	0	5	5	1	0.7
1980	*KC-A	12	7	.632	**75**	0	0	0	**33**	128^{1}	129	5	27	37	11.0	3.09	131	.265	.305	0	—	0	14	14	3	2.9

YEAR	TM/L	W	L	PCT	G	GS	CG	SH	SV	IP	H	HR	BB	SO	RAT	ERA	ERA+	OAV	OOB	BH	AVG	PB	PR	/A	PD	TPI
1981	*KC-A	1	4	.200	40	0	0	0	18	62^1	59	1	15	20	10.8	1.73	208	.258	.306	0	—	0	13	13	3	2.2
1982	KC-A★	9	7	.563	72	0	0	0	**35**	136^2	126	12	12	46	9.1	2.57	159	.252	.270	0	—	0	23	23	6	4.5
1983	KC-A★	5	3	.625	**69**	0	0	0	**45**	139	118	6	11	48	8.4	1.94	210	.229	.245	0	—	0	**33**	**33**	2	4.2
1984	*KC-A☆	6	3	.667	72	0	0	0	**44**	129^1	121	10	12	41	9.3	2.64	152	.247	.265	0	—	0	19	20	3	2.9
1985	*KC-A	8	9	.471	**84**	0	0	0	**37**	129	142	8	16	54	11.1	2.37	175	.280	.303	0	—	0	25	26	1	4.6
1986	KC-A	3	7	.300	62	0	0	0	12	81^1	92	2	24	36	13.2	2.77	154	.291	.347	0	—	0	13	13	2	2.0
1987	KC-A	4	1	.800	47	0	0	0	8	49	58	3	10	17	12.7	2.76	165	.287	.324	0	—	0	9	10	2	1.3
1988	KC-A	0	1	.000	20	0	0	0	1	25^1	32	0	5	9	13.1	3.55	112	.305	.336	0	—	0	1	1	1	0.1
	StL-N	2	0	1.000	33	0	0	0	0	38	54	4	6	19	14.2	6.16	56	.344	.368	0	.000	0	-11	-11	0	-0.5
1989	StL-N	3	1	.750	63	0	0	0	6	78^1	78	2	14	37	10.6	2.64	137	.261	.294	1	.250	0	7	9	2	0.8
1990	SF-N	0	1	.000	5	0	0	0	0	6^2	13	1	3	2	21.6	13.50	27	.419	.471	0	.000	-0	-7	-7	-0	-0.9
Total	12	56	46	.549	674	0	0	0	244	1043^1	1064	59	162	379	10.6	2.76	146	.267	.297	1	.167	0	144	147	25	24.8

● CHARLIE RABE Rabe, Charles Henry b: 5/6/32, Boyce, Tex. BL/TL, 6'1", 180 lbs. Deb: 9/21/57

YEAR	TM/L	W	L	PCT	G	GS	CG	SH	SV	IP	H	HR	BB	SO	RAT	ERA	ERA+	OAV	OOB	BH	AVG	PB	PR	/A	PD	TPI
1957	Cin-N	0	1	.000	2	1	0	0	0	8^1	5	2	0	6	5.4	2.16	190	.167	.167	0	.000	-0	2	2	-0	0.1
1958	Cin-N	0	3	.000	9	1	0	0	0	18^2	25	3	9	10	16.4	4.34	96	.321	.391	0	.000	-1	-1	-0	0	-0.1
Total	2	0	4	.000	11	2	0	0	0	27	30	5	9	16	13.0	3.67	113	.278	.333	0	.000	-1	1	1	0	0.0

● STEVE RACHUNOK Rachunok, Stephen Stepanovich "The Mad Russian" b: 12/5/16, Rittman, Ohio BR/TR, 6'4.5", 205 lbs. Deb: 9/17/40

YEAR	TM/L	W	L	PCT	G	GS	CG	SH	SV	IP	H	HR	BB	SO	RAT	ERA	ERA+	OAV	OOB	BH	AVG	PB	PR	/A	PD	TPI
1940	Bro-N	0	1	.000	2	1	1	0	0	10	9	0	5	10	12.6	4.50	89	.243	.333	0	.000	0	-1	-1	0	0.0

● MIKE RACZKA Raczka, Michael b: 11/16/62, New Britain, Conn. BL/TL, 6', 200 lbs. Deb: 8/15/92

YEAR	TM/L	W	L	PCT	G	GS	CG	SH	SV	IP	H	HR	BB	SO	RAT	ERA	ERA+	OAV	OOB	BH	AVG	PB	PR	/A	PD	TPI
1992	Oak-A	0	0	—	8	0	0	0	0	6^1	8	0	5	2	18.5	8.53	44	.308	.419	0	—	0	-3	-3	-0	0.1

● DICK RADATZ Radatz, Richard Raymond "The Monster" b: 4/2/37, Detroit, Mich. BR/TR, 6'5", 235 lbs. Deb: 4/10/62

YEAR	TM/L	W	L	PCT	G	GS	CG	SH	SV	IP	H	HR	BB	SO	RAT	ERA	ERA+	OAV	OOB	BH	AVG	PB	PR	/A	PD	TPI
1962	Bos-A	9	6	.600	**62**	0	0	0	**24**	124^2	95	9	40	144	10.0	2.24	184	.211	.281	3	.097	-2	**24**	**26**	-2	3.7
1963	Bos-A★	15	6	.714	66	0	0	0	25	132^1	94	9	51	162	10.2	1.97	192	.201	.286	2	.069	-2	**24**	**27**	-2	**5.0**
1964	Bos-A★	16	9	.640	79	0	0	0	**29**	157	103	13	58	181	9.6	2.29	168	.186	.271	6	.162	-0	23	**27**	-2	**5.1**
1965	Bos-A	9	11	.450	63	0	0	0	22	124^1	104	11	53	121	11.7	3.91	95	.227	.314	5	.185	1	-6	-3	-1	-0.4
1966	Bos-A	0	2	.000	16	0	0	0	4	19	24	3	11	19	16.6	4.74	80	.304	.389	0	.000	-0	-3	-2	-1	-0.4
	Cle-A	0	3	.000	39	0	0	0	10	56^2	49	6	34	49	13.7	4.61	75	.233	.348	1	.111	-0	-7	-7	-1	-0.8
	Yr	0	5	.000	55	0	0	0	14	75^2	73	9	45	68	14.4	4.64	76	.253	.359	1	.091	-1	-10	-9	-2	-1.2
1967	Cle-A	0	0	—	3	0	0	0	0	3	5	1	2	1	21.0	6.00	54	.357	.438	0	—	0	-1	-1	0	0.0
	Chi-N	1	0	1.000	20	0	0	0	5	23^1	12	4	24	18	15.8	6.56	54	.154	.383	1	.250	0	-8	-8	-0	-0.7
1969	Det-A	2	2	.500	11	0	0	0	0	18^2	14	3	5	18	9.2	3.38	111	.212	.268	0	.000	-0	1	1	0	0.1
	Mon-N	0	4	.000	22	0	0	0	3	34^2	32	6	18	32	13.2	5.71	64	.244	.340	1	.250	0	-8	-8	-1	-1.0
Total	7	52	43	.547	381	0	0	0	122	693^2	532	65	296	745	11.1	3.13	122	.212	.303	19	.131	-3	38	53	-9	10.6

● CHARLEY RADBOURN Radbourn, Charles Gardner "Old Hoss" b: 12/11/1854, Rochester, N.Y. d: 2/5/1897, Bloomington, Ill. BR/TR, 5'9", 168 lbs. Deb: 5/5/1880 H♦

YEAR	TM/L	W	L	PCT	G	GS	CG	SH	SV	IP	H	HR	BB	SO	RAT	ERA	ERA+	OAV	OOB	BH	AVG	PB	PR	/A	PD	TPI
1881	Pro-N	25	11	**.694**	41	36	34	3	0	325^1	309	1	64	117	10.3	2.43	109	**.235**	.270	59	.219	-1	12	8	3	0.9
1882	Pro-N	33	20	.623	55	52	51	**6**	0	474	429	6	51	**201**	9.1	2.09	135	.226	.246	78	.239	-1	**43**	**38**	1	**3.4**
1883	Pro-N	**48**	25	.658	**76**	68	66	4	1	632^1	563	7	56	315	**8.8**	2.05	151	.227	**.244**	108	.283	14	**76**	**73**	5	**8.4**
1884	*Pro-N	**59**	12	**.831**	**75**	73	**73**	11	1	**678^2**	528	18	98	**441**	8.3	**1.38**	**206**	.205	.234	83	.230	5	121	111	-4	**9.9**
1885	Pro-N	28	21	.571	49	49	49	2	0	445^2	423	4	83	154	10.2	2.20	122	.241	.275	58	.233	11	31	24	4	3.7
1886	Bos-N	27	31	.466	58	58	57	3	0	509^1	521	18	111	218	11.2	3.00	106	.254	.292	60	.237	8	17	11	2	1.9
1887	Bos-N	24	23	.511	50	50	48	1	0	425	505	20	133	87	13.8	4.55	89	.286	.340	40	.229	2	-23	-23	-3	-2.1
1888	Bos-N	7	16	.304	24	24	24	1	0	207	187	8	45	64	10.4	2.87	99	.234	.282	17	.215	1	-0	-0	-1	-0.1
1889	Bos-N	20	11	.645	33	31	28	1	0	277	282	14	72	99	11.8	3.67	113	.256	.306	23	.189	-1	11	15	2	1.4
1890	Bos-P	27	12	.692	41	38	36	1	0	343	352	8	100	80	12.1	3.31	133	.254	.309	39	.253	0	35	42	2	3.7
1891	Cin-N	11	13	.458	26	24	23	2	0	218	236	13	62	54	12.8	4.25	79	.266	.323	17	.177	-1	-22	-21	-3	-2.1
Total	11	309	195	.613	528	503	489	35	2	4535^1	4335	117	875	1830	10.4	2.67	120	.241	.278	585	.235	39	302	271	7	29.0

● GEORGE RADBOURN Radbourn, George B. "Dordy" b: 4/8/1856, Bloomington, Ill. d: 1/1/04, Bloomington, Ill. 160 lbs. Deb: 5/30/1883

YEAR	TM/L	W	L	PCT	G	GS	CG	SH	SV	IP	H	HR	BB	SO	RAT	ERA	ERA+	OAV	OOB	BH	AVG	PB	PR	/A	PD	TPI
1883	Det-N	1	2	.333	3	3	2	0	0	22	38	1	7	2	18.4	6.55	47	.345	.385	2	.167	-1	-8	-8	-0	-0.8

● ROY RADEBAUGH Radebaugh, Roy b: 2/22/1884, Champaign, Ill. d: 1/17/45, Cedar Rapids, Iowa BR/TR, 5'7", 160 lbs. Deb: 9/22/11

YEAR	TM/L	W	L	PCT	G	GS	CG	SH	SV	IP	H	HR	BB	SO	RAT	ERA	ERA+	OAV	OOB	BH	AVG	PB	PR	/A	PD	TPI
1911	StL-N	0	0	—	2	1	0	0	0	10	6	0	4	1	9.0	2.70	125	.176	.263	0	.000	-0	1	1	0	0.0

● DREW RADER Rader, Drew Leon "Lefty" b: 5/14/01, Elmira, N.Y. d: 6/5/75, Catskill, N.Y. BR/TL, 6'2", 187 lbs. Deb: 7/18/21

YEAR	TM/L	W	L	PCT	G	GS	CG	SH	SV	IP	H	HR	BB	SO	RAT	ERA	ERA+	OAV	OOB	BH	AVG	PB	PR	/A	PD	TPI
1921	Pit-N	0	0	—	1	0	0	0	0	2	2	0	0	0	9.0	0.00	—	.286	.286	0	.000	-0	1	1	-0	0.0

● PAUL RADFORD Radford, Paul Revere "Shorty" b: 10/14/1861, Roxbury, Mass. d: 2/21/45, Boston, Mass. BR/TR, 5'6", 148 lbs. Deb: 5/1/1883 ♦

YEAR	TM/L	W	L	PCT	G	GS	CG	SH	SV	IP	H	HR	BB	SO	RAT	ERA	ERA+	OAV	OOB	BH	AVG	PB	PR	/A	PD	TPI
1884	*Pro-N	0	2	.000	2	2	1	0	0	13	27	0	3	2	20.8	7.62	37	.403	.429	70	.197	0	-7	-7	-0	-0.7
1885	Pro-N	0	2	.000	3	2	2	0	0	18^1	34	1	8	3	20.6	7.85	34	.378	.429	90	.243	1	-10	-11	0	-0.8
1887	NY-a	0	0	—	2	0	0	0	0	5	15	1	3	4	32.4	18.00	24	.789	.818	129	.265	1	-8	-8	-0	0.0
1890	Cle-P	0	0	—	1	0	0	0	0	5	7	1	1	3	14.4	3.60	110	.318	.348	136	.292	0	0	0	1	0.1
1891	Bos-a	0	0	—	1	0	0	0	0	1	0	0	0	0	0.0	0.00	—	.000	.000	118	.259	0	0	0	-0	0.0
1893	Was-N	0	0	—	1	0	0	0	0	1	2	2	2	1	36.0	18.00	26	.400	.571	106	.228	0	-1	-1	0	0.0
Total	6	0	4	.000	10	4	3	0	0	43^1	85	5	17	13	21.2	8.52	37	.413	.457	1206	.242	2	-25	-26	0	-1.4

● SCOTT RADINSKY Radinsky, Scott David b: 3/3/68, Glendale, Cal. BL/TL, 6'3", 204 lbs. Deb: 4/9/90

YEAR	TM/L	W	L	PCT	G	GS	CG	SH	SV	IP	H	HR	BB	SO	RAT	ERA	ERA+	OAV	OOB	BH	AVG	PB	PR	/A	PD	TPI
1990	Chi-A	6	1	.857	62	0	0	0	4	52^1	47	1	36	46	14.6	4.82	79	.241	.365	0	—	0	-5	-6	0	-0.7
1991	Chi-A	5	5	.500	67	0	0	0	8	71^1	53	4	23	49	9.7	2.02	197	.206	.274	0	—	0	16	15	1	2.4
1992	Chi-A	3	7	.300	68	0	0	0	15	59^1	54	3	34	48	13.7	2.73	141	.243	.349	0	—	0	8	7	0	1.6
1993	*Chi-A	8	2	.800	73	0	0	0	4	54^2	61	3	19	44	13.3	4.28	98	.268	.327	0	—	0	0	-1	0	0.0
1995	Chi-A	2	1	.667	46	0	0	0	1	38	46	7	17	14	14.9	5.45	82	.309	.380	0	—	0	-3	-4	0	-0.3
1996	*LA-N	5	1	.833	58	0	0	0	1	52^1	52	2	17	48	11.9	2.41	160	.264	.322	0	.000	-0	11	8	0	0.9
1997	LA-N	5	1	.833	75	0	0	0	3	62^1	54	4	21	44	11.0	2.89	133	.236	.303	0	.000	-0	9	7	-0	0.6
1998	LA-N	6	6	.500	62	0	0	0	13	61^2	63	5	20	45	12.7	2.63	148	.272	.340	0	—	0	11	9	-0	1.8
Total	8	40	24	.625	511	0	0	0	49	452	430	29	187	338	12.5	3.25	122	.252	.329	0	.000	-1	47	36	1	6.3

● BRAD RADKE Radke, Brad William b: 10/27/72, Eau Claire, Wis. BR/TR, 6'2", 180 lbs. Deb: 4/29/95

YEAR	TM/L	W	L	PCT	G	GS	CG	SH	SV	IP	H	HR	BB	SO	RAT	ERA	ERA+	OAV	OOB	BH	AVG	PB	PR	/A	PD	TPI
1995	Min-A	11	14	.440	29	28	2	1	0	181	195	32	47	75	12.2	5.32	90	.275	.323	0	—	0	-12	-11	-1	-1.3
1996	Min-A	11	16	.407	35	35	3	0	0	232	231	40	57	148	11.3	4.46	115	.256	.304	0	—	0	14	17	-3	1.4
1997	Min-A	20	10	.667	35	35	4	1	0	239^2	238	28	48	174	10.9	3.87	120	.257	.296	0	.000	-0	19	21	1	2.4
1998	Min-A★	12	14	.462	32	32	5	1	0	213^2	238	23	43	146	12.2	4.30	109	.283	.325	0	.000	-0	8	9	1	1.1
Total	4	54	54	.500	131	130	14	3	0	866^1	902	123	195	543	11.6	4.44	108	.267	.311	0	.000	-1	28	36	-2	3.6

● HAL RAETHER Raether, Harold Herman "Bud" b: 10/10/32, Lake Mills, Wis. BR/TR, 6'1", 185 lbs. Deb: 7/4/54

YEAR	TM/L	W	L	PCT	G	GS	CG	SH	SV	IP	H	HR	BB	SO	RAT	ERA	ERA+	OAV	OOB	BH	AVG	PB	PR	/A	PD	TPI
1954	Phi-A	0	0	—	1	0	0	0	0	2	1	0	4	0	22.5	4.50	87	.200	.556	0	—	0	-0	-0	0	0.0
1957	KC-A	0	0	—	1	0	0	0	0	2	2	1	0	0	9.0	9.00	44	.250	.250	0	—	0	-1	-1	-0	0.0
Total	2	0	0	—	2	0	0	0	0	4	3	1	4	0	15.8	6.75	58	.231	.412	0	—	0	-1	-1	0	0.0

● KEN RAFFENSBERGER Raffensberger, Kenneth David b: 8/8/17, York, Pa. BR/TL, 6'2", 185 lbs. Deb: 4/25/39

YEAR	TM/L	W	L	PCT	G	GS	CG	SH	SV	IP	H	HR	BB	SO	RAT	ERA	ERA+	OAV	OOB	BH	AVG	PB	PR	/A	PD	TPI
1939	StL-N	0	0	—	1	0	0	0	0	1	2	0	0	1	18.0	0.00	—	.400	.400	0	—	0	0	0	0	0.0
1940	Chi-N	7	9	.438	43	10	3	0	3	114^2	120	10	29	55	11.9	3.38	111	.271	.319	5	.167	-1	6	5	-1	0.5
1941	Chi-N	0	1	.000	10	1	0	0	0	18	17	0	7	5	12.0	4.50	78	.262	.333	0	.000	-1	-2	-2	1	-0.1
1943	Phi-N	0	1	.000	1	1	1	0	0	8	7	0	2	3	10.1	1.13	300	.241	.290	0	.000	-0	2	2	-0	0.2
1944	Phi-N★	13	20	.394	37	31	18	3	0	258^2	257	9	45	136	10.6	3.06	118	.252	.285	11	.138	-3	16	16	-3	1.3
1945	Phi-N	0	3	.000	5	4	1	0	0	24^1	28	3	14	6	15.5	4.44	86	.283	.372	0	.000	-1	-2	-2	0	-0.3
1946	Phi-N	8	15	.348	39	23	14	2	**6**	196	203	10	39	73	11.2	3.63	95	.265	.302	10	.167	-1	-5	-4	-3	-0.8

YEAR	TM/L	W	L	PCT	G	GS	CG	SH	SV	IP	H	HR	BB	SO	RAT	ERA	ERA+	OAV	OOB	BH	AVG	PB	PR	/A	PD	TPI
1947	Phi-N	2	6	.250	10	7	3	1	0	41	50	4	8	16	13.0	5.49	73	.307	.343	4	.267	0	-7	-7	1	-1.0
	Cin-N	6	5	.545	19	15	7	0	1	106^2	132	11	29	38	13.6	4.13	99	.305	.348	6	.162	-1	-1	-0	-1	-0.2
	Yr	8	11	.421	29	22	10	1	1	147^2	182	15	37	54	13.3	4.51	90	.305	.345	10	.192	-0	-7	-7	0	-1.2
1948	Cin-N	11	12	.478	40	24	7	4	0	180^1	187	15	37	57	11.2	3.84	102	.259	.296	7	.113	-3	2	1	-2	-0.3
1949	Cin-N	18	17	.514	41	38	20	**5**	0	284	289	23	80	103	11.8	3.39	123	.264	.315	16	.178	0	21	25	-3	2.6
1950	Cin-N	14	19	.424	38	35	18	4	0	239	271	34	40	87	11.8	4.26	100	.279	.308	11	.134	-2	-3	-1	-2	-0.4
1951	Cin-N	16	17	.485	42	33	14	5	5	248^2	232	30	38	81	**10.0**	3.44	119	.246	.279	10	.122	-3	14	18	-4	1.5
1952	Cin-N	17	13	.567	38	33	18	**6**	1	247	247	18	45	93	10.7	2.81	134	.261	.295	8	.107	-2	25	27	-2	2.7
1953	Cin-N	7	14	.333	26	26	9	1	0	174	200	23	33	47	12.1	3.93	111	.289	.322	8	.140	-1	7	8	2	0.9
1954	Cin-N	0	2	.000	6	1	0	0	0	10^1	15	2	3	5	15.7	7.84	53	.333	.375	1	.500	0	-4	-4	-0	-0.7
Total	15	119	154	.436	396	282	133	31	16	2151^2	2257	192	449	806	11.4	3.60	110	.267	.306	97	.141	-17	71	82	-18	5.9

● AL RAFFO Raffo, Albert Martin b: 11/27/41, San Francisco, Cal. BR/TR, 6'5", 210 lbs. Deb: 4/29/69

YEAR	TM/L	W	L	PCT	G	GS	CG	SH	SV	IP	H	HR	BB	SO	RAT	ERA	ERA+	OAV	OOB	BH	AVG	PB	PR	/A	PD	TPI
1969	Phi-N	1	3	.250	45	0	0	0	1	72^1	81	6	25	38	13.7	4.11	86	.286	.353	1	.167	0	-4	-5	1	-0.2

● PAT RAGAN Ragan, Don Carlos Patrick b: 11/15/1888, Blanchard, Iowa d: 9/4/56, Los Angeles, Cal. BR/TR, 5'10.5", 185 lbs. Deb: 4/21/09 C

YEAR	TM/L	W	L	PCT	G	GS	CG	SH	SV	IP	H	HR	BB	SO	RAT	ERA	ERA+	OAV	OOB	BH	AVG	PB	PR	/A	PD	TPI
1909	Cin-N	0	1	.000	2	0	0	0	0	8	7	0	4	2	12.4	3.38	77	.259	.355	1	.500	0	-1	-1	-0	-0.1
	Chi-N	0	0	—	2	0	0	0	0	3^2	4	0	1	2	12.3	2.45	104	.286	.333	0	.000	-0	0	0	-0	0.0
	Yr	0	1	.000	4	0	0	0	0	11^2	11	0	5	4	12.3	3.09	84	.268	.348	1	.250	0	-1	-1	-0	-0.1
1911	Bro-N	4	3	.571	22	7	5	1	1	93^2	81	0	31	39	11.0	2.11	158	.252	.321	4	.138	-1	13	13	-1	0.7
1912	Bro-N	7	18	.280	36	26	12	1	1	208	211	7	65	101	12.1	3.63	92	.270	.329	4	.060	-7	-5	-7	-1	-1.5
1913	Bro-N	15	18	.455	44	32	14	0	0	264^2	284	10	64	109	12.0	3.77	87	.281	.327	15	.165	-2	-17	-14	2	-1.7
1914	Bro-N	10	15	.400	38	25	14	1	3	208^1	214	5	85	106	13.0	2.98	96	.270	.343	10	.133	-3	-4	-3	0	-0.7
1915	Bro-N	1	0	1.000	5	0	0	0	0	19^2	11	0	8	7	8.7	0.92	304	.164	.253	1	.167	-0	4	4	0	0.1
	Bos-N	16	12	.571	33	26	13	3	0	227	208	2	59	81	10.9	2.46	105	.255	.311	12	.150	-0	7	3	-2	0.0
	Yr	17	12	.586	38	26	13	3	0	246^2	219	2	67	88	10.7	2.34	112	.248	.306	13	.151	-1	11	7	-2	0.1
1916	Bos-N	9	9	.500	28	23	14	3	0	182	143	3	47	94	9.4	2.08	120	.218	.270	13	.217	3	11	8	1	1.3
1917	Bos-N	6	9	.400	30	13	5	1	1	147^2	138	6	35	61	10.6	2.93	87	.250	.295	6	.125	-1	-4	-6	0	-0.8
1918	Bos-N	8	17	.320	30	25	15	2	0	206^1	212	4	54	68	11.8	3.23	83	.270	.320	13	.183	-2	-11	-12	-0	-1.6
1919	Bos-N	0	2	.000	4	3	0	0	0	12^2	16	0	3	3	13.5	7.11	40	.281	.317	1	.250	0	-6	-6	0	-0.8
	NY-N	1	0	1.000	7	1	1	0	0	22^2	19	0	14	7	13.1	1.59	177	.247	.363	3	.429	1	3	3	0	0.3
	Yr	1	2	.333	11	4	1	0	0	35^1	35	0	17	10	13.2	3.57	79	.261	.344	4	.364	1	-3	-3	0	-0.5
	Chi-A	0	0	—	1	0	0	0	0	1	1	0	0	0	9.0	0.00	—	.250	.250	0	—	0	0	0	0	0.0
1923	Phi-N	0	0	—	1	0	0	0	0	3	6	1	0	0	18.0	6.00	77	.400	.400	1	.500	0	-1	-0	-0	0.0
Total	11	77	104	.425	283	181	93	12	6	1608^1	1555	38	470	680	11.5	2.99	97	.260	.317	84	.154	-13	-8	-18	-2	-4.8

● BRADY RAGGIO Raggio, Brady John b: 9/17/72, Los Angeles, Cal. BR/TR, 6'4", 210 lbs. Deb: 4/15/97

YEAR	TM/L	W	L	PCT	G	GS	CG	SH	SV	IP	H	HR	BB	SO	RAT	ERA	ERA+	OAV	OOB	BH	AVG	PB	PR	/A	PD	TPI
1997	StL-N	1	2	.333	15	4	0	0	0	31^1	44	1	16	21	17.5	6.89	60	.336	.412	0	.000	-0	-9	-10	0	-0.8
1998	StL-N	1	1	.500	4	1	0	0	0	7	22	1	3	3	33.4	15.43	27	.579	.619	0	.000	-0	-9	-9	0	-1.7
Total	2	2	3	.400	19	5	0	0	0	38^1	66	2	19	24	20.4	8.45	49	.391	.458	0	.000	-0	-18	-18	0	-2.5

● FRANK RAGLAND Ragland, Frank Roland b: 5/26/04, Water Valley, Miss. d: 7/28/59, Paris, Miss. BR/TR, 6'1", 186 lbs. Deb: 4/17/32

YEAR	TM/L	W	L	PCT	G	GS	CG	SH	SV	IP	H	HR	BB	SO	RAT	ERA	ERA+	OAV	OOB	BH	AVG	PB	PR	/A	PD	TPI
1932	Was-A	1	0	1.000	12	1	0	0	0	37^2	54	5	21	11	18.6	7.41	58	.346	.433	3	.273	1	-12	-13	0	-0.2
1933	Phi-N	0	4	.000	11	5	0	0	0	38^1	51	1	10	4	14.6	6.81	56	.317	.360	2	.200	-0	-15	-13	1	-1.1
Total	2	1	4	.200	23	6	0	0	0	76	105	6	31	15	16.6	7.11	58	.331	.398	5	.238	1	-27	-25	1	-1.3

● ERIC RAICH Raich, Eric James b: 11/1/51, Detroit, Mich. BR/TR, 6'4", 225 lbs. Deb: 5/24/75

YEAR	TM/L	W	L	PCT	G	GS	CG	SH	SV	IP	H	HR	BB	SO	RAT	ERA	ERA+	OAV	OOB	BH	AVG	PB	PR	/A	PD	TPI
1975	Cle-A	7	8	.467	18	17	2	0	0	92^2	118	12	31	34	14.6	5.54	68	.320	.374	0	—	0	-18	-18	-1	-2.6
1976	Cle-A	0	0	—	1	0	0	0	0	2^2	7	1	0	1	23.6	16.88	21	.467	.467	0	—	0	-4	-4	-0	0.0
Total	2	7	8	.467	19	17	2	0	0	95^1	125	13	31	35	14.8	5.85	64	.326	.377	0	—	0	-22	-22	-1	-2.6

● CHUCK RAINEY Rainey, Charles David b: 7/14/54, San Diego, Cal. BR/TR, 5'11", 190 lbs. Deb: 4/8/79

YEAR	TM/L	W	L	PCT	G	GS	CG	SH	SV	IP	H	HR	BB	SO	RAT	ERA	ERA+	OAV	OOB	BH	AVG	PB	PR	/A	PD	TPI
1979	Bos-A	8	5	.615	20	16	4	1	1	103^2	97	7	41	41	12.2	3.82	116	.250	.326	0	—	0	5	7	1	0.8
1980	Bos-A	8	3	.727	16	13	2	1	0	87	92	7	41	43	14.0	4.86	87	.273	.355	0	—	0	-8	-6	-1	-0.8
1981	Bos-A	0	1	.000	11	2	0	0	0	40	39	2	13	20	11.7	2.70	143	.252	.310	0	—	0	4	5	1	0.1
1982	Bos-A	7	5	.583	27	25	3	3	0	129	146	14	63	57	14.7	5.02	86	.294	.376	0	—	0	-14	-10	1	-0.8
1983	Chi-N	14	13	.519	34	34	1	1	0	191	219	17	74	84	13.9	4.48	85	.295	.361	9	.161	1	-18	-15	3	-1.6
1984	Chi-N	5	7	.417	17	16	0	0	0	88^1	102	4	38	45	14.5	4.28	91	.290	.362	3	.097	-1	-7	-4	1	-0.5
	Oak-A	1	1	.500	16	0	0	0	1	30^2	43	2	17	10	17.6	6.75	55	.333	.411	0	—	0	-9	-10	-0	-0.7
Total	6	43	35	.551	141	106	10	6	2	669^2	738	53	287	300	13.9	4.50	90	.284	.358	12	.138	-1	-47	-33	5	-3.5

● DAVE RAJSICH Rajsich, David Christopher b: 9/28/51, Youngstown, Ohio BL/TL, 6'5", 175 lbs. Deb: 7/2/78 F

YEAR	TM/L	W	L	PCT	G	GS	CG	SH	SV	IP	H	HR	BB	SO	RAT	ERA	ERA+	OAV	OOB	BH	AVG	PB	PR	/A	PD	TPI
1978	NY-A	0	0	—	4	2	0	0	0	13^1	16	0	6	9	14.9	4.05	89	.320	.393	0	—	0	-0	-1	-0	0.0
1979	Tex-A	1	3	.250	27	3	0	0	0	53^2	56	7	18	32	12.4	3.52	118	.267	.325	0	—	0	4	4	1	0.3
1980	Tex-A	2	1	.667	24	1	0	0	2	48^1	56	7	22	35	15.1	5.96	65	.295	.377	0	—	0	-10	-11	0	-0.7
Total	3	3	4	.429	55	6	0	0	2	115^1	128	14	46	76	13.8	4.60	86	.284	.355	0	—	0	-7	-8	1	-0.4

● JASON RAKERS Rakers, Jason Paul b: 6/29/73, Pittsburgh, Pa. BR/TR, 6'2", 197 lbs. Deb: 5/6/98

YEAR	TM/L	W	L	PCT	G	GS	CG	SH	SV	IP	H	HR	BB	SO	RAT	ERA	ERA+	OAV	OOB	BH	AVG	PB	PR	/A	PD	TPI
1998	Cle-A	0	0	—	1	0	0	0	0	1	0	0	3	0	27.0	9.00	53	.000	.600	0	—	0	-0	-0	0	-0.1

● ED RAKOW Rakow, Edward Charles "Rock" b: 5/30/36, Pittsburgh, Pa. BB/TR, 5'11", 178 lbs. Deb: 4/22/60

YEAR	TM/L	W	L	PCT	G	GS	CG	SH	SV	IP	H	HR	BB	SO	RAT	ERA	ERA+	OAV	OOB	BH	AVG	PB	PR	/A	PD	TPI
1960	LA-N	0	1	.000	9	2	0	0	0	22	30	5	11	9	16.8	7.36	54	.323	.394	2	.333	0	-9	-8	-0	-0.3
1961	KC-A	2	8	.200	45	11	1	0	1	124^2	131	14	49	81	13.6	4.76	88	.269	.346	3	.103	-2	-10	-8	1	-0.7
1962	KC-A	14	17	.452	42	35	11	2	1	235^1	232	31	98	159	12.8	4.25	99	.260	.336	8	.098	-5	-7	-1	2	-0.4
1963	KC-A	9	10	.474	34	26	7	1	0	174^1	173	18	61	104	12.3	3.92	99	.261	.328	6	.105	-2	-6	-0	1	-0.1
1964	Det-A	8	9	.471	42	13	1	0	3	152^1	155	14	59	96	13.0	3.72	98	.266	.340	0	.000	-4	-2	-1	2	-0.3
1965	Det-A	0	0	—	6	0	0	0	0	13^1	14	2	11	10	16.9	6.08	57	.280	.410	0	.000	-0	-4	-4	-1	-0.1
1967	Atl-N	3	2	.600	17	3	0	0	0	39^1	36	4	15	25	11.9	5.26	63	.240	.313	0	.000	-1	-8	-8	-1	-1.2
Total	7	36	47	.434	195	90	20	3	5	761^1	771	88	304	484	13.0	4.33	92	.264	.339	19	.084	-13	-46	-31	4	-3.1

● JOHN RALEIGH Raleigh, John Austin b: 4/21/1890, Elkhorn, Wis. d: 8/24/55, Escondido, Cal. BR/TL, Deb: 8/4/09

YEAR	TM/L	W	L	PCT	G	GS	CG	SH	SV	IP	H	HR	BB	SO	RAT	ERA	ERA+	OAV	OOB	BH	AVG	PB	PR	/A	PD	TPI
1909	StL-N	1	10	.091	15	10	3	0	0	80^2	85	0	21	26	12.2	3.79	67	.285	.339	2	.087	-2	-11	-11	0	-1.6
1910	StL-N	0	0	—	3	1	0	0	0	5	8	0	0	2	14.4	9.00	33	.364	.364	0	.000	-0	-3	-3	0	0.0
Total	2	1	10	.091	18	11	3	0	0	85^2	93	0	21	28	12.3	4.10	62	.291	.340	2	.083	-2	-14	-15	0	-1.6

● PEP RAMBERT Rambert, Elmer Donald b: 8/1/16, Cleveland, Ohio d: 11/16/74, W.Palm Beach, Fla. BR/TR, 6', 175 lbs. Deb: 9/23/39

YEAR	TM/L	W	L	PCT	G	GS	CG	SH	SV	IP	H	HR	BB	SO	RAT	ERA	ERA+	OAV	OOB	BH	AVG	PB	PR	/A	PD	TPI
1939	Pit-N	0	0	—	2	0	0	0	0	3^2	7	0	1	4	19.6	9.82	39	.389	.421	0	—	0	-2	-2	0	0.0
1940	Pit-N	0	1	.000	3	1	0	0	0	8^1	12	0	4	0	20.5	7.56	50	.333	.442	0	.000	0	-3	-3	0	-0.4
Total	2	0	1	.000	5	1	0	0	0	12	19	0	5	4	20.3	8.25	46	.352	.435	0	.000	0	-6	-6	0	-0.4

● PETE RAMBO Rambo, Warren Dawson b: 11/1/06, Thorofare, N.J. d: 6/19/91, Camden, N.J. BR/TR, 5'9", 150 lbs. Deb: 9/16/26

YEAR	TM/L	W	L	PCT	G	GS	CG	SH	SV	IP	H	HR	BB	SO	RAT	ERA	ERA+	OAV	OOB	BH	AVG	PB	PR	/A	PD	TPI
1926	Phi-N	0	0	—	1	0	0	0	0	3^2	6	0	4	4	24.5	14.73	28	.353	.476	1	1.000	0	-4	-4	0	0.0

● ALLAN RAMIREZ Ramirez, Daniel Allan b: 5/1/57, Victoria, Tex. BR/TR, 5'10", 180 lbs. Deb: 6/8/83

YEAR	TM/L	W	L	PCT	G	GS	CG	SH	SV	IP	H	HR	BB	SO	RAT	ERA	ERA+	OAV	OOB	BH	AVG	PB	PR	/A	PD	TPI
1983	Bal-A	4	4	.500	11	10	1	0	0	57	46	6	30	20	12.0	3.47	114	.229	.329	0	—	0	4	3	0	0.4

● ROBERTO RAMIREZ Ramirez, Roberto Sanchez b: 8/17/72, Veracruz, Mexico BL/TL, 6', 171 lbs. Deb: 6/12/98

YEAR	TM/L	W	L	PCT	G	GS	CG	SH	SV	IP	H	HR	BB	SO	RAT	ERA	ERA+	OAV	OOB	BH	AVG	PB	PR	/A	PD	TPI
1998	SD-N	1	0	1.000	21	0	0	0	0	14^2	12	4	12	17	14.7	6.14	62	.211	.348	0	—	0	-3	-4	-0	-0.2

● EDGAR RAMOS Ramos, Edgar Jose (Malave) b: 3/6/75, Cumana, Venezuela BR/TR, 6'4", 190 lbs. Deb: 5/21/97

YEAR	TM/L	W	L	PCT	G	GS	CG	SH	SV	IP	H	HR	BB	SO	RAT	ERA	ERA+	OAV	OOB	BH	AVG	PB	PR	/A	PD	TPI
1997	Phi-N	0	2	.000	4	2	0	0	0	14	15	3	6	4	14.1	5.14	82	.288	.373	0	.000	-0	-1	-1	-0	-0.2

● **PEDRO RAMOS** Ramos, Pedro (Guerra) "Pete" b: 4/28/35, Pinar Del Rio, Cuba BB/TR, 6', 185 lbs. Deb: 4/11/55 ♦

YEAR	TM/L	W	L	PCT	G	GS	CG	SH	SV	IP	H	HR	BB	SO	RAT	ERA	ERA+	OAV	OOB	BH	AVG	PB	PR	/A	PD	TPI
1955	Was-A	5	11	.313	45	9	3	1	5	130	121	13	39	34	11.8	3.88	99	.253	.323	3	.079	-3	1	-1	-1	-0.5
1956	Was-A	12	10	.545	37	18	4	0	0	152	178	23	76	54	15.2	5.27	82	.299	.381	9	.205	0	-19	-16	-0	-2.0
1957	Was-A	12	16	.429	43	30	7	1	0	231	251	43	69	91	12.7	4.79	81	.271	.327	13	.171	-1	-26	-23	-0	-2.6
1958	Was-A	14	18	.438	43	37	10	4	3	259^{1}	277	38	77	132	12.5	4.23	90	.273	.327	21	.239	1	-13	-12	-1	-1.3
1959	Was-A☆	13	19	.406	37	35	11	0	0	233^{2}	233	29	52	95	11.3	4.16	94	.257	.304	11	.147	-0	-8	-6	-1	-0.8
1960	Was-A	11	18	.379	43	36	14	1	2	274	254	24	99	160	11.8	3.45	113	.245	.315	10	.116	-2	13	13	0	1.2
1961	Min-A	11	20	.355	42	34	9	3	2	264^{1}	265	39	79	174	11.8	3.95	107	.258	.313	16	.172	1	2	9	-3	0.8
1962	Cle-A	10	12	.455	37	27	7	2	1	201^{1}	189	28	85	96	12.5	3.71	104	.246	.326	10	.147	2	6	4	0	0.6
1963	Cle-A	9	8	.529	36	22	5	0	0	184^{2}	156	29	41	169	9.8	3.12	116	.226	.273	6	.109	1	10	10	-2	0.8
1964	Cle-A	7	10	.412	36	19	3	1	0	133	144	18	26	98	11.8	5.14	70	.273	.312	7	.179	2	-22	-23	-1	-2.5
	NY-A	1	0	1.000	13	0	0	0	8	21^{2}	13	1	0	21	5.4	1.25	291	.183	.183	0	.000	-1	6	6	-1	0.6
	Yr	8	10	.444	49	19	3	1	8	154^{2}	157	19	26	119	10.6	4.60	78	.259	.290	7	.159	1	-17	-17	-2	-1.9
1965	NY-A	5	5	.500	65	0	0	0	19	92^{1}	80	7	27	68	10.5	2.92	116	.237	.296	1	.083	-1	5	5	-1	0.6
1966	NY-A	3	9	.250	52	1	0	0	13	89^{2}	98	10	18	58	11.7	3.61	92	.283	.321	2	.154	-0	-2	-3	-0	-0.5
1967	Phi-N	0	0	—	6	0	0	0	0	8	14	1	8	1	27.0	9.00	38	.412	.545	0	.000	-0	-5	-5	1	0.1
1969	Pit-N	0	1	.000	5	0	0	0	0	6	8	2	0	4	12.0	6.00	58	.320	.320	0	.000	-0	-2	-2	0	-0.3
	Cin-N	4	3	.571	38	0	0	0	2	66^{1}	73	8	24	40	13.8	5.16	73	.284	.357	0	.000	-1	-12	-10	-0	-1.1
	Yr	4	4	.500	43	0	0	0	2	72^{1}	81	10	24	44	13.7	5.23	72	.287	.354	0	.000	-1	-13	-12	-0	-1.4
1970	Was-A	0	0	—	4	0	0	0	0	8^{1}	10	2	4	10	15.1	7.56	47	.294	.368	0	.000	0	-4	-4	0	0.0
Total	15	117	160	.422	582	268	73	13	55	2355^{2}	2364	315	724	1305	12.1	4.08	95	.261	.320	109	.155	-0	-68	-58	-9	-6.9

● **WILLIE RAMSDELL** Ramsdell, James Willard "The Knuck" b: 4/4/16, Williamsburg, Kan. d: 10/8/69, Wichita, Kan. BR/TR, 5'10", 180 lbs. Deb: 9/24/47

YEAR	TM/L	W	L	PCT	G	GS	CG	SH	SV	IP	H	HR	BB	SO	RAT	ERA	ERA+	OAV	OOB	BH	AVG	PB	PR	/A	PD	TPI
1947	Bro-N	1	1	.500	2	0	0	0	0	2^{2}	4	0	3	3	27.0	6.75	61	.333	.500	1	1.000	0	-1	-1	0	-0.4
1948	Bro-N	4	4	.500	27	1	0	0	4	50^{1}	48	6	41	34	16.5	5.19	77	.251	.391	1	.091	-1	-7	-7	1	-1.0
1950	Bro-N	1	2	.333	5	0	0	0	1	6^{1}	7	0	2	2	14.2	2.84	144	.292	.370	0	.000	-0	1	1	0	0.4
	Cin-N	7	12	.368	27	22	8	1	0	157^{1}	151	17	75	83	13.0	3.72	114	.255	.341	10	.200	1	7	9	-1	0.9
	Yr	8	14	.364	32	22	8	1	1	163^{2}	158	17	77	85	13.0	3.68	115	.256	.341	10	.189	0	8	10	-1	1.3
1951	Cin-N	9	17	.346	31	31	10	1	0	196	204	18	70	88	12.9	4.04	101	.266	.333	9	.155	-1	-2	1	-2	-0.2
1952	Chi-N	2	3	.400	19	4	0	0	0	67	41	5	24	30	9.4	2.42	159	.173	.263	1	.056	-1	10	11	-1	0.6
Total	5	24	39	.381	111	58	18	2	5	479^{2}	455	46	215	240	12.9	3.83	107	.250	.335	22	.156	-2	9	14	-2	0.3

● **TOAD RAMSEY** Ramsey, Thomas A. b: 8/8/1864, Indianapolis, Ind. d: 3/27/06, Indianapolis, Ind. BR/TL, Deb: 9/5/1885

YEAR	TM/L	W	L	PCT	G	GS	CG	SH	SV	IP	H	HR	BB	SO	RAT	ERA	ERA+	OAV	OOB	BH	AVG	PB	PR	/A	PD	TPI
1885	Lou-a	3	6	.333	9	9	9	0	0	79	44	1	28	83	8.3	1.94	167	.150	.227	4	.129	-2	12	11	-0	0.8
1886	Lou-a	38	27	.585	67	67	**66**	3	0	**588**^{2}	447	3	207	499	10.2	2.45	149	**.198**	.269	58	.241	-3	66	**78**	-3	6.5
1887	Lou-a	37	27	.578	65	64	61	0	0	561	544	9	167	**355**	11.7	3.43	128	.242	.299	43	.191	-10	54	60	-9	3.5
1888	Lou-a	8	30	.211	40	40	37	1	0	342^{1}	362	10	86	228	12.1	3.42	90	.262	.310	17	.120	-7	-13	-13	-4	-2.1
1889	Lou-a	1	16	.059	18	18	15	0	0	140	175	7	71	60	15.9	5.59	69	.297	.374	15	.263	0	-27	-27	-2	-2.5
	StL-a	3	1	.750	5	3	3	0	0	41	44	0	10	33	12.1	3.95	107	.265	.311	5	.294	0	-0	1	-1	0.1
	Yr	4	17	.190	23	21	18	0	0	181	219	7	81	93	15.0	5.22	75	.289	.358	20	.270	1	-28	-26	-2	-2.4
1890	StL-a	24	17	.585	44	40	34	1	0	348^{2}	325	10	102	257	11.2	3.69	117	.239	.296	33	.228	-1	7	24	-7	1.5
Total	6	114	124	.479	248	241	225	5	0	2100^{2}	1941	40	671	1515	11.4	3.29	117	.234	.295	175	.204	-22	97	134	-25	7.8

● **RIBS RANEY** Raney, Frank Robert Donald (b: Frank Robert Donald Raniszewski) b: 2/16/23, Detroit, Mich. BR/TR, 6'4", 190 lbs. Deb: 9/18/49

YEAR	TM/L	W	L	PCT	G	GS	CG	SH	SV	IP	H	HR	BB	SO	RAT	ERA	ERA+	OAV	OOB	BH	AVG	PB	PR	/A	PD	TPI
1949	StL-A	1	2	.333	3	3	1	0	0	16^{1}	23	2	12	5	19.3	7.71	59	.333	.432	0	.000	-1	-6	-6	-0	-0.9
1950	StL-A	0	1	.000	1	0	0	0	0	2	2	0	2	2	18.0	4.50	110	.250	.400	0	.000	-0	0	0	0	0.0
Total	2	1	3	.250	4	3	1	0	0	18^{1}	25	2	14	7	19.1	7.36	62	.325	.429	0	.000	-1	-6	-6	-0	-0.9

● **PAT RAPP** Rapp, Patrick Leland b: 7/13/67, Jennings, La. BR/TR, 6'3", 215 lbs. Deb: 7/10/92

YEAR	TM/L	W	L	PCT	G	GS	CG	SH	SV	IP	H	HR	BB	SO	RAT	ERA	ERA+	OAV	OOB	BH	AVG	PB	PR	/A	PD	TPI
1992	SF-N	0	2	.000	3	2	0	0	0	10	8	0	6	3	13.5	7.20	46	.235	.366	0	.000	-0	-4	-4	0	-0.7
1993	Fla-N	4	6	.400	16	16	1	0	0	94	101	7	39	57	13.6	4.02	107	.281	.355	6	.194	0	0	3	0	0.4
1994	Fla-N	7	8	.467	24	23	2	1	0	133^{1}	132	13	69	75	14.0	3.85	114	.266	.364	5	.122	-2	5	8	-1	0.5
1995	Fla-N	14	7	.667	28	28	3	2	0	167^{1}	158	10	76	102	13.0	3.44	122	.253	.340	6	.107	-3	14	14	-1	1.3
1996	Fla-N	8	16	.333	30	29	0	0	0	162^{1}	184	12	91	86	15.4	5.10	80	.301	.394	7	.121	-2	-16	-19	0	-2.5
1997	Fla-N	4	6	.400	19	19	1	1	0	108^{2}	121	11	51	64	14.5	4.47	90	.286	.367	5	.143	0	-3	-5	-0	-0.4
	SF-N	1	2	.333	8	6	0	0	0	33	37	5	21	28	16.4	6.00	69	.294	.403	0	.000	-1	-7	-7	-0	-0.7
	Yr	5	8	.385	27	25	1	1	0	141^{2}	158	16	72	92	14.7	4.83	84	.285	.369	5	.106	-1	-10	-12	-0	-1.1
1998	KC-A	12	13	.480	32	32	1	1	0	188^{1}	208	24	107	132	15.5	5.30	93	.285	.384	0	.000	-0	-14	-8	0	-0.9
Total	7	50	60	.455	160	155	8	5	0	897	949	82	460	547	14.5	4.52	96	.279	.370	29	.122	-7	-24	-19	-2	-3.0

● **VIC RASCHI** Raschi, Victor John Angelo b: 3/28/19, W.Springfield, Mass. d: 10/14/88, Groveland, N.Y. BR/TR, 6'1", 205 lbs. Deb: 9/23/46

YEAR	TM/L	W	L	PCT	G	GS	CG	SH	SV	IP	H	HR	BB	SO	RAT	ERA	ERA+	OAV	OOB	BH	AVG	PB	PR	/A	PD	TPI
1946	NY-A	2	0	1.000	2	2	2	0	0	16	14	0	5	11	10.7	3.94	88	.230	.288	1	.250	0	-1	-1	0	-0.1
1947	*NY-A	7	2	.778	15	14	6	1	0	104^{2}	89	11	38	51	11.0	3.87	91	.226	.296	10	.250	2	-2	-4	-0	-0.2
1948	NY-A★	19	8	.704	36	31	18	6	1	222^{2}	208	15	74	124	11.5	3.84	106	.247	.310	19	.235	2	11	6	-1	0.7
1949	*NY-A★	21	10	.677	38	37	21	3	0	274^{2}	247	16	138	124	12.8	3.34	121	.241	.334	13	.157	1	26	21	1	2.3
1950	*NY-A★	21	8	**.724**	33	32	17	2	1	256^{2}	232	19	116	155	12.3	4.00	107	.243	.327	17	.198	1	17	8	-3	0.7
1951	*NY-A	21	10	.677	35	34	15	4	0	258^{1}	233	20	103	**164**	11.9	3.27	117	.242	.319	15	.176	-2	24	16	-3	1.2
1952	*NY-A★	16	6	.727	31	31	13	4	0	223	174	13	91	127	10.9	2.78	119	.216	.300	13	.188	3	22	13	-4	1.1
1953	*NY-A	13	6	.684	28	26	7	4	1	181	150	11	55	76	**10.2**	3.33	111	.224	**.283**	9	.143	-2	13	7	-2	0.3
1954	StL-N	8	9	.471	30	29	6	2	0	179	182	24	71	73	12.7	4.73	87	.268	.337	9	.141	-2	-13	-12	1	-1.1
1955	StL-N	0	1	.000	1	1	0	0	0	1^{2}	5	0	1	1	32.4	21.60	19	.556	.600	0	—	0	-3	-3	-0	-1.0
	KC-A	4	6	.400	20	18	1	0	0	101^{1}	132	10	35	38	14.9	5.42	77	.312	.366	6	.182	-0	-16	-14	1	-1.1
Total	10	132	66	.667	269	255	106	26	3	1819	1666	139	727	944	12.0	3.72	105	.244	.319	112	.184	3	78	38	-9	2.8

● **DENNIS RASMUSSEN** Rasmussen, Dennis Lee b: 4/18/59, Los Angeles, Cal. BL/TL, 6'7", 230 lbs. Deb: 9/16/83 F

YEAR	TM/L	W	L	PCT	G	GS	CG	SH	SV	IP	H	HR	BB	SO	RAT	ERA	ERA+	OAV	OOB	BH	AVG	PB	PR	/A	PD	TPI
1983	SD-N	0	0	—	4	1	0	0	0	13^{2}	10	1	8	13	11.9	1.98	176	.200	.310	0	.000	-0	3	2	1	0.0
1984	NY-A	9	6	.600	24	24	1	0	0	147^{2}	127	16	60	110	11.6	4.57	83	.234	.315	0	—	0	-10	-13	-1	-1.0
1985	NY-A	3	5	.375	22	16	2	0	0	101^{2}	97	10	42	63	12.4	3.98	100	.255	.331	0	—	0	2	0	0	0.2
1986	NY-A	18	6	.750	31	31	3	1	0	202	160	28	74	131	10.5	3.88	105	.217	.290	0	—	0	7	5	-1	0.5
1987	NY-A	9	7	.563	26	25	2	0	0	146	145	31	55	89	12.6	4.75	92	.260	.331	0	—	0	-5	-6	-0	-0.5
	Cin-N	4	1	.800	7	7	0	0	0	45^{1}	39	5	12	39	10.3	3.97	107	.229	.284	1	.067	-1	1	1	0	0.1
1988	Cin-N	2	6	.250	11	11	1	1	0	56^{1}	68	8	22	27	14.7	5.75	62	.300	.367	5	.227	1	-14	-14	0	-1.6
	SD-N	14	4	.778	20	20	6	0	0	148^{1}	131	9	36	85	10.3	2.55	133	.238	.287	9	.188	2	15	14	2	2.2
	Yr	16	10	.615	31	31	7	1	0	204^{2}	199	17	58	112	11.4	3.43	100	.254	.308	14	.200	3	0	0	2	0.6
1989	SD-N	10	10	.500	33	33	1	0	0	183^{2}	190	18	72	87	13.0	4.26	82	.270	.340	11	.169	1	-16	-16	-1	-1.6
1990	SD-N	11	15	.423	32	32	3	1	0	187^{2}	217	28	62	86	13.5	4.51	85	.292	.349	18	.290	5	-15	-14	0	-1.3
1991	SD-N	6	13	.316	24	24	1	1	0	146^{2}	155	12	49	75	12.6	3.74	101	.271	.331	6	.136	1	-1	1	2	0.4
1992	Chi-N	0	0	—	3	1	0	0	0	5	7	2	2	0	18.0	10.80	33	.350	.435	0	—	0	-4	-4	0	0.0
	KC-A	4	1	.800	5	5	1	1	0	37^{2}	25	0	6	12	7.4	1.43	283	.197	.233	0	—	0	10	11	1	1.5
1993	KC-A	1	2	.333	9	4	0	0	0	29	40	4	14	12	17.1	7.45	61	.328	.401	0	—	0	-10	-9	-0	-0.8
1995	KC-A	0	1	.000	5	1	0	0	0	10	13	3	8	6	18.9	9.00	53	.302	.412	0	—	0	-5	-5	-0	-0.4
Total	12	91	77	.542	256	235	21	5	0	1460^{2}	1424	175	522	835	12.2	4.15	93	.257	.324	50	.193	8	-42	-45	2	-2.3

● **ERIC RASMUSSEN** Rasmussen, Eric Ralph (Born Harold Ralph Rasmussen) b: 3/22/52, Racine, Wis. BR/TR, 6'3", 205 lbs. Deb: 7/21/75

YEAR	TM/L	W	L	PCT	G	GS	CG	SH	SV	IP	H	HR	BB	SO	RAT	ERA	ERA+	OAV	OOB	BH	AVG	PB	PR	/A	PD	TPI
1975	StL-N	5	5	.500	14	13	2	1	0	81	86	8	20	59	11.8	3.78	99	.264	.306	4	.154	-0	-1	-0	-0	-0.1
1976	StL-N	6	12	.333	43	17	2	1	0	150^{1}	139	10	54	76	11.7	3.53	100	.247	.315	4	.105	-1	-1	0	3	0.2
1977	StL-N	11	17	.393	34	34	11	3	0	233	223	24	63	120	11.2	3.48	111	.254	.308	10	.139	0	11	10	-1	1.0
1978	StL-N	2	5	.286	10	10	2	1	0	60^{1}	61	4	20	32	12.1	4.18	84	.270	.329	2	.111	-1	-4	-4	0	-0.6
	SD-N	12	10	.545	27	24	3	2	0	146^{1}	154	16	43	59	12.2	4.06	82	.277	.331	7	.152	-1	-8	-12	1	-1.6
	Yr	14	15	.483	37	34	5	3	0	206^{2}	215	20	63	91	12.1	4.09	83	.274	.329	9	.141	-2	-12	-16	1	-2.2
1979	SD-N	6	9	.400	45	20	5	3	3	156^{2}	142	9	42	54	10.6	3.27	108	.244	.295	2	.056	-2	8	4	-1	0.2

YEAR	TM/L	W	L	PCT	G	GS	CG	SH	SV	IP	H	HR	BB	SO	RAT	ERA	ERA+	OAV	OOB	BH	AVG	PB	PR	/A	PD	TPI
1980	SD-N	4	11	.267	40	14	0	0	1	111^1	130	9	33	50	13.4	4.37	79	.295	.349	2	.095	-1	-9	-12	-0	-1.6
1982	StL-N	1	2	.333	8	3	0	0	0	18^1	21	2	8	15	14.2	4.42	82	.288	.358	0	.000	-0	-2	-2	0	-0.2
1983	StL-N	0	0	—	6	0	0	0	1	7^2	16	1	4	6	23.5	11.74	31	.444	.500	0	—	0	-7	-7	0	-0.2
	KC-A	3	6	.333	11	9	2	1	0	52^2	61	4	22	18	14.2	4.78	85	.289	.356	0	—	0	-4	-4	-0	-0.6
Total	8	50	77	.394	238	144	27	12	5	1017^2	1033	87	309	489	12.0	3.85	94	.266	.321	31	.119	-5	-17	-27	2	-3.5
● **HANS RASMUSSEN**	Rasmussen, Henry Florian b: 4/18/1895, Chicago, Ill. d: 1/1/49, Chicago, Ill. BR/TR, 6'6", 220 lbs. Deb: 8/11/15																									
1915	Chi-F	0	0	—	2	0	0	0	0	2	3	0	2	2	22.5	13.50	19	.600	.714	0	.000	-0	-2	-2	0	0.0
● **GARY RATH**	Rath, Alfred Gary b: 1/10/73, Gulfport, Miss. BL/TL, 6'2", 185 lbs. Deb: 6/2/98																									
1998	LA-N	0	0	—	3	0	0	0	0	3^1	3	1	2	4	13.5	10.80	36	.250	.357	0	—	0	-2	-3	-0	0.0
● **FRED RATH**	Rath, Frederick Helsher Sr. b: 9/1/43, Little Rock, Ark. BR/TR, 6'3", 200 lbs. Deb: 9/10/68 F																									
1968	Chi-A	0	0	—	5	0	0	0	0	11^1	8	0	3	3	9.5	1.59	191	.182	.250	0	—	0	2	2	0	0.0
1969	Chi-A	0	2	.000	3	2	0	0	0	11^2	11	4	8	4	14.7	7.71	50	.256	.373	0	.000	-0	-5	-5	0	-0.7
Total	2	0	2	.000	8	2	0	0	0	23	19	4	11	7	12.1	4.70	73	.218	.313	0	.000	-0	-4	-3	0	-0.7
● **FRED RATH**	Rath, Frederick Helsher Jr. b: 1/5/73, Dallas, Tex. BR/TR, 6'3", 220 lbs. Deb: 7/29/98 F																									
1998	Col-N	0	0	—	2	0	0	0	0	5^1	6	0	2	2	13.5	1.69	300	.300	.364	0	.000	-0	2	2	-0	0.0
● **STEVE RATZER**	Ratzer, Steven Wayne b: 9/9/53, Paterson, N.J. BR/TR, 6'1", 192 lbs. Deb: 10/5/80																									
1980	Mon-N	0	0	—	1	1	0	0	0	4	9	0	2	0	24.8	11.25	32	.450	.500	0	.000	-0	-3	-3	0	0.0
1981	Mon-N	1	1	.500	12	0	0	0	0	17^1	23	2	7	4	15.6	6.23	56	.311	.370	0	.000	-0	-5	-5	1	-0.5
Total	2	1	1	.500	13	1	0	0	0	21^1	32	2	9	4	17.3	7.17	49	.340	.398	0	.000	-0	-9	-9	1	-0.5
● **DOUG RAU**	Rau, Douglas James b: 12/15/48, Columbus, Tex. BL/TL, 6'2", 175 lbs. Deb: 9/2/72																									
1972	LA-N	2	2	.500	7	3	2	0	0	32^2	18	1	11	19	8.3	2.20	151	.159	.240	1	.143	1	5	4	0	0.6
1973	LA-N	4	2	.667	31	3	0	0	3	63^2	64	5	28	51	13.1	3.96	87	.259	.337	1	.091	-1	-2	-4	-0	-0.5
1974	*LA-N	13	11	.542	36	35	3	1	0	198^1	191	20	70	126	12.0	3.72	91	.251	.318	9	.141	-1	-2	-7	-0	-0.9
1975	LA-N	15	9	.625	38	38	8	2	0	257^2	227	18	61	151	10.2	3.11	109	.236	.283	17	.195	2	15	8	-1	0.9
1976	LA-N	16	12	.571	34	32	8	3	0	231	221	18	69	98	11.6	2.57	132	.258	.318	9	.150	1	24	21	-0	2.6
1977	*LA-N	14	8	.636	32	32	4	2	0	212^1	232	15	49	126	12.2	3.43	111	.282	.327	10	.141	-0	11	9	-1	0.7
1978	*LA-N	15	9	.625	30	30	7	2	0	199	219	17	68	95	13.1	3.26	108	.284	.344	9	.143	-1	7	6	-2	0.3
1979	LA-N	1	5	.167	11	11	1	1	0	56	73	3	22	28	15.9	5.30	69	.320	.390	2	.143	1	-10	-10	0	-0.9
1981	Cal-A	1	2	.333	3	3	0	0	0	10^1	14	2	4	3	15.7	8.71	42	.341	.400	0	—	0	-6	-6	-0	-1.3
Total	9	81	60	.574	222	187	33	11	3	1261	1259	99	382	697	11.9	3.35	104	.262	.320	58	.154	2	41	21	-6	1.5
● **BOB RAUCH**	Rauch, Robert John b: 6/16/49, Brookings, S.D. BR/TR, 6'4", 200 lbs. Deb: 6/29/72																									
1972	NY-N	0	1	.000	19	0	0	0	1	27	27	3	21	23	16.0	5.00	67	.273	.400	0	.000	-0	-5	-5	0	-0.2
● **LANCE RAUTZHAN**	Rautzhan, Clarence George b: 8/20/52, Pottsville, Pa. BR/TL, 6'1", 195 lbs. Deb: 7/23/77																									
1977	*LA-N	4	1	.800	25	0	0	0	2	20^2	25	0	7	13	13.9	4.35	88	.313	.368	0	.000	-0	-1	-1	0	-0.3
1978	*LA-N	2	1	.667	43	0	0	0	4	61^1	61	1	19	25	11.9	2.93	120	.263	.321	0	.000	-0	4	4	2	0.4
1979	LA-N	0	2	.000	12	0	0	0	1	9^2	9	0	11	5	19.6	7.45	49	.273	.467	0	—	0	-4	-4	0	-0.8
	Mil-A	0	0	—	3	0	0	0	0	3	3	0	10	2	39.0	9.00	46	.300	.650	0	—	0	-2	-2	0	0.0
Total	3	6	4	.600	83	0	0	0	7	94^2	98	1	47	45	14.0	3.90	93	.276	.364	0	.000	-1	-2	-3	2	-0.7
● **SHANE RAWLEY**	Rawley, Shane William b: 7/27/55, Racine, Wis. BR/TL, 6', 180 lbs. Deb: 4/6/78																									
1978	Sea-A	4	9	.308	52	2	0	0	4	111^1	114	7	51	66	13.7	4.12	92	.275	.362	0	—	0	-4	-4	1	-0.3
1979	Sea-A	5	9	.357	48	3	0	0	11	84^1	88	2	40	48	13.8	3.84	113	.278	.361	0	—	0	3	5	1	0.8
1980	Sea-A	7	7	.500	59	0	0	0	13	113^2	103	3	63	68	13.4	3.33	124	.257	.363	0	—	0	9	10	2	1.6
1981	Sea-A	4	6	.400	46	0	0	0	8	68^1	64	1	38	35	13.6	3.95	97	.257	.358	0	—	0	-2	-1	0	-0.3
1982	NY-A	11	10	.524	47	17	3	0	3	164	165	10	54	111	12.1	4.06	98	.267	.328	0	—	0	0	-1	1	0.1
1983	NY-A	14	14	.500	34	33	13	2	1	238^1	246	19	79	124	12.4	3.78	103	.269	.329	0	—	0	8	3	0	0.5
1984	NY-A	2	3	.400	11	10	0	0	0	42	46	0	27	24	15.6	6.21	61	.272	.372	0	—	0	-10	-11	-0	-0.9
	Phi-N	10	6	.625	18	18	3	0	0	120^1	117	13	27	58	10.8	3.81	95	.257	.300	5	.116	-2	-3	-2	-1	-0.6
1985	Phi-N	13	8	.619	36	31	6	2	0	198^2	188	16	81	106	12.3	3.31	111	.249	.323	8	.138	0	6	8	1	1.0
1986	Phi-N☆	11	7	.611	23	23	7	1	0	157^2	166	13	50	73	12.4	3.54	109	.270	.326	9	.173	0	3	5	-0	0.6
1987	Phi-N	17	11	.607	36	36	4	1	0	229^2	250	23	86	123	13.4	4.39	97	.279	.346	12	.152	-0	-8	-4	-1	-0.6
1988	Phi-N	8	16	.333	32	32	4	1	0	198	220	27	78	87	13.7	4.18	85	.286	.355	6	.105	-1	-16	-14	-0	-1.7
1989	Min-A	5	12	.294	27	25	1	0	0	145	167	19	60	68	14.1	5.21	79	.293	.361	0	—	0	-21	-17	-1	-1.9
Total	12	111	118	.485	469	230	41	7	40	1871^1	1934	153	734	991	13.0	4.02	97	.271	.341	40	.138	-3	-36	-22	2	-1.7
● **CARL RAY**	Ray, Carl Grady b: 1/31/1889, Danbury, N.C. d: 4/3/70, Walnut Cove, N.C. BL/TL, 5'11", 170 lbs. Deb: 9/25/15																									
1915	Phi-A	0	1	.000	2	1	0	0	0	7^1	11	0	6	6	25.8	4.91	60	.333	.488	0	.000	0	-2	-2	-0	-0.2
1916	Phi-A	0	1	.000	3	1	0	0	0	9^1	9	0	14	5	23.1	4.82	59	.257	.480	0	.000	-0	-2	-2	-0	-0.3
Total	2	0	2	.000	5	2	0	0	0	16^2	20	0	20	11	24.3	4.86	59	.294	.484	0	.000	-0	-4	-4	-1	-0.5
● **JIM RAY**	Ray, James Francis "Sting" b: 12/1/44, Rock Hill, S.C. BR/TR, 6'1", 195 lbs. Deb: 9/16/65																									
1965	Hou-N	0	2	.000	3	2	0	0	0	7^2	11	1	6	7	20.0	10.57	32	.355	.459	0	.000	-0	-6	-6	0	-1.2
1966	Hou-N	0	0	—	1	0	0	0	0	0	0	0	1	0	—	∞	—	—	1.000	0	—	0	-1	-1	0	-0.1
1968	Hou-N	2	3	.400	41	2	1	0	1	80^2	65	5	25	71	10.2	2.68	110	.220	.283	1	.067	-1	3	2	-1	0.0
1969	Hou-N	8	2	.800	40	13	0	0	0	115	105	11	48	115	12.1	3.91	90	.245	.324	3	.115	-1	-4	-5	-1	-0.6
1970	Hou-N	6	3	.667	52	2	0	0	5	105	97	13	49	67	12.5	3.26	119	.251	.336	5	.185	-0	9	7	0	0.6
1971	Hou-N	10	4	.714	47	1	0	0	3	97^2	72	3	31	46	9.7	2.12	159	.211	.281	3	.167	0	15	14	-2	1.8
1972	Hou-N	10	9	.526	54	0	0	0	8	90^1	77	10	44	50	12.4	4.28	79	.227	.321	1	.063	-1	-8	-9	-1	-2.3
1973	Hou-N	6	4	.600	42	0	0	0	6	69	65	5	38	25	13.8	4.43	82	.253	.356	3	.231	0	-6	-6	-1	-1.0
1974	Det-A	1	3	.250	28	0	0	0	2	52^1	49	4	29	26	13.6	4.47	85	.254	.354	0	—	0	-5	-4	0	-0.5
Total	9	43	30	.589	308	20	1	0	25	617^2	541	52	271	407	12.0	3.61	97	.238	.323	16	.137	-3	-4	-8	-6	-3.3
● **FARMER RAY**	Ray, Robert Henry b: 9/17/1886, Ft.Lyon, Colo. d: 3/11/63, Electra, Tex. BL/TR, 5'11", 160 lbs. Deb: 6/13/10																									
1910	StL-A	4	10	.286	21	16	11	0	0	140^2	146	3	49	35	12.9	3.58	69	.285	.356	7	.175	0	-17	-17	-3	-1.9
● **CURT RAYDON**	Raydon, Curtis Lowell b: 11/18/33, Bloomington, Ill. BR/TR, 6'4", 190 lbs. Deb: 4/15/58																									
1958	Pit-N	8	4	.667	31	20	2	1	1	134^1	118	18	61	85	12.3	3.62	107	.236	.326	1	.026	-2	5	4	-3	-0.2
● **BUGS RAYMOND**	Raymond, Arthur Lawrence b: 2/24/1882, Chicago, Ill. d: 9/7/12, Chicago, Ill. BR/TR, 5'10", 180 lbs. Deb: 9/23/04																									
1904	Det-A	0	1	.000	5	2	1	0	0	14^2	14	0	6	7	13.5	3.07	83	.250	.344	0	.000	-1	-1	-1	1	0.0
1907	StL-N	2	4	.333	8	6	6	1	0	64^2	56	3	21	34	10.9	1.67	150	.230	.294	2	.091	-0	6	6	0	0.6
1908	StL-N	15	25	.375	48	37	23	5	2	324^1	236	2	95	145	9.6	2.03	116	.207	.277	17	.189	1	12	12	3	2.1
1909	NY-N	18	12	.600	39	30	18	2	0	270	239	7	87	121	11.1	2.47	104	.245	.311	13	.146	0	4	3	2	0.5
1910	NY-N	4	11	.267	19	11	6	0	0	99^1	106	2	40	55	14.0	3.81	78	.280	.362	5	.156	-1	-9	-9	2	-1.1
1911	NY-N	6	4	.600	17	9	4	1	0	81^2	73	1	33	39	11.9	3.31	102	.248	.328	5	.200	-0	1	1	1	0.1
Total	6	45	57	.441	136	95	58	9	2	854^2	724	15	282	401	10.9	2.49	105	.235	.306	42	.160	-0	13	11	9	2.2
● **HARRY RAYMOND**	Raymond, Harry H. "Jack" b: 2/20/1862, Utica, N.Y. d: 3/21/25, San Diego, Cal. 5'9", 179 lbs. Deb: 9/9/1888 ♦																									
1889	Lou-a	1	0	1.000	1	1	1	0	0	9	8	0	11	1	19.0	1.00	385	.229	.413	123	.239	0	3	3	-0	0.2
● **CLAUDE RAYMOND**	Raymond, Joseph Claude Marc "Frenchy" b: 5/7/37, St.Jean, Que., Canada BR/TR, 5'10", 175 lbs. Deb: 4/15/59																									
1959	Chi-A	0	0	—	3	0	0	0	0	4	5	2	2	1	15.8	9.00	42	.333	.412	0	—	0	-2	-2	0	0.0
1961	Mil-N	1	0	1.000	13	0	0	0	2	20^1	22	2	9	13	14.2	3.98	94	.275	.356	0	.000	-0	0	-1	0	0.0
1962	Mil-N	5	5	.500	26	0	0	0	10	42^2	37	5	15	40	11.4	2.74	138	.236	.310	0	.000	-1	6	5	-1	1.2
1963	Mil-N	4	6	.400	45	0	0	0	5	53^1	57	12	27	44	14.9	5.40	60	.268	.361	2	.500	2	-13	-13	1	-2.3

YEAR	TM/L	W	L	PCT	G	GS	CG	SH	SV	IP	H	HR	BB	SO	RAT	ERA	ERA+	OAV	OOB	BH	AVG	PB	PR	/A	PD	TPI
1964	Hou-N	5	5	.500	38	0	0	0	0	79^2	64	3	22	56	10.1	2.82	121	.229	.292	1	.071	-0	6	5	1	0.7
1965	Hou-N	7	4	.636	33	7	2	0	5	96^1	87	6	16	79	10.1	2.90	116	.244	.286	3	.115	-1	7	5	-0	0.5
1966	Hou-N☆	7	5	.583	62	0	0	0	16	92	85	10	25	73	11.2	3.13	109	.242	.300	1	.111	-0	5	3	-2	0.3
1967	Hou-N	0	4	.000	21	0	0	0	5	31	31	5	7	17	11.6	3.19	104	.256	.308	1	.200	0	1	0	-0	0.1
	Atl-N	4	1	.800	28	0	0	0	5	34^1	33	2	11	14	11.5	2.62	127	.260	.319	0	.000	-0	3	3	0	0.5
	Yr	4	5	.444	49	0	0	0	10	65^1	64	7	18	31	11.3	2.89	115	.255	.305	1	.143	0	4	3	-0	0.6
1968	Atl-N	3	5	.375	36	0	0	0	10	60^1	56	4	18	37	11.2	2.83	106	.256	.315	1	.143	-0	1	1	0	0.2
1969	Atl-N	2	2	.500	33	0	0	0	1	48	56	4	13	15	13.3	5.25	69	.298	.350	2	.286	0	-9	-9	-1	-0.8
	Mon-N	1	2	.333	15	0	0	0	1	22	21	2	8	11	12.7	4.09	90	.256	.337	0	.000	-0	-1	-1	-0	-0.1
	Yr	3	4	.429	48	0	0	0	2	70	77	6	21	26	12.9	4.89	74	.281	.337	2	.182	-0	-10	-10	-0	-0.9
1970	Mon-N	6	7	.462	59	0	0	0	23	83^1	76	13	27	68	11.3	4.43	93	.240	.303	0	.000	-1	-4	-3	-1	-0.8
1971	Mon-N	1	7	.125	37	0	0	0	0	53^2	81	5	25	29	17.8	4.70	75	.373	.438	0	.000	-0	-7	-7	-1	-0.9
Total	12	46	53	.465	449	7	2	0	83	721	711	75	225	497	12.0	3.66	96	.261	.324	11	.109	-2	-7	-13	-0	-1.4

● BARRY RAZIANO Raziano, Barry John b: 2/5/47, New Orleans, La. BB/TR, 5'10", 175 lbs. Deb: 8/18/73

YEAR	TM/L	W	L	PCT	G	GS	CG	SH	SV	IP	H	HR	BB	SO	RAT	ERA	ERA+	OAV	OOB	BH	AVG	PB	PR	/A	PD	TPI
1973	KC-A	0	0	—	2	0	0	0	0	5	6	1	1	0	14.4	5.40	76	.316	.381	0	—	0	-1	-1	0	0.0
1974	Cal-A	1	2	.333	13	0	0	0	1	16^2	15	1	8	9	12.4	6.48	53	.246	.333	0	—	0	-5	-6	-0	-0.7
Total	2	1	2	.333	15	0	0	0	1	21^2	21	2	9	9	12.9	6.23	58	.262	.344	0	—	0	-6	-6	-0	-0.7

● RIP REAGAN Reagan, Arthur (b: Arthur Edgar Ragan) b: 6/5/1878, Lincoln, Ill. d: 6/8/53, Kansas City, Mo. BR/TR, 5'11", 170 lbs. Deb: 9/19/03

YEAR	TM/L	W	L	PCT	G	GS	CG	SH	SV	IP	H	HR	BB	SO	RAT	ERA	ERA+	OAV	OOB	BH	AVG	PB	PR	/A	PD	TPI
1903	Cin-N	0	2	.000	3	2	2	0	0	18	40	0	7	7	24.0	6.00	59	.455	.500	2	.250	0	-5	-5	-0	-0.4

● JIM REARDON Reardon, James Matthew b: 1866, Hoosick Falls, N.Y. d: 2/25/1891, Hoosick Falls, N.Y Deb: 7/17/1886

YEAR	TM/L	W	L	PCT	G	GS	CG	SH	SV	IP	H	HR	BB	SO	RAT	ERA	ERA+	OAV	OOB	BH	AVG	PB	PR	/A	PD	TPI
1886	StL-N	0	1	.000	1	1	1	0	0	8	10	1	5	0	16.9	6.75	48	.323	.417	1	.250	0	-3	-3	-0	-0.3
	Cin-a	0	1	.000	1	1	0	0	0	2	5	0	4	0	40.5	18.00	20	.500	.643	0	.000	-1	-3	-3	0	-0.9
Total	1	0	2	.000	2	2	1	0	0	10	15	1	9	0	21.6	9.00	36	.366	.480	1	.143	-1	-6	-6	-0	-1.2

● JEFF REARDON Reardon, Jeffrey James b: 10/1/55, Dalton, Mass. BR/TR, 6'1", 195 lbs. Deb: 8/25/79

YEAR	TM/L	W	L	PCT	G	GS	CG	SH	SV	IP	H	HR	BB	SO	RAT	ERA	ERA+	OAV	OOB	BH	AVG	PB	PR	/A	PD	TPI
1979	NY-N	1	2	.333	18	0	0	0	2	20^2	12	2	9	10	9.1	1.74	209	.174	.269	0	—	0	5	4	-0	0.7
1980	NY-N	8	7	.533	61	0	0	0	6	110^1	96	10	47	101	11.7	2.61	136	.231	.310	0	.000	-1	12	12	-2	1.3
1981	NY-N	1	0	1.000	18	0	0	0	2	28^2	27	2	12	28	12.6	3.45	101	.245	.325	0	.000	-0	0	0	-1	-0.1
	*Mon-N	2	0	1.000	25	0	0	0	6	41^2	21	3	9	21	6.7	1.30	269	.148	.204	0	.000	-0	10	10	-1	0.6
	Yr	3	0	1.000	43	0	0	0	8	70^1	48	5	21	49	9.0	2.18	160	.189	.254	0	.000	-1	10	10	-2	0.5
1982	Mon-N	7	4	.636	75	0	0	0	26	109	87	6	36	86	10.3	2.06	176	.221	.289	1	.100	-0	19	19	-1	2.6
1983	Mon-N	7	9	.438	66	0	0	0	21	92	87	7	44	78	12.9	3.03	118	.250	.336	1	.125	-0	6	6	-2	0.9
1984	Mon-N	7	7	.500	68	0	0	0	23	87	70	5	37	79	11.4	2.90	118	.220	.307	0	.000	-1	7	5	-2	0.8
1985	Mon-N★	2	8	.200	63	0	0	0	**41**	87^2	68	7	26	67	9.8	3.18	107	.209	.270	2	.286	0	4	2	-1	0.4
1986	Mon-N☆	7	9	.438	62	0	0	0	35	89	83	12	26	67	11.1	3.94	94	.251	.307	1	.125	-0	-2	-3	-0	-0.7
1987	*Min-A	8	8	.500	63	0	0	0	31	80^1	70	14	28	83	11.3	4.48	103	.232	.303	0	—	0	-0	1	-1	0.2
1988	Min-A☆	2	4	.333	63	0	0	0	42	73	68	6	15	56	10.5	2.47	165	.245	.289	0	—	0	12	13	-2	2.0
1989	Min-A	5	4	.556	65	0	0	0	31	73	68	8	12	46	10.2	4.07	102	.246	.285	0	—	0	-2	1	-2	-0.5
1990	*Bos-A	5	3	.625	47	0	0	0	21	51^1	39	5	19	33	10.3	3.16	129	.206	.282	0	—	0	4	5	-1	0.8
1991	Bos-A★	1	4	.200	57	0	0	0	40	59^1	54	9	16	44	10.8	3.03	142	.236	.289	0	—	0	7	8	-2	1.1
1992	Bos-A	2	2	.500	46	0	0	0	27	42^1	53	6	7	32	13.0	4.25	99	.308	.339	0	—	0	-1	-0	-0	-0.2
	*Atl-N	3	0	1.000	14	0	0	0	3	15^2	14	0	2	7	9.8	1.15	318	.241	.279	0	—	0	4	4	-0	1.0
1993	Cin-N	4	6	.400	58	0	0	0	8	61^2	66	4	10	35	11.8	4.09	98	.270	.313	0	.000	-0	-0	-0	-1	-0.2
1994	NY-A	1	0	1.000	11	0	0	0	2	9^2	17	3	3	4	18.6	8.38	55	.386	.426	0	—	0	-4	-4	-0	-0.4
Total	16	73	77	.487	880	0	0	0	367	1132^1	1000	109	358	877	11.0	3.16	121	.236	.299	5	.088	-3	80	83	-19	10.3

● FRANK REBERGER Reberger, Frank Beall "Crane" b: 6/7/44, Caldwell, Idaho BL/TR, 6'5", 200 lbs. Deb: 6/6/68 C

YEAR	TM/L	W	L	PCT	G	GS	CG	SH	SV	IP	H	HR	BB	SO	RAT	ERA	ERA+	OAV	OOB	BH	AVG	PB	PR	/A	PD	TPI
1968	Chi-N	0	1	.000	3	1	0	0	0	6	9	1	2	3	16.5	4.50	70	.346	.393	0	—	0	-1	-1	0	-0.1
1969	SD-N	1	2	.333	67	0	0	0	6	87^2	83	6	41	65	12.9	3.59	98	.258	.345	1	.200	0	-1	2	0	0.2
1970	SF-N	7	8	.467	45	18	3	0	2	152	178	13	98	117	16.8	5.57	71	.293	.397	11	.234	1	-26	-27	-0	-2.3
1971	SF-N	3	0	1.000	13	7	0	0	0	43^2	37	5	19	21	12.0	3.92	87	.228	.317	3	.231	0	-2	-3	-0	-0.1
1972	SF-N	3	4	.429	20	11	2	0	0	99^1	97	10	37	52	12.6	3.99	87	.257	.332	8	.229	2	-6	-6	1	0.0
Total	5	14	15	.483	148	37	5	0	8	388^2	404	35	197	258	14.3	4.52	81	.270	.361	23	.230	4	-35	-36	4	-2.3

● JOHN RECCIUS Reccius, John b: 10/29/1859, Louisville, Ky. d: 9/1/30, Louisville, Ky. 5'6.5", Deb: 5/2/1882 F♦

YEAR	TM/L	W	L	PCT	G	GS	CG	SH	SV	IP	H	HR	BB	SO	RAT	ERA	ERA+	OAV	OOB	BH	AVG	PB	PR	/A	PD	TPI
1882	Lou-a	4	6	.400	13	10	9	1	0	95	106	3	22	31	12.1	3.03	82	.264	.303	63	.237	3	-4	-6	-1	-0.4
1883	Lou-a	0	0	—	1	0	0	0	0	4	10	0	0	0	22.5	2.25	133	.455	.455	9	.143	-0	0	0	0	0.0
Total	2	4	6	.400	14	10	9	1	0	99	116	3	22	31	12.5	3.00	83	.274	.310	72	.219	3	-3	-6	-1	-0.4

● PHIL RECCIUS Reccius, Phillip b: 6/7/1862, Louisville, Ky. d: 2/15/03, Louisville, Ky. 5'9", 163 lbs. Deb: 9/25/1882 F♦

YEAR	TM/L	W	L	PCT	G	GS	CG	SH	SV	IP	H	HR	BB	SO	RAT	ERA	ERA+	OAV	OOB	BH	AVG	PB	PR	/A	PD	TPI
1884	Lou-a	6	7	.462	18	11	11	0	0	129^1	118	2	19	46	9.8	2.71	114	.228	.261	63	.240	2	8	5	0	0.6
1885	Lou-a	0	4	.000	7	5	4	0	1	40	46	0	11	10	13.0	3.82	84	.253	.299	97	.241	1	-3	-3	1	-0.1
1886	Lou-a	0	1	.000	1	1	0	0	0	3	7	0	3	0	30.0	9.00	40	.467	.556	4	.308	0	-2	-2	-0	-0.4
1887	Cle-a	0	0	—	1	0	0	0	0	7	8	0	5	0	16.7	7.71	56	.320	.433	47	.205	-0	-3	-3	0	0.0
Total	4	6	12	.333	27	17	15	0	1	179^1	179	2	38	56	11.1	3.26	97	.242	.284	225	.231	4	1	-2	1	0.1

● PHIL REDDING Redding, Philip Hayden b: 1/28/1889, Crystal Springs, Miss. d: 3/31/28, Greenwood, Miss. BL/TR, 5'11.5", 190 lbs. Deb: 9/14/12

YEAR	TM/L	W	L	PCT	G	GS	CG	SH	SV	IP	H	HR	BB	SO	RAT	ERA	ERA+	OAV	OOB	BH	AVG	PB	PR	/A	PD	TPI
1912	StL-N	2	1	.667	3	3	2	0	0	25^1	31	2	11	9	14.9	4.97	69	.313	.382	0	.000	-1	-4	-4	-0	-0.5
1913	StL-N	0	0	—	1	0	0	0	0	2^2	2	0	1	1	10.1	6.75	48	.286	.375	0	.000	-0	-1	-1	0	0.0
Total	2	2	1	.667	4	3	2	0	0	28	33	2	12	10	14.5	5.14	66	.311	.381	0	.000	-1	-5	-5	-0	-0.5

● PETE REDFERN Redfern, Peter Irvine b: 8/25/54, Glendale, Cal. BR/TR, 6'2", 195 lbs. Deb: 5/15/76

YEAR	TM/L	W	L	PCT	G	GS	CG	SH	SV	IP	H	HR	BB	SO	RAT	ERA	ERA+	OAV	OOB	BH	AVG	PB	PR	/A	PD	TPI
1976	Min-A	8	8	.500	23	23	1	1	0	118	105	6	63	74	13.0	3.51	102	.241	.341	0	—	0	0	1	-1	-0.1
1977	Min-A	6	9	.400	30	28	1	0	0	137^1	164	13	66	73	15.3	5.18	77	.304	.384	0	—	0	-17	-18	1	-1.6
1978	Min-A	0	2	.000	3	2	0	0	0	9^2	10	2	6	4	14.9	6.52	59	.294	.400	0	—	0	-3	-3	0	-0.6
1979	Min-A	7	3	.700	40	6	0	0	1	108^1	106	8	35	85	11.8	3.49	126	.258	.318	0	—	0	9	11	-1	0.5
1980	Min-A	7	7	.500	23	16	2	0	2	104^2	117	11	33	73	12.9	4.56	96	.283	.336	0	—	0	-6	-2	-1	-0.4
1981	Min-A	9	8	.529	24	23	3	0	0	141^2	140	12	52	77	12.3	4.07	97	.261	.328	0	—	0	-6	-2	-1	-0.6
1982	Min-A	5	11	.313	27	13	2	0	0	94^1	122	16	51	40	16.6	6.58	64	.322	.404	0	—	0	-26	-25	0	-3.5
Total	7	42	48	.467	170	111	9	1	3	714	764	68	306	426	13.6	4.54	89	.278	.353	0	—	0	-50	-38	-2	-6.3

● HOWIE REED Reed, Howard Dean "Diz" b: 12/21/36, Dallas, Tex. d: 12/7/84, Corpus Christi, Tex. BR/TR, 6'1", 210 lbs. Deb: 9/13/58

YEAR	TM/L	W	L	PCT	G	GS	CG	SH	SV	IP	H	HR	BB	SO	RAT	ERA	ERA+	OAV	OOB	BH	AVG	PB	PR	/A	PD	TPI
1958	KC-A	1	0	1.000	3	1	1	0	0	10^1	5	0	4	5	7.8	0.87	449	.132	.214	0	.000	0	3	3	-0	0.3
1959	KC-A	0	3	.000	6	3	0	0	0	20^2	26	3	10	11	15.7	7.40	54	.313	.387	0	.000	-0	-8	-8	-1	-1.0
1960	KC-A	0	0	—	1	0	0	0	0	1^2	2	1	0	1	10.8	0.00	—	.286	.286	0	.000	-0	1	1	-0	0.0
1964	LA-N	3	4	.429	26	7	0	0	1	90	79	4	36	52	11.5	3.20	101	.236	.310	2	.100	-0	1	3	0	0.1
1965	*LA-N	7	5	.583	38	5	0	0	1	78	73	6	27	47	11.9	3.12	105	.243	.312	0	.000	0	4	1	1	0.3
1966	LA-N	0	0	—	1	0	0	0	0	1^2	1	0	0	0	5.4	0.00	—	.167	.167	0	.000	-0	1	1	0	0.0
	Cal-A	0	1	.000	19	1	0	0	1	43	39	5	15	17	11.3	2.93	115	.247	.312	0	.000	-1	2	2	-0	-0.1
1967	Hou-N	1	1	.500	4	2	0	0	0	18^1	19	0	2	9	10.3	3.44	96	.268	.288	0	.000	-0	-0	-0	-0	-0.1
1969	Mon-N	6	7	.462	31	15	2	1	1	106	119	7	50	59	14.5	4.84	76	.290	.369	4	.125	1	-15	-14	2	-1.2
1970	Mon-N	6	5	.545	57	1	0	0	5	89	81	7	40	42	12.4	3.13	131	.252	.339	0	.000	-0	9	10	0	1.2
1971	Mon-N	2	3	.400	43	0	0	0	0	56^2	66	8	24	25	14.3	4.29	82	.296	.364	0	.000	-0	-5	-5	0	-0.4
Total	10	26	29	.473	229	35	3	1	9	515^1	510	41	208	268	12.7	3.72	96	.261	.334	6	.066	-1	-5	-9	3	-0.9

● JERRY REED Reed, Jerry Maxwell b: 10/8/55, Bryson City, N.C. BR/TR, 6'1", 190 lbs. Deb: 9/11/81

YEAR	TM/L	W	L	PCT	G	GS	CG	SH	SV	IP	H	HR	BB	SO	RAT	ERA	ERA+	OAV	OOB	BH	AVG	PB	PR	/A	PD	TPI
1981	Phi-N	0	1	.000	4	0	0	0	0	4^2	7	0	6	5	25.1	7.71	47	.333	.481	0	—	0	-2	-2	0	-0.4
1982	Phi-N	1	0	1.000	7	0	0	0	0	8^2	11	0	3	1	15.6	5.19	71	.324	.395	0	—	0	-2	-1	-0	-0.2
	Cle-A	1	1	.500	6	1	0	0	0	15^2	15	1	3	10	10.3	3.45	118	.250	.286	0	—	0	1	1	0	0.1

YEAR	TM/L	W	L	PCT	G	GS	CG	SH	SV	IP	H	HR	BB	SO	RAT	ERA	ERA+	OAV	OOB	BH	AVG	PB	PR	/A	PD	TPI
1983	Cle-A	0	0	—	7	0	0	0	0	21^{1}	26	4	9	11	14.8	7.17	59	.310	.376	0	—	0	-7	-7	1	0.1
1985	Cle-A	3	5	.375	33	5	0	0	8	72^{1}	67	12	19	37	11.1	4.11	101	.245	.302	0	—	0	0	0	1	0.1
1986	Sea-A	4	0	1.000	11	4	0	0	0	34^{2}	38	3	13	16	13.2	3.12	136	.273	.336	0	—	0	4	4	-0	0.4
1987	Sea-A	1	2	.333	39	1	0	0	7	81^{2}	79	7	24	51	11.7	3.42	138	.255	.315	0	—	0	9	12	-0	0.2
1988	Sea-A	1	1	.500	46	0	0	0	1	86^{1}	82	8	33	48	12.2	3.96	105	.256	.330	0	—	0	0	2	1	0.0
1989	Sea-A	7	7	.500	52	1	0	0	0	101^{2}	89	10	43	50	11.8	3.19	126	.235	.314	0	—	0	8	9	-0	1.0
1990	Sea-A	0	1	.000	4	0	0	0	0	7^{1}	8	1	3	2	13.5	4.91	81	.286	.355	0	—	0	-1	-1	0	-0.1
	Bos-A	2	1	.667	29	0	0	0	2	45	55	1	16	17	14.2	4.80	85	.302	.359	0	—	0	-4	-4	-0	-0.5
	Yr	2	2	.500	33	0	0	0	2	52^{1}	63	2	19	19	14.1	4.82	84	.300	.358	0	—	0	-5	-4	0	-0.6
Total	9	20	19	.513	238	12	0	0	18	479^{1}	477	47	172	248	12.4	3.94	107	.261	.328	0	—	0	6	14	2	0.7

● RICK REED

Reed, Richard Allen b: 8/16/64, Huntington, W.Va. BR/TR, 6', 205 lbs. Deb: 8/8/88

YEAR	TM/L	W	L	PCT	G	GS	CG	SH	SV	IP	H	HR	BB	SO	RAT	ERA	ERA+	OAV	OOB	BH	AVG	PB	PR	/A	PD	TPI
1988	Pit-N	1	0	1.000	2	2	0	0	0	12	10	1	2	6	9.0	3.00	113	.233	.267	0	.000	-0	1	1	0	0.0
1989	Pit-N	1	4	.200	15	7	0	0	0	54^{2}	62	5	11	34	12.3	5.60	60	.290	.330	1	.077	-0	-13	-14	-0	-1.2
1990	Pit-N	2	3	.400	13	8	1	1	1	53^{2}	62	6	12	27	12.6	4.36	83	.279	.319	4	.250	1	-3	-4	-1	-0.3
1991	Pit-N	0	0	—	1	1	0	0	0	4^{1}	8	1	1	2	18.7	10.38	34	.400	.429	1	.500	1	-3	-3	-0	0.1
1992	KC-A	3	7	.300	19	18	1	1	0	100^{1}	105	10	20	49	11.7	3.68	110	.271	.316	0	—	0	3	4	1	0.3
1993	KC-A	0	0	—	1	0	0	0	0	3^{2}	6	0	1	3	19.6	9.82	47	.375	.444	0	—	0	-2	-2	0	-0.2
	Tex-A	1	0	1.000	2	0	0	0	0	4	6	1	1	2	18.0	2.25	184	.375	.444	0	—	0	1	1	0	0.3
	Yr	1	0	1.000	3	0	0	0	0	7^{2}	12	1	2	5	17.6	5.87	74	.364	.417	0	—	0	-1	-1	0	0.1
1994	Tex-A	1	1	.500	4	3	0	0	0	16^{2}	17	3	7	12	13.5	5.94	81	.254	.333	0	—	0	-2	-2	0	-0.2
1995	Cin-N	0	0	—	4	3	0	0	0	17	18	5	3	10	11.1	5.82	71	.273	.304	0	.000	-0	-3	-3	-0	-0.1
1997	NY-N	13	9	.591	33	31	2	0	0	208^{1}	186	19	31	113	9.6	2.89	139	.239	.273	10	.175	4	30	26	-0	2.9
1998	NY-N☆	16	11	.593	31	31	2	1	0	212^{1}	208	30	29	153	10.3	3.48	120	.261	.292	8	.125	-1	18	16	1	2.0
Total	10	38	35	.521	125	104	6	3	1	687	688	81	118	411	10.8	3.75	107	.262	.299	24	.151	4	26	19	1	3.6

● BOB REED

Reed, Robert Edward b: 1/12/45, Boston, Mass. BR/TR, 5'10", 175 lbs. Deb: 9/5/69

YEAR	TM/L	W	L	PCT	G	GS	CG	SH	SV	IP	H	HR	BB	SO	RAT	ERA	ERA+	OAV	OOB	BH	AVG	PB	PR	/A	PD	TPI
1969	Det-A	0	0	—	8	1	0	0	0	14^{2}	9	0	8	9	10.4	1.84	203	.184	.298	1	.500	0	3	3	0	0.1
1970	Det-A	2	4	.333	16	4	0	0	2	46^{1}	54	5	14	26	13.2	4.86	77	.292	.342	1	.083	-0	-6	-6	-1	-0.8
Total	2	2	4	.333	24	5	0	0	2	61	63	5	22	35	12.5	4.13	90	.269	.332	2	.143	-0	-3	-3	-0	-0.7

● RON REED

Reed, Ronald Lee b: 11/2/42, LaPorte, Ind. BR/TR, 6'6", 215 lbs. Deb: 9/26/66

YEAR	TM/L	W	L	PCT	G	GS	CG	SH	SV	IP	H	HR	BB	SO	RAT	ERA	ERA+	OAV	OOB	BH	AVG	PB	PR	/A	PD	TPI
1966	Atl-N	1	1	.500	2	2	0	0	0	8^{1}	7	1	4	6	11.9	2.16	168	.226	.314	0	.000	-0	1	1	-0	0.3
1967	Atl-N	1	1	.500	3	3	0	0	0	21^{1}	21	1	3	11	11.0	2.95	112	.262	.306	0	.000	-1	1	1	1	0.1
1968	Atl-N★	11	10	.524	35	28	6	1	0	201^{2}	189	10	49	111	10.9	3.35	89	.246	.297	10	.161	1	-8	-8	0	-0.7
1969	*Atl-N	18	10	.643	36	33	7	1	0	241^{1}	227	24	56	160	10.8	3.47	104	.246	.294	10	.125	-2	3	4	-1	0.1
1970	Atl-N	7	10	.412	21	18	6	0	0	134^{2}	140	16	39	68	12.1	4.41	97	.266	.319	4	.091	-2	-5	-2	1	-0.4
1971	Atl-N	13	14	.481	32	32	8	1	0	222^{1}	221	26	54	129	11.2	3.72	100	.261	.306	11	.149	-3	-6	-0	-1	-0.4
1972	Atl-N	11	15	.423	31	30	11	1	0	213	222	18	60	111	12.2	3.93	96	.270	.325	13	.178	-1	-11	-3	1	-0.4
1973	Atl-N	4	11	.267	20	19	2	0	1	116^{1}	133	7	31	64	12.9	4.41	89	.287	.335	9	.200	-0	-10	-6	1	-0.6
1974	Atl-N	10	11	.476	28	28	6	2	0	186	171	16	41	78	10.4	3.39	112	.243	.286	6	.105	-3	5	8	-2	0.3
1975	Atl-N	4	5	.444	10	10	1	0	0	74^{2}	93	1	16	40	13.1	4.22	89	.304	.339	6	.231	1	-5	-4	-0	-0.3
	StL-N	9	8	.529	24	24	7	2	0	175^{2}	181	4	37	99	11.4	3.23	116	.263	.305	9	.161	-0	8	10	-1	0.8
	Yr	13	13	.500	34	34	8	2	0	250^{1}	274	5	53	139	11.9	3.52	107	.275	.314	15	.183	1	3	7	-1	0.5
1976	*Phi-N	8	7	.533	59	4	1	0	14	128	88	8	32	96	8.6	2.46	144	.193	.249	4	.167	-0	15	15	-1	2.1
1977	*Phi-N	7	5	.583	60	3	0	0	15	124^{1}	101	9	37	84	10.1	2.75	145	.223	.283	2	.111	-0	16	17	-1	1.9
1978	*Phi-N	3	4	.429	66	0	0	0	17	108^{2}	87	6	23	85	9.5	2.24	160	.223	.275	0	.000	-0	16	16	-2	1.4
1979	Phi-N	13	8	.619	61	0	0	0	5	102	110	9	32	58	12.7	4.15	92	.278	.335	3	.300	1	-5	-4	-0	-0.6
1980	*Phi-N	7	5	.583	55	0	0	0	9	91^{1}	88	4	30	54	11.7	4.04	94	.253	.314	3	.300	1	-4	-3	1	-0.2
1981	*Phi-N	5	3	.625	39	0	0	0	8	61^{1}	54	6	17	40	10.6	3.08	118	.237	.293	3	.500	1	3	4	-1	0.7
1982	Phi-N	5	5	.500	57	2	0	0	14	98	85	4	24	57	10.3	2.66	138	.235	.289	4	.333	2	10	11	2	1.7
1983	*Phi-N	9	1	.900	61	0	0	0	8	95^{2}	89	5	34	73	11.7	3.48	102	.248	.315	1	.167	-0	2	1	-2	-0.1
1984	Chi-A	0	6	.000	51	0	0	0	12	73	67	7	14	57	10.1	3.08	135	.248	.288	0	.000	-0	7	9	0	1.0
Total	19	146	140	.510	751	236	55	8	103	2477^{2}	2374	182	633	1481	11.1	3.46	107	.252	.303	98	.158	-6	32	68	-3	6.7

● STEVE REED

Reed, Steven Vincent b: 3/11/66, Los Angeles, Cal. BR/TR, 6'2", 202 lbs. Deb: 8/30/92

YEAR	TM/L	W	L	PCT	G	GS	CG	SH	SV	IP	H	HR	BB	SO	RAT	ERA	ERA+	OAV	OOB	BH	AVG	PB	PR	/A	PD	TPI
1992	SF-N	1	0	1.000	18	0	0	0	0	15^{2}	13	2	3	11	9.8	2.30	144	.220	.270	0	—	0	2	2	1	0.2
1993	Col-N	9	5	.643	64	0	0	0	3	84^{1}	80	13	30	51	12.1	4.48	106	.259	.330	0	.000	-1	-4	3	0	0.3
1994	Col-N	3	2	.600	**61**	0	0	0	3	64	79	9	26	51	15.6	3.94	126	.306	.383	0	.000	-0	2	7	-1	0.4
1995	*Col-N	5	2	.714	71	0	0	0	3	84	61	8	21	79	8.9	2.14	251	.203	.257	1	.333	0	19	**30**	1	2.6
1996	Col-N	4	3	.571	70	0	0	0	0	75	66	11	19	51	10.9	3.96	132	.239	.302	1	.333	0	2	10	-1	0.8
1997	Col-N	4	6	.400	63	0	0	0	6	62^{1}	49	10	27	43	11.7	4.04	128	.219	.316	0	.000	-0	1	8	0	1.3
1998	SF-N	2	1	.667	50	0	0	0	1	54^{2}	30	4	19	50	8.7	1.48	274	.160	.251	1	.333	0	17	16	-1	0.8
	*Cle-A	2	2	.500	20	0	0	0	0	25^{2}	26	4	8	23	12.3	6.66	72	.260	.321	0	—	0	-6	-5	0	-0.8
Total	7	30	21	.588	417	0	0	0	16	465^{2}	404	61	153	359	11.3	3.54	139	.236	.308	3	.143	-1	33	71	-0	5.6

● BILL REEDER

Reeder, William Edgar b: 2/20/22, Dike, Texas BR/TR, 6'5", 205 lbs. Deb: 4/23/49

YEAR	TM/L	W	L	PCT	G	GS	CG	SH	SV	IP	H	HR	BB	SO	RAT	ERA	ERA+	OAV	OOB	BH	AVG	PB	PR	/A	PD	TPI
1949	StL-N	1	1	.500	21	1	0	0	0	33^{2}	33	2	30	21	17.1	5.08	82	.270	.418	0	.000	-0	-4	-3	-0	-0.2

● STAN REES

Rees, Stanley Milton "Nellie" b: 2/25/1899, Cynthiana, Ky. d: 8/30/37, Lexington, Ky. BL/TL, 6'3", 190 lbs. Deb: 6/12/18

YEAR	TM/L	W	L	PCT	G	GS	CG	SH	SV	IP	H	HR	BB	SO	RAT	ERA	ERA+	OAV	OOB	BH	AVG	PB	PR	/A	PD	TPI
1918	Was-A	1	0	1.000	2	0	0	0	0	2	3	0	4	1	31.5	0.00	—	.500	.700	0	—	0	1	1	0	0.3

● BOBBY REEVES

Reeves, Robert Edwin "Gunner" b: 6/24/04, Hill City, Tenn. d: 6/4/93, Chattanooga, Tenn. BR/TR, 5'11", 170 lbs. Deb: 6/9/26 ♦

YEAR	TM/L	W	L	PCT	G	GS	CG	SH	SV	IP	H	HR	BB	SO	RAT	ERA	ERA+	OAV	OOB	BH	AVG	PB	PR	/A	PD	TPI
1931	Bos-A	0	0	—	1	0	0	0	0	7^{1}	6	0	1	0	8.6	3.68	117	.214	.241	14	.167	0	1	1	0	0.0

● MIKE REGAN

Regan, Michael John b: 11/19/1888, Phoenix, N.Y. d: 5/22/61, Albany, N.Y. BR/TR, 5'10", 160 lbs. Deb: 5/13/17

YEAR	TM/L	W	L	PCT	G	GS	CG	SH	SV	IP	H	HR	BB	SO	RAT	ERA	ERA+	OAV	OOB	BH	AVG	PB	PR	/A	PD	TPI
1917	Cin-N	11	10	.524	32	26	16	1	0	216	228	4	41	50	11.4	2.71	97	.273	.310	15	.200	1	0	-2	3	0.2
1918	Cin-N	5	5	.500	22	6	4	3	2	80	77	0	29	15	11.9	3.26	82	.262	.328	8	.296	2	-4	-5	-1	-0.5
1919	Cin-N	0	0	—	1	0	0	0	0	2^{1}	1	0	0	1	3.9	0.00	—	.143	.143	0	.000	-0	1	1	-0	0.0
Total	3	16	15	.516	55	32	20	4	2	298^{1}	306	4	70	66	11.5	2.84	93	.269	.314	23	.223	3	-4	-7	2	-0.3

● PHIL REGAN

Regan, Philip Raymond "The Vulture" b: 4/6/37, Otsego, Mich. BR/TR, 6'3", 200 lbs. Deb: 7/19/60 MC

YEAR	TM/L	W	L	PCT	G	GS	CG	SH	SV	IP	H	HR	BB	SO	RAT	ERA	ERA+	OAV	OOB	BH	AVG	PB	PR	/A	PD	TPI
1960	Det-A	0	4	.000	17	7	0	0	1	68	70	11	25	38	12.8	4.50	88	.267	.336	1	.059	-1	-5	-4	-1	-0.4
1961	Det-A	10	7	.588	32	16	6	0	2	120	134	19	41	46	13.2	5.25	78	.281	.339	3	.075	-2	-16	-15	-3	-2.4
1962	Det-A	11	9	.550	35	23	6	0	0	171^{1}	169	23	64	87	12.3	4.04	101	.254	.320	13	.206	1	-1	0	-2	-0.1
1963	Det-A	15	9	.625	38	27	5	1	1	189	179	33	59	115	11.7	3.86	97	.245	.308	9	.143	-1	-5	-2	-3	-0.6
1964	Det-A	5	10	.333	32	21	2	0	1	146^{2}	162	21	49	91	13.3	5.03	73	.282	.344	13	.317	5	-23	-22	-0	-1.6
1965	Det-A	1	5	.167	16	7	1	0	0	51^{2}	57	6	20	37	13.4	5.05	69	.282	.347	1	.083	-0	-9	-9	-0	-1.1
1966	*LA-N☆	14	1	.933	65	0	0	0	**21**	116^{2}	85	6	24	88	8.4	1.62	203	.207	.251	3	.143	0	**26**	**22**	1	3.8
1967	LA-N	6	9	.400	55	3	0	0	6	96^{1}	108	2	32	53	13.3	2.99	104	.284	.343	1	.100	-0	4	1	1	0.2
1968	LA-N	2	0	1.000	5	0	0	0	0	7^{2}	10	1	1	7	12.9	3.52	78	.313	.333	0	.000	-0	-0	-1	-0	-0.2
	Chi-N	10	5	.667	68	0	0	0	25	127	109	9	24	60	9.6	2.20	144	.232	.272	3	.150	0	11	14	0	2.4
	Yr	12	5	.706	73	0	0	0	**25**	134^{2}	119	10	25	67	9.8	2.27	138	.237	.276	3	.143	0	11	13	-0	2.2
1969	Chi-N	12	6	.667	71	0	0	0	17	112	120	6	35	56	12.6	3.70	109	.282	.339	1	.067	-0	-1	4	0	0.8
1970	Chi-N	5	9	.357	54	0	0	0	12	75^{2}	81	8	32	31	13.6	4.76	95	.287	.362	0	.000	-1	-6	-2	2	-0.3
1971	Chi-N	5	5	.500	48	1	0	0	6	73^{1}	84	4	33	28	14.6	3.93	100	.301	.379	0	.000	-1	-4	0	1	0.0
1972	Chi-N	0	1	.000	5	0	0	0	0	4	6	0	2	2	18.0	2.25	169	.400	.471	0	—	0	1	1	-0	0.2
	Chi-A	0	1	.000	10	0	0	0	0	13^{1}	18	1	6	4	16.9	4.05	77	.346	.424	1	1.000	0	-1	-1	0	0.0
Total	13	96	81	.542	551	105	20	1	92	1372^{2}	1392	150	447	743	12.2	3.84	97	.265	.325	49	.153	1	-31	-16	-4	0.7

● EARL REID

Reid, Earl Percy b: 6/8/13, Bangor, Ala. d: 5/11/84, Cullman, Ala. BL/TR, 6'3", 190 lbs. Deb: 5/8/46

YEAR	TM/L	W	L	PCT	G	GS	CG	SH	SV	IP	H	HR	BB	SO	RAT	ERA	ERA+	OAV	OOB	BH	AVG	PB	PR	/A	PD	TPI
1946	Bos-N	1	0	1.000	2	0	0	0	0	3	4	0	3	2	21.0	3.00	114	.308	.438	0	—	0	0	0	-0	0.0

● **BILL REIDY** Reidy, William Joseph b: 10/9/1873, Cleveland, Ohio d: 10/14/15, Cleveland, Ohio BR/TR, 5'10", 175 lbs. Deb: 7/21/1896

YEAR	TM/L	W	L	PCT	G	GS	CG	SH	SV	IP	H	HR	BB	SO	RAT	ERA	ERA+	OAV	OOB	BH	AVG	PB	PR	/A	PD	TPI
1896	NY-N	0	1	.000	2	1	1	0	0	13	24	0	2	1	20.1	7.62	55	.393	.439	0	.000	-1	-5	-5	0	-0.3
1899	Bro-N	1	0	1.000	2	1	1	0	1	7	9	0	2	2	14.1	2.57	152	.310	.355	0	.000	-1	1	1	0	0.1
1901	Mil-A	16	20	.444	37	33	28	2	0	301^1	364	14	62	50	13.0	4.21	85	.295	.333	16	.143	-6	-18	-21	-3	-2.7
1902	StL-A	3	5	.375	12	9	7	0	0	95	111	0	13	16	12.4	4.45	79	.292	.327	8	.195	-0	-9	-10	1	-0.6
1903	StL-A	1	4	.200	5	5	5	1	0	43	53	1	7	8	13.2	3.98	73	.301	.339	1	.067	-2	-5	-5	-1	-0.8
	Bro-N	6	7	.462	15	13	11	0	0	104	130	0	14	21	13.0	3.46	92	.315	.346	9	.243	1	-2	-3	-1	-0.4
1904	Bro-N	0	4	.000	6	4	2	0	1	38^1	49	0	6	11	13.4	4.46	62	.293	.326	5	.156	-0	-7	-7	-1	-0.8
Total	6	27	41	.397	79	66	55	3	2	601^2	740	15	106	109	13.1	4.17	82	.301	.337	39	.159	-9	-46	-50	-5	-5.5

● **ART REINHART** Reinhart, Arthur Conrad b: 5/29/1899, Ackley, Iowa d: 11/11/46, Houston, Tex. BL/TL, 6'1", 170 lbs. Deb: 4/26/19

YEAR	TM/L	W	L	PCT	G	GS	CG	SH	SV	IP	H	HR	BB	SO	RAT	ERA	ERA+	OAV	OOB	BH	AVG	PB	PR	/A	PD	TPI
1919	StL-N	0	0	—	1	0	0	0	0	0	0	0	0	0	—	—	—	—	1.000	0	—	0	0	0	0	0.0
1925	StL-N	11	5	.688	20	16	15	1	0	144^2	149	7	47	26	12.4	3.05	142	.278	.341	22	.328	5	20	20	-0	2.5
1926	*StL-N	10	5	.667	27	11	9	0	0	143	159	5	47	26	13.2	4.22	93	.295	.355	20	.317	4	-6	-5	1	0.0
1927	StL-N	5	2	.714	21	9	4	2	1	81^2	82	5	36	15	13.0	4.19	94	.267	.344	10	.313	2	-2	-2	-1	-0.1
1928	StL-N	4	6	.400	23	9	3	1	2	75^1	80	3	27	12	12.8	2.87	140	.272	.333	4	.167	-0	9	9	-1	1.1
Total	5	30	18	.625	92	45	31	4	3	444^2	470	20	157	79	12.9	3.60	113	.280	.345	56	.301	10	20	23	-1	3.5

● **JACK REIS** Reis, Harrie Crane b: 6/14/1890, Cincinnati, Ohio d: 7/20/39, Cincinnati, Ohio BR/TR, 5'10.5", 160 lbs. Deb: 9/9/11

YEAR	TM/L	W	L	PCT	G	GS	CG	SH	SV	IP	H	HR	BB	SO	RAT	ERA	ERA+	OAV	OOB	BH	AVG	PB	PR	/A	PD	TPI
1911	StL-N	0	0	—	3	0	0	0	0	9^1	5	0	8	4	12.5	0.96	350	.156	.325	0	.000	-0	3	3	0	0.0

● **LAURIE REIS** Reis, Lawrence P. b: 11/20/1858, Illinois d: 1/24/21, Chicago, Ill. BR/TR, 160 lbs. Deb: 10/1/1877

YEAR	TM/L	W	L	PCT	G	GS	CG	SH	SV	IP	H	HR	BB	SO	RAT	ERA	ERA+	OAV	OOB	BH	AVG	PB	PR	/A	PD	TPI
1877	Chi-N	3	1	.750	4	4	4	1	0	36	29	1	6	11	8.8	0.75	396	.213	.246	2	.125	-2	8	9	-0	0.7
1878	Chi-N	1	3	.250	4	4	4	0	0	36	55	0	4	8	14.8	3.25	75	.335	.351	3	.150	-1	-4	-3	-1	-0.5
Total	2	4	4	.500	8	8	8	1	0	72	84	1	10	19	11.8	2.00	135	.280	.303	5	.139	-2	4	6	-2	0.2

● **BOBBY REIS** Reis, Robert Joseph Thomas b: 1/2/09, Woodside, N.Y. d: 5/1/73, St.Paul, Minn. BR/TR, 6'1", 175 lbs. Deb: 9/19/31 ♦

YEAR	TM/L	W	L	PCT	G	GS	CG	SH	SV	IP	H	HR	BB	SO	RAT	ERA	ERA+	OAV	OOB	BH	AVG	PB	PR	/A	PD	TPI
1935	Bro-N	3	2	.600	14	2	1	0	2	41^1	46	0	24	7	15.5	2.83	140	.277	.372	21	.247	1	5	5	1	0.8
1936	Bos-N	6	5	.545	35	5	3	0	0	138^2	152	7	74	25	15.0	4.48	86	.283	.375	13	.217	1	-7	-10	4	-0.2
1937	Bos-N	0	0	—	4	0	0	0	0	5	3	0	5	0	14.4	1.80	199	.158	.333	21	.244	1	1	1	-0	0.0
1938	Bos-N	1	6	.143	16	2	1	0	0	57^2	61	5	41	20	16.9	4.99	69	.271	.397	9	.184	-0	-8	-10	0	-1.0
Total	4	10	13	.435	69	9	5	0	2	242^2	262	12	144	52	15.5	4.27	88	.277	.379	70	.233	3	-8	-14	5	-0.4

● **TOMMY REIS** Reis, Thomas Edward b: 8/6/14, Newport, Ky. BR/TR, 6'2", 180 lbs. Deb: 4/27/38

YEAR	TM/L	W	L	PCT	G	GS	CG	SH	SV	IP	H	HR	BB	SO	RAT	ERA	ERA+	OAV	OOB	BH	AVG	PB	PR	/A	PD	TPI
1938	Phi-N	0	1	.000	4	0	0	0	0	4^2	8	0	8	2	30.9	19.29	20	.364	.533	0	.000	-0	-8	-8	0	-1.3
	Bos-N	0	0	—	4	0	0	0	0	6^1	8	1	1	4	12.8	7.11	48	.296	.321	0	—	0	-2	-3	-0	0.0
	Yr	0	1	.000	8	0	0	0	0	11	16	1	9	6	20.5	12.27	30	.327	.431	0	.000	-0	-10	-11	-0	-1.3

● **BUGS REISIGL** Reisigl, Jacob b: 12/12/1887, Brooklyn, N.Y. d: 2/24/57, Amsterdam, N.Y. BR/TR, 5'10.5", 175 lbs. Deb: 9/20/11

YEAR	TM/L	W	L	PCT	G	GS	CG	SH	SV	IP	H	HR	BB	SO	RAT	ERA	ERA+	OAV	OOB	BH	AVG	PB	PR	/A	PD	TPI
1911	Cle-A	0	1	.000	2	1	1	0	0	13	13	1	3	6	11.1	6.23	55	.271	.314	0	.000	-1	-4	-4	-0	-0.3

● **DOC REISLING** Reisling, Frank Carl b: 7/25/1874, Martins Ferry, O. d: 3/4/55, Tulsa, Okla. BR/TR, 5'10", 180 lbs. Deb: 9/10/04

YEAR	TM/L	W	L	PCT	G	GS	CG	SH	SV	IP	H	HR	BB	SO	RAT	ERA	ERA+	OAV	OOB	BH	AVG	PB	PR	/A	PD	TPI
1904	Bro-N	3	4	.429	7	7	6	1	0	51	45	0	10	19	11.3	2.12	130	.238	.308	2	.154	0	4	4	0	0.5
1905	Bro-N	0	1	.000	2	0	0	0	0	3	3	0	4	2	21.0	3.00	96	.273	.467	0	.000	0	0	-0	0	0.0
1909	Was-A	2	4	.333	10	6	6	1	0	66^2	70	0	17	22	11.7	2.43	100	.270	.315	4	.167	0	0	0	-1	-0.1
1910	Was-A	10	10	.500	30	20	13	2	1	191	185	3	44	57	11.0	2.54	98	.264	.312	12	.200	2	-1	-1	0	0.1
Total	4	15	19	.441	49	33	25	4	1	311^2	303	3	75	100	11.3	2.45	103	.261	.314	18	.184	2	3	2	-1	0.5

● **BRYAN REKAR** Rekar, Bryan Robert b: 6/3/72, Oak Lawn, Ill. BR/TR, 6'3", 205 lbs. Deb: 7/19/95

YEAR	TM/L	W	L	PCT	G	GS	CG	SH	SV	IP	H	HR	BB	SO	RAT	ERA	ERA+	OAV	OOB	BH	AVG	PB	PR	/A	PD	TPI
1995	Col-N	4	6	.400	15	14	1	0	0	85	95	11	24	60	12.9	4.98	108	.282	.335	1	.038	-2	-8	4	1	0.2
1996	Col-N	2	4	.333	14	11	0	0	0	58^1	87	11	26	25	18.2	8.95	58	.345	.417	4	.267	1	-31	-24	-0	-2.0
1997	Col-N	1	0	1.000	2	2	0	0	0	9^1	11	3	6	4	16.4	5.79	89	.282	.378	1	.250	0	-2	-1	-0	-0.1
1998	TB-A	2	8	.200	16	15	1	0	0	86^2	95	16	21	55	12.3	4.98	98	.282	.328	0	—	0	-3	-1	-1	-0.2
Total	4	9	18	.333	47	42	2	0	0	239^1	288	41	77	144	14.1	5.98	87	.298	.356	6	.133	-2	-43	-21	0	-2.1

● **MIKE REMLINGER** Remlinger, Michael John b: 3/23/66, Middletown, N.Y. BL/TL, 6', 195 lbs. Deb: 6/15/91

YEAR	TM/L	W	L	PCT	G	GS	CG	SH	SV	IP	H	HR	BB	SO	RAT	ERA	ERA+	OAV	OOB	BH	AVG	PB	PR	/A	PD	TPI
1991	SF-N	2	1	.667	8	6	1	1	0	35	36	5	20	19	14.4	4.37	82	.271	.366	0	.000	-0	-3	-3	-0	-0.3
1994	NY-N	1	5	.167	10	9	0	0	0	54^2	55	9	35	33	15.0	4.61	91	.261	.368	0	.000	-1	-2	-3	-1	-0.5
1995	NY-N	0	1	.000	5	0	0	0	0	5^2	7	1	2	6	14.3	6.35	64	.292	.346	0	.000	-0	-1	-1	-0	-0.2
	Cin-N	0	0	—	2	0	0	0	0	1	2	0	3	1	45.0	9.00	46	.500	.714	0	—	0	-1	-1	0	0.0
	Yr	0	1	.000	7	0	0	0	0	6^2	9	1	5	7	18.9	6.75	60	.321	.424	0	.000	-0	-2	-2	-0	-0.2
1996	Cin-N	0	1	.000	19	4	0	0	0	27^1	24	4	19	19	15.1	5.60	76	.242	.380	1	.143	0	-4	-4	0	-0.1
1997	Cin-N	8	8	.500	69	12	2	0	2	124	100	11	60	145	12.1	4.14	103	.223	.324	2	.095	0	1	2	1	0.3
1998	Cin-N	8	15	.348	35	28	1	1	0	164^1	164	23	87	144	14.0	4.82	90	.266	.362	5	.106	-2	-11	-9	-2	-1.4
Total	6	19	31	.380	148	59	4	2	2	412	388	53	226	367	13.8	4.63	91	.253	.355	8	.081	-3	-21	-19	-1	-2.2

● **WIN REMMERSWAAL** Remmerswaal, Wilhelmus Abraham b: 3/8/54, The Hague, Holland BR/TR, 6'2", 160 lbs. Deb: 8/3/79

YEAR	TM/L	W	L	PCT	G	GS	CG	SH	SV	IP	H	HR	BB	SO	RAT	ERA	ERA+	OAV	OOB	BH	AVG	PB	PR	/A	PD	TPI
1979	Bos-A	1	0	1.000	8	0	0	0	0	20^1	26	1	12	16	17.3	7.08	62	.317	.411	0	—	0	-6	-6	-0	-0.7
1980	Bos-A	2	1	.667	14	0	0	0	0	35^1	39	4	9	20	12.2	4.58	92	.295	.340	0	—	0	-2	-1	-1	-0.2
Total	2	3	1	.750	22	0	0	0	0	55^2	65	5	21	36	14.1	5.50	78	.304	.369	0	—	0	-9	-7	-1	-0.9

● **ALEX REMNEAS** Remneas, Alexander Norman b: 2/21/1886, Minneapolis, Minn. d: 8/27/75, Phoenix, Ariz. BR/TR, 6'1", 180 lbs. Deb: 4/15/12

YEAR	TM/L	W	L	PCT	G	GS	CG	SH	SV	IP	H	HR	BB	SO	RAT	ERA	ERA+	OAV	OOB	BH	AVG	PB	PR	/A	PD	TPI
1912	Det-A	0	0	—	1	0	0	0	0	1^2	5	0	0	0	27.0	27.00	12	.455	.455	0	—	0	-4	-4	0	0.0
1915	StL-A	0	0	—	2	0	0	0	0	6	3	0	3	5	10.5	1.50	191	.136	.269	0	.000	-0	1	1	0	0.0
Total	2	0	0	—	3	0	0	0	0	7^2	8	0	3	5	14.1	7.04	42	.242	.324	0	.000	0	-3	-3	0	0.0

● **ERWIN RENFER** Renfer, Erwin Arthur b: 12/11/1891, Elgin, Ill. d: 10/26/57, Sycamore, Ill. BR/TR, 6', 180 lbs. Deb: 9/18/13

YEAR	TM/L	W	L	PCT	G	GS	CG	SH	SV	IP	H	HR	BB	SO	RAT	ERA	ERA+	OAV	OOB	BH	AVG	PB	PR	/A	PD	TPI
1913	Det-A	0	1	.000	1	1	0	0	0	6	5	0	3	1	13.5	6.00	49	.227	.346	0	.000	-0	-2	-2	0	-0.3

● **LADDIE RENFROE** Renfroe, Cohen Williams b: 5/9/62, Natchez, Miss. BB/TR, 5'11", 200 lbs. Deb: 7/3/91

YEAR	TM/L	W	L	PCT	G	GS	CG	SH	SV	IP	H	HR	BB	SO	RAT	ERA	ERA+	OAV	OOB	BH	AVG	PB	PR	/A	PD	TPI
1991	Chi-N	0	1	.000	4	0	0	0	0	4^2	11	1	2	4	25.1	13.50	29	.440	.481	0	.000	-0	-5	-5	0	-0.9

● **MARSHALL RENFROE** Renfroe, Marshall Daniel b: 5/25/36, Century, Fla. d: 12/10/70, Pensacola, Fla. BL/TL, 6', 180 lbs. Deb: 9/27/59

YEAR	TM/L	W	L	PCT	G	GS	CG	SH	SV	IP	H	HR	BB	SO	RAT	ERA	ERA+	OAV	OOB	BH	AVG	PB	PR	/A	PD	TPI
1959	SF-N	0	0	—	1	1	0	0	0	2	3	1	3	3	27.0	27.00	14	.333	.500	0	.000	-0	-5	-5	-0	0.0

● **HAL RENIFF** Reniff, Harold Eugene "Porky" b: 7/2/38, Warren, Ohio BR/TR, 6', 215 lbs. Deb: 6/8/61

YEAR	TM/L	W	L	PCT	G	GS	CG	SH	SV	IP	H	HR	BB	SO	RAT	ERA	ERA+	OAV	OOB	BH	AVG	PB	PR	/A	PD	TPI
1961	NY-A	2	0	1.000	25	0	0	0	2	45^1	31	1	31	21	12.3	2.58	144	.197	.330	0	.000	-1	7	6	-1	0.2
1962	NY-A	0	0	—	2	0	0	0	0	3^2	6	0	5	1	29.5	7.36	51	.400	.571	0	—	0	-1	-1	-0	0.0
1963	*NY-A	4	3	.571	48	0	0	0	18	89^1	63	3	42	56	10.8	2.62	134	.202	.301	0	.000	-1	10	9	3	1.2
1964	*NY-A	6	4	.600	41	0	0	0	9	69^1	47	3	30	38	10.0	3.12	116	.199	.289	1	.100	-1	4	4	0	0.6
1965	NY-A	3	4	.429	51	0	0	0	3	85^1	74	4	48	74	13.4	3.80	90	.232	.341	0	.000	-0	-3	-4	-0	-0.4
1966	NY-A	3	7	.300	56	0	0	0	9	95^1	80	2	49	79	12.7	3.21	104	.229	.333	4	.286	1	2	1	-1	0.2
1967	NY-A	0	2	.000	24	0	0	0	0	40	40	1	14	24	12.8	4.27	73	.256	.329	0	.000	-0	-5	-5	-1	-0.3
	NY-N	3	3	.500	29	0	0	0	4	43	42	1	23	21	13.8	3.35	101	.266	.363	0	.000	-0	0	0	-1	-0.1
Total	7	21	23	.477	276	0	0	0	45	471^1	383	14	242	314	12.3	3.27	106	.225	.327	5	.096	-2	14	10	-0	1.4

● **JIM RENINGER** Reninger, James David b: 3/7/15, Aurora, Ill. d: 8/23/93, N.Fort Myers, Fla. BR/TR, 6'3", 210 lbs. Deb: 9/17/38

YEAR	TM/L	W	L	PCT	G	GS	CG	SH	SV	IP	H	HR	BB	SO	RAT	ERA	ERA+	OAV	OOB	BH	AVG	PB	PR	/A	PD	TPI
1938	Phi-A	0	2	.000	4	4	1	0	0	22^2	28	3	14	9	16.7	7.15	68	.295	.385	0	.000	-0	-6	-6	0	-0.4
1939	Phi-A	0	2	.000	4	2	0	0	0	16^1	24	3	12	3	19.8	7.71	61	.369	.468	1	.167	-0	-6	-5	0	-0.5
Total	2	0	4	.000	8	6	1	0	0	39	52	6	26	12	18.0	7.38	65	.325	.419	1	.077	-1	-12	-11	0	-0.9

● **STEVE RENKO** Renko, Steven b: 12/10/44, Kansas City, Kan. BR/TR, 6'5", 230 lbs. Deb: 6/27/69

YEAR	TM/L	W	L	PCT	G	GS	CG	SH	SV	IP	H	HR	BB	SO	RAT	ERA	ERA+	OAV	OOB	BH	AVG	PB	PR	/A	PD	TPI
1969	Mon-N	6	7	.462	18	15	4	0	0	103^1	94	14	50	68	12.7	4.01	92	.243	.333	6	.167	1	-5	-4	-1	-0.4

YEAR	TM/L	W	L	PCT	G	GS	CG	SH	SV	IP	H	HR	BB	SO	RAT	ERA	ERA+	OAV	OOB	BH	AVG	PB	PR	/A	PD	TPI
1970	Mon-N	13	11	.542	41	33	7	1	1	222^2	203	27	104	142	12.7	4.32	95	.241	.329	16	.200	2	-7	-5	-0	-0.3
1971	Mon-N	15	14	.517	40	37	9	3	0	275^2	256	24	135	129	12.9	3.75	94	.247	.336	21	.210	4	-9	-7	-2	-0.4
1972	Mon-N	1	10	.091	30	12	0	0	0	97	96	11	67	66	15.1	5.20	68	.262	.376	7	.292	1	-19	-18	1	-1.7
1973	Mon-N	15	11	.577	36	34	9	0	1	249^2	201	26	108	164	11.2	2.81	136	.218	.300	24	.273	7	24	28	-2	3.6
1974	Mon-N	12	16	.429	37	35	8	1	0	227^2	222	17	81	138	12.0	4.03	95	.257	.321	17	.210	3	-10	-5	3	0.1
1975	Mon-N	6	12	.333	31	25	3	1	1	170^1	175	20	76	99	13.3	4.07	94	.265	.341	15	.278	5	-8	-5	-0	0.0
1976	Mon-N	0	1	.000	5	1	0	0	0	13	15	2	3	4	12.5	5.54	67	.288	.327	1	.333	0	-3	-3	-1	-0.2
	Chi-N	8	11	.421	28	27	4	1	0	163^1	164	12	43	112	11.4	3.86	100	.258	.305	5	.094	-3	-6	0	-1	-0.5
	Yr	8	12	.400	33	28	4	1	0	176^1	179	14	46	116	11.5	3.98	97	.260	.307	6	.107	-3	-9	-3	-2	-0.7
1977	Chi-N	2	2	.500	13	8	0	0	1	51^1	51	10	21	34	12.8	4.56	96	.258	.332	2	.167	0	-4	-1	-1	-0.2
	Chi-A	5	0	1.000	8	8	0	0	0	53^1	55	3	17	36	12.3	3.54	115	.274	.333	0	—	0	3	3	0	0.3
1978	Oak-A	6	12	.333	27	25	3	1	0	151	152	10	67	89	13.2	4.29	85	.265	.344	0	—	0	-9	-11	-0	-0.8
1979	Bos-A	11	9	.550	27	27	4	1	0	171	174	22	53	99	12.1	4.11	107	.260	.317	0	—	0	2	6	-1	0.3
1980	Bos-A	9	9	.500	32	23	1	0	0	165^1	180	17	56	90	12.9	4.19	101	.281	.340	0	—	0	-3	0	-1	-0.2
1981	Cal-A	8	4	.667	22	15	0	0	1	102	93	7	42	50	12.0	3.44	106	.250	.328	0	—	0	2	2	-2	0.1
1982	Cal-A	11	6	.647	31	23	4	0	0	156	163	17	51	81	12.4	4.44	91	.269	.327	0	—	0	-6	-7	-2	-0.8
1983	KC-A	6	11	.353	25	17	1	0	1	121^1	144	9	36	54	13.4	4.30	95	.293	.341	0	—	0	-3	-3	-1	-0.5
Total	15	134	146	.479	451	365	57	9	6	2494	2438	248	1010	1455	12.5	3.99	98	.256	.329	114	.215	21	-62	-27	-9	-1.6

● ANDY REPLOGLE Replogle, Andrew David b: 10/7/53, South Bend, Ind. BR/TR, 6'5", 205 lbs. Deb: 4/11/78

YEAR	TM/L	W	L	PCT	G	GS	CG	SH	SV	IP	H	HR	BB	SO	RAT	ERA	ERA+	OAV	OOB	BH	AVG	PB	PR	/A	PD	TPI
1978	Mil-A	9	5	.643	32	18	3	2	0	149^1	177	14	47	41	13.6	3.92	96	.301	.353	0	—	0	-3	-3	-2	-0.5
1979	Mil-A	0	0	—	3	0	0	0	0	8	13	0	2	2	16.9	5.63	74	.382	.417	0	—	0	-1	-1	0	0.0
Total	2	9	5	.643	35	18	3	2	0	157^1	190	14	49	43	13.7	4.00	95	.305	.357	0	—	0	-4	-4	-2	-0.5

● XAVIER RESCIGNO Rescigno, Xavier Frederick "Mr. X" b: 10/13/13, New York, N.Y. BR/TR, 5'10.5", 175 lbs. Deb: 4/22/43

YEAR	TM/L	W	L	PCT	G	GS	CG	SH	SV	IP	H	HR	BB	SO	RAT	ERA	ERA+	OAV	OOB	BH	AVG	PB	PR	/A	PD	TPI
1943	Pit-N	6	9	.400	37	14	5	1	2	132^2	125	6	45	41	11.7	2.98	117	.252	.317	5	.143	0	6	7	-2	0.6
1944	Pit-N	10	8	.556	48	6	2	0	5	124	146	9	34	45	13.1	4.35	85	.291	.337	2	.091	-1	-10	-9	-0	-1.3
1945	Pit-N	3	5	.375	44	1	0	0	9	78^2	95	6	34	29	14.9	5.72	69	.303	.372	2	.133	-0	-17	-16	-0	-1.8
Total	3	19	22	.463	129	21	7	1	16	335^1	366	21	113	115	13.0	4.13	89	.279	.338	9	.125	-1	-21	-17	-3	-2.5

● GEORGE RETTGER Rettger, George Edward b: 7/29/1868, Cleveland, Ohio d: 6/5/21, Lakewood, Ohio BR/TR, 5'11", 175 lbs. Deb: 8/13/1891

YEAR	TM/L	W	L	PCT	G	GS	CG	SH	SV	IP	H	HR	BB	SO	RAT	ERA	ERA+	OAV	OOB	BH	AVG	PB	PR	/A	PD	TPI
1891	StL-a	7	3	.700	14	12	10	1	1	92^2	85	4	51	49	14.0	3.40	124	.235	.343	3	.071	-3	3	8	-1	0.4
1892	Cle-N	1	3	.250	6	5	3	0	0	38	32	2	31	12	15.2	4.26	80	.219	.360	2	.133	-0	-4	-4	-0	-0.4
	Cin-N	1	0	1.000	1	1	1	0	0	9	8	0	10	1	19.0	4.00	82	.229	.413	1	.125	-0	-1	-1	-0	-0.1
	Yr	2	3	.400	7	6	4	0	0	47	40	2	41	13	15.7	4.21	80	.220	.366	3	.130	-0	-5	-4	-0	-0.5
Total	2	9	6	.600	21	18	14	1	1	139^2	125	6	92	62	14.6	3.67	107	.231	.352	6	.092	-3	-1	4	-1	-0.1

● OTTO RETTIG Rettig, Adolph John b: 1/29/1894, New York, N.Y. d: 6/16/77, Stuart, Fla. BR/TR, 5'11", 165 lbs. Deb: 7/19/22

YEAR	TM/L	W	L	PCT	G	GS	CG	SH	SV	IP	H	HR	BB	SO	RAT	ERA	ERA+	OAV	OOB	BH	AVG	PB	PR	/A	PD	TPI
1922	Phi-A	1	2	.333	4	4	1	0	0	18^1	18	0	12	3	15.2	4.91	87	.265	.383	0	.000	-1	-2	-1	0	-0.3

● ED REULBACH Reulbach, Edward Marvin "Big Ed" b: 12/1/1882, Detroit, Mich. d: 7/17/61, Glens Falls, N.Y. BR/TR, 6'1", 190 lbs. Deb: 5/16/05

YEAR	TM/L	W	L	PCT	G	GS	CG	SH	SV	IP	H	HR	BB	SO	RAT	ERA	ERA+	OAV	OOB	BH	AVG	PB	PR	/A	PD	TPI
1905	Chi-N	18	14	.563	34	29	28	5	1	291^2	208	1	73	152	9.2	1.42	210	**.201**	.266	14	.127	-6	51	51	-1	4.8
1906	*Chi-N	19	4	**.826**	33	24	20	6	3	218	129	2	92	94	9.7	1.65	160	**.175**	.278	13	.157	-2	24	24	3	2.8
1907	*Chi-N	17	4	**.810**	27	22	16	4	0	192	147	1	64	96	10.3	1.69	148	.217	.294	11	.175	0	17	17	1	2.1
1908	*Chi-N	24	7	**.774**	46	35	25	7	1	297^2	227	4	106	133	10.4	2.03	116	.214	.292	23	.232	7	11	11	-1	1.7
1909	Chi-N	19	10	.655	35	32	23	6	0	262^2	194	1	82	105	9.8	1.78	143	.212	.285	12	.140	-1	24	22	4	2.9
1910	*Chi-N	12	8	.600	24	23	14	1	0	173^1	161	1	49	55	11.4	3.12	92	.250	.312	6	.107	-3	-2	-5	1	-0.8
1911	Chi-N	16	9	.640	33	29	15	2	0	221^2	191	3	103	79	12.1	2.96	112	.236	.325	6	.090	-1	11	9	3	1.0
1912	Chi-N	10	6	.625	39	19	8	0	4	169	161	7	60	75	12.2	3.78	88	.259	.332	6	.109	-3	-7	-9	4	-0.6
1913	Chi-N	1	3	.250	10	3	1	0	0	38^2	41	1	21	10	14.7	4.42	72	.281	.375	3	.250	0	-5	-5	0	-0.5
	Bro-N	7	6	.538	15	12	8	2	0	110	77	3	34	46	9.4	2.05	161	.202	.274	3	.103	0	14	15	-1	1.7
	Yr	8	9	.471	25	15	9	2	0	148^2	118	4	55	56	10.7	2.66	123	.223	.301	6	.146	0	9	10	-1	1.2
1914	Bro-N	11	18	.379	44	29	14	3	3	256	228	5	83	119	11.3	2.64	108	.242	.310	9	.122	-0	4	6	1	0.8
1915	New-F	21	10	.677	33	30	23	4	1	270	233	3	69	117	10.2	2.23	115	.236	.287	18	.196	-2	15	10	1	1.1
1916	Bos-N	7	6	.538	21	11	6	0	0	109^1	99	1	41	47	11.9	2.47	101	.251	.328	3	.091	-1	2	0	5	0.5
1917	Bos-N	0	1	.000	5	2	0	0	0	22^1	21	0	15	9	14.9	2.82	90	.256	.378	0	.000	1	-0	-1	1	0.2
Total	13	182	106	.632	399	300	201	40	13	2632^1	2117	33	892	1137	10.7	2.28	122	.224	.299	127	.147	-11	159	146	22	17.7

● PAUL REUSCHEL Reuschel, Paul Richard b: 1/12/47, Quincy, Ill. BR/TR, 6'4", 225 lbs. Deb: 7/25/75 F

YEAR	TM/L	W	L	PCT	G	GS	CG	SH	SV	IP	H	HR	BB	SO	RAT	ERA	ERA+	OAV	OOB	BH	AVG	PB	PR	/A	PD	TPI
1975	Chi-N	1	3	.250	28	0	0	0	5	36	44	1	13	12	14.5	3.50	110	.312	.374	0	.000	-0	0	1	0	0.2
1976	Chi-N	4	2	.667	50	2	0	0	3	87	94	12	33	55	13.2	4.55	85	.278	.344	2	.154	-0	-10	-7	1	-0.4
1977	Chi-N	5	6	.455	69	0	0	0	4	107	105	9	40	62	12.2	4.37	100	.262	.329	0	.000	-1	-6	0	2	0.1
1978	Chi-N	2	0	1.000	16	0	0	0	0	28	29	4	13	13	13.8	5.14	78	.269	.352	0	.000	-0	-5	-3	-0	-0.3
	Cle-A	2	4	.333	18	6	1	0	0	89^2	95	5	22	24	11.9	3.11	120	.271	.318	0	—	0	6	6	1	0.5
1979	Cle-A	2	1	.667	17	1	0	0	1	45^1	73	7	11	22	16.7	7.94	54	.365	.398	0	—	0	-19	-19	1	-1.1
Total	5	16	16	.500	198	9	1	0	13	393	440	38	132	188	13.2	4.51	89	.286	.344	2	.063	-2	-32	-21	5	-1.0

● RICK REUSCHEL Reuschel, Rickey Eugene b: 5/16/49, Quincy, Ill. BR/TR, 6'3", 235 lbs. Deb: 6/19/72 F

YEAR	TM/L	W	L	PCT	G	GS	CG	SH	SV	IP	H	HR	BB	SO	RAT	ERA	ERA+	OAV	OOB	BH	AVG	PB	PR	/A	PD	TPI
1972	Chi-N	10	8	.556	21	18	5	4	0	129	127	3	29	87	11.0	2.93	130	.259	.303	6	.136	-1	7	13	-0	1.6
1973	Chi-N	14	15	.483	36	36	7	3	0	237	244	15	62	168	11.8	3.00	131	.263	.312	9	.123	-3	17	25	4	3.0
1974	Chi-N	13	12	.520	41	38	8	2	0	240^2	262	18	83	160	13.1	4.30	89	.276	.338	19	.221	2	-18	-13	5	-0.6
1975	Chi-N	11	17	.393	38	37	6	0	1	234	244	17	67	155	12.2	3.73	103	.268	.323	16	.208	2	-3	3	3	0.8
1976	Chi-N	14	12	.538	38	37	9	2	1	260	260	17	64	146	11.5	3.46	111	.265	.315	19	.229	4	1	11	3	1.9
1977	Chi-N★	20	10	.667	39	37	8	4	1	252	233	13	74	166	11.1	2.79	157	.247	.305	18	.207	1	31	**45**	3	5.8
1978	Chi-N	14	15	.483	35	35	9	1	0	242^2	235	16	54	115	10.9	3.41	118	.254	.299	10	.137	-1	4	17	2	2.0
1979	Chi-N	18	12	.600	36	36	5	1	0	239	251	16	75	125	12.7	3.62	114	.274	.335	13	.165	1	3	13	5	2.1
1980	Chi-N	11	13	.458	38	38	6	0	0	257	281	13	76	140	12.6	3.40	115	.286	.340	13	.159	-1	6	15	5	1.8
1981	Chi-N	4	7	.364	13	13	1	0	0	85^2	87	4	23	53	12.0	3.47	107	.267	.323	2	.080	-1	0	2	2	0.3
	*NY-A	4	4	.500	12	11	3	0	0	70^2	75	4	10	22	11.0	2.67	134	.280	.308	0	—	0	8	7	1	0.9
1983	Chi-N	1	1	.500	4	4	0	0	0	20^2	18	1	10	9	12.2	3.92	97	.234	.322	1	.143	-0	-1	-0	1	0.1
1984	Chi-N	5	5	.500	19	14	1	0	0	92^1	123	7	23	43	14.5	5.17	76	.339	.383	7	.241	2	-16	-13	1	-1.0
1985	Pit-N	14	8	.636	31	26	9	1	1	194	153	7	52	138	9.6	2.27	157	.215	.272	10	.169	2	28	28	4	4.0
1986	Pit-N	9	16	.360	35	34	4	2	0	215^2	232	20	57	125	12.4	3.96	97	.274	.326	11	.157	0	-6	-3	3	0.0
1987	Pit-N★	8	6	.571	25	25	9	3	0	177	163	12	35	80	10.4	2.75	150	.246	.290	9	.150	2	26	27	1	2.3
	*SF-N	5	3	.625	9	8	3	1	0	50	44	1	7	27	9.5	4.32	89	.230	.265	2	.105	-0	-1	-3	0	-0.4
	Yr	13	9	.591	34	33	**12**	**4**	0	227	207	13	42	107	**10.0**	3.09	131	.239	.276	11	.139	2	25	24	1	1.9
1988	SF-N	19	11	.633	36	36	7	2	0	245	242	11	42	92	10.7	3.12	104	.260	.297	8	.110	-1	9	4	-2	0.0
1989	*SF-N★	17	8	.680	32	32	2	0	0	208^1	195	18	54	111	10.8	2.94	115	.247	.297	10	.164	1	13	10	-0	1.3
1990	SF-N	3	6	.333	15	13	0	0	1	87	102	8	31	49	13.9	3.93	93	.297	.357	4	.154	0	-1	-3	0	-0.2
1991	SF-N	0	2	.000	4	1	0	0	0	10^2	17	0	7	4	20.3	4.22	85	.370	.453	0	.000	-0	-1	-1	-0	-0.2
Total	19	214	191	.528	557	529	102	26	5	3548^1	3588	221	935	2015	11.7	3.37	114	.264	.316	187	.168	8	108	183	39	25.5

● JERRY REUSS Reuss, Jerry b: 6/19/49, St.Louis, Mo. BL/TL, 6'5", 217 lbs. Deb: 9/27/69

YEAR	TM/L	W	L	PCT	G	GS	CG	SH	SV	IP	H	HR	BB	SO	RAT	ERA	ERA+	OAV	OOB	BH	AVG	PB	PR	/A	PD	TPI
1969	StL-N	1	0	1.000	1	1	0	0	0	7	2	0	3	3	9.0	0.00	—	.091	.259	1	.333	0	3	3	0	0.6
1970	StL-N	7	8	.467	20	20	5	2	0	127^1	132	9	49	74	12.9	4.10	100	.271	.339	2	.050	-3	-1	0	-0	-0.2
1971	StL-N	14	14	.500	36	35	7	2	0	211	228	15	109	131	14.7	4.78	75	.279	.368	8	.123	0	-31	-28	-2	-3.5
1972	Hou-N	9	13	.409	33	30	4	1	1	192	177	14	83	174	12.7	4.17	81	.246	.332	7	.106	-1	-15	-17	-1	-2.0
1973	Hou-N	16	13	.552	41	40	12	3	0	279^1	271	17	117	177	12.6	3.74	97	.256	.332	13	.137	-1	-2	-3	-2	-0.7
1974	*Pit-N	16	11	.593	35	35	14	1	0	260	259	20	101	105	12.5	3.50	99	.261	.329	13	.151	0	4	-1	-2	-0.3
1975	*Pit-N★	18	11	.621	32	32	15	6	0	237^1	224	10	78	131	11.5	2.54	139	.253	.314	14	.197	2	28	26	2	3.7
1976	Pit-N	14	9	.609	31	29	11	3	2	209^1	209	16	51	108	11.3	3.53	99	.256	.301	16	.242	6	-1	-1	-2	0.3

YEAR	TM/L	W	L	PCT	G	GS	CG	SH	SV	IP	H	HR	BB	SO	RAT	ERA	ERA+	OAV	OOB	BH	AVG	PB	PR	/A	PD	TPI
1977	Pit-N	10	13	.435	33	33	8	2	0	208	225	11	71	116	13.0	4.11	97	.280	.341	12	.171	1	-5	-3	1	-0.1
1978	Pit-N	3	2	.600	23	12	3	1	0	82^2	97	5	23	42	13.4	4.90	76	.297	.348	5	.185	0	-12	-11	-0	-0.6
1979	LA-N	7	14	.333	39	21	4	1	3	160	178	4	60	83	13.6	3.54	103	.282	.347	7	.167	1	3	2	1	0.5
1980	LA-N★	18	6	.750	37	29	10	**6**	3	229^1	193	12	40	111	9.1	2.51	139	.227	.261	6	.088	-1	28	25	1	2.7
1981	*LA-N	10	4	.714	22	22	8	2	0	152^2	138	6	27	51	10.0	2.30	144	.243	.282	10	.196	0	20	17	3	1.9
1982	LA-N	18	11	.621	39	37	8	4	0	254^2	232	11	50	138	10.0	3.11	111	.240	.278	17	.221	3	14	10	2	1.6
1983	*LA-N	12	11	.522	32	31	7	0	0	223^1	233	12	50	143	11.5	2.94	122	.271	.313	20	.282	5	17	16	4	2.7
1984	LA-N	5	7	.417	30	15	2	0	1	99	102	4	31	44	12.1	3.82	92	.266	.321	4	.167	1	-3	-3	-0	-0.3
1985	*LA-N	14	10	.583	34	33	5	3	0	212^2	210	13	58	84	11.5	2.92	119	.260	.312	10	.135	-1	16	13	-2	1.1
1986	LA-N	2	6	.250	19	13	0	0	1	74	96	13	17	29	14.0	5.84	59	.313	.353	5	.250	2	-17	-20	1	-1.7
1987	LA-N	0	0	—	1	0	0	0	0	2	2	0	0	2	9.0	4.50	88	.333	.333	0	—	0	-0	-0	-0	0.0
	Cin-N	0	5	.000	7	7	0	0	0	34^2	52	2	12	10	16.9	7.79	54	.351	.404	1	.125	0	-14	-14	-1	-1.6
	Yr	0	5	.000	8	7	0	0	0	36^2	54	2	12	12	16.4	7.61	56	.348	.399	1	.125	0	-14	-14	-1	-1.6
	Cal-A	4	5	.444	17	16	1	1	0	82^1	112	16	17	37	14.3	5.25	82	.327	.362	0	—	0	-7	-9	2	-0.7
1988	Chi-A	13	9	.591	32	29	2	0	0	183	183	15	43	73	11.3	3.44	115	.263	.309	0	—	0	11	11	0	1.2
1989	Chi-A	8	5	.615	23	19	1	1	0	106^2	135	12	21	27	13.4	5.06	75	.308	.344	0	—	0	-14	-15	-2	-1.8
	Mil-A	1	4	.200	7	7	0	0	0	33^2	36	7	13	13	13.4	5.35	72	.273	.342	0	—	0	-5	-6	-0	-0.7
	Yr	9	9	.500	30	26	1	1	0	140^1	171	19	34	40	13.2	5.13	74	.295	.336	0	—	0	-19	-21	-2	-2.5
1990	Pit-N	0	0	—	4	1	0	0	0	7^2	8	1	3	1	12.9	3.52	103	.267	.333	0	—	0	0	0	0	0.0
Total	22	220	191	.535	628	547	127	39	11	3669^2	3734	245	1127	1907	12.1	3.64	100	.265	.322	171	.167	15	16	-7	2	2.1

● TODD REVENIG

Revenig, Todd Michael b: 6/28/69, Brainerd, Minn. BR/TR, 6′1″, 185 lbs. Deb: 8/24/92

YEAR	TM/L	W	L	PCT	G	GS	CG	SH	SV	IP	H	HR	BB	SO	RAT	ERA	ERA+	OAV	OOB	BH	AVG	PB	PR	/A	PD	TPI
1992	Oak-A	0	0	—	2	0	0	0	0	2	2	0	0	1	9.0	0.00	—	.286	.286	0	—	0	1	1	-0	0.4

● CARLOS REYES

Reyes, Carlos Alberto b: 4/4/69, Miami, Fla. BB/TR, 6′1″, 190 lbs. Deb: 4/7/94

YEAR	TM/L	W	L	PCT	G	GS	CG	SH	SV	IP	H	HR	BB	SO	RAT	ERA	ERA+	OAV	OOB	BH	AVG	PB	PR	/A	PD	TPI
1994	Oak-A	0	3	.000	27	9	0	0	1	78	71	10	44	57	13.5	4.15	107	.242	.345	0	—	0	6	2	-1	0.5
1995	Oak-A	4	6	.400	40	1	0	0	0	69	71	10	28	48	13.6	5.09	88	.264	.344	0	—	0	-3	-5	1	-0.4
1996	Oak-A	7	10	.412	46	10	0	0	0	122^1	134	19	61	78	14.5	4.78	103	.281	.365	0	—	0	3	2	-1	0.2
1997	Oak-A	3	4	.429	37	6	0	0	0	77^1	101	13	25	43	14.9	5.82	78	.316	.369	0	—	0	-11	-11	0	-0.8
1998	SD-N	2	2	.500	22	0	0	0	1	27^2	23	4	6	24	10.1	3.58	107	.235	.292	0	—	0	2	1	0	0.1
	Bos-A	1	1	.500	24	0	0	0	0	38^1	35	2	14	23	11.7	3.52	131	.246	.318	0	—	0	5	5	0	0.2
Total	5	17	26	.395	196	26	0	0	2	412^2	435	58	178	273	13.7	4.71	97	.272	.350	0	—	0	2	-6	-1	-0.2

● DENNIS REYES

Reyes, Dennis (Valarde) b: 4/19/77, Higuera De Zaragoza, Mex. BL/TL, 6′3″, 246 lbs. Deb: 7/13/97

YEAR	TM/L	W	L	PCT	G	GS	CG	SH	SV	IP	H	HR	BB	SO	RAT	ERA	ERA+	OAV	OOB	BH	AVG	PB	PR	/A	PD	TPI
1997	LA-N	2	3	.400	14	5	0	0	0	47	51	4	18	36	13.4	3.83	101	.280	.348	0	.000	-1	2	0	2	0.1
1998	LA-N	0	4	.000	11	3	0	0	0	28^2	27	1	20	33	14.8	4.71	83	.255	.373	0	.000	-1	-2	-3	0	-0.3
	Cin-N	3	1	.750	8	7	0	0	0	38^2	35	2	27	44	14.7	4.42	98	.255	.382	1	.083	-0	-1	-0	0	-0.1
	Yr	3	5	.375	19	10	0	0	0	67^1	62	3	47	77	14.7	4.54	91	.254	.377	1	.059	-1	-2	-3	0	-0.4
Total	2	5	8	.385	33	15	0	0	0	114^1	113	7	65	113	14.2	4.25	95	.266	.366	1	.038	-2	-0	-3	2	-0.3

● ALBERTO REYES

Reyes, Rafael Alberto b: 4/10/71, San Cristobal, D.R. BR/TR, 6′1″, 195 lbs. Deb: 4/27/95

YEAR	TM/L	W	L	PCT	G	GS	CG	SH	SV	IP	H	HR	BB	SO	RAT	ERA	ERA+	OAV	OOB	BH	AVG	PB	PR	/A	PD	TPI
1995	Mil-A	1	1	.500	27	0	0	0	1	33^1	19	3	18	29	10.8	2.43	205	.167	.296	0	—	0	8	9	0	0.4
1996	Mil-A	1	0	1.000	5	0	0	0	0	5^2	8	1	2	2	15.9	7.94	65	.320	.370	0	—	0	-2	-2	-0	-0.4
1997	Mil-A	1	2	.333	19	0	0	0	1	29^2	32	4	9	28	13.3	5.46	84	.274	.341	0	—	0	-3	-3	0	-0.2
1998	Mil-N	5	1	.833	50	0	0	0	0	57	55	9	31	58	13.9	3.95	109	.253	.352	1	.200	0	2	2	-0	0.2
Total	4	8	4	.667	101	0	0	0	2	125^2	114	17	60	117	13.0	4.08	112	.241	.336	1	.200	0	5	7	0	0.0

● ALLIE REYNOLDS

Reynolds, Allie Pierce "Superchief" b: 2/10/15, Bethany, Okla. d: 12/26/94, Oklahoma City, Okla. BR/TR, 6′, 195 lbs. Deb: 9/17/42

YEAR	TM/L	W	L	PCT	G	GS	CG	SH	SV	IP	H	HR	BB	SO	RAT	ERA	ERA+	OAV	OOB	BH	AVG	PB	PR	/A	PD	TPI
1942	Cle-A	0	0	—	2	0	0	0	0	5	5	0	4	2	16.2	0.00	—	.250	.375	0	.000	-0	2	2	-0	0.0
1943	Cle-A	11	12	.478	34	21	11	3	3	198^2	140	3	109	**151**	11.6	2.99	104	**.202**	.316	10	.149	-1	7	3	-0	0.1
1944	Cle-A	11	8	.579	28	21	5	1	1	158	141	2	91	84	13.4	3.30	100	.240	.346	7	.123	-3	2	-0	-1	-0.4
1945	Cle-A†	18	12	.600	44	30	16	2	4	247^1	227	7	130	112	13.2	3.20	101	.247	.343	8	.094	-7	5	1	-1	-0.7
1946	Cle-A	11	15	.423	31	28	9	3	0	183^1	180	10	108	107	14.2	3.88	85	.259	.359	14	.222	1	-8	-12	-1	-1.5
1947	*NY-A	19	8	**.704**	34	30	17	4	2	241^2	207	23	123	129	12.4	3.20	110	.227	.322	13	.146	-2	13	9	-2	0.6
1948	NY-A	16	7	.696	39	31	11	1	3	236^1	240	17	111	101	13.5	3.77	108	.268	.351	16	.193	0	14	8	-3	0.4
1949	*NY-A☆	17	6	.739	35	31	4	2	1	213^2	200	15	123	105	13.8	4.00	101	.250	.353	17	.218	6	5	1	-0	0.6
1950	*NY-A★	16	12	.571	35	29	14	2	2	240^2	215	12	138	160	13.5	3.74	115	.242	.349	15	.185	1	22	15	-1	1.5
1951	*NY-A	17	8	.680	40	26	16	**7**	7	221	171	12	100	126	11.2	3.05	125	**.213**	.304	14	.184	0	26	19	-3	1.8
1952	*NY-A☆	20	8	.714	35	29	24	**6**	6	244^1	194	10	97	**160**	11.0	**2.06**	**161**	.218	.300	13	.153	-1	**44**	34	-1	3.9
1953	*NY-A★	13	7	.650	41	15	5	1	13	145	140	9	61	86	12.8	3.41	108	.253	.333	5	.122	1	9	4	-2	0.5
1954	NY-A†	13	4	.765	36	18	5	4	7	157^1	133	13	66	100	11.6	3.32	104	.233	.316	8	.160	-0	7	2	-0	0.1
Total	13	182	107	.630	434	309	137	36	49	2492^1	2193	133	1261	1423	12.7	3.30	110	.238	.333	140	.163	-5	149	87	-16	6.9

● ARCHIE REYNOLDS

Reynolds, Archie Edward b: 1/3/46, Glendale, Cal. BR/TR, 6′2″, 205 lbs. Deb: 8/15/68

YEAR	TM/L	W	L	PCT	G	GS	CG	SH	SV	IP	H	HR	BB	SO	RAT	ERA	ERA+	OAV	OOB	BH	AVG	PB	PR	/A	PD	TPI
1968	Chi-N	0	1	.000	7	1	0	0	0	13^1	14	1	7	6	14.9	6.75	47	.259	.355	1	.500	1	-6	-5	-0	-0.4
1969	Chi-N	0	1	.000	2	2	0	0	0	7^1	11	1	7	4	22.1	2.45	164	.379	.500	0	.000	0	1	1	0	0.2
1970	Chi-N	0	2	.000	7	1	0	0	0	15	17	2	9	9	16.2	6.60	68	.298	.403	0	.000	0	-4	-3	-0	-0.4
1971	Cal-A	0	3	.000	15	1	0	0	0	27^1	32	2	18	15	16.5	4.61	70	.305	.407	0	.000	-0	-3	-4	0	-0.4
1972	Mil-A	0	1	.000	5	2	0	0	0	18^2	26	2	8	13	16.4	7.23	42	.338	.400	2	.500	1	-9	-9	-1	-0.4
Total	5	0	8	.000	36	7	0	0	0	81^2	100	8	49	47	16.6	5.73	61	.311	.405	3	.273	2	-21	-21	-1	-1.4

● CHARLIE REYNOLDS

Reynolds, Charles E. b: 7/31/1857, Allegany, N.Y. d: 5/1/13, Buffalo, N.Y. Deb: 5/18/1882

YEAR	TM/L	W	L	PCT	G	GS	CG	SH	SV	IP	H	HR	BB	SO	RAT	ERA	ERA+	OAV	OOB	BH	AVG	PB	PR	/A	PD	TPI
1882	Phi-a	1	1	.500	2	2	1	0	0	12	18	0	3	4	15.8	5.25	57	.327	.362	1	.125	-1	-3	-3	-1	-0.5

● CRAIG REYNOLDS

Reynolds, Gordon Craig b: 12/27/52, Houston, Tex. BL/TR, 6′1″, 175 lbs. Deb: 8/1/75 ◆

YEAR	TM/L	W	L	PCT	G	GS	CG	SH	SV	IP	H	HR	BB	SO	RAT	ERA	ERA+	OAV	OOB	BH	AVG	PB	PR	/A	PD	TPI
1986	*Hou-N	0	0	—	1	0	0	0	0	1	3	0	2	1	45.0	27.00	13	.500	.625	78	.249	0	-3	-3	0	0.0
1989	Hou-N	0	0	—	1	0	0	0	0	1	3	0	1	0	45.0	27.00	13	.500	.625	38	.201	0	-3	-3	0	0.0
Total	2	0	0	—	2	0	0	0	0	2	6	0	3	1	45.0	27.00	13	.500	.625	1142	.256	0	-5	-5	0	0.0

● KEN REYNOLDS

Reynolds, Kenneth Lee b: 1/4/47, Trevose, Pa. BL/TL, 6′, 180 lbs. Deb: 9/5/70

YEAR	TM/L	W	L	PCT	G	GS	CG	SH	SV	IP	H	HR	BB	SO	RAT	ERA	ERA+	OAV	OOB	BH	AVG	PB	PR	/A	PD	TPI
1970	Phi-N	0	0	—	4	0	0	0	0	2^1	3	0	4	1	27.0	0.00	—	.333	.538	0	—	0	1	1	0	0.0
1971	Phi-N	5	9	.357	35	25	2	1	0	162^1	163	11	82	81	13.9	4.49	78	.269	.361	10	.200	2	-19	-17	-1	-1.3
1972	Phi-N	2	15	.118	33	23	2	0	0	154^1	149	17	60	87	12.2	4.26	84	.258	.329	8	.200	1	-14	-11	-0	-1.1
1973	Mil-A	0	1	.000	2	1	0	0	0	7^1	5	1	10	3	19.6	7.36	51	.200	.444	0	—	0	-3	-3	1	-0.2
1975	StL-N	0	1	.000	10	0	0	0	0	17	12	0	11	7	12.2	1.59	236	.214	.343	0	.000	-0	4	4	1	0.3
1976	SD-N	0	3	.000	19	2	0	0	1	32^1	38	0	29	18	18.6	6.40	51	.309	.441	0	.000	-1	-10	-11	-0	-1.1
Total	6	7	29	.194	103	51	4	1	1	375^2	370	29	196	197	13.8	4.46	80	.265	.358	18	.186	2	-41	-38	0	-3.4

● SHANE REYNOLDS

Reynolds, Richard Shane b: 3/26/68, Bastrop, La. BR/TR, 6′3″, 210 lbs. Deb: 7/20/92

YEAR	TM/L	W	L	PCT	G	GS	CG	SH	SV	IP	H	HR	BB	SO	RAT	ERA	ERA+	OAV	OOB	BH	AVG	PB	PR	/A	PD	TPI
1992	Hou-N	1	3	.250	8	5	0	0	0	25^1	42	2	6	10	17.1	7.11	47	.385	.417	2	.500	1	-10	-11	0	-1.3
1993	Hou-N	0	0	—	5	1	0	0	0	11	11	0	6	10	13.9	0.82	473	.256	.347	1	.500	0	4	4	-0	0.0
1994	Hou-N	8	5	.615	33	14	1	1	0	124	128	10	21	110	11.3	3.05	130	.263	.302	3	.091	-2	16	12	0	1.0
1995	Hou-N	10	11	.476	30	30	3	2	0	189^1	196	15	37	175	11.2	3.47	111	.263	.300	8	.127	-2	15	8	3	1.0
1996	Hou-N	16	10	.615	35	35	4	1	0	239	227	20	44	204	10.5	3.65	106	.249	.290	14	.184	4	15	6	-1	0.9
1997	*Hou-N	9	10	.474	30	30	2	0	0	181	189	19	47	152	11.9	4.23	95	.267	.315	6	.113	-0	-1	-5	1	-0.4
1998	*Hou-N	19	8	.704	35	35	3	1	0	233^1	257	25	53	209	12.0	3.51	116	.280	.320	13	.159	1	19	14	4	2.0
Total	7	63	47	.573	176	150	13	5	0	1003	1050	91	214	870	11.5	3.67	107	.268	.309	47	.150	3	58	29	8	3.2

● BOB REYNOLDS

Reynolds, Robert Allen b: 1/21/47, Seattle, Wash. BR/TR, 6′, 205 lbs. Deb: 9/19/69

YEAR	TM/L	W	L	PCT	G	GS	CG	SH	SV	IP	H	HR	BB	SO	RAT	ERA	ERA+	OAV	OOB	BH	AVG	PB	PR	/A	PD	TPI
1969	Mon-N	0	0	—	1	1	0	0	0	1^1	3	0	3	2	40.5	20.25	18	.429	.600	0	—	0	-2	-2	0	0.0
1971	StL-N	0	0	—	4	0	0	0	0	7	15	2	6	4	28.3	10.29	35	.441	.537	0	.000	-0	-5	-5	-0	0.0
	Mil-A	0	1	.000	3	0	0	0	0	6	4	0	3	4	10.5	3.00	116	.222	.333	0	.000	-0	0	0	0	0.0

YEAR	TM/L	W	L	PCT	G	GS	CG	SH	SV	IP	H	HR	BB	SO	RAT	ERA	ERA+	OAV	OOB	BH	AVG	PB	PR	/A	PD	TPI
1972	Bal-A	0	0	—	3	0	0	0	0	9^2	8	0	7	5	14.0	1.86	165	.258	.395	0	.000	-0	1	1	-0	0.0
1973	*Bal-A	7	5	.583	42	1	0	0	9	111	88	3	31	77	9.6	1.95	192	.219	.275	0	—	0	23	22	-2	2.5
1974	*Bal-A	7	5	.583	54	0	0	0	7	69^1	75	4	14	43	11.7	2.73	127	.278	.316	0	—	0	7	6	-0	1.0
1975	Bal-A	0	1	.000	7	0	0	0	0	6	11	1	1	1	18.0	9.00	39	.423	.444	0	—	0	-3	-4	-0	-0.1
	Det-A	0	2	.000	21	0	0	0	3	34^2	40	8	14	26	14.3	4.67	86	.288	.357	0	—	0	-3	-3	0	-0.5
	Cle-A	0	2	.000	5	0	0	0	2	9^2	11	0	3	5	13.0	4.66	81	.289	.341	0	—	0	-1	-1	-0	-0.2
	Yr	0	5	.000	33	0	0	0	5	50^1	62	9	18	32	14.3	5.19	75	.301	.357	0	—	0	-8	-7	-0	-0.8
Total	6	14	16	.467	140	2	0	0	21	254^2	255	18	82	167	12.0	3.15	116	.264	.324	0	.000	-0	16	14	-3	2.7

● ROSS REYNOLDS

Reynolds, Ross Ernest "Doc" b: 8/20/1887, Barksdale, Tex. d: 6/23/70, Ada, Okla. BR/TR, 6'2", 185 lbs. Deb: 5/2/14

YEAR	TM/L	W	L	PCT	G	GS	CG	SH	SV	IP	H	HR	BB	SO	RAT	ERA	ERA+	OAV	OOB	BH	AVG	PB	PR	/A	PD	TPI
1914	Det-A	5	3	.625	26	7	3	1	0	78	62	0	39	31	12.3	2.08	135	.230	.340	1	.048	-2	6	6	-1	0.3
1915	Det-A	0	1	.000	4	2	0	0	0	11^1	17	0	5	2	18.3	6.35	48	.378	.451	0	.000	-0	-4	-4	0	-0.3
Total	2	5	4	.556	30	9	3	1	0	89^1	79	0	44	33	13.1	2.62	108	.251	.355	1	.042	-2	1	2	-1	0.0

● ARMANDO REYNOSO

Reynoso, Armando Martin (Gutierrez) b: 5/1/66, San Luis Potosi, Mex. BR/TR, 6', 196 lbs. Deb: 8/11/91

YEAR	TM/L	W	L	PCT	G	GS	CG	SH	SV	IP	H	HR	BB	SO	RAT	ERA	ERA+	OAV	OOB	BH	AVG	PB	PR	/A	PD	TPI
1991	Atl-N	2	1	.667	6	5	0	0	0	23^1	26	4	10	10	15.0	6.17	63	.299	.390	0	.000	-0	-6	-6	2	-0.5
1992	Atl-N	1	0	1.000	3	1	0	0	1	7^2	11	2	2	2	16.4	4.70	78	.393	.452	0	.000	-0	-1	-1	0	-0.1
1993	Col-N	12	11	.522	30	30	4	0	0	189	206	22	63	117	13.2	4.00	119	.277	.340	8	.127	-1	1	16	2	1.9
1994	Col-N	3	4	.429	9	9	1	0	0	52^1	54	5	22	25	14.1	4.82	103	.278	.369	3	.176	-0	-4	1	2	0.3
1995	*Col-N	7	7	.500	20	18	0	0	0	93	116	12	36	40	15.2	5.32	101	.316	.385	4	.133	-2	-12	1	3	0.2
1996	Col-N	8	9	.471	30	30	0	0	0	168^2	195	27	49	88	13.5	4.96	105	.291	.348	9	.173	-1	-14	5	2	0.6
1997	NY-N	6	3	.667	16	16	1	1	0	91^1	95	7	29	47	12.8	4.53	89	.275	.342	7	.241	3	-3	-5	1	-0.1
1998	NY-N	7	3	.700	11	11	0	0	0	68^1	64	4	32	40	13.3	3.82	109	.256	.352	5	.167	0	3	3	3	0.7
Total	8	46	38	.548	125	120	6	1	1	693^2	767	83	243	369	13.7	4.61	104	.286	.355	36	.157	-1	-36	13	15	3.0

● FLINT RHEM

Rhem, Charles Flint "Shad" b: 1/24/01, Rhems, S.C. d: 7/30/69, Columbia, S.C. BR/TR, 6'2", 180 lbs. Deb: 9/6/24

YEAR	TM/L	W	L	PCT	G	GS	CG	SH	SV	IP	H	HR	BB	SO	RAT	ERA	ERA+	OAV	OOB	BH	AVG	PB	PR	/A	PD	TPI
1924	StL-N	2	2	.500	6	3	3	0	1	32^1	31	1	17	20	13.4	4.45	85	.254	.345	2	.167	-0	-2	-2	0	-0.3
1925	StL-N	8	13	.381	30	24	8	1	1	170	204	16	58	66	14.1	4.92	88	.299	.357	14	.237	1	-12	-11	0	-1.1
1926	*StL-N	**20**	7	.741	34	34	20	1	0	258	241	12	75	72	11.1	3.21	122	.250	.305	18	.188	-2	18	20	1	1.8
1927	StL-N	10	12	.455	27	26	9	2	0	169^1	189	6	54	51	13.1	4.41	90	.285	.342	4	.068	-5	-9	-9	-3	-1.8
1928	*StL-N	11	8	.579	28	22	9	0	3	169^2	199	13	71	47	14.5	4.14	97	.296	.365	11	.164	-1	-3	-3	2	-0.3
1930	*StL-N	12	8	.600	26	19	9	0	0	139^2	173	11	37	47	13.7	4.45	113	.306	.352	12	.231	-1	8	9	-3	0.7
1931	*StL-N	11	10	.524	33	26	10	2	1	207^1	214	17	60	72	12.0	3.56	111	.268	.321	9	.130	-4	7	9	-2	0.2
1932	StL-N	4	2	.667	6	6	5	1	0	50	48	3	10	18	10.4	3.06	129	.257	.294	3	.188	0	5	5	0	0.6
	Phi-N	11	7	.611	26	20	10	0	1	168^2	177	13	49	35	12.1	3.74	118	.269	.319	7	.113	-5	3	13	-0	0.7
	Yr	15	9	.625	32	26	15	1	1	218^2	225	16	59	53	11.7	3.58	120	.266	.314	10	.128	-5	7	18	-0	1.3
1933	Phi-N	5	14	.263	28	19	3	0	2	125	182	10	33	27	15.6	6.62	58	.340	.381	4	.087	-4	-46	-39	-0	-5.5
1934	StL-N	1	0	1.000	5	1	0	0	1	15^2	26	0	7	6	19.0	4.60	92	.394	.452	0	.000	-0	-1	-1	-0	-0.1
	Bos-N	8	8	.500	25	20	5	1	0	152^2	164	5	38	56	11.9	3.60	106	.273	.317	3	.058	-5	8	4	1	0.0
	Yr	9	8	.529	30	21	5	1	1	168^1	190	5	45	62	12.6	3.69	105	.285	.331	3	.056	-5	7	3	1	-0.1
1935	Bos-N	0	5	.000	10	6	0	0	0	40^1	61	4	11	10	16.1	5.36	71	.341	.379	0	.000	-1	-6	-7	0	-0.8
1936	StL-N	2	1	.667	10	4	0	0	0	26^2	49	2	9	7	19.6	6.75	58	.405	.446	1	.125	-0	-8	-8	-1	-0.9
Total	12	105	97	.520	294	230	91	8	10	1725^1	1958	113	529	534	13.1	4.20	98	.287	.340	88	.144	-28	-39	-20	-3	-6.8

● BILLY RHINES

Rhines, William Pearl "Bunker" b: 3/14/1869, Ridgway, Pa. d: 1/30/22, Ridgway, Pa. BR/TR, 5'11", 168 lbs. Deb: 4/22/1890

YEAR	TM/L	W	L	PCT	G	GS	CG	SH	SV	IP	H	HR	BB	SO	RAT	ERA	ERA+	OAV	OOB	BH	AVG	PB	PR	/A	PD	TPI
1890	Cin-N	28	17	.622	46	45	45	6	0	401^1	337	6	113	182	**10.4**	**1.95**	**182**	.221	**.281**	29	.188	-5	**72**	72	1	6.5
1891	Cin-N	17	24	.415	48	43	40	1	1	372^2	364	4	124	138	12.3	2.87	117	.246	.314	18	.122	-9	20	21	3	1.3
1892	Cin-N	3	7	.300	11	9	6	0	0	74^2	102	0	36	10	17.1	5.42	60	.313	.388	5	.185	1	-18	-18	-1	-1.8
1893	Lou-N	1	4	.200	5	5	3	0	0	31	49	3	19	0	20.6	8.71	51	.348	.436	1	.091	-2	-14	-15	0	-1.6
1895	Cin-N	19	10	.655	38	33	25	0	0	267^2	322	4	76	72	14.1	4.81	103	.293	.351	25	.221	-4	-1	5	-0	0.1
1896	Cin-N	8	6	.571	19	17	11	3	0	143	128	1	48	32	**11.6**	**2.45**	**188**	**.238**	**.311**	10	.192	-3	30	34	0	2.5
1897	Cin-N	21	15	.583	41	32	26	1	0	288^2	311	4	86	65	12.9	4.08	112	.273	.333	17	.159	-6	7	15	-2	0.7
1898	Pit-N	12	16	.429	31	29	27	2	0	258	289	0	61	48	12.7	3.52	101	.281	.329	15	.150	-4	2	1	5	0.2
1899	Pit-N	4	4	.500	9	9	4	0	0	54	59	3	13	6	12.7	6.00	64	.277	.330	10	.435	4	-13	-13	-1	-1.2
Total	9	113	103	.523	248	222	187	13	1	1891	1961	25	576	553	12.6	3.48	114	.262	.324	130	.177	-27	87	100	4	6.7

● BOB RHOADS

Rhoads, Robert Barton "Dusty" b: 10/4/1879, Wooster, Ohio d: 2/12/67, San Bernardino, Cal. BR/TR, 6'1", 215 lbs. Deb: 4/19/02

YEAR	TM/L	W	L	PCT	G	GS	CG	SH	SV	IP	H	HR	BB	SO	RAT	ERA	ERA+	OAV	OOB	BH	AVG	PB	PR	/A	PD	TPI
1902	Chi-N	4	8	.333	16	12	12	1	1	118	131	1	42	43	13.7	3.20	84	.281	.348	10	.222	0	-6	-7	-1	-0.7
1903	StL-N	5	8	.385	17	13	12	1	0	129	154	3	47	52	14.2	4.60	71	.303	.366	7	.140	-2	-19	-19	-1	-1.9
	Cle-A	2	3	.400	5	5	5	0	0	41	55	2	3	21	13.2	5.27	54	.320	.339	2	.118	-1	-10	-11	-0	-1.2
1904	Cle-A	10	9	.526	22	19	18	0	0	175^1	175	1	48	72	11.7	2.87	88	.261	.315	18	.196	0	-5	-7	-1	-0.8
1905	Cle-A	16	9	.640	28	26	24	4	0	235	219	4	55	61	10.9	2.83	93	.249	.300	21	.221	4	-5	-5	0	-0.1
1906	Cle-A	22	10	.688	38	34	31	7	0	315	259	5	92	89	10.2	1.80	145	.227	.288	19	.161	-3	31	29	-2	2.4
1907	Cle-A	15	14	.517	35	31	23	5	1	275	258	0	84	76	11.7	2.29	109	.250	.316	17	.185	-1	8	7	-1	0.4
1908	Cle-A	18	12	.600	37	30	20	1	0	270	229	2	73	62	10.3	1.77	135	.239	.298	20	.222	4	19	19	2	2.9
1909	Cle-A	5	9	.357	20	15	9	2	0	133^1	124	1	50	46	12.2	2.90	88	.281	.361	7	.163	-0	-6	-5	1	-0.5
Total	8	97	82	.542	218	185	154	21	2	1691^2	1604	19	494	522	11.5	2.61	100	.256	.316	121	.188	-0	6	0	-3	0.5

● RICK RHODEN

Rhoden, Richard Alan b: 5/16/53, Boynton Beach, Fla. BR/TR, 6'3", 195 lbs. Deb: 7/5/74

YEAR	TM/L	W	L	PCT	G	GS	CG	SH	SV	IP	H	HR	BB	SO	RAT	ERA	ERA+	OAV	OOB	BH	AVG	PB	PR	/A	PD	TPI
1974	LA-N	1	0	1.000	4	0	0	0	0	9	5	1	4	7	9.0	2.00	170	.161	.257	1	.500	0	2	1	-0	0.2
1975	LA-N	3	3	.500	26	11	1	0	0	99^1	94	8	32	40	11.5	3.08	110	.253	.314	2	.071	-2	6	4	0	0.0
1976	LA-N★	12	3	.800	27	26	10	3	0	181	165	17	53	77	10.9	2.98	113	.242	.298	20	.308	7	10	8	-2	1.2
1977	*LA-N	16	10	.615	31	31	4	1	0	216^1	223	20	63	122	12.0	3.74	102	.270	.323	18	.231	5	4	2	-3	0.4
1978	*LA-N	10	8	.556	30	23	6	3	0	164^2	160	13	51	79	11.7	3.66	96	.255	.314	7	.135	-0	-2	-3	-1	-0.5
1979	Pit-N	0	1	.000	1	1	0	0	0	5	5	0	2	2	12.6	7.20	54	.263	.333	1	1.000	0	-2	-2	0	-0.2
1980	Pit-N	7	5	.583	20	19	2	0	0	126^2	133	9	40	70	12.5	3.84	95	.273	.332	15	.375	6	-3	-3	0	0.4
1981	Pit-N	9	4	.692	21	21	4	2	0	136^1	147	6	53	76	13.3	3.89	92	.283	.352	9	.188	1	-6	-5	1	-0.3
1982	Pit-N	11	14	.440	35	35	6	1	0	230^1	239	14	70	128	12.2	4.14	89	.267	.321	22	.265	8	-14	-11	2	0.0
1983	Pit-N	13	13	.500	36	35	7	2	1	244^1	256	13	68	153	12.0	3.09	120	.276	.327	13	.151	-2	14	17	1	1.6
1984	Pit-N	14	9	.609	33	33	6	3	0	238^1	216	13	62	136	10.5	2.72	132	.243	.293	28	.333	10	23	**23**	2	3.5
1985	Pit-N	10	15	.400	35	35	2	0	0	213^1	254	18	69	128	13.9	4.47	80	.296	.352	14	.189	2	-21	-21	-0	-2.1
1986	Pit-N☆	15	12	.556	34	34	12	1	0	253^2	211	17	76	159	10.3	2.84	135	.228	.288	25	.278	9	25	28	1	4.0
1987	NY-A	16	10	.615	30	29	4	0	0	181^2	184	22	61	107	12.3	3.86	113	.268	.330	0	—	0	12	10	-0	1.4
1988	NY-A	12	12	.500	30	30	5	1	0	197	206	20	56	94	12.3	4.29	92	.269	.325	0	.000	-0	-7	-8	-1	-0.9
1989	Hou-N	2	6	.250	20	17	0	0	0	96^2	108	7	41	41	14.2	4.28	79	.289	.364	6	.207	1	-8	-10	1	-0.6
Total	16	151	125	.547	413	380	69	17	1	2593^2	2606	198	801	1419	12.0	3.50	103	.264	.321	181	.238	45	33	32	1	8.1

● ARTHUR RHODES

Rhodes, Arthur Lee b: 10/24/69, Waco, Tex. BL/TL, 6'2", 206 lbs. Deb: 8/21/91

YEAR	TM/L	W	L	PCT	G	GS	CG	SH	SV	IP	H	HR	BB	SO	RAT	ERA	ERA+	OAV	OOB	BH	AVG	PB	PR	/A	PD	TPI
1991	Bal-A	0	3	.000	8	8	0	0	0	36	47	4	23	23	17.5	8.00	49	.320	.412	0	—	0	-16	-16	-1	-0.9
1992	Bal-A	7	5	.583	15	15	2	1	0	94^1	87	6	38	77	12.0	3.63	111	.249	.325	0	—	0	3	4	0	0.4
1993	Bal-A	5	6	.455	17	17	0	0	0	85^2	91	16	49	49	14.8	6.51	69	.274	.369	0	—	0	-21	-19	-1	-2.4
1994	Bal-A	3	5	.375	10	10	3	2	0	52^2	51	8	30	47	14.2	5.81	86	.254	.356	0	—	0	-6	-5	-1	-0.8
1995	Bal-A	2	5	.286	19	9	0	0	0	75^1	68	13	48	77	13.9	6.21	76	.239	.349	0	—	0	-13	-12	-1	-1.0
1996	*Bal-A	9	1	.900	28	2	0	0	1	53	48	6	23	62	12.1	4.08	121	.241	.320	0	—	0	5	5	-1	0.7
1997	*Bal-A	10	3	.769	53	0	0	0	1	95^1	75	9	26	102	9.9	3.02	146	.218	.281	0	.000	-0	16	15	1	1.9
1998	Bal-A	4	4	.500	45	0	0	0	4	77	65	8	34	83	11.7	3.51	129	.233	.318	1	.500	0	10	9	-1	0.8
Total	8	40	32	.556	195	61	5	3	6	569^1	532	70	271	520	12.8	4.81	93	.249	.336	1	.333	0	-20	-20	-5	-1.3

● CHARLIE RHODES

Rhodes, Charles Anderson "Dusty" b: 4/7/1885, Caney, Kan. d: 10/26/18, Caney, Kan. BR/TR, 5'7", 180 lbs. Deb: 7/26/06

YEAR	TM/L	W	L	PCT	G	GS	CG	SH	SV	IP	H	HR	BB	SO	RAT	ERA	ERA+	OAV	OOB	BH	AVG	PB	PR	/A	PD	TPI
1906	StL-N	3	4	.429	9	6	3	0	0	45	37	0	20	32	12.6	3.40	77	.223	.328	3	.188	-0	-4	-4	0	-0.6
1908	Cin-N	0	0	—	1	0	0	0	0	4	1	0	2	4	9.0	0.00	—	.077	.250	0	.000	-0	1	1	0	0.0

YEAR	TM/L	W	L	PCT	G	GS	CG	SH	SV	IP	H	HR	BB	SO	RAT	ERA	ERA+	OAV	OOB	BH	AVG	PB	PR	/A	PD	TPI
	StL-N	1	2	.333	4	4	3	0	0	33	23	2	12	15	9.8	3.00	79	.200	.281	3	.250	1	-2	-2	1	-0.1
	Yr	1	2	.333	5	4	3	0	0	37	24	2	14	19	9.5	2.68	88	.186	.271	3	.231	1	-1	-1	1	-0.1
1909	StL-N	3	5	.375	12	10	4	0	0	61	55	0	33	25	13.3	3.98	63	.256	.360	4	.211	1	-9	-10	2	-0.9
Total	3	7	11	.389	26	20	10	0	0	143	116	2	67	76	12.1	3.46	73	.228	.329	10	.208	2	-15	-15	4	-1.6

● GORDON RHODES Rhodes, John Gordon "Dusty" b: 8/11/07, Winnemucca, Nev. d: 3/24/60, Long Beach, Cal. BR/TR, 6', 187 lbs. Deb: 4/29/29

YEAR	TM/L	W	L	PCT	G	GS	CG	SH	SV	IP	H	HR	BB	SO	RAT	ERA	ERA+	OAV	OOB	BH	AVG	PB	PR	/A	PD	TPI
1929	NY-A	0	4	.000	10	4	0	0	0	42^{2}	57	3	16	13	15.8	4.85	80	.333	.397	3	.300	1	-3	-5	-1	-0.4
1930	NY-A	0	0	—	3	0	0	0	0	2	3	0	4	1	31.5	9.00	48	.500	.700	0	—	0	-1	-1	0	0.0
1931	NY-A	6	3	.667	18	11	4	0	0	87	82	3	52	36	13.9	3.41	116	.235	.334	6	.214	1	9	5	0	0.6
1932	NY-A	1	2	.333	10	2	1	0	0	24	25	0	21	15	17.3	7.88	52	.275	.411	2	.286	0	-9	-10	1	-0.8
	Bos-A	1	8	.111	12	11	4	0	0	79^{1}	79	5	31	22	12.5	5.11	88	.261	.329	2	.074	-2	-6	-5	-0	-0.7
	Yr	2	10	.167	22	13	5	0	0	103^{1}	104	5	52	37	13.6	5.75	76	.264	.350	4	.118	-2	-15	-16	1	-1.5
1933	Bos-A	12	15	.444	34	29	14	0	0	232	242	13	93	85	13.0	4.03	109	.265	.334	23	.267	4	6	9	-1	1.3
1934	Bos-A	12	12	.500	44	31	10	0	2	219	247	10	98	79	14.3	4.56	105	.285	.360	10	.133	-3	-2	6	1	0.3
1935	Bos-A	2	10	.167	34	19	1	0	2	146^{1}	195	14	60	44	15.7	5.41	88	.324	.387	7	.146	-4	-16	-11	-1	-1.1
1936	Phi-A	9	20	.310	35	28	13	1	1	216^{1}	266	26	102	61	15.4	5.74	89	.304	.378	16	.213	-2	-17	-15	-3	-2.0
Total	8	43	74	.368	200	135	47	1	5	1048^{2}	1196	74	477	356	14.4	4.85	95	.286	.361	69	.194	-5	-37	-28	-3	-2.8

● BILL RHODES Rhodes, William Clarence b: Pottstown, Pa. Deb: 6/14/1893

YEAR	TM/L	W	L	PCT	G	GS	CG	SH	SV	IP	H	HR	BB	SO	RAT	ERA	ERA+	OAV	OOB	BH	AVG	PB	PR	/A	PD	TPI
1893	Lou-N	5	12	.294	20	19	17	0	0	151^{2}	244	10	66	22	19.0	7.60	58	.352	.416	9	.129	-4	-49	-54	-2	-4.4

● DENNIS RIBANT Ribant, Dennis Joseph b: 9/20/41, Detroit, Mich. BR/TR, 5'11", 175 lbs. Deb: 8/9/64

YEAR	TM/L	W	L	PCT	G	GS	CG	SH	SV	IP	H	HR	BB	SO	RAT	ERA	ERA+	OAV	OOB	BH	AVG	PB	PR	/A	PD	TPI
1964	NY-N	1	5	.167	14	7	1	1	1	57^{2}	65	8	9	35	11.5	5.15	69	.281	.308	2	.100	-0	-10	-10	-1	-1.1
1965	NY-N	1	3	.250	19	1	0	0	3	35^{1}	29	5	6	13	8.9	3.82	92	.228	.263	0	.000	-1	-1	-1	-0	-0.3
1966	NY-N	11	9	.550	39	26	10	1	3	188^{1}	184	20	40	84	10.8	3.20	114	.254	.294	12	.197	0	8	9	0	1.1
1967	Pit-N	9	8	.529	38	22	2	0	0	172	186	16	40	75	12.0	4.08	82	.280	.324	16	.267	5	-14	-14	2	-0.6
1968	Det-A	2	2	.500	14	0	0	0	1	24^{1}	20	1	10	7	11.5	2.22	136	.217	.301	1	.200	0	2	2	-1	0.4
	Chi-A	0	2	.000	17	0	0	0	1	31^{1}	42	3	17	20	17.5	6.03	50	.318	.404	0	.000	-1	-11	-10	0	-0.8
	Yr	2	4	.333	31	0	0	0	2	55^{2}	62	4	27	27	14.7	4.37	69	.276	.358	1	.083	-0	-9	-8	-0	-0.4
1969	StL-N	0	0	—	1	0	0	0	0	1^{1}	4	1	1	0	33.8	13.50	26	.571	.625	0	—	0	-1	-1	-0	0.0
	Cin-N	0	0	—	7	0	0	0	0	8^{1}	6	1	3	7	9.7	1.08	348	.188	.257	0	—	0	2	2	-0	0.0
	Yr	0	0	—	8	0	0	0	0	9^{2}	10	2	4	7	13.0	2.79	134	.250	.318	0	—	0	1	1	-0	0.0
Total	6	24	29	.453	149	56	13	2	9	518^{2}	536	55	126	241	11.6	3.87	90	.267	.312	31	.195	4	-24	-23	0	-1.3

● FRANK RICCELLI Riccelli, Frank Joseph b: 2/24/53, Syracuse, N.Y. BL/TL, 6'3", 205 lbs. Deb: 9/11/76

YEAR	TM/L	W	L	PCT	G	GS	CG	SH	SV	IP	H	HR	BB	SO	RAT	ERA	ERA+	OAV	OOB	BH	AVG	PB	PR	/A	PD	TPI
1976	SF-N	1	1	.500	4	3	0	0	0	16	16	1	5	11	11.8	5.63	64	.258	.313	1	.167	-0	-4	-4	-0	-0.4
1978	Hou-N	0	0	—	2	0	0	0	0	3	1	0	0	1	3.0	0.00	—	.100	.100	0	—	0	1	1	-0	0.0
1979	Hou-N	2	2	.500	11	2	0	0	0	22	22	0	18	20	16.4	4.09	86	.262	.392	2	.333	1	-1	-1	1	-0.1
Total	3	3	3	.500	17	5	0	0	0	41	39	1	23	32	13.6	4.39	81	.250	.346	3	.250	1	-3	-4	0	-0.5

● CHUCK RICCI Ricci, Charles Mark b: 11/20/68, Abington, Pa. BR/TR, 6'2", 180 lbs. Deb: 9/8/95

YEAR	TM/L	W	L	PCT	G	GS	CG	SH	SV	IP	H	HR	BB	SO	RAT	ERA	ERA+	OAV	OOB	BH	AVG	PB	PR	/A	PD	TPI
1995	Phi-N	1	0	1.000	7	0	0	0	0	10	9	0	3	9	11.7	1.80	235	.273	.351	0	—	0	3	3	-0	0.2

● SAM RICE Rice, Edgar Charles b: 2/20/1890, Morocco, Ind. d: 10/13/74, Rossmoor, Md. BL/TR, 5'9", 150 lbs. Deb: 8/7/15 H♦

YEAR	TM/L	W	L	PCT	G	GS	CG	SH	SV	IP	H	HR	BB	SO	RAT	ERA	ERA+	OAV	OOB	BH	AVG	PB	PR	/A	PD	TPI
1915	Was-A	1	0	1.000	4	2	1	0	0	18	13	0	9	9	11.0	2.00	148	.213	.314	3	.375	1	2	2	0	0.2
1916	Was-A	0	1	.000	5	1	0	0	0	21^{1}	18	0	10	3	11.8	2.95	95	.237	.326	59	.299	2	-0	-0	-0	0.1
Total	2	1	1	.500	9	3	1	0	0	39^{1}	31	0	19	12	11.4	2.52	114	.226	.321	2987	.322	2	2	2	0	0.3

● PAT RICE Rice, Patrick Edward b: 11/2/63, Rapid City, S.Dak. BR/TR, 6'2", 200 lbs. Deb: 5/18/91

YEAR	TM/L	W	L	PCT	G	GS	CG	SH	SV	IP	H	HR	BB	SO	RAT	ERA	ERA+	OAV	OOB	BH	AVG	PB	PR	/A	PD	TPI
1991	Sea-A	1	1	.500	7	2	0	0	0	21	18	3	10	12	12.4	3.00	137	.234	.330	0	—	0	3	3	-0	0.2

● WOODY RICH Rich, Woodrow Earl b: 3/9/16, Morganton, N.C. d: 4/18/83, Morganton, N.C. BL/TR, 6'2", 185 lbs. Deb: 4/22/39

YEAR	TM/L	W	L	PCT	G	GS	CG	SH	SV	IP	H	HR	BB	SO	RAT	ERA	ERA+	OAV	OOB	BH	AVG	PB	PR	/A	PD	TPI
1939	Bos-A	4	3	.571	21	12	3	0	1	77	78	2	35	24	13.8	4.91	96	.264	.352	7	.259	0	-2	-2	1	0.0
1940	Bos-A	1	0	1.000	3	1	1	0	0	11^{2}	9	2	1	8	7.7	0.77	583	.214	.233	0	.000	-1	5	5	-0	0.3
1941	Bos-A	0	0	—	2	1	0	0	0	3^{2}	8	1	2	4	24.5	17.18	24	.421	.476	0	—	0	-5	-5	0	0.0
1944	Bos-N	1	1	.500	7	2	1	0	0	25	32	3	12	6	16.9	5.76	66	.327	.416	1	.125	-1	-6	-5	0	-0.4
Total	4	6	4	.600	33	16	5	0	1	117^{1}	127	8	50	42	14.2	5.06	89	.280	.361	8	.205	-1	-9	-7	2	-0.1

● J.R. RICHARD Richard, James Rodney b: 3/7/50, Vienna, La. BR/TR, 6'8", 222 lbs. Deb: 9/5/71

YEAR	TM/L	W	L	PCT	G	GS	CG	SH	SV	IP	H	HR	BB	SO	RAT	ERA	ERA+	OAV	OOB	BH	AVG	PB	PR	/A	PD	TPI
1971	Hou-N	2	1	.667	4	4	1	0	0	21	17	1	16	29	14.1	3.43	98	.215	.347	0	.000	-1	0	-0	0	-0.1
1972	Hou-N	1	0	1.000	4	1	0	0	0	6	10	0	8	8	30.0	13.50	25	.385	.556	0	—	0	-7	-7	0	-0.9
1973	Hou-N	6	2	.750	16	10	2	1	0	72	54	2	38	75	11.6	4.00	91	.210	.314	5	.179	-0	-3	-3	-1	-0.4
1974	Hou-N	2	3	.400	15	9	0	0	0	64^{2}	58	3	36	42	13.2	4.18	83	.243	.344	3	.143	0	-4	-5	-1	-0.4
1975	Hou-N	12	10	.545	33	31	7	1	0	203	178	8	138	176	14.2	4.39	77	.238	.359	15	.203	4	-17	-23	-2	-2.0
1976	Hou-N	20	15	.571	39	39	14	3	0	291	221	14	151	214	11.6	2.75	116	**.212**	.314	14	.140	0	24	14	-1	1.6
1977	Hou-N	18	12	.600	36	36	13	3	0	267	212	18	104	214	10.7	2.97	120	.218	.293	20	.230	6	28	18	3	2.9
1978	Hou-N	18	11	.621	36	36	16	3	0	275^{1}	192	12	141	**303**	11.0	3.11	107	**.196**	.299	18	.178	1	14	6	2	1.0
1979	Hou-N	18	13	.581	38	38	19	4	0	292^{1}	220	13	98	**313**	9.9	**2.71**	130	**.209**	.278	12	.126	-0	**33**	**26**	-1	2.5
1980	Hou-N★	10	4	.714	17	17	4	4	0	113^{2}	65	2	40	119	8.3	1.90	173	.166	.244	6	.154	1	21	18	-1	2.2
Total	10	107	71	.601	238	221	76	19	0	1606	1227	73	770	1493	11.3	3.15	108	.212	.306	93	.168	12	91	44	0	6.4

● DUANE RICHARDS Richards, Duane Lee b: 12/16/36, Spartanburg, Ind. BR/TR, 6'3", 200 lbs. Deb: 9/25/60

YEAR	TM/L	W	L	PCT	G	GS	CG	SH	SV	IP	H	HR	BB	SO	RAT	ERA	ERA+	OAV	OOB	BH	AVG	PB	PR	/A	PD	TPI
1960	Cin-N	0	0	—	2	0	0	0	0	3	5	0	2	2	21.0	9.00	42	.385	.467	0	—	0	-2	-2	0	0.0

● RUSTY RICHARDS Richards, Russell Earl b: 1/27/65, Houston, Tex. BL/TR, 6'4", 200 lbs. Deb: 9/20/89

YEAR	TM/L	W	L	PCT	G	GS	CG	SH	SV	IP	H	HR	BB	SO	RAT	ERA	ERA+	OAV	OOB	BH	AVG	PB	PR	/A	PD	TPI
1989	Atl-N	0	0	—	2	2	0	0	0	9^{1}	10	2	6	4	16.4	4.82	76	.278	.395	0	.000	-0	-1	-1	0	0.0
1990	Atl-N	0	0	—	1	0	0	0	0	1	2	1	1	0	27.0	27.00	15	.400	.500	0	—	0	-3	-3	0	0.0
Total	2	0	0	—	3	2	0	0	0	10^{1}	12	3	7	4	17.4	6.97	53	.293	.408	0	.000	-0	-4	-4	0	0.0

● HARDY RICHARDSON Richardson, Abram Harding "Old True Blue" b: 4/21/1855, Clarksboro, N.J. d: 1/14/31, Utica, N.Y. BR/TR, 5'9.5", 170 lbs. Deb: 5/1/1879 ♦

YEAR	TM/L	W	L	PCT	G	GS	CG	SH	SV	IP	H	HR	BB	SO	RAT	ERA	ERA+	OAV	OOB	BH	AVG	PB	PR	/A	PD	TPI
1885	Buf-N	0	0	—	1	0	0	0	0	4	5	0	3	1	18.0	2.25	132	.294	.400	136	.319	0	0	0	0	0.0
1886	Det-N	3	0	1.000	4	0	0	0	0	12	11	1	10	5	15.8	4.50	74	.208	.333	189	.351	2	-2	-2	-0	-0.3
Total	2	3	0	1.000	5	0	0	0	0	16	16	1	13	6	16.3	3.94	82	.229	.349	1688	.299	3	-1	-1	0	-0.3

● DANNY RICHARDSON Richardson, Daniel b: 1/25/1863, Elmira, N.Y. d: 9/12/26, New York, N.Y. BR/TR, 5'8", 165 lbs. Deb: 5/22/1884 M♦

YEAR	TM/L	W	L	PCT	G	GS	CG	SH	SV	IP	H	HR	BB	SO	RAT	ERA	ERA+	OAV	OOB	BH	AVG	PB	PR	/A	PD	TPI
1885	NY-N	7	1	.875	9	8	7	1	0	75	58	0	18	21	9.1	2.40	111	.205	.252	52	.263	2	4	2	-1	0.3
1886	NY-N	0	2	.000	5	1	1	0	0	25	33	1	11	17	15.8	5.76	56	.320	.386	55	.232	1	-7	-7	1	-0.3
1887	NY-N	0	0	—	1	0	0	0	0	0	0	0	1	0	—	—	—	—	1.000	125	.278	0	0	0	0	0.0
Total	3	7	3	.700	15	9	8	1	0	100	91	1	30	38	10.9	3.24	86	.236	.291	1129	.254	3	-3	-5	-0	0.0

● GORDIE RICHARDSON Richardson, Gordon Clark b: 7/19/38, Colquitt, Ga. BR/TL, 6', 185 lbs. Deb: 7/26/64

YEAR	TM/L	W	L	PCT	G	GS	CG	SH	SV	IP	H	HR	BB	SO	RAT	ERA	ERA+	OAV	OOB	BH	AVG	PB	PR	/A	PD	TPI
1964	*StL-N	4	2	.667	19	6	1	0	1	47	40	2	15	28	10.7	2.30	166	.231	.296	1	.077	-0	6	8	-1	0.9
1965	NY-N	2	2	.500	35	0	0	0	2	52^{1}	41	5	16	43	10.1	3.78	93	.224	.294	0	.000	-1	-1	-1	-0	-0.2
1966	NY-N	0	2	.000	15	1	0	0	1	18^{2}	24	7	6	15	14.5	9.16	40	.312	.361	0	.000	-0	-12	-11	-0	-1.3
Total	3	6	6	.500	69	7	1	0	4	118	105	14	37	86	11.1	4.04	90	.242	.307	1	.048	-1	-6	-5	-2	-0.6

● JEFF RICHARDSON Richardson, Jeffrey Scott b: 8/29/63, Wichita, Kan. BR/TR, 6'3", 185 lbs. Deb: 9/19/90

YEAR	TM/L	W	L	PCT	G	GS	CG	SH	SV	IP	H	HR	BB	SO	RAT	ERA	ERA+	OAV	OOB	BH	AVG	PB	PR	/A	PD	TPI
1990	Cal-A	0	0	—	1	0	0	0	0	0^{1}	1	0	0	0	27.0	0.00	—	.500	.500	0	—	0	0	0	0	0.2

● JACK RICHARDSON Richardson, John William b: 10/3/1891, Central City, Ill. d: 1/18/70, Marion, Ill. BB/TR, 6'3", 197 lbs. Deb: 9/17/15

YEAR	TM/L	W	L	PCT	G	GS	CG	SH	SV	IP	H	HR	BB	SO	RAT	ERA	ERA+	OAV	OOB	BH	AVG	PB	PR	/A	PD	TPI
1915	Phi-A	0	1	.000	3	3	2	0	0	24	21	0	14	11	13.5	2.63	111	.253	.367	0	.000	-1	1	1	-0	-0.1

YEAR	TM/L	W	L	PCT	G	GS	CG	SH	SV	IP	H	HR	BB	SO	RAT	ERA	ERA+	OAV	OOB	BH	AVG	PB	PR	/A	PD	TPI
1916	Phi-A	0	0	—	1	0	0	0	0	0^2	2	0	1	1	40.5	40.50	7	.667	.750	0	—	0	-3	-3	-0	0.0
Total	2	0	1	.000	4	3	2	0	0	24^2	23	0	15	12	14.2	3.65	80	.267	.382	0	.000	-1	-2	-2	-0	-0.1

● PETE RICHERT Richert, Peter Gerard b: 10/29/39, Floral Park, N.Y. BL/TL, 6′, 184 lbs. Deb: 4/12/62

YEAR	TM/L	W	L	PCT	G	GS	CG	SH	SV	IP	H	HR	BB	SO	RAT	ERA	ERA+	OAV	OOB	BH	AVG	PB	PR	/A	PD	TPI
1962	LA-N	5	4	.556	19	12	1	0	0	81^1	77	6	45	75	13.6	3.87	94	.249	.346	2	.080	-1	1	-2	1	-0.3
1963	LA-N	5	3	.625	20	12	1	0	0	78	80	7	28	54	12.6	4.50	67	.262	.326	4	.182	1	-11	-13	-1	-1.3
1964	LA-N	2	3	.400	8	6	1	1	0	34^2	38	2	18	25	15.1	4.15	78	.271	.363	1	.091	-0	-2	-4	1	-0.4
1965	Was-A★	15	12	.556	34	29	6	0	0	194	146	18	84	161	10.8	2.60	134	.210	.297	10	.156	-0	19	19	-0	2.5
1966	Was-A★	14	14	.500	36	34	7	0	0	245^2	196	36	69	195	9.7	3.37	103	.215	.271	14	.163	2	2	2	-2	0.2
1967	Was-A	2	6	.250	11	10	1	1	0	54^1	49	5	15	41	10.8	4.64	68	.237	.291	1	.059	-1	-8	-9	-1	-1.5
	Bal-A	7	10	.412	26	19	5	1	2	132^1	107	11	41	90	10.1	2.99	105	.220	.282	4	.108	-1	4	2	1	0.3
	Yr	9	16	.360	37	29	6	2	2	186^2	156	16	56	131	10.3	3.47	91	.223	.282	5	.093	-2	-5	-7	-1	-1.2
1968	Bal-A	6	3	.667	36	0	0	0	6	62^1	51	7	12	47	9.5	3.47	84	.225	.273	2	.200	0	-3	-4	1	-0.5
1969	*Bal-A	7	4	.636	44	0	0	0	12	57^1	42	7	14	54	8.8	2.20	162	.202	.252	1	.125	-0	9	9	-1	2.0
1970	*Bal-A	7	2	.778	50	0	0	0	13	54^2	36	5	24	66	10.0	1.98	185	.194	.289	0	.000	-0	11	10	0	2.1
1971	*Bal-A	3	5	.375	35	0	0	0	4	36^1	26	3	22	35	12.1	3.47	97	.205	.327	0	.000	-0	-0	-0	0	-0.1
1972	LA-N	2	3	.400	37	0	0	0	6	52	42	3	18	38	10.6	2.25	148	.219	.289	3	.500	1	7	6	-0	0.8
1973	LA-N	3	3	.500	39	0	0	0	7	51	44	5	19	31	11.3	3.18	108	.234	.308	1	.200	0	3	1	1	0.3
1974	StL-N	0	0	—	13	0	0	0	1	11^1	10	1	11	4	16.7	2.38	150	.244	.404	0	—	0	2	2	-0	0.0
	Phi-N	2	1	.667	21	0	0	0	0	20^1	15	0	4	9	8.4	2.21	171	.205	.247	0	—	0	3	4	-0	0.5
	Yr	2	1	.667	34	0	0	0	1	31^2	25	1	15	13	11.4	2.27	163	.216	.305	0	—	0	5	5	-1	0.5
Total	13	80	73	.523	429	122	22	3	51	1165^2	959	116	424	925	10.8	3.19	106	.223	.295	43	.145	-1	34	24	-3	4.6

● LEW RICHIE Richie, Lewis A. b: 8/23/1883, Ambler, Pa. d: 8/15/36, South Mountain, Pa. BR/TR, 5′8″, 165 lbs. Deb: 5/8/06

YEAR	TM/L	W	L	PCT	G	GS	CG	SH	SV	IP	H	HR	BB	SO	RAT	ERA	ERA+	OAV	OOB	BH	AVG	PB	PR	/A	PD	TPI
1906	Phi-N	9	11	.450	33	22	14	3	0	205^2	170	3	79	65	11.2	2.41	109	.230	.309	3	.050	-3	5	5	-3	-0.2
1907	Phi-N	6	6	.500	25	12	9	2	0	117	88	0	38	40	10.1	1.77	137	.215	.290	7	.163	0	9	8	-1	0.8
1908	Phi-N	7	10	.412	25	15	13	2	1	157^2	125	1	49	58	10.3	1.83	133	.233	.304	11	.212	2	9	10	-1	1.2
1909	Phi-N	1	1	.500	11	1	0	0	1	45	40	0	18	11	12.0	2.00	130	.263	.349	4	.250	1	3	3	-1	0.2
	Bos-N	7	7	.500	22	13	9	2	2	131^2	118	2	44	42	11.1	2.32	121	.247	.312	5	.114	-2	4	7	-3	0.2
	Yr	8	8	.500	33	14	9	2	3	176^2	158	2	62	53	11.3	2.24	123	.250	.318	9	.150	-1	7	10	-4	0.4
1910	Bos-N	0	3	.000	4	2	0	0	0	16^1	20	0	9	7	16.0	2.76	121	.317	.403	0	.000	-1	1	1	1	0.2
	*Chi-N	11	4	.733	30	11	8	3	4	130	117	1	51	53	11.8	2.70	107	.257	.336	9	.225	3	5	3	1	0.6
	Yr	11	7	.611	34	13	8	3	4	146^1	137	1	60	60	12.3	2.71	108	.264	.344	9	.205	2	5	4	1	0.8
1911	Chi-N	15	11	.577	36	29	18	4	1	253	213	6	103	78	11.3	2.31	143	.235	.315	14	.154	-3	31	28	0	2.4
1912	Chi-N	16	8	.667	39	27	15	4	0	238	222	5	74	69	11.4	2.95	113	.261	.324	10	.132	-3	12	10	-2	0.3
1913	Chi-N	2	4	.333	16	5	0	0	0	65	77	3	30	15	15.0	5.82	55	.304	.380	2	.118	-0	-19	-19	-1	-1.7
Total	8	74	65	.532	241	137	86	20	9	1359^1	1190	21	495	438	11.4	2.54	115	.246	.320	65	.147	-7	60	58	-11	4.0

● BERYL RICHMOND Richmond, Beryl Justice b: 8/24/07, Glen Easton, W.Va. d: 4/24/80, Cameron, W.Va. BB/TL, 6′1″, 185 lbs. Deb: 4/21/33

YEAR	TM/L	W	L	PCT	G	GS	CG	SH	SV	IP	H	HR	BB	SO	RAT	ERA	ERA+	OAV	OOB	BH	AVG	PB	PR	/A	PD	TPI
1933	Chi-N	0	0	—	4	0	0	0	0	4^2	10	0	2	2	23.1	1.93	170	.455	.500	0	.000	-0	1	1	-0	0.0
1934	Cin-N	1	2	.333	6	2	1	0	0	19^1	23	0	10	9	15.4	3.72	110	.303	.384	0	.000	-1	1	1	-0	0.0
Total	2	1	2	.333	10	2	1	0	0	24	33	0	12	11	16.9	3.38	116	.337	.409	0	.000	-1	1	1	-0	0.0

● LEE RICHMOND Richmond, J Lee b: 5/5/1857, Sheffield, Ohio d: 10/1/29, Toledo, Ohio TL, 5′10″, 155 lbs. Deb: 9/27/1879 ♦

YEAR	TM/L	W	L	PCT	G	GS	CG	SH	SV	IP	H	HR	BB	SO	RAT	ERA	ERA+	OAV	OOB	BH	AVG	PB	PR	/A	PD	TPI
1879	Bos-N	1	0	1.000	1	1	1	0	0	9	4	0	1	11	5.0	2.00	124	.114	.139	2	.333	0	0	0	0	0.1
1880	Wor-N	32	32	.500	**74**	66	57	5	**3**	590^2	541	7	74	243	9.4	2.15	121	.232	.255	70	.227	-4	15	29	-6	1.9
1881	Wor-N	25	26	.490	53	52	50	3	0	462^1	547	7	68	156	12.0	3.39	89	.284	.309	63	.250	-1	-31	-19	2	-1.5
1882	Wor-N	14	33	.298	48	46	44	0	0	411	525	11	88	123	13.4	3.74	83	.294	.327	64	.281	7	-39	-29	3	-1.7
1883	Pro-N	3	7	.300	12	12	8	0	0	92	122	2	27	13	14.6	3.33	93	.314	.358	55	.284	3	-2	-2	-0	0.0
1886	Cin-a	0	2	.000	3	2	1	0	0	18	24	0	11	6	18.5	8.00	44	.308	.407	8	.276	0	-9	-9	-0	-0.7
Total	6	75	100	.429	191	179	161	8	3	1583	1763	27	269	552	11.6	3.06	95	.269	.298	262	.257	7	-66	-28	-1	-1.9

● RAY RICHMOND Richmond, Raymond Sinclair b: 6/15/1896, Fillmore, Ill. d: 10/21/69, DeSoto, Mo. BR/TR, 6′, 175 lbs. Deb: 9/25/20

YEAR	TM/L	W	L	PCT	G	GS	CG	SH	SV	IP	H	HR	BB	SO	RAT	ERA	ERA+	OAV	OOB	BH	AVG	PB	PR	/A	PD	TPI
1920	StL-A	2	0	1.000	2	2	1	0	0	17	18	0	9	4	14.3	6.35	62	.273	.360	1	.167	-0	-5	-5	0	-0.4
1921	StL-A	0	1	.000	6	2	0	0	0	14^1	21	1	13	6	23.2	11.30	40	.362	.500	0	.000	-1	-11	-11	0	-0.7
Total	2	2	1	.667	8	4	1	0	0	31^1	39	1	22	10	18.4	8.62	48	.315	.430	1	.100	-1	-16	-15	0	-1.1

● REGGIE RICHTER Richter, Emil Henry b: 9/14/1888, Dusseldorf, Germany d: 8/2/34, Winfield, Ill. BR/TR, 6′2″, 180 lbs. Deb: 5/30/11

YEAR	TM/L	W	L	PCT	G	GS	CG	SH	SV	IP	H	HR	BB	SO	RAT	ERA	ERA+	OAV	OOB	BH	AVG	PB	PR	/A	PD	TPI
1911	Chi-N	1	3	.250	22	5	0	0	2	54^2	62	1	20	34	14.0	3.13	106	.307	.378	1	.100	-1	**2**	**1**	-0	0.0

● DICK RICKETTS Ricketts, Richard James b: 12/4/33, Pottstown, Pa. d: 3/6/88, Rochester, N.Y. BL/TR, 6′7″, 215 lbs. Deb: 6/14/59 F

YEAR	TM/L	W	L	PCT	G	GS	CG	SH	SV	IP	H	HR	BB	SO	RAT	ERA	ERA+	OAV	OOB	BH	AVG	PB	PR	/A	PD	TPI
1959	StL-N	1	6	.143	12	9	0	0	0	55^2	68	7	30	25	15.8	5.82	73	.301	.383	1	.056	-2	-12	-10	-2	-1.4

● ELMER RIDDLE Riddle, Elmer Ray b: 7/31/14, Columbus, Ga. d: 5/14/84, Columbus, Ga. BR/TR, 5′11.5″, 170 lbs. Deb: 10/1/39 F

YEAR	TM/L	W	L	PCT	G	GS	CG	SH	SV	IP	H	HR	BB	SO	RAT	ERA	ERA+	OAV	OOB	BH	AVG	PB	PR	/A	PD	TPI
1939	Cin-N	0	0	—	1	0	0	0	0	2	1	0	0	0	4.5	0.00	—	.143	.143	0	—	0	1	1	-0	0.0
1940	*Cin-N	1	2	.333	15	1	1	0	2	33^2	30	0	17	9	12.6	1.87	202	.250	.343	1	.143	0	7	7	0	0.7
1941	Cin-N	19	4	**.826**	33	22	15	4	1	216^2	180	8	59	80	10.1	**2.24**	**160**	.224	.282	16	.225	3	33	33	-1	3.6
1942	Cin-N	7	11	.389	29	19	7	1	0	158^1	157	7	79	78	13.6	3.69	89	.260	.349	15	.259	3	-7	-7	-1	-0.6
1943	Cin-N	**21**	11	.656	36	33	19	5	3	260^1	235	6	107	69	11.9	2.63	126	.245	.322	18	.194	1	22	20	-1	2.5
1944	Cin-N	2	2	.500	4	4	2	0	0	26^2	25	0	12	6	12.5	4.05	86	.250	.330	1	.125	-0	-1	-2	1	-0.2
1945	Cin-N	1	4	.200	12	3	0	0	0	29^2	39	4	27	5	20.0	8.19	46	.333	.458	3	.273	1	-14	-15	0	-1.9
1947	Cin-N	1	0	1.000	16	3	0	0	0	30^1	42	5	31	8	22.0	8.31	49	.333	.468	0	.000	-0	-14	-14	-1	-0.5
1948	Pit-N☆	12	10	.545	28	27	12	3	1	191	184	20	81	63	12.6	3.49	117	.250	.327	12	.188	1	10	12	0	1.5
1949	Pit-N	1	8	.111	16	12	1	0	1	74^1	81	9	45	24	15.7	5.33	79	.281	.386	3	.136	-1	-11	-9	-2	-1.2
Total	10	65	52	.556	190	124	57	13	8	1023	974	59	458	342	12.8	3.40	107	.252	.335	69	.204	7	26	25	-4	3.9

● DENNY RIDDLEBERGER Riddleberger, Dennis Michael b: 11/22/45, Clifton Forge, Va. BR/TL, 6′3″, 195 lbs. Deb: 9/15/70

YEAR	TM/L	W	L	PCT	G	GS	CG	SH	SV	IP	H	HR	BB	SO	RAT	ERA	ERA+	OAV	OOB	BH	AVG	PB	PR	/A	PD	TPI
1970	Was-A	0	0	—	8	0	0	0	0	9^1	7	1	2	5	8.7	0.96	369	.219	.265	0	—	0	3	3	-0	0.0
1971	Was-A	3	1	.750	57	0	0	0	1	69^2	67	9	32	56	12.9	3.23	102	.260	.344	0	.000	0	2	1	-0	0.0
1972	Cle-A	1	3	.250	38	0	0	0	0	54	45	5	22	34	11.5	2.50	129	.237	.322	0	.000	-0	3	4	-0	0.3
Total	3	4	4	.500	103	0	0	0	1	133	119	15	56	95	12.0	2.77	119	.248	.330	0	.000	-0	8	8	-1	0.3

● DORSEY RIDDLEMOSER Riddlemoser, Dorsey Lee b: 3/25/1875, Frederick, Md. d: 5/11/54, Frederick, Md. BR/TR, Deb: 8/22/1899

YEAR	TM/L	W	L	PCT	G	GS	CG	SH	SV	IP	H	HR	BB	SO	RAT	ERA	ERA+	OAV	OOB	BH	AVG	PB	PR	/A	PD	TPI
1899	Was-N	0	0	—	1	0	0	0	0	2	7	0	2	0	40.5	18.00	22	.538	.600	0	.000	-0	-3	-3	0	0.0

● JACK RIDGWAY Ridgway, Jacob A. b: 7/23/1889, Philadelphia, Pa. d: 2/23/28, Philadelphia, Pa. BL/TR, 5′11″, 174 lbs. Deb: 5/20/14

YEAR	TM/L	W	L	PCT	G	GS	CG	SH	SV	IP	H	HR	BB	SO	RAT	ERA	ERA+	OAV	OOB	BH	AVG	PB	PR	/A	PD	TPI
1914	Bal-F	0	1	.000	4	1	0	0	0	9	20	1	3	2	24.0	11.00	28	.444	.490	0	.000	-0	-8	-8	0	-0.7

● STEVE RIDZIK Ridzik, Stephen George b: 4/29/29, Yonkers, N.Y. BR/TR, 5′11″, 170 lbs. Deb: 9/4/50

YEAR	TM/L	W	L	PCT	G	GS	CG	SH	SV	IP	H	HR	BB	SO	RAT	ERA	ERA+	OAV	OOB	BH	AVG	PB	PR	/A	PD	TPI
1950	Phi-N	0	0	—	1	0	0	0	0	3	3	1	1	2	12.0	6.00	67	.300	.364	0	—	0	-1	-1	-0	0.0
1952	Phi-N	4	2	.667	24	9	2	0	0	92^2	74	10	37	43	10.9	3.01	121	.218	.297	3	.136	0	7	7	-2	0.2
1953	Phi-N	9	6	.600	42	12	1	0	0	124	119	15	48	53	12.5	3.77	112	.256	.332	7	.194	2	7	6	-1	0.8
1954	Phi-N	4	5	.444	35	6	0	0	0	80^2	72	7	44	45	12.9	4.13	98	.233	.329	5	.227	1	-1	-1	0	0.0
1955	Phi-N	0	1	.000	3	1	0	0	0	11	7	1	8	6	14.7	2.45	162	.179	.360	0	.000	-1	2	2	-0	0.1
	Cin-N	0	3	.000	13	2	0	0	0	30	35	4	14	6	15.0	4.50	94	.299	.379	1	.167	-0	-2	-1	-1	-0.2
	Yr	0	4	.000	16	3	0	0	0	41	42	5	22	12	14.3	3.95	105	.264	.357	1	.100	-1	0	1	-1	-0.1
1956	NY-N	6	2	.750	41	5	1	1	0	92^1	80	7	65	53	14.6	3.80	99	.240	.371	7	.250	1	-0	-0	-0	0.0
1957	NY-N	0	2	.000	15	0	0	0	0	26^2	19	3	19	13	13.5	4.73	83	.213	.364	1	.200	-0	-3	-2	0	-0.1
1958	Cle-A	0	2	.000	6	0	0	0	0	8^2	9	1	5	6	14.5	2.08	176	.257	.350	0	.000	-0	2	2	0	0.4
1963	Was-A	5	6	.455	20	10	0	0	1	89^2	82	16	35	47	12.2	4.82	77	.240	.319	5	.172	0	-12	-11	-0	-1.3
1964	Was-A	5	5	.500	49	3	0	0	2	112	96	10	31	60	10.8	2.89	128	.236	.301	6	.222	1	9	10	-1	0.9
1965	Was-A	6	4	.600	63	0	0	0	8	109^2	108	18	43	72	13.0	4.02	86	.257	.335	3	.167	0	-7	-7	0	-0.6

YEAR	TM/L	W	L	PCT	G	GS	CG	SH	SV	IP	H	HR	BB	SO	RAT	ERA	ERA+	OAV	OOB	BH	AVG	PB	PR	/A	PD	TPI
1966	Phi-N	0	0	—	2	0	0	0	0	2^1	5	0	1	0	23.1	7.71	47	.455	.500	0	—	0	-1	-1	-0	0.0
Total	12	39	38	.506	314	48	4	1	11	782^2	709	93	351	406	12.6	3.79	101	.243	.332	38	.192	4	2	3	-4	0.2

● ELMER RIEGER Rieger, Elmer Jay b: 2/25/1889, Perris, Cal. d: 10/21/59, Los Angeles, Cal. BB/TR, 6', 175 lbs. Deb: 4/20/10

YEAR	TM/L	W	L	PCT	G	GS	CG	SH	SV	IP	H	HR	BB	SO	RAT	ERA	ERA+	OAV	OOB	BH	AVG	PB	PR	/A	PD	TPI
1910	StL-N	0	2	.000	13	1	0	0	0	21^1	26	1	7	9	14.3	5.48	54	.325	.386	0	.000	0	-6	-6	0	-0.5

● BRAD RIGBY Rigby, Bradley Kenneth b: 5/14/73, Milwaukee, Wis. BR/TR, 6'6", 203 lbs. Deb: 6/28/97

YEAR	TM/L	W	L	PCT	G	GS	CG	SH	SV	IP	H	HR	BB	SO	RAT	ERA	ERA+	OAV	OOB	BH	AVG	PB	PR	/A	PD	TPI
1997	Oak-A	1	7	.125	14	14	0	0	0	77^2	92	14	22	34	13.4	4.87	93	.302	.353	0	.000	-0	-3	-3	1	-0.2

● DAVE RIGHETTI Righetti, David Allan b: 11/28/58, San Jose, Cal. BL/TL, 6'3", 198 lbs. Deb: 9/16/79

YEAR	TM/L	W	L	PCT	G	GS	CG	SH	SV	IP	H	HR	BB	SO	RAT	ERA	ERA+	OAV	OOB	BH	AVG	PB	PR	/A	PD	TPI
1979	NY-A	0	1	.000	3	3	0	0	0	17^1	10	2	10	13	10.4	3.63	112	.182	.308	0	—	0	1	1	0	0.3
1981	*NY-A	8	4	.667	15	15	2	0	0	105^1	75	1	38	89	9.7	2.05	174	.196	.269	0	—	0	19	18	-1	2.0
1982	NY-A	11	10	.524	33	27	4	0	1	183	155	11	108	163	13.2	3.79	105	.229	.340	0	—	0	6	4	-2	0.4
1983	NY-A	14	8	.636	31	31	7	2	0	217	194	12	67	169	10.9	3.44	113	.237	.297	0	—	0	15	11	-1	0.9
1984	NY-A	5	6	.455	64	0	0	0	31	96^1	79	5	37	90	10.8	2.34	162	.223	.296	0	—	0	18	16	-0	2.7
1985	NY-A	12	7	.632	74	0	0	0	29	107	96	5	45	92	11.9	2.78	144	.241	.318	0	—	0	16	15	-1	3.3
1986	NY-A★	8	8	.500	74	0	0	0	**46**	106^2	88	4	35	83	10.5	2.45	167	.226	.293	0	—	0	20	19	-1	4.3
1987	NY-A★	8	6	.571	60	0	0	0	31	95	95	9	44	77	13.4	3.51	125	.262	.346	0	—	0	10	9	-0	1.9
1988	NY-A	5	4	.556	60	0	0	0	25	87	86	5	37	70	12.8	3.52	112	.257	.332	0	—	0	4	4	-1	0.6
1989	NY-A	2	6	.250	55	0	0	0	25	69	73	3	26	51	13.0	3.00	129	.277	.344	0	—	0	7	7	-0	1.1
1990	NY-A	1	1	.500	53	0	0	0	36	53	48	8	26	43	12.9	3.57	111	.234	.326	0	—	0	2	2	-1	0.2
1991	SF-N	2	7	.222	61	0	0	0	24	71^2	64	4	28	51	11.9	3.39	106	.240	.319	0	.000	-0	2	2	1	0.3
1992	SF-N	2	7	.222	54	4	0	0	3	78^1	79	4	36	47	13.2	5.06	65	.269	.348	1	.143	-0	-14	-15	-2	-2.0
1993	SF-N	1	1	.500	51	0	0	0	1	47^1	58	11	17	31	14.5	5.70	69	.305	.365	1	1.000	0	-9	-9	-0	-0.4
1994	Oak-A	0	0	—	7	0	0	0	0	7	13	3	9	4	29.6	16.71	26	.419	.561	0	—	0	-9	-10	0	0.2
	Tor-A	0	1	.000	13	0	0	0	0	13^1	9	2	10	10	12.8	6.75	71	.188	.328	0	—	0	-3	-3	0	-0.2
	Yr	0	1	.000	20	0	0	0	0	20^1	22	5	19	14	18.1	10.18	46	.272	.410	0	—	0	-12	-12	0	0.0
1995	Chi-A	3	2	.600	10	9	0	0	0	49^1	65	6	18	29	15.1	4.20	106	.325	.381	0	—	0	3	1	-1	0.1
Total	16	82	79	.509	718	89	13	2	252	1403^2	1287	95	591	1112	12.2	3.46	113	.244	.323	2	.182	0	89	71	-10	15.7

● RON RIGHTNOWAR Rightnowar, Ronald Gene b: 9/5/64, Toledo, Ohio BR/TR, 6'3", 190 lbs. Deb: 5/20/95

YEAR	TM/L	W	L	PCT	G	GS	CG	SH	SV	IP	H	HR	BB	SO	RAT	ERA	ERA+	OAV	OOB	BH	AVG	PB	PR	/A	PD	TPI
1995	Mil-A	2	1	.667	34	0	0	0	1	36^2	35	3	18	22	14.2	5.40	92	.271	.382	0	—	0	-3	-2	1	-0.1

● JOHNNY RIGNEY Rigney, John Dungan b: 10/28/14, Oak Park, Ill. d: 10/21/84, Lombard, Ill. BR/TR, 6'2", 190 lbs. Deb: 4/21/37

YEAR	TM/L	W	L	PCT	G	GS	CG	SH	SV	IP	H	HR	BB	SO	RAT	ERA	ERA+	OAV	OOB	BH	AVG	PB	PR	/A	PD	TPI
1937	Chi-A	2	5	.286	22	4	0	0	1	90^2	107	10	46	38	15.5	4.96	93	.290	.373	5	.167	-0	-3	-4	-1	-0.3
1938	Chi-A	9	9	.500	38	12	7	1	1	167	164	16	72	84	12.8	3.56	138	.256	.333	8	.145	-3	23	25	0	2.0
1939	Chi-A	15	8	.652	35	29	11	2	0	218^2	208	10	84	119	12.1	3.70	128	.247	.316	16	.200	-1	22	25	-2	2.0
1940	Chi-A	14	18	.438	39	33	19	2	3	280^2	240	22	90	141	10.6	3.11	142	.230	.292	20	.215	1	40	41	-1	4.2
1941	Chi-A	13	13	.500	30	29	18	3	0	237	224	21	92	119	12.1	3.84	107	.249	.320	17	.202	2	8	7	-0	0.8
1942	Chi-A	3	3	.500	7	7	6	0	0	59	40	2	16	34	8.7	3.20	112	.185	.245	1	.053	-1	3	3	0	0.1
1946	Chi-A	5	5	.500	15	11	3	2	0	82^2	76	6	35	51	12.3	4.03	85	.240	.319	4	.154	-1	-5	-6	-1	-0.8
1947	Chi-A	2	3	.400	11	7	2	0	0	50^2	42	3	15	19	10.1	1.95	187	.228	.286	0	.000	-2	10	10	1	0.8
Total	8	63	64	.496	197	132	66	10	5	1186^1	1101	90	450	605	11.9	3.59	121	.244	.314	71	.177	-6	98	100	-3	8.8

● JOSE RIJO Rijo, Jose Antonio (Abreu) b: 5/13/65, San Cristobal, D.R. BR/TR, 6'2", 200 lbs. Deb: 4/5/84

YEAR	TM/L	W	L	PCT	G	GS	CG	SH	SV	IP	H	HR	BB	SO	RAT	ERA	ERA+	OAV	OOB	BH	AVG	PB	PR	/A	PD	TPI
1984	NY-A	2	8	.200	24	5	0	0	2	62^1	74	5	33	47	15.6	4.76	80	.298	.383	0	—	0	-5	-7	1	-0.9
1985	Oak-A	6	4	.600	12	9	0	0	0	63^2	57	6	28	65	12.2	3.53	109	.239	.322	0	—	0	4	2	-1	0.8
1986	Oak-A	9	11	.450	39	26	4	0	1	193^2	172	24	108	176	13.2	4.65	83	.237	.339	0	—	0	-10	-17	-1	-1.0
1987	Oak-A	2	7	.222	21	14	1	0	0	82^1	106	10	41	67	16.3	5.90	70	.305	.381	0	—	0	-13	-16	0	-1.1
1988	Cin-N	13	8	.619	49	19	0	0	0	162	120	7	63	160	10.3	2.39	150	.209	.291	2	.054	-2	19	21	0	2.6
1989	Cin-N	7	6	.538	19	19	1	1	0	111	101	6	48	86	12.2	2.84	127	.249	.332	8	.211	1	8	9	-0	1.2
1990	*Cin-N	14	8	.636	29	29	7	1	0	197	151	10	78	152	10.6	2.70	146	.212	.292	10	.161	-0	24	27	1	3.1
1991	Cin-N	15	6	**.714**	30	30	3	1	0	204^1	165	8	55	172	**9.8**	2.51	151	.219	**.274**	14	.209	1	27	29	-0	3.0
1992	Cin-N	15	10	.600	33	33	2	0	0	211	185	15	44	171	9.9	2.56	141	.238	.282	14	.194	1	22	24	1	3.2
1993	Cin-N	14	9	.609	36	36	2	1	0	257^1	218	19	62	**227**	9.9	2.48	162	.230	.278	22	.268	7	45	44	3	4.8
1994	Cin-N†	9	6	.600	26	26	2	0	0	172^1	177	16	52	171	12.2	3.08	134	.265	.322	10	.204	2	22	20	2	1.9
1995	Cin-N	5	4	.556	14	14	0	0	0	69	76	6	22	62	12.8	4.17	99	.285	.339	3	.136	-0	0	-0	0	-0.1
Total	12	111	87	.561	332	260	22	4	3	1786	1602	132	634	1556	11.4	3.16	122	.240	.309	83	.193	10	142	140	5	17.5

● GEORGE RILEY Riley, George Michael b: 10/6/56, Philadelphia, Pa. BL/TL, 6'2", 210 lbs. Deb: 9/15/79

YEAR	TM/L	W	L	PCT	G	GS	CG	SH	SV	IP	H	HR	BB	SO	RAT	ERA	ERA+	OAV	OOB	BH	AVG	PB	PR	/A	PD	TPI
1979	Chi-N	0	1	.000	4	1	0	0	0	13	16	1	6	5	16.6	5.54	74	.320	.414	0	.000	-0	-3	-2	0	-0.1
1980	Chi-N	0	4	.000	22	0	0	0	0	36	41	2	20	18	15.8	5.75	68	.293	.389	0	.000	-0	-9	-7	1	-0.7
1984	SF-N	1	0	1.000	5	4	0	0	0	29^1	39	1	7	12	14.7	3.99	88	.315	.361	1	.100	-0	-1	-2	-0	-0.1
1986	Mon-N	0	0	—	10	0	0	0	0	8^2	7	0	8	5	16.6	4.15	89	.212	.381	0	—	0	-0	-0	-0	0.0
Total	4	1	5	.167	41	5	0	0	0	87	103	4	41	40	15.6	4.97	76	.297	.382	1	.077	-1	-13	-11	1	-0.9

● ANDY RINCON Rincon, Andrew John b: 3/5/59, Monterey Park, Cal. BR/TR, 6'3", 195 lbs. Deb: 9/15/80

YEAR	TM/L	W	L	PCT	G	GS	CG	SH	SV	IP	H	HR	BB	SO	RAT	ERA	ERA+	OAV	OOB	BH	AVG	PB	PR	/A	PD	TPI
1980	StL-N	3	1	.750	4	4	1	0	0	31	23	1	7	22	8.7	2.61	141	.215	.263	3	.250	0	3	4	0	0.6
1981	StL-N	3	1	.750	5	5	1	1	0	35^2	27	0	5	13	8.6	1.77	201	.214	.256	3	.231	1	7	7	-0	0.9
1982	StL-N	2	3	.400	11	6	1	0	0	40	35	1	25	11	13.5	4.72	77	.241	.353	1	.100	-0	-5	-5	-1	-0.6
Total	3	8	5	.615	20	15	3	1	0	106^2	85	2	37	46	10.5	3.12	116	.225	.297	7	.200	1	5	6	-1	0.9

● RICARDO RINCON Rincon, Ricardo (Espinoza) b: 4/13/70, Veracruz, Mexico BL/TL, 6', 190 lbs. Deb: 4/3/97

YEAR	TM/L	W	L	PCT	G	GS	CG	SH	SV	IP	H	HR	BB	SO	RAT	ERA	ERA+	OAV	OOB	BH	AVG	PB	PR	/A	PD	TPI
1997	Pit-N	4	8	.333	62	0	0	0	4	60	51	5	24	71	11.6	3.45	124	.230	.310	0	.000	-0	5	6	-0	1.0
1998	Pit-N	0	2	.000	60	0	0	0	14	65	50	6	29	64	10.9	2.91	149	.208	.294	0	.000	-0	10	10	0	0.6
Total	2	4	10	.286	122	0	0	0	18	125	101	11	53	135	11.2	3.17	136	.219	.302	0	.000	-0	15	16	-0	1.6

● JEFF RINEER Rineer, Jeffrey Alan b: 7/3/55, Lancaster, Pa. BL/TL, 6'4", 205 lbs. Deb: 9/30/79

YEAR	TM/L	W	L	PCT	G	GS	CG	SH	SV	IP	H	HR	BB	SO	RAT	ERA	ERA+	OAV	OOB	BH	AVG	PB	PR	/A	PD	TPI
1979	Bal-A	0	0	—	1	0	0	0	0	1	0	0	0	0	0.0	0.00	—	.000	.000	0	—	0	0	0	0	0.4

● JIMMY RING Ring, James Joseph b: 2/15/1895, Brooklyn, N.Y. d: 7/6/65, New York, N.Y. BR/TR, 6'1", 170 lbs. Deb: 4/13/17

YEAR	TM/L	W	L	PCT	G	GS	CG	SH	SV	IP	H	HR	BB	SO	RAT	ERA	ERA+	OAV	OOB	BH	AVG	PB	PR	/A	PD	TPI
1917	Cin-N	3	7	.300	24	7	3	0	2	88	90	2	35	33	12.9	4.40	60	.272	.343	2	.077	-2	-16	-17	0	-2.2
1918	Cin-N	9	5	.643	21	18	13	4	0	142^1	130	5	48	26	11.4	2.85	94	.247	.314	6	.120	-3	-1	-3	-3	-0.9
1919	*Cin-N	10	9	.526	32	18	12	2	3	183	150	1	51	61	10.0	2.26	123	.232	.291	6	.097	-5	13	10	3	0.9
1920	Cin-N	17	16	.515	42	33	18	1	1	266^2	268	4	92	73	12.3	3.54	86	.264	.329	19	.198	-0	-12	-15	1	-1.8
1921	Phi-N	10	19	.345	34	30	21	0	1	246	258	8	88	88	12.8	4.24	100	.274	.340	12	.145	-4	-13	-0	3	-0.2
1922	Phi-N	12	18	.400	40	33	17	0	1	249^1	292	19	103	116	14.4	4.58	102	.297	.365	13	.148	-5	-13	2	4	0.2
1923	Phi-N	18	16	.529	39	36	23	0	0	304^1	336	13	115	112	13.4	3.87	119	.283	.347	12	.106	-9	4	25	3	1.8
1924	Phi-N	10	12	.455	32	31	16	1	0	215^1	236	9	108	72	14.5	3.97	112	.286	.371	17	.230	-1	-2	12	2	1.3
1925	Phi-N	14	16	.467	38	37	21	1	0	270	325	14	119	93	14.8	4.37	109	.297	.367	11	.109	-7	-3	12	2	0.7
1926	NY-N	11	10	.524	39	23	5	0	2	183^1	207	12	74	76	13.8	4.57	82	.290	.357	8	.143	-3	-15	-17	-1	-2.1
1927	StL-N	0	4	.000	13	3	1	0	0	33	39	3	17	13	15.5	6.55	60	.300	.385	3	.375	1	-10	-10	1	-0.8
1928	Phi-N	4	17	.190	35	25	4	0	1	176	220	14	103	70	16.6	6.44	66	.320	.410	11	.183	-2	-48	-42	1	-4.3
Total	12	118	149	.442	389	294	154	9	11	2357^1	2551	104	953	833	13.5	4.13	95	.281	.351	120	.147	-40	-116	-52	16	-7.4

● DANNY RIOS Rios, Daniel b: 11/11/72, Madrid, Spain BR/TR, 6'2", 190 lbs. Deb: 5/30/97

YEAR	TM/L	W	L	PCT	G	GS	CG	SH	SV	IP	H	HR	BB	SO	RAT	ERA	ERA+	OAV	OOB	BH	AVG	PB	PR	/A	PD	TPI
1997	NY-A	0	0	—	2	0	0	0	0	2^1	9	3	2	1	46.3	19.29	23	.563	.632	0	—	0	-4	-4	0	0.0
1998	KC-A	0	1	.000	5	0	0	0	0	7^1	9	1	6	6	19.6	6.14	80	.300	.432	0	—	0	-1	-1	-0	-0.1
Total	2	0	1	.000	7	0	0	0	0	9^2	18	4	8	7	26.1	9.31	51	.391	.500	0	—	0	-5	-5	-0	-0.1

● ALLEN RIPLEY Ripley, Allen Stevens b: 10/18/52, Norwood, Mass. BR/TR, 6'3", 190 lbs. Deb: 4/10/78 F

YEAR	TM/L	W	L	PCT	G	GS	CG	SH	SV	IP	H	HR	BB	SO	RAT	ERA	ERA+	OAV	OOB	BH	AVG	PB	PR	/A	PD	TPI
1978	Bos-A	2	5	.286	15	11	1	0	0	73	92	10	22	26	14.4	5.55	74	.311	.364	0	—	0	-14	-12	-1	-1.9

YEAR TM/L	W	L	PCT	G	GS	CG	SH	SV	IP	H	HR	BB	SO	RAT	ERA	ERA+	OAV	OOB	BH	AVG	PB	PR	/A	PD	TPI
1979 Bos-A	3	1	.750	16	3	0	0	1	64^2	77	9	25	34	14.6	5.15	86	.295	.363	0	—	0	-7	-5	-1	-0.9
1980 SF-N	9	10	.474	23	20	2	0	0	112^2	119	10	36	65	12.7	4.15	85	.274	.335	6	.150	-0	-7	-8	0	-1.2
1981 SF-N	4	4	.500	19	14	1	0	0	90^2	103	5	27	47	13.2	4.07	84	.289	.345	4	.133	-1	-6	-6	1	-0.6
1982 Chi-N	5	7	.417	28	19	0	0	0	122^2	130	12	38	57	12.5	4.26	88	.285	.343	5	.132	-1	-9	-7	1	-0.7
Total 5	23	27	.460	101	67	4	0	1	463^2	521	46	148	229	13.3	4.52	83	.289	.348	15	.139	-3	-43	-38	-0	-5.3
● **WALT RIPLEY** Ripley, Walter Franklin b: 11/26/16, Worcester, Mass. d: 10/7/90, Attleboro, Mass. BR/TR, 6', 168 lbs. Deb: 8/17/35 F																									
1935 Bos-A	0	0	—	2	0	0	0	0	4	7	0	3	0	22.5	9.00	53	.412	.500	0	—	0	-2	-2	-0	0.0
● **RAY RIPPELMEYER** Rippelmeyer, Raymond Roy b: 7/9/33, Valmeyer, Ill. BR/TR, 6'3", 200 lbs. Deb: 4/14/62 C																									
1962 Was-A	1	2	.333	18	1	0	0	0	39^1	47	7	17	17	14.6	5.49	74	.294	.362	3	.500	2	-7	-6	2	0.0
● **CHARLIE RIPPLE** Ripple, Charles Dawson b: 12/1/21, Bolton, N.C. d: 5/6/79, Wilmington, N.C. BL/TL, 6'2", 210 lbs. Deb: 9/25/44																									
1944 Phi-N	0	0	—	1	1	0	0	0	2^1	6	0	4	2	38.6	15.43	23	.500	.625	1	1.000	0	-3	-3	-0	0.0
1945 Phi-N	0	1	.000	4	0	0	0	0	7^2	7	0	10	5	20.0	7.04	54	.241	.436	0	.000	-0	-3	-3	-0	-0.3
1946 Phi-N	1	0	1.000	6	0	0	0	0	3^1	5	0	6	3	29.7	10.80	32	.385	.579	0	—	0	-3	-3	-0	-0.7
Total 3	1	1	.500	11	1	0	0	0	13^1	18	0	20	10	25.7	9.45	39	.333	.514	1	.500	0	-9	-9	-0	-1.0
● **BILL RISLEY** Risley, William Charles b: 5/29/67, Chicago, Ill. BR/TR, 6'2", 215 lbs. Deb: 7/8/92																									
1992 Mon-N	1	0	1.000	1	1	0	0	0	5	4	0	1	2	9.0	1.80	193	.235	.278	0	.000	-0	1	1	0	0.2
1993 Mon-N	0	0	—	2	0	0	0	0	3	2	1	2	2	15.0	6.00	70	.200	.385	0	—	0	-1	-1	0	0.0
1994 Sea-A	9	6	.600	37	0	0	0	0	52^1	31	7	19	61	8.6	3.44	142	.170	.249	0	—	0	8	8	-0	2.0
1995 *Sea-A	2	1	.667	45	0	0	0	1	60^1	55	7	18	65	11.0	3.13	151	.244	.303	0	—	0	11	11	-1	0.4
1996 Tor-A	0	1	.000	25	0	0	0	0	41^2	33	7	25	29	12.5	3.89	129	.221	.333	0	—	0	5	5	-1	0.1
1997 Tor-A	0	1	.000	3	0	0	0	0	4^1	3	2	2	2	10.4	8.31	55	.188	.278	0	—	0	-2	-2	-0	-0.4
1998 Tor-A	3	4	.429	44	0	0	0	0	54^2	52	7	34	42	14.8	5.27	88	.259	.377	0	—	0	-4	-4	-1	-0.5
Total 7	15	13	.536	157	1	0	0	1	221^1	180	31	101	203	11.7	3.98	119	.225	.316	0	.000	-0	18	19	-3	1.8
● **JAY RITCHIE** Ritchie, Jay Seay b: 11/20/36, Salisbury, N.C. BR/TR, 6'4", 190 lbs. Deb: 8/4/64																									
1964 Bos-A	1	1	.500	21	0	0	0	0	46	43	4	14	35	11.2	2.74	141	.249	.305	1	.111	-1	5	6	-0	0.2
1965 Bos-A	1	2	.333	44	0	0	0	2	71	83	3	26	55	13.9	3.17	118	.302	.364	1	.200	0	2	4	0	0.2
1966 Atl-N	0	1	.000	22	0	0	0	4	35^1	32	3	12	33	11.2	4.08	89	.241	.303	2	.500	1	-2	-2	0	0.0
1967 Atl-N	4	6	.400	52	0	0	0	2	82^1	75	6	29	57	11.8	3.17	105	.245	.319	3	.300	1	2	1	1	0.4
1968 Cin-N	2	3	.400	28	2	0	0	0	56^2	68	7	13	32	13.0	4.61	69	.293	.333	0	.000	-1	-10	-9	-1	-1.0
Total 5	8	13	.381	167	2	0	0	8	291^1	301	23	94	212	12.4	3.49	101	.269	.329	7	.200	1	-3	1	0	-0.2
● **TODD RITCHIE** Ritchie, Todd Everett b: 11/7/71, Portsmouth, Va. BR/TR, 6'3", 205 lbs. Deb: 4/3/97																									
1997 Min-A	2	3	.400	42	0	0	0	0	74^2	87	11	28	44	14.1	4.58	102	.290	.355	0	.000	-0	-0	1	-0	0.0
1998 Min-A	0	0	—	15	0	0	0	0	24	30	1	9	21	14.6	5.63	83	.288	.345	0	—	0	-3	-2	-1	-0.1
Total 2	2	3	.400	57	0	0	0	0	98^2	117	12	37	65	14.2	4.83	96	.290	.352	0	.000	-0	-3	-2	-1	-0.1
● **WALLY RITCHIE** Ritchie, Wallace Reid b: 7/12/65, Glendale, Cal. BL/TL, 6'2", 180 lbs. Deb: 5/1/87																									
1987 Phi-N	3	2	.600	49	0	0	0	3	62^1	60	8	29	45	13.0	3.75	113	.254	.338	1	.250	0	2	3	-0	0.3
1988 Phi-N	0	0	—	19	0	0	0	0	26	19	1	17	8	12.8	3.12	114	.207	.336	0	—	0	1	1	-0	0.0
1991 Phi-N	1	2	.333	39	0	0	0	0	50^1	44	4	17	26	11.3	2.50	146	.234	.304	0	.000	-0	7	7	-0	0.3
1992 Phi-N	2	1	.667	40	0	0	0	1	39	44	3	17	19	14.1	3.00	116	.288	.359	0	.000	0	2	2	-0	0.1
Total 4	6	5	.545	147	0	0	0	4	177^2	167	16	80	98	12.7	3.14	121	.250	.333	1	.125	0	12	13	-1	0.7
● **REGGIE RITTER** Ritter, Reggie Blake b: 1/23/60, Malvern, Ark. BL/TR, 6'2", 195 lbs. Deb: 5/17/86																									
1986 Cle-A	0	0	—	5	0	0	0	0	10	14	1	4	6	17.1	6.30	66	.341	.413	0	—	0	-2	-2	0	0.2
1987 Cle-A	1	1	.500	14	0	0	0	0	26^2	33	5	16	11	16.5	6.08	74	.300	.389	0	—	0	-5	-5	0	-0.3
Total 2	1	1	.500	19	0	0	0	0	36^2	47	6	20	17	16.7	6.14	72	.311	.395	0	—	0	-7	-7	0	-0.1
● **HANK RITTER** Ritter, William Herbert b: 10/12/1893, McCoysville, Pa. d: 9/3/64, Akron, Ohio BR/TR, 6', 180 lbs. Deb: 8/3/12																									
1912 Phi-N	0	0	—	3	0	0	0	0	6	5	0	5	1	15.0	4.50	81	.192	.323	0	.000	-0	-1	-1	-0	0.0
1914 NY-N	1	0	1.000	1	0	0	0	0	8	4	0	4	4	9.0	1.13	236	.160	.276	0	.000	-0	1	1	-0	0.1
1915 NY-N	2	1	.667	22	1	0	0	2	58^1	66	4	15	35	13.3	4.63	55	.291	.348	2	.125	-1	-12	-13	-0	-0.9
1916 NY-N	1	0	1.000	3	0	0	0	0	5	3	0	0	3	7.2	0.00	—	.200	.250	0	—	0	1	1	0	0.3
Total 4	4	1	.800	29	1	0	0	2	77^1	78	4	24	43	12.6	3.96	67	.266	.334	2	.100	-1	-10	-11	-1	-0.5
● **JIM RITTWAGE** Rittwage, James Michael b: 10/23/44, Cleveland, Ohio BR/TR, 6'3", 190 lbs. Deb: 9/7/70																									
1970 Cle-A	1	1	.500	8	3	1	0	0	26	18	0	21	16	13.5	4.15	95	.194	.342	3	.375	1	-1	-1	0	0.1
● **KEVIN RITZ** Ritz, Kevin D b: 6/8/65, Eatontown, N.J. BR/TR, 6'4", 220 lbs. Deb: 7/15/89																									
1989 Det-A	4	6	.400	12	12	1	0	0	74	75	2	44	56	14.6	4.38	87	.265	.366	0	—	0	-4	-5	0	-0.5
1990 Det-A	0	4	.000	4	4	0	0	0	7^1	14	0	14	3	34.4	11.05	36	.400	.571	0	—	0	-6	-6	1	-2.1
1991 Det-A	0	3	.000	11	5	0	0	0	15^1	17	1	22	9	24.1	11.74	35	.288	.494	0	—	0	-13	-13	0	-2.1
1992 Det-A	2	5	.286	23	11	0	0	0	80^1	88	4	44	57	15.1	5.60	71	.278	.372	0	—	0	-15	-15	0	-1.2
1994 Col-N	5	6	.455	15	15	0	0	0	73^2	88	5	35	53	15.5	5.62	88	.298	.386	0	.000	-2	-12	-5	1	-0.8
1995 *Col-N	11	11	.500	31	28	0	0	2	173^1	171	16	65	120	12.6	4.21	128	.259	.332	9	.188	-1	-1	23	3	2.9
1996 Col-N	17	11	.607	35	35	2	0	0	213	236	24	105	105	14.9	5.28	99	.282	.370	15	.231	2	-25	-2	4	0.4
1997 Col-N	6	8	.429	18	18	1	0	0	107^1	142	16	46	56	15.8	5.87	88	.330	.396	2	.057	-2	-20	-8	1	-1.1
1998 Col-N	0	2	.000	2	2	0	0	0	9	17	1	2	3	20.0	11.00	46	.395	.435	1	.333	0	-7	-6	0	-0.9
Total 9	45	56	.446	151	130	4	0	2	753^1	848	69	377	462	15.0	5.35	92	.287	.374	27	.158	-3	-102	-38	10	-5.4
● **BEN RIVERA** Rivera, Bienvenido Santana b: 1/11/68, San Pedro De Macoris, D.R. BR/TR, 6'6", 210 lbs. Deb: 4/9/92																									
1992 Atl-N	0	1	.000	8	0	0	0	0	15^1	21	1	13	11	21.1	4.70	78	.339	.468	0	.000	-0	-2	-2	0	-0.1
Phi-N	7	3	.700	20	14	4	1	0	102	78	8	32	66	9.9	2.82	124	.211	.278	3	.094	-1	8	8	-0	0.6
Yr	7	4	.636	28	14	4	1	0	117^1	99	9	45	77	11.2	3.07	114	.228	.304	3	.091	-1	6	6	0	0.5
1993 *Phi-N	13	9	.591	30	28	1	1	0	163	175	16	85	123	14.7	5.02	79	.273	.363	5	.098	-2	-18	-19	-2	-2.6
1994 Phi-N	3	4	.429	9	7	0	0	0	38	40	7	22	19	14.9	6.87	62	.274	.373	0	.000	-1	-11	-11	0	-1.7
Total 3	23	17	.575	67	49	5	2	0	318^1	314	32	152	219	13.5	4.52	85	.258	.345	8	.086	-3	-23	-24	-2	-3.8
● **MARIANO RIVERA** Rivera, Mariano b: 11/29/69, Panama City, Panama BR/TR, 6'4", 170 lbs. Deb: 5/23/95																									
1995 *NY-A	5	3	.625	19	10	0	0	0	67	71	11	30	51	13.8	5.51	84	.266	.344	0	—	0	-6	-7	1	-0.6
1996 *NY-A	8	3	.727	61	0	0	0	5	107^2	73	1	34	130	9.1	2.09	236	.189	.258	0	—	0	**35**	**34**	0	3.2
1997 *NY-A★	6	4	.600	66	0	0	0	43	71^2	65	5	20	68	10.7	1.88	236	.237	.289	0	—	0	21	20	1	4.8
1998 *NY-A	3	0	1.000	54	0	0	0	36	61^1	48	3	17	36	9.7	1.91	233	.215	.274	0	—	0	19	17	1	2.6
Total 4	22	10	.688	200	10	0	0	84	307^2	257	20	101	285	10.6	2.75	169	.223	.289	0	—	0	69	65	3	10.0
● **ROBERTO RIVERA** Rivera, Roberto (Diaz) b: 1/1/69, Bayamon, P.R. BL/TL, 6', 175 lbs. Deb: 9/3/95																									
1995 Chi-N	0	0	—	7	0	0	0	0	5	8	1	2	2	18.0	5.40	76	.381	.435	0	—	0	-1	-1	0	0.0
● **TINK RIVIERE** Riviere, Arthur Bernard b: 8/2/1899, Liberty, Tex. d: 9/27/65, Liberty, Tex. BR/TR, 5'10", 167 lbs. Deb: 4/15/21																									
1921 StL-N	1	0	1.000	18	2	0	0	0	38^1	45	2	20	15	15.7	6.10	60	.280	.366	3	.375	2	-10	-10	-2	-0.2
1925 Chi-A	0	0	—	3	0	0	0	0	4^2	6	0	7	1	27.0	13.50	31	.429	.636	0	.000	-0	-5	-5	1	0.0
Total 2	1	0	1.000	21	2	0	0	0	43	51	2	27	16	17.0	6.91	54	.291	.395	3	.333	2	-15	-15	-1	-0.2
● **EPPA RIXEY** Rixey, Eppa "Jeptha" b: 5/3/1891, Culpeper, Va. d: 2/28/63, Cincinnati, Ohio BR/TL, 6'5", 210 lbs. Deb: 6/21/12 H																									
1912 Phi-N	10	10	.500	23	20	10	3	0	162	147	2	54	59	11.3	2.50	145	.256	.322	9	.170	-2	16	20	-1	2.0
1913 Phi-N	9	5	.643	35	19	9	1	2	155^2	148	4	56	75	12.1	3.12	107	.258	.331	9	.191	-0	1	4	-0	0.3
1914 Phi-N	2	11	.154	24	15	2	0	0	103	124	0	45	41	15.0	4.37	67	.313	.387	1	.038	-1	-18	-16	0	-2.0
1915 *Phi-N	11	12	.478	29	22	10	2	1	176^2	163	2	64	88	11.7	2.39	115	.250	.319	9	.164	-0	7	7	0	0.9

YEAR	TM/L	W	L	PCT	G	GS	CG	SH	SV	IP	H	HR	BB	SO	RAT	ERA	ERA+	OAV	OOB	BH	AVG	PB	PR	/A	PD	TPI
1916	Phi-N	22	10	.688	38	33	20	3	0	287	239	2	74	134	10.0	1.85	143	.229	.284	15	.155	-2	25	26	3	3.2
1917	Phi-N	16	21	.432	39	36	23	4	1	281^1	249	1	67	121	10.3	2.27	124	.241	.290	18	.191	-1	14	17	4	2.6
1919	Phi-N	6	12	.333	23	18	11	1	0	154	160	4	50	63	12.4	3.97	81	.278	.339	7	.149	-2	-18	-13	2	-1.4
1920	Phi-N	11	22	.333	41	34	25	0	2	284^1	288	5	69	109	11.4	3.48	98	.274	.321	25	.248	1	-11	-2	3	0.3
1921	Cin-N	19	18	.514	40	37	21	2	1	301	324	1	66	76	11.8	2.78	129	.282	.324	13	.129	-5	**34**	27	3	2.8
1922	Cin-N	**25**	13	.658	40	38	26	2	0	**313^1**	337	13	45	80	11.1	3.53	113	.275	.303	21	.193	-1	20	16	-0	1.5
1923	Cin-N	20	15	.571	42	37	23	3	1	309	334	3	65	97	11.7	2.80	138	.280	.320	17	.159	-5	41	37	2	3.4
1924	Cin-N	15	14	.517	35	29	15	**4**	1	238^1	219	3	47	57	10.1	2.76	137	.246	.285	18	.214	1	29	27	-1	3.1
1925	Cin-N	21	11	.656	39	36	22	2	1	287^1	302	8	47	69	11.2	2.88	143	.273	.307	22	.214	-1	44	39	-2	3.6
1926	Cin-N	14	8	.636	37	29	14	3	0	233	231	12	58	61	11.2	3.40	109	.265	.313	19	.226	0	11	8	-2	0.5
1927	Cin-N	12	10	.545	34	29	11	1	1	219^2	240	3	43	42	11.7	3.48	109	.287	.325	20	.247	4	11	7	-1	1.0
1928	Cin-N	19	18	.514	43	37	17	3	2	291^1	317	4	67	58	12.0	3.43	115	.288	.330	18	.173	-1	18	17	-0	1.8
1929	Cin-N	10	13	.435	35	24	11	0	1	201	235	6	60	37	13.3	4.16	110	.296	.348	15	.231	0	12	9	-1	0.8
1930	Cin-N	9	13	.409	32	21	5	0	0	164	207	11	47	37	14.3	5.10	95	.317	.370	11	.200	-1	-2	-5	0	-0.6
1931	Cin-N	4	7	.364	22	17	4	0	0	126^2	143	4	30	22	12.3	3.91	96	.291	.332	6	.150	-1	-1	-2	4	0.1
1932	Cin-N	5	5	.500	25	11	6	2	0	111^2	108	3	16	14	10.3	2.66	145	.254	.288	9	.265	1	15	15	1	1.4
1933	Cin-N	6	3	.667	16	12	5	1	0	94^1	118	1	12	10	12.4	3.15	108	.298	.319	9	.257	2	2	3	1	0.6
Total	21	266	251	.515	692	554	290	37	14	4494^2	4633	92	1082	1350	11.6	3.15	116	.272	.318	291	.191	-15	251	248	16	25.9

● **TODD RIZZO** Rizzo, Todd Michael b: 5/24/71, Media, Pa. BR/TL, 6'3", 220 lbs. Deb: 4/2/98

YEAR	TM/L	W	L	PCT	G	GS	CG	SH	SV	IP	H	HR	BB	SO	RAT	ERA	ERA+	OAV	OOB	BH	AVG	PB	PR	/A	PD	TPI
1998	Chi-A	0	0	—	9	0	0	0	0	6^2	12	0	6	3	24.3	13.50	34	.387	.486	0	—	0	-7	-7	-0	0.0

● **JOE ROA** Roa, Joseph Rodger b: 10/11/71, Southfield, Mich. BR/TR, 6'1", 194 lbs. Deb: 9/20/95

YEAR	TM/L	W	L	PCT	G	GS	CG	SH	SV	IP	H	HR	BB	SO	RAT	ERA	ERA+	OAV	OOB	BH	AVG	PB	PR	/A	PD	TPI
1995	Cle-A	0	1	.000	1	1	0	0	0	6	9	1	2	0	16.5	6.00	78	.360	.407	0	—	0	-1	-1	0	-0.1
1996	Cle-A	0	0	—	1	0	0	0	0	1^2	4	0	3	0	37.8	10.80	45	.500	.636	0	—	0	-1	-1	-0	0.0
1997	SF-N	2	5	.286	28	3	0	0	0	65^2	86	8	20	34	14.8	5.21	79	.333	.386	2	.133	-0	-7	-8	2	-0.6
Total	3	2	6	.250	30	4	0	0	0	73^1	99	9	25	34	15.5	5.40	78	.340	.396	2	.133	-0	-9	-10	2	-0.7

● **JOHN ROACH** Roach, John F. b: Farrandsville, Pa. BR/TL, 5'9", 175 lbs. Deb: 5/14/1887

YEAR	TM/L	W	L	PCT	G	GS	CG	SH	SV	IP	H	HR	BB	SO	RAT	ERA	ERA+	OAV	OOB	BH	AVG	PB	PR	/A	PD	TPI
1887	NY-N	0	1	.000	1	1	1	0	0	8	18	0	4	3	25.9	11.25	33	.419	.479	1	.250	-0	-6	-7	-0	-0.5

● **SKEL ROACH** Roach, Rudolph Charles (b: Rudolph Charles Weichbrodt) b: 10/20/1871, Danzig, Germany d: 3/9/58, Oak Park, Ill. BR/TR, 6'2", Deb: 8/9/1899

YEAR	TM/L	W	L	PCT	G	GS	CG	SH	SV	IP	H	HR	BB	SO	RAT	ERA	ERA+	OAV	OOB	BH	AVG	PB	PR	/A	PD	TPI
1899	Chi-N	1	0	1.000	1	1	1	0	0	9	13	0	1	0	14.0	3.00	125	.333	.350	0	.000	-1	1	1	-0	0.0

● **BRUCE ROBBINS** Robbins, Bruce Duane b: 9/10/59, Portland, Ind. BL/TL, 6'1", 190 lbs. Deb: 7/28/79

YEAR	TM/L	W	L	PCT	G	GS	CG	SH	SV	IP	H	HR	BB	SO	RAT	ERA	ERA+	OAV	OOB	BH	AVG	PB	PR	/A	PD	TPI
1979	Det-A	3	3	.500	10	8	0	0	0	46	45	3	21	22	12.9	3.91	111	.265	.346	0	—	0	2	2	-1	0.1
1980	Det-A	4	2	.667	15	6	0	0	0	51^2	60	12	28	23	15.3	6.62	62	.287	.371	0	—	0	-15	-14	0	-1.6
Total	2	7	5	.583	25	14	0	0	0	97^2	105	15	49	45	14.2	5.34	79	.277	.360	0	—	0	-13	-12	-0	-1.5

● **BERT ROBERGE** Roberge, Bertrand Roland b: 10/3/54, Lewiston, Maine BR/TR, 6'4", 190 lbs. Deb: 5/28/79

YEAR	TM/L	W	L	PCT	G	GS	CG	SH	SV	IP	H	HR	BB	SO	RAT	ERA	ERA+	OAV	OOB	BH	AVG	PB	PR	/A	PD	TPI
1979	Hou-N	3	0	1.000	26	0	0	0	4	32	20	0	17	13	10.4	1.69	208	.196	.311	0	.000	-0	7	6	-0	0.7
1980	Hou-N	2	0	1.000	14	0	0	0	0	24^1	24	2	10	9	13.3	5.92	56	.261	.346	0	.000	-0	-6	-7	-0	-0.6
1982	Hou-N	1	2	.333	22	0	0	0	3	25^2	29	0	6	18	12.3	4.21	79	.284	.324	0	.000	-0	-2	-3	0	-0.3
1984	Chi-A	3	3	.500	21	0	0	0	0	40^2	36	2	15	25	12.0	3.76	111	.240	.321	0	—	0	1	2	1	0.2
1985	Mon-N	3	3	.500	42	0	0	0	2	68	58	5	22	34	10.9	3.44	99	.232	.299	0	.000	-0	1	-0	0	0.0
1986	Mon-N	0	4	.000	21	0	0	0	1	28^2	33	2	10	20	13.8	6.28	59	.295	.358	0	.000	-0	-8	-8	-0	-1.1
Total	6	12	12	.500	146	0	0	0	10	219^1	200	11	80	119	11.8	3.98	90	.248	.321	0	.000	-1	-7	-10	1	-1.1

● **SID ROBERSON** Roberson, Sidney Dean b: 9/9/71, Jacksonville, Fla. BL/TL, 5'9", 170 lbs. Deb: 5/20/95

YEAR	TM/L	W	L	PCT	G	GS	CG	SH	SV	IP	H	HR	BB	SO	RAT	ERA	ERA+	OAV	OOB	BH	AVG	PB	PR	/A	PD	TPI
1995	Mil-A	6	4	.600	26	13	0	0	0	84^1	102	16	37	40	15.7	5.76	86	.307	.390	0	—	0	-10	-7	-2	-0.9

● **DALE ROBERTS** Roberts, Dale "Mountain Man" b: 4/12/42, Owenton, Ky. BR/TL, 6'4", 180 lbs. Deb: 9/9/67

YEAR	TM/L	W	L	PCT	G	GS	CG	SH	SV	IP	H	HR	BB	SO	RAT	ERA	ERA+	OAV	OOB	BH	AVG	PB	PR	/A	PD	TPI
1967	NY-A	0	0	—	2	0	0	0	0	2	3	0	2	0	31.5	9.00	35	.429	.636	0	—	0	-1	-1	0	0.0

● **DAVE ROBERTS** Roberts, David Arthur b: 9/11/44, Gallipolis, Ohio BL/TL, 6'2", 197 lbs. Deb: 7/6/69

YEAR	TM/L	W	L	PCT	G	GS	CG	SH	SV	IP	H	HR	BB	SO	RAT	ERA	ERA+	OAV	OOB	BH	AVG	PB	PR	/A	PD	TPI
1969	SD-N	0	3	.000	22	5	0	0	1	48^2	65	5	19	19	16.1	4.81	74	.322	.388	4	.267	1	-7	-7	0	-0.3
1970	SD-N	8	14	.364	43	21	3	2	1	181^2	182	16	43	102	11.2	3.81	104	.261	.305	9	.153	1	5	3	-0	0.5
1971	SD-N	14	17	.452	37	34	14	2	0	269^2	238	9	61	135	10.1	2.10	157	.240	.288	19	.221	2	41	36	1	4.6
1972	Hou-N	12	7	.632	35	28	7	3	2	192	227	18	57	111	13.4	4.50	75	.296	.346	16	.239	6	-22	-24	-1	-1.9
1973	Hou-N	17	11	.607	39	36	12	6	0	249^1	264	15	62	119	11.8	2.85	127	.271	.316	11	.129	-3	22	22	-1	2.0
1974	Hou-N	10	12	.455	34	30	8	2	1	204	216	6	65	72	12.5	3.40	102	.276	.333	16	.219	5	5	1	2	0.9
1975	Hou-N	8	14	.364	32	27	7	0	1	198^1	182	16	73	101	11.7	4.27	79	.244	.313	9	.143	-0	-14	-20	1	-1.9
1976	Det-A	16	17	.485	36	36	18	4	0	252	254	16	63	79	11.5	4.00	93	.264	.312	0	—	0	-13	-8	2	-1.1
1977	Det-A	4	10	.286	22	22	5	0	0	129^1	143	20	41	46	12.9	5.15	83	.274	.330	0	—	0	-16	-12	-0	-1.5
	Chi-N	1	1	.500	17	6	1	0	1	53	55	1	12	23	11.5	3.23	136	.275	.319	1	.059	-2	4	7	2	0.3
1978	Chi-N	6	8	.429	35	20	2	1	1	142^1	159	17	56	54	13.8	5.25	77	.288	.357	17	.327	6	-26	-19	1	-1.1
1979	SF-N	0	2	.000	26	1	0	0	3	42	42	3	18	23	13.1	2.57	136	.262	.341	0	.000	-1	5	4	1	0.2
	*Pit-N	5	2	.714	21	3	0	0	1	38^2	47	1	12	15	14.0	3.26	119	.318	.373	0	.000	-1	2	3	0	0.5
	Yr	5	4	.556	47	4	0	0	4	80^2	89	4	30	38	13.4	2.90	127	.287	.352	0	.000	-1	7	7	1	0.7
1980	Pit-N	0	1	.000	2	0	0	0	0	2^1	2	0	1	1	11.6	3.86	94	.250	.333	0	—	0	-0	-0	-0	0.0
	Sea-A	2	3	.400	37	4	0	0	3	80^1	86	7	27	47	12.8	4.37	95	.270	.329	0	—	0	-3	-2	-1	-0.3
1981	NY-N	0	3	.000	7	4	0	0	0	15^1	26	5	5	10	18.2	9.39	37	.366	.408	1	.250	0	-10	-10	0	-1.6
Total	13	103	125	.452	445	277	77	20	15	2099	2188	155	615	957	12.2	3.78	97	.270	.324	103	.194	15	-27	-28	7	-0.7

● **JIM ROBERTS** Roberts, James Newson "Big Jim" b: 10/13/1895, Artesia, Miss. d: 6/24/84, Columbus, Miss. BR/TR, 6'3", 205 lbs. Deb: 7/27/24

YEAR	TM/L	W	L	PCT	G	GS	CG	SH	SV	IP	H	HR	BB	SO	RAT	ERA	ERA+	OAV	OOB	BH	AVG	PB	PR	/A	PD	TPI
1924	Bro-N	0	3	.000	11	5	0	0	0	25^1	41	1	8	10	18.1	7.46	50	.360	.411	1	.143	-0	-10	-10	-0	-1.1
1925	Bro-N	0	0	—	1	0	0	0	0	1	1	0	0	0	9.0	0.00	—	.500	.500	0	—	0	0	0	0	0.0
Total	2	0	3	.000	12	5	0	0	0	26^1	42	1	8	10	17.8	7.18	52	.362	.413	1	.143	-0	-10	-10	-0	-1.1

● **LEON ROBERTS** Roberts, Leon Kauffman b: 1/22/51, Vicksburg, Mich. BR/TR, 6'3", 200 lbs. Deb: 9/3/74 ♦

YEAR	TM/L	W	L	PCT	G	GS	CG	SH	SV	IP	H	HR	BB	SO	RAT	ERA	ERA+	OAV	OOB	BH	AVG	PB	PR	/A	PD	TPI
1984	KC-A	0	0	—	1	0	0	0	0	1	4	1	1	1	45.0	27.00	15	.571	.625	10	.222	0	-3	-3	0	0.0

● **RAY ROBERTS** Roberts, Raymond b: 8/25/1895, Cruger, Miss. d: 1/30/62, Cruger, Miss. BL/TR, 5'11", 180 lbs. Deb: 9/12/19

YEAR	TM/L	W	L	PCT	G	GS	CG	SH	SV	IP	H	HR	BB	SO	RAT	ERA	ERA+	OAV	OOB	BH	AVG	PB	PR	/A	PD	TPI
1919	Phi-A	0	2	.000	3	2	0	0	0	14	21	0	3	2	15.4	7.71	44	.368	.400	1	.250	-0	-7	-7	-0	-0.8

● **ROBIN ROBERTS** Roberts, Robin Evan b: 9/30/26, Springfield, Ill. BB/TR, 6', 190 lbs. Deb: 6/18/48 H

YEAR	TM/L	W	L	PCT	G	GS	CG	SH	SV	IP	H	HR	BB	SO	RAT	ERA	ERA+	OAV	OOB	BH	AVG	PB	PR	/A	PD	TPI
1948	Phi-N	7	9	.438	20	20	9	0	0	146^2	148	10	61	84	13.1	3.19	124	.278	.356	11	.250	4	12	12	-2	1.5
1949	Phi-N	15	15	.500	43	31	11	3	4	226^2	229	15	75	95	12.3	3.69	107	.273	.337	5	.075	-3	9	6	-3	0.1
1950	*Phi-N★	20	11	.645	40	39	21	**5**	1	304^1	282	29	77	146	10.7	3.02	134	.248	.297	12	.118	-4	**38**	35	0	2.9
1951	Phi-N★	21	15	.583	44	39	22	6	2	**315**	284	20	64	127	10.0	3.03	127	.237	**.278**	15	.172	5	33	29	-3	**3.4**
1952	Phi-N☆	**28**	7	.800	39	37	**30**	3	2	**330**	292	22	45	148	9.3	2.59	141	.234	.263	14	.125	2	**42**	**39**	-3	4.0
1953	Phi-N★	**23**	16	.590	44	41	**33**	5	2	**346^2**	324	30	61	**198**	10.0	2.75	153	.242	.276	22	.179	2	59	**56**	-1	6.1
1954	Phi-N★	**23**	15	.605	45	38	**29**	4	4	**336^2**	289	35	56	**185**	**9.4**	2.97	136	.231	**.267**	15	.123	-3	41	40	-4	3.6
1955	Phi-N★	**23**	14	.622	41	38	**26**	1	3	**305**	292	41	53	160	10.2	3.28	121	.246	**.280**	27	.252	14	26	24	-5	3.7
1956	Phi-N☆	19	18	.514	43	37	**22**	1	3	297^1	328	46	40	157	11.2	4.45	84	.282	.307	20	.200	4	-22	-24	-0	-2.4
1957	Phi-N	10	22	.313	39	32	14	2	2	249^2	246	40	43	128	10.5	4.07	93	.252	.284	13	.162	0	-5	-7	0	-0.8
1958	Phi-N	17	14	.548	35	34	21	1	0	269^2	270	30	51	130	10.8	3.24	122	.259	.294	20	.202	4	21	22	-2	2.5
1959	Phi-N	15	17	.469	35	35	19	2	0	257^1	267	34	35	137	10.7	4.27	96	.263	.291	17	.191	3	-9	-5	0	-0.2
1960	Phi-N	12	16	.429	35	33	13	2	1	237^1	256	31	34	122	11.1	4.02	97	.275	.302	12	.152	-1	-7	-4	-3	-0.8
1961	Phi-N	1	10	.091	26	18	2	0	0	117	154	19	23	54	13.8	5.85	70	.326	.360	3	.091	-2	-24	-23	-2	-2.2
1962	Bal-A	10	9	.526	27	25	6	0	0	191^1	176	17	41	102	10.4	2.78	133	.244	.289	10	.192	2	25	20	-1	2.0
1963	Bal-A	14	13	.519	35	35	9	2	0	251^1	230	35	40	124	9.8	3.33	104	.240	**.272**	16	.203	2	8	4	-2	0.5

YEAR	TM/L	W	L	PCT	G	GS	CG	SH	SV	IP	H	HR	BB	SO	RAT	ERA	ERA+	OAV	OOB	BH	AVG	PB	PR	/A	PD	TPI
1964	Bal-A	13	7	.650	31	31	8	4	0	204	203	18	52	109	11.4	2.91	123	.261	.310	9	.132	-1	16	15	-2	1.1
1965	Bal-A	5	7	.417	20	15	5	1	0	114^{2}	110	17	20	63	10.3	3.38	103	.252	.286	6	.171	1	1	1	-1	0.1
	Hou-N	5	2	.714	10	10	3	2	0	76	61	1	10	34	8.4	1.89	177	.216	.243	5	.238	3	14	12	-2	1.4
1966	Hou-N	3	5	.375	13	12	1	1	1	63^{2}	79	7	10	26	12.7	3.82	90	.307	.336	1	.063	-1	-1	-3	-1	-0.5
	Chi-N	2	3	.400	11	9	1	0	0	48^{1}	62	8	11	28	13.6	6.14	60	.313	.349	2	.200	1	-14	-13	0	-1.1
	Yr	5	8	.385	24	21	2	1	1	112	141	15	21	54	13.0	4.82	73	.307	.337	3	.115	-0	-15	-16	-0	-1.6
Total	19	286	245	.539	676	609	305	45	25	4688^{2}	4582	505	902	2357	10.6	3.41	113	.255	.293	255	.167	34	264	236	-35	24.9

● CHARLIE ROBERTSON Robertson, Charles Culbertson b: 1/31/1896, Dexter, Tex. d: 8/23/84, Fort Worth, Tex. BL/TR, 6', 175 lbs. Deb: 5/13/19

YEAR	TM/L	W	L	PCT	G	GS	CG	SH	SV	IP	H	HR	BB	SO	RAT	ERA	ERA+	OAV	OOB	BH	AVG	PB	PR	/A	PD	TPI
1919	Chi-A	0	1	.000	1	1	0	0	0	2	5	0	0	1	22.5	9.00	35	.556	.556	0	—	0	-1	-1	-0	-0.5
1922	Chi-A	14	15	.483	37	34	21	3	0	272	294	9	89	83	12.8	3.64	112	.286	.345	16	.184	-2	12	13	-5	0.6
1923	Chi-A	13	18	.419	38	34	18	1	0	255	262	8	104	91	13.1	3.81	104	.272	.346	21	.247	0	5	4	-2	0.3
1924	Chi-A	4	10	.286	17	14	5	0	0	97^{1}	108	2	54	29	15.0	4.99	83	.293	.383	6	.182	-1	-8	-9	-2	-1.4
1925	Chi-A	8	12	.400	24	23	6	2	0	137	181	8	47	27	15.1	5.26	79	.327	.381	10	.222	0	-13	-17	-2	-2.1
1926	StL-A	1	2	.333	8	7	1	0	0	28	38	4	21	13	19.6	8.36	51	.333	.445	3	.300	1	-13	-13	0	-1.0
1927	Bos-N	7	17	.292	28	21	6	0	0	154^{1}	188	2	46	49	13.9	4.72	79	.308	.360	12	.240	1	-14	-17	-1	-2.4
1928	Bos-N	2	5	.286	13	7	3	0	1	59^{1}	73	5	16	17	13.5	5.31	74	.308	.352	0	.000	-1	-9	-9	-1	-1.1
Total	8	49	80	.380	166	141	60	6	1	1005	1149	38	377	310	13.8	4.44	90	.296	.361	68	.208	-2	-42	-49	-13	-7.6

● JERRY ROBERTSON Robertson, Jerry Lee b: 10/13/43, Winchester, Kan. d: 3/24/96, Burlington, Kan. BB/TR, 6'2", 205 lbs. Deb: 4/8/69

YEAR	TM/L	W	L	PCT	G	GS	CG	SH	SV	IP	H	HR	BB	SO	RAT	ERA	ERA+	OAV	OOB	BH	AVG	PB	PR	/A	PD	TPI
1969	Mon-N	5	16	.238	38	27	3	0	1	179^{2}	186	17	81	133	13.6	3.96	93	.272	.352	5	.089	-3	-7	-6	-3	-1.1
1970	Det-A	0	0	—	11	0	0	0	0	14^{2}	19	1	5	11	14.7	3.68	101	.306	.358	0	—	0	0	0	-0	0.0
Total	2	5	16	.238	49	27	3	0	1	194^{1}	205	18	86	144	13.7	3.94	93	.274	.352	5	.089	-3	-7	-6	-3	-1.1

● DICK ROBERTSON Robertson, Preston b: 1891, Washington, D.C. d: 10/2/44, New Orleans, La. BR/TR, 5'9", 160 lbs. Deb: 9/16/13

YEAR	TM/L	W	L	PCT	G	GS	CG	SH	SV	IP	H	HR	BB	SO	RAT	ERA	ERA+	OAV	OOB	BH	AVG	PB	PR	/A	PD	TPI
1913	Cin-N	0	1	.000	2	1	1	0	0	10	13	0	9	1	19.8	7.20	45	.342	.468	0	.000	-0	-4	-4	-0	-0.4
1918	Bro-N	3	6	.333	13	9	7	1	0	87	87	0	28	18	11.9	2.59	108	.272	.330	9	.300	2	2	2	-0	0.4
1919	Was-A	0	1	.000	7	4	0	0	0	27^{2}	25	1	9	7	11.1	2.28	141	.253	.315	0	.000	-1	3	3	0	0.0
Total	3	3	8	.273	22	14	8	1	0	124^{2}	125	1	46	26	12.3	2.89	101	.274	.340	9	.225	0	0	0	-1	0.0

● RICH ROBERTSON Robertson, Richard Paul b: 10/14/44, Albany, Cal. BR/TR, 6'2", 210 lbs. Deb: 9/10/66

YEAR	TM/L	W	L	PCT	G	GS	CG	SH	SV	IP	H	HR	BB	SO	RAT	ERA	ERA+	OAV	OOB	BH	AVG	PB	PR	/A	PD	TPI
1966	SF-N	0	0	—	1	0	0	0	0	2^{1}	3	0	2	2	19.3	7.71	48	.300	.417	0	—	0	-1	-1	-0	0.0
1967	SF-N	0	0	—	1	0	0	0	0	2	3	0	0	1	13.5	4.50	73	.333	.333	0	—	0	-0	-0	0	0.0
1968	SF-N	2	0	1.000	3	1	0	0	0	9	9	0	3	8	12.0	6.00	49	.265	.324	1	.500	0	-3	-3	0	-0.6
1969	SF-N	1	3	.250	17	7	1	1	0	44^{1}	53	4	21	20	15.2	5.48	64	.298	.375	0	.000	-1	-9	-10	0	-0.9
1970	SF-N	8	9	.471	41	26	6	0	1	183^{2}	199	22	96	121	14.5	4.85	82	.277	.363	6	.102	-1	-16	-18	-0	-1.6
1971	SF-N	2	2	.500	23	6	1	0	1	61	66	5	31	32	14.6	4.57	74	.267	.354	1	.067	-1	-8	-8	-1	-0.7
Total	6	13	14	.481	86	40	8	1	2	302^{1}	333	31	153	184	14.6	4.94	76	.278	.362	8	.093	-2	-38	-40	-1	-3.8

● RICH ROBERTSON Robertson, Richard Wayne b: 9/15/68, Nacogdoches, Tex. BL/TL, 6'4", 175 lbs. Deb: 4/30/93

YEAR	TM/L	W	L	PCT	G	GS	CG	SH	SV	IP	H	HR	BB	SO	RAT	ERA	ERA+	OAV	OOB	BH	AVG	PB	PR	/A	PD	TPI
1993	Pit-N	0	1	.000	9	0	0	0	0	9	15	0	4	5	19.0	6.00	67	.385	.442	0	—	0	-2	-2	-0	-0.2
1994	Pit-N	0	0	—	8	0	0	0	0	15^{2}	20	2	10	8	17.2	6.89	63	.313	.405	1	.250	0	-5	-4	-0	0.0
1995	Min-A	2	0	1.000	25	4	1	0	0	51^{2}	48	4	31	38	13.8	3.83	124	.253	.357	0	—	0	5	5	-1	0.1
1996	Min-A	7	17	.292	36	31	5	**3**	0	186^{1}	197	22	116	114	15.6	5.12	100	.273	.380	0	—	0	-3	-0	2	0.1
1997	Min-A	8	12	.400	31	26	0	0	0	147	169	19	70	69	15.0	5.69	82	.292	.374	1	.200	0	-18	-17	-2	-2.1
1998	Ana-A	0	0	—	5	0	0	0	0	5^{2}	11	3	2	3	20.6	15.88	30	.393	.433	0	—	0	-7	-7	1	0.0
Total	6	17	30	.362	114	61	6	3	0	415^{1}	460	50	233	237	15.3	5.40	90	.284	.379	2	.222	0	-30	-25	-1	-2.1

● DEWEY ROBINSON Robinson, Dewey Everett b: 4/28/55, Evanston, Ill. BR/TR, 6', 180 lbs. Deb: 4/6/79 C

YEAR	TM/L	W	L	PCT	G	GS	CG	SH	SV	IP	H	HR	BB	SO	RAT	ERA	ERA+	OAV	OOB	BH	AVG	PB	PR	/A	PD	TPI
1979	Chi-A	0	1	.000	11	0	0	0	0	14^{1}	11	1	9	5	12.6	6.28	68	.212	.328	0	—	0	-3	-3	-0	-0.2
1980	Chi-A	1	1	.500	15	0	0	0	0	35	26	2	16	28	10.8	3.09	131	.215	.307	0	—	0	4	4	0	0.2
1981	Chi-A	1	0	1.000	4	0	0	0	0	4	5	1	3	2	18.0	4.50	79	.357	.471	0	—	0	-0	-0	-0	-0.1
Total	3	2	2	.500	30	0	0	0	0	53^{1}	42	4	28	35	11.8	4.05	100	.225	.326	0	—	0	0	0	0	-0.1

● DON ROBINSON Robinson, Don Allen b: 6/8/57, Ashland, Ky. BR/TR, 6'4", 231 lbs. Deb: 4/10/78

YEAR	TM/L	W	L	PCT	G	GS	CG	SH	SV	IP	H	HR	BB	SO	RAT	ERA	ERA+	OAV	OOB	BH	AVG	PB	PR	/A	PD	TPI
1978	Pit-N	14	6	.700	35	32	9	1	1	228^{1}	203	20	57	135	10.4	3.47	107	.236	.286	20	.235	2	3	6	-1	0.6
1979	*Pit-N	8	8	.500	29	25	4	0	0	160^{2}	171	12	52	96	12.7	3.87	100	.277	.337	10	.204	1	-2	0	-3	-0.2
1980	Pit-N	7	10	.412	29	24	3	2	1	160^{1}	157	14	45	103	11.6	3.99	91	.257	.314	19	.333	6	-7	-6	0	-0.6
1981	Pit-N	0	3	.000	16	2	0	0	2	38^{1}	47	4	23	17	16.4	5.87	61	.313	.405	3	.250	1	-10	-10	1	-0.7
1982	Pit-N	15	13	.536	38	30	6	0	0	227	213	26	103	165	12.6	4.28	87	.250	.333	24	.282	8	-17	-15	-2	-1.0
1983	Pit-N	2	2	.500	9	6	0	0	0	36^{1}	43	5	21	28	15.9	4.46	83	.297	.386	2	.154	1	-3	-3	0	-0.2
1984	Pit-N	5	6	.455	51	1	0	0	10	122	99	6	49	110	10.9	3.02	119	.226	.304	9	.290	4	8	8	0	1.3
1985	Pit-N	5	11	.313	44	6	0	0	3	95^{1}	95	6	42	65	13.1	3.87	92	.255	.334	5	.238	3	-3	-3	-0	-0.3
1986	Pit-N	3	4	.429	50	0	0	0	14	69^{1}	61	5	27	53	11.7	3.38	114	.237	.315	4	.667	2	3	4	0	0.7
1987	Pit-N	6	6	.500	42	0	0	0	12	65^{1}	66	6	22	53	12.1	3.86	107	.267	.327	1	.143	0	2	2	0	0.4
	*SF-N	5	1	.833	25	0	0	0	7	42^{2}	39	1	18	26	12.0	2.74	140	.239	.315	3	.273	2	6	5	-1	1.0
	Yr	11	7	.611	67	0	0	0	19	108	105	7	40	79	12.1	3.42	117	.255	.322	4	.222	2	8	7	-1	1.4
1988	SF-N	10	5	.667	51	19	3	2	6	176^{2}	152	11	49	122	10.4	2.45	133	.231	.287	9	.173	3	20	16	-2	1.6
1989	*SF-N	12	11	.522	34	32	5	1	0	197	184	22	37	96	10.2	3.43	98	.248	.285	15	.185	4	2	-1	-4	-0.2
1990	SF-N	10	7	.588	26	25	4	0	0	157^{2}	173	18	41	78	12.3	4.57	80	.280	.326	9	.143	1	-14	-16	-2	-1.6
1991	SF-N	5	9	.357	34	16	0	0	1	121^{1}	123	12	50	78	12.9	4.38	82	.265	.337	6	.150	0	-9	-11	-0	-1.2
1992	Cal-A	1	0	1.000	3	3	0	0	0	16^{1}	19	1	3	9	12.1	2.20	181	.292	.324	0	—	0	3	3	-1	0.1
	Phi-N	1	4	.200	8	8	0	0	0	43^{2}	49	6	4	17	11.1	6.18	56	.290	.310	7	.389	3	-13	-13	-1	-1.1
Total	15	109	106	.507	524	229	34	6	57	1958^{1}	1894	175	643	1251	11.8	3.79	96	.255	.317	146	.231	41	-34	-34	-14	-0.8

● HUMBERTO ROBINSON Robinson, Humberto Valentino b: 6/25/30, Colon, Panama BR/TR, 6'1", 155 lbs. Deb: 4/20/55

YEAR	TM/L	W	L	PCT	G	GS	CG	SH	SV	IP	H	HR	BB	SO	RAT	ERA	ERA+	OAV	OOB	BH	AVG	PB	PR	/A	PD	TPI
1955	Mil-N	3	1	.750	13	2	1	0	2	38	31	1	25	19	14.2	3.08	122	.235	.373	1	.077	-1	4	3	0	0.2
1956	Mil-N	0	0	—	1	0	0	0	0	2	1	0	2	0	13.5	0.00	—	.167	.375	0	—	0	1	1	0	0.0
1958	Mil-N	2	4	.333	19	0	0	0	1	41^{2}	30	4	13	26	9.7	3.02	116	.203	.276	1	.167	1	4	2	1	0.5
1959	Cle-A	1	0	1.000	5	0	0	0	0	8^{2}	9	0	4	6	13.5	4.15	89	.281	.361	0	—	0	-0	-0	0	0.0
	Phi-N	2	4	.333	31	4	1	0	1	73	70	6	24	32	11.6	3.33	123	.251	.310	3	.231	1	5	6	0	0.7
1960	Phi-N	0	4	.000	33	1	0	0	0	49^{2}	48	6	22	31	12.7	3.44	113	.255	.333	1	.167	-0	2	2	0	0.2
Total	5	8	13	.381	102	7	2	0	4	213	189	17	90	114	12.0	3.25	119	.241	.323	6	.158	0	16	14	2	1.6

● JEFF ROBINSON Robinson, Jeffrey Daniel b: 12/13/60, Santa Ana, Cal. BR/TR, 6'4", 200 lbs. Deb: 4/7/84

YEAR	TM/L	W	L	PCT	G	GS	CG	SH	SV	IP	H	HR	BB	SO	RAT	ERA	ERA+	OAV	OOB	BH	AVG	PB	PR	/A	PD	TPI
1984	SF-N	7	15	.318	34	33	1	1	0	171^{2}	195	12	52	102	13.3	4.56	77	.288	.345	7	.115	-2	-19	-20	0	-2.5
1985	SF-N	0	0	—	8	0	0	0	0	12^{1}	16	2	10	8	19.0	5.11	67	.333	.448	0	—	0	-2	-2	-0	0.0
1986	SF-N	6	3	.667	64	0	0	0	8	104^{1}	92	8	32	90	10.8	3.36	105	.234	.293	1	.067	-1	4	2	-1	0.0
1987	SF-N	6	8	.429	63	0	0	0	10	96^{2}	69	10	48	82	11.0	2.79	138	.207	.309	2	.111	-1	14	11	1	1.7
	Pit-N	2	1	.667	18	0	0	0	4	26^{2}	20	1	6	19	8.8	3.04	135	.215	.263	1	.250	1	3	3	0	0.6
	Yr	8	9	.471	81	0	0	0	14	123^{1}	89	11	54	101	10.4	2.85	137	.206	.295	3	.136	0	17	14	1	2.3
1988	Pit-N	11	5	.688	75	0	0	0	9	124^{2}	113	6	39	87	11.2	3.03	112	.244	.307	3	.188	0	6	5	0	0.8
1989	Pit-N	7	13	.350	50	19	0	0	4	141^{1}	161	14	59	95	14.1	4.58	73	.283	.351	8	.229	2	-17	-19	1	-2.3
1990	NY-A	3	6	.333	54	4	1	0	0	88^{2}	82	8	34	43	11.9	3.45	115	.248	.320	0	—	0	4	5	2	0.7
1991	Cal-A	0	3	.000	39	0	0	0	3	57	56	9	29	57	13.7	5.37	76	.259	.352	0	—	0	-8	-8	0	-0.4
1992	Chi-N	4	3	.571	49	5	0	0	1	78	76	5	40	46	13.6	3.00	120	.263	.356	0	.000	-1	4	5	1	0.4
Total	9	46	57	.447	454	62	2	1	39	901^{1}	880	75	349	629	12.5	3.79	95	.258	.330	22	.137	-1	-10	-18	4	-1.0

● JEFF ROBINSON Robinson, Jeffrey Mark b: 12/14/61, Ventura, Cal. BR/TR, 6'6", 240 lbs. Deb: 4/12/87

YEAR	TM/L	W	L	PCT	G	GS	CG	SH	SV	IP	H	HR	BB	SO	RAT	ERA	ERA+	OAV	OOB	BH	AVG	PB	PR	/A	PD	TPI
1987	*Det-A	9	6	.600	29	21	2	1	0	127^{1}	132	16	54	98	13.6	5.37	79	.262	.342	0	—	0	-13	-16	-1	-1.6
1988	Det-A	13	6	.684	24	23	6	2	0	172	121	19	72	114	10.3	2.98	128	**.197**	.284	0	—	0	19	16	-0	1.7
1989	Det-A	4	5	.444	16	16	1	1	0	78	76	10	46	40	14.2	4.73	81	.259	.361	0	—	0	-7	-8	-1	-0.9

YEAR	TM/L	W	L	PCT	G	GS	CG	SH	SV	IP	H	HR	BB	SO	RAT	ERA	ERA+	OAV	OOB	BH	AVG	PB	PR	/A	PD	TPI
1990	Det-A	10	9	.526	27	27	1	1	0	145	141	23	88	76	14.6	5.96	66	.255	.364	0	—	0	-33	-32	-1	-3.7
1991	Bal-A	4	9	.308	21	19	0	0	0	104^1	119	12	51	65	15.2	5.18	76	.289	.375	0	—	0	-13	-14	-1	-1.4
1992	Tex-A	4	4	.500	16	4	0	0	0	45^2	50	6	21	18	14.0	5.72	66	.281	.357	0	—	0	-9	-10	-0	-1.4
	Pit-N	3	1	.750	8	7	0	0	0	36^1	33	2	15	14	12.1	4.46	77	.244	.325	1	.091	-1	-4	-4	0	-0.5
Total	6	47	40	.540	141	117	10	5	0	708^2	672	88	347	425	13.2	4.79	82	.250	.341	1	.091	-1	-60	-68	-4	-7.8

● **JACK ROBINSON** Robinson, John Edward b: 2/20/21, Orange, N.J. BR/TR, 6′, 175 lbs. Deb: 5/4/49

YEAR	TM/L	W	L	PCT	G	GS	CG	SH	SV	IP	H	HR	BB	SO	RAT	ERA	ERA+	OAV	OOB	BH	AVG	PB	PR	/A	PD	TPI
1949	Bos-A	0	0	—	3	0	0	0	0	4	4	0	1	1	13.5	2.25	194	.267	.353	0	—	0	1	1	0	0.0

● **HANK ROBINSON** Robinson, John Henry "Rube" (b: John Henry Roberson) b: 8/16/1889, Floyd, Ark. d: 7/3/65, N.Little Rock, Ark BR/TL, 5′11.5″, 160 lbs. Deb: 9/2/11

YEAR	TM/L	W	L	PCT	G	GS	CG	SH	SV	IP	H	HR	BB	SO	RAT	ERA	ERA+	OAV	OOB	BH	AVG	PB	PR	/A	PD	TPI
1911	Pit-N	0	1	.000	5	0	0	0	0	13	13	0	5	8	13.2	2.77	124	.283	.365	0	.000	-0	1	1	1	0.1
1912	Pit-N	12	7	.632	33	16	11	0	2	175	146	3	30	79	**9.6**	2.26	144	.237	.284	15	.254	3	22	19	-1	2.1
1913	Pit-N	14	9	.609	43	22	8	1	0	196^1	184	1	41	50	10.6	2.38	127	.255	.301	11	.180	-1	18	14	-2	1.3
1914	StL-N	7	8	.467	26	16	6	1	0	126	128	1	32	30	11.7	3.00	93	.274	.325	6	.171	-0	-3	-3	2	-0.2
1915	StL-N	7	8	.467	32	15	6	1	0	143	128	1	35	57	10.7	2.45	114	.245	.301	5	.106	-2	5	5	1	0.4
1918	NY-A	2	4	.333	11	3	1	0	0	48	47	0	16	14	12.4	3.00	94	.269	.340	0	.000	-2	-1	-1	-0	-0.4
Total	6	42	37	.532	150	72	32	3	2	701^1	646	6	159	238	10.7	2.53	118	.253	.305	37	.170	-3	42	36	1	3.3

● **KENNY ROBINSON** Robinson, Kenneth Neal b: 11/3/69, Barberton, Ohio BR/TR, 5′7″, 175 lbs. Deb: 7/20/95

YEAR	TM/L	W	L	PCT	G	GS	CG	SH	SV	IP	H	HR	BB	SO	RAT	ERA	ERA+	OAV	OOB	BH	AVG	PB	PR	/A	PD	TPI
1995	Tor-A	1	2	.333	21	0	0	0	0	39	25	7	22	31	11.3	3.69	128	.179	.299	0	—	0	4	4	-1	0.2
1996	KC-A	1	0	1.000	5	0	0	0	0	6	9	0	3	5	18.0	6.00	83	.346	.414	0	—	0	-1	-1	-0	-0.1
1997	Tor-A	0	0	—	3	0	0	0	0	3^1	1	1	1	4	5.4	2.70	170	.100	.182	0	—	0	1	1	1	0.1
Total	3	2	2	.500	29	0	0	0	0	48^1	35	8	26	40	11.7	3.91	121	.199	.309	0	—	0	4	4	-0	0.2

● **RON ROBINSON** Robinson, Ronald Dean b: 3/24/62, Exeter, Cal. BR/TR, 6′4″, 235 lbs. Deb: 8/14/84

YEAR	TM/L	W	L	PCT	G	GS	CG	SH	SV	IP	H	HR	BB	SO	RAT	ERA	ERA+	OAV	OOB	BH	AVG	PB	PR	/A	PD	TPI
1984	Cin-N	1	2	.333	12	5	1	0	0	39^2	35	3	13	24	10.9	2.72	139	.232	.293	0	.000	-1	4	5	0	0.2
1985	Cin-N	7	7	.500	33	12	0	0	1	108^1	107	11	32	76	11.6	3.99	95	.259	.314	2	.091	-1	-5	-2	1	-0.4
1986	Cin-N	10	3	.769	70	0	0	0	14	116^2	110	10	43	117	12.0	3.24	119	.253	.323	1	.071	-1	6	8	1	1.1
1987	Cin-N	7	5	.583	48	18	0	0	4	154	148	14	43	99	11.2	3.68	115	.256	.308	7	.194	0	7	10	-2	0.5
1988	Cin-N	3	7	.300	17	16	0	0	0	78^2	88	5	26	38	13.3	4.12	87	.285	.344	5	.200	1	-6	-5	-0	-0.5
1989	Cin-N	5	3	.625	15	15	0	0	0	83^1	80	8	28	36	11.9	3.35	108	.252	.317	6	.214	1	1	2	-0	0.3
1990	Cin-N	2	2	.500	6	5	0	0	0	31^1	36	2	14	14	14.4	4.88	81	.295	.368	1	.091	-1	-4	-3	-0	-0.4
	Mil-A	12	5	.706	22	22	7	2	0	148^1	158	5	37	57	12.2	2.91	133	.275	.326	0	—	0	16	16	-0	1.7
1991	Mil-A	0	1	.000	1	1	0	0	0	4^1	6	0	3	0	20.8	6.23	64	.353	.476	0	—	0	-1	-1	0	-0.1
1992	Mil-A	1	4	.200	8	8	0	0	0	35^1	51	3	14	12	17.1	5.86	65	.331	.394	0	—	0	-8	-8	-0	-0.9
Total	9	48	39	.552	232	102	8	2	19	800	819	61	253	473	12.3	3.63	107	.267	.326	22	.153	-2	12	21	-1	1.5

● **BILL ROBINSON** Robinson, William (b: William Anderson) b: Taylorsville, Ky. Deb: 8/12/1889

YEAR	TM/L	W	L	PCT	G	GS	CG	SH	SV	IP	H	HR	BB	SO	RAT	ERA	ERA+	OAV	OOB	BH	AVG	PB	PR	/A	PD	TPI
1889	Lou-a	0	1	.000	1	1	1	0	0	8	10	2	6	2	18.0	10.13	38	.294	.400	1	.333	0	-6	-6	0	-0.4

● **YANK ROBINSON** Robinson, William H. b: 9/19/1859, Philadelphia, Pa. d: 8/25/1894, St.Louis, Mo. BR/TR, 5′6.5″, 170 lbs. Deb: 8/24/1882 ♦

YEAR	TM/L	W	L	PCT	G	GS	CG	SH	SV	IP	H	HR	BB	SO	RAT	ERA	ERA+	OAV	OOB	BH	AVG	PB	PR	/A	PD	TPI
1882	Det-N	0	0	—	1	0	0	0	0	2	0	0	1	0	4.5	0.00	—	.000	.125	7	.179	-0	1	1	0	0.0
1884	Bal-U	3	3	.500	11	3	3	0	0	75	96	1	18	61	13.7	3.48	77	.292	.329	111	.267	-0	-9	-7	-3	-0.7
1886	*StL-a	0	1	.000	1	1	1	0	0	9	10	0	7	1	17.0	3.00	115	.286	.405	132	.274	0	0	0	-0	0.1
1887	*StL-a	0	0	—	1	0	0	0	1	3	3	0	3	0	21.0	3.00	151	.333	.538	131	.305	0	0	1	-0	0.0
Total	4	3	4	.429	14	4	4	0	1	89	109	1	29	62	14.1	3.34	85	.287	.339	825	.241	0	-7	-5	-3	-0.6

● **CHICK ROBITAILLE** Robitaille, Joseph Anthony b: 3/2/1879, Whitehall, N.Y. d: 7/30/47, Waterford, N.Y. BR/TR, 5′8″, 150 lbs. Deb: 9/2/04

YEAR	TM/L	W	L	PCT	G	GS	CG	SH	SV	IP	H	HR	BB	SO	RAT	ERA	ERA+	OAV	OOB	BH	AVG	PB	PR	/A	PD	TPI
1904	Pit-N	4	3	.571	9	8	8	0	0	66	52	1	13	34	9.0	1.91	144	.208	.250	2	.095	-2	6	6	-1	0.3
1905	Pit-N	8	5	.615	17	12	10	0	0	120^1	126	1	28	32	11.7	2.92	103	.276	.322	6	.133	-2	1	1	-0	-0.1
Total	2	12	8	.600	26	20	18	0	0	186^1	178	2	41	66	10.8	2.56	114	.252	.297	8	.121	-4	7	7	-1	0.2

● **ARMANDO ROCHE** Roche, Armando (Baez) b: 12/7/26, Havana, Cuba BR/TR, 6′, 190 lbs. Deb: 5/10/45

YEAR	TM/L	W	L	PCT	G	GS	CG	SH	SV	IP	H	HR	BB	SO	RAT	ERA	ERA+	OAV	OOB	BH	AVG	PB	PR	/A	PD	TPI
1945	Was-A	0	0	—	2	0	0	0	0	6	10	0	2	0	18.0	6.00	52	.400	.444	0	.000	-0	-2	-2	0	0.0

● **MIKE ROCHFORD** Rochford, Michael Joseph b: 3/14/63, Methuen, Mass. BL/TL, 6′4″, 205 lbs. Deb: 9/3/88

YEAR	TM/L	W	L	PCT	G	GS	CG	SH	SV	IP	H	HR	BB	SO	RAT	ERA	ERA+	OAV	OOB	BH	AVG	PB	PR	/A	PD	TPI
1988	Bos-A	0	0	—	2	0	0	0	0	2^1	4	0	1	1	19.3	0.00	—	.364	.417	0	—	0	1	1	0	0.0
1989	Bos-A	0	0	—	4	0	0	0	0	4	4	1	4	1	18.0	6.75	61	.267	.421	0	—	0	-1	-1	-0	0.0
1990	Bos-A	0	1	.000	2	1	0	0	0	4	10	1	4	0	31.5	18.00	23	.526	.609	0	—	0	-6	-6	-0	-1.1
Total	3	0	1	.000	8	1	0	0	0	10^1	18	2	9	2	23.5	9.58	43	.400	.500	0	—	0	-7	-6	0	-1.1

● **JOHN ROCKER** Rocker, John Loy b: 10/17/74, Statesboro, Ga. BR/TL, 6′4″, 210 lbs. Deb: 5/5/98

YEAR	TM/L	W	L	PCT	G	GS	CG	SH	SV	IP	H	HR	BB	SO	RAT	ERA	ERA+	OAV	OOB	BH	AVG	PB	PR	/A	PD	TPI
1998	*Atl-N	1	3	.250	47	0	0	0	2	38	22	4	22	42	11.1	2.13	198	.172	.307	0	—	0	9	9	0	0.9

● **RICH RODAS** Rodas, Richard Martin b: 11/7/59, Roseville, Cal. BL/TL, 6′1″, 180 lbs. Deb: 9/6/83

YEAR	TM/L	W	L	PCT	G	GS	CG	SH	SV	IP	H	HR	BB	SO	RAT	ERA	ERA+	OAV	OOB	BH	AVG	PB	PR	/A	PD	TPI
1983	LA-N	0	0	—	7	0	0	0	0	4^2	4	0	3	5	13.5	1.93	186	.222	.333	0	—	0	1	1	-0	0.0
1984	LA-N	0	0	—	3	0	0	0	0	5	5	2	1	1	10.8	5.40	65	.250	.286	0	.000	-0	-1	-1	0	0.0
Total	2	0	0	—	10	0	0	0	0	9^2	9	2	4	6	12.1	3.72	96	.237	.310	0	.000	-0	-0	-0	0	0.0

● **EDUARDO RODRIGUEZ** Rodriguez, Eduardo (Reyes) b: 3/6/52, Barceloneta, P.R. BR/TR, 6′, 185 lbs. Deb: 6/20/73

YEAR	TM/L	W	L	PCT	G	GS	CG	SH	SV	IP	H	HR	BB	SO	RAT	ERA	ERA+	OAV	OOB	BH	AVG	PB	PR	/A	PD	TPI
1973	Mil-A	9	7	.563	30	6	2	0	5	76^1	71	6	47	49	14.1	3.30	114	.247	.357	1	1.000	1	4	4	-0	0.9
1974	Mil-A	7	4	.636	43	6	0	0	4	111^2	97	7	51	58	12.3	3.63	100	.241	.333	0	—	0	-0	-0	0	0.0
1975	Mil-A	7	0	1.000	43	1	0	0	7	87^2	77	9	44	65	12.9	3.49	110	.235	.334	0	—	0	3	3	-2	0.1
1976	Mil-A	5	13	.278	45	12	3	0	8	136	124	10	65	77	12.7	3.64	96	.249	.339	0	—	0	-2	-2	-1	-0.3
1977	Mil-A	5	6	.455	42	5	1	1	4	142^2	126	15	56	104	11.7	4.35	93	.236	.311	0	—	0	-5	-5	-1	-0.4
1978	Mil-A	5	5	.500	32	8	0	0	2	105^1	107	9	26	51	11.5	3.93	96	.262	.310	0	—	0	-2	-2	-0	-0.2
1979	KC-A	4	1	.800	29	1	1	0	2	74^1	79	9	34	26	14.0	4.84	88	.276	.359	0	—	0	-5	-5	-1	-0.5
Total	7	42	36	.538	264	39	7	1	32	734	681	65	323	430	12.6	3.89	98	.248	.332	1	1.000	1	-7	-7	-5	-0.4

● **FELIX RODRIGUEZ** Rodriguez, Felix Antonio b: 12/5/72, Monte Cristi, D.R. BR/TR, 6′1″, 170 lbs. Deb: 5/13/95

YEAR	TM/L	W	L	PCT	G	GS	CG	SH	SV	IP	H	HR	BB	SO	RAT	ERA	ERA+	OAV	OOB	BH	AVG	PB	PR	/A	PD	TPI
1995	LA-N	1	1	.500	11	0	0	0	0	10^2	11	2	5	5	13.5	2.53	150	.275	.356	0	—	0	2	1	-0	0.2
1997	Cin-N	0	0	—	26	1	0	0	0	46	48	2	28	34	16.0	4.30	99	.271	.389	0	.000	-0	-1	-0	-1	-0.1
1998	Ari-N	0	2	.000	43	0	0	0	5	44	44	5	29	36	15.1	6.14	70	.259	.370	0	—	0	-9	-9	1	-0.4
Total	3	1	3	.250	80	1	0	0	5	100^2	103	9	62	75	15.4	4.92	86	.266	.377	0	.000	-0	-8	-8	-0	-0.3

● **FREDDY RODRIGUEZ** Rodriguez, Fernando Pedro (Borrego) b: 4/29/24, Havana, Cuba BR/TR, 6′, 180 lbs. Deb: 4/18/58

YEAR	TM/L	W	L	PCT	G	GS	CG	SH	SV	IP	H	HR	BB	SO	RAT	ERA	ERA+	OAV	OOB	BH	AVG	PB	PR	/A	PD	TPI
1958	Chi-N	0	0	—	7	0	0	0	2	7^1	8	2	5	5	17.2	7.36	53	.267	.389	0	.000	-0	-3	-3	-0	-0.2
1959	Phi-N	0	0	—	1	0	0	0	0	2	4	1	0	1	22.5	13.50	30	.400	.455	0	—	0	-2	-2	-0	0.0
Total	2	0	0	—	8	0	0	0	2	9^1	12	3	5	6	18.3	8.68	46	.300	.404	0	.000	-0	-5	-5	-0	-0.2

● **FRANK RODRIGUEZ** Rodriguez, Francisco b: 12/11/72, Brooklyn, N.Y. BR/TR, 6′, 190 lbs. Deb: 4/26/95

YEAR	TM/L	W	L	PCT	G	GS	CG	SH	SV	IP	H	HR	BB	SO	RAT	ERA	ERA+	OAV	OOB	BH	AVG	PB	PR	/A	PD	TPI
1995	Bos-A	0	2	.000	9	2	0	0	0	15^1	21	3	10	14	18.2	10.57	46	.323	.413	0	—	0	-10	-10	1	-1.0
	Min-A	5	6	.455	16	16	0	0	0	90^1	93	8	47	45	14.4	5.38	89	.269	.364	0	—	0	-7	-6	2	-0.4
	Yr	5	8	.385	25	18	0	0	0	105^2	114	11	57	59	15.0	6.13	78	.277	.372	0	—	0	-17	-16	3	-1.4
1996	Min-A	13	14	.481	38	33	3	0	2	206^2	218	27	78	110	13.1	5.05	101	.272	.340	0	—	0	-1	1	1	0.1
1997	Min-A	3	6	.333	43	15	0	0	0	142^1	147	12	60	65	13.3	4.62	101	.271	.348	0	.000	-0	-1	1	1	0.1
1998	Min-A	4	6	.400	20	11	0	0	0	70	88	6	30	62	15.6	6.56	72	.303	.375	0	—	0	-15	-14	0	-1.7
Total	4	25	34	.424	126	77	3	0	2	524^2	567	56	225	296	13.9	5.35	91	.277	.354	0	.000	-0	-34	-28	5	-2.9

● **NERIO RODRIGUEZ** Rodriguez, Nerio b: 3/22/73, San Pedro De Macoris, D.R. BR/TR, 6′1″, 195 lbs. Deb: 8/18/96

YEAR	TM/L	W	L	PCT	G	GS	CG	SH	SV	IP	H	HR	BB	SO	RAT	ERA	ERA+	OAV	OOB	BH	AVG	PB	PR	/A	PD	TPI
1996	Bal-A	0	1	.000	8	1	0	0	0	16^2	18	2	7	12	14.0	4.32	114	.265	.342	0	—	0	1	1	-1	0.0
1997	Bal-A	2	1	.667	6	2	0	0	0	22	21	2	8	11	12.3	4.91	90	.250	.323	0	—	0	-1	-1	0	0.1

YEAR	TM/L	W	L	PCT	G	GS	CG	SH	SV	IP	H	HR	BB	SO	RAT	ERA	ERA+	OAV	OOB	BH	AVG	PB	PR	/A	PD	TPI
1998	Bal-A	1	3	.250	6	4	0	0	0	19	25	0	9	8	16.1	8.05	56	.321	.391	0	—	0	-7	-7	-1	-1.1
	Tor-A	1	0	1.000	7	0	0	0	0	8^1	10	1	8	3	20.5	9.72	48	.286	.432	0	—	0	-5	-5	-0	-0.5
	Yr	2	3	.400	13	4	0	0	0	27^1	35	1	17	11	17.5	8.56	53	.304	.398	0	—	0	-12	-12	-1	-1.6
Total	3	4	5	.444	27	7	0	0	0	66	74	5	32	34	14.9	6.27	73	.279	.363	0	—	0	-11	-12	-1	-1.5
● **RICK RODRIGUEZ**	Rodriguez, Ricardo b: 9/21/60, Oakland, Cal. BR/TR, 6'3", 190 lbs. Deb: 9/17/86																									
1986	Oak-A	1	2	.333	3	3	0	0	0	16^1	17	4	7	2	13.2	6.61	58	.262	.333	0	—	0	-4	-5	0	-0.5
1987	Oak-A	1	0	1.000	15	0	0	0	0	24^1	32	1	15	9	17.8	2.96	139	.337	.432	0	—	0	4	3	1	0.2
1988	Cle-A	1	2	.333	10	5	0	0	0	33	43	4	17	9	16.6	7.09	58	.323	.404	0	—	0	-11	-11	1	-0.8
1990	SF-N	0	0	—	3	0	0	0	0	3^1	5	0	2	2	18.9	8.10	45	.357	.438	0	—	0	-2	-2	0	0.0
Total	4	3	4	.429	31	8	0	0	0	77	97	9	41	22	16.4	5.73	71	.316	.400	0	—	0	-13	-14	2	-1.1
● **RICH RODRIGUEZ**	Rodriguez, Richard Anthony b: 3/1/63, Downey, Cal. BL/TL, 6', 200 lbs. Deb: 6/30/90																									
1990	SD-N	1	1	.500	32	0	0	0	1	47^2	52	2	16	22	13.0	2.83	135	.287	.348	0	.000	-0	5	5	1	0.3
1991	SD-N	3	1	.750	64	1	0	0	0	80	66	8	44	40	12.4	3.26	116	.234	.337	0	.000	-1	4	5	-0	0.2
1992	SD-N	6	3	.667	61	1	0	0	0	91	77	4	29	64	10.5	2.37	151	.229	.290	0	.000	-0	11	12	1	1.2
1993	SD-N	2	3	.400	34	0	0	0	2	30	34	2	9	22	13.2	3.30	125	.281	.336	0	—	0	2	3	-1	0.4
	Fla-N	0	1	.000	36	0	0	0	1	46	39	8	24	21	12.5	4.11	105	.229	.328	0	.000	-0	-0	1	1	0.1
	Yr	2	4	.333	70	0	0	0	3	76	73	10	33	43	12.7	3.79	112	.250	.328	0	.000	-0	2	4	0	0.5
1994	StL-N	3	5	.375	56	0	0	0	0	60^1	62	6	26	43	13.3	4.03	103	.270	.346	0	.000	-0	1	1	-1	-0.1
1995	StL-N	0	0	—	1	0	0	0	0	1^2	0	0	0	0	0.0	0.00	—	.000	.000	0	—	0	1	1	-0	0.0
1997	*SF-N	4	3	.571	71	0	0	0	1	65^1	65	7	21	32	12.0	3.17	130	.264	.325	1	.333	1	7	7	1	0.9
1998	SF-N	4	0	1.000	68	0	0	0	2	65^2	69	7	20	44	12.2	3.70	110	.272	.325	1	.167	-0	4	3	1	0.2
Total	8	23	17	.575	423	2	0	0	7	487^2	464	44	189	288	12.1	3.27	121	.254	.326	2	.077	-1	36	38	2	3.2
● **ROSARIO RODRIGUEZ**	Rodriguez, Rosario Isabel (Echavarria) b: 7/8/69, Los Mochis, Mexico BR/TL, 6', 185 lbs. Deb: 9/1/89																									
1989	Cin-N	1	1	.500	7	0	0	0	0	4^1	3	0	3	0	12.5	4.15	87	.188	.316	0	—	0	-0	-0	0	-0.1
1990	Cin-N	0	0	—	9	0	0	0	0	10^1	15	3	2	8	15.7	6.10	65	.357	.400	0	—	0	-3	-2	0	0.0
1991	*Pit-N	1	1	.500	18	0	0	0	6	15^1	14	1	8	10	13.5	4.11	87	.246	.348	0	.000	-0	-1	-1	0	-0.2
Total	3	2	2	.500	34	0	0	0	6	30	32	4	13	18	14.1	4.80	77	.278	.362	0	.000	-0	-4	-4	1	-0.3
● **ROBERTO RODRIQUEZ**	Rodriquez, Roberto (Munoz) b: 11/29/41, Caracas, Venez. BR/TR, 6'3", 185 lbs. Deb: 5/13/67																									
1967	KC-A	1	1	.500	15	5	0	0	2	40^1	42	4	14	29	12.7	3.57	89	.268	.331	0	.000	-1	-2	-2	-0	-0.3
1970	Oak-A	0	0	—	6	0	0	0	0	12^1	10	2	3	8	9.5	2.92	121	.227	.277	0	.000	-0	1	1	-0	0.0
	SD-N	0	0	—	10	0	0	0	3	16^1	26	1	5	8	17.1	6.61	60	.366	.408	0	.000	-0	-5	-5	0	-0.2
	Chi-N	3	2	.600	26	0	0	0	2	43^1	50	6	15	46	13.5	5.82	77	.289	.346	1	.125	1	-9	-6	0	-0.6
	Yr	3	2	.600	36	0	0	0	5	59^2	76	7	20	54	14.5	6.03	72	.311	.364	1	.091	0	-13	-11	0	-0.8
Total	2	4	3	.571	57	5	0	0	7	112^1	128	13	37	91	13.3	4.81	80	.288	.344	1	.048	-1	-14	-12	-0	-1.1
● **PREACHER ROE**	Roe, Elwin Charles b: 2/26/15, Ash Flat, Ark. BR/TL, 6'2", 170 lbs. Deb: 8/22/38																									
1938	StL-N	0	0	—	1	0	0	0	0	2^2	6	0	2	1	27.0	13.50	29	.429	.500	0	.000	-0	-3	-3	-0	0.0
1944	Pit-N	13	11	.542	39	25	7	1	1	185^1	182	7	59	88	11.8	3.11	120	.253	.311	7	.132	-2	10	13	-1	1.2
1945	Pit-N†	14	13	.519	33	31	15	3	1	235	228	11	46	**148**	10.5	2.87	137	.259	.296	8	.107	-3	24	28	1	2.8
1946	Pit-N	3	8	.273	21	10	1	0	2	70	83	5	25	28	14.1	5.14	69	.294	.356	1	.067	-1	-13	-13	-0	-1.9
1947	Pit-N	4	15	.211	38	22	4	1	2	144	156	19	63	59	13.7	5.25	80	.276	.348	5	.125	-2	-19	-16	-1	-2.2
1948	Bro-N	12	8	.600	34	22	8	2	2	177^2	156	14	33	86	9.7	2.63	152	.233	.271	5	.098	-2	26	27	-1	2.6
1949	*Bro-N★	15	6	**.714**	30	27	13	3	1	212^2	201	25	44	109	10.5	2.79	147	.252	.293	8	.114	-2	29	31	-2	2.4
1950	Bro-N☆	19	11	.633	36	32	16	2	1	250^2	245	34	66	125	11.3	3.30	124	.257	.308	14	.154	-3	23	22	-2	1.9
1951	Bro-N☆	22	3	**.880**	34	33	19	2	0	257^2	247	30	64	113	10.9	3.04	129	.258	.304	10	.112	-5	26	25	-1	1.7
1952	*Bro-N†	11	2	.846	27	25	8	2	0	158^2	163	16	39	83	11.6	3.12	117	.270	.317	4	.070	-3	11	9	-1	0.2
1953	*Bro-N	11	3	.786	25	24	9	1	0	157	171	27	40	85	12.2	4.36	98	.278	.323	3	.053	-4	-1	-2	1	-0.5
1954	Bro-N	3	4	.429	15	10	1	0	0	63	69	11	23	31	13.1	5.00	82	.279	.341	3	.143	-0	-7	-6	-0	-0.7
Total	12	127	84	.602	333	261	101	17	10	1914^1	1907	199	504	956	11.4	3.43	116	.261	.310	68	.110	-27	108	115	-9	7.5
● **CLAY ROE**	Roe, James Clay "Shad" b: 1/7/04, Greenbriar, Tenn. d: 4/4/56, Cleveland, Miss. BL/TL, 6'1", 180 lbs. Deb: 10/3/23																									
1923	Was-A	0	1	.000	1	1	0	0	0	1^2	0	0	6	2	32.4	0.00	—	.000	.500	0	—	0	1	1	-0	0.5
● **ED ROEBUCK**	Roebuck, Edward Jack b: 7/3/31, East Millsboro, Pa. BR/TR, 6'2", 185 lbs. Deb: 4/18/55																									
1955	*Bro-N	5	6	.455	47	0	0	0	12	84	96	14	24	33	13.2	4.71	86	.288	.342	2	.111	-1	-6	-6	1	-0.9
1956	*Bro-N	5	4	.556	43	0	0	0	1	89^1	83	15	29	60	11.5	3.93	101	.251	.315	6	.333	2	-2	0	1	0.3
1957	Bro-N	8	2	.800	44	1	0	0	8	96^1	70	9	46	73	11.0	2.71	154	.205	.303	5	.238	2	13	**16**	2	2.3
1958	LA-N	0	1	.000	32	0	0	0	5	44	45	9	15	26	12.7	3.48	118	.271	.339	2	.500	1	2	3	-0	0.2
1960	LA-N	8	3	.727	58	0	0	0	8	116^2	109	13	38	77	11.3	2.78	143	.256	.317	4	.167	-0	13	15	2	1.8
1961	LA-N	2	0	1.000	5	0	0	0	0	9	12	1	2	9	14.0	5.00	87	.324	.359	0	.000	-0	-1	-1	0	-0.2
1962	LA-N	10	2	.833	64	0	0	0	9	119^1	102	11	54	72	12.2	3.09	117	.232	.325	6	.214	1	11	7	0	0.9
1963	LA-N	2	4	.333	29	0	0	0	0	40^1	54	4	21	26	17.2	4.24	71	.321	.403	1	.250	0	-4	-5	1	-0.7
	Was-A	2	1	.667	26	0	0	0	4	57^1	63	5	29	25	14.8	3.30	113	.284	.372	2	.182	0	2	3	1	0.2
1964	Was-A	0	0	—	2	0	0	0	0	1	0	0	2	0	18.0	9.00	41	.000	.333	0	—	0	-1	-1	0	0.0
	Phi-N	5	3	.625	60	0	0	0	12	77^1	55	7	25	42	9.8	2.21	157	.196	.272	0	.000	-1	11	11	1	1.5
1965	Phi-N	5	3	.625	44	0	0	0	3	50^1	55	2	15	29	13.4	3.40	102	.288	.355	0	.000	-0	1	0	-1	-0.1
1966	Phi-N	0	2	.000	6	0	0	0	0	6	9	0	2	5	16.5	6.00	60	.333	.379	0	—	0	-2	-2	-0	-0.5
Total	11	52	31	.627	460	1	0	0	62	791	753	90	302	477	12.3	3.35	114	.254	.329	28	.204	3	38	41	7	4.8
● **MIKE ROESLER**	Roesler, Michael Joseph b: 9/12/63, Fort Wayne, Ind. BR/TR, 6'5", 195 lbs. Deb: 8/9/89																									
1989	Cin-N	0	1	.000	17	0	0	0	0	25	22	4	9	14	11.2	3.96	91	.239	.307	0	—	0	-1	-1	-1	-0.1
1990	Pit-N	1	0	1.000	5	0	0	0	0	6	5	1	2	4	10.5	3.00	121	.217	.280	0	.000	-0	1	0	-0	0.0
Total	2	1	1	.500	22	0	0	0	0	31	27	5	11	18	11.0	3.77	96	.235	.302	0	.000	-0	-1	-1	-1	-0.1
● **OSCAR ROETTGER**	Roettger, Oscar Frederick Louis "Okkie" b: 2/19/1900, St.Louis, Mo. d: 7/4/86, St.Louis, Mo. BR/TR, 6', 170 lbs. Deb: 7/7/23 F♦																									
1923	NY-A	0	0	—	5	0	0	0	1	11^2	16	3	12	7	22.4	8.49	46	.340	.483	0	.000	-0	-6	-6	0	-0.1
1924	NY-A	0	0	—	1	0	0	0	0	0	1	0	2	0	—	—	—	1.000	1.000	0	—	0	0	0	0	0.0
Total	2	0	0	—	6	0	0	0	1	11^2	17	3	14	7	24.7	8.49	46	.354	.508	14	.212	-0	-6	-6	0	-0.1
● **JOE ROGALSKI**	Rogalski, Joseph Anthony b: 7/16/15, Ashland, Wis. d: 11/20/51, Ashland, Wis. BR/TR, 6'2", 187 lbs. Deb: 9/14/38																									
1938	Det-A	0	0	—	2	0	0	0	0	7	12	0	0	2	15.4	2.57	194	.400	.400	0	.000	-0	2	2	-0	0.0
● **KEVIN ROGERS**	Rogers, Charles Kevin b: 8/20/68, Cleveland, Miss. BB/TL, 6'2", 190 lbs. Deb: 9/4/92																									
1992	SF-N	0	2	.000	6	6	0	0	0	34	37	4	13	26	13.5	4.24	78	.280	.349	2	.222	0	-3	-4	-1	-0.2
1993	SF-N	2	2	.500	64	0	0	0	0	80^2	71	3	28	62	11.5	2.68	146	.236	.309	0	.000	-0	12	11	-1	0.4
1994	SF-N	0	0	—	9	0	0	0	0	10^1	10	1	6	7	13.9	3.48	115	.250	.348	0	—	0	1	1	-0	0.0
Total	3	2	4	.333	79	6	0	0	0	125	118	8	47	95	12.2	3.17	118	.249	.324	2	.167	-0	10	8	-2	0.2
● **JIMMY ROGERS**	Rogers, James Randall b: 1/3/67, Tulsa, Okla. BR/TR, 6'2", 190 lbs. Deb: 7/30/95																									
1995	Tor-A	2	4	.333	19	0	0	0	0	23^2	21	4	18	13	14.8	5.70	83	.239	.368	0	—	0	-3	-3	-0	-0.6
● **KENNY ROGERS**	Rogers, Kenneth Scott b: 11/10/64, Savannah, Ga. BL/TL, 6'1", 205 lbs. Deb: 4/6/89																									
1989	Tex-A	3	4	.429	73	0	0	0	2	73^2	60	2	42	63	13.0	2.93	135	.232	.348	0	—	0	8	8	2	1.0
1990	Tex-A	10	6	.625	69	3	0	0	15	97^2	93	6	42	74	12.5	3.13	125	.249	.326	0	—	0	8	9	2	1.7
1991	Tex-A	10	10	.500	63	9	0	0	5	109^2	121	14	61	73	15.4	5.42	74	.281	.378	0	—	0	-16	-17	-0	-2.8
1992	Tex-A	3	6	.333	**81**	0	0	0	6	78^2	80	7	26	70	12.1	3.09	123	.261	.319	0	—	0	7	6	1	1.1
1993	Tex-A	16	10	.615	35	33	5	0	0	208^1	210	18	71	140	12.3	4.10	101	.263	.326	0	—	0	5	1	4	0.8
1994	Tex-A	11	8	.579	24	24	6	2	0	167^1	169	24	52	120	12.0	4.46	108	.260	.318	0	—	0	6	7	2	0.9

YEAR	TM/L	W	L	PCT	G	GS	CG	SH	SV	IP	H	HR	BB	SO	RAT	ERA	ERA+	OAV	OOB	BH	AVG	PB	PR	/A	PD	TPI
1995	Tex-A★	17	7	.708	31	31	3	1	0	208	192	26	76	140	11.7	3.38	143	.243	.311	0	—	0	31	34	1	3.6
1996	*NY-A	12	8	.600	30	30	2	1	0	179	179	16	83	92	13.6	4.68	106	.261	.347	0	—	0	6	5	2	0.7
1997	NY-A	6	7	.462	31	22	1	0	0	145	161	18	62	78	14.3	5.65	79	.280	.357	0	.000	-0	-17	-19	5	-1.0
1998	Oak-A	16	8	.667	34	34	7	1	0	238^2	215	19	67	138	10.9	3.17	144	.242	.301	0	.000	-0	39	37	7	4.0
Total	10	104	74	.584	471	186	24	5	28	1506	1480	150	582	988	12.6	4.03	110	.257	.330	0	.000	-1	78	70	27	10.0
● LEE ROGERS Rogers, Lee Otis "Buck" b: 10/8/13, Tuscaloosa, Ala. d: 11/23/95, Little Rock, Ark. BR/TL, 5'11", 170 lbs. Deb: 4/27/38																										
1938	Bos-A	1	1	.500	14	2	0	0	0	27^2	32	4	18	7	16.3	6.51	76	.302	.403	0	.000	-0	-5	-5	1	-0.2
	Bro-N	0	2	.000	12	2	0	0	0	23^2	23	0	10	11	12.9	5.70	68	.256	.337	0	.000	0	-5	-5	1	-0.2
Total	1	1	3	.250	26	4	0	0	0	51^1	55	4	28	18	14.7	6.14	73	.281	.373	0	.000	0	-10	-10	2	-0.4
● BUCK ROGERS Rogers, Orlin Woodrow "Lefty" b: 11/5/12, Spring Garden, Va. BR/TL, 5'8.5", 164 lbs. Deb: 9/15/35																										
1935	Was-A	0	1	.000	2	1	0	0	0	10	16	0	6	7	19.8	7.20	60	.340	.415	0	.000	-1	-3	-3	-0	-0.3
● STEVE ROGERS Rogers, Stephen Douglas b: 10/26/49, Jefferson City, Mo. BR/TR, 6'1", 182 lbs. Deb: 7/18/73																										
1973	Mon-N	10	5	.667	17	17	7	3	0	134	93	5	49	64	9.6	1.54	247	.199	.276	4	.098	-1	31	34	1	4.1
1974	Mon-N☆	15	22	.405	38	38	11	1	0	253^2	255	19	80	154	12.1	4.47	86	.265	.324	11	.139	-1	-24	-18	3	-2.2
1975	Mon-N	11	12	.478	35	35	12	3	0	251^2	248	13	88	137	12.2	3.29	116	.260	.325	13	.169	1	9	15	0	1.5
1976	Mon-N	7	17	.292	33	32	8	4	1	230	212	10	69	150	11.2	3.21	116	.250	.309	11	.149	-2	7	13	5	1.7
1977	Mon-N	17	16	.515	40	40	17	4	0	301^2	272	16	81	206	10.7	3.10	123	.242	.296	10	.104	-5	27	24	4	2.3
1978	Mon-N★	13	10	.565	30	29	11	1	1	219	186	12	64	126	10.4	2.47	143	.235	.294	8	.113	-2	27	26	1	2.6
1979	Mon-N★	13	12	.520	37	37	13	**5**	0	248^2	232	14	78	143	11.4	3.00	122	.251	.312	12	.156	1	20	18	2	2.1
1980	Mon-N	16	11	.593	37	37	**14**	4	0	281	247	16	85	147	10.7	2.98	120	.238	.298	13	.160	1	19	18	-1	1.7
1981	*Mon-N	12	8	.600	22	22	7	3	0	160^2	149	7	41	87	10.8	3.42	102	.248	.298	8	.145	-1	1	1	-1	0.0
1982	Mon-N★	19	8	.704	35	35	14	4	0	277	245	12	65	179	10.3	**2.40**	**151**	.237	.286	11	.129	0	**37**	**38**	0	3.7
1983	Mon-N☆	17	12	.586	36	36	13	**5**	0	273	258	14	78	146	11.2	3.23	111	.252	.308	12	.146	-1	12	11	-2	0.8
1984	Mon-N	6	15	.286	31	28	1	0	0	169^1	171	12	78	64	13.3	4.31	80	.267	.348	7	.143	1	-13	-17	0	-1.8
1985	Mon-N	2	4	.333	8	7	1	0	0	38	51	1	20	18	16.8	5.68	60	.329	.406	2	.143	0	-9	-10	1	-1.2
Total	13	158	152	.510	399	393	129	37	2	2837^2	2619	151	876	1621	11.2	3.17	115	.248	.308	122	.138	-8	146	154	14	15.3
● TOM ROGERS Rogers, Thomas Andrew "Shotgun" b: 2/12/1892, Sparta, Tenn. d: 3/7/36, Nashville, Tenn. BR/TR, 6'0.5", 180 lbs. Deb: 4/14/17																										
1917	StL-A	3	6	.333	24	8	3	0	0	108^2	112	2	44	27	13.2	3.89	67	.277	.352	5	.172	-1	-15	-16	-0	-1.4
1918	StL-A	8	10	.444	29	16	11	0	2	154	148	3	49	29	11.7	3.27	84	.267	.330	13	.245	2	-8	-9	2	-0.7
1919	StL-A	0	1	.000	2	0	0	0	0	1	7	0	0	1	63.0	27.00	12	.700	.700	0	—	0	-3	-3	0	-1.6
	Phi-A	4	12	.250	23	18	7	1	0	140	152	9	60	37	13.8	4.31	80	.292	.369	11	.224	-0	-17	-14	4	-1.0
	Yr	4	13	.235	25	18	7	1	0	141	159	9	60	38	14.2	4.47	77	.300	.374	11	.224	-0	-19	-16	4	-2.6
1921	*NY-A	0	1	.000	5	0	0	0	1	11	12	1	9	0	18.0	7.36	58	.300	.440	1	.333	0	-4	-4	1	-0.3
Total	4	15	30	.333	83	42	21	1	3	414^2	431	15	162	94	13.1	3.95	75	.282	.354	30	.224	1	-46	-45	6	-5.0
● CLINT ROGGE Rogge, Francis Clinton b: 7/19/1889, Memphis, Mich. d: 1/6/69, Mt.Clemens, Mich. BL/TR, 5'10", 185 lbs. Deb: 4/11/15																										
1915	Pit-F	17	11	.607	37	31	17	5	0	254^1	240	6	93	93	12.1	2.55	106	.257	.330	14	.173	-1	5	5	1	0.5
1921	Cin-N	1	2	.333	6	2	0	0	0	35^1	43	2	9	12	13.2	4.08	88	.307	.349	1	.100	0	-1	-2	0	-0.1
Total	2	18	13	.581	43	33	17	5	0	289^2	283	8	102	105	12.2	2.73	103	.264	.332	15	.165	-1	4	3	1	0.4
● GARRY ROGGENBURK Roggenburk, Garry Earl b: 4/16/40, Cleveland, Ohio BR/TL, 6'6", 195 lbs. Deb: 4/20/63																										
1963	Min-A	2	4	.333	36	2	0	0	4	50	47	3	22	24	13.3	2.16	169	.253	.347	1	.143	0	8	8	1	1.2
1965	Min-A	1	0	1.000	12	0	0	0	2	21	21	1	12	6	14.1	3.43	104	.266	.363	0	.000	-0	0	0	-1	0.0
1966	Min-A	1	2	.333	12	0	0	0	1	12^1	14	4	10	3	17.5	5.84	62	.292	.414	0	—	0	-3	-3	0	-0.7
	Bos-A	0	0	—	1	0	0	0	0	0^1	1	0	1	0	54.0	0.00	—	.500	.667	0	—	0	0	0	0	0.0
	Yr	1	2	.333	13	0	0	0	1	12^2	15	4	11	3	18.5	5.68	63	.300	.426	0	—	0	-3	-3	0	-0.7
1968	Bos-A	0	0	—	4	0	0	0	0	8^1	9	0	3	4	13.0	2.16	146	.257	.316	0	—	0	1	1	-0	0.0
1969	Bos-A	0	1	.000	7	0	0	0	0	9^2	13	1	5	8	17.7	8.38	45	.342	.432	0	.000	-0	-5	-5	0	-0.5
	Sea-A	2	2	.500	7	4	1	0	0	24^1	27	6	11	11	14.4	4.44	82	.276	.355	1	.125	-0	-2	-2	-0	-0.4
	Yr	2	3	.400	14	4	1	0	0	34	40	7	16	19	15.1	5.56	66	.292	.370	1	.100	-1	-7	-7	0	-0.9
Total	5	6	9	.400	79	6	1	0	7	126	132	15	64	56	14.5	3.64	99	.272	.364	2	.100	-1	-1	-1	0	-0.4
● SAUL ROGOVIN Rogovin, Saul Walter b: 10/10/23, Brooklyn, N.Y. d: 1/23/95, New York, N.Y. BR/TR, 6'2", 205 lbs. Deb: 4/28/49																										
1949	Det-A	0	1	.000	5	0	0	0	0	5^2	13	1	7	2	31.8	14.29	29	.464	.571	0	—	0	-6	-6	-0	-0.9
1950	Det-A	2	1	.667	11	5	1	0	0	40	39	5	26	11	15.1	4.50	104	.258	.374	3	.188	0	0	1	-1	0.0
1951	Det-A	1	1	.500	5	4	0	0	0	24	23	4	7	5	11.3	5.25	80	.247	.300	2	.286	1	-3	-3	0	-0.1
	Chi-A	11	7	.611	22	22	17	3	0	192^2	166	11	67	77	10.9	2.48	163	.234	.301	15	.203	-0	35	33	-1	2.9
	Yr	12	8	.600	27	26	17	3	0	216^2	189	15	74	82	11.0	**2.78**	**146**	.235	.301	17	.210	1	32	**31**	-0	2.8
1952	Chi-A	14	9	.609	33	30	12	3	1	231^2	224	14	79	121	11.9	3.85	95	.255	.318	17	.202	3	-4	-5	-0	-0.2
1953	Chi-A	7	12	.368	22	19	4	1	1	131	151	17	48	62	13.8	5.22	77	.289	.351	5	.135	-0	-18	-17	-0	-2.2
1955	Bal-A	1	8	.111	14	12	1	0	0	71	79	5	27	35	13.7	4.56	84	.288	.356	2	.091	-1	-5	-6	-0	-0.9
	Phi-N	5	3	.625	12	11	5	2	0	73	60	3	17	27	9.5	3.08	129	.230	.277	6	.250	2	8	7	-1	0.9
1956	Phi-N	7	6	.538	22	18	3	0	0	106^2	122	22	27	48	12.6	4.98	75	.282	.325	4	.111	-2	-14	-15	-1	-1.9
1957	Phi-N	0	0	—	4	0	0	0	0	8	11	1	3	0	15.8	9.00	42	.333	.389	0	—	0	-5	-5	-0	0.0
Total	8	48	48	.500	150	121	43	9	2	883^2	888	83	308	388	12.3	4.06	96	.262	.326	54	.180	2	-12	-16	-4	-2.4
● LES ROHR Rohr, Leslie Norvin b: 3/5/46, Lowestoft, England BL/TL, 6'5", 205 lbs. Deb: 9/19/67																										
1967	NY-N	2	1	.667	3	3	0	0	0	17	13	1	9	15	11.6	2.12	160	.224	.328	0	.000	-1	2	2	-1	0.3
1968	NY-N	0	2	.000	2	1	0	0	0	6	9	0	7	5	24.0	4.50	67	.333	.471	0	—	0	-1	-1	0	-0.3
1969	NY-N	0	0	—	1	0	0	0	0	1^1	5	0	1	0	40.5	20.25	18	.625	.667	0	—	0	-2	-2	-0	0.0
Total	3	2	3	.400	6	4	0	0	0	24^1	27	1	17	20	16.3	3.70	90	.290	.400	0	.000	-0	-1	-1	-1	0.0
● BILLY ROHR Rohr, William Joseph b: 7/1/45, San Diego, Cal. BL/TL, 6'3", 170 lbs. Deb: 4/14/67																										
1967	Bos-A	2	3	.400	10	8	2	1	0	42^1	43	4	22	16	14.2	5.10	68	.256	.349	0	.000	-1	-9	-8	-0	-0.9
1968	Cle-A	1	0	1.000	17	0	0	0	1	18^1	18	5	10	5	13.7	6.87	43	.265	.359	0	.000	-0	-8	-8	0	-0.6
Total	2	3	3	.500	27	8	2	1	1	60^2	61	9	32	21	14.1	5.64	59	.258	.352	0	.000	-1	-17	-16	-0	-1.5
● MEL ROJAS Rojas, Melquiades (Medrano) b: 12/10/66, Haina, D.R. BR/TR, 5'11", 185 lbs. Deb: 8/1/90																										
1990	Mon-N	3	1	.750	23	0	0	0	1	40	34	5	24	26	13.5	3.60	101	.234	.351	0	.000	-0	1	0	-0	-0.1
1991	Mon-N	3	3	.500	37	0	0	0	6	48	42	4	13	37	10.5	3.75	96	.228	.283	0	.000	-0	-0	-1	-0	-0.2
1992	Mon-N	7	1	.875	68	0	0	0	10	100^2	71	2	34	70	9.6	1.43	242	.199	.272	1	.067	-1	**23**	**23**	-0	2.1
1993	Mon-N	5	8	.385	66	0	0	0	10	88^1	80	6	30	48	11.6	2.95	141	.242	.313	1	.083	-1	11	12	-1	1.7
1994	Mon-N	3	2	.600	58	0	0	0	16	84	71	11	21	84	10.3	3.32	127	.227	.284	2	.200	0	8	8	0	0.8
1995	Mon-N	1	4	.200	59	0	0	0	30	67^2	69	2	29	61	14.0	4.12	104	.262	.351	0	.000	-1	0	1	-0	0.1
1996	Mon-N	7	4	.636	74	0	0	0	36	81	56	5	28	92	9.6	3.22	134	.193	.269	3	.375	1	9	10	1	2.1
1997	Chi-N	0	4	.000	54	0	0	0	13	59	54	11	30	61	13.6	4.42	97	.244	.348	0	.000	-0	-1	-1	-1	-0.2
	NY-N	0	2	.000	23	0	0	0	2	26^1	24	4	6	32	10.9	5.13	79	.235	.291	0	—	0	-3	-3	-0	-0.3
	Yr	0	6	.000	77	0	0	0	15	85^1	78	15	36	93	12.2	4.64	91	.237	.316	0	.000	-0	-4	-4	-1	-0.5
1998	NY-N	5	2	.714	50	0	0	0	2	58	68	9	30	41	15.7	6.05	69	.305	.395	0	—	0	-12	-12	1	-1.3
Total	9	34	31	.523	512	0	0	0	126	653	569	59	245	552	11.7	3.51	115	.234	.313	7	.119	-2	36	37	-1	4.7
● MINNIE ROJAS Rojas, Minervino Alejandro (Landin) b: 11/26/38, Remidios, Las Villas, Cuba BR/TR, 6'1", 170 lbs. Deb: 5/30/66																										
1966	Cal-A	7	4	.636	47	2	0	0	10	84^1	83	9	15	37	10.6	2.88	117	.262	.297	1	.071	-0	5	4	-1	0.5
1967	Cal-A	12	9	.571	72	0	0	0	**27**	121^2	106	7	38	83	10.9	2.52	125	.232	.296	1	.059	-1	10	8	-2	1.6
1968	Cal-A	4	3	.571	38	0	0	0	6	55	55	11	15	33	11.5	4.25	68	.252	.300	1	.100	-0	-8	-8	-1	-1.4
Total	3	23	16	.590	157	2	0	0	43	261	244	27	68	153	10.9	3.00	105	.246	.297	3	.073	-2	7	5	-4	0.7

YEAR	TM/L	W	L	PCT	G	GS	CG	SH	SV	IP	H	HR	BB	SO	RAT	ERA	ERA+	OAV	OOB	BH	AVG	PB	PR	/A	PD	TPI
● **COOKIE ROJAS**	Rojas, Octavio Victor (Rivas) b: 3/6/39, Havana, Cuba BR/TR, 5'10", 170 lbs. Deb: 4/10/62 MC♦																									
1967	Phi-N	0	0	—	1	0	0	0	0	1	1	0	0	0	9.0	0.00	—	.200	.200	137	.259	0	0	0	-0	0.0
● **JIM ROLAND**	Roland, James Ivan b: 12/14/42, Franklin, N.C. BR/TL, 6'3", 190 lbs. Deb: 9/20/62																									
1962	Min-A	0	0	—	1	0	0	0	0	2	1	0	0	1	4.5	0.00	—	.143	.143	0	—	0	1	1	-0	0.0
1963	Min-A	4	1	.800	10	7	2	1	0	49	32	4	27	34	10.8	2.57	142	.185	.295	0	.000	-2	6	6	0	0.4
1964	Min-A	2	6	.250	30	13	1	0	3	94^{1}	76	12	55	63	12.9	4.10	87	.218	.332	4	.148	-1	-5	-6	-1	-0.7
1966	Min-A	0	0	—	1	0	0	0	0	2	0	0	0	1	0.0	0.00	—	.000	.000	0	—	0	1	1	-0	0.0
1967	Min-A	0	1	.000	25	0	0	0	2	35^{2}	33	3	17	16	12.6	3.03	114	.244	.329	0	.000	-0	1	2	-0	0.0
1968	Min-A	4	1	.800	28	4	1	0	0	61^{2}	55	3	24	36	11.8	3.50	88	.238	.315	0	.000	-1	-4	-3	1	-0.2
1969	Oak-A	5	1	.833	39	3	2	0	1	86^{1}	59	2	46	48	11.6	2.19	157	.197	.316	2	.095	-1	14	12	0	0.7
1970	Oak-A	3	3	.500	28	2	0	0	2	43^{1}	28	2	23	26	10.6	2.70	131	.181	.287	0	.000	-0	5	4	1	0.6
1971	Oak-A	1	3	.250	31	0	0	0	1	45^{1}	34	4	19	30	11.5	3.18	105	.214	.317	0	.000	-0	1	1	-1	0.0
1972	Oak-A	0	0	—	2	0	0	0	0	2^{1}	5	0	0	0	19.3	3.86	74	.455	.455	0	—	0	-0	-0	0	0.0
	NY-A	0	1	.000	16	0	0	0	0	25	27	3	16	13	15.8	5.04	58	.287	.396	0	.000	-0	-6	-6	-0	-0.3
	Tex-A	0	0	—	5	0	0	0	0	3^{1}	7	1	2	4	27.0	8.10	37	.412	.500	0	—	0	-2	-2	-0	0.0
	Yr	0	1	.000	23	0	0	0	0	30^{2}	39	4	18	17	17.0	5.28	56	.317	.408	0	.000	-0	-8	-8	-0	-0.3
Total	10	19	17	.528	216	29	6	1	9	450^{1}	357	34	229	272	12.1	3.22	106	.218	.321	6	.071	-5	12	10	-1	0.5
● **JOSE ROMAN**	Roman, Jose Rafael (Sarita) b: 5/21/63, Santo Domingo, D.R. BR/TR, 6', 175 lbs. Deb: 9/5/84																									
1984	Cle-A	0	2	.000	3	2	0	0	0	6	9	1	11	3	30.0	18.00	23	.391	.588	0	—	0	-9	-9	-0	-2.0
1985	Cle-A	0	4	.000	5	3	0	0	0	16^{1}	13	3	14	12	14.9	6.61	63	.200	.342	0	—	0	-4	-4	-0	-0.9
1986	Cle-A	1	2	.333	6	5	0	0	0	22	23	3	17	9	16.8	6.55	63	.280	.410	0	—	0	-6	-6	-1	-0.7
Total	3	1	8	.111	14	10	0	0	0	44^{1}	45	7	42	24	17.9	8.12	51	.265	.413	0	—	0	-20	-20	-1	-3.6
● **RON ROMANICK**	Romanick, Ronald James b: 11/6/60, Burley, Idaho BR/TR, 6'4", 195 lbs. Deb: 4/5/84																									
1984	Cal-A	12	12	.500	33	33	8	2	0	229^{2}	240	23	61	87	12.0	3.76	105	.270	.320	0	—	0	6	5	-2	0.3
1985	Cal-A	14	9	.609	31	31	6	1	0	195	210	29	62	64	12.7	4.11	100	.280	.338	0	—	0	1	0	-3	-0.3
1986	Cal-A	5	8	.385	18	18	1	1	0	106^{1}	124	13	44	38	14.2	5.50	75	.297	.364	0	—	0	-16	-16	-1	-1.8
Total	3	31	29	.517	82	82	15	4	0	531	574	65	167	189	12.7	4.24	96	.279	.336	0	—	0	-9	-11	-6	-1.8
● **JIM ROMANO**	Romano, James King b: 4/6/27, Brooklyn, N.Y. d: 9/12/90, New York, N.Y. BR/TR, 6'4", 190 lbs. Deb: 9/21/50																									
1950	Bro-N	0	0	—	3	1	0	0	0	6^{1}	8	0	2	8	14.2	5.68	72	.296	.345	0	.000	-0	-1	-1	0	0.0
● **DUTCH ROMBERGER**	Romberger, Allen Isaiah b: 5/26/27, Klingerstown, Pa. d: 5/26/83, Weikert, Pa. BR/TR, 6', 185 lbs. Deb: 5/31/54																									
1954	Phi-A	1	1	.500	10	0	0	0	0	15^{2}	28	3	12	6	23.0	11.49	34	.406	.494	0	.000	0	-14	-13	-0	-1.5
● **RAMON ROMERO**	Romero, Ramon (De Los Santos) b: 1/8/59, San Pedro De Macoris, D.R. BL/TL, 6'4", 170 lbs. Deb: 9/18/84																									
1984	Cle-A	0	0	—	1	0	0	0	0	3	0	0	0	3	3.0	0.00	—	.000	.111	0	—	0	1	1	-0	-0.1
1985	Cle-A	2	3	.400	19	10	0	0	0	64^{1}	69	13	38	38	15.7	6.58	63	.276	.382	0	—	0	-17	-17	-1	-1.2
Total	2	2	3	.400	20	10	0	0	0	67^{1}	69	13	38	41	15.1	6.28	66	.267	.374	0	—	0	-16	-16	-1	-1.3
● **EDDIE ROMMEL**	Rommel, Edwin Americus b: 9/13/1897, Baltimore, Md. d: 8/26/70, Baltimore, Md. BR/TR, 6'2", 197 lbs. Deb: 4/19/20 CU																									
1920	Phi-A	7	7	.500	33	12	8	2	1	173^{2}	165	5	43	43	11.0	2.85	141	.259	.309	11	.216	-0	18	23	5	2.2
1921	Phi-A	16	23	.410	46	32	20	0	3	285^{1}	312	21	87	71	12.6	3.94	113	.284	.337	18	.191	-2	11	16	3	2.0
1922	Phi-A	**27**	13	.675	**51**	33	22	3	2	294	294	21	63	54	11.1	3.28	130	.267	.309	17	.181	-3	25	32	3	4.0
1923	Phi-A	18	19	.486	**56**	31	19	3	5	297^{2}	306	14	108	76	12.6	3.27	126	.271	.336	24	.238	1	24	28	6	**4.0**
1924	Phi-A	18	15	.545	43	34	21	3	1	278	302	8	94	72	12.9	3.95	108	.284	.344	15	.158	-6	9	10	8	1.2
1925	Phi-A	**21**	10	.677	52	28	14	1	3	261	285	10	95	67	13.3	3.69	126	.281	.346	15	.185	-1	20	28	5	3.3
1926	Phi-A	11	11	.500	37	26	12	3	0	219	225	10	54	52	11.5	3.08	135	.268	.314	6	.098	-4	23	26	2	2.3
1927	Phi-A	11	3	.786	30	17	8	2	1	146^{2}	166	6	48	33	13.3	4.36	98	.286	.343	8	.157	-2	-4	-2	3	-0.1
1928	Phi A	13	5	.722	43	11	6	0	4	173^{2}	177	11	26	37	10.6	3.06	131	.266	.295	12	.255	3	19	18	3	2.3
1929	*Phi-A	12	2	.857	32	6	4	0	4	113^{2}	135	10	34	25	13.5	2.85	148	.294	.344	8	.205	-0	18	17	1	2.0
1930	Phi-A	9	4	.692	35	9	5	0	3	130^{1}	142	11	27	35	11.7	4.28	109	.277	.315	10	.263	3	5	6	1	0.9
1931	*Phi-A	7	5	.583	25	10	8	1	0	118	136	5	27	18	12.5	2.97	151	.291	.331	14	.259	2	18	20	-0	1.9
1932	Phi-A	1	2	.333	17	0	0	0	2	65^{1}	84	6	18	16	14.1	5.51	82	.315	.358	6	.300	2	-7	-7	2	0.0
Total	13	171	119	.590	500	249	147	18	29	2556^{1}	2729	138	724	599	12.3	3.54	122	.277	.329	164	.199	-7	179	217	42	26.0
● **ENRIQUE ROMO**	Romo, Enrique (Navarro) b: 7/15/47, Santa Rosalia, Mex BR/TR, 5'11", 185 lbs. Deb: 4/7/77 F																									
1977	Sea-A	8	10	.444	58	3	0	0	16	114^{1}	93	8	39	105	10.8	2.83	145	.227	.302	0	—	0	16	16	1	3.0
1978	Sea-A	11	7	.611	56	0	0	0	10	107^{1}	88	12	39	62	11.1	3.69	103	.227	.306	0	—	0	1	1	-1	0.1
1979	*Pit-N	10	5	.667	84	0	0	0	5	129^{1}	122	11	43	106	11.7	2.99	130	.253	.318	2	.167	-0	11	13	2	1.7
1980	Pit-N	5	5	.500	74	0	0	0	11	123^{2}	117	10	28	82	10.6	3.27	111	.252	.296	5	.455	3	4	5	1	0.9
1981	Pit-N	1	3	.250	33	0	0	0	9	41^{2}	47	5	18	23	14.0	4.54	79	.288	.359	0	.000	-0	-5	-4	-0	-0.7
1982	Pit-N	9	3	.750	45	0	0	0	1	86^{2}	81	11	36	58	12.3	4.36	85	.245	.322	3	.300	1	-7	-6	-0	-0.8
Total	6	44	33	.571	350	3	0	0	52	603	548	57	203	436	11.4	3.45	111	.245	.312	10	.270	4	19	25	2	4.2
● **VICENTE ROMO**	Romo, Vicente (Navarro) "Huevo" b: 4/12/43, Santa Rosalia, Mex. BR/TR, 6'1", 195 lbs. Deb: 4/11/68 F																									
1968	LA-N	0	0	—	1	0	0	0	0	1	1	0	0	0	9.0	0.00	—	.250	.250	0	—	0	0	0	-0	0.0
	Cle-A	5	3	.625	40	1	0	0	12	83^{1}	43	5	32	54	8.3	1.62	183	.154	.245	2	.143	-0	13	12	-0	1.7
1969	Cle-A	1	1	.500	3	0	0	0	0	8	7	0	3	7	11.3	2.25	167	.233	.303	1	.500	0	1	1	-0	0.4
	Bos-A	7	9	.438	52	11	4	1	11	127^{1}	116	14	50	89	11.8	3.18	120	.247	.321	4	.129	-1	6	9	0	1.2
	Yr	8	10	.444	55	11	4	1	11	135^{1}	123	14	53	96	11.8	3.13	122	.246	.319	5	.152	-0	7	10	0	1.6
1970	Bos-A	7	3	.700	48	10	0	0	6	108	115	14	43	71	13.2	4.08	97	.273	.340	4	.148	0	-4	-1	1	0.0
1971	Chi-A	1	7	.125	45	2	0	0	5	72	52	5	37	48	11.1	3.38	106	.202	.303	4	.364	1	1	2	1	0.5
1972	Chi-A	3	0	1.000	28	0	0	0	1	51^{2}	47	5	18	46	11.5	3.31	94	.246	.314	0	.000	-1	-1	-1	1	-0.1
1973	SD-N	2	3	.400	49	1	0	0	7	87^{2}	85	11	46	51	13.4	3.70	94	.260	.351	2	.125	-0	-0	-2	0	-0.1
1974	SD-N	5	5	.500	54	1	0	0	9	71	78	6	37	26	14.8	4.56	78	.290	.380	0	.000	-1	-7	-8	2	-1.2
1982	LA-N	1	2	.333	15	6	0	0	1	35^{2}	25	1	14	24	10.3	3.03	114	.195	.285	1	.200	0	2	2	1	0.2
Total	8	32	33	.492	335	32	4	1	52	645^{2}	569	61	280	416	11.9	3.36	106	.239	.322	18	.149	-1	10	13	5	2.6
● **JOHN ROMONOSKY**	Romonosky, John b: 7/7/29, Harrisburg, Ill. BR/TR, 6'2", 195 lbs. Deb: 9/6/53																									
1953	StL-N	0	0	—	2	2	0	0	0	7^{2}	9	1	4	3	16.4	4.70	91	.281	.378	0	.000	-0	-0	-0	-0	-0.1
1958	Was-A	2	4	.333	18	5	1	0	0	55^{1}	52	6	28	38	13.0	6.51	59	.243	.331	4	.308	2	-17	-17	0	-1.3
1959	Was-A	1	0	1.000	12	2	0	0	0	38^{1}	36	4	19	22	13.6	3.29	119	.254	.354	2	.182	0	2	3	-0	0.1
Total	3	3	4	.429	32	9	1	0	0	101^{1}	97	11	51	63	13.5	5.15	75	.250	.343	6	.231	2	-15	-14	-0	-1.3
● **GILBERTO RONDON**	Rondon, Gilberto b: 11/18/53, Bronx, N.Y. BR/TR, 6'2", 200 lbs. Deb: 4/10/76 F																									
1976	Hou-N	2	2	.500	19	7	0	0	0	53^{2}	70	6	39	21	18.3	5.70	56	.315	.418	4	.286	1	-13	-15	-1	-1.0
1979	Chi-A	0	0	—	4	0	0	0	0	9^{2}	11	2	6	3	15.8	3.72	114	.282	.378	0	—	0	1	1	-0	0.0
Total	2	2	2	.500	23	7	0	0	0	63^{1}	81	8	45	24	17.9	5.40	62	.310	.412	4	.286	1	-13	-14	-1	-1.0
● **JIM ROOKER**	Rooker, James Phillip b: 9/23/42, Lakeview, Ore. BR/TL, 6', 201 lbs. Deb: 6/30/68																									
1968	Det-A	0	0	—	2	0	0	0	0	4^{2}	4	0	1	4	9.6	3.86	78	.235	.278	0	.000	-0	-0	-0	0	0.0
1969	KC-A	4	16	.200	28	22	8	1	0	158^{1}	136	13	73	108	11.9	3.75	98	.229	.315	16	.281	8	-2	-1	-1	0.6
1970	KC-A	10	15	.400	38	29	6	3	1	203^{2}	190	11	102	117	12.9	3.54	106	.252	.341	14	.200	3	4	5	-0	0.9
1971	KC-A	2	7	.222	20	7	1	1	0	54	59	2	24	31	14.0	5.33	64	.284	.361	0	.000	-1	-11	-11	-1	-1.9
1972	KC-A	5	6	.455	18	10	4	2	0	72	78	3	24	44	12.9	4.38	69	.280	.339	2	.100	-1	-11	-11	1	-1.6
1973	Pit-N	10	6	.625	41	18	6	3	5	170^{1}	143	12	52	122	10.4	2.85	123	.229	.290	12	.245	3	15	13	1	1.6
1974	*Pit-N	15	11	.577	33	33	15	1	0	262^{2}	228	11	83	139	10.8	2.78	124	.238	.301	29	.305	11	25	20	1	3.2
1975	*Pit-N	13	11	.542	28	28	7	1	0	196^{2}	177	16	76	102	11.7	2.97	119	.238	.311	6	.095	-3	14	12	0	1.2
1976	Pit-N	15	8	.652	30	29	10	1	1	198^{2}	201	12	72	92	12.5	3.35	104	.263	.328	16	.216	3	3	3	-1	0.6

YEAR	TM/L	W	L	PCT	G	GS	CG	SH	SV	IP	H	HR	BB	SO	RAT	ERA	ERA+	OAV	OOB	BH	AVG	PB	PR	/A	PD	TPI
1977	Pit-N	14	9	.609	30	30	7	2	0	204^1	196	24	64	89	11.5	3.08	129	.253	.310	13	.186	0	19	20	-2	2.0
1978	Pit-N	9	11	.450	28	28	1	0	0	163^1	160	13	81	76	13.4	4.24	87	.259	.348	9	.161	0	-12	-10	1	-1.0
1979	*Pit-N	4	7	.364	19	17	1	0	0	103^2	106	11	39	44	12.6	4.60	84	.266	.331	4	.121	-1	-10	-8	-1	-1.0
1980	Pit-N	2	2	.500	4	4	0	0	0	18	16	0	12	8	14.0	3.50	104	.262	.384	1	.143	1	0	0	0	0.2
Total	13	103	109	.486	319	255	66	15	7	1810^1	1694	128	703	976	12.0	3.46	104	.249	.321	122	.201	23	34	30	-2	4.8
● CHARLIE ROOT Root, Charles Henry "Chinski" b: 3/17/1899, Middletown, Ohio d: 11/5/70, Hollister, Cal. BR/TR, 5'10.5", 190 lbs. Deb: 4/18/23 C																										
1923	StL-A	0	4	.000	27	2	0	0	0	60	68	4	18	27	13.8	5.70	73	.302	.369	1	.077	-1	-11	-10	-1	-0.7
1926	Chi-N	18	17	.514	42	32	21	2	2	271^1	267	10	62	127	11.1	2.82	136	.264	.310	13	.143	-4	30	31	-1	3.2
1927	Chi-N	**26**	15	.634	**48**	36	21	4	2	**309**	296	16	117	145	12.3	3.76	103	.254	.326	27	.221	3	6	4	-4	0.3
1928	Chi-N	14	18	.438	40	30	13	1	2	237	214	15	73	122	11.2	3.57	108	.242	.305	13	.178	-0	11	7	-3	0.6
1929	*Chi-N	19	6	**.760**	43	31	19	4	5	272	286	12	83	124	12.3	3.47	133	.275	.330	15	.156	0	38	35	-4	2.4
1930	Chi-N	16	14	.533	37	30	15	**4**	3	220^1	247	17	63	124	12.9	4.33	113	.281	.334	21	.262	5	16	14	-3	1.7
1931	Chi-N	17	14	.548	39	31	19	3	2	251	240	7	71	131	11.4	3.48	111	.252	.309	20	.222	3	11	11	-3	1.2
1932	*Chi-N	15	10	.600	39	23	11	0	3	216^1	211	10	55	96	11.3	3.58	105	.253	.303	13	.171	-1	7	5	-3	0.1
1933	Chi-N	15	10	.600	35	30	20	2	0	242^1	232	14	61	86	11.3	2.60	126	.252	.306	8	.094	-4	20	18	-3	1.0
1934	Chi-N	4	7	.364	34	9	2	0	0	117^2	141	8	53	46	15.2	4.28	90	.298	.375	7	.175	2	-3	-5	-1	-0.4
1935	*Chi-N	15	8	.652	38	18	11	1	2	201^1	193	15	47	94	10.9	3.08	127	.252	.298	14	.203	2	21	19	-3	1.9
1936	Chi-N	3	6	.333	33	4	0	0	1	73^2	81	3	20	32	12.6	4.15	96	.280	.331	5	.333	1	-1	-1	-1	-0.1
1937	Chi-N	13	5	.722	43	15	5	0	5	178^2	173	18	32	74	10.5	3.38	118	.253	.290	12	.179	0	11	12	-1	1.1
1938	*Chi-N	8	7	.533	44	11	5	0	8	160^2	163	10	30	70	10.9	2.86	134	.258	.294	8	.167	-0	17	17	-2	1.4
1939	Chi-N	8	8	.500	35	16	8	0	4	167^1	189	11	34	65	12.1	4.03	98	.286	.323	10	.175	2	-2	-2	-3	-0.3
1940	Chi-N	2	4	.333	36	8	1	0	1	112	118	9	33	50	12.2	3.86	97	.265	.317	4	.129	-1	-0	-1	-0	-0.2
1941	Chi-N	8	7	.533	19	15	6	0	0	106^2	133	8	37	46	14.3	5.40	65	.306	.360	5	.152	2	-21	-22	-1	-2.6
Total	17	201	160	.557	632	341	177	21	40	3197^1	3252	187	889	1459	11.9	3.59	110	.264	.318	196	.180	8	148	129	-35	10.6
● JOHN ROPER Roper, John Christopher b: 11/21/71, Southern Pines, N.C. BR/TR, 6', 175 lbs. Deb: 5/16/93																										
1993	Cin-N	2	5	.286	16	15	0	0	0	80	92	10	36	54	14.8	5.62	72	.295	.375	5	.179	-0	-14	-14	-0	-1.1
1994	Cin-N	6	2	.750	16	15	0	0	0	92	90	16	30	51	12.1	4.50	92	.255	.320	6	.182	0	-3	-4	-0	-0.3
1995	Cin-N	0	0	—	2	2	0	0	0	7	13	3	4	6	21.9	10.29	40	.406	.472	0	.000	-0	-5	-5	0	0.0
	SF-N	0	0	—	1	0	0	0	0	1	2	0	2	0	36.0	27.00	15	.500	.667	0	—	0	-3	-3	-0	0.0
	Yr	0	0	—	3	2	0	0	0	8	15	3	6	6	23.6	12.38	33	.417	.500	0	.000	-0	-7	-7	-0	0.0
Total	3	8	7	.533	35	32	0	0	0	180	197	29	72	111	13.9	5.35	76	.281	.355	11	.177	0	-24	-25	-1	-1.4
● RAFAEL ROQUE Roque, Rafael Antonio b: 1/1/72, Cotui, D.R. BL/TL, 6'4", 186 lbs. Deb: 8/1/98																										
1998	Mil-N	4	2	.667	9	9	0	0	0	48	42	9	24	34	12.6	4.88	88	.237	.332	1	.077	-1	-3	-3	1	-0.4
● JOSE ROSADO Rosado, Jose Antonio b: 11/9/74, Newark, N.J. BL/TL, 6', 175 lbs. Deb: 6/12/96																										
1996	KC-A	8	6	.571	16	16	2	1	0	106^2	101	7	26	64	11.1	3.21	156	.249	.300	0	—	0	21	21	-0	2.4
1997	KC-A★	9	12	.429	33	33	2	0	0	203^1	208	26	73	129	12.6	4.69	100	.264	.330	0	.000	-0	-3	0	-1	0.0
1998	KC-A	8	11	.421	38	25	2	1	1	174^2	180	25	57	135	12.5	4.69	105	.260	.321	1	.500	0	-1	4	1	0.5
Total	3	25	29	.463	87	74	6	2	1	484^2	489	58	156	328	12.2	4.36	111	.260	.321	1	.250	0	17	26	-0	2.9
● BRIAN ROSE Rose, Brian Leonard b: 2/13/76, New Bedford, Mass. BR/TR, 6'3", 215 lbs. Deb: 7/25/97																										
1997	Bos-A	0	0	—	1	1	0	0	0	3	5	0	2	3	21.0	12.00	39	.357	.438	0	—	0	-2	-2	-0	0.0
1998	Bos-A	1	4	.200	8	8	0	0	0	37^2	43	9	14	18	14.1	6.93	67	.285	.353	0	—	0	-10	-10	-0	-1.0
Total	2	1	4	.200	9	9	0	0	0	40^2	48	9	16	21	14.6	7.30	63	.291	.361	0	—	0	-12	-12	-0	-1.0
● CHUCK ROSE Rose, Charles Alfred b: 9/1/1885, Macon, Mo. d: 8/4/61, Salina, Kan. BL/TL, 5'8.5", 158 lbs. Deb: 9/13/09																										
1909	StL-A	1	2	.333	3	3	3	0	0	25	32	1	7	6	15.1	5.40	45	.330	.393	0	.000	-1	-8	-8	-1	-1.0
● DON ROSE Rose, Donald Gary b: 3/19/47, Covina, Cal. BR/TR, 6'3", 195 lbs. Deb: 9/15/71																										
1971	NY-N	0	0	—	1	0	0	0	0	2	2	0	0	1	9.0	0.00	—	.286	.286	0	—	0	1	1	-0	0.0
1972	Cal-A	1	4	.200	16	4	0	0	0	42^2	49	9	19	39	14.3	4.22	69	.283	.354	2	.200	1	-5	-6	-0	-0.6
1974	SF-N	0	0	—	2	0	0	0	0	1	4	0	1	0	45.0	9.00	42	.667	.714	0	—	0	-1	-1	0	0.0
Total	3	1	4	.200	19	4	0	0	0	45^2	55	9	20	40	14.8	4.14	71	.296	.364	2	.200	1	-5	-6	-1	-0.6
● ZEKE ROSEBRAUGH Rosebraugh, Eli Ethelbert b: 9/8/1870, Charleston, Ill. d: 7/16/30, Fresno, Cal. TL , Deb: 9/21/1898																										
1898	Pit-N	0	2	.000	4	2	2	0	0	21^2	23	0	9	6	14.5	3.32	107	.271	.361	3	.375	1	1	1	-0	0.1
1899	Pit-N	0	1	.000	2	2	0	0	0	6	14	0	3	2	27.0	9.00	42	.452	.514	0	.000	-0	-3	-3	-0	-0.5
Total	2	0	3	.000	6	4	2	0	0	27^2	37	0	12	8	17.2	4.55	79	.319	.402	3	.300	1	-3	-3	-0	-0.4
● CHIEF ROSEMAN Roseman, James John b: 1856, New York, N.Y. d: 7/4/38, Brooklyn, N.Y. BR/TR, 5'7", 167 lbs. Deb: 5/1/1882 M♦																										
1885	NY-a	0	1	.000	1	1	0	0	0	1	3	0	2	0	45.0	27.00	11	.333	.455	114	.278	0	-3	-3	0	-1.2
1886	NY-a	0	0	—	1	0	0	0	0	7	6	0	0	0	7.7	5.14	66	.240	.240	127	.227	0	-1	-1	0	0.0
1887	NY-a	0	0	—	2	0	0	0	0	8	11	0	5	1	20.3	7.88	54	.407	.529	55	.228	-0	-3	-3	-0	0.0
Total	3	0	1	.000	4	1	0	0	0	16	20	0	7	1	16.3	7.88	48	.328	.414	726	.263	0	-7	-7	-0	-1.2
● STEVE ROSENBERG Rosenberg, Steven Allen b: 10/31/64, Brooklyn, N.Y. BL/TL, 6', 186 lbs. Deb: 6/4/88																										
1988	Chi-A	0	1	.000	33	0	0	0	1	46	53	5	19	28	14.1	4.30	92	.298	.365	0	—	0	-2	-2	-0	-0.1
1989	Chi-A	4	13	.235	38	21	2	0	0	142	148	14	58	77	13.1	4.94	77	.273	.344	0	—	0	-17	-18	0	-1.9
1990	Chi-A	1	0	1.000	6	0	0	0	0	10	10	2	5	4	13.5	5.40	71	.256	.341	0	—	0	-2	-2	0	-0.1
1991	SD-N	1	1	.500	10	0	0	0	0	11^2	11	3	5	6	12.3	6.94	55	.250	.327	0	.000	-0	-4	-4	-0	-0.7
Total	4	6	15	.286	87	21	2	0	1	209^2	222	24	87	115	13.3	4.94	78	.276	.348	0	.000	-0	-24	-26	-0	-2.8
● WAYNE ROSENTHAL Rosenthal, Wayne Scott b: 2/19/65, Brooklyn, N.Y. BR/TR, 6'5", 220 lbs. Deb: 6/26/91																										
1991	Tex-A	1	4	.200	36	0	0	0	1	70^1	72	9	36	61	13.9	5.25	77	.257	.344	0	—	0	-9	-10	-1	-0.7
1992	Tex-A	0	0	—	6	0	0	0	0	4^2	7	1	2	1	17.4	7.71	49	.333	.391	0	—	0	-2	-2	0	0.0
Total	2	1	4	.200	42	0	0	0	1	75	79	10	38	62	14.2	5.40	74	.262	.347	0	—	0	-11	-12	-1	-0.7
● STEVE ROSER Roser, Emerson Corey b: 1/25/18, Rome, N.Y. BR/TR, 6'4", 220 lbs. Deb: 5/5/44																										
1944	NY-A	4	3	.571	16	6	1	0	1	84	80	3	34	34	12.2	3.86	90	.256	.329	3	.100	-2	-4	-3	-1	-0.5
1945	NY-A	0	0	—	11	0	0	0	0	27	27	1	8	11	11.7	3.67	94	.262	.315	1	.125	-0	-1	-1	0	0.0
1946	NY-A	1	1	.500	4	1	0	0	0	3^1	7	0	4	1	29.7	16.20	21	.438	.550	0	—	0	-5	-5	-0	-2.0
	Bos-N	1	1	.500	14	1	0	0	1	35	33	1	18	18	13.1	3.60	95	.250	.340	0	.000	-1	-1	-1	-0	-0.1
Total	3	6	5	.545	45	8	1	0	2	149^1	147	5	64	64	12.7	4.04	86	.261	.336	4	.093	-3	-10	-9	-1	-2.6
● BUSTER ROSS Ross, Chester Franklin b: 3/11/03, Kuttawa, Ky. d: 4/24/82, Mayfield, Ky. BL/TL, 6'1", 195 lbs. Deb: 6/15/24																										
1924	Bos-A	4	3	.571	30	2	1	1	1	93^1	109	3	30	16	13.4	3.47	126	.307	.361	5	.200	-0	8	9	-1	0.5
1925	Bos-A	3	8	.273	33	8	0	0	0	94^1	119	9	40	15	15.6	6.20	73	.313	.386	3	.125	-1	-19	-17	-1	-1.8
1926	Bos-A	0	1	.000	1	0	0	0	0	2^2	5	0	4	0	30.4	16.88	24	.385	.529	0	.000	-0	-4	-4	0	-0.8
Total	3	7	12	.368	64	10	1	1	1	190^1	233	12	74	31	14.8	5.01	89	.311	.377	8	.160	-2	-15	-12	-2	-2.1
● CLIFF ROSS Ross, Clifford Davis b: 8/3/28, Philadelphia, Pa. BL/TL, 6'4", 195 lbs. Deb: 9/11/54																										
1954	Cin-N	0	0	—	4	0	0	0	1	2^2	0	0	0	1	0.0	0.00	—	.000	.000	0	—	0	1	1	0	0.1
● ERNIE ROSS Ross, Ernest Bertram "Curly" b: 3/31/1880, Toronto, Ont., Can. d: 3/28/50, Toronto, Ont., Can. BL/TL, 5'8", 150 lbs. Deb: 9/17/02																										
1902	Bal-A	1	1	.500	2	2	2	0	0	17	20	0	12	2	17.5	7.41	51	.294	.407	0	.000	-1	-7	-7	-1	-0.7
● BOB ROSS Ross, Floyd Robert b: 11/2/28, Fullerton, Cal. BR/TL, 6', 165 lbs. Deb: 6/16/50																										
1950	Was-A	0	1	.000	6	2	0	0	0	12^2	15	1	15	2	21.3	8.53	53	.300	.462	0	.000	-0	-6	-6	0	-0.4
1951	Was-A	0	1	.000	11	1	0	0	0	31^2	36	3	21	23	16.2	6.54	63	.295	.399	1	.111	-0	-8	-9	-1	-0.3

YEAR	TM/L	W	L	PCT	G	GS	CG	SH	SV	IP	H	HR	BB	SO	RAT	ERA	ERA+	OAV	OOB	BH	AVG	PB	PR	/A	PD	TPI
1956	Phi-N	0	0	—	3	0	0	0	0	3^1	4	1	2	4	16.2	8.10	46	.333	.429	0	—	0	-2	-2	0	0.0
Total	3	0	2	.000	20	3	0	0	0	47^2	55	5	38	29	17.6	7.17	58	.299	.419	1	.083	-1	-16	-16	-0	-0.7
● GARY ROSS	Ross, Gary Douglas b: 9/16/47, McKeesport, Pa. BR/TR, 6'1", 190 lbs. Deb: 6/28/68																									
1968	Chi-N	1	1	.500	13	5	1	0	0	41	44	1	25	31	15.1	4.17	76	.288	.388	1	.091	-1	-5	-5	0	-0.3
1969	Chi-N	0	0	—	2	1	0	0	0	2	1	0	2	2	13.5	13.50	30	.143	.333	0	—	0	-2	-2	-0	0.0
	SD-N	3	12	.200	46	7	0	0	3	109^2	104	5	56	58	13.5	4.19	84	.252	.348	0	.000	-2	-7	-8	2	-1.1
	Yr	3	12	.200	48	8	0	0	3	111^2	105	5	58	60	13.5	4.35	81	.250	.348	0	.000	-2	-9	-10	2	-1.1
1970	SD-N	2	3	.400	33	2	0	0	1	62^1	72	8	36	39	16.0	5.20	76	.305	.404	4	.500	2	-8	-8	1	-0.4
1971	SD-N	1	3	.250	13	0	0	0	0	24^1	27	0	11	13	14.4	2.96	111	.300	.382	0	.000	-0	1	1	0	0.1
1972	SD-N	4	3	.571	60	0	0	0	3	91^2	87	2	49	46	13.7	2.45	134	.261	.363	2	.154	-0	10	8	1	0.8
1973	SD-N	4	4	.500	58	0	0	0	0	76^1	93	8	33	44	15.3	5.42	64	.304	.379	0	.000	-0	-15	-17	0	-1.6
1974	SD-N	0	0	—	9	0	0	0	0	18	23	1	6	11	14.5	4.50	79	.315	.367	0	.000	-0	-2	-2	0	0.0
1975	Cal-A	0	1	.000	1	1	0	0	0	5	6	1	1	4	12.6	5.40	66	.273	.304	0	—	0	-1	-1	-0	-0.1
1976	Cal-A	8	16	.333	34	31	7	2	0	225	224	12	58	100	11.5	3.00	111	.258	.308	0	—	0	13	8	5	1.4
1977	Cal-A	2	4	.333	14	12	0	0	0	58^1	83	10	11	30	14.8	5.55	70	.337	.371	0	—	0	-10	-11	1	-0.9
Total	10	25	47	.347	283	59	8	2	7	713^2	764	48	288	378	13.6	3.92	89	.278	.352	7	.115	-2	-26	-36	9	-2.1
● GEORGE ROSS	Ross, George Sidney b: 6/27/1892, San Rafael, Cal. d: 4/22/35, Amityville, N.Y. BL/TL, 5'10.5", 175 lbs. Deb: 6/27/18																									
1918	NY-N	0	0	—	1	0	0	0	1	2^1	2	0	3	2	19.3	0.00	—	.222	.417	0	.000	-0	1	1	0	0.1
● BUCK ROSS	Ross, Lee Ravon b: 2/2/15, Norwood, N.C. d: 11/23/78, Charlotte, N.C. BR/TR, 6'2", 170 lbs. Deb: 5/7/36																									
1936	Phi-A	9	14	.391	30	27	12	1	0	200^2	253	17	83	47	15.1	5.83	88	.304	.367	12	.169	-1	-18	-16	-2	-1.7
1937	Phi-A	5	10	.333	28	22	7	1	0	147^1	183	12	63	37	15.1	4.89	96	.306	.373	5	.102	-3	-4	-3	0	-0.5
1938	Phi-A	9	16	.360	29	28	10	0	0	184^1	218	23	80	54	14.5	5.32	91	.289	.357	12	.190	-0	-11	-10	-0	-1.1
1939	Phi-A	6	14	.300	29	28	6	1	0	174	216	17	95	43	16.1	6.00	78	.302	.384	12	.207	-1	-27	-25	-2	-2.5
1940	Phi-A	5	10	.333	24	19	10	0	1	156^1	160	15	60	43	12.7	4.38	102	.256	.322	7	.132	-2	0	1	-1	-0.2
1941	Phi-A	0	1	.000	1	1	0	0	0	4	10	2	2	0	27.0	18.00	23	.435	.480	0	.000	-0	-6	-6	0	-0.9
	Chi-A	3	8	.273	20	11	7	0	0	108^1	99	6	43	30	11.9	3.16	130	.239	.312	7	.219	1	12	11	-2	1.0
	Yr	3	9	.250	21	12	7	0	0	112^1	109	8	45	30	12.4	3.69	111	.249	.321	7	.212	1	6	5	-2	0.1
1942	Chi-A	5	7	.417	22	14	4	2	1	113^1	118	6	39	37	12.5	5.00	72	.264	.323	6	.158	0	-17	-18	-3	-1.9
1943	Chi-A	11	7	.611	21	21	7	1	0	149^1	140	6	56	41	11.9	3.19	105	.253	.324	4	.087	-1	2	2	-1	0.0
1944	Chi-A	2	7	.222	20	9	2	0	0	90^1	97	7	35	20	13.4	5.18	66	.280	.350	2	.077	-2	-18	-18	-2	-2.0
1945	Chi-A	1	1	.500	13	2	0	0	0	37^1	51	3	17	8	16.4	5.79	57	.327	.393	2	.182	-0	-10	-10	-1	-0.6
Total	10	56	95	.371	237	182	65	6	2	1365^1	1545	114	573	360	14.0	4.94	88	.283	.351	69	.154	-11	-97	-91	-13	-10.4
● MARK ROSS	Ross, Mark Joseph b: 8/8/57, Galveston, Tex. BR/TR, 6', 195 lbs. Deb: 9/12/82																									
1982	Hou-N	0	0	—	4	0	0	0	0	6	3	0	0	4	4.5	1.50	221	.143	.143	0	—	0	1	1	0	0.0
1984	Hou-N	1	0	1.000	2	0	0	0	0	2^1	1	0	0	1	3.9	0.00	—	.125	.125	0	—	0	1	1	-0	0.4
1985	Hou-N	0	2	.000	8	0	0	0	1	13	12	2	2	3	9.7	4.85	71	.240	.269	0	.000	-0	-2	-2	0	-0.3
1987	Pit-N	0	0	—	1	0	0	0	0	1	1	1	0	0	9.0	9.00	46	.250	.250	0	—	0	-1	-1	0	0.0
1988	Tor-A	0	0	—	3	0	0	0	0	7^1	5	0	4	4	11.0	4.91	80	.185	.290	0	—	0	-1	-1	-0	0.0
1990	Pit-N	1	0	1.000	9	0	0	0	0	12^2	11	2	4	5	10.7	3.55	102	.244	.306	0	.000	-0	0	0	0	0.0
Total	6	2	2	.500	27	0	0	0	1	42^1	33	5	10	17	9.1	3.83	93	.213	.261	0	.000	-0	-0	-1	0	0.1
● JOE ROSSELLI	Rosselli, Joseph Donald b: 5/28/72, Burbank, Cal. BR/TL, 6'1", 170 lbs. Deb: 4/30/95																									
1995	SF-N	2	1	.667	9	5	0	0	0	30	39	5	20	7	17.7	8.70	47	.342	.440	2	.200	0	-15	-15	-0	-1.3
● FRANK ROSSO	Rosso, Francis James b: 3/1/21, Agawam, Mass. d: 1/26/80, Springfield, Mass. BR/TR, 5'11", 180 lbs. Deb: 9/15/44																									
1944	NY-N	0	0	—	2	0	0	0	0	4	11	0	3	1	31.5	9.00	41	.550	.609	0	—	0	-2	-2	0	0.0
● MARV ROTBLATT	Rotblatt, Marvin "Rotty" b: 10/18/27, Chicago, Ill. BB/TL, 5'7", 160 lbs. Deb: 7/4/48																									
1948	Chi-A	0	1	.000	7	2	0	0	0	18^1	19	0	23	4	21.1	7.85	54	.271	.457	0	.000	-0	-7	-7	-1	-0.4
1950	Chi-A	0	0	—	2	0	0	0	0	8^2	11	2	5	6	16.6	6.23	72	.344	.432	0	.000	-0	-2	-2	0	0.0
1951	Chi-A	4	2	.667	26	2	0	0	2	47^2	44	4	23	20	12.8	3.40	119	.244	.333	0	.000	-2	4	3	1	0.3
Total	3	4	3	.571	35	4	0	0	2	74^2	74	6	51	30	15.3	4.82	86	.262	.379	0	.000	-2	-5	-6	1	-0.1
● JACK ROTHROCK	Rothrock, John Huston b: 3/14/05, Long Beach, Cal. d: 2/2/80, San Bernardino, Cal BB/TR, 5'11.5", 165 lbs. Deb: 7/28/25 ♦																									
1928	Bos-A	0	0	—	1	0	0	0	0	1	0	0	0	0	0.0	0.00	—	.000	.000	92	.267	0	0	0	0	0.0
● LARRY ROTHSCHILD	Rothschild, Lawrence Lee b: 3/12/54, Chicago, Ill. BL/TR, 6'2", 180 lbs. Deb: 9/11/81 MC																									
1981	Det-A	0	0	—	5	0	0	0	1	5^2	4	0	6	1	15.9	1.59	237	.200	.385	0	—	0	1	1	0	0.1
1982	Det-A	0	0	—	2	0	0	0	0	2^2	4	1	2	0	20.3	13.50	30	.333	.429	0	—	0	-3	-3	-0	0.0
Total	2	0	0	—	7	0	0	0	1	8^1	8	1	8	1	17.3	5.40	72	.250	.400	0	—	0	-1	-1	0	0.1
● GENE ROUNSAVILLE	Rounsaville, Virle Gene b: 9/27/44, Konawa, Okla. BR/TR, 6'3", 205 lbs. Deb: 4/7/70																									
1970	Chi-A	0	1	.000	8	0	0	0	0	6^1	10	1	2	3	17.1	9.95	39	.357	.400	0	—	0	-4	-4	-0	-0.6
● JACK ROWAN	Rowan, John Albert b: 6/16/1887, New Castle, Pa. d: 9/29/66, Dayton, Ohio BR/TR, 6'1", 210 lbs. Deb: 9/6/06																									
1906	Det-A	0	1	.000	1	1	1	0	0	9	15	0	6	0	21.0	11.00	25	.375	.457	1	.250	0	-8	-8	-0	-0.6
1908	Cin-N	3	3	.500	8	7	4	1	0	49^1	46	0	16	24	11.3	1.82	126	.253	.313	1	.071	-0	3	3	1	0.3
1909	Cin-N	11	12	.478	38	23	14	0	0	225^2	185	0	104	81	11.6	2.79	93	.233	.324	6	.092	-1	-5	-5	-5	-1.1
1910	Cin-N	14	13	.519	42	30	18	4	1	261	242	4	105	108	12.3	2.93	99	.254	.334	19	.229	3	3	-0	-4	-0.2
1911	Phi-N	2	4	.333	12	6	2	0	0	45^2	59	3	20	17	15.8	4.73	73	.316	.385	1	.077	-1	-7	-7	1	-0.8
	Chi-N	0	0	—	1	0	0	0	0	2	1	0	2	0	18.0	4.50	74	.143	.400	0	.000	-0	-0	-0	0	0.0
	Yr	2	4	.333	13	6	2	0	0	47^2	60	3	22	17	15.7	4.72	73	.308	.381	1	.071	-1	-7	-7	1	-0.8
1913	Cin-N	0	4	.000	5	5	5	0	0	39	37	0	9	21	10.8	3.00	108	.264	.313	2	.182	1	1	1	-0	0.2
1914	Cin-N	1	3	.250	12	2	0	0	2	39	38	1	10	16	11.1	3.46	85	.262	.310	0	.000	-1	-3	-2	-1	-0.4
Total	7	31	40	.437	119	74	44	5	3	670^2	623	8	272	267	12.2	3.07	92	.255	.333	30	.151	1	-16	-19	-9	-2.6
● DAVE ROWE	Rowe, David Elwood b: 10/9/1854, Harrisburg, Pa. d: 12/9/30, Glendale, Cal. BR/TR, 5'9", 180 lbs. Deb: 5/30/1877 FM♦																									
1877	Chi-N	0	1	.000	1	1	0	0	0	1	3	0	2	0	45.0	18.00	17	.600	.714	2	.286	0	-2	-2	0	-0.9
1882	Cle-N	0	1	.000	1	1	1	0	0	9	29	3	7	0	36.0	12.00	23	.492	.545	25	.258	0	-9	-9	-0	-0.6
1883	Bal-a	0	0	—	1	0	0	0	0	4	12	1	2	1	31.5	20.25	17	.500	.538	80	.313	0	-8	-7	-0	0.0
1884	StL-U	1	0	1.000	1	1	1	0	0	9	10	0	0	2	10.0	2.00	120	.263	.263	142	.293	0	0	0	0	0.1
Total	4	1	2	.333	4	3	2	0	0	23	54	4	11	3	25.4	9.78	28	.429	.474	383	.263	0	-18	-18	-0	-1.4
● DON ROWE	Rowe, Donald Howard b: 4/3/36, Brawley, Cal. BL/TL, 6', 180 lbs. Deb: 4/9/63 C																									
1963	NY-N	0	0	—	26	1	0	0	0	54^2	59	6	21	27	13.3	4.28	81	.280	.348	3	.231	0	-6	-5	-1	-0.1
● KEN ROWE	Rowe, Kenneth Darrell b: 12/31/33, Ferndale, Mich. BR/TR, 6'2", 185 lbs. Deb: 4/14/63 C																									
1963	LA-N	1	1	.500	14	0	0	0	1	27^2	28	2	11	12	13.0	2.93	103	.264	.339	0	.000	-1	1	0	-0	-0.1
1964	Bal-A	1	0	1.000	6	0	0	0	0	4^1	10	1	1	4	22.8	8.31	43	.455	.478	0	—	0	-2	-2	0	-0.4
1965	Bal-A	0	0	—	6	0	0	0	0	13^1	17	0	2	3	12.8	3.38	103	.321	.345	1	1.000	0	0	0	-1	0.0
Total	3	2	1	.667	26	0	0	0	1	45^1	55	3	14	19	13.9	3.57	90	.304	.357	1	.167	-0	-1	-2	-1	-0.5
● SCHOOLBOY ROWE	Rowe, Lynwood Thomas b: 1/11/10, Waco, Tex. d: 1/8/61, ElDorado, Ark. BR/TR, 6'4.5", 210 lbs. Deb: 4/15/33 C♦																									
1933	Det-A	7	4	.636	19	15	8	1	0	123^1	129	7	31	75	11.7	3.58	121	.269	.315	11	.220	-0	10	10	2	0.9
1934	*Det-A	24	8	.750	45	30	20	3	1	266	259	12	81	149	11.5	3.45	127	.256	.312	33	.303	12	31	28	-0	4.0
1935	*Det-A☆	19	13	.594	42	34	21	**6**	3	275^2	272	11	68	140	11.2	3.69	113	.255	**.301**	34	.312	14	23	15	-2	2.6
1936	Det-A★	19	10	.655	41	35	19	4	3	245^1	266	15	64	115	12.2	4.51	110	.275	.321	23	.256	7	14	12	2	2.0
1937	Det-A	1	4	.200	10	2	1	0	0	31^1	49	7	9	6	16.9	8.62	54	.350	.393	2	.200	-0	-14	-14	0	-1.6
1938	Det-A	0	2	.000	4	3	0	0	0	21	20	1	11	4	13.3	3.00	167	.256	.348	1	.167	-0	4	5	1	0.4

YEAR	TM/L	W	L	PCT	G	GS	CG	SH	SV	IP	H	HR	BB	SO	RAT	ERA	ERA+	OAV	OOB	BH	AVG	PB	PR	/A	PD	TPI
1939	Det-A	10	12	.455	28	24	8	1	0	164	192	17	61	51	14.0	4.99	98	.291	.353	15	.246	2	-7	-2	0	0.0
1940	*Det-A	16	3	**.842**	27	23	11	1	0	169	170	15	43	61	11.4	3.46	137	.259	.305	18	.269	5	17	24	-0	2.9
1941	Det-A	8	6	.571	27	14	4	0	1	139	155	6	33	54	12.2	4.14	110	.278	.318	15	.273	5	0	6	1	1.1
1942	Det-A	1	0	1.000	2	1	0	0	0	10^1	9	0	2	7	9.6	0.00	—	.220	.256	0	.000	-1	4	5	0	0.4
	Bro-N	1	0	1.000	9	2	0	0	0	30^1	36	2	12	6	14.5	5.34	61	.288	.355	4	.211	0	-7	-7	0	-0.2
1943	Phi-N	14	8	.636	27	25	11	3	1	199	196	7	29	52	10.3	2.94	115	.249	.279	36	.300	16	10	10	0	3.1
1946	Phi-N	11	4	.733	17	16	9	2	0	136	112	3	21	51	9.2	2.12	162	.224	.263	11	.180	2	20	20	-2	2.3
1947	Phi-N★	14	10	.583	31	28	15	1	1	195^2	232	22	45	74	12.9	4.32	93	.292	.333	22	.278	10	-6	-7	-1	0.1
1948	Phi-N	10	10	.500	30	20	8	0	2	148	167	5	31	46	12.2	4.07	97	.281	.319	10	.192	2	-2	-2	1	0.0
1949	Phi-N	3	7	.300	23	6	2	0	0	65^1	68	2	17	22	12.0	4.82	82	.300	.354	4	.235	2	-6	-6	1	-0.6
Total	15	158	101	.610	382	278	137	22	12	2219^1	2332	132	558	913	11.8	3.87	110	.269	.315	239	.263	76	93	96	2	17.4
● MIKE ROWLAND	Rowland, Michael Evan b: 1/31/53, Chicago, Ill. BR/TR, 6'3", 205 lbs. Deb: 7/25/80																									
1980	SF-N	1	1	.500	19	0	0	0	0	27	20	2	8	8	9.7	2.33	152	.206	.274	0	—	0	4	4	-0	0.2
1981	SF-N	0	1	.000	9	1	0	0	0	15^2	13	1	6	8	11.5	3.45	100	.232	.317	1	1.000	0	0	-0	-0	0.0
Total	2	1	2	.333	28	1	0	0	0	42^2	33	3	14	16	10.3	2.74	128	.216	.290	1	1.000	0	4	4	-0	0.2
● CHARLIE ROY	Roy, Charles Robert b: 6/22/1884, Beaulieu, Minn. d: 2/10/50, Blackfoot, Idaho BR/TR, 5'10", 190 lbs. Deb: 6/27/06 F																									
1906	Phi-N	0	1	.000	7	1	0	0	0	18^1	24	0	5	6	14.7	4.91	53	.316	.366	0	.000	-1	-5	-5	-0	-0.3
● EMIL ROY	Roy, Emil Arthur b: 5/26/07, Brighton, Mass. d: 1/5/97, Crystal River, Fla. BR/TR, 5'11", 180 lbs. Deb: 9/30/33																									
1933	Phi-A	0	1	.000	1	1	0	0	0	2^1	4	0	4	3	30.9	27.00	16	.364	.533	0	—	0	-6	-6	-0	-1.2
● JEAN-PIERRE ROY	Roy, Jean-Pierre b: 6/26/20, Montreal, Que., Can. BB/TR, 5'10", 160 lbs. Deb: 5/5/46																									
1946	Bro-N	0	0	—	3	1	0	0	0	6^1	5	2	5	6	14.2	9.95	34	.200	.333	0	.000	-0	-5	-5	-0	-0.1
● LUTHER ROY	Roy, Luther Franklin b: 7/29/02, Ooltewah, Tenn. d: 7/24/63, Grand Rapids, Mich. BR/TR, 5'10.5", 161 lbs. Deb: 6/12/24 F																									
1924	Cle-A	0	5	.000	16	5	2	0	0	48^2	62	3	31	14	17.2	7.77	55	.318	.412	4	.267	-0	-19	-19	1	-1.5
1925	Cle-A	0	0	—	6	1	0	0	0	10	14	1	11	1	22.5	3.60	123	.368	.510	0	.000	-0	1	1	-0	-0.1
1927	Chi-N	3	1	.750	11	0	0	0	0	19^2	14	0	11	5	11.9	2.29	169	.209	.329	1	.333	0	4	3	0	0.7
1929	Phi-N	3	6	.333	21	12	1	0	0	88^2	137	11	37	16	18.0	8.42	62	.350	.411	9	.281	2	-37	-32	1	-2.2
	Bro-N	0	0	—	2	0	0	0	0	3^2	4	0	2	0	14.7	4.91	94	.286	.375	0	.000	-0	-0	-0	0	0.0
	Yr	3	6	.333	23	12	1	0	0	92^1	141	11	39	16	17.5	8.29	62	.346	.403	9	.273	2	-37	-32	1	-2.2
Total	4	6	12	.333	56	18	3	0	0	170^2	231	15	92	36	17.2	7.17	66	.328	.408	14	.264	2	-51	-47	1	-3.1
● NORMIE ROY	Roy, Norman Brooks "Jumbo" b: 11/15/28, Newton, Mass. BR/TR, 6', 200 lbs. Deb: 4/23/50																									
1950	Bos-N	4	3	.571	19	6	2	0	1	59^2	72	7	39	25	17.0	5.13	75	.305	.408	3	.167	0	-7	-8	0	-0.9
● DICK ROZEK	Rozek, Richard Louis b: 3/27/27, Cedar Rapids, Iowa BL/TL, 6'0.5", 190 lbs. Deb: 4/29/50																									
1950	Cle-A	0	0	—	12	2	0	0	0	25^1	28	3	19	14	16.7	4.97	87	.283	.398	0	.000	-1	-1	-2	-1	-0.1
1951	Cle-A	0	0	—	7	1	0	0	0	15^1	18	1	11	5	17.6	2.93	129	.286	.400	1	.333	0	2	1	-1	0.0
1952	Cle-A	1	0	1.000	10	1	0	0	0	12^2	11	0	13	5	17.1	4.97	67	.224	.387	0	.000	-0	-2	-2	-0	-0.2
1953	Phi-A	0	0	—	2	0	0	0	0	10^2	8	3	9	2	14.3	5.06	85	.222	.378	0	.000	-0	-1	-1	-0	0.0
1954	Phi-A	0	0	—	2	0	0	0	0	1^1	0	0	3	0	27.0	6.75	58	.000	.571	0	—	0	-0	-0	-0	0.0
Total	5	1	0	1.000	33	4	0	0	0	65^1	65	7	55	26	16.8	4.55	88	.260	.397	1	.083	-1	-3	-4	-2	-0.3
● DAVE ROZEMA	Rozema, David Scott b: 8/5/56, Grand Rapids, Mich. BR/TR, 6'4", 200 lbs. Deb: 4/11/77																									
1977	Det-A	15	7	.682	28	28	16	1	0	218^1	222	25	34	92	10.8	3.09	139	.265	.299	0	—	0	23	29	0	2.8
1978	Det-A	9	12	.429	28	28	11	2	0	209^1	205	17	41	57	10.7	3.14	123	.260	.298	0	—	0	15	17	-1	1.5
1979	Det-A	4	4	.500	16	16	4	1	0	97^1	101	12	30	33	12.7	3.51	123	.270	.334	0	—	0	8	9	0	0.6
1980	Det-A	6	9	.400	42	13	2	1	4	144^2	152	11	49	49	12.8	3.92	105	.277	.342	0	—	0	2	3	1	0.3
1981	Det-A	5	5	.500	28	9	2	2	3	104	99	12	25	46	11.0	3.63	104	.256	.306	0	—	0	0	2	-1	0.1
1982	Det-A	3	0	1.000	8	2	0	0	1	27^2	17	2	7	15	8.1	1.63	250	.179	.243	0	—	0	8	7	1	0.9
1983	Det-A	8	3	.727	29	16	1	0	2	105	100	10	29	63	11.1	3.43	114	.248	.300	0	—	0	7	6	1	0.7
1984	Det-A	7	6	.538	29	16	0	0	0	101	110	13	18	48	11.6	3.74	105	.274	.309	0	—	0	3	2	1	0.3
1985	Tex-A	3	7	.300	34	4	0	0	7	88	100	10	22	42	12.7	4.19	101	.287	.333	0	—	0	-0	0	1	0.1
1986	Tex-A	0	0	—	6	0	0	0	0	10^2	19	1	3	3	18.6	5.91	73	.404	.440	0	—	0	-2	-2	0	0.0
Total	10	60	53	.531	248	132	36	7	17	1106	1125	113	258	448	11.5	3.47	117	.266	.313	0	—	0	63	73	3	7.3
● JORGE RUBIO	Rubio, Jorge Jesus (Chavez) b: 4/23/45, Mexicali, Mexico BR/TR, 6'3", 200 lbs. Deb: 4/21/66																									
1966	Cal-A	2	1	.667	7	4	1	1	0	27^1	22	2	16	27	12.8	2.96	113	.220	.333	0	.000	-1	1	1	-0	0.0
1967	Cal-A	0	2	.000	3	3	0	0	0	15	18	2	9	4	18.6	3.60	87	.316	.443	1	.333	1	-1	-1	0	0.0
Total	2	2	3	.400	10	7	1	1	0	42^1	40	4	25	31	14.9	3.19	103	.255	.374	1	.091	-0	1	0	-0	0.0
● DAVE RUCKER	Rucker, David Michael b: 9/1/57, San Bernardino, Cal BL/TL, 6'1", 190 lbs. Deb: 4/12/81																									
1981	Det-A	0	0	—	2	0	0	0	0	4	3	0	1	2	11.3	6.75	56	.188	.278	0	—	0	-1	-1	-0	0.0
1982	Det-A	5	6	.455	27	4	1	0	0	64	62	4	23	31	12.2	3.38	120	.251	.320	0	—	0	5	5	0	0.8
1983	Det-A	1	2	.333	4	3	0	0	0	9	18	2	8	6	27.0	17.00	23	.419	.519	0	—	0	-13	-13	0	-2.7
	StL-N	5	3	.625	34	0	0	0	0	37	36	1	18	22	13.4	2.43	149	.263	.353	0	.000	-0	5	5	0	1.0
1984	StL-N	2	3	.400	50	0	0	0	0	73	62	0	34	38	12.0	2.10	166	.237	.327	1	.143	-0	12	11	-1	0.6
1985	Phi-N	3	2	.600	39	3	0	0	1	79^1	83	6	40	41	14.2	4.31	85	.279	.368	4	.333	2	-6	-6	0	-0.1
1986	Phi-N	0	2	.000	19	0	0	0	0	25	34	4	14	14	17.3	5.76	67	.340	.421	0	.000	-0	-6	-5	0	-0.4
1988	Pit-N	0	2	.000	31	0	0	0	0	28^1	39	2	9	16	15.2	4.76	71	.328	.375	0	.000	-0	-4	-4	-0	-0.3
Total	7	16	20	.444	206	10	1	0	1	319^2	337	19	147	170	13.9	3.94	94	.276	.357	5	.192	1	-8	-9	0	-1.1
● NAP RUCKER	Rucker, George b: 9/30/1884, Crabapple, Ga. d: 12/19/70, Alpharetta, Ga. BR/TL, 5'11", 190 lbs. Deb: 4/15/07																									
1907	Bro-N	15	13	.536	37	30	26	4	0	275^1	242	3	80	131	10.8	2.06	114	.242	.303	15	.155	-1	13	9	-1	0.7
1908	Bro-N	17	19	.472	42	37	30	6	1	333^1	265	1	125	199	11.0	2.08	113	.231	.317	21	.179	-1	11	10	4	1.5
1909	Bro-N	13	19	.406	38	33	28	6	1	309^1	245	6	101	201	10.5	2.24	116	.228	.303	12	.119	-5	12	12	-2	0.5
1910	Bro-N	17	18	.486	41	39	**27**	**6**	0	**320^1**	293	5	84	147	10.8	2.58	117	.251	.306	23	.209	-1	16	16	-2	1.3
1911	Bro-N	22	18	.550	48	33	23	5	4	315^2	255	12	110	190	10.6	2.71	123	.226	.300	21	.202	2	24	22	2	3.0
1912	Bro-N	18	21	.462	45	34	23	**6**	4	297^2	272	6	72	151	10.5	2.21	152	.250	.298	25	.245	2	40	38	2	**5.2**
1913	Bro-N	14	15	.483	41	33	16	4	3	260	236	3	67	111	10.7	2.87	115	.249	.304	21	.241	2	10	12	-4	1.1
1914	Bro-N	7	6	.538	16	16	5	0	0	103^2	113	2	27	35	12.3	3.39	84	.275	.323	9	.265	2	-7	-6	0	-0.5
1915	Bro-N	9	4	.692	19	15	7	1	1	122^2	134	3	28	38	12.0	2.42	115	.279	.322	9	.214	1	4	5	1	0.8
1916	*Bro-N	2	1	.667	9	3	1	0	0	37^1	34	0	7	14	10.1	1.69	159	.241	.282	1	.091	-1	4	4	0	0.2
Total	10	134	134	.500	336	273	186	38	14	2375^1	2089	41	701	1217	10.8	2.42	119	.243	.306	157	.195	1	127	121	1	13.8
● ERNIE RUDOLPH	Rudolph, Ernest William b: 2/13/09, Black River Falls, Wis. BL/TR, 5'8", 165 lbs. Deb: 6/16/45																									
1945	Bro-N	1	0	1.000	7	0	0	0	0	8^2	12	1	7	3	19.7	5.19	72	.333	.442	0	—	1	-1	-1	0	-0.1
● DON RUDOLPH	Rudolph, Frederick Donald b: 8/16/31, Baltimore, Md. d: 9/12/68, Granada Hills, Cal BL/TL, 5'11", 195 lbs. Deb: 9/21/57																									
1957	Chi-A	1	0	1.000	5	0	0	0	0	12	6	2	2	2	6.0	2.25	166	.146	.186	1	.500	1	2	2	-0	0.2
1958	Chi-A	1	0	1.000	7	0	0	0	1	7	4	0	5	2	11.6	2.57	141	.190	.346	0	—	0	1	1	0	0.2
1959	Chi-A	0	0	—	4	0	0	0	1	3	4	0	2	0	18.0	0.00	—	.333	.429	0	—	0	1	1	0	0.1
	Cin-N	0	0	—	5	0	0	0	0	7^1	13	1	3	8	19.6	4.91	83	.394	.444	0	.000	-0	-1	-1	0	0.0
1962	Cle-A	0	0	—	1	0	0	0	0	0^1	1	0	0	0	27.0	0.00	—	1.000	1.000	0	—	0	0	0	0	0.0
	Was-A	8	10	.444	37	23	6	2	0	176^1	187	13	42	68	11.8	3.62	111	.274	.319	10	.175	1	7	8	-1	0.8
	Yr	8	10	.444	38	23	6	2	0	176^2	188	13	42	68	11.9	3.62	112	.275	.320	10	.175	1	7	8	-1	0.8
1963	Was-A	7	19	.269	37	26	4	0	1	174	189	28	36	70	11.9	4.55	82	.275	.317	8	.178	2	-18	-16	-1	-2.1
1964	Was-A	1	3	.250	28	8	0	0	0	70^1	81	10	12	32	11.9	4.09	90	.290	.320	1	.067	-1	-4	-3	-0	-0.3
Total	6	18	32	.360	124	57	10	2	3	450^1	485	54	102	182	11.9	4.00	96	.276	.319	20	.167	3	-11	-8	-1	-1.1

● DICK RUDOLPH Rudolph, Richard "Baldy" b: 8/25/1887, New York, N.Y. d: 10/20/49, Bronx, N.Y. BR/TR, 5'9.5", 160 lbs. Deb: 9/30/10 C

YEAR	TM/L	W	L	PCT	G	GS	CG	SH	SV	IP	H	HR	BB	SO	RAT	ERA	ERA+	OAV	OOB	BH	AVG	PB	PR	/A	PD	TPI
1910	NY-N	0	1	.000	3	1	1	0	2	12	21	0	2	9	17.3	7.50	40	.350	.371	1	.250	0	-6	-6	-0	-0.7
1911	NY-N	0	0	—	1	0	0	0	0	2	2	0	0	0	9.0	9.00	37	.250	.250	1	1.000	0	-1	-1	-0	0.0
1913	Bos-N	14	13	.519	33	22	17	2	0	249^1	258	4	59	109	11.5	2.92	112	.276	.320	21	.239	4	8	10	5	1.9
1914	*Bos-N	26	10	.722	42	36	31	6	0	336^1	288	9	61	138	**9.4**	2.35	117	.238	.276	15	.125	-1	16	15	2	1.7
1915	Bos-N	22	19	.537	44	43	30	3	1	341^1	304	4	64	147	9.9	2.37	109	.242	.282	23	.198	6	14	8	1	1.7
1916	Bos-N	19	12	.613	41	38	27	5	3	312	266	7	38	133	**8.9**	2.16	115	.235	**.261**	16	.158	1	16	11	6	1.9
1917	Bos-N	13	13	.500	31	30	22	5	0	242^2	252	1	54	96	11.5	3.41	75	.272	.314	20	.230	3	-19	-23	1	-2.1
1918	Bos-N	9	10	.474	21	20	15	3	0	154	144	2	30	48	10.2	2.57	104	.255	.292	10	.185	-1	3	2	1	0.3
1919	Bos-N	13	18	.419	37	32	24	2	2	273^2	282	2	54	76	11.1	2.17	132	.276	.314	17	.193	3	23	21	0	2.9
1920	Bos-N	4	8	.333	18	11	3	0	0	89	104	4	24	24	13.3	4.04	75	.294	.346	5	.185	-0	-9	-10	0	-1.2
1922	Bos-N	0	2	.000	3	3	1	0	0	16	22	2	5	3	15.2	5.06	79	.328	.375	2	.400	1	-2	-2	0	-0.1
1923	Bos-N	1	2	.333	4	4	1	1	0	19^1	27	0	10	3	17.7	3.72	107	.333	.413	0	.000	-1	1	1	0	0.0
1927	Bos-N	0	0	—	1	0	0	0	0	1^1	1	0	1	0	13.5	0.00	—	.200	.333	0	—	0	1	1	-0	0.0
Total	13	121	108	.528	279	240	172	27	8	2049	1971	35	402	786	10.5	2.66	104	.258	.298	131	.188	14	44	25	15	6.3

● MATT RUEBEL Ruebel, Matthew Alexander b: 10/16/69, Cincinnati, Ohio BL/TL, 6'2", 180 lbs. Deb: 5/21/96

YEAR	TM/L	W	L	PCT	G	GS	CG	SH	SV	IP	H	HR	BB	SO	RAT	ERA	ERA+	OAV	OOB	BH	AVG	PB	PR	/A	PD	TPI
1996	Pit-N	1	1	.500	26	7	0	0	1	58^2	64	7	25	22	14.6	4.60	95	.277	.363	3	.231	1	-3	-2	0	0.0
1997	Pit-N	3	2	.600	44	0	0	0	0	62^2	77	8	27	50	15.7	6.32	68	.301	.378	0	.000	-1	-15	-14	-0	-1.1
1998	TB-A	0	2	.000	7	1	0	0	0	8^2	11	3	4	6	15.6	6.23	79	.314	.385	0	—	0	-2	-1	-0	-0.3
Total	3	4	5	.444	77	8	0	0	1	130	152	18	56	78	15.2	5.54	79	.291	.372	3	.150	-0	-19	-17	-1	-1.4

● KIRK RUETER Rueter, Kirk Wesley b: 12/1/70, Hoyleton, Ill. BL/TL, 6'3", 195 lbs. Deb: 7/7/93

YEAR	TM/L	W	L	PCT	G	GS	CG	SH	SV	IP	H	HR	BB	SO	RAT	ERA	ERA+	OAV	OOB	BH	AVG	PB	PR	/A	PD	TPI
1993	Mon-N	8	0	1.000	14	14	1	0	0	85^2	85	5	18	31	10.8	2.73	153	.264	.303	2	.077	-1	12	14	2	1.3
1994	Mon-N	7	3	.700	20	20	0	0	0	92^1	106	11	23	50	12.8	5.17	82	.294	.340	4	.118	-1	-10	-10	0	-1.0
1995	Mon-N	5	3	.625	9	9	1	1	0	47^1	38	3	9	28	9.1	3.23	133	.224	.267	0	.000	-2	5	6	1	0.8
1996	Mon-N	5	6	.455	16	16	0	0	0	78^2	91	12	22	30	13.2	4.58	94	.294	.345	3	.120	-1	-3	-2	2	-0.1
	SF-N	1	2	.333	4	3	0	0	0	23^1	18	0	5	16	8.9	1.93	212	.207	.250	1	.143	0	6	6	-0	0.7
	Yr	6	8	.429	20	19	0	0	0	102	109	12	27	46	12.0	3.97	107	.273	.319	4	.125	-1	3	3	2	0.6
1997	*SF-N	13	6	.684	32	32	0	0	0	190^2	194	17	51	115	11.6	3.45	120	.264	.313	9	.138	-1	16	14	5	1.7
1998	SF-N	16	9	.640	33	33	1	0	0	187^2	193	27	57	102	12.3	4.36	93	.265	.324	14	.209	1	-3	-6	2	-0.4
Total	6	55	29	.655	128	127	3	1	0	705^2	725	75	185	372	11.8	3.89	107	.267	.317	33	.138	-4	24	21	11	3.0

● DUTCH RUETHER Ruether, Walter Henry b: 9/13/1893, Alameda, Cal. d: 5/16/70, Phoenix, Ariz. BL/TL, 6'1.5", 180 lbs. Deb: 4/13/17 ♦

YEAR	TM/L	W	L	PCT	G	GS	CG	SH	SV	IP	H	HR	BB	SO	RAT	ERA	ERA+	OAV	OOB	BH	AVG	PB	PR	/A	PD	TPI
1917	Chi-N	2	0	1.000	10	4	1	0	0	36^1	37	0	12	23	12.9	2.48	117	.285	.359	12	.273	2	1	2	1	0.4
	Cin-N	1	2	.333	7	4	1	1	0	35^2	43	0	14	12	14.9	3.53	74	.323	.396	5	.208	1	-3	-4	-0	-0.2
	Yr	3	2	.600	17	8	2	1	0	72	80	0	26	35	13.5	3.00	92	.301	.367	17	.250	3	-2	-2	0	0.2
1918	Cin-N	0	1	.000	2	2	1	0	0	10	10	0	3	10	12.6	2.70	99	.244	.311	0	.000	-0	0	-0	-0	-0.1
1919	*Cin-N	19	6	**.760**	33	29	20	3	0	242^2	195	1	83	78	10.6	1.82	153	.223	.295	24	.261	6	30	26	-3	3.1
1920	Cin-N	16	12	.571	37	33	23	5	3	265^2	235	2	96	99	11.5	2.47	123	.247	.321	20	.192	-1	20	17	0	1.7
1921	Bro-N	10	13	.435	36	27	12	1	2	211^1	247	7	67	78	13.7	4.26	91	.299	.356	34	.351	11	-11	-9	-1	0.2
1922	Bro-N	21	12	.636	35	35	26	2	0	267^1	290	11	92	89	13.1	3.53	115	.282	.345	26	.208	6	17	16	-0	2.2
1923	Bro-N	15	14	.517	34	34	20	0	0	275	308	11	86	87	13.1	4.22	92	.287	.343	32	.274	4	-7	-10	-2	-0.6
1924	Bro-N	8	13	.381	30	21	13	2	3	168	190	4	45	63	12.9	3.91	96	.282	.332	15	.242	2	-1	-3	1	0.0
1925	*Was-A	18	7	.720	30	29	16	1	0	223^1	241	5	105	68	14.3	3.87	109	.281	.365	36	.333	6	13	9	-3	1.6
1926	Was-A	12	6	.667	23	23	9	0	0	169^1	214	5	66	48	15.1	4.84	80	.311	.375	23	.250	4	-15	-18	-2	-1.4
	*NY-A	2	3	.400	5	5	1	0	0	36	32	0	18	8	12.8	3.50	110	.248	.345	2	.095	-2	2	1	-1	-0.1
	Yr	14	9	.609	28	28	10	0	0	205^1	246	5	84	56	14.5	4.60	84	.300	.366	25	.221	3	-13	-17	-3	-1.5
1927	NY-A	13	6	.684	27	26	12	3	0	184	202	8	52	45	12.8	3.38	114	.287	.343	21	.262	5	16	10	0	1.4
Total	11	137	95	.591	309	272	155	18	8	2124^2	2244	54	739	708	12.9	3.50	104	.277	.342	250	.258	45	60	36	-9	8.2

● SCOTT RUFFCORN Ruffcorn, Scott Patrick b: 12/29/69, Austin, Tex. BR/TR, 6'4", 210 lbs. Deb: 6/19/93

YEAR	TM/L	W	L	PCT	G	GS	CG	SH	SV	IP	H	HR	BB	SO	RAT	ERA	ERA+	OAV	OOB	BH	AVG	PB	PR	/A	PD	TPI
1993	Chi-A	0	2	.000	3	2	0	0	0	10	9	2	10	2	17.1	8.10	52	.265	.432	0	—	0	-4	-4	-1	-0.7
1994	Chi-A	0	2	.000	2	2	0	0	0	6^1	15	1	5	3	28.4	12.79	36	.455	.526	0	—	0	-6	-6	-0	-1.1
1995	Chi-A	0	0	—	4	0	0	0	0	8	10	0	13	5	28.1	7.88	57	.333	.556	0	—	0	-3	-3	0	0.0
1996	Chi-A	0	1	.000	3	1	0	0	0	6^1	10	1	6	3	22.7	11.37	42	.370	.485	0	—	0	-4	-5	-0	-0.5
1997	Phi-N	0	3	.000	18	4	0	0	0	39^2	42	4	36	33	19.3	7.71	55	.275	.434	0	.000	-0	-15	-15	-1	-1.1
Total	5	0	8	.000	30	9	0	0	0	70^1	86	8	70	46	21.1	8.57	51	.310	.463	0	.000	-0	-33	-33	-1	-3.4

● BRUCE RUFFIN Ruffin, Bruce Wayne b: 10/4/63, Lubbock, Tex BB/TL, 6'2", 209 lbs. Deb: 6/28/86

YEAR	TM/L	W	L	PCT	G	GS	CG	SH	SV	IP	H	HR	BB	SO	RAT	ERA	ERA+	OAV	OOB	BH	AVG	PB	PR	/A	PD	TPI
1986	Phi-N	9	4	.692	21	21	6	0	0	146^1	138	6	44	70	11.3	2.46	157	.251	.308	4	.073	-3	20	23	-1	1.5
1987	Phi-N	11	14	.440	35	35	3	1	0	204^2	236	17	73	93	13.7	4.35	97	.298	.359	4	.055	-5	-6	-3	-1	-0.8
1988	Phi-N	6	10	.375	55	15	3	0	3	144^1	151	7	80	82	14.6	4.43	80	.275	.370	4	.121	-0	-16	-14	1	-1.5
1989	Phi-N	6	10	.375	24	23	1	0	0	125^2	152	10	62	70	15.3	4.44	80	.301	.377	6	.176	2	-13	-13	2	-1.1
1990	Phi-N	6	13	.316	32	25	2	1	0	149	178	14	62	79	14.6	5.38	71	.297	.364	3	.068	-2	-26	-26	0	-3.1
1991	Phi-N	4	7	.364	31	15	1	1	0	119	125	6	38	85	12.4	3.78	97	.272	.329	0	.000	-1	-1	-2	-0	-0.3
1992	Mil-A	1	6	.143	25	6	1	0	0	58	66	7	41	45	16.6	6.67	57	.293	.402	0	—	0	-18	-18	-0	-2.0
1993	Col-N	6	5	.545	59	12	0	0	2	139^2	145	10	69	126	13.9	3.87	123	.269	.352	2	.080	-1	3	14	-0	0.9
1994	Col-N	4	5	.444	56	0	0	0	16	55^2	55	6	30	65	13.9	4.04	123	.253	.347	1	.250	0	1	6	1	1.2
1995	*Col-N	0	1	.000	37	0	0	0	11	34	26	1	19	23	11.9	2.12	254	.222	.331	0	.000	-0	8	12	0	1.0
1996	Col-N	7	5	.583	71	0	0	0	24	69^2	55	5	29	74	10.9	4.00	130	.212	.291	0	.000	0	2	9	0	2.0
1997	Col-N	0	2	.000	23	0	0	0	7	22	18	3	18	31	14.7	5.32	97	.220	.360	0	—	0	-3	-0	0	-0.1
Total	12	60	82	.423	469	152	17	3	63	1268	1345	92	565	843	13.6	4.19	98	.275	.351	24	.081	-10	-49	-13	1	-2.3

● JOHNNY RUFFIN Ruffin, Johnny Renando b: 7/29/71, Butler, Ala. BR/TR, 6'3", 172 lbs. Deb: 8/8/93

YEAR	TM/L	W	L	PCT	G	GS	CG	SH	SV	IP	H	HR	BB	SO	RAT	ERA	ERA+	OAV	OOB	BH	AVG	PB	PR	/A	PD	TPI
1993	Cin-N	2	1	.667	21	0	0	0	2	37^2	36	4	11	30	11.5	3.58	112	.247	.304	1	.333	0	2	2	0	0.2
1994	Cin-N	7	2	.778	51	0	0	0	1	70	57	7	27	44	10.8	3.09	134	.223	.297	0	.000	-1	9	8	-1	0.8
1995	Cin-N	0	0	—	10	0	0	0	0	13^1	4	0	11	11	10.1	1.35	305	.093	.278	0	.000	-0	4	4	0	0.0
1996	Cin-N	1	3	.250	49	0	0	0	0	62^1	71	10	37	69	15.9	5.49	77	.292	.390	2	.500	1	-9	-9	-0	-0.5
Total	4	10	6	.625	131	0	0	0	3	183^1	168	21	86	154	12.6	3.88	107	.244	.331	3	.176	-0	6	5	-1	0.5

● RED RUFFING Ruffing, Charles Herbert b: 5/3/04, Granville, Ill. d: 2/17/86, Mayfield Hts., O. BR/TR, 6'1.5", 205 lbs. Deb: 5/31/24 CH♦

YEAR	TM/L	W	L	PCT	G	GS	CG	SH	SV	IP	H	HR	BB	SO	RAT	ERA	ERA+	OAV	OOB	BH	AVG	PB	PR	/A	PD	TPI
1924	Bos-A	0	0	—	8	2	0	0	0	23	29	0	9	10	16.0	6.65	66	.333	.414	1	.143	-0	-6	-6	-1	0.0
1925	Bos-A	9	18	.333	37	27	13	3	1	217^1	253	10	75	64	13.7	5.01	91	.299	.357	17	.215	-0	-15	-11	-1	-1.2
1926	Bos-A	6	15	.286	37	22	6	0	2	166	169	4	68	58	13.1	4.39	93	.274	.351	10	.196	0	-7	-6	-1	-0.8
1927	Bos-A	5	13	.278	26	18	10	0	2	158^1	160	7	87	77	14.3	4.66	91	.277	.375	14	.255	1	-9	-8	0	-0.6
1928	Bos-A	10	25	.286	42	34	**25**	1	2	289^1	303	8	96	118	12.7	3.89	106	.275	.339	38	.314	11	5	7	-3	1.7
1929	Bos-A	9	22	.290	35	30	18	1	1	244^1	280	17	118	109	14.7	4.86	88	.297	.376	35	.307	5	-17	-16	-1	-1.0
1930	Bos-A	0	3	.000	4	3	1	0	0	24	32	1	6	14	14.6	6.38	72	.323	.368	3	.273	1	-5	-5	-1	-0.5
	NY-A	15	5	.750	34	25	12	2	1	197^2	200	10	62	117	12.0	4.14	104	.260	.317	37	.374	17	11	3	-2	1.6
	Yr	15	8	.652	38	28	13	2	1	221^2	232	11	68	131	12.3	4.38	99	.267	.322	40	.364	18	7	-1	-3	1.1
1931	NY-A	16	14	.533	37	30	19	1	2	237	240	11	87	132	12.6	4.41	90	.256	.323	36	.330	11	-1	-12	-3	-0.3
1932	*NY-A	18	7	.720	35	29	22	3	2	259	219	16	115	**190**	11.7	3.09	132	**.226**	.311	38	.306	14	40	28	-2	3.5
1933	NY-A	9	14	.391	35	28	18	0	3	235	230	7	93	122	12.5	3.91	99	.258	.330	29	.252	8	10	-1	-0	0.7
1934	NY-A★	19	11	.633	36	31	19	5	0	256^1	232	18	104	149	11.8	3.93	103	.236	.310	28	.248	7	16	4	-3	0.7
1935	NY-A	16	11	.593	30	29	19	2	0	222	201	17	76	81	11.3	3.12	130	.239	.303	37	.339	14	33	23	-2	3.5
1936	*NY-A	20	12	.625	33	33	25	3	0	271	274	22	90	102	12.2	3.85	121	.263	.323	37	.291	16	36	24	2	3.9
1937	*NY-A	20	7	.741	31	31	22	4	0	256^1	242	17	68	131	10.9	2.98	149	.247	.296	26	.202	3	47	42	-4	3.7
1938	*NY-A☆	**21**	7	**.750**	31	31	22	3	0	247^1	246	16	82	127	11.9	3.31	137	.258	.317	24	.224	10	**41**	34	-2	**4.0**
1939	*NY-A★	21	7	.750	28	28	22	**5**	0	233^1	211	15	75	95	11.1	2.93	149	.240	.301	35	.307	9	44	37	-2	4.7
1940	NY-A★	15	12	.556	30	30	20	3	0	226	218	24	76	97	11.8	3.38	119	.252	.314	11	.124	-3	25	16	-3	1.1

YEAR	TM/L	W	L	PCT	G	GS	CG	SH	SV	IP	H	HR	BB	SO	RAT	ERA	ERA+	OAV	OOB	BH	AVG	PB	PR	/A	PD	TPI
1941	*NY-A☆	15	6	.714	23	23	13	2	0	185^{2}	177	13	54	60	11.2	3.54	111	.252	.306	27	.303	12	13	8	-3	1.6
1942	*NY-A☆	14	7	.667	24	24	16	4	0	193^{2}	183	10	41	80	10.5	3.21	107	.250	.292	20	.250	7	10	5	-2	1.0
1945	NY-A	7	3	.700	11	11	8	1	0	87^{1}	85	2	20	24	10.9	2.89	120	.251	.294	10	.217	1	5	6	-2	0.5
1946	NY-A	5	1	.833	8	8	4	2	0	61	37	2	23	19	8.9	1.77	195	.171	.251	3	.120	-1	12	11	-1	0.9
1947	Chi-A	3	5	.375	9	9	1	0	0	53	63	7	16	11	13.4	6.11	60	.290	.339	5	.208	-0	-14	-14	-0	-1.8
Total	22	273	225	.548	624	536	335	45	16	4344	4284	254	1541	1987	12.2	3.80	109	.258	.323	521	.269	143	272	174	-34	26.9

● **VERN RUHLE** Ruhle, Vernon Gerald b: 1/25/51, Coleman, Mich. BR/TR, 6'1", 187 lbs. Deb: 9/9/74 C

YEAR	TM/L	W	L	PCT	G	GS	CG	SH	SV	IP	H	HR	BB	SO	RAT	ERA	ERA+	OAV	OOB	BH	AVG	PB	PR	/A	PD	TPI
1974	Det-A	2	0	1.000	5	3	1	0	0	33	35	1	6	10	11.5	2.73	139	.273	.311	0	—	0	3	4	-1	-0.1
1975	Det-A	11	12	.478	32	31	8	3	0	190	199	17	65	67	12.8	4.03	100	.266	.330	0	—	0	-5	-0	-2	-0.5
1976	Det-A	9	12	.429	32	32	5	1	0	199^{2}	227	19	59	88	13.1	3.92	95	.288	.340	0	—	0	-9	-5	-0	-0.7
1977	Det-A	3	5	.375	14	10	0	0	0	66^{1}	83	9	15	27	13.7	5.70	75	.305	.348	0	—	0	-12	-10	-1	-1.1
1978	Hou-N	3	3	.500	13	10	2	2	0	68	57	0	20	27	10.3	2.12	156	.224	.283	1	.056	-1	11	9	-1	0.6
1979	Hou-N	2	6	.250	13	10	2	2	0	66^{1}	64	9	8	33	10.0	4.07	86	.249	.277	1	.053	-1	-2	-4	-1	-0.6
1980	*Hou-N	12	4	.750	28	22	6	2	0	159^{1}	148	7	29	55	10.2	2.37	139	.251	.289	12	.245	4	22	16	-2	1.9
1981	*Hou-N	4	6	.400	20	15	1	0	1	102	97	6	20	39	10.4	2.91	113	.250	.289	6	.250	3	7	4	-2	0.6
1982	Hou-N	9	13	.409	31	21	3	2	1	149	169	12	24	56	11.9	3.93	84	.289	.321	4	.098	-0	-5	-10	-1	-1.5
1983	Hou-N	8	5	.615	41	9	0	0	3	114^{2}	107	13	36	43	11.5	3.69	92	.249	.312	2	.105	0	-1	-4	0	-0.3
1984	Hou-N	1	9	.100	40	6	0	0	2	90^{1}	112	5	29	60	14.3	4.58	72	.309	.365	1	.083	0	-10	-13	1	-1.3
1985	Cle-A	2	10	.167	42	16	1	0	3	125	139	16	30	54	12.3	4.32	96	.283	.326	0	—	0	-2	-3	-0	-0.3
1986	*Cal-A	1	3	.250	16	3	0	0	1	47^{2}	46	5	7	23	10.2	4.15	99	.247	.278	0	—	0	0	-0	1	0.0
Total	13	67	88	.432	327	188	29	12	11	1411^{1}	1483	119	348	582	11.9	3.73	97	.270	.318	27	.148	6	-5	-16	-8	-3.3

● **SEAN RUNYAN** Runyan, Sean David b: 6/21/74, Fort Smith, Ark. BL/TL, 6'3", 200 lbs. Deb: 3/31/98

YEAR	TM/L	W	L	PCT	G	GS	CG	SH	SV	IP	H	HR	BB	SO	RAT	ERA	ERA+	OAV	OOB	BH	AVG	PB	PR	/A	PD	TPI
1998	Det-A	1	4	.200	**88**	0	0	0	1	50^{1}	47	7	28	39	13.8	3.58	132	.255	.360	0	—	0	6	6	-1	0.4

● **GLENDON RUSCH** Rusch, Glendon James b: 11/7/74, Seattle, Wash. BL/TL, 6'2", 170 lbs. Deb: 4/6/97

YEAR	TM/L	W	L	PCT	G	GS	CG	SH	SV	IP	H	HR	BB	SO	RAT	ERA	ERA+	OAV	OOB	BH	AVG	PB	PR	/A	PD	TPI
1997	KC-A	6	9	.400	30	27	1	0	0	170^{1}	206	28	52	116	14.0	5.50	86	.301	.357	0	.000	-0	-18	-15	-2	-1.3
1998	KC-A	6	15	.286	29	24	1	1	1	154^{2}	191	22	50	94	14.3	5.88	83	.304	.359	0	.000	-0	-21	-17	0	-1.9
Total	2	12	24	.333	59	51	2	1	1	325	397	50	102	210	14.1	5.68	85	.302	.358	0	.000	-1	-39	-32	-2	-3.2

● **ANDY RUSH** Rush, Jesse Howard b: 12/26/1889, Longton, Kan. d: 3/16/69, Fresno, Cal. BR/TR, 6'3", 180 lbs. Deb: 4/16/25

YEAR	TM/L	W	L	PCT	G	GS	CG	SH	SV	IP	H	HR	BB	SO	RAT	ERA	ERA+	OAV	OOB	BH	AVG	PB	PR	/A	PD	TPI
1925	Bro-N	0	1	.000	4	2	0	0	0	9^{2}	16	3	5	4	19.6	9.31	45	.364	.429	0	.000	-0	-5	-6	0	-0.5

● **BOB RUSH** Rush, Robert Ransom b: 12/21/25, Battle Creek, Mich BR/TR, 6'4", 205 lbs. Deb: 4/22/48

YEAR	TM/L	W	L	PCT	G	GS	CG	SH	SV	IP	H	HR	BB	SO	RAT	ERA	ERA+	OAV	OOB	BH	AVG	PB	PR	/A	PD	TPI
1948	Chi-N	5	11	.313	36	16	4	0	0	133^{1}	153	8	37	72	12.9	3.92	100	.287	.335	5	.128	-2	1	-0	1	-0.1
1949	Chi-N	10	18	.357	35	27	9	1	4	201	197	10	79	80	12.4	4.07	99	.255	.324	2	.032	-7	-1	-1	1	-0.7
1950	Chi-N☆	13	20	.394	39	34	19	1	1	254^{2}	261	11	93	93	12.7	3.71	113	.265	.332	15	.167	-1	12	14	2	1.8
1951	Chi-N	11	12	.478	37	29	12	2	2	211^{1}	212	16	68	129	12.1	3.83	107	.254	.312	13	.191	-0	3	6	1	0.7
1952	Chi-N★	17	13	.567	34	32	17	4	0	250^{1}	205	14	81	157	10.5	2.70	143	.216	.282	28	.292	7	29	32	2	**5.0**
1953	Chi-N	9	14	.391	29	28	8	1	0	166^{2}	177	17	66	84	13.4	4.54	98	.270	.341	6	.111	-2	-5	-2	1	-0.3
1954	Chi-N	13	15	.464	33	32	11	0	0	236^{1}	213	12	103	124	12.2	3.77	111	.243	.326	23	.277	7	8	11	3	2.3
1955	Chi-N	13	11	.542	33	33	14	3	0	234	204	19	73	130	10.7	3.50	117	.234	.295	9	.110	-3	14	15	1	1.2
1956	Chi-N	13	10	.565	32	32	13	1	0	239^{2}	210	30	59	104	10.2	3.19	118	.233	.282	8	.098	-3	15	15	-2	0.9
1957	Chi-N	6	16	.273	31	29	5	0	0	205^{1}	211	16	66	103	12.2	4.38	88	.265	.323	14	.203	2	-12	-12	-2	-1.1
1958	*Mil-N	10	6	.625	28	20	5	2	0	147^{1}	142	13	31	84	10.6	3.42	103	.253	.293	9	.200	2	9	2	-2	0.2
1959	Mil-N	5	6	.455	31	9	1	1	0	101^{1}	102	5	23	64	11.2	2.40	148	.257	.299	6	.188	0	17	13	-1	1.3
1960	Mil-N	2	0	1.000	10	0	0	0	1	15	24	2	5	8	17.4	4.20	82	.369	.414	1	.333	1	-1	-1	-0	-0.1
	Chi-A	0	0	—	9	0	0	0	0	14^{1}	16	4	5	12	13.2	5.65	67	.302	.362	1	1.000	0	-3	-3	0	0.1
Total	13	127	152	.455	417	321	118	16	8	2410^{2}	2327	177	789	1244	11.8	3.65	109	.251	.313	140	.173	0	88	90	7	11.2

● **AMOS RUSIE** Rusie, Amos Wilson "The Hoosier Thunderbolt" b: 5/30/1871, Mooresville, Ind. d: 12/6/42, Seattle, Wash. BR/TR, 6'1", 200 lbs. Deb: 5/9/1889 H

YEAR	TM/L	W	L	PCT	G	GS	CG	SH	SV	IP	H	HR	BB	SO	RAT	ERA	ERA+	OAV	OOB	BH	AVG	PB	PR	/A	PD	TPI
1889	Ind-N	12	10	.545	33	22	19	1	0	225	246	12	116	109	14.8	5.32	78	.270	.358	18	.175	-3	-33	-29	-2	-2.5
1890	NY-N	29	34	.460	67	62	56	4	1	548^{2}	436	3	289	**341**	12.3	2.56	137	**.212**	.316	79	.278	10	62	58	6	**6.9**
1891	NY-N	33	20	.623	61	57	52	**6**	1	500^{1}	391	6	262	**337**	12.1	2.55	125	**.207**	.310	54	.245	4	44	36	2	3.7
1892	NY-N	32	31	.508	65	62	59	2	0	541	410	7	270	304	11.5	2.84	113	.202	.299	54	.211	-0	27	23	6	2.7
1893	NY-N	33	21	.611	**56**	52	**50**	**4**	1	**482**	451	15	218	**208**	12.8	3.23	144	**.240**	.324	57	.269	3	**77**	**76**	3	**7.2**
1894	*NY-N	**36**	13	.735	54	50	45	**3**	1	444	426	10	200	**195**	**12.8**	**2.78**	**189**	**.250**	**.330**	52	.280	3	126	122	8	**11.0**
1895	NY-N	23	23	.500	49	47	42	**4**	0	393^{1}	384	9	159	**201**	12.6	3.73	124	.252	.325	44	.246	-5	46	40	3	3.3
1897	NY-N	28	10	.737	38	37	35	2	0	322^{1}	314	6	87	135	11.5	**2.54**	164	.253	.308	40	.278	3	64	58	2	6.1
1898	NY-N	20	11	.645	37	36	33	4	1	300	288	6	103	114	12.0	3.03	115	.251	.317	29	.210	-1	19	15	-0	1.2
1901	Cin-N	0	1	.000	3	2	2	0	0	22	43	1	3	6	18.8	8.59	37	.406	.422	1	.125	-0	-13	-13	0	-0.5
Total	10	246	174	.586	463	427	393	30	5	3778^{2}	3389	75	1707	1950	12.4	3.07	130	.234	.319	428	.247	12	418	384	27	39.1

● **SCOTT RUSKIN** Ruskin, Scott Drew b: 6/8/63, Jacksonville, Fla. BR/TL, 6'2", 185 lbs. Deb: 4/9/90

YEAR	TM/L	W	L	PCT	G	GS	CG	SH	SV	IP	H	HR	BB	SO	RAT	ERA	ERA+	OAV	OOB	BH	AVG	PB	PR	/A	PD	TPI
1990	Pit-N	2	2	.500	44	0	0	0	2	47^{2}	50	2	28	34	15.1	3.02	120	.269	.370	2	.333	2	4	3	0	0.4
	Mon-N	1	0	1.000	23	0	0	0	0	27^{2}	25	2	10	23	11.4	2.28	160	.243	.310	0	.000	-0	5	4	0	0.2
	Yr	3	2	.600	67	0	0	0	2	75^{1}	75	4	38	57	13.5	2.75	132	.256	.341	2	.250	1	9	7	0	0.6
1991	Mon-N	4	4	.500	64	0	0	0	6	63^{2}	57	4	30	46	12.7	4.24	85	.241	.333	0	.000	0	-4	-4	-0	-0.6
1992	Cin-N	4	3	.571	57	0	0	0	0	53^{2}	56	6	20	43	12.9	5.03	72	.275	.342	0	.000	-0	-9	-9	0	-1.1
1993	Cin-N	0	0	—	4	0	0	0	0	1	3	1	2	0	45.0	18.00	22	.500	.625	0	—	0	-2	-2	0	0.0
Total	4	11	9	.550	192	0	0	0	8	193^{2}	191	15	90	146	13.3	3.95	92	.260	.345	2	.154	1	-6	-7	1	-1.1

● **JOHN RUSS** Russ, John b: 4/1/1858, Cannelton, Ind. d: 1/18/12, Louisville, Ky. Deb: 7/4/1882 ♦

YEAR	TM/L	W	L	PCT	G	GS	CG	SH	SV	IP	H	HR	BB	SO	RAT	ERA	ERA+	OAV	OOB	BH	AVG	PB	PR	/A	PD	TPI
1882	Bal-a	0	0	—	1	0	0	0	0	3	3	0	1	0	12.0	3.00	92	.250	.308	1	.333	0	-0	-0	-0	0.0

● **ALLAN RUSSELL** Russell, Allan E. "Rubberarm" b: 7/31/1893, Baltimore, Md. d: 10/20/72, Baltimore, Md. BB/TR, 5'11", 165 lbs. Deb: 9/13/15 F

YEAR	TM/L	W	L	PCT	G	GS	CG	SH	SV	IP	H	HR	BB	SO	RAT	ERA	ERA+	OAV	OOB	BH	AVG	PB	PR	/A	PD	TPI
1915	NY-A	1	2	.333	5	3	1	0	0	27	21	1	21	21	14.3	2.67	110	.228	.377	2	.250	0	1	1	-0	0.1
1916	NY-A	6	10	.375	34	19	8	1	6	171^{1}	138	8	75	104	11.6	3.20	90	.232	.324	2	.044	-3	-7	-6	0	-0.9
1917	NY-A	7	8	.467	25	10	6	0	2	104^{1}	89	3	39	55	11.6	2.24	120	.236	.319	10	.323	3	5	5	-1	1.1
1918	NY-A	7	11	.389	27	18	7	2	4	141	139	6	73	54	13.9	3.26	87	.267	.363	7	.167	-1	-7	-7	-1	-1.1
1919	NY-A	5	5	.500	23	9	4	1	1	90^{2}	89	6	32	50	12.2	3.47	92	.251	.317	7	.233	0	-2	-3	0	-0.2
	Bos-A	10	4	.714	21	11	9	1	4	121^{1}	105	0	39	63	10.8	2.52	120	.246	.310	5	.122	-1	10	7	-1	0.6
	Yr	15	9	.625	44	20	13	2	**5**	212	194	6	71	113	11.3	2.93	106	.248	.311	12	.169	-1	7	4	-0	0.4
1920	Bos-A	5	6	.455	16	10	7	0	1	107^{2}	100	3	38	53	11.8	3.01	121	.251	.321	5	.122	-2	9	8	1	0.6
1921	Bos-A	6	11	.353	39	14	7	0	3	173	204	10	77	60	15.1	4.11	103	.303	.382	7	.123	-5	3	2	0	-0.3
1922	Bos-A	6	7	.462	34	11	1	0	2	125^{2}	152	6	57	34	15.3	5.01	82	.314	.392	3	.079	-3	-14	-13	2	-1.2
1923	Was-A	10	7	.588	52	5	4	0	**9**	181^{1}	177	9	77	67	12.7	3.03	124	.270	.348	10	.200	2	19	15	-3	1.2
1924	*Was-A	5	1	.833	37	0	0	0	8	82^{1}	83	1	45	17	14.1	4.37	92	.282	.379	5	.278	2	-1	-3	-0	-0.1
1925	Was-A	2	4	.333	32	2	0	0	2	68^{2}	85	6	37	25	16.1	5.77	73	.315	.399	2	.143	-1	-10	-12	2	-0.8
Total	11	70	76	.479	345	112	54	5	42	1394^{1}	1382	59	610	603	13.1	3.52	99	.269	.351	65	.157	-10	5	-4	-0	-1.0

● **LEFTY RUSSELL** Russell, Clarence Dickson b: 7/8/1890, Baltimore, Md. d: 1/22/62, Baltimore, Md. BL/TL, 6'1", 165 lbs. Deb: 10/1/10 F

YEAR	TM/L	W	L	PCT	G	GS	CG	SH	SV	IP	H	HR	BB	SO	RAT	ERA	ERA+	OAV	OOB	BH	AVG	PB	PR	/A	PD	TPI
1910	Phi-A	1	0	1.000	1	1	1	1	0	9	8	0	2	5	10.0	0.00	—	.258	.303	0	.000	-0	3	2	0	0.3
1911	Phi-A	0	3	.000	7	2	0	0	0	31^{2}	45	1	18	7	19.3	7.67	41	.357	.456	5	.385	1	-15	-16	1	-1.0
1912	Phi-A	0	2	.000	5	2	1	0	0	17^{1}	18	1	14	9	18.2	7.27	42	.265	.412	0	.000	-0	-8	-8	0	-0.8
Total	3	1	5	.167	13	5	2	1	0	58	71	2	34	21	17.5	6.36	47	.316	.423	5	.250	0	-20	-22	1	-1.5

● **REB RUSSELL** Russell, Ewell Albert b: 4/12/1889, Jackson, Miss. d: 9/30/73, Indianapolis, Ind BL/TL, 5'11", 185 lbs. Deb: 4/18/13 ♦

YEAR	TM/L	W	L	PCT	G	GS	CG	SH	SV	IP	H	HR	BB	SO	RAT	ERA	ERA+	OAV	OOB	BH	AVG	PB	PR	/A	PD	TPI
1913	Chi-A	22	16	.579	**52**	36	26	8	4	316^{2}	250	2	79	122	9.5	1.90	154	.219	.273	20	.189	3	36	36	-5	4.2
1914	Chi-A	7	12	.368	38	23	8	1	1	167^{1}	168	3	33	79	11.0	2.90	92	.268	.308	17	.266	4	-3	-4	0	-0.1
1915	Chi-A	11	10	.524	41	25	10	3	2	229^{1}	215	0	47	90	10.5	2.59	115	.249	.292	21	.244	4	9	10	-2	1.1

YEAR	TM/L	W	L	PCT	G	GS	CG	SH	SV	IP	H	HR	BB	SO	RAT	ERA	ERA+	OAV	OOB	BH	AVG	PB	PR	/A	PD	TPI
1916	Chi-A	18	11	.621	56	25	16	5	3	264^1	207	1	42	112	**8.5**	2.42	114	.220	**.254**	13	.143	-4	12	10	-2	0.5
1917	*Chi-A	15	5	**.750**	35	24	11	5	3	189^1	170	1	32	54	9.6	1.95	136	.245	.279	19	.279	5	15	15	-1	2.2
1918	Chi-A	7	5	.583	19	15	10	2	0	124^2	117	0	33	38	10.8	2.60	105	.252	.302	7	.140	-1	2	2	-1	-0.2
1919	Chi-A	0	0	—	1	0	0	0	0	0	1	0	1	0	—	—	—	1.000	1.000	0	—	0	0	0	0	0.0
Total	7	80	59	.576	242	148	81	24	13	1291^2	1128	7	267	495	9.8	2.33	120	.238	.281	262	.268	10	72	69	-11	7.7
● **JACK RUSSELL**	Russell, Jack Erwin b: 10/24/05, Paris, Tex. d: 11/3/90, Clearwater, Fla. BR/TR, 6'1.5", 178 lbs. Deb: 5/5/26																									
1926	Bos-A	0	5	.000	36	5	1	0	0	98	94	2	24	17	10.9	3.58	114	.268	.316	4	.190	-0	5	5	4	0.6
1927	Bos-A	4	9	.308	34	15	4	1	0	147	172	5	40	25	13.3	4.10	103	.298	.348	6	.125	-3	1	2	1	0.0
1928	Bos-A	11	14	.440	32	26	10	2	0	201^1	233	6	41	27	12.4	3.84	107	.294	.332	13	.210	-0	4	6	1	0.8
1929	Bos-A	6	18	.250	35	32	13	0	0	227^1	263	12	40	37	12.1	3.92	109	.290	.322	9	.129	-4	8	9	4	0.8
1930	Bos-A	9	20	.310	35	30	15	0	0	229^2	302	11	53	35	14.0	5.45	85	.321	.359	14	.177	-3	-20	-21	2	-2.2
1931	Bos-A	10	18	.357	36	31	13	0	0	232	298	7	65	45	14.2	5.16	83	.310	.355	16	.195	-0	-20	-22	3	-1.8
1932	Bos-A	1	7	.125	11	6	1	0	0	39^2	61	2	15	7	17.2	6.81	66	.343	.394	1	.091	-1	-10	-10	0	-1.7
	Cle-A	5	7	.417	18	11	6	0	1	113	146	5	27	27	13.9	4.70	101	.310	.349	12	.300	2	-3	1	1	0.4
	Yr	6	14	.300	29	17	7	0	1	152^2	207	7	42	34	14.7	5.25	89	.319	.361	13	.255	1	-13	-10	2	-1.3
1933	*Was-A	12	6	.667	50	3	2	0	**13**	124	119	3	32	28	11.0	2.69	156	.255	.305	5	.147	-1	**22**	**21**	4	3.4
1934	Was-A☆	5	10	.333	**54**	9	3	0	**7**	157^2	179	6	56	38	13.5	4.17	104	.287	.348	7	.159	3	6	3	3	0.7
1935	Was-A	4	9	.308	43	7	2	0	3	126	170	10	37	30	14.9	5.71	76	.324	.371	7	.200	1	-18	-20	3	-1.4
1936	Was-A	3	2	.600	18	5	1	0	3	49^2	66	3	25	6	16.5	6.34	75	.317	.391	0	.000	-2	-7	-9	1	-0.9
	Bos-A	0	3	.000	23	2	0	0	0	40	57	2	16	9	16.4	5.62	94	.345	.403	2	.286	0	-3	-1	2	0.1
	Yr	3	5	.375	41	7	1	0	3	89^2	123	5	41	15	16.5	6.02	83	.330	.396	2	.091	-2	-10	-10	3	-0.8
1937	Det-A	2	5	.286	25	0	0	0	4	40^1	63	4	20	10	18.7	7.59	62	.362	.431	0	.000	-0	-13	-13	1	-2.0
1938	*Chi-N	6	1	.857	42	0	0	0	3	102^1	100	1	30	29	11.5	3.34	115	.258	.313	7	.219	1	5	6	3	0.8
1939	Chi-N	4	3	.571	39	0	0	0	3	68^2	78	3	24	32	13.4	3.67	107	.282	.339	0	.000	-2	**2**	2	2	0.1
1940	StL-N	3	4	.429	26	0	0	0	1	54	53	1	26	16	13.2	2.50	160	.252	.335	0	.000	-2	8	9	1	1.1
Total	15	85	141	.376	557	182	71	3	38	2050^2	2454	83	571	418	13.4	4.46	97	.299	.346	103	.167	-11	-33	-33	36	-1.2
● **JEFF RUSSELL**	Russell, Jeffrey Lee b: 9/2/61, Cincinnati, Ohio BR/TR, 6'3", 210 lbs. Deb: 8/13/83																									
1983	Cin-N	4	5	.444	10	10	2	0	0	68^1	58	7	22	40	10.5	3.03	126	.233	.295	3	.143	1	5	6	-0	0.8
1984	Cin-N	6	18	.250	33	30	4	2	0	181^2	186	15	65	101	12.6	4.26	89	.263	.329	8	.140	-0	-14	-10	1	-1.1
1985	Tex-A	3	6	.333	13	13	0	0	0	62	85	10	27	44	16.5	7.55	56	.324	.392	0	—	0	-23	-23	1	-2.6
1986	Tex-A	5	2	.714	37	0	0	0	2	82	74	11	31	54	11.6	3.40	126	.244	.316	0	—	0	7	8	2	0.8
1987	Tex-A	5	4	.556	52	2	0	0	3	97^1	109	9	52	56	15.1	4.44	101	.285	.373	0	—	0	0	0	1	0.2
1988	Tex-A★	10	9	.526	34	24	5	0	0	188^2	183	15	66	88	12.2	3.82	107	.257	.326	0	.000	-0	3	6	2	0.7
1989	Tex-A★	6	4	.600	71	0	0	0	**38**	72^2	45	4	24	77	8.9	1.98	200	.182	.263	0	—	0	15	16	2	3.8
1990	Tex-A	1	5	.167	27	0	0	0	10	25^1	23	1	16	16	13.9	4.26	92	.253	.364	0	—	0	-1	-1	0	-0.3
1991	Tex-A	6	4	.600	68	0	0	0	30	79^1	71	11	26	52	11.1	3.29	122	.235	.298	0	—	0	7	7	2	1.3
1992	Tex-A	2	3	.400	51	0	0	0	28	56^2	51	3	22	43	11.9	1.91	199	.238	.315	0	—	0	13	12	1	2.1
	*Oak-A	2	0	1.000	8	0	0	0	2	9^2	4	0	3	5	6.5	0.00	—	.125	.200	0	—	0	4	4	-0	0.9
	Yr	4	3	.571	59	0	0	0	30	66^1	55	3	25	48	10.9	1.63	233	.220	.291	0	—	0	17	16	0	3.0
1993	Bos-A	1	4	.200	51	0	0	0	33	46^2	39	1	14	45	10.4	2.70	171	.231	.293	0	—	0	8	10	1	2.2
1994	Bos-A	0	5	.000	29	0	0	0	12	28	30	3	13	18	14.1	5.14	98	.270	.352	0	—	0	-1	-0	-1	-0.2
	Cle-A	1	1	.500	13	0	0	0	5	12^2	13	2	3	10	11.4	4.97	95	.265	.308	0	—	0	-0	-0	-0	-0.1
	Yr	1	6	.143	42	0	0	0	17	40^2	43	5	16	28	13.1	5.09	97	.264	.330	0	—	0	-1	-1	-1	-0.3
1995	Tex-A	1	0	1.000	37	0	0	0	20	32^2	36	3	9	21	12.4	3.03	159	.277	.324	0	—	0	6	7	-1	0.8
1996	*Tex-A	3	3	.500	55	0	0	0	3	56	58	5	22	23	13.5	3.38	155	.269	.347	0	—	0	10	12	-0	1.1
Total	14	56	73	.434	589	79	11	2	186	1099^2	1065	100	415	693	12.3	3.75	111	.255	.326	11	.139	1	40	52	9	10.4
● **JOHN RUSSELL**	Russell, John Albert b: 10/20/1894, San Mateo, Cal. d: 11/19/30, Ely, Nev. BL/TL, 6'2", 195 lbs. Deb: 7/4/17																									
1917	Bro-N	0	1	.000	5	1	1	0	0	16	12	1	6	1	10.1	4.50	62	.222	.300	1	.250	0	-3	-3	-0	-0.2
1918	Bro-N	0	0	—	1	0	0	0	0	1	2	0	1	0	27.0	18.00	15	.500	.600	0	—	0	-2	-2	-0	0.0
1921	Chi-A	2	5	.286	11	9	4	0	0	66^1	82	3	35	15	16.0	5.29	80	.314	.397	10	.400	3	-7	-8	-1	-0.4
1922	Chi-A	0	1	.000	4	1	0	0	1	6^2	7	0	4	3	14.9	6.75	60	.280	.379	0	.000	-0	-2	-2	0	-0.3
Total	4	2	7	.222	21	11	5	0	1	90	103	4	46	19	15.0	5.40	73	.299	.384	11	.367	3	-14	-14	-1	-0.9
● **JOHN RUSSELL**	Russell, John William b: 1/5/61, Oklahoma City, Okla. BR/TR, 6', 200 lbs. Deb: 6/22/84 ♦																									
1989	Atl-N	0	0	—	1	0	0	0	0	0^1	0	0	0	0	0.0	0.00	—	.000	.000	29	.182	0	0	0	0	0.0
● **MARIUS RUSSO**	Russo, Marius Ugo "Lefty" b: 7/19/14, Brooklyn, N.Y. BR/TL, 6'1", 190 lbs. Deb: 6/6/39																									
1939	NY-A	8	3	.727	21	11	9	2	2	116	86	6	41	55	9.9	2.41	181	.210	.283	10	.244	1	29	25	2	2.5
1940	NY-A	14	8	.636	30	24	15	0	1	189^1	181	17	55	87	11.3	3.28	123	.249	.303	12	.188	2	23	16	3	2.2
1941	*NY-A☆	14	10	.583	28	27	17	3	1	209^2	195	8	87	105	12.1	3.09	127	.247	.322	18	.231	3	25	20	2	2.5
1942	NY-A	4	1	.800	9	5	2	0	0	45^1	41	2	14	15	11.1	2.78	124	.244	.306	4	.235	1	4	3	0	0.5
1943	*NY-A	5	10	.333	24	14	5	1	1	101^2	89	7	45	42	12.0	3.72	87	.235	.319	6	.194	1	-5	-6	0	-0.7
1946	NY-A	0	2	.000	8	3	0	0	0	18^2	26	1	11	7	17.8	4.34	80	.333	.416	0	.000	-1	-2	-2	0	-0.2
Total	6	45	34	.570	120	84	48	6	5	680^2	618	41	253	311	11.6	3.13	124	.242	.312	50	.213	8	74	57	8	6.8
● **DICK RUSTECK**	Rusteck, Richard Frank b: 7/12/41, Chicago, Ill. BR/TL, 6'1", 175 lbs. Deb: 6/10/66																									
1966	NY-N	1	2	.333	8	3	1	1	0	24	24	1	8	9	12.0	3.00	121	.276	.337	0	.000	-1	2	2	-0	0.1
● **BABE RUTH**	Ruth, George Herman "The Bambino" or "The Sultan Of Swat" b: 2/6/1895, Baltimore, Md. d: 8/16/48, New York, N.Y. BL/TL, 6'2", 215 lbs. Deb: 7/11/14 CH♦																									
1914	Bos-A	2	1	.667	4	3	1	0	0	23	21	1	7	3	11.0	3.91	69	.236	.292	2	.200	0	-3	-3	-0	-0.4
1915	*Bos-A	18	8	.692	32	28	16	1	0	217^2	166	3	85	112	10.6	2.44	114	.212	.294	29	.315	16	12	8	1	2.8
1916	*Bos-A	23	12	.657	44	41	23	**9**	1	323^2	230	0	118	170	9.9	**1.75**	**158**	**.201**	.280	37	.272	14	**39**	37	0	**5.9**
1917	Bos-A	24	13	.649	41	38	**35**	6	2	326^1	244	2	108	128	10.0	2.01	128	.211	.284	40	.325	17	24	21	2	4.8
1918	*Bos-A	13	7	.650	20	19	18	1	0	166^1	125	1	49	40	9.5	2.22	121	.214	.277	95	.300	12	10	9	4	2.9
1919	Bos-A	9	5	.643	17	15	12	0	1	133^1	148	2	58	30	14.0	2.97	102	.290	.365	139	.322	14	4	1	0	1.5
1920	NY-A	1	0	1.000	1	1	0	0	0	4	3	0	2	0	11.3	4.50	85	.200	.294	172	.376	1	-0	-0	-0	0.0
1921	*NY-A	2	0	1.000	2	1	0	0	0	9	14	1	9	2	23.0	9.00	47	.350	.469	204	.378	2	-5	-5	0	-0.7
1930	NY-A	1	0	1.000	1	1	1	0	0	9	11	0	2	3	13.0	3.00	143	.306	.342	186	.359	1	2	1	1	0.3
1933	NY-A★	1	0	1.000	1	1	1	0	0	9	12	0	3	0	15.0	5.00	78	.308	.357	138	.301	1	-1	-1	-0	0.0
Total	10	94	46	.671	163	148	107	17	4	1221^1	974	10	441	488	10.6	2.28	122	.221	.297	2873	.342	78	81	67	8	17.1
● **JOHNNY RUTHERFORD**	Rutherford, John William "Doc" b: 5/5/25, Belleville, Ont., Canada BL/TR, 5'10.5", 170 lbs. Deb: 4/30/52																									
1952	*Bro-N	7	7	.500	22	11	4	0	2	97^1	97	9	29	29	11.8	4.25	86	.262	.319	9	.290	2	-6	-7	1	-0.6
● **DICK RUTHVEN**	Ruthven, Richard David b: 3/27/51, Sacramento, Cal. BR/TR, 6'3", 190 lbs. Deb: 4/17/73																									
1973	Phi-N	6	9	.400	25	23	3	1	1	128^1	125	10	75	98	14.2	4.21	90	.257	.360	5	.132	-1	-8	-6	1	-0.7
1974	Phi-N	9	13	.409	35	35	6	0	0	212^2	182	11	116	153	12.7	4.02	94	.231	.332	13	.191	-1	-10	-6	-1	-0.8
1975	Phi-N	2	2	.500	11	7	0	0	0	40^2	37	2	22	26	13.3	4.20	89	.243	.343	2	.154	-0	-3	-2	-0	-0.3
1976	Atl-N☆	14	17	.452	36	36	8	4	0	240^1	255	14	90	142	13.2	4.19	90	.275	.345	13	.171	-0	-19	-11	2	-1.1
1977	Atl-N	7	13	.350	25	23	6	2	0	151	158	14	62	84	13.2	4.23	105	.267	.338	12	.267	3	-5	4	-2	0.6
1978	Atl-N	2	6	.250	13	13	2	1	0	81	78	8	28	45	11.8	4.11	98	.257	.319	2	.083	-2	-5	-1	-0	-0.2
	*Phi-N	13	5	.722	20	20	9	2	0	150^2	136	13	28	75	9.9	2.99	119	.248	.285	15	.283	4	10	10	-0	1.6
	Yr	15	11	.577	33	33	11	3	0	231^2	214	21	56	120	10.5	3.38	111	.250	.297	17	.221	3	5	9	-1	1.4
1979	Phi-N	7	5	.583	20	20	3	2	0	122^1	121	10	37	58	11.8	4.27	90	.256	.313	6	.146	-0	-7	-6	-2	-0.7
1980	*Phi-N	17	10	.630	33	33	6	1	0	223^1	241	9	74	86	12.8	3.55	107	.283	.342	16	.235	4	1	6	-0	1.0
1981	*Phi-N★	12	7	.632	23	22	5	0	0	146^2	162	10	54	80	13.4	5.15	70	.281	.346	7	.140	-0	-27	-25	-1	-3.0
1982	Phi-N	11	11	.500	33	31	8	2	0	204^1	189	18	59	115	11.2	3.79	97	.246	.305	7	.109	-2	-4	-3	-2	-0.8

YEAR	TM/L	W	L	PCT	G	GS	CG	SH	SV	IP	H	HR	BB	SO	RAT	ERA	ERA+	OAV	OOB	BH	AVG	PB	PR	/A	PD	TPI
1983	Phi-N	1	3	.250	7	7	0	0	0	33^{2}	46	5	10	26	15.0	5.61	64	.333	.378	1	.111	-0	-7	-8	0	-0.8
	Chi-N	12	9	.571	25	25	5	2	0	149^{1}	156	17	28	73	11.3	4.10	92	.269	.306	12	.226	2	-8	-5	2	-0.3
	Yr	13	12	.520	32	32	5	2	0	183	202	22	38	99	12.0	4.38	86	.279	.318	13	.210	2	-15	-13	2	-1.1
1984	Chi-N	6	10	.375	23	22	0	0	0	126^{2}	154	14	41	55	14.1	5.04	77	.302	.359	7	.159	0	-21	-16	-0	-1.8
1985	Chi-N	4	7	.364	20	15	0	0	0	87^{1}	103	6	37	26	14.4	4.53	88	.299	.367	5	.208	0	-9	-5	-1	-0.8
1986	Chi-N	0	0	—	6	0	0	0	0	10^{2}	12	4	6	3	15.2	5.06	80	.293	.383	0	.000	-0	-2	-1	-0	0.0
Total	14	123	127	.492	355	332	61	17	1	2109	2155	165	767	1145	12.6	4.14	92	.267	.333	123	.183	6	-123	-75	-4	-8.1
● **CYCLONE RYAN**	Ryan, Daniel R. b: 1866, Cappagh White, Ireland d: 1/30/17, Medfield, Mass. TR , 6′, 200 lbs. Deb: 8/8/1887 ♦																									
1887	NY-a	0	1	.000	2	1	0	0	0	2^{1}	5	1	6	0	42.4	23.14	18	.455	.647	7	.219	-0	-5	-5	-0	-1.2
1891	Bos-N	0	0	—	1	0	0	0	0	3	2	0	1	0	9.0	0.00	—	.182	.250	0	.000	-0	1	1	0	0.0
Total	2	0	1	.000	3	1	0	0	0	5^{1}	7	1	7	0	23.6	10.13	39	.318	.483	7	.212	-0	-4	-4	0	-1.2
● **JACK RYAN**	Ryan, Jack "Gulfport" b: 9/19/1884, Lawrenceville, Ill. d: 10/16/49, Handsboro, Miss. BR/TR, 5′10″, 165 lbs. Deb: 7/2/08																									
1908	Cle-A	1	1	.500	8	1	1	0	1	35^{2}	27	3	2	7	7.6	2.27	105	.220	.238	1	.091	0	0	0	-0	0.1
1909	Bos-A	3	3	.500	13	8	2	0	0	59^{1}	64	0	20	24	13.3	3.34	75	.288	.358	4	.211	0	-6	-6	-1	-0.6
1911	Bro-N	0	1	.000	3	1	0	0	0	6	9	1	4	1	21.0	3.00	111	.375	.483	0	.000	-0	0	0	0	0.0
Total	3	4	5	.444	24	10	3	0	1	101	100	4	26	32	11.8	2.94	85	.271	.329	5	.161	1	-5	-5	-0	-0.5
● **JIMMY RYAN**	Ryan, James Edward "Pony" b: 2/11/1863, Clinton, Mass. d: 10/26/23, Chicago, Ill. BR/TL, 5′9″, 162 lbs. Deb: 10/8/1885 ♦																									
1886	*Chi-N	0	0	—	5	0	0	0	1	23^{1}	19	2	13	15	12.3	4.63	78	.257	.368	100	.306	1	-3	-3	0	0.1
1887	Chi-N	2	1	.667	8	3	2	0	0	45	53	3	17	14	15.2	4.20	107	.305	.386	145	.285	2	-1	1	2	0.3
1888	Chi-N	4	0	1.000	8	2	1	0	0	38^{1}	47	2	12	11	13.9	3.05	99	.297	.347	182	.332	4	-1	-0	0	0.2
1891	Chi-N	0	0	—	2	0	0	0	1	5^{2}	11	0	2	2	20.6	1.59	210	.393	.433	140	.277	1	1	1	-0	0.0
1893	Chi-N	0	0	—	1	0	0	0	0	4^{2}	3	0	0	1	5.8	0.00	—	.176	.176	102	.299	0	2	2	0	0.0
Total	5	6	1	.857	24	5	3	0	2	117	133	7	44	43	14.1	3.62	105	.295	.365	2502	.306	9	-1	2	2	0.6
● **JOHN RYAN**	Ryan, John A. b: Birmingham, Mich. TR , Deb: 4/19/1884																									
1884	Bal-U	3	2	.600	6	6	5	0	0	51	61	1	16	33	13.6	3.35	80	.277	.326	2	.080	-3	-5	-4	-0	-0.6
● **JOHNNY RYAN**	Ryan, John Joseph b: 10/1853, Philadelphia, Pa. d: 3/22/02, Philadelphia, Pa. 5′7.5″, 150 lbs. Deb: 8/19/1873 ♦																									
1874	Bal-n	0	0	—	1	0	0	0	0	3^{1}	13	0	0	0	35.1	16.20	14	.565	.565	35	.193	-0	-5	-5		0.0
1875	NH-n	1	5	.167	10	6	4	0	0	59^{1}	70	1	9	1	12.0	3.19	65	.255	.279	23	.158	-1	-6	-7		-0.7
1876	Lou-N	0	0	—	1	0	0	0	0	8	22	0	0	1	24.8	5.63	48	.449	.449	61	.253	-0	-3	-3	-0	0.0
Total	2 n	1	5	.167	11	6	4	0	0	62^{2}	83	1	9	1	13.2	3.88	54	.279	.301	60	.179	-1	-12	-12		-0.7
● **KEN RYAN**	Ryan, Kenneth Frederick b: 10/24/68, Pawtucket, R.I. BR/TR, 6′3″, 230 lbs. Deb: 8/31/92																									
1992	Bos-A	0	0	—	7	0	0	0	1	7	4	2	5	5	11.6	6.43	66	.174	.321	0	—	0	-2	-2	0	0.0
1993	Bos-A	7	2	.778	47	0	0	0	1	50	43	2	29	49	13.5	3.60	128	.235	.349	0	—	0	4	6	0	0.9
1994	Bos-A	2	3	.400	42	0	0	0	13	48	46	1	17	32	12.0	2.44	206	.256	.323	0	—	0	13	14	-1	1.9
1995	Bos-A	0	4	.000	28	0	0	0	7	32^{2}	34	4	24	34	16.3	4.96	98	.268	.388	0	—	0	-1	-0	-1	-0.1
1996	Phi-N	3	5	.375	62	0	0	0	8	89	71	4	45	70	11.8	2.43	177	.223	.321	1	.143	-0	18	19	0	1.8
1997	Phi-N	1	0	1.000	22	0	0	0	0	20^{2}	31	5	13	10	20.0	9.58	44	.344	.438	0	—	0	-12	-12	-0	-0.5
1998	Phi-N	0	0	—	17	1	0	0	0	22^{2}	21	1	20	16	16.7	4.37	100	.253	.404	0	.000	-0	-0	-0	0	0.0
Total	7	13	14	.481	225	1	0	0	30	270	250	19	153	216	13.7	3.77	121	.249	.353	1	.125	-0	19	24	-1	4.0
● **NOLAN RYAN**	Ryan, Lynn Nolan b: 1/31/47, Refugio, Tex. BR/TR, 6′2″, 195 lbs. Deb: 9/11/66																									
1966	NY-N	0	1	.000	2	1	0	0	0	3	5	1	3	6	24.0	15.00	24	.357	.471	0	—	0	-4	-4	0	-0.9
1968	NY-N	6	9	.400	21	18	3	0	0	134	93	12	75	133	11.6	3.09	98	.200	.317	5	.114	-1	-2	-1	-2	-0.5
1969	*NY-N	6	3	.667	25	10	2	0	1	89^{1}	60	3	53	92	11.5	3.53	104	.189	.307	3	.103	-1	1	1	-2	-0.3
1970	NY-N	7	11	.389	27	19	5	2	1	131^{2}	86	10	97	125	12.8	3.42	118	.188	.335	8	.178	-1	9	9	-1	1.0
1971	NY-N	10	14	.417	30	26	3	0	0	152	125	8	116	137	15.2	3.97	86	.219	.365	6	.128	-0	-8	-9	-1	-1.6
1972	Cal-A☆	19	16	.543	39	39	20	**9**	0	284	166	14	157	**329**	10.6	2.28	128	**.171**	.292	13	.135	0	25	20	-2	2.4
1973	Cal-A★	21	16	.568	41	39	26	4	1	326	238	18	162	**383**	11.2	2.87	123	.203	.304	0	—	0	34	24	-2	2.9
1974	Cal-A	22	16	.579	42	41	26	3	0	**332^{2}**	221	18	202	**367**	11.7	2.89	119	**.190**	.314	0	—	0	27	20	2	2.8
1975	Cal-A☆	14	12	.538	28	28	10	5	0	198	152	13	132	186	13.2	3.45	103	.213	.342	0	—	0	7	2	-2	0.5
1976	Cal-A	17	18	.486	39	39	21	**7**	0	284^{1}	193	13	183	**327**	12.1	3.36	99	**.195**	.323	0	—	0	5	-1	0	0.3
1977	Cal-A†	19	16	.543	37	37	**22**	4	0	299	198	12	204	**341**	12.4	2.77	141	**.193**	.331	0	—	0	**43**	**38**	0	4.2
1978	Cal-A	10	13	.435	31	31	14	3	0	234^{2}	183	12	148	**260**	12.8	3.72	97	.220	.340	0	—	0	1	-3	1	0.1
1979	*Cal-A★	16	14	.533	34	34	17	**5**	0	222^{2}	169	15	114	**223**	11.7	3.60	113	**.212**	.314	0	—	0	15	12	-0	1.6
1980	*Hou-N	11	10	.524	35	35	4	2	0	233^{2}	205	10	98	200	11.8	3.35	98	.236	.316	6	.086	-1	6	-2	-1	-0.5
1981	*Hou-N★	11	5	.688	21	21	5	3	0	149	99	2	68	140	10.1	**1.69**	**195**	**.188**	.281	11	.216	3	**30**	**27**	-1	**3.3**
1982	Hou-N	16	12	.571	35	35	10	3	0	250^{1}	196	20	109	245	11.3	3.16	105	**.213**	.302	10	.120	-1	12	4	-0	0.3
1983	Hou-N	14	9	.609	29	29	5	2	0	196^{1}	134	9	101	183	11.0	2.98	114	**.195**	.302	5	.072	-4	14	9	-0	0.6
1984	Hou-N	12	11	.522	30	30	5	2	0	183^{2}	143	12	69	197	10.6	3.04	109	.211	.288	6	.098	-2	11	6	-3	0.3
1985	Hou-N★	10	12	.455	35	35	4	0	0	232	205	12	95	209	12.0	3.80	91	.239	.322	7	.111	-1	-5	-9	-3	-1.2
1986	*Hou-N	12	8	.600	30	30	1	0	0	178	119	14	82	194	10.4	3.34	108	.188	.285	6	.102	-2	8	5	-1	0.1
1987	Hou-N	8	16	.333	34	34	0	0	0	211^{2}	154	14	87	**270**	10.4	**2.76**	**142**	**.199**	.284	4	.062	-3	**31**	**27**	-1	2.5
1988	Hou-N	12	11	.522	33	33	4	1	0	220	186	18	87	**228**	11.5	3.52	94	.227	.307	4	.057	-3	-2	-5	-3	-1.1
1989	Tex-A★	16	10	.615	32	32	6	2	0	239^{1}	162	17	98	**301**	10.1	3.20	124	**.187**	.276	0	—	0	18	20	-1	1.9
1990	Tex-A	13	9	.591	30	30	5	2	0	204	137	18	74	**232**	**9.6**	3.44	114	**.188**	**.269**	0	—	0	11	11	-2	0.9
1991	Tex-A	12	6	.667	27	27	2	2	0	173	102	12	72	203	**9.3**	2.91	138	**.172**	**.267**	0	—	0	23	21	-1	2.0
1992	Tex-A	5	9	.357	27	27	2	0	0	157^{1}	138	9	69	157	12.5	3.72	102	.238	.331	0	—	0	4	1	-1	0.0
1993	Tex-A	5	5	.500	13	13	0	0	0	66^{1}	54	5	40	46	12.9	4.88	85	.220	.331	0	—	0	-4	-5	-2	-0.8
Total	27	324	292	.526	807	773	222	61	3	5386	3923	321	2795	5714	11.5	3.19	111	.204	.309	94	.110	-17	309	218	-29	20.8
● **ROSY RYAN**	Ryan, Wilfred Patrick Dolan b: 3/15/1898, Worcester, Mass. d: 12/10/80, Scottsdale, Ariz. BL/TR, 6′, 185 lbs. Deb: 9/7/19																									
1919	NY-N	1	2	.333	4	3	1	0	0	20^{1}	20	0	9	7	13.3	3.10	91	.260	.345	0	.000	-1	-0	-1	-1	-0.2
1920	NY-N	0	1	.000	3	1	1	0	0	15^{1}	14	1	4	5	10.6	1.76	170	.259	.310	0	.000	-1	2	2	0	0.1
1921	NY-N	7	10	.412	36	16	5	0	3	147^{1}	140	6	32	58	10.6	3.73	98	.255	.297	9	.200	1	1	-1	-1	-0.2
1922	*NY-N	17	12	.586	46	22	12	1	3	191^{2}	194	5	74	75	12.7	3.01	133	.269	.338	12	.194	1	23	21	-1	2.8
1923	*NY-N	16	5	.762	**45**	15	7	0	4	172^{2}	169	8	46	58	11.3	3.49	109	.257	.308	11	.208	0	10	6	0	0.7
1924	*NY-N	8	6	.571	37	9	2	0	5	124^{2}	137	1	37	36	12.7	4.26	86	.285	.339	5	.139	-1	-5	-8	-2	-1.2
1925	Bos-N	2	8	.200	37	7	1	0	2	122^{2}	152	7	52	48	15.0	6.31	64	.303	.368	11	.282	3	-28	-31	-1	-2.0
1926	Bos-N	0	2	.000	7	2	0	0	0	19	29	1	7	1	17.1	7.58	47	.392	.444	1	.200	-0	-8	-9	-0	-0.8
1928	NY-A	0	0	—	3	0	0	0	0	6	17	1	1	5	27.0	16.50	23	.486	.500	0	.000	-1	-8	-8	-0	-0.1
1933	Bro-N	1	1	.500	30	0	0	0	2	61^{1}	69	3	16	22	12.9	4.55	71	.276	.327	2	.154	0	-8	-9	-0	-0.4
Total	10	52	47	.525	248	75	29	1	19	881	941	33	278	315	12.6	4.14	91	.277	.333	51	.190	1	-22	-38	-5	-1.3
● **MIKE RYBA**	Ryba, Dominic Joseph b: 6/9/03, DeLancey, Pa. d: 12/13/71, Brookline Station, Mo. BR/TR, 5′11.5″, 195 lbs. Deb: 9/22/35 C																									
1935	StL-N	1	1	.500	2	1	1	0	0	16	15	0	1	6	9.0	3.38	121	.242	.254	2	.400	1	1	1	0	0.2
1936	StL-N	5	1	.833	14	0	0	0	0	45	55	3	16	25	14.6	5.40	73	.294	.356	3	.167	-0	-7	-7	-1	-1.0
1937	StL-N	9	6	.600	38	8	5	0	0	135	152	8	40	57	12.9	4.13	96	.284	.336	15	.313	4	-3	-2	0	0.2
1938	StL-N	1	1	.500	3	0	0	0	0	5	8	0	1	0	16.2	5.40	73	.348	.375	0	—	0	-1	-1	0	-0.3
1941	Bos-A	7	3	.700	40	3	0	0	6	121	143	14	42	54	13.8	4.46	93	.297	.353	8	.216	1	-4	-4	2	0.0
1942	Bos-A	3	3	.500	18	0	0	0	3	44^{1}	49	5	13	16	12.8	3.86	97	.278	.332	5	.294	1	-1	-1	1	0.0
1943	Bos-A	7	5	.583	40	8	4	1	2	143^{2}	142	4	57	50	12.5	3.26	102	.262	.333	8	.186	0	1	1	-1	0.0
1944	Bos-A	12	7	.632	42	7	2	0	2	138	119	7	39	50	10.3	3.33	102	.233	.287	6	.146	-0	2	1	3	0.4
1945	Bos-A	7	6	.538	34	9	4	1	2	123	122	5	33	44	11.5	2.49	137	.259	.310	9	.250	2	12	13	-1	1.5
1946	*Bos-A	0	1	.000	9	0	0	0	1	12^{2}	12	1	5	5	12.1	3.55	103	.261	.333	2	1.000	1	-0	0	-0	0.1
Total	10	52	34	.605	240	36	16	2	16	783^{2}	817	47	247	307	12.3	3.66	100	.269	.326	58	.235	9	-1	1	3	1.1

YEAR	TM/L	W	L	PCT	G	GS	CG	SH	SV	IP	H	HR	BB	SO	RAT	ERA	ERA+	OAV	OOB	BH	AVG	PB	PR	/A	PD	TPI
● **GARY RYERSON**	Ryerson, Gary Lawrence b: 6/7/48, Los Angeles, Cal. BR/TL, 6′1″, 175 lbs. Deb: 6/28/72																									
1972	Mil-A	3	8	.273	20	14	4	1	0	102	119	9	21	45	12.4	3.62	84	.290	.324	1	.042	-1	-6	-7	-1	-1.0
1973	Mil-A	0	1	.000	9	4	0	0	0	23	32	0	7	10	15.3	7.83	48	.327	.371	0	—	0	-10	-10	0	-0.3
Total	2	3	9	.250	29	18	4	1	0	125	151	9	28	55	12.9	4.39	72	.297	.333	1	.042	-1	-17	-17	-1	-1.3
● **BRET SABERHAGEN**	Saberhagen, Bret William b: 4/11/64, Chicago Heights, Ill. BR/TR, 6′1″, 195 lbs. Deb: 4/4/84																									
1984	*KC-A	10	11	.476	38	18	2	1	1	157^2	138	13	36	73	10.0	3.48	116	.237	.283	0	—	0	9	10	0	1.2
1985	*KC-A	20	6	.769	32	32	10	1	0	235^1	211	19	38	158	**9.6**	2.87	145	.241	**.273**	0	—	0	33	34	2	3.8
1986	KC-A	7	12	.368	30	25	4	2	0	156	165	15	29	112	11.3	4.15	102	.268	.303	0	—	0	0	2	1	0.3
1987	KC-A★	18	10	.643	33	33	15	4	0	257	246	27	53	163	10.7	3.36	135	.252	.295	0	—	0	31	34	1	3.4
1988	KC-A	14	16	.467	35	35	9	0	0	260^2	271	18	59	171	11.5	3.80	105	.269	.312	0	—	0	5	5	0	0.6
1989	KC-A	**23**	6	**.793**	36	35	**12**	4	0	**262^1**	209	13	43	193	**8.7**	**2.16**	**178**	.217	**.252**	0	—	0	**50**	**49**	0	**5.5**
1990	KC-A★	5	9	.357	20	20	5	0	0	135	146	9	28	87	11.7	3.27	117	.279	.316	0	—	0	10	8	3	1.2
1991	KC-A	13	8	.619	28	28	7	2	0	196^1	165	12	45	136	10.0	3.07	134	.228	.281	0	—	0	22	23	1	2.4
1992	NY-N	3	5	.375	17	15	1	1	0	97^2	84	6	27	81	10.6	3.50	99	.233	.294	3	.107	-1	0	-0	3	0.2
1993	NY-N	7	7	.500	19	19	4	1	0	139^1	131	11	17	93	9.8	3.29	122	.250	.278	5	.111	-0	12	11	3	1.3
1994	NY-N☆	14	4	**.778**	24	24	4	0	0	177^1	169	13	13	143	9.4	2.74	152	.254	.273	10	.172	1	29	28	2	3.1
1995	NY-N	5	5	.500	16	16	3	0	0	110	105	13	20	71	10.6	3.35	121	.251	.293	4	.114	-1	10	8	2	0.8
	*Col-N	2	1	.667	9	9	0	0	0	43	60	8	13	29	16.3	6.28	86	.323	.382	1	.071	-1	-10	-4	0	-0.3
	Yr	7	6	.538	25	25	3	0	0	153	165	21	33	100	11.9	4.18	106	.269	.312	5	.102	-2	0	4	2	0.5
1997	Bos-A	0	1	.000	6	6	0	0	0	26	30	5	10	14	14.5	6.58	70	.288	.362	0	.000	-0	-6	-6	-0	-0.2
1998	*Bos-A	15	8	.652	31	31	0	0	0	175	181	22	29	100	11.1	3.96	117	.264	.300	0	.000	-0	13	13	-1	1.3
Total	14	156	109	.589	374	346	76	16	1	2428^2	2311	204	460	1624	10.5	3.35	124	.251	.291	23	.124	-2	209	215	18	24.6
● **BRIAN SACKINSKY**	Sackinsky, Brian Walter b: 6/22/71, Pittsburgh, Pa. BR/TR, 6′4″, 220 lbs. Deb: 4/20/96																									
1996	Bal-A	0	0	—	3	0	0	0	0	4^2	6	1	3	2	17.4	3.86	128	.316	.409	0	—	0	1	1	-0	0.0
● **RAY SADECKI**	Sadecki, Raymond Michael b: 12/26/40, Kansas City, Kan. BL/TL, 5′11″, 180 lbs. Deb: 5/19/60																									
1960	StL-N	9	9	.500	26	26	7	1	0	157^1	148	15	86	95	13.4	3.78	109	.249	.345	12	.211	-0	-0	6	-2	0.4
1961	StL-N	14	10	.583	31	31	13	0	0	222^2	196	28	102	114	12.2	3.72	118	.238	.324	22	.253	2	8	17	-5	1.3
1962	StL-N	6	8	.429	22	17	4	1	1	102^1	121	13	43	50	14.7	5.54	77	.296	.367	3	.081	-2	-18	-14	-2	-2.1
1963	StL-N	10	10	.500	36	28	4	1	1	193^1	198	25	78	136	13.0	4.10	87	.266	.339	9	.141	-1	-17	-12	-3	-1.6
1964	*StL-N	20	11	.645	37	32	9	2	1	220	232	16	60	119	12.0	3.68	103	.273	.322	12	.160	2	-4	3	-3	0.3
1965	StL-N	6	15	.286	36	28	4	0	1	172^2	192	26	64	122	13.3	5.21	74	.284	.346	11	.200	2	-32	-26	-2	-3.0
1966	StL-N	2	1	.667	5	3	1	0	0	24^1	16	2	9	21	9.2	2.22	162	.188	.266	3	.429	2	4	4	0	0.7
	SF-N	3	7	.300	26	19	3	1	0	105	125	20	39	62	14.4	5.40	68	.293	.358	11	.324	5	-21	-20	-2	-1.4
	Yr	5	8	.385	31	22	4	1	0	129^1	141	22	48	83	13.4	4.80	76	.276	.343	14	.341	7	-17	-17	-2	-0.7
1967	SF-N	12	6	.667	35	24	10	2	0	188	165	8	58	145	10.9	2.78	118	.238	.301	18	.247	4	13	11	-1	1.4
1968	SF-N	12	18	.400	38	36	13	6	0	254	225	14	70	206	10.6	2.91	101	.237	.292	8	.094	-1	2	1	-2	-0.3
1969	SF-N	5	8	.385	29	17	4	3	0	138^1	137	18	53	104	12.5	4.23	83	.259	.329	5	.125	2	-10	-11	2	-0.6
1970	NY-N	8	4	.667	28	19	4	0	0	138^2	134	18	52	89	12.1	3.89	103	.255	.322	8	.205	1	2	2	-2	0.0
1971	NY-N	7	7	.500	34	20	5	2	0	163^1	139	10	44	120	10.3	2.92	117	.229	.285	10	.200	1	10	9	-2	0.6
1972	NY-N	2	1	.667	34	2	0	0	0	75^2	73	3	31	38	12.6	3.09	109	.257	.334	2	.154	-0	3	2	-1	-0.1
1973	*NY-N	5	4	.556	31	11	1	0	1	116^2	109	11	41	87	11.6	3.39	107	.248	.314	7	.226	1	3	3	-3	0.1
1974	NY-N	8	8	.500	34	10	3	1	0	103	107	7	35	46	12.6	3.41	105	.274	.337	7	.259	1	2	2	-0	0.3
1975	StL-N	1	0	1.000	8	0	0	0	0	11	13	0	7	8	16.4	3.27	115	.289	.385	0	—	0	0	1	-0	0.0
	Atl-N	2	3	.400	25	5	0	0	1	66^1	73	3	21	24	13.3	4.21	90	.286	.350	3	.200	0	-4	-3	-1	-0.3
	Yr	3	3	.500	33	5	0	0	1	77^1	86	3	28	32	13.7	4.07	93	.285	.353	3	.200	0	-4	-3	-1	-0.3
	KC-A	1	0	1.000	5	0	0	0	0	3	5	0	3	0	24.0	3.00	128	.333	.444	0	—	0	0	0	-0	-0.1
1976	KC-A	0	0	—	3	0	0	0	0	4^2	7	0	3	1	19.3	0.00	—	.368	.455	0	—	0	2	2	-0	-0.1
	Mil-A	2	0	1.000	36	0	0	0	1	37^1	38	2	20	27	14.7	4.34	81	.262	.363	0	—	0	-3	-4	-1	-0.2
	Yr	2	0	1.000	39	0	0	0	1	42	45	2	23	28	15.2	3.86	91	.274	.374	0	—	0	-2	-2	-1	-0.3
1977	NY-N	0	1	.000	4	0	0	0	0	3	3	1	3	0	18.0	6.00	62	.300	.462	0	—	0	-1	-1	-0	-0.2
Total	18	135	131	.508	563	328	85	20	7	2500^2	2456	240	922	1614	12.3	3.78	97	.258	.326	151	.191	19	-61	-32	-30	-4.9
● **JIM SADOWSKI**	Sadowski, James Michael b: 8/7/51, Pittsburgh, Pa. BR/TR, 6′3″, 195 lbs. Deb: 4/27/74																									
1974	Pit-N	0	1	.000	4	0	0	0	0	9	7	1	9	1	16.0	6.00	57	.233	.410	0	.000	0	-2	-3	1	-0.2
● **BOB SADOWSKI**	Sadowski, Robert b: 2/19/38, Pittsburgh, Pa. BR/TR, 6′2″, 195 lbs. Deb: 6/19/63 F																									
1963	Mil-N	5	7	.417	19	18	5	1	0	116^2	99	8	30	72	10.3	2.62	123	.231	.289	2	.057	-2	9	8	1	0.6
1964	Mil-N	9	10	.474	51	18	5	0	5	166^2	159	18	56	96	12.0	4.10	86	.251	.319	8	.154	0	-11	-11	3	-1.0
1965	Mil-N	5	9	.357	34	13	3	0	3	123	117	11	35	78	11.3	4.32	82	.250	.306	3	.086	-2	-11	-11	-1	-1.5
1966	Bos-A	1	1	.500	11	5	0	0	0	33^1	41	4	9	11	13.8	5.40	70	.311	.359	0	.000	-1	-7	-6	-0	-0.4
Total	4	20	27	.426	115	54	13	1	8	439^2	416	41	130	257	11.5	3.87	90	.250	.311	13	.101	-4	-20	-20	2	-2.3
● **TED SADOWSKI**	Sadowski, Theodore b: 4/1/36, Pittsburgh, Pa. d: 7/18/93, Shaler Twsp., Pa. BR/TR, 6′1.5″, 190 lbs. Deb: 9/2/60 F																									
1960	Was-A	1	0	1.000	9	1	0	0	1	17^1	17	4	9	12	14.0	5.19	75	.258	.355	0	.000	-0	-3	-3	-0	-0.2
1961	Min-A	0	2	.000	15	1	0	0	0	33	49	6	11	12	16.6	6.82	62	.348	.399	0	.000	-1	-10	-9	1	-0.5
1962	Min-A	1	1	.500	19	0	0	0	0	34	37	6	11	15	13.0	5.03	81	.301	.363	2	.500	1	-4	-4	0	-0.1
Total	3	2	3	.400	43	2	0	0	1	84^1	103	16	31	39	14.6	5.76	71	.312	.376	2	.154	-0	-17	-16	1	-0.8
● **A. J. SAGER**	Sager, Anthony Joseph b: 3/3/65, Columbus, Ohio BR/TR, 6′4″, 220 lbs. Deb: 4/4/94																									
1994	SD-N	1	4	.200	22	3	0	0	0	46^2	62	4	16	26	15.4	5.98	69	.325	.383	1	.100	0	-9	-10	2	-0.7
1995	Col-N	0	0	—	10	0	0	0	0	14^2	19	1	7	10	16.0	7.36	73	.311	.382	0	.000	-0	-5	-3	1	0.0
1996	Det-A	4	5	.444	22	9	0	0	0	79	91	10	29	52	13.9	5.01	101	.294	.358	0	—	0	-0	0	-0	0.0
1997	Det-A	3	4	.429	38	1	0	0	3	84	81	10	24	53	11.4	4.18	110	.258	.313	0	—	0	4	4	0	0.3
1998	Det-A	4	2	.667	31	3	0	0	2	59^1	79	7	23	23	15.6	6.52	72	.325	.386	0	.000	-0	-12	-12	1	-1.0
Total	5	12	15	.444	123	16	0	0	5	283^2	332	32	99	164	13.9	5.36	88	.297	.357	1	.071	-0	-23	-21	4	-1.4
● **JOHNNY SAIN**	Sain, John Franklin b: 9/25/17, Havana, Ark. BR/TR, 6′2″, 200 lbs. Deb: 4/24/42 C																									
1942	Bos-N	4	7	.364	40	3	0	0	6	97	79	8	63	68	13.6	3.90	86	.228	.354	2	.074	-2	-6	-6	1	-0.8
1946	Bos-N	20	14	.588	37	34	**24**	3	2	265	225	8	87	129	10.7	2.21	155	.230	.294	28	.298	5	35	36	3	**5.9**
1947	Bos-N★	21	12	.636	38	35	22	3	1	266	265	19	79	132	11.8	3.52	111	.255	.310	37	.346	12	16	11	1	2.6
1948	*Bos-N★	**24**	15	.615	42	39	**28**	4	1	**314^2**	297	19	83	137	11.0	2.60	147	.245	.296	25	.217	3	**47**	43	-2	5.3
1949	Bos-N	10	17	.370	37	36	16	1	0	243	285	15	75	73	13.5	4.81	78	.291	.344	20	.206	1	-21	-28	-2	-2.7
1950	Bos-N	20	13	.606	37	37	25	3	0	278^1	294	34	70	96	11.8	3.94	98	.269	.314	21	.206	4	6	-3	-2	-0.2
1951	Bos-N	5	13	.278	26	22	6	1	1	160^1	195	16	45	63	13.6	4.21	87	.299	.347	11	.212	3	-4	-10	0	-0.7
	*NY-A	2	1	.667	7	4	1	0	1	37	41	5	8	21	11.9	4.14	93	.281	.318	4	.286	1	-0	-1	1	0.0
1952	*NY-A	11	6	.647	35	16	8	0	7	148^1	149	15	38	57	11.5	3.46	96	.261	.310	19	.268	7	4	-2	-1	0.3
1953	*NY-A☆	14	7	.667	40	19	10	1	9	189	189	16	45	84	11.3	3.00	123	.262	.308	17	.250	5	21	15	-0	2.1
1954	NY-A	6	6	.500	45	0	0	0	**22**	77	66	11	15	33	9.5	3.16	109	.229	.267	6	.353	3	5	2	-0	0.7
1955	NY-A	0	0	—	3	0	0	0	0	5^1	6	4	1	5	11.8	6.75	55	.300	.333	0	.000	-0	-2	-2	0	0.0
	KC-A	2	5	.286	25	0	0	0	1	44^2	54	10	10	12	12.9	5.44	77	.297	.333	0	.000	-1	-7	-6	-1	-1.1
	Yr	2	5	.286	28	0	0	0	1	50	60	14	11	17	12.8	5.58	74	.297	.333	0	.000	-1	-9	-8	-1	-1.1
Total	11	139	116	.545	412	245	140	16	51	2125^2	2145	180	619	910	11.8	3.49	106	.261	.315	190	.245	40	94	50	-2	11.4
● **RANDY ST.CLAIRE**	St.Claire, Randy Anthony b: 8/23/60, Glens Falls, N.Y. BR/TR, 6′2″, 190 lbs. Deb: 9/11/84 F																									
1984	Mon-N	0	0	—	4	0	0	0	0	8	11	0	2	4	15.8	4.50	76	.344	.400	0	—	0	-1	-1	-0	0.0
1985	Mon-N	5	3	.625	42	0	0	0	0	68^2	69	3	26	25	12.6	3.93	86	.265	.334	1	.200	1	-3	-4	0	-0.3
1986	Mon-N	2	0	1.000	11	0	0	0	1	19	13	2	6	21	9.0	2.37	156	.186	.250	0	.000	-0	3	3	1	0.4
1987	Mon-N	3	3	.500	44	0	0	0	7	67	64	9	20	43	11.4	4.03	104	.249	.306	2	.333	0	0	1	-0	0.1

YEAR	TM/L	W	L	PCT	G	GS	CG	SH	SV	IP	H	HR	BB	SO	RAT	ERA	ERA+	OAV	OOB	BH	AVG	PB	PR	/A	PD	TPI
1988	Mon-N	0	0	—	6	0	0	0	0	7^1	11	2	5	6	19.6	6.14	59	.344	.432	0	—	0	-2	-2	0	0.0
	Cin-N	1	0	1.000	10	0	0	0	0	13^2	13	3	5	8	11.9	2.63	136	.241	.305	0	.000	-0	1	1	-0	0.1
	Yr	1	0	1.000	16	0	0	0	0	21	24	5	10	14	14.6	3.86	93	.276	.351	0	.000	-0	-1	-1	0	0.1
1989	Min-A	1	0	1.000	14	0	0	0	1	22^1	19	4	10	14	12.5	5.24	79	.226	.323	0	—	0	-3	-3	0	-0.1
1991	*Atl-N	0	0	—	19	0	0	0	0	28^2	31	4	9	30	12.6	4.08	95	.282	.336	1	.500	0	-1	-1	0	0.1
1992	Atl-N	0	0	—	10	0	0	0	0	15^1	17	1	8	7	14.7	5.87	62	.283	.368	0	—	0	-4	-4	0	0.0
1994	Tor-A	0	0	—	2	0	0	0	0	2	4	0	2	2	27.0	9.00	54	.444	.545	0	—	0	-1	-1	0	0.0
Total	9	12	6	.667	162	0	0	0	9	252	252	28	93	160	12.5	4.14	92	.260	.328	4	.267	1	-11	-10	2	0.3
● JIM ST.VRAIN	St.Vrain, James Marcellin b: 6/6/1883, Ralls County, Mo. d: 6/12/37, Butte, Montana BR/TL, 5'9", 175 lbs. Deb: 4/20/02																									
1902	Chi-N	4	6	.400	12	11	10	1	0	95	88	0	25	51	11.2	2.08	130	.246	.304	3	.097	-2	7	7	0	0.5
● MIKE SAIPE	Saipe, Michael Eric b: 9/10/73, San Diego, Cal. BR/TR, 6'1", 190 lbs. Deb: 6/25/98																									
1998	Col-N	0	1	.000	2	2	0	0	0	10	22	5	0	2	21.6	10.80	47	.431	.453	0	.000	0	-7	-6	0	-0.5
● LUIS SALAZAR	Salazar, Luis Ernesto (Garcia) b: 5/19/56, Barcelona, Venez. BR/TR, 5'9", 180 lbs. Deb: 8/15/80 ♦																									
1987	SD-N	0	0	—	2	0	0	0	0	2	2	0	1	0	13.5	4.50	88	.250	.333	48	.254	0	-0	-0	0	0.0
● FREDDY SALE	Sale, Frederick Link b: 5/2/02, Chester, S.C. d: 5/27/56, Hermosa Beach, Cal BR/TR, 5'9", 160 lbs. Deb: 6/30/24																									
1924	Pit-N	0	0	—	1	0	0	0	0	1	2	0	0	0	18.0	0.00	—	.500	.500	0	—	0	0	0	-0	0.0
● HARRY SALISBURY	Salisbury, Henry H. b: 5/15/1855, Providence, R.I. d: 3/29/33, Chicago, Ill. BL, 5'8.5", 162 lbs. Deb: 8/28/1879																									
1879	Tro-N	4	6	.400	10	10	9	0	0	89	103	0	11	31	11.5	2.22	112	.265	.285	2	.056	-4	3	3	2	0.0
1882	Pit-a	20	18	.526	38	38	38	1	0	335	315	1	37	135	9.5	2.63	99	.232	.253	22	.152	-6	2	-1	-2	-0.8
Total	2	24	24	.500	48	48	47	1	0	424	418	1	48	166	9.9	2.55	102	.239	.260	24	.133	-10	5	2	-1	-0.8
● BILL SALISBURY	Salisbury, William Ansel "Solly" b: 11/12/1876, Algona, Iowa d: 1/17/52, Rowena, Ore. BR/TR, 6', 180 lbs. Deb: 4/19/02																									
1902	Phi-N	0	0	—	2	1	0	0	0	6	15	1	2	0	27.0	13.50	21	.469	.514	0	.000	-0	-7	-7	-1	-0.1
● ROGER SALKELD	Salkeld, Roger William b: 3/6/71, Burbank, Cal. BR/TR, 6'5", 215 lbs. Deb: 9/8/93 F																									
1993	Sea-A	0	0	—	3	2	0	0	0	14^1	13	0	4	13	11.3	2.51	175	.232	.295	0	—	0	3	3	0	0.0
1994	Sea-A	2	5	.286	13	13	0	0	0	59	76	7	45	46	18.6	7.17	68	.314	.424	0	—	0	-16	-15	-1	-1.5
1996	Cin-N	8	5	.615	29	19	1	1	0	116	114	18	54	82	13.5	5.20	81	.261	.351	1	.031	-3	-13	-13	-0	-1.5
Total	3	10	10	.500	45	34	1	1	0	189^1	203	25	103	141	14.9	5.61	79	.277	.372	1	.031	-3	-25	-25	-1	-3.0
● SLIM SALLEE	Sallee, Harry Franklin "Scatter" b: 2/3/1885, Higginsport, Ohio d: 3/23/50, Higginsport, Ohio BL/TL, 6'3", 180 lbs. Deb: 4/16/08																									
1908	StL-N	3	8	.273	25	12	7	1	0	128^2	144	1	36	39	12.8	3.15	75	.274	.324	2	.049	-3	-11	-11	-0	-1.3
1909	StL-N	10	11	.476	32	27	12	1	0	219	223	3	59	55	11.8	2.42	104	.264	.315	8	.113	-2	4	3	-0	0.0
1910	StL-N	7	8	.467	18	13	9	1	2	115	112	4	24	46	10.7	2.97	100	.251	.290	4	.108	-2	1	0	0	-0.2
1911	StL-N	15	9	.625	36	30	18	1	3	245	234	6	64	74	11.1	2.76	123	.257	.309	15	.169	-2	18	17	-3	1.1
1912	StL-N	16	17	.485	48	32	20	3	**6**	294	289	6	72	108	11.2	2.60	132	.266	.315	14	.136	-4	26	27	-2	2.3
1913	StL-N	19	15	.559	50	29	18	3	5	276	257	11	60	106	10.5	2.71	119	.255	.301	20	.211	2	15	16	1	2.2
1914	StL-N	18	17	.514	46	29	18	3	**6**	282^1	252	5	72	105	10.6	2.10	133	.246	.302	21	.231	2	22	22	-2	2.9
1915	StL-N	13	17	.433	46	33	17	2	3	275^1	245	6	57	91	10.0	2.84	98	.238	.280	11	.120	-3	-3	-2	-1	-0.7
1916	StL-N	5	5	.500	16	7	4	2	1	70	75	2	23	28	12.9	3.47	76	.290	.352	3	.167	-0	-7	-6	-1	-1.1
	NY-N	9	4	.692	15	11	7	2	0	111^2	96	2	10	35	8.5	1.37	178	.234	.252	9	.257	2	15	13	-3	1.6
	Yr	14	9	.609	31	18	11	4	1	181^2	171	4	33	63	10.1	2.18	115	.255	.290	12	.226	2	9	7	-4	0.5
1917	*NY-N	18	7	.720	34	24	18	1	**4**	215^2	199	4	34	54	9.8	2.17	118	.249	.280	17	.221	1	13	9	-4	0.8
1918	NY-N	8	8	.500	18	16	12	1	2	132	122	3	12	33	**9.1**	2.25	117	.241	**.259**	5	.122	-2	8	6	-2	0.3
1919	*Cin-N	21	7	.750	29	28	22	4	0	227^2	221	4	20	24	9.6	2.06	135	.258	.276	14	.189	2	22	18	-5	2.0
1920	Cin-N	5	6	.455	21	12	6	0	2	116	129	4	16	13	11.4	3.34	91	.293	.320	6	.171	-1	-3	-4	-3	-0.8
	NY-N	1	0	1.000	5	2	1	0	0	17	16	0	0	2	8.5	1.59	189	.239	.239	1	.333	1	3	3	-0	0.2
	Yr	6	6	.500	26	14	7	0	2	133	145	4	16	15	10.9	3.11	97	.284	.306	7	.184	-0	0	-1	-4	-0.6
1921	NY-N	6	4	.600	37	0	0	0	2	96^1	115	7	14	23	12.1	3.64	101	.307	.332	8	.364	2	1	0	-2	0.1
Total	14	174	143	.549	476	305	189	25	36	2821^2	2729	68	573	836	10.7	2.56	114	.258	.299	158	.171	-8	125	109	-26	9.4
● ROGER SALMON	Salmon, Roger Elliott b: 5/11/1891, Newark, N.J. d: 6/17/74, Belfast, Me. BL/TL, 6'2", 170 lbs. Deb: 5/3/12																									
1912	Phi-A	1	0	1.000	2	1	0	0	0	5	7	0	4	5	19.8	9.00	34	.318	.423	0	.000	-0	-3	-3	-0	-0.5
● GUS SALVE	Salve, Augustus William b: 12/29/1885, Boston, Mass. d: 3/29/71, Providence, R.I. BL/TL, 6', 190 lbs. Deb: 9/14/08																									
1908	Phi-A	0	1	.000	2	1	1	0	0	15^1	17	1	9	6	15.8	4.11	62	.266	.365	0	.000	-1	-3	-3	-1	-0.3
● JACK SALVESON	Salveson, John Theodore b: 1/5/14, Fullerton, Cal. d: 12/28/74, Norwalk, Cal. BR/TR, 6'0.5", 180 lbs. Deb: 6/3/33																									
1933	NY-N	0	2	.000	8	2	2	0	0	30^2	30	4	14	8	12.9	3.82	84	.252	.331	1	.111	-1	-2	-2	0	-0.2
1934	NY-N	3	1	.750	12	4	0	0	0	38^1	43	2	13	18	13.1	3.52	110	.281	.337	3	.300	0	2	1	1	0.2
1935	Pit-N	0	1	.000	5	0	0	0	0	7	11	1	5	2	21.9	9.00	46	.306	.405	0	.000	-0	-4	-4	1	-0.4
	Chi-A	1	2	.333	20	2	2	0	1	66^2	79	6	23	22	13.8	4.86	95	.298	.354	6	.300	2	-3	-2	-0	0.1
1943	Cle-A	5	3	.625	23	11	4	3	3	86	87	5	26	24	11.9	3.35	93	.266	.322	6	.231	2	-0	-2	0	0.0
1945	Cle-A	0	0	—	19	0	0	0	0	44	52	3	6	11	12.1	3.68	88	.294	.321	4	.400	3	-2	-2	1	0.4
Total	5	9	9	.500	87	19	8	3	4	272^2	302	21	87	85	12.9	3.99	91	.280	.336	20	.260	7	-8	-11	2	0.1
● MANNY SALVO	Salvo, Manuel "Gyp" b: 6/30/12, Sacramento, Cal. d: 2/7/97, Vallejo, Cal. BR/TR, 6'4", 210 lbs. Deb: 4/22/39																									
1939	NY-N	4	10	.286	32	18	4	0	1	136	150	11	75	69	15.2	4.63	85	.285	.380	4	.098	-2	-11	-11	-1	-1.0
1940	Bos-N	10	9	.526	21	20	14	**5**	0	160^2	151	9	43	60	11.0	3.08	121	.248	.300	6	.103	-3	14	11	-1	0.8
1941	Bos-N	7	16	.304	35	27	11	2	0	195	192	9	93	67	13.3	4.06	88	.255	.340	7	.113	-0	-9	-11	-0	-1.2
1942	Bos-N	7	8	.467	25	14	6	1	0	130^2	129	7	41	25	12.0	3.03	110	.260	.322	5	.122	-1	4	4	-1	0.2
1943	Bos-N	0	1	.000	1	1	0	0	0	5	5	0	6	1	19.8	7.20	47	.250	.423	2	1.000	2	-2	-2	-0	-0.2
	Phi-N	0	0	—	1	0	0	0	0	0^1	2	0	1	0	81.0	27.00	12	.667	.750	0	—	0	-1	-1	0	0.0
	Bos-N	5	6	.455	20	13	5	1	0	93^2	94	6	25	25	11.5	3.27	105	.261	.311	6	.214	0	1	2	-1	0.2
	Yr	5	7	.417	22	14	5	1	0	99	101	6	32	26	12.2	3.55	96	.264	.322	8	.267	2	-2	-1	-1	0.0
Total	5	33	50	.398	135	93	40	9	1	721^1	723	42	284	247	12.8	3.69	98	.261	.334	30	.129	-4	-4	-7	-3	-1.2
● JOE SAMBITO	Sambito, Joseph Charles b: 6/28/52, Brooklyn, N.Y. BL/TL, 6'1", 190 lbs. Deb: 7/20/76																									
1976	Hou-N	3	2	.600	20	4	1	1	1	53^1	45	4	14	26	10.0	3.54	90	.237	.289	2	.222	1	-0	-2	1	0.0
1977	Hou-N	5	5	.500	54	1	0	0	7	89	77	6	24	67	10.2	2.33	153	.235	.287	2	.154	-0	16	12	1	1.5
1978	Hou-N	4	9	.308	62	0	0	0	11	88	85	5	32	96	12.0	3.07	108	.260	.326	1	.167	0	5	2	1	0.6
1979	Hou-N★	8	7	.533	63	0	0	0	22	91^1	80	8	23	83	10.5	1.77	198	.235	.292	2	.286	2	**20**	18	1	4.1
1980	*Hou-N	8	4	.667	64	0	0	0	17	90^1	65	3	22	75	8.9	2.19	150	.200	.255	0	.000	-1	14	11	0	1.8
1981	*Hou-N	5	5	.500	49	0	0	0	10	63^2	43	4	22	41	9.5	1.84	179	.192	.270	0	.000	-1	12	10	1	2.0
1982	Hou-N	0	0	—	9	0	0	0	4	12^2	7	0	2	7	6.4	0.71	467	.159	.196	0	.000	-0	4	4	0	0.3
1984	Hou-N	0	0	—	32	0	0	0	0	47^2	39	5	16	26	10.4	3.02	110	.228	.294	0	.000	-0	3	2	-1	-0.1
1985	NY-N	0	0	—	8	0	0	0	0	10^2	21	1	8	3	24.5	12.66	27	.420	.500	0	—	0	-11	-11	0	0.0
1986	*Bos-A	2	0	1.000	53	0	0	0	12	44^2	54	4	16	30	14.5	4.84	86	.298	.362	0	—	0	-3	-3	0	-0.3
1987	Bos-A	2	6	.250	47	0	0	0	0	37^2	46	8	16	35	14.8	6.93	65	.301	.367	0	—	0	-10	-10	0	-1.9
Total	11	37	38	.493	461	5	1	1	84	629	562	48	195	489	11.0	3.03	115	.241	.302	7	.135	2	49	32	4	8.0
● BILL SAMPEN	Sampen, William Albert b: 1/18/63, Lincoln, Ill. BR/TR, 6'2", 195 lbs. Deb: 4/10/90																									
1990	Mon-N	12	7	.632	59	4	0	0	2	90^1	94	7	33	69	12.9	2.99	122	.268	.334	0	.000	-1	8	7	-1	1.2
1991	Mon-N	9	5	.643	43	8	0	0	0	92^1	96	13	46	52	14.1	4.00	91	.273	.362	3	.231	0	-3	-4	-1	-0.6
1992	Mon-N	1	4	.200	44	1	0	0	0	63^1	62	4	29	23	13.1	3.13	111	.268	.352	0	.000	-1	3	2	1	0.2
	KC-A	0	2	.000	8	1	0	0	0	19^2	21	0	3	14	12.4	3.66	111	.292	.346	0	—	0	1	1	0	0.1
1993	KC-A	2	2	.500	18	0	0	0	0	18^1	25	1	9	9	18.7	5.89	78	.338	.437	0	—	0	-3	-3	0	-0.9

YEAR	TM/L	W	L	PCT	G	GS	CG	SH	SV	IP	H	HR	BB	SO	RAT	ERA	ERA+	OAV	OOB	BH	AVG	PB	PR	/A	PD	TPI
1994	Cal-A	1	1	.500	10	0	0	0	0	15^1	14	1	13	9	17.6	6.46	76	.241	.405	0	—	0	-3	-3	0	-0.3
Total	5	25	21	.543	182	14	0	0	2	299^1	312	26	133	176	13.9	3.73	100	.274	.358	3	.111	-1	2	0	-1	-0.3
● BENJ SAMPSON Sampson, Benjamin Damon b: 4/27/75, Des Moines, Iowa BR/TL, 6'2", 210 lbs. Deb: 9/9/98																										
1998	Min-A	1	0	1.000	5	2	0	0	0	17^1	10	0	7	16	8.8	1.56	301	.172	.262	0	—	0	6	6	-0	0.3
● JOE SAMUELS Samuels, Joseph Jonas "Skabotch" b: 3/21/05, Scranton, Pa. d: 10/28/96, Bath, N.Y. BR/TR, 6'1.5", 196 lbs. Deb: 4/23/30																										
1930	Det-A	0	0	—	2	0	0	0	0	6	10	1	6	1	24.0	16.50	29	.417	.533	0	.000	-0	-8	-8	-0	0.0
● ROGER SAMUELS Samuels, Roger Howard b: 1/5/61, San Jose, Cal. BL/TL, 6'5", 210 lbs. Deb: 7/20/88																										
1988	SF-N	1	2	.333	15	0	0	0	0	23^1	17	4	7	22	9.6	3.47	94	.202	.272	0	.000	-0	-0	-1	0	-0.1
1989	Pit-N	0	0	—	5	0	0	0	0	3^2	9	1	4	2	31.9	9.82	34	.474	.565	0	—	0	-3	-3	-0	0.0
Total	2	1	2	.333	20	0	0	0	0	27	26	5	11	24	12.7	4.33	76	.252	.330	0	.000	-0	-3	-3	0	-0.1
● ALEX SANCHEZ Sanchez, Alex Anthony b: 4/8/66, Concord, Cal. BR/TR, 6'2", 185 lbs. Deb: 5/23/89																										
1989	Tor-A	0	1	.000	4	3	0	0	0	11^2	16	1	14	4	23.1	10.03	38	.356	.508	0	—	0	-8	-8	1	-0.5
● ISRAEL SANCHEZ Sanchez, Israel (Matos) b: 8/20/63, Falcon Lasvias, Cuba BL/TL, 5'9", 170 lbs. Deb: 7/7/88																										
1988	KC-A	3	2	.600	19	1	0	0	1	35^2	36	0	18	14	13.6	4.54	88	.265	.351	0	—	0	-2	-2	0	-0.3
1990	KC-A	0	0	—	11	0	0	0	0	9^2	16	1	3	5	18.6	8.38	46	.381	.435	0	—	0	-5	-5	-0	0.0
Total	2	3	2	.600	30	1	0	0	1	45^1	52	1	21	19	14.7	5.36	74	.292	.370	0	—	0	-7	-7	0	-0.3
● JESUS SANCHEZ Sanchez, Jesus Paulino b: 10/11/74, Nizao, D.R. BL/TL, 5'10", 153 lbs. Deb: 3/31/98																										
1998	Fla-N	7	9	.438	35	29	0	0	0	173	178	18	91	137	14.2	4.47	91	.272	.364	7	.135	-1	-5	-7	2	-0.5
● LUIS SANCHEZ Sanchez, Luis Mercedes (b: Luis Mercedes Escoba (Sanchez)) b: 8/24/53, Cariaco, Ven. BR/TR, 6'2", 210 lbs. Deb: 4/10/81																										
1981	Cal-A	0	2	.000	17	0	0	0	2	33^2	39	4	11	13	13.6	2.94	124	.287	.345	0	—	0	3	3	-0	0.2
1982	*Cal-A	7	4	.636	46	0	0	0	5	92^2	89	3	34	58	12.6	3.21	126	.259	.339	0	—	0	9	9	1	1.1
1983	Cal-A	10	8	.556	56	1	0	0	7	98^1	92	6	40	49	12.4	3.66	110	.254	.333	0	—	0	4	4	2	0.9
1984	Cal-A	9	7	.563	49	0	0	0	11	83^2	84	10	33	62	12.9	3.33	119	.268	.343	0	—	0	6	6	-0	1.2
1985	Cal-A	2	0	1.000	26	0	0	0	2	61^1	67	9	27	34	13.9	5.72	72	.283	.358	0	—	0	-11	-11	0	-0.3
Total	5	28	21	.571	194	1	0	0	27	369^2	371	32	145	216	12.9	3.75	107	.267	.342	0	—	0	11	10	2	3.1
● RAUL SANCHEZ Sanchez, Raul Guadalupe (Rodriguez) b: 12/12/30, Marianao, Cuba BR/TR, 6', 150 lbs. Deb: 4/17/52																										
1952	Was-A	1	1	.500	3	2	1	1	0	12^2	13	0	7	6	14.2	3.55	100	.260	.351	0	.000	-1	0	0	0	-0.1
1957	Cin-N	3	2	.600	38	0	0	0	5	62^1	61	7	25	37	13.0	4.76	86	.262	.344	2	.286	1	-6	-5	1	-0.3
1960	Cin-N	1	0	1.000	8	0	0	0	0	14^2	12	1	11	5	16.0	4.91	78	.226	.388	1	.500	0	-2	-2	0	-0.1
Total	3	5	3	.625	49	2	1	1	5	89^2	86	8	43	48	13.7	4.62	86	.256	.352	3	.214	0	-8	-6	1	-0.5
● BEN SANDERS Sanders, Alexander Bennett b: 2/16/1865, Catharpin, Va. d: 8/29/30, Memphis, Tenn. BR/TR, 6', 210 lbs. Deb: 6/6/1888 ♦																										
1888	Phi-N	19	10	.655	31	29	28	**8**	0	275^1	240	3	33	121	9.0	1.90	157	.228	.253	58	.246	5	29	33	4	4.2
1889	Phi-N	19	18	.514	44	39	34	1	1	349^2	406	9	96	123	13.0	3.55	122	.282	.328	47	.278	6	18	31	-2	3.0
1890	Phi-P	19	18	.514	43	40	37	2	1	346^2	412	13	69	107	12.7	3.76	114	.283	.320	59	.312	9	18	20	1	2.4
1891	Phi-a	11	5	.688	19	18	15	0	0	145	157	3	37	40	12.5	3.79	101	.267	.319	39	.250	2	-1	1	-1	0.2
1892	Lou-N	12	19	.387	31	31	30	3	0	268^1	281	6	62	77	11.6	3.22	95	.259	.300	54	.273	10	2	-5	-1	0.5
Total	5	80	70	.533	168	157	144	14	2	1385	1496	34	297	468	11.8	3.24	116	.266	.306	257	.271	33	66	79	1	10.3
● DEE SANDERS Sanders, Dee Wilma b: 4/8/21, Quitman, Tex. BR/TR, 6'3", 195 lbs. Deb: 8/12/45																										
1945	StL-A	0	0	—	2	0	0	0	0	1^1	7	0	1	1	54.0	40.50	9	.700	.727	0	—	0	-6	-5	0	0.0
● KEN SANDERS Sanders, Kenneth George "Daffy" b: 7/8/41, St.Louis, Mo. BR/TR, 5'11", 185 lbs. Deb: 8/6/64																										
1964	KC-A	0	2	.000	21	0	0	0	1	27	23	2	17	18	13.7	3.67	104	.232	.350	0	—	0	-0	0	1	0.1
1966	Bos-A	3	6	.333	24	0	0	0	2	47^1	36	2	28	33	12.5	3.80	100	.214	.333	0	.000	-0	-2	0	-0	0.0
	KC-A	3	4	.429	38	1	0	0	1	65^1	59	7	48	41	14.9	3.72	91	.250	.379	2	.250	0	-2	-2	1	-0.1
	Yr	6	10	.375	62	1	0	0	3	112^2	95	9	76	74	13.7	3.75	95	.233	.355	2	.143	0	-4	-2	1	-0.1
1968	Oak-A	0	1	.000	7	0	0	0	0	10^2	8	1	8	6	13.5	3.38	84	.229	.372	0	—	0	-0	-1	0	-0.1
1970	Mil-A	5	2	.714	50	0	0	0	13	92^1	64	1	25	64	9.1	1.75	216	.201	.268	3	.231	1	20	21	1	2.4
1971	Mil-A	7	12	.368	**83**	0	0	0	**31**	136^1	111	9	34	80	9.8	1.91	181	.227	.282	0	.000	-1	**23**	**24**	2	4.7
1972	Mil-A	2	9	.182	62	0	0	0	17	92^1	88	10	31	51	11.8	3.12	97	.245	.309	1	.143	0	-1	-1	1	0.0
1973	Min-A	2	4	.333	27	0	0	0	8	44^1	53	4	21	19	15.4	6.09	65	.299	.380	0	—	0	-11	-11	0	-1.7
	Cle-A	5	1	.833	15	0	0	0	5	27^1	18	2	9	14	8.9	1.65	238	.188	.257	0	—	0	7	7	0	1.8
	Yr	7	5	.583	42	0	0	0	13	71^2	71	6	30	33	12.7	4.40	90	.255	.328	0	—	0	-5	-4	0	0.1
1974	Cle-A	0	1	.000	9	0	0	0	1	11	21	5	5	4	21.3	9.82	37	.404	.456	0	—	0	-8	-8	0	-0.7
	Cal-A	0	0	—	9	0	0	0	1	9^2	10	0	3	4	12.1	2.79	123	.278	.333	0	—	0	1	1	1	0.5
	Yr	0	1	.000	18	0	0	0	2	20^2	31	5	8	8	17.0	6.53	54	.352	.406	0	—	0	-7	-7	1	-0.2
1975	NY-N	1	1	.500	29	0	0	0	5	43	31	2	14	8	9.4	2.30	150	.205	.273	0	.000	-0	6	5	-0	0.4
1976	NY-N	1	2	.333	31	0	0	0	1	47	39	4	12	16	10.0	2.87	115	.231	.286	0	.000	-0	3	2	1	0.2
	KC-A	0	0	—	3	0	0	0	0	3	3	0	3	2	18.0	0.00	—	.273	.429	0	—	0	1	1	-0	-0.1
Total	10	29	45	.392	408	1	0	0	86	656^2	564	49	258	360	11.5	2.97	118	.235	.314	6	.115	-0	38	39	7	7.4
● ROY SANDERS Sanders, Roy Garvin "Butch" or "Pepe" b: 8/1/1892, Stafford, Kan. d: 1/17/50, Kansas City, Mo. BR/TR, 6'0.5", 195 lbs. Deb: 4/16/17																										
1917	Cin-N	0	1	.000	2	2	1	0	0	14	12	0	16	3	18.6	4.50	58	.273	.475	0	.000	-1	-3	-3	1	-0.2
1918	Pit-N	7	9	.438	28	14	6	1	1	156	135	1	52	55	10.9	2.60	111	.239	.305	8	.151	-1	3	5	2	0.6
Total	2	7	10	.412	30	16	7	1	1	170	147	1	68	58	11.5	2.75	104	.241	.321	8	.136	-2	0	2	2	0.4
● ROY SANDERS Sanders, Roy Lee "Simon" b: 6/10/1894, Missouri d: 7/8/63, Louisville, Ky. BR/TR, 6', 185 lbs. Deb: 8/6/18																										
1918	NY-A	0	2	.000	6	2	0	0	0	25^2	28	0	16	8	16.1	4.21	67	.301	.414	0	.000	-1	-4	-4	-1	-0.5
1920	StL-A	1	1	.500	8	1	0	0	0	17^1	20	1	17	2	19.7	5.19	75	.313	.463	0	.000	-1	-3	-2	-1	-0.4
Total	2	1	3	.250	14	3	0	0	0	43	48	1	33	10	17.6	4.60	71	.306	.435	0	.000	-2	-7	-6	-1	-0.9
● SCOTT SANDERS Sanders, Scott Gerald b: 3/25/69, Hannibal, Mo. BR/TR, 6'4", 220 lbs. Deb: 8/6/93																										
1993	SD-N	3	3	.500	9	9	0	0	0	52^1	54	4	23	37	13.4	4.13	100	.265	.342	1	.063	-1	-1	0	-1	-0.2
1994	SD-N	4	8	.333	23	20	0	0	1	111	103	10	48	109	12.6	4.78	86	.245	.329	4	.125	-0	-7	-8	1	-0.8
1995	SD-N	5	5	.500	17	15	1	0	0	90	79	14	31	88	11.2	4.30	94	.228	.296	8	.296	2	-1	-3	-2	-0.2
1996	*SD-N	9	5	.643	46	16	0	0	0	144	117	10	48	157	10.4	3.38	118	.221	.288	7	.194	2	13	9	-1	0.9
1997	Sea-A	3	6	.333	33	6	0	0	2	65^1	73	16	38	62	15.7	6.47	69	.280	.377	0	—	0	-14	-14	-2	-1.9
	Det-A	3	8	.273	14	14	1	1	0	74^1	79	14	24	58	12.6	5.33	86	.276	.334	0	—	0	-6	-6	-0	-0.8
	Yr	6	14	.300	47	20	1	1	2	139^2	152	30	62	120	13.9	5.86	77	.274	.348	0	—	0	-20	-21	-2	-2.7
1998	Det-A	0	2	.000	3	2	0	0	0	9^2	24	1	6	6	27.9	17.69	27	.471	.526	0	—	0	-14	-14	0	-1.8
	SD-N	3	1	.750	23	0	0	0	0	30^2	33	5	5	26	11.2	4.11	93	.270	.299	0	—	0	0	-1	0	-0.1
Total	6	30	38	.441	168	82	2	1	3	577^1	562	74	223	543	12.5	4.74	88	.253	.325	20	.180	3	-29	-37	-5	-4.9
● WAR SANDERS Sanders, Warren Williams b: 8/2/1877, Maynardville, Tenn. d: 8/3/62, Chattanooga, Tenn. BR/TL, 5'10", 160 lbs. Deb: 4/18/03																										
1903	StL-N	1	6	.143	8	6	3	0	0	40	48	0	21	9	16.0	6.07	54	.286	.372	1	.067	-2	-12	-12	-1	-1.9
1904	StL-N	1	2	.333	4	3	1	0	0	19	25	1	1	11	12.8	4.74	57	.298	.314	0	.000	-1	-4	-4	0	-0.6
Total	2	2	8	.200	12	9	4	0	0	59	73	1	22	20	14.9	5.64	55	.290	.354	1	.048	-2	-17	-17	-0	-2.5
● SCOTT SANDERSON Sanderson, Scott Douglas b: 7/22/56, Dearborn, Mich. BR/TR, 6'5", 200 lbs. Deb: 8/6/78																										
1978	Mon-N	4	2	.667	10	9	1	1	0	61	52	3	21	50	10.9	2.51	140	.232	.301	2	.105	-1	7	7	-1	0.5
1979	Mon-N	9	8	.529	34	24	5	3	1	168	148	16	54	138	11.0	3.43	107	.236	.300	8	.160	-0	6	4	-2	0.2
1980	Mon-N	16	11	.593	33	33	7	3	0	211^1	206	18	56	125	11.3	3.11	115	.257	.308	5	.078	-3	12	11	-2	0.8
1981	*Mon-N	9	7	.563	22	22	4	1	0	137^1	122	10	31	77	10.1	2.95	118	.236	.281	4	.114	2	8	8	-2	1.0
1982	Mon-N	12	12	.500	32	32	7	0	0	224	212	24	58	158	11.0	3.46	105	.251	.301	8	.140	1	4	5	-3	0.2

YEAR	TM/L	W	L	PCT	G	GS	CG	SH	SV	IP	H	HR	BB	SO	RAT	ERA	ERA+	OAV	OOB	BH	AVG	PB	PR	/A	PD	TPI
1983	Mon-N	6	7	.462	18	16	0	0	1	81^1	98	12	20	55	13.1	4.65	77	.303	.344	4	.143	-0	-9	-10	-1	-1.5
1984	*Chi-N	8	5	.615	24	24	3	0	0	140^2	140	5	24	76	10.6	3.14	125	.264	.298	5	.119	-1	7	12	1	1.1
1985	Chi-N	5	6	.455	19	19	2	0	0	121	100	13	27	80	9.4	3.12	128	.228	.273	2	.065	-2	6	12	1	1.0
1986	Chi-N	9	11	.450	37	28	1	1	1	169^2	165	21	37	124	10.8	4.19	96	.255	.297	3	.059	-3	-9	-3	-1	-0.8
1987	Chi-N	8	9	.471	32	22	0	0	2	144^2	156	23	50	106	13.0	4.29	100	.274	.336	3	.075	-1	-3	-0	-1	-0.2
1988	Chi-N	1	2	.333	11	0	0	0	0	15^1	13	1	3	6	9.4	5.28	68	.232	.271	0	—	0	-3	-3	-0	-0.6
1989	*Chi-N	11	9	.550	37	23	2	0	0	146^1	155	16	31	86	11.6	3.94	95	.273	.313	2	.047	-2	-7	-3	-2	-0.8
1990	*Oak-A	17	11	.607	34	34	2	1	0	206^1	205	27	66	128	12.0	3.88	96	.255	.315	0	—	0	1	-4	-2	-0.6
1991	NY-A☆	16	10	.615	34	34	2	2	0	208	200	22	29	130	10.0	3.81	109	.252	.281	0	—	0	7	8	-3	0.6
1992	NY-A	12	11	.522	33	33	2	1	0	193^1	220	28	64	104	13.4	4.93	79	.286	.344	0	—	0	-21	-22	-2	-2.5
1993	Cal-A	7	11	.389	21	21	4	1	0	135^1	153	15	27	66	12.3	4.46	101	.289	.329	0	—	0	-2	1	-1	-0.2
	SF-N	4	2	.667	11	8	0	0	0	48^2	48	12	7	36	10.4	3.51	111	.255	.286	0	.000	-1	3	2	0	0.1
1994	Chi-A	8	4	.667	18	14	1	0	0	92	110	20	12	36	12.1	5.09	92	.296	.322	0	—	0	-3	-4	1	-0.4
1995	Cal-A	1	3	.250	7	7	0	0	0	39^1	48	6	4	23	12.4	4.12	114	.298	.323	0	—	0	3	3	-0	0.2
1996	Cal-A	0	2	.000	5	4	0	0	0	18	39	5	4	7	22.5	7.50	67	.433	.469	0	—	0	-5	-5	0	-0.4
Total	19	163	143	.533	472	407	43	14	5	2561^2	2590	297	625	1611	11.4	3.84	102	.263	.310	46	.097	-12	-1	19	-21	-2.3

● FRED SANFORD Sanford, John Frederick b: 8/9/19, Garfield, Utah BB/TR, 6′1″, 200 lbs. Deb: 5/5/43

YEAR	TM/L	W	L	PCT	G	GS	CG	SH	SV	IP	H	HR	BB	SO	RAT	ERA	ERA+	OAV	OOB	BH	AVG	PB	PR	/A	PD	TPI
1943	StL-A	0	0	—	3	0	0	0	0	9^1	7	0	4	2	10.6	1.93	172	.219	.306	0	—	0	1	1	0	0.0
1946	StL-A	2	1	.667	3	3	2	2	0	22	19	0	9	8	11.5	2.05	182	.235	.311	2	.286	1	4	4	-0	0.7
1947	StL-A	7	16	.304	34	23	9	0	4	186^2	186	17	76	62	12.6	3.71	104	.261	.332	11	.204	-0	-0	3	-1	0.2
1948	StL-A	12	21	.364	42	33	9	1	2	227	250	19	91	79	13.6	4.64	98	.279	.347	11	.151	-2	-9	-2	1	-0.4
1949	NY-A	7	3	.700	29	11	3	0	0	95^1	100	9	57	51	14.8	3.87	105	.270	.367	4	.118	-2	3	2	-0	-0.1
1950	NY-A	5	4	.556	26	12	2	0	0	112^2	103	9	79	54	14.6	4.55	94	.252	.374	8	.229	1	0	-3	3	0.1
1951	NY-A	0	3	.000	11	2	0	0	0	26^2	15	2	25	10	13.5	3.71	103	.169	.351	0	.000	-1	1	0	1	0.0
	Was-A	2	3	.400	7	7	0	0	0	37	51	5	27	12	19.0	6.57	62	.329	.429	1	.071	-1	-10	-10	-1	-1.3
	StL-A	2	4	.333	9	7	1	0	0	27^1	37	6	23	7	19.8	10.21	43	.308	.420	2	.286	1	-18	-18	-0	-2.9
	Yr	4	10	.286	27	16	1	0	0	91	103	13	75	29	17.6	6.82	60	.283	.405	3	.115	-1	-27	-27	-0	-4.2
Total	7	37	55	.402	164	98	26	3	6	744	768	67	391	285	14.1	4.45	94	.268	.357	39	.170	-4	-28	-21	2	-3.7

● JACK SANFORD Sanford, John Stanley b: 5/18/29, Wellesley Hills, Mass. BR/TR, 6′, 190 lbs. Deb: 9/16/56 C

YEAR	TM/L	W	L	PCT	G	GS	CG	SH	SV	IP	H	HR	BB	SO	RAT	ERA	ERA+	OAV	OOB	BH	AVG	PB	PR	/A	PD	TPI
1956	Phi-N	1	0	1.000	3	1	0	0	0	13	7	0	13	6	14.5	1.38	269	.184	.404	1	.333	0	3	3	0	0.3
1957	Phi-N★	19	8	.704	33	33	15	3	0	236^2	194	22	94	**188**	11.1	3.08	124	**.221**	.298	15	.169	-1	21	19	-1	1.9
1958	Phi-N	10	13	.435	38	27	7	2	0	186^1	197	15	81	106	13.6	4.44	89	.274	.350	10	.169	1	-10	-10	-2	-1.1
1959	SF-N	15	12	.556	36	31	10	0	1	222^1	198	22	70	132	11.1	3.16	121	.235	.300	8	.111	-1	20	16	-1	1.6
1960	SF-N	12	14	.462	37	34	11	**6**	0	219	199	11	99	125	12.3	3.82	91	.243	.326	13	.176	1	-1	-8	-1	-0.9
1961	SF-N	13	9	.591	38	33	6	0	0	217^1	203	22	87	112	12.2	4.22	90	.249	.325	16	.216	6	-5	-10	-1	-0.4
1962	*SF-N	24	7	.774	39	38	13	2	0	265^1	233	23	92	147	11.1	3.43	111	.234	.301	15	.153	0	15	11	2	1.3
1963	SF-N	16	13	.552	42	42	11	0	0	284^1	273	21	76	158	11.2	3.51	91	.251	.303	13	.138	3	-7	-10	3	-0.4
1964	SF-N	5	7	.417	18	17	3	1	1	106^1	91	7	37	64	11.2	3.30	108	.228	.300	4	.133	1	3	3	1	0.4
1965	SF-N	4	5	.444	23	16	0	0	2	91	92	11	30	43	12.8	3.96	91	.256	.325	3	.120	-0	-4	-4	-1	-0.4
	Cal-A	1	2	.333	9	5	0	0	1	29^1	35	2	10	13	13.8	4.60	74	.324	.381	1	.143	-0	-4	-4	1	-0.4
1966	Cal-A	13	7	.650	50	6	0	0	5	108	108	11	27	54	11.6	3.83	88	.271	.323	3	.136	1	-5	-6	1	-0.9
1967	Cal-A	3	2	.600	12	9	0	0	1	48^1	53	6	7	21	11.2	4.47	70	.288	.314	3	.200	1	-7	-7	1	-0.5
	KC-A	1	2	.333	10	1	0	0	0	22	24	1	14	13	16.4	6.55	49	.296	.412	0	.000	-0	-8	-8	1	-1.0
	Yr	4	4	.500	22	10	0	0	1	70^1	77	7	21	34	12.8	5.12	62	.288	.345	3	.167	1	-15	-15	2	-1.5
Total	12	137	101	.576	388	293	76	14	11	2049^1	1907	174	737	1182	11.8	3.69	98	.247	.316	105	.158	12	11	-14	3	-0.5

● MO SANFORD Sanford, Meredith Leroy b: 12/24/66, Americus, Ga. BR/TR, 6′6″, 220 lbs. Deb: 8/9/91

YEAR	TM/L	W	L	PCT	G	GS	CG	SH	SV	IP	H	HR	BB	SO	RAT	ERA	ERA+	OAV	OOB	BH	AVG	PB	PR	/A	PD	TPI
1991	Cin-N	1	2	.333	5	5	0	0	0	28	19	3	15	31	11.3	3.86	99	.186	.297	0	.000	-1	-1	-0	-0	-0.1
1993	Col-N	1	2	.333	11	6	0	0	0	35^2	37	4	27	36	16.1	5.30	90	.278	.400	0	.000	-1	-5	-2	-1	-0.3
1995	Min-A	0	0	—	11	0	0	0	0	18^2	16	7	16	17	16.4	5.30	90	.225	.382	0	—	0	-1	-1	-1	-0.1
Total	3	2	4	.333	27	11	0	0	0	82^1	72	14	58	84	14.5	4.81	92	.235	.362	0	.000	-2	-7	-3	-2	-0.5

● JULIO SANTANA Santana, Julio Franklin b: 1/20/73, San Pedro De Macoris, D.R. BR/TR, 6′, 175 lbs. Deb: 4/6/97

YEAR	TM/L	W	L	PCT	G	GS	CG	SH	SV	IP	H	HR	BB	SO	RAT	ERA	ERA+	OAV	OOB	BH	AVG	PB	PR	/A	PD	TPI
1997	Tex-A	4	6	.400	30	14	0	0	0	104	141	16	49	64	16.8	6.75	71	.323	.396	1	.500	0	-25	-23	1	-1.7
1998	Tex-A	0	0	—	3	0	0	0	0	5^1	7	0	4	1	18.6	8.44	57	.304	.407	0	—	0	-2	-2	0	0.0
	TB-A	5	6	.455	32	19	1	0	0	140^1	144	18	58	60	13.3	4.23	116	.270	.347	0	.000	-0	6	10	-3	0.4
	Yr	5	6	.455	35	19	1	0	0	145^2	151	18	62	61	13.5	4.39	112	.272	.350	0	.000	-0	4	8	-3	0.4
Total	2	9	12	.429	65	33	1	0	0	249^2	292	34	111	125	14.9	5.37	90	.294	.370	1	.167	-0	-21	-14	-2	-1.3

● MARINO SANTANA Santana, Marino (Castro) b: 5/10/72, San Jose De Los Llanos, D.R. BR/TR, 6′1″, 175 lbs. Deb: 9/4/98

YEAR	TM/L	W	L	PCT	G	GS	CG	SH	SV	IP	H	HR	BB	SO	RAT	ERA	ERA+	OAV	OOB	BH	AVG	PB	PR	/A	PD	TPI
1998	Det-A	0	0	—	7	0	0	0	0	7^1	9	1	8	10	22.1	3.68	128	.310	.474	0	—	0	1	1	0	0.0

● JOSE SANTIAGO Santiago, Jose Guillermo (Guzman) "Pants" b: 9/4/28, Coamo, P.R. BR/TR, 5′10″, 175 lbs. Deb: 4/17/54

YEAR	TM/L	W	L	PCT	G	GS	CG	SH	SV	IP	H	HR	BB	SO	RAT	ERA	ERA+	OAV	OOB	BH	AVG	PB	PR	/A	PD	TPI
1954	Cle-A	0	0	—	1	0	0	0	0	1^2	0	0	2	1	10.8	0.00	—	.000	.286	0	—	0	1	1	-0	0.0
1955	Cle-A	2	0	1.000	17	0	0	0	0	32^2	31	1	14	19	13.8	2.48	161	.256	.357	2	.500	1	5	5	0	0.4
1956	KC-A	1	2	.333	9	5	0	0	0	21^2	36	8	17	9	24.1	8.31	52	.387	.504	2	.400	0	-10	-10	0	-1.0
Total	3	3	2	.600	27	5	0	0	0	56	67	9	33	29	17.7	4.66	88	.306	.420	4	.444	2	-4	-3	0	-0.6

● JOSE SANTIAGO Santiago, Jose Rafael (Alfonso) b: 8/15/40, Juana Diaz, P.R. BR/TR, 6′2″, 185 lbs. Deb: 9/9/63

YEAR	TM/L	W	L	PCT	G	GS	CG	SH	SV	IP	H	HR	BB	SO	RAT	ERA	ERA+	OAV	OOB	BH	AVG	PB	PR	/A	PD	TPI
1963	KC-A	1	0	1.000	4	0	0	0	0	7	8	4	2	6	12.9	9.00	43	.276	.323	0	—	0	-4	-4	0	-0.5
1964	KC-A	0	6	.000	34	8	0	0	0	83^2	84	9	35	64	13.2	4.73	81	.258	.337	0	.000	-2	-10	-9	-1	-0.8
1965	KC-A	0	0	—	4	0	0	0	0	5	8	1	4	8	21.6	9.00	39	.364	.462	0	—	0	-3	-3	0	0.0
1966	Bos-A	12	13	.480	35	28	7	1	2	172	155	17	58	119	11.3	3.66	104	.238	.302	11	.196	0	-4	3	-1	0.3
1967	*Bos-A	12	4	.750	50	11	2	0	5	145^1	138	14	47	109	11.6	3.59	97	.251	.313	8	.190	2	-6	-2	0	0.1
1968	Bos-A†	9	4	.692	18	18	7	2	0	124	96	9	42	86	10.2	2.25	140	.215	.287	7	.163	1	10	13	-0	1.4
1969	Bos-A	0	0	—	10	0	0	0	0	7^2	11	2	4	4	17.6	3.52	108	.324	.395	0	—	0	0	0	-0	0.0
1970	Bos-A	0	2	.000	8	0	0	0	1	11^1	18	0	8	8	20.6	10.32	38	.353	.441	2	.667	1	-8	-8	-0	-1.3
Total	8	34	29	.540	163	65	16	3	8	556	518	56	200	404	11.8	3.74	96	.246	.314	28	.173	2	-26	-10	-2	-0.8

● JOSE SANTIAGO Santiago, Jose Rafael (Fuentes) b: 11/5/74, Fajardo, P.R. BR/TR, 6′3″, 200 lbs. Deb: 6/7/97

YEAR	TM/L	W	L	PCT	G	GS	CG	SH	SV	IP	H	HR	BB	SO	RAT	ERA	ERA+	OAV	OOB	BH	AVG	PB	PR	/A	PD	TPI
1997	KC-A	0	0	—	4	0	0	0	0	4^2	7	0	2	1	19.3	1.93	244	.333	.417	0	—	0	1	1	-0	-0.1
1998	KC-A	0	0	—	2	0	0	0	0	2	4	0	0	2	18.0	9.00	55	.444	.444	0	—	0	-1	-1	0	0.0
Total	2	0	0	—	6	0	0	0	0	6^2	11	0	2	3	18.9	4.05	118	.367	.424	0	—	0	0	1	-0	-0.1

● AL SANTORINI Santorini, Alan Joel b: 5/19/48, Irvington, N.J. BR/TR, 6′, 190 lbs. Deb: 9/10/68

YEAR	TM/L	W	L	PCT	G	GS	CG	SH	SV	IP	H	HR	BB	SO	RAT	ERA	ERA+	OAV	OOB	BH	AVG	PB	PR	/A	PD	TPI
1968	Atl-N	0	1	.000	1	1	0	0	0	3	4	1	0	0	12.0	0.00	—	.286	.286	0	—	0	1	1	-0	0.4
1969	SD-N	8	14	.364	32	30	2	1	0	184^2	194	11	73	111	13.4	3.95	90	.270	.343	7	.111	-1	-7	-8	1	-1.0
1970	SD-N	1	8	.111	21	12	0	0	1	75^2	91	11	43	41	16.3	6.07	66	.294	.385	0	.000	-2	-17	-18	-1	-2.1
1971	SD-N	0	2	.000	18	3	0	0	0	38^1	43	4	11	21	12.7	3.76	88	.285	.333	2	.400	1	-1	-2	-1	-0.1
	StL-N	0	2	.000	19	5	0	0	2	49^2	51	2	19	21	12.9	3.81	95	.270	.340	3	.300	1	-2	-1	-0	0.0
	Yr	0	4	.000	37	8	0	0	2	88	94	6	30	42	12.8	3.78	92	.275	.335	5	.333	1	-3	-3	-1	-0.1
1972	StL-N	8	11	.421	30	19	3	3	0	133^2	136	6	46	72	12.3	4.11	83	.263	.324	3	.075	-2	-10	-10	-1	-1.7
1973	StL-N	0	0	—	6	0	0	0	0	8^1	14	1	2	2	18.4	5.40	67	.400	.447	0	.000	-0	-2	-2	-0	0.0
Total	6	17	38	.309	127	70	5	4	3	493^1	533	36	194	268	13.5	4.29	83	.276	.346	15	.109	-4	-38	-40	-3	-4.5

● MANNY SARMIENTO Sarmiento, Manuel Eduardo (Aponte) b: 2/2/56, Cagua, Venez. BR/TR, 6′, 170 lbs. Deb: 7/30/76

YEAR	TM/L	W	L	PCT	G	GS	CG	SH	SV	IP	H	HR	BB	SO	RAT	ERA	ERA+	OAV	OOB	BH	AVG	PB	PR	/A	PD	TPI
1976	*Cin-N	5	1	.833	22	0	0	0	0	43^2	36	1	12	20	10.1	2.06	170	.222	.280	0	.000	-1	7	7	-1	0.7
1977	Cin-N	0	0	—	24	0	0	0	1	40^1	28	6	11	23	8.7	2.45	160	.196	.253	0	.000	-0	7	7	-1	-0.1
1978	Cin-N	9	7	.563	63	4	0	0	5	127^1	109	16	54	72	11.6	4.38	81	.234	.315	0	.000	-1	-11	-12	-1	-1.7
1979	Cin-N	0	4	.000	23	1	0	0	0	38^2	47	2	7	23	12.8	4.66	80	.311	.346	0	.000	-1	-4	-4	-0	-0.5

YEAR	TM/L	W	L	PCT	G	GS	CG	SH	SV	IP	H	HR	BB	SO	RAT	ERA	ERA+	OAV	OOB	BH	AVG	PB	PR	/A	PD	TPI
1980	Sea-A	0	1	.000	9	0	0	0	1	14^2	14	2	6	15	12.3	3.68	112	.255	.328	0	—	0	1	1	-0	0.0
1982	Pit-N	9	4	.692	35	17	4	0	1	164^2	153	7	46	81	10.9	3.39	109	.246	.298	9	.191	1	4	6	-2	0.3
1983	Pit-N	3	5	.375	52	0	0	0	4	84^1	74	8	36	49	11.7	2.99	124	.243	.324	0	.000	-1	6	7	-1	0.5
Total	7	26	22	.542	228	22	4	0	12	513^2	461	42	172	283	11.1	3.49	106	.242	.306	9	.103	-3	9	11	-6	-0.8

● KEVIN SAUCIER Saucier, Kevin Andrew b: 8/9/56, Pensacola, Fla. BR/TL, 6′1″, 196 lbs. Deb: 10/1/78

YEAR	TM/L	W	L	PCT	G	GS	CG	SH	SV	IP	H	HR	BB	SO	RAT	ERA	ERA+	OAV	OOB	BH	AVG	PB	PR	/A	PD	TPI
1978	Phi-N	0	1	.000	1	0	0	0	0	2	4	0	1	2	27.0	18.00	20	.400	.500	0	—	0	-3	-3	-0	-0.9
1979	Phi-N	1	4	.200	29	2	0	0	1	62^1	68	4	33	21	15.0	4.19	91	.291	.385	1	.100	-1	-3	-3	0	-0.2
1980	*Phi-N	7	3	.700	40	0	0	0	0	50	50	2	20	25	13.3	3.42	111	.281	.366	0	.000	-1	1	2	0	0.3
1981	Det-A	4	2	.667	38	0	0	0	13	49	26	1	21	23	9.6	1.65	228	.160	.277	0	—	0	11	12	0	2.0
1982	Det-A	3	1	.750	31	1	0	0	5	40^1	35	0	29	23	14.7	3.12	130	.254	.391	0	—	0	4	4	0	0.5
Total	5	15	11	.577	139	3	0	0	19	203^2	183	7	104	94	13.3	3.31	116	.253	.359	1	.056	-2	10	12	1	1.7

● TONY SAUNDERS Saunders, Anthony Scott b: 4/29/74, Baltimore, Md. BL/TL, 6′2″, 205 lbs. Deb: 4/5/97

YEAR	TM/L	W	L	PCT	G	GS	CG	SH	SV	IP	H	HR	BB	SO	RAT	ERA	ERA+	OAV	OOB	BH	AVG	PB	PR	/A	PD	TPI
1997	*Fla-N	4	6	.400	22	21	0	0	0	111^1	99	12	64	102	13.3	4.61	87	.244	.350	3	.081	-1	-5	-7	-1	-0.7
1998	TB-A	6	15	.286	31	31	2	0	0	192^1	191	15	111	172	14.5	4.12	119	.265	.368	2	1.000	1	11	17	-1	1.6
Total	2	10	21	.323	53	52	2	0	0	303^2	290	27	175	274	14.0	4.30	106	.258	.362	5	.128	0	6	9	-2	0.9

● DENNIS SAUNDERS Saunders, Dennis James b: 1/4/49, Alhambra, Cal. BB/TR, 6′3″, 195 lbs. Deb: 5/21/70

YEAR	TM/L	W	L	PCT	G	GS	CG	SH	SV	IP	H	HR	BB	SO	RAT	ERA	ERA+	OAV	OOB	BH	AVG	PB	PR	/A	PD	TPI
1970	Det-A	1	1	.500	8	0	0	0	1	14	16	1	5	8	14.1	3.21	116	.286	.355	0	.000	-1	1	1	1	0.1

● RICH SAUVEUR Sauveur, Richard Daniel b: 11/23/63, Arlington, Va. BL/TL, 6′4″, 170 lbs. Deb: 7/1/86

YEAR	TM/L	W	L	PCT	G	GS	CG	SH	SV	IP	H	HR	BB	SO	RAT	ERA	ERA+	OAV	OOB	BH	AVG	PB	PR	/A	PD	TPI
1986	Pit-N	0	0	—	3	3	0	0	0	12	17	3	6	6	18.8	6.00	64	.354	.446	1	.333	0	-3	-3	1	0.1
1988	Mon-N	0	0	—	4	0	0	0	0	3	3	1	2	3	15.0	6.00	60	.250	.357	0	—	0	-1	-1	0	0.0
1991	NY-N	0	0	—	6	0	0	0	0	3^1	7	1	2	4	24.3	10.80	34	.467	.529	0	—	0	-3	-3	0	0.0
1992	KC-A	0	1	.000	8	0	0	0	0	14^1	15	1	8	7	15.7	4.40	92	.273	.385	0	—	0	-1	-1	-0	-0.1
1996	Chi-A	0	0	—	3	0	0	0	0	3	3	1	5	1	27.0	15.00	32	.333	.600	0	—	0	-3	-3	0	0.1
Total	5	0	1	.000	24	3	0	0	0	35^2	45	7	23	21	18.4	6.56	60	.324	.437	1	.333	0	-11	-10	1	0.1

● JACK SAVAGE Savage, John Joseph b: 4/22/64, Louisville, Ky. BR/TR, 6′3″, 190 lbs. Deb: 9/14/87

YEAR	TM/L	W	L	PCT	G	GS	CG	SH	SV	IP	H	HR	BB	SO	RAT	ERA	ERA+	OAV	OOB	BH	AVG	PB	PR	/A	PD	TPI
1987	LA-N	0	0	—	3	0	0	0	0	3^1	4	0	0	0	10.8	2.70	147	.286	.286	0	—	0	1	0	-0	0.0
1990	Min-A	0	2	.000	17	0	0	0	1	26	37	3	11	12	16.6	8.31	50	.339	.400	0	—	0	-13	-12	-0	-0.9
Total	2	0	2	.000	20	0	0	0	1	29^1	41	3	11	12	16.0	7.67	54	.333	.388	0	—	0	-12	-12	-0	-0.9

● BOB SAVAGE Savage, John Robert b: 12/1/21, Manchester, N.H. BR/TR, 6′2″, 180 lbs. Deb: 6/24/42

YEAR	TM/L	W	L	PCT	G	GS	CG	SH	SV	IP	H	HR	BB	SO	RAT	ERA	ERA+	OAV	OOB	BH	AVG	PB	PR	/A	PD	TPI
1942	Phi-A	0	1	.000	8	3	0	0	0	30^2	24	0	31	10	16.1	3.23	117	.220	.393	1	.111	0	1	2	-0	0.0
1946	Phi-A	3	15	.167	40	19	7	1	2	164	164	5	93	78	14.2	4.06	87	.259	.355	5	.122	1	-10	-9	-3	-1.2
1947	Phi-A	8	10	.444	44	8	2	1	2	146	135	8	55	56	11.7	3.76	101	.245	.314	2	.050	-4	-1	1	-2	-0.5
1948	Phi-A	5	1	.833	33	1	1	0	5	75^1	98	9	33	26	15.7	6.21	69	.318	.384	1	.077	-1	-16	-16	-1	-1.4
1949	StL-A	0	0	—	4	0	0	0	0	7	12	1	3	1	19.3	6.43	70	.400	.455	0	.000	-0	-2	-1	0	0.0
Total	5	16	27	.372	129	31	10	2	9	423	433	23	215	171	13.8	4.32	88	.265	.352	9	.087	-3	-27	-24	-6	-3.1

● DON SAVIDGE Savidge, Donald Snyder b: 8/28/08, Berwick, Pa. d: 3/22/83, Santa Barbara, Cal BR/TR, 6′1″, 180 lbs. Deb: 8/6/29 F

YEAR	TM/L	W	L	PCT	G	GS	CG	SH	SV	IP	H	HR	BB	SO	RAT	ERA	ERA+	OAV	OOB	BH	AVG	PB	PR	/A	PD	TPI
1929	Was-A	0	0	—	3	0	0	0	0	6	12	1	2	2	21.0	9.00	47	.414	.452	0	—	0	-3	-3	0	0.0

● RALPH SAVIDGE Savidge, Ralph Austin "The Human Whipcord" b: 2/3/1879, Jerseytown, Pa. d: 7/22/59, Berwick, Pa. BR/TR, 6′2″, 210 lbs. Deb: 9/22/08 F

YEAR	TM/L	W	L	PCT	G	GS	CG	SH	SV	IP	H	HR	BB	SO	RAT	ERA	ERA+	OAV	OOB	BH	AVG	PB	PR	/A	PD	TPI
1908	Cin-N	0	1	.000	4	1	1	0	0	21	18	0	8	7	11.1	2.57	90	.247	.321	0	.000	-1	-0	-1	-1	-0.2
1909	Cin-N	0	0	—	1	0	0	0	0	4	10	1	3	2	31.5	22.50	12	.588	.667	0	.000	-0	-9	-9	0	0.0
Total	2	0	1	.000	5	1	1	0	0	25	28	1	11	9	14.4	5.76	41	.311	.392	0	.000	-1	-9	-9	-1	-0.2

● MOE SAVRANSKY Savransky, Morris b: 1/13/29, Cleveland, Ohio BL/TL, 5′11″, 175 lbs. Deb: 4/23/54

YEAR	TM/L	W	L	PCT	G	GS	CG	SH	SV	IP	H	HR	BB	SO	RAT	ERA	ERA+	OAV	OOB	BH	AVG	PB	PR	/A	PD	TPI
1954	Cin-N	0	2	.000	16	0	0	0	0	24	23	6	8	7	12.4	4.88	86	.247	.320	1	.500	1	-2	-2	1	0.0

● RICK SAWYER Sawyer, Richard Clyde b: 4/7/48, Bakersfield, Cal. BR/TR, 6′2″, 205 lbs. Deb: 4/28/74

YEAR	TM/L	W	L	PCT	G	GS	CG	SH	SV	IP	H	HR	BB	SO	RAT	ERA	ERA+	OAV	OOB	BH	AVG	PB	PR	/A	PD	TPI
1974	NY-A	0	0	—	1	0	0	0	0	1^2	2	0	1	1	16.2	16.20	22	.500	.600	0	—	0	-2	-2	0	0.1
1975	NY-A	0	0	—	4	0	0	0	0	6	7	0	2	3	13.5	3.00	123	.304	.360	0	—	0	1	0	-0	0.0
1976	SD-N	5	3	.625	13	11	4	2	0	81^2	84	2	38	33	13.6	2.53	129	.272	.353	5	.208	1	9	7	-0	0.7
1977	SD-N	7	6	.538	56	9	0	0	0	111	136	15	55	45	16.1	5.84	61	.316	.402	3	.150	1	-24	-28	1	-2.7
Total	4	12	9	.571	74	20	4	2	0	200^1	229	17	96	82	15.0	4.49	76	.299	.382	8	.182	2	-17	-24	1	-1.9

● WILL SAWYER Sawyer, Willard Newton b: 7/29/1864, Brimfield, Ohio d: 1/5/36, Kent, Ohio BL/TL, Deb: 7/21/1883

YEAR	TM/L	W	L	PCT	G	GS	CG	SH	SV	IP	H	HR	BB	SO	RAT	ERA	ERA+	OAV	OOB	BH	AVG	PB	PR	/A	PD	TPI
1883	Cle-N	4	10	.286	17	15	15	0	0	141	119	1	47	76	10.6	2.36	133	**.217**	.279	1	.021	-7	12	12	-3	0.1

● BILL SAYLES Sayles, William Nisbeth b: 7/27/17, Portland, Ore. d: 11/20/96, Lincoln City, Ore. BR/TR, 6′2″, 175 lbs. Deb: 7/17/39

YEAR	TM/L	W	L	PCT	G	GS	CG	SH	SV	IP	H	HR	BB	SO	RAT	ERA	ERA+	OAV	OOB	BH	AVG	PB	PR	/A	PD	TPI
1939	Bos-A	0	0	—	5	0	0	0	0	14	14	1	13	9	17.4	7.07	67	.264	.409	1	.143	-0	-4	-4	0	0.0
1943	NY-N	1	3	.250	18	3	1	0	0	53	60	1	23	38	14.1	4.75	72	.284	.355	4	.308	1	-8	-8	-0	-0.5
	Bro-N	0	0	—	5	0	0	0	0	11^2	13	0	10	5	17.7	7.71	44	.271	.397	1	.500	0	-6	-6	-0	0.0
	Yr	1	3	.250	23	3	1	0	0	64^2	73	1	33	43	14.8	5.29	65	.282	.363	5	.333	1	-14	-13	-1	-0.5
Total	2	1	3	.250	28	3	1	0	0	78^2	87	2	46	52	15.2	5.61	65	.279	.372	6	.273	1	-17	-17	-0	-0.5

● PHIL SAYLOR Saylor, Philip Andrew "Lefty" b: 1/2/1871, Van Wert Co., Ohio d: 7/23/37, W.Alexandria, O. TL , Deb: 7/11/1891

YEAR	TM/L	W	L	PCT	G	GS	CG	SH	SV	IP	H	HR	BB	SO	RAT	ERA	ERA+	OAV	OOB	BH	AVG	PB	PR	/A	PD	TPI
1891	Phi-N	0	0	—	1	0	0	0	0	3	2	1	0	0	6.0	6.00	57	.182	.182	0	.000	-0	-1	-1	-0	0.0

● FRANK SCANLAN Scanlan, Frank Aloysius b: 4/28/1890, Syracuse, N.Y. d: 4/9/69, Brooklyn, N.Y. BL/TL, 6′1.5″, 175 lbs. Deb: 8/6/09 F

YEAR	TM/L	W	L	PCT	G	GS	CG	SH	SV	IP	H	HR	BB	SO	RAT	ERA	ERA+	OAV	OOB	BH	AVG	PB	PR	/A	PD	TPI
1909	Phi-N	0	0	—	6	0	0	0	1	11	8	0	5	5	10.6	1.64	159	.211	.302	0	.000	-1	1	1	-0	-0.1

● BOB SCANLAN Scanlan, Robert Guy b: 8/9/66, Los Angeles, Cal. BR/TR, 6′8″, 210 lbs. Deb: 5/7/91

YEAR	TM/L	W	L	PCT	G	GS	CG	SH	SV	IP	H	HR	BB	SO	RAT	ERA	ERA+	OAV	OOB	BH	AVG	PB	PR	/A	PD	TPI
1991	Chi-N	7	8	.467	40	13	0	0	1	111	114	5	40	44	12.7	3.89	100	.268	.335	1	.042	-2	-3	-0	-0	-0.2
1992	Chi-N	3	6	.333	69	0	0	0	14	87^1	76	4	30	42	11.0	2.89	125	.235	.302	0	.000	-0	6	7	1	1.0
1993	Chi-N	4	5	.444	70	0	0	0	0	75^1	79	6	28	44	13.1	4.54	88	.278	.349	1	.500	0	-4	-5	-1	-0.6
1994	Mil-A	2	6	.250	30	12	0	0	2	103	117	11	28	65	13.0	4.11	122	.288	.340	0	—	0	8	11	-0	0.7
1995	Mil-A	4	7	.364	17	14	0	0	0	83^1	101	9	44	29	16.4	6.59	76	.304	.397	0	—	0	-17	-15	0	-1.6
1996	Det-A	0	0	—	8	0	0	0	0	11	16	1	9	3	21.3	10.64	47	.348	.464	0	—	0	-7	-7	-0	0.0
	KC-A	0	1	.000	9	0	0	0	0	11^1	13	1	3	3	13.5	3.18	158	.295	.354	0	—	0	2	2	-0	0.2
	Yr	0	1	.000	17	0	0	0	0	22^1	29	2	12	6	16.9	6.85	73	.319	.404	0	—	0	-5	-5	-0	0.2
1998	Hou-N	0	1	.000	27	0	0	0	0	26^1	24	4	13	9	13.0	3.08	132	.245	.339	0	—	0	3	3	-1	0.0
Total	7	20	34	.370	270	39	0	0	17	508^2	540	41	195	239	13.4	4.39	98	.276	.348	2	.067	-2	-11	-4	-1	-0.5

● DOC SCANLAN Scanlan, William Dennis b: 3/7/1881, Syracuse, N.Y. d: 5/29/49, Brooklyn, N.Y. BL/TR, 5′8″, 165 lbs. Deb: 9/24/03 F

YEAR	TM/L	W	L	PCT	G	GS	CG	SH	SV	IP	H	HR	BB	SO	RAT	ERA	ERA+	OAV	OOB	BH	AVG	PB	PR	/A	PD	TPI
1903	Pit-N	0	1	.000	1	1	1	0	0	9	5	0	6	0	11.0	4.00	81	.167	.306	0	.000	0	-1	-1	-0	-0.1
1904	Pit-N	1	3	.250	4	3	1	0	0	22	21	0	20	10	17.6	4.91	56	.236	.387	0	.000	-1	-5	-5	-0	-0.9
	Bro-N	6	6	.500	13	12	11	3	0	104	94	0	40	40	11.8	2.16	127	.242	.316	5	.143	-2	7	7	-2	0.4
	Yr	7	9	.438	17	15	12	3	0	126	115	0	60	50	12.6	2.64	104	.240	.327	5	.122	-2	1	1	-2	-0.5
1905	Bro-N	14	12	.538	33	28	22	2	0	249^2	220	4	104	135	12.0	2.92	99	.237	.319	16	.167	-2	2	-1	-2	-0.4
1906	Bro-N	18	13	.581	38	33	28	6	2	288	230	5	127	120	11.3	3.19	79	.214	.301	18	.186	3	-18	-21	-7	-2.7
1907	Bro-N	6	8	.429	17	15	10	2	0	107	90	1	61	59	13.0	3.20	73	.239	.349	9	.265	5	-9	-10	-2	-0.9
1909	Bro-N	8	7	.533	19	17	12	2	0	141^1	125	2	65	72	12.4	2.93	88	.252	.343	12	.273	5	-5	-5	-1	-0.1
1910	Bro-N	9	11	.450	34	25	14	0	2	217^1	175	1	116	103	12.3	2.61	116	.234	.341	14	.203	1	10	10	-2	0.8
1911	Bro-N	3	10	.231	22	15	3	0	1	113^2	101	2	69	45	13.9	3.64	92	.256	.374	4	.121	-2	-3	-4	-1	-0.7
Total	8	65	71	.478	181	149	102	15	5	1252	1061	15	608	584	12.3	3.00	93	.234	.330	78	.188	8	-21	-31	-17	-4.6

● PAT SCANTLEBURY Scantlebury, Patricio Athelstan b: 11/11/17, Gatun, Canal Zone d: 5/24/91, Glen Ridge, N.J. BL/TL, 6′1″, 180 lbs. Deb: 4/19/56

YEAR	TM/L	W	L	PCT	G	GS	CG	SH	SV	IP	H	HR	BB	SO	RAT	ERA	ERA+	OAV	OOB	BH	AVG	PB	PR	/A	PD	TPI
1956	Cin-N	0	1	.000	6	2	0	0	0	19	24	5	5	10	13.7	6.63	60	.293	.333	0	.000	-0	-6	-6	-0	-0.3

YEAR	TM/L	W	L	PCT	G	GS	CG	SH	SV	IP	H	HR	BB	SO	RAT	ERA	ERA+	OAV	OOB	BH	AVG	PB	PR	/A	PD	TPI
● **RANDY SCARBERY**	Scarbery, Randy James b: 6/22/52, Fresno, Cal. BB/TR, 6'1", 185 lbs. Deb: 4/16/79																									
1979	Chi-A	2	8	.200	45	5	0	0	4	101^1	102	9	34	45	12.3	4.62	92	.262	.326	0	—	0	-5	-4	0	-0.4
1980	Chi-A	1	2	.333	15	0	0	0	2	28^2	24	1	7	18	10.4	4.08	99	.238	.300	0	—	0	-0	-0	-0	0.0
Total	2	3	10	.231	60	5	0	0	6	130	126	10	41	63	11.9	4.50	93	.257	.320	0	—	0	-5	-4	-0	-0.4
● **RAY SCARBOROUGH**	Scarborough, Ray Wilson (b: Rae Wilson Scarborough) b: 7/23/17, Mt.Gilead, N.C. d: 7/1/82, Mount Olive, N.C. BR/TR, 6', 185 lbs. Deb: 6/26/42 C																									
1942	Was-A	2	1	.667	17	5	1	1	0	63^1	68	2	32	16	14.2	4.12	89	.272	.355	4	.190	0	-3	-3	1	-0.1
1943	Was-A	4	4	.500	24	6	2	0	3	86	93	2	46	43	14.5	2.83	113	.273	.359	8	.333	2	5	4	0	0.6
1946	Was-A	7	11	.389	32	20	6	1	1	155^2	176	8	74	46	14.5	4.05	83	.286	.364	7	.140	-2	-9	-12	2	-1.3
1947	Was-A	6	13	.316	33	18	8	2	0	161	165	5	67	63	13.0	3.41	109	.267	.339	6	.120	-3	5	6	-0	0.3
1948	Was-A	15	8	.652	31	26	9	0	1	185^1	166	10	72	76	11.7	2.82	154	.233	.307	14	.219	-0	30	31	1	3.8
1949	Was-A	13	11	.542	34	27	11	1	0	199^2	204	10	88	81	13.5	4.60	93	.265	.346	13	.194	-0	-9	-8	1	-0.7
1950	Was-A	3	5	.375	8	8	4	2	0	58^1	62	1	22	24	13.3	4.01	112	.276	.345	2	.100	-1	4	3	1	0.3
	Chi-A☆	10	13	.435	27	23	8	1	1	149^1	160	10	62	70	13.6	5.30	85	.274	.347	8	.174	-1	-12	-14	-1	-1.9
	Yr	13	18	.419	35	31	12	3	1	207^2	222	11	84	94	13.4	4.94	91	.273	.344	10	.152	-3	-8	-10	-0	-1.6
1951	Bos-A	12	9	.571	37	22	8	0	0	184	201	21	61	71	13.5	5.09	88	.275	.342	13	.191	-2	-20	-13	1	-1.5
1952	Bos-A	1	5	.167	28	8	1	1	4	76^2	79	8	35	29	13.9	4.81	82	.266	.351	4	.222	0	-10	-7	0	-0.6
	*NY-A	5	1	.833	9	4	1	0	0	34	27	4	15	13	11.4	2.91	114	.223	.314	5	.357	2	3	2	-0	0.4
	Yr	6	6	.500	37	12	2	1	4	110^2	106	12	50	42	12.8	4.23	89	.251	.332	9	.281	2	-7	-6	0	-0.2
1953	NY-A	2	2	.500	25	1	0	0	0	54^2	52	4	26	20	13.5	3.29	112	.250	.345	1	.083	-0	4	2	0	0.2
	Det-A	0	2	.000	13	0	0	0	2	20^2	34	3	11	12	20.9	8.27	49	.354	.436	0	.000	-0	-10	-10	-0	-1.1
	Yr	2	4	.333	38	1	0	0	2	75^1	86	7	37	32	15.1	4.66	81	.279	.362	1	.071	-0	-6	-7	-0	-0.9
Total	10	80	85	.485	318	168	59	9	12	1428^2	1487	88	611	564	13.5	4.13	97	.267	.344	85	.186	-6	-22	-19	4	-1.6
● **MAC SCARCE**	Scarce, Guerrant McCurdy b: 4/8/49, Danville, Va. BL/TL, 6'3", 200 lbs. Deb: 7/10/72																									
1972	Phi-N	1	2	.333	31	0	0	0	4	36^2	30	6	20	40	12.8	3.44	105	.222	.331	0	.000	-1	0	1	1	0.1
1973	Phi-N	1	8	.111	52	0	0	0	12	70^2	54	3	47	57	13.0	2.42	157	.220	.347	0	.000	-1	10	11	-1	1.5
1974	Phi-N	3	8	.273	58	0	0	0	5	70^1	72	6	35	50	13.9	4.99	76	.275	.365	0	.000	-1	-11	-9	-1	-1.7
1975	NY-N	0	0	—	1	0	0	0	0	0	1	0	0	0	—	—	—	1.000	1.000	0	—	0	0	0	0	0.0
1978	Min-A	1	1	.500	17	0	0	0	0	32	35	5	15	17	14.9	3.94	97	.292	.384	0	—	0	-1	-0	-1	-0.1
Total	5	6	19	.240	159	0	0	0	21	209^2	192	20	117	164	13.6	3.69	102	.251	.357	0	.000	-2	-2	2	-2	-0.2
● **AL SCHACHT**	Schacht, Alexander b: 11/11/1892, New York, N.Y. d: 7/14/84, Waterbury, Conn. BR/TR, 5'11", 142 lbs. Deb: 9/18/19 C																									
1919	Was-A	2	0	1.000	2	2	1	0	0	15	14	0	4	4	10.8	2.40	134	.233	.281	0	.000	0	1	1	-0	0.2
1920	Was-A	6	4	.600	22	11	5	1	1	99^1	130	2	30	19	14.6	4.44	84	.319	.367	5	.192	1	-7	-8	2	-0.4
1921	Was-A	6	6	.500	29	5	2	0	1	82^2	110	2	27	15	15.1	4.90	84	.332	.386	5	.227	1	-6	-7	-3	-1.1
Total	3	14	10	.583	53	18	8	1	2	197	254	4	61	38	14.5	4.48	86	.318	.368	10	.196	2	-11	-14	-2	-1.3
● **SID SCHACHT**	Schacht, Sidney b: 2/3/18, Bogota, N.J. d: 3/30/91, Ft.Lauderdale, Fla. BR/TR, 5'11", 170 lbs. Deb: 4/23/50																									
1950	StL-A	0	0	—	8	1	0	0	0	10^2	24	5	14	7	32.1	16.03	31	.429	.543	0	.000	-0	-14	-13	-0	0.0
1951	StL-A	0	0	—	6	0	0	0	1	6	14	1	5	4	28.5	21.00	21	.452	.528	0	—	0	-11	-11	-0	-0.4
	Bos-N	0	2	.000	5	0	0	0	0	4^2	6	0	2	1	15.4	1.93	191	.300	.364	0	—	0	1	1	-0	0.3
Total	2	0	2	.000	19	1	0	0	1	21^1	44	6	21	12	27.4	14.34	31	.411	.508	0	.000	-0	-24	-23	-1	-0.1
● **HAL SCHACKER**	Schacker, Harold b: 4/6/25, Brooklyn, N.Y. BR/TR, 6', 190 lbs. Deb: 5/9/45																									
1945	Bos-N	0	1	.000	6	0	0	0	0	15^1	14	2	9	6	13.5	5.28	73	.241	.343	0	.000	0	-3	-2	-0	-0.2
● **GERMANY SCHAEFER**	Schaefer, Herman A. b: 2/4/1877, Chicago, Ill. d: 5/16/19, Saranac Lake, N.Y. BR/TR, 5'9", 175 lbs. Deb: 10/5/01 ♦																									
1912	Was-A	0	0	—	1	0	0	0	0	0^2	1	0	0	0	13.5	0.00	—	.333	.333	41	.247	0	0	0	-0	0.0
1913	Was-A	0	0	—	1	0	0	0	0	0^1	2	1	0	0	54.0	54.00	5	.667	.667	32	.320	0	-2	-2	0	0.0
Total	2	0	0	—	2	0	0	0	0	1	3	1	0	0	27.0	18.00	18	.500	.500	972	.257	0	-2	-2	0	0.0
● **HARRY SCHAEFFER**	Schaeffer, Harry Edward "Lefty" b: 6/23/24, Reading, Pa. BL/TL, 6'2.5", 175 lbs. Deb: 7/28/52																									
1952	NY-A	0	1	.000	5	2	0	0	0	17	18	2	18	15	19.1	5.29	63	.265	.419	0	.000	-0	-3	-4	0	-0.2
● **MARK SCHAEFFER**	Schaeffer, Mark Philip b: 6/5/48, Santa Monica, Cal. BL/TL, 6'5", 215 lbs. Deb: 4/18/72																									
1972	SD-N	2	0	1.000	41	0	0	0	1	41	52	3	28	25	18.0	4.61	71	.319	.425	0	.000	-0	-5	-6	1	-0.3
● **JOE SCHAFFERNOTH**	Schaffernoth, Joseph Arthur b: 8/6/37, Trenton, N.J. BR/TR, 6'4.5", 195 lbs. Deb: 4/15/59																									
1959	Chi-N	1	0	1.000	5	1	0	0	0	7^2	11	1	4	3	17.6	8.22	48	.355	.429	0	.000	-0	-4	-4	-0	-0.5
1960	Chi-N	2	3	.400	33	0	0	0	3	55	46	2	17	33	10.5	2.78	136	.235	.299	2	.286	0	6	6	0	0.7
1961	Chi-N	0	4	.000	21	0	0	0	0	38^1	43	7	18	23	14.6	6.34	66	.293	.373	0	.000	-1	-10	-9	0	-0.9
	Cle-A	0	1	.000	15	0	0	0	0	17	16	2	14	9	16.4	4.76	83	.242	.383	0	.000	-0	-1	-2	1	0.0
Total	3	3	8	.273	74	1	0	0	3	118	116	12	53	68	13.1	4.58	86	.264	.347	2	.125	-1	-9	-8	1	-0.7
● **ART SCHALLOCK**	Schallock, Arthur Lawrence b: 4/25/24, Mill Valley, Cal. BL/TL, 5'9", 160 lbs. Deb: 7/16/51																									
1951	NY-A	3	1	.750	11	6	1	0	0	46^1	50	3	20	19	13.8	3.88	99	.272	.346	5	.294	1	1	-0	0	0.1
1952	NY-A	0	0	—	2	0	0	0	0	2	3	0	2	1	22.5	9.00	37	.375	.500	0	—	0	-1	-1	-0	0.0
1953	*NY-A	0	0	—	7	1	0	0	1	21^1	30	2	15	13	19.4	2.95	125	.345	.447	2	.333	0	2	2	-0	0.0
1954	NY-A	0	1	.000	6	1	1	0	0	17^1	20	3	11	9	16.6	4.15	83	.282	.386	0	.000	-0	-1	-1	-0	-0.2
1955	NY-A	0	0	—	2	0	0	0	0	3	4	1	1	2	15.0	6.00	62	.333	.385	0	—	0	-1	-1	0	0.0
	Bal-A	3	5	.375	30	6	1	0	0	80^1	92	2	42	33	15.2	4.15	92	.294	.381	2	.105	-1	-2	-3	-1	-0.4
	Yr	3	5	.375	32	6	1	0	0	83^1	96	3	43	35	15.2	4.21	90	.295	.381	2	.105	-1	-2	-4	-1	-0.4
Total	5	6	7	.462	58	14	3	0	1	170^1	199	11	91	77	15.6	4.02	94	.295	.383	9	.200	1	-1	-5	-1	-0.5
● **CHARLEY SCHANZ**	Schanz, Charles Murrell b: 6/8/19, Anacortes, Wash. d: 5/28/92, Sacramento, Cal. BR/TR, 6'3.5", 215 lbs. Deb: 4/20/44																									
1944	Phi-N	13	16	.448	40	30	13	1	3	241^1	231	6	103	84	12.7	3.32	109	.254	.334	12	.148	-1	8	8	-0	0.8
1945	Phi-N	4	15	.211	35	21	5	1	5	144^2	165	5	87	56	16.2	4.35	88	.285	.387	6	.154	-0	-9	-8	1	-1.0
1946	Phi-N	6	6	.500	32	15	4	0	4	116^1	130	8	71	47	15.9	5.80	59	.286	.389	3	.083	-2	-31	-31	1	-3.2
1947	Phi-N	2	4	.333	34	6	1	0	2	101^2	107	7	47	42	13.9	4.16	96	.295	.380	4	.148	-1	-1	-2	0	-0.2
1950	Bos-A	3	2	.600	14	0	0	0	0	22^2	25	3	24	14	19.9	8.34	59	.281	.439	1	.091	-1	-9	-9	0	-1.6
Total	5	28	43	.394	155	72	23	2	14	626^2	658	29	332	243	14.6	4.34	86	.275	.369	26	.134	-5	-43	-42	1	-5.2
● **JOHN SCHAPPERT**	Schappert, John b: Brooklyn, N.Y. d: 7/29/16, Rockaway Beach, N.Y. BR/TR, 5'10", 170 lbs. Deb: 5/3/1882																									
1882	StL-a	8	7	.533	15	14	13	0	0	128	131	2	32	38	11.5	3.52	80	.248	.291	9	.180	0	-12	-10	-2	-1.1
● **BILL SCHARDT**	Schardt, Wilburt "Big Bill" b: 1/20/1886, Cleveland, Ohio d: 7/20/64, Vermilion, Ohio BR/TR, 6'4", 210 lbs. Deb: 4/14/11																									
1911	Bro-N	5	15	.250	39	22	10	1	4	195^1	190	4	91	77	13.3	3.59	93	.266	.355	10	.169	0	-4	-6	0	-0.5
1912	Bro-N	0	1	.000	7	0	0	0	1	20^2	25	1	6	7	14.4	4.35	77	.321	.384	0	.000	-1	-2	-2	2	0.0
Total	2	5	16	.238	46	22	10	1	5	216	215	5	97	84	13.4	3.67	91	.271	.358	10	.154	-1	-6	-8	2	-0.5
● **JEFF SCHATTINGER**	Schattinger, Jeffrey Charles b: 10/25/55, Fresno, Cal. BL/TR, 6'5", 200 lbs. Deb: 9/21/81																									
1981	KC-A	0	0	—	1	0	0	0	0	3	2	0	1	1	15.0	0.00	—	.182	.357	0	—	0	1	1	-0	0.0
● **DAN SCHATZEDER**	Schatzeder, Daniel Ernest b: 12/1/54, Elmhurst, Ill. BL/TL, 6', 195 lbs. Deb: 9/4/77																									
1977	Mon-N	2	1	.667	6	3	1	1	0	21^2	16	0	13	14	12.0	2.49	153	.203	.315	2	.333	0	3	3	-0	0.5
1978	Mon-N	7	7	.500	29	18	2	0	0	143^2	108	10	68	69	11.2	3.07	115	.213	.308	10	.222	3	8	7	-2	0.8
1979	Mon-N	10	5	.667	32	21	3	0	1	162	136	17	59	106	10.9	2.83	129	.225	.295	11	.216	4	16	15	-3	1.5
1980	Det-A	11	13	.458	32	26	9	2	0	192^2	178	23	58	94	11.2	4.02	102	.246	.304	0	—	0	0	2	-2	0.0
1981	Det-A	6	8	.429	17	14	1	0	0	71^1	74	13	29	20	13.2	6.06	62	.265	.339	0	—	0	-19	-18	-0	-3.1
1982	SF-N	1	4	.200	13	3	0	0	0	33^1	47	3	12	18	15.9	7.29	49	.333	.386	1	.125	-0	-14	-14	0	-1.8

YEAR	TM/L	W	L	PCT	G	GS	CG	SH	SV	IP	H	HR	BB	SO	RAT	ERA	ERA+	OAV	OOB	BH	AVG	PB	PR	/A	PD	TPI
	Mon-N	0	2	.000	26	1	0	0	0	36	37	1	12	15	12.8	3.50	104	.276	.345	2	.400	1	0	1	-0	0.1
	Yr	1	6	.143	39	4	0	0	0	69^1	84	4	24	33	14.3	5.32	68	.304	.364	3	.231	1	-13	-13	0	-1.7
1983	Mon-N	5	2	.714	58	2	0	0	2	87	88	3	25	48	12.2	3.21	112	.265	.326	2	.200	0	4	4	-1	0.2
1984	Mon-N	7	7	.500	36	14	1	1	1	136	112	13	36	89	9.9	2.71	126	.224	.278	11	.314	5	13	11	-3	1.3
1985	Mon-N	3	5	.375	24	15	1	0	0	104^1	101	13	31	64	11.4	3.80	89	.259	.314	6	.194	3	-2	-5	0	0.0
1986	Mon-N	3	2	.600	30	1	0	0	1	59	53	6	19	33	11.0	3.20	115	.240	.300	9	.429	6	3	3	-1	0.8
	Phi-N	3	3	.500	25	0	0	0	1	29^1	28	3	16	14	13.5	3.38	114	.252	.346	1	.200	0	1	2	-0	0.3
	Yr	6	5	.545	55	1	0	0	2	88^1	81	9	35	47	11.8	3.26	115	.243	.314	10	.385	7	4	5	-1	1.1
1987	Phi-N	3	1	.750	26	0	0	0	0	37^2	40	4	14	28	12.9	4.06	104	.278	.342	2	.167	0	0	1	-1	0.0
	*Min-A	3	1	.750	30	1	0	0	0	43^2	64	8	18	30	17.1	6.39	72	.342	.403	0	—	0	-9	-9	-0	-0.7
1988	Cle-A	0	2	.000	15	0	0	0	3	16	26	6	2	10	16.3	9.56	43	.351	.377	0	—	0	-10	-10	-0	-1.5
	Min-A	0	1	.000	10	0	0	0	0	10^1	8	1	5	7	12.2	1.74	234	.216	.326	0	—	0	3	3	0	0.1
	Yr	0	3	.000	25	0	0	0	3	26^1	34	7	7	17	14.4	6.49	63	.304	.350	0	—	0	-7	-7	-0	-1.4
1989	Hou-N	4	1	.800	36	0	0	0	1	56^2	64	2	28	46	15.1	4.45	76	.287	.374	0	.000	-1	-6	-7	0	-0.7
1990	Hou-N	1	3	.250	45	2	0	0	0	64	61	2	23	37	11.8	2.39	155	.261	.327	1	.250	0	10	9	-0	0.5
	NY-N	0	0	—	6	0	0	0	0	5^2	5	0	0	2	7.9	0.00	—	.263	.263	0	—	0	2	2	-0	0.0
	Yr	1	3	.250	51	2	0	0	0	69^2	66	2	23	39	11.5	2.20	169	.256	.317	1	.250	0	12	12	-0	0.5
1991	KC-A	0	0	—	8	0	0	0	0	6^2	11	0	7	4	24.3	9.45	44	.367	.486	0	—	0	-4	-4	-0	0.0
Total	15	69	68	.504	504	121	18	4	10	1317	1257	128	475	748	12.0	3.74	99	.253	.321	58	.240	22	1	-4	-13	-1.7

● RUBE SCHAUER Schauer, Alexander John (b: Dimitri Ivanovich Dimitrihoff)
b: 3/19/1891, Odessa, Russia d: 4/15/57, Minneapolis, Minn. BR/TR, 6′2″, 192 lbs. Deb: 8/27/13

YEAR	TM/L	W	L	PCT	G	GS	CG	SH	SV	IP	H	HR	BB	SO	RAT	ERA	ERA+	OAV	OOB	BH	AVG	PB	PR	/A	PD	TPI
1913	NY-N	0	1	.000	3	1	1	0	0	12	14	0	9	7	17.3	7.50	42	.292	.404	0	.000	-0	-6	-6	0	-0.4
1914	NY-N	0	0	—	6	0	0	0	0	22^1	16	2	8	6	9.7	3.22	82	.205	.279	1	.143	-0	-1	-1	-1	-0.1
1915	NY-N	2	8	.200	32	7	4	0	0	105^1	101	4	35	65	11.8	3.50	73	.258	.322	2	.077	-2	-9	-11	-0	-1.3
1916	NY-N	1	4	.200	19	3	1	0	0	45^2	44	0	16	24	12.2	2.96	82	.257	.328	2	.222	0	-2	-3	-0	-0.3
1917	Phi-A	7	16	.304	33	21	10	0	1	215	209	6	69	62	11.8	3.14	88	.263	.324	11	.145	-2	-11	-9	0	-1.2
Total	5	10	29	.256	93	32	16	0	1	400^1	384	12	137	164	11.9	3.35	80	.259	.324	16	.132	-4	-29	-30	-1	-3.3

● OWEN SCHEETZ Scheetz, Owen Franklin b: 12/24/13, New Bedford, Ohio d: 9/28/94, Kirkersville, O. BR/TR, 6′1″, 200 lbs. Deb: 4/22/43

YEAR	TM/L	W	L	PCT	G	GS	CG	SH	SV	IP	H	HR	BB	SO	RAT	ERA	ERA+	OAV	OOB	BH	AVG	PB	PR	/A	PD	TPI
1943	Was-A	0	0	—	6	0	0	0	1	9	16	0	4	5	20.0	7.00	46	.381	.435	0	.000	-0	-4	-4	0	-0.1

● LEFTY SCHEGG Schegg, Gilbert Eugene (b: Gilbert Eugene Price)
b: 8/28/1889, Leesville, Ohio d: 2/27/63, Niles, Ohio BL/TL, 5′11″, 180 lbs. Deb: 8/20/12

YEAR	TM/L	W	L	PCT	G	GS	CG	SH	SV	IP	H	HR	BB	SO	RAT	ERA	ERA+	OAV	OOB	BH	AVG	PB	PR	/A	PD	TPI
1912	Was-A	0	0	—	2	1	0	0	0	5^1	7	0	4	3	18.6	3.38	99	.333	.440	0	.000	-0	-0	-0	-1	-0.1

● CARL SCHEIB Scheib, Carl Alvin b: 1/1/27, Gratz, Pa. BR/TR, 6′1″, 192 lbs. Deb: 9/6/43

YEAR	TM/L	W	L	PCT	G	GS	CG	SH	SV	IP	H	HR	BB	SO	RAT	ERA	ERA+	OAV	OOB	BH	AVG	PB	PR	/A	PD	TPI
1943	Phi-A	0	1	.000	6	0	0	0	0	18^2	24	4	3	3	13.5	4.34	78	.308	.341	0	.000	-1	-2	-2	-1	-0.2
1944	Phi-A	0	0	—	15	0	0	0	0	36^1	36	1	11	13	12.6	4.21	83	.257	.329	3	.300	1	-3	-3	1	0.2
1945	Phi-A	0	0	—	4	0	0	0	0	8^2	6	0	4	2	10.4	3.12	110	.207	.303	0	.000	-0	0	0	0	0.0
1947	Phi-A	4	6	.400	21	12	6	2	0	116	121	11	55	26	13.8	5.04	76	.274	.357	6	.133	-2	-17	-16	-2	-1.6
1948	Phi-A	14	8	.636	32	24	15	1	0	198^2	219	14	76	44	13.4	3.94	109	.286	.351	31	.298	7	8	8	1	1.9
1949	Phi-A	9	12	.429	38	23	11	2	0	182^2	191	16	118	43	15.3	5.12	80	.275	.382	17	.236	3	-19	-21	-3	-2.0
1950	Phi-A	3	10	.231	43	8	1	0	3	106	138	13	70	37	17.7	7.22	63	.317	.411	13	.250	2	-31	-31	-1	-3.2
1951	Phi-A	1	12	.077	46	11	3	0	10	143	132	7	71	49	13.3	4.47	96	.250	.347	21	.396	8	-6	-3	4	1.0
1952	Phi-A	11	7	.611	30	19	8	1	2	158	153	21	50	42	11.8	4.39	90	.253	.314	18	.220	-1	-12	-8	0	-0.8
1953	Phi-A	3	7	.300	28	8	3	0	2	96	99	9	29	25	12.7	4.88	88	.261	.325	8	.195	-1	-9	-6	-0	-0.7
1954	Phi-A	0	1	.000	1	1	0	0	0	2	5	0	1	1	31.5	22.50	17	.500	.583	0	—	0	-4	-4	-0	-1.1
	StL-N	0	1	.000	3	1	0	0	0	4^2	6	3	5	5	21.2	11.57	36	.300	.440	0	.000	-0	-4	-4	0	-0.7
Total	11	45	65	.409	267	107	47	6	17	1070^2	1130	99	493	290	13.9	4.88	85	.274	.355	117	.250	16	-100	-89	0	-7.2

● FRANK SCHEIBECK Scheibeck, Frank S. b: 6/28/1865, Detroit, Mich. d: 10/22/56, Detroit, Mich. BR/TR, 5′7″, 145 lbs. Deb: 5/9/1887 ♦

YEAR	TM/L	W	L	PCT	G	GS	CG	SH	SV	IP	H	HR	BB	SO	RAT	ERA	ERA+	OAV	OOB	BH	AVG	PB	PR	/A	PD	TPI
1887	Cle-a	0	1	.000	1	1	1	0	0	9	17	1	4	3	22.0	12.00	36	.362	.423	2	.222	0	-8	-8	-0	-0.5

● JACK SCHEIBLE Scheible, John G. b: 2/16/1866, Youngstown, Ohio d: 8/9/1897, Youngstown, Ohio TL , Deb: 9/8/1893

YEAR	TM/L	W	L	PCT	G	GS	CG	SH	SV	IP	H	HR	BB	SO	RAT	ERA	ERA+	OAV	OOB	BH	AVG	PB	PR	/A	PD	TPI
1893	Cle-N	1	1	.500	2	2	2	1	0	18	15	0	11	1	13.0	2.00	244	.221	.329	1	.143	-0	5	6	-0	0.5
1894	Phi-N	0	1	.000	1	1	0	0	0	0^1	6	0	2	0	243.0	189.00	3	.857	.900	0	—	0	-7	-7	-0	-3.9
Total	2	1	2	.333	3	3	2	1	0	18^1	21	0	13	1	17.2	5.40	91	.280	.393	1	.143	-0	-1	-1	-0	-3.4

● RICH SCHEID Scheid, Richard Paul b: 2/3/65, Staten Island, N.Y. BL/TL, 6′3″, 185 lbs. Deb: 9/11/92

YEAR	TM/L	W	L	PCT	G	GS	CG	SH	SV	IP	H	HR	BB	SO	RAT	ERA	ERA+	OAV	OOB	BH	AVG	PB	PR	/A	PD	TPI
1992	Hou-N	0	1	.000	7	1	0	0	0	12	14	2	6	8	15.0	6.00	56	.280	.357	0	.000	-0	-3	-4	-0	-0.3
1994	Fla-N	1	3	.250	8	5	0	0	0	32^1	35	6	8	17	12.5	3.34	131	.269	.321	0	.000	-1	3	4	-1	0.3
1995	Fla-N	0	0	—	6	0	0	0	0	10^1	14	1	7	10	18.3	6.10	69	.341	.438	0	.000	-0	-2	-2	1	0.1
Total	3	1	4	.200	21	6	0	0	0	54^2	63	9	21	35	14.2	4.45	92	.285	.352	0	.000	-1	-2	-2	0	0.1

● JIM SCHELLE Schelle, Gerard Anthony b: 4/13/17, Baltimore, Md. d: 5/4/90, Weymouth, Mass. BR/TR, 6′3″, 204 lbs. Deb: 7/23/39

YEAR	TM/L	W	L	PCT	G	GS	CG	SH	SV	IP	H	HR	BB	SO	RAT	ERA	ERA+	OAV	OOB	BH	AVG	PB	PR	/A	PD	TPI
1939	Phi-A	0	0	—	1	0	0	0	0	0	1	0	3	0	—	∞	—	1.000	1.000	0	—	0	-3	-3	0	-0.2

● FRED SCHEMANSKE Schemanske, Frederick George "Buck" b: 4/28/03, Detroit, Mich. d: 2/18/60, Detroit, Mich. BR/TR, 6′2″, 190 lbs. Deb: 9/15/23 ♦

YEAR	TM/L	W	L	PCT	G	GS	CG	SH	SV	IP	H	HR	BB	SO	RAT	ERA	ERA+	OAV	OOB	BH	AVG	PB	PR	/A	PD	TPI
1923	Was-A	0	0	—	1	0	0	0	0	1	3	0	0	0	27.0	27.00	14	.600	.600	2	1.000	1	-3	-3	-0	0.1

● BILL SCHENCK Schenck, William G. b: 7/1854, Brooklyn, N.Y. d: 1/29/34, Brooklyn, N.Y. 5′7″, 171 lbs. Deb: 5/29/1882 ♦

YEAR	TM/L	W	L	PCT	G	GS	CG	SH	SV	IP	H	HR	BB	SO	RAT	ERA	ERA+	OAV	OOB	BH	AVG	PB	PR	/A	PD	TPI
1882	Lou-a	1	0	1.000	2	1	1	0	0	10	6	0	1	4	6.3	0.90	275	.162	.184	60	.260	0	2	2	-0	0.1

● JOHN SCHENEBERG Scheneberg, John Bluford b: 11/20/1887, Guyandotte, W.Va. d: 9/26/50, Huntington, W.Va. BB/TR, 6′1″, 180 lbs. Deb: 9/23/13

YEAR	TM/L	W	L	PCT	G	GS	CG	SH	SV	IP	H	HR	BB	SO	RAT	ERA	ERA+	OAV	OOB	BH	AVG	PB	PR	/A	PD	TPI
1913	Pit-N	0	1	.000	1	1	0	0	0	6	10	0	2	1	18.0	6.00	50	.400	.444	1	.500	0	-2	-2	0	-0.2
1920	StL-A	0	0	—	1	0	0	0	0	2	7	0	1	0	36.0	27.00	15	.583	.615	0	—	0	-5	-5	-0	0.0
Total	2	0	1	.000	2	1	0	0	0	8	17	0	3	1	22.5	11.25	29	.459	.500	1	.500	0	-7	-7	0	-0.2

● FRED SCHERMAN Scherman, Frederick John b: 7/25/44, Dayton, Ohio BL/TL, 6′1″, 195 lbs. Deb: 4/26/69

YEAR	TM/L	W	L	PCT	G	GS	CG	SH	SV	IP	H	HR	BB	SO	RAT	ERA	ERA+	OAV	OOB	BH	AVG	PB	PR	/A	PD	TPI
1969	Det-A	1	0	1.000	4	0	0	0	0	4	6	2	0	3	13.5	6.75	55	.333	.333	0	—	0	-1	-1	0	-0.3
1970	Det-A	4	4	.500	48	0	0	0	1	69^2	61	5	28	58	11.6	3.23	115	.237	.315	2	.167	-0	4	4	0	0.4
1971	Det-A	11	6	.647	69	1	1	0	20	113	91	11	49	46	11.5	2.71	133	.226	.318	5	.208	1	9	11	1	2.3
1972	*Det-A	7	3	.700	57	3	0	0	12	94	91	5	53	53	14.3	3.64	86	.269	.376	2	.091	-1	-6	-5	-1	-0.9
1973	Det-A	2	2	.500	34	0	0	0	1	61^2	59	6	30	28	13.4	4.23	97	.258	.351	0	—	0	-3	-1	-1	-0.2
1974	Hou-N	2	5	.286	53	0	0	0	4	61^1	67	5	26	35	14.7	4.11	84	.284	.372	0	.000	-0	-3	-4	-0	-0.6
1975	Hou-N	0	1	.000	16	0	0	0	0	16^1	21	4	4	13	14.3	4.96	68	.318	.366	0	.000	-0	-2	-3	0	-0.2
	Mon-N	4	3	.571	34	7	0	0	0	76^1	84	3	41	43	15.3	3.54	108	.283	.379	1	.063	-1	1	2	1	0.2
	Yr	4	4	.500	50	7	0	0	0	92^2	105	7	45	56	15.1	3.79	99	.288	.373	1	.059	-1	-2	-0	1	0.0
1976	Mon-N	2	2	.500	31	0	0	0	1	40	42	5	14	18	13.3	4.95	75	.261	.331	1	.250	0	-6	-5	-1	-0.6
Total	8	33	26	.559	346	11	1	0	39	536^1	522	46	245	297	13.4	3.66	99	.260	.350	11	.134	-1	-9	-3	-1	0.1

● BILL SCHERRER Scherrer, William Joseph b: 1/20/58, Tonawanda, N.Y. BL/TL, 6′4″, 180 lbs. Deb: 9/7/82

YEAR	TM/L	W	L	PCT	G	GS	CG	SH	SV	IP	H	HR	BB	SO	RAT	ERA	ERA+	OAV	OOB	BH	AVG	PB	PR	/A	PD	TPI
1982	Cin-N	0	1	.000	5	2	0	0	0	17^1	17	0	0	7	8.8	2.60	142	.250	.250	1	.500	1	2	2	-0	0.2
1983	Cin-N	2	3	.400	73	0	0	0	10	92	73	6	33	57	10.4	2.74	139	.225	.296	1	.091	-0	9	11	1	0.8
1984	Cin-N	1	1	.500	36	0	0	0	1	52^1	64	6	15	35	13.6	4.99	76	.300	.346	0	.000	-0	-8	-7	0	-0.3
	*Det-A	1	0	1.000	18	0	0	0	0	19	14	1	8	16	10.4	1.89	207	.206	.289	0	—	0	4	4	-0	0.2
1985	Det-A	3	2	.600	48	0	0	0	0	66	62	10	41	46	14.2	4.36	93	.248	.356	0	—	0	-2	-2	1	-0.1
1986	Det-A	0	1	.000	13	0	0	0	0	21	19	3	22	16	18.0	7.29	57	.244	.416	0	—	0	-7	-7	0	-0.3
1987	Cin-N	1	1	.500	23	0	0	0	0	33	43	3	16	24	16.1	4.36	97	.328	.401	0	.000	-0	-1	-0	-0	-0.1
1988	Bal-A	0	1	.000	4	0	0	0	0	4	8	2	3	3	24.8	13.50	29	.400	.478	0	—	0	-4	-4	-0	-0.7

YEAR	TM/L	W	L	PCT	G	GS	CG	SH	SV	IP	H	HR	BB	SO	RAT	ERA	ERA+	OAV	OOB	BH	AVG	PB	PR	/A	PD	TPI
	Phi-N	0	0	—	8	0	0	0	0	6^2	7	0	2	3	12.2	5.40	66	.269	.321	0	—	0	-1	-1	0	0.0
Total	7	8	10	.444	228	2	0	0	11	311^1	307	31	140	207	13.0	4.08	96	.260	.340	2	.118	-0	-8	-5	1	-0.3
● DUTCH SCHESLER	Schesler, Charles b: 6/1/1900, Frankfurt, Germany d: 11/19/53, Harrisburg, Pa. BR/TR, 6'2", 185 lbs. Deb: 4/16/31																									
1931	Phi-N	0	0	—	17	0	0	0	0	38^1	65	4	18	14	20.4	7.28	58	.385	.455	1	.111	-0	-15	-13	0	0.0
● LOU SCHETTLER	Schettler, Louis Martin b: 6/12/1886, Pittsburgh, Pa. d: 5/1/60, Youngstown, Ohio BR/TR, 5'11", 160 lbs. Deb: 4/25/10																									
1910	Phi-N	2	6	.250	27	7	3	0	1	107	96	2	51	62	12.5	3.20	98	.247	.337	7	.171	-1	-2	-1	-1	-0.3
● CURT SCHILLING	Schilling, Curtis Montague b: 11/14/66, Anchorage, Alaska BR/TR, 6'4", 215 lbs. Deb: 9/7/88																									
1988	Bal-A	0	3	.000	4	4	0	0	0	14^2	22	3	10	4	20.3	9.82	40	.355	.452	0	—	0	-10	-10	-1	-1.4
1989	Bal-A	0	1	.000	5	1	0	0	0	8^2	10	2	3	6	13.5	6.23	61	.286	.342	0	—	0	-2	-2	-0	-0.3
1990	Bal-A	1	2	.333	35	0	0	0	3	46	38	1	19	32	11.2	2.54	149	.229	.308	0	—	0	7	6	-1	0.4
1991	Hou-N	3	5	.375	56	0	0	0	8	75^2	79	2	39	71	14.0	3.81	92	.271	.358	1	.333	0	-1	-3	-1	-0.4
1992	Phi-N	14	11	.560	42	26	10	4	2	226^1	165	11	59	147	**8.9**	2.35	149	**.201**	**.256**	10	.156	-0	29	29	-3	3.0
1993	*Phi-N	16	7	.696	34	34	7	2	0	235^1	234	23	57	186	11.3	4.02	99	.259	.305	11	.147	-1	1	-1	0	-0.2
1994	Phi-N	2	8	.200	13	13	1	0	0	82^1	87	10	28	58	12.9	4.48	96	.270	.334	3	.107	-1	-2	-2	-1	-0.4
1995	Phi-N	7	5	.583	17	17	1	0	0	116	96	12	26	114	9.7	3.57	118	.220	.268	7	.175	0	8	8	-2	0.6
1996	Phi-N	9	10	.474	26	26	**8**	2	0	183^1	149	16	50	182	9.9	3.19	135	.223	.280	11	.175	-0	21	23	-3	1.8
1997	Phi-N★	17	11	.607	35	35	7	2	0	254^1	208	25	58	**319**	9.6	2.97	143	.224	.273	14	.173	-0	35	36	1	3.9
1998	Phi-N☆	15	14	.517	35	35	**15**	2	0	**268^2**	236	23	61	**300**	10.2	3.25	134	.236	.284	10	.132	-1	29	33	1	3.3
Total	11	84	77	.522	302	191	49	12	13	1511^1	1324	128	410	1419	10.5	3.36	121	.235	.290	67	.156	-3	114	117	-9	10.3
● RED SCHILLINGS	Schillings, Elbert Isaiah b: 3/29/1900, Deport, Tex. d: 1/7/54, Oklahoma City, Okla BR/TR, 5'10", 180 lbs. Deb: 9/11/22																									
1922	Phi-A	0	0	—	4	0	0	0	0	8	10	1	11	4	23.6	6.75	63	.313	.488	0	.000	-0	-2	-2	-0	0.0
● CALVIN SCHIRALDI	Schiraldi, Calvin Drew b: 6/16/62, Houston, Tex. BR/TR, 6'4", 200 lbs. Deb: 9/1/84																									
1984	NY-N	0	2	.000	5	3	0	0	0	17^1	20	3	10	16	15.6	5.71	62	.286	.375	0	.000	-0	-4	-4	0	-0.4
1985	NY-N	2	1	.667	10	4	0	0	0	26^1	43	4	11	21	19.5	8.89	39	.368	.435	1	.125	-0	-15	-16	0	-1.6
1986	*Bos-A	4	2	.667	25	0	0	0	9	51	36	5	15	55	9.2	1.41	295	.201	.267	0	—	0	16	16	-1	2.2
1987	Bos-A	8	5	.615	62	1	0	0	6	83^2	75	15	40	93	12.5	4.41	103	.240	.328	0	—	0	0	1	-0	0.2
1988	Chi-N	9	13	.409	29	27	2	1	1	166^1	166	13	63	140	12.5	4.38	82	.257	.325	6	.100	-2	-17	-14	-2	-2.2
1989	Chi-N	3	6	.333	54	0	0	0	4	78^2	60	7	50	54	12.7	3.78	100	.209	.328	0	.000	-1	-2	-0	-1	-0.2
	SD-N	3	1	.750	5	4	0	0	0	21^1	12	1	13	17	10.5	2.53	138	.162	.287	1	.143	1	2	2	-0	0.5
	Yr	6	7	.462	59	4	0	0	4	100	72	8	63	71	12.2	3.51	105	.198	.316	1	.063	0	-0	2	-2	0.3
1990	SD-N	3	8	.273	42	8	0	0	1	104	105	11	60	74	14.4	4.41	87	.264	.362	4	.190	2	-7	-7	-1	-0.6
1991	Tex-A	0	1	.000	3	0	0	0	0	4^2	5	3	5	1	19.3	11.57	35	.263	.417	0	—	0	-4	-4	0	-0.6
Total	8	32	39	.451	235	47	2	1	21	553^1	522	62	267	471	13.0	4.28	90	.248	.336	12	.111	-1	-32	-26	-5	-2.7
● BIFF SCHLITZER	Schlitzer, Victor Joseph b: 12/4/1884, Rochester, N.Y. d: 1/4/48, Wellesley Hills, Mass. BR/TR, 5'11", 175 lbs. Deb: 4/17/08																									
1908	Phi-A	6	8	.429	24	18	11	2	0	131	110	1	45	57	10.8	3.16	81	.234	.303	9	.196	-1	-11	-9	-2	-1.3
1909	Phi-A	0	3	.000	4	3	0	0	0	13^1	13	0	7	6	15.5	5.40	45	.245	.365	1	.250	0	-4	-4	-1	-0.8
	Bos-A	4	4	.500	13	8	5	0	1	69^2	68	0	17	23	11.1	3.49	72	.234	.279	5	.185	0	-8	-8	-1	-0.8
	Yr	4	7	.364	17	11	5	0	1	83	81	0	24	29	11.5	3.80	65	.234	.286	6	.194	1	-12	-12	-1	-1.6
1914	Buf-F	0	0	—	3	0	0	0	0	3^1	7	3	2	1	24.3	16.20	18	.438	.500	1	1.000	0	-5	-5	0	0.0
Total	3	10	15	.400	44	29	16	2	1	217^1	198	4	71	87	11.4	3.60	71	.239	.303	16	.205	0	-28	-26	-1	-2.9
● GEORGE SCHMEES	Schmees, George Edward "Rocky" b: 9/6/24, Cincinnati, Ohio BL/TL, 6', 190 lbs. Deb: 4/15/52 ♦																									
1952	Bos-A	0	0	—	2	1	0	0	0	6	9	0	2	2	16.5	3.00	131	.346	.393	13	.203	0	0	1	1	0.1
● AL SCHMELZ	Schmelz, Alan George b: 11/12/43, Whittier, Cal. BR/TR, 6'4", 210 lbs. Deb: 9/7/67																									
1967	NY-N	0	0	—	2	0	0	0	0	3	4	1	1	2	15.0	3.00	113	.364	.417	0		0	0	0	0	0.0
● BUTCH SCHMIDT	Schmidt, Charles John "Butcher Boy" b: 7/19/1886, Baltimore, Md. d: 9/4/52, Baltimore, Md. BL/TL, 6'1.5", 200 lbs. Deb: 5/11/09 ♦																									
1909	NY-A	0	0	—	1	0	0	0	0	5	10	0	1	2	19.8	7.20	35	.435	.458	0	.000	-0	-3	-3	-0	-0.1
● CURT SCHMIDT	Schmidt, Curtis Allen b: 3/16/70, Miles City, Mont. BR/TR, 6'6", 200 lbs. Deb: 4/28/95																									
1995	Mon-N	0	0	—	11	0	0	0	0	10^1	15	1	9	7	22.6	6.97	62	.357	.491	0	—	0	-3	-3	-0	0.0
● DAVE SCHMIDT	Schmidt, David Joseph b: 4/22/57, Niles, Mich. BR/TR, 6'1", 185 lbs. Deb: 5/1/81																									
1981	Tex-A	0	1	.000	14	1	0	0	1	31^2	31	1	11	13	12.2	3.13	111	.258	.326	0	—	0	2	1	0	0.1
1982	Tex-A	4	6	.400	33	8	0	0	6	109^2	118	5	25	69	12.1	3.20	121	.279	.327	0	—	0	11	8	-0	1.0
1983	Tex-A	3	3	.500	31	0	0	0	2	46^1	42	3	14	29	11.1	3.88	103	.241	.302	0	—	0	1	1	0	0.2
1984	Tex-A	6	6	.500	43	0	0	0	12	70^1	69	3	20	46	11.4	2.56	162	.262	.314	0	—	0	11	12	1	2.5
1985	Tex-A	7	6	.538	51	4	1	1	5	85^2	81	6	22	46	10.8	3.15	134	.246	.293	0	—	0	9	10	1	1.6
1986	Chi-A	3	6	.333	49	1	0	0	8	92^1	94	10	27	67	12.3	3.31	130	.264	.325	0	—	0	9	10	-1	0.9
1987	Bal-A	10	5	.667	35	14	2	2	1	124	128	13	26	70	11.3	3.77	117	.263	.302	0	—	0	9	9	-1	0.8
1988	Bal-A	8	5	.615	41	9	0	0	2	129^2	129	14	38	67	11.8	3.40	115	.262	.319	0	—	0	8	7	2	1.0
1989	Bal-A	10	13	.435	38	26	2	0	0	156^2	196	24	36	46	13.4	5.69	67	.310	.349	0	—	0	-31	-33	1	-4.1
1990	Mon-N	3	3	.500	34	0	0	0	13	48	58	3	13	22	13.3	4.31	85	.297	.341	0	.000	-0	-3	-4	0	-0.6
1991	Mon-N	0	1	.000	4	0	0	0	0	4^1	9	2	2	3	22.8	10.38	35	.429	.478	0	—	0	-3	-3	0	-0.6
1992	Sea-A	0	0	—	3	0	0	0	0	3^1	7	1	3	1	27.0	18.90	21	.438	.526	0	—	0	-6	-6	-0	0.0
Total	12	54	55	.495	376	63	5	3	50	902	962	85	237	479	12.1	3.88	103	.274	.323	0	.000	-0	17	13	3	2.8
● FREDDY SCHMIDT	Schmidt, Frederick Albert b: 2/9/16, Hartford, Conn. BR/TR, 6'1", 185 lbs. Deb: 4/25/44																									
1944	*StL-N	7	3	.700	37	9	3	2	5	114^1	94	5	58	58	12.0	3.15	112	.222	.317	7	.206	-0	6	5	-1	0.3
1946	StL-N	1	0	1.000	16	0	0	0	0	27^1	27	0	15	14	14.8	3.29	105	.276	.388	0	.000	-0	0	0	0	0.0
1947	StL-N	0	0	—	2	0	0	0	0	4	5	1	1	2	13.5	2.25	184	.333	.375	0	—	0	1	1	-0	0.0
	Phi-N	5	8	.385	29	5	0	0	0	76^2	76	4	43	24	14.4	4.70	85	.285	.392	1	.050	-2	-5	-6	-1	-1.1
	Chi-N	0	0	—	1	1	0	0	0	3	4	0	5	0	27.0	9.00	44	.333	.529	0	.000	-0	-2	-2	-0	0.0
	Yr	5	8	.385	32	6	0	0	0	83^2	85	5	49	26	14.4	4.73	85	.285	.386	1	.045	-2	-6	-7	-1	-1.1
Total	3	13	11	.542	85	15	3	2	5	225^1	206	10	122	98	13.4	3.75	98	.252	.355	8	.140	-2	-0	-1	-1	-0.8
● PETE SCHMIDT	Schmidt, Friedrich Christoph Herman b: 7/23/1890, Lowden, Iowa d: 3/11/73, Pembroke, Ont., Can BR/TR, 5'11", 175 lbs. Deb: 7/14/13																									
1913	StL-A	0	0	—	1	0	0	0	1	2	3	0	2	0	22.5	4.50	65	.333	.455	0	—	0	-0	-0	-0	-0.1
● HENRY SCHMIDT	Schmidt, Henry Martin b: 6/26/1873, Brownsville, Tex. d: 4/23/26, Nashville, Tenn. BR/TR, 5'11", 170 lbs. Deb: 4/17/03																									
1903	Bro-N	22	13	.629	40	36	29	5	2	301	321	5	120	96	13.8	3.83	83	.280	.359	21	.196	3	-19	-21	6	-1.3
● JASON SCHMIDT	Schmidt, Jason David b: 1/29/73, Kelso, Wash. BR/TR, 6'5", 185 lbs. Deb: 4/28/95																									
1995	Atl-N	2	2	.500	9	2	0	0	0	25	27	2	18	19	16.6	5.76	74	.287	.407	1	.200	0	-4	-4	0	-0.5
1996	Atl-N	3	4	.429	13	11	0	0	0	58^2	69	8	32	48	15.5	6.75	65	.296	.381	0	.000	-2	-17	-15	-1	-1.7
	Pit-N	2	2	.500	6	6	1	0	0	37^2	39	2	21	26	14.8	4.06	107	.271	.371	1	.083	-1	1	1	-0	0.0
	Yr	5	6	.455	19	17	1	0	0	96^1	108	10	53	74	15.2	5.70	77	.282	.372	1	.032	-2	-16	-14	-1	-1.7
1997	Pit-N	10	9	.526	32	32	2	0	0	187^2	193	16	76	136	13.3	4.60	93	.265	.342	6	.107	-1	-8	-7	-1	-0.9
1998	Pit-N	11	14	.440	33	33	0	0	0	214^1	228	24	71	158	12.7	4.07	106	.275	.336	6	.097	-2	4	6	-4	0.0
Total	4	28	31	.475	93	84	3	0	0	523^1	556	52	218	387	13.6	4.64	93	.274	.350	14	.091	-6	-25	-19	-6	-3.1
● JEFF SCHMIDT	Schmidt, Jeffrey Thomas b: 2/21/71, Northfield, Minn. BR/TR, 6'5", 205 lbs. Deb: 5/17/96																									
1996	Cal-A	2	0	1.000	9	0	0	0	0	8	13	2	8	2	23.6	7.88	64	.394	.512	0	—	0	-3	-3	-0	-0.5
● WILLARD SCHMIDT	Schmidt, Willard Raymond b: 5/29/28, Hays, Kan. BR/TR, 6'1", 187 lbs. Deb: 4/19/52																									
1952	StL-N	2	3	.400	18	3	0	0	1	34^2	36	6	18	30	14.5	5.19	72	.267	.361	1	.125	-0	-6	-6	1	-0.7

YEAR	TM/L	W	L	PCT	G	GS	CG	SH	SV	IP	H	HR	BB	SO	RAT	ERA	ERA+	OAV	OOB	BH	AVG	PB	PR	/A	PD	TPI
1953	StL-N	0	2	.000	6	2	0	0	0	17^{2}	21	1	13	11	17.8	9.17	46	.288	.402	0	.000	-1	-10	-10	-0	-0.9
1955	StL-N	7	6	.538	20	15	8	1	0	129^{2}	89	7	57	86	10.3	2.78	146	.197	.291	5	.119	-3	18	19	1	1.5
1956	StL-N	6	8	.429	33	21	2	0	1	147^{2}	131	18	78	52	12.8	3.84	99	.246	.344	10	.233	1	-1	-1	2	0.2
1957	StL-N	10	3	.769	40	8	1	0	0	116^{2}	146	13	49	63	15.2	4.78	83	.312	.380	7	.212	0	-12	-11	1	-1.0
1958	Cin-N	3	5	.375	41	2	0	0	0	69^{1}	60	8	33	41	12.2	2.86	145	.235	.325	1	.091	-1	8	10	1	1.1
1959	Cin-N	3	2	.600	36	4	0	0	0	70^{2}	80	4	30	40	14.1	3.95	103	.296	.369	1	.083	0	-0	1	1	0.2
Total	7	31	29	.517	194	55	11	1	2	586^{1}	563	57	278	323	13.1	3.93	101	.258	.344	25	.163	-2	-1	2	6	0.4

● **CRAZY SCHMIT** Schmit, Frederick M. "Germany" b: 2/13/1866, Chicago, Ill. d: 10/5/40, Chicago, Ill. BL/TL, 5'10.5", 165 lbs. Deb: 4/21/1890

YEAR	TM/L	W	L	PCT	G	GS	CG	SH	SV	IP	H	HR	BB	SO	RAT	ERA	ERA+	OAV	OOB	BH	AVG	PB	PR	/A	PD	TPI
1890	Pit-N	1	9	.100	11	10	9	1	0	83^{1}	108	3	42	35	17.1	5.83	57	.304	.390	2	.061	-3	-21	-23	-0	-2.3
1892	Bal-N	1	4	.200	6	6	6	0	0	47^{1}	37	0	26	17	12.0	3.23	106	.207	.307	2	.105	-1	0	1	1	0.1
1893	Bal-N	3	2	.600	9	6	4	0	0	49	67	1	22	10	16.7	6.61	72	.316	.386	5	.238	-0	-11	-10	-1	-0.8
	NY-N	0	2	.000	4	4	1	0	0	20^{2}	30	0	17	5	21.3	7.40	63	.330	.445	4	.444	2	-6	-6	0	-0.3
	Yr	3	4	.429	13	10	5	0	0	69^{2}	97	1	39	15	17.8	6.85	69	.318	.399	9	.300	1	-17	-16	-1	-1.1
1899	Cle-N	2	17	.105	20	19	16	0	0	138^{1}	197	3	62	24	17.8	5.86	63	.334	.410	11	.157	-2	-31	-33	2	-3.4
1901	Bal-A	0	2	.000	4	3	1	0	0	22^{2}	25	0	16	2	16.3	1.99	195	.278	.387	2	.222	0	4	5	0	0.5
Total	5	7	36	.163	54	48	37	1	0	361^{1}	464	7	185	93	16.8	5.45	69	.306	.391	26	.161	-4	-64	-68	2	-6.2

● **JOHNNY SCHMITZ** Schmitz, John Albert "Bear Tracks" b: 11/27/20, Wausau, Wis. BR/TL, 6', 170 lbs. Deb: 9/6/41

YEAR	TM/L	W	L	PCT	G	GS	CG	SH	SV	IP	H	HR	BB	SO	RAT	ERA	ERA+	OAV	OOB	BH	AVG	PB	PR	/A	PD	TPI
1941	Chi-N	2	0	1.000	5	3	1	0	0	20^{2}	12	0	9	11	9.6	1.31	269	.182	.289	4	.571	2	5	5	1	0.8
1942	Chi-N	3	7	.300	23	10	1	0	2	86^{2}	70	3	45	51	12.3	3.43	93	.230	.335	4	.154	-1	-1	-2	4	0.1
1946	Chi-N☆	11	11	.500	41	31	14	2	2	224^{1}	184	6	94	**135**	11.2	2.61	127	**.221**	.302	9	.129	-2	20	18	2	1.8
1947	Chi-N	13	18	.419	38	28	10	3	4	207	209	8	80	97	12.7	3.22	123	.262	.330	9	.132	-2	19	17	2	2.4
1948	Chi-N★	18	13	.581	34	30	18	2	1	242	186	11	97	100	10.6	2.64	148	**.215**	.295	11	.131	-2	35	34	5	4.6
1949	Chi-N	11	13	.458	36	31	9	3	3	207	227	11	92	75	14.0	4.35	93	.287	.363	10	.143	-1	-7	-7	5	-0.3
1950	Chi-N	10	16	.385	39	27	8	3	0	193	217	23	91	75	14.5	4.99	84	.284	.363	8	.119	-3	-18	-17	5	-1.7
1951	Chi-N	1	2	.333	8	3	0	0	0	18	22	1	15	6	18.5	8.00	51	.301	.420	1	.167	-0	-8	-8	1	-1.0
	Bro-N	1	4	.200	16	7	0	0	0	55^{2}	55	4	28	20	13.7	5.34	74	.259	.351	4	.222	2	-9	-9	1	-0.4
	Yr	2	6	.250	24	10	0	0	0	73^{2}	77	5	43	26	14.9	5.99	66	.270	.370	5	.208	1	-17	-17	2	-1.4
1952	Bro-N	1	1	.500	10	3	1	0	0	33^{1}	29	3	18	11	13.0	4.32	84	.238	.340	1	.125	-0	-2	-3	1	0.0
	NY-A	1	1	.500	5	2	1	0	1	15	15	0	9	3	15.0	3.60	92	.263	.373	3	.600	2	0	-0	0	0.2
	Cin-N	1	0	1.000	3	0	0	0	0	5	3	0	3	3	10.8	0.00	—	.188	.316	0	—	0	2	2	0	0.4
1953	NY-A	0	0	—	3	0	0	0	2	4^{1}	2	1	3	0	10.4	2.08	178	.143	.294	0	—	0	1	1	0	0.1
	Was-A	2	7	.222	24	13	5	0	4	107^{2}	118	9	37	39	13.3	3.68	106	.286	.351	2	.059	-4	4	3	1	-0.1
	Yr	2	7	.222	27	13	5	0	6	112	120	10	40	39	13.2	3.62	108	.282	.349	2	.059	-4	5	3	1	0.0
1954	Was-A	11	8	.579	29	23	12	2	1	185^{1}	176	6	64	56	11.8	2.91	122	.255	.321	7	.117	-3	17	13	2	1.2
1955	Was-A	7	10	.412	32	21	6	1	1	165	187	8	54	49	13.5	3.71	103	.291	.352	10	.185	0	5	2	2	0.5
1956	Bos-A	0	0	—	2	0	0	0	0	4^{1}	5	0	4	0	18.7	0.00	—	.278	.409	0	.000	-0	2	2	0	0.0
	Bal-A	0	3	.000	18	3	0	0	0	38^{1}	49	3	14	15	15.0	3.99	98	.318	.379	0	.000	-1	1	-0	1	-0.1
	Yr	0	3	.000	20	3	0	0	0	42^{2}	54	3	18	15	15.4	3.59	111	.314	.382	0	.000	-2	3	2	1	-0.1
Total	13	93	114	.449	366	235	86	16	21	1812^{2}	1766	97	757	746	12.7	3.55	107	.258	.335	83	.141	-14	66	50	35	8.5

● **CHARLIE SCHMUTZ** Schmutz, Charles Otto "King" b: 1/1/1890, San Diego, Cal. d: 6/27/62, Seattle, Wash. BR/TR, 6'1.5", 195 lbs. Deb: 5/13/14

YEAR	TM/L	W	L	PCT	G	GS	CG	SH	SV	IP	H	HR	BB	SO	RAT	ERA	ERA+	OAV	OOB	BH	AVG	PB	PR	/A	PD	TPI
1914	Bro-N	1	3	.250	18	5	1	0	0	57^{1}	57	1	13	21	11.1	3.30	87	.265	.310	3	.188	1	-3	-3	0	-0.1
1915	Bro-N	0	0	—	1	0	0	0	0	4	7	0	1	1	18.0	6.75	41	.438	.471	0	.000	-0	-2	-2	0	0.0
Total	2	1	3	.250	19	5	1	0	0	61^{1}	64	1	14	22	11.6	3.52	81	.277	.321	3	.176	0	-5	-5	1	-0.1

● **FRANK SCHNEIBERG** Schneiberg, Frank Frederick b: 3/12/1882, Milwaukee, Wis. d: 5/18/48, Milwaukee, Wis. TR , Deb: 6/8/10

YEAR	TM/L	W	L	PCT	G	GS	CG	SH	SV	IP	H	HR	BB	SO	RAT	ERA	ERA+	OAV	OOB	BH	AVG	PB	PR	/A	PD	TPI
1910	Bro-N	0	0	—	1	0	0	0	0	1	5	0	4	0	81.0	63.00	5	.625	.750	0	—	0	-7	-7	-0	0.0

● **DAN SCHNEIDER** Schneider, Daniel Louis b: 8/29/42, Evansville, Ind. BL/TL, 6'3", 170 lbs. Deb: 5/12/63

YEAR	TM/L	W	L	PCT	G	GS	CG	SH	SV	IP	H	HR	BB	SO	RAT	ERA	ERA+	OAV	OOB	BH	AVG	PB	PR	/A	PD	TPI
1963	Mil-N	1	0	1.000	30	3	0	0	0	43^{2}	36	2	20	19	11.5	3.09	104	.225	.311	0	.000	-1	1	1	-1	-0.2
1964	Mil-N	1	2	.333	13	5	0	0	0	36^{1}	38	6	13	14	12.6	5.45	65	.270	.331	0	.000	-1	-8	-8	1	-0.6
1966	Atl-N	0	0	—	14	0	0	0	0	26^{1}	35	1	5	11	14.0	3.42	106	.324	.360	4	.500	1	1	1	-0	0.1
1967	Hou-N	0	2	.000	54	0	0	0	2	52^{2}	60	5	27	39	15.2	4.96	67	.296	.384	1	.200	0	-9	-10	1	-0.3
1969	Hou-N	0	1	.000	6	0	0	0	0	7^{1}	16	2	5	3	25.8	13.50	26	.485	.553	0	.000	-0	-8	-8	0	-0.9
Total	5	2	5	.286	117	8	0	0	2	166^{1}	185	16	70	86	14.0	4.71	72	.287	.359	5	.172	-0	-24	-24	1	-1.9

● **JEFF SCHNEIDER** Schneider, Jeffrey Theodore b: 12/6/52, Bremerton, Wash. BB/TL, 6'3", 195 lbs. Deb: 8/12/81

YEAR	TM/L	W	L	PCT	G	GS	CG	SH	SV	IP	H	HR	BB	SO	RAT	ERA	ERA+	OAV	OOB	BH	AVG	PB	PR	/A	PD	TPI
1981	Bal-A	0	0	—	11	0	0	0	1	24	27	4	12	17	15.0	4.88	74	.290	.377	0	—	0	-3	-3	-0	-0.1

● **PETE SCHNEIDER** Schneider, Peter Joseph b: 8/20/1895, Los Angeles, Cal. d: 6/1/57, Los Angeles, Cal. BR/TR, 6'1", 194 lbs. Deb: 6/20/14

YEAR	TM/L	W	L	PCT	G	GS	CG	SH	SV	IP	H	HR	BB	SO	RAT	ERA	ERA+	OAV	OOB	BH	AVG	PB	PR	/A	PD	TPI
1914	Cin-N	5	13	.278	29	15	11	1	1	144^{1}	143	1	56	62	12.8	2.81	104	.269	.347	8	.178	1	-0	2	-1	0.2
1915	Cin-N	14	19	.424	48	35	16	5	2	275^{2}	254	4	104	108	11.9	2.48	115	.251	.325	23	.245	5	8	12	-1	2.0
1916	Cin-N	10	19	.345	44	31	16	2	1	274^{1}	259	4	82	117	11.6	2.69	96	.255	.319	21	.236	2	-2	-3	-3	-0.3
1917	Cin-N	20	19	.513	46	42	24	0	1	333^{2}	311	4	117	138	11.8	2.10	124	.255	.326	19	.167	0	23	19	-5	1.8
1918	Cin-N	10	15	.400	33	30	17	2	0	217	213	2	117	51	14.1	3.53	76	.272	.374	24	.289	6	-18	-21	-3	-2.0
1919	NY-A	0	1	.000	7	4	0	0	0	29	19	0	22	11	13.7	3.41	94	.192	.355	1	.111	-1	-1	-1	-1	-0.2
Total	6	59	86	.407	207	157	84	10	4	1274	1199	16	498	487	12.4	2.66	102	.257	.336	96	.221	14	9	8	-13	1.5

● **KARL SCHNELL** Schnell, Karl Otto b: 9/20/1899, Los Angeles, Cal. d: 5/31/92, Palo Alto, Cal. BR/TR, 6'1", 176 lbs. Deb: 4/24/22

YEAR	TM/L	W	L	PCT	G	GS	CG	SH	SV	IP	H	HR	BB	SO	RAT	ERA	ERA+	OAV	OOB	BH	AVG	PB	PR	/A	PD	TPI
1922	Cin-N	0	0	—	10	0	0	0	0	20	21	0	18	5	17.5	2.70	148	.300	.443	1	.250	0	3	3	0	0.0
1923	Cin-N	0	0	—	1	0	0	0	0	1	2	0	2	0	36.0	36.00	11	.667	.800	0	—	0	-4	-4	-0	0.0
Total	2	0	0	—	11	0	0	0	0	21	23	0	20	5	18.4	4.29	93	.315	.462	1	.250	0	-0	-1	0	0.0

● **GERRY SCHOEN** Schoen, Gerald Thomas b: 1/15/47, New Orleans, La. BR/TR, 6'3", 215 lbs. Deb: 9/14/68

YEAR	TM/L	W	L	PCT	G	GS	CG	SH	SV	IP	H	HR	BB	SO	RAT	ERA	ERA+	OAV	OOB	BH	AVG	PB	PR	/A	PD	TPI
1968	Was-A	0	1	.000	1	1	0	0	0	3^{2}	6	1	1	1	17.2	7.36	40	.400	.438	0	.000	-0	-2	-2	-0	-0.4

● **JUMBO SCHOENECK** Schoeneck, Louis N. b: 3/3/1862, Chicago, Ill. d: 1/20/30, Chicago, Ill. BR/TR, 6'3", 223 lbs. Deb: 4/20/1884 ♦

YEAR	TM/L	W	L	PCT	G	GS	CG	SH	SV	IP	H	HR	BB	SO	RAT	ERA	ERA+	OAV	OOB	BH	AVG	PB	PR	/A	PD	TPI
1888	Ind-N	0	0	—	2	0	0	0	0	4^{1}	5	0	1	1	12.5	0.00	—	.227	.261	40	.237	0	1	1	-0	0.0

● **MIKE SCHOOLER** Schooler, Michael Ralph b: 8/10/62, Anaheim, Cal. BR/TR, 6'3", 220 lbs. Deb: 6/10/88

YEAR	TM/L	W	L	PCT	G	GS	CG	SH	SV	IP	H	HR	BB	SO	RAT	ERA	ERA+	OAV	OOB	BH	AVG	PB	PR	/A	PD	TPI
1988	Sea-A	5	8	.385	40	0	0	0	15	48^{1}	45	4	24	54	13.0	3.54	118	.245	.335	0	—	0	2	3	-0	0.7
1989	Sea-A	1	7	.125	67	0	0	0	33	77	81	2	19	69	11.9	2.81	144	.266	.314	0	—	0	9	10	1	1.8
1990	Sea-A	1	4	.200	49	0	0	0	30	56	47	5	16	45	10.3	2.25	176	.227	.286	0	.000	-0	10	11	0	1.9
1991	Sea-A	3	3	.500	34	0	0	0	7	34^{1}	25	2	10	31	9.2	3.67	112	.198	.257	0	—	0	2	2	-0	0.3
1992	Sea-A	2	7	.222	53	0	0	0	13	51^{2}	55	7	24	33	13.9	4.70	84	.275	.356	0	—	0	-4	-4	1	-0.8
1993	Tex-A	3	0	1.000	17	0	0	0	0	24^{1}	30	3	10	16	14.8	5.55	75	.303	.367	0	—	0	-3	-4	-0	-0.4
Total	6	15	29	.341	260	0	0	0	98	291^{2}	283	23	103	248	12.1	3.49	116	.253	.318	0	.000	-0	16	18	1	3.5

● **ED SCHORR** Schorr, Edward Walter b: 2/14/1891, Bremen, Ohio d: 9/12/69, Atlantic City, N.J. BR/TR, 6'2.5", 180 lbs. Deb: 4/26/15

YEAR	TM/L	W	L	PCT	G	GS	CG	SH	SV	IP	H	HR	BB	SO	RAT	ERA	ERA+	OAV	OOB	BH	AVG	PB	PR	/A	PD	TPI
1915	Chi-N	0	0	—	2	0	0	0	0	6	9	0	5	3	21.0	7.50	37	.409	.519	1	.500	0	-3	-3	0	0.0

● **GENE SCHOTT** Schott, Arthur Eugene b: 7/14/13, Batavia, Ohio d: 11/16/92, Sun City Center, Fla. BR/TR, 6'2", 185 lbs. Deb: 4/16/35 ♦

YEAR	TM/L	W	L	PCT	G	GS	CG	SH	SV	IP	H	HR	BB	SO	RAT	ERA	ERA+	OAV	OOB	BH	AVG	PB	PR	/A	PD	TPI
1935	Cin-N	8	11	.421	33	19	9	1	0	159	153	5	64	49	12.3	3.91	102	.253	.326	12	.200	1	2	1	3	0.5
1936	Cin-N	11	11	.500	31	22	8	0	1	180	184	7	73	65	13.1	3.80	101	.262	.335	18	.300	7	4	0	1	0.9
1937	Cin-N	4	13	.235	37	16	7	2	1	154^{1}	150	2	48	56	11.6	2.97	125	.253	.310	7	.143	-1	16	13	1	1.3
1938	Cin-N	5	5	.500	31	4	0	0	2	83	89	8	32	21	13.2	4.45	82	.279	.347	3	.125	-1	-6	-7	1	-0.9
1939	Phi-N	0	1	.000	4	0	0	0	0	11	14	0	5	1	17.2	4.91	82	.326	.420	2	.333	1	-1	-1	-1	0.0
Total	5	28	41	.406	136	61	24	3	4	587^{1}	590	22	222	192	12.6	3.72	103	.261	.329	42	.211	6	15	6	6	1.8

YEAR	TM/L	W	L	PCT	G	GS	CG	SH	SV	IP	H	HR	BB	SO	RAT	ERA	ERA+	OAV	OOB	BH	AVG	PB	PR	/A	PD	TPI
● PETE SCHOUREK Schourek, Peter Alan b: 5/10/69, Austin, Tex. BL/TL, 6'5", 205 lbs. Deb: 4/9/91																										
1991	NY-N	5	4	.556	35	8	1	1	2	86^1	82	7	43	67	13.2	4.27	85	.248	.338	3	.136	0	-6	-6	1	-0.5
1992	NY-N	6	8	.429	22	21	0	0	0	136	137	9	44	60	12.1	3.64	95	.261	.321	2	.048	-3	-2	-3	-2	-0.8
1993	NY-N	5	12	.294	41	18	0	0	0	128^1	168	13	45	72	15.1	5.96	67	.319	.376	7	.219	2	-27	-28	-0	-3.1
1994	Cin-N	7	2	.778	22	10	0	0	0	81^1	90	11	29	69	13.5	4.09	101	.287	.353	4	.174	1	1	0	0	0.2
1995	*Cin-N	18	7	.720	29	29	2	0	0	190^1	158	17	45	160	10.0	3.22	128	.228	.283	13	.220	2	20	19	0	2.5
1996	Cin-N	4	5	.444	12	12	0	0	0	67^1	79	7	24	54	14.2	6.01	70	.293	.357	5	.263	1	-13	-13	0	-1.4
1997	Cin-N	5	8	.385	18	17	0	0	0	84^2	78	18	38	59	12.8	5.42	79	.241	.328	4	.167	1	-11	-11	-1	-1.4
1998	Hou-N	7	6	.538	15	15	0	0	0	80	82	10	36	59	13.7	4.50	90	.269	.354	4	.211	1	-2	-4	-1	-0.6
	*Bos-A	1	3	.250	10	8	0	0	0	44	45	7	14	36	12.3	4.30	108	.273	.333	0	—	0	2	2	-1	0.0
Total	8	58	55	.513	204	138	3	1	2	898^1	919	99	318	636	12.7	4.44	90	.266	.333	42	.175	4	-39	-44	-4	-5.1
● BARNEY SCHREIBER Schreiber, David Henry b: 5/8/1882, Waverly, Ohio d: 10/6/64, Chillicothe, Ohio BL/TL, 6', 185 lbs. Deb: 5/15/11																										
1911	Cin-N	0	0	—	3	0	0	0	1	10	19	2	2	5	18.9	5.40	61	.413	.438	0	.000	-0	-2	-2	-0	-0.1
● PAUL SCHREIBER Schreiber, Paul Frederick "Von" b: 10/8/02, Jacksonville, Fla. d: 1/28/82, Sarasota, Fla. BR/TR, 6'2", 180 lbs. Deb: 9/2/22 C																										
1922	Bro-N	0	0	—	1	0	0	0	0	1	2	0	0	0	18.0	0.00	—	.500	.500	0	—	0	0	0	0	0.0
1923	Bro-N	0	0	—	9	0	0	0	1	15	16	1	8	4	15.6	4.20	92	.276	.382	0	.000	-0	-0	-1	-0	-0.1
1945	NY-A	0	0	—	2	0	0	0	0	4^1	4	0	2	1	12.5	4.15	83	.267	.353	0	.000	-0	-0	-0	1	0.1
Total	3	0	0	—	12	0	0	0	1	20^1	22	1	10	5	15.0	3.98	96	.286	.382	0	.000	-0	-0	-0	1	0.0
● AL SCHROLL Schroll, Albert Bringhurst "Bull" b: 3/22/32, New Orleans, La. BR/TR, 6'2", 210 lbs. Deb: 4/20/58																										
1958	Bos-A	0	0	—	5	0	0	0	0	10	6	1	4	7	9.0	4.50	89	.176	.263	1	1.000	0	-1	-1	0	0.1
1959	Phi-N	1	1	.500	3	0	0	0	0	9^1	12	1	6	4	17.4	8.68	47	.353	.450	1	.250	0	-5	-5	0	-0.8
	Bos-A	1	4	.200	14	5	1	0	0	46	47	3	22	26	13.7	4.70	86	.269	.354	1	.111	0	-4	-3	-1	-0.3
1960	Chi-N	0	0	—	2	0	0	0	0	2^2	3	1	5	2	27.0	10.13	37	.273	.500	1	1.000	0	-2	-2	-0	0.0
1961	Min-A	4	4	.500	11	8	2	0	0	50	53	5	27	24	14.8	5.22	81	.266	.360	5	.278	2	-7	-5	-0	-0.6
Total	4	6	9	.400	35	13	3	0	0	118	121	11	64	63	14.3	5.34	77	.267	.362	9	.273	4	-19	-16	-1	-1.6
● KEN SCHROM Schrom, Kenneth Marvin b: 11/23/54, Grangeville, Idaho BR/TR, 6'2", 195 lbs. Deb: 8/8/80																										
1980	Tor-A	1	0	1.000	17	0	0	0	1	31	32	2	19	13	14.8	5.23	82	.274	.375	0	—	0	-4	-3	0	-0.1
1982	Tor-A	1	0	1.000	6	0	0	0	0	15^1	13	3	15	8	16.4	5.87	76	.232	.394	0	—	0	-3	-2	-1	-0.6
1983	Min-A	15	8	.652	33	28	6	1	0	196^1	196	14	80	80	13.1	3.71	114	.266	.345	0	—	0	8	12	-3	0.9
1984	Min-A	5	11	.313	25	21	3	0	0	137	156	15	41	49	13.0	4.47	94	.285	.336	0	—	0	-7	-4	-2	-0.8
1985	Min-A	9	12	.429	29	26	6	0	0	160^2	164	28	59	74	12.5	4.99	88	.272	.337	0	—	0	-15	-10	1	-1.2
1986	Cle-A☆	14	7	.667	34	33	3	1	0	206	217	34	49	87	12.1	4.54	91	.271	.322	0	—	0	-8	-9	-3	-1.1
1987	Cle-A	6	13	.316	32	29	4	1	0	153^2	185	29	57	61	14.3	6.50	70	.298	.360	0	—	0	-35	-34	-2	-3.6
Total	7	51	51	.500	176	137	22	3	1	900	963	125	320	372	13.1	4.81	89	.276	.342	0	—	0	-65	-51	-10	-6.5
● RON SCHUELER Schueler, Ronald Richard b: 4/18/48, Catharine, Kan. BR/TR, 6'4", 205 lbs. Deb: 4/16/72 C																										
1972	Atl-N	5	8	.385	37	18	3	0	2	144^2	122	16	60	96	11.4	3.67	103	.227	.307	8	.190	0	-3	2	-1	0.1
1973	Atl-N	8	7	.533	39	20	4	2	2	186	179	24	66	124	11.9	3.87	102	.255	.319	11	.177	-1	-4	1	-1	-0.1
1974	Phi-N	11	16	.407	44	27	5	0	1	203^1	202	17	98	109	13.5	3.72	102	.264	.351	6	.118	-2	-2	1	-2	-0.4
1975	Phi-N	4	4	.500	46	6	1	0	0	92^2	88	6	40	69	12.5	5.24	71	.258	.338	2	.154	-0	-17	-16	1	-1.2
1976	Phi-N	1	0	1.000	35	0	0	0	3	49^2	44	4	16	43	11.2	2.90	122	.243	.312	0	.000	-0	3	4	-1	0.0
1977	Min-A	8	7	.533	52	7	0	0	3	134^2	131	16	61	77	13.2	4.41	90	.260	.347	0	—	0	-5	-6	2	-0.4
1978	Chi-A	3	5	.375	30	7	0	0	0	81^2	76	10	39	39	13.4	4.30	88	.251	.350	0	—	0	-5	-5	0	-0.4
1979	Chi-A	0	1	.000	8	1	0	0	0	19^2	19	3	13	6	15.6	7.32	58	.264	.391	0	—	0	-7	-7	-0	-0.3
Total	8	40	48	.455	291	86	13	2	11	912^1	861	96	393	563	12.6	4.08	94	.253	.334	27	.159	-3	-40	-25	-2	-2.7
● DAVE SCHULER Schuler, David Paul b: 10/4/53, Framingham, Mass. BR/TL, 6'4", 210 lbs. Deb: 9/17/79																										
1979	Cal-A	0	0	—	1	0	0	0	0	1^2	2	1	0	0	10.8	10.80	38	.333	.333	0	—	0	-1	-1	-0	0.2
1980	Cal-A	0	1	.000	8	0	0	0	0	12^2	13	3	2	7	10.7	3.55	111	.271	.300	0	—	0	1	1	-0	0.0
1985	Atl-N	0	0	—	9	0	0	0	0	10^2	19	4	3	10	18.6	6.75	57	.404	.440	0	—	0	-4	-3	-0	0.0
Total	3	0	1	.000	18	0	0	0	0	25	34	8	5	17	14.0	5.40	72	.337	.368	0	—	0	-4	-4	-1	0.2
● ERIK SCHULLSTROM Schullstrom, Erik Paul b: 3/25/69, San Diego, Cal. BR/TR, 6'5", 220 lbs. Deb: 7/18/94																										
1994	Min-A	0	0	—	9	0	0	0	1	13	13	0	5	13	13.2	2.77	176	.260	.339	0	—	0	3	3	-0	0.0
1995	Min-A	0	0	—	37	0	0	0	0	47	66	8	22	21	17.0	6.89	69	.332	.401	0	—	0	-11	-11	-0	0.0
Total	2	0	0	—	46	0	0	0	1	60	79	8	27	34	16.2	6.00	80	.317	.388	0	—	0	-8	-8	-1	0.0
● BUDDY SCHULTZ Schultz, Charles Budd b: 9/19/50, Cleveland, Ohio BR/TL, 6', 175 lbs. Deb: 9/3/75																										
1975	Chi-N	2	0	1.000	6	0	0	0	0	5^2	11	0	5	4	25.4	6.35	60	.367	.457	0	—	0	-2	-2	-0	-0.5
1976	Chi-N	1	1	.500	29	0	0	0	2	23^2	37	3	9	15	17.5	6.08	63	.356	.407	0	.000	-0	-7	-6	1	-0.6
1977	StL-N	6	1	.857	40	3	0	0	1	85^1	76	5	24	66	10.5	2.32	166	.245	.299	2	.167	0	15	14	-1	1.1
1978	StL-N	2	4	.333	62	0	0	0	6	83	68	6	36	70	11.3	3.80	93	.226	.309	1	.200	1	-2	-3	-1	-0.2
1979	StL-N	4	3	.571	31	0	0	0	3	42^1	40	7	14	38	11.5	4.46	84	.256	.318	0	.000	-0	-3	-3	-0	-0.6
Total	5	15	9	.625	168	3	0	0	12	240	232	21	88	193	12.0	3.68	101	.257	.324	3	.120	0	1	1	-1	-0.8
● BARNEY SCHULTZ Schultz, George Warren b: 8/15/26, Beverly, N.J. BR/TR, 6'2", 200 lbs. Deb: 4/12/55 C																										
1955	StL-N	1	2	.333	19	0	0	0	4	29^2	28	5	15	19	14.3	7.89	52	.259	.370	0	.000	-1	-13	-13	1	-1.4
1959	Det-A	1	2	.333	13	0	0	0	0	18^1	17	1	14	17	15.7	4.42	92	.254	.390	2	1.000	1	-1	-1	-0	0.0
1961	Chi-N	7	6	.538	41	0	0	0	7	66^2	57	6	25	59	11.6	2.70	155	.228	.308	1	.100	-1	10	11	-0	2.1
1962	Chi-N	5	5	.500	51	0	0	0	5	77^2	66	7	23	58	10.8	3.82	108	.231	.297	0	.000	-0	1	3	0	0.3
1963	Chi-N	1	0	1.000	15	0	0	0	2	27^1	25	5	9	18	11.2	3.62	97	.263	.327	0	.000	-0	-1	-0	0	0.0
	StL-N	2	0	1.000	24	0	0	0	1	35^1	36	5	8	26	11.7	3.57	99	.263	.313	0	—	0	-1	-0	-0	0.0
	Yr	3	0	1.000	39	0	0	0	3	62^2	61	10	17	44	11.5	3.59	98	.263	.319	0	.000	-0	-2	-0	0	0.0
1964	*StL-N	1	3	.250	30	0	0	0	14	49^1	35	1	11	29	8.4	1.64	232	.201	.249	1	.167	-0	10	12	-1	1.7
1965	StL-N	2	2	.500	34	0	0	0	2	42^1	39	8	11	38	10.6	3.83	100	.242	.291	0	.000	-0	-1	0	0	0.0
Total	7	20	20	.500	227	0	0	0	35	346^2	303	38	116	264	11.3	3.63	109	.237	.308	4	.121	-1	4	12	-0	2.7
● BOB SCHULTZ Schultz, Robert Duffy b: 11/27/23, Louisville, Ky. d: 3/31/79, Nashville, Tenn. BR/TL, 6'3", 200 lbs. Deb: 4/20/51																										
1951	Chi-N	3	6	.333	17	10	2	0	0	77^1	75	9	51	27	14.9	5.24	78	.251	.364	4	.138	-1	-11	-10	-1	-1.2
1952	Chi-N	6	3	.667	29	5	1	0	0	74	63	3	51	31	14.1	4.01	96	.232	.357	4	.222	0	-2	-1	-2	-0.3
1953	Chi-N	0	2	.000	7	2	0	0	0	11^2	13	2	11	4	19.3	5.40	82	.289	.439	0	.000	-0	-1	-1	-1	-0.3
	Pit-N	0	2	.000	11	2	0	0	0	18^2	26	3	10	5	18.3	8.20	55	.321	.409	0	.000	0	-8	-8	-0	-0.7
	Yr	0	4	.000	18	4	0	0	0	30^1	39	5	21	9	18.4	7.12	63	.307	.413	0	.000	-0	-10	-9	-1	-1.0
1955	Det-A	0	0	—	1	0	0	0	0	1^1	2	0	2	0	27.0	20.25	19	.333	.500	0	—	0	-2	-2	-0	0.0
Total	4	9	13	.409	65	19	3	0	0	183	179	17	125	67	15.3	5.16	79	.255	.372	8	.154	-1	-25	-23	-4	-2.5
● WEBB SCHULTZ Schultz, Webb Carl b: 1/31/1898, Wautoma, Wis. d: 7/26/86, Delavan, Wis. BR/TR, 5'11", 172 lbs. Deb: 8/3/24																										
1924	Chi-A	0	0	—	1	0	0	0	0	1	1	0	0	0	9.0	9.00	46	.250	.250	0	—	0	-1	-1	-0	0.0
● MIKE SCHULTZ Schultz, William Michael b: 12/17/20, Syracuse, N.Y. BL/TL, 6'1", 175 lbs. Deb: 4/20/47																										
1947	Cin-N	0	0	—	1	0	0	0	0	2	4	0	2	0	27.0	4.50	91	.444	.545	0	—	0	-0	-0	-0	0.0
● JOHN SCHULTZE Schultze, John F. b: Burlington, N.J. 6'0.5", 165 lbs. Deb: 5/6/1891																										
1891	Phi-N	0	1	.000	6	1	0	0	0	15	18	1	11	4	17.4	6.60	52	.286	.392	1	.167	-0	-5	-5	-1	-0.3
● AL SCHULZ Schulz, Albert Christopher b: 5/12/1889, Toledo, Ohio d: 12/13/31, Gallipolis, Ohio BR/TL, 6', 182 lbs. Deb: 9/25/12																										
1912	NY-A	1	1	.500	3	1	1	0	0	16^1	11	0	11	8	12.1	2.20	163	.183	.310	0	.000	-0	2	3	1	0.3
1913	NY-A	7	14	.333	38	22	9	0	0	193	197	4	69	77	12.6	3.73	80	.266	.333	11	.175	0	-17	-16	-1	-1.7

YEAR	TM/L	W	L	PCT	G	GS	CG	SH	SV	IP	H	HR	BB	SO	RAT	ERA	ERA+	OAV	OOB	BH	AVG	PB	PR	/A	PD	TPI
1914	NY-A	1	3	.250	6	4	1	0	0	28^1	27	0	10	18	12.4	4.76	58	.237	.310	0	.000	-0	-6	-6	1	-0.8
	Buf-F	9	12	.429	27	23	10	0	2	171	160	3	77	87	12.6	3.37	88	.259	.343	10	.179	-1	-9	-8	2	-0.8
1915	Buf-F	21	14	.600	42	38	25	5	0	309^2	264	8	149	160	12.2	3.08	91	.238	.332	18	.165	-4	-12	-10	1	-1.3
1916	Cin-N	8	19	.296	44	22	10	0	2	215	208	4	93	95	12.8	3.14	83	.268	.350	8	.125	-3	-12	-13	0	-2.0
Total	5	47	63	.427	160	110	56	5	4	933^1	867	19	409	445	12.5	3.32	85	.254	.337	47	.155	-9	-55	-50	3	-6.3

● WALT SCHULZ Schulz, Walter Frederick b: 4/16/1900, St.Louis, Mo. d: 2/27/28, Prescott, Ark. BR/TR, 6', 170 lbs. Deb: 9/24/20

YEAR	TM/L	W	L	PCT	G	GS	CG	SH	SV	IP	H	HR	BB	SO	RAT	ERA	ERA+	OAV	OOB	BH	AVG	PB	PR	/A	PD	TPI
1920	StL-N	0	0	—	2	0	0	0	0	6	10	0	2	0	18.0	6.00	50	.370	.414	0	.000	-0	-2	-2	0	0.0

● DON SCHULZE Schulze, Donald Arthur b: 9/27/62, Roselle, Ill. BR/TR, 6'3", 225 lbs. Deb: 9/13/83

YEAR	TM/L	W	L	PCT	G	GS	CG	SH	SV	IP	H	HR	BB	SO	RAT	ERA	ERA+	OAV	OOB	BH	AVG	PB	PR	/A	PD	TPI
1983	Chi-N	0	1	.000	4	3	0	0	0	14	19	1	7	8	17.4	7.07	54	.322	.403	0	.000	0	-5	-5	0	-0.3
1984	Chi-N	0	0	—	1	1	0	0	0	3	8	0	1	2	27.0	12.00	33	.571	.600	0	—	0	-3	-3	0	0.0
	Cle-A	3	6	.333	19	14	2	0	0	85^2	105	9	27	39	13.9	4.83	85	.302	.352	0	—	0	-8	-7	-0	-0.7
1985	Cle-A	4	10	.286	19	18	1	0	0	94^1	128	10	19	37	14.4	6.01	69	.322	.360	0	—	0	-20	-20	1	-2.4
1986	Cle-A	4	4	.500	19	13	1	0	0	84^2	88	9	34	33	13.5	5.00	83	.266	.343	0	—	0	-8	-8	-1	-0.7
1987	NY-N	1	2	.333	5	4	0	0	0	21^2	24	4	6	5	12.9	6.23	61	.296	.352	0	.000	0	-5	-6	1	-0.6
1989	NY-A	1	1	.500	2	2	0	0	0	11	12	1	5	5	14.7	4.09	95	.300	.391	0	—	0	-0	-0	-0	-0.1
	SD-N	2	1	.667	7	4	0	0	0	24^1	38	6	6	15	16.3	5.55	63	.352	.386	0	.000	-0	-6	-6	1	-0.6
Total	6	15	25	.375	76	59	4	0	0	338^2	422	40	105	144	14.3	5.47	74	.306	.361	0	.000	0	-54	-54	1	-5.4

● HAL SCHUMACHER Schumacher, Harold Henry "Prince Hal" b: 11/23/10, Hinckley, N.Y. d: 4/21/93, Cooperstown, N.Y. BR/TR, 6', 190 lbs. Deb: 4/15/31

YEAR	TM/L	W	L	PCT	G	GS	CG	SH	SV	IP	H	HR	BB	SO	RAT	ERA	ERA+	OAV	OOB	BH	AVG	PB	PR	/A	PD	TPI
1931	NY-N	1	1	.500	8	2	1	0	1	18^1	31	3	14	11	22.1	10.80	34	.387	.479	1	.143	-0	-14	-14	1	-1.4
1932	NY-N	5	6	.455	27	13	2	1	0	101^1	119	3	39	38	14.2	3.55	104	.288	.352	7	.226	1	4	2	2	0.5
1933	*NY-N☆	19	12	.613	35	33	21	7	1	258^2	199	9	84	96	9.9	2.16	149	**.214**	.280	21	.214	1	34	30	3	4.2
1934	NY-N	23	10	.697	41	36	18	2	2	297	299	16	89	112	11.8	3.18	122	.259	.313	28	.239	10	29	23	3	3.5
1935	NY-N★	19	9	.679	33	33	19	3	0	261^2	235	11	70	79	10.7	2.89	133	.238	.292	21	.196	2	33	28	7	3.7
1936	*NY-N	11	13	.458	35	30	9	3	1	215^1	234	15	69	75	12.7	3.47	112	.280	.336	16	.216	2	13	10	4	1.6
1937	*NY-N	13	12	.520	38	29	10	1	1	217^2	222	12	89	100	12.9	3.60	108	.264	.335	18	.222	3	8	7	1	1.1
1938	NY-N	13	8	.619	28	28	12	3	0	185	178	12	50	54	11.2	3.50	108	.248	.299	16	.239	4	6	5	2	1.2
1939	NY-N	13	10	.565	29	27	8	0	0	181^2	199	14	89	58	14.4	4.81	82	.276	.358	14	.203	1	-18	-18	-0	-1.9
1940	NY-N	13	13	.500	34	30	12	1	1	227	218	14	96	123	12.4	3.25	119	.251	.325	15	.192	2	15	16	4	2.4
1941	NY-N	12	10	.545	30	26	12	3	1	206	187	11	79	63	11.8	3.36	110	.243	.317	10	.152	-1	6	8	-1	0.6
1942	NY-N	12	13	.480	29	29	12	3	0	216	208	12	82	49	12.2	3.04	111	.251	.321	13	.173	1	7	8	2	1.2
1946	NY-N	4	4	.500	24	13	2	0	1	96^2	95	8	52	48	13.7	3.91	88	.255	.347	1	.038	-2	-5	-5	3	-0.4
Total	13	158	121	.566	391	329	138	27	7	2482^1	2424	140	902	906	12.1	3.36	111	.255	.321	181	.202	24	117	100	30	16.3

● HACK SCHUMANN Schumann, Carl J. b: 8/13/1884, Buffalo, N.Y. d: 3/25/46, Mill Grove, N.Y. TR, 6'2", 230 lbs. Deb: 9/19/06

YEAR	TM/L	W	L	PCT	G	GS	CG	SH	SV	IP	H	HR	BB	SO	RAT	ERA	ERA+	OAV	OOB	BH	AVG	PB	PR	/A	PD	TPI
1906	Phi-A	0	2	.000	4	2	1	0	0	18	21	0	8	9	15.5	4.00	68	.296	.383	0	.000	-1	-3	-3	-0	-0.4

● FERDIE SCHUPP Schupp, Ferdinand Maurice b: 1/16/1891, Louisville, Ky. d: 12/16/71, Los Angeles, Cal. BR/TR, 5'10", 150 lbs. Deb: 4/19/13

YEAR	TM/L	W	L	PCT	G	GS	CG	SH	SV	IP	H	HR	BB	SO	RAT	ERA	ERA+	OAV	OOB	BH	AVG	PB	PR	/A	PD	TPI
1913	NY-N	0	0	—	5	1	0	0	0	12	10	0	3	2	9.8	0.75	416	.244	.295	1	.333	1	3	3	-0	0.1
1914	NY-N	0	0	—	8	0	0	0	1	17	19	0	9	9	15.9	5.82	46	.306	.411	0	.000	-0	-6	-6	-0	-0.1
1915	NY-N	1	0	1.000	23	1	0	0	0	54^2	57	1	29	28	14.7	5.10	50	.281	.379	2	.200	0	-14	-15	0	-0.2
1916	NY-N	9	3	.750	30	11	8	4	1	140^1	79	1	37	86	7.8	0.90	271	.167	.235	4	.098	-2	27	24	-3	1.6
1917	*NY-N	21	7	**.750**	36	32	25	6	0	272	202	7	70	147	9.1	1.95	131	**.209**	.265	15	.161	1	23	18	-3	1.7
1918	NY-N	0	1	.000	10	2	1	0	0	33^1	42	1	27	22	19.4	7.56	35	.328	.456	1	.111	-0	-18	-18	0	-0.6
1919	NY-N	1	3	.250	9	4	0	0	1	32	32	2	18	17	14.1	5.63	50	.269	.365	2	.333	0	-10	-10	-1	-1.3
	StL-N	4	4	.500	10	10	6	0	0	69^2	55	2	30	37	11.1	3.75	75	.221	.307	1	.050	-0	-6	-7	-1	-0.9
	Yr	5	7	.417	19	14	6	0	1	101^2	87	4	48	54	12.0	4.34	64	.236	.326	3	.115	-0	-16	-17	-2	-2.2
1920	StL-N	16	13	.552	38	37	17	0	0	250^2	246	5	127	119	13.7	3.52	85	.265	.358	22	.256	6	-11	-15	-2	-1.3
1921	StL-N	2	0	1.000	9	4	1	0	1	37^1	42	5	21	22	15.7	4.10	89	.276	.371	4	.286	0	-1	-2	-0	-0.1
	Bro-N	3	4	.429	20	7	1	0	2	61	75	2	27	26	15.3	4.57	85	.310	.384	1	.083	-1	-5	-5	0	-0.6
	Yr	5	4	.556	29	11	2	0	3	98^1	117	7	48	48	15.3	4.39	87	.295	.374	5	.192	-0	-7	-6	-0	-0.7
1922	Chi-A	4	4	.500	18	12	3	1	0	74	79	4	66	38	17.9	6.08	67	.284	.425	5	.217	1	-17	-17	-0	-1.5
Total	10	61	39	.610	216	121	62	11	6	1054	938	30	464	553	12.3	3.32	87	.244	.331	58	.182	5	-35	-51	-10	-3.2

● WAYNE SCHURR Schurr, Wayne Allen b: 8/6/37, Garrett, Ind. BR/TR, 6'4", 185 lbs. Deb: 4/15/64

YEAR	TM/L	W	L	PCT	G	GS	CG	SH	SV	IP	H	HR	BB	SO	RAT	ERA	ERA+	OAV	OOB	BH	AVG	PB	PR	/A	PD	TPI
1964	Chi-N	0	0	—	26	0	0	0	0	48^1	57	3	11	29	12.7	3.72	100	.298	.337	0	.000	-0	-1	-0	-0	-0.1

● CARL SCHUTZ Schutz, Carl James b: 8/22/71, Hammond, La. BL/TL, 5'11", 208 lbs. Deb: 9/3/96

YEAR	TM/L	W	L	PCT	G	GS	CG	SH	SV	IP	H	HR	BB	SO	RAT	ERA	ERA+	OAV	OOB	BH	AVG	PB	PR	/A	PD	TPI
1996	Atl-N	0	0	—	3	0	0	0	0	3^1	3	0	2	5	13.5	2.70	163	.273	.385	0	—	0	1	1	-0	0.0

● MIKE SCHWABE Schwabe, Michael Scott b: 7/12/64, Ft.Dodge, Iowa BR/TR, 6'4", 200 lbs. Deb: 5/27/89

YEAR	TM/L	W	L	PCT	G	GS	CG	SH	SV	IP	H	HR	BB	SO	RAT	ERA	ERA+	OAV	OOB	BH	AVG	PB	PR	/A	PD	TPI
1989	Det-A	2	4	.333	13	4	0	0	0	44^2	58	6	16	13	15.1	6.04	63	.307	.364	0	—	0	-11	-11	1	-1.2
1990	Det-A	0	0	—	1	0	0	0	0	3^2	5	0	0	1	12.3	2.45	161	.357	.357	0	—	0	1	1	0	0.0
Total	2	2	4	.333	14	4	0	0	0	48^1	63	6	16	14	14.9	5.77	66	.310	.364	0	—	0	-10	-10	1	-1.2

● DON SCHWALL Schwall, Donald Bernard b: 3/2/36, Wilkes-Barre, Pa. BR/TR, 6'6", 200 lbs. Deb: 5/21/61

YEAR	TM/L	W	L	PCT	G	GS	CG	SH	SV	IP	H	HR	BB	SO	RAT	ERA	ERA+	OAV	OOB	BH	AVG	PB	PR	/A	PD	TPI
1961	Bos-A★	15	7	.682	25	25	10	2	0	178^2	167	8	110	91	14.3	3.22	129	.255	.368	11	.180	-0	16	19	1	2.2
1962	Bos-A	9	15	.375	33	32	5	1	0	182^1	180	18	121	89	15.4	4.94	84	.260	.378	9	.136	-2	-20	-16	0	-2.1
1963	Pit-N	6	12	.333	33	24	3	2	0	167^2	158	13	74	86	12.8	3.33	99	.255	.340	8	.160	-0	-1	-1	2	0.1
1964	Pit-N	4	3	.571	15	9	0	0	0	49^2	53	1	15	36	12.3	4.35	81	.269	.321	5	.263	2	-4	-5	0	-0.4
1965	Pit-N	9	6	.600	43	1	0	0	4	77	77	5	30	55	12.7	2.92	120	.269	.343	0	.000	-2	5	5	2	1.0
1966	Pit-N	3	2	.600	11	4	0	0	0	41^2	31	3	21	24	11.4	2.16	165	.209	.312	1	.100	-0	7	7	0	0.8
	Atl-N	3	3	.500	11	8	0	0	0	45^1	44	2	19	27	12.9	4.37	83	.256	.337	0	.000	-0	-4	-4	-0	-0.6
	Yr	6	5	.545	22	12	0	0	0	87	75	5	40	51	12.1	3.31	109	.234	.322	1	.043	-2	3	3	0	0.2
1967	Atl-N	0	0	—	1	0	0	0	0	0^2	0	0	1	0	13.5	0.00	—	.000	.500	0	—	0	0	0	0	0.0
Total	7	49	48	.505	172	103	18	5	4	743	710	50	391	408	13.7	3.72	102	.257	.354	34	.145	-5	-1	5	4	1.0

● BLACKIE SCHWAMB Schwamb, Ralph Richard b: 8/6/26, Lancaster, Cal. d: 12/21/89, Los Angeles, Cal. BR/TR, 6'5.5", 198 lbs. Deb: 7/25/48

YEAR	TM/L	W	L	PCT	G	GS	CG	SH	SV	IP	H	HR	BB	SO	RAT	ERA	ERA+	OAV	OOB	BH	AVG	PB	PR	/A	PD	TPI
1948	StL-A	1	1	.500	12	5	0	0	0	31^2	44	3	21	7	18.5	8.53	53	.331	.422	3	.300	1	-15	-14	0	-0.6

● JEFF SCHWARZ Schwarz, Jeffrey William b: 5/20/64, Fort Pierce, Fla. BR/TR, 6'5", 190 lbs. Deb: 4/24/93

YEAR	TM/L	W	L	PCT	G	GS	CG	SH	SV	IP	H	HR	BB	SO	RAT	ERA	ERA+	OAV	OOB	BH	AVG	PB	PR	/A	PD	TPI
1993	Chi-A	2	2	.500	41	0	0	0	0	51	35	1	38	41	13.4	3.71	113	.201	.353	0	—	0	3	3	-1	0.1
1994	Chi-A	0	0	—	9	0	0	0	0	11^1	9	0	16	14	19.9	6.35	73	.205	.417	0	—	0	-2	-2	-0	0.1
	Cal-A	0	0	—	4	0	0	0	0	6^2	5	0	6	4	14.9	4.05	121	.250	.423	0	—	0	1	0	-0	-0.1
	Yr	0	0	—	13	0	0	0	0	18	14	0	22	18	18.0	5.50	86	.219	.419	0	—	0	-1	-2	-0	0.0
Total	2	2	2	.500	54	0	0	0	0	69	49	1	60	59	14.6	4.17	104	.206	.372	0	—	0	2	1	-2	0.1

● RUDY SCHWENCK Schwenck, Rudolph Christian b: 4/6/1884, Louisville, Ky. d: 11/27/41, Anchorage, Ky. BL/TL, 6', 174 lbs. Deb: 9/23/09

YEAR	TM/L	W	L	PCT	G	GS	CG	SH	SV	IP	H	HR	BB	SO	RAT	ERA	ERA+	OAV	OOB	BH	AVG	PB	PR	/A	PD	TPI
1909	Chi-N	1	1	.500	3	2	0	0	0	4	16	0	3	3	45.0	13.50	19	.308	.357	1	.250	0	-5	-5	1	-1.6

● HAL SCHWENK Schwenk, Harold Edward b: 8/23/1890, Schuylkill Haven, Pa. d: 9/3/55, Kansas City, Mo. BL/TL, 6', 185 lbs. Deb: 9/4/13

YEAR	TM/L	W	L	PCT	G	GS	CG	SH	SV	IP	H	HR	BB	SO	RAT	ERA	ERA+	OAV	OOB	BH	AVG	PB	PR	/A	PD	TPI
1913	StL-A	1	0	1.000	1	1	1	0	0	11	12	0	4	3	13.1	3.27	90	.333	.400	1	.333	1	-0	-0	-0	0.0

● JIM SCOGGINS Scoggins, Lynn J. "Lefty" b: 7/19/1891, Killeen, Tex. d: 8/16/23, Columbia, S.C. BL/TL, 5'11", 165 lbs. Deb: 8/26/13

YEAR	TM/L	W	L	PCT	G	GS	CG	SH	SV	IP	H	HR	BB	SO	RAT	ERA	ERA+	OAV	OOB	BH	AVG	PB	PR	/A	PD	TPI
1913	Chi-A	0	1	.000	1	1	0	0	0	0	0	0	1	0	—	—	—	.000	.500	0	—	0	0	0	0	0.0

● HERB SCORE Score, Herbert Jude b: 6/7/33, Rosedale, N.Y. BL/TL, 6'2", 185 lbs. Deb: 4/15/55

YEAR	TM/L	W	L	PCT	G	GS	CG	SH	SV	IP	H	HR	BB	SO	RAT	ERA	ERA+	OAV	OOB	BH	AVG	PB	PR	/A	PD	TPI
1955	Cle-A☆	16	10	.615	33	32	11	2	0	227^1	158	18	154	**245**	12.4	2.85	140	.194	.323	10	.119	-4	28	29	-4	2.2
1956	Cle-A★	20	9	.690	35	33	16	**5**	0	249^1	162	18	129	**263**	**10.6**	2.53	**166**	**.186**	.292	16	.184	1	**45**	**46**	-4	4.8
1957	Cle-A	2	1	.667	5	5	3	1	0	36	18	0	26	39	11.3	2.00	186	.149	.304	1	.091	-0	7	7	0	0.5
1958	Cle-A	2	3	.400	12	5	2	1	3	41	29	1	34	48	13.8	3.95	92	.197	.348	1	.091	-0	-1	-1	-1	-0.3

YEAR	TM/L	W	L	PCT	G	GS	CG	SH	SV	IP	H	HR	BB	SO	RAT	ERA	ERA+	OAV	OOB	BH	AVG	PB	PR	/A	PD	TPI
1959	Cle-A	9	11	.450	30	25	9	1	0	160^2	123	28	115	147	13.4	4.71	78	**.210**	.341	5	.096	-3	-15	-18	-3	-2.6
1960	Chi-A	5	10	.333	23	22	5	1	0	113^2	91	10	87	78	14.3	3.72	102	.226	.366	3	.100	-0	2	1	-1	0.0
1961	Chi-A	1	2	.333	8	5	1	0	0	24^1	22	3	24	14	17.0	6.66	59	.259	.422	0	.000	-1	-7	-7	0	-0.8
1962	Chi-A	0	0	—	4	0	0	0	0	6	6	1	4	3	15.0	4.50	87	.261	.370	0	—	0	-0	-0	0	0.0
Total	8	55	46	.545	150	127	47	11	3	858^1	609	79	573	837	12.5	3.36	117	.200	.328	36	.128	-8	59	55	-12	3.8

● DICK SCOTT

Scott, Amos Richard b: 2/5/1883, Bethel, Ohio d: 1/18/11, Chicago, Ill. BR/TR, 6′, 180 lbs. Deb: 6/26/01

YEAR	TM/L	W	L	PCT	G	GS	CG	SH	SV	IP	H	HR	BB	SO	RAT	ERA	ERA+	OAV	OOB	BH	AVG	PB	PR	/A	PD	TPI
1901	Cin-N	0	2	.000	3	2	2	0	0	21	26	2	9	7	16.3	5.14	62	.302	.388	0	.000	-1	-4	-5	-1	-0.5

● DARRYL SCOTT

Scott, Darryl Nelson b: 8/6/68, Fresno, Cal. BR/TR, 6′1″, 185 lbs. Deb: 5/31/93

YEAR	TM/L	W	L	PCT	G	GS	CG	SH	SV	IP	H	HR	BB	SO	RAT	ERA	ERA+	OAV	OOB	BH	AVG	PB	PR	/A	PD	TPI
1993	Cal-A	1	2	.333	16	0	0	0	0	20	19	1	11	13	13.9	5.85	77	.250	.352	0	—	0	-3	-3	-1	-0.5

● ED SCOTT

Scott, Edward b: 8/12/1870, Walbridge, Ohio d: 11/1/33, Toledo, Ohio BR/TR, 6′3″, Deb: 4/19/00

YEAR	TM/L	W	L	PCT	G	GS	CG	SH	SV	IP	H	HR	BB	SO	RAT	ERA	ERA+	OAV	OOB	BH	AVG	PB	PR	/A	PD	TPI
1900	Cin-N	17	20	.459	42	35	31	0	1	315	370	10	65	87	12.8	3.86	95	.292	.334	19	.154	-5	-6	-6	9	-0.2
1901	Cle-A	6	6	.500	17	16	11	0	1	124^2	149	2	38	23	14.0	4.40	81	.293	.350	10	.208	1	-10	-12	2	-0.7
Total	2	23	26	.469	59	51	42	0	2	439^2	519	12	103	110	13.2	4.01	91	.292	.338	29	.170	-4	-16	-18	11	-0.9

● GEORGE SCOTT

Scott, George William b: 11/17/1896, Trenton, Mo. BR/TR, 6′1″, 175 lbs. Deb: 9/13/20

YEAR	TM/L	W	L	PCT	G	GS	CG	SH	SV	IP	H	HR	BB	SO	RAT	ERA	ERA+	OAV	OOB	BH	AVG	PB	PR	/A	PD	TPI
1920	StL-N	0	0	—	2	0	0	0	0	6	4	0	3	1	10.5	4.50	66	.200	.304	0	.000	-0	-1	-1	-0	-0.1

● JIM SCOTT

Scott, James "Death Valley Jim" b: 4/23/1888, Deadwood, S.Dak. d: 4/7/57, Jacumba, Cal. BR/TR, 6′1″, 235 lbs. Deb: 4/25/09 U

YEAR	TM/L	W	L	PCT	G	GS	CG	SH	SV	IP	H	HR	BB	SO	RAT	ERA	ERA+	OAV	OOB	BH	AVG	PB	PR	/A	PD	TPI
1909	Chi-A	12	12	.500	36	29	20	4	0	250^1	194	0	93	135	10.9	2.30	102	.223	.310	9	.106	-1	5	1	-1	-0.2
1910	Chi-A	8	18	.308	41	23	14	2	1	229^2	182	5	86	135	10.7	2.43	99	.226	.303	15	.203	2	2	-1	3	0.4
1911	Chi-A	14	11	.560	39	26	13	3	0	222	195	3	81	128	11.4	2.39	135	.240	.311	11	.155	-2	24	21	-4	1.5
1912	Chi-A	2	2	.500	6	4	2	1	0	37^2	36	0	15	23	12.4	2.15	149	.265	.342	0	.000	-2	5	4	-0	0.2
1913	Chi-A	20	21	.488	48	38	25	4	1	312^1	252	2	86	158	10.0	1.90	154	.221	.281	7	.072	-7	36	36	-0	3.9
1914	Chi-A	14	18	.438	43	33	12	2	1	253^1	228	5	75	138	10.9	2.84	94	.246	.306	14	.163	-0	-3	-4	3	-0.4
1915	Chi-A	24	11	.686	48	35	23	**7**	2	296^1	256	3	78	120	10.3	2.03	146	.238	.292	12	.126	-5	30	31	2	3.4
1916	Chi-A	7	14	.333	32	21	8	1	3	165^1	155	3	53	71	11.5	2.72	101	.258	.321	6	.115	-3	2	1	-1	-0.4
1917	Chi-A	6	7	.462	24	17	6	2	1	125	126	0	42	37	12.5	1.87	142	.272	.341	5	.119	-2	11	11	0	1.0
Total	9	107	114	.484	317	226	123	26	9	1892	1624	21	609	945	10.9	2.30	120	.238	.305	79	.129	-21	111	99	3	9.4

● JACK SCOTT

Scott, John William b: 4/18/1892, Ridgeway, N.C. d: 11/30/59, Durham, N.C. BL/TR, 6′2.5″, 199 lbs. Deb: 9/6/16

YEAR	TM/L	W	L	PCT	G	GS	CG	SH	SV	IP	H	HR	BB	SO	RAT	ERA	ERA+	OAV	OOB	BH	AVG	PB	PR	/A	PD	TPI
1916	Pit-N	0	0	—	1	0	0	0	0	5	5	1	3	4	14.4	10.80	25	.278	.381	0	.000	0	-5	-5	0	0.0
1917	Bos-N	1	2	.333	7	3	3	0	0	39^2	36	0	5	21	10.0	1.82	141	.255	.295	2	.125	-1	4	3	-1	0.1
1919	Bos-N	6	6	.500	19	12	7	0	1	103^2	109	3	39	44	12.9	3.13	91	.275	.341	7	.175	-1	-2	-3	-3	-0.7
1920	Bos-N	10	21	.323	44	33	22	3	1	291	308	6	85	94	12.6	3.53	87	.277	.336	21	.212	0	-13	-15	-4	-2.0
1921	Bos-N	15	13	.536	**47**	28	16	2	3	233^2	258	9	57	83	12.4	3.70	99	.283	.330	30	.341	10	2	-1	-1	0.7
1922	Cin-N	0	0	—	1	0	0	0	0	1	2	0	1	0	27.0	9.00	44	.500	.600	0	.000	-0	-1	-1	-0	0.0
	*NY-N	8	2	.800	17	10	5	0	2	79^2	83	7	23	37	12.2	4.41	91	.265	.320	8	.267	1	-3	-4	-1	-0.4
	Yr	8	2	.800	18	10	5	0	2	80^2	85	7	24	37	12.4	4.46	90	.268	.324	8	.258	1	-3	-4	-1	-0.4
1923	*NY-N	16	7	.696	40	25	9	3	1	220	223	15	65	79	11.9	3.89	98	.267	.323	25	.316	7	3	-2	-2	0.3
1925	NY-N	14	15	.483	36	28	18	2	3	239^2	251	10	55	87	11.6	3.15	128	.269	.313	21	.241	6	30	24	2	3.3
1926	NY-N	13	15	.464	**50**	22	13	0	5	226	242	13	53	82	11.9	4.34	86	.276	.319	28	.337	9	-13	-15	-1	-0.9
1927	Phi-N	9	21	.300	**48**	25	17	1	1	233^1	304	15	69	69	14.5	5.09	81	.330	.379	33	.289	8	-30	-25	-0	-2.0
1928	NY-N	4	1	.800	16	3	3	0	1	50^1	59	3	11	17	12.9	3.58	109	.295	.338	4	.267	1	2	2	0	0.3
1929	NY-N	7	6	.538	30	6	2	0	1	91^2	89	12	27	40	11.4	3.53	130	.260	.314	8	.308	3	12	11	1	1.6
Total	12	103	109	.486	356	195	115	11	19	1814^2	1969	94	493	657	12.4	3.85	96	.281	.332	187	.275	44	-13	-30	-9	0.3

● LEFTY SCOTT

Scott, Marshall b: 7/15/15, Roswell, N.Mex. d: 3/3/64, Houston, Tex. BR/TL, 6′0.5″, 165 lbs. Deb: 6/15/45

YEAR	TM/L	W	L	PCT	G	GS	CG	SH	SV	IP	H	HR	BB	SO	RAT	ERA	ERA+	OAV	OOB	BH	AVG	PB	PR	/A	PD	TPI
1945	Phi-N	0	2	.000	8	2	0	0	0	22^1	29	1	12	5	16.5	4.43	86	.312	.390	0	.000	-0	-2	-1	-1	-0.2

● MIKE SCOTT

Scott, Michael Warren b: 4/26/55, Santa Monica, Cal. BR/TR, 6′3″, 215 lbs. Deb: 4/18/79

YEAR	TM/L	W	L	PCT	G	GS	CG	SH	SV	IP	H	HR	BB	SO	RAT	ERA	ERA+	OAV	OOB	BH	AVG	PB	PR	/A	PD	TPI
1979	NY-N	1	3	.250	18	9	0	0	0	52^1	59	4	20	21	13.6	5.33	68	.289	.353	0	.000	-1	-9	-10	-0	-0.8
1980	NY-N	1	1	.500	6	6	1	1	0	29^1	40	1	8	13	14.7	4.30	83	.331	.372	1	.111	0	-2	-2	-0	-0.1
1981	NY-N	5	10	.333	23	23	1	0	0	136	130	11	34	54	10.9	3.90	89	.261	.309	3	.073	-2	-6	-6	3	-0.5
1982	NY-N	7	13	.350	37	22	1	0	3	147	185	13	60	63	15.1	5.14	71	.321	.387	7	.146	0	-25	-25	4	-2.7
1983	Hou-N	10	6	.625	24	24	2	2	0	145	143	8	46	73	12.0	3.72	91	.258	.320	8	.167	1	-2	-5	0	-0.4
1984	Hou-N	5	11	.313	31	29	0	0	0	154	179	7	43	83	13.1	4.68	71	.293	.343	6	.128	-0	-19	-23	-0	-2.2
1985	Hou-N	18	8	.692	36	35	4	2	0	221^2	194	20	80	137	11.2	3.29	105	.235	.304	11	.153	2	7	4	-2	0.6
1986	*Hou-N★	18	10	.643	37	37	7	**5**	0	**275^1**	182	17	72	**306**	**8.4**	**2.22**	**162**	**.186**	**.244**	12	.126	-2	**46**	**42**	2	**4.3**
1987	Hou-N★	16	13	.552	36	36	8	3	0	247^2	199	21	79	233	10.2	3.23	121	.217	**.282**	10	.125	-1	23	19	0	1.9
1988	Hou-N	14	8	.636	32	32	8	5	0	218^2	162	19	53	190	9.2	2.92	114	.204	.261	6	.085	-3	13	10	-1	0.6
1989	Hou-N†	**20**	10	.667	33	32	9	2	0	229	180	23	62	172	9.6	3.10	109	.212	.268	10	.133	-0	10	7	-2	0.6
1990	Hou-N	9	13	.409	32	32	4	2	0	205^2	194	27	66	121	11.4	3.81	98	.246	.305	7	.130	-0	-0	-2	-2	-0.4
1991	Hou-N	0	2	.000	2	2	0	0	0	7	11	2	4	3	20.6	12.86	27	.367	.457	0	.000	-0	-7	-7	-0	-1.3
Total	13	124	108	.534	347	319	45	22	3	2068^2	1858	173	627	1469	11.0	3.54	100	.240	.300	81	.124	-6	28	1	3	-0.4

● MILT SCOTT

Scott, Milton Parker "Mikado Milt" b: 1/17/1866, Chicago, Ill. d: 11/3/38, Baltimore, Md. BR , 5′9″, 160 lbs. Deb: 9/30/1882 ♦

YEAR	TM/L	W	L	PCT	G	GS	CG	SH	SV	IP	H	HR	BB	SO	RAT	ERA	ERA+	OAV	OOB	BH	AVG	PB	PR	/A	PD	TPI
1886	Bal-a	0	0	—	1	0	0	0	0	3	2	0	2	0	15.0	3.00	114	.125	.263	92	.190	-0	0	0	-0	0.0

● MICKEY SCOTT

Scott, Ralph Robert b: 7/25/47, Weimar, Germany BL/TL, 6′1″, 165 lbs. Deb: 5/6/72

YEAR	TM/L	W	L	PCT	G	GS	CG	SH	SV	IP	H	HR	BB	SO	RAT	ERA	ERA+	OAV	OOB	BH	AVG	PB	PR	/A	PD	TPI
1972	Bal-A	0	1	.000	15	0	0	0	0	23	23	2	5	11	11.3	2.74	112	.277	.326	0	.000	1	1	1	-0	0.1
1973	Bal-A	0	0	—	1	0	0	0	0	1^2	2	1	2	2	21.6	5.40	69	.286	.444	0	—	0	-0	-0	-0	0.1
	Mon-N	1	2	.333	22	0	0	0	0	24	27	3	9	11	14.3	5.25	73	.287	.362	0	.000	-0	-4	-4	0	-0.5
1975	Cal-A	4	2	.667	50	0	0	0	1	68^1	59	8	18	31	10.3	3.29	108	.233	.287	0	—	0	4	2	-1	0.7
1976	Cal-A	3	0	1.000	33	0	0	0	3	39	47	3	12	10	13.6	3.23	103	.307	.358	0	—	0	1	0	-1	0.0
1977	Cal-A	0	2	.000	12	0	0	0	0	16	19	1	4	5	12.9	5.63	70	.302	.343	0	—	0	-3	-3	0	-0.2
Total	5	8	7	.533	133	0	0	0	4	172	177	18	50	70	12.1	3.72	94	.271	.327	0	.000	0	-2	-4	-1	0.2

● DICK SCOTT

Scott, Richard Lewis b: 3/15/33, Portsmouth, N.H. BR/TL, 6′2″, 185 lbs. Deb: 5/8/63

YEAR	TM/L	W	L	PCT	G	GS	CG	SH	SV	IP	H	HR	BB	SO	RAT	ERA	ERA+	OAV	OOB	BH	AVG	PB	PR	/A	PD	TPI
1963	LA-N	0	0	—	9	0	0	0	2	12	17	6	3	6	15.0	6.75	45	.340	.377	0	—	0	-5	-5	0	-0.2
1964	Chi-N	0	0	—	3	0	0	0	0	4^1	10	2	1	1	22.8	12.46	30	.417	.440	0	—	0	-4	-4	0	0.0
Total	2	0	0	—	12	0	0	0	2	16^1	27	8	4	7	17.1	8.27	39	.365	.397	0	—	0	-9	-9	0	-0.2

● TIM SCOTT

Scott, Timothy Dale b: 11/16/66, Hanford, Cal. BR/TR, 6′2″, 205 lbs. Deb: 6/25/91

YEAR	TM/L	W	L	PCT	G	GS	CG	SH	SV	IP	H	HR	BB	SO	RAT	ERA	ERA+	OAV	OOB	BH	AVG	PB	PR	/A	PD	TPI
1991	SD-N	0	0	—	2	0	0	0	0	1	2	0	0	1	18.0	9.00	42	.400	.400	0	—	0	-1	-1	0	0.0
1992	SD-N	4	1	.800	34	0	0	0	0	37^2	39	4	21	30	14.6	5.26	68	.267	.363	0	—	0	-7	-7	-1	-0.9
1993	SD-N	2	0	1.000	24	0	0	0	0	37^2	38	1	15	30	13.6	2.39	173	.260	.345	0	.000	-0	7	7	0	0.3
	Mon-N	5	2	.714	32	0	0	0	1	34	31	3	19	35	13.2	3.71	113	.242	.340	0	.000	-0	1	2	-0	0.3
	Yr	7	2	.778	56	0	0	0	1	71^2	69	4	34	65	12.9	3.01	138	.246	.328	0	.000	-0	8	9	-0	0.6
1994	Mon-N	5	2	.714	40	0	0	0	1	53^1	51	0	18	37	12.0	2.70	156	.251	.318	0	.000	-0	9	9	-2	0.9
1995	Mon-N	2	0	1.000	62	0	0	0	2	63^1	52	6	23	57	11.5	3.98	108	.222	.308	1	.250	0	1	2	-1	0.0
1996	Mon-N	3	5	.375	45	0	0	0	1	46^1	41	3	21	37	12.4	3.11	139	.238	.328	0	.000	-0	6	6	-1	0.9
	SF-N	2	2	.500	20	0	0	0	0	19^2	24	5	9	10	15.6	8.24	50	.316	.395	0	.000	-0	-9	-9	1	-1.5
	Yr	5	7	.417	65	0	0	0	1	66	65	8	30	47	13.1	4.64	92	.258	.339	0	.000	-1	-3	-3	-0	-0.6
1997	SD-N	1	1	.500	14	0	0	0	0	18^1	25	2	5	14	16.2	7.85	49	.321	.384	0	—	0	-7	-8	1	-0.7
	Col-N	0	0	—	3	0	0	0	0	2^2	5	0	2	2	23.6	10.13	51	.455	.538	0	—	0	-2	-1	0	0.0
	Yr	1	1	.500	17	0	0	0	0	21	30	2	7	16	15.9	8.14	50	.323	.370	0	—	0	-9	-10	1	-0.7
Total	7	24	13	.649	276	0	0	0	5	314	308	24	133	253	13.2	4.13	100	.257	.340	1	.067	-1	-2	0	-3	-0.7

● SCOTT SCUDDER Scudder, William Scott b: 2/14/68, Paris, Tex. BR/TR, 6′2″, 185 lbs. Deb: 6/6/89

YEAR	TM/L	W	L	PCT	G	GS	CG	SH	SV	IP	H	HR	BB	SO	RAT	ERA	ERA+	OAV	OOB	BH	AVG	PB	PR	/A	PD	TPI
1989	Cin-N	4	9	.308	23	17	0	0	0	100^1	91	14	61	66	13.7	4.49	80	.239	.346	4	.167	1	-11	-10	-1	-1.2
1990	*Cin-N	5	5	.500	21	10	0	0	0	71^2	74	12	30	42	13.4	4.90	81	.265	.343	1	.056	-1	-9	-8	-1	-1.1
1991	Cin-N	6	9	.400	27	14	0	0	1	101^1	91	6	56	51	13.6	4.35	87	.246	.354	3	.103	-0	-8	-6	-1	-1.0
1992	Cle-A	6	10	.375	23	22	0	0	0	109	134	10	55	66	15.8	5.28	74	.303	.383	0	—	0	-16	-17	0	-2.1
1993	Cle-A	0	1	.000	2	1	0	0	0	4	5	0	4	1	22.5	9.00	48	.333	.500	0	—	0	-2	-2	-0	-0.4
Total	5	21	34	.382	96	64	0	0	1	386^1	395	42	206	226	14.3	4.80	79	.266	.360	8	.113	-0	-46	-42	-3	-5.8

● ROD SCURRY Scurry, Rodney Grant b: 3/17/56, Sacramento, Cal. d: 11/5/92, Reno, Nev. BL/TL, 6′2″, 180 lbs. Deb: 4/17/80

YEAR	TM/L	W	L	PCT	G	GS	CG	SH	SV	IP	H	HR	BB	SO	RAT	ERA	ERA+	OAV	OOB	BH	AVG	PB	PR	/A	PD	TPI
1980	Pit-N	0	2	.000	20	0	0	0	0	37^2	23	2	17	28	10.0	2.15	169	.176	.280	1	.250	0	6	6	-0	0.3
1981	Pit-N	4	5	.444	27	7	0	0	7	74	74	6	40	65	14.2	3.77	95	.261	.358	3	.158	0	-2	-1	-1	-0.3
1982	Pit-N	4	5	.444	76	0	0	0	14	103^2	79	3	64	94	12.8	1.74	213	.212	.334	5	.238	1	21	23	-1	2.6
1983	Pit-N	4	9	.308	61	0	0	0	7	68	63	6	53	67	15.9	5.56	67	.249	.387	0	.000	-1	-15	-14	-0	-2.8
1984	Pit-N	5	6	.455	43	0	0	0	4	46^1	28	1	22	48	9.7	2.53	143	.175	.275	0	.000	-0	5	6	0	1.4
1985	Pit-N	0	1	.000	30	0	0	0	2	47^2	42	4	28	43	13.2	3.21	111	.236	.340	0	.000	-0	2	2	0	0.0
	NY-A	1	0	1.000	5	0	0	0	1	12^2	5	2	10	17	10.7	2.84	141	.125	.300	0	—	0	2	2	-0	0.1
1986	NY-A	1	2	.333	31	0	0	0	2	39^1	38	1	22	36	14.2	3.66	112	.252	.354	0	—	0	2	2	0	0.2
1988	Sea-A	0	2	.000	39	0	0	0	2	31^1	32	6	18	33	15.5	4.02	103	.258	.370	0	—	0	-0	0	0	-0.1
Total	8	19	32	.373	332	7	0	0	39	460^2	384	31	274	431	13.2	3.24	115	.227	.341	9	.164	0	22	25	-0	1.4

● JOHNNIE SEALE Seale, Johnny Ray "Durango Kid" b: 11/14/38, Edgewater, Colo. BL/TL, 5′10″, 155 lbs. Deb: 9/20/64

YEAR	TM/L	W	L	PCT	G	GS	CG	SH	SV	IP	H	HR	BB	SO	RAT	ERA	ERA+	OAV	OOB	BH	AVG	PB	PR	/A	PD	TPI
1964	Det-A	1	0	1.000	4	0	0	0	0	10	6	1	4	5	9.0	3.60	102	.171	.256	0	.000	-0	0	0	1	0.0
1965	Det-A	0	0	—	4	0	0	0	0	3	7	1	2	3	27.0	12.00	29	.500	.563	0	—	0	-3	-3	-0	0.0
Total	2	1	0	1.000	8	0	0	0	0	13	13	2	6	8	13.2	5.54	65	.265	.345	0	.000	-0	-3	-3	0	0.0

● KIM SEAMAN Seaman, Kim Michael b: 5/6/57, Pascagoula, Miss. BL/TL, 6′4″, 205 lbs. Deb: 9/28/79

YEAR	TM/L	W	L	PCT	G	GS	CG	SH	SV	IP	H	HR	BB	SO	RAT	ERA	ERA+	OAV	OOB	BH	AVG	PB	PR	/A	PD	TPI
1979	StL-N	0	0	—	1	0	0	0	0	2	0	0	2	3	9.0	0.00	—	.000	.250	0	—	0	1	1	0	0.0
1980	StL-N	3	2	.600	26	0	0	0	4	23^2	16	2	13	10	11.0	3.42	108	.188	.296	0	.000	-0	0	1	-0	0.1
Total	2	3	2	.600	27	0	0	0	4	25^2	16	2	15	13	10.9	3.16	117	.176	.292	0	.000	-0	1	2	-0	0.1

● RUDY SEANEZ Seanez, Rudy Caballero b: 10/20/68, Brawley, Cal. BR/TR, 5′10″, 185 lbs. Deb: 9/7/89

YEAR	TM/L	W	L	PCT	G	GS	CG	SH	SV	IP	H	HR	BB	SO	RAT	ERA	ERA+	OAV	OOB	BH	AVG	PB	PR	/A	PD	TPI
1989	Cle-A	0	0	—	5	0	0	0	0	5	1	0	4	7	9.0	3.60	110	.071	.278	0	—	-0	0	0	-0	0.0
1990	Cle-A	2	1	.667	24	0	0	0	0	27^1	22	2	25	24	15.8	5.60	70	.220	.381	0	—	0	-5	-5	-1	-0.5
1991	Cle-A	0	0	—	5	0	0	0	0	5	10	2	7	7	30.6	16.20	26	.385	.515	0	—	0	-7	-7	-0	0.0
1993	SD-N	0	0	—	3	0	0	0	0	3^1	8	1	2	1	27.0	13.50	31	.471	.526	0	—	0	-4	-3	0	0.0
1994	LA-N	1	1	.500	17	0	0	0	0	23^2	24	2	9	18	12.9	2.66	147	.273	.347	0	.000	-0	4	3	0	0.2
1995	LA-N	1	3	.250	37	0	0	0	3	34^2	39	5	18	29	15.1	6.75	56	.285	.372	0	.000	-0	-10	-11	-0	-1.4
1998	*Atl-N	4	1	.800	34	0	0	0	2	36	25	2	16	50	10.3	2.75	154	.195	.285	0	.000	-0	6	6	-0	0.7
Total	7	8	6	.571	125	0	0	0	5	135	129	14	81	136	14.2	5.13	78	.253	.359	0	.000	-0	-15	-17	-1	-1.0

● RAY SEARAGE Searage, Raymond Mark b: 5/1/55, Freeport, N.Y. BL/TL, 6′1″, 180 lbs. Deb: 6/11/81

YEAR	TM/L	W	L	PCT	G	GS	CG	SH	SV	IP	H	HR	BB	SO	RAT	ERA	ERA+	OAV	OOB	BH	AVG	PB	PR	/A	PD	TPI
1981	NY-N	1	0	1.000	26	0	0	0	1	36^2	34	2	17	16	12.5	3.68	95	.252	.336	1	1.000	0	-1	-1	-0	0.0
1984	Mil-A	2	1	.667	21	0	0	0	6	38^1	20	0	16	29	8.7	0.70	546	.155	.253	0	—	0	14	13	-0	1.4
1985	Mil-A	1	4	.200	33	0	0	0	1	38	54	2	24	36	18.5	5.92	70	.338	.424	0	—	0	-7	-7	-1	-1.0
1986	Mil-A	0	1	.000	17	0	0	0	1	22	29	6	9	10	16.0	6.95	62	.315	.382	0	—	0	-7	-6	0	-0.4
	Chi-A	1	0	1.000	29	0	0	0	0	29	15	1	19	26	10.6	0.62	694	.156	.296	0	—	0	11	12	0	0.3
	Yr	1	1	.500	46	0	0	0	1	51	44	7	28	36	12.7	3.35	129	.233	.332	0	—	0	5	5	0	-0.1
1987	Chi-A	2	3	.400	58	0	0	0	2	55^2	56	9	24	33	13.1	4.20	109	.264	.342	0	—	0	2	2	-0	0.1
1989	LA-N	3	4	.429	41	0	0	0	0	35^2	29	1	18	24	11.9	3.53	97	.225	.320	0	—	0	-0	-0	1	0.0
1990	LA-N	1	0	1.000	29	0	0	0	0	32^1	30	1	10	19	11.1	2.78	131	.250	.308	0	.000	-0	4	3	1	0.1
Total	7	11	13	.458	254	0	0	0	11	287^2	267	22	137	193	12.7	3.50	114	.249	.336	1	.333	0	15	15	0	0.5

● STEVE SEARCY Searcy, William Steven b: 6/4/64, Knoxville, Tenn. BL/TL, 6′1″, 185 lbs. Deb: 8/29/88

YEAR	TM/L	W	L	PCT	G	GS	CG	SH	SV	IP	H	HR	BB	SO	RAT	ERA	ERA+	OAV	OOB	BH	AVG	PB	PR	/A	PD	TPI
1988	Det-A	0	2	.000	2	2	0	0	0	8	8	3	4	5	13.5	5.63	68	.242	.324	0	—	0	-1	-2	-0	-0.2
1989	Det-A	1	1	.500	8	2	0	0	0	22^1	27	3	12	11	15.7	6.04	63	.307	.390	0	—	0	-5	-6	-0	-0.5
1990	Det-A	2	7	.222	16	12	1	0	0	75^1	76	9	51	66	15.2	4.66	85	.270	.381	0	—	0	-6	-6	-0	-0.7
1991	Det-A	1	2	.333	16	5	0	0	0	40^2	52	8	30	32	18.1	8.41	49	.313	.418	0	—	0	-19	-19	-0	-1.2
	Phi-N	2	1	.667	18	0	0	0	0	30^1	29	2	14	21	12.8	4.15	88	.252	.333	0	.000	-0	-2	-2	-0	-0.2
1992	Phi-N	0	0	—	10	0	0	0	0	10^1	13	0	8	5	18.3	6.10	57	.325	.438	0	—	0	-3	-3	0	0.0
Total	5	6	13	.316	70	21	1	0	0	187	205	25	119	140	15.6	5.68	69	.283	.384	0	.000	-0	-37	-37	-1	-2.8

● TOM SEATON Seaton, Thomas Gordon b: 8/30/1887, Blair, Neb. d: 4/10/40, ElPaso, Tex. BB/TR, 6′, 175 lbs. Deb: 4/13/12

YEAR	TM/L	W	L	PCT	G	GS	CG	SH	SV	IP	H	HR	BB	SO	RAT	ERA	ERA+	OAV	OOB	BH	AVG	PB	PR	/A	PD	TPI
1912	Phi-N	16	12	.571	44	27	16	2	2	255	246	8	106	118	12.7	3.28	111	.261	.342	18	.217	-0	4	10	-2	0.8
1913	Phi-N	**27**	12	.692	52	35	21	5	1	**322^1**	262	6	136	**168**	11.4	2.60	128	.226	.313	12	.109	-5	22	26	2	2.7
1914	Bro-F	25	14	.641	44	38	26	7	2	302^2	299	6	102	172	12.3	3.03	95	.259	.326	22	.206	2	-5	-5	0	-0.4
1915	Bro-F	11	11	.500	32	24	13	0	3	189^1	199	6	99	86	14.3	4.42	62	.273	.362	16	.242	3	-36	-36	1	-3.5
	New-F	2	6	.250	12	10	7	0	1	75	61	1	21	28	10.1	2.28	112	.224	.285	4	.154	-0	4	2	1	0.3
	Yr	13	17	.433	44	34	20	0	4	264^1	260	7	120	114	13.0	3.81	70	.259	.339	20	.217	3	-32	-33	2	-3.2
1916	Chi-N	6	6	.500	31	12	4	0	1	121	108	3	43	45	11.5	3.27	89	.246	.319	7	.184	0	-9	-5	1	-0.4
1917	Chi-N	5	4	.556	16	9	3	1	1	74^2	60	0	23	27	10.1	2.53	115	.227	.292	5	.238	1	1	3	1	0.6
Total	6	92	65	.586	231	155	90	15	11	1340	1235	30	530	644	12.1	3.12	99	.249	.327	84	.186	0	-19	-5	4	0.1

● TOM SEATS Seats, Thomas Edward b: 9/24/10, Farmington, N.C. d: 5/10/92, San Ramon, Cal. BR/TL, 5′11″, 190 lbs. Deb: 5/4/40

YEAR	TM/L	W	L	PCT	G	GS	CG	SH	SV	IP	H	HR	BB	SO	RAT	ERA	ERA+	OAV	OOB	BH	AVG	PB	PR	/A	PD	TPI
1940	Det-A	2	2	.500	26	2	0	0	1	55^2	67	4	21	25	14.2	4.69	101	.290	.349	1	.083	-1	-2	0	0	-0.1
1945	Bro-N	10	7	.588	31	18	6	2	0	121^2	127	8	37	44	12.5	4.36	86	.261	.320	9	.209	0	-8	-8	0	-1.0
Total	2	12	9	.571	57	20	6	2	1	177^1	194	12	58	69	13.0	4.47	91	.271	.329	10	.182	-1	-10	-8	0	-1.1

● TOM SEAVER Seaver, George Thomas "Tom Terrific" b: 11/17/44, Fresno, Cal. BR/TR, 6′1″, 206 lbs. Deb: 4/13/67 H

YEAR	TM/L	W	L	PCT	G	GS	CG	SH	SV	IP	H	HR	BB	SO	RAT	ERA	ERA+	OAV	OOB	BH	AVG	PB	PR	/A	PD	TPI
1967	NY-N★	16	13	.552	35	34	18	2	0	251	224	19	78	170	11.0	2.76	123	.241	.303	11	.143	2	17	18	0	2.3
1968	NY-N★	16	12	.571	36	35	14	5	1	277^2	224	15	48	205	9.1	2.20	137	.222	.262	15	.158	0	24	25	2	3.1
1969	*NY-N☆	**25**	7	**.781**	36	35	18	5	0	273^1	202	24	82	208	9.6	2.21	166	**.207**	.273	11	.121	-0	42	44	2	5.6
1970	NY-N★	18	12	.600	37	36	19	2	0	290^2	230	21	83	**283**	9.8	**2.82**	**143**	.214	.273	17	.179	4	**40**	**39**	2	**4.5**
1971	NY-N☆	20	10	.667	36	35	21	4	0	286^1	210	18	61	**289**	**8.6**	**1.76**	**194**	.206	**.253**	18	.196	4	**54**	**52**	1	**6.5**
1972	NY-N☆	21	12	.636	35	35	13	3	0	262	215	23	77	249	10.2	2.92	115	.224	.285	13	.146	4	16	13	2	2.3
1973	*NY-N★	19	10	.655	36	36	**18**	3	0	290	219	23	64	**251**	**8.9**	**2.08**	**174**	**.206**	**.254**	15	.161	3	**51**	**50**	-0	**5.4**
1974	NY-N	11	11	.500	32	32	12	5	0	236	199	19	75	201	10.6	3.20	111	.230	.293	7	.099	-2	11	9	2	0.9
1975	NY-N★	**22**	9	.710	36	36	15	5	0	280^1	217	11	88	**243**	9.9	2.38	145	.214	.280	17	.179	3	39	33	2	4.3
1976	NY-N★	14	11	.560	35	34	13	5	0	271	211	14	77	**235**	9.7	2.59	127	.213	.273	7	.085	-2	**27**	21	1	1.9
1977	NY-N	7	3	.700	13	13	5	3	0	96	79	7	28	72	10.0	3.00	125	.221	.277	5	.161	-0	10	8	1	0.8
	Cin-N★	14	3	.824	20	20	14	4	0	165^1	120	12	38	124	8.6	2.34	168	.201	.249	12	.218	4	29	29	-1	3.3
	Yr	21	6	.778	33	33	19	**7**	0	261^1	199	19	66	196	**9.1**	2.58	149	**.208**	**.259**	17	.198	4	39	37	-0	4.1
1978	Cin-N☆	16	14	.533	36	36	8	1	0	259^2	218	26	89	226	10.6	2.88	123	.227	.292	9	.122	-0	20	19	-2	2.0
1979	*Cin-N	16	6	**.727**	32	32	9	**5**	0	215	187	16	61	131	10.4	3.14	119	.236	.291	12	.158	2	14	14	0	1.6
1980	Cin-N	10	8	.556	26	26	5	1	0	168	140	24	59	101	10.7	3.64	98	.225	.293	6	.130	1	-1	-1	1	0.1
1981	Cin-N★	**14**	2	**.875**	23	23	6	1	0	166^1	120	10	66	87	10.2	2.54	140	.205	.289	11	.200	4	17	19	-1	2.1
1982	Cin-N	5	13	.278	21	21	0	0	0	111^1	136	14	44	62	14.8	5.50	67	.302	.368	6	.176	1	-23	-22	-1	-3.2
1983	NY-N	9	14	.391	34	34	5	2	0	231	201	18	86	135	11.3	3.55	102	.235	.308	10	.156	2	2	2	-1	0.3
1984	Chi-A	15	11	.577	34	33	10	4	0	236^2	216	27	61	131	10.6	3.95	105	.240	.290	0	—	0	1	5	1	0.7
1985	Chi-A	16	11	.593	35	33	6	1	0	238^2	223	22	69	134	11.3	3.17	136	.248	.307	0	—	0	26	30	2	3.5
1986	Chi-A	2	6	.250	12	12	1	0	0	72	66	9	27	31	12.3	4.38	99	.242	.321	0	—	0	-2	-1	-1	-0.2
	Bos-A	5	7	.417	16	16	1	0	0	104^1	114	8	29	72	12.5	3.80	110	.278	.329	0	—	0	4	4	-0	0.4

YEAR	TM/L	W	L	PCT	G	GS	CG	SH	SV	IP	H	HR	BB	SO	RAT	ERA	ERA+	OAV	OOB	BH	AVG	PB	PR	/A	PD	TPI
	Yr	7	13	.350	28	28	2	0	0	176^{1}	180	17	56	103	12.1	4.03	105	.261	.318	0	—	0	3	4	-1	0.2
Total	20	311	205	.603	656	647	231	61	1	4782^{2}	3971	380	1390	3640	10.2	2.86	127	.226	.285	202	.154	28	419	411	13	48.2

● BOB SEBRA Sebra, Robert Bush b: 12/11/61, Ridgewood, N.J. BR/TR, 6'2", 200 lbs. Deb: 6/26/85

YEAR	TM/L	W	L	PCT	G	GS	CG	SH	SV	IP	H	HR	BB	SO	RAT	ERA	ERA+	OAV	OOB	BH	AVG	PB	PR	/A	PD	TPI
1985	Tex-A	0	2	.000	7	4	0	0	0	20^{1}	26	4	14	13	18.1	7.52	56	.306	.410	0	—	0	-8	-7	-0	-0.6
1986	Mon-N	5	5	.500	17	13	3	1	0	91^{1}	82	9	25	66	10.8	3.55	104	.239	.296	6	.207	1	2	1	-1	0.2
1987	Mon-N	6	15	.286	36	27	4	1	0	177^{1}	184	15	67	156	12.9	4.42	95	.272	.340	8	.157	0	-7	-4	-1	-0.5
1988	Phi-N	1	2	.333	3	3	0	0	0	11^{1}	15	0	10	7	19.9	7.94	45	.333	.455	0	.000	-0	-6	-6	-0	-1.2
1989	Phi-N	2	3	.400	6	5	0	0	0	34^{1}	41	6	10	21	14.4	4.46	80	.295	.359	0	.000	-0	-4	-3	-0	-0.5
	Cin-N	0	0	—	15	0	0	0	1	21	24	2	18	14	19.3	6.43	56	.296	.441	0	.000	-0	-7	-7	-0	-0.1
	Yr	2	3	.400	21	5	0	0	1	55^{1}	65	8	28	35	15.6	5.20	68	.289	.375	0	.000	-1	-11	-10	-0	-0.6
1990	Mil-A	1	2	.333	10	0	0	0	0	11	20	1	5	4	21.3	8.18	47	.408	.473	0	—	0	-5	-5	1	-1.2
Total	6	15	29	.341	94	52	7	2	1	366^{2}	392	37	149	281	13.6	4.71	84	.276	.351	14	.146	-0	-34	-31	-2	-3.9

● DOC SECHRIST Sechrist, Theodore O'Hara b: 2/10/1876, Williamstown, Ky. d: 4/2/50, Louisville, Ky. BR/TR, 5'9", 160 lbs. Deb: 4/28/1899

YEAR	TM/L	W	L	PCT	G	GS	CG	SH	SV	IP	H	HR	BB	SO	RAT	ERA	ERA+	OAV	OOB	BH	AVG	PB	PR	/A	PD	TPI
1899	NY-N	0	0	—	1	0	0	0	0	0	0	0	2	0	—	—	—	—	1.000	0	—	0	0	0	0	0.0

● DON SECRIST Secrist, Donald Laverne b: 2/26/44, Seattle, Wash. BL/TL, 6'2", 195 lbs. Deb: 4/11/69

YEAR	TM/L	W	L	PCT	G	GS	CG	SH	SV	IP	H	HR	BB	SO	RAT	ERA	ERA+	OAV	OOB	BH	AVG	PB	PR	/A	PD	TPI
1969	Chi-A	0	1	.000	19	0	0	0	0	40	35	7	14	23	11.2	6.07	63	.227	.296	1	.143	0	-11	-10	0	-0.2
1970	Chi-A	0	0	—	9	0	0	0	0	14^{2}	19	2	12	9	19.0	5.52	71	.333	.449	0	—	0	-3	-3	-0	0.0
Total	2	0	1	.000	28	0	0	0	0	54^{2}	54	9	26	32	13.3	5.93	65	.256	.340	1	.143	0	-14	-13	-0	-0.2

● DUKE SEDGWICK Sedgwick, Henry Kenneth b: 6/1/1898, Martins Ferry, O. d: 12/4/82, Clearwater, Fla. BR/TR, 6', 175 lbs. Deb: 7/12/21

YEAR	TM/L	W	L	PCT	G	GS	CG	SH	SV	IP	H	HR	BB	SO	RAT	ERA	ERA+	OAV	OOB	BH	AVG	PB	PR	/A	PD	TPI
1921	Phi-N	1	3	.250	16	5	1	0	0	71^{1}	81	3	32	21	14.8	4.92	86	.283	.363	5	.208	-1	-9	-5	-1	-0.5
1923	Was-A	0	1	.000	5	2	1	0	0	16	27	1	6	4	18.6	7.88	48	.415	.465	0	.000	-1	-7	-7	1	-0.4
Total	2	1	4	.200	21	7	2	0	0	87^{1}	108	4	38	25	15.5	5.46	76	.308	.382	5	.172	-2	-16	-13	-0	-0.9

● CHARLIE SEE See, Charles Henry "Chad" b: 10/13/1896, Pleasantville, N.Y d: 7/19/48, Bridgeport, Conn. BL/TR, 5'10.5", 175 lbs. Deb: 8/6/19 ♦

YEAR	TM/L	W	L	PCT	G	GS	CG	SH	SV	IP	H	HR	BB	SO	RAT	ERA	ERA+	OAV	OOB	BH	AVG	PB	PR	/A	PD	TPI
1920	Cin-N	0	0	—	1	0	0	0	0	6	6	0	4	3	15.0	6.00	51	.286	.400	25	.305	0	-2	-2	-0	0.0

● CHUCK SEELBACH Seelbach, Charles Frederick b: 3/20/48, Lakewood, Ohio BR/TR, 6', 180 lbs. Deb: 6/29/71

YEAR	TM/L	W	L	PCT	G	GS	CG	SH	SV	IP	H	HR	BB	SO	RAT	ERA	ERA+	OAV	OOB	BH	AVG	PB	PR	/A	PD	TPI
1971	Det-A	0	0	—	5	0	0	0	0	4	6	2	7	1	31.5	13.50	27	.375	.583	0	—	0	-4	-4	-0	0.0
1972	*Det-A	9	8	.529	61	3	0	0	14	112	96	6	39	76	11.1	2.89	109	.238	.310	3	.143	1	2	3	-1	0.7
1973	Det-A	1	0	1.000	5	0	0	0	0	7	7	1	2	2	11.6	3.86	106	.250	.300	0	—	0	-0	0	1	-0.4
1974	Det-A	0	0	—	4	0	0	0	0	7^{2}	9	2	3	0	15.3	4.70	81	.300	.382	0	—	0	-1	-1	-0	-0.3
Total	4	10	8	.556	75	3	0	0	14	130^{2}	118	11	51	79	12.0	3.38	96	.247	.326	3	.143	1	-3	-2	-0	-0.0

● EMMETT SEERY Seery, John Emmett b: 2/13/1861, Princeville, Ill. d: 8/7/30, Saranac Lake, N.Y. BL/TR, Deb: 4/17/1884 ♦

YEAR	TM/L	W	L	PCT	G	GS	CG	SH	SV	IP	H	HR	BB	SO	RAT	ERA	ERA+	OAV	OOB	BH	AVG	PB	PR	/A	PD	TPI
1886	StL-N	0	0	—	2	0	0	0	0	7	8	1	3	2	14.1	7.71	42	.320	.393	108	.238	0	-3	-3	-0	0.0

● HERMAN SEGELKE Segelke, Herman Neils b: 4/24/58, San Mateo, Cal. BR/TR, 6'4", 200 lbs. Deb: 4/7/82

YEAR	TM/L	W	L	PCT	G	GS	CG	SH	SV	IP	H	HR	BB	SO	RAT	ERA	ERA+	OAV	OOB	BH	AVG	PB	PR	/A	PD	TPI
1982	Chi-N	0	0	—	3	0	0	0	0	4^{1}	6	1	6	4	24.9	8.31	45	.316	.480	0	—	0	-2	-2	0	0.0

● DIEGO SEGUI Segui, Diego Pablo (Gonzalez) b: 8/17/37, Holguin, Cuba BR/TR, 6', 190 lbs. Deb: 4/12/62 F

YEAR	TM/L	W	L	PCT	G	GS	CG	SH	SV	IP	H	HR	BB	SO	RAT	ERA	ERA+	OAV	OOB	BH	AVG	PB	PR	/A	PD	TPI
1962	KC-A	8	5	.615	37	13	2	0	6	116^{2}	89	16	46	71	10.5	3.86	109	.211	.291	8	.235	2	1	5	0	0.7
1963	KC-A	9	6	.600	38	23	4	1	0	167	173	17	73	116	13.4	3.77	103	.267	.343	12	.218	1	-3	2	1	0.4
1964	KC-A	8	17	.320	40	35	5	2	0	217	219	30	94	155	13.0	4.56	84	.260	.335	11	.155	0	-23	-18	2	-1.7
1965	KC-A	5	15	.250	40	25	5	1	0	163	166	18	67	119	13.0	4.64	75	.261	.334	9	.191	2	-21	-21	-1	-2.2
1966	Was-A	3	7	.300	21	13	1	1	0	72	82	8	24	54	13.3	5.00	69	.291	.346	2	.111	-1	-13	-12	-1	-1.7
1967	KC-A	3	4	.429	36	3	0	0	1	70	62	4	31	52	12.2	3.09	103	.238	.324	0	.000	-1	1	1	-0	-0.1
1968	Oak-A	6	5	.545	52	0	0	0	6	83	51	7	32	72	9.0	2.39	118	.173	.255	1	.111	0	5	4	-1	0.5
1969	Sea-A	12	6	.667	66	8	2	0	12	142^{1}	127	14	61	113	12.0	3.35	108	.238	.319	4	.148	-0	4	4	1	0.7
1970	Oak-A	10	10	.500	47	19	3	2	2	162	130	9	68	95	11.1	**2.56**	**138**	.222	.305	5	.116	-2	21	18	-1	1.8
1971	*Oak-A	10	8	.556	26	21	5	0	0	146^{1}	122	13	63	81	11.6	3.14	106	.229	.316	4	.085	-1	5	3	-1	0.2
1972	Oak-A	0	1	.000	7	3	0	0	0	22^{2}	25	2	7	11	12.7	3.57	80	.287	.340	1	.143	-0	-1	-2	-0	-0.1
	StL-N	3	1	.750	33	0	0	0	9	55^{2}	47	2	32	54	12.8	3.07	111	.229	.333	1	.143	0	2	2	1	0.3
1973	StL-N	7	6	.538	65	0	0	0	17	100^{1}	78	6	53	93	11.8	2.78	131	.211	.310	0	.000	-1	10	10	-1	1.3
1974	Bos-A	6	8	.429	58	0	0	0	10	108	106	9	49	76	13.0	4.00	96	.257	.337	0	—	0	-5	-2	-1	-0.8
1975	*Bos-A	2	5	.286	33	1	1	0	6	71	71	10	43	45	14.5	4.82	85	.270	.373	0	—	0	-8	-6	-1	-0.7
1977	Sea-A	0	7	.000	40	7	0	0	2	110^{2}	108	20	43	91	12.4	5.69	72	.251	.321	0	—	0	-20	-19	0	-1.1
Total	15	92	111	.453	639	171	28	7	71	1807^{2}	1656	185	786	1298	12.2	3.81	96	.243	.323	58	.151	-1	-43	-32	-3	-2.5

● JOSE SEGURA Segura, Jose Altagracia (Mota) b: 1/26/63, Fundacion, D.R. BR/TR, 5'11", 180 lbs. Deb: 4/10/88

YEAR	TM/L	W	L	PCT	G	GS	CG	SH	SV	IP	H	HR	BB	SO	RAT	ERA	ERA+	OAV	OOB	BH	AVG	PB	PR	/A	PD	TPI
1988	Chi-A	0	0	—	4	0	0	0	0	8^{2}	19	1	8	2	28.0	13.50	29	.432	.519	0	—	0	-9	-9	0	0.0
1989	Chi-A	0	1	.000	7	0	0	0	0	6	13	2	3	4	24.0	15.00	25	.464	.516	0	—	0	-7	-7	0	-1.0
1991	SF-N	0	1	.000	11	0	0	0	0	16^{1}	20	1	5	10	13.8	4.41	81	.303	.352	0	—	0	-1	-2	-0	-0.1
Total	3	0	2	.000	22	0	0	0	0	31	52	4	16	16	19.7	9.00	41	.377	.442	0	—	0	-18	-18	0	-1.1

● SOCKS SEIBOLD Seibold, Harry b: 4/3/1896, Philadelphia, Pa. d: 9/21/65, Philadelphia, Pa. BR/TR, 5'8.5", 162 lbs. Deb: 9/18/15 ♦

YEAR	TM/L	W	L	PCT	G	GS	CG	SH	SV	IP	H	HR	BB	SO	RAT	ERA	ERA+	OAV	OOB	BH	AVG	PB	PR	/A	PD	TPI
1916	Phi-A	1	1	.500	3	2	1	1	0	21^{2}	22	0	9	5	12.9	4.15	69	.272	.344	2	.167	-0	-3	-3	1	-0.2
1917	Phi-A	4	16	.200	33	15	9	1	1	160	141	1	85	55	12.9	3.94	70	.243	.343	13	.220	2	-23	-21	-1	-2.5
1919	Phi-A	2	3	.400	14	4	1	0	0	45^{2}	58	2	26	19	17.3	5.32	64	.322	.419	2	.154	-1	-11	-10	0	-1.0
1929	Bos-N	12	17	.414	33	27	16	1	1	205^{2}	228	17	80	54	13.6	4.73	99	.285	.352	20	.286	4	-0	-1	-1	0.2
1930	Bos-N	15	16	.484	36	33	20	1	2	251	288	16	85	70	13.4	4.12	120	.290	.348	19	.211	0	24	23	-3	2.1
1931	Bos-N	10	18	.357	33	29	10	3	0	206^{1}	226	12	65	50	12.8	4.67	81	.279	.335	9	.129	-4	-18	-20	0	-2.7
1932	Bos-N	3	10	.231	28	20	6	1	0	136^{2}	173	12	41	33	14.2	4.68	80	.309	.358	7	.152	-2	-12	-14	2	-1.1
1933	Bos-N	1	4	.200	11	5	1	0	1	36^{2}	43	0	14	10	14.0	3.68	83	.295	.356	1	.111	0	-1	-3	0	-0.3
Total	8	48	85	.361	191	135	64	8	5	1063^{2}	1179	60	405	296	13.5	4.43	91	.284	.350	76	.192	-0	-45	-48	-1	-5.5

● KEVIN SEITZER Seitzer, Kevin Lee b: 3/26/62, Springfield, Ill. BR/TR, 5'11", 190 lbs. Deb: 9/3/86 ♦

YEAR	TM/L	W	L	PCT	G	GS	CG	SH	SV	IP	H	HR	BB	SO	RAT	ERA	ERA+	OAV	OOB	BH	AVG	PB	PR	/A	PD	TPI
1993	Oak-A	0	0	—	1	0	0	0	0	0^{1}	0	0	0	1	0.0	0.00	—	.000	.000	65	.255	0	0	0	0	0.0

● AARON SELE Sele, Aaron Helmer b: 6/25/70, Golden Valley, Minn. BR/TR, 6'5", 218 lbs. Deb: 6/23/93

YEAR	TM/L	W	L	PCT	G	GS	CG	SH	SV	IP	H	HR	BB	SO	RAT	ERA	ERA+	OAV	OOB	BH	AVG	PB	PR	/A	PD	TPI
1993	Bos-A	7	2	.778	18	18	0	0	0	111^{2}	100	5	48	93	12.5	2.74	168	.237	.325	0	—	0	20	23	-2	1.4
1994	Bos-A	8	7	.533	22	22	2	0	0	143^{1}	140	13	60	105	13.1	3.83	131	.261	.345	0	—	0	15	19	-1	1.4
1995	Bos-A	3	1	.750	6	6	0	0	0	32^{1}	32	3	14	21	13.6	3.06	159	.252	.340	0	—	0	6	6	-0	0.5
1996	Bos-A	7	11	.389	29	29	1	0	0	157^{1}	192	14	67	137	15.3	5.32	95	.303	.377	0	—	0	-6	-4	-0	-0.5
1997	Bos-A	13	12	.520	33	33	1	0	0	177^{1}	196	25	80	122	14.8	5.38	86	.279	.365	0	.000	-0	-16	-15	0	-1.7
1998	*Tex-A☆	19	11	.633	33	33	3	2	0	212^{2}	239	14	84	167	14.2	4.23	114	.283	.357	1	.250	0	10	14	-1	1.7
Total	6	57	44	.564	141	141	7	2	0	834^{2}	899	74	353	645	14.1	4.37	111	.275	.356	1	.167	0	29	44	-4	2.8

● EPP SELL Sell, Lester Elwood b: 4/26/1897, Llewellyn, Pa. d: 2/19/61, Reading, Pa. BR/TR, 6', 175 lbs. Deb: 9/1/22

YEAR	TM/L	W	L	PCT	G	GS	CG	SH	SV	IP	H	HR	BB	SO	RAT	ERA	ERA+	OAV	OOB	BH	AVG	PB	PR	/A	PD	TPI
1922	StL-N	4	2	.667	7	5	0	0	0	33	47	2	6	5	15.0	6.82	57	.338	.374	4	.333	1	-10	-11	1	-1.3
1923	StL-N	0	1	.000	5	1	0	0	0	15	16	1	8	2	14.4	6.00	65	.291	.381	0	.000	-1	-3	-3	-0	-0.3
Total	2	4	3	.571	12	6	0	0	0	48	63	3	14	7	14.8	6.56	59	.325	.376	4	.211	0	-13	-14	0	-1.6

● JEFF SELLERS Sellers, Jeffrey Doyle b: 5/11/64, Compton, Cal. BR/TR, 6'1", 175 lbs. Deb: 9/15/85

YEAR	TM/L	W	L	PCT	G	GS	CG	SH	SV	IP	H	HR	BB	SO	RAT	ERA	ERA+	OAV	OOB	BH	AVG	PB	PR	/A	PD	TPI
1985	Bos-A	2	0	1.000	4	4	1	0	0	22^{1}	24	1	7	6	12.5	3.63	118	.273	.326	0	—	0	1	2	-0	0.1
1986	Bos-A	3	7	.300	14	13	1	0	0	82	90	13	40	51	14.6	4.94	84	.282	.367	0	—	0	-7	-7	0	-0.7
1987	Bos-A	7	8	.467	25	22	4	2	0	139^{2}	161	10	61	99	14.5	5.28	86	.298	.373	0	—	0	-13	-12	1	-1.2
1988	Bos-A	1	7	.125	18	12	1	0	0	85^{2}	89	9	56	70	15.5	4.83	85	.268	.379	0	—	0	-8	-7	-0	-0.9
Total	4	13	22	.371	61	51	7	2	0	329^{2}	364	33	164	226	14.7	4.97	87	.285	.370	0	—	0	-27	-24	0	-2.7

● DAVE SELLS

Sells, David Wayne b: 9/18/46, Vacaville, Cal. BR/TR, 5'11", 175 lbs. Deb: 8/2/72

YEAR	TM/L	W	L	PCT	G	GS	CG	SH	SV	IP	H	HR	BB	SO	RAT	ERA	ERA+	OAV	OOB	BH	AVG	PB	PR	/A	PD	TPI
1972	Cal-A	2	0	1.000	10	0	0	0	0	16	11	0	5	2	9.0	2.81	103	.196	.262	0	—	0	0	0	0	0.1
1973	Cal-A	7	2	.778	51	0	0	0	10	68	72	2	35	25	14.8	3.71	96	.277	.373	0	—	0	1	-1	0	0.4
1974	Cal-A	2	3	.400	20	0	0	0	2	39	48	3	16	14	15.5	3.69	93	.312	.387	0	—	0	-0	-1	0	0.3
1975	Cal-A	0	0	—	4	0	0	0	0	8^{1}	9	3	8	7	18.4	8.64	41	.250	.386	0	—	0	-5	-5	0	0.0
	LA-N	0	2	.000	5	0	0	0	0	7	6	2	3	1	11.6	3.86	88	.222	.300	1	1.000	1	-0	-0	0	0.0
Total	4	11	7	.611	90	0	0	0	12	138^{1}	146	10	67	49	14.4	3.90	88	.274	.363	1	1.000	1	-4	-7	1	0.8

● DICK SELMA

Selma, Richard Jay b: 11/4/43, Santa Ana, Cal. BR/TR, 5'11", 175 lbs. Deb: 9/2/65

YEAR	TM/L	W	L	PCT	G	GS	CG	SH	SV	IP	H	HR	BB	SO	RAT	ERA	ERA+	OAV	OOB	BH	AVG	PB	PR	/A	PD	TPI
1965	NY-N	2	1	.667	4	4	1	1	0	26^{2}	22	2	9	26	10.8	3.71	95	.229	.302	2	.222	0	-1	-1	1	0.0
1966	NY-N	4	6	.400	30	7	0	0	1	80^{2}	84	11	39	58	14.1	4.24	86	.274	.361	1	.071	0	-6	-5	2	-0.4
1967	NY-N	2	4	.333	38	4	0	0	2	81^{1}	71	3	36	52	12.1	2.77	122	.241	.328	2	.091	-1	6	6	1	0.4
1968	NY-N	9	10	.474	33	23	4	3	0	169^{2}	148	11	54	117	11.0	2.76	110	.233	.298	12	.207	2	4	5	2	1.0
1969	SD-N	2	2	.500	4	3	1	0	0	22	19	3	9	20	11.5	4.09	86	.229	.304	2	.286	0	-1	-1	0	-0.2
	Chi-N	10	8	.556	36	25	4	2	1	168^{2}	137	13	72	161	11.3	3.63	111	.222	.307	8	.154	-0	-1	7	-1	0.6
	Yr	12	10	.545	40	28	5	2	1	190^{2}	156	16	81	181	11.3	3.68	108	.223	.307	10	.169	-0	-2	6	-1	0.4
1970	Phi-N	8	9	.471	73	0	0	0	22	134^{1}	108	8	59	153	11.5	2.75	145	.226	.317	3	.150	0	**19**	**19**	2	3.0
1971	Phi-N	0	2	.000	17	0	0	0	1	24^{2}	21	2	8	15	11.3	3.28	107	.231	.307	1	1.000	0	0	1	0	0.1
1972	Phi-N	2	9	.182	46	10	1	0	3	98^{2}	91	13	73	58	15.4	5.56	65	.249	.381	4	.200	1	-23	-22	1	-2.3
1973	Phi-N	1	1	.500	6	0	0	0	0	8	6	1	5	4	12.4	5.63	67	.240	.367	0	—	0	-2	-2	1	-0.3
1974	Cal-A	2	2	.500	18	0	0	0	1	23	22	2	17	15	15.7	5.09	68	.272	.404	0	—	0	-4	-4	1	-0.2
	Mil-A	0	0	—	2	0	0	0	0	2^{1}	5	0	0	2	23.1	19.29	19	.455	.500	0	—	0	-4	-4	-0	0.0
	Yr	2	2	.500	20	0	0	0	1	25^{1}	27	2	17	17	16.0	6.39	54	.290	.405	0	—	0	-8	-8	1	-0.2
Total	10	42	54	.438	307	76	11	6	31	840	734	69	381	681	12.2	3.62	100	.238	.327	35	.172	2	-11	-2	8	1.7

● FRANK SELMAN

Selman, Frank C. (a.k.a. Frank C. Williams 1871-75) b: Baltimore, Md. Deb: 5/4/1871 ♦

YEAR	TM/L	W	L	PCT	G	GS	CG	SH	SV	IP	H	HR	BB	SO	RAT	ERA	ERA+	OAV	OOB	BH	AVG	PB	PR	/A	PD	TPI
1873	Mar-n	0	1	.000	1	1	1	0	0	9	21	0	0	0	21.0	8.00	40	.350	.350	1	.333	0	-5	-5		-0.3

● CARROLL SEMBERA

Sembera, Carroll William b: 7/26/41, Shiner, Tex. BR/TR, 6', 155 lbs. Deb: 9/28/65

YEAR	TM/L	W	L	PCT	G	GS	CG	SH	SV	IP	H	HR	BB	SO	RAT	ERA	ERA+	OAV	OOB	BH	AVG	PB	PR	/A	PD	TPI
1965	Hou-N	0	1	.000	2	1	0	0	0	7^{1}	5	0	3	4	9.8	3.68	91	.185	.267	0	.000	-0	-0	-0	0	0.0
1966	Hou-N	1	2	.333	24	0	0	0	1	33	36	3	16	21	14.2	3.00	114	.288	.369	0	.000	-0	2	2	0	0.1
1967	Hou-N	2	6	.250	45	0	0	0	3	59^{2}	66	7	19	48	13.0	4.83	69	.269	.325	1	.143	-0	-10	-10	1	-1.3
1969	Mon-N	0	2	.000	23	0	0	0	2	33	28	1	24	15	14.7	3.55	104	.246	.386	1	.250	0	0	0	-0	0.0
1970	Mon-N	0	0	—	5	0	0	0	0	6^{2}	14	2	11	6	35.1	18.90	22	.424	.578	0	—	0	-11	-11	0	0.0
Total	5	3	11	.214	99	1	0	0	6	139^{2}	149	13	73	94	14.6	4.70	74	.274	.364	2	.133	-0	-18	-19	1	-1.2

● FRANK SEMINARA

Seminara, Frank Peter b: 5/16/67, Brooklyn, N.Y. BR/TR, 6'2", 205 lbs. Deb: 6/2/92

YEAR	TM/L	W	L	PCT	G	GS	CG	SH	SV	IP	H	HR	BB	SO	RAT	ERA	ERA+	OAV	OOB	BH	AVG	PB	PR	/A	PD	TPI
1992	SD-N	9	4	.692	19	18	0	0	0	100^{1}	98	5	46	61	13.2	3.68	97	.257	.342	4	.118	-1	-2	-1	2	-0.1
1993	SD-N	3	3	.500	18	7	0	0	0	46^{1}	53	5	21	22	15.0	4.47	93	.294	.377	2	.200	0	-2	-2	0	-0.2
1994	NY-N	0	2	.000	10	1	0	0	0	17	20	2	8	7	14.8	5.82	72	.303	.378	0	.000	-0	-3	-3	-1	-0.4
Total	3	12	9	.571	47	26	0	0	0	163^{2}	171	12	75	90	13.9	4.12	92	.273	.356	6	.128	-1	-7	-6	1	-0.7

● RAY SEMPROCH

Semproch, Roman Anthony "Baby" b: 1/7/31, Cleveland, Ohio BR/TR, 5'11", 180 lbs. Deb: 4/15/58

YEAR	TM/L	W	L	PCT	G	GS	CG	SH	SV	IP	H	HR	BB	SO	RAT	ERA	ERA+	OAV	OOB	BH	AVG	PB	PR	/A	PD	TPI
1958	Phi-N	13	11	.542	36	30	12	2	0	204^{1}	211	25	58	92	12.1	3.92	101	.264	.319	7	.095	-5	1	1	-1	-0.4
1959	Phi-N	3	10	.231	30	18	2	0	3	111^{2}	119	12	59	54	14.6	5.40	76	.277	.368	6	.176	-0	-18	-16	1	-1.7
1960	Det-A	3	0	1.000	17	0	0	0	0	27	29	2	16	9	15.0	4.00	99	.269	.363	0	.000	-0	-0	-0	1	0.1
1961	LA-A	0	0	—	2	0	0	0	0	1	1	0	3	1	36.0	9.00	50	.333	.667	0	—	0	-1	-0	0	0.0
Total	4	19	21	.475	85	48	14	2	3	344	360	39	136	156	13.2	4.42	91	.269	.340	13	.116	-5	-18	-16	1	-2.0

● STEVE SENTENEY

Senteney, Stephen Leonard b: 8/7/55, Indianapolis, Ind. d: 6/19/89, Colusa, Cal. BR/TR, 6'2", 205 lbs. Deb: 6/6/82

YEAR	TM/L	W	L	PCT	G	GS	CG	SH	SV	IP	H	HR	BB	SO	RAT	ERA	ERA+	OAV	OOB	BH	AVG	PB	PR	/A	PD	TPI
1982	Tor-A	0	0	—	11	0	0	0	0	22	23	5	6	20	11.9	4.91	91	.247	.293	0	—	0	-2	-1	-0	-0.1

● MANNY SEOANE

Seoane, Manuel Modesto b: 6/26/55, Tampa, Fla. BR/TR, 6'3", 187 lbs. Deb: 9/18/77

YEAR	TM/L	W	L	PCT	G	GS	CG	SH	SV	IP	H	HR	BB	SO	RAT	ERA	ERA+	OAV	OOB	BH	AVG	PB	PR	/A	PD	TPI
1977	Phi-N	0	0	—	2	1	0	0	0	6	11	0	3	4	21.0	6.00	67	.407	.467	1	.500	0	-1	-1	-0	0.0
1978	Chi-N	1	0	1.000	7	1	0	0	0	8^{1}	11	0	6	5	18.4	5.40	75	.297	.395	0	—	0	-2	-1	-0	-0.2
Total	2	1	0	1.000	9	2	0	0	0	14^{1}	22	0	9	9	19.5	5.65	71	.344	.425	1	.500	0	-3	-3	-1	-0.2

● BILLY SERAD

Serad, William I. b: 1863, Philadelphia, Pa. d: 11/1/25, Chester, Pa. BR/TR, 5'7", 156 lbs. Deb: 5/5/1884

YEAR	TM/L	W	L	PCT	G	GS	CG	SH	SV	IP	H	HR	BB	SO	RAT	ERA	ERA+	OAV	OOB	BH	AVG	PB	PR	/A	PD	TPI
1884	Buf-N	16	20	.444	37	37	34	2	0	308	373	21	111	150	14.1	4.27	74	.281	.336	24	.175	-7	-44	-38	-3	-4.2
1885	Buf-N	7	21	.250	30	29	27	0	0	241^{1}	299	5	80	90	14.1	4.10	73	.293	.344	16	.154	-6	-34	-30	-3	-3.5
1887	Cin-a	10	11	.476	22	21	20	2	1	187^{1}	201	7	80	34	13.9	4.08	106	.266	.343	14	.177	-4	4	5	-1	0.1
1888	Cin-a	2	3	.400	6	5	5	0	0	50^{2}	62	1	19	4	15.5	3.55	89	.291	.366	3	.130	-1	-3	-2	-1	-0.4
Total	4	35	55	.389	95	92	86	4	1	787^{1}	935	34	290	278	14.2	4.13	82	.282	.342	57	.166	-17	-77	-64	-7	-8.0

● DAN SERAFINI

Serafini, Daniel Joseph b: 1/25/74, San Francisco, Cal. BB/TL, 6'1", 185 lbs. Deb: 6/25/96

YEAR	TM/L	W	L	PCT	G	GS	CG	SH	SV	IP	H	HR	BB	SO	RAT	ERA	ERA+	OAV	OOB	BH	AVG	PB	PR	/A	PD	TPI
1996	Min-A	0	1	.000	1	1	0	0	0	4^{1}	7	1	2	1	20.8	10.38	49	.368	.455	0	—	0	-3	-3	-0	-0.4
1997	Min-A	2	1	.667	6	4	1	0	0	26^{1}	27	1	11	15	13.0	3.42	136	.273	.345	0	—	0	3	4	-1	0.3
1998	Min-A	7	4	.636	28	9	0	0	0	75	95	10	29	46	15.0	6.48	72	.310	.372	0	.000	-0	-15	-15	-1	-1.9
Total	3	9	6	.600	35	14	1	0	0	105^{2}	129	12	42	62	14.7	5.88	80	.304	.370	0	.000	-0	-15	-14	-2	-2.0

● GARY SERUM

Serum, Gary Wayne b: 10/24/56, Fargo, N.D. BR/TR, 6'1", 180 lbs. Deb: 7/22/77

YEAR	TM/L	W	L	PCT	G	GS	CG	SH	SV	IP	H	HR	BB	SO	RAT	ERA	ERA+	OAV	OOB	BH	AVG	PB	PR	/A	PD	TPI
1977	Min-A	0	0	—	8	0	0	0	0	22^{2}	22	4	10	14	13.5	4.37	91	.268	.362	0	—	0	-1	-1	-0	0.0
1978	Min-A	9	9	.500	34	23	6	1	1	184^{1}	188	14	44	80	11.5	4.10	93	.266	.311	0	—	0	-7	-6	0	-0.6
1979	Min-A	1	3	.250	20	5	0	0	0	64	93	10	20	31	15.9	6.61	66	.354	.399	0	—	0	-17	-16	0	-0.9
Total	3	10	12	.455	62	28	6	1	1	271	303	28	74	125	12.7	4.72	84	.288	.337	0	—	0	-25	-23	-0	-1.5

● SCOTT SERVICE

Service, Scott David b: 2/26/67, Cincinnati, Ohio BR/TR, 6'6", 226 lbs. Deb: 9/5/88

YEAR	TM/L	W	L	PCT	G	GS	CG	SH	SV	IP	H	HR	BB	SO	RAT	ERA	ERA+	OAV	OOB	BH	AVG	PB	PR	/A	PD	TPI
1988	Phi-N	0	0	—	5	0	0	0	0	5^{1}	7	0	1	6	15.2	1.69	211	.333	.391	0	—	0	1	1	-0	0.0
1992	Mon-N	0	0	—	5	0	0	0	0	7	15	1	5	11	25.7	14.14	25	.417	.488	0	.000	-0	-8	-8	-0	0.0
1993	Col-N	0	0	—	3	0	0	0	0	4^{2}	8	1	1	3	19.3	9.64	49	.400	.455	0	—	0	-3	-3	0	0.0
	Cin-N	2	2	.500	26	0	0	0	2	41^{1}	36	5	15	40	11.3	3.70	109	.235	.308	1	.143	-0	2	1	-0	0.1
	Yr	2	2	.500	29	0	0	0	2	46	44	6	16	43	11.9	4.30	95	.250	.316	1	.143	-0	-1	-1	0	0.1
1994	Cin-N	1	2	.333	6	0	0	0	0	7^{1}	8	2	3	5	13.5	7.36	56	.267	.333	0	—	0	-3	-3	0	-0.9
1995	SF-N	3	1	.750	28	0	0	0	0	31	18	4	20	30	11.6	3.19	128	.176	.323	0	.000	-0	3	3	-0	0.3
1996	Cin-N	1	0	1.000	34	1	0	0	0	48	51	7	18	46	14.1	3.94	107	.277	.361	0	.000	-1	1	2	0	0.0
1997	Cin-N	0	0	—	4	0	0	0	0	5^{1}	11	1	1	3	20.3	11.81	36	.458	.480	0	—	0	-5	-4	0	0.0
	KC-A	0	3	.000	12	0	0	0	0	17	17	1	5	19	11.6	4.76	99	.274	.328	0	—	0	-0	-0	-0	0.0
1998	KC-A	6	4	.600	73	0	0	0	4	82^{2}	70	7	34	95	12.3	3.48	141	.231	.327	0	.000	-0	11	13	1	1.6
Total	8	13	12	.520	196	1	0	0	6	249^{2}	241	29	103	258	13.1	4.33	102	.258	.344	1	.063	-1	-0	2	1	1.1

● MERLE SETTLEMIRE

Settlemire, Edgar Merle "Lefty" b: 1/19/03, Santa Fe, Ohio d: 6/12/88, Russells Point, Ohio BL/TL, 5'9", 156 lbs. Deb: 4/13/28

YEAR	TM/L	W	L	PCT	G	GS	CG	SH	SV	IP	H	HR	BB	SO	RAT	ERA	ERA+	OAV	OOB	BH	AVG	PB	PR	/A	PD	TPI
1928	Bos-A	0	6	.000	30	9	0	0	0	82^{1}	116	2	34	12	17.1	5.47	75	.345	.415	3	.176	-1	-13	-12	2	-0.6

● AL SEVERINSEN

Severinsen, Albert Henry b: 11/9/44, Brooklyn, N.Y. BR/TR, 6'3", 220 lbs. Deb: 7/1/69

YEAR	TM/L	W	L	PCT	G	GS	CG	SH	SV	IP	H	HR	BB	SO	RAT	ERA	ERA+	OAV	OOB	BH	AVG	PB	PR	/A	PD	TPI
1969	Bal-A	1	1	.500	12	0	0	0	0	19^{2}	14	2	10	13	11.0	2.29	156	.206	.308	1	.333	0	3	3	0	0.3
1971	SD-N	2	5	.286	59	0	0	0	8	70	77	4	30	31	14.0	3.47	95	.292	.368	0	.000	-0	-0	-1	1	0.0
1972	SD-N	0	1	.000	17	0	0	0	1	21^{1}	13	1	7	9	9.3	2.53	130	.173	.262	0	.000	-0	2	2	0	0.1
Total	3	3	7	.300	88	0	0	0	9	111	104	7	47	53	12.6	3.08	108	.256	.338	1	.200	0	5	3	2	0.4

● ED SEWARD

Seward, Edward William (b: Edward William Sourhardt)
b: 6/29/1867, Cleveland, Ohio d: 7/30/47, Cleveland, Ohio TR, 5'7", 175 lbs. Deb: 9/30/1885 U♦

YEAR	TM/L	W	L	PCT	G	GS	CG	SH	SV	IP	H	HR	BB	SO	RAT	ERA	ERA+	OAV	OOB	BH	AVG	PB	PR	/A	PD	TPI
1885	Pro-N	0	0	—	1	0	0	0	0	6	2	0	0	1	3.0	0.00	—	.100	.100	0	.000	-0	2	2	1	0.0

YEAR	TM/L	W	L	PCT	G	GS	CG	SH	SV	IP	H	HR	BB	SO	RAT	ERA	ERA+	OAV	OOB	BH	AVG	PB	PR	/A	PD	TPI
1887	Phi-a	25	25	.500	55	52	52	3	0	470^2	445	7	140	155	11.6	4.13	104	.244	.306	50	.188	-4	9	8	-2	0.0
1888	Phi-a	35	19	.648	57	57	57	**6**	0	518^2	388	4	127	**272**	9.3	2.01	149	.200	.258	32	.142	-4	61	56	3	4.9
1889	Phi-a	21	15	.583	39	38	35	3	0	320	353	8	101	102	13.1	3.97	95	.271	.330	31	.217	6	-4	-6	-2	-0.2
1890	Phi-a	6	12	.333	21	19	15	1	0	154	165	4	72	55	14.3	4.73	81	.266	.349	10	.139	-1	-15	-15	-0	-1.5
1891	Cle-N	2	1	.667	3	3	0	0	0	16^1	16	0	11	4	14.9	3.86	90	.246	.355	4	.211	0	-1	-1	-1	-0.1
Total	6	89	72	.553	176	169	159	13	0	1485^2	1369	23	451	589	11.4	3.40	108	.237	.300	127	.174	-3	51	43	-2	3.1

● FRANK SEWARD Seward, Frank Martin b: 4/7/21, Pennsauken, N.J. BR/TR, 6'3", 200 lbs. Deb: 9/28/43

YEAR	TM/L	W	L	PCT	G	GS	CG	SH	SV	IP	H	HR	BB	SO	RAT	ERA	ERA+	OAV	OOB	BH	AVG	PB	PR	/A	PD	TPI
1943	NY-N	0	1	.000	1	1	1	0	0	9	12	0	5	2	17.0	3.00	115	.324	.405	0	.000	-1	0	0	-0	-0.1
1944	NY-N	3	2	.600	25	7	2	0	0	78^1	98	8	32	16	15.2	5.40	68	.306	.373	2	.083	-2	-16	-15	-1	-1.2
Total	2	3	3	.500	26	8	3	0	0	87^1	110	8	37	18	15.4	5.15	71	.308	.376	2	.071	-2	-15	-15	-2	-1.3

● RIP SEWELL Sewell, Truett Banks b: 5/11/07, Decatur, Ala. d: 9/3/89, Plant City, Fla. BL/TR, 6'1", 180 lbs. Deb: 6/14/32 C

YEAR	TM/L	W	L	PCT	G	GS	CG	SH	SV	IP	H	HR	BB	SO	RAT	ERA	ERA+	OAV	OOB	BH	AVG	PB	PR	/A	PD	TPI
1932	Det-A	0	0	—	5	0	0	0	0	10^2	19	2	8	2	22.8	12.66	37	.388	.474	1	.500	0	-10	-9	0	0.0
1938	Pit-N	0	1	.000	17	0	0	0	1	38^1	41	3	21	17	15.0	4.23	90	.275	.372	1	.083	-1	-2	-2	1	0.0
1939	Pit-N	10	9	.526	52	12	5	1	2	176^1	177	10	73	69	12.8	4.08	94	.265	.339	11	.200	1	-3	-5	3	-0.1
1940	Pit-N	16	5	.762	33	23	14	2	1	189^2	169	6	67	60	11.3	2.80	136	.238	.307	14	.192	2	22	21	2	2.7
1941	Pit-N	14	17	.452	39	32	18	2	2	249	225	18	84	76	11.3	3.72	97	.235	.299	16	.174	0	-2	-3	2	-0.1
1942	Pit-N	17	15	.531	40	33	18	5	2	248	259	13	72	69	12.1	3.41	99	.265	.317	13	.149	-2	-3	-1	-0	-0.3
1943	Pit-N★	**21**	9	.700	35	31	**25**	2	3	265^1	267	6	75	65	11.7	2.54	137	.260	.312	30	.286	6	25	28	1	**4.0**
1944	Pit-N★	21	12	.636	38	33	24	3	2	286	263	15	99	87	11.5	3.18	117	.240	.304	25	.223	3	14	17	-1	2.1
1945	Pit-N†	11	9	.550	33	24	9	1	1	188	212	9	91	60	14.6	4.07	97	.279	.357	20	.313	6	-6	-3	-0	0.3
1946	Pit-N★	8	12	.400	25	20	11	2	0	149^1	140	6	53	33	11.7	3.68	96	.245	.310	9	.180	0	-4	-3	-1	-0.4
1947	Pit-N	6	4	.600	24	12	4	1	0	121	121	11	36	36	11.9	3.57	118	.263	.321	5	.125	-1	7	9	1	0.7
1948	Pit-N	13	3	.813	21	17	7	0	0	121^2	126	9	37	36	12.1	3.48	117	.262	.317	6	.143	1	6	8	-0	1.1
1949	Pit-N	6	1	.857	28	6	2	1	1	76	82	8	32	26	13.5	3.91	108	.280	.351	1	.063	-0	1	2	-1	0.1
Total	13	143	97	.596	390	243	137	20	15	2119^1	2101	116	748	636	12.2	3.48	107	.256	.320	152	.203	16	45	60	7	10.1

● ELMER SEXAUER Sexauer, Elmer George b: 5/21/26, St.Louis Co., Mo. BR/TR, 6'4", 220 lbs. Deb: 9/6/48

YEAR	TM/L	W	L	PCT	G	GS	CG	SH	SV	IP	H	HR	BB	SO	RAT	ERA	ERA+	OAV	OOB	BH	AVG	PB	PR	/A	PD	TPI
1948	Bro-N	0	0	—	2	0	0	0	0	0^2	0	0	2	0	27.0	13.50	30	.000	.500	0	—	0	-1	-1	-0	0.0

● FRANK SEXTON Sexton, Frank Joseph b: 7/8/1872, Brockton, Mass. d: 1/4/38, Brighton, Mass. 160 lbs. Deb: 6/21/1895

YEAR	TM/L	W	L	PCT	G	GS	CG	SH	SV	IP	H	HR	BB	SO	RAT	ERA	ERA+	OAV	OOB	BH	AVG	PB	PR	/A	PD	TPI
1895	Bos-N	1	5	.167	7	5	4	0	0	49	59	2	22	14	15.2	5.69	90	.294	.369	5	.227	-1	-5	-3	-1	-0.4

● GORDON SEYFRIED Seyfried, Gordon Clay b: 7/4/37, Long Beach, Cal. BR/TR, 6', 185 lbs. Deb: 9/13/63

YEAR	TM/L	W	L	PCT	G	GS	CG	SH	SV	IP	H	HR	BB	SO	RAT	ERA	ERA+	OAV	OOB	BH	AVG	PB	PR	/A	PD	TPI
1963	Cle-A	0	1	.000	3	1	0	0	0	7^1	9	0	3	1	14.7	1.23	295	.300	.364	0	.000	-0	2	2	0	0.3
1964	Cle-A	0	0	—	2	0	0	0	0	2^1	4	0	0	0	15.4	0.00	—	.444	.444	0	—	0	1	1	-0	0.0
Total	2	0	1	.000	5	1	0	0	0	9^2	13	0	3	1	14.9	0.93	388	.333	.381	0	.000	-0	3	3	0	0.3

● JAKE SEYMOUR Seymour, Jacob (b: Jacob Semer) b: 1854, Pittsburgh, Pa. d: 8/1/1897, Allegheny, Pa. Deb: 9/23/1882

YEAR	TM/L	W	L	PCT	G	GS	CG	SH	SV	IP	H	HR	BB	SO	RAT	ERA	ERA+	OAV	OOB	BH	AVG	PB	PR	/A	PD	TPI
1882	Pit-a	0	1	.000	1	1	1	0	0	8	16	0	2	2	20.3	7.88	33	.390	.419	0	.000	-1	-5	-5	-0	-0.4

● CY SEYMOUR Seymour, James Bentley b: 12/9/1872, Albany, N.Y. d: 9/20/19, New York, N.Y. BL/TL, 6', 200 lbs. Deb: 4/22/1896 ♦

YEAR	TM/L	W	L	PCT	G	GS	CG	SH	SV	IP	H	HR	BB	SO	RAT	ERA	ERA+	OAV	OOB	BH	AVG	PB	PR	/A	PD	TPI
1896	NY-N	2	4	.333	11	8	4	0	0	70^1	75	8	51	33	16.5	6.40	66	.271	.390	7	.219	-1	-16	-17	1	-1.1
1897	NY-N	18	14	.563	38	33	28	2	1	277^2	254	4	164	149	14.2	3.37	123	**.242**	.355	33	.241	1	29	24	8	3.0
1898	NY-N	25	19	.568	45	43	39	4	0	356^2	313	4	213	**239**	14.1	3.18	109	.234	.353	82	.276	7	17	12	8	2.7
1899	NY-N	14	18	.438	32	32	31	0	0	268^1	247	5	170	142	14.7	3.56	106	.245	.364	52	.327	8	9	6	5	1.9
1900	NY-N	2	1	.667	13	7	2	0	0	53	58	4	54	19	20.7	6.96	52	.278	.447	12	.300	1	-19	-20	1	-0.7
1902	Cin-N	0	0	—	1	0	0	0	0	3	4	0	3	2	21.0	9.00	33	.308	.438	83	.340	0	-2	-2	-0	0.0
Total	6	61	56	.521	140	123	104	6	1	1029	951	25	655	584	14.8	3.76	101	.244	.365	1723	.303	16	18	3	23	5.8

● JOHN SHAFFER Shaffer, John W. "Cannon Ball" b: 2/18/1864, Lock Haven, Pa. d: 11/21/26, Endicott, N.Y. Deb: 9/13/1886

YEAR	TM/L	W	L	PCT	G	GS	CG	SH	SV	IP	H	HR	BB	SO	RAT	ERA	ERA+	OAV	OOB	BH	AVG	PB	PR	/A	PD	TPI
1886	NY-a	5	3	.625	8	8	8	1	0	69	40	0	29	36	9.1	1.96	174	.164	.255	6	.240	1	11	11	-1	1.1
1887	NY-a	2	11	.154	13	13	13	0	0	112	148	3	53	22	17.0	6.19	69	.310	.391	8	.167	-3	-24	-24	2	-2.0
Total	2	7	14	.333	21	21	21	1	0	181	188	3	82	58	14.0	4.57	86	.260	.346	14	.192	-2	-12	-13	1	-0.9

● GUS SHALLIX Shallix, August (b: August Schallick)
b: 3/29/1858, Paderborn, Westphalia, Germany d: 10/28/37, Cincinnati, Ohio BR/TR, 5'11", 165 lbs. Deb: 6/22/1884

YEAR	TM/L	W	L	PCT	G	GS	CG	SH	SV	IP	H	HR	BB	SO	RAT	ERA	ERA+	OAV	OOB	BH	AVG	PB	PR	/A	PD	TPI
1884	Cin-a	11	10	.524	23	23	23	0	0	199^2	163	6	53	78	10.9	3.70	90	.212	.286	3	.036	-10	-10	-8	1	-1.5
1885	Cin-a	6	4	.600	13	12	7	0	0	91^1	95	1	33	15	13.9	3.25	100	.265	.349	5	.128	-2	-0	0	1	-0.1
Total	2	17	14	.548	36	35	30	0	0	291	258	7	86	93	11.8	3.56	93	.229	.306	8	.065	-12	-10	-8	2	-1.6

● GREG SHANAHAN Shanahan, Paul Gregory b: 12/11/47, Eureka, Cal. BR/TR, 6'2", 190 lbs. Deb: 9/4/73

YEAR	TM/L	W	L	PCT	G	GS	CG	SH	SV	IP	H	HR	BB	SO	RAT	ERA	ERA+	OAV	OOB	BH	AVG	PB	PR	/A	PD	TPI
1973	LA-N	0	0	—	7	0	0	0	1	15^2	14	2	4	11	10.3	3.45	100	.230	.277	0	.000	0	0	-0	-0	0.0
1974	LA-N	0	0	—	4	0	0	0	0	7	7	1	5	2	15.4	3.86	88	.259	.375	0	—	0	-0	-0	0	0.0
Total	2	0	0	—	11	0	0	0	1	22^2	21	3	9	13	11.9	3.57	96	.239	.309	0	.000	0	0	-0	0	0.0

● HARVEY SHANK Shank, Harvey Tillman b: 7/29/46, Toronto, Ont., Can. BR/TR, 6'4", 220 lbs. Deb: 5/16/70

YEAR	TM/L	W	L	PCT	G	GS	CG	SH	SV	IP	H	HR	BB	SO	RAT	ERA	ERA+	OAV	OOB	BH	AVG	PB	PR	/A	PD	TPI
1970	Cal-A	0	0	—	1	0	0	0	0	3	2	0	2	1	12.0	0.00	—	.182	.308	0	—	0	1	1	-0	0.0

● BILL SHANNER Shanner, Wilfred William b: 11/4/1894, Oakland City, Ind. d: 12/18/86, Evansville, Ind. BL/TR, Deb: 10/1/20

YEAR	TM/L	W	L	PCT	G	GS	CG	SH	SV	IP	H	HR	BB	SO	RAT	ERA	ERA+	OAV	OOB	BH	AVG	PB	PR	/A	PD	TPI
1920	Phi-A	0	0	—	1	0	0	0	0	4	6	2	1	1	15.8	6.75	60	.353	.389	0	.000	-0	-1	-1	0	0.0

● BOBBY SHANTZ Shantz, Robert Clayton b: 9/26/25, Pottstown, Pa. BR/TL, 5'6", 142 lbs. Deb: 5/1/49 F

YEAR	TM/L	W	L	PCT	G	GS	CG	SH	SV	IP	H	HR	BB	SO	RAT	ERA	ERA+	OAV	OOB	BH	AVG	PB	PR	/A	PD	TPI
1949	Phi-A	6	8	.429	33	7	4	1	2	127	100	9	74	58	12.5	3.40	121	.221	.334	7	.189	1	11	10	4	1.5
1950	Phi-A	8	14	.364	36	23	6	1	0	214^2	251	18	85	93	14.4	4.61	99	.294	.362	11	.167	-0	-1	-1	4	0.2
1951	Phi-A☆	18	10	.643	32	25	13	3	0	205^1	213	15	70	77	12.6	3.94	108	.270	.333	18	.250	2	4	8	3	1.5
1952	Phi-A★	**24**	7	**.774**	33	33	27	5	0	279^2	230	21	63	152	**9.6**	2.48	160	.225	**.272**	19	.198	2	37	**46**	2	**5.5**
1953	Phi-A	5	9	.357	16	16	6	0	0	105^2	107	10	26	58	11.3	4.09	105	.263	.307	9	.237	1	-1	2	2	0.6
1954	Phi-A	1	0	1.000	2	1	0	0	0	8	12	2	3	3	18.0	7.88	50	.364	.432	1	.333	0	-4	-4	0	-0.3
1955	KC-A	5	10	.333	23	17	4	1	0	125	124	8	66	58	13.8	4.54	92	.264	.356	6	.146	-2	-8	-5	1	-0.6
1956	KC-A	2	7	.222	45	2	1	0	9	101^1	95	12	37	67	12.0	4.35	99	.248	.319	2	.091	-1	-2	-0	1	0.0
1957	*NY-A☆	11	5	.688	30	21	9	1	5	173	157	15	40	72	10.6	**2.45**	**147**	.248	.299	10	.179	2	26	22	6	3.1
1958	NY-A	7	6	.538	33	13	3	0	0	126	127	8	35	80	11.7	3.36	105	.262	.315	8	.229	2	6	2	3	0.8
1959	NY-A	7	3	.700	33	4	2	2	3	94^2	64	4	33	66	9.2	2.38	153	.189	.261	5	.217	2	16	13	1	1.7
1960	*NY-A	5	4	.556	42	0	0	0	11	67^2	57	5	24	54	11.0	2.79	128	.235	.309	1	.100	-0	8	6	1	1.0
1961	Pit-N	6	3	.667	43	6	2	1	2	89^1	91	5	26	61	12.2	3.32	120	.271	.331	7	.438	3	7	7	2	1.1
1962	Hou-N	1	1	.500	3	3	1	0	0	20^2	15	1	5	14	8.7	1.31	286	.208	.260	0	.000	-1	6	6	2	0.7
	StL-N	5	3	.625	28	0	0	0	4	57^2	45	7	20	47	10.3	2.18	195	.211	.282	2	.154	-0	11	13	1	2.0
	Yr	6	4	.600	31	3	1	0	4	78^1	60	8	25	61	9.9	1.95	211	.210	.276	2	.095	-1	17	19	3	2.7
1963	StL-N	6	4	.600	55	0	0	0	11	79^1	55	6	17	70	8.4	2.61	136	.192	.243	1	.143	0	6	8	3	1.6
1964	StL-N	1	3	.250	16	0	0	0	0	17^1	14	2	7	12	10.9	3.12	122	.226	.304	0	—	0	1	1	1	0.4
	Chi-N	0	1	.000	20	0	0	0	1	11^1	15	2	6	12	16.7	5.56	67	.319	.396	0	—	0	-3	-2	0	-0.2
	Phi-N	1	1	.500	14	0	0	0	0	32	23	1	6	18	8.2	2.25	154	.204	.244	0	.000	-0	5	4	2	0.5
	Yr	2	5	.286	50	0	0	0	1	60^2	52	5	19	42	10.5	3.12	116	.233	.293	0	.000	0	3	3	4	0.7
Total	16	119	99	.546	537	171	78	15	48	1935^2	1795	151	643	1072	11.5	3.38	119	.248	.313	107	.195	11	125	137	39	21.1

● GEORGE SHARROTT Sharrott, George Oscar b: 11/2/1869, Staten Island, N.Y. d: 1/6/32, Jamaica, N.Y. BL/TL, 5'8", 164 lbs. Deb: 7/27/1893

YEAR	TM/L	W	L	PCT	G	GS	CG	SH	SV	IP	H	HR	BB	SO	RAT	ERA	ERA+	OAV	OOB	BH	AVG	PB	PR	/A	PD	TPI
1893	Bro-N	4	6	.400	13	10	10	0	1	95	114	3	58	24	17.1	5.87	75	.289	.390	9	.231	0	-13	-15	-1	-1.2
1894	Bro-N	0	1	.000	2	2	1	0	0	9	7	0	5	2	15.0	7.00	71	.212	.366	1	.333	0	-2	-2	-0	-0.2
Total	2	4	7	.364	15	12	11	0	1	104	121	3	63	26	16.9	5.97	75	.283	.388	10	.238	0	-14	-17	-1	-1.4

● **JACK SHARROTT** Sharrott, John Henry b: 8/13/1869, Bangor, Me. d: 12/31/27, Los Angeles, Cal. BR/TR, 5'9", 165 lbs. Deb: 4/22/1890 ♦

YEAR	TM/L	W	L	PCT	G	GS	CG	SH	SV	IP	H	HR	BB	SO	RAT	ERA	ERA+	OAV	OOB	BH	AVG	PB	PR	/A	PD	TPI
1890	NY-N	11	10	.524	25	19	18	0	0	184	162	3	88	84	12.7	2.89	121	.229	.322	22	.202	-2	14	13	3	1.2
1891	NY-N	5	5	.500	10	9	6	0	1	69^1	47	2	35	41	11.2	2.60	123	.185	.294	10	.333	4	6	5	1	1.0
1892	NY-N	0	0	—	1	0	0	0	0	2	2	0	1	1	13.5	4.50	72	.250	.333	1	.125	-0	-0	-0	-0	0.0
1893	Phi-N	4	2	.667	12	4	2	0	0	56	53	1	33	11	14.5	4.50	102	.242	.352	38	.250	0	1	0	0	0.1
Total	4	20	17	.541	48	32	26	0	1	311^1	264	6	157	137	12.7	3.12	116	.222	.322	71	.237	2	21	17	3	2.3

● **JOE SHAUTE** Shaute, Joseph Benjamin "Lefty" b: 8/1/1899, Peckville, Pa. d: 2/21/70, Scranton, Pa. BL/TL, 6', 190 lbs. Deb: 7/6/22

YEAR	TM/L	W	L	PCT	G	GS	CG	SH	SV	IP	H	HR	BB	SO	RAT	ERA	ERA+	OAV	OOB	BH	AVG	PB	PR	/A	PD	TPI
1922	Cle-A	0	0	—	2	0	0	0	0	3^2	7	2	3	3	24.5	19.64	20	.389	.476	0	.000	-0	-6	-6	-0	-0.1
1923	Cle-A	10	8	.556	33	16	7	0	0	172	176	4	53	61	12.0	3.51	113	.275	.332	11	.162	-4	9	9	-2	0.3
1924	Cle-A	20	17	.541	46	34	21	2	2	283	317	8	83	68	12.9	3.75	114	.287	.340	34	.318	9	15	16	-2	2.6
1925	Cle-A	4	12	.250	26	17	10	1	4	131	160	6	44	34	14.1	5.43	81	.304	.358	16	.302	3	-15	-15	-2	-1.4
1926	Cle-A	14	10	.583	34	25	15	1	1	206^2	215	9	65	47	12.3	3.53	115	.278	.337	20	.274	4	11	12	-5	1.2
1927	Cle-A	9	16	.360	45	28	14	0	2	230^1	255	9	75	63	13.0	4.22	100	.286	.343	27	.325	6	-2	-0	-2	0.3
1928	Cle-A	13	17	.433	36	31	21	1	2	253^2	295	9	68	81	13.1	4.04	102	.299	.348	21	.228	3	-0	3	1	0.7
1929	Cle-A	8	8	.500	26	24	8	0	0	162	211	6	52	43	14.7	4.28	104	.320	.370	17	.293	3	-1	3	-3	0.3
1930	Cle-A	0	0	—	4	0	0	0	0	4^2	8	0	4	2	23.1	15.43	31	.333	.429	0	—	0	-6	-5	0	0.0
1931	Bro-N	11	8	.579	25	19	6	0	0	128^2	162	9	32	50	13.6	4.83	79	.305	.346	8	.178	-0	-14	-14	0	-1.9
1932	Bro-N	7	7	.500	34	9	1	0	4	117	147	8	21	32	13.1	4.54	84	.301	.333	9	.200	1	-9	-9	-2	-1.1
1933	Bro-N	3	4	.429	41	4	0	0	2	108^1	125	4	31	26	13.0	3.49	92	.287	.336	6	.222	1	-2	-3	1	0.0
1934	Cin-N	0	2	.000	8	1	0	0	1	17^1	19	1	3	2	11.4	4.15	98	.268	.297	1	.250	0	-0	-0	-1	-0.1
Total	13	99	109	.476	360	208	103	5	18	1818^1	2097	75	534	512	13.1	4.15	99	.293	.345	170	.258	25	-18	-12	-14	0.8

● **JEFF SHAVER** Shaver, Jeffrey Thomas b: 7/30/63, Beaver, Pa. BR/TR, 6'3", 195 lbs. Deb: 7/6/88

YEAR	TM/L	W	L	PCT	G	GS	CG	SH	SV	IP	H	HR	BB	SO	RAT	ERA	ERA+	OAV	OOB	BH	AVG	PB	PR	/A	PD	TPI
1988	Oak-A	0	0	—	1	0	0	0	0	1	0	0	0	0	9.0	0.00	—	.000	.333	0	—	0	0	0	0	0.3

● **DON SHAW** Shaw, Donald Wellington b: 2/23/44, Pittsburgh, Pa. BL/TL, 6', 185 lbs. Deb: 4/11/67

YEAR	TM/L	W	L	PCT	G	GS	CG	SH	SV	IP	H	HR	BB	SO	RAT	ERA	ERA+	OAV	OOB	BH	AVG	PB	PR	/A	PD	TPI
1967	NY-N	4	5	.444	40	0	0	0	3	51^1	40	5	23	44	11.0	2.98	114	.219	.306	0	.000	0	2	2	-1	0.4
1968	NY-N	0	0	—	7	0	0	0	0	12^1	3	1	5	11	5.8	0.73	414	.086	.200	0	—	0	3	3	0	0.0
1969	Mon-N	2	5	.286	35	1	0	0	1	65^2	61	9	37	45	13.7	5.21	71	.254	.358	0	.000	-0	-12	-11	1	-1.1
1971	StL-N	7	2	.778	45	0	0	0	2	51	45	1	31	19	13.6	2.65	136	.237	.347	0	.000	-0	5	5	-0	0.9
1972	StL-N	0	1	.000	8	0	0	0	0	3	5	1	3	0	24.0	9.00	38	.417	.533	0	.000	-0	-2	-2	-0	-0.6
	Oak-A	0	1	.000	3	0	0	0	0	5^1	12	2	2	4	23.6	16.88	17	.500	.538	0	—	0	-8	-8	-0	-1.2
Total	5	13	14	.481	138	1	0	0	6	188^2	166	19	101	123	12.9	4.01	87	.243	.343	0	.000	-0	-12	-11	-0	-1.6

● **DUPEE SHAW** Shaw, Frederick Lander b: 5/31/1859, Charlestown, Mass. d: 6/11/38, Wakefield, Mass. BL/TL, 5'8", 165 lbs. Deb: 6/18/1883

YEAR	TM/L	W	L	PCT	G	GS	CG	SH	SV	IP	H	HR	BB	SO	RAT	ERA	ERA+	OAV	OOB	BH	AVG	PB	PR	/A	PD	TPI
1883	Det-N	10	15	.400	26	25	23	1	0	227	238	3	44	73	11.2	2.50	124	.256	.290	29	.206	-3	16	15	0	1.2
1884	Det-N	9	18	.333	28	28	25	0	0	227^2	219	8	72	142	11.5	3.04	95	.237	.292	26	.191	-1	-2	-4	2	-0.3
	Bos-U	21	15	.583	39	38	35	5	0	315^2	227	1	37	309	7.5	1.77	135	.188	.212	37	.242	-5	**24**	22	-0	1.5
1885	Pro-N	23	26	.469	49	49	47	6	0	399^2	343	7	99	194	10.0	2.57	105	.209	.254	22	.133	-10	11	5	-2	-0.6
1886	Was-N	13	31	.295	45	44	43	1	0	385^2	384	12	91	177	11.1	3.34	98	.250	.291	13	.088	-10	-1	-2	-1	-1.3
1887	Was-N	7	13	.350	21	20	20	0	0	181^1	263	8	46	47	15.5	6.45	63	.328	.366	13	.186	-2	-48	-48	-2	-4.0
1888	Was-N	0	3	.000	3	3	3	0	0	25	36	2	7	8	15.5	6.48	43	.333	.374	0	.000	-1	-10	-10	-1	-1.1
Total	6	83	121	.407	211	207	196	13	0	1762	1710	41	396	950	10.8	3.10	96	.239	.279	140	.170	-32	-10	-23	-5	-4.6

● **JIM SHAW** Shaw, James Aloysius "Grunting Jim" b: 8/19/1893, Pittsburgh, Pa. d: 1/27/62, Washington, D.C. BR/TR, 6', 180 lbs. Deb: 9/15/13

YEAR	TM/L	W	L	PCT	G	GS	CG	SH	SV	IP	H	HR	BB	SO	RAT	ERA	ERA+	OAV	OOB	BH	AVG	PB	PR	/A	PD	TPI
1913	Was-A	0	1	.000	2	1	0	0	0	13	8	0	7	14	11.1	2.08	142	.205	.340	0	.000	-0	1	1	1	0.2
1914	Was-A	15	17	.469	48	31	15	5	**4**	257	198	3	137	164	12.0	2.70	104	.216	.324	10	.118	-3	1	3	1	0.2
1915	Was-A	6	11	.353	25	18	7	1	1	133	102	2	76	78	12.2	2.50	119	.220	.333	10	.233	1	6	7	-1	0.9
1916	Was-A	3	8	.273	26	9	5	2	1	106^1	86	1	50	44	11.7	2.62	106	.227	.320	5	.156	-0	2	2	-3	-0.1
1917	Was-A	15	14	.517	47	31	15	2	1	266^1	233	1	123	118	12.1	3.21	82	.242	.328	14	.154	-2	-16	-17	-3	-2.4
1918	Was-A	16	12	.571	41	30	14	4	1	241^1	201	2	90	129	10.9	2.42	113	.228	.300	11	.133	-5	9	8	-5	-0.1
1919	Was-A	17	17	.500	**45**	37	23	3	**5**	**306^2**	274	5	101	128	11.2	2.73	118	.244	.309	17	.160	-1	17	16	-6	1.1
1920	Was-A	11	18	.379	38	32	17	0	1	236^1	285	12	87	88	14.3	4.27	87	.314	.376	14	.189	0	-12	-14	-4	-1.8
1921	Was-A	1	0	1.000	15	5	0	0	3	40^1	59	2	17	4	17.0	7.36	56	.345	.404	5	.417	2	-14	-15	0	-0.3
Total	9	84	98	.462	287	194	96	17	17	1600^1	1446	28	688	767	12.1	3.07	99	.247	.329	86	.163	-8	-4	-7	-19	-2.3

● **JEFF SHAW** Shaw, Jeffrey Lee b: 7/7/66, Washington Court House, Ohio BR/TR, 6'2", 200 lbs. Deb: 4/30/90

YEAR	TM/L	W	L	PCT	G	GS	CG	SH	SV	IP	H	HR	BB	SO	RAT	ERA	ERA+	OAV	OOB	BH	AVG	PB	PR	/A	PD	TPI
1990	Cle-A	3	4	.429	12	9	0	0	0	48^2	73	11	20	25	17.2	6.66	59	.356	.413	0	—	0	-15	-15	0	-1.7
1991	Cle-A	0	5	.000	29	1	0	0	1	72^1	72	6	27	31	12.8	3.36	124	.262	.337	0	—	0	6	6	0	0.4
1992	Cle-A	0	1	.000	2	1	0	0	0	7^2	7	2	4	3	12.9	8.22	48	.259	.355	0	—	0	-4	-4	0	-0.3
1993	Mon-N	2	7	.222	55	8	0	0	0	95^2	91	12	32	50	12.2	4.14	101	.254	.327	1	.067	-1	-1	0	1	0.0
1994	Mon-N	5	2	.714	46	0	0	0	1	67^1	67	8	15	47	11.2	3.88	109	.254	.299	2	.286	1	3	3	1	0.4
1995	Mon-N	1	6	.143	50	0	0	0	3	62^1	58	4	26	45	12.6	4.62	93	.250	.333	0	.000	-0	-3	-2	1	-0.2
	Chi-A	0	0	—	9	0	0	0	0	9^2	12	2	1	6	13.0	6.52	68	.316	.350	0	—	0	-2	-2	0	0.4
1996	Cin-N	8	6	.571	78	0	0	0	4	104^2	99	8	29	69	11.2	2.49	170	.252	.307	0	.000	-0	20	**20**	1	2.6
1997	Cin-N	4	2	.667	78	0	0	0	**42**	94^2	79	7	12	74	8.7	2.38	179	.227	.255	0	.000	-0	**19**	**20**	1	2.8
1998	Cin-N	2	4	.333	39	0	0	0	23	49^2	40	2	12	29	9.6	1.81	239	.231	.285	0	.000	-0	13	14	0	2.7
	LA-N★	1	4	.200	34	0	0	0	25	35^1	35	6	7	26	10.7	2.55	153	.252	.288	0	—	0	7	5	1	1.4
	Yr	3	8	.273	73	0	0	0	48	85	75	8	19	55	10.0	2.12	196	.238	.281	0	.000	-0	20	19	1	4.1
Total	9	26	41	.388	432	19	0	0	99	648	633	68	185	405	11.7	3.56	118	.258	.316	3	.079	-1	43	46	5	8.5

● **BOB SHAW** Shaw, Robert John b: 6/29/33, Bronx, N.Y. BR/TR, 6'2", 195 lbs. Deb: 8/11/57 C

YEAR	TM/L	W	L	PCT	G	GS	CG	SH	SV	IP	H	HR	BB	SO	RAT	ERA	ERA+	OAV	OOB	BH	AVG	PB	PR	/A	PD	TPI
1957	Det-A	0	1	.000	7	0	0	0	0	9^2	11	2	7	4	16.8	7.45	52	.289	.400	0	.000	-0	-4	-4	-0	-0.4
1958	Det-A	1	2	.333	11	2	0	0	0	26^2	32	2	13	17	15.2	5.06	80	.302	.378	3	.375	1	-4	-3	1	-0.2
	Chi-A	4	2	.667	29	3	0	0	1	64	67	8	28	18	13.6	4.64	78	.271	.350	0	.000	-1	-6	-7	2	-0.6
	Yr	5	4	.556	40	5	0	0	1	90^2	99	10	41	35	14.1	4.76	79	.280	.358	3	.136	-0	-10	-10	2	-0.8
1959	*Chi-A	18	6	**.750**	47	26	8	3	3	230^2	217	15	54	89	10.8	2.69	140	.249	.297	9	.123	-2	30	27	1	2.6
1960	Chi-A	13	13	.500	36	32	7	1	0	192^2	221	16	62	46	13.4	4.06	93	.292	.348	8	.138	-0	-4	-6	-1	-0.9
1961	Chi-A	3	4	.429	14	10	3	0	0	71^1	85	11	20	31	13.4	3.79	103	.302	.351	0	.000	-1	2	1	-0	-0.1
	KC-A	9	10	.474	26	24	6	0	0	150^1	165	13	58	60	13.8	4.31	97	.281	.352	11	.200	-1	-5	-2	0	-0.3
	Yr	12	14	.462	40	34	9	0	0	221^2	250	24	78	91	13.6	4.14	99	.286	.349	11	.151	-2	-3	-1	-0	-0.4
1962	Mil-N★	15	9	.625	38	29	12	3	2	225	223	20	44	124	11.2	2.80	136	.260	.305	10	.137	1	29	25	-0	2.6
1963	Mil-N	7	11	.389	48	16	3	3	13	159	144	10	55	105	11.5	2.66	121	.243	.312	5	.122	0	11	10	-2	1.2
1964	SF-N	7	6	.538	61	1	0	0	11	93^1	105	5	31	57	13.6	3.76	95	.286	.350	0	.000	-1	-2	-2	-2	-0.6
1965	SF-N	16	9	.640	42	33	6	1	2	235	213	17	53	148	10.3	2.64	136	.236	.280	8	.101	-3	23	25	1	2.4
1966	SF-N	1	4	.200	13	6	0	0	0	31^2	45	9	7	21	14.8	6.25	59	.324	.356	0	.000	-1	-9	-9	-1	-1.4
	NY-N	11	10	.524	26	25	7	2	0	167^2	171	12	42	104	11.8	3.92	93	.261	.313	13	.260	3	-6	-5	1	-0.2
	Yr	12	14	.462	39	31	7	2	0	199^1	216	21	49	125	12.3	4.29	85	.272	.320	13	.232	2	-15	-14	0	-1.6
1967	NY-N	3	9	.250	23	13	3	1	0	98^2	105	9	28	49	12.3	4.29	79	.273	.326	1	.040	-2	-10	-10	-1	-1.4
	Chi-N	0	2	.000	9	3	0	0	0	22^1	33	0	9	7	18.5	6.04	59	.351	.430	1	.250	0	-7	-6	-1	-0.6
	Yr	3	11	.214	32	16	3	1	0	121	138	9	37	56	13.3	4.61	74	.286	.342	2	.069	-1	-17	-16	-2	-2.0
Total	11	108	98	.524	430	223	55	14	32	1778	1837	149	511	880	12.2	3.52	105	.267	.323	69	.133	-7	38	34	-2	2.1

● **SAM SHAW** Shaw, Samuel E. b: 5/1864, Baltimore, Md. BR/TR, 5'5", 140 lbs. Deb: 5/3/1888

YEAR	TM/L	W	L	PCT	G	GS	CG	SH	SV	IP	H	HR	BB	SO	RAT	ERA	ERA+	OAV	OOB	BH	AVG	PB	PR	/A	PD	TPI
1888	Bal-a	2	4	.333	6	6	6	0	0	53	65	2	15	22	14.3	3.40	88	.291	.347	3	.150	-1	-2	-2	-1	-0.4
1893	Chi-N	1	0	1.000	2	2	1	0	0	16	12	2	13	1	19.1	5.63	82	.203	.420	2	.286	-0	-2	-2	-0	-0.1
Total	2	3	4	.429	8	8	7	0	0	69	77	4	28	23	15.4	3.91	86	.273	.365	5	.185	-1	-4	-4	-1	-0.5

● **BOB SHAWKEY** Shawkey, James Robert b: 12/4/1890, Sigel, Pa. d: 12/31/80, Syracuse, N.Y. BR/TR, 5'11", 168 lbs. Deb: 7/16/13 MC

YEAR	TM/L	W	L	PCT	G	GS	CG	SH	SV	IP	H	HR	BB	SO	RAT	ERA	ERA+	OAV	OOB	BH	AVG	PB	PR	/A	PD	TPI
1913	Phi-A	6	5	.545	18	15	8	1	0	111^1	92	2	50	52	11.7	2.34	118	.207	.291	6	.136	-2	7	5	1	0.4

YEAR	TM/L	W	L	PCT	G	GS	CG	SH	SV	IP	H	HR	BB	SO	RAT	ERA	ERA+	OAV	OOB	BH	AVG	PB	PR	/A	PD	TPI
1914	*Phi-A	15	8	.652	38	31	18	5	2	237	223	4	75	89	11.4	2.73	96	.262	.323	17	.205	2	0	-3	-2	-0.3
1915	Phi-A	6	6	.500	17	13	7	1	0	100	103	3	38	56	12.8	4.05	72	.278	.346	4	.129	-1	-12	-12	0	-1.4
	NY-A	4	7	.364	16	9	5	1	0	85^2	78	2	35	31	12.1	3.26	90	.265	.347	7	.241	1	-3	-3	-1	-0.3
	Yr	10	13	.435	33	22	12	2	0	185^2	181	5	73	87	12.4	3.68	80	.272	.345	11	.183	1	-15	-16	-1	-1.7
1916	NY-A	24	14	.632	53	27	21	4	**8**	276^2	204	4	81	122	9.5	2.21	131	.209	.273	17	.183	-1	19	21	0	2.9
1917	NY-A	13	15	.464	32	26	16	2	0	236^1	207	2	72	97	10.9	2.44	110	.243	.306	16	.190	-0	6	7	3	1.1
1918	NY-A	1	1	.500	3	2	1	1	0	16	7	0	10	3	9.6	1.13	251	.143	.288	3	.750	2	3	3	0	0.7
1919	NY-A	20	11	.645	41	27	22	3	**5**	261^1	218	7	92	122	10.8	2.72	117	.231	.303	22	.234	-0	15	14	-1	1.5
1920	NY-A	20	13	.606	38	31	20	5	2	267^2	246	10	85	126	11.2	**2.45**	**156**	.248	.308	23	.230	-0	40	41	-3	4.3
1921	*NY-A	18	12	.600	38	31	18	3	2	245	245	15	86	126	12.4	4.08	104	.263	.329	27	.300	4	6	4	-4	0.4
1922	*NY-A	20	12	.625	39	34	22	3	1	299^2	286	16	98	130	11.5	2.91	138	.256	.316	21	.183	-3	38	36	-0	3.2
1923	*NY-A	16	11	.593	36	31	17	1	1	258^2	232	17	102	125	11.8	3.51	112	**.246**	.322	20	.202	-3	14	12	-1	0.8
1924	NY-A	16	11	.593	38	25	10	1	0	207^2	226	11	74	114	13.1	4.12	101	.286	.350	22	.319	8	3	1	-1	0.7
1925	NY-A	6	14	.300	33	19	9	1	0	186	209	12	67	81	13.6	4.11	104	.294	.359	10	.147	-4	6	3	-1	-0.2
1926	*NY-A	8	7	.533	29	10	3	1	3	104^1	102	8	37	63	12.2	3.62	106	.263	.330	9	.257	2	5	3	-0	0.5
1927	NY-A	2	3	.400	19	2	0	0	4	43^2	44	1	16	23	12.6	2.89	134	.262	.330	1	.091	-1	6	5	0	0.5
Total	15	195	150	.565	488	333	197	33	28	2937	2722	114	1018	1360	11.6	3.09	114	.251	.319	225	.214	4	151	136	-10	14.8

● SPEC SHEA

Shea, Francis Joseph "The Naugatuck Nugget" (b: Francis Joseph O'shea) b: 10/2/20, Naugatuck, Conn. BR/TR, 6', 195 lbs. Deb: 4/19/47

YEAR	TM/L	W	L	PCT	G	GS	CG	SH	SV	IP	H	HR	BB	SO	RAT	ERA	ERA+	OAV	OOB	BH	AVG	PB	PR	/A	PD	TPI
1947	*NY-A★	14	5	.737	27	23	13	3	1	178^2	127	10	89	89	11.1	3.07	115	**.200**	.303	11	.196	2	13	9	-3	0.8
1948	NY-A	9	10	.474	28	22	8	3	1	155^2	117	10	87	71	11.9	3.41	120	**.208**	.316	7	.149	1	15	12	-2	1.1
1949	NY-A	1	1	.500	20	3	0	0	1	52^1	48	5	43	22	15.6	5.33	76	.250	.387	3	.250	1	-7	-7	-0	-0.2
1951	NY-A	5	5	.500	25	11	2	2	0	95^2	112	11	50	38	15.6	4.33	88	.300	.389	6	.214	1	-2	-5	-0	-0.4
1952	Was-A	11	7	.611	22	21	12	2	0	169	144	6	92	65	12.7	2.93	121	.231	.331	15	.238	2	14	12	-1	1.3
1953	Was-A	12	7	.632	23	23	11	1	0	164^2	151	11	75	38	12.6	3.94	99	.244	.329	11	.177	-1	1	-1	-1	-0.3
1954	Was-A	2	9	.182	23	11	1	0	0	71^1	97	9	34	22	16.8	6.18	58	.340	.414	1	.050	-2	-19	-21	1	-2.9
1955	Was-A	2	2	.500	27	4	1	1	2	56^1	53	4	27	16	12.9	3.99	96	.251	.339	4	.400	2	-0	-1	-1	0.0
Total	8	56	46	.549	195	118	48	12	5	943^2	849	66	497	361	13.0	3.80	99	.243	.340	58	.195	6	14	-3	-8	-0.6

● JOHN SHEA

Shea, John Michael Joseph "Lefty" b: 12/27/04, Everett, Mass. d: 11/30/56, Malden, Mass. BL/TL, 5'10.5", 171 lbs. Deb: 6/30/28

YEAR	TM/L	W	L	PCT	G	GS	CG	SH	SV	IP	H	HR	BB	SO	RAT	ERA	ERA+	OAV	OOB	BH	AVG	PB	PR	/A	PD	TPI
1928	Bos-A	0	0	—	1	0	0	0	0	1	1	0	1	0	18.0	18.00	23	.250	.400	0	—	0	-2	-2	0	0.0

● MIKE SHEA

Shea, Michael Joseph b: 3/10/1867, New Orleans, La. d: 8/22/27, New Orleans, La. TR, 5'10", 170 lbs. Deb: 4/20/1887

YEAR	TM/L	W	L	PCT	G	GS	CG	SH	SV	IP	H	HR	BB	SO	RAT	ERA	ERA+	OAV	OOB	BH	AVG	PB	PR	/A	PD	TPI
1887	Cin-a	1	1	.500	2	2	2	0	0	16^2	26	0	10	0	19.4	7.02	62	.333	.409	2	.250	0	-5	-5	1	-0.3

● RED SHEA

Shea, Patrick Henry b: 11/29/1898, Ware, Mass. d: 11/17/81, Stafford Springs, Conn. BR/TR, 6', 165 lbs. Deb: 5/6/18

YEAR	TM/L	W	L	PCT	G	GS	CG	SH	SV	IP	H	HR	BB	SO	RAT	ERA	ERA+	OAV	OOB	BH	AVG	PB	PR	/A	PD	TPI
1918	Phi-A	0	0	—	3	0	0	0	0	9	14	0	2	2	16.0	4.00	73	.378	.410	0	.000	-0	-1	-1	-0	-0.1
1921	NY-N	5	2	.714	9	2	1	0	0	32	28	2	2	10	9.3	3.09	119	.239	.270	1	.111	-1	2	2	-1	0.3
1922	NY-N	0	3	.000	11	2	0	0	0	23	22	2	11	5	12.9	4.70	85	.256	.340	0	.000	-1	-2	-2	1	-0.2
Total	3	5	5	.500	23	4	1	0	0	64	64	4	15	17	11.5	3.80	97	.267	.318	1	.053	-2	-0	-1	-0	0.0

● STEVE SHEA

Shea, Steven Francis b: 12/5/42, Worcester, Mass. BR/TR, 6'3", 215 lbs. Deb: 7/14/68

YEAR	TM/L	W	L	PCT	G	GS	CG	SH	SV	IP	H	HR	BB	SO	RAT	ERA	ERA+	OAV	OOB	BH	AVG	PB	PR	/A	PD	TPI
1968	Hou-N	4	4	.500	30	0	0	0	6	34^2	27	0	11	15	10.6	3.38	88	.229	.311	0	.000	-1	-2	-2	1	-0.4
1969	Mon-N	0	0	—	10	0	0	0	0	15^2	18	2	8	11	14.9	2.87	128	.300	.382	0	—	0	1	1	0	0.0
Total	2	4	4	.500	40	0	0	0	6	50^1	45	2	19	26	12.0	3.22	99	.253	.335	0	.000	-1	-0	-0	1	-0.4

● AL SHEALY

Shealy, Albert Berley b: 3/20/1900, Chapin, S.C. d: 3/7/67, Hagerstown, Md. BR/TR, 5'11", 175 lbs. Deb: 4/13/28

YEAR	TM/L	W	L	PCT	G	GS	CG	SH	SV	IP	H	HR	BB	SO	RAT	ERA	ERA+	OAV	OOB	BH	AVG	PB	PR	/A	PD	TPI
1928	NY-A	8	6	.571	23	12	3	0	2	96	124	4	42	39	15.7	5.06	74	.308	.375	9	.237	2	-11	-14	0	-1.6
1930	Chi-N	0	0	—	24	0	0	0	0	27	37	2	14	14	17.0	8.00	61	.327	.402	3	.600	1	-9	-9	-0	0.1
Total	2	8	6	.571	47	12	3	0	2	123	161	6	56	53	16.0	5.71	70	.313	.381	12	.279	4	-20	-23	-0	-1.5

● JOHN SHEARON

Shearon, John M. b: 1870, Pittsburgh, Pa. d: 2/1/23, Bradford, Pa. Deb: 7/28/1891 ♦

YEAR	TM/L	W	L	PCT	G	GS	CG	SH	SV	IP	H	HR	BB	SO	RAT	ERA	ERA+	OAV	OOB	BH	AVG	PB	PR	/A	PD	TPI
1891	Cle-N	1	3	.250	6	5	4	0	0	46	57	2	24	19	16.0	3.52	98	.292	.373	30	.242	-0	-1	-0	-0	0.0

● GEORGE SHEARS

Shears, George Penfield b: 4/13/1890, Marshall, Mo. d: 11/12/78, Loveland, Colo. BR/TL, 6'3", 180 lbs. Deb: 4/24/12

YEAR	TM/L	W	L	PCT	G	GS	CG	SH	SV	IP	H	HR	BB	SO	RAT	ERA	ERA+	OAV	OOB	BH	AVG	PB	PR	/A	PD	TPI
1912	NY-A	0	0	—	4	0	0	0	0	15	24	1	11	9	21.0	5.40	67	.364	.455	1	.167	0	-3	-3	0	0.0

● TOM SHEEHAN

Sheehan, Thomas Clancy b: 3/31/1894, Grand Ridge, Ill. d: 10/29/82, Chillicothe, Ohio BR/TR, 6'2.5", 190 lbs. Deb: 7/14/15 MC

YEAR	TM/L	W	L	PCT	G	GS	CG	SH	SV	IP	H	HR	BB	SO	RAT	ERA	ERA+	OAV	OOB	BH	AVG	PB	PR	/A	PD	TPI
1915	Phi-A	4	9	.308	15	13	8	1	0	102	131	1	38	22	15.0	4.15	71	.335	.395	4	.118	-3	-14	-14	-1	-1.9
1916	Phi-A	1	16	.059	38	17	8	0	0	188	197	2	94	54	14.0	3.69	78	.287	.374	7	.125	-2	-18	-17	3	-1.4
1921	NY-A	1	0	1.000	12	1	0	0	1	33	43	1	19	7	17.2	5.45	78	.326	.414	5	.625	2	-4	-4	2	0.2
1924	Cin-N	9	11	.450	39	14	8	2	1	166^2	170	5	54	52	12.1	3.24	116	.269	.328	18	.310	4	12	10	-2	1.2
1925	Cin-N	1	0	1.000	10	3	1	0	1	29	37	3	12	5	15.2	8.07	51	.298	.360	1	.200	1	-12	-13	-1	-0.4
	Pit-N	1	1	.500	23	0	0	0	2	57^1	63	2	13	13	11.9	2.67	167	.286	.326	3	.150	-1	10	11	-0	0.3
	Yr	2	1	.667	33	3	1	0	3	86^1	100	5	25	18	13.0	4.48	97	.291	.339	4	.160	-0	-2	-1	-1	-0.1
1926	Pit-N	0	2	.000	9	2	1	0	0	31	36	0	12	16	14.5	6.68	59	.298	.370	1	.111	-1	-10	-9	-0	-0.6
Total	6	17	39	.304	146	50	26	3	5	607	677	14	242	169	13.7	4.00	86	.294	.362	39	.205	0	-36	-36	1	-2.6

● ROLLIE SHELDON

Sheldon, Roland Frank b: 12/17/36, Putnam, Conn. BR/TR, 6'4", 190 lbs. Deb: 4/23/61

YEAR	TM/L	W	L	PCT	G	GS	CG	SH	SV	IP	H	HR	BB	SO	RAT	ERA	ERA+	OAV	OOB	BH	AVG	PB	PR	/A	PD	TPI
1961	NY-A	11	5	.688	35	21	6	2	0	162^2	149	17	55	84	11.4	3.60	103	.246	.311	7	.125	-2	8	2	1	0.1
1962	NY-A	7	8	.467	34	16	2	0	1	118	136	12	28	54	12.6	5.49	68	.289	.331	2	.077	0	-20	-23	-2	-2.7
1964	*NY-A	5	2	.714	19	12	3	0	1	102^1	92	18	18	57	9.8	3.61	100	.243	.279	3	.088	-2	0	0	1	-0.1
1965	NY-A	0	0	—	3	0	0	0	0	6^1	5	0	1	7	8.5	1.42	240	.238	.273	0	.000	-0	1	1	0	0.0
	KC-A	10	8	.556	32	29	4	1	0	186^2	180	22	56	105	11.7	3.95	88	.251	.312	4	.078	-3	-10	-10	-1	-1.2
	Yr	10	8	.556	35	29	4	1	0	193	185	22	57	112	11.6	3.87	90	.251	.310	4	.077	-3	-9	-8	0	-1.2
1966	KC-A	4	7	.364	14	13	1	1	0	69	73	3	26	26	13.0	3.13	109	.275	.342	2	.087	-1	2	2	0	0.2
	Bos-A	1	6	.143	23	10	1	0	0	79^2	106	15	23	38	14.8	4.97	77	.320	.368	2	.111	-1	-14	-10	-1	-0.9
	Yr	5	13	.278	37	23	2	1	0	148^2	179	18	49	64	13.9	4.12	88	.297	.352	4	.098	-2	-11	-8	1	-0.7
Total	5	38	36	.514	160	101	17	4	2	724^2	741	87	207	371	11.9	4.09	89	.266	.320	20	.096	-9	-32	-36	0	-4.6

● FRANK SHELLENBACK

Shellenback, Frank Victor b: 12/16/1898, Joplin, Mo. d: 8/17/69, Newton, Mass. BR/TR, 6'2", 192 lbs. Deb: 5/8/18 C

YEAR	TM/L	W	L	PCT	G	GS	CG	SH	SV	IP	H	HR	BB	SO	RAT	ERA	ERA+	OAV	OOB	BH	AVG	PB	PR	/A	PD	TPI
1918	Chi-A	9	12	.429	28	21	10	2	2	182^2	180	1	74	47	12.7	2.66	103	.262	.338	7	.130	-1	2	2	-5	-0.5
1919	Chi-A	1	3	.250	8	4	2	0	0	35	40	1	16	10	14.4	5.14	62	.303	.378	1	.091	-0	-7	-8	-0	-0.8
Total	2	10	15	.400	36	25	12	2	2	217^2	220	2	90	57	13.0	3.06	92	.269	.344	8	.123	-1	-5	-6	-5	-1.3

● JIM SHELLENBACK

Shellenback, James Philip b: 11/18/43, Riverside, Cal. BL/TL, 6'2", 200 lbs. Deb: 9/15/66 C

YEAR	TM/L	W	L	PCT	G	GS	CG	SH	SV	IP	H	HR	BB	SO	RAT	ERA	ERA+	OAV	OOB	BH	AVG	PB	PR	/A	PD	TPI
1966	Pit-N	0	0	—	2	0	0	0	0	3	3	2	3	0	18.0	9.00	40	.300	.462	0	—	0	-2	-2	0	0.0
1967	Pit-N	1	1	.500	6	2	1	0	0	23^1	23	1	12	11	13.9	2.70	125	.250	.343	1	.167	0	2	2	-0	0.1
1969	Pit-N	0	0	—	8	0	0	0	0	16^2	14	1	4	7	9.7	3.24	108	.233	.281	0	.000	-0	1	0	1	0.1
	Was-A	4	7	.364	30	11	2	0	1	84^2	87	8	48	50	14.5	4.04	86	.268	.364	5	.185	-0	-4	-5	2	-0.5
1970	Was-A	6	7	.462	39	14	2	1	0	117^1	107	6	51	57	12.1	3.68	97	.246	.325	2	.067	-2	0	-2	-1	-0.4
1971	Was-A	3	11	.214	40	15	3	1	0	120	123	10	49	47	13.1	3.53	94	.267	.342	5	.167	0	-1	-3	-1	-0.2
1972	Tex-A	2	4	.333	22	6	0	0	1	57	46	6	16	30	10.1	3.47	87	.221	.283	1	.100	-0	-3	-3	-1	-0.4
1973	Tex-A	0	0	—	2	0	0	0	0	1^2	0	0	0	3	0.0	0.00	—	.000	.000	0	—	0	1	1	0	0.1
1974	Tex-A	0	0	—	11	0	0	0	0	24^2	30	5	12	14	15.7	5.84	61	.306	.387	0	—	0	-6	-6	0	-0.8
1977	Min-A	0	0	—	5	0	0	0	0	5^2	10	1	5	3	23.8	7.94	50	.385	.484	0	—	0	-2	-2	0	0.0
Total	9	16	30	.348	165	48	8	2	2	454	443	40	200	222	12.9	3.81	89	.258	.338	14	.135	-2	-14	-21	3	-1.2

● BERT SHEPARD

Shepard, Bert Robert b: 6/28/20, Dana, Ind. BL/TL, 5'11", 185 lbs. Deb: 8/4/45

YEAR	TM/L	W	L	PCT	G	GS	CG	SH	SV	IP	H	HR	BB	SO	RAT	ERA	ERA+	OAV	OOB	BH	AVG	PB	PR	/A	PD	TPI
1945	Was-A	0	0	—	1	0	0	0	0	5^1	3	0	1	2	8.4	1.69	184	.167	.250	0	.000	-0	1	1	0	0.0

● KEITH SHEPHERD Shepherd, Keith Wayne b: 1/21/68, Wabash, Ind. BR/TR, 6'2", 205 lbs. Deb: 9/6/92

YEAR	TM/L	W	L	PCT	G	GS	CG	SH	SV	IP	H	HR	BB	SO	RAT	ERA	ERA+	OAV	OOB	BH	AVG	PB	PR	/A	PD	TPI
1992	Phi-N	1	1	.500	12	0	0	0	2	22	19	0	6	10	10.2	3.27	107	.244	.298	0	—	0	1	1	0	0.1
1993	Col-N	1	3	.250	14	1	0	0	1	19^1	26	4	4	7	14.4	6.98	68	.333	.373	0	.000	-0	-6	-5	-0	-0.9
1995	Bos-A	0	0	—	2	0	0	0	0	1	4	0	2	0	54.0	36.00	14	.571	.667	0	—	0	-3	-3	0	-0.2
1996	Bal-A	0	1	.000	13	0	0	0	0	20^2	31	6	18	17	21.3	8.71	57	.341	.450	0	—	0	-9	-9	-0	-0.3
Total	4	2	5	.286	41	1	0	0	3	63	80	10	30	34	15.9	6.71	65	.315	.389	0	.000	-0	-18	-16	0	-1.3

● BILL SHERDEL Sherdel, William Henry "Wee Willie" b: 8/15/1896, McSherrystown, Pa d: 11/14/68, McSherrystown, Pa BL/TL, 5'10", 160 lbs. Deb: 4/22/18

YEAR	TM/L	W	L	PCT	G	GS	CG	SH	SV	IP	H	HR	BB	SO	RAT	ERA	ERA+	OAV	OOB	BH	AVG	PB	PR	/A	PD	TPI
1918	StL-N	6	12	.333	35	16	9	1	0	182^1	174	3	49	40	11.2	2.71	100	.259	.313	15	.242	3	1	-0	-2	0.2
1919	StL-N	5	9	.357	36	11	7	0	1	137^1	137	3	42	52	11.9	3.47	80	.270	.328	13	.271	2	-9	-10	1	-0.7
1920	StL-N	11	10	.524	43	7	4	0	**6**	170	183	1	40	74	12.4	3.28	91	.297	.350	14	.222	2	-3	-6	1	-0.4
1921	StL-N	9	8	.529	38	8	5	1	1	144^1	137	7	38	57	11.1	3.18	115	.247	.299	5	.114	-2	10	8	1	0.6
1922	StL-N	17	13	.567	47	31	15	3	2	242	298	12	62	79	13.6	3.87	100	.303	.348	17	.193	1	6	-0	-3	-0.3
1923	StL-N	15	13	.536	39	26	14	0	2	225	270	15	59	78	13.4	4.32	90	.296	.343	28	.337	9	-8	-10	-3	-0.6
1924	StL-N	8	9	.471	35	10	6	0	1	168^2	188	9	38	57	12.3	3.42	111	.291	.335	15	.200	2	8	7	-2	0.7
1925	StL-N	15	6	**.714**	32	21	17	2	1	200	216	8	42	53	11.7	3.11	139	.277	.316	15	.205	2	26	27	-1	2.6
1926	*StL-N	16	12	.571	34	29	17	3	0	234^2	255	15	49	59	11.9	3.49	112	.278	.318	22	.244	2	9	11	-3	1.1
1927	StL-N	17	12	.586	39	28	18	0	**6**	232^1	241	17	48	59	11.3	3.53	112	.269	.308	14	.194	1	10	11	-4	1.0
1928	*StL-N	21	10	.677	38	27	20	0	**5**	248^2	251	17	56	72	11.2	2.86	140	.261	.303	19	.226	4	31	32	-5	3.7
1929	StL-N	10	15	.400	33	22	11	1	0	195^2	278	14	58	69	15.5	5.93	79	.337	.382	16	.229	2	-26	-28	-2	-2.8
1930	StL-N	3	2	.600	13	7	1	0	0	64	86	5	13	29	14.1	4.64	108	.325	.358	2	.105	-1	2	3	-1	0.0
	Bos-N	6	5	.545	21	14	7	0	1	119^1	131	10	30	26	12.3	4.75	104	.283	.329	4	.095	-4	3	2	-1	-0.2
	Yr	9	7	.563	34	21	8	0	1	183^1	217	15	43	55	12.9	4.71	105	.298	.339	6	.098	-5	5	5	-1	-0.2
1931	Bos-N	6	10	.375	27	16	8	0	0	137^2	163	13	35	34	13.0	4.25	89	.294	.337	14	.304	4	-6	-7	-2	-0.6
1932	Bos-N	0	0	—	1	0	0	0	0	1^2	3	0	1	0	21.6	0.00	—	.375	.444	0	—	0	1	1	-0	0.0
	StL-N	0	0	—	3	0	0	0	0	5^2	7	0	1	1	12.7	4.76	83	.304	.333	1	1.000	1	-1	-1	0	0.1
	Yr	0	0	—	4	0	0	0	0	7^1	10	0	2	1	14.7	3.68	106	.323	.364	1	1.000	1	0	0	0	0.1
Total	15	165	146	.531	514	273	159	11	26	2709^1	3018	149	661	839	12.4	3.72	103	.285	.330	214	.223	27	55	38	-25	4.4

● ROY SHERID Sherid, Royden Richard b: 1/25/07, Norristown, Pa. d: 2/28/82, Parker Ford, Pa. BR/TR, 6'2", 185 lbs. Deb: 5/11/29

YEAR	TM/L	W	L	PCT	G	GS	CG	SH	SV	IP	H	HR	BB	SO	RAT	ERA	ERA+	OAV	OOB	BH	AVG	PB	PR	/A	PD	TPI
1929	NY-A	6	6	.500	33	15	9	0	1	154^2	165	6	55	51	13.1	3.61	107	.277	.343	9	.180	-1	11	4	-1	0.2
1930	NY-A	12	13	.480	37	21	8	0	4	184	214	13	87	59	15.0	5.23	82	.289	.368	7	.101	-6	-12	-19	-1	-2.7
1931	NY-A	5	5	.500	17	8	3	0	2	74^1	94	4	24	39	14.7	5.69	70	.306	.362	10	.333	2	-11	-14	0	-1.4
Total	3	23	24	.489	87	44	20	0	7	413	473	23	166	149	14.2	4.71	87	.288	.358	26	.174	-4	-12	-29	-2	-3.9

● JOE SHERMAN Sherman, Joel Powers b: 11/4/1890, Yarmouth, Mass. d: 12/21/87, Cape Coral, Fla. BR/TR, 6', 165 lbs. Deb: 9/24/15

YEAR	TM/L	W	L	PCT	G	GS	CG	SH	SV	IP	H	HR	BB	SO	RAT	ERA	ERA+	OAV	OOB	BH	AVG	PB	PR	/A	PD	TPI
1915	Phi-A	1	0	1.000	2	1	1	0	0	15	15	0	1	5	10.8	2.40	122	.259	.295	2	.333	1	1	1	-0	0.0

● DAN SHERMAN Sherman, Lester Daniel "Babe" b: 5/9/1890, Hubbardsville, N.Y. d: 9/16/55, Highland Park, Mich. BR/TR, 5'6", 145 lbs. Deb: 6/4/14

YEAR	TM/L	W	L	PCT	G	GS	CG	SH	SV	IP	H	HR	BB	SO	RAT	ERA	ERA+	OAV	OOB	BH	AVG	PB	PR	/A	PD	TPI
1914	Chi-F	0	1	.000	1	1	0	0	0	0^1	0	0	2	0	54.0	0.00	—	.000	.667	0	—	0	0	0	0	0.3

● TIM SHERRILL Sherrill, Timothy Shawn b: 9/10/65, Harrison, Ark. BL/TL, 5'11", 170 lbs. Deb: 8/14/90

YEAR	TM/L	W	L	PCT	G	GS	CG	SH	SV	IP	H	HR	BB	SO	RAT	ERA	ERA+	OAV	OOB	BH	AVG	PB	PR	/A	PD	TPI
1990	StL-N	0	0	—	8	0	0	0	0	4^1	10	0	3	3	27.0	6.23	61	.476	.542	0	—	0	-1	-1	0	0.0
1991	StL-N	0	0	—	10	0	0	0	0	14^1	20	2	3	4	15.7	8.16	46	.339	.391	0	—	0	-7	-7	0	0.0
Total	2	0	0	—	18	0	0	0	0	18^2	30	2	6	7	18.3	7.71	48	.375	.432	0	—	0	-8	-8	0	0.0

● FRED SHERRY Sherry, Fred Peter (b: Fred Peter Schuerholz) b: 1/13/1889, Honesdale, Pa. d: 7/27/75, Honesdale, Pa. BR/TR, 6', 170 lbs. Deb: 4/25/11

YEAR	TM/L	W	L	PCT	G	GS	CG	SH	SV	IP	H	HR	BB	SO	RAT	ERA	ERA+	OAV	OOB	BH	AVG	PB	PR	/A	PD	TPI
1911	Was-A	0	4	.000	10	3	2	0	0	52^1	63	1	19	20	14.1	4.30	76	.310	.369	3	.158	-0	-6	-6	0	-0.4

● LARRY SHERRY Sherry, Lawrence b: 7/25/35, Los Angeles, Cal. BR/TR, 6'2", 204 lbs. Deb: 4/17/58 FC

YEAR	TM/L	W	L	PCT	G	GS	CG	SH	SV	IP	H	HR	BB	SO	RAT	ERA	ERA+	OAV	OOB	BH	AVG	PB	PR	/A	PD	TPI
1958	LA-N	0	0	—	5	0	0	0	0	4^1	10	0	7	2	37.4	12.46	33	.476	.621	0	—	0	-4	-4	0	0.0
1959	*LA-N	7	2	.778	23	9	1	1	3	94^1	75	9	43	72	11.4	2.19	193	.218	.308	7	.219	2	18	21	-1	2.2
1960	LA-N	14	10	.583	57	3	1	0	7	142^1	125	14	82	114	13.5	3.79	105	.238	.347	6	.162	1	-1	3	1	0.6
1961	LA-N	4	4	.500	53	1	0	0	15	94^2	90	10	39	79	12.6	3.90	111	.252	.333	2	.154	-0	1	5	-2	0.3
1962	LA-N	7	3	.700	58	0	0	0	11	90	81	8	44	71	13.1	3.20	113	.241	.339	2	.118	-0	7	4	-0	0.5
1963	LA-N	2	6	.250	36	3	0	0	3	79^2	82	8	24	47	12.4	3.73	81	.265	.325	1	.111	1	-4	-6	-0	-0.6
1964	Det-A	7	5	.583	38	0	0	0	11	66^1	52	7	37	58	12.5	3.66	100	.216	.327	0	.000	-2	-0	-0	-0	-0.2
1965	Det-A	3	6	.333	39	0	0	0	5	78^1	71	5	40	46	12.9	3.10	112	.254	.349	3	.300	2	3	3	0	0.6
1966	Det-A	8	5	.615	55	0	0	0	20	77^2	66	8	36	63	12.2	3.82	91	.232	.325	4	.400	2	-3	-3	-1	-0.5
1967	Det-A	0	1	.000	20	0	0	0	1	28	35	3	7	20	13.8	6.43	51	.289	.333	0	.000	-0	-10	-10	0	-0.4
	Hou-N	1	2	.333	29	0	0	0	6	40^2	53	4	13	32	14.8	4.87	68	.327	.381	0	.000	-1	-7	-7	1	-0.7
1968	Cal-A	0	0	—	3	0	0	0	0	3	7	2	2	2	27.0	6.00	49	.467	.529	0	—	0	-1	-1	-0	0.0
Total	11	53	44	.546	416	16	2	1	82	799^1	747	78	374	606	13.0	3.67	101	.249	.339	25	.169	4	0	5	-2	1.8

● BEN SHIELDS Shields, Benjamin Cowan "Big Ben" or "Lefty" b: 6/17/03, Huntersville, N.C d: 1/24/82, Woodruff, S.C. BR/TL, 6'1.5", 195 lbs. Deb: 4/17/24

YEAR	TM/L	W	L	PCT	G	GS	CG	SH	SV	IP	H	HR	BB	SO	RAT	ERA	ERA+	OAV	OOB	BH	AVG	PB	PR	/A	PD	TPI
1924	NY-A	0	0	—	2	0	0	0	0	2	6	0	2	3	36.0	27.00	15	.545	.615	0	—	0	-5	-5	-0	0.0
1925	NY-A	3	0	1.000	4	2	2	0	0	24	24	2	12	5	14.3	4.88	87	.267	.365	1	.125	-1	-1	-2	-1	-0.3
1930	Bos-A	0	0	—	3	0	0	0	0	10	16	0	6	1	19.8	9.00	51	.400	.478	0	.000	-1	-5	-5	0	0.0
1931	Phi-N	1	0	1.000	4	0	0	0	0	5^1	9	1	7	0	27.0	15.19	28	.391	.533	0	.000	-0	-7	-6	-0	-1.0
Total	4	4	0	1.000	13	2	2	0	0	41^1	55	3	27	9	18.3	8.27	53	.335	.435	1	.077	-2	-18	-18	-1	-1.3

● CHARLIE SHIELDS Shields, Charles Jessamine b: 12/10/1879, Jackson, Tenn. d: 8/27/53, Memphis, Tenn. BL/TL, Deb: 4/23/02

YEAR	TM/L	W	L	PCT	G	GS	CG	SH	SV	IP	H	HR	BB	SO	RAT	ERA	ERA+	OAV	OOB	BH	AVG	PB	PR	/A	PD	TPI
1902	Bal-A	4	11	.267	23	15	10	1	1	142^1	201	7	32	28	14.9	4.24	89	.333	.368	8	.167	-1	-10	-7	-4	-1.1
	StL-A	3	0	1.000	4	4	3	0	0	30	37	1	7	6	13.2	3.30	107	.303	.341	6	.462	2	1	1	-1	0.3
	Yr	7	11	.389	27	19	13	1	1	172^1	238	8	39	34	14.5	4.07	92	.327	.361	14	.230	1	-10	-7	-5	-0.8
1907	StL-N	0	2	.000	3	2	0	0	0	6^2	12	0	7	1	28.4	9.45	26	.444	.583	0	.000	-0	-5	-5	0	-1.2
Total	2	7	13	.350	30	21	13	1	1	179	250	8	46	35	15.1	4.27	86	.332	.374	14	.222	1	-15	-12	-4	-2.0

● STEVE SHIELDS Shields, Stephen Mack b: 11/30/58, Gadsden, Ala. BR/TR, 6'5", 230 lbs. Deb: 6/1/85

YEAR	TM/L	W	L	PCT	G	GS	CG	SH	SV	IP	H	HR	BB	SO	RAT	ERA	ERA+	OAV	OOB	BH	AVG	PB	PR	/A	PD	TPI
1985	Atl-N	1	2	.333	23	6	0	0	0	68	86	9	32	29	15.8	5.16	75	.320	.394	2	.111	-1	-12	-10	-1	-0.6
1986	Atl-N	0	0	—	6	0	0	0	0	12^2	13	4	7	6	14.2	7.11	56	.271	.364	0	.000	-0	-5	-4	-0	0.0
	KC-A	0	0	—	3	0	0	0	0	8^2	3	1	4	2	7.3	2.08	205	.111	.226	0	—	0	2	2	-0	-0.1
1987	Sea-A	2	0	1.000	20	0	0	0	3	30	43	7	12	22	16.5	6.60	71	.333	.390	0	—	0	-7	-6	0	-0.8
1988	NY-A	5	5	.500	39	0	0	0	0	82^1	96	8	30	55	14.0	4.37	90	.298	.362	0	—	0	-4	-4	0	-0.4
1989	Min-A	0	1	.000	11	0	0	0	0	17^1	28	3	6	12	17.7	7.79	53	.354	.400	0	—	0	-8	-7	0	-0.5
Total	5	8	8	.500	102	6	0	0	3	219	269	32	91	126	14.9	5.26	77	.308	.375	2	.105	-1	-33	-29	-1	-2.4

● VINCE SHIELDS Shields, Vincent William
b: 11/18/1900, Fredericton, N.B., Canada d: 10/17/52, Plaster Rock, N.B., Canada BL/TR, 5'11", 185 lbs. Deb: 9/20/24

YEAR	TM/L	W	L	PCT	G	GS	CG	SH	SV	IP	H	HR	BB	SO	RAT	ERA	ERA+	OAV	OOB	BH	AVG	PB	PR	/A	PD	TPI
1924	StL-N	1	1	.500	2	1	0	0	0	12	10	1	3	4	12.0	3.00	126	.227	.320	2	.400	0	1	1	-1	0.2

● GARLAND SHIFFLETT Shifflett, Garland Jessie "Duck" b: 3/28/35, Elkton, Va. BR/TR, 5'10.5", 165 lbs. Deb: 4/22/57

YEAR	TM/L	W	L	PCT	G	GS	CG	SH	SV	IP	H	HR	BB	SO	RAT	ERA	ERA+	OAV	OOB	BH	AVG	PB	PR	/A	PD	TPI
1957	Was-A	0	0	—	6	1	0	0	0	8	6	0	10	2	18.0	10.13	38	.222	.432	0	—	0	-6	-6	-0	0.0
1964	Min-A	0	2	.000	10	0	0	0	1	17^2	22	1	7	8	15.3	4.58	78	.297	.366	0	.000	-0	-2	-2	0	-0.2
Total	2	0	2	.000	16	1	0	0	1	25^2	28	1	17	10	16.1	6.31	58	.277	.387	0	.000	-0	-8	-8	0	-0.2

● STEVE SHIFFLETT Shifflett, Stephen Earl b: 1/5/66, Kansas City, Mo. BR/TR, 6'1", 205 lbs. Deb: 7/3/92

YEAR	TM/L	W	L	PCT	G	GS	CG	SH	SV	IP	H	HR	BB	SO	RAT	ERA	ERA+	OAV	OOB	BH	AVG	PB	PR	/A	PD	TPI
1992	KC-A	1	4	.200	34	0	0	0	0	52	55	6	17	25	12.8	2.60	156	.279	.343	0	—	0	8	8	0	0.8

● ZAK SHINALL Shinall, Zakary Sebastien b: 10/14/68, St.Louis, Mo. BR/TR, 6'3", 215 lbs. Deb: 5/12/93

YEAR	TM/L	W	L	PCT	G	GS	CG	SH	SV	IP	H	HR	BB	SO	RAT	ERA	ERA+	OAV	OOB	BH	AVG	PB	PR	/A	PD	TPI
1993	Sea-A	0	0	—	1	0	0	0	0	2^2	4	1	2	0	20.3	3.38	130	.333	.429	0	—	0	0	0	0	0.0

YEAR	TM/L	W	L	PCT	G	GS	CG	SH	SV	IP	H	HR	BB	SO	RAT	ERA	ERA+	OAV	OOB	BH	AVG	PB	PR	/A	PD	TPI
● RAZOR SHINES	Shines, Anthony Raymond "Ray" b: 7/18/56, Durham, N.C. BB/TR, 6'1", 210 lbs. Deb: 9/9/83 ♦																									
1985	Mon-N	0	0	–	1	0	0	0	0	1	1	0	0	0	9.0	0.00	–	.250	.250	6	.120	-0	0	0	-0	0.0
● DAVE SHIPANOFF	Shipanoff, David Noel b: 11/13/59, Edmonton, Alberta, Can. BR/TR, 6'2", 185 lbs. Deb: 8/9/85																									
1985	Phi-N	1	2	.333	26	0	0	0	3	36^1	33	3	16	26	12.4	3.22	114	.231	.313	0	.000	-0	1	2	-0	0.1
● JOE SHIPLEY	Shipley, Joseph Clark "Moses" b: 5/9/35, Morristown, Tenn. BR/TR, 6'4", 210 lbs. Deb: 7/14/58																									
1958	SF-N	0	0	–	1	0	0	0	0	1^1	3	0	3	0	54.0	33.75	11	.429	.667	0	—	0	-4	-4	-0	0.0
1959	SF-N	0	0	–	10	1	0	0	0	18	16	2	17	11	17.0	4.50	85	.239	.400	0	.000	-0	-1	-1	-0	-0.1
1960	SF-N	0	0	–	15	0	0	0	0	20	20	2	9	9	14.4	5.40	64	.274	.376	0	—	0	-4	-4	1	0.1
1963	Chi-A	0	1	.000	3	0	0	0	0	4^2	9	0	6	3	28.9	5.79	61	.409	.536	0	.000	-0	-1	-1	0	-0.3
Total	4	0	1	.000	29	1	0	0	0	44	48	4	35	23	18.2	5.93	61	.284	.424	0	.000	-1	-10	-11	0	-0.3
● DUKE SHIREY	Shirey, Clair Lee b: 6/20/1898, Jersey Shore, Pa. d: 9/1/62, Hagerstown, Md. BR/TR, 6'1", 175 lbs. Deb: 9/28/20																									
1920	Was-A	0	1	.000	2	1	0	0	0	4	5	0	2	0	18.0	6.75	55	.313	.421	0	.000	-0	-1	-1	-0	-0.3
● TEX SHIRLEY	Shirley, Alvis Newman b: 4/25/18, Birthright, Tex. d: 11/7/93, DeSoto, Tex. BB/TR, 6'1", 175 lbs. Deb: 9/6/41																									
1941	Phi-A	0	1	.000	5	0	0	0	1	7^1	8	1	6	1	17.2	2.45	171	.286	.412	0	.000	-0	1	1	0	0.2
1942	Phi-A	0	1	.000	15	1	0	0	1	35^2	37	0	22	10	15.4	5.30	71	.272	.381	0	.000	-1	-7	-6	-1	-0.4
1944	*StL-A	5	4	.556	23	11	2	1	0	80^1	59	4	64	35	13.9	4.15	87	.203	.348	4	.143	-2	-6	-5	-1	-0.8
1945	StL-A	8	12	.400	32	24	10	2	0	183^2	191	8	93	77	14.0	3.63	97	.274	.360	20	.286	2	-5	-2	-1	-0.1
1946	StL-A	6	12	.333	27	18	7	0	0	139^2	148	7	105	45	16.4	4.96	75	.273	.391	10	.196	-0	-23	-19	-1	-2.3
Total	5	19	30	.388	102	54	19	3	2	446^2	443	20	290	168	14.9	4.25	85	.261	.371	34	.214	-1	-39	-31	-3	-3.4
● BOB SHIRLEY	Shirley, Robert Charles b: 6/25/54, Cushing, Okla. BR/TL, 5'11", 185 lbs. Deb: 4/10/77																									
1977	SD-N	12	18	.400	39	35	1	0	0	214	215	22	100	146	13.4	3.70	96	.259	.341	9	.122	-2	5	-4	1	-0.6
1978	SD-N	8	11	.421	50	20	2	0	5	166	164	10	61	102	12.4	3.69	90	.262	.330	5	.125	-0	-2	-7	2	-0.6
1979	SD-N	8	16	.333	49	25	4	1	0	205	196	15	59	117	11.5	3.38	104	.257	.316	5	.091	-2	8	3	0	0.2
1980	SD-N	11	12	.478	59	12	3	0	7	137	143	12	54	67	12.9	3.55	97	.276	.344	1	.033	-2	-2	-2	-2	-0.3
1981	StL-N	6	4	.600	28	11	1	0	1	79^1	78	6	34	36	12.8	4.08	87	.260	.337	3	.136	-1	-5	-5	-1	-0.8
1982	Cin-N	8	13	.381	41	20	1	0	0	152^2	138	17	73	89	12.6	3.60	103	.248	.338	6	.143	-1	0	2	1	0.2
1983	NY-A	5	8	.385	25	17	1	1	0	108	122	10	36	53	13.2	5.08	77	.293	.350	0	—	0	-12	-14	1	-1.3
1984	NY-A	3	3	.500	41	7	1	0	0	114^1	119	8	38	48	12.4	3.38	112	.274	.333	0	—	0	8	5	0	0.5
1985	NY-A	5	5	.500	48	8	2	0	2	109	103	5	26	55	10.7	2.64	151	.251	.295	0	—	0	18	16	-1	1.4
1986	NY-A	0	4	.000	39	6	0	0	3	105^1	108	13	40	64	12.9	5.04	81	.271	.342	0	—	0	-10	-11	1	-0.3
1987	NY-A	1	0	1.000	12	1	0	0	0	34	36	4	16	12	13.8	4.50	97	.277	.356	0	—	0	-0	-0	-1	0.0
	KC-A	0	0	–	3	0	0	0	0	7^1	10	5	6	1	19.6	14.73	31	.323	.432	0	—	0	-8	-8	-0	-0.2
	Yr	1	0	1.000	15	1	0	0	0	41^1	46	9	22	13	14.8	6.31	70	.275	.360	0	—	0	-9	-9	-1	-0.2
Total	11	67	94	.416	434	162	16	2	18	1432	1432	127	543	790	12.5	3.82	96	.264	.334	29	.110	-8	2	-24	5	-1.8
● STEVE SHIRLEY	Shirley, Steven Brian b: 10/12/56, San Francisco, Cal. BL/TL, 6', 185 lbs. Deb: 6/21/82																									
1982	LA-N	1	1	.500	11	0	0	0	0	12^2	15	0	7	8	15.6	4.26	81	.300	.386	1	1.000	0	-1	-1	-0	-0.1
● GEORGE SHOCH	Shoch, George Quintus b: 1/6/1859, Philadelphia, Pa. d: 9/30/37, Philadelphia, Pa. BR/TR, 5'6", 158 lbs. Deb: 9/10/1886 ♦																									
1888	Was-N	0	0	–	1	0	0	0	0	3	2	0	1	0	9.0	0.00	–	.167	.231	58	.183	0	1	1	-0	0.0
● URBAN SHOCKER	Shocker, Urban James (b: Urbain Jacques Shockcor) b: 8/22/1890, Cleveland, Ohio d: 9/9/28, Denver, Colo. BR/TR, 5'10", 170 lbs. Deb: 4/24/16																									
1916	NY-A	4	3	.571	12	9	4	1	0	82^1	67	2	32	43	11.5	2.62	110	.230	.319	4	.190	1	2	2	-0	0.3
1917	NY-A	8	5	.615	26	13	7	0	1	145	124	4	46	68	10.6	2.61	103	.241	.303	8	.178	-1	1	1	2	0.2
1918	StL-A	6	5	.545	14	9	7	0	2	94^2	69	0	40	33	10.5	1.81	152	.209	.296	11	.324	4	10	10	1	1.8
1919	StL-A	13	11	.542	30	25	14	5	0	211	193	6	55	86	10.7	2.69	123	.244	.296	8	.138	-0	13	15	-1	1.4
1920	StL-A	20	10	.667	38	28	22	5	**5**	245^2	224	10	70	107	10.9	2.71	145	.248	.305	18	.225	2	30	33	-0	4.0
1921	StL-A	**27**	12	.692	47	38	30	4	4	326^2	345	21	86	132	12.0	3.55	126	.270	.319	27	.260	5	26	34	3	4.3
1922	StL-A	24	17	.585	48	38	29	2	3	348	365	22	57	**149**	11.0	2.97	139	.272	.304	22	.191	2	41	45	-3	4.8
1923	StL-A	20	12	.625	43	35	24	3	5	277^1	292	12	49	109	**11.2**	3.41	122	.272	**.306**	16	.200	2	18	24	-3	2.4
1924	StL-A	16	13	.552	40	33	17	4	1	246^1	270	11	52	88	11.9	4.20	107	.277	.315	16	.239	5	1	9	-2	1.2
1925	NY-A	12	12	.500	41	30	15	2	2	244^1	278	17	58	74	12.5	3.65	117	.294	.336	11	.172	5	20	17	-2	1.7
1926	*NY-A	19	11	.633	41	32	18	0	2	258^1	272	13	71	59	12.0	3.38	114	.269	.318	13	.171	1	18	14	-2	1.3
1927	NY-A	18	6	.750	31	27	13	2	0	200	207	8	41	35	11.2	2.84	136	.268	.306	13	.241	3	29	23	-2	2.5
1928	NY-A	0	0	–	1	0	0	0	0	2	3	0	0	0	13.5	0.00	–	.429	.429	0	—	0	1	1	-0	0.0
Total	13	187	117	.615	412	317	200	28	25	2681^2	2709	126	657	983	11.4	3.17	124	.265	.311	167	.209	28	210	226	-9	25.9
● MILT SHOFFNER	Shoffner, Milburn James b: 11/13/05, Sherman, Tex. d: 1/19/78, Madison, Ohio BL/TL, 6'1.5", 184 lbs. Deb: 7/20/29																									
1929	Cle-A	2	3	.400	11	3	1	0	0	44^2	46	4	22	15	14.3	5.04	88	.284	.380	0	.000	-2	-4	-3	-0	-0.5
1930	Cle-A	3	4	.429	24	10	1	0	0	84^2	129	8	50	17	19.1	7.97	61	.362	.442	7	.212	1	-31	-30	-0	-1.8
1931	Cle-A	2	3	.400	12	4	1	0	0	41	55	4	26	12	18.2	7.24	64	.320	.415	1	.077	-1	-13	-12	-0	-1.3
1937	Bos-N	3	1	.750	6	5	3	1	1	42^2	38	1	9	13	10.1	2.53	142	.239	.284	2	.125	1	7	5	1	0.6
1938	Bos-N	8	7	.533	26	15	9	1	1	139^2	147	7	36	49	11.9	3.54	97	.270	.317	12	.211	3	4	-2	-2	-0.1
1939	Bos-N	4	6	.400	25	11	7	0	1	132^1	133	4	42	51	12.0	3.13	118	.265	.324	7	.159	-0	12	8	0	0.6
	Cin-N	2	2	.500	10	3	0	0	0	37^2	43	3	11	6	13.4	3.35	115	.289	.346	1	.091	-1	2	2	-0	0.1
	Yr	6	8	.429	35	14	7	0	1	170	176	7	53	57	12.2	3.18	117	.270	.327	8	.145	-1	14	10	0	0.7
1940	Cin-N	1	0	1.000	20	0	0	0	0	54^1	56	3	18	17	12.3	5.63	67	.268	.326	2	.125	-1	-11	-11	-1	-0.3
Total	7	25	26	.490	134	51	22	2	3	577	647	34	214	180	13.6	4.59	85	.287	.352	32	.156	-0	-35	-43	-2	-2.7
● ERNIE SHORE	Shore, Ernest Grady b: 3/24/1891, East Bend, N.C. d: 9/24/80, Winston-Salem, N.C. BR/TR, 6'4", 220 lbs. Deb: 6/20/12																									
1912	NY-N	0	0	–	1	0	0	0	1	1	8	1	1	1	81.0	27.00	13	.667	.692	0	—	0	-3	-3	-0	-0.5
1914	Bos-A	10	5	.667	20	16	10	1	1	139^2	103	1	34	51	9.2	2.00	135	.204	.261	5	.102	-3	12	11	2	1.1
1915	*Bos-A	19	8	.704	38	32	17	4	0	247	207	3	66	102	10.1	1.64	169	.228	.283	8	.101	-3	36	31	4	3.5
1916	*Bos-A	16	10	.615	38	28	10	3	1	225^2	221	1	49	62	10.9	2.63	105	.259	.302	7	.091	-5	5	3	5	0.4
1917	Bos-A	13	10	.565	29	27	14	1	1	226^2	201	1	55	57	10.6	2.22	116	.240	.297	13	.167	-1	11	9	3	1.1
1919	NY-A	5	8	.385	20	13	3	0	0	95	105	4	44	24	14.2	4.17	77	.288	.366	4	.143	-2	-10	-10	0	-1.4
1920	NY-A	2	2	.500	14	5	2	0	1	44^1	61	1	21	12	16.8	4.87	78	.333	.405	2	.182	0	-5	-5	1	-0.4
Total	7	65	43	.602	160	121	56	9	5	979^1	906	12	270	309	11.1	2.47	113	.247	.304	39	.121	-14	45	36	14	3.8
● RAY SHORE	Shore, Raymond Everett b: 6/9/21, Cincinnati, Ohio d: 8/13/96, St.Louis, Mo. BR/TR, 6'3", 210 lbs. Deb: 9/21/46 C																									
1946	StL-A	0	0	–	1	0	0	0	0	1	3	0	1	1	36.0	18.00	21	.500	.571	0	—	0	-2	-2	0	0.0
1948	StL-A	1	2	.333	17	4	0	0	0	38	40	2	35	12	18.7	6.39	71	.270	.422	0	.000	-1	-9	-8	-0	-0.6
1949	StL-A	0	1	.000	13	0	0	0	0	23^1	27	3	31	13	23.1	10.80	42	.297	.484	0	.000	-1	-17	-16	1	-0.6
Total	3	1	3	.250	31	4	0	0	0	62^1	70	5	67	26	20.6	8.23	55	.286	.450	0	.000	-2	-28	-26	1	-1.2
● BILL SHORES	Shores, William David b: 5/26/04, Abilene, Tex. d: 2/19/84, Purcell, Okla. BR/TR, 6', 185 lbs. Deb: 4/11/28																									
1928	Phi-A	1	1	.500	3	2	1	0	0	14	13	0	7	5	12.9	3.21	125	.250	.339	0	.000	-1	1	1	-0	0.0
1929	Phi-A	11	6	.647	39	13	5	1	7	152^2	150	9	59	49	12.5	3.60	118	.262	.334	5	.125	-2	11	11	-1	0.9
1930	*Phi-A	12	4	.750	31	19	7	1	0	159	169	11	70	48	13.7	4.19	112	.276	.353	11	.193	-2	8	9	0	0.5
1931	Phi-A	0	3	.000	6	2	0	0	0	16	26	3	10	2	20.3	5.06	89	.361	.439	1	.333	0	-1	-1	0	-0.1
1933	NY-N	2	1	.667	8	3	1	0	0	36^2	41	4	14	20	13.5	3.93	82	.291	.355	3	.273	1	-2	-3	1	0.0
1936	Chi-A	0	0	–	9	0	0	0	0	17	26	1	8	5	17.0	9.53	55	.356	.420	1	.200	-0	-8	-8	-0	0.0
Total	6	26	15	.634	96	39	14	2	7	395^1	425	28	168	129	13.6	4.17	105	.279	.353	21	.174	-4	8	8	1	1.3
● CHRIS SHORT	Short, Christopher Joseph b: 9/19/37, Milford, Del. d: 8/1/91, Wilmington, Del. BR/TL, 6'4", 205 lbs. Deb: 4/19/59																									
1959	Phi-N	0	0	–	3	2	0	0	0	14^1	19	3	10	8	18.8	8.16	50	.317	.423	0	.000	-1	-7	-6	-0	-0.1

YEAR	TM/L	W	L	PCT	G	GS	CG	SH	SV	IP	H	HR	BB	SO	RAT	ERA	ERA+	OAV	OOB	BH	AVG	PB	PR	/A	PD	TPI
1960	Phi-N	6	9	.400	42	10	2	0	3	107^1	101	8	52	54	13.1	3.94	99	.249	.339	0	.000	-3	-2	-1	0	-0.4
1961	Phi-N	6	12	.333	39	16	1	0	1	127^1	157	12	71	80	16.3	5.94	69	.304	.391	6	.162	-1	-27	-26	-1	-3.3
1962	Phi-N	11	9	.550	47	12	4	0	3	142	149	13	56	91	13.5	3.42	113	.272	.348	8	.222	1	8	7	0	1.1
1963	Phi-N	9	12	.429	38	27	6	3	0	198	185	12	69	160	11.7	2.95	109	.248	.315	7	.106	-2	7	6	4	0.8
1964	Phi-N★	17	9	.654	42	31	12	4	2	220^2	174	10	51	181	9.3	2.20	158	.217	.268	7	.108	-1	33	31	-1	3.5
1965	Phi-N	18	11	.621	47	40	15	5	2	297^1	260	18	89	237	10.7	2.82	123	.235	.295	13	.131	-2	24	21	-3	1.5
1966	Phi-N	20	10	.667	42	39	19	4	0	272	257	28	68	177	11.1	3.54	102	.250	.302	22	.208	1	2	2	0	0.3
1967	Phi-N★	9	11	.450	29	26	8	2	1	199^1	163	9	74	142	10.9	2.39	142	.225	.300	6	.091	-2	22	22	0	2.1
1968	Phi-N	19	13	.594	42	36	9	2	1	269^2	236	25	81	202	10.9	2.94	102	.236	.299	12	.152	0	1	2	-1	0.2
1969	Phi-N	0	0	—	2	2	0	0	0	10	11	2	4	5	14.4	7.20	49	.282	.364	0	.000	-0	-4	-4	0	0.0
1970	Phi-N	9	16	.360	36	34	7	2	1	199	211	13	66	133	12.8	4.30	93	.272	.334	3	.049	-5	-6	-7	-2	-1.5
1971	Phi-N	7	14	.333	31	26	5	2	1	173	182	22	63	95	12.9	3.85	92	.274	.339	4	.083	-1	-7	-6	-1	-0.9
1972	Phi-N	1	1	.500	19	0	0	0	1	23	24	3	8	20	12.5	3.91	92	.267	.327	0	—	0	-1	-1	-0	-0.1
1973	Mil-A	3	5	.375	42	7	0	0	2	72	86	5	44	44	16.5	5.13	73	.299	.395	0	—	0	-10	-11	0	-1.2
Total	15	135	132	.506	501	308	88	24	18	2325	2215	183	806	1629	11.9	3.43	103	.252	.319	88	.126	-17	33	30	-4	2.0

● BILL SHORT
Short, William Ross b: 11/27/37, Kingston, N.Y. BL/TL, 5'9", 170 lbs. Deb: 4/23/60

YEAR	TM/L	W	L	PCT	G	GS	CG	SH	SV	IP	H	HR	BB	SO	RAT	ERA	ERA+	OAV	OOB	BH	AVG	PB	PR	/A	PD	TPI
1960	NY-A	3	5	.375	10	10	2	0	0	47	49	5	30	14	15.3	4.79	75	.282	.390	3	.200	1	-5	-6	-1	-0.9
1962	Bal-A	0	0	—	5	0	0	0	0	4	8	0	6	3	33.8	15.75	23	.381	.536	0	.000	-0	-5	-5	0	0.0
1966	Bal-A	2	3	.400	6	6	1	1	0	37^2	34	2	10	27	10.5	2.87	116	.239	.289	1	.091	-1	2	2	1	0.2
	Bos-A	0	0	—	8	0	0	0	0	8^1	10	1	2	2	13.0	4.32	88	.294	.333	0	.000	-0	-1	-0	0	0.0
	Yr	2	3	.400	14	6	1	1	0	46	44	3	12	29	11.0	3.13	109	.247	.295	1	.083	-1	2	1	1	0.2
1967	Pit-N	0	0	—	6	0	0	0	1	2^1	1	0	1	1	7.7	3.86	87	.143	.250	0	.000	-0	-0	-0	0	0.0
1968	NY-N	0	3	.000	34	0	0	0	1	30^1	24	0	14	24	11.6	4.75	64	.220	.315	0	.000	-0	-6	-6	1	-0.6
1969	Cin-N	0	0	—	4	0	0	0	0	2^1	4	0	1	0	19.3	15.43	24	.400	.455	0	.000	-0	-3	-3	-0	0.0
Total	6	5	11	.313	73	16	3	1	2	132	130	8	64	71	13.4	4.70	73	.262	.349	4	.125	-1	-18	-19	2	-1.3

● CLYDE SHOUN
Shoun, Clyde Mitchell "Hardrock" b: 3/20/12, Mountain City, Tenn. d: 3/20/68, Mountain Home, Tenn. BL/TL, 6'1", 188 lbs. Deb: 8/7/35

YEAR	TM/L	W	L	PCT	G	GS	CG	SH	SV	IP	H	HR	BB	SO	RAT	ERA	ERA+	OAV	OOB	BH	AVG	PB	PR	/A	PD	TPI
1935	Chi-N	1	0	1.000	5	1	0	0	0	12^2	14	2	5	5	13.5	2.84	138	.298	.365	0	.000	-0	2	2	-0	0.0
1936	Chi-N	0	0	—	4	0	0	0	0	4^1	3	0	6	1	18.7	12.46	32	.200	.429	0	—	0	-4	-4	0	0.0
1937	Chi-N	7	7	.500	37	9	2	0	0	93	118	9	45	43	15.8	5.61	71	.309	.382	4	.138	-1	-18	-17	-1	-2.4
1938	StL-N	6	6	.500	40	12	3	0	1	117^1	130	8	43	37	13.3	4.14	96	.283	.345	8	.258	0	-5	-2	-1	-0.3
1939	StL-N	3	1	.750	**53**	2	0	0	**9**	103	98	4	42	50	12.4	3.76	109	.248	.323	3	.115	-1	2	**4**	-1	0.1
1940	StL-N	13	11	.542	**54**	19	13	1	5	197^1	193	13	46	82	11.0	3.92	102	.255	.299	12	.190	-1	-2	1	-0	0.0
1941	StL-N	3	5	.375	26	6	0	0	0	70	98	9	20	34	15.2	5.66	67	.337	.379	4	.182	0	-16	-15	1	-1.4
1942	StL-N	0	0	—	2	0	0	0	0	1^2	1	0	0	0	5.4	0.00	—	.167	.167	0	—	0	1	1	-0	0.0
	Cin-N	1	3	.250	34	0	0	0	0	72^2	55	2	24	32	9.8	2.23	147	.216	.283	4	.308	1	9	9	1	0.6
	Yr	1	3	.250	36	0	0	0	0	74^1	56	2	24	32	9.7	2.18	151	.215	.281	4	.308	1	9	9	1	0.6
1943	Cin-N	14	5	.737	45	5	2	0	7	147	131	5	46	61	10.8	3.06	108	.241	.300	13	.310	4	5	4	1	1.0
1944	Cin-N	13	10	.565	38	21	12	1	2	202^2	193	10	42	55	10.6	3.02	116	.248	.290	15	.224	1	13	11	-3	0.9
1946	Cin-N	1	6	.143	27	5	0	0	0	79	87	3	26	20	13.0	4.10	82	.292	.351	2	.095	-1	-6	-7	-2	-0.9
1947	Cin-N	0	0	—	10	0	0	0	0	14^1	16	2	5	7	13.8	5.02	82	.320	.393	0	—	0	-2	-1	0	0.0
	Bos-N	5	3	.625	26	3	1	1	1	73^2	73	6	21	23	11.5	4.40	89	.254	.305	3	.158	-1	-3	-4	-1	-0.6
	Yr	5	3	.625	36	3	1	1	1	88	89	8	26	30	11.8	4.50	87	.263	.316	3	.158	-1	-4	-6	-1	-0.6
1948	Bos-N	5	1	.833	36	2	1	0	4	74	77	7	20	25	11.8	4.01	96	.267	.315	4	.190	0	-0	-1	-2	-0.3
1949	Bos-N	0	0	—	1	0	0	0	0	1	1	0	0	0	9.0	0.00	—	.250	.250	0	—	0	0	0	-0	0.0
	Chi-A	1	1	.500	16	0	0	0	0	23^1	37	1	13	8	19.3	5.79	72	.370	.442	1	.200	0	-4	-4	0	-0.3
Total	14	73	59	.553	454	85	34	3	29	1287	1325	81	404	483	12.2	3.91	96	.267	.324	73	.202	1	-27	-25	-9	-3.6

● BRIAN SHOUSE
Shouse, Brian Douglas b: 9/26/68, Effingham, Ill. BL/TL, 5'11", 180 lbs. Deb: 7/31/93

YEAR	TM/L	W	L	PCT	G	GS	CG	SH	SV	IP	H	HR	BB	SO	RAT	ERA	ERA+	OAV	OOB	BH	AVG	PB	PR	/A	PD	TPI
1993	Pit-N	0	0	—	6	0	0	0	0	4	7	1	2	3	20.3	9.00	45	.368	.429	0	—	0	-2	-2	0	0.0
1998	Bos-A	0	1	.000	7	0	0	0	0	8	9	2	4	5	14.6	5.63	82	.281	.361	0	—	0	-1	-1	0	-0.1
Total	2	0	1	.000	13	0	0	0	0	12	16	3	6	8	16.5	6.75	66	.314	.386	0	—	0	-3	-3	0	-0.1

● ERIC SHOW
Show, Eric Vaughn b: 5/19/56, Riverside, Cal. d: 3/16/94, Dulzura, Cal. BR/TR, 6'1", 185 lbs. Deb: 9/2/81

YEAR	TM/L	W	L	PCT	G	GS	CG	SH	SV	IP	H	HR	BB	SO	RAT	ERA	ERA+	OAV	OOB	BH	AVG	PB	PR	/A	PD	TPI
1981	SD-N	1	3	.250	15	0	0	0	3	23	17	2	9	22	10.6	3.13	104	.213	.300	0	—	0	1	0	0	0.1
1982	SD-N	10	6	.625	47	14	2	2	3	150	117	10	48	88	10.2	2.64	130	.217	.287	6	.146	-1	16	13	2	1.5
1983	SD-N	15	12	.556	35	33	4	2	0	200^2	201	25	74	120	12.6	4.17	84	.263	.333	11	.172	1	-12	-15	-2	-2.0
1984	*SD-N	15	9	.625	32	32	3	1	0	206^2	175	18	88	104	11.6	3.40	105	.234	.317	17	.246	6	4	4	-1	1.0
1985	SD-N	12	11	.522	35	35	5	2	0	233	212	27	87	141	11.7	3.09	114	.243	.316	10	.127	-1	13	11	-3	0.7
1986	SD-N	9	5	.643	24	22	2	0	0	136^1	109	11	69	94	12.0	2.97	123	.225	.326	7	.163	1	11	10	-2	0.9
1987	SD-N	8	16	.333	34	34	5	3	0	206^1	188	26	85	117	12.3	3.84	103	.241	.323	5	.071	-4	6	3	-1	-0.2
1988	SD-N	16	11	.593	32	32	13	1	0	234^2	201	22	53	144	10.0	3.26	104	.231	.280	12	.148	-0	5	4	-4	-0.1
1989	SD-N	8	6	.571	16	16	1	0	0	106^1	113	9	39	66	13.0	4.23	83	.274	.340	8	.235	2	-9	-9	-1	-1.0
1990	SD-N	6	8	.429	39	12	0	0	1	106^1	131	16	41	55	14.9	5.76	66	.306	.372	5	.200	1	-23	-23	-1	-2.7
1991	Oak-A	1	2	.333	23	5	0	0	0	51^2	62	5	17	20	13.8	5.92	65	.298	.351	0	—	0	-10	-12	-1	-0.6
Total	11	101	89	.532	332	235	35	11	7	1655	1526	171	610	971	11.9	3.66	98	.247	.319	81	.160	3	1	-13	-13	-2.4

● LEV SHREVE
Shreve, Leven Lawrence b: 1/14/1869, Louisville, Ky. d: 10/18/42, Detroit, Mich. BR/TR, 5'11", 150 lbs. Deb: 5/2/1887

YEAR	TM/L	W	L	PCT	G	GS	CG	SH	SV	IP	H	HR	BB	SO	RAT	ERA	ERA+	OAV	OOB	BH	AVG	PB	PR	/A	PD	TPI
1887	Bal-a	3	1	.750	5	5	4	1	0	38	33	0	19	13	12.6	3.79	108	.228	.321	4	.167	-1	2	1	0	0.0
	Ind-N	5	9	.357	14	14	14	1	0	122	141	5	65	22	15.5	4.72	88	.278	.365	13	.265	0	-9	-8	-2	-0.8
1888	Ind-N	11	24	.314	35	35	34	1	0	297^2	352	23	93	101	13.7	4.63	64	.288	.342	21	.183	-1	-59	-55	0	-5.4
1889	Ind-N	0	3	.000	3	3	1	0	0	15^2	25	3	12	5	21.8	13.79	30	.352	.452	0	.000	-1	-17	-17	0	-1.9
Total	3	19	37	.339	57	57	53	3	0	473^1	551	31	189	141	14.3	4.89	70	.283	.351	38	.195	-3	-82	-78	-1	-8.1

● HARRY SHRIVER
Shriver, Harry Graydon "Pop" b: 9/2/1896, Wadestown, W.Va. d: 1/21/70, Morgantown, W.Va. BR/TR, 6'2", 180 lbs. Deb: 4/14/22

YEAR	TM/L	W	L	PCT	G	GS	CG	SH	SV	IP	H	HR	BB	SO	RAT	ERA	ERA+	OAV	OOB	BH	AVG	PB	PR	/A	PD	TPI
1922	Bro-N	4	6	.400	25	13	4	2	0	108^1	114	5	48	38	13.6	2.99	136	.287	.367	1	.037	-3	13	13	-2	0.5
1923	Bro-N	0	0	—	1	1	0	0	0	4	8	0	0	1	18.0	6.75	58	.444	.444	0	.000	-0	-1	-1	-0	0.0
Total	2	4	6	.400	26	14	4	2	0	112^1	122	5	48	39	13.8	3.12	130	.294	.370	1	.036	-3	12	12	-3	0.5

● PAUL SHUEY
Shuey, Paul Kenneth b: 9/16/70, Lima, Ohio BR/TR, 6'3", 215 lbs. Deb: 5/8/94

YEAR	TM/L	W	L	PCT	G	GS	CG	SH	SV	IP	H	HR	BB	SO	RAT	ERA	ERA+	OAV	OOB	BH	AVG	PB	PR	/A	PD	TPI
1994	Cle-A	0	1	.000	14	0	0	0	5	11^2	14	1	12	16	20.1	8.49	56	.280	.419	0	—	0	-5	-5	-0	-0.7
1995	Cle-A	0	2	.000	7	0	0	0	0	6^1	5	0	5	5	14.2	4.26	110	.238	.385	0	—	0	0	0	0	0.0
1996	*Cle-A	5	2	.714	42	0	0	0	4	53^2	45	6	26	44	11.9	2.85	171	.231	.321	0	—	0	13	12	-0	1.5
1997	Cle-A	4	2	.667	40	0	0	0	2	45	52	5	28	46	16.2	6.20	76	.294	.393	0	.000	-0	-8	-8	1	-0.9
1998	*Cle-A	5	4	.556	43	0	0	0	2	51	44	6	25	58	12.7	3.00	159	.229	.327	0	.000	-0	9	10	-0	1.6
Total	5	14	11	.560	146	0	0	0	13	167^2	160	18	96	169	14.0	4.24	113	.252	.354	0	.000	-0	9	10	-0	1.5

● TOOTS SHULTZ
Shultz, Wallace Luther b: 10/10/1888, Homestead, Pa. d: 1/30/59, McKeesport, Pa. BR/TR, 5'10", 175 lbs. Deb: 5/5/11

YEAR	TM/L	W	L	PCT	G	GS	CG	SH	SV	IP	H	HR	BB	SO	RAT	ERA	ERA+	OAV	OOB	BH	AVG	PB	PR	/A	PD	TPI
1911	Phi-N	0	3	.000	5	3	2	0	0	25	30	5	15	9	17.6	9.36	37	.300	.412	2	.250	0	-17	-16	0	-1.5
1912	Phi-N	1	4	.200	22	4	1	0	1	59	75	2	35	20	17.2	4.58	79	.333	.430	5	.238	0	-8	-6	0	-0.4
Total	2	1	7	.125	27	7	3	0	1	84	105	7	50	29	17.4	6.00	60	.323	.424	7	.241	0	-24	-23	1	-1.9

● HARRY SHUMAN
Shuman, Harry b: 3/5/15, Philadelphia, Pa. d: 10/25/96, Philadelphia, Pa. BR/TR, 6'2", 195 lbs. Deb: 9/14/42

YEAR	TM/L	W	L	PCT	G	GS	CG	SH	SV	IP	H	HR	BB	SO	RAT	ERA	ERA+	OAV	OOB	BH	AVG	PB	PR	/A	PD	TPI
1942	Pit-N	0	0	—	1	0	0	0	0	2	0	0	1	1	4.5	0.00	—	.000	.167	0	—	0	1	1	-0	0.0
1943	Pit-N	0	0	—	11	0	0	0	0	22	30	0	8	5	16.4	5.32	65	.337	.404	0	.000	-0	-5	-4	0	0.0
1944	Phi-N	0	0	—	18	0	0	0	0	26^2	26	1	11	4	12.5	4.05	89	.245	.316	0	.000	-0	-1	-1	0	0.0
Total	3	0	0	—	30	0	0	0	0	50^2	56	1	20	10	13.9	4.44	80	.280	.351	0	.000	-0	-5	-5	0	0.0

● PAUL SIEBERT
Siebert, Paul Edward b: 6/5/53, Minneapolis, Minn. BL/TL, 6'2", 205 lbs. Deb: 9/7/74 F

YEAR	TM/L	W	L	PCT	G	GS	CG	SH	SV	IP	H	HR	BB	SO	RAT	ERA	ERA+	OAV	OOB	BH	AVG	PB	PR	/A	PD	TPI
1974	Hou-N	1	1	.500	5	5	1	1	0	25^1	21	3	11	10	11.4	3.55	97	.236	.320	0	.000	-1	0	-0	1	0.0
1975	Hou-N	0	2	.000	7	2	0	0	2	18^1	20	0	6	6	13.3	2.95	114	.294	.360	0	.000	-0	1	1	0	0.1

YEAR	TM/L	W	L	PCT	G	GS	CG	SH	SV	IP	H	HR	BB	SO	RAT	ERA	ERA+	OAV	OOB	BH	AVG	PB	PR	/A	PD	TPI
1976	Hou-N	0	2	.000	19	0	0	0	0	25^2	29	0	18	10	16.8	3.16	101	.296	.410	0	.000	-0	1	0	-1	-0.1
1977	SD-N	0	0	—	4	0	0	0	0	3^2	3	1	4	1	17.2	2.45	144	.214	.389	0	—	0	1	0	-0	0.0
	NY-N	2	1	.667	25	0	0	0	0	28	27	0	13	20	13.2	3.86	97	.257	.345	0	.000	-0	0	-0	-0	-0.1
	Yr	2	1	.667	29	0	0	0	0	31^2	30	1	17	21	13.6	3.69	101	.250	.348	0	.000	-0	1	0	-0	-0.1
1978	NY-N	0	2	.000	27	0	0	0	1	28	30	2	21	12	16.7	5.14	68	.283	.406	0	.000	-0	-5	-5	0	-0.4
Total	5	3	8	.273	87	7	1	1	3	129	130	6	73	59	14.4	3.77	92	.271	.372	0	.000	-2	-2	-4	0	-0.5
● **SONNY SIEBERT**	Siebert, Wilfred Charles b: 1/14/37, St.Marys, Mo. BR/TR, 6'3", 198 lbs. Deb: 4/26/64 C																									
1964	Cle-A	7	9	.438	41	14	3	1	3	156	142	15	57	144	11.6	3.23	111	.243	.313	13	.265	5	7	6	-2	1.1
1965	Cle-A	16	8	.667	39	27	4	1	1	188^2	139	14	46	191	9.1	2.43	143	.206	**.262**	7	.106	-2	22	22	1	2.7
1966	Cle-A★	16	8	**.667**	34	32	11	1	1	241	193	25	62	163	9.7	2.80	123	.221	.278	11	.129	-2	17	17	2	1.7
1967	Cle-A	10	12	.455	34	26	7	1	4	185^1	136	17	54	136	9.5	2.38	137	.202	.268	7	.135	1	18	18	-2	2.3
1968	Cle-A	12	10	.545	31	30	8	4	0	206	145	12	88	146	10.5	2.97	100	.198	.290	11	.157	1	0	-0	1	0.2
1969	Cle-A	0	1	.000	2	2	0	0	0	14	10	1	8	6	11.6	3.21	117	.196	.305	1	.250	0	1	1	-0	0.1
	Bos-A	14	10	.583	43	22	2	0	5	163^1	151	21	68	127	12.3	3.80	100	.245	.324	8	.151	1	-3	0	2	0.3
	Yr	14	11	.560	45	24	2	0	5	177^1	161	22	76	133	12.2	3.76	101	.241	.322	9	.158	1	-3	1	2	0.4
1970	Bos-A	15	8	.652	33	33	7	2	0	222^2	207	29	60	142	11.0	3.44	115	.248	.303	10	.130	-2	7	13	0	1.1
1971	Bos-A☆	16	10	.615	32	32	12	4	0	235^1	220	20	60	131	10.8	2.91	127	.245	.294	21	.266	10	15	21	1	3.5
1972	Bos-A	12	12	.500	32	30	7	3	0	196^1	204	17	59	123	12.4	3.80	84	.264	.322	17	.236	6	-16	-13	1	-0.8
1973	Bos-A	0	1	.000	2	2	0	0	0	2^1	5	1	1	5	23.1	7.71	52	.417	.462	0	—	0	-1	-1	-0	-0.3
	Tex-A	7	11	.389	25	20	1	1	2	119^2	120	11	37	76	12.0	3.99	93	.258	.317	0	—	0	-2	-4	2	-0.3
	Yr	7	12	.368	27	20	1	1	2	122	125	12	38	81	12.2	4.06	92	.262	.320	0	—	0	-3	-4	2	-0.6
1974	StL-N	8	8	.500	28	20	5	3	0	133^2	150	8	51	68	13.7	3.84	93	.288	.355	5	.114	-2	-3	-4	-1	-0.7
1975	SD-N	3	2	.600	6	6	0	0	0	26^2	37	2	10	10	16.2	4.39	79	.330	.390	3	.375	2	-2	-3	0	-0.3
	Oak-A	4	4	.500	17	13	0	0	0	61	60	4	31	44	13.4	3.69	98	.252	.338	0	.000	-0	1	-0	-1	-0.2
Total	12	140	114	.551	399	307	67	21	16	2152	1919	197	692	1512	11.1	3.21	110	.238	.303	114	.173	18	57	73	5	10.4
● **DWIGHT SIEBLER**	Siebler, Dwight Leroy b: 8/5/37, Columbus, Neb. BR/TR, 6'2", 184 lbs. Deb: 8/26/63																									
1963	Min-A	2	1	.667	7	5	2	0	0	38^2	25	6	12	22	8.8	2.79	130	.182	.253	2	.133	-0	4	4	-1	0.1
1964	Min-A	0	0	—	9	0	0	0	0	11	10	1	6	10	13.1	4.91	73	.256	.356	0	—	0	-2	-2	-0	0.0
1965	Min-A	0	0	—	7	1	0	0	0	15	11	2	11	15	13.2	4.20	85	.193	.324	0	.000	-0	-1	-1	0	0.0
1966	Min-A	2	2	.500	23	2	0	0	0	49^2	47	6	14	24	11.2	3.44	104	.253	.308	0	.000	-1	-0	1	-1	-0.1
1967	Min-A	0	0	—	2	0	0	0	0	3	4	0	1	0	15.0	3.00	115	.364	.417	0	—	0	0	0	-0	0.0
Total	5	4	3	.571	48	8	2	0	1	117^1	97	15	44	71	11.0	3.45	104	.226	.300	2	.074	-1	1	2	-2	0.0
● **CANDY SIERRA**	Sierra, Ulises (Pizarro) b: 3/27/67, Rio Piedras, P.R. BR/TR, 6'2", 190 lbs. Deb: 4/6/88																									
1988	SD-N	0	1	.000	15	0	0	0	0	23^2	36	2	11	20	17.9	5.70	60	.379	.443	0	.000	-0	-6	-6	-0	-0.3
	Cin-N	0	0	—	1	0	0	0	0	4	5	0	1	4	13.5	4.50	80	.294	.333	0	.000	-0	-0	-0	0	0.0
	Yr	0	1	.000	16	0	0	0	0	27^2	41	2	12	24	17.2	5.53	62	.363	.424	0	.000	-0	-6	-6	0	-0.3
● **ED SIEVER**	Siever, Edward Tilden b: 4/2/1877, Goddard, Kan. d: 2/4/20, Detroit, Mich. BL/TL, 5'11.5", 190 lbs. Deb: 4/26/01																									
1901	Det-A	18	14	.563	38	33	30	2	0	288^2	334	9	65	85	12.7	3.24	119	.286	.328	18	.168	-5	14	19	-1	1.2
1902	Det-A	8	11	.421	25	23	17	4	1	188^1	166	0	32	36	9.6	**1.91**	**191**	.237	.272	10	.152	-4	35	36	-4	2.6
1903	StL-A	13	14	.481	31	27	24	1	0	254	245	6	39	90	10.2	2.48	117	.253	.285	13	.140	-4	14	12	2	1.0
1904	StL-A	10	15	.400	29	24	19	2	0	217	235	3	65	77	12.6	2.65	93	.277	.330	11	.155	-1	-1	-4	1	-0.6
1906	Det-A	14	11	.560	30	25	20	1	0	222^2	240	5	45	71	11.9	2.71	102	.278	.321	12	.156	-3	-0	1	-2	-0.4
1907	*Det-A	18	11	.621	39	33	22	3	1	274^2	256	1	52	88	10.5	2.16	120	.249	.293	15	.160	-3	12	14	-3	0.7
1908	Det-A	2	6	.250	11	9	4	1	0	61^2	74	0	13	23	12.7	3.50	69	.302	.337	3	.167	-1	-8	-7	1	-1.1
Total	7	83	82	.503	203	174	136	14	2	1507	1550	24	311	470	11.3	2.60	116	.266	.308	82	.156	-21	64	70	-8	3.4
● **WALTER SIGNER**	Signer, Walter Donald Aloysius b: 10/12/10, New York, N.Y. d: 7/23/74, Greenwich, Conn. BR/TR, 6', 185 lbs. Deb: 9/18/43																									
1943	Chi-N	2	1	.667	4	2	1	0	0	25	24	3	4	5	10.1	2.88	116	.245	.275	2	.250	0	1	1	-0	0.2
1945	Chi-N	0	0	—	6	0	0	0	1	8	11	1	5	0	18.0	3.38	108	.256	.333	0	.000	-0	0	0	-0	0.0
Total	2	2	1	.667	10	2	1	0	1	33	35	4	9	5	12.0	3.00	114	.248	.293	2	.222	0	2	2	-0	0.2
● **SETH SIGSBY**	Sigsby, Seth De Witt (b: Seth De Witt) b: 4/30/1874, Cobleskill, N.Y. d: 9/15/53, Schenectady, N.Y 6', 175 lbs. Deb: 6/27/1893																									
1893	NY-N	0	0	—	1	0	0	0	0	3	1	0	4	2	18.0	9.00	52	.100	.400	0	.000	-0	-1	-1	-0	0.0
● **JOSE SILVA**	Silva, Jose Leonel b: 12/19/73, Tijuana, Mex. BR/TR, 6'5", 210 lbs. Deb: 9/10/96																									
1996	Tor-A	0	0	—	2	0	0	0	0	2	5	1	0	0	22.5	13.50	37	.455	.455	0	—	0	-2	-2	0	0.0
1997	Pit-N	2	1	.667	11	4	0	0	0	36^1	52	4	16	30	17.1	5.94	72	.347	.413	1	.143	-0	-7	-7	-1	-0.6
1998	Pit-N	6	7	.462	18	18	1	0	0	100^1	104	7	30	64	12.1	4.40	98	.271	.325	1	.037	-1	-2	-1	0	-0.2
Total	3	8	8	.500	31	22	1	0	0	138^2	161	12	46	94	13.6	4.93	88	.295	.352	2	.059	-1	-11	-9	-0	-0.8
● **AL SIMA**	Sima, Albert b: 10/7/21, Mahwah, N.J. d: 8/17/93, Suffern, N.Y. BR/TL, 6', 187 lbs. Deb: 6/28/50																									
1950	Was-A	4	5	.444	17	9	1	0	0	77	89	9	26	23	13.6	4.79	94	.291	.348	3	.115	-2	-2	-3	-1	-0.6
1951	Was-A	3	7	.300	18	8	1	0	0	77	79	5	41	26	14.0	4.79	85	.261	.349	3	.176	1	-6	-6	-1	-0.6
1953	Was-A	2	3	.400	31	5	1	0	1	68^1	63	7	31	25	12.8	3.42	114	.249	.338	2	.118	-1	4	4	1	0.2
1954	Chi-A	0	1	.000	5	1	0	0	1	7	11	1	2	1	16.7	5.14	73	.393	.433	0	.000	-0	-1	-1	-0	-0.2
	Phi-A	2	5	.286	29	7	1	0	2	79^1	101	9	32	36	15.1	5.22	75	.309	.370	1	.050	-2	-13	-12	-1	-1.3
	Yr	2	6	.250	34	8	1	0	3	86^1	112	10	34	37	15.2	5.21	75	.314	.373	1	.045	-2	-14	-13	-1	-1.5
Total	4	11	21	.344	100	30	4	0	4	308^2	343	31	132	111	14.0	4.61	89	.282	.354	9	.110	-5	-18	-17	-2	-2.5
● **BILL SIMAS**	Simas, William Anthony b: 11/28/71, Hanford, Cal. BL/TR, 6'3", 220 lbs. Deb: 8/15/95																									
1995	Chi-A	1	1	.500	14	0	0	0	0	14	15	1	10	16	16.7	2.57	173	.273	.394	0	—	0	3	3	-0	0.3
1996	Chi-A	2	8	.200	64	0	0	0	2	72^2	75	5	39	65	14.5	4.58	103	.265	.360	0	—	0	3	1	-0	0.2
1997	Chi-A	3	1	.750	40	0	0	0	1	41^1	46	6	24	38	15.7	4.14	106	.279	.377	0	—	0	2	1	-0	0.1
1998	Chi-A	4	3	.571	60	0	0	0	18	70^2	54	12	22	56	9.8	3.57	128	.206	.270	0	—	0	8	8	-0	1.0
Total	4	10	13	.435	178	0	0	0	21	198^2	190	24	95	175	13.2	3.99	115	.248	.337	0	—	0	17	13	-1	1.6
● **CURT SIMMONS**	Simmons, Curtis Thomas b: 5/19/29, Egypt, Pa. BL/TL, 6', 187 lbs. Deb: 9/28/47																									
1947	Phi-N	1	0	1.000	1	1	1	0	0	9	5	0	6	9	11.0	1.00	401	.161	.297	1	.500	0	3	3	-0	0.4
1948	Phi-N	7	13	.350	31	22	7	0	0	170	169	8	108	86	14.8	4.87	81	.266	.374	7	.137	-1	-17	-17	1	-1.8
1949	Phi-N	4	10	.286	38	14	2	0	1	131^1	133	7	55	83	13.0	4.59	86	.275	.350	7	.171	-1	-8	-9	-0	-1.0
1950	Phi-N	17	8	.680	31	27	11	2	1	214^2	178	19	88	146	11.2	3.40	119	.223	.302	12	.156	-1	18	16	-0	1.5
1952	Phi-N★	14	8	.636	28	28	15	**6**	0	201^1	170	11	70	141	10.8	2.82	130	.227	.294	11	.164	2	20	19	-3	1.9
1953	Phi-N★	16	13	.552	32	30	19	4	0	238	211	17	82	138	11.2	3.21	131	.236	.302	13	.140	-3	28	26	-3	2.4
1954	Phi-N	14	15	.483	34	33	21	3	1	253	226	14	98	125	11.7	2.81	144	.239	.314	16	.176	-1	35	35	-3	3.3
1955	Phi-N	8	8	.500	25	22	3	0	0	130	148	15	50	58	13.9	4.92	81	.290	.356	8	.174	-1	-13	-14	-1	-1.6
1956	Phi-N	15	10	.600	33	27	14	0	0	198	186	17	65	88	11.5	3.36	111	.248	.311	17	.236	3	9	8	-1	1.3
1957	Phi-N★	12	11	.522	32	29	9	2	0	212	214	11	50	92	11.3	3.44	111	.264	.309	17	.239	4	10	9	-3	1.0
1958	Phi-N	7	14	.333	29	27	7	1	1	168^1	196	11	40	78	12.8	4.38	90	.293	.336	12	.203	0	-8	-8	-1	-1.0
1959	Phi-N	0	0	—	7	0	0	0	0	10	16	2	0	4	15.3	4.50	91	.400	.415	0	—	0	-1	-0	0	0.0
1960	Phi-N	0	0	—	4	2	0	0	0	4	13	3	6	4	42.8	18.00	22	.542	.633	0	—	0	-6	-6	1	0.0
	StL-N	7	4	.636	23	17	3	1	0	152	149	11	31	63	10.7	2.66	154	.257	.295	10	.213	1	19	24	0	1.8
	Yr	7	4	.636	27	19	3	1	0	156	162	14	37	67	11.5	3.06	134	.269	.311	10	.213	1	12	18	1	1.8
1961	StL-N	9	10	.474	30	29	6	2	0	195^2	203	14	64	99	12.5	3.13	**141**	.269	.329	20	.303	5	20	**28**	-0	3.0
1962	StL-N	10	10	.500	31	22	9	4	0	154	167	18	32	74	11.8	3.51	122	.280	.320	8	.160	0	7	13	-1	1.5
1963	StL-N	15	9	.625	32	32	11	6	0	232^2	209	13	48	127	10.2	2.48	143	.239	.283	13	.160	0	21	28	-4	2.5
1964	*StL-N	18	9	.667	34	34	12	3	0	244	233	24	49	104	10.6	3.43	111	.249	.290	10	.106	-3	3	10	-1	0.6
1965	StL-N	9	15	.375	34	32	5	0	0	203	229	19	54	96	12.7	4.08	94	.283	.331	3	.047	-5	-12	-5	-2	-1.3
1966	StL-N	1	1	.500	10	5	1	0	0	33^1	35	3	14	14	13.2	4.59	78	.269	.340	1	.125	0	-4	-4	-1	-0.2

YEAR	TM/L	W	L	PCT	G	GS	CG	SH	SV	IP	H	HR	BB	SO	RAT	ERA	ERA+	OAV	OOB	BH	AVG	PB	PR	/A	PD	TPI
	Chi-N	4	7	.364	19	10	3	1	0	77^1	79	7	21	24	11.8	4.07	90	.268	.319	2	.111	-0	-4	-3	2	-0.4
	Yr	5	8	.385	29	15	4	1	0	110^2	114	10	35	38	12.2	4.23	86	.268	.325	3	.115	-0	-8	-7	1	-0.6
1967	Chi-N	3	7	.300	17	14	3	0	0	82	100	10	23	31	13.7	4.94	72	.300	.349	4	.143	-1	-14	-13	-0	-1.5
	Cal-A	2	1	.667	14	4	1	1	1	34^2	44	1	9	13	14.3	2.60	121	.321	.372	2	.222	1	2	2	-1	0.2
Total	20	193	183	.513	569	461	163	36	5	3348^1	3313	255	1063	1697	11.9	3.54	111	.259	.319	194	.171	1	109	142	-21	12.6
● **PAT SIMMONS**	Simmons, Patrick Clement (b: Patrick Clement Simoni) b: 11/29/08, Watervliet, N.Y. d: 7/3/68, Albany, N.Y. BR/TR, 5′11″, 172 lbs. Deb: 4/18/28																									
1928	Bos-A	0	2	.000	31	3	0	0	1	69	69	4	38	16	14.1	4.04	102	.271	.367	2	.133	-1	0	1	-0	-0.1
1929	Bos-A	0	0	—	2	0	0	0	1	7	6	0	3	2	11.6	0.00	—	.231	.310	0	.000	0	3	3	0	0.1
Total	2	0	2	.000	33	3	0	0	2	76	75	4	41	18	13.9	3.67	112	.267	.362	2	.125	-1	3	4	-0	0.0
● **DOUG SIMONS**	Simons, Douglas Eugene b: 9/15/66, Bakersfield, Cal. BL/TL, 6′, 170 lbs. Deb: 4/9/91																									
1991	NY-N	2	3	.400	42	1	0	0	1	60^2	55	5	19	38	11.3	5.19	70	.246	.310	0	.000	-0	-10	-10	2	-0.7
1992	Mon-N	0	0	—	7	0	0	0	0	5^1	15	3	2	6	30.4	23.63	15	.500	.545	0	—	0	-12	-12	-0	0.0
Total	2	2	3	.400	49	1	0	0	1	66	70	8	21	44	12.8	6.68	54	.276	.338	0	.000	-0	-22	-22	2	-0.7
● **JOE SIMPSON**	Simpson, Joe Allen b: 12/31/51, Purcell, Okla. BL/TL, 6′3″, 175 lbs. Deb: 9/2/75 ◆																									
1983	KC-A	0	0	—	2	0	0	0	0	3	4	0	2	1	18.0	3.00	136	.308	.400	20	.168	0	0	0	-0	0.0
● **STEVE SIMPSON**	Simpson, Steven Edward b: 8/30/48, St.Joseph, Mo. d: 11/2/89, Omaha, Neb. BR/TR, 6′3″, 200 lbs. Deb: 9/10/72																									
1972	SD-N	0	2	.000	9	0	0	0	2	11^1	10	0	8	9	14.3	4.76	69	.238	.360	0	—	0	-2	-2	-0	-0.4
● **DUKE SIMPSON**	Simpson, Thomas Leo b: 9/15/27, Columbus, Ohio BR/TR, 6′1.5″, 190 lbs. Deb: 5/6/53																									
1953	Chi-N	1	2	.333	30	1	0	0	0	45	60	8	25	21	17.2	8.00	56	.314	.396	2	.250	0	-19	-18	-0	-1.0
● **WAYNE SIMPSON**	Simpson, Wayne Kirby b: 12/2/48, Los Angeles, Cal. BR/TR, 6′3″, 220 lbs. Deb: 4/9/70																									
1970	Cin-N☆	14	3	.824	26	26	10	2	0	176	125	15	81	119	11.0	3.02	134	**.198**	.298	6	.094	-4	20	20	2	1.6
1971	Cin-N	4	7	.364	22	21	1	0	0	117^1	106	9	77	61	14.3	4.76	71	.244	.361	1	.031	-2	-17	-18	2	-1.6
1972	Cin-N	8	5	.615	24	22	1	0	0	130^1	124	17	49	70	12.1	4.14	78	.247	.316	3	.063	-3	-10	-13	3	-1.8
1973	KC-A	3	4	.429	16	10	1	0	0	59^2	66	1	35	29	15.4	5.73	72	.284	.381	0	—	0	-13	-11	-0	-1.1
1975	Phi-N	1	0	1.000	7	5	0	0	0	30^2	31	1	11	19	12.6	3.23	116	.263	.331	2	.222	0	1	2	0	0.1
1977	Cal-A	6	12	.333	27	23	0	0	0	122	154	14	62	55	16.5	5.83	67	.308	.392	0	—	0	-24	-26	-1	-3.3
Total	6	36	31	.537	122	107	13	2	0	636	606	57	315	353	13.4	4.37	85	.251	.343	12	.078	-8	-42	-47	0	-6.1
● **PETE SIMS**	Sims, Clarence b: 5/24/1891, Crown City, Ohio d: 12/2/68, Dallas, Tex. BR/TR, 5′11.5″, 165 lbs. Deb: 9/16/15																									
1915	StL-A	1	0	1.000	3	2	0	0	0	8^1	6	0	6	4	13.0	4.32	66	.214	.353	1	1.000	1	-1	-1	-0	-0.1
● **STEVE SINCLAIR**	Sinclair, Steven Scott b: Victoria, B.C., Canada BL/TL, 6′2″, 190 lbs. Deb: 4/25/98																									
1998	Tor-A	0	2	.000	24	0	0	0	0	15	13	0	5	8	10.8	3.60	129	.232	.295	0	—	0	2	2	0	0.2
● **BERT SINCOCK**	Sincock, Herbert Sylvester b: 9/8/1887, Barkerville, B.C., Canada d: 8/1/46, Houghton, Mich. BL/TL, 5′10.5″, 165 lbs. Deb: 6/25/08																									
1908	Cin-N	0	0	—	1	0	0	0	0	4^2	3	0	0	1	5.8	3.86	60	.176	.176	0	.000	-0	-1	-1	-0	0.0
● **BILL SINGER**	Singer, William Robert "The Singer Throwing Machine" b: 4/24/44, Los Angeles, Cal. BR/TR, 6′4″, 200 lbs. Deb: 9/24/64																									
1964	LA-N	0	1	.000	2	2	0	0	0	14	11	0	12	3	14.8	3.21	101	.216	.365	1	.167	0	1	0	-0	0.0
1965	LA-N	0	0	—	2	0	0	0	0	1	2	0	2	1	36.0	0.00	—	.400	.571	0	—	0	0	0	0	0.0
1966	LA-N	0	0	—	3	0	0	0	0	4	4	0	2	4	13.5	0.00	—	.286	.375	0	—	0	2	1	0	0.0
1967	LA-N	12	8	.600	32	29	7	3	0	204^1	185	5	61	169	11.2	2.64	117	.239	.301	6	.090	-3	17	10	1	0.7
1968	LA-N	13	17	.433	37	36	12	6	0	256^1	227	14	78	227	10.9	2.88	96	.237	.298	12	.148	3	3	-3	0	0.0
1969	LA-N★	20	12	.625	41	40	16	2	1	315^2	244	22	74	247	9.4	2.34	142	.210	.263	11	.102	-4	44	35	-2	2.8
1970	LA-N	8	5	.615	16	16	5	3	0	106^1	79	10	32	93	9.6	3.13	122	.203	.267	5	.132	-0	11	8	-1	0.8
1971	LA-N	10	17	.370	31	31	8	1	0	203^1	195	19	71	144	12.0	4.16	78	.252	.318	6	.103	-0	-16	-21	-1	-2.7
1972	LA-N	6	16	.273	26	25	4	3	0	169^1	148	8	60	101	11.3	3.67	91	.237	.309	4	.073	-3	-4	-6	1	-1.0
1973	Cal-A★	20	14	.588	40	40	19	2	0	315^2	280	15	130	241	11.9	3.22	110	.235	.314	0	—	0	21	11	-2	1.0
1974	Cal-A	7	4	.636	14	14	8	0	0	108^2	102	3	43	77	12.1	2.98	115	.250	.323	0	—	0	8	5	0	0.6
1975	Cal-A	7	15	.318	29	27	8	0	1	179	171	18	81	78	13.0	4.98	71	.257	.343	0	—	0	-24	-28	-1	-3.1
1976	Tex-A	4	1	.800	10	10	2	1	0	64^2	56	4	27	34	12.2	3.48	103	.239	.331	0	—	0	0	1	-1	0.0
	Min-A	9	9	.500	26	26	5	3	0	172	177	9	69	63	13.2	3.77	95	.274	.349	0	—	0	-5	-4	-2	-0.5
	Yr	13	10	.565	36	36	7	4	0	236^2	233	13	96	97	12.7	3.69	97	.262	.338	0	—	0	-4	-3	-2	-0.5
1977	Tor-A	2	8	.200	13	12	0	0	0	59^2	71	5	39	33	16.9	6.79	62	.296	.399	0	—	0	-18	-17	-0	-2.3
Total	14	118	127	.482	322	308	94	24	2	2174	1952	132	781	1515	11.6	3.39	99	.240	.311	45	.109	-7	39	-8	-7	-3.7
● **ELMER SINGLETON**	Singleton, Bert Elmer "Smoky" b: 6/26/18, Ogden, Utah d: 1/5/96, Ogden, Utah BR/TR, 6′2″, 174 lbs. Deb: 8/20/45																									
1945	Bos-N	1	4	.200	7	5	1	0	0	37^1	35	1	14	14	12.1	4.82	79	.248	.321	0	.000	-1	-4	-4	-0	-0.6
1946	Bos-N	0	1	.000	15	2	0	0	1	33^2	27	3	21	17	13.1	3.74	92	.221	.340	0	.000	-1	-1	-1	0	-0.1
1947	Pit-N	2	2	.500	36	3	0	0	1	67	70	9	39	24	14.9	6.31	67	.267	.366	4	.308	1	-17	-16	0	-0.7
1948	Pit-N	4	6	.400	38	5	1	0	2	92^1	90	11	40	53	12.8	4.97	82	.253	.330	2	.087	-2	-10	-9	1	-1.0
1950	Was-A	1	2	.333	21	1	0	0	0	36^1	39	4	17	19	13.9	5.20	86	.291	.371	3	.429	1	-3	-3	1	0.0
1957	Chi-N	0	1	.000	5	2	0	0	0	13^1	20	3	2	6	14.9	6.75	57	.333	.355	0	.000	-0	-4	-4	0	-0.3
1958	Chi-N	1	0	1.000	2	0	0	0	0	4^2	1	0	1	2	3.9	0.00	—	.071	.133	0	.000	-0	2	2	-0	0.4
1959	Chi-N	2	1	.667	21	1	0	0	0	43	40	2	12	25	10.9	2.72	145	.252	.304	0	.000	-1	6	6	1	0.4
Total	8	11	17	.393	145	19	2	0	4	327^2	322	33	146	160	13.0	4.83	83	.258	.338	9	.132	-3	-32	-29	3	-1.9
● **JOHN SINGLETON**	Singleton, John Edward "Sheriff" b: 11/27/1896, Gallipolis, Ohio d: 10/23/37, Dayton, Ohio BR/TR, 5′11″, 171 lbs. Deb: 6/8/22																									
1922	Phi-N	1	10	.091	22	9	3	1	0	93	127	6	38	27	16.5	5.90	79	.346	.415	5	.139	-2	-19	-13	-1	-1.5
● **MIKE SIROTKA**	Sirotka, Michael Robert b: 5/13/71, Houston, Tex. BL/TL, 6′1″, 190 lbs. Deb: 7/19/95																									
1995	Chi-A	1	2	.333	6	6	0	0	0	34^1	39	2	17	19	14.7	4.19	106	.298	.378	0	—	0	2	1	-0	0.1
1996	Chi-A	1	2	.333	15	4	0	0	0	26^1	34	3	12	11	15.7	7.18	66	.315	.383	0	—	0	-6	-7	-1	-0.7
1997	Chi-A	3	0	1.000	7	4	0	0	0	32	36	4	5	24	11.8	2.25	195	.290	.323	0	.000	-0	8	8	-0	0.6
1998	Chi-A	14	15	.483	33	33	5	0	0	211^2	255	30	47	128	12.9	5.06	90	.300	.338	0	.000	-0	-10	-12	0	-1.3
Total	4	19	19	.500	61	47	5	0	0	304^1	364	39	81	182	13.2	4.85	94	.300	.345	0	.000	-0	-6	-10	-1	-1.3
● **DOUG SISK**	Sisk, Douglas Randall b: 9/26/57, Renton, Wash. BR/TR, 6′2″, 210 lbs. Deb: 9/6/82																									
1982	NY-N	0	1	.000	8	0	0	0	1	8^2	5	1	4	4	10.4	1.04	349	.172	.294	0	—	0	2	2	0	0.3
1983	NY-N	5	4	.556	67	0	0	0	11	104^1	88	1	59	33	13.0	2.24	162	.235	.346	3	.500	1	16	16	-1	1.7
1984	NY-N	1	3	.250	50	0	0	0	15	77^2	57	1	54	32	13.2	2.09	169	.215	.354	1	.091	-0	13	12	0	1.1
1985	NY-N	4	5	.444	42	0	0	0	2	73	86	3	40	26	15.8	5.30	65	.291	.379	0	.000	-1	-14	-15	1	-1.9
1986	*NY-N	4	2	.667	41	0	0	0	1	70^2	77	0	31	31	14.4	3.06	116	.282	.366	0	.000	-0	5	4	-1	0.2
1987	NY-N	3	1	.750	55	0	0	0	3	78	83	5	22	37	12.5	3.46	109	.270	.325	0	.000	-1	5	3	1	0.2
1988	Bal-A	3	3	.500	52	0	0	0	0	94^1	109	3	45	26	14.9	3.72	105	.306	.387	0	—	0	3	2	1	0.2
1990	Atl-N	0	0	—	3	0	0	0	0	2^1	1	0	4	1	19.3	3.86	105	.143	.455	0	—	0	-0	0	0	0.0
1991	Atl-N	2	1	.667	14	0	0	0	0	14^1	21	1	8	5	18.2	5.02	77	.333	.408	0	—	0	-2	-2	0	-0.3
Total	9	22	20	.524	332	0	0	0	33	523^1	527	15	267	195	14.0	3.27	112	.268	.361	4	.105	-1	29	23	2	1.5
● **TOMMIE SISK**	Sisk, Tommie Wayne b: 4/12/42, Ardmore, Okla. BR/TR, 6′3″, 195 lbs. Deb: 7/19/62																									
1962	Pit-N	0	2	.000	5	3	1	0	0	17^2	18	1	8	6	13.8	4.08	97	.257	.342	1	.200	0	-0	-0	-0	-0.1
1963	Pit-N	1	3	.250	57	4	1	0	1	108	85	6	45	73	10.9	2.92	113	.222	.305	1	.063	-0	4	5	1	0.2
1964	Pit-N	1	4	.200	42	1	0	0	0	61^1	91	4	29	35	18.0	6.16	57	.364	.436	0	.000	-1	-18	-18	2	-1.3
1965	Pit-N	7	3	.700	38	12	1	1	0	111^1	103	6	50	66	12.4	3.40	103	.248	.330	2	.061	-2	2	1	-1	-0.2
1966	Pit-N	10	5	.667	34	23	4	1	1	150	146	14	52	60	12.1	4.14	86	.256	.323	5	.098	-1	-9	-9	0	-1.0
1967	Pit-N	13	13	.500	37	31	11	2	1	207^2	196	6	78	85	12.0	3.34	101	.253	.324	7	.101	-2	1	1	1	-0.1

YEAR	TM/L	W	L	PCT	G	GS	CG	SH	SV	IP	H	HR	BB	SO	RAT	ERA	ERA+	OAV	OOB	BH	AVG	PB	PR	/A	PD	TPI
1968	Pit-N	5	5	.500	33	11	0	0	1	96	101	3	35	41	13.0	3.28	89	.282	.351	2	.083	-1	-3	-4	0	-0.5
1969	SD-N	2	13	.133	53	13	1	0	6	143	160	11	48	59	13.2	4.78	74	.285	.342	3	.120	0	-19	-20	0	-2.0
1970	Chi-A	1	1	.500	17	1	0	0	0	33^1	37	6	13	16	13.5	5.40	72	.276	.340	1	.250	0	-6	-6	1	-0.2
Total	9	40	49	.449	316	99	19	4	10	928^1	937	57	358	441	12.7	3.92	88	.266	.337	22	.094	-7	-48	-50	3	-5.2

● DAVE SISLER Sisler, David Michael b: 10/16/31, St.Louis, Mo. BR/TR, 6'4", 200 lbs. Deb: 4/21/56 F

YEAR	TM/L	W	L	PCT	G	GS	CG	SH	SV	IP	H	HR	BB	SO	RAT	ERA	ERA+	OAV	OOB	BH	AVG	PB	PR	/A	PD	TPI
1956	Bos-A	9	8	.529	39	14	3	0	3	142^1	120	13	72	93	12.6	4.62	100	.227	.328	5	.119	-2	-7	0	0	-0.2
1957	Bos-A	7	8	.467	22	19	5	0	1	122^1	135	15	61	55	14.6	4.71	85	.280	.363	7	.167	-0	-12	-10	1	-1.1
1958	Bos-A	8	9	.471	30	25	4	1	0	149^1	157	22	79	71	14.3	4.94	81	.276	.366	9	.196	0	-19	-16	-1	-1.6
1959	Bos-A	0	0	—	3	0	0	0	0	6^2	9	3	1	3	13.5	6.75	60	.310	.333	1	.500	0	-2	-2	-0	0.0
	Det-A	1	3	.250	32	0	0	0	7	51^2	46	4	36	29	14.5	4.01	101	.242	.366	1	.200	-0	-1	0	-1	0.0
	Yr	1	3	.250	35	0	0	0	7	58^1	55	7	37	32	14.3	4.32	94	.251	.362	2	.286	0	-3	-2	-1	0.0
1960	Det-A	7	5	.583	41	0	0	0	6	80	56	3	45	47	11.6	2.47	160	.199	.314	2	.125	-0	12	13	1	2.2
1961	Was-A	2	8	.200	45	1	0	0	11	60^1	55	6	48	30	15.8	4.18	96	.251	.393	0	.000	0	-1	-1	0	-0.2
1962	Cin-N	4	3	.571	35	0	0	0	1	43^2	44	4	26	27	14.4	3.92	103	.270	.370	0	—	0	0	1	-1	0.0
Total	7	38	44	.463	247	59	12	1	29	656^1	622	70	368	355	13.8	4.33	95	.253	.354	25	.157	-2	-31	-15	1	-0.9

● GEORGE SISLER Sisler, George Harold "Georgeous George" b: 3/24/1893, Manchester, Ohio d: 3/26/73, Richmond Heights, Mo. BL/TL, 5'11", 170 lbs. Deb: 6/28/15 FMCH♦

YEAR	TM/L	W	L	PCT	G	GS	CG	SH	SV	IP	H	HR	BB	SO	RAT	ERA	ERA+	OAV	OOB	BH	AVG	PB	PR	/A	PD	TPI
1915	StL-A	4	4	.500	15	8	6	0	0	70	62	0	38	41	13.4	2.83	101	.247	.355	78	.285	3	1	0	0	0.2
1916	StL-A	1	2	.333	3	3	3	1	0	27	18	0	6	12	8.3	1.00	275	.198	.255	177	.305	1	5	5	1	0.9
1918	StL-A	0	0	—	2	1	0	0	1	8	10	0	4	4	16.9	4.50	61	.286	.375	154	.341	1	-2	-2	0	0.0
1920	StL-A	0	0	—	1	0	0	0	1	1	0	0	0	2	0.0	0.00	—	.000	.000	257	.407	1	0	0	0	0.1
1925	StL-A	0	0	—	1	0	0	0	0	2	1	0	1	1	9.0	0.00	—	.167	.286	224	.345	0	1	1	0	0.0
1926	StL-A	0	0	—	1	0	0	0	1	2	0	0	2	3	9.0	0.00	—	.000	.286	178	.290	0	1	1	0	0.1
1928	Bos-N	0	0	—	1	0	0	0	0	1	0	0	1	0	9.0	0.00	—	.000	.333	167	.340	0	0	0	-0	0.0
Total	7	5	6	.455	24	12	9	1	3	111	91	0	52	63	12.1	2.35	123	.231	.330	2812	.340	7	8	7	1	1.3

● CARL SITTON Sitton, Carl Vetter b: 9/22/1882, Pendleton, S.C. d: 9/11/31, Valdosta, Ga. BR/TR, 5'10.5", 170 lbs. Deb: 4/24/09

YEAR	TM/L	W	L	PCT	G	GS	CG	SH	SV	IP	H	HR	BB	SO	RAT	ERA	ERA+	OAV	OOB	BH	AVG	PB	PR	/A	PD	TPI
1909	Cle-A	3	2	.600	14	5	3	0	0	50	50	1	16	16	12.2	2.88	89	.263	.327	2	.154	0	-2	-2	-1	-0.2

● PETE SIVESS Sivess, Peter b: 9/23/13, South River, N.J. BR/TR, 6'3.5", 195 lbs. Deb: 6/13/36

YEAR	TM/L	W	L	PCT	G	GS	CG	SH	SV	IP	H	HR	BB	SO	RAT	ERA	ERA+	OAV	OOB	BH	AVG	PB	PR	/A	PD	TPI
1936	Phi-N	3	4	.429	17	6	2	0	0	65	84	6	36	22	16.8	4.57	99	.310	.393	3	.120	-2	-4	-0	-2	-0.4
1937	Phi-N	1	1	.500	6	2	1	0	0	23	30	5	11	4	16.0	7.04	62	.330	.402	0	.000	-1	-8	-7	-1	-0.6
1938	Phi-N	3	6	.333	39	8	2	0	3	116	143	12	69	32	16.5	5.51	71	.306	.397	6	.188	-1	-22	-21	-1	-1.7
Total	3	7	11	.389	62	16	5	0	3	204	257	23	116	58	16.5	5.38	77	.310	.396	9	.143	-4	-34	-28	-3	-2.7

● JIM SIWY Siwy, James Gerard b: 9/20/58, Central Falls, R.I BR/TR, 6'4", 200 lbs. Deb: 8/20/82

YEAR	TM/L	W	L	PCT	G	GS	CG	SH	SV	IP	H	HR	BB	SO	RAT	ERA	ERA+	OAV	OOB	BH	AVG	PB	PR	/A	PD	TPI
1982	Chi-A	0	0	—	2	1	0	0	0	7	10	1	5	3	19.3	10.29	39	.385	.484	0	—	0	-5	-5	-0	0.0
1984	Chi-A	0	0	—	1	0	0	0	0	4^1	3	0	2	1	10.4	2.08	200	.231	.333	0	—	0	1	1	0	-0.2
Total	2	0	0	—	3	1	0	0	0	11^1	13	1	7	4	15.9	7.15	57	.333	.435	0	—	0	-4	-4	-0	-0.2

● JOE SKALSKI Skalski, Joseph Douglas b: 9/26/64, Burnham, Ill. BR/TR, 6'3", 190 lbs. Deb: 4/10/89

YEAR	TM/L	W	L	PCT	G	GS	CG	SH	SV	IP	H	HR	BB	SO	RAT	ERA	ERA+	OAV	OOB	BH	AVG	PB	PR	/A	PD	TPI
1989	Cle-A	0	2	.000	2	1	0	0	0	6^2	7	0	4	3	17.6	6.75	59	.259	.394	0	—	0	-2	-2	-0	-0.5

● DAVE SKAUGSTAD Skaugstad, David Wendell b: 1/10/40, Algona, Iowa BL/TL, 6'1", 179 lbs. Deb: 9/25/57

YEAR	TM/L	W	L	PCT	G	GS	CG	SH	SV	IP	H	HR	BB	SO	RAT	ERA	ERA+	OAV	OOB	BH	AVG	PB	PR	/A	PD	TPI
1957	Cin-N	0	0	—	2	0	0	0	0	5^2	4	0	6	4	15.9	1.59	259	.190	.370	0	.000	0	1	2	0	0.0

● DAVE SKEELS Skeels, David b: 12/29/1892, Addy, Wash. d: 12/2/26, Spokane, Wash. BL/TR, 6'1", 187 lbs. Deb: 9/14/10

YEAR	TM/L	W	L	PCT	G	GS	CG	SH	SV	IP	H	HR	BB	SO	RAT	ERA	ERA+	OAV	OOB	BH	AVG	PB	PR	/A	PD	TPI
1910	Det-A	0	0	—	1	1	0	0	0	6	9	0	4	2	21.0	12.00	22	.333	.438	0	.000	-0	-6	-6	0	0.0

● CRAIG SKOK Skok, Craig Richard b: 9/1/47, Dobbs Ferry, N.Y. BR/TL, 6', 190 lbs. Deb: 5/4/73

YEAR	TM/L	W	L	PCT	G	GS	CG	SH	SV	IP	H	HR	BB	SO	RAT	ERA	ERA+	OAV	OOB	BH	AVG	PB	PR	/A	PD	TPI
1973	Bos-A	0	1	.000	11	0	0	0	1	28^2	35	2	11	22	14.4	6.28	64	.304	.365	0	—	0	-8	-7	-0	-0.3
1976	Tex-A	0	1	.000	9	0	0	0	0	5	13	2	3	5	28.8	12.60	28	.481	.533	0	—	0	-5	-5	0	-1.0
1978	Atl-N	3	2	.600	43	0	0	0	2	62	64	8	27	28	13.2	4.35	93	.266	.340	2	.250	0	-5	-2	-0	-0.2
1979	Atl-N	1	3	.250	44	0	0	0	2	54^1	58	7	17	30	12.9	3.98	102	.282	.345	0	.000	-0	-1	0	0	0.1
Total	4	4	7	.364	107	0	0	0	5	150	170	19	58	85	13.9	4.86	83	.289	.355	2	.182	0	-20	-14	-0	-1.4

● JOHN SKOPEC Skopec, John S. "Buckshot" b: 5/8/1880, Chicago, Ill. d: 10/20/12, Chicago, Ill. BR/TL, 5'10", 190 lbs. Deb: 4/25/01

YEAR	TM/L	W	L	PCT	G	GS	CG	SH	SV	IP	H	HR	BB	SO	RAT	ERA	ERA+	OAV	OOB	BH	AVG	PB	PR	/A	PD	TPI
1901	Chi-A	6	3	.667	9	9	6	0	0	68^1	62	1	45	24	15.1	3.16	110	.239	.369	10	.333	3	4	2	3	0.8
1903	Det-A	2	2	.500	6	5	3	0	0	39^1	46	0	13	14	14.0	3.43	85	.291	.353	2	.154	-0	-2	-2	0	-0.2
Total	2	8	5	.615	15	14	9	0	0	107^2	108	1	58	38	14.7	3.26	101	.259	.363	12	.279	3	2	0	3	0.6

● JOHN SLAGLE Slagle, John A. b: Lawrence, Ind. BL/TR, Deb: 4/30/1891

YEAR	TM/L	W	L	PCT	G	GS	CG	SH	SV	IP	H	HR	BB	SO	RAT	ERA	ERA+	OAV	OOB	BH	AVG	PB	PR	/A	PD	TPI
1891	Cin-a	0	0	—	1	0	0	0	1	1^1	3	0	1	1	27.0	0.00	—	.429	.500	0	.000	-0	1	1	0	0.1

● ROGER SLAGLE Slagle, Roger Lee b: 11/4/53, Wichita, Kan. BR/TR, 6'3", 190 lbs. Deb: 9/7/79

YEAR	TM/L	W	L	PCT	G	GS	CG	SH	SV	IP	H	HR	BB	SO	RAT	ERA	ERA+	OAV	OOB	BH	AVG	PB	PR	/A	PD	TPI
1979	NY-A	0	0	—	1	0	0	0	0	2	0	0	0	2	0.0	0.00	—	.000	.000	0	—	0	1	1	0	0.0

● WALT SLAGLE Slagle, Walter Jennings b: 12/15/1878, Kenton, Ohio d: 6/17/74, San Gabriel, Cal. BB/TR, 6', 165 lbs. Deb: 5/4/10

YEAR	TM/L	W	L	PCT	G	GS	CG	SH	SV	IP	H	HR	BB	SO	RAT	ERA	ERA+	OAV	OOB	BH	AVG	PB	PR	/A	PD	TPI
1910	Cin-N	0	0	—	1	0	0	0	0	1	0	0	3	0	36.0	9.00	32	.000	.571	0	—	0	-1	-1	-0	0.0

● CY SLAPNICKA Slapnicka, Cyril Charles b: 3/23/1886, Cedar Rapids, Iowa d: 10/20/79, Cedar Rapids, Iowa BB/TR, 5'10", 165 lbs. Deb: 9/26/11

YEAR	TM/L	W	L	PCT	G	GS	CG	SH	SV	IP	H	HR	BB	SO	RAT	ERA	ERA+	OAV	OOB	BH	AVG	PB	PR	/A	PD	TPI
1911	Chi-N	0	2	.000	3	2	1	0	0	24	21	0	7	10	11.6	3.38	98	.236	.313	2	.222	-0	0	-0	1	0.1
1918	Pit-N	1	4	.200	7	6	4	0	1	49^1	50	2	22	3	14.0	4.74	61	.269	.362	1	.071	-1	-11	-10	-0	-1.1
Total	2	1	6	.143	10	8	5	0	1	73^1	71	2	29	13	13.3	4.30	70	.258	.346	3	.130	-1	-11	-10	0	-1.0

● JOHN SLAPPEY Slappey, John Henry b: 8/8/1898, Albany, Ga. d: 6/10/57, Marietta, Ga. BL/TL, 6'4", 170 lbs. Deb: 8/23/20

YEAR	TM/L	W	L	PCT	G	GS	CG	SH	SV	IP	H	HR	BB	SO	RAT	ERA	ERA+	OAV	OOB	BH	AVG	PB	PR	/A	PD	TPI
1920	Phi-A	0	1	.000	3	1	0	0	0	6^1	15	0	4	1	27.0	7.11	57	.441	.500	1	.500	1	-2	-2	-0	-0.2

● JIM SLATON Slaton, James Michael b: 6/19/50, Long Beach, Cal. BR/TR, 6', 185 lbs. Deb: 4/14/71

YEAR	TM/L	W	L	PCT	G	GS	CG	SH	SV	IP	H	HR	BB	SO	RAT	ERA	ERA+	OAV	OOB	BH	AVG	PB	PR	/A	PD	TPI
1971	Mil-A	10	8	.556	26	23	5	4	0	147^2	140	16	71	63	12.9	3.78	92	.253	.339	5	.109	-1	-5	-5	-2	-0.9
1972	Mil-A	1	6	.143	9	8	0	0	0	44	50	3	21	17	14.7	5.52	55	.287	.367	1	.091	-1	-12	-12	1	-1.8
1973	Mil-A	13	15	.464	38	38	13	3	0	276^1	266	30	99	134	11.9	3.71	101	.251	.316	0	—	0	3	1	-3	-0.2
1974	Mil-A	13	16	.448	40	35	10	3	0	250	255	22	102	126	13.0	3.92	92	.268	.341	0	—	0	-9	-9	0	-0.9
1975	Mil-A	11	18	.379	37	33	10	3	0	217	238	28	90	119	13.7	4.52	85	.276	.346	0	—	0	-18	-17	1	-2.0
1976	Mil-A	14	15	.483	38	38	12	2	0	292^2	287	14	94	138	11.9	3.44	101	.259	.320	0	—	0	2	2	-0	0.3
1977	Mil-A☆	10	14	.417	32	31	7	1	0	221	223	25	77	104	12.7	3.58	113	.266	.336	0	—	0	12	12	0	1.2
1978	Det-A	17	11	.607	35	34	11	2	0	233^2	235	27	85	92	12.6	4.12	94	.263	.332	0	—	0	-9	-7	-1	-0.9
1979	Mil-A	15	9	.625	32	31	12	3	0	213	229	15	54	80	12.0	3.63	115	.278	.323	0	—	0	14	13	1	1.3
1980	Mil-A	1	1	.500	3	3	0	0	0	16^1	17	3	5	4	12.1	4.41	88	.270	.324	0	—	0	-1	-1	0	-0.1
1981	*Mil-A	5	7	.417	24	21	0	0	0	117^1	120	10	50	47	13.2	4.37	78	.273	.350	0	—	0	-9	-12	-0	-0.9
1982	*Mil-A	10	6	.625	39	7	0	0	6	117^2	117	14	41	59	12.2	3.29	115	.264	.327	0	—	0	10	6	-0	0.8
1983	Mil-A	14	6	.700	46	0	0	0	5	112^1	112	12	56	38	13.7	4.33	86	.272	.363	0	—	0	-3	-7	-0	-1.2
1984	Cal-A	7	10	.412	32	22	5	1	0	163	192	22	56	67	13.8	4.97	80	.295	.353	0	—	0	-18	-18	0	-1.6
1985	Cal-A	6	10	.375	29	24	1	0	1	148^1	162	22	63	60	13.8	4.37	94	.284	.357	0	—	0	-4	-4	-0	-0.4
1986	Cal-A	4	6	.400	14	12	0	0	0	73^1	84	9	29	31	14.1	5.65	73	.295	.364	0	—	0	-12	-13	1	-1.4
	Det-A	0	0	—	22	0	0	0	2	40	46	5	11	12	13.0	4.05	102	.287	.337	0	—	0	1	0	0	0.0
	Yr	4	6	.400	36	12	0	0	2	113^1	130	14	40	43	13.6	5.08	81	.287	.346	0	—	0	-11	-12	1	-1.4
Total	16	151	158	.489	496	360	86	22	14	2683^2	2773	277	1004	1191	12.8	4.03	94	.270	.337	6	.105	-2	-58	-70	-4	-8.7

● PHIL SLATTERY Slattery, Philip Ryan b: 2/25/1893, Harper, Iowa d: 3/2/68, Long Beach, Cal. BR/TL, 5'11", 160 lbs. Deb: 9/16/15

YEAR	TM/L	W	L	PCT	G	GS	CG	SH	SV	IP	H	HR	BB	SO	RAT	ERA	ERA+	OAV	OOB	BH	AVG	PB	PR	/A	PD	TPI
1915	Pit-N	0	0	—	3	0	0	0	0	8	5	0	1	1	9.0	0.00	—	.185	.267	0	.000	-0	2	2	-1	-0.1

YEAR	TM/L	W	L	PCT	G	GS	CG	SH	SV	IP	H	HR	BB	SO	RAT	ERA	ERA+	OAV	OOB	BH	AVG	PB	PR	/A	PD	TPI
● **BARNEY SLAUGHTER**	Slaughter, Byron Atkins b: 10/6/1884, Smyrna, Del. d: 5/17/61, Philadelphia, Pa. BR/TR, 5'11.5", 165 lbs. Deb: 8/9/10																									
1910	Phi-N	0	1	.000	8	1	0	0	1	18	21	0	11	7	16.0	5.50	57	.318	.416	1	.200	0	-5	-5	0	-0.3
● **STERLING SLAUGHTER**	Slaughter, Sterling Feore b: 11/18/41, Danville, Ill. BR/TR, 5'11", 165 lbs. Deb: 4/19/64																									
1964	Chi-N	2	4	.333	20	6	1	0	0	51^2	64	8	32	32	16.7	5.75	65	.305	.397	1	.083	-0	-13	-12	-1	-1.4
● **BILL SLAYBACK**	Slayback, William Grover b: 2/21/48, Hollywood, Cal. BR/TR, 6'4", 200 lbs. Deb: 6/26/72																									
1972	Det-A	5	6	.455	23	13	3	1	0	81^2	74	4	25	65	11.0	3.20	98	.239	.298	4	.174	-0	-1	-0	1	0.0
1973	Det-A	0	0	—	3	0	0	0	0	2	5	0	0	1	27.0	4.50	91	.417	.462	0	—	0	-0	-0	-0	0.0
1974	Det-A	1	3	.250	16	4	0	0	0	54^2	57	1	26	23	14.2	4.77	80	.273	.361	0	—	0	-7	-6	-0	-0.5
Total	3	6	9	.400	42	17	3	1	0	138^1	136	5	51	89	12.5	3.84	89	.256	.327	4	.174	-0	-8	-7	0	-0.5
● **STEVE SLAYTON**	Slayton, Foster Herbert b: 4/26/02, Barre, Vt. d: 12/20/84, Manchester, N.H. BR/TR, 6', 163 lbs. Deb: 7/21/28																									
1928	Bos-A	0	0	—	3	0	0	0	0	7	6	0	3	2	11.6	3.86	107	.240	.321	0	.000	-0	0	0	-0	0.0
● **LOU SLEATER**	Sleater, Louis Mortimer b: 9/8/26, St.Louis, Mo. BL/TL, 5'10", 185 lbs. Deb: 4/25/50																									
1950	StL-A	0	0	—	1	0	0	0	0	1	0	0	0	1	0.0	0.00	—	.000	.000	0	—	0	1	1	0	0.0
1951	StL-A	1	9	.100	20	8	4	0	1	81	88	7	53	33	16.2	5.11	86	.271	.381	7	.226	0	-9	-6	-1	-0.8
1952	StL-A	0	1	.000	4	2	0	0	0	8^2	9	1	5	1	14.5	7.27	54	.265	.359	0	.000	-0	-3	-3	0	-0.4
	Was-A	4	2	.667	14	9	3	1	0	57	56	4	30	22	13.9	3.63	98	.260	.356	1	.050	-2	0	-0	-1	-0.4
	Yr	4	3	.571	18	11	3	1	0	65^2	65	5	35	23	14.0	4.11	88	.261	.357	1	.045	-2	-3	-4	-1	-0.8
1955	KC-A	1	1	.500	16	1	0	0	0	25^2	33	3	21	11	18.9	7.71	54	.324	.439	2	.154	-1	-11	-10	-0	-0.8
1956	Mil-N	2	2	.500	25	1	0	0	2	45^2	42	6	27	32	13.6	3.15	110	.240	.342	5	.500	2	3	2	1	0.5
1957	Det-A	3	3	.500	41	0	0	0	2	69^1	61	9	28	43	11.7	3.76	102	.237	.315	5	.250	3	0	1	-0	0.4
1958	Det-A	0	0	—	4	0	0	0	0	5^1	3	2	6	4	15.2	6.75	60	.158	.360	1	1.000	1	-2	-2	0	0.2
	Bal-A	1	0	1.000	6	0	0	0	0	7	14	0	2	5	20.6	12.86	28	.438	.471	0	.000	-1	-7	-7	0	-0.9
	Yr	1	0	1.000	10	0	0	0	0	12^1	17	2	8	9	18.2	10.22	37	.333	.424	1	.143	0	-9	-9	0	-0.7
Total	7	12	18	.400	131	21	7	1	5	300^2	306	32	172	152	14.5	4.70	83	.263	.362	21	.204	3	-28	-26	-2	-2.2
● **LEFTY SLOAT**	Sloat, Dwain Clifford b: 12/1/18, Nokomis, Ill. BR/TL, 6', 168 lbs. Deb: 4/24/48																									
1948	Bro-N	0	1	.000	4	1	0	0	0	7^1	7	0	8	1	18.4	6.14	65	.280	.455	0	.000	-0	-2	-2	1	-0.2
1949	Chi-N	0	0	—	5	1	0	0	0	9	14	0	3	3	17.0	7.00	58	.400	.447	0	—	0	-3	-3	0	0.0
Total	2	0	1	.000	9	2	0	0	0	16^1	21	0	11	4	17.6	6.61	61	.350	.451	0	.000	-0	-5	-5	1	-0.2
● **HEATHCLIFF SLOCUMB**	Slocumb, Heath b: 6/7/66, Jamaica, N.Y. BR/TR, 6'3", 220 lbs. Deb: 4/11/91																									
1991	Chi-N	2	1	.667	52	0	0	0	1	62^2	53	3	30	34	12.4	3.45	113	.231	.328	0	.000	-0	2	3	0	0.1
1992	Chi-N	0	3	.000	30	0	0	0	1	36	52	3	21	27	18.5	6.50	55	.351	.435	0	.000	-0	-12	-12	-0	-1.1
1993	Chi-N	1	0	1.000	10	0	0	0	0	10^2	7	0	4	4	9.3	3.38	118	.189	.268	0	.000	-0	1	1	0	0.1
	Cle-A	3	1	.750	20	0	0	0	0	27^1	28	3	16	18	14.5	4.28	101	.272	.370	0	—	0	0	0	-0	0.0
1994	Phi-N	5	1	.833	52	0	0	0	0	72^1	75	0	28	58	13.1	2.86	150	.262	.332	1	.250	0	11	11	0	0.9
1995	Phi-N★	5	6	.455	61	0	0	0	32	65^1	64	2	35	63	13.8	2.89	146	.257	.351	0	.000	-0	9	10	2	2.5
1996	Bos-A	5	5	.500	75	0	0	0	31	83^1	68	2	55	88	13.6	3.02	168	.222	.346	0	—	0	18	19	1	3.3
1997	Bos-A	0	5	.000	49	0	0	0	17	46^2	58	4	34	36	18.3	5.79	80	.312	.426	0	—	0	-6	-6	-0	-0.9
	*Sea-A	0	4	.000	27	0	0	0	10	28^1	26	2	15	28	13.3	4.13	109	.241	.339	0	—	0	1	1	-0	0.2
	Yr	0	9	.000	76	0	0	0	27	75	84	6	49	64	16.1	5.16	89	.281	.384	0	—	0	-5	-5	-0	-0.7
1998	Sea-A	2	5	.286	57	0	0	0	3	67^2	72	5	44	51	15.6	5.32	87	.275	.381	0	—	0	-5	-5	0	-0.5
Total	8	23	31	.426	433	0	0	0	95	500^1	503	24	282	407	14.4	3.99	110	.263	.362	1	.091	-1	19	23	3	4.6
● **JOE SLUSARSKI**	Slusarski, Joseph Andrew b: 12/19/66, Indianapolis, Ind. BR/TR, 6'4", 195 lbs. Deb: 4/11/91																									
1991	Oak-A	5	7	.417	20	19	1	0	0	109^1	121	14	52	60	14.6	5.27	73	.283	.366	0	—	0	-14	-17	-1	-1.6
1992	Oak-A	5	5	.500	15	14	0	0	0	76	85	15	27	38	14.0	5.45	69	.284	.355	0	—	0	-13	-14	-1	-1.7
1993	Oak-A	0	0	—	2	1	0	0	0	8^2	9	1	11	1	20.8	5.19	78	.300	.488	0	—	0	-1	-1	0	0.0
1995	Mil-A	1	1	.500	12	0	0	0	0	15	21	3	6	6	17.4	5.40	92	.333	.408	0	—	0	-1	-1	-0	-0.1
Total	4	11	13	.458	49	34	1	0	0	209	236	33	96	105	14.8	5.34	73	.288	.371	0	—	0	-29	-34	-2	-3.4
● **AARON SMALL**	Small, Aaron James b: 11/23/71, Oxnard, Cal. BR/TR, 6'5", 200 lbs. Deb: 6/11/94																									
1994	Tor-A	0	0	—	1	0	0	0	0	2	5	1	2	0	31.5	9.00	54	.500	.583	0	—	0	-1	-1	0	0.0
1995	Fla-N	1	0	1.000	7	0	0	0	0	6^1	7	1	6	5	18.5	1.42	296	.269	.406	0	—	0	2	2	0	0.3
1996	Oak-A	1	3	.250	12	3	0	0	0	28^2	37	3	22	17	18.8	8.16	60	.308	.420	0	—	0	-10	-10	0	-1.1
1997	Oak-A	9	5	.643	71	0	0	0	4	96^2	109	6	40	57	14.2	4.28	106	.294	.367	0	.000	-0	3	3	0	0.4
1998	Oak-A	1	1	.500	24	0	0	0	0	36	51	3	14	19	17.0	7.25	63	.333	.400	0	—	0	-10	-11	-1	-0.5
	Ari-N	3	1	.750	23	0	0	0	0	31^2	32	5	8	14	11.7	3.69	117	.269	.320	0	—	0	2	2	-1	0.1
Total	5	15	10	.600	138	3	0	0	4	201^1	241	19	92	112	15.2	5.23	87	.302	.379	0	.000	-0	-15	-15	-1	-0.8
● **MARK SMALL**	Small, Mark Allen b: 11/12/67, Portland, Ore. BR/TR, 6'3", 205 lbs. Deb: 4/5/96																									
1996	Hou-N	0	1	.000	16	0	0	0	0	24^1	33	1	13	16	17.4	5.92	65	.308	.388	0	.000	-0	-5	-6	-1	-0.3
● **WALT SMALLWOOD**	Smallwood, Walter Clayton b: 4/24/1893, Dayton, Md. d: 4/29/67, Baltimore, Md. BR/TR, 6'2", 190 lbs. Deb: 9/19/17																									
1917	NY-A	0	0	—	2	0	0	0	0	2	1	0	1	1	9.0	0.00	—	.167	.286	0	—	0	1	1	0	0.0
1919	NY-A	0	0	—	6	0	0	0	0	21^2	20	1	9	6	12.9	4.98	64	.263	.356	0	.000	-1	-4	-4	-0	-0.1
Total	2	0	0	—	8	0	0	0	0	23^2	21	1	10	7	12.5	4.56	69	.256	.351	0	.000	-1	-4	-4	-0	-0.1
● **JOHN SMILEY**	Smiley, John Patrick b: 3/17/65, Phoenixville, Pa. BL/TL, 6'4", 200 lbs. Deb: 9/1/86																									
1986	Pit-N	1	0	1.000	12	0	0	0	0	11^2	4	2	4	9	6.2	3.86	99	.105	.190	0	—	0	-0	-0	0	0.0
1987	Pit-N	5	5	.500	63	0	0	0	4	75	69	7	50	58	14.3	5.76	71	.244	.357	1	.143	0	-14	-14	0	-1.7
1988	Pit-N	13	11	.542	34	32	5	1	0	205	185	15	46	129	10.3	3.25	105	.241	.287	5	.079	-2	5	3	-1	0.1
1989	Pit-N	12	8	.600	28	28	8	1	0	205^1	174	22	49	123	9.9	2.81	120	.226	.276	9	.138	1	16	13	-2	1.0
1990	*Pit-N	9	10	.474	26	25	2	0	0	149^1	161	15	36	86	12.0	4.64	78	.275	.319	6	.122	-0	-14	-17	0	-1.9
1991	*Pit-N★	**20**	8	**.714**	33	32	2	1	0	207^2	194	17	44	129	10.4	3.08	116	.251	.294	7	.100	-2	14	11	-0	1.2
1992	Min-A	16	9	.640	34	34	5	2	0	241	205	17	65	163	10.3	3.21	126	.231	.288	0	—	0	19	23	0	2.2
1993	Cin-N	3	9	.250	18	18	2	0	0	105^2	117	15	31	60	12.8	5.62	72	.286	.339	8	.250	2	-19	-19	0	-1.6
1994	Cin-N	11	10	.524	24	24	1	1	0	158^2	169	18	37	112	11.9	3.86	107	.275	.320	11	.200	3	6	5	-1	0.7
1995	*Cin-N★	12	5	.706	28	27	1	0	0	176^2	173	11	39	124	11.0	3.46	119	.263	.308	9	.164	2	14	13	-0	1.3
1996	Cin-N	13	14	.481	35	34	2	2	0	217^1	207	20	54	171	11.0	3.64	116	.256	.306	13	.191	2	14	14	-1	1.7
1997	Cin-N	9	10	.474	20	20	0	0	0	117	139	17	31	94	13.5	5.23	81	.296	.347	4	.100	-2	-13	-13	-2	-2.0
	Cle-A	2	4	.333	6	6	0	0	0	37^1	45	9	10	26	13.5	5.54	85	.304	.352	0	—	0	-4	-4	-0	-0.5
Total	12	126	103	.550	361	280	28	8	4	1907^2	1842	185	496	1284	11.2	3.80	102	.255	.307	73	.145	3	24	15	-6	0.5
● **SMITH**	Smith Deb: 6/5/1884																									
1884	Bal-U	0	0	—	1	1	0	0	0	6	12	0	2	2	21.0	9.00	30	.387	.424	1	.200	-1	-4	-4	-0	-0.1
● **SMITH**	Smith Deb: 5/31/1886																									
1886	Cin-a	0	1	.000	1	1	1	0	0	9	8	0	10	1	18.0	4.00	88	.229	.400	1	.250	-0	-1	-0	-0	-0.1
● **AL SMITH**	Smith, Alfred John b: 10/12/07, Belleville, Ill. d: 4/28/77, Brownsville, Tex. BL/TL, 5'11", 180 lbs. Deb: 5/5/34 C																									
1934	NY-N	3	5	.375	30	4	0	0	5	66^2	70	2	21	27	12.3	4.32	90	.266	.320	4	.286	1	-2	-3	-0	-0.4
1935	NY-N	10	8	.556	40	10	4	1	5	124	125	6	32	44	11.9	3.41	113	.263	.319	4	.118	-0	8	6	-1	0.7
1936	*NY-N	14	13	.519	43	30	9	**4**	2	209^1	217	16	69	89	12.5	3.78	103	.274	.335	10	.137	-1	6	3	-1	0.1
1937	*NY-N	5	4	.556	33	9	2	0	0	85^2	91	8	30	41	12.9	4.20	93	.275	.339	3	.120	-2	-3	-3	-1	-0.5
1938	Phi-N	1	4	.200	37	1	0	0	1	86	115	7	40	46	16.2	6.28	62	.320	.388	0	.000	-2	-24	-23	0	-1.4
1939	Phi-N	0	0	—	5	0	0	0	0	9	11	1	5	2	18.0	4.00	100	.314	.429	0	.000	-0	-0	0	0	0.0
1940	Cle-A	15	7	.682	31	24	11	1	2	183	187	12	55	46	12.2	3.44	122	.270	.329	19	.306	7	19	16	2	2.6

YEAR	TM/L	W	L	PCT	G	GS	CG	SH	SV	IP	H	HR	BB	SO	RAT	ERA	ERA+	OAV	OOB	BH	AVG	PB	PR	/A	PD	TPI
1941	Cle-A	12	13	.480	29	27	13	2	0	206^2	204	12	75	76	12.2	3.83	103	.256	.321	11	.155	2	7	2	2	0.6
1942	Cle-A	10	15	.400	30	24	7	1	0	168^1	163	9	71	66	12.8	3.96	87	.251	.329	15	.250	3	-6	-9	-1	-1.0
1943	Cle-A☆	17	7	.708	29	27	14	3	1	208^1	186	7	72	72	11.1	2.55	122	.239	.303	14	.206	3	17	13	-0	1.9
1944	Cle-A	7	13	.350	28	26	7	1	0	181^2	197	6	69	44	13.3	3.42	96	.280	.347	10	.156	-1	0	-2	1	-0.2
1945	Cle-A	5	12	.294	21	19	8	3	1	133^2	141	8	48	34	12.9	3.84	85	.275	.340	12	.293	4	-7	-9	2	-0.4
Total	12	99	101	.495	356	201	75	16	17	1662^1	1707	94	587	587	12.6	3.72	99	.267	.332	102	.191	14	17	-10	4	2.0

● AL SMITH Smith, Alfred Kendricks b: 12/13/03, Norristown, Pa. d: 8/11/95, San Diego, Cal. BR/TR, 6', 170 lbs. Deb: 6/18/26

YEAR	TM/L	W	L	PCT	G	GS	CG	SH	SV	IP	H	HR	BB	SO	RAT	ERA	ERA+	OAV	OOB	BH	AVG	PB	PR	/A	PD	TPI
1926	NY-N	0	0	—	1	0	0	0	0	2	4	0	2	0	27.0	9.00	42	.444	.545	0	—	0	-1	-1	-0	0.0

● ART SMITH Smith, Arthur Laird b: 6/21/06, Boston, Mass. d: 11/22/95, Norwalk, Conn. BR/TR, 6', 175 lbs. Deb: 6/9/32

YEAR	TM/L	W	L	PCT	G	GS	CG	SH	SV	IP	H	HR	BB	SO	RAT	ERA	ERA+	OAV	OOB	BH	AVG	PB	PR	/A	PD	TPI
1932	Chi-A	0	1	.000	3	2	0	0	0	7	17	1	4	1	27.0	11.57	37	.500	.553	0	.000	-0	-6	-6	1	-0.6

● BILLY SMITH Smith, Billy Lavern b: 9/13/54, LaMarque, Tex. BR/TR, 6'7", 200 lbs. Deb: 6/9/81

YEAR	TM/L	W	L	PCT	G	GS	CG	SH	SV	IP	H	HR	BB	SO	RAT	ERA	ERA+	OAV	OOB	BH	AVG	PB	PR	/A	PD	TPI
1981	*Hou-N	1	1	.500	10	1	0	0	1	20^2	20	3	3	3	10.0	3.05	108	.263	.291	0	.000	-0	1	1	0	0.0

● BRYN SMITH Smith, Bryn Nelson b: 8/11/55, Marietta, Ga. BR/TR, 6'2", 205 lbs. Deb: 9/8/81

YEAR	TM/L	W	L	PCT	G	GS	CG	SH	SV	IP	H	HR	BB	SO	RAT	ERA	ERA+	OAV	OOB	BH	AVG	PB	PR	/A	PD	TPI
1981	Mon-N	1	0	1.000	7	0	0	0	0	13	14	1	3	9	11.8	2.77	126	.280	.321	0	.000	-0	1	1	-0	0.0
1982	Mon-N	2	4	.333	47	1	0	0	3	79^1	81	5	23	50	11.8	4.20	87	.264	.315	0	.000	-0	-5	-5	0	-0.4
1983	Mon-N	6	11	.353	49	12	5	3	3	155^1	142	13	43	101	11.0	2.49	144	.248	.306	5	.167	0	20	19	0	2.1
1984	Mon-N	12	13	.480	28	28	4	2	0	179	178	15	51	101	11.7	3.32	103	.259	.313	7	.132	1	5	2	2	0.6
1985	Mon-N	18	5	.783	32	32	4	2	0	222^1	193	12	41	127	9.5	2.91	116	.232	.269	14	.194	3	17	12	-1	1.4
1986	Mon-N	10	8	.556	30	30	1	0	0	187^1	182	15	63	105	12.1	3.94	94	.251	.316	8	.138	1	-5	-5	3	0.0
1987	Mon-N	10	9	.526	26	26	2	0	0	150^1	164	16	31	94	11.8	4.37	96	.274	.312	6	.136	-0	-5	-3	-0	-0.3
1988	Mon-N	12	10	.545	32	32	1	0	0	198	179	15	32	122	10.0	3.00	120	.243	.284	6	.109	-1	10	13	-2	1.1
1989	Mon-N	10	11	.476	33	32	3	1	0	215^2	177	16	54	129	9.8	2.84	124	.223	.276	4	.065	-2	16	17	2	1.6
1990	StL-N	9	8	.529	26	25	0	0	0	141^1	160	11	30	78	12.4	4.27	89	.286	.327	10	.256	3	-7	-7	-1	-0.5
1991	StL-N	12	9	.571	31	31	3	0	0	198^2	188	16	45	94	10.9	3.85	97	.251	.300	16	.246	3	-4	-3	-1	-0.1
1992	StL-N	4	2	.667	13	1	0	0	0	21^1	20	3	5	9	11.8	4.64	73	.247	.315	0	.000	-0	-3	-3	0	-0.8
1993	Col-N	2	4	.333	11	5	0	0	0	29^2	47	2	11	9	18.5	8.49	56	.362	.424	0	.000	-0	-15	-12	1	-2.0
Total	13	108	94	.535	365	255	23	8	6	1791^1	1725	140	432	1028	11.1	3.53	104	.253	.302	76	.153	7	25	25	4	2.7

● CHARLIE SMITH Smith, Charles Edwin b: 4/20/1880, Cleveland, Ohio d: 1/3/29, Wickliffe, Ohio BR/TR, 6'1", 185 lbs. Deb: 8/6/02 F

YEAR	TM/L	W	L	PCT	G	GS	CG	SH	SV	IP	H	HR	BB	SO	RAT	ERA	ERA+	OAV	OOB	BH	AVG	PB	PR	/A	PD	TPI
1902	Cle-A	2	1	.667	3	3	2	1	0	20	23	0	5	5	12.6	4.05	85	.287	.329	1	.125	-0	-1	-1	0	-0.2
1906	Was-A	9	16	.360	33	22	17	2	0	235^1	250	2	75	105	12.7	2.91	91	.275	.336	16	.184	-1	-6	-7	-3	-1.1
1907	Was-A	10	20	.333	36	31	21	3	0	258^2	254	0	51	119	10.6	2.61	93	.259	.297	12	.143	-3	-2	-6	3	-0.6
1908	Was-A	9	13	.409	26	23	14	1	1	183	166	2	60	83	11.3	2.41	95	.247	.311	8	.123	-2	-0	-3	-1	-0.6
1909	Was-A	3	12	.200	23	15	7	1	0	145^2	140	4	37	72	11.2	3.27	74	.250	.303	7	.156	-1	-13	-14	0	-1.4
	Bos-A	3	0	1.000	3	3	2	0	0	25	23	2	2	11	9.4	2.16	116	.237	.260	3	.300	1	1	1	0	0.2
	Yr	6	12	.333	26	18	9	1	0	170^2	163	6	39	83	10.7	3.11	78	.247	.290	10	.182	-0	-12	-13	1	-1.2
1910	Bos-A	11	6	.647	24	18	11	0	1	156^1	141	4	35	53	10.2	2.30	111	.248	.294	5	.114	-2	4	4	-2	-0.1
1911	Bos-A	0	0	—	1	1	0	0	0	2	2	1	1	0	13.5	9.00	36	.250	.333	0	—	0	-1	-1	0	0.0
	Chi-N	3	2	.600	7	5	3	1	0	38	31	0	7	11	9.2	1.42	233	.228	.271	1	.077	-1	8	8	-1	0.8
1912	Chi-N	7	4	.636	20	5	1	0	1	94	92	2	31	47	12.1	4.21	79	.269	.335	9	.257	1	-8	-9	1	-0.8
1913	Chi-N	7	9	.438	20	17	8	1	0	137^2	138	2	34	47	11.5	2.55	125	.274	.325	4	.089	-3	10	10	0	0.7
1914	Chi-N	2	4	.333	16	5	1	0	0	53^2	49	3	15	17	10.9	3.86	72	.251	.308	1	.091	-1	-6	-6	-1	-0.9
Total	10	66	87	.431	212	148	87	10	3	1349^1	1309	22	353	570	11.3	2.81	94	.259	.311	67	.150	-13	-15	-24	-2	-4.0

● POP SMITH Smith, Charles Marvin b: 10/12/1856, Digby, N.S., Canada d: 4/18/27, Boston, Mass. BR/TR, 5'11", 170 lbs. Deb: 5/1/1880 U◆

YEAR	TM/L	W	L	PCT	G	GS	CG	SH	SV	IP	H	HR	BB	SO	RAT	ERA	ERA+	OAV	OOB	BH	AVG	PB	PR	/A	PD	TPI
1883	Col-a	0	0	—	3	0	0	0	0	5^2	10	0	0	0	15.9	6.35	48	.357	.357	106	.262	1	-2	-2	-0	0.0

● POP-BOY SMITH Smith, Clarence Ossie b: 5/23/1892, Newport, Tenn. d: 2/16/24, Sweetwater, Tex. BR/TR, 6'1", 176 lbs. Deb: 4/19/13

YEAR	TM/L	W	L	PCT	G	GS	CG	SH	SV	IP	H	HR	BB	SO	RAT	ERA	ERA+	OAV	OOB	BH	AVG	PB	PR	/A	PD	TPI
1913	Chi-A	0	1	.000	15	2	0	0	0	32	31	0	11	13	12.7	3.38	87	.261	.338	0	.000	-1	-2	-2	1	0.0
1916	Cle-A	1	2	.333	5	3	0	0	1	25^2	25	1	11	4	13.0	3.86	78	.253	.333	2	.286	0	-3	-2	-0	-0.3
1917	Cle-A	0	1	.000	6	0	0	0	0	8^2	14	0	4	3	19.7	8.31	34	.368	.442	0	.000	-0	-5	-5	1	-0.5
Total	3	1	4	.200	26	5	0	0	1	66^1	70	1	26	20	13.7	4.21	70	.273	.352	2	.154	-1	-10	-9	2	-0.8

● CLAY SMITH Smith, Clay Jamieson b: 9/11/14, Cambridge, Kan. BR/TR, 6'2", 190 lbs. Deb: 9/13/38

YEAR	TM/L	W	L	PCT	G	GS	CG	SH	SV	IP	H	HR	BB	SO	RAT	ERA	ERA+	OAV	OOB	BH	AVG	PB	PR	/A	PD	TPI
1938	Cle-A	0	0	—	4	0	0	0	0	11	18	1	2	3	16.4	6.55	71	.367	.392	0	.000	-0	-2	-2	0	0.0
1940	*Det-A	1	1	.500	14	1	0	0	0	28^1	32	3	13	14	14.6	5.08	94	.283	.362	0	.000	-1	-2	-1	1	-0.1
Total	2	1	1	.500	18	1	0	0	0	39^1	50	4	15	17	15.1	5.49	86	.309	.371	0	.000	-1	-4	-3	1	-0.1

● DAN SMITH Smith, Daniel Scott b: 4/20/69, St.Paul, Minn. BL/TL, 6'5", 190 lbs. Deb: 9/12/92

YEAR	TM/L	W	L	PCT	G	GS	CG	SH	SV	IP	H	HR	BB	SO	RAT	ERA	ERA+	OAV	OOB	BH	AVG	PB	PR	/A	PD	TPI
1992	Tex-A	0	3	.000	4	2	0	0	0	14^1	18	1	8	5	16.3	5.02	76	.321	.406	0	—	0	-2	-2	-0	-0.4
1994	Tex-A	1	2	.333	13	0	0	0	0	14^2	18	2	12	9	18.4	4.30	112	.281	.395	0	—	0	1	1	-0	0.1
Total	2	1	5	.167	17	2	0	0	0	29	36	3	20	14	17.4	4.66	92	.300	.400	0	—	0	-1	-1	-1	-0.3

● DARYL SMITH Smith, Daryl Clinton b: 7/29/60, Baltimore, Md. BR/TR, 6'4", 185 lbs. Deb: 9/18/90

YEAR	TM/L	W	L	PCT	G	GS	CG	SH	SV	IP	H	HR	BB	SO	RAT	ERA	ERA+	OAV	OOB	BH	AVG	PB	PR	/A	PD	TPI
1990	KC-A	0	1	.000	2	1	0	0	0	6^2	5	0	4	6	12.2	4.05	95	.238	.360	0	—	0	-0	-0	-0	0.0

● DAVE SMITH Smith, David Merwin b: 12/17/14, Sellers, S.C. d: 4/1/98, Whiteville, N.C. BR/TR, 5'10", 170 lbs. Deb: 6/16/38

YEAR	TM/L	W	L	PCT	G	GS	CG	SH	SV	IP	H	HR	BB	SO	RAT	ERA	ERA+	OAV	OOB	BH	AVG	PB	PR	/A	PD	TPI
1938	Phi-A	2	1	.667	21	0	0	0	0	44^1	50	0	28	13	16.0	5.08	95	.284	.385	0	.000	-1	-1	-1	-0	-0.2
1939	Phi-A	0	0	—	1	0	0	0	0	0	1	0	2	0	—	—	—	1.000	1.000	0	—	0	0	0	0	0.0
Total	2	2	1	.667	22	0	0	0	0	44^1	51	0	30	13	16.6	5.08	95	.288	.394	0	.000	-1	-1	-1	-0	-0.2

● DAVE SMITH Smith, David Stanley b: 1/21/55, Richmond, Cal. BR/TR, 6'1", 195 lbs. Deb: 4/11/80

YEAR	TM/L	W	L	PCT	G	GS	CG	SH	SV	IP	H	HR	BB	SO	RAT	ERA	ERA+	OAV	OOB	BH	AVG	PB	PR	/A	PD	TPI
1980	*Hou-N	7	5	.583	57	0	0	0	10	102^2	90	1	32	85	11.0	1.93	170	.237	.304	0	.000	-1	19	15	-1	1.8
1981	*Hou-N	5	3	.625	42	0	0	0	8	75	54	2	23	52	9.5	2.76	119	.198	.265	2	.250	0	6	4	-0	0.6
1982	Hou-N	5	4	.556	49	1	0	0	11	63^1	69	4	31	28	14.2	3.84	86	.285	.366	0	.000	-0	-2	-4	-1	-0.7
1983	Hou-N	3	1	.750	42	0	0	0	6	72^2	72	2	36	41	13.4	3.10	110	.258	.343	0	.000	-1	4	2	-2	-0.1
1984	Hou-N	5	4	.556	53	0	0	0	5	77^1	60	5	20	45	9.4	2.21	150	.214	.269	0	.000	-0	12	10	-1	1.1
1985	Hou-N	9	5	.643	64	0	0	0	27	79^1	69	3	17	40	9.9	2.27	153	.235	.280	0	.000	0	12	11	-1	2.4
1986	*Hou-N☆	4	7	.364	54	0	0	0	33	56	39	5	22	46	10.0	2.73	132	.200	.284	0	.000	-0	6	5	0	1.6
1987	Hou-N	2	3	.400	50	0	0	0	24	60	39	0	21	73	9.2	1.65	237	.182	.258	1	.500	1	16	15	-0	2.3
1988	Hou-N	4	5	.444	51	0	0	0	27	57^1	60	1	19	38	12.6	2.67	124	.268	.328	0	.000	-0	5	4	-0	1.0
1989	Hou-N	3	4	.429	52	0	0	0	25	58	49	1	19	31	10.7	2.64	128	.233	.300	0	.000	-0	6	5	1	1.0
1990	Hou-N★	6	6	.500	49	0	0	0	23	60^1	45	4	20	50	9.7	2.39	156	.210	.278	0	.000	0	9	9	-1	2.2
1991	Chi-N	0	6	.000	35	0	0	0	17	33	39	6	19	16	16.1	6.00	65	.302	.396	0	.000	-0	-8	-8	-0	-2.0
1992	Chi-N	0	0	—	11	0	0	0	0	14^1	15	0	4	3	11.9	2.51	143	.273	.322	0	—	0	2	2	-0	0.0
Total	13	53	53	.500	609	1	0	0	216	809^1	700	34	283	548	11.1	2.67	130	.234	.303	3	.068	-2	87	71	-7	11.2

● DAVE SMITH Smith, David Wayne b: 8/30/57, Tomball, Tex. BR/TR, 6'1", 190 lbs. Deb: 9/18/84

YEAR	TM/L	W	L	PCT	G	GS	CG	SH	SV	IP	H	HR	BB	SO	RAT	ERA	ERA+	OAV	OOB	BH	AVG	PB	PR	/A	PD	TPI
1984	Cal-A	0	0	—	1	0	0	0	0	1	4	1	0	0	36.0	18.00	22	.571	.571	0	—	0	-2	-2	0	0.0
1985	Cal-A	0	0	—	4	0	0	0	0	5	5	1	1	3	10.8	7.20	57	.278	.316	0	—	0	-2	-2	0	0.0
Total	2	0	0	—	5	0	0	0	0	6	9	2	1	3	15.0	9.00	45	.360	.385	0	—	0	-3	-3	0	0.0

● DOUG SMITH Smith, Douglass Weldon b: 5/25/1892, Millers Falls, Mass. d: 9/18/73, Greenfield, Mass. BL/TL, 5'10", 168 lbs. Deb: 7/10/12

YEAR	TM/L	W	L	PCT	G	GS	CG	SH	SV	IP	H	HR	BB	SO	RAT	ERA	ERA+	OAV	OOB	BH	AVG	PB	PR	/A	PD	TPI
1912	Bos-A	0	0	—	1	0	0	0	0	3	4	0	0	1	12.0	3.00	113	.364	.364	0	—	0	0	0	-0	0.0

● EDDIE SMITH Smith, Edgar b: 12/14/13, Mansfield, N.J. d: 1/2/94, Willingboro, N.J. BB/TL, 5'10", 174 lbs. Deb: 9/20/36

YEAR	TM/L	W	L	PCT	G	GS	CG	SH	SV	IP	H	HR	BB	SO	RAT	ERA	ERA+	OAV	OOB	BH	AVG	PB	PR	/A	PD	TPI
1936	Phi-A	1	1	.500	2	2	2	0	0	19	22	3	8	7	14.2	1.89	269	.275	.341	1	.125	-1	7	7	0	0.6
1937	Phi-A	4	17	.190	38	23	14	1	5	196^2	178	18	90	79	12.4	3.94	120	.242	.327	17	.233	1	15	17	-2	1.7
1938	Phi-A	3	10	.231	43	7	0	0	4	130^2	151	13	76	78	15.9	5.92	82	.287	.381	12	.286	3	-16	-16	0	-1.1

YEAR	TM/L	W	L	PCT	G	GS	CG	SH	SV	IP	H	HR	BB	SO	RAT	ERA	ERA+	OAV	OOB	BH	AVG	PB	PR	/A	PD	TPI
1939	Phi-A	1	0	1.000	3	0	0	0	0	3^{2}	7	0	2	3	22.1	9.82	48	.412	.474	0	—	0	-2	-2	-0	-0.4
	Chi-A	9	11	.450	29	22	7	1	0	176^{2}	161	11	90	67	13.0	3.67	129	.247	.342	6	.115	-1	19	21	-2	1.7
	Yr	10	11	.476	32	22	7	1	0	180^{1}	168	11	92	70	13.2	3.79	125	.251	.346	6	.115	-1	17	19	-2	1.3
1940	Chi-A	14	9	.609	32	28	12	0	0	207^{1}	179	16	95	119	12.0	3.21	138	.228	.313	15	.217	2	27	28	-1	2.9
1941	Chi-A★	13	17	.433	34	33	21	1	1	263^{1}	243	13	114	111	12.4	3.18	129	.246	.328	19	.216	4	28	27	0	3.2
1942	Chi-A☆	7	20	.259	29	28	18	2	1	215	223	17	86	78	13.1	3.98	90	.269	.341	9	.123	-2	-8	-9	2	-1.0
1943	Chi-A	11	11	.500	25	25	14	2	0	187^{2}	197	2	76	66	13.3	3.69	90	.277	.351	11	.159	-1	-8	-7	1	-0.9
1946	Chi-A	8	11	.421	24	21	3	1	1	145^{1}	135	9	60	59	12.3	2.85	120	.246	.325	8	.178	0	11	9	-0	1.2
1947	Chi-A	1	3	.250	15	5	0	0	0	33^{1}	40	1	24	12	17.3	7.29	50	.299	.405	1	.167	-0	-13	-13	-1	-1.5
	Bos-A	1	3	.250	8	3	0	0	0	17	18	3	18	15	19.1	7.41	52	.269	.424	1	.167	0	-7	-7	-0	-1.3
	Yr	2	6	.250	23	8	0	0	0	50^{1}	58	4	42	27	17.9	7.33	51	.289	.412	2	.167	-0	-20	-20	-1	-2.8
Total	10	73	113	.392	282	197	91	8	12	1595^{2}	1554	106	739	694	13.1	3.82	108	.256	.340	100	.188	5	51	53	-3	5.1

● EDGAR SMITH Smith, Edgar Eugene b: 6/12/1862, Providence, R.I. d: 11/3/1892, Providence, R.I. BR/TR, 5'10", 160 lbs. Deb: 5/25/1883 ♦

YEAR	TM/L	W	L	PCT	G	GS	CG	SH	SV	IP	H	HR	BB	SO	RAT	ERA	ERA+	OAV	OOB	BH	AVG	PB	PR	/A	PD	TPI
1883	Phi-N	0	1	.000	1	1	0	0	0	7	18	0	3	2	27.0	15.43	20	.409	.447	3	.750	1	-10	-10	-0	-0.7
1884	Was-a	0	2	.000	3	2	2	0	0	22	27	0	5	4	13.5	4.91	62	.276	.317	5	.088	-1	-4	-5	-0	-0.4
1885	Pro-N	1	0	1.000	1	1	1	0	0	9	9	0	0	1	9.0	1.00	268	.273	.273	1	.250	0	2	2	0	0.2
1890	Cle-N	1	4	.200	6	6	5	0	0	44	42	1	10	11	10.8	4.30	83	.244	.290	7	.292	2	-4	-3	2	0.0
Total	4	2	7	.222	11	10	8	0	0	82	96	1	18	18	12.7	5.05	65	.277	.316	18	.184	2	-15	-16	1	-0.9

● ELMER SMITH Smith, Elmer Ellsworth b: 3/23/1868, Pittsburgh, Pa. d: 11/3/45, Pittsburgh, Pa. BL/TL, 5'11", 178 lbs. Deb: 9/10/1886 ♦

YEAR	TM/L	W	L	PCT	G	GS	CG	SH	SV	IP	H	HR	BB	SO	RAT	ERA	ERA+	OAV	OOB	BH	AVG	PB	PR	/A	PD	TPI
1886	Cin-a	4	4	.500	9	9	8	0	0	72^{2}	57	1	44	40	12.9	3.72	95	.211	.328	8	.286	4	-2	-2	-2	0.0
1887	Cin-a	34	17	.667	52	52	49	3	0	447^{1}	400	5	126	176	**10.8**	**2.94**	**148**	**.230**	**.286**	47	.253	5	68	**70**	-5	6.0
1888	Cin-a	22	17	.564	40	40	37	5	0	348^{1}	309	1	89	154	10.8	2.74	116	.229	.286	29	.225	4	13	17	-5	1.4
1889	Cin-a	9	12	.429	29	22	16	0	0	203	253	11	101	104	16.0	4.88	80	.296	.375	23	.277	6	-23	-22	-4	-1.6
1892	Pit-N	6	7	.462	17	13	12	1	0	134	140	2	58	51	13.4	3.63	91	.258	.331	140	.274	6	-5	-5	-1	-0.1
1894	Pit-N	0	0	—	1	0	0	0	0	4	6	0	1	0	18.0	4.50	116	.333	.400	174	.356	0	0	0	-0	0.0
1898	Cin-N	0	0	—	1	0	0	0	0	1	2	0	3	0	45.0	18.00	21	.400	.625	166	.342	0	-2	-2	-0	0.0
Total	7	75	57	.568	149	136	122	9	0	1210^{1}	1167	20	422	525	12.1	3.35	113	.244	.311	1454	.310	25	48	58	-19	5.7

● BILL SMITH Smith, F. William b: 1863, New Orleans, La. TR , 5'8", 152 lbs. Deb: 7/6/1886

YEAR	TM/L	W	L	PCT	G	GS	CG	SH	SV	IP	H	HR	BB	SO	RAT	ERA	ERA+	OAV	OOB	BH	AVG	PB	PR	/A	PD	TPI
1886	Det-N	5	4	.556	9	9	9	0	0	77	81	0	30	36	13.0	4.09	81	.259	.324	7	.184	-1	-7	-7	-1	-0.8

● FRANK SMITH Smith, Frank Elmer "Nig" or "Piano Mover" (b: Frank Elmer Schmidt)
b: 10/28/1879, Pittsburgh, Pa. d: 11/3/52, Pittsburgh, Pa. BR/TR, 5'10.5", 194 lbs. Deb: 4/22/04

YEAR	TM/L	W	L	PCT	G	GS	CG	SH	SV	IP	H	HR	BB	SO	RAT	ERA	ERA+	OAV	OOB	BH	AVG	PB	PR	/A	PD	TPI
1904	Chi-A	16	9	.640	26	23	22	4	0	202^{1}	157	0	58	107	10.1	2.09	117	.215	.284	18	.250	4	11	8	-2	1.3
1905	Chi-A	19	13	.594	39	31	27	4	0	291^{2}	215	0	107	171	10.2	2.13	116	.208	.287	24	.226	7	17	11	0	2.0
1906	Chi-A	5	5	.500	20	13	8	1	1	122	124	3	37	53	12.2	3.39	75	.267	.327	12	.293	5	-10	-12	1	-0.3
1907	Chi-A	23	10	.697	41	37	29	3	0	310	280	3	111	139	11.4	2.47	97	.243	.311	18	.196	5	3	-2	3	0.6
1908	Chi-A	16	17	.485	41	35	24	3	1	297^{2}	213	2	73	129	8.7	2.03	114	.203	.256	20	.189	2	12	10	3	1.7
1909	Chi-A	25	17	.595	**51**	40	**37**	7	1	**365**	278	1	70	**177**	8.7	1.80	130	.214	.257	22	.173	6	27	22	10	**4.6**
1910	Chi-A	4	9	.308	19	15	9	3	0	128^{2}	91	1	40	50	9.3	2.03	118	.204	.272	8	.186	2	7	5	4	1.2
	Bos-A	1	2	.333	4	3	2	0	0	28	22	0	11	8	10.9	4.82	53	.234	.321	1	.111	-0	-7	-7	-0	-0.7
	Yr	5	11	.313	23	18	11	3	0	156^{2}	113	1	51	58	9.5	2.53	96	.208	.277	9	.173	2	-0	-2	4	0.5
1911	Bos-A	0	0	—	1	1	0	0	0	2^{1}	6	0	3	1	34.7	15.43	21	.500	.600	0	—	0	-3	-3	0	0.1
	Cin-N	10	14	.417	34	18	10	0	1	176^{1}	198	1	55	67	13.1	3.98	83	.289	.345	12	.214	3	-11	-13	4	-0.9
1912	Cin-N	1	1	.500	7	3	1	0	0	22^{2}	34	1	15	5	19.5	6.35	53	.370	.458	0	.000	-0	-7	-8	-0	-0.6
1914	Bal-F	10	8	.556	39	22	9	1	2	174^{2}	180	8	47	83	11.7	2.99	101	.259	.306	12	.203	0	-2	1	2	0.3
1915	Bal-F	4	4	.500	17	9	2	0	0	88^{2}	108	5	31	37	14.1	4.67	61	.312	.369	5	.172	0	-19	-18	0	-1.4
	Bro-F	5	2	.714	15	5	4	1	0	63	69	2	18	24	12.4	3.14	87	.290	.340	4	.200	0	-3	-3	1	-0.2
	Yr	9	6	.600	32	14	6	1	0	151^{2}	177	7	49	61	13.4	4.04	70	.303	.357	9	.184	1	-22	-21	1	-1.6
Total	11	139	111	.556	354	255	184	27	6	2273	1975	27	676	1051	10.7	2.59	99	.237	.297	156	.204	35	15	-10	26	7.7

● FRANK SMITH Smith, Frank Thomas b: 4/4/28, Pierrepont Manor, N.Y. BR/TR, 6'3", 200 lbs. Deb: 4/18/50

YEAR	TM/L	W	L	PCT	G	GS	CG	SH	SV	IP	H	HR	BB	SO	RAT	ERA	ERA+	OAV	OOB	BH	AVG	PB	PR	/A	PD	TPI
1950	Cin-N	2	7	.222	38	4	0	0	3	90^{2}	73	12	39	55	11.9	3.87	109	.216	.312	2	.095	-2	3	4	-1	0.1
1951	Cin-N	5	5	.500	50	0	0	0	11	76	65	7	22	34	10.8	3.20	128	.230	.295	0	.000	-1	6	7	0	1.1
1952	Cin-N	12	11	.522	53	2	1	0	7	122^{1}	109	13	41	77	11.6	3.75	101	.242	.315	5	.172	0	-0	0	-2	-0.1
1953	Cin-N	8	1	.889	50	1	0	0	2	83^{2}	89	15	25	42	12.6	5.49	79	.272	.330	2	.154	-1	-11	-11	1	-1.0
1954	Cin-N	5	8	.385	50	0	0	0	20	81	60	15	29	51	10.2	2.67	157	.211	.291	1	.100	1	13	14	0	2.9
1955	StL-N	3	1	.750	28	0	0	0	1	39	27	3	23	17	12.7	3.23	126	.205	.344	0	.000	-1	3	4	-0	0.3
1956	Cin-N	0	0	—	2	0	0	0	0	3	3	2	2	1	15.0	12.00	33	.300	.417	0	—	0	-3	-3	-0	0.0
Total	7	35	33	.515	271	7	1	0	44	495^{2}	426	67	181	277	11.6	3.81	107	.234	.313	10	.115	-3	11	16	-2	3.3

● FRED SMITH Smith, Frederick b: 11/24/1878, New Diggings, Wis. d: 2/4/64, Los Angeles, Cal. BL/TR, 6', 186 lbs. Deb: 6/14/07

YEAR	TM/L	W	L	PCT	G	GS	CG	SH	SV	IP	H	HR	BB	SO	RAT	ERA	ERA+	OAV	OOB	BH	AVG	PB	PR	/A	PD	TPI
1907	Cin-N	2	7	.222	18	9	5	0	1	85^{1}	90	3	24	19	12.4	2.85	91	.274	.331	3	.107	-2	-4	-2	0	-0.4

● FRED SMITH Smith, Frederick C. b: 3/25/1863, Greene, N.Y. d: 1/9/41, Syracuse, N.Y. BL/TR, 5'11", 156 lbs. Deb: 4/18/1890

YEAR	TM/L	W	L	PCT	G	GS	CG	SH	SV	IP	H	HR	BB	SO	RAT	ERA	ERA+	OAV	OOB	BH	AVG	PB	PR	/A	PD	TPI
1890	Tol-a	19	13	.594	35	34	31	2	0	286	273	13	90	116	11.8	3.27	121	.244	.307	21	.167	-2	19	22	3	2.0

● GEORGE SMITH Smith, George Allen "Columbia George" b: 5/31/1892, Byram, Conn. d: 1/7/65, Greenwich, Conn. BR/TR, 6'2", 163 lbs. Deb: 8/9/16

YEAR	TM/L	W	L	PCT	G	GS	CG	SH	SV	IP	H	HR	BB	SO	RAT	ERA	ERA+	OAV	OOB	BH	AVG	PB	PR	/A	PD	TPI
1916	NY-N	3	0	1.000	9	1	0	0	0	20^{2}	14	0	6	9	9.1	2.61	93	.197	.269	0	.000	-0	0	-0	0	0.0
1917	NY-N	0	3	.000	14	1	1	0	0	38	38	1	11	16	11.8	2.84	90	.270	.327	0	.000	-1	-1	-1	-0	-0.2
1918	Cin-N	2	3	.400	10	6	4	1	0	55^{1}	71	3	11	19	13.3	4.07	66	.329	.361	0	.000	-2	-8	-9	1	-0.9
	NY-N	2	3	.400	5	2	1	0	0	26^{2}	26	0	6	4	11.1	4.05	65	.255	.303	2	.250	0	-4	-4	-1	-0.8
	Bro-N	4	1	.800	8	5	4	0	0	50	43	0	5	18	9.0	2.34	119	.249	.278	3	.200	0	2	2	1	0.4
	Yr	8	7	.533	23	13	9	1	0	132	140	3	22	41	11.2	3.41	79	.285	.318	5	.125	-2	-9	-10	0	-1.3
1919	NY-N	0	2	.000	3	2	0	0	0	11	18	1	4	0	18.0	5.73	49	.383	.431	0	.000	-0	-3	-4	-0	-0.7
	Phi-N	5	11	.313	31	19	11	1	0	184^{2}	194	7	46	42	11.8	3.22	100	.278	.326	8	.133	-3	-6	0	-1	-0.4
	Yr	5	13	.278	34	21	11	1	0	195^{2}	212	8	50	42	12.2	3.36	95	.285	.332	8	.127	-4	-10	-3	-1	-1.1
1920	Phi-N	13	18	.419	43	28	10	1	2	250^{2}	265	10	51	51	11.6	3.45	99	.283	.324	7	.097	-6	-9	-1	-2	-0.9
1921	Phi-N	4	20	.167	39	28	12	1	1	221^{1}	303	12	52	45	14.6	4.76	89	.335	.373	4	.056	-8	-24	-13	-2	-2.1
1922	Phi-N	5	14	.263	42	16	6	1	0	194	250	16	35	44	13.5	4.78	98	.316	.350	5	.076	-7	-15	-2	-2	-1.0
1923	Bro-N	3	6	.333	25	7	3	0	1	91	99	4	28	15	12.9	3.66	106	.278	.336	5	.192	-1	3	2	-2	-0.1
Total	8	41	81	.336	229	115	52	5	4	1143^{1}	1321	54	255	263	12.6	3.89	94	.298	.340	34	.097	-29	-63	-31	-8	-6.7

● HEINIE SMITH Smith, George Henry b: 10/24/1871, Pittsburgh, Pa. d: 6/25/39, Buffalo, N.Y. BR/TR, 5'9.5", 160 lbs. Deb: 9/8/1897 M♦

YEAR	TM/L	W	L	PCT	G	GS	CG	SH	SV	IP	H	HR	BB	SO	RAT	ERA	ERA+	OAV	OOB	BH	AVG	PB	PR	/A	PD	TPI
1901	NY-N	0	1	.000	2	1	1	0	0	13^{1}	24	0	5	5	21.6	8.10	41	.387	.457	6	.207	0	-7	-7	-0	-0.4

● GERMANY SMITH Smith, George J. b: 4/21/1863, Pittsburgh, Pa. d: 12/1/27, Altoona, Pa. BR/TR, 6', 175 lbs. Deb: 4/17/1884 ♦

YEAR	TM/L	W	L	PCT	G	GS	CG	SH	SV	IP	H	HR	BB	SO	RAT	ERA	ERA+	OAV	OOB	BH	AVG	PB	PR	/A	PD	TPI
1884	Alt-U	0	0	—	1	0	0	0	0	1	3	0	0	1	27.0	9.00	30	.500	.500	34	.315	0	-1	-1	0	0.0

● GEORGE SMITH Smith, George Shelby b: 10/27/01, Louisville, Ky. d: 5/26/81, Richmond, Va. BR/TR, 6'1", 175 lbs. Deb: 4/21/26

YEAR	TM/L	W	L	PCT	G	GS	CG	SH	SV	IP	H	HR	BB	SO	RAT	ERA	ERA+	OAV	OOB	BH	AVG	PB	PR	/A	PD	TPI
1926	Det-A	1	2	.333	23	1	0	0	1	44	55	3	33	15	18.4	6.95	58	.318	.433	0	.000	-0	-14	-14	-1	-0.9
1927	Det-A	4	1	.800	29	0	0	0	0	71^{1}	62	3	50	32	14.4	3.91	108	.240	.368	7	.368	3	2	2	-1	0.4
1928	Det-A	1	1	.500	39	2	0	0	3	106	103	3	50	54	13.0	4.42	93	.263	.346	3	.111	-2	-4	-4	-2	-0.5
1929	Det-A	3	2	.600	14	2	1	0	0	35^{2}	42	1	36	13	19.7	5.80	74	.307	.451	5	.417	2	-6	-6	1	-0.4
1930	Bos-A	1	2	.333	27	2	0	0	0	73^{2}	92	7	49	21	17.3	6.60	70	.317	.418	8	.333	2	-16	-16	0	-0.3
Total	5	10	8	.556	132	7	1	0	3	330^{2}	354	17	218	135	15.7	5.28	81	.283	.392	23	.264	4	-39	-38	-2	-1.7

● HAL SMITH Smith, Harold Laverne b: 6/30/02, Creston, Iowa d: 9/27/92, Ft.Lauderdale, Fla. BR/TR, 6'3", 195 lbs. Deb: 9/14/32

YEAR	TM/L	W	L	PCT	G	GS	CG	SH	SV	IP	H	HR	BB	SO	RAT	ERA	ERA+	OAV	OOB	BH	AVG	PB	PR	/A	PD	TPI
1932	Pit-N	1	0	1.000	2	1	1	1	0	12	9	0	2	4	8.3	0.75	508	.209	.244	0	.000	-0	4	4	0	0.3
1933	Pit-N	8	7	.533	28	19	8	2	1	145	149	5	31	40	11.5	2.86	116	.261	.305	6	.128	-2	8	7	-2	0.4

YEAR	TM/L	W	L	PCT	G	GS	CG	SH	SV	IP	H	HR	BB	SO	RAT	ERA	ERA+	OAV	OOB	BH	AVG	PB	PR	/A	PD	TPI
1934	Pit-N	3	4	.429	20	5	1	0	0	50	72	3	18	15	16.9	7.20	57	.343	.405	1	.059	-2	-17	-17	-0	-2.2
1935	Pit-N	0	0	—	1	0	0	0	0	3	2	0	1	0	9.0	3.00	137	.200	.273	0	—	0	0	0	-0	0.0
Total	4	12	11	.522	51	25	10	3	1	210	232	8	52	59	12.6	3.77	94	.279	.328	7	.104	-4	-5	-5	-2	-1.5

● HARRY SMITH

Smith, Harrison Morton b: 8/15/1889, Union, Neb. d: 7/26/64, Dunbar, Neb. BR/TR, 5'9", 160 lbs. Deb: 10/6/12

YEAR	TM/L	W	L	PCT	G	GS	CG	SH	SV	IP	H	HR	BB	SO	RAT	ERA	ERA+	OAV	OOB	BH	AVG	PB	PR	/A	PD	TPI
1912	Chi-A	1	0	1.000	1	1	0	0	0	5	6	0	0	1	10.8	1.80	178	.333	.333	0	.000	-0	1	1	-0	0.1

● JACK SMITH

Smith, Jack Hatfield b: 11/15/35, Pikeville, Ky. BR/TR, 6', 185 lbs. Deb: 9/10/62

YEAR	TM/L	W	L	PCT	G	GS	CG	SH	SV	IP	H	HR	BB	SO	RAT	ERA	ERA+	OAV	OOB	BH	AVG	PB	PR	/A	PD	TPI
1962	LA-N	0	0	—	8	0	0	0	1	10	10	0	4	7	12.6	4.50	81	.263	.333	0	.000	-0	-1	-1	-0	-0.1
1963	LA-N	0	0	—	4	0	0	0	0	8^1	10	2	2	5	15.1	7.56	40	.303	.378	0	.000	-0	-4	-4	0	0.0
1964	Mil-N	2	2	.500	22	0	0	0	0	31	28	3	11	19	11.3	3.77	93	.237	.302	1	.333	0	-1	-1	1	0.0
Total	3	2	2	.500	34	0	0	0	1	49^1	48	5	17	31	12.2	4.56	76	.254	.322	1	.167	-0	-5	-6	1	-0.1

● JAKE SMITH

Smith, Jacob (b: Jacob Schmidt) b: 6/10/1887, Dravosburg, Pa d: 11/7/48, E.McKeesport, Pa. BB/TL, 6'5", 200 lbs. Deb: 10/3/11

YEAR	TM/L	W	L	PCT	G	GS	CG	SH	SV	IP	H	HR	BB	SO	RAT	ERA	ERA+	OAV	OOB	BH	AVG	PB	PR	/A	PD	TPI
1911	Phi-N	0	0	—	2	0	0	0	0	5	3	0	2	1	9.0	0.00	—	.176	.263	0	.000	-0	2	2	0	0.0

● PHENOMENAL SMITH

Smith, John Francis (b: John Francis Gammon)
b: 12/12/1864, Philadelphia, Pa. d: 4/3/52, Manchester, N.H. BL/TL, 5'6.5", 161 lbs. Deb: 4/18/1884

YEAR	TM/L	W	L	PCT	G	GS	CG	SH	SV	IP	H	HR	BB	SO	RAT	ERA	ERA+	OAV	OOB	BH	AVG	PB	PR	/A	PD	TPI
1884	Bal-U	3	4	.429	9	8	5	0	0	62	86	2	17	13	15.0	3.48	77	.308	.348	5	.147	-4	-7	-6	-1	-0.9
	Phi-a	0	1	.000	1	1	1	0	0	9	14	0	1	3	15.0	4.00	85	.368	.385	1	.250	-0	-1	-1	0	0.0
	Pit-a	0	1	.000	1	1	1	0	0	8	11	0	2	4	15.8	9.00	37	.306	.359	0	.000	-1	-5	-5	0	-0.5
	Yr	0	2	.000	2	2	2	0	0	17	25	0	3	7	15.4	6.35	53	.338	.372	1	.125	-1	-6	-6	0	-0.5
1885	Bro-a	0	1	.000	1	1	1	0	0	8	12	0	6	2	21.4	12.38	27	.300	.404	1	.333	0	-8	-8	0	-0.6
	Phi-a	0	1	.000	1	1	0	0	0	4	7	0	4	7	27.0	9.00	38	.368	.500	0	.000	-0	-3	-2	0	-0.4
	Yr	0	2	.000	2	2	1	0	0	12	19	0	10	9	22.5	11.25	30	.317	.423	1	.200	-0	-11	-11	0	-1.0
1886	Det-N	1	1	.500	3	3	3	0	0	25	16	0	8	15	8.6	2.16	153	.174	.240	1	.111	-1	3	3	-1	0.1
1887	Bal-a	25	30	.455	58	55	54	1	0	491^1	526	7	176	206	13.1	3.79	108	.261	.325	48	.234	8	28	17	-1	2.0
1888	Bal-a	14	19	.424	35	32	31	0	0	292	249	5	137	152	12.6	3.61	83	.222	.320	27	.248	8	-18	-20	-4	-1.5
	Phi-a	2	1	.667	3	3	3	0	0	22	21	0	10	19	12.7	2.86	104	.241	.320	3	.333	1	0	0	-0	0.1
	Yr	16	20	.444	38	35	34	0	0	314	270	5	147	171	12.0	3.55	84	.219	.303	30	.254	9	-17	-20	-4	-1.4
1889	Phi-a	2	3	.400	5	5	5	0	0	43	53	2	25	12	17.0	4.40	86	.294	.389	3	.188	0	-3	-3	-1	-0.3
1890	Phi-N	8	12	.400	24	20	19	1	0	204	209	5	89	81	13.5	4.28	85	.257	.336	24	.279	4	-16	-14	-2	-0.9
	Pit-N	1	3	.250	5	5	5	0	0	44	39	0	13	15	10.8	3.07	107	.231	.290	7	.412	2	2	1	-0	0.3
	Yr	9	15	.375	29	25	24	1	0	248	248	5	102	96	12.7	4.06	88	.251	.321	31	.301	6	-14	-13	-3	-0.6
1891	Phi-N	1	1	.500	3	2	0	0	0	19	20	1	8	3	13.3	4.26	80	.260	.329	3	.375	1	-2	-2	-1	-0.1
Total	8	57	78	.422	149	137	128	2	0	1231^1	1263	22	496	532	13.2	3.87	93	.254	.329	123	.243	19	-28	-38	-10	-2.7

● CHICK SMITH

Smith, John William (b: Jan Smadt) b: 12/2/1892, Dayton, Ky. d: 10/11/35, Dayton, Ky. BL/TL, 5'8", 165 lbs. Deb: 4/12/13

YEAR	TM/L	W	L	PCT	G	GS	CG	SH	SV	IP	H	HR	BB	SO	RAT	ERA	ERA+	OAV	OOB	BH	AVG	PB	PR	/A	PD	TPI
1913	Cin-N	0	1	.000	5	1	0	0	0	17^2	15	1	11	11	13.2	3.57	91	.238	.351	0	.000	-1	-1	-1	0	-0.1

● LEE SMITH

Smith, Lee Arthur b: 12/4/57, Shreveport, La. BR/TR, 6'6", 225 lbs. Deb: 9/1/80

YEAR	TM/L	W	L	PCT	G	GS	CG	SH	SV	IP	H	HR	BB	SO	RAT	ERA	ERA+	OAV	OOB	BH	AVG	PB	PR	/A	PD	TPI
1980	Chi-N	2	0	1.000	18	0	0	0	0	21^2	21	0	14	17	14.5	2.91	135	.259	.368	0	—	0	2	2	-0	0.2
1981	Chi-N	3	6	.333	40	1	0	0	1	66^2	57	2	31	50	12.0	3.51	105	.239	.330	0	.000	-1	-0	1	-0	0.0
1982	Chi-N	2	5	.286	72	5	0	0	17	117	105	5	37	99	11.2	2.69	139	.245	.309	1	.063	-0	12	14	-1	1.1
1983	Chi-N★	4	10	.286	66	0	0	0	**29**	103^1	70	5	41	91	9.8	1.65	229	.194	.279	1	.111	-0	23	25	-1	4.6
1984	*Chi-N	9	7	.563	69	0	0	0	33	101	98	6	35	86	11.9	3.65	107	.255	.317	1	.077	-1	-1	3	0	0.5
1985	Chi-N	7	4	.636	65	0	0	0	33	97^2	87	9	32	112	11.1	3.04	131	.242	.305	0	.000	-0	6	10	-1	1.7
1986	Chi-N	9	9	.500	66	0	0	0	31	90^1	69	7	42	93	11.1	3.09	131	.215	.306	0	.000	-1	6	10	-0	2.4
1987	Chi-N★	4	10	.286	62	0	0	0	36	83^2	84	4	32	96	12.5	3.12	137	.259	.326	0	.000	-0	9	11	-1	2.4
1988	*Bos-A	4	5	.444	64	0	0	0	29	83^2	72	7	37	96	11.8	2.80	147	.225	.307	0	—	0	11	12	-1	1.9
1989	Bos-A	6	1	.857	64	0	0	0	25	70^2	53	6	33	96	11.0	3.57	115	.209	.301	0	—	0	2	4	-1	0.2
1990	Bos-A	2	1	.667	11	0	0	0	4	14^1	13	0	9	17	13.8	1.88	216	.236	.344	0	—	0	3	3	0	0.8
	StL-N	3	4	.429	53	0	0	0	27	68^2	58	3	20	70	10.2	2.10	182	.227	.284	0	.000	-0	13	13	-2	2.1
1991	StL-N☆	6	3	.667	67	0	0	0	**47**	73	70	5	13	67	10.2	2.34	159	.249	.282	0	—	0	11	11	-1	2.5
1992	StL-N☆	4	9	.308	70	0	0	0	**43**	75	62	4	26	60	10.6	3.12	109	.221	.287	0	—	0	3	2	-1	0.5
1993	StL-N☆	2	4	.333	55	0	0	0	43	50	49	11	9	49	10.4	4.50	88	.251	.284	0	.000	-0	-3	-3	-1	-0.9
	NY-A	0	0	—	8	0	0	0	3	8	4	0	5	11	10.1	0.00	—	.148	.281	0	—	0	4	4	0	0.2
1994	Bal-A★	1	4	.200	41	0	0	0	**33**	38^1	34	6	11	42	10.6	3.29	152	.239	.294	0	—	0	6	7	-1	1.9
1995	Cal-A☆	0	5	.000	52	0	0	0	37	49^1	42	3	25	43	12.4	3.47	135	.237	.335	0	—	0	7	7	-1	1.4
1996	Cal-A	0	0	—	11	0	0	0	0	11	8	0	3	6	9.0	2.45	204	.205	.262	0	—	0	3	3	-0	0.0
	Cin-N	3	4	.429	43	0	0	0	2	44^1	49	4	23	35	14.8	4.06	104	.277	.363	0	—	0	1	1	-0	0.1
1997	Mon-N	0	1	.000	25	0	0	0	5	21^2	28	2	8	15	15.4	5.82	72	.308	.370	0	—	0	-4	-4	0	-0.3
Total	18	71	92	.436	1022	6	0	0	478	1289^1	1133	89	486	1251	11.4	3.03	132	.237	.308	3	.047	-4	115	137	-11	23.3

● ROY SMITH

Smith, Le Roy Purdy b: 9/6/61, Mt.Vernon, N.Y. BR/TR, 6'3", 200 lbs. Deb: 6/23/84

YEAR	TM/L	W	L	PCT	G	GS	CG	SH	SV	IP	H	HR	BB	SO	RAT	ERA	ERA+	OAV	OOB	BH	AVG	PB	PR	/A	PD	TPI
1984	Cle-A	5	5	.500	22	14	0	0	0	86^1	91	14	40	55	13.8	4.59	89	.270	.349	0	—	0	-6	-5	-2	-0.7
1985	Cle-A	1	4	.200	12	11	1	0	0	62^1	84	8	17	28	14.7	5.34	77	.321	.364	0	—	0	-8	-8	-1	-0.8
1986	Min-A	0	2	.000	5	0	0	0	0	10^1	13	1	5	8	16.5	6.97	62	.295	.380	0	—	0	-3	-3	-0	-0.6
1987	Min-A	1	0	1.000	7	1	0	0	0	16^1	20	3	6	8	15.4	4.96	93	.290	.364	0	—	0	-0	-0	-0	-0.1
1988	Min-A	3	0	1.000	9	4	0	0	0	37	29	3	12	17	10.2	2.68	152	.210	.278	0	—	0	5	6	-1	0.4
1989	Min-A	10	6	.625	32	26	2	0	1	172^1	180	22	51	92	12.3	3.92	106	.269	.326	0	—	0	-1	4	-3	-0.2
1990	Min-A	5	10	.333	32	23	1	1	0	153^1	191	20	47	87	14.0	4.81	86	.313	.362	0	—	0	-15	-11	-2	-1.3
1991	Bal-A	5	4	.556	17	14	0	0	0	80^1	99	9	24	25	13.9	5.60	71	.311	.362	0	—	0	-13	-15	-1	-1.3
Total	8	30	31	.492	136	93	4	1	1	618^1	707	80	202	320	13.4	4.60	90	.289	.346	0	—	0	-42	-33	-9	-4.4

● MARK SMITH

Smith, Mark Christopher b: 11/23/55, Arlington, Va. BR/TR, 6'2", 215 lbs. Deb: 8/12/83

YEAR	TM/L	W	L	PCT	G	GS	CG	SH	SV	IP	H	HR	BB	SO	RAT	ERA	ERA+	OAV	OOB	BH	AVG	PB	PR	/A	PD	TPI
1983	Oak-A	1	0	1.000	8	1	0	0	0	14^2	24	0	6	10	19.0	6.75	57	.387	.449	0	—	0	-4	-5	-0	0.0

● MIKE SMITH

Smith, Michael Anthony b: 2/23/61, Jackson, Miss. BR/TR, 6'1", 195 lbs. Deb: 4/6/84

YEAR	TM/L	W	L	PCT	G	GS	CG	SH	SV	IP	H	HR	BB	SO	RAT	ERA	ERA+	OAV	OOB	BH	AVG	PB	PR	/A	PD	TPI
1984	Cin-N	1	0	1.000	8	0	0	0	0	10^1	12	1	5	7	14.8	5.23	72	.286	.362	0	—	0	-2	-2	-0	-0.2
1985	Cin-N	0	0	—	2	0	0	0	0	3^1	2	2	1	2	8.1	5.40	70	.167	.231	0	—	0	-1	-1	-0	0.0
1986	Cin-N	0	0	—	2	1	0	0	0	3^1	7	0	1	1	21.6	13.50	29	.412	.444	0	—	0	-4	-4	-0	0.0
1988	Mon-N	0	0	—	5	0	0	0	0	8^2	6	0	5	4	11.4	3.12	115	.207	.324	0	.000	-0	0	0	-0	0.0
1989	Pit-N	0	1	.000	16	0	0	0	0	24	28	1	10	12	14.3	3.75	89	.301	.369	0	.000	-0	-1	-1	1	0.0
Total	5	1	1	.500	33	1	0	0	1	49^2	55	4	22	26	14.0	4.71	75	.285	.358	0	.000	-1	-7	-6	0	-0.2

● MIKE SMITH

Smith, Michael Anthony b: 10/31/63, San Antonio, Tex. BR/TR, 6'3", 180 lbs. Deb: 6/30/89

YEAR	TM/L	W	L	PCT	G	GS	CG	SH	SV	IP	H	HR	BB	SO	RAT	ERA	ERA+	OAV	OOB	BH	AVG	PB	PR	/A	PD	TPI
1989	Bal-A	2	0	1.000	13	1	0	0	0	20	25	3	14	12	17.5	7.65	50	.313	.415	0	—	0	-8	-9	0	-0.6
1990	Bal-A	0	0	—	2	0	0	0	0	3	4	2	1	2	15.0	12.00	32	.308	.357	0	—	0	-3	-3	0	0.0
Total	2	2	0	1.000	15	1	0	0	0	23	29	5	15	14	17.2	8.22	46	.312	.407	0	—	0	-11	-11	0	-0.6

● PETE SMITH

Smith, Peter John b: 2/27/66, Abington, Mass. BR/TR, 6'2", 200 lbs. Deb: 9/8/87

YEAR	TM/L	W	L	PCT	G	GS	CG	SH	SV	IP	H	HR	BB	SO	RAT	ERA	ERA+	OAV	OOB	BH	AVG	PB	PR	/A	PD	TPI
1987	Atl-N	1	2	.333	6	6	0	0	0	31^2	39	3	14	11	15.1	4.83	90	.307	.376	1	.091	-1	-3	-2	-1	-0.3
1988	Atl-N	7	15	.318	32	32	5	3	0	195^1	183	15	88	124	12.5	3.69	100	.250	.331	6	.113	-1	-5	-0	-3	-0.4
1989	Atl-N	5	14	.263	28	27	1	0	0	142	144	13	57	115	12.7	4.75	77	.263	.333	4	.098	-0	-20	-17	-1	-2.3
1990	Atl-N	5	6	.455	13	13	3	0	0	77	77	11	24	56	11.8	4.79	84	.260	.316	2	.087	-1	-9	-6	-1	-1.0
1991	Atl-N	1	3	.250	14	10	0	0	0	48	48	5	22	29	13.1	5.06	77	.262	.341	2	.167	0	-7	-6	1	-0.4
1992	*Atl-N	7	0	1.000	12	11	2	1	0	79	63	3	28	43	10.4	2.05	178	.217	.286	1	.038	-1	13	14	-0	1.1
1993	Atl-N	4	8	.333	20	14	0	0	0	90^2	92	15	36	53	12.9	4.37	92	.270	.343	6	.222	1	-3	-4	0	-0.3
1994	NY-N	4	10	.286	21	21	1	0	0	131^1	145	25	42	62	13.0	5.55	75	.285	.342	5	.135	0	-20	-20	1	-1.7
1995	Cin-N	1	2	.333	11	2	0	0	0	24^1	30	8	7	14	14.1	6.66	62	.319	.373	0	.000	0	-7	-7	0	-0.7
1997	SD-N	7	6	.538	37	15	0	0	1	118	120	16	52	68	13.2	4.81	81	.267	.345	5	.167	1	-8	-12	1	-1.0

YEAR	TM/L	W	L	PCT	G	GS	CG	SH	SV	IP	H	HR	BB	SO	RAT	ERA	ERA+	OAV	OOB	BH	AVG	PB	PR	/A	PD	TPI
1998	SD-N	3	2	.600	10	8	0	0	0	43^1	45	5	18	36	13.7	4.78	80	.266	.347	1	.071	-0	-3	-5	0	-0.5
	Bal-A	2	3	.400	27	4	0	0	0	45	57	7	16	29	14.6	6.20	73	.311	.367	0	.000	-0	-8	-8	1	-0.7
Total	11	47	71	.398	231	163	12	4	1	1025^2	1043	126	404	640	12.8	4.55	86	.266	.336	33	.118	-2	-79	-72	-1	-8.2

● **PETE SMITH** Smith, Peter Luke b: 3/19/40, Natick, Mass. BR/TR, 6'2", 190 lbs. Deb: 9/13/62

YEAR	TM/L	W	L	PCT	G	GS	CG	SH	SV	IP	H	HR	BB	SO	RAT	ERA	ERA+	OAV	OOB	BH	AVG	PB	PR	/A	PD	TPI
1962	Bos-A	0	1	.000	1	1	0	0	0	3^2	7	3	2	1	22.1	19.64	21	.438	.500	0	.000	-0	-6	-6	0	-0.9
1963	Bos-A	0	0	—	6	1	0	0	0	15	11	2	6	6	10.2	3.60	105	.212	.293	0	.000	-0	0	0	0	0.0
Total	2	0	1	.000	7	2	0	0	0	18^2	18	5	8	7	12.5	6.75	57	.265	.342	0	.000	-0	-6	-6	0	-0.9

● **REX SMITH** Smith, Rex (b: Henry W. Schmidt) b: 1864, Louisville, Ky. d: 6/21/1895, Louisville, Ky. Deb: 7/11/1886

YEAR	TM/L	W	L	PCT	G	GS	CG	SH	SV	IP	H	HR	BB	SO	RAT	ERA	ERA+	OAV	OOB	BH	AVG	PB	PR	/A	PD	TPI
1886	Phi-a	0	1	.000	1	1	1	0	0	9	15	0	5	4	20.0	7.00	50	.385	.455	0	.000	-1	-4	-3	-0	-0.3

● **ED SMITH** Smith, Rhesa Edward b: 2/21/1879, Mentone, Ind. d: 3/20/55, Tarpon Springs, Fla. BR/TR, 5'11", 170 lbs. Deb: 4/27/06

YEAR	TM/L	W	L	PCT	G	GS	CG	SH	SV	IP	H	HR	BB	SO	RAT	ERA	ERA+	OAV	OOB	BH	AVG	PB	PR	/A	PD	TPI
1906	StL-A	8	11	.421	19	18	13	0	0	154^2	153	3	53	45	12.5	3.72	69	.261	.331	11	.204	2	-18	-20	1	-1.9

● **BOB SMITH** Smith, Robert Ashley (a.k.a. Robert M. Brown In 1914)
b: 7/20/1890, Woodbury, Vt. d: 12/27/65, West Los Angeles, Cal. BR/TR, 5'11", 160 lbs. Deb: 4/19/13

YEAR	TM/L	W	L	PCT	G	GS	CG	SH	SV	IP	H	HR	BB	SO	RAT	ERA	ERA+	OAV	OOB	BH	AVG	PB	PR	/A	PD	TPI
1913	Chi-A	0	0	—	1	0	0	0	0	2	3	0	3	1	27.0	13.50	22	.273	.429	0	—	0	-2	-2	-0	0.0
1914	Buf-F	0	0	—	15	1	0	0	3	36^2	39	3	16	13	14.0	3.44	86	.281	.363	2	.222	0	-2	-2	1	0.1
1915	Buf-F	0	0	—	1	0	0	0	0	1	1	0	2	0	36.0	18.00	16	.333	.667	0	—	0	-2	-2	0	0.0
Total	3	0	0	—	17	1	0	0	3	39^2	43	3	21	14	15.2	4.31	69	.281	.379	2	.222	0	-6	-6	1	0.1

● **BOB SMITH** Smith, Robert Eldridge b: 4/22/1895, Rogersville, Tenn. d: 7/19/87, Waycross, Ga. BR/TR, 5'10", 175 lbs. Deb: 4/19/23 ♦

YEAR	TM/L	W	L	PCT	G	GS	CG	SH	SV	IP	H	HR	BB	SO	RAT	ERA	ERA+	OAV	OOB	BH	AVG	PB	PR	/A	PD	TPI
1925	Bos-N	5	3	.625	13	10	6	0	0	92^2	110	6	36	19	14.2	4.47	90	.304	.367	49	.282	3	-2	-5	-0	-0.1
1926	Bos-N	10	13	.435	33	23	14	4	1	201^1	199	10	75	44	12.2	3.75	94	.269	.336	25	.298	7	2	-5	2	0.5
1927	Bos-N	10	18	.357	41	31	16	1	3	260^2	297	9	75	81	12.9	3.76	99	.301	.351	27	.248	4	4	-1	2	0.6
1928	Bos-N	13	17	.433	38	26	14	0	2	244^1	274	11	74	59	12.9	3.87	101	.289	.342	23	.250	3	3	1	3	0.7
1929	Bos-N	11	17	.393	34	29	19	1	3	231	256	20	71	65	12.8	4.68	100	.285	.338	17	.172	-1	1	0	1	0.1
1930	Bos-N	10	14	.417	38	24	14	2	5	219^2	247	25	85	84	13.7	4.26	116	.290	.357	19	.235	-1	17	16	2	1.6
1931	Chi-N	15	12	.556	36	29	18	2	2	240^1	239	10	62	63	11.3	3.22	120	.256	.303	19	.218	2	17	17	1	2.0
1932	*Chi-N	4	3	.571	34	11	4	1	2	119	148	4	36	35	14.1	4.61	82	.303	.355	10	.238	2	-10	-11	1	-0.4
1933	Cin-N	4	4	.500	16	6	4	0	0	73^2	75	3	11	18	10.5	2.20	154	.260	.287	5	.200	0	9	10	-0	1.0
	Bos-N	4	3	.571	14	4	3	1	1	58^2	68	3	7	16	11.5	3.22	95	.296	.316	4	.200	1	1	-1	1	0.0
	Yr	8	7	.533	30	10	7	1	1	132^1	143	6	18	34	10.9	2.65	123	.276	.300	9	.200	1	10	9	1	1.0
1934	Bos-N	6	9	.400	39	5	3	0	5	121^2	133	9	36	26	12.5	4.66	82	.277	.328	9	.250	1	-8	-11	1	-1.1
1935	Bos-N	8	18	.308	46	20	8	2	5	203^1	232	13	61	58	13.1	3.94	96	.285	.337	17	.270	2	2	-3	-1	-0.2
1936	Bos-N	6	7	.462	35	11	5	2	8	136	142	3	35	36	11.8	3.77	102	.264	.311	10	.222	0	4	1	1	0.2
1937	Bos-N	0	1	.000	18	0	0	0	3	44	52	6	6	14	12.3	4.09	88	.295	.326	2	.200	0	-1	-2	-1	-0.1
Total	13	106	139	.433	435	229	128	16	40	2246^1	2472	132	670	618	12.7	3.94	100	.283	.335	409	.242	23	40	4	12	4.8

● **BOB SMITH** Smith, Robert Gilchrist b: 2/1/31, Woodsville, N.H. BR/TL, 6'1.5", 190 lbs. Deb: 4/29/55

YEAR	TM/L	W	L	PCT	G	GS	CG	SH	SV	IP	H	HR	BB	SO	RAT	ERA	ERA+	OAV	OOB	BH	AVG	PB	PR	/A	PD	TPI
1955	Bos-A	0	0	—	1	0	0	0	0	1^2	1	0	1	1	10.8	0.00	—	.200	.333	0	—	0	1	1	-0	0.0
1957	StL-N	0	0	—	6	0	0	0	1	9^2	12	0	6	11	17.7	4.66	85	.267	.365	0	.000	-0	-1	-1	0	0.0
	Pit-N	2	4	.333	20	4	2	0	0	55	48	2	25	35	12.1	3.11	122	.229	.314	1	.077	-1	5	4	-1	0.2
	Yr	2	4	.333	26	4	2	0	1	64^2	60	2	31	46	12.8	3.34	114	.234	.319	1	.067	-1	4	3	-1	0.2
1958	Pit-N	2	2	.500	35	4	0	0	1	61	61	6	31	24	13.9	4.43	87	.262	.353	1	.091	-1	-3	-4	1	-0.2
1959	Pit-N	0	0	—	20	0	0	0	0	28^1	32	1	17	12	15.6	3.49	111	.291	.386	0	.000	-0	1	1	-0	-0.1
	Det-A	0	3	.000	9	0	0	0	0	11	20	5	3	10	18.8	8.18	50	.417	.451	0	.000	-0	-5	-5	0	-1.2
Total	4	4	9	.308	91	8	2	0	2	166^2	174	14	83	93	14.1	4.05	95	.267	.354	2	.069	-2	-2	-3	-0	-1.3

● **BOB SMITH** Smith, Robert Walkay "Riverboat" b: 5/13/27, Clarence, Mo. BL/TL, 6', 185 lbs. Deb: 4/22/58

YEAR	TM/L	W	L	PCT	G	GS	CG	SH	SV	IP	H	HR	BB	SO	RAT	ERA	ERA+	OAV	OOB	BH	AVG	PB	PR	/A	PD	TPI
1958	Bos-A	4	3	.571	17	7	1	0	0	66^2	61	4	45	43	14.3	3.78	106	.248	.364	2	.105	-1	-0	2	1	0.1
1959	Chi-N	0	0	—	1	0	0	0	0	0^2	5	0	2	0	94.5	81.00	5	.833	.875	0	—	0	-6	-6	0	0.0
	Cle-A	0	1	.000	12	3	0	0	0	29^1	31	2	12	17	13.2	5.22	71	.282	.352	0	.000	-1	-4	-5	0	-0.2
Total	2	4	4	.500	30	10	1	0	0	96^2	97	6	59	60	14.5	4.75	82	.268	.371	2	.080	-2	-10	-9	1	-0.1

● **RUFUS SMITH** Smith, Rufus Frazier "Shirt" b: 1/24/05, Guilford College, N.C. d: 8/21/84, Aiken, S.C. BR/TL, 5'8", 165 lbs. Deb: 10/2/27

YEAR	TM/L	W	L	PCT	G	GS	CG	SH	SV	IP	H	HR	BB	SO	RAT	ERA	ERA+	OAV	OOB	BH	AVG	PB	PR	/A	PD	TPI
1927	Det-A	0	0	—	1	1	0	0	0	8	8	0	3	2	13.5	3.38	125	.242	.324	0	.000	-1	1	1	-0	-0.1

● **SHERRY SMITH** Smith, Sherrod Malone b: 2/18/1891, Monticello, Ga. d: 9/12/49, Reidsville, Ga. BR/TL, 6'1", 170 lbs. Deb: 5/11/11

YEAR	TM/L	W	L	PCT	G	GS	CG	SH	SV	IP	H	HR	BB	SO	RAT	ERA	ERA+	OAV	OOB	BH	AVG	PB	PR	/A	PD	TPI
1911	Pit-N	0	0	—	1	0	0	0	0	0^2	4	0	1	0	67.5	54.00	6	.667	.714	0	—	0	-4	-4	-0	0.0
1912	Pit-N	0	0	—	3	0	0	0	1	4	6	0	1	3	15.8	6.75	48	.600	.636	0	—	0	-1	-2	-0	-0.1
1915	Bro-N	14	8	.636	29	20	11	2	2	173^2	169	3	42	52	11.2	2.59	107	.264	.315	14	.246	3	3	4	-0	0.7
1916	*Bro-N	14	10	.583	36	25	15	4	1	219	193	5	45	67	9.9	2.34	114	.239	.282	21	.273	5	7	8	0	1.6
1917	Bro-N	12	12	.500	38	23	15	0	3	211^1	210	5	51	58	11.2	3.32	84	.265	.311	15	.195	2	-14	-12	3	-0.8
1919	Bro-N	7	12	.368	30	19	13	2	1	173	181	3	29	40	11.1	2.24	133	.278	.313	8	.148	-2	13	14	3	1.7
1920	*Bro-N	11	9	.550	33	13	6	2	3	136^1	134	1	27	33	10.8	1.85	173	.264	.304	10	.233	2	19	21	5	4.0
1921	Bro-N	7	11	.389	35	17	9	0	4	175^1	232	4	34	36	13.7	3.90	100	.319	.350	13	.228	1	-2	-0	5	0.5
1922	Bro-N	4	8	.333	28	8	3	1	2	108^2	128	6	35	15	14.1	4.56	89	.309	.373	9	.257	2	-5	-6	1	-0.3
	Cle-A	1	0	1.000	2	2	1	0	0	15^2	18	0	3	4	12.1	3.45	116	.295	.328	2	.333	1	1	1	0	0.1
1923	Cle-A	9	6	.600	30	16	10	1	1	124	129	4	37	23	12.2	3.27	121	.269	.324	11	.244	1	10	10	2	1.3
1924	Cle-A	12	14	.462	39	27	20	2	1	247^2	267	5	42	34	11.5	3.02	142	.277	.312	18	.202	-1	33	35	3	3.4
1925	Cle-A	11	14	.440	31	30	**22**	1	1	237	296	11	48	30	13.3	4.86	91	.306	.342	28	.304	7	-12	-12	-0	-0.4
1926	Cle-A	11	10	.524	27	24	16	1	0	188^1	214	8	31	25	11.9	3.73	109	.292	.324	14	.215	2	6	7	3	1.2
1927	Cle-A	1	4	.200	11	2	1	0	1	38	53	2	14	8	15.9	5.45	77	.342	.396	2	.167	-0	-6	-5	0	-0.6
Total	14	114	118	.491	373	226	142	16	21	2052^2	2234	57	440	428	11.9	3.32	108	.282	.324	165	.233	22	48	59	26	12.3

● **TOM SMITH** Smith, Thomas Edward b: 12/5/1871, Boston, Mass. d: 3/2/29, Dorchester, Mass. BR/TR, 5'7.5", 165 lbs. Deb: 6/6/1894

YEAR	TM/L	W	L	PCT	G	GS	CG	SH	SV	IP	H	HR	BB	SO	RAT	ERA	ERA+	OAV	OOB	BH	AVG	PB	PR	/A	PD	TPI
1894	Bos-N	0	0	—	2	0	0	0	1	6	8	2	6	2	27.0	15.00	38	.320	.514	0	.000	-0	-6	-6	-0	-0.2
1895	Phi-N	2	3	.400	11	7	4	0	0	68	76	1	53	21	18.0	6.88	70	.278	.408	8	.242	-0	-16	-16	-1	-0.9
1896	Lou-N	2	3	.400	11	5	4	0	0	55	73	2	25	14	16.7	5.40	80	.316	.392	8	.205	-0	-6	-7	1	-0.4
1898	StL-N	0	1	.000	1	1	1	0	0	9	9	0	5	1	16.0	2.00	189	.257	.381	1	.500	1	2	2	0	0.3
Total	4	4	7	.364	25	13	9	0	1	138	166	5	89	38	17.7	6.33	72	.294	.406	17	.224	-0	-27	-27	-0	-1.2

● **TRAVIS SMITH** Smith, Travis William b: 11/7/72, Springfield, Ore. BR/TR, 5'10", 170 lbs. Deb: 6/21/98

YEAR	TM/L	W	L	PCT	G	GS	CG	SH	SV	IP	H	HR	BB	SO	RAT	ERA	ERA+	OAV	OOB	BH	AVG	PB	PR	/A	PD	TPI
1998	Mil-N	0	0	—	1	0	0	0	0	2	1	0	0	1	4.5	0.00	—	.143	.143	0	.000	-0	1	1	-0	0.0

● **BILL SMITH** Smith, William Garland b: 6/8/34, Washington, D.C. d: 3/30/97, Clinton, Md. BL/TL, 6', 190 lbs. Deb: 9/13/58

YEAR	TM/L	W	L	PCT	G	GS	CG	SH	SV	IP	H	HR	BB	SO	RAT	ERA	ERA+	OAV	OOB	BH	AVG	PB	PR	/A	PD	TPI
1958	StL-N	0	1	.000	2	1	0	0	0	9^2	12	0	4	4	14.9	6.52	63	.324	.390	0	.000	-0	-3	-3	0	-0.2
1959	StL-N	0	0	—	6	0	0	0	1	8^1	11	0	3	4	15.1	1.08	393	.333	.389	0	.000	-0	3	3	-0	0.1
1962	Phi-N	1	5	.167	24	5	0	0	0	50^1	59	8	10	26	12.5	4.29	90	.295	.332	2	.182	1	-2	-2	-0	-0.2
Total	3	1	6	.143	32	6	0	0	1	68^1	82	8	17	34	13.2	4.21	94	.304	.347	2	.143	0	-2	-2	-0	-0.3

● **WILLIE SMITH** Smith, Willie b: 2/11/39, Anniston, Ala. BL/TL, 6', 190 lbs. Deb: 6/18/63 ♦

YEAR	TM/L	W	L	PCT	G	GS	CG	SH	SV	IP	H	HR	BB	SO	RAT	ERA	ERA+	OAV	OOB	BH	AVG	PB	PR	/A	PD	TPI
1963	Det-A	1	0	1.000	11	2	0	0	2	21^2	24	2	13	16	15.4	4.57	82	.300	.398	1	.125	-0	-2	-2	0	-0.2
1964	LA-A	1	4	.200	15	1	0	0	0	31^2	34	5	10	20	12.8	2.84	116	.293	.354	108	.301	6	3	2	0	0.5
1968	Cle-A	0	0	—	2	0	0	0	0	5	2	0	1	1	5.4	0.00	—	.125	.176	6	.143	0	2	2	0	0.0
	Chi-N	0	0	—	1	0	0	0	0	2^2	0	0	0	2	0.0	0.00	—	.000	.000	39	.275	0	1	1	0	0.1
Total	3	2	4	.333	29	3	0	0	2	61	60	7	24	39	12.5	3.10	110	.273	.347	410	.248	6	3	2	1	0.4

● **WILLIE SMITH** Smith, Willie Everett b: 8/27/67, Savannah, Ga. BR/TR, 6'6", 250 lbs. Deb: 4/25/94

YEAR	TM/L	W	L	PCT	G	GS	CG	SH	SV	IP	H	HR	BB	SO	RAT	ERA	ERA+	OAV	OOB	BH	AVG	PB	PR	/A	PD	TPI
1994	StL-N	1	1	.500	8	0	0	0	0	7	9	4	3	7	15.4	9.00	46	.300	.364	0	—	0	-4	-4	-0	-0.9

YEAR	TM/L	W	L	PCT	G	GS	CG	SH	SV	IP	H	HR	BB	SO	RAT	ERA	ERA+	OAV	OOB	BH	AVG	PB	PR	/A	PD	TPI
● **ZANE SMITH**	Smith, Zane William b: 12/28/60, Madison, Wis. BL/TL, 6'2", 195 lbs. Deb: 9/10/84																									
1984	Atl-N	1	0	1.000	3	3	0	0	0	20	16	1	13	16	13.0	2.25	171	.219	.337	5	.556	2	3	4	0	0.4
1985	Atl-N	9	10	.474	42	18	2	2	0	147	135	4	80	85	13.3	3.80	101	.254	.355	6	.162	-0	-3	1	2	0.3
1986	Atl-N	8	16	.333	38	32	3	1	1	204^2	209	8	105	139	14.0	4.05	98	.275	.367	5	.085	-3	-7	-2	3	-0.2
1987	Atl-N	15	10	.600	36	36	9	3	0	242	245	19	91	130	12.7	4.09	106	.266	.335	10	.132	-1	-0	7	1	0.8
1988	Atl-N	5	10	.333	23	22	3	0	0	140^1	159	8	44	59	13.2	4.30	86	.292	.348	7	.167	0	-13	-10	3	-0.6
1989	Atl-N	1	12	.077	17	17	0	0	0	99	102	5	33	58	12.5	4.45	82	.267	.329	5	.179	-0	-11	-9	2	-0.9
	Mon-N	0	1	.000	31	0	0	0	2	48	39	2	19	35	11.1	1.50	235	.220	.299	1	.250	0	11	11	1	0.5
	Yr	1	13	.071	48	17	0	0	2	147	141	7	52	93	11.9	3.49	103	.249	.313	6	.188	0	0	2	3	-0.4
1990	Mon-N	6	7	.462	22	21	1	0	0	139^1	141	11	41	80	11.9	3.23	113	.266	.322	7	.175	1	9	6	1	0.8
	*Pit-N	6	2	.750	11	10	3	2	0	76	55	4	9	50	7.6	1.30	278	.203	.229	4	.143	1	21	20	-0	2.2
	Yr	12	9	.571	33	31	4	2	0	215^1	196	15	50	130	10.3	2.55	143	.243	.287	11	.162	2	30	26	1	3.0
1991	*Pit-N	16	10	.615	35	35	6	3	0	228	234	15	29	120	10.5	3.20	112	.268	.293	13	.183	3	12	9	1	1.4
1992	Pit-N	8	8	.500	23	22	4	3	0	141	138	8	19	56	10.1	3.06	112	.261	.289	6	.122	-0	7	6	1	0.7
1993	Pit-N	3	7	.300	14	14	1	0	0	83	97	5	22	32	12.9	4.55	89	.298	.343	2	.080	-2	-5	-5	-1	-0.7
1994	Pit-N	10	8	.556	25	24	2	1	0	157	162	18	34	57	11.2	3.27	132	.270	.309	12	.211	1	16	18	3	2.3
1995	*Bos-A	8	8	.500	24	21	0	0	0	110^2	144	7	23	47	13.7	5.61	87	.316	.351	0	—	0	-11	-9	0	-1.1
1996	Pit-N	4	6	.400	16	16	1	1	0	83^1	104	7	21	47	13.9	5.08	86	.309	.356	4	.154	-1	-8	-7	-0	-0.8
Total	13	100	115	.465	360	291	35	16	3	1919^1	1980	122	583	1011	12.2	3.74	105	.271	.327	87	.158	0	20	41	17	5.1
● **ROGER SMITHBERG**	Smithberg, Roger Craig b: 3/21/66, Elgin, Ill. BR/TR, 6'3", 205 lbs. Deb: 9/1/93																									
1993	Oak-A	1	2	.333	13	0	0	0	3	19^2	13	2	7	4	9.6	2.75	148	.197	.284	0	—	0	3	3	1	0.6
1994	Oak-A	0	0	—	2	0	0	0	0	2^1	6	1	1	3	27.0	15.43	29	.500	.538	0	—	0	-3	-3	0	0.0
Total	2	1	2	.333	15	0	0	0	3	22	19	3	8	7	11.5	4.09	101	.244	.322	0	—	0	1	0	1	0.6
● **MIKE SMITHSON**	Smithson, Billy Mike b: 1/21/55, Centerville, Tenn. BL/TR, 6'8", 215 lbs. Deb: 8/27/82																									
1982	Tex-A	3	4	.429	8	8	3	0	0	46^2	51	5	13	24	12.9	5.01	77	.282	.340	0	—	0	-5	-6	-1	-0.8
1983	Tex-A	10	14	.417	33	33	10	0	0	223^1	233	14	71	135	12.6	3.91	102	.269	.330	0	—	0	4	2	1	0.4
1984	Min-A	15	13	.536	36	36	10	1	0	252	246	35	54	144	11.0	3.68	114	.252	.296	0	—	0	9	15	-1	1.4
1985	Min-A	15	14	.517	37	37	8	3	0	257	264	25	78	127	12.5	4.34	101	.270	.333	0	—	0	-6	2	-2	0.0
1986	Min-A	13	14	.481	34	33	8	1	0	198	234	26	57	114	13.9	4.77	90	.294	.352	0	—	0	-13	-10	1	-1.3
1987	Min-A	4	7	.364	21	20	0	0	0	109	126	17	38	53	14.3	5.94	78	.286	.355	0	—	0	-18	-16	-1	-1.5
1988	*Bos-A	9	6	.600	31	18	1	0	0	126^2	149	25	37	73	13.6	5.97	69	.292	.347	0	—	0	-28	-26	-1	-2.8
1989	Bos-A	7	14	.333	40	19	1	1	2	143^2	170	21	35	61	13.5	4.95	83	.297	.348	0	—	0	-17	-14	-1	-2.1
Total	8	76	86	.469	240	204	41	6	2	1356^1	1473	168	383	731	12.8	4.58	92	.277	.334	0	—	0	-74	-53	-4	-6.7
● **LEFTY SMOLL**	Smoll, Clyde Hetrick b: 4/17/14, Quakertown, Pa. d: 8/31/85, Quakertown, Pa. BB/TL, 5'10", 175 lbs. Deb: 4/26/40																									
1940	Phi-N	2	8	.200	33	9	0	0	0	109	145	6	36	31	15.3	5.37	73	.322	.378	5	.161	-1	-18	-18	-2	-1.7
● **JOHN SMOLTZ**	Smoltz, John Andrew b: 5/15/67, Detroit, Mich. BR/TR, 6'3", 210 lbs. Deb: 7/23/88																									
1988	Atl-N	2	7	.222	12	12	0	0	0	64	74	10	33	37	15.3	5.48	67	.285	.369	2	.118	-0	-14	-13	-1	-1.7
1989	Atl-N★	12	11	.522	29	29	5	0	0	208	160	15	72	168	10.1	2.94	124	.212	.282	7	.113	1	13	16	2	2.1
1990	Atl-N	14	11	.560	34	34	6	2	0	231^1	206	20	90	170	11.6	3.85	105	.240	.313	12	.162	1	-2	5	1	0.7
1991	*Atl-N	14	13	.519	36	36	5	0	0	229^2	206	16	77	148	11.2	3.80	102	.243	.308	7	.108	-1	-3	2	0	0.2
1992	*Atl-N★	15	12	.556	35	35	9	3	0	246^2	206	17	80	**215**	10.6	2.85	129	.224	.289	12	.160	2	18	22	-1	2.6
1993	*Atl-N★	15	11	.577	35	35	3	1	0	243^2	208	23	100	208	11.6	3.62	111	.230	.311	13	.183	3	11	11	-0	1.3
1994	Atl-N	6	10	.375	21	21	1	0	0	134^2	120	15	48	113	11.5	4.14	102	.239	.310	6	.162	2	1	1	0	0.3
1995	*Atl-N	12	7	.632	29	29	2	1	0	192^2	166	15	72	193	11.3	3.18	134	.232	.306	6	.107	-1	21	23	-1	1.9
1996	*Atl-N★	**24**	8	**.750**	35	35	6	2	0	**253^2**	199	19	55	**276**	**9.1**	2.94	149	.216	**.261**	17	.218	4	36	41	1	5.4
1997	*Atl-N	15	12	.556	35	35	7	2	0	**256**	234	21	63	241	10.5	3.02	138	.242	.289	18	.228	6	33	33	1	3.9
1998	*Atl-N	17	3	**.850**	26	26	2	2	0	167^2	145	10	44	173	10.4	2.90	146	.231	.286	10	.196	3	25	25	0	3.2
Total	11	146	105	.582	327	327	46	13	0	2228	1924	181	734	1942	10.9	3.36	120	.232	.297	110	.165	19	140	168	2	19.9
● **HARRY SMYTHE**	Smythe, William Henry b: 10/24/04, Augusta, Ga. d: 8/28/80, Augusta, Ga. BL/TL, 5'10.5", 179 lbs. Deb: 7/21/29																									
1929	Phi-N	4	6	.400	19	7	2	0	1	68^2	94	3	15	12	14.4	5.24	99	.330	.365	5	.192	-1	-4	-0	2	0.0
1930	Phi-N	0	3	.000	25	3	0	0	2	49^2	84	3	31	9	21.4	7.79	70	.368	.450	4	.286	-0	-16	-13	-1	-0.8
1934	NY-A	0	2	.000	8	0	0	0	1	15	24	1	8	7	19.2	7.80	52	.381	.451	1	.200	-0	-6	-6	-1	-0.7
	Bro-N	1	1	.500	8	0	0	0	0	21^1	30	3	8	5	16.5	5.91	66	.337	.398	3	.333	1	-4	-5	1	-0.2
Total	3	5	12	.294	60	10	2	0	4	154^2	232	10	62	33	17.4	6.40	78	.349	.408	13	.241	0	-29	-24	2	-1.7
● **NATE SNELL**	Snell, Nathaniel b: 9/2/52, Orangeburg, S.C. BR/TR, 6'4", 190 lbs. Deb: 9/20/84																									
1984	Bal-A	1	1	.500	5	0	0	0	0	7^2	8	1	1	7	10.6	2.35	165	.258	.281	0	—	0	1	1	-0	0.3
1985	Bal-A	3	2	.600	43	0	0	0	5	100^1	100	4	30	41	11.8	2.69	150	.260	.315	0	—	0	16	15	1	0.9
1986	Bal-A	2	1	.667	34	0	0	0	0	72^1	69	9	22	29	11.4	3.86	107	.257	.316	0	—	0	3	2	1	0.3
1987	Det-A	1	2	.333	22	2	0	0	0	38^2	39	5	19	19	13.5	3.96	107	.267	.352	0	—	0	2	1	-1	0.1
Total	4	7	6	.538	104	2	0	0	5	219	216	19	72	96	11.9	3.29	125	.260	.321	0	—	0	22	20	1	1.6
● **FRANK SNOOK**	Snook, Frank Walter b: 3/28/49, Somerville, N.J. BR/TR, 6'2", 180 lbs. Deb: 7/13/73																									
1973	SD-N	0	2	.000	18	0	0	0	1	27^1	19	4	18	13	12.2	3.62	96	.200	.327	0	.000	-0	0	-0	1	0.0
● **COLONEL SNOVER**	Snover, Colonel Lester "Bosco" b: 5/16/1895, Hallstead, Pa. d: 4/30/69, Rochester, N.Y. BL/TL, 6'0.5", 200 lbs. Deb: 9/18/19																									
1919	NY-N	0	1	.000	2	1	0	0	0	9	7	0	3	4	11.0	1.00	281	.212	.297	0	.000	0	2	2	-0	0.2
● **BRIAN SNYDER**	Snyder, Brian Robert b: 2/20/58, Flemington, N.J. BL/TL, 6'3", 185 lbs. Deb: 5/25/85																									
1985	Sea-A	1	2	.333	15	6	0	0	1	35^1	44	2	19	23	16.3	6.37	66	.306	.390	0	—	0	-9	-8	1	-0.6
1989	Oak-A	0	0	—	2	0	0	0	0	0^2	2	1	2	1	54.0	27.00	14	.500	.667	0	—	0	-2	-2	0	0.2
Total	2	1	2	.333	17	6	0	0	1	36	46	3	21	24	17.0	6.75	62	.311	.400	0	—	0	-10	-10	1	-0.4
● **GENE SNYDER**	Snyder, Gene Walter b: 3/31/31, York, Pa. d: 6/2/96, York, Pa. BR/TL, 5'11", 175 lbs. Deb: 4/26/59																									
1959	LA-N	1	1	.500	11	2	0	0	0	26^1	32	1	20	20	17.8	5.47	77	.299	.409	0	.000	-0	-4	-4	-0	-0.3
● **GEORGE SNYDER**	Snyder, George T. b: 8/1848, Philadelphia, Pa. d: 8/2/05, Philadelphia, Pa. Deb: 9/30/1882																									
1882	Phi-a	1	0	1.000	1	1	1	0	0	9	4	0	2	0	6.0	0.00	—	.125	.176	1	.333	0	3	3	0	0.3
● **JOHN SNYDER**	Snyder, John Michael b: 8/16/74, Southfield, Mich. BR/TR, 6'3", 185 lbs. Deb: 6/30/98																									
1998	Chi-A	7	2	.778	15	14	1	0	0	86^1	96	14	23	52	12.6	4.80	95	.286	.335	0	—	0	-1	-2	1	-0.1
● **BILL SNYDER**	Snyder, William Nicholas b: 1/28/1898, Mansfield, Ohio d: 10/8/34, Vicksburg, Mich. BR/TR, Deb: 9/4/19																									
1919	Was-A	0	1	.000	2	1	0	0	0	8	6	0	3	5	10.1	1.13	285	.200	.273	0	.000	-0	2	2	-0	0.2
1920	Was-A	2	1	.667	16	4	1	0	1	54	59	1	28	17	15.5	4.17	90	.280	.380	6	.316	1	-2	-3	-1	-0.1
Total	2	2	2	.500	18	5	1	0	1	62	65	1	31	22	14.8	3.77	97	.270	.367	6	.286	1	-0	-1	-1	0.1
● **STEVE SODERSTROM**	Soderstrom, Stephen Andrew b: 4/3/72, Turlock, Cal. BR/TR, 6'3", 215 lbs. Deb: 9/17/96																									
1996	SF-N	2	0	1.000	3	3	0	0	0	13^2	16	1	6	9	15.8	5.27	78	.302	.393	0	.000	-1	-2	-2	-0	-0.3
● **CLINT SODOWSKY**	Sodowsky, Clint Rea b: 7/13/72, Ponca City, Okla. BL/TR, 6'3", 180 lbs. Deb: 9/4/95																									
1995	Det-A	2	2	.500	6	6	0	0	0	23^1	24	4	18	14	16.2	5.01	95	.258	.378	0	—	0	-1	-1	-0	-0.1
1996	Det-A	1	3	.250	7	7	0	0	0	24^1	40	5	20	9	23.3	11.84	43	.370	.481	0	—	0	-19	-18	-0	-2.1
1997	Pit-N	2	2	.500	45	0	0	0	0	52	49	6	34	51	14.7	3.63	118	.249	.365	1	.500	0	3	4	-0	0.3
1998	Ari-N	3	6	.333	45	6	0	0	0	77^2	86	5	39	42	15.3	5.68	76	.283	.377	3	.300	1	-12	-12	-0	-1.1
Total	4	8	13	.381	103	19	0	0	0	177^1	199	20	111	116	16.3	5.84	76	.283	.390	4	.333	1	-29	-27	-1	-3.0

YEAR	TM/L	W	L	PCT	G	GS	CG	SH	SV	IP	H	HR	BB	SO	RAT	ERA	ERA+	OAV	OOB	BH	AVG	PB	PR	/A	PD	TPI
● RAY SOFF Soff, Raymond John b: 10/31/58, Adrian, Mich. BR/TR, 6′, 185 lbs. Deb: 7/17/86																										
1986	StL-N	4	2	.667	30	0	0	0	0	38^1	37	4	13	22	11.7	3.29	111	.255	.316	0	.000	-0	2	1	0	0.2
1987	StL-N	1	0	1.000	12	0	0	0	0	15^1	18	3	5	9	14.1	6.46	64	.295	.358	0	.000	-0	-4	-4	-0	-0.2
Total	2	5	2	.714	42	0	0	0	0	53^2	55	7	18	31	12.4	4.19	90	.267	.329	0	.000	-0	-2	-2	0	0.0
● JULIO SOLANO Solano, Julio Cesar b: 1/8/60, Aqua Blanca, D.R. BR/TR, 6′1″, 160 lbs. Deb: 4/5/83																										
1983	Hou-N	0	2	.000	4	0	0	0	0	6	5	1	4	3	13.5	6.00	57	.217	.333	0	—	0	-2	-2	0	-0.5
1984	Hou-N	1	3	.250	31	0	0	0	0	50^2	31	3	18	33	8.7	1.95	170	.179	.257	1	.333	0	9	8	-1	0.5
1985	Hou-N	2	2	.500	20	0	0	0	0	33^2	34	5	13	17	12.6	3.48	100	.262	.329	0	.000	-0	0	-0	-1	-0.1
1986	Hou-N	3	1	.750	16	1	0	0	0	32	39	5	22	21	18.0	7.59	47	.310	.424	0	.000	-1	-14	-14	-0	-1.7
1987	Hou-N	0	0	—	11	0	0	0	0	20	25	5	9	12	15.3	7.65	51	.298	.366	0	.000	-0	-8	-8	0	0.0
1988	Sea-A	0	0	—	17	0	0	0	3	22	22	3	12	10	13.9	4.09	102	.268	.362	0	—	0	-0	0	0	-0.2
1989	Sea-A	0	0	—	7	0	0	0	0	9^2	6	1	4	6	10.2	5.59	72	.176	.282	0	—	0	-2	-2	0	-0.2
Total	7	6	8	.429	106	1	0	0	3	174	162	23	82	102	12.8	4.55	79	.248	.336	1	.077	-1	-16	-18	-2	-2.2
● MARCELINO SOLIS Solis, Marcelino b: 7/19/30, San Luis Potosi, Mexico BL/TL, 6′1″, 185 lbs. Deb: 7/16/58																										
1958	Chi-N	3	3	.500	15	4	0	0	0	52	74	5	20	15	17.0	6.06	65	.339	.405	5	.250	1	-12	-12	-0	-1.1
● EDDIE SOLOMON Solomon, Eddie "Buddy" b: 2/9/51, Perry, Ga. d: 1/12/86, Macon, Ga. BR/TR, 6′3″, 190 lbs. Deb: 9/2/73																										
1973	LA-N	0	0	—	4	0	0	0	0	6^1	10	3	4	6	21.3	7.11	48	.357	.455	0	.000	-0	-2	-3	-0	0.0
1974	*LA-N	0	0	—	4	0	0	0	1	6	5	1	2	2	10.5	1.50	227	.217	.280	0	—	0	1	1	0	0.1
1975	Chi-N	0	0	—	6	0	0	0	0	6^2	7	1	6	3	17.6	1.35	285	.269	.406	0	—	0	2	2	0	0.0
1976	StL-N	1	1	.500	26	2	0	0	0	37	45	2	16	19	15.1	4.86	73	.306	.378	2	.400	1	-6	-5	1	-0.1
1977	Atl-N	6	6	.500	18	16	0	0	0	88^2	110	10	34	54	14.8	4.57	97	.305	.368	4	.129	-1	-6	-1	-0	-0.3
1978	Atl-N	4	6	.400	37	8	0	0	2	106	98	12	50	64	12.7	4.08	99	.247	.335	4	.138	-1	-6	-0	-0	-0.1
1979	Atl-N	7	14	.333	31	30	4	0	0	186	184	19	51	96	11.7	4.21	96	.254	.308	13	.203	1	-10	-3	-1	-0.4
1980	Pit-N	7	3	.700	26	12	2	0	0	100^1	96	8	37	35	12.3	2.69	135	.253	.325	7	.219	1	10	11	-0	1.1
1981	Pit-N	8	6	.571	22	17	2	0	1	127	133	10	27	38	11.6	3.12	115	.278	.321	7	.163	-1	5	7	-1	0.5
1982	Pit-N	2	6	.250	11	10	0	0	0	46^2	69	9	18	18	17.0	6.75	55	.347	.404	2	.133	-1	-16	-16	-2	-2.4
	Chi-A	1	0	1.000	6	0	0	0	0	7^1	7	1	2	2	11.0	3.68	110	.241	.290	0	—	0	0	0	-0	0.0
Total	10	36	42	.462	191	95	8	0	4	718	764	76	247	337	12.9	4.00	97	.274	.337	39	.177	-1	-28	-8	-3	-1.6
● JOE SOMMER Sommer, Joseph John b: 11/20/1858, Covington, Ky. d: 1/16/38, Cincinnati, Ohio BR/TR, Deb: 7/8/1880 ♦																										
1883	Cin-a	0	0	—	1	0	0	0	0	5	9	0	1	2	18.0	5.40	60	.360	.385	115	.278	0	-1	-1	-0	0.0
1885	Bal-a	0	0	—	2	0	0	0	1	3	6	0	0	0	18.0	9.00	36	.429	.429	118	.251	0	-2	-2	-0	-0.1
1886	Bal-a	0	0	—	1	0	0	0	0	4	14	0	3	1	38.3	18.00	19	.519	.567	117	.209	-0	-6	-6	-0	0.0
1887	Bal-a	0	0	—	1	0	0	0	0	1	2	0	1	0	27.0	9.00	46	.333	.429	123	.266	0	-1	-1	-0	0.0
1890	Cle-N	0	0	—	1	0	0	0	0	1	2	1	2	0	36.0	0.00	—	.400	.571	8	.229	-0	0	0	-0	0.0
Total	5	0	0	—	6	0	0	0	1	14	33	1	7	3	25.7	9.64	35	.429	.476	911	.248	1	-10	-10	-1	-0.1
● RUDY SOMMERS Sommers, Rudolph b: 10/30/1886, Cincinnati, Ohio d: 3/18/49, Louisville, Ky. BB/TL, 5′11″, 165 lbs. Deb: 9/8/12																										
1912	Chi-N	0	1	.000	1	0	0	0	0	3	4	0	2	2	18.0	3.00	111	.333	.429	0	.000	0	0	0	-0	0.0
1914	Bro-F	2	7	.222	23	8	2	0	2	82	88	2	34	40	13.7	4.06	71	.282	.358	6	.250	2	-11	-11	-1	-1.0
1926	Bos-A	0	0	—	2	0	0	0	0	2	3	0	3	0	27.0	13.50	30	.333	.500	0	—	0	-2	-2	0	0.0
1927	Bos-A	0	0	—	7	0	0	0	0	14	18	2	14	2	20.6	8.36	51	.353	.492	1	.500	0	-7	-6	1	0.1
Total	4	2	8	.200	33	8	2	0	2	101	113	4	53	44	15.1	4.81	64	.294	.384	7	.259	2	-19	-19	-0	-0.9
● ANDY SOMMERVILLE Sommerville, Andrew Henry (b: Henry Travers Summersgill) b: 2/6/1876, Brooklyn, N.Y. d: 6/16/31, Richmond Hill, N.Y. Deb: 8/8/1894																										
1894	Bro-N	0	1	.000	1	1	0	0	0	0^1	1	0	5	0	162.0	162.00	3	.500	.857	0	—	0	-6	-6	0	-3.6
● DON SONGER Songer, Donald C. b: 1/31/1900, Walnut, Kan. d: 10/3/62, Kansas City, Mo. BL/TL, 6′, 165 lbs. Deb: 9/21/24																										
1924	Pit-N	0	0	—	4	1	0	0	1	9^1	14	1	3	3	16.4	6.75	57	.333	.378	0	.000	-0	-3	-3	0	-0.1
1925	Pit-N	0	1	.000	8	0	0	0	0	11^2	14	0	8	4	17.0	2.31	193	.298	.400	0	.000	-0	3	3	-0	0.2
1926	Pit-N	7	8	.467	35	15	5	1	2	126^1	118	4	52	27	12.9	3.13	126	.252	.340	4	.105	-2	10	11	1	1.1
1927	Pit-N	0	0	—	2	0	0	0	0	4^2	10	0	4	1	28.9	11.57	36	.526	.625	0	.000	-0	-4	-4	-0	0.0
	NY-N	3	5	.375	22	1	0	0	1	50^1	48	4	31	9	14.3	2.86	135	.261	.370	3	.300	1	6	6	1	1.0
	Yr	3	5	.375	24	1	0	0	1	55	58	4	35	10	15.4	3.60	108	.284	.392	3	.273	1	2	2	1	1.0
Total	4	10	14	.417	71	17	5	1	4	202^1	204	9	98	44	14.0	3.38	117	.268	.361	7	.132	-2	11	13	2	2.2
● LARY SORENSEN Sorensen, Lary Alan b: 10/4/55, Detroit, Mich. BR/TR, 6′2″, 210 lbs. Deb: 6/7/77																										
1977	Mil-A	7	10	.412	23	20	9	0	0	142^1	147	10	36	57	11.6	4.36	93	.270	.316	0	—	0	-5	-5	1	-0.4
1978	Mil-A★	18	12	.600	37	36	17	3	1	280^2	277	14	50	78	10.6	3.21	117	.259	.295	0	—	0	17	17	1	1.8
1979	Mil-A	15	14	.517	34	34	16	2	0	235^1	250	30	42	63	11.3	3.98	105	.275	.310	0	—	0	6	5	1	0.6
1980	Mil-A	12	10	.545	35	29	8	2	1	195^2	242	13	45	54	13.3	3.68	105	.311	.351	0	—	0	8	4	1	0.7
1981	StL-N	7	7	.500	23	23	3	1	0	140^1	149	3	26	52	11.3	3.27	109	.271	.305	3	.065	-3	3	4	0	0.1
1982	Cle-A	10	15	.400	32	30	6	1	0	189^1	251	19	55	62	14.7	5.61	73	.322	.369	0	—	0	-32	-32	-1	-3.7
1983	Cle-A	12	11	.522	36	34	8	1	0	222^2	238	21	65	76	12.3	4.24	100	.276	.328	0	—	0	-5	-0	2	0.1
1984	Oak-A	6	13	.316	46	21	2	0	1	183^1	240	21	44	63	14.2	4.91	76	.317	.359	0	—	0	-19	-24	-1	-2.3
1985	Chi-N	3	7	.300	45	3	0	0	0	82^1	86	8	24	34	12.5	4.26	94	.274	.333	0	.000	-0	-6	-3	-0	-0.3
1987	Mon-N	3	4	.429	23	5	0	0	1	47^2	56	7	12	21	13.4	4.72	89	.286	.336	0	.000	-1	-3	-3	-1	-0.5
1988	SF-N	0	0	—	12	0	0	0	2	16^2	24	1	3	9	14.6	4.86	67	.329	.355	0	.000	-0	-3	-3	-0	-0.1
Total	11	93	103	.474	346	235	69	10	6	1736^1	1960	147	402	569	12.4	4.15	95	.287	.329	3	.049	-4	-38	-38	1	-4.0
● VIC SORRELL Sorrell, Victor Garland b: 4/9/01, Morrisville, N.C. d: 5/4/72, Raleigh, N.C. BR/TR, 5′10″, 180 lbs. Deb: 4/22/28																										
1928	Det-A	8	11	.421	29	23	8	0	0	171	182	9	83	67	14.2	4.79	86	.277	.363	6	.109	-5	-14	-13	-3	-1.9
1929	Det-A	14	15	.483	36	31	13	1	1	226	270	15	106	81	15.1	5.18	83	.302	.377	12	.145	-6	-23	-22	-1	-3.0
1930	Det-A	16	11	.593	35	30	14	2	1	233^1	245	13	106	97	13.5	3.86	124	.274	.351	15	.188	-3	21	24	-3	1.8
1931	Det-A	13	14	.481	35	32	19	1	1	245	267	8	114	99	14.0	4.15	110	.278	.355	14	.159	-4	6	12	1	0.8
1932	Det-A	14	14	.500	32	31	13	1	0	234^1	234	11	77	84	12.1	4.03	117	.259	.319	9	.118	-4	12	17	-2	1.3
1933	Det-A	11	15	.423	36	28	13	1	1	232^2	233	18	78	75	12.1	3.79	114	.260	.321	11	.149	-2	13	13	-0	1.0
1934	Det-A	6	9	.400	28	19	6	1	2	129^2	146	13	45	46	13.5	4.79	92	.283	.345	4	.108	-1	-4	-6	2	-0.5
1935	Det-A	4	3	.571	12	6	4	0	0	51^1	65	2	25	22	16.1	4.03	103	.319	.398	0	.000	-3	2	1	0	-0.2
1936	Det-A	6	7	.462	30	14	5	1	3	131^1	153	9	64	37	15.0	5.28	94	.294	.373	6	.154	1	-3	-5	2	-0.2
1937	Det-A	0	2	.000	7	2	0	0	1	17	25	3	8	11	17.5	9.00	52	.338	.402	0	.000	-0	-8	-8	0	-0.9
Total	10	92	101	.477	280	216	95	8	10	1671^2	1820	101	706	619	13.7	4.43	102	.279	.351	77	.139	-27	-0	14	-4	-1.8
● ELIAS SOSA Sosa, Elias (Martinez) b: 6/10/50, LaVega, D.R. BR/TR, 6′2″, 190 lbs. Deb: 9/8/72																										
1972	SF-N	0	1	.000	8	0	0	0	3	15^2	10	0	12	10	12.6	2.30	152	.189	.338	0	.000	-0	2	2	-0	0.2
1973	SF-N	10	4	.714	71	1	0	0	18	107	95	7	41	70	11.8	3.28	116	.241	.318	1	.071	-0	5	6	-1	0.9
1974	SF-N	9	7	.563	68	0	0	0	6	101	94	8	45	48	12.5	3.48	109	.252	.334	1	.067	-1	2	4	-1	0.4
1975	StL-N	0	3	.000	14	1	0	0	0	27^1	22	3	14	15	12.2	3.95	95	.227	.330	1	.125	-0	-1	-1	-0	-0.1
	Atl-N	2	2	.500	43	0	0	0	2	62^1	70	3	29	31	14.7	4.48	84	.294	.378	1	.143	-0	-6	-5	-0	-0.4
	Yr	2	5	.286	57	1	0	0	2	89^2	92	6	43	46	13.9	4.32	87	.271	.358	2	.133	-1	-7	-5	-0	-0.5
1976	Atl-N	4	4	.500	21	0	0	0	3	35^1	41	3	13	32	14.0	5.35	71	.287	.350	1	.143	-0	-7	-6	-0	-1.5
	LA-N	2	4	.333	24	0	0	0	1	33^2	30	0	12	20	11.2	3.48	97	.242	.309	0	—	0	0	-0	0	-0.1
	Yr	6	8	.429	45	0	0	0	4	69	71	3	25	52	12.5	4.43	81	.263	.325	1	.143	-0	-7	-6	-0	-1.6
1977	*LA-N	2	2	.500	44	0	0	0	1	63^2	42	7	12	47	7.8	1.98	193	.189	.234	1	.250	0	14	13	-0	0.8
1978	Oak-A	8	2	.800	68	0	0	0	14	109	106	5	44	61	12.5	2.64	138	.264	.338	0	—	0	14	12	0	1.5
1979	Mon-N	8	7	.533	62	0	0	0	18	96^2	77	2	37	59	10.8	1.96	187	.219	.297	2	.154	0	19	18	-1	3.3
1980	Mon-N	9	6	.600	67	0	0	0	9	93^2	104	5	19	58	11.9	3.07	116	.286	.323	1	.091	-1	5	5	-0	0.8

YEAR	TM/L	W	L	PCT	G	GS	CG	SH	SV	IP	H	HR	BB	SO	RAT	ERA	ERA+	OAV	OOB	BH	AVG	PB	PR	/A	PD	TPI
1981	*Mon-N	1	2	.333	32	0	0	0	3	39^1	46	3	8	18	12.6	3.66	95	.297	.335	2	1.000	1	-1	-1	0	0.1
1982	Det-A	3	3	.500	38	0	0	0	4	61	64	11	18	24	12.4	4.43	92	.270	.327	0	—	0	-2	-2	1	-0.2
1983	SD-N	1	4	.200	41	1	0	0	1	72^1	72	7	30	45	13.1	4.35	80	.268	.348	1	.143	-0	-6	-7	-1	-0.6
Total	12	59	51	.536	601	3	0	0	83	918	873	64	334	538	12.0	3.32	111	.255	.325	12	.130	-3	37	39	-3	5.1

● **JOSE SOSA** Sosa, Jose Ynocencio (b: Jose Ynocencio (Sosa)) b: 12/28/52, Santo Domingo, D.R. BR/TR, 5′11″, 158 lbs. Deb: 7/22/75

YEAR	TM/L	W	L	PCT	G	GS	CG	SH	SV	IP	H	HR	BB	SO	RAT	ERA	ERA+	OAV	OOB	BH	AVG	PB	PR	/A	PD	TPI
1975	Hou-N	1	3	.250	25	2	0	0	1	47	51	5	23	31	14.4	4.02	84	.291	.377	3	.333	2	-2	-3	-1	-0.2
1976	Hou-N	0	0	—	9	0	0	0	0	11^2	16	0	6	5	19.3	6.94	46	.340	.446	0	—	0	-4	-5	1	0.1
Total	2	1	3	.250	34	2	0	0	1	58^2	67	5	29	36	15.3	4.60	72	.302	.392	3	.333	2	-7	-8	-0	-0.1

● **ALLEN SOTHORON** Sothoron, Allen Sutton b: 4/27/1893, Bradford, Ohio d: 6/17/39, St.Louis, Mo. BB/TR, 5′11″, 182 lbs. Deb: 9/17/14 MC

YEAR	TM/L	W	L	PCT	G	GS	CG	SH	SV	IP	H	HR	BB	SO	RAT	ERA	ERA+	OAV	OOB	BH	AVG	PB	PR	/A	PD	TPI
1914	StL-A	0	0	—	1	0	0	0	0	6	6	0	4	3	15.0	6.00	45	.261	.370	0	.000	-0	-2	-2	-0	0.0
1915	StL-A	0	1	.000	3	1	0	0	0	3^2	8	0	5	2	31.9	7.36	39	.400	.520	0	.000	-0	-2	-2	0	-0.4
1917	StL-A	14	19	.424	48	32	17	3	4	276^2	259	2	96	85	11.8	2.83	92	.251	.320	20	.217	3	-5	-7	-1	-0.6
1918	StL-A	12	12	.500	29	24	14	2	0	209	152	3	67	71	9.6	1.94	141	**.205**	.274	10	.159	-2	20	19	-3	1.6
1919	StL-A	20	12	.625	40	30	21	3	3	270	256	4	87	106	11.8	2.20	151	.246	.311	17	.175	-2	31	34	-7	3.0
1920	StL-A	8	15	.348	36	26	12	1	2	218^1	263	6	89	81	14.8	4.70	83	.307	.376	16	.222	-1	-22	-19	-2	-2.1
1921	StL-A	1	2	.333	5	4	1	0	0	27^2	33	0	8	9	13.7	5.20	86	.314	.368	1	.111	-1	-3	-2	-0	-0.3
	Bos-A	0	2	.000	2	2	0	0	0	6	15	0	5	2	30.0	13.50	31	.455	.526	1	.500	1	-6	-6	0	-1.2
	Cle-A	12	4	.750	22	16	10	2	0	144^2	146	0	58	61	13.1	3.24	132	.279	.358	16	.276	2	17	17	-2	1.5
	Yr	13	8	.619	29	22	11	2	0	178^1	194	0	71	72	13.7	3.89	111	.293	.367	18	.261	2	8	8	-2	0.0
1922	Cle-A	1	3	.250	6	4	2	0	0	25^1	26	1	14	8	14.9	6.39	63	.274	.378	4	.444	1	-7	-7	-0	-0.8
1924	StL-N	10	16	.385	29	28	16	**4**	0	196^2	209	9	84	62	13.9	3.57	106	.275	.354	14	.194	-2	7	5	-3	0.0
1925	StL-N	10	10	.500	28	22	8	2	0	155^2	173	7	63	67	14.0	4.05	107	.280	.353	11	.196	-1	4	5	-4	0.0
1926	StL-N	3	3	.500	15	4	1	0	0	42^2	37	2	16	19	11.2	4.22	93	.247	.319	3	.231	0	-2	-1	-1	-0.3
Total	11	91	99	.479	264	193	102	17	9	1582^1	1583	34	596	576	12.7	3.31	105	.264	.336	113	.207	-2	29	30	-24	0.4

● **MARIO SOTO** Soto, Mario Melvin b: 7/12/56, Bani, D.R. BR/TR, 6′, 185 lbs. Deb: 7/21/77

YEAR	TM/L	W	L	PCT	G	GS	CG	SH	SV	IP	H	HR	BB	SO	RAT	ERA	ERA+	OAV	OOB	BH	AVG	PB	PR	/A	PD	TPI
1977	Cin-N	2	6	.250	12	10	2	1	0	60^2	60	12	26	44	13.2	5.34	74	.258	.340	1	.077	-0	-10	-10	0	-1.1
1978	Cin-N	1	0	1.000	5	1	0	0	0	18	13	1	13	13	13.0	2.50	142	.197	.329	0	.000	-0	2	2	-0	0.0
1979	*Cin-N	3	2	.600	25	0	0	0	0	37^1	33	2	30	32	15.4	5.30	70	.243	.383	4	.571	2	-7	-7	-1	-0.7
1980	Cin-N	10	8	.556	53	12	3	1	4	190^1	126	11	84	182	10.0	3.07	116	**.187**	.279	2	.043	-4	11	11	0	0.6
1981	Cin-N	12	9	.571	25	25	10	3	0	175	142	13	61	151	10.6	3.29	108	.220	.290	4	.068	-4	4	5	-0	0.0
1982	Cin-N★	14	13	.519	35	34	13	2	0	257^2	202	19	71	274	**9.7**	2.79	132	.215	**.273**	14	.167	1	23	26	-1	2.7
1983	Cin-N★	17	13	.567	34	34	**18**	3	0	273^2	207	28	95	242	10.1	2.70	141	.208	.280	11	.125	-2	28	**34**	-1	3.3
1984	Cin-N★	18	7	.720	33	33	**13**	0	0	237^1	181	26	87	185	10.4	3.53	107	.209	.286	18	.207	3	2	7	-3	0.7
1985	Cin-N	12	15	.444	36	36	9	1	0	256^2	196	30	104	214	10.6	3.58	106	.211	.292	11	.133	-2	0	6	-1	0.3
1986	Cin-N	5	10	.333	19	19	1	1	0	105	113	15	46	67	13.7	4.71	82	.280	.355	3	.111	-1	-12	-10	-1	-1.4
1987	Cin-N	3	2	.600	6	6	0	0	0	31^2	34	7	12	11	13.1	5.12	83	.279	.343	1	.083	-1	-4	-3	0	-0.5
1988	Cin-N	3	7	.300	14	14	3	1	0	87	88	8	28	34	12.2	4.66	77	.267	.328	1	.045	-1	-12	-10	-1	-1.3
Total	12	100	92	.521	297	224	72	13	4	1730^1	1395	172	657	1449	10.8	3.47	108	.220	.296	70	.132	-10	27	51	-8	2.6

● **MARK SOUZA** Souza, Kenneth Mark b: 2/1/55, Redwood City, Cal. BL/TL, 6′, 180 lbs. Deb: 4/22/80

YEAR	TM/L	W	L	PCT	G	GS	CG	SH	SV	IP	H	HR	BB	SO	RAT	ERA	ERA+	OAV	OOB	BH	AVG	PB	PR	/A	PD	TPI
1980	Oak-A	0	0	—	5	0	0	0	0	7	9	1	5	2	18.0	7.71	49	.310	.412	0	—	0	-3	-3	-0	0.4

● **JOHN SOWDERS** Sowders, John b: 12/10/1866, Louisville, Ky. d: 7/29/39, Indianapolis, Ind BR/TL, 6′, Deb: 6/28/1887 F♦

YEAR	TM/L	W	L	PCT	G	GS	CG	SH	SV	IP	H	HR	BB	SO	RAT	ERA	ERA+	OAV	OOB	BH	AVG	PB	PR	/A	PD	TPI
1887	Ind-N	0	0	—	1	0	0	0	0	3	11	0	5	0	48.0	21.00	20	.500	.593	0	.000	-0	-6	-6	-0	0.0
1889	KC-a	6	16	.273	25	23	20	0	1	185	204	9	105	104	15.4	4.82	87	.271	.366	19	.218	-2	-20	-13	-2	-1.4
1890	Bro-P	19	16	.543	39	37	28	1	0	309	358	3	161	91	15.4	3.82	117	.278	.363	25	.189	-5	14	22	-2	1.3
Total	3	25	32	.439	65	60	48	1	1	497	573	12	271	195	15.6	4.29	102	.278	.366	44	.199	-7	-11	4	-4	-0.1

● **BILL SOWDERS** Sowders, William Jefferson "Little Bill"
b: 11/29/1864, Louisville, Ky. d: 2/2/51, Indianapolis, Ind. BR/TR, 6′, 155 lbs. Deb: 4/24/1888 F

YEAR	TM/L	W	L	PCT	G	GS	CG	SH	SV	IP	H	HR	BB	SO	RAT	ERA	ERA+	OAV	OOB	BH	AVG	PB	PR	/A	PD	TPI
1888	Bos-N	19	15	.559	36	35	34	2	0	317	278	3	73	132	10.2	2.07	138	.226	.275	18	.148	-4	27	27	1	2.3
1889	Bos-N	1	2	.333	7	4	3	0	3	42	53	3	23	10	16.7	5.14	81	.299	.386	4	.235	-0	-5	-5	1	-0.3
	Pit-N	6	5	.545	13	11	9	0	0	52^2	94	1	29	33	21.7	7.35	51	.376	.449	13	.271	2	-19	-21	2	-2.7
	Yr	7	7	.500	20	15	12	0	**3**	94^2	147	4	52	43	19.3	6.37	62	.343	.419	17	.262	2	-25	-26	3	-3.0
1890	Pit-N	3	8	.273	15	11	9	0	0	106	117	1	24	30	12.1	4.42	75	.271	.313	9	.180	-2	-10	-13	-2	-1.4
Total	3	29	30	.492	71	61	55	2	3	517^2	542	8	149	205	12.3	3.34	94	.260	.314	44	.186	-4	-7	-11	2	-2.1

● **BOB SPADE** Spade, Robert b: 1/4/1877, Akron, Ohio d: 9/7/24, Cincinnati, Ohio BR/TR, 5′10″, 190 lbs. Deb: 9/22/07

YEAR	TM/L	W	L	PCT	G	GS	CG	SH	SV	IP	H	HR	BB	SO	RAT	ERA	ERA+	OAV	OOB	BH	AVG	PB	PR	/A	PD	TPI
1907	Cin-N	1	2	.333	3	3	3	1	0	27	21	0	9	7	10.3	1.00	260	.219	.292	2	.286	1	4	5	-1	0.7
1908	Cin-N	17	12	.586	35	28	22	2	1	249^1	230	2	85	74	11.6	2.74	84	.250	.317	17	.195	1	-11	-12	-4	-1.8
1909	Cin-N	5	5	.500	14	13	8	0	0	98	91	0	39	31	12.3	2.85	91	.236	.313	10	.294	4	-3	-3	-4	-0.3
1910	Cin-N	1	2	.333	3	3	1	0	0	17^1	35	1	9	1	23.4	6.75	43	.479	.542	0	.000	-1	-7	-7	-0	-1.1
	StL-A	1	3	.250	7	5	2	1	0	34^2	34	1	17	8	13.5	4.41	56	.270	.361	3	.273	2	-7	-7	-1	-0.7
Total	4	25	24	.510	62	52	36	4	1	426^1	411	4	159	121	12.3	2.96	82	.257	.329	32	.222	7	-23	-25	-9	-3.2

● **WARREN SPAHN** Spahn, Warren Edward b: 4/23/21, Buffalo, N.Y. BL/TL, 6′, 175 lbs. Deb: 4/19/42 CH

YEAR	TM/L	W	L	PCT	G	GS	CG	SH	SV	IP	H	HR	BB	SO	RAT	ERA	ERA+	OAV	OOB	BH	AVG	PB	PR	/A	PD	TPI
1942	Bos-N	0	0	—	4	2	1	0	0	15^2	25	0	11	7	20.7	5.74	58	.368	.456	1	.167	-0	-4	-4	-0	0.0
1946	Bos-N	8	5	.615	24	16	8	0	1	125^2	107	6	36	67	10.3	2.94	117	.228	.285	7	.163	-1	7	7	-2	0.4
1947	Bos-N★	21	10	.677	40	35	22	**7**	3	**289^2**	245	15	84	123	**10.3**	**2.33**	**167**	.226	**.283**	16	.163	1	**56**	**50**	-2	5.1
1948	*Bos-N	15	12	.556	36	35	16	3	1	257	237	19	77	114	11.0	3.71	103	.242	.298	15	.167	2	7	3	0	0.5
1949	Bos-N★	**21**	14	.600	38	38	**25**	4	0	**302^1**	283	27	86	**151**	11.1	3.07	123	.245	.299	18	.162	-0	33	24	-2	2.3
1950	Bos-N☆	**21**	17	.553	41	39	25	1	1	293	248	22	111	**191**	11.1	3.16	122	.227	.299	23	.217	4	32	22	0	3.1
1951	Bos-N☆	22	14	.611	39	36	**26**	**7**	0	310^2	278	20	109	**164**	11.2	2.98	123	.238	.304	22	.190	5	34	24	-2	2.9
1952	Bos-N☆	14	19	.424	40	35	19	5	3	290	263	19	73	**183**	10.6	2.98	121	.240	.291	18	.161	2	24	20	1	2.7
1953	Mil-N★	**23**	7	.767	35	32	24	5	3	265^2	211	14	70	148	**9.6**	**2.10**	**187**	**.217**	**.270**	23	.219	5	**65**	54	2	**6.6**
1954	Mil-N★	21	12	.636	39	34	23	1	3	283^1	262	24	86	136	11.1	3.14	118	.245	.302	21	.208	6	29	18	1	2.7
1955	Mil-N	17	14	.548	39	32	16	1	1	245^2	249	25	65	110	11.6	3.26	115	.265	.314	17	.210	5	21	14	0	2.1
1956	Mil-N★	20	11	.645	39	35	20	3	3	281^1	249	25	52	128	9.7	2.78	124	.238	.276	22	.210	6	**31**	21	-1	2.9
1957	*Mil-N☆	**21**	11	.656	39	35	**18**	4	3	271	241	23	78	111	10.7	2.69	130	.237	.293	13	.138	1	**36**	24	0	3.0
1958	*Mil-N★	**22**	11	**.667**	38	36	**23**	2	1	**290**	257	29	76	150	**10.4**	3.07	115	.237	.288	36	.333	18	28	14	4	**3.9**
1959	Mil-N☆	**21**	15	.583	40	36	**21**	**4**	0	**292**	282	21	70	143	10.9	2.96	120	.253	.298	24	.231	7	32	19	-1	2.8
1960	Mil-N	**21**	10	.677	40	33	**18**	4	2	267^2	254	24	74	154	11.2	3.50	98	.250	.303	14	.147	3	8	-2	3	0.3
1961	Mil-N★	**21**	13	.618	38	34	**21**	**4**	0	262^2	236	24	64	115	**10.4**	**3.02**	124	.243	**.293**	21	.223	10	**30**	21	3	**3.9**
1962	Mil-N☆	18	14	.563	34	34	**22**	0	0	269^1	248	25	55	118	10.2	3.04	125	.246	.287	18	.184	4	27	23	1	3.1
1963	Mil-N☆	23	7	.767	33	33	**22**	7	0	259^2	241	23	49	102	10.1	2.60	124	.248	.284	16	.178	5	20	18	4	3.2
1964	Mil-N	6	13	.316	38	25	4	1	4	173^2	204	23	52	78	13.4	5.29	67	.297	.348	11	.186	2	-34	-34	-1	-3.5
1965	NY-N	4	12	.250	20	19	5	0	0	126	140	18	35	56	12.6	4.36	81	.281	.331	4	.114	1	-11	-12	0	-1.2
	SF-N	3	4	.429	16	11	3	0	0	71^2	70	8	21	34	11.6	3.39	106	.256	.312	3	.143	0	1	2	1	0.2
	Yr	7	16	.304	36	30	8	0	0	197^2	210	26	56	90	12.2	4.01	89	.271	.321	7	.125	2	-10	-10	1	-1.0
Total	21	363	245	.597	750	665	382	63	29	5243^2	4830	434	1434	2583	10.8	3.09	118	.244	.297	363	.194	88	470	330	9	47.0

● **AL SPALDING** Spalding, Albert Goodwill b: 9/2/1850, Byron, Ill. d: 9/9/15, San Diego, Cal. BR/TR, 6′1″, 170 lbs. Deb: 5/5/1871 MH♦

YEAR	TM/L	W	L	PCT	G	GS	CG	SH	SV	IP	H	HR	BB	SO	RAT	ERA	ERA+	OAV	OOB	BH	AVG	PB	PR	/A	PD	TPI
1871	Bos-n	**19**	10	.655	31	31	22	**1**	0	257^1	333	2	38	23	13.0	3.36	124	.268	.290	39	.271	2	25	23		1.6
1872	Bos-n	**38**	8	**.826**	48	48	41	**3**	0	404^2	417	0	27	27	9.9	1.87	195	.244	.255	84	.354	18	**80**	**80**		**7.8**
1873	Bos-n	**41**	14	**.745**	**60**	55	47	1	2	**497^2**	643	5	28	31	12.1	2.46	135	.283	.292	106	.329	21	**44**	**47**		**5.4**
1874	Bos-n	**52**	16	**.765**	**71**	69	**65**	**4**	0	**617^1**	755	1	19	31	11.3	1.92	112	.273	.278	119	.329	21	18	16		**2.9**
1875	Bos-n	**54**	5	**.915**	**72**	62	52	**7**	**9**	570^2	573	1	18	75	9.3	1.59	135	.245	.251	107	.312	22	**40**	35		**4.7**
1876	Chi-N	**47**	12	**.797**	61	60	53	8	0	528^2	542	6	26	39	9.7	1.75	139	.247	.256	91	.312	9	33	41	4	4.6

YEAR TM/L	W	L	PCT	G	GS	CG	SH	SV	IP	H	HR	BB	SO	RAT	ERA	ERA+	OAV	OOB	BH	AVG	PB	PR	/A	PD	TPI
1877 Chi-N	1	0	1.000	4	1	0	0	1	11	17	0	0	2	13.9	3.27	91	.321	.321	65	.256	0	-1	-0	1	0.0
Total 5 n	204	53	.794	282	265	227	16	11	2347^{2}	2721	9	130	187	10.9	2.10	136	.264	.273	455	.323	85	206	199		22.4
Total 2	48	12	.800	65	61	53	8	1	539^{2}	559	6	26	41	9.8	1.78	138	.249	.257	158	.287	9	32	40	5	4.6
● BILL SPANSWICK Spanswick, William Henry b: 7/8/38, Springfield, Mass. BL/TL, 6'3", 195 lbs. Deb: 4/18/64																									
1964 Bos-A	2	3	.400	29	7	0	0	0	65^{1}	75	9	44	55	16.8	6.89	56	.306	.418	4	.286	1	-24	-22	1	-1.3
● STEVE SPARKS Sparks, Steven William b: 7/2/65, Tulsa, Okla. BR/TR, 6', 180 lbs. Deb: 4/28/95																									
1995 Mil-A	9	11	.450	33	27	3	0	0	202	210	17	86	96	13.4	4.63	108	.274	.351	0	—	0	2	8	4	0.8
1996 Mil-A	4	7	.364	20	13	1	0	0	88^{2}	103	19	52	21	16.0	6.60	79	.297	.393	0	—	0	-16	-14	2	-1.4
1998 Ana-A	9	4	.692	22	20	0	0	0	128^{2}	130	14	58	90	13.5	4.34	108	.263	.346	0	.000	0	4	5	3	0.8
Total 3	22	22	.500	75	60	4	0	0	419^{1}	443	50	196	207	14.0	4.96	100	.275	.359	0	.000	0	-10	-1	9	0.2
● TULLY SPARKS Sparks, Thomas Frank b: 12/12/1874, Etna, Ga. d: 7/15/37, Anniston, Ala. BR/TR, Deb: 9/15/1897																									
1897 Phi-N	0	1	.000	1	1	1	0	0	8	12	0	4	0	18.0	10.13	41	.343	.410	0	.000	-1	-5	-5	0	-0.4
1899 Pit-N	8	6	.571	28	17	8	0	0	170	180	1	82	53	14.4	3.86	99	.271	.360	8	.129	-2	-0	-1	-1	-0.3
1901 Mil-A	7	17	.292	29	26	18	0	0	210	228	5	93	62	14.4	3.51	102	.273	.356	12	.169	-1	4	2	-0	0.1
1902 NY-N	4	10	.286	15	13	11	0	1	115	123	2	40	40	13.1	3.76	75	.273	.338	5	.135	-1	-12	-12	3	-1.2
Bos-A	7	9	.438	17	15	15	1	0	142^{2}	151	4	40	37	12.5	3.47	103	.272	.329	8	.154	-1	2	2	0	0.0
1903 Phi-N	11	15	.423	28	28	27	0	0	248	248	3	56	88	11.3	2.72	120	.263	.310	10	.109	-5	15	15	-2	0.7
1904 Phi-N	7	16	.304	26	25	19	3	0	200^{2}	208	1	43	67	11.5	2.65	101	.260	.302	8	.105	-5	2	1	-4	-0.8
1905 Phi-N	14	11	.560	34	26	20	3	1	259^{2}	217	2	73	98	10.4	2.18	134	.236	.298	12	.128	-2	24	21	-6	1.1
1906 Phi-N	19	16	.543	42	37	29	6	3	316^{2}	244	4	62	114	9.0	2.16	121	.211	.257	16	.154	0	17	16	-4	1.4
1907 Phi-N	22	8	.733	33	31	24	3	1	265	221	2	51	90	9.5	2.00	121	.228	.271	3	.034	-8	14	12	-5	-0.1
1908 Phi-N	16	15	.516	33	31	24	2	2	263^{1}	251	3	51	85	10.6	2.60	93	.257	.300	4	.052	-5	-7	-5	-2	-1.5
1909 Phi-N	6	11	.353	24	16	6	1	0	121^{2}	126	4	32	40	11.9	2.96	88	.280	.332	5	.139	-1	-5	-5	-1	-0.9
1910 Phi-N	0	2	.000	3	3	0	0	0	15	22	2	2	4	15.6	6.00	52	.324	.361	0	.000	-1	-5	-5	0	-0.6
Total 12	121	137	.469	313	269	202	19	8	2335^{2}	2231	33	629	778	11.4	2.79	105	.253	.309	91	.114	-33	42	37	-20	-2.5
● JOE SPARMA Sparma, Joseph Blase b: 2/4/42, Massillon, Ohio d: 5/14/86, Columbus, Ohio BR/TR, 6', 195 lbs. Deb: 5/20/64																									
1964 Det-A	5	6	.455	21	11	3	2	0	84	62	4	45	71	11.8	3.00	122	.207	.316	4	.160	1	6	6	1	1.0
1965 Det-A	13	8	.619	30	28	6	0	0	167	142	13	75	127	11.9	3.18	109	.228	.314	7	.135	-0	5	6	-1	0.6
1966 Det-A	2	7	.222	29	13	0	0	0	91^{2}	103	14	52	61	15.5	5.30	66	.288	.383	5	.217	1	-19	-19	-2	-1.8
1967 Det-A	16	9	.640	37	37	11	5	0	217^{2}	186	20	85	153	11.5	3.76	87	.227	.306	4	.054	-5	-13	-12	-2	-2.1
1968 *Det-A	10	10	.500	34	31	7	1	0	182^{1}	169	14	77	110	12.5	3.70	81	.246	.328	8	.133	-1	-15	-14	-2	-1.9
1969 Det-A	6	8	.429	23	16	3	2	0	92^{2}	78	5	77	41	15.2	4.76	78	.231	.375	4	.138	-1	-12	-11	-1	-1.6
1970 Mon-N	0	4	.000	9	6	1	0	0	29^{1}	34	7	25	23	18.7	7.06	58	.296	.430	0	.000	-0	-10	-10	-0	-1.2
Total 7	52	52	.500	183	142	31	10	0	864^{2}	774	77	436	586	12.9	3.94	86	.239	.334	32	.119	-6	-57	-53	-7	-7.0
● TRIS SPEAKER Speaker, Tristram E "The Grey Eagle" b: 4/4/1888, Hubbard, Tex. d: 12/8/58, Lake Whitney, Tex. BL/TL, 5'11.5", 193 lbs. Deb: 9/14/07 MH♦																									
1914 Bos-A	0	0	—	1	0	0	0	0	1	2	0	0	0	18.0	9.00	30	.500	.500	193	.338	1	-1	-1	0	0.0
● CLIFF SPECK Speck, Robert Clifford b: 8/8/56, Portland, Ore. BR/TR, 6'4", 195 lbs. Deb: 7/30/86																									
1986 Atl-N	2	1	.667	13	1	0	0	0	28^{1}	25	2	15	21	13.0	4.13	96	.238	.339	0	.000	-0	-1	-0	0	0.0
● BY SPEECE Speece, Byron Franklin b: 1/6/1897, West Baden, Ind. d: 9/29/74, Elgin, Ore. BR/TR, 5'11", 170 lbs. Deb: 4/21/24																									
1924 *Was-A	2	1	.667	21	1	0	0	0	54^{1}	60	0	27	15	14.7	2.65	152	.303	.392	3	.150	-1	**10**	**8**	1	0.4
1925 Cle-A	3	5	.375	28	3	3	0	1	90^{1}	106	0	28	26	13.6	4.28	103	.297	.353	5	.161	-2	1	1	0	0.0
1926 Cle-A	0	0	—	2	0	0	0	0	3	1	0	2	1	9.0	0.00	—	.125	.300	0	—	0	1	1	0	0.0
1930 Phi-N	0	0	—	11	0	0	0	0	19^{2}	41	1	4	9	20.6	13.27	41	.432	.455	1	.333	0	-18	-17	-0	0.0
Total 4	5	6	.455	62	4	3	0	1	167^{1}	208	1	61	51	14.7	4.73	93	.316	.378	9	.167	-2	-6	-6	2	0.4
● FLOYD SPEER Speer, Floyd Vernie b: 1/27/13, Booneville, Ark. d: 3/22/69, Little Rock, Ark. BR/TR, 6', 180 lbs. Deb: 4/25/43																									
1943 Chi-A	0	0	—	1	0	0	0	0	1	1	0	2	1	27.0	9.00	37	.250	.500	0	—	0	-1	-1	0	0.0
1944 Chi-A	0	0	—	2	0	0	0	0	2	4	0	0	1	18.0	9.00	38	.500	.500	0	—	0	-1	-1	0	0.0
Total 2	0	0	—	3	0	0	0	0	3	5	0	2	2	21.0	9.00	38	.417	.500	0	—	0	-2	-2	0	0.0
● KID SPEER Speer, George Nathan b: 6/16/1886, Corning, Mo. d: 1/13/46, Edmonton, Alberta, Canada BL/TL, 5'9", 152 lbs. Deb: 4/24/09																									
1909 Det-A	4	4	.500	12	8	4	0	1	76^{1}	88	2	13	12	12.4	2.83	89	.293	.331	3	.120	-0	-3	-3	1	-0.3
● JUSTIN SPEIER Speier, Justin James b: 11/6/73, Daly City, Cal. BR/TR, 6'4", 200 lbs. Deb: 5/27/98 F																									
1998 Chi-N	0	0	—	1	0	0	0	0	1^{1}	2	0	1	2	20.3	13.50	32	.333	.429	0	—	0	-1	-1	0	0.0
Fla-N	0	3	.000	18	0	0	0	0	19^{1}	25	7	12	15	17.2	8.38	49	.325	.416	0	—	0	-9	-9	-0	-1.2
Yr	0	3	.000	19	0	0	0	0	20^{2}	27	7	13	17	17.4	8.71	47	.325	.417	0	—	0	-10	-11	-0	-1.2
● HACK SPENCER Spencer, Fred Calvin b: 4/25/1885, St.Cloud, Minn. d: 2/5/69, St.Anthony, Minn. BR/TR, 5'10.5", 172 lbs. Deb: 4/18/12																									
1912 StL-A	0	0	—	1	0	0	0	0	1^{2}	2	0	0	0	10.8	0.00	—	.286	.286	0	—	0	1	1	0	0.0
● GEORGE SPENCER Spencer, George Elwell b: 7/7/26, Columbus, Ohio BR/TR, 6'1", 215 lbs. Deb: 8/17/50																									
1950 NY-N	1	0	1.000	10	1	1	0	0	25^{1}	12	3	7	5	6.8	2.49	165	.141	.207	0	.000	-1	5	5	0	0.1
1951 *NY-N	10	4	.714	57	4	2	0	6	132	125	21	56	36	12.4	3.75	104	.254	.332	4	.125	-1	3	2	1	0.3
1952 NY-N	3	5	.375	35	4	0	0	3	60	57	13	21	27	12.2	5.55	67	.251	.323	2	.200	0	-12	-12	-0	-1.6
1953 NY-N	0	0	—	1	0	0	0	0	2^{1}	3	0	2	1	19.3	7.71	56	.300	.417	0	—	0	-1	-1	-0	0.0
1954 NY-N	1	0	1.000	6	0	0	0	0	12^{1}	9	1	8	4	12.4	3.65	111	.209	.333	0	.000	-0	1	1	0	0.1
1955 NY-N	0	0	—	1	0	0	0	0	1^{2}	1	1	3	0	21.6	5.40	75	.167	.444	0	—	0	-0	-0	0	0.0
1958 Det-A	1	0	1.000	7	0	0	0	0	10	11	0	4	5	13.5	2.70	149	.289	.357	0	—	0	1	1	0	0.2
1960 Det-A	0	1	.000	5	0	0	0	0	7^{2}	10	1	5	4	17.6	3.52	112	.323	.417	0	.000	-0	0	0	-0	0.0
Total 8	16	10	.615	122	9	3	0	9	251^{1}	228	40	106	82	12.1	4.05	96	.245	.324	6	.120	-2	-3	-4	2	-0.9
● GLENN SPENCER Spencer, Glenn Edward b: 9/11/05, Corning, N.Y. d: 12/30/58, Binghamton, N.Y. BR/TR, 5'11", 155 lbs. Deb: 4/11/28																									
1928 Pit-N	0	0	—	4	0	0	0	0	5^{2}	4	0	3	2	11.1	1.59	256	.200	.304	0	.000	-0	2	2	-0	-0.1
1930 Pit-N	8	9	.471	41	10	5	0	4	156^{2}	185	16	63	60	14.4	5.40	92	.305	.372	6	.113	-4	-7	-7	-2	-1.2
1931 Pit-N	11	12	.478	38	18	11	1	3	186^{2}	180	8	65	51	12.1	3.42	112	.260	.328	5	.096	-3	9	9	-0	0.7
1932 Pit-N	4	8	.333	39	13	5	1	1	137^{2}	167	10	44	35	14.0	4.97	77	.288	.341	6	.162	-1	-17	-18	-1	-1.6
1933 NY-N	0	2	.000	17	3	1	0	0	47^{1}	52	3	26	14	15.0	5.13	63	.284	.376	2	.167	-0	-9	-10	0	-0.4
Total 5	23	31	.426	139	44	22	2	8	534	588	37	201	162	13.5	4.53	91	.282	.349	19	.123	-9	-23	-25	-3	-2.6
● STAN SPENCER Spencer, Stanley Roger b: 8/2/68, Vancouver, Wash. BR/TR, 6'4", 205 lbs. Deb: 8/27/98																									
1998 SD-N	1	0	1.000	6	5	0	0	0	30^{2}	29	5	4	31	10.0	4.70	81	.244	.274	1	.111	-0	-2	-3	-1	-0.1
● BOB SPICER Spicer, Robert Oberton b: 4/11/25, Richmond, Va. BL/TR, 5'10", 173 lbs. Deb: 4/17/55																									
1955 KC-A	0	0	—	2	0	0	0	0	2^{2}	9	2	4	2	47.3	33.75	12	.529	.636	0	.000	-0	-9	-9	-0	0.0
1956 KC-A	0	0	—	2	0	0	0	0	2^{1}	6	1	1	0	30.9	19.29	22	.545	.615	0	—	0	-4	-4	0	0.0
Total 2	0	0	—	4	0	0	0	0	5	15	3	5	2	39.6	27.00	16	.536	.629	0	.000	-0	-13	-13	0	0.0
● DAN SPILLNER Spillner, Daniel Ray b: 11/27/51, Casper, Wyo. BR/TR, 6'1", 190 lbs. Deb: 5/21/74																									
1974 SD-N	9	11	.450	30	25	5	2	0	148	153	15	70	95	13.6	4.01	89	.267	.346	1	.023	-4	-7	-8	-1	-1.5
1975 SD-N	5	13	.278	37	25	3	0	1	166^{2}	194	14	63	104	14.0	4.27	81	.293	.356	6	.133	1	-12	-15	-0	-1.4
1976 SD-N	2	11	.154	32	14	0	0	0	106^{2}	120	11	55	57	14.8	5.06	65	.291	.374	1	.040	-1	-19	-21	1	-2.4
1977 SD-N	7	6	.538	76	0	0	0	6	123	130	12	60	74	14.0	3.73	95	.280	.363	2	.118	1	2	-3	-2	-0.4
1978 SD-N	1	0	1.000	17	0	0	0	0	25^{2}	32	2	7	16	13.7	4.56	73	.317	.361	0	—	0	-3	-4	-0	-0.1
Cle-A	3	1	.750	36	0	0	0	3	56^{1}	54	2	21	48	12.1	3.67	102	.254	.323	0	—	0	1	0	-1	-0.1
1979 Cle-A	9	5	.643	49	13	3	0	1	157^{2}	153	16	64	97	12.6	4.62	92	.256	.331	0	—	0	-7	-6	-1	-0.6

YEAR	TM/L	W	L	PCT	G	GS	CG	SH	SV	IP	H	HR	BB	SO	RAT	ERA	ERA+	OAV	OOB	BH	AVG	PB	PR	/A	PD	TPI
1980	Cle-A	16	11	.593	34	30	7	1	0	194^1	225	23	74	100	14.0	5.28	77	.288	.352	0	—	0	-27	-26	-2	-3.3
1981	Cle-A	4	4	.500	32	5	1	0	7	97^1	86	3	39	59	11.6	3.14	115	.240	.314	0	—	0	6	5	0	0.5
1982	Cle-A	12	10	.545	65	0	0	0	21	133^2	117	9	45	90	10.9	2.49	164	.235	.299	0	—	0	**24**	**24**	-3	4.2
1983	Cle-A	2	9	.182	60	0	0	0	8	92^1	117	7	38	48	15.3	5.07	84	.315	.382	0	—	0	-10	-9	-1	-1.2
1984	Cle-A	0	5	.000	14	8	0	0	1	51	70	3	22	23	16.2	5.65	72	.332	.395	0	—	0	-9	-9	1	-0.7
	Chi-A	1	0	1.000	22	0	0	0	1	48^1	51	7	14	26	12.3	4.10	101	.276	.330	0	—	0	-1	0	-0	0.0
	Yr	1	5	.167	36	8	0	0	2	99^1	121	10	36	49	14.3	4.89	84	.301	.360	0	—	0	-10	-9	1	-0.7
1985	Chi-A	4	3	.571	52	3	0	0	1	91^2	83	10	33	41	11.4	3.44	126	.245	.312	0	—	0	7	9	-3	0.4
Total	12	75	89	.457	556	123	19	3	50	1492^2	1585	134	605	878	13.3	4.21	91	.275	.345	10	.077	-3	-55	-62	-12	-6.6

● SCIPIO SPINKS Spinks, Scipio Ronald b: 7/12/47, Chicago, Ill. BR/TR, 6'1", 185 lbs. Deb: 9/16/69

1969	Hou-N	0	0	—	1	0	0	0	0	2	1	0	1	4	9.0	0.00	—	.143	.250	0	—	0	1	1	0	0.0
1970	Hou-N	0	1	.000	5	2	0	0	0	13^2	17	5	9	6	17.1	9.88	39	.293	.388	0	.000	-0	-9	-9	-1	-0.6
1971	Hou-N	1	0	1.000	5	3	1	0	0	29^1	22	2	13	26	11.0	3.68	91	.210	.303	2	.222	0	-1	-1	0	0.0
1972	StL-N	5	5	.500	16	16	6	0	0	118	96	5	59	93	12.0	2.67	127	.221	.317	7	.167	-1	10	10	1	0.8
1973	StL-N	1	5	.167	8	8	0	0	0	38^2	39	4	25	25	14.9	4.89	75	.269	.376	2	.182	1	-5	-5	1	-0.6
Total	5	7	11	.389	35	29	7	0	0	201^2	175	16	107	154	12.7	3.70	94	.234	.332	11	.169	0	-4	-5	1	-0.4

● PAUL SPLITTORFF Splittorff, Paul William b: 10/8/46, Evansville, Ind. BL/TL, 6'3", 210 lbs. Deb: 9/23/70

1970	KC-A	0	1	.000	2	1	0	0	0	8^2	16	1	5	10	21.8	7.27	51	.390	.457	1	.500	0	-3	-3	0	-0.3
1971	KC-A	8	9	.471	22	22	6	3	0	144^1	129	4	35	80	10.5	2.68	128	.243	.295	5	.104	-1	13	12	2	1.5
1972	KC-A	12	12	.500	35	33	12	2	0	216	189	11	67	140	10.8	3.13	97	.241	.304	16	.225	4	-2	-2	4	0.6
1973	KC-A	20	11	.645	38	38	12	3	0	262	279	19	78	110	12.4	3.98	103	.272	.327	0	—	0	-5	4	1	0.0
1974	KC-A	13	19	.406	36	36	8	1	0	226	252	23	75	90	13.1	4.10	93	.285	.342	0	—	0	-12	-7	0	-1.3
1975	KC-A	9	10	.474	35	23	6	3	1	159	156	10	56	76	12.1	3.17	121	.255	.319	0	—	0	11	12	2	1.5
1976	*KC-A	11	8	.579	26	23	5	1	0	158^2	169	11	59	59	13.1	3.97	88	.277	.343	0	—	0	-8	-8	1	-0.8
1977	*KC-A	16	6	**.727**	37	37	6	2	0	229	243	11	83	99	12.9	3.69	109	.278	.342	0	—	0	9	9	-0	0.7
1978	*KC-A	19	13	.594	39	38	13	2	0	262	244	22	60	76	10.5	3.40	112	.247	.293	0	—	0	11	12	1	1.5
1979	KC-A	15	17	.469	36	35	11	0	0	240	248	25	77	77	12.4	4.24	101	.268	.328	0	—	0	-1	1	-2	-0.2
1980	*KC-A	14	11	.560	34	33	4	0	0	204	236	17	43	53	12.4	4.15	98	.296	.333	0	—	0	-3	-2	-0	-0.3
1981	KC-A	5	5	.500	21	15	1	0	0	99	111	12	23	48	12.3	4.36	83	.294	.337	0	—	0	-8	-8	1	-0.7
1982	KC-A	10	10	.500	29	28	0	0	0	162	166	14	57	74	12.6	4.28	95	.266	.330	0	—	0	-4	-4	0	-0.4
1983	KC-A	13	8	.619	27	27	4	0	0	156	159	9	52	61	12.2	3.63	112	.262	.322	0	—	0	7	8	0	0.9
1984	KC-A	1	3	.250	12	3	0	0	0	28	47	3	10	4	18.3	7.71	52	.376	.422	0	—	0	-12	-11	1	-1.3
Total	15	166	143	.537	429	392	88	17	1	2554^2	2644	192	780	1057	12.2	3.81	101	.270	.326	22	.182	3	-6	10	10	1.4

● PAUL SPOLJARIC Spoljaric, Paul Nikola b: 9/24/70, Kelowna, B.C., Canada BR/TL, 6'3", 205 lbs. Deb: 4/6/94

1994	Tor-A	0	1	.000	2	1	0	0	0	2^1	5	3	9	2	54.0	38.57	12	.417	.667	0	—	0	-9	-9	-0	-1.9
1996	Tor-A	2	2	.500	28	0	0	0	1	38	30	6	19	38	12.1	3.08	162	.214	.317	0	—	0	8	8	0	0.8
1997	Tor-A	0	3	.000	37	0	0	0	3	48	37	3	21	43	11.3	3.19	144	.215	.308	0	.000	-0	7	7	1	0.6
	*Sea-A	0	0	—	20	0	0	0	0	22^2	24	1	15	27	15.9	4.76	94	.276	.388	0	—	0	-1	-1	-0	0.0
	Yr	0	3	.000	57	0	0	0	3	70^2	61	4	36	70	12.5	3.69	123	.232	.327	0	.000	-0	7	7	1	0.6
1998	Sea-A	4	6	.400	53	6	0	0	0	83^1	85	14	55	89	15.2	6.48	71	.263	.372	0	—	0	-17	-17	-0	-1.7
Total	4	6	12	.333	140	7	0	0	4	194^1	181	27	119	199	14.2	5.19	90	.247	.356	0	.000	-0	-11	-11	1	-2.2

● CARL SPONGBERG Spongberg, Carl Gustav b: 5/21/1884, Idaho Falls, Idaho d: 7/21/38, Los Angeles, Cal. BR/TR, 6'2", 208 lbs. Deb: 8/1/08

1908	Chi-N	0	0	—	1	0	0	0	0	7	9	1	6	4	21.9	9.00	26	.321	.472	2	.667	1	-5	-5	0	0.1

● KARL SPOONER Spooner, Karl Benjamin b: 6/23/31, Oriskany Falls, N.Y. d: 4/10/84, Vero Beach, Fla. BR/TL, 6', 185 lbs. Deb: 9/22/54

1954	Bro-N	2	0	1.000	2	2	2	2	0	18	7	0	6	27	6.5	0.00	—	.113	.191	1	.167	0	8	8	-0	1.1
1955	*Bro-N	8	6	.571	29	14	2	1	2	98^2	79	8	41	78	11.4	3.65	111	.215	.302	8	.286	3	4	5	-0	0.8
Total	2	10	6	.625	31	16	4	3	2	116^2	86	8	47	105	10.6	3.09	132	.200	.286	9	.265	3	12	13	-1	1.9

● JERRY SPRADLIN Spradlin, Jerry Carl b: 6/14/67, Fullerton, Cal. BB/TR, 6'7", 230 lbs. Deb: 7/2/93

1993	Cin-N	2	1	.667	37	0	0	0	2	49	44	4	9	24	9.7	3.49	115	.249	.285	0	.000	-0	3	3	-1	0.0
1994	Cin-N	0	0	—	6	0	0	0	0	8	12	2	2	4	15.8	10.13	41	.353	.389	0	—	0	-5	-5	0	0.0
1996	Cin-N	0	0	—	1	0	0	0	0	0^1	0	0	0	0	0.0	0.00	—	.000	.000	0	—	0	0	0	0	0.0
1997	Phi-N	4	8	.333	76	0	0	0	1	81^2	86	9	27	67	12.6	4.74	90	.274	.333	0	.000	-0	-5	-5	-1	-0.7
1998	Phi-N	4	4	.500	69	0	0	0	1	81^2	63	9	20	76	9.4	3.53	124	.216	.272	1	1.000	1	6	8	-0	0.7
Total	5	10	13	.435	189	0	0	0	4	220^2	205	24	58	171	10.8	4.20	101	.251	.303	1	.250	0	-1	1	-3	0.0

● HOMER SPRAGINS Spragins, Homer Franklin b: 11/9/20, Grenada, Miss. BR/TR, 6'1", 190 lbs. Deb: 9/13/47

1947	Phi-N	0	0	—	4	0	0	0	0	5^1	3	0	3	3	10.1	6.75	59	.158	.273	0	—	0	-2	-2	0	0.0

● CHARLIE SPRAGUE Sprague, Charles Wellington b: 10/10/1864, Cleveland, Ohio d: 12/31/12, Des Moines, Iowa BL/TL, 5'11", 150 lbs. Deb: 9/17/1887 ♦

1887	Chi-N	1	0	1.000	3	3	2	0	0	22	24	1	13	9	16.8	4.91	91	.276	.394	2	.154	-1	-2	-1	-1	-0.2
1889	Cle-N	0	2	.000	2	2	2	0	0	17	27	0	10	8	20.6	8.47	48	.351	.438	1	.143	-0	-8	-8	-0	-0.6
1890	Tol-a	9	5	.643	19	12	9	0	0	122^2	111	0	78	59	15.2	3.89	102	.234	.363	47	.236	3	-0	1	-2	0.1
Total	3	10	7	.588	24	17	13	0	0	161^2	162	1	101	76	16.0	4.51	89	.254	.376	50	.228	1	-11	-9	-2	-0.7

● ED SPRAGUE Sprague, Edward Nelson Sr. b: 9/16/45, Boston, Mass. BR/TR, 6'4", 195 lbs. Deb: 4/10/68 F

1968	Oak-A	3	4	.429	47	1	0	0	4	68^2	51	5	34	34	11.4	3.28	86	.209	.311	0	.000	-1	-2	-3	1	-0.4
1969	Oak-A	1	1	.500	27	0	0	0	2	46^1	47	4	31	20	15.5	4.47	77	.267	.383	1	.200	0	-4	-5	2	0.0
1971	Cin-N	1	0	1.000	7	0	0	0	0	11	8	0	1	7	7.4	0.00	—	.195	.214	0	.000	-0	4	4	-1	0.3
1972	Cin-N	3	3	.500	33	1	0	0	0	56^2	55	6	26	25	13.3	4.13	78	.261	.350	0	.000	-1	-4	-6	-1	-0.7
1973	Cin-N	1	3	.250	28	0	0	0	1	38^2	35	3	22	19	13.7	5.12	66	.246	.355	0	.000	-0	-6	-7	0	-0.7
	StL-N	0	0	—	8	0	0	0	0	8	8	1	4	2	13.5	2.25	162	.276	.364	0	—	0	1	1	0	0.0
	Yr	1	3	.250	36	0	0	0	1	46^2	43	4	26	21	13.3	4.63	74	.247	.345	0	.000	-0	-5	-6	1	-0.7
	Mil-A	0	1	.000	7	0	0	0	1	9^2	13	0	14	3	27.0	9.31	40	.317	.509	0	—	0	-6	-6	-0	-0.6
1974	Mil-A	7	2	.778	20	10	3	0	0	94	94	3	31	57	12.4	2.39	151	.266	.332	0	—	0	13	13	-1	1.2
1975	Mil-A	1	7	.125	18	11	0	0	1	67^1	81	5	40	21	16.4	4.68	82	.297	.390	0	—	0	-7	-6	-1	-0.8
1976	Mil-A	0	2	.000	3	0	0	0	0	7^2	14	0	3	0	20.0	7.04	50	.438	.486	0	—	0	-3	-3	1	-0.6
Total	8	17	23	.425	198	23	3	0	9	408	406	27	206	188	13.9	3.84	89	.263	.356	1	.045	-1	-15	-19	2	-2.3

● JACK SPRING Spring, Jack Russell b: 3/11/33, Spokane, Wash. BR/TL, 6'1", 180 lbs. Deb: 4/16/55

1955	Phi-N	0	1	.000	2	0	0	0	0	2^2	2	2	1	2	10.1	6.75	59	.200	.273	0	.000	-0	-1	-1	-0	-0.3
1957	Bos-A	0	0	—	1	0	0	0	0	1	0	0	0	2	0.0	0.00	—	.000	.000	0	—	0	0	0	0	0.0
1958	Was-A	0	0	—	3	1	0	0	0	7	16	1	7	1	29.6	14.14	27	.457	.548	0	.000	-0	-8	-8	0	0.0
1961	LA-A	3	0	1.000	18	4	0	0	0	38	35	4	15	27	12.6	4.26	106	.243	.327	0	.000	-1	-1	1	-0	0.0
1962	LA-A	4	2	.667	57	0	0	0	6	65	66	7	30	31	13.6	4.02	96	.270	.355	1	.091	-1	-0	-1	1	-0.1
1963	LA-A	3	0	1.000	45	0	0	0	2	38^1	40	3	9	13	11.5	3.05	112	.268	.310	1	.333	0	2	2	1	0.2
1964	LA-A	1	0	1.000	6	0	0	0	0	3^1	3	1	3	0	16.2	2.70	122	.273	.429	0	—	0	0	0	-0	0.0
	Chi-N	0	0	—	7	0	0	0	0	6	4	0	2	1	9.0	6.00	62	.200	.273	0	—	0	-2	-2	0	0.0
	StL-N	0	0	—	2	0	0	0	0	3	8	1	1	0	27.0	3.00	127	.471	.500	0	—	0	0	0	0	0.0
	Yr	0	0	—	9	0	0	0	0	9	12	1	3	1	15.0	5.00	75	.316	.366	0	—	0	-1	-1	0	0.0
1965	Cle-A	1	2	.333	14	0	0	0	0	21^2	21	2	10	9	12.9	3.74	93	.259	.341	1	.333	0	-1	-1	-1	-0.1
Total	8	12	5	.706	155	5	0	0	8	186	195	21	78	86	13.5	4.26	90	.273	.349	3	.107	-1	-9	-9	1	-0.3

● BRAD SPRINGER Springer, Bradford Louis b: 5/9/04, Detroit, Mich. d: 1/4/70, Birmingham, Mich. BL/TL, 6', 155 lbs. Deb: 5/1/25

1925	StL-A	0	0	—	2	0	0	0	0	3	1	0	7	0	24.0	3.00	156	.200	.667	0	—	0	0	1	0	0.0
1926	Cin-N	0	0	—	1	0	0	0	0	1^1	2	0	2	1	33.8	6.75	55	.286	.500	0	.000	-0	-0	-0	0	0.0
Total	2	0	0	—	3	0	0	0	0	4^1	3	0	9	1	27.0	4.15	105	.250	.591	0	.000	-0	0	0	0	0.0

YEAR	TM/L	W	L	PCT	G	GS	CG	SH	SV	IP	H	HR	BB	SO	RAT	ERA	ERA+	OAV	OOB	BH	AVG	PB	PR	/A	PD	TPI
● DENNIS SPRINGER	Springer, Dennis Leroy b: 2/12/65, Fresno, Cal. BR/TR, 5'10", 185 lbs. Deb: 9/14/95																									
1995	Phi-N	0	3	.000	4	4	0	0	0	22^1	21	3	9	15	12.5	4.84	87	.256	.337	1	.125	-0	-2	-2	-1	-0.3
1996	Cal-A	5	6	.455	20	15	2	1	0	94^2	91	24	43	64	13.3	5.51	91	.251	.340	0	—	0	-5	-5	-1	-0.6
1997	Ana-A	9	9	.500	32	28	3	1	0	194^2	199	32	73	75	13.0	5.18	88	.267	.340	0	.000	-0	-13	-13	-1	-1.1
1998	TB-A	3	11	.214	29	17	1	0	0	115^2	120	21	60	46	14.9	5.45	90	.271	.374	0	.000	-0	-10	-7	-1	-0.8
Total	4	17	29	.370	85	64	6	2	0	427^1	431	80	185	200	13.6	5.31	89	.264	.349	1	.083	-1	-31	-27	-4	-2.8
● ED SPRINGER	Springer, Edward H. b: 2/9/1861, California d: 4/24/26, Los Angeles Co., Cal. 6'2", 187 lbs. Deb: 7/12/1889																									
1889	Lou-a	0	1	.000	1	1	1	0	0	5	8	0	2	1	21.6	9.00	43	.348	.444	0	.000	-0	-3	-3	-0	-0.4
● RUSS SPRINGER	Springer, Russell Paul b: 11/7/68, Alexandria, La. BR/TR, 6'4", 195 lbs. Deb: 4/17/92																									
1992	NY-A	0	0	—	14	0	0	0	0	16	18	0	10	12	16.3	6.19	63	.281	.387	0	—	0	-4	-4	-0	0.0
1993	Cal-A	1	6	.143	14	9	1	0	0	60	73	11	32	31	16.2	7.20	63	.303	.391	0	—	0	-19	-18	-1	-2.0
1994	Cal-A	2	2	.500	18	5	0	0	2	45^2	53	9	14	28	13.2	5.52	89	.291	.342	0	—	0	-4	-3	-1	-0.4
1995	Cal-A	1	2	.333	19	6	0	0	1	51^2	60	11	25	38	15.7	6.10	77	.290	.380	0	—	0	-8	-8	-0	-0.4
	Phi-N	0	0	—	14	0	0	0	0	26^2	22	5	10	32	11.5	3.71	114	.227	.312	0	.000	-0	1	2	1	0.0
1996	Phi-N	3	10	.231	51	7	0	0	0	96^2	106	12	38	94	13.5	4.66	93	.272	.338	1	.059	-1	-5	-4	-1	-0.7
1997	*Hou-N	3	3	.500	54	0	0	0	3	55^1	48	4	27	74	12.8	4.23	94	.232	.332	0	.000	-0	-0	-1	0	-0.2
1998	Ari-N	4	3	.571	26	0	0	0	0	32^2	29	4	14	37	12.1	4.13	104	.232	.314	0	.000	-0	0	1	-1	0.0
	Atl-N	1	1	.500	22	0	0	0	0	20	22	0	16	19	17.1	4.05	104	.301	.427	0	—	0	0	0	-0	0.0
	Yr	5	4	.556	48	0	0	0	0	52^2	51	4	30	56	13.8	4.10	104	.256	.354	0	.000	-0	1	1	-1	0.0
Total	7	15	27	.357	232	27	1	0	6	404^2	431	56	186	365	14.1	5.18	85	.272	.354	1	.050	-2	-38	-36	-4	-3.7
● CHARLIE SPROULL	Sproull, Charles William b: 1/9/19, Taylorsville, Ga. d: 1/13/80, Rockford, Ill. BR/TR, 6'3", 185 lbs. Deb: 4/19/45																									
1945	Phi-N	4	10	.286	34	19	2	0	1	130^1	158	10	80	47	16.4	5.94	65	.298	.390	5	.143	-1	-31	-31	-1	-3.1
● BOB SPROUT	Sprout, Robert Samuel b: 12/5/41, Florin, Pa. BL/TL, 6', 165 lbs. Deb: 9/27/61																									
1961	LA-A	0	0	—	1	1	0	0	0	4	4	0	3	2	15.8	4.50	100	.267	.389	0	—	0	-0	0	-0	0.0
● BOBBY SPROWL	Sprowl, Robert John b: 4/14/56, Sandusky, Ohio BL/TL, 6'2", 190 lbs. Deb: 9/5/78																									
1978	Bos-A	0	2	.000	3	3	0	0	0	12^2	12	3	10	10	15.6	6.39	64	.245	.373	0	—	0	-4	-3	-0	-0.5
1979	Hou-N	0	0	—	3	0	0	0	0	4	1	0	2	3	6.8	0.00	—	.083	.214	0	—	0	2	2	-0	0.0
1980	Hou-N	0	0	—	1	0	0	0	0	1	1	0	1	3	18.0	0.00	—	.250	.400	0	—	0	0	0	0	0.0
1981	Hou-N	0	1	.000	15	1	0	0	0	28^2	40	1	14	18	17.0	5.97	55	.333	.403	1	.167	-0	-8	-9	-0	-0.3
Total	4	0	3	.000	22	4	0	0	0	46^1	54	4	27	34	15.7	5.44	65	.292	.382	1	.167	-0	-10	-10	-1	-0.8
● MIKE SQUIRES	Squires, Michael Lynn b: 3/5/52, Kalamazoo, Mich. BL/TL, 5'11", 185 lbs. Deb: 9/1/75 C♦																									
1984	Chi-A	0	0	—	1	0	0	0	0	0^1	0	0	0	0	0.0	0.00	—	.000	.000	15	.183	0	0	0	0	0.0
● GEORGE STABLEIN	Stablein, George Charles b: 10/29/57, Inglewood, Cal. BR/TR, 6'4", 185 lbs. Deb: 9/20/80																									
1980	SD-N	0	1	.000	4	2	0	0	0	11^2	16	0	3	4	14.7	3.09	111	.340	.380	0	.000	-0	1	0	-0	0.0
● EDDIE STACK	Stack, William Edward b: 10/24/1887, Chicago, Ill. d: 8/28/58, Chicago, Ill. BR/TR, 6', 175 lbs. Deb: 6/7/10																									
1910	Phi-N	6	7	.462	20	16	8	1	0	117	115	7	34	48	11.8	4.00	78	.266	.326	3	.083	-3	-13	-11	-1	-1.6
1911	Phi-N	5	5	.500	13	10	5	0	0	77^2	67	3	41	36	13.2	3.59	96	.234	.342	2	.083	-2	-2	-1	0	-0.3
1912	Bro-N	7	5	.583	28	17	4	0	1	142	139	3	55	45	12.9	3.36	100	.264	.343	7	.135	-3	1	-0	-1	-0.4
1913	Bro-N	4	4	.500	23	9	4	1	0	87	79	0	32	34	11.6	2.38	138	.250	.321	4	.160	-1	8	9	-2	0.4
	Chi-N	4	2	.667	11	7	3	1	1	51	56	1	15	28	12.9	4.24	75	.280	.336	1	.063	-1	-6	-6	-1	-0.9
	Yr	8	6	.571	34	16	7	2	1	138	135	1	47	62	12.0	3.07	106	.261	.325	5	.122	-2	2	3	-3	-0.5
1914	Chi-N	0	1	.000	7	1	0	0	0	16^1	13	0	11	9	13.2	4.96	56	.220	.343	0	.000	-0	-4	-4	0	-0.2
Total	5	26	24	.520	102	60	24	3	2	491	469	14	188	200	12.4	3.52	93	.258	.334	17	.108	-10	-15	-14	-4	-3.0
● GENERAL STAFFORD	Stafford, James Joseph "Jamsey" b: 7/9/1868, Webster, Mass. d: 9/18/23, Worcester, Mass. BR/TR, 5'8", 165 lbs. Deb: 8/27/1890 F♦																									
1890	Buf-P	3	9	.250	12	12	11	0	0	98	123	8	43	21	15.6	5.14	80	.294	.366	7	.143	-2	-10	-11	-1	-1.1
● JOHN STAFFORD	Stafford, John Henry "Doc" b: 4/8/1870, Dudley, Mass. d: 7/3/40, Worcester, Mass. BR/TR, 5'10", 170 lbs. Deb: 6/15/1893 F																									
1893	Cle-N	0	1	.000	2	0	0	0	0	7	12	1	7	4	24.4	14.14	35	.364	.475	0	.000	-1	-7	-7	-0	-0.7
● BILL STAFFORD	Stafford, William Charles b: 8/13/39, Catskill, N.Y. BR/TR, 6'2", 193 lbs. Deb: 4/17/60																									
1960	*NY-A	3	1	.750	11	8	2	1	0	60	50	3	18	36	10.4	2.25	159	.226	.287	1	.045	-2	11	9	1	0.4
1961	*NY-A	14	9	.609	36	25	8	3	2	195	168	13	59	101	10.7	2.68	139	.232	.294	12	.179	2	29	23	-1	2.6
1962	*NY-A	14	9	.609	35	33	7	2	0	213^1	188	23	77	109	11.3	3.67	102	.233	.303	17	.218	3	7	2	-1	0.3
1963	NY-A	4	8	.333	28	14	0	0	3	89^2	104	16	42	52	15.0	6.02	58	.287	.366	7	.292	3	-24	-25	-0	-3.0
1964	NY-A	5	0	1.000	31	1	0	0	4	60^2	50	4	22	39	11.0	2.67	136	.231	.308	1	.077	-1	6	6	0	0.5
1965	NY-A	3	8	.273	22	15	1	0	0	111^1	93	16	31	71	10.2	3.56	96	.229	.286	0	.000	-3	-1	-2	-0	-0.5
1966	KC-A	0	4	.000	9	8	0	0	0	39^2	42	2	12	31	12.7	4.99	68	.273	.333	0	.000	-1	-7	-7	-1	-0.8
1967	KC-A	0	1	.000	14	0	0	0	0	16	12	0	9	10	11.8	1.69	189	.214	.323	0	.000	-0	3	3	0	0.2
Total	8	43	40	.518	186	104	18	6	9	785^2	707	77	270	449	11.4	3.52	103	.240	.308	38	.155	0	24	9	-2	-0.3
● CHICK STAHL	Stahl, Charles Sylvester b: 1/10/1873, Avilla, Ind. d: 3/28/07, W.Baden, Ind. BL/TL, 5'10", 160 lbs. Deb: 4/19/1897 M♦																									
1899	Bos-N	0	0	—	1	0	0	0	0	2	2	0	3	0	22.5	9.00	46	.250	.455	202	.351	0	-1	-1	0	0.0
● GERRY STALEY	Staley, Gerald Lee b: 8/21/20, Brush Prairie, Wash. BR/TR, 6', 195 lbs. Deb: 4/20/47																									
1947	StL-N	1	0	1.000	18	1	1	0	0	29^1	33	2	8	14	12.9	2.76	150	.287	.339	0	.000	-1	4	4	1	0.1
1948	StL-N	4	4	.500	31	3	0	0	0	52	61	5	21	23	14.2	6.92	59	.288	.352	2	.222	1	-17	-16	1	-2.0
1949	StL-N	10	10	.500	45	17	5	2	6	171^1	154	7	41	55	10.4	2.73	152	**.238**	.286	5	.122	-0	25	27	3	3.5
1950	StL-N	13	13	.500	42	22	7	1	3	169^2	201	14	61	62	14.3	4.99	86	.300	.365	8	.145	-1	-16	-13	3	-1.6
1951	StL-N	19	13	.594	42	30	10	4	3	227	244	14	74	67	12.9	3.81	104	.275	.337	13	.160	-1	4	4	2	0.6
1952	StL-N☆	17	14	.548	35	33	15	0	0	239^2	238	21	52	93	11.2	3.27	114	.256	.301	13	.153	-2	12	12	4	1.6
1953	StL-N☆	18	9	.667	40	32	10	1	4	230	243	31	54	88	12.3	3.99	107	.269	.322	8	.103	-5	8	7	2	0.5
1954	StL-N	7	13	.350	48	20	3	1	2	155^2	198	21	47	50	14.5	5.26	78	.308	.361	5	.139	-0	-21	-20	2	-2.1
1955	Cin-N	5	8	.385	30	18	2	0	0	119^2	146	22	28	40	13.3	4.66	91	.309	.351	2	.056	-4	-8	-6	1	-0.8
	NY-A	0	0	—	2	0	0	0	0	2	5	1	1	0	27.0	13.50	28	.417	.462	0	—	0	-2	-2	0	0.0
1956	NY-A	0	0	—	1	0	0	0	0	0^1	4	0	0	1	108.0	108.00	4	.800	.800	0	.000	-0	-4	-4	0	0.0
	Chi-A	8	3	.727	26	10	5	0	0	101^2	98	11	20	25	11.0	2.92	140	.251	.298	3	.094	-2	14	13	1	1.1
	Yr	8	3	.727	27	10	5	0	0	102	102	11	20	26	11.3	3.26	126	.258	.304	3	.091	-3	10	9	1	1.1
1957	Chi-A	5	1	.833	47	0	0	0	7	105	95	7	27	44	10.5	2.06	182	.244	.293	1	.045	-1	**20**	**20**	2	1.4
1958	Chi-A	4	5	.444	50	0	0	0	8	85^1	81	10	24	27	11.1	3.16	115	.259	.312	0	.000	-1	6	4	3	0.7
1959	*Chi-A	8	5	.615	**67**	0	0	0	14	116^1	111	5	25	54	10.5	2.24	167	.259	.300	2	.154	0	**21**	**20**	-0	2.6
1960	Chi-A★	13	8	.619	64	0	0	0	10	115^1	94	8	25	52	9.5	2.42	156	.227	.276	4	.235	1	**19**	**17**	3	**3.7**
1961	Chi-A	0	3	.000	16	0	0	0	0	18	17	3	5	8	11.0	5.00	78	.246	.297	0	—	0	-2	-2	0	-0.3
	KC-A	1	1	.500	23	0	0	0	2	30	32	4	10	16	13.2	3.60	116	.278	.346	0	.000	0	1	2	1	0.2
	Det-A	1	1	.500	13	0	0	0	2	13^1	15	1	6	8	14.2	3.38	121	.288	.362	0	.000	-0	1	1	0	0.2
	Yr	2	5	.286	52	0	0	0	4	61^1	64	8	21	32	12.5	3.96	103	.267	.326	0	.000	0	0	1	1	0.1
Total	15	134	111	.547	640	186	58	9	61	1981^2	2070	187	529	727	12.1	3.70	108	.270	.322	66	.126	-16	65	68	29	9.4
● HARRY STALEY	Staley, Henry Eli b: 11/3/1866, Jacksonville, Ill. d: 1/12/10, Battle Creek, Mich BR/TR, 5'10", 175 lbs. Deb: 6/23/1888																									
1888	Pit-N	12	12	.500	25	24	24	2	0	207^1	185	6	53	89	10.6	2.69	99	.235	.289	11	.129	-4	4	-1	-1	-0.5
1889	Pit-N	21	26	.447	49	47	46	1	1	420	433	11	116	159	11.9	3.51	107	.258	.309	30	.161	-7	23	11	2	0.6
1890	Pit-P	21	25	.457	46	46	44	3	0	387^2	392	5	74	145	**11.1**	3.23	121	.251	**.290**	34	.207	1	43	29	-2	2.5
1891	Pit-N	4	5	.444	9	7	6	0	0	71^2	77	4	11	25	11.3	2.89	114	.265	.296	7	.226	1	4	3	-0	0.4
	Bos-N	20	8	.714	31	30	26	1	0	252^1	236	11	69	114	11.0	2.50	146	.238	.290	17	.167	-2	24	33	-1	2.7

YEAR	TM/L	W	L	PCT	G	GS	CG	SH	SV	IP	H	HR	BB	SO	RAT	ERA	ERA+	OAV	OOB	BH	AVG	PB	PR	/A	PD	TPI
	Yr	24	13	.649	40	37	32	1	0	324	313	15	80	139	**11.0**	2.58	138	.244	**.290**	24	.180	-1	28	36	-1	3.1
1892	*Bos-N	22	10	.688	37	35	31	3	0	299^{2}	273	10	97	93	11.2	3.03	116	.233	.293	16	.131	-6	8	16	-2	0.7
1893	Bos-N	18	10	.643	36	31	23	0	0	263	344	22	81	61	14.7	5.13	96	.307	.356	30	.265	3	-14	-6	-1	-0.4
1894	Bos-N	12	10	.545	27	21	18	0	1	208^{2}	305	15	61	32	16.0	6.81	83	.337	.382	20	.235	0	-35	-26	-3	-2.1
1895	StL-N	6	13	.316	23	16	13	0	0	158^{2}	223	8	39	28	15.0	5.22	93	.327	.365	9	.134	-6	-8	-7	-2	-1.2
Total	8	136	119	.533	283	257	231	10	2	2269	2468	92	601	746	12.4	3.80	105	.269	.317	174	.182	-19	51	51	-9	2.7

● TRACY STALLARD Stallard, Evan Tracy b: 8/31/37, Coeburn, Va. BR/TR, 6'5", 205 lbs. Deb: 9/24/60

YEAR	TM/L	W	L	PCT	G	GS	CG	SH	SV	IP	H	HR	BB	SO	RAT	ERA	ERA+	OAV	OOB	BH	AVG	PB	PR	/A	PD	TPI
1960	Bos-A	0	0	—	4	0	0	0	0	4	0	0	2	6	4.5	0.00	—	.000	.133	0	—	0	2	2	0	0.0
1961	Bos-A	2	7	.222	43	14	1	0	2	132^{2}	110	15	96	109	14.0	4.88	85	.229	.359	3	.083	-2	-13	-11	-2	-1.1
1962	Bos-A	0	0	—	1	0	0	0	0	1	0	0	0	0	0.0	0.00	—	.000	.000	0	—	0	0	0	-0	0.0
1963	NY-N	6	17	.261	39	23	5	0	1	154^{2}	156	23	77	110	13.6	4.71	74	.262	.347	3	.063	-3	-24	-21	-1	-3.3
1964	NY-N	10	20	.333	36	34	11	2	0	225^{2}	213	20	73	118	11.6	3.79	94	.252	.316	15	.190	2	-6	-5	-2	-0.7
1965	StL-N	11	8	.579	40	26	4	1	0	194^{1}	172	25	70	99	11.5	3.38	114	.235	.307	6	.088	-4	3	10	-2	0.3
1966	StL-N	1	5	.167	20	7	0	0	1	52^{1}	65	9	25	35	15.8	5.68	63	.305	.383	0	.000	-2	-12	-12	0	-1.5
Total	7	30	57	.345	183	104	21	3	4	764^{2}	716	92	343	477	12.7	4.17	90	.248	.332	27	.110	-9	-50	-37	-7	-6.3

● CHARLEY STANCEU Stanceu, Charles b: 1/9/16, Canton, Ohio d: 4/3/69, Canton, Ohio BR/TR, 6'2", 190 lbs. Deb: 4/16/41

YEAR	TM/L	W	L	PCT	G	GS	CG	SH	SV	IP	H	HR	BB	SO	RAT	ERA	ERA+	OAV	OOB	BH	AVG	PB	PR	/A	PD	TPI
1941	NY-A	3	3	.500	22	2	0	0	0	48	58	3	35	21	17.6	5.63	70	.296	.405	0	.000	-2	-8	-9	-1	-1.2
1946	NY-A	0	0	—	3	0	0	0	0	4	6	0	5	3	24.8	9.00	38	.316	.458	0	—	0	-2	-2	0	0.0
	Phi-N	2	4	.333	14	11	1	0	0	70^{1}	71	4	39	23	14.1	4.22	81	.270	.364	0	.000	-2	-6	-6	-1	-0.8
Total	2	5	7	.417	39	13	1	0	0	122^{1}	135	7	79	47	15.8	4.93	74	.282	.385	0	.000	-4	-17	-18	-2	-2.0

● PETE STANDRIDGE Standridge, Alfred Peter b: 4/25/1891, Black Diamond, Wash. d: 8/2/63, San Francisco, Cal. BR/TR, 5'10.5", 165 lbs. Deb: 9/19/11

YEAR	TM/L	W	L	PCT	G	GS	CG	SH	SV	IP	H	HR	BB	SO	RAT	ERA	ERA+	OAV	OOB	BH	AVG	PB	PR	/A	PD	TPI
1911	StL-N	0	0	—	2	0	0	0	0	4^{2}	10	0	4	3	28.9	9.64	35	.435	.536	0	.000	-0	-3	-3	0	0.0
1915	Chi-N	4	1	.800	29	3	2	0	0	112^{1}	120	2	36	42	12.7	3.61	77	.274	.332	9	.225	3	-11	-10	0	-0.2
Total	2	4	1	.800	31	3	2	0	0	117	130	2	40	45	13.3	3.85	73	.282	.343	9	.220	3	-14	-14	0	-0.2

● AL STANEK Stanek, Albert Wilfred "Lefty" b: 12/24/43, Springfield, Mass. BL/TL, 5'11.5", 190 lbs. Deb: 4/26/63

YEAR	TM/L	W	L	PCT	G	GS	CG	SH	SV	IP	H	HR	BB	SO	RAT	ERA	ERA+	OAV	OOB	BH	AVG	PB	PR	/A	PD	TPI
1963	SF-N	0	0	—	11	0	0	0	0	13^{1}	10	1	12	5	14.9	4.73	68	.217	.379	0	.000	-0	-2	-2	1	0.1

● KEVIN STANFIELD Stanfield, Kevin Bruce b: 12/19/55, Huron, S.Dak. BL/TL, 6', 190 lbs. Deb: 9/14/79

YEAR	TM/L	W	L	PCT	G	GS	CG	SH	SV	IP	H	HR	BB	SO	RAT	ERA	ERA+	OAV	OOB	BH	AVG	PB	PR	/A	PD	TPI
1979	Min-A	0	0	—	3	0	0	0	0	3	2	0	0	0	6.0	6.00	73	.200	.200	0	—	0	-1	-1	0	0.0

● LEE STANGE Stange, Albert Lee b: 10/27/36, Chicago, Ill. BR/TR, 5'10", 170 lbs. Deb: 4/15/61 C

YEAR	TM/L	W	L	PCT	G	GS	CG	SH	SV	IP	H	HR	BB	SO	RAT	ERA	ERA+	OAV	OOB	BH	AVG	PB	PR	/A	PD	TPI
1961	Min-A	1	0	1.000	7	0	0	0	0	12^{1}	15	1	10	10	18.2	2.92	145	.294	.410	0	.000	-0	2	2	0	0.1
1962	Min-A	4	3	.571	44	6	1	0	3	95	98	14	39	70	13.1	4.45	92	.271	.343	1	.059	-1	-5	-4	-0	-0.4
1963	Min-A	12	5	.706	32	20	7	2	0	164^{2}	145	21	43	100	10.3	2.62	139	.233	.283	5	.096	-1	18	19	-0	1.7
1964	Min-A	3	6	.333	14	11	2	0	0	79^{2}	78	13	19	54	11.0	4.74	75	.255	.298	1	.040	-1	-10	-10	1	-1.1
	Cle-A	4	8	.333	23	14	0	0	0	91^{2}	98	14	31	78	12.8	4.12	87	.270	.329	2	.080	-1	-5	-5	-0	-0.8
	Yr	7	14	.333	37	25	2	0	0	171^{1}	176	27	50	132	11.9	4.41	81	.262	.314	3	.060	-2	-15	-16	0	-1.9
1965	Cle-A	8	4	.667	41	12	4	2	0	132	122	13	26	80	10.2	3.34	104	.247	.286	3	.107	1	2	2	-2	0.1
1966	Cle-A	1	0	1.000	8	2	1	0	0	16	17	1	3	8	11.8	2.81	122	.279	.323	1	.250	0	1	1	-0	0.1
	Bos-A	7	9	.438	28	19	8	2	0	153^{1}	140	17	43	77	10.8	3.35	114	.246	.300	3	.063	-3	2	8	-1	0.3
	Yr	8	9	.471	36	21	9	2	0	169^{1}	157	18	46	85	10.8	3.30	114	.248	.300	4	.077	-3	3	9	-2	0.4
1967	*Bos-A	8	10	.444	35	24	6	2	1	181^{2}	171	14	32	101	10.2	2.77	126	.246	.282	3	.061	-3	9	14	-3	0.9
1968	Bos-A	5	5	.500	50	2	1	0	12	103	89	10	25	53	10.0	3.93	80	.237	.286	2	.133	0	-11	-9	-1	-1.3
1969	Bos-A	6	9	.400	41	15	2	0	3	137	137	14	56	59	13.1	3.68	103	.256	.333	3	.086	-2	-1	2	-2	-0.1
1970	Bos-A	2	2	.500	20	0	0	0	2	27^{1}	34	5	12	14	15.8	5.60	71	.301	.378	0	.000	-0	-6	-5	0	-0.8
	Chi-A	1	0	1.000	16	0	0	0	0	22^{1}	28	5	5	14	13.3	5.24	74	.295	.330	0	.000	-0	-4	-3	-0	-0.2
	Yr	3	2	.600	36	0	0	0	2	49^{2}	62	10	17	28	14.3	5.44	72	.291	.343	0	.000	-0	-10	-8	-0	-1.0
Total	10	62	61	.504	359	125	32	8	21	1216	1172	142	344	718	11.3	3.56	102	.252	.306	24	.079	-11	-8	12	-9	-1.5

● DON STANHOUSE Stanhouse, Donald Joseph b: 2/12/51, DuQuoin, Ill. BR/TR, 6'2", 195 lbs. Deb: 4/19/72

YEAR	TM/L	W	L	PCT	G	GS	CG	SH	SV	IP	H	HR	BB	SO	RAT	ERA	ERA+	OAV	OOB	BH	AVG	PB	PR	/A	PD	TPI
1972	Tex-A	2	9	.182	24	16	1	0	0	104^{2}	83	8	73	78	13.5	3.78	80	.223	.351	4	.129	-0	-8	-9	2	-0.8
1973	Tex-A	1	7	.125	21	5	1	0	1	70	70	5	44	42	14.9	4.76	78	.262	.371	0	—	0	-7	-8	2	-0.6
1974	Tex-A	1	1	.500	18	0	0	0	0	31^{1}	38	4	17	26	16.4	4.88	73	.302	.393	0	—	0	-4	-5	1	0.0
1975	Mon-N	0	0	—	4	3	0	0	0	13	19	1	11	5	20.8	8.31	46	.345	.455	1	.333	0	-7	-6	-0	0.0
1976	Mon-N	9	12	.429	34	26	8	1	1	184	182	7	92	79	13.6	3.77	99	.263	.352	11	.212	2	-5	-1	3	0.4
1977	Mon-N	10	10	.500	47	16	1	1	10	158^{1}	147	12	84	89	13.4	3.41	112	.251	.349	9	.191	1	9	7	-1	0.9
1978	Bal-A	6	9	.400	56	0	0	0	24	74^{2}	60	0	52	42	13.5	2.89	121	.230	.358	0	—	0	7	5	0	1.4
1979	*Bal-A☆	7	3	.700	52	0	0	0	21	72^{2}	49	4	51	34	12.5	2.85	141	.202	.342	0	—	0	11	9	1	1.9
1980	LA-N	2	2	.500	21	0	0	0	7	25	30	4	16	5	16.6	5.04	69	.306	.404	0	.000	0	-4	-4	1	-0.8
1982	Bal-A	0	1	.000	17	0	0	0	0	26^{2}	29	3	15	8	15.5	5.40	75	.276	.377	0	—	0	-4	-4	0	-0.1
Total	10	38	54	.413	294	66	11	2	64	760^{1}	707	48	455	408	13.9	3.84	95	.252	.359	25	.185	4	-13	-16	8	2.3

● ROB STANIFER Stanifer, Robert Wayne b: 3/10/72, Easley, S.C. BR/TR, 6'3", 205 lbs. Deb: 5/3/97

YEAR	TM/L	W	L	PCT	G	GS	CG	SH	SV	IP	H	HR	BB	SO	RAT	ERA	ERA+	OAV	OOB	BH	AVG	PB	PR	/A	PD	TPI
1997	Fla-N	1	2	.333	36	0	0	0	1	45	43	9	16	28	12.4	4.60	88	.261	.337	2	.667	2	-2	-3	-0	-0.1
1998	Fla-N	2	4	.333	38	0	0	0	1	48	54	5	22	30	14.3	5.63	73	.277	.350	0	.000	-1	-7	-8	-1	-1.0
Total	2	3	6	.333	74	0	0	0	2	93	97	14	38	58	13.4	5.13	79	.269	.344	2	.250	1	-9	-11	-1	-1.1

● JOE STANKA Stanka, Joe Donald b: 7/23/31, Hammon, Okla. BR/TR, 6'5", 201 lbs. Deb: 9/2/59

YEAR	TM/L	W	L	PCT	G	GS	CG	SH	SV	IP	H	HR	BB	SO	RAT	ERA	ERA+	OAV	OOB	BH	AVG	PB	PR	/A	PD	TPI
1959	Chi-A	1	0	1.000	2	0	0	0	0	5^{1}	2	1	4	3	10.1	3.38	111	.111	.273	1	.333	0	0	0	-0	0.0

● BUCK STANLEY Stanley, John Leonard b: 11/13/1889, Washington, D.C. d: 8/13/40, Norfolk, Va. BL/TL, 5'10", 160 lbs. Deb: 9/12/11 F

YEAR	TM/L	W	L	PCT	G	GS	CG	SH	SV	IP	H	HR	BB	SO	RAT	ERA	ERA+	OAV	OOB	BH	AVG	PB	PR	/A	PD	TPI
1911	Phi-N	0	0	—	4	0	0	0	0	11^{1}	14	0	9	5	18.3	6.35	54	.326	.442	0	.000	-1	-4	-4	-1	-0.1

● JOE STANLEY Stanley, Joseph Bernard b: 4/2/1881, Washington, D.C. d: 9/13/67, Detroit, Mich. BB/TR, 5'9.5", 150 lbs. Deb: 9/11/1897 F♦

YEAR	TM/L	W	L	PCT	G	GS	CG	SH	SV	IP	H	HR	BB	SO	RAT	ERA	ERA+	OAV	OOB	BH	AVG	PB	PR	/A	PD	TPI
1897	Was-N	0	0	—	1	0	0	0	0	0^{2}	0	0	0	0	0.0	0.00	—	.000	.000	0	.000	-0	0	0	-0	0.0
1903	Bos-N	0	0	—	1	0	0	0	0	4	4	0	4	4	20.3	9.00	36	.286	.474	77	.250	0	-3	-3	-0	0.0
1906	Was-A	0	0	—	1	0	0	0	0	3	3	1	1	0	15.0	12.00	22	.273	.385	36	.163	-0	-3	-3	-0	0.0
Total	3	0	0	—	3	0	0	0	0	7^{2}	7	1	5	4	16.4	9.39	33	.259	.412	148	.213	0	-5	-5	-1	0.0

● BOB STANLEY Stanley, Robert William b: 11/10/54, Portland, Maine BR/TR, 6'4", 215 lbs. Deb: 4/16/77

YEAR	TM/L	W	L	PCT	G	GS	CG	SH	SV	IP	H	HR	BB	SO	RAT	ERA	ERA+	OAV	OOB	BH	AVG	PB	PR	/A	PD	TPI
1977	Bos-A	8	7	.533	41	13	3	1	3	151	176	10	43	44	13.2	3.99	112	.294	.344	0	—	0	1	8	4	0.8
1978	Bos-A	15	2	.882	52	3	0	0	10	141^{2}	142	5	34	38	11.2	2.60	158	.266	.312	0	—	0	18	24	2	3.2
1979	Bos-A★	16	12	.571	40	30	9	4	1	216^{2}	250	14	44	56	12.4	3.99	111	.294	.332	0	—	0	5	10	2	1.3
1980	Bos-A	10	8	.556	52	17	5	1	14	175	186	11	52	71	12.6	3.39	124	.278	.337	0	—	0	12	16	3	2.1
1981	Bos-A	10	8	.556	35	1	0	0	0	98^{2}	110	3	38	28	14.0	3.83	101	.294	.368	0	—	0	-2	0	3	0.3
1982	Bos-A	12	7	.632	48	0	0	0	14	168^{1}	161	11	50	83	11.5	3.10	**139**	.255	.313	0	—	0	18	23	4	3.1
1983	Bos-A★	8	10	.444	64	0	0	0	33	145^{1}	145	7	38	65	11.5	2.85	153	.266	.317	0	—	0	20	24	-1	3.7
1984	Bos-A	9	10	.474	57	0	0	0	22	106^{2}	113	9	23	52	11.6	3.54	117	.267	.308	0	—	0	5	7	3	1.7
1985	Bos-A	6	6	.500	48	0	0	0	10	87^{2}	76	7	30	46	11.1	2.87	149	.237	.306	0	—	0	12	14	0	2.0
1986	*Bos-A	6	6	.500	66	1	0	0	16	82^{1}	109	9	22	54	14.3	4.37	95	.322	.364	0	—	0	-2	-2	1	-0.3
1987	Bos-A	4	15	.211	34	20	4	1	0	152^{2}	198	17	42	67	14.2	5.01	91	.321	.366	0	—	0	-9	-8	1	-0.9
1988	*Bos-A	6	4	.600	57	0	0	0	5	101^{2}	90	6	29	57	11.2	3.19	129	.242	.309	0	—	0	9	10	-0	0.9
1989	Bos-A	5	2	.714	43	0	0	0	4	79^{1}	102	4	26	32	14.6	4.88	84	.321	.374	0	—	0	-9	-7	1	-0.6
Total	13	115	97	.542	637	85	21	7	132	1707	1858	113	471	693	12.5	3.64	117	.282	.334	0	—	0	80	121	22	17.3

● MIKE STANTON Stanton, Michael Thomas b: 9/25/52, Phenix City, Ala. BB/TR, 6'2", 205 lbs. Deb: 7/9/75

YEAR	TM/L	W	L	PCT	G	GS	CG	SH	SV	IP	H	HR	BB	SO	RAT	ERA	ERA+	OAV	OOB	BH	AVG	PB	PR	/A	PD	TPI
1975	Hou-N	0	2	.000	7	2	0	0	1	17^{1}	20	1	20	16	20.8	7.27	46	.290	.449	1	.250	0	-7	-8	0	-0.8
1980	Cle-A	1	3	.250	51	0	0	0	5	85^{2}	98	5	44	74	15.2	5.46	75	.297	.385	0	—	0	-14	-13	1	-0.6

YEAR	TM/L	W	L	PCT	G	GS	CG	SH	SV	IP	H	HR	BB	SO	RAT	ERA	ERA+	OAV	OOB	BH	AVG	PB	PR	/A	PD	TPI
1981	Cle-A	3	3	.500	24	0	0	0	2	43^1	43	4	18	34	12.7	4.36	83	.262	.335	0	—	0	-3	-4	-1	-0.5
1982	Sea-A	2	4	.333	56	1	0	0	7	71^1	70	5	21	49	11.5	4.16	102	.260	.314	0	—	0	-1	1	1	0.1
1983	Sea-A	2	3	.400	50	0	0	0	7	65	65	3	28	47	13.0	3.32	128	.273	.352	0	—	0	5	7	-0	0.5
1984	Sea-A	4	4	.500	54	0	0	0	8	61	55	3	22	55	11.7	3.54	113	.241	.313	0	—	0	3	3	-1	0.4
1985	Sea-A	1	2	.333	24	0	0	0	1	29	32	4	21	17	17.4	5.28	80	.278	.403	0	—	0	-4	-3	1	-0.3
	Chi-A	0	1	.000	11	0	0	0	0	11^2	15	2	8	12	17.7	9.26	47	.294	.390	0	—	0	-7	-6	-0	-0.5
	Yr	1	3	.250	35	0	0	0	1	40^2	47	6	29	29	16.8	6.42	66	.278	.384	0	—	0	-10	-10	1	-0.8
Total	7	13	22	.371	277	3	0	0	31	384^1	398	27	182	304	13.8	4.61	88	.272	.356	1	.250	0	-27	-24	1	-1.7

● MIKE STANTON Stanton, William Michael b: 6/2/67, Houston, Tex. BL/TL, 6′1″, 190 lbs. Deb: 8/24/89

YEAR	TM/L	W	L	PCT	G	GS	CG	SH	SV	IP	H	HR	BB	SO	RAT	ERA	ERA+	OAV	OOB	BH	AVG	PB	PR	/A	PD	TPI
1989	Atl-N	0	1	.000	20	0	0	0	7	24	17	0	8	27	9.4	1.50	243	.207	.278	0	—	0	5	6	-0	0.5
1990	Atl-N	0	3	.000	7	0	0	0	2	7	16	1	4	7	27.0	18.00	22	.444	.512	0	—	0	-11	-11	0	-3.6
1991	*Atl-N	5	5	.500	74	0	0	0	7	78	62	6	21	54	9.7	2.88	135	.217	.273	3	.500	2	7	9	1	1.5
1992	*Atl-N	5	4	.556	65	0	0	0	8	63^2	59	6	20	44	11.5	4.10	89	.247	.310	1	.500	0	-4	-3	0	-0.4
1993	*Atl-N	4	6	.400	63	0	0	0	27	52	51	4	29	43	13.8	4.67	86	.255	.349	0	—	0	-4	-4	0	-1.0
1994	Atl-N	3	1	.750	49	0	0	0	3	45^2	41	2	26	35	13.8	3.55	120	.248	.361	2	.667	1	3	4	1	0.5
1995	Atl-N	1	1	.500	26	0	0	0	1	19^1	31	3	6	13	17.7	5.59	76	.369	.418	0	—	0	-3	-3	0	-0.3
	*Bos-A	1	0	1.000	22	0	0	0	0	21	17	3	8	10	10.7	3.00	162	.224	.298	0	—	0	4	4	-0	0.0
1996	Bos-A	4	3	.571	59	0	0	0	1	56^1	58	9	23	46	12.9	3.83	132	.275	.346	0	—	0	7	8	-0	0.7
	*Tex-A	0	1	.000	22	0	0	0	0	22^1	20	2	4	14	9.7	3.22	162	.241	.276	0	—	0	4	5	-1	-0.2
	Yr	4	4	.500	81	0	0	0	1	78^2	78	11	27	60	12.0	3.66	140	.264	.325	0	—	0	12	13	-1	0.5
1997	*NY-A	6	1	.857	64	0	0	0	3	66^2	50	3	34	70	11.7	2.57	173	.205	.310	0	—	0	15	14	-0	1.4
1998	*NY-A	4	1	.800	67	0	0	0	6	79	71	13	26	69	11.5	5.47	81	.239	.309	0	.000	-0	-7	-9	-1	-0.7
Total	10	33	27	.550	538	0	0	0	65	535	493	52	209	432	12.1	3.95	108	.246	.322	6	.500	3	17	20	0	-1.6

● DAVE STAPLETON Stapleton, David Earl b: 10/16/61, Miami, Ariz. BL/TL, 6′1″, 185 lbs. Deb: 9/14/87

YEAR	TM/L	W	L	PCT	G	GS	CG	SH	SV	IP	H	HR	BB	SO	RAT	ERA	ERA+	OAV	OOB	BH	AVG	PB	PR	/A	PD	TPI
1987	Mil-A	2	0	1.000	4	0	0	0	0	14^2	13	0	3	14	9.8	1.84	248	.241	.281	0	—	0	4	4	-0	0.5
1988	Mil-A	0	0	—	6	0	0	0	0	13^2	20	1	9	6	19.8	5.93	67	.339	.435	0	—	0	-3	-3	-0	0.0
Total	2	2	0	1.000	10	0	0	0	0	28^1	33	1	12	20	14.6	3.81	112	.292	.365	0	—	0	1	1	-0	0.5

● CON STARKEL Starkel, Conrad b: 11/16/1880, Germany d: 1/19/33, Tacoma, Wash. BR/TR, 6′, 200 lbs. Deb: 4/19/06

YEAR	TM/L	W	L	PCT	G	GS	CG	SH	SV	IP	H	HR	BB	SO	RAT	ERA	ERA+	OAV	OOB	BH	AVG	PB	PR	/A	PD	TPI
1906	Was-A	0	0	—	1	0	0	0	0	3	7	1	2	1	27.0	18.00	15	.467	.529	0	—	0	-5	-5	0	0.0

● RAY STARR Starr, Raymond Francis "Iron Man" b: 4/23/06, Nowata, Okla. d: 2/9/63, Baylis, Ill. BR/TR, 6′1″, 178 lbs. Deb: 9/11/32

YEAR	TM/L	W	L	PCT	G	GS	CG	SH	SV	IP	H	HR	BB	SO	RAT	ERA	ERA+	OAV	OOB	BH	AVG	PB	PR	/A	PD	TPI
1932	StL-N	1	1	.500	3	2	1	1	0	20	19	2	10	6	13.5	2.70	146	.284	.385	1	.250	0	3	3	1	0.3
1933	NY-N	0	1	.000	6	2	0	0	0	13^1	19	0	10	2	20.3	5.40	59	.339	.448	0	.000	-0	-3	-3	-0	-0.3
	Bos-N	0	1	.000	9	1	0	0	0	28	32	4	9	15	13.5	3.86	79	.296	.356	1	.143	0	-2	-2	0	0.0
	Yr	0	2	.000	15	3	0	0	0	41^1	51	4	19	17	15.5	4.35	71	.309	.384	1	.100	-0	-5	-6	0	-0.3
1941	Cin-N	3	2	.600	7	4	3	2	0	34	28	1	6	11	9.3	2.65	136	.219	.259	2	.182	-0	4	4	0	0.5
1942	Cin-N☆	15	13	.536	37	33	17	4	0	276^2	228	10	106	83	11.0	2.67	123	.226	.301	8	.091	-5	20	19	-2	1.2
1943	Cin-N	11	10	.524	36	33	9	2	1	217^1	201	9	91	42	12.3	3.64	91	.248	.328	9	.122	-4	-6	-8	-0	-1.2
1944	Pit-N	6	5	.545	27	12	5	0	3	89^2	116	6	36	25	15.4	5.02	74	.314	.377	3	.136	1	-14	-13	-1	-1.5
1945	Pit-N	0	2	.000	4	0	0	0	0	6^2	10	0	4	0	18.9	9.45	42	.370	.452	1	1.000	1	-4	-4	0	-0.9
	Chi-N	1	0	1.000	9	1	0	0	0	13^1	17	1	7	5	16.2	7.43	49	.298	.375	1	.500	0	-5	-6	0	-0.3
	Yr	1	2	.333	13	1	0	0	0	20	27	1	11	5	17.1	8.10	46	.321	.400	2	.667	1	-10	-10	0	-1.2
Total	7	37	35	.514	138	88	35	9	4	699	670	33	279	189	12.4	3.53	96	.255	.329	26	.123	-7	-8	-11	-1	-2.2

● DICK STARR Starr, Richard Eugene b: 3/2/21, Kittanning, Pa. BR/TR, 6′3″, 190 lbs. Deb: 9/5/47

YEAR	TM/L	W	L	PCT	G	GS	CG	SH	SV	IP	H	HR	BB	SO	RAT	ERA	ERA+	OAV	OOB	BH	AVG	PB	PR	/A	PD	TPI
1947	NY-A	1	0	1.000	4	1	1	0	0	12^1	12	1	8	1	14.6	1.46	242	.250	.357	1	.333	1	3	3	0	0.3
1948	NY-A	0	0	—	1	0	0	0	0	2	0	0	2	2	9.0	4.50	91	.000	.250	0	—	0	-0	-0	0	0.0
1949	StL-A	1	7	.125	30	8	1	1	0	83^1	96	6	48	44	15.7	4.32	105	.292	.384	2	.087	-1	-1	2	-1	0.0
1950	StL-A	7	5	.583	32	16	4	1	2	123^2	140	11	74	30	16.1	5.02	99	.287	.389	5	.139	-3	-6	-1	-1	-0.4
1951	StL-A	2	5	.286	15	9	0	0	0	62	66	10	42	26	16.0	7.40	59	.273	.385	4	.222	0	-23	-21	-1	-2.0
	Was-A	1	7	.125	11	11	1	0	0	61^1	76	12	24	17	14.7	5.58	73	.304	.365	3	.176	1	-10	-10	-2	-1.2
	Yr	3	12	.200	26	20	1	0	0	123^1	142	22	66	43	15.2	6.49	65	.287	.371	7	.200	1	-33	-31	-2	-3.2
Total	5	12	24	.333	93	45	7	2	2	344^2	390	40	198	120	15.6	5.25	86	.286	.381	15	.155	-2	-37	-27	-4	-3.3

● HERMAN STARRETTE Starrette, Herman Paul b: 11/20/38, Statesville, N.C. BR/TR, 6′, 175 lbs. Deb: 7/1/63 C

YEAR	TM/L	W	L	PCT	G	GS	CG	SH	SV	IP	H	HR	BB	SO	RAT	ERA	ERA+	OAV	OOB	BH	AVG	PB	PR	/A	PD	TPI
1963	Bal-A	0	1	.000	18	0	0	0	0	26	26	1	7	13	12.1	3.46	100	.271	.333	0	.000	0	0	0	1	0.1
1964	Bal-A	1	0	1.000	5	0	0	0	0	11	9	0	6	5	12.3	1.64	218	.250	.357	0	.000	-0	2	2	-0	0.1
1965	Bal-A	0	0	—	4	0	0	0	0	9	8	0	3	3	11.0	1.00	347	.258	.324	0	.000	-0	2	2	0	0.0
Total	3	1	1	.500	27	0	0	0	0	46	43	1	16	21	11.9	2.54	137	.264	.337	0	.000	-0	5	5	1	0.2

● ED STAUFFER Stauffer, Charles Edward b: 1/10/1898, Emsworth, Pa. d: 7/2/79, St.Petersburg, Fla BR/TR, 5′11″, 185 lbs. Deb: 4/26/23

YEAR	TM/L	W	L	PCT	G	GS	CG	SH	SV	IP	H	HR	BB	SO	RAT	ERA	ERA+	OAV	OOB	BH	AVG	PB	PR	/A	PD	TPI
1923	Chi-N	0	0	—	1	0	0	0	0	2	5	0	1	0	27.0	13.50	30	.556	.600	0	—	0	-2	-2	0	0.0
1925	StL-A	0	1	.000	20	1	0	0	0	30^1	34	1	21	13	16.3	5.34	87	.283	.390	1	.250	-0	-3	-2	-1	-0.2
Total	2	0	1	.000	21	1	0	0	0	32^1	39	1	22	13	17.0	5.85	79	.302	.404	1	.250	-0	-5	-4	-1	-0.2

● BILL STEARNS Stearns, William E. b: 3/20/1853, Washington, D.C. d: 12/30/1898, Washington, D.C. TR , Deb: 6/26/1871

YEAR	TM/L	W	L	PCT	G	GS	CG	SH	SV	IP	H	HR	BB	SO	RAT	ERA	ERA+	OAV	OOB	BH	AVG	PB	PR	/A	PD	TPI
1871	Oly-n	2	0	1.000	2	2	2	0	0	18	10	0	8	0	9.0	2.50	167	.149	.240	0	.000	-1	3	3		0.1
1872	Nat-n	0	11	.000	11	11	11	0	0	99	193	2	3	2	17.8	6.18	75	.339	.343	12	.267	-3	-28	-17		-1.4
1873	Was-n	7	25	.219	32	32	32	0	0	283	481	7	15	4	15.8	4.55	74	.330	.337	24	.180	-6	-41	-38		-3.2
1874	Har-n	3	14	.176	22	18	14	0	0	158^2	237	0	15	14	14.3	2.95	78	.297	.310	21	.159	-5	-14	-12		-1.3
1875	Was-n	1	14	.067	17	16	14	0	0	141	246	3	4	3	16.0	4.02	59	.332	.336	20	.256	-0	-28	-26		-2.2
Total	5 n	13	64	.169	84	79	73	0	0	699^2	1167	12	45	23	15.6	4.26	56	.321	.330	77	.194	-16	-158	-147		-8.0

● CHARLIE STECHER Stecher, Charles b: Bordentown, N.J. Deb: 9/6/1890

YEAR	TM/L	W	L	PCT	G	GS	CG	SH	SV	IP	H	HR	BB	SO	RAT	ERA	ERA+	OAV	OOB	BH	AVG	PB	PR	/A	PD	TPI
1890	Phi-a	0	10	.000	10	10	9	0	0	68	111	1	60	18	24.5	10.32	37	.356	.479	7	.241	1	-49	-49	2	-4.4

● ELMER STEELE Steele, Elmer Rae b: 5/17/1886, Poughkeepsie, N.Y. d: 3/9/66, Rhinebeck, N.Y. BB/TR, 5′11″, 200 lbs. Deb: 9/12/07

YEAR	TM/L	W	L	PCT	G	GS	CG	SH	SV	IP	H	HR	BB	SO	RAT	ERA	ERA+	OAV	OOB	BH	AVG	PB	PR	/A	PD	TPI
1907	Bos-A	0	1	.000	4	1	0	0	0	11^1	11	0	1	10	9.5	1.59	162	.256	.273	0	.000	-1	1	1	0	0.1
1908	Bos-A	5	7	.417	16	13	9	1	0	118	85	1	13	37	7.7	1.83	134	.209	.239	2	.051	-4	7	8	-1	0.3
1909	Bos-A	4	4	.500	16	8	2	0	1	75^2	75	1	15	32	10.8	2.85	88	.255	.294	5	.227	1	-3	-3	1	-0.1
1910	Pit-N	0	3	.000	3	3	2	0	0	24	19	0	3	7	8.3	2.25	138	.221	.247	0	.000	-1	2	2	1	0.3
1911	Pit-N	9	9	.500	31	16	7	2	2	166	153	5	31	52	10.2	2.60	132	.256	.297	11	.180	-0	15	15	2	1.7
	Bro-N	0	0	—	5	2	0	0	0	23	24	0	5	9	11.3	3.13	107	.258	.296	0	.000	-1	1	1	0	-0.1
	Yr	9	9	.500	36	18	7	2	2	189	177	5	36	61	10.1	2.67	128	.255	.292	11	.157	-1	15	16	2	1.6
Total	5	18	24	.429	75	43	20	3	3	418	367	7	68	147	9.5	2.41	122	.241	.278	18	.127	-6	23	25	3	2.2

● BOB STEELE Steele, Robert Wesley b: 1/5/1894, Cassburn, Ont., Can. d: 1/27/62, Ocala, Fla. BB/TL, 5′10.5″, 175 lbs. Deb: 4/17/16

YEAR	TM/L	W	L	PCT	G	GS	CG	SH	SV	IP	H	HR	BB	SO	RAT	ERA	ERA+	OAV	OOB	BH	AVG	PB	PR	/A	PD	TPI
1916	StL-N	5	15	.250	29	21	7	1	0	148	156	6	42	67	12.2	3.41	78	.285	.340	10	.196	-1	-13	-13	-3	-2.0
1917	StL-N	1	3	.250	12	6	1	0	0	42	33	1	19	23	11.1	3.21	84	.223	.311	5	.385	2	-2	-2	-1	-0.1
	Pit-N	5	11	.313	27	19	13	1	1	179^2	158	0	53	82	10.8	2.76	103	.237	.298	17	.224	1	-1	2	-2	0.0
	Yr	6	14	.300	39	25	14	1	1	221^2	191	1	72	105	10.9	2.84	99	.235	.301	22	.247	2	-3	-1	-2	-0.1
1918	Pit-N	2	3	.400	10	4	2	1	1	49	44	2	17	21	11.6	3.31	87	.240	.312	2	.125	-0	-3	-2	-0	-0.3
	NY-N	3	5	.375	12	7	5	1	1	66	56	1	11	24	9.5	2.59	101	.226	.267	6	.286	2	1	0	-2	0.0
	Yr	5	8	.385	22	11	7	2	2	115	100	3	28	45	10.3	2.90	94	.231	.282	8	.216	2	-2	-2	-3	-0.3
1919	NY-N	0	1	.000	1	0	0	0	0	3	3	0	2	0	15.0	6.00	47	.250	.357	0	.000	-0	-1	-1	-0	-0.3
Total	4	16	38	.296	91	57	28	4	3	487^2	450	10	144	217	11.2	3.05	90	.249	.310	40	.225	3	-19	-16	-8	-2.7

● BILL STEELE Steele, William Mitchell "Big Bill" b: 10/5/1885, Milford, Pa. d: 10/19/49, Overland, Mo. BR/TR, 5′11″, 200 lbs. Deb: 9/10/10

YEAR	TM/L	W	L	PCT	G	GS	CG	SH	SV	IP	H	HR	BB	SO	RAT	ERA	ERA+	OAV	OOB	BH	AVG	PB	PR	/A	PD	TPI
1910	StL-N	4	4	.500	9	8	8	0	1	71^2	71	1	24	25	12.7	3.27	91	.264	.338	8	.258	1	-2	-2	1	0.0

YEAR	TM/L	W	L	PCT	G	GS	CG	SH	SV	IP	H	HR	BB	SO	RAT	ERA	ERA+	OAV	OOB	BH	AVG	PB	PR	/A	PD	TPI
1911	StL-N	18	19	.486	43	34	23	1	3	287^{1}	287	8	113	115	12.8	3.73	91	.269	.345	21	.208	4	-10	-11	3	-0.6
1912	StL-N	9	13	.409	40	25	7	0	2	194	245	5	66	67	14.8	4.69	73	.322	.381	11	.180	1	-27	-27	4	-2.2
1913	StL-N	4	4	.500	12	9	2	0	0	54	58	3	18	10	13.2	5.00	65	.286	.353	1	.056	-1	-11	-11	-1	-1.6
1914	StL-N	1	2	.333	17	2	0	0	0	53^{1}	55	3	7	16	11.0	2.70	104	.274	.308	5	.294	2	1	1	1	0.3
	Bro-N	1	1	.500	8	1	0	0	1	16^{1}	17	1	7	3	13.2	5.51	52	.258	.329	1	.333	1	-5	-5	-0	-0.6
	Yr	2	3	.400	25	3	0	0	1	69^{2}	72	4	14	19	11.1	3.36	84	.267	.303	6	.300	2	-4	-4	1	-0.3
Total	5	37	43	.463	129	79	40	1	7	676^{2}	733	21	235	236	13.3	4.02	82	.286	.352	47	.203	8	-55	-55	8	-4.7

● **BILL STEEN** Steen, William John b: 11/11/1887, Pittsburgh, Pa. d: 3/13/79, Signal Hill, Cal. BR/TR, 6'0.5", 180 lbs. Deb: 4/15/12

YEAR	TM/L	W	L	PCT	G	GS	CG	SH	SV	IP	H	HR	BB	SO	RAT	ERA	ERA+	OAV	OOB	BH	AVG	PB	PR	/A	PD	TPI
1912	Cle-A	9	8	.529	26	16	6	1	0	143^{1}	163	3	45	61	13.1	3.77	90	.298	.352	13	.271	2	-7	-6	-1	-0.5
1913	Cle-A	4	5	.444	22	13	7	2	2	128^{1}	113	3	49	57	11.6	2.45	124	.237	.313	7	.171	-0	7	8	-0	0.5
1914	Cle-A	9	14	.391	30	22	13	1	0	200^{2}	201	0	68	97	12.2	2.60	111	.272	.337	14	.200	1	3	6	0	0.8
1915	Cle-A	1	4	.200	10	7	2	0	0	45^{1}	51	1	15	22	13.5	4.96	61	.290	.352	3	.188	-0	-10	-10	2	-0.8
	Det-A	5	1	.833	20	7	3	0	4	79^{1}	83	0	22	28	12.0	2.72	111	.269	.319	5	.179	-1	2	3	2	0.3
	Yr	6	5	.545	30	14	5	0	4	124^{2}	134	1	37	50	12.4	3.54	86	.275	.328	8	.182	-1	-8	-7	4	-0.5
Total	4	28	32	.467	108	65	31	4	6	597	611	7	199	265	12.4	3.05	101	.272	.334	42	.207	1	-6	2	2	0.3

● **MILT STEENGRAFE** Steengrafe, Milton Henry b: 5/26/1900, San Francisco, Cal d: 6/2/77, Oklahoma City, Okla. BR/TR, 6', 170 lbs. Deb: 5/5/24

YEAR	TM/L	W	L	PCT	G	GS	CG	SH	SV	IP	H	HR	BB	SO	RAT	ERA	ERA+	OAV	OOB	BH	AVG	PB	PR	/A	PD	TPI
1924	Chi-A	0	0	—	3	0	0	0	0	5^{2}	15	0	4	3	30.2	12.71	32	.484	.543	0	.000	-0	-5	-5	0	0.0
1926	Chi-A	1	1	.500	13	1	0	0	0	38^{1}	43	1	19	10	15.0	3.99	97	.295	.383	0	.000	-2	0	-1	-1	-0.3
Total	2	1	1	.500	16	1	0	0	0	44	58	1	23	13	17.0	5.11	76	.328	.411	0	.000	-2	-5	-6	-1	-0.3

● **KENNIE STEENSTRA** Steenstra, Kenneth Gregory b: 10/13/70, Springfield, Mo. BR/TR, 6'5", 220 lbs. Deb: 5/21/98

YEAR	TM/L	W	L	PCT	G	GS	CG	SH	SV	IP	H	HR	BB	SO	RAT	ERA	ERA+	OAV	OOB	BH	AVG	PB	PR	/A	PD	TPI
1998	Chi-N	0	0	—	4	0	0	0	0	3^{1}	7	2	1	4	21.6	10.80	40	.412	.444	0	—	0	-2	-2	-0	0.0

● **MORRIE STEEVENS** Steevens, Morris Dale b: 10/7/40, Salem, Ill. BL/TL, 6'2", 175 lbs. Deb: 4/13/62

YEAR	TM/L	W	L	PCT	G	GS	CG	SH	SV	IP	H	HR	BB	SO	RAT	ERA	ERA+	OAV	OOB	BH	AVG	PB	PR	/A	PD	TPI
1962	Chi-N	0	1	.000	12	1	0	0	0	15	10	0	11	5	13.2	2.40	173	.196	.349	0	.000	-0	3	3	0	0.2
1964	Phi-N	0	0	—	4	0	0	0	0	2^{2}	5	0	1	3	20.3	3.38	103	.385	.429	0	—	0	0	0	0	0.0
1965	Phi-N	0	1	.000	6	0	0	0	0	2^{2}	5	1	4	3	30.4	16.88	20	.417	.563	0	—	0	-4	-4	-0	-1.3
Total	3	0	2	.000	22	1	0	0	0	20^{1}	20	1	16	11	16.4	4.43	90	.263	.398	0	.000	-0	-1	-1	0	-1.1

● **ED STEIN** Stein, Edward F. b: 9/5/1869, Detroit, Mich. d: 5/10/28, Detroit, Mich. BR/TR, 5'11", 170 lbs. Deb: 7/24/1890

YEAR	TM/L	W	L	PCT	G	GS	CG	SH	SV	IP	H	HR	BB	SO	RAT	ERA	ERA+	OAV	OOB	BH	AVG	PB	PR	/A	PD	TPI
1890	Chi-N	12	6	.667	20	18	14	1	0	160^{2}	147	9	83	65	13.5	3.81	96	.236	.336	9	.153	-2	-4	-3	-1	-0.5
1891	Chi-N	7	6	.538	14	10	9	1	0	101	99	7	57	38	14.1	3.74	89	.247	.343	7	.163	-1	-4	-5	2	-0.4
1892	Bro-N	27	16	.628	48	42	38	6	1	377^{1}	310	6	150	190	11.3	2.84	111	.215	.296	31	.215	4	19	14	2	1.8
1893	Bro-N	19	15	.559	37	34	28	1	0	298^{1}	294	4	119	81	12.7	3.77	117	.250	.323	25	.212	-3	30	22	2	1.7
1894	Bro-N	26	14	.650	44	40	37	2	1	350	388	10	170	84	14.7	4.63	107	.278	.362	38	.259	5	27	12	-0	1.3
1895	Bro-N	15	13	.536	32	27	24	1	1	255^{1}	282	9	93	55	13.4	4.72	93	.276	.340	26	.250	2	2	-9	1	-0.5
1896	Bro-N	3	6	.333	17	10	6	0	0	90^{1}	130	6	51	16	18.2	4.88	84	.334	.414	10	.256	0	-5	-8	0	-0.5
1898	Bro-N	0	2	.000	3	2	2	0	0	23	39	0	9	6	18.8	5.48	65	.371	.421	4	.400	1	-5	-5	-0	-0.3
Total	8	109	78	.583	215	183	158	12	3	1656	1689	51	732	535	13.5	3.97	103	.258	.338	150	.226	5	59	22	5	2.6

● **IRV STEIN** Stein, Irvin Michael b: 5/21/11, Madisonville, La. d: 1/7/81, Covington, La. BR/TR, 6'2", 170 lbs. Deb: 7/7/32

YEAR	TM/L	W	L	PCT	G	GS	CG	SH	SV	IP	H	HR	BB	SO	RAT	ERA	ERA+	OAV	OOB	BH	AVG	PB	PR	/A	PD	TPI
1932	Phi-A	0	0	—	1	0	0	0	0	3	7	2	1	0	24.0	12.00	38	.500	.533	0	.000	-0	-3	-2	0	0.0

● **BLAKE STEIN** Stein, William Blake b: 8/3/73, McComb, Miss. BR/TR, 6'7", 210 lbs. Deb: 5/10/98

YEAR	TM/L	W	L	PCT	G	GS	CG	SH	SV	IP	H	HR	BB	SO	RAT	ERA	ERA+	OAV	OOB	BH	AVG	PB	PR	/A	PD	TPI
1998	Oak-A	5	9	.357	24	20	1	1	0	117^{1}	117	22	71	89	14.8	6.37	72	.255	.361	0	.000	-0	-22	-24	-1	-2.4

● **RANDY STEIN** Stein, William Randolph b: 3/7/53, Pomona, Cal. BR/TR, 6'4", 210 lbs. Deb: 4/17/78

YEAR	TM/L	W	L	PCT	G	GS	CG	SH	SV	IP	H	HR	BB	SO	RAT	ERA	ERA+	OAV	OOB	BH	AVG	PB	PR	/A	PD	TPI
1978	Mil-A	3	2	.600	31	1	0	0	1	72^{2}	78	5	39	42	15.0	5.33	71	.280	.376	0	—	0	-13	-13	0	-0.8
1979	Sea-A	2	3	.400	23	1	0	0	0	41^{1}	48	7	27	39	16.5	5.88	74	.291	.394	0	—	0	-8	-7	-1	-0.8
1981	Sea-A	0	1	.000	5	0	0	0	0	9^{1}	18	1	8	6	25.1	10.61	36	.429	.520	0	—	0	-7	-7	0	-0.7
1982	Chi-N	0	0	—	6	0	0	0	0	10^{1}	7	2	7	6	12.2	3.48	107	.200	.333	0	—	0	0	0	-0	0.0
Total	4	5	6	.455	65	2	0	0	1	133^{2}	151	15	81	93	16.0	5.72	69	.290	.390	0	—	0	-27	-26	-1	-2.3

● **RAY STEINEDER** Steineder, Raymond J. b: 11/13/1895, Salem, N.J. d: 8/25/82, Vineland, N.J. BR/TR, 6'0.5", 160 lbs. Deb: 7/16/23

YEAR	TM/L	W	L	PCT	G	GS	CG	SH	SV	IP	H	HR	BB	SO	RAT	ERA	ERA+	OAV	OOB	BH	AVG	PB	PR	/A	PD	TPI
1923	Pit-N	2	0	1.000	15	2	1	0	0	55	58	3	18	23	12.8	4.75	85	.278	.341	7	.467	3	-5	-4	-1	0.0
1924	Pit-N	0	1	.000	5	0	0	0	0	2^{2}	6	0	5	0	37.1	13.50	28	.400	.550	0	—	0	-3	-3	0	-0.9
	Phi-N	1	1	.500	9	0	0	0	0	28^{2}	31	1	16	11	14.8	4.40	101	.284	.376	3	.300	0	-2	0	0	0.1
	Yr	1	2	.333	14	0	0	0	0	31^{1}	37	1	21	11	16.7	5.17	85	.298	.400	3	.300	0	-5	-3	0	-0.8
Total	2	3	2	.600	29	2	1	0	0	86^{1}	95	4	39	34	14.2	4.90	85	.285	.364	10	.400	3	-9	-7	-1	-0.8

● **RICK STEIRER** Steirer, Ricky Francis b: 8/27/56, Baltimore, Md. BR/TR, 6'4", 200 lbs. Deb: 8/5/82

YEAR	TM/L	W	L	PCT	G	GS	CG	SH	SV	IP	H	HR	BB	SO	RAT	ERA	ERA+	OAV	OOB	BH	AVG	PB	PR	/A	PD	TPI
1982	Cal-A	1	0	1.000	10	1	0	0	0	26^{1}	25	2	11	14	12.6	3.76	108	.243	.322	0	—	0	1	1	0	0.1
1983	Cal-A	3	2	.600	19	5	0	0	0	61^{2}	77	3	18	25	14.3	4.82	83	.302	.355	0	—	0	-5	-6	1	-0.3
1984	Cal-A	0	1	.000	1	1	0	0	0	2^{2}	6	0	2	2	27.0	16.88	24	.500	.571	0	—	0	-4	-4	0	-0.8
Total	3	4	3	.571	30	7	0	0	0	90^{2}	108	5	31	41	14.2	4.86	83	.292	.353	0	—	0	-8	-8	1	-1.0

● **BILL STELLBERGER** Stellberger, William F. b: 4/22/1865, Detroit, Mich. d: 11/9/36, Detroit, Mich. BL/TL, Deb: 10/1/1885

YEAR	TM/L	W	L	PCT	G	GS	CG	SH	SV	IP	H	HR	BB	SO	RAT	ERA	ERA+	OAV	OOB	BH	AVG	PB	PR	/A	PD	TPI
1885	Pro-N	0	1	.000	1	1	1	0	0	8	14	0	4	0	20.3	7.88	34	.389	.450	0	.000	-1	-4	-5	0	-0.4

● **JEFF STEMBER** Stember, Jeffrey Alan b: 3/2/58, Elizabeth, N.J. BR/TR, 6'5", 220 lbs. Deb: 8/5/80

YEAR	TM/L	W	L	PCT	G	GS	CG	SH	SV	IP	H	HR	BB	SO	RAT	ERA	ERA+	OAV	OOB	BH	AVG	PB	PR	/A	PD	TPI
1980	SF-N	0	0	—	1	1	0	0	0	3	2	1	2	0	12.0	3.00	118	.167	.286	0	.000	-0	0	0	-0	0.0

● **BILL STEMMEYER** Stemmeyer, William "Cannon Ball" b: 5/6/1865, Cleveland, Ohio d: 5/3/45, Cleveland, Ohio BR/TR, 6'2", 190 lbs. Deb: 10/3/1885

YEAR	TM/L	W	L	PCT	G	GS	CG	SH	SV	IP	H	HR	BB	SO	RAT	ERA	ERA+	OAV	OOB	BH	AVG	PB	PR	/A	PD	TPI
1885	Bos-N	1	1	.500	2	2	2	1	0	11	7	0	11	8	14.7	0.00	—	.194	.383	3	.429	1	3	3	0	0.8
1886	Bos-N	22	18	.550	41	41	41	0	0	348^{2}	300	11	144	239	11.5	3.02	106	.218	.292	41	.277	9	11	7	-3	1.2
1887	Bos-N	6	8	.429	15	14	14	0	**1**	119^{1}	138	4	41	41	13.7	5.20	78	.274	.331	12	.255	2	-15	-15	-2	-1.3
1888	Cle-a	0	2	.000	2	2	2	0	0	16	37	0	9	7	26.4	9.00	34	.435	.495	4	.400	1	-11	-11	-0	-0.8
Total	4	29	29	.500	60	59	59	1	1	495	482	15	205	295	12.5	3.67	92	.241	.312	60	.283	14	-11	-16	-4	-0.1

● **DAVE STENHOUSE** Stenhouse, David Rotchford b: 9/12/33, Westerly, R.I. BR/TR, 6', 195 lbs. Deb: 4/18/62 F

YEAR	TM/L	W	L	PCT	G	GS	CG	SH	SV	IP	H	HR	BB	SO	RAT	ERA	ERA+	OAV	OOB	BH	AVG	PB	PR	/A	PD	TPI
1962	Was-A★	11	12	.478	34	26	9	2	0	197	169	24	90	123	11.9	3.65	110	.234	.320	3	.052	-5	7	8	2	0.6
1963	Was-A	3	9	.250	16	16	2	1	0	87	90	12	45	47	14.1	4.55	82	.260	.347	2	.080	-1	-9	-8	0	-1.1
1964	Was-A	2	7	.222	26	14	1	0	1	88	80	12	39	44	12.3	4.81	77	.239	.320	6	.300	2	-12	-11	-0	-0.9
Total	3	16	28	.364	76	56	12	3	1	372	339	48	174	214	12.5	4.14	94	.241	.327	11	.107	-4	-14	-11	1	-1.4

● **BUZZ STEPHEN** Stephen, Louis Roberts b: 7/13/44, Porterville, Cal. BR/TR, 6'4", 205 lbs. Deb: 9/20/68

YEAR	TM/L	W	L	PCT	G	GS	CG	SH	SV	IP	H	HR	BB	SO	RAT	ERA	ERA+	OAV	OOB	BH	AVG	PB	PR	/A	PD	TPI
1968	Min-A	1	1	.500	2	2	0	0	0	11^{1}	11	0	7	4	15.1	4.76	65	.275	.396	0	.000	-0	-2	-2	0	-0.4

● **BRYAN STEPHENS** Stephens, Bryan Maris b: 7/14/20, Fayetteville, Ark d: 11/21/91, Santa Ana, Cal. BR/TR, 6'4", 175 lbs. Deb: 5/15/47

YEAR	TM/L	W	L	PCT	G	GS	CG	SH	SV	IP	H	HR	BB	SO	RAT	ERA	ERA+	OAV	OOB	BH	AVG	PB	PR	/A	PD	TPI
1947	Cle-A	5	10	.333	31	5	1	0	1	92	79	6	39	34	11.7	4.01	87	.230	.312	3	.111	-2	-3	-5	-1	-1.1
1948	StL-A	3	6	.333	43	12	2	0	3	122^{2}	141	14	67	35	15.6	6.02	76	.289	.379	4	.125	-1	-24	-20	-1	-1.5
Total	2	8	16	.333	74	17	3	0	4	214^{2}	220	20	106	69	13.9	5.16	79	.264	.352	7	.119	-3	-27	-26	-2	-2.6

● **CLARENCE STEPHENS** Stephens, Clarence Wright b: 8/19/1863, Cincinnati, Ohio d: 2/28/45, Cincinnati, Ohio TR , Deb: 10/8/1886

YEAR	TM/L	W	L	PCT	G	GS	CG	SH	SV	IP	H	HR	BB	SO	RAT	ERA	ERA+	OAV	OOB	BH	AVG	PB	PR	/A	PD	TPI
1886	Cin-a	1	0	1.000	1	1	1	0	0	8	9	0	5	6	16.9	5.63	63	.273	.385	3	.600	1	-2	-2	0	-0.1
1891	Cin-N	0	1	.000	1	1	1	0	0	8	9	1	3	3	13.5	7.88	43	.273	.333	0	.000	-0	-4	-4	-0	-0.4
1892	Cin-N	0	1	.000	1	1	0	0	0	7	12	0	4	1	20.6	1.29	254	.364	.432	0	.000	-0	2	2	0	0.2
Total	3	1	2	.333	3	3	2	0	0	23	30	1	12	10	16.8	5.09	67	.303	.384	3	.300	0	-4	-4	0	-0.3

● **BEN STEPHENS** Stephens, George Benjamin b: 9/28/1867, Romeo, Mich. d: 8/5/1896, Armada, Mich. 5'10.5", 170 lbs. Deb: 8/5/1892

YEAR	TM/L	W	L	PCT	G	GS	CG	SH	SV	IP	H	HR	BB	SO	RAT	ERA	ERA+	OAV	OOB	BH	AVG	PB	PR	/A	PD	TPI
1892	Bal-N	1	1	.500	5	2	2	0	1	29	37	2	9	7	14.6	2.79	123	.298	.351	0	.000	-2	2	2	-0	0.0

YEAR	TM/L	W	L	PCT	G	GS	CG	SH	SV	IP	H	HR	BB	SO	RAT	ERA	ERA+	OAV	OOB	BH	AVG	PB	PR	/A	PD	TPI
1893	Was-N	0	6	.000	9	6	6	0	0	63^2	83	1	31	14	16.7	5.80	80	.306	.386	3	.103	-4	-8	-8	1	-0.8
1894	Was-N	0	0	—	3	2	1	0	0	11	19	1	8	1	22.9	4.91	107	.373	.467	1	.250	-0	1	0	0	0.0
Total	3	1	7	.125	17	10	9	0	1	103^2	139	4	48	22	16.8	4.86	90	.312	.386	4	.087	-5	-6	-6	1	-0.8

● EARL STEPHENSON
Stephenson, Chester Earl b: 7/31/47, Benson, N.C. BL/TL, 6'3", 175 lbs. Deb: 4/7/71

YEAR	TM/L	W	L	PCT	G	GS	CG	SH	SV	IP	H	HR	BB	SO	RAT	ERA	ERA+	OAV	OOB	BH	AVG	PB	PR	/A	PD	TPI
1971	Chi-N	1	0	1.000	16	0	0	0	1	20^1	24	1	11	11	15.5	4.43	89	.316	.402	0	.000	-0	-2	-1	0	-0.1
1972	Mil-A	3	5	.375	35	8	1	0	0	80^1	79	5	33	33	12.9	3.25	93	.262	.340	0	.000	-2	-2	-2	0	-0.4
1977	Bal-A	0	0	—	1	0	0	0	0	3	5	1	0	2	15.0	9.00	42	.357	.357	0	—	0	-2	-2	-0	0.6
1978	Bal-A	0	0	—	2	0	0	0	0	9^2	10	0	5	4	14.0	2.79	125	.294	.385	0	—	0	1	1	-0	0.3
Total	4	4	5	.444	54	8	1	0	1	113^1	118	7	49	50	13.5	3.57	91	.277	.356	0	.000	-2	-4	-4	-0	0.4

● GARRETT STEPHENSON
Stephenson, Garrett Charles b: 1/2/72, Takoma Park, Md. BR/TR, 6'4", 185 lbs. Deb: 7/25/96

YEAR	TM/L	W	L	PCT	G	GS	CG	SH	SV	IP	H	HR	BB	SO	RAT	ERA	ERA+	OAV	OOB	BH	AVG	PB	PR	/A	PD	TPI
1996	Bal-A	0	1	.000	3	0	0	0	0	6^1	13	1	3	3	24.2	12.79	38	.433	.500	0	—	0	-5	-6	0	-0.6
1997	Phi-N	8	6	.571	20	18	2	0	0	117	104	11	38	81	11.2	3.15	135	.244	.310	3	.094	-1	14	14	0	1.5
1998	Phi-N	0	2	.000	6	6	0	0	0	23	31	3	19	17	19.6	9.00	48	.316	.427	1	.167	0	-12	-12	-0	-0.9
Total	3	8	9	.471	29	24	2	0	0	146^1	148	15	60	101	13.0	4.49	96	.267	.343	4	.105	-1	-4	-3	-0	0.0

● JERRY STEPHENSON
Stephenson, Jerry Joseph b: 10/6/43, Detroit, Mich. BL/TR, 6'2", 185 lbs. Deb: 4/14/63 F

YEAR	TM/L	W	L	PCT	G	GS	CG	SH	SV	IP	H	HR	BB	SO	RAT	ERA	ERA+	OAV	OOB	BH	AVG	PB	PR	/A	PD	TPI
1963	Bos-A	0	0	—	1	1	0	0	0	2^1	5	0	2	3	27.0	7.71	49	.556	.636	0	.000	-0	-1	-1	-0	0.0
1965	Bos-A	1	5	.167	15	8	0	0	0	52	62	7	33	49	16.6	6.23	60	.287	.384	3	.231	0	-16	-14	0	-1.4
1966	Bos-A	2	5	.286	15	11	1	0	0	66^1	68	6	44	50	15.3	5.83	65	.264	.373	2	.118	-1	-18	-15	0	-1.5
1967	*Bos-A	3	1	.750	8	6	0	0	1	39^2	32	4	16	24	11.1	3.86	90	.227	.310	4	.250	0	-3	-2	0	-0.1
1968	Bos-A	2	8	.200	23	7	2	0	0	68^2	81	4	42	51	16.4	5.64	56	.295	.392	6	.353	2	-20	-19	1	-2.4
1969	Sea-A	0	0	—	2	0	0	0	0	2^2	6	0	3	1	33.8	10.13	36	.429	.556	0	—	0	-2	-2	0	0.0
1970	LA-N	0	0	—	3	0	0	0	0	6^2	11	0	5	6	21.6	9.45	41	.379	.471	0	.000	-0	-4	-4	-0	0.0
Total	7	8	19	.296	67	33	3	0	1	238^1	265	21	145	184	15.7	5.70	62	.281	.381	15	.231	2	-64	-57	1	-5.4

● JOHN STERLING
Sterling, John A. b: Philadelphia, Pa. Deb: 10/12/1890

YEAR	TM/L	W	L	PCT	G	GS	CG	SH	SV	IP	H	HR	BB	SO	RAT	ERA	ERA+	OAV	OOB	BH	AVG	PB	PR	/A	PD	TPI
1890	Phi-a	0	1	.000	1	1	1	0	0	5	16	1	4	1	37.8	21.60	18	.516	.583	0	.000	-0	-10	-10	-0	-1.0

● RANDY STERLING
Sterling, Randall Wayne b: 4/21/51, Key West, Fla. BB/TR, 6'2", 195 lbs. Deb: 9/16/74

YEAR	TM/L	W	L	PCT	G	GS	CG	SH	SV	IP	H	HR	BB	SO	RAT	ERA	ERA+	OAV	OOB	BH	AVG	PB	PR	/A	PD	TPI
1974	NY-N	1	1	.500	3	2	0	0	0	9^1	13	0	3	2	16.4	4.82	74	.351	.415	0	.000	0	-1	-1	0	-0.2

● DAVE STEVENS
Stevens, David James b: 3/4/70, Fullerton, Cal. BR/TR, 6'3", 210 lbs. Deb: 5/20/94

YEAR	TM/L	W	L	PCT	G	GS	CG	SH	SV	IP	H	HR	BB	SO	RAT	ERA	ERA+	OAV	OOB	BH	AVG	PB	PR	/A	PD	TPI
1994	Min-A	5	2	.714	24	0	0	0	0	45	55	6	23	24	15.8	6.80	72	.302	.383	0	—	0	-10	-10	-0	-1.2
1995	Min-A	5	4	.556	56	0	0	0	10	65^2	74	14	32	47	14.7	5.07	94	.285	.365	0	—	0	-3	-2	0	-0.3
1996	Min-A	3	3	.500	49	0	0	0	11	58	58	12	25	29	12.9	4.66	110	.264	.339	0	—	0	2	3	-0	0.2
1997	Min-A	1	3	.250	6	6	0	0	0	23	41	8	17	16	22.7	9.00	52	.383	.468	0	—	0	-11	-11	-0	-1.5
	Chi-N	0	2	.000	10	0	0	0	0	9^1	13	0	9	13	22.2	9.64	45	.333	.469	0	.000	-0	-6	-6	-0	-1.0
1998	Chi-N	1	2	.333	31	0	0	0	0	38	42	6	17	31	14.2	4.74	92	.288	.366	1	.250	0	-2	-2	-1	-0.2
Total	5	15	16	.484	176	6	0	0	21	239	283	46	123	160	15.4	5.80	82	.297	.379	1	.200	0	-30	-27	-2	-4.0

● JIM STEVENS
Stevens, James Arthur "Steve" b: 8/25/1889, Williamsburg, Md. d: 9/25/66, Baltimore, Md. BR/TR, 5'11", 180 lbs. Deb: 8/24/14

YEAR	TM/L	W	L	PCT	G	GS	CG	SH	SV	IP	H	HR	BB	SO	RAT	ERA	ERA+	OAV	OOB	BH	AVG	PB	PR	/A	PD	TPI
1914	Was-A	0	0	—	2	0	0	0	0	3	4	0	2	0	21.0	9.00	31	.364	.500	0	.000	-0	-2	-2	-0	0.0

● DAVE STEWART
Stewart, David Keith b: 2/19/57, Oakland, Cal. BR/TR, 6'2", 200 lbs. Deb: 9/22/78 C

YEAR	TM/L	W	L	PCT	G	GS	CG	SH	SV	IP	H	HR	BB	SO	RAT	ERA	ERA+	OAV	OOB	BH	AVG	PB	PR	/A	PD	TPI
1978	LA-N	0	0	—	1	0	0	0	0	2	1	0	0	1	4.5	0.00	—	.167	.167	0	—	0	1	1	-0	0.0
1981	*LA-N	4	3	.571	32	0	0	0	6	43^1	40	3	14	29	11.2	2.49	133	.250	.310	2	.400	2	5	4	0	1.0
1982	LA-N	9	8	.529	45	14	0	0	1	146^1	137	14	49	80	11.6	3.81	91	.249	.313	7	.179	1	-3	-6	-1	-0.6
1983	LA-N	5	2	.714	46	1	0	0	8	76	67	4	33	54	12.1	2.96	121	.237	.321	1	.143	-0	6	5	-1	0.5
	Tex-A	5	2	.714	8	8	2	0	0	59	50	2	17	24	10.5	2.14	188	.233	.295	0	—	0	13	12	0	1.5
1984	Tex-A	7	14	.333	32	27	3	0	0	192^1	193	26	87	119	13.3	4.73	88	.258	.339	0	—	0	-16	-12	-1	-1.4
1985	Tex-A	0	6	.000	42	5	0	0	4	81^1	86	13	37	64	13.8	5.42	78	.273	.353	0	—	0	-12	-11	0	-0.8
	Phi-N	0	0	—	4	0	0	0	0	4^1	5	0	4	2	18.7	6.23	59	.278	.409	0	—	0	-1	-1	-0	0.0
1986	Phi-N	0	0	—	8	0	0	0	0	12^1	15	1	4	9	13.9	6.57	59	.306	.358	0	—	0	-4	-4	-0	0.0
	Oak-A	9	5	.643	29	17	4	1	0	149^1	137	15	65	102	12.4	3.74	103	.241	.322	0	—	0	7	2	-0	0.2
1987	Oak-A	**20**	13	.606	37	37	8	1	0	261^1	224	24	105	205	11.5	3.68	112	.229	.307	0	—	0	22	13	-3	1.5
1988	*Oak-A	21	12	.636	37	37	**14**	2	0	**275^2**	240	14	110	192	11.5	3.23	117	.234	.310	0	—	0	22	17	-3	1.7
1989	*Oak-A★	21	9	.700	36	36	8	0	0	257^2	260	23	69	155	11.7	3.32	111	.263	.315	0	—	0	16	10	-1	1.2
1990	*Oak-A	22	11	.667	36	36	**11**	**4**	0	**267**	226	16	83	166	10.6	2.56	145	.231	.294	0	—	0	40	34	-2	4.1
1991	Oak-A	11	11	.500	35	35	2	1	0	226	245	24	105	144	14.3	5.18	74	.278	.361	0	—	0	-27	-34	-2	-3.0
1992	*Oak-A	12	10	.545	31	31	2	0	0	199^1	175	25	79	130	11.8	3.66	102	.237	.318	0	—	0	6	2	-3	0.1
1993	*Tor-A	12	8	.600	26	26	0	0	0	162	146	23	72	96	12.3	4.44	97	.242	.326	0	—	0	-2	-2	-2	-0.5
1994	Tor-A	7	8	.467	22	22	1	0	0	133^1	151	26	62	111	14.6	5.87	82	.285	.364	0	—	0	-16	-16	-2	-1.6
1995	Oak-A	3	7	.300	16	16	0	0	0	81	101	11	39	58	15.8	6.89	65	.305	.382	0	—	0	-20	-22	0	-2.1
Total	16	168	129	.566	523	348	55	9	19	2629^2	2499	264	1034	1741	12.3	3.95	99	.251	.325	10	.196	2	37	-7	-21	1.8

● FRANK STEWART
Stewart, Frank "Stewy" b: 9/8/06, Minneapolis, Minn. BR/TR, 6'1.5", 180 lbs. Deb: 10/2/27

YEAR	TM/L	W	L	PCT	G	GS	CG	SH	SV	IP	H	HR	BB	SO	RAT	ERA	ERA+	OAV	OOB	BH	AVG	PB	PR	/A	PD	TPI
1927	Chi-A	0	1	.000	1	1	0	0	0	4	5	0	4	0	20.3	9.00	45	.357	.500	0	.000	-0	-2	-2	1	-0.4

● JOE STEWART
Stewart, Joseph Lawrence "Ace" b: 3/11/1879, Monroe, N.C. d: 2/9/13, Youngstown, Ohio TR , 5'11", 175 lbs. Deb: 9/13/04

YEAR	TM/L	W	L	PCT	G	GS	CG	SH	SV	IP	H	HR	BB	SO	RAT	ERA	ERA+	OAV	OOB	BH	AVG	PB	PR	/A	PD	TPI
1904	Bos-N	0	0	—	2	0	0	0	0	9^1	12	0	4	1	16.4	9.64	29	.286	.362	1	.200	-0	-7	-7	-0	0.0

● SAMMY STEWART
Stewart, Samuel Lee b: 10/28/54, Asheville, N.C. BR/TR, 6'3", 208 lbs. Deb: 9/1/78

YEAR	TM/L	W	L	PCT	G	GS	CG	SH	SV	IP	H	HR	BB	SO	RAT	ERA	ERA+	OAV	OOB	BH	AVG	PB	PR	/A	PD	TPI
1978	Bal-A	1	1	.500	2	2	0	0	0	11^1	10	0	3	11	10.3	3.18	110	.238	.289	0	—	0	1	0	0	0.4
1979	*Bal-A	8	5	.615	31	3	1	0	1	117^2	96	11	71	71	13.2	3.52	114	.232	.351	0	—	0	9	6	3	1.0
1980	Bal-A	7	7	.500	33	3	2	0	3	118^2	103	9	60	78	12.5	3.56	111	.235	.330	0	—	0	6	5	-0	0.6
1981	Bal-A	4	8	.333	29	3	0	0	4	112^1	89	8	57	57	11.9	2.32	**156**	.225	.327	0	—	0	17	16	-0	1.8
1982	Bal-A	10	9	.526	38	12	1	1	5	139	140	9	62	69	13.2	4.14	97	.263	.342	0	—	0	-1	-2	1	-0.2
1983	*Bal-A	9	4	.692	58	1	0	0	7	144^1	138	7	67	95	12.8	3.62	109	.253	.336	0	—	0	7	5	-1	0.4
1984	Bal-A	7	4	.636	60	0	0	0	13	93	81	7	47	56	12.5	3.29	118	.241	.336	0	—	0	7	6	0	0.8
1985	Bal-A	5	7	.417	56	1	0	0	9	129^2	117	15	66	77	12.8	3.61	112	.246	.339	0	—	0	8	6	-1	0.6
1986	Bos-A	4	1	.800	27	0	0	0	0	63^2	64	7	48	47	15.8	4.38	95	.266	.388	0	—	0	-1	-2	-0	-0.2
1987	Cle-A	4	2	.667	25	0	0	0	3	27	25	4	21	25	15.7	5.67	80	.234	.364	0	—	0	-4	-3	0	-0.7
Total	10	59	48	.551	359	25	4	1	45	956^2	863	77	502	586	13.0	3.59	110	.245	.341	0	—	0	49	39	1	4.5

● BUNKY STEWART
Stewart, Veston Goff b: 1/7/31, Jasper, N.C. BL/TL, 6', 155 lbs. Deb: 5/4/52

YEAR	TM/L	W	L	PCT	G	GS	CG	SH	SV	IP	H	HR	BB	SO	RAT	ERA	ERA+	OAV	OOB	BH	AVG	PB	PR	/A	PD	TPI
1952	Was-A	0	0	—	1	0	0	0	0	1	2	0	1	1	27.0	18.00	20	.500	.600	0	—	0	-2	-2	0	0.0
1953	Was-A	0	2	.000	2	2	1	0	0	15^1	17	1	11	3	17.0	4.70	83	.283	.403	1	.200	-0	-1	-1	-0	-0.2
1954	Was-A	0	2	.000	29	2	0	0	0	50^2	67	3	27	27	17.4	7.64	47	.324	.412	0	.000	-0	-22	-23	1	-0.8
1955	Was-A	0	0	—	7	1	0	0	0	15^1	18	0	6	10	14.1	4.11	93	.295	.358	0	.000	-0	-0	-0	0	0.0
1956	Was-A	5	7	.417	33	9	1	0	3	105	111	15	82	36	17.0	5.57	78	.276	.405	7	.250	-0	-16	-15	1	-1.4
Total	5	5	11	.313	72	14	2	0	3	187^1	215	19	127	77	16.9	6.01	67	.293	.404	8	.211	-0	-42	-41	2	-2.4

● LEFTY STEWART
Stewart, Walter Cleveland b: 9/23/1900, Sparta, Tenn. d: 9/26/74, Knoxville, Tenn. BR/TL, 5'10", 160 lbs. Deb: 4/20/21

YEAR	TM/L	W	L	PCT	G	GS	CG	SH	SV	IP	H	HR	BB	SO	RAT	ERA	ERA+	OAV	OOB	BH	AVG	PB	PR	/A	PD	TPI
1921	Det-A	0	0	—	5	0	0	0	1	9	20	0	5	4	25.0	12.00	36	.455	.510	0	.000	-0	-8	-8	0	-0.2
1927	StL-A	8	11	.421	27	19	11	0	1	155^2	187	7	43	43	13.4	4.28	102	.310	.357	15	.306	3	-2	1	2	0.5
1928	StL-A	7	9	.438	29	17	7	1	3	142^2	173	5	32	25	13.1	4.67	90	.310	.350	14	.275	3	-10	-7	-0	-0.5
1929	StL-A	9	6	.600	23	18	8	1	0	149^2	137	11	49	47	11.4	3.25	136	.246	.312	6	.118	-4	17	20	-0	1.3
1930	StL-A	20	12	.625	35	33	23	1	0	271	281	21	70	79	11.7	3.45	141	.268	.315	22	.244	2	36	43	0	4.7
1931	StL-A	14	17	.452	36	33	20	1	0	258	287	17	85	89	13.1	4.40	105	.277	.334	22	.250	6	-0	7	1	1.4
1932	StL-A	15	19	.441	41	32	18	2	1	259^2	269	22	99	86	12.9	4.61	105	.270	.338	12	.146	-2	-4	7	-1	0.6

YEAR	TM/L	W	L	PCT	G	GS	CG	SH	SV	IP	H	HR	BB	SO	RAT	ERA	ERA+	OAV	OOB	BH	AVG	PB	PR	/A	PD	TPI
1933	*Was-A	15	6	.714	34	31	11	1	0	230^{2}	227	19	60	69	11.2	3.82	109	.256	.304	11	.143	1	12	9	1	0.8
1934	Was-A	7	11	.389	24	22	7	1	0	152	184	8	36	36	13.1	4.03	107	.303	.343	7	.156	-1	8	5	-0	0.3
1935	Was-A	0	1	.000	1	1	0	0	0	2^{2}	8	1	2	1	33.8	13.50	32	.533	.588	0	.000	-0	-3	-3	-0	-0.6
	Cle-A	6	6	.500	24	10	2	0	2	91	122	6	17	24	13.8	5.44	83	.312	.342	6	.200	-1	-10	-9	-1	-1.3
	Yr	6	7	.462	25	11	2	0	2	93^{2}	130	7	19	25	14.4	5.67	79	.320	.352	6	.194	-1	-13	-12	-1	-1.9
Total	10	101	98	.508	279	216	107	8	8	1722	1895	117	498	503	12.6	4.19	108	.281	.332	115	.204	6	35	64	0	7.0

● MACK STEWART

Stewart, William Macklin b: 9/23/14, Stevenson, Ala. d: 3/21/60, Macon, Ga. BR/TR, 6′, 167 lbs. Deb: 7/7/44

YEAR	TM/L	W	L	PCT	G	GS	CG	SH	SV	IP	H	HR	BB	SO	RAT	ERA	ERA+	OAV	OOB	BH	AVG	PB	PR	/A	PD	TPI
1944	Chi-N	0	0	—	8	0	0	0	0	12^{1}	11	1	4	3	10.9	1.46	242	.239	.300	0	.000	-0	3	3	-0	0.0
1945	Chi-N	0	1	.000	16	1	0	0	0	28^{1}	37	0	14	9	16.2	4.76	77	.322	.395	1	.333	0	-3	-4	0	-0.1
Total	2	0	1	.000	24	1	0	0	0	40^{2}	48	1	18	12	14.6	3.76	96	.298	.369	1	.250	0	-0	-1	0	-0.1

● PHIL STIDHAM

Stidham, Phillip Wayne b: 11/18/68, Tulsa, Okla. BR/TR, 6′, 180 lbs. Deb: 6/4/94

YEAR	TM/L	W	L	PCT	G	GS	CG	SH	SV	IP	H	HR	BB	SO	RAT	ERA	ERA+	OAV	OOB	BH	AVG	PB	PR	/A	PD	TPI
1994	Det-A	0	0	—	5	0	0	0	0	4^{1}	12	3	4	4	33.2	24.92	19	.571	.640	0	—	0	-10	-10	-0	0.0

● DAVE STIEB

Stieb, David Andrew b: 7/22/57, Santa Ana, Cal. BR/TR, 6′1″, 195 lbs. Deb: 6/29/79

YEAR	TM/L	W	L	PCT	G	GS	CG	SH	SV	IP	H	HR	BB	SO	RAT	ERA	ERA+	OAV	OOB	BH	AVG	PB	PR	/A	PD	TPI
1979	Tor-A	8	8	.500	18	18	7	1	0	129^{1}	139	11	48	52	13.3	4.31	101	.276	.344	0	—	0	-1	0	3	0.3
1980	Tor-A★	12	15	.444	34	32	14	4	0	242^{2}	232	12	83	108	11.9	3.71	116	.260	.327	0	.000	-0	9	16	5	2.2
1981	Tor-A★	11	10	.524	25	25	11	2	0	183^{2}	148	10	61	89	10.8	3.19	124	.223	.299	0	—	0	10	15	2	1.9
1982	Tor-A	17	14	.548	38	38	**19**	**5**	0	**288^{1}**	271	27	75	141	11.0	3.25	138	.248	.299	0	—	0	27	**39**	4	4.2
1983	Tor-A★	17	12	.586	36	36	14	4	0	278	223	21	93	187	10.7	3.04	141	.219	.293	0	—	0	31	**39**	1	3.9
1984	Tor-A★	16	8	.667	35	35	11	2	0	**267**	215	19	88	198	10.6	2.83	**145**	**.221**	.293	0	—	0	34	**37**	1	3.3
1985	*Tor-A★	14	13	.519	36	36	8	2	0	265	206	22	96	167	10.6	**2.48**	**170**	**.213**	.290	0	—	0	**49**	**51**	5	**5.5**
1986	Tor-A	7	12	.368	37	34	1	1	1	205	239	29	87	127	15.0	4.74	89	.297	.376	0	—	0	-13	-12	1	-0.8
1987	Tor-A	13	9	.591	33	31	3	1	0	185	164	16	87	115	12.6	4.09	110	.239	.331	0	—	0	8	8	1	1.0
1988	Tor-A★	16	8	.667	32	31	8	4	0	207^{1}	157	15	79	147	10.8	3.04	129	.210	.296	0	—	0	21	21	1	2.3
1989	*Tor-A	17	8	.680	33	33	3	2	0	206^{2}	164	12	76	101	11.0	3.35	112	.219	.302	0	—	0	12	10	0	1.2
1990	Tor-A★	18	6	.750	33	33	2	2	0	208^{2}	179	11	64	125	10.9	2.93	134	.230	.297	0	—	0	23	23	3	2.9
1991	Tor-A	4	3	.571	9	9	1	0	0	59^{2}	52	4	23	29	11.6	3.17	133	.243	.322	0	—	0	6	7	1	0.8
1992	Tor-A	4	6	.400	21	14	1	0	0	96^{1}	98	9	43	45	13.5	5.04	81	.275	.359	0	—	0	-12	-10	2	-0.9
1993	Chi-A	1	3	.250	4	4	0	0	0	22^{1}	27	1	14	11	16.5	6.04	69	.300	.394	0	—	0	-4	-5	-0	-0.6
1998	Tor-A	1	2	.333	19	3	0	0	2	50^{1}	58	6	17	27	14.3	4.83	96	.284	.354	0	.000	-0	-1	-1	-0	-0.1
Total	16	176	137	.562	443	412	103	30	3	2895^{1}	2572	225	1034	1669	11.6	3.44	122	.239	.314	0	.000	-0	198	240	29	27.1

● FRED STIELY

Stiely, Fred Warren "Lefty" b: 6/1/01, Pillow, Pa. d: 1/6/81, Valley View, Pa. BL/TL, 5′8″, 170 lbs. Deb: 10/6/29

YEAR	TM/L	W	L	PCT	G	GS	CG	SH	SV	IP	H	HR	BB	SO	RAT	ERA	ERA+	OAV	OOB	BH	AVG	PB	PR	/A	PD	TPI
1929	StL-A	1	0	1.000	1	1	1	0	0	9	11	0	3	2	15.0	0.00	—	.297	.366	2	.667	1	4	4	0	0.7
1930	StL-A	0	1	.000	4	2	1	0	0	19	27	4	8	5	17.1	8.53	57	.346	.414	3	.429	1	-8	-8	-0	-0.2
1931	StL-A	0	0	—	4	0	0	0	0	6^{2}	7	0	3	2	14.9	6.75	69	.269	.367	0	—	0	-2	-2	-0	0.0
Total	3	1	1	.500	9	3	2	0	0	34^{2}	45	4	14	9	16.1	5.97	79	.319	.392	5	.500	2	-6	-5	-1	0.5

● DICK STIGMAN

Stigman, Richard Lewis b: 1/24/36, Nimrod, Minn. BR/TL, 6′3″, 200 lbs. Deb: 4/22/60

YEAR	TM/L	W	L	PCT	G	GS	CG	SH	SV	IP	H	HR	BB	SO	RAT	ERA	ERA+	OAV	OOB	BH	AVG	PB	PR	/A	PD	TPI
1960	Cle-A☆	5	11	.313	41	18	3	0	9	133^{2}	118	13	87	104	13.8	4.51	83	.238	.352	8	.222	2	-9	-11	-2	-1.4
1961	Cle-A	2	5	.286	22	6	0	0	0	64^{1}	65	9	25	48	12.6	4.62	85	.264	.332	2	.125	-1	-4	-5	0	-0.5
1962	Min-A	12	5	.706	40	15	6	0	3	142^{2}	122	19	64	116	11.9	3.66	112	.233	.319	2	.044	-4	5	7	-2	0.2
1963	Min-A	15	15	.500	33	33	15	3	0	241	210	32	81	193	10.9	3.25	112	.231	.294	9	.107	-2	10	11	-4	0.6
1964	Min-A	6	15	.286	32	29	5	1	0	190	160	31	70	159	11.1	4.03	89	.225	.299	7	.101	-3	-8	-9	-3	-1.5
1965	Min-A	4	2	.667	33	8	0	0	4	70	59	14	33	70	11.8	4.37	81	.227	.314	2	.133	-0	-7	-6	-1	-0.7
1966	Bos-A	2	1	.667	34	10	1	1	0	81	85	15	46	65	14.7	5.44	70	.268	.363	2	.118	-1	-18	-15	-1	-0.7
Total	7	46	54	.460	235	119	30	5	16	922^{2}	819	133	406	755	12.0	4.03	93	.237	.318	32	.113	-8	-32	-29	-13	-4.0

● ROLLIE STILES

Stiles, Rolland Mays "Lena" b: 11/17/06, Ratcliff, Ark. BR/TR, 6′1.5″, 180 lbs. Deb: 6/19/30

YEAR	TM/L	W	L	PCT	G	GS	CG	SH	SV	IP	H	HR	BB	SO	RAT	ERA	ERA+	OAV	OOB	BH	AVG	PB	PR	/A	PD	TPI
1930	StL-A	3	6	.333	20	7	3	0	0	102	136	10	41	25	15.7	5.91	82	.337	.399	10	.270	0	-14	-12	-1	-0.9
1931	StL-A	3	1	.750	34	2	0	0	0	81	112	2	60	32	19.3	7.22	64	.352	.458	1	.045	-2	-26	-23	-0	-1.2
1933	StL-A	3	7	.300	31	9	6	1	1	115	154	4	47	29	15.9	5.01	93	.327	.390	2	.061	-3	-9	-5	-1	-0.7
Total	3	9	14	.391	85	18	9	1	1	298	402	16	148	86	16.8	5.92	80	.337	.412	13	.141	-5	-49	-40	-2	-2.8

● ARCHIE STIMMEL

Stimmel, Archibald May "Lumbago" b: 5/30/1873, Woodsboro, Md. d: 8/18/58, Frederick, Md. BR/TR, 6′, 175 lbs. Deb: 7/3/00

YEAR	TM/L	W	L	PCT	G	GS	CG	SH	SV	IP	H	HR	BB	SO	RAT	ERA	ERA+	OAV	OOB	BH	AVG	PB	PR	/A	PD	TPI
1900	Cin-N	1	1	.500	2	1	1	0	0	13	18	1	4	2	15.2	6.92	53	.327	.373	1	.200	-0	-5	-5	-0	-0.6
1901	Cin-N	4	14	.222	20	18	14	1	0	153^{1}	170	10	44	55	13.3	4.11	78	.279	.339	5	.081	-5	-13	-15	-3	-2.2
1902	Cin-N	0	4	.000	4	3	3	0	0	26	37	1	12	7	17.7	3.46	87	.333	.408	2	.200	-0	-2	-1	-0	-0.2
Total	3	5	19	.208	26	22	18	1	0	192^{1}	225	12	60	64	14.0	4.21	76	.290	.352	8	.104	-5	-20	-21	-3	-3.0

● CARL STIMSON

Stimson, Carl Remus b: 7/18/1894, Hamburg, Iowa d: 11/9/36, Omaha, Neb. BB/TR, 6′5″, 190 lbs. Deb: 6/6/23

YEAR	TM/L	W	L	PCT	G	GS	CG	SH	SV	IP	H	HR	BB	SO	RAT	ERA	ERA+	OAV	OOB	BH	AVG	PB	PR	/A	PD	TPI
1923	Bos-A	0	0	—	2	0	0	0	0	4	12	0	5	1	40.5	22.50	18	.750	.818	0	.000	-0	-8	-8	0	0.0

● HARRY STINE

Stine, Harry C. b: 2/20/1864, Shenandoah, Pa. d: 6/5/24, Niagara Falls, N.Y TL, 5′6″, 150 lbs. Deb: 7/22/1890

YEAR	TM/L	W	L	PCT	G	GS	CG	SH	SV	IP	H	HR	BB	SO	RAT	ERA	ERA+	OAV	OOB	BH	AVG	PB	PR	/A	PD	TPI
1890	Phi-a	0	1	.000	1	1	1	0	0	8	17	0	4	1	23.6	9.00	43	.415	.467	0	.000	-0	-5	-5	-0	-0.4

● LEE STINE

Stine, Lee Elbert b: 11/17/13, Stillwater, Okla. BR/TR, 5′11″, 185 lbs. Deb: 4/17/34

YEAR	TM/L	W	L	PCT	G	GS	CG	SH	SV	IP	H	HR	BB	SO	RAT	ERA	ERA+	OAV	OOB	BH	AVG	PB	PR	/A	PD	TPI
1934	Chi-A	0	0	—	4	0	0	0	0	11	11	2	10	8	18.0	8.18	58	.268	.423	0	.000	0	-5	-4	-0	0.0
1935	Chi-A	0	0	—	1	0	0	0	0	2	2	1	3	1	22.5	9.00	51	.286	.500	0	—	0	-1	-1	-0	0.1
1936	Cin-N	3	8	.273	40	13	5	1	2	121^{2}	157	6	41	26	15.2	5.03	76	.318	.379	8	.296	3	-14	-16	2	-0.9
1938	NY-A	0	0	—	4	0	0	0	0	8^{2}	9	0	1	4	10.4	1.04	437	.333	.357	1	.500	0	4	3	-0	0.0
Total	4	3	8	.273	49	13	5	1	2	143^{1}	179	9	55	39	15.3	5.09	78	.315	.384	9	.300	4	-16	-18	2	-0.8

● JACK STIVETTS

Stivetts, John Elmer "Happy Jack" b: 3/31/1868, Ashland, Pa. d: 4/18/30, Ashland, Pa. BR/TR, 6′2″, 185 lbs. Deb: 6/26/1889 ♦

YEAR	TM/L	W	L	PCT	G	GS	CG	SH	SV	IP	H	HR	BB	SO	RAT	ERA	ERA+	OAV	OOB	BH	AVG	PB	PR	/A	PD	TPI
1889	StL-a	12	7	.632	26	20	18	2	2	191^{2}	153	4	68	143	**10.6**	**2.25**	**188**	**.212**	**.285**	18	.228	-1	34	42	0	3.3
1890	StL-a	27	21	.563	54	46	41	3	0	419^{1}	399	14	179	289	12.8	3.52	123	.243	.324	65	.288	14	16	37	3	4.9
1891	StL-a	33	22	.600	**64**	56	40	3	1	440	357	15	232	**259**	12.4	2.86	147	.214	.317	92	.305	9	42	**66**	3	**7.7**
1892	*Bos-N	35	16	.686	54	48	45	3	1	415^{2}	346	12	171	180	11.4	3.03	116	.217	.297	71	.296	15	12	22	1	3.7
1893	Bos-N	20	12	.625	38	34	29	1	1	283^{2}	315	17	115	61	14.0	4.41	112	.273	.344	51	.297	7	8	17	-2	1.7
1894	Bos-N	26	14	.650	45	39	30	0	0	338	429	27	127	76	15.2	4.90	116	.306	.369	80	.328	10	16	29	-3	3.0
1895	Bos-N	17	17	.500	38	34	30	0	0	291	341	15	89	111	13.7	4.64	110	.288	.344	30	.190	-7	5	15	-1	0.5
1896	Bos-N	22	14	.611	42	36	31	2	0	329	353	20	99	71	12.6	4.10	111	.272	.327	77	.347	12	9	16	-3	2.1
1897	*Bos-N	11	4	.733	18	15	10	0	0	129^{1}	147	5	43	27	13.6	3.41	131	.284	.345	73	.367	7	13	15	1	2.1
1898	Bos-N	0	1	.000	2	1	1	0	0	12	17	2	7	1	18.0	8.25	45	.333	.414	28	.252	0	-6	-6	0	-0.3
1899	Cle-N	0	4	.000	7	4	3	0	0	38	48	0	25	5	17.8	5.68	65	.308	.410	8	.205	1	-8	-8	2	-0.5
Total	11	203	132	.606	388	333	278	14	5	2887^{2}	2905	131	1155	1223	13.0	3.74	121	.255	.329	593	.298	65	141	247	0	28.2

● CHUCK STOBBS

Stobbs, Charles Klein b: 7/2/29, Wheeling, W.Va. BL/TL, 6′1″, 185 lbs. Deb: 9/15/47

YEAR	TM/L	W	L	PCT	G	GS	CG	SH	SV	IP	H	HR	BB	SO	RAT	ERA	ERA+	OAV	OOB	BH	AVG	PB	PR	/A	PD	TPI
1947	Bos-A	0	1	.000	4	0	0	0	0	9	10	0	10	5	20.0	6.00	65	.294	.455	0	.000	-0	-2	-2	-0	-0.2
1948	Bos-A	0	0	—	6	0	0	0	0	7	9	0	7	4	20.6	6.43	68	.321	.457	0	.000	-0	-2	-2	0	0.0
1949	Bos-A	11	6	.647	26	19	10	0	0	152	145	10	75	70	13.1	4.03	108	.254	.343	11	.208	0	3	6	-1	0.5
1950	Bos-A	12	7	.632	32	21	6	0	1	169^{1}	158	17	88	78	13.3	5.10	96	.250	.346	14	.246	3	-10	-4	1	0.0
1951	Bos-A	10	9	.526	34	25	6	0	0	170	180	15	74	75	13.7	4.76	94	.271	.349	11	.180	-2	-12	-6	-2	-1.0
1952	Chi-A	7	12	.368	38	17	2	0	1	135	118	9	72	73	13.0	3.13	116	.237	.339	3	.079	-1	8	8	1	1.0
1953	Was-A	11	8	.579	27	20	8	0	0	153	146	11	44	67	11.2	3.29	118	.246	.299	10	.227	1	12	10	-0	1.3
1954	Was-A	11	11	.500	31	24	10	3	0	182	189	6	67	67	12.7	4.10	87	.270	.335	7	.137	0	-8	-11	1	-1.1
1955	Was-A	4	14	.222	41	16	2	0	3	140^{1}	169	13	57	60	14.6	5.00	77	.302	.368	6	.171	2	-16	-18	1	-1.8
1956	Was-A	15	15	.500	37	33	15	1	1	240	264	29	54	97	12.0	3.60	120	.279	.318	15	.179	-2	15	19	1	2.1
1957	Was-A	8	20	.286	42	31	5	2	1	211^{2}	235	28	80	114	13.6	5.36	73	.279	.345	16	.211	1	-37	-34	-3	-4.2
1958	Was-A	2	6	.250	19	8	0	0	0	56^{2}	87	7	16	23	16.7	6.04	63	.369	.413	0	.000	-2	-14	-14	0	-1.9

YEAR	TM/L	W	L	PCT	G	GS	CG	SH	SV	IP	H	HR	BB	SO	RAT	ERA	ERA+	OAV	OOB	BH	AVG	PB	PR	/A	PD	TPI
	StL-N	1	3	.250	17	0	0	0	1	39^{2}	40	4	14	25	12.3	3.63	114	.261	.323	1	.250	0	1	2	1	0.3
1959	Was-A	1	8	.111	41	7	0	0	7	90^{2}	82	13	24	50	10.7	2.98	131	.238	.291	2	.105	-1	9	9	-0	0.9
1960	Was-A	12	7	.632	40	13	1	1	2	119^{1}	115	13	38	72	11.8	3.32	117	.252	.313	3	.088	-2	7	8	-2	0.8
1961	Min-A	2	3	.400	24	3	0	0	2	44^{2}	56	8	15	17	14.7	7.46	57	.311	.371	3	.375	1	-17	-16	-1	-1.7
Total	15	107	130	.451	459	238	65	7	19	1920^{1}	2003	183	735	897	13.0	4.29	95	.269	.338	102	.176	-1	-63	-46	-3	-5.0

● WES STOCK Stock, Wesley Gay b: 4/10/34, Longview, Wash. BR/TR, 6'2", 188 lbs. Deb: 4/19/59 C

YEAR	TM/L	W	L	PCT	G	GS	CG	SH	SV	IP	H	HR	BB	SO	RAT	ERA	ERA+	OAV	OOB	BH	AVG	PB	PR	/A	PD	TPI
1959	Bal-A	0	0	—	7	0	0	0	1	12^{2}	16	1	2	8	12.8	3.55	107	.302	.327	0	.000	-0	0	0	-0	0.0
1960	Bal-A	2	2	.500	17	0	0	0	2	34^{1}	26	2	14	23	10.7	2.88	132	.218	.306	0	.000	-1	4	4	1	0.4
1961	Bal-A	5	0	1.000	35	1	0	0	3	71^{2}	58	3	27	47	10.9	3.01	128	.225	.303	0	.000	-1	8	7	2	0.6
1962	Bal-A	3	2	.600	53	0	0	0	3	65	50	7	36	34	12.0	4.43	83	.217	.326	0	.000	-0	-3	-5	3	-0.1
1963	Bal-A	7	0	1.000	47	0	0	0	1	75^{1}	69	11	31	55	11.9	3.94	88	.246	.321	0	.000	-1	-3	-4	1	-0.4
1964	Bal-A	2	0	1.000	14	0	0	0	0	20^{2}	17	5	8	14	10.9	3.92	91	.233	.309	0	.000	-0	-1	-1	0	-0.1
	KC-A	6	3	.667	50	0	0	0	5	93	69	10	34	101	10.4	1.94	197	.213	.296	3	.200	0	17	19	-1	2.0
	Yr	8	3	.727	64	0	0	0	5	113^{2}	86	15	42	115	10.5	2.30	164	.216	.297	3	.158	-0	17	19	-0	1.9
1965	KC-A	0	4	.000	62	2	0	0	4	99^{2}	96	18	40	52	12.6	5.24	67	.251	.328	0	.000	-1	-20	-19	2	-0.8
1966	KC-A	2	2	.500	35	0	0	0	3	44	30	3	21	31	11.0	2.66	128	.199	.309	0	.000	-0	4	4	-0	0.3
1967	KC-A	0	0	—	1	0	0	0	0	1	3	0	2	0	45.0	18.00	18	.500	.625	0	—	0	-2	-2	0	0.0
Total	9	27	13	.675	321	3	0	0	22	517^{1}	434	60	215	365	11.6	3.60	101	.231	.315	3	.051	-4	6	3	7	1.9

● OTIS STOCKSDALE Stocksdale, Otis Hinkley "Old Gray Fox"
b: 8/7/1871, Arcadia, Md. d: 3/15/33, Pennsville, N.J. BL/TR, 5'10.5", 180 lbs. Deb: 7/24/1893

YEAR	TM/L	W	L	PCT	G	GS	CG	SH	SV	IP	H	HR	BB	SO	RAT	ERA	ERA+	OAV	OOB	BH	AVG	PB	PR	/A	PD	TPI
1893	Was-N	2	8	.200	11	11	7	0	0	69	111	4	32	12	19.3	8.22	56	.352	.420	12	.300	2	-27	-28	1	-2.5
1894	Was-N	5	9	.357	18	14	11	0	0	117^{1}	176	10	42	10	17.8	5.06	104	.342	.407	23	.324	1	3	3	1	0.3
1895	Was-N	6	11	.353	20	17	11	0	1	136	199	7	52	23	17.1	6.09	79	.336	.397	23	.311	2	-20	-19	-0	-1.5
	Bos-N	2	2	.500	4	4	1	0	0	23	31	2	8	2	15.3	5.87	87	.316	.368	4	.267	-0	-3	-2	-0	-0.3
	Yr	8	13	.381	24	21	12	0	1	159	230	9	60	25	16.4	6.06	80	.329	.382	27	.303	2	-23	-21	-1	-1.8
1896	Bal-N	0	1	.000	1	0	0	0	0	1^{2}	4	0	2	1	37.8	16.20	26	.444	.583	1	.333	1	-2	-2	-0	-0.7
Total	4	15	31	.326	54	46	30	0	1	347	521	23	136	48	17.8	6.20	80	.341	.405	63	.310	5	-49	-48	1	-4.7

● BOB STODDARD Stoddard, Robert Lyle b: 3/8/57, San Jose, Cal. BR/TR, 6'1", 200 lbs. Deb: 9/4/81

YEAR	TM/L	W	L	PCT	G	GS	CG	SH	SV	IP	H	HR	BB	SO	RAT	ERA	ERA+	OAV	OOB	BH	AVG	PB	PR	/A	PD	TPI
1981	Sea-A	2	1	.667	5	5	1	0	0	34^{2}	35	3	9	22	11.7	2.60	148	.269	.321	0	—	0	4	5	-0	0.4
1982	Sea-A	3	3	.500	9	9	2	1	0	67^{1}	48	7	18	24	9.2	2.41	176	.205	.271	0	—	0	12	14	0	1.2
1983	Sea-A	9	17	.346	35	23	2	1	0	175^{2}	182	29	58	87	12.5	4.41	97	.274	.336	0	—	0	-7	-3	3	-0.1
1984	Sea-A	2	3	.400	27	6	0	0	0	79	86	10	37	39	14.2	5.13	78	.278	.359	0	—	0	-10	-10	1	-0.5
1985	Det-A	0	0	—	8	0	0	0	1	13^{1}	15	3	5	11	13.5	6.75	60	.268	.328	0	—	0	-4	-4	1	0.0
1986	SD-N	1	0	1.000	18	0	0	0	1	23^{1}	20	1	11	17	12.3	2.31	158	.227	.320	0	.000	-0	4	3	-0	0.1
1987	KC-A	1	3	.250	17	2	0	0	1	40	51	3	22	23	17.1	4.27	107	.313	.404	0	—	0	1	1	1	0.2
Total	7	18	27	.400	119	45	5	2	3	433^{1}	437	56	160	223	12.7	4.03	103	.266	.336	0	.000	-0	0	6	5	1.3

● TIM STODDARD Stoddard, Timothy Paul b: 1/24/53, E.Chicago, Ind. BR/TR, 6'7", 250 lbs. Deb: 9/7/75

YEAR	TM/L	W	L	PCT	G	GS	CG	SH	SV	IP	H	HR	BB	SO	RAT	ERA	ERA+	OAV	OOB	BH	AVG	PB	PR	/A	PD	TPI
1975	Chi-A	0	0	—	1	0	0	0	0	1	2	1	0	0	18.0	9.00	43	.400	.400	0	—	0	-1	-1	0	0.0
1978	Bal-A	0	1	.000	8	0	0	0	0	18	22	3	8	14	16.0	6.00	58	.301	.386	0	—	0	-4	-5	0	0.0
1979	*Bal-A	3	1	.750	29	0	0	0	3	58	44	3	19	47	9.8	1.71	235	.212	.278	0	—	0	16	15	-0	1.2
1980	Bal-A	5	3	.625	64	0	0	0	26	86	72	2	38	64	11.6	2.51	157	.233	.319	0	—	0	15	14	-1	2.1
1981	Bal-A	4	2	.667	31	0	0	0	7	37^{1}	38	6	18	32	14.0	3.86	94	.268	.358	0	—	0	-1	-1	-0	-0.2
1982	Bal-A	3	4	.429	50	0	0	0	12	56	53	4	29	42	13.3	4.02	100	.249	.342	0	—	0	0	0	-0	0.0
1983	Bal-A	4	3	.571	47	0	0	0	9	57^{2}	65	10	29	50	14.8	6.09	65	.293	.377	0	—	0	-13	-14	0	-1.9
1984	*Chi-N	10	6	.625	58	0	0	0	7	92	77	9	57	87	13.2	3.82	102	.236	.352	1	.091	-1	-2	1	-1	0.0
1985	SD-N	1	6	.143	44	0	0	0	1	60	63	3	37	42	15.0	4.65	76	.269	.369	0	.000	-1	-7	-7	-1	-1.0
1986	SD-N	1	3	.250	30	0	0	0	0	45^{1}	33	6	34	47	13.3	3.77	97	.200	.337	1	.250	1	-0	-1	0	0.1
	NY-A	4	1	.800	24	0	0	0	0	49^{1}	41	6	23	34	11.7	3.83	107	.232	.320	0	—	0	2	1	0	0.1
1987	NY-A	4	3	.571	57	0	0	0	8	92^{2}	83	13	30	78	11.0	3.50	125	.235	.295	0	—	0	10	9	-1	0.7
1988	NY-A	2	2	.500	28	0	0	0	3	55	62	5	27	33	14.9	6.38	62	.286	.370	0	—	0	-15	-15	0	-1.0
1989	Cle-A	0	0	—	14	0	0	0	0	21^{1}	25	1	7	12	13.5	2.95	134	.313	.368	0	—	0	2	2	0	-0.1
Total	13	41	35	.539	485	0	0	0	76	729^{2}	680	72	356	582	12.9	3.95	100	.250	.339	2	.100	-0	2	-0	-3	-0.0

● ART STOKES Stokes, Arthur Milton b: 9/13/1896, Emmitsburg, Md. d: 6/3/62, Titusville, Pa. BR/TR, 5'10.5", 155 lbs. Deb: 5/5/25

YEAR	TM/L	W	L	PCT	G	GS	CG	SH	SV	IP	H	HR	BB	SO	RAT	ERA	ERA+	OAV	OOB	BH	AVG	PB	PR	/A	PD	TPI
1925	Phi-A	1	1	.500	12	0	0	0	0	24^{1}	24	0	10	7	13.3	4.07	114	.270	.356	0	.000	-0	1	2	-0	0.0

● DICK STONE Stone, Charles Richard b: 12/5/11, Oklahoma City, Okla d: 2/18/80, Oklahoma City, Okla. BL/TL, 5'9", 153 lbs. Deb: 8/26/45

YEAR	TM/L	W	L	PCT	G	GS	CG	SH	SV	IP	H	HR	BB	SO	RAT	ERA	ERA+	OAV	OOB	BH	AVG	PB	PR	/A	PD	TPI
1945	Was-A	0	0	—	3	0	0	0	0	5	6	0	2	0	14.4	0.00	—	.316	.381	0	—	0	2	2	0	0.0

● DEAN STONE Stone, Darrah Dean b: 9/1/30, Moline, Ill. BL/TL, 6'4", 205 lbs. Deb: 9/13/53

YEAR	TM/L	W	L	PCT	G	GS	CG	SH	SV	IP	H	HR	BB	SO	RAT	ERA	ERA+	OAV	OOB	BH	AVG	PB	PR	/A	PD	TPI
1953	Was-A	0	1	.000	3	1	0	0	0	8^{2}	13	0	5	5	18.7	8.31	47	.361	.439	0	.000	-0	-4	-4	-0	-0.4
1954	Was-A★	12	10	.545	31	23	10	2	0	178^{2}	161	7	69	87	11.6	3.22	110	.240	.312	5	.096	-0	10	7	-3	0.5
1955	Was-A	6	13	.316	43	24	5	1	1	180	180	14	114	84	14.9	4.15	92	.267	.375	2	.043	-4	-4	-6	-2	-1.1
1956	Was-A	5	7	.417	41	21	2	0	3	132	148	10	93	86	16.9	6.27	69	.282	.397	3	.088	-1	-31	-29	-1	-2.5
1957	Was-A	0	0	—	3	0	0	0	0	3^{1}	5	0	2	3	18.9	8.10	48	.357	.438	0	—	0	-2	-2	-0	0.0
	Bos-A	1	3	.250	17	8	0	0	1	51^{1}	56	5	35	32	16.0	5.08	78	.284	.392	0	.000	-1	-7	-6	1	-0.5
	Yr	1	3	.250	20	8	0	0	1	54^{2}	61	5	37	35	16.1	5.27	76	.288	.394	0	.000	-1	-9	-8	1	-0.5
1959	StL-N	0	1	.000	18	1	0	0	1	30	30	4	16	17	13.8	4.20	101	.273	.365	0	.000	-0	-1	0	-0	-0.1
1962	Hou-N	3	2	.600	15	7	2	2	0	52^{1}	61	4	20	31	14.1	4.47	84	.295	.360	4	.250	1	-3	-4	0	-0.2
	Chi-A	1	0	1.000	27	0	0	0	5	30^{1}	28	3	9	23	11.3	3.26	120	.255	.317	1	.500	1	2	2	-0	0.2
1963	Bal-A	1	2	.333	17	0	0	0	1	19^{1}	23	0	10	12	15.4	5.12	68	.307	.388	0	—	0	-3	-4	0	-0.5
Total	8	29	39	.426	215	85	19	5	12	686	705	47	373	380	14.3	4.47	86	.269	.363	15	.088	-6	-43	-46	-5	-4.6

● DWIGHT STONE Stone, Dwight Ely b: 8/2/1886, Holt Co., Neb. d: 6/3/76, Glendale, Cal. BR/TR, 6'1.5", 170 lbs. Deb: 4/13/13

YEAR	TM/L	W	L	PCT	G	GS	CG	SH	SV	IP	H	HR	BB	SO	RAT	ERA	ERA+	OAV	OOB	BH	AVG	PB	PR	/A	PD	TPI
1913	StL-A	2	6	.250	18	7	4	1	0	91	94	0	46	37	14.5	3.56	82	.267	.363	9	.273	2	-6	-6	1	-0.2
1914	KC-F	8	14	.364	39	22	6	0	0	186^{2}	205	8	77	88	14.0	4.34	64	.281	.356	7	.121	-4	-30	-32	1	-3.7
Total	2	10	20	.333	57	29	10	1	0	277^{2}	299	8	123	125	14.2	4.08	69	.276	.358	16	.176	-2	-36	-39	2	-3.9

● ARNIE STONE Stone, Edwin Arnold b: 10/9/1892, North Creek, N.Y. d: 7/29/48, Hudson Falls, N.Y BR/TL, 6', 180 lbs. Deb: 7/30/23

YEAR	TM/L	W	L	PCT	G	GS	CG	SH	SV	IP	H	HR	BB	SO	RAT	ERA	ERA+	OAV	OOB	BH	AVG	PB	PR	/A	PD	TPI
1923	Pit-N	0	1	.000	9	0	0	0	0	12^{1}	19	0	4	2	16.8	8.03	50	.352	.397	0	.000	-0	-6	-6	-1	-0.4
1924	Pit-N	4	2	.667	26	2	1	0	0	64	57	0	15	7	10.1	2.95	130	.259	.306	2	.133	-1	6	6	0	0.4
Total	2	4	3	.571	35	2	1	0	0	76^{1}	76	0	19	9	11.2	3.77	102	.277	.324	2	.125	-1	1	1	-0	0.0

● GEORGE STONE Stone, George Heard b: 7/9/46, Ruston, La. BL/TL, 6'3", 205 lbs. Deb: 9/15/67

YEAR	TM/L	W	L	PCT	G	GS	CG	SH	SV	IP	H	HR	BB	SO	RAT	ERA	ERA+	OAV	OOB	BH	AVG	PB	PR	/A	PD	TPI
1967	Atl-N	0	0	—	2	1	0	0	0	7^{1}	8	0	1	5	11.0	4.91	68	.267	.290	0	.000	-0	-1	-1	0	0.0
1968	Atl-N	7	4	.636	17	10	2	0	0	75	63	9	19	52	9.8	2.76	108	.222	.271	9	.333	3	2	2	-1	0.5
1969	*Atl-N	13	10	.565	36	20	3	0	3	165^{1}	166	20	48	102	11.9	3.65	99	.260	.317	11	.186	1	-1	-1	-1	0.0
1970	Atl-N	11	11	.500	35	30	9	2	0	207^{1}	218	27	50	131	11.9	3.86	111	.267	.314	17	.236	4	4	10	3	1.6
1971	Atl-N	6	8	.429	27	24	4	2	0	172^{2}	186	19	35	110	11.8	3.60	103	.274	.315	11	.177	-0	-3	2	-0	0.1
1972	Atl-N	6	11	.353	31	16	2	1	1	111	143	18	44	63	15.5	5.51	69	.315	.380	5	.200	1	-25	-21	1	-2.8
1973	*NY-N	12	3	.800	27	20	2	0	1	148	157	16	31	77	11.4	2.80	129	.274	.311	13	.271	2	14	13	1	1.7
1974	NY-N	2	7	.222	15	13	1	0	0	77	103	10	21	29	14.5	5.03	71	.322	.364	3	.115	-1	-12	-13	0	-1.4
1975	NY-N	3	3	.500	13	11	1	0	0	57	75	3	21	21	15.2	5.05	68	.323	.379	3	.167	0	-9	-10	1	-0.9
Total	9	60	57	.513	203	145	24	5	5	1020^{2}	1119	122	270	590	12.4	3.89	96	.278	.326	72	.212	10	-31	-19	4	-1.2

● ROCKY STONE Stone, John Vernon b: 8/23/18, Redding, Cal. d: 11/12/86, Fountain Valley, Cal. BR/TR, 6', 200 lbs. Deb: 5/2/43

YEAR	TM/L	W	L	PCT	G	GS	CG	SH	SV	IP	H	HR	BB	SO	RAT	ERA	ERA+	OAV	OOB	BH	AVG	PB	PR	/A	PD	TPI
1943	Cin-N	0	1	.000	13	0	0	0	0	24^{2}	23	0	8	11	11.3	4.38	76	.237	.295	1	.250	0	-3	-3	-1	-0.2

● STEVE STONE

Stone, Steven Michael b: 7/14/47, Euclid, Ohio BR/TR, 5'10", 175 lbs. Deb: 4/8/71

YEAR	TM/L	W	L	PCT	G	GS	CG	SH	SV	IP	H	HR	BB	SO	RAT	ERA	ERA+	OAV	OOB	BH	AVG	PB	PR	/A	PD	TPI
1971	SF-N	5	9	.357	24	19	2	2	0	110^2	110	9	55	63	13.7	4.15	82	.259	.349	0	.000	-2	-8	-9	2	-1.2
1972	SF-N	6	8	.429	27	16	4	1	0	123^2	97	11	49	85	10.8	2.98	117	.218	.298	4	.118	-1	6	7	0	0.7
1973	Chi-A	6	11	.353	36	22	3	0	1	176^1	163	11	82	138	12.9	4.24	93	.245	.335	0	—	0	-8	-5	0	-0.5
1974	Chi-N	8	6	.571	38	23	1	0	0	169^2	185	19	64	90	13.4	4.14	92	.278	.345	7	.121	-3	-10	-6	1	-0.7
1975	Chi-N	12	8	.600	33	32	6	1	0	214^1	198	24	80	139	11.9	3.95	97	.245	.317	8	.111	-2	-8	-3	0	-0.4
1976	Chi-N	3	6	.333	17	15	1	1	0	75	70	6	21	33	11.3	4.08	95	.250	.309	3	.143	-1	-5	-2	-1	-0.4
1977	Chi-A	15	12	.556	31	31	8	0	0	207^1	228	25	80	124	13.6	4.51	90	.281	.350	0	—	0	-10	-10	-0	-1.1
1978	Chi-A	12	12	.500	30	30	6	1	0	212	196	19	84	118	12.0	4.37	87	.247	.321	0	—	0	-14	-13	-1	-1.5
1979	*Bal-A	11	7	.611	32	32	3	0	0	186	173	31	73	96	12.0	3.77	106	.248	.320	0	—	0	9	5	1	0.6
1980	Bal-A★	**25**	7	**.781**	37	37	9	1	0	250^2	224	22	101	149	11.9	3.23	122	.240	.319	0	—	0	22	20	-2	2.2
1981	Bal-A	4	7	.364	15	12	0	0	0	62^2	63	7	27	30	13.1	4.60	79	.266	.343	0	—	0	-7	-7	-0	-1.1
Total	11	107	93	.535	320	269	43	7	1	1788^1	1707	184	716	1065	12.4	3.97	97	.253	.328	22	.100	-9	-32	-22	-0	-3.4

● TIGE STONE

Stone, William Arthur b: 9/18/01, Macon, Ga. d: 1/1/60, Jacksonville, Fla. BR/TR, 5'8", 145 lbs. Deb: 8/23/23 ♦

YEAR	TM/L	W	L	PCT	G	GS	CG	SH	SV	IP	H	HR	BB	SO	RAT	ERA	ERA+	OAV	OOB	BH	AVG	PB	PR	/A	PD	TPI
1923	StL-N	0	0	—	1	0	0	0	0	3	5	1	3	1	24.0	12.00	33	.455	.571	1	1.000	0	-3	-3	0	0.1

● BILL STONEMAN

Stoneman, William Hambly b: 4/7/44, Oak Park, Ill. BR/TR, 5'10", 170 lbs. Deb: 7/16/67

YEAR	TM/L	W	L	PCT	G	GS	CG	SH	SV	IP	H	HR	BB	SO	RAT	ERA	ERA+	OAV	OOB	BH	AVG	PB	PR	/A	PD	TPI
1967	Chi-N	2	4	.333	28	2	0	0	4	63	51	7	22	52	10.4	3.29	108	.223	.291	0	.000	-1	1	2	-1	0.0
1968	Chi-N	0	1	.000	18	0	0	0	0	29^1	35	6	14	18	15.3	5.52	57	.310	.391	0	.000	-0	-8	-8	-0	-0.3
1969	Mon-N	11	19	.367	42	36	8	5	0	235^2	233	26	123	185	14.1	4.39	84	.261	.358	4	.055	-3	-21	-19	-1	-2.6
1970	Mon-N	7	15	.318	40	30	5	3	0	207^2	209	26	109	176	14.4	4.59	90	.263	.361	6	.100	-2	-13	-11	-1	-1.4
1971	Mon-N	17	16	.515	39	39	20	3	0	294^2	243	20	146	251	12.0	3.15	112	.225	.321	12	.129	-1	10	12	0	1.4
1972	Mon-N★	12	14	.462	36	35	13	4	0	250^2	213	15	102	171	11.4	2.98	119	.229	.308	6	.080	-4	13	16	0	1.1
1973	Mon-N	4	8	.333	29	17	0	0	1	96^2	120	12	55	48	16.9	6.80	56	.310	.404	1	.050	-1	-34	-32	0	-3.6
1974	Cal-A	1	8	.111	13	11	0	0	0	58^2	78	8	31	33	17.0	6.14	56	.322	.404	0	—	0	-16	-18	0	-2.3
Total	8	54	85	.388	245	170	46	15	5	1236^1	1182	120	602	934	13.3	4.08	90	.253	.344	29	.086	-13	-68	-57	-3	-7.7

● LIL STONER

Stoner, Ulysses Simpson Grant b: 2/28/1899, Bowie, Tex. d: 6/26/66, Enid, Okla. BR/TR, 5'9.5", 180 lbs. Deb: 4/15/22

YEAR	TM/L	W	L	PCT	G	GS	CG	SH	SV	IP	H	HR	BB	SO	RAT	ERA	ERA+	OAV	OOB	BH	AVG	PB	PR	/A	PD	TPI
1922	Det-A	4	4	.500	17	7	2	0	0	62^2	76	3	35	18	16.4	7.04	55	.315	.409	2	.100	-1	-21	-22	1	-2.3
1924	Det-A	11	11	.500	36	25	10	1	0	215^2	271	13	65	66	14.2	4.72	87	.316	.367	15	.195	1	-12	-14	-1	-1.2
1925	Det-A	10	9	.526	34	18	8	0	1	152	166	6	53	51	13.5	4.26	101	.283	.352	16	.291	4	2	1	-3	0.1
1926	Det-A	7	10	.412	32	22	7	0	0	159^2	179	11	63	57	13.8	5.47	74	.291	.359	9	.170	-2	-26	-25	-0	-2.4
1927	Det-A	10	13	.435	38	24	13	0	5	215	251	9	77	63	13.9	3.98	106	.301	.362	8	.108	-6	4	6	-2	-0.2
1928	Det-A	5	8	.385	36	11	4	0	4	126^1	151	16	42	29	14.0	4.35	95	.296	.353	7	.179	-1	-4	-3	-2	-0.6
1929	Det-A	3	3	.500	24	3	1	0	4	53	57	2	31	12	15.3	5.26	82	.288	.390	1	.067	-2	-6	-6	2	-0.7
1930	Pit-N	0	0	—	5	0	0	0	0	5^2	7	2	3	1	15.9	4.76	105	.318	.400	0	—	0	0	0	0	0.0
1931	Phi-N	0	0	—	7	1	0	0	0	13^2	22	0	5	2	17.8	6.59	64	.373	.422	0	.000	-1	-4	-4	-0	-0.1
Total	9	50	58	.463	229	111	45	1	14	1003^2	1180	62	374	299	14.2	4.76	87	.301	.366	58	.172	-7	-66	-67	-5	-7.4

● JIM STOOPS

Stoops, James Wellington b: 6/30/72, Edison, N.J. BR/TR, 6'2", 180 lbs. Deb: 9/9/98

YEAR	TM/L	W	L	PCT	G	GS	CG	SH	SV	IP	H	HR	BB	SO	RAT	ERA	ERA+	OAV	OOB	BH	AVG	PB	PR	/A	PD	TPI
1998	Col-N	1	0	1.000	3	0	0	0	0	4	5	1	3	0	20.3	2.25	225	.385	.529	0	—	0	1	1	0	0.3

● MEL STOTTLEMYRE

Stottlemyre, Melvin Leon Jr. b: 12/28/63, Prosser, Wash. BR/TR, 6', 190 lbs. Deb: 7/17/90 F

YEAR	TM/L	W	L	PCT	G	GS	CG	SH	SV	IP	H	HR	BB	SO	RAT	ERA	ERA+	OAV	OOB	BH	AVG	PB	PR	/A	PD	TPI
1990	KC-A	0	1	.000	13	2	0	0	0	31^1	35	3	12	14	13.5	4.88	78	.280	.343	0	—	0	-3	-4	0	-0.1

● MEL STOTTLEMYRE

Stottlemyre, Melvin Leon Sr. b: 11/13/41, Hazleton, Mo. BR/TR, 6'2", 190 lbs. Deb: 8/12/64 FC

YEAR	TM/L	W	L	PCT	G	GS	CG	SH	SV	IP	H	HR	BB	SO	RAT	ERA	ERA+	OAV	OOB	BH	AVG	PB	PR	/A	PD	TPI
1964	*NY-A	9	3	.750	13	12	5	2	0	96	77	3	35	49	10.7	2.06	176	.219	.294	9	.243	2	17	17	1	2.5
1965	NY-A☆	20	9	.690	37	37	**18**	4	0	**291**	250	18	88	155	10.7	2.63	129	.233	.295	13	.131	1	27	25	6	3.2
1966	NY-A★	12	20	.375	37	35	9	3	1	251	239	18	82	146	11.5	3.80	87	.253	.313	11	.138	1	-10	-13	4	-1.1
1967	NY-A	15	15	.500	36	36	10	4	0	255	235	20	88	151	11.5	2.96	105	.248	.313	8	.098	-3	8	5	6	0.8
1968	NY-A★	21	12	.636	36	36	19	6	0	278^2	243	21	65	140	10.0	2.45	118	.234	.281	13	.143	2	16	14	2	2.2
1969	NY-A★	20	14	.588	39	39	**24**	3	0	303	267	19	97	113	11.0	2.82	123	.239	.303	18	.178	5	27	22	8	3.8
1970	NY-A★	15	13	.536	37	37	14	0	0	271	262	23	84	126	11.7	3.09	114	.255	.315	16	.188	9	19	13	2	2.5
1971	NY-A	16	12	.571	35	35	19	7	0	269^2	234	16	69	132	10.2	2.87	113	.233	.285	16	.170	2	18	11	3	1.7
1972	NY-A	14	18	.438	36	36	9	7	0	260	250	13	85	110	11.7	3.22	92	.254	.316	16	.200	3	-5	-8	3	-0.3
1973	NY-A	16	16	.500	38	38	19	4	0	273	259	13	79	95	11.3	3.07	119	.253	.310	0	—	0	23	18	2	2.2
1974	NY-A	6	7	.462	16	15	6	0	0	113	119	7	37	40	12.7	3.58	98	.272	.335	0	—	0	0	-1	-1	-0.2
Total	11	164	139	.541	360	356	152	40	1	2661^1	2435	171	809	1257	11.1	2.97	112	.245	.304	120	.160	21	139	102	36	17.3

● TODD STOTTLEMYRE

Stottlemyre, Todd Vernon b: 5/20/65, Sunnyside, Wash. BL/TR, 6'3", 195 lbs. Deb: 4/6/88 F

YEAR	TM/L	W	L	PCT	G	GS	CG	SH	SV	IP	H	HR	BB	SO	RAT	ERA	ERA+	OAV	OOB	BH	AVG	PB	PR	/A	PD	TPI
1988	Tor-A	4	8	.333	28	16	0	0	0	98	109	15	46	67	14.6	5.69	69	.283	.366	0	—	0	-19	-19	-0	-2.1
1989	*Tor-A	7	7	.500	27	18	0	0	0	127^2	137	11	44	63	13.1	3.88	97	.282	.348	0	—	0	0	-2	-1	-0.3
1990	Tor-A	13	17	.433	33	33	4	0	0	203	214	18	69	115	12.9	4.34	91	.274	.339	0	—	0	-10	-9	1	-1.1
1991	*Tor-A	15	8	.652	34	34	1	0	0	219	194	21	75	116	11.5	3.78	111	.235	.308	0	—	0	8	10	-0	0.8
1992	*Tor-A	12	11	.522	28	27	6	2	0	174	175	20	63	98	12.8	4.50	91	.262	.334	0	—	0	-11	-8	-1	-1.2
1993	*Tor-A	11	12	.478	30	28	1	1	0	176^2	204	11	69	98	14.1	4.84	89	.292	.358	0	—	0	-10	-10	-1	-1.2
1994	Tor-A	7	7	.500	26	19	3	1	1	140^2	149	19	48	105	13.1	4.22	114	.275	.342	0	—	0	9	9	-1	0.7
1995	Oak-A	14	7	.667	31	31	2	0	0	209^2	228	26	80	205	13.5	4.55	98	.276	.344	0	.000	-0	4	-2	-1	-0.3
1996	*StL-N	14	11	.560	34	33	5	2	0	223^1	191	30	93	194	11.6	3.87	108	.231	.312	15	.227	4	9	8	1	1.2
1997	StL-N	12	9	.571	28	28	0	0	0	181	155	16	65	160	11.5	3.88	107	.231	.310	13	.236	6	6	5	-1	1.1
1998	StL-N	9	9	.500	23	23	3	0	0	161^1	146	20	51	147	11.2	3.51	119	.240	.303	12	.226	2	13	12	1	1.6
	*Tex-A	5	4	.556	10	10	0	0	0	60^1	68	5	30	57	14.6	4.33	112	.282	.362	0	—	0	2	3	-1	0.2
Total	11	123	110	.528	332	300	25	6	1	1974^2	1970	212	733	1425	12.7	4.23	100	.261	.332	40	.229	12	1	-1	-3	-0.6

● ALLYN STOUT

Stout, Allyn McClelland "Fish Hook" b: 10/31/04, Peoria, Ill. d: 12/22/74, Sikeston, Mo. BR/TR, 5'10", 167 lbs. Deb: 5/16/31

YEAR	TM/L	W	L	PCT	G	GS	CG	SH	SV	IP	H	HR	BB	SO	RAT	ERA	ERA+	OAV	OOB	BH	AVG	PB	PR	/A	PD	TPI
1931	StL-N	6	0	1.000	30	3	1	0	3	72^2	87	2	34	40	15.1	4.21	93	.305	.381	2	.105	-1	-3	-2	1	-0.2
1932	StL-N	4	5	.444	36	3	1	0	1	73^2	87	5	28	32	14.5	4.40	89	.305	.375	2	.100	-1	-4	-4	1	-0.5
1933	StL-N	0	0	—	1	0	0	0	0	2	1	0	1	1	9.0	0.00	—	.167	.286	0	—	0	1	1	0	0.0
	Cin-N	2	3	.400	23	5	2	0	0	71^1	85	3	26	29	14.0	3.79	90	.295	.354	4	.182	-0	-4	-3	-1	-0.3
	Yr	2	3	.400	24	5	2	0	0	73^1	86	3	27	30	13.9	3.68	92	.293	.352	4	.182	-0	-3	-2	-1	-0.3
1934	Cin-N	6	8	.429	41	16	4	0	1	140^2	170	10	47	51	14.1	4.86	84	.297	.354	8	.186	0	-13	-12	-0	-1.1
1935	NY-N	1	4	.200	40	2	0	0	5	88	99	7	37	29	14.3	4.91	79	.289	.365	2	.133	0	-9	-10	-1	-0.7
1943	Bos-N	1	0	1.000	9	0	0	0	1	9^1	17	1	4	3	20.3	6.75	51	.378	.429	0	.000	-0	-3	-3	-0	-0.5
Total	6	20	20	.500	180	29	8	0	11	457^2	546	28	177	185	14.5	4.54	85	.299	.365	18	.149	-3	-35	-34	-1	-3.3

● JESSE STOVALL

Stovall, Jesse Cramer "Scout" b: 7/24/1875, Leeds, Mo. d: 7/12/55, San Diego, Cal. BL/TR, 6', 175 lbs. Deb: 8/31/03 F

YEAR	TM/L	W	L	PCT	G	GS	CG	SH	SV	IP	H	HR	BB	SO	RAT	ERA	ERA+	OAV	OOB	BH	AVG	PB	PR	/A	PD	TPI
1903	Cle-A	5	1	.833	6	6	6	2	0	57	44	0	21	12	10.7	2.05	139	.213	.294	1	.045	-2	6	5	-1	0.2
1904	Det-A	2	13	.133	22	17	13	1	0	146^2	170	3	45	41	14.2	4.42	58	.291	.358	11	.196	0	-30	-30	0	-2.8
Total	2	7	14	.333	28	23	19	3	0	203^2	214	3	66	53	13.2	3.76	70	.270	.341	12	.154	-2	-24	-25	-0	-2.6

● HARRY STOVEY

Stovey, Harry Duffield (b: Harry Duffield Stowe)
b: 12/20/1856, Philadelphia, Pa. d: 9/20/37, New Bedford, Mass BR/TR, 5'11.5", 175 lbs. Deb: 5/1/1880 M♦

YEAR	TM/L	W	L	PCT	G	GS	CG	SH	SV	IP	H	HR	BB	SO	RAT	ERA	ERA+	OAV	OOB	BH	AVG	PB	PR	/A	PD	TPI
1880	Wor-N	0	0	—	2	0	0	0	0	6	8	0	3	3	16.5	4.50	58	.308	.379	94	.265	0	-1	-1	-0	0.0
1883	Phi-a	0	0	—	1	0	0	0	0	3	5	0	0	4	15.0	9.00	39	.357	.357	128	.304	0	-2	-2	-0	0.0
1886	Phi-a	0	0	—	1	0	0	0	0	0^1	2	0	0	0	54.0	27.00	13	.667	.667	144	.294	0	-1	-1	0	0.0
Total	3	0	0	—	4	0	0	0	0	9^1	15	0	3	7	17.4	6.75	43	.349	.391	1771	.289	1	-4	-4	-0	0.0

● HAL STOWE

Stowe, Harold Rudolph b: 8/29/37, Gastonia, N.C. BL/TL, 6', 170 lbs. Deb: 9/30/60

YEAR	TM/L	W	L	PCT	G	GS	CG	SH	SV	IP	H	HR	BB	SO	RAT	ERA	ERA+	OAV	OOB	BH	AVG	PB	PR	/A	PD	TPI
1960	NY-A	0	0	—	1	0	0	0	0	1	0	0	1	0	9.0	9.00	40	.000	.500	0	—	0	-1	-1	-0	0.0

YEAR	TM/L	W	L	PCT	G	GS	CG	SH	SV	IP	H	HR	BB	SO	RAT	ERA	ERA+	OAV	OOB	BH	AVG	PB	PR	/A	PD	TPI
● **MIKE STRAHLER**	Strahler, Michael Wayne b: 3/14/47, Chicago, Ill. BR/TR, 6'4", 180 lbs. Deb: 9/12/70																									
1970	LA-N	1	1	.500	6	0	0	0	1	18^2	13	1	10	11	11.1	1.45	265	.194	.299	2	.250	0	5	5	0	0.6
1971	LA-N	0	0	—	6	0	0	0	0	12^2	10	1	8	7	12.8	2.84	114	.217	.333	0	.000	-0	1	1	-0	0.0
1972	LA-N	1	2	.333	19	2	1	0	0	47	42	5	22	25	12.4	3.26	102	.237	.325	2	.182	1	1	0	-0	0.1
1973	Det-A	4	5	.444	22	11	1	0	0	80^1	84	7	39	37	13.9	4.37	94	.273	.356	0	—	0	-5	-3	-1	-0.3
Total	4	6	8	.429	53	13	2	0	1	158^2	149	14	79	80	13.0	3.57	105	.249	.339	4	.200	1	2	3	-1	0.4
● **DICK STRAHS**	Strahs, Richard Bernard b: 12/4/23, Evanston, Ill. d: 5/26/88, Las Vegas, Nev. BL/TR, 6', 192 lbs. Deb: 7/24/54																									
1954	Chi-A	0	0	—	9	0	0	0	1	14^1	16	0	8	8	15.1	5.65	66	.271	.358	0	.000	-0	-3	-3	0	0.0
● **LES STRAKER**	Straker, Lester Paul (Bolnalda) b: 10/10/59, Ciudad Bolivar, Venezuela BR/TR, 6'1", 193 lbs. Deb: 4/11/87																									
1987	*Min-A	8	10	.444	31	26	1	0	0	154^1	150	24	59	76	12.3	4.37	106	.257	.328	0	—	0	1	4	-2	0.3
1988	Min-A	2	5	.286	16	14	1	1	1	82^2	86	8	25	23	12.1	3.92	104	.276	.329	0	—	0	0	1	0	0.1
Total	2	10	15	.400	47	40	2	1	1	237	236	32	84	99	12.2	4.22	105	.264	.328	0	—	0	2	5	-1	0.4
● **BOB STRAMPE**	Strampe, Robert Edwin b: 6/13/50, Janesville, Wis. BB/TR, 6'1", 185 lbs. Deb: 5/10/72																									
1972	Det-A	0	0	—	7	0	0	0	0	4^2	6	0	7	4	25.1	11.57	27	.300	.481	0	—	0	-4	-4	-0	0.0
● **PAUL STRAND**	Strand, Paul Edward b: 12/19/1893, Carbonado, Wash. d: 7/2/74, Salt Lake City, Utah BR/TL, 6'0.5", 190 lbs. Deb: 5/15/13 ♦																									
1913	Bos-N	0	0	—	7	0	0	0	0	17	22	1	12	6	18.0	2.12	155	.393	.500	1	.167	-0	2	2	0	0.0
1914	Bos-N	6	2	.750	16	3	1	0	0	55^1	47	1	23	33	11.5	2.44	113	.235	.317	8	.333	2	2	2	-0	0.5
1915	Bos-N	1	1	.500	6	2	2	0	1	22^2	26	0	3	13	11.5	2.38	109	.295	.319	2	.091	-0	1	1	-1	-0.1
Total	3	7	3	.700	29	5	3	0	1	95	95	2	38	52	12.7	2.37	119	.276	.350	49	.224	2	5	5	-1	0.4
● **SCOTT STRATTON**	Stratton, C. Scott b: 10/2/1869, Campbellsburg, Ky. d: 3/8/39, Louisville, Ky. BL/TR, 6', 180 lbs. Deb: 4/21/1888 ♦																									
1888	Lou-a	10	17	.370	33	28	28	2	0	269^2	287	7	53	97	11.8	3.64	85	.263	.306	64	.257	5	-17	-17	-1	-1.0
1889	Lou-a	3	13	.188	19	17	13	0	1	133^2	157	6	42	42	13.9	3.23	119	.284	.342	66	.288	4	9	9	2	1.4
1890	*Lou-a	34	14	**.708**	50	49	44	4	0	431	398	3	61	207	**9.9**	**2.36**	**163**	.238	**.270**	61	.323	16	**72**	**71**	6	**8.9**
1891	Pit-N	0	2	.000	2	2	2	0	0	18^1	16	0	5	5	10.3	2.45	134	.225	.276	1	.125	-1	2	2	1	0.2
	Lou-a	6	13	.316	20	20	20	1	0	172	204	10	34	52	12.8	4.08	90	.285	.324	27	.235	1	-7	-8	3	-0.4
1892	Lou-N	21	19	.525	42	40	39	2	0	351^2	342	1	70	93	10.8	2.92	105	.245	.285	56	.256	10	14	6	2	1.8
1893	Lou-N	12	23	.343	37	35	34	1	0	314^2	445	8	100	43	15.8	5.43	81	.323	.373	49	.226	3	-27	-36	6	-2.1
1894	Lou-N	1	5	.167	7	5	4	0	0	43	72	3	13	3	18.4	8.37	61	.367	.415	12	.324	2	-15	-16	0	-1.2
	Chi-N	8	5	.615	15	12	11	0	0	119^1	198	5	40	23	18.2	6.03	93	.365	.412	36	.375	7	-9	-6	0	0.1
	Yr	9	10	.474	22	17	15	0	0	162^1	270	8	53	26	18.1	6.65	82	.364	.409	48	.361	8	-24	-21	1	-1.1
1895	Chi-N	2	3	.400	5	5	3	0	0	30	51	1	14	4	20.7	9.60	53	.370	.442	7	.292	1	-16	-15	1	-1.5
Total	8	97	114	.460	230	213	198	10	1	1883^1	2170	44	432	569	12.8	3.87	99	.280	.323	379	.274	48	7	-10	20	6.2
● **MONTY STRATTON**	Stratton, Monty Franklin Pierce "Gander" b: 5/21/12, Celeste, Tex. d: 9/29/82, Greenville, Tex. BR/TR, 6'5", 180 lbs. Deb: 6/2/34 C																									
1934	Chi-A	0	0	—	1	0	0	0	0	3^1	4	0	1	0	13.5	5.40	88	.333	.385	0	.000	-0	-0	-0	-0	0.0
1935	Chi-A	1	2	.333	5	5	2	0	0	38	40	0	9	8	12.1	4.03	115	.274	.325	2	.143	-1	2	3	0	0.1
1936	Chi-A	5	7	.417	16	14	3	0	0	95	117	8	46	37	15.5	5.21	100	.305	.381	8	.216	1	-2	-0	2	0.2
1937	Chi-A†	15	5	.750	22	21	14	5	0	164^2	142	6	37	69	**9.9**	2.40	**191**	.234	**.280**	12	.200	-0	41	40	1	4.5
1938	Chi-A	15	9	.625	26	22	17	0	2	186^1	186	18	56	82	12.0	4.01	122	.255	.315	21	.266	5	16	18	0	2.6
Total	5	36	23	.610	70	62	36	5	2	487^1	489	32	149	196	12.0	3.71	130	.261	.319	43	.224	5	56	61	3	7.4
● **ED STRATTON**	Stratton, William Edward b: Baltimore, Md. Deb: 5/14/1873																									
1873	Mar-n	0	3	.000	3	3	3	0	0	27	75	1	1	0	25.3	8.33	39	.412	.415	2	.125	-1	-15	-15		-1.0
● **JOE STRAUSS**	Strauss, Joseph "Dutch" or "The Socker" (b: Joseph Strasser) b: 11/16/1858, Cincinnati, Ohio d: 6/24/06, Cincinnati, Ohio BR/TR, Deb: 7/27/1884 ♦																									
1886	Lou-a	0	0	—	2	0	0	0	1	4	6	0	3	0	20.3	4.50	81	.231	.310	64	.215	-0	-0	-0	-0	0.0
● **OSCAR STREIT**	Streit, Oscar William b: 7/7/1873, Florence, Ala. d: 10/10/35, Birmingham, Ala. BL/TL, 6'5", 190 lbs. Deb: 4/21/1899																									
1899	Bos-N	1	0	1.000	2	1	1	0	0	14^2	15	1	15	0	19.6	6.75	62	.263	.432	0	.000	-1	-5	-4	0	-0.3
1902	Cle-A	0	7	.000	8	7	4	0	0	51^2	72	3	25	10	17.4	5.23	66	.330	.407	4	.211	1	-9	-10	-1	-1.1
Total	2	1	7	.125	10	8	5	0	0	66^1	87	4	40	10	17.9	5.56	65	.316	.412	4	.154	-0	-14	-14	-1	-1.4
● **ED STRELECKI**	Strelecki, Edward Harold b: 4/10/05, Newark, N.J. d: 1/9/68, Newark, N.J. BR/TR, 5'11.5", 180 lbs. Deb: 4/16/28																									
1928	StL-A	0	2	.000	22	2	1	0	1	50^1	49	4	17	8	12.0	4.29	98	.269	.335	2	.200	0	-1	-1	-0	0.0
1929	StL-A	1	1	.500	7	0	0	0	0	11	12	1	6	2	15.5	4.91	90	.279	.380	0	.000	-0	-1	-1	0	-0.1
1931	Cin-N	0	0	—	13	0	0	0	0	24^1	37	2	9	3	18.1	9.25	40	.394	.462	1	.200	0	-15	-15	0	0.1
Total	3	1	3	.250	42	2	1	0	1	85^2	98	7	32	13	14.2	5.78	71	.307	.379	3	.176	0	-17	-16	1	0.0
● **PHIL STREMMEL**	Stremmel, Philip b: 4/16/1880, Zanesville, Ohio d: 12/26/47, Chicago, Ill. BR/TR, 6', 175 lbs. Deb: 9/16/09																									
1909	StL-A	0	2	.000	2	2	2	0	0	18	20	0	4	6	12.5	4.50	54	.308	.357	0	.000	-1	-4	-4	0	-0.4
1910	StL-A	0	2	.000	5	2	2	0	0	29	31	0	16	7	14.6	3.72	66	.287	.379	1	.125	-0	-4	-4	2	-0.1
Total	2	0	4	.000	7	4	4	0	0	47	51	0	20	13	13.8	4.02	61	.295	.371	1	.071	-1	-8	-8	2	-0.5
● **CUB STRICKER**	Stricker, John A. (b: John A. Streaker) b: 2/15/1860, Philadelphia, Pa. d: 11/19/37, Philadelphia, Pa. BR/TR, 5'3", 138 lbs. Deb: 5/2/1882 M♦																									
1882	Phi-a	1	0	1.000	2	0	0	0	0	7	3	0	1	2	5.1	1.29	232	.120	.154	59	.217	-0	1	1	-0	0.1
1884	Phi-a	0	0	—	1	0	0	0	0	3	6	0	1	1	21.0	6.00	56	.333	.368	92	.231	0	-1	-1	-0	0.0
1887	Cle-a	0	0	—	3	0	0	0	1	5^2	5	0	7	2	19.1	3.18	137	.238	.429	141	.264	0	1	1	0	0.1
1888	Cle-a	1	0	1.000	2	0	0	0	0	12	16	0	2	5	14.3	4.50	69	.308	.345	115	.233	0	-2	-2	-0	-0.1
Total	4	2	0	1.000	8	0	0	0	1	27^2	30	0	11	10	13.7	3.58	94	.259	.328	1106	.239	1	-1	-1	-0	0.1
● **JIM STRICKLAND**	Strickland, James Michael b: 6/12/46, Los Angeles, Cal. BL/TL, 6', 175 lbs. Deb: 5/19/71																									
1971	Min-A	1	0	1.000	24	0	0	0	1	31^1	20	2	18	21	11.5	1.44	247	.183	.310	0	.000	0	7	7	0	0.3
1972	Min-A	3	1	.750	25	0	0	0	3	36	28	7	19	30	11.8	2.50	128	.214	.313	1	.333	1	2	3	0	0.5
1973	Min-A	0	1	.000	7	0	0	0	0	5^1	11	0	5	6	27.0	11.81	34	.440	.533	0	—	0	-5	-5	0	-0.7
1975	Cle-A	0	0	—	4	0	0	0	1	4^2	4	0	2	3	13.5	1.93	196	.222	.333	0	—	0	1	1	-0	0.0
Total	4	4	2	.667	60	0	0	0	5	77^1	63	9	44	60	12.8	2.68	128	.223	.333	1	.250	1	6	7	0	0.1
● **BILL STRICKLAND**	Strickland, William Goss b: 3/29/08, Nashville, Ga. BR/TR, 6'2", 170 lbs. Deb: 9/16/37																									
1937	StL-A	0	0	—	9	0	0	0	0	21^1	28	2	15	6	19.0	5.91	82	.341	.455	1	.167	-0	-3	-3	-0	0.0
● **ELMER STRICKLETT**	Stricklett, Elmer Griffin "Spitball" b: 8/29/1876, Glasco, Kan. d: 6/7/64, Santa Cruz, Cal. BR/TR, 5'6", 140 lbs. Deb: 4/22/04																									
1904	Chi-A	0	1	.000	1	1	0	0	0	7	12	0	2	3	18.0	10.29	24	.375	.412	0	.000	-0	-6	-6	0	-0.6
1905	Bro-N	9	18	.333	33	28	25	1	1	237^1	259	0	71	77	13.0	3.34	87	.282	.343	13	.148	-1	-9	-12	9	-0.4
1906	Bro-N	14	18	.438	41	35	28	5	5	291^2	273	2	77	88	11.0	2.72	93	.253	.306	20	.206	5	-3	-6	9	0.9
1907	Bro-N	12	14	.462	29	26	25	4	0	229^2	211	1	65	69	11.1	2.27	103	.255	.315	12	.148	1	5	2	7	1.1
Total	4	35	51	.407	104	90	78	10	6	765^2	755	3	215	237	11.7	2.84	91	.264	.322	45	.167	4	-12	-22	25	1.0
● **JOHN STRIKE**	Strike, John b: 1865, Pennsylvania Deb: 9/24/1886																									
1886	Phi-N	1	1	.500	2	2	1	0	0	15	19	1	7	11	15.6	4.80	69	.311	.382	0	.000	-1	-2	-2	-1	-0.4
● **JAKE STRIKER**	Striker, Wilbur Scott b: 10/23/33, New Washington, O. BL/TL, 6'2", 200 lbs. Deb: 9/25/59																									
1959	Cle-A	1	0	1.000	1	1	0	0	0	6^2	8	0	4	5	16.2	2.70	136	.296	.387	0	.000	1	1	1	0	0.2
1960	Chi-A	0	0	—	2	0	0	0	0	3^2	5	1	1	1	17.2	4.91	77	.357	.438	0	—	0	-0	-0	-0	0.0
Total	2	1	0	1.000	3	1	0	0	0	10^1	13	1	5	6	16.5	3.48	107	.317	.404	0	.000	1	0	0	-0	0.2

● NICK STRINCEVICH
Strincevich, Nicholas "Jumbo" b: 3/1/15, Gary, Ind. BR/TR, 6'1", 180 lbs. Deb: 4/23/40

YEAR	TM/L	W	L	PCT	G	GS	CG	SH	SV	IP	H	HR	BB	SO	RAT	ERA	ERA+	OAV	OOB	BH	AVG	PB	PR	/A	PD	TPI
1940	Bos-N	4	8	.333	32	14	5	0	1	128^{2}	142	17	63	54	14.9	5.53	67	.278	.367	5	.116	-2	-24	-26	-2	-2.5
1941	Bos-N	0	0	—	3	0	0	0	0	3^{1}	7	0	6	1	37.8	10.80	33	.412	.583	0	—	0	-3	-3	0	0.0
	Pit-N	1	2	.333	12	3	0	0	0	31	35	4	13	12	14.2	5.23	69	.280	.353	3	.429	1	-5	-6	0	-0.4
	Yr	1	2	.333	15	3	0	0	0	34^{1}	42	4	19	13	16.3	5.77	63	.294	.380	3	.429	1	-8	-8	0	-0.4
1942	Pit-N	0	0	—	7	1	0	0	0	22^{1}	19	2	9	10	11.7	2.82	120	.229	.312	0	.000	-1	1	1	-0	-0.1
1944	Pit-N	14	7	.667	40	26	11	0	2	190	190	5	37	47	10.9	3.08	121	.257	.296	9	.158	-1	11	13	5	1.9
1945	Pit-N	16	10	.615	36	29	18	1	2	228^{1}	235	7	49	74	11.3	3.31	119	.260	.301	17	.202	0	12	16	-2	1.6
1946	Pit-N	10	15	.400	32	22	11	3	1	176	185	7	44	49	11.9	3.58	98	.268	.316	8	.154	1	-3	-1	-2	-0.3
1947	Pit-N	1	6	.143	32	7	1	0	0	89	111	9	37	22	15.2	5.26	80	.316	.385	1	.048	-2	-12	-10	-0	-0.9
1948	Pit-N	0	0	—	3	0	0	0	0	4^{1}	8	0	2	1	20.8	8.31	49	.444	.500	0	—	0	-2	-2	0	0.0
	Phi-N	0	1	.000	6	1	0	0	0	16^{2}	26	1	10	4	19.4	9.18	43	.347	.424	0	.000	-1	-10	-10	-1	-0.6
	Yr	0	1	.000	9	1	0	0	0	21	34	1	12	5	19.7	9.00	44	.366	.438	0	.000	-1	-12	-12	-0	-0.6
Total	8	46	49	.484	203	103	46	4	6	889^{2}	958	52	270	274	12.7	4.05	93	.273	.329	43	.158	-4	-34	-26	-0	-1.3

● JOHN STROHMAYER
Strohmayer, John Emery b: 10/13/46, Belle Fourche, S.D. BR/TR, 6'1", 181 lbs. Deb: 4/29/70

YEAR	TM/L	W	L	PCT	G	GS	CG	SH	SV	IP	H	HR	BB	SO	RAT	ERA	ERA+	OAV	OOB	BH	AVG	PB	PR	/A	PD	TPI
1970	Mon-N	3	1	.750	42	0	0	0	0	76	85	7	39	74	14.9	4.86	85	.279	.364	1	.167	-0	-7	-6	-0	-0.3
1971	Mon-N	7	5	.583	27	14	2	0	1	114	124	16	31	56	12.6	4.34	81	.281	.333	8	.229	1	-11	-10	-1	-1.1
1972	Mon-N	1	2	.333	48	0	0	0	3	76^{2}	73	6	31	50	12.3	3.52	101	.256	.331	0	.000	-0	-1	0	1	0.1
1973	Mon-N	0	1	.000	17	3	0	0	0	34^{2}	34	4	22	15	14.8	5.19	73	.260	.370	1	.200	0	-6	-5	-0	-0.1
	NY-N	0	0	—	7	0	0	0	0	10	13	2	4	5	15.3	8.10	45	.310	.370	0	—	0	-5	-5	0	0.0
	Yr	0	1	.000	24	3	0	0	0	44^{2}	47	6	26	20	14.7	5.84	65	.270	.365	1	.200	0	-11	-10	-0	-0.1
1974	NY-N	0	0	—	1	0	0	0	0	1	0	0	1	0	9.0	0.00	—	.000	.250	0	—	0	0	0	0	0.0
Total	5	11	9	.550	142	17	2	0	4	312^{1}	329	35	128	200	13.4	4.47	83	.272	.346	10	.200	1	-29	-26	-0	-1.4

● BRENT STROM
Strom, Brent Terry b: 10/14/48, San Diego, Cal. BR/TL, 6'3", 190 lbs. Deb: 7/31/72 C

YEAR	TM/L	W	L	PCT	G	GS	CG	SH	SV	IP	H	HR	BB	SO	RAT	ERA	ERA+	OAV	OOB	BH	AVG	PB	PR	/A	PD	TPI
1972	NY-N	0	3	.000	11	5	0	0	0	30^{1}	34	7	15	20	14.5	6.82	49	.296	.377	0	.000	-1	-11	-12	-1	-1.2
1973	Cle-A	2	10	.167	27	18	2	0	0	123	134	18	47	91	13.5	4.61	85	.278	.346	0	—	0	-11	-9	1	-0.8
1975	SD-N	8	8	.500	18	16	6	2	0	120^{1}	103	6	33	56	10.3	2.54	137	.233	.289	3	.100	-1	14	12	0	1.6
1976	SD-N	12	16	.429	36	33	8	1	0	210^{2}	188	15	73	103	11.2	3.29	99	.239	.305	4	.063	-2	5	-0	0	-0.3
1977	SD-N	0	2	.000	8	3	0	0	0	16^{2}	23	5	12	8	18.9	12.42	28	.329	.427	1	.333	0	-16	-16	-0	-1.6
Total	5	22	39	.361	100	75	16	3	0	501	482	51	180	278	12.0	3.95	88	.254	.321	8	.078	-3	-19	-26	0	-2.3

● FLOYD STROMME
Stromme, Floyd Marvin "Rock" b: 8/1/16, Cooperstown, N.Dak. d: 2/7/93, Wenatchee, Wash. BR/TR, 5'11", 170 lbs. Deb: 7/5/39

YEAR	TM/L	W	L	PCT	G	GS	CG	SH	SV	IP	H	HR	BB	SO	RAT	ERA	ERA+	OAV	OOB	BH	AVG	PB	PR	/A	PD	TPI
1939	Cle-A	0	1	.000	5	0	0	0	0	13	13	1	13	4	18.0	4.85	91	.265	.419	1	.333	0	-0	-1	-0	0.0

● SAILOR STROUD
Stroud, Ralph Vivian b: 5/15/1885, Ironia, N.J. d: 4/11/70, Stockton, Cal. BR/TR, 6', 160 lbs. Deb: 4/29/10

YEAR	TM/L	W	L	PCT	G	GS	CG	SH	SV	IP	H	HR	BB	SO	RAT	ERA	ERA+	OAV	OOB	BH	AVG	PB	PR	/A	PD	TPI
1910	Det-A	5	9	.357	28	15	7	3	1	130^{1}	123	9	41	63	11.8	3.25	81	.257	.325	1	.026	-4	-11	-9	-4	-1.8
1915	NY-N	12	9	.571	32	22	8	0	1	184	194	3	35	62	11.5	2.79	92	.281	.321	9	.161	-1	-1	-5	0	-0.6
1916	NY-N	3	2	.600	10	4	0	0	1	46^{2}	47	1	9	16	11.0	2.70	90	.266	.305	1	.071	-1	-0	-1	-0	-0.3
Total	3	20	20	.500	70	41	15	3	3	361	364	13	85	141	11.5	2.94	88	.271	.321	11	.101	-6	-12	-15	-4	-2.7

● STEAMBOAT STRUSS
Struss, Clarence Herbert b: 2/24/09, Riverdale, Ill. d: 9/12/85, Grand Rapids, Mich. BR/TR, 5'11", 163 lbs. Deb: 9/30/34

YEAR	TM/L	W	L	PCT	G	GS	CG	SH	SV	IP	H	HR	BB	SO	RAT	ERA	ERA+	OAV	OOB	BH	AVG	PB	PR	/A	PD	TPI
1934	Pit-N	0	1	.000	1	1	0	0	0	7	7	0	6	3	16.7	6.43	64	.250	.382	1	.333	0	-2	-2	0	-0.2

● DUTCH STRYKER
Stryker, Sterling Alpa b: 7/29/1895, Atlantic Highlands, N.J. d: 11/5/64, Red Bank, N.J. BR/TR, 5'11.5", 180 lbs. Deb: 4/16/24

YEAR	TM/L	W	L	PCT	G	GS	CG	SH	SV	IP	H	HR	BB	SO	RAT	ERA	ERA+	OAV	OOB	BH	AVG	PB	PR	/A	PD	TPI
1924	Bos-N	3	8	.273	20	10	2	0	0	73^{1}	90	4	22	22	13.9	6.01	64	.314	.365	5	.217	-0	-17	-18	2	-2.1
1926	Bro-N	0	0	—	2	0	0	0	0	2	8	0	1	0	40.5	27.00	14	.571	.600	0	—	0	-5	-5	-0	0.0
Total	2	3	8	.273	22	10	2	0	0	75^{1}	98	4	23	22	14.6	6.57	58	.326	.375	5	.217	-0	-23	-23	2	-2.1

● JOHNNY STUART
Stuart, John Davis "Stud" b: 4/27/01, Clinton, Tenn. d: 5/13/70, Charleston, W.Va. BR/TR, 5'11", 170 lbs. Deb: 7/27/22

YEAR	TM/L	W	L	PCT	G	GS	CG	SH	SV	IP	H	HR	BB	SO	RAT	ERA	ERA+	OAV	OOB	BH	AVG	PB	PR	/A	PD	TPI
1922	StL-N	0	0	—	2	1	0	0	0	2	2	0	2	1	22.5	9.00	43	.222	.417	0	—	0	-1	-1	-0	0.0
1923	StL-N	9	5	.643	37	10	7	1	3	149^{2}	139	11	70	55	13.1	4.27	91	.252	.345	14	.246	1	-4	-6	-1	-0.6
1924	StL-N	9	11	.450	28	22	13	0	0	159	167	12	60	54	13.1	4.75	80	.273	.343	11	.204	-1	-16	-17	-3	-2.2
1925	StL-N	2	2	.500	15	1	1	0	0	47	52	6	24	14	14.9	6.13	71	.278	.366	4	.250	1	-10	-9	-0	-0.6
Total	4	20	18	.526	82	34	21	1	3	357^{2}	360	29	156	124	13.4	4.76	82	.265	.348	29	.228	1	-31	-34	-5	-3.4

● MARLIN STUART
Stuart, Marlin Henry b: 8/8/18, Paragould, Ark. d: 6/16/94, Paragould, Ark. BL/TR, 6'2", 185 lbs. Deb: 4/26/49

YEAR	TM/L	W	L	PCT	G	GS	CG	SH	SV	IP	H	HR	BB	SO	RAT	ERA	ERA+	OAV	OOB	BH	AVG	PB	PR	/A	PD	TPI
1949	Det-A	0	2	.000	14	2	0	0	0	29^{2}	39	3	35	14	22.4	9.10	46	.348	.503	2	.333	1	-16	-16	0	-0.9
1950	Det-A	3	1	.750	19	1	0	0	2	43^{2}	59	6	22	19	16.9	5.56	84	.330	.406	1	.083	-1	-5	-4	0	-0.5
1951	Det-A	4	6	.400	29	15	5	0	1	124	119	9	71	46	14.3	3.77	111	.258	.365	10	.233	1	5	6	0	0.6
1952	Det-A	3	2	.600	30	9	2	0	1	91^{1}	91	8	48	32	14.0	4.93	77	.265	.360	2	.087	-1	-13	-11	-0	-0.7
	StL-A	1	2	.333	12	2	0	0	1	26	26	3	9	13	12.1	4.15	94	.260	.321	0	.000	-1	-1	-1	-1	-0.2
	Yr	4	4	.500	42	11	2	0	2	117^{1}	117	11	57	45	13.3	4.76	81	.262	.346	2	.069	-2	-14	-12	-1	-0.9
1953	StL-A	8	2	.800	60	2	0	0	7	114^{1}	136	6	44	46	14.2	3.94	107	.300	.363	5	.192	-1	1	3	-0	0.2
1954	Bal-A	1	2	.333	22	0	0	0	2	38^{1}	46	2	15	13	14.8	4.46	80	.303	.373	0	.000	-0	-3	-4	0	-0.3
	NY-A	3	0	1.000	10	0	0	0	1	18^{1}	28	0	12	2	19.6	5.40	64	.350	.435	2	.333	0	-3	-4	0	-0.6
	Yr	4	2	.667	32	0	0	0	3	56^{2}	74	2	27	15	16.0	4.76	74	.315	.385	2	.222	0	-7	-8	1	-0.9
Total	6	23	17	.575	196	31	7	0	15	485^{2}	544	37	256	185	15.1	4.65	87	.289	.378	22	.176	-1	-36	-31	-0	-2.4

● GEORGE STUELAND
Stueland, George Anton b: 3/2/1899, Algona, Iowa d: 9/9/64, Onawa, Iowa BB/TR, 6'1.5", 174 lbs. Deb: 9/15/21

YEAR	TM/L	W	L	PCT	G	GS	CG	SH	SV	IP	H	HR	BB	SO	RAT	ERA	ERA+	OAV	OOB	BH	AVG	PB	PR	/A	PD	TPI
1921	Chi-N	0	1	.000	2	1	0	0	0	11	11	0	7	4	14.7	5.73	67	.282	.391	1	.333	0	-2	-2	0	-0.2
1922	Chi-N	9	4	.692	35	11	4	0	0	113	129	9	49	44	14.6	5.81	72	.292	.369	4	.129	-2	-22	-20	-1	-2.2
1923	Chi-N	0	1	.000	6	0	0	0	0	8	11	0	5	2	18.0	5.63	71	.478	.571	0	—	0	-1	-1	0	-0.1
1925	Chi-N	0	0	—	2	0	0	0	0	3	2	0	3	2	15.0	3.00	144	.182	.357	1	1.000	0	0	0	0	0.1
Total	4	9	6	.600	45	12	4	0	0	135	153	9	64	52	14.8	5.73	73	.297	.380	6	.171	-1	-25	-24	-1	-2.4

● PAUL STUFFEL
Stuffel, Paul Harrington "Stu" b: 3/22/27, Canton, Ohio BR/TR, 6'2", 185 lbs. Deb: 9/16/50

YEAR	TM/L	W	L	PCT	G	GS	CG	SH	SV	IP	H	HR	BB	SO	RAT	ERA	ERA+	OAV	OOB	BH	AVG	PB	PR	/A	PD	TPI
1950	Phi-N	0	0	—	3	0	0	0	0	5	4	0	1	3	10.8	1.80	225	.211	.286	0	—	0	1	1	0	0.0
1952	Phi-N	1	0	1.000	2	1	0	0	0	6	5	0	7	3	18.0	3.00	122	.217	.400	0	.000	-0	0	0	0	0.1
1953	Phi-N	0	0	—	2	0	0	0	0	0	0	0	4	0	—	∞	—	—	1.000	0	—	0	-4	-4	0	-0.4
Total	3	1	0	1.000	7	1	0	0	0	11	9	0	12	6	18.0	5.73	67	.214	.400	0	.000	-0	-2	-2	0	-0.3

● EVERETT STULL
Stull, Everett James b: 8/24/71, Fort Riley, Kan. BR/TR, 6'3", 200 lbs. Deb: 4/14/97

YEAR	TM/L	W	L	PCT	G	GS	CG	SH	SV	IP	H	HR	BB	SO	RAT	ERA	ERA+	OAV	OOB	BH	AVG	PB	PR	/A	PD	TPI
1997	Mon-N	0	1	.000	3	0	0	0	0	3^{1}	7	1	4	2	29.7	16.20	26	.438	.550	0	—	0	-4	-4	-0	-1.0

● GEORGE STULTZ
Stultz, George Irvin b: 6/30/1873, Louisville, Ky. d: 3/19/55, Louisville, Ky. 5'10", 150 lbs. Deb: 9/22/1894

YEAR	TM/L	W	L	PCT	G	GS	CG	SH	SV	IP	H	HR	BB	SO	RAT	ERA	ERA+	OAV	OOB	BH	AVG	PB	PR	/A	PD	TPI
1894	Bos-N	1	0	1.000	1	1	1	0	0	9	4	0	5	1	9.0	0.00	—	.133	.257	1	.333	-0	5	6	1	0.6

● JIM STUMP
Stump, James Gilbert b: 2/10/32, Lansing, Mich. BR/TR, 6', 188 lbs. Deb: 8/29/57

YEAR	TM/L	W	L	PCT	G	GS	CG	SH	SV	IP	H	HR	BB	SO	RAT	ERA	ERA+	OAV	OOB	BH	AVG	PB	PR	/A	PD	TPI
1957	Det-A	1	0	1.000	6	0	0	0	0	13^{1}	11	0	8	2	12.8	2.03	190	.220	.328	1	.500	0	3	3	0	0.2
1959	Det-A	0	0	—	5	0	0	0	0	11^{1}	12	1	4	6	12.7	2.38	170	.279	.340	1	1.000	1	2	2	0	0.1
Total	2	1	0	1.000	11	0	0	0	0	24^{2}	23	1	12	8	12.8	2.19	180	.247	.333	2	.667	1	4	5	0	0.3

● JOHN STUPER
Stuper, John Anton b: 5/9/57, Butler, Pa. BR/TR, 6'2", 200 lbs. Deb: 6/1/82

YEAR	TM/L	W	L	PCT	G	GS	CG	SH	SV	IP	H	HR	BB	SO	RAT	ERA	ERA+	OAV	OOB	BH	AVG	PB	PR	/A	PD	TPI
1982	*StL-N	9	7	.563	23	21	2	0	0	136^{2}	137	8	55	53	12.6	3.36	108	.266	.337	5	.119	-1	4	4	-3	0.0
1983	StL-N	12	11	.522	40	30	6	1	1	198	202	15	71	81	12.5	3.68	98	.265	.329	8	.136	-1	-1	-1	-1	-0.4
1984	StL-N	3	5	.375	15	12	0	0	0	61^{1}	73	4	20	19	13.9	5.28	66	.297	.354	1	.063	-1	-12	-12	0	-1.5
1985	Cin-N	8	5	.615	33	13	1	0	0	99	116	8	37	38	13.9	4.55	83	.303	.364	1	.059	-0	-10	-8	0	-1.1
Total	4	32	28	.533	111	76	9	1	1	495	528	35	183	191	13.0	3.96	92	.277	.341	15	.112	-3	-20	-18	-4	-3.0

YEAR	TM/L	W	L	PCT	G	GS	CG	SH	SV	IP	H	HR	BB	SO	RAT	ERA	ERA+	OAV	OOB	BH	AVG	PB	PR	/A	PD	TPI
● **TOM STURDIVANT**	Sturdivant, Thomas Virgil "Snake" b: 4/28/30, Gordon, Kan. BL/TR, 6'1", 186 lbs. Deb: 4/14/55																									
1955	*NY-A	1	3	.250	33	1	0	0	0	68^1	48	6	42	48	12.1	3.16	118	.203	.329	1	.083	-1	6	4	-0	0.1
1956	*NY-A	16	8	.667	32	17	6	2	5	158^1	134	15	52	110	10.8	3.30	117	.224	**.291**	20	.313	4	15	10	-2	1.7
1957	*NY-A	16	6	**.727**	28	28	7	2	0	201^2	170	14	80	118	11.3	2.54	141	.232	.311	13	.183	1	28	23	-2	2.3
1958	NY-A	3	6	.333	15	10	0	0	0	70^2	77	6	38	41	15.0	4.20	84	.274	.366	4	.190	0	-3	-5	-2	-0.7
1959	NY-A	0	2	.000	7	3	0	0	0	25^1	20	4	9	16	10.3	4.97	73	.222	.293	0	.000	-1	-3	-4	0	-0.3
	KC-A	2	6	.250	36	3	0	0	5	71^2	70	9	34	57	13.8	4.65	86	.258	.354	1	.059	-2	-6	-5	1	-0.6
	Yr	2	8	.200	43	6	0	0	5	97	90	13	43	73	12.9	4.73	83	.249	.338	1	.043	-3	-9	-9	2	-0.9
1960	Bos-A	3	3	.500	40	3	0	0	1	101^1	106	16	45	67	13.6	4.97	81	.279	.358	4	.182	-1	-12	-10	-0	-0.7
1961	Was-A	2	6	.250	15	10	1	1	0	80	67	6	40	39	12.4	4.61	87	.233	.332	2	.077	-1	-5	-5	1	-0.5
	Pit-N	5	2	.714	13	11	6	1	1	85^2	81	6	17	45	10.4	2.84	141	.249	.289	8	.250	1	11	11	-1	0.8
1962	Pit-N	9	5	.643	49	12	2	1	2	125^1	120	12	39	76	11.6	3.73	105	.260	.321	6	.182	0	3	3	0	0.3
1963	Pit-N	0	0	—	3	0	0	0	0	8^1	8	1	4	6	13.0	6.48	51	.267	.353	0	.000	-0	-3	-3	0	0.0
	Det-A	1	2	.333	28	0	0	0	2	55	43	7	24	36	11.1	3.76	99	.221	.309	0	.000	-1	-1	-0	1	-0.1
	KC-A	1	2	.333	17	3	0	0	0	53	47	3	17	26	11.0	3.74	104	.237	.301	0	.000	-1	-1	1	0	-0.1
	Yr	2	4	.333	45	3	0	0	2	108	90	10	41	62	11.0	3.75	102	.226	.300	0	.000	-2	-1	1	1	-0.2
1964	KC-A	0	0	—	3	0	0	0	0	3^2	4	0	1	1	17.2	9.82	39	.308	.438	1	1.000	0	-3	-2	-0	0.0
	NY-N	0	0	—	16	0	0	0	1	28^2	34	2	7	18	13.5	5.97	60	.306	.358	0	.000	-0	-8	-8	-0	-0.1
Total	10	59	51	.536	335	101	22	7	17	1137	1029	107	449	704	12.0	3.74	102	.244	.322	60	.183	-1	18	10	-4	2.1
● **TANYON STURTZE**	Sturtze, Tanyon James b: 10/12/70, Worcester, Mass. BR/TR, 6'5", 190 lbs. Deb: 5/3/95																									
1995	Chi-N	0	0	—	2	0	0	0	0	2	2	1	1	0	13.5	9.00	46	.250	.333	0	—	0	-1	-1	-0	0.0
1996	Chi-N	1	0	1.000	6	0	0	0	0	11	16	3	5	7	17.2	9.00	48	.348	.412	0	.000	-0	-6	-6	0	-0.4
1997	Tex-A	1	1	.500	9	5	0	0	0	32^2	45	6	18	18	17.4	8.27	58	.338	.417	0	—	0	-13	-13	-1	-0.7
Total	3	2	1	.667	17	5	0	0	0	45^2	63	10	24	25	17.1	8.47	55	.337	.412	0	.000	-0	-20	-19	-1	-1.1
● **DICK SUCH**	Such, Richard Stanley b: 10/15/44, Sanford, N.C. BL/TR, 6'4", 190 lbs. Deb: 4/6/70 C																									
1970	Was-A	1	5	.167	21	5	0	0	0	50	48	8	45	41	17.3	7.56	47	.258	.410	3	.231	1	-21	-22	0	-2.2
● **CHARLEY SUCHE**	Suche, Charles Morris b: 8/5/15, Cranes Mill, Tex. d: 2/11/84, San Antonio, Tex. BR/TL, 6'2", 190 lbs. Deb: 9/18/38																									
1938	Cle-A	0	0	—	1	0	0	0	0	1^1	4	0	3	1	47.3	27.00	17	.571	.700	1	1.000	1	-3	-3	0	0.1
● **JIM SUCHECKI**	Suchecki, James Joseph b: 8/25/26, Chicago, Ill. BR/TR, 5'11", 185 lbs. Deb: 5/20/50																									
1950	Bos-A	0	0	—	4	0	0	0	0	4	3	0	4	3	15.8	4.50	109	.231	.412	0	—	0	0	0	-0	0.0
1951	StL-A	0	6	.000	29	6	0	0	0	89^2	113	8	42	47	15.7	5.42	81	.299	.371	2	.100	-2	-13	-10	-1	-0.8
1952	Pit-N	0	0	—	5	0	0	0	0	10	14	1	4	6	17.1	5.40	74	.326	.396	0	.000	0	-2	-2	-0	0.0
Total	3	0	6	.000	38	6	0	0	0	103^2	130	9	50	56	15.8	5.38	81	.300	.374	2	.091	-2	-15	-12	-1	-0.8
● **WILLIE SUDHOFF**	Sudhoff, John William "Wee Willie" b: 9/17/1874, St.Louis, Mo. d: 5/25/17, St.Louis, Mo. BR/TR, 5'7", 165 lbs. Deb: 8/20/1897																									
1897	StL-N	2	7	.222	11	9	9	0	0	92^2	126	8	21	19	14.3	4.47	99	.321	.356	10	.238	-1	-2	-1	2	0.0
1898	StL-N	11	27	.289	41	38	35	0	1	315	355	11	102	65	13.8	4.34	87	.282	.349	19	.158	-6	-26	-19	8	-1.8
1899	Cle-N	3	8	.273	11	10	8	0	0	86^1	131	3	25	10	17.0	6.98	53	.347	.399	2	.065	-2	-30	-32	2	-2.9
	StL-N	12	10	.545	25	23	16	0	0	178^1	193	5	62	29	13.6	4.04	99	.276	.347	13	.203	-0	-4	-1	4	0.3
	Yr	15	18	.455	36	33	24	0	0	264^2	324	8	87	39	14.5	5.00	78	.299	.359	15	.158	-3	-34	-33	7	-2.6
1900	StL-N	6	8	.429	16	14	13	2	0	127	128	3	37	29	12.3	2.76	132	.261	.323	20	.189	-0	13	12	1	1.2
1901	StL-N	17	11	.607	38	26	25	1	2	276^1	281	4	92	78	12.7	3.52	90	.262	.331	19	.176	3	-6	-10	2	-0.4
1902	StL-A	12	12	.500	30	25	20	0	0	220	213	6	67	42	11.9	2.86	123	.254	.319	13	.169	-2	17	16	3	1.7
1903	StL-A	21	15	.583	38	35	30	5	0	293^2	262	4	56	104	10.0	2.27	128	.238	.281	20	.182	-1	23	21	3	2.7
1904	StL-A	8	15	.348	27	24	20	1	0	222^1	232	8	54	63	12.0	3.76	66	.269	.320	14	.165	0	-29	-32	5	-2.5
1905	StL-A	10	20	.333	32	30	23	1	0	244	222	8	78	70	11.5	2.99	85	.244	.313	16	.186	2	-9	-12	4	-0.8
1906	Was-A	0	2	.000	9	5	0	0	0	19^2	30	1	9	7	18.8	9.15	29	.353	.427	3	.429	1	-14	-14	1	-1.1
Total	10	102	135	.430	278	239	199	10	3	2075^1	2173	61	603	516	12.6	3.60	91	.269	.329	149	.178	-7	-65	-74	35	-3.6
● **JOE SUGDEN**	Sugden, Joseph b: 7/31/1870, Philadelphia, Pa. d: 6/28/59, Philadelphia, Pa. BB/TR, 5'10", 180 lbs. Deb: 7/20/1893 C♦																									
1902	StL-A	0	0	—	1	0	0	0	0	1	1	0	0	0	9.0	0.00	—	.250	.250	50	.250	0	0	0	0	0.0
● **GEORGE SUGGS**	Suggs, George Franklin b: 7/7/1882, Kinston, N.C. d: 4/4/49, Kinston, N.C. BR/TR, 5'7.5", 168 lbs. Deb: 4/21/08																									
1908	Det-A	1	1	.500	6	1	1	0	1	27	32	0	2	8	11.3	1.67	145	.299	.312	2	.200	0	2	2	-1	0.1
1909	Det-A	1	3	.250	9	4	2	0	1	44^1	34	1	10	18	9.5	2.03	124	.228	.290	1	.067	-1	2	2	-0	0.1
1910	Cin-N	20	12	.625	35	30	23	2	3	266	248	6	48	91	10.5	2.40	121	.253	.297	14	.165	2	19	15	1	2.1
1911	Cin-N	15	13	.536	36	29	17	1	0	260^2	258	3	79	91	12.0	3.00	110	.268	.330	23	.256	6	12	9	3	1.9
1912	Cin-N	19	16	.543	42	36	25	5	3	303	320	6	56	104	11.5	2.94	114	.278	.318	17	.160	-1	16	14	1	1.5
1913	Cin-N	8	15	.348	36	22	9	2	2	199	220	6	35	73	11.8	4.03	81	.292	.329	17	.254	2	-18	-17	3	-1.3
1914	Bal-F	24	14	.632	46	38	26	6	4	319^1	322	6	57	132	11.0	2.90	104	.266	.304	21	.212	2	-1	5	6	1.3
1915	Bal-F	11	17	.393	35	25	12	0	3	232^2	288	12	68	71	14.0	4.14	69	.318	.370	17	.221	0	-36	-33	2	-3.5
Total	8	99	91	.521	245	185	115	16	17	1652	1722	40	355	588	11.7	3.11	100	.277	.322	112	.204	11	-5	-1	14	2.2
● **ED SUKLA**	Sukla, Edward Anthony (b: Edward Anthony Suckla) b: 3/3/43, Long Beach, Cal. BR/TR, 5'11", 170 lbs. Deb: 9/17/64																									
1964	LA-A	0	1	.000	2	0	0	0	0	2^2	2	1	1	3	10.1	6.75	49	.200	.273	0	—	0	-1	-1	0	-0.3
1965	Cal-A	2	3	.400	25	0	0	0	3	32	32	3	10	15	12.1	4.50	76	.264	.326	0	—	0	-4	-4	1	-0.6
1966	Cal-A	1	1	.500	12	0	0	0	1	16^2	18	4	6	8	13.0	6.48	52	.281	.343	0	.000	-0	-6	-6	-1	-0.8
Total	3	3	5	.375	39	0	0	0	4	51^1	52	8	17	26	12.3	5.26	64	.267	.329	0	.000	-0	-10	-11	0	-1.7
● **CHARLIE SULLIVAN**	Sullivan, Charles Edward b: 5/23/03, Yadkin Valley, N.C d: 5/28/35, Maiden, N.C. BL/TR, 6'1", 185 lbs. Deb: 4/21/28																									
1928	Det-A	0	2	.000	3	2	0	0	0	12^1	18	1	6	2	17.5	6.57	63	.360	.429	0	.000	-1	-3	-3	0	-0.5
1930	Det-A	1	5	.167	40	3	2	0	5	93^2	112	9	53	38	16.0	6.53	73	.311	.401	7	.292	2	-20	-18	1	-0.9
1931	Det-A	3	2	.600	31	4	2	0	0	95	109	6	46	28	14.8	4.93	93	.288	.366	4	.167	-1	-6	-4	-0	-0.3
Total	3	4	9	.308	74	9	4	0	5	201	239	16	105	68	15.5	5.78	81	.303	.386	11	.212	-0	-29	-25	1	-1.7
● **FLEURY SULLIVAN**	Sullivan, Florence P. b: 1862, E.St.Louis, Ill. d: 2/15/1897, E.St.Louis, Ill. Deb: 5/3/1884																									
1884	Pit-a	16	35	.314	51	51	51	2	0	441	496	15	96	189	12.5	4.20	80	.268	.311	29	.153	-9	-47	-41	1	-4.5
● **FRANK SULLIVAN**	Sullivan, Franklin Leal b: 1/23/30, Hollywood, Cal. BR/TR, 6'6.5", 215 lbs. Deb: 7/31/53																									
1953	Bos-A	1	1	.500	14	0	0	0	0	25^2	24	3	11	17	12.6	5.61	75	.264	.350	1	.250	0	-5	-4	-0	-0.3
1954	Bos-A	15	12	.556	36	26	11	3	1	206^1	185	18	66	124	11.2	3.14	131	.240	.305	7	.103	-3	13	22	1	2.7
1955	Bos-A★	**18**	13	.581	35	35	16	3	0	**260**	235	23	100	129	11.8	2.91	147	.241	.316	10	.112	-4	30	40	1	4.2
1956	Bos-A☆	14	7	.667	34	33	12	1	0	242	253	22	82	116	12.8	3.42	135	.268	.332	12	.141	-5	20	32	0	2.0
1957	Bos-A	14	11	.560	31	30	14	3	0	240^2	206	16	48	127	**9.8**	2.73	146	.230	**.275**	13	.165	-2	28	34	2	**3.5**
1958	Bos-A	13	9	.591	32	29	10	2	3	199^1	216	12	49	103	12.1	3.57	112	.278	.324	11	.164	-1	4	10	-1	0.9
1959	Bos-A	9	11	.450	30	26	5	2	1	177^2	172	17	67	107	12.5	3.95	103	.258	.332	12	.200	-1	-2	2	-1	0.0
1960	Bos-A	6	16	.273	40	22	4	0	1	153^2	164	12	52	98	13.0	5.10	79	.269	.332	5	.125	-1	-21	-18	-1	-2.5
1961	Phi-N	3	16	.158	49	18	1	1	6	159^1	161	19	55	114	12.5	4.29	95	.262	.327	5	.152	0	-5	-4	1	-0.3
1962	Phi-N	0	2	.000	19	0	0	0	0	23	38	2	12	12	20.3	6.26	62	.396	.473	0	—	0	-6	-6	0	-0.4
	Min-A	4	1	.800	21	0	0	0	5	33^1	33	3	13	10	12.4	3.24	126	.258	.326	0	.000	-0	3	3	0	0.5
1963	Min-A	0	1	.000	10	0	0	0	1	11	15	1	4	2	15.5	5.73	64	.349	.404	0	—	0	-3	-3	0	-0.2
Total	11	97	100	.492	351	219	73	15	18	1732	1702	148	559	959	12.0	3.60	116	.257	.320	76	.144	-17	59	108	3	10.1
● **HARRY SULLIVAN**	Sullivan, Harry Andrew b: 4/12/1888, Rockford, Ill. d: 9/22/19, Rockford, Ill. BL/TL, Deb: 8/11/09																									
1909	StL-N	0	0	—	2	1	0	0	0	1	4	1	2	1	54.0	36.00	7	.500	.600	0	.000	-0	-4	-4	-0	0.0
● **JIM SULLIVAN**	Sullivan, James E. b: 4/25/1869, Charlestown, Mass. d: 11/30/01, Roxbury, Mass. BR/TR, 5'10", 155 lbs. Deb: 4/22/1891																									
1891	Bos-N	0	0	—	1	0	0	0	0	0^1	2	0	5	0	189.0	81.00	5	.667	.875	0	—	0	-3	-3	-0	0.0

YEAR	TM/L	W	L	PCT	G	GS	CG	SH	SV	IP	H	HR	BB	SO	RAT	ERA	ERA+	OAV	OOB	BH	AVG	PB	PR	/A	PD	TPI
	Col-a	0	1	.000	1	1	1	0	0	9	10	1	5	1	16.0	4.00	87	.270	.372	0	.000	-1	-0	-1	1	-0.1
1895	Bos-N	11	9	.550	21	19	16	0	0	179^1	236	10	58	46	15.6	4.82	106	.312	.373	15	.176	-6	-1	6	-2	-0.2
1896	Bos-N	11	12	.478	31	26	21	1	1	225^1	268	12	68	33	13.7	4.03	113	.293	.346	19	.216	-2	8	13	-3	0.5
1897	*Bos-N	4	5	.444	13	9	8	1	2	89	91	1	26	17	12.0	3.94	113	.263	.318	6	.182	-3	4	5	-1	0.1
Total	4	26	27	.491	67	55	46	2	3	503	607	24	162	97	14.2	4.35	108	.295	.354	40	.190	-11	8	20	-6	0.3

● JIM SULLIVAN Sullivan, James Richard b: 4/5/1894, Mine Run, Va. d: 2/12/72, Burtonsville, Md. BR/TR, 5'11", 165 lbs. Deb: 9/27/21

YEAR	TM/L	W	L	PCT	G	GS	CG	SH	SV	IP	H	HR	BB	SO	RAT	ERA	ERA+	OAV	OOB	BH	AVG	PB	PR	/A	PD	TPI
1921	Phi-A	0	2	.000	2	2	2	0	0	17	20	0	7	8	14.3	3.18	140	.294	.360	0	.000	-1	2	2	-0	0.1
1922	Phi-A	0	2	.000	20	2	1	0	0	51^1	76	3	25	15	17.9	5.44	78	.373	.443	1	.091	-1	-8	-7	-0	-0.3
1923	Cle-A	0	1	.000	3	0	0	0	0	5	10	0	5	4	28.8	14.40	28	.476	.593	0	.000	-0	-6	-6	0	-0.9
Total	3	0	5	.000	25	4	3	0	0	73^1	106	3	37	27	17.8	5.52	78	.362	.437	1	.056	-2	-12	-10	-1	-1.1

● JOE SULLIVAN Sullivan, Joe b: 9/26/10, Mason City, Ill. d: 4/8/85, Sequim, Wash. BL/TL, 5'11", 175 lbs. Deb: 4/20/35

YEAR	TM/L	W	L	PCT	G	GS	CG	SH	SV	IP	H	HR	BB	SO	RAT	ERA	ERA+	OAV	OOB	BH	AVG	PB	PR	/A	PD	TPI
1935	Det-A	6	6	.500	25	12	5	0	0	125^2	119	4	71	53	13.8	3.51	119	.244	.344	7	.163	-1	13	9	-1	0.6
1936	Det-A	2	5	.286	26	4	1	0	1	79^2	111	4	40	32	17.3	6.78	73	.331	.406	5	.179	-1	-15	-16	-1	-1.3
1939	Bos-N	6	9	.400	31	11	7	0	2	113^2	114	3	50	46	13.1	3.64	101	.266	.346	12	.300	3	3	1	0	0.4
1940	Bos-N	10	14	.417	36	22	7	0	1	177^1	157	9	89	64	12.9	3.55	105	.240	.339	14	.197	-0	6	3	0	0.4
1941	Bos-N	2	2	.500	16	2	0	0	0	52^1	60	3	26	11	15.1	4.13	86	.290	.374	1	.067	-1	-3	-3	1	-0.3
	Pit-N	4	1	.800	16	4	0	0	1	39^1	40	2	22	10	14.2	2.97	121	.258	.350	4	.364	1	3	3	0	0.5
	Yr	6	3	.667	32	6	0	0	1	91^2	100	5	48	21	14.5	3.63	99	.275	.359	5	.192	-0	0	-0	1	0.2
Total	5	30	37	.448	150	55	20	0	5	588	601	25	298	216	14.0	4.01	99	.265	.355	43	.207	1	7	-3	0	0.3

● JOHN SULLIVAN Sullivan, John Jeremiah "Lefty" b: 5/31/1894, Chicago, Ill. d: 7/7/58, Chicago, Ill. BL/TL, 5'11", 165 lbs. Deb: 7/18/19

YEAR	TM/L	W	L	PCT	G	GS	CG	SH	SV	IP	H	HR	BB	SO	RAT	ERA	ERA+	OAV	OOB	BH	AVG	PB	PR	/A	PD	TPI
1919	Chi-A	0	1	.000	4	2	1	0	0	15	24	0	8	9	19.8	4.20	76	.364	.440	0	.000	-0	-2	-2	-1	-0.2

● MARTY SULLIVAN Sullivan, Martin C. b: 10/20/1862, Lowell, Mass. d: 1/6/1894, Lowell, Mass. BR/TR, Deb: 4/30/1887 ♦

YEAR	TM/L	W	L	PCT	G	GS	CG	SH	SV	IP	H	HR	BB	SO	RAT	ERA	ERA+	OAV	OOB	BH	AVG	PB	PR	/A	PD	TPI
1887	Chi-N	0	0	—	1	0	0	0	0	2^1	6	0	1	1	27.0	7.71	58	.500	.538	134	.284	0	-1	-1	-0	0.0

● MIKE SULLIVAN Sullivan, Michael Joseph "Big Mike" b: 10/23/1866, Boston, Mass. d: 6/14/06, Boston, Mass. BL, 6'1", 210 lbs. Deb: 6/17/1889

YEAR	TM/L	W	L	PCT	G	GS	CG	SH	SV	IP	H	HR	BB	SO	RAT	ERA	ERA+	OAV	OOB	BH	AVG	PB	PR	/A	PD	TPI
1889	Was-N	0	3	.000	9	3	3	0	0	41	47	2	32	15	18.0	7.24	54	.280	.404	1	.053	-2	-15	-15	-0	-1.0
1890	Chi-N	5	6	.455	12	12	10	0	0	96	108	3	58	33	15.9	4.59	80	.276	.374	5	.125	-3	-11	-10	-0	-1.2
1891	Phi-a	0	2	.000	2	2	2	0	0	18	17	2	10	7	15.0	3.50	109	.239	.357	0	.000	-1	0	1	-0	-0.1
	NY-N	1	2	.333	3	3	3	0	0	24	24	0	8	11	12.4	3.38	95	.250	.314	2	.200	-0	-0	-0	0	-0.1
1892	Cin-N	12	4	.750	21	16	15	0	0	166^1	179	8	74	56	14.2	3.08	106	.264	.344	13	.176	-2	4	3	-2	-0.1
1893	Cin-N	8	11	.421	27	18	14	0	1	183^2	200	5	103	40	15.7	5.05	95	.269	.370	16	.203	-3	-8	-5	-0	-0.7
1894	Was-N	2	10	.167	20	12	11	0	1	117^2	166	10	74	21	19.0	6.58	80	.329	.422	9	.158	-4	-16	-17	-0	-1.5
	Cle-N	6	5	.545	13	11	9	0	0	90^2	128	4	47	19	17.7	6.35	86	.329	.405	13	.295	0	-10	-9	-1	-0.8
	Yr	8	15	.348	33	23	20	0	1	208^1	294	14	121	40	18.1	6.48	83	.326	.407	22	.218	-4	-27	-26	-1	-2.3
1895	Cle-N	1	2	.333	4	3	2	0	0	31	42	1	16	5	17.1	8.42	59	.318	.396	2	.133	-2	-13	-12	-1	-0.9
1896	NY-N	10	13	.435	25	22	18	0	0	185^1	188	3	71	42	13.2	4.66	90	.261	.338	16	.208	-3	-6	-9	0	-1.2
1897	NY-N	8	7	.533	23	16	11	1	2	148^2	183	6	71	35	16.2	5.09	82	.300	.386	18	.273	0	-13	-15	1	-1.1
1898	Bos-N	0	1	.000	3	2	0	0	0	12	19	1	9	1	21.8	12.00	31	.358	.460	1	.333	0	-11	-11	-0	-0.7
1899	Bos-N	1	0	1.000	1	1	1	0	0	9	10	1	4	1	15.0	5.00	83	.278	.366	1	.333	0	-1	-1	-0	-0.1
Total	11	54	66	.450	163	121	99	1	4	1123^1	1311	46	577	286	15.8	5.11	84	.285	.375	97	.196	-21	-100	-102	-5	-9.5

● PAT SULLIVAN Sullivan, Patrick J. b: 12/22/1862, Milwaukee, Wis. TR, 5'11", 165 lbs. Deb: 8/30/1884 ♦

YEAR	TM/L	W	L	PCT	G	GS	CG	SH	SV	IP	H	HR	BB	SO	RAT	ERA	ERA+	OAV	OOB	BH	AVG	PB	PR	/A	PD	TPI
1884	KC-U	0	1	.000	1	1	0	0	0	7	15	1	5	1	25.7	11.57	19	.405	.476	22	.193	-0	-7	-7	-0	-0.6

● LEFTY SULLIVAN Sullivan, Paul Thomas b: 9/7/16, Nashville, Tenn. d: 11/1/88, Scottsdale, Ariz. BL/TL, 6'3", 204 lbs. Deb: 5/6/39

YEAR	TM/L	W	L	PCT	G	GS	CG	SH	SV	IP	H	HR	BB	SO	RAT	ERA	ERA+	OAV	OOB	BH	AVG	PB	PR	/A	PD	TPI
1939	Cle-A	0	1	.000	7	1	0	0	0	12^2	9	0	9	4	13.5	4.26	103	.214	.365	0	.000	-0	1	0	-1	-0.1

● SUTER SULLIVAN Sullivan, Suter G. b: 10/14/1872, Baltimore, Md. d: 4/19/25, Baltimore, Md. 6', 170 lbs. Deb: 7/24/1898 ♦

YEAR	TM/L	W	L	PCT	G	GS	CG	SH	SV	IP	H	HR	BB	SO	RAT	ERA	ERA+	OAV	OOB	BH	AVG	PB	PR	/A	PD	TPI
1898	StL-N	0	0	—	1	0	0	0	0	6	10	0	4	3	21.0	1.50	253	.370	.452	32	.222	0	1	2	-0	0.0

● TOM SULLIVAN Sullivan, Thomas b: 3/1/1860, New York, N.Y. d: 4/12/47, Cincinnati, Ohio Deb: 9/27/1884

YEAR	TM/L	W	L	PCT	G	GS	CG	SH	SV	IP	H	HR	BB	SO	RAT	ERA	ERA+	OAV	OOB	BH	AVG	PB	PR	/A	PD	TPI
1884	Col-a	2	2	.500	4	4	4	0	0	31	42	2	3	12	13.1	4.06	75	.318	.333	1	.091	-1	-3	-4	-1	-0.5
1886	Lou-a	2	7	.222	9	9	8	0	0	75	94	6	33	27	15.5	3.96	92	.305	.376	3	.111	-2	-4	-3	0	-0.4
1888	KC-a	8	16	.333	24	24	24	0	0	214^2	227	2	68	84	13.4	3.40	101	.262	.332	10	.109	-6	-8	1	5	0.0
1889	KC-a	2	8	.200	10	10	10	0	0	87^1	111	2	48	24	17.1	5.67	74	.300	.391	5	.152	-1	-18	-14	-1	-1.3
Total	4	14	33	.298	47	47	46	0	0	408	474	12	152	147	14.5	4.04	89	.282	.354	19	.117	-9	-33	-20	4	-2.2

● TOM SULLIVAN Sullivan, Thomas Augustin b: 10/18/1895, Boston, Mass. d: 9/23/62, Boston, Mass. BL/TL, 5'11", 178 lbs. Deb: 5/15/22

YEAR	TM/L	W	L	PCT	G	GS	CG	SH	SV	IP	H	HR	BB	SO	RAT	ERA	ERA+	OAV	OOB	BH	AVG	PB	PR	/A	PD	TPI
1922	Phi-N	0	0	—	3	0	0	0	0	8	16	0	5	2	24.8	11.25	41	.410	.489	1	.250	1	-6	-6	0	0.1

● SLEEPER SULLIVAN Sullivan, Thomas Jefferson "Old Iron Hands" b: St.Louis, Mo. d: 9/25/1899, Camden, N.J. BR/TR, 175 lbs. Deb: 5/3/1881 ♦

YEAR	TM/L	W	L	PCT	G	GS	CG	SH	SV	IP	H	HR	BB	SO	RAT	ERA	ERA+	OAV	OOB	BH	AVG	PB	PR	/A	PD	TPI
1884	StL-U	1	0	1.000	1	1	0	0	0	6	10	0	0	3	15.0	4.50	53	.345	.345	1	.111	-1	-1	-1	-0	-0.2

● BILL SULLIVAN Sullivan, William F. b: 12/1868, Providence, R.I. d: 10/8/05, Providence, R.I. BR/TR, Deb: 4/19/1890

YEAR	TM/L	W	L	PCT	G	GS	CG	SH	SV	IP	H	HR	BB	SO	RAT	ERA	ERA+	OAV	OOB	BH	AVG	PB	PR	/A	PD	TPI
1890	Syr-a	1	4	.200	6	6	4	0	0	42	51	2	27	13	18.0	7.93	45	.291	.404	2	.091	-2	-19	-21	-0	-1.8

● SCOTT SULLIVAN Sullivan, William Scott b: 3/13/71, Tuscaloosa, Ala. BR/TR, 6'3", 210 lbs. Deb: 5/6/95

YEAR	TM/L	W	L	PCT	G	GS	CG	SH	SV	IP	H	HR	BB	SO	RAT	ERA	ERA+	OAV	OOB	BH	AVG	PB	PR	/A	PD	TPI
1995	Cin-N	0	0	—	3	0	0	0	0	3^2	4	0	2	2	14.7	4.91	84	.286	.375	0	.000	-0	-0	-0	0	0.0
1996	Cin-N	0	0	—	7	0	0	0	0	8	7	0	5	3	14.6	2.25	188	.250	.382	0	.000	-0	2	2	0	0.0
1997	Cin-N	5	3	.625	59	0	0	0	1	97^1	79	12	30	96	10.7	3.24	132	.220	.293	0	.000	-1	10	11	-1	0.7
1998	Cin-N	5	5	.500	67	0	0	0	1	102	98	14	36	86	12.6	5.21	83	.253	.330	1	.091	-1	-11	-10	-0	-1.0
Total	4	10	8	.556	136	0	0	0	2	211	188	26	73	187	11.9	4.18	103	.238	.316	1	.050	-2	1	3	-1	-0.3

● ED SUMMERS Summers, Oron Edgar "Kickapoo Ed" or "Chief" b: 12/5/1884, Ladoga, Ind. d: 5/12/53, Indianapolis, Ind. BB/TR, 6'2", 180 lbs. Deb: 4/16/08

YEAR	TM/L	W	L	PCT	G	GS	CG	SH	SV	IP	H	HR	BB	SO	RAT	ERA	ERA+	OAV	OOB	BH	AVG	PB	PR	/A	PD	TPI
1908	*Det-A	24	12	.667	40	32	23	5	1	301	271	3	55	103	10.3	1.64	147	.242	.290	14	.124	-6	25	26	-1	2.4
1909	*Det-A	19	9	.679	35	32	24	3	1	281^2	243	4	52	107	9.7	2.24	113	.227	.269	10	.106	-4	8	9	1	0.5
1910	Det-A	13	12	.520	30	25	18	1	0	220^1	211	8	60	82	11.3	2.53	104	.254	.308	14	.184	-0	-0	2	1	0.3
1911	Det-A	11	11	.500	30	20	13	0	1	179^1	189	3	51	65	12.6	3.66	95	.274	.334	16	.254	1	-6	-4	-1	-0.5
1912	Det-A	1	1	.500	3	3	1	0	0	16^2	16	1	3	5	10.3	4.86	67	.250	.284	3	.500	1	-3	-3	0	-0.2
Total	5	68	45	.602	138	112	79	9	3	999	930	19	221	362	10.8	2.42	111	.246	.296	57	.162	-9	23	30	-0	2.5

● BILLY SUNDAY Sunday, William Ashley "Parson" or "The Evangelist"
b: 11/19/1862, Ames, Iowa d: 11/6/35, Chicago, Ill. BL/TR, 5'10", 160 lbs. Deb: 5/22/1883 ♦

YEAR	TM/L	W	L	PCT	G	GS	CG	SH	SV	IP	H	HR	BB	SO	RAT	ERA	ERA+	OAV	OOB	BH	AVG	PB	PR	/A	PD	TPI
1890	Pit-N	0	0	—	1	0	0	0	0	0	2	0	0	0	—	∞	—	1.000	1.000	92	.257	0	-2	-2	0	-0.2

● GORDIE SUNDIN Sundin, Gordon Vincent b: 10/10/37, Minneapolis, Minn. BR/TR, 6'4", 215 lbs. Deb: 9/19/56

YEAR	TM/L	W	L	PCT	G	GS	CG	SH	SV	IP	H	HR	BB	SO	RAT	ERA	ERA+	OAV	OOB	BH	AVG	PB	PR	/A	PD	TPI
1956	Bal-A	0	0	—	1	0	0	0	0	0	0	0	2	0	—	∞	—	—	1.000	0	—	0	-1	-1	0	-0.1

● STEVE SUNDRA Sundra, Stephen Richard "Smokey" b: 3/27/10, Luxor, Pa. d: 3/23/52, Cleveland, Ohio BR/TR, 6'2", 190 lbs. Deb: 4/17/36

YEAR	TM/L	W	L	PCT	G	GS	CG	SH	SV	IP	H	HR	BB	SO	RAT	ERA	ERA+	OAV	OOB	BH	AVG	PB	PR	/A	PD	TPI
1936	NY-A	0	0	—	1	0	0	0	0	2	2	0	2	1	18.0	0.00	—	.286	.444	0	.000	-0	1	1	-0	0.0
1938	NY-A	6	4	.600	25	8	3	0	0	93^2	107	7	43	33	14.4	4.80	94	.291	.365	6	.182	1	-0	-3	1	-0.1
1939	*NY-A	11	1	.917	24	11	8	1	0	120^2	110	7	56	27	12.4	2.76	158	.240	.323	13	.265	4	25	21	1	2.2
1940	NY-A	4	6	.400	27	8	2	0	2	99^1	121	11	42	26	14.9	5.53	73	.299	.366	4	.138	-1	-13	-16	0	-1.5
1941	Was-A	9	13	.409	28	23	11	0	0	168^1	203	11	61	50	14.2	5.29	76	.294	.352	13	.217	2	-21	-23	-1	-2.4
1942	Was-A	1	3	.250	6	4	2	0	0	33^2	43	1	15	5	15.8	5.61	65	.305	.376	2	.167	-0	-7	-7	-0	-0.8
	StL-A	8	3	.727	20	13	6	0	0	110^2	122	2	29	26	12.3	3.82	97	.275	.319	9	.225	3	-2	-1	-0	0.1
	Yr	9	6	.600	26	17	8	0	0	144^1	165	3	44	31	13.0	4.24	87	.282	.332	11	.212	2	-9	-9	-0	-0.7
1943	StL-A	15	11	.577	32	29	13	3	0	208	212	10	66	44	12.0	3.25	103	.266	.322	16	.219	1	1	2	-0	0.4
1944	StL-A	2	0	1.000	3	3	2	0	0	19	15	1	4	1	9.0	1.42	253	.211	.253	0	.000	-0	4	5	-0	0.5

YEAR	TM/L	W	L	PCT	G	GS	CG	SH	SV	IP	H	HR	BB	SO	RAT	ERA	ERA+	OAV	OOB	BH	AVG	PB	PR	/A	PD	TPI
1946	StL-A	0	0	—	2	0	0	0	0	4	9	0	3	1	27.0	11.25	33	.409	.480	0	—	0	-3	-3	0	0.0
Total	9	56	41	.577	168	99	47	4	2	859^1	944	50	321	214	13.3	4.17	94	.277	.340	63	.209	10	-16	-24	1	-1.6

● TOM SUNKEL

Sunkel, Thomas Jacob "Lefty" b: 8/9/12, Paris, Ill. BL/TL, 6'1", 190 lbs. Deb: 8/26/37

YEAR	TM/L	W	L	PCT	G	GS	CG	SH	SV	IP	H	HR	BB	SO	RAT	ERA	ERA+	OAV	OOB	BH	AVG	PB	PR	/A	PD	TPI
1937	StL-N	0	0	—	9	1	0	0	1	29^1	24	0	11	9	10.7	2.76	144	.214	.285	1	.111	-1	4	4	-0	-0.1
1939	StL-N	4	4	.500	20	11	2	1	0	85^1	79	4	56	54	14.3	4.22	98	.242	.354	9	.321	2	-3	-1	-1	0.0
1941	NY-N	1	1	.500	2	2	1	1	0	15^1	7	0	12	14	11.7	2.93	126	.140	.317	2	.333	0	1	1	-0	0.2
1942	NY-N	3	6	.333	19	11	3	0	0	63^2	65	5	41	29	15.0	4.81	70	.269	.375	2	.105	-1	-11	-10	-2	-1.6
1943	NY-N	0	1	.000	1	1	0	0	0	2^2	4	1	3	0	23.6	10.13	34	.308	.438	0	—	0	-2	-2	0	-0.5
1944	Bro-N	1	3	.250	12	3	0	0	1	24	39	1	10	6	18.4	7.50	47	.368	.422	0	.000	-1	-10	-11	-1	-1.7
Total	6	9	15	.375	63	29	6	2	2	220^1	218	11	133	112	14.4	4.53	83	.256	.358	14	.212	0	-21	-19	-4	-3.7

● JEFF SUPPAN

Suppan, Jeffrey Scot b: 1/2/75, Oklahoma City, Okla. BR/TR, 6'1", 200 lbs. Deb: 7/17/95

YEAR	TM/L	W	L	PCT	G	GS	CG	SH	SV	IP	H	HR	BB	SO	RAT	ERA	ERA+	OAV	OOB	BH	AVG	PB	PR	/A	PD	TPI
1995	Bos-A	1	2	.333	8	3	0	0	0	22^2	29	4	5	19	13.5	5.96	82	.312	.347	0	—	0	-3	-3	-0	-0.3
1996	Bos-A	1	1	.500	8	4	0	0	0	22^2	29	3	13	13	17.1	7.54	67	.330	.422	0	—	0	-6	-6	-0	-0.5
1997	Bos-A	7	3	.700	23	22	0	0	0	112^1	140	12	36	67	14.4	5.69	81	.305	.361	0	.000	-0	-14	-13	-2	-1.1
1998	Ari-N	1	7	.125	13	13	1	0	0	66	82	12	21	39	14.2	6.68	64	.301	.354	6	.273	1	-18	-17	1	-1.5
	KC-A	0	0	—	4	1	0	0	0	12^2	9	1	1	12	7.1	0.71	691	.200	.217	0	—	0	6	6	0	-0.1
Total	4	10	13	.435	56	43	1	0	0	236^1	289	32	76	150	14.1	5.90	78	.302	.357	6	.250	1	-36	-34	-0	-3.5

● RICK SURHOFF

Surhoff, Richard Clifford b: 10/3/62, Bronx, N.Y. BR/TR, 6'3", 210 lbs. Deb: 9/8/85 F

YEAR	TM/L	W	L	PCT	G	GS	CG	SH	SV	IP	H	HR	BB	SO	RAT	ERA	ERA+	OAV	OOB	BH	AVG	PB	PR	/A	PD	TPI
1985	Phi-N	1	0	1.000	2	0	0	0	0	1	2	0	0	1	18.0	0.00	—	.500	.500	0	—	0	0	0	0	0.4
	Tex-A	0	1	.000	7	0	0	0	2	8^1	12	2	3	8	16.2	7.56	56	.343	.395	0	—	0	-3	-3	-0	-0.5
Total	1	1	1	.500	9	0	0	0	2	9^1	14	2	3	9	16.4	6.75	62	.359	.405	0	—	0	-3	-3	-0	-0.1

● MAX SURKONT

Surkont, Matthew Constantine b: 6/16/22, Central Falls, R.I. d: 10/8/86, Largo, Fla. BR/TR, 6', 205 lbs. Deb: 4/19/49

YEAR	TM/L	W	L	PCT	G	GS	CG	SH	SV	IP	H	HR	BB	SO	RAT	ERA	ERA+	OAV	OOB	BH	AVG	PB	PR	/A	PD	TPI
1949	Chi-A	3	5	.375	44	2	0	0	4	96	92	9	60	38	14.5	4.78	87	.255	.366	1	.045	-1	-6	-7	-1	-0.8
1950	Bos-N	5	2	.714	9	6	2	0	0	55^2	63	5	20	21	13.7	3.23	119	.285	.350	10	.435	5	6	4	-1	0.9
1951	Bos-N	12	16	.429	37	33	11	2	1	237	230	21	89	110	12.4	3.99	92	.252	.323	11	.151	0	-1	-8	-3	-1.1
1952	Bos-N	12	13	.480	31	29	12	3	0	215	201	19	76	125	11.7	3.77	96	.245	.311	7	.111	-1	-1	-4	-1	-0.6
1953	Mil-N	11	5	.688	28	24	11	2	0	170	168	22	64	83	12.3	4.18	94	.255	.321	16	.286	7	2	-5	1	0.3
1954	Pit-N	9	18	.333	33	29	11	0	0	208^1	216	25	78	78	12.9	4.41	95	.268	.335	10	.167	0	-8	-5	0	-0.5
1955	Pit-N	7	14	.333	35	22	5	0	2	166^1	194	23	78	84	14.9	5.57	74	.298	.376	7	.140	-1	-28	-27	-2	-3.2
1956	Pit-N	0	0	—	1	0	0	0	0	2	2	0	3	1	22.5	4.50	84	.333	.556	0	—	0	-0	-0	0	0.0
	StL-N	0	0	—	5	0	0	0	0	5^2	10	3	2	5	19.1	9.53	40	.417	.462	0	.000	-0	-4	-4	-0	0.0
	NY-N	2	2	.500	8	4	1	0	1	32	24	5	9	18	9.3	4.78	79	.202	.258	1	.111	-0	-4	-4	-0	-0.5
	Yr	2	2	.500	14	4	1	0	1	39^2	36	8	14	24	11.3	5.45	69	.240	.305	1	.100	-0	-7	-7	-1	-0.5
1957	NY-N	0	1	.000	5	0	0	0	0	6^1	9	2	2	8	15.6	9.95	40	.321	.367	0	—	0	-4	-4	0	-0.6
Total	9	61	76	.445	236	149	53	7	8	1194^1	1209	134	481	571	12.9	4.38	89	.262	.335	63	.176	8	-48	-63	-5	-6.1

● GEORGE SUSCE

Susce, George Daniel b: 9/13/31, Pittsburgh, Pa. BR/TR, 6'1", 180 lbs. Deb: 4/15/55 F

YEAR	TM/L	W	L	PCT	G	GS	CG	SH	SV	IP	H	HR	BB	SO	RAT	ERA	ERA+	OAV	OOB	BH	AVG	PB	PR	/A	PD	TPI
1955	Bos-A	9	7	.563	29	15	6	1	1	144^1	123	12	49	60	11.2	3.06	140	.232	.306	7	.143	-2	15	20	-0	1.8
1956	Bos-A	2	4	.333	21	6	0	0	0	69^2	71	14	44	26	15.4	6.20	74	.262	.373	4	.222	1	-16	-12	-0	-0.8
1957	Bos-A	7	3	.700	29	5	0	0	1	88^1	93	6	41	40	14.0	4.28	93	.274	.358	3	.120	-1	-5	-3	-1	-0.5
1958	Bos-A	0	0	—	2	0	0	0	0	2	6	1	1	0	31.5	18.00	22	.600	.636	0	—	0	-3	-3	-0	0.0
	Det-A	4	3	.571	27	10	2	0	1	90^2	90	7	26	42	11.8	3.67	110	.259	.316	3	.125	-1	1	4	-2	0.0
	Yr	4	3	.571	29	10	2	0	1	92^2	96	8	27	42	12.2	3.98	101	.268	.325	3	.125	-1	-2	1	-2	0.0
1959	Det-A	0	0	—	9	0	0	0	0	14^2	24	4	9	9	21.5	12.89	32	.358	.449	0	.000	-0	-15	-14	-0	0.0
Total	5	22	17	.564	117	36	8	1	3	409^2	407	44	170	177	13.1	4.42	95	.260	.340	17	.145	-2	-23	-9	-4	0.5

● RICK SUTCLIFFE

Sutcliffe, Richard Lee b: 6/21/56, Independence, Mo. BL/TR, 6'7", 215 lbs. Deb: 9/29/76

YEAR	TM/L	W	L	PCT	G	GS	CG	SH	SV	IP	H	HR	BB	SO	RAT	ERA	ERA+	OAV	OOB	BH	AVG	PB	PR	/A	PD	TPI
1976	LA-N	0	0	—	1	1	0	0	0	5	2	0	1	3	5.4	0.00	—	.125	.176	0	.000	-0	2	2	-0	0.0
1978	LA-N	0	0	—	2	0	0	0	0	1^2	2	0	1	0	21.6	0.00	—	.286	.444	0	—	0	1	1	0	0.0
1979	LA-N	17	10	.630	39	30	5	1	0	242	217	16	97	117	11.8	3.46	105	.243	.319	21	.247	5	7	5	-2	0.8
1980	LA-N	3	9	.250	42	10	1	1	5	110	122	10	55	59	14.6	5.56	63	.285	.368	4	.148	-0	-24	-25	-1	-2.9
1981	LA-N	2	2	.500	14	6	0	0	0	47	41	5	20	16	12.1	4.02	83	.238	.325	2	.182	1	-3	-4	0	-0.2
1982	Cle-A	14	8	.636	34	27	6	1	1	216	174	16	98	142	11.5	**2.96**	138	**.226**	.317	0	—	0	**27**	27	1	2.7
1983	Cle-A☆	17	11	.607	36	35	10	2	0	243^1	251	23	102	160	13.3	4.29	99	.268	.344	0	—	0	-6	-1	2	-0.2
1984	Cle-A	4	5	.444	15	15	2	0	0	94^1	111	7	46	58	15.2	5.15	79	.298	.378	0	—	0	-12	-11	-0	-1.0
	*Chi-N	16	1	**.941**	20	20	7	3	0	150^1	123	9	39	155	9.8	2.69	145	.220	.272	14	.250	3	15	20	2	2.8
1985	Chi-N	8	8	.500	20	20	6	3	0	130	119	12	44	102	11.5	3.18	125	.240	.306	10	.233	2	6	12	1	1.8
1986	Chi-N	5	14	.263	28	27	4	1	0	176^2	166	18	96	122	13.4	4.64	87	.252	.348	11	.208	2	-18	-12	1	-0.8
1987	Chi-N★	**18**	10	.643	34	34	6	1	0	237^1	223	24	106	174	12.6	3.68	116	.252	.335	12	.148	2	11	16	4	2.4
1988	Chi-N	13	14	.481	32	32	12	2	0	226	232	18	70	144	12.1	3.86	93	.269	.325	12	.160	3	-10	-6	1	-0.3
1989	*Chi-N★	16	11	.593	35	34	5	1	0	229	202	18	69	153	10.7	3.66	103	.240	.299	10	.143	1	-4	3	1	0.6
1990	Chi-N	0	2	.000	5	5	0	0	0	21^1	25	2	12	7	15.6	5.91	69	.305	.394	0	.000	0	-5	-4	0	-0.3
1991	Chi-N	6	5	.545	19	18	0	0	0	96^2	96	4	45	52	13.1	4.10	95	.264	.345	3	.094	-1	-4	-2	0	-0.4
1992	Bal-A	16	15	.516	36	36	5	2	0	237^1	251	20	74	109	12.6	4.47	90	.273	.332	0	—	0	-14	-12	-2	-1.8
1993	Bal-A	10	10	.500	29	28	3	0	0	166	212	23	74	80	15.8	5.75	78	.314	.386	0	—	0	-26	-24	1	-2.5
1994	StL-N	6	4	.600	16	14	0	0	0	67^2	93	11	32	26	16.9	6.52	64	.331	.403	3	.130	-1	-17	-18	1	-2.1
Total	18	171	139	.552	457	392	72	18	6	2697^2	2662	236	1081	1679	12.6	4.08	97	.260	.334	102	.181	17	-77	-34	10	-1.4

● HARRY SUTER

Suter, Harry Richard "Handsome Harry" or "Rube"
b: 9/15/1887, Independence, Mo. d: 7/24/71, Topeka, Kan. BL/TL, 5'10", 190 lbs. Deb: 4/16/09

YEAR	TM/L	W	L	PCT	G	GS	CG	SH	SV	IP	H	HR	BB	SO	RAT	ERA	ERA+	OAV	OOB	BH	AVG	PB	PR	/A	PD	TPI
1909	Chi-A	2	3	.400	18	7	3	1	1	87^1	72	2	28	53	10.7	2.47	95	.199	.264	3	.094	-1	0	-1	-1	-0.3

● DARRELL SUTHERLAND

Sutherland, Darrell Wayne b: 11/14/41, Glendale, Cal. BR/TR, 6'4", 169 lbs. Deb: 6/28/64 F

YEAR	TM/L	W	L	PCT	G	GS	CG	SH	SV	IP	H	HR	BB	SO	RAT	ERA	ERA+	OAV	OOB	BH	AVG	PB	PR	/A	PD	TPI
1964	NY-N	0	3	.000	10	4	0	0	0	26^2	32	1	12	9	15.5	7.76	46	.302	.383	1	.200	0	-13	-12	1	-1.1
1965	NY-N	3	1	.750	18	2	0	0	0	48	33	4	17	16	10.1	2.81	125	.199	.289	2	.154	0	4	4	2	0.5
1966	NY-N	2	0	1.000	31	0	0	0	1	44^1	60	6	25	23	17.7	4.87	75	.339	.426	2	.667	1	-6	-6	1	-0.1
1968	Cle-A	0	0	—	3	0	0	0	0	3^1	6	0	4	2	27.0	8.10	37	.375	.500	0	—	0	-2	-2	-0	0.0
Total	4	5	4	.556	62	6	0	0	1	122^1	131	11	58	50	14.5	4.78	75	.282	.371	5	.238	1	-17	-17	3	-0.7

● SUDS SUTHERLAND

Sutherland, Harvey Scott b: 2/20/1894, Beaverton, Ore. d: 5/11/72, Portland, Ore. BR/TR, 6', 180 lbs. Deb: 4/14/21

YEAR	TM/L	W	L	PCT	G	GS	CG	SH	SV	IP	H	HR	BB	SO	RAT	ERA	ERA+	OAV	OOB	BH	AVG	PB	PR	/A	PD	TPI
1921	Det-A	6	2	.750	13	8	3	0	0	58	80	1	18	18	15.2	4.97	86	.328	.374	11	.407	2	-4	-4	2	-0.1

● DIZZY SUTHERLAND

Sutherland, Howard Alvin b: 4/9/22, Washington, D.C. d: 8/26/79, Washington, D.C. BL/TL, 6', 200 lbs. Deb: 9/20/49

YEAR	TM/L	W	L	PCT	G	GS	CG	SH	SV	IP	H	HR	BB	SO	RAT	ERA	ERA+	OAV	OOB	BH	AVG	PB	PR	/A	PD	TPI
1949	Was-A	0	1	.000	1	1	0	0	0	1	2	0	6	0	72.0	45.00	9	.400	.727	0	—	0	-5	-5	0	-1.7

● BRUCE SUTTER

Sutter, Howard Bruce b: 1/8/53, Lancaster, Pa. BR/TR, 6'2", 190 lbs. Deb: 5/9/76

YEAR	TM/L	W	L	PCT	G	GS	CG	SH	SV	IP	H	HR	BB	SO	RAT	ERA	ERA+	OAV	OOB	BH	AVG	PB	PR	/A	PD	TPI
1976	Chi-N	6	3	.667	52	0	0	0	10	83^1	63	4	26	73	9.6	2.70	143	.209	.272	0	.000	-1	7	11	-0	1.3
1977	Chi-N†	7	3	.700	62	0	0	0	31	107^1	69	5	23	129	7.8	1.34	327	.183	.232	3	.150	-0	31	**36**	1	5.6
1978	Chi-N★	8	10	.444	64	0	0	0	27	99	82	10	34	106	10.6	3.18	127	.220	.287	1	.077	-0	4	9	0	2.2
1979	Chi-N★	6	6	.500	62	0	0	0	**37**	101^1	67	3	32	110	8.8	2.22	185	.186	.252	3	.250	0	17	**21**	1	**4.3**
1980	Chi-N★	5	8	.385	60	0	0	0	**28**	102^1	90	5	34	76	11.0	2.64	148	.242	.307	1	.111	-1	11	14	-0	2.6
1981	StL-N★	3	5	.375	48	0	0	0	**25**	82^1	64	5	24	57	9.7	2.62	136	.218	.279	0	.000	-1	8	9	-1	1.2
1982	*StL-N	9	8	.529	70	0	0	0	**36**	102^1	88	8	34	61	11.0	2.90	125	.235	.303	1	.125	-0	8	8	0	1.9
1983	StL-N	9	10	.474	60	0	0	0	21	89^1	90	8	30	64	12.2	4.23	86	.262	.324	0	.000	-1	-6	-6	2	-1.4
1984	StL-N☆	5	7	.417	71	0	0	0	**45**	122^2	109	9	23	77	9.8	1.54	225	.245	.284	0	.000	-1	**28**	**26**	1	**4.4**
1985	Atl-N	7	7	.500	58	0	0	0	23	88^1	91	13	29	52	12.5	4.48	86	.267	.330	0	.000	-0	-9	-6	-0	-1.3
1986	Atl-N	2	0	1.000	16	0	0	0	3	18^2	17	3	9	16	12.5	4.34	92	.243	.329	0	.000	-0	-1	-1	0	-0.1

YEAR	TM/L	W	L	PCT	G	GS	CG	SH	SV	IP	H	HR	BB	SO	RAT	ERA	ERA+	OAV	OOB	BH	AVG	PB	PR	/A	PD	TPI
1988	Atl-N	1	4	.200	38	0	0	0	14	45^1	49	4	11	40	12.1	4.76	77	.275	.321	0	.000	0	-7	-5	-0	-0.9
Total	12	68	71	.489	661	0	0	0	300	1042^1	879	77	309	861	10.4	2.83	135	.230	.289	9	.088	-5	91	116	4	19.8
● **JACK SUTTHOFF**	Sutthoff, John Gerhard "Sunny Jack" b: 6/29/1873, Cincinnati, Ohio d: 8/3/42, Cincinnati, Ohio BL/TR, 5'9", 175 lbs. Deb: 9/15/1898																									
1898	Was-N	0	0	—	2	1	0	0	0	8^1	16	1	8	3	25.9	12.96	28	.400	.500	1	.333	0	-9	-9	0	0.0
1899	StL-N	1	2	.333	3	3	3	0	0	24	29	1	15	8	16.5	4.13	97	.299	.393	1	.100	-1	-1	-0	0	-0.1
1901	Cin-N	1	6	.143	10	4	4	0	0	70^1	82	2	39	12	15.7	5.50	58	.289	.378	3	.107	-2	-17	-18	-1	-1.7
1903	Cin-N	16	9	.640	30	27	21	3	0	224^2	207	2	79	76	12.1	2.80	127	.246	.323	12	.143	-3	12	19	-1	1.4
1904	Cin-N	5	6	.455	12	10	8	0	0	90	83	1	43	27	12.9	2.30	127	.255	.348	6	.182	-0	4	6	-2	0.5
	Phi-N	6	13	.316	19	18	17	0	0	163^2	172	2	71	46	13.9	3.68	73	.272	.354	10	.164	-0	-17	-18	-1	-2.1
	Yr	11	19	.367	31	28	25	0	0	253^2	255	3	114	73	13.4	3.19	87	.266	.349	16	.170	-1	-13	-12	-3	-1.6
1905	Phi-N	3	4	.429	13	6	4	1	0	77^2	82	2	36	26	14.1	3.82	76	.290	.378	2	.080	-1	-7	-8	0	-0.7
Total	6	32	40	.444	89	69	57	4	0	658^2	671	11	291	198	13.6	3.54	89	.268	.352	35	.143	-7	-35	-28	-5	-2.7
● **DON SUTTON**	Sutton, Donald Howard b: 4/2/45, Clio, Ala. BR/TR, 6'1", 185 lbs. Deb: 4/14/66 H																									
1966	LA-N	12	12	.500	37	35	6	2	0	225^2	192	19	52	209	9.9	2.99	110	.228	.276	15	.183	1	15	8	-0	0.9
1967	LA-N	11	15	.423	37	34	11	3	1	232^2	223	18	57	169	11.1	3.95	79	.250	.300	10	.133	-0	-15	-22	-2	-2.5
1968	LA-N	11	15	.423	35	27	7	2	1	207^2	179	6	59	162	10.4	2.60	106	.232	.288	11	.177	1	9	4	-1	0.5
1969	LA-N	17	18	.486	41	41	11	4	0	293^1	269	25	91	217	11.1	3.47	96	.242	.301	15	.153	-1	4	-5	0	-0.6
1970	LA-N	15	13	.536	38	38	10	4	0	260^1	251	38	78	201	11.7	4.08	94	.249	.310	13	.155	3	-1	-7	-1	-0.5
1971	LA-N	17	12	.586	38	37	12	4	1	265^1	231	10	55	194	9.9	2.54	127	.238	.282	19	.216	3	27	20	-1	2.5
1972	LA-N★	19	9	.679	33	33	18	**9**	0	272^2	186	13	63	207	**8.4**	2.08	160	**.189**	**.240**	13	.143	-1	42	38	-0	3.9
1973	LA-N★	18	10	.643	33	33	14	3	0	256^1	196	18	56	200	9.0	2.42	142	.209	.258	10	.119	-2	35	29	-1	2.9
1974	*LA-N	19	9	.679	40	40	10	5	0	276	241	23	80	179	10.7	3.23	105	.229	.288	18	.184	1	12	5	-1	0.4
1975	LA-N★	16	13	.552	35	35	11	4	0	254^1	202	17	62	175	9.4	2.87	119	.213	**.264**	11	.138	-1	21	15	-1	1.4
1976	LA-N	21	10	.677	35	34	15	4	0	267^2	231	22	82	161	10.6	3.06	111	.234	.295	7	.083	-3	13	10	-3	0.5
1977	*LA-N★	14	8	.636	33	33	9	3	0	240^1	207	23	69	150	10.4	3.18	120	.233	.291	11	.151	1	19	17	-1	1.4
1978	*LA-N	15	11	.577	34	34	12	2	0	238^1	228	29	54	154	10.8	3.55	99	.250	.295	6	.083	-3	1	-1	-2	-0.7
1979	LA-N	12	15	.444	33	32	6	1	1	226	201	21	61	146	10.5	3.82	95	.239	.291	11	.143	-2	-2	-5	-1	-0.8
1980	LA-N	13	5	.722	32	31	4	2	1	212^1	163	20	47	128	**9.0**	**2.20**	159	.211	**.258**	5	.078	-4	33	30	-0	2.1
1981	Hou-N	11	9	.550	23	23	6	3	0	158^2	132	6	29	104	**9.2**	2.61	126	.230	**.268**	7	.137	0	16	12	0	1.6
1982	Hou-N	13	8	.619	27	27	4	0	0	195	169	10	46	139	10.0	3.00	111	.232	.279	11	.162	-0	13	7	-1	0.6
	*Mil-A	4	1	.800	7	7	2	1	0	54^2	55	8	18	36	12.0	3.29	115	.263	.322	0	—	0	5	3	1	0.7
1983	Mil-A	8	13	.381	31	31	4	0	0	220^1	209	21	54	134	10.9	4.08	91	.246	.295	0	—	0	-1	-9	-1	-0.5
1984	Mil-A	14	12	.538	33	33	1	0	0	212^2	224	24	51	143	11.8	3.77	102	.266	.310	0	—	0	5	2	-2	0.2
1985	Oak-A	13	8	.619	29	29	1	1	0	194^1	194	19	51	91	11.3	3.89	99	.256	.302	0	—	0	6	-1	-0	0.3
	Cal-A	2	2	.500	5	5	0	0	0	31^2	27	6	8	16	9.9	3.69	111	.233	.282	0	—	0	2	1	-1	0.1
	Yr	15	10	.600	34	34	1	1	0	226	221	25	59	107	11.2	3.86	101	.251	.298	0	—	0	7	1	-1	0.4
1986	*Cal-A	15	11	.577	34	34	3	1	0	207	192	31	49	116	10.6	3.74	110	.242	.288	0	—	0	10	9	-3	0.8
1987	Cal-A	11	11	.500	35	34	1	0	0	191^2	199	38	41	99	11.6	4.70	92	.269	.313	0	—	0	-5	-8	-3	-0.9
1988	LA-N	3	6	.333	16	16	0	0	0	87^1	91	7	30	44	12.6	3.92	85	.270	.332	2	.087	-1	-5	-6	-1	-0.7
Total	23	324	256	.559	774	756	178	58	5	5282^1	4692	472	1343	3574	10.4	3.26	108	.236	.287	195	.144	-7	259	146	-26	13.6
● **EZRA SUTTON**	Sutton, Ezra Ballou b: 9/17/1850, Palmyra, N.Y. d: 6/20/07, Braintree, Mass. BR/TR, 5'8.5", 153 lbs. Deb: 5/4/1871 ♦																									
1875	Ath-n	0	0	—	2	0	0	0	0	6	14	0	0	0	21.0	10.50	23	.412	.412	116	.324	1	-6	-5		0.0
● **JOHN SUTTON**	Sutton, Johnny Ike b: 11/13/52, Dallas, Tex. BR/TR, 5'11", 185 lbs. Deb: 4/7/77																									
1977	StL-N	2	1	.667	14	0	0	0	0	24^1	28	1	9	9	13.7	2.59	149	.315	.378	0	.000	-0	4	3	0	0.4
1978	Min-A	0	0	—	17	0	0	0	0	44^1	46	3	15	18	12.6	3.45	111	.264	.326	0	—	0	2	2	-0	-0.2
Total	2	2	1	.667	31	0	0	0	0	68^2	74	4	24	27	13.0	3.15	122	.281	.344	0	.000	-0	5	5	0	0.2
● **MAC SUZUKI**	Suzuki, Makoto b: 5/31/75, Kobe, Japan BR/TR, 6'3", 195 lbs. Deb: 7/7/96																									
1996	Sea-A	0	0	—	1	0	0	0	0	1^1	2	0	2	1	27.0	20.25	24	.333	.500	0	—	0	-2	-2	0	0.0
1998	Sea-A	1	2	.333	6	5	0	0	0	26^1	34	3	15	19	16.7	7.18	64	.304	.386	0	—	0	-7	-7	-0	-0.7
Total	2	1	2	.333	7	5	0	0	0	27^2	36	3	17	20	17.2	7.81	59	.305	.393	0	—	0	-10	-10	-0	-0.7
● **BILL SWABACH**	Swabach, William Deb: 7/9/1887																									
1887	NY-N	0	2	.000	2	2	2	0	0	16	27	1	6	6	19.1	5.06	74	.346	.400	0	.000	-1	-2	-2	0	-0.3
● **BILL SWAGGERTY**	Swaggerty, William David b: 12/5/56, Sanford, Fla. BR/TR, 6'2", 186 lbs. Deb: 8/13/83																									
1983	Bal-A	1	1	.500	7	2	0	0	0	21^2	23	1	6	7	12.0	2.91	136	.267	.315	0	—	0	3	3	1	0.4
1984	Bal-A	3	2	.600	23	6	0	0	0	57	68	7	21	18	14.1	5.21	74	.302	.362	0	—	0	-8	-8	-1	-0.7
1985	Bal-A	0	0	—	1	0	0	0	0	1^2	3	0	2	2	27.0	5.40	75	.375	.500	0	—	0	-0	-0	-0	0.1
1986	Bal-A	0	0	—	1	0	0	0	0	1	6	0	1	1	63.0	18.00	23	.750	.778	0	—	0	-2	-2	0	0.1
Total	4	4	3	.571	32	8	0	0	0	81^1	100	8	30	28	14.4	4.76	82	.306	.364	0	—	0	-7	-8	0	-0.1
● **CY SWAIM**	Swaim, John Hillary b: 3/11/1874, Cadwallader, Ohio d: 12/27/45, Eustis, Fla. 6'6", 180 lbs. Deb: 5/3/1897																									
1897	Was-N	9	11	.450	26	19	14	0	0	184	219	5	59	52	14.1	4.60	94	.293	.353	16	.225	-3	-6	-5	-4	-1.0
1898	Was-N	3	11	.214	16	13	9	0	1	101^1	119	4	28	30	13.4	4.26	86	.290	.342	5	.143	-3	-7	-7	-1	-1.1
Total	2	12	22	.353	42	32	23	0	1	285^1	338	9	87	82	13.8	4.48	92	.292	.349	21	.198	-6	-13	-12	-5	-2.1
● **CRAIG SWAN**	Swan, Craig Steven b: 11/30/50, Van Nuys, Cal. BR/TR, 6'3", 215 lbs. Deb: 9/3/73																									
1973	NY-N	0	1	.000	3	1	0	0	0	8^1	16	2	2	4	19.4	8.64	42	.432	.462	0	.000	-0	-5	-5	-0	-0.5
1974	NY-N	1	3	.250	7	5	0	0	0	30^1	28	1	21	10	14.5	4.45	80	.255	.374	4	.364	1	-3	-3	0	-0.2
1975	NY-N	1	3	.250	6	6	0	0	0	31	38	4	13	19	15.1	6.39	54	.302	.371	0	.000	-1	-10	-10	-1	-1.2
1976	NY-N	6	9	.400	23	22	2	1	0	132^1	129	11	44	89	12.1	3.54	93	.254	.320	4	.103	-1	-1	-4	-1	-0.5
1977	NY-N	9	10	.474	26	24	2	1	0	146^2	153	10	56	71	12.9	4.23	88	.268	.334	9	.188	-0	-5	-8	-2	-1.2
1978	NY-N	9	6	.600	29	28	5	1	0	207^1	164	12	58	125	**9.7**	**2.43**	**143**	.219	.277	10	.154	-0	26	24	1	1.8
1979	NY-N	14	13	.519	35	35	10	3	0	251^1	241	20	57	145	10.7	3.29	110	.255	.299	10	.123	-1	12	10	-1	0.8
1980	NY-N	5	9	.357	21	21	4	1	0	128^1	117	20	30	79	10.3	3.58	99	.247	.292	7	.219	2	0	-0	-2	-0.1
1981	NY-N	0	2	.000	5	3	0	0	0	13^2	10	0	1	9	7.2	3.29	106	.204	.220	0	.000	-0	0	0	-0	0.0
1982	NY-N	11	7	.611	37	21	2	0	1	166^1	165	13	37	67	10.9	3.35	108	.256	.297	8	.182	3	5	5	-1	0.7
1983	NY-N	2	8	.200	27	18	0	0	1	96^1	112	14	42	43	14.4	5.51	66	.299	.369	2	.077	-2	-20	-20	-1	-2.2
1984	NY-N	1	0	1.000	10	0	0	0	0	18^2	18	5	7	10	12.1	8.20	43	.247	.313	0	—	0	-10	-10	-0	-0.5
	Cal-A	0	1	.000	2	1	0	0	0	5	8	3	0	2	14.4	10.80	37	.348	.348	0	—	0	-4	-4	0	-0.6
Total	12	59	72	.450	231	185	25	7	2	1235^2	1199	115	368	673	11.5	3.74	95	.256	.312	54	.151	1	-13	-24	-10	-3.7
● **DUCKY SWAN**	Swan, Harry Gordon b: 8/11/1887, Lancaster, Pa. d: 5/8/46, Pittsburgh, Pa. BR/TR, 5'10", 165 lbs. Deb: 4/28/14																									
1914	KC-F	0	0	—	1	0	0	0	0	1	0	0	1	1	9.0	0.00	—	.000	.250	0	—	0	0	0	-0	0.0
● **RUSS SWAN**	Swan, Russell Howard b: 1/3/64, Fremont, Cal. BL/TL, 6'4", 215 lbs. Deb: 8/3/89																									
1989	SF-N	0	2	.000	2	2	0	0	0	6^2	11	4	4	2	20.3	10.80	31	.393	.469	0	.000	-0	-5	-6	0	-1.2
1990	SF-N	0	1	.000	2	1	0	0	0	2^1	6	0	4	1	38.6	3.86	94	.429	.556	0	.000	-0	-0	-0	0	0.0
	Sea-A	2	3	.400	11	8	0	0	0	47	42	3	18	15	11.5	3.64	109	.244	.316	0	—	0	1	2	0	0.1
1991	Sea-A	6	2	.750	63	0	0	0	2	78^2	81	8	28	33	12.5	3.43	120	.269	.331	0	—	0	6	6	1	0.6
1992	Sea-A	3	10	.231	55	9	1	0	9	104^1	104	8	45	45	13.1	4.74	84	.262	.342	0	—	0	-9	-9	2	-1.0
1993	Sea-A	3	3	.500	23	0	0	0	0	19^2	25	2	18	10	20.6	9.15	48	.316	.455	0	—	0	-11	-10	1	-2.6
1994	Cle-A	0	1	.000	12	0	0	0	0	8	13	1	7	2	22.5	11.25	42	.382	.488	0	—	0	-6	-6	0	-0.6
Total	6	14	22	.389	168	20	1	0	11	266^2	282	26	124	108	13.9	4.83	84	.275	.356	0	.000	-0	-24	-23	3	-4.7
● **RED SWANSON**	Swanson, Arthur Leonard b: 10/15/36, Baton Rouge, La. BR/TR, 6'1.5", 175 lbs. Deb: 9/10/55																									
1955	Pit-N	0	0	—	1	0	0	0	0	2	2	1	3	0	22.5	18.00	23	.286	.500	0	—	0	-3	-3	-0	0.0

YEAR	TM/L	W	L	PCT	G	GS	CG	SH	SV	IP	H	HR	BB	SO	RAT	ERA	ERA+	OAV	OOB	BH	AVG	PB	PR	/A	PD	TPI
1956	Pit-N	0	0	—	9	0	0	0	0	11^2	21	1	8	5	22.4	10.03	38	.438	.518	0	—	0	-8	-8	1	0.1
1957	Pit-N	3	3	.500	32	8	1	0	0	72^2	68	9	31	29	12.4	3.72	102	.248	.327	0	.000	-1	1	1	-1	-0.2
Total	3	3	3	.500	42	8	1	0	0	86^1	91	11	42	34	14.0	4.90	77	.277	.360	0	.000	-1	-10	-11	-0	-0.1
● **ED SWARTWOOD**	Swartwood, Cyrus Edward b: 1/12/1859, Rockford, Ill. d: 5/15/24, Pittsburgh, Pa. BL/TR, 5'11", 198 lbs. Deb: 8/11/1881 U♦																									
1884	Pit-a	0	0	—	1	0	0	0	0	2^1	6	0	1	0	27.0	11.57	29	.400	.438	115	.288	0	-2	-2	-0	0.0
1890	Tol-a	0	0	—	1	0	0	0	0	3	2	0	0	1	6.0	3.00	132	.182	.182	151	.327	0	0	0	-0	0.0
Total	2	0	0	—	2	0	0	0	0	5^1	8	0	1	1	15.2	6.75	55	.308	.333	861	.299	1	-2	-2	-0	0.0
● **BUD SWARTZ**	Swartz, Sherwin Merle b: 6/13/29, Tulsa, Okla. d: 6/24/91, Los Angeles, Cal. BL/TL, 6'2.5", 180 lbs. Deb: 7/12/47																									
1947	StL-A	0	0	—	5	0	0	0	0	5^1	9	1	7	1	27.0	6.75	57	.360	.500	1	1.000	0	-2	-2	-0	0.0
● **MONTY SWARTZ**	Swartz, Vernon Monroe "Dazzy" b: 1/1/1897, Farmersville, Ohio d: 1/13/80, Germantown, Ohio BR/TR, 5'11", 182 lbs. Deb: 10/3/20																									
1920	Cin-N	0	1	.000	1	1	1	0	0	12	17	0	2	2	14.3	4.50	68	.333	.358	2	.500	1	-2	-2	0	-0.1
● **DAVE SWARTZBAUGH**	Swartzbaugh, David Theodore b: 2/11/68, Middletown, Ohio BR/TR, 6'2", 195 lbs. Deb: 9/3/95																									
1995	Chi-N	0	0	—	7	0	0	0	0	7^1	5	0	3	5	9.8	0.00	—	.208	.296	0	—	0	3	3	-0	0.0
1996	Chi-N	0	2	.000	6	5	0	0	0	24	26	3	14	13	15.0	6.38	68	.277	.370	0	.000	-0	-6	-5	0	-0.4
1997	Chi-N	0	1	.000	2	2	0	0	0	8	12	1	7	4	22.5	9.00	48	.364	.488	0	.000	-0	-4	-4	-0	-0.5
Total	3	0	3	.000	15	7	0	0	0	39^1	43	4	24	22	15.6	5.72	75	.285	.386	0	.000	-1	-7	-6	0	-0.9
● **PARK SWARTZEL**	Swartzel, Park B. b: 11/21/1865, Knightstown, Ind. d: 1/3/40, Los Angeles, Cal. BR/TR, 5'10", Deb: 4/17/1889																									
1889	KC-a	19	27	.413	48	47	45	0	1	410^1	481	21	117	147	13.6	4.32	97	.283	.338	25	.144	-9	-22	-6	9	-0.5
● **CHARLIE SWEENEY**	Sweeney, Charles J. b: 4/13/1863, San Francisco, Cal d: 4/4/02, San Francisco, Cal. BR/TR, 5'10.5", 181 lbs. Deb: 5/11/1882 ♦																									
1883	Pro-N	7	7	.500	20	18	14	0	0	146^2	142	3	28	48	10.4	3.13	99	.237	.272	19	.218	-1	0	-1	1	-0.1
1884	Pro-N	17	8	.680	27	24	22	4	1	221	153	4	29	145	**7.4**	1.55	184	**.187**	**.215**	50	.298	8	35	32	1	4.0
	StL-U	24	7	.774	33	32	31	2	0	271	207	2	13	192	7.3	1.83	131	.197	.207	54	.316	6	19	17	5	2.4
1885	StL-N	11	21	.344	35	35	32	2	0	275	276	6	50	84	10.7	3.93	70	.250	.282	55	.206	-0	-34	-36	0	-3.3
1886	StL-N	5	6	.455	11	11	11	0	0	93	108	9	39	28	14.2	4.16	78	.285	.352	16	.250	1	-9	-10	0	-0.8
1887	Cle-a	0	3	.000	3	3	3	0	0	24	42	0	13	8	20.6	8.25	53	.372	.437	30	.226	0	-11	-10	0	-0.8
Total	5	64	52	.552	129	123	113	8	1	1030^2	928	24	172	505	9.6	2.87	98	.228	.260	224	.251	14	1	-8	8	1.4
● **BILL SWEENEY**	Sweeney, William J. b: Philadelphia, Pa. d: 8/2/03, Philadelphia, Pa. TR, Deb: 6/27/1882																									
1882	Phi-a	9	10	.474	20	20	18	0	0	170	178	4	42	48	11.6	2.91	102	.252	.294	14	.159	-3	-4	1	-1	-0.2
1884	Bal-U	**40**	21	.656	**62**	60	**58**	4	0	**538**	522	13	74	374	10.0	2.59	103	.238	.263	71	.240	-16	-9	5	1	-0.7
Total	2	49	31	.613	82	80	76	4	0	708	700	17	116	422	10.4	2.67	103	.241	.270	85	.221	-19	-13	7	1	-0.9
● **LES SWEETLAND**	Sweetland, Lester Leo (Born Leo Sweetland) b: 8/15/01, St.Ignace, Mich. d: 3/4/74, Melbourne, Fla. BR/TL, 5'11.5", 155 lbs. Deb: 7/4/27																									
1927	Phi-N	2	10	.167	21	13	6	0	0	103^2	147	3	53	21	17.6	6.16	67	.348	.425	12	.316	3	-26	-23	5	-1.5
1928	Phi-N	3	15	.167	37	18	5	0	2	135^1	163	15	97	23	18.3	6.58	65	.306	.426	9	.191	1	-39	-35	2	-3.6
1929	Phi-N	13	11	.542	43	25	10	2	2	204^1	255	23	87	47	15.5	5.11	102	.316	.389	26	.292	3	-9	2	4	0.8
1930	Phi-N	7	15	.318	34	25	8	1	0	167	271	24	60	36	18.1	7.71	71	.373	.425	16	.281	4	-51	-42	1	-3.7
1931	Chi-N	8	7	.533	26	14	9	0	0	130^1	156	3	61	32	15.3	5.04	77	.297	.375	15	.268	5	-17	-17	0	-1.3
Total	5	33	58	.363	161	95	38	3	4	740^2	992	68	358	159	16.9	6.10	77	.329	.407	78	.272	16	-142	-116	12	-9.3
● **STEVE SWETONIC**	Swetonic, Stephen Albert b: 8/13/03, Mt.Pleasant, Pa. d: 4/22/74, Canonsburg, Pa. BR/TR, 5'11", 185 lbs. Deb: 4/17/29 ♦																									
1929	Pit-N	8	10	.444	41	12	3	0	5	143^2	172	6	50	35	14.2	4.82	99	.299	.360	13	.271	3	-2	-1	2	0.3
1930	Pit-N	6	6	.500	23	6	3	1	5	96^2	107	7	27	35	12.5	4.47	111	.276	.323	4	.111	-3	5	5	-1	0.3
1931	Pit-N	0	2	.000	14	0	0	0	1	27^2	28	0	16	8	14.3	3.90	99	.264	.361	1	.143	-0	-0	-0	-0	0.0
1932	Pit-N	11	6	.647	24	19	11	**4**	0	162^2	134	11	55	39	10.5	2.82	135	**.221**	.286	5	.093	-4	19	18	-1	1.2
1933	Pit-N	12	12	.500	31	21	8	3	0	164^2	166	10	64	37	12.7	3.50	95	.260	.330	11	.200	1	-3	-3	-1	-0.5
Total	5	37	36	.507	133	58	25	8	11	595^1	607	34	212	154	12.5	3.81	107	.262	.326	34	.170	-3	20	19	-2	1.3
● **BILL SWIFT**	Swift, William Charles b: 10/27/61, Portland, Maine BR/TR, 6', 180 lbs. Deb: 6/7/85																									
1985	Sea-A	6	10	.375	23	21	0	0	0	120^2	131	8	48	55	13.7	4.77	88	.279	.352	0	—	0	-8	-8	0	-0.9
1986	Sea-A	2	9	.182	29	17	1	0	0	115^1	148	5	55	55	16.4	5.46	78	.319	.399	0	—	0	-16	-16	1	-1.2
1988	Sea-A	8	12	.400	38	24	6	1	0	174^2	199	10	65	47	14.0	4.59	91	.294	.363	0	—	0	-12	-8	2	-0.9
1989	Sea-A	7	3	.700	37	16	0	0	1	130	140	7	38	45	12.5	4.43	91	.278	.331	0	—	0	-8	-6	5	-0.1
1990	Sea-A	6	4	.600	55	8	0	0	6	128	135	4	21	42	11.5	2.39	166	.272	.311	0	—	0	22	22	0	1.8
1991	Sea-A	1	2	.333	71	0	0	0	17	90^1	74	3	26	48	10.1	1.99	207	.224	.283	0	—	0	21	21	3	1.6
1992	SF-N	10	4	.714	30	22	3	2	1	164^2	144	6	43	77	10.4	**2.08**	159	.239	.293	8	.157	1	26	22	2	2.3
1993	SF-N	21	8	.724	34	34	1	1	0	232^2	195	18	55	157	9.9	2.82	138	.226	.278	21	.262	6	31	28	2	4.2
1994	SF-N	8	7	.533	17	17	0	0	0	109^1	109	10	31	62	11.6	3.38	119	.262	.315	6	.188	2	10	8	-1	1.1
1995	*Col-N	9	3	.750	19	19	0	0	0	105^2	122	12	43	68	14.1	4.94	109	.296	.364	7	.194	0	-9	5	3	0.8
1996	Col-N	1	1	.500	7	3	0	0	2	18^1	23	1	5	5	13.7	5.40	97	.307	.350	2	.333	0	-2	-0	0	0.0
1997	Col-N	4	6	.400	14	13	0	0	0	65^1	85	11	26	29	15.6	6.34	82	.317	.382	4	.211	1	-16	-8	2	-0.8
1998	Sea-A	11	9	.550	29	26	0	0	0	144^2	183	21	51	77	15.2	5.85	79	.306	.370	0	.000	-0	-19	-20	2	-2.1
Total	13	94	78	.547	403	220	11	4	27	1599^2	1688	116	507	767	12.6	3.95	106	.273	.334	48	.210	10	19	40	23	5.8
● **BILL SWIFT**	Swift, William Vincent b: 1/10/08, Elmira, N.Y. d: 2/23/69, Bartow, Fla. BR/TR, 6'1.5", 192 lbs. Deb: 4/12/32																									
1932	Pit-N	14	10	.583	39	23	11	0	4	214^1	205	15	26	64	9.8	3.61	106	.248	.272	15	.192	-1	6	5	-4	0.0
1933	Pit-N	14	10	.583	37	29	13	2	0	218^1	214	11	36	64	10.5	3.13	106	.251	.285	20	.244	3	5	5	-2	0.6
1934	Pit-N	11	13	.458	37	24	13	1	0	212^2	244	15	46	81	12.6	3.98	103	.284	.326	18	.214	2	2	3	-1	0.3
1935	Pit-N	15	8	.652	39	21	11	3	1	203^2	193	6	37	74	10.2	2.70	152	.247	.282	19	.244	3	30	32	-4	3.2
1936	Pit-N	16	16	.500	45	31	17	0	2	262^1	275	18	63	92	11.8	4.01	101	.265	.310	31	.295	9	0	1	-5	0.5
1937	Pit-N	9	10	.474	36	17	9	0	3	164	160	14	34	84	10.8	3.95	98	.256	.297	9	.167	-1	-1	-2	-3	-0.5
1938	Pit-N	7	5	.583	36	9	2	0	4	150	155	9	40	77	11.9	3.24	117	.271	.323	10	.200	2	9	9	-1	0.8
1939	Pit-N	5	7	.417	36	8	2	1	4	129^2	150	6	28	56	12.6	3.89	99	.293	.333	10	.238	2	0	-1	-3	-0.2
1940	Bos-N	1	1	.500	4	0	0	0	1	9^1	12	0	7	7	18.3	2.89	129	.308	.413	0	.000	-0	1	1	0	0.2
1941	Bro-N	3	0	1.000	9	0	0	0	1	22	26	4	7	9	13.5	3.27	112	.289	.340	1	.200	-0	1	1	-0	0.1
1943	Chi-A	0	2	.000	18	1	0	0	0	51^1	48	5	27	28	14.2	4.21	79	.246	.355	1	.100	0	-5	-5	-2	-0.4
Total	11	95	82	.537	336	163	78	7	20	1637^2	1682	103	351	636	11.4	3.58	108	.263	.305	134	.227	18	49	49	-25	4.6
● **OAD SWIGART**	Swigart, Oadis Vaughn b: 2/13/15, Archie, Mo. d: 8/8/97, St.Joseph, Mo. BL/TR, 6', 175 lbs. Deb: 9/14/39																									
1939	Pit-N	1	1	.500	3	3	1	1	0	24^1	27	1	6	8	12.2	4.44	87	.293	.337	2	.250	0	-1	-2	-0	-0.1
1940	Pit-N	0	2	.000	7	2	0	0	0	22^1	27	1	10	9	14.9	4.43	86	.297	.366	1	.200	-0	-1	-2	0	-0.1
Total	2	1	3	.250	10	5	1	1	0	46^2	54	2	16	17	13.5	4.44	86	.295	.352	3	.231	0	-3	-3	0	-0.2
● **AD SWIGLER**	Swigler, Adam William "Doc" b: 9/21/1895, Philadelphia, Pa. d: 2/5/75, Philadelphia, Pa. BR/TR, 5'10", 180 lbs. Deb: 9/25/17																									
1917	NY-N	0	1	.000	1	1	0	0	0	6	7	0	8	4	22.5	6.00	43	.333	.517	0	.000	-0	-2	-2	0	-0.3
● **GREG SWINDELL**	Swindell, Forest Gregory b: 1/2/65, Fort Worth, Tex. BR/TL, 6'3", 225 lbs. Deb: 8/21/86																									
1986	Cle-A	5	2	.714	9	9	1	0	0	61^2	57	9	15	46	10.7	4.23	98	.243	.291	0	—	0	-0	-1	1	0.1
1987	Cle-A	3	8	.273	16	15	4	1	0	102^1	112	18	37	97	13.2	5.10	89	.283	.346	0	—	0	-7	-7	-0	-0.7
1988	Cle-A	18	14	.563	33	33	12	4	0	242	234	18	45	180	10.4	3.20	129	.252	.287	0	—	0	21	25	-1	2.9
1989	Cle-A★	13	6	.684	28	28	5	2	0	184^1	170	16	51	129	10.8	3.37	118	.246	.298	0	—	0	11	12	-0	1.0
1990	Cle-A	12	9	.571	34	34	3	0	0	214^2	245	27	47	135	12.3	4.40	89	.288	.326	0	—	0	-12	-12	-2	-1.2
1991	Cle-A	9	16	.360	33	33	7	0	0	238	241	21	31	169	10.4	3.48	119	.263	.289	0	—	0	16	18	-1	1.6
1992	Cin-N	12	8	.600	31	30	5	3	0	213^2	210	14	41	138	10.7	2.70	133	.260	.297	10	.125	-2	19	21	-1	1.8
1993	Hou-N	12	13	.480	31	30	1	1	0	190^1	215	24	40	124	12.1	4.16	93	.283	.319	11	.183	0	-3	-6	0	-0.7
1994	Hou-N	8	9	.471	24	24	1	0	0	148^1	175	20	26	74	12.3	4.37	90	.302	.333	11	.250	3	-3	-7	-2	-0.6

YEAR	TM/L	W	L	PCT	G	GS	CG	SH	SV	IP	H	HR	BB	SO	RAT	ERA	ERA+	OAV	OOB	BH	AVG	PB	PR	/A	PD	TPI
1995	Hou-N	10	9	.526	33	26	1	1	0	153	180	21	39	96	13.0	4.47	86	.297	.342	12	.240	4	-5	-10	2	-0.6
1996	Hou-N	0	3	.000	8	4	0	0	0	23	35	5	11	15	18.4	7.83	49	.340	.409	2	.333	1	-9	-10	-0	-1.0
	Cle-A	1	1	.500	13	2	0	0	0	28^{2}	31	8	8	21	12.2	6.59	74	.279	.328	0	—	0	-5	-5	0	-0.3
1997	Min-A	7	4	.636	65	1	0	0	1	115^{2}	102	12	25	75	10.0	3.58	130	.238	.284	0	—	0	13	14	-0	1.1
1998	Min-A	3	3	.500	52	0	0	0	2	66^{1}	67	10	18	45	11.9	3.66	128	.263	.319	0	—	0	7	8	-0	0.6
	*Bos-A	2	3	.400	29	0	0	0	0	24	25	3	13	18	14.3	3.38	137	.278	.369	0	—	0	3	3	0	0.6
	Yr	5	6	.455	81	0	0	0	2	90^{1}	92	13	31	63	12.3	3.59	130	.263	.323	0	—	0	11	11	0	1.2
Total	13	115	108	.516	439	269	40	12	3	2006	2099	226	447	1362	11.5	3.87	105	.271	.312	46	.192	7	46	44	-5	4.6
● **JOSH SWINDELL** Swindell, Joshua Ernest b: 7/5/1883, Rose Hill, Kan. d: 3/19/69, Fruita, Colo. BR/TR, 6', 180 lbs. Deb: 9/16/11 ♦																										
1911	Cle-A	0	1	.000	4	1	1	0	0	17^{1}	19	0	4	6	12.5	2.08	164	.257	.304	1	.250	-0	2	3	-0	0.1
● **PAUL SWINGLE** Swingle, Paul Christopher b: 12/21/66, Inglewood, Cal. BR/TR, 6', 185 lbs. Deb: 9/7/93																										
1993	Cal-A	0	1	.000	9	0	0	0	0	9^{2}	15	2	6	6	19.6	8.38	54	.357	.438	0	—	0	-4	-4	-0	-0.4
● **LEN SWORMSTEDT** Swormstedt, Leonard Jordan b: 10/6/1878, Cincinnati, Ohio d: 7/19/64, Salem, Mass. BR/TR, 5'11.5", 165 lbs. Deb: 9/29/01																										
1901	Cin-N	2	1	.667	3	3	3	0	0	26	19	2	5	13	9.0	1.73	185	.202	.257	0	.000	-1	5	4	0	0.3
1902	Cin-N	0	2	.000	2	2	2	0	0	18	22	1	5	3	13.5	4.00	75	.301	.346	0	.000	-1	-2	-2	-0	-0.3
1906	Bos-A	1	1	.500	3	2	2	0	0	21	17	0	0	6	7.7	1.29	214	.224	.234	1	.125	-1	3	3	-1	0.2
Total	3	3	4	.429	8	7	7	0	0	65	58	3	10	22	9.8	2.22	136	.239	.277	1	.043	-3	5	6	-1	0.2
● **BOB SYKES** Sykes, Robert Joseph b: 12/11/54, Neptune, N.J. BB/TL, 6'2", 200 lbs. Deb: 4/9/77																										
1977	Det-A	5	7	.417	32	20	3	0	0	132^{2}	141	15	50	58	13.1	4.41	97	.271	.337	0	—	0	-5	-2	-0	-0.5
1978	Det-A	6	6	.500	22	10	3	2	2	93^{2}	99	14	34	58	12.9	3.94	98	.275	.339	0	—	0	-2	-1	-2	-0.5
1979	StL-N	4	3	.571	13	11	0	0	0	67	86	11	34	35	16.3	6.18	61	.315	.393	2	.095	-0	-18	-18	-1	-1.7
1980	StL-N	6	10	.375	27	19	4	3	0	126	134	12	54	50	13.4	4.64	79	.277	.350	4	.103	-2	-15	-13	-2	-1.9
1981	StL-N	2	0	1.000	22	1	0	0	0	37^{1}	37	2	18	14	13.5	4.58	78	.266	.354	0	.000	0	-5	-4	1	-0.1
Total	5	23	26	.469	116	61	10	5	2	456^{2}	497	54	190	215	13.6	4.65	84	.280	.351	6	.097	-2	-44	-38	-4	-4.7
● **LOU SYLVESTER** Sylvester, Louis J. b: 2/14/1855, Springfield, Ill. BR/TR, 5'3", 165 lbs. Deb: 4/18/1884 ♦																										
1884	Cin-U	0	1	.000	6	1	1	0	1	32^{2}	32	0	6	7	10.5	3.58	72	.239	.271	89	.267	-0	-4	-4	-1	-0.2
● **JEFF TABAKA** Tabaka, Jeffrey Jon b: 1/17/64, Barberton, Ohio BR/TL, 6'2", 195 lbs. Deb: 4/19/94																										
1994	Pit-N	0	0	—	5	0	0	0	0	4	4	1	8	2	27.0	18.00	24	.250	.500	0	—	0	-6	-6	-0	0.0
	SD-N	3	1	.750	34	0	0	0	1	37	28	0	19	30	11.4	3.89	106	.209	.307	1	1.000	1	1	1	-0	0.2
	Yr	3	1	.750	39	0	0	0	1	41	32	1	27	32	13.0	5.27	78	.213	.333	1	1.000	1	-5	-5	-0	0.2
1995	SD-N	0	0	—	10	0	0	0	0	6^{1}	10	1	5	6	21.3	7.11	57	.370	.469	0	—	0	-2	-2	-0	0.0
	Hou-N	1	0	1.000	24	0	0	0	0	24^{1}	17	1	12	19	10.7	2.22	174	.202	.302	0	.000	-0	5	4	-0	0.1
	Yr	1	0	1.000	34	0	0	0	0	30^{2}	27	2	17	25	12.9	3.23	121	.243	.344	0	.000	-0	3	2	-0	0.1
1996	Hou-N	0	2	.000	18	0	0	0	1	20^{1}	28	5	14	18	19.9	6.64	58	.322	.433	0	.000	-0	-5	-6	-1	-0.6
1997	Cin-N	0	0	—	3	0	0	0	0	2	1	1	1	1	18.0	4.50	95	.143	.400	0	—	0	-0	-0	-0	0.0
1998	Pit-N	2	2	.500	37	0	0	0	0	50^{2}	37	6	22	40	11.4	3.02	143	.204	.308	0	.000	-0	7	7	0	0.5
Total	5	6	5	.545	131	0	0	0	2	144^{2}	125	15	81	116	13.4	4.23	97	.233	.344	1	.250	1	-0	-2	-1	0.2
● **LEFTY TABER** Taber, Edward Timothy b: 1/11/1900, Rock Island, Ill. d: 11/5/83, Lincoln, Neb. BL/TL, 6', 180 lbs. Deb: 9/4/26																										
1926	Phi-N	0	0	—	6	0	0	0	0	8^{1}	8	0	5	0	16.2	7.56	55	.242	.375	0	.000	-0	-3	-3	-0	0.0
1927	Phi-N	0	1	.000	3	1	0	0	0	3^{1}	8	0	5	0	37.8	18.90	22	.533	.667	0	.000	-0	-6	-5	0	-1.2
Total	2	0	1	.000	9	1	0	0	0	11^{2}	16	0	10	0	22.4	10.80	38	.333	.475	0	.000	-0	-9	-9	0	-1.2
● **JOHN TABER** Taber, John Pardon b: 6/28/1868, Acushnet, Mass. d: 2/21/40, Boston, Mass. BR/TR, 5'8", Deb: 4/30/1890																										
1890	Bos-N	0	1	.000	2	1	1	0	1	13	11	0	8	3	13.2	4.15	90	.220	.328	0	.000	-1	-1	-1	0	-0.1
● **JEFF TACKETT** Tackett, Jeffrey Wilson b: 12/1/65, Fresno, Cal. BR/TR, 6'2", 200 lbs. Deb: 9/11/91 ♦																										
1993	Bal-A	0	0	—	1	0	0	0	0	1	1	0	1	0	18.0	0.00	—	.250	.400	15	.172	0	0	0	0	0.0
● **JOHN TAFF** Taff, John Gallatin b: 6/3/1890, Austin, Tex. d: 5/15/61, Houston, Tex. BR/TR, 6', 170 lbs. Deb: 5/11/13																										
1913	Phi-A	0	1	.000	7	1	0	0	1	17^{2}	22	0	5	9	13.8	6.62	42	.293	.338	1	.200	-0	-7	-8	0	-0.5
● **DOUG TAITT** Taitt, Douglas John "Poco" b: 8/3/02, Bay City, Mich. d: 12/12/70, Portland, Ore. BL/TR, 6', 176 lbs. Deb: 4/10/28 ♦																										
1928	Bos-A	0	0	—	1	0	0	0	0	1	2	0	2	1	36.0	27.00	15	.400	.571	144	.299	0	-3	-3	0	0.0
● **FRED TALBOT** Talbot, Frederick Lealand "Bubby" b: 6/28/41, Washington, D.C. BR/TR, 6'2", 195 lbs. Deb: 9/28/63																										
1963	Chi-A	0	0	—	1	0	0	0	0	3	2	0	4	2	18.0	3.00	117	.222	.462	0	.000	-0	0	0	0	0.0
1964	Chi-A	4	5	.444	17	12	3	2	0	75^{1}	83	7	20	34	12.8	3.70	93	.288	.343	5	.263	3	-1	-2	-1	0.0
1965	KC-A	10	12	.455	39	33	2	1	0	198	188	25	86	117	12.7	4.14	84	.251	.333	14	.200	3	-15	-14	-1	-1.2
1966	KC-A	4	4	.500	11	11	0	0	0	67^{2}	65	6	28	37	12.6	4.79	71	.248	.325	3	.150	0	-10	-10	-0	-1.1
	NY-A	7	7	.500	23	19	3	0	0	124^{1}	123	16	45	48	12.4	4.13	81	.262	.331	5	.143	1	-10	-11	-0	-1.1
	Yr	11	11	.500	34	30	3	0	0	192	188	22	73	85	12.4	4.36	77	.256	.326	8	.145	1	-20	-22	-0	-2.2
1967	NY-A	6	8	.429	29	22	2	0	0	138^{2}	132	20	54	61	12.5	4.22	74	.252	.329	6	.158	3	-15	-17	2	-1.0
1968	NY-A	1	9	.100	29	11	1	0	0	99	89	6	42	67	12.1	3.36	86	.241	.322	2	.118	1	-4	-5	1	-0.4
1969	NY-A	0	0	—	8	0	0	0	0	12^{1}	13	1	6	7	13.9	5.11	68	.283	.365	0	.000	-0	-2	-2	0	0.0
	Sea-A	5	8	.385	25	16	1	1	0	114^{2}	125	12	41	67	13.3	4.16	87	.278	.343	6	.162	2	-7	-7	0	-0.5
	Oak-A	1	2	.333	12	2	0	0	1	19	22	2	7	9	13.7	5.21	66	.297	.358	1	.333	0	-3	-4	0	-0.6
	Yr	6	10	.375	45	18	1	1	1	146	160	15	54	83	13.2	4.38	82	.277	.339	7	.171	2	-12	-13	0	-1.1
1970	Oak-A	0	1	.000	1	0	0	0	0	1^{2}	2	1	1	0	16.2	10.80	33	.286	.375	0	—	0	-1	-1	0	-0.5
Total	8	38	56	.404	195	126	12	4	1	853^{2}	844	96	334	449	12.7	4.12	81	.260	.334	42	.174	13	-68	-74	2	-6.4
● **ROY TALCOTT** Talcott, Le Roy Everett b: 1/16/20, Brookline, Mass. BR/TR, 6'1.5", 180 lbs. Deb: 6/24/43																										
1943	Bos-N	0	0	—	1	0	0	0	0	0^{2}	1	0	2	0	40.5	27.00	13	.333	.600	0	—	0	-2	-2	0	0.0
● **JEFF TAM** Tam, Jeffrey Eugene b: 8/19/70, Fullerton, Cal. BR/TR, 6'1", 202 lbs. Deb: 6/30/98																										
1998	NY-N	1	1	.500	15	0	0	0	0	14^{1}	13	2	4	8	11.9	6.28	66	.241	.317	0	.000	-0	-3	-3	0	-0.4
● **VITO TAMULIS** Tamulis, Vitautis Casimirus b: 7/11/11, Cambridge, Mass. d: 5/5/74, Nashville, Tenn. BL/TL, 5'9", 170 lbs. Deb: 9/25/34																										
1934	NY-A	1	0	1.000	1	1	1	1	0	9	7	0	1	5	8.0	0.00	—	.219	.242	1	.250	0	4	4	0	0.5
1935	NY-A	10	5	.667	30	19	9	3	1	160^{2}	178	7	55	57	13.2	4.09	99	.280	.339	14	.246	4	7	-1	-1	0.2
1938	StL-A	0	3	.000	3	2	0	0	0	15^{1}	26	2	10	11	21.1	7.63	65	.366	.444	2	.400	1	-5	-5	0	-0.6
	Bro-N	12	6	.667	38	18	9	0	2	159^{2}	181	11	40	70	12.6	3.83	102	.288	.333	7	.127	-3	-1	1	-2	-0.3
1939	Bro-N	9	8	.529	39	17	8	1	4	158^{2}	177	10	45	83	13.0	4.37	92	.287	.343	10	.182	-1	-8	-6	0	-0.7
1940	Bro-N	8	5	.615	41	12	4	1	2	154^{1}	147	5	34	55	10.7	3.09	129	.244	.288	6	.130	-1	13	16	-1	1.0
1941	Phi-N	0	1	.000	6	1	0	0	0	12	21	1	7	5	21.8	9.00	41	.382	.460	0	.000	-0	-7	-7	0	-0.5
	Bro-N	0	0	—	12	0	0	0	1	22	21	1	10	8	12.7	3.68	100	.244	.323	0	.000	-1	-0	-0	0	-0.1
	Yr	0	1	.000	18	1	0	0	1	34	42	2	17	13	15.6	5.56	66	.296	.371	0	.000	-1	-7	-7	0	-0.6
Total	6	40	28	.588	170	70	31	6	10	691^{2}	758	37	202	294	12.7	3.97	101	.278	.331	40	.175	-1	3	4	-2	-0.5
● **FRANK TANANA** Tanana, Frank Daryl b: 7/3/53, Detroit, Mich. BL/TL, 6'3", 195 lbs. Deb: 9/9/73																										
1973	Cal-A	2	2	.500	4	4	2	1	0	26^{1}	20	2	8	22	9.6	3.08	115	.200	.259	0	—	0	2	1	0	0.3
1974	Cal-A	14	19	.424	39	35	12	4	0	268^{2}	262	27	77	180	11.6	3.12	110	.255	.312	0	—	0	15	10	0	1.6
1975	Cal-A	16	9	.640	34	33	16	5	0	257^{1}	211	21	73	**269**	10.2	2.62	135	.226	.288	0	—	0	33	26	3	3.3
1976	Cal-A★	19	10	.655	34	34	23	2	0	288^{1}	212	24	73	261	**9.2**	2.43	137	.203	**.261**	0	—	0	35	29	1	3.2
1977	Cal-A†	15	9	.625	31	31	20	**7**	0	241^{1}	201	19	61	205	10.2	**2.54**	**154**	.227	.286	0	—	0	41	37	1	3.7
1978	Cal-A☆	18	12	.600	33	33	10	4	0	239	239	26	60	137	11.6	3.65	99	.258	.309	0	—	0	3	-1	-2	-0.4
1979	*Cal-A	7	5	.583	18	17	2	1	0	90^{1}	93	9	25	46	12.0	3.89	105	.264	.317	0	—	0	3	2	-1	0.4

YEAR	TM/L	W	L	PCT	G	GS	CG	SH	SV	IP	H	HR	BB	SO	RAT	ERA	ERA+	OAV	OOB	BH	AVG	PB	PR	/A	PD	TPI
1980	Cal-A	11	12	.478	32	31	7	0	0	204	223	18	45	113	12.2	4.15	95	.277	.322	0	—	0	-3	-5	-1	-0.6
1981	Bos-A	4	10	.286	24	23	5	2	0	141^1	142	17	43	78	12.0	4.01	96	.265	.324	0	—	0	-6	-2	1	-0.2
1982	Tex-A	7	18	.280	30	30	7	0	0	194^1	199	16	55	87	12.1	4.21	92	.264	.320	0	—	0	-3	-7	-0	-0.7
1983	Tex-A	7	9	.438	29	22	3	0	0	159^1	144	14	49	108	11.3	3.16	127	.240	.304	0	—	0	16	15	3	1.8
1984	Tex-A	15	15	.500	35	35	9	1	0	246^1	234	30	81	141	11.7	3.25	127	.245	.308	0	—	0	20	24	1	2.7
1985	Tex-A	2	7	.222	13	13	0	0	0	77^2	89	15	23	52	13.1	5.91	72	.287	.338	0	—	0	-15	-15	0	-1.5
	Det-A	10	7	.588	20	20	4	0	0	137^1	131	13	34	107	10.9	3.34	122	.250	.298	0	—	0	12	11	1	1.4
	Yr	12	14	.462	33	33	4	0	0	215	220	28	57	159	11.7	4.27	97	.262	.311	0	—	0	-3	-3	1	-0.1
1986	Det-A	12	9	.571	32	31	3	1	0	188^1	196	23	65	119	12.6	4.16	99	.268	.330	0	—	0	0	-1	1	0.1
1987	*Det-A	15	10	.600	34	34	5	3	0	218^2	216	27	56	146	11.4	3.91	108	.256	.306	0	—	0	13	8	1	0.9
1988	Det-A	14	11	.560	32	32	2	0	0	203	213	25	64	127	12.5	4.21	91	.267	.324	0	—	0	-6	-9	1	-0.7
1989	Det-A	10	14	.417	33	33	6	1	0	223^2	227	21	74	147	12.4	3.58	107	.265	.329	0	—	0	7	6	2	1.0
1990	Det-A	9	8	.529	34	29	1	0	1	176^1	190	25	66	114	13.5	5.31	75	.280	.352	0	—	0	-27	-26	1	-2.2
1991	Det-A	13	12	.520	33	33	3	2	0	217^1	217	26	78	107	12.3	3.77	110	.265	.330	0	.000	-0	8	9	1	1.1
1992	Det-A	13	11	.542	32	31	3	0	0	186^2	188	22	90	91	13.7	4.39	90	.267	.356	0	—	0	-9	-9	1	-1.0
1993	NY-N	7	15	.318	29	29	0	0	0	183	198	26	48	104	12.5	4.48	90	.278	.332	9	.155	0	-9	-9	-1	-1.1
	NY-A	0	2	.000	3	3	0	0	0	19^2	18	2	7	12	11.4	3.20	130	.222	.284	0	—	0	2	2	-1	0.2
Total	21	240	236	.504	638	616	143	34	1	4188^1	4063	448	1255	2773	11.7	3.66	106	.254	.314	9	.153	0	134	95	14	13.3

● JESSE TANNEHILL

Tannehill, Jesse Niles "Powder" b: 7/14/1874, Dayton, Ky. d: 9/22/56, Dayton, Ky. BB/TL, 5′8″, 150 lbs. Deb: 6/17/1894 FC♦

YEAR	TM/L	W	L	PCT	G	GS	CG	SH	SV	IP	H	HR	BB	SO	RAT	ERA	ERA+	OAV	OOB	BH	AVG	PB	PR	/A	PD	TPI
1894	Cin-N	1	1	.500	5	2	1	0	1	29	37	1	16	7	16.8	7.14	78	.306	.391	0	.000	-2	-6	-5	-1	-0.5
1897	Pit-N	9	9	.500	21	16	11	1	1	142	172	1	24	40	12.9	4.25	98	.297	.333	49	.266	3	1	-1	3	0.3
1898	Pit-N	25	13	.658	43	38	34	5	2	326^2	338	2	63	93	11.4	2.95	121	.265	.306	44	.289	7	24	22	3	3.5
1899	Pit-N	24	14	.632	40	35	32	3	1	313	354	4	51	61	12.0	2.73	140	.285	.320	34	.258	5	39	38	4	4.8
1900	Pit-N	20	6	.769	29	27	23	2	0	234	247	3	43	50	11.8	2.88	126	.271	.316	37	.336	8	21	19	1	2.7
1901	Pit-N	18	10	.643	32	30	25	4	1	252^1	240	1	36	118	10.2	**2.18**	150	.249	.283	33	.244	5	32	31	-3	3.2
1902	Pit-N	20	6	.769	26	24	23	2	0	231	203	0	25	100	9.3	1.95	140	.236	.266	43	.291	7	21	20	-0	3.1
1903	NY-A	15	15	.500	32	31	22	2	0	239^2	258	3	34	106	11.3	3.27	96	.274	.307	26	.234	5	-8	-4	2	0.3
1904	Bos-A	21	11	.656	33	31	30	4	0	281^2	256	5	33	116	9.6	2.04	131	.243	.275	24	.197	3	17	20	3	3.0
1905	Bos-A	22	9	.710	37	32	27	6	0	271^2	238	7	59	113	10.3	2.48	109	.237	.288	21	.226	6	5	6	2	1.6
1906	Bos-A	13	11	.542	27	26	18	2	0	196^1	207	9	39	82	11.7	3.16	87	.274	.318	22	.278	6	-10	-9	0	-0.4
1907	Bos-A	6	7	.462	18	16	10	2	1	131	131	3	20	29	10.7	2.47	104	.263	.298	10	.196	1	1	1	0	0.3
1908	Bos-A	0	0	—	1	1	0	0	0	5	4	0	3	2	12.6	3.60	68	.200	.304	1	.500	0	-1	-1	0	0.1
	Was-A	2	4	.333	10	9	5	0	0	71^2	77	0	23	14	13.3	3.77	61	.278	.346	11	.256	2	-11	-12	1	-0.6
	Yr	2	4	.333	11	10	5	0	0	76^2	81	0	26	16	13.3	3.76	61	.273	.343	12	.267	2	-12	-12	2	-0.5
1909	Was-A	1	1	.500	3	2	2	1	0	21	19	1	5	8	10.7	3.43	71	.268	.325	6	.167	0	-2	-2	1	-0.1
1911	Cin-N	0	0	—	1	0	0	0	0	4^1	6	0	3	1	18.7	6.23	53	.316	.409	0	.000	-0	-1	-1	0	0.0
Total	15	197	117	.627	358	320	263	34	7	2750^1	2787	40	477	940	11.1	2.79	115	.263	.303	361	.256	55	123	124	16	21.3

● BRUCE TANNER

Tanner, Bruce Matthew b: 12/9/61, New Castle, Pa. BL/TR, 6′3″, 220 lbs. Deb: 6/12/85 F

YEAR	TM/L	W	L	PCT	G	GS	CG	SH	SV	IP	H	HR	BB	SO	RAT	ERA	ERA+	OAV	OOB	BH	AVG	PB	PR	/A	PD	TPI
1985	Chi-A	1	2	.333	10	4	0	0	0	27	34	1	13	9	16.3	5.33	81	.309	.392	0	—	0	-4	-3	1	-0.4

● KEVIN TAPANI

Tapani, Kevin Ray b: 2/18/64, Des Moines, Iowa BR/TR, 6′, 187 lbs. Deb: 7/4/89

YEAR	TM/L	W	L	PCT	G	GS	CG	SH	SV	IP	H	HR	BB	SO	RAT	ERA	ERA+	OAV	OOB	BH	AVG	PB	PR	/A	PD	TPI
1989	NY-N	0	0	—	3	0	0	0	0	7^1	5	1	4	2	11.0	3.68	89	.192	.300	0	.000	-0	-0	-0	0	0.0
	Min-A	2	2	.500	5	5	0	0	0	32^2	34	2	8	21	11.6	3.86	107	.266	.309	0	—	0	0	1	-0	-0.2
1990	Min-A	12	8	.600	28	28	1	1	0	159^1	164	12	29	101	11.0	4.07	102	.264	.299	0	—	0	-3	2	0	0.0
1991	*Min-A	16	9	.640	34	34	4	1	0	244	225	23	40	135	9.8	2.99	143	.245	.278	0	—	0	30	35	-0	3.3
1992	Min-A	16	11	.593	34	34	4	1	0	220	226	17	48	138	11.4	3.97	102	.269	.313	0	—	0	-1	2	-0	0.1
1993	Min-A	12	15	.444	36	35	3	1	0	225^2	243	21	57	150	12.2	4.43	98	.272	.320	0	—	0	-3	-2	1	-0.1
1994	Min-A	11	7	.611	24	24	4	1	0	156	181	13	39	91	12.9	4.62	105	.291	.337	0	—	0	3	4	1	0.6
1995	Min-A	6	11	.353	20	20	3	1	0	133^2	155	21	34	88	13.0	4.92	97	.290	.337	0	—	0	-3	-2	-1	-0.3
	*LA-N	4	2	.667	13	11	0	0	0	57	72	8	14	43	13.7	5.05	75	.306	.348	3	.176	0	-6	-8	0	-0.7
1996	Chi-A	13	10	.565	34	34	1	0	0	225^1	236	34	76	150	12.6	4.59	103	.268	.328	0	—	0	10	4	-1	0.4
1997	Chi-N	9	3	.750	13	13	1	1	0	85	77	7	23	55	10.8	3.39	127	.242	.297	3	.136	-0	8	9	-1	1.1
1998	*Chi-N	19	9	.679	35	34	2	2	0	219	244	30	62	136	12.8	4.85	90	.284	.336	10	.133	1	-15	-12	-1	-1.3
Total	10	120	87	.580	279	272	23	9	0	1765	1862	189	434	1110	11.9	4.22	104	.271	.317	16	.138	1	21	33	-0	2.9

● RANDY TATE

Tate, Randall Lee b: 10/23/52, Florence, Ala. BR/TR, 6′3″, 190 lbs. Deb: 4/14/75

YEAR	TM/L	W	L	PCT	G	GS	CG	SH	SV	IP	H	HR	BB	SO	RAT	ERA	ERA+	OAV	OOB	BH	AVG	PB	PR	/A	PD	TPI
1975	NY-N	5	13	.278	26	23	2	0	0	137^2	121	8	86	99	13.9	4.45	78	.240	.356	0	.000	-4	-13	-15	0	-2.3

● STU TATE

Tate, Stuart Douglas b: 6/17/62, Huntsville, Ala. BR/TR, 6′3″, 205 lbs. Deb: 9/20/89

YEAR	TM/L	W	L	PCT	G	GS	CG	SH	SV	IP	H	HR	BB	SO	RAT	ERA	ERA+	OAV	OOB	BH	AVG	PB	PR	/A	PD	TPI
1989	SF-N	0	0	—	2	0	0	0	0	2^2	3	0	0	4	10.1	3.38	100	.250	.250	0	—	0	0	-0	-0	0.0

● AL TATE

Tate, Walter Alvin b: 7/1/18, Coleman, Okla. d: 5/8/93, Bountiful, Utah BR/TR, 6′, 180 lbs. Deb: 9/27/46

YEAR	TM/L	W	L	PCT	G	GS	CG	SH	SV	IP	H	HR	BB	SO	RAT	ERA	ERA+	OAV	OOB	BH	AVG	PB	PR	/A	PD	TPI
1946	Pit-N	0	1	.000	2	1	1	0	0	9	8	0	7	2	15.0	5.00	70	.267	.405	1	.333	0	-2	-1	0	-0.1

● RAMON TATIS

Tatis, Ramon Francisco (Medrano) b: 1/5/73, Guayubin, D.R. BL/TL, 6′2″, 185 lbs. Deb: 4/6/97

YEAR	TM/L	W	L	PCT	G	GS	CG	SH	SV	IP	H	HR	BB	SO	RAT	ERA	ERA+	OAV	OOB	BH	AVG	PB	PR	/A	PD	TPI
1997	Chi-N	1	1	.500	56	0	0	0	0	55^2	66	13	29	33	15.8	5.34	81	.308	.398	0	.000	-0	-7	-6	1	-0.1
1998	TB-A	0	0	—	22	0	0	0	0	11^2	23	2	16	5	30.9	13.89	35	.418	.556	0	—	0	-12	-12	1	-0.1
Total	2	1	1	.500	78	0	0	0	0	67^1	89	15	45	38	18.4	6.82	65	.331	.434	0	.000	-0	-19	-18	1	-0.2

● KEN TATUM

Tatum, Kenneth Ray b: 4/25/44, Alexandria, La. BR/TR, 6′2″, 205 lbs. Deb: 5/28/69

YEAR	TM/L	W	L	PCT	G	GS	CG	SH	SV	IP	H	HR	BB	SO	RAT	ERA	ERA+	OAV	OOB	BH	AVG	PB	PR	/A	PD	TPI
1969	Cal-A	7	2	.778	45	0	0	0	22	86^1	51	1	39	65	9.8	1.36	257	.172	.277	6	.286	4	**22**	20	-0	3.8
1970	Cal-A	7	4	.636	62	0	0	0	17	88^2	68	12	26	50	10.0	2.94	123	.208	.277	2	.182	1	8	7	0	1.1
1971	Bos-A	2	4	.333	36	1	0	0	9	53^2	50	3	25	21	13.9	4.19	88	.255	.362	3	.300	2	-4	-3	0	-0.2
1972	Bos-A	0	2	.000	22	0	0	0	4	29^1	32	3	15	15	15.0	3.07	105	.283	.377	0	.000	0	-0	0	-0	0.0
1973	Bos-A	0	0	—	1	0	0	0	0	4	6	2	3	0	20.3	9.00	45	.462	.563	0	—	0	-2	-2	-0	0.0
1974	Chi-A	0	0	—	10	1	0	0	0	20^2	23	3	9	5	13.9	4.79	78	.274	.344	0	.000	-0	-3	-2	1	0.0
Total	6	16	12	.571	176	2	0	0	52	282^2	230	24	117	156	11.7	2.93	122	.224	.314	11	.244	7	20	20	0	4.7

● WALT TAUSCHER

Tauscher, Walter Edward b: 11/22/01, LaSalle, Ill. d: 11/27/92, Winter Park, Fla. BR/TR, 6′1″, 186 lbs. Deb: 4/19/28

YEAR	TM/L	W	L	PCT	G	GS	CG	SH	SV	IP	H	HR	BB	SO	RAT	ERA	ERA+	OAV	OOB	BH	AVG	PB	PR	/A	PD	TPI
1928	Pit-N	0	0	—	17	0	0	0	1	29^1	28	0	12	7	13.2	4.91	83	.280	.374	1	.167	-0	-3	-3	-0	-0.1
1931	Was-A	1	0	1.000	6	0	0	0	0	12	24	2	4	5	21.0	7.50	57	.429	.467	0	—	0	-4	-4	2	-0.2
Total	2	1	0	1.000	23	0	0	0	1	41^1	52	2	16	12	15.5	5.66	73	.333	.406	1	.167	-0	-7	-7	1	-0.3

● JULIAN TAVAREZ

Tavarez, Julian (Carmen) b: 5/22/73, Santiago, D.R. BR/TR, 6′2″, 165 lbs. Deb: 8/7/93

YEAR	TM/L	W	L	PCT	G	GS	CG	SH	SV	IP	H	HR	BB	SO	RAT	ERA	ERA+	OAV	OOB	BH	AVG	PB	PR	/A	PD	TPI
1993	Cle-A	2	2	.500	8	7	0	0	0	37	53	7	13	19	16.5	6.57	66	.340	.398	0	—	0	-9	-9	-0	-0.8
1994	Cle-A	0	1	.000	1	1	0	0	0	1^2	6	1	1	0	37.8	21.60	22	.500	.538	0	—	0	-3	-3	-0	-1.0
1995	*Cle-A	10	2	.833	57	0	0	0	0	85	76	7	21	68	10.6	2.44	193	.235	.287	0	—	0	22	21	0	2.6
1996	*Cle-A	4	7	.364	51	4	0	0	0	80^2	101	9	22	46	13.8	5.36	91	.315	.360	0	—	0	-3	-4	-1	-0.5
1997	*SF-N	6	4	.600	**89**	0	0	0	0	88^1	91	6	34	38	13.1	3.87	107	.277	.351	0	.000	-0	3	3	-0	0.2
1998	SF-N	5	3	.625	60	0	0	0	1	85^1	96	5	36	52	14.8	3.80	107	.298	.383	1	.111	-0	4	3	-1	0.1
Total	6	27	19	.587	266	12	0	0	1	378	423	35	127	223	13.5	4.19	106	.289	.353	1	.100	-1	13	10	-2	0.6

● ARLAS TAYLOR

Taylor, Arlas Walter "Lefty" or "Foxy" b: 3/16/1896, Warrick County, Ind. d: 9/10/58, Dade City, Fla. BR/TL, 5′11″, Deb: 9/15/21

YEAR	TM/L	W	L	PCT	G	GS	CG	SH	SV	IP	H	HR	BB	SO	RAT	ERA	ERA+	OAV	OOB	BH	AVG	PB	PR	/A	PD	TPI
1921	Phi-A	0	1	.000	1	1	0	0	0	2	7	1	2	1	40.5	22.50	20	.636	.692	0	—	0	-4	-4	-0	-1.0

● BEN TAYLOR

Taylor, Benjamin Harrison b: 4/2/1889, Paoli, Ind. d: 11/3/46, Martin County, Ind. BR/TR, 5′11″, 163 lbs. Deb: 6/28/12

YEAR	TM/L	W	L	PCT	G	GS	CG	SH	SV	IP	H	HR	BB	SO	RAT	ERA	ERA+	OAV	OOB	BH	AVG	PB	PR	/A	PD	TPI
1912	Cin-N	0	0	—	2	0	0	0	0	5^2	9	0	3	2	20.6	3.18	106	.360	.448	0	.000	0	0	0	-0	0.0

● BRUCE TAYLOR

Taylor, Bruce Bell b: 4/16/53, Holden, Mass. BR/TR, 6′, 178 lbs. Deb: 8/5/77

YEAR	TM/L	W	L	PCT	G	GS	CG	SH	SV	IP	H	HR	BB	SO	RAT	ERA	ERA+	OAV	OOB	BH	AVG	PB	PR	/A	PD	TPI
1977	Det-A	1	0	1.000	19	0	0	0	2	29^1	23	2	10	19	10.4	3.38	127	.219	.293	0	—	0	2	3	0	0.0

YEAR	TM/L	W	L	PCT	G	GS	CG	SH	SV	IP	H	HR	BB	SO	RAT	ERA	ERA+	OAV	OOB	BH	AVG	PB	PR	/A	PD	TPI
1978	Det-A	0	0	—	1	0	0	0	0	1	0	0	0	0	0.0	0.00	—	.000	.000	0	—	0	0	0	0	0.0
1979	Det-A	1	2	.333	10	0	0	0	0	18^2	16	1	7	8	12.1	4.82	90	.242	.333	0	—	0	-1	-1	0	-0.3
Total	3	2	2	.500	30	0	0	0	2	49	39	3	17	27	10.8	3.86	111	.224	.304	0	—	0	1	2	0	-0.3

● CHUCK TAYLOR Taylor, Charles Gilbert b: 4/18/42, Murfreesboro, Tenn. BR/TR, 6′2″, 195 lbs. Deb: 5/27/69

YEAR	TM/L	W	L	PCT	G	GS	CG	SH	SV	IP	H	HR	BB	SO	RAT	ERA	ERA+	OAV	OOB	BH	AVG	PB	PR	/A	PD	TPI
1969	StL-N	7	5	.583	27	13	5	1	0	126^2	108	8	30	62	10.0	2.56	140	.235	.287	7	.179	1	15	14	-2	1.2
1970	StL-N	6	7	.462	56	7	1	1	8	124^1	116	5	31	64	10.8	3.11	132	.256	.306	3	.115	-1	13	14	1	1.5
1971	StL-N	3	1	.750	43	1	0	0	3	71^1	72	7	25	46	12.4	3.53	102	.267	.331	2	.167	0	-1	1	0	0.1
1972	NY-N	0	0	—	20	0	0	0	2	31	44	2	9	9	15.7	5.52	61	.341	.388	0	.000	-0	-7	-7	1	0.0
	Mil-A	0	0	—	5	0	0	0	1	11^2	8	0	3	5	9.3	1.54	196	.200	.273	1	.500	0	2	2	0	0.1
1973	Mon-N	2	0	1.000	8	0	0	0	0	20^1	17	3	2	10	8.4	1.77	215	.230	.250	0	.000	-0	4	5	1	0.5
1974	Mon-N	6	2	.750	61	0	0	0	11	107^2	101	8	25	43	10.8	2.17	177	.256	.305	3	.300	1	17	20	-0	2.0
1975	Mon-N	2	2	.500	54	0	0	0	6	74	72	6	24	29	11.8	3.53	108	.264	.326	0	.000	-0	1	2	0	0.1
1976	Mon-N	2	3	.400	31	0	0	0	0	40	38	4	13	14	11.5	4.50	83	.273	.336	0	.000	-0	-4	-3	-0	-0.5
Total	8	28	20	.583	305	21	6	2	31	607	576	43	162	282	11.1	3.07	123	.258	.312	16	.158	0	40	47	1	5.0

● DORN TAYLOR Taylor, Donald Clyde b: 8/11/58, Abington, Pa. BR/TR, 6′2″, 180 lbs. Deb: 4/30/87

YEAR	TM/L	W	L	PCT	G	GS	CG	SH	SV	IP	H	HR	BB	SO	RAT	ERA	ERA+	OAV	OOB	BH	AVG	PB	PR	/A	PD	TPI
1987	Pit-N	2	3	.400	14	8	0	0	0	53^1	48	10	28	37	13.0	5.74	72	.247	.345	3	.167	-0	-10	-10	-1	-0.8
1989	Pit-N	1	1	.500	9	0	0	0	0	10^2	14	0	5	3	16.0	5.06	66	.333	.404	0	.000	-0	-2	-2	-0	-0.4
1990	Bal-A	0	1	.000	4	0	0	0	0	3^2	4	0	2	4	14.7	2.45	155	.250	.333	0	—	0	1	1	-0	0.3
Total	3	3	5	.375	27	8	0	0	0	67^2	66	10	35	44	13.6	5.45	73	.262	.354	3	.158	-0	-11	-11	-1	-0.9

● ED TAYLOR Taylor, Edgar Ruben "Rube" b: 3/23/1877, Palestine, Tex. d: 1/31/12, Dallas, Tex. TL , Deb: 8/8/03

YEAR	TM/L	W	L	PCT	G	GS	CG	SH	SV	IP	H	HR	BB	SO	RAT	ERA	ERA+	OAV	OOB	BH	AVG	PB	PR	/A	PD	TPI
1903	StL-N	0	0	—	1	0	0	0	0	3	0	0	0	1	0.0	0.00	—	.000	.000	0	.000	-0	1	1	0	0.0

● GARY TAYLOR Taylor, Gary William b: 10/19/45, Detroit, Mich. BR/TR, 6′2″, 190 lbs. Deb: 9/2/69

YEAR	TM/L	W	L	PCT	G	GS	CG	SH	SV	IP	H	HR	BB	SO	RAT	ERA	ERA+	OAV	OOB	BH	AVG	PB	PR	/A	PD	TPI
1969	Det-A	0	1	.000	7	0	0	0	0	10^1	10	2	6	3	13.9	5.23	71	.244	.340	0	.000	-0	-2	-2	0	-0.2

● HARRY TAYLOR Taylor, Harry Evans b: 12/2/35, San Angelo, Tex. BR/TR, 6′, 185 lbs. Deb: 9/17/57

YEAR	TM/L	W	L	PCT	G	GS	CG	SH	SV	IP	H	HR	BB	SO	RAT	ERA	ERA+	OAV	OOB	BH	AVG	PB	PR	/A	PD	TPI
1957	KC-A	0	0	—	2	0	0	0	0	8^2	11	0	4	4	16.6	3.12	127	.314	.400	1	.250	0	1	1	-0	0.0

● HARRY TAYLOR Taylor, James Harry b: 5/20/19, E.Glenn, Ind. BR/TR, 6′1″, 175 lbs. Deb: 9/22/46

YEAR	TM/L	W	L	PCT	G	GS	CG	SH	SV	IP	H	HR	BB	SO	RAT	ERA	ERA+	OAV	OOB	BH	AVG	PB	PR	/A	PD	TPI
1946	Bro-N	0	0	—	4	0	0	0	1	4^2	5	0	1	6	11.6	3.86	88	.313	.353	0	—	0	-0	-0	0	0.0
1947	*Bro-N	10	5	.667	33	20	10	2	1	162	130	10	83	58	12.1	3.11	133	**.225**	.327	8	.129	-2	17	18	1	1.5
1948	Bro-N	2	7	.222	17	13	2	0	0	80^2	90	8	61	32	17.2	5.36	75	.288	.408	6	.273	1	-13	-12	2	-0.9
1950	Bos-A	2	0	1.000	3	2	2	1	0	19	13	0	8	8	9.9	1.42	345	.197	.284	2	.286	0	7	7	0	0.8
1951	Bos-A	4	9	.308	31	8	1	0	2	81^1	100	6	42	22	15.8	5.75	78	.307	.388	3	.103	-3	-15	-12	1	-1.8
1952	Bos-A	1	0	1.000	2	1	1	0	0	10	6	1	6	1	11.7	1.80	219	.176	.317	1	.250	0	2	2	0	0.2
Total	6	19	21	.475	90	44	16	3	4	357^2	344	25	201	127	14.0	4.10	102	.258	.359	20	.161	-3	-2	4	4	-0.2

● JACK TAYLOR Taylor, John Budd "Brewery Jack" b: 5/23/1873, Staten Island, N.Y d: 2/7/1900, Staten Island, N.Y. BR/TR, 6′1″, 190 lbs. Deb: 9/16/1891

YEAR	TM/L	W	L	PCT	G	GS	CG	SH	SV	IP	H	HR	BB	SO	RAT	ERA	ERA+	OAV	OOB	BH	AVG	PB	PR	/A	PD	TPI
1891	NY-N	0	1	.000	1	1	1	0	0	8	4	1	3	3	7.9	1.13	285	.143	.226	0	.000	0	2	2	-0	0.2
1892	Phi-N	1	0	1.000	3	3	2	0	0	26	28	2	10	7	13.2	1.38	234	.264	.328	2	.167	-0	5	5	-1	0.0
1893	Phi-N	10	9	.526	25	16	14	0	1	170	187	8	77	41	14.5	4.24	108	.271	.353	20	.215	-2	8	6	2	0.5
1894	Phi-N	23	13	.639	41	34	31	1	1	298	347	13	96	76	13.9	4.08	125	.288	.349	48	.333	9	41	34	2	3.7
1895	Phi-N	26	14	.650	41	37	33	1	1	335	403	7	83	93	13.5	4.49	107	.293	.340	45	.290	7	11	11	4	1.9
1896	Phi-N	20	21	.488	45	41	35	1	1	359	459	17	112	97	14.8	4.79	90	.308	.365	29	.185	-6	-17	-19	4	-1.8
1897	Phi-N	16	20	.444	40	37	35	2	2	317^1	376	5	76	88	13.6	4.23	99	.292	.345	35	.252	2	3	-1	3	0.3
1898	StL-N	15	29	.341	**50**	47	**42**	0	1	**397^1**	465	14	83	89	13.0	3.90	97	.290	.335	38	.242	3	-13	-5	8	0.7
1899	Cin-N	9	10	.474	24	18	15	2	2	168^1	197	7	41	34	13.3	4.12	95	.291	.341	17	.250	-0	-5	-4	-1	-0.5
Total	9	120	117	.506	270	234	208	7	9	2079	2466	74	581	528	13.7	4.23	103	.291	.346	234	.252	11	36	34	21	5.0

● JACK TAYLOR Taylor, John W. b: 1/14/1874, New Straitsville, Ohio d: 3/4/38, Columbus, Ohio BR/TR, 5′10″, 170 lbs. Deb: 9/25/1898

YEAR	TM/L	W	L	PCT	G	GS	CG	SH	SV	IP	H	HR	BB	SO	RAT	ERA	ERA+	OAV	OOB	BH	AVG	PB	PR	/A	PD	TPI
1898	Chi-N	5	0	1.000	5	5	5	0	0	41	32	0	10	11	9.4	2.20	163	.213	.267	3	.200	1	6	6	-0	0.8
1899	Chi-N	18	21	.462	41	39	39	1	0	354^2	380	6	84	67	12.3	3.76	100	.274	.325	37	.266	10	4	-0	1	1.0
1900	Chi-N	10	17	.370	28	26	25	2	1	222^1	226	4	58	57	11.8	2.55	141	.263	.316	19	.235	2	28	26	-3	2.7
1901	Chi-N	13	19	.406	33	31	30	0	0	275^2	341	5	44	68	12.8	3.36	96	.302	.332	23	.217	2	-1	-4	2	0.0
1902	Chi-N	23	11	.676	36	33	33	7	1	324^2	271	2	43	83	**9.0**	**1.33**	**203**	.227	**.260**	44	.237	3	**52**	**49**	4	**6.3**
1903	Chi-N	21	14	.600	37	33	33	1	1	312^1	277	2	57	83	9.8	2.45	128	.235	.273	28	.222	4	28	24	1	2.9
1904	StL-N	20	19	.513	41	39	**39**	2	1	352	297	5	82	103	10.0	2.22	121	.220	.271	28	.211	4	20	19	1	2.6
1905	StL-N	15	21	.417	37	34	34	3	1	309	302	10	85	102	11.6	3.44	87	.259	.315	23	.190	4	-15	-16	-2	-1.5
1906	StL-N	8	9	.471	17	17	17	1	0	155	133	3	47	27	10.9	2.15	122	.227	.292	11	.208	3	8	8	1	1.4
	Chi-N	12	3	.800	17	16	15	2	0	147^1	116	1	39	34	9.8	1.83	144	.223	.285	11	.208	2	13	13	-0	1.5
	Yr	20	12	.625	34	33	32	3	0	302^1	249	4	86	61	10.2	1.99	132	.224	.283	22	.208	5	21	21	0	2.9
1907	Chi-N	7	5	.583	18	13	8	0	0	123	127	3	33	22	11.8	3.29	76	.268	.318	9	.191	0	-11	-11	1	-1.0
Total	10	152	139	.522	310	286	278	19	5	2617	2502	41	582	657	10.9	2.66	115	.250	.298	236	.223	35	134	116	5	16.7

● KERRY TAYLOR Taylor, Kerry Thomas b: 1/25/71, Bemidji, Minn. BR/TR, 6′3″, 200 lbs. Deb: 4/13/93

YEAR	TM/L	W	L	PCT	G	GS	CG	SH	SV	IP	H	HR	BB	SO	RAT	ERA	ERA+	OAV	OOB	BH	AVG	PB	PR	/A	PD	TPI
1993	SD-N	0	5	.000	36	7	0	0	0	68^1	72	5	49	45	16.5	6.45	64	.277	.399	0	.000	-1	-18	-18	-1	-1.3
1994	SD-N	0	0	—	1	1	0	0	0	4^1	9	1	1	3	22.8	8.31	49	.409	.458	0	.000	-0	-2	-2	-0	0.0
Total	2	0	5	.000	37	8	0	0	0	72^2	81	6	50	48	16.8	6.56	63	.287	.404	0	.000	-2	-20	-20	-1	-1.3

● DUMMY TAYLOR Taylor, Luther Haden b: 2/21/1875, Oskaloosa, Kan. d: 8/22/58, Jacksonville, Ill. BR/TR, 6′1″, 160 lbs. Deb: 8/27/00

YEAR	TM/L	W	L	PCT	G	GS	CG	SH	SV	IP	H	HR	BB	SO	RAT	ERA	ERA+	OAV	OOB	BH	AVG	PB	PR	/A	PD	TPI
1900	NY-N	4	3	.571	11	7	6	0	0	62^1	74	0	24	16	14.9	2.45	147	.294	.367	3	.136	-1	9	8	-2	0.5
1901	NY-N	18	27	.400	**45**	43	37	4	0	353^1	377	8	112	136	12.9	3.18	104	.271	.333	18	.132	-8	5	5	1	-0.2
1902	Cle-A	1	3	.250	4	4	4	1	0	34	37	0	8	8	12.4	1.59	217	.278	.329	1	.100	-0	8	7	1	0.9
	NY-N	7	15	.318	26	25	18	0	0	200^2	194	4	55	87	11.8	2.29	123	.254	.317	6	.092	-5	11	12	-1	0.6
1903	NY-N	13	13	.500	33	31	18	1	0	244^2	306	6	89	94	14.7	4.23	79	.314	.374	12	.146	-2	-26	-24	-1	-2.4
1904	NY-N	21	15	.583	37	36	29	5	0	296^1	231	6	75	138	9.6	2.34	117	.214	.270	16	.157	-1	13	13	3	1.6
1905	NY-N	16	9	.640	32	28	18	4	0	213^1	200	5	51	91	10.9	2.66	110	.247	.298	9	.130	-1	8	6	1	0.6
1906	NY-N	17	9	.654	31	27	13	2	0	213	186	4	57	91	10.5	2.20	119	.233	.289	14	.184	0	10	10	-1	1.1
1907	NY-N	11	7	.611	28	21	11	3	1	171	145	1	46	56	10.2	2.42	102	.232	.288	6	.125	-1	1	1	-1	-0.1
1908	NY-N	8	5	.615	27	15	6	1	2	127^2	127	5	34	50	11.6	2.33	104	.253	.306	8	.229	2	1	1	-0	0.3
Total	9	116	106	.523	274	237	160	21	3	1916^1	1877	39	551	767	11.7	2.75	107	.256	.314	93	.144	-17	40	39	0	2.9

● WILEY TAYLOR Taylor, Philip Wiley b: 3/18/1888, Wamego, Kan. d: 7/8/54, Westmoreland, Kan. BR/TR, 6′1″, 175 lbs. Deb: 9/6/11

YEAR	TM/L	W	L	PCT	G	GS	CG	SH	SV	IP	H	HR	BB	SO	RAT	ERA	ERA+	OAV	OOB	BH	AVG	PB	PR	/A	PD	TPI
1911	Det-A	0	2	.000	3	2	1	0	0	19	18	0	10	9	13.7	3.79	91	.247	.345	0	.000	-1	-1	-1	-1	-0.2
1912	Chi-A	0	1	.000	3	3	0	0	0	20	21	0	14	4	15.7	4.95	65	.309	.427	0	.000	-1	-4	-4	0	-0.2
1913	StL-A	0	2	.000	5	4	1	0	0	31^2	33	0	16	12	13.9	4.83	61	.280	.366	0	.000	-1	-7	-7	0	-0.5
1914	StL-A	2	5	.286	16	8	2	1	0	50	41	0	25	20	12.2	3.42	79	.209	.305	2	.167	-0	-4	-4	-0	-0.6
Total	4	2	10	.167	27	17	4	1	0	120^2	113	0	65	45	13.5	4.10	72	.248	.346	2	.061	-3	-15	-15	-0	-1.5

● SCOTT TAYLOR Taylor, Rodney Scott b: 8/2/67, Defiance, Ohio BL/TL, 6′1″, 185 lbs. Deb: 9/17/92

YEAR	TM/L	W	L	PCT	G	GS	CG	SH	SV	IP	H	HR	BB	SO	RAT	ERA	ERA+	OAV	OOB	BH	AVG	PB	PR	/A	PD	TPI
1992	Bos-A	1	1	.500	4	1	0	0	0	14^2	13	4	4	7	10.4	4.91	86	.245	.298	0	—	0	-2	-1	0	-0.1
1993	Bos-A	0	1	.000	16	0	0	0	0	11	14	1	12	8	22.1	8.18	56	.311	.466	0	—	0	-5	-4	-0	-0.8
Total	2	1	2	.333	20	1	0	0	0	25^2	27	5	16	15	15.4	6.31	69	.276	.383	0	—	0	-6	-5	-0	-0.9

● RON TAYLOR Taylor, Ronald Wesley b: 12/13/37, Toronto, Ont., Can. BR/TR, 6′1″, 195 lbs. Deb: 4/11/62

YEAR	TM/L	W	L	PCT	G	GS	CG	SH	SV	IP	H	HR	BB	SO	RAT	ERA	ERA+	OAV	OOB	BH	AVG	PB	PR	/A	PD	TPI
1962	Cle-A	2	2	.500	8	4	1	0	0	33^1	36	6	13	15	13.5	5.94	65	.281	.352	3	.273	0	-7	-8	-0	-0.8
1963	StL-N	9	7	.563	54	9	2	0	11	133^1	119	10	30	91	10.3	2.84	125	.243	.293	1	.031	-3	7	11	-3	0.9
1964	*StL-N	8	4	.667	63	2	0	0	7	101^1	109	15	33	69	12.7	4.62	82	.274	.331	2	.133	-0	-12	-9	2	-1.0
1965	StL-N	2	1	.667	25	0	0	0	1	43^2	43	6	15	26	12.2	4.53	85	.261	.326	2	.400	0	-5	-3	0	-0.2

YEAR	TM/L	W	L	PCT	G	GS	CG	SH	SV	IP	H	HR	BB	SO	RAT	ERA	ERA+	OAV	OOB	BH	AVG	PB	PR	/A	PD	TPI
	Hou-N	1	5	.167	32	1	0	0	4	57^{2}	68	5	16	37	13.9	6.40	52	.305	.365	0	.000	-1	-18	-19	-1	-2.4
	Yr	3	6	.333	57	1	0	0	5	101^{1}	111	11	31	63	13.1	5.60	64	.283	.343	2	.111	-1	-23	-23	-1	-2.6
1966	Hou-N	2	3	.400	36	1	0	0	0	64^{2}	89	5	10	29	14.5	5.71	60	.333	.369	2	.167	0	-15	-16	-1	-1.3
1967	NY-N	4	6	.400	50	0	0	0	8	73	60	1	23	46	10.4	2.34	145	.230	.295	0	.000	-1	8	8	0	1.3
1968	NY-N	1	5	.167	58	0	0	0	13	76^{2}	64	4	18	49	9.7	2.70	112	.228	.277	0	.000	-1	2	3	1	0.3
1969	*NY-N	9	4	.692	59	0	0	0	13	76	61	7	24	42	10.2	2.72	134	.228	.294	1	.250	0	7	8	0	1.7
1970	NY-N	5	4	.556	57	0	0	0	13	66^{1}	65	5	16	28	11.0	3.93	102	.265	.310	0	.000	-0	1	1	0	0.1
1971	NY-N	2	2	.500	45	0	0	0	2	69	71	7	11	32	10.8	3.65	93	.269	.301	1	.250	0	-1	-2	-0	-0.1
1972	SD-N	0	0	—	4	0	0	0	0	5	9	5	0	0	16.2	12.60	26	.375	.375	0	—	0	-5	-5	0	0.0
Total	11	45	43	.511	491	17	3	0	72	800	794	76	209	464	11.5	3.93	91	.264	.316	12	.103	-5	-39	-32	-2	-1.5

● SCOTT TAYLOR

Taylor, Scott Michael b: 10/3/66, Topeka, Kan. BR/TR, 6'3", 200 lbs. Deb: 7/28/95

YEAR	TM/L	W	L	PCT	G	GS	CG	SH	SV	IP	H	HR	BB	SO	RAT	ERA	ERA+	OAV	OOB	BH	AVG	PB	PR	/A	PD	TPI
1995	Tex-A	1	2	.333	3	3	0	0	0	15^{1}	25	6	5	10	17.6	9.39	51	.379	.423	0	—	0	-8	-8	0	-1.1

● TERRY TAYLOR

Taylor, Terry Derrell b: 7/28/64, Crestview, Fla. BR/TR, 6'1", 180 lbs. Deb: 8/19/88

YEAR	TM/L	W	L	PCT	G	GS	CG	SH	SV	IP	H	HR	BB	SO	RAT	ERA	ERA+	OAV	OOB	BH	AVG	PB	PR	/A	PD	TPI
1988	Sea-A	0	1	.000	5	5	0	0	0	23	26	2	11	9	14.5	6.26	66	.295	.374	0	—	0	-6	-5	-1	-0.6

● PETE TAYLOR

Taylor, Vernon Charles b: 11/26/27, Severn, Md. BR/TR, 6'1", 170 lbs. Deb: 5/2/52

YEAR	TM/L	W	L	PCT	G	GS	CG	SH	SV	IP	H	HR	BB	SO	RAT	ERA	ERA+	OAV	OOB	BH	AVG	PB	PR	/A	PD	TPI
1952	StL-A	0	0	—	1	0	0	0	0	2	4	0	3	0	31.5	13.50	29	.500	.636	0	—	0	-2	-2	0	0.0

● WADE TAYLOR

Taylor, Wade Eric b: 10/19/65, Mobile, Ala. BR/TR, 6'1", 185 lbs. Deb: 6/2/91

YEAR	TM/L	W	L	PCT	G	GS	CG	SH	SV	IP	H	HR	BB	SO	RAT	ERA	ERA+	OAV	OOB	BH	AVG	PB	PR	/A	PD	TPI
1991	NY-A	7	12	.368	23	22	0	0	0	116^{1}	144	13	53	72	15.8	6.27	66	.314	.393	0	—	0	-28	-27	1	-3.6

● BILLY TAYLOR

Taylor, William Henry "Bollicky Bill"
b: 1855, Washington, D.C. d: 5/14/1900, Jacksonville, Fla. BR/TR, 5'11.5", 204 lbs. Deb: 5/21/1881 ♦

YEAR	TM/L	W	L	PCT	G	GS	CG	SH	SV	IP	H	HR	BB	SO	RAT	ERA	ERA+	OAV	OOB	BH	AVG	PB	PR	/A	PD	TPI
1881	Wor-N	0	1	.000	1	1	1	0	0	8	15	0	6	0	23.6	7.88	38	.366	.447	3	.107	-0	-5	-4	-0	-0.4
	Cle-N	0	0	—	1	0	0	0	0	3	0	0	1	2	3.0	0.00	—	.000	.100	25	.243	-0	1	1	-0	0.0
	Yr	0	1	.000	2	1	1	0	0	11	15	0	7	2	18.0	5.73	51	.300	.386	28	.214	-0	-4	-3	-0	-0.4
1882	Pit-a	0	1	.000	1	0	0	0	0	5	11	0	4	1	27.0	16.20	16	.407	.484	84	.281	0	-8	-8	-0	-0.8
1883	Pit-a	4	7	.364	19	9	8	0	0	127	166	4	34	41	14.2	5.39	60	.296	.337	96	.260	3	-29	-31	-2	-1.9
1884	StL-U	25	4	.862	33	29	29	2	**4**	263	222	2	40	154	9.0	1.68	143	.213	.243	68	.366	13	22	21	-1	**2.8**
	Phi-a	18	12	.600	30	30	30	1	0	260	232	3	44	130	10.0	2.53	134	.219	.258	28	.252	3	21	25	2	2.9
1885	Phi-a	1	5	.167	6	6	6	0	0	52^{1}	68	0	9	11	13.4	3.27	105	.343	.375	4	.190	-1	-0	1	-1	-0.1
1886	Bal-a	1	6	.143	8	8	8	0	0	72^{1}	87	1	20	37	13.6	5.72	60	.284	.332	12	.308	1	-18	-18	-0	-1.2
1887	Phi-a	1	0	1.000	1	1	1	0	0	9	10	1	7	0	17.0	3.00	143	.286	.405	1	.250	-0	1	1	-0	0.1
Total	7	50	36	.581	100	84	83	3	4	799^{2}	811	11	165	376	11.2	3.17	96	.248	.287	323	.277	20	-14	-13	-4	1.4

● BILLY TAYLOR

Taylor, William Howell b: 10/16/61, Monticello, Fla. BR/TR, 6'8", 200 lbs. Deb: 4/5/94

YEAR	TM/L	W	L	PCT	G	GS	CG	SH	SV	IP	H	HR	BB	SO	RAT	ERA	ERA+	OAV	OOB	BH	AVG	PB	PR	/A	PD	TPI
1994	Oak-A	1	3	.250	41	0	0	0	1	46^{1}	38	4	18	48	11.3	3.50	127	.220	.301	0	—	0	7	5	-0	0.8
1996	Oak-A	6	3	.667	55	0	0	0	17	60^{1}	52	5	25	67	12.1	4.33	114	.231	.319	0	—	0	4	4	1	0.7
1997	Oak-A	3	4	.429	72	0	0	0	23	73	70	3	36	66	13.7	3.82	118	.254	.350	0	—	0	6	6	1	0.9
1998	Oak-A	4	9	.308	70	0	0	0	33	73	71	7	22	58	11.8	3.58	128	.255	.317	0	—	0	9	8	-0	1.8
Total	4	14	19	.424	238	0	0	0	74	252^{2}	231	19	101	239	12.3	3.81	121	.243	.324	0	—	0	26	22	1	4.2

● BUD TEACHOUT

Teachout, Arthur John b: 2/27/04, Los Angeles, Cal. d: 5/11/85, Laguna Beach, Cal BR/TL, 6'2", 183 lbs. Deb: 5/12/30

YEAR	TM/L	W	L	PCT	G	GS	CG	SH	SV	IP	H	HR	BB	SO	RAT	ERA	ERA+	OAV	OOB	BH	AVG	PB	PR	/A	PD	TPI
1930	Chi-N	11	4	.733	40	16	6	0	0	153	178	16	48	59	13.3	4.06	120	.296	.348	17	.270	3	16	14	-1	1.3
1931	Chi-N	1	2	.333	27	3	1	0	0	61^{1}	79	6	28	14	15.8	5.72	67	.305	.375	5	.238	0	-13	-13	1	-0.4
1932	StL-N	0	0	—	1	0	0	0	0	1	2	0	0	0	18.0	0.00	—	.400	.400	0	—	0	0	0	-0	0.0
Total	3	12	6	.667	68	19	7	0	0	215^{1}	259	22	76	73	14.0	4.51	102	.299	.356	22	.262	3	3	2	0	0.9

● GEORGE TEBEAU

Tebeau, George E. "White Wings" b: 12/26/1861, St.Louis, Mo. d: 2/4/23, Denver, Colo. BR/TR, 5'9", 175 lbs. Deb: 4/16/1887 F♦

YEAR	TM/L	W	L	PCT	G	GS	CG	SH	SV	IP	H	HR	BB	SO	RAT	ERA	ERA+	OAV	OOB	BH	AVG	PB	PR	/A	PD	TPI
1887	Cin-a	0	1	.000	1	1	1	0	0	8	21	0	3	1	28.1	13.50	32	.488	.532	94	.296	0	-8	-8	0	-0.5
1090	Tol-a	0	0	—	1	0	0	0	0	5	9	0	5	0	25.2	9.00	44	.375	.483	102	.268	0	-3	-3	-0	0.0
Total	2	0	1	.000	2	1	1	0	0	13	30	0	8	1	27.0	11.77	36	.448	.513	622	.269	1	-11	-11	0	-0.5

● PATSY TEBEAU

Tebeau, Oliver Wendell b: 12/5/1864, St.Louis, Mo. d: 5/15/18, St.Louis, Mo. BR/TR, 5'8", 163 lbs. Deb: 9/20/1887 FM♦

YEAR	TM/L	W	L	PCT	G	GS	CG	SH	SV	IP	H	HR	BB	SO	RAT	ERA	ERA+	OAV	OOB	BH	AVG	PB	PR	/A	PD	TPI
1896	*Cle-N	0	0	—	1	0	0	0	0	0	1	0	0	0	—	—	—	1.000	1.000	146	.269	0	0	0	0	0.0

● AL TEDROW

Tedrow, Allen Seymour b: 12/14/1891, Westerville, Ohio d: 1/23/58, Westerville, Ohio BR/TL, 6', 180 lbs. Deb: 9/15/14

YEAR	TM/L	W	L	PCT	G	GS	CG	SH	SV	IP	H	HR	BB	SO	RAT	ERA	ERA+	OAV	OOB	BH	AVG	PB	PR	/A	PD	TPI
1914	Cle-A	1	2	.333	4	3	1	0	0	22^{1}	19	0	14	4	14.5	1.21	239	.235	.367	1	.167	0	4	4	-0	0.6

● KENT TEKULVE

Tekulve, Kenton Charles b: 3/5/47, Cincinnati, Ohio BR/TR, 6'4", 180 lbs. Deb: 5/20/74

YEAR	TM/L	W	L	PCT	G	GS	CG	SH	SV	IP	H	HR	BB	SO	RAT	ERA	ERA+	OAV	OOB	BH	AVG	PB	PR	/A	PD	TPI
1974	Pit-N	1	1	.500	8	0	0	0	0	9	12	1	5	6	18.0	6.00	57	.343	.439	0	—	0	-2	-3	1	-0.5
1975	*Pit-N	1	2	.333	34	0	0	0	5	56	43	2	23	28	10.8	2.25	157	.215	.299	1	.091	-0	9	8	2	0.7
1976	Pit-N	5	3	.625	64	0	0	0	9	102^{2}	91	3	25	68	10.2	2.45	142	.241	.288	0	.000	-1	12	12	2	1.2
1977	Pit-N	10	1	.909	72	0	0	0	7	103	89	5	33	59	10.7	3.06	130	.236	.299	3	.250	0	10	11	3	1.6
1978	Pit-N	8	7	.533	**91**	0	0	0	31	135	115	5	55	77	11.5	2.33	159	.228	.306	2	.095	-1	**19**	21	3	3.5
1979	*Pit-N	10	8	.556	**94**	0	0	0	31	134^{1}	109	5	49	75	10.7	2.75	141	.222	.296	2	.133	-0	15	17	2	3.1
1980	Pit-N☆	8	12	.400	78	0	0	0	21	93	96	6	40	47	13.3	3.39	107	.267	.342	0	.000	-1	2	3	1	0.6
1981	Pit-N	5	5	.500	45	0	0	0	3	65	61	1	17	34	10.9	2.49	144	.250	.302	0	.000	-0	7	8	1	1.4
1982	Pit-N	12	8	.600	**85**	0	0	0	20	128^{2}	113	7	46	66	11.3	2.87	129	.237	.309	1	.071	-1	10	12	2	2.2
1983	Pit-N	7	5	.583	76	0	0	0	18	99	78	1	36	52	10.4	1.64	226	.223	.296	0	.000	-1	22	23	1	3.5
1984	Pit-N	3	9	.250	72	0	0	0	13	88	86	4	33	36	12.3	2.66	135	.262	.331	0	.000	-1	9	9	3	1.6
1985	Pit-N	0	0	—	3	0	0	0	0	3^{1}	7	1	5	4	32.4	16.20	22	.467	.600	0	—	0	-5	-5	0	0.0
	Phi-N	4	10	.286	58	0	0	0	14	72^{1}	67	4	25	36	11.7	2.99	123	.246	.314	0	.000	-0	5	6	0	1.3
	Yr	4	10	.286	61	0	0	0	14	75^{2}	74	5	30	40	12.6	3.57	103	.258	.332	0	.000	-0	0	1	0	1.3
1986	Phi-N	11	5	.688	73	0	0	0	4	110	99	2	25	57	10.1	2.54	152	.240	.283	0	.000	-0	14	16	0	2.4
1987	Phi-N	6	4	.600	**90**	0	0	0	3	105	96	8	29	60	10.7	3.09	137	.243	.295	0	.000	0	12	13	1	1.4
1988	Phi-N	3	7	.300	70	0	0	0	4	80	87	3	22	43	12.5	3.60	99	.276	.327	0	.000	-0	-1	-0	1	0.0
1989	Cin-N	0	3	.000	37	0	0	0	1	52	56	5	23	31	13.7	5.02	72	.272	.345	1	.500	0	-9	-8	0	-0.4
Total	16	94	90	.511	1050	0	0	0	184	1436^{1}	1305	63	491	779	11.4	2.85	131	.244	.309	10	.083	-6	128	141	22	23.6

● AMAURY TELEMACO

Telemaco, Amaury (Regalado) b: 1/19/74, Higuey, D.R. BR/TR, 6'4", 220 lbs. Deb: 5/16/96

YEAR	TM/L	W	L	PCT	G	GS	CG	SH	SV	IP	H	HR	BB	SO	RAT	ERA	ERA+	OAV	OOB	BH	AVG	PB	PR	/A	PD	TPI
1996	Chi-N	5	7	.417	25	17	0	0	0	97^{1}	108	20	31	64	13.1	5.46	79	.281	.339	3	.103	-1	-13	-12	-1	-1.5
1997	Chi-N	0	3	.000	10	5	0	0	0	38	47	4	11	29	13.7	6.16	70	.303	.349	2	.222	0	-8	-8	0	-0.5
1998	Chi-N	1	1	.500	14	0	0	0	0	27^{2}	23	5	13	18	11.7	3.90	112	.219	.305	1	.167	-0	1	1	0	0.1
	Ari-N	6	9	.400	27	18	0	0	0	121	127	13	33	60	12.2	3.94	109	.271	.325	2	.069	-1	4	5	-1	0.4
	Yr	7	10	.412	41	18	0	0	0	148^{2}	150	18	46	78	12.1	3.93	110	.262	.321	3	.086	-1	5	6	-1	0.5
Total	3	12	20	.375	76	40	0	0	0	284	305	42	88	171	12.7	4.75	91	.274	.331	8	.110	-2	-17	-14	-1	-1.5

● ANTHONY TELFORD

Telford, Anthony Charles b: 3/6/66, San Jose, Cal. BR/TR, 6', 175 lbs. Deb: 8/19/90

YEAR	TM/L	W	L	PCT	G	GS	CG	SH	SV	IP	H	HR	BB	SO	RAT	ERA	ERA+	OAV	OOB	BH	AVG	PB	PR	/A	PD	TPI
1990	Bal-A	3	3	.500	8	8	0	0	0	36^{1}	43	4	19	20	15.6	4.95	77	.295	.380	0	—	0	-4	-5	0	-0.5
1991	Bal-A	0	0	—	9	1	0	0	0	26^{2}	27	3	6	24	11.1	4.05	98	.265	.306	0	—	0	0	-0	-0	0.0
1993	Bal-A	0	0	—	3	0	0	0	0	7^{1}	11	3	1	6	16.0	9.82	46	.344	.382	0	—	0	-4	-4	0	-0.3
1997	Mon-N	4	6	.400	65	0	0	0	1	89	77	11	33	61	11.6	3.24	130	.236	.316	3	.200	0	10	9	2	1.2
1998	Mon-N	3	6	.333	77	0	0	0	1	91	85	9	36	59	12.4	3.86	106	.247	.326	1	.250	0	4	2	1	0.3
Total	5	10	15	.400	162	9	0	0	2	250^{1}	243	30	95	170	12.5	3.99	102	.256	.330	4	.211	1	5	3	3	0.7

● DAVE TELGHEDER

Telgheder, David William b: 11/11/66, Middletown, N.Y. BR/TR, 6'3", 212 lbs. Deb: 6/12/93

YEAR	TM/L	W	L	PCT	G	GS	CG	SH	SV	IP	H	HR	BB	SO	RAT	ERA	ERA+	OAV	OOB	BH	AVG	PB	PR	/A	PD	TPI
1993	NY-N	6	2	.750	24	7	0	0	0	75^{2}	82	10	21	35	12.7	4.76	84	.276	.332	1	.067	-0	-6	-6	-1	-0.7
1994	NY-N	0	1	.000	6	0	0	0	0	10	11	2	8	4	17.1	7.20	58	.282	.404	0	—	0	-3	-3	-1	-0.3
1995	NY-N	1	2	.333	7	4	0	0	0	25^{2}	34	4	7	16	14.4	5.61	72	.318	.360	2	.333	1	-4	-4	1	-0.4
1996	Oak-A	4	7	.364	16	14	1	1	0	79^{1}	92	12	26	43	13.5	4.65	106	.292	.348	0	—	0	3	2	0	0.3

YEAR	TM/L	W	L	PCT	G	GS	CG	SH	SV	IP	H	HR	BB	SO	RAT	ERA	ERA+	OAV	OOB	BH	AVG	PB	PR	/A	PD	TPI
1997	Oak-A	4	6	.400	20	19	0	0	0	101	134	15	35	55	15.2	6.06	75	.324	.379	0	.000	-0	-17	-17	3	-1.2
1998	Oak-A	0	1	.000	8	2	0	0	0	20	19	4	6	5	12.1	3.60	127	.235	.303	0	—	0	2	2	-0	0.2
Total	6	15	19	.441	81	46	1	1	0	311^{2}	372	47	103	158	14.0	5.23	85	.297	.355	3	.130	-0	-25	-27	2	-2.1

● TOM TELLMANN Tellmann, Thomas John b: 3/29/54, Warren, Pa. BR/TR, 6′3″, 195 lbs. Deb: 6/9/79

YEAR	TM/L	W	L	PCT	G	GS	CG	SH	SV	IP	H	HR	BB	SO	RAT	ERA	ERA+	OAV	OOB	BH	AVG	PB	PR	/A	PD	TPI
1979	SD-N	0	0	—	1	0	0	0	0	2^{2}	7	1	0	1	23.6	16.88	21	.467	.467	0	.000	-0	-4	-4	0	0.0
1980	SD-N	3	0	1.000	6	2	2	0	1	22^{1}	23	0	8	9	12.5	1.61	213	.264	.326	1	.125	-0	5	5	0	0.6
1983	Mil-A	9	4	.692	44	0	0	0	8	99^{2}	95	7	35	48	11.9	2.80	133	.259	.327	0	—	0	14	10	3	2.1
1984	Mil-A	6	3	.667	50	0	0	0	4	81	82	6	31	28	12.7	2.78	138	.272	.342	0	—	0	11	10	1	1.1
1985	Oak-A	0	0	—	11	0	0	0	0	21^{1}	33	3	9	8	18.1	5.06	76	.347	.410	0	—	0	-2	-3	0	0.1
Total	5	18	7	.720	112	2	2	0	13	227	240	17	83	94	13.0	3.05	123	.277	.343	1	.111	-0	24	18	4	3.9

● CHUCK TEMPLETON Templeton, Charles Sherman b: 6/1/32, Detroit, Mich. d: 10/9/97, Irving, Tex. BR/TL, 6′3″, 210 lbs. Deb: 9/9/55

YEAR	TM/L	W	L	PCT	G	GS	CG	SH	SV	IP	H	HR	BB	SO	RAT	ERA	ERA+	OAV	OOB	BH	AVG	PB	PR	/A	PD	TPI
1955	Bro-N	0	1	.000	4	0	0	0	0	4^{2}	5	2	5	3	21.2	11.57	35	.294	.478	0	—	0	-4	-4	0	-0.7
1956	Bro-N	0	1	.000	6	2	0	0	0	16^{1}	20	2	10	8	16.5	6.61	60	.294	.385	0	.000	-0	-5	-5	-0	-0.3
Total	2	0	2	.000	10	2	0	0	0	21	25	4	15	11	17.6	7.71	52	.294	.406	0	.000	-0	-9	-9	-0	-1.0

● JOHN TENER Tener, John Kinley b: 7/25/1863, County Tyrone, Ireland d: 5/19/46, Pittsburgh, Pa. BR/TR, 6′4″, 180 lbs. Deb: 6/8/1885 ♦

YEAR	TM/L	W	L	PCT	G	GS	CG	SH	SV	IP	H	HR	BB	SO	RAT	ERA	ERA+	OAV	OOB	BH	AVG	PB	PR	/A	PD	TPI
1888	Chi-N	7	5	.583	12	12	11	1	0	102	90	6	25	39	10.9	2.74	111	.228	.288	9	.196	-0	1	3	1	0.4
1889	Chi-N	15	15	.500	35	30	28	1	0	287	302	16	105	105	13.0	3.64	114	.262	.328	41	.273	5	12	17	3	2.1
1890	Pit-P	3	11	.214	14	14	13	0	0	117	160	6	70	30	18.1	7.31	53	.312	.400	12	.190	2	-40	-44	4	-3.1
Total	3	25	31	.446	61	56	52	2	0	506	552	28	200	174	13.7	4.30	90	.268	.339	62	.236	6	-27	-23	8	-0.6

● JIM TENNANT Tennant, James McDonnell b: 3/3/07, Shepherdstown, W.Va d: 4/16/67, Trumbull, Conn. BR/TR, 6′1″, 190 lbs. Deb: 9/28/29

YEAR	TM/L	W	L	PCT	G	GS	CG	SH	SV	IP	H	HR	BB	SO	RAT	ERA	ERA+	OAV	OOB	BH	AVG	PB	PR	/A	PD	TPI
1929	NY-N	0	0	—	1	0	0	0	0	1	1	0	0	1	9.0	0.00	—	.333	.333	0	—	0	1	1	0	0.0

● FRED TENNEY Tenney, Fred Clay b: 7/9/1859, Marlborough, N.H. d: 6/15/19, Fall River, Mass. Deb: 4/28/1884 ♦

YEAR	TM/L	W	L	PCT	G	GS	CG	SH	SV	IP	H	HR	BB	SO	RAT	ERA	ERA+	OAV	OOB	BH	AVG	PB	PR	/A	PD	TPI
1884	Bos-U	3	1	.750	4	4	4	0	0	35	31	0	5	18	9.3	2.31	103	.221	.248	2	.118	-3	0	0	-1	-0.3
	Wil-U	0	1	.000	1	1	1	0	0	8	6	0	4	10	11.3	1.13	237	.194	.286	0	.000	-1	1	1	0	0.1
	Yr	3	2	.600	5	5	5	0	0	43	37	0	9	28	9.6	2.09	116	.216	.256	2	.100	-3	2	2	-1	-0.2

● FRED TENNEY Tenney, Frederick b: 11/26/1871, Georgetown, Mass. d: 7/3/52, Boston, Mass. BL/TL, 5′9″, 155 lbs. Deb: 6/16/1894 M♦

YEAR	TM/L	W	L	PCT	G	GS	CG	SH	SV	IP	H	HR	BB	SO	RAT	ERA	ERA+	OAV	OOB	BH	AVG	PB	PR	/A	PD	TPI
1905	Bos-N	0	0	—	1	0	0	0	0	2	5	0	1	0	27.0	4.50	69	.417	.462	158	.288	0	-0	-0	0	0.0

● BOB TERLECKI Terlecki, Robert Joseph b: 2/14/45, Trenton, N.J. BR/TR, 5′8″, 185 lbs. Deb: 8/16/72

YEAR	TM/L	W	L	PCT	G	GS	CG	SH	SV	IP	H	HR	BB	SO	RAT	ERA	ERA+	OAV	OOB	BH	AVG	PB	PR	/A	PD	TPI
1972	Phi-N	0	0	—	9	0	0	0	0	13^{1}	16	2	10	5	17.6	4.73	76	.308	.419	0	—	0	-2	-2	0	0.0

● GREG TERLECKY Terlecky, Gregory John b: 3/20/52, Culver City, Cal. BR/TR, 6′3″, 200 lbs. Deb: 6/12/75

YEAR	TM/L	W	L	PCT	G	GS	CG	SH	SV	IP	H	HR	BB	SO	RAT	ERA	ERA+	OAV	OOB	BH	AVG	PB	PR	/A	PD	TPI
1975	StL-N	0	1	.000	20	0	0	0	0	30^{1}	38	4	12	13	14.8	4.45	84	.306	.368	1	.333	0	-3	-2	0	0.0

● JEFF TERPKO Terpko, Jeffrey Michael b: 10/16/50, Sayre, Pa. BR/TR, 6′, 180 lbs. Deb: 9/21/74

YEAR	TM/L	W	L	PCT	G	GS	CG	SH	SV	IP	H	HR	BB	SO	RAT	ERA	ERA+	OAV	OOB	BH	AVG	PB	PR	/A	PD	TPI
1974	Tex-A	0	0	—	3	0	0	0	0	7	6	0	4	3	12.9	1.29	277	.231	.333	0	—	0	2	2	-0	0.2
1976	Tex-A	3	3	.500	32	0	0	0	0	52^{2}	42	3	29	24	12.1	2.39	150	.223	.327	0	—	0	7	7	-0	0.6
1977	Mon-N	0	1	.000	13	0	0	0	0	20^{2}	28	2	15	14	18.7	5.66	67	.346	.448	0	.000	-0	-4	-4	-0	-0.2
Total	3	3	4	.429	48	0	0	0	0	80^{1}	76	5	48	41	13.9	3.14	116	.258	.362	0	.000	-0	4	5	-1	0.6

● WALT TERRELL Terrell, Charles Walter b: 5/11/58, Jeffersonville, Ind BL/TR, 6′2″, 205 lbs. Deb: 9/8/82

YEAR	TM/L	W	L	PCT	G	GS	CG	SH	SV	IP	H	HR	BB	SO	RAT	ERA	ERA+	OAV	OOB	BH	AVG	PB	PR	/A	PD	TPI
1982	NY-N	0	3	.000	3	3	0	0	0	21	22	2	14	8	15.4	3.43	106	.268	.375	2	.400	1	0	0	-0	0.1
1983	NY-N	8	8	.500	21	20	4	2	0	133^{2}	123	7	55	59	12.1	3.57	102	.251	.329	8	.182	3	1	1	-0	0.4
1984	NY-N	11	12	.478	33	33	3	1	0	215	232	16	80	114	13.2	3.52	101	.282	.348	6	.080	-4	2	0	0	-0.3
1985	Det-A	15	10	.600	34	34	5	3	0	229	221	9	95	130	12.6	3.85	106	.255	.332	0	—	0	7	6	3	0.9
1986	Det-A	15	12	.556	34	33	9	2	0	217^{1}	199	30	98	93	12.4	4.56	90	.245	.329	0	—	0	-9	-10	2	-1.0
1987	*Det-A	17	10	.630	35	35	10	1	0	244^{2}	254	30	94	143	12.9	4.05	104	.268	.336	0	—	0	11	5	-1	0.7
1988	Det-A	7	16	.304	29	29	11	1	0	206^{1}	199	20	78	84	12.2	3.97	96	.258	.328	0	—	0	-0	-4	1	0.0
1989	SD-N	5	13	.278	19	19	4	1	0	123^{1}	134	14	26	63	11.7	4.01	87	.277	.314	4	.100	-0	-7	-7	3	-0.7
	NY-A	6	5	.545	13	13	1	1	0	83	102	9	24	30	13.9	5.20	74	.307	.358	0	—	0	-12	-12	-0	-1.4
1990	Pit-N	2	7	.222	16	16	0	0	0	82^{2}	98	13	33	34	14.7	5.88	62	.295	.366	3	.107	-1	-19	-21	1	-2.0
	Det-A	6	4	.600	13	12	0	0	0	75^{1}	86	7	24	30	14.1	4.54	87	.290	.359	0	—	0	-5	-5	-1	-0.7
1991	Det-A	12	14	.462	35	33	8	2	0	218^{2}	257	16	79	80	13.9	4.24	98	.301	.361	0	—	0	-4	-2	-1	-0.3
1992	Det-A	7	10	.412	36	14	1	0	0	136^{2}	163	14	48	61	14.1	5.20	76	.298	.358	0	—	0	-19	-19	1	-2.0
Total	11	111	124	.472	321	294	56	14	0	1986^{2}	2090	187	748	929	13.0	4.22	93	.274	.341	23	.120	-1	-54	-68	8	-6.3

● JERRY TERRELL Terrell, Jerry Wayne b: 7/13/46, Waseca, Minn. BR/TR, 6′, 170 lbs. Deb: 4/14/73 ♦

YEAR	TM/L	W	L	PCT	G	GS	CG	SH	SV	IP	H	HR	BB	SO	RAT	ERA	ERA+	OAV	OOB	BH	AVG	PB	PR	/A	PD	TPI
1979	KC-A	0	0	—	1	0	0	0	0	1	0	0	0	0	0.0	0.00	—	.000	.000	12	.300	0	0	0	0	0.0
1980	KC-A	0	0	—	1	0	0	0	0	1	1	0	1	0	18.0	0.00	—	.250	.400	1	.063	-0	0	0	0	0.0
Total	2	0	0	—	2	0	0	0	0	2	1	0	1	0	9.0	0.00	—	.143	.250	412	.253	0	1	1	0	0.0

● JOHN TERRY Terry, John Burchard b: 11/1/1879, Waterbury, Conn. d: 4/27/33, Kansas City, Mo. Deb: 9/17/02

YEAR	TM/L	W	L	PCT	G	GS	CG	SH	SV	IP	H	HR	BB	SO	RAT	ERA	ERA+	OAV	OOB	BH	AVG	PB	PR	/A	PD	TPI
1902	Det-A	0	1	.000	1	1	1	0	0	5	8	0	1	0	16.2	3.60	101	.364	.391	0	.000	-0	-0	0	-0	-0.1
1903	StL-A	1	1	.500	3	1	1	0	0	17^{2}	21	0	4	2	14.3	2.55	114	.296	.359	0	.000	-1	1	1	-0	-0.1
Total	2	1	2	.333	4	2	2	0	0	22^{2}	29	0	5	2	14.7	2.78	111	.312	.366	0	.000	-2	1	1	-1	-0.2

● YANK TERRY Terry, Lancelot Yank b: 2/11/11, Bedford, Ind. d: 11/4/79, Bloomington, Ind. BR/TR, 6′1″, 180 lbs. Deb: 8/3/40

YEAR	TM/L	W	L	PCT	G	GS	CG	SH	SV	IP	H	HR	BB	SO	RAT	ERA	ERA+	OAV	OOB	BH	AVG	PB	PR	/A	PD	TPI
1940	Bos-A	1	0	1.000	4	1	0	0	0	19^{1}	24	2	11	9	16.3	8.84	51	.304	.389	2	.250	0	-10	-9	0	-0.4
1942	Bos-A	6	5	.545	20	11	3	0	1	85	82	5	43	37	13.4	3.92	95	.248	.339	3	.111	-1	-2	-2	-0	-0.4
1943	Bos-A	7	9	.438	30	22	7	0	1	163^{2}	147	8	63	63	11.6	3.52	94	.242	.314	3	.067	-3	-4	-4	0	-0.6
1944	Bos-A	6	10	.375	27	17	3	0	0	132^{2}	142	10	65	30	14.2	4.21	81	.276	.361	11	.234	1	-11	-12	0	-1.2
1945	Bos-A	0	4	.000	12	4	1	0	0	56^{2}	68	8	14	28	13.0	4.13	82	.296	.336	2	.111	-2	-5	-5	-1	-0.5
Total	5	20	28	.417	93	55	14	0	2	457^{1}	463	33	196	167	13.1	4.09	85	.263	.339	21	.145	-4	-32	-31	-1	-3.1

● RALPH TERRY Terry, Ralph Willard b: 1/9/36, Big Cabin, Okla. BR/TR, 6′3″, 195 lbs. Deb: 8/6/56

YEAR	TM/L	W	L	PCT	G	GS	CG	SH	SV	IP	H	HR	BB	SO	RAT	ERA	ERA+	OAV	OOB	BH	AVG	PB	PR	/A	PD	TPI
1956	NY-A	1	2	.333	3	3	0	0	0	13^{1}	17	2	11	8	18.9	9.45	41	.347	.467	1	.167	-0	-8	-8	-0	-1.3
1957	NY-A	1	1	.500	7	2	1	1	0	20^{2}	18	1	8	7	11.3	3.05	118	.240	.313	1	.250	0	2	1	0	0.2
	KC-A	4	11	.267	21	19	3	1	0	130^{2}	119	15	47	80	11.7	3.38	117	.239	.310	6	.143	-2	6	8	0	0.7
	Yr	5	12	.294	28	21	4	2	0	151^{1}	137	16	55	87	11.7	3.33	117	.239	.310	7	.152	-2	8	10	0	0.9
1958	KC-A	11	13	.458	40	33	8	3	2	216^{2}	217	29	61	134	11.6	4.24	92	.262	.314	14	.197	-0	-11	-8	-2	-1.1
1959	KC-A	2	4	.333	9	7	2	0	0	46^{1}	56	9	19	35	14.8	5.24	76	.308	.376	3	.176	-1	-7	-6	1	-0.7
	NY-A	3	7	.300	24	16	5	1	0	127^{1}	130	7	30	55	11.5	3.39	107	.270	.316	4	.098	-3	7	4	-0	-0.1
	Yr	5	11	.313	33	23	7	1	0	173^{2}	186	16	49	90	12.3	3.89	96	.280	.331	7	.121	-3	-0	-3	0	-0.8
1960	*NY-A	10	8	.556	35	23	7	3	1	166^{2}	149	15	52	92	11.1	3.40	105	.237	.300	6	.122	-2	9	3	0	0.1
1961	*NY-A	16	3	.842	31	27	9	2	0	188^{1}	162	19	42	86	9.8	3.15	118	.232	.277	15	.227	2	18	12	1	1.4
1962	*NY-A☆	**23**	12	.657	43	39	14	3	2	**298^{2}**	257	40	57	176	**9.6**	3.19	117	.231	.270	20	.189	1	26	18	-4	1.7
1963	*NY-A	17	15	.531	40	37	**18**	3	1	268	246	29	39	114	**9.7**	3.22	109	.242	.273	7	.080	-6	12	9	-1	0.2
1964	*NY-A	7	11	.389	27	14	2	1	4	115	130	20	31	77	12.7	4.54	80	.283	.329	7	.200	1	-12	-12	-0	-1.7
1965	Cle-A	11	6	.647	30	26	6	2	0	165^{2}	154	22	23	84	9.7	3.69	94	.242	.269	7	.143	2	-4	-4	-4	-0.6
1966	KC-A	1	5	.167	15	10	0	0	0	64	65	7	15	33	11.4	3.80	89	.263	.308	3	.214	1	-3	-3	-1	-0.2
	NY-N	0	1	.000	11	1	0	0	1	24^{2}	27	1	11	14	13.9	4.74	77	.293	.369	1	.167	-0	-3	-3	-0	-0.2
1967	NY-N	0	0	—	2	0	0	0	0	3^{1}	1	0	0	5	2.7	0.00	—	.091	.091	0	—	0	1	1	0	0.0
Total	12	107	99	.519	338	257	75	20	11	1849^{1}	1748	216	446	1000	10.8	3.62	102	.249	.296	95	.160	-6	32	13	-11	-1.6

● SCOTT TERRY Terry, Scott Ray b: 11/21/59, Hobbs, N.Mex. BR/TR, 5′11″, 195 lbs. Deb: 4/9/86

YEAR	TM/L	W	L	PCT	G	GS	CG	SH	SV	IP	H	HR	BB	SO	RAT	ERA	ERA+	OAV	OOB	BH	AVG	PB	PR	/A	PD	TPI
1986	Cin-N	1	2	.333	28	3	0	0	0	55^{2}	66	8	32	32	15.8	6.14	63	.300	.389	1	.250	0	-15	-14	0	-0.7
1987	StL-N	0	0	—	11	0	0	0	0	13^{1}	13	0	8	9	14.2	3.38	123	.260	.362	0	.000	-0	1	1	0	0.0

YEAR	TM/L	W	L	PCT	G	GS	CG	SH	SV	IP	H	HR	BB	SO	RAT	ERA	ERA+	OAV	OOB	BH	AVG	PB	PR	/A	PD	TPI
1988	StL-N	9	6	.600	51	11	1	0	3	129^{1}	119	5	34	65	10.6	2.92	119	.247	.297	7	.250	2	8	8	0	1.2
1989	StL-N	8	10	.444	31	24	1	0	2	148^{2}	142	14	43	69	11.4	3.57	102	.253	.310	7	.156	2	-1	1	2	0.5
1990	StL-N	2	6	.250	50	2	0	0	2	72	75	7	27	35	13.3	4.75	80	.264	.337	5	.455	2	-8	-7	0	-0.6
1991	StL-N	4	4	.500	65	0	0	0	1	80^{1}	76	1	32	52	12.1	2.80	133	.249	.320	1	.143	-0	8	8	1	0.9
Total	6	24	28	.462	236	40	2	0	8	499^{1}	491	35	176	262	12.1	3.73	98	.258	.323	21	.216	6	-7	-3	4	1.3

● ADONIS TERRY Terry, William H b: 8/7/1864, Westfield, Mass. d: 2/24/15, Milwaukee, Wis. BR/TR, 5'11.5", 168 lbs. Deb: 5/1/1884 U♦

YEAR	TM/L	W	L	PCT	G	GS	CG	SH	SV	IP	H	HR	BB	SO	RAT	ERA	ERA+	OAV	OOB	BH	AVG	PB	PR	/A	PD	TPI
1884	Bro-a	19	35	.352	56	55	54	2	0	476	486	10	72	230	10.7	3.55	93	.248	.277	55	.233	3	-16	-12	-3	-1.2
1885	Bro-a	6	17	.261	25	23	23	0	1	209	213	9	42	96	11.2	4.26	77	.262	.301	45	.170	-3	-24	-22	1	-2.1
1886	Bro-a	18	16	.529	34	34	32	5	0	288^{1}	263	1	115	162	12.3	3.09	113	.231	.310	71	.237	2	12	13	4	1.8
1887	Bro-a	16	16	.500	40	35	35	1	**3**	318	331	10	99	138	12.4	4.02	107	.262	.320	103	.293	7	10	10	5	1.6
1888	Bro-a	13	8	.619	23	23	20	2	0	195	145	2	67	138	10.2	2.03	147	**.199**	.275	29	.252	3	22	21	1	2.2
1889	*Bro-a	22	15	.595	41	39	35	2	0	326	285	6	126	186	11.8	3.29	113	.228	.307	48	.300	12	20	16	6	2.9
1890	*Bro-N	26	16	.619	46	44	38	1	0	370	362	3	133	185	12.4	2.94	117	.248	.318	101	.278	15	26	20	1	3.1
1891	Bro-N	6	16	.273	25	22	18	1	1	194	207	5	80	65	13.6	4.22	78	.263	.336	19	.209	3	-19	-20	-1	-1.5
1892	Bal-N	0	1	.000	1	1	1	0	0	9	7	0	7	3	14.0	4.00	86	.206	.341	0	.000	-1	-1	-1	0	-0.1
	Pit-N	18	7	.720	30	26	24	2	1	240	185	3	106	95	11.2	2.51	131	.204	.293	16	.160	1	21	21	1	2.1
	Yr	18	8	.692	31	27	25	2	1	249	192	3	113	98	11.3	2.57	129	.204	.295	16	.154	1	20	20	1	2.0
1893	Pit-N	12	8	.600	26	19	14	0	0	170	177	5	99	52	15.2	4.45	102	.260	.363	18	.254	2	4	2	0	0.4
1894	Pit-N	0	1	.000	1	1	0	0	0	0^{2}	2	0	4	0	81.0	67.50	8	.500	.750	0	—	0	-5	-5	0	-2.1
	Chi-N	5	11	.313	23	21	16	0	0	163^{1}	232	12	123	39	20.4	5.84	96	.330	.441	33	.347	4	-9	-4	-1	0.0
	Yr	5	12	.294	24	22	16	0	0	164	234	12	127	39	20.7	6.09	92	.331	.444	33	.347	4	-14	-9	-1	-2.1
1895	Chi-N	21	14	.600	38	34	31	0	0	311^{1}	346	4	131	88	14.3	4.80	106	.277	.354	30	.219	-6	-1	10	2	0.5
1896	Chi-N	15	14	.517	30	28	25	1	0	235^{2}	273	6	88	75	14.2	4.43	102	.288	.354	26	.263	2	-2	3	-2	0.3
1897	Chi-N	0	1	.000	1	1	1	0	0	8	11	0	6	1	21.4	10.13	44	.324	.452	0	.000	-1	-5	-5	0	-0.4
Total	14	197	196	.501	440	406	367	17	6	3514^{1}	3525	76	1298	1553	12.7	3.74	103	.253	.323	594	.249	45	34	43	15	7.5

● DICK TERWILLIGER Terwilliger, Richard Martin b: 6/27/06, Sand Lake, Mich. d: 1/21/69, Greenville, Mich. BR/TR, 5'11", 178 lbs. Deb: 8/18/32

YEAR	TM/L	W	L	PCT	G	GS	CG	SH	SV	IP	H	HR	BB	SO	RAT	ERA	ERA+	OAV	OOB	BH	AVG	PB	PR	/A	PD	TPI
1932	StL-N	0	0	—	1	0	0	0	0	3	1	0	2	2	12.0	0.00	—	.143	.400	0	.000	-0	1	1	0	0.0

● JEFF TESREAU Tesreau, Charles Monroe b: 3/5/1889, Silver Mine, Mo. d: 9/24/46, Hanover, N.H. BR/TR, 6'2", 218 lbs. Deb: 4/12/12

YEAR	TM/L	W	L	PCT	G	GS	CG	SH	SV	IP	H	HR	BB	SO	RAT	ERA	ERA+	OAV	OOB	BH	AVG	PB	PR	/A	PD	TPI
1912	*NY-N	17	7	.708	36	28	19	3	1	243	177	2	106	119	10.9	**1.96**	**172**	**.204**	.298	12	.146	-2	39	38	1	3.3
1913	*NY-N	22	13	.629	41	38	17	1	0	282	222	7	119	167	11.1	2.17	144	**.220**	.306	21	.221	2	32	30	1	3.9
1914	NY-N	26	10	.722	42	41	26	**8**	1	322^{1}	238	8	128	189	10.4	2.37	112	**.209**	.293	28	.239	6	15	10	-2	1.5
1915	NY-N	19	16	.543	43	39	24	8	3	306	235	4	75	176	9.3	2.29	112	.215	.269	24	.233	6	16	9	1	1.8
1916	NY-N	14	14	.500	40	32	23	5	2	268^{1}	249	9	65	113	10.7	2.92	83	.250	.300	18	.191	2	-9	-14	-0	-1.4
1917	*NY-N	13	8	.619	33	20	11	1	2	183^{2}	168	6	58	85	11.2	3.09	83	.249	.312	14	.230	2	-8	-11	2	-1.0
1918	NY-N	4	4	.500	12	9	3	1	0	73^{2}	61	1	21	31	10.0	2.32	113	.227	.283	7	.318	2	4	3	1	0.6
Total	7	115	72	.615	247	207	123	27	9	1679	1350	37	572	880	10.5	2.43	114	.223	.295	124	.216	17	89	63	3	8.7

● JAY TESSMER Tessmer, Jay Weldon b: 12/26/71, Meadville, Pa. BR/TR, 6'3", 190 lbs. Deb: 8/27/98

YEAR	TM/L	W	L	PCT	G	GS	CG	SH	SV	IP	H	HR	BB	SO	RAT	ERA	ERA+	OAV	OOB	BH	AVG	PB	PR	/A	PD	TPI
1998	NY-A	1	0	1.000	7	0	0	0	0	8^{2}	4	1	4	6	8.3	3.12	143	.143	.250	0	—	0	1	1	-0	0.2

● BOB TEWKSBURY Tewksbury, Robert Alan b: 11/30/60, Concord, N.H. BR/TR, 6'4", 200 lbs. Deb: 4/11/86

YEAR	TM/L	W	L	PCT	G	GS	CG	SH	SV	IP	H	HR	BB	SO	RAT	ERA	ERA+	OAV	OOB	BH	AVG	PB	PR	/A	PD	TPI
1986	NY-A	9	5	.643	23	20	2	0	0	130^{1}	144	8	31	49	12.4	3.31	123	.282	.329	0	—	0	12	11	2	1.3
1987	NY-A	1	4	.200	8	6	0	0	0	33^{1}	47	5	7	12	14.9	6.75	65	.338	.374	0	—	0	-9	-9	0	-1.0
	Chi-N	0	4	.000	7	3	0	0	0	18	32	1	13	10	22.5	6.50	66	.421	.506	0	.000	-1	-5	-4	-1	-0.9
1988	Chi-N	0	0	—	1	1	0	0	0	3^{1}	6	1	2	1	21.6	8.10	45	.400	.471	0	.000	-0	-2	-2	0	-0.3
1989	StL-N	1	0	1.000	7	4	1	1	0	30	25	2	10	17	11.1	3.30	110	.225	.301	1	.111	-0	1	1	-0	0.0
1990	StL-N	10	9	.526	28	20	3	2	1	145^{1}	151	7	15	50	10.5	3.47	110	.267	.290	7	.171	1	5	6	-1	0.8
1991	StL-N	11	12	.478	30	30	3	0	0	191	206	13	38	75	11.7	3.25	114	.281	.321	9	.155	1	9	10	0	1.3
1992	StL-N★	16	5	**.762**	33	32	5	0	0	233	217	15	20	91	9.3	2.16	157	.248	.267	6	.086	-2	35	32	0	2.7
1993	StL-N	17	10	.630	32	32	2	0	0	213^{2}	258	15	20	97	12.0	3.83	103	.301	.322	14	.203	2	5	3	3	0.9
1994	StL-N	12	10	.545	24	24	4	1	0	155^{2}	190	19	22	79	12.4	5.32	78	.304	.330	10	.185	1	-19	-20	2	-2.1
1995	Tex-A	8	7	.533	21	21	4	1	0	129^{2}	169	8	20	53	13.3	4.58	105	.319	.348	0	.000	-0	2	4	1	0.5
1996	SD-N	10	10	.500	36	33	1	0	0	206^{2}	224	17	43	126	11.8	4.31	92	.275	.314	2	.031	-5	-2	-8	4	-0.7
1997	Min-A	8	13	.381	26	26	5	2	0	168^{2}	200	12	31	92	12.4	4.22	110	.297	.329	1	.200	0	7	8	3	1.2
1998	Min-A	7	13	.350	26	25	1	0	0	148^{1}	174	19	20	60	12.1	4.79	98	.292	.322	0	.000	-0	-2	-2	2	0.0
Total	13	110	102	.519	302	277	31	7	1	1807	2043	142	292	812	11.8	3.92	104	.287	.319	50	.132	-3	37	29	17	4.0

● GRANT THATCHER Thatcher, Ulysses Grant b: 2/23/1877, Maytown, Pa. d: 3/17/36, Lancaster, Pa. TR, 5'10.5", 180 lbs. Deb: 9/9/03

YEAR	TM/L	W	L	PCT	G	GS	CG	SH	SV	IP	H	HR	BB	SO	RAT	ERA	ERA+	OAV	OOB	BH	AVG	PB	PR	/A	PD	TPI
1903	Bro-N	3	1	.750	4	4	4	0	0	28	33	1	7	9	12.9	2.89	110	.292	.333	2	.182	0	1	1	-0	0.1
1904	Bro-N	1	0	1.000	1	0	0	0	0	9	9	0	2	4	11.0	4.00	69	.281	.324	1	.250	0	-1	-1	-0	-0.1
Total	2	4	1	.800	5	4	4	0	0	37	42	1	9	13	12.4	3.16	98	.290	.331	3	.200	0	-0	-0	-0	0.0

● GREG THAYER Thayer, Gregory Allen b: 10/23/49, Cedar Rapids, Iowa BR/TR, 5'11", 182 lbs. Deb: 4/7/78

YEAR	TM/L	W	L	PCT	G	GS	CG	SH	SV	IP	H	HR	BB	SO	RAT	ERA	ERA+	OAV	OOB	BH	AVG	PB	PR	/A	PD	TPI
1978	Min-A	1	1	.500	20	0	0	0	0	45	40	5	30	30	14.6	3.80	100	.258	.388	0	—	0	-0	0	-0	0.0

● JACK THEIS Theis, John Louis b: 7/23/1891, Georgetown, Ohio d: 7/6/41, Georgetown, Ohio BR/TR, 6', 190 lbs. Deb: 7/5/20

YEAR	TM/L	W	L	PCT	G	GS	CG	SH	SV	IP	H	HR	BB	SO	RAT	ERA	ERA+	OAV	OOB	BH	AVG	PB	PR	/A	PD	TPI
1920	Cin-N	0	0	—	1	0	0	0	0	2	1	0	3	0	18.0	0.00	—	.143	.400	0	—	0	1	1	-0	0.0

● DUANE THEISS Theiss, Duane Charles b: 11/20/53, Zanesville, Ohio BR/TR, 6'3", 185 lbs. Deb: 8/5/77

YEAR	TM/L	W	L	PCT	G	GS	CG	SH	SV	IP	H	HR	BB	SO	RAT	ERA	ERA+	OAV	OOB	BH	AVG	PB	PR	/A	PD	TPI
1977	Atl-N	1	1	.500	17	0	0	0	0	20^{2}	26	1	16	7	18.7	6.53	68	.338	.457	0	.000	-0	-6	-5	0	-0.4
1978	Atl-N	0	0	—	3	0	0	0	0	6^{1}	3	0	3	3	9.9	1.42	285	.158	.304	0	.000	-0	2	2	0	0.0
Total	2	1	1	.500	20	0	0	0	0	27	29	1	19	10	16.7	5.33	82	.302	.427	0	.000	-0	-5	-3	0	-0.4

● JUG THESENGA Thesenga, Arnold Joseph b: 4/27/14, Jefferson, S.Dak. BR/TR, 6', 200 lbs. Deb: 9/1/44

YEAR	TM/L	W	L	PCT	G	GS	CG	SH	SV	IP	H	HR	BB	SO	RAT	ERA	ERA+	OAV	OOB	BH	AVG	PB	PR	/A	PD	TPI
1944	Was-A	0	0	—	5	1	0	0	0	12^{1}	18	0	12	2	21.9	5.11	64	.340	.462	0	.000	-0	-2	-3	0	0.0

● BERT THIEL Thiel, Maynard Bert b: 5/4/26, Marion, Wis. BR/TR, 5'10", 185 lbs. Deb: 4/17/52

YEAR	TM/L	W	L	PCT	G	GS	CG	SH	SV	IP	H	HR	BB	SO	RAT	ERA	ERA+	OAV	OOB	BH	AVG	PB	PR	/A	PD	TPI
1952	Bos-N	1	1	.500	4	0	0	0	0	7	11	1	4	6	21.9	7.71	47	.344	.447	0	—	0	-3	-3	-0	-0.8

● HENRY THIELMAN Thielman, Henry Joseph b: 10/3/1880, St.Cloud, Minn. d: 9/2/42, New York, N.Y. BR/TR, 5'11", 175 lbs. Deb: 4/17/02 F♦

YEAR	TM/L	W	L	PCT	G	GS	CG	SH	SV	IP	H	HR	BB	SO	RAT	ERA	ERA+	OAV	OOB	BH	AVG	PB	PR	/A	PD	TPI
1902	NY-N	0	1	.000	2	2	0	0	0	6	8	0	6	5	21.0	1.50	187	.320	.452	1	.111	-0	1	1	0	0.2
	Cin-N	9	15	.375	25	23	22	0	1	211	201	2	78	49	12.7	3.24	92	.251	.332	12	.132	-4	-11	-6	-1	-1.1
	Yr	9	16	.360	27	25	22	0	1	217	209	2	84	54	12.9	3.19	94	.253	.336	13	.130	-4	-10	-5	-0	-0.9
1903	Bro-N	0	3	.000	4	3	3	0	0	29	31	3	14	10	14.6	4.66	69	.330	.427	5	.217	1	-4	-5	1	-0.2
Total	2	9	19	.321	31	28	25	0	1	246	240	5	98	64	13.1	3.37	90	.261	.346	18	.146	-3	-14	-9	0	-1.1

● JAKE THIELMAN Thielman, John Peter b: 5/20/1879, St.Cloud, Minn. d: 1/28/28, Minneapolis, Minn. BR/TR, 5'11", 175 lbs. Deb: 4/23/05 F

YEAR	TM/L	W	L	PCT	G	GS	CG	SH	SV	IP	H	HR	BB	SO	RAT	ERA	ERA+	OAV	OOB	BH	AVG	PB	PR	/A	PD	TPI
1905	StL-N	15	16	.484	32	29	26	0	0	242	265	4	62	87	12.6	3.50	85	.281	.333	21	.231	8	-13	-14	3	-0.5
1906	StL-N	0	1	.000	1	1	0	0	0	5	5	0	2	0	12.6	3.60	73	.263	.333	1	.500	0	-1	-1	-0	-0.1
1907	Cle-A	11	8	.579	20	18	18	3	0	166	151	2	34	56	10.4	2.33	107	.245	.292	12	.203	1	4	3	-3	0.2
1908	Cle-A	4	3	.571	11	8	5	0	0	61^{2}	59	2	9	15	10.5	3.65	65	.260	.300	8	.348	4	-9	-9	2	-0.4
	Bos-A	0	0	—	1	0	0	0	0	0^{2}	3	1	0	0	40.5	40.50	6	.600	.600	0	—	0	-3	-3	-0	0.0
	Yr	4	3	.571	12	8	5	0	0	62^{1}	62	3	9	15	10.3	4.04	59	.263	.290	8	.348	4	-11	-11	1	-0.4
Total	4	30	28	.517	65	56	49	3	0	475^{1}	483	9	107	158	11.6	3.16	86	.267	.316	42	.240	13	-21	-23	2	-0.8

● DAVE THIES Thies, David Robert b: 3/21/37, Minneapolis, Minn. BR/TR, 6'4", 205 lbs. Deb: 4/20/63

YEAR	TM/L	W	L	PCT	G	GS	CG	SH	SV	IP	H	HR	BB	SO	RAT	ERA	ERA+	OAV	OOB	BH	AVG	PB	PR	/A	PD	TPI
1963	KC-A	0	1	.000	9	2	0	0	0	25^{1}	26	2	12	9	14.2	4.62	84	.274	.367	2	.333	1	-3	-2	0	0.0

● JAKE THIES Thies, Vernon Arthur b: 4/1/26, St.Louis, Mo. BR/TR, 5'11", 170 lbs. Deb: 4/24/54

YEAR	TM/L	W	L	PCT	G	GS	CG	SH	SV	IP	H	HR	BB	SO	RAT	ERA	ERA+	OAV	OOB	BH	AVG	PB	PR	/A	PD	TPI
1954	Pit-N	3	9	.250	33	18	3	1	0	130^{1}	120	13	49	57	11.9	3.87	108	.244	.317	1	.030	-2	3	5	0	0.2

YEAR	TM/L	W	L	PCT	G	GS	CG	SH	SV	IP	H	HR	BB	SO	RAT	ERA	ERA+	OAV	OOB	BH	AVG	PB	PR	/A	PD	TPI
1955	Pit-N	0	1	.000	1	1	0	0	0	3^2	5	0	3	0	22.1	4.91	84	.357	.500	0	—	0	-0	-0	-0	-0.1
Total	2	3	10	.231	34	19	3	1	0	134	125	13	52	57	12.2	3.90	107	.248	.323	1	.030	-2	3	4	0	0.1

● BOBBY THIGPEN Thigpen, Robert Thomas b: 7/17/63, Tallahassee, Fla. BR/TR, 6'3", 195 lbs. Deb: 8/6/86

YEAR	TM/L	W	L	PCT	G	GS	CG	SH	SV	IP	H	HR	BB	SO	RAT	ERA	ERA+	OAV	OOB	BH	AVG	PB	PR	/A	PD	TPI
1986	Chi-A	2	0	1.000	20	0	0	0	7	35^2	26	1	12	20	9.8	1.77	244	.205	.279	0	—	0	10	10	-0	0.8
1987	Chi-A	7	5	.583	51	0	0	0	16	89	86	10	24	52	11.4	2.73	168	.256	.311	0	—	0	17	18	0	2.8
1988	Chi-A	5	8	.385	68	0	0	0	34	90	96	6	33	62	13.3	3.30	120	.273	.342	0	—	0	7	7	0	1.4
1989	Chi-A	2	6	.250	61	0	0	0	34	79	62	10	40	47	11.7	3.76	101	.218	.316	0	—	0	1	0	-1	0.1
1990	Chi-A★	4	6	.400	**77**	0	0	0	**57**	88^2	60	5	32	70	9.4	1.83	209	.195	.274	0	—	0	20	20	0	4.4
1991	Chi-A	7	5	.583	67	0	0	0	30	69^2	63	10	38	47	13.6	3.49	114	.245	.351	0	—	0	5	4	1	1.1
1992	Chi-A	1	3	.250	55	0	0	0	22	55	58	4	33	45	15.4	4.75	81	.275	.381	0	—	0	-5	-5	1	-0.6
1993	Chi-A	0	0	—	25	0	0	0	1	34^2	51	5	12	19	17.7	5.71	73	.349	.417	0	—	0	-5	-6	-1	0.1
	*Phi-N	3	1	.750	17	0	0	0	0	19^1	23	2	9	10	15.4	6.05	66	.307	.388	0	.000	-0	-4	-4	-0	-0.8
1994	Sea-A	0	2	.000	7	0	0	0	0	7^2	12	3	5	4	20.0	9.39	52	.353	.436	0	—	0	-4	-4	-0	-0.9
Total	9	31	36	.463	448	0	0	0	201	568^2	537	56	238	376	12.6	3.43	118	.252	.334	0	.000	-0	41	39	0	8.4

● J. J. THOBE Thobe, John Joseph b: 11/19/70, Covington, Ky. BR/TR, 6'6", 200 lbs. Deb: 9/18/95 F

YEAR	TM/L	W	L	PCT	G	GS	CG	SH	SV	IP	H	HR	BB	SO	RAT	ERA	ERA+	OAV	OOB	BH	AVG	PB	PR	/A	PD	TPI
1995	Mon-N	0	0	—	4	0	0	0	0	4	6	0	3	0	20.3	9.00	48	.333	.429	0	—	0	-2	-2	-0	0.0

● TOM THOBE Thobe, Thomas Neal b: 9/3/69, Covington, Ky. BL/TL, 6'6", 195 lbs. Deb: 9/12/95 F

YEAR	TM/L	W	L	PCT	G	GS	CG	SH	SV	IP	H	HR	BB	SO	RAT	ERA	ERA+	OAV	OOB	BH	AVG	PB	PR	/A	PD	TPI
1995	Atl-N	0	0	—	3	0	0	0	0	3^1	7	0	0	2	18.9	10.80	39	.412	.412	0	—	0	-2	-2	-0	0.0
1996	Atl-N	0	1	.000	4	0	0	0	0	6	5	1	0	1	7.5	1.50	293	.217	.217	0	.000	-0	2	2	-1	0.2
Total	2	0	1	.000	7	0	0	0	0	9^1	12	1	0	3	11.6	4.82	90	.300	.300	0	.000	-0	-1	-0	-1	0.2

● DICK THOENEN Thoenen, Richard Crispin b: 1/9/44, Mexico, Mo. BR/TR, 6'6", 215 lbs. Deb: 9/16/67

YEAR	TM/L	W	L	PCT	G	GS	CG	SH	SV	IP	H	HR	BB	SO	RAT	ERA	ERA+	OAV	OOB	BH	AVG	PB	PR	/A	PD	TPI
1967	Phi-N	0	0	—	1	0	0	0	0	1	2	0	0	0	18.0	9.00	38	.500	.500	0	—	0	-1	-1	0	0.0

● TOMMY THOMAS Thomas, Alphonse b: 12/23/1899, Baltimore, Md. d: 4/27/88, Dallastown, Pa. BR/TR, 5'10", 175 lbs. Deb: 4/17/26

YEAR	TM/L	W	L	PCT	G	GS	CG	SH	SV	IP	H	HR	BB	SO	RAT	ERA	ERA+	OAV	OOB	BH	AVG	PB	PR	/A	PD	TPI
1926	Chi-A	15	12	.556	44	32	13	2	2	249	225	7	110	127	12.1	3.80	102	**.244**	.325	16	.186	-1	6	2	-3	-0.2
1927	Chi-A	19	16	.543	40	36	24	3	1	**307^2**	271	16	94	107	10.7	2.98	136	.244	.303	14	.147	-3	40	36	-4	2.9
1928	Chi-A	17	16	.515	36	32	24	3	2	283	277	14	76	129	11.4	3.08	131	.259	.310	21	.219	3	30	30	-3	3.3
1929	Chi-A	14	18	.438	36	31	**24**	2	1	259^2	270	17	60	62	11.4	3.19	134	.269	.310	25	.255	2	30	32	-3	3.4
1930	Chi-A	5	13	.278	34	27	7	0	0	169	229	13	44	58	14.6	5.22	89	.323	.364	7	.125	-4	-11	-11	0	-1.3
1931	Chi-A	10	14	.417	43	36	11	2	2	245^1	298	17	69	72	13.6	4.73	90	.292	.340	21	.241	1	-10	-13	-1	-1.0
1932	Chi-A	3	3	.500	12	3	1	0	0	43^2	55	6	15	11	14.6	6.18	70	.307	.364	1	.077	-1	-8	-9	-0	-1.1
	Was-A	8	7	.533	18	14	7	1	0	117	114	5	46	36	12.3	3.54	122	.255	.325	10	.238	1	12	10	-2	1.0
	Yr	11	10	.524	30	17	8	1	0	160^2	169	11	61	47	12.9	4.26	101	.270	.334	11	.200	0	4	1	-2	-0.1
1933	*Was-A	7	7	.500	35	14	2	0	3	135	149	9	49	35	13.3	4.80	87	.273	.336	10	.238	1	-8	-9	-2	-0.9
1934	Was-A	8	9	.471	33	18	7	1	1	133^1	154	9	58	42	14.5	5.47	79	.294	.368	7	.184	-0	-14	-17	-2	-2.0
1935	Was-A	0	0	—	1	0	0	0	0	0^1	3	0	0	0	81.0	54.00	8	.750	.750	0	—	0	-2	-2	0	0.0
	Phi-N	0	1	.000	4	1	0	0	0	12	15	2	5	3	15.0	5.25	86	.313	.377	0	.000	-0	-2	-1	-0	-0.1
1936	StL-A	11	9	.550	36	21	8	1	0	179^2	219	25	72	40	14.8	5.26	102	.297	.362	8	.138	-3	-4	2	-2	-0.3
1937	StL-A	0	1	.000	17	2	0	0	0	30^2	46	2	10	10	16.7	7.04	69	.348	.399	0	.000	-1	-8	-8	0	-0.3
	Bos-A	0	2	.000	9	0	0	0	0	11	16	2	4	4	17.2	4.09	116	.340	.404	1	.250	-0	1	1	-0	0.1
	Yr	0	3	.000	26	2	0	0	0	41^2	62	4	14	14	16.6	6.26	77	.344	.395	1	.125	-1	-8	-7	-0	-0.2
Total	12	117	128	.478	398	267	128	15	12	2176^1	2341	144	712	736	12.7	4.11	104	.275	.333	141	.195	-5	52	43	-22	3.5

● BLAINE THOMAS Thomas, Blaine M. "Baldy" b: 8/1888, Glendora, Cal. d: 8/21/15, Glendora, Cal. BR/TR, 5'10", 165 lbs. Deb: 8/25/11

YEAR	TM/L	W	L	PCT	G	GS	CG	SH	SV	IP	H	HR	BB	SO	RAT	ERA	ERA+	OAV	OOB	BH	AVG	PB	PR	/A	PD	TPI
1911	Bos-A	0	0	—	2	2	0	0	0	4^2	3	0	7	0	21.2	0.00	—	.273	.579	1	.500	0	2	2	0	0.0

● CARL THOMAS Thomas, Carl Leslie b: 5/28/32, Minneapolis, Minn. BR/TR, 6'5", 245 lbs. Deb: 4/19/60

YEAR	TM/L	W	L	PCT	G	GS	CG	SH	SV	IP	H	HR	BB	SO	RAT	ERA	ERA+	OAV	OOB	BH	AVG	PB	PR	/A	PD	TPI
1960	Cle-A	1	0	1.000	4	0	0	0	0	9^2	8	1	10	5	17.7	7.45	50	.229	.413	1	.333	1	-4	-4	0	-0.3

● LEFTY THOMAS Thomas, Clarence Fletcher b: 10/4/03, Glade Spring, Va. d: 3/21/52, Charlottesville, Va. BL/TL, 6', 183 lbs. Deb: 9/26/25

YEAR	TM/L	W	L	PCT	G	GS	CG	SH	SV	IP	H	HR	BB	SO	RAT	ERA	ERA+	OAV	OOB	BH	AVG	PB	PR	/A	PD	TPI
1925	Was-A	0	2	.000	2	2	1	0	0	13	14	0	7	10	14.5	2.08	204	.264	.350	0	.000	-1	3	3	0	0.3
1926	Was-A	0	0	—	6	0	0	0	0	8^2	8	0	10	3	18.7	5.19	74	.267	.450	0	.000	0	-1	-1	-1	0.0
Total	2	0	2	.000	8	2	1	0	0	21^2	22	0	17	13	16.2	3.32	123	.265	.390	0	.000	-1	2	2	-1	0.3

● CLAUDE THOMAS Thomas, Claude Alfred "Lefty" b: 5/15/1890, Stanberry, Mo. d: 3/6/46, Sulphur, Okla. BL/TL, 6'1", 180 lbs. Deb: 9/14/16

YEAR	TM/L	W	L	PCT	G	GS	CG	SH	SV	IP	H	HR	BB	SO	RAT	ERA	ERA+	OAV	OOB	BH	AVG	PB	PR	/A	PD	TPI
1916	Was-A	1	2	.333	7	4	1	1	0	28^1	27	1	12	7	13.0	4.13	68	.265	.353	1	.100	-1	-4	-4	-0	-0.5

● FAY THOMAS Thomas, Fay Wesley "Scow" b: 10/10/04, Holyrood, Kan. d: 8/16/90, Chatsworth, Cal. BR/TR, 6'2", 195 lbs. Deb: 6/27/27

YEAR	TM/L	W	L	PCT	G	GS	CG	SH	SV	IP	H	HR	BB	SO	RAT	ERA	ERA+	OAV	OOB	BH	AVG	PB	PR	/A	PD	TPI
1927	NY-N	0	0	—	9	0	0	0	0	16^1	19	3	4	11	13.2	3.31	117	.302	.353	0	.000	-0	1	1	-0	-0.1
1931	Cle-A	2	4	.333	16	2	1	0	0	48^2	63	2	32	25	17.8	5.18	89	.323	.421	2	.154	-1	-4	-3	-1	-0.4
1932	Bro-N	0	1	.000	7	2	0	0	0	17	22	0	8	9	15.9	7.41	51	.306	.375	0	.000	-0	-7	-7	0	-0.4
1935	StL-A	7	15	.318	49	19	4	0	1	147	165	11	89	67	15.7	4.78	100	.289	.388	4	.105	-3	-5	0	2	0.0
Total	4	9	20	.310	81	23	5	0	1	229	269	16	133	112	16.0	4.95	93	.299	.392	6	.107	-4	-15	-9	1	-0.9

● FROSTY THOMAS Thomas, Forrest b: 5/23/1881, Faucett, Mo. d: 3/18/70, St.Joseph, Mo. BR/TR, 6', 185 lbs. Deb: 5/1/05

YEAR	TM/L	W	L	PCT	G	GS	CG	SH	SV	IP	H	HR	BB	SO	RAT	ERA	ERA+	OAV	OOB	BH	AVG	PB	PR	/A	PD	TPI
1905	Det-A	0	1	.000	2	1	0	0	0	6	10	0	3	5	21.0	7.50	36	.370	.452	0	.000	0	-3	-3	0	-0.4

● LARRY THOMAS Thomas, Larry Wayne b: 10/25/69, Miami, Fla. BR/TL, 6'1", 190 lbs. Deb: 8/11/95

YEAR	TM/L	W	L	PCT	G	GS	CG	SH	SV	IP	H	HR	BB	SO	RAT	ERA	ERA+	OAV	OOB	BH	AVG	PB	PR	/A	PD	TPI
1995	Chi-A	0	0	—	17	0	0	0	0	13^2	8	1	6	12	9.2	1.32	338	.167	.259	0	—	0	5	5	-0	0.3
1996	Chi-A	2	3	.400	57	0	0	0	0	30^2	32	1	14	20	14.4	3.23	147	.281	.374	0	—	0	6	5	0	1.1
1997	Chi-A	0	0	—	5	0	0	0	0	3^1	3	1	2	0	13.5	8.10	54	.250	.357	0	—	0	-1	-1	0	0.3
Total	3	2	3	.400	79	0	0	0	0	47^2	43	3	22	32	12.8	3.02	153	.247	.342	0	—	0	10	9	-0	1.7

● BUD THOMAS Thomas, Luther Baxter b: 9/9/10, Faber, Va. BR/TR, 6', 180 lbs. Deb: 9/13/32

YEAR	TM/L	W	L	PCT	G	GS	CG	SH	SV	IP	H	HR	BB	SO	RAT	ERA	ERA+	OAV	OOB	BH	AVG	PB	PR	/A	PD	TPI
1932	Was-A	0	0	—	2	0	0	0	0	3	1	0	2	1	9.0	0.00	—	.100	.250	0	—	0	1	1	-0	0.0
1933	Was-A	0	0	—	2	0	0	0	0	4	11	1	2	1	31.5	15.75	27	.550	.609	0	.000	-0	-5	-5	0	0.0
1937	Phi-A	8	15	.348	35	26	6	1	0	169^2	208	15	52	54	13.8	4.99	95	.295	.344	6	.128	-1	-7	-5	-3	-0.9
1938	Phi-A	9	14	.391	42	29	7	1	0	212^1	259	23	62	48	13.7	4.92	98	.299	.347	9	.130	-3	-3	-2	-1	-0.5
1939	Phi-A	0	1	.000	2	2	0	0	0	4	8	2	1	0	20.3	15.75	30	.421	.450	0	.000	-0	-5	-5	0	-0.9
	Was-A	0	0	—	4	0	0	0	0	9	11	0	2	0	13.0	6.00	72	.306	.342	0	.000	-0	-1	-2	0	0.0
	Det-A	7	0	1.000	27	0	0	0	1	47^1	45	7	20	14	12.4	4.18	117	.254	.330	1	.111	-1	2	4	0	0.4
	Yr	7	1	.875	33	2	0	0	1	60^1	64	9	23	14	13.0	5.22	92	.276	.341	1	.071	-2	-4	-3	0	-0.5
1940	Det-A	0	1	.000	3	0	0	0	0	4	8	1	3	0	24.8	9.00	53	.421	.500	0	—	0	-2	-2	1	-0.3
1941	Det-A	1	3	.250	26	1	0	0	2	72^2	74	4	22	17	11.9	4.21	108	.260	.313	2	.105	-1	-1	3	2	0.2
Total	7	25	34	.424	143	58	13	2	3	526	625	53	166	135	13.6	4.96	96	.292	.345	18	.120	-7	-20	-13	-1	-2.0

● MIKE THOMAS Thomas, Michael Steven b: 9/2/69, Sacramento, Cal. BL/TL, 6'2", 205 lbs. Deb: 7/12/95

YEAR	TM/L	W	L	PCT	G	GS	CG	SH	SV	IP	H	HR	BB	SO	RAT	ERA	ERA+	OAV	OOB	BH	AVG	PB	PR	/A	PD	TPI
1995	Mil-A	0	0	—	1	0	0	0	0	1^1	2	0	1	0	20.3	0.00	—	.333	.429	0	—	0	1	1	0	-0.4

● MYLES THOMAS Thomas, Myles Lewis b: 10/22/1897, State College, Pa. d: 12/12/63, Toledo, Ohio BR/TR, 5'9.5", 170 lbs. Deb: 4/18/26

YEAR	TM/L	W	L	PCT	G	GS	CG	SH	SV	IP	H	HR	BB	SO	RAT	ERA	ERA+	OAV	OOB	BH	AVG	PB	PR	/A	PD	TPI
1926	*NY-A	6	6	.500	33	13	3	0	0	140^1	140	6	65	38	13.3	4.23	91	.271	.356	5	.116	-3	-3	-6	1	-0.7
1927	NY-A	7	4	.636	21	9	1	0	0	88^2	111	4	43	25	15.7	4.87	79	.322	.398	9	.333	2	-7	-10	0	-0.9
1928	NY-A	1	0	1.000	12	1	0	0	0	31^2	33	3	9	10	11.9	3.41	110	.277	.328	4	.400	1	2	1	-0	0.1
1929	NY-A	0	2	.000	5	1	0	0	0	15	27	1	9	3	21.6	10.80	36	.409	.480	1	.143	-1	-11	-12	1	-1.2
	Was-A	7	8	.467	22	14	7	0	2	125^1	139	3	48	33	13.4	3.52	121	.288	.352	14	.292	2	10	10	0	1.3
	Yr	7	10	.412	27	15	7	0	2	140^1	166	4	57	36	14.3	4.30	98	.302	.368	15	.273	1	-1	-2	1	0.1
1930	Was-A	2	2	.500	12	2	0	0	0	33^2	49	3	15	12	17.1	8.29	55	.358	.421	2	.182	-1	-14	-14	-1	-1.4
Total	5	23	22	.511	105	40	11	0	2	434^2	499	20	189	121	14.3	4.64	87	.299	.372	35	.240	0	-23	-30	1	-2.8

YEAR	TM/L	W	L	PCT	G	GS	CG	SH	SV	IP	H	HR	BB	SO	RAT	ERA	ERA+	OAV	OOB	BH	AVG	PB	PR	/A	PD	TPI
● **ROY THOMAS**	Thomas, Roy Allen b: 3/24/1874, Norristown, Pa. d: 11/20/59, Norristown, Pa. BL/TL, 5'11", 150 lbs. Deb: 4/14/1899 FC♦																									
1900	Phi-N	0	0	—	1	0	0	0	0	2^2	4	0	0	0	13.5	3.38	107	.333	.333	168	.316	0	0	0	-0	0.0
● **ROY THOMAS**	Thomas, Roy Justin b: 6/22/53, Quantico, Va. BR/TR, 6'6", 200 lbs. Deb: 9/21/77																									
1977	Hou-N	0	0	—	4	0	0	0	0	6^1	5	0	3	4	11.4	2.84	125	.208	.296	0	—	0	1	1	0	0.0
1978	StL-N	1	1	.500	16	1	0	0	3	28^1	21	0	16	16	11.8	3.81	92	.216	.327	1	.250	0	-1	-1	1	0.0
1979	StL-N	3	4	.429	26	6	0	0	1	77	66	9	24	44	10.5	2.92	129	.237	.298	1	.059	-1	7	7	1	0.6
1980	StL-N	2	3	.400	24	5	0	0	0	55	59	3	25	22	14.2	4.75	78	.274	.358	2	.154	-0	-7	-6	1	-0.5
1983	Sea-A	3	1	.750	43	0	0	0	1	88^2	95	3	32	77	13.1	3.45	123	.275	.340	0	—	0	6	8	-0	0.1
1984	Sea-A	3	2	.600	21	1	0	0	1	49^2	52	8	37	42	16.9	5.26	76	.280	.410	0	—	0	-7	-7	0	-0.6
1985	Sea-A	7	0	1.000	40	0	0	0	1	93^2	66	8	48	70	11.1	3.36	125	.202	.309	0	—	0	8	9	-1	0.5
1987	Sea-A	1	0	1.000	8	0	0	0	0	20^2	23	2	11	14	15.2	5.23	90	.299	.393	0	—	0	-2	-1	-1	-0.2
Total	8	20	11	.645	182	13	0	0	7	419^1	387	33	196	289	12.8	3.82	105	.250	.339	4	.118	-1	5	9	1	-0.1
● **STAN THOMAS**	Thomas, Stanley Brown b: 7/11/49, Rumford, Me. BR/TR, 6'2", 185 lbs. Deb: 7/5/74																									
1974	Tex-A	0	0	—	12	0	0	0	0	13^2	22	1	6	8	18.4	6.59	54	.379	.438	0	—	0	-5	-5	0	0.0
1975	Tex-A	4	4	.500	46	1	0	0	3	81^1	72	2	34	46	12.1	3.10	121	.239	.322	0	—	0	6	6	0	0.7
1976	Cle-A	4	4	.500	37	7	2	0	6	105^2	88	5	41	54	11.3	2.30	152	.229	.310	0	—	0	14	14	3	1.6
1977	Sea-A	2	6	.250	13	9	1	0	0	58^1	74	8	25	14	15.7	6.02	68	.310	.382	0	—	0	-13	-12	-0	-1.4
	NY-A	1	0	1.000	3	0	0	0	0	6^1	7	0	4	1	15.6	7.11	55	.280	.379	0	—	0	-2	-2	-0	-0.3
	Yr	3	6	.333	16	9	1	0	0	64^2	81	8	29	15	15.3	6.12	67	.300	.368	0	—	0	-15	-15	-1	-1.7
Total	4	11	14	.440	111	17	3	0	9	265^1	263	16	110	123	13.0	3.70	101	.261	.340	0	—	0	1	1	3	0.6
● **TOM THOMAS**	Thomas, Thomas R. "Savage Tom" b: 12/27/1873, Shawnee, Ohio d: 9/23/42, Shawnee, Ohio BR/TR, 6'4", 195 lbs. Deb: 9/20/1894																									
1894	Cle-N	0	0	—	1	0	0	0	1	0^1	0	0	2	0	54.0	27.00	20	.000	.667	0	—	0	-1	-1	0	-0.3
1899	StL-N	1	1	.500	4	2	2	0	0	25	22	1	4	8	9.4	2.52	158	.237	.268	3	.250	0	4	4	0	0.3
1900	StL-N	2	2	.500	5	1	1	0	0	26^1	38	2	4	7	14.7	3.76	97	.336	.364	1	.091	-1	-0	-0	-1	-0.2
Total	3	3	3	.500	10	3	3	0	1	51^2	60	3	10	15	12.4	3.31	115	.290	.326	4	.174	-1	3	3	-1	-0.2
● **ERSKINE THOMASON**	Thomason, Melvin Erskine b: 8/13/48, Laurens, S.C. BR/TR, 6'1", 190 lbs. Deb: 9/18/74																									
1974	Phi-N	0	0	—	1	0	0	0	0	1	0	0	0	1	0.0	0.00	—	.000	.000	0	—	0	0	0	0	0.0
● **ART THOMPSON**	Thompson, Arthur J. Deb: 6/17/1884																									
1884	Was-U	0	1	.000	1	1	1	0	0	8	10	0	3	8	14.6	6.75	36	.286	.342	0	.000	-1	-4	-4	0	-0.4
● **FORREST THOMPSON**	Thompson, David Forrest b: 3/3/18, Mooresville, N.C. d: 2/26/79, Charlotte, N.C. BL/TL, 5'11", 195 lbs. Deb: 4/26/48																									
1948	Was-A	6	10	.375	46	7	0	0	4	131^1	134	9	54	40	13.0	3.84	113	.262	.334	10	.286	2	7	7	-0	1.1
1949	Was-A	1	3	.250	9	1	1	0	0	16^1	22	1	9	8	17.6	4.41	97	.328	.416	3	.600	2	-0	-0	0	0.1
Total	2	7	13	.350	55	8	1	0	4	147^2	156	10	63	48	13.5	3.90	111	.270	.344	13	.325	4	6	7	-0	1.2
● **JUNIOR THOMPSON**	Thompson, Eugene Earl b: 6/7/17, Latham, Ill. BR/TR, 6'1", 185 lbs. Deb: 4/26/39																									
1939	*Cin-N	13	5	.722	42	11	5	3	2	152^1	130	6	55	87	11.1	2.54	151	.236	.309	11	.229	0	23	22	-1	2.3
1940	*Cin-N	16	9	.640	33	31	17	3	0	225^1	197	10	96	103	11.8	3.32	114	.233	.313	18	.228	3	13	12	-1	1.4
1941	Cin-N	6	6	.500	27	15	4	0	1	109	117	6	57	46	14.6	4.87	74	.272	.361	7	.233	1	-15	-15	2	-1.3
1942	Cin-N	4	7	.364	29	10	1	0	0	101^2	86	5	53	35	12.5	3.36	98	.226	.324	8	.267	2	-1	-1	4	0.5
1946	NY-N	4	6	.400	39	1	0	0	4	62^2	36	5	40	31	10.9	1.29	266	.190	.332	1	.143	0	15	15	2	2.8
1947	NY-N	4	2	.667	15	0	0	0	0	35^2	36	3	27	13	16.1	4.29	95	.279	.408	0	.000	-1	-1	-1	1	-0.1
Total	6	47	35	.573	185	68	27	6	7	686^2	602	35	328	315	12.3	3.26	113	.239	.329	45	.225	6	35	32	6	5.6
● **FULLER THOMPSON**	Thompson, Fuller Weidner b: 5/1/1889, Los Angeles, Cal. d: 2/19/72, Los Angeles, Cal. BR/TR, 5'11.5", 164 lbs. Deb: 8/19/11																									
1911	Bos-N	0	0	—	3	0	0	0	0	4^2	5	0	2	0	13.5	3.86	99	.294	.368	0	—	0	-0	-0	0	0.0
● **HARRY THOMPSON**	Thompson, Harold b: 9/9/1889, Nanticoke, Pa. d: 2/14/51, Reno, Nev. BL/TL, 5'8", 150 lbs. Deb: 4/24/19																									
1919	Was-A	0	3	.000	12	2	0	0	1	43^1	48	0	8	10	12.0	3.53	91	.293	.333	8	.250	0	-1	-2	0	0.0
	Phi-A	0	1	.000	3	0	0	0	0	12	16	4	3	1	14.3	6.75	51	.327	.365	0	.000	-1	-5	-4	0	-0.4
	Yr	0	4	.000	15	2	0	0	1	55^1	64	4	11	11	12.2	4.23	77	.298	.332	8	.211	0	-6	-6	1	-0.4
● **LEE THOMPSON**	Thompson, John Dudley "Lefty" b: 2/26/1898, Smithfield, Utah d: 2/17/63, Santa Barbara, Cal BL/TL, 6'1", 185 lbs. Deb: 9/4/21																									
1921	Chi-A	0	3	.000	4	4	0	0	0	20^2	32	0	6	4	16.5	8.27	51	.333	.373	2	.286	0	-9	-9	-1	-1.0
● **GUS THOMPSON**	Thompson, John Gustav b: 6/22/1877, Humboldt, Iowa d: 3/28/58, Kalispell, Mont. 6'2", 185 lbs. Deb: 8/31/03																									
1903	*Pit-N	2	2	.500	5	4	3	0	0	43	52	1	16	22	14.4	3.56	91	.295	.358	4	.250	0	-1	-2	-1	-0.2
1906	StL-N	2	11	.154	17	12	8	0	0	103	111	2	25	36	12.3	4.28	61	.285	.336	6	.176	-1	-19	-19	1	-2.2
Total	2	4	13	.235	22	16	11	0	0	146	163	3	41	58	12.9	4.07	69	.288	.343	10	.200	-0	-20	-20	0	-2.4
● **JOCKO THOMPSON**	Thompson, John Samuel b: 1/17/17, Beverly, Mass. d: 2/3/88, Olney, Md. BL/TL, 6', 185 lbs. Deb: 9/21/48																									
1948	Phi-N	1	0	1.000	2	2	1	0	0	13	10	0	9	7	13.2	2.77	142	.233	.365	0	.000	0	2	2	-0	0.1
1949	Phi-N	1	3	.250	8	5	1	0	0	31^1	38	6	11	12	14.1	6.89	57	.314	.371	2	.182	-0	-10	-10	-0	-1.1
1950	Phi-N	0	0	—	2	0	0	0	0	4	1	0	4	2	11.3	0.00	—	.077	.294	0	—	0	2	2	0	0.0
1951	Phi-N	4	8	.333	29	14	3	2	1	119^1	102	12	59	60	12.3	3.85	100	.231	.325	4	.103	-1	2	0	-1	-0.2
Total	4	6	11	.353	41	21	5	2	1	167^2	151	18	83	81	12.7	4.24	91	.244	.336	6	.113	-1	-5	-7	-1	-1.2
● **JUSTIN THOMPSON**	Thompson, Justin Willard b: 3/8/73, San Antonio, Tex. BL/TL, 6'4", 215 lbs. Deb: 5/27/96																									
1996	Det-A	1	6	.143	11	11	0	0	0	59	62	7	31	44	14.5	4.58	110	.267	.358	0	—	0	3	3	1	0.4
1997	Det-A★	15	11	.577	32	32	4	0	0	223^1	188	20	66	151	10.3	3.02	152	.233	.292	0	.000	-0	38	39	0	4.2
1998	Det-A	11	15	.423	34	34	5	0	0	222	227	20	79	149	12.5	4.05	116	.267	.331	1	.143	-0	15	16	0	1.7
Total	3	27	32	.458	77	77	9	0	0	504^1	477	47	176	344	11.8	3.66	128	.253	.318	1	.111	-0	56	58	2	6.3
● **MARK THOMPSON**	Thompson, Mark Radford b: 4/7/71, Russellville, Ky. BR/TR, 6'2", 205 lbs. Deb: 7/26/94																									
1994	Col-N	1	1	.500	2	2	0	0	0	9	16	2	8	5	25.0	9.00	55	.400	.510	0	.000	-0	-5	-4	-0	-0.7
1995	*Col-N	2	3	.400	21	5	0	0	0	51	73	7	22	30	16.9	6.53	82	.349	.414	5	.385	1	-13	-6	1	-0.4
1996	Col-N	9	11	.450	34	28	3	1	0	169^2	189	25	74	99	14.6	5.30	98	.285	.368	8	.138	-2	-21	-2	-1	-0.5
1997	Col-N	3	3	.500	6	6	0	0	0	29^2	40	8	13	9	17.3	7.89	66	.323	.404	2	.182	1	-12	-9	0	-1.4
1998	Col-N	1	2	.333	6	6	0	0	0	23^1	36	8	12	14	20.4	7.71	66	.379	.473	1	.143	-0	-9	-7	-0	-0.8
Total	5	16	20	.444	69	47	3	1	0	282^2	354	50	129	157	16.1	6.11	85	.313	.395	16	.172	-2	-60	-28	-1	-3.8
● **MIKE THOMPSON**	Thompson, Michael Wayne b: 9/6/49, Denver, Colo. BR/TR, 6'3", 190 lbs. Deb: 5/19/71																									
1971	Was-A	1	6	.143	16	12	0	0	0	66^2	53	3	54	41	14.9	4.86	68	.222	.372	2	.118	0	-10	-12	0	-1.1
1973	StL-N	0	0	—	2	2	0	0	0	4	1	0	5	3	13.5	0.00	—	.077	.333	0	.000	-0	2	2	-0	0.0
1974	StL-N	0	3	.000	19	4	0	0	0	38^1	37	1	35	25	17.4	5.63	63	.274	.430	0	.000	-1	-9	-9	0	-0.7
	Atl-N	0	0	—	1	1	0	0	0	4	7	0	2	2	20.3	4.50	84	.412	.474	1	1.000	0	-0	-0	0	0.1
	Yr	0	3	.000	20	5	0	0	0	42^1	44	1	37	27	17.2	5.53	65	.286	.424	1	.111	-1	-9	-9	0	-0.6
1975	Atl-N	0	6	.000	16	10	0	0	0	51^2	60	2	32	42	16.0	4.70	80	.305	.402	1	.071	-1	-6	-5	1	-0.6
Total	4	1	15	.063	54	29	0	0	0	164^2	158	6	128	113	15.9	4.86	73	.263	.396	4	.098	-1	-24	-24	1	-2.3
● **RICH THOMPSON**	Thompson, Richard Neil b: 11/1/58, New York, N.Y. BR/TR, 6'3", 225 lbs. Deb: 4/28/85																									
1985	Cle-A	3	8	.273	57	0	0	0	5	80	95	8	48	30	16.8	6.30	66	.303	.405	0	—	0	-19	-19	-2	-2.6
1989	Mon-N	0	2	.000	19	1	0	0	0	33	27	2	11	15	10.9	2.18	162	.241	.320	0	.000	0	5	5	-0	0.3
1990	Mon-N	0	0	—	1	0	0	0	0	1	1	0	0	0	9.0	0.00	—	.250	.250	0	—	0	0	0	0	0.0
Total	3	3	10	.231	77	1	0	0	5	114	123	10	59	45	15.0	5.05	78	.286	.382	0	.000	0	-14	-14	-2	-2.3
● **TOMMY THOMPSON**	Thompson, Thomas Carl b: 11/7/1889, Spring City, Tenn. d: 1/16/63, LaJolla, Cal. BR/TR, 5'9.5", 170 lbs. Deb: 6/5/12 F																									
1912	NY-A	0	2	.000	7	2	1	0	0	32^2	43	0	13	15	16.3	6.06	59	.341	.415	3	.300	1	-10	-9	-1	-0.5

● WILL THOMPSON Thompson, Will McLain b: 8/30/1870, Pittsburgh, Pa. d: 6/9/62, Pittsburgh, Pa. BR/TR, 5′11.5″, 190 lbs. Deb: 7/9/1892

YEAR	TM/L	W	L	PCT	G	GS	CG	SH	SV	IP	H	HR	BB	SO	RAT	ERA	ERA+	OAV	OOB	BH	AVG	PB	PR	/A	PD	TPI
1892	Pit-N	0	1	.000	1	1	0	0	0	3	3	0	5	0	27.0	3.00	110	.250	.500	0	—	0	0	0	0	0.1

● JOHN THOMSON Thomson, John Carl b: 10/1/73, Vicksburg, Miss. BR/TR, 6′3″, 175 lbs. Deb: 5/11/97

YEAR	TM/L	W	L	PCT	G	GS	CG	SH	SV	IP	H	HR	BB	SO	RAT	ERA	ERA+	OAV	OOB	BH	AVG	PB	PR	/A	PD	TPI
1997	Col-N	7	9	.438	27	27	2	1	0	166^1	193	15	51	106	13.5	4.71	110	.296	.352	10	.213	-0	-9	9	-0	0.7
1998	Col-N	8	11	.421	26	26	2	0	0	161	174	21	49	106	12.6	4.81	105	.282	.337	6	.120	-3	-10	5	-1	0.0
Total	2	15	20	.429	53	53	4	1	0	327^1	367	36	100	212	13.0	4.76	108	.289	.345	16	.165	-3	-20	13	-1	0.7

● HANK THORMAHLEN Thormahlen, Herbert Ehler "Lefty" b: 7/5/1896, Jersey City, N.J. d: 2/6/55, Los Angeles, Cal. BL/TL, 6′, 180 lbs. Deb: 9/29/17

YEAR	TM/L	W	L	PCT	G	GS	CG	SH	SV	IP	H	HR	BB	SO	RAT	ERA	ERA+	OAV	OOB	BH	AVG	PB	PR	/A	PD	TPI
1917	NY-A	0	1	.000	1	1	0	0	0	8	9	0	4	5	15.8	2.25	119	.281	.378	0	.000	-0	0	0	-0	0.0
1918	NY-A	7	3	.700	16	12	5	2	0	112^2	85	1	52	22	11.4	2.48	114	.217	.318	3	.077	-3	4	4	0	0.0
1919	NY-A	12	8	.600	30	25	13	2	1	188^2	155	10	61	62	10.5	2.62	122	.228	.295	11	.186	-0	13	12	-1	1.0
1920	NY-A	9	6	.600	29	15	6	0	1	143^1	178	5	43	35	14.0	4.14	92	.312	.362	10	.222	1	-6	-5	1	-0.3
1921	Bos-A	1	7	.125	23	9	3	0	0	96^1	101	3	34	17	13.2	4.48	94	.277	.349	4	.174	-1	-2	-3	-0	-0.2
1925	Bro-N	0	3	.000	5	2	0	0	0	16	22	0	9	7	18.6	3.94	106	.333	.429	1	.200	0	1	0	0	0.2
Total	6	29	28	.509	104	64	27	4	2	565	550	19	203	148	12.3	3.33	105	.261	.332	29	.168	-3	10	9	0	0.7

● PAUL THORMODSGARD Thormodsgard, Paul Gayton b: 11/10/53, San Francisco, Cal. BR/TR, 6′2″, 190 lbs. Deb: 4/10/77

YEAR	TM/L	W	L	PCT	G	GS	CG	SH	SV	IP	H	HR	BB	SO	RAT	ERA	ERA+	OAV	OOB	BH	AVG	PB	PR	/A	PD	TPI
1977	Min-A	11	15	.423	37	37	8	1	0	218	236	25	65	94	12.6	4.62	86	.280	.333	0	—	0	-14	-16	-1	-1.6
1978	Min-A	1	6	.143	12	12	1	0	0	66	81	7	17	23	13.5	5.05	76	.308	.352	0	—	0	-9	-9	-1	-1.0
1979	Min-A	0	0	—	1	0	0	0	0	1	3	1	0	1	27.0	9.00	49	.500	.500	0	—	0	-1	-1	0	0.0
Total	3	12	21	.364	50	49	9	1	0	285	320	33	82	118	12.8	4.74	83	.288	.339	0	—	0	-24	-25	-2	-2.6

● JOHN THORNTON Thornton, John b: 1870, Washington, D.C. 5′10.5″, 175 lbs. Deb: 8/14/1889 ♦

YEAR	TM/L	W	L	PCT	G	GS	CG	SH	SV	IP	H	HR	BB	SO	RAT	ERA	ERA+	OAV	OOB	BH	AVG	PB	PR	/A	PD	TPI
1889	Was-N	0	1	.000	1	1	1	0	0	9	8	0	7	3	15.0	5.00	79	.229	.357	0	.000	-1	-1	-1	-0	-0.2
1891	Phi-N	15	16	.484	37	32	23	1	2	269	268	3	115	52	13.1	3.68	93	.250	.328	17	.138	-7	-10	-8	2	-1.3
1892	Phi-N	0	2	.000	3	2	1	0	0	12	16	1	17	2	24.8	12.75	25	.308	.478	5	.385	1	-13	-13	0	-1.3
Total	3	15	19	.441	41	35	25	1	2	290	292	4	139	57	13.7	4.10	83	.252	.337	22	.154	-7	-24	-22	2	-2.8

● WALTER THORNTON Thornton, Walter Miller b: 2/18/1875, Lewiston, Maine d: 7/14/60, Los Angeles, Cal. BL/TL, 6′1″, 180 lbs. Deb: 7/1/1895 ♦

YEAR	TM/L	W	L	PCT	G	GS	CG	SH	SV	IP	H	HR	BB	SO	RAT	ERA	ERA+	OAV	OOB	BH	AVG	PB	PR	/A	PD	TPI
1895	Chi-N	2	0	1.000	7	2	2	0	1	40	58	3	31	13	21.1	6.07	84	.333	.448	7	.318	2	-6	-4	-1	-0.1
1896	Chi-N	2	1	.667	5	5	2	0	0	23^2	30	1	13	10	16.4	5.70	80	.306	.387	8	.364	2	-4	-3	-1	-0.2
1897	Chi-N	6	7	.462	16	16	15	0	0	130^1	164	4	51	55	15.3	4.70	95	.305	.371	85	.321	4	-6	-3	0	0.1
1898	Chi-N	13	10	.565	28	25	21	2	0	215^1	226	4	56	56	12.5	3.34	107	.268	.327	62	.295	6	6	6	-1	0.9
Total	4	23	18	.561	56	48	40	2	1	409^1	478	12	151	134	14.5	4.18	97	.289	.359	162	.312	13	-8	-6	-2	0.7

● BOB THORPE Thorpe, Robert Joseph b: 1/12/35, San Diego, Cal. d: 3/17/60, San Diego, Cal. BR/TR, 6′1″, 170 lbs. Deb: 4/17/55

YEAR	TM/L	W	L	PCT	G	GS	CG	SH	SV	IP	H	HR	BB	SO	RAT	ERA	ERA+	OAV	OOB	BH	AVG	PB	PR	/A	PD	TPI
1955	Chi-N	0	0	—	2	0	0	0	0	3	4	0	0	0	12.0	3.00	136	.333	.333	0	—	0	0	0	0	0.0

● GEORGE THROOP Throop, George Lynford b: 11/24/50, Pasadena, Cal. BR/TR, 6′7″, 205 lbs. Deb: 9/7/75

YEAR	TM/L	W	L	PCT	G	GS	CG	SH	SV	IP	H	HR	BB	SO	RAT	ERA	ERA+	OAV	OOB	BH	AVG	PB	PR	/A	PD	TPI
1975	KC-A	0	0	—	7	0	0	0	2	9	8	1	2	8	10.0	4.00	96	.250	.294	0	—	0	-0	-0	0	-0.1
1977	KC-A	0	0	—	4	0	0	0	1	5^1	1	1	4	1	8.4	3.38	120	.059	.238	0	—	0	0	0	0	0.0
1978	KC-A	1	0	1.000	1	0	0	0	0	3	2	0	3	2	15.0	0.00	—	.222	.417	0	—	0	1	1	0	0.3
1979	KC-A	0	0	—	4	0	0	0	0	2^2	7	0	5	1	40.5	13.50	32	.467	.600	0	—	0	-3	-3	-0	-0.1
	Hou-N	1	0	1.000	14	0	0	0	0	22^1	23	4	11	15	14.1	3.22	109	.271	.361	0	.000	-0	1	1	-0	0.0
Total	4	2	0	1.000	30	0	0	0	3	42^1	41	6	25	27	14.2	3.83	97	.259	.364	0	.000	-0	-0	-1	0	0.1

● LOU THUMAN Thuman, Louis Charles Frank b: 12/13/16, Baltimore, Md. BR/TR, 6′2″, 185 lbs. Deb: 9/8/39

YEAR	TM/L	W	L	PCT	G	GS	CG	SH	SV	IP	H	HR	BB	SO	RAT	ERA	ERA+	OAV	OOB	BH	AVG	PB	PR	/A	PD	TPI
1939	Was-A	0	0	—	3	0	0	0	0	4	5	0	2	1	15.8	9.00	48	.278	.350	0	—	0	-2	-2	0	0.0
1940	Was-A	0	1	.000	2	0	0	0	0	5	10	0	7	0	30.6	14.40	29	.400	.531	0	.000	-0	-6	-6	0	-0.8
Total	2	0	1	.000	5	0	0	0	0	9	15	0	9	1	24.0	12.00	35	.349	.462	0	.000	-0	-8	-8	0	-0.8

● MIKE THURMAN Thurman, Michael Richard b: 7/22/73, Corvallis, Ore. BR/TR, 6′4″, 190 lbs. Deb: 9/2/97

YEAR	TM/L	W	L	PCT	G	GS	CG	SH	SV	IP	H	HR	BB	SO	RAT	ERA	ERA+	OAV	OOB	BH	AVG	PB	PR	/A	PD	TPI
1997	Mon-N	1	0	1.000	5	2	0	0	0	11^2	8	3	4	8	10.0	5.40	78	.186	.271	1	.500	0	-2	-2	0	0.0
1998	Mon-N	4	5	.444	14	13	0	0	0	67	60	7	26	32	12.0	4.70	87	.238	.317	0	.000	-2	-4	-4	-0	-0.7
Total	2	5	5	.500	19	15	0	0	0	78^2	68	10	30	40	11.7	4.81	86	.231	.310	1	.040	-2	-5	-6	0	-0.7

● MARK THURMOND Thurmond, Mark Anthony b: 9/12/56, Houston, Tex. BL/TL, 6′, 193 lbs. Deb: 5/14/83

YEAR	TM/L	W	L	PCT	G	GS	CG	SH	SV	IP	H	HR	BB	SO	RAT	ERA	ERA+	OAV	OOB	BH	AVG	PB	PR	/A	PD	TPI
1983	SD-N	7	3	.700	21	18	2	0	0	115^1	104	7	33	49	10.8	2.65	131	.248	.306	2	.054	-2	12	11	1	0.8
1984	*SD-N	14	8	.636	32	29	1	1	0	178^2	174	12	55	57	11.5	2.97	120	.256	.311	11	.190	1	12	12	2	1.8
1985	SD-N	7	11	.389	36	23	1	1	2	138^1	154	9	44	57	13.1	3.97	89	.291	.349	3	.088	-2	-6	-7	1	-0.9
1986	SD-N	3	7	.300	17	15	2	1	0	70^2	96	7	27	32	15.7	6.50	56	.325	.382	6	.250	1	-22	-22	0	-2.6
	Det-A	4	1	.800	25	4	0	0	3	51^2	44	7	17	17	10.6	1.92	215	.234	.298	0	—	0	13	13	-1	1.2
1987	*Det-A	0	1	.000	48	0	0	0	5	61^2	83	5	24	21	15.6	4.23	100	.331	.389	0	—	0	2	-0	-0	0.0
1988	Bal-A	1	8	.111	43	6	0	0	3	74^2	80	10	27	29	13.1	4.58	85	.277	.343	0	—	0	-5	-6	-1	-0.7
1989	Bal-A	2	4	.333	49	2	0	0	4	90	102	6	17	34	12.0	3.90	97	.288	.323	0	—	0	-0	-1	-1	-0.1
1990	SF-N	2	3	.400	43	0	0	0	4	56^2	53	6	18	24	11.3	3.34	109	.257	.317	0	.000	-1	3	2	1	0.3
Total	8	40	46	.465	314	97	6	3	21	837^2	890	69	262	320	12.5	3.69	100	.277	.333	22	.139	-1	9	1	2	-0.2

● SLOPPY THURSTON Thurston, Hollis John b: 6/2/1899, Fremont, Neb. d: 9/14/73, Los Angeles, Cal. BR/TR, 5′11″, 165 lbs. Deb: 4/19/23

YEAR	TM/L	W	L	PCT	G	GS	CG	SH	SV	IP	H	HR	BB	SO	RAT	ERA	ERA+	OAV	OOB	BH	AVG	PB	PR	/A	PD	TPI
1923	StL-A	0	0	—	2	1	0	0	0	4	8	0	2	0	22.5	6.75	62	.421	.476	0	—	0	-1	-1	-0	0.0
	Chi-A	7	8	.467	44	12	8	0	4	191^2	223	11	36	55	12.2	3.05	130	.308	.341	25	.316	6	20	19	-0	2.0
	Yr	7	8	.467	46	13	8	0	4	195^2	231	11	38	55	12.4	3.13	127	.310	.345	25	.316	6	19	18	-1	2.0
1924	Chi-A	20	14	.588	38	36	**28**	1	1	291	330	17	60	37	12.2	3.80	108	.290	.329	31	.254	4	14	10	1	1.6
1925	Chi-A	10	14	.417	36	25	9	0	1	183	250	14	47	35	14.9	5.95	70	.335	.378	24	.286	7	-32	-37	2	-3.1
1926	Chi-A	6	8	.429	31	13	6	1	3	134^1	164	10	36	35	13.5	5.02	77	.311	.356	19	.311	6	-15	-17	-1	-1.3
1927	Was-A	13	13	.500	29	28	13	2	0	205^1	254	16	60	38	13.9	4.47	91	.308	.356	29	.315	9	-8	-9	-1	-0.2
1930	Bro-N	6	4	.600	24	11	5	2	1	106	110	4	17	26	10.8	3.40	145	.266	.295	10	.200	-0	19	18	2	1.5
1931	Bro-N	9	9	.500	24	17	11	0	0	143	175	3	39	23	13.5	3.97	96	.301	.346	13	.217	2	-2	-2	-1	-0.1
1932	Bro-N	12	8	.600	28	20	10	2	0	153	174	14	38	35	12.5	4.06	94	.287	.330	17	.304	5	-3	-4	1	0.1
1933	Bro-N	6	8	.429	32	15	5	0	3	131^1	171	4	34	22	14.5	4.52	71	.319	.366	7	.159	-1	-17	-19	2	-1.9
Total	9	89	86	.509	288	178	95	8	13	1542^2	1859	93	369	306	13.1	4.24	94	.304	.346	175	.270	38	-25	-42	3	-1.4

● LUIS TIANT Tiant, Luis Clemente (Vega) b: 11/23/40, Marianao, Cuba BR/TR, 5′11″, 190 lbs. Deb: 7/19/64

YEAR	TM/L	W	L	PCT	G	GS	CG	SH	SV	IP	H	HR	BB	SO	RAT	ERA	ERA+	OAV	OOB	BH	AVG	PB	PR	/A	PD	TPI
1964	Cle-A	10	4	.714	19	16	9	3	1	127	94	13	47	105	10.1	2.83	127	.207	.284	5	.111	-1	11	11	0	1.1
1965	Cle-A	11	11	.500	41	30	10	2	1	196^1	166	20	66	152	10.8	3.53	99	.228	.295	6	.088	-2	-2	-1	-0	-0.3
1966	Cle-A	12	11	.522	46	16	7	**5**	8	155	121	16	50	145	10.0	2.79	123	.213	.279	4	.111	-1	11	11	-1	1.5
1967	Cle-A	12	9	.571	33	29	9	1	2	213^2	177	24	67	219	10.3	2.74	119	.221	.282	18	.254	5	12	13	-2	1.5
1968	Cle-A★	21	9	.700	34	32	19	**9**	0	258^1	152	16	73	264	8.0	**1.60**	**185**	**.168**	**.233**	7	.080	-5	**40**	39	-3	4.2
1969	Cle-A	9	20	.310	38	37	9	1	0	249^2	229	37	129	156	13.2	3.71	101	.246	.343	19	.235	6	-3	1	-1	0.7
1970	*Min-A	7	3	.700	18	17	2	1	0	92^2	84	12	41	50	12.3	3.40	109	.246	.330	13	.406	5	3	3	-0	0.9
1971	Bos-A	1	7	.125	21	10	1	0	0	72^1	73	8	32	59	13.2	4.85	76	.259	.337	3	.158	-0	-11	-9	-0	-1.0
1972	Bos-A	15	6	.714	43	19	12	6	3	179	128	7	65	123	9.7	**1.91**	**168**	.202	.277	6	.107	-2	23	26	-1	3.0
1973	Bos-A	20	13	.606	35	35	23	0	0	272	217	32	78	206	**10.0**	3.34	120	.219	**.281**	0	—	0	14	20	-1	2.0
1974	Bos-A★	22	13	.629	38	38	25	**7**	0	311^1	281	21	82	176	10.6	2.92	132	.241	.293	0	—	0	24	32	-3	3.0
1975	*Bos-A	18	14	.563	35	35	18	2	0	260	262	25	72	142	11.7	4.02	101	.264	.316	0	.000	-0	-7	2	-3	-0.2
1976	Bos-A★	21	12	.636	38	38	19	3	0	279	274	25	64	131	11.0	3.06	128	.260	.304	0	.000	-0	14	26	-2	2.8
1977	Bos-A	12	8	.600	32	32	3	3	0	188^2	210	26	51	124	12.5	4.53	99	.279	.327	0	—	0	-10	-1	-2	-1.0
1978	Bos-A	13	8	.619	32	31	12	5	0	212^1	185	26	57	114	10.5	3.31	124	.234	.290	0	—	0	11	19	-2	0.8
1979	NY-A	13	8	.619	30	30	5	1	0	195^2	190	22	53	104	11.2	3.91	104	.251	.300	0	—	0	7	4	-0	0.5
1980	NY-A	8	9	.471	25	25	3	0	0	136^1	139	10	50	84	12.5	4.89	80	.265	.330	0	—	0	-13	-15	1	-1.4
1981	Pit-N	2	5	.286	9	9	1	0	0	57^1	54	3	19	32	11.5	3.92	92	.243	.303	3	.188	1	-3	-2	-1	-0.3

YEAR	TM/L	W	L	PCT	G	GS	CG	SH	SV	IP	H	HR	BB	SO	RAT	ERA	ERA+	OAV	OOB	BH	AVG	PB	PR	/A	PD	TPI
1982	Cal-A	2	2	.500	6	5	0	0	0	29^2	39	3	8	30	14.3	5.76	70	.310	.351	0	—	0	-6	-6	-1	-0.7
Total	19	229	172	.571	573	484	187	49	15	3486^1	3075	346	1104	2416	10.9	3.30	113	.236	.298	84	.164	5	116	173	-21	17.1
● JAY TIBBS Tibbs, Jay Lindsey b: 1/4/62, Birmingham, Ala. BR/TR, 6'3", 185 lbs. Deb: 7/15/84																										
1984	Cin-N	6	2	.750	14	14	3	1	0	100^2	87	4	33	40	10.7	2.86	132	.238	.302	5	.139	-1	8	10	-1	0.6
1985	Cin-N	10	16	.385	35	34	5	2	0	218	216	14	83	98	12.3	3.92	97	.262	.329	6	.092	-3	-8	-3	1	-0.6
1986	Mon-N	7	9	.438	35	31	3	2	0	190^1	181	12	70	117	12.0	3.97	93	.256	.326	7	.130	-0	-5	-6	-1	-0.5
1987	Mon-N	4	5	.444	19	12	0	0	0	83	95	10	34	54	14.0	4.99	84	.289	.355	3	.120	0	-8	-7	-1	-0.7
1988	Bal-A	4	15	.211	30	24	1	0	0	158^2	184	18	63	82	14.2	5.39	72	.293	.360	0	—	0	-25	-26	0	-2.7
1989	Bal-A	5	0	1.000	10	8	1	0	0	54^1	62	2	20	30	13.6	2.82	135	.287	.347	0	—	0	6	6	-0	0.5
1990	Bal-A	2	7	.222	10	10	0	0	0	50^2	55	8	14	23	12.3	5.68	67	.279	.327	0	—	0	-10	-11	0	-1.5
	Pit-N	1	0	1.000	5	0	0	0	0	7	7	0	2	4	11.6	2.57	141	.259	.310	0	—	0	1	1	0	0.1
Total	7	39	54	.419	158	133	13	5	0	862^2	887	68	319	448	12.6	4.20	91	.269	.335	21	.117	-4	-41	-36	-1	-4.8
● DICK TIDROW Tidrow, Richard William b: 5/14/47, San Francisco, Cal. BR/TR, 6'4", 213 lbs. Deb: 4/18/72																										
1972	Cle-A	14	15	.483	39	34	10	3	0	237^1	200	21	70	123	10.5	2.77	116	.230	.291	7	.100	-3	8	12	-4	0.7
1973	Cle-A	14	16	.467	42	40	13	2	0	274^2	289	31	95	138	12.8	4.42	89	.270	.334	0	—	0	-19	-15	-2	-1.7
1974	Cle-A	1	3	.250	4	4	0	0	0	19	21	4	13	8	17.1	7.11	51	.276	.396	0	—	0	-7	-7	0	-1.2
	NY-A	11	9	.550	33	25	5	0	1	190^2	205	14	53	100	12.4	3.87	91	.279	.331	0	—	0	-5	-7	-2	-0.8
	Yr	12	12	.500	37	29	5	0	1	209^2	226	18	66	108	12.7	4.16	85	.278	.335	0	—	0	-13	-15	-1	-2.0
1975	NY-A	6	3	.667	37	0	0	0	5	69^1	65	5	31	38	12.9	3.12	118	.256	.344	0	—	0	5	4	-1	0.5
1976	*NY-A	4	5	.444	47	2	0	0	10	92^1	80	5	24	65	10.2	2.63	130	.233	.285	0	—	0	9	8	-1	0.8
1977	*NY-A	11	4	.733	49	7	0	0	5	151	143	20	41	83	11.1	3.16	125	.250	.303	0	—	0	15	13	-1	1.3
1978	*NY-A	7	11	.389	31	25	4	0	0	185^1	191	13	53	73	12.1	3.84	94	.267	.322	0	—	0	-2	-4	-2	-0.4
1979	NY-A	2	1	.667	14	0	0	0	2	22^2	38	5	4	7	16.7	7.94	51	.409	.433	0	—	0	-9	-10	1	-1.0
	Chi-N	11	5	.688	63	0	0	0	4	102^2	86	5	42	68	11.4	2.72	151	.231	.313	2	.200	0	12	16	1	2.7
1980	Chi-N	6	5	.545	**84**	0	0	0	6	116	97	10	53	97	12.0	2.79	140	.229	.322	0	.000	-0	10	14	-1	1.4
1981	Chi-N	3	10	.231	51	0	0	0	9	74^2	73	6	30	39	12.5	5.06	73	.256	.329	0	.000	-1	-13	-11	-1	-2.3
1982	Chi-N	8	3	.727	65	0	0	0	6	103^2	106	6	29	62	12.0	3.39	110	.265	.319	0	.000	-1	2	4	-2	0.2
1983	*Chi-A	2	4	.333	50	1	0	0	7	91^2	86	13	34	66	11.9	4.22	99	.242	.310	0	—	0	-2	-0	1	-0.2
1984	NY-N	0	0	—	11	0	0	0	0	15^2	25	5	7	8	18.4	9.19	38	.357	.416	0	—	0	-10	-10	0	0.0
Total	13	100	94	.515	620	138	32	5	55	1746^2	1705	163	579	975	12.0	3.68	101	.257	.321	9	.095	-5	-5	7	-11	0.0
● BOBBY TIEFENAUER Tiefenauer, Bobby Gene b: 10/10/29, Desloge, Mo. BR/TR, 6'2", 185 lbs. Deb: 7/14/52 C																										
1952	StL-N	0	0	—	6	0	0	0	0	8	12	1	7	3	21.4	7.88	47	.343	.452	0	.000	-0	-4	-4	0	0.0
1955	StL-N	1	4	.200	18	0	0	0	0	32^2	31	6	10	16	12.4	4.41	92	.261	.338	0	.000	-0	-1	-1	0	-0.2
1960	Cle-A	0	1	.000	6	0	0	0	0	9	8	0	3	2	11.0	2.00	187	.242	.306	0	.000	0	2	2	-0	0.2
1961	StL-N	0	0	—	3	0	0	0	0	4^1	9	0	4	3	27.0	6.23	71	.450	.542	0	—	0	-1	-1	-0	0.0
1962	Hou-N	2	4	.333	43	0	0	0	1	85	91	6	21	60	12.1	4.34	86	.277	.324	1	.111	0	-4	-6	-2	-0.5
1963	Mil-N	1	1	.500	12	0	0	0	2	29^2	20	1	4	22	7.3	1.21	265	.194	.224	0	.000	-0	7	7	1	0.6
1964	Mil-N	4	6	.400	46	0	0	0	13	73	61	6	15	48	9.7	3.21	110	.225	.273	0	.000	-1	3	3	-1	0.2
1965	Mil-N	0	1	.000	6	0	0	0	0	7	8	1	3	7	15.4	7.71	46	.286	.375	0	—	0	-3	-3	0	-0.4
	NY-A	1	1	.500	10	0	0	0	2	20^1	19	3	5	15	11.1	3.54	96	.253	.309	0	.000	-0	-0	-0	-0	0.0
	Cle-A	0	5	.000	15	0	0	0	4	22^1	24	3	10	13	14.1	4.84	72	.273	.354	0	.000	-0	-3	-3	-0	-0.9
	Yr	1	6	.143	25	0	0	0	6	42^2	43	6	15	28	12.4	4.22	82	.259	.324	0	.000	-0	-4	-4	0	-0.9
1967	Cle-A	0	1	.000	5	0	0	0	0	11^1	9	0	3	6	9.5	0.79	411	.225	.279	0	—	0	3	3	-1	0.2
1968	Chi-N	0	1	.000	9	0	0	0	1	13^1	20	2	2	9	14.9	6.08	52	.351	.373	0	.000	-0	-5	-4	-0	-0.4
Total	10	9	25	.265	179	0	0	0	23	316	312	29	87	204	11.7	3.84	94	.260	.317	1	.026	-1	-7	-9	-2	-1.2
● VERLE TIEFENTHALER Tiefenthaler, Verle Matthew b: 7/11/37, Breda, Iowa BL/TR, 6'1", 190 lbs. Deb: 4/19/62																										
1962	Chi-A	0	0	—	3	0	0	0	0	3^2	6	1	7	1	31.9	9.82	40	.353	.542	0	—	0	-2	-2	-0	0.0
● EDDIE TIEMEYER Tiemeyer, Edward Carl b: 5/9/1885, Cincinnati, Ohio d: 9/27/46, Cincinnati, Ohio BR/TR, 5'11.5", 185 lbs. Deb: 8/19/06 ♦																										
1906	Cin-N	0	0	—	1	0	0	0	0	1	1	0	1	1	18.0	0.00	—	.500	.667	2	.182	0	0	0	-0	0.0
● MIKE TIERNAN Tiernan, Michael Joseph "Silent Mike" b: 1/21/1867, Trenton, N.J. d: 11/9/18, New York, N.Y. BL/TL, 5'11", 165 lbs. Deb: 4/30/1887 ♦																										
1887	NY-N	1	2	.333	5	0	0	0	1	19^2	33	2	7	3	18.8	8.69	43	.398	.451	117	.287	2	-10	-11	-0	-1.2
● LES TIETJE Tietje, Leslie William "Toots" b: 9/11/11, Sumner, Iowa d: 10/2/96, Rochester, Minn. BR/TR, 6'0.5", 178 lbs. Deb: 9/18/33																										
1933	Chi-A	2	0	1.000	3	3	1	0	0	22^1	16	1	15	9	12.5	2.42	175	.203	.330	1	.125	0	5	5	0	0.4
1934	Chi-A	5	14	.263	34	22	6	1	0	176	174	20	96	81	13.9	4.81	98	.257	.351	1	.017	-7	-6	-1	2	-0.7
1935	Chi-A	9	15	.375	30	21	9	1	0	169^2	184	14	81	64	14.2	4.30	108	.277	.357	12	.197	-1	3	6	-2	0.5
1936	Chi-A	0	0	—	2	0	0	0	0	2^1	6	0	5	3	42.4	27.00	19	.462	.611	0	—	0	-6	-6	-0	0.0
	StL-A	3	5	.375	14	7	2	0	0	50^1	65	2	30	16	17.3	6.62	81	.310	.401	1	.067	-1	-9	-7	1	-0.9
	Yr	3	5	.375	16	7	2	0	0	52^2	71	2	35	19	18.5	7.52	71	.318	.415	1	.067	-1	-15	-13	1	-0.9
1937	StL-A	1	2	.333	5	4	2	0	0	30	32	0	17	5	14.7	4.20	115	.283	.377	0	.000	-2	1	2	-1	0.0
1938	StL-A	2	5	.286	17	8	2	1	0	62	83	8	38	15	17.6	7.55	66	.327	.414	2	.111	-1	-19	-18	-0	-1.7
Total	6	22	41	.349	105	65	22	3	0	512^2	560	45	282	193	14.9	5.11	93	.279	.369	17	.099	-12	-31	-19	0	-2.4
● RAY TIFT Tift, Raymond Frank b: 6/21/1884, Fitchburg, Mass. d: 3/29/45, Verona, N.J. TL , Deb: 8/7/07																										
1907	NY-A	0	0	—	4	1	0	0	0	19	33	0	4	6	17.5	4.74	59	.384	.411	0	.000	-0	-5	-4	-1	-0.1
● JOHNNY TILLMAN Tillman, John Lawrence "Ducky" b: 10/6/1893, Bridgeport, Conn. d: 4/7/64, Harrisburg, Pa. BB/TR, 5'11", 170 lbs. Deb: 9/20/15																										
1915	StL-A	1	0	1.000	2	1	0	0	0	10	6	0	4	6	9.0	0.90	318	.176	.263	0	.000	-0	2	2	0	0.2
● THAD TILLOTSON Tillotson, Thaddeus Asa b: 12/20/40, Merced, Cal. BR/TR, 6'2.5", 195 lbs. Deb: 4/14/67																										
1967	NY-A	3	9	.250	43	5	1	0	2	98^1	99	9	39	62	12.8	4.03	78	.261	.333	1	.063	-0	-9	-10	0	-1.2
1968	NY-A	1	0	1.000	7	0	0	0	0	10^1	11	0	7	1	15.7	4.35	67	.282	.391	0	.000	-0	-2	-2	0	-0.1
Total	2	4	9	.308	50	5	1	0	2	108^2	110	9	46	63	13.1	4.06	77	.263	.339	1	.059	-1	-10	-11	1	-1.3
● GARY TIMBERLAKE Timberlake, Gary Dale b: 8/8/48, Laconia, Ind. BR/TL, 6'2", 205 lbs. Deb: 6/18/69																										
1969	Sea-A	0	0	—	2	2	0	0	0	6	7	0	9	4	24.0	7.50	48	.269	.457	0	.000	-0	-3	-3	-0	0.0
● MIKE TIMLIN Timlin, Michael August b: 3/10/66, Midland, Tex. BR/TR, 6'4", 210 lbs. Deb: 4/8/91																										
1991	*Tor-A	11	6	.647	63	3	0	0	3	108^1	94	6	50	85	12.0	3.16	133	.233	.319	0	—	0	11	13	1	1.9
1992	*Tor-A	0	2	.000	26	0	0	0	1	43^2	45	0	20	35	13.6	4.12	99	.271	.353	0	—	0	-1	-0	0	-0.1
1993	*Tor-A	4	2	.667	54	0	0	0	1	55^2	63	7	27	49	14.7	4.69	92	.284	.364	0	—	0	-2	-2	1	-0.1
1994	Tor-A	0	1	.000	34	0	0	0	2	40	41	5	20	38	14.2	5.17	93	.261	.352	0	—	0	-2	-2	0	0.0
1995	Tor-A	4	3	.571	31	0	0	0	5	42	38	1	17	36	12.2	2.14	220	.242	.324	0	—	0	12	12	1	2.1
1996	Tor-A	1	6	.143	59	0	0	0	31	56^2	47	4	18	52	10.6	3.65	137	.229	.298	0	—	0	8	8	-0	1.7
1997	Tor-A	3	2	.600	38	0	0	0	9	47	41	6	15	36	10.9	2.87	160	.243	.308	0	—	0	9	9	1	1.2
	*Sea-A	3	2	.600	26	0	0	0	1	25^2	28	2	5	9	11.6	3.86	117	.280	.314	0	—	0	2	2	0	0.3
	Yr	6	4	.600	64	0	0	0	10	72^2	69	8	20	45	11.0	3.22	141	.255	.306	0	—	0	11	11	1	1.5
1998	Sea-A	3	3	.500	70	0	0	0	19	79^1	78	5	16	60	11.0	2.95	157	.264	.308	0	—	0	15	15	1	1.7
Total	8	29	27	.518	401	3	0	0	72	498^1	475	36	188	400	12.2	3.52	128	.253	.325	0	—	0	53	55	5	8.7
● TOM TIMMERMANN Timmermann, Thomas Henry b: 5/12/40, Breese, Ill. BR/TR, 6'4", 215 lbs. Deb: 6/18/69																										
1969	Det-A	4	3	.571	31	1	1	0	1	55^2	50	1	26	42	12.6	2.75	136	.238	.328	1	.111	-0	5	6	-1	0.6
1970	Det-A	6	7	.462	61	0	0	0	27	85^1	90	3	34	49	13.3	4.11	91	.273	.344	0	.000	-2	-4	-4	-0	-1.0
1971	Det-A	7	6	.538	52	2	0	0	4	84	82	6	37	51	13.1	3.86	93	.262	.346	1	.053	-1	-4	-2	0	-0.5
1972	Det-A	8	10	.444	34	25	3	2	0	149^2	121	12	41	88	10.0	2.89	109	.216	.276	6	.136	-0	3	4	-2	0.3
1973	Det-A	1	1	.500	17	1	0	0	1	39	39	4	11	21	11.5	3.69	111	.258	.309	0	—	0	1	2	-1	-0.2

YEAR	TM/L	W	L	PCT	G	GS	CG	SH	SV	IP	H	HR	BB	SO	RAT	ERA	ERA+	OAV	OOB	BH	AVG	PB	PR	/A	PD	TPI
	Cle-A	8	7	.533	29	15	4	0	2	124^1	117	15	54	62	12.6	4.92	80	.251	.332	0	—	0	-15	-14	-0	-1.6
	Yr	9	8	.529	46	16	4	0	3	163^1	156	19	65	83	12.3	4.63	86	.252	.327	0	—	0	-15	-12	-1	-1.8
1974	Cle-A	1	1	.500	4	0	0	0	0	10	9	1	5	2	12.6	5.40	67	.250	.341	0	—	0	-2	-2	1	-0.3
Total	6	35	35	.500	228	44	8	2	35	548	508	42	208	315	12.0	3.78	96	.246	.319	8	.091	-4	-16	-10	-3	-2.7
● BEN TINCUP Tincup, Austin Ben b: 12/14/1890, Adair, Okla. d: 7/5/80, Claremore, Okla. BL/TR, 6'1", 180 lbs. Deb: 5/22/14 C♦																										
1914	Phi-N	8	10	.444	28	17	9	3	2	155	165	0	62	108	13.4	2.61	113	.286	.359	9	.170	-1	3	6	1	0.7
1915	Phi-N	0	0	—	10	0	0	0	0	31	26	1	9	10	10.2	2.03	135	.263	.324	0	.000	-1	2	2	0	-0.1
1918	Phi-N	0	1	.000	8	1	0	0	0	16^2	24	0	6	6	16.2	7.56	40	.329	.380	1	.125	-0	-9	-8	1	-0.4
1928	Chi-N	0	0	—	2	0	0	0	0	9	14	0	1	3	15.0	7.00	55	.378	.395	0	.000	-0	-3	-3	0	0.0
Total	4	8	11	.421	48	18	9	3	2	211^2	229	1	78	127	13.2	3.10	95	.291	.358	10	.135	-3	-6	-3	3	0.2
● BUD TINNING Tinning, Lyle Forrest b: 3/12/06, Pilger, Neb. d: 1/17/61, Evansville, Ind. BB/TR, 5'11", 198 lbs. Deb: 4/20/32																										
1932	*Chi-N	5	3	.625	24	7	2	0	0	93^1	93	3	24	30	11.5	2.80	135	.263	.313	2	.087	-1	11	10	0	0.7
1933	Chi-N	13	6	.684	32	21	10	3	1	175^1	169	3	60	59	12.0	3.18	103	.255	.320	14	.209	1	3	2	-2	0.0
1934	Chi-N	4	6	.400	39	7	1	1	3	129^1	134	9	46	44	12.6	3.34	116	.269	.332	7	.179	-1	10	8	-1	0.4
1935	StL-N	0	0	—	4	0	0	0	0	7^2	9	1	5	2	17.6	5.87	70	.300	.417	0	.000	-0	-2	-2	0	0.0
Total	4	22	15	.595	99	35	13	4	4	405^2	405	16	135	135	12.2	3.19	113	.262	.325	23	.177	-1	23	18	-4	1.1
● DAN TIPPLE Tipple, Daniel E. "Big Dan" or "Rusty" b: 2/13/1890, Rockford, Ill. d: 3/26/60, Omaha, Neb. BR/TR, 6', 176 lbs. Deb: 9/18/15																										
1915	NY-A	1	1	.500	3	2	2	0	0	19	14	1	11	14	11.8	0.95	310	.203	.313	0	.000	-1	4	4	-1	0.2
● JACK TISING Tising, Johnnie Joseph b: 10/9/03, High Point, Mo. d: 9/5/67, Leadville, Colo. BL/TR, 6'2", 180 lbs. Deb: 4/24/36																										
1936	Pit-N	1	3	.250	10	6	1	0	0	47	52	5	24	27	14.6	4.21	96	.272	.353	3	.273	0	-1	-1	-0	-0.1
● CANNONBALL TITCOMB Titcomb, Ledell b: 8/21/1866, W.Baldwin, Me. d: 6/8/50, Kingston, N.H. BL/TL, 5'6", 157 lbs. Deb: 5/5/1886																										
1886	Phi-N	0	5	.000	5	5	5	0	0	41	43	1	24	24	14.7	3.73	88	.244	.335	1	.063	-2	-2	-2	1	-0.3
1887	Phi-a	1	2	.333	3	3	3	0	0	24	31	1	19	16	18.8	6.75	64	.298	.407	0	.000	-1	-7	-7	-1	-0.7
	NY-N	4	3	.571	9	9	9	0	0	72	68	3	37	34	13.3	3.88	97	.233	.321	2	.069	-4	2	-1	-1	-0.5
1888	*NY-N	14	8	.636	23	23	22	4	0	197	149	4	46	129	9.1	2.24	122	.201	.253	10	.122	-4	13	11	-4	0.2
1889	NY-N	1	2	.333	3	3	3	0	0	26	27	1	16	7	15.6	6.58	60	.260	.369	1	.083	-1	-7	-8	-0	-0.7
1890	Roc-a	10	9	.526	20	19	19	1	0	168^2	168	6	97	73	14.9	3.74	95	.251	.358	8	.107	-5	3	-3	-3	-1.0
Total	5	30	29	.508	63	62	61	5	0	528^2	486	16	239	283	12.7	3.47	96	.233	.318	22	.098	-18	2	-9	-8	-3.0
● DAVE TOBIK Tobik, David Vance b: 3/2/53, Euclid, Ohio BR/TR, 6'1", 195 lbs. Deb: 8/26/78																										
1978	Det-A	0	0	—	5	0	0	0	0	12	12	1	3	11	11.3	3.75	103	.261	.306	0	—	0	0	0	-0	-0.2
1979	Det-A	3	5	.375	37	0	0	0	3	68^2	59	12	25	48	11.0	4.33	100	.231	.300	0	—	0	-1	-0	-1	-0.3
1980	Det-A	1	0	1.000	17	1	0	0	0	61	61	7	21	34	12.1	3.98	103	.266	.328	0	—	0	0	1	-0	-0.1
1981	Det-A	2	2	.500	27	0	0	0	1	60^1	47	7	33	32	11.9	2.69	140	.215	.317	0	—	0	7	7	-1	0.2
1982	Det-A	4	9	.308	51	1	0	0	9	98^2	86	8	38	63	11.4	3.56	114	.241	.316	0	—	0	6	6	-1	0.7
1983	Tex-A	2	1	.667	27	0	0	0	9	44	36	2	13	30	10.0	3.68	109	.222	.280	0	—	0	2	2	0	0.3
1984	Tex-A	1	6	.143	24	0	0	0	5	42^1	44	5	17	30	13.2	3.61	115	.265	.337	0	—	0	2	2	1	0.2
1985	Sea-A	1	0	1.000	8	0	0	0	1	9	10	2	3	8	13.0	6.00	70	.286	.342	0	—	0	-2	-2	-0	-0.2
Total	8	14	23	.378	196	2	0	0	28	396	355	44	153	256	11.6	3.70	110	.242	.314	0	—	0	13	16	-3	0.6
● JIM TOBIN Tobin, James Anthony "Abba Dabba" b: 12/27/12, Oakland, Cal. d: 5/19/69, Oakland, Cal. BR/TR, 6', 185 lbs. Deb: 4/30/37 F♦																										
1937	Pit-N	6	3	.667	20	8	7	0	1	87	74	1	28	37	10.7	3.00	129	.226	.289	15	.441	7	9	8	-2	1.4
1938	Pit-N	14	12	.538	40	33	14	2	0	241^1	254	17	66	70	12.2	3.47	109	.270	.321	25	.243	7	9	9	-2	1.3
1939	Pit-N	9	9	.500	25	19	8	0	0	145^1	194	7	33	43	14.2	4.52	85	.319	.356	18	.243	5	-10	-11	-1	-0.8
1940	Bos-N	7	3	.700	15	11	9	0	0	96^1	102	8	24	29	11.8	3.83	97	.264	.307	12	.279	3	0	-1	-1	0.2
1941	Bos-N	12	12	.500	33	26	20	3	0	238	229	12	60	61	10.9	3.10	115	.253	.300	19	.184	3	14	12	4	2.0
1942	Bos-N	12	21	.364	37	33	**28**	1	0	**287**^{2}	283	20	96	71	12.0	3.97	84	.257	.320	28	.246	14	-21	-20	6	-0.1
1943	Bos-N	14	14	.500	33	30	24	1	0	250	241	12	69	52	11.2	2.66	128	.251	.303	30	.280	6	20	21	2	3.5
1944	Bos-N★	18	19	.486	43	36	**28**	5	3	299^1	271	18	97	83	11.2	3.01	127	.240	.302	22	.190	5	20	27	7	4.7
1945	Bos-N	9	14	.391	27	25	16	0	0	196^2	220	10	56	38	12.9	3.84	100	.282	.334	11	.143	5	-1	-0	2	0.7
	*Det-A	4	5	.444	14	6	2	0	1	58^1	61	2	28	14	14.3	3.55	99	.274	.365	3	.120	0	-1	-0	1	0.1
Total	9	105	112	.484	287	227	156	12	5	1900	1929	107	557	498	11.9	3.44	106	.262	.316	183	.230	54	39	45	16	13.0
● PAT TOBIN Tobin, Marion Brooks b: 1/28/16, Hermitage, Ark. d: 1/21/75, Shreveport, La. BR/TR, 6'1", 198 lbs. Deb: 8/21/41																										
1941	Phi-A	0	0	—	1	0	0	0	0	1	4	0	2	0	54.0	36.00	12	.571	.667	0	—	0	-4	-4	0	0.0
● FRANK TODD Todd, George Franklin b: 10/18/1869, Aberdeen, Md. d: 8/11/19, Havre De Grace, Md. TL , Deb: 7/14/1898																										
1898	Lou-N	0	2	.000	4	2	0	0	0	11	23	0	8	5	27.0	13.91	26	.418	.508	1	.200	0	-13	-13	-1	-1.6
● JACKSON TODD Todd, Jackson A b: 11/20/51, Tulsa, Okla. BR/TR, 6'2", 180 lbs. Deb: 5/5/77																										
1977	NY-N	3	6	.333	19	10	0	0	0	71^2	78	8	20	39	12.6	4.77	78	.273	.325	1	.059	-1	-7	-8	0	-1.0
1979	Tor-A	0	1	.000	12	1	0	0	0	32^1	40	7	7	14	13.4	5.85	74	.299	.338	0	—	0	-6	-5	0	-0.2
1980	Tor-A	5	2	.714	12	12	4	0	0	85	90	14	30	44	12.9	4.02	107	.276	.341	0	—	0	0	3	1	0.1
1981	Tor-A	2	7	.222	21	13	3	0	0	97^2	94	10	31	41	11.9	3.96	99	.251	.315	0	—	0	-3	-0	1	-0.1
Total	4	10	16	.385	64	36	7	0	0	286^2	302	39	88	138	12.5	4.40	92	.270	.328	1	.059	-1	-16	-11	2	-1.2
● JIM TODD Todd, James Richard b: 9/21/47, Lancaster, Pa. BL/TR, 6'2", 190 lbs. Deb: 4/29/74																										
1974	Chi-N	4	2	.667	43	6	0	0	3	88	82	7	41	42	12.9	3.89	98	.252	.341	1	.063	-1	-3	-1	1	-0.1
1975	*Oak-A	8	3	.727	58	0	0	0	12	122	104	4	33	50	10.3	2.29	159	.234	.292	0	—	0	20	18	4	2.3
1976	Oak-A	7	8	.467	49	0	0	0	4	82^2	87	6	34	22	13.8	3.81	88	.276	.358	0	—	0	-3	-4	2	-0.6
1977	Chi-N	1	1	.500	20	0	0	0	0	30^2	47	1	19	17	20.0	9.10	48	.336	.422	0	.000	-0	-18	-16	0	-0.9
1978	Sea-A	3	4	.429	49	2	0	0	3	106^2	113	4	61	37	14.7	3.88	98	.280	.375	0	—	0	-1	-1	0	0.0
1979	Oak-A	2	5	.286	51	0	0	0	2	81	108	12	51	26	17.9	6.56	62	.329	.423	0	—	0	-21	-23	0	-1.4
Total	6	25	23	.521	270	8	0	0	24	511	541	34	239	194	14.0	4.23	89	.277	.360	1	.059	-2	-25	-26	7	-0.7
● HAL TOENES Toenes, William Harrel b: 10/8/17, Mobile, Ala. BR/TR, 5'11.5", 175 lbs. Deb: 9/17/47																										
1947	Was-A	0	1	.000	3	1	0	0	0	6^2	11	0	2	5	17.6	6.75	55	.379	.419	0	.000	0	-2	-2	-0	-0.3
● FREDDIE TOLIVER Toliver, Freddie Lee b: 2/3/61, Natchez, Miss. BR/TR, 6'1", 170 lbs. Deb: 9/15/84																										
1984	Cin-N	0	0	—	3	1	0	0	0	10	7	0	7	4	12.6	0.90	420	.206	.341	0	.000	-0	3	3	-0	0.0
1985	Phi-N	0	4	.000	11	3	0	0	1	25	27	2	17	23	15.8	4.68	79	.273	.379	2	.500	1	-3	-3	-0	-0.4
1986	Phi-N	0	2	.000	5	5	0	0	0	25^2	28	0	11	20	13.7	3.51	110	.286	.358	0	.000	-0	1	1	0	0.1
1987	Phi-N	1	1	.500	10	4	0	0	0	30^1	34	2	17	25	15.4	5.64	75	.291	.385	0	.000	-1	-5	-5	0	-0.3
1988	Min-A	7	6	.538	21	19	0	0	0	114^2	116	8	52	69	13.3	4.24	96	.270	.350	0	—	0	-3	-2	0	-0.2
1989	Min-A	1	3	.250	7	5	0	0	0	29	39	2	15	11	17.1	7.76	53	.317	.396	0	—	0	-12	-12	1	-1.2
	SD-N	0	0	—	9	0	0	0	0	14	17	5	9	14	17.4	7.07	49	.321	.429	0	—	0	-6	-6	-0	0.0
1993	Pit-N	1	0	1.000	12	0	0	0	0	21^2	20	2	8	14	12.5	3.74	108	.267	.353	0	.000	-0	1	1	-1	0.0
Total	7	10	16	.385	78	37	0	0	1	270^1	288	21	136	180	14.3	4.73	85	.280	.367	2	.111	-0	-25	-22	1	-2.0
● DICK TOMANEK Tomanek, Richard Carl "Bones" b: 1/6/31, Avon Lake, Ohio BL/TL, 6'1", 175 lbs. Deb: 9/25/53																										
1953	Cle-A	1	0	1.000	1	1	1	0	0	9	6	1	6	6	13.0	2.00	188	.176	.317	0	.000	-1	2	2	-0	0.1
1954	Cle-A	0	0	—	1	0	0	0	0	1^2	1	1	1	0	10.8	5.40	68	.167	.286	0	—	0	-0	-0	0	0.0
1957	Cle-A	2	1	.667	34	2	0	0	0	69^2	67	13	37	55	13.6	5.68	65	.248	.341	3	.231	0	-15	-15	0	-0.5
1958	Cle-A	2	3	.400	18	6	2	0	0	57^2	61	8	28	42	14.2	5.62	65	.276	.363	2	.118	0	-12	-13	0	-0.9
	KC-A	5	5	.500	36	2	1	0	5	72^1	69	5	28	50	12.1	3.61	108	.252	.321	3	.231	1	1	2	-0	0.4
	Yr	7	8	.467	54	8	3	0	5	130	130	13	56	92	12.9	4.50	84	.261	.336	5	.167	1	-11	-10	0	-0.5

YEAR	TM/L	W	L	PCT	G	GS	CG	SH	SV	IP	H	HR	BB	SO	RAT	ERA	ERA+	OAV	OOB	BH	AVG	PB	PR	/A	PD	TPI
1959	KC-A	0	1	.000	16	0	0	0	2	20^2	27	6	12	13	17.9	6.53	61	.310	.406	1	.500	0	-6	-6	0	-0.3
Total	5	10	10	.500	106	11	4	0	7	231	231	34	112	166	13.6	4.95	77	.259	.346	9	.180	1	-30	-30	1	-1.2

● **ANDY TOMASIC** Tomasic, Andrew John b: 12/10/19, Hokendauqua, Pa. BR/TR, 6', 175 lbs. Deb: 4/28/49

YEAR	TM/L	W	L	PCT	G	GS	CG	SH	SV	IP	H	HR	BB	SO	RAT	ERA	ERA+	OAV	OOB	BH	AVG	PB	PR	/A	PD	TPI
1949	NY-N	0	1	.000	2	0	0	0	0	5	9	2	5	2	25.2	18.00	22	.375	.483	0	.000	-0	-8	-8	-0	-1.1

● **ANDY TOMBERLIN** Tomberlin, Andy Lee b: 11/7/66, Monroe, N.C. BL/TL, 5'11", 160 lbs. Deb: 8/12/93 ◆

YEAR	TM/L	W	L	PCT	G	GS	CG	SH	SV	IP	H	HR	BB	SO	RAT	ERA	ERA+	OAV	OOB	BH	AVG	PB	PR	/A	PD	TPI
1994	Bos-A	0	0	—	1	0	0	0	0	2	1	0	1	1	9.0	0.00	—	.143	.250	7	.194	0	1	1	-0	0.0

● **BRETT TOMKO** Tomko, Brett Daniel b: 4/7/73, Cleveland, O. BR/TR, 6'4", 215 lbs. Deb: 5/27/97

YEAR	TM/L	W	L	PCT	G	GS	CG	SH	SV	IP	H	HR	BB	SO	RAT	ERA	ERA+	OAV	OOB	BH	AVG	PB	PR	/A	PD	TPI
1997	Cin-N	11	7	.611	22	19	0	0	0	126	106	14	47	95	11.2	3.43	124	.233	.311	5	.139	-0	11	12	-2	1.3
1998	Cin-N	13	12	.520	34	34	1	0	0	210^2	198	22	64	162	11.5	4.44	97	.247	.308	7	.108	-2	-5	-3	-1	-0.5
Total	2	24	19	.558	56	53	1	0	0	336^2	304	36	111	257	11.4	4.06	106	.242	.309	12	.119	-2	6	9	-3	0.8

● **DAVE TOMLIN** Tomlin, David Allen b: 6/22/49, Maysville, Ky. BL/TL, 6'3", 185 lbs. Deb: 9/2/72

YEAR	TM/L	W	L	PCT	G	GS	CG	SH	SV	IP	H	HR	BB	SO	RAT	ERA	ERA+	OAV	OOB	BH	AVG	PB	PR	/A	PD	TPI
1972	Cin-N	0	0	—	3	0	0	0	0	4	7	2	1	2	18.0	9.00	36	.412	.444	0	—	0	-2	-3	0	0.0
1973	*Cin-N	1	2	.333	16	0	0	0	1	27^2	24	5	15	20	12.7	4.88	70	.238	.336	0	.000	-0	-4	-5	0	-0.5
1974	SD-N	2	0	1.000	47	0	0	0	2	58	59	4	30	29	14.1	4.34	82	.271	.364	0	.000	-0	-5	-5	1	-0.2
1975	SD-N	4	2	.667	67	0	0	0	1	83	87	5	31	48	13.0	3.25	107	.275	.344	1	.200	1	3	2	3	0.6
1976	SD-N	0	1	.000	49	1	0	0	0	73	62	4	20	43	10.2	2.84	115	.235	.291	0	.000	-1	5	4	2	0.2
1977	SD-N	4	4	.500	76	0	0	0	3	101^2	98	3	32	55	11.7	3.01	118	.259	.320	2	.286	0	10	6	1	0.6
1978	Cin-N	9	1	.900	57	0	0	0	4	62^1	88	3	30	32	17.5	5.78	61	.326	.399	1	.200	0	-15	-15	1	-2.5
1979	*Cin-N	2	2	.500	53	0	0	0	1	58^1	59	3	18	30	12.0	2.62	142	.269	.328	1	.500	0	7	7	0	0.5
1980	Cin-N	3	0	1.000	27	0	0	0	0	26	38	2	11	6	17.0	5.54	65	.355	.415	0	—	0	-6	-6	0	-0.5
1982	Mon-N	0	0	—	1	0	0	0	0	2	1	0	1	2	9.0	4.50	81	.167	.286	0	—	0	-0	-0	-0	0.0
1983	Pit-N	0	0	—	5	0	0	0	0	4	6	0	1	5	15.8	6.75	55	.316	.350	0	—	0	-1	-1	-0	0.0
1985	Pit-N	0	0	—	1	0	0	0	0	1	1	0	1	0	18.0	0.00	—	.333	.500	0	—	0	0	0	-0	0.0
1986	Mon-N	0	0	—	7	0	0	0	0	10^1	13	1	7	6	18.3	5.23	71	.317	.429	0	—	0	-2	-2	0	0.0
Total	13	25	12	.676	409	1	0	0	12	511^1	543	32	198	278	13.3	3.82	92	.277	.347	5	.147	1	-9	-17	9	-1.8

● **RANDY TOMLIN** Tomlin, Randy Leon b: 6/14/66, Bainbridge, Md. BL/TL, 5'11", 170 lbs. Deb: 8/6/90

YEAR	TM/L	W	L	PCT	G	GS	CG	SH	SV	IP	H	HR	BB	SO	RAT	ERA	ERA+	OAV	OOB	BH	AVG	PB	PR	/A	PD	TPI
1990	Pit-N	4	4	.500	12	12	2	0	0	77^2	62	5	12	42	8.7	2.55	142	.221	.256	1	.040	-1	11	9	1	0.9
1991	*Pit-N	8	7	.533	31	27	4	2	0	175	170	9	54	104	11.8	2.98	120	.254	.316	10	.192	1	14	11	2	1.3
1992	*Pit-N	14	9	.609	35	33	1	1	0	208^2	226	11	42	90	11.8	3.41	101	.282	.322	9	.138	-0	2	1	3	0.4
1993	Pit-N	4	8	.333	18	18	1	0	0	98^1	109	11	15	44	11.8	4.85	83	.291	.327	6	.182	0	-9	-9	1	-0.8
1994	Pit-N	0	3	.000	10	4	0	0	0	20^2	23	1	10	17	14.4	3.92	110	.291	.371	3	.500	1	1	1	0	0.2
Total	5	30	31	.492	106	94	8	3	0	580^1	590	37	133	297	11.5	3.43	106	.268	.314	29	.160	1	18	13	7	2.0

● **CHUCK TOMPKINS** Tompkins, Charles Herbert b: 9/1/1889, Prescott, Ark. d: 9/20/75, Prescott, Ark. BR/TR, 6', 185 lbs. Deb: 6/25/12

YEAR	TM/L	W	L	PCT	G	GS	CG	SH	SV	IP	H	HR	BB	SO	RAT	ERA	ERA+	OAV	OOB	BH	AVG	PB	PR	/A	PD	TPI
1912	Cin-N	0	0	—	1	0	0	0	0	3	5	0	0	1	15.0	0.00	—	.357	.357	1	1.000	0	1	1	-0	0.0

● **RON TOMPKINS** Tompkins, Ronald Everett "Stretch" b: 11/27/44, San Diego, Cal. BR/TR, 6'4", 198 lbs. Deb: 9/9/65

YEAR	TM/L	W	L	PCT	G	GS	CG	SH	SV	IP	H	HR	BB	SO	RAT	ERA	ERA+	OAV	OOB	BH	AVG	PB	PR	/A	PD	TPI
1965	KC-A	0	0	—	5	1	0	0	0	10^1	9	0	3	4	11.3	3.48	100	.237	.310	0	.000	-0	-0	0	0	0.0
1971	Chi-N	0	2	.000	35	0	0	0	3	39^2	31	3	21	20	12.5	4.08	96	.214	.325	0	—	0	-3	-1	1	0.1
Total	2	0	2	.000	40	1	0	0	3	50	40	3	24	24	12.2	3.96	97	.219	.322	0	.000	-0	-3	-1	1	0.1

● **TOMMY TOMS** Toms, Thomas Howard b: 10/15/51, Charlottesville, Va BR/TR, 6'4", 195 lbs. Deb: 5/4/75

YEAR	TM/L	W	L	PCT	G	GS	CG	SH	SV	IP	H	HR	BB	SO	RAT	ERA	ERA+	OAV	OOB	BH	AVG	PB	PR	/A	PD	TPI
1975	SF-N	0	1	.000	7	0	0	0	0	10^1	13	1	6	6	16.5	6.10	62	.317	.404	0	—	0	-3	-3	-0	-0.2
1976	SF-N	0	1	.000	7	0	0	0	1	8^2	13	1	1	4	14.5	6.23	58	.351	.368	0	—	0	-3	-3	0	-0.3
1977	SF-N	0	1	.000	4	0	0	0	0	4^1	7	0	2	2	18.7	2.08	188	.333	.391	0	—	0	1	1	-0	0.2
Total	3	0	3	.000	18	0	0	0	1	23^1	33	2	9	12	16.2	5.40	70	.333	.389	0	—	0	-5	-4	0	-0.3

● **FRED TONEY** Toney, Fred Alexandra b: 12/11/1888, Nashville, Tenn. d: 3/11/53, Nashville, Tenn. BR/TR, 6'1", 195 lbs. Deb: 4/15/11

YEAR	TM/L	W	L	PCT	G	GS	CG	SH	SV	IP	H	HR	BB	SO	RAT	ERA	ERA+	OAV	OOB	BH	AVG	PB	PR	/A	PD	TPI
1911	Chi-N	1	1	.500	18	4	1	0	0	67	55	2	35	27	12.8	2.42	137	.229	.339	2	.111	-1	7	7	1	0.1
1912	Chi-N	1	2	.333	9	2	0	0	0	24	21	0	11	9	12.4	5.25	63	.247	.340	0	.000	-0	-5	-5	-1	-0.6
1913	Chi-N	2	2	.500	7	5	2	0	0	39	52	1	22	12	17.3	6.00	53	.327	.412	3	.250	1	-12	-12	0	-1.0
1915	Cin-N	17	6	.739	36	23	18	6	2	222^2	160	1	73	108	9.5	1.58	181	.207	.278	7	.095	-5	29	32	1	3.1
1916	Cin-N	14	17	.452	41	38	21	3	1	300	247	7	78	146	10.0	2.28	114	.231	.288	12	.121	-4	11	11	-4	0.2
1917	Cin-N	24	16	.600	43	42	31	7	1	339^2	300	4	77	123	10.1	2.20	119	.238	.286	13	.112	-6	19	16	-5	0.7
1918	Cin-N	6	10	.375	21	19	9	1	2	136^2	148	2	31	32	11.8	2.90	92	.282	.322	9	.214	0	-2	-3	1	-0.3
	NY-N	6	2	.750	11	9	7	1	1	85^1	55	1	7	19	6.8	1.69	156	.192	.216	6	.188	-1	10	9	-1	0.7
	Yr	12	12	.500	32	28	16	2	**3**	222	203	3	38	51	9.9	2.43	109	.250	.285	15	.203	-0	8	5	0	0.4
1919	NY-N	13	6	.684	24	20	14	4	1	181	157	6	35	40	9.6	1.84	152	.235	.276	15	.227	1	22	19	-3	1.9
1920	NY-N	21	11	.656	42	37	17	4	1	278^1	266	8	57	81	10.6	2.65	113	.259	.302	23	.240	3	15	11	-2	1.2
1921	*NY-N	18	11	.621	42	32	16	1	3	249^1	274	14	65	63	12.4	3.61	102	.289	.338	18	.209	2	5	2	-1	0.3
1922	NY-N	5	6	.455	13	12	6	0	0	86^1	91	5	31	10	12.9	4.17	96	.277	.343	2	.067	-3	-1	-2	-2	-0.6
1923	StL-N	11	12	.478	29	28	16	1	0	196^2	211	8	61	48	12.7	3.84	102	.282	.341	8	.116	-5	3	1	3	0.0
Total	12	139	102	.577	336	271	158	28	12	2206	2037	59	583	718	10.9	2.69	113	.251	.305	118	.159	-18	102	85	-12	5.7

● **DOC TONKIN** Tonkin, Harry Glenville b: 8/11/1881, Concord, N.H. d: 5/30/59, Miami, Fla. BL/TL, 5'9", 165 lbs. Deb: 8/19/07

YEAR	TM/L	W	L	PCT	G	GS	CG	SH	SV	IP	H	HR	BB	SO	RAT	ERA	ERA+	OAV	OOB	BH	AVG	PB	PR	/A	PD	TPI
1907	Was-A	0	0	—	1	0	0	0	0	2^2	6	0	5	0	37.1	6.75	36	.462	.611	2	1.000	1	-1	-1	0	0.1

● **STEVE TOOLE** Toole, Stephen John b: 4/9/1859, New Orleans, La. d: 3/28/19, Pittsburgh, Pa. BR/TL, 6', 170 lbs. Deb: 4/20/1886 U

YEAR	TM/L	W	L	PCT	G	GS	CG	SH	SV	IP	H	HR	BB	SO	RAT	ERA	ERA+	OAV	OOB	BH	AVG	PB	PR	/A	PD	TPI
1886	Bro-a	6	6	.500	13	12	11	0	0	104	100	0	64	48	14.9	4.41	79	.246	.359	20	.351	4	-11	-11	2	-0.5
1887	Bro-a	14	10	.583	24	24	22	1	0	194	186	1	106	48	14.1	4.31	100	.254	.358	24	.233	-1	-0	-0	-1	-0.2
1888	KC-a	5	6	.455	12	10	10	0	0	91^2	124	4	50	35	17.6	6.68	51	.312	.395	10	.208	-0	-37	-33	0	-2.9
1890	Bro-a	2	4	.333	6	6	6	0	0	53^1	47	0	39	10	15.2	4.05	96	.229	.363	6	.300	2	-1	-1	0	0.1
Total	4	27	26	.509	55	52	49	1	0	443	457	5	259	141	15.1	4.79	81	.262	.367	60	.263	5	-49	-44	2	-3.5

● **RUPE TOPPIN** Toppin, Ruperto b: 12/7/41, Panama City, Panama BR/TR, 6', 185 lbs. Deb: 7/28/62

YEAR	TM/L	W	L	PCT	G	GS	CG	SH	SV	IP	H	HR	BB	SO	RAT	ERA	ERA+	OAV	OOB	BH	AVG	PB	PR	/A	PD	TPI
1962	KC-A	0	0	—	2	0	0	0	0	2	1	0	5	1	27.0	13.50	31	.167	.545	1	1.000	0	-2	-2	-0	0.0

● **RED TORKELSON** Torkelson, Chester Leroy b: 3/19/1894, Chicago, Ill. d: 9/22/64, Chicago, Ill. BR/TR, 6', 175 lbs. Deb: 8/29/17

YEAR	TM/L	W	L	PCT	G	GS	CG	SH	SV	IP	H	HR	BB	SO	RAT	ERA	ERA+	OAV	OOB	BH	AVG	PB	PR	/A	PD	TPI
1917	Cle-A	2	1	.667	4	3	0	0	0	22^1	33	1	13	10	19.3	7.66	37	.333	.421	2	.222	-0	-12	-12	0	-1.3

● **PABLO TORREALBA** Torrealba, Pablo Arnoldo (Torrealba) b: 4/28/48, Barquisimeto, Ven. BL/TL, 5'9", 175 lbs. Deb: 4/9/75

YEAR	TM/L	W	L	PCT	G	GS	CG	SH	SV	IP	H	HR	BB	SO	RAT	ERA	ERA+	OAV	OOB	BH	AVG	PB	PR	/A	PD	TPI
1975	Atl-N	0	1	.000	6	0	0	0	0	6^2	7	0	3	5	13.5	1.35	279	.250	.323	1	1.000	0	2	2	1	0.4
1976	Atl-N	0	2	.000	30	0	0	0	2	53	67	0	22	33	15.6	3.57	106	.315	.387	0	.000	-0	-0	1	1	0.1
1977	Oak-A	4	6	.400	41	10	3	0	2	116^2	127	5	38	51	12.9	2.62	153	.279	.337	0	—	0	19	18	2	1.7
1978	Chi-A	2	4	.333	25	3	1	1	1	57^1	69	6	39	23	17.4	4.71	81	.301	.410	0	—	0	-6	-6	-1	-0.8
1979	Chi-A	0	0	—	3	0	0	0	0	5^2	5	1	2	1	11.1	1.59	268	.250	.318	0	—	0	2	2	0	0.0
Total	5	6	13	.316	111	13	4	1	5	239^1	275	12	104	113	14.6	3.27	120	.291	.366	1	.200	-0	16	17	2	1.4

● **ANGEL TORRES** Torres, Angel Rafael (Ruiz) b: 10/24/52, Las Ciengas, Azua, D.R. BL/TL, 5'11", 168 lbs. Deb: 9/12/77

YEAR	TM/L	W	L	PCT	G	GS	CG	SH	SV	IP	H	HR	BB	SO	RAT	ERA	ERA+	OAV	OOB	BH	AVG	PB	PR	/A	PD	TPI
1977	Cin-N	0	0	—	5	0	0	0	0	8^1	7	2	8	8	16.2	2.16	182	.233	.395	0	—	0	2	2	0	0.0

● **DILSON TORRES** Torres, Dilson Dario b: 5/31/70, Sur Edo Aragua, Venez. BR/TR, 6'3", 200 lbs. Deb: 4/29/95

YEAR	TM/L	W	L	PCT	G	GS	CG	SH	SV	IP	H	HR	BB	SO	RAT	ERA	ERA+	OAV	OOB	BH	AVG	PB	PR	/A	PD	TPI
1995	KC-A	1	2	.333	24	2	0	0	0	44^1	56	6	17	28	15.0	6.09	79	.311	.374	0	—	0	-7	-6	2	-0.2

● **GIL TORRES** Torres, Don Gilberto (Nunez) b: 8/23/15, Regla, Cuba d: 1/10/83, Regla, Cuba BR/TR, 6', 155 lbs. Deb: 4/25/40 F◆

YEAR	TM/L	W	L	PCT	G	GS	CG	SH	SV	IP	H	HR	BB	SO	RAT	ERA	ERA+	OAV	OOB	BH	AVG	PB	PR	/A	PD	TPI
1940	Was-A	0	0	—	2	0	0	0	0	2^2	3	0	0	1	10.1	0.00	—	.273	.273	0	—	0	1	1	0	0.0
1946	Was-A	0	0	—	3	0	0	0	1	7	9	0	3	2	15.4	7.71	43	.310	.375	47	.254	1	-3	-3	-0	-0.1
Total	2	0	0	—	5	0	0	0	1	9^2	12	0	3	3	14.0	5.59	64	.300	.349	320	.252	1	-2	-2	-0	-0.1

YEAR	TM/L	W	L	PCT	G	GS	CG	SH	SV	IP	H	HR	BB	SO	RAT	ERA	ERA+	OAV	OOB	BH	AVG	PB	PR	/A	PD	TPI
● **HECTOR TORRES**	Torres, Hector Epitacio (Marroquin) b: 9/16/45, Monterrey, Mexico BR/TR, 6', 175 lbs. Deb: 4/10/68 C♦																									
1972	Mon-N	0	0	—	1	0	0	0	0	0^2	5	0	0	0	67.5	27.00	13	.714	.714	28	.155	0	-2	-2	0	0.0
● **SALOMON TORRES**	Torres, Salomon (Ramirez) b: 3/11/72, San Pedro De Macoris, D.R. BR/TR, 5'11", 165 lbs. Deb: 8/29/93																									
1993	SF-N	3	5	.375	8	8	0	0	0	44^2	37	5	27	23	13.1	4.03	97	.231	.346	3	.231	0	0	-1	1	0.0
1994	SF-N	2	8	.200	16	14	1	0	0	84^1	95	10	34	42	14.5	5.44	74	.292	.372	4	.154	-0	-12	-13	-2	-1.5
1995	SF-N	0	1	.000	4	1	0	0	0	8	13	4	7	2	22.5	9.00	45	.394	.500	0	.000	-0	-4	-4	0	-0.5
	Sea-A	3	8	.273	16	13	1	0	0	72	87	12	42	45	16.4	6.00	79	.291	.382	0	—	0	-10	-10	1	-1.1
1996	Sea-A	3	3	.500	10	7	1	1	0	49	44	5	23	36	12.9	4.59	108	.242	.337	0	—	0	2	2	-1	0.1
1997	Sea-A	0	0	—	2	0	0	0	0	3^1	7	0	3	0	29.7	27.00	17	.412	.524	0	—	0	-8	-8	0	0.0
	Mon-N	0	0	—	12	0	0	0	0	22^1	25	2	12	11	15.7	7.25	58	.284	.382	0	.000	-1	-8	-8	1	0.0
Total	5	11	25	.306	68	43	3	1	0	283^2	308	38	148	159	15.0	5.71	76	.279	.372	7	.152	-1	-40	-43	0	-3.0
● **MIKE TORREZ**	Torrez, Michael Augustine b: 8/28/46, Topeka, Kan. BR/TR, 6'5", 220 lbs. Deb: 9/10/67																									
1967	StL-N	0	1	.000	3	1	0	0	0	5^2	5	0	1	5	11.1	3.18	103	.238	.304	0	.000	-0	0	0	-0	0.0
1968	StL-N	2	1	.667	5	2	0	0	0	19^1	20	1	12	6	15.4	2.79	104	.286	.398	2	.286	0	0	0	0	0.1
1969	StL-N	10	4	.714	24	15	3	0	0	107^2	96	7	62	61	13.5	3.59	99	.240	.346	3	.073	-2	-0	-0	0	-0.2
1970	StL-N	8	10	.444	30	28	5	1	0	179^1	168	12	103	100	13.8	4.22	98	.248	.350	17	.270	4	-3	-2	-0	0.2
1971	StL-N	1	2	.333	9	6	0	0	0	36	41	2	30	8	18.0	6.00	60	.304	.434	1	.143	1	-10	-10	0	-0.6
	Mon-N	0	0	—	1	0	0	0	0	3	4	0	1	2	15.0	0.00	—	.308	.357	0	—	0	1	1	0	0.0
	Yr	1	2	.333	10	6	0	0	0	39	45	2	31	10	17.5	5.54	65	.300	.420	1	.143	1	-9	-8	1	-0.6
1972	Mon-N	16	12	.571	34	33	13	0	0	243^1	215	15	103	112	12.0	3.33	107	.242	.325	15	.176	0	3	6	2	1.0
1973	Mon-N	9	12	.429	35	34	3	1	0	208	207	17	115	90	14.1	4.46	86	.262	.359	12	.174	-1	-18	-15	2	-1.3
1974	Mon-N	15	8	.652	32	30	6	1	0	186^1	184	10	84	92	13.1	3.57	107	.257	.337	8	.125	-3	1	5	5	0.8
1975	Bal-A	20	9	**.690**	36	36	16	2	0	270^2	238	15	133	119	12.5	3.06	115	.239	.332	0	—	0	22	14	1	1.4
1976	Oak-A	16	12	.571	39	39	13	4	0	266^1	231	15	87	115	10.9	2.50	134	.235	.301	0	—	0	30	25	-1	2.7
1977	Oak-A	3	1	.750	4	4	2	0	0	26^1	23	3	11	12	12.0	4.44	91	.242	.327	0	—	0	-1	-1	-0	-0.2
	*NY-A	14	12	.538	31	31	15	2	0	217	212	20	75	90	12.2	3.82	103	.259	.326	0	—	0	6	3	-2	0.1
	Yr	17	13	.567	35	35	17	2	0	243^1	235	23	86	102	12.1	3.88	102	.256	.324	0	—	0	5	2	-2	-0.1
1978	Bos-A	16	13	.552	36	36	15	2	0	250	272	19	99	120	13.5	3.96	104	.281	.349	0	—	0	-6	4	-2	0.2
1979	Bos-A	16	13	.552	36	36	12	1	0	252^1	254	20	121	125	13.6	4.49	98	.264	.349	0	—	0	-8	-2	-0	-0.4
1980	Bos-A	9	16	.360	36	32	6	1	0	207^1	256	18	75	97	14.4	5.08	83	.313	.371	0	—	0	-24	-20	2	-2.0
1981	Bos-A	10	3	.769	22	22	2	0	0	127^1	130	10	51	54	12.8	3.68	105	.267	.337	0	—	0	-0	3	-1	0.1
1982	Bos-A	9	9	.500	31	31	1	0	0	175^2	196	20	74	84	14.1	5.23	82	.282	.356	0	—	0	-22	-18	-2	-1.9
1983	NY-N	10	17	.370	39	34	5	0	0	222^1	227	16	113	94	13.8	4.37	83	.271	.358	3	.046	-5	-18	-18	0	-2.5
1984	NY-N	1	5	.167	9	8	0	0	0	37^2	55	3	18	16	17.9	5.02	70	.369	.444	3	.300	1	-6	-6	0	-0.8
	Oak-A	0	0	—	2	0	0	0	0	2^1	9	0	3	2	46.3	27.00	14	.563	.632	0	—	0	-6	-6	-0	0.3
Total	18	185	160	.536	494	458	117	15	0	3044	3043	223	1371	1404	13.2	3.96	97	.264	.345	64	.155	-4	-60	-38	3	-3.0
● **LOU TOST**	Tost, Louis Eugene b: 6/1/11, Cumberland, Wash. d: 2/22/67, Santa Clara, Cal. BL/TL, 6', 175 lbs. Deb: 4/20/42																									
1942	Bos-N	10	10	.500	35	22	5	1	0	147^2	146	12	52	43	12.3	3.53	94	.256	.322	9	.176	0	-4	-3	-1	-0.5
1943	Bos-N	0	1	.000	3	1	0	0	0	6^2	10	2	4	3	18.9	5.40	63	.357	.438	0	.000	-0	-1	-1	0	-0.2
1947	Pit-N	0	0	—	1	0	0	0	0	1	3	0	0	0	27.0	9.00	47	.600	.600	0	—	0	-1	-1	0	0.0
Total	3	10	11	.476	39	23	5	1	0	155^1	159	14	56	46	12.7	3.65	92	.263	.330	9	.173	-0	-6	-5	-1	-0.7
● **PAUL TOTH**	Toth, Paul Louis b: 6/30/35, McRoberts, Ky. BR/TR, 6'1", 175 lbs. Deb: 4/22/62																									
1962	StL-N	1	0	1.000	6	1	1	0	0	16^2	18	1	4	5	11.9	5.40	79	.295	.338	2	.400	0	-3	-2	-0	-0.1
	Chi-N	3	1	.750	6	4	1	0	0	34	29	2	10	11	10.9	4.24	98	.240	.308	2	.182	0	-1	-0	-0	-0.1
	Yr	4	1	.800	12	5	2	0	0	50^2	47	3	14	16	11.2	4.62	91	.257	.317	4	.250	1	-4	-2	-1	-0.2
1963	Chi-N	5	9	.357	27	14	3	2	0	130^2	115	9	35	66	10.5	3.10	113	.240	.294	1	.026	-3	3	6	-1	0.2
1964	Chi-N	0	2	.000	4	2	0	0	0	10^2	15	2	5	0	16.9	8.44	44	.341	.408	1	.333	0	-6	-6	1	-0.8
Total	3	9	12	.429	43	21	5	2	0	192	177	14	54	82	11.0	3.80	97	.251	.308	6	.103	-2	-7	-2	-1	-0.8
● **CLAY TOUCHSTONE**	Touchstone, Clayland Maffitt b: 1/24/03, Moores, Pa. d: 4/28/49, Beaumont, Tex. BR/TR, 5'9", 175 lbs. Deb: 9/4/28																									
1928	Bos-N	0	0	—	5	0	0	0	0	8	15	0	2	1	20.3	4.50	87	.417	.462	0	.000	-0	-0	-1	0	0.0
1929	Bos-N	0	0	—	1	0	0	0	0	2^2	6	1	0	1	20.3	16.88	28	.429	.429	1	1.000	0	-4	-4	-0	0.0
1945	Chi-A	0	0	—	6	0	0	0	0	10	14	1	6	4	18.9	5.40	61	.311	.404	0	.000	-0	-2	-2	0	0.0
Total	3	0	0	—	12	0	0	0	0	20^2	35	2	8	6	19.6	6.53	57	.368	.429	1	.250	0	-6	-6	0	0.0
● **CESAR TOVAR**	Tovar, Cesar Leonardo "Pepito" (b: Cesar Leonard Perez (Tovar)) b: 7/3/40, Caracas, Venez. d: 7/14/94, Caracas, Venez. BR/TR, 5'9", 155 lbs. Deb: 4/12/65 ♦																									
1968	Min-A	0	0	—	1	1	0	0	0	1	0	0	1	1	9.0	0.00	—	.000	.250	167	.272	0	0	0	0	0.0
● **IRA TOWNSEND**	Townsend, Ira Dance "Pat" b: 1/9/1894, Weimar, Tex. d: 7/21/65, Schulenburg, Tex. BR/TR, 6'1", 180 lbs. Deb: 8/25/20																									
1920	Bos-N	0	0	—	4	1	0	0	0	6^2	10	0	2	1	17.6	1.35	226	.370	.433	0	.000	-0	1	1	-0	0.0
1921	Bos-N	0	0	—	4	0	0	0	0	7^1	11	1	4	0	20.9	6.14	59	.344	.447	0	.000	-0	-2	-2	0	0.0
Total	2	0	0	—	8	1	0	0	0	14	21	1	6	1	19.3	3.86	87	.356	.441	0	.000	-1	-1	-1	0	0.0
● **HAPPY TOWNSEND**	Townsend, John b: 4/9/1879, Townsend, Del. d: 12/21/63, Wilmington, Del. BR/TR, 6', 190 lbs. Deb: 4/19/01																									
1901	Phi-N	9	6	.600	19	16	14	2	0	143^2	118	3	64	72	11.7	3.45	99	**.223**	.312	7	.109	-4	-2	-1	-2	-0.7
1902	Was-A	8	16	.333	27	26	22	0	0	220^1	233	12	89	71	13.7	4.45	83	.272	.349	23	.264	3	-21	-18	-1	-1.4
1903	Was-A	2	11	.154	20	13	10	0	0	126^2	145	3	48	54	14.4	4.76	66	.287	.359	2	.045	-4	-25	-23	0	-2.4
1904	Was-A	5	26	.161	36	34	31	2	0	291^1	319	3	100	143	13.2	3.58	74	.279	.342	20	.168	-2	-32	-30	-1	-3.3
1905	Was-A	7	16	.304	34	24	22	0	0	263	247	2	84	102	11.8	2.63	100	.250	.318	15	.181	1	1	0	-3	-0.1
1906	Cle-A	3	7	.300	17	12	8	1	0	92^2	92	1	31	31	12.5	2.91	90	.262	.332	4	.133	-1	-2	-3	-0	-0.5
Total	6	34	82	.293	153	125	107	5	0	1137^2	1154	24	416	473	12.9	3.59	83	.264	.336	71	.166	-8	-82	-75	-7	-8.4
● **LEO TOWNSEND**	Townsend, Leo Alphonse "Lefty" b: 1/15/1891, Mobile, Ala. d: 12/3/76, Mobile, Ala. BL/TL, 5'10", 160 lbs. Deb: 9/8/20																									
1920	Bos-N	2	2	.500	7	1	1	0	0	24^1	18	1	2	0	7.4	1.48	206	.220	.238	1	.167	0	4	4	0	0.7
1921	Bos-N	0	1	.000	1	1	0	0	0	1^1	2	0	3	0	33.8	27.00	14	.400	.625	0	—	0	-3	-3	0	-1.2
Total	2	2	3	.400	8	2	1	0	0	25^2	20	1	5	0	8.8	2.81	110	.230	.272	1	.167	0	1	1	0	-0.5
● **BILL TOZER**	Tozer, William Louis b: 7/3/1882, St.Louis, Mo. d: 2/23/55, Belmont, Cal. BR/TR, 6', 200 lbs. Deb: 4/16/08																									
1908	Cin-N	0	0	—	4	0	0	0	0	10^2	11	0	4	5	13.5	1.69	137	.268	.348	0	.000	-0	1	1	0	0.0
● **STEVE TRACHSEL**	Trachsel, Stephen Christopher b: 10/31/70, Oxnard, Cal. BR/TR, 6'4", 205 lbs. Deb: 9/19/93																									
1993	Chi-N	0	2	.000	3	3	0	0	0	19^2	16	4	3	14	8.7	4.58	87	.219	.250	1	.167	0	-1	-1	0	0.0
1994	Chi-N	9	7	.563	22	22	1	0	0	146	133	19	54	108	11.7	3.21	130	.242	.314	8	.186	1	16	15	2	1.8
1995	Chi-N	7	13	.350	30	29	2	0	0	160^2	174	25	76	117	14.0	5.15	80	.277	.355	13	.265	3	-17	-19	-2	-1.9
1996	Chi-N★	13	9	.591	31	31	3	2	0	205	181	30	62	132	11.0	3.03	143	.235	.299	7	.106	-2	27	30	0	2.8
1997	Chi-N	8	12	.400	34	34	0	0	0	201^1	225	32	69	160	13.4	4.51	95	.287	.348	7	.117	-0	-7	-5	0	-0.4
1998	Chi-N	15	8	.652	33	33	1	0	0	208	204	27	84	149	12.8	4.46	98	.260	.337	17	.266	6	-5	-2	2	0.6
Total	6	52	51	.505	153	152	7	2	0	940^2	933	137	348	680	12.5	4.09	104	.260	.329	53	.184	9	12	18	2	2.9
● **FRED TRAUTMAN**	Trautman, Frederick Orlando b: 3/24/1892, Bucyrus, Ohio d: 2/15/64, Bucyrus, Ohio BR/TR, 6'1", 175 lbs. Deb: 4/27/15																									
1915	New-F	0	0	—	1	0	0	0	0	3	4	0	1	2	18.0	6.00	43	.364	.462	0	.000	-0	-1	-1	-0	0.0
● **JOHN TRAUTWEIN**	Trautwein, John Howard b: 8/7/62, Lafayette Hill, Pa. BR/TR, 6'3", 205 lbs. Deb: 4/7/88																									
1988	Bos-A	0	1	.000	9	0	0	0	0	16	26	2	9	8	20.3	9.00	46	.382	.462	0	—	0	-9	-9	0	-0.7
● **ALLAN TRAVERS**	Travers, Aloysius Joseph "Joe" b: 5/7/1892, Philadelphia, Pa. d: 4/19/68, Philadelphia, Pa. BR/TR, 6'1", 180 lbs. Deb: 5/18/12																									
1912	Det-A	0	1	.000	1	1	1	0	0	8	26	0	7	1	37.1	15.75	21	.605	.660	0	.000	-0	-11	-11	1	-0.8

YEAR TM/L	W	L	PCT	G	GS	CG	SH	SV	IP	H	HR	BB	SO	RAT	ERA	ERA+	OAV	OOB	BH	AVG	PB	PR	/A	PD	TPI
● **BILL TRAVERS** Travers, William Edward b: 10/27/52, Norwood, Mass. BL/TL, 6'6", 200 lbs. Deb: 5/19/74																									
1974 Mil-A	2	3	.400	23	1	0	0	0	53	59	6	30	31	15.3	4.92	73	.296	.391	0	—	0	-8	-8	0	-0.6
1975 Mil-A	6	11	.353	28	23	5	0	1	136^1	130	15	60	57	13.3	4.29	89	.251	.342	0	—	0	-8	-7	-1	-0.9
1976 Mil-A☆	15	16	.484	34	34	15	3	0	240	211	21	95	120	11.8	2.81	124	.237	.316	0	—	0	19	18	-1	2.3
1977 Mil-A	4	12	.250	19	19	2	1	0	121^2	140	13	57	49	15.1	5.25	77	.291	.374	0	—	0	-16	-16	0	-1.8
1978 Mil-A	12	11	.522	28	28	8	3	0	175^2	184	20	58	66	12.7	4.41	85	.268	.331	0	—	0	-13	-13	1	-1.4
1979 Mil-A	14	8	.636	30	27	9	2	0	187^1	196	33	45	74	11.7	3.89	107	.270	.315	0	—	0	7	6	-2	0.4
1980 Mil-A	12	6	.667	29	25	7	1	0	154^1	147	20	47	62	11.7	3.91	99	.249	.311	0	—	0	2	-1	-1	0.1
1981 Cal-A	0	1	.000	4	4	0	0	0	9^2	14	2	4	5	16.8	8.38	44	.333	.391	0	—	0	-5	-5	-0	-0.5
1983 Cal-A	0	3	.000	10	7	0	0	0	42^2	58	4	19	24	16.7	5.91	68	.331	.403	0	—	0	-9	-9	0	-0.5
Total 9	65	71	.478	205	168	46	10	1	1120^2	1139	134	415	488	12.8	4.10	93	.264	.335	0	—	0	-30	-34	-3	-2.9
● **HARRY TREKELL** Trekell, Harry Roy b: 11/18/1892, Buda, Ill. d: 11/4/65, Spokane, Wash. BR/TR, 6'1.5", 170 lbs. Deb: 8/16/13																									
1913 StL-N	0	1	.000	7	1	1	0	0	30	25	2	8	15	10.5	4.50	72	.221	.285	1	.111	-0	-4	-4	-0	-0.2
● **BILL TREMEL** Tremel, William Leonard "Mumbles" b: 7/4/29, Lilly, Pa. BR/TR, 5'11", 180 lbs. Deb: 6/12/54																									
1954 Chi-N	1	2	.333	33	0	0	0	4	51^1	45	3	28	21	12.8	4.21	100	.243	.343	2	.250	0	-1	-0	-1	-0.1
1955 Chi-N	3	0	1.000	23	0	0	0	2	38^2	33	2	18	13	11.9	3.72	110	.239	.327	2	.286	0	1	2	-1	0.1
1956 Chi-N	0	0	—	1	0	0	0	0	1	3	0	0	0	27.0	9.00	42	.600	.600	0	—	0	-1	-1	-0	0.0
Total 3	4	2	.667	57	0	0	0	6	91	81	5	46	34	12.6	4.05	102	.247	.340	4	.267	1	-0	1	-2	0.0
● **BOB TRICE** Trice, Robert Lee b: 8/28/26, Newton, Ga. d: 9/16/88, Weirton, W.Va. BR/TR, 6'3", 190 lbs. Deb: 9/13/53																									
1953 Phi-A	2	1	.667	3	3	1	0	0	23	25	4	6	4	12.1	5.48	78	.275	.320	1	.143	0	-4	-3	1	-0.2
1954 Phi-A	7	8	.467	19	18	8	1	0	119	146	14	48	22	14.7	5.60	70	.305	.369	12	.286	4	-25	-22	0	-2.0
1955 KC-A	0	0	—	4	0	0	0	0	10	14	4	6	2	18.0	9.00	46	.326	.408	2	.667	1	-6	-5	1	0.1
Total 3	9	9	.500	26	21	9	1	0	152	185	22	60	28	14.5	5.80	69	.302	.365	15	.288	5	-34	-31	2	-2.1
● **JOE TRIMBLE** Trimble, Joseph Gerard b: 10/12/30, Providence, R.I. BR/TR, 6'1", 190 lbs. Deb: 4/29/55																									
1955 Bos-A	0	0	—	2	0	0	0	0	2	0	0	3	1	13.5	0.00	—	.000	.375	0	—	0	1	1	0	0.0
1957 Pit-N	0	2	.000	5	4	0	0	0	19^2	23	7	13	9	16.9	8.24	46	.291	.398	1	.143	-0	-10	-10	0	-0.8
Total 2	0	2	.000	7	4	0	0	0	21^2	23	7	16	10	16.6	7.48	51	.274	.396	1	.143	-0	-9	-9	0	-0.8
● **KEN TRINKLE** Trinkle, Kenneth Wayne b: 12/15/19, Paoli, Ind. d: 5/10/76, Paoli, Ind. BR/TR, 6'1.5", 175 lbs. Deb: 4/25/43																									
1943 NY-N	1	5	.167	11	6	1	0	0	45^2	51	3	15	10	13.2	3.74	92	.276	.333	3	.250	1	-2	-2	1	0.0
1946 NY-N	7	14	.333	**48**	13	2	0	2	151	146	8	74	49	13.2	3.87	89	.253	.340	3	.079	-2	-8	-7	-0	-1.2
1947 NY-N	8	4	.667	**62**	0	0	0	10	93^2	100	3	48	37	14.3	3.75	109	.278	.364	3	.188	-0	3	3	2	0.6
1948 NY-N	4	5	.444	53	0	0	0	7	70^2	66	6	41	20	14.0	3.18	124	.244	.350	2	.250	0	6	6	1	1.0
1949 Phi-N	1	1	.500	42	0	0	0	2	74^1	79	3	30	14	13.6	4.00	99	.299	.377	0	.000	-0	0	-0	1	0.1
Total 5	21	29	.420	216	19	3	0	21	435^1	442	23	208	130	13.6	3.74	100	.267	.352	11	.138	-2	0	0	6	0.5
● **RICKY TRLICEK** Trlicek, Richard Alan b: 4/26/69, Houston, Tex. BR/TR, 6'2", 200 lbs. Deb: 4/8/92																									
1992 Tor-A	0	0	—	2	0	0	0	0	1^2	2	0	2	1	21.6	10.80	38	.286	.444	0	—	0	-1	-1	-0	-0.1
1993 LA-N	1	2	.333	41	0	0	0	1	64	59	3	21	41	11.5	4.08	94	.244	.309	1	.250	0	-0	-2	1	0.0
1994 Bos-A	1	1	.500	12	1	0	0	0	22^1	32	5	16	7	19.3	8.06	62	.330	.425	0	—	0	-8	-8	-0	-0.7
1996 NY-N	0	1	.000	5	0	0	0	0	5^1	3	0	3	3	11.8	3.38	119	.214	.389	0	—	0	0	0	0	0.1
1997 Bos-A	3	4	.429	18	0	0	0	0	23^1	26	2	18	10	17.4	4.63	100	.289	.413	0	—	0	-0	0	0	0.0
NY-N	0	0	—	9	0	0	0	0	9	10	2	5	4	15.0	8.00	50	.303	.395	0	—	0	-4	-4	0	0.0
Total 5	5	8	.385	87	1	0	0	1	125^2	132	12	65	66	14.4	5.23	80	.273	.364	1	.250	0	-13	-14	1	-0.7
● **RICH TROEDSON** Troedson, Richard La Monte b: 5/1/50, Palo Alto, Cal. BL/TL, 6'1", 170 lbs. Deb: 4/9/73																									
1973 SD-N	7	9	.438	50	18	2	0	1	152^1	167	12	59	81	13.4	4.25	82	.284	.351	7	.175	0	-10	-13	2	-1.1
1974 SD-N	1	1	.500	15	1	0	0	1	18^2	24	6	8	11	15.9	8.68	41	.300	.371	0	.000	-0	-10	-11	0	-1.1
Total 2	8	10	.444	65	19	2	0	2	171	191	18	67	92	13.7	4.74	73	.286	.353	7	.171	-0	-21	-24	2	-2.2
● **MIKE TROMBLEY** Trombley, Michael Scott b: 4/14/67, Springfield, Mass. BR/TR, 6'2", 208 lbs. Deb: 8/19/92																									
1992 Min-A	3	2	.600	10	7	0	0	0	46^1	43	5	17	38	11.8	3.30	123	.247	.318	0	—	0	3	4	0	0.3
1993 Min-A	6	6	.500	44	10	0	0	2	114^1	131	15	41	85	13.8	4.88	89	.290	.353	0	—	0	-7	-7	1	-0.5
1994 Min-A	2	0	1.000	24	0	0	0	0	48^1	56	10	18	32	14.3	6.33	77	.287	.356	0	—	0	-8	-8	-1	-0.3
1995 Min-A	4	8	.333	20	18	0	0	0	97^2	107	18	42	68	14.0	5.62	85	.273	.348	0	—	0	-10	-9	-1	-1.1
1996 Min-A	5	1	.833	43	0	0	0	6	68^2	61	2	25	57	11.9	3.01	170	.236	.315	0	—	0	15	16	-0	1.3
1997 Min-A	2	3	.400	67	0	0	0	1	82^1	77	7	31	74	12.0	4.37	106	.248	.320	0	.000	-0	2	3	-0	0.1
1998 Min-A	6	5	.545	77	1	0	0	1	96^2	90	16	41	89	12.7	3.63	129	.247	.332	0	—	0	11	11	-1	1.1
Total 7	28	25	.528	285	36	0	0	10	554^1	565	73	215	443	13.0	4.48	104	.263	.336	0	.000	-0	6	10	-2	0.9
● **HAL TROSKY** Trosky, Harold Arthur Jr. "Hoot" (b: Harold Arthur Troyavesky Jr.) b: 9/29/36, Cleveland, Ohio BR/TR, 6'3", 205 lbs. Deb: 9/25/58 F																									
1958 Chi-A	1	0	1.000	2	0	0	0	0	3	5	0	2	1	21.0	6.00	61	.385	.467	0	—	0	-1	-1	0	-0.2
● **BILL TROTTER** Trotter, William Felix b: 8/10/08, Cisne, Ill. d: 8/26/84, Arlington, Mass. BR/TR, 6'2", 195 lbs. Deb: 4/23/37																									
1937 StL-A	2	9	.182	34	12	3	0	1	122^1	150	14	50	37	15.2	5.81	83	.304	.376	1	.030	-3	-16	-13	-2	-1.4
1938 StL-A	0	1	.000	1	1	1	0	0	8	8	0	0	1	9.0	5.63	88	.242	.242	0	.000	-0	-1	-1	1	0.0
1939 StL-A	6	13	.316	41	13	4	0	0	156^2	205	16	54	61	15.2	5.34	91	.318	.376	4	.108	-1	-13	-8	1	-0.8
1940 StL-A	7	6	.538	36	4	1	0	2	98	117	5	31	29	13.7	3.77	122	.300	.353	1	.045	-2	7	**9**	1	0.9
1941 StL-A	4	2	.667	29	0	0	0	0	49^2	68	2	19	17	16.1	5.98	72	.332	.394	0	.000	-1	-10	-9	1	-1.0
1942 StL-A	0	1	.000	3	0	0	0	0	2	5	0	2	0	31.5	18.00	21	.385	.467	0	—	0	-3	-3	0	-1.2
Was-A	3	1	.750	17	0	0	0	0	40^2	52	4	14	13	14.6	5.75	63	.304	.357	0	.000	-0	-9	-9	0	-0.8
Yr	3	2	.600	20	0	0	0	0	42^2	57	4	16	13	15.4	6.33	58	.310	.365	0	.000	-0	-13	-13	1	-2.0
1944 StL-N	0	1	.000	2	1	0	0	0	6	14	5	4	0	27.0	13.50	26	.467	.529	0	.000	-0	-7	-7	0	-0.8
Total 7	22	34	.393	163	31	9	0	3	483^1	619	46	174	158	15.0	5.40	85	.313	.373	6	.055	-7	-52	-42	2	-5.1
● **DIZZY TROUT** Trout, Paul Howard b: 6/29/15, Sandcut, Ind. d: 2/28/72, Harvey, Ill. BR/TR, 6'2.5", 195 lbs. Deb: 4/25/39 F																									
1939 Det-A	9	10	.474	33	22	6	0	2	162	168	5	74	72	13.7	3.61	135	.270	.351	12	.211	-0	18	23	-1	2.2
1940 *Det-A	3	7	.300	33	10	1	0	2	100^2	125	4	54	64	16.3	4.47	106	.307	.392	4	.129	-2	-1	3	2	0.3
1941 Det-A	9	9	.500	37	18	6	1	2	151^2	144	7	84	88	13.6	3.74	122	.252	.350	9	.180	0	7	14	1	1.6
1942 Det-A	12	18	.400	35	29	13	1	0	223	214	15	89	91	12.4	3.43	115	.249	.322	16	.213	2	6	13	4	2.3
1943 Det-A	**20**	12	.625	44	30	18	**5**	6	246^2	204	6	101	111	11.1	2.48	142	.227	.305	20	.220	2	22	29	4	4.7
1944 Det-A☆	27	14	.659	49	40	**33**	**7**	0	**352^1**	314	9	83	144	10.2	**2.12**	**168**	.237	.284	36	.271	12	**51**	**57**	7	**9.1**
1945 *Det-A	18	15	.545	41	31	18	4	2	246^1	252	8	79	97	12.1	3.14	112	.267	.324	25	.245	4	6	10	3	2.1
1946 Det-A	17	13	.567	38	32	23	5	3	276^1	244	11	97	151	11.2	2.34	156	.238	.306	20	.194	3	36	40	4	5.3
1947 Det-A☆	10	11	.476	32	26	9	2	2	186^1	186	6	65	74	12.3	3.48	108	.261	.325	11	.162	3	5	6	3	1.4
1948 Det-A	10	14	.417	32	23	11	2	2	183^2	193	6	73	91	13.1	3.43	127	.269	.338	15	.217	2	18	19	2	2.6
1949 Det-A	3	6	.333	33	0	0	0	3	59^1	68	2	21	19	13.5	4.40	95	.292	.350	2	.143	0	-1	-2	2	-0.1
1950 Det-A	13	5	.722	34	20	11	1	4	184^2	190	13	64	88	12.6	3.75	125	.267	.332	12	.190	1	17	19	3	2.1
1951 Det-A	9	14	.391	42	22	7	0	5	191^2	172	13	75	89	11.6	4.04	103	.240	.312	14	.269	5	2	3	4	1.2
1952 Det-A	1	5	.167	10	2	0	0	1	27	30	4	19	20	16.3	5.33	71	.286	.395	3	.333	1	-5	-5	1	-0.8
Bos-A	9	8	.529	26	17	2	0	1	133^2	133	3	68	57	13.7	3.64	108	.263	.354	6	.136	-1	1	5	1	0.5
Yr	10	13	.435	36	19	2	0	2	160^2	163	7	87	77	14.2	3.92	100	.267	.361	9	.170	-1	-4	-0	2	-0.3
1957 Bal-A	0	0	—	2	0	0	0	0	0^1	4	0	0	0	108.0	81.00	4	.800	.800	0	—	0	-3	-3	0	0.0
Total 15	170	161	.514	521	322	158	28	35	2725^2	2641	112	1046	1256	12.3	3.23	124	.255	.325	205	.213	31	177	232	38	34.5
● **STEVE TROUT** Trout, Steven Russell b: 7/30/57, Detroit, Mich. BL/TL, 6'4", 195 lbs. Deb: 7/1/78 F																									
1978 Chi-A	3	0	1.000	4	3	1	0	0	22^1	19	0	11	11	12.1	4.03	94	.229	.319	0	—	0	-1	-1	-0	-0.1
1979 Chi-A	11	8	.579	34	18	6	2	4	155	165	10	59	76	13.3	3.89	109	.273	.343	0	—	0	6	6	2	0.9

YEAR	TM/L	W	L	PCT	G	GS	CG	SH	SV	IP	H	HR	BB	SO	RAT	ERA	ERA+	OAV	OOB	BH	AVG	PB	PR	/A	PD	TPI
1980	Chi-A	9	16	.360	32	30	7	2	0	199^2	229	14	49	89	12.9	3.70	109	.290	.338	0	—	0	8	7	3	1.1
1981	Chi-A	8	7	.533	20	18	3	0	0	124^2	122	7	38	54	11.8	3.47	103	.261	.322	0	—	0	3	2	0	0.3
1982	Chi-A	6	9	.400	25	19	2	0	0	120^1	130	9	50	62	13.6	4.26	95	.273	.344	0	—	0	-3	-3	0	-0.3
1983	Chi-N	10	14	.417	34	32	1	0	0	180	217	13	59	80	13.9	4.65	82	.305	.360	12	.194	1	-20	-17	2	-1.8
1984	*Chi-N	13	7	.650	32	31	6	2	0	190	205	7	59	81	12.6	3.41	115	.285	.341	8	.131	-1	4	10	4	1.3
1985	Chi-N	9	7	.563	24	24	3	1	0	140^2	142	8	63	44	13.2	3.39	118	.270	.350	5	.109	-2	3	9	2	1.1
1986	Chi-N	5	7	.417	37	25	0	0	0	161	184	6	78	69	14.7	4.75	85	.298	.378	9	.209	1	-19	-13	1	-0.7
1987	Chi-N	6	3	.667	11	11	3	2	0	75	72	3	27	32	12.0	3.00	143	.260	.328	4	.154	-1	9	11	0	1.2
	NY-A	0	4	.000	14	9	0	0	0	46^1	51	4	37	27	17.3	6.60	66	.274	.397	0	—	0	-11	-11	0	-0.7
1988	Sea-A	4	7	.364	15	13	0	0	0	56^1	86	6	31	14	19.5	7.83	53	.361	.445	0	—	0	-24	-23	0	-3.8
1989	Sea-A	4	3	.571	19	3	0	0	0	30	43	3	17	17	18.0	6.60	61	.333	.411	0	—	0	-9	-9	0	-1.9
Total	12	88	92	.489	301	236	32	9	4	1501^1	1665	90	578	656	13.6	4.18	96	.286	.354	38	.160	-2	-55	-30	14	-3.4

● BOB TROWBRIDGE

Trowbridge, Robert b: 6/27/30, Hudson, N.Y. d: 4/3/80, Hudson, N.Y. BR/TR, 6'1", 190 lbs. Deb: 4/22/56

YEAR	TM/L	W	L	PCT	G	GS	CG	SH	SV	IP	H	HR	BB	SO	RAT	ERA	ERA+	OAV	OOB	BH	AVG	PB	PR	/A	PD	TPI
1956	Mil-N	3	2	.600	19	4	1	0	0	50^2	38	4	34	40	13.1	2.66	130	.210	.341	0	.000	-1	6	4	0	0.4
1957	*Mil-N	7	5	.583	32	16	3	1	1	126	118	9	52	75	12.2	3.64	96	.248	.323	4	.103	-2	3	-2	-1	-0.4
1958	Mil-N	1	3	.250	27	4	0	0	0	55	53	4	26	31	13.1	3.93	90	.252	.338	1	.111	-1	0	-2	1	-0.3
1959	Mil-N	1	0	1.000	16	0	0	0	1	30^1	45	2	10	22	16.3	5.93	60	.344	.390	0	.000	-0	-7	-8	-0	-0.4
1960	KC-A	1	3	.250	22	1	0	0	2	68^1	70	6	34	33	13.8	4.61	86	.281	.370	1	.056	-1	-6	-5	0	-0.4
Total	5	13	13	.500	116	25	4	1	5	330^1	324	25	156	201	13.2	3.95	91	.260	.344	6	.078	-5	-3	-13	-1	-1.1

● BUN TROY

Troy, Robert b: 8/27/1888, Bad Wurzach, Ger. d: 10/7/18, Petit Maujouym, France BR/TR, 6'4", 195 lbs. Deb: 9/15/12

YEAR	TM/L	W	L	PCT	G	GS	CG	SH	SV	IP	H	HR	BB	SO	RAT	ERA	ERA+	OAV	OOB	BH	AVG	PB	PR	/A	PD	TPI
1912	Det-A	0	1	.000	1	1	0	0	0	6^2	9	0	3	1	17.6	5.40	60	.346	.433	0	.000	-0	-2	-2	-0	-0.2

● VIRGIL TRUCKS

Trucks, Virgil Oliver "Fire" b: 4/26/17, Birmingham, Ala. BR/TR, 5'11", 198 lbs. Deb: 9/27/41 C

YEAR	TM/L	W	L	PCT	G	GS	CG	SH	SV	IP	H	HR	BB	SO	RAT	ERA	ERA+	OAV	OOB	BH	AVG	PB	PR	/A	PD	TPI
1941	Det-A	0	0	—	1	0	0	0	0	2	4	0	0	3	18.0	9.00	50	.500	.500	0	—	0	-1	-1	0	0.0
1942	Det-A	14	8	.636	28	20	8	2	0	167^2	147	3	74	91	12.0	2.74	144	.231	.314	8	.123	-4	17	23	-2	2.3
1943	Det-A	16	10	.615	33	25	10	2	2	202^2	170	11	52	118	9.9	2.84	124	.225	.276	13	.181	-2	10	15	2	1.6
1945	*Det-A	0	0	—	1	1	0	0	0	5^1	3	0	2	3	8.4	1.69	208	.176	.263	0	.000	-0	1	1	0	0.0
1946	Det-A	14	9	.609	32	29	15	2	0	236^2	217	23	75	161	11.2	3.23	113	.241	.302	17	.179	-1	7	11	-1	0.8
1947	Det-A	10	12	.455	36	26	8	2	2	180^2	186	14	79	108	13.3	4.53	83	.263	.339	19	.271	2	-17	-15	-1	-1.6
1948	Det-A	14	13	.519	43	26	7	0	2	211^2	190	14	85	123	11.8	3.78	115	.240	.315	13	.165	-3	12	14	-1	1.1
1949	Det-A★	19	11	.633	41	32	17	**6**	4	275	209	16	124	**153**	11.0	2.81	148	.211	.301	12	.120	-6	42	41	-3	3.3
1950	Det-A	3	1	.750	7	7	2	1	0	48^1	45	6	21	25	12.5	3.54	133	.243	.324	3	.150	-1	6	6	1	0.4
1951	Det-A	13	8	.619	37	18	6	1	1	153^2	153	9	75	89	13.6	4.33	96	.262	.350	13	.236	-0	-4	-3	2	-0.2
1952	Det-A	5	19	.208	35	29	8	3	1	197	190	12	82	129	12.7	3.97	96	.251	.330	12	.188	-0	-7	-4	2	-0.2
1953	StL-A	5	4	.556	16	12	4	2	2	88	83	4	32	47	12.2	3.07	137	.249	.322	4	.160	-1	9	11	-1	0.9
	Chi-A	15	6	.714	24	21	13	3	1	176^1	151	14	67	102	11.3	2.86	141	.232	.306	15	.238	2	22	23	1	2.9
	Yr	20	10	.667	40	33	17	5	3	264^1	234	18	99	149	11.4	2.93	139	.237	.308	19	.216	1	31	34	0	3.8
1954	Chi-A★	19	12	.613	40	33	16	**5**	3	264^2	224	13	95	152	10.9	2.79	134	.228	.297	17	.183	-1	27	28	1	3.2
1955	Chi-A	13	8	.619	32	26	7	3	0	175	176	19	61	91	12.3	3.96	100	.260	.323	8	.125	-3	0	-0	0	0.3
1956	Det-A	6	5	.545	22	16	3	1	1	120	104	15	63	43	13.0	3.83	108	.239	.343	11	.244	1	4	4	1	0.2
1957	KC-A	9	7	.563	48	7	0	0	7	116	106	12	62	55	13.2	3.03	131	.248	.346	4	.143	-1	10	12	0	1.6
1958	KC-A	0	1	.000	16	0	0	0	3	22	18	2	15	15	13.5	2.05	191	.222	.344	0	.000	-0	4	5	0	0.3
	NY-A	2	1	.667	25	0	0	0	1	39^2	40	1	24	26	15.0	4.54	78	.265	.373	2	.250	0	-3	-4	-0	-0.4
	Yr	2	2	.500	41	0	0	0	4	61^2	58	3	39	41	14.4	3.65	100	.249	.361	2	.222	0	1	0	-0	-0.1
Total	17	177	135	.567	517	328	124	33	30	2682^1	2416	188	1088	1534	11.9	3.39	117	.240	.317	171	.180	-19	141	167	-5	15.9

● MIKE TRUJILLO

Trujillo, Michael Andrew b: 1/12/60, Denver, Colo. BR/TR, 6'1", 180 lbs. Deb: 4/14/85

YEAR	TM/L	W	L	PCT	G	GS	CG	SH	SV	IP	H	HR	BB	SO	RAT	ERA	ERA+	OAV	OOB	BH	AVG	PB	PR	/A	PD	TPI
1985	Bos-A	4	4	.500	27	7	1	0	1	84	112	7	23	19	14.8	4.82	89	.320	.367		—	0	-6	-5	2	-0.6
1986	Bos-A	0	0	—	3	0	0	0	0	5^2	7	0	6	4	20.6	9.53	44	.304	.448	0	—	0	-3	-3	1	0.0
	Sea-A	3	2	.600	11	4	1	1	1	41^1	32	5	15	19	10.2	2.40	177	.215	.287	0	—	0	8	8	-0	0.9
	Yr	3	2	.600	14	4	1	1	1	47	39	5	21	23	11.5	3.26	130	.227	.311	0	—	0	5	5	0	0.9
1987	Sea-A	4	4	.500	28	7	0	0	1	65^2	70	12	26	36	13.4	6.17	76	.277	.349	0	—	0	-12	-11	-1	-1.6
1988	Det-A	0	0	—	6	0	0	0	0	12^1	11	2	5	5	11.7	5.11	75	.234	.308	0	—	0	-2	-2	0	0.3
1989	Det-A	1	2	.333	8	4	1	0	0	25^2	35	3	13	13	16.8	5.96	64	.333	.407	0	—	0	-6	-6	0	-0.5
Total	5	12	12	.500	83	22	3	1	3	234^2	267	29	88	96	13.8	5.02	86	.288	.353	0	—	0	-21	-19	2	-1.5

● ED TRUMBULL

Trumbull, Edward J. (b: Edward J. Trembly) b: 11/3/1860, Chicopee, Mass. d: 1/14/37, Kingston, Pa. Deb: 5/10/1884 ♦

YEAR	TM/L	W	L	PCT	G	GS	CG	SH	SV	IP	H	HR	BB	SO	RAT	ERA	ERA+	OAV	OOB	BH	AVG	PB	PR	/A	PD	TPI
1884	Was-a	1	9	.100	10	10	10	0	0	84	108	4	31	43	15.0	4.71	64	.295	.352	10	.116	-2	-14	-16	-1	-1.7

● GEORGE TSAMIS

Tsamis, George Alex b: 6/14/67, Campbell, Cal. BR/TL, 6'2", 190 lbs. Deb: 4/26/93

YEAR	TM/L	W	L	PCT	G	GS	CG	SH	SV	IP	H	HR	BB	SO	RAT	ERA	ERA+	OAV	OOB	BH	AVG	PB	PR	/A	PD	TPI
1993	Min-A	1	2	.333	41	0	0	0	1	68^1	86	9	27	30	15.3	6.19	70	.317	.385	0	—	0	-14	-14	1	-0.5

● JOHN TSITOURIS

Tsitouris, John Philip b: 5/4/36, Monroe, N.C. BR/TR, 6', 175 lbs. Deb: 6/13/57

YEAR	TM/L	W	L	PCT	G	GS	CG	SH	SV	IP	H	HR	BB	SO	RAT	ERA	ERA+	OAV	OOB	BH	AVG	PB	PR	/A	PD	TPI
1957	Det-A	1	0	1.000	2	0	0	0	0	3^1	8	0	2	2	27.0	8.10	48	.500	.556	0	.000	-0	-2	-2	0	-0.4
1958	KC-A	0	0	—	1	1	0	0	0	3	2	0	2	1	12.0	3.00	130	.182	.308	0	.000	0	0	0	0	0.0
1959	KC-A	4	3	.571	24	10	0	0	0	83^1	90	3	35	50	13.8	4.97	81	.271	.346	3	.150	-1	-10	-9	-1	-0.8
1960	KC-A	0	2	.000	14	2	0	0	0	33	38	3	21	12	16.8	6.55	61	.297	.427	0	.000	-1	-10	-9	0	-0.6
1962	Cin-N	1	0	1.000	4	2	1	1	0	21^1	13	0	7	7	9.7	0.84	477	.181	.280	0	.000	-1	7	8	-0	0.2
1963	Cin-N	12	8	.600	30	21	8	3	0	191	167	20	38	113	10.2	3.16	106	.232	.281	5	.081	-3	3	4	-3	-0.3
1964	Cin-N	9	13	.409	37	24	6	1	2	175^1	178	20	75	146	13.2	3.80	95	.263	.340	11	.190	2	-5	-4	-1	-0.3
1965	Cin-N	6	9	.400	31	20	3	0	1	131	134	18	65	91	14.3	4.95	76	.265	.359	3	.070	-2	-20	-17	-1	-2.2
1966	Cin-N	0	0	—	1	0	0	0	0	1	3	0	1	0	36.0	18.00	22	.750	.800	0	—	0	-2	-2	0	0.0
1967	Cin-N	1	0	1.000	2	1	0	0	0	8	4	1	6	4	11.3	3.38	111	.154	.313	0	—	0	0	0	0	0.1
1968	Cin-N	0	3	.000	3	3	0	0	0	12^2	16	6	8	6	17.8	7.11	44	.302	.403	0	.000	0	-6	-6	0	-1.1
Total	11	34	38	.472	149	84	18	5	3	663	653	71	260	432	12.9	4.13	88	.257	.335	22	.111	-6	-44	-36	-5	-5.4

● TOMMY TUCKER

Tucker, Thomas Joseph "Foghorn" b: 10/28/1863, Holyoke, Mass. d: 10/22/35, Montague, Mass. BB/TR, 5'11", 165 lbs. Deb: 4/16/1887 ♦

YEAR	TM/L	W	L	PCT	G	GS	CG	SH	SV	IP	H	HR	BB	SO	RAT	ERA	ERA+	OAV	OOB	BH	AVG	PB	PR	/A	PD	TPI
1888	Bal-a	0	0	—	1	0	0	0	0	2^1	4	0	0	2	15.4	3.86	77	.364	.364	149	.287	0	-0	-0	-0	0.0
1891	Bos-N	0	0	—	1	0	0	0	0	1	3	0	0	0	27.0	9.00	41	.500	.500	148	.270	0	-1	-1	-0	0.0
Total	2	0	0	—	2	0	0	0	0	3^1	7	0	0	2	18.9	5.40	59	.412	.412	1882	.290	0	-1	-1	-0	0.0

● TOM TUCKEY

Tuckey, Thomas H. "Tabasco Tom" b: 10/7/1883, Birmingham, England d: 10/17/50, New York, N.Y. TL, 6'3", Deb: 8/11/08

YEAR	TM/L	W	L	PCT	G	GS	CG	SH	SV	IP	H	HR	BB	SO	RAT	ERA	ERA+	OAV	OOB	BH	AVG	PB	PR	/A	PD	TPI
1908	Bos-N	3	3	.500	8	8	3	1	0	72	60	2	20	26	10.5	2.50	96	.265	.336	1	.050	-2	-1	-1	0	-0.2
1909	Bos-N	0	9	.000	17	10	4	0	0	90^2	104	1	22	16	12.8	4.27	66	.295	.342	4	.138	-1	-17	-15	1	-1.4
Total	2	3	12	.200	25	18	7	1	0	162^2	164	3	42	42	11.8	3.49	76	.284	.340	5	.102	-3	-18	-15	1	-1.6

● JOHN TUDOR

Tudor, John Thomas b: 2/2/54, Schenectady, N.Y. BL/TL, 6', 185 lbs. Deb: 8/16/79

YEAR	TM/L	W	L	PCT	G	GS	CG	SH	SV	IP	H	HR	BB	SO	RAT	ERA	ERA+	OAV	OOB	BH	AVG	PB	PR	/A	PD	TPI
1979	Bos-A	1	2	.333	6	6	1	0	0	28	39	2	9	11	15.4	6.43	69	.345	.393	0	—	0	-7	-6	1	-0.5
1980	Bos-A	8	5	.615	16	13	5	0	0	92^1	81	4	31	45	11.2	3.02	140	.238	.307	0	—	0	10	12	2	1.4
1981	Bos-A	4	3	.571	18	11	2	0	1	78^2	74	11	28	44	12.0	4.58	85	.252	.323	0	—	0	-8	-6	1	-0.8
1982	Bos-A	13	10	.565	32	30	6	1	0	195^2	215	20	59	146	13.0	3.63	119	.280	.338	0	—	0	10	15	2	1.4
1983	Bos-A	13	12	.520	34	34	7	2	0	242	236	32	81	136	11.9	4.09	106	.255	.317	0	—	0	-1	7	-1	0.2
1984	Pit-N	12	11	.522	32	32	6	1	0	212	200	19	56	117	10.9	3.27	110	.248	.297	16	.211	2	8	8	-1	1.0
1985	*StL-N	21	8	.724	36	36	14	**10**	0	275	209	14	49	169	**8.6**	1.93	183	.209	**.249**	13	.138	1	51	49	1	5.5
1986	StL-N	13	7	.650	30	30	3	0	0	219	197	22	53	107	10.3	2.92	125	.244	.291	11	.153	-0	19	18	1	1.6
1987	*StL-N	10	2	.833	16	16	0	0	0	96	100	11	32	54	12.5	3.84	108	.272	.333	7	.200	1	3	3	1	0.6
1988	StL-N	6	5	.545	21	21	4	1	0	145^1	131	5	31	55	10.1	2.29	152	.247	.290	5	.109	-1	19	19	1	1.5
	*LA-N	4	3	.571	9	9	1	0	0	52^1	58	5	10	32	11.7	2.41	138	.284	.318	0	.000	-1	6	5	0	0.6
	Yr	10	8	.556	30	30	5	1	0	197^2	189	10	41	87	10.5	2.32	148	.255	.294	5	.085	-2	25	24	1	2.1
1989	LA-N	0	0	—	6	3	0	0	0	14^1	17	1	6	9	14.4	3.14	109	.309	.377	0	.000	-0	1	0	0	0.0

YEAR TM/L	W	L	PCT	G	GS	CG	SH	SV	IP	H	HR	BB	SO	RAT	ERA	ERA+	OAV	OOB	BH	AVG	PB	PR	/A	PD	TPI
1990 StL-N	12	4	.750	25	22	1	1	0	146^1	120	10	30	63	9.3	2.40	159	.225	.269	7	.152	0	23	23	2	2.7
Total 12	117	72	.619	281	263	50	16	1	1797	1677	156	475	988	10.9	3.12	123	.248	.301	59	.154	3	132	146	9	15.2
● OSCAR TUERO Tuero, Oscar (Monzon) (b: Oscar Tuero Monzon) b: 12/17/1898, Canada d: 10/21/60, Houston, Tex. BR/TR, 5'8.5", 158 lbs. Deb: 5/30/18																									
1918 StL-N	1	2	.333	11	3	2	0	0	44^1	32	0	10	13	9.1	1.02	267	.208	.269	3	.250	0	9	8	-1	0.5
1919 StL-N	5	7	.417	**45**	16	4	0	**4**	154^2	137	4	42	45	11.0	3.20	87	.242	.306	8	.205	1	-5	-7	-0	-0.5
1920 StL-N	0	0	—	2	0	0	0	0	0^2	5	0	1	0	81.0	54.00	6	.833	.857	0	—	0	-4	-4	-0	0.0
Total 3	6	9	.400	58	19	6	0	4	199^2	174	4	53	58	10.8	2.88	96	.240	.303	11	.216	1	-0	-2	-1	0.0
● BOB TUFTS Tufts, Robert Malcolm b: 11/2/55, Medford, Mass. BL/TL, 6'5", 215 lbs. Deb: 8/10/81																									
1981 SF-N	0	0	—	11	0	0	0	0	15^1	20	1	6	12	15.8	3.52	97	.308	.375	0	.000	-0	-0	-0	1	0.1
1982 KC-A	2	0	1.000	10	0	0	0	2	20	24	3	3	13	12.1	4.50	91	.293	.318	0	—	0	-1	-1	-1	-0.2
1983 KC-A	0	0	—	6	0	0	0	0	6^2	16	1	5	3	29.7	8.10	50	.444	.524	0	—	0	-3	-3	0	0.0
Total 3	2	0	1.000	27	0	0	0	2	42	60	5	14	28	16.3	4.71	81	.328	.382	0	.000	-0	-4	-4	0	-0.1
● LEE TUNNELL Tunnell, Byron Lee b: 10/30/60, Tyler, Tex. BR/TR, 6'1", 180 lbs. Deb: 9/4/82																									
1982 Pit-N	1	1	.500	5	3	0	0	0	18^1	17	1	5	4	11.8	3.93	94	.254	.324	0	.000	-0	-1	-0	0	-0.1
1983 Pit-N	11	6	.647	35	25	5	3	0	177^2	167	15	58	95	11.5	3.65	102	.252	.314	7	.121	-1	-0	1	2	0.2
1984 Pit-N	1	7	.125	26	6	0	0	1	68^1	81	6	40	51	15.9	5.27	68	.298	.388	1	.083	-1	-13	-13	1	-1.3
1985 Pit-N	4	10	.286	24	23	0	0	0	132^1	126	11	57	74	12.5	4.01	89	.251	.329	4	.085	-2	-6	-6	1	-0.8
1987 *StL-N	4	4	.500	32	9	0	0	0	74^1	90	5	34	49	15.1	4.84	86	.307	.381	4	.235	0	-6	-6	0	-0.5
1989 Min-A	1	0	1.000	10	0	0	0	0	12	18	1	6	7	18.0	6.00	69	.340	.407	0	—	0	-3	-2	-0	-0.6
Total 6	22	28	.440	132	66	5	3	1	483	499	39	200	280	13.1	4.23	88	.270	.343	16	.116	-4	-29	-27	4	-3.1
● GEORGE TURBEVILLE Turbeville, George Elkins b: 8/24/14, Turbeville, S.C. d: 10/5/83, Salisbury, N.C. BR/TL, 6'1", 175 lbs. Deb: 7/20/35																									
1935 Phi-A	0	3	.000	19	6	2	0	0	63^2	74	2	69	20	20.2	7.63	60	.312	.467	2	.105	-2	-22	-22	-1	-1.1
1936 Phi-A	2	5	.286	12	6	2	0	0	43^2	42	6	32	10	16.5	6.39	80	.258	.398	2	.143	-1	-7	-6	-0	-0.8
1937 Phi-A	0	4	.000	31	3	0	0	0	77^1	80	2	56	17	15.8	4.77	99	.266	.381	6	.231	0	-1	-1	-1	-0.1
Total 3	2	12	.143	62	15	4	0	0	184^2	196	10	157	47	17.5	6.14	77	.280	.416	10	.169	-2	-30	-29	-2	-2.0
● LUCAS TURK Turk, Lucas Newton "Harlem" or "Chief" b: 5/2/1898, Homer, Ga. d: 1/11/94, Homer, Ga. BR/TR, 6', 165 lbs. Deb: 6/7/22																									
1922 Was-A	0	0	—	5	0	0	0	0	11^2	16	0	5	1	16.2	6.94	56	.340	.404	1	.250	0	-4	-4	-1	-0.1
● BOB TURLEY Turley, Robert Lee "Bullet Bob" b: 9/19/30, Troy, Ill. BR/TR, 6'2", 215 lbs. Deb: 9/29/51 C																									
1951 StL-A	0	1	.000	1	1	0	0	0	7^1	11	0	3	5	17.2	7.36	60	.355	.412	0	.000	-0	-3	-2	0	-0.3
1953 StL-A	2	6	.250	10	7	3	1	0	60^1	39	4	44	61	12.7	3.28	128	.184	.329	5	.278	1	5	6	-1	0.9
1954 Bal-A☆	14	15	.483	35	35	14	0	0	247^1	178	7	181	**185**	13.3	3.46	104	**.203**	.343	11	.136	-3	7	3	-1	0.1
1955 *NY-A☆	17	13	.567	36	34	13	6	1	246^2	168	16	177	210	12.8	3.06	122	**.193**	.333	11	.134	-0	25	19	-2	1.9
1956 *NY-A	8	4	.667	27	21	5	1	1	132	138	13	103	91	16.7	5.05	77	.273	.400	8	.174	-0	-13	-17	-1	-1.5
1957 *NY-A	13	6	.684	32	23	9	4	3	176^1	120	17	85	152	10.9	2.71	133	**.194**	.300	5	.088	-2	21	17	-0	1.6
1958 *NY-A★	**21**	7	**.750**	33	31	**19**	6	1	245^1	178	24	128	168	11.5	2.97	119	**.206**	.313	12	.136	-1	22	15	-2	1.4
1959 NY-A	8	11	.421	33	22	7	3	0	154^1	141	15	83	111	13.2	4.32	84	.245	.343	4	.087	-2	-8	-11	-1	-1.5
1960 *NY-A	9	3	.750	34	24	4	1	5	173^1	138	14	87	87	11.9	3.27	110	.222	.322	4	.073	-4	12	6	-1	-0.1
1961 NY-A	3	5	.375	15	12	1	0	0	72	74	11	51	48	16.1	5.75	65	.269	.391	2	.095	-1	-14	-16	-1	-1.7
1962 NY-A	3	3	.500	24	8	0	0	1	69	68	8	47	42	15.5	4.57	82	.263	.384	0	.000	-1	-5	-6	1	-0.6
1963 LA-A	2	7	.222	19	12	3	2	0	87^1	71	5	51	70	12.8	3.30	104	.222	.332	4	.160	1	3	1	-0	0.2
Bos-A	1	4	.200	11	7	0	0	0	41^1	42	6	28	35	15.5	6.10	62	.256	.368	3	.214	0	-11	-11	-0	-1.2
Yr	3	11	.214	30	19	3	2	0	128^2	113	11	79	105	13.5	4.20	84	.232	.340	7	.179	1	-8	-9	-1	-1.0
Total 12	101	85	.543	310	237	78	24	12	1712^2	1366	140	1068	1265	13.1	3.64	101	.220	.340	69	.126	-12	41	4	-9	-0.8
● TUCK TURNER Turner, George A. b: 2/13/1873, W.New Brighton, N.Y. d: 7/16/45, Staten Island, N.Y. BB/TL, 5'6.5", 155 lbs. Deb: 8/18/1893 ♦																									
1894 Phi-N	0	0	—	1	0	0	0	0	6	9	1	2	3	18.0	7.50	68	.346	.414	141	.416	1	-1	-2	-0	0.0
● JIM TURNER Turner, James Riley "Milkman Jim" b: 8/6/03, Antioch, Tenn. d: 11/29/98, Nashville, Tenn. BL/TR, 6', 185 lbs. Deb: 4/30/37 C																									
1937 Bos-N	20	11	.645	33	30	**24**	**5**	1	256^2	228	13	52	69	**9.8**	**2.38**	**150**	.235	**.274**	24	.250	4	**44**	34	-0	**4.5**
1938 Bos-N☆	14	18	.438	35	34	22	3	0	268	267	21	54	71	10.9	3.46	99	.259	.299	22	.229	4	10	-1	4	0.7
1939 Bos-N	4	11	.267	25	22	9	0	0	157^2	181	10	51	50	13.5	4.28	86	.293	.351	13	.236	2	-6	-10	1	-0.5
1940 *Cin-N	14	7	.667	24	23	11	0	0	187	187	9	32	53	10.5	2.89	131	.264	.296	18	.240	3	20	19	-1	2.2
1941 Cin-N	6	4	.600	23	10	3	0	0	113	120	5	24	34	11.5	3.11	116	.277	.317	6	.146	-1	7	6	2	0.6
1942 Cin-N	0	0	—	3	0	0	0	0	3^1	5	1	3	0	21.6	10.80	30	.333	.444	0	.000	-0	-3	-3	0	0.0
*NY-A	1	1	.500	5	0	0	0	1	7	4	0	1	2	6.4	1.29	268	.167	.200	0	.000	-0	2	2	0	0.6
1943 NY-A	3	0	1.000	18	0	0	0	1	43^1	44	1	13	15	11.8	3.53	91	.260	.313	1	.077	-1	-1	-2	-0	-0.3
1944 NY-A	4	4	.500	35	0	0	0	7	41^2	42	3	22	13	13.8	3.46	101	.264	.354	2	.200	0	-0	0	-1	0.0
1945 NY-A	3	4	.429	30	0	0	0	**10**	54^1	45	4	31	22	12.6	3.64	95	.225	.329	1	.091	-1	-2	-1	1	-0.2
Total 9	69	60	.535	231	119	69	8	20	1132	1123	67	283	329	11.3	3.22	111	.260	.307	87	.218	12	70	45	6	7.6
● KEN TURNER Turner, Kenneth Charles b: 8/17/43, Framingham, Mass. BR/TL, 6'2", 190 lbs. Deb: 6/11/67																									
1967 Cal-A	1	2	.333	13	1	0	0	0	17^1	16	4	4	6	10.9	4.15	76	.239	.292	0	.000	-0	-2	-2	0	-0.3
● TED TURNER Turner, Theodore Holhot b: 5/4/1892, Lawrenceburg, Ky. d: 2/4/58, Lexington, Ky. BR/TR, 6', 180 lbs. Deb: 4/20/20																									
1920 Chi-N	0	0	—	1	0	0	0	0	1^1	2	0	1	0	20.3	13.50	24	.400	.500	0	.000	-0	-2	-2	-0	0.0
● TINK TURNER Turner, Thomas Lovatt b: 2/20/1890, Swarthmore, Pa. d: 2/25/62, Philadelphia, Pa. BR/TR, 6'1", 190 lbs. Deb: 9/24/15																									
1915 Phi-A	0	1	.000	1	1	0	0	0	2	5	1	3	0	36.0	22.50	13	.500	.615	0	—	0	-4	-4	0	-1.1
● MATT TURNER Turner, William Matthew b: 2/18/67, Lexington, Ky. BR/TR, 6'5", 215 lbs. Deb: 4/23/93																									
1993 Fla-N	4	5	.444	55	0	0	0	0	68	55	7	26	59	10.9	2.91	148	.227	.305	0	.000	-0	9	11	0	1.3
1994 Cle-A	1	0	1.000	9	0	0	0	1	12^2	13	0	7	5	16.3	2.13	221	.241	.359	0	—	0	4	4	-1	0.2
Total 2	5	5	.500	64	0	0	0	1	80^2	68	7	33	64	11.7	2.79	157	.230	.315	0	.000	-0	12	14	-0	1.5
● ELMER TUTWILER Tutwiler, Elmer Strange b: 11/19/05, Carbon Hill, Ala. d: 5/3/76, Pensacola, Fla. BR/TR, 5'11", 158 lbs. Deb: 8/20/28																									
1928 Pit-N	0	0	—	2	0	0	0	0	3^2	4	0	0	1	9.8	4.91	83	.267	.267	0	.000	-0	-0	-0	-0	0.0
● TWINK TWINING Twining, Howard Earle "Doc" b: 5/30/1894, Horsham, Pa. d: 6/14/73, Lansdale, Pa. BR/TR, 6', 168 lbs. Deb: 7/9/16																									
1916 Cin-N	0	0	—	1	0	0	0	0	2	4	1	1	0	27.0	13.50	19	.444	.545	0	—	0	-2	-2	0	0.0
● LARRY TWITCHELL Twitchell, Lawrence Grant b: 2/18/1864, Cleveland, Ohio d: 8/23/30, Cleveland, Ohio BR/TR, 6', 185 lbs. Deb: 4/30/1886 ♦																									
1886 Det-N	0	2	.000	4	4	2	0	0	25	35	1	12	6	16.9	6.48	51	.347	.416	1	.063	-2	-9	-9	1	-0.6
1887 *Det-N	11	1	.917	15	12	11	0	**1**	112^1	120	3	36	24	13.3	4.33	94	.268	.336	88	.333	4	-3	-3	-1	-0.2
1888 Det-N	0	0	—	2	0	0	0	0	4	6	1	0	3	13.5	6.75	41	.375	.375	128	.244	0	-2	-2	0	-0.1
1889 Cle-N	0	0	—	1	0	0	0	0	1	0	0	1	0	9.0	0.00	—	.000	.250	151	.275	0	0	0	-0	0.0
1890 Buf-P	5	7	.417	13	12	12	0	0	104^1	112	3	72	29	17.2	4.57	90	.262	.387	38	.221	1	-4	-5	2	-0.2
1891 Col-a	1	1	.500	6	1	1	0	0	31	29	1	13	8	13.1	4.06	85	.240	.328	62	.277	2	-1	-2	-0	0.0
1894 Lou-N	0	0	—	1	0	0	0	0	3	5	1	1	0	18.0	6.00	85	.357	.400	56	.267	0	-0	-0	0	0.0
Total 7	17	11	.607	42	29	26	0	2	280^2	307	10	135	70	15.1	4.62	85	.272	.363	676	.263	7	-19	-21	1	-1.1
● WAYNE TWITCHELL Twitchell, Wayne Lee b: 3/10/48, Portland, Ore. BR/TR, 6'6", 220 lbs. Deb: 9/7/70																									
1970 Mil-A	0	0	—	2	0	0	0	0	1^2	3	0	1	5	21.6	10.80	35	.333	.400	0	—	0	-1	-1	0	0.0
1971 Phi-N	1	0	1.000	6	1	0	0	0	16	8	1	10	15	10.7	0.00	—	.145	.288	0	.000	-0	6	6	-0	0.3
1972 Phi-N	5	9	.357	49	15	1	1	1	139^2	138	6	56	112	12.6	4.06	88	.259	.332	2	.071	-2	-9	-7	-1	-1.0
1973 Phi-N★	13	9	.591	34	28	10	5	0	223^1	172	16	99	169	11.3	2.50	152	.219	.314	7	.097	-4	29	32	-3	2.3
1974 Phi-N	6	9	.400	25	18	2	0	0	112^1	122	11	65	72	15.5	5.21	73	.276	.377	6	.171	-1	-20	-18	-2	-2.3
1975 Phi-N	5	10	.333	36	20	0	0	0	134^1	132	10	78	101	14.1	4.42	84	.261	.361	3	.088	-2	-12	-10	-3	-1.5

YEAR	TM/L	W	L	PCT	G	GS	CG	SH	SV	IP	H	HR	BB	SO	RAT	ERA	ERA+	OAV	OOB	BH	AVG	PB	PR	/A	PD	TPI
1976	Phi-N	3	1	.750	26	2	0	0	1	61^2	55	3	18	67	11.1	1.75	203	.241	.305	1	.167	0	12	12	0	0.9
1977	Phi-N	0	5	.000	12	8	0	0	0	45^2	50	3	25	37	14.8	4.53	88	.287	.377	1	.091	-0	-3	-3	1	-0.3
	Mon-N	6	5	.545	22	22	2	0	0	139	116	18	49	93	11.0	4.21	90	.230	.304	8	.205	2	-5	-6	-1	-0.3
	Yr	6	10	.375	34	30	2	0	0	184^2	166	21	74	130	11.9	4.29	90	.244	.323	9	.180	2	-8	-9	-0	-0.6
1978	Mon-N	4	12	.250	33	15	0	0	0	112	121	16	71	69	15.8	5.38	65	.286	.395	2	.083	-1	-22	-23	-1	-3.2
1979	NY-N	5	3	.625	33	2	0	0	0	63^2	55	6	55	44	16.1	5.23	70	.243	.400	3	.375	1	-11	-11	-0	-1.2
	Sea-A	0	2	.000	4	2	0	0	0	13^2	11	2	10	5	15.1	5.27	83	.220	.371	0	—	0	-2	-1	-0	-0.2
Total	10	48	65	.425	282	133	15	6	2	1063	983	92	537	789	13.2	3.98	94	.250	.346	33	.127	-6	-38	-31	-10	-6.5

● JEFF TWITTY Twitty, Jeffrey Dean b: 11/10/57, Lancaster, S.C. BL/TL, 6'2", 185 lbs. Deb: 7/5/80

YEAR	TM/L	W	L	PCT	G	GS	CG	SH	SV	IP	H	HR	BB	SO	RAT	ERA	ERA+	OAV	OOB	BH	AVG	PB	PR	/A	PD	TPI
1980	KC-A	2	1	.667	13	0	0	0	0	22^1	33	4	7	9	16.1	6.04	67	.351	.396	0	—	0	-5	-5	0	-0.6

● CY TWOMBLY Twombly, Edwin Parker b: 6/15/1897, Groveland, Mass. d: 12/3/74, Savannah, Ga. BR/TR, 5'10.5", 170 lbs. Deb: 6/25/21

YEAR	TM/L	W	L	PCT	G	GS	CG	SH	SV	IP	H	HR	BB	SO	RAT	ERA	ERA+	OAV	OOB	BH	AVG	PB	PR	/A	PD	TPI
1921	Chi-A	1	2	.333	7	4	0	0	0	27^2	26	1	25	7	17.2	5.86	72	.283	.445	0	.000	-2	-5	-5	1	-0.5

● LEFTY TYLER Tyler, George Albert b: 12/14/1889, Derry, N.H. d: 9/29/53, Lowell, Mass. BL/TL, 6', 175 lbs. Deb: 9/20/10 F

YEAR	TM/L	W	L	PCT	G	GS	CG	SH	SV	IP	H	HR	BB	SO	RAT	ERA	ERA+	OAV	OOB	BH	AVG	PB	PR	/A	PD	TPI
1910	Bos-N	0	0	—	2	0	0	0	0	11^1	11	1	6	6	13.5	2.38	140	.275	.370	2	.500	1	1	1	-0	0.1
1911	Bos-N	7	10	.412	28	20	10	1	0	165^1	150	11	109	90	14.6	5.06	76	.243	.365	10	.164	-1	-31	-23	3	-1.8
1912	Bos-N	12	22	.353	42	31	15	1	0	256^1	262	8	126	144	14.0	4.18	86	.276	.367	19	.198	-1	-22	-17	4	-1.8
1913	Bos-N	16	17	.485	39	34	**28**	4	2	290^1	245	2	108	143	11.3	2.79	118	.235	.313	21	.206	4	13	16	7	2.9
1914	*Bos-N	16	13	.552	38	34	21	5	2	271^1	247	7	101	140	12.0	2.69	103	.249	.327	19	.202	1	3	2	-2	0.1
1915	Bos-N	10	9	.526	32	24	15	1	0	204^2	182	6	84	89	11.9	2.86	91	.243	.324	23	.261	8	-2	-6	-1	0.2
1916	Bos-N	17	9	.654	34	28	21	6	1	249^1	200	6	58	117	9.4	2.02	123	.226	.276	19	.204	7	17	13	2	2.5
1917	Bos-N	14	12	.538	32	28	22	4	1	239	203	1	86	98	11.1	2.52	101	.240	.314	31	.231	4	5	1	3	1.1
1918	*Chi-N	19	8	.704	33	30	22	6	1	269^1	218	1	67	102	9.7	2.00	139	.226	.279	21	.210	1	23	23	3	3.0
1919	Chi-N	2	2	.500	6	5	3	0	0	30	20	0	13	9	9.9	2.10	137	.196	.287	1	.143	1	3	3	1	0.6
1920	Chi-N	11	12	.478	27	27	18	2	0	193	193	6	57	57	11.8	3.31	97	.268	.324	17	.262	4	-4	-2	3	0.5
1921	Chi-N	3	2	.600	10	6	4	0	0	50	59	2	14	8	13.1	3.24	118	.294	.340	6	.231	1	3	3	-1	0.3
Total	12	127	116	.523	323	267	179	30	7	2230	1990	51	829	1003	11.6	2.95	101	.245	.320	189	.217	30	9	11	21	7.7

● JIM TYNG Tyng, James Alexander b: 3/27/1856, Philadelphia, Pa. d: 10/30/31, New York, N.Y. 5'9", 155 lbs. Deb: 9/23/1879

YEAR	TM/L	W	L	PCT	G	GS	CG	SH	SV	IP	H	HR	BB	SO	RAT	ERA	ERA+	OAV	OOB	BH	AVG	PB	PR	/A	PD	TPI
1879	Bos-N	1	2	.333	3	3	3	0	0	27	35	0	6	7	13.7	5.00	50	.292	.325	5	.357	1	-8	-8	0	-0.5
1888	Phi-N	0	0	—	1	0	0	0	1	4	8	0	2	2	24.8	4.50	66	.381	.458	0	.000	-0	-1	-1	0	0.0
Total	2	1	2	.333	4	3	3	0	1	31	43	0	8	9	15.1	4.94	51	.305	.347	5	.333	1	-8	-8	0	-0.5

● DAVE TYRIVER Tyriver, David Burton b: 10/31/37, Oshkosh, Wis. d: 10/28/88, Oshkosh, Wis. BR/TR, 6' ", 175 lbs. Deb: 8/21/62

YEAR	TM/L	W	L	PCT	G	GS	CG	SH	SV	IP	H	HR	BB	SO	RAT	ERA	ERA+	OAV	OOB	BH	AVG	PB	PR	/A	PD	TPI
1962	Cle-A	0	0	—	4	0	0	0	0	10^2	10	2	7	7	15.2	4.22	92	.250	.375	0	.000	-0	-0	-0	0	0.0

● JIMMY UCHRINSCKO Uchrinscko, James Emerson b: 10/20/1900, W.Newton, Pa. d: 3/17/95, Mt.Pleasant, Pa. BL/TR, 6', 180 lbs. Deb: 7/20/26

YEAR	TM/L	W	L	PCT	G	GS	CG	SH	SV	IP	H	HR	BB	SO	RAT	ERA	ERA+	OAV	OOB	BH	AVG	PB	PR	/A	PD	TPI
1926	Was-A	0	0	—	3	0	0	0	0	8	13	0	8	0	23.6	10.13	38	.433	.553	0	.000	-0	-5	-6	0	0.0

● BOB UHL Uhl, Robert Ellwood "Lefty" b: 9/17/13, San Francisco, Cal. d: 8/21/90, Santa Rosa, Cal. BB/TL, 5'11", 175 lbs. Deb: 5/8/38

YEAR	TM/L	W	L	PCT	G	GS	CG	SH	SV	IP	H	HR	BB	SO	RAT	ERA	ERA+	OAV	OOB	BH	AVG	PB	PR	/A	PD	TPI
1938	Chi-A	0	0	—	1	0	0	0	0	2	1	0	0	0	4.5	0.00	—	.167	.167	0	—	0	1	1	-0	0.0
1940	Det-A	0	0	—	1	0	0	0	0	0	4	0	2	0	—	∞	—	1.000	1.000	0	—	0	-4	-4	0	-0.3
Total	2	0	0	—	2	0	0	0	0	2	5	0	2	0	31.5	18.00	27	.500	.583	0	—	0	-3	-3	-0	-0.3

● GEORGE UHLE Uhle, George Ernest "The Bull" b: 9/18/1898, Cleveland, Ohio d: 2/26/85, Lakewood, Ohio BR/TR, 6', 190 lbs. Deb: 4/30/19 C♦

YEAR	TM/L	W	L	PCT	G	GS	CG	SH	SV	IP	H	HR	BB	SO	RAT	ERA	ERA+	OAV	OOB	BH	AVG	PB	PR	/A	PD	TPI
1919	Cle-A	10	5	.667	26	12	7	1	0	127	129	1	43	50	12.7	2.91	115	.261	.329	13	.302	3	5	6	0	1.0
1920	*Cle-A	4	5	.444	27	6	2	0	1	84^2	98	3	29	27	14.4	5.21	73	.296	.367	11	.344	2	-13	-13	0	-1.0
1921	Cle-A	16	13	.552	41	28	13	2	2	238	288	9	63	63	13.4	4.01	106	.306	.352	23	.245	3	7	7	-3	0.7
1922	Cle-A	22	16	.579	50	40	23	**5**	3	287^1	328	6	89	82	13.5	4.07	98	.290	.348	29	.266	9	-1	-2	-3	0.1
1923	Cle-A	**26**	16	.619	54	44	**29**	1	5	**357^2**	378	8	102	109	12.4	3.77	105	.271	.326	52	.361	16	8	8	0	2.4
1924	Cle-A	9	15	.375	28	25	15	0	1	196^1	238	6	75	57	14.9	4.77	90	.306	.376	33	.308	7	-12	-11	1	-0.4
1925	Cle-A	13	11	.542	29	26	17	1	0	210^2	218	5	78	68	13.0	4.10	108	.268	.339	29	.287	6	7	7	-3	1.0
1926	Cle-A	**27**	11	**.711**	39	36	**32**	3	1	**318^1**	300	7	118	159	12.2	2.83	143	.253	.328	30	.227	4	42	43	-0	**5.2**
1927	Cle-A	8	9	.471	25	22	10	1	1	153^1	187	3	59	69	15.0	4.34	97	.310	.379	21	.266	4	-3	-2	-1	0.0
1928	Cle-A	12	17	.414	31	28	18	2	1	214^1	252	8	48	74	12.9	4.07	102	.300	.344	28	.286	7	-1	2	3	1.1
1929	Det-A	15	11	.577	32	30	23	1	0	249	283	9	58	100	12.4	4.08	105	.287	.328	37	.343	8	4	6	-3	1.1
1930	Det-A	12	12	.500	33	29	18	1	3	239	239	18	75	117	12.0	3.65	131	.264	.323	36	.308	8	26	30	-3	3.2
1931	Det-A	11	12	.478	29	18	15	2	2	193	190	10	49	63	11.3	3.50	131	.255	.304	22	.244	5	19	23	-1	2.9
1932	Det-A	6	6	.500	33	15	6	1	5	146^2	152	15	42	51	12.1	4.48	105	.266	.320	10	.182	1	-0	4	-1	0.3
1933	Det-A	0	0	—	1	0	0	0	0	0^2	2	1	0	1	27.0	27.00	16	.500	.500	0	—	0	-2	-2	0	0.0
	NY-N	1	1	.500	6	1	0	0	0	13^2	16	1	6	4	14.5	7.90	41	.302	.373	0	.000	-0	-7	-7	0	-0.9
	NY-A	6	1	.857	12	6	4	0	0	61	63	4	20	26	12.7	5.16	75	.257	.321	8	.400	4	-6	-9	-1	-0.5
1934	NY-A	2	4	.333	10	2	0	0	0	16^1	30	3	7	10	20.4	9.92	41	.400	.451	3	.600	2	-10	-11	-0	-2.7
1936	Cle-A	0	1	.000	7	0	0	0	0	12^2	26	2	5	5	22.0	8.53	59	.419	.463	8	.381	4	-5	-5	-1	0.0
Total	17	200	166	.546	513	368	232	21	25	3119^2	3417	119	966	1135	13.0	3.99	105	.281	.340	393	.289	92	60	74	-15	13.5

● JERRY UJDUR Ujdur, Gerald Raymond b: 3/5/57, Duluth, Minn. BR/TR, 6'1", 195 lbs. Deb: 8/17/80

YEAR	TM/L	W	L	PCT	G	GS	CG	SH	SV	IP	H	HR	BB	SO	RAT	ERA	ERA+	OAV	OOB	BH	AVG	PB	PR	/A	PD	TPI
1980	Det-A	1	0	1.000	9	2	0	0	0	21^1	36	5	10	8	19.8	7.59	54	.383	.448	0	—	0	-8	-8	-1	-0.6
1981	Det-A	0	0	—	4	4	0	0	0	14	19	2	5	5	15.4	6.43	59	.322	.375	0	—	0	-4	-4	0	0.0
1982	Det-A	10	10	.500	25	25	7	0	0	178	150	29	69	86	11.2	3.69	110	.230	.306	0	—	0	8	7	-1	0.6
1983	Det-A	0	4	.000	11	6	0	0	0	34	41	6	20	13	16.4	7.15	55	.293	.385	0	—	0	-12	-12	-1	-1.2
1984	Cle-A	1	2	.333	4	3	0	0	0	14^1	22	1	6	6	18.8	6.91	59	.355	.429	0	—	0	-5	-4	-1	-0.9
Total	5	12	16	.429	53	40	7	0	0	261^2	268	43	110	118	13.2	4.78	84	.266	.342	0	—	0	-21	-22	-3	-2.1

● SANDY ULLRICH Ullrich, Carlos Santiago (Castello) b: 7/25/21, Havana, Cuba BR/TR, 6'1", 180 lbs. Deb: 5/3/44

YEAR	TM/L	W	L	PCT	G	GS	CG	SH	SV	IP	H	HR	BB	SO	RAT	ERA	ERA+	OAV	OOB	BH	AVG	PB	PR	/A	PD	TPI
1944	Was-A	0	0	—	3	0	0	0	0	9^2	17	2	4	2	20.5	9.31	35	.386	.449	1	.333	0	-6	-7	0	0.0
1945	Was-A	3	3	.500	28	6	0	0	1	81^1	91	3	34	26	13.8	4.54	68	.276	.343	6	.273	1	-11	-13	1	-0.7
Total	2	3	3	.500	31	6	0	0	1	91	108	5	38	28	14.5	5.04	62	.289	.356	7	.280	1	-17	-19	2	-0.7

● DUTCH ULRICH Ulrich, Frank W. b: 11/18/1899, Baltimore, Md. d: 2/11/29, Baltimore, Md. BR/TR, 6'2", 195 lbs. Deb: 4/18/25

YEAR	TM/L	W	L	PCT	G	GS	CG	SH	SV	IP	H	HR	BB	SO	RAT	ERA	ERA+	OAV	OOB	BH	AVG	PB	PR	/A	PD	TPI
1925	Phi-N	3	3	.500	21	4	2	1	0	65	73	6	12	29	11.9	3.05	157	.285	.320	2	.125	-1	9	12	1	1.0
1926	Phi-N	8	13	.381	45	16	8	1	1	147^2	178	9	37	52	13.2	4.08	101	.304	.347	12	.245	1	-4	1	-0	0.3
1927	Phi-N	8	11	.421	32	18	14	1	1	193^1	201	6	40	42	11.2	3.17	131	.271	.308	9	.123	-6	16	21	-2	1.1
Total	3	19	27	.413	98	38	24	3	2	406	452	21	89	123	12.0	3.48	122	.286	.324	23	.167	-5	21	34	-2	2.4

● ARNOLD UMBACH Umbach, Arnold William b: 12/6/42, Williamsburg, Va. BR/TR, 6'1", 180 lbs. Deb: 10/3/64

YEAR	TM/L	W	L	PCT	G	GS	CG	SH	SV	IP	H	HR	BB	SO	RAT	ERA	ERA+	OAV	OOB	BH	AVG	PB	PR	/A	PD	TPI
1964	Mil-N	1	0	1.000	1	1	0	0	0	8^1	11	0	4	7	16.2	3.24	109	.333	.405	0	.000	0	0	0	-0	0.0
1966	Atl-N	0	2	.000	22	3	0	0	0	40^2	40	1	18	23	13.3	3.10	117	.256	.341	1	.200	0	2	2	-0	0.1
Total	2	1	2	.333	23	4	0	0	0	49	51	1	22	30	13.8	3.12	116	.270	.352	1	.125	0	3	3	-0	0.1

● JIM UMBARGER Umbarger, James Harold b: 2/17/53, Burbank, Cal. BL/TL, 6'6", 200 lbs. Deb: 4/8/75

YEAR	TM/L	W	L	PCT	G	GS	CG	SH	SV	IP	H	HR	BB	SO	RAT	ERA	ERA+	OAV	OOB	BH	AVG	PB	PR	/A	PD	TPI
1975	Tex-A	8	7	.533	56	12	3	2	2	131	134	11	59	50	13.4	4.12	91	.276	.357	0	—	0	-5	-5	1	-0.5
1976	Tex-A	10	12	.455	30	30	10	3	0	197^1	208	12	54	105	12.0	3.15	114	.274	.324	0	—	0	8	10	-0	1.0
1977	Oak-A	1	5	.167	12	8	1	0	0	44	62	3	28	24	19.2	6.55	61	.354	.454	0	—	0	-12	-12	0	-1.3
	Tex-A	1	1	.500	3	2	0	0	0	13	14	2	4	5	12.5	5.54	74	.275	.327	0	—	0	-2	-2	-0	-0.3
	Yr	2	6	.250	15	10	1	0	0	57	76	5	32	29	17.1	6.32	64	.326	.408	0	—	0	-14	-14	0	-1.6
1978	Tex-A	5	8	.385	32	9	1	0	1	97^2	116	9	36	60	14.2	4.88	77	.299	.362	0	—	0	-12	-12	1	-1.5
Total	4	25	33	.431	133	61	15	5	3	483	534	37	181	244	13.5	4.14	90	.287	.354	0	—	0	-23	-22	2	-2.6

YEAR	TM/L	W	L	PCT	G	GS	CG	SH	SV	IP	H	HR	BB	SO	RAT	ERA	ERA+	OAV	OOB	BH	AVG	PB	PR	/A	PD	TPI
● JIM UMBRICHT	Umbricht, James b: 9/17/30, Chicago, Ill. d: 4/8/64, Houston, Tex. BR/TR, 6'4", 215 lbs. Deb: 9/26/59																									
1959	Pit-N	0	0	—	1	1	0	0	0	7	7	3	4	3	14.1	6.43	60	.259	.355	0	.000	-0	-2	-2	0	0.0
1960	Pit-N	1	2	.333	17	3	0	0	1	40^{2}	40	5	27	26	14.8	5.09	74	.270	.383	2	.333	0	-6	-6	-1	-0.5
1961	Pit-N	0	0	—	1	0	0	0	0	3^{1}	5	0	2	1	18.9	2.70	148	.333	.412	1	1.000	0	0	0	-0	0.0
1962	Hou-N	4	0	1.000	34	0	0	0	2	67	51	3	17	55	9.4	2.01	185	.213	.270	1	.111	-0	14	13	1	0.8
1963	Hou-N	4	3	.571	35	3	0	0	0	76	52	6	21	48	8.8	2.61	121	.195	.256	1	.111	-0	6	5	1	0.5
Total	5	9	5	.643	88	7	0	0	3	194	155	17	71	133	10.6	3.06	115	.222	.297	5	.179	-0	13	10	0	0.8
● WILLIE UNDERHILL	Underhill, Willie Vern b: 9/6/04, Yowell, Tex. d: 10/26/70, Bay City, Tex. BR/TR, 6'2", 185 lbs. Deb: 9/8/27																									
1927	Cle-A	0	2	.000	4	1	0	0	0	8^{1}	12	0	11	4	24.8	9.72	43	.375	.535	0	.000	-0	-5	-5	0	-0.9
1928	Cle-A	1	2	.333	11	3	1	0	0	28	33	0	20	16	17.4	4.50	92	.306	.419	4	.364	2	-1	-1	0	0.1
Total	2	1	4	.200	15	4	1	0	0	36^{1}	45	0	31	20	19.1	5.70	73	.321	.448	4	.333	1	-7	-6	0	-0.8
● FRED UNDERWOOD	Underwood, Frederick Theodore b: 10/14/1868, St.Louis Co., Mo. d: 1/26/06, Kansas City, Mo. 170 lbs. Deb: 7/18/1894																									
1894	Bro-N	2	4	.333	7	6	5	0	0	47	80	1	30	10	21.4	7.85	63	.372	.453	7	.389	2	-13	-15	-0	-1.1
● PAT UNDERWOOD	Underwood, Patrick John b: 2/9/57, Kokomo, Ind. BL/TL, 6', 175 lbs. Deb: 5/31/79 F																									
1979	Det-A	6	4	.600	27	15	1	0	0	121^{2}	126	17	29	83	11.6	4.59	94	.269	.314	0	—	0	-5	-4	-1	-0.4
1980	Det-A	3	6	.333	49	7	0	0	5	112^{2}	121	12	35	60	12.6	3.59	114	.277	.333	0	—	0	6	6	-0	0.3
1982	Det-A	4	8	.333	33	12	2	0	3	99	108	17	22	43	11.8	4.73	86	.269	.307	0	—	0	-7	-7	1	-0.8
1983	Det-A	0	0	—	4	0	0	0	0	10^{1}	11	1	6	2	14.8	8.71	45	.289	.386	0	—	0	-5	-6	-0	0.0
Total	4	13	18	.419	113	34	3	0	8	343^{2}	366	47	92	188	12.1	4.43	94	.272	.320	0	—	0	-12	-10	-1	-0.9
● TOM UNDERWOOD	Underwood, Thomas Gerald b: 12/22/53, Kokomo, Ind. BR/TL, 5'11", 170 lbs. Deb: 8/19/74 F																									
1974	Phi-N	1	0	1.000	7	0	0	0	0	13	15	1	5	8	13.8	4.85	78	.313	.377	0	.000	-0	-2	-2	-0	-0.2
1975	Phi-N	14	13	.519	35	35	7	2	0	219^{1}	221	12	84	123	12.8	4.14	90	.262	.333	9	.122	-2	-13	-10	-4	-1.7
1976	*Phi-N	10	5	.667	33	25	3	0	2	155^{2}	154	9	63	94	12.6	3.53	101	.260	.332	5	.109	-1	-0	0	-2	-0.3
1977	Phi-N	3	2	.600	14	0	0	0	1	33^{1}	44	2	18	20	16.7	5.13	78	.328	.408	0	.000	-0	-5	-4	-0	-0.6
	StL-N	6	9	.400	19	17	1	0	0	100	104	7	57	66	14.6	4.95	78	.278	.375	4	.133	-0	-12	-12	-1	-1.7
	Yr	9	11	.450	33	17	1	0	1	133^{1}	148	9	75	86	15.1	4.99	78	.290	.382	4	.121	-0	-16	-16	-2	-2.3
1978	Tor-A	6	14	.300	31	30	7	1	0	197^{2}	201	23	87	139	13.2	4.10	96	.263	.340	0	—	0	-7	-4	-3	-0.7
1979	Tor-A	9	16	.360	33	32	12	1	0	227	213	23	95	127	12.6	3.69	118	.253	.335	0	—	0	13	17	-0	1.6
1980	*NY-A	13	9	.591	38	27	2	2	2	187	163	15	66	116	11.2	3.66	107	.237	.307	0	—	0	8	5	-0	0.7
1981	NY-A	1	4	.200	9	6	0	0	0	32^{2}	32	2	13	29	12.4	4.41	81	.262	.333	0	—	0	-3	-3	-0	-0.4
	*Oak-A	3	2	.600	16	5	1	0	1	51	37	4	25	46	11.3	3.18	109	.202	.305	0	—	0	3	2	0	0.2
	Yr	4	6	.400	25	11	1	0	1	83^{2}	69	6	38	75	11.7	3.66	96	.226	.316	0	—	0	-0	-1	-0	-0.2
1982	Oak-A	10	6	.625	56	10	2	0	7	153	136	11	68	79	12.1	3.29	119	.241	.324	0	—	0	13	10	-2	1.0
1983	Oak-A	9	7	.563	51	15	0	0	4	144^{2}	156	13	50	62	12.9	4.04	95	.277	.338	0	—	0	0	-3	-3	-0.5
1984	Bal-A	1	0	1.000	37	1	0	0	1	71^{2}	78	8	31	39	13.7	3.52	110	.282	.354	0	—	0	4	3	1	0.3
Total	11	86	87	.497	379	203	35	6	18	1586	1554	130	662	948	12.7	3.89	100	.259	.336	18	.117	-4	0	-0	-15	-2.3
● WOODY UPCHURCH	Upchurch, Jefferson Woodrow b: 4/13/11, Buies Creek, N.C. d: 10/23/71, Buies Creek, N.C. BR/TL, 6', 180 lbs. Deb: 9/14/35																									
1935	Phi-A	0	2	.000	3	3	1	0	0	21^{1}	23	3	12	2	14.8	5.06	90	.271	.361	2	.286	0	-1	-1	-0	-0.1
1936	Phi-A	0	2	.000	7	2	1	0	0	22^{1}	36	7	14	6	20.1	9.67	53	.353	.431	1	.143	-0	-12	-11	-1	-0.9
Total	2	0	4	.000	10	5	2	0	0	43^{2}	59	10	26	8	17.5	7.42	65	.316	.399	3	.214	-0	-13	-13	-1	-1.0
● JOHN UPHAM	Upham, John Leslie b: 12/29/41, Windsor, Ont., Can. BL/TL, 6', 180 lbs. Deb: 4/16/67 ♦																									
1967	Chi-N	0	1	.000	5	0	0	0	0	1^{1}	4	1	2	2	40.5	33.75	11	.571	.667	2	.667	1	-5	-4	0	-2.4
1968	Chi-N	0	0	—	2	0	0	0	0	7	2	0	3	2	7.7	0.00	—	.087	.222	2	.200	0	2	2	0	0.0
Total	2	0	1	.000	7	0	0	0	0	8^{1}	6	1	5	4	13.0	5.40	60	.200	.333	4	.308	1	-2	-2	0	-2.4
● BILL UPHAM	Upham, William Lawrence b: 4/4/1888, Akron, Ohio d: 9/14/59, Newark, N.J. BB/TR, 6', 178 lbs. Deb: 4/10/15																									
1915	Bro-F	7	8	.467	33	11	4	2	4	121	129	0	40	46	12.6	3.35	81	.274	.331	4	.111	-2	-8	-8	2	-1.1
1918	Bos-N	1	1	.500	3	2	2	0	0	20^{2}	28	2	1	8	12.6	5.23	51	.326	.333	2	.222	0	-6	-6	-0	-0.5
Total	2	8	9	.471	36	13	6	2	4	141^{2}	157	2	41	54	12.6	3.62	75	.282	.332	6	.133	-2	-14	-14	2	-1.6
● JERRY UPP	Upp, George Henry b: 12/10/1883, Sandusky, Ohio d: 6/30/37, Sandusky, Ohio TL, Deb: 9/2/09																									
1909	Cle-A	2	1	.667	7	4	2	0	0	26^{2}	26	0	12	13	12.8	1.69	152	.260	.339	2	.222	0	2	3	1	0.4
● CECIL UPSHAW	Upshaw, Cecil Lee b: 10/22/42, Spearsville, La. d: 2/7/95, Lawrenceville, Ga. BR/TR, 6'6", 205 lbs. Deb: 10/1/66																									
1966	Atl-N	0	0	—	1	0	0	0	0	3	0	0	3	2	9.0	0.00	—	.000	.273	1	1.000	0	1	1	-0	0.0
1967	Atl-N	2	3	.400	30	0	0	0	8	45^{1}	42	4	8	31	10.7	2.58	129	.247	.297	1	.167	1	4	4	0	0.6
1968	Atl-N	8	7	.533	52	0	0	0	13	116^{2}	98	6	24	74	9.7	2.47	121	.229	.276	4	.174	0	7	7	-0	1.1
1969	*Atl-N	6	4	.600	62	0	0	0	27	105^{1}	102	7	29	57	11.3	2.91	124	.259	.311	5	.238	2	8	8	1	1.5
1971	Atl-N	11	6	.647	49	0	0	0	17	82	95	5	28	56	13.7	3.51	106	.292	.352	0	.000	-2	-0	2	-1	0.2
1972	Atl-N	3	5	.375	42	0	0	0	13	53^{2}	50	5	19	23	11.7	3.69	103	.249	.317	1	.143	-0	-1	1	1	0.2
1973	Atl-N	0	1	.000	5	0	0	0	0	3^{2}	8	0	2	3	24.5	9.82	40	.444	.500	0	—	0	-3	-2	0	-0.6
	Hou-N	2	3	.400	35	0	0	0	1	38^{1}	38	3	15	21	12.7	4.46	81	.259	.331	0	.000	-0	-3	-4	1	-0.4
	Yr	2	4	.333	40	0	0	0	1	42	46	3	17	24	13.7	4.93	74	.277	.348	0	.000	-0	-6	-6	1	-1.0
1974	Cle-A	0	1	.000	7	0	0	0	0	8	10	1	4	7	15.8	3.38	107	.345	.424	0	—	0	0	0	-0	0.0
	NY-A	1	5	.167	36	0	0	0	6	59^{2}	53	1	24	27	12.1	3.02	117	.254	.339	0	—	0	4	3	1	0.5
	Yr	1	6	.143	43	0	0	0	6	67^{2}	63	2	28	34	12.5	3.06	116	.262	.347	0	—	0	4	4	1	0.5
1975	Chi-A	1	1	.500	29	0	0	0	1	47^{1}	49	5	21	22	14.1	3.23	120	.271	.359	0	—	0	3	3	-0	0.1
Total	9	34	36	.486	348	0	0	0	86	563	545	37	177	323	11.9	3.13	112	.258	.322	12	.160	1	19	23	2	3.2
● BILL UPTON	Upton, William Ray b: 6/18/29, Esther, Mo. d: 1/2/87, San Diego, Cal. BR/TR, 6', 167 lbs. Deb: 4/13/54 F																									
1954	Phi-A	0	0	—	2	0	0	0	1	5	6	1	1	2	12.6	1.80	217	.300	.333	0	—	0	1	1	0	0.1
● JACK URBAN	Urban, Jack Elmer b: 12/5/28, Omaha, Neb. BR/TR, 5'8", 155 lbs. Deb: 6/13/57																									
1957	KC-A	7	4	.636	31	13	3	0	0	129^{1}	111	7	45	55	10.9	3.34	118	.237	.305	11	.282	2	6	9	2	1.1
1958	KC-A	8	11	.421	30	24	5	1	1	132	150	17	51	54	13.8	5.93	66	.286	.351	7	.152	-2	-32	-30	-1	-4.0
1959	StL-N	0	0	—	8	0	0	0	0	10^{2}	18	1	7	4	21.1	9.28	46	.409	.490	0	.000	-0	-6	-6	-0	0.0
Total	3	15	15	.500	69	37	8	1	1	272	279	25	103	113	12.7	4.83	82	.269	.337	18	.209	0	-32	-27	-0	-2.9
● TOM URBANI	Urbani, Thomas James b: 1/21/68, Santa Cruz, Cal. BL/TL, 6'1", 190 lbs. Deb: 4/21/93																									
1993	StL-N	1	3	.250	18	9	0	0	0	62	73	4	26	33	14.4	4.65	85	.296	.363	3	.188	1	-4	-5	0	-0.2
1994	StL-N	3	7	.300	20	10	0	0	0	80^{1}	98	12	21	43	13.7	5.15	81	.302	.350	6	.250	1	-8	-9	0	-0.8
1995	StL-N	3	5	.375	24	13	0	0	0	82^{2}	99	11	21	52	13.3	3.70	113	.305	.351	6	.316	3	4	4	1	0.9
1996	StL-N	1	0	1.000	3	2	0	0	0	11^{2}	15	3	4	1	14.7	7.71	54	.319	.373	1	.167	-0	-5	-5	-1	-0.4
	Det-A	2	2	.500	16	2	0	0	0	23^{2}	31	8	14	20	17.9	8.37	60	.310	.405	0	—	0	-9	-9	0	-1.2
Total	4	10	17	.370	81	36	0	0	0	260^{1}	316	38	86	149	14.1	4.98	84	.303	.360	16	.246	6	-22	-23	1	-1.7
● UGUETH URBINA	Urbina, Ugueth Urtain (Villarreal) b: 2/15/74, Caracas, Venez. BR/TR, 6'2", 185 lbs. Deb: 5/9/95																									
1995	Mon-N	2	2	.500	7	4	0	0	0	23^{1}	26	6	14	15	15.4	6.17	70	.280	.374	2	.333	0	-5	-5	1	-0.6
1996	Mon-N	10	5	.667	33	17	0	0	0	114	102	18	44	108	11.6	3.71	116	.234	.306	3	.103	-1	6	8	-1	0.7
1997	Mon-N	5	8	.385	63	0	0	0	27	64^{1}	52	9	29	84	11.5	3.78	111	.214	.300	0	.000	-1	3	3	0	0.7
1998	Mon-N★	6	3	.667	64	0	0	0	34	69^{1}	37	2	33	94	9.1	1.30	316	.157	.260	0	.000	-1	23	22	-1	4.3
Total	4	23	18	.561	167	21	0	0	61	271	217	35	120	301	11.3	3.32	127	.215	.300	5	.109	-2	27	27	-1	5.1
● JOHN URREA	Urrea, John Godoy b: 2/9/55, Los Angeles, Cal. BR/TR, 6'3", 205 lbs. Deb: 4/10/77																									
1977	StL-N	7	6	.538	41	12	2	1	4	139^{2}	126	13	35	81	10.4	3.16	122	.244	.292	4	.138	2	12	11	1	1.2
1978	StL-N	4	9	.308	27	12	1	0	0	98^{2}	108	4	47	61	14.8	5.38	65	.284	.373	3	.125	-1	-20	-20	0	-2.5

YEAR	TM/L	W	L	PCT	G	GS	CG	SH	SV	IP	H	HR	BB	SO	RAT	ERA	ERA+	OAV	OOB	BH	AVG	PB	PR	/A	PD	TPI
1979	StL-N	0	0	—	3	2	0	0	0	11^1	13	0	9	5	17.5	3.97	95	.310	.431	1	.250	0	-0	-0	0	0.0
1980	StL-N	4	1	.800	30	1	0	0	3	64^2	57	2	41	36	13.9	3.48	106	.239	.356	3	.231	0	1	2	-1	0.0
1981	SD-N	2	2	.500	38	0	0	0	2	49	43	1	28	19	13.6	2.39	136	.239	.351	1	.250	0	6	5	-1	0.3
Total	5	17	18	.486	139	27	3	1	9	363^1	347	20	160	202	12.9	3.74	97	.256	.339	12	.162	2	-2	-4	-1	-1.0
● BOB VAIL	Vail, Robert Garfield "Doc" b: 9/24/1881, Linneus, Maine d: 3/22/42, Philadelphia, Pa. BR/TR, 5'10", 165 lbs. Deb: 8/27/08																									
1908	Pit-N	1	2	.333	4	1	0	0	0	15	15	0	7	9	13.8	6.00	38	.268	.359	1	.333	1	-6	-6	-1	-1.1
● ISMAEL VALDES	Valdes, Ismael (Alvarez) b: 8/21/73, Victoria, Mex. BR/TR, 6'3", 185 lbs. Deb: 6/15/94																									
1994	LA-N	3	1	.750	21	1	0	0	0	28^1	21	2	10	28	9.8	3.18	123	.206	.277	0	.000	-0	3	2	1	0.4
1995	*LA-N	13	11	.542	33	27	6	2	1	197^2	168	17	51	150	10.0	3.05	124	.228	.279	6	.097	-3	25	16	1	1.6
1996	*LA-N	15	7	.682	33	33	0	0	0	225	219	20	54	173	11.0	3.32	116	.251	.296	10	.143	-1	22	13	-0	1.1
1997	LA-N	10	11	.476	30	30	0	0	0	196^2	171	16	47	140	10.1	2.65	145	.234	.283	5	.088	-2	34	26	0	2.5
1998	LA-N	11	10	.524	27	27	2	2	0	174	171	17	66	122	12.4	3.98	98	.256	.324	8	.167	1	5	-2	-0	-0.1
Total	5	52	40	.565	144	118	8	4	1	821^2	750	72	228	613	10.8	3.23	119	.241	.295	29	.121	-5	89	56	2	5.5
● MARC VALDES	Valdes, Marc Christopher b: 12/20/71, Dayton, Ohio BR/TR, 6', 170 lbs. Deb: 8/28/95																									
1995	Fla-N	0	0	—	3	3	0	0	0	7	17	1	9	2	34.7	14.14	30	.459	.574	0	.000	-0	-8	-8	-0	-0.1
1996	Fla-N	1	3	.250	11	8	0	0	0	48^2	63	5	23	13	16.1	4.81	85	.315	.388	0	.000	-1	-3	-4	-1	-0.5
1997	Mon-N	4	4	.500	48	7	0	0	2	95	84	2	39	54	12.4	3.13	134	.240	.330	2	.105	-1	11	11	-1	0.8
1998	Mon-N	1	3	.250	20	4	0	0	0	36^1	41	6	21	28	15.6	7.43	55	.285	.380	2	.400	1	-13	-13	0	-1.2
Total	4	6	10	.375	82	22	0	0	2	187	205	14	92	97	14.8	4.81	86	.280	.369	4	.100	-1	-13	-14	-1	-1.0
● CARLOS VALDEZ	Valdez, Carlos Luis (Lorenzo) b: 12/26/71, Bani, D.R. BR/TR, 5'11", 165 lbs. Deb: 7/18/95																									
1995	SF-N	0	1	.000	11	0	0	0	0	14^2	19	1	8	7	17.2	6.14	67	.322	.412	0	.000	-0	-3	-3	-0	-0.2
1998	Bos-A	1	0	1.000	4	0	0	0	0	3^1	1	0	5	4	16.2	0.00	—	.100	.400	0	—	0	2	2	-0	0.5
Total	2	1	1	.500	15	0	0	0	0	18	20	1	13	11	17.0	5.00	84	.290	.410	0	.000	-0	-1	-2	-0	0.3
● EFRAIN VALDEZ	Valdez, Efrain Antonio b: 7/11/66, Nizao Bani, D.R. BL/TL, 5'11", 180 lbs. Deb: 8/13/90																									
1990	Cle-A	1	1	.500	13	0	0	0	0	23^2	20	2	14	13	12.9	3.04	129	.233	.340	0	—	0	2	2	-0	0.2
1991	Cle-A	0	0	—	7	0	0	0	0	6	5	0	3	1	13.5	1.50	277	.238	.360	0	—	0	2	2	0	0.0
1998	Ari-N	0	0	—	6	0	0	0	0	4^1	7	2	1	2	16.6	4.15	104	.368	.400	0	—	0	0	0	0	0.0
Total	3	1	1	.500	26	0	0	0	0	34	32	4	18	16	13.5	2.91	138	.254	.352	0	—	0	4	4	0	0.2
● RAFAEL VALDEZ	Valdez, Rafael Emilio (Diaz) b: 12/17/67, Nizao Bani, D.R. BR/TR, 5'11", 165 lbs. Deb: 4/18/90																									
1990	SD-N	0	1	.000	3	0	0	0	0	5^2	11	4	2	3	20.6	11.12	34	.393	.433	0	.000	-0	-5	-5	-0	-0.7
● RENE VALDEZ	Valdez, Rene Gutierrez (b: Rene Gutierrez (Valdez)) b: 6/2/29, Guanabacoa, Cuba BR/TR, 6'3", 175 lbs. Deb: 4/21/57																									
1957	Bro-N	1	1	.500	5	1	0	0	0	13	13	1	7	10	13.8	5.54	75	.265	.357	0	.000	0	-2	-2	-0	-0.3
● SERGIO VALDEZ	Valdez, Sergio Sanchez (b: Sergio Sanchez (Valdez)) b: 9/7/64, Elias Pina, D.R. BR/TR, 6'1", 190 lbs. Deb: 9/10/86																									
1986	Mon-N	0	4	.000	5	5	0	0	0	25	39	2	11	20	18.4	6.84	54	.361	.425	1	.125	-0	-9	-9	-0	-1.2
1989	Atl-N	1	2	.333	19	1	0	0	0	32^2	31	5	17	26	13.2	6.06	60	.246	.336	1	1.000	0	-9	-9	-1	-0.8
1990	Atl-N	0	0	—	6	0	0	0	0	5^1	6	0	3	3	15.2	6.75	60	.273	.360	0	—	0	-2	-2	0	0.0
	Cle-A	6	6	.500	24	13	0	0	0	102^1	109	17	35	63	12.8	4.75	82	.276	.336	0	—	0	-10	-9	-0	-1.0
1991	Cle-A	1	0	1.000	6	0	0	0	0	16^1	15	3	5	11	11.0	5.51	75	.238	.294	0	—	0	-3	-2	-1	-0.2
1992	Mon-N	0	2	.000	27	0	0	0	0	37^1	25	2	12	32	8.9	2.41	144	.185	.252	0	.000	-0	5	4	0	0.2
1993	Mon-N	0	0	—	4	0	0	0	0	3	4	1	1	2	15.0	9.00	46	.308	.357	0	—	0	-2	-2	-0	0.0
1994	Bos-A	0	1	.000	12	1	0	0	0	14^1	25	4	8	4	20.7	8.16	62	.391	.458	0	—	0	-5	-5	0	-0.3
1995	SF-N	4	5	.444	13	11	1	0	0	66^1	78	12	17	29	13.3	4.75	86	.298	.348	2	.095	-1	-4	-5	0	-0.6
Total	8	12	20	.375	116	31	1	0	0	302^2	332	46	109	190	13.3	5.06	78	.279	.343	4	.121	-1	-39	-38	-1	-3.9
● CORKY VALENTINE	Valentine, Harold Lewis b: 1/4/29, Troy, Ohio BR/TR, 6'1", 203 lbs. Deb: 4/17/54																									
1954	Cin-N	12	11	.522	36	28	7	3	1	194^1	211	24	60	73	12.7	4.45	94	.282	.339	9	.138	-2	-8	-5	-2	-0.9
1955	Cin-N	2	1	.667	10	5	0	0	0	26^2	29	5	16	14	15.5	7.43	57	.276	.377	0	.000	-1	-10	-9	1	-0.9
Total	2	14	12	.538	46	33	7	3	1	221	240	29	76	87	13.1	4.81	87	.282	.344	9	.125	-3	-18	-15	-1	-1.8
● JOHN VALENTINE	Valentine, John Gill b: 11/21/1855, Brooklyn, N.Y. d: 10/10/03, Central Islip, N.Y Deb: 5/3/1883																									
1883	Col-a	2	10	.167	13	12	11	0	0	102	130	0	17	13	13.0	3.53	87	.291	.317	17	.283	3	-3	-5	1	-0.1
● VITO VALENTINETTI	Valentinetti, Vito John b: 9/16/28, W.New York, N.J. BR/TR, 6', 195 lbs. Deb: 6/20/54																									
1954	Chi-A	0	0	—	1	0	0	0	0	1	4	1	2	1	54.0	54.00	7	.571	.667	0	—	0	-6	-6	0	0.0
1956	Chi-N	6	4	.600	42	2	0	0	1	95^1	84	10	36	26	11.4	3.78	100	.243	.317	2	.100	-1	-0	-0	-1	-0.3
1957	Chi-N	0	0	—	9	0	0	0	0	12	12	1	7	8	14.3	2.25	172	.255	.352	0	.000	0	2	2	-0	0.0
	Cle-A	2	2	.500	11	2	1	0	0	23^2	26	3	13	9	15.2	4.94	75	.289	.385	1	.200	-0	-3	-3	0	-0.5
1958	Det-A	1	0	1.000	15	0	0	0	2	18^2	18	4	5	10	11.6	3.38	120	.257	.316	0	—	0	1	1	-0	0.1
	Was-A	4	6	.400	23	10	2	0	0	95^2	106	16	49	33	14.8	5.08	75	.286	.373	9	.321	2	-14	-13	2	-0.9
	Yr	5	6	.455	38	10	2	0	2	114^1	124	20	54	43	14.2	4.80	80	.281	.362	9	.321	2	-13	-12	1	-0.8
1959	Was-A	0	2	.000	7	1	0	0	0	10^2	16	0	10	7	22.8	10.13	39	.356	.482	0	—	0	-7	-7	0	-1.1
Total	5	13	14	.481	108	15	3	0	3	257	266	35	122	94	13.8	4.73	81	.273	.358	12	.218	1	-27	-26	0	-2.7
● FERNANDO VALENZUELA	Valenzuela, Fernando (Anguamea) b: 11/1/60, Navojoa, Mexico BL/TL, 5'11", 195 lbs. Deb: 9/15/80																									
1980	LA-N	2	0	1.000	10	0	0	0	1	17^2	8	0	5	16	6.6	0.00	—	.136	.203	0	.000	-0	7	7	0	0.9
1981	*LA-N★	13	7	.650	25	25	**11**	**8**	0	**192^1**	140	11	61	**180**	9.5	2.48	134	.205	.271	16	.250	3	22	18	2	2.5
1982	LA-N★	19	13	.594	37	37	18	4	0	285	247	13	83	199	10.5	2.87	121	.236	.294	16	.168	1	23	19	5	2.7
1983	*LA-N☆	15	10	.600	35	35	9	4	0	257	245	16	99	189	12.2	3.75	96	.255	.327	17	.187	2	-3	-4	4	0.2
1984	LA-N★	12	17	.414	34	34	12	2	0	261	218	14	106	240	11.2	3.03	116	.229	.308	15	.190	4	16	14	4	2.5
1985	*LA-N★	17	10	.630	35	35	14	5	0	272^1	211	14	101	208	10.3	2.45	142	.214	.288	21	.216	4	35	31	2	3.6
1986	LA-N★	**21**	11	.656	34	34	**20**	3	0	269^1	226	18	85	242	10.4	3.14	110	.226	.288	24	.220	5	17	9	4	1.9
1987	LA-N	14	14	.500	34	34	**12**	1	0	251	254	25	124	190	13.7	3.98	100	.262	.349	13	.141	-1	3	-0	3	0.2
1988	LA-N	5	8	.385	23	22	3	0	1	142^1	142	11	76	64	13.8	4.24	79	.268	.360	8	.182	1	-12	-14	3	-0.8
1989	LA-N	10	13	.435	31	31	3	0	0	196^2	185	11	98	116	13.0	3.43	99	.251	.340	12	.182	1	1	-0	2	0.2
1990	LA-N	13	13	.500	33	33	5	2	0	204	223	19	77	115	13.2	4.59	80	.276	.339	21	.304	8	-18	-21	-0	-1.6
1991	Cal-A	0	2	.000	2	2	0	0	0	6^2	14	3	3	5	23.0	12.15	34	.452	.500	0	—	0	-6	-6	0	-1.2
1993	Bal-A	8	10	.444	32	31	5	2	0	178^2	179	18	79	78	13.2	4.94	91	.266	.346	0	—	0	-12	-9	2	-0.7
1994	Phi-N	1	2	.333	8	7	0	0	0	45	42	8	7	19	9.8	3.00	143	.247	.277	3	.250	1	6	6	0	0.5
1995	SD-N	8	3	.727	29	15	0	0	0	90^1	101	16	34	57	13.5	4.98	81	.289	.352	8	.250	3	-8	-10	3	-0.4
1996	*SD-N	13	8	.619	33	31	0	0	0	171^2	177	17	67	95	12.8	3.62	110	.269	.336	9	.143	-1	11	7	2	0.8
1997	SD-N	2	8	.200	13	13	1	0	0	66^1	84	10	32	51	16.3	4.75	82	.309	.390	3	.176	0	-4	-6	1	-0.7
	StL-N	0	4	.000	5	5	0	0	0	22^2	22	2	14	10	14.7	5.56	75	.253	.363	1	.200	0	-3	-4	1	-0.5
	Yr	2	12	.143	18	18	1	0	0	89	106	12	46	61	15.5	4.96	80	.290	.371	4	.182	0	-7	-10	2	-1.2
Total	17	173	153	.531	453	424	113	31	2	2930	2718	226	1151	2074	12.0	3.54	103	.248	.321	187	.200	32	73	36	36	10.1
● JULIO VALERA	Valera, Julio Enrique (Torres) b: 10/13/68, Aguadilla, P.R. BR/TR, 6'2", 215 lbs. Deb: 9/1/90																									
1990	NY-N	1	1	.500	3	3	0	0	0	13	20	1	7	4	18.7	6.92	54	.351	.422	1	.200	0	-5	-5	-1	-0.6
1991	NY-N	0	0	—	2	0	0	0	0	2	1	0	4	3	22.5	0.00	—	.143	.455	0	—	0	1	1	0	0.0
1992	Cal-A	8	11	.421	30	28	4	2	0	188	188	15	64	113	12.2	3.73	107	.262	.324	0	—	0	4	5	-2	0.2
1993	Cal-A	3	6	.333	19	5	0	0	4	53	77	8	15	28	16.0	6.62	68	.344	.390	0	—	0	-14	-12	-0	-2.0
1996	KC-A	3	2	.600	31	2	0	0	1	61^1	75	7	27	31	15.3	6.46	78	.307	.381	0	—	0	-10	-10	-0	-0.7
Total	5	15	20	.429	85	38	4	2	5	317^1	361	31	117	179	13.7	4.85	88	.289	.353	1	.200	0	-23	-21	-4	-3.1

YEAR	TM/L	W	L	PCT	G	GS	CG	SH	SV	IP	H	HR	BB	SO	RAT	ERA	ERA+	OAV	OOB	BH	AVG	PB	PR	/A	PD	TPI
● **CLAY Van ALSTYNE**	Van Alstyne, Clayton Emory "Spike" b: 5/24/1900, Stuyvesant, N.Y. d: 1/5/60, Hudson, N.Y. BR/TR, 5′11″, 180 lbs. Deb: 8/20/27																									
1927	Was-A	0	0	—	2	0	0	0	0	3	3	0	0	0	9.0	3.00	136	.250	.250	0	—	0	0	0	-0	0.0
1928	Was-A	0	0	—	4	0	0	0	0	21^1	26	0	13	5	16.9	5.48	73	.329	.430	2	.250	1	-3	-3	1	0.2
Total	2	0	0	—	6	0	0	0	0	24^1	29	0	13	5	15.9	5.18	78	.319	.410	2	.250	1	-3	-3	1	0.2
● **RUSS Van ATTA**	Van Atta, Russell "Sheriff" b: 6/21/06, Augusta, N.J. d: 10/10/86, Andover, N.J. BL/TL, 6′, 184 lbs. Deb: 4/25/33																									
1933	NY-A	12	4	.750	26	22	10	2	1	157	160	8	63	76	12.8	4.18	93	.262	.332	17	.283	4	2	-5	0	-0.1
1934	NY-A	3	5	.375	28	9	0	0	0	88	107	3	46	39	15.9	6.34	64	.307	.390	6	.207	1	-18	-22	-1	-1.6
1935	NY-A	0	0	—	5	0	0	0	0	4^2	5	0	4	3	17.4	3.86	105	.263	.391	0	.000	-0	0	0	-0	0.0
	StL-A	9	16	.360	53	17	1	0	3	170^1	201	10	87	87	15.4	5.34	90	.292	.374	9	.214	-1	-17	-10	-1	-1.5
	Yr	9	16	.360	**58**	17	1	0	3	175	206	10	91	90	15.4	5.30	90	.291	.375	9	.209	-1	-16	-10	-2	-1.5
1936	StL-A	4	7	.364	**52**	9	2	0	2	122^2	164	9	68	59	17.2	6.60	81	.320	.401	5	.172	-1	-21	-17	1	-1.2
1937	StL-A	1	2	.333	16	6	1	0	0	58^2	74	2	32	34	16.3	5.52	87	.307	.388	6	.462	3	-6	-5	1	0.2
1938	StL-A	4	7	.364	25	12	3	1	0	104	118	7	61	35	15.6	6.06	82	.289	.382	4	.133	-1	-15	-13	0	-1.1
1939	StL-A	0	0	—	2	1	0	0	0	7	9	0	7	6	21.9	11.57	42	.310	.459	0	.000	-0	-5	-5	-0	0.0
Total	7	33	41	.446	207	76	17	3	6	712^1	838	39	368	339	15.4	5.60	82	.293	.376	47	.228	5	-80	-78	-1	-5.3
● **OZZIE Van BRABANT**	Van Brabant, Camille Oscar b: 9/28/26, Kingsville, Ont., Canada BR/TR, 6′1″, 165 lbs. Deb: 4/13/54																									
1954	Phi-A	0	2	.000	9	2	0	0	0	26^2	35	3	18	10	18.2	7.09	55	.347	.450	1	.200	0	-10	-9	1	-0.5
1955	KC-A	0	0	—	2	0	0	0	0	2	4	1	2	1	27.0	18.00	23	.400	.500	0	—	0	-3	-3	-0	0.0
Total	2	0	2	.000	11	2	0	0	0	28^2	39	4	20	11	18.8	7.85	50	.351	.455	1	.200	0	-13	-13	1	-0.5
● **DAZZY VANCE**	Vance, Clarence Arthur b: 3/4/1891, Orient, Iowa d: 2/16/61, Homosassa Springs, Fla. BR/TR, 6′2″, 200 lbs. Deb: 4/16/15 H																									
1915	Pit-N	0	1	.000	1	1	0	0	0	2^2	3	0	5	0	30.4	10.13	27	.375	.643	0	.000	-0	-2	-2	0	-0.6
	NY-A	0	3	.000	8	3	1	0	0	28	23	1	16	18	13.2	3.54	83	.232	.350	2	.667	2	-2	-2	-0	0.0
1918	NY-A	0	0	—	2	0	0	0	0	2^1	9	0	2	0	42.4	15.43	18	.692	.733	0	—	0	-3	-3	-0	0.0
1922	Bro-N	18	12	.600	36	31	16	**5**	0	245^2	259	9	94	**134**	13.2	3.70	110	.276	.347	20	.225	1	11	10	0	1.3
1923	Bro-N	18	15	.545	37	35	21	3	0	280^1	263	10	100	**197**	12.0	3.50	111	.250	.322	7	.084	-3	16	12	0	0.9
1924	Bro-N	**28**	6	.824	35	34	**30**	3	0	308^1	238	11	77	**262**	**9.5**	**2.16**	**173**	**.213**	**.269**	16	.151	-2	**58**	**54**	1	**5.7**
1925	Bro-N	**22**	9	.710	31	31	26	**4**	0	265^1	247	8	66	**221**	11.0	3.53	118	.250	.304	14	.143	-0	22	19	1	2.1
1926	Bro-N	9	10	.474	24	22	12	0	1	169	172	7	58	**140**	12.3	3.89	98	.271	.333	10	.182	-1	-1	-1	2	-0.1
1927	Bro-N	16	15	.516	34	32	**25**	2	1	273^1	242	12	69	**184**	10.4	2.70	147	**.239**	.291	15	.167	-2	37	38	-2	3.8
1928	Bro-N	22	10	.688	38	32	24	**4**	2	280^1	226	11	72	**200**	**9.8**	**2.09**	**191**	**.221**	**.277**	17	.177	2	**59**	**59**	1	**7.0**
1929	Bro-N	14	13	.519	31	26	17	1	0	231^1	244	15	47	126	11.7	3.89	119	.274	.316	10	.135	-2	21	19	1	1.7
1930	Bro-N	17	15	.531	35	31	20	**4**	0	258^2	241	15	55	173	**10.5**	**2.61**	**188**	**.246**	**.289**	12	.135	-5	**68**	**66**	-1	**6.6**
1931	Bro-N	11	13	.458	30	29	12	2	0	218^2	221	12	53	150	11.3	3.38	113	.261	.304	9	.134	-2	12	11	1	0.9
1932	Bro-N	12	11	.522	27	24	9	1	1	175^2	171	10	57	103	11.7	4.20	91	.256	.315	5	.089	-4	-6	-7	-0	-1.2
1933	StL-N	6	2	.750	28	11	2	0	3	99	105	3	28	67	12.2	3.55	98	.267	.318	5	.179	-1	-2	-1	-1	-0.2
1934	Cin-N	0	2	.000	6	2	0	0	0	18	28	1	11	9	20.0	7.50	54	.350	.435	1	.250	0	-7	-7	0	-0.6
	*StL-N	1	1	.500	19	4	1	0	1	59	62	4	14	33	11.9	3.66	115	.271	.318	2	.133	-0	3	4	-0	0.1
	Yr	1	3	.250	25	6	1	0	1	77	90	5	25	42	13.7	4.56	92	.290	.347	3	.158	0	-4	-3	-0	-0.5
1935	Bro-N	3	2	.600	20	0	0	0	2	51	55	3	16	28	13.1	4.41	90	.268	.330	1	.059	-2	-2	-2	-0	-0.4
Total	16	197	140	.585	442	348	216	29	11	2966^2	2809	132	840	2045	11.3	3.24	125	.251	.308	146	.150	-18	281	266	3	27.0
● **SANDY VANCE**	Vance, Gene Covington b: 1/5/47, Lamar, Colo. BR/TR, 6′2″, 180 lbs. Deb: 4/26/70																									
1970	LA-N	7	7	.500	20	18	2	0	0	115	109	9	37	45	11.5	3.13	122	.248	.308	7	.189	1	12	9	-3	0.8
1971	LA-N	2	1	.667	10	3	0	0	0	26	38	1	9	11	16.3	6.92	47	.355	.405	0	.000	-0	-10	-11	-0	-1.2
Total	2	9	8	.529	30	21	2	0	0	141	147	10	46	56	12.4	3.83	97	.269	.327	7	.167	0	2	-2	-3	-0.4
● **JOE VANCE**	Vance, Joseph Albert "Sandy" b: 9/16/05, Devine, Tex. d: 7/4/78, Devine, Tex. BR/TR, 6′1.5″, 190 lbs. Deb: 4/18/35																									
1935	Chi-A	2	2	.500	10	0	0	0	0	31	36	1	21	12	16.5	6.68	69	.295	.399	2	.182	-1	-8	-7	1	-0.8
1937	NY-A	1	0	1.000	2	2	0	0	0	15	11	2	9	3	12.0	3.00	148	.204	.317	0	.000	-1	3	2	1	0.1
1938	NY-A	0	0	—	3	1	0	0	0	11^1	20	2	4	2	19.1	7.15	63	.408	.453	3	.750	2	-3	-3	0	0.2
Total	3	3	2	.600	15	3	0	0	0	57^1	67	5	34	17	15.9	5.81	79	.298	.390	5	.250	1	-8	-8	1	-0.5
● **CHRIS Van CUYK**	Van Cuyk, Christian Gerald b: 1/3/27, Kimberly, Wis. d: 11/3/92, Hudson, Fla. BL/TL, 6′6″, 215 lbs. Deb: 7/16/50 F																									
1950	Bro-N	1	3	.250	12	4	1	0	0	33^1	33	3	12	21	12.4	4.86	84	.266	.336	1	.100	-1	-3	-3	-1	-0.4
1951	Bro-N	1	2	.333	9	6	0	0	0	29^1	33	4	11	16	14.7	5.52	71	.295	.378	2	.250	0	-5	-5	-0	-0.4
1952	Bro-N	5	6	.455	23	16	4	0	1	97^2	104	12	40	66	13.7	5.16	71	.271	.347	8	.242	2	-16	-17	-1	-1.7
Total	3	7	11	.389	44	26	5	0	1	160^1	170	19	63	103	13.6	5.16	73	.274	.351	11	.216	1	-23	-25	-2	-2.5
● **JOHNNY Van CUYK**	Van Cuyk, John Henry b: 7/7/21, Little Chute, Wis. BL/TL, 6′1″, 190 lbs. Deb: 9/18/47 F																									
1947	Bro-N	0	0	—	2	0	0	0	0	3^1	5	0	1	2	16.2	5.40	77	.357	.400	0	—	0	-0	-0	0	0.0
1948	Bro-N	0	0	—	3	0	0	0	0	5	4	1	1	1	9.0	3.60	111	.200	.238	0	—	0	0	0	0	0.0
1949	Bro-N	0	0	—	2	0	0	0	0	2	3	0	1	0	18.0	9.00	46	.429	.500	0	—	0	-1	-1	-0	0.0
Total	3	0	0	—	7	0	0	0	0	10^1	12	1	3	3	13.1	5.23	78	.293	.341	0	—	0	-1	-1	0	0.0
● **ED VANDE BERG**	Vande Berg, Edward John b: 10/26/58, Redlands, Cal. BR/TL, 6′2″, 180 lbs. Deb: 4/7/82																									
1982	Sea-A	9	4	.692	**78**	0	0	0	5	76	54	5	32	60	10.4	2.37	179	.207	.298	0	—	0	14	16	2	2.9
1983	Sea-A	2	4	.333	68	0	0	0	5	64^1	59	6	22	49	11.5	3.36	127	.246	.312	0	—	0	5	6	0	0.5
1984	Sea-A	8	12	.400	50	17	2	0	7	130^1	165	18	50	71	14.8	4.76	84	.313	.373	0	—	0	-11	-11	-0	-1.7
1985	Sea-A	2	1	.667	76	0	0	0	3	67^2	71	4	31	34	13.7	3.72	113	.274	.354	0	—	0	3	4	1	0.2
1986	LA-N	1	5	.167	60	0	0	0	0	71^1	83	8	33	42	14.8	3.41	101	.290	.366	0	.000	-0	2	0	1	0.1
1987	Cle-A	1	0	1.000	55	0	0	0	0	72^1	96	9	21	40	14.6	5.10	89	.325	.370	0	—	0	-5	-5	0	0.0
1988	Tex-A	2	2	.500	26	0	0	0	2	37	44	2	11	18	13.4	4.14	99	.308	.357	0	—	0	-1	-0	-1	-0.2
Total	7	25	28	.472	413	17	2	0	22	519	572	52	200	314	13.5	3.92	104	.284	.351	0	.000	-0	8	10	3	1.8
● **HY VANDENBERG**	Vandenberg, Harold Harris b: 3/17/06, Abilene, Kan. d: 7/31/94, Bloomington, Minn. BR/TR, 6′4″, 220 lbs. Deb: 6/8/35																									
1935	Bos-A	0	0	—	3	0	0	0	0	5^1	15	1	4	2	32.1	20.25	23	.500	.559	1	1.000	0	-9	-9	0	0.0
1937	NY-N	0	1	.000	1	1	1	0	0	8	10	0	6	2	18.0	7.88	49	.313	.421	0	.000	-1	-4	-4	1	-0.3
1938	NY-N	0	1	.000	6	1	0	0	0	18	28	2	12	7	20.0	7.50	50	.368	.455	0	.000	-1	-7	-7	1	-0.3
1939	NY-N	0	0	—	2	1	0	0	0	6^1	10	0	6	3	22.7	5.68	69	.345	.457	0	.000	-0	-1	-1	0	0.0
1940	NY-N	1	1	.500	13	3	1	0	1	32^1	27	2	16	17	12.2	3.90	100	.227	.324	1	.125	-0	-0	-0	-0	-0.1
1944	Chi-N	7	4	.636	35	9	2	0	2	126^1	123	8	51	54	12.5	3.63	97	.255	.327	9	.237	1	-0	-1	0	-0.1
1945	*Chi-N	7	3	.700	30	7	3	1	2	95^1	91	4	33	35	12.1	3.49	105	.259	.330	4	.125	-1	3	2	0	0.1
Total	7	15	10	.600	90	22	7	1	5	291^2	304	17	128	120	13.5	4.32	85	.271	.349	15	.169	-1	-19	-21	2	-0.7
● **JOHNNY VANDER MEER**	Vander Meer, John Samuel "Double No-Hit" or "The Dutch Master" b: 11/2/14, Prospect Park, N.J. d: 10/6/97, Tampa, Fla. BB/TL, 6′1″, 190 lbs. Deb: 4/22/37																									
1937	Cin-N	3	5	.375	19	10	4	0	0	84^1	63	0	69	52	14.3	3.84	97	.209	.359	5	.217	1	1	-1	2	0.2
1938	Cin-N★	15	10	.600	32	29	16	3	0	225^1	177	12	103	125	11.3	3.12	117	**.213**	.302	15	.181	-2	17	13	-1	1.0
1939	Cin-N☆	5	9	.357	30	21	8	0	0	129	128	7	95	102	15.7	4.67	82	.264	.387	4	.111	-1	-11	-12	-1	-1.4
1940	*Cin-N	3	1	.750	10	7	2	0	1	48	38	3	41	41	15.0	3.75	101	.211	.360	6	.300	2	1	0	0	0.2
1941	Cin-N	16	13	.552	33	32	18	6	0	226^1	172	8	126	**202**	11.9	2.82	127	.214	.321	10	.132	-3	20	19	2	2.3
1942	Cin-N★	18	12	.600	33	33	21	4	0	244	188	6	102	**186**	10.7	2.43	135	.208	.290	11	.147	-1	24	23	1	2.9
1943	Cin-N★	15	16	.484	36	36	21	3	0	289	228	5	162	**174**	12.2	2.87	116	.224	.332	13	.137	-2	17	14	3	1.6
1946	Cin-N	10	12	.455	29	25	11	4	0	204^1	175	11	78	94	11.1	3.17	105	.233	.305	18	.247	2	5	4	-2	0.5
1947	Cin-N	9	14	.391	30	29	9	3	0	186	186	11	87	79	13.4	4.40	93	.261	.343	5	.088	-3	-7	-6	-1	-1.0
1948	Cin-N	17	14	.548	33	33	14	3	0	232	204	15	124	120	12.8	3.41	115	.239	.336	11	.141	0	14	13	-1	1.6
1949	Cin-N	5	10	.333	28	24	7	3	0	159^2	172	12	85	76	14.6	4.90	85	.281	.370	4	.077	-3	-15	-13	1	-1.2
1950	Chi-N	3	4	.429	32	6	0	0	1	73^2	60	10	59	41	14.8	3.79	111	.221	.363	2	.125	-0	3	3	-0	0.3

YEAR	TM/L	W	L	PCT	G	GS	CG	SH	SV	IP	H	HR	BB	SO	RAT	ERA	ERA+	OAV	OOB	BH	AVG	PB	PR	/A	PD	TPI
1951	Cle-A	0	1	.000	1	1	0	0	0	3	8	0	1	2	27.0	18.00	21	.500	.529	0	.000	-0	-5	-5	1	-0.9
Total	13	119	121	.496	346	286	131	29	2	2104^{2}	1799	100	1132	1294	12.6	3.44	107	.232	.332	104	.152	-9	63	53	3	6.1

● BEN Van DYKE Van Dyke, Benjamin Harrison b: 8/15/1888, Clintonville, Pa. d: 10/22/73, Sarasota, Fla. BR/TL, 6'1", 150 lbs. Deb: 5/11/09

YEAR	TM/L	W	L	PCT	G	GS	CG	SH	SV	IP	H	HR	BB	SO	RAT	ERA	ERA+	OAV	OOB	BH	AVG	PB	PR	/A	PD	TPI
1909	Phi-N	0	0	—	2	0	0	0	0	7^{1}	7	0	4	5	13.5	3.68	71	.269	.367	0	.000	-0	-1	-1	-0	-0.1
1912	Bos-A	0	0	—	3	1	0	0	0	14^{1}	13	0	7	8	13.2	3.14	108	.245	.344	1	.250	-0	0	0	-1	-0.1
Total	2	0	0	—	5	1	0	0	0	21^{2}	20	0	11	13	13.3	3.32	94	.253	.352	1	.143	-0	-1	-0	-1	-0.2

● TIM Van EGMOND Van Egmond, Timothy Layne b: 5/31/69, Shreveport, La. BR/TR, 6'2", 185 lbs. Deb: 6/26/94

YEAR	TM/L	W	L	PCT	G	GS	CG	SH	SV	IP	H	HR	BB	SO	RAT	ERA	ERA+	OAV	OOB	BH	AVG	PB	PR	/A	PD	TPI
1994	Bos-A	2	3	.400	7	7	1	0	0	38^{1}	38	7	21	22	13.9	6.34	79	.255	.347	0	—	0	-7	-6	-1	-0.7
1995	Bos-A	0	1	.000	4	1	0	0	0	6^{2}	9	2	6	5	20.3	9.45	52	.310	.429	0	—	0	-4	-3	0	-0.4
1996	Mil-A	3	5	.375	12	9	0	0	0	54^{2}	58	6	23	33	13.5	5.27	98	.274	.347	0	—	0	-2	-0	0	-0.1
Total	3	5	9	.357	23	17	1	0	0	99^{2}	105	15	50	60	14.1	5.96	86	.269	.354	0	—	0	-12	-9	-1	-1.2

● ELAM VANGILDER Vangilder, Elam Russell b: 4/23/1896, Cape Girardeau, Mo d: 4/30/77, Cape Girardeau, Mo BR/TR, 6'1", 192 lbs. Deb: 9/18/19

YEAR	TM/L	W	L	PCT	G	GS	CG	SH	SV	IP	H	HR	BB	SO	RAT	ERA	ERA+	OAV	OOB	BH	AVG	PB	PR	/A	PD	TPI
1919	StL-A	1	0	1.000	3	1	1	0	0	13	15	0	3	6	12.5	2.08	160	.306	.346	2	.667	1	2	2	1	0.3
1920	StL-A	3	8	.273	24	13	4	0	0	104^{2}	131	7	40	25	15.0	5.50	71	.310	.373	4	.133	-2	-20	-18	-0	-1.8
1921	StL-A	11	12	.478	31	21	10	1	0	180^{1}	196	10	67	48	13.2	3.94	114	.278	.342	13	.200	-2	7	11	-0	1.0
1922	StL-A	19	13	.594	43	30	19	3	4	245	248	13	48	63	11.1	3.42	121	.270	.310	32	.344	13	17	20	-3	3.4
1923	StL-A	16	17	.485	41	35	20	4	1	282^{1}	276	11	120	74	12.8	3.06	136	.266	.345	24	.218	-0	29	**35**	-3	3.4
1924	StL-A	5	10	.333	43	18	5	0	1	145^{1}	183	10	55	49	15.3	5.64	80	.317	.385	13	.295	3	-23	-18	2	-1.2
1925	StL-A	14	8	.636	52	16	4	1	6	193^{1}	225	11	92	61	15.0	4.70	99	.303	.385	13	.183	-3	-7	-1	-0	-0.3
1926	StL-A	9	11	.450	42	19	8	1	1	181	196	12	98	40	14.7	5.17	83	.285	.376	11	.190	1	-23	-18	-2	-1.8
1927	StL-A	10	12	.455	44	23	12	3	1	203	245	13	102	62	15.6	4.79	91	.310	.392	19	.279	2	-15	-10	-4	-1.0
1928	Det-A	11	10	.524	38	11	7	0	5	156^{1}	163	4	67	43	13.4	3.91	105	.272	.348	15	.259	2	2	3	0	0.6
1929	Det-A	0	1	.000	6	0	0	0	0	11^{1}	16	1	7	3	18.3	6.35	68	.348	.434	0	.000	-0	-3	-3	1	-0.1
Total	11	99	102	.493	367	187	90	13	19	1715^{2}	1894	92	699	474	13.8	4.28	100	.288	.360	146	.243	15	-33	3	-9	2.5

● GEORGE Van HALTREN Van Haltren, George Edward Martin "Rip"
b: 3/30/1866, St.Louis, Mo. d: 9/29/45, Oakland, Cal. BL/TL, 5'11", 170 lbs. Deb: 6/27/1887 M♦

YEAR	TM/L	W	L	PCT	G	GS	CG	SH	SV	IP	H	HR	BB	SO	RAT	ERA	ERA+	OAV	OOB	BH	AVG	PB	PR	/A	PD	TPI
1887	Chi-N	11	7	.611	20	18	18	1	**1**	161	177	7	66	76	14.5	3.86	116	.277	.359	35	.203	-2	4	11	-0	0.8
1888	Chi-N	13	13	.500	30	24	24	4	1	245^{2}	263	15	60	139	12.3	3.52	86	.267	.318	90	.283	11	-18	-13	2	-0.1
1890	Bro-P	15	10	.600	28	25	23	0	2	223	272	8	89	48	15.4	4.28	104	.288	.362	126	.335	10	-1	4	3	1.3
1891	Bal-a	0	1	.000	6	1	0	0	0	23	38	1	10	7	20.3	5.09	73	.358	.433	180	.318	3	-3	-3	-0	0.0
1892	Bal-N	0	0	—	4	0	0	0	0	14^{2}	28	1	7	5	21.5	9.20	37	.389	.443	168	.302	2	-10	-9	0	0.1
1895	NY-N	0	0	—	1	0	0	0	0	5	13	0	2	1	30.6	12.60	37	.481	.548	177	.340	0	-4	-4	-0	0.0
1896	NY-N	1	0	1.000	2	0	0	0	0	8	5	1	1	3	6.8	2.25	187	.179	.207	197	.351	1	2	2	-0	0.2
1900	NY-N	0	0	—	1	0	0	0	0	3	1	0	3	0	12.0	0.00	—	.100	.308	180	.315	0	1	1	-0	0.0
1901	NY-N	0	0	—	1	0	0	0	0	6	12	0	6	2	28.5	3.00	110	.414	.528	182	.335	0	0	0	1	0.1
Total	9	40	31	.563	93	68	65	5	4	689^{1}	809	33	244	281	14.5	4.05	96	.285	.353	2532	.316	25	-30	-12	6	2.4

● WILLIAM Van LANDINGHAM Van Landingham, William Joseph b: 7/16/70, Columbia, Tenn. BR/TR, 6'2", 210 lbs. Deb: 5/21/94

YEAR	TM/L	W	L	PCT	G	GS	CG	SH	SV	IP	H	HR	BB	SO	RAT	ERA	ERA+	OAV	OOB	BH	AVG	PB	PR	/A	PD	TPI
1994	SF-N	8	2	.800	16	14	0	0	0	84	70	4	43	56	12.3	3.54	113	.223	.320	2	.065	-2	6	4	-0	0.2
1995	SF-N	6	3	.667	18	18	1	0	0	122^{2}	124	14	40	95	12.2	3.67	111	.264	.324	7	.152	0	7	6	0	0.5
1996	SF-N	9	14	.391	32	32	0	0	0	181^{2}	196	17	78	97	14.0	5.40	76	.276	.355	8	.131	-1	-24	-26	-3	-3.1
1997	SF-N	4	7	.364	18	17	0	0	0	89	80	11	59	52	14.1	4.96	83	.237	.351	3	.115	-0	-7	-8	-2	-1.1
Total	4	27	26	.509	84	81	1	0	0	477^{1}	470	46	220	300	13.3	4.54	90	.257	.340	20	.122	-3	-18	-25	-5	-3.5

● TODD Van POPPEL Van Poppel, Todd Matthew b: 12/9/71, Hinsdale, Ill. BR/TR, 6'5", 210 lbs. Deb: 9/11/91

YEAR	TM/L	W	L	PCT	G	GS	CG	SH	SV	IP	H	HR	BB	SO	RAT	ERA	ERA+	OAV	OOB	BH	AVG	PB	PR	/A	PD	TPI
1991	Oak-A	0	0	—	1	1	0	0	0	4^{2}	7	1	2	6	17.4	9.64	40	.368	.429	0	—	0	-3	-3	0	0.3
1993	Oak-A	6	6	.500	16	16	0	0	0	84	76	10	62	47	15.0	5.04	81	.243	.371	0	—	0	-7	-9	-1	-1.2
1994	Oak-A	7	10	.412	23	23	0	0	0	116^{2}	108	20	89	83	15.4	6.09	73	.250	.382	0	—	0	-17	-22	-1	-2.5
1995	Oak-A	4	8	.333	36	14	1	0	0	138^{1}	125	16	56	122	12.0	4.88	92	.244	.323	0	—	0	-3	-6	-2	-0.6
1996	Oak-A	1	5	.167	28	6	0	0	1	63	86	13	33	37	17.3	7.71	64	.333	.413	0	—	0	-19	-20	-1	-1.6
	Det-A	2	4	.333	9	9	1	1	0	36^{1}	53	11	29	16	20.6	11.39	44	.338	.444	0	—	0	-26	-26	0	-2.9
	Yr	3	9	.250	37	15	1	1	1	99^{1}	139	24	62	53	18.3	9.06	55	.329	.416	0	—	0	-45	-45	-1	-4.5
1998	Tex-A	1	2	.333	4	4	0	0	0	19^{1}	26	5	10	10	17.2	8.84	55	.313	.394	0	.000	-0	-9	-9	-1	-1.0
	Pit-N	1	2	.333	18	7	0	0	0	47	53	4	18	32	13.6	5.36	81	.286	.350	3	.250	1	-6	-5	-1	-0.3
Total	6	22	37	.373	135	80	2	1	1	509^{1}	534	80	299	353	14.9	6.24	72	.272	.372	3	.214	1	-89	-99	-7	-9.8

● BEN Van RYN Van Ryn, Benjamin Ashley b: 8/9/71, Fort Wayne, Ind. BL/TL, 6'5", 185 lbs. Deb: 5/9/96

YEAR	TM/L	W	L	PCT	G	GS	CG	SH	SV	IP	H	HR	BB	SO	RAT	ERA	ERA+	OAV	OOB	BH	AVG	PB	PR	/A	PD	TPI
1996	Cal-A	0	0	—	1	0	0	0	0	1	1	0	1	0	18.0	0.00	—	.250	.400	0	—	0	1	1	0	0.0
1998	Chi-N	0	0	—	9	0	0	0	0	8	9	0	6	6	18.0	3.38	129	.290	.421	0	.000	-0	1	1	-0	0.0
	SD-N	0	1	.000	6	0	0	0	0	2^{2}	3	0	4	1	27.0	10.13	38	.273	.500	0	—	0	-2	-2	-0	-0.6
	Yr	0	1	.000	15	0	0	0	0	10^{2}	12	0	10	7	19.4	5.06	83	.273	.418	0	.000	-0	-1	-1	-0	-0.6
	Tor-A	0	1	.000	10	0	0	0	0	4	6	0	2	3	18.0	9.00	52	.400	.471	0	—	0	-2	-2	-0	-0.4
Total	2	0	2	.000	26	0	0	0	0	15^{2}	19	0	13	10	19.5	5.74	76	.311	.447	0	.000	-0	-2	-2	-0	-1.0

● IKE Van ZANDT Van Zandt, Charles Isaac b: 2/1876, Brooklyn, N.Y. d: 9/14/08, Nashua, N.H. BL , Deb: 8/5/01 ♦

YEAR	TM/L	W	L	PCT	G	GS	CG	SH	SV	IP	H	HR	BB	SO	RAT	ERA	ERA+	OAV	OOB	BH	AVG	PB	PR	/A	PD	TPI
1901	NY-N	0	0	—	2	0	0	0	0	12^{2}	16	0	8	2	17.8	7.11	47	.308	.410	1	.167	-0	-5	-5	-1	-0.1
1905	StL-A	0	0	—	1	0	0	0	0	6^{2}	2	0	2	3	6.8	0.00	—	.095	.208	75	.233	0	2	2	0	0.0
Total	2	0	0	—	3	0	0	0	0	19^{1}	18	0	10	5	14.0	4.66	65	.247	.353	76	.224	-0	-3	-3	-1	-0.1

● ANDY VARGA Varga, Andrew William b: 12/11/30, Chicago, Ill. d: 11/4/92, Orlando, Fla. BR/TL, 6'4", 187 lbs. Deb: 9/9/50

YEAR	TM/L	W	L	PCT	G	GS	CG	SH	SV	IP	H	HR	BB	SO	RAT	ERA	ERA+	OAV	OOB	BH	AVG	PB	PR	/A	PD	TPI
1950	Chi-N	0	0	—	1	0	0	0	0	1	0	0	1	0	9.0	0.00	—	.000	.333	0	—	0	0	0	-0	0.0
1951	Chi-N	0	0	—	2	0	0	0	0	3	2	0	6	1	24.0	3.00	136	.200	.500	0	—	0	0	0	-0	0.0
Total	2	0	0	—	3	0	0	0	0	4	2	0	7	1	20.3	2.25	183	.167	.474	0	—	0	1	1	-0	0.0

● ROBERTO VARGAS Vargas, Roberto Enrique (Velez) b: 5/29/29, Santurce, P.R. BL/TL, 5'11", 170 lbs. Deb: 4/17/55

YEAR	TM/L	W	L	PCT	G	GS	CG	SH	SV	IP	H	HR	BB	SO	RAT	ERA	ERA+	OAV	OOB	BH	AVG	PB	PR	/A	PD	TPI
1955	Mil-N	0	0	—	25	0	0	0	2	24^{2}	39	4	14	13	19.7	8.76	43	.355	.432	1	.500	0	-13	-14	1	-0.1

● BILL VARGUS Vargus, William Fay b: 11/11/1899, N.Scituate, Mass. d: 2/12/79, Hyannis, Mass. BL/TL, 6', 165 lbs. Deb: 6/23/25

YEAR	TM/L	W	L	PCT	G	GS	CG	SH	SV	IP	H	HR	BB	SO	RAT	ERA	ERA+	OAV	OOB	BH	AVG	PB	PR	/A	PD	TPI
1925	Bos-N	1	1	.500	11	2	1	0	0	36^{1}	45	1	13	5	14.9	3.96	101	.302	.366	3	.250	0	1	0	0	0.0
1926	Bos-N	0	0	—	4	0	0	0	0	3	4	0	1	0	15.0	3.00	118	.333	.385	0	—	0	0	0	0	0.0
Total	2	1	1	.500	15	2	1	0	0	39^{1}	49	1	14	5	14.9	3.89	102	.304	.367	3	.250	0	2	0	0	0.0

● DIKE VARNEY Varney, Lawrence Delano (b: Lawrence Delano De Varney)
b: 8/9/1880, Dover, N.H. d: 4/23/50, Long Island City, N.Y. BL/TL, 6', 165 lbs. Deb: 7/3/02

YEAR	TM/L	W	L	PCT	G	GS	CG	SH	SV	IP	H	HR	BB	SO	RAT	ERA	ERA+	OAV	OOB	BH	AVG	PB	PR	/A	PD	TPI
1902	Cle-A	1	1	.500	3	3	0	0	0	14^{2}	14	0	12	7	19.0	6.14	56	.250	.425	1	.167	-0	-4	-4	0	-0.5

● CAL VASBINDER Vasbinder, Moses Calhoun b: 7/19/1880, Scio, Ohio d: 12/22/50, Cadiz, Ohio BR/TR, 6'2", Deb: 4/27/02

YEAR	TM/L	W	L	PCT	G	GS	CG	SH	SV	IP	H	HR	BB	SO	RAT	ERA	ERA+	OAV	OOB	BH	AVG	PB	PR	/A	PD	TPI
1902	Cle-A	0	0	—	2	0	0	0	0	5	5	1	8	2	23.4	9.00	38	.263	.481	1	.500	0	-3	-3	0	0.0

● RAFAEL VASQUEZ Vasquez, Rafael b: 6/28/58, LaRomana, D.R. BR/TR, 6', 160 lbs. Deb: 4/6/79

YEAR	TM/L	W	L	PCT	G	GS	CG	SH	SV	IP	H	HR	BB	SO	RAT	ERA	ERA+	OAV	OOB	BH	AVG	PB	PR	/A	PD	TPI
1979	Sea-A	1	0	1.000	9	0	0	0	0	16	23	4	6	9	16.9	5.06	86	.354	.417	0	—	0	-2	-1	-0	-0.1

● PORTER VAUGHAN Vaughan, Cecil Porter "Lefty" b: 5/11/19, Stevensville, Va. BR/TL, 6'1", 178 lbs. Deb: 6/16/40

YEAR	TM/L	W	L	PCT	G	GS	CG	SH	SV	IP	H	HR	BB	SO	RAT	ERA	ERA+	OAV	OOB	BH	AVG	PB	PR	/A	PD	TPI
1940	Phi-A	2	9	.182	18	15	5	0	2	99^{1}	104	9	61	46	15.2	5.35	83	.264	.367	8	.235	0	-11	-10	-1	-1.0
1941	Phi-A	0	2	.000	5	3	1	0	0	22^{2}	32	3	12	6	17.5	7.94	53	.327	.400	1	.143	-0	-10	-9	-0	-0.7
1946	Phi-A	0	0	—	1	0	0	0	0	0	1	0	1	0	—	—	—	1.000	1.000	0	—	-0	0	0	0	0.0
Total	3	2	11	.154	24	18	6	0	2	122	137	12	74	52	15.8	5.83	75	.278	.375	9	.220	-0	-20	-19	-1	-1.7

YEAR	TM/L	W	L	PCT	G	GS	CG	SH	SV	IP	H	HR	BB	SO	RAT	ERA	ERA+	OAV	OOB	BH	AVG	PB	PR	/A	PD	TPI
● **CHARLIE VAUGHAN**	Vaughan, Charles Wayne b: 10/6/47, Mercedes, Tex. BR/TL, 6'1.5", 185 lbs. Deb: 9/3/66																									
1966	Atl-N	1	0	1.000	1	1	0	0	0	7	8	0	3	6	14.1	2.57	141	.296	.367	1	.250	0	1	1	0	0.1
1969	Atl-N	0	0	—	1	0	0	0	0	1	1	0	3	1	36.0	18.00	20	.250	.571	0	—	0	-2	-2	0	0.0
Total	2	1	0	1.000	2	1	0	0	0	8	9	0	6	7	16.9	4.50	81	.290	.405	1	.250	0	-1	-1	0	0.1
● **ROY VAUGHN**	Vaughn, Clarence Leroy b: 9/4/11, Sedalia, Mo. d: 3/1/37, Martinsville, Va. BB/TR, 6'0.5", 178 lbs. Deb: 7/1/34																									
1934	Phi-A	0	0	—	2	0	0	0	0	4^{1}	3	1	3	1	12.5	2.08	211	.176	.300	0	.000	-0	1	1	-0	0.0
● **DE WAYNE VAUGHN**	Vaughn, De Wayne Mathew b: 7/22/59, Oklahoma City, Okla BR/TR, 5'11", 180 lbs. Deb: 4/17/88																									
1988	Tex-A	0	0	—	8	0	0	0	0	15^{1}	24	4	4	8	16.4	7.63	53	.348	.384	0	—	0	-6	-6	-1	-0.1
● **FARMER VAUGHN**	Vaughn, Harry Francis b: 3/1/1864, Ruraldale, Ohio d: 2/21/14, Cincinnati, Ohio BR/TR, 6'3", 177 lbs. Deb: 10/7/1886 ♦																									
1891	Cin-a	0	0	—	1	0	0	0	0	7	12	0	1	0	18.0	3.86	107	.364	.400	45	.257	0	-0	0	-0	0.0
● **HIPPO VAUGHN**	Vaughn, James Leslie b: 4/9/1888, Weatherford, Tex. d: 5/29/66, Chicago, Ill. BB/TL, 6'4", 215 lbs. Deb: 6/19/08																									
1908	NY-A	0	0	—	2	0	0	0	0	2^{1}	1	0	4	2	19.3	3.86	64	.167	.500	0	.000	-0	-0	-0	0	0.0
1910	NY-A	13	11	.542	30	25	18	5	1	221^{2}	190	1	58	107	10.5	1.83	146	.237	.297	10	.133	-2	17	20	-0	2.0
1911	NY-A	8	10	.444	26	19	10	0	0	145^{2}	158	2	54	74	13.5	4.39	82	.284	.354	7	.143	-1	-17	-13	1	-1.4
1912	NY-A	2	8	.200	15	10	5	1	0	63	66	1	37	46	14.9	5.14	70	.264	.361	2	.095	-2	-13	-11	1	-1.5
	Was-A	4	3	.571	12	8	4	0	0	81	75	0	43	49	13.6	2.89	115	.253	.356	6	.200	-1	4	4	2	0.4
	Yr	6	11	.353	27	18	9	1	0	144	141	1	80	95	14.1	3.88	89	.258	.357	8	.157	-2	-9	-7	3	-1.1
1913	Chi-N	5	1	.833	7	6	5	2	0	56	37	0	27	36	10.6	1.45	220	.182	.284	4	.190	-1	11	11	0	1.1
1914	Chi-N	21	13	.618	42	35	23	4	1	293^{2}	236	1	109	165	10.8	2.05	135	.222	.299	14	.144	-0	24	24	-0	2.7
1915	Chi-N	20	12	.625	41	34	18	4	1	269^{2}	240	4	77	148	10.9	2.87	97	.238	.299	14	.163	1	-4	-3	-1	-0.3
1916	Chi-N	17	15	.531	44	35	21	4	1	294	269	4	67	144	10.5	2.20	132	.250	.298	14	.135	-4	14	23	1	2.2
1917	Chi-N	23	13	.639	41	38	27	5	0	295^{2}	255	3	91	195	10.8	2.01	144	.235	.300	16	.160	-1	23	29	3	4.1
1918	*Chi-N	**22**	10	.688	35	33	27	**8**	0	**290^{1}**	216	4	76	**148**	9.3	**1.74**	**161**	**.208**	.266	23	.240	4	**33**	**34**	-1	**4.4**
1919	Chi-N	21	14	.600	38	37	25	4	1	**306^{2}**	264	3	62	**141**	9.7	1.79	161	.234	.278	17	.173	-0	**38**	**37**	-3	4.2
1920	Chi-N	19	16	.543	40	38	24	4	0	301	301	8	81	131	11.7	2.54	126	.264	.318	22	.216	4	20	22	-2	2.7
1921	Chi-N	3	11	.214	17	14	7	0	0	109^{1}	153	8	31	30	15.6	6.01	64	.341	.390	10	.244	2	-27	-27	-1	-2.7
Total	13	178	137	.565	390	332	214	41	5	2730	2461	39	817	1416	11.1	2.49	120	.244	.306	159	.173	-1	123	152	-1	17.9
● **JAVIER VAZQUEZ**	Vazquez, Javier Carlos b: 6/25/76, Ponce, P.R. BR/TR, 6'2", 180 lbs. Deb: 4/3/98																									
1998	Mon-N	5	15	.250	33	32	0	0	0	172^{1}	196	31	68	139	14.4	6.06	68	.292	.366	9	.173	1	-35	-37	1	-3.4
● **AL VEACH**	Veach, Alvis Lindel b: 8/6/09, Maylene, Ala. d: 9/6/90, Charlotte, N.C. BR/TR, 5'11", 178 lbs. Deb: 9/22/35																									
1935	Phi-A	0	2	.000	2	2	1	0	0	10	20	1	9	3	26.1	11.70	39	.417	.509	0	.000	-1	-8	-8	0	-1.1
● **BOBBY VEACH**	Veach, Robert Hayes b: 6/29/1888, Island, Ky. d: 8/7/45, Detroit, Mich. BL/TR, 5'11", 160 lbs. Deb: 8/6/12 ♦																									
1918	Det-A	0	0	—	1	0	0	0	1	2	2	0	2	0	18.0	4.50	59	.286	.444	139	.279	0	-0	-0	-0	-0.1
● **PEEK-A-BOO VEACH**	Veach, William Walter b: 6/15/1862, Indianapolis, Ind d: 11/12/37, Indianapolis, Ind. Deb: 8/24/1884 ♦																									
1884	KC-U	3	9	.250	12	12	12	0	0	104	95	1	10	62	9.1	2.42	92	.227	.245	11	.134	-3	0	-2	1	-0.4
1887	Lou-a	0	1	.000	1	1	1	0	0	9	5	1	8	2	13.0	4.00	110	.172	.351	0	.000	-0	0	0	-0	0.0
Total	2	3	10	.231	13	13	13	0	0	113	100	2	18	64	9.4	2.55	94	.223	.253	76	.215	-4	1	-2	1	-0.4
● **BOB VEALE**	Veale, Robert Andrew b: 10/28/35, Birmingham, Ala. BB/TL, 6'6", 212 lbs. Deb: 4/16/62																									
1962	Pit-N	2	2	.500	11	6	2	0	1	45^{2}	39	2	25	42	12.6	3.74	105	.235	.335	4	.250	1	1	1	-0	0.1
1963	Pit-N	5	2	.714	34	7	3	2	3	77^{2}	59	1	40	68	11.6	1.04	316	.215	.317	2	.087	-0	19	**19**	0	1.9
1964	Pit-N	18	12	.600	40	38	14	1	0	279^{2}	222	8	124	**250**	11.2	2.74	128	.217	.303	15	.156	-0	25	24	-1	2.4
1965	Pit-N☆	17	12	.586	39	37	14	7	0	266	221	5	119	276	11.7	2.84	124	.225	.313	8	.086	-4	21	20	-2	1.5
1966	Pit-N☆	16	12	.571	38	37	12	3	0	268^{1}	228	18	102	229	11.2	3.02	118	.232	.307	13	.138	-2	18	17	-2	1.2
1967	Pit-N	16	8	.667	33	31	6	1	0	203	184	12	119	179	13.7	3.64	93	.245	.352	3	.043	-5	-6	-6	1	-1.1
1968	Pit-N	13	14	.481	36	33	13	4	0	245^{1}	187	13	94	171	10.4	2.05	142	.211	.288	9	.110	-2	25	24	-2	2.3
1969	Pit-N	13	14	.481	34	34	9	1	0	225^{2}	232	8	91	213	13.0	3.23	108	.267	.338	4	.051	-5	9	6	-0	0.1
1970	Pit-N	10	15	.400	34	32	5	1	0	202	189	15	94	178	12.7	3.92	100	.246	.331	11	.164	1	3	-0	-2	-0.1
1971	*Pit-N	6	0	1.000	37	0	0	0	2	46^{1}	59	5	24	40	16.1	6.99	48	.314	.392	3	.333	1	-18	-19	-2	-2.5
1972	Pit-N	0	0	—	5	0	0	0	0	9	10	0	7	6	17.0	6.00	55	.313	.436	0	.000	-0	-3	-3	-0	-0.1
	Bos-A	2	0	1.000	6	0	0	0	2	8	2	0	3	10	5.6	0.00	—	.083	.185	0	.000	-0	3	3	0	1.0
1973	Bos-A	2	3	.400	32	0	0	0	11	36^{1}	37	2	12	25	12.1	3.47	116	.268	.327	0	—	0	1	2	1	0.5
1974	Bos-A	0	1	.000	18	0	0	0	2	13	15	2	4	16	13.2	5.54	69	.283	.333	0	—	0	-3	-2	-0	-0.3
Total	13	120	95	.558	397	255	78	20	21	1926	1684	91	858	1703	12.0	3.07	113	.236	.320	72	.114	-17	96	86	-9	6.9
● **LOU VEDDER**	Vedder, Louis Edward b: 4/20/1897, Oakville, Mich. d: 3/9/90, Lake Placid, Fla. BR/TR, 5'10.5", 175 lbs. Deb: 9/18/20																									
1920	Det-A	0	0	—	1	0	0	0	0	2	0	0	0	1	0.0	0.00	—	.000	.000	0	—	0	1	1	0	0.0
● **AL VEIGEL**	Veigel, Allen Francis b: 1/30/17, Dover, Ohio BR/TR, 6'1", 180 lbs. Deb: 9/21/39																									
1939	Bos-N	0	1	.000	2	2	0	0	0	2^{2}	3	0	5	1	27.0	6.75	55	.250	.471	0	.000	-0	-1	-1	-0	-0.3
● **BUCKY VEIL**	Veil, Frederick William b: 8/2/1881, Tyrone, Pa. d: 4/16/31, Altoona, Pa. BR/TR, 5'10", 165 lbs. Deb: 4/19/03																									
1903	*Pit-N	5	3	.625	12	6	4	0	0	70^{2}	70	1	36	20	13.8	3.82	85	.269	.362	6	.207	-0	-4	-5	-0	-0.5
1904	Pit-N	0	0	—	1	1	0	0	0	4^{2}	4	0	4	1	17.4	5.79	47	.250	.429	1	1.000	0	-2	-2	0	0.1
Total	2	5	3	.625	13	7	4	0	0	75^{1}	74	1	40	21	14.0	3.94	81	.268	.367	7	.233	0	-6	-6	-0	-0.4
● **CARLOS VELAZQUEZ**	Velazquez, Carlos (Quinones) b: 3/22/48, Loiza, P.R. BR/TR, 5'11", 180 lbs. Deb: 7/20/73																									
1973	Mil-A	2	2	.500	18	0	0	0	2	38^{1}	46	5	10	12	13.1	2.58	146	.297	.339	0	—	0	5	5	0	0.6
● **DARIO VERAS**	Veras, Dario Antonio b: 3/13/73, Santiago, D.R. BR/TR, 6'2", 165 lbs. Deb: 7/31/96																									
1996	*SD-N	3	1	.750	23	0	0	0	0	29	24	3	10	23	10.9	2.79	142	.231	.304	0	—	0	5	4	0	0.5
1997	SD-N	2	1	.667	23	0	0	0	0	24^{2}	28	5	12	21	15.3	5.11	76	.280	.368	0	—	0	-2	-3	-1	-0.4
1998	Bos-A	0	1	.000	7	0	0	0	0	8	12	0	7	2	22.5	10.13	46	.343	.465	0	—	0	-5	-5	-0	-0.5
Total	3	5	3	.625	53	0	0	0	0	61^{2}	64	8	29	46	14.2	4.67	86	.268	.357	0	—	0	-3	-5	-1	-0.4
● **JOE VERBANIC**	Verbanic, Joseph Michael b: 4/24/43, Washington, Pa. BR/TR, 6', 155 lbs. Deb: 7/22/66																									
1966	Phi-N	1	1	.500	17	0	0	0	0	14	12	2	10	7	14.1	5.14	70	.226	.349	0	—	0	-2	-2	-0	-0.3
1967	NY-A	4	3	.571	28	6	1	1	2	80^{1}	74	6	21	39	10.9	2.80	112	.249	.303	2	.111	-0	4	3	2	0.4
1968	NY-A	6	7	.462	40	11	2	1	4	97	104	6	41	40	14.0	3.15	92	.284	.366	2	.080	1	2	-3	1	-0.4
1970	NY-A	1	0	1.000	7	0	0	0	0	15^{2}	20	1	12	8	19.0	4.60	76	.323	.440	1	.333	0	-2	-2	1	0.0
Total	4	12	11	.522	92	17	3	2	6	207	210	15	84	94	13.2	3.26	95	.270	.348	5	.109	-1	-2	-4	4	-0.3
● **AL VERDEL**	Verdel, Albert Alfred "Stumpy" b: 6/10/21, Punxsutawney, Pa. d: 4/16/91, Sarasota, Fla. BR/TR, 5'9.5", 186 lbs. Deb: 4/20/44																									
1944	Phi-N	0	0	—	1	0	0	0	0	1	0	0	0	0	0.0	0.00	—	.000	.000	0	—	0	0	0	-0	0.0
● **TOMMY VEREKER**	Vereker, John James b: 12/2/1893, Baltimore, Md. d: 4/2/74, Baltimore, Md. 5'10", 185 lbs. Deb: 6/17/15																									
1915	Bal-F	0	0	—	2	0	0	0	0	3	3	1	2	1	18.0	15.00	19	.273	.429	0	—	0	-4	-4	0	0.0
● **DAVE VERES**	Veres, David Scott b: 10/19/66, Montgomery, Ala. BR/TR, 6'2", 195 lbs. Deb: 5/10/94																									
1994	Hou-N	3	3	.500	32	0	0	0	1	41	39	4	7	28	10.3	2.41	164	.247	.283	1	.500	1	8	7	-1	1.0
1995	Hou-N	5	1	.833	72	0	0	0	1	103^{1}	89	5	30	94	10.7	2.26	171	.241	.304	0	.000	-1	**22**	18	-1	0.9
1996	Mon-N	6	3	.667	68	0	0	0	4	77^{2}	85	10	32	81	14.3	4.17	103	.277	.357	3	.375	1	0	1	-0	0.2
1997	Mon-N	2	3	.400	53	0	0	0	1	62	68	5	27	47	14.1	3.48	120	.278	.354	1	1.000	0	5	5	-1	0.4
1998	Col-N	3	1	.750	63	0	0	0	8	76^{1}	67	6	27	74	11.3	2.83	179	.233	.303	1	.333	0	12	19	1	1.3
Total	5	19	11	.633	288	0	0	0	15	360^{1}	348	30	123	324	12.1	3.02	142	.254	.323	6	.316	2	47	50	-1	3.8

YEAR	TM/L	W	L	PCT	G	GS	CG	SH	SV	IP	H	HR	BB	SO	RAT	ERA	ERA+	OAV	OOB	BH	AVG	PB	PR	/A	PD	TPI
● **RANDY VERES** Veres, Randolph Ruhland b: 11/25/65, Sacramento, Cal. BR/TR, 6'3", 210 lbs. Deb: 7/1/89																										
1989	Mil-A	0	1	.000	3	1	0	0	0	8^1	9	0	4	8	14.0	4.32	89	.290	.371	0	—	0	-0	-0	0	0.0
1990	Mil-A	0	3	.000	26	0	0	0	1	41^2	38	5	16	16	11.9	3.67	105	.247	.322	0	—	0	1	1	1	0.2
1994	Chi-N	1	1	.500	10	0	0	0	0	9^2	12	3	2	5	14.0	5.59	74	.308	.357	0	.000	-0	-1	-2	0	-0.3
1995	Fla-N	4	4	.500	47	0	0	0	1	48^2	46	6	22	31	12.8	3.88	108	.251	.335	0	.000	-0	2	2	-1	0.1
1996	Det-A	0	4	.000	25	0	0	0	0	30^1	38	6	23	28	18.7	8.31	61	.306	.423	0	—	0	-11	-11	-1	-1.2
1997	KC-A	4	0	1.000	24	0	0	0	1	35^1	36	4	7	28	11.7	3.31	142	.273	.324	0	—	0	5	5	0	0.5
Total	6	9	13	.409	135	1	0	0	3	174	179	24	74	116	13.5	4.60	95	.270	.350	0	.000	-0	-5	-5	-1	-0.7
● **JOHN VERHOEVEN** Verhoeven, John C b: 7/3/53, Long Beach, Cal. BR/TR, 6'5", 200 lbs. Deb: 7/6/76																										
1976	Cal-A	0	2	.000	21	0	0	0	4	37^1	35	2	14	23	11.8	3.38	99	.252	.320	0	—	0	1	-0	1	0.2
1977	Cal-A	0	2	.000	3	0	0	0	0	4^2	4	0	4	3	17.4	3.86	101	.222	.391	0	—	0	0	0	0	0.2
	Chi-A	0	0	—	6	0	0	0	0	10^1	9	0	2	6	9.6	2.61	156	.231	.268	0	—	0	2	2	1	0.1
	Yr	0	2	.000	9	0	0	0	0	15	13	0	6	9	11.4	3.00	134	.224	.297	0	—	0	2	2	1	0.3
1980	Min-A	3	4	.429	44	0	0	0	0	99^2	109	10	29	42	12.7	3.97	110	.289	.345	0	—	0	1	4	0	-0.1
1981	Min-A	0	0	—	25	0	0	0	0	52	57	4	14	16	12.6	3.98	99	.288	.341	0	—	0	-2	-0	0	-0.2
Total	4	3	8	.273	99	0	0	0	4	204	214	16	63	90	12.5	3.79	106	.278	.337	0	—	0	1	5	2	0.2
● **JOE VERNON** Vernon, Joseph Henry b: 11/25/1889, Mansfield, Mass. d: 3/13/55, Philadelphia, Pa. BR/TR, 5'11", 160 lbs. Deb: 7/20/12																										
1912	Chi-N	0	0	—	1	0	0	0	0	4	4	0	6	1	24.8	11.25	30	.286	.524	0	.000	-0	-3	-4	-0	-0.1
1914	Bro-F	0	0	—	1	1	0	0	0	3^1	4	0	5	0	24.3	10.80	27	.308	.500	0	.000	-0	-3	-3	0	0.0
Total	2	0	0	—	2	1	0	0	0	7^1	8	0	11	1	24.5	11.05	28	.296	.513	0	.000	-0	-6	-6	-0	-0.1
● **BOB VESELIC** Veselic, Robert Michael b: 9/27/55, Pittsburgh, Pa. d: 12/26/95, Los Angeles, Cal. BR/TR, 6', 175 lbs. Deb: 9/18/80																										
1980	Min-A	0	0	—	1	0	0	0	0	4	3	1	1	2	9.0	4.50	97	.214	.267	0	—	0	-0	-0	-0	-0.3
1981	Min-A	1	1	.500	5	0	0	0	0	22^2	22	1	12	13	13.5	3.18	124	.250	.340	0	—	0	1	2	-1	-0.1
Total	2	1	1	.500	6	0	0	0	0	26^2	25	2	13	15	12.8	3.38	119	.245	.330	0	—	0	1	2	-1	-0.4
● **LEE VIAU** Viau, Leon A. b: 7/5/1866, Corinth, Vt. d: 12/17/47, Hopewell, N.J. BR/TR, 5'4", 160 lbs. Deb: 4/22/1888																										
1888	Cin-a	27	14	.659	42	42	42	1	0	387^2	331	7	110	164	10.7	2.65	120	.222	.285	13	.087	-11	18	23	-2	0.7
1889	Cin-a	22	20	.524	47	42	38	1	1	373	379	8	136	152	12.7	3.79	103	.255	.322	21	.143	-9	3	5	-3	-0.6
1890	Cin-N	7	5	.583	13	10	7	1	0	90	97	8	39	41	13.7	4.50	79	.266	.339	5	.139	-2	-9	-9	1	-1.1
	Cle-N	4	9	.308	13	13	13	1	0	107	101	4	42	30	12.4	3.36	106	.242	.318	7	.163	-2	2	3	-1	0.0
	Yr	11	14	.440	26	23	20	2	0	197	198	12	81	71	13.0	3.88	92	.253	.327	12	.152	-4	-7	-7	0	-1.1
1891	Cle-N	18	17	.514	45	38	31	0	0	343^2	367	3	138	130	13.6	3.01	115	.263	.336	23	.160	-3	13	17	1	1.2
1892	Cle-N	0	1	.000	1	1	0	0	0	1	5	0	1	0	54.0	36.00	9	.625	.667	0	—	0	-4	-4	0	-1.5
	Lou-N	4	11	.267	16	15	14	1	0	130^2	156	7	56	36	14.6	3.99	77	.285	.351	13	.197	1	-10	-13	2	-0.9
	Bos-N	1	0	1.000	1	1	1	0	0	9	5	0	4	1	9.0	0.00	—	.156	.250	0	.000	-0	3	4	-0	0.3
	Yr	5	12	.294	18	17	15	1	0	140^2	166	7	61	37	14.5	3.97	78	.282	.350	13	.188	1	-11	-14	2	-2.1
Total	5	83	77	.519	178	162	146	5	1	1442	1441	37	526	554	12.6	3.33	105	.251	.320	82	.139	-27	16	25	-1	-1.9
● **RUBE VICKERS** Vickers, Harry Porter b: 5/17/1878, St.Marys, Ont., Can d: 12/9/58, Belleville, Mich. BL/TR, 6'2", 225 lbs. Deb: 9/21/02																										
1902	Cin-N	0	3	.000	3	3	3	0	0	21	31	0	8	6	17.1	6.00	50	.341	.400	4	.364	1	-8	-7	-1	-0.8
1903	Bro-N	0	1	.000	4	1	0	0	0	14	27	0	9	5	23.8	10.93	29	.415	.493	1	.100	-1	-12	-12	1	-0.6
1907	Phi-A	2	2	.500	10	4	3	1	0	50^1	44	1	12	21	10.2	3.40	77	.238	.288	3	.150	-1	-5	-4	0	-0.4
1908	Phi-A	18	19	.486	53	34	21	6	1	317	264	0	71	156	9.8	2.21	116	.231	.282	17	.160	-1	6	12	-3	1.0
1909	Phi-A	2	2	.500	18	3	1	0	1	55^2	60	0	19	25	13.1	3.40	71	.274	.338	1	.063	-1	-6	-6	-1	-0.8
Total	5	22	27	.449	88	45	29	7	2	458	426	1	119	213	11.0	2.93	88	.250	.305	26	.160	-3	-24	-17	-4	-1.6
● **TOM VICKERY** Vickery, Thomas Gill "Vinegar Tom" b: 5/5/1867, Milford, N.J. d: 3/21/21, Burlington, N.J. TR, 6', 170 lbs. Deb: 4/21/1890																										
1890	Phi-N	24	22	.522	46	46	41	2	0	382	405	8	184	162	14.6	3.44	106	.264	.353	33	.208	-4	6	9	-2	0.3
1891	Chi-N	6	5	.545	14	12	7	0	0	79^2	72	4	44	39	13.7	4.07	82	.232	.337	7	.179	-2	-6	-7	1	-0.8
1892	Bal-N	8	10	.444	24	21	17	0	0	176	189	3	87	49	14.6	3.53	97	.264	.351	18	.243	2	-5	-2	-2	-0.1
1893	Phi-N	4	5	.444	13	11	7	0	0	80	100	1	37	15	16.1	5.40	85	.297	.376	11	.314	1	-7	-7	2	-0.3
Total	4	42	42	.500	97	90	72	2	0	717^2	766	16	352	265	14.6	3.75	98	.264	.354	69	.225	-3	-12	-6	-1	-0.9
● **RON VILLONE** Villone, Ronald Thomas b: 1/16/70, Englewood, N.J. BL/TL, 6'3", 230 lbs. Deb: 4/28/95																										
1995	Sea-A	0	2	.000	19	0	0	0	0	19^1	20	6	23	26	20.5	7.91	60	.270	.449	0	—	0	-7	-7	-0	-0.7
	SD-N	2	1	.667	19	0	0	0	1	25^2	24	5	11	37	12.3	4.21	96	.242	.318	0	.000	-0	-0	-1	-0	-0.1
1996	SD-N	1	1	.500	21	0	0	0	0	18^1	17	2	7	19	12.3	2.95	135	.243	.321	0	—	0	3	2	0	0.2
	Mil-A	0	0	—	23	0	0	0	2	24^2	14	4	18	19	13.1	3.28	158	.175	.353	0	—	0	5	5	-1	-0.3
1997	Mil-A	1	0	1.000	50	0	0	0	0	52^2	54	4	36	40	15.6	3.42	135	.271	.386	0	.000	-0	7	7	0	0.1
1998	Cle-A	0	0	—	25	0	0	0	0	27	30	3	22	15	18.0	6.00	80	.297	.432	0	—	0	-4	-4	0	-0.3
Total	4	4	4	.500	157	0	0	0	3	167^2	159	24	117	156	15.3	4.40	104	.255	.381	0	.000	-0	3	3	-1	-1.1
● **BOB VINES** Vines, Robert Earl b: 2/25/1897, Waxahachie, Tex. d: 10/18/82, Orlando, Fla. BR/TR, 6'4", 184 lbs. Deb: 9/3/24																										
1924	StL-N	0	0	—	2	0	0	0	0	10^2	23	1	0	0	19.4	9.28	41	.426	.426	0	.000	-1	-6	-7	-0	-0.1
1925	Phi-N	0	0	—	3	0	0	0	0	4	9	0	3	0	27.0	11.25	42	.450	.522	0	—	0	-3	-3	0	0.0
Total	2	0	0	—	5	0	0	0	0	14^2	32	1	3	0	21.5	9.82	41	.432	.455	0	.000	-1	-10	-9	-0	-0.1
● **DAVE VINEYARD** Vineyard, David Kent b: 2/25/41, Clay, W.Va. BR/TR, 6'3", 195 lbs. Deb: 7/18/64																										
1964	Bal-A	2	5	.286	19	6	1	0	0	54	57	5	27	50	14.0	4.17	86	.274	.357	2	.167	0	-3	-4	-1	-0.5
● **BILL VINTON** Vinton, William Miller b: 4/27/1865, Winthrop, Mass. d: 9/3/1893, Pawtucket, R.I. BR/TR, 6'1", 160 lbs. Deb: 7/3/1884																										
1884	Phi-N	10	10	.500	21	21	20	0	0	182	166	6	35	105	9.9	2.23	134	.220	.255	9	.115	-6	15	15	3	1.1
1885	Phi-N	3	6	.333	9	9	8	0	0	77	90	0	23	21	13.2	3.04	92	.269	.317	2	.067	-3	-2	-2	0	-0.5
	Phi-a	4	3	.571	7	7	6	2	0	55	46	1	15	34	10.6	2.45	140	.200	.261	4	.154	-0	5	6	-0	0.6
Total	2	17	19	.472	37	37	34	2	0	314	302	7	73	160	10.9	2.46	122	.229	.272	15	.112	-10	18	19	3	1.2
● **FRANK VIOLA** Viola, Frank John b: 4/19/60, Hempstead, N.Y. BL/TL, 6'4", 209 lbs. Deb: 6/6/82																										
1982	Min-A	4	10	.286	22	22	3	1	0	126	152	22	38	84	13.6	5.21	81	.302	.351	0	—	0	-16	-14	-1	-1.4
1983	Min-A	7	15	.318	35	34	4	0	0	210	242	34	92	127	14.7	5.49	77	.287	.363	0	—	0	-33	-29	-1	-2.7
1984	Min-A	18	12	.600	35	35	10	4	0	257^2	225	28	73	149	10.5	3.21	131	.233	.290	0	—	0	22	28	-3	2.8
1985	Min-A	18	14	.563	36	36	9	0	0	250^2	262	26	68	135	11.9	4.09	108	.268	.316	0	—	0	1	9	-2	0.8
1986	Min-A	16	13	.552	37	37	7	1	0	245^2	257	37	83	191	12.6	4.51	96	.268	.329	0	—	0	-9	-5	-3	-0.9
1987	*Min-A	17	10	.630	36	36	7	1	0	251^2	230	29	66	197	10.8	2.90	159	.241	.294	0	—	0	44	48	-1	**4.6**
1988	Min-A★	**24**	7	**.774**	35	35	7	2	0	255^1	236	20	54	193	10.3	2.64	154	.245	.288	0	—	0	38	**40**	-1	**4.6**
1989	Min-A	8	12	.400	24	24	7	1	0	175^2	171	17	47	138	11.3	3.79	109	.256	.308	0	—	0	2	7	0	0.7
	NY-N	5	5	.500	12	12	2	1	0	85^1	75	5	27	73	10.9	3.38	97	.236	.298	3	.130	-0	1	-1	-1	-0.2
1990	NY-N★	20	12	.625	35	35	7	3	0	**249^2**	227	15	60	182	10.4	2.67	140	.242	.289	13	.153	-1	**31**	30	-0	**3.6**
1991	NY-N★	13	15	.464	35	35	3	0	0	231^1	259	25	54	132	12.2	3.97	92	.286	.327	9	.127	-1	-7	-8	-1	-1.2
1992	Bos-A	13	12	.520	35	35	6	1	0	238	214	13	89	121	11.7	3.44	122	.242	.316	0	—	0	13	20	3	1.8
1993	Bos-A	11	8	.579	29	29	2	1	0	183^2	180	12	72	91	12.6	3.14	147	.259	.334	0	—	0	24	30	0	2.9
1994	Bos-A	1	1	.500	6	6	0	0	0	31	34	2	17	9	14.8	4.65	108	.296	.386	0	—	0	1	1	-0	-0.2
1995	Cin-N	0	1	.000	3	3	0	0	0	14^1	20	3	3	4	14.4	6.28	66	.333	.365	1	.167	0	-3	-3	-0	-0.2
1996	Tor-A	1	3	.250	6	6	0	0	0	30^1	43	6	21	18	19.6	7.71	65	.350	.452	0	—	0	-9	-9	-0	-0.9
Total	15	176	150	.540	421	420	74	16	0	2836^1	2827	294	864	1844	11.9	3.73	112	.260	.317	26	.141	-2	99	143	-12	14.1
● **JAKE VIRTUE** Virtue, Jacob Kitchline "Guesses" b: 3/2/1865, Philadelphia, Pa. d: 2/3/43, Camden, N.J. BB/TL, 5'9.5", 165 lbs. Deb: 7/21/1890 ♦																										
1893	Cle-N	0	0	—	1	0	0	0	0	5	3	0	3	2	10.8	1.80	271	.167	.286	100	.265	0	2	2	-0	0.0
1894	Cle-N	0	0	—	1	0	0	0	0	0	0	0	1	0	—	—	—	—	1.000	23	.258	0	0	0	0	0.0
Total	2	0	0	—	2	0	0	0	0	5	3	0	4	2	12.6	1.80	271	.167	.318	483	.274	0	2	2	-0	0.0

YEAR	TM/L	W	L	PCT	G	GS	CG	SH	SV	IP	H	HR	BB	SO	RAT	ERA	ERA+	OAV	OOB	BH	AVG	PB	PR	/A	PD	TPI
● JOE VITELLI Vitelli, Antonio Joseph b: 4/12/08, McKees Rocks, Pa. d: 2/7/67, Pittsburgh, Pa. BR/TR, 6'1", 195 lbs. Deb: 5/30/44 ♦																										
1944	Pit-N	0	0	—	4	0	0	0	0	7	5	1	7	2	16.7	2.57	145	.185	.371	0	.000	-0	1	1	0	0.0
● JOE VITKO Vitko, Joseph John b: 2/1/70, Somerville, N.J. BR/TR, 6'8", 210 lbs. Deb: 9/18/92																										
1992	NY-N	0	1	.000	3	1	0	0	0	4^{2}	12	1	1	6	25.1	13.50	26	.444	.464	0	—	0	-5	-5	-0	-0.9
● OLLIE VOIGT Voigt, Olen Edward "Ode" b: 1/29/1900, Wheaton, Ill. d: 4/7/70, Scottsdale, Ariz. BL/TR, 6'1", 170 lbs. Deb: 4/19/24																										
1924	StL-A	1	0	1.000	8	1	0	0	0	16^{1}	21	1	13	4	18.7	5.51	82	.356	.472	1	.250	1	-2	-2	1	0.1
● BILL VOISELLE Voiselle, William Symmes "Big Bill" or "Ninety-Six" b: 1/29/19, Greenwood, S.C. BR/TR, 6'4", 200 lbs. Deb: 9/1/42																										
1942	NY-N	0	1	.000	2	1	0	0	0	9	6	1	4	5	10.0	2.00	168	.176	.263	0	.000	0	1	1	0	0.2
1943	NY-N	1	2	.333	4	4	3	0	0	31	18	1	14	19	9.3	2.03	170	.154	.244	1	.111	-1	5	5	-1	0.3
1944	NY-N☆	21	16	.568	43	41	25	1	0	**312^{2}**	276	31	118	**161**	11.5	3.02	121	.232	.303	22	.210	3	20	22	-3	2.5
1945	NY-N	14	14	.500	41	35	14	4	0	232^{1}	249	15	97	115	13.6	4.49	87	.273	.345	10	.127	-3	-18	-15	-0	-1.9
1946	NY-N	9	15	.375	36	25	10	2	0	178	171	14	85	89	12.9	3.74	92	.248	.330	9	.164	-1	-7	-6	-0	-0.9
1947	NY-N	1	4	.200	11	5	1	0	0	42^{2}	44	4	22	20	14.1	4.64	88	.284	.376	2	.133	-1	-3	-3	-0	-0.4
	Bos-N	8	7	.533	22	20	7	0	0	131^{1}	146	10	51	59	13.6	4.32	90	.280	.345	9	.170	-1	-4	-6	1	-0.6
	Yr	9	11	.450	33	25	8	0	0	174	190	14	73	79	13.7	4.40	90	.280	.351	11	.162	-1	-7	-9	1	-1.0
1948	*Bos-N	13	13	.500	37	30	9	2	2	215^{2}	226	18	90	89	13.3	3.63	106	.272	.345	7	.097	-4	8	5	-3	-0.1
1949	Bos-N	7	8	.467	30	22	5	4	1	169^{1}	170	14	78	63	13.2	4.04	94	.263	.343	7	.115	-2	0	-5	1	-0.5
1950	Chi-N	0	4	.000	19	7	0	0	0	51^{1}	64	7	29	25	16.5	5.79	73	.303	.390	1	.077	-1	-9	-9	-1	-0.8
Total	9	74	84	.468	245	190	74	13	3	1373^{1}	1370	115	588	645	12.9	3.83	98	.258	.334	68	.147	-10	-6	-10	-6	-2.2
● JAKE VOLZ Volz, Jacob Phillip "Silent Jake" b: 4/4/1878, San Antonio, Tex. d: 8/11/62, San Antonio, Tex. BR/TR, 5'10", 175 lbs. Deb: 9/28/01																										
1901	Bos-A	1	0	1.000	1	1	1	0	0	7	6	2	9	5	19.3	9.00	39	.231	.429	0	.000	-1	-4	-4	-1	-0.5
1905	Bos-N	0	2	.000	3	2	0	0	0	8^{2}	12	0	8	1	21.8	10.38	30	.364	.500	0	.000	-0	-7	-7	-1	-1.3
1908	Cin-N	1	2	.333	7	4	1	0	0	22^{2}	16	1	12	6	11.9	3.57	65	.195	.313	1	.250	0	-3	-3	-1	-0.5
Total	3	2	4	.333	11	7	2	0	0	38^{1}	34	3	29	12	15.5	6.10	44	.241	.382	1	.100	-1	-14	-14	-2	-2.3
● TONY Von FRICKEN Von Fricken, Anthony b: 5/30/1870, Brooklyn, N.Y. d: 3/22/47, Troy, N.Y. BB/TR, 5'11.5", 160 lbs. Deb: 5/9/1890																										
1890	Bos-N	0	1	.000	1	1	1	0	0	8	23	0	8	2	34.9	10.13	37	.489	.564	0	.000	-1	-6	-6	-0	-0.5
● BRUCE Von HOFF Von Hoff, Bruce Frederick b: 11/17/43, Oakland, Cal. BR/TR, 6', 187 lbs. Deb: 9/28/65																										
1965	Hou-N	0	0	—	3	0	0	0	0	3	3	0	2	1	15.0	9.00	37	.250	.357	0	—	0	-2	-2	-0	0.0
1967	Hou-N	0	3	.000	10	10	0	0	0	50^{1}	52	3	28	22	14.3	4.83	69	.268	.360	1	.067	-1	-8	-8	-1	-0.6
Total	2	0	3	.000	13	10	0	0	0	53^{1}	55	3	30	23	14.3	5.06	65	.267	.360	1	.067	-1	-10	-10	-1	-0.6
● DAVE Von OHLEN Von Ohlen, David b: 10/25/58, Flushing, N.Y. BL/TL, 6'2", 200 lbs. Deb: 5/13/83																										
1983	StL-N	3	2	.600	46	0	0	0	2	68^{1}	71	3	25	21	13.0	3.29	110	.280	.351	1	.143	0	3	2	-0	0.2
1984	StL-N	1	0	1.000	27	0	0	0	1	34^{2}	39	0	8	19	12.2	3.12	111	.300	.341	1	1.000	0	2	1	1	0.2
1985	Cle-A	3	2	.600	26	0	0	0	0	43^{1}	47	3	20	12	13.9	2.91	142	.288	.366	0	—	0	6	6	1	0.7
1986	Oak-A	0	3	.000	24	0	0	0	1	15^{1}	18	0	7	4	14.7	3.52	110	.300	.373	0	—	0	1	1	0	0.2
1987	Oak-A	0	0	—	4	0	0	0	0	6	10	1	1	3	16.5	7.50	55	.400	.423	0	—	0	-2	-2	-0	0.0
Total	5	7	7	.500	127	0	0	0	4	167^{2}	185	7	61	59	13.4	3.33	113	.293	.358	2	.250	1	9	8	1	1.3
● CY VORHEES Vorhees, Henry Bert b: 9/30/1874, Lodi, Ohio d: 2/8/10, Perry, Ohio 6'3", 200 lbs. Deb: 4/17/02																										
1902	Phi-N	3	3	.500	10	5	3	1	0	53^{2}	63	1	20	24	14.1	3.86	73	.292	.354	7	.350	2	-6	-6	-1	-0.5
	Was-A	0	1	.000	1	1	1	0	0	8	10	0	2	1	13.5	4.50	82	.303	.343	2	.667	1	-1	-1	-0	0.0
Total	1	3	4	.429	11	6	4	1	0	61^{2}	73	1	22	25	14.0	3.94	74	.293	.353	9	.391	3	-7	-7	-1	-0.5
● ED VOSBERG Vosberg, Edward John b: 9/28/61, Tucson, Ariz. BL/TL, 6'1", 190 lbs. Deb: 9/17/86																										
1986	SD-N	0	1	.000	5	3	0	0	0	13^{2}	17	1	9	8	17.1	6.59	55	.304	.400	0	.000	-0	-4	-4	-0	-0.4
1990	SF-N	1	1	.500	18	0	0	0	0	24^{1}	21	3	12	12	12.2	5.55	66	.233	.324	0	—	0	-5	-5	0	-0.4
1994	Oak-A	0	2	.000	16	0	0	0	0	13^{2}	16	2	5	12	13.8	3.95	112	.320	.382	0	—	0	1	1	1	0.3
1995	Tex-A	5	5	.500	44	0	0	0	4	36	32	3	16	36	12.0	3.00	161	.241	.322	0	—	0	7	7	-1	1.8
1996	*Tex-A	1	1	.500	52	0	0	0	8	44	51	4	21	32	14.7	3.27	160	.298	.375	0	—	0	8	10	1	0.7
1997	Tex-A	1	2	.333	42	0	0	0	0	41	44	3	15	29	13.4	4.61	104	.277	.347	0	—	0	-0	1	-1	-0.1
	Fla-N	1	1	.500	17	0	0	0	1	12	15	0	6	8	18.0	3.75	107	.313	.421	0	—	0	1	0	-0	0.0
Total	6	9	13	.409	194	3	0	0	13	184^{2}	196	16	84	137	13.9	4.14	111	.277	.358	0	.000	-0	8	9	0	1.9
● ALEX VOSS Voss, Alexander b: 5/16/1858, Roswell, Ga. d: 8/31/06, Cincinnati, Ohio BR/TR, 6'1", 180 lbs. Deb: 4/17/1884 ♦																										
1884	Was-U	5	14	.263	27	20	18	0	0	186^{1}	206	2	32	112	11.5	3.57	67	.262	.291	47	.192	-9	-23	-24	3	-2.2
	KC-U	0	6	.000	7	6	6	0	0	53	74	2	7	17	13.8	4.25	53	.310	.329	4	.089	-4	-11	-12	1	-1.3
	Yr	5	20	.200	34	26	24	0	0	239^{1}	280	4	39	129	12.0	3.72	63	.273	.300	51	.176	-13	-34	-36	3	-3.5
● RIP VOWINKEL Vowinkel, John Henry b: 11/18/1884, Oswego, N.Y. d: 7/13/66, Oswego, N.Y. BR/TR, 5'10", 195 lbs. Deb: 9/5/05																										
1905	Cin-N	3	3	.500	6	6	4	0	0	45^{1}	52	2	10	7	12.5	4.17	79	.302	.344	1	.071	-0	-6	-4	-2	-0.7
● PETE VUCKOVICH Vuckovich, Peter Dennis b: 10/27/52, Johnstown, Pa. BR/TR, 6'4", 220 lbs. Deb: 8/3/75 C																										
1975	Chi-A	0	1	.000	4	2	0	0	0	10^{1}	17	0	7	5	20.9	13.06	30	.386	.471	0	—	0	-11	-11	0	-0.9
1976	Chi-A	7	4	.636	33	7	1	0	0	110^{1}	122	3	60	62	15.2	4.65	77	.287	.380	0	—	0	-14	-13	0	-1.3
1977	Tor-A	7	7	.500	53	8	3	1	8	148	143	13	59	123	12.6	3.47	121	.257	.333	0	—	0	10	12	1	1.2
1978	StL-N	12	12	.500	45	23	6	2	1	198^{1}	187	9	59	149	11.3	2.54	138	.253	.310	8	.138	-1	23	21	2	2.6
1979	StL-N	15	10	.600	34	32	9	0	0	233	229	22	64	145	11.4	3.59	105	.260	.312	12	.152	-2	4	4	-1	0.1
1980	StL-N	12	9	.571	32	30	7	3	1	222^{1}	203	18	68	132	11.1	3.40	109	.247	.306	13	.183	1	5	7	-1	0.8
1981	*Mil-A	**14**	4	**.778**	24	23	2	1	0	149^{2}	137	9	57	84	11.9	3.55	96	.249	.324	0	—	0	2	-2	1	0.0
1982	*Mil-A	18	6	**.750**	30	30	9	1	0	223^{2}	234	14	102	105	13.7	3.34	113	.275	.356	0	—	0	18	11	1	1.2
1983	Mil-A	0	2	.000	3	3	0	0	0	14^{2}	15	0	10	10	16.0	4.91	76	.259	.377	0	—	0	-1	-2	-0	-0.2
1985	Mil-A	6	10	.375	22	22	1	0	0	112^{2}	134	16	48	55	15.1	5.51	76	.298	.374	0	—	0	-17	-17	-1	-2.1
1986	Mil-A	2	4	.333	6	6	0	0	0	32^{1}	33	3	11	12	12.8	3.06	141	.273	.343	0	—	0	4	5	0	0.8
Total	11	93	69	.574	286	186	38	8	10	1455^{1}	1454	107	545	882	12.6	3.66	103	.264	.334	33	.159	-2	22	16	2	2.2
● PAUL WACHTEL Wachtel, Paul Horine b: 4/30/1888, Myersville, Md. d: 12/15/64, San Antonio, Tex. BR/TR, 5'11", 175 lbs. Deb: 9/18/17																										
1917	Bro-N	0	0	—	2	0	0	0	0	6	9	0	4	3	19.5	10.50	27	.375	.464	1	.333	0	-5	-5	-0	0.0
● CHARLIE WACKER Wacker, Charles James b: 12/8/1883, Jeffersonville, Ind d: 8/7/48, Evansville, Ind. BL/TL, 5'9", Deb: 4/28/09																										
1909	Pit-N	0	0	—	1	0	0	0	0	2	2	0	1	0	13.5	0.00	—	.400	.500	0	—	0	1	1	0	0.0
● RUBE WADDELL Waddell, George Edward b: 10/13/1876, Bradford, Pa. d: 4/1/14, San Antonio, Tex. BR/TL, 6'1.5", 196 lbs. Deb: 9/8/1897 H																										
1897	Lou-N	0	1	.000	2	1	1	0	0	14	17	0	6	5	15.4	3.21	133	.298	.375	0	.000	-1	2	2	0	0.0
1899	Lou-N	7	2	.778	10	9	9	1	1	79	69	4	14	44	10.4	3.08	125	.235	.288	8	.235	-0	7	7	-1	0.6
1900	*Pit-N	8	13	.381	29	22	16	2	0	208^{2}	176	3	55	130	10.5	**2.37**	**153**	**.229**	.291	14	.173	-2	31	29	1	2.4
1901	Pit-N	0	2	.000	2	2	0	0	0	7^{2}	10	0	9	4	23.5	9.39	35	.313	.476	0	.000	-0	-5	-5	0	-0.9
	Chi-N	14	14	.500	29	28	26	0	0	243^{2}	239	5	66	168	11.6	2.81	115	.255	.310	25	.255	6	14	12	3	2.2
	Yr	14	16	.467	31	30	26	0	0	251^{1}	249	5	75	172	11.9	3.01	108	.256	.316	25	.248	6	9	6	4	1.3
1902	Phi-A	24	7	.774	33	27	26	3	0	276^{1}	224	7	64	**210**	9.7	2.05	179	.222	.276	32	.286	7	47	50	-0	**5.9**
1903	Phi-A	21	16	.568	39	38	**34**	4	0	324	274	3	85	**302**	10.2	2.44	125	.229	.284	14	.122	-6	19	22	0	1.7
1904	Phi-A	25	19	.568	46	46	39	8	0	383	307	5	91	**349**	9.7	1.62	**165**	.221	.275	17	.122	-7	**42**	45	2	4.9
1905	Phi-A	**27**	10	**.730**	**46**	34	27	7	0	328^{2}	231	5	90	**287**	9.1	**1.48**	**180**	**.200**	.263	20	.172	-1	**43**	**43**	-0	4.9
1906	Phi-A	15	17	.469	43	34	22	8	0	272^{2}	221	1	92	**196**	10.7	2.21	123	.225	.297	14	.163	-0	15	16	-2	1.6
1907	Phi-A	19	13	.594	44	33	20	7	0	284^{2}	234	2	73	**232**	10.2	2.15	121	.227	.287	12	.119	-5	12	14	-2	0.8
1908	StL-A	19	14	.576	43	36	25	5	3	285^{2}	223	0	90	232	10.1	1.89	127	.213	.281	10	.110	-1	16	16	-1	1.7

YEAR TM/L	W	L	PCT	G	GS	CG	SH	SV	IP	H	HR	BB	SO	RAT	ERA	ERA+	OAV	OOB	BH	AVG	PB	PR	/A	PD	TPI
1909 StL-A	11	14	.440	31	28	16	5	0	220^1	204	1	57	141	10.9	2.37	102	.267	.323	5	.067	-5	3	1	-1	-0.6
1910 StL-A	3	1	.750	10	2	0	0	1	33	31	1	11	16	11.7	3.55	70	.242	.307	1	.111	-0	-4	-4	-1	-0.6
Total 13	193	143	.574	407	340	261	50	5	2961^1	2460	37	803	2316	10.3	2.16	135	.228	.288	172	.161	-17	240	247	-0	24.6

● TOM WADDELL Waddell, Thomas David b: 9/17/58, Dundee, Scotland BR/TR, 6'1", 185 lbs. Deb: 4/15/84

YEAR TM/L	W	L	PCT	G	GS	CG	SH	SV	IP	H	HR	BB	SO	RAT	ERA	ERA+	OAV	OOB	BH	AVG	PB	PR	/A	PD	TPI
1984 Cle-A	7	4	.636	58	0	0	0	6	97	68	12	37	59	9.8	3.06	133	.202	.283	0	—	0	10	11	-1	1.1
1985 Cle-A	8	6	.571	49	9	1	0	9	112^2	104	20	39	53	11.5	4.87	85	.246	.312	0	—	0	-9	-9	0	-1.1
1987 Cle-A	0	1	.000	6	0	0	0	0	5^2	7	1	7	6	23.8	14.29	32	.292	.469	0	—	0	-6	-6	-0	-0.9
Total 3	15	11	.577	113	9	1	0	15	215^1	179	33	83	118	11.1	4.30	96	.229	.305	0	—	0	-5	-4	-1	-0.9

● BEN WADE Wade, Benjamin Styron b: 11/26/22, Morehead City, N.C BR/TR, 6'3", 205 lbs. Deb: 4/30/48 F

YEAR TM/L	W	L	PCT	G	GS	CG	SH	SV	IP	H	HR	BB	SO	RAT	ERA	ERA+	OAV	OOB	BH	AVG	PB	PR	/A	PD	TPI
1948 Chi-N	0	1	.000	2	0	0	0	0	5	4	0	4	1	14.4	7.20	54	.211	.348	0	.000	-0	-2	-2	0	-0.3
1952 Bro-N	11	9	.550	37	24	5	1	3	180	166	19	94	118	13.1	3.60	101	.246	.340	7	.117	1	3	1	-2	0.0
1953 *Bro-N	7	5	.583	32	0	0	0	3	90^1	79	15	33	65	11.6	3.79	113	.232	.308	4	.167	0	5	5	-2	0.4
1954 Bro-N	1	1	.500	23	0	0	0	3	45	62	9	21	25	16.6	8.20	50	.339	.407	0	.000	-1	-21	-21	-1	-1.2
StL-N	0	0	—	13	0	0	0	0	23	27	3	15	19	17.2	5.48	75	.303	.415	0	.000	-0	-4	-3	0	0.0
Yr	1	1	.500	36	0	0	0	3	68	89	12	36	44	16.8	7.28	56	.319	.401	0	.000	-1	-24	-24	-1	-1.2
1955 Pit-N	0	1	.000	11	1	0	0	1	28	26	3	14	7	13.2	3.21	128	.252	.347	0	.000	-0	3	3	-0	0.1
Total 5	19	17	.528	118	25	5	1	10	371^1	364	49	181	235	13.4	4.34	90	.259	.347	11	.112	-0	-16	-18	-5	-1.0

● TERRELL WADE Wade, Hawatha Terrell b: 1/25/73, Rembert, S.C. BL/TL, 6'3", 205 lbs. Deb: 9/12/95

YEAR TM/L	W	L	PCT	G	GS	CG	SH	SV	IP	H	HR	BB	SO	RAT	ERA	ERA+	OAV	OOB	BH	AVG	PB	PR	/A	PD	TPI
1995 Atl-N	0	1	.000	3	0	0	0	0	4	3	1	4	3	15.8	4.50	95	.214	.389	0	—	0	-0	-0	-0	0.0
1996 *Atl-N	5	0	1.000	44	8	0	0	1	69^2	57	9	47	79	13.6	2.97	148	.227	.351	2	.154	-0	10	11	0	0.7
1997 Atl-N	2	3	.400	12	9	0	0	0	42	60	6	16	35	16.7	5.36	78	.349	.411	3	.250	1	-5	-5	-0	-0.5
1998 TB-A	1	1	.500	2	2	0	0	0	10^2	14	3	2	8	13.5	5.06	97	.318	.348	0	—	0	-0	-0	-0	-0.1
Total 4	8	5	.615	61	19	0	0	1	126^1	134	19	69	125	14.7	3.99	109	.279	.373	5	.200	1	4	5	-1	0.1

● JAKE WADE Wade, Jacob Fields "Whistling Jake" b: 4/1/12, Morehead City, N.C. BL/TL, 6'2", 175 lbs. Deb: 4/22/36 F

YEAR TM/L	W	L	PCT	G	GS	CG	SH	SV	IP	H	HR	BB	SO	RAT	ERA	ERA+	OAV	OOB	BH	AVG	PB	PR	/A	PD	TPI
1936 Det-A	4	5	.444	13	11	4	1	0	78^1	93	7	52	30	16.8	5.29	94	.296	.398	5	.172	-0	-2	-3	-1	-0.4
1937 Det-A	7	10	.412	33	25	7	1	0	165^1	160	13	107	69	14.7	5.39	87	.257	.368	11	.186	-1	-14	-13	1	-1.2
1938 Det-A	3	2	.600	27	2	0	0	0	70	73	9	48	23	15.6	6.56	76	.268	.378	1	.048	-2	-14	-12	0	-0.9
1939 Bos-A	1	4	.200	20	6	1	0	0	47^2	68	1	37	21	19.8	6.23	76	.358	.463	0	.000	-2	-9	-8	-0	-0.9
StL-A	0	2	.000	4	2	1	0	0	16^1	26	1	19	9	24.8	11.02	44	.356	.489	0	.000	-1	-12	-11	0	-1.0
Yr	1	6	.143	24	8	2	0	0	64	94	2	56	30	21.1	7.45	64	.357	.470	0	.000	-3	-20	-19	0	-1.9
1942 Chi-A	5	5	.500	15	10	3	0	0	85^2	84	2	56	32	14.7	4.10	88	.255	.363	7	.241	1	-4	-5	1	-0.3
1943 Chi-A	3	7	.300	21	9	3	1	0	83^2	66	3	54	41	13.3	3.01	111	.222	.349	4	.148	-0	3	3	-1	0.2
1944 Chi-A	2	4	.333	19	5	1	0	2	74^2	75	3	41	35	14.0	4.82	71	.261	.354	7	.292	1	-12	-12	-2	-1.0
1946 NY-A	2	1	.667	13	1	0	0	1	35^1	33	2	14	22	12.2	2.29	151	.250	.327	1	.111	-0	5	5	0	0.4
Was-A	0	0	—	6	0	0	0	0	11^1	12	1	12	9	19.1	4.76	70	.279	.436	0	.000	-0	-2	-2	0	0.0
Yr	2	1	.667	19	1	0	0	1	46^2	45	3	26	31	13.7	2.89	118	.256	.351	1	.100	-0	3	3	1	0.4
Total 8	27	40	.403	171	71	20	3	3	668^1	690	42	440	291	15.3	5.00	84	.269	.378	36	.167	-5	-60	-58	-1	-5.1

● JACK WADSWORTH Wadsworth, John L. b: 12/17/1867, Wellington, Ohio d: 7/8/41, Elyria, Ohio BL/TR, 180 lbs. Deb: 5/1/1890

YEAR TM/L	W	L	PCT	G	GS	CG	SH	SV	IP	H	HR	BB	SO	RAT	ERA	ERA+	OAV	OOB	BH	AVG	PB	PR	/A	PD	TPI
1890 Cle-N	2	16	.111	20	19	19	0	0	169^2	202	6	81	26	15.3	5.20	69	.287	.365	12	.176	-3	-31	-30	-1	-2.7
1893 Bal-N	0	3	.000	3	3	0	0	0	16	37	0	8	2	25.3	11.25	42	.440	.489	3	.429	1	-12	-12	-1	-1.3
1894 Lou-N	4	18	.182	22	22	20	0	0	173	261	10	103	57	19.1	7.60	67	.344	.425	19	.257	0	-44	-48	-0	-3.9
1895 Lou-N	0	1	.000	2	0	0	0	0	9	24	0	7	2	31.0	16.00	29	.480	.544	1	.250	-0	-11	-11	0	-0.8
Total 4	6	38	.136	47	44	39	0	0	367^2	524	16	199	87	17.9	6.85	64	.328	.406	35	.229	-2	-97	-101	-1	-8.7

● CHARLIE WAGNER Wagner, Charles Thomas "Broadway" b: 12/3/12, Reading, Pa. BR/TR, 5'11", 170 lbs. Deb: 4/19/38 C

YEAR TM/L	W	L	PCT	G	GS	CG	SH	SV	IP	H	HR	BB	SO	RAT	ERA	ERA+	OAV	OOB	BH	AVG	PB	PR	/A	PD	TPI
1938 Bos-A	1	3	.250	13	6	1	0	0	36^2	47	5	24	14	17.7	8.35	59	.309	.407	2	.167	-1	-14	-14	-1	-1.3
1939 Bos-A	3	1	.750	9	5	0	0	0	38^1	49	3	14	13	14.8	4.23	112	.320	.377	1	.071	-2	2	2	-0	0.0
1940 Bos-A	1	0	1.000	12	1	0	0	0	29^1	45	5	8	13	16.3	5.52	81	.344	.381	1	.200	-0	-4	-3	-0	-0.1
1941 Bos-A	12	8	.600	29	25	12	3	0	187^1	175	14	85	51	12.5	3.07	136	.245	.326	10	.159	-1	22	23	-0	2.1
1942 Bos-A	14	11	.560	29	26	17	2	0	205^1	184	5	95	52	12.4	3.29	113	.247	.336	5	.077	-5	8	10	1	0.7
1946 Bos-A	1	0	1.000	8	4	0	0	0	30^2	32	6	19	14	15.0	5.87	62	.276	.378	1	.091	-1	-8	-8	-0	-0.3
Total 6	32	23	.582	100	67	30	5	0	527^2	532	38	245	157	13.4	3.91	104	.264	.346	20	.118	-9	6	10	-1	1.1

● GARY WAGNER Wagner, Gary Edward b: 6/28/40, Bridgeport, Ill. BR/TR, 6'4", 191 lbs. Deb: 4/18/65

YEAR TM/L	W	L	PCT	G	GS	CG	SH	SV	IP	H	HR	BB	SO	RAT	ERA	ERA+	OAV	OOB	BH	AVG	PB	PR	/A	PD	TPI
1965 Phi-N	7	7	.500	59	0	0	0	7	105	87	6	49	91	11.8	3.00	115	.233	.325	1	.077	-0	6	5	1	0.8
1966 Phi-N	0	1	.000	5	1	0	0	0	6^1	8	1	5	2	18.5	8.53	42	.333	.448	0	—	0	-3	-3	-0	-0.5
1967 Phi-N	0	0	—	1	0	0	0	0	2	1	0	0	1	4.5	0.00	—	.167	.167	0	—	0	1	1	0	0.0
1968 Phi-N	4	4	.500	44	0	0	0	8	78	69	0	31	43	12.1	3.00	100	.243	.328	1	.083	-1	-0	0	1	0.0
1969 Phi-N	0	3	.000	9	2	0	0	0	19^1	31	3	7	8	17.7	7.91	45	.365	.413	0	.000	-0	-9	-9	-1	-1.4
Bos-A	1	3	.250	6	1	0	0	0	16^1	18	1	15	9	18.2	6.06	63	.300	.440	0	.000	-0	-4	-4	-0	-0.9
1970 Bos-A	3	1	.750	38	0	0	0	7	40^1	36	3	19	20	12.7	3.35	118	.232	.324	1	.167	-0	2	3	-1	0.3
Total 6	15	19	.441	162	4	0	0	22	267^1	250	14	126	174	13.0	3.70	93	.253	.343	3	.081	-2	-9	-8	1	-1.7

● HECTOR WAGNER Wagner, Hector Raul Guerrero (b: Hector Raul Guerrero (Wagner)) b: 11/26/68, San Juan, D.R. BR/TR, 6'3", 185 lbs. Deb: 9/10/90

YEAR TM/L	W	L	PCT	G	GS	CG	SH	SV	IP	H	HR	BB	SO	RAT	ERA	ERA+	OAV	OOB	BH	AVG	PB	PR	/A	PD	TPI
1990 KC-A	0	2	.000	5	5	0	0	0	23^1	32	4	11	14	16.6	8.10	47	.323	.391	0	—	0	-11	-11	0	-0.7
1991 KC-A	1	1	.500	2	2	0	0	0	10	16	2	3	5	17.1	7.20	57	.348	.388	0	—	0	-3	-3	-0	-0.6
Total 2	1	3	.250	7	7	0	0	0	33^1	48	6	14	19	16.7	7.83	50	.331	.390	0	—	0	-14	-14	0	-1.3

● HONUS WAGNER Wagner, John Peter "The Flying Dutchman"
b: 2/24/1874, Chartiers, Pa. d: 12/6/55, Carnegie, Pa. BR/TR, 5'11", 200 lbs. Deb: 7/19/1897 FMCH♦

YEAR TM/L	W	L	PCT	G	GS	CG	SH	SV	IP	H	HR	BB	SO	RAT	ERA	ERA+	OAV	OOB	BH	AVG	PB	PR	/A	PD	TPI
1900 *Pit-N	0	0	—	1	0	0	0	0	3	3	0	4	1	21.0	0.00	—	.250	.438	201	.381	1	1	1	-0	0.0
1902 Pit-N	0	0	—	1	0	0	0	0	5^1	4	0	2	5	10.1	0.00	—	.211	.286	176	.330	1	2	2	-0	0.0
Total 2	0	0	—	2	0	0	0	0	8^1	7	0	6	6	14.0	0.00	—	.226	.351	3415	.327	1	3	3	-0	0.0

● MARK WAGNER Wagner, Mark Duane b: 3/4/54, Conneaut, Ohio BR/TR, 6'1", 175 lbs. Deb: 8/20/76 ♦

YEAR TM/L	W	L	PCT	G	GS	CG	SH	SV	IP	H	HR	BB	SO	RAT	ERA	ERA+	OAV	OOB	BH	AVG	PB	PR	/A	PD	TPI
1984 Oak-A	0	0	—	1	0	0	0	0	1^2	2	0	1	1	16.2	0.00	—	.400	.500	20	.230	0	1	1	-0	0.0

● MATT WAGNER Wagner, Matthew William b: 4/4/72, Cedar Falls, Ia. BR/TR, 6'5", 215 lbs. Deb: 6/5/96

YEAR TM/L	W	L	PCT	G	GS	CG	SH	SV	IP	H	HR	BB	SO	RAT	ERA	ERA+	OAV	OOB	BH	AVG	PB	PR	/A	PD	TPI
1996 Sea-A	3	5	.375	15	14	1	0	0	80	91	15	38	41	14.8	6.86	72	.285	.367	0	—	0	-17	-17	-1	-1.4

● PAUL WAGNER Wagner, Paul Alan b: 11/14/67, Milwaukee, Wis. BR/TR, 6'1", 202 lbs. Deb: 7/26/92

YEAR TM/L	W	L	PCT	G	GS	CG	SH	SV	IP	H	HR	BB	SO	RAT	ERA	ERA+	OAV	OOB	BH	AVG	PB	PR	/A	PD	TPI
1992 Pit-N	2	0	1.000	6	1	0	0	0	13	9	0	5	5	9.7	0.69	497	.191	.269	1	.333	0	4	4	0	0.7
1993 Pit-N	8	8	.500	44	17	1	1	2	141^1	143	15	42	114	11.8	4.27	95	.263	.317	8	.190	0	-4	-3	-1	-0.4
1994 Pit-N	7	8	.467	29	17	1	0	0	119^2	136	7	50	86	14.6	4.59	94	.293	.372	6	.162	-0	-5	-4	2	-0.2
1995 Pit-N	5	16	.238	33	25	3	1	1	165	174	18	72	120	13.8	4.80	90	.273	.353	9	.214	2	-11	-9	1	-0.8
1996 Pit-N	4	8	.333	16	15	1	0	0	81^2	86	10	39	81	14.1	5.40	81	.275	.361	1	.040	-2	-11	-9	1	-1.3
1997 Pit-N	0	0	—	14	0	0	0	0	16	17	3	13	9	16.9	3.94	109	.274	.400	0	.000	-0	0	1	0	0.0
Mil-A	1	0	1.000	2	0	0	0	0	2	3	1	0	0	13.5	9.00	51	.375	.375	0	—	0	-1	-1	0	-0.4
1998 Mil-N	1	5	.167	13	9	0	0	0	55^2	67	10	31	37	16.0	7.11	60	.302	.390	3	.158	-0	-18	-17	-0	-1.6
Total 7	28	45	.384	157	84	6	2	3	594^1	635	64	252	452	13.7	4.83	88	.277	.353	28	.166	-0	-45	-40	3	-4.0

● BILLY WAGNER Wagner, William Edward b: 7/25/71, Tannersville, Va. BL/TL, 5'10", 180 lbs. Deb: 9/13/95

YEAR TM/L	W	L	PCT	G	GS	CG	SH	SV	IP	H	HR	BB	SO	RAT	ERA	ERA+	OAV	OOB	BH	AVG	PB	PR	/A	PD	TPI
1995 Hou-N	0	0	—	1	0	0	0	0	0^1	0	0	0	0	0.0	0.00	—	.000	.000	0	—	0	0	0	0	0.0
1996 Hou-N	2	2	.500	37	0	0	0	9	51^2	28	6	30	67	10.6	2.44	158	.165	.300	0	.000	-1	10	8	-1	0.7
1997 *Hou-N	7	8	.467	62	0	0	0	23	66^1	49	5	30	106	11.1	2.85	140	.204	.300	0	.000	-0	10	8	0	2.3
1998 *Hou-N	4	3	.571	58	0	0	0	30	60	46	6	25	97	10.7	2.70	151	.211	.292	1	.333	0	10	9	-1	1.7
Total 4	13	13	.500	158	0	0	0	62	178^1	123	17	85	270	10.8	2.67	149	.196	.297	1	.111	-0	31	26	-1	4.7

● BULL WAGNER Wagner, William George b: 12/25/1887, Lilley, Mich. d: 10/2/67, Muskegon, Mich. BR/TR, 6'0.5", 225 lbs. Deb: 6/2/13

YEAR	TM/L	W	L	PCT	G	GS	CG	SH	SV	IP	H	HR	BB	SO	RAT	ERA	ERA+	OAV	OOB	BH	AVG	PB	PR	/A	PD	TPI
1913	Bro-N	4	2	.667	18	1	0	0	0	70^2	77	5	30	11	14.0	5.48	60	.285	.363	6	.231	0	-18	-17	-2	-1.4
1914	Bro-N	0	1	.000	6	0	0	0	0	12^1	14	0	12	4	19.7	6.57	44	.311	.466	0	.000	-0	-5	-5	-0	-0.4
Total	2	4	3	.571	24	1	0	0	0	83	91	5	42	15	14.9	5.64	57	.289	.380	6	.222	0	-23	-22	-2	-1.8

● DAVE WAINHOUSE Wainhouse, David Paul b: 11/7/67, Toronto, Ont., Can. BL/TR, 6'2", 190 lbs. Deb: 8/3/91

YEAR	TM/L	W	L	PCT	G	GS	CG	SH	SV	IP	H	HR	BB	SO	RAT	ERA	ERA+	OAV	OOB	BH	AVG	PB	PR	/A	PD	TPI
1991	Mon-N	0	1	.000	2	0	0	0	0	2^2	2	0	4	1	20.3	6.75	54	.222	.462	0	—	0	-1	-1	-0	-0.3
1993	Sea-A	0	0	—	3	0	0	0	0	2^1	7	1	5	2	50.1	27.00	16	.500	.650	0	—	0	-6	-6	-0	0.0
1996	Pit-N	1	0	1.000	17	0	0	0	0	23^2	22	3	10	16	12.2	5.70	76	.250	.327	0	.000	-0	-4	-4	1	-0.1
1997	Pit-N	0	1	.000	25	0	0	0	0	28	34	2	17	21	17.4	8.04	53	.301	.406	0	.000	-0	-12	-12	-0	-0.4
1998	Col-N	1	0	1.000	10	0	0	0	0	11	15	1	5	3	18.0	4.91	103	.341	.431	0	.000	-0	-1	0	1	0.1
Total	5	2	2	.500	57	0	0	0	0	67^2	80	7	41	43	16.9	7.32	60	.299	.403	0	.000	-0	-23	-22	1	-0.7

● RICK WAITS Waits, Michael Richard b: 5/15/52, Atlanta, Ga. BL/TL, 6'3", 195 lbs. Deb: 9/17/73

YEAR	TM/L	W	L	PCT	G	GS	CG	SH	SV	IP	H	HR	BB	SO	RAT	ERA	ERA+	OAV	OOB	BH	AVG	PB	PR	/A	PD	TPI
1973	Tex-A	0	0	—	1	0	0	0	1	1	1	0	1	0	18.0	9.00	41	.333	.500	0	—	0	-1	-1	0	-0.1
1975	Cle-A	6	2	.750	16	7	3	0	1	70^1	57	3	25	34	10.6	2.94	128	.221	.292	0	—	0	7	7	0	0.8
1976	Cle-A	7	9	.438	26	22	4	2	0	123^2	143	7	54	65	14.3	4.00	87	.297	.368	0	—	0	-7	-7	1	-0.9
1977	Cle-A	9	7	.563	37	16	1	0	2	135^1	132	8	64	62	13.1	3.99	99	.262	.347	0	—	0	1	-1	-0	-0.1
1978	Cle-A	13	15	.464	34	33	15	2	0	230^1	206	16	86	97	11.5	3.20	117	.240	.310	0	—	0	14	14	3	2.0
1979	Cle-A	16	13	.552	34	34	8	3	0	231	230	26	91	91	12.7	4.44	96	.264	.336	0	—	0	-6	-5	2	-0.4
1980	Cle-A	13	14	.481	33	33	9	2	0	224^1	231	18	82	109	12.6	4.45	91	.270	.335	0	—	0	-10	-10	-1	-1.1
1981	Cle-A	8	10	.444	22	21	5	1	0	126^1	173	7	44	51	15.5	4.92	74	.330	.383	0	—	0	-18	-18	2	-2.1
1982	Cle-A	2	13	.133	25	21	2	0	0	115	128	13	57	44	14.6	5.40	76	.290	.372	0	—	0	-17	-17	1	-1.8
1983	Cle-A	0	1	.000	8	0	0	0	0	19^2	23	1	9	13	14.6	4.58	93	.307	.381	0	—	0	-1	-1	0	0.0
	Mil-A	0	2	.000	10	2	0	0	0	30	39	1	11	20	15.0	5.10	73	.320	.376	0	—	0	-3	-5	-0	-0.3
	Yr	0	3	.000	18	2	0	0	0	49^2	62	2	20	33	14.9	4.89	80	.308	.371	0	—	0	-5	-5	-0	-0.3
1984	Mil-A	2	4	.333	47	1	0	0	3	73	84	7	24	49	13.3	3.58	108	.297	.352	0	—	0	3	2	0	0.3
1985	Mil-A	3	2	.600	24	0	0	0	1	47	67	3	20	24	16.7	6.51	64	.340	.401	0	.000	-0	-12	-12	0	-1.2
Total	12	79	92	.462	317	190	47	10	8	1427	1514	110	568	659	13.2	4.25	92	.277	.346	0	.000	-0	-50	-53	8	-4.9

● TIM WAKEFIELD Wakefield, Timothy Stephen b: 8/2/66, Melbourne, Fla. BR/TR, 6'2", 204 lbs. Deb: 7/31/92

YEAR	TM/L	W	L	PCT	G	GS	CG	SH	SV	IP	H	HR	BB	SO	RAT	ERA	ERA+	OAV	OOB	BH	AVG	PB	PR	/A	PD	TPI
1992	*Pit-N	8	1	.889	13	13	4	1	0	92	76	3	35	51	11.0	2.15	160	.232	.309	2	.071	-1	14	13	1	1.3
1993	Pit-N	6	11	.353	24	20	3	2	0	128^1	145	14	75	59	16.1	5.61	72	.291	.393	7	.163	1	-22	-22	-1	-2.5
1995	*Bos-A	16	8	.667	27	27	6	1	0	195^1	163	22	68	119	11.1	2.95	165	.227	.302	0	—	0	38	42	-1	4.5
1996	Bos-A	14	13	.519	32	32	6	0	0	211^2	238	38	90	140	14.5	5.14	99	.280	.357	0	—	0	-4	-2	-2	-0.4
1997	Bos-A	12	15	.444	35	29	4	2	0	201^1	193	24	87	151	13.2	4.25	109	.256	.346	0	.000	-0	7	9	-1	0.9
1998	*Bos-A	17	8	.680	36	33	2	0	0	216	211	30	79	146	12.7	4.58	101	.252	.327	0	.000	0	2	1	-1	0.0
Total	6	73	56	.566	167	154	25	6	0	1044^2	1026	131	434	666	13.1	4.24	108	.258	.340	9	.122	-0	35	40	-6	3.8

● BILL WAKEFIELD Wakefield, William Sumner b: 5/24/41, Kansas City, Mo. BR/TR, 6', 175 lbs. Deb: 4/18/64

YEAR	TM/L	W	L	PCT	G	GS	CG	SH	SV	IP	H	HR	BB	SO	RAT	ERA	ERA+	OAV	OOB	BH	AVG	PB	PR	/A	PD	TPI
1964	NY-N	3	5	.375	62	4	0	0	2	119^2	103	10	61	61	13.0	3.61	99	.235	.341	4	.167	-0	-1	-0	0	0.0

● RUBE WALBERG Walberg, George Elvin b: 7/27/1896, Pine City, Minn. d: 10/27/78, Tempe, Ariz. BL/TL, 6'1.5", 190 lbs. Deb: 4/29/23

YEAR	TM/L	W	L	PCT	G	GS	CG	SH	SV	IP	H	HR	BB	SO	RAT	ERA	ERA+	OAV	OOB	BH	AVG	PB	PR	/A	PD	TPI
1923	NY-N	0	0	—	2	0	0	0	0	5	4	0	1	1	9.0	1.80	212	.211	.250	0	.000	-0	1	1	-0	0.0
	Phi-A	4	8	.333	26	10	4	0	0	115	122	10	60	38	14.4	5.32	77	.280	.369	13	.317	3	-17	-16	1	-1.1
1924	Phi-A	0	0	—	6	2	0	0	0	7	10	0	10	3	25.7	12.86	33	.345	.513	1	.500	0	-7	-7	0	0.0
1925	Phi-A	8	14	.364	53	20	7	0	7	191^2	197	11	77	82	13.0	3.99	117	.269	.340	10	.156	-4	9	14	1	1.2
1926	Phi-A	12	10	.545	40	19	5	2	2	151	168	4	60	72	13.9	2.80	149	.292	.365	7	.152	-2	20	23	-1	2.8
1927	Phi-A	16	12	.571	46	33	14	0	4	249^1	257	18	91	136	12.7	3.93	108	.271	.337	18	.207	3	6	9	-0	1.2
1928	Phi-A	17	12	.586	38	30	15	3	1	235^2	236	19	64	112	11.6	3.55	113	.265	.317	18	.209	1	13	12	1	1.5
1929	*Phi-A	18	11	.621	40	33	20	3	4	267^2	256	22	99	94	11.9	3.60	118	.254	.320	23	.223	-0	19	19	-2	1.6
1930	*Phi-A	13	12	.520	38	30	12	2	1	205^1	207	6	85	100	12.9	4.69	100	.262	.335	12	.164	-3	-1	-0	-1	-0.4
1931	*Phi-A	20	12	.625	44	35	19	1	3	**291**	298	16	109	106	12.6	3.74	120	.266	.331	13	.124	-6	21	24	-1	1.6
1932	Phi-A	17	10	.630	41	34	19	3	1	272	305	16	103	96	13.5	4.73	96	.282	.344	16	.170	-3	-8	-6	-0	-0.8
1933	Phi-A	9	13	.409	40	20	10	1	4	201	224	12	95	68	14.3	4.88	88	.278	.354	9	.132	-1	-13	-13	1	-1.4
1934	Bos-A	6	7	.462	30	10	2	0	1	104^2	118	5	41	38	13.8	4.04	119	.284	.350	6	.188	-1	5	9	1	1.0
1935	Bos-A	5	9	.357	44	10	4	0	3	142^2	152	10	54	44	13.1	3.91	121	.273	.340	6	.162	-2	9	13	1	0.9
1936	Bos-A	5	4	.556	24	9	5	0	0	100^1	98	7	36	49	12.1	4.40	121	.257	.323	5	.156	-1	7	10	1	0.7
1937	Bos-A	5	7	.417	32	11	3	0	1	104^2	143	7	46	46	16.5	5.59	85	.332	.400	5	.147	-1	-11	-10	-0	-1.1
Total	15	155	141	.524	544	306	139	15	32	2644	2795	163	1031	1085	13.1	4.16	107	.273	.341	162	.179	-18	53	82	-2	7.7

● DOC WALDBAUER Waldbauer, Albert Charles b: 2/22/1892, Richmond, Va. d: 7/16/69, Yakima, Wash. BR/TR, 6', 172 lbs. Deb: 9/24/17

YEAR	TM/L	W	L	PCT	G	GS	CG	SH	SV	IP	H	HR	BB	SO	RAT	ERA	ERA+	OAV	OOB	BH	AVG	PB	PR	/A	PD	TPI
1917	Was-A	0	0	—	2	0	0	0	1	5	10	0	2	2	21.6	7.20	36	.476	.522	0	.000	-0	-3	-3	0	-0.1

● BOB WALK Walk, Robert Vernon b: 11/26/56, Van Nuys, Cal. BR/TR, 6'4", 208 lbs. Deb: 5/26/80

YEAR	TM/L	W	L	PCT	G	GS	CG	SH	SV	IP	H	HR	BB	SO	RAT	ERA	ERA+	OAV	OOB	BH	AVG	PB	PR	/A	PD	TPI
1980	*Phi-N	11	7	.611	27	27	2	0	0	151^2	163	8	71	94	14.0	4.57	83	.276	.356	7	.140	-0	-16	-13	-1	-1.5
1981	Atl-N	1	4	.200	12	8	0	0	0	43^1	41	6	23	16	13.3	4.57	78	.250	.342	1	.143	-0	-5	-5	-1	-0.6
1982	*Atl-N	11	9	.550	32	27	3	1	0	164^1	179	19	59	84	13.4	4.87	77	.280	.347	10	.196	2	-23	-21	-2	-2.4
1983	Atl-N	0	0	—	1	1	0	0	0	3^2	7	0	2	4	22.1	7.36	53	.412	.474	0	.000	-0	-2	-1	0	0.0
1984	Pit-N	1	1	.500	2	2	0	0	0	10^1	8	1	4	10	10.5	2.61	138	.200	.273	0	.000	-0	1	1	-0	0.1
1985	Pit-N	2	3	.400	9	9	1	1	0	58^2	60	3	18	40	12.0	3.68	97	.265	.320	0	.000	-1	-1	-1	-1	-0.3
1986	Pit-N	7	8	.467	44	15	1	1	2	141^2	129	14	64	78	12.5	3.75	102	.251	.337	6	.154	0	-0	1	2	0.3
1987	Pit-N	8	2	.800	39	12	1	1	0	117	107	11	51	78	12.4	3.31	124	.245	.329	6	.231	1	10	10	1	1.0
1988	Pit-N★	12	10	.545	32	32	1	1	0	212^2	183	6	65	81	10.6	2.71	126	.230	.290	6	.087	-2	17	16	0	1.5
1989	Pit-N	13	10	.565	33	31	2	0	0	196	208	15	65	83	12.7	4.41	76	.271	.331	13	.186	3	-20	-23	1	-2.2
1990	*Pit-N	7	5	.583	26	24	1	1	1	129^2	136	17	36	73	12.2	3.75	97	.270	.324	6	.162	1	1	-2	-1	-0.2
1991	*Pit-N	9	2	.818	25	20	0	0	0	115	104	10	35	67	11.3	3.60	99	.240	.304	8	.205	2	1	-0	-0	0.2
1992	*Pit-N	10	6	.625	36	19	1	0	2	135	132	10	43	60	12.1	3.20	108	.258	.323	4	.093	-2	5	4	1	0.4
1993	Pit-N	13	14	.481	32	32	3	0	0	187	214	23	70	80	13.9	5.68	71	.294	.360	7	.121	-2	-34	-34	-1	-4.3
Total	14	105	81	.565	350	259	16	6	5	1666	1671	143	606	848	12.5	4.03	91	.263	.330	74	.145	1	-66	-67	-1	-8.0

● ED WALKER Walker, Edward Harrison b: 8/11/1874, Cambois, England d: 9/29/47, Akron, Ohio BL/TL, 6'5", 242 lbs. Deb: 9/26/02

YEAR	TM/L	W	L	PCT	G	GS	CG	SH	SV	IP	H	HR	BB	SO	RAT	ERA	ERA+	OAV	OOB	BH	AVG	PB	PR	/A	PD	TPI
1902	Cle-A	0	1	.000	1	1	1	0	0	8	11	0	3	1	15.8	3.38	102	.324	.378	1	.333	0	0	0	0	0.0
1903	Cle-A	0	1	.000	3	3	0	0	0	12	13	0	10	4	17.3	5.25	54	.277	.404	0	.000	-0	-3	-3	-1	-0.3
Total	2	0	2	.000	4	4	1	0	0	20	24	0	13	5	16.6	4.50	69	.296	.394	1	.167	0	-3	-3	-1	-0.3

● DIXIE WALKER Walker, Ewart Gladstone b: 6/1/1887, Brownsville, Pa. d: 11/14/65, Leeds, Ala. BL/TR, 6', 192 lbs. Deb: 9/17/09 F

YEAR	TM/L	W	L	PCT	G	GS	CG	SH	SV	IP	H	HR	BB	SO	RAT	ERA	ERA+	OAV	OOB	BH	AVG	PB	PR	/A	PD	TPI
1909	Was-A	3	1	.750	4	4	4	0	0	36	31	0	6	25	9.3	2.50	97	.217	.248	2	.154	-0	-0	-0	-0	-0.1
1910	Was-A	11	11	.500	29	26	16	3	0	199^1	177	2	68	84	11.4	3.30	76	.245	.317	9	.130	-3	-17	-18	-1	-2.3
1911	Was-A	8	13	.381	32	24	15	2	0	185^2	205	2	50	65	12.7	3.39	97	.286	.339	20	.303	4	-1	-2	-1	0.0
1912	Was-A	3	6	.333	9	8	5	0	0	60	72	2	18	29	14.1	5.25	64	.300	.359	2	.125	1	-13	-13	-0	-1.5
Total	4	25	31	.446	74	62	40	5	0	481	485	6	142	203	12.1	3.52	82	.266	.326	33	.201	2	-31	-33	-3	-3.9

● MYSTERIOUS WALKER Walker, Frederick Mitchell b: 3/21/1884, Utica, Neb. d: 2/1/58, Oak Park, Ill. BR/TR, 5'10.5", 185 lbs. Deb: 6/28/10

YEAR	TM/L	W	L	PCT	G	GS	CG	SH	SV	IP	H	HR	BB	SO	RAT	ERA	ERA+	OAV	OOB	BH	AVG	PB	PR	/A	PD	TPI
1910	Cin-N	0	0	—	1	0	0	0	0	3	4	0	4	1	24.0	3.00	97	.333	.500	0	.000	-0	0	-0	0	0.0
1912	Cle-A	0	0	—	1	0	0	0	0	1	0	0	1	0	9.0	0.00	—	.000	.200	0	—	0	0	0	-0	0.0
1913	Bro-N	1	3	.250	11	8	3	0	0	58^1	44	3	35	35	13.0	3.55	93	.233	.367	3	.167	-0	-2	-2	2	0.0
1914	Pit-F	4	16	.200	35	21	12	0	0	169^1	197	3	74	79	14.6	4.31	67	.294	.367	6	.113	-3	-27	-27	3	-2.8
1915	Bro-F	2	4	.333	13	7	2	0	1	65^2	61	3	22	28	11.4	3.70	73	.242	.303	6	.222	0	-7	-7	1	-0.5
Total	5	7	23	.233	61	36	17	0	1	297^1	306	9	136	143	13.6	4.00	73	.272	.354	15	.152	-3	-36	-36	6	-3.3

YEAR	TM/L	W	L	PCT	G	GS	CG	SH	SV	IP	H	HR	BB	SO	RAT	ERA	ERA+	OAV	OOB	BH	AVG	PB	PR	/A	PD	TPI
● **GEORGE WALKER**	Walker, George A. b: 1863, Hamilton, Ontario, Canada TR , 5′9″, 184 lbs. Deb: 8/1/1888																									
1888	Bal-a	1	3	.250	4	4	4	1	0	35	36	2	14	18	12.9	5.91	50	.257	.325	1	.077	-1	-11	-11	-0	-1.1
● **LUKE WALKER**	Walker, James Luke b: 9/2/43, DeKalb, Tex. BL/TL, 6′1.5″, 192 lbs. Deb: 9/7/65																									
1965	Pit-N	0	0	—	2	0	0	0	0	5	2	0	1	5	5.4	0.00	—	.118	.167	0	—	0	2	2	0	0.0
1966	Pit-N	0	1	.000	10	1	0	0	0	10	8	0	15	7	21.6	4.50	79	.205	.436	0	.000	-0	-1	-1	-0	-0.1
1968	Pit-N	0	3	.000	39	2	0	0	3	61^2	42	1	39	66	12.0	2.04	143	.190	.314	0	.000	-1	6	6	1	0.4
1969	Pit-N	4	6	.400	31	15	3	1	0	118^2	98	5	57	96	11.9	3.64	96	.226	.319	0	.000	-3	-1	-2	1	-0.4
1970	*Pit-N	15	6	.714	42	19	5	3	3	163	129	6	89	124	12.1	3.04	128	.219	.323	6	.130	-1	18	16	-0	1.8
1971	*Pit-N	10	8	.556	28	24	4	2	0	159^2	157	9	53	86	11.9	3.55	95	.262	.324	1	.022	-3	-2	-3	-2	-0.8
1972	*Pit-N	4	6	.400	26	12	2	0	2	92^2	98	4	34	48	12.8	3.40	98	.278	.342	2	.083	-1	1	-1	-0	-0.3
1973	Pit-N	7	12	.368	37	18	2	1	1	122	129	9	66	74	14.5	4.65	76	.270	.360	2	.067	-2	-13	-15	-1	-2.5
1974	Det-A	5	5	.500	28	9	0	0	0	92	100	9	54	52	15.3	4.99	76	.278	.375	0	—	0	-14	-12	-0	-1.3
Total	9	45	47	.489	243	100	16	7	9	824^2	763	43	408	558	12.9	3.65	97	.247	.337	11	.059	-11	-3	-11	-2	-3.2
● **JAMIE WALKER**	Walker, James Ross b: 7/1/71, McMinnville, Tenn. BL/TL, 6′2″, 190 lbs. Deb: 4/2/97																									
1997	KC-A	3	3	.500	50	0	0	0	0	43	46	6	20	24	14.4	5.44	87	.271	.358	0	—	0	-4	-4	0	-0.4
1998	KC-A	0	1	.000	6	2	0	0	0	17^1	30	5	3	15	18.2	9.87	50	.380	.417	0	—	0	-10	-10	1	-0.6
Total	2	3	4	.429	56	2	0	0	0	60^1	76	11	23	39	15.5	6.71	71	.305	.375	0	—	0	-14	-13	1	-1.0
● **ROY WALKER**	Walker, James Roy "Dixie" b: 4/13/1893, Lawrenceburg, Tenn d: 2/10/62, New Orleans, La. BR/TR, 6′1.5″, 180 lbs. Deb: 9/16/12																									
1912	Cle-A	0	0	—	1	0	0	0	0	2	0	0	2	1	9.0	0.00	—	.000	.250	0	—	0	1	1	-0	0.0
1915	Cle-A	4	9	.308	25	15	4	0	1	131	122	1	65	57	13.3	3.98	77	.261	.360	5	.132	-2	-15	-14	-2	-1.8
1917	Chi-N	0	1	.000	2	1	0	0	0	7	8	0	5	4	16.7	3.86	75	.286	.394	0	.000	-0	-1	-1	-0	-0.1
1918	Chi-N	1	3	.250	13	7	2	0	1	43^1	50	1	15	20	13.7	2.70	103	.298	.359	0	.000	-1	0	0	0	-0.1
1921	StL-N	11	12	.478	38	23	11	0	3	170^2	194	10	53	52	13.1	4.22	87	.293	.347	11	.204	-0	-8	-10	-1	-1.4
1922	StL-N	1	2	.333	12	2	0	0	0	32	34	1	15	14	13.8	4.78	81	.293	.374	1	.143	-0	-2	-3	-1	-0.4
Total	6	17	27	.386	91	48	17	0	5	386	408	13	155	148	13.3	3.99	85	.282	.355	17	.153	-4	-26	-26	-5	-3.8
● **JERRY WALKER**	Walker, Jerry Allen b: 2/12/39, Ada, Okla. BB/TR, 6′1″, 195 lbs. Deb: 7/6/57 C																									
1957	Bal-A	1	0	1.000	13	3	1	1	1	27^2	24	1	14	13	12.4	2.93	123	.245	.339	0	.000	-1	3	2	-0	0.0
1958	Bal-A	0	0	—	6	0	0	0	0	10^1	16	2	5	6	18.3	6.97	52	.340	.404	0	.000	-0	-4	-4	-0	0.0
1959	Bal-A★	11	10	.524	30	22	7	2	4	182	160	13	52	100	10.6	2.92	130	.240	.297	11	.169	-1	19	18	-0	1.9
1960	Bal-A	3	4	.429	29	18	1	0	5	118	107	15	56	48	12.7	3.74	102	.247	.337	14	.368	5	2	1	1	0.6
1961	KC-A	8	14	.364	36	24	4	0	2	168	161	23	96	56	14.3	4.82	87	.253	.359	16	.250	3	-15	-12	1	-1.1
1962	KC-A	8	9	.471	31	21	3	1	0	143^1	165	27	78	57	15.7	5.90	72	.288	.381	15	.263	5	-31	-27	1	-2.2
1963	Cle-A	6	6	.500	39	2	0	0	1	88	92	15	36	41	13.3	4.91	74	.265	.338	2	.105	-0	-13	-13	-0	-1.7
1964	Cle-A	0	1	.000	6	0	0	0	0	9^2	9	1	4	5	12.1	4.66	77	.257	.333	0	.000	-0	-1	-1	-0	-0.2
Total	8	37	44	.457	190	90	16	4	13	747	734	97	341	326	13.3	4.36	90	.259	.343	58	.230	10	-39	-36	1	-2.7
● **MARTY WALKER**	Walker, Martin Van Buren "Buddy" b: 3/27/1899, Philadelphia, Pa. d: 4/24/78, Philadelphia, Pa. BL/TL, 6′, 170 lbs. Deb: 9/30/28																									
1928	Phi-N	0	1	.000	1	1	0	0	0	0	2	0	3	0	—	∞	—	1.000	1.000	0	—	0	-2	-2	0	-0.2
● **MIKE WALKER**	Walker, Michael Aaron b: 6/23/65, Houston, Tex. BR/TR, 6′3″, 205 lbs. Deb: 6/16/92																									
1992	Sea-A	0	3	.000	5	3	0	0	0	14^2	21	4	9	5	18.4	7.36	54	.333	.417	0	—	0	-6	-6	0	-0.9
● **MIKE WALKER**	Walker, Michael Charles b: 10/4/66, Chicago, Ill. BR/TR, 6′1″, 195 lbs. Deb: 9/9/88																									
1988	Cle-A	0	1	.000	3	1	0	0	0	8^2	8	0	10	7	18.7	7.27	57	.258	.439	0	—	0	-3	-3	0	-0.4
1990	Cle-A	2	6	.250	18	11	0	0	0	75^2	82	6	42	34	15.5	4.88	80	.277	.378	0	—	0	-8	-8	-0	-0.8
1991	Cle-A	0	1	.000	5	0	0	0	0	4^1	6	0	2	2	18.7	2.08	200	.316	.409	0	—	0	1	1	0	0.2
1995	Chi-N	1	3	.250	42	0	0	0	1	44^2	45	2	24	20	13.9	3.22	127	.259	.348	0	.000	-0	5	4	-0	0.3
1996	Det-A	0	0	—	20	0	0	0	1	27^2	40	10	17	13	18.9	8.46	60	.351	.439	0	—	0	-11	-10	-1	-0.1
Total	5	3	11	.214	88	12	0	0	2	161	181	18	95	76	15.9	5.09	82	.285	.385	0	.000	-0	-16	-16	-1	-0.8
● **PETE WALKER**	Walker, Peter Brian b: 4/8/69, Beverly, Mass. BR/TR, 6′2″, 195 lbs. Deb: 6/7/95																									
1995	NY-N	1	0	1.000	13	0	0	0	0	17^2	24	3	5	5	14.8	4.58	88	.329	.372	0	—	0	-1	-1	-0	-0.1
1996	SD-N	0	0	—	1	0	0	0	0	0^2	0	0	3	1	40.5	0.00	—	.000	.600	0	—	0	0	0	0	0.0
Total	2	1	0	1.000	14	0	0	0	0	18^1	24	3	8	6	15.7	4.42	91	.320	.386	0	—	0	-0	-1	-0	-0.1
● **TOM WALKER**	Walker, Robert Thomas b: 11/7/48, Tampa, Fla. BR/TR, 6′1″, 188 lbs. Deb: 4/23/72																									
1972	Mon-N	2	2	.500	46	0	0	0	2	74^2	71	4	22	42	11.3	2.89	123	.248	.304	0	.000	-0	5	5	-0	0.3
1973	Mon-N	7	5	.583	54	0	0	0	4	91^2	95	7	42	68	13.7	3.63	105	.274	.357	0	.000	-1	0	2	-0	0.2
1974	Mon-N	4	5	.444	33	8	1	0	2	91^2	96	7	28	70	12.4	3.83	100	.266	.322	3	.188	0	-2	0	-1	0.0
1975	Det-A	3	8	.273	36	9	1	0	0	115^1	116	16	40	60	12.6	4.45	90	.261	.329	0	—	0	-9	-6	-2	-0.9
1976	StL-N	1	2	.333	10	0	0	0	3	19^2	22	2	3	11	11.4	4.12	86	.265	.291	2	.400	1	-1	-1	-1	-0.2
1977	Mon-N	1	1	.500	11	0	0	0	0	19	15	2	7	10	10.4	4.74	80	.221	.293	0	.000	-0	-2	-2	-0	-0.2
	Cal-A	0	0	—	1	0	0	0	0	2	3	2	0	1	13.5	9.00	43	.375	.375	0	—	0	-1	-1	-0	0.0
Total	6	18	23	.439	191	17	2	0	11	414	418	40	142	262	12.4	3.87	99	.262	.326	5	.152	-0	-10	-3	-3	-0.8
● **TOM WALKER**	Walker, Thomas William b: 8/1/1881, Philadelphia, Pa. d: 7/10/44, Woodbury Heights, N.J. BR/TR, 5′11″, 170 lbs. Deb: 9/27/02																									
1902	Phi-A	0	1	.000	1	1	1	0	0	8	10	0	0	2	12.4	5.63	65	.303	.324	1	.250	-0	-2	-2	1	-0.1
1904	Cin-N	15	8	.652	24	24	22	2	0	217	196	2	53	64	11.1	2.24	131	.238	.299	9	.117	-4	12	17	-2	1.0
1905	Cin-N	9	7	.563	23	19	12	1	0	144^2	171	3	44	28	13.7	3.24	102	.305	.362	7	.137	-1	-4	1	-0	-0.1
Total	3	24	16	.600	48	44	35	3	0	369^2	377	5	97	94	12.1	2.70	114	.266	.325	17	.129	-6	6	16	-1	0.8
● **BILL WALKER**	Walker, William Henry b: 10/7/03, E.St.Louis, Ill. d: 6/14/66, E.St.Louis, Ill. BR/TL, 6′, 175 lbs. Deb: 9/13/27																									
1927	NY-N	0	0	—	3	0	0	0	0	4	6	0	5	4	24.8	9.00	43	.429	.579	0	—	0	-2	-2	-0	0.0
1928	NY-N	3	6	.333	22	8	1	0	0	76^1	79	9	31	39	13.1	4.72	83	.275	.348	2	.091	-2	-6	-7	-0	-0.9
1929	NY-N	14	7	.667	29	23	13	1	0	177^2	188	11	57	65	12.6	**3.09**	148	.274	.334	7	.115	-3	32	29	-3	2.3
1930	NY-N	17	15	.531	39	34	13	2	1	245^1	258	19	88	105	12.9	3.93	121	.268	.334	16	.186	-1	29	22	-1	2.1
1931	NY-N	16	9	.640	37	28	19	**6**	3	239^1	212	6	64	121	10.5	**2.26**	**164**	.231	.283	5	.065	-6	**43**	**38**	-4	2.8
1932	NY-N	8	12	.400	31	22	9	0	2	163	177	23	55	74	13.0	4.14	90	.274	.334	7	.135	-2	-5	-8	2	-0.9
1933	StL-N	9	10	.474	29	20	6	2	0	158	168	8	67	41	13.4	3.42	102	.273	.346	7	.132	-2	-1	1	1	0.0
1934	*StL-N	12	4	.750	24	19	10	1	0	153	160	11	66	76	13.4	3.12	136	.270	.345	5	.093	-4	16	19	-1	1.2
1935	StL-N★	13	8	.619	37	25	8	2	1	193^1	222	7	78	79	14.2	3.82	107	.288	.357	6	.102	-4	4	6	-1	0.2
1936	StL-N	5	6	.455	21	13	4	1	1	79^2	106	5	27	22	15.3	5.87	67	.318	.373	7	.280	2	-16	-17	1	-1.8
Total	10	97	77	.557	272	192	83	15	8	1489^2	1576	99	538	626	12.9	3.59	114	.271	.335	62	.127	-23	93	83	-7	5.0
● **JIM WALKUP**	Walkup, James Elton b: 12/14/09, Havana, Ark. d: 2/7/97, Danville, Ark. BR/TR, 6′1″, 170 lbs. Deb: 9/22/34																									
1934	StL-A	0	0	—	3	0	0	0	0	8^1	6	0	5	6	11.9	2.16	231	.200	.314	1	.333	0	2	3	-0	0.0
1935	StL-A	6	9	.400	55	20	4	1	0	181^1	226	17	104	44	16.5	6.25	77	.305	.392	6	.128	-3	-36	-29	-1	-2.4
1936	StL-A	0	3	.000	5	2	0	0	0	15^2	20	0	6	5	14.9	8.04	67	.308	.366	0	.000	-1	-5	-5	1	-0.7
1937	StL-A	9	12	.429	27	18	6	0	0	150^1	218	16	83	46	18.0	7.36	66	.347	.423	14	.241	-1	-46	-42	2	-4.4
1938	StL-A	1	12	.077	18	13	1	0	0	94	127	13	53	28	17.5	6.80	73	.329	.414	4	.138	-2	-21	-19	0	-2.1
1939	StL-A	0	1	.000	1	0	0	0	0	0^2	2	0	1	0	40.5	0.00	—	.500	.600	0	—	0	0	0	0	0.6
	Det-A	0	1	.000	7	0	0	0	0	12	15	3	8	5	17.3	7.50	65	.319	.418	1	.500	0	-4	-3	0	-0.2
	Yr	0	2	.000	8	0	0	0	0	12^2	17	3	9	5	18.5	7.11	69	.333	.433	1	.500	0	-3	-3	0	0.4
Total	6	16	38	.296	116	53	11	1	0	462^1	614	49	260	134	17.1	6.74	72	.323	.406	26	.182	-6	-110	-96	1	-9.2
● **JIM WALKUP**	Walkup, James Huey b: 11/3/1895, Havana, Ark. d: 6/12/90, Duncan, Okla. BR/TL, 5′8″, 150 lbs. Deb: 4/30/27																									
1927	Det-A	0	0	—	2	0	0	0	0	1^2	3	0	0	0	16.2	5.40	78	.429	.429	0	.000	-0	-0	-0	0	0.0

YEAR	TM/L	W	L	PCT	G	GS	CG	SH	SV	IP	H	HR	BB	SO	RAT	ERA	ERA+	OAV	OOB	BH	AVG	PB	PR	/A	PD	TPI
● **DONNE WALL**	Wall, Donnell Lee b: 7/11/67, Potosi, Mo. BR/TR, 6'1", 180 lbs. Deb: 9/2/95																									
1995	Hou-N	3	1	.750	6	5	0	0	0	24^{1}	33	5	5	16	14.1	5.55	70	.320	.352	0	.000	-1	-4	-5	-0	-0.7
1996	Hou-N	9	8	.529	26	23	2	1	0	150	170	17	34	99	12.6	4.56	85	.286	.331	9	.205	2	-6	-12	-0	-1.0
1997	Hou-N	2	5	.286	8	8	0	0	0	41^{2}	53	8	16	25	15.3	6.26	64	.315	.382	1	.100	-0	-10	-11	-0	-1.4
1998	*SD-N	5	4	.556	46	1	0	0	1	70^{1}	50	6	32	56	10.6	2.43	157	.202	.295	2	.286	0	14	11	0	1.4
Total	4	19	18	.514	86	37	2	1	1	286^{1}	306	36	87	196	12.6	4.37	89	.275	.333	12	.182	2	-5	-16	-0	-1.7
● **MURRAY WALL**	Wall, Murray Wesley b: 9/19/26, Dallas, Tex. d: 10/8/71, Lone Oak, Tex. BR/TR, 6'3", 185 lbs. Deb: 7/4/50																									
1950	Bos-N	0	0	—	1	0	0	0	0	4	6	0	2	2	18.0	9.00	43	.333	.400	0	.000	-0	-2	-2	-0	0.0
1957	Bos-A	3	0	1.000	11	0	0	0	1	24^{1}	21	3	2	13	8.5	3.33	120	.233	.250	2	.333	0	1	2	1	0.4
1958	Bos-A	8	9	.471	52	1	0	0	10	114^{1}	109	14	33	53	11.6	3.62	111	.255	.316	3	.107	-2	2	5	3	0.9
1959	Bos-A	1	4	.200	15	0	0	0	3	31^{2}	31	5	15	8	13.1	5.40	75	.267	.351	0	.000	-1	-5	-5	1	-0.8
	Was-A	0	0	—	1	0	0	0	0	1^{1}	3	1	0	0	20.3	6.75	58	.600	.600	0	.000	-0	-0	-0	0	0.0
	Bos-A	1	1	.500	11	0	0	0	0	17^{1}	26	2	11	6	19.7	5.71	71	.371	.463	0	.000	-0	-4	-3	-0	-0.4
	Yr	2	5	.286	27	0	0	0	3	50^{1}	60	8	26	14	15.6	5.54	73	.313	.397	0	.000	-1	-9	-8	1	-1.2
Total	4	13	14	.481	91	1	0	0	14	193	196	25	63	82	12.4	4.20	96	.270	.333	5	.109	-3	-8	-4	5	0.1
● **STAN WALL**	Wall, Stanley Arthur b: 6/16/51, Butler, Mo. BL/TL, 6'1", 175 lbs. Deb: 7/19/75																									
1975	LA-N	0	1	.000	10	0	0	0	0	16	12	0	7	6	11.3	1.69	201	.222	.323	0	—	0	3	3	0	0.2
1976	LA-N	2	2	.500	31	0	0	0	1	50	50	5	15	27	12.1	3.60	94	.269	.330	0	.000	-0	-1	-1	-1	-0.2
1977	LA-N	2	3	.400	25	0	0	0	0	32	36	3	13	22	14.1	5.34	72	.279	.350	0	.000	-0	-5	-5	-1	-0.8
Total	3	4	6	.400	66	0	0	0	1	98	98	8	35	55	12.6	3.86	91	.266	.336	0	.000	-1	-2	-4	-1	-0.8
● **DAVE WALLACE**	Wallace, David William b: 9/7/47, Waterbury, Conn. BR/TR, 5'10", 185 lbs. Deb: 7/18/73																									
1973	Phi-N	0	0	—	4	0	0	0	0	3^{2}	13	1	2	2	36.8	22.09	17	.591	.625	0	—	0	-8	-7	0	0.0
1974	Phi-N	0	1	.000	3	0	0	0	0	3	4	2	3	3	21.0	9.00	42	.308	.438	0	—	0	-2	-2	0	-0.5
1978	Tor-A	0	0	—	6	0	0	0	0	14	12	1	11	7	14.8	3.86	102	.245	.383	0	—	0	-0	0	-0	0.0
Total	3	0	1	.000	13	0	0	0	0	20^{2}	29	4	16	12	19.6	7.84	49	.345	.450	0	—	0	-9	-9	0	-0.5
● **DEREK WALLACE**	Wallace, Derek Robert b: 9/1/71, Van Nuys, Cal. BR/TR, 6'3", 200 lbs. Deb: 8/13/96																									
1996	NY-N	2	3	.400	19	0	0	0	3	24^{2}	29	2	14	15	15.7	4.01	100	.290	.377	0	—	0	1	-0	-0	0.0
● **HUCK WALLACE**	Wallace, Harry Clinton "Lefty" b: 7/27/1882, Richmond, Ind. d: 7/6/51, Cleveland, Ohio BL/TL, 5'6", 160 lbs. Deb: 6/5/12																									
1912	Phi-N	0	0	—	4	0	0	0	0	4^{2}	7	0	4	4	21.2	0.00	—	.350	.458	0	—	0	2	2	0	0.0
● **LEFTY WALLACE**	Wallace, James Harold b: 8/12/21, Evansville, Ind. d: 7/28/82, Evansville, Ind. BL/TL, 5'11", 160 lbs. Deb: 5/5/42																									
1942	Bos-N	1	3	.250	19	3	1	0	0	49^{1}	39	3	24	20	11.9	3.83	87	.217	.316	2	.143	-0	-3	-3	-1	-0.3
1945	Bos-N	1	0	1.000	5	3	1	0	0	20	18	1	9	4	12.6	4.50	85	.240	.329	0	.000	-1	-2	-1	0	-0.1
1946	Bos-N	3	3	.500	27	8	2	0	0	75^{1}	76	5	31	27	12.9	4.18	82	.253	.325	1	.056	-1	-6	-6	2	-0.4
Total	3	5	6	.455	51	14	4	0	0	144^{2}	133	9	64	51	12.5	4.11	84	.240	.323	3	.079	-2	-11	-10	1	-0.8
● **JEFF WALLACE**	Wallace, Jeffrey Allen b: 4/12/76, Wheeling, W.Va. BL/TL, 6'2", 240 lbs. Deb: 8/21/97																									
1997	Pit-N	0	0	—	11	0	0	0	0	12	8	0	8	14	12.0	0.75	571	.200	.333	0	—	0	5	5	0	0.0
● **MIKE WALLACE**	Wallace, Michael Sherman b: 2/3/51, Gastonia, N.C. BL/TL, 6'2", 204 lbs. Deb: 6/27/73																									
1973	Phi-N	1	1	.500	20	3	1	0	1	33^{1}	38	1	15	20	14.3	3.78	100	.304	.379	0	.000	-0	-0	0	-0	-0.1
1974	Phi-N	1	0	1.000	8	0	0	0	0	8^{1}	12	0	2	1	15.1	5.40	70	.324	.359	0	—	0	-2	-2	-0	-0.2
	NY-A	6	0	1.000	23	1	0	0	0	52^{1}	42	3	35	34	13.2	2.41	146	.222	.344	0	—	0	7	6	-1	0.6
1975	NY-A	0	0	—	3	0	0	0	0	4^{1}	11	1	1	2	24.9	14.54	25	.458	.480	0	—	0	-5	-5	0	0.1
	StL-N	0	0	—	9	0	0	0	0	8^{2}	9	0	5	6	14.5	2.08	181	.281	.378	0	—	0	1	2	0	0.0
1976	StL-N	3	2	.600	49	0	0	0	2	66^{1}	66	3	39	40	14.2	4.07	87	.264	.363	1	.333	0	-4	-4	0	-0.3
1977	Tex-A	0	0	—	5	0	0	0	0	8^{1}	10	1	10	2	21.6	7.56	54	.323	.488	0	—	0	-3	-3	0	0.0
Total	5	11	3	.786	117	4	1	0	3	181^{2}	188	9	107	105	14.6	3.91	93	.273	.371	1	.143	0	-6	-6	-1	0.1
● **BOBBY WALLACE**	Wallace, Rhoderick John b: 11/4/1873, Pittsburgh, Pa. d: 11/3/60, Torrance, Cal. BR/TR, 5'8", 170 lbs. Deb: 9/15/1894 MUCH♦																									
1894	Cle-N	2	1	.667	4	3	2	0	0	26	28	1	20	10	17.0	5.19	105	.272	.395	2	.154	-1	0	1	1	0.0
1895	Cle-N	12	14	.462	30	28	22	1	1	228^{2}	271	3	87	63	14.4	4.09	122	.290	.356	21	.214	-3	17	23	3	2.0
1896	*Cle-N	10	7	.588	22	16	13	2	0	145^{1}	167	2	49	46	13.6	3.34	136	.286	.345	35	.235	0	16	19	-0	1.8
1902	StL-A	0	0	—	1	1	0	0	0	2	3	0	0	1	13.5	0.00	—	.333	.333	141	.285	0	1	1	0	0.0
Total	4	24	22	.522	57	48	37	3	1	402	469	6	156	120	14.3	3.87	125	.288	.355	2309	.268	-3	35	44	4	3.8
● **TIM WALLACH**	Wallach, Timothy Charles b: 9/14/57, Huntington Park, Cal. BR/TR, 6'3", 200 lbs. Deb: 9/6/80 ♦																									
1987	Mon-N★	0	0	—	1	0	0	0	0	1	1	0	0	0	9.0	0.00	—	.333	.333	177	.298	1	0	0	-0	0.0
1989	Mon-N★	0	0	—	1	0	0	0	0	1	2	0	0	0	18.0	9.00	39	.500	.500	159	.277	0	-1	-1	-0	0.0
Total	2	0	0	—	2	0	0	0	0	2	3	0	0	0	13.5	4.50	86	.429	.429	2085	.257	1	-0	-0	-0	0.0
● **RED WALLER**	Waller, John Francis b: 6/16/1883, Washington, D.C. d: 2/9/15, Secaucus, N.J. Deb: 4/27/09																									
1909	NY-N	0	0	—	1	0	0	0	0	1	3	0	0	1	36.0	0.00	—	.429	.500	0	—	0	0	0	0	0.0
● **AUGIE WALSH**	Walsh, August Sothley b: 8/17/04, Wilmington, Del. d: 11/12/85, San Rafael, Cal. BR/TR, 6', 175 lbs. Deb: 10/2/27																									
1927	Phi-N	0	1	.000	1	1	1	0	0	10	12	3	5	0	15.3	4.50	92	.333	.415	1	.250	-0	-1	-0	-0	-0.1
1928	Phi-N	4	9	.308	38	11	2	0	2	122^{1}	160	13	40	38	15.1	6.18	69	.321	.378	10	.256	2	-30	-26	-2	-2.4
Total	2	4	10	.286	39	12	3	0	2	132^{1}	172	16	45	38	15.1	6.05	70	.322	.380	11	.256	2	-30	-26	-2	-2.5
● **CONNIE WALSH**	Walsh, Cornelius R. b: 4/23/1882, St.Louis, Mo. d: 4/5/53, St.Louis, Mo. Deb: 9/16/07																									
1907	Pit-N	0	0	—	1	0	0	0	0	1	1	0	1	0	18.0	9.00	27	.250	.400	0	—	0	-1	-1	-0	0.0
● **DAVE WALSH**	Walsh, David Peter b: 9/25/60, Arlington, Mass. BL/TL, 6'1", 185 lbs. Deb: 8/13/90																									
1990	LA-N	1	0	1.000	20	0	0	0	1	16^{1}	15	1	6	15	11.6	3.86	95	.242	.309	0	—	0	-0	-0	0	0.0
● **ED WALSH**	Walsh, Edward Arthur b: 2/11/05, Meriden, Conn. d: 10/31/37, Meriden, Conn. BR/TR, 6'1", 180 lbs. Deb: 7/4/28 F																									
1928	Chi-A	4	7	.364	14	10	3	0	0	78	86	2	42	32	15.3	4.96	82	.290	.387	3	.111	-2	-8	-8	-1	-1.2
1929	Chi-A	6	11	.353	24	20	7	0	0	129	156	9	64	31	15.6	5.65	76	.312	.394	10	.233	2	-20	-20	1	-1.9
1930	Chi-A	1	4	.200	37	4	0	0	0	103^{2}	131	8	30	37	14.3	5.38	86	.316	.367	9	.265	1	-8	-9	1	-0.2
1932	Chi-A	0	2	.000	4	4	1	0	0	20^{1}	26	3	13	7	17.3	8.41	51	.299	.390	2	.286	0	-9	-9	-0	-0.7
Total	4	11	24	.314	79	38	11	0	0	331	399	22	149	107	15.3	5.57	78	.307	.384	24	.216	1	-45	-45	1	-4.0
● **ED WALSH**	Walsh, Edward Augustine "Big Ed" b: 5/14/1881, Plains, Pa. d: 5/26/59, Pompano Beach, Fla BR/TR, 6'1", 193 lbs. Deb: 5/7/04 FMUCH																									
1904	Chi-A	6	3	.667	18	8	6	1	1	110^{2}	90	1	32	57	10.2	2.60	94	.223	.285	9	.220	3	-0	-2	0	0.2
1905	Chi-A	8	3	.727	22	13	9	1	0	136^{2}	121	0	29	71	10.1	2.17	113	.239	.284	9	.155	-0	7	4	0	0.4
1906	*Chi-A	17	13	.567	41	31	24	**10**	2	278^{1}	215	1	58	171	9.1	1.88	135	.217	.265	14	.141	-2	25	21	8	3.0
1907	Chi-A	24	18	.571	**56**	46	**37**	5	**4**	**422^{1}**	341	3	87	206	9.3	**1.60**	**150**	.223	.269	25	.162	-1	**44**	**37**	22	**6.4**
1908	Chi-A	**40**	15	**.727**	**66**	49	**42**	**11**	**6**	**464**	343	2	56	**269**	7.9	1.42	163	.203	.232	27	.172	2	**50**	**46**	14	**8.1**
1909	Chi-A	15	11	.577	31	28	20	**8**	2	230^{1}	166	0	50	127	**8.6**	1.41	166	.203	**.253**	18	.214	4	**27**	24	7	4.4
1910	Chi-A	18	20	.474	**45**	36	33	7	**5**	**369^{2}**	242	5	61	258	**7.5**	**1.27**	**189**	**.187**	**.226**	30	.217	4	**52**	46	10	**7.1**
1911	Chi-A	27	18	.600	**56**	37	33	5	**4**	**368^{2}**	327	4	72	**255**	9.9	2.22	145	.239	**.280**	34	.215	-2	46	41	15	6.2
1912	Chi-A	27	17	.614	**62**	41	32	6	**10**	**393**	332	6	94	254	9.8	2.15	149	.231	.279	33	.243	6	51	46	7	6.6
1913	Chi-A	8	3	.727	16	14	7	1	1	97^{2}	91	1	39	34	12.3	2.58	113	.243	.321	5	.156	-1	4	4	1	0.4
1914	Chi-A	2	3	.400	8	5	3	1	0	44^{2}	33	0	20	15	10.9	2.82	95	.212	.305	1	.063	-1	-0	-1	-1	-0.1
1915	Chi-A	3	0	1.000	3	3	3	1	0	27	19	0	7	12	8.7	1.33	223	.202	.257	4	.364	1	5	5	-1	0.6
1916	Chi-A	0	1	.000	2	1	0	0	0	3^{1}	4	0	3	3	18.9	2.70	102	.286	.412	0	—	0	0	0	0	0.0
1917	Bos-N	0	1	.000	4	3	1	0	0	18	22	0	9	4	16.0	3.50	73	.314	.400	1	.250	1	-2	-2	0	0.0
Total	14	195	126	.607	430	315	250	57	35	2964^{1}	2346	23	617	1736	9.2	1.82	145	.218	.264	210	.193	14	310	270	83	43.3

YEAR	TM/L	W	L	PCT	G	GS	CG	SH	SV	IP	H	HR	BB	SO	RAT	ERA	ERA+	OAV	OOB	BH	AVG	PB	PR	/A	PD	TPI
● JUNIOR WALSH Walsh, James Gerald b: 3/7/19, Newark, N.J. d: 11/12/90, Olyphant, Pa. BR/TR, 5'11", 185 lbs. Deb: 9/14/46																										
1946	Pit-N	0	1	.000	4	2	0	0	0	10^1	9	0	10	2	17.4	5.23	67	.237	.408	0	.000	-1	-2	-2	-0	-0.2
1948	Pit-N	1	0	1.000	2	0	0	0	0	4^1	4	1	5	0	18.7	10.38	39	.235	.409	0	.000	-0	-3	-3	0	-0.5
1949	Pit-N	1	4	.200	9	7	1	1	0	42^2	40	5	16	24	11.8	5.06	83	.244	.311	0	.000	-1	-5	-4	-1	-0.6
1950	Pit-N	1	1	.500	38	2	0	0	2	62^1	56	6	34	33	13.1	5.05	87	.246	.346	1	.167	1	-6	-5	0	-0.1
1951	Pit-N	1	4	.200	36	1	0	0	0	73^1	92	9	46	32	17.1	6.87	61	.304	.397	1	.143	0	-24	-22	0	-1.3
Total	5	4	10	.286	89	12	1	1	2	193	201	21	111	91	14.7	5.88	72	.268	.365	2	.065	-1	-40	-35	-0	-2.7
● JIM WALSH Walsh, James Thomas b: 7/10/1894, Roxbury, Mass. d: 5/13/67, Boston, Mass. BL/TL, 5'11", 175 lbs. Deb: 8/25/21																										
1921	Det-A	0	0	—	3	0	0	0	0	4	2	0	1	3	6.8	2.25	190	.125	.176	0	—	0	1	1	-0	0.0
● DEE WALSH Walsh, Leo Thomas b: 3/28/1890, St.Louis, Mo. d: 7/14/71, St.Louis, Mo. BB/TR, 5'9.5", 165 lbs. Deb: 4/10/13 ♦																										
1915	StL-A	0	0	—	1	0	0	0	0	2	2	0	2	0	18.0	13.50	21	.222	.364	33	.220	0	-2	-2	-0	0.0
● JIMMY WALSH Walsh, Michael Timothy "Runt" b: 3/25/1886, Lima, Ohio d: 1/21/47, Baltimore, Md. BR/TR, 5'9", 174 lbs. Deb: 4/25/10 ♦																										
1911	Phi-N	0	1	.000	1	0	0	0	0	2^2	7	1	1	1	27.0	13.50	26	.500	.533	78	.270	0	-3	-3	-0	-0.7
● GENE WALTER Walter, Gene Winston b: 11/22/60, Chicago, Ill. BL/TL, 6'4", 200 lbs. Deb: 8/9/85																										
1985	SD-N	0	2	.000	15	0	0	0	3	22	12	0	8	18	8.2	2.05	173	.158	.238	0	.000	0	4	4	0	0.5
1986	SD-N	2	2	.500	57	0	0	0	1	98	89	7	49	84	13.0	3.86	95	.247	.343	2	.200	1	-2	-2	1	0.1
1987	NY-N	1	2	.333	21	0	0	0	0	19^2	18	1	13	11	14.6	3.20	118	.243	.364	0	.000	0	2	1	-0	0.2
1988	NY-N	0	1	.000	19	0	0	0	0	16^2	21	0	11	14	17.3	3.78	85	.309	.405	0	—	0	-1	-1	-0	-0.1
	Sea-A	1	0	1.000	16	0	0	0	0	26^1	21	0	15	13	13.0	5.13	81	.216	.333	0	—	0	-3	-3	-0	-0.3
Total	4	4	7	.364	128	0	0	0	4	182^2	161	8	96	140	13.0	3.74	98	.238	.339	2	.167	1	0	1	0	0.4
● BERNIE WALTER Walter, James Bernard b: 8/15/08, Dover, Tenn. d: 10/30/88, Nashville, Tenn. BR/TR, 6'1", 175 lbs. Deb: 8/16/30																										
1930	Pit-N	0	0	—	1	0	0	0	0	1	0	0	0	1	0.0	0.00	—	.000	.000	0	—	0	1	1	0	0.0
● CHARLIE WALTERS Walters, Charles Leonard b: 2/21/47, Minneapolis, Minn. BR/TR, 6'4", 190 lbs. Deb: 4/11/69																										
1969	Min-A	0	0	—	6	0	0	0	0	6^2	6	1	3	2	13.5	5.40	68	.240	.345	0	—	0	-1	-1	-0	0.0
● MIKE WALTERS Walters, Michael Charles b: 10/18/57, St.Louis, Mo. BR/TR, 6'5", 203 lbs. Deb: 7/8/83																										
1983	Min-A	1	1	.500	23	0	0	0	2	59	52	4	20	21	11.3	4.12	103	.243	.314	0	—	0	-0	1	0	-0.1
1984	Min-A	0	3	.000	23	0	0	0	2	29	31	1	14	10	14.3	3.72	113	.287	.374	0	—	0	1	2	-0	-0.1
Total	2	1	4	.200	46	0	0	0	4	88	83	5	34	31	12.3	3.99	106	.258	.334	0	—	0	0	2	-0	-0.2
● BUCKY WALTERS Walters, William Henry b: 4/19/09, Philadelphia, Pa. d: 4/20/91, Abington, Pa. BR/TR, 6'1", 180 lbs. Deb: 9/18/31 MC♦																										
1934	Phi-N	0	0	—	2	1	0	0	0	7	8	1	2	7	14.1	1.29	367	.296	.367	78	.260	0	2	3	1	0.1
1935	Phi-N	9	9	.500	24	22	8	2	0	151	168	9	68	40	14.5	4.17	109	.289	.370	24	.250	1	-3	6	2	1.1
1936	Phi-N	11	21	.344	40	33	15	**4**	0	258	284	11	115	66	14.1	4.26	107	.277	.353	29	.240	2	-7	8	9	2.2
1937	Phi-N★	14	15	.483	37	34	15	3	0	246^1	292	14	86	87	13.9	4.75	91	.295	.353	38	.277	4	-23	-11	5	-0.2
1938	Phi-N	4	8	.333	12	12	9	1	0	82^2	91	8	42	28	14.8	5.23	74	.276	.363	10	.286	3	-13	-12	0	-1.2
	Cin-N	11	6	.647	27	22	11	2	1	168^1	168	5	66	65	12.6	3.69	99	.255	.324	9	.141	-0	2	-1	2	0.1
	Yr	15	14	.517	39	34	20	3	1	251	259	13	108	93	13.2	4.20	89	.261	.335	19	.192	3	-11	-13	3	-1.1
1939	*Cin-N☆	**27**	11	.711	39	36	**31**	2	0	**319**	250	15	109	**137**	10.3	**2.29**	**168**	**.220**	.291	39	.325	13	**58**	**55**	4	**8.5**
1940	*Cin-N★	**22**	10	.688	36	36	**29**	3	0	**305**	241	19	92	115	10.0	**2.48**	**153**	**.220**	.283	24	.205	2	**46**	**44**	-1	4.7
1941	Cin-N★	19	15	.559	37	35	**27**	5	2	**302**	292	10	88	129	11.4	2.83	127	.255	.309	20	.189	2	27	26	2	3.3
1942	Cin-N★	15	14	.517	34	32	21	2	0	253^2	223	8	73	109	10.7	2.66	123	.231	.289	24	.242	6	18	18	1	3.0
1943	Cin-N	15	15	.500	34	34	21	5	0	246^1	244	8	109	80	12.9	3.54	94	.264	.342	24	.267	8	-4	-6	1	0.2
1944	Cin-N★	**23**	8	.742	34	32	27	6	1	285	233	10	87	77	10.2	2.40	145	**.219**	.281	30	.280	8	**38**	**34**	1	**4.7**
1945	Cin-N	10	10	.500	22	22	12	3	0	168	166	6	51	45	11.7	2.68	140	.259	.316	14	.230	5	21	20	-0	2.9
1946	Cin-N	10	7	.588	22	22	10	2	0	151^1	146	9	64	60	12.6	2.56	131	.258	.336	7	.127	-1	14	13	2	1.6
1947	Cin-N	8	8	.500	20	20	5	2	0	122	137	15	49	43	13.9	5.75	71	.278	.347	12	.267	3	-23	-22	-1	-2.3
1948	Cin-N	0	3	.000	7	5	1	0	0	35	42	6	18	19	15.4	4.63	84	.316	.397	4	.267	0	-3	-3	1	-0.1
1950	Bos-N	0	0	—	1	0	0	0	0	4	5	0	2	0	15.8	4.50	86	.313	.389	0	.000	-0	-0	-0	-0	0.0
Total	16	198	160	.553	428	398	242	42	4	3104^2	2990	154	1121	1107	12.1	3.30	115	.253	.321	477	.243	57	152	168	27	28.6
● BRUCE WALTON Walton, Bruce Kenneth b: 12/25/62, Bakersfield, Cal. BR/TR, 6'2", 195 lbs. Deb: 5/11/91																										
1991	Oak-A	1	0	1.000	12	0	0	0	0	13	11	3	6	10	12.5	6.23	62	.229	.327	0	—	0	-3	-3	-0	-0.2
1992	Oak-A	0	0	—	7	0	0	0	0	10	17	1	3	7	18.0	9.90	38	.378	.417	0	—	0	-7	-7	-0	0.0
1993	Mon-N	0	0	—	4	0	0	0	0	5^2	11	1	3	0	22.2	9.53	44	.407	.467	0	.000	-0	-3	-3	0	0.0
1994	Col-N	1	0	1.000	4	0	0	0	0	5^1	6	1	3	1	15.2	8.44	59	.273	.360	0	—	0	-3	-2	-0	-0.3
Total	4	2	0	1.000	27	0	0	0	0	34	45	6	15	18	16.1	8.21	49	.317	.386	0	.000	-0	-16	-16	-1	-0.5
● DICK WANTZ Wantz, Richard Carter b: 4/11/40, South Gate, Cal. d: 5/13/65, Inglewood, Cal. BR/TR, 6'5", 175 lbs. Deb: 4/13/65																										
1965	Cal-A	0	0	—	1	0	0	0	0	1	3	0	0	2	27.0	18.00	19	.500	.500	0	—	0	-2	-2	0	0.0
● STEVE WAPNICK Wapnick, Steven Lee b: 9/25/65, Panorama City, Cal. BR/TR, 6'2", 200 lbs. Deb: 4/14/90																										
1990	Det-A	0	0	—	4	0	0	0	0	7	8	0	10	6	23.1	6.43	62	.296	.486	0	—	0	-2	-2	-0	0.0
1991	Chi-A	0	1	.000	6	0	0	0	0	5	2	0	4	1	10.8	1.80	221	.111	.273	0	—	0	1	1	-0	0.2
Total	2	0	1	.000	10	0	0	0	0	12	10	0	14	7	18.0	4.50	88	.222	.407	0	—	0	-1	-1	-0	0.2
● BRYAN WARD Ward, Bryan Matthew b: 1/25/72, Bristol, Pa. BL/TL, 6'2", 210 lbs. Deb: 7/3/98																										
1998	Chi-A	1	2	.333	28	0	0	0	1	27	30	4	7	17	12.3	3.33	137	.278	.322	0	—	0	4	4	-1	0.3
● COLIN WARD Ward, Colin Norval b: 11/22/60, Los Angeles, Cal. BL/TL, 6'3", 190 lbs. Deb: 9/21/85																										
1985	SF-N	0	0	—	6	2	0	0	0	12^1	10	0	7	8	12.4	4.38	78	.233	.340	0	.000	-0	-1	-1	0	0.0
● JOHNNY WARD Ward, John b: East St.Louis, Ill. Deb: 9/19/1885																										
1885	Pro-N	0	1	.000	1	1	1	0	0	8	10	0	1	3	12.4	4.50	60	.286	.306	0	.000	-0	-1	-2	-0	-0.2
● JOHN WARD Ward, John Montgomery b: 3/3/1860, Bellefonte, Pa. d: 3/4/25, Augusta, Ga. BL/TR, 5'9", 165 lbs. Deb: 7/15/1878 MH♦																										
1878	Pro-N	22	13	.629	37	37	37	6	0	334	308	3	34	116	9.2	**1.51**	**146**	.231	.251	27	.196	2	**30**	26	2	2.6
1879	Pro-N	**47**	19	**.712**	70	60	58	2	**1**	587	571	5	36	**239**	9.3	2.15	110	.239	.250	104	.286	17	23	13	4	2.9
1880	Pro-N	39	24	.619	70	67	59	**8**	1	595	501	5	45	230	8.3	1.74	127	.217	.232	81	.228	1	**42**	31	5	3.4
1881	Pro-N	18	18	.500	39	35	32	3	0	330	326	2	53	119	10.3	2.13	125	.242	.271	87	.244	3	24	19	5	2.5
1882	Pro-N	19	12	.613	33	32	29	4	**1**	278	261	6	36	72	9.6	2.59	109	.232	.256	87	.245	1	10	7	4	1.0
1883	NY-N	16	13	.552	34	25	24	1	0	277	278	3	31	121	10.0	2.70	115	.246	.267	97	.255	6	14	12	4	1.8
1884	NY-N	3	3	.500	9	5	5	0	0	60^2	72	2	18	23	13.4	3.41	87	.280	.327	122	.253	1	-3	-3	1	-0.1
Total	7	164	102	.617	292	261	244	24	3	2461^2	2317	26	253	920	9.4	2.10	118	.235	.254	2104	.275	31	138	105	24	14.1
● DICK WARD Ward, Richard Ole b: 5/21/09, Herrick, S.Dak. d: 5/30/66, Freeland, Wash. BR/TR, 6'1", 198 lbs. Deb: 5/3/34																										
1934	Chi-N	0	0	—	3	0	0	0	0	6	9	0	2	1	16.5	3.00	129	.375	.423	0	.000	-0	1	1	-0	0.0
1935	StL-N	0	0	—	1	0	0	0	0	0	0	0	1	0	—	—	—	—	1.000	0	—	0	0	0	0	0.0
Total	2	0	0	—	4	0	0	0	0	6	9	0	3	1	18.0	3.00	129	.375	.444	0	.000	-0	1	1	-0	0.0
● COLBY WARD Ward, Robert Colby b: 1/2/64, Lansing, Mich. BR/TR, 6'2", 185 lbs. Deb: 7/27/90																										
1990	Cle-A	1	3	.250	22	0	0	0	1	36	31	3	21	23	13.3	4.25	92	.238	.349	0	—	0	-1	-1	-0	-0.1
● DUANE WARD Ward, Roy Duane b: 5/28/64, Park View, N.Mex. BR/TR, 6'4", 210 lbs. Deb: 4/12/86																										
1986	Atl-N	0	1	.000	10	0	0	0	0	16	22	2	8	8	16.9	7.31	54	.349	.423	0	.000	-0	-6	-6	1	-0.3
	Tor-A	0	1	.000	2	1	0	0	0	2	3	0	4	1	36.0	13.50	31	.300	.533	0	—	0	-2	-2	0	-0.8
1987	Tor-A	1	0	1.000	12	1	0	0	0	11^2	14	0	12	10	20.1	6.94	65	.326	.473	0	—	0	-3	-3	0	-0.3

YEAR	TM/L	W	L	PCT	G	GS	CG	SH	SV	IP	H	HR	BB	SO	RAT	ERA	ERA+	OAV	OOB	BH	AVG	PB	PR	/A	PD	TPI
1988	Tor-A	9	3	.750	64	0	0	0	15	111^{2}	101	5	60	91	13.4	3.30	119	.245	.347	0	—	0	8	8	-0	0.9
1989	*Tor-A	4	10	.286	66	0	0	0	15	114^{2}	94	4	58	122	12.3	3.77	100	.230	.333	0	—	0	1	0	2	0.2
1990	Tor-A	2	8	.200	73	0	0	0	11	127^{2}	101	9	42	112	10.2	3.45	114	.221	.288	0	—	0	6	7	1	0.6
1991	*Tor-A	7	6	.538	**81**	0	0	0	23	107^{1}	80	3	33	132	9.6	2.77	152	.207	.273	0	—	0	16	17	0	2.5
1992	*Tor-A	7	4	.636	79	0	0	0	12	101^{1}	76	5	39	103	10.3	1.95	209	.207	.285	0	—	0	**22**	**24**	-0	2.9
1993	*Tor-A★	2	3	.400	71	0	0	0	**45**	71^{2}	49	4	25	97	9.4	2.13	202	.193	.268	0	—	0	17	17	-1	2.9
1995	Tor-A	0	1	.000	4	0	0	0	0	2^{2}	11	0	5	3	57.4	27.00	17	.579	.680	0	—	0	-7	-7	-0	-1.7
Total	9	32	37	.464	462	2	0	0	121	666^{2}	551	32	286	679	11.5	3.28	123	.228	.314	0	.000	-0	53	55	2	6.9

● **JON WARDEN** Warden, Jonathan Edgar "Warbler" b: 10/1/46, Columbus, Ohio BB/TL, 6′, 205 lbs. Deb: 4/11/68

YEAR	TM/L	W	L	PCT	G	GS	CG	SH	SV	IP	H	HR	BB	SO	RAT	ERA	ERA+	OAV	OOB	BH	AVG	PB	PR	/A	PD	TPI
1968	Det-A	4	1	.800	28	0	0	0	3	37^{1}	30	5	15	25	10.8	3.62	83	.217	.294	0	.000	-0	-3	-3	-1	-0.5

● **CURT WARDLE** Wardle, Curtis Ray b: 11/16/60, Downey, Cal. BL/TL, 6′5″, 220 lbs. Deb: 8/30/84

YEAR	TM/L	W	L	PCT	G	GS	CG	SH	SV	IP	H	HR	BB	SO	RAT	ERA	ERA+	OAV	OOB	BH	AVG	PB	PR	/A	PD	TPI
1984	Min-A	0	0	—	2	0	0	0	0	4	3	2	0	5	6.8	4.50	93	.200	.200	0	—	0	-0	-0	0	-0.3
1985	Min-A	1	3	.250	35	0	0	0	1	49	49	9	28	47	14.3	5.51	80	.266	.366	0	—	0	-7	-6	1	-0.8
	Cle-A	7	6	.538	15	12	0	0	0	66	78	11	34	37	15.4	6.68	62	.297	.379	0	—	0	-19	-19	-1	-3.0
	Yr	8	9	.471	50	12	0	0	1	115	127	20	62	84	14.9	6.18	69	.283	.371	0	—	0	-26	-25	-0	-3.8
Total	2	8	9	.471	52	12	0	0	1	119	130	22	62	89	14.7	6.13	69	.281	.369	0	—	0	-26	-25	0	-4.1

● **JEFF WARE** Ware, Jeffrey Allan b: 11/11/70, Norfolk, Va. BR/TR, 6′3″, 190 lbs. Deb: 9/2/95

YEAR	TM/L	W	L	PCT	G	GS	CG	SH	SV	IP	H	HR	BB	SO	RAT	ERA	ERA+	OAV	OOB	BH	AVG	PB	PR	/A	PD	TPI
1995	Tor-A	2	1	.667	5	5	0	0	0	26^{1}	28	2	21	18	17.1	5.47	86	.277	.407	0	—	0	-2	-2	0	-0.2
1996	Tor-A	1	5	.167	13	4	0	0	0	32^{2}	35	6	31	11	18.7	9.09	55	.271	.420	0	—	0	-15	-15	0	-2.0
Total	2	3	6	.333	18	9	0	0	0	59	63	8	52	29	18.0	7.47	65	.274	.414	0	—	0	-17	-17	0	-2.2

● **JACK WARHOP** Warhop, John Milton "Chief" or "Crab" (b: John Milton Wauhop)
b: 7/4/1884, Hinton, W.Va. d: 10/4/60, Freeport, Ill. BR/TR, 5′9.5″, 168 lbs. Deb: 9/19/08

YEAR	TM/L	W	L	PCT	G	GS	CG	SH	SV	IP	H	HR	BB	SO	RAT	ERA	ERA+	OAV	OOB	BH	AVG	PB	PR	/A	PD	TPI
1908	NY-A	1	2	.333	5	4	3	0	0	36^{1}	40	0	8	11	12.9	4.46	56	.292	.349	1	.063	-1	-8	-8	0	-0.7
1909	NY-A	13	15	.464	36	23	21	3	2	243^{1}	197	2	81	95	11.2	2.40	105	.233	.319	11	.128	-2	2	3	1	0.3
1910	NY-A	14	14	.500	37	27	20	0	2	243	219	1	79	75	11.7	3.00	89	.246	.320	14	.177	-1	-13	-9	-4	-1.6
1911	NY-A	12	13	.480	31	25	17	1	0	209^{2}	239	6	44	71	12.8	4.16	86	.286	.333	12	.156	-4	-19	-13	-2	-1.9
1912	NY-A	10	19	.345	39	22	16	0	3	258	256	3	59	110	11.5	2.86	126	.266	.319	19	.207	-1	13	21	-3	1.9
1913	NY-A	4	5	.444	15	7	1	0	0	62^{1}	69	1	33	11	16.5	3.75	80	.292	.406	3	.130	-0	-6	-5	-2	-0.9
1914	NY-A	8	15	.348	37	23	15	0	0	216^{2}	182	8	44	56	9.8	2.37	117	.235	.286	10	.141	-1	9	9	-2	0.7
1915	NY-A	7	9	.438	21	19	12	0	0	143^{1}	164	7	52	34	14.3	3.96	74	.309	.384	7	.137	-2	-16	-16	-3	-2.0
Total	8	69	92	.429	221	150	105	4	7	1412^{2}	1366	28	400	463	12.0	3.12	96	.262	.328	77	.156	-12	-38	-19	-13	-4.2

● **CY WARMOTH** Warmoth, Wallace Walter b: 2/2/1893, Bone Gap, Ill. d: 6/20/57, Mt.Carmel, Ill. BL/TL, 5′11″, 158 lbs. Deb: 8/31/16

YEAR	TM/L	W	L	PCT	G	GS	CG	SH	SV	IP	H	HR	BB	SO	RAT	ERA	ERA+	OAV	OOB	BH	AVG	PB	PR	/A	PD	TPI
1916	StL-N	0	0	—	3	0	0	0	0	5	12	0	4	1	30.6	14.40	18	.500	.586	0	.000	-0	-7	-7	-0	-0.1
1922	Was-A	1	0	1.000	5	1	1	0	0	19	15	0	9	8	11.4	1.42	272	.205	.293	1	.143	-0	6	5	-0	0.2
1923	Was-A	7	5	.583	21	13	3	0	0	105	103	4	76	45	15.4	4.29	88	.261	.381	8	.222	2	-4	-6	0	-0.4
Total	3	8	5	.615	29	14	4	0	0	129	130	4	89	54	15.4	4.26	88	.264	.379	9	.200	1	-5	-7	-0	-0.3

● **LON WARNEKE** Warneke, Lonnie "The Arkansas Hummingbird" b: 3/28/09, Mt.Ida, Ark. d: 6/23/76, Hot Springs, Ark. BR/TR, 6′2″, 185 lbs. Deb: 4/18/30 U

YEAR	TM/L	W	L	PCT	G	GS	CG	SH	SV	IP	H	HR	BB	SO	RAT	ERA	ERA+	OAV	OOB	BH	AVG	PB	PR	/A	PD	TPI
1930	Chi-N	0	0	—	1	0	0	0	0	1^{1}	2	0	5	0	47.3	33.75	14	.400	.700	0	—	0	-4	-4	0	0.0
1931	Chi-N	2	4	.333	20	7	3	0	0	64^{1}	67	1	37	27	15.0	3.22	120	.269	.370	5	.263	1	5	5	-1	0.4
1932	*Chi-N	**22**	6	**.786**	35	32	25	**4**	0	277	247	12	64	106	10.2	**2.37**	**159**	.237	.283	19	.192	-0	**46**	**43**	-0	4.1
1933	Chi-N★	18	13	.581	36	34	**26**	4	1	287^{1}	262	8	75	133	10.6	2.00	163	.244	.295	30	.300	10	43	40	3	6.2
1934	Chi-N★	22	10	.688	43	35	23	3	3	291^{1}	273	16	66	143	10.5	3.21	121	.244	.287	22	.195	-1	27	21	0	2.1
1935	*Chi-N	20	13	.606	42	30	20	1	4	261^{2}	257	19	50	120	10.7	3.06	128	.257	.294	20	.220	1	28	25	-1	3.0
1936	Chi-N★	16	13	.552	40	29	13	**4**	1	240^{1}	246	10	76	113	12.2	3.45	116	.264	.322	17	.202	0	15	14	-1	1.5
1937	StL-N	18	11	.621	36	33	18	2	0	238^{2}	280	32	69	87	13.2	4.53	88	.287	.335	21	.262	4	-16	-14	-3	-1.4
1938	StL-N	13	8	.619	31	26	12	4	0	197	199	14	64	89	12.1	3.97	100	.256	.314	23	.324	5	-4	-0	-2	0.3
1939	StL-N☆	13	7	.650	34	21	6	2	2	162	160	14	49	59	11.7	3.78	109	.259	.316	10	.192	1	3	6	-0	0.7
1940	StL-N	16	10	.615	33	31	17	1	0	232	235	17	47	85	11.1	3.14	127	.257	.296	18	.209	2	18	22	1	2.6
1941	StL-N☆	17	9	.654	37	30	12	4	0	246	227	19	82	83	11.4	3.15	120	.249	.313	9	.117	-2	13	17	-2	1.3
1942	StL-N	6	4	.600	12	12	5	0	0	82	76	8	15	31	10.0	3.29	104	.238	.272	10	.333	3	0	1	-1	0.3
	Chi-N	5	7	.417	15	12	8	1	2	99	97	2	21	28	10.7	2.27	141	.259	.298	6	.188	-0	11	10	-0	1.2
	Yr	11	11	.500	27	24	13	1	2	181	173	10	36	59	10.4	2.73	121	.249	.286	16	.258	2	12	11	-1	1.5
1943	Chi-N	4	5	.444	21	10	4	0	0	88^{1}	82	3	18	30	10.2	3.16	106	.246	.285	5	.192	1	2	2	1	0.4
1945	Chi-N	0	1	.000	9	1	0	0	0	14	16	0	1	6	10.9	3.86	95	.267	.279	0	.000	0	-0	-0	0	0.0
Total	15	192	121	.613	445	343	192	30	13	2782^{1}	2726	175	739	1140	11.3	3.18	119	.255	.304	215	.223	27	188	188	-5	22.7

● **ED WARNER** Warner, Edward Emory b: 6/20/1889, Fitchburg, Mass. d: 2/5/54, New York, N.Y. BR/TL, 5′10.5″, 165 lbs. Deb: 7/2/12

YEAR	TM/L	W	L	PCT	G	GS	CG	SH	SV	IP	H	HR	BB	SO	RAT	ERA	ERA+	OAV	OOB	BH	AVG	PB	PR	/A	PD	TPI
1912	Pit-N	1	1	.500	11	3	1	1	0	45	40	0	18	13	12.2	3.60	91	.242	.328	2	.133	-1	-1	-2	1	-0.1

● **JACK WARNER** Warner, Jack Dyer b: 7/12/40, Brandywine, W.Va. BR/TR, 5′11″, 190 lbs. Deb: 4/10/62

YEAR	TM/L	W	L	PCT	G	GS	CG	SH	SV	IP	H	HR	BB	SO	RAT	ERA	ERA+	OAV	OOB	BH	AVG	PB	PR	/A	PD	TPI
1962	Chi-N	0	0	—	7	0	0	0	0	7	9	3	0	3	11.6	7.71	54	.321	.321	0	—	0	-3	-3	0	0.0
1963	Chi-N	0	1	.000	8	0	0	0	0	22^{2}	21	1	8	7	11.5	2.78	126	.256	.322	1	.250	0	1	2	-0	0.1
1964	Chi-N	0	0	—	7	0	0	0	0	9^{1}	12	0	4	6	15.4	2.89	128	.333	.400	0	—	0	1	1	0	0.0
1965	Chi-N	0	1	.000	11	0	0	0	0	15^{2}	22	1	9	7	17.8	8.62	43	.355	.437	0	.000	-0	-9	-9	0	-0.5
Total	4	0	2	.000	33	0	0	0	0	54^{2}	64	5	21	23	14.0	5.10	72	.308	.371	1	.200	0	-10	-9	0	-0.4

● **MIKE WARREN** Warren, Michael Bruce b: 3/26/61, Inglewood, Cal. BR/TR, 6′1″, 175 lbs. Deb: 6/12/83

YEAR	TM/L	W	L	PCT	G	GS	CG	SH	SV	IP	H	HR	BB	SO	RAT	ERA	ERA+	OAV	OOB	BH	AVG	PB	PR	/A	PD	TPI
1983	Oak-A	5	3	.625	12	9	3	1	0	65^{2}	51	4	18	30	9.6	4.11	94	.215	.273	0	—	0	-0	-2	-1	0.2
1984	Oak-A	3	6	.333	24	12	0	0	0	90	104	11	44	61	15.1	4.90	76	.291	.373	0	—	0	-9	-12	-2	-0.7
1985	Oak-A	1	4	.200	16	6	0	0	0	49	52	13	38	48	17.3	6.61	58	.261	.390	0	—	0	-13	-15	-1	-0.9
Total	3	9	13	.409	52	27	3	1	0	204^{2}	207	28	100	139	13.9	5.06	75	.261	.349	0	—	0	-23	-28	-4	-1.4

● **TOMMY WARREN** Warren, Thomas Gentry b: 7/5/17, Tulsa, Okla. d: 1/2/68, Tulsa, Okla. BB/TL, 6′1″, 190 lbs. Deb: 4/18/44

YEAR	TM/L	W	L	PCT	G	GS	CG	SH	SV	IP	H	HR	BB	SO	RAT	ERA	ERA+	OAV	OOB	BH	AVG	PB	PR	/A	PD	TPI
1944	Bro-N	1	4	.200	22	4	2	0	0	68^{2}	74	4	40	18	14.9	4.98	71	.270	.363	11	.256	2	-10	-11	0	-0.6

● **DAN WARTHEN** Warthen, Daniel Dean b: 12/1/52, Omaha, Neb. BB/TL, 6′, 200 lbs. Deb: 5/18/75 C

YEAR	TM/L	W	L	PCT	G	GS	CG	SH	SV	IP	H	HR	BB	SO	RAT	ERA	ERA+	OAV	OOB	BH	AVG	PB	PR	/A	PD	TPI
1975	Mon-N	8	6	.571	40	18	2	0	3	167^{2}	130	8	87	128	11.7	3.11	123	.217	.317	6	.118	-2	9	13	1	0.9
1976	Mon-N	2	10	.167	23	16	2	1	0	90	76	8	66	67	14.4	5.30	70	.232	.364	0	.000	-3	-18	-16	0	-2.2
1977	Mon-N	2	3	.400	12	6	1	0	0	35	33	7	38	26	18.3	7.97	48	.262	.433	1	.111	-0	-16	-16	1	-1.9
	Phi-N	0	1	.000	3	0	0	0	0	3^{2}	4	0	5	1	22.1	0.00	—	.267	.450	0	—	0	2	2	-0	0.4
	Yr	2	4	.333	15	6	1	0	0	38^{2}	37	7	43	27	18.6	7.22	53	.201	.432	1	.111	-0	-14	15	0	1.6
1978	Hou-N	0	1	.000	5	1	0	0	0	10^{2}	10	3	2	2	10.1	4.22	78	.250	.286	0	.000	-0	-1	-1	-0	-0.1
Total	4	12	21	.364	83	41	5	1	3	307	253	26	198	224	13.3	4.31	88	.228	.347	7	.079	-6	-23	-18	1	-2.9

● **JOHN WASDIN** Wasdin, John Truman b: 8/5/72, Fort Belvoir, Va. BR/TR, 6′2″, 190 lbs. Deb: 8/24/95

YEAR	TM/L	W	L	PCT	G	GS	CG	SH	SV	IP	H	HR	BB	SO	RAT	ERA	ERA+	OAV	OOB	BH	AVG	PB	PR	/A	PD	TPI
1995	Oak-A	1	1	.500	5	2	0	0	0	17^{1}	14	4	3	6	9.3	4.67	96	.215	.261	0	—	0	0	-0	-1	0.0
1996	Oak-A	8	7	.533	25	21	1	0	0	131^{1}	145	24	50	75	13.6	5.96	83	.283	.352	0	—	0	-14	-15	-1	-1.5
1997	Bos-A	4	6	.400	53	7	0	0	0	124^{2}	121	18	38	84	11.7	4.40	105	.251	.310	0	—	0	2	3	-2	0.1
1998	*Bos-A	6	4	.600	47	8	0	0	0	96	111	14	27	59	13.1	5.25	88	.288	.337	0	—	0	-6	-7	0	-0.5
Total	4	19	18	.514	130	38	1	0	0	369^{1}	391	60	118	224	12.6	5.19	91	.271	.330	0	—	0	-18	-19	-3	-1.9

● **GEORGE WASHBURN** Washburn, George Edward b: 10/6/14, Solon, Me. d: 1/5/79, Baton Rouge, La. BL/TR, 6′1″, 175 lbs. Deb: 5/4/41

YEAR	TM/L	W	L	PCT	G	GS	CG	SH	SV	IP	H	HR	BB	SO	RAT	ERA	ERA+	OAV	OOB	BH	AVG	PB	PR	/A	PD	TPI
1941	NY-A	0	1	.000	1	1	0	0	0	2	2	0	5	1	31.5	13.50	29	.286	.583	0	.000	-0	-2	-2	0	-0.7

● **GREG WASHBURN** Washburn, Gregory James b: 12/3/46, Coal City, Ill. BR/TR, 6′, 190 lbs. Deb: 6/7/69

YEAR	TM/L	W	L	PCT	G	GS	CG	SH	SV	IP	H	HR	BB	SO	RAT	ERA	ERA+	OAV	OOB	BH	AVG	PB	PR	/A	PD	TPI
1969	Cal-A	0	2	.000	8	2	0	0	0	11^{1}	21	0	5	4	21.4	7.94	44	.404	.466	0	—	0	-5	-6	0	-0.9

● **JARROD WASHBURN** Washburn, Jarrod Michael b: 8/13/74, LaCrosse, Wis. BL/TL, 6'1", 190 lbs. Deb: 6/2/98

YEAR	TM/L	W	L	PCT	G	GS	CG	SH	SV	IP	H	HR	BB	SO	RAT	ERA	ERA+	OAV	OOB	BH	AVG	PB	PR	/A	PD	TPI
1998	Ana-A	6	3	.667	15	11	0	0	0	74	70	11	27	48	12.2	4.62	101	.248	.321	0	.000	-0	0	1	-1	0.0

● **LIBE WASHBURN** Washburn, Libeus b: 6/16/1874, Lyme, N.H. d: 3/22/40, Malone, N.Y. BB/TL, 5'10", 180 lbs. Deb: 5/30/02 ♦

YEAR	TM/L	W	L	PCT	G	GS	CG	SH	SV	IP	H	HR	BB	SO	RAT	ERA	ERA+	OAV	OOB	BH	AVG	PB	PR	/A	PD	TPI
1903	Phi-N	0	4	.000	4	4	4	0	0	35	44	0	11	9	14.1	4.37	75	.326	.377	3	.167	-0	-4	-4	-1	-0.5

● **RAY WASHBURN** Washburn, Ray Clark b: 5/31/38, Pasco, Wash. BR/TR, 6'1", 205 lbs. Deb: 9/20/61

YEAR	TM/L	W	L	PCT	G	GS	CG	SH	SV	IP	H	HR	BB	SO	RAT	ERA	ERA+	OAV	OOB	BH	AVG	PB	PR	/A	PD	TPI
1961	StL-N	1	1	.500	3	2	1	0	0	20^1	10	1	7	12	8.0	1.77	248	.152	.243	1	.125	-1	5	6	0	0.5
1962	StL-N	12	9	.571	34	25	2	1	0	175^2	187	25	58	109	12.7	4.10	104	.273	.332	10	.179	1	-3	3	1	0.5
1963	StL-N	5	3	.625	11	11	4	2	0	64^1	50	5	14	47	9.1	3.08	115	.212	.259	1	.053	-1	2	3	0	0.4
1964	StL-N	3	4	.429	15	10	0	0	2	60	60	7	17	28	12.3	4.05	94	.264	.329	2	.133	-0	-3	-2	1	-0.1
1965	StL-N	9	11	.450	28	16	1	1	2	119^1	114	15	28	67	10.8	3.62	106	.254	.300	5	.152	0	-1	3	-1	0.4
1966	StL-N	11	9	.550	27	26	4	1	0	170	183	15	44	98	12.1	3.76	95	.280	.326	5	.093	-1	-3	-3	1	-0.4
1967	*StL-N	10	7	.588	27	27	3	1	0	186^1	190	14	42	98	11.4	3.53	93	.265	.309	6	.091	-2	-3	-5	2	-0.4
1968	*StL-N	14	8	.636	31	30	8	4	0	215	191	9	47	124	10.0	2.26	128	.239	.283	5	.083	0	17	15	-2	1.4
1969	StL-N	3	8	.273	28	16	2	0	1	132^1	133	9	49	80	12.4	3.06	117	.261	.327	3	.081	-2	8	8	1	0.5
1970	*Cin-N	4	4	.500	35	3	0	0	0	66^1	90	7	48	37	18.7	6.92	58	.324	.423	0	.000	-1	-21	-21	1	-2.2
Total	10	72	64	.529	239	166	25	10	5	1209^2	1208	107	354	700	11.8	3.53	101	.261	.316	38	.105	-7	-3	6	4	0.6

● **BUCK WASHER** Washer, William b: 10/11/1882, Akron, Ohio d: 12/8/55, Akron, Ohio BR/TR, 5'10", 175 lbs. Deb: 4/25/05

YEAR	TM/L	W	L	PCT	G	GS	CG	SH	SV	IP	H	HR	BB	SO	RAT	ERA	ERA+	OAV	OOB	BH	AVG	PB	PR	/A	PD	TPI
1905	Phi-N	0	0	—	1	0	0	0	0	3	4	0	5	0	27.0	6.00	49	.333	.529	0	.000	-0	-1	-1	0	0.0

● **GARY WASLEWSKI** Waslewski, Gary Lee b: 7/21/41, Meriden, Conn. BR/TR, 6'4", 195 lbs. Deb: 6/11/67

YEAR	TM/L	W	L	PCT	G	GS	CG	SH	SV	IP	H	HR	BB	SO	RAT	ERA	ERA+	OAV	OOB	BH	AVG	PB	PR	/A	PD	TPI
1967	*Bos-A	2	2	.500	12	8	0	0	0	42	34	3	20	20	11.8	3.21	108	.225	.320	1	.091	-1	0	1	0	0.1
1968	Bos-A	4	7	.364	34	11	2	0	2	105^1	108	9	40	59	13.2	3.67	86	.269	.344	1	.038	-2	-8	-6	2	-0.7
1969	StL-N	0	2	.000	12	0	0	0	1	20^2	19	3	8	16	12.2	3.92	91	.244	.322	0	.000	-0	-1	-1	1	0.0
	Mon-N	3	7	.300	30	14	3	1	1	109^1	102	5	63	63	14.2	3.29	112	.252	.364	1	.033	-2	4	5	1	0.2
	Yr	3	9	.250	42	14	3	1	2	130	121	8	71	79	13.8	3.39	108	.250	.355	1	.032	-2	3	4	1	0.2
1970	Mon-N	0	2	.000	6	4	0	0	0	24^2	23	3	15	19	13.9	5.11	80	.247	.352	0	.000	-0	-3	-3	1	-0.2
	NY-A	2	2	.500	26	5	0	0	0	55	42	4	27	27	11.9	3.11	113	.219	.327	1	.100	-1	4	2	1	0.2
1971	NY-A	0	1	.000	24	0	0	0	1	35^2	28	2	16	17	11.4	3.28	98	.214	.304	0	.000	-0	1	-0	-0	0.0
1972	Oak-A	0	3	.000	8	0	0	0	0	17^2	12	3	8	8	10.2	2.04	140	.190	.282	0	.000	-0	2	2	0	0.3
Total	6	11	26	.297	152	42	5	1	5	410^1	368	32	197	229	12.9	3.44	100	.243	.338	4	.045	-6	-2	1	4	-0.1

● **STEVE WATERBURY** Waterbury, Steven Craig b: 4/6/52, Carbondale, Ill. BR/TR, 6'5", 190 lbs. Deb: 9/14/76

YEAR	TM/L	W	L	PCT	G	GS	CG	SH	SV	IP	H	HR	BB	SO	RAT	ERA	ERA+	OAV	OOB	BH	AVG	PB	PR	/A	PD	TPI
1976	StL-N	0	0	—	5	0	0	0	0	6	7	0	3	4	15.0	6.00	59	.304	.385	0	—	0	-2	-2	-0	0.0

● **FRED WATERS** Waters, Fred Warren b: 2/2/27, Benton, Miss. d: 8/28/89, Pensacola, Fla. BL/TL, 5'11", 185 lbs. Deb: 9/20/55

YEAR	TM/L	W	L	PCT	G	GS	CG	SH	SV	IP	H	HR	BB	SO	RAT	ERA	ERA+	OAV	OOB	BH	AVG	PB	PR	/A	PD	TPI
1955	Pit-N	0	0	—	2	0	0	0	0	5	7	1	2	0	16.2	3.60	114	.318	.375	0	.000	-0	0	0	0	0.0
1956	Pit-N	2	2	.500	23	5	1	0	0	51	48	3	30	14	13.9	2.82	134	.258	.364	1	.050	-1	5	5	1	0.1
Total	2	2	2	.500	25	5	1	0	0	56	55	4	32	14	14.1	2.89	131	.264	.365	1	.048	-1	6	6	1	0.1

● **BOB WATKINS** Watkins, Robert Cecil b: 3/12/48, San Francisco, Cal. BR/TR, 6'1", 170 lbs. Deb: 9/6/69

YEAR	TM/L	W	L	PCT	G	GS	CG	SH	SV	IP	H	HR	BB	SO	RAT	ERA	ERA+	OAV	OOB	BH	AVG	PB	PR	/A	PD	TPI
1969	Hou-N	0	0	—	5	0	0	0	0	15^2	13	1	13	11	14.9	5.17	68	.241	.388	0	.000	-0	-3	-3	-0	-0.1

● **SCOTT WATKINS** Watkins, Scott Allen b: 5/15/70, Tulsa, Okla. BL/TL, 6'3", 180 lbs. Deb: 8/1/95

YEAR	TM/L	W	L	PCT	G	GS	CG	SH	SV	IP	H	HR	BB	SO	RAT	ERA	ERA+	OAV	OOB	BH	AVG	PB	PR	/A	PD	TPI
1995	Min-A	0	0	—	27	0	0	0	0	21^2	22	2	11	11	13.7	5.40	88	.278	.367	0	—	0	-2	-2	0	0.0

● **ALLEN WATSON** Watson, Allen Kenneth b: 11/18/70, Jamaica, N.Y. BL/TL, 6'3", 190 lbs. Deb: 7/8/93

YEAR	TM/L	W	L	PCT	G	GS	CG	SH	SV	IP	H	HR	BB	SO	RAT	ERA	ERA+	OAV	OOB	BH	AVG	PB	PR	/A	PD	TPI
1993	StL-N	6	7	.462	16	15	0	0	0	86	90	11	28	49	12.7	4.60	86	.271	.333	6	.231	2	-5	-6	-1	-0.7
1994	StL-N	6	5	.545	22	22	0	0	0	115^2	130	15	53	74	14.9	5.52	75	.286	.370	6	.158	1	-17	-18	-1	-1.4
1995	StL-N	7	9	.438	21	19	0	0	0	114^1	126	17	41	49	13.5	4.96	84	.285	.352	15	.417	6	-10	-10	1	-0.5
1996	SF-N	8	12	.400	29	29	2	0	0	185^2	189	28	69	128	12.7	4.61	89	.273	.343	15	.231	4	-8	-11	-2	-0.7
1997	Ana-A	12	12	.500	35	34	0	0	0	199	220	37	73	141	13.6	4.93	93	.279	.346	0	—	0	-8	-8	1	-0.8
1998	Ana-A	6	7	.462	28	14	1	0	0	92^1	122	12	34	64	15.5	6.04	78	.323	.383	0	—	0	-14	-14	0	-1.6
Total	6	45	52	.464	151	133	3	0	0	793	877	120	298	505	13.7	5.04	85	.284	.353	42	.255	14	-63	-66	-2	-5.7

● **DOC WATSON** Watson, Charles John b: 1/30/1886, Kensington, Ohio d: 12/30/49, San Diego, Cal. BR/TL, 6', 170 lbs. Deb: 9/3/13

YEAR	TM/L	W	L	PCT	G	GS	CG	SH	SV	IP	H	HR	BB	SO	RAT	ERA	ERA+	OAV	OOB	BH	AVG	PB	PR	/A	PD	TPI
1913	Chi-N	1	0	1.000	1	1	1	0	0	9	8	0	6	1	15.0	1.00	318	.242	.375	0	.000	0	2	2	-1	0.2
1914	Chi-F	9	8	.529	26	18	10	3	1	172	145	2	49	69	10.3	2.04	130	.236	.295	5	.093	-5	16	12	1	0.5
	StL-F	3	4	.429	9	7	4	2	0	56	41	1	24	18	11.1	1.93	158	.211	.311	2	.125	-1	6	7	-1	0.6
	Yr	12	12	.500	35	25	14	5	1	228	186	3	73	87	10.4	2.01	137	.229	.296	7	.100	-6	22	19	-2	1.1
1915	StL-F	9	9	.500	33	20	6	0	0	135^2	132	1	58	45	12.9	3.98	72	.273	.355	5	.125	-3	-19	-17	-4	-2.8
Total	3	22	21	.512	69	46	21	5	1	372^2	326	4	137	133	11.5	2.70	104	.246	.322	12	.107	-9	5	4	-7	-1.5

● **MULE WATSON** Watson, John Reeves b: 10/15/1896, Homer, La. d: 8/25/49, Shreveport, La. BR/TR, 6'1.5", 185 lbs. Deb: 7/4/18

YEAR	TM/L	W	L	PCT	G	GS	CG	SH	SV	IP	H	HR	BB	SO	RAT	ERA	ERA+	OAV	OOB	BH	AVG	PB	PR	/A	PD	TPI
1918	Phi-A	7	10	.412	21	19	11	3	0	141^2	139	0	44	30	11.8	3.37	87	.288	.350	6	.128	-3	-9	-7	-2	-1.3
1919	Phi-A	0	1	.000	4	2	0	0	0	14^1	17	2	7	6	15.1	6.91	50	.309	.387	0	.000	-1	-6	-6	1	-0.3
1920	Bos-N	0	0	—	1	0	0	0	0	3	0	0	0	0	0.0	0.00	—	.000	.000	0	.000	-0	1	1	0	0.0
	Pit-N	0	0	—	5	0	0	0	0	11^1	15	2	7	1	17.5	8.74	37	.326	.415	0	.000	-0	-7	-7	0	-0.1
	Bos-N	5	4	.556	12	10	4	2	0	71^2	79	0	17	16	12.2	3.77	81	.298	.343	3	.130	-1	-5	-6	-0	-0.8
	Yr	5	4	.556	18	10	4	2	0	86	94	2	24	17	12.5	4.29	72	.294	.345	3	.111	-2	-11	-12	-0	-0.9
1921	Bos-N	14	13	.519	44	31	15	1	2	259^1	269	11	57	48	11.6	3.85	95	.270	.314	12	.138	-4	-2	-6	-1	-1.0
1922	Bos-N	8	14	.364	41	27	8	1	1	201	262	9	59	53	14.6	4.70	85	.317	.366	13	.197	-0	-13	-16	-0	-1.5
1923	Bos-N	1	2	.333	11	4	1	0	1	31^1	42	2	20	10	17.8	5.17	77	.339	.431	2	.250	-0	-4	-4	0	-0.4
	*NY-N	8	5	.615	17	15	8	0	0	108^1	117	11	21	26	11.5	3.41	112	.280	.316	8	.174	-1	7	5	1	0.3
	Yr	9	7	.563	28	19	9	0	1	139^2	159	13	41	36	13.0	3.80	101	.293	.344	10	.185	-1	3	1	-1	-0.1
1924	*NY-N	7	4	.636	22	16	6	1	0	99^2	122	7	24	18	13.3	3.79	97	.303	.343	9	.257	4	1	-1	-1	0.2
Total	7	50	53	.485	178	124	53	8	4	941^2	1062	44	256	208	12.8	4.03	89	.293	.342	53	.165	-8	-38	-45	-3	-4.9

● **MILT WATSON** Watson, Milton Wilson "Mule" b: 1/10/1890, Flovilla, Ga. d: 4/10/62, Pine Bluff, Ark. BR/TR, 6'1", 180 lbs. Deb: 7/26/16

YEAR	TM/L	W	L	PCT	G	GS	CG	SH	SV	IP	H	HR	BB	SO	RAT	ERA	ERA+	OAV	OOB	BH	AVG	PB	PR	/A	PD	TPI
1916	StL-N	4	6	.400	18	13	5	2	0	103	109	3	33	27	12.8	3.06	86	.283	.346	7	.219	0	-5	-5	1	-0.5
1917	StL-N	10	13	.435	41	20	5	3	0	161^1	149	3	51	45	11.7	3.51	77	.252	.321	5	.098	-4	-14	-15	1	-2.3
1918	Phi-N	5	7	.417	23	11	6	0	0	112^2	126	1	36	29	13.1	3.43	87	.293	.350	3	.075	-4	-8	-5	-1	-1.1
1919	Phi-N	2	4	.333	8	4	3	0	0	47	51	3	19	12	13.8	5.17	62	.282	.356	1	.063	-2	-12	-10	0	-1.3
Total	4	21	30	.412	90	48	19	5	0	424	435	10	139	113	12.5	3.57	79	.274	.339	16	.115	-9	-40	-35	-0	-5.2

● **MOTHER WATSON** Watson, Walter L. b: 1/27/1865, Middleport, Ohio d: 11/23/1898, Middleport, Ohio 5'9", 145 lbs. Deb: 5/19/1887

YEAR	TM/L	W	L	PCT	G	GS	CG	SH	SV	IP	H	HR	BB	SO	RAT	ERA	ERA+	OAV	OOB	BH	AVG	PB	PR	/A	PD	TPI
1887	Cin-a	0	1	.000	2	2	1	0	0	14	22	0	6	1	18.0	5.79	75	.328	.384	1	.125	-0	-2	-2	-1	-0.2

● **EDDIE WATT** Watt, Edward Dean b: 4/4/41, Lamoni, Iowa BR/TR, 5'10", 197 lbs. Deb: 4/12/66

YEAR	TM/L	W	L	PCT	G	GS	CG	SH	SV	IP	H	HR	BB	SO	RAT	ERA	ERA+	OAV	OOB	BH	AVG	PB	PR	/A	PD	TPI
1966	Bal-A	9	7	.563	43	13	1	0	4	145^2	123	11	44	102	10.6	3.83	87	.230	.295	14	.304	6	-6	-8	-2	-0.5
1967	Bal-A	3	5	.375	49	0	0	0	8	103^2	67	5	37	93	9.3	2.26	140	.183	.263	4	.182	2	11	10	0	1.2
1968	Bal-A	5	5	.500	59	0	0	0	11	83^1	63	1	35	72	10.8	2.27	129	.209	.295	0	.000	-0	7	6	0	0.9
1969	*Bal-A	5	2	.714	56	0	0	0	16	71	49	3	26	46	9.8	1.65	216	.194	.274	0	.000	-0	16	15	-0	2.2
1970	*Bal-A	7	7	.500	53	0	0	0	12	55^1	44	3	29	33	12.7	3.25	112	.239	.358	1	.125	-0	3	2	0	0.7
1971	*Bal-A	3	1	.750	35	0	0	0	11	39^2	39	1	8	26	10.7	1.82	185	.260	.297	0	.000	-0	7	7	-1	1.1
1972	Bal-A	2	3	.400	38	0	0	0	7	45^2	30	2	20	23	10.2	2.17	142	.191	.291	0	.000	-0	5	5	-0	0.7
1973	*Bal-A	3	4	.429	30	0	0	0	5	71	62	8	21	38	10.8	3.30	113	.235	.296	0	—	0	4	3	-1	0.3
1974	Phi-N	1	1	.500	42	0	0	0	6	38^1	39	3	26	23	15.7	3.99	95	.275	.394	0	.000	-0	-2	-1	0	-0.1
1975	Chi-N	0	1	.000	6	0	0	0	0	6	14	0	8	6	34.5	13.50	28	.452	.575	0	—	0	-7	-6	0	-0.9
Total	10	38	36	.514	411	13	1	0	80	659^2	530	37	254	462	11.0	2.91	116	.222	.304	19	.190	6	38	33	-3	5.6

YEAR	TM/L	W	L	PCT	G	GS	CG	SH	SV	IP	H	HR	BB	SO	RAT	ERA	ERA+	OAV	OOB	BH	AVG	PB	PR	/A	PD	TPI
● FRANK WATT	Watt, Frank Marion "Kilo" b: 12/15/02, Washington, D.C. d: 8/31/56, Washington, D.C. BR/TR, 6'1", 205 lbs. Deb: 4/14/31 F																									
1931	Phi-N	5	5	.500	38	12	5	0	2	122^2	147	5	49	25	14.6	4.84	88	.296	.362	8	.205	0	-13	-8	-2	-0.8
● JIM WAUGH	Waugh, James Elden b: 11/25/33, Lancaster, Ohio BR/TR, 6'3", 185 lbs. Deb: 4/19/52																									
1952	Pit-N	1	6	.143	17	7	1	0	0	52^1	61	4	32	18	16.3	6.36	63	.285	.383	1	.100	-0	-15	-14	-0	-1.6
1953	Pit-N	4	5	.444	29	11	1	0	0	90^1	108	21	56	23	16.3	6.48	69	.295	.389	5	.227	0	-22	-20	-1	-1.7
Total	2	5	11	.313	46	18	2	0	0	142^2	169	25	88	41	16.3	6.43	67	.291	.387	6	.188	0	-37	-34	-1	-3.3
● FRANK WAYENBERG	Wayenberg, Frank b: 8/27/1898, Franklin, Kan. d: 4/16/75, Zanesville, Ohio BR/TR, 6'0.5", 172 lbs. Deb: 8/25/24																									
1924	Cle-A	0	0	—	2	1	0	0	0	6^2	7	0	5	3	17.6	5.40	79	.259	.394	1	.500	0	-1	-1	-0	0.0
● GARY WAYNE	Wayne, Gary Anthony b: 11/30/62, Dearborn, Mich. BL/TL, 6'3", 192 lbs. Deb: 4/7/89																									
1989	Min-A	3	4	.429	60	0	0	0	1	71	55	4	36	41	11.7	3.30	126	.212	.311	0	—	0	5	7	-0	0.3
1990	Min-A	1	1	.500	38	0	0	0	1	38^2	38	5	13	28	12.1	4.19	99	.255	.319	0	—	0	-1	-0	-0	-0.1
1991	Min-A	1	0	1.000	8	0	0	0	1	12^1	11	1	4	7	11.7	5.11	84	.244	.320	0	—	0	-1	-1	-0	-0.1
1992	Min-A	3	3	.500	41	0	0	0	0	48	46	2	19	29	12.8	2.63	154	.260	.342	0	—	0	7	8	1	1.0
1993	Col-N	5	3	.625	65	0	0	0	1	62^1	68	8	26	49	13.7	5.05	94	.276	.348	1	1.000	0	-7	-2	-0	-0.2
1994	LA-N	1	3	.250	19	0	0	0	0	17^1	19	2	6	10	14.5	4.67	84	.279	.364	0	.000	-0	-1	-1	0	-0.3
Total	6	14	14	.500	231	0	0	0	4	249^2	237	22	104	164	12.7	3.93	109	.251	.332	1	.500	0	1	10	1	0.6
● KEN WEAFER	Weafer, Kenneth Albert "Al" b: 2/6/14, Woburn, Mass. BR/TR, 6'0.5", 183 lbs. Deb: 5/29/36																									
1936	Bos-N	0	0	—	1	0	0	0	0	3	6	1	3	0	27.0	12.00	32	.375	.474	0	.000	-0	-3	-3	-0	0.0
● DAVE WEATHERS	Weathers, John David b: 9/25/69, Lawrenceburg, Tenn. BR/TR, 6'3", 205 lbs. Deb: 8/2/91																									
1991	Tor-A	1	0	1.000	15	0	0	0	0	14^2	15	1	17	13	20.9	4.91	86	.263	.447	0	—	0	-1	-1	-0	-0.1
1992	Tor-A	0	0	—	2	0	0	0	0	3^1	5	1	2	3	18.9	8.10	50	.385	.467	0	—	0	-2	-1	-0	0.0
1993	Fla-N	2	3	.400	14	6	0	0	0	45^2	57	3	13	34	14.0	5.12	84	.306	.355	1	.100	-1	-5	-4	-0	-0.5
1994	Fla-N	8	12	.400	24	24	0	0	0	135	166	13	59	72	15.3	5.27	83	.306	.379	3	.068	-2	-16	-13	-1	-2.0
1995	Fla-N	4	5	.444	28	15	0	0	0	90^1	104	8	52	60	16.0	5.98	70	.295	.394	4	.154	-1	-18	-18	-1	-1.6
1996	Fla-N	2	2	.500	31	8	0	0	0	71^1	85	7	28	40	14.8	4.54	90	.302	.374	3	.158	1	-3	-4	-0	-0.1
	*NY-A	0	2	.000	11	4	0	0	0	17^1	23	1	14	13	20.3	9.35	53	.315	.438	0	—	0	-8	-8	0	-0.8
1997	NY-A	0	1	.000	10	0	0	0	0	9	15	1	7	4	22.0	10.00	44	.375	.468	0	—	0	-5	-6	-0	-0.5
	Cle-A	1	2	.333	9	1	0	0	0	16^2	23	2	8	14	17.3	7.56	62	.343	.421	0	—	0	-6	-5	-0	-0.8
	Yr	1	3	.250	19	1	0	0	0	25^2	38	3	15	18	18.9	8.42	55	.355	.439	0	—	0	-11	-11	-0	-1.3
1998	Cin-N	2	4	.333	16	9	0	0	0	62^1	86	3	27	51	16.5	6.21	70	.330	.394	1	.067	0	-14	-13	-1	-1.1
	Mil-N	4	1	.800	28	0	0	0	0	47^2	44	3	14	43	11.3	3.21	134	.246	.308	1	.125	-0	5	6	0	0.5
	Yr	6	5	.545	44	9	0	0	0	110	130	6	41	94	14.2	4.91	88	.294	.357	2	.087	0	-8	-7	-1	-0.6
Total	8	24	32	.429	188	67	0	0	0	513^1	623	43	241	347	15.5	5.51	78	.304	.383	13	.107	-3	-73	-68	-3	-7.0
● FLOYD WEAVER	Weaver, David Floyd b: 5/12/41, Ben Franklin, Tex. BR/TR, 6'4", 195 lbs. Deb: 9/30/62																									
1962	Cle-A	1	0	1.000	1	1	0	0	0	5	3	1	0	8	5.4	1.80	215	.167	.167	1	.500	0	1	1	-0	0.3
1965	Cle-A	2	2	.500	32	1	0	0	1	61^1	61	10	24	37	13.2	5.43	64	.265	.347	1	.091	0	-13	-13	-0	-0.9
1970	Chi-A	1	2	.333	31	3	0	0	0	61^2	52	7	31	51	12.4	4.38	89	.233	.332	0	.000	-1	-5	-3	-1	-0.3
1971	Mil-A	0	1	.000	21	0	0	0	0	27^1	33	3	18	12	17.1	7.24	48	.320	.426	0	—	0	-11	-11	0	-0.4
Total	4	4	5	.444	85	5	0	0	1	155^1	149	21	73	108	13.3	5.21	70	.260	.351	2	.100	-0	-28	-27	-1	-1.3
● HARRY WEAVER	Weaver, Harry Abraham b: 2/26/1892, Clarendon, Pa. d: 5/30/83, Rochester, N.Y. BR/TR, 5'11", 160 lbs. Deb: 9/18/15																									
1915	Phi-A	0	2	.000	2	2	2	0	0	18	18	1	10	1	14.5	3.00	98	.290	.397	1	.167	0	-0	-0	1	0.1
1916	Phi-A	0	0	—	3	0	0	0	0	8	14	0	5	2	21.4	10.13	28	.424	.500	1	.500	0	-6	-6	0	0.0
1917	Chi-N	1	1	.500	4	2	1	1	0	19^2	17	0	7	8	11.0	2.75	106	.230	.296	1	.200	-0	-0	0	1	0.1
1918	Chi-N	2	2	.500	8	3	1	1	1	32^2	27	1	7	9	9.4	2.20	126	.227	.270	2	.250	0	2	2	1	0.4
1919	Chi-N	0	1	.000	2	1	0	0	0	3^1	6	0	2	1	24.3	10.80	27	.375	.474	0	.000	-0	-3	-3	-0	-0.7
Total	5	3	6	.333	19	8	4	2	1	81^2	82	2	31	21	12.7	3.64	79	.270	.341	5	.227	0	-8	-7	2	-0.1
● JIM WEAVER	Weaver, James Brian "Fluff" b: 2/19/39, Lancaster, Pa. BL/TL, 6', 178 lbs. Deb: 8/13/67																									
1967	Cal-A	3	0	1.000	13	2	0	0	1	30^1	26	2	9	20	10.7	2.67	118	.232	.295	0	.000	-1	2	2	2	0.3
1968	Cal-A	0	1	.000	14	0	0	0	0	22^2	22	4	10	8	12.7	2.38	122	.259	.337	0	.000	-0	2	1	-1	0.0
Total	2	3	1	.750	27	2	0	0	1	53	48	6	19	28	11.5	2.55	119	.244	.313	0	.000	-1	3	3	1	0.3
● JIM WEAVER	Weaver, James Dement "Big Jim" b: 11/25/03, Obion County, Tenn. d: 12/12/83, Lakeland, Fla. BR/TR, 6'6", 230 lbs. Deb: 8/27/28																									
1928	Was-A	0	0	—	3	0	0	0	0	6	2	0	6	2	13.5	1.50	267	.143	.429	0	.000	-0	2	2	0	0.0
1931	NY-A	2	1	.667	17	5	2	0	0	57^2	66	1	29	28	15.0	5.31	75	.280	.361	1	.050	-3	-6	-9	0	-0.6
1934	StL-A	2	0	1.000	5	5	2	0	0	19^2	17	3	20	11	16.9	6.41	78	.236	.402	1	.143	-0	-4	-3	1	-0.2
	Chi-N	11	9	.550	27	20	8	1	0	159	163	5	54	98	12.5	3.91	99	.263	.326	3	.058	-5	3	-1	-1	-0.6
1935	Pit-N	14	8	.636	33	22	11	**4**	0	176^1	177	9	58	87	12.1	3.42	120	.254	.313	4	.071	-4	12	13	1	1.2
1936	Pit-N	14	8	.636	38	31	11	1	0	225^2	239	12	74	108	12.5	4.31	94	.272	.329	8	.101	-5	-7	-6	-2	-1.2
1937	Pit-N	8	5	.615	32	9	2	1	0	109^2	106	2	31	44	11.2	3.20	121	.255	.307	4	.148	-0	9	8	-2	0.7
1938	StL-A	0	1	.000	1	1	0	0	0	7	9	0	9	4	23.1	9.00	55	.321	.486	0	.000	-0	-3	-3	-0	-0.3
	Cin-N	6	4	.600	30	15	2	0	3	129^1	109	6	54	64	11.4	3.13	117	.227	.306	9	.205	0	9	7	-1	0.5
1939	Cin-N	0	0	—	3	0	0	0	0	3	3	0	1	3	12.0	3.00	128	.250	.308	0	.000	-0	0	0	0	0.0
Total	8	57	36	.613	189	108	38	7	3	893^1	891	38	336	449	12.5	3.88	102	.258	.326	30	.104	-17	14	9	-4	-0.5
● ERIC WEAVER	Weaver, James Eric b: 8/4/73, Springfield, Ill. BR/TR, 6'5", 230 lbs. Deb: 5/30/98																									
1998	LA-N	2	0	1.000	7	0	0	0	0	9^2	5	1	6	5	10.2	0.93	418	.179	.324	0	.000	-0	4	3	-0	0.6
● MONTE WEAVER	Weaver, Montie Morton "Prof" b: 6/15/06, Helton, N.C. d: 6/14/94, Orlando, Fla. BL/TR, 6', 170 lbs. Deb: 9/20/31																									
1931	Was-A	1	0	1.000	3	1	1	0	0	10	11	0	6	6	15.3	4.50	95	.268	.362	0	.000	-0	-0	-0	0	0.0
1932	Was-A	22	10	.688	43	30	13	1	2	234	236	9	112	83	13.4	4.08	106	.261	.342	27	.287	6	10	6	-2	1.0
1933	*Was-A	10	5	.667	23	21	12	1	0	152^1	147	3	53	45	11.9	3.25	129	.257	.322	7	.125	-3	17	16	-1	1.0
1934	Was-A	11	15	.423	31	31	11	0	0	204^2	255	16	63	51	14.0	4.79	90	.306	.355	13	.162	-2	-7	-11	-2	-1.5
1935	Was-A	1	1	.500	5	2	0	0	0	12	16	1	6	4	16.5	5.25	82	.320	.393	1	.333	0	-1	-1	0	-0.2
1936	Was-A	6	4	.600	26	5	3	0	1	91	92	3	38	15	12.9	4.35	110	.262	.334	5	.200	1	7	4	-0	0.4
1937	Was-A	12	9	.571	30	26	9	0	0	188^2	197	21	70	44	12.7	4.20	105	.266	.330	14	.206	1	9	5	1	0.6
1938	Was-A	7	6	.538	31	18	7	0	0	139	157	9	74	43	15.2	5.24	86	.282	.370	12	.267	4	-7	-11	-1	-0.6
1939	Bos-A	1	0	1.000	9	1	1	0	1	20^1	26	0	13	6	17.7	6.64	71	.321	.421	0	.000	-1	-5	-4	-1	-0.3
Total	9	71	50	.587	201	135	57	2	4	1052	1137	62	435	297	13.5	4.36	101	.276	.345	79	.209	5	24	3	-6	0.4
● ORLIE WEAVER	Weaver, Orville Forest b: 6/4/1886, Newport, Ky. d: 11/28/70, New Orleans, La. BR/TR, 6', 180 lbs. Deb: 9/14/10																									
1910	Chi-N	1	1	.500	7	2	2	0	0	32	34	2	15	22	14.1	3.66	79	.270	.352	2	.154	-1	-2	-3	-1	-0.3
1911	Chi-N	2	2	.500	6	3	1	1	0	43^2	29	0	17	20	10.3	2.06	161	.196	.296	1	.059	-1	7	6	-0	0.3
	Bos-N	3	12	.200	27	17	4	0	0	121	140	9	84	50	17.2	6.47	59	.303	.418	5	.122	-2	-41	-36	-2	-4.1
	Yr	5	14	.263	33	20	5	1	0	164^2	169	9	101	70	15.1	5.30	70	.275	.384	6	.103	-4	-35	-29	-3	-3.8
Total	2	6	15	.286	40	22	7	1	0	196^2	203	11	116	92	15.1	5.03	71	.276	.383	8	.113	-4	-37	-32	-4	-4.1
● ROGER WEAVER	Weaver, Roger Edward b: 10/6/54, Amsterdam, N.Y. BR/TR, 6'3", 190 lbs. Deb: 6/6/80																									
1980	Det-A	3	4	.429	19	6	0	0	0	63^2	56	5	34	42	12.9	4.10	100	.247	.347	0	—	0	-0	0	1	-0.1
● SAM WEAVER	Weaver, Samuel H. b: 7/10/1855, Philadelphia, Pa. d: 2/1/14, Philadelphia, Pa. BR/TR, 5'10", 175 lbs. Deb: 10/25/1875																									
1875	Phi-n	1	0	1.000	1	1	1	0	0	6	6	0	2	2	12.0	1.50	152	.240	.296	1	.250	0	0	1		0.1
1878	Mil-N	12	31	.279	45	43	39	1	0	383	371	2	21	95	**9.2**	1.95	135	.237	**.247**	34	.200	-3	15	**29**	0	**2.7**
1882	Phi-a	26	15	.634	42	41	41	2	0	371	374	6	35	104	9.9	2.74	109	.245	.262	36	.232	1	-2	10	1	1.1
1883	Lou-a	24	22	.522	46	46	45	4	0	400^2	451	3	35	105	10.9	3.71	81	.266	.281	37	.192	0	-18	-32	-1	-3.0

YEAR	TM/L	W	L	PCT	G	GS	CG	SH	SV	IP	H	HR	BB	SO	RAT	ERA	ERA+	OAV	OOB	BH	AVG	PB	PR	/A	PD	TPI
1884	Phi-U	5	10	.333	17	17	14	0	0	136	206	3	11	40	14.4	5.76	40	.328	.339	18	.214	-5	-50	-52	-1	-4.4
1886	Phi-a	0	2	.000	2	2	1	0	0	11	30	0	2	2	27.0	14.73	24	.423	.446	1	.143	-1	-14	-14	-0	-1.4
Total	5	67	80	.456	152	149	140	7	0	1301^2	1432	14	104	346	10.6	3.22	88	.261	.275	126	.207	-7	-69	-54	-1	-5.0
● LEFTY WEBB	Webb, Cleon Earl b: 3/1/1885, Mt.Gilead, Ohio d: 1/12/58, Circleville, Ohio BB/TL, 5'11", 165 lbs. Deb: 5/23/10																									
1910	Pit-N	2	1	.667	7	3	2	0	0	27	29	0	9	6	13.3	5.67	55	.266	.333	2	.200	-0	-8	-8	-0	-0.8
● HANK WEBB	Webb, Henry Gaylon Matthew b: 5/21/50, Copiague, N.Y. BR/TR, 6'3", 175 lbs. Deb: 9/5/72																									
1972	NY-N	0	0	—	6	2	0	0	0	18^1	18	1	9	15	13.3	4.42	76	.261	.346	0	.000	-1	-2	-2	1	0.0
1973	NY-N	0	0	—	2	0	0	0	0	1^2	2	1	2	1	21.6	10.80	33	.286	.444	0	—	0	-1	-1	-0	0.0
1974	NY-N	0	2	.000	3	2	0	0	0	10	15	1	10	8	23.4	7.20	49	.341	.473	0	.000	-0	-4	-4	-0	-0.7
1975	NY-N	7	6	.538	29	15	3	1	0	115	102	12	62	38	12.9	4.07	85	.236	.333	8	.258	2	-6	-8	-1	-0.7
1976	NY-N	0	1	.000	8	0	0	0	0	16	17	2	7	7	14.6	4.50	73	.274	.366	0	.000	0	-2	-2	0	-0.1
1977	LA-N	0	0	—	5	0	0	0	0	8	5	1	1	2	7.9	2.25	170	.192	.250	0	—	0	1	1	-0	0.0
Total	6	7	9	.438	53	19	3	1	0	169	159	18	91	71	13.6	4.31	80	.248	.346	8	.200	1	-13	-16	-1	-1.5
● RED WEBB	Webb, Samuel Henry b: 9/25/24, Washington, D.C. d: 2/7/96, Hyattsville, Md. BL/TR, 6', 175 lbs. Deb: 9/15/48																									
1948	NY-N	2	1	.667	5	3	2	0	0	28	27	2	10	9	12.2	3.21	122	.248	.317	2	.222	0	2	2	0	0.2
1949	NY-N	1	1	.500	20	0	0	0	0	44^2	41	3	21	9	12.5	4.03	99	.248	.333	4	.400	2	0	-0	2	0.4
Total	2	3	2	.600	25	3	2	0	0	72^2	68	5	31	18	12.4	3.72	107	.248	.327	6	.316	2	2	2	2	0.6
● BILL WEBB	Webb, William Frederick b: 12/12/13, Atlanta, Ga. d: 6/1/94, Austell, Ga. BR/TR, 6'2", 180 lbs. Deb: 5/15/43																									
1943	Phi-N	0	0	—	1	0	0	0	0	1	1	1	1	0	18.0	9.00	37	.333	.500	0	—	0	-1	-1	-0	0.0
● LES WEBBER	Webber, Lester Elmer b: 5/6/15, Kelseyville, Cal. d: 11/13/86, Santa Maria, Cal. BR/TR, 6'0.5", 185 lbs. Deb: 5/17/42																									
1942	Bro-N	3	2	.600	19	3	1	0	1	51^2	46	2	22	23	11.8	2.96	110	.230	.306	1	.071	-1	2	2	1	0.1
1943	Bro-N	2	2	.500	54	0	0	0	**10**	115^2	112	6	69	24	14.5	3.81	88	.264	.373	3	.120	-1	-6	-6	2	-0.2
1944	Bro-N	7	8	.467	48	9	1	0	3	140^1	157	9	64	42	14.2	4.94	72	.282	.357	8	.205	1	-21	-22	4	-1.7
1945	Bro-N	7	3	.700	17	7	5	0	0	75^1	69	3	25	30	11.3	3.58	105	.237	.300	2	.091	-1	2	1	-1	0.0
1946	Bro-N	3	3	.500	11	4	0	0	0	43	34	5	15	16	10.3	2.30	147	.225	.295	1	.100	-1	5	5	-1	0.6
	Cle-A	1	1	.500	4	2	0	0	0	5^1	13	0	5	5	30.4	23.63	14	.464	.545	0	.000	0	-12	-12	0	-2.8
1948	Cle-A	0	0	—	1	0	0	0	0	0^2	3	0	1	1	54.0	40.50	10	.750	.800	0	—	0	-3	-3	0	0.0
Total	6	23	19	.548	154	25	7	0	14	432	434	25	201	141	13.4	4.19	83	.262	.345	15	.135	-2	-32	-34	5	-4.0
● CHARLIE WEBER	Weber, Charles P. "Count" b: 10/22/1868, Cincinnati, Ohio d: 6/13/14, Beaumont, Tex. Deb: 7/30/1898																									
1898	Was-N	0	1	.000	1	1	0	0	0	4	9	0	1	0	27.0	15.75	23	.450	.522	0	.000	-0	-5	-5	-0	-0.8
● NEIL WEBER	Weber, Neil Aaron b: 12/6/72, Newport Beach, Cal. BL/TL, 6'5", 215 lbs. Deb: 9/11/98																									
1998	Ari-N	0	0	—	4	0	0	0	0	2^1	5	0	3	4	30.9	11.57	37	.417	.533	0	—	0	-2	-2	0	0.0
● MIKE WEGENER	Wegener, Michael Denis b: 10/8/46, Denver, Colo. BR/TR, 6'4", 215 lbs. Deb: 4/9/69																									
1969	Mon-N	5	14	.263	32	26	4	1	0	165^2	150	10	96	124	13.6	4.40	84	.243	.349	13	.241	2	-15	-13	1	-1.0
1970	Mon-N	3	6	.333	25	16	1	0	0	104^1	100	16	56	35	13.8	5.26	78	.252	.350	4	.118	-2	-14	-13	-1	-1.2
Total	2	8	20	.286	57	42	5	1	0	270	250	26	152	159	13.7	4.73	81	.247	.349	17	.193	0	-29	-27	1	-2.2
● BILL WEGMAN	Wegman, William Edward b: 12/19/62, Cincinnati, Ohio BR/TR, 6'5", 220 lbs. Deb: 9/14/85																									
1985	Mil-A	2	0	1.000	3	3	0	0	0	17^2	17	3	3	6	10.2	3.57	117	.246	.278	0	—	0	1	1	-0	0.1
1986	Mil-A	5	12	.294	35	32	2	0	0	198^1	217	32	43	82	12.1	5.13	84	.279	.323	0	—	0	-21	-18	-1	-1.4
1987	Mil-A	12	11	.522	34	33	7	0	0	225	229	31	53	102	11.5	4.24	108	.265	.312	0	—	0	5	8	-0	0.7
1988	Mil-A	13	13	.500	32	31	4	1	0	199	207	24	50	84	11.8	4.12	97	.265	.313	0	—	0	-3	-3	-1	-0.5
1989	Mil-A	2	6	.250	11	8	0	0	0	51	69	6	21	27	15.9	6.71	57	.321	.381	0	—	0	-16	-16	1	-2.0
1990	Mil-A	2	2	.500	8	5	1	1	0	29^2	37	6	6	20	13.0	4.85	80	.298	.331	0	—	0	-3	-3	-1	-0.4
1991	Mil-A	15	7	.682	28	28	7	2	0	193^1	176	16	40	89	10.4	2.84	140	.242	.288	0	—	0	27	24	2	2.9
1992	Mil-A	13	14	.481	35	35	7	0	0	261^2	251	28	55	127	10.8	3.20	120	.250	.295	0	—	0	22	19	4	2.2
1993	Mil-A	4	14	.222	20	18	5	0	0	120^2	135	13	34	50	12.8	4.48	95	.291	.342	0	—	0	-2	-3	1	-0.3
1994	Mil-A	8	4	.667	19	19	0	0	0	115^2	140	14	26	59	13.1	4.51	111	.303	.343	0	—	0	4	7	2	0.7
1995	Mil-A	5	7	.417	37	4	0	0	2	70^2	89	14	21	50	14.4	5.35	93	.312	.366	0	—	0	-5	-3	-1	-0.5
Total	11	81	90	.474	262	216	33	4	2	1482^2	1567	187	352	696	11.9	4.16	102	.271	.318	0	—	0	8	12	6	1.5
● BIGGS WEHDE	Wehde, Wilbur b: 11/23/06, Holstein, Iowa d: 9/21/70, Sioux Falls, S.Dak. BR/TR, 5'10.5", 180 lbs. Deb: 9/15/30																									
1930	Chi-A	0	0	—	4	0	0	0	0	6^1	7	1	7	3	21.3	9.95	46	.304	.484	0	.000	-0	-4	-4	1	0.1
1931	Chi-A	1	0	1.000	8	0	0	0	0	16	19	0	10	3	17.4	6.75	63	.333	.449	0	.000	-0	-4	-4	1	-0.2
Total	2	1	0	1.000	12	0	0	0	0	22^1	26	1	17	6	18.5	7.66	57	.325	.460	0	.000	-1	-8	-8	1	-0.1
● HERM WEHMEIER	Wehmeier, Herman Ralph b: 2/18/27, Cincinnati, Ohio d: 5/21/73, Dallas, Tex. BR/TR, 6'2", 200 lbs. Deb: 9/7/45																									
1945	Cin-N	0	1	.000	2	2	0	0	0	5	10	0	4	0	25.2	12.60	30	.435	.519	0	.000	-0	-5	-5	0	-0.7
1947	Cin-N	0	0	—	1	0	0	0	0	1	0	0	0	0	0.0	0.00	—	.000	.000	0	—	0	0	0	-0	0.0
1948	Cin-N	11	8	.579	33	24	6	0	0	147^1	179	21	75	56	15.6	5.86	67	.299	.379	5	.091	-3	-31	-32	-0	-3.8
1949	Cin-N	11	12	.478	33	29	11	1	0	213^1	202	20	117	80	13.8	4.68	89	.253	.353	20	.256	2	-15	-12	-2	-1.1
1950	Cin-N	10	18	.357	41	32	12	0	4	230	255	27	135	121	15.4	5.67	75	.281	.376	14	.152	-3	-39	-37	-3	-4.4
1951	Cin-N	7	10	.412	39	22	10	2	2	184^2	167	15	89	93	12.7	3.70	110	.241	.330	17	.288	3	5	8	-2	0.8
1952	Cin-N	9	11	.450	33	26	6	1	0	190^1	197	23	103	83	14.5	5.15	73	.269	.365	12	.188	2	-30	-29	-4	-2.9
1953	Cin-N	1	6	.143	28	10	2	0	0	81^2	100	20	47	32	16.2	7.16	61	.299	.385	4	.200	-0	-26	-25	-1	-1.9
1954	Cin-N	0	3	.000	12	3	0	0	2	33^2	36	6	21	13	15.5	6.68	63	.271	.374	0	.000	-1	-10	-9	1	-0.8
	Phi-N	10	8	.556	25	17	10	2	0	138	117	10	51	49	11.0	3.85	105	.231	.302	6	.120	-2	3	3	-0	0.1
	Yr	10	11	.476	37	20	10	2	2	171^2	153	16	72	62	11.8	4.40	92	.238	.316	6	.102	-3	-6	-6	1	-0.7
1955	Phi-N	10	12	.455	31	29	10	1	0	193^2	176	21	67	85	11.4	4.41	90	.241	.307	20	.278	4	-8	-10	-1	-0.7
1956	Phi-N	0	2	.000	3	3	0	0	0	20	18	2	11	8	13.0	4.05	92	.240	.337	0	.000	-1	-1	-1	-1	-0.2
	StL-N	12	9	.571	34	19	7	2	1	170^2	150	16	71	68	11.7	3.69	102	.240	.319	13	.224	4	2	2	-1	0.5
	Yr	12	11	.522	37	22	7	2	1	190^2	168	18	82	76	11.8	3.73	101	.240	.320	13	.197	3	1	1	-2	0.3
1957	StL-N	10	7	.588	36	18	5	0	0	165	165	25	54	91	12.1	4.31	92	.253	.312	12	.203	0	-8	-6	-0	-0.6
1958	StL-N	0	1	.000	3	3	0	0	0	6	13	2	2	4	22.5	13.50	31	.448	.484	1	.500	1	-6	-6	0	-0.8
	Det-A	1	0	1.000	7	3	0	0	0	22^2	21	2	5	11	10.3	2.38	169	.241	.283	0	.000	-1	3	4	-0	0.1
Total	13	92	108	.460	361	240	79	9	9	1803	1806	210	852	794	13.4	4.80	84	.260	.344	124	.196	5	-165	-156	-14	-16.4
● DAVE WEHRMEISTER	Wehrmeister, David Thomas b: 11/9/52, Berwyn, Ill. BR/TR, 6'4", 195 lbs. Deb: 4/16/76																									
1976	SD-N	0	4	.000	7	4	0	0	0	19^1	27	0	11	10	17.7	7.45	44	.333	.413	0	.000	-1	-8	-9	0	-1.6
1977	SD-N	1	3	.250	30	6	0	0	0	69^2	81	8	44	32	16.5	6.07	58	.293	.396	2	.167	0	-17	-20	-0	-1.0
1978	SD-N	1	0	1.000	4	0	0	0	0	7^1	8	1	5	2	16.0	6.14	54	.276	.382	0	—	0	-2	-2	-0	-0.3
1981	NY-A	0	0	—	5	0	0	0	0	7	6	0	7	7	16.7	5.14	69	.240	.406	0	—	0	-1	-1	0	0.1
1984	Phi-N	0	0	—	7	0	0	0	0	15	18	1	7	13	15.6	7.20	50	.300	.382	0	.000	-0	-6	-6	0	0.0
1985	Chi-A	2	2	.500	23	0	0	0	2	39^1	35	4	10	32	11.0	3.43	126	.241	.304	0	—	0	3	4	-0	0.4
Total	6	4	9	.308	76	10	0	0	2	157^2	175	14	84	96	15.2	5.65	65	.284	.376	2	.100	-1	-31	-34	0	-2.4
● DICK WEIK	Weik, Richard Henry "Legs" b: 11/17/27, Waterloo, Iowa d: 4/21/91, Harvey, Ill. BR/TR, 6'3.5", 184 lbs. Deb: 9/8/48 ♦																									
1948	Was-A	1	2	.333	3	3	0	0	0	12^2	14	1	22	8	25.6	5.68	76	.311	.537	3	.750	2	-2	-2	-0	-0.2
1949	Was-A	3	12	.200	27	14	2	2	1	95^1	78	5	103	58	17.1	5.38	79	.230	.410	5	.179	-1	-13	-12	1	-1.6
1950	Was-A	1	3	.250	14	5	1	0	0	44	38	2	47	26	17.4	4.30	105	.236	.409	2	.154	-1	1	1	-1	-0.1
	Cle-A	1	3	.250	11	2	0	0	0	26	18	1	26	16	15.6	3.81	114	.205	.391	1	.200	0	2	2	0	0.2
	Yr	2	6	.250	25	7	1	0	0	70	56	3	73	42	16.7	4.11	108	.225	.402	3	.167	-1	4	2	-1	0.1
1953	Det-A	0	1	.000	12	1	0	0	0	19^1	32	3	23	6	25.6	13.97	29	.386	.519	1	.500	1	-21	-21	0	-0.9

YEAR	TM/L	W	L	PCT	G	GS	CG	SH	SV	IP	H	HR	BB	SO	RAT	ERA	ERA+	OAV	OOB	BH	AVG	PB	PR	/A	PD	TPI
1954	Det-A	0	1	.000	9	1	0	0	0	16^1	23	3	16	9	22.0	7.16	52	.354	.488	0	.000	-0	-6	-6	-1	-0.4
Total 5		6	22	.214	76	26	3	2	1	213^2	203	15	237	123	18.6	5.90	72	.260	.433	12	.226	1	-39	-39	0	-3.0

● ED WEILAND
Weiland, Edwin Nicholas b: 11/26/14, Evanston, Ill. d: 7/12/71, Chicago, Ill. BL/TR, 5'11", 180 lbs. Deb: 5/1/40 F

YEAR	TM/L	W	L	PCT	G	GS	CG	SH	SV	IP	H	HR	BB	SO	RAT	ERA	ERA+	OAV	OOB	BH	AVG	PB	PR	/A	PD	TPI
1940	Chi-A	0	0	—	5	0	0	0	0	14^1	15	5	7	3	13.8	8.79	50	.263	.344	1	.200	-0	-7	-7	-0	-0.1
1942	Chi-A	0	0	—	5	0	0	0	0	9^2	18	0	3	4	19.6	7.45	48	.383	.420	0	.000	-0	-4	-4	-0	-0.1
Total 2		0	0	—	10	0	0	0	0	24	33	5	10	7	16.1	8.25	50	.317	.377	1	.143	-0	-11	-11	-1	-0.2

● BOB WEILAND
Weiland, Robert George "Lefty" b: 12/14/05, Chicago, Ill. d: 11/9/88, Chicago, Ill. BL/TL, 6'4", 215 lbs. Deb: 9/30/28 F

YEAR	TM/L	W	L	PCT	G	GS	CG	SH	SV	IP	H	HR	BB	SO	RAT	ERA	ERA+	OAV	OOB	BH	AVG	PB	PR	/A	PD	TPI
1928	Chi-A	1	0	1.000	1	1	1	0	0	9	7	0	5	9	13.0	0.00	—	.212	.333	1	.333	0	4	4	0	0.5
1929	Chi-A	2	4	.333	15	9	1	0	1	62	62	3	43	25	15.7	5.81	74	.268	.390	2	.111	-1	-11	-10	-1	-1.1
1930	Chi-A	0	4	.000	14	3	0	0	0	32^2	38	1	21	15	16.8	6.61	70	.297	.404	0	.000	-1	-7	-7	-0	-0.8
1931	Chi-A	2	7	.222	15	8	3	0	0	75	75	4	46	38	15.0	5.16	83	.259	.368	4	.182	-1	-7	-8	1	-0.6
1932	Bos-A	6	16	.273	43	27	7	0	1	195^2	231	11	97	63	15.4	4.51	100	.295	.377	9	.148	-1	-1	-0	3	0.2
1933	Bos-A	8	14	.364	39	27	12	0	3	216^1	197	19	100	97	12.6	3.87	113	.244	.331	7	.108	-4	10	12	-2	0.6
1934	Bos-A	1	5	.167	11	7	2	0	0	55^2	63	4	27	29	14.6	5.50	87	.293	.372	2	.105	-1	-6	-4	0	-0.4
	Cle-A	1	5	.167	16	7	2	0	0	70	71	5	30	42	13.0	4.11	111	.262	.336	3	.125	-0	3	3	-1	0.2
	Yr	2	10	.167	27	14	4	0	0	125^2	134	9	57	71	13.7	4.73	99	.276	.352	5	.116	-1	-3	-1	-0	0.2
1935	StL-A	0	2	.000	14	4	0	0	0	32	39	4	31	11	20.0	9.56	50	.298	.436	0	.000	-1	-18	-17	-1	-1.0
1937	StL-N	15	14	.517	41	34	21	2	0	264^1	283	14	94	105	13.0	3.54	112	.276	.339	15	.169	0	11	13	-2	1.1
1938	StL-N	16	11	.593	35	29	11	1	1	228^1	248	14	67	117	12.6	3.59	110	.272	.324	11	.138	-3	5	9	-1	0.6
1939	StL-N	10	12	.455	32	23	6	3	1	146^1	146	4	50	63	12.4	3.57	115	.264	.331	3	.065	-4	6	9	-1	0.7
1940	StL-N	0	0	—	1	0	0	0	0	0	0	0	0	0	27.0	27.00	15	.600	.600	0	—	0	-3	-3	-0	0.0
Total 12		62	94	.397	277	179	66	7	7	1388^1	1463	85	611	614	13.7	4.24	100	.272	.350	57	.129	-16	-13	2	-4	0.0

● CARL WEILMAN
Weilman, Carl Woolworth "Zeke" (b: Carl Woolworth Weilenmann)
b: 11/29/1889, Hamilton, Ohio d: 5/25/24, Hamilton, Ohio BL/TL, 6'5.5", 187 lbs. Deb: 8/24/12

YEAR	TM/L	W	L	PCT	G	GS	CG	SH	SV	IP	H	HR	BB	SO	RAT	ERA	ERA+	OAV	OOB	BH	AVG	PB	PR	/A	PD	TPI
1912	StL-A	2	4	.333	8	6	5	2	1	48^1	42	0	3	24	8.4	2.79	119	.227	.239	2	.118	-1	3	3	0	0.3
1913	StL-A	10	19	.345	39	28	17	2	0	251^2	262	2	60	79	11.7	3.40	86	.281	.328	12	.146	-3	-13	-13	1	-1.6
1914	StL-A	17	12	.586	44	36	20	3	1	299	260	0	84	119	10.7	2.08	130	.237	.298	15	.149	-1	22	21	1	2.1
1915	StL-A	18	19	.486	47	31	19	3	4	295^2	240	6	83	125	9.9	2.34	122	.229	.287	23	.230	2	19	17	-1	2.3
1916	StL-A	17	18	.486	46	31	19	1	2	276	237	3	76	91	10.5	2.15	128	.242	.301	14	.154	-1	21	18	-3	1.9
1917	StL-A	1	2	.333	5	3	0	0	0	19	19	1	6	9	11.8	1.89	137	.268	.325	0	.000	-1	2	1	1	0.3
1919	StL-A	10	6	.625	20	20	12	3	0	148	133	3	45	44	11.0	2.07	160	.244	.305	9	.191	0	19	21	-0	2.2
1920	StL-A	9	13	.409	30	24	13	1	2	183^1	201	6	51	65	11.6	4.47	88	.291	.351	11	.175	-2	-14	-11	1	-1.3
Total 8		84	93	.475	239	179	105	15	10	1521	1394	22	418	536	10.9	2.67	112	.251	.307	86	.170	-7	59	56	1	6.2

● JAKE WEIMER
Weimer, Jacob "Tornado Jake" b: 11/29/1873, Ottumwa, Iowa d: 6/19/28, Chicago, Ill. BR/TL, 5'11", 175 lbs. Deb: 4/17/03

YEAR	TM/L	W	L	PCT	G	GS	CG	SH	SV	IP	H	HR	BB	SO	RAT	ERA	ERA+	OAV	OOB	BH	AVG	PB	PR	/A	PD	TPI
1903	Chi-N	20	8	.714	35	33	27	3	0	282	241	4	104	128	11.4	2.30	136	**.225**	.301	21	.196	2	30	26	-1	2.4
1904	Chi-N	20	14	.588	37	37	31	5	0	307	229	1	97	177	9.8	1.91	140	.204	.272	21	.183	-1	28	26	3	2.9
1905	Chi-N	18	12	.600	33	30	26	2	1	250^1	212	1	80	107	10.9	2.26	132	.229	.299	19	.207	2	21	20	-1	2.4
1906	Cin-N	20	14	.588	41	39	31	6	1	304^2	263	0	99	141	11.1	2.22	124	.236	.306	29	.269	6	14	18	1	2.9
1907	Cin-N	11	14	.440	29	26	19	3	0	209	165	6	63	67	10.8	2.41	108	.226	.308	14	.194	2	1	4	2	1.0
1908	Cin-N	8	7	.533	15	15	9	2	0	116^2	110	2	50	36	12.8	2.39	96	.255	.341	11	.244	2	-0	-1	1	0.2
1909	NY-N	0	0	—	1	0	0	0	0	3	7	0	1	2	24.0	9.00	28	.467	.500	0	.000	-0	-2	-2	-0	0.0
Total 7		97	69	.584	191	180	143	21	2	1472^2	1227	14	493	657	11.0	2.23	125	.227	.300	115	.213	11	92	93	5	11.8

● LEFTY WEINERT
Weinert, Phillip Walter b: 4/21/02, Philadelphia, Pa. d: 4/17/73, Rockledge, Fla. BL/TL, 6'1", 195 lbs. Deb: 9/24/19

YEAR	TM/L	W	L	PCT	G	GS	CG	SH	SV	IP	H	HR	BB	SO	RAT	ERA	ERA+	OAV	OOB	BH	AVG	PB	PR	/A	PD	TPI
1919	Phi-N	0	0	—	1	0	0	0	0	4	11	0	2	0	29.3	18.00	18	.478	.520	2	1.000	1	-7	-7	-0	0.2
1920	Phi-N	1	1	.500	10	2	0	0	0	22	27	1	19	10	19.2	6.14	56	.333	.465	0	.000	-1	-7	-7	-0	-0.7
1921	Phi-N	1	0	1.000	8	0	0	0	0	12^1	8	1	5	2	10.2	1.46	290	.216	.326	1	1.000	0	3	4	-1	0.3
1922	Phi-N	8	11	.421	34	22	10	0	1	166^2	189	10	70	58	14.3	3.40	137	.289	.362	14	.241	-0	13	23	-2	2.3
1923	Phi-N	4	17	.190	38	20	8	0	1	156	207	14	81	46	17.1	5.42	85	.327	.410	19	.322	2	-25	-14	-3	-1.7
1924	Phi-N	0	1	.000	8	1	0	0	0	14^2	10	0	11	7	12.9	2.45	182	.204	.350	0	.000	-1	2	3	0	0.2
1927	Chi-N	1	1	.500	5	3	1	0	0	19^2	21	2	5	12	12.4	4.58	84	.259	.310	1	.200	0	-1	-2	-0	-0.2
1928	Chi-N	1	0	1.000	10	1	0	0	0	17	24	0	9	8	18.0	5.29	73	.393	.479	0	.000	-0	-2	-3	-1	-0.2
1931	NY-A	2	2	.500	17	0	0	0	0	24^2	31	2	19	24	20.1	6.20	64	.316	.451	0	.000	-0	-5	-6	-0	-0.8
Total 9		18	33	.353	131	49	19	0	2	437	528	26	222	160	15.9	4.59	97	.308	.393	37	.261	2	-29	-7	-6	-0.6

● ROY WEIR
Weir, William Franklin "Bill" b: 2/25/11, Portland, Maine d: 9/30/89, Anaheim, Cal. BL/TL, 5'8.5", 170 lbs. Deb: 6/25/36

YEAR	TM/L	W	L	PCT	G	GS	CG	SH	SV	IP	H	HR	BB	SO	RAT	ERA	ERA+	OAV	OOB	BH	AVG	PB	PR	/A	PD	TPI
1936	Bos-N	4	3	.571	12	7	3	2	0	57^1	53	0	24	29	12.1	2.83	136	.241	.316	5	.278	2	8	6	1	1.0
1937	Bos-N	1	1	.500	10	4	1	0	0	33	27	0	19	8	12.5	3.82	94	.227	.333	0	.000	-1	0	-1	-1	-0.1
1938	Bos-N	1	0	1.000	5	0	0	0	0	13^1	14	4	6	3	13.5	6.75	51	.269	.345	1	.333	0	-4	-5	0	-0.3
1939	Bos-N	0	0	—	2	0	0	0	0	2^2	1	0	1	2	6.8	0.00	—	.125	.222	0	.000	-0	1	1	0	0.6
Total 4		6	4	.600	29	11	4	2	0	106^1	95	4	50	42	12.3	3.55	104	.238	.323	6	.188	1	5	2	0	0.6

● CURT WELCH
Welch, Curtis Benton b: 2/10/1862, Williamsport, O. d: 8/29/1896, E.Liverpool, Ohio BR/TR, 5'10", 175 lbs. Deb: 5/1/1884 ♦

YEAR	TM/L	W	L	PCT	G	GS	CG	SH	SV	IP	H	HR	BB	SO	RAT	ERA	ERA+	OAV	OOB	BH	AVG	PB	PR	/A	PD	TPI
1890	Phi-a	0	0	—	1	0	0	0	0	1	6	0	0	1	54.0	54.00	7	.667	.667	106	.268	0	-6	-6	0	0.0

● TED WELCH
Welch, Floyd John b: 10/17/1892, Coyville, Kan. d: 1/6/43, Great Bend, Kan. BL/TR, 5'9.5", 160 lbs. Deb: 5/15/14

YEAR	TM/L	W	L	PCT	G	GS	CG	SH	SV	IP	H	HR	BB	SO	RAT	ERA	ERA+	OAV	OOB	BH	AVG	PB	PR	/A	PD	TPI
1914	StL-F	0	0	—	3	0	0	0	0	6	6	0	3	2	18.0	6.00	51	.273	.429	0	.000	-0	-2	-2	-0	0.0

● JOHNNY WELCH
Welch, John Vernon b: 12/2/06, Washington, D.C. d: 9/2/40, St.Louis, Mo. BL/TR, 6'3", 184 lbs. Deb: 5/22/26

YEAR	TM/L	W	L	PCT	G	GS	CG	SH	SV	IP	H	HR	BB	SO	RAT	ERA	ERA+	OAV	OOB	BH	AVG	PB	PR	/A	PD	TPI
1926	Chi-N	0	0	—	3	0	0	0	0	4^1	7	0	1	0	12.5	2.08	185	.357	.400	1	1.000	0	1	1	-0	0.0
1927	Chi-N	0	0	—	1	0	0	0	0	1	1	0	0	0	27.0	9.00	43	.000	.500	0	—	0	-1	-1	0	0.0
1928	Chi-N	0	0	—	3	0	0	0	0	4	13	0	0	2	29.3	15.75	24	.591	.591	0	—	0	-5	-5	0	0.0
1931	Chi-N	2	1	.667	8	3	1	0	0	33^2	39	2	10	7	13.4	3.74	103	.291	.345	5	.417	2	0	0	0	0.2
1932	Bos-A	4	6	.400	20	8	3	1	0	72^1	93	3	38	26	16.7	5.23	86	.312	.395	9	.250	2	-6	-6	0	-0.5
1933	Bos-A	4	9	.308	47	7	1	0	3	129	142	6	67	68	14.7	4.60	95	.283	.370	6	.162	-1	-5	-3	1	-0.3
1934	Bos-A	13	15	.464	41	22	8	0	0	206^1	223	14	76	91	13.4	4.49	107	.274	.342	15	.203	-1	0	7	1	0.7
1935	Bos-A	10	9	.526	31	19	10	1	2	143	155	4	53	48	13.3	4.47	106	.273	.339	9	.180	-0	4	0	0	0.5
1936	Bos-A	2	1	.667	9	3	1	0	0	32^2	43	4	8	14	14.1	5.51	96	.305	.342	3	.273	1	-2	-1	-0	0.0
	Pit-N	0	0	—	9	1	0	0	1	22	22	3	4	5	11.5	4.50	90	.265	.315	2	.286	-1	-1	-1	0	0.0
Total 9		35	41	.461	172	63	24	3	6	648^1	735	36	222	255	14.1	4.66	99	.285	.355	50	.219	3	-18	-4	1	0.6

● MICKEY WELCH
Welch, Michael Francis "Smiling Mickey" (b: Michael Francis Walsh)
b: 7/4/1859, Brooklyn, N.Y. d: 7/30/41, Concord, N.H. BR/TR, 5'8", 160 lbs. Deb: 5/1/1880 H

YEAR	TM/L	W	L	PCT	G	GS	CG	SH	SV	IP	H	HR	BB	SO	RAT	ERA	ERA+	OAV	OOB	BH	AVG	PB	PR	/A	PD	TPI
1880	Tro-N	34	30	.531	65	64	64	4	0	574	575	7	80	123	10.3	2.54	99	.249	.274	72	.287	10	-11	-1	-7	0.3
1881	Tro-N	21	18	.538	40	40	40	4	0	368	371	7	78	104	11.0	2.67	111	.255	.293	30	.203	-4	4	12	-6	0.1
1882	Tro-N	14	16	.467	33	33	30	5	0	281	334	7	62	53	12.7	3.46	82	.280	.315	37	.245	1	-17	-20	-3	-1.9
1883	NY-N	25	23	.521	54	52	46	4	0	426	431	11	66	144	10.5	2.73	114	.244	.272	75	.234	3	20	18	-6	1.3
1884	NY-N	39	21	.650	65	65	62	4	0	557^1	528	12	146	345	10.9	2.50	119	.237	.284	60	.241	9	30	29	-5	2.9
1885	NY-N	44	11	**.800**	56	55	55	7	1	492	372	4	131	258	9.2	1.66	160	.203	.256	41	.206	5	63	55	-8	5.0
1886	NY-N	33	22	.600	59	59	56	1	0	500	514	13	163	272	12.2	2.99	108	.259	.315	46	.216	1	18	12	-2	0.8
1887	NY-N	22	15	.595	40	40	39	2	0	346	339	7	91	115	11.3	3.36	112	.253	.303	36	.243	4	28	16	-2	1.3
1888	*NY-N	26	19	.578	47	47	47	5	0	425^1	328	12	108	167	9.5	1.93	142	.207	.263	32	.189	1	44	38	-4	3.3
1889	*NY-N	27	12	.692	45	41	39	3	2	375	340	14	149	125	12.0	3.02	130	.234	.310	30	.192	-2	41	38	-3	2.8
1890	NY-N	17	14	.548	37	37	33	2	0	292^1	268	5	122	97	12.8	2.99	117	.236	.317	20	.177	1	8	13	-3	0.8
1891	NY-N	5	9	.357	22	15	14	0	1	160	177	7	97	46	16.0	4.27	75	.270	.373	10	.141	-4	-16	-19	-3	-1.9
1892	NY-N	0	0	—	1	1	0	0	0	5	11	0	4	1	27.0	14.40	22	.423	.500	1	.333	0	-6	-6	-0	0.0
Total 13		307	210	.594	564	549	525	41	4	4802	4588	106	1297	1850	11.1	2.71	114	.242	.292	492	.224	21	216	196	-52	14.8

YEAR	TM/L	W	L	PCT	G	GS	CG	SH	SV	IP	H	HR	BB	SO	RAT	ERA	ERA+	OAV	OOB	BH	AVG	PB	PR	/A	PD	TPI
● MIKE WELCH	Welch, Michael Paul b: 8/25/72, Haverill, Mass. BL/TR, 6′2″, 210 lbs. Deb: 7/17/98																									
1998	Phi-N	0	2	.000	10	2	0	0	0	20^2	26	7	7	15	15.2	8.27	53	.310	.376	0	.000	-0	-9	-9	0	-0.8
● BOB WELCH	Welch, Robert Lynn b: 11/3/56, Detroit, Mich. BR/TR, 6′3″, 190 lbs. Deb: 6/20/78																									
1978	*LA-N	7	4	.636	23	13	4	3	3	111^1	92	6	26	66	9.6	2.02	174	.229	.277	5	.172	0	19	18	-1	1.8
1979	LA-N	5	6	.455	25	12	1	0	5	81^1	82	7	32	64	12.9	3.98	91	.265	.340	3	.158	-0	-2	-3	-1	-0.5
1980	LA-N★	14	9	.609	32	32	3	2	0	213^2	190	15	79	141	11.5	3.29	106	.242	.314	17	.243	3	7	5	-1	0.8
1981	*LA-N	9	5	.643	23	23	2	1	0	141^1	141	11	41	88	11.8	3.44	96	.259	.315	10	.222	2	1	-2	-1	-0.1
1982	LA-N	16	11	.593	36	36	9	3	0	235^2	199	19	81	176	10.9	3.36	103	.229	.299	12	.141	-1	6	3	-1	0.0
1983	*LA-N	15	12	.556	31	31	4	3	0	204	164	13	72	156	10.5	2.65	136	.222	.294	7	.096	-2	22	21	-0	2.5
1984	LA-N	13	13	.500	31	29	3	1	0	178^2	191	11	58	126	12.6	3.78	93	.273	.331	4	.078	-3	-4	-5	2	-0.8
1985	*LA-N	14	4	.778	23	23	8	3	0	167^1	141	16	35	96	9.8	2.31	150	.225	.273	9	.180	1	24	22	1	2.6
1986	LA-N	7	13	.350	33	33	7	3	0	235^2	227	14	55	183	11.0	3.28	105	.251	.299	8	.105	-0	11	4	-1	0.2
1987	LA-N	15	9	.625	35	35	6	**4**	0	251^2	204	21	86	196	10.5	3.22	123	.221	.291	13	.157	1	24	21	2	2.2
1988	*Oak-A	17	9	.654	36	36	4	2	0	244^2	237	22	81	158	12.1	3.64	104	.257	.323	0	—	0	9	4	0	0.6
1989	*Oak-A	17	8	.680	33	33	1	0	0	209^2	191	13	78	137	11.8	3.00	122	.241	.314	0	—	0	20	16	-1	1.8
1990	*Oak-A★	**27**	6	**.818**	35	35	2	2	0	238	214	26	77	127	11.2	2.95	126	.242	.306	0	—	0	25	20	0	3.0
1991	Oak-A	12	13	.480	35	35	7	1	0	220	220	25	91	101	13.2	4.58	84	.263	.343	0	—	0	-12	-18	-1	-1.9
1992	*Oak-A	11	7	.611	20	20	0	0	0	123^2	114	13	43	47	11.6	3.27	114	.247	.314	0	—	0	9	6	-1	1.0
1993	Oak-A	9	11	.450	30	28	0	0	0	166^2	208	25	56	63	14.6	5.29	77	.310	.370	0	—	0	-18	-23	1	-2.1
1994	Oak-A	3	6	.333	25	8	0	0	0	68^2	79	10	43	44	16.1	7.08	63	.290	.389	0	.000	-0	-17	-20	-1	-2.2
Total	17	211	146	.591	506	462	61	28	8	3092	2894	267	1034	1969	11.7	3.47	106	.249	.314	88	.151	2	126	70	-4	8.9
● DON WELCHEL	Welchel, Donald Ray b: 2/3/57, Atlanta, Tex. BR/TR, 6′4″, 205 lbs. Deb: 9/15/82																									
1982	Bal-A	1	0	1.000	2	0	0	0	0	4^1	6	0	2	3	16.6	8.31	49	.300	.364	0	—	0	-2	-2	-0	-0.4
1983	Bal-A	0	2	.000	11	0	0	0	0	26^2	33	1	10	16	14.5	5.40	73	.297	.355	0	—	0	-4	-4	-0	-0.3
Total	2	1	2	.333	13	0	0	0	0	31	39	1	12	19	14.8	5.81	68	.298	.357	0	—	0	-6	-6	-0	-0.7
● DAVID WELLS	Wells, David Lee b: 5/20/63, Torrance, Cal. BL/TL, 6′4″, 225 lbs. Deb: 6/30/87																									
1987	Tor-A	4	3	.571	18	2	0	0	1	29^1	37	0	12	32	15.0	3.99	113	.311	.374	0	—	0	2	2	0	0.4
1988	Tor-A	3	5	.375	41	0	0	0	4	64^1	65	12	31	56	13.7	4.62	85	.269	.356	0	—	0	-5	-5	-0	-0.6
1989	*Tor-A	7	4	.636	54	0	0	0	2	86^1	66	5	28	78	9.8	2.40	157	.207	.271	0	—	0	14	13	0	1.7
1990	Tor-A	11	6	.647	43	25	0	0	3	189	165	14	45	115	10.1	3.14	125	.235	.283	0	—	0	16	17	1	1.4
1991	*Tor-A	15	10	.600	40	28	2	0	1	198^1	188	24	49	106	10.8	3.72	113	.251	.299	0	—	0	8	11	1	1.3
1992	*Tor-A	7	9	.438	41	14	0	0	2	120	138	16	36	62	13.7	5.40	76	.289	.349	0	—	0	-19	-18	-0	-2.3
1993	Det-A	11	9	.550	32	30	0	0	0	187	183	26	42	139	11.2	4.19	102	.254	.301	0	—	0	3	2	-1	0.1
1994	Det-A	5	7	.417	16	16	5	1	0	111^1	113	13	24	71	11.2	3.96	122	.260	.302	0	—	0	10	11	-1	0.9
1995	Det-A★	10	3	.769	18	18	3	0	0	130^1	120	17	37	83	11.0	3.04	157	.242	.298	0	—	0	24	25	-0	2.2
	*Cin-N	6	5	.545	11	11	3	0	0	72^2	74	6	16	50	11.1	3.59	115	.265	.305	4	.143	-1	5	4	-1	0.4
1996	*Bal-A	11	14	.440	34	34	3	0	0	224^1	247	32	51	130	12.2	5.14	96	.285	.330	0	—	0	-4	-5	2	-0.3
1997	*NY-A	16	10	.615	32	32	5	2	0	218	239	24	45	156	12.0	4.21	106	.278	.318	0	—	0	9	6	-1	0.6
1998	*NY-A★	18	4	**.818**	30	30	8	**5**	0	214^1	195	29	29	163	**9.4**	3.49	128	.239	**.266**	1	.250	0	28	23	-1	2.0
Total	12	124	89	.582	410	240	29	8	13	1845^1	1830	218	445	1241	11.3	3.96	111	.258	.306	5	.156	-1	91	86	-1	7.8
● ED WELLS	Wells, Edwin Lee "Satchelfoot" b: 6/7/1900, Ashland, Ohio d: 5/1/86, Montgomery, Ala. BL/TL, 6′1.5″, 183 lbs. Deb: 6/16/23																									
1923	Det-A	0	0	—	7	0	0	0	0	10	11	0	6	6	15.3	5.40	72	.306	.405	0	.000	-0	-2	-2	-0	0.0
1924	Det-A	6	8	.429	29	15	5	0	4	102	117	2	42	33	14.1	4.06	101	.291	.360	7	.212	-1	2	1	1	0.1
1925	Det-A	6	9	.400	35	14	5	0	2	134^1	190	8	62	45	17.0	6.23	69	.345	.413	12	.279	3	-27	-29	1	-2.5
1926	Det-A	12	10	.545	36	26	9	**4**	0	178	201	7	76	58	14.1	4.15	98	.297	.370	15	.205	0	-2	-2	-3	-0.4
1927	Det-A	0	1	.000	8	1	0	0	1	20	28	3	5	5	14.8	6.75	62	.333	.371	2	.286	0	-6	-6	1	-0.2
1929	NY-A	13	9	.591	31	23	10	3	0	193^1	179	19	81	78	12.1	4.33	89	.248	.324	17	.230	2	-2	-10	-4	-1.2
1930	NY-A	12	3	.800	27	21	7	0	0	150^2	185	11	49	46	14.2	5.20	83	.302	.358	15	.259	0	-9	-15	-2	-1.4
1931	NY-A	9	5	.643	27	10	6	0	2	116^2	130	7	37	34	13.0	4.32	92	.286	.341	10	.222	1	1	-5	-2	-0.5
1932	NY-A	3	3	.500	22	0	0	0	2	31^2	38	1	12	13	14.2	4.26	96	.302	.362	0	.000	-1	1	-1	-0	-0.2
1933	StL-A	6	14	.300	36	22	10	0	1	203^2	230	13	63	58	13.0	4.20	111	.278	.330	14	.197	-1	2	10	-3	0.5
1934	StL-A	1	7	.125	33	8	2	0	1	92	108	7	35	27	14.0	4.79	104	.292	.353	1	.045	-2	-3	2	1	0.1
Total	11	68	69	.496	291	140	54	7	13	1232^1	1417	78	468	403	13.9	4.65	91	.291	.355	93	.215	1	-46	-55	-10	-5.7
● JOHN WELLS	Wells, John Frederick b: 11/25/22, Junction City, Kan. d: 10/23/93, Olean, N.Y. BR/TR, 5′11.5″, 180 lbs. Deb: 9/14/44																									
1944	Bro-N	0	2	.000	4	2	0	0	0	15	18	1	11	7	17.4	5.40	66	.316	.426	1	.250	0	-3	-3	-0	-0.4
● BOB WELLS	Wells, Robert Lee b: 11/1/66, Yakima, Wash. BR/TR, 6′, 180 lbs. Deb: 5/16/94																									
1994	Phi-N	1	0	1.000	6	0	0	0	0	5	4	0	3	3	14.4	1.80	238	.235	.381	0	—	0	1	1	-0	0.2
	Sea-A	1	0	1.000	1	0	0	0	0	4	4	0	1	3	11.3	2.25	217	.250	.294	0	—	0	1	1	-0	0.3
1995	*Sea-A	4	3	.571	30	4	0	0	0	76^2	88	11	39	38	15.3	5.75	82	.284	.369	0	—	0	-9	-9	-0	-0.7
1996	Sea-A	12	7	.632	36	16	1	1	0	130^2	141	25	46	94	13.3	5.30	93	.274	.340	0	—	0	-5	-5	-1	-0.7
1997	*Sea-A	2	0	1.000	46	1	0	0	2	67^1	88	11	18	51	14.6	5.75	78	.314	.362	0	—	0	-9	-9	-0	-0.3
1998	Sea-A	2	2	.500	30	0	0	0	0	51^2	54	12	16	29	12.5	6.10	76	.261	.320	0	—	0	-8	-8	-0	-0.6
Total	5	22	12	.647	149	21	1	1	2	335^1	379	59	123	218	13.9	5.53	86	.282	.349	0	—	0	-28	-29	-2	-1.8
● TERRY WELLS	Wells, Terry b: 9/10/63, Kankakee, Ill. BL/TL, 6′3″, 205 lbs. Deb: 7/3/90																									
1990	LA-N	1	2	.333	5	5	0	0	0	20^2	25	4	14	18	17.0	7.84	47	.287	.386	0	.000	-1	-9	-10	-1	-1.3
● CHRIS WELSH	Welsh, Christopher Charles b: 4/14/55, Wilmington, Del. BL/TL, 6′2″, 185 lbs. Deb: 4/12/81																									
1981	SD-N	6	7	.462	22	19	4	2	0	123^2	122	9	41	51	11.9	3.78	86	.264	.325	6	.146	0	-4	-7	1	-0.6
1982	SD-N	8	8	.500	28	20	3	1	0	139^1	146	16	63	48	13.7	4.91	70	.268	.347	11	.262	4	-20	-23	1	-2.0
1983	SD-N	0	1	.000	7	1	0	0	0	14^1	13	2	2	5	9.4	2.51	139	.236	.263	0	.000	-0	2	2	-0	0.0
	Mon-N	0	1	.000	16	5	0	0	0	44^2	46	5	18	17	13.7	5.04	71	.267	.351	4	.286	1	-7	-7	1	0.1
	Yr	0	2	.000	23	6	0	0	0	59	59	7	20	22	12.7	4.42	81	.260	.331	4	.222	1	-5	-6	1	0.1
1985	Tex-A	2	5	.286	25	6	0	0	0	76^1	101	11	25	31	15.3	4.13	102	.316	.372	0	—	0	0	1	-1	0.0
1986	Cin-N	6	9	.400	24	24	1	0	0	139^1	163	9	40	40	13.3	4.78	81	.301	.353	5	.119	0	-16	-14	-1	-1.4
Total	5	22	31	.415	122	75	8	3	0	537^2	591	52	189	192	13.3	4.45	81	.282	.346	26	.182	5	-46	-49	2	-3.9
● DICK WELTEROTH	Welteroth, Richard John b: 8/3/27, Williamsport, Pa. BR/TR, 5′11″, 165 lbs. Deb: 5/16/48																									
1948	Was-A	2	1	.667	33	2	0	0	1	65^1	73	6	50	16	17.1	5.51	79	.286	.405	1	.100	-1	-9	-8	-0	-0.5
1949	Was-A	2	5	.286	52	2	0	0	2	95^1	107	6	89	37	18.6	7.36	58	.296	.437	1	.059	-1	-34	-33	0	-2.3
1950	Was-A	0	0	—	5	0	0	0	0	6	5	0	6	2	16.5	3.00	150	.217	.379	0	—	0	1	1	0	0.0
Total	3	4	6	.400	90	4	0	0	3	166^2	185	12	145	55	17.9	6.48	66	.290	.422	2	.074	-2	-41	-40	-0	-2.8
● TONY WELZER	Welzer, Anton Frank b: 4/5/1899, Germany d: 3/18/71, Milwaukee, Wis. BR/TR, 5′11″, 160 lbs. Deb: 4/13/26																									
1926	Bos-A	4	3	.571	39	5	1	1	0	139	167	5	53	29	14.4	4.86	84	.308	.373	8	.211	2	-13	-12	4	0.0
1927	Bos-A	6	11	.353	37	19	8	0	1	171^2	214	10	71	56	15.2	4.72	89	.318	.386	4	.095	-2	-11	-9	1	-0.9
Total	2	10	14	.417	76	24	9	1	1	310^2	381	15	124	85	14.8	4.78	87	.313	.380	12	.150	-0	-24	-22	4	-0.9
● TURK WENDELL	Wendell, Steven John b: 5/19/67, Pittsfield, Mass. BB/TR, 6′2″, 190 lbs. Deb: 6/17/93																									
1993	Chi-N	1	2	.333	7	4	0	0	0	22^2	24	0	8	15	12.7	4.37	91	.273	.333	1	.143	-0	-1	-1	0	-0.1
1994	Chi-N	0	1	.000	6	2	0	0	0	14^1	22	3	10	9	20.1	11.93	35	.349	.438	0	.000	0	-12	-12	0	-0.7
1995	Chi-N	3	1	.750	43	0	0	0	0	60^1	71	11	24	50	14.5	4.92	83	.298	.367	0	.000	-0	-5	-5	1	-0.2
1996	Chi-N	4	5	.444	70	0	0	0	18	79^1	58	8	44	75	11.9	2.84	153	.201	.313	1	.500	1	12	13	0	1.9
1997	Chi-N	3	5	.375	52	0	0	0	4	60	53	4	39	54	14.0	4.20	102	.238	.354	0	.000	-0	0	1	0	0.1
	NY-N	0	0	—	13	0	0	0	1	16^1	15	3	14	10	16.5	4.96	81	.250	.400	0	.000	-0	-1	-2	1	0.0

YEAR	TM/L	W	L	PCT	G	GS	CG	SH	SV	IP	H	HR	BB	SO	RAT	ERA	ERA+	OAV	OOB	BH	AVG	PB	PR	/A	PD	TPI
	Yr	3	5	.375	65	0	0	0	5	76^1	68	7	53	64	14.4	4.36	97	.237	.358	0	.000	-0	-1	-1	1	0.1
1998	NY-N	5	1	.833	66	0	0	0	4	76^2	62	4	33	58	11.4	2.93	142	.221	.307	0	.000	-0	11	10	0	0.8
Total	6	16	15	.516	257	6	0	0	27	329^2	305	33	172	271	13.3	4.10	103	.246	.342	2	.074	-1	4	4	3	1.8

● DON WENGERT Wengert, Donald Paul b: 11/6/69, Sioux City, Iowa BR/TR, 6'2", 205 lbs. Deb: 4/30/95

YEAR	TM/L	W	L	PCT	G	GS	CG	SH	SV	IP	H	HR	BB	SO	RAT	ERA	ERA+	OAV	OOB	BH	AVG	PB	PR	/A	PD	TPI
1995	Oak-A	1	1	.500	19	0	0	0	0	29^2	30	3	12	16	13.0	3.34	134	.263	.339	0	—	0	5	4	-1	0.2
1996	Oak-A	7	11	.389	36	25	1	1	0	161^1	200	29	60	75	14.8	5.58	88	.307	.371	0	—	0	-11	-12	-2	-1.3
1997	Oak-A	5	11	.313	49	12	1	0	2	134	177	21	41	68	15.2	6.04	75	.321	.377	0	—	0	-22	-23	0	-2.3
1998	SD-N	0	0	—	10	0	0	0	1	13^2	21	2	5	5	17.1	5.93	65	.356	.406	0	.000	-0	-3	-3	-0	-0.1
	Chi-N	1	5	.167	21	6	0	0	0	49^2	55	8	23	41	14.7	5.07	86	.279	.363	0	.000	-1	-5	-4	-0	-0.6
	Yr	1	5	.167	31	6	0	0	1	63^1	76	10	28	46	15.2	5.26	81	.297	.373	0	.000	-2	-7	-7	-1	-0.7
Total	4	14	28	.333	135	43	2	1	3	388^1	483	63	141	205	14.9	5.52	84	.307	.371	0	.000	-2	-35	-38	-4	-4.1

● BUTCH WENSLOFF Wensloff, Charles William b: 12/3/15, Sausalito, Cal. BR/TR, 5'11", 185 lbs. Deb: 5/2/43

YEAR	TM/L	W	L	PCT	G	GS	CG	SH	SV	IP	H	HR	BB	SO	RAT	ERA	ERA+	OAV	OOB	BH	AVG	PB	PR	/A	PD	TPI
1943	NY-A	13	11	.542	29	27	18	1	1	223^1	179	7	70	105	10.1	2.54	127	.219	.282	14	.177	-0	19	17	-1	1.7
1947	*NY-A	3	1	.750	11	5	1	0	0	51^2	41	3	22	18	11.0	2.61	135	.217	.299	5	.263	1	6	5	-1	0.4
1948	Cle-A	0	1	.000	1	0	0	0	0	1^2	2	1	3	2	27.0	10.80	38	.286	.500	0	—	0	-1	-1	-0	-0.5
Total	3	16	13	.552	41	32	19	1	1	276^2	222	11	95	125	10.3	2.60	126	.219	.287	19	.194	0	24	21	-2	1.6

● FRED WENZ Wenz, Frederick Charles "Fireball" b: 8/26/41, Bound Brook, N.J. BR/TR, 6'3", 214 lbs. Deb: 6/4/68

YEAR	TM/L	W	L	PCT	G	GS	CG	SH	SV	IP	H	HR	BB	SO	RAT	ERA	ERA+	OAV	OOB	BH	AVG	PB	PR	/A	PD	TPI
1968	Bos-A	0	0	—	1	0	0	0	0	1	0	0	2	3	18.0	0.00	—	.000	.400	0	—	0	0	0	0	0.0
1969	Bos-A	1	0	1.000	8	0	0	0	0	11	9	7	10	11	15.5	5.73	66	.225	.380	0	—	0	-3	-2	0	-0.2
1970	Phi-N	2	0	1.000	22	0	0	0	1	30^1	27	2	13	24	12.2	4.45	90	.237	.320	0	.000	-1	-1	-2	-1	-0.2
Total	3	3	0	1.000	31	0	0	0	1	42^1	36	9	25	38	13.2	4.68	84	.229	.339	0	.000	-0	-4	-4	-1	-0.4

● PERRY WERDEN Werden, Percival Wheritt b: 7/21/1865, St.Louis, Mo. d: 1/9/34, Minneapolis, Minn. BR/TR, 6'2", 220 lbs. Deb: 4/24/1884 ◆

YEAR	TM/L	W	L	PCT	G	GS	CG	SH	SV	IP	H	HR	BB	SO	RAT	ERA	ERA+	OAV	OOB	BH	AVG	PB	PR	/A	PD	TPI
1884	StL-U	12	1	.923	16	16	12	1	0	141^1	113	1	22	51	8.6	1.97	121	.204	.235	18	.237	-4	7	7	1	0.2

● BILL WERLE Werle, William George "Bugs" b: 12/21/20, Oakland, Cal. BL/TL, 6'2.5", 182 lbs. Deb: 4/22/49 C

YEAR	TM/L	W	L	PCT	G	GS	CG	SH	SV	IP	H	HR	BB	SO	RAT	ERA	ERA+	OAV	OOB	BH	AVG	PB	PR	/A	PD	TPI
1949	Pit-N	12	13	.480	35	29	10	2	0	221	243	22	51	106	12.3	4.24	99	.278	.324	9	.117	-3	-5	-1	1	-0.3
1950	Pit-N	8	16	.333	48	22	6	0	8	215^1	249	25	65	78	13.4	4.60	95	.290	.344	13	.194	1	-11	-5	4	-0.1
1951	Pit-N	8	6	.571	59	9	2	0	6	149^2	181	20	51	57	14.3	5.65	75	.304	.364	12	.300	3	-28	-24	3	-1.5
1952	Pit-N	0	0	—	5	0	0	0	0	4	9	1	1	1	22.5	9.00	44	.429	.455	0	—	0	-2	-2	0	0.0
	StL-N	1	2	.333	19	0	0	0	1	39	40	6	15	23	12.9	4.85	77	.268	.339	1	.111	-0	-5	-5	1	-0.3
	Yr	1	2	.333	24	0	0	0	1	43	49	7	16	24	13.8	5.23	71	.288	.353	1	.111	-0	-7	-7	2	-0.3
1953	Bos-A	0	1	.000	5	0	0	0	0	11^2	7	1	1	4	6.2	1.54	273	.179	.200	0	.000	-0	3	3	1	0.4
1954	Bos-A	0	1	.000	14	0	0	0	0	24^2	41	5	10	14	19.3	4.38	94	.376	.438	0	.000	-0	-2	-1	-0	-0.1
Total	6	29	39	.426	185	60	18	2	15	665^1	770	80	194	283	13.4	4.69	90	.291	.345	35	.176	1	-50	-34	10	-1.9

● GEORGE WERLEY Werley, George William b: 9/8/38, St.Louis, Mo. BR/TR, 6'2", 196 lbs. Deb: 9/29/56

YEAR	TM/L	W	L	PCT	G	GS	CG	SH	SV	IP	H	HR	BB	SO	RAT	ERA	ERA+	OAV	OOB	BH	AVG	PB	PR	/A	PD	TPI
1956	Bal-A	0	0	—	1	0	0	0	0	1	1	0	2	0	27.0	9.00	44	.250	.500	0	—	0	-1	-1	0	0.0

● JOHNNY WERTS Werts, Henry Levi b: 4/20/1898, Pomaria, S.C. d: 9/24/90, Newberry, S.C. BR/TR, 5'10", 180 lbs. Deb: 4/14/26

YEAR	TM/L	W	L	PCT	G	GS	CG	SH	SV	IP	H	HR	BB	SO	RAT	ERA	ERA+	OAV	OOB	BH	AVG	PB	PR	/A	PD	TPI
1926	Bos-N	11	9	.550	32	23	7	1	0	189^1	212	6	47	65	12.8	3.28	108	.287	.338	17	.266	4	11	6	2	1.2
1927	Bos-N	4	10	.286	42	15	4	0	1	164^1	204	5	52	39	14.2	4.55	82	.315	.369	7	.163	-0	-11	-15	-1	-1.3
1928	Bos-N	0	2	.000	10	2	0	0	0	18^1	31	2	8	5	19.1	10.31	38	.369	.424	1	.333	0	-13	-13	0	-1.1
1929	Bos-N	0	0	—	4	0	0	0	1	6	13	1	4	2	25.5	10.50	45	.433	.500	1	1.000	0	-4	-4	-0	-0.1
Total	4	15	21	.417	88	40	11	1	2	378	460	14	111	111	13.9	4.29	85	.307	.360	26	.234	4	-17	-27	1	-1.3

● BILL WERTZ Wertz, William Charles b: 1/15/67, Cleveland, Ohio BR/TR, 6'6", 220 lbs. Deb: 5/22/93

YEAR	TM/L	W	L	PCT	G	GS	CG	SH	SV	IP	H	HR	BB	SO	RAT	ERA	ERA+	OAV	OOB	BH	AVG	PB	PR	/A	PD	TPI
1993	Cle-A	2	3	.400	34	0	0	0	0	59^2	54	5	32	53	13.1	3.62	119	.238	.335	0	—	0	5	5	-2	0.2
1994	Cle-A	0	0	—	1	0	0	0	0	4^1	9	0	1	1	20.8	10.38	45	.409	.435	0	—	0	-3	-3	-0	0.0
Total	2	2	3	.400	35	0	0	0	0	64	63	5	33	54	13.6	4.08	107	.253	.343	0	—	0	2	2	-2	0.2

● DAVID WEST West, David Lee b: 9/1/64, Memphis, Tenn. BL/TL, 6'6", 230 lbs. Deb: 9/24/88

YEAR	TM/L	W	L	PCT	G	GS	CG	SH	SV	IP	H	HR	BB	SO	RAT	ERA	ERA+	OAV	OOB	BH	AVG	PB	PR	/A	PD	TPI
1988	NY-N	1	0	1.000	2	1	0	0	0	6	6	0	3	3	13.5	3.00	107	.273	.360	2	1.000	1	0	0	-0	0.2
1989	NY-N	0	2	.000	11	2	0	0	0	24^1	25	4	14	19	14.8	7.40	44	.260	.360	1	.200	0	-11	-11	-1	-0.9
	Min-A	3	2	.600	10	5	0	0	0	39^1	48	5	19	31	15.8	6.41	65	.306	.388	0	—	0	-11	-10	-1	-1.3
1990	Min-A	7	9	.438	29	27	2	0	0	146^1	142	21	78	92	13.8	5.10	81	.256	.352	0	—	0	-19	-15	-1	-2.0
1991	*Min-A	4	4	.500	15	12	0	0	0	71^1	66	13	28	52	12.0	4.54	94	.244	.317	0	—	0	-4	-2	0	-0.2
1992	Min-A	1	3	.250	9	3	0	0	0	28^1	32	3	20	19	16.8	6.99	58	.276	.387	0	—	0	-10	-9	-0	-1.2
1993	*Phi-N	6	4	.600	76	0	0	0	3	86^1	60	6	51	87	12.1	2.92	136	.194	.318	2	.400	1	11	10	-2	1.0
1994	Phi-N	4	10	.286	31	14	0	0	0	99	74	7	61	83	12.4	3.55	121	.205	.322	2	.071	-2	7	8	-2	0.7
1995	Phi-N	3	2	.600	8	8	0	0	0	38	34	5	19	25	12.8	3.79	111	.241	.335	1	.125	1	2	2	-1	0.2
1996	Phi-N	2	2	.500	7	6	0	0	0	28^1	31	0	11	22	13.3	4.76	90	.272	.336	2	.286	1	-2	-1	-0	-0.1
1998	Bos-A	0	0	—	6	0	0	0	0	2	7	1	7	4	63.0	27.00	17	.538	.700	0	—	0	-5	-5	0	0.0
Total	10	31	38	.449	204	78	2	0	3	569^1	525	65	311	437	13.5	4.66	88	.244	.343	10	.182	2	-41	-34	-7	-3.6

● FRANK WEST West, J. Franklin b: 1/1874, Johnstown, Pa. d: 9/6/32, Wilmerding, Pa. 180 lbs. Deb: 7/11/1894

YEAR	TM/L	W	L	PCT	G	GS	CG	SH	SV	IP	H	HR	BB	SO	RAT	ERA	ERA+	OAV	OOB	BH	AVG	PB	PR	/A	PD	TPI
1894	Bos-N	0	0	—	1	0	0	0	0	3	5	0	2	1	21.0	9.00	63	.357	.438	0	.000	-0	-1	-1	-0	0.0

● HI WEST West, James Hiram b: 8/8/1884, Roseville, Ill. d: 5/25/63, Los Angeles, Cal. BR/TR, 6', 185 lbs. Deb: 9/8/05

YEAR	TM/L	W	L	PCT	G	GS	CG	SH	SV	IP	H	HR	BB	SO	RAT	ERA	ERA+	OAV	OOB	BH	AVG	PB	PR	/A	PD	TPI
1905	Cle-A	2	2	.500	6	4	4	1	0	33	43	0	10	15	15.3	4.09	64	.316	.376	1	.077	-1	-5	-5	-2	-0.9
1911	Cle-A	3	4	.429	13	8	3	0	1	64^2	84	1	18	17	14.6	3.76	91	.343	.395	3	.130	-2	-3	-2	-1	-0.5
Total	2	5	6	.455	19	12	7	1	1	97^2	127	1	28	32	14.8	3.87	81	.333	.388	4	.111	-3	-8	-8	-3	-1.4

● LEFTY WEST West, Weldon Edison b: 9/3/15, Gibsonville, N.C. d: 7/23/79, Hendersonville, N.C. BR/TL, 6', 165 lbs. Deb: 4/30/44

YEAR	TM/L	W	L	PCT	G	GS	CG	SH	SV	IP	H	HR	BB	SO	RAT	ERA	ERA+	OAV	OOB	BH	AVG	PB	PR	/A	PD	TPI
1944	StL-A	0	0	—	11	0	0	0	0	24^1	34	1	19	11	20.0	6.29	57	.366	.478	1	.143	-0	-8	-7	-0	-0.1
1945	StL-A	3	4	.429	24	8	1	0	0	74^1	71	2	31	38	12.3	3.63	97	.245	.318	2	.074	-3	-2	-1	-2	-0.5
Total	2	3	4	.429	35	8	1	0	0	98^2	105	3	50	49	14.2	4.29	83	.274	.359	3	.088	-3	-10	-8	-2	-0.6

● HUYLER WESTERVELT Westervelt, Huyler b: 10/1/1870, Piermont, N.Y. 5'9", 170 lbs. Deb: 4/21/1894

YEAR	TM/L	W	L	PCT	G	GS	CG	SH	SV	IP	H	HR	BB	SO	RAT	ERA	ERA+	OAV	OOB	BH	AVG	PB	PR	/A	PD	TPI
1894	NY-N	7	10	.412	23	18	11	1	0	141	170	4	76	35	16.0	5.04	104	.295	.382	8	.143	-5	4	3	0	-0.1

● MICKEY WESTON Weston, Michael Lee b: 3/26/61, Flint, Mich. BR/TR, 6'1", 187 lbs. Deb: 6/18/89

YEAR	TM/L	W	L	PCT	G	GS	CG	SH	SV	IP	H	HR	BB	SO	RAT	ERA	ERA+	OAV	OOB	BH	AVG	PB	PR	/A	PD	TPI
1989	Bal-A	1	0	1.000	7	0	0	0	1	13	18	1	2	7	14.5	5.54	68	.346	.382	0	—	0	-2	-3	-0	-0.2
1990	Bal-A	0	1	.000	9	2	0	0	0	21	28	6	6	9	14.6	7.71	49	.322	.366	0	—	0	-9	-9	-0	-0.3
1991	Tor-A	0	0	—	2	0	0	0	0	2	1	0	1	1	9.0	0.00	—	.143	.250	0	—	0	1	1	-0	0.0
1992	Phi-N	0	1	.000	1	1	0	0	0	3^2	7	1	1	0	22.1	12.27	28	.412	.474	0	.000	-0	-4	-4	-0	-0.7
1993	NY-N	0	0	—	4	0	0	0	0	5^2	11	0	1	2	20.6	7.94	51	.393	.433	0	—	0	-2	-2	0	0.0
Total	5	1	2	.333	23	3	0	0	1	45^1	65	8	11	19	15.7	7.15	53	.340	.385	0	.000	-0	-16	-17	-1	-1.2

● JOHN WETTELAND Wetteland, John Karl b: 8/21/66, San Mateo, Cal. BR/TR, 6'2", 195 lbs. Deb: 5/31/89

YEAR	TM/L	W	L	PCT	G	GS	CG	SH	SV	IP	H	HR	BB	SO	RAT	ERA	ERA+	OAV	OOB	BH	AVG	PB	PR	/A	PD	TPI
1989	LA-N	5	8	.385	31	12	0	0	1	102^2	81	8	34	96	10.1	3.77	91	.218	.284	3	.143	-0	-3	-4	-1	-0.6
1990	LA-N	2	4	.333	22	5	0	0	0	43	44	6	17	36	13.6	4.81	76	.263	.346	1	.143	1	-5	-6	-1	-0.7
1991	LA-N	1	0	1.000	6	0	0	0	0	9	5	0	3	9	9.0	0.00	—	.161	.257	0	—	0	4	4	0	0.4
1992	Mon-N	4	4	.500	67	0	0	0	37	83^1	64	6	36	99	11.2	2.92	119	.213	.305	1	.200	0	5	5	-1	0.9
1993	Mon-N	9	3	.750	70	0	0	0	43	85^1	58	3	28	113	9.3	1.37	304	.188	.260	0	.000	-0	25	27	-1	5.7
1994	Mon-N	4	6	.400	52	0	0	0	25	63^2	46	5	21	68	9.9	2.83	149	.202	.278	1	.250	0	10	10	-1	2.0
1995	*NY-A	1	5	.167	60	0	0	0	31	61^1	40	6	14	66	7.9	2.93	157	.185	.235	0	—	0	12	11	-1	1.9
1996	*NY-A☆	2	3	.400	62	0	0	0	**43**	63^2	54	9	21	69	10.6	2.83	175	.224	.286	0	—	0	15	15	-0	2.7
1997	Tex-A	7	2	.778	61	0	0	0	31	65	43	5	21	63	8.9	1.94	247	.182	.249	1	1.000	1	19	21	-1	4.3

YEAR	TM/L	W	L	PCT	G	GS	CG	SH	SV	IP	H	HR	BB	SO	RAT	ERA	ERA+	OAV	OOB	BH	AVG	PB	PR	/A	PD	TPI
1998	★Tex-A★	3	1	.750	63	0	0	0	42	62	47	6	14	72	8.9	2.03	238	.203	.249	0	—	0	18	19	-0	3.3
Total	10	38	36	.514	494	17	0	0	253	639	482	54	209	691	9.9	2.73	152	.207	.276	7	.167	1	101	101	-7	19.9

● BUZZ WETZEL
Wetzel, Charles Edward b: 8/25/1894, Jay, Okla. d: 3/7/41, Globe, Ariz. BR/TR, 6'1", 162 lbs. Deb: 7/25/27

YEAR	TM/L	W	L	PCT	G	GS	CG	SH	SV	IP	H	HR	BB	SO	RAT	ERA	ERA+	OAV	OOB	BH	AVG	PB	PR	/A	PD	TPI
1927	Phi-A	0	0	—	2	1	0	0	0	4^2	8	0	5	0	25.1	7.71	55	.400	.520	1	1.000	0	-2	-2	0	0.1

● SHORTY WETZEL
Wetzel, George William b: 1868, Philadelphia, Pa. d: 2/25/1899, Dayton, Ohio Deb: 8/26/1885

YEAR	TM/L	W	L	PCT	G	GS	CG	SH	SV	IP	H	HR	BB	SO	RAT	ERA	ERA+	OAV	OOB	BH	AVG	PB	PR	/A	PD	TPI
1885	Bal-a	0	2	.000	2	2	1	0	0	17	27	0	9	6	20.6	8.47	38	.333	.419	0	.000	-1	-10	-10	1	-0.8

● STEFAN WEVER
Wever, Stefan Matthew b: 4/22/58, Marburg, W.Ger. BR/TR, 6'8", 245 lbs. Deb: 9/17/82

YEAR	TM/L	W	L	PCT	G	GS	CG	SH	SV	IP	H	HR	BB	SO	RAT	ERA	ERA+	OAV	OOB	BH	AVG	PB	PR	/A	PD	TPI
1982	NY-A	0	1	.000	1	1	0	0	0	2^2	6	1	3	2	30.4	27.00	15	.429	.529	0	—	0	-7	-7	-0	-1.2

● GUS WEYHING
Weyhing, August "Cannonball" b: 9/29/1866, Louisville, Ky. d: 9/4/55, Louisville, Ky. BR/TR, 5'10", 145 lbs. Deb: 5/2/1887 F

YEAR	TM/L	W	L	PCT	G	GS	CG	SH	SV	IP	H	HR	BB	SO	RAT	ERA	ERA+	OAV	OOB	BH	AVG	PB	PR	/A	PD	TPI
1887	Phi-a	26	28	.481	55	55	53	2	0	466^1	465	12	167	193	12.9	4.27	101	.253	.328	42	.201	-9	2	1	-2	-0.8
1888	Phi-a	28	18	.609	47	47	45	3	0	404	314	4	111	204	10.4	2.25	133	.207	.279	40	.217	4	36	33	1	3.7
1889	Phi-a	30	21	.588	54	53	50	4	0	449	382	15	212	213	12.6	2.95	128	.223	.321	25	.131	-15	45	42	-3	2.1
1890	Bro-P	30	16	.652	49	46	38	3	0	390	419	10	179	177	14.2	3.60	124	.263	.343	27	.164	-6	27	37	-9	1.9
1891	Phi-a	31	20	.608	52	51	51	3	0	450	428	12	161	219	12.4	3.18	120	.242	.316	22	.111	-16	27	32	-5	1.0
1892	Phi-N	32	21	.604	59	49	46	6	**3**	469^2	411	9	168	202	11.4	2.66	122	.226	.298	29	.136	-10	33	30	-9	1.1
1893	Phi-N	23	16	.590	42	40	33	2	0	345^1	399	10	145	101	14.7	4.74	96	.281	.356	22	.150	-9	-3	-6	-2	-1.5
1894	Phi-N	16	14	.533	38	34	25	2	1	266^1	365	12	116	81	16.8	5.81	88	.322	.393	20	.174	-9	-14	-21	-3	-2.5
1895	Phi-N	0	2	.000	2	2	0	0	0	9	23	0	13	5	36.0	20.00	24	.469	.581	0	.000	-1	-15	-15	0	-1.7
	Pit-N	1	0	1.000	1	1	1	0	0	9	10	0	5	3	15.0	1.00	452	.278	.366	1	.250	0	4	4	1	0.4
	Lou-N	7	19	.269	28	25	22	1	0	213	285	9	66	53	15.2	5.41	86	.316	.367	20	.225	-0	-15	-18	0	-1.6
	Yr	8	21	.276	31	28	23	1	0	231	318	9	84	61	16.0	5.81	80	.322	.380	21	.216	-1	-26	-30	1	-2.9
1896	Lou-N	2	3	.400	5	5	4	0	0	42	62	6	15	9	16.9	6.64	65	.339	.395	2	.133	-1	-11	-11	0	-0.9
1898	Was-N	15	26	.366	45	42	39	0	0	361	428	10	84	92	13.2	4.51	81	.292	.338	25	.177	-5	-36	-34	-2	-3.8
1899	Was-N	17	21	.447	43	38	34	2	0	334^2	414	8	76	96	13.9	4.54	86	.303	.352	26	.206	-1	-26	-24	-6	-2.8
1900	StL-N	3	2	.600	7	5	3	0	0	46^2	60	2	21	6	15.8	4.63	79	.311	.381	2	.095	-2	-5	-5	-1	-0.7
	Bro-N	3	4	.429	8	8	3	0	0	48	66	1	20	8	16.5	4.31	89	.325	.391	4	.222	-0	-3	-3	-1	-0.4
	Yr	6	6	.500	15	13	6	0	0	94^2	126	3	41	14	16.1	4.47	84	.317	.384	6	.154	-3	-8	-8	-1	-1.1
1901	Cle-A	0	0	—	2	1	0	0	0	11^1	20	0	5	0	23.0	7.94	45	.377	.468	0	.000	-1	-5	-6	-0	-0.1
	Cin-N	0	1	.000	1	1	1	0	0	9	11	0	2	3	15.0	3.00	107	.297	.366	0	.000	-0	0	0	-0	-0.1
Total	14	264	232	.532	538	503	448	28	4	4324^1	4562	120	1566	1665	13.3	3.89	102	.264	.335	307	.166	-83	41	38	-39	-6.7

● JOHN WEYHING
Weyhing, John b: 6/24/1869, Louisville, Ky. d: 6/20/1890, Louisville, Ky. BL/TL, 6'2", 185 lbs. Deb: 7/13/1888 F

YEAR	TM/L	W	L	PCT	G	GS	CG	SH	SV	IP	H	HR	BB	SO	RAT	ERA	ERA+	OAV	OOB	BH	AVG	PB	PR	/A	PD	TPI
1888	Cin-a	3	4	.429	8	8	7	0	0	65^2	52	0	17	30	9.6	1.23	257	.210	.263	3	.130	-2	13	14	-1	1.1
1889	Col-a	0	0	—	1	0	0	0	0	1	1	0	4	0	45.0	27.00	13	.250	.625	0	—	0	-3	-3	-0	0.0
Total	2	3	4	.429	9	8	7	0	0	66^2	53	0	21	30	10.1	1.62	196	.210	.274	3	.130	-2	11	12	-1	1.1

● LEE WHEAT
Wheat, Leroy William b: 9/15/29, Edwardsville, Ill BR/TR, 6'4", 200 lbs. Deb: 4/21/54

YEAR	TM/L	W	L	PCT	G	GS	CG	SH	SV	IP	H	HR	BB	SO	RAT	ERA	ERA+	OAV	OOB	BH	AVG	PB	PR	/A	PD	TPI
1954	Phi-A	0	2	.000	8	1	0	0	0	28^1	38	1	9	7	15.2	5.72	68	.304	.356	1	.125	-0	-6	-6	-0	-0.4
1955	KC-A	0	0	—	3	0	0	0	0	2	8	1	3	1	49.5	22.50	19	.533	.611	0	—	0	-4	-4	0	0.0
Total	2	0	2	.000	11	1	0	0	0	30^1	46	2	12	8	17.5	6.82	57	.329	.386	1	.125	-0	-10	-10	-0	-0.4

● CHARLIE WHEATLEY
Wheatley, Charles b: 6/27/1893, Rosedale, Kan. d: 12/10/82, Tulsa, Okla. BR/TR, 5'11", 174 lbs. Deb: 9/6/12

YEAR	TM/L	W	L	PCT	G	GS	CG	SH	SV	IP	H	HR	BB	SO	RAT	ERA	ERA+	OAV	OOB	BH	AVG	PB	PR	/A	PD	TPI
1912	Det-A	1	4	.200	5	5	2	0	0	35	45	1	17	14	16.5	6.17	53	.331	.413	0	.000	-2	-11	-11	0	-1.4

● WOODY WHEATON
Wheaton, Elwood Pierce b: 10/3/14, Philadelphia, Pa. d: 12/11/95, Lancaster, Pa. BL/TL, 5'8.5", 160 lbs. Deb: 9/28/43 ♦

YEAR	TM/L	W	L	PCT	G	GS	CG	SH	SV	IP	H	HR	BB	SO	RAT	ERA	ERA+	OAV	OOB	BH	AVG	PB	PR	/A	PD	TPI
1944	Phi-A	0	1	.000	11	1	1	0	0	38	36	1	20	15	13.5	3.55	98	.255	.352	11	.186	0	-1	-0	-1	-0.1

● RIP WHEELER
Wheeler, Floyd Clark b: 3/2/1898, Marion, Ky. d: 9/18/68, Marion, Ky. BR/TR, 6', 180 lbs. Deb: 9/30/21

YEAR	TM/L	W	L	PCT	G	GS	CG	SH	SV	IP	H	HR	BB	SO	RAT	ERA	ERA+	OAV	OOB	BH	AVG	PB	PR	/A	PD	TPI
1921	Pit-N	0	0	—	1	0	0	0	0	3	6	0	1	0	24.0	9.00	43	.500	.571	0	.000	-0	-2	-2	0	0.0
1922	Pit-N	0	0	—	1	0	0	0	0	1	1	0	2	0	27.0	0.00	—	.333	.600	0	—	0	0	0	0	0.0
1923	Chi-N	1	2	.333	3	3	1	0	0	24	28	2	5	5	13.5	4.88	82	.298	.353	1	.111	-1	-2	-2	1	-0.2
1924	Chi-N	3	6	.333	29	4	0	0	0	101^1	103	8	21	16	11.0	3.91	100	.265	.303	7	.219	-1	-0	-0	0	-0.1
Total	4	4	8	.333	34	7	1	0	0	129^1	138	10	29	21	11.9	4.18	94	.278	.323	8	.190	-2	-4	-4	2	-0.3

● GEORGE WHEELER
Wheeler, George L. (b: George L. Heroux)
b: 8/3/1869, Methuen, Mass. d: 3/23/46, Santa Ana, Cal. BB/TR, 5'9", 180 lbs. Deb: 9/18/1896

YEAR	TM/L	W	L	PCT	G	GS	CG	SH	SV	IP	H	HR	BB	SO	RAT	ERA	ERA+	OAV	OOB	BH	AVG	PB	PR	/A	PD	TPI
1896	Phi-N	1	1	.500	3	2	2	0	0	16^1	18	0	5	2	13.8	3.86	112	.277	.347	1	.111	-1	1	1	0	0.0
1897	Phi-N	11	10	.524	26	19	17	0	0	191	229	3	62	35	13.9	3.96	106	.295	.349	16	.203	-1	8	5	1	0.4
1898	Phi-N	6	8	.429	15	13	10	0	0	112^1	155	1	36	20	15.8	4.17	82	.325	.380	8	.186	-1	-7	-9	3	-0.8
1899	Phi-N	3	1	.750	6	5	3	0	0	39	44	1	13	3	13.8	6.00	61	.284	.351	4	.235	1	-9	-10	0	-0.7
Total	4	21	20	.512	50	39	32	0	0	358^2	446	5	116	60	14.5	4.24	92	.303	.359	29	.196	-2	-8	-13	4	-1.1

● HARRY WHEELER
Wheeler, Harry Eugene b: 3/3/1858, Versailles, Ind. d: 10/9/1900, Cincinnati, Ohio BR/TR, 5'11", 165 lbs. Deb: 6/19/1878 M♦

YEAR	TM/L	W	L	PCT	G	GS	CG	SH	SV	IP	H	HR	BB	SO	RAT	ERA	ERA+	OAV	OOB	BH	AVG	PB	PR	/A	PD	TPI
1878	Pro-N	6	1	.857	7	6	6	0	0	62	70	1	25	25	13.8	3.48	63	.275	.339	4	.148	-1	-8	-9	-2	-1.0
1879	Cin-N	0	1	.000	1	1	0	0	0	1	6	0	4	0	90.0	81.00	3	.667	.769	0	.000	-0	-9	-9	-0	-2.5
1882	Cin-a	1	2	.333	4	1	1	0	0	21^2	21	0	12	10	13.7	5.40	49	.239	.330	86	.250	1	-7	-7	-0	-0.7
1883	Col-a	0	1	.000	1	1	0	0	0	5	13	0	2	0	27.0	7.20	43	.448	.484	84	.226	0	-2	-2	-0	-0.3
1884	KC-U	0	1	.000	1	1	1	0	0	8	7	0	0	6	7.9	1.13	199	.219	.219	16	.258	-0	1	1	0	0.1
Total	5	7	6	.538	14	10	8	0	0	97^2	117	1	43	41	14.7	4.70	50	.283	.351	256	.228	-1	-24	-26	-2	-4.4

● GARY WHEELOCK
Wheelock, Gary Richard b: 11/29/51, Bakersfield, Cal. BR/TR, 6'3", 205 lbs. Deb: 9/17/76

YEAR	TM/L	W	L	PCT	G	GS	CG	SH	SV	IP	H	HR	BB	SO	RAT	ERA	ERA+	OAV	OOB	BH	AVG	PB	PR	/A	PD	TPI
1976	Cal-A	0	0	—	2	0	0	0	0	2	6	0	1	2	36.0	27.00	12	.500	.571	0	—	0	-5	-5	-0	0.0
1977	Sea-A	6	9	.400	17	17	2	0	0	88^1	94	16	26	47	12.4	4.89	84	.268	.322	0	—	0	-8	-8	-1	-1.2
1980	Sea-A	0	0	—	1	1	0	0	0	3	4	0	1	1	15.0	6.00	69	.333	.385	0	—	0	-1	-1	0	0.0
Total	3	6	9	.400	20	18	2	0	0	93^1	104	16	28	50	13.0	5.40	76	.277	.333	0	—	0	-14	-14	-1	-1.2

● JACK WHILLOCK
Whillock, Jack Franklin b: 11/4/42, Clinton, Ark. BR/TR, 6'3", 195 lbs. Deb: 8/29/71

YEAR	TM/L	W	L	PCT	G	GS	CG	SH	SV	IP	H	HR	BB	SO	RAT	ERA	ERA+	OAV	OOB	BH	AVG	PB	PR	/A	PD	TPI
1971	Det-A	0	2	.000	7	0	0	0	1	8	10	0	2	6	13.5	5.63	64	.323	.364	0	.000	-0	-2	-2	0	-0.5

● MATT WHISENANT
Whisenant, Matthew Michael b: 6/8/71, Los Angeles, Cal. BR/TL, 6'3", 215 lbs. Deb: 7/4/97

YEAR	TM/L	W	L	PCT	G	GS	CG	SH	SV	IP	H	HR	BB	SO	RAT	ERA	ERA+	OAV	OOB	BH	AVG	PB	PR	/A	PD	TPI
1997	Fla-N	0	0	—	4	0	0	0	0	2^2	4	0	6	4	33.8	16.88	24	.333	.556	0	—	0	-4	-4	-0	0.0
	KC-A	1	0	1.000	24	0	0	0	0	19	15	0	12	16	14.2	2.84	166	.211	.349	0	—	0	4	4	0	0.2
1998	KC-A	2	1	.667	70	0	0	0	2	60^2	61	3	33	45	14.4	4.90	100	.271	.372	0	—	0	-2	0	0	0.0
Total	2	3	1	.750	98	0	0	0	2	82^1	80	3	51	65	15.0	4.81	100	.260	.375	0	—	0	-2	0	0	0.2

● PAT WHITAKER
Whitaker, William H. b: 11/1864, St.Louis, Mo. d: 7/15/02, St.Louis, Mo. TR, Deb: 10/11/1888

YEAR	TM/L	W	L	PCT	G	GS	CG	SH	SV	IP	H	HR	BB	SO	RAT	ERA	ERA+	OAV	OOB	BH	AVG	PB	PR	/A	PD	TPI
1888	Bal-a	1	1	.500	2	2	2	0	0	14	13	0	6	5	13.5	5.14	58	.236	.333	0	.000	-1	-3	-3	2	-0.3
1889	Bal-a	1	0	1.000	1	1	1	0	0	9	10	0	4	1	14.0	2.00	197	.270	.341	1	.250	-0	2	2	0	0.2
Total	2	2	1	.667	3	3	3	0	0	23	23	0	10	6	13.7	3.91	86	.250	.337	1	.100	-1	-1	-1	2	-0.1

● BILL WHITBY
Whitby, William Edward b: 7/29/43, Crewe, Va. BR/TR, 6'1", 190 lbs. Deb: 6/17/64

YEAR	TM/L	W	L	PCT	G	GS	CG	SH	SV	IP	H	HR	BB	SO	RAT	ERA	ERA+	OAV	OOB	BH	AVG	PB	PR	/A	PD	TPI
1964	Min-A	0	0	—	4	0	0	0	0	6^1	8	3	1	2	12.8	8.53	42	.308	.333	0	.000	-0	-3	-3	-0	0.0

● BOB WHITCHER
Whitcher, Robert Arthur b: 4/29/17, Berlin, N.H. d: 5/8/97, Akron, Ohio BL/TL, 5'8", 165 lbs. Deb: 8/20/45

YEAR	TM/L	W	L	PCT	G	GS	CG	SH	SV	IP	H	HR	BB	SO	RAT	ERA	ERA+	OAV	OOB	BH	AVG	PB	PR	/A	PD	TPI
1945	Bos-N	0	2	.000	6	3	0	0	0	15^2	12	1	12	6	13.8	2.87	133	.235	.381	1	.333	0	2	2	-0	0.2

● ABE WHITE
White, Adel b: 5/16/04, Winder, Ga. d: 10/1/78, Atlanta, Ga. BR/TL, 6', 185 lbs. Deb: 7/10/37

YEAR	TM/L	W	L	PCT	G	GS	CG	SH	SV	IP	H	HR	BB	SO	RAT	ERA	ERA+	OAV	OOB	BH	AVG	PB	PR	/A	PD	TPI
1937	StL-N	0	1	.000	5	0	0	0	0	9^1	14	1	3	2	16.4	6.75	59	.341	.386	1	1.000	0	-3	-3	-0	-0.2

● ERNIE WHITE White, Ernest Daniel b: 9/5/16, Pacolet Mills, S.C d: 5/22/74, Augusta, Ga. BR/TL, 5′11.5″, 175 lbs. Deb: 5/9/40 C

YEAR	TM/L	W	L	PCT	G	GS	CG	SH	SV	IP	H	HR	BB	SO	RAT	ERA	ERA+	OAV	OOB	BH	AVG	PB	PR	/A	PD	TPI
1940	StL-N	1	1	.500	8	1	0	0	0	21^2	29	0	14	15	18.3	4.15	96	.315	.411	3	.429	1	-1	-0	1	0.1
1941	StL-N	17	7	.708	32	25	12	3	2	210	169	12	70	117	10.5	2.40	157	.217	.287	15	.190	0	29	32	-4	3.3
1942	*StL-N	7	5	.583	26	19	7	1	2	128^1	113	11	41	67	10.9	2.52	136	.232	.294	8	.195	0	11	13	-2	1.0
1943	*StL-N	5	5	.500	14	10	5	1	0	78^2	78	4	33	28	12.8	3.78	89	.257	.332	6	.214	0	-3	-4	-1	-0.5
1946	Bos-N	0	1	.000	12	1	0	0	0	23^2	22	1	12	8	12.9	4.18	82	.256	.347	1	.250	0	-2	-2	-1	-0.1
1947	Bos-N	0	0	—	1	1	0	0	0	4	1	0	1	1	4.5	0.00	—	.083	.154	1	1.000	0	2	2	-0	0.0
1948	Bos-N	0	2	.000	15	0	0	0	2	23	13	0	17	8	11.7	1.96	196	.167	.316	0	.000	-0	5	5	-1	0.4
Total	7	30	21	.588	108	57	24	5	6	489^1	425	28	188	244	11.5	2.78	130	.231	.306	34	.209	2	41	45	-8	4.2

● GABE WHITE White, Gabriel Allen b: 11/20/71, Sebring, Fla. BL/TL, 6′2″, 200 lbs. Deb: 5/27/94

YEAR	TM/L	W	L	PCT	G	GS	CG	SH	SV	IP	H	HR	BB	SO	RAT	ERA	ERA+	OAV	OOB	BH	AVG	PB	PR	/A	PD	TPI
1994	Mon-N	1	1	.500	7	5	0	0	1	23^2	24	4	11	17	13.7	6.08	69	.261	.346	0	.000	-0	-5	-5	-0	-0.4
1995	Mon-N	1	2	.333	19	1	0	0	0	25^2	26	7	9	25	12.6	7.01	61	.260	.327	0	.000	-0	-8	-8	-0	-0.9
1997	Cin-N	2	2	.500	12	6	0	0	1	41	39	6	8	25	10.5	4.39	97	.253	.294	1	.111	-0	-1	-1	-1	-0.2
1998	Cin-N	5	5	.500	69	3	0	0	9	98^2	86	17	27	83	10.4	4.01	108	.231	.285	1	.167	-0	2	3	-1	0.3
Total	4	9	10	.474	107	15	0	0	11	189	175	34	55	150	11.1	4.76	90	.244	.301	2	.091	-1	-11	-10	-2	-1.2

● DEKE WHITE White, George Frederick b: 9/8/1872, Albany, N.Y. d: 11/5/57, Ilion, N.Y. BB/TL, Deb: 9/14/1895

YEAR	TM/L	W	L	PCT	G	GS	CG	SH	SV	IP	H	HR	BB	SO	RAT	ERA	ERA+	OAV	OOB	BH	AVG	PB	PR	/A	PD	TPI
1895	Phi-N	1	0	1.000	3	1	1	0	1	17^1	17	1	13	6	16.6	9.87	49	.254	.390	1	.125	-1	-10	-10	-0	-0.6

● DOC WHITE White, Guy Harris b: 4/9/1879, Washington, D.C. d: 2/19/69, Silver Spring, Md. BL/TL, 6′1″, 150 lbs. Deb: 4/22/01 ♦

YEAR	TM/L	W	L	PCT	G	GS	CG	SH	SV	IP	H	HR	BB	SO	RAT	ERA	ERA+	OAV	OOB	BH	AVG	PB	PR	/A	PD	TPI
1901	Phi-N	14	13	.519	31	27	22	0	0	236^2	241	2	56	132	11.8	3.19	106	.262	.314	27	.276	5	3	5	3	1.3
1902	Phi-N	16	20	.444	36	35	34	3	1	306	277	3	72	185	10.6	2.53	111	.241	.294	47	.263	4	9	10	2	2.0
1903	Chi-A	17	16	.515	37	36	29	3	0	300	258	4	69	114	10.2	2.13	132	.232	.285	20	.202	6	28	23	3	3.3
1904	Chi-A	16	12	.571	30	30	23	7	0	228	201	6	68	115	11.0	1.78	138	.238	.301	12	.158	0	21	17	1	2.4
1905	Chi-A	17	13	.567	36	33	25	4	0	260^1	204	2	58	120	9.4	1.76	140	.218	.270	15	.167	0	26	20	0	2.4
1906	*Chi-A	18	6	.750	28	24	20	7	0	219^1	160	2	38	95	**8.3**	**1.52**	**167**	.207	**.249**	12	.185	4	29	25	2	3.6
1907	Chi-A	**27**	13	.675	46	35	24	6	1	291	270	3	38	141	9.7	2.26	106	.248	.278	20	.222	4	9	4	5	1.6
1908	Chi-A	18	13	.581	41	37	24	5	0	296	262	3	69	126	10.3	2.55	91	.240	.291	25	.229	4	-5	-8	7	0.4
1909	Chi-A	11	9	.550	24	21	14	3	0	177^2	149	1	31	77	9.5	1.72	136	.226	.269	45	.234	6	15	12	-1	2.1
1910	Chi-A	15	13	.536	33	29	20	2	1	236^2	219	2	50	111	10.7	2.66	90	.243	.291	25	.198	2	-4	-7	2	-0.3
1911	Chi-A	10	14	.417	34	29	16	4	2	214^1	219	2	35	72	11.0	2.98	108	.271	.309	20	.256	3	9	6	-1	0.8
1912	Chi-A	8	10	.444	32	19	9	1	0	172	172	1	47	57	11.9	3.24	99	.267	.325	7	.125	-1	1	-1	-1	-0.3
1913	Chi-A	2	4	.333	19	8	2	0	0	103	106	2	39	39	13.1	3.50	84	.278	.353	3	.120	-1	-6	-7	2	-0.2
Total	13	189	156	.548	427	363	262	45	5	3041	2738	33	670	1384	10.4	2.39	112	.242	.292	278	.217	37	134	99	25	19.1

● HAL WHITE White, Harold George b: 3/18/19, Utica, N.Y. BR/TR, 5′10″, 170 lbs. Deb: 4/22/41

YEAR	TM/L	W	L	PCT	G	GS	CG	SH	SV	IP	H	HR	BB	SO	RAT	ERA	ERA+	OAV	OOB	BH	AVG	PB	PR	/A	PD	TPI
1941	Det-A	0	0	—	4	0	0	0	0	9	11	0	6	2	17.0	6.00	76	.306	.405	0	.000	-0	-2	-1	0	0.0
1942	Det-A	12	12	.500	34	25	12	4	1	216^2	212	6	82	93	12.4	2.91	136	.252	.323	13	.169	-1	18	25	0	2.6
1943	Det-A	7	12	.368	32	24	7	2	2	177^2	150	6	71	58	11.2	3.39	104	.228	.304	8	.140	-1	-2	3	0	0.2
1946	Det-A	1	1	.500	11	1	1	0	0	27^1	34	5	15	12	16.1	5.60	65	.312	.395	0	.000	-1	-6	-6	1	-0.4
1947	Det-A	4	5	.444	35	5	0	0	2	84^2	91	5	47	33	14.9	3.61	104	.279	.373	3	.167	0	1	1	1	0.3
1948	Det-A	2	1	.667	27	0	0	0	1	42^2	46	2	26	17	15.4	6.12	71	.272	.372	2	.154	0	-9	-8	-1	-0.6
1949	Det-A	1	0	1.000	9	0	0	0	2	12	5	0	4	4	6.8	0.00	—	.125	.205	1	.333	0	6	6	1	0.7
1950	Det-A	9	6	.600	42	8	3	1	1	111	96	7	65	53	13.1	4.54	103	.239	.347	4	.121	-2	0	2	0	0.0
1951	Det-A	3	4	.429	38	4	0	0	4	76	74	7	49	23	14.8	4.74	88	.264	.378	4	.250	0	-5	-5	2	-0.3
1952	Det-A	1	8	.111	41	0	0	0	5	63^1	53	1	39	18	13.1	3.69	103	.237	.350	2	.182	-0	-0	1	1	0.2
1953	StL-A	0	0	—	10	0	0	0	0	10^1	8	1	3	2	10.5	2.61	161	.205	.279	0	.000	0	2	2	0	0.1
	StL-N	6	5	.545	49	0	0	0	7	84^2	84	5	39	32	13.1	2.98	143	.272	.353	0	.000	-2	12	12	1	1.5
1954	StL-N	0	0	—	4	0	0	0	0	5	11	2	4	2	28.8	19.80	21	.440	.533	0	.000	-0	-9	-9	-0	0.0
Total	12	46	54	.460	336	67	23	7	25	920^1	875	47	450	349	13.1	3.78	106	.253	.342	37	.145	-7	6	23	6	4.3

● DEACON WHITE White, James Laurie b: 12/7/1847, Caton, N.Y. d: 7/7/39, Aurora, Ill. BL/TR, 5′11″, 175 lbs. Deb: 5/4/1871 FM♦

YEAR	TM/L	W	L	PCT	G	GS	CG	SH	SV	IP	H	HR	BB	SO	RAT	ERA	ERA+	OAV	OOB	BH	AVG	PB	PR	/A	PD	TPI
1876	Chi-N	0	0	—	1	0	0	0	1	2	1	0	0	3	4.5	0.00	—	.143	.143	104	.343	0	1	1	0	0.1
1890	Buf-P	0	0	—	1	0	0	0	0	8	18	0	2	0	22.5	9.00	46	.429	.455	114	.260	0	-4	-4	-1	0.0
Total	2	0	0	—	2	0	0	0	1	10	19	0	2	3	18.9	7.20	53	.388	.412	1619	.303	1	-4	-4	-0	0.1

● LARRY WHITE White, Larry David b: 9/25/58, San Fernando, Cal. BR/TR, 6′5″, 190 lbs. Deb: 9/20/83

YEAR	TM/L	W	L	PCT	G	GS	CG	SH	SV	IP	H	HR	BB	SO	RAT	ERA	ERA+	OAV	OOB	BH	AVG	PB	PR	/A	PD	TPI
1983	LA-N	0	0	—	4	0	0	0	0	7	4	0	3	5	9.0	1.29	279	.174	.269	0	—	0	2	2	0	0.0
1984	LA-N	0	1	.000	7	1	0	0	0	12	9	2	6	10	11.3	3.00	118	.209	.306	0	.000	-0	1	1	-0	0.0
Total	2	0	1	.000	11	1	0	0	0	19	13	2	9	15	10.4	2.37	150	.197	.293	0	.000	-0	3	3	-0	0.0

● KIRBY WHITE White, Oliver Kirby "Red" or "Buck" b: 1/3/1884, Hillsboro, Ohio d: 4/22/43, Hillsboro, Ohio BL/TR, 6′, 190 lbs. Deb: 5/4/09

YEAR	TM/L	W	L	PCT	G	GS	CG	SH	SV	IP	H	HR	BB	SO	RAT	ERA	ERA+	OAV	OOB	BH	AVG	PB	PR	/A	PD	TPI
1909	Bos-N	6	13	.316	23	19	11	1	0	148^1	134	5	80	53	13.0	3.22	88	.245	.343	8	.160	-1	-10	-7	-1	-1.0
1910	Bos-N	1	2	.333	3	3	3	0	0	26	15	2	12	6	10.4	1.38	240	.188	.316	2	.333	1	5	6	0	0.8
	Pit-N	10	9	.526	30	21	7	3	2	153^1	142	2	75	42	13.0	3.46	90	.258	.352	12	.261	3	-7	-6	-3	-0.7
	Yr	11	11	.500	33	24	10	3	2	179^1	157	4	87	48	12.5	3.16	99	.248	.343	14	.269	4	-3	-1	-3	0.1
1911	Pit-N	0	1	.000	2	1	0	0	0	3	3	1	1	1	12.0	9.00	38	.250	.308	0	.000	-0	-2	-2	0	-0.5
Total	3	17	25	.405	58	44	21	4	2	330^2	294	10	168	102	12.8	3.24	93	.247	.345	22	.214	3	-15	-9	-4	-1.4

● RICK WHITE White, Richard Allen b: 12/23/68, Springfield, Ohio BR/TR, 6′4″, 215 lbs. Deb: 4/6/94

YEAR	TM/L	W	L	PCT	G	GS	CG	SH	SV	IP	H	HR	BB	SO	RAT	ERA	ERA+	OAV	OOB	BH	AVG	PB	PR	/A	PD	TPI
1994	Pit-N	4	5	.444	43	5	0	0	6	75^1	79	9	17	38	12.2	3.82	113	.280	.334	1	.077	-1	3	4	-1	0.4
1995	Pit-N	2	3	.400	15	9	0	0	0	55	66	3	18	29	14.1	4.75	91	.299	.357	1	.067	-1	-3	-3	0	-0.3
1998	TB-A	2	6	.250	38	3	0	0	0	68^2	66	8	23	39	11.9	3.80	129	.253	.318	1	.333	0	6	8	0	0.9
Total	3	8	14	.364	96	17	0	0	6	199	211	20	58	106	12.6	4.07	111	.276	.335	3	.097	-1	6	10	-0	1.0

● STEVE WHITE White, Stephen Vincent b: 12/21/1884, Dorchester, Mass. d: 1/29/75, Braintree, Mass. BR/TR, 5′10″, 160 lbs. Deb: 5/29/12

YEAR	TM/L	W	L	PCT	G	GS	CG	SH	SV	IP	H	HR	BB	SO	RAT	ERA	ERA+	OAV	OOB	BH	AVG	PB	PR	/A	PD	TPI
1912	Was-A	0	0	—	1	0	0	0	0	0^2	2	1	0	1	27.0	0.00	—	.667	.667	0	—	0	0	0	-0	0.0
	Bos-N	0	0	—	3	0	0	0	0	6	9	0	5	2	22.5	6.00	60	.429	.556	0	.000	-0	-2	-2	0	0.0
Total	1	0	0	—	4	0	0	0	0	6^2	11	1	5	3	23.0	5.40	66	.458	.567	0	.000	-0	-1	-1	-0	0.0

● BILL WHITE White, William Dighton b: 5/1/1860, Bridgeport, Ohio d: 12/29/24, Bellaire, Ohio TR , Deb: 5/3/1884 ♦

YEAR	TM/L	W	L	PCT	G	GS	CG	SH	SV	IP	H	HR	BB	SO	RAT	ERA	ERA+	OAV	OOB	BH	AVG	PB	PR	/A	PD	TPI
1886	Lou-a	0	0	—	1	0	0	0	0	1	2	0	2	1	36.0	9.00	40	.400	.571	143	.257	0	-1	-1	0	0.0

● WILL WHITE White, William Henry "Whoop-La" b: 10/11/1854, Caton, N.Y. d: 8/31/11, Port Carling, Ont., Canada BB/TR, 5′9.5″, 175 lbs. Deb: 7/20/1877 FM

YEAR	TM/L	W	L	PCT	G	GS	CG	SH	SV	IP	H	HR	BB	SO	RAT	ERA	ERA+	OAV	OOB	BH	AVG	PB	PR	/A	PD	TPI
1877	Bos-N	2	1	.667	3	3	3	1	0	27	27	0	2	7	9.7	3.00	94	.243	.257	3	.200	-1	-1	-1	-1	-0.2
1878	Cin-N	30	21	.588	52	52	52	5	0	468	477	1	45	169	10.0	1.79	119	.252	.269	28	.142	-8	27	18	-2	0.7
1879	Cin-N	43	31	.581	**76**	75	**75**	4	0	**680**	676	10	68	232	9.8	1.99	117	.238	.256	40	.136	-17	**38**	26	-7	0.2
1880	Cin-N	18	42	.300	62	62	58	3	0	517^1	550	9	56	161	10.5	2.14	116	.255	.273	35	.169	-9	13	20	-7	0.5
1881	Det-N	0	2	.000	2	2	2	0	0	18	24	0	2	5	13.0	5.00	58	.296	.313	0	.000	-1	-4	-4	-1	-0.5
1882	Cin-a	**40**	12	**.769**	54	54	**52**	**8**	0	**480**	411	3	71	122	9.0	1.54	172	.216	.244	55	.266	6	**61**	**59**	13	**7.3**
1883	Cin-a	**43**	22	.662	65	64	64	**6**	0	577	473	16	104	141	9.0	**2.09**	155	.209	.244	54	.225	3	**78**	**74**	-3	**6.6**
1884	Cin-a	34	18	.654	52	52	52	**7**	0	456	479	16	74	118	11.6	3.32	101	.255	.296	35	.190	-2	-3	1	-6	-0.8
1885	Cin-a	18	15	.545	34	34	33	2	0	293^1	295	9	64	80	11.8	3.53	92	.255	.309	20	.169	-3	-9	-9	-3	-1.4
1886	Cin-a	1	2	.333	3	3	3	0	0	26	28	1	10	6	15.2	4.15	85	.280	.379	1	.111	-1	-2	-2	-0	-0.2
Total	10	229	166	.580	403	401	394	36	0	3542^2	3440	65	496	1041	10.2	2.28	120	.239	.268	271	.183	-33	198	179	-18	12.2

● JOHN WHITEHEAD Whitehead, John Henderson "Silent John" b: 4/27/09, Coleman, Tex. d: 10/20/64, Bonham, Tex. BR/TR, 6′2″, 195 lbs. Deb: 4/19/35

YEAR	TM/L	W	L	PCT	G	GS	CG	SH	SV	IP	H	HR	BB	SO	RAT	ERA	ERA+	OAV	OOB	BH	AVG	PB	PR	/A	PD	TPI
1935	Chi-A	13	13	.500	28	27	18	1	0	222^1	209	17	101	72	12.6	3.72	124	.250	.332	12	.146	-5	18	22	3	2.0
1936	Chi-A	13	13	.500	34	32	15	1	1	230^2	254	9	98	70	13.9	4.64	112	.276	.349	21	.241	1	10	14	3	1.7
1937	Chi-A	11	8	.579	26	24	8	4	0	165^2	191	14	56	45	13.7	4.07	113	.294	.354	13	.224	1	10	10	-1	0.9
1938	Chi-A	10	11	.476	32	24	10	2	2	183^1	218	12	80	38	14.8	4.76	103	.299	.370	6	.100	-4	1	3	-1	-0.1

YEAR	TM/L	W	L	PCT	G	GS	CG	SH	SV	IP	H	HR	BB	SO	RAT	ERA	ERA+	OAV	OOB	BH	AVG	PB	PR	/A	PD	TPI
1939	Chi-A	0	3	.000	7	4	0	0	0	32	60	4	5	9	18.3	8.16	58	.408	.428	0	.000	-1	-13	-12	0	-1.0
	StL-A	1	3	.250	26	4	0	0	1	66	88	10	17	9	14.6	5.86	83	.321	.365	1	.059	-1	-9	-7	1	-0.4
	Yr	1	6	.143	33	8	0	0	1	98	148	14	22	18	15.8	6.61	73	.352	.387	1	.038	-3	-22	-20	1	-1.4
1940	StL-A	1	3	.250	15	4	1	1	0	40	46	3	14	11	13.5	5.40	85	.286	.343	2	.167	-1	-5	-4	-1	-0.4
1942	StL-A	0	0	—	4	0	0	0	0	4	8	0	1	0	22.5	6.75	55	.421	.476	0	—	0	-1	-1	0	0.0
Total	7	49	54	.476	172	119	52	9	4	944	1074	69	372	254	14.0	4.60	105	.287	.355	55	.169	-11	11	24	5	2.7

● MILT WHITEHEAD Whitehead, Milton P. b: 1862, Canada d: 8/15/01, Highland, Cal. BB , Deb: 4/20/1884 ♦

YEAR	TM/L	W	L	PCT	G	GS	CG	SH	SV	IP	H	HR	BB	SO	RAT	ERA	ERA+	OAV	OOB	BH	AVG	PB	PR	/A	PD	TPI
1884	StL-U	0	1	.000	1	1	1	0	0	8	14	0	2	2	18.0	9.00	27	.359	.390	83	.211	-0	-6	-6	0	-0.5

● EARL WHITEHILL Whitehill, Earl Oliver b: 2/7/1900, Cedar Rapids, Iowa d: 10/22/54, Omaha, Neb. BL/TL, 5'9.5", 174 lbs. Deb: 9/15/23 C

YEAR	TM/L	W	L	PCT	G	GS	CG	SH	SV	IP	H	HR	BB	SO	RAT	ERA	ERA+	OAV	OOB	BH	AVG	PB	PR	/A	PD	TPI
1923	Det-A	2	0	1.000	8	3	1	0	0	33	22	2	15	19	10.9	2.73	142	.188	.296	4	.364	1	5	4	-0	0.3
1924	Det-A	17	9	.654	35	32	16	2	0	233	260	8	79	65	13.6	3.86	106	.288	.353	19	.213	1	10	6	-0	0.7
1925	Det-A	11	11	.500	35	33	15	1	2	239^1	267	13	88	83	13.7	4.66	92	.293	.361	19	.218	0	-7	-9	-1	-0.8
1926	Det-A	16	13	.552	36	34	13	0	0	252^1	271	7	79	109	12.8	3.99	102	.277	.336	23	.253	4	1	2	-1	0.5
1927	Det-A	16	14	.533	41	31	17	3	3	236	238	4	105	95	13.4	3.36	125	.267	.350	16	.205	-0	21	22	-3	2.3
1928	Det-A	11	16	.407	31	30	12	1	0	196^1	214	8	78	93	13.4	4.31	95	.277	.344	13	.194	-1	-6	-4	1	-0.6
1929	Det-A	14	15	.483	38	28	18	1	1	245^1	267	16	96	103	13.4	4.62	93	.280	.348	23	.256	5	-10	-9	-0	-0.5
1930	Det-A	17	13	.567	34	31	16	0	1	220^2	248	8	80	109	13.7	4.24	113	.285	.351	16	.193	-4	10	14	-2	1.0
1931	Det-A	13	16	.448	34	34	22	0	0	271^1	287	22	118	81	13.6	4.08	112	.274	.351	15	.155	-5	9	15	2	1.1
1932	Det-A	16	12	.571	33	31	17	3	0	244	255	17	93	81	13.0	4.54	104	.269	.337	22	.244	1	-2	5	-2	0.4
1933	*Was-A	22	8	.733	39	37	19	2	1	270	271	9	100	96	12.5	3.33	125	.262	.329	24	.222	2	28	25	-2	2.5
1934	Was-A	14	11	.560	32	31	15	0	0	235	269	10	94	96	14.0	4.52	96	.290	.357	17	.200	4	-1	-5	-0	-0.2
1935	Was-A	14	13	.519	34	34	19	1	0	279^1	318	16	104	102	13.8	4.29	101	.289	.354	19	.183	-1	5	1	1	0.1
1936	Was-A	14	11	.560	28	28	14	0	0	212^1	252	17	89	63	14.5	4.87	98	.294	.362	13	.169	-0	4	-2	-1	-0.3
1937	Cle-A	8	8	.500	33	22	6	1	2	147	189	9	80	53	16.8	6.49	71	.322	.409	11	.224	1	-31	-31	1	-2.5
1938	Cle-A	9	8	.529	26	23	4	0	0	160^1	187	18	83	60	15.7	5.56	83	.289	.378	7	.125	-2	-14	-16	-2	-1.6
1939	Chi-N	4	7	.364	24	11	2	1	1	89^1	102	8	50	42	15.8	5.14	77	.292	.389	3	.103	-2	-12	-12	-1	-1.6
Total	17	218	185	.541	541	473	226	16	11	3564^2	3917	192	1431	1350	13.8	4.36	100	.282	.353	264	.204	4	10	6	-9	0.8

● CHARLIE WHITEHOUSE Whitehouse, Charles Evis "Lefty"
b: 1/25/1894, Charleston, Ill. d: 7/19/60, Indianapolis, Ind BB/TL, 6', 152 lbs. Deb: 8/29/14

YEAR	TM/L	W	L	PCT	G	GS	CG	SH	SV	IP	H	HR	BB	SO	RAT	ERA	ERA+	OAV	OOB	BH	AVG	PB	PR	/A	PD	TPI
1914	Ind-F	2	0	1.000	8	2	2	0	0	26	34	0	5	10	13.8	4.85	64	.324	.360	0	.000	-1	-6	-5	-0	-0.5
1915	New-F	2	2	.500	11	3	1	0	0	39^2	46	0	17	18	15.4	4.31	59	.299	.386	0	.000	-1	-7	-8	-1	-0.9
1919	Was-A	0	1	.000	6	1	0	0	0	12	13	1	6	5	14.3	4.50	71	.283	.365	0	.000	-0	-2	-2	-0	-0.2
Total	3	4	3	.571	25	6	3	0	0	77^2	93	1	28	33	14.7	4.52	63	.305	.375	0	.000	-2	-14	-14	-1	-1.6

● GIL WHITEHOUSE Whitehouse, Gilbert Arthur b: 10/15/1893, Somerville, Mass. d: 2/14/26, Brewer, Me. BB/TR, 5'10", 170 lbs. Deb: 6/20/12 ♦

YEAR	TM/L	W	L	PCT	G	GS	CG	SH	SV	IP	H	HR	BB	SO	RAT	ERA	ERA+	OAV	OOB	BH	AVG	PB	PR	/A	PD	TPI
1915	New-F	0	0	—	1	0	0	0	0	1	0	0	1	0	9.0	0.00	—	.000	.250	27	.225	0	0	0	-0	0.0

● LEN WHITEHOUSE Whitehouse, Leonard Joseph b: 9/10/57, Burlington, Vt. BL/TL, 5'11", 175 lbs. Deb: 9/1/81

YEAR	TM/L	W	L	PCT	G	GS	CG	SH	SV	IP	H	HR	BB	SO	RAT	ERA	ERA+	OAV	OOB	BH	AVG	PB	PR	/A	PD	TPI
1981	Tex-A	0	1	.000	2	1	0	0	0	3^1	8	1	2	2	27.0	16.20	21	.500	.556	0	—	0	-5	-5	-0	-0.9
1983	Min-A	7	1	.875	60	0	0	0	2	73^2	70	6	44	44	14.2	4.15	102	.261	.369	0	—	0	-1	1	-1	-0.3
1984	Min-A	2	2	.500	30	0	0	0	1	31^1	29	3	17	18	13.8	3.16	133	.254	.361	0	—	0	3	4	-0	0.1
1985	Min-A	0	0	—	5	0	0	0	1	7^1	12	4	2	4	17.2	11.05	40	.353	.389	0	—	0	-6	-5	-0	-0.5
Total	4	9	4	.692	97	1	0	0	4	115^2	119	14	65	68	14.6	4.67	90	.275	.375	0	—	0	-8	-6	-1	-1.6

● WALLY WHITEHURST Whitehurst, Walter Richard b: 4/11/64, Shreveport, La. BR/TR, 6'3", 195 lbs. Deb: 7/17/89

YEAR	TM/L	W	L	PCT	G	GS	CG	SH	SV	IP	H	HR	BB	SO	RAT	ERA	ERA+	OAV	OOB	BH	AVG	PB	PR	/A	PD	TPI
1989	NY-N	0	1	.000	9	1	0	0	0	14	17	2	5	9	14.1	4.50	73	.293	.349	0	.000	0	-2	-2	-0	-0.1
1990	NY-N	1	0	1.000	38	0	0	0	2	65^2	63	5	9	46	9.9	3.29	114	.251	.277	2	.250	0	4	3	0	0.1
1991	NY-N	7	12	.368	36	20	0	0	1	133^1	142	12	25	87	11.5	4.18	87	.274	.313	6	.182	1	-7	-8	1	-0.8
1992	NY-N	3	9	.250	44	11	0	0	0	97	99	4	33	70	12.6	3.62	96	.264	.330	4	.182	1	-1	-2	1	-0.1
1993	SD-N	4	7	.364	21	19	0	0	0	105^2	109	11	30	57	12.1	3.83	108	.276	.332	2	.083	-2	2	4	0	0.2
1994	SD-N	4	7	.364	13	13	0	0	0	64	84	8	26	43	15.6	4.92	83	.319	.383	2	.105	0	-5	-6	0	-0.8
1996	NY-A	1	1	.500	2	2	0	0	0	8	11	1	2	1	14.6	6.75	73	.324	.361	0	—	0	-2	-2	0	-0.3
Total	7	20	37	.351	163	66	0	0	3	487^2	525	43	130	313	12.3	4.02	94	.277	.328	16	.150	1	-11	-12	2	-1.8

● MARK WHITEN Whiten, Mark Anthony b: 11/25/66, Pensacola, Fla. BB/TR, 6'3", 215 lbs. Deb: 7/12/90 ♦

YEAR	TM/L	W	L	PCT	G	GS	CG	SH	SV	IP	H	HR	BB	SO	RAT	ERA	ERA+	OAV	OOB	BH	AVG	PB	PR	/A	PD	TPI
1998	Cle-A	0	0	—	1	0	0	0	0	1	1	0	2	3	36.0	9.00	53	.250	.571	64	.283	0	-0	-0	0	0.0

● SEAN WHITESIDE Whiteside, David Sean b: 4/19/71, Lakeland, Fla. BL/TL, 6'4", 190 lbs. Deb: 4/29/95

YEAR	TM/L	W	L	PCT	G	GS	CG	SH	SV	IP	H	HR	BB	SO	RAT	ERA	ERA+	OAV	OOB	BH	AVG	PB	PR	/A	PD	TPI
1995	Det-A	0	0	—	2	0	0	0	0	3^2	7	1	4	2	27.0	14.73	32	.438	.550	0	—	0	-4	-4	-0	0.0

● MATT WHITESIDE Whiteside, Matthew Christopher b: 8/8/67, Charleston, Mo. BR/TR, 6', 205 lbs. Deb: 8/5/92

YEAR	TM/L	W	L	PCT	G	GS	CG	SH	SV	IP	H	HR	BB	SO	RAT	ERA	ERA+	OAV	OOB	BH	AVG	PB	PR	/A	PD	TPI
1992	Tex-A	1	1	.500	20	0	0	0	4	28	26	1	11	13	11.9	1.93	197	.245	.316	0	—	0	6	6	-0	0.7
1993	Tex-A	2	1	.667	60	0	0	0	1	73	78	7	23	39	12.6	4.32	96	.281	.338	0	—	0	0	-1	-1	0.2
1994	Tex-A	2	2	.500	47	0	0	0	1	61	68	6	28	37	14.3	5.02	96	.286	.363	0	—	0	-1	-1	-1	-0.1
1995	Tex-A	5	4	.556	40	0	0	0	3	53	48	5	19	46	11.5	4.08	118	.242	.312	0	—	0	4	4	-1	0.6
1996	Tex-A	0	1	.000	14	0	0	0	0	32^1	43	8	11	15	15.0	6.68	78	.321	.372	0	—	0	-6	-5	-0	-0.3
1997	Tex-A	4	1	.800	42	1	0	0	0	72^2	85	4	26	44	14.1	5.08	94	.296	.361	0	—	0	-4	-2	2	-0.1
1998	Phi-N	1	1	.500	10	0	0	0	0	18	27	6	5	14	16.0	8.50	51	.338	.376	0	.000	-0	-9	-8	0	-0.8
Total	7	15	11	.577	233	1	0	0	9	338	375	37	123	208	13.4	4.82	95	.284	.348	0	.000	-0	-10	-9	-1	0.2

● JESSE WHITING Whiting, Jesse W. b: 5/30/1879, Philadelphia, Pa. d: 10/28/37, Philadelphia, Pa. Deb: 9/27/02

YEAR	TM/L	W	L	PCT	G	GS	CG	SH	SV	IP	H	HR	BB	SO	RAT	ERA	ERA+	OAV	OOB	BH	AVG	PB	PR	/A	PD	TPI
1902	Phi-N	0	1	.000	1	1	1	0	0	9	13	0	6	0	19.0	5.00	56	.333	.422	1	.333	0	-2	-2	0	-0.2
1906	Bro-N	1	1	.500	3	2	2	1	0	24^2	26	0	6	7	12.0	2.92	86	.286	.337	3	.300	1	-1	-1	1	0.1
1907	Bro-N	0	0	—	1	0	0	0	0	3	3	0	3	2	18.0	12.00	20	.273	.429	0	.000	-0	-3	-3	0	0.0
Total	3	1	2	.333	5	3	3	1	0	36^2	42	0	15	9	14.2	4.17	62	.298	.369	4	.267	0	-6	-6	1	-0.1

● ART WHITNEY Whitney, Arthur Wilson b: 1/16/1858, Brockton, Mass. d: 8/15/43, Lowell, Mass. BR/TR, 5'8", 155 lbs. Deb: 5/1/1880 F♦

YEAR	TM/L	W	L	PCT	G	GS	CG	SH	SV	IP	H	HR	BB	SO	RAT	ERA	ERA+	OAV	OOB	BH	AVG	PB	PR	/A	PD	TPI
1882	Det-N	0	1	.000	3	2	1	0	0	18	31	1	8	11	19.5	6.00	49	.373	.429	21	.183	-1	-6	-6	-1	-0.3
1886	Pit-a	0	0	—	1	0	0	0	0	6	7	0	3	2	15.0	3.00	113	.304	.385	122	.239	0	0	0	-0	0.0
1889	*NY-N	0	1	.000	1	0	0	0	0	6	7	0	3	3	15.0	3.00	131	.280	.357	103	.218	0	1	1	-0	0.1
Total	3	0	2	.000	5	2	1	0	0	30	45	1	14	16	17.7	4.80	67	.344	.407	820	.223	-1	-5	-5	-1	-0.2

● JIM WHITNEY Whitney, James Evans "Grasshopper Jim" b: 11/10/1857, Conklin, N.Y. d: 5/21/1891, Binghamton, N.Y. BL/TR, 6'2", 172 lbs. Deb: 5/2/1881 ♦

YEAR	TM/L	W	L	PCT	G	GS	CG	SH	SV	IP	H	HR	BB	SO	RAT	ERA	ERA+	OAV	OOB	BH	AVG	PB	PR	/A	PD	TPI
1881	Bos-N	**31**	33	.484	**66**	63	**57**	6	0	**552**^{1}	548	6	90	162	10.4	2.48	107	.248	.277	72	.255	11	18	11	-4	1.9
1882	Bos-N	24	21	.533	49	48	46	3	0	420	404	3	41	180	9.5	2.64	109	.237	.255	81	.323	23	12	11	1	3.1
1883	Bos-N	37	21	.638	62	56	54	1	**2**	514	492	7	35	**345**	9.2	2.24	138	.238	.251	115	.281	20	51	49	0	6.0
1884	Bos-N	23	14	.622	38	37	35	6	0	336	272	12	27	270	8.0	2.09	138	.207	.223	70	.259	10	33	30	4	4.0
1885	Bos-N	18	32	.360	51	50	50	2	0	441^1	503	14	37	200	11.0	2.98	90	.272	.286	68	.234	7	-8	-14	6	-0.2
1886	KC-N	12	32	.273	46	44	42	3	0	393	465	9	55	167	11.9	4.49	84	.284	.308	59	.239	5	-51	-31	6	-1.7
1887	Was-N	24	21	.533	47	47	46	2	0	404^2	430	16	42	146	10.9	3.22	126	.259	.284	53	.264	9	38	38	4	4.6
1888	Was-N	18	21	.462	39	39	37	3	0	325	317	7	54	79	10.5	3.05	92	.245	.280	24	.170	-1	-7	-9	-1	-1.1
1889	Ind-N	2	7	.222	9	8	7	0	0	70	106	4	19	16	16.3	6.81	61	.339	.380	12	.375	5	-22	-21	-1	-1.5
1890	Phi-a	2	2	.500	6	4	3	0	0	40	61	1	11	6	16.4	5.17	74	.341	.382	5	.238	-0	-6	-6	-0	-0.5
Total	10	191	204	.484	413	396	377	26	2	3496^1	3598	79	411	1571	10.4	2.97	105	.253	.275	559	.261	89	60	55	15	14.6

● BILL WHITROCK Whitrock, William Franklin b: 3/4/1870, Cincinnati, Ohio d: 7/26/35, Derby, Conn. TR , 5'7.5", 170 lbs. Deb: 5/3/1890

YEAR	TM/L	W	L	PCT	G	GS	CG	SH	SV	IP	H	HR	BB	SO	RAT	ERA	ERA+	OAV	OOB	BH	AVG	PB	PR	/A	PD	TPI
1890	StL-a	5	6	.455	16	11	10	0	1	105	104	2	40	39	12.9	3.51	123	.251	.327	7	.146	-3	4	9	0	0.6
1893	Lou-N	2	5	.286	8	8	5	0	0	46^2	64	3	19	8	16.8	8.10	54	.317	.387	7	.280	1	-18	-19	0	-1.8
1894	Lou-N	0	1	.000	1	1	0	0	0	4	8	0	2	0	22.5	9.00	57	.400	.455	0	.000	-0	-2	-2	-0	-0.3

YEAR	TM/L	W	L	PCT	G	GS	CG	SH	SV	IP	H	HR	BB	SO	RAT	ERA	ERA+	OAV	OOB	BH	AVG	PB	PR	/A	PD	TPI
	Cin-N	2	6	.250	10	8	8	0	0	70^1	110	7	39	9	20.2	6.65	84	.351	.438	13	.217	-2	-10	-9	0	-0.8
	Yr	2	7	.222	11	9	8	0	0	74^1	118	7	41	9	20.3	6.78	82	.354	.439	13	.210	-3	-12	-10	0	-1.1
1896	Phi-N	0	1	.000	2	1	1	0	0	9	10	0	3	1	13.0	3.00	144	.278	.333	0	.000	-0	1	1	-0	0.1
Total	4	9	19	.321	37	29	24	0	1	235	296	12	103	57	16.0	5.44	87	.300	.378	27	.196	-5	-24	-18	1	-2.2

● ED WHITSON

Whitson, Eddie Lee b: 5/19/55, Johnson City, Tenn. BR/TR, 6′3″, 195 lbs. Deb: 9/4/77

YEAR	TM/L	W	L	PCT	G	GS	CG	SH	SV	IP	H	HR	BB	SO	RAT	ERA	ERA+	OAV	OOB	BH	AVG	PB	PR	/A	PD	TPI
1977	Pit-N	1	0	1.000	5	2	0	0	0	15^2	11	0	9	10	11.5	3.45	116	.204	.317	0	.000	-0	1	1	-0	0.0
1978	Pit-N	5	6	.455	43	0	0	0	4	74^1	66	5	37	64	12.7	3.27	113	.243	.338	2	.182	-0	3	4	-1	0.5
1979	Pit-N	2	3	.400	19	7	0	0	1	57^2	53	6	36	31	14.0	4.37	89	.238	.346	0	.000	-1	-4	-3	-1	-0.4
	SF-N	5	8	.385	18	17	2	0	0	100^1	98	5	39	62	12.6	3.95	89	.254	.329	5	.156	-1	-2	-5	-0	-0.7
	Yr	7	11	.389	37	24	2	0	1	158	151	11	75	93	13.1	4.10	89	.248	.334	5	.111	-2	-6	-8	-1	-1.1
1980	SF-N☆	11	13	.458	34	34	6	2	0	211^2	222	7	56	90	12.0	3.10	114	.271	.321	6	.091	-4	12	10	-2	0.5
1981	SF-N	6	9	.400	22	22	2	1	0	123	130	10	47	65	13.1	4.02	85	.273	.340	3	.091	-1	-7	-8	-2	-1.2
1982	Cle-A	4	2	.667	40	9	1	1	2	107^2	91	6	58	61	12.5	3.26	125	.231	.330	0	—	0	10	10	-2	0.4
1983	SD-N	5	7	.417	31	21	2	0	1	144^1	143	23	50	81	12.1	4.30	81	.256	.318	8	.182	1	-11	-13	-4	-1.3
1984	*SD-N	14	8	.636	31	31	1	0	0	189	181	16	42	103	10.8	3.24	110	.255	.299	3	.049	-5	7	7	1	0.4
1985	NY-A	10	8	.556	30	30	2	2	0	158^2	201	19	43	89	14.0	4.88	82	.309	.354	0	—	0	-13	-15	-2	-1.5
1986	NY-A	5	2	.714	14	4	0	0	0	37	54	5	23	27	18.7	7.54	54	.335	.418	0	—	0	-14	-14	-0	-2.1
	SD-N	1	7	.125	17	12	0	0	0	75^2	85	8	37	46	14.5	5.59	65	.287	.366	3	.167	-0	-16	-16	0	-1.5
1987	SD-N	10	13	.435	36	34	3	1	0	205^2	197	36	64	135	11.6	4.73	84	.251	.310	8	.123	-1	-15	-18	-2	-2.1
1988	SD-N	13	11	.542	34	33	3	1	0	205^1	202	17	45	118	10.9	3.77	90	.259	.301	11	.167	1	-7	-9	-1	-0.9
1989	SD-N	16	11	.593	33	33	5	1	0	227	198	22	48	117	10.0	2.66	132	.235	.281	10	.139	1	21	21	-2	2.4
1990	SD-N	14	9	.609	32	32	6	3	0	228^2	215	13	47	127	10.4	2.60	147	.251	.291	10	.149	1	30	31	3	3.4
1991	SD-N	4	6	.400	13	12	2	0	0	78^2	93	13	17	40	12.6	5.03	75	.299	.335	3	.125	-1	-12	-11	-1	-1.3
Total	15	126	123	.506	452	333	35	12	8	2240^1	2240	211	698	1266	11.9	3.79	97	.261	.319	72	.125	-11	-17	-28	-14	-5.4

● WALT WHITTAKER

Whittaker, Walter Elton "Doc" b: 6/11/1894, Chelsea, Mass. d: 8/9/65, Pembroke, Mass. BL/TR, 5′9.5″, 165 lbs. Deb: 7/6/16

YEAR	TM/L	W	L	PCT	G	GS	CG	SH	SV	IP	H	HR	BB	SO	RAT	ERA	ERA+	OAV	OOB	BH	AVG	PB	PR	/A	PD	TPI
1916	Phi-A	0	0	—	1	0	0	0	0	2	3	0	2	0	22.5	4.50	63	.375	.500	0	—	0	-0	-0	0	0.0

● KEVIN WICKANDER

Wickander, Kevin Dean b: 1/4/65, Fort Dodge, Iowa BL/TL, 6′2″, 202 lbs. Deb: 8/10/89

YEAR	TM/L	W	L	PCT	G	GS	CG	SH	SV	IP	H	HR	BB	SO	RAT	ERA	ERA+	OAV	OOB	BH	AVG	PB	PR	/A	PD	TPI
1989	Cle-A	0	0	—	2	0	0	0	0	2^2	6	0	2	0	27.0	3.38	117	.462	.533	0	—	0	0	0	-0	-0.1
1990	Cle-A	0	1	.000	10	0	0	0	0	12^1	14	0	4	10	13.9	3.65	107	.304	.373	0	—	0	0	0	-0	0.0
1992	Cle-A	2	0	1.000	44	0	0	0	1	41	39	1	28	38	15.6	3.07	127	.258	.388	0	—	0	4	4	0	0.3
1993	Cle-A	0	0	—	11	0	0	0	0	8^2	15	3	3	3	18.7	4.15	104	.366	.409	0	—	0	0	0	-0	0.0
	Cin-N	1	0	1.000	33	0	0	0	0	25^1	32	5	19	20	18.8	6.75	60	.308	.424	0	.000	-0	-8	-8	-0	-0.3
1995	Det-A	0	0	—	21	0	0	0	1	17^1	18	1	9	9	14.5	2.60	183	.273	.368	0	—	0	4	4	0	0.1
	Mil-A	0	0	—	8	0	0	0	0	6	1	0	3	2	6.0	0.00	—	.059	.200	0	—	0	3	3	-0	-0.1
	Yr	0	0	—	29	0	0	0	1	23^1	19	1	12	11	12.0	1.93	250	.224	.320	0	—	0	7	7	0	0.0
1996	Mil-A	2	0	1.000	21	0	0	0	0	25^1	26	2	17	19	15.3	4.97	104	.265	.374	0	—	0	0	1	0	0.0
Total	6	5	1	.833	150	0	0	0	2	138^2	151	12	85	101	15.8	4.02	108	.282	.388	0	.000	-0	4	5	-1	-0.1

● KEMP WICKER

Wicker, Kemp Caswell (b: Kemp Caswell Whicker)
b: 8/13/06, Kernersville, N.C. d: 6/11/73, Kernersville, N.C BR/TL, 5′11″, 182 lbs. Deb: 8/14/36

YEAR	TM/L	W	L	PCT	G	GS	CG	SH	SV	IP	H	HR	BB	SO	RAT	ERA	ERA+	OAV	OOB	BH	AVG	PB	PR	/A	PD	TPI
1936	NY-A	1	2	.333	7	0	0	0	0	20	31	2	11	5	18.9	7.65	61	.356	.429	1	.143	-0	-6	-7	0	-0.8
1937	*NY-A	7	3	.700	16	10	6	1	0	88	107	8	26	14	13.6	4.40	101	.296	.343	4	.114	-3	2	0	-2	-0.4
1938	NY-A	1	0	1.000	1	0	0	0	0	1	0	0	1	0	9.0	0.00	—	.000	.250	0	—	0	1	1	-0	0.5
1941	Bro-N	1	2	.333	16	2	0	0	1	32	30	3	14	8	12.4	3.66	100	.252	.331	1	.250	0	-0	0	-0	0.0
Total	4	10	7	.588	40	12	6	1	1	141	168	13	52	27	14.0	4.66	92	.294	.353	6	.130	-2	-3	-5	-2	-0.7

● BOB WICKER

Wicker, Robert Kitridge b: 5/25/1877, Bono, Ind. d: 1/22/55, Evanston, Ill. BL/TR, 5′11″, 210 lbs. Deb: 8/11/01

YEAR	TM/L	W	L	PCT	G	GS	CG	SH	SV	IP	H	HR	BB	SO	RAT	ERA	ERA+	OAV	OOB	BH	AVG	PB	PR	/A	PD	TPI
1901	StL-N	0	0	—	1	0	0	0	0	3	4	0	1	2	15.0	0.00	—	.308	.357	1	.333	0	1	1	-0	0.0
1902	StL-N	5	12	.294	22	16	14	1	0	152^1	159	1	45	78	12.2	3.19	86	.269	.322	18	.234	1	-7	-8	3	-0.4
1903	StL-N	0	0	—	1	0	0	0	0	5	4	0	3	3	12.6	0.00	—	.174	.269	0	.000	-0	2	2	1	0.0
	Chi-N	20	9	.690	32	27	24	1	1	247	236	3	74	110	11.4	3.02	104	.253	.311	24	.245	6	7	3	-5	0.4
	Yr	20	9	.690	33	27	24	1	1	252	240	3	77	113	11.4	2.96	106	.252	.309	24	.240	6	9	5	-4	0.4
1904	Chi-N	17	9	.654	30	27	23	4	0	229	201	6	58	99	10.3	2.67	100	.232	.282	34	.219	1	2	-0	-5	-0.5
1905	Chi-N	13	6	.684	22	22	17	4	0	178	139	3	47	86	9.5	2.02	147	.221	.276	10	.139	-2	19	19	-3	1.4
1906	Chi-N	3	5	.375	10	8	5	0	0	72^1	70	0	19	25	11.1	2.99	88	.257	.306	2	.100	-1	-3	-3	-1	-0.5
	Cin-N	6	11	.353	20	17	14	0	0	150	150	3	46	69	11.8	2.70	102	.263	.319	9	.180	2	-1	1	-4	-0.1
	Yr	9	16	.360	30	25	19	0	0	222^1	220	3	65	94	11.6	2.79	97	.261	.315	11	.157	1	-4	-2	-5	-0.6
Total	6	64	52	.552	138	117	97	10	1	1036^2	963	16	293	472	11.0	2.73	105	.247	.301	98	.205	6	20	16	-15	0.3

● DAVE WICKERSHAM

Wickersham, David Clifford b: 9/27/35, Erie, Pa. BR/TR, 6′3″, 190 lbs. Deb: 9/18/60

YEAR	TM/L	W	L	PCT	G	GS	CG	SH	SV	IP	H	HR	BB	SO	RAT	ERA	ERA+	OAV	OOB	BH	AVG	PB	PR	/A	PD	TPI
1960	KC-A	0	0	—	5	0	0	0	2	8^1	4	0	1	3	5.4	1.08	369	.148	.179	0	.000	-0	3	3	0	0.1
1961	KC-A	2	1	.667	17	0	0	0	2	21	25	0	5	10	13.7	5.14	81	.309	.364	2	.667	1	-3	-2	0	-0.2
1962	KC-A	11	4	.733	30	9	3	0	1	110	105	13	43	61	12.8	4.17	101	.257	.340	2	.057	-3	-2	1	1	-0.1
1963	KC-A	12	15	.444	38	34	4	1	1	237^2	244	21	79	118	12.6	4.09	95	.268	.333	11	.138	-3	-12	-5	1	-0.8
1964	Det-A	19	12	.613	40	36	11	1	1	254	224	28	81	164	11.2	3.44	106	.232	.299	6	.073	-5	5	6	-0	0.1
1965	Det-A	9	14	.391	34	27	8	3	0	195^1	179	12	61	109	11.6	3.78	92	.241	.308	4	.069	-4	-7	-7	1	-1.0
1966	Det-A	8	3	.727	38	14	3	0	1	140^2	139	14	54	93	12.9	3.20	109	.261	.338	2	.044	-3	4	4	1	0.1
1967	Det-A	4	5	.444	36	4	0	0	4	85^1	72	6	33	44	11.5	2.74	119	.235	.318	0	.000	-2	5	5	1	0.5
1968	Pit-N	1	0	1.000	11	0	0	0	1	20^2	21	0	13	9	14.8	3.48	84	.276	.382	1	.333	0	-1	-1	-0	-0.1
1969	KC-A	2	3	.400	34	0	0	0	5	50	58	6	14	27	13.3	3.96	93	.294	.347	0	.000	0	-2	-2	0	-0.1
Total	10	68	57	.544	283	124	29	5	18	1123	1071	100	384	638	12.1	3.66	100	.252	.323	28	.086	-18	-11	2	4	-1.5

● BOB WICKMAN

Wickman, Robert Joe b: 2/6/69, Green Bay, Wis. BR/TR, 6′1″, 212 lbs. Deb: 8/24/92

YEAR	TM/L	W	L	PCT	G	GS	CG	SH	SV	IP	H	HR	BB	SO	RAT	ERA	ERA+	OAV	OOB	BH	AVG	PB	PR	/A	PD	TPI
1992	NY-A	6	1	.857	8	8	0	0	0	50^1	51	2	20	21	13.1	4.11	95	.273	.349	0	—	0	-1	-1	0	-0.1
1993	NY-A	14	4	.778	41	19	1	1	4	140	156	13	69	70	14.8	4.63	90	.284	.369	0	—	0	-5	-7	-1	-0.6
1994	NY-A	5	4	.556	**53**	0	0	0	6	70	54	3	27	56	10.5	3.09	148	.213	.292	0	—	0	13	12	-0	1.6
1995	*NY-A	2	4	.333	63	1	0	0	1	80	77	6	33	51	12.9	4.05	114	.253	.336	0	—	0	6	5	0	0.4
1996	NY-A	4	1	.800	58	0	0	0	0	79	94	7	34	61	15.2	4.67	106	.299	.377	0	—	0	3	2	3	0.4
	Mil-A	3	0	1.000	12	0	0	0	0	16^2	12	3	10	14	11.9	3.24	160	.200	.314	0	—	0	3	4	-0	0.4
	Yr	7	1	.875	70	0	0	0	0	95^2	106	10	44	75	14.1	4.42	113	.277	.351	0	—	0	6	6	3	0.8
1997	Mil-A	7	6	.538	74	0	0	0	1	95^2	89	8	41	78	12.5	2.73	169	.252	.335	0	—	0	20	20	1	2.5
1998	Mil-N	6	9	.400	72	0	0	0	25	82^1	79	5	39	71	13.3	3.72	116	.262	.355	0	.000	-0	5	5	1	1.2
Total	7	47	29	.618	381	28	1	1	37	614	612	47	273	422	13.3	3.88	115	.264	.347	0	.000	-0	44	39	4	5.8

● AL WIDMAR

Widmar, Albert Joseph b: 3/20/25, Cleveland, Ohio BR/TR, 6′3″, 185 lbs. Deb: 4/25/47 C

YEAR	TM/L	W	L	PCT	G	GS	CG	SH	SV	IP	H	HR	BB	SO	RAT	ERA	ERA+	OAV	OOB	BH	AVG	PB	PR	/A	PD	TPI
1947	Bos-A	0	0	—	2	0	0	0	0	1^1	1	1	2	1	20.3	13.50	29	.200	.429	0	—	0	-1	-1	0	0.0
1948	StL-A	2	6	.250	49	0	0	0	1	82^2	88	4	48	34	14.8	4.46	102	.275	.370	3	.300	1	-2	1	2	0.3
1950	StL-A	7	15	.318	36	26	8	1	4	194^2	211	16	74	78	13.3	4.76	104	.271	.337	10	.149	-3	-4	4	1	0.2
1951	StL-A	4	9	.308	26	16	4	0	0	107^2	157	19	52	28	17.6	6.52	67	.344	.414	5	.167	-1	-29	-25	1	-2.6
1952	Chi-A	0	0	—	1	0	0	0	0	2	4	1	0	2	18.0	4.50	81	.444	.444	0	—	0	-0	-0	-0	0.0
Total	5	13	30	.302	114	42	12	1	5	388^1	461	41	176	143	14.9	5.21	90	.294	.367	18	.168	-4	-36	-22	3	-2.1

● WILD BILL WIDNER

Widner, William Waterfield b: 6/3/1867, Cincinnati, Ohio d: 12/10/08, Cincinnati, Ohio BR/TR, 6′, 180 lbs. Deb: 6/8/1887

YEAR	TM/L	W	L	PCT	G	GS	CG	SH	SV	IP	H	HR	BB	SO	RAT	ERA	ERA+	OAV	OOB	BH	AVG	PB	PR	/A	PD	TPI
1887	Cin-a	1	0	1.000	1	1	1	0	0	9	11	2	2	0	14.0	5.00	87	.275	.326	1	.250	-0	-1	-1	0	0.0
1888	Was-N	5	7	.417	13	13	13	0	0	115	111	7	22	33	10.9	2.82	100	.247	.291	12	.200	-1	0	-0	-0	-0.1
1889	Col-a	12	20	.375	41	34	25	2	1	294	368	11	85	63	14.4	5.20	70	.297	.351	28	.211	-2	-44	-52	0	-4.2
1890	Col-a	4	8	.333	13	10	8	1	0	96	103	3	24	14	12.2	3.28	109	.266	.314	8	.195	-1	6	3	2	0.4

YEAR	TM/L	W	L	PCT	G	GS	CG	SH	SV	IP	H	HR	BB	SO	RAT	ERA	ERA+	OAV	OOB	BH	AVG	PB	PR	/A	PD	TPI
1891	Cin-a	0	1	.000	1	1	1	0	0	8	13	0	4	0	21.4	7.88	52	.351	.442	1	.250	-0	-4	-3	-0	-0.3
Total	5	22	36	.379	69	59	48	3	1	522	606	23	137	110	13.3	4.36	79	.281	.333	50	.207	-3	-42	-52	2	-4.2

● **TED WIEAND** Wieand, Franklin Delano Roosevelt b: 4/4/33, Walnutport, Pa. BR/TR, 6'2", 195 lbs. Deb: 9/27/58

YEAR	TM/L	W	L	PCT	G	GS	CG	SH	SV	IP	H	HR	BB	SO	RAT	ERA	ERA+	OAV	OOB	BH	AVG	PB	PR	/A	PD	TPI
1958	Cin-N	0	0	—	1	0	0	0	0	2	4	1	0	2	18.0	9.00	46	.400	.400	0	—	0	-1	-1	-0	0.0
1960	Cin-N	0	1	.000	5	0	0	0	0	4^1	4	2	5	3	18.7	10.38	37	.250	.429	0	—	0	-3	-3	-0	-0.6
Total	2	0	1	.000	6	0	0	0	0	6^1	8	3	5	5	18.5	9.95	39	.308	.419	0	—	0	-4	-4	-0	-0.6

● **CHARLIE WIEDEMEYER** Wiedemeyer, Charles John "Chick" b: 1/31/14, Chicago, Ill. d: 10/27/79, Lake Geneva, Fla. BL/TL, 6'3", 180 lbs. Deb: 9/9/34

YEAR	TM/L	W	L	PCT	G	GS	CG	SH	SV	IP	H	HR	BB	SO	RAT	ERA	ERA+	OAV	OOB	BH	AVG	PB	PR	/A	PD	TPI
1934	Chi-N	0	0	—	4	1	0	0	0	8^1	16	0	4	2	22.7	9.72	40	.432	.500	0	.000	-0	-5	-5	0	0.0

● **STUMP WIEDMAN** Wiedman, George Edward b: 2/17/1861, Rochester, N.Y. d: 3/2/05, New York, N.Y. BR/TR, 5'7.5", 165 lbs. Deb: 8/26/1880 U♦

YEAR	TM/L	W	L	PCT	G	GS	CG	SH	SV	IP	H	HR	BB	SO	RAT	ERA	ERA+	OAV	OOB	BH	AVG	PB	PR	/A	PD	TPI
1880	Buf-N	0	9	.000	17	13	9	0	0	113^2	141	1	9	25	11.9	3.40	72	.291	.304	8	.103	-5	-13	-12	-1	-1.3
1881	Det-N	8	5	.615	13	13	13	1	0	115	108	1	12	26	**9.4**	**1.80**	**162**	.238	**.258**	12	.255	0	12	14	-2	1.3
1882	Det-N	25	20	.556	46	45	43	4	0	411	391	10	39	161	9.4	2.63	112	.236	.253	42	.218	-5	12	14	-0	0.7
1883	Det-N	20	24	.455	52	47	41	3	**2**	402^1	435	8	72	183	11.3	3.53	88	.257	.288	58	.185	-8	-18	-19	0	-2.2
1884	Det-N	4	21	.160	26	26	24	0	0	212^2	257	9	57	96	13.3	3.72	78	.273	.314	49	.163	-4	-18	-20	-1	-2.1
1885	Det-N	14	24	.368	38	38	37	3	0	330	343	7	63	149	11.1	3.14	91	.252	.286	24	.157	-4	-12	-11	-3	-1.7
1886	KC-N	12	36	.250	51	51	48	1	0	427^2	549	11	112	168	13.9	4.50	84	.303	.344	30	.168	-10	-57	-35	4	-3.5
1887	Det-N	13	7	.650	21	21	20	0	0	183	221	9	60	56	14.3	5.36	76	.296	.356	17	.207	-2	-26	-27	-0	-2.4
	NY-a	4	8	.333	12	12	11	1	0	97	122	3	25	37	13.7	4.64	92	.292	.333	7	.152	-2	-4	-4	1	-0.4
	NY-N	0	1	.000	1	1	1	0	0	8	10	0	2	4	13.5	1.13	335	.286	.324	1	.333	0	3	2	-0	0.2
1888	NY-N	1	1	.500	2	2	2	0	0	18	17	2	8	5	13.5	3.50	78	.230	.321	0	.000	-0	-1	-2	-0	-0.2
Total	9	101	156	.393	279	269	249	13	2	2318^1	2594	61	459	910	11.9	3.60	89	.268	.302	248	.177	-41	-120	-98	-2	-11.6

● **JACK WIENEKE** Wieneke, John b: 3/10/1894, Saltsburg, Pa. d: 3/16/33, Pleasant Ridge, Mich. BR/TL, 6', 182 lbs. Deb: 7/4/21

YEAR	TM/L	W	L	PCT	G	GS	CG	SH	SV	IP	H	HR	BB	SO	RAT	ERA	ERA+	OAV	OOB	BH	AVG	PB	PR	/A	PD	TPI
1921	Chi-A	0	1	.000	10	3	0	0	0	25^1	39	4	17	10	20.3	8.17	52	.351	.442	1	.111	-1	-11	-11	0	-0.4

● **BOB WIESLER** Wiesler, Robert George b: 8/13/30, St.Louis, Mo. BB/TL, 6'2", 195 lbs. Deb: 8/3/51

YEAR	TM/L	W	L	PCT	G	GS	CG	SH	SV	IP	H	HR	BB	SO	RAT	ERA	ERA+	OAV	OOB	BH	AVG	PB	PR	/A	PD	TPI
1951	NY-A	0	2	.000	4	3	0	0	0	9^1	13	0	11	3	23.1	13.50	28	.361	.511	0	.000	-1	-10	-10	0	-1.6
1954	NY-A	3	2	.600	6	5	0	0	0	30^1	28	0	30	25	17.2	4.15	83	.259	.420	3	.273	-1	-1	-2	-1	-0.3
1955	NY-A	0	2	.000	16	7	0	0	0	53	39	1	49	22	15.1	3.91	96	.212	.380	2	.143	-1	0	-1	1	0.0
1956	Was-A	3	12	.200	37	21	3	0	0	123	141	11	112	49	18.7	6.44	67	.300	.438	3	.091	-3	-31	-29	1	-3.1
1957	Was-A	1	1	.500	3	2	1	0	0	16^1	15	2	11	9	14.9	4.41	88	.250	.375	1	.167	0	-1	-1	0	-0.1
1958	Was-A	0	0	—	4	0	0	0	0	9^1	14	2	5	5	19.3	6.75	56	.359	.444	0	.000	-0	-3	-3	1	0.0
Total	6	7	19	.269	70	38	4	0	0	241^1	250	16	218	113	17.7	5.74	70	.279	.423	9	.130	-3	-46	-46	3	-5.1

● **WHITEY WIETELMANN** Wietelmann, William Frederick b: 3/15/19, Zanesville, Ohio BB/TR, 6', 170 lbs. Deb: 9/6/39 C♦

YEAR	TM/L	W	L	PCT	G	GS	CG	SH	SV	IP	H	HR	BB	SO	RAT	ERA	ERA+	OAV	OOB	BH	AVG	PB	PR	/A	PD	TPI
1945	Bos-N	0	0	—	1	0	0	0	0	1	6	0	2	0	72.0	54.00	7	.667	.727	116	.271	0	-6	-6	-0	0.0
1946	Bos-N	0	0	—	3	0	0	0	0	6^2	9	1	4	2	18.9	8.10	42	.310	.412	16	.205	0	-3	-3	-0	0.0
Total	2	0	0	—	4	0	0	0	0	7^2	15	1	6	2	25.8	14.09	25	.395	.489	409	.232	1	-9	-9	-0	0.0

● **JIMMY WIGGS** Wiggs, James Alvin "Big Jim" b: 9/1/1876, Trondheim, Norway d: 1/20/63, Xenia, Ohio BB/TR, 6'4", 200 lbs. Deb: 4/23/03

YEAR	TM/L	W	L	PCT	G	GS	CG	SH	SV	IP	H	HR	BB	SO	RAT	ERA	ERA+	OAV	OOB	BH	AVG	PB	PR	/A	PD	TPI
1903	Cin-N	0	1	.000	2	1	0	0	0	5	12	0	2	2	27.0	5.40	66	.500	.556	0	.000	-0	-1	-1	-0	-0.2
1905	Det-A	3	3	.500	7	7	4	0	0	41^1	30	0	29	37	13.1	3.27	84	.205	.341	2	.133	-0	-3	-2	-0	-0.4
1906	Det-A	0	0	—	4	1	0	0	0	10^1	11	1	7	7	17.4	5.23	53	.275	.408	1	.333	0	-3	-3	0	0.1
Total	3	3	4	.429	13	9	4	0	0	56^2	53	1	38	46	15.1	3.81	74	.252	.377	3	.158	-0	-7	-6	0	-0.5

● **BILL WIGHT** Wight, William Robert "Lefty" b: 4/12/22, Rio Vista, Cal. BL/TL, 6'1", 180 lbs. Deb: 4/17/46

YEAR	TM/L	W	L	PCT	G	GS	CG	SH	SV	IP	H	HR	BB	SO	RAT	ERA	ERA+	OAV	OOB	BH	AVG	PB	PR	/A	PD	TPI
1946	NY-A	2	2	.500	14	4	1	0	0	40^1	44	1	30	11	16.7	4.46	77	.289	.410	0	.000	-1	-4	-5	0	-0.5
1947	NY-A	1	0	1.000	1	1	1	0	0	9	8	0	2	3	10.0	1.00	353	.242	.286	0	.000	0	3	3	0	0.4
1948	Chi-A	9	20	.310	34	32	7	1	1	223^1	238	9	135	68	15.1	4.80	89	.278	.377	6	.082	-7	-13	-13	1	-2.0
1949	Chi-A	15	13	.536	35	33	14	3	1	245	254	9	96	78	12.9	3.31	126	.275	.343	14	.165	-1	24	24	0	2.3
1950	Chi-A	10	16	.385	30	28	13	3	0	206	213	10	79	62	12.8	3.58	125	.270	.336	0	.000	-9	23	21	2	1.6
1951	Bos-A	7	7	.500	34	17	4	2	0	118^1	128	5	63	38	14.5	5.10	88	.282	.369	3	.073	-4	-13	-8	1	-1.2
1952	Bos-A	2	1	.667	10	2	0	0	0	24^1	14	3	14	5	10.7	2.96	133	.169	.296	1	.143	-0	2	3	0	0.3
	Det-A	5	9	.357	23	19	8	3	0	143^2	167	7	55	65	13.9	3.88	98	.291	.354	11	.220	1	-3	-1	2	0.2
	Yr	7	10	.412	33	21	8	3	0	168	181	10	69	70	13.4	3.75	102	.275	.344	12	.211	1	-1	1	2	0.5
1953	Det-A	0	3	.000	13	4	0	0	0	25^1	35	4	14	10	17.4	8.88	46	.333	.412	3	.429	1	-14	-14	-1	-1.3
	Cle-A	2	1	.667	20	0	0	0	1	26^2	29	1	16	14	15.2	3.71	101	.282	.378	0	.000	-1	1	0	0	0.0
	Yr	2	4	.333	33	4	0	0	1	52	64	5	30	24	16.3	6.23	63	.308	.395	3	.250	0	-13	-13	-0	-1.3
1955	Cle-A	0	0	—	17	0	0	0	1	24	24	0	9	9	12.4	2.63	152	.261	.327	0	—	0	4	4	2	0.2
	Bal-A	6	8	.429	19	14	8	2	2	117^1	111	6	39	54	11.6	2.45	155	.252	.315	3	.083	-2	20	18	2	2.1
	Yr	6	8	.429	36	14	8	2	3	141^1	135	6	48	63	11.7	2.48	155	.254	.317	3	.083	-2	23	21	4	2.3
1956	Bal-A	9	12	.429	35	26	7	1	0	174^2	198	7	72	84	14.2	4.02	98	.289	.362	12	.200	-1	3	-2	-1	-0.3
1957	Bal-A	6	6	.500	27	17	2	0	0	121	122	4	54	50	13.4	3.64	99	.271	.354	1	.029	-3	2	-1	-1	-0.5
1958	Cin-N	0	1	.000	7	0	0	0	0	6^2	7	1	4	5	14.9	4.05	102	.292	.393	0	—	0	-0	0	0	0.0
	StL-N	3	0	1.000	28	1	1	0	2	57^1	64	7	32	18	15.1	5.02	82	.290	.379	1	.100	-0	-7	-6	1	-0.3
	Yr	3	1	.750	35	1	1	0	2	64	71	8	36	23	15.0	4.92	84	.290	.381	1	.100	-0	-7	-6	1	-0.3
Total	12	77	99	.438	347	198	66	15	8	1563	1656	74	714	574	13.7	3.95	103	.277	.355	55	.115	-28	27	22	9	1.0

● **FRED WIGINGTON** Wigington, Fred Thomas b: 12/16/1897, Rogers, Neb. d: 5/8/80, Mesa, Ariz. BR/TR, 5'10", 168 lbs. Deb: 4/20/23

YEAR	TM/L	W	L	PCT	G	GS	CG	SH	SV	IP	H	HR	BB	SO	RAT	ERA	ERA+	OAV	OOB	BH	AVG	PB	PR	/A	PD	TPI
1923	StL-N	0	0	—	4	0	0	0	0	8^1	11	0	5	2	17.3	3.24	121	.367	.457	0	.000	-0	1	1	0	0.0

● **SANDY WIHTOL** Wihtol, Alexander Ames b: 6/1/55, Palo Alto, Cal. BR/TR, 6'1", 195 lbs. Deb: 9/7/79

YEAR	TM/L	W	L	PCT	G	GS	CG	SH	SV	IP	H	HR	BB	SO	RAT	ERA	ERA+	OAV	OOB	BH	AVG	PB	PR	/A	PD	TPI
1979	Cle-A	0	0	—	5	0	0	0	0	10^2	10	0	3	6	11.0	3.38	126	.238	.289	0	—	0	1	1	0	0.0
1980	Cle-A	1	0	1.000	17	0	0	0	1	35^1	35	2	14	20	13.0	3.57	114	.257	.336	0	—	0	2	2	-1	0.0
1982	Cle-A	0	0	—	6	0	0	0	0	11^2	9	1	7	8	13.1	4.63	88	.220	.347	0	—	0	-1	-1	-0	0.0
Total	3	1	0	1.000	28	0	0	0	1	57^2	54	3	24	34	12.6	3.75	110	.247	.329	0	—	0	2	2	-1	0.0

● **MILT WILCOX** Wilcox, Milton Edward b: 4/20/50, Honolulu, Hawaii BR/TR, 6'2", 185 lbs. Deb: 9/5/70

YEAR	TM/L	W	L	PCT	G	GS	CG	SH	SV	IP	H	HR	BB	SO	RAT	ERA	ERA+	OAV	OOB	BH	AVG	PB	PR	/A	PD	TPI
1970	*Cin-N	3	1	.750	5	2	1	1	1	22^1	19	2	7	13	10.9	2.42	167	.229	.297	1	.200	0	4	4	0	0.8
1971	Cin-N	2	2	.500	18	3	0	0	1	43^1	43	2	17	21	12.9	3.32	101	.269	.346	0	.000	-1	1	0	0	-0.1
1972	Cle-A	7	14	.333	32	27	4	2	0	156	145	18	72	90	12.8	3.40	94	.251	.339	9	.200	1	-6	-3	-3	-0.6
1973	Cle-A	8	10	.444	26	19	4	0	0	134^1	143	14	68	82	14.7	5.83	67	.275	.367	0	—	0	-30	-29	1	-3.2
1974	Cle-A	2	2	.500	41	2	1	0	4	71^1	74	10	24	33	13.0	4.67	77	.271	.341	0	—	0	-8	-8	1	-0.5
1975	Chi-N	0	1	.000	25	0	0	0	0	38^1	50	4	17	21	16.0	5.63	68	.323	.393	1	.333	0	-9	-8	0	-0.1
1977	Det-A	6	2	.750	20	13	1	0	0	106^1	96	13	37	82	11.3	3.64	118	.241	.307	0	—	0	5	8	-0	0.5
1978	Det-A	13	12	.520	29	27	16	2	0	215^1	208	22	68	132	11.9	3.76	103	.255	.318	0	—	0	0	2	1	0.4
1979	Det-A	12	10	.545	33	29	7	0	0	196^1	201	18	73	109	13.1	4.35	99	.267	.341	0	—	0	-3	-1	3	0.2
1980	Det-A	13	11	.542	32	31	13	1	0	198^2	201	24	68	97	12.5	4.48	92	.262	.327	0	—	0	-10	-8	1	-0.8
1981	Det-A	12	9	.571	24	24	8	1	0	166^1	152	10	52	79	11.4	3.03	124	.247	.312	0	—	0	12	14	1	1.7
1982	Det-A	12	10	.545	29	29	9	1	0	193^2	187	18	85	112	13.0	3.62	112	.257	.340	0	—	0	10	9	3	1.2
1983	Det-A	11	10	.524	26	26	9	2	0	186	164	19	74	101	11.7	3.97	98	.237	.314	0	—	0	2	-1	3	0.3
1984	*Det-A	17	8	.680	33	33	0	0	0	193^2	183	13	66	119	11.9	4.00	98	.252	.321	0	—	0	-0	-2	1	0.0
1985	Det-A	1	3	.250	8	8	0	0	0	39	51	6	14	20	15.0	4.85	84	.315	.369	0	—	0	-3	-3	0	-0.1
1986	Sea-A	0	8	.000	13	10	0	0	0	55^2	74	11	28	26	16.7	5.50	77	.327	.404	0	—	0	-8	-8	0	-0.9
Total	16	119	113	.513	394	283	73	10	6	2016^2	1991	204	770	1137	12.7	4.07	96	.260	.334	11	.177	0	-44	-33	14	-1.2

● **RANDY WILES** Wiles, Randall E b: 9/10/51, Fort Belvoir, Va. BL/TL, 6'1", 185 lbs. Deb: 8/7/77

YEAR	TM/L	W	L	PCT	G	GS	CG	SH	SV	IP	H	HR	BB	SO	RAT	ERA	ERA+	OAV	OOB	BH	AVG	PB	PR	/A	PD	TPI
1977	Chi-A	1	1	.500	5	0	0	0	0	2^2	5	1	3	0	27.0	10.13	40	.417	.533	0	—	0	-2	-2	0	-1.1

YEAR TM/L	W	L	PCT	G	GS	CG	SH	SV	IP	H	HR	BB	SO	RAT	ERA	ERA+	OAV	OOB	BH	AVG	PB	PR	/A	PD	TPI
● MARK WILEY	Wiley, Mark Eugene b: 2/28/48, National City, Cal. BR/TR, 6'1", 200 lbs. Deb: 6/17/75 C																								
1975 Min-A	1	3	.250	15	3	1	0	2	38^{2}	50	4	13	15	14.9	6.05	63	.325	.381	0	—	0	-10	-10	-1	-1.1
1978 SD-N	1	0	1.000	4	1	0	0	0	7^{2}	11	1	1	1	14.1	5.87	57	.324	.343	0	.000	-0	-2	-2	-0	-0.3
Tor-A	0	0	—	2	0	0	0	0	2^{2}	3	0	1	2	13.5	6.75	58	.273	.333	0	—	0	-1	-1	-0	0.0
Total 2	2	3	.400	21	4	1	0	2	49	64	5	15	18	14.7	6.06	62	.322	.372	0	.000	-0	-13	-13	-1	-1.4
● HARRY WILHELM	Wilhelm, Harry Lester b: 4/7/1874, Uniontown, Pa. d: 2/20/44, Republic, Pa. BR/TR, 5'7", 155 lbs. Deb: 8/12/1899																								
1899 Lou-N	1	1	.500	5	3	2	0	0	25	36	1	3	6	14.4	6.12	63	.336	.360	3	.250	2	-6	-6	0	-0.2
● KAISER WILHELM	Wilhelm, Irvin Key b: 1/26/1874, Wooster, Ohio d: 5/22/36, Rochester, N.Y. BR/TR, 6', 162 lbs. Deb: 4/18/03 MUC																								
1903 Pit-N	5	3	.625	12	9	7	1	0	86	88	0	25	20	12.1	3.24	100	.264	.321	3	.088	-2	0	-0	2	-0.1
1904 Bos-N	14	20	.412	39	36	30	3	0	288	316	8	74	73	12.4	3.69	75	.285	.333	7	.070	-8	-30	-30	1	-3.9
1905 Bos-N	3	23	.115	34	28	23	0	0	242^{1}	287	7	75	76	13.6	4.53	68	.295	.349	16	.160	-2	-41	-39	2	-3.7
1908 Bro-N	16	22	.421	42	36	33	6	0	332	266	3	83	99	9.6	1.87	125	.217	.271	12	.108	-4	18	18	3	1.9
1909 Bro-N	3	13	.188	22	17	14	1	0	163	176	3	59	45	13.1	3.26	80	.289	.353	13	.228	2	-12	-12	1	-0.8
1910 Bro-N	3	7	.300	15	5	0	0	0	68^{1}	88	3	18	17	14.1	4.74	64	.314	.358	6	.316	2	-13	-13	1	-1.4
1914 Bal-F	12	17	.414	47	27	11	1	5	243^{2}	263	10	81	113	12.7	4.03	75	.291	.349	21	.250	1	-31	-27	3	-2.6
1915 Bal-F	0	0	—	1	0	0	0	0	1	0	0	0	0	0.0	0.00	—	.000	.000	0	—	0	0	0	-0	0.0
1921 Phi-N	0	0	—	4	0	0	0	0	8	11	0	3	1	15.8	3.38	125	.393	.452	0	.000	-0	0	1	-0	0.0
Total 9	56	105	.348	216	158	118	12	5	1432^{1}	1495	34	418	444	12.2	3.44	81	.274	.328	78	.154	-12	-108	-102	11	-10.6
● HOYT WILHELM	Wilhelm, James Hoyt b: 7/26/23, Huntersville, N.C. BR/TR, 6', 195 lbs. Deb: 4/19/52 H																								
1952 NY-N	15	3	**.833**	**71**	0	0	0	11	159^{1}	127	12	57	108	10.7	**2.43**	**152**	.220	.296	6	.158	0	23	23	1	2.9
1953 NY-N☆	7	8	.467	**68**	0	0	0	15	145	127	13	77	71	12.9	3.04	141	.238	.339	5	.152	1	**20**	**20**	-1	2.3
1954 *NY-N	12	4	.750	57	0	0	0	7	111^{1}	77	5	52	64	10.8	2.10	192	.198	.300	1	.048	-2	**24**	**24**	1	3.4
1955 NY-N	4	1	.800	59	0	0	0	0	103	104	10	40	71	12.8	3.93	102	.266	.337	3	.158	-1	1	1	3	0.2
1956 NY-N	4	9	.308	64	0	0	0	8	89^{1}	97	7	43	71	14.3	3.83	99	.280	.362	2	.222	0	-1	-0	2	0.1
1957 StL-N	1	4	.200	40	0	0	0	11	55	52	7	21	29	12.4	4.25	93	.254	.332	0	.000	-1	-2	-2	-0	-0.3
Cle-A	1	0	1.000	2	0	0	0	1	3^{2}	2	1	1	0	9.8	2.45	151	.154	.267	0	—	0	1	1	-0	0.1
1958 Cle-A	2	7	.222	30	6	1	0	5	90^{1}	70	4	35	57	10.6	2.49	146	.215	.294	2	.095	-1	13	12	1	1.2
Bal-A	1	3	.250	9	4	3	1	0	40^{2}	25	2	10	35	8.0	1.99	180	.179	.238	1	.091	-1	8	7	-0	0.6
Yr	3	10	.231	39	10	4	1	5	131	95	6	45	92	9.7	2.34	155	.203	.274	3	.094	-2	21	19	1	1.8
1959 Bal-A★	15	11	.577	32	27	13	3	0	226	178	13	77	139	10.6	**2.19**	**173**	.224	.301	4	.053	-6	**42**	**40**	-1	3.7
1960 Bal-A	11	8	.579	41	11	3	1	7	147	125	13	39	107	10.1	3.31	115	.228	.280	3	.071	-3	9	8	1	0.9
1961 Bal-A★	9	7	.563	51	1	0	0	18	109^{2}	89	5	41	87	11.0	2.30	167	.219	.296	1	.050	-1	21	19	1	3.2
1962 Bal-A†	7	10	.412	52	0	0	0	15	93	64	5	34	90	9.8	1.94	191	.197	.279	2	.125	-0	21	18	0	3.8
1963 Chi-A	5	8	.385	55	3	0	0	21	136^{1}	106	8	30	111	9.2	2.64	133	.215	.265	2	.069	-1	15	13	1	1.6
1964 Chi-A	12	9	.571	73	0	0	0	27	131^{1}	94	7	30	95	8.6	1.99	174	.202	.254	3	.143	-0	24	21	-1	4.2
1965 Chi-A	7	7	.500	66	0	0	0	20	144	88	11	32	106	7.6	1.81	176	.177	.229	0	.000	-2	**26**	**22**	-1	2.5
1966 Chi-A	5	2	.714	46	0	0	0	6	81^{1}	50	6	17	61	7.5	1.66	191	.178	.227	1	.125	0	16	14	-1	1.3
1967 Chi-A	8	3	.727	49	0	0	0	12	89	58	2	34	76	9.7	1.31	236	.183	.270	1	.077	-1	**19**	**18**	-1	2.6
1968 Chi-A	4	4	.500	72	0	0	0	12	93^{2}	69	4	24	72	9.1	1.73	175	.205	.262	0	.000	-0	13	13	-1	1.5
1969 Cal-A	5	7	.417	44	0	0	0	10	65^{2}	45	4	18	53	9.0	2.47	141	.194	.261	0	.000	-1	8	7	-0	1.4
Atl-N	2	0	1.000	8	0	0	0	4	12^{1}	5	0	4	14	7.3	0.73	494	.119	.213	0	.000	-0	4	4	0	1.0
1970 Atl-N☆	6	4	.600	50	0	0	0	13	78^{1}	69	7	39	67	12.5	3.10	138	.234	.325	1	.091	-0	8	10	0	1.6
Chi-N	0	1	.000	3	0	0	0	0	3^{2}	4	1	3	1	17.2	9.82	46	.286	.412	0	—	0	-2	-2	0	-0.4
Yr	6	5	.545	53	0	0	0	13	82	73	8	42	68	12.6	3.40	126	.234	.325	1	.091	-0	6	8	1	1.2
1971 Atl-N	0	0	—	3	0	0	0	0	2^{1}	6	2	1	1	27.0	15.43	24	.500	.538	0	—	0	-3	-3	0	0.0
LA-N	0	1	.000	9	0	0	0	3	17^{2}	6	1	4	15	5.1	1.02	317	.111	.172	0	.000	-0	5	4	-0	0.4
Yr	0	1	.000	12	0	0	0	3	20	12	3	5	16	7.6	2.70	122	.182	.239	0	.000	-0	2	1	0	0.4
1972 LA-N	0	1	.000	16	0	0	0	1	25^{1}	20	0	15	9	12.4	4.62	72	.217	.327	0	.000	-0	-3	-4	0	-0.1
Total 21	143	122	.540	1070	52	20	5	227	2254^{1}	1757	150	778	1610	10.4	2.52	146	.216	.290	38	.088	-21	310	288	5	39.7
● LEFTY WILKIE	Wilkie, Aldon Jay b: 10/30/14, Zealandia, Sask., Canada d: 8/5/92, Tualatin, Ore. BL/TL, 5'11.5", 175 lbs. Deb: 4/22/41																								
1941 Pit-N	2	4	.333	26	6	2	1	2	79	90	1	40	16	14.9	4.56	79	.289	.372	7	.292	1	-8	-8	1	-0.4
1942 Pit-N	6	7	.462	35	6	3	0	1	107^{1}	112	4	37	18	12.6	4.19	81	.269	.330	10	.263	2	-10	-10	2	-0.7
1946 Pit-N	0	0	—	7	0	0	0	0	7^{2}	13	0	3	3	18.8	10.57	33	.382	.432	0	—	0	-6	-6	-0	0.0
Total 3	8	11	.421	68	12	5	1	3	194	215	5	80	37	13.8	4.59	76	.283	.352	17	.274	3	-25	-24	3	-1.1
● DEAN WILKINS	Wilkins, Dean Allan b: 8/24/66, Blue Island, Ill. BR/TR, 6'1", 170 lbs. Deb: 8/21/89																								
1989 Chi-N	1	0	1.000	11	0	0	0	0	15^{2}	13	2	9	14	12.6	4.60	82	.228	.333	0	.000	-0	-2	-1	0	-0.1
1990 Chi-N	0	0	—	7	0	0	0	1	7^{1}	11	1	7	3	23.3	9.82	42	.333	.463	0	—	0	-5	-5	-0	-0.1
1991 Hou-N	2	1	.667	7	0	0	0	1	8	16	0	10	4	29.3	11.25	31	.410	.531	0	.000	-0	-7	-7	-0	-2.2
Total 3	3	1	.750	25	0	0	0	2	31	40	3	26	21	19.5	7.55	50	.310	.429	0	.000	-0	-14	-13	-0	-2.4
● ERIC WILKINS	Wilkins, Eric Lamoine b: 12/9/56, St.Louis, Mo. BR/TR, 6'1", 190 lbs. Deb: 4/11/79																								
1979 Cle-A	2	4	.333	16	14	0	0	0	69^{2}	77	4	38	52	15.4	4.39	97	.289	.386	0	—	0	-1	-1	0	-0.1
● MARC WILKINS	Wilkins, Marc Allen b: 10/21/70, Mansfield, Ohio BR/TR, 5'11", 200 lbs. Deb: 5/11/96																								
1996 Pit-N	4	3	.571	47	2	0	0	1	75	75	6	36	62	14.0	3.84	113	.266	.361	2	.222	0	3	4	-0	0.4
1997 Pit-N	9	5	.643	70	0	0	0	2	75^{2}	65	7	33	47	12.1	3.69	116	.242	.333	0	.000	-0	4	5	-2	0.7
1998 Pit-N	0	0	—	16	0	0	0	0	15^{1}	13	1	9	17	14.1	3.52	123	.236	.364	0	—	0	1	1	-0	0.0
Total 3	13	8	.619	133	2	0	0	3	166	153	14	78	126	13.2	3.74	116	.252	.349	2	.154	0	9	11	-2	1.1
● ROY WILKINSON	Wilkinson, Roy Hamilton b: 5/8/1893, Canandaigua, N.Y. d: 7/2/56, Louisville, Ky. BR/TR, 6'1", 170 lbs. Deb: 4/29/18																								
1918 Cle-A	0	0	—	1	0	0	0	0	1	0	0	0	0	0.0	0.00	—	.000	.000	0	—	0	0	0	-0	0.0
1919 *Chi-A	1	1	.500	4	1	1	1	0	22	21	0	10	5	12.7	2.05	156	.266	.348	3	.375	2	3	3	1	0.5
1920 Chi-A	7	9	.438	34	12	8	0	2	145	162	6	48	30	13.2	4.03	93	.297	.356	7	.146	-3	-4	-4	-3	-0.9
1921 Chi-A	4	20	.167	36	23	11	0	3	198^{1}	259	4	78	50	15.5	5.13	83	.334	.397	8	.123	-4	-19	-20	5	-1.8
1922 Chi-A	0	1	.000	4	1	0	0	1	14^{1}	24	1	6	3	19.5	8.79	46	.393	.456	0	.000	-0	-8	-8	-0	-0.6
Total 5	12	31	.279	79	37	20	1	6	380^{2}	466	11	142	88	14.5	4.66	86	.318	.381	18	.145	-5	-27	-28	4	-2.8
● BILL WILKINSON	Wilkinson, William Carl b: 8/10/64, Greybull, Wyoming BR/TL, 5'10", 160 lbs. Deb: 6/13/85 F																								
1985 Sea-A	0	2	.000	2	2	0	0	0	6	8	2	6	5	21.0	13.50	31	.333	.467	0	—	0	-6	-6	0	-1.3
1987 Sea-A	3	4	.429	56	0	0	0	10	76^{1}	61	8	21	73	9.7	3.66	129	.223	.278	0	—	0	7	9	-1	0.8
1988 Sea-A	2	2	.500	30	0	0	0	2	31	28	3	15	25	12.5	3.48	119	.233	.319	0	—	0	2	2	-1	0.1
Total 3	5	8	.385	88	2	0	0	12	113^{1}	97	13	42	103	11.0	4.13	110	.232	.302	0	—	0	2	5	-1	-0.4
● TED WILKS	Wilks, Theodore "Cork" b: 11/13/15, Fulton, N.Y. d: 8/21/89, Houston, Tex. BR/TR, 5'9.5", 178 lbs. Deb: 4/25/44 C																								
1944 *StL-N	17	4	**.810**	36	21	16	4	0	207^{2}	173	12	49	70	**9.7**	2.64	133	.227	**.275**	9	.141	-1	22	20	-4	1.4
1945 StL-N	4	7	.364	18	16	4	1	0	98^{1}	103	9	29	28	12.2	2.93	128	.270	.324	4	.133	-0	10	9	-2	0.7
1946 *StL-N	8	0	1.000	40	4	0	0	1	95	88	13	38	40	12.1	3.41	101	.248	.324	5	.208	0	0	0	-1	0.0
1947 StL-N	4	0	1.000	37	0	0	0	5	50^{1}	57	10	11	28	12.5	5.01	83	.279	.323	1	.167	0	-5	-5	-0	-0.4
1948 StL-N	6	6	.500	57	2	1	0	13	130^{2}	113	5	39	71	10.5	2.62	156	.235	.293	5	.167	0	**19**	**21**	-1	2.2
1949 StL-N	10	3	.769	**59**	0	0	0	**9**	118^{1}	105	7	38	71	10.9	3.73	112	.240	.301	1	.037	-3	4	6	-2	0.1
1950 StL-N	2	0	1.000	18	0	0	0	0	24^{1}	27	4	9	15	13.7	6.66	65	.287	.356	0	.000	-1	-7	-6	0	-0.5
1951 StL-N	0	0	—	17	0	0	0	1	18	19	1	5	5	12.0	3.00	132	.279	.329	0	.000	-0	2	2	-1	0.0
Pit-N	3	5	.375	48	1	1	0	12	82^{2}	69	6	24	43	10.3	2.83	149	.231	.292	1	.083	-1	10	13	1	1.6
Yr	3	5	.375	**65**	1	1	0	**13**	100^{2}	88	7	29	48	10.6	2.86	146	.240	.299	1	.077	-1	12	15	0	1.6
1952 Pit-N	5	5	.500	44	0	0	0	4	72^{1}	65	9	31	24	12.2	3.61	111	.245	.329	1	.125	-0	1	3	-1	0.3
Cle-A	0	0	—	7	0	0	0	1	11^{2}	8	0	7	6	11.6	3.86	87	.186	.300	0	—	0	-0	-1	0	0.0

YEAR	TM/L	W	L	PCT	G	GS	CG	SH	SV	IP	H	HR	BB	SO	RAT	ERA	ERA+	OAV	OOB	BH	AVG	PB	PR	/A	PD	TPI
1953	Cle-A	0	0	—	4	0	0	0	0	3^2	5	0	3	2	19.6	7.36	51	.278	.381	0	—	0	-1	-1	-0	0.0
Total	10	59	30	.663	385	44	22	5	46	913	832	76	283	403	11.1	3.26	118	.244	.304	27	.131	-5	55	61	-11	5.4
● ED WILLETT	Willett, Robert Edgar b: 3/7/1884, Norfolk, Va. d: 5/10/34, Wellington, Kan. BR/TR, 6′, 183 lbs. Deb: 9/5/06																									
1906	Det-A	0	3	.000	3	3	3	0	0	25	24	0	8	16	12.2	3.96	70	.255	.327	0	.000	-1	-4	-3	1	-0.4
1907	Det-A	1	5	.167	10	6	1	0	0	48^2	47	0	20	27	12.8	3.70	70	.255	.335	1	.077	-1	-6	-6	1	-0.7
1908	Det-A	15	8	.652	30	23	18	2	1	197^1	186	2	60	77	11.9	2.28	106	.261	.331	11	.164	-2	2	3	5	0.6
1909	*Det-A	21	10	.677	41	34	25	3	1	292^2	239	5	76	89	10.1	2.34	108	.221	.281	22	.196	3	5	6	-1	0.8
1910	Det-A	16	11	.593	37	25	18	4	0	224^1	175	2	74	65	10.7	2.37	111	.217	.296	11	.133	-2	4	7	7	1.3
1911	Det-A	13	14	.481	38	27	15	2	1	231^1	261	5	80	86	13.8	3.66	95	.295	.363	22	.268	7	-8	-5	3	0.4
1912	Det-A	17	15	.531	37	31	28	1	0	284^1	281	3	84	89	12.1	3.29	99	.262	.326	19	.165	-2	1	-1	5	0.3
1913	Det-A	13	14	.481	34	30	19	0	0	242	237	0	89	59	12.5	3.09	95	.260	.333	26	.283	7	-4	-5	3	0.7
1914	StL-F	4	17	.190	27	22	14	0	0	175	208	5	56	73	14.1	4.27	71	.295	.355	15	.234	2	-27	-24	5	-1.9
1915	StL-F	2	3	.400	17	2	1	0	2	52^2	61	2	18	19	14.0	4.61	62	.295	.360	3	.200	0	-11	-10	0	-1.0
Total	10	102	100	.505	274	203	142	12	5	1773^1	1719	24	565	600	12.1	3.08	94	.258	.326	130	.199	11	-48	-38	28	0.1
● CARL WILLEY	Willey, Carlton Francis b: 6/6/31, Cherryfield, Me. BR/TR, 6′, 175 lbs. Deb: 4/30/58																									
1958	*Mil-N	9	7	.563	23	19	9	**4**	0	140	110	14	53	74	10.6	2.70	130	.215	.291	5	.104	-2	19	13	-2	0.9
1959	Mil-N	5	9	.357	26	15	5	2	0	117	126	12	31	51	12.2	4.15	85	.273	.322	4	.103	-1	-3	-8	-1	-1.1
1960	Mil-N	6	7	.462	28	21	2	1	0	144^2	136	19	65	109	12.9	4.35	79	.248	.335	7	.146	1	-10	-15	-1	-1.2
1961	Mil-N	6	12	.333	35	22	4	0	0	159^2	147	20	65	91	12.1	3.83	98	.247	.323	1	.019	-6	4	-2	3	-0.5
1962	Mil-N	2	5	.286	30	6	0	0	1	73^1	95	9	20	40	14.2	5.40	70	.319	.364	3	.273	1	-12	-13	-0	-1.1
1963	NY-N	9	14	.391	30	28	7	4	0	183	149	24	69	101	10.9	3.10	113	.220	.296	6	.111	-1	4	8	0	0.9
1964	NY-N	0	2	.000	14	3	0	0	0	30	37	5	8	14	13.8	3.60	99	.301	.348	0	.000	-0	-0	-0	-1	-0.2
1965	NY-N	1	2	.333	13	3	1	0	0	28	30	2	15	13	15.1	4.18	84	.270	.367	0	.000	-1	-2	-2	-0	-0.3
Total	8	38	58	.396	199	117	28	11	1	875^2	830	105	326	493	12.1	3.76	95	.250	.320	26	.099	-9	1	-17	-3	-2.6
● NICK WILLHITE	Willhite, Jon Nicholas b: 1/27/41, Tulsa, Okla. BL/TL, 6′2″, 195 lbs. Deb: 6/16/63																									
1963	LA-N	2	3	.400	8	8	1	1	0	38	44	5	10	28	12.8	3.79	80	.286	.329	3	.300	1	-2	-3	-1	-0.4
1964	LA-N	2	4	.333	10	7	2	0	0	43^2	43	4	13	24	11.5	3.71	87	.264	.318	0	.000	-0	-1	-2	1	-0.2
1965	Was-A	0	0	—	5	0	0	0	0	6^1	10	2	4	3	19.9	7.11	49	.345	.424	0	—	0	-3	-3	-0	0.0
	LA-N	2	2	.500	15	6	0	0	1	42	47	7	22	28	15.2	5.36	61	.288	.380	4	.400	3	-8	-10	-0	-0.6
1966	LA-N	0	0	—	6	0	0	0	0	4^1	3	0	5	4	16.6	2.08	159	.214	.421	0	—	0	1	1	0	0.0
1967	Cal-A	0	2	.000	10	7	0	0	0	39^1	39	8	16	22	12.6	4.35	72	.258	.329	0	.000	-1	-5	-5	-0	-0.4
	NY-N	0	1	.000	4	1	0	0	0	8^1	9	1	5	9	15.1	8.64	39	.257	.350	0	.000	-0	-5	-5	0	-0.5
Total	5	6	12	.333	58	29	3	1	1	182	195	27	75	118	13.5	4.55	70	.275	.346	7	.163	2	-23	-27	0	-2.1
● ALBERT WILLIAMS	Williams, Albert Hamilton (De Souza) b: 5/6/54, Laguna De Perlas, Nic. BR/TR, 6′4″, 190 lbs. Deb: 5/7/80																									
1980	Min-A	6	2	.750	18	9	3	0	1	77	73	9	30	35	12.0	3.51	124	.253	.323	0	—	0	5	7	-1	0.2
1981	Min-A	6	10	.375	23	22	4	0	0	150	160	11	52	76	12.8	4.08	97	.276	.337	0	—	0	-7	-2	-2	-0.7
1982	Min-A	9	7	.563	26	26	3	0	0	153^2	166	18	55	61	12.9	4.22	101	.276	.337	0	—	0	-2	0	0	0.0
1983	Min-A	11	14	.440	36	29	4	1	1	193^1	196	21	68	68	12.5	4.14	103	.262	.327	0	—	0	-2	2	-2	0.1
1984	Min-A	3	5	.375	17	11	1	0	0	68^2	75	9	22	22	13.6	5.77	73	.284	.355	0	—	0	-14	-12	0	-1.3
Total	5	35	38	.479	120	97	15	1	2	642^2	670	68	227	262	12.7	4.24	99	.270	.334	0	—	0	-20	-4	-4	-1.7
● AL WILLIAMS	Williams, Almon Edward b: 5/11/14, Valhermoso Springs, Ala. d: 7/19/69, Groves, Tex. BR/TR, 6′3″, 200 lbs. Deb: 4/19/37																									
1937	Phi-A	4	1	.800	16	8	2	0	1	75^1	88	0	49	27	16.5	5.38	88	.300	.402	2	.083	-2	-6	-6	0	-0.5
1938	Phi-A	0	7	.000	30	8	1	0	0	93^1	128	6	54	25	17.6	6.94	70	.324	.407	1	.040	-3	-22	-22	-0	-1.5
Total	2	4	8	.333	46	16	3	0	1	168^2	216	6	103	52	17.1	6.24	77	.314	.405	3	.061	-5	-29	-27	0	-2.0
● GUS WILLIAMS	Williams, Augustine H. b: 1870, New York, N.Y. d: 10/14/1890, New York, N.Y. 5′11″, 170 lbs. Deb: 4/18/1890																									
1890	Bro-a	0	1	.000	2	2	1	0	0	12	13	0	12	2	18.8	7.50	52	.265	.410	2	.500	1	-5	-5	-1	-0.3
● BRIAN WILLIAMS	Williams, Brian O'Neal b: 2/15/69, Lancaster, S.C. BR/TR, 6′2″, 195 lbs. Deb: 9/16/91																									
1991	Hou-N	0	1	.000	2	2	0	0	0	12	11	2	4	4	12.0	3.75	94	.250	.327	0	.000	-0	-0	-0	0	-0.1
1992	Hou-N	7	6	.538	16	16	0	0	0	96^1	92	10	42	54	12.5	3.92	86	.255	.333	4	.133	-0	-4	-6	0	-0.8
1993	Hou-N	4	4	.500	42	5	0	0	3	82	76	7	38	56	13.0	4.83	80	.248	.338	2	.200	0	-7	-9	2	-0.6
1994	Hou-N	6	5	.545	20	13	0	0	0	78^1	112	9	41	49	18.0	5.74	69	.343	.422	6	.261	1	-13	-16	-1	-1.8
1995	SD-N	3	10	.231	44	6	0	0	0	72	79	3	38	75	15.6	6.00	67	.279	.380	1	.071	-1	-15	-16	0	-2.5
1996	Det-A	3	10	.231	40	17	2	1	2	121	145	21	85	72	17.6	6.77	75	.304	.415	0	—	0	-24	-23	-0	-2.0
1997	Bal-A	0	0	—	13	0	0	0	0	24	20	0	18	14	14.3	3.00	147	.220	.349	0	—	0	4	4	-0	0.2
Total	7	23	36	.390	177	59	2	1	5	485^2	535	52	266	324	15.3	5.34	77	.283	.378	13	.162	0	-59	-66	1	-7.6
● CHARLIE WILLIAMS	Williams, Charles Prosek b: 10/11/47, Flushing, N.Y. BR/TR, 6′2″, 200 lbs. Deb: 4/23/71																									
1971	NY-N	5	6	.455	31	9	1	0	0	90^1	92	7	41	53	13.5	4.78	71	.267	.348	2	.087	-1	-13	-14	-1	-1.8
1972	SF-N	0	2	.000	3	2	0	0	0	9^1	14	3	3	3	16.4	8.68	40	.333	.378	0	.000	-0	-5	-5	-0	-1.0
1973	SF-N	3	0	1.000	12	2	0	0	0	23	32	2	7	11	15.3	6.65	57	.330	.375	1	.333	0	-8	-7	0	-0.8
1974	SF-N	1	3	.250	39	7	0	0	0	100^1	93	6	31	48	11.3	2.78	137	.250	.311	3	.136	-1	9	11	3	0.6
1975	SF-N	5	3	.625	55	2	0	0	3	98	94	2	66	45	15.1	3.49	109	.261	.381	2	.125	0	1	3	2	0.5
1976	SF-N	2	0	1.000	48	2	0	0	1	85	80	4	39	34	12.8	2.96	122	.256	.343	1	.125	-0	5	6	1	0.2
1977	SF-N	6	5	.545	55	8	1	0	0	119^1	116	9	60	41	13.5	4.00	98	.262	.354	4	.222	0	-1	-1	-0	-0.1
1978	SF-N	1	3	.250	25	1	0	0	0	48	60	5	28	22	16.7	5.44	63	.314	.405	0	.000	-1	-10	-11	0	-0.9
Total	8	23	22	.511	268	33	2	0	4	573^1	581	38	275	257	13.7	3.97	93	.269	.355	13	.134	-2	-22	-17	3	-3.3
● LEFTY WILLIAMS	Williams, Claude Preston b: 3/9/1893, Aurora, Mo. d: 11/4/59, Laguna Beach, Cal. BR/TL, 5′9″, 160 lbs. Deb: 9/17/13																									
1913	Det-A	1	3	.250	5	4	3	0	1	29	34	0	4	9	12.1	4.97	59	.286	.315	1	.100	-0	-7	-7	-1	-1.0
1914	Det-A	0	1	.000	1	1	0	0	0	1	3	0	2	0	45.0	0.00	—	.429	.556	0	—	0	0	0	-0	0.4
1916	Chi-A	13	7	.650	43	26	10	2	1	224^1	220	5	65	138	11.8	2.89	96	.267	.327	10	.135	-0	-1	-3	-4	-0.8
1917	*Chi-A	17	8	.680	45	29	8	1	1	230	221	3	81	85	12.2	2.97	89	.252	.321	6	.090	-3	-8	-8	-5	-1.7
1918	Chi-A	6	4	.600	15	14	7	2	1	105^2	76	0	47	30	10.9	2.73	100	.209	.308	5	.132	-2	1	0	-2	-0.5
1919	*Chi-A	23	11	.676	41	40	27	5	1	297	265	7	58	125	10.1	2.64	121	.244	.289	17	.181	1	20	18	-5	1.5
1920	Chi-A	22	14	.611	39	38	25	0	0	299	302	15	90	128	12.2	3.91	96	.271	.332	22	.218	0	-4	-5	-3	-0.8
Total	7	82	48	.631	189	152	80	10	5	1186	1121	30	347	515	11.5	3.13	99	.255	.316	61	.159	-4	1	-4	-21	-2.9
● MUTT WILLIAMS	Williams, David Carter b: 7/31/1891, Ozark, Ark. d: 3/30/62, Fayetteville, Ark. BR/TR, 6′3.5″, 195 lbs. Deb: 10/4/13																									
1913	Was-A	1	0	1.000	1	1	0	0	0	4	4	1	2	1	13.5	4.50	66	.286	.375	1	.500	0	-1	-1	0	-0.1
1914	Was-A	0	0	—	5	0	0	0	1	7	5	0	4	3	11.6	5.14	55	.227	.346	0	—	0	-2	-2	-0	-0.1
Total	2	1	0	1.000	6	1	0	0	1	11	9	1	6	4	12.3	4.91	58	.250	.357	1	.500	0	-3	-2	-0	-0.2
● DAVE WILLIAMS	Williams, David Owen b: 2/7/1881, Scranton, Pa. d: 4/25/18, Hot Springs, Ark. BR/TL, 5′11.5″, 167 lbs. Deb: 7/2/02																									
1902	Bos-A	0	0	—	3	0	0	0	0	18^2	22	0	11	7	16.4	5.30	67	.293	.391	3	.333	1	-4	-4	-1	0.0
● DON WILLIAMS	Williams, Donald Fred b: 9/14/31, Floyd, Va. BR/TR, 6′2″, 180 lbs. Deb: 9/12/58																									
1958	Pit-N	0	0	—	2	0	0	0	0	4	6	1	1	3	15.8	6.75	57	.375	.412	0	—	0	-1	-1	0	0.0
1959	Pit-N	0	0	—	6	0	0	0	0	12	17	1	3	3	15.0	6.75	57	.362	.400	1	.333	1	-4	-4	-1	0.0
1962	KC-A	0	0	—	3	0	0	0	0	4	6	0	0	1	15.8	9.00	47	.353	.389	0	.000	-0	-2	-2	-0	0.0
Total	3	0	0	—	11	0	0	0	0	20	29	2	4	7	15.3	7.20	55	.363	.400	1	.250	1	-7	-7	-1	0.0
● DON WILLIAMS	Williams, Donald Reid "Dino" b: 9/2/35, Los Angeles, Cal. d: 12/20/91, LaJolla, Cal. BR/TR, 6′5″, 218 lbs. Deb: 8/4/63																									
1963	Min-A	0	0	—	3	0	0	0	0	4^1	8	1	6	2	29.1	10.38	35	.381	.519	0	—	0	-3	-3	0	0.0

YEAR TM/L	W	L	PCT	G	GS	CG	SH	SV	IP	H	HR	BB	SO	RAT	ERA	ERA+	OAV	OOB	BH	AVG	PB	PR	/A	PD	TPI
● DALE WILLIAMS Williams, Elisha Alphonso b: 10/6/1855, Ludlow, Ky. d: 10/22/39, Covington, Ky. BR/TR, 5'9", 175 lbs. Deb: 8/12/1876																									
1876 Cin-N	1	8	.111	9	9	9	0	0	83	123	1	4	9	13.8	4.23	52	.339	.346	7	.200	-2	-18	-19	-0	-1.6
● FRANK WILLIAMS Williams, Frank Lee b: 2/13/58, Seattle, Wash. BR/TR, 6'1", 190 lbs. Deb: 4/5/84																									
1984 SF-N	9	4	.692	61	1	1	1	3	106^1	88	2	51	91	12.0	3.55	99	.226	.321	4	.222	1	0	-1	4	0.5
1985 SF-N	2	4	.333	49	0	0	0	0	73	65	5	35	54	13.1	4.19	82	.242	.342	0	.000	-0	-5	-6	0	-0.5
1986 SF-N	3	1	.750	36	0	0	0	1	52^1	35	0	21	33	10.3	1.20	292	.212	.316	1	.500	0	15	13	1	1.1
1987 Cin-N	4	0	1.000	85	0	0	0	2	105^2	101	5	39	60	12.1	2.30	185	.254	.324	0	.000	-1	21	23	1	0.9
1988 Cin-N	3	2	.600	60	0	0	0	1	62^2	59	6	35	43	13.8	2.59	139	.252	.354	0	.000	-0	6	7	0	0.6
1989 Det-A	3	3	.500	42	0	0	0	1	71^2	70	5	46	33	14.9	3.64	105	.254	.366	0	—	0	2	1	-0	0.1
Total 6	24	14	.632	333	1	1	1	8	471^2	418	23	227	314	12.7	3.00	124	.242	.336	5	.172	1	39	38	5	2.7
● WOODY WILLIAMS Williams, Gregory Scott b: 8/19/66, Houston, Tex. BR/TR, 6', 190 lbs. Deb: 5/14/93																									
1993 Tor-A	3	1	.750	30	0	0	0	0	37	40	2	22	24	15.3	4.38	99	.274	.373	0	—	0	-0	-0	1	0.0
1994 Tor-A	1	3	.250	38	0	0	0	0	59^1	44	5	33	56	12.0	3.64	132	.205	.316	0	—	0	8	8	-0	0.4
1995 Tor-A	1	2	.333	23	3	0	0	0	53^2	44	6	28	41	12.4	3.69	128	.220	.322	0	—	0	6	6	0	0.3
1996 Tor-A	4	5	.444	12	10	1	0	0	59	64	8	21	43	13.1	4.73	106	.278	.341	0	—	0	2	2	-0	0.2
1997 Tor-A	9	14	.391	31	31	0	0	0	194^2	201	31	66	124	12.6	4.35	106	.269	.332	1	.500	0	5	5	-4	0.2
1998 Tor-A	10	9	.526	32	32	1	1	0	209^2	196	36	81	151	12.0	4.46	104	.245	.316	2	.333	1	4	4	-2	0.2
Total 6	28	34	.452	166	76	2	1	0	613^1	589	88	251	439	12.5	4.30	108	.252	.328	3	.375	1	24	25	-5	1.3
● JOHNNIE WILLIAMS Williams, John Brodie "Honolulu Johnnie" b: 7/16/1889, Honolulu, Hawaii d: 9/8/63, Long Beach, Cal. BR/TR, 6', 180 lbs. Deb: 4/21/14																									
1914 Det-A	0	2	.000	4	3	1	0	0	11^1	17	0	5	4	17.5	6.35	44	.378	.440	0	.000	-0	-5	-4	-0	-0.8
● LEON WILLIAMS Williams, Leon Theo "Lefty" b: 12/2/05, Macon, Ga. d: 11/20/84, Atlanta, Ga. BL/TL, 5'10.5", 154 lbs. Deb: 6/2/26																									
1926 Bro-N	0	0	—	8	0	0	0	0	8^1	16	0	2	3	19.4	5.40	71	.421	.450	1	.200	0	-1	-1	1	0.1
● MARSH WILLIAMS Williams, Marshall McDiarmid "Cap" b: 2/21/1893, Faison, N.C. d: 2/22/35, Tucson, Ariz. BR/TR, 6', 180 lbs. Deb: 7/7/16																									
1916 Phi-A	0	6	.000	10	4	3	0	0	51^1	71	4	31	17	17.9	7.89	36	.350	.436	2	.105	-1	-29	-29	-1	-3.0
● MATT WILLIAMS Williams, Matthew Evan b: 7/25/59, Houston, Tex. BR/TR, 6'1", 200 lbs. Deb: 8/2/83																									
1983 Tor-A	1	1	.500	4	3	0	0	0	8	13	5	7	5	23.6	14.63	29	.361	.477	0	—	0	-9	-9	0	-1.6
1985 Tex-A	2	1	.667	6	3	0	0	0	26	20	3	10	22	10.4	2.42	175	.211	.286	0	—	0	5	5	-1	0.4
Total 2	3	2	.600	10	6	0	0	0	34	33	8	17	27	13.5	5.29	80	.252	.342	0	—	0	-4	-4	-0	-1.2
● MIKE WILLIAMS Williams, Michael Darren b: 7/29/69, Radford, Va. BR/TR, 6'2", 199 lbs. Deb: 6/30/92																									
1992 Phi-N	1	1	.500	5	5	1	0	0	28^2	29	3	7	5	11.3	5.34	65	.259	.303	4	.400	1	-6	-6	-0	-0.3
1993 Phi-N	1	3	.250	17	4	0	0	0	51	50	5	22	33	12.7	5.29	75	.253	.327	1	.083	-1	-7	-8	-0	-0.6
1994 Phi-N	2	4	.333	12	8	0	0	0	50^1	61	7	20	29	14.5	5.01	86	.310	.373	2	.167	0	-4	-4	0	-0.4
1995 Phi-N	3	3	.500	33	8	0	0	0	87^2	78	10	29	57	11.3	3.29	129	.239	.306	2	.125	-0	9	9	1	0.6
1996 Phi-N	6	14	.300	32	29	0	0	0	167	188	25	67	103	14.1	5.44	79	.290	.362	8	.157	-1	-23	-21	3	-1.9
1997 KC-A	0	2	.000	10	0	0	0	1	14	20	1	8	10	18.6	6.43	73	.333	.420	0	—	0	-3	-3	-0	-0.5
1998 Pit-N	4	2	.667	37	1	0	0	0	51	39	1	16	59	9.7	1.94	223	.211	.274	0	.000	-0	13	13	1	1.5
Total 7	17	29	.370	146	55	1	0	1	449^2	465	52	169	296	12.9	4.58	92	.269	.338	17	.163	-0	-21	-19	4	-1.6
● MITCH WILLIAMS Williams, Mitchell Steven "Wild Thing" b: 11/17/64, Santa Ana, Cal. BL/TL, 6'4", 205 lbs. Deb: 4/9/86																									
1986 Tex-A	8	6	.571	**80**	0	0	0	8	98	69	8	79	90	14.6	3.58	120	.202	.369	0	—	0	6	8	-1	1.0
1987 Tex-A	8	6	.571	85	1	0	0	6	108^2	63	9	94	129	13.6	3.23	138	.175	.355	0	—	0	15	15	1	1.9
1988 Tex-A	2	7	.222	67	0	0	0	18	68	48	4	47	61	13.4	4.63	88	.203	.349	0	—	0	-5	-4	0	-0.7
1989 *Chi-N★	4	4	.500	**76**	0	0	0	36	81^2	71	6	52	67	14.4	2.76	136	.238	.366	1	.200	1	7	9	-1	1.7
1990 Chi-N	1	8	.111	59	2	0	0	16	66^1	60	4	50	55	15.1	3.93	104	.239	.368	0	.000	-1	-1	1	-1	0.0
1991 Phi-N	12	5	.706	69	0	0	0	30	88^1	56	4	62	84	12.8	2.34	156	.182	.333	0	.000	0	13	13	-1	3.1
1992 Phi-N	5	8	.385	66	0	0	0	29	81	69	4	64	74	15.4	3.78	92	.240	.389	1	.250	0	-2	-3	-1	-0.6
1993 *Phi-N	3	7	.300	65	0	0	0	43	62	56	3	44	60	14.8	3.34	119	.245	.371	1	1.000	0	5	4	-1	1.1
1994 Hou-N	1	4	.200	25	0	0	0	6	20	21	4	24	21	20.7	7.65	52	.269	.447	0	—	0	-8	-8	-0	-2.2
1995 Cal-A	1	2	.333	20	0	0	0	0	10^2	13	1	21	9	30.4	6.75	70	.317	.563	0	—	0	-2	-2	0	-0.5
1997 KC-A	0	1	.000	7	0	0	0	0	6^2	11	2	7	10	24.3	10.80	44	.367	.486	0	—	0	-5	-5	-0	-0.7
Total 11	45	58	.437	619	3	0	0	192	691^1	537	49	544	660	14.7	3.65	110	.218	.371	3	.188	1	23	29	-6	4.1
● STEAMBOAT WILLIAMS Williams, Rees Gephardt b: 1/31/1892, Cascade, Mont. d: 6/29/79, Deer River, Minn. BL/TR, 5'11", 170 lbs. Deb: 7/12/14																									
1914 StL-N	0	1	.000	5	1	0	0	0	11	13	1	6	2	15.5	6.55	43	.295	.380	0	.000	-0	-5	-5	-0	-0.4
1916 StL-N	6	7	.462	36	8	5	0	1	105	121	6	27	25	12.8	4.20	63	.291	.336	5	.208	1	-18	-18	-0	-2.2
Total 2	6	8	.429	41	9	5	0	1	116	134	7	33	27	13.0	4.42	60	.291	.340	5	.200	1	-23	-23	-0	-2.6
● RICK WILLIAMS Williams, Richard Allen b: 11/9/52, Merced, Cal. BR/TR, 6'1", 180 lbs. Deb: 6/12/78																									
1978 Hou-N	1	2	.333	17	1	0	0	0	34^2	43	2	10	17	13.8	4.67	71	.301	.346	0	.000	-1	-4	-5	0	-0.5
1979 Hou-N	4	7	.364	31	16	2	2	0	121^1	122	6	30	37	11.4	3.26	108	.261	.308	8	.258	3	6	3	0	0.6
Total 2	5	9	.357	48	17	2	2	0	156	165	8	40	54	11.9	3.58	97	.270	.317	8	.222	2	2	-2	1	0.1
● ACE WILLIAMS Williams, Robert Fulton b: 3/18/17, Montclair, N.J. BR/TL, 6'2", 174 lbs. Deb: 7/15/40																									
1940 Bos-N	0	0	—	5	0	0	0	0	9	21	0	12	5	34.0	16.00	23	.375	.493	0	.000	-0	-12	-12	0	0.0
1946 Bos-N	0	0	—	1	0	0	0	0	0	1	0	1	0	—	—	—	1.000	1.000	0	—	0	0	0	0	0.0
Total 2	0	0	—	6	0	0	0	0	9	22	0	13	5	36.0	16.00	23	.386	.507	0	.000	-0	-12	-12	0	0.0
● SHAD WILLIAMS Williams, Shad Clayton b: 3/10/71, Fresno, Cal. BR/TR, 6', 198 lbs. Deb: 5/18/96																									
1996 Cal-A	0	2	.000	13	2	0	0	0	28^1	42	7	21	26	20.6	8.89	56	.341	.445	0	—	0	-12	-12	-1	-0.8
1997 Ana-A	0	0	—	1	0	0	0	0	1	1	0	1	0	18.0	0.00	—	.250	.400	0	—	0	1	1	0	0.0
Total 2	0	2	.000	14	2	0	0	0	29^1	43	7	22	26	20.6	8.59	58	.339	.444	0	—	0	-12	-12	-1	-0.8
● STAN WILLIAMS Williams, Stanley Wilson b: 9/14/36, Enfield, N.H. BR/TR, 6'5", 230 lbs. Deb: 5/17/58 C																									
1958 LA-N	9	7	.563	27	21	3	2	0	119	99	10	65	80	12.9	4.01	102	.228	.338	2	.050	-3	-1	1	0	-0.1
1959 *LA-N	5	5	.500	35	15	2	0	0	124^2	102	12	86	89	14.2	3.97	106	.228	.363	7	.194	1	-0	4	0	0.3
1960 LA-N★	14	10	.583	38	30	9	2	1	207^1	162	26	72	175	10.4	3.00	133	.210	.282	9	.141	0	18	22	1	2.6
1961 LA-N	15	12	.556	41	35	6	2	0	235^1	213	21	108	205	12.5	3.90	111	.242	.329	13	.167	-1	3	12	-1	1.1
1962 LA-N	14	12	.538	40	28	4	1	1	185^2	184	16	98	108	13.7	4.46	81	.253	.341	5	.076	-2	-11	-17	-1	-2.4
1963 *NY-A	9	8	.529	29	21	6	1	0	146	137	7	57	98	12.3	3.21	110	.249	.326	5	.102	-1	7	5	1	0.5
1964 NY-A	1	5	.167	21	10	1	0	0	82	76	7	38	54	12.5	3.84	94	.248	.330	3	.143	-0	-2	-2	1	-0.1
1965 Cle-A	0	0	—	3	0	0	0	0	4^1	6	1	3	1	18.7	6.23	56	.353	.450	0	—	0	-1	-1	0	0.0
1967 Cle-A	6	4	.600	16	8	2	1	1	79	64	6	24	75	10.1	2.62	125	.218	.279	2	.091	-1	5	6	-2	0.4
1968 Cle-A	13	11	.542	44	24	6	2	9	194^1	163	14	51	147	10.4	2.50	118	.225	.285	9	.161	1	10	10	-1	1.5
1969 Cle-A	6	14	.300	61	15	3	0	12	178^1	155	25	67	139	11.8	3.94	96	.235	.317	4	.100	-1	-6	-3	-1	-0.5
1970 *Min-A	10	1	.909	68	0	0	0	15	113^1	85	8	32	76	9.7	1.99	187	.208	.274	0	.000	-2	22	22	-2	2.2
1971 Min-A	4	5	.444	46	1	0	0	4	78	63	7	44	47	13.3	4.15	86	.220	.340	0	.000	-1	-6	-5	-1	-0.8
StL-N	3	0	1.000	10	0	0	0	0	12^2	13	0	2	8	12.1	1.42	253	.265	.321	0	.000	-0	3	3	0	0.8
1972 Bos-A	0	0	—	3	0	0	0	0	4^1	5	0	1	3	12.5	6.23	52	.294	.333	0	—	0	-2	-1	0	0.0
Total 14	109	94	.537	482	208	42	11	43	1764^1	1527	160	748	1305	12.0	3.48	108	.232	.317	59	.118	-10	39	53	-4	5.5
● TED WILLIAMS Williams, Theodore Samuel "The Kid', "The Thumper" or "The Splendid Splinter" b: 8/30/18, San Diego, Cal. BL/TR, 6'3", 205 lbs. Deb: 4/20/39 MH♦																									
1940 Bos-A★	0	0	—	1	0	0	0	0	2	3	0	0	1	13.5	4.50	100	.333	.333	193	.344	1	-0	-0	0	0.0

YEAR	TM/L	W	L	PCT	G	GS	CG	SH	SV	IP	H	HR	BB	SO	RAT	ERA	ERA+	OAV	OOB	BH	AVG	PB	PR	/A	PD	TPI
● TOM WILLIAMS Williams, Thomas C. b: 8/19/1870, Minersville, Ohio d: 7/27/40, Columbus, Ohio Deb: 5/1/1892																										
1892	Cle-N	1	0	1.000	2	1	1	0	0	9	9	1	1	3	10.0	3.00	113	.250	.270	1	.100	-1	0	0	-0	0.0
1893	Cle-N	1	1	.500	5	2	2	0	0	24	33	1	10	6	16.5	4.88	100	.317	.383	5	.278	0	-1	0	0	0.0
Total	2	2	1	.667	7	3	3	0	0	33	42	2	11	9	14.7	4.36	102	.300	.355	6	.214	-0	-0	0	-0	0.0
● TODD WILLIAMS Williams, Todd Michael b: 2/13/71, Syracuse, N.Y. BR/TR, 6'3", 185 lbs. Deb: 4/29/95																										
1995	LA-N	2	2	.500	16	0	0	0	0	19^1	19	3	7	8	12.1	5.12	74	.264	.329	1	.500	0	-2	-3	1	-0.4
1998	Cin-N	0	1	.000	6	0	0	0	0	9^1	15	1	6	4	20.3	7.71	56	.341	.420	0	.000	-0	-4	-4	-0	-0.4
Total	2	2	3	.400	22	0	0	0	0	28^2	34	4	13	12	14.8	5.97	66	.293	.364	1	.250	0	-6	-6	0	-0.8
● POP WILLIAMS Williams, Walter Merrill b: 5/19/1874, Bowdoinham, Me. d: 8/4/59, Topsham, Maine BL/TR, 5'11", 190 lbs. Deb: 9/14/1898																										
1898	Was-N	0	2	.000	2	2	2	0	0	17	32	0	7	3	20.6	8.47	43	.395	.443	3	.375	1	-9	-9	-1	-0.7
1902	Chi-N	11	16	.407	31	31	26	1	0	254^1	259	1	63	94	11.7	2.51	107	.264	.313	23	.198	1	8	5	3	1.1
1903	Chi-N	0	1	.000	1	1	1	0	0	5	9	0	0	2	16.2	5.40	58	.409	.409	0	.000	0	-1	-1	-0	-0.2
	Phi-N	1	1	.500	2	2	2	0	0	18	21	0	6	8	14.0	3.00	109	.304	.368	2	.286	0	1	1	1	0.2
	Bos-N	4	5	.444	10	10	9	1	0	83	97	3	37	20	15.5	4.12	78	.295	.381	10	.238	-0	-8	-8	-1	-0.8
	Yr	5	7	.417	13	13	12	1	0	106	127	3	43	30	15.2	3.99	81	.302	.378	12	.235	0	-8	-9	0	-0.8
Total	3	16	25	.390	46	46	40	2	0	377^1	418	4	113	127	13.1	3.20	90	.282	.340	38	.217	4	-10	-13	2	-0.4
● WASH WILLIAMS Williams, Washington J. b: Philadelphia, Pa. d: 1/1890, Philadelphia, Pa. 5'11", 180 lbs. Deb: 8/5/1884 ♦																										
1885	Chi-N	0	0	—	1	1	0	0	0	2	2	0	5	0	31.5	13.50	22	.400	.700	1	.250	-0	-2	-2	0	0.0
● NED WILLIAMSON Williamson, Edward Nagle b: 10/24/1857, Philadelphia, Pa. d: 3/3/1894, Mountain Valley Springs, Ark BR/TR, 5'11", 210 lbs. Deb: 5/1/1878 ♦																										
1881	Chi-N	1	1	.500	3	1	1	0	0	18	14	0	0	2	7.0	2.00	137	.209	.209	92	.268	1	2	1	-0	0.1
1882	Chi-N	0	0	—	1	0	0	0	0	3	9	0	1	0	30.0	6.00	48	.500	.526	98	.282	0	-1	-1	0	0.0
1883	Chi-N	0	0	—	1	0	0	0	0	1	1	0	1	1	18.0	9.00	35	.167	.286	111	.276	0	-1	-1	0	0.0
1884	Chi-N	0	0	—	2	0	0	0	0	2	8	0	2	0	45.0	18.00	17	.500	.556	116	.278	1	-3	-3	0	0.0
1885	*Chi-N	0	0	—	2	0	0	0	**2**	6	2	0	0	3	3.0	0.00	—	.080	.080	97	.238	0	2	2	0	0.2
1886	*Chi-N	0	0	—	2	0	0	0	1	3	2	0	0	1	6.0	0.00	—	.143	.143	93	.216	0	1	1	-0	0.1
1887	Chi-N	0	0	—	1	0	0	0	0	2	2	0	1	0	13.5	9.00	50	.222	.300	117	.267	0	-1	-1	0	0.0
Total	7	1	1	.500	12	1	1	0	3	35	38	1	5	7	11.1	3.34	90	.245	.269	1159	.255	3	-2	-1	0	0.4
● MARK WILLIAMSON Williamson, Mark Alan b: 7/21/59, Corpus Christi, Tex. BR/TR, 6', 172 lbs. Deb: 4/8/87																										
1987	Bal-A	8	9	.471	61	2	0	0	3	125	122	12	41	73	12.0	4.03	109	.261	.324	0	—	0	6	5	1	0.8
1988	Bal-A	5	8	.385	37	10	2	0	2	117^2	125	14	40	69	12.8	4.90	80	.272	.333	0	—	0	-12	-13	-0	-1.3
1989	Bal-A	10	5	.667	65	0	0	0	9	107^1	105	4	30	55	11.5	2.93	129	.261	.315	0	—	0	11	10	-1	1.5
1990	Bal-A	8	2	.800	49	0	0	0	1	85^1	65	8	28	60	9.8	2.21	171	.215	.282	0	—	0	16	15	1	1.8
1991	Bal-A	5	5	.500	65	0	0	0	4	80^1	87	9	35	53	13.7	4.48	88	.275	.348	0	—	0	-3	-5	-0	-0.6
1992	Bal-A	0	0	—	12	0	0	0	1	18^2	16	1	10	14	12.5	0.96	417	.239	.338	0	—	0	6	6	-1	0.0
1993	Bal-A	7	5	.583	48	1	0	0	0	88	106	5	25	45	13.4	4.91	91	.304	.350	0	—	0	-6	-4	-0	-0.6
1994	Bal-A	3	1	.750	28	2	0	0	1	67^1	75	9	17	28	12.6	4.01	125	.278	.325	0	—	0	6	7	-1	0.2
Total	8	46	35	.568	365	15	2	0	21	689^2	701	62	226	397	12.2	3.86	107	.266	.326	0	—	0	24	22	-1	1.8
● AL WILLIAMSON Williamson, Silas Albert b: 2/20/1900, Buckville, Ark. d: 11/29/78, Hot Springs, Ark. BR/TR, 5'11", 160 lbs. Deb: 4/27/28																										
1928	Chi-A	0	0	—	1	0	0	0	0	2	1	0	0	0	4.5	0.00	—	.167	.167	0	—	0	1	1	0	0.0
● CARL WILLIS Willis, Carl Blake b: 12/28/60, Danville, Va. BL/TR, 6'4", 213 lbs. Deb: 6/9/84																										
1984	Det-A	0	2	.000	10	2	0	0	0	16	25	1	5	4	16.9	7.31	54	.362	.405	0	—	0	-6	-6	0	-0.6
	Cin-N	0	1	.000	7	0	0	0	1	9^2	8	1	2	3	9.3	3.72	101	.222	.263	0	—	0	-0	0	0	0.0
1985	Cin-N	1	0	1.000	11	0	0	0	1	13^2	21	3	5	6	17.1	9.22	41	.344	.394	0	.000	0	-9	-8	-0	-0.7
1986	Cin-N	1	3	.250	29	0	0	0	0	52^1	54	4	32	24	15.0	4.47	87	.278	.383	1	.333	0	-4	-4	1	-0.2
1988	Chi-A	0	0	—	6	0	0	0	0	12	17	3	7	6	18.0	8.25	48	.362	.444	0	—	0	-6	-6	-0	0.0
1991	*Min-A	8	3	.727	40	0	0	0	2	89	76	4	19	53	9.7	2.63	162	.232	.276	0	—	0	14	16	-1	1.8
1992	Min-A	7	3	.700	59	0	0	0	1	79^1	73	4	11	45	9.5	2.72	149	.246	.273	0	—	0	11	12	-1	1.3
1993	Min-A	3	0	1.000	53	0	0	0	5	58	56	2	17	44	11.3	3.10	140	.259	.313	0	—	0	8	8	-0	0.4
1994	Min-A	2	4	.333	49	0	0	0	3	59^1	89	6	12	37	15.3	5.92	82	.335	.363	0	—	0	-7	-7	-1	-0.7
1995	Min-A	0	0	—	3	0	0	0	0	0^2	5	0	5	0	135.0	94.50	5	.833	.909	0	—	0	-7	-7	0	0.0
Total	9	22	16	.579	267	2	0	0	13	390	424	28	115	222	12.5	4.25	100	.279	.330	1	.250	0	-6	-1	-3	1.3
● LEFTY WILLIS Willis, Charles William b: 11/4/05, Leetown, W.Va. d: 5/10/62, Bethesda, Md. BL/TL, 6'1", 175 lbs. Deb: 10/3/25																										
1925	Phi-A	0	0	—	1	1	0	0	0	5	9	2	2	3	19.8	10.80	43	.409	.458	0	.000	-1	-4	-3	0	0.0
1926	Phi-A	0	0	—	13	1	0	0	1	32^1	31	0	12	13	12.2	1.39	300	.270	.344	2	.222	-0	9	10	-0	0.0
1927	Phi-A	3	1	.750	15	2	1	0	0	27	32	2	11	7	14.3	5.67	75	.308	.374	0	.000	-1	-5	-4	1	-0.5
Total	3	3	1	.750	29	4	1	0	1	64^1	72	4	25	23	13.7	3.92	108	.299	.367	2	.111	-1	1	2	1	-0.5
● DALE WILLIS Willis, Dale Jerome b: 5/29/38, Calhoun, Ga. BR/TR, 5'11", 165 lbs. Deb: 4/14/63																										
1963	KC-A	0	2	.000	25	0	0	0	1	44^2	46	3	25	47	15.1	5.04	77	.266	.371	1	.167	-0	-7	-6	1	-0.2
● JIM WILLIS Willis, James Gladden b: 3/20/27, Doyline, La. BL/TR, 6'3", 175 lbs. Deb: 4/22/53																										
1953	Chi-N	2	1	.667	13	3	2	0	0	43^1	37	1	17	15	11.8	3.12	143	.228	.313	0	.000	-1	6	6	1	0.4
1954	Chi-N	0	1	.000	14	1	0	0	0	23	22	1	18	5	16.8	3.91	107	.256	.402	0	.000	-1	0	1	1	0.0
Total	2	2	2	.500	27	4	2	0	0	66^1	59	2	35	20	13.6	3.39	129	.238	.346	0	.000	-2	6	7	2	0.4
● JOE WILLIS Willis, Joseph Denk b: 4/9/1890, Coal Grove, Ohio d: 12/4/66, Ironton, Ohio BR/TL, 6'1", 185 lbs. Deb: 5/3/11																										
1911	StL-A	0	1	.000	1	1	0	0	0	7	8	0	3	0	14.1	5.14	66	.308	.379	0	.000	0	-1	-1	-1	-0.2
	StL-N	0	1	.000	2	2	1	0	0	15	13	0	4	5	10.2	4.20	80	.232	.283	0	.000	-1	-1	-1	0	-0.1
1912	StL-N	4	9	.308	31	17	4	0	2	129^2	143	3	62	55	14.6	4.44	77	.288	.372	6	.158	-2	-15	-15	-1	-1.5
1913	StL-N	0	0	—	7	0	0	0	1	9^2	9	0	11	6	18.6	7.45	43	.257	.435	0	.000	-0	-5	-5	-0	-0.2
Total	3	4	11	.267	41	20	5	0	3	161^1	173	3	80	66	14.4	4.63	74	.282	.369	6	.125	-2	-22	-22	-1	-2.0
● LES WILLIS Willis, Lester Evans "Wimpy" or "Lefty" b: 1/17/08, Nacogdoches, Tex. d: 1/22/82, Jasper, Tex. BL/TL, 5'9.5", 195 lbs. Deb: 4/28/47																										
1947	Cle-A	0	2	.000	22	2	0	0	1	44	58	3	24	10	16.8	3.48	100	.324	.404	1	.091	-1	1	0	-1	-0.2
● MIKE WILLIS Willis, Michael Henry b: 12/26/50, Oklahoma City, Okla BL/TL, 6'2", 210 lbs. Deb: 4/13/77																										
1977	Tor-A	2	6	.250	43	3	0	0	5	107^1	105	15	38	59	12.0	3.94	106	.260	.324	0	—	0	1	3	1	0.3
1978	Tor-A	3	7	.300	44	2	1	0	7	100^2	104	11	39	52	12.8	4.56	86	.271	.338	0	—	0	-9	-7	0	-0.8
1979	Tor-A	0	3	.000	17	1	0	0	0	26^2	35	1	16	8	17.6	8.44	51	.333	.426	0	—	0	-13	-12	0	-1.2
1980	Tor-A	2	1	.667	20	0	0	0	3	26^1	25	3	11	14	12.6	1.71	252	.248	.327	0	—	0	7	8	0	0.7
1981	Tor-A	0	4	.000	20	0	0	0	0	35	43	6	20	16	16.5	5.91	67	.301	.390	0	—	0	-9	-8	0	-0.8
Total	5	7	21	.250	144	6	1	0	15	296	312	36	124	149	13.3	4.59	89	.274	.347	0	—	0	-22	-16	1	-1.8
● RON WILLIS Willis, Ronald Earl b: 7/12/43, Willisville, Tenn. d: 11/21/77, Memphis, Tenn. BR/TR, 6'2", 195 lbs. Deb: 9/20/66																										
1966	StL-N	0	0	—	4	0	0	0	1	3	1	0	1	2	6.0	0.00	—	.100	.182	0	—	0	1	1	-0	0.1
1967	*StL-N	6	5	.545	65	0	0	0	10	81	76	3	43	42	13.6	2.67	123	.257	.357	3	.375	1	6	6	2	1.3
1968	*StL-N	2	3	.400	48	0	0	0	4	63^2	50	4	28	39	11.2	3.39	85	.213	.299	0	.000	-1	-3	-4	1	-0.4
1969	StL-N	1	2	.333	26	0	0	0	0	32^1	26	4	19	23	12.8	4.18	86	.224	.338	1	1.000	0	-2	-2	1	0.0
	Hou-N	0	0	—	3	0	0	0	0	2^1	3	0	0	2	11.6	0.00	—	.300	.300	0	—	0	1	1	-0	0.0
	Yr	1	2	.333	29	0	0	0	0	34^2	29	4	19	25	12.5	3.89	92	.223	.322	1	1.000	0	-1	-1	1	0.0
1970	SD-N	2	2	.500	42	0	0	0	4	56	53	4	28	20	13.7	4.02	99	.247	.344	0	.000	-1	0	-0	1	0.1
Total	5	11	12	.478	188	0	0	0	19	238^1	209	15	119	128	12.7	3.32	102	.237	.334	4	.160	0	4	2	5	1.1

● VIC WILLIS Willis, Victor Gazaway b: 4/12/1876, Cecil Co., Md. d: 8/3/47, Elkton, Md. BR/TR, 6'2", 185 lbs. Deb: 4/20/1898 H

YEAR	TM/L	W	L	PCT	G	GS	CG	SH	SV	IP	H	HR	BB	SO	RAT	ERA	ERA+	OAV	OOB	BH	AVG	PB	PR	/A	PD	TPI
1898	Bos-N	25	13	.658	41	38	29	1	0	311	264	5	148	160	12.8	2.84	130	.228	.331	17	.145	-6	27	30	-0	2.5
1899	Bos-N	27	8	.771	41	38	35	**5**	2	342^2	277	6	117	120	11.1	2.50	**167**	**.221**	.303	29	.216	-4	52	**63**	0	5.3
1900	Bos-N	10	17	.370	32	29	22	2	0	236	258	11	106	53	14.3	4.19	98	.277	.359	12	.136	-6	-13	-2	-2	-0.9
1901	Bos-N	20	17	.541	38	35	33	**6**	0	305^1	262	6	78	133	10.3	2.36	**153**	.230	.286	20	.187	-1	33	**43**	-1	4.6
1902	Bos-N	27	20	.574	**51**	46	**45**	4	**3**	**410**	372	6	101	**225**	10.7	2.20	129	.242	.295	23	.153	-6	27	29	4	3.1
1903	Bos-N	12	18	.400	33	32	29	2	0	278	256	3	88	125	11.5	2.98	108	.251	.317	24	.188	-1	9	7	3	0.8
1904	Bos-N	18	25	.419	43	43	**39**	2	0	350	357	7	109	196	12.3	2.85	97	.266	.327	27	.182	1	-4	-4	7	0.4
1905	Bos-N	12	29	.293	41	41	36	4	0	342	340	7	107	149	12.1	3.21	97	.265	.328	20	.153	-3	-8	-4	6	-0.1
1906	Pit-N	23	13	.639	41	36	32	6	1	322	295	0	76	124	10.5	1.73	154	.250	.298	20	.174	-1	32	34	5	4.5
1907	Pit-N	21	11	.656	39	37	27	6	1	292^2	234	4	69	107	9.5	2.34	104	.219	.271	14	.136	-2	4	3	2	0.3
1908	Pit-N	23	11	.676	41	38	25	7	0	304^2	239	2	69	97	9.3	2.07	111	.213	.262	17	.165	-1	10	8	1	0.7
1909	*Pit-N	22	11	.667	39	35	24	4	1	289^2	243	3	83	95	10.3	2.24	122	.231	.289	14	.136	-2	12	16	1	1.6
1910	StL-N	9	12	.429	33	23	12	1	3	212	224	6	61	67	12.1	3.35	89	.275	.326	11	.167	-2	-8	-9	2	-0.8
Total	13	249	205	.548	513	471	388	50	11	3996	3621	66	1212	1651	11.2	2.63	118	.243	.307	248	.166	-33	172	208	27	22.0

● CLAUDE WILLOUGHBY Willoughby, Claude William "Flunky" or "Weeping Willie" b: 11/14/1898, Buffalo, Kan. d: 8/14/73, McPherson, Kan. BR/TR, 5'9.5", 165 lbs. Deb: 9/18/25

YEAR	TM/L	W	L	PCT	G	GS	CG	SH	SV	IP	H	HR	BB	SO	RAT	ERA	ERA+	OAV	OOB	BH	AVG	PB	PR	/A	PD	TPI
1925	Phi-N	2	1	.667	3	3	1	0	0	23	26	0	11	6	14.9	1.96	244	.295	.380	0	.000	-1	6	7	-1	0.7
1926	Phi-N	8	12	.400	47	19	6	0	1	168	218	7	71	37	15.8	5.95	70	.327	.396	11	.212	-1	-40	-34	3	-3.3
1927	Phi-N	3	7	.300	35	6	1	1	2	97^2	126	7	53	14	16.7	6.54	63	.321	.404	2	.077	-2	-28	-26	-1	-2.6
1928	Phi-N	6	5	.545	35	13	5	1	1	130^2	180	6	83	26	18.3	5.30	81	.340	.432	6	.150	-1	-19	-15	-1	-1.2
1929	Phi-N	15	14	.517	49	34	14	1	4	243^1	288	15	108	50	14.8	4.99	104	.296	.370	13	.143	-5	-7	5	4	0.5
1930	Phi-N	4	17	.190	41	24	5	1	1	153	241	17	68	38	18.3	7.59	72	.369	.430	5	.104	-4	-44	-36	2	-3.9
1931	Pit-N	0	2	.000	9	2	1	0	0	25^2	32	4	12	4	15.4	6.31	61	.305	.376	2	.286	0	-7	-7	0	-0.4
Total	7	38	58	.396	219	101	33	4	9	841^1	1111	56	406	175	16.4	5.84	81	.326	.401	39	.143	-14	-140	-106	8	-10.2

● JIM WILLOUGHBY Willoughby, James Arthur b: 1/31/49, Salinas, Cal. BR/TR, 6'2", 185 lbs. Deb: 9/5/71

YEAR	TM/L	W	L	PCT	G	GS	CG	SH	SV	IP	H	HR	BB	SO	RAT	ERA	ERA+	OAV	OOB	BH	AVG	PB	PR	/A	PD	TPI
1971	SF-N	0	1	.000	2	1	0	0	0	4	8	0	1	3	20.3	9.00	38	.400	.429	0	.000	-0	-2	-2	0	-0.5
1972	SF-N	6	4	.600	11	11	7	0	0	87^2	72	8	14	40	9.0	2.36	148	.222	.259	5	.185	0	11	11	0	1.4
1973	SF-N	4	5	.444	39	12	1	1	1	123	138	21	37	60	13.0	4.68	82	.295	.350	4	.143	1	-14	-12	-1	-0.8
1974	SF-N	1	4	.200	18	4	0	0	0	40^2	51	7	9	12	13.3	4.65	82	.304	.339	1	.100	-0	-5	-4	1	-0.4
1975	*Bos-A	5	2	.714	24	0	0	0	8	48^1	46	6	16	29	11.9	3.54	115	.247	.314	0	—	0	1	3	0	0.3
1976	Bos-A	3	12	.200	54	0	0	0	10	99	94	4	31	37	12.1	2.82	139	.256	.328	0	.000	-0	8	12	1	2.2
1977	Bos-A	6	2	.750	31	0	0	0	2	54^2	54	5	18	33	12.2	4.94	91	.258	.323	0	—	0	-5	-3	1	-0.3
1978	Chi-A	1	6	.143	59	0	0	0	13	93^1	95	6	19	36	11.4	3.86	99	.275	.320	0	—	0	-1	-1	2	0.1
Total	8	26	36	.419	238	28	8	1	34	550^2	558	57	145	250	11.8	3.79	102	.267	.321	10	.149	1	-8	4	5	2.0

● FRANK WILLS Wills, Frank Lee b: 10/26/58, New Orleans, La. BR/TR, 6'2", 202 lbs. Deb: 7/31/83

YEAR	TM/L	W	L	PCT	G	GS	CG	SH	SV	IP	H	HR	BB	SO	RAT	ERA	ERA+	OAV	OOB	BH	AVG	PB	PR	/A	PD	TPI
1983	KC-A	2	1	.667	6	4	0	0	0	34^2	35	2	15	23	13.0	4.15	98	.259	.333	0	—	0	-0	-0	-0	-0.1
1984	KC-A	2	3	.400	10	5	0	0	0	37	39	3	13	21	12.6	5.11	79	.271	.331	0	—	0	-5	-4	-1	-0.6
1985	Sea-A	5	11	.313	24	18	1	0	1	123	122	18	68	67	14.1	6.00	70	.266	.365	0	—	0	-25	-24	0	-2.7
1986	Cle-A	4	4	.500	26	0	0	0	4	40^1	43	6	16	32	13.2	4.91	84	.272	.339	0	—	0	-3	-3	0	-0.6
1987	Cle-A	0	1	.000	6	0	0	0	1	5^1	3	0	7	4	16.9	5.06	89	.176	.417	0	—	0	-0	-0	0	-0.1
1988	Tor-A	0	0	—	10	0	0	0	0	20^2	22	2	6	19	12.2	5.23	75	.272	.322	0	—	0	-3	-3	1	0.0
1989	Tor-A	3	1	.750	24	4	0	0	0	71^1	65	4	30	41	12.1	3.66	103	.242	.320	0	—	0	2	1	-0	0.1
1990	Tor-A	6	4	.600	44	4	0	0	0	99	101	13	38	72	12.7	4.73	83	.266	.334	0	—	0	-9	-9	0	-0.8
1991	Tor-A	0	1	.000	4	0	0	0	0	4^1	8	2	5	2	29.1	16.62	25	.421	.560	0	—	0	-6	-6	0	-1.1
Total	9	22	26	.458	154	35	1	0	6	435^2	438	50	198	281	13.3	5.06	80	.264	.344	0	—	0	-50	-50	0	-5.9

● TED WILLS Wills, Theodore Carl b: 2/9/34, Fresno, Cal. BL/TL, 6'2", 200 lbs. Deb: 5/24/59

YEAR	TM/L	W	L	PCT	G	GS	CG	SH	SV	IP	H	HR	BB	SO	RAT	ERA	ERA+	OAV	OOB	BH	AVG	PB	PR	/A	PD	TPI
1959	Bos-A	2	6	.250	9	8	2	0	0	56^1	68	9	24	24	14.9	5.27	77	.302	.372	4	.250	1	-9	-8	-0	-0.9
1960	Bos-A	1	1	.500	15	0	0	0	1	30^1	38	4	16	28	16.9	7.42	55	.317	.410	2	.250	1	-12	-11	-0	-0.6
1961	Bos-A	3	2	.600	17	0	0	0	0	19^2	24	2	19	11	19.7	5.95	70	.304	.439	0	.000	-0	-4	-4	0	-0.9
1962	Bos-A	0	0	—	1	0	0	0	0	0	2	0	1	0	—	∞	—	1.000	1.000	0	—	0	-1	-1	0	-0.1
	Cin-N	0	2	.000	26	5	0	0	3	61	61	12	23	58	13.1	5.31	76	.266	.346	5	.313	1	-9	-9	-0	-0.3
1965	Chi-A	2	0	1.000	15	0	0	0	1	19	17	2	14	12	15.2	2.84	112	.258	.395	0	.000	0	1	1	0	0.1
Total	5	8	11	.421	83	13	2	0	5	186^1	210	29	97	133	15.3	5.51	72	.291	.383	11	.250	3	-34	-32	1	-2.7

● PAUL WILMET Wilmet, Paul Richard b: 11/8/58, Green Bay, Wis. BR/TR, 5'11", 170 lbs. Deb: 7/25/89

YEAR	TM/L	W	L	PCT	G	GS	CG	SH	SV	IP	H	HR	BB	SO	RAT	ERA	ERA+	OAV	OOB	BH	AVG	PB	PR	/A	PD	TPI
1989	Tex-A	0	0	—	3	0	0	0	0	2^1	5	0	2	1	27.0	15.43	26	.417	.500	0	—	0	-3	-3	0	0.0

● WHITEY WILSHERE Wilshere, Vernon Sprague b: 8/3/12, Poplar Ridge, N.Y. d: 5/23/85, Cooperstown, N.Y. BL/TL, 6', 180 lbs. Deb: 6/24/34

YEAR	TM/L	W	L	PCT	G	GS	CG	SH	SV	IP	H	HR	BB	SO	RAT	ERA	ERA+	OAV	OOB	BH	AVG	PB	PR	/A	PD	TPI
1934	Phi-A	0	1	.000	9	2	0	0	0	21^2	39	0	15	19	22.8	12.05	36	.394	.478	0	.000	-0	-18	-18	-1	-0.8
1935	Phi-A	9	9	.500	27	18	7	3	1	142^1	136	8	78	80	14.2	4.05	112	.253	.358	4	.093	-4	6	8	-0	0.5
1936	Phi-A	1	2	.333	5	3	0	0	0	18^1	21	1	19	4	19.6	6.87	74	.288	.435	0	.000	-0	-4	-4	-0	-0.5
Total	3	10	12	.455	41	23	7	3	1	182^1	196	9	112	103	15.7	5.28	87	.276	.383	4	.080	-4	-15	-14	-1	-0.8

● TERRY WILSHUSEN Wilshusen, Terry Wayne b: 3/22/49, Atascadero, Cal. BR/TR, 6'2", 210 lbs. Deb: 4/7/73

YEAR	TM/L	W	L	PCT	G	GS	CG	SH	SV	IP	H	HR	BB	SO	RAT	ERA	ERA+	OAV	OOB	BH	AVG	PB	PR	/A	PD	TPI
1973	Cal-A	0	0	—	1	0	0	0	0	0^1	0	0	2	0	81.0	81.00	4	.000	.750	0	—	0	-3	-3	0	0.4

● DON WILSON Wilson, Donald Edward b: 2/12/45, Monroe, La. d: 1/5/75, Houston, Tex. BR/TR, 6'3", 205 lbs. Deb: 9/29/66

YEAR	TM/L	W	L	PCT	G	GS	CG	SH	SV	IP	H	HR	BB	SO	RAT	ERA	ERA+	OAV	OOB	BH	AVG	PB	PR	/A	PD	TPI
1966	Hou-N	1	0	1.000	1	0	0	0	0	6	5	1	1	7	9.0	3.00	114	.238	.273	1	.500	1	0	0	0	0.1
1967	Hou-N	10	9	.526	31	28	7	3	0	184	141	10	69	159	10.6	2.79	119	.209	.289	6	.091	-2	12	11	-2	0.7
1968	Hou-N	13	16	.448	33	30	9	3	0	208^2	187	9	70	175	11.3	3.28	90	.236	.302	15	.214	4	-7	-7	-2	-0.8
1969	Hou-N	16	12	.571	34	34	13	1	0	225	210	16	97	235	12.6	4.00	89	.245	.328	8	.099	-1	-10	-11	-0	-1.5
1970	Hou-N	11	6	.647	29	27	3	0	0	184^1	188	15	66	94	12.7	3.91	99	.259	.327	8	.116	-2	3	-1	-3	-0.6
1971	Hou-N★	16	10	.615	35	34	18	3	0	268	195	15	79	180	9.4	2.45	137	**.202**	.268	14	.154	-1	30	27	-3	2.2
1972	Hou-N	15	10	.600	33	33	13	3	0	228^1	196	16	66	172	10.4	2.68	125	.233	.290	8	.105	-2	20	17	1	1.7
1973	Hou-N	11	16	.407	37	32	10	3	2	239^1	187	21	92	149	10.8	3.20	114	.213	.293	14	.177	1	12	12	-2	1.1
1974	Hou-N	11	13	.458	33	27	5	4	0	204^2	170	16	100	112	12.0	3.08	112	.227	.321	13	.206	2	12	9	-3	1.0
Total	9	104	92	.531	266	245	78	20	2	1748^1	1479	119	640	1283	11.2	3.15	109	.228	.301	87	.146	-1	73	57	-14	3.9

● DUANE WILSON Wilson, Duane Lewis b: 6/29/34, Wichita, Kan. BL/TL, 6'1", 185 lbs. Deb: 7/3/58

YEAR	TM/L	W	L	PCT	G	GS	CG	SH	SV	IP	H	HR	BB	SO	RAT	ERA	ERA+	OAV	OOB	BH	AVG	PB	PR	/A	PD	TPI
1958	Bos-A	0	0	—	2	2	0	0	0	6^1	10	0	7	3	24.2	5.68	70	.400	.531	0	.000	-0	-1	-1	0	0.0

● FIN WILSON Wilson, Finis Elbert b: 12/9/1889, East Fork, Ky. d: 3/9/69, Coral Gables, Fla. BL/TL, 6'1", 194 lbs. Deb: 9/26/14

YEAR	TM/L	W	L	PCT	G	GS	CG	SH	SV	IP	H	HR	BB	SO	RAT	ERA	ERA+	OAV	OOB	BH	AVG	PB	PR	/A	PD	TPI
1914	Bro-F	0	1	.000	2	1	1	0	0	7	7	0	11	4	23.1	7.71	37	.269	.486	1	.500	1	-4	-4	-0	-0.4
1915	Bro-F	1	8	.111	18	11	5	0	0	102^1	85	2	53	47	12.5	3.78	72	.249	.356	11	.314	2	-12	-12	-0	-0.7
Total	2	1	9	.100	20	12	6	0	0	109^1	92	2	64	51	13.2	4.03	68	.250	.367	12	.324	3	-16	-16	-0	-1.1

● ZEKE WILSON Wilson, Frank Ealton b: 12/24/1869, Benton, Ala. d: 4/26/28, Montgomery, Ala. BR/TR, 5'10", 165 lbs. Deb: 4/23/1895

YEAR	TM/L	W	L	PCT	G	GS	CG	SH	SV	IP	H	HR	BB	SO	RAT	ERA	ERA+	OAV	OOB	BH	AVG	PB	PR	/A	PD	TPI
1895	Bos-N	2	4	.333	6	6	4	0	0	45	54	1	27	5	16.2	5.20	98	.293	.384	6	.316	1	-2	-0	1	0.1
	Cle-N	3	1	.750	8	7	3	0	0	44^2	63	3	20	16	17.1	4.23	118	.328	.397	2	.111	-2	3	4	-0	0.0
	Yr	5	5	.500	14	13	7	0	0	89^2	117	4	47	21	16.7	4.72	107	.311	.391	8	.216	-2	1	3	1	0.1
1896	Cle-N	17	9	.654	33	29	20	1	1	240	265	9	81	56	13.3	4.01	113	.278	.339	27	.270	2	9	14	6	1.8
1897	Cle-N	16	11	.593	34	30	26	1	0	263^2	323	9	83	69	14.2	4.16	108	.299	.354	26	.224	-3	4	10	1	0.6
1898	Cle-N	13	18	.419	33	31	28	1	0	254^2	307	4	51	45	12.9	3.60	100	.296	.333	21	.178	-3	0	0	4	0.1
1899	StL-N	1	1	.500	5	2	2	0	0	26	30	0	4	3	12.5	4.50	88	.288	.327	0	.000	-1	-2	-1	1	-0.1
Total	5	52	44	.542	119	105	83	3	1	874	1042	26	266	194	13.8	4.03	106	.293	.347	82	.215	-8	13	25	14	2.5

YEAR	TM/L	W	L	PCT	G	GS	CG	SH	SV	IP	H	HR	BB	SO	RAT	ERA	ERA+	OAV	OOB	BH	AVG	PB	PR	/A	PD	TPI
● **GARY WILSON**	Wilson, Gary Morris b: 1/1/70, Arcata, Cal. BR/TR, 6'3", 190 lbs. Deb: 4/28/95																									
1995	Pit-N	0	1	.000	10	0	0	0	0	14^1	13	2	5	8	12.6	5.02	86	.241	.328	0	—	0	-1	-1	-0	-0.1
● **GARY WILSON**	Wilson, Gary Steven b: 11/21/54, Camden, Ark. BR/TR, 6'2", 185 lbs. Deb: 4/13/79																									
1979	Hou-N	0	0	—	6	0	0	0	0	7^1	15	2	6	6	25.8	12.27	29	.441	.525	0	—	0	-7	-7	-0	0.0
● **GLENN WILSON**	Wilson, Glenn Dwight b: 12/22/58, Baytown, Tex. BR/TR, 6'1", 190 lbs. Deb: 4/15/82 ◆																									
1987	Phi-N	0	0	—	1	0	0	0	0	1	0	0	0	1	0.0	0.00	—	.000	.000	150	.264	0	0	0	0	0.0
● **TEX WILSON**	Wilson, Gomer Russell b: 7/8/01, Trenton, Tex. d: 9/15/46, Sulphur Springs, Tex. BR/TL, 5'10", 170 lbs. Deb: 9/2/24																									
1924	Bro-N	0	0	—	2	0	0	0	0	3^2	7	0	1	1	19.6	14.73	25	.412	.444	0	.000	-0	-4	-4	0	0.0
● **HIGHBALL WILSON**	Wilson, Howard Paul b: 8/9/1878, Philadelphia, Pa. d: 10/16/34, Havre De Grace, Md TR, Deb: 9/13/1899																									
1899	Cle-N	0	1	.000	1	1	1	0	0	8	12	0	5	1	19.1	9.00	41	.343	.425	1	.333	0	-5	-5	-0	-0.4
1902	Phi-A	7	4	.636	13	10	8	0	0	96^1	103	1	19	18	12.2	2.43	151	.274	.324	6	.171	-1	12	13	-1	1.1
1903	Was-A	7	18	.280	30	28	25	1	0	242^1	269	7	43	56	12.0	3.31	95	.280	.318	17	.200	2	-9	-5	-4	-0.6
1904	Was-A	0	3	.000	3	3	3	0	0	25	33	0	4	11	14.0	4.68	57	.317	.355	2	.222	1	-6	-6	0	-0.5
Total	4	14	26	.350	47	42	37	1	0	371^2	417	8	71	86	12.3	3.29	99	.283	.325	26	.197	2	-7	-2	-5	-0.4
● **JIM WILSON**	Wilson, James Alger b: 2/20/22, San Diego, Cal. d: 9/2/86, Newport Beach, Cal BR/TR, 6'1.5", 200 lbs. Deb: 4/18/45																									
1945	Bos-A	6	8	.429	23	21	8	2	0	144^1	121	7	88	50	13.1	3.30	103	.228	.339	13	.245	2	1	2	-2	0.1
1946	Bos-A	0	0	—	1	0	0	0	0	0^2	2	1	0	0	27.0	27.00	14	.500	.500	0	—	0	-2	-2	-0	0.0
1948	StL-A	0	0	—	4	0	0	0	0	2^2	5	0	5	1	33.8	13.50	34	.417	.588	0	—	0	-3	-3	0	0.0
1949	Phi-A	0	0	—	2	0	0	0	0	5	7	2	5	2	21.6	14.40	29	.350	.480	0	.000	-0	-6	-6	0	-0.1
1951	Bos-N	7	7	.500	20	15	5	0	1	110	131	14	40	33	14.3	5.40	68	.294	.357	7	.179	0	-18	-21	-1	-2.4
1952	Bos-N	12	14	.462	33	33	14	0	0	234	234	19	90	104	12.6	4.23	85	.262	.333	14	.163	-0	-13	-16	-1	-1.8
1953	Mil-N	4	9	.308	20	18	5	0	0	114	107	16	43	71	12.1	4.34	90	.243	.315	6	.167	1	-1	-5	1	-0.3
1954	Mil-N☆	8	2	.800	27	19	6	4	0	127^2	129	12	36	52	12.0	3.52	106	.266	.323	7	.159	0	8	3	1	0.3
1955	Bal-A☆	12	18	.400	34	31	14	4	0	235^1	200	17	87	96	11.1	3.44	111	.228	.300	15	.169	-2	14	10	-0	1.0
1956	Bal-A	4	2	.667	7	7	1	0	0	48^1	49	5	16	31	12.5	5.03	78	.268	.333	4	.267	2	-5	-6	0	-0.4
	Chi-A★	9	12	.429	28	21	6	3	0	159^2	149	15	70	82	12.5	4.06	101	.248	.329	19	.306	4	2	1	-0	0.5
	Yr	13	14	.481	35	28	7	3	0	208	198	20	86	113	12.4	4.28	95	.252	.327	23	.299	6	-3	-5	0	0.1
1957	Chi-A	15	8	.652	30	29	12	**5**	0	201^2	189	22	65	100	11.5	3.48	107	.249	.310	10	.147	-0	7	6	-2	0.4
1958	Chi-A	9	9	.500	28	23	4	1	1	155^2	156	21	63	70	12.7	4.10	89	.268	.341	4	.078	-3	-6	-8	-1	-1.3
Total	12	86	89	.491	257	217	75	19	2	1539	1479	151	608	692	12.4	4.01	93	.254	.327	99	.181	4	-21	-45	-5	-4.0
● **JACK WILSON**	Wilson, John Francis "Black Jack" b: 4/12/12, Portland, Ore. d: 4/19/95, Edmonds, Wash. BR/TR, 5'11", 210 lbs. Deb: 9/9/34																									
1934	Phi-A	0	1	.000	2	2	1	0	0	9	15	1	9	2	24.0	12.00	37	.405	.522	0	.000	-0	-8	-8	-0	-0.6
1935	Bos-A	3	4	.429	23	6	2	0	1	64	72	0	36	19	15.5	4.22	112	.290	.385	5	.313	2	2	4	1	0.7
1936	Bos-A	6	8	.429	43	9	2	0	3	136^1	152	4	86	74	15.8	4.42	120	.284	.384	11	.220	-0	9	13	0	1.1
1937	Bos-A	16	10	.615	51	21	14	1	7	221^1	209	13	119	137	13.5	3.70	128	.248	.343	14	.165	-3	23	26	1	2.5
1938	Bos-A	15	15	.500	37	27	11	3	1	194^2	200	16	91	96	13.5	4.30	115	.262	.342	15	.221	0	11	14	-1	1.7
1939	Bos-A	11	11	.500	36	22	6	0	2	177^1	198	10	75	80	13.9	4.67	101	.281	.351	10	.159	-4	-1	1	-0	-0.2
1940	Bos-A	12	6	.667	41	16	9	0	5	157^2	170	17	87	102	14.8	5.08	89	.270	.362	18	.273	4	-12	-10	-2	-0.8
1941	Bos-A	4	13	.235	27	12	4	1	1	116^1	140	7	70	55	16.6	5.03	83	.300	.397	7	.159	-1	-11	-11	2	-1.3
1942	Was-A	1	4	.200	12	6	1	0	0	42	57	2	23	18	17.4	6.64	55	.322	.403	2	.118	-1	-14	-14	-1	-1.6
	Det-A	0	0	—	9	0	0	0	0	13	20	3	5	7	17.3	4.85	81	.351	.403	0	.000	-0	-2	-1	0	0.0
	Yr	1	4	.200	21	6	1	0	0	55	77	5	28	25	17.2	6.22	60	.328	.399	2	.111	-1	-16	-15	-0	-1.6
Total	9	68	72	.486	281	121	50	5	20	1131^2	1233	73	601	590	14.7	4.59	102	.276	.364	82	.199	-3	-4	13	1	1.5
● **JOHN WILSON**	Wilson, John Nicodemus b: 6/15/1890, Boonsboro, Md. d: 9/23/54, Annapolis, Md. BR/TL, 6'1", 185 lbs. Deb: 6/11/13																									
1913	Was-A	0	0	—	3	0	0	0	0	4	4	0	3	1	15.8	4.50	66	.267	.389	0	—	0	-1	-1	0	0.0
● **JOHN WILSON**	Wilson, John Samuel b: 4/25/03, Coal City, Ala. d: 8/27/80, Chattanooga, Tenn. BR/TR, 6'2", 164 lbs. Deb: 5/9/27																									
1927	Bos-A	0	2	.000	5	2	2	0	0	25^1	31	1	13	8	15.6	3.55	119	.326	.407	1	.111	-1	2	2	-0	0.0
1928	Bos-A	0	0	—	2	0	0	0	0	5	6	0	6	1	21.6	9.00	46	.333	.500	0	.000	-0	-3	-3	0	0.0
Total	2	0	2	.000	7	2	2	0	0	30^1	37	1	19	9	16.6	4.45	94	.327	.424	1	.100	-1	-1	-1	-0	0.0
● **MAX WILSON**	Wilson, Max b: 6/3/16, Haw River, N.C. d: 1/2/77, Greensboro, N.C. BL/TL, 5'7", 160 lbs. Deb: 9/10/40																									
1940	Phi-N	0	0	—	3	0	0	0	0	7	16	1	2	3	23.1	12.86	30	.444	.474	0	.000	-0	-7	-7	0	0.0
1946	Was-A	0	1	.000	9	0	0	0	0	12^2	16	1	9	8	17.8	7.11	47	.320	.424	0	.000	0	-5	-5	-0	-0.4
Total	2	0	1	.000	12	0	0	0	0	19^2	32	2	11	11	19.7	9.15	39	.372	.443	0	.000	-0	-12	-12	-0	-0.4
● **PAUL WILSON**	Wilson, Paul Anthony b: 3/28/73, Orlando, Fla. BR/TR, 6'5", 235 lbs. Deb: 4/4/96																									
1996	NY-N	5	12	.294	26	26	1	0	0	149	157	15	71	109	14.4	5.38	75	.268	.357	4	.080	-2	-19	-23	-2	-2.5
● **PETE WILSON**	Wilson, Peter Alex b: 10/9/1885, Springfield, Mass. d: 6/5/57, St.Petersburg, Fla TL, Deb: 9/15/08																									
1908	NY-A	3	3	.500	6	6	4	1	0	39	27	0	33	28	14.1	3.46	72	.191	.349	1	.071	-1	-5	-4	-0	-0.7
1909	NY-A	6	5	.545	14	13	7	1	0	93^2	82	2	43	44	12.4	3.17	80	.230	.320	4	.118	-1	-7	-7	-1	-1.0
Total	2	9	8	.529	20	19	11	2	0	132^2	109	2	76	72	12.9	3.26	77	.219	.329	5	.104	-2	-12	-11	-1	-1.7
● **EARL WILSON**	Wilson, Robert Earl (Name Changed From Wilson, Earl Lawrence) b: 10/2/34, Ponchatoula, La. BR/TR, 6'3", 216 lbs. Deb: 7/28/59																									
1959	Bos-A	1	1	.500	9	4	0	0	0	23^2	21	2	31	17	19.8	6.08	67	.241	.441	4	.500	2	-6	-5	0	-0.2
1960	Bos-A	3	2	.600	13	9	2	0	0	65	61	4	48	40	15.1	4.71	86	.247	.369	4	.174	-0	-6	-5	0	-0.3
1962	Bos-A	12	8	.600	31	28	4	1	0	191^1	163	21	111	137	13.2	3.90	106	.231	.340	12	.174	3	1	5	-1	0.7
1963	Bos-A	11	16	.407	37	34	6	3	0	210^2	184	18	105	123	12.4	3.76	101	.234	.325	15	.208	5	-3	1	1	0.7
1964	Bos-A	11	12	.478	33	31	5	0	0	202^1	213	37	73	166	12.8	4.49	86	.269	.332	15	.205	8	-20	-14	0	-0.7
1965	Bos-A	13	14	.481	36	36	8	1	0	230^2	221	27	77	164	11.8	3.98	94	.250	.313	14	.177	8	-13	-7	-1	0.0
1966	Bos-A	5	5	.500	15	14	5	1	0	100^2	88	14	36	67	11.3	3.84	99	.235	.306	8	.250	3	-5	-0	-0	0.3
	Det-A	13	6	.684	23	23	8	2	0	163^1	126	16	38	133	9.3	2.59	134	.213	.265	15	.234	9	15	16	2	3.2
	Yr	18	11	.621	38	37	13	3	0	264	214	30	74	200	10.0	3.07	117	.220	.278	23	.240	12	11	16	2	3.5
1967	Det-A	**22**	11	.667	39	38	12	0	0	264	216	34	92	184	10.6	3.27	100	.224	.294	20	.185	7	-1	-0	2	0.9
1968	*Det-A	13	12	.520	34	33	10	3	0	224^1	192	20	65	168	10.3	2.85	106	.231	.287	20	.227	10	3	4	1	1.7
1969	Det-A	12	10	.545	35	35	5	1	0	214^2	209	23	69	150	11.8	3.31	113	.256	.317	10	.132	-0	7	10	1	1.1
1970	Det-A	4	6	.400	18	16	4	1	0	96	87	15	32	74	11.3	4.41	85	.238	.303	6	.194	2	-7	-7	-0	-0.5
	SD-N	1	6	.143	15	9	0	0	0	65	82	5	19	29	14.3	4.85	82	.309	.360	1	.059	0	-6	-6	-1	-0.7
Total	11	121	109	.526	338	310	69	13	0	2051^2	1863	236	796	1452	11.8	3.69	99	.242	.315	144	.195	57	-39	-10	2	6.2
● **ROY WILSON**	Wilson, Roy Edward "Lefty" b: 9/13/1896, Foster, Iowa d: 12/3/69, Clarion, Iowa BL/TL, 6', 175 lbs. Deb: 4/18/28																									
1928	Chi-A	0	0	—	1	0	0	0	0	3^1	2	0	3	2	13.5	0.00	—	.167	.333	0	.000	-0	1	2	0	0.0
● **STEVE WILSON**	Wilson, Stephen Douglas b: 12/13/64, Victoria, B.C., Can. BL/TL, 6'4", 195 lbs. Deb: 9/16/88																									
1988	Tex-A	0	0	—	3	0	0	0	0	7^2	7	1	4	1	12.9	5.87	70	.259	.355	0	—	0	-2	-2	-0	-0.1
1989	*Chi-N	6	4	.600	53	8	0	0	2	85^2	83	6	31	65	12.1	4.20	89	.257	.324	1	.063	-1	-7	-4	0	-0.6
1990	Chi-N	4	9	.308	45	15	1	0	1	139	140	17	43	95	12.0	4.79	85	.259	.316	6	.162	0	-15	-11	-1	-1.0
1991	Chi-N	0	0	—	8	0	0	0	0	12^1	13	1	5	9	13.1	4.38	89	.277	.346	0	.000	-0	-1	-1	-0	-0.1
	LA-N	0	0	—	11	0	0	0	2	8^1	1	0	4	5	5.4	0.00	—	.042	.179	0	.000	-0	3	3	-0	0.1
	Yr	0	0	—	19	0	0	0	2	20^2	14	1	9	14	10.0	2.61	144	.194	.284	0	.000	-0	2	3	-1	0.0
1992	LA-N	2	5	.286	60	0	0	0	0	66^2	74	6	29	54	14.0	4.18	82	.282	.356	1	.333	0	-5	-5	-0	-0.6
1993	LA-N	1	0	1.000	25	0	0	0	1	25^2	30	2	14	23	15.8	4.56	84	.288	.378	0	.000	-0	-1	-2	0	-0.1
Total	6	13	18	.419	205	23	1	0	6	345^1	348	33	130	252	12.6	4.40	87	.262	.330	8	.133	-1	-28	-22	-2	-2.4

YEAR	TM/L	W	L	PCT	G	GS	CG	SH	SV	IP	H	HR	BB	SO	RAT	ERA	ERA+	OAV	OOB	BH	AVG	PB	PR	/A	PD	TPI
● TREVOR WILSON	Wilson, Trevor Kirk b: 6/7/66, Torrance, Cal. BL/TL, 6', 195 lbs. Deb: 9/5/88																									
1988	SF-N	0	2	.000	4	4	0	0	0	22	25	1	8	15	13.5	4.09	80	.298	.359	2	.286	1	-2	-2	-1	-0.2
1989	SF-N	2	3	.400	14	4	0	0	0	39^1	28	2	24	22	12.8	4.35	78	.207	.344	2	.250	1	-4	-4	-0	-0.4
1990	SF-N	8	7	.533	27	17	3	2	0	110^1	87	11	49	66	11.2	4.00	91	.218	.305	4	.138	0	-3	-4	2	-0.4
1991	SF-N	13	11	.542	44	29	2	1	0	202	173	13	77	139	11.4	3.56	100	.234	.310	12	.235	5	3	0	3	0.8
1992	SF-N	8	14	.364	26	26	1	1	0	154	152	18	64	88	13.0	4.21	79	.265	.345	3	.077	-1	-12	-15	1	-2.0
1993	SF-N	7	5	.583	22	18	1	0	0	110	110	8	40	57	12.8	3.60	109	.275	.350	4	.138	1	5	4	-1	0.4
1995	SF-N	3	4	.429	17	17	0	0	0	82^2	82	8	38	38	13.5	3.92	104	.269	.357	7	.233	1	2	2	1	0.3
1998	Ana-A	0	0	—	15	0	0	0	0	7^2	8	0	5	6	16.4	3.52	133	.267	.389	0	—	0	1	1	0	0.0
Total	8	41	46	.471	169	115	7	4	0	728	665	61	305	431	12.3	3.87	94	.249	.332	34	.176	7	-8	-20	5	-1.5
● WALTER WILSON	Wilson, Walter Wood b: 11/24/13, Glenn, Ga. d: 4/17/94, Bremen, Ga. BL/TR, 6'4", 190 lbs. Deb: 4/17/45																									
1945	Det-A	1	3	.250	25	4	1	0	0	70^1	76	4	35	28	14.6	4.61	76	.284	.373	1	.053	-2	-10	-9	1	-0.6
● WILLY WILSON	Wilson, William b: 1/7/1884, Columbus, Ohio d: 10/28/25, Seattle, Wash. BR/TR, Deb: 10/3/06																									
1906	Was-A	0	1	.000	1	1	1	0	0	7	3	0	2	1	7.7	2.57	102	.130	.231	0	.000	-0	0	0	0	0.0
● MUTT WILSON	Wilson, William Clarence "Lank" b: 7/20/1896, Kiser, N.C. d: 8/31/62, Wildwood, Fla. BR/TR, 6'3", 167 lbs. Deb: 9/11/20																									
1920	Det-A	1	1	.500	3	2	1	0	0	13	12	0	5	4	11.8	3.46	108	.240	.309	1	.250	-0	0	0	-1	0.0
● BILL WILSON	Wilson, William Donald b: 11/6/28, Central City, Neb. BR/TR, 6'2", 200 lbs. Deb: 9/24/50 ♦																									
1955	KC-A	0	0	—	1	0	0	0	0	1	1	0	1	1	18.0	0.00	—	.250	.400	61	.223	0	0	0	0	0.0
● BILL WILSON	Wilson, William Harlan b: 9/21/42, Pomeroy, Ohio d: 8/11/93, Broken Arrow, Okla. BR/TR, 6'2", 200 lbs. Deb: 4/8/69																									
1969	Phi-N	2	5	.286	37	0	0	0	6	62^1	53	6	36	48	13.0	3.32	107	.231	.338	0	.000	-0	2	2	-1	0.0
1970	Phi-N	1	0	1.000	37	0	0	0	0	58^1	57	5	33	41	13.9	4.78	83	.263	.360	1	.250	0	-5	-5	-0	-0.1
1971	Phi-N	4	6	.400	38	0	0	0	7	58^2	39	4	22	40	9.5	3.07	115	.188	.268	1	.100	-1	3	3	2	0.7
1972	Phi-N	1	1	.500	23	0	0	0	0	30	26	1	11	18	11.1	3.30	109	.234	.303	0	—	0	1	1	0	0.1
1973	Phi-N	1	3	.250	44	0	0	0	4	48^2	54	7	29	24	15.3	6.66	57	.293	.390	0	.000	-0	-16	-15	-0	-1.5
Total	5	9	15	.375	179	0	0	0	17	258	229	23	131	171	12.6	4.22	88	.241	.335	2	.083	-1	-16	-15	0	-0.8
● HOOKS WILTSE	Wiltse, George Leroy b: 9/7/1880, Hamilton, N.Y. d: 1/21/59, Long Beach, N.Y. BR/TL, 6', 185 lbs. Deb: 4/21/04 FC																									
1904	NY-N	13	3	.813	24	16	14	2	3	164^2	150	8	61	105	11.8	2.84	96	.240	.313	15	.224	3	-2	-2	3	0.4
1905	NY-N	15	6	.714	32	19	18	1	3	197	158	5	61	120	10.2	2.47	119	.219	.284	20	.278	7	12	10	5	2.4
1906	NY-N	16	11	.593	38	26	21	4	6	249^1	227	3	58	125	10.4	2.27	115	.241	.288	18	.191	2	10	9	-1	1.2
1907	NY-N	13	12	.520	33	21	14	3	2	190^1	171	3	48	79	10.6	2.18	114	.241	.294	9	.134	0	6	6	2	1.1
1908	NY-N	23	14	.622	44	38	30	7	2	330	266	4	73	118	9.5	2.24	108	.224	.274	26	.236	6	5	7	-0	1.4
1909	NY-N	20	11	.645	37	30	22	4	3	269^1	228	9	51	119	9.5	2.00	128	.233	.275	19	.200	2	18	17	-2	1.9
1910	NY-N	14	12	.538	36	30	18	2	2	235^1	232	4	52	88	10.9	2.72	109	.261	.303	13	.176	0	8	7	-3	0.4
1911	*NY-N	12	9	.571	30	24	11	4	0	187^1	177	7	39	92	10.5	3.27	103	.251	.292	13	.188	1	3	2	0	0.1
1912	NY-N	9	6	.600	28	17	5	0	3	134	140	7	28	58	11.4	3.16	107	.273	.312	15	.326	4	4	3	2	0.8
1913	*NY-N	0	0	—	17	2	0	0	3	57^2	53	1	8	25	9.7	1.56	200	.237	.266	5	.208	0	11	10	0	0.2
1914	NY-N	1	1	.500	20	0	0	0	1	38	41	2	12	19	12.6	2.84	93	.289	.344	2	.667	2	-0	-1	0	0.1
1915	Bro-F	3	5	.375	18	3	1	0	5	59^1	49	1	7	17	8.8	2.28	120	.226	.257	1	.045	-3	3	3	-1	0.1
Total	12	139	90	.607	357	226	154	27	33	2112^1	1892	54	498	965	10.4	2.47	112	.241	.290	156	.210	22	77	72	5	10.1
● HAL WILTSE	Wiltse, Harold James "Whitey" b: 8/6/03, Clay City, Ill. d: 11/2/83, Bunkie, La. BL/TL, 5'9", 168 lbs. Deb: 4/13/26																									
1926	Bos-A	8	15	.348	37	29	9	1	0	196^1	201	6	99	59	14.0	4.22	97	.273	.363	5	.085	-5	-4	-3	0	-0.7
1927	Bos-A	10	18	.357	36	29	13	1	1	219	276	5	76	47	14.6	5.10	83	.321	.379	16	.208	-2	-23	-21	1	-2.3
1928	Bos-A	0	2	.000	2	2	1	0	0	12	16	1	1	5	15.0	9.00	46	.314	.364	0	.000	-1	-7	-7	-0	-0.8
	StL-A	2	5	.286	26	5	0	0	0	72	93	4	35	23	16.4	5.25	80	.316	.395	5	.227	0	-10	-8	0	-0.7
	Yr	2	7	.222	28	7	1	0	0	84	109	5	36	28	15.9	5.79	72	.313	.382	5	.192	-1	-16	-15	-0	-1.5
1931	Phi-N	0	0	—	1	0	0	0	0	1	3	0	0	0	27.0	9.00	47	.600	.600	0	—	0	-1	-1	0	0.0
Total	4	20	40	.333	102	65	23	2	1	500^1	589	16	211	134	14.7	4.87	85	.303	.375	26	.160	-7	-44	-40	2	-4.5
● SNAKE WILTSE	Wiltse, Lewis De Witt b: 12/5/1871, Bouckville, N.Y. d: 8/25/28, Harrisburg, Pa. BR/TL, Deb: 5/5/01 F																									
1901	Pit-N	1	4	.200	7	5	3	0	0	44^1	57	2	13	10	15.2	4.26	77	.310	.371	3	.158	-1	-5	-5	1	-0.5
	Phi-A	13	5	.722	19	19	18	2	0	166	185	1	35	40	12.3	3.58	105	.279	.322	25	.373	8	2	4	1	1.2
1902	Phi-A	8	8	.500	19	17	13	0	1	138	182	7	41	28	14.9	5.15	71	.318	.368	10	.175	-0	-24	-23	-1	-2.3
	Bal-A	7	11	.389	19	18	18	0	0	164	215	4	51	37	15.0	5.10	74	.316	.371	39	.295	6	-28	-24	-0	-1.7
	Yr	15	19	.441	38	35	31	0	1	302	397	11	92	65	14.8	5.13	73	.316	.366	49	.259	5	-52	-47	-1	-4.0
1903	NY-A	0	3	.000	4	3	2	0	1	25	35	1	6	6	15.1	5.40	58	.330	.372	2	.222	0	-7	-6	-0	-0.7
Total	3	29	31	.483	68	62	54	2	2	537^1	674	15	146	121	14.2	4.59	80	.305	.356	79	.278	13	-62	-55	0	-4.0
● FRED WINCHELL	Winchell, Frederick Russell (b: Frederick Cook) b: 1/23/1882, Arlington, Mass. d: 8/8/58, Toronto, Ont., Can. TR, 5'8", Deb: 9/16/09																									
1909	Cle-A	0	3	.000	4	3	0	0	1	14^1	16	0	2	7	11.3	6.28	41	.296	.321	1	.200	0	-6	-6	-0	-1.2
● SCOTT WINCHESTER	Winchester, Scott J. b: 4/20/73, Midland, Mich. BR/TR, 6'2", 210 lbs. Deb: 9/8/97																									
1997	Cin-N	0	0	—	5	0	0	0	0	6	9	1	2	3	18.0	6.00	71	.360	.429	0	—	0	-1	-1	0	0.0
1998	Cin-N	3	6	.333	16	16	1	0	0	79	101	12	27	40	15.0	5.81	74	.312	.372	3	.130	-1	-14	-13	-0	-1.3
Total	2	3	6	.333	21	16	1	0	0	85	110	13	29	43	15.2	5.82	74	.315	.376	3	.130	-1	-15	-14	-0	-1.3
● ED WINEAPPLE	Wineapple, Edward "Lefty" b: 8/10/05, Boston, Mass. d: 7/23/96, Delray Beach, Fla. BL/TL, 6', 210 lbs. Deb: 9/15/29																									
1929	Was-A	0	0	—	1	0	0	0	0	4	7	0	3	1	22.5	4.50	94	.467	.556	0	.000	-0	-0	-0	-0	0.0
● RALPH WINEGARNER	Winegarner, Ralph Lee b: 10/29/09, Benton, Kan. d: 4/14/88, Wichita, Kan. BR/TR, 6', 182 lbs. Deb: 9/20/30 C♦																									
1932	Cle-A	1	0	1.000	5	1	1	0	0	17^1	7	0	13	5	10.4	1.04	457	.123	.286	1	.143	-0	7	7	-0	0.3
1934	Cle-A	5	4	.556	22	6	4	0	0	78^1	91	1	39	32	15.2	5.51	82	.289	.371	10	.196	1	-9	-8	-0	-0.7
1935	Cle-A	2	2	.500	25	4	2	0	0	67^1	89	10	29	41	15.9	5.75	78	.313	.379	26	.310	4	-10	-9	0	0.0
1936	Cle-A	0	0	—	9	0	0	0	0	14^2	18	0	6	3	14.7	4.91	103	.295	.358	2	.125	-1	0	0	-0	-0.1
1949	StL-A	0	0	—	9	0	0	0	0	16^2	24	2	2	8	14.0	7.56	60	.329	.347	2	.400	2	-6	-6	-0	0.1
Total	5	8	6	.571	70	11	7	0	0	194^1	229	13	89	89	14.9	5.33	86	.290	.364	51	.276	5	-18	-16	-1	-0.4
● JIM WINFORD	Winford, James Head "Cowboy" b: 10/9/09, Shelbyville, Tenn. d: 12/16/70, Miami, Okla. BR/TR, 6'1", 180 lbs. Deb: 9/10/32																									
1932	StL-N	1	1	.500	4	1	0	0	0	8^1	9	0	5	4	15.1	6.48	61	.273	.368	2	.667	1	-2	-2	0	-0.4
1934	StL-N	0	2	.000	5	1	0	0	0	12^2	17	0	6	3	17.8	7.82	54	.327	.417	0	.000	0	-5	-5	0	-0.6
1935	StL-N	0	0	—	2	1	0	0	0	11^1	13	1	5	7	14.3	3.97	103	.283	.353	0	.000	-0	0	0	-1	-0.1
1936	StL-N	11	10	.524	39	23	10	1	3	192	203	10	68	72	12.9	3.80	104	.269	.333	5	.085	-4	5	3	-4	-0.5
1937	StL-N	2	4	.333	16	4	0	0	0	46^1	56	2	27	17	16.1	5.83	68	.311	.401	1	.125	-1	-10	-10	-0	-1.1
1938	Bro-N	0	1	.000	2	1	0	0	0	5^2	9	1	4	4	20.6	11.12	35	.346	.433	0	.000	0	-5	-5	-0	-0.6
Total	6	14	18	.438	68	31	10	1	3	276^1	307	14	115	107	14.0	4.56	87	.281	.353	8	.108	-3	-17	-18	-5	-3.3
● ERNIE WINGARD	Wingard, Ernest James "Jim" b: 10/17/1900, Prattville, Ala. d: 1/17/77, Prattville, Ala. BL/TL, 6'2", 176 lbs. Deb: 5/1/24																									
1924	StL-A	13	12	.520	36	26	14	0	1	218	215	6	85	23	12.5	3.51	129	.262	.334	18	.234	2	17	24	-3	2.4
1925	StL-A	9	10	.474	32	18	8	0	0	145	183	10	77	20	16.3	5.52	85	.319	.403	15	.288	3	-18	-14	2	-1.0
1926	StL-A	5	8	.385	39	16	7	0	3	169	188	9	76	30	14.3	3.57	120	.290	.369	14	.230	1	8	14	3	1.4
1927	StL-A	2	13	.133	38	17	7	0	0	156^1	213	7	79	28	16.9	6.56	66	.340	.415	10	.179	2	-42	-38	2	-2.7
Total	4	29	43	.403	145	77	36	0	4	688^1	799	32	317	101	14.8	4.64	96	.299	.377	57	.232	7	-34	-14	4	0.1
● TED WINGFIELD	Wingfield, Frederick Davis b: 8/7/1899, Bedford, Va. d: 7/18/75, Johnson City, Tenn. BR/TR, 5'11", 168 lbs. Deb: 9/23/23																									
1923	Was-A	0	0	—	1	0	0	0	0	1	0	0	0	1	0.0	0.00	—	.000	.000	0	—	0	0	0	0	0.0

YEAR	TM/L	W	L	PCT	G	GS	CG	SH	SV	IP	H	HR	BB	SO	RAT	ERA	ERA+	OAV	OOB	BH	AVG	PB	PR	/A	PD	TPI
1924	Was-A	0	0	—	4	0	0	0	0	7	9	0	4	2	16.7	2.57	157	.300	.382	0	.000	-0	1	1	0	0.0
	Bos-A	0	2	.000	4	3	2	0	0	25^2	23	0	8	4	10.9	2.45	178	.240	.298	3	.333	1	5	5	0	0.5
	Yr	0	2	.000	8	3	2	0	0	32^2	32	0	12	6	12.1	2.48	173	.254	.319	3	.273	0	6	7	-0	0.5
1925	Bos-A	12	19	.387	41	27	18	2	2	254^1	267	11	92	30	13.0	3.96	115	.278	.346	23	.245	1	12	16	7	2.5
1926	Bos-A	11	16	.407	43	20	9	1	3	190^2	220	11	50	30	12.8	4.44	92	.298	.344	15	.217	-0	-9	-8	2	-0.8
1927	Bos-A	1	7	.125	20	8	2	0	0	74^2	105	2	27	1	16.3	5.06	83	.357	.417	4	.222	0	-8	-7	2	-0.4
Total	5	24	44	.353	113	58	31	3	5	553^1	624	24	181	68	13.3	4.18	103	.294	.353	45	.234	1	3	9	11	1.8

● LAVE WINHAM Winham, Lafayette Sharkey "Lefty" b: 10/23/1881, Brooklyn, N.Y. d: 9/12/51, Brooklyn, N.Y. BL/TL, 5'11", 200 lbs. Deb: 4/21/02

YEAR	TM/L	W	L	PCT	G	GS	CG	SH	SV	IP	H	HR	BB	SO	RAT	ERA	ERA+	OAV	OOB	BH	AVG	PB	PR	/A	PD	TPI
1902	Bro-N	0	0	—	1	0	0	0	0	3	4	0	2	1	18.0	0.00	—	.308	.400	0	.000	-0	1	1	0	0.0
1903	Pit-N	3	1	.750	5	4	3	1	0	36	33	0	21	22	13.5	2.25	144	.231	.329	1	.071	-1	4	4	-1	0.1
Total	2	3	1	.750	6	4	3	1	0	39	37	0	23	23	13.8	2.08	154	.237	.335	1	.063	-2	5	5	-1	0.1

● GEORGE WINKELMAN Winkelman, George Edward b: 2/18/1865, Washington, D.C. d: 5/19/60, Washington, D.C. BL/TL, Deb: 8/4/1883 ♦

YEAR	TM/L	W	L	PCT	G	GS	CG	SH	SV	IP	H	HR	BB	SO	RAT	ERA	ERA+	OAV	OOB	BH	AVG	PB	PR	/A	PD	TPI
1886	Was-N	0	1	.000	1	1	0	0	0	6	12	0	5	4	25.5	10.50	31	.400	.486	1	.200	-0	-5	-5	-0	-0.5

● GEORGE WINN Winn, George Benjamin "Breezy" or "Lefty" b: 10/26/1897, Perry, Ga. d: 11/1/69, Roberta, Ga. BL/TL, 5'11", 170 lbs. Deb: 4/29/19

YEAR	TM/L	W	L	PCT	G	GS	CG	SH	SV	IP	H	HR	BB	SO	RAT	ERA	ERA+	OAV	OOB	BH	AVG	PB	PR	/A	PD	TPI
1919	Bos-A	0	0	—	3	0	0	0	0	4^2	6	0	1	0	13.5	7.71	39	.353	.389	0	.000	-0	-2	-2	-0	0.0
1922	Cle-A	1	2	.333	8	3	1	0	0	33^2	44	2	5	7	13.1	4.54	88	.317	.340	3	.333	1	-2	-2	0	-0.1
1923	Cle-A	0	0	—	1	0	0	0	0	2	0	0	1	0	4.5	0.00	—	.000	.143	0	—	0	1	1	-0	0.0
Total	3	1	2	.333	12	3	1	0	0	40^1	50	2	7	7	12.7	4.69	83	.309	.337	3	.300	1	-3	-4	-0	-0.1

● JIM WINN Winn, James Francis b: 9/23/59, Stockton, Cal. BR/TR, 6'3", 210 lbs. Deb: 4/10/83

YEAR	TM/L	W	L	PCT	G	GS	CG	SH	SV	IP	H	HR	BB	SO	RAT	ERA	ERA+	OAV	OOB	BH	AVG	PB	PR	/A	PD	TPI
1983	Pit-N	0	0	—	7	0	0	0	0	11	12	2	6	3	14.7	7.36	50	.267	.353	0	—	0	-5	-4	0	0.0
1984	Pit-N	1	0	1.000	9	0	0	0	1	18^2	19	2	9	11	13.5	3.86	93	.264	.346	0	.000	-0	-1	-1	0	0.0
1985	Pit-N	3	6	.333	30	7	0	0	0	75^2	77	4	31	22	13.1	5.23	68	.266	.341	2	.111	-0	-14	-14	2	-1.4
1986	Pit-N	3	5	.375	50	3	0	0	3	88	85	9	38	70	12.8	3.58	107	.258	.338	1	.063	-1	1	2	1	0.3
1987	Chi-A	4	6	.400	56	0	0	0	6	94	95	10	62	44	15.6	4.79	96	.271	.390	0	—	0	-3	-2	3	-0.1
1988	Min-A	1	0	1.000	9	0	0	0	0	21	33	4	10	9	18.4	6.00	68	.355	.417	0	—	0	-5	-5	0	-0.4
Total	6	12	17	.414	161	10	0	0	10	308^1	321	31	156	159	14.2	4.67	85	.272	.362	3	.086	-1	-26	-23	6	-1.6

● TOM WINSETT Winsett, John Thomas "Long Tom" b: 11/24/09, McKenzie, Tenn. d: 7/20/87, Memphis, Tenn. BL/TR, 6'2", 190 lbs. Deb: 4/20/30 ♦

YEAR	TM/L	W	L	PCT	G	GS	CG	SH	SV	IP	H	HR	BB	SO	RAT	ERA	ERA+	OAV	OOB	BH	AVG	PB	PR	/A	PD	TPI
1937	Bro-N	0	0	—	1	0	0	0	0	1	3	0	2	0	45.0	18.00	22	.600	.714	83	.237	0	-2	-2	-0	0.0

● DARRIN WINSTON Winston, Darrin Alexander b: 7/6/66, Passaic, N.J. BR/TL, 6', 195 lbs. Deb: 9/10/97

YEAR	TM/L	W	L	PCT	G	GS	CG	SH	SV	IP	H	HR	BB	SO	RAT	ERA	ERA+	OAV	OOB	BH	AVG	PB	PR	/A	PD	TPI
1997	Phi-N	2	0	1.000	7	1	0	0	0	12	8	4	3	8	9.8	5.25	81	.178	.260	1	.500	1	-1	-1	-0	-0.2
1998	Phi-N	2	2	.500	27	0	0	0	1	25	31	7	6	11	14.0	6.12	71	.298	.348	0	.000	-0	-5	-5	-0	-0.7
Total	2	4	2	.667	34	1	0	0	1	37	39	11	9	19	12.6	5.84	74	.262	.321	1	.333	1	-7	-6	-1	-0.9

● HANK WINSTON Winston, Henry Rudolph b: 6/15/04, Youngsville, N.C. d: 2/4/74, Jacksonville, Fla. BL/TR, 6'3.5", 226 lbs. Deb: 9/30/33

YEAR	TM/L	W	L	PCT	G	GS	CG	SH	SV	IP	H	HR	BB	SO	RAT	ERA	ERA+	OAV	OOB	BH	AVG	PB	PR	/A	PD	TPI
1933	Phi-A	0	0	—	1	0	0	0	0	6^2	7	0	6	2	17.6	6.75	63	.280	.419	0	.000	-0	-2	-2	0	0.0
1936	Bro-N	1	3	.250	14	0	0	0	0	32^1	40	2	16	8	15.9	6.12	67	.301	.380	1	.091	-1	-8	-7	-0	-0.8
Total	2	1	3	.250	15	0	0	0	0	39	47	2	22	10	16.2	6.23	67	.297	.387	1	.071	-1	-9	-9	0	-0.8

● GEORGE WINTER Winter, George Lovington "Sassafras"
b: 4/27/1878, New Providence, Pa d: 5/26/51, Franklin Lakes, N.J. TR, 5'8", 155 lbs. Deb: 6/15/01

YEAR	TM/L	W	L	PCT	G	GS	CG	SH	SV	IP	H	HR	BB	SO	RAT	ERA	ERA+	OAV	OOB	BH	AVG	PB	PR	/A	PD	TPI
1901	Bos-A	16	12	.571	28	28	26	1	0	241	234	4	66	63	11.4	2.80	126	.252	.304	19	.190	-4	23	20	-1	1.5
1902	Bos-A	11	9	.550	20	20	18	0	0	168^1	149	2	53	51	11.2	2.99	119	.238	.305	10	.164	-2	11	11	-0	0.8
1903	Bos-A	9	8	.529	24	19	14	0	0	178^1	182	4	37	64	11.4	3.08	99	.263	.307	7	.106	-4	-2	-1	-1	-0.6
1904	Bos-A	8	4	.667	20	16	12	1	0	135^2	126	4	27	31	10.5	2.32	115	.247	.293	5	.116	-2	4	5	-2	0.1
1905	Bos-A	16	17	.485	35	27	24	2	0	264^1	249	5	54	119	10.5	2.96	91	.251	.293	24	.261	3	-9	-8	1	-0.5
1906	Bos-A	6	18	.250	29	22	18	1	2	207^2	215	8	38	72	11.2	4.12	67	.270	.308	17	.246	2	-33	-32	-0	-3.3
1907	Bos-A	12	15	.444	35	27	21	4	1	256^2	198	2	61	88	9.2	2.07	124	.215	.267	21	.223	1	14	14	-2	1.5
1908	Bos-A	4	14	.222	22	17	8	0	0	147^2	150	3	34	55	11.5	3.05	81	.274	.321	9	.184	-1	-11	-10	-0	-1.3
	*Det-A	1	5	.167	7	6	5	0	1	56^1	49	0	7	25	9.4	1.60	151	.240	.276	2	.111	-1	5	5	1	0.6
	Yr	5	19	.208	29	23	13	0	1	204	199	3	41	80	10.7	2.65	93	.263	.304	11	.164	-2	-6	-4	1	-0.7
Total	8	83	102	.449	220	182	146	9	4	1656	1552	32	377	568	10.7	2.87	101	.250	.297	114	.193	-8	2	7	-4	-1.2

● CLARENCE WINTERS Winters, Clarence John b: 9/7/1898, Detroit, Mich. d: 6/29/45, Detroit, Mich. Deb: 8/28/24

YEAR	TM/L	W	L	PCT	G	GS	CG	SH	SV	IP	H	HR	BB	SO	RAT	ERA	ERA+	OAV	OOB	BH	AVG	PB	PR	/A	PD	TPI
1924	Bos-A	0	1	.000	4	2	0	0	0	7	22	0	4	3	33.4	20.57	21	.512	.553	1	.333	0	-13	-13	-0	-1.3

● JESSE WINTERS Winters, Jesse Franklin "Buck" or "T-Bone"
b: 12/22/1893, Stephenville, Tex. d: 6/5/86, Abilene, Texas BR/TR, 6'1", 165 lbs. Deb: 5/3/19

YEAR	TM/L	W	L	PCT	G	GS	CG	SH	SV	IP	H	HR	BB	SO	RAT	ERA	ERA+	OAV	OOB	BH	AVG	PB	PR	/A	PD	TPI
1919	NY-N	1	2	.333	16	2	0	0	3	28	39	1	13	6	17.7	5.46	51	.339	.420	0	.000	-0	-8	-8	-0	-1.1
1920	NY-N	0	0	—	21	0	0	0	0	46^1	37	1	28	14	13.4	3.50	86	.233	.361	0	.000	-1	-2	-3	1	0.0
1921	Phi-N	5	10	.333	18	14	10	0	0	114	142	4	28	22	13.7	3.63	116	.310	.355	5	.128	-3	2	8	2	0.8
1922	Phi-N	6	6	.500	34	9	4	0	2	138^1	176	8	56	29	15.4	5.33	87	.319	.386	11	.256	0	-19	-10	1	-0.7
1923	Phi-N	1	6	.143	21	6	1	0	1	78^1	116	7	39	23	18.3	7.35	63	.348	.423	4	.160	-1	-29	-24	-1	-1.9
Total	5	13	24	.351	110	31	15	0	6	405	510	21	164	94	15.4	5.04	83	.316	.385	20	.171	-5	-56	-39	2	-2.9

● ALAN WIRTH Wirth, Alan Lee b: 12/8/56, Mesa, Ariz. BR/TR, 6'4", 190 lbs. Deb: 4/9/78

YEAR	TM/L	W	L	PCT	G	GS	CG	SH	SV	IP	H	HR	BB	SO	RAT	ERA	ERA+	OAV	OOB	BH	AVG	PB	PR	/A	PD	TPI
1978	Oak-A	5	6	.455	16	14	2	1	0	81^1	72	6	34	31	12.1	3.43	106	.252	.337	0	—	0	3	2	-1	0.3
1979	Oak-A	1	0	1.000	5	1	0	0	0	12	14	2	8	7	17.3	6.00	67	.298	.411	0	—	0	-2	-3	0	0.2
1980	Oak-A	0	0	—	2	0	0	0	0	2	3	0	0	1	13.5	4.50	84	.333	.333	0	—	0	-0	-0	-0	0.7
Total	3	6	6	.500	23	15	2	1	0	95^1	89	8	42	39	12.7	3.78	98	.260	.348	0	—	0	1	-1	-1	1.2

● ARCHIE WISE Wise, Archibald Edwin b: 7/31/12, Waxahachie, Tex. d: 2/2/78, Dallas, Tex. BR/TR, 6', 165 lbs. Deb: 7/24/32

YEAR	TM/L	W	L	PCT	G	GS	CG	SH	SV	IP	H	HR	BB	SO	RAT	ERA	ERA+	OAV	OOB	BH	AVG	PB	PR	/A	PD	TPI
1932	Chi-A	0	0	—	2	0	0	0	0	7^1	8	1	5	2	17.2	4.91	88	.258	.378	0	.000	-1	-0	-0	0	-0.1

● RICK WISE Wise, Richard Charles b: 9/13/45, Jackson, Mich. BR/TR, 6'2", 195 lbs. Deb: 4/18/64

YEAR	TM/L	W	L	PCT	G	GS	CG	SH	SV	IP	H	HR	BB	SO	RAT	ERA	ERA+	OAV	OOB	BH	AVG	PB	PR	/A	PD	TPI
1964	Phi-N	5	3	.625	25	8	0	0	0	69	78	7	25	39	13.8	4.04	86	.277	.342	5	.294	2	-4	-4	-2	-0.4
1966	Phi-N	5	6	.455	22	13	3	0	0	99^1	100	5	24	58	11.5	3.71	97	.262	.311	0	.000	-4	-1	-1	-1	-0.6
1967	Phi-N	11	11	.500	36	25	6	3	0	181^1	177	8	45	111	11.2	3.28	104	.259	.308	11	.208	3	2	3	1	0.7
1968	Phi-N	9	15	.375	30	30	7	1	0	182	210	12	37	97	12.5	4.55	66	.292	.332	14	.241	7	-32	-31	1	-3.2
1969	Phi-N	15	13	.536	33	31	14	4	0	220	215	17	61	144	11.4	3.23	110	.257	.309	20	.270	7	9	8	1	1.9
1970	Phi-N	13	14	.481	35	34	5	1	0	220^1	253	15	65	113	13.1	4.17	96	.287	.338	15	.200	5	-3	-4	1	0.1
1971	Phi-N☆	17	14	.548	38	37	17	4	0	272^1	261	20	70	155	11.1	2.88	123	.254	.304	23	.237	10	18	20	0	3.4
1972	StL-N	16	16	.500	35	35	20	2	0	269	250	16	71	142	10.8	3.11	109	.251	.301	16	.172	1	10	9	2	1.4
1973	StL-N★	16	12	.571	35	34	14	5	0	259	259	18	59	144	11.2	3.37	108	.257	.300	17	.193	6	8	8	-1	1.4
1974	Bos-A	3	4	.429	9	9	1	0	0	49	47	2	16	25	11.8	3.86	100	.251	.314	0	—	0	-1	-0	-0	-0.1
1975	*Bos-A	19	12	.613	35	35	17	1	0	255^1	262	34	72	141	11.9	3.95	103	.263	.315	0	—	0	-5	4	-1	0.1
1976	Bos-A	14	11	.560	34	34	11	4	0	224^1	218	18	48	93	10.8	3.53	111	.255	.296	0	—	0	-0	9	2	1.2
1977	Bos-A	11	5	.688	26	20	4	2	0	128^1	151	19	28	85	12.8	4.77	94	.291	.332	0	—	0	-10	-4	1	-0.4
1978	Cle-A	9	19	.321	33	31	9	1	0	211^2	226	22	59	106	12.2	4.34	86	.275	.325	0	—	0	-14	-14	-0	-1.7
1979	Cle-A	15	10	.600	34	34	9	2	0	231^2	229	24	68	108	11.6	3.73	114	.256	.309	0	—	0	12	13	4	1.7
1980	SD-N	6	8	.429	27	27	1	0	0	154^1	172	14	37	59	12.2	3.67	93	.285	.326	8	.138	-1	-1	-4	-1	-0.5
1981	SD-N	4	8	.333	18	18	0	0	0	98	116	10	19	27	12.4	3.77	86	.296	.328	1	.040	-2	-3	-6	0	-0.8
1982	SD-N	0	0	—	1	0	0	0	0	2	3	0	0	0	13.5	9.00	38	.333	.333	0	—	0	-1	-1	0	0.0
Total	18	188	181	.509	506	455	138	30	0	3127	3227	261	804	1647	11.7	3.69	100	.267	.315	130	.195	34	-15	2	9	4.2

● ROY WISE Wise, Roy Ogden b: 11/18/24, Springfield, Ill. BB/TR, 6'2", 170 lbs. Deb: 5/13/44

YEAR	TM/L	W	L	PCT	G	GS	CG	SH	SV	IP	H	HR	BB	SO	RAT	ERA	ERA+	OAV	OOB	BH	AVG	PB	PR	/A	PD	TPI
1944	Pit-N	0	0	—	2	0	0	0	0	3	4	0	3	1	21.0	9.00	41	.333	.467	0	—	0	-2	-2	-0	0.0

YEAR	TM/L	W	L	PCT	G	GS	CG	SH	SV	IP	H	HR	BB	SO	RAT	ERA	ERA+	OAV	OOB	BH	AVG	PB	PR	/A	PD	TPI
● **BILL WISE**	Wise, William E. b: 3/15/1861, Washington, D.C. d: 5/5/40, Washington, D.C. Deb: 5/2/1882																									
1882	Bal-a	1	2	.333	3	3	3	0	0	26	30	1	4	9	11.8	2.77	99	.270	.296	2	.100	-1	-0	-0	-0	-0.1
1884	Was-U	23	18	.561	50	41	34	4	0	364^1	383	5	60	268	10.9	3.04	79	.252	.281	79	.233	-8	-24	-26	5	-2.4
1886	Was-N	0	1	.000	1	1	0	0	0	3	6	0	2	0	24.0	9.00	37	.400	.471	0	.000	-0	-2	-2	-0	-0.4
Total	3	24	21	.533	54	45	37	4	0	393^1	419	6	66	277	11.1	3.07	79	.255	.284	81	.224	-9	-26	-28	4	-2.9
● **JACK WISNER**	Wisner, John Henry b: 11/5/1899, Grand Rapids, Mich. d: 12/15/81, Jackson, Mich. BR/TR, 6'3", 195 lbs. Deb: 9/12/19																									
1919	Pit-N	1	0	1.000	4	1	1	0	0	18^2	12	0	7	4	9.6	0.96	313	.185	.274	0	.000	-1	4	4	-0	0.1
1920	Pit-N	1	3	.250	17	2	1	0	0	44^2	46	1	10	13	11.5	3.43	94	.274	.318	0	.000	-1	-1	-1	1	-0.1
1925	NY-N	0	0	—	25	0	0	0	0	40^1	33	4	14	13	10.9	3.79	106	.228	.304	0	.000	-1	2	1	0	-0.1
1926	NY-N	2	2	.500	5	3	2	0	0	28	21	4	10	5	10.0	3.54	106	.208	.279	2	.200	-0	1	1	-0	0.0
Total	4	4	5	.444	51	6	4	0	0	131^2	112	9	41	35	10.7	3.21	111	.234	.300	2	.065	-3	6	5	1	-0.1
● **WHITEY WISTERT**	Wistert, Francis Michael b: 2/20/12, Chicago, Ill. d: 4/23/85, Painesville, Ohio BR/TR, 6'4", 210 lbs. Deb: 9/11/34																									
1934	Cin-N	0	1	.000	2	1	0	0	0	8	5	1	5	1	11.3	1.13	363	.185	.313	0	.000	-0	3	3	-0	0.2
● **JAY WITASICK**	Witasick, Gerald Alfonse b: 8/28/72, Baltimore, Md. BR/TR, 6'4", 205 lbs. Deb: 7/7/96																									
1996	Oak-A	1	1	.500	12	0	0	0	0	13	12	5	5	12	11.8	6.23	79	.245	.315	0	—	0	-2	-2	-0	-0.3
1997	Oak-A	0	0	—	8	0	0	0	0	11	14	2	6	8	16.4	5.73	79	.304	.385	0	—	0	-1	-1	-0	0.0
1998	Oak-A	1	3	.250	7	3	0	0	0	27	36	9	15	29	17.0	6.33	72	.310	.389	0	—	0	-5	-5	-0	-0.5
Total	3	2	4	.333	27	3	0	0	0	51	62	16	26	49	15.5	6.18	75	.294	.371	0	—	0	-8	-9	-1	-0.8
● **SHANNON WITHEM**	Withem, Shannon Bolt b: 9/21/72, Ann Arbor, Mich. BR/TR, 6'3", 185 lbs. Deb: 9/18/98																									
1998	Tor-A	0	0	—	1	0	0	0	0	3	3	0	2	2	15.0	3.00	155	.250	.357	0	—	0	1	1	0	0.0
● **CHARLES WITHEROW**	Witherow, Charles Samuel Deb: 7/1/1875																									
1875	Was-n	0	1	.000	1	1	0	0	0	1	4	0	0	0	36.0	18.00	13	.444	.444	0	.000	-0	-2	-2		-0.9
● **ROY WITHERUP**	Witherup, Foster Leroy b: 7/26/1886, N.Washington, Pa. d: 12/23/41, New Bethlehem, Pa. BR/TR, 6', 185 lbs. Deb: 5/14/06																									
1906	Bos-N	0	3	.000	8	3	3	0	0	46	59	2	19	14	15.5	6.26	43	.322	.389	2	.133	-1	-19	-18	-1	-1.2
1908	Was-A	2	4	.333	6	6	4	0	0	48^1	51	0	8	31	11.2	2.98	77	.264	.297	3	.167	-1	-3	-4	0	-0.5
1909	Was-A	1	5	.167	12	8	5	0	0	68	79	1	20	26	13.1	4.24	57	.306	.356	1	.053	-2	-13	-14	-2	-1.5
Total	3	3	12	.200	26	17	12	0	0	162^1	189	3	47	71	13.2	4.44	55	.298	.348	6	.115	-3	-35	-36	-2	-3.2
● **GEORGE WITT**	Witt, George Adrian "Red" b: 11/9/33, Long Beach, Cal. BR/TR, 6'3", 200 lbs. Deb: 9/21/57																									
1957	Pit-N	0	1	.000	1	1	0	0	0	1^1	4	1	5	1	60.8	40.50	9	.500	.692	0	—	0	-5	-5	0	-1.6
1958	Pit-N	9	2	.818	18	15	5	3	0	106	78	2	59	81	11.8	1.61	240	.209	.320	6	.154	-1	28	27	-0	2.5
1959	Pit-N	0	7	.000	15	11	0	0	0	50^2	58	7	32	30	16.2	6.93	56	.293	.394	0	.000	-1	-17	-17	-0	-2.1
1960	*Pit-N	1	2	.333	10	6	0	0	0	30	33	3	12	15	13.5	4.20	89	.300	.369	0	.000	-1	-1	-1	-0	-0.3
1961	Pit-N	0	1	.000	9	1	0	0	0	15^2	17	5	5	9	12.6	6.32	63	.274	.328	1	.500	1	-4	-4	-1	-0.2
1962	LA-A	1	1	.500	5	2	0	0	0	10	15	4	5	10	18.0	8.10	48	.349	.417	1	.333	0	-5	-5	-0	-0.8
	Hou-N	0	2	.000	8	2	0	0	0	15^1	20	2	9	10	17.6	7.04	53	.339	.435	1	.250	0	-5	-6	0	-0.6
Total	6	11	16	.407	66	38	5	3	0	229	225	24	127	156	14.0	4.32	89	.263	.361	9	.130	-2	-10	-12	-2	-3.1
● **MIKE WITT**	Witt, Michael Atwater b: 7/20/60, Fullerton, Cal. BR/TR, 6'7", 192 lbs. Deb: 4/11/81																									
1981	Cal-A	8	9	.471	22	21	7	1	0	129	123	9	47	75	12.6	3.28	111	.251	.330	0	—	0	5	5	-1	0.5
1982	*Cal-A	8	6	.571	33	26	5	1	0	179^2	177	8	47	85	11.6	3.51	116	.260	.314	0	—	0	11	11	-0	0.7
1983	Cal-A	7	14	.333	43	19	2	0	5	154	173	14	75	77	14.8	4.91	82	.293	.379	0	—	0	-14	-15	0	-1.9
1984	Cal-A	15	11	.577	34	34	9	2	0	246^2	227	17	84	196	11.5	3.47	114	.244	.310	0	—	0	14	14	-1	1.3
1985	Cal-A	15	9	.625	35	35	6	1	0	250	228	22	98	180	11.9	3.56	115	.243	.317	0	—	0	16	15	0	1.4
1986	*Cal-A☆	18	10	.643	34	34	14	3	0	269	218	22	73	208	9.8	2.84	144	.221	.277	0	—	0	40	38	2	4.0
1987	Cal-A☆	16	14	.533	36	36	10	0	0	247	252	34	84	192	12.4	4.01	107	.261	.323	0	—	0	12	8	-1	1.1
1988	Cal-A	13	16	.448	34	34	12	2	0	249^2	263	14	87	133	12.8	4.15	93	.272	.335	0	—	0	-5	-8	-0	-0.7
1989	Cal-A	9	15	.375	33	33	5	0	0	220	252	26	48	123	12.4	4.54	84	.292	.330	0	—	0	-16	-18	4	-1.3
1990	Cal-A	0	3	.000	10	0	0	0	1	20^1	19	1	13	14	14.6	1.77	216	.250	.367	0	—	0	5	5	1	0.9
	NY-A	5	6	.455	16	16	2	1	0	96^2	87	8	34	60	11.6	4.47	89	.240	.312	0	—	0	-6	-5	0	-0.5
	Yr	5	9	.357	26	16	2	1	1	117	106	9	47	74	12.1	4.00	99	.240	.319	0	—	0	-1	-1	1	0.4
1991	NY-A	0	1	.000	2	2	0	0	0	5^1	8	1	1	0	15.2	10.13	41	.320	.346	0	—	0	-4	-4	0	-0.5
1993	NY-A	3	2	.600	9	9	0	0	0	41	39	7	22	30	14.0	5.27	79	.248	.352	0	—	0	-4	-5	0	-0.3
Total	12	117	116	.502	341	299	72	11	6	2108^1	2066	183	713	1373	12.1	3.83	105	.257	.322	0	—	0	55	41	4	4.7
● **BOBBY WITT**	Witt, Robert Andrew b: 5/11/64, Arlington, Mass. BR/TR, 6'2", 205 lbs. Deb: 4/10/86																									
1986	Tex-A	11	9	.550	31	31	0	0	0	157^2	130	18	143	174	15.8	5.48	78	.223	.379	0	—	0	-23	-21	0	-2.4
1987	Tex-A	8	10	.444	26	25	1	0	0	143	114	10	140	160	16.2	4.91	91	.219	.388	0	.000	-0	-7	-7	0	-0.7
1988	Tex-A	8	10	.444	22	22	13	2	0	174^1	134	13	101	148	12.2	3.92	104	.216	.326	0	—	0	1	3	-1	0.0
1989	Tex-A	12	13	.480	31	31	5	1	0	194^1	182	14	114	166	13.8	5.14	77	.248	.351	0	—	0	-27	-25	-0	-2.9
1990	Tex-A	17	10	.630	33	32	7	1	0	222	197	12	110	221	12.6	3.36	116	.238	.330	0	—	0	13	14	-1	1.5
1991	Tex-A	3	7	.300	17	16	1	1	0	88^2	84	4	74	82	16.1	6.09	66	.254	.392	0	—	0	-20	-20	-1	-2.0
1992	Tex-A	9	13	.409	25	25	0	0	0	161^1	152	14	95	100	13.9	4.46	85	.254	.358	0	—	0	-9	-12	-0	-1.4
	*Oak-A	1	1	.500	6	6	0	0	0	31^2	31	2	19	25	14.2	3.41	110	.265	.368	0	—	0	2	1	0	0.2
	Yr	10	14	.417	31	31	0	0	0	193	183	16	114	125	13.8	4.29	88	.252	.354	0	—	0	-8	-11	-0	-1.2
1993	Oak-A	14	13	.519	35	33	5	1	0	220	226	16	91	131	13.1	4.21	97	.269	.343	0	—	0	3	-3	2	0.2
1994	Oak-A	8	10	.444	24	24	5	3	0	135^2	151	22	70	111	15.0	5.04	88	.283	.371	0	—	0	-4	-9	-1	-0.8
1995	Fla-N	2	7	.222	19	19	1	0	0	110^2	104	8	47	95	12.4	3.90	108	.251	.330	2	.063	-2	3	4	0	0.1
	Tex-A	3	4	.429	10	10	1	0	0	61^1	81	4	21	46	15.1	4.55	106	.324	.379	0	—	0	1	2	-1	0.1
1996	*Tex-A	16	12	.571	33	32	2	0	0	199^2	235	28	96	157	15.0	5.41	97	.295	.372	0	—	0	-9	-4	1	-0.4
1997	Tex-A	12	12	.500	34	32	3	0	0	209	245	33	74	121	13.8	4.82	99	.294	.353	2	.333	2	-6	-1	-0	0.0
1998	Tex-A	5	4	.556	14	13	0	0	0	69^1	95	14	33	30	16.6	7.66	63	.328	.396	0	.000	-0	-23	-22	-2	-2.4
	StL-N	2	5	.286	17	5	0	0	0	47^1	55	7	20	28	14.6	4.94	85	.289	.363	2	.200	1	-4	-4	1	-0.4
Total	13	131	140	.483	377	356	44	9	0	2226	2216	219	1248	1795	14.1	4.73	91	.261	.358	6	.120	0	-109	-105	-3	-11.3
● **JOHNNIE WITTIG**	Wittig, John Carl "Hans" b: 6/16/14, Baltimore, Md. BR/TR, 6', 180 lbs. Deb: 8/4/38																									
1938	NY-N	2	3	.400	13	6	2	0	0	39^1	41	4	26	14	15.3	4.81	78	.263	.368	0	.000	-1	-4	-5	-1	-0.8
1939	NY-N	0	2	.000	5	2	1	0	0	16^2	18	0	14	4	17.8	7.56	52	.281	.418	0	.000	-1	-7	-7	0	-0.7
1941	NY-N	3	5	.375	25	9	0	0	0	85^1	111	5	45	47	16.6	5.59	66	.319	.398	5	.200	-0	-19	-18	-2	-1.7
1943	NY-N	5	15	.250	40	22	4	1	4	164	172	14	76	56	13.6	4.23	82	.273	.352	5	.098	-3	-15	-14	-3	-2.3
1949	Bos-A	0	0	—	1	0	0	0	0	2	2	0	2	0	18.0	9.00	48	.286	.444	0	—	0	-1	-1	0	0.0
Total	5	10	25	.286	84	39	7	1	4	307^1	344	23	163	121	14.9	4.89	73	.286	.372	10	.110	-6	-46	-44	-6	-5.5
● **MARK WOHLERS**	Wohlers, Mark Edward b: 1/23/70, Holyoke, Mass. BR/TR, 6'4", 207 lbs. Deb: 8/17/91																									
1991	*Atl-N	3	1	.750	17	0	0	0	2	19^2	17	1	13	13	14.6	3.20	121	.239	.372	0	.000	-0	1	1	0	0.3
1992	*Atl-N	1	2	.333	32	0	0	0	4	35^1	28	0	14	17	11.0	2.55	144	.235	.321	0	.000	-0	4	4	0	0.5
1993	*Atl-N	6	2	.750	46	0	0	0	0	48	37	2	22	45	11.3	4.50	89	.218	.311	0	—	0	-2	-3	0	-0.3
1994	Atl-N	7	2	.778	51	0	0	0	1	51	51	1	33	58	14.8	4.59	92	.264	.372	1	1.000	0	-2	-2	0	-0.2
1995	*Atl-N	7	3	.700	65	0	0	0	25	64^2	51	2	24	90	10.6	2.09	204	.211	.285	0	.000	-0	15	16	-1	3.2
1996	*Atl-N★	2	4	.333	77	0	0	0	39	77^1	71	8	21	100	10.9	3.03	145	.240	.295	0	.000	-0	10	12	-1	1.7
1997	*Atl-N	5	7	.417	71	0	0	0	33	69^1	57	4	38	92	12.3	3.50	119	.224	.325	0	.000	-0	5	5	-1	1.1
1998	Atl-N	0	1	.000	27	0	0	0	8	20^1	18	2	33	22	23.0	10.18	42	.231	.464	0	—	0	-13	-13	-0	-1.5
Total	8	31	22	.585	386	0	0	0	112	385^2	330	20	198	437	12.5	3.69	113	.232	.329	1	.083	-1	17	21	-2	4.8
● **STEVE WOJCIECHOWSKI**	Wojciechowski, Steven Joseph b: 7/29/70, Blue Island, Ill. BL/TL, 6'2", 185 lbs. Deb: 7/18/95																									
1995	Oak-A	2	3	.400	14	7	0	0	0	48^2	51	7	28	13	14.8	5.18	86	.273	.370	0	—	0	-3	-4	-0	-0.3

YEAR	TM/L	W	L	PCT	G	GS	CG	SH	SV	IP	H	HR	BB	SO	RAT	ERA	ERA+	OAV	OOB	BH	AVG	PB	PR	/A	PD	TPI
1996	Oak-A	5	5	.500	16	15	0	0	0	79^{2}	97	10	28	30	14.3	5.65	87	.300	.360	0	—	0	-6	-6	-1	-0.7
1997	Oak-A	0	2	.000	2	2	0	0	0	10^{1}	17	2	1	5	15.7	7.84	58	.386	.400	0	—	0	-4	-4	0	-0.5
Total	3	7	10	.412	32	24	0	0	0	138^{2}	165	19	57	48	14.6	5.65	84	.298	.366	0	—	0	-12	-14	-1	-1.5

● **PETE WOJEY** Wojey, Peter Paul b: 12/1/19, Stowe, Pa. d: 4/23/91, Mobile, Ala. BR/TR, 5'11", 185 lbs. Deb: 7/2/54

YEAR	TM/L	W	L	PCT	G	GS	CG	SH	SV	IP	H	HR	BB	SO	RAT	ERA	ERA+	OAV	OOB	BH	AVG	PB	PR	/A	PD	TPI
1954	Bro-N	1	1	.500	14	1	0	0	1	27^{2}	24	3	14	21	13.0	3.25	126	.242	.348	0	.000	-0	3	3	1	0.2
1956	Det-A	0	0	—	2	0	0	0	0	4	2	0	1	1	6.8	2.25	183	.167	.231	0	—	0	1	1	0	0.0
1957	Det-A	0	0	—	2	0	0	0	0	1^{1}	1	0	0	0	6.8	0.00	—	.200	.200	0	—	0	1	1	0	0.0
Total	3	1	1	.500	18	1	0	0	1	33	27	3	15	22	12.0	3.00	136	.233	.331	0	.000	-0	4	4	1	0.2

● **ED WOJNA** Wojna, Edward David b: 8/20/60, Bridgeport, Conn. BR/TR, 6'1", 185 lbs. Deb: 6/16/85

YEAR	TM/L	W	L	PCT	G	GS	CG	SH	SV	IP	H	HR	BB	SO	RAT	ERA	ERA+	OAV	OOB	BH	AVG	PB	PR	/A	PD	TPI
1985	SD-N	2	4	.333	15	7	0	0	0	42	53	6	19	18	16.1	5.79	61	.312	.391	2	.167	-0	-10	-11	0	-1.3
1986	SD-N	2	2	.500	7	7	1	0	0	39	42	2	16	19	13.6	3.23	113	.268	.339	2	.143	-0	2	2	-1	0.1
1987	SD-N	0	3	.000	5	3	0	0	0	18^{1}	25	2	6	13	15.7	5.89	67	.333	.390	0	.000	-1	-4	-4	1	-0.5
1989	Cle-A	0	1	.000	9	3	0	0	0	33	31	0	14	10	12.3	4.09	97	.254	.331	0	—	0	-1	-0	1	0.0
Total	4	4	10	.286	36	20	1	0	0	132^{1}	151	10	55	60	14.4	4.62	81	.288	.361	4	.129	-1	-13	-13	1	-1.7

● **BOB WOLCOTT** Wolcott, Robert William b: 9/8/73, Huntington Beach, Cal. BR/TR, 6', 190 lbs. Deb: 8/18/95

YEAR	TM/L	W	L	PCT	G	GS	CG	SH	SV	IP	H	HR	BB	SO	RAT	ERA	ERA+	OAV	OOB	BH	AVG	PB	PR	/A	PD	TPI
1995	*Sea-A	3	2	.600	7	6	0	0	0	36^{2}	43	6	14	19	14.5	4.42	107	.297	.366	0	—	0	1	1	-1	0.1
1996	Sea-A	7	10	.412	30	28	1	0	0	149^{1}	179	26	54	78	14.5	5.73	86	.297	.361	0	—	0	-12	-13	-0	-1.2
1997	Sea-A	5	6	.455	19	18	0	0	0	100	129	22	29	58	14.7	6.03	75	.314	.366	0	.000	-0	-16	-17	-0	-1.6
1998	Ari-N	1	3	.250	6	6	0	0	0	33	32	7	13	21	12.3	7.09	61	.252	.321	2	.222	0	-10	-10	-1	-1.0
Total	4	16	21	.432	62	58	1	0	0	319	383	61	110	176	14.3	5.81	81	.298	.360	2	.200	0	-38	-39	-2	-3.7

● **ERNIE WOLF** Wolf, Ernest Adolph b: 2/2/1889, Newark, N.J. d: 5/23/64, Atlantic Highlands, N.J. BR/TR, 5'11", 174 lbs. Deb: 9/10/12

YEAR	TM/L	W	L	PCT	G	GS	CG	SH	SV	IP	H	HR	BB	SO	RAT	ERA	ERA+	OAV	OOB	BH	AVG	PB	PR	/A	PD	TPI
1912	Cle-A	0	0	—	1	0	0	0	0	5^{2}	8	0	4	1	19.1	6.35	54	.348	.444	0	.000	-0	-2	-2	-0	-0.1

● **WALLY WOLF** Wolf, Walter Beck b: 1/5/42, Los Angeles, Cal. BR/TR, 6'0.5", 191 lbs. Deb: 9/27/69

YEAR	TM/L	W	L	PCT	G	GS	CG	SH	SV	IP	H	HR	BB	SO	RAT	ERA	ERA+	OAV	OOB	BH	AVG	PB	PR	/A	PD	TPI
1969	Cal-A	0	0	—	2	0	0	0	0	2^{1}	3	1	3	2	23.1	11.57	30	.333	.500	0	—	0	-2	-2	-0	0.0
1970	Cal-A	0	0	—	4	0	0	0	0	5^{1}	3	1	4	5	11.8	5.06	71	.176	.333	0	—	0	-1	-1	-0	0.0
Total	2	0	0	—	6	0	0	0	0	7^{2}	6	2	7	7	15.3	7.04	51	.231	.394	0	—	0	-3	-3	-0	0.0

● **LEFTY WOLF** Wolf, Walter Francis b: 6/10/1900, Hartford, Conn. d: 9/25/71, New Orleans, La. BR/TL, 5'10", 163 lbs. Deb: 7/4/21

YEAR	TM/L	W	L	PCT	G	GS	CG	SH	SV	IP	H	HR	BB	SO	RAT	ERA	ERA+	OAV	OOB	BH	AVG	PB	PR	/A	PD	TPI
1921	Phi-A	0	0	—	8	0	0	0	0	15	15	0	16	11	19.8	7.20	62	.273	.452	1	.250	-0	-5	-5	-0	0.0

● **JIMMY WOLF** Wolf, William Van Winkle "Chicken" b: 5/12/1862, Louisville, Ky. d: 5/16/03, Louisville, Ky. BR/TR, 5'9", 190 lbs. Deb: 5/2/1882 M♦

YEAR	TM/L	W	L	PCT	G	GS	CG	SH	SV	IP	H	HR	BB	SO	RAT	ERA	ERA+	OAV	OOB	BH	AVG	PB	PR	/A	PD	TPI
1882	Lou-a	0	0	—	1	0	0	0	0	6	11	0	3	1	21.0	9.00	28	.367	.424	95	.299	0	-4	-4	-0	0.0
1885	Lou-a	0	0	—	1	0	0	0	0	1	1	0	0	1	9.0	9.00	36	.200	.200	141	.292	0	-1	-1	-0	0.0
1886	Lou-a	0	0	—	1	0	0	0	0	3	7	0	0	0	21.0	15.00	24	.350	.350	148	.272	0	-4	-4	-0	0.0
Total	3	0	0	—	3	0	0	0	0	10	19	0	3	2	19.8	10.80	27	.345	.379	1440	.290	1	-9	-9	-0	0.0

● **CHUCK WOLFE** Wolfe, Charles Hunt b: 2/15/1897, Wolfsburg, Pa. d: 11/27/57, Schellsburg, Pa. BL/TR, 5'7", 175 lbs. Deb: 8/2/23

YEAR	TM/L	W	L	PCT	G	GS	CG	SH	SV	IP	H	HR	BB	SO	RAT	ERA	ERA+	OAV	OOB	BH	AVG	PB	PR	/A	PD	TPI
1923	Phi-A	0	0	—	3	0	0	0	0	9^{2}	6	1	8	1	13.0	3.72	110	.194	.359	1	.333	0	0	0	-0	0.0

● **ED WOLFE** Wolfe, Edward Anthony b: 1/2/29, Los Angeles, Cal. BR/TR, 6'3", 185 lbs. Deb: 4/19/52

YEAR	TM/L	W	L	PCT	G	GS	CG	SH	SV	IP	H	HR	BB	SO	RAT	ERA	ERA+	OAV	OOB	BH	AVG	PB	PR	/A	PD	TPI
1952	Pit-N	0	0	—	3	0	0	0	0	3^{2}	7	1	5	1	31.9	7.36	54	.467	.619	0	—	0	-1	-1	0	0.0

● **BARNEY WOLFE** Wolfe, Wilbert Otto b: 1/9/1876, Independence, Pa. d: 2/27/53, N.Charleroi, Pa. BR/TR, 6'1", Deb: 4/24/03

YEAR	TM/L	W	L	PCT	G	GS	CG	SH	SV	IP	H	HR	BB	SO	RAT	ERA	ERA+	OAV	OOB	BH	AVG	PB	PR	/A	PD	TPI
1903	NY-A	6	9	.400	20	16	12	1	0	148^{1}	143	1	26	48	10.6	2.97	105	.253	.293	4	.075	-4	-0	2	-0	-0.2
1904	NY-A	0	3	.000	7	3	2	0	0	33^{2}	31	1	4	8	9.9	3.21	85	.246	.280	0	.000	-1	-2	-2	0	-0.3
	Was-A	6	10	.375	17	16	13	2	0	126^{2}	131	0	22	44	11.7	3.27	81	.268	.314	5	.119	-2	-9	-9	-2	-1.4
	Yr	6	13	.316	24	19	15	2	0	160^{1}	162	1	26	52	11.2	3.26	82	.263	.304	5	.096	-3	-12	-10	-2	-1.7
1905	Was-A	9	14	.391	28	23	17	1	1	182	162	1	37	52	10.2	2.57	103	.240	.287	8	.127	-1	2	2	-2	-0.2
1906	Was-A	0	3	.000	4	3	2	0	0	20	17	0	10	8	13.0	4.05	65	.233	.341	2	.286	0	-3	-3	0	-0.4
Total	4	21	39	.350	76	61	46	4	1	510^{2}	484	3	99	160	10.8	2.96	94	.251	.298	19	.109	-8	-13	-10	-4	-2.5

● **BILL WOLFE** Wolfe, William b: Jersey City, N.J. Deb: 9/10/02

YEAR	TM/L	W	L	PCT	G	GS	CG	SH	SV	IP	H	HR	BB	SO	RAT	ERA	ERA+	OAV	OOB	BH	AVG	PB	PR	/A	PD	TPI
1902	Phi-N	0	1	.000	1	1	1	0	0	9	11	0	4	3	16.0	4.00	70	.297	.381	1	.333	0	-1	-1	0	-0.1

● **ROGER WOLFF** Wolff, Roger Francis b: 4/10/11, Evansville, Ill. d: 3/23/94, Chester, Ill. BR/TR, 6'0.5", 208 lbs. Deb: 9/20/41

YEAR	TM/L	W	L	PCT	G	GS	CG	SH	SV	IP	H	HR	BB	SO	RAT	ERA	ERA+	OAV	OOB	BH	AVG	PB	PR	/A	PD	TPI
1941	Phi-A	0	2	.000	2	2	2	0	0	17	15	0	4	2	10.1	3.18	132	.231	.275	1	.200	-0	2	2	-0	0.2
1942	Phi-A	12	15	.444	32	25	15	2	3	214^{1}	206	16	69	94	11.7	3.32	114	.249	.309	6	.088	-3	8	11	0	1.0
1943	Phi-A	10	15	.400	41	26	13	2	6	221	232	11	72	91	12.5	3.54	96	.274	.334	9	.122	-4	-6	-4	-3	-1.1
1944	Was-A	4	15	.211	33	21	5	0	2	155	186	9	60	73	14.6	4.99	65	.295	.362	12	.218	1	-27	-30	2	-3.1
1945	Was-A	20	10	.667	33	29	21	4	2	250	200	7	53	108	**9.1**	2.12	146	.215	**.258**	9	.107	-5	35	27	-1	2.7
1946	Was-A	5	8	.385	21	17	6	0	0	122	115	8	30	50	11.1	2.58	130	.249	.302	4	.103	-1	12	10	-1	0.9
1947	Cle-A	0	0	—	7	2	0	0	0	16	15	1	10	5	15.2	3.94	88	.259	.386	0	.000	-0	-0	-1	1	0.0
	Pit-N	1	4	.200	13	6	1	0	0	30	49	4	18	7	20.4	8.70	49	.368	.447	0	.000	-1	-15	-15	-1	-2.1
Total	7	52	69	.430	182	128	63	8	13	1025^{1}	1018	56	316	430	11.9	3.41	100	.258	.316	41	.122	-13	8	1	-3	-1.5

● **MELLIE WOLFGANG** Wolfgang, Meldon John "Red" b: 3/20/1890, Albany, N.Y. d: 6/30/47, Albany, N.Y. BR/TR, 5'9", 160 lbs. Deb: 4/18/14

YEAR	TM/L	W	L	PCT	G	GS	CG	SH	SV	IP	H	HR	BB	SO	RAT	ERA	ERA+	OAV	OOB	BH	AVG	PB	PR	/A	PD	TPI
1914	Chi-A	9	5	.643	24	11	9	2	0	119^{1}	96	0	32	50	9.7	1.89	142	.219	.272	7	.175	-0	11	11	4	1.7
1915	Chi-A	2	2	.500	17	2	0	0	0	53^{2}	39	0	12	21	8.7	1.84	161	.211	.263	2	.118	-1	7	7	-1	0.2
1916	Chi-A	4	6	.400	27	14	6	1	0	127	103	2	42	36	10.4	1.98	139	.228	.296	9	.225	0	12	11	1	1.0
1917	Chi-A	0	0	—	5	0	0	0	0	17^{2}	18	1	6	3	12.7	5.09	52	.305	.379	0	.000	-1	-5	-5	-0	-0.1
1918	Chi-A	0	1	.000	4	0	0	0	0	8^{1}	12	0	3	1	16.2	5.40	51	.333	.385	1	.500	0	-2	-2	0	-0.2
Total	5	15	14	.517	77	27	15	3	0	326	268	3	95	111	10.1	2.18	127	.229	.289	19	.184	-1	23	21	4	2.6

● **HARRY WOLTER** Wolter, Harry Meigs b: 7/11/1884, Monterey, Cal. d: 7/7/70, Palo Alto, Cal. BL/TL, 5'10", 175 lbs. Deb: 5/14/07 ♦

YEAR	TM/L	W	L	PCT	G	GS	CG	SH	SV	IP	H	HR	BB	SO	RAT	ERA	ERA+	OAV	OOB	BH	AVG	PB	PR	/A	PD	TPI
1907	Pit-N	0	0	—	1	0	0	0	0	2	3	0	2	0	22.5	4.50	54	.333	.455	0	.000	-0	-0	-0	-0	0.0
	StL-N	0	2	.000	3	3	1	0	0	23	27	1	18	8	18.4	4.30	58	.318	.448	16	.340	1	-5	-5	-1	-0.4
	Yr	0	2	.000	4	3	1	0	0	25	30	1	20	8	18.7	4.32	58	.319	.448	16	.333	1	-5	-5	-1	-0.4
1909	Bos-A	4	4	.500	11	6	0	0	0	59	66	0	30	21	15.3	3.51	71	.303	.397	29	.240	2	-7	-7	-1	-0.8
Total	2	4	6	.400	15	9	1	0	0	84	96	1	50	29	16.3	3.75	67	.308	.413	514	.270	3	-12	-12	-2	-1.2

● **RYNIE WOLTERS** Wolters, Reinder Albertus b: 3/17/1842, Schantz, Holland d: 1/3/17, Newark, N.J. TR , 6', 165 lbs. Deb: 5/18/1871

YEAR	TM/L	W	L	PCT	G	GS	CG	SH	SV	IP	H	HR	BB	SO	RAT	ERA	ERA+	OAV	OOB	BH	AVG	PB	PR	/A	PD	TPI
1871	Mut-n	16	16	.500	**32**	32	**31**	**1**	0	**283**	345	7	39	22	12.2	3.43	110	**.263**	.285	51	.370	20	25	11		1.9
1872	Cle-n	3	6	.333	12	8	5	0	0	75^{1}	115	3	7	4	14.6	6.09	58	.304	.317	16	.232	-0	-21	-21		-1.6
1873	Res-n	0	1	.000	1	1	1	0	0	9	13	0	1	1	14.0	0.00	—	.220	.233	0	.000	-1	3	3		0.2
Total	3 n	19	23	.452	45	41	37	1	0	367^{1}	473	10	47	27	12.7	3.90	86	.271	.290	67	.318	19	-26	-22		0.5

● **DOOLEY WOMACK** Womack, Horace Guy b: 8/25/39, Columbia, S.C. BL/TR, 6', 170 lbs. Deb: 4/14/66

YEAR	TM/L	W	L	PCT	G	GS	CG	SH	SV	IP	H	HR	BB	SO	RAT	ERA	ERA+	OAV	OOB	BH	AVG	PB	PR	/A	PD	TPI
1966	NY-A	7	3	.700	42	1	0	0	4	75	52	6	23	50	9.4	2.64	126	.198	.270	1	.200	0	7	6	2	1.1
1967	NY-A	5	6	.455	65	0	0	0	18	97	80	6	35	57	10.9	2.41	130	.230	.306	4	.286	1	9	8	4	1.8
1968	NY-A	3	7	.300	45	0	0	0	2	61^{2}	53	6	29	27	12.1	3.21	90	.244	.336	1	.200	0	-2	-2	2	-0.1
1969	Hou-N	2	1	.667	30	0	0	0	0	51^{1}	49	1	20	32	12.6	3.51	101	.259	.340	1	.167	-0	0	0	2	0.2
	Sea-A	2	1	.667	9	0	0	0	0	14^{1}	15	0	3	8	11.3	2.51	145	.273	.310	0	.000	-0	2	2	0	0.4
1970	Oak-A	0	0	—	2	0	0	0	0	3	4	2	1	3	15.0	15.00	24	.308	.357	0	—	0	-4	-4	0	0.0
Total	5	19	18	.514	193	1	0	0	24	302^{1}	253	21	111	177	11.1	2.95	110	.233	.310	7	.226	1	12	9	11	3.4

● **SPADES WOOD** Wood, Charles Asher b: 1/13/09, Spartanburg, S.C. d: 5/18/86, Wichita, Kan. BL/TL, 5'10.5", 150 lbs. Deb: 8/16/30

YEAR	TM/L	W	L	PCT	G	GS	CG	SH	SV	IP	H	HR	BB	SO	RAT	ERA	ERA+	OAV	OOB	BH	AVG	PB	PR	/A	PD	TPI
1930	Pit-N	4	3	.571	9	7	4	2	0	58	61	4	32	23	14.4	5.12	97	.270	.360	5	.250	1	-1	-1	-2	-0.2

YEAR	TM/L	W	L	PCT	G	GS	CG	SH	SV	IP	H	HR	BB	SO	RAT	ERA	ERA+	OAV	OOB	BH	AVG	PB	PR	/A	PD	TPI
1931	Pit-N	2	6	.250	15	10	2	0	0	64	69	2	46	33	16.3	6.05	64	.273	.387	5	.227	1	-16	-16	-0	-1.6
Total	2	6	9	.400	24	17	6	2	0	122	130	6	78	56	15.4	5.61	78	.271	.375	10	.238	1	-16	-17	-2	-1.8
● GEORGE WOOD Wood, George A. "Dandy" b: 11/9/1858, Boston, Mass. d: 4/4/24, Harrisburg, Pa. BL/TR, 5'10.5", 175 lbs. Deb: 5/1/1880 MU♦																										
1883	Det-N	0	0	—	1	0	0	0	0	5	8	0	3	0	19.8	7.20	43	.348	.423	133	.302	0	-2	-2	0	0.1
1885	Det-N	0	0	—	1	0	0	0	0	4	5	0	1	1	13.5	0.00	—	.333	.375	105	.290	0	1	1	-0	0.0
1888	Phi-N	0	0	—	2	0	0	0	**2**	2	3	0	1	0	18.0	4.50	66	.300	.364	99	.229	1	-0	-0	0	-0.1
1889	Phi-N	0	0	—	1	0	0	0	0	1	2	0	0	2	18.0	18.00	24	.400	.400	106	.251	0	-2	-2	0	0.0
Total	4	0	0	—	5	0	0	0	2	12	18	0	5	3	17.3	5.25	59	.340	.397	1467	.273	1	-3	-3	0	0.0
● JOE WOOD Wood, Joe "Smokey Joe" (b: Howard Ellsworth Wood) b: 10/25/1889, Kansas City, Mo. d: 7/27/85, West Haven, Conn BR/TR, 5'11", 180 lbs. Deb: 8/24/08 F♦																										
1908	Bos-A	1	1	.500	6	2	1	1	0	22^2	14	0	16	11	12.3	2.38	103	.161	.298	0	.000	-1	0	0	-0	-0.1
1909	Bos-A	11	7	.611	24	19	13	4	0	160^2	121	1	43	88	9.5	2.18	114	.209	.270	9	.164	-0	5	6	-4	0.2
1910	Bos-A	12	13	.480	35	17	14	3	0	196^2	155	3	56	145	10.1	1.69	151	.220	.287	18	.261	5	18	19	2	3.3
1911	Bos-A	23	17	.575	44	33	25	5	3	275^2	226	2	76	231	10.2	2.02	162	.223	.284	23	.261	9	40	38	2	**6.5**
1912	*Bos-A	**34**	5	**.872**	43	38	**35**	**10**	1	344	267	2	82	258	9.4	1.91	178	.216	.272	36	.290	11	54	57	8	8.6
1913	Bos-A	11	5	.688	23	18	12	1	2	145^2	120	0	61	123	11.7	2.29	129	.229	.319	15	.268	4	10	11	4	2.1
1914	Bos-A	10	3	.769	18	14	11	1	0	113^1	94	1	34	67	10.2	2.62	103	.229	.288	6	.140	-0	2	1	1	0.2
1915	Bos-A	15	5	**.750**	25	16	10	3	2	157^1	120	1	44	63	9.4	**1.49**	187	.216	.275	14	.259	4	25	23	1	3.6
1917	Cle-A	0	1	.000	5	1	0	0	1	15^2	17	0	7	2	13.8	3.45	82	.309	.387	0	.000	-1	-1	-1	0	-0.2
1919	Cle-A	0	0	—	1	0	0	0	1	0^2	0	0	0	0	0.0	0.00	—	.000	.000	49	.255	0	0	0	0	0.1
1920	*Cle-A	0	0	—	1	0	0	0	0	2	4	0	2	1	27.0	22.50	17	.444	.545	37	.270	0	-4	-4	0	0.0
Total	11	117	57	.672	225	158	121	28	10	1434^1	1138	10	421	989	10.1	2.03	146	.220	.285	553	.283	31	150	149	14	24.3
● JOHN WOOD Wood, John B. b: 1871, 5'7", 142 lbs. Deb: 5/9/1896																										
1896	StL-N	0	0	—	1	0	0	0	0	0	1	0	2	0	—	∞	—	1.000	1.000	0	—	0	-1	-1	0	-0.1
● JOE WOOD Wood, Joseph Frank b: 5/20/16, Shohola, Pa. BR/TR, 6', 190 lbs. Deb: 5/1/44 F																										
1944	Bos-A	0	1	.000	3	1	0	0	0	9^2	13	0	3	5	14.9	6.52	52	.317	.364	0	.000	-0	-3	-3	0	-0.3
● KERRY WOOD Wood, Kerry Lee b: 6/16/77, Irving, Tex. BR/TR, 6'5", 225 lbs. Deb: 4/12/98																										
1998	*Chi-N	13	6	.684	26	26	1	1	0	166^2	117	14	85	233	11.5	3.40	128	**.196**	.307	7	.130	-0	15	18	-2	1.7
● PETE WOOD Wood, Peter Burke b: 2/1/1857, Hamilton, Ont., Can. d: 3/15/23, Chicago, Ill. TR, 5'7", 185 lbs. Deb: 7/15/1885 F																										
1885	Buf-N	8	15	.348	24	22	21	0	0	198^2	235	8	66	38	13.6	4.44	67	.280	.332	23	.221	-1	-36	-32	-1	-3.1
1889	Phi-N	1	1	.500	3	2	2	0	0	19	28	0	3	8	14.7	5.21	83	.333	.356	0	.000	-1	-3	-2	-0	-0.3
Total	2	9	16	.360	27	24	23	0	0	217^2	263	8	69	46	13.7	4.51	69	.285	.334	23	.205	-2	-38	-34	-1	-3.4
● WILBUR WOOD Wood, Wilbur Forrester b: 10/22/41, Cambridge, Mass. BR/TL, 6', 180 lbs. Deb: 6/30/61																										
1961	Bos-A	0	0	—	6	1	0	0	0	13	14	2	7	7	14.5	5.54	75	.269	.356	0	.000	-0	-2	-2	-0	-0.1
1962	Bos-A	0	0	—	1	1	0	0	0	7^2	6	0	3	3	10.6	3.52	117	.214	.290	0	.000	-0	0	1	0	0.0
1963	Bos-A	0	5	.000	25	6	0	0	0	64^2	67	10	13	28	11.6	3.76	101	.270	.314	0	.000	-1	-1	0	-1	-0.2
1964	Bos-A	0	0	—	4	0	0	0	0	5^2	13	1	3	5	25.4	17.47	22	.433	.485	0	.000	-0	-9	-9	0	0.0
	Pit-N	0	2	.000	3	2	1	0	0	17^1	16	0	11	7	15.1	3.63	97	.246	.372	0	.000	-0	-0	-0	-1	-0.1
1965	Pit-N	1	1	.500	34	1	0	0	0	51^1	44	3	16	29	10.7	3.16	111	.237	.300	0	.000	-1	2	2	-1	-0.1
1967	Chi-A	4	2	.667	51	8	0	0	4	95^1	95	2	28	47	11.7	2.45	126	.260	.315	1	.063	-0	8	7	-1	0.4
1968	Chi-A	13	12	.520	**88**	2	0	0	16	159	127	8	33	74	9.2	1.87	162	.222	.268	2	.091	-1	**20**	**20**	-0	3.9
1969	Chi-A	10	11	.476	**76**	0	0	0	15	119^2	113	13	40	73	11.7	3.01	128	.248	.313	0	.000	-1	8	11	1	2.1
1970	Chi-A	9	13	.409	**77**	0	0	0	21	121^2	118	7	36	85	11.5	2.81	139	.258	.315	2	.111	-1	12	15	2	3.2
1971	Chi-A☆	22	13	.629	44	42	22	7	1	334	272	21	62	210	9.2	1.91	**188**	.222	.264	5	.052	-5	**57**	**62**	2	**6.6**
1972	Chi-A★	**24**	17	.585	49	49	20	8	0	**376^2**	325	28	74	193	9.7	2.51	125	.235	.277	17	.136	-2	23	26	4	3.1
1973	Chi-A	**24**	20	.545	49	48	21	4	0	**359^1**	381	25	91	199	12.0	3.46	114	.270	.318	0	—	0	14	20	1	2.3
1974	Chi-A☆	20	19	.513	42	42	22	1	0	320^1	305	27	80	169	11.1	3.60	104	.254	.305	0	—	0	1	5	3	0.7
1975	Chi-A	16	20	.444	43	43	14	2	0	291^1	309	26	92	140	12.5	4.11	94	.272	.329	0	—	0	-11	-8	1	-0.8
1976	Chi-A	4	3	.571	7	7	5	1	0	56^1	51	3	11	31	9.9	2.24	159	.242	.279	0	—	0	8	8	1	1.1
1977	Chi-A	7	8	.467	24	18	5	1	0	122^2	139	10	50	42	14.6	4.99	82	.293	.373	0	—	0	-13	-12	2	-1.1
1978	Chi-A	10	10	.500	28	27	4	0	0	168	187	23	74	69	14.1	5.20	73	.285	.361	0	—	0	-27	-26	2	-2.5
Total	17	164	156	.512	651	297	114	24	57	2684	2582	209	724	1411	11.3	3.24	112	.254	.308	27	.084	-14	92	120	15	18.5
● BRAD WOODALL Woodall, David Bradley b: 6/25/69, Atlanta, Ga. BB/TL, 6', 175 lbs. Deb: 7/22/94																										
1994	Atl-N	0	1	.000	1	1	0	0	0	6	5	2	2	2	10.5	4.50	94	.227	.292	1	.500	0	-0	-0	1	0.1
1995	Atl-N	1	1	.500	9	0	0	0	0	10^1	13	1	8	5	18.3	6.10	70	.310	.420	1	1.000	0	-2	-2	0	-0.3
1996	Atl-N	2	2	.500	8	3	0	0	0	19^2	28	4	4	20	14.6	7.32	60	.333	.364	1	.200	0	-7	-6	-0	-1.1
1998	Mil-N	7	9	.438	31	20	0	0	0	138	145	25	47	85	12.9	4.96	87	.273	.338	9	.237	3	-11	-10	1	-0.6
Total	4	10	13	.435	49	24	0	0	0	174	191	32	61	112	13.3	5.28	82	.281	.345	12	.261	4	-20	-19	1	-1.9
● STEVE WOODARD Woodard, Steven Larry b: 5/15/75, Hartselle, Ala. BL/TR, 6'4", 225 lbs. Deb: 7/28/97																										
1997	Mil-A	3	3	.500	7	7	0	0	0	36^2	39	5	6	32	11.5	5.15	89	.269	.307	0	—	0	-2	-2	-1	-0.4
1998	Mil-N	10	12	.455	34	26	0	0	0	165^2	170	19	33	135	11.5	4.18	103	.264	.309	7	.140	-1	1	2	-2	0.0
Total	2	13	15	.464	41	33	0	0	0	202^1	209	24	39	167	11.5	4.36	100	.265	.309	7	.140	-1	-2	-0	-3	-0.4
● GENE WOODBURN Woodburn, Eugene Stewart b: 8/20/1886, Bellaire, Ohio d: 1/18/61, Sandusky, Ohio BR/TR, 6', 175 lbs. Deb: 7/27/11																										
1911	StL-N	1	5	.167	11	6	1	0	0	38^1	22	0	40	23	16.0	5.40	63	.167	.382	1	.167	1	-9	-9	1	-1.0
1912	StL-N	1	4	.200	20	5	1	0	0	48^1	60	0	42	25	19.7	5.59	61	.306	.438	0	.000	-2	-12	-12	-1	-1.3
Total	2	2	9	.182	31	11	2	0	0	86^2	82	0	82	48	18.1	5.50	62	.250	.414	1	.053	-0	-20	-20	0	-2.3
● FRED WOODCOCK Woodcock, Fred Wayland b: 5/17/1868, Winchendon, Mass. d: 8/11/43, Ashburnham, Mass. BL/TL, 6'2", 190 lbs. Deb: 5/17/1892																										
1892	Pit-N	1	2	.333	5	4	3	0	0	33	42	1	17	8	16.6	3.55	93	.298	.381	3	.200	0	-1	-1	0	0.0
● GEORGE WOODEND Woodend, George Anthony b: 12/9/17, Hartford, Conn. d: 2/6/80, Hartford, Conn. BR/TR, 6', 200 lbs. Deb: 4/22/44																										
1944	Bos-N	0	0	—	3	0	0	0	0	2	5	0	5	0	45.0	13.50	28	.556	.714	0	—	0	-2	-2	0	0.0
● HAL WOODESHICK Woodeshick, Harold Joseph b: 8/24/32, Wilkes-Barre, Pa. BR/TL, 6'3", 200 lbs. Deb: 9/14/56																										
1956	Det-A	0	2	.000	2	2	0	0	0	5^1	12	1	3	1	25.3	13.50	30	.444	.500	0	—	0	-6	-6	0	-1.3
1958	Cle-A	6	6	.500	14	9	3	0	0	71^2	71	4	25	27	12.8	3.64	100	.265	.341	4	.167	-1	1	0	3	0.2
1959	Was-A	2	4	.333	31	3	0	0	0	61	58	2	36	30	14.0	3.69	106	.253	.357	0	.000	-1	1	2	1	0.1
1960	Was-A	4	5	.444	41	14	1	0	4	115	131	7	60	46	15.2	4.70	83	.289	.375	2	.069	-2	-11	-10	2	-0.8
1961	Was-A	3	2	.600	7	6	1	0	0	40^1	38	3	24	24	14.5	4.02	100	.257	.371	2	.125	-1	0	-0	1	0.0
	Det-A	1	1	.500	12	2	0	0	0	18^1	25	3	17	13	20.6	7.85	52	.316	.438	0	.000	-0	-8	-8	1	-0.7
	Yr	4	3	.571	19	8	1	0	0	58^2	63	6	41	37	16.0	5.22	77	.273	.382	2	.100	-1	-8	-8	2	-0.7
1962	Hou-N	5	16	.238	31	26	2	1	0	139^1	161	3	54	82	14.1	4.39	85	.290	.356	3	.081	-1	-7	-10	0	-1.5
1963	Hou-N★	11	9	.550	55	0	0	0	10	114	75	3	42	94	9.7	1.97	160	.186	.273	3	.130	-0	17	15	3	3.3
1964	Hou-N	2	9	.182	61	0	0	0	**23**	78^1	73	3	32	58	12.9	2.76	124	.249	.337	0	.000	-0	7	6	2	1.3
1965	Hou-N	3	4	.429	27	0	0	0	3	32^1	27	3	18	22	12.5	3.06	110	.227	.328	1	.167	-0	2	1	1	0.3
	StL-N	3	2	.600	51	0	0	0	15	59^2	47	1	27	37	11.5	1.81	212	.221	.314	0	.000	-1	11	13	2	2.0
	Yr	6	6	.500	78	0	0	0	18	92	74	4	45	59	11.8	2.25	163	.223	.319	1	.071	-1	13	15	2	2.3
1966	StL-N	2	1	.667	59	0	0	0	4	70^1	57	5	23	30	10.4	1.92	187	.224	.290	1	.200	0	13	13	3	1.1
1967	*StL-N	2	1	.667	36	0	0	0	2	41^2	41	2	28	20	15.6	5.18	63	.252	.371	0	.000	-0	-8	-9	1	-0.7
Total	11	44	62	.415	427	62	7	1	61	847^1	816	40	389	484	13.2	3.56	102	.254	.342	16	.092	-7	13	7	18	3.3

YEAR	TM/L	W	L	PCT	G	GS	CG	SH	SV	IP	H	HR	BB	SO	RAT	ERA	ERA+	OAV	OOB	BH	AVG	PB	PR	/A	PD	TPI
● **DAN WOODMAN**	Woodman, Daniel Courtenay "Cocoa" b: 7/8/1893, Danvers, Mass. d: 12/14/62, Danvers, Mass. BR/TR, 5'8", 160 lbs. Deb: 7/10/14																									
1914	Buf-F	0	0	—	13	0	0	0	1	33^2	30	0	11	13	11.2	2.41	123	.246	.313	1	.143	-1	2	2	-1	-0.1
1915	Buf-F	0	0	—	5	1	0	0	0	15^1	14	0	9	1	13.5	4.11	68	.246	.348	1	.250	-0	-2	-2	1	0.1
Total	2	0	0	—	18	1	0	0	1	49	44	0	20	14	11.9	2.94	99	.246	.325	2	.182	-1	-1	-0	0	0.0
● **CLARENCE WOODS**	Woods, Clarence Cofield b: 6/11/1892, Woods Ridge, Ohio County, Ind. d: 7/2/69, Rising Sun, Ind. BR/TR, 6'5", 230 lbs. Deb: 8/8/14																									
1914	Ind-F	0	0	—	2	0	0	0	1	2	1	0	2	1	13.5	4.50	69	.167	.375	0	—	0	-0	-0	0	0.0
● **PINKY WOODS**	Woods, George Rowland b: 5/22/15, Waterbury, Conn. d: 10/30/82, Los Angeles, Cal. BR/TR, 6'5", 225 lbs. Deb: 6/20/43																									
1943	Bos-A	5	6	.455	23	12	2	0	1	100^2	109	6	55	32	14.8	4.92	67	.284	.375	8	.222	-0	-18	-18	-0	-1.9
1944	Bos-A	4	8	.333	38	20	5	1	0	170^2	171	4	88	56	14.0	3.27	104	.266	.360	7	.146	-1	3	2	2	0.2
1945	Bos-A	4	7	.364	24	12	3	0	2	107^1	108	3	63	36	14.4	4.19	81	.268	.368	9	.214	1	-10	-9	1	-0.7
Total	3	13	21	.382	85	44	10	1	3	378^2	388	13	206	124	14.3	3.97	85	.272	.366	24	.190	-1	-25	-25	3	-2.4
● **JOHN WOODS**	Woods, John Fulton "Abe" b: 1/18/1898, Princeton, W.Va. d: 10/4/46, Norfolk, Va. BR/TR, 6', 175 lbs. Deb: 9/16/24																									
1924	Bos-A	0	0	—	1	0	0	0	0	1	0	0	3	0	27.0	0.00	—	.000	.500	0	—	0	0	0	-0	0.0
● **WALT WOODS**	Woods, Walter Sydney b: 4/28/1875, Rye, N.H. d: 10/30/51, Portsmouth, N.H. BR/TR, 5'9.5", 165 lbs. Deb: 4/20/1898																									
1898	Chi-N	9	13	.409	27	22	18	3	0	215	224	7	59	26	12.3	3.14	114	.266	.322	27	.175	-4	11	11	1	0.6
1899	Lou-N	9	13	.409	26	21	17	0	0	186^1	216	9	37	21	12.6	3.28	117	.290	.329	19	.151	-3	12	12	5	1.3
1900	Pit-N	0	0	—	1	0	0	0	0	3	9	0	1	1	30.0	21.00	17	.500	.526	0	.000	-0	-6	-6	-0	0.0
Total	3	18	26	.409	54	43	35	3	0	404^1	449	16	97	48	12.5	3.34	111	.280	.328	46	.164	-7	17	17	5	1.9
● **DICK WOODSON**	Woodson, Richard Lee b: 3/30/45, Oelwein, Iowa BR/TR, 6'5", 207 lbs. Deb: 4/8/69																									
1969	*Min-A	7	5	.583	44	10	2	0	1	110^1	99	11	49	66	12.3	3.67	99	.237	.322	2	.074	-1	-1	-0	1	-0.1
1970	*Min-A	1	2	.333	21	0	0	0	1	30^2	29	2	19	22	14.1	3.82	98	.244	.348	0	.000	-0	-0	-0	0	0.0
1972	Min-A	14	14	.500	36	36	9	3	0	251^2	193	19	101	150	10.6	2.72	118	.211	.291	7	.080	-5	10	14	1	1.1
1973	Min-A	10	8	.556	23	23	4	2	0	141^1	137	12	68	53	13.2	3.95	100	.254	.339	0	—	0	-2	0	-2	-0.2
1974	Min-A	1	1	.500	5	4	0	0	0	27	30	5	4	12	11.7	4.33	86	.273	.304	0	—	0	-2	-2	1	-0.3
	NY-A	1	2	.333	8	3	0	0	0	28	34	6	12	12	15.1	5.79	61	.301	.373	0	—	0	-7	-7	-1	-0.6
	Yr	2	3	.400	13	7	0	0	0	55	64	11	16	24	13.3	5.07	71	.286	.336	0	—	0	-9	-9	-0	-0.9
Total	5	34	32	.515	137	76	15	5	2	589	522	55	253	315	12.0	3.47	102	.236	.317	9	.077	-7	-2	5	-0	-0.1
● **KERRY WOODSON**	Woodson, Walter Browne b: 5/18/69, Jacksonville, Fla. BR/TR, 6'2", 190 lbs. Deb: 7/19/92																									
1992	Sea-A	0	1	.000	8	1	0	0	0	13^2	12	0	11	6	16.5	3.29	121	.245	.403	0	—	0	1	1	0	0.1
● **FRANK WOODWARD**	Woodward, Frank Russell b: 5/17/1894, New Haven, Conn. d: 6/11/61, New Haven, Conn. BR/TR, 5'10", 175 lbs. Deb: 4/17/18																									
1918	Phi-N	0	0	—	2	0	0	0	0	6	6	0	4	4	15.0	6.00	50	.250	.357	1	.333	0	-2	-2	-0	0.0
1919	Phi-N	6	9	.400	17	12	6	0	0	100^2	109	5	35	27	13.3	4.74	68	.291	.359	6	.207	1	-20	-17	-2	-2.4
	StL-N	3	5	.375	17	7	2	0	1	72	65	1	28	18	11.8	2.63	106	.248	.323	1	.048	-2	2	1	-0	-0.1
	Yr	9	14	.391	34	19	8	0	1	172^2	174	6	63	45	12.4	3.86	79	.271	.337	7	.140	-1	-18	-16	-2	-2.5
1921	Was-A	0	0	—	3	1	0	0	0	10^2	11	0	3	4	11.8	5.91	70	.282	.333	1	.333	0	-2	-2	0	0.0
1922	Was-A	0	0	—	1	0	0	0	0	2^1	3	0	3	2	23.1	11.57	33	.375	.545	0	.000	-0	-2	-2	0	0.0
1923	Chi-A	0	1	.000	2	1	0	0	0	2	5	0	1	0	27.0	13.50	29	.500	.545	0	—	0	-2	-2	0	-0.7
Total	5	9	15	.375	42	21	8	0	1	193^2	199	6	74	55	13.0	4.23	74	.277	.350	9	.158	-1	-26	-24	-2	-3.2
● **BOB WOODWARD**	Woodward, Robert John b: 9/28/62, Hanover, N.H. BR/TR, 6'3", 185 lbs. Deb: 9/5/85																									
1985	Bos-A	1	0	1.000	5	2	0	0	0	26^2	17	0	9	16	9.5	1.69	254	.168	.250	0	—	0	7	8	-1	-0.1
1986	Bos-A	2	3	.400	9	6	0	0	0	35^2	46	4	11	14	14.6	5.30	79	.313	.365	0	—	0	-4	-5	0	-0.5
1987	Bos-A	1	1	.500	9	6	0	0	0	37	53	6	15	15	16.8	7.05	64	.338	.399	0	—	0	-11	-10	-1	-0.6
1988	Bos-A	0	0	—	1	0	0	0	0	0^2	2	0	1	0	40.5	13.50	30	.500	.600	0	—	0	-1	-1	0	0.0
Total	4	4	4	.500	24	14	0	0	0	100	118	10	36	45	14.2	5.04	86	.289	.352	0	—	0	-9	-8	-1	-1.2
● **FLOYD WOOLDRIDGE**	Wooldridge, Floyd Lewis b: 8/25/28, Jerico Springs, Mo BR/TR, 6'1", 185 lbs. Deb: 5/1/55																									
1955	StL-N	2	4	.333	18	8	2	0	0	57^2	64	9	27	14	14.4	4.84	84	.281	.359	4	.222	0	-5	-5	-1	-0.6
● **JUNIOR WOOTEN**	Wooten, Earl Hazwell b: 1/16/24, Pelzer, S.C. BR/TL, 5'11", 160 lbs. Deb: 9/16/47 ♦																									
1948	Was-A	0	0	—	1	0	0	0	0	2	2	0	2	1	18.0	9.00	48	.250	.400	66	.256	0	-1	-1	0	0.0
● **FRED WORDEN**	Worden, Frederick Bamford b: 9/4/1894, St.Louis, Mo. d: 11/9/41, St.Louis, Mo. BR/TR, Deb: 9/28/14																									
1914	Phi-A	0	0	—	1	0	0	0	0	2	8	0	0	1	36.0	18.00	15	.615	.615	0	.000	-0	-3	-3	0	0.0
● **HOGE WORKMAN**	Workman, Harry Hall b: 9/25/1899, Huntington, W.Va. d: 5/20/72, Ft.Myers, Fla. BR/TR, 5'11", 170 lbs. Deb: 6/27/24																									
1924	Bos-A	0	0	—	11	0	0	0	0	18	25	2	11	7	19.0	8.50	51	.325	.422	0	.000	-0	-9	-8	0	0.0
● **RALPH WORKS**	Works, Ralph Talmadge "Judge" b: 3/16/1888, Payson, Ill. d: 8/8/41, Pasadena, Cal. BL/TR, 6'2.5", 185 lbs. Deb: 5/1/09																									
1909	*Det-A	4	1	.800	16	4	4	0	2	64	62	0	17	31	11.3	1.97	128	.261	.313	1	.059	-2	4	4	-1	0.1
1910	Det-A	3	6	.333	18	10	5	0	1	85^2	73	1	39	36	12.2	3.57	74	.235	.328	8	.267	1	-10	-9	-1	-0.9
1911	Det-A	11	5	.688	30	15	9	3	0	167^1	173	3	67	68	13.2	3.87	89	.268	.342	9	.148	-3	-10	-8	-4	-1.4
1912	Det-A	5	10	.333	27	16	9	1	1	157	185	1	66	64	14.8	4.24	77	.308	.383	8	.143	-3	-16	-17	0	-1.7
	Cin-N	1	1	.500	3	1	1	0	0	9^2	4	0	5	5	9.3	2.79	120	.133	.278	1	.200	-0	1	1	-0	0.1
1913	Cin-N	0	1	.000	5	2	0	0	0	15	15	0	8	4	15.6	7.80	42	.242	.356	1	.167	-0	-8	-8	0	-0.4
Total	5	24	24	.500	99	48	28	4	4	498^2	512	5	202	208	13.3	3.79	83	.271	.348	28	.160	-8	-39	-37	-6	-4.2
● **TIM WORRELL**	Worrell, Timothy Howard b: 7/5/67, Pasadena, Cal. BR/TR, 6'4", 220 lbs. Deb: 6/25/93 F																									
1993	SD-N	2	7	.222	21	16	0	0	0	100^2	104	11	43	52	13.1	4.92	84	.269	.342	1	.032	-3	-10	-9	-1	-1.0
1994	SD-N	0	1	.000	3	3	0	0	0	14^2	9	0	5	14	8.6	3.68	112	.170	.241	1	.500	1	1	1	0	0.1
1995	SD-N	1	0	1.000	9	0	0	0	0	13^1	16	2	6	13	15.5	4.73	85	.291	.371	0	.000	-0	-1	-1	0	-0.1
1996	*SD-N	9	7	.563	50	11	0	0	1	121	109	9	39	99	11.5	3.05	130	.236	.304	3	.150	-0	16	12	-2	1.3
1997	SD-N	4	8	.333	60	10	0	0	3	106^1	116	14	50	81	14.6	5.16	75	.280	.367	3	.200	1	-11	-15	1	-1.4
1998	Det-A	2	6	.250	15	9	0	0	0	61^2	66	11	19	47	12.6	5.98	79	.270	.326	0	—	0	-9	-9	0	-0.9
	Cle-A	0	0	—	3	0	0	0	0	5^1	6	0	2	2	13.5	5.06	94	.300	.364	0	—	0	-0	-0	1	0.0
	Oak-A	0	1	.000	25	0	0	0	0	36	34	5	8	33	10.5	4.00	114	.241	.282	0	—	0	3	2	-0	0.1
	Yr	2	7	.222	43	9	0	0	0	103	106	16	29	82	11.8	5.24	89	.259	.308	0	—	0	-7	-7	1	-0.8
Total	6	18	30	.375	186	49	0	0	4	459	460	52	172	341	12.7	4.51	92	.259	.330	8	.116	-1	-12	-19	-1	-1.9
● **TODD WORRELL**	Worrell, Todd Roland b: 9/28/59, Arcadia, Cal. BR/TR, 6'5", 222 lbs. Deb: 8/28/85 F																									
1985	*StL-N	3	0	1.000	17	0	0	0	5	21^2	17	2	7	17	10.0	2.91	122	.215	.279	0	.000	-0	2	2	-0	0.2
1986	StL-N	9	10	.474	74	0	0	0	**36**	103^2	86	9	41	73	11.1	2.08	175	.229	.307	1	.143	0	**19**	**18**	-2	4.2
1987	*StL-N	8	6	.571	75	0	0	0	33	94^2	86	8	34	92	11.4	2.66	156	.242	.308	1	.100	-0	15	16	0	3.1
1988	StL-N★	5	9	.357	68	0	0	0	32	90	69	7	34	78	10.4	3.00	116	.214	.291	0	.000	-0	4	5	-0	1.0
1989	StL-N	3	5	.375	47	0	0	0	20	51^2	42	4	26	41	11.8	2.96	123	.222	.316	0	.000	-0	3	4	1	0.9
1992	StL-N	5	3	.625	67	0	0	0	3	64	45	4	25	64	10.0	2.11	161	.198	.281	0	—	0	10	9	-1	1.0
1993	LA-N	1	1	.500	35	0	0	0	5	38^2	46	6	11	31	13.3	6.05	63	.313	.361	0	—	0	-9	-10	-0	-0.7
1994	LA-N	6	5	.545	38	0	0	0	11	42	37	4	12	44	10.7	4.29	91	.236	.294	0	—	0	-0	-2	-0	-0.5
1995	LA-N†	4	1	.800	59	0	0	0	32	62^1	50	4	19	61	10.1	2.02	188	.221	.285	0	.000	-0	15	12	1	2.1
1996	*LA-N★	4	6	.400	72	0	0	0	**44**	65^1	70	5	15	66	12.0	3.03	127	.265	.310	0	—	0	9	6	-1	1.5
1997	LA-N	2	6	.250	65	0	0	0	35	59^2	60	12	23	61	12.5	5.28	73	.250	.316	0	—	0	-7	-9	1	-2.0
Total	11	50	52	.490	617	0	0	0	256	693^2	608	65	247	628	11.2	3.09	121	.235	.304	2	.074	-1	60	51	-2	10.8

YEAR	TM/L	W	L	PCT	G	GS	CG	SH	SV	IP	H	HR	BB	SO	RAT	ERA	ERA+	OAV	OOB	BH	AVG	PB	PR	/A	PD	TPI
● RICH WORTHAM	Wortham, Richard Cooper b: 10/22/53, Odessa, Tex. BR/TL, 6′, 185 lbs. Deb: 5/3/78																									
1978	Chi-A	3	2	.600	8	8	2	0	0	59	59	1	23	25	12.5	3.05	125	.267	.336	0	—	0	5	5	-0	0.4
1979	Chi-A	14	14	.500	34	33	5	0	0	204	195	21	100	119	13.1	4.90	87	.255	.343	0	—	0	-15	-15	-2	-1.9
1980	Chi-A	4	7	.364	41	10	0	0	1	92	102	4	58	45	15.9	5.97	67	.285	.389	0	—	0	-20	-20	1	-2.0
1983	Oak-A	0	0	—	1	0	0	0	0	0	3	0	1	0	—	∞	—	1.000	1.000	0	—	0	-1	-1	0	0.1
Total	4	21	23	.477	84	51	7	0	1	355	359	26	182	189	13.9	4.89	84	.266	.356	0	—	0	-32	-31	-1	-3.4
● AL WORTHINGTON	Worthington, Allan Fulton "Red" b: 2/5/29, Birmingham, Ala. BR/TR, 6′2″, 205 lbs. Deb: 7/6/53 C																									
1953	NY-N	4	8	.333	20	17	5	2	0	102	103	6	54	52	14.0	3.44	125	.258	.349	2	.065	-2	10	10	0	0.8
1954	NY-N	0	2	.000	10	1	0	0	0	18	21	0	15	8	18.0	3.50	115	.333	.462	0	.000	-1	1	1	0	0.1
1956	NY-N	7	14	.333	28	24	4	0	0	165^2	158	20	74	95	12.8	3.97	95	.254	.338	12	.235	2	-4	-3	2	0.0
1957	NY-N	8	11	.421	55	12	1	1	4	157^2	140	19	56	90	11.5	4.22	93	.237	.309	4	.100	-2	-6	-5	0	-0.8
1958	SF-N	11	7	.611	54	12	1	0	6	151^1	152	17	57	76	12.5	3.63	105	.255	.322	8	.182	0	5	3	0	0.4
1959	SF-N	2	3	.400	42	3	0	0	2	73^1	68	8	37	45	13.5	3.68	103	.253	.354	1	.077	-1	2	1	1	0.1
1960	Bos-A	0	1	.000	6	0	0	0	0	11^2	17	1	11	7	21.6	7.71	52	.340	.459	0	.000	-0	-5	-5	0	-0.4
	Chi-A	1	1	.500	4	0	0	0	0	5^1	3	0	4	1	11.8	3.38	112	.176	.333	2	1.000	1	0	0	0	0.2
	Yr	1	2	.333	10	0	0	0	0	17	20	1	15	8	18.5	6.35	62	.299	.427	2	.667	1	-5	-5	0	-0.2
1963	Cin-N	4	4	.500	50	0	0	0	10	81^1	75	6	31	55	12.1	2.99	112	.248	.324	1	.083	-0	3	3	2	0.6
1964	Cin-N	1	0	1.000	6	0	0	0	0	7	14	0	2	6	21.9	10.29	35	.400	.447	0	—	0	-5	-5	-0	-0.7
	Min-A	5	6	.455	41	0	0	0	14	72^1	47	4	28	59	9.3	1.37	261	.183	.263	1	.063	-1	18	18	1	3.4
1965	*Min-A	10	7	.588	62	0	0	0	21	80^1	57	4	41	59	11.3	2.13	167	.207	.316	1	.100	0	12	13	2	3.6
1966	Min-A	6	3	.667	65	0	0	0	16	91^1	66	6	27	93	9.3	2.46	146	.199	.261	3	.273	1	10	11	1	1.8
1967	Min-A	8	9	.471	59	0	0	0	16	92	77	6	38	80	11.3	2.84	122	.229	.309	0	.000	-1	4	6	0	1.4
1968	Min-A	4	5	.444	54	0	0	0	**18**	76^1	67	1	32	57	11.7	2.71	114	.238	.315	0	.000	-1	2	3	0	0.5
1969	*Min-A	4	1	.800	46	0	0	0	3	61	65	7	20	51	12.5	4.57	80	.278	.335	0	.000	-1	-6	-6	-1	-0.7
Total	14	75	82	.478	602	69	11	3	110	1246^2	1130	105	527	834	12.2	3.39	110	.243	.323	35	.137	-5	41	46	7	10.3
● GENE WRIGHT	Wright, Clarence Eugene "Big Gene" b: 12/11/1878, Cleveland, Ohio d: 10/29/30, Barberton, Ohio BR/TR, 6′2″, 185 lbs. Deb: 10/5/01																									
1901	Bro-N	1	0	1.000	1	1	1	0	0	9	6	0	1	6	7.0	1.00	335	.188	.212	1	.333	0	2	2	-0	0.3
1902	Cle-A	7	10	.412	21	18	15	1	1	148	150	6	75	52	14.2	3.95	87	.263	.357	10	.143	-2	-6	-8	-2	-1.2
1903	Cle-A	3	10	.231	15	12	8	0	0	101^2	122	1	58	42	16.3	5.75	50	.296	.388	9	.209	2	-32	-33	2	-3.1
	StL-A	3	5	.375	8	8	7	1	0	61	73	2	16	37	13.7	3.69	79	.296	.348	3	.143	-1	-5	-5	1	-0.6
	Yr	6	15	.286	23	20	15	1	0	162^2	195	3	74	79	15.1	4.98	58	.294	.368	12	.188	2	-36	-38	3	-3.7
1904	StL-A	0	1	.000	1	1	0	0	0	4	10	0	2	3	27.0	13.50	18	.476	.522	0	.000	-0	-5	-5	1	-0.8
Total	4	14	26	.350	46	40	31	2	1	323^2	361	9	152	140	14.7	4.50	70	.282	.365	23	.167	-1	-45	-49	1	-5.4
● CLYDE WRIGHT	Wright, Clyde b: 2/20/41, Jefferson City, Tenn. BR/TL, 6′1″, 185 lbs. Deb: 6/15/66 F																									
1966	Cal-A	4	7	.364	20	13	3	1	0	91^1	92	11	25	37	11.6	3.74	90	.265	.316	3	.103	-1	-3	-4	0	-0.6
1967	Cal-A	5	5	.500	20	11	1	0	0	77^1	76	5	24	35	11.8	3.26	96	.260	.319	6	.273	2	-0	-1	0	0.1
1968	Cal-A	10	6	.625	41	13	2	1	3	125^2	123	13	44	71	12.1	3.94	74	.256	.321	8	.216	2	-13	-14	-1	-1.8
1969	Cal-A	1	8	.111	37	5	0	0	0	63^2	66	4	30	31	13.7	4.10	85	.278	.362	2	.182	0	-3	-4	0	-0.5
1970	Cal-A★	22	12	.647	39	39	7	2	0	260^2	226	24	88	110	11.1	2.83	128	.232	.300	18	.171	3	26	23	-2	3.0
1971	Cal-A	16	17	.485	37	37	10	2	0	276^2	225	17	82	135	10.1	2.99	108	.226	.287	14	.154	2	14	8	4	1.5
1972	Cal-A	18	11	.621	35	35	15	2	0	251	229	14	80	87	11.2	2.98	98	.246	.308	18	.217	7	2	-2	3	0.9
1973	Cal-A	11	19	.367	37	36	13	1	0	257	273	26	76	65	12.3	3.68	96	.273	.326	0	—	0	4	-4	4	0.2
1974	Mil-A	9	20	.310	38	32	15	0	0	232	264	22	54	64	12.3	4.42	82	.284	.323	0	—	0	-21	-21	2	-2.2
1975	Tex-A	4	6	.400	25	14	1	0	0	93^1	105	7	47	32	14.8	4.44	85	.294	.378	0	—	0	-7	-7	2	-0.5
Total	10	100	111	.474	329	235	67	9	3	1728^2	1679	143	550	667	11.7	3.50	96	.256	.316	69	.183	14	-1	-27	13	0.1
● DAVE WRIGHT	Wright, David William b: 8/27/1875, Dennison, Ohio d: 1/18/46, Dennison, Ohio BR/TR, 6′, 185 lbs. Deb: 7/22/1895																									
1895	Pit-N	0	0	—	1	0	0	0	0	2	6	0	1	0	31.5	27.00	17	.500	.538	0	.000	-0	-5	-5	0	0.0
1897	Chi-N	1	0	1.000	1	1	1	0	0	7	17	1	2	4	27.0	15.43	29	.459	.512	1	.333	0	-9	-9	0	-0.7
Total	2	1	0	1.000	2	1	1	0	0	9	23	1	3	4	28.0	18.00	25	.469	.519	1	.250	0	-14	-14	0	-0.7
● GEORGE WRIGHT	Wright, George b: 1/28/1847, Yonkers, N.Y. d: 8/21/37, Boston, Mass. BR/TR, 5′9.5″, 150 lbs. Deb: 5/5/1871 FMH♦																									
1875	Bos-n	0	1	.000	2	0	0	0	0	4	5	0	0	0	11.3	6.75	32	.294	.294	136	.333	1	-2	-2		-0.3
1876	Bos-N	0	0	—	1	0	0	0	0	1	1	0	0	1	9.0	0.00	—	.250	.250	100	.299	0	0	0	0	0.0
● ED WRIGHT	Wright, Henderson Edward b: 5/15/19, Dyersburg, Tenn. d: 11/19/95, Dyersburg, Tenn. BR/TR, 6′1″, 180 lbs. Deb: 7/29/45																									
1945	Bos-N	8	3	.727	15	12	7	1	0	111^1	104	7	33	24	11.1	2.51	153	.254	.310	5	.128	-2	16	16	-1	1.2
1946	Bos-N	12	9	.571	36	21	8	2	0	176^1	164	8	71	44	12.1	3.52	97	.250	.325	18	.305	6	-2	-2	0	0.4
1947	Bos-N	3	3	.500	23	6	1	0	0	64^2	80	9	35	14	16.3	6.40	61	.305	.391	3	.130	-0	-17	-18	-0	-1.5
1948	Bos-N	0	0	—	3	0	0	0	0	4^2	9	0	2	2	21.2	1.93	199	.474	.524	0	—	0	1	1	0	0.0
1952	Phi-A	2	1	.667	24	0	0	0	1	41^1	55	6	20	9	17.0	6.53	61	.320	.400	1	.143	-0	-13	-12	-0	-0.9
Total	5	25	16	.610	101	39	16	3	1	398^1	412	30	161	93	13.1	4.00	92	.271	.344	27	.211	3	-15	-14	-2	-0.8
● JIM WRIGHT	Wright, James "Jiggs" b: 9/19/1900, Hyde, England d: 4/10/63, Oakland, Cal. BR/TR, 6′2.5″, 195 lbs. Deb: 9/14/27																									
1927	StL-A	1	0	1.000	2	1	1	0	0	12	8	0	4	4	9.0	4.50	97	.182	.250	0	.000	-0	-0	-0	-0	-0.1
1928	StL-A	0	0	—	2	0	0	0	0	2	3	0	2	2	22.5	13.50	31	.375	.500	0	—	0	-2	-2	0	0.0
Total	2	1	0	1.000	4	1	1	0	0	14	11	0	6	6	10.9	5.79	75	.212	.293	0	.000	-0	-3	-2	0	-0.1
● JIM WRIGHT	Wright, James Clifton b: 12/21/50, Reed City, Mich. BR/TR, 6′1″, 165 lbs. Deb: 4/15/78																									
1978	Bos-A	8	4	.667	24	16	5	3	0	116	122	8	24	56	11.9	3.57	115	.276	.323	0	—	0	2	7	-2	0.5
1979	Bos-A	1	0	1.000	11	1	0	0	0	23	19	5	7	15	11.3	5.09	87	.226	.309	0	—	0	-2	-2	-0	-0.4
Total	2	9	4	.692	35	17	5	3	0	139	141	13	31	71	11.8	3.82	109	.268	.321	0	—	0	0	5	-2	0.1
● JIM WRIGHT	Wright, James Leon b: 3/3/55, St.Joseph, Mo. BR/TR, 6′5″, 205 lbs. Deb: 4/22/81 C																									
1981	KC-A	2	3	.400	17	4	0	0	0	52	57	5	21	27	13.8	3.46	104	.277	.349	0	—	0	1	1	-1	0.0
1982	KC-A	0	0	—	7	0	0	0	0	23^2	32	3	6	9	14.5	5.32	77	.320	.358	0	—	0	-3	-3	-1	-0.1
Total	2	2	3	.400	24	4	0	0	0	75^2	89	8	27	36	14.0	4.04	93	.291	.352	0	—	0	-2	-2	-1	-0.1
● RICKY WRIGHT	Wright, James Richard b: 11/22/58, Paris, Tex. BL/TL, 6′3″, 175 lbs. Deb: 7/28/82																									
1982	LA-N	2	1	.667	14	5	0	0	0	32^2	28	1	20	24	13.2	3.03	114	.233	.343	1	.125	0	2	2	0	0.2
1983	LA-N	0	0	—	6	0	0	0	0	6^1	5	0	2	5	9.9	2.84	126	.227	.292	0	—	0	1	1	-0	0.0
	Tex-A	0	0	—	1	0	0	0	0	2	0	0	1	2	4.5	0.00	—	.000	.167	0	—	0	1	1	-0	0.2
1984	Tex-A	0	2	.000	8	1	0	0	0	14^2	20	3	11	6	19.0	6.14	68	.357	.463	0	—	0	-3	-3	0	-0.5
1985	Tex-A	0	0	—	5	0	0	0	0	7^2	5	0	5	7	11.7	4.70	90	.185	.313	0	—	0	-0	-0	0	-0.1
1986	Tex-A	1	0	1.000	21	1	0	0	0	39^1	44	1	21	23	14.9	5.03	85	.284	.369	0	—	0	-4	-3	1	0.0
Total	5	3	3	.500	55	7	0	0	0	102^2	102	5	60	67	14.2	4.30	92	.265	.364	1	.125	0	-4	-4	1	-0.2
● JAMEY WRIGHT	Wright, Jamey Alan b: 12/24/74, Oklahoma City, Okla. BR/TR, 6′6″, 205 lbs. Deb: 7/3/96																									
1996	Col-N	4	4	.500	16	15	0	0	0	91^1	105	8	41	45	15.1	4.93	106	.298	.382	2	.077	-1	-7	3	1	0.2
1997	Col-N	8	12	.400	26	26	1	0	0	149^2	198	19	71	59	16.8	6.25	83	.327	.408	6	.125	-2	-34	-18	-0	-2.2
1998	Col-N	9	14	.391	34	34	1	0	0	206^1	235	24	95	86	14.9	5.67	89	.294	.377	10	.175	1	-33	-14	1	-1.2
Total	3	21	30	.412	76	75	2	0	0	447^1	538	51	207	190	15.6	5.71	90	.306	.389	18	.137	-2	-74	-29	2	-3.2
● JARET WRIGHT	Wright, Jaret Samuel b: 12/29/75, Anaheim, Cal. BR/TR, 6′2″, 220 lbs. Deb: 6/24/97 F																									
1997	*Cle-A	8	3	.727	16	16	0	0	0	90^1	81	9	35	63	12.1	4.38	107	.238	.318	0	.000	-0	2	3	-0	0.3
1998	*Cle-A	12	10	.545	32	32	1	1	0	192^2	207	22	87	140	14.2	4.72	101	.277	.361	3	.429	1	-2	1	0	0.2
Total	2	20	13	.606	48	48	1	1	0	283	288	31	122	203	13.5	4.61	103	.265	.347	3	.300	1	0	4	0	0.5

YEAR	TM/L	W	L	PCT	G	GS	CG	SH	SV	IP	H	HR	BB	SO	RAT	ERA	ERA+	OAV	OOB	BH	AVG	PB	PR	/A	PD	TPI

● KEN WRIGHT   Wright, Kenneth Warren   b: 9/4/46, Pensacola, Fla.   BR/TR, 6'2", 210 lbs.   Deb: 4/10/70

1970	KC-A	1	2	.333	47	0	0	0	3	53¹	49	2	29	30	14.3	5.23	71	.261	.379	0	.000	-0	-9	-9	-0	-0.6
1971	KC-A	3	6	.333	21	12	1	1	1	78	66	6	47	56	13.4	3.69	93	.230	.344	2	.091	-1	-2	-2	1	-0.3
1972	KC-A	1	2	.333	17	0	0	0	4	18¹	15	0	15	18	15.2	4.91	62	.231	.383	0	.000	-0	-4	-4	0	-0.9
1973	KC-A	6	5	.545	25	12	1	0	0	80²	60	6	82	75	15.8	4.91	84	.210	.386	0	—	-0	-10	-7	-1	-1.1
1974	NY-A	0	0	—	3	0	0	0	0	5²	5	0	7	2	19.1	3.18	111	.227	.414	0	—	0	0	0	0	0.1
Total	5	11	15	.423	113	24	2	1	8	236	195	14	180	181	14.7	4.54	81	.230	.372	2	.071	-2	-24	-22	-1	-2.8

● MEL WRIGHT   Wright, Melvin James   b: 5/11/28, Manila, Ark.   d: 5/16/83, Houston, Tex.   BR/TR, 6'3", 210 lbs.   Deb: 4/17/54   C

1954	StL-N	0	0	—	9	0	0	0	0	10¹	16	2	11	4	25.3	10.45	39	.348	.492	0	.000	-0	-7	-7	-0	-0.9
1955	StL-N	2	2	.500	29	0	0	0	0	36¹	44	4	9	18	13.4	6.19	66	.308	.353	0	.000	-1	-9	-9	-0	-0.9
1960	Chi-N	0	1	.000	9	0	0	0	2	16¹	17	1	3	8	11.0	4.96	76	.279	.313	0	.000	-0	-2	-2	-1	-0.3
1961	Chi-N	0	1	.000	11	0	0	0	0	21	42	3	4	6	19.7	10.71	39	.416	.438	0	.000	-0	-16	-15	1	-0.6
Total	4	2	4	.333	58	0	0	0	2	84	119	10	27	36	16.0	7.61	53	.339	.391	0	.000	-2	-34	-33	1	-1.8

● BOB WRIGHT   Wright, Robert Cassius   b: 12/13/1891, Decatur Co., Ind.   d: 7/30/93, Carmichael, Cal.   BR/TR, 6'1.5", 175 lbs.   Deb: 9/21/15

| 1915 | Chi-N | 0 | 0 | — | 2 | 0 | 0 | 0 | 0 | 4 | 6 | 0 | 0 | 3 | 13.5 | 2.25 | 123 | .353 | .353 | 0 | — | 0 | 0 | 0 | 0 | 0.0 |

● ROY WRIGHT   Wright, Roy Earl   b: 9/26/33, Buchtel, Ohio   BR/TR, 6'2", 170 lbs.   Deb: 9/30/56

| 1956 | NY-N | 0 | 1 | .000 | 1 | 1 | 0 | 0 | 0 | 2² | 8 | 1 | 2 | 0 | 33.8 | 16.88 | 22 | .533 | .588 | 0 | .000 | -0 | -4 | -4 | 0 | -0.9 |

● RASTY WRIGHT   Wright, Wayne Bromley   b: 11/5/1895, Ceredo, W.Va.   d: 6/12/48, Columbus, Ohio   BR/TR, 5'11", 160 lbs.   Deb: 6/22/17

1917	StL-A	0	1	.000	16	1	0	0	0	39²	48	0	10	5	13.4	5.45	48	.300	.345	2	.200	0	-12	-13	0	-0.2
1918	StL-A	8	2	.800	18	13	6	1	0	111¹	99	1	18	25	9.9	2.51	109	.244	.285	10	.294	3	3	3	-1	0.5
1919	StL-A	0	5	.000	24	5	2	0	0	63¹	79	1	20	14	14.2	5.54	60	.315	.368	1	.083	-1	-16	-16	0	-1.2
1922	StL-A	9	7	.563	31	16	5	0	5	154	148	7	50	44	12.0	2.92	142	.262	.331	7	.140	-2	19	21	1	2.0
1923	StL-A	7	4	.636	20	8	4	0	0	82²	107	6	34	26	15.9	6.42	65	.317	.387	6	.222	0	-22	-21	0	-2.2
Total	5	24	19	.558	109	43	17	1	5	451	481	15	132	114	12.6	4.05	87	.280	.338	26	.195	1	-28	-26	-1	-1.1

● HARRY WRIGHT   Wright, William Henry   b: 1/10/1835, Sheffield, England   d: 10/3/1895, Atlantic City, N.J.   BR/TR, 5'9.5", 157 lbs.   Deb: 5/5/1871   FMH♦

1871	Bos-n	1	0	1.000	9	0	0	0	3	18²	34	0	4	0	18.3	6.27	66	.337	.362	44	.299		-4	-4		-0.2
1872	Bos-n	1	0	1.000	7	0	0	0	4	25²	26	0	0	1	9.1	2.10	173	.239	.239	52	.250	-0	4	4		0.2
1873	Bos-n	2	2	.500	13	5	0	0	4	38¹	65	0	7	0	16.9	4.23	78	.330	.353	67	.252	2	-4	-4		-0.3
1874	Bos-n	0	2	.000	6	2	0	0	3	16²	24	0	4	0	15.1	2.16	100	.324	.359	58	.315	2	-0	-0		0.1
Total	4 n	4	4	.500	35	7	0	0	14	99¹	149	0	15	1	14.9	3.71	58	.310	.331	222	.274	5	-17	-17		-0.2

● LUCKY WRIGHT   Wright, William Simmons "William The Red" or "Deacon"   b: 2/21/1880, Tontogany, Ohio   d: 7/6/41, Tontogany, Ohio   BR/TR, 6', 178 lbs.   Deb: 4/18/09

| 1909 | Cle-A | 0 | 4 | .000 | 5 | 4 | 3 | 0 | 0 | 28 | 21 | 0 | 7 | 5 | 9.6 | 3.21 | 80 | .223 | .277 | 1 | .000 | -1 | -2 | -2 | -0 | -0.4 |

● FRANK WURM   Wurm, Frank James   b: 4/27/24, Cambridge, N.Y.   d: 9/19/93, Glens Falls, N.Y.   BB/TL, 6'1", 175 lbs.   Deb: 9/4/44

| 1944 | Bro-N | 0 | 0 | — | 1 | 1 | 0 | 0 | 0 | 0¹ | 1 | 0 | 5 | 1 | 162.0 | 108.00 | 3 | .500 | .857 | 0 | — | 0 | -4 | -4 | 0 | 0.0 |

● JOHN WYATT   Wyatt, John Thomas   b: 4/19/35, Chicago, Ill.   d: 4/6/98, Omaha, Neb.   BR/TR, 5'11.5", 200 lbs.   Deb: 9/8/61

1961	KC-A	0	0	—	5	0	0	0	0	7¹	8	0	4	6	16.0	2.45	170	.296	.406	0	—	0	1	1	0	0.1
1962	KC-A	10	7	.588	59	9	0	0	11	125	121	12	80	106	14.8	4.46	95	.253	.366	3	.103	-2	-7	-3	-1	-0.7
1963	KC-A	6	4	.600	63	0	0	0	21	92	83	12	43	81	12.3	3.13	125	.239	.323	0	.000	-1	5	8	-1	1.1
1964	KC-A★	9	8	.529	81	0	0	0	20	128	111	23	52	74	11.5	3.59	106	.236	.314	0	.000	-1	1	3	-1	0.3
1965	KC-A	2	6	.250	65	0	0	0	18	88²	78	8	53	70	13.7	3.25	107	.241	.354	0	.000	-0	2	2	0	0.3
1966	KC-A	0	3	.000	19	0	0	0	2	23²	19	3	16	25	14.1	5.32	64	.213	.346	0	—	0	-5	-5	-1	-0.6
	Bos-A	3	4	.429	42	0	0	0	8	71²	59	3	27	63	11.3	3.14	121	.229	.311	0	.000	-1	2	5	-1	0.4
	Yr	3	7	.300	61	0	0	0	10	95¹	78	6	43	88	11.8	3.68	101	.223	.316	0	.000	-1	-3	-0	-1	-0.2
1967	*Bos-A	10	7	.588	60	0	0	0	20	93¹	71	6	39	68	10.8	2.60	134	.217	.304	1	.083	-0	7	9	1	2.2
1968	Bos-A	1	2	.333	8	0	0	0	0	10²	9	2	6	11	13.5	4.22	75	.231	.348	0	—	0	-1	-1	-0	-0.3
	NY-A	0	2	.000	7	0	0	0	0	8¹	7	1	9	6	17.3	2.16	134	.219	.390	0	.000	-0	1	1	-0	0.2
	Det-A	1	0	1.000	22	0	0	0	2	30¹	26	2	11	25	11.3	2.37	127	.236	.311	0	.000	-0	2	2	0	0.1
	Yr	2	4	.333	37	0	0	0	2	49¹	42	5	26	42	12.6	2.74	110	.230	.329	0	.000	-0	2	2	-0	-0.0
1969	Oak-A	0	1	.000	4	0	0	0	0	8¹	8	0	6	5	17.3	5.40	64	.250	.400	0	.000	-0	-2	-2	-0	-0.2
Total	9	42	44	.488	435	9	0	0	103	687¹	600	72	346	540	12.7	3.47	108	.237	.334	4	.048	-6	6	21	-2	2.9

● WHIT WYATT   Wyatt, John Whitlow   b: 9/27/07, Kensington, Ga.   BR/TR, 6'1", 185 lbs.   Deb: 9/16/29   C

1929	Det-A	0	1	.000	4	4	1	0	0	25¹	30	1	18	14	17.4	6.75	64	.309	.422	1	.100	-1	-7	-7	1	-0.3
1930	Det-A	4	5	.444	21	7	2	0	0	85²	76	6	35	68	12.0	3.57	134	.239	.320	12	.353	3	10	12	0	1.4
1931	Det-A	0	2	.000	4	1	0	0	0	20¹	30	2	12	8	19.0	8.85	52	.361	.448	2	.286	0	-10	-10	-1	-0.8
1932	Det-A	9	13	.409	43	22	10	0	1	205²	228	12	102	82	14.6	5.03	93	.286	.369	15	.192	-0	-13	-8	-1	-0.8
1933	Det-A	0	1	.000	10	0	0	0	0	17	20	1	9	9	16.4	4.24	102	.299	.397	0	.000	-0	0	0	-0	0.0
	Chi-A	3	4	.429	26	7	2	0	1	87²	91	7	45	31	14.2	4.62	92	.266	.355	6	.214	0	-3	-4	0	-0.2
	Yr	3	5	.375	36	7	2	0	1	104²	111	8	54	40	14.4	4.56	93	.270	.358	6	.200	0	-3	-4	-0	-0.2
1934	Chi-A	4	11	.267	23	6	2	0	2	67²	83	10	37	36	16.1	7.18	66	.303	.388	6	.231	0	-20	-18	0	-3.2
1935	Chi-A	4	3	.571	30	5	1	0	5	52	65	6	25	22	15.9	6.75	69	.308	.387	3	.231	1	-13	-12	1	-1.4
1936	Chi-A	0	0	—	3	0	0	1	0	3	3	0	0	2	9.0	0.00	—	.273	.273	0	—	0	2	2	-0	0.1
1937	Cle-A	2	3	.400	29	4	2	0	0	73	67	3	40	52	13.2	4.44	104	.244	.340	3	.389	3	1	1	0	0.3
1939	Bro-N☆	8	3	.727	16	14	6	2	0	109	88	3	39	52	10.7	2.31	174	.224	.297	6	.167	-0	19	21	1	2.1
1940	Bro-N★	15	14	.517	37	34	16	5	0	239¹	233	19	62	124	11.3	3.46	116	.254	.304	14	.175	-0	10	14	-2	1.3
1941	*Bro-N★	22	10	.688	38	35	23	7	1	288¹	223	10	82	176	9.6	2.34	157	.212	.270	26	.239	7	41	42	-1	5.3
1942	Bro-N☆	19	7	.731	31	30	16	0	0	217¹	185	9	63	104	10.0	2.73	119	.225	.286	14	.182	1	14	13	-1	1.4
1943	Bro-N	14	5	.737	26	26	13	3	0	180²	139	5	43	80	9.1	2.49	135	.207	.255	17	.283	4	18	17	-2	2.1
1944	Bro-N	2	6	.250	9	9	1	0	0	37²	51	1	6	14	15.5	7.17	50	.311	.379	2	.154	-0	-15	-15	-0	-2.6
1945	Phi-N	0	7	.000	10	10	2	0	0	51¹	72	3	14	10	15.1	5.26	73	.330	.371	2	.125	0	-8	-8	1	-0.9
Total	16	106	95	.527	360	210	97	17	13	1761	1684	98	642	872	12.1	3.79	105	.251	.319	133	.219	18	27	39	-6	3.8

● WELDON WYCKOFF   Wyckoff, John Weldon   b: 2/19/1892, Williamsport, Pa.   d: 5/8/61, Sheboygan Falls, Wis.   BR/TR, 6'1", 175 lbs.   Deb: 4/19/13

1913	Phi-A	2	4	.333	17	14	4	0	0	61²	56	1	46	31	15.3	4.38	63	.233	.363	4	.190	-0	-10	-11	0	-1.0
1914	*Phi-A	11	7	.611	32	20	11	0	2	185	153	2	103	86	12.6	3.02	87	.228	.334	11	.140	-0	-6	-8	-5	-1.3
1915	Phi-A	10	22	.313	43	34	20	1	0	276	238	1	165	157	13.3	3.52	83	.246	.359	12	.125	-4	-18	-18	-2	-2.2
1916	Phi-A	0	1	.000	7	2	1	0	0	21¹	20	1	20	4	17.3	5.48	52	.247	.402	3	.375	1	-6	-6	0	-0.2
	Bos-A	0	0	—	8	0	0	0	0	22²	19	0	18	18	14.7	4.76	58	.232	.370	1	.000	-0	-5	-5	-1	-0.2
	Yr	0	1	.000	15	2	1	0	0	44	39	1	38	22	15.8	5.11	55	.238	.381	4	.286	1	-11	-11	-1	-0.4
1917	Bos-A	0	0	—	1	0	0	0	0	5	4	0	4	1	16.2	1.80	143	.222	.391	0	.000	0	0	0	0	0.0
1918	Bos-A	0	0	—	1	0	0	0	0	2	4	0	1	2	22.5	0.00	—	.400	.455	0	—	0	1	1	-0	0.0
Total	6	23	34	.404	109	63	36	1	3	573²	494	5	357	299	13.6	3.55	79	.239	.355	31	.149	-4	-44	-48	-3	-4.9

● FRANK WYMAN   Wyman, Frank H.   b: 5/10/1862, Haverhill, Mass.   d: 2/4/16, Everett, Mass.   Deb: 6/10/1884   ♦

| 1884 | KC-U | 0 | 1 | .000 | 3 | 1 | 1 | 0 | 0 | 21 | 37 | 0 | 3 | 9 | 17.1 | 6.86 | 33 | .363 | .381 | 27 | .218 | -1 | -10 | -11 | -1 | -0.5 |

● EARLY WYNN   Wynn, Early "Gus"   b: 1/6/20, Hartford, Ala.   BB/TR, 6', 200 lbs.   Deb: 9/13/39   CH♦

1939	Was-A	0	2	.000	3	3	1	0	0	20¹	26	0	10	1	15.9	5.75	76	.313	.387	1	.167	0	-3	-3	-1	-0.3
1941	Was-A	3	1	.750	5	5	4	0	0	40	35	1	10	15	10.1	1.57	257	.233	.275	2	.133	-0	11	11	0	1.1
1942	Was-A	10	16	.385	30	28	10	1	0	190	246	3	73	58	15.3	5.12	71	.314	.374	15	.217	2	-31	-31	0	-3.6
1943	Was-A	18	12	.600	37	33	12	3	0	256²	232	15	83	89	11.1	2.91	110	.240	.301	29	.296	7	11	8	-2	1.6
1944	Was-A	8	17	.320	33	25	19	2	2	207²	221	3	67	65	12.6	3.38	96	.277	.334	19	.207	2	1	-3	-2	-0.4

YEAR	TM/L	W	L	PCT	G	GS	CG	SH	SV	IP	H	HR	BB	SO	RAT	ERA	ERA+	OAV	OOB	BH	AVG	PB	PR	/A	PD	TPI
1946	Was-A	8	5	.615	17	12	9	0	0	107	112	8	33	36	12.4	3.11	108	.267	.325	15	.319	7	5	3	-0	1.1
1947	Was-A☆	17	15	.531	33	31	22	2	0	247	251	13	90	73	12.6	3.64	102	.262	.329	33	.275	7	2	2	-1	0.9
1948	Was-A	8	19	.296	33	31	15	1	0	198	236	18	94	49	15.0	5.82	75	.295	.370	23	.217	3	-34	-32	-1	-3.4
1949	Cle-A	11	7	.611	26	23	6	0	0	164^2	186	8	57	62	13.3	4.15	96	.282	.340	10	.143	-2	1	-3	1	-0.3
1950	Cle-A	18	8	.692	32	28	14	2	0	213^2	166	20	101	143	**11.4**	**3.20**	135	**.212**	**.305**	18	.234	7	33	27	0	3.6
1951	Cle-A	20	13	.606	37	34	21	3	1	**274^1**	227	18	107	133	11.1	3.02	126	.225	.301	20	.185	2	**34**	23	-1	2.6
1952	Cle-A	23	12	.657	42	33	19	4	3	285^2	239	23	132	153	11.7	2.90	115	.231	.318	22	.222	5	25	14	-1	2.1
1953	Cle-A	17	12	.586	36	34	16	1	0	251^2	234	19	107	138	12.3	3.93	95	.245	.324	25	.275	9	2	-5	-1	0.2
1954	*Cle-A	**23**	11	.676	40	36	20	3	2	**270^2**	225	21	83	155	10.2	2.73	135	.225	.284	17	.183	1	30	29	-3	3.3
1955	Cle-A★	17	11	.607	32	31	16	6	0	230	207	19	80	122	11.3	2.82	142	.240	.307	15	.179	1	29	30	-3	3.3
1956	Cle-A★	20	9	.690	38	35	18	4	2	277^2	233	19	91	158	10.7	2.72	154	.228	.294	23	.228	3	44	46	1	5.1
1957	Cle-A★	14	17	.452	40	37	13	1	1	263	270	32	104	**184**	13.0	4.31	86	.265	.336	10	.116	-2	-15	-17	-1	-2.1
1958	Chi-A★	14	16	.467	40	34	11	4	2	239^2	214	27	104	**179**	12.2	4.13	88	.242	.325	15	.200	3	-10	-13	-2	-1.5
1959	*Chi-A★	**22**	10	.688	37	37	14	5	0	**255^2**	202	20	119	179	11.6	3.17	119	.216	.310	22	.244	9	20	17	-1	2.8
1960	Chi-A★	13	12	.520	36	35	13	**4**	1	237^1	220	20	112	158	12.7	3.49	108	.247	.334	15	.200	7	10	8	-2	1.2
1961	Chi-A	8	2	.800	17	16	5	0	0	110^1	88	11	47	64	11.1	3.51	112	.220	.304	6	.162	-0	6	5	-2	0.2
1962	Chi-A	7	15	.318	27	26	11	3	0	167^2	171	15	56	91	12.3	4.46	88	.264	.326	7	.130	0	-9	-10	-2	-1.4
1963	Cle-A	1	2	.333	20	5	1	0	1	55^1	50	2	15	29	10.6	2.28	159	.250	.302	3	.273	1	8	8	-0	0.5
Total	23	300	244	.551	691	612	290	49	15	4564	4291	338	1775	2334	12.1	3.54	106	.248	.321	365	.214	72	170	112	-25	16.6

● **BILLY WYNNE** Wynne, Billy Vernon b: 7/31/43, Willlamston, N.C. BL/TR, 6′5″, 206 lbs. Deb: 8/6/67

YEAR	TM/L	W	L	PCT	G	GS	CG	SH	SV	IP	H	HR	BB	SO	RAT	ERA	ERA+	OAV	OOB	BH	AVG	PB	PR	/A	PD	TPI
1967	NY-N	0	0	—	6	1	0	0	0	8^2	12	0	2	4	14.5	3.12	109	.324	.359	0	.000	-0	0	0	-0	0.0
1968	Chi-A	0	0	—	1	0	0	0	0	2	2	0	2	1	18.0	4.50	67	.250	.400	0	—	0	-0	-0	-0	0.0
1969	Chi-A	7	7	.500	20	20	6	1	0	128^2	143	14	50	67	13.7	4.06	95	.283	.351	5	.122	-1	-6	-3	0	-0.3
1970	Chi-A	1	4	.200	12	9	0	0	0	44	54	8	22	19	15.8	5.32	73	.298	.377	1	.077	-1	-8	-7	1	-0.7
1971	Cal-A	0	0	—	3	0	0	0	0	3^2	6	0	2	6	19.6	4.91	66	.375	.444	0	—	0	-1	-1	0	0.0
Total	5	8	11	.421	42	30	6	1	0	187	217	22	78	97	14.4	4.33	88	.290	.361	6	.109	-2	-15	-11	1	-1.0

● **BILL WYNNE** Wynne, William Andrew b: 3/27/1869, Neuse, N.C. d: 8/7/51, Raleigh, N.C. BR/TR, 5′11.5″, 161 lbs. Deb: 8/31/1894

YEAR	TM/L	W	L	PCT	G	GS	CG	SH	SV	IP	H	HR	BB	SO	RAT	ERA	ERA+	OAV	OOB	BH	AVG	PB	PR	/A	PD	TPI
1894	Was-N	0	1	.000	1	1	1	0	0	8	10	0	8	2	22.5	6.75	78	.303	.465	0	.000	-0	-1	-1	-0	-0.1

● **HANK WYSE** Wyse, Henry Washington "Hooks" b: 3/1/18, Lunsford, Ark. BR/TR, 5′11.5″, 185 lbs. Deb: 9/7/42

YEAR	TM/L	W	L	PCT	G	GS	CG	SH	SV	IP	H	HR	BB	SO	RAT	ERA	ERA+	OAV	OOB	BH	AVG	PB	PR	/A	PD	TPI
1942	Chi-N	2	1	.667	4	4	1	1	0	28	33	1	6	8	12.5	1.93	166	.287	.322	1	.125	-0	4	4	-0	0.4
1943	Chi-N	9	7	.563	38	15	8	2	5	156	159	4	34	45	11.3	2.94	113	.264	.306	4	.080	-4	8	7	3	0.7
1944	Chi-N	16	15	.516	41	34	14	3	1	257^1	277	9	57	86	11.8	3.15	112	.278	.318	16	.178	-1	13	11	0	1.1
1945	*Chi-N†	22	10	.688	38	34	23	2	0	278^1	272	17	55	77	10.7	2.68	136	.256	.296	17	.168	-2	**35**	30	2	3.2
1946	Chi-N	14	12	.538	40	27	12	2	1	201^1	206	7	52	52	11.7	2.68	124	.265	.313	18	.243	1	16	14	2	2.2
1947	Chi-N	6	9	.400	37	19	5	1	1	142	158	12	64	53	14.3	4.31	92	.286	.363	5	.111	-1	-4	-6	1	-0.5
1950	Phi-A	9	14	.391	41	23	4	0	0	170^2	192	16	87	33	15.1	5.85	78	.287	.376	9	.153	-3	-24	-25	0	-3.0
1951	Phi-A	1	2	.333	9	1	0	0	0	14^2	24	0	8	5	19.6	7.98	54	.381	.451	1	.250	-0	-6	-6	-0	-1.0
	Was-A	0	0	—	3	2	0	0	0	9^1	17	0	10	3	27.0	9.64	42	.378	.500	0	.000	-1	-6	-6	0	-0.1
	Yr	1	2	.333	12	3	0	0	0	24	41	0	18	8	22.5	8.63	49	.380	.472	1	.125	-1	-12	-12	0	-1.1
Total	8	79	70	.530	251	159	67	11	8	1257^2	1338	66	373	362	12.4	3.52	105	.274	.329	71	.163	-11	36	24	9	3.0

● **BIFF WYSONG** Wysong, Harlan b: 4/13/05, Clarksville, Ohio d: 8/8/51, Xenia, Ohio BL/TL, 6′3″, 195 lbs. Deb: 8/10/30

YEAR	TM/L	W	L	PCT	G	GS	CG	SH	SV	IP	H	HR	BB	SO	RAT	ERA	ERA+	OAV	OOB	BH	AVG	PB	PR	/A	PD	TPI
1930	Cin-N	0	1	.000	1	1	0	0	0	2^1	6	0	3	1	34.7	19.29	25	.545	.643	0	—	0	-4	-4	-0	-0.9
1931	Cin-N	0	2	.000	12	2	0	0	0	21^2	25	2	23	5	19.9	7.89	47	.298	.449	1	.250	0	-10	-10	-1	-0.8
1932	Cin-N	1	0	1.000	7	0	0	0	0	12^1	13	0	8	5	15.3	3.65	106	.277	.382	0	.000	-0	0	0	0	0.0
Total	3	1	3	.250	20	3	0	0	0	36^1	44	2	34	11	19.3	7.18	54	.310	.443	1	.167	-0	-13	-13	-0	-1.7

● **ESTEBAN YAN** Yan, Esteban Luis b: 6/22/74, Campina Del Seibo, D.R. BR/TR, 6′4″, 230 lbs. Deb: 5/20/96

YEAR	TM/L	W	L	PCT	G	GS	CG	SH	SV	IP	H	HR	BB	SO	RAT	ERA	ERA+	OAV	OOB	BH	AVG	PB	PR	/A	PD	TPI
1996	Bal-A	0	0	—	4	0	0	0	0	9^1	13	3	3	7	15.4	5.79	85	.333	.381	0	—	0	-1	-1	-0	0.0
1997	Bal-A	0	1	.000	3	2	0	0	0	9^2	20	3	7	4	27.0	15.83	28	.417	.509	0	—	0	-12	-12	-0	-0.9
1998	TB-A	5	4	.556	64	0	0	0	1	88^2	78	11	41	77	12.6	3.86	127	.236	.329	0	—	0	8	10	0	0.9
Total	3	5	5	.500	71	2	0	0	1	107^2	111	17	51	88	14.1	5.10	95	.266	.355	0	—	0	-5	-3	-0	0.0

● **RUSTY YARNALL** Yarnall, Waldo William b: 10/22/02, Chicago, Ill. d: 10/9/85, Lowell, Mass. BR/TR, 6′, 175 lbs. Deb: 6/30/26

YEAR	TM/L	W	L	PCT	G	GS	CG	SH	SV	IP	H	HR	BB	SO	RAT	ERA	ERA+	OAV	OOB	BH	AVG	PB	PR	/A	PD	TPI
1926	Phi-N	0	1	.000	1	0	0	0	0	1	3	0	1	0	36.0	18.00	23	.500	.571	0	.000	-0	-2	-2	0	-0.9

● **RUBE YARRISON** Yarrison, Byron Wardsworth b: 3/9/1896, Montgomery, Pa. d: 4/22/77, Williamsport, Pa. BR/TR, 5′11″, 165 lbs. Deb: 4/13/22

YEAR	TM/L	W	L	PCT	G	GS	CG	SH	SV	IP	H	HR	BB	SO	RAT	ERA	ERA+	OAV	OOB	BH	AVG	PB	PR	/A	PD	TPI
1922	Phi-A	1	2	.333	18	1	0	0	0	33^2	50	4	12	10	17.1	8.29	51	.362	.421	1	.167	-0	-16	-15	-0	-1.2
1924	Bro-N	0	2	.000	3	2	0	0	0	11	12	0	3	2	13.1	6.55	57	.267	.327	0	.000	-0	-3	-3	0	-0.5
Total	2	1	4	.200	21	3	0	0	0	44^2	62	4	15	12	16.1	7.86	53	.339	.398	1	.125	-0	-19	-19	0	-1.7

● **EMIL YDE** Yde, Emil Ogden b: 1/28/1900, Great Lakes, Ill. d: 12/4/68, Leesburg, Fla. BB/TL, 5′11″, 165 lbs. Deb: 4/21/24

YEAR	TM/L	W	L	PCT	G	GS	CG	SH	SV	IP	H	HR	BB	SO	RAT	ERA	ERA+	OAV	OOB	BH	AVG	PB	PR	/A	PD	TPI
1924	Pit-N	16	3	**.842**	33	22	14	**4**	0	194	171	3	62	53	11.1	2.83	136	.244	.311	21	.239	2	22	22	1	2.3
1925	*Pit-N	17	9	.654	33	28	13	0	0	207	254	11	75	41	14.4	4.13	108	.309	.369	17	.191	-2	3	8	-0	0.6
1926	Pit-N	8	7	.533	37	22	12	1	0	187^1	181	3	81	34	12.7	3.65	108	.260	.339	17	.230	3	4	6	0	0.7
1927	*Pit-N	1	3	.250	9	2	0	0	0	29^2	45	1	15	9	18.8	9.71	42	.375	.453	3	.167	-0	-19	-18	1	-1.9
1929	Det-A	7	3	.700	29	6	4	1	0	86^2	100	8	63	23	16.9	5.30	81	.296	.406	16	.333	2	-10	-10	-1	-0.7
Total	5	49	25	.662	141	80	43	6	0	704^2	751	26	296	160	13.5	4.02	102	.281	.355	74	.233	5	-0	7	1	1.0

● **JOE YEAGER** Yeager, Joseph F. "Little Joe" b: 8/28/1875, Philadelphia, Pa. d: 7/2/37, Detroit, Mich. BR/TR, 5′10″, 160 lbs. Deb: 4/22/1898 ♦

YEAR	TM/L	W	L	PCT	G	GS	CG	SH	SV	IP	H	HR	BB	SO	RAT	ERA	ERA+	OAV	OOB	BH	AVG	PB	PR	/A	PD	TPI
1898	Bro-N	12	22	.353	36	33	32	0	0	291^1	333	4	80	70	12.9	3.65	98	.285	.334	23	.172	-3	-1	-2	5	0.0
1899	Bro-N	2	2	.500	10	4	2	1	1	47^2	56	1	16	6	14.0	4.72	83	.292	.352	9	.191	1	-5	-4	1	-0.2
1900	Bro-N	1	1	.500	2	2	2	0	0	17	21	1	5	2	13.8	6.88	56	.304	.351	3	.333	0	-6	-6	-0	-0.5
1901	Det-A	12	11	.522	26	25	22	2	1	199^2	209	4	46	38	11.9	2.61	147	.266	.313	37	.296	5	23	27	2	3.5
1902	Det-A	6	12	.333	19	15	14	0	0	140	171	5	41	28	13.9	4.82	76	.301	.353	39	.242	3	-19	-18	3	-1.4
1903	Det-A	0	1	.000	1	1	1	0	0	9	15	0	0	1	15.0	4.00	73	.366	.366	103	.256	0	-1	-1	0	-0.1
Total	6	33	49	.402	94	80	73	3	2	704^2	805	15	188	145	13.0	3.74	99	.285	.334	467	.252	6	-9	-4	11	1.3

● **AL YEARGIN** Yeargin, James Almond b: 10/16/01, Mauldin, S.C. d: 5/8/37, Greenville, S.C. BR/TR, 5′11″, 170 lbs. Deb: 10/1/22

YEAR	TM/L	W	L	PCT	G	GS	CG	SH	SV	IP	H	HR	BB	SO	RAT	ERA	ERA+	OAV	OOB	BH	AVG	PB	PR	/A	PD	TPI
1922	Bos-N	0	1	.000	1	1	1	0	0	7	5	1	2	1	9.0	1.29	311	.192	.250	0	.000	-0	2	2	0	0.2
1924	Bos-N	1	11	.083	32	12	6	0	0	141^1	162	7	42	34	13.2	5.09	75	.293	.346	6	.143	-2	-19	-20	4	-1.3
Total	2	1	12	.077	33	13	7	0	0	148^1	167	8	44	35	13.0	4.91	78	.288	.342	6	.133	-2	-17	-18	4	-1.1

● **LARRY YELLEN** Yellen, Lawrence Alan b: 1/4/43, Brooklyn, N.Y. BR/TR, 5′11″, 190 lbs. Deb: 9/26/63

YEAR	TM/L	W	L	PCT	G	GS	CG	SH	SV	IP	H	HR	BB	SO	RAT	ERA	ERA+	OAV	OOB	BH	AVG	PB	PR	/A	PD	TPI
1963	Hou-N	0	0	—	1	1	0	0	0	5	7	0	1	3	14.4	3.60	88	.280	.308	0	.000	-0	-0	-0	0	0.0
1964	Hou-N	0	0	—	13	1	0	0	0	21	27	4	10	9	15.9	6.86	50	.297	.366	0	.000	-0	-8	-8	-0	0.0
Total	2	0	0	—	14	2	0	0	0	26	34	4	11	12	15.6	6.23	54	.293	.354	0	.000	-0	-8	-8	0	0.0

● **CHIEF YELLOWHORSE** Yellowhorse, Moses J. b: 1/28/1898, Pawnee, Okla. d: 4/10/64, Pawnee, Okla. BR/TR, 5′10″, 180 lbs. Deb: 4/15/21

YEAR	TM/L	W	L	PCT	G	GS	CG	SH	SV	IP	H	HR	BB	SO	RAT	ERA	ERA+	OAV	OOB	BH	AVG	PB	PR	/A	PD	TPI
1921	Pit-N	5	3	.625	10	4	1	0	1	48^1	45	1	13	19	10.8	2.98	129	.254	.305	0	.000	-2	4	5	-2	0.3
1922	Pit-N	3	1	.750	28	4	2	0	0	77^2	92	0	20	24	13.2	4.52	90	.305	.352	6	.316	1	-4	-4	-1	-0.1
Total	2	8	4	.667	38	8	3	0	1	126	137	1	33	43	12.3	3.93	101	.286	.335	6	.167	-2	1	1	-3	0.2

● **CARROLL YERKES** Yerkes, Charles Carroll "Lefty" b: 6/13/03, McSherrystown, Pa. d: 12/20/50, Oakland, Cal. BR/TL, 5′11″, 180 lbs. Deb: 5/31/27

YEAR	TM/L	W	L	PCT	G	GS	CG	SH	SV	IP	H	HR	BB	SO	RAT	ERA	ERA+	OAV	OOB	BH	AVG	PB	PR	/A	PD	TPI
1927	Phi-A	0	0	—	1	0	0	0	0	1	0	0	1	0	9.0	0.00	—	.000	.333	0	—	0	0	0	0	0.0
1928	Phi-A	0	1	.000	2	1	1	0	0	8^2	7	0	2	1	9.3	2.08	193	.233	.281	0	.000	-0	2	2	1	0.2
1929	Phi-A	1	0	1.000	19	2	0	0	1	37^1	47	0	13	11	14.7	4.58	92	.329	.389	0	.000	-2	-1	-1	2	0.0
1932	Chi-N	0	0	—	2	0	0	0	0	9	5	2	3	4	8.0	3.00	126	.167	.242	1	.333	0	1	1	-0	0.0

YEAR	TM/L	W	L	PCT	G	GS	CG	SH	SV	IP	H	HR	BB	SO	RAT	ERA	ERA+	OAV	OOB	BH	AVG	PB	PR	/A	PD	TPI
1933	Chi-N	0	0	—	1	0	0	0	0	2	2	0	1	0	13.5	4.50	73	.286	.375	0	—	0	-0	-0	0	0.0
Total	5	1	1	.500	25	3	1	0	1	58	61	2	20	16	12.7	3.88	106	.288	.352	1	.063	-2	2	1	3	0.2

● STAN YERKES
Yerkes, Stanley Lewis "Yank" b: 11/28/1874, Cheltenham, Pa. d: 7/28/40, Boston, Mass. BR/TR, 5'10", 165 lbs. Deb: 5/3/01

YEAR	TM/L	W	L	PCT	G	GS	CG	SH	SV	IP	H	HR	BB	SO	RAT	ERA	ERA+	OAV	OOB	BH	AVG	PB	PR	/A	PD	TPI
1901	Bal-A	0	1	.000	1	1	1	0	0	8	12	0	2	4	15.8	6.75	57	.343	.378	1	.333	0	-3	-3	0	-0.2
	StL-N	3	1	.750	4	4	4	0	0	34	35	2	6	15	11.1	3.18	100	.265	.302	1	.083	-1	1	0	-0	-0.1
1902	StL-N	12	21	.364	39	37	27	1	0	272^{2}	341	1	79	81	13.9	3.66	75	.306	.353	12	.132	-3	-27	-28	-2	-3.6
1903	StL-N	0	1	.000	1	1	0	0	0	5	8	0	0	3	14.4	1.80	181	.333	.333	0	.000	-0	1	1	-0	0.1
Total	3	15	24	.385	45	43	32	1	0	319^{2}	396	3	87	103	13.7	3.66	77	.303	.348	14	.130	-4	-28	-30	-3	-3.8

● RICH YETT
Yett, Richard Martin b: 10/6/62, Pomona, Cal. BR/TR, 6'2", 187 lbs. Deb: 4/13/85

YEAR	TM/L	W	L	PCT	G	GS	CG	SH	SV	IP	H	HR	BB	SO	RAT	ERA	ERA+	OAV	OOB	BH	AVG	PB	PR	/A	PD	TPI
1985	Min-A	0	0	—	1	1	0	0	0	0^{1}	1	0	2	0	81.0	27.00	16	.333	.600	0	—	0	-1	-1	0	-0.2
1986	Cle-A	5	3	.625	39	3	1	1	1	78^{2}	84	10	37	50	14.0	5.15	80	.275	.355	0	—	0	-8	-9	-1	-0.9
1987	Cle-A	3	9	.250	37	11	2	0	1	97^{2}	96	21	49	59	13.6	5.25	86	.257	.347	0	—	0	-9	-8	-1	-0.9
1988	Cle-A	9	6	.600	23	22	0	0	0	134^{1}	146	11	55	71	13.5	4.62	89	.275	.344	0	—	0	-10	-8	-2	-1.0
1989	Cle-A	5	6	.455	32	12	1	0	0	99	111	10	47	47	14.5	5.00	79	.283	.363	0	—	0	-12	-11	-1	-1.4
1990	Min-A	0	0	—	4	0	0	0	0	4^{1}	6	1	1	2	14.5	2.08	200	.353	.389	0	—	0	1	1	0	-0.3
Total	6	22	24	.478	136	49	4	1	2	414^{1}	444	53	191	229	13.9	4.95	84	.274	.353	0	—	0	-39	-36	-5	-4.7

● EARL YINGLING
Yingling, Earl Hershey "Chink" b: 10/29/1888, Chillicothe, Ohio d: 10/2/62, Columbus, Ohio BL/TL, 5'11.5", 180 lbs. Deb: 4/12/11

YEAR	TM/L	W	L	PCT	G	GS	CG	SH	SV	IP	H	HR	BB	SO	RAT	ERA	ERA+	OAV	OOB	BH	AVG	PB	PR	/A	PD	TPI
1911	Cle-A	1	0	1.000	4	3	1	0	0	22^{1}	30	1	9	6	16.1	4.43	77	.326	.392	3	.273	0	-3	-3	0	-0.1
1912	Bro-N	6	11	.353	25	16	12	0	0	163	186	10	56	51	13.4	3.59	93	.293	.351	16	.250	3	-3	-4	-1	-0.2
1913	Bro-N	8	8	.500	26	13	8	2	0	146^{2}	158	2	10	40	10.4	2.58	128	.280	.295	23	.383	8	10	12	-1	2.0
1914	Cin-N	9	13	.409	34	27	8	3	0	198	207	6	54	80	12.1	3.45	85	.274	.328	23	.192	1	-15	-12	-2	-1.2
1918	Was-A	1	2	.333	5	2	2	0	0	38	30	0	12	15	9.9	2.13	128	.238	.304	7	.467	3	3	3	1	0.7
Total	5	25	34	.424	94	61	31	5	0	568	611	19	141	192	12.1	3.22	98	.281	.328	72	.267	16	-8	-4	-3	1.2

● JOE YINGLING
Yingling, Joseph Granville b: 7/23/1866, Westminster, Md. d: 10/24/46, Manchester, Md. BR/TL, 5'7.5", 145 lbs. Deb: 5/28/1886 ♦

YEAR	TM/L	W	L	PCT	G	GS	CG	SH	SV	IP	H	HR	BB	SO	RAT	ERA	ERA+	OAV	OOB	BH	AVG	PB	PR	/A	PD	TPI
1886	Was-N	0	0	—	1	0	0	0	0	3	7	0	1	1	24.0	12.00	27	.412	.444	0	.000	-0	-3	-3	0	0.0

● LEN YOCHIM
Yochim, Leonard Joseph b: 10/16/28, New Orleans, La. BL/TL, 6'2", 200 lbs. Deb: 9/18/51 F

YEAR	TM/L	W	L	PCT	G	GS	CG	SH	SV	IP	H	HR	BB	SO	RAT	ERA	ERA+	OAV	OOB	BH	AVG	PB	PR	/A	PD	TPI
1951	Pit-N	1	1	.500	2	2	0	0	0	8^{2}	10	0	11	5	22.8	8.31	51	.278	.458	0	.000	-0	-4	-4	0	-0.7
1954	Pit-N	0	1	.000	10	1	0	0	0	19^{2}	30	2	8	7	17.4	7.32	57	.361	.418	1	.500	0	-7	-7	1	-0.2
Total	2	1	2	.333	12	3	0	0	0	28^{1}	40	2	19	12	19.1	7.62	55	.336	.432	1	.200	-0	-11	-11	1	-0.9

● RAY YOCHIM
Yochim, Raymond Austin Aloysius b: 7/19/22, New Orleans, La. BR/TR, 6'1", 170 lbs. Deb: 5/2/48 F

YEAR	TM/L	W	L	PCT	G	GS	CG	SH	SV	IP	H	HR	BB	SO	RAT	ERA	ERA+	OAV	OOB	BH	AVG	PB	PR	/A	PD	TPI
1948	StL-N	0	0	—	1	0	0	0	0	1	0	0	3	1	27.0	0.00	—	.000	.500	0	—	0	0	0	0	0.0
1949	StL-N	0	0	—	3	0	0	0	0	2^{1}	3	1	4	3	27.0	15.43	27	.273	.467	0	—	0	-3	-3	-0	0.0
Total	2	0	0	—	4	0	0	0	0	3^{1}	3	1	7	4	27.0	10.80	38	.214	.476	0	—	0	-3	-2	-0	0.0

● LEFTY YORK
York, James Edward b: 11/1/1892, West Fork, Ark. d: 4/9/61, York, Pa. BL/TL, 5'10", 185 lbs. Deb: 9/12/19

YEAR	TM/L	W	L	PCT	G	GS	CG	SH	SV	IP	H	HR	BB	SO	RAT	ERA	ERA+	OAV	OOB	BH	AVG	PB	PR	/A	PD	TPI
1919	Phi-A	0	2	.000	2	2	0	0	0	4^{1}	13	0	5	2	37.4	24.92	14	.500	.581	0	.000	-0	-10	-10	0	-2.4
1921	Chi-N	5	9	.357	40	11	4	1	1	139	170	5	63	57	15.4	4.73	81	.308	.384	5	.128	-2	-15	-14	-3	-1.8
Total	2	5	11	.313	42	13	4	1	1	143^{1}	183	5	68	59	16.1	5.34	71	.317	.393	5	.125	-2	-25	-24	-3	-4.2

● JIM YORK
York, James Harlan b: 8/27/47, Maywood, Cal. BR/TR, 6'3", 200 lbs. Deb: 9/21/70

YEAR	TM/L	W	L	PCT	G	GS	CG	SH	SV	IP	H	HR	BB	SO	RAT	ERA	ERA+	OAV	OOB	BH	AVG	PB	PR	/A	PD	TPI
1970	KC-A	1	1	.500	4	0	0	0	0	8	5	2	2	6	7.9	3.38	111	.179	.233	0	.000	-0	0	0	-0	0.0
1971	KC-A	5	5	.500	53	0	0	0	3	93^{1}	70	7	44	103	11.3	2.89	119	.203	.299	2	.118	1	6	6	-0	0.7
1972	Hou-N	0	1	.000	26	0	0	0	0	36	45	3	18	25	16.0	5.25	64	.321	.403	0	.000	-0	-7	-8	0	-0.2
1973	Hou-N	3	4	.429	41	0	0	0	6	53	65	4	20	22	14.6	4.42	82	.305	.368	0	.000	-0	-4	-5	0	-0.7
1974	Hou-N	2	2	.500	28	0	0	0	1	38^{1}	48	1	19	15	16.0	3.29	105	.298	.376	0	.000	-1	1	1	0	0.0
1975	Hou-N	4	4	.500	19	4	0	0	0	46^{2}	43	1	25	17	14.1	3.86	87	.251	.363	1	.091	-0	-1	-3	-1	-0.6
1976	NY-A	1	0	1.000	3	0	0	0	0	9^{2}	14	1	4	6	17.7	5.59	61	.333	.404	0	—	0	-2	-2	-0	-0.2
Total	7	16	17	.485	174	4	0	0	10	285	290	19	132	194	13.7	3.79	91	.264	.349	3	.075	-1	-7	-10	-1	-1.0

● MIKE YORK
York, Michael David b: 9/6/64, Oak Park, Ill. BR/TR, 6'1", 187 lbs. Deb: 8/17/90

YEAR	TM/L	W	L	PCT	G	GS	CG	SH	SV	IP	H	HR	BB	SO	RAT	ERA	ERA+	OAV	OOB	BH	AVG	PB	PR	/A	PD	TPI
1990	Pit-N	1	1	.500	4	1	0	0	0	12^{2}	13	0	5	4	13.5	2.84	127	.277	.358	1	.333	0	1	1	0	0.2
1991	Cle-A	1	4	.200	14	4	0	0	0	34^{2}	45	2	19	19	17.1	6.75	62	.333	.423	0	—	0	-10	-10	-0	-1.3
Total	2	2	5	.286	18	5	0	0	0	47^{1}	58	2	24	23	16.2	5.70	70	.319	.407	1	.333	0	-9	-9	-0	-1.1

● MASATO YOSHII
Yoshii, Masato b: 4/20/65, Osaka, Japan BR/TR, 6'2", 210 lbs. Deb: 4/5/98

YEAR	TM/L	W	L	PCT	G	GS	CG	SH	SV	IP	H	HR	BB	SO	RAT	ERA	ERA+	OAV	OOB	BH	AVG	PB	PR	/A	PD	TPI
1998	NY-N	6	8	.429	29	29	1	0	0	171^{2}	166	22	53	117	11.8	3.93	106	.255	.316	3	.063	-2	6	4	-1	0.0

● GUS YOST
Yost, August 6'5", Deb: 6/12/1893

YEAR	TM/L	W	L	PCT	G	GS	CG	SH	SV	IP	H	HR	BB	SO	RAT	ERA	ERA+	OAV	OOB	BH	AVG	PB	PR	/A	PD	TPI
1893	Chi-N	0	1	.000	1	1	0	0	0	2^{2}	3	0	8	1	37.1	13.50	34	.273	.579	0	.000	-0	-3	-3	0	-0.6

● FLOYD YOUMANS
Youmans, Floyd Everett b: 5/11/64, Tampa, Fla. BR/TR, 6'1", 190 lbs. Deb: 7/1/85

YEAR	TM/L	W	L	PCT	G	GS	CG	SH	SV	IP	H	HR	BB	SO	RAT	ERA	ERA+	OAV	OOB	BH	AVG	PB	PR	/A	PD	TPI
1985	Mon-N	4	3	.571	14	12	0	0	0	77	57	3	49	54	12.5	2.45	138	.206	.327	1	.053	-0	10	8	-2	0.5
1986	Mon-N	13	12	.520	33	32	6	2	0	219	145	14	118	202	11.0	3.53	104	.188	.299	12	.160	2	4	4	-3	0.2
1987	Mon-N	9	8	.529	23	23	3	3	0	116^{1}	112	13	47	94	12.4	4.64	91	.251	.324	6	.150	1	-7	-6	-0	-0.7
1988	Mon-N	3	6	.333	14	13	1	1	0	84	64	8	41	54	11.5	3.21	112	.213	.311	4	.154	-0	2	4	-1	0.3
1989	Phi-N	1	5	.167	10	10	0	0	0	42^{2}	50	7	25	20	16.2	5.70	62	.299	.397	1	.077	-1	-10	-10	0	-1.3
Total	5	30	34	.469	94	90	10	6	0	539	428	45	280	424	12.0	3.74	100	.218	.319	24	.139	1	-1	-1	-6	-1.0

● ANTHONY YOUNG
Young, Anthony Wayne b: 1/19/66, Houston, Tex. BR/TR, 6'2", 210 lbs. Deb: 8/5/91

YEAR	TM/L	W	L	PCT	G	GS	CG	SH	SV	IP	H	HR	BB	SO	RAT	ERA	ERA+	OAV	OOB	BH	AVG	PB	PR	/A	PD	TPI
1991	NY-N	2	5	.286	10	8	0	0	0	49^{1}	48	4	12	20	11.1	3.10	117	.257	.305	2	.143	0	3	3	-1	0.3
1992	NY-N	2	14	.125	52	13	1	0	15	121	134	8	31	64	12.3	4.17	83	.285	.331	3	.111	-1	-9	-9	-0	-1.5
1993	NY-N	1	16	.059	39	10	1	0	3	100^{1}	103	8	42	62	13.1	3.77	107	.265	.339	2	.143	-0	3	3	0	0.4
1994	Chi-N	4	6	.400	20	19	0	0	0	114^{2}	103	12	46	65	11.7	3.92	106	.246	.320	6	.176	0	4	3	1	0.3
1995	Chi-N	3	4	.429	32	1	0	0	2	41^{1}	47	5	14	15	13.9	3.70	111	.288	.356	2	.667	1	2	2	-1	0.3
1996	Hou-N	3	3	.500	28	0	0	0	0	33^{1}	36	4	22	19	16.7	4.59	84	.279	.400	0	.000	-0	-1	-3	0	-0.4
Total	6	15	48	.238	181	51	2	0	20	460	471	41	167	245	12.7	3.89	99	.268	.335	15	.160	-0	2	-1	-1	-0.6

● PETE YOUNG
Young, Bryan Owen b: 3/19/68, Meadville, Miss. BR/TR, 6', 225 lbs. Deb: 6/5/92

YEAR	TM/L	W	L	PCT	G	GS	CG	SH	SV	IP	H	HR	BB	SO	RAT	ERA	ERA+	OAV	OOB	BH	AVG	PB	PR	/A	PD	TPI
1992	Mon-N	0	0	—	13	0	0	0	0	20^{1}	18	0	9	11	12.4	3.98	87	.247	.337	0	—	0	-1	-1	-0	0.0
1993	Mon-N	1	0	1.000	4	0	0	0	0	5^{1}	4	1	0	3	6.8	3.38	124	.211	.211	0	.000	-0	0	0	0	0.1
Total	2	1	0	1.000	17	0	0	0	0	25^{2}	22	1	9	14	11.2	3.86	94	.239	.314	0	.000	-0	-1	-1	-0	0.1

● CHARLIE YOUNG
Young, Charles "Cy" b: 1/12/1893, Philadelphia, Pa. d: 5/12/52, Riverside, N.J. BB/TR, 5'10.5", 155 lbs. Deb: 9/5/15

YEAR	TM/L	W	L	PCT	G	GS	CG	SH	SV	IP	H	HR	BB	SO	RAT	ERA	ERA+	OAV	OOB	BH	AVG	PB	PR	/A	PD	TPI
1915	Bal-F	2	3	.400	9	5	1	0	0	35	39	0	21	13	16.5	5.91	49	.289	.400	2	.222	0	-12	-12	2	-1.3

● CLIFF YOUNG
Young, Clifford Raphael b: 8/2/64, Willis, Tex. d: 11/4/93, Montgomery Co., Tex. BL/TL, 6'4", 200 lbs. Deb: 7/14/90

YEAR	TM/L	W	L	PCT	G	GS	CG	SH	SV	IP	H	HR	BB	SO	RAT	ERA	ERA+	OAV	OOB	BH	AVG	PB	PR	/A	PD	TPI
1990	Cal-A	1	1	.500	17	0	0	0	0	30^{2}	40	2	7	19	14.1	3.52	108	.325	.366	0	—	0	1	1	-0	0.2
1991	Cal-A	1	0	1.000	11	0	0	0	0	12^{2}	12	3	3	6	10.7	4.26	96	.261	.306	0	—	0	-0	-0	0	0.0
1993	Cle-A	3	3	.500	21	7	0	0	1	60^{1}	74	9	18	31	14.2	4.62	94	.298	.353	0	—	0	-2	-2	-1	-0.2
Total	3	5	4	.556	49	7	0	0	1	103^{2}	126	14	28	56	13.7	4.25	97	.302	.352	0	—	0	-1	-1	-1	0.0

● CURT YOUNG
Young, Curtis Allen b: 4/16/60, Saginaw, Mich. BR/TL, 6'1", 180 lbs. Deb: 6/24/83

YEAR	TM/L	W	L	PCT	G	GS	CG	SH	SV	IP	H	HR	BB	SO	RAT	ERA	ERA+	OAV	OOB	BH	AVG	PB	PR	/A	PD	TPI
1983	Oak-A	0	1	.000	8	2	0	0	0	9	17	1	5	5	23.0	16.00	24	.386	.460	0	—	0	-12	-12	-0	-1.0
1984	Oak-A	9	4	.692	20	17	2	1	0	108^{2}	118	9	31	41	13.0	4.06	92	.274	.334	0	—	0	-1	-4	-1	-0.3
1985	Oak-A	0	4	.000	19	7	0	0	0	46	57	15	22	19	15.7	7.24	53	.300	.376	0	—	0	-16	-17	-1	-1.0
1986	Oak-A	13	9	.591	29	27	5	2	0	198	176	19	57	116	10.9	3.45	112	.236	.297	0	—	0	16	9	0	1.1

YEAR	TM/L	W	L	PCT	G	GS	CG	SH	SV	IP	H	HR	BB	SO	RAT	ERA	ERA+	OAV	OOB	BH	AVG	PB	PR	/A	PD	TPI
1987	Oak-A	13	7	.650	31	31	6	0	0	203	194	38	44	124	10.7	4.08	101	.252	.295	0	.000	-0	8	1	0	0.1
1988	*Oak-A	11	8	.579	26	26	1	0	0	156^1	162	23	50	69	12.4	4.14	91	.275	.336	0	—	0	-3	-6	-1	-0.8
1989	Oak-A	5	9	.357	25	20	1	0	0	111	117	10	47	55	13.5	3.73	99	.264	.338	0	—	0	2	-1	-1	0.1
1990	*Oak-A	9	6	.600	26	21	0	0	0	124^1	124	17	53	56	13.0	4.85	77	.266	.344	0	—	0	-13	-16	1	-1.5
1991	Oak-A	4	2	.667	41	1	0	0	0	68^1	74	8	34	27	14.5	5.00	77	.278	.364	0	—	0	-7	-9	1	-0.6
1992	KC-A	1	2	.333	10	2	0	0	0	24^1	29	1	7	7	13.3	5.18	78	.293	.340	0	—	0	-3	-3	-0	-0.4
	NY-A	3	0	1.000	13	5	0	0	0	43^1	51	1	10	13	13.1	3.32	118	.298	.344	0	—	0	3	3	0	0.2
	Yr	4	2	.667	23	7	0	0	0	67^2	80	2	17	20	13.2	3.99	99	.295	.341	0	—	0	-0	-0	0	-0.2
1993	Oak-A	1	1	.500	3	3	0	0	0	14^2	14	5	6	4	12.3	4.30	95	.241	.313	0	—	0	0	-0	0	0.0
Total	11	69	53	.566	251	162	15	3	0	1107	1133	147	366	536	12.5	4.31	90	.265	.328	0	.000	-0	-26	-55	-1	-4.1

● CY YOUNG Young, Denton True b: 3/29/1867, Gilmore, Ohio d: 11/4/55, Newcomerstown, Ohio BR/TR, 6′2″, 210 lbs. Deb: 8/6/1890 MH

YEAR	TM/L	W	L	PCT	G	GS	CG	SH	SV	IP	H	HR	BB	SO	RAT	ERA	ERA+	OAV	OOB	BH	AVG	PB	PR	/A	PD	TPI
1890	Cle-N	9	7	.563	17	16	16	0	0	147^2	145	6	30	39	11.2	3.47	103	.249	.295	8	.123	-6	2	2	1	-0.3
1891	Cle-N	27	22	.551	55	46	43	0	2	423^2	431	4	140	147	12.3	2.85	122	.254	.314	29	.167	-3	24	29	-1	2.4
1892	*Cle-N	**36**	12	**.750**	53	49	48	**9**	0	453	363	8	118	168	**9.8**	**1.93**	**176**	.211	**.266**	31	.158	-8	**68**	**74**	5	**6.6**
1893	Cle-N	34	16	.680	53	46	42	1	1	422^2	442	10	103	102	**11.8**	3.36	145	.261	**.307**	44	.235	-6	61	71	4	6.4
1894	Cle-N	26	21	.553	52	47	44	2	1	408^2	488	19	106	108	13.2	3.94	139	.293	.337	40	.215	-8	63	69	7	5.6
1895	*Cle-N	**35**	10	.778	47	40	36	**4**	0	369^2	363	10	75	121	**10.9**	3.26	153	.253	**.294**	30	.214	-4	62	71	8	7.0
1896	*Cle-N	28	15	.651	51	46	42	**5**	**3**	414^1	477	7	62	**140**	11.9	3.24	140	.286	.316	52	.289	7	52	60	8	6.4
1897	Cle-N	21	19	.525	46	38	35	2	0	335^2	391	7	49	88	12.0	3.78	119	.289	.318	34	.222	-4	20	27	3	2.3
1898	Cle-N	25	13	.658	46	41	40	1	0	377^2	387	6	41	101	10.4	2.53	143	.263	.287	39	.253	5	45	46	7	5.3
1899	StL-N	26	16	.619	44	42	**40**	4	1	369^1	368	10	44	111	**10.2**	2.58	154	.260	**.285**	32	.216	-1	**52**	57	6	**6.2**
1900	StL-N	19	19	.500	41	35	32	**4**	0	321^1	337	7	36	115	10.5	3.00	121	.269	.291	22	.177	-2	25	23	0	2.1
1901	Bos-A	**33**	10	.767	43	41	38	**5**	0	371^1	324	6	37	**158**	**8.9**	**1.62**	**217**	**.232**	**.256**	32	.209	0	**84**	**79**	1	**8.3**
1902	Bos-A	**32**	11	.744	**45**	43	**41**	3	0	**384^2**	350	6	53	160	9.7	2.15	166	.243	.276	34	.230	2	**61**	**61**	-6	5.8
1903	*Bos-A	**28**	9	**.757**	40	35	**34**	**7**	**2**	**341^2**	294	6	37	176	9.0	2.08	146	.232	.259	44	.321	12	34	**36**	-3	**4.9**
1904	Bos-A	26	16	.619	43	41	40	**10**	1	380	327	6	29	200	**8.5**	1.97	136	.233	**.251**	33	.223	2	27	30	-5	3.1
1905	Bos-A	18	19	.486	38	33	31	4	0	320^2	248	3	30	210	**8.0**	1.82	148	.215	**.241**	18	.150	-2	30	31	-2	3.3
1906	Bos-A	13	21	.382	39	34	28	0	2	287^2	288	3	25	140	10.0	3.19	86	.263	.285	16	.154	-2	-16	-14	-1	-2.0
1907	Bos-A	21	15	.583	43	37	33	6	2	343^1	286	3	51	147	**9.0**	1.99	129	.229	**.263**	27	.216	0	21	22	-6	1.8
1908	Bos-A	21	11	.656	36	33	30	3	2	299	230	1	37	150	8.1	1.26	195	.213	.240	26	.226	1	38	40	-6	4.1
1909	Cle-A	19	15	.559	35	34	30	3	0	294^1	267	4	59	109	10.2	2.26	113	.250	.294	21	.196	-0	7	10	-1	0.9
1910	Cle-A	7	10	.412	21	20	14	1	0	163^1	149	0	27	58	9.9	2.53	102	.252	.289	8	.145	-0	-0	1	1	0.2
1911	Cle-A	3	4	.429	7	7	4	0	0	46^1	54	2	13	20	13.2	3.88	88	.298	.349	1	.063	-2	-3	-2	-0	-0.5
	Bos-N	4	5	.444	11	11	8	2	0	80	83	4	15	35	11.4	3.71	103	.268	.308	2	.080	-2	-3	1	0	-0.1
Total	22	511	316	.618	906	815	749	76	17	7356	7092	138	1217	2803	10.4	2.63	138	.252	.287	623	.210	-22	753	819	19	79.8

● HARLEY YOUNG Young, Harlan Edward "Cy The Third" b: 9/28/1883, Portland, Ind. d: 3/26/75, Jacksonville, Fla. BR/TR, 6′2″, Deb: 4/21/08

YEAR	TM/L	W	L	PCT	G	GS	CG	SH	SV	IP	H	HR	BB	SO	RAT	ERA	ERA+	OAV	OOB	BH	AVG	PB	PR	/A	PD	TPI
1908	Pit-N	0	2	.000	8	3	0	0	0	48^1	40	0	10	17	10.2	2.23	103	.234	.296	1	.083	-1	1	0	1	0.0
	Bos-N	0	1	.000	6	2	1	0	0	27^1	29	0	4	12	11.9	3.29	73	.269	.313	2	.200	0	-3	-3	-0	-0.1
	Yr	0	3	.000	14	5	1	0	0	75^2	69	0	14	29	10.2	2.62	89	.243	.286	3	.136	-0	-2	-2	1	-0.1

● IRV YOUNG Young, Irving Melrose "Young Cy" or "Cy The Second" b: 7/21/1877, Columbia Falls, Maine d: 1/14/35, Brewer, Maine BL/TL, 5′10″, 170 lbs. Deb: 4/14/05

YEAR	TM/L	W	L	PCT	G	GS	CG	SH	SV	IP	H	HR	BB	SO	RAT	ERA	ERA+	OAV	OOB	BH	AVG	PB	PR	/A	PD	TPI
1905	Bos-N	20	21	.488	43	42	**41**	7	0	**378**	337	6	71	156	9.9	2.90	107	.241	.282	14	.103	-8	4	8	4	0.4
1906	Bos-N	16	25	.390	43	41	**37**	4	0	**358^1**	349	7	83	151	11.0	2.91	92	.263	.309	12	.096	-7	-11	-9	3	-1.5
1907	Bos-N	10	23	.303	40	32	22	3	1	245^1	287	5	58	86	13.1	3.96	64	.306	.354	13	.162	-1	-41	-38	1	-4.9
1908	Bos-N	4	9	.308	16	11	7	1	0	85	94	2	19	32	12.2	2.86	84	.289	.332	5	.156	-1	-5	-4	-1	-0.9
	Pit-N	4	3	.571	16	7	3	1	1	89^2	73	1	21	31	9.9	2.01	115	.225	.283	6	.200	1	4	3	-1	0.3
	Yr	8	12	.400	32	18	10	2	1	174^2	167	3	40	63	10.9	2.42	97	.257	.305	11	.177	0	-1	-1	-2	-0.6
1910	Chi-A	4	8	.333	27	17	7	4	0	135^2	122	0	39	64	10.9	2.72	88	.247	.306	5	.114	-2	-3	-5	-0	-0.7
1911	Chi-A	5	6	.455	24	11	3	1	2	92^2	99	2	25	40	12.0	4.37	74	.229	.271	5	.179	-0	-11	-12	1	-1.2
Total	6	63	95	.399	209	161	120	21	4	1384^2	1361	23	316	560	11.1	3.11	88	.260	.307	60	.126	-18	-62	-57	6	-8.5

● J. B. YOUNG Young, J. B. b: Mt.Carmel, Pa. Deb: 6/10/1892

YEAR	TM/L	W	L	PCT	G	GS	CG	SH	SV	IP	H	HR	BB	SO	RAT	ERA	ERA+	OAV	OOB	BH	AVG	PB	PR	/A	PD	TPI
1892	StL-N	0	0	—	1	0	0	0	0	2	9	0	2	1	49.5	22.50	14	.600	.647	0	.000	-0	-4	-4	-0	0.0

● KIP YOUNG Young, Kip Lane b: 10/29/54, Georgetown, Ohio BR/TR, 5′11″, 175 lbs. Deb: 7/21/78

YEAR	TM/L	W	L	PCT	G	GS	CG	SH	SV	IP	H	HR	BB	SO	RAT	ERA	ERA+	OAV	OOB	BH	AVG	PB	PR	/A	PD	TPI
1978	Det-A	6	7	.462	14	13	7	0	0	105^2	94	9	30	49	10.7	2.81	137	.246	.304	0	—	0	11	12	-2	1.1
1979	Det-A	2	2	.500	13	7	0	0	0	43^2	60	11	11	22	14.8	6.39	68	.323	.364	0	—	0	-11	-10	1	-0.9
Total	2	8	9	.471	27	20	7	0	0	149^1	154	20	41	71	11.9	3.86	104	.271	.324	0	—	0	1	2	-1	0.2

● MATT YOUNG Young, Matthew John b: 8/9/58, Pasadena, Cal. BL/TL, 6′3″, 205 lbs. Deb: 4/6/83

YEAR	TM/L	W	L	PCT	G	GS	CG	SH	SV	IP	H	HR	BB	SO	RAT	ERA	ERA+	OAV	OOB	BH	AVG	PB	PR	/A	PD	TPI
1983	Sea-A★	11	15	.423	33	32	5	2	0	203^2	178	17	79	130	11.7	3.27	130	.236	.315	0	—	0	18	22	2	2.8
1984	Sea-A	6	8	.429	22	22	1	0	0	113^1	141	11	57	73	15.8	5.72	70	.307	.384	0	—	0	-22	-22	1	-2.2
1985	Sea-A	12	19	.387	37	35	5	2	1	218^1	242	23	76	136	13.4	4.91	86	.282	.345	0	—	0	-18	-17	-2	-2.3
1986	Sea-A	8	6	.571	65	5	1	0	13	103^2	108	9	46	82	14.1	3.82	111	.272	.359	0	—	0	4	5	-1	0.5
1987	LA-N	5	8	.385	47	0	0	0	11	54^1	62	3	17	42	13.1	4.47	89	.288	.341	0	.000	-0	-2	-3	-2	-0.9
1989	*Oak-A	1	4	.200	26	4	0	0	0	37^1	42	2	31	27	17.6	6.75	55	.286	.410	0	—	0	-12	-13	0	-1.3
1990	Sea-A	8	18	.308	34	33	7	1	0	225^1	198	15	107	176	12.4	3.51	113	.237	.328	0	—	0	10	11	-0	1.2
1991	Bos-A	3	7	.300	19	16	0	0	0	88^2	92	4	53	69	14.9	5.18	83	.266	.367	0	—	0	-11	-9	-0	-1.0
1992	Bos-A	0	4	.000	28	8	1	0	0	70^2	69	7	42	57	14.5	4.58	92	.257	.363	0	—	0	-5	-3	-1	-0.3
1993	Cle-A	1	6	.143	22	8	0	0	0	74^1	75	8	57	65	16.3	5.21	83	.266	.395	0	—	0	-7	-7	0	-0.6
Total	10	55	95	.367	333	163	20	5	25	1189^2	1207	99	565	857	13.7	4.40	94	.265	.350	0	.000	-0	-46	-35	-3	-4.1

● TIM YOUNG Young, Timothy R. b: 10/15/73, Gulfport, Miss. BL/TL, 5′9″, 170 lbs. Deb: 9/5/98

YEAR	TM/L	W	L	PCT	G	GS	CG	SH	SV	IP	H	HR	BB	SO	RAT	ERA	ERA+	OAV	OOB	BH	AVG	PB	PR	/A	PD	TPI
1998	Mon-N	0	0	—	10	0	0	0	0	6	6	0	4	7	15.0	6.00	68	.250	.357	0	—	0	-1	-1	0	0.0

● CHIEF YOUNGBLOOD Youngblood, Albert Clyde b: 6/13/1900, Hillsboro, Tex. d: 7/6/68, Amarillo, Tex. BL/TR, 6′3″, 202 lbs. Deb: 7/16/22

YEAR	TM/L	W	L	PCT	G	GS	CG	SH	SV	IP	H	HR	BB	SO	RAT	ERA	ERA+	OAV	OOB	BH	AVG	PB	PR	/A	PD	TPI
1922	Was-A	0	0	—	2	0	0	0	0	4^1	9	0	7	0	37.4	14.54	27	.429	.600	0	.000	-0	-5	-5	0	0.0

● DUCKY YOUNT Yount, Herbert Macon "Hub" b: 12/7/1885, Iredell Co., N.C. d: 5/9/70, Winston-Salem, N.C. BR/TR, 6′2″, 178 lbs. Deb: 5/20/14

YEAR	TM/L	W	L	PCT	G	GS	CG	SH	SV	IP	H	HR	BB	SO	RAT	ERA	ERA+	OAV	OOB	BH	AVG	PB	PR	/A	PD	TPI
1914	Bal-F	1	1	.500	13	1	1	0	0	41^1	44	2	19	19	14.2	4.14	73	.280	.365	1	.083	-1	-6	-5	1	-0.3

● LARRY YOUNT Yount, Lawrence King b: 2/15/50, Houston, Tex. BR/TR, 6′2″, 185 lbs. Deb: 9/15/71 F

YEAR	TM/L	W	L	PCT	G	GS	CG	SH	SV	IP	H	HR	BB	SO	RAT	ERA	ERA+	OAV	OOB	BH	AVG	PB	PR	/A	PD	TPI
1971	Hou-N	0	0	—	1	0	0	0	0	0	0	0	0	0	—	—	—	—	—	0	—	0	0	0	0	0.0

● CARL YOWELL Yowell, Carl Columbus "Sundown" b: 12/20/02, Madison, Va. d: 7/27/85, Jacksonville, Tex. BL/TL, 6′4″, 180 lbs. Deb: 9/5/24

YEAR	TM/L	W	L	PCT	G	GS	CG	SH	SV	IP	H	HR	BB	SO	RAT	ERA	ERA+	OAV	OOB	BH	AVG	PB	PR	/A	PD	TPI
1924	Cle-A	1	1	.500	4	2	2	0	0	27	37	1	13	8	16.7	6.67	64	.343	.413	2	.182	-1	-7	-7	-0	-0.5
1925	Cle-A	2	3	.400	12	4	1	0	0	36^1	40	1	17	12	14.4	4.46	99	.310	.395	1	.125	-1	-0	-0	0	-0.1
Total	2	3	4	.429	16	6	3	0	0	63^1	77	2	30	20	15.3	5.40	81	.325	.403	3	.158	-1	-8	-7	0	-0.6

● EDDIE YUHAS Yuhas, John Edward b: 8/5/24, Youngstown, Ohio d: 7/6/86, Winston-Salem, N.C BR/TR, 6′1″, 180 lbs. Deb: 4/17/52

YEAR	TM/L	W	L	PCT	G	GS	CG	SH	SV	IP	H	HR	BB	SO	RAT	ERA	ERA+	OAV	OOB	BH	AVG	PB	PR	/A	PD	TPI
1952	StL-N	12	2	.857	54	2	0	0	6	99^1	90	5	35	39	11.5	2.72	137	.243	.312	4	.190	1	11	11	-1	1.6
1953	StL-N	0	0	—	2	0	0	0	0	1	3	0	0	0	27.0	18.00	24	.500	.500	0	—	0	-2	-2	-0	0.0
Total	2	12	2	.857	56	2	0	0	6	100^1	93	5	35	39	11.7	2.87	130	.247	.315	4	.190	1	10	9	-1	1.6

● ADRIAN ZABALA Zabala, Adrian (Rodriguez) b: 8/26/16, San Antonio De Los Banos, Cuba BL/TL, 5′11″, 165 lbs. Deb: 8/11/45

YEAR	TM/L	W	L	PCT	G	GS	CG	SH	SV	IP	H	HR	BB	SO	RAT	ERA	ERA+	OAV	OOB	BH	AVG	PB	PR	/A	PD	TPI
1945	NY-N	2	4	.333	11	5	1	0	0	43^1	46	2	20	14	13.7	4.78	82	.284	.363	3	.231	1	-5	-4	0	-0.4
1949	NY-N	2	3	.400	15	4	2	1	1	41	44	5	10	13	12.1	5.27	76	.278	.325	1	.077	-1	-6	-6	-1	-0.9
Total	2	4	7	.364	26	9	3	1	1	84^1	90	7	30	27	12.9	5.02	79	.281	.345	4	.154	-0	-10	-10	-1	-1.3

YEAR	TM/L	W	L	PCT	G	GS	CG	SH	SV	IP	H	HR	BB	SO	RAT	ERA	ERA+	OAV	OOB	BH	AVG	PB	PR	/A	PD	TPI
● ZIP ZABEL	Zabel, George Washington b: 2/18/1891, Wetmore, Kan. d: 5/31/70, Beloit, Wis. BR/TR, 6'1.5", 185 lbs. Deb: 10/5/13																									
1913	Chi-N	1	0	1.000	1	1	0	0	0	5	3	0	1	0	7.2	0.00	—	.167	.211	0	.000	0	2	2	0	0.4
1914	Chi-N	4	4	.500	29	7	2	0	3	128	104	5	45	50	10.6	2.18	128	.235	.309	7	.184	-1	9	9	-1	0.4
1915	Chi-N	7	10	.412	36	17	8	3	0	163	124	3	84	60	11.7	3.20	87	.218	.323	4	.074	-4	-8	-8	3	-0.8
Total	3	12	14	.462	66	25	10	3	3	296	231	8	130	110	11.2	2.71	103	.224	.315	11	.117	-4	2	3	2	0.0
● CHINK ZACHARY	Zachary, Albert Myron (b: Albert Myron Zarski) b: 10/19/17, Brooklyn, N.Y. BR/TR, 5'11", 182 lbs. Deb: 4/23/44																									
1944	Bro-N	0	2	.000	4	2	0	0	0	10^1	10	2	7	3	15.7	9.58	37	.238	.360	0	.000	-0	-7	-7	-0	-1.1
● TOM ZACHARY	Zachary, Jonathan Thompson Walton (a.k.a. Zach Walton In 1918) b: 5/7/1896, Graham, N.C. d: 1/24/69, Burlington, N.C. BL/TL, 6'1", 187 lbs. Deb: 7/11/18																									
1918	Phi-A	2	0	1.000	2	2	0	0	0	8	9	0	7	1	18.0	5.63	52	.321	.457	2	.500	1	-3	-2	-0	-0.5
1919	Was-A	1	5	.167	17	7	0	0	0	61^2	68	0	20	9	13.0	2.92	110	.292	.350	5	.333	2	2	2	-1	0.3
1920	Was-A	15	16	.484	44	31	19	3	2	262^2	289	7	78	53	12.7	3.77	99	.285	.339	29	.261	6	1	-1	0	0.4
1921	Was-A	18	16	.529	39	30	17	2	1	250	314	10	59	53	13.6	3.96	104	.319	.361	23	.256	3	9	4	-0	0.8
1922	Was-A	15	10	.600	32	25	13	1	1	184^2	190	6	43	37	11.5	3.12	124	.275	.321	21	.296	5	19	15	0	2.4
1923	Was-A	10	16	.385	35	29	10	0	0	204^1	270	9	63	40	14.8	4.49	84	.321	.372	15	.192	-0	-12	-17	-1	-1.9
1924	*Was-A	15	9	.625	33	27	13	1	2	202^2	198	5	53	45	11.3	2.75	147	.264	.315	22	.306	4	33	29	2	3.7
1925	*Was-A	12	15	.444	38	33	11	1	2	217^2	247	10	74	58	13.4	3.85	110	.296	.355	12	.174	-2	13	9	-0	0.8
1926	StL-A	14	15	.483	34	31	18	3	0	247^1	264	14	97	53	13.4	3.60	119	.288	.359	23	.267	4	11	19	3	2.7
1927	StL-A	4	6	.400	13	12	6	0	0	78^1	110	4	27	13	15.7	4.37	100	.345	.396	3	.107	-2	-2	-0	-1	-0.3
	Was-A	4	7	.364	15	14	5	1	0	102^2	116	2	30	13	13.0	3.94	103	.290	.343	5	.139	-2	2	1	-3	-0.3
	Yr	8	13	.381	28	26	11	1	0	181	226	6	57	26	14.2	4.13	102	.314	.366	8	.125	-4	0	1	-3	-0.6
1928	Was-A	6	9	.400	20	14	5	1	0	102^2	130	5	40	19	15.0	5.44	74	.322	.384	10	.303	1	-16	-16	1	-1.7
	*NY-A	3	3	.500	7	6	3	0	1	45^2	54	1	15	7	13.6	3.94	95	.320	.375	2	.133	-0	1	-1	1	-0.1
	Yr	9	12	.429	27	20	8	1	1	148^1	184	6	55	26	14.5	4.98	79	.321	.380	12	.250	1	-15	-17	2	-1.8
1929	NY-A	12	0	1.000	26	11	7	2	2	119^2	131	5	30	35	12.3	2.48	155	.277	.323	10	.238	1	23	18	-3	1.5
1930	NY-A	1	1	.500	3	3	0	0	0	16^2	18	0	9	1	14.6	6.48	66	.269	.355	2	.250	1	-3	-4	1	-0.3
	Bos-N	11	5	.688	24	22	10	1	0	151^1	192	9	50	57	14.4	4.58	108	.317	.369	13	.241	2	7	6	-1	0.6
1931	Bos-N	11	15	.423	33	28	16	3	2	229	243	8	53	64	11.7	3.10	122	.272	.314	14	.167	-1	19	17	2	2.0
1932	Bos-N	12	11	.522	32	24	12	1	0	212	231	5	55	67	12.2	3.10	121	.280	.326	21	.273	5	18	16	-2	1.9
1933	Bos-N	7	9	.438	26	20	6	2	2	125	134	1	35	22	12.2	3.53	87	.276	.325	5	.119	-2	-3	-6	0	-1.0
1934	Bos-N	1	2	.333	5	4	2	1	0	24	27	1	8	4	13.1	3.38	113	.278	.333	0	.000	-1	2	1	-0	0.0
	Bro-N	5	6	.455	22	12	4	0	2	101^2	122	5	21	28	12.8	4.43	88	.301	.339	7	.184	1	-4	-6	-1	-0.5
	Yr	6	8	.429	27	16	6	1	2	125^2	149	6	29	32	12.9	4.23	92	.297	.338	7	.152	-0	-2	-5	-1	-0.5
1935	Bro-N	7	12	.368	25	21	9	1	4	158	193	10	35	33	13.1	3.59	111	.297	.335	7	.135	-1	8	7	0	0.7
1936	Bro-N	0	0	—	1	0	0	0	0	0^1	2	0	1	0	81.0	54.00	8	1.000	1.000	0	—	0	-2	-2	0	0.0
	Phi-N	0	3	.000	7	2	0	0	1	20^1	28	2	11	8	17.3	7.97	57	.329	.406	3	.333	1	-9	-8	0	-0.9
	Yr	0	3	.000	8	2	0	0	1	20^2	30	2	12	8	18.3	8.71	52	.345	.424	3	.333	1	-11	-10	0	-0.9
Total	19	186	191	.493	533	408	186	24	22	3126^1	3580	119	914	720	13.1	3.73	106	.294	.345	254	.226	25	116	82	-2	10.3
● CHRIS ZACHARY	Zachary, William Christopher b: 2/19/44, Knoxville, Tenn. BL/TR, 6'2", 200 lbs. Deb: 4/11/63																									
1963	Hou-N	2	2	.500	22	7	0	0	0	57	62	5	22	42	13.7	4.89	64	.272	.344	0	.000	-1	-10	-11	1	-0.7
1964	Hou-N	0	1	.000	1	1	0	0	0	4	6	1	1	2	15.8	9.00	38	.333	.368	0	.000	-0	-2	-2	0	-0.4
1965	Hou-N	0	2	.000	4	2	0	0	0	10^2	12	0	6	4	15.2	4.22	80	.273	.360	0	.000	-0	-1	-1	-0	-0.2
1966	Hou-N	3	5	.375	10	8	0	0	0	55	44	1	32	37	12.6	3.44	100	.221	.332	4	.222	1	1	-0	-1	0.0
1967	Hou-N	1	6	.143	9	7	0	0	0	36^1	42	5	12	18	13.9	5.70	58	.290	.352	1	.100	-0	-9	-10	-0	-1.7
1969	KC-A	0	1	.000	8	2	0	0	0	18^1	27	4	7	6	16.7	7.85	47	.346	.400	1	.500	0	-9	-8	-0	-0.4
1971	StL-N	3	10	.231	23	12	1	1	0	89^2	114	3	26	48	14.5	5.32	68	.316	.368	8	.242	1	-18	-17	0	-2.2
1972	*Det-A	1	1	.500	25	1	0	0	1	38^1	27	2	15	21	10.1	1.41	223	.201	.287	1	.500	1	7	7	-0	0.5
1973	Pit-N	0	1	.000	6	0	0	0	1	12	10	1	1	6	8.3	3.00	117	.222	.239	0	.000	-0	1	1	-0	0.0
Total	9	10	29	.256	108	40	1	1	2	321^1	344	22	122	184	13.4	4.57	74	.275	.344	15	.181	1	-41	-42	-1	-5.1
● PAT ZACHRY	Zachry, Patrick Paul b: 4/24/52, Richmond, Tex. BR/TR, 6'5", 180 lbs. Deb: 4/11/76																									
1976	*Cin-N	14	7	.667	38	28	6	1	0	204	170	8	83	143	11.3	2.74	128	.228	.307	7	.113	-2	17	17	-2	1.4
1977	Cin-N	3	7	.300	12	12	3	0	0	75	78	7	29	36	13.0	5.04	78	.273	.342	3	.136	-1	-9	-9	1	-1.0
	NY-N	7	6	.538	19	19	2	1	0	119^2	129	14	48	63	13.5	3.76	99	.278	.350	6	.143	-1	2	-0	-2	-0.3
	Yr	10	13	.435	31	31	5	1	0	194^2	207	21	77	99	13.3	4.25	90	.274	.344	9	.141	-2	-7	-10	-0	-1.3
1978	NY-N☆	10	6	.625	21	21	5	2	0	138	120	9	60	78	11.8	3.33	105	.236	.318	3	.070	-2	4	2	1	0.2
1979	NY-N	5	1	.833	7	7	1	0	0	42^2	44	3	21	17	14.1	3.59	101	.267	.356	2	.125	-1	1	0	0	0.0
1980	NY-N	6	10	.375	28	26	7	3	0	164^2	145	16	58	88	11.4	3.01	118	.240	.312	2	.043	-4	11	10	-2	0.4
1981	NY-N	7	14	.333	24	24	3	0	0	139	151	13	56	76	13.7	4.14	84	.282	.354	6	.158	0	-10	-10	1	-1.4
1982	NY-N	6	9	.400	36	16	2	0	1	137^2	149	10	57	69	13.5	4.05	90	.279	.349	3	.079	-2	-7	-6	0	-0.9
1983	*LA-N	6	1	.857	40	1	0	0	0	61^1	63	4	21	36	12.5	2.49	144	.278	.341	2	.500	1	8	7	0	0.9
1984	LA-N	5	6	.455	58	0	0	0	2	82^2	84	3	51	55	14.9	3.81	93	.267	.372	2	.333	1	-2	-3	1	-0.2
1985	Phi-N	0	0	—	10	0	0	0	0	12^2	14	1	11	8	17.8	4.26	86	.280	.410	0	.000	-0	-1	-1	1	0.0
Total	10	69	67	.507	293	154	29	7	3	1177^1	1147	88	495	669	12.7	3.52	102	.259	.336	36	.113	-11	13	8	-1	-0.9
● GEORGE ZACKERT	Zackert, George Carl "Zeke" b: 12/24/1884, Buchanan Co., Mo. d: 2/18/77, Burlington, Iowa BL/TL, 6', 177 lbs. Deb: 9/22/11																									
1911	StL-N	0	2	.000	4	1	0	0	0	7^1	17	0	6	6	28.2	11.05	31	.486	.561	0	.000	-0	-6	-6	1	-1.3
1912	StL-N	0	0	—	1	0	0	0	0	1	2	0	1	0	36.0	18.00	19	.667	.800	0	—	0	-2	-2	0	0.0
Total	2	0	2	.000	5	1	0	0	0	8^1	19	0	7	6	29.2	11.88	28	.500	.587	0	.000	-0	-8	-8	1	-1.3
● GEOFF ZAHN	Zahn, Geoffrey Clayton b: 12/19/45, Baltimore, Md. BL/TL, 6'1", 180 lbs. Deb: 9/2/73																									
1973	LA-N	1	0	1.000	6	1	0	0	0	13^1	5	2	2	9	4.7	1.35	255	.116	.156	0	.000	-0	3	3	0	0.2
1974	LA-N	3	5	.375	21	10	1	0	0	79^2	78	3	16	33	10.8	2.03	167	.254	.295	4	.174	-0	14	12	0	1.1
1975	LA-N	0	1	.000	2	0	0	0	0	3	2	0	5	1	21.0	9.00	38	.222	.500	0	—	0	-2	-2	-0	-0.5
	Chi-N	2	7	.222	16	10	0	0	1	62^2	67	2	26	21	13.4	4.45	86	.282	.352	2	.133	-1	-6	-4	1	-0.5
	Yr	2	8	.200	18	10	0	0	1	65^2	69	2	31	22	13.7	4.66	82	.279	.360	2	.133	-1	-8	-6	1	-1.0
1976	Chi-N	0	1	.000	3	2	0	0	0	8^1	16	0	2	4	20.5	10.80	36	.410	.452	0	.000	-0	-7	-6	0	-0.7
1977	Min-A	12	14	.462	34	32	7	1	0	198	234	20	66	88	13.9	4.68	85	.299	.358	0	—	0	-14	-15	2	-1.4
1978	Min-A	14	14	.500	35	35	12	1	0	252^1	260	18	81	106	12.3	3.03	126	.274	.334	0	—	0	20	22	-0	2.3
1979	Min-A	13	7	.650	26	24	4	0	0	169	181	13	41	58	11.8	3.57	123	.279	.322	0	—	0	12	15	2	1.5
1980	Min-A	14	18	.438	38	35	13	5	0	232^2	273	17	66	96	13.2	4.41	99	.302	.351	0	—	0	-10	-1	0	-0.7
1981	Cal-A	10	11	.476	25	25	9	0	0	161^1	181	18	43	52	12.5	4.41	83	.285	.330	0	—	0	-13	-14	0	-1.6
1982	*Cal-A	18	8	.692	34	34	12	4	0	229^1	225	18	65	81	11.5	3.73	109	.259	.314	0	—	0	9	8	-1	0.7
1983	Cal-A	9	11	.450	29	28	11	3	0	203	212	22	51	81	11.7	3.33	121	.269	.314	0	—	0	17	16	-2	1.3
1984	Cal-A	13	10	.565	28	27	9	**5**	0	199^1	200	11	48	61	11.2	3.12	127	.263	.308	0	—	0	19	19	1	2.2
1985	Cal-A	2	2	.500	7	7	1	1	0	37	44	5	14	14	14.1	4.38	94	.299	.360	0	—	0	-1	-1	1	0.0
Total	13	111	109	.505	304	270	79	20	1	1849	1978	149	526	705	12.3	3.74	107	.278	.329	6	.140	-2	43	51	4	3.9
● PAUL ZAHNISER	Zahniser, Paul Vernon b: 9/6/1896, Sac City, Iowa d: 9/26/64, Klamath Falls, Ore. BR/TR, 5'10.5", 170 lbs. Deb: 5/18/23																									
1923	Was-A	9	10	.474	33	21	10	1	0	177	201	7	76	52	14.2	3.86	97	.291	.364	5	.096	-1	2	-2	-2	-0.5
1924	Was-A	5	7	.417	24	14	5	1	0	92	98	2	49	28	14.8	4.40	92	.283	.378	4	.129	-2	-2	-4	-2	-0.7
1925	Bos-A	5	12	.294	37	21	7	1	0	176^2	232	6	89	30	16.4	5.15	88	.327	.403	8	.138	-4	-15	-12	-2	-1.5
1926	Bos-A	6	18	.250	30	24	7	1	0	172	213	5	69	35	14.9	4.97	82	.321	.387	8	.163	-1	-18	-17	3	-1.8
1929	Cin-N	0	0	—	1	0	0	0	0	1	2	1	1	0	27.0	27.00	17	.400	.500	0	—	0	-2	-2	-0	0.0
Total	5	25	47	.347	125	80	29	4	1	618^2	746	21	284	145	15.1	4.66	88	.309	.384	25	.132	-8	-35	-37	-3	-4.5

YEAR	TM/L	W	L	PCT	G	GS	CG	SH	SV	IP	H	HR	BB	SO	RAT	ERA	ERA+	OAV	OOB	BH	AVG	PB	PR	/A	PD	TPI
● **CARL ZAMLOCH** Zamloch, Carl Eugene b: 10/6/1889, Oakland, Cal. d: 8/19/63, Santa Barbara, Cal BR/TR, 6'1", 176 lbs. Deb: 5/7/13																										
1913	Det-A	1	6	.143	17	5	3	0	1	69^2	66	1	23	28	11.9	2.45	119	.257	.325	4	.182	-1	4	4	-1	0.2
● **OSCAR ZAMORA** Zamora, Oscar Jose (Sosa) b: 9/23/44, Camaguey, Cuba BR/TR, 5'10", 178 lbs. Deb: 6/18/74																										
1974	Chi-N	3	9	.250	56	0	0	0	10	83^2	82	6	19	38	10.9	3.12	122	.264	.306	2	.182	-0	5	6	-0	1.0
1975	Chi-N	5	2	.714	52	0	0	0	10	71	84	17	15	28	12.5	5.07	76	.298	.333	1	.167	-0	-11	-10	-0	-1.3
1976	Chi-N	5	3	.625	40	2	0	0	3	55	70	8	17	27	14.4	5.24	74	.317	.368	0	.000	-1	-11	-8	-1	-1.4
1978	Hou-N	0	0	—	10	0	0	0	0	15	20	2	7	6	16.2	7.20	46	.328	.397	0	.000	-0	-6	-6	0	0.0
Total	4	13	14	.481	158	2	0	0	23	224^2	256	33	58	99	12.6	4.53	84	.293	.337	3	.107	-2	-23	-18	-1	-1.7
● **DOM ZANNI** Zanni, Dominick Thomas b: 3/1/32, Bronx, N.Y. BR/TR, 5'11", 180 lbs. Deb: 9/28/58																										
1958	SF-N	1	0	1.000	1	0	0	0	0	4	7	1	1	3	18.0	2.25	169	.412	.444	0	.000	-0	1	1	-0	0.1
1959	SF-N	0	0	—	9	0	0	0	0	11	12	2	8	11	17.2	6.55	58	.273	.396	0	—	0	-3	-3	1	0.1
1961	SF-N	1	0	1.000	8	0	0	0	0	13^2	13	1	12	11	16.5	3.95	96	.277	.424	0	—	0	0	-0	0	0.0
1962	Chi-A	6	5	.545	44	2	0	0	5	86^1	67	12	31	66	10.3	3.75	104	.214	.287	5	.278	2	2	1	2	0.6
1963	Chi-A	0	0	—	5	0	0	0	0	4^1	5	1	4	2	18.7	8.31	42	.294	.429	0	—	0	-2	-2	0	0.0
	Cin-N	1	1	.500	31	1	0	0	5	43	39	2	21	40	13.4	4.19	80	.247	.350	1	.333	0	-4	-4	1	-0.2
1965	Cin-N	0	0	—	8	0	0	0	0	13^1	7	1	5	10	8.1	1.35	278	.159	.245	0	.000	-0	3	4	0	0.0
1966	Cin-N	0	0	—	5	0	0	0	0	7^1	5	0	3	5	11.0	0.00	—	.192	.300	1	1.000	0	3	3	-0	0.0
Total	7	9	6	.600	111	3	0	0	10	183	155	20	85	148	12.1	3.79	99	.233	.326	7	.280	2	-1	-1	4	0.6
● **JEFF ZASKE** Zaske, Lloyd Jeffrey b: 10/6/60, Seattle, Wash. BR/TR, 6'5", 180 lbs. Deb: 7/21/84																										
1984	Pit-N	0	0	—	3	0	0	0	0	5	4	0	1	2	9.0	0.00	—	.211	.250	0	—	0	2	2	0	0.0
● **CLINT ZAVARAS** Zavaras, Clinton Wayne b: 1/4/67, Denver, Colo. BR/TR, 6'1", 175 lbs. Deb: 6/3/89																										
1989	Sea-A	1	6	.143	10	10	0	0	0	52	49	4	30	31	14.0	5.19	78	.253	.358	0	—	0	-8	-7	-0	-1.1
● **ZAY** Zay Deb: 10/7/1886 ♦																										
1886	Bal-a	0	1	.000	1	1	0	0	0	2	4	0	4	2	36.0	9.00	38	.333	.500	0	.000	-0	-1	-1	-0	-0.4
● **MATT ZEISER** Zeiser, Matthew J. b: 9/25/1888, Chicago, Ill. d: 6/10/42, Chicago, Ill BR/TR, 5'10", 170 lbs. Deb: 4/27/14																										
1914	Bos-A	0	0	—	2	0	0	0	0	10	9	0	8	0	16.2	1.80	150	.281	.439	0	.000	-0	1	1	-1	-0.1
● **BILL ZEPP** Zepp, William Clinton b: 7/22/46, Detroit, Mich. BR/TR, 6'2", 185 lbs. Deb: 8/12/69																										
1969	Min-A	0	0	—	4	0	0	0	0	5^1	6	1	4	2	16.9	6.75	54	.286	.400	0	.000	-0	-2	-2	-0	0.0
1970	*Min-A	9	4	.692	43	20	1	1	2	151	154	9	51	64	12.8	3.22	116	.266	.335	6	.136	-1	8	8	-2	0.4
1971	Det-A	1	1	.500	16	4	0	0	2	31^2	41	2	17	15	17.3	5.12	70	.328	.421	0	.000	-0	-6	-5	0	-0.4
Total	3	10	5	.667	63	24	1	1	4	188	201	12	72	81	13.6	3.64	102	.278	.353	6	.122	-2	1	1	-2	0.0
● **GEORGE ZETTLEIN** Zettlein, George "Charmer" b: 7/18/1844, Brooklyn, N.Y. d: 5/23/05, Patchogue, N.Y. BR/TR, 5'9", 162 lbs. Deb: 5/8/1871																										
1871	Chi-n	18	9	.667	28	28	25	0	0	240^2	298	6	25	22	**12.1**	**2.73**	**168**	.267	**.283**	32	.250	-7	**40**	**50**		**2.9**
1872	Tro-n	14	8	.636	25	22	17	2	1	187^2	207	2	8	17	10.3	2.16	168	.250	.257	29	.257	1	31	31		2.4
	Eck-n	1	8	.111	9	9	8	0	0	75^1	106	1	6	8	13.4	2.75	123	.300	.312	3	.088	-4	7	5		0.2
	Yr	15	16	.484	34	31	25	2	1	263	313	3	14	25	11.2	2.33	153	.265	.274	32	.218	-4	38	36		2.6
1873	Phi-n	36	15	.706	51	51	49	0	0	460	593	3	41	28	12.4	2.70	122	.283	.297	50	.207	-8	28	31		1.9
1874	Chi-n	27	30	.474	57	57	57	3	0	515^2	640	3	43	26	11.9	2.43	92	.273	.286	47	.193	-9	-14	-12		-1.6
1875	Chi-n	17	14	.548	31	31	29	6	0	282	266	0	6	18	8.7	1.28	178	.230	.234	29	.218	-3	30	31		2.5
	Phi-n	12	8	.600	21	21	20	1	0	181^1	209	0	10	13	10.9	2.08	109	.264	.273	15	.181	-4	3	4		-0.1
	Yr	29	22	.569	52	52	49	**7**	0	463^1	475	0	16	31	9.5	1.59	143	.244	.250	44	.204	-7	33	35		2.4
1876	Phi-N	4	20	.167	28	25	23	1	2	234	358	2	6	10	14.0	3.88	62	.331	.334	27	.211	-5	-41	-38	-1	-3.4
Total	5 n	125	92	.576	222	219	205	12	1	1942^2	2319	15	139	132	11.4	2.32	128	.267	.278	205	.210	-35	125	138		8.2
● **BOB ZICK** Zick, Robert George b: 4/26/27, Chicago, Ill. BL/TR, 6', 168 lbs. Deb: 5/2/54																										
1954	Chi-N	0	0	—	8	0	0	0	0	16^1	23	1	7	9	16.5	8.27	51	.343	.405	1	.250	0	-8	-7	-0	0.0
● **GEORGE ZIEGLER** Ziegler, George J. b: 1872, Chicago, Ill. d: 7/22/16, Kankakee, Ill. Deb: 6/19/1890																										
1890	Pit-N	0	1	.000	1	1	0	0	0	6	12	0	0	1	18.0	10.50	31	.400	.400	0	.000	-0	-5	-5	-0	-0.5
● **STEVE ZIEM** Ziem, Stephen Graeling b: 10/24/61, Milwaukee, Wis. BR/TR, 6'2", 210 lbs. Deb: 4/30/87																										
1987	Atl-N	0	1	.000	2	0	0	0	0	2^1	4	0	1	0	19.3	7.71	56	.364	.417	0	—	0	-1	-1	-0	-0.3
● **WALTER ZINK** Zink, Walter Noble b: 11/21/1899, Pittsfield, Mass. d: 6/12/64, Quincy, Mass. BR/TR, 6', 165 lbs. Deb: 7/6/21																										
1921	NY-N	0	0	—	2	0	0	0	0	4	4	0	3	1	15.8	2.25	163	.235	.350	0	.000	-0	1	1	-0	0.0
● **JIMMY ZINN** Zinn, James Edward b: 1/21/1895, Benton, Ark. d: 2/26/91, Memphis, Tenn. BL/TR, 6'0.5", 195 lbs. Deb: 9/4/19																										
1919	Phi-A	1	3	.250	5	3	2	0	0	25^2	38	1	10	9	17.2	6.31	54	.365	.426	4	.308	2	-9	-8	-0	-0.9
1920	Pit-N	1	1	.500	6	3	2	0	0	31	32	2	5	18	11.0	3.48	92	.260	.295	3	.200	0	-1	-1	-0	0.0
1921	Pit-N	7	6	.538	32	9	5	1	4	127^1	159	3	30	49	13.5	3.68	104	.318	.359	11	.224	0	2	2	-2	0.0
1922	Pit-N	0	0	—	5	0	0	0	1	9^2	11	1	2	3	12.1	1.86	219	.297	.333	0	.000	-0	2	2	-0	0.0
1929	Cle-A	4	6	.400	18	11	6	1	2	105^1	150	8	33	29	15.9	5.04	88	.340	.390	16	.381	7	-9	-7	-0	0.0
Total	5	13	16	.448	66	26	15	2	7	299	390	15	80	108	14.4	4.30	92	.324	.369	34	.283	9	-15	-12	-3	-0.9
● **BILL ZINSER** Zinser, William Francis b: 1/6/18, Astoria, N.Y. d: 2/16/93, Englewood, Fla. BR/TR, 6'1", 185 lbs. Deb: 8/19/44																										
1944	Was-A	0	0	—	2	0	0	0	0	0^2	1	0	5	1	81.0	27.00	12	.333	.750	0	—	0	-2	-2	0	0.0
● **ED ZMICH** Zmich, Edward Albert b: 10/1/1884, Cleveland, Ohio d: 8/20/50, Cleveland, Ohio BL/TL, 6', 180 lbs. Deb: 7/23/10																										
1910	StL-N	0	5	.000	9	6	2	0	0	36	38	0	29	19	17.5	6.25	48	.304	.446	1	.077	-1	-13	-13	1	-1.6
1911	StL-N	1	0	1.000	4	0	0	0	0	12^2	8	0	8	4	12.1	2.13	158	.182	.321	0	.000	-1	2	2	-1	0.0
Total	2	1	5	.167	13	6	2	0	0	48^2	46	0	37	23	16.1	5.18	60	.272	.414	1	.059	-2	-11	-11	0	-1.6
● **SAM ZOLDAK** Zoldak, Samuel Walter "Sad Sam" b: 12/8/18, Brooklyn, N.Y. d: 8/25/66, New Hyde Park, N.Y BL/TL, 5'11.5", 185 lbs. Deb: 5/13/44																										
1944	StL-A	0	0	—	18	0	0	0	0	38^2	49	1	19	15	15.8	3.72	97	.310	.384	2	.333	0	-1	-1	0	0.0
1945	StL-A	3	2	.600	26	1	1	0	0	69^2	74	3	18	19	11.9	3.36	105	.267	.312	1	.050	-2	0	1	-1	-0.3
1946	StL-A	9	11	.450	35	21	9	2	2	170^1	166	11	57	51	11.8	3.43	109	.256	.317	9	.173	-0	1	6	1	0.7
1947	StL-A	9	10	.474	35	19	6	1	1	171	162	7	76	36	12.5	3.47	112	.254	.334	10	.172	-1	4	8	3	1.0
1948	StL-A	2	4	.333	11	9	0	0	0	54	64	4	19	13	14.0	4.67	98	.296	.356	6	.273	0	-2	-1	0	0.0
	Cle-A	9	6	.600	23	12	4	1	0	105^2	104	6	24	17	10.9	2.81	144	.261	.303	5	.139	-2	17	15	2	1.9
	Yr	11	10	.524	34	21	4	1	0	159^2	168	10	43	30	11.9	3.44	123	.273	.321	11	.190	-2	15	14	2	1.9
1949	Cle-A	1	2	.333	27	0	0	0	0	53	60	4	18	11	13.2	4.25	94	.291	.348	3	.375	1	-0	-1	3	0.3
1950	Cle-A	4	2	.667	33	3	0	0	4	63^2	64	6	21	15	12.2	3.96	109	.259	.320	3	.188	0	4	3	-0	0.2
1951	Phi-A	6	10	.375	26	18	8	1	0	128	127	9	24	18	10.6	3.16	135	.257	.292	7	.156	-3	14	16	-2	1.3
1952	Phi-A	0	6	.000	16	10	2	0	1	75^1	86	3	25	12	13.3	4.06	97	.290	.345	4	.174	-1	-3	-1	2	0.1
Total	9	43	53	.448	250	93	30	5	8	929^1	956	54	301	207	12.2	3.54	112	.267	.325	50	.175	-7	34	45	7	5.2
● **BILL ZUBER** Zuber, William Henry "Goober" b: 3/26/13, Middle Amana, Iowa d: 11/2/82, Cedar Rapids, Iowa BR/TR, 6'2", 195 lbs. Deb: 9/16/36																										
1936	Cle-A	1	1	.500	2	2	1	0	0	13^2	14	0	15	5	19.1	6.59	76	.269	.433	1	.200	-0	-2	-2	-0	-0.3
1938	Cle-A	0	3	.000	15	0	0	0	1	28^2	33	0	20	14	16.6	5.02	92	.295	.402	0	.000	-1	-1	-1	-0	-0.2
1939	Cle-A	2	0	1.000	16	1	0	0	0	31^2	41	2	19	16	17.3	5.97	74	.323	.415	1	.200	1	-5	-6	1	-0.2
1940	Cle-A	1	1	.500	17	0	0	0	0	24	25	3	14	12	14.6	5.63	75	.260	.355	1	.333	0	-3	-4	-0	-0.3
1941	Was-A	6	4	.600	36	7	1	0	2	96^1	110	5	61	51	16.2	5.42	75	.291	.392	0	.000	-3	-14	-15	-1	-1.8
1942	Was-A	9	9	.500	37	7	3	1	1	126^2	115	5	82	64	14.0	3.84	95	.243	.355	6	.154	0	-3	-3	-3	-0.5
1943	NY-A	8	4	.667	20	13	7	0	1	118	100	3	74	57	13.3	3.89	83	.234	.347	7	.184	2	-8	-9	-2	-0.8

YEAR	TM/L	W	L	PCT	G	GS	CG	SH	SV	IP	H	HR	BB	SO	RAT	ERA	ERA+	OAV	OOB	BH	AVG	PB	PR	/A	PD	TPI
1944	NY-A	5	7	.417	22	13	2	1	0	107	101	5	54	59	13.1	4.21	83	.255	.346	4	.129	-2	-9	-9	-1	-1.1
1945	NY-A	5	11	.313	21	14	7	0	1	127	121	2	56	50	12.5	3.19	109	.259	.338	7	.167	-1	2	4	-1	0.2
1946	NY-A	0	1	.000	3	0	0	0	0	5²	10	2	3	3	20.6	12.71	27	.385	.448	0	.000	-0	-6	-6	-0	-0.9
	*Bos-A	5	1	.833	15	7	2	1	0	56²	37	4	39	29	12.1	2.54	144	.187	.321	2	.111	-1	6	7	-0	0.6
	Yr	5	2	.714	18	7	2	1	0	62¹	47	6	42	32	12.9	3.47	105	.210	.335	2	.100	-1	0	1	-0	-0.3
1947	Bos-A	1	0	1.000	20	1	0	0	0	50²	60	4	31	23	16.2	5.33	73	.311	.406	2	.154	-0	-9	-8	-0	-0.2
Total	11	43	42	.506	224	65	23	3	6	786	767	35	468	383	14.2	4.28	87	.260	.362	31	.135	-6	-51	-50	-8	-5.5

● GEORGE ZUVERINK

Zuverink, George b: 8/20/24, Holland, Mich. BR/TR, 6'4", 200 lbs. Deb: 4/21/51

YEAR	TM/L	W	L	PCT	G	GS	CG	SH	SV	IP	H	HR	BB	SO	RAT	ERA	ERA+	OAV	OOB	BH	AVG	PB	PR	/A	PD	TPI
1951	Cle-A	0	0	—	16	0	0	0	0	25¹	24	2	13	14	13.5	5.33	71	.253	.349	0	—	0	-3	-4	0	0.0
1952	Cle-A	0	0	—	1	0	0	0	0	1¹	1	0	0	1	6.8	0.00	—	.200	.200	0	—	0	1	0	0	0.0
1954	Cin-N	0	0	—	2	0	0	0	0	6	10	1	1	2	16.5	9.00	47	.385	.407	1	.500	0	-3	-3	-0	0.0
	Det-A	9	13	.409	35	25	9	2	4	203	201	22	62	70	12.0	3.59	103	.257	.318	8	.125	-3	3	2	3	0.2
1955	Det-A	0	5	.000	14	1	0	0	0	28¹	38	6	14	13	16.8	6.99	55	.309	.384	0	.000	-1	-10	-10	0	-1.5
	Bal-A	4	3	.571	28	5	0	0	4	86¹	80	5	17	31	10.5	2.19	174	.264	.312	5	.217	1	17	16	1	1.5
	Yr	4	8	.333	42	6	0	0	4	114²	118	11	31	44	12.0	3.38	113	.276	.331	5	.185	0	7	6	1	0.0
1956	Bal-A	7	6	.538	**62**	0	0	0	**16**	97¹	112	6	34	33	13.8	4.16	94	.294	.356	2	.118	-1	-0	-3	1	-0.4
1957	Bal-A	10	6	.625	**56**	0	0	0	9	112²	105	9	39	36	11.8	2.48	145	.257	.327	3	.130	-0	16	14	1	2.2
1958	Bal-A	2	2	.500	45	0	0	0	7	69	74	4	17	22	12.7	3.39	106	.286	.344	2	.222	1	3	2	1	0.4
1959	Bal-A	0	1	.000	6	0	0	0	0	13	15	1	6	1	14.5	4.15	91	.306	.382	0	—	1	-0	-1	0	0.0
Total	8	32	36	.471	265	31	9	2	40	642¹	660	56	203	223	12.5	3.54	105	.271	.334	21	.148	-2	23	13	7	2.4

The Annual Record

This section contains the season-by-season standings and records for all teams since 1871, plus 28 statistical categories for each team's batting and baserunning, and 26 categories for its pitching and fielding. In those years in which major league play consisted of more than one league, the statistics are presented in the order of the leagues' founding: that is, the National Association comes first; the National League record precedes those of all its rivals; the American Association precedes the Union Association and Players League; and the American League follows the National League but precedes the Federal League.

This edition includes an additional page for each league season, thus doubling the size of the Annual Record. The additional page will present daily highlights and team rosters. An asterisk following a date signifies a non-major league event. The rosters are complete for all years of major league play until the expansion of 1961, with the exception of the 1884 Union Association, which featured massive player movement, and the 12-team National League of 1892-1899. For those league years the criteria for listing a player here are 60 at bats or 15 innings pitched. For the AL since 1961 and the NL since 1962, the criteria becomes 200 at bats or 50 innings pitched. Substitute players are listed at their main positions, up to two if they played in 10 or more games at the position; if a man played fewer than 10 games at his main position, he is shown with a slash preceding his position.

On the statistical page, the figure for the leading team in a given category is displayed in boldface. Where data are unavailable, the statistical column is blank. Also presented here are the top three to five players/pitchers in up to 48 categories per season. When fewer than 48 categories are shown, it means that official records are lacking; that data is not reconstructible at present; or that available data is not meaningful, such as for Relief Runs or Relief Ranking in the early years of this century. When fewer than five individuals appear in a given category, credible standouts are lacking, as in the case of Stolen Base Wins in most years. The criterion used for identifying pitching leaders is a minimum of one inning pitched per scheduled game; for batters the criterion employed is the one officially in place at the time or, in the absence of any known practice, 3.1 plate appearances per scheduled game.

Ties in counting stats are common, and occasionally they are so numerous that space does not permit listing all the players by name; ties for fifth place are not shown. Highly uncommon are ties in stats based on a large array of data, as with batting averages, on base percentages, earned run averages, and sabermetric stats such as Runs Created, Total Average, or the various Linear Weights measures. Where rounding off has created the appearance of a tie, the true leader—as extra decimal places for a complete calculation would have revealed—is listed first. An example is the AL batting race of 1949, in which George Kell and Ted Williams are both shown as hitting .343; Kell in fact hit .3429 and Williams .3428. Both men are credited with batting averages of .343, but Kell, the actual leader, is listed first. (This procedure does not hold for calculated stats based on pitchers' won-lost percentages, where the narrow array of data frequently produces actual ties.)

For additional useful information about a team in a given year, we refer the reader to the various registers and the rosters. Team abbreviations used in the Annual Record are to be found on the last page of this book.

Following are the abbreviations employed in the team statistical reviews of the Annual Record, aside from those that are defined adequately in the introductions to the Player or Pitcher Registers, plus brief descriptions of what the less common statistics measure. For information about formulas and computation, see the Glossary.

Batting and Baserunning

PCT	Percentage of games won
GB	Games Behind the league or division leader
OR	Opponents' Runs scored
PRO	Production (On Base Percentage plus Slugging Average)
PRO+	Normalized and park-adjusted Production. A figure of 100 is a league-average performance.
BR	Batting Runs (Linear Weights measure of runs contributed beyond what a league-average batter or team might have contributed, defined as zero.)
/A	Adjusted (Signifies that the stat to the immediate left, in this instance Batting Runs, is here normalized to league average and adjusted for home-park factor. A mark of 100 is a league-average performance. Pitcher batting is removed from all league batting statistics before normalization for a variety of reasons expanded upon in the Glossary.)

PF   Park Factor (Calculated separately for batters and pitchers: above 100 signifies a park favorable to hitters, below 100 signifies a park favorable to pitchers; see Glossary for further data and technical information.)

CHI   Clutch Hitting Index (Calculated for individuals, actual RBI over expected RBI, adjusted for league average and position in batting order; calculated for teams, actual runs scored divided by Batting Runs. Marks above the median of 100 are superior. See Glossary for precise formula.)

RC   Runs Created (Bill James's formulation for run contribution from a variety of batting and baserunning events; many different formulas are applied, depending on data available; see Glossary.)

SBA   Stolen Base Average (Stolen bases divided by attempts; availability dependent upon CS, as shown above.)

SBR   Stolen Base Runs (Linear Weights measure of runs contributed *beyond* what a league-average base stealer or team might have gained, defined as zero; individual SBRs are calculated on the basis of a 66.7 percent success rate, the rate necessary to produce benefit, while team SBRs are normalized to the success rate for the league in that season; availability dependent upon CS.)

Pitching and Fielding

SH   Shutouts (Individual and combined when calculated for teams; individual only for top five leaders.)

H/G   Hits allowed per Game (Game defined as nine innings.)

CPI   Clutch Pitching Index (Expected runs over actual runs, with 100 being a league-average performance and marks above 100 indicating better than expected results. See Glossary.)

E   Errors

DP   Double Plays

FW   Fielding Wins (Fielding Runs divided by the number of runs required to create an additional win beyond average; average is defined as a team record of .500 because a league won-lost average must be .500. For more technical data about Runs Per Win and Fielding Run formulas, see Glossary.)

PW   Pitching Wins (Adjusted Pitching Runs divided by the number of runs required to create an additional win beyond average; average is defined as a team record of .500 because a league won-lost average must be .500. For more technical data about Runs Per Win and Pitching Run formulas, see Glossary.)

BW   Batting Wins (Adjusted Batting Runs divided by the number of runs required to create an additional win beyond average; average is defined as a team record of .500 because a league won-lost average must be .500. For more technical data about Runs Per Win and Batting Run formulas, see Glossary.)

SBW   Stolen Base Wins (Stolen Base Runs divided by the number of runs required to create an additional win beyond average; average is defined as a team record of .500 because a league won-lost average must be .500. For more technical data about Runs Per Win and Stolen Base Run formulas, see Glossary.)

DIF   Differential (Difference between the team's actual won-lost record and that predicted by the total of its Pitching Wins, Batting Wins, Fielding Wins, and Stolen Base Wins; indicates the extent to which a team outperformed or underperformed its talent.)

Other stats carried only on an individual basis in the Annual Record portion of *Total Baseball* are as follows (definitions supplied only when not available from Player or Pitcher Register introductions):

Total Average   Tom Boswell's formulation for offensive contribution from a variety of batting and baserunning events; calculated to make use of the maximum available data.

Fielding Runs

Total Player Rating

Bases on Balls Per Game   Game defined as nine innings; league leaders calculated on the basis of fewest walks per nine innings.

Strikeouts Per Game   Game defined as nine innings; league leaders calculated on the basis of most strikeouts per nine innings.

Starter Runs   Identical to Pitching Runs but confined to starting pitchers, defined as pitchers who average more than three innings per appearance.

Relief Runs   Identical to Pitching Runs but confined to relief pitchers.

Relief Ranking   Adjusted Relief Runs, weighted for the greater value of a bullpen "closer" who limits his opponents' scoring in the late innings; see Glossary for formula. Relief Runs will tend to benefit long and middle relievers, who are effective over many innings, while Relief Ranking will tend to benefit relievers with perhaps fewer innings but more saves and decisions.

Total Pitcher Index

Total Baseball Ranking   The "MVP" of statistics, this ranks pitchers and position players by the total runs contributed in all their endeavors, revealing the most valuable performers in a given year. For rare individuals like Babe Ruth in his Red Sox years, or Bob Caruthers, both of whom played a position in the field when they were not pitching, the TPR will sum up their records in both endeavors.

How to Read a Team Line

TEAM	G	W	L	PCT	GB	R	OR	AB	H	2B	3B	HR	BB	SO	AVG	OBP	SLG	PRO	PRO+	BR	/A	PF	CHI	RC	SB	CS	SBA	SBR
EAST																												
NY	160	100	60	.625		703	532	5408	1387	251	24	152	544	842	.256	.328	.396	.724	120	95	131	95	97	717	140	51	73	11
PIT	160	85	75	.531	15	651	616	5379	1327	240	45	110	553	947	.247	.321	.369	.690	105	33	42	99	99	648	119	60	66	0
MON	163	81	81	.500	20	628	592	5573	1400	260	48	107	454	1053	.251	.311	.373	.684	98	12	-18	105	97	636	189	89	68	3
CHI	163	77	85	.475	24	660	694	5675	1481	262	46	113	403	910	.261	.312	.383	.695	100	31	1	105	99	673	120	46	72	8
STL	162	76	86	.469	25	578	633	5518	1373	207	33	71	484	827	.249	.312	.337	.649	92	-47	-53	101	98	601	234	64	79	32
PHI	162	65	96	.404	35.5	597	734	5403	1294	246	31	106	489	981	.239	.308	.355	.663	94	-22	-35	102	100	599	112	49	70	4
WEST																												
LA	162	94	67	.584		628	544	5431	1346	217	25	99	437	947	.248	.308	.352	.660	99	-32	-14	97	107	590	131	46	74	12
CIN	161	87	74	.540	7	641	596	5426	1334	246	25	122	479	922	.246	.311	.368	.679	97	6	-19	104	102	639	207	56	79	29
SD	161	83	78	.516	11	594	583	5366	1325	205	35	94	494	892	.247	.313	.351	.664	99	-19	-8	98	99	594	123	50	71	7
SF	162	83	79	.512	11.5	670	626	5450	1353	227	44	113	550	1023	.248	.321	.368	.689	109	32	61	96	101	650	121	78	61	-11
HOU	162	82	80	.506	12.5	617	631	5494	1338	239	31	96	474	840	.244	.308	.351	.659	99	-32	-9	96	103	604	198	71	74	17
ATL	160	54	106	.338	39.5	555	741	5440	1319	228	28	96	432	848	.242	.301	.348	.649	88	-56	-84	105	99	549	95	69	58	-13
TOT	969					7522		65563	16277	2828	415	1279	5793	11032	.248	.313	.363	.675							1789	729	71	99

TEAM	CG	SH	SV	IP	H	H/G	HR	BB	SO	RAT	ERA	ERA+	OAV	OOB	PR	/A	PF	CPI	FA	E	DP	FW	PW	BW	SBW	DIF
EAST																										
NY	31	22	46	1439	1253	7.8	78	404	1100	10.6	2.91	111	.235	.293	86	50	93	97	.981	115	127	.9	5.4	14.1	.3	-.7
PIT	12	11	46	1440²	1349	8.4	108	469	790	11.6	3.47	98	.250	.314	-3	-10	99	101	.980	125	128	.3	-1.1	4.5	-.9	2.1
MON	18	12	43	1482²	1310	8.0	122	476	923	11.1	3.08	117	.238	.303	60	84	104	105	.978	142	145	-.5	9.1	-1.9	-.6	-6.0
CHI	30	10	29	1464¹	1494	9.2	115	490	897	12.4	3.84	94	.265	.327	-64	-38	105	102	.980	125	128	.5	-4.1	.1	-.0	-.4
STL	17	14	42	1470²	1387	8.5	91	486	881	11.6	3.47	100	.252	.314	-4	1	101	99	.981	121	131	.6	.1	-5.7	2.6	-2.6
PHI	16	6	36	1433	1447	9.1	118	628	859	13.3	4.14	86	.265	.344	-110	-92	103	102	.976	145	139	-.7	-9.9	-3.8	-.5	-.6
WEST																										
LA	32	24	49	1463¹	1291	7.9	84	473	1029	11.0	2.96	112	.237	.301	78	59	97	102	.977	142	126	-.5	6.4	-1.5	.4	8.8
CIN	24	13	43	1455	1271	7.9	121	504	934	11.1	3.35	107	.237	.306	16	38	104	98	.980	125	131	.4	4.1	-2.0	2.2	1.9
SD	30	9	39	1449	1332	8.3	112	439	885	11.1	3.28	104	.247	.306	27	19	99	102	.981	120	147	.6	2.0	-.9	-.1	.8
SF	25	13	42	1462¹	1323	8.1	99	422	875	10.9	3.39	96	.242	.300	10	-20	95	93	.980	129	145	.2	-2.2	6.6	-2.1	-.5
HOU	21	15	40	1474²	1339	8.2	123	478	1049	11.3	3.41	97	.242	.307	7	-14	96	99	.978	138	124	-.3	-1.5	-1.0	.9	2.9
ATL	14	4	25	1446	1481	9.2	108	524	810	12.7	4.09	90	.268	.336	-103	-67	107	100	.976	151	138	-1.1	-7.2	-9.1	-2.3	-6.3
TOT	270	153	480	17480²		8.4				11.6	3.45		.248	.313					.979	1578	1609					

The Los Angeles Dodgers had a miracle season in 1988, winning the National League pennant and the World Series against seemingly far superior opponents, the New York Mets and the Oakland Athletics, respectively. But their first miracle was to win the National League's Western Division title after finishing 73-89 in each of the previous two seasons. How did they win the West so easily? With mirrors, mostly, for they had below-average fielding and hitting that should have partially negated their outstanding pitching.

Let's just track the Dodgers' performance in some of the key categories to show how illuminating a close examination of team data in the Annual Record can be. The Dodgers' on base percentage (OBP) and slugging average (SLG) reveal them to have been a weak hitting club, though their Adjusted Production (PRO+) is a bit better, for they scored more runs in their park than might have been expected from the total run-scoring picture at Chavez Ravine (Park Factor 97). However, their Clutch Hitting Index (CHI) was the best in their division. Their Stolen Base Average was above average, but still only accounted for 12 extra runs over the course of the season, so this wasn't the secret of their success.

The pitching numbers are superlative—fewest runs allowed in the West and lowest ERA—despite the fact that Cincinnati held opponents to the same batting average (OAV) and San Francisco to the same on base percentage (OOB). Their Clutch Pitching Index (CPI) suggests that Dodgers hurlers pulled their belts a notch tighter when men were on base, and their Home Runs allowed (HR) gives another tip that they knew how to stay away from the big inning. And maybe all those Shutouts (SH) are indicative of the many games they won while scoring few runs themselves.

Look at their batting (which cost them 1.5 wins in the BW, or Batting Wins, column) and baserunning and fielding (which are a virtual wash at +0.4 and −0.5, respectively, in the SBW and FW columns), and notice that their pitching, good as it was, only supplied 6.4 wins beyond average (.500). On balance, then, their offense and defense combined to produce only five wins beyond average. They should have finished with a record of 86–76, or five games beyond the 81–81 league average. Instead they finished 94–67, eight wins beyond their expectations, as indicated in the Differential (DIF) column. Maybe it was manager Tommy Lasorda's doing after all.

March 17 The National Association of Professional Base Ball Players is formed in New York. Each club will play best-of-five series with the other clubs. The championship will be awarded to the team winning the most series against the other teams and not on a total wins or percentage basis. Teams represented are: Athletics of Philadelphia, Boston Red Stockings (who hired Harry Wright to represent them after the Cincinnati Reds disbanded); Chicago White Stockings, Eckford of Brooklyn, Forest Citys of Cleveland; Forest Citys of Rockford, Illinois, Atlantics of Brooklyn, Mutuals of New York, Nationals of Washington, D.C., Olympics of Washington, D.C., Kekiongas of Fort Wayne, Indiana, and the Union Club of Troy, New York, also known as the Haymakers.

April 29 The new ball grounds in Chicago, located at Randolph and Michigan on the lakefront, are opened as the White Stockings and a picked nine play before 1,500 people. The *New York Clipper* says: "They will have accommodations on their grounds to seat 6,500 people. With the single exception of being somewhat narrow, they will have one of the finest ballparks in the country."

May 4 The first National Association game is played at Fort Wayne, Indiana, between the Kekiongas and the Forest Citys of Cleveland. Bobby Mathews shuts out the Cleveland team, 2-0, one of only four shutouts in 1871.

May 8 The visiting Boston Reds demolish the Brooklyn Atlantics, 25–0, at Union Grounds, the single worst defeat the Brooklyn club will suffer in its brief history.

May 16 The first professional game ever played in Boston is played between the Red Stockings and the visiting Haymakers before 5,000. Boston has Harry Wright playing shortstop in place of his injured brother George. George will miss half the games played by the Reds, severely hampering their pennant chances. Troy wins, 29-14.

May 25 The heavily favored Mutuals are soundly defeated by the Haymakers of Troy, at a game played on Brooklyn's Union Grounds, 25–10. Troy's player-manager Lipman Pike collects six hits.

June 5 The eagerly awaited series opens between the White Stockings and the Mutuals before 10,000 at the Union Grounds in Brooklyn. Five of the old Eckfords play for Chicago while five of last year's Atlantics play for the Mutuals. Fielding decides the game, as Chicago makes 19 errors to "only" seven for the Mutuals. New York wins, 8–5.

July 6* An early baseball game between a black team and a white team takes place in Chicago, when the black Uniques beat the white Alerts, 17-16.

August 28 At the Union Grounds in Brooklyn, the Chicago White Stockings clinch the season's series with a 6–4 victory. The Whites could have insured a fifth and deciding game of the series played on their own grounds by losing today's game.

October 7 The Chicago Fire breaks out at 10 p.m. As the Rockford club travels toward Chicago the next day, they see the glow of the fire, turn around, and return home. Chicago loses its ballpark and equipment in the Fire. The Whites are leading in the pennant race and must defeat the Haymakers in their remaining three games to clinch.

October 30 The final championship match takes place on the Union Grounds in Brooklyn between the Athletics and the Chicago White Stockings. The Championship Committee decrees that today's game will decide the winner of the pennant. The 4-1 victory by the Athletics gives them the championship for 1871.

ATHLETICS		BOSTON		CHICAGO		CLEVELAND		KEKIONGAS	
M	D.McBride	M	H.Wright	M	J.Wood	M	C.Pabor	M	B.Lennon
1B	W.Fisler	1B	C.Gould	1B	B.McAtee	1B	J.Carleton	H.Deane
2B	A.Reach	2B	R.Barnes	2B	J.Wood	2B	G.Kimball	1B	J.Foran
SS	J.Radcliff	SS	G.Wright	SS	E.Duffy	SS	J.Bass	2B	T.Carey
3B	L.Meyerle	3B	H.Schafer	3B	E.Pinkham	3B	E.Sutton	SS	W.Goldsmith
LF	N.Cuthbert	LF	F.Cone	LF	F.Treacey	LF	C.Pabor	3B	F.Selman
CF	C.Sensenderfer	CF	H.Wright	CF	T.Foley	CF	A.Allison	LF	E.Mincher
RF	G.Heubel	RF	D.Birdsall	RF	J.Simmons	RF	E.White	CF	S.Armstrong
C	F.Malone	C	C.McVey	C	C.Hodes	C	D.White	RF	B.Kelly
								C	B.Lennon
O	G.Bechtel	O	F.Barrows	O	M.King	2	C.Johnson		
/1	T.Pratt	2	S.Jackson	/3	M.Brannock	/2	J.Quest	/O	P.Donnelly
/O	N.Berkenstock			P	G.Zettlein	/O	J.Battin	/S	J.Hallinan
/O	T.Berry	P	A.Spalding			/O	G.Ewell	/O	H.Deane
								/C	J.Quinn
P	D.McBride					P	A.Pratt	/C	H.Kohler
								/O	J.McDermott
								/C	B.Barrett
								/1	N.Phelps
								/1	C.Bierman
								P	B.Mathews

MUTUALS		OLYMPICS		ROCKFORD		TROY	
M	B.Ferguson	M	N.Young	M	S.Hastings	M	L.Pike
1B	J.Start	1B	E.Mills	1B	D.Mack	M	B.Craver
2B	D.Higham	2B	A.Leonard	2B	B.Addy	1B	C.Flynn
SS	D.Pearce	SS	D.Force	SS	C.Fulmer	2B	B.Craver
3B	B.Ferguson	3B	F.Waterman	3B	C.Anson	SS	D.Flowers
LF	J.Hatfield	LF	H.Berthrong	LF	R.Ham	3B	S.Bellan
CF	D.Eggler	CF	G.Hall	CF	G.Bird	LF	S.King
RF	D.Patterson	RF	J.Glenn	RF	G.Stires	CF	T.York
C	C.Mills	C	D.Allison	C	S.Hastings	RF	L.Pike
						C	M.McGeary
3	C.Smith	/O	H.Burroughs	/S	P.Sager		
		/O	T.Beals	/O	A.Barker	/1	N.Connor
P	R.Wolters	/2	C.Sweasy			/2	E.Beavens
		/2	W.White	P	C.Fisher	/S	D.Abercrombie
/P	F.Fleet	/3	F.Norton				
						P	J.McMullin
		P	A.Brainard				
		P	B.Stearns				

TEAM	G	W	L	PCT	GB	R	OR	AB	H	2B	3B	HR	BB	SO	AVG	OBP	SLG	PRO	PRO+	BR	/A	PF	CHI	RC	SB	CS	SBA	SBR
ATH	28	21	7	.750		376	266	1281	410	66	27	9	46	23	.320	.344	.435	.779	125	38	42	99	107	206	56	12	82	10
BOS	31	20	10	.667	2	401	303	1372	426	70	37	3	60	19	.310	.339	.422	.761	115	33	21	103	108	216	73	16	82	12
CHI	28	19	9	.679	2	302	241	1196	323	52	21	10	60	22	.270	.305	.374	.679	86	-7	-38	111	104	150	69	21	77	8
MUT	33	16	17	.485	7.5	302	313	1404	403	43	21	1	33	15	.287	.303	.350	.653	97	-20	8	91	94	159	46	15	75	5
OLY	32	15	15	.500	7	310	303	1353	375	54	26	6	48	13	.277	.302	.369	.671	98	-12	4	95	97	160	48	13	79	7
TRO	29	13	15	.464	8	351	362	1248	384	51	34	6	49	19	.308	.334	.417	.751	114	25	20	101	106	184	62	24	72	4
CLE	29	10	19	.345	11.5	249	341	1186	328	35	40	7	26	25	.277	.292	.391	.683	102	-7	8	95	89	136	18	8	69	1
KEK	19	7	12	.368	9.5	137	243	746	178	19	8	2	33	9	.239	.271	.294	.565	63	-34	-37	102	91	63	16	4	80	2
ROK	25	4	21	.160	15.5	231	287	1036	274	44	25	3	38	30	.264	.291	.364	.655	92	-16	-5	96	97	121	53	10	84	10
TOT	127					2659		10822	3101	434	239	47	393	175	.287	.312	.384	.695							441	123	78	59

TEAM	CG	SH	SV	IP	H	H/G	HR	BB	SO	RAT	ERA	ERA+	OAV	OOB	PR	/A	PF	CPI	FA	E	DP	FW	PW	BW	SBW	DIF
ATH	27	0	0	249	329	11.9	3	53	16	13.8	4.95	81	.284	.315	-20	-26	95	85	.845	194	13	1.1	-1.7	2.7	.2	4.6
BOS	22	1	3	276	367	12.0	2	42	23	13.3	3.55	117	.273	.296	20	18	99	101	.834	243	24	-.3	1.2	1.4	.4	2.4
CHI	25	0	1	251	308	11.0	6	28	22	12.0	2.76	166	.264	.281	41	51	109	121	.829	229	16	-.8	3.3	-2.5	.0	4.8
MUT	32	1	0	293	373	11.5	7	42	22	12.7	3.72	102	.271	.292	16	2	90	98	.840	235	14	1.0	.1	.5	-.0	-2.0
OLY	32	0	0	282	371	11.8	4	45	13	13.3	4.37	95	.281	.305	-5	-6	99	90	.850	218	20	1.5	-.4	.3	.0	-1.4
TRO	28	0	0	250	431	15.5	4	75	12	18.2	5.51	76	.342	.378	-36	-36	100	118	.845	198	22	1.3	-2.3	1.3	-.2	-1.1
CLE	23	0	0	254	346	12.3	13	53	34	14.1	4.11	100	.283	.312	3	0	98	107	.818	234	15	-.6	.0	.5	-.4	-4.0
KEK	19	1	0	169	261	13.9	5	21	17	15.0	5.17	88	.305	.322	-18	-11	108	93	.803	163	8	-.9	-.7	-2.4	-.3	1.8
ROK	23	1	0	226	315	13.9	3	34	16	13.9	4.30	95	.282	.303	-2	-5	97	91	.821	220	14	-1.5	-.3	-.3	.2	-6.6
TOT	231	4	4	2250		12.4				14.0	4.22		.287	.312					.833	1934	146					

Runs
Barnes-Bos 66
Birdsall-Bos 51
Radcliff-Ath 47
Cuthbert-Ath 47
Waterman-Oly 46

Hits
McVey-Bos 66
Meyerle-Ath....... 64
Barnes-Bos....... 63
Start-Mut 58
King-Tro 57

Doubles
Anson-Rok 11

Triples
Bass-Cle 10
Wolters-Mut 9
Barnes-Bos 9
Pratt-Cle 8

Home Runs
Treacey-Chi 4
Pike-Tro 4
Meyerle-Ath 4

Total Bases
Meyerle-Ath 91
Barnes-Bos 91
Pike-Tro 85
McVey-Bos 85
King-Tro 79

Runs Batted In
Wolters-Mut 44
McVey-Bos 43
Meyerle-Ath 40
Pike-Tro 39

Runs Produced
Barnes-Bos 100
McVey-Bos 86
Meyerle-Ath 81
King-Tro 79
Pike-Tro 78

Bases On Balls
Pinkham-Chi 18
H.Wright-Bos 13
Barnes-Bos 13
Wood-Chi 11

Batting Average
Meyerle-Ath 492
McVey-Bos 431
Barnes-Bos 401
King-Tro 396
Wood-Chi 378

On Base Percentage
Meyerle-Ath 500
G.Wright-Bos 453
Barnes-Bos 447
McVey-Bos 435
Wood-Chi........425

Slugging Average
Meyerle-Ath 700
Pike-Tro 654
Bass-Cle 640
Barnes-Bos 580
Treacey-Chi 573

Production
Meyerle-Ath 1.200
G.Wright-Bos 1.078
Pike-Tro 1.054
Barnes-Bos 1.027
McVey-Bos.......991

Adjusted Production
Meyerle-Ath........ 243
G.Wright-Bos 200
Pike-Tro 194
Wolters-Mut 189
Barnes-Bos 186

Batter Runs
Meyerle-Ath 22.6
Barnes-Bos 18.9
Pike-Tro 15.5
McVey-Bos 15.5
Wood-Chi 14.2

Adjusted Batter Runs
Meyerle-Ath 23.2
Wolters-Mut 17.2
Barnes-Bos.......17.0
Pike-Tro........14.9
McVey-Bos 13.9

Clutch Hitting Index
Goldsmith-Kek 169
Barrows-Bos 150
McMullin-Tro 149
Brainard-Oly 143
Fisher-Rok 137

Runs Created
Meyerle-Ath 49
Barnes-Bos 42
McVey-Bos 41
Wood-Chi 40
Pike-Tro 33

Total Average
Meyerle-Ath 1.470
G.Wright-Bos 1.306
Wood-Chi 1.198
Barnes-Bos 1.079
Pike-Tro........1.071

Stolen Bases
McGeary-Tro 20
Wood-Chi 18
Cuthbert-Ath 16
Leonard-Oly 14
Eggler-Mut 14

Stolen Base Average
Wood-Chi 90.0
Cuthbert-Ath 88.9
McGeary-Tro 83.3

Stolen Base Runs
Wood-Chi 4.2
McGeary-Tro 3.6
Mack-Rok 3.6
Cuthbert-Ath......3.6
Cone-Bos 3.0

Fielding Runs
Force-Oly 17.6
Barnes-Bos 13.4
Pinkham-Chi 9.4
Malone-Ath 9.1
Wood-Chi 8.6

Total Player Rating
Barnes-Bos 1.8
Force-Oly 1.3
Wood-Chi 1.3
G.Wright-Bos 1.1
McVey-Bos 1.0

Wins
Spalding-Bos 19
Zettlein-Chi 18
McBride-Ath 18
Wolters-Mut 16

Win Percentage
McBride-Ath .... .783
Zettlein-Chi .... .667
Spalding-Bos ...... .655
Wolters-Mut....... .500

Games
Wolters-Mut 32
Spalding-Bos 31
Brainard-Oly 30
McMullin-Tro 29

Complete Games
Wolters-Mut 31
Brainard-Oly 30
McMullin-Tro 28
Zettlein-Chi 25
McBride-Ath 25

Shutouts
Wolters-Mut......... 1
Spalding-Bos 1
Mathews-Kek 1
Fisher-Rok 1

Saves
H.Wright-Bos 3
Pinkham-Chi 1

Innings Pitched
Wolters-Mut 283.0
Brainard-Oly 264.0
Spalding-Bos ...257.1
McMullin-Tro 249.0
Zettlein-Chi 240.2

Fewest Hits/Game
Wolters-Mut 10.97
Zettlein-Chi 11.14
McBride-Ath 11.55
Spalding-Bos 11.65
Pratt-Cle 11.86

Fewest BB/Game
Zettlein-Chi 93
Mathews-Kek..... 1.12
Wolters-Mut 1.24
Brainard-Oly 1.26
Fisher-Rok 1.31

Strikeouts
Pratt-Cle 34
Spalding-Bos 23
Zettlein-Chi 22
Wolters-Mut 22
Mathews-Kek 17

Strikeouts/Game
Pratt-Cle 1.36
Mathews-Kek ..... .91
Zettlein-Chi ...... .82
Spalding-Bos ..... .80
Wolters-Mut .... .70

Ratio
Zettlein-Chi...... 12.08
Wolters-Mut 12.21
Spalding-Bos 12.98
McBride-Ath 13.18
Brainard-Oly 13.57

Earned Run Average
Zettlein-Chi 2.73
Spalding-Bos 3.36
Wolters-Mut 3.43
Pratt-Cle 3.77
Fisher-Rok 4.35

Adjusted ERA
Zettlein-Chi 168
Spalding-Bos 124
Wolters-Mut...... 110
Pratt-Cle 110
Fisher-Rok........ 94

Opponents' Batting Avg.
Wolters-Mut ...... .263
Zettlein-Chi ...... .267
Spalding-Bos ..... .268
Pratt-Cle .... .277
McBride-Ath ..... .280

Opponents' On Base Pct.
Zettlein-Chi........283
Wolters-Mut ...... .285
Spalding-Bos ..... .290
Fisher-Rok .... .302
McBride-Ath ..... .307

Starter Runs
Zettlein-Chi 39.8
Wolters-Mut 24.7
Spalding-Bos 24.7
Pratt-Cle 11.3
Stearns-Oly 3.4

Adjusted Starter Runs
Zettlein-Chi 49.7
Spalding-Bos 22.9
Wolters-Mut 11.2
Pratt-Cle 9.0
Stearns-Oly 3.3

Clutch Pitching Index
Zettlein-Chi....... 124
McMullin-Tro ... 118
Pratt-Cle 110
Spalding-Bos 101
Wolters-Mut 99

Relief Runs
Pinkham-Chi 8

Adjusted Relief Runs
Pinkham-Chi 1.3

Relief Ranking
Pinkham-Chi.......1.4

Total Pitcher Index
Zettlein-Chi 2.9
Wolters-Mut....... 1.9
Spalding-Bos 1.6
Pratt-Cle 1.0
Stearns-Oly 1

Total Baseball Ranking
Zettlein-Chi....... 2.8
Wolters-Mut 1.9
Barnes-Bos 1.8
Spalding-Bos 1.4
Force-Oly 1.3

March 4 The National Association of Professional Base Ball Players holds its annual convention in Cleveland. Eight clubs send delegates. Bob Ferguson, Atlantics infielder/manager, is elected president. Each team is required to play a series of five games with each club. Whoever wins the most games will be declared champion. The rules will now permit the snap of the wrist in pitching.

April 13 A gathering of Cincinnatians takes place on the old Union Grounds to witness the auction of the trophies of the famous Cincinnati Red Stockings Base Ball Club. Balls from the Reds' victories of 1869 and 1870 sell for an average of $2–$4 each.

May 29 The first game to be played in Chicago since the Great Fire is played on the new grounds of the Chicago Base Ball Association before an enthusiastic crowd of 4,000. Baltimore defeats Cleveland, 5-3.

June 15 During the Athletics-Atlantics game, Tom Barlow bunts the ball and reaches first safely. The New York *Clipper* describes the play: "After the first two strikers had been retired, Barlow, amid much laughter and applause, 'blocked' a ball in front of the home plate and reached first base before the ball did." That is one of only three hits off Dick McBride, as the Athletics win, 11–1.

July 26 The National Association holds a special meeting, resolving that, because some teams have dropped out of the race (Troy, Nationals, and Olympics), nine games will be played between contending teams this season instead of five.

August 19 After the defeat of the Forest Citys of Cleveland by Boston, 18-7, at Cleveland, the club disbands. There are now only six clubs left playing for the pennant.

September 1 Albert Thake, 22-year-old left fielder of the Brooklyn Atlantics, drowns off Fort Hamilton, in New York Harbor, while fishing. A benefit game is arranged by Bob Ferguson between the old Brooklyn Atlantics and members of the 1869 Cincinnati Red Stockings.

September 14 An unusual play highlights the Athletics-Boston match in Philadelphia. With the Athletics leading, 4–1, in the seventh inning, and runners on first and second, Fergy Malone pops up to shortstop George Wright. Wright catches the ball in his hat and then throws the ball to third base after which it is thrown to second base. Wright claims a double play has been completed, as a batter cannot be retired with a "hat catch," and thus runners Cap Anson and Bob Reach are forced out. The umpire finally gives Malone another at-bat, declaring nobody out. The Athletics win, 6–4.

October 8 The "Grand Base Ball Tournament" begins, a series of games played on the Union Grounds in Brooklyn among the three major professional clubs: Mutuals, Athletics, and the Reds of Boston. First prize will be $1,800. Today's game ends in a tie: Mutuals 7, Boston 7. The tournament will end October 17 with Philadelphia and Boston splitting the prize money.

October 22 The Boston Red Stockings win the championship of the season, winning their 39th game by defeating the Eckfords, 4-3.

ATHLETICS		ATLANTICS		BALTIMORE		BOSTON		CLEVELAND		ECKFORDS	
M	D.McBride	M	B.Ferguson	M	B.Craver	M	H.Wright	M	S.Hastings	M	A.Allison
1B	D.Mack	1B	H.Dehlman	M	E.Mills	1B	C.Gould	M	D.White	M	J.Wood
2B	W.Fisler	2B	J.Hall	1B	E.Mills	2B	R.Barnes	1B	J.Simmons	M	P.Martin
SS	M.McGeary	SS	J.Burdock	2B	T.Carey	SS	G.Wright	2B	C.Sweasy	1B	A.Allison
3B	C.Anson	3B	B.Ferguson	SS	J.Radcliff	3B	H.Schafer	SS	J.Holdsworth	2B	C.Nelson
LF	N.Cuthbert	LF	A.Thake	3B	D.Force	LF	A.Leonard	3B	E.Sutton	SS	Ja.Snyder
CF	F.Treacey	CF	J.Remsen	LF	T.York	CF	H.Wright	LF	C.Pabor	3B	J.Clinton
RF	L.Meyerle	RF	J.McDonald	CF	G.Hall	RF	F.Rogers	CF	A.Allison	LF	C.Gedney
C	F.Malone	C	T.Barlow	RF	L.Pike	C	C.McVey	RF	R.Wolters	CF	D.Patterson
				C	B.Craver			C	D.White	RF	D.Hunt
O	A.Reach	O	E.Booth			C	D.Birdsall			C	D.Allison
/S	D.Flowers	2	E.Beavens	CO	D.Higham			C	S.Hastings		
/O	C.Sensenderfer	/O	Barrett	C	S.Hastings	P	A.Spalding	/1	J.Carleton	3	F.Fleet
		/2	C.Lowe					/O	Mullen	/3	M.Swandell
P	D.McBride	/O	H.Doscher	P	B.Mathews					/O	Ji.Snyder
		/2	J.Kenney	P	C.Fisher			P	A.Pratt	/2	J.Wood
		/O	O.Brown					P	R.Wolters	/1	Kavanaugh
		/O	S.Jackson							/1	B.Allison
		/O	J.Bass							/2	A.Martin
		/2	D.Clare							/C	Bestick
		/O	H.Worth							/C	Leutz
		/2	J.Galvin							/O	G.Fletcher
		/O	Higby							/C	N.Jewett
										/S	J.Holdsworth
		P	J.Britt							/S	McDonald
										P	P.Martin
										P	G.Zettlein
										P	J.McDermott
										P	M.Malone
										/P	O'Rourke

MANSFIELDS		MUTUALS		NATIONALS		OLYMPICS		TROY	
M	J.Clapp	M	D.Pearce	M	W.White	M	F.Waterman	M	J.Wood
1B	T.Murnane	M	J.Hatfield	1B	P.Hines	1B	C.Flynn	1B	B.McAtee
2B	E.Booth	1B	J.Start	2B	H.Hollingshead	2B	T.Beals	2B	J.Wood
SS	J.O'Rourke	2B	J.Hatfield	SS	J.Doyle	SS	W.Goldsmith	SS	S.Bellan
3B	G.Fields	SS	D.Pearce	3B	W.White	3B	F.Waterman	3B	D.Force
LF	J.Tipper	3B	B.Boyd	LF	E.Mincher	LF	J.Glenn	LF	S.King
CF	F.McCarton	LF	J.McMullin	CF	S.Studley	CF	G.Heubel	CF	C.Gedney
RF	C.Bentley	CF	D.Eggler	RF	O.Bielaski	RF	V.Robinson	RF	P.Martin
C	J.Clapp	RF	G.Bechtel	C	B.Lennon	C	F.Selman	C	D.Allison
		C	N.Hicks						
OP	F.Buttery			O1	D.Coughlin	/S	B.Reach	/S	C.Hodes
OS	H.Allen	3S	C.Fulmer	/O	J.Glenn	/O	H.Burroughs	/O	C.Nelson
/2	A.Brainard	/O	C.Mills	/1	J.Miller	/O	D.Hurley	/O	M.King
/O	B.Arnold			/S	Spencer	/C	B.Barrett		
		P	C.Cummings	/O	B.Yeatman			P	G.Zettlein
P	C.Bentley					P	A.Brainard		
				P	B.Stearns				

TEAM	G	W	L	PCT	GB	R	OR	AB	H	2B	3B	HR	BB	SO	AVG	OBP	SLG	PRO	PRO+	BR	/A	PF	CHI	RC	SB	CS	SBA	SBR
BOS	48	39	8	.830		521	236	2122	672	106	30	7	29	26	.317	.326	.405	.731	120	61	34	105	100	293	47	14	77	6
BAL	58	35	19	.648	7.5	617	434	2576	752	105	30	14	27	28	.292	.299	.372	.671	103	22	-4	105	107	294	36	18	67	0
MUT	56	34	20	.630	8.5	523	362	2431	674	85	12	4	55	52	.277	.293	.327	.620	99	-18	15	94	102	241	58	21	73	5
ATH	47	30	14	.682	7.5	539	349	2141	679	79	25	4	69	47	.317	.338	.383	.721	124	60	58	100	102	287	58	31	65	-1
TRO	25	15	10	.600	13	273	191	1098	330	58	8	5	7	14	.301	.305	.382	.687	111	15	11	101	109	127	9	7	56	-2
ATL	37	9	28	.243	25	237	473	1460	374	37	10	0	19	24	.256	.266	.295	.561	64	-41	-89	117	87	117	19	14	58	-3
CLE	22	6	16	.273	20.5	174	254	943	272	28	5	0	17	13	.288	.301	.329	.630	102	-4	7	95	97	96	12	3	80	2
MAN	24	5	19	.208	22.5	220	348	1022	294	29	9	1	5	12	.288	.291	.337	.628	101	-6	6	94	103	100	5	3	63	0
ECK	29	3	26	.103	27	152	413	1070	241	24	6	0	14	29	.225	.235	.259	.494	64	-55	-30	85	86	66	8	4	67	0
OLY	9	2	7	.222	18	54	140	365	91	10	3	0	4	4	.249	.257	.293	.550	75	-12	-9	95	81	26	0	3	0	-2
NAT	11	0	11	.0	21	80	190	451	108	6	1	0	1	3	.239	.241	.257	.498	47	-22	-35	117	108	29				
TOT	183					3390		15679	4487	567	139	35	247	252	.286	.297	.347	.644							252	118	68	5

TEAM	CG	SH	SV	IP	H	H/G	HR	BB	SO	RAT	ERA	ERA+	OAV	OOB	PR	/A	PF	CPI	FA	E	DP	FW	PW	BW	SBW	DIF
BOS	41	4	4	430¹	443	9.3	0	27	28	9.8	1.88	194	.243	.254	84	85	100	124	.876	278	43	4.5	5.9	2.4	.4	2.3
BAL	48	1	1	516	573	10.0	3	63	75	11.1	2.90	127	.245	.264	43	44	101	85	.829	432	22	.4	3.1	-.3	-.0	4.8
MUT	54	3	1	512	623	11.0	2	32	44	11.5	2.99	113	.272	.282	37	22	93	105	.867	326	33	5.2	1.5	1.0	.3	-1.0
ATH	47	1	0	419¹	508	10.9	3	26	44	11.5	2.85	124	.265	.275	37	32	98	103	.858	298	20	3.1	2.2	4.0	-.0	-1.2
TRO	17	2	1	225	277	11.1	2	10	18	11.5	2.60	140	.265	.276	26	26	100	117	.859	154	9	1.9	1.8	.8	-.2	-1.8
ATL	37	0	0	336	570	15.3	6	19	13	15.8	4.34	104	.328	.335	-26	-26	124	117	.810	358	14	-4.0	1.4	-6.2	-.2	.5
CLE	15	0	0	199	285	12.9	6	24	11	14.0	5.74	62	.290	.307	-47	-48	98	70	.816	184	17	-.9	-3.3	.5	.1	-1.4
MAN	21	0	0	211	373	15.9	5	14	5	16.5	5.67	63	.332	.340	-48	-49	99	94	.806	224	8	-2.2	-3.4	.4	-.0	-1.8
ECK	28	0	0	259¹	494	17.1	6	24	11	18.0	5.52	61	.348	.358	-54	-61	93	109	.797	284	5	-3.3	-4.2	-2.1	-.0	-1.8
OLY	9	0	0	79	148	16.9	0	5	1	17.4	6.38	56	.333	.341	-24	-24	99	82	.786	96	7	-1.4	-1.7	-.6	-.2	1.4
NAT	11	0	0	99	193	17.5	2	3	2	17.8	6.18	75	.339	.343	-28	-17	127	90	.774	120	2	-1.9	-1.2	-2.4	-.0	.0
TOT	328	11	7	3286		12.3				13.0	3.64		.286	.297					.836	2754	180					

Runs
Eggler-Mut 94
G.Wright-Bos 87
Cuthbert-Ath 83
Barnes-Bos 81
Hatfield-Mut 76

Hits
Barnes-Bos 99
Eggler-Mut 98
Force-Tro-Bal 94
Hatfield-Mut 92
Anson-Ath 90

Doubles
Barnes-Bos 28
Eggler-Mut 20
Hall-Bal 17
G.Wright-Bos 16

Triples
Gould-Bos 8
Anson-Ath 7
G.Wright-Bos 6
Hall-Bal 6

Home Runs
Pike-Bal 6
Gedney-Tro-Eck 3

Total Bases
Barnes-Bos 134
Pike-Bal 127
G.Wright-Bos 120
Eggler-Mut 118
Hall-Bal 116

Runs Batted In
Pike-Bal 60
Start-Mut 50
Anson-Ath 50
Fisler-Ath 48

Runs Produced
Cuthbert-Ath 129
Barnes-Bos 124
Pike-Bal 121
Hatfield-Mut 120
G.Wright-Bos 117

Bases On Balls
Mack-Ath 23
Anson-Ath 16
McMullin-Mut 11

Batting Average
Barnes-Bos ...... .432
Force-Tro-Bal ... .418
Anson-Ath .... .415
Hastings-Cle-Bal .362
McGeary-Ath ..... .360

On Base Percentage
Anson-Ath .... .455
Barnes-Bos ...... .454
Force-Tro-Bal ... .423
Hastings-Cle-Bal .376
McGeary-Ath ..... .366

Slugging Average
Barnes-Bos ...... .585
Anson-Ath .... .525
Wood-Tro-Eck .... .503
Force-Tro-Bal ... .493
Meyerle-Ath ..... .486

Production
Barnes-Bos 1.039
Anson-Ath .... .980
Force-Tro-Bal ... .916
Wood-Tro-Eck .... .839
G.Wright-Bos .... .816

Adjusted Production
Barnes-Bos 206
Anson-Ath 200
Force-Tro-Bal 176
Wood-Tro-Eck 158
Meyerle-Ath 147

Batter Runs
Barnes-Bos 30.8
Anson-Ath 26.0
Force-Tro-Bal ... 20.5
G.Wright-Bos 13.7
Hall-Bal 12.8

Adjusted Batter Runs
Barnes-Bos 26.6
Anson-Ath 25.7
Force-Tro-Bal ... 18.6
Eggler-Mut 16.2
Hatfield-Mut 12.6

Clutch Hitting Index
Start-Mut 168
White-Cle 150
Zettlein-Tro-Eck . 144
Cuthbert-Ath 135
Boyd-Mut 135

Runs Created
Barnes-Bos 65
Anson-Ath 52
Force-Tro-Bal 49
Eggler-Mut 47
G.Wright-Bos 45

Total Average
Barnes-Bos 1.133
Anson-Ath .... .963
Force-Tro-Bal ... .866
Wood-Tro-Eck .... .828
G.Wright-Bos .... .769

Stolen Bases
Eggler-Mut 18
G.Wright-Bos 14
Cuthbert-Ath 14
McGeary-Ath 13

Stolen Base Average
Eggler-Mut 78.3

Stolen Base Runs
Eggler-Mut 2.4
Barnes-Bos 2.4
Bechtel-Mut 2.1

Fielding Runs
Ferguson-Atl 36.3
Barnes-Bos 25.4
G.Wright-Bos 21.8
Eggler-Mut 15.4
York-Bal 10.5

Total Player Rating
Barnes-Bos 3.4
Eggler-Mut 2.5
G.Wright-Bos 2.3
Ferguson-Atl 1.7
Force-Tro-Bal 1.7

Wins
Spalding-Bos 38
Cummings-Mut 33
McBride-Ath 30
Mathews-Bal 25
Zettlein-Tro-Eck .. 15

Win Percentage
Spalding-Bos .... .826
McBride-Ath ..... .682
Cummings-Mut .... .623
Mathews-Bal ..... .581
Zettlein-Tro-Eck .500

Games
Cummings-Mut 55
Mathews-Bal 49
Spalding-Bos 48
McBride-Ath 47
Britt-Atl 37

Complete Games
Cummings-Mut 53
McBride-Ath 47
Spalding-Bos 41
Mathews-Bal 39
Britt-Atl 37

Shutouts
Spalding-Bos 3
Cummings-Mut 3
Zettlein-Tro-Eck ... 2
McBride-Ath 1
Fisher-Bal 1

Saves
H.Wright-Bos 4
Zettlein-Tro-Eck ... 1
McMullin-Mut 1
Fisher-Bal 1

Innings Pitched
Cummings-Mut ... 497.0
McBride-Ath 419.1
Mathews-Bal 406.0
Spalding-Bos ... 404.2
Britt-Atl 336.0

Fewest Hits/Game
Fisher-Bal 7.61
Spalding-Bos 9.27
Mathews-Bal 10.64
Zettlein-Tro-Eck 10.71
McBride-Ath 10.90

Fewest BB/Game
Stearns-Nat ...... .27
Buttery-Man ...... .33
P.Martin-Tro-Eck . .44
Zettlein-Tro-Eck . .48
Britt-Atl .... .51

Strikeouts
Mathews-Bal 55
McBride-Ath 44
Cummings-Mut 43
Spalding-Bos 27
Zettlein-Tro-Eck .. 25

Strikeouts/Game
Fisher-Bal 1.64
Mathews-Bal 1.22
McBride-Ath ...... .94
Zettlein-Tro-Eck . .86
Cummings-Mut ..... .78

Ratio
Fisher-Bal 8.51
Spalding-Bos 9.87
Zettlein-Tro-Eck 11.19
McBride-Ath 11.46
Cummings-Mut ... 11.50

Earned Run Average
Fisher-Bal 1.80
Spalding-Bos 1.87
Zettlein-Tro-Eck . 2.33
McBride-Ath 2.85
Cummings-Mut 2.97

Adjusted ERA
Fisher-Bal 204
Spalding-Bos 195
Zettlein-Tro-Eck . 153
McBride-Ath 124
Mathews-Bal 115

Opponents' Batting Avg.
Fisher-Bal .... .197
Spalding-Bos ..... .244
Mathews-Bal ...... .257
McBride-Ath ...... .265
Zettlein-Tro-Eck .265

Opponents' On Base Pct.
Fisher-Bal .... .216
Spalding-Bos ..... .255
Zettlein-Tro-Eck .274
McBride-Ath ...... .275
Mathews-Bal ...... .277

Starter Runs
Spalding-Bos 79.7
Zettlein-Tro-Eck . 38.4
Cummings-Mut 37.0
McBride-Ath 36.6
Fisher-Bal 22.5

Adjusted Starter Runs
Spalding-Bos 80.2
Zettlein-Tro-Eck . 36.2
McBride-Ath 32.4
Fisher-Bal 22.8
Cummings-Mut 22.1

Clutch Pitching Index
Zettlein-Tro-Eck . 127
Spalding-Bos 126
Britt-Atl 117
P.Martin-Tro-Eck . 115
Buttery-Man 109

Relief Runs
H.Wright-Bos 4.4

Adjusted Relief Runs
H.Wright-Bos 4.4

Relief Ranking
H.Wright-Bos 3.1

Total Pitcher Index
Spalding-Bos 7.8
McBride-Ath 2.7
Zettlein-Tro-Eck .. 2.5
Fisher-Bal 1.5
Cummings-Mut 9

Total Baseball Ranking
Spalding-Bos 7.6
Barnes-Bos 3.4
McBride-Ath 2.7
Eggler-Mut 2.5
Zettlein-Tro-Eck .. 2.5

March 3 Delegates from the existing professional clubs of the country assemble in Baltimore to establish a permanent Professional Association. A constitution is adopted along with Henry Chadwick's code of rules. For the first time a uniform ball must be used in all games.

May 5 Two thousand spectators pay 50¢ at the Union Grounds in Brooklyn and watch Baltimore play the Mutuals. Baltimore scores three in the first inning without a base hit and wins, 6–1.

June 11 The largest crowd of the year, 10,000, jams the Jefferson Street Grounds at 25th Street and Jefferson to see the Athletics play the Philadelphias. The Philadelphias score five runs in the seventh to win, 7–5.

June 14 In Boston, 2,000 spectators watch the Reds suffer a shutout for the first time in their history. Dick McBride of the Athletics holds the champions to only two hits.

July 4 The Resolutes of Elizabeth, New Jersey, upset the Red Stockings, 11–2, in a morning game. The afternoon game is close for six innings but Boston scores five runs in the seventh, two in the eighth, and 21 in the ninth to roll to a 32–3 win.

July 10 In Philadelphia, 3,000 people see the Philadelphias, favorites for this year's pennant, and Boston, last year's champions, play a wild game with the home team winning, 18–17. The teams have decided to cut short the number of games they will play in August due to poor attendance during that month.

July 21 One thousand people witness an extraordinary game in Philadelphia between the Athletics and the Lord Baltimores. Lipman Pike's three-base hit and Tom York's groundout tie the game at the end of nine innings. The Athletics' three runs in the top of the 10th and two in the top of the 11th are matched by Baltimore, and it is not until the 13th that Everett Mills scores the winning run for the Baltimores on John Radcliffe's hit, winning, 12–11.

July 24 Brooklyn's Bob Ferguson umpires a close game between the Mutuals and the Baltimores that ends in a three-run rally by the Mutes in the last of the ninth to win, 11–10. A police escort is needed to get the umpire to the clubhouse. Nat Hicks of the Mutuals and Ferguson get into an altercation, the end result of which is the striking of Hicks's left arm with a bat wielded by the umpire. The men are reconciled after the game, but Hicks's arm is broken in two places, and he will not play for the next two months.

July 30 The Philadelphia Athletics play their first game in three weeks after spending a holiday at Cape May, New Jersey, to rest from the rigors of the season. They are roughly handled at Boston, with the Reds defeating them, 24–10.

August 16 At Baltimore's Newington Park, Baltimore outfielder Lipman Pike races against a horse named "Clarence." Pike has a short lead after 75 yards when the trotter breaks into a run. Pike holds on to win in 10 seconds flat.

October 22 The Boston Red Stockings clinch the pennant for 1873 by defeating the Washington Nationals, 11–8, in Washington. George Wright leads the attack with a triple and two singles.

November 6 The first game under the proposed new rule of 10 men and 10 innings is played between the Athletics and the Phillies as a benefit for Ned Cuthbert. The majority present thought the 10th man (a so-called "right shortstop") was an unnecessary innovation.

	ATHLETICS		ATLANTICS		BALTIMORE		BOSTON		MARYLANDS
M	D.McBride	M	B.Ferguson	M	C.McVey	M	H.Wright	M	B.Smith
1B	C.Anson	1B	H.Dehlman	M	T.Carey	1B	J.O'Rourke	1B	B.Lennon
2B	W.Fisler	2B	J.Burdock	1B	E.Mills	2B	R.Barnes	2B	M.Simpson
SS	M.McGeary	SS	D.Pearce	2B	T.Carey	SS	G.Wright	SS	L.Say
3B	E.Sutton	3B	B.Ferguson	SS	J.Radcliff	3B	H.Schafer	3B	H.Kohler
LF	J.McMullin	LF	C.Pabor	3B	D.Force	LF	A.Leonard	LF	M.Hooper
CF	T.Murnane	CF	J.Remsen	LF	T.York	CF	H.Wright	CF	J.Smith
RF	C.Fisher	RF	B.Boyd	CF	G.Hall	RF	B.Addy	RF	B.French
C	J.Clapp	C	T.Barlow	RF	L.Pike	C	D.White	C	B.Smith
				C	C.McVey				
O	C.Sensenderfer	O	E.Booth			1	J.Manning	/O	J.Sheppard
/2	A.Reach	/O	H.Doscher	CS	B.Craver	/O	D.Birdsall	/2	J.Kernan
/O	J.Battin	/1	H.Kessler	CO	S.Hastings	/1	F.Rogers	/S	R.Woodhead
				/S	B.Barrett	/2	C.Sweasy	/2	W.Goldsmith
P	D.McBride	P	J.Britt					/O	T.Johns
				P	C.Cummings	P	A.Spalding	/O	Jones
				P	A.Brainard			/S	G.Popplein
								/O	Eland
								P	E.Stratton
								P	F.Selman
								P	Mc Doolan

	MUTUALS		PHILADELPHIA		RESOLUTES		WASHINGTON
M	J.Hatfield	M	F.Malone	M	D.Allison	M	N.Young
M	J.Start	1B	D.Mack	1B	M.Campbell	1B	J.Glenn
1B	J.Start	2B	J.Wood	2B	B.Laughlin	2B	T.Beals
2B	C.Nelson	SS	C.Fulmer	SS	F.Wordsworth	SS	J.Gerhardt
SS	J.Holdsworth	3B	L.Meyerle	3B	A.Nevin	3B	W.White
3B	J.Hatfield	LF	N.Cuthbert	LF	E.Booth	LF	P.Hines
LF	C.Gedney	CF	F.Treacey	CF	A.Allison	CF	H.Hollingshead
CF	D.Eggler	RF	G.Bechtel	RF	H.Austin	RF	O.Bielaski
RF	P.Martin	C	F.Malone	C	D.Allison	C	P.Snyder
C	N.Hicks						
		1	J.Devlin	2S	F.Fleet	S2	J.Donnelly
O2	D.Higham	2	B.Addy	/C	J.Farrow	/S	F.Waterman
C	D.Allison	/1	J.Ryan	/3	J.Clinton	/O	E.Atkinson
/3	S.Bellan			/1	M.Swandell	/S	B.Reach
/1	N.Phelps	P	G.Zettlein	/2	F.Crane	/S	H.Wall
P	B.Mathews			P	H.Campbell	P	B.Stearns
						P	Greyson
				/P	L.Lovett		
				/P	R.Wolters		

TEAM	G	W	L	PCT	GB	R	OR	AB	H	2B	3B	HR	BB	SO	AVG	OBP	SLG	PRO	PRO+	BR	/A	PF	CHI	RC	SB	CS	SBA	SBR
BOS	60	43	16	.729		739	460	2755	930	146	44	12	62	24	.338	.352	.436	.788	128	122	64	108	105	428	39	27	59	-5
PHI	53	36	17	.679	4	526	396	2325	645	83	20	8	62	39	.277	.296	.341	.637	91	-17	-35	104	110	243	44	14	76	5
BAL	57	34	22	.607	7.5	644	451	2562	810	106	38	9	41	25	.316	.327	.398	.725	121	57	60	100	108	340	22	11	67	0
MUT	53	29	24	.547	11	424	385	2214	622	51	36	5	42	22	.281	.294	.343	.637	94	-16	-13	99	94	227	15	6	71	1
ATH	52	28	23	.549	11	474	403	2266	683	71	20	4	35	32	.301	.312	.356	.668	96	8	-28	108	98	251	29	24	55	-6
ATL	55	17	37	.315	23.5	366	549	2210	588	42	23	6	53	43	.266	.283	.314	.597	92	-46	-2	89	87	198	19	11	63	-1
WAS	39	8	31	.205	25	283	485	1563	408	38	19	2	19	33	.261	.270	.313	.583	80	-41	-32	97	99	132	5	5	50	-2
RES	23	2	21	.87	23	98	299	868	204	18	8	0	8	22	.235	.242	.274	.516	62	-43	-33	92	71	58	5	2	67	0
MAR	6	0	6	.0	16.5	26	152	211	33	1	0	0	0	3	.156	.156	.161	.317	-4	-25	-22	77	139	5				
TOT	199					3580		16974	4923	556	208	46	322	243	.290	.303	.355	.659							175	99	64	-7

TEAM	CG	SH	SV	IP	H	H/G	HR	BB	SO	RAT	ERA	ERA+	OAV	OOB	PR	/A	PF	CPI	FA	E	DP	FW	PW	BW	SBW	DIF
BOS	47	1	6	536	708	11.9	5	35	31	12.5	2.59	128	.287	.297	40	44	102	118	.838	465	46	.8	3.1	4.5	-.3	5.4
PHI	50	0	0	481	627	11.7	3	44	28	12.6	2.77	119	.284	.298	26	28	101	110	.848	379	43	2.3	2.0	-2.5	.4	7.3
BAL	55	1	0	508²	680	12.0	4	42	37	12.8	3.01	108	.285	.297	14	14	100	101	.855	366	33	4.6	1.0	4.2	.0	-3.9
MUT	48	2	0	477	539	10.2	5	69	76	11.5	2.62	121	.254	.278	33	29	97	88	.821	419	28	.3	2.1	-.9	.1	1.0
ATH	44	3	2	475	553	10.5	4	58	41	11.6	3.03	113	.257	.276	12	20	105	75	.842	383	30	1.7	1.4	-2.0	-.4	1.7
ATL	52	1	0	500	737	13.3	8	42	15	14.0	3.98	76	.303	.315	-40	-52	93	93	.820	505	30	-3.3	-3.7	-.1	-.0	-2.9
WAS	39	0	0	346	593	14.9	10	22	7	16.0	4.71	113	.335	.343	-56	-52	103	103	.818	334	27	-1.1	-3.7	-2.3	-.0	-4.4
RES	22	0	0	207	342	14.9	6	9	8	15.3	3.22	104	.310	.316	1	3	103	123	.787	247	9	-3.2	-2.3	-2.3	.0	-4.2
MAR	6	0	0	54	144	24.0	1	1	0	24.2	8.00	40	.393	.395	-28	-29	100	97	.761	74	0	-1.3	-2.1	-1.6	.0	1.9
TOT	363	8	8	3584²		12.4				13.2	3.25		.290	.303					.831	3172	246					

Runs
Barnes-Bos	125
G.Wright-Bos	99
Spalding-Bos	83
Eggler-Mut	82
Leonard-Bos	81

Hits
Barnes-Bos	137
G.Wright-Bos	126
White-Bos	121
Spalding-Bos	106
Anson-Ath	101

Doubles
Barnes-Bos	29
G.Wright-Bos	19
O'Rourke-Bos	19
Mills-Bal	19
Carey-Bal	19

Triples
Mills-Bal	9
G.Wright-Bos	8
Pike-Bal	8
Holdsworth-Mut	8
Barnes-Bos	8

Home Runs
Pike-Bal	4
G.Wright-Bos	3
Meyerle-Phi	3

Total Bases
Barnes-Bos	188
G.Wright-Bos	170
White-Bos	148
Pike-Bal	132
Spalding-Bos	131

Runs Batted In
White-Bos	66
Barnes-Bos	62
Leonard-Bos	61
Spalding-Bos	60
Meyerle-Phi	58

Runs Produced
Barnes-Bos	185
G.Wright-Bos	146
White-Bos	145
Spalding-Bos	142
Leonard-Bos	142

Bases On Balls
Barnes-Bos	18
Mack-Phi	15
O'Rourke-Bos	14
Malone-Phi	14

Batting Average
Barnes-Bos	.425
Anson-Ath	.398
White-Bos	.390
G.Wright-Bos	.388
McVey-Bal	.380

On Base Percentage
Barnes-Bos	.456
Anson-Ath	.409
G.Wright-Bos	.402
Force-Bal	.391
White-Bos	.390

Slugging Average
Barnes-Bos	.584
G.Wright-Bos	.523
McVey-Bal	.484
Meyerle-Phi	.479
White-Bos	.477

Production
Barnes-Bos	1.040
G.Wright-Bos	.925
McVey-Bal	.874
White-Bos	.868
Anson-Ath	.858

Adjusted Production
Barnes-Bos	191
G.Wright-Bos	160
McVey-Bal	159
Pabor-Atl	153
White-Bos	144

Batter Runs
Barnes-Bos	41.9
G.Wright-Bos	28.1
White-Bos	20.4
Anson-Ath	16.8
O'Rourke-Bos	15.9

Adjusted Batter Runs
Barnes-Bos	32.8
G.Wright-Bos	20.3
Pabor-Atl	16.4
White-Bos	13.5
McVey-Bal	13.5

Clutch Hitting Index
Cummings-Bal	168
McBride-Ath	156
Donnelly-Was	136
Hollingshead-Was	131
Addy-Phi-Bos	131

Runs Created
Barnes-Bos	91
G.Wright-Bos	69
White-Bos	61
O'Rourke-Bos	49
Pike-Bal	47

Total Average
Barnes-Bos	1.132
G.Wright-Bos	.863
McVey-Bal	.808
White-Bos	.796
Meyerle-Phi	.771

Stolen Bases
Cuthbert-Phi	13
Barnes-Bos	13
McMullin-Ath	9
Wood-Phi	8
Pike-Bal	8

Stolen Base Average

Stolen Base Runs
Cuthbert-Phi	2.7
McMullin-Ath	2.1
Pike-Bal	1.8

Fielding Runs
Ferguson-Atl	31.5
Barnes-Bos	19.9
Fulmer-Phi	18.5
Gedney-Mut	14.6
G.Wright-Bos	14.5

Total Player Rating
Barnes-Bos	3.4
G.Wright-Bos	2.2
Ferguson-Atl	1.8
York-Bal	1.2
Mills-Bal	1.1

Wins
Spalding-Bos	41
Zettlein-Phi	36
Mathews-Mut	29
Cummings-Bal	28
McBride-Ath	24

Win Percentage
Spalding-Bos	.745
Zettlein-Phi	.706
Cummings-Bal	.667
McBride-Ath	.558
Mathews-Mut	.558

Games
Spalding-Bos	60
Britt-Atl	54
Mathews-Mut	52
Zettlein-Phi	51
McBride-Ath	46

Complete Games
Britt-Atl	51
Zettlein-Phi	49
Spalding-Bos	47
Mathews-Mut	47
Cummings-Bal	42

Shutouts
McBride-Ath	3
Mathews-Mut	2
Spalding-Bos	1
Cummings-Bal	1
Britt-Atl	1

Saves
H.Wright-Bos	4
Spalding-Bos	2
Fisher-Ath	2

Innings Pitched
Spalding-Bos	497.2
Britt-Atl	480.2
Zettlein-Phi	460.0
Mathews-Mut	443.0
McBride-Ath	382.2

Fewest Hits/Game
Fisher-Ath	9.60
Mathews-Mut	9.93
McBride-Ath	10.65
Cummings-Bal	11.19
Zettlein-Phi	11.60

Fewest BB/Game
H.Campbell-Res	.38
Stearns-Was	.48
Spalding-Bos	.51
Brainard-Bal	.75
Britt-Atl	.75

Strikeouts
Mathews-Mut	75
Cummings-Bal	34
Spalding-Bos	31
Zettlein-Phi	28
McBride-Ath	25

Strikeouts/Game
Mathews-Mut	1.52
Fisher-Ath	1.49
Cummings-Bal	.80
McBride-Ath	.59
Spalding-Bos	.56

Ratio
Fisher-Ath	10.67
Mathews-Mut	11.19
McBride-Ath	11.76
Cummings-Bal	11.97
Spalding-Bos	12.13

Earned Run Average
Fisher-Ath	1.81
Spalding-Bos	2.46
Mathews-Mut	2.56
Cummings-Bal	2.66
Zettlein-Phi	2.70

Adjusted ERA
Fisher-Ath	188
Spalding-Bos	135
Mathews-Mut	124
Cummings-Bal	122
Zettlein-Phi	122

Opponents' Batting Avg.
Fisher-Ath	.227
Mathews-Mut	.251
McBride-Ath	.263
Cummings-Bal	.274
Zettlein-Phi	.283

Opponents' On Base Pct.
Fisher-Ath	.246
Mathews-Mut	.274
McBride-Ath	.282
Cummings-Bal	.287
Spalding-Bos	.292

Starter Runs
Spalding-Bos	43.8
Mathews-Mut	34.0
Zettlein-Phi	28.2
Cummings-Bal	25.0
Fisher-Ath	13.5

Adjusted Starter Runs
Spalding-Bos	47.4
Zettlein-Phi	30.5
Mathews-Mut	29.7
Cummings-Bal	25.0
Fisher-Ath	15.0

Clutch Pitching Index
H.Campbell-Res	123
Spalding-Bos	119
Zettlein-Phi	111
Greyson-Was	108
Brainard-Bal	103

Relief Runs

Adjusted Relief Runs

Relief Ranking

Total Pitcher Index
Spalding-Bos	5.4
Zettlein-Phi	1.9
Mathews-Mut	1.8
Cummings-Bal	1.7
Fisher-Ath	.8

Total Baseball Ranking
Spalding-Bos	5.1
Barnes-Bos	3.4
G.Wright-Bos	2.2
Zettlein-Phi	1.9
Mathews-Mut	1.7

January 29 A. G. Spalding arrives in England where he will call on sporting editors and athletes pursuing his plan to bring two baseball clubs to England this summer to exhibit American baseball and to play some cricket matches.

February 27 The first match of American baseball ever played in England takes place at the Kennington Oval Cricket Field in London.

March 2 The fourth meeting of the Professional Association takes place at the United States Hotel in Boston. New rules include the adoption of the batter's box and the prohibition of any player betting on his own team (expulsion) or any other team (forfeiture of pay).

March 14 A. G. Spalding comes home from his visit to England after arranging the tour of the Athletic and Boston teams this summer. Plans call for the teams to depart from the U.S. on July 16, play baseball and cricket matches in England during August, and leave Liverpool for home Aug. 26. The full number of championship matches during the regular baseball season will be played.

May 5 Tommy Bond pitches for the Atlantics in their 1874 opener. It is his first appearance in the National Association. Bond will later win 40 or more games in three consecutive seasons in the NL. Today he limits Baltimore to four hits as the Atlantics win the game, played at the Union Grounds, 24–3.

May 13 The first professional championship match in Chicago, by a Chicago team, since the Great Fire is played before 4,000 spectators. George Zettlein and the White Stockings defeat the Athletics of Philadelphia, 4-0. The Athletics have 10 hits and 21 base runners and yet fail to score.

June 15 Candy Cummings strikes out six consecutive Chicago White Stocking batters during an 8–6 victory at Philadelphia.

June 18 One of the poorest games of baseball ever played between two professional clubs occurs in New York as the Mutuals defeat the Chicago White Stockings, 38–1. Of the 33 hits collected by the Mutes, Tom Carey makes six and scores six runs. Chicago had just two hits and commits 36 errors.

July 10 Joe Start, the Mutual first baseman, misses the train to Hartford, and the Mutes are forced to play with only eight players. Hartford wins, 13–4.

August 3 The American visitors play their first game of baseball in London at the Lord's Cricket Grounds as Boston defeats the Athletics, 24-7. In the morning, a cricket match between the Americans and the Marylebone Club is started. At the completion of the match on the 4th, the Americans are victorious, 107-105. The American ballplayers will play in seven cricket matches during the

tour and will win all seven. However, the Americans field 18 players while their opponents use 11.

September 9 The stockholders of the Philadelphias baseball club vote, 26–15 to expel player John J. Radcliffe. Umpire William McLean has testified that Radcliffe approached him before the game at Chicago on July 15 and offered him $175 if he would help Chicago win the game. Four other players were in on the plot: Candy Cummings, Nat Hicks, Bill Craver, and Denny Mack.

September 14 To the surprise of 1,000 Boston spectators, Chicago bats Spalding all over the lot with 10 runs on 22 hits while George Zettlein limits the Reds to no runs on four hits. Boston's George Wright makes three errors.

September 16* The Globes, Louisville's first black baseball team, play a charity game for yellow fever sufferers, shaming a pair of local white clubs into following suit to avoid, in the words of the *Louisville Courier-Journal,* being "outdone by the darkly-complected portion of the human race."

November 1 The season ends today with the Boston Red Stockings being declared the champions with a record of 43-17. Boston actually had a record of 52-18 but the Committee throws out the Baltimore games because the team did not complete its schedule.

ATHLETICS		ATLANTICS		BALTIMORE		BOSTON		CHICAGO		HARTFORD		MUTUALS		PHILADELPHIA	
M	D.McBride	M	B.Ferguson	M	W.White	M	H.Wright	M	F.Malone	M	L.Pike	M	T.Carey	M	N.Hicks
1B	W.Fisler	1B	H.Dehlman	1B	C.Gould	1B	J.O'Rourke	M	J.Wood	1B	E.Mills	M	D.Higham	1B	D.Mack
2B	J.Battin	2B	J.Farrow	2B	J.Manning	2B	R.Barnes	1B	J.Glenn	2B	B.Addy	1B	J.Start	2B	B.Craver
SS	E.Sutton	SS	D.Pearce	SS	L.Say	SS	G.Wright	2B	L.Meyerle	SS	T.Barlow	2B	C.Nelson	SS	C.Fulmer
3B	C.Anson	3B	B.Ferguson	3B	W.White	3B	H.Schafer	SS	J.Peters	3B	B.Boyd	SS	T.Carey	3B	J.Holdsworth
LF	C.Gedney	LF	E.Booth	LF	J.Ryan	LF	A.Leonard	3B	D.Force	LF	J.Tipper	3B	J.Burdock	LF	T.York
CF	J.McMullin	CF	B.Clack	CF	H.Deane	CF	G.Hall	LF	N.Cuthbert	LF	L.Pike	LF	J.Hatfield	CF	D.Eggler
RF	J.Clapp	RF	J.Chapman	RF	O.Bielaski	RF	C.McVey	CF	P.Hines	RF	B.Barnie	CF	J.Remsen	RF	G.Bechtel
C	M.McGeary	C	J.Knowdell	C	P.Snyder	C	D.White	RF	F.Treacey	C	S.Hastings	RF	D.Allison	C	N.Hicks
								C	F.Malone			C	D.Higham		
O	T.Murnane	C2	F.Fleet	S	J.Gerhardt	O	H.Wright			3O	S.Brady			O	J.Radcliff
O	A.Reach	O	C.Hodes	/C	F.Selman	2	T.Beals	1O	J.Devlin	/O	O.Shaffer	/O	N.Phelps	O	C.Pabor
/C	T.Miller	O	P.McGee	1	Z.Taylor			/C	Gilroy	/O	J.Farrell	/O	B.Geer	/O	J.Donnelly
/O	C.Sensenderfer	/C	H.Kessler	/2	C.Sweasy	P	A.Spalding	/C	T.Connell	/3	J.Manning	/1	D.Patterson	/1	E.McKenna
		2	C.Sweasy	/S	J.Smith					/O	O'Neal	/O	O.Shaffer	/S	Quinlan
P	D.McBride	/2	B.West	/S	Brown			P	G.Zettlein						
		/2	A.Martin	/C	Jones					P	C.Fisher	P	B.Mathews	P	C.Cummings
		/2	J.Clinton	/3	B.Smiley			/P	D.Collins	P	B.Stearns				
		/2	J.Hall	/2	Wood										
		/2	Gavern	/O	F.Boardman										
		/C	M.Ledwith	/1	H.Kohler										
		/C	C.Snow	/O	H.Reed										
				/O	H.Reville										
		P	T.Bond	/C	L.Carl										
				P	A.Brainard										
				P	J.Manning										

TEAM	G	W	L	PCT	GB	R	OR	AB	H	2B	3B	HR	BB	SO	AVG	OBP	SLG	PRO	PRO+	BR	/A	PF	CHI	RC	SB	CS	SBA	SBR
BOS	71	52	18	.743		735	415	3130	979	121	61	17	33	27	.313	.320	.407	.727	128	115	77	106	108	418	45	18	71	3
MUT	65	42	23	.646	7.5	501	377	2729	714	89	28	7	36	39	.262	.271	.322	.593	90	-20	-35	103	105	253	36	3	92	9
ATH	55	33	22	.600	11.5	441	344	2258	647	83	18	6	24	49	.287	.294	.347	.641	99	19	-18	109	103	237	36	14	72	3
PHI	58	29	29	.500	17	476	428	2435	677	78	50	2	28	33	.278	.286	.354	.640	103	19	3	104	103	248	27	18	60	-3
CHI	59	28	31	.475	18.5	418	480	2462	685	87	4	4	32	54	.278	.287	.322	.609	97	-4	-8	101	94	232	32	12	73	2
ATL	56	22	33	.400	22.5	301	450	2169	498	45	8	1	31	51	.230	.240	.259	.499	71	-84	-49	88	97	136	11	4	73	1
HAR	53	16	37	.302	27.5	371	471	2143	591	85	18	2	30	56	.276	.286	.335	.621	97	4	-16	105	94	207	27	17	61	-2
BAL	47	9	38	.191	31.5	227	505	1778	435	45	7	1	22	36	.245	.254	.280	.534	75	-49	-47	99	83	127	12	5	71	1
TOT	232					3470		19104	5226	633	194	40	236	345	.274	.282	.333	.616		226	91						71	13

TEAM	CG	SH	SV	IP	H	H/G	HR	BB	SO	RAT	ERA	ERA+	OAV	OOB	PR	/A	PF	CPI	FA	E	DP	FW	PW	BW	SBW	DIF
BOS	65	4	3	634	779	11.1	1	23	30	11.4	1.93	112	.274	.280	18	16	99	108	.850	490	53	4.7	1.2	6.0	.1	5.0
MUT	62	4	0	586	663	10.2	3	41	100	10.8	1.89	119	.261	.273	19	23	103	98	.846	443	22	4.5	1.8	-2.7	.6	5.3
ATH	55	0	0	487	514	9.5	6	32	36	10.1	1.64	140	.240	.251	29	36	106	77	.839	396	34	2.8	2.8	-1.4	.0	1.3
PHI	56	3	0	522	673	11.6	4	19	61	11.9	1.93	114	.278	.284			101	116	.809	518	38	-2.1	1.2	.2	-.4	1.0
CHI	58	3	0	533²	684	11.5	7	45	26	12.3	2.65	84	.279	.292	-28	-25	102	93	.809	477	27	.4	-1.9	-.6	.0	.7
ATL	56	1	0	506	618	11.0	15	11	39	11.2	2.06	99	.266	.269	7	-1	94	97	.820	504	14	-2.2	-.0	-3.8	-.0	.6
HAR	45	0	0	481	655	12.3	1	27	34	12.8	2.51	92	.285	.293	-17	-11	105	99	.793	532	17	-4.8	-.9	-1.2	-.3	-3.3
BAL	42	0	0	420	640	13.7	3	38	19	14.5	3.09	72	.305	.318	-42	-41	102	107	.807	450	15	-3.2	-3.2	-3.6	-.0	-4.4
TOT	439	15	3	4169²		11.3				11.8	2.18		.274	.282					.825	3810	220					

Runs
McVey-Bos	91
O'Rourke-Bos	82
Spalding-Bos	80
G.Wright-Bos	76
White-Bos	75

Hits
McVey-Bos	123
Spalding-Bos	119
Leonard-Bos	108
White-Bos	106
O'Rourke-Bos	104

Doubles
Pike-Har	22
McVey-Bos	21
Meyerle-Chi	19
Craver-Phi	19
Leonard-Bos	18

Triples
G.Wright-Bos	15
Craver-Phi	11
Holdsworth-Phi	9

Home Runs
O'Rourke-Bos	5
White-Bos	3
McVey-Bos	3
Clapp-Ath	3

Total Bases
McVey-Bos	165
O'Rourke-Bos	150
G.Wright-Bos	149

Runs Batted In
McVey-Bos	71
O'Rourke-Bos	61
Craver-Phi	56
Spalding-Bos	54
White-Bos	52

Runs Produced
McVey-Bos	159
O'Rourke-Bos	138
Spalding-Bos	134
White-Bos	124
Craver-Phi	124

Bases On Balls
Nelson-Mut	9
McMullin-Ath	8
Barnes-Bos	8

Batting Average
Meyerle-Chi	.394
McVey-Bos	.359
Pike-Har	.355
Manning-Bal-Har	.346
McMullin-Ath	.346

On Base Percentage
Meyerle-Chi	.401
Pike-Har	.368
McMullin-Ath	.366
McVey-Bos	.360
Barnes-Bos	.360

Slugging Average
Pike-Har	.504
Craver-Phi	.498
Meyerle-Chi	.488
McVey-Bos	.481
G.Wright-Bos	.476

Production
Meyerle-Chi	.889
Pike-Har	.872
Craver-Phi	.851
McVey-Bos	.842
G.Wright-Bos	.816

Adjusted Production
Meyerle-Chi	182
Pike-Har	168
Craver-Phi	164
McVey-Bos	158
G.Wright-Bos	150

Batter Runs
McVey-Bos	24.3
Meyerle-Chi	22.6
Craver-Phi	19.7
G.Wright-Bos	19.5
Pike-Har	19.3

Adjusted Batter Runs
Meyerle-Chi	22.0
McVey-Bos	19.6
Craver-Phi	17.3
Pike-Har	16.2
G.Wright-Bos	15.3

Clutch Hitting Index
McBride-Ath	152
Malone-Chi	140
York-Phi	139
Fisher-Har	135
Fulmer-Phi	130

Runs Created
McVey-Bos	62
G.Wright-Bos	52
O'Rourke-Bos	52
Meyerle-Chi	51
Craver-Phi	49

Total Average
Meyerle-Chi	.822
Pike-Har	.817
Craver-Phi	.804
McVey-Bos	.774
G.Wright-Bos	.739

Stolen Bases
O'Rourke-Bos	11
Leonard-Bos	11
Craver-Phi	11
McGeary-Ath	10
Barlow-Har	9

Stolen Base Average

Stolen Base Runs
O'Rourke-Bos	2.7
Cuthbert-Chi	2.4

Fielding Runs
White-Bal	24.6
Barnes-Bos	19.1
Pike-Har	13.6
Ryan-Bal	12.7
Force-Chi	11.1

Total Player Rating
Pike-Har	2.3
Barnes-Bos	1.9
Craver-Phi	1.7
McVey-Bos	1.6
White-Bal	1.5

Wins
Spalding-Bos	52
Mathews-Mut	42
McBride-Ath	33
Cummings-Phi	28
Zettlein-Chi	27

Win Percentage
Spalding-Bos	.765
Mathews-Mut	.656
McBride-Ath	.600
Cummings-Phi	.519
Zettlein-Chi	.474

Games
Spalding-Bos	71
Mathews-Mut	65
Zettlein-Chi	57
McBride-Ath	55
Bond-Atl	55

Complete Games
Spalding-Bos	65
Mathews-Mut	62
Zettlein-Chi	57
McBride-Ath	55
Bond-Atl	55

Shutouts
Spalding-Bos	4
Mathews-Mut	4
Zettlein-Chi	3
Cummings-Phi	3
Bond-Atl	1

Saves
H.Wright-Bos	3

Innings Pitched
Spalding-Bos	617.1
Mathews-Mut	578.0
Zettlein-Chi	515.2
Bond-Atl	497.0
McBride-Ath	487.0

Fewest Hits/Game
McBride-Ath	9.50
Mathews-Mut	10.15
Bond-Atl	10.97
Spalding-Bos	11.01
Zettlein-Chi	11.17

Fewest BB/Game
Bond-Atl	.14
Spalding-Bos	.28
Cummings-Phi	.34
Fisher-Har	.36
McBride-Ath	.59

Strikeouts
Mathews-Mut	100
Cummings-Phi	61
Bond-Atl	39
McBride-Ath	36
Spalding-Bos	30

Strikeouts/Game
Mathews-Mut	1.56
Cummings-Phi	1.14
Stearns-Har	.79
Bond-Atl	.71
McBride-Ath	.67

Ratio
McBride-Ath	10.09
Mathews-Mut	10.79
Bond-Atl	11.12
Spalding-Bos	11.28
Cummings-Phi	11.81

Earned Run Average
McBride-Ath	1.64
Mathews-Mut	1.88
Spalding-Bos	1.92
Cummings-Phi	1.96
Bond-Atl	2.03

Adjusted ERA
McBride-Ath	140
Mathews-Mut	119
Cummings-Phi	113
Spalding-Bos	112
Fisher-Har	102

Opponents' Batting Avg.
McBride-Ath	.240
Mathews-Mut	.261
Bond-Atl	.266
Spalding-Bos	.273
Zettlein-Chi	.273

Opponents' On Base Pct.
McBride-Ath	.251
Bond-Atl	.268
Mathews-Mut	.273
Spalding-Bos	.278
Cummings-Phi	.282

Starter Runs
McBride-Ath	29.1
Mathews-Mut	19.1
Spalding-Bos	17.7
Cummings-Phi	12.1
Bond-Atl	8.5

Adjusted Starter Runs
McBride-Ath	35.7
Mathews-Mut	22.8
Spalding-Bos	16.0
Cummings-Phi	13.6
Bechtel-Phi	2.6

Clutch Pitching Index
Cummings-Phi	113
Brainard-Bal	111
Spalding-Bos	106
Stearns-Har	99
Bond-Atl	98

Relief Runs

Adjusted Relief Runs

Relief Ranking

Total Pitcher Index
Spalding-Bos	2.9
McBride-Ath	1.8
Mathews-Mut	1.5
Bond-Atl	.9
Cummings-Phi	.4

Total Baseball Ranking
Spalding-Bos	2.8
Pike-Har	2.3
Barnes-Bos	1.9
McBride-Ath	1.8
Craver-Phi	1.7

January 9* The first game of baseball played on ice this winter in the New York area takes place at Prospect Park in Brooklyn. Only two outs per team constitute an inning.

May 26 The Centennial club of Philadelphia becomes the first professional club of 1875 to disband. The Centennials also become the first team to sell a ballplayer. The rival Athletics wanted Bill Craver and George Bechtel, so the Athletics paid an official of the Centennials to have the two players released and transferred to the Athletic club.

June 5 In St. Louis, the Boston Reds suffer their first defeat of the season after 21 victories and one draw. The Browns'

George Bradley holds the Reds to eight hits. After Bradley makes the last putout, the crowd rushes on the field and lifts him to their shoulders.

June 19 Henry Chadwick has this to say about today's game: "the finest display of baseball playing and the most exciting contest yet recorded in the annals of the national game." The Chicago Whites and the Dark Blues of Hartford battle 10 scoreless innings before Jim Devlin scores on a fly out by Paul Hines in the 11th to win for Chicago, 1–0.

July 28 Philadelphia's Joseph E. Borden, also known by the name Josephs, pitches the first no-hitter in major league

history, beating the Chicago White Stockings, 4-0. The game takes one hour and 35 minutes to play.

September 11* The first baseball game played with women professionals takes place in Springfield, Illinois. The diamond is half-sized and a 9-foot high canvas surrounds the entire field. The uniforms are similar to the male version except the pants are shorter. Final score: "Blondes" 42, "Brunettes" 38.

October 24 The *Chicago Tribune* calls for the formation of an organization of major professional teams: Chicago, Cincinnati, Louisville, Philadelphia, New York, Boston, and Hartford.

	ATHLETICS		ATLANTICS		BOSTON		CENTENNIALS		CHICAGO		HARTFORD		MUTUALS
M	D.McBride	M	C.Pabor	M	H.Wright	M	B.Craver	M	J.Wood	M	B.Ferguson	M	N.Hicks
M	C.Anson	M	B.Boyd	1B	C.McVey	1B	J.Abadie	1B	J.Devlin	1B	E.Mills	1B	J.Start
1B	W.Fisler	1B	F.Crane	2B	R.Barnes	2B	E.Somerville	2B	J.Miller	2B	J.Burdock	2B	C.Nelson
2B	B.Craver	2B	F.Fleet	SS	G.Wright	SS	B.Craver	SS	J.Peters	SS	T.Carey	SS	J.Hallinan
SS	D.Force	SS	H.Kessler	3B	H.Schafer	3B	G.Trenwith	3B	W.White	3B	B.Ferguson	3B	J.Gerhardt
3B	E.Sutton	3B	A.Nichols	LF	A.Leonard	LF	F.Treacey	LF	J.Glenn	LF	T.York	LF	C.Gedney
LF	G.Hall	LF	C.Pabor	CF	J.O'Rourke	CF	F.Warner	CF	P.Hines	CF	J.Remsen	CF	J.Holdsworth
CF	D.Eggler	CF	B.Clack	RF	J.Manning	RF	C.Mason	RF	O.Bielaski	RF	A.Allison	RF	E.Booth
RF	G.Bechtel	RF	B.Boyd	C	D.White	C	T.McGinley	C	S.Hastings	C	D.Allison	C	N.Hicks
C	J.Clapp	C	J.Knowdell										
				O	T.Beals	/S	J.Radcliff	CO	D.Higham	CO	B.Harbidge	O	P.McGee
1O	C.Anson	S	M.Moore	1	J.Latham	/O	L.Lovett	OP	M.Golden	/C	P.Quinn	/C	D.Higham
2O	J.Richmond	O	P.McGee	/1	F.Heifer	/C	S.Field	CO	P.Quinn	/O	S.Brady	/C	B.Barnie
O	A.Rocap	/2	D.Patterson	/O	H.Wright			/2	G.Keerl	/O	C.Jones	/3	A.Metcalf
/O	A.Reach	/2	A.Martin			P	G.Bechtel	/3	F.Waterman			/O	N.Phelps
/C	W.Coon	/2	T.Smith	P	A.Spalding			/3	W.Foley	P	C.Cummings	/O	J.Hatfield
/C	Gilroy	/1	O.Brown					/3	M.Brannock	P	T.Bond		
		/O	Stoddard					/O	Brady			P	B.Mathews
P	D.McBride	/O	J.Dailey										
P	L.Knight	/C	B.Gilligan					P	G.Zettlein				
		/O	P.Quinn										
		/C	D.Bushong										
		/O	F.Thompson										
		/1	J.Abadie										
		/2	T.Barlow										
		/3	Boland										
		/O	W.Fulmer										
		/2	Hellings										
		/2	H.Munn										
		/O	W.Rexter										
		/O	Shaffer										
		/O	Sheridan										
		/1	O.Walker										
		P	J.Cassidy										
		P	J.Clinton										
		P	J.O'Neill										
		/P	H.Arundel										
		/P	Edwards										

	NEW HAVEN		PHILADELPHIA		RED STOCKINGS		ST. LOUIS		WASHINGTON		WESTERNS
M	C.Gould	M	M.McGeary	M	C.Sweasy	M	D.Pearce	M	H.Hollingshead	M	J.Simmons
M	J.Latham	M	B.Addy	1B	C.Hautz	1B	H.Dehlman	M	B.Parks	1B	J.Carbine
M	C.Pabor	1B	T.Murnane	2B	C.Sweasy	2B	J.Battin	1B	A.Allison	2B	J.Miller
1B	C.Gould	2B	L.Meyerle	SS	B.Redmon	SS	D.Pearce	2B	S.Brady	SS	J.Hallinan
2B	E.Somerville	SS	C.Fulmer	3B	T.McSorley	3B	B.Hague	SS	J.Dailey	3B	W.Goldsmith
SS	S.Wright	3B	M.McGeary	LF	A.Croft	LF	N.Cuthbert	3B	H.Doscher	LF	C.Jones
3B	H.Luff	LF	F.Treacey	CF	B.Morgan	CF	J.Pike	LF	B.Parks	CF	J.Simmons
LF	J.Ryan	CF	J.McMullin	RF	T.Oran	RF	J.Chapman	CF	H.Hollingshead	RF	B.Riley
CF	J.Tipper	RF	B.Addy	C	S.Flint	C	T.Miller	RF	L.Ressler	C	P.Quinn
RF	J.McKelvey	C	P.Snyder					C	A.Thompson		
C	T.McGinley			/3	J.Ellick	O	C.Waitt			OC	B.Barnie
		1	F.Malone	/C	P.Dillon	C	G.Seward	C	McCloskey	/O	J.Hall
O2	B.Geer	O	O.Shaffer	/S	J.Dillon			/S	L.Say		
1	J.Latham	/3	B.Crowley			P	G.Bradley	/O	C.Mason	P	M.Golden
C	S.Bancker			P	J.Blong	P	P.Galvin	/O	J.Lowry		
/3	G.Trenwith	P	C.Fisher					/1	Terry		
/O	C.Pabor	P	G.Zettlein			/P	F.Fleet	/C	S.Field		
/1	J.Cassidy	P	J.Borden					/C	J.Gilmore		
/C	J.Keenan							/O	R.Stevens		
/O	Sullivan	/P	S.Weaver					/1	F.Selman		
/S	T.Barlow	/P	B.Parks								
/O	L.Dole							P	B.Stearns		
/O	Evans										
/2	F.Goldsmith							/P	Witherow		
/C	R.Harrison										
/S	J.Smith										
/S	Booth										
P	T.Nichols										
/P	G.Knight										

TEAM	G	W	L	PCT	GB	R	OR	AB	H	2B	3B	HR	BB	SO	AVG	OBP	SLG	PRO	PRO+	BR	/A	PF	CHI	RC	SB	CS	SBA	SBR
BOS	82	71	8	.899		831	343	3515	1128	167	51	15	33	52	.321	.327	.410	.737	153	191	164	104	111	494	93	37	72	6
HAR	86	54	28	.659	18.5	557	343	3356	871	92	35	2	34	64	.260	.267	.310	.577	97	7	-20	105	104	284	65	33	66	0
ATH	77	53	20	.726	15	699	402	3250	941	124	57	7	38	55	.290	.298	.369	.667	120	102	35	111	113	365	75	46	62	-5
STL	70	39	29	.574	26.5	386	369	2674	643	85	29	0	32	102	.240	.249	.294	.543	99	-23	13	91	96	210	108	36	75	11
PHI	70	37	31	.544	28.5	470	376	2721	683	67	27	5	21	58	.251	.257	.301	.558	92	-12	-28	104	113	220	105	51	67	1
MUT	71	30	38	.441	35.5	328	425	2685	633	82	21	7	19	47	.236	.241	.290	.531	82	-36	-57	105	85	185	20	24	45	-8
CHI	69	30	37	.448	35	379	416	2685	699	83	16	0	21	65	.260	.266	.303	.569	99	-1	-5	101	90	220	69	50	58	-9
NH	47	7	40	.149	48	170	397	1714	373	41	13	2	14	62	.218	.224	.260	.484	80	-49	-22	87	77	103	35	16	69	1
WAS	28	5	23	.179	40.5	107	338	1004	194	14	8	0	6	42	.193	.198	.223	.421	50	-49	-45	96	98	47	23	7	77	3
RS	19	4	15	.211	37	60	161	688	137	20	1	0	12	45	.199	.213	.231	.444	62	-28	-20	90	74	37	27	9	75	3
CEN	14	2	12	.143	36.5	70	138	530	125	22	3	0	10	25	.236	.250	.289	.539	97	-5	1	92	88	40	4			
ATL	44	2	42	.45	51.5	132	438	1562	304	33	6	2	8	36	.195	.199	.227	.426	57	-74	-53	87	77	69	1	5	17	-3
WES	13	1	12	.77	37	45	88	449	81	9	6	0	1	22	.180	.182	.227	.409	41	-24	-27	105	97	17	4	6	40	-2
TOT	345					4234		26833	6812	839	273	40	249	675	.254	.261	.310	.571							629	320	66	-3

TEAM	CG	SH	SV	IP	H	H/G	HR	BB	SO	RAT	ERA	ERA+	OAV	OOB	PR	/A	PF	CPI	FA	E	DP	FW	PW	BW	SBW	DIF
BOS	60	10	17	732	751	9.2	2	33	110	9.6	1.87	115	.248	.256	29	22	96	110	.870	483	56	4.3	1.9	14.0	.5	10.8
HAR	83	13	0	770	708	8.3	4	11	152	8.4	1.57	150	.228	.231	56	67	105	94	.881	438	47	7.8	5.7	-1.7	.0	1.2
ATH	75	6	0	687	776	10.2	4	39	45	10.7	2.40	100	.268	.278	-13	-1	107	111	.876	419	51	5.7	-.0	3.0	-.4	8.3
STL	67	5	1	630	636	9.1	3	21	71	9.4	2.10	96	.243	.247	9	-6	90	87	.869	425	36	3.0	-.5	1.1	1.0	.4
PHI	64	5	0	628	652	9.3	6	30	42	9.8	2.12	107	.243	.251	7	11	102	93	.848	477	32	.5	.9	-2.4	.1	3.8
MUT	70	3	0	636²	718	10.1	4	21	77	10.4	2.46	95	.258	.264	-17	-9	105	95	.838	526	30	-1.5	-.8	-4.9	-.7	3.8
CHI	65	7	0	625	649	9.3	0	26	55	9.7	1.63	139	.243	.250	42	45	102	115	.853	478	30	.1	3.8	-.4	-.7	-6.3
NH	40	0	0	425	501	10.6	5	21	54	11.1	2.65	78	.254	.262	-20	-27	93	87	.814	447	24	-5.7	-2.3	-1.9	.1	-6.7
WAS	23	0	0	250²	397	14.3	6	10	6	14.6	3.77	63	.311	.317	-43	-39	107	112	.791	285	8	-4.3	-3.3	-3.8	.3	2.2
RS	16	2	0	171	209	11.0	0	3	21	11.2	2.63	83	.267	.269	-8	-8	98	94	.833	150	6	-.8	-.7	-1.7	.3	-2.5
CEN	14	0	0	126	169	12.1	0	5	6	12.4	2.71	80	.274	.280	-7	-8	98	103	.769	164	5	-3.2	-.7	.0	.0	-1.2
ATL	31	0	0	396	535	12.2	6	17	16	12.5	3.16	66	.285	.291	-41	-47	94	103	.801	432	20	-6.0	-4.0	-4.5	-.2	-5.2
WES	13	0	0	113	111	8.8	0	12	20	9.8	1.83	133	.225	.243	5	8	110	84	.860	78	5	.6	.7	-2.3	-.1	-4.3
TOT	621	51	18	6190¹		9.9				10.3	2.23		.254	.261					.849	4802	350					

Runs		Hits		Doubles		Triples		Home Runs		Total Bases	
Barnes-Bos	115	Barnes-Bos	143	McVey-Bos	36	Craver-Cen-Ath	13	O'Rourke-Bos	6	McVey-Bos	201
G.Wright-Bos	106	McVey-Bos	138	White-Bos	23	Pike-StL	12	Start-Mut	4	G.Wright-Bos	176
O'Rourke-Bos	97	G.Wright-Bos	136	Pike-StL	22	Hall-Ath	12	Hall-Ath	4	Barnes-Bos	174
McVey-Bos	89	White-Bos	136	Force-Ath	22	McVey-Bos	9	Hallinan-Wes-Mut	3	White-Bos	168
Leonard-Bos	87	Leonard-Bos	127			Meyerle-Phi	8	McVey-Bos	3	Leonard-Bos	156

Runs Batted In		Runs Produced		Bases On Balls		Batting Average		On Base Percentage		Slugging Average	
McVey-Bos	87	McVey-Bos	173	Dehlman-StL	11	White-Bos	.367	Barnes-Bos	.375	McVey-Bos	.517
Leonard-Bos	74	Barnes-Bos	172	Barnes-Bos	9	Barnes-Bos	.364	White-Bos	.372	Pike-StL	.494
O'Rourke-Bos	72	G.Wright-Bos	165	Nelson-Mut	9	McVey-Bos	.355	McVey-Bos	.356	Craver-Cen-Ath	.455
Hall-Ath	62	O'Rourke-Bos	163	Hastings-Chi	9	Pike-StL	.346	Pike-StL	.352	White-Bos	.453
G.Wright-Bos	61	Leonard-Bos	160	Harbidge-Har	9	G.Wright-Bos	.333	G.Wright-Bos	.337	Barnes-Bos	.443

Production		Adjusted Production		Batter Runs		Adjusted Batter Runs		Clutch Hitting Index		Runs Created	
McVey-Bos	.873	Pike-StL	210	McVey-Bos	36.9	Pike-StL	34.3	Chapman-StL	189	McVey-Bos	76
Pike-StL	.846	McVey-Bos	193	Barnes-Bos	31.4	McVey-Bos	33.4	McBride-Ath	164	Barnes-Bos	75
White-Bos	.824	White-Bos	178	White-Bos	30.0	Barnes-Bos	28.0	Leonard-Bos	148	White-Bos	62
Barnes-Bos	.818	Barnes-Bos	177	Pike-StL	27.1	White-Bos	26.9	Addy-Phi	142	G.Wright-Bos	62
Craver-Cen-Ath	.779	G.Wright-Bos	159	G.Wright-Bos	25.1	G.Wright-Bos	22.0	Clapp-Ath	136	Pike-StL	58

Total Average		Stolen Bases		Stolen Base Average		Stolen Base Runs		Fielding Runs		Total Player Rating	
McVey-Bos	.833	Murnane-Phi	30	Cuthbert-StL	94.7	Barnes-Bos	5.1	Barnes-Bos	19.2	Barnes-Bos	4.3
Pike-StL	.800	Barnes-Bos	29	Barnes-Bos	82.9	Cuthbert-StL	4.8	Clapp-Ath	18.1	White-Bos	3.6
Barnes-Bos	.797	Pike-StL	25	McGeary-Phi	82.6	Murnane-Phi	3.6	D.Allison-Har	17.3	McVey-Bos	3.4
White-Bos	.708	Dehlman-StL	23	O'Rourke-Bos	77.3	McGeary-Phi	3.3	White-Bos	14.5	Pike-StL	2.9
Craver-Cen-Ath	.694	Burdock-Har	20	Murnane-Phi	76.9	Battin-StL	2.7	Sutton-Ath	13.9	G.Wright-Bos	2.0

Wins		Win Percentage		Games		Complete Games		Shutouts		Saves	
Spalding-Bos	54	Spalding-Bos	.915	Spalding-Bos	72	Mathews-Mut	69	Zettlein-Chi-Phi	7	Spalding-Bos	9
McBride-Ath	44	Manning-Bos	.889	Mathews-Mut	70	McBride-Ath	59	Spalding-Bos	7	Manning-Bos	6
Cummings-Har	35	McBride-Ath	.759	McBride-Ath	60	Bradley-StL	57	Cummings-Har	7	McVey-Bos	1
Bradley-StL	33	Cummings-Har	.745	Bradley-StL	60	Spalding-Bos	52	McBride-Ath	6	Heifer-Bos	1
		Zettlein-Chi-Phi	.569	Zettlein-Chi-Phi	52	Zettlein-Chi-Phi	49	Bond-Har	6	Galvin-StL	1

Innings Pitched		Fewest Hits/Game		Fewest BB/Game		Strikeouts		Strikeouts/Game		Ratio	
Mathews-Mut	625.2	Borden-Phi	6.41	Cummings-Har	.09	Cummings-Har	82	Manning-Bos	2.13	Borden-Phi	7.36
Spalding-Bos	570.2	Galvin-StL	7.69	Blong-RS	.14	Spalding-Bos	75	Bond-Har	1.79	Galvin-StL	7.84
McBride-Ath	538.0	Bond-Har	7.72	Galvin-StL	.15	Mathews-Mut	75	Cummings-Har	1.77	Bond-Har	7.90
Bradley-StL	535.2	Cummings-Har	8.59	Bond-Har	.18	Bond-Har	70	Nichols-NH	1.50	Cummings-Har	8.68
Zettlein-Chi-Phi	463.1	Fisher-Phi	8.67	Fisher-Phi	.23	Bradley-StL	60	Golden-Wes-Chi	1.32	Fisher-Phi	8.90

Earned Run Average		Adjusted ERA		Opponents' Batting Avg.		Opponents' On Base Pct.		Starter Runs		Adjusted Starter Runs	
Galvin-StL	1.16	Galvin-StL	173	Borden-Phi	.181	Borden-Phi	.203	Spalding-Bos	40.1	Bond-Har	36.7
Bond-Har	1.41	Bond-Har	167	Galvin-StL	.209	Galvin-StL	.212	Zettlein-Chi-Phi	32.6	Spalding-Bos	34.9
Borden-Phi	1.50	Borden-Phi	152	Bond-Har	.216	Bond-Har	.219	Bond-Har	32.1	Zettlein-Chi-Phi	34.9
Zettlein-Chi-Phi	1.59	Cummings-Har	146	Fisher-Phi	.229	Fisher-Phi	.233	Cummings-Har	28.9	Cummings-Har	34.3
Spalding-Bos	1.59	Zettlein-Chi-Phi	143	Cummings-Har	.235	Cummings-Har	.236	Fisher-Phi	9.5	Golden-Wes-Chi	12.6

Clutch Pitching Index		Relief Runs	Adjusted Relief Runs	Relief Ranking		Total Pitcher Index		Total Baseball Ranking	
Stearns-Was	123					Spalding-Bos	4.7	Spalding-Bos	4.3
Spalding-Bos	122					Bond-Har	3.7	Barnes-Bos	4.3
Zettlein-Chi-Phi	118					Cummings-Har	2.8	Bond-Har	4.0
Devlin-Chi	117					Zettlein-Chi-Phi	2.4	White-Bos	3.6
McBride-Ath	113					Devlin-Chi	1.3	McVey-Bos	3.2

January 12 Al Spalding, pitching star of the National Association, moves from his home in Rockford, IL, with his brother J. Walter Spalding, to Chicago to "open a large emporium where they will sell all kinds of baseball goods." This will be the start of the Spalding sporting goods enterprise.

February 2 Chicago president William Hulbert organizes a meeting in New York to establish a new league. To win the support of four eastern clubs, Hulbert proposes that Morgan Bulkeley of the Hartford club be president and Nick Young of Washington be secretary. The National League is officially organized.

April 22 In the first National League game, Boston is a 6-5 winner over Philadelphia at Athletic Park. Jim O'Rourke makes the first hit and Joseph Borden, pitching under the name Josephs, is the winning pitcher.

April 24 Chicago manager Al Spalding pitches the NL's first shutout, 4–0, at Louisville.

May 2 Chicago's Ross Barnes, the great batting star of the National Association, hits the first NL homer, an inside-the-park drive off William "Cherokee" Fisher against the Cincinnati Red Stockings in Cincinnati. Barnes also hits a triple and a single, steals two bases, and scores four runs.

May 10 Chicago plays its first National League home game as Albert Spalding shuts out the Cincinnati Reds, 6-0.

May 13 Dick Higham of the Hartford Dark Blues hits into the first NL triple play against New York. It is the only bright spot for the Mutuals, who lose 28–3.

June 14 George Hall of the Athletics hits three triples and a home run in a 20-5 shellacking of Cincinnati. Teammate Ezra Sutton also hits three triples, the only time two players have done this in the same game.

June 27 Little Davey Force of the Athletics goes 6-for-6 against Spalding of Chicago, and Philadelphia scores four runs in the ninth to pull out a 14–13 victory. He is the first major leaguer to collect six hits in a nine-inning game.

July 8 The *Boston Herald* carries the midseason averages showing hits and errors per game (not per at bat nor per chance). Chicago's Ross Barnes is the top batter with 2.1 hits per game, and Dave Eggler of the Athletics is the leading fielder with .19 errors per game.

July 15 George Bradley of St. Louis pitches the National League's first no-hitter, defeating Hartford and Tommy Bond, 2-0. It is his third shutout over Hartford in the three-game series.

July 25 For the second consecutive game, Cal McVey of Chicago collects six hits in seven trips.

August 4 Louisville, trailing Chicago by a wide margin with rain threatening in the fifth, decides to stall. They make error after error until the umpire forfeits the game to Chicago. The contest would later be ruled "no game."

September 9 Curveballer Candy Cummings of Hartford wins two games over Cincinnati, 14-4, in the morning and 8-1 in the afternoon. This marks the first time two games are played in the same day.

September 16 After only 200 watch the New York Mutuals lose to Cincinnati, the club announces that they, like the Athletics, will not make their western trip.

October 6 Louisville closes out its season with an 11–2 loss to Hartford. Jim Devlin, injured severely during yesterday's game, does not pitch for the first time this season. He will still lead the league in games (68), complete games (66), and innings pitched (622).

October 23 The *Chicago Tribune* publishes season-ending batting percentages based on the new method of dividing number of at bats into number of hits. Ross Barnes is the batting leader with a .429 average.

December 10 After a five-day league meeting in Cleveland, these results are announced: the Philadelphia Athletics and New York Mutuals are expelled by unanimous vote; a uniform and lively baseball is agreed upon.

	BOSTON		CHICAGO		CINCINNATI		HARTFORD		LOUISVILLE		NEW YORK		PHILADELPHIA		ST.LOUIS
M	H.Wright	M	A.Spalding	M	C.Gould	M	B.Ferguson	M	J.Chapman	M	B.Craver	M	A.Wright	M	M.Graffen
1B	T.Murnane	1B	C.McVey	1B	C.Gould	1B	E.Mills	1B	J.Gerhardt	1B	J.Start	1B	E.Sutton	1B	G.McManus
2B	J.Morrill	2B	R.Barnes	2B	C.Sweasy	2B	J.Burdock	2B	E.Somerville	2B	B.Craver	2B	W.Fisler	1B	H.Dehlman
SS	G.Wright	SS	J.Peters	SS	H.Kessler	SS	T.Carey	SS	C.Fulmer	SS	J.Hallinan	SS	D.Force	2B	M.McGeary
3B	H.Schafer	3B	C.Anson	3B	W.Foley	3B	B.Ferguson	3B	B.Hague	3B	A.Nichols	3B	L.Meyerle	SS	J.Battin
LF	A.Leonard	LF	J.Glenn	LF	R.Snyder	LF	T.York	LF	J.Ryan	LF	F.Treacey	LF	G.Hall	3B	N.Cuthbert
CF	J.O'Rourke	CF	P.Hines	CF	C.Jones	CF	J.Remsen	CF	S.Hastings	CF	J.Holdsworth	CF	D.Eggler	CF	L.Pike
RF	J.Manning	RF	O.Bielaski	RF	D.Pierson	RF	D.Higham	RF	A.Allison	RF	E.Booth	RF	W.Coon	RF	J.Blong
C	L.Brown	C	D.White	C	A.Booth	C	D.Allison	C	P.Snyder	C	N.Hicks	C	F.Malone	C	J.Clapp
O	F.Whitney	O	B.Addy	O	B.Clack	C	B.Harbidge	O	J.Chapman	/O	M.Hayes	2	B.Fouser		
/O	T.McGinley	/O	F.Andrus	/C	S.Field	/O	J.Cassidy	/O	J.Clinton	/O	G.Bechtel	/O	W.Ritterson	S	D.Pearce
/S	S.Wright							O	G.Bechtel	/O	J.Shandley	/C	D.Bushong		
/O	B.Parks	P	A.Spalding	P	D.Dean	P	T.Bond	C	B.Holbert	/O	J.Maloney	/C	P.Curren	P	G.Bradley
/O	H.Wright			P	C.Fisher	P	C.Cummings	/O	D.Collins	/S	P.Treacey	/C	L.Paul		
				P	D.Williams			/1	J.Carbine	/2	G.Fair	/O	J.Bergh		
P	J.Borden							/2	J.Hatfield	/C	N.Phelps		
P	F.Bradley					P	J.Devlin	/1	G.Heubel	/C	J.Ward		
								/2	J.McGuinness	/C	J.Mullen		
/P	D.McBride					/P	F.Pearce	/2	B.West	/O	F.Warner		
/P	T.Nichols							/S	D.Force				
								/O	N.Phelps	P	L.Knight		
								/2	G.Seward	P	G.Zettlein		
								/C	B.Valentine				
								/P	F.Lafferty		
								P	B.Mathews				
								/P	T.Larkin				

TEAM	G	W	L	PCT	GB	R	OR	AB	H	2B	3B	HR	BB	SO	AVG	OBP	SLG	PRO	PRO+	BR	/A	PF	CHI	RC	SB	CS	SBA	SBR
CHI	66	52	14	.788		624	257	2748	926	131	32	8	70	45	.337	.353	.417	.770	140	160	93	112	107	415				
STL	64	45	19	.703	6	386	229	2478	642	73	27	2	59	63	.259	.276	.313	.589	102	-6	14	95	103	219				
HAR	69	47	21	.691	6	429	261	2664	711	96	22	2	39	78	.267	.277	.322	.599	92	1	-33	108	106	244				
BOS	70	39	31	.557	15	471	450	2722	723	96	24	9	58	98	.266	.281	.328	.609	102	11	4	102	110	257				
LOU	69	30	36	.455	22	280	344	2570	641	68	14	6	24	98	.249	.256	.294	.550	71	-42	-105	118	81	198				
NY	57	21	35	.375	26	260	412	2180	494	39	15	2	18	35	.227	.233	.261	.494	75	-76	-45	87	103	136				
PHI	60	14	45	.237	34.5	378	534	2387	646	79	35	7	27	36	.271	.279	.342	.621	108	16	19	99	100	233				
CIN	65	9	56	.138	42.5	238	579	2372	555	51	12	4	41	136	.234	.247	.271	.518	86	-63	-22	86	80	163				
TOT	260					3066		20121	5338	633	181	40	336	589	.265	.277	.321	.598										

TEAM	CG	SH	SV	IP	H	H/G	HR	BB	SO	RAT	ERA	ERA+	OAV	OOB	PR	/A	PF	CPI	FA	E	DP	FW	PW	BW	SBW	DIF
CHI	58	9	4	592¹	608	9.2	6	29	51	9.7	1.76	139	.247	.256	36	45	106	100	.899	282	33	6.0	4.0	8.2		.9
STL	63	16	0	577	472	7.4	3	39	103	8.0	1.22	175	.210	.224	70	59	93	74	.902	268	33	6.1	5.2	1.2		.5
HAR	69	11	0	624	570	8.2	2	27	114	8.6	1.67	142	.227	.235	44	49	103	72	.888	337	27	4.0	4.3	-2.9		7.6
BOS	49	3	7	632	732	10.4	7	104	77	11.9	2.51	90	.268	.295	-14	-18	98	106	.860	442	42	-1.1	-1.6	.4		6.3
LOU	67	5	0	643	605	8.5	3	38	125	9.0	1.69	160	.229	.240	44	73	118	75	.875	397	44	.9	6.4	-9.2		-1.1
NY	56	2	0	530	718	12.2	8	24	37	12.6	2.94	73	.302	.309	-37	-47	93	114	.825	473	18	-6.8	-4.1	-4.0		7.9
PHI	53	1	2	550	783	12.8	2	41	22	13.5	3.22	75	.310	.321	-56	-49	105	112	.839	456	32	-5.0	-4.3	1.7		-7.9
CIN	57	0	0	591	850	12.9	9	34	60	13.5	3.62	61	.313	.322	-86	-94	95	103	.841	469	45	-4.1	-8.3	-1.9		-9.2
TOT	472	47	13	4739¹		10.1				10.8	2.31		.265	.277					.866	3124	274					

Runs		Hits		Doubles		Triples		Home Runs		Total Bases	
Barnes-Chi	126	Barnes-Chi	138	Hines-Chi	21	Barnes-Chi	14	Hall-Phi	5	Barnes-Chi	190
G.Wright-Bos	72	Peters-Chi	111	Higham-Har	21	Hall-Phi	13	Jones-Cin	4	Hall-Phi	146
Peters-Chi	70	Anson-Chi	110	Barnes-Chi	21	Pike-StL	10			Anson-Chi	139
White-Chi	66	McVey-Chi	107	Pike-StL	19	Meyerle-Phi	8			Hines-Chi	134
Burdock-Har	66	White-Chi	104								

Runs Batted In		Runs Produced		Bases On Balls		Batting Average		On Base Percentage		Slugging Average	
White-Chi	60	Barnes-Chi	184	Barnes-Chi	20	Barnes-Chi	.429	Barnes-Chi	.462	Barnes-Chi	.590
Hines-Chi	59	White-Chi	125	O'Rourke-Bos	15	Hall-Phi	.366	Hall-Phi	.384	Hall-Phi	.545
Barnes-Chi	59	Anson-Chi	120	Burdock-Har	13	Anson-Chi	.356	Anson-Chi	.380	Pike-StL	.472
Anson-Chi	59	Hines-Chi	119	Glenn-Chi	12	Peters-Chi	.351	White-Chi	.358	Anson-Chi	.450
McVey-Chi	53	Peters-Chi	116	Anson-Chi	12	McVey-Chi	.347	O'Rourke-Bos	.358	Meyerle-Phi	.449

Production		Adjusted Production		Batter Runs		Adjusted Batter Runs		Clutch Hitting Index		Runs Created	
Barnes-Chi	1.052	Barnes-Chi	222	Barnes-Chi	50.0	Barnes-Chi	38.7	Battin-StL	150	Barnes-Chi	90
Hall-Phi	.929	Hall-Phi	208	Hall-Phi	29.1	Hall-Phi	29.7	White-Chi	142	Hall-Phi	57
Anson-Chi	.830	Pike-StL	178	Anson-Chi	24.2	Pike-StL	23.1	McVey-Chi	140	Anson-Chi	54
Pike-StL	.813	Meyerle-Phi	165	Pike-StL	19.7	Jones-Cin	18.9	Anson-Chi	138	Peters-Chi	48
Meyerle-Phi	.797	Jones-Cin	162	O'Rourke-Bos	19.1	O'Rourke-Bos	18.1	McGeary-StL	135	O'Rourke-Bos	48

Total Average		Stolen Bases	Stolen Base Average	Stolen Base Runs	Fielding Runs		Total Player Rating	
Barnes-Chi	1.141				Somerville-Lou	29.7	Barnes-Chi	3.7
Hall-Phi	.906				Force-Phi-NY	21.3	Anson-Chi	2.6
Anson-Chi	.759				Battin-StL	13.6	Hall-Phi	2.4
Pike-StL	.738				G.Wright-Bos	13.1	Battin-StL	2.2
Meyerle-Phi	.698				Anson-Chi	12.8	G.Wright-Bos	2.1

Wins		Win Percentage		Games		Complete Games		Shutouts		Saves	
Spalding-Chi	47	Spalding-Chi	.797	Devlin-Lou	68	Devlin-Lou	66	Bradley-StL	16	Manning-Bos	5
Bradley-StL	45	Manning-Bos	.783	Bradley-StL	64	Bradley-StL	63	Spalding-Chi	8	Zettlein-Phi	2
Bond-Har	31	Bond-Har	.705	Spalding-Chi	61	Mathews-NY	55	Bond-Har	6	McVey-Chi	2
Devlin-Lou	30	Bradley-StL	.703	Mathews-NY	56	Spalding-Chi	53	Devlin-Lou	5		
Mathews-NY	21	Cummings-Har	.667	Bond-Har	45	Bond-Har	45	Cummings-Har	5		

Innings Pitched		Fewest Hits/Game		Fewest BB/Game		Strikeouts		Strikeouts/Game		Ratio	
Devlin-Lou	622.0	Bradley-StL	7.38	Zettlein-Phi	.23	Devlin-Lou	122	Bond-Har	1.94	Bradley-StL	7.98
Bradley-StL	573.0	Bond-Har	7.83	Fisher-Cin	.24	Bradley-StL	103	Devlin-Lou	1.77	Bond-Har	8.12
Spalding-Chi	528.2	Devlin-Lou	8.19	Bond-Har	.29	Bond-Har	88	Bradley-StL	1.62	Devlin-Lou	8.73
Mathews-NY	516.0	Cummings-Har	8.96	Mathews-NY	.42	Spalding-Chi	39	Borden-Bos	1.40	Cummings-Har	9.54
Bond-Har	408.0	Spalding-Chi	9.23	Williams-Cin	.43	Mathews-NY	37	Fisher-Cin	1.14	Spalding-Chi	9.67

Earned Run Average		Adjusted ERA		Opponents' Batting Avg.		Opponents' On Base Pct.		Starter Runs		Adjusted Starter Runs	
Bradley-StL	1.23	Bradley-StL	174	Bradley-StL	.211	Bradley-StL	.224	Bradley-StL	68.9	Devlin-Lou	79.8
Devlin-Lou	1.56	Devlin-Lou	174	Bond-Har	.220	Bond-Har	.227	Devlin-Lou	51.5	Bradley-StL	57.9
Cummings-Har	1.67	Cummings-Har	142	Devlin-Lou	.224	Devlin-Lou	.235	Spalding-Chi	32.5	Spalding-Chi	40.5
Bond-Har	1.68	Bond-Har	141	Cummings-Har	.239	Cummings-Har	.251	Bond-Har	28.6	Bond-Har	31.5
Spalding-Chi	1.75	Spalding-Chi	139	Spalding-Chi	.247	Spalding-Chi	.256	Cummings-Har	15.4	Cummings-Har	16.9

Clutch Pitching Index		Relief Runs	Adjusted Relief Runs	Relief Ranking	Total Pitcher Index		Total Baseball Ranking	
Knight-Phi	126				Devlin-Lou	7.3	Devlin-Lou	7.3
Mathews-NY	116				Bradley-StL	5.8	Bradley-StL	5.8
Borden-Bos	108				Spalding-Chi	4.6	Spalding-Chi	4.4
Dean-Cin	108				Bond-Har	3.2	Barnes-Chi	3.7
Zettlein-Phi	107				McVey-Chi	.8	Bond-Har	3.2

January 6 Joe Battin reportedly will not sign with the St. Louis Brown Stockings because of the new NL policy of charging players $30 for uniforms and, during road trips, deducting 50¢ a day from salaries to help offset the cost of meals.

February 3 Cherokee Fisher admits he was paid $100 to lose a game last September while pitching for the West Ends in Milwaukee.

February 20* The International Association is organized at a meeting of representatives of 17 clubs held in Pittsburgh. Although set up as an alternative to the NL, the IA will go down in history as the first minor league. A day later, the IA adopts a $10 admission fee, with an additional $10 required to enter the pennant race. Candy Cummings, pitcher-manager of the Live Oaks of Lynn, Mass., is elected president.

March 5 The Hartford club completes arrangements to play its NL home games in Brooklyn. The club will still be called "Hartford."

March 22 The NL publishes its game schedule, the first league-wide schedule ever issued. The failure of the Athletics and the Mutuals to finish the 1876 season has convinced the league of the necessity of agreeing on a schedule.

April 26* The IA's opening game is played in Lynn, MA. The Manchester, NH, team beats the Live Oaks, 14–3.

May 2* The Allegheny (IA) club of Pittsburgh upsets the Boston Red Stockings behind the brilliant work of Jim Galvin. Not only does he pitch a one-hit shutout, he hits a homer, said to be the first ball to clear the fence at Pittsburgh's Union Park.

May 17 At a special meeting, the league adopts a livelier version of the Spalding ball for all games.

June 5 Making his last start as a pitcher, Chicago's Al Spalding fails to retire any of the five Cincinnati batters he faces. Spalding's old Rockford teammate, Bob Addy, literally knocks Spalding out of the box with a line drive to the chest.

June 10 The St. Louis Browns and Cincinnati Reds stage a Sunday exhibition game, the only Sunday game between NL teams that would be played until 1892.

June 18 Lacking the funds to start their scheduled eastern trip, the Cincinnati club disbands. Cincinnati stockholders move to reorganize the club three days later.

June 25 Hard luck continues to dog the Cincinnati club, as a heavy windstorm nearly destroys the pavilion at the Cincinnati Baseball Park.

July 3 The reorganized Cincinnati Red Stockings reappear in action versus the Louisville Grays, losing 6-3. Whether their games will count or not in the NL standings will not be resolved until the NL meeting in December.

July 13 After pitching in 88 consecutive games since the start of the NL, an all-time record, George Bradley steps aside for Cal McVey, and Chicago beats Hartford 6-3. The revamped lineup shows Bradley at third base, Spalding at first base, and Cap Anson catching.

August 6 The NL rule calls for the home team to submit three names of approved local men as a possible umpire for each game, with the visiting team choosing one of them at random. Today

in Louisville, Chicago's Cal McVey reaches into the hat and picks out a slip bearing the name of Dan Devinney, who accused St. Louis of trying to bribe him five days earlier. Disgusted, McVey then grabs the hat and finds that all three slips have Devinney's name on them. The incensed White Stockings demand a new umpire and then snap the Grays' six-game winning streak, 7-2.

August 8 After St. Louis catcher John Clapp has his cheek smashed by a foul tip, replacement Mike Dorgan goes behind the plate wearing a mask. This is perhaps the first use of a catcher's mask in an official NL game.

September 6* Sam "Buck" Weaver of Milwaukee no-hits the Mutuals of Janesville, to win the Wisconsin state championship. The Janesville battery consists of future stars John Montgomery Ward and Albert Bushong.

October 26 Louisville club vice president Charles Chase confronts George Hall and Jim Devlin with charges that they threw road games in August and September. Both admit to throwing non-league games and implicate teammates Al Nichols and Bill Craver. The Louisville club formally expels Devlin, Hall, and Nichols for selling games and tampering with other players and expels Craver for "disobedience to positive orders." Craver will deny any wrongdoing.

December 4 At the formal meeting in Cleveland, the NL directors meet and confirm the expulsions of the four Louisville players. The directors also vote to throw out all Cincinnati games from the standings on the grounds that Cincinnati never paid its $100 dues.

	BOSTON		CHICAGO		CINCINNATI		HARTFORD		LOUISVILLE		ST. LOUIS
M	H.Wright	M	A.Spalding	M	L.Pike	M	B.Ferguson	M	J.Chapman	M	G.McManus
1B	D.White	1B	A.Spalding	M	B.Addy	1B	J.Start	1B	J.Latham	1B	H.Dehlman
2B	G.Wright	2B	R.Barnes	M	J.Manning	2B	J.Burdock	2B	J.Gerhardt	2B	M.McGeary
SS	E.Sutton	SS	J.Peters	1B	C.Gould	SS	T.Carey	SS	B.Craver	SS	D.Force
3B	J.Morrill	3B	C.Anson	2B	J.Hallinan	3B	B.Ferguson	3B	B.Hague	3B	J.Battin
LF	A.Leonard	LF	J.Glenn	SS	J.Manning	LF	T.York	LF	G.Hall	LF	J.Blong
CF	J.O'Rourke	CF	D.Eggler	3B	W.Foley	CF	J.Holdsworth	CF	B.Crowley	CF	J.Remsen
RF	H.Schafer	RF	P.Hines	LF	C.Jones	RF	J.Cassidy	RF	O.Shaffer	RF	M.Dorgan
C	L.Brown	C	C.McVey	CF	L.Pike	C	B.Harbidge	C	P.Snyder	C	J.Clapp
				RF	B.Addy						
O	T.Murnane	2O	H.Smith	C	S.Hastings	C	D.Allison	/2	A.Nichols	1O	A.Croft
/O	H.Wright	O	J.Hallinan			/O	L.Taylor	/O	F.Lafferty	/S	D.Pearce
		O	C.Eden	SC	A.Booth	/O	J.Bass	/2	J.Haldeman	/O	L.Lee
P	T.Bond	O	C.Waitt	S2	L.Meyerle	/2	J.Bunce	/2	H.Little	/O	H.Little
		/O	J.Quinn	O	N.Cuthbert	/O	J.Maloney			/O	T.Loftus
/P	W.White	/O	C.Jones	C	G.Miller	/O	J.Pike	P	J.Devlin	/O	E.McKenna
		/O	D.Rowe	/C	H.Smith					/O	J.Gleason
		/3	C.Fisher	/C	N.Hicks	P	T.Larkin			/S	T.Newell
				/1	C.Sullivan						
		P	G.Bradley	/O	J.Ryan					P	T.Nichols
		P	L.Reis	/C	H.Kessler						
				/S	B.Redmon						
				P	C.Cummings						
				P	B.Mathews						
				P	B.Mitchell						

TEAM	G	W	L	PCT	GB	R	OR	AB	H	2B	3B	HR	BB	SO	AVG	OBP	SLG	PRO	PRO+	BR	/A	PF	CHI	RC	SB	CS	SBA	SBR
BOS	61	42	18	.700		419	263	2368	700	91	37	4	65	121	.296	.314	.370	.684	114	47	33	104	104	283				
LOU	61	35	25	.583	7	339	288	2355	659	75	36	9	58	140	.280	.297	.354	.651	92	19	-47	118	92	254				
HAR	60	31	27	.534	10	341	311	2358	637	63	31	4	30	97	.270	.279	.328	.607	105	-17	18	89	103	222				
STL	60	28	32	.467	14	284	318	2178	531	51	36	1	57	147	.244	.263	.302	.565	84	-46	-31	95	102	177				
CHI	60	26	33	.441	15.5	366	375	2273	633	79	30	0	57	111	.278	.296	.340	.636	92	8	-33	112	105	234				
CIN	58	15	42	.263	25.5	291	485	2135	545	72	34	6	78	110	.255	.282	.329	.611	107	-11	24	89	94	203				
TOT	180					2040		13667	3705	431	204	24	345	726	.271	.289	.338	.627										

TEAM	CG	SH	SV	IP	H	H/G	HR	BB	SO	RAT	ERA	ERA+	OAV	OOB	PR	/A	PF	CPI	FA	E	DP	FW	PW	BW	SBW	DIF
BOS	61	7	0	548	557	9.1	5	38	177	9.8	2.15	130	.249	.261	40	40	100	98	.889	290	36	1.2	3.6	2.9		4.3
LOU	61	4	0	559	617	9.9	4	41	141	10.6	2.25	147	.270	.283	34	65	118	119	.904	267	37	2.4	5.8	-4.2		1.0
HAR	59	4	0	544	572	9.5	2	56	99	10.4	2.32	105	.253	.271	30	7	87	97	.885	313	32	-.2	.6	1.6		-.0
STL	52	1	0	541	582	9.7	2	92	132	11.2	2.66	98	.262	.291	9	-4	93	102	.892	281	29	1.4	-.4	-2.8		-.3
CHI	45	3	3	534	630	10.6	7	58	92	11.6	3.37	88	.274	.292	-33	-24	106	87	.883	313	43	-.2	-2.1	-2.9		1.7
CIN	48	1	1	515	747	13.1	4	61	85	14.1	4.19	63	.318	.335	-79	-89	94	102	.851	394	33	-4.7	-7.9	2.1		-3.0
TOT	326	20	4	3241		10.3				11.2	2.81		.271	.289					.884	1858	210					

Runs		Hits		Doubles		Triples		Home Runs		Total Bases	
O'Rourke-Bos	68	D.White-Bos	103	Anson-Chi	19		11	Pike-Cin	4	D.White-Bos	145
G.Wright-Bos	58	McVey-Chi	98	York-Har	16	Jones-Cin-Chi-Cin	10	Shaffer-Lou	3	McVey-Chi	121
McVey-Chi	58	O'Rourke-Bos	96	Manning-Cin	16	Hall-Lou	8	Jones-Cin-Chi-Cin	2	O'Rourke-Bos	118
Start-Har	55	Cassidy-Har	95	G.Wright-Bos	15	Brown-Bos	8	D.White-Bos	2	Hall-Lou	118
		Start-Har	90	Hall-Lou	15			Snyder-Lou	2	Cassidy-Har	115

Runs Batted In		Runs Produced		Bases On Balls		Batting Average		On Base Percentage		Slugging Average	
D.White-Bos	49	D.White-Bos	98	O'Rourke-Bos	20	D.White-Bos	.387	O'Rourke-Bos	.407	D.White-Bos	.545
Peters-Chi	41	McVey-Chi	94	Jones-Cin-Chi-Cin	15	Cassidy-Har	.378	D.White-Bos	.405	Jones-Cin-Chi-Cin	.471
Sutton-Bos	39	G.Wright-Bos	93	Hall-Lou	12	McVey-Chi	.368	McVey-Chi	.387	Cassidy-Har	.458
Jones-Cin-Chi-Cin	38	O'Rourke-Bos	91	Booth-Cin	12	O'Rourke-Bos	.362	Cassidy-Har	.386	McVey-Chi	.455
York-Har	37	Jones-Cin-Chi-Cin	89	Force-StL	11	Anson-Chi	.337	Anson-Chi	.360	O'Rourke-Bos	.445

Production		Adjusted Production		Batter Runs		Adjusted Batter Runs		Clutch Hitting Index		Runs Created	
D.White-Bos	.950	D.White-Bos	190	D.White-Bos	28.2	D.White-Bos	25.8	Ferguson-Har	142	D.White-Bos	60
O'Rourke-Bos	.852	Cassidy-Har	184	O'Rourke-Bos	21.2	Cassidy-Har	23.7	Peters-Chi	139	O'Rourke-Bos	49
Cassidy-Har	.844	Jones-Cin-Chi-Cin	175	McVey-Chi	18.9	Jones-Cin-Chi-Cin	21.2	Bond-Bos	139	McVey-Chi	48
McVey-Chi	.842	O'Rourke-Bos	162	Cassidy-Har	17.6	O'Rourke-Bos	18.9	Croft-StL	139	Cassidy-Har	45
Jones-Cin-Chi-Cin	.824	Manning-Cin	157	Jones-Cin-Chi-Cin	15.6	Manning-Cin	16.4	Addy-Cin	138	Hall-Lou	43

Total Average		Stolen Bases	Stolen Base Average	Stolen Base Runs	Fielding Runs		Total Player Rating	
D.White-Bos	.939				Gerhardt-Lou	19.8	Jones-Cin-Chi-Cin	2.7
O'Rourke-Bos	.817				Peters-Chi	19.1	D.White-Bos	2.3
Jones-Cin-Chi-Cin	.776				Ferguson-Har	17.2	Peters-Chi	1.8
McVey-Chi	.768				Brown-Bos	15.4	Gerhardt-Lou	1.7
Cassidy-Har	.756				Snyder-Lou	15.2	Brown-Bos	1.6

Wins		Win Percentage		Games		Complete Games		Shutouts		Saves	
Bond-Bos	40	Bond-Bos	.702	Devlin-Lou	61	Devlin-Lou	61	Bond-Bos	6	McVey-Chi	2
Devlin-Lou	35	Devlin-Lou	.583	Bond-Bos	58	Bond-Bos	58	Larkin-Har	4	Spalding-Chi	1
Larkin-Har	29	Larkin-Har	.537	Larkin-Har	56	Larkin-Har	55	Devlin-Lou	4	Manning-Cin	1
Nichols-StL	18	Nichols-StL	.439	Bradley-Chi	50	Nichols-StL	35	Bradley-Chi	2		
Bradley-Chi	18	Bradley-Chi	.439	Nichols-StL	42	Bradley-Chi	35				

Innings Pitched		Fewest Hits/Game		Fewest BB/Game		Strikeouts		Strikeouts/Game		Ratio	
Devlin-Lou	559.0	Bond-Bos	9.16	Bond-Bos	.62	Bond-Bos	170	Mitchell-Cin	3.69	Bond-Bos	9.78
Bond-Bos	521.0	Larkin-Har	9.16	Devlin-Lou	.66	Devlin-Lou	141	Bond-Bos	2.94	Larkin-Har	10.11
Larkin-Har	501.0	Nichols-StL	9.67	Cummings-Cin	.75	Larkin-Har	96	Blong-StL	2.45	Devlin-Lou	10.59
Bradley-Chi	394.0	Blong-StL	9.75	Bradley-Chi	.89	Nichols-StL	80	Devlin-Lou	2.27	Nichols-StL	11.03
Nichols-StL	350.0	Devlin-Lou	9.93	Larkin-Har	.95	Bradley-Chi	59	Nichols-StL	2.06	Bradley-Chi	11.22

Earned Run Average		Adjusted ERA		Opponents' Batting Avg.		Opponents' On Base Pct.		Starter Runs		Adjusted Starter Runs	
Bond-Bos	2.11	Devlin-Lou	147	Larkin-Har	.245	Bond-Bos	.261	Bond-Bos	40.5	Devlin-Lou	65.4
Larkin-Har	2.14	Bond-Bos	133	Bond-Bos	.249	Larkin-Har	.264	Larkin-Har	37.3	Bond-Bos	40.5
Devlin-Lou	2.25	Larkin-Har	114	Blong-StL	.262	Devlin-Lou	.283	Devlin-Lou	34.4	Larkin-Har	16.3
Nichols-StL	2.60	Nichols-StL	100	Nichols-StL	.263	Bradley-Chi	.286	Reis-Chi	8.2	Reis-Chi	8.9
Blong-StL	2.74	Blong-StL	95	Bradley-Chi	.269	Nichols-StL	.289	Nichols-StL	8.2		

Clutch Pitching Index		Relief Runs	Adjusted Relief Runs	Relief Ranking	Total Pitcher Index		Total Baseball Ranking	
Mathews-Cin	123				Devlin-Lou	5.9	Devlin-Lou	5.9
Devlin-Lou	119				Bond-Bos	3.5	Bond-Bos	3.4
Booth-Cin	104				Larkin-Har	1.8	Jones-Cin-Chi-Cin	2.7
Nichols-StL	104				Reis-Chi	.7	D.White-Bos	2.3
Blong-StL	101				Spalding-Chi	.0	Peters-Chi	1.8

January 16 The Grays, a new club that Benjamin Douglas put together in Providence, is finally organized with Henry Root as president, Douglas is hired as manager, and veteran Tom Carey is signed as captain.

February 9* Official averages compiled by the IA list Rochester's Steve Brady as the first-ever minor league batting champion with a .373 average.

March 27* The National Association of Amateur Base Ball Players disbands. This organization had traced its roots back to the first National Association founded in 1858.

April 1* The NL signs an agreement with six of the stronger IA clubs agreeing to drop their demand of a $100 guarantee for exhibition games and agree to split the gate receipts 50/50.

April 20 Chicago's new Lake Front Park is opened with a practice game. This field with its very short right field fence (180 feet from the plate) will house the White Stockings (NL) for eight years.

April 24 John "Bud" Fowler, a young black hurler with the Chelsea team, wins a 2–1 exhibition game from the Boston Nationals, the 1877 NL champs. Fowler will sign with the Lynn Live Oaks of the International Association. There are claims that Fowler played professionally in New Castle, Pennsylvania, as early as 1872.

May 8 Providence center fielder Paul Hines pulls off a spectacular and, perhaps, unassisted triple play. With men on second base and third base and none out in the eighth inning, Boston's Jack Burdock lines one over shortstop as both runners go. Hines, racing in, catches the ball and keeps going until he touches third base. This retires the runner who started on third base, but did it retire the runner who started on second base but had already rounded third base? To make sure, Hines throws back to Charley Sweasy to touch second base. This touches off a lively debate over whether the triple play was unassisted or not, a debate that still continues over a century later.

May 9 Sam Weaver pitches a no-hitter to lead the Milwaukee Cream Citys to their first NL win, beating Indianapolis, 2–1, one run scoring after a walk. One scorer gave a hit to John Clapp of the Blues, but Weaver is generally credited with a no-hitter.

May 14 A crowd of 1,500 attends the first NL game in Milwaukee and sees the Grays end the Cincinnati Reds' six-game winning streak with an 8-5 decision.

July 15 John Montgomery Ward makes his NL debut pitching for Providence in Cincinnati. The first game is a fiasco, the Grays losing, 13-9, thanks to 17 battery errors by Monte Ward and Brown. But the 18-year-old rookie will pitch every inning of every league game for the Grays for the rest of the season.

August 26* The Manchester IA club plays an exhibition at the state reform school. During the game, their dressing room is robbed of jewelry and $48 in cash.

September 14 The Red Stockings and Blues play an exhibition game in which they experiment with calling every pitch a ball or a strike and allowing only six balls for a walk. (The rules up to this time provide for the umpire to call a "warning pitch" on the first wide delivery). The reaction is favorable.

September 30 The NL season ends with a Providence win over Boston. For the first time ever, a league completes its entire schedule.

November 9 The official NL averages give Milwaukee's Abner Dalrymple the batting championship with a .356 average. These figures do not include tie games, however, and counting ties, Providence's Paul Hines would have the lead .358 to .354. The calculations giving Hines the batting crown, as well as research showing he led in RBIs, were not made until long after his death in 1935, so Hines did not know he was the major league's first Triple Crown winner.

December 4 The full NL meets and admits the Stars of Syracuse, Buffalo, and Cleveland. Indianapolis resigns, and the Milwaukee club is given 20 days to pay its creditors and resign honorably or be expelled. New rules include the following: The pitcher's box is narrowed from six feet wide to four feet wide. Every pitch is called either a ball, a strike, or a foul, and nine balls are required for a walk, as opposed to the old rule in which every third bad pitch was a called ball and three called balls gave the batter his base. A system of fines is established against pitchers who hit batsmen with pitches. Pitchers are barred from turning their backs completely to the batters during delivery. Batting-order rules are altered to make the first batter in a new inning follow the last batter in the previous inning, rather than the last man to be retired, who might have been put out on the basepaths.

	BOSTON		CHICAGO		CINCINNATI		INDIANAPOLIS		MILWAUKEE		PROVIDENCE
M	H.Wright	M	B.Ferguson	M	C.McVey	M	J.Clapp	M	J.Chapman	M	T.York
1B	J.Morrill	1B	J.Start	1B	C.Sullivan	1B	A.Croft	1B	J.Goodman	1B	T.Murnane
2B	J.Burdock	2B	B.McClellan	2B	J.Gerhardt	2B	J.Quest	2B	J.Peters	2B	C.Sweasy
SS	G.Wright	SS	B.Ferguson	SS	B.Geer	SS	F.Warner	SS	B.Redmon	SS	T.Carey
3B	E.Sutton	3B	F.Hankinson	3B	C.McVey	3B	N.Williamson	3B	W.Foley	3B	B.Hague
LF	A.Leonard	LF	C.Anson	LF	C.Jones	LF	J.Clapp	LF	A.Dalrymple	LF	T.York
CF	J.O'Rourke	CF	J.Remsen	CF	L.Pike	CF	R.McKelvy	CF	M.Golden	CF	P.Hines
RF	J.Manning	RF	J.Cassidy	RF	K.Kelly	RF	O.Shaffer	RF	B.Holbert	RF	D.Higham
C	P.Snyder	C	B.Harbidge	C	D.White	C	S.Flint	C	C.Bennett	C	L.Brown
/O	H.Schafer	O	J.Hallinan	O	B.Dickerson	S	C.Nelson	2O	G.Creamer	C	D.Allison
		/C	P.Powers			/O	J.Hallinan	O	B.Morgan	/2	L.Pike
P	T.Bond	/C	B.Traffley	P	W.White			/C	J.Knowdell		
		/O	B.Sullivan	P	B.Mitchell	P	T.Nolan	/C	J.Ellick	P	J.Ward
		/2	A.Spalding			P	J.McCormick	/3	F.Bliss	P	T.Nichols
						P	T.Healey	/C	A.Jennings	P	H.Wheeler
		P	T.Larkin								
		P	L.Reis					P	S.Weaver	/P	T.Healey
										/P	F.Corey
										/P	C.Fisher

TEAM	G	W	L	PCT	GB	R	OR	AB	H	2B	3B	HR	BB	SO	AVG	OBP	SLG	PRO	PRO+	BR	/A	PF	CHI	RC	SB	CS	SBA	SBR
BOS	60	41	19	.683		298	241	2220	535	75	25	2	35	154	.241	.253	.300	.553	79	-35	-56	108	110	173				
CIN	61	37	23	.617	4	333	281	2281	629	67	22	5	58	141	.276	.294	.331	.625	120	21	53	91	98	227				
PRO	62	33	27	.550	8	353	337	2298	604	107	30	8	50	218	.263	.279	.346	.625	109	19	20	100	104	227				
CHI	61	30	30	.500	11	371	331	2333	677	91	20	3	88	157	.290	.316	.350	.666	115	56	31	107	96	265				
IND	63	24	36	.400	17	293	328	2300	542	76	15	3	64	197	.236	.256	.286	.542	95	-43	-6	87	105	173				
MIL	61	15	45	.250	26	256	386	2212	552	65	20	2	69	214	.250	.272	.300	.572	86	-18	-38	107	88	185				
TOT	184					1904		13644	3539	481	132	23	364	1081	.259	.279	.319	.598										

TEAM	CG	SH	SV	IP	H	H/G	HR	BB	SO	RAT	ERA	ERA+	OAV	OOB	PR	/A	PF	CPI	FA	E	DP	FW	PW	BW	SBW	DIF
BOS	58	9	0	544	595	9.8	6	38	184	10.5	2.32	102	.272	.284	-1	2	102	111	.914	228	48	3.5	.2	-5.2		12.5
CIN	61	6	0	548	546	9.0	2	63	220	10.0	1.84	116	.248	.269	28	17	92	108	.900	269	37	1.5	1.6	5.0		-1.1
PRO	59	6	0	556	609	9.9	5	86	173	11.3	2.38	93	.265	.291	-5	-11	96	108	.892	311	42	-.5	-1.0	1.9		2.7
CHI	61	1	0	551	577	9.4	4	35	175	10.0	2.37	102	.253	.265	-4	3	105	85	.891	304	37	-.4	.3	2.9		-2.8
IND	59	2	1	578	621	9.7	3	87	182	11.0	2.32	87	.262	.288	-1	-19	88	106	.898	290	37	.9	-1.8	-.6		-4.6
MIL	54	1	0	547	589	9.7	3	55	147	10.6	2.60	101	.255	.272	-18	1	114	82	.866	376	32	-4.4	.0	-3.6		-7.1
TOT	352	25	1	3324		9.6				10.6	2.30		.259	.279					.893	1778	233					

Runs		Hits		Doubles		Triples		Home Runs		Total Bases	
Higham-Pro	60	Start-Chi	100	Higham-Pro	22	York-Pro	10	Hines-Pro	4	York-Pro	125
Start-Chi	58	Dalrymple-Mil	96	Brown-Pro	21	O'Rourke-Bos	7	Jones-Cin	3	Start-Chi	125
York-Pro	56	Hines-Pro	92	York-Pro	19	Jones-Cin	7	McVey-Cin	2	Hines-Pro	125
Anson-Chi	55	Ferguson-Chi	91	Shaffer-Ind	19			McKelvy-Ind	2	Shaffer-Ind	121
Dalrymple-Mil	52			O'Rourke-Bos	17					Higham-Pro	117

Runs Batted In		Runs Produced		Bases On Balls		Batting Average		On Base Percentage		Slugging Average	
Hines-Pro	50	Anson-Chi	95	Remsen-Chi	17	Dalrymple-Mil	.354	Ferguson-Chi	.375	Hines-Pro	.486
Brown-Pro	43	Hines-Pro	88	Larkin-Chi	17	Hines-Pro	.358	Anson-Chi	.372	York-Pro	.465
Anson-Chi	40	Higham-Pro	88	Shaffer-Ind	13	Ferguson-Chi	.351	Shaffer-Ind	.369	Shaffer-Ind	.455
Jones-Cin	39	Jones-Cin	86	Clapp-Ind	13	Start-Chi	.351	Dalrymple-Mil	.368	Brown-Pro	.453
Ferguson-Chi	39	Brown-Pro	86	Anson-Chi	13	Anson-Chi	.341	Hines-Pro	.363	Jones-Cin	.441

Production		Adjusted Production		Batter Runs		Adjusted Batter Runs		Clutch Hitting Index		Runs Created	
Hines-Pro	.849	Shaffer-Ind	196	Hines-Pro	20.0	Shaffer-Ind	27.8	McClellan-Chi	165	Hines-Pro	47
Shaffer-Ind	.824	Hines-Pro	177	Shaffer-Ind	19.6	Hines-Pro	20.2	Harbidge-Chi	151	Shaffer-Ind	46
Start-Chi	.794	Jones-Cin	163	Start-Chi	17.2	Jones-Cin	17.4	Hague-Pro	142	Start-Chi	46
York-Pro	.793	York-Pro	159	Dalrymple-Mil	16.4	York-Pro	16.3	McKelvy-Ind	140	Dalrymple-Mil	43
Dalrymple-Mil	.789	Brown-Pro	153	York-Pro	16.1	Clapp-Ind	14.5	Bond-Bos	131	York-Pro	42

Total Average		Stolen Bases		Stolen Base Average		Stolen Base Runs		Fielding Runs		Total Player Rating	
Hines-Pro	.770							Burdock-Bos	21.3	Shaffer-Ind	2.9
Shaffer-Ind	.761							Hague-Pro	18.7	Ferguson-Chi	2.8
York-Pro	.715							Ferguson-Chi	15.9	Burdock-Bos	2.2
Brown-Pro	.692							Kelly-Cin	11.1	Jones-Cin	1.9
Start-Chi	.686							Wright-Bos	10.5	Hines-Pro	1.8

Wins		Win Percentage		Games		Complete Games		Shutouts		Saves	
Bond-Bos	40	Bond-Bos	.678	Bond-Bos	59	Bond-Bos	57	Bond-Bos	9	Healey-Pro-Ind	1
W.White-Cin	30	Ward-Pro	.629	Larkin-Chi	56	Larkin-Chi	56	Ward-Pro	6		
Larkin-Chi	29	W.White-Cin	.588	W.White-Cin	52	W.White-Cin	52	W.White-Cin	5		
Ward-Pro	22	Larkin-Chi	.527	Weaver-Mil	45	Weaver-Mil	39				
Nolan-Ind	13			Nolan-Ind	38						

Innings Pitched		Fewest Hits/Game		Fewest BB/Game		Strikeouts		Strikeouts/Game		Ratio	
Bond-Bos	532.2	Mitchell-Cin	7.76	Weaver-Mil	.49	Bond-Bos	182	Mitchell-Cin	5.74	Weaver-Mil	9.21
Larkin-Chi	506.0	Ward-Pro	8.30	Larkin-Chi	.55	W.White-Cin	169	Wheeler-Pro	3.63	Ward-Pro	9.22
W.White-Cin	468.0	Weaver-Mil	8.72	Bond-Bos	.56	Larkin-Chi	163	W.White-Cin	3.25	Larkin-Chi	9.64
Weaver-Mil	383.0	Larkin-Chi	9.09	Nichols-Pro	.73	Nolan-Ind	125	Nolan-Ind	3.24	Mitchell-Cin	9.79
Nolan-Ind	347.0	W.White-Cin	9.17	W.White-Cin	.87	Ward-Pro	116	Ward-Pro	3.13	W.White-Cin	10.04

Earned Run Average		Adjusted ERA		Opponents' Batting Avg.		Opponents' On Base Pct.		Starter Runs		Adjusted Starter Runs	
Ward-Pro	1.51	Ward-Pro	146	Mitchell-Cin	.223	Weaver-Mil	.247	Ward-Pro	29.5	Weaver-Mil	28.6
McCormick-Ind	1.69	Weaver-Mil	134	Ward-Pro	.231	Ward-Pro	.251	W.White-Cin	26.8	Ward-Pro	25.7
W.White-Cin	1.79	McCormick-Ind	120	Weaver-Mil	.237	Larkin-Chi	.257	Weaver-Mil	15.1	Bond-Bos	17.6
Weaver-Mil	1.95	W.White-Cin	119	Larkin-Chi	.246	Mitchell-Cin	.265	Bond-Bos	14.4	W.White-Cin	17.6
Bond-Bos	2.06	Bond-Bos	114	W.White-Cin	.252	W.White-Cin	.269	McCormick-Ind	8.0	Larkin-Chi	10.2

Clutch Pitching Index		Relief Runs		Adjusted Relief Runs		Relief Ranking		Total Pitcher Index		Total Baseball Ranking	
McCormick-Ind	152							Weaver-Mil	2.7	Shaffer-Ind	2.9
Healey-Pro-Ind	122							Ward-Pro	2.6	Ferguson-Chi	2.8
Bond-Bos	119							Larkin-Chi	1.8	Ward-Pro	2.6
W.White-Cin	114							Bond-Bos	1.3	Weaver-Mil	2.4
Nichols-Pro	112							W.White-Cin	.7	Burdock-Bos	2.2

January 26 Troy receives notification of its admission into the NL. The Trojans are already committed to salaries totaling $10,240 for 11 players and a manager.

February 14 The Milwaukee NL club's property (Cream Citys) is sold to satisfy a bankruptcy judgment of $125.61.

February 18* At the International Association meeting, the 1878 pennant is awarded to Buffalo with a 24-8 record; Syracuse was 23-9. With no Canadian clubs in attendance, the league changes its name to the National Association.

March 25 Despite some vocal opposition from some members, the NL votes to retain its 50 cent minimum admission price. It also reinstitutes the rule making outs of fouls on third strikes caught on the first bounce.

April 1* The Northwest League is formed with Davenport, Omaha, Dubuque, and Rockford. This league refuses to affiliate with the NA or NL, setting its sights at limited attendance and salary standards. In this sense, it is the first minor league.

April 4 The Providence Grays vote to establish a "bull pen" in center field for which 15¢ admissions can be purchased starting in the fifth inning. This will become a very popular ticket, with a daily rush in the fifth.

May 30 John Ward of Providence beats Buffalo, 4-0, and saves his own shutout with the innovative tactic of backing up home plate on a throw coming in from the outfield.

June 2* J. Lee Richmond, Brown University baseball star, makes his pro debut with the Worcester Brown Stockings by no-hitting Chicago in a 7-inning game, 11–0. A week later, Richmond pitches Brown to the College Championship by beating Yale, 3–2. Worcester will join the NL in 1880.

July 4* A holiday crowd of more than 5,000 turns out in Philadelphia to see a widely advertised game between two women's teams, the New York Blue Stockings and the Philadelphia Red Stockings. The teams, connected with variety theaters, are playing for "the championship of the U.S." The Blue Stockings win, 36–24, in a loosely played game cut short when the unruly crowd gets out of control.

July 26 Syracuse's Harry McCormick hits a home run in the first and then makes it stand up by beating Boston's Tommy Bond, 1-0. This will be the only time in major league history that a pitcher wins his own 1-0 game with a first-inning home run.

August 5 After Providence pitcher Bobby Mathews gives up six runs in the first two innings, he switches positions with third base Monte Ward, who pitches shutout ball the rest of the way to rally the Grays to a 7–6 win. Captain George Wright would successfully employ this pitching scheme several more times in the season.

August 7 An unusual base-path occurrence is the feature in Syracuse. Mike Dorgan, the Star runner from second base, passes Hick Carpenter, the man from third base, and crosses the plate before Carpenter is tagged out. There is as yet no specific rule about passing preceding runners, but the umpire calls both men out. The Stars beat Boston, 6–5.

September 29 Will White pitches his 74th complete game of the season for Cincinnati, beating Cleveland, 13-1. He will finish with 75 complete games and 680 innings pitched, establishing ML season records that will never be broken.

September 30 From the second day of the NL meeting, word leaks out of a secret agreement among the owners allowing each club to "reserve" 5 players with whom the other clubs agree not to negotiate to keep their salaries at or below current levels.

December 4 NL owners again vote to retain the 50 cent minimum admission charge despite opposition from Troy and Buffalo. The following rule changes are made: the number of balls for a walk is reduced from nine to eight. the catcher must catch the third strike on the fly to put the batter out (the first bounce no longer counting), the final outs of the last half inning need no longer be completed if the team batting last is already ahead.

	BOSTON		BUFFALO		CHICAGO		CINCINNATI		CLEVELAND		PROVIDENCE		SYRACUSE		TROY
M	H.Wright	M	J.Clapp	M	C.Anson	M	D.White	M	J.McCormick	M	G.Wright	M	M.Dorgan	M	H.Phillips
1B	E.Cogswell	1B	O.Walker	M	S.Flint	M	C.McVey	1B	B.Phillips	1B	J.Start	1B	B.Holbert	M	B.Ferguson
2B	J.Burdock	2B	C.Fulmer	1B	C.Anson	1B	C.McVey	2B	J.Glasscock	2B	M.McGeary	M	J.Macullar	1B	D.Brouthers
SS	E.Sutton	SS	D.Force	2B	J.Quest	2B	J.Gerhardt	SS	T.Carey	SS	G.Wright	1B	H.Carpenter	2B	T.Hawkes
3B	J.Morrill	3B	H.Richardson	SS	J.Peters	SS	R.Barnes	3B	F.Warner	3B	B.Hague	2B	J.Farrell	SS	E.Caskin
LF	C.Jones	LF	J.Hornung	3B	N.Williamson	3B	W.Foley	LF	B.Riley	LF	T.York	SS	J.Macullar	3B	H.Doscher
CF	J.O'Rourke	CF	D.Eggler	LF	A.Dalrymple	LF	B.Dickerson	CF	G.Strief	CF	P.Hines	3B	R.Woodhead	LF	T.Mansell
RF	S.Houck	RF	B.Crowley	CF	G.Gore	CF	P.Hotaling	RF	C.Eden	RF	J.O'Rourke	LF	M.Mansell	CF	A.Hall
C	P.Snyder	C	J.Clapp	RF	O.Shaffer	RF	K.Kelly	C	D.Kennedy	C	L.Brown	CF	J.Richmond	RF	J.Evans
				C	S.Flint	C	D.White					RF	B.Purcell	C	C.Reilley
O	B.Hawes	OP	B.McGunnigle					CO	B.Gilligan	C	E.Gross	C	B.Holbert		
		/C	J.Rowe	O1	J.Remsen	S	M.Burke	3	J.Allen	2	J.Farrell			1O	A.Clapp
P	T.Bond	/1	S.Libby	/1	L.Brown	O	B.Purcell	/C	H.Hoffman	/3	D.Sullivan	1O	M.Dorgan	3	B.Ferguson
P	C.Foley			/O	B.Harbidge	/O	J.Neagle	/O	L.Stockwell	/C	R.Kemmler	2	G.Creamer	S	C.Nelson
		P	P.Galvin	/3	J.Stedronsky	/O	J.Magner	/O	F.Gunkle	/O	D.O'Leary	1	J.McGuinness	O	S.Taylor
/P	J.Tyng			/3	H.Doscher	/O	H.Wheeler			/C	D.Allison	/3	J.Allen	S	J.Shoupe
/P	L.Richmond			/C	T.Dolan			P	J.McCormick	/1	B.White	/C	K.Kelly	/O	J.Cassidy
						P	W.White	P	B.Mitchell			/O	G.Adams	/C	K.Kelly
				P	T.Larkin					P	J.Ward	/C	F.Decker	/C	B.Holbert
				P	F.Hankinson					P	B.Mathews	/O	C.Osterhout		
												/O	T.Mansell	P	G.Bradley
														P	H.Salisbury
												P	H.McCormick	P	F.Goldsmith
														/P	P.McManus
														/P	G.Gardner

TEAM	G	W	L	PCT	GB	R	OR	AB	H	2B	3B	HR	BB	SO	AVG	OBP	SLG	PRO	PRO+	BR	/A	PF	CHI	RC	SB	CS	SBA	SBR
PRO	85	59	25	.702		612	355	3392	1003	142	55	12	91	172	.296	.314	.381	.695	134	110	119	98	103	416				
BOS	84	54	30	.643	5	562	348	3217	883	138	51	20	90	222	.274	.294	.368	.662	118	68	56	102	107	357				
BUF	79	46	32	.590	10	394	365	2906	733	105	54	2	78	314	.252	.272	.328	.600	98	1	-9	102	95	265				
CHI	83	46	33	.582	10.5	437	411	3116	808	167	32	5	73	294	.259	.276	.336	.612	98	14	-13	106	96	297				
CIN	81	43	37	.538	14	485	464	3085	813	127	53	8	66	207	.264	.279	.347	.626	115	27	50	95	105	306				
CLE	82	27	55	.329	31	322	461	2987	666	116	29	4	37	214	.223	.232	.285	.517	73	-83	-80	99	96	203				
SYR	71	22	48	.314	30	276	462	2611	592	61	19	4	28	238	.227	.235	.270	.505	78	-82	-51	98	98	170				
TRO	77	19	56	.253	35.5	321	543	2841	673	102	24	4	45	182	.237	.249	.294	.543	87	-54	-31	93	93	213				
TOT	321					3409		24155	6171	958	317	58	508	1843	.255	.271	.329	.599										

TEAM	CG	SH	SV	IP	H	H/G	HR	BB	SO	RAT	ERA	ERA+	OAV	OOB	PR	/A	PF	CPI	FA	E	DP	FW	PW	BW	SBW	DIF
PRO	73	3	2	776	765	8.9	9	62	329	9.6	2.18	108	.243	.258	27	15	94	99	.902	382	41	1.8	1.4	11.0		2.8
BOS	80	13	0	753	757	9.0	9	46	230	9.6	2.19	114	.251	.262	26	25	100	107	.913	319	58	4.9	2.3	5.2		-.3
BUF	78	8	0	713	698	8.8	3	47	198	9.4	2.34	112	.242	.254	13	22	105	87	.906	331	62	2.9	2.0	-.8		2.9
CHI	82	6	0	744	762	9.2	5	57	211	9.9	2.46	105	.244	.258	3	9	103	86	.900	381	52	1.3	.8	-1.2		5.5
CIN	79	4	0	726	756	9.4	11	81	246	10.4	2.29	102	.248	.267	16	4	93	104	.877	454	48	-3.1	.4	4.6		1.1
CLE	79	3	0	741	818	9.9	4	116	287	11.3	2.65	95	.265	.292	-12	-12	100	111	.889	406	42	-.3	-1.1	-7.4		-5.3
SYR	64	5	0	649	775	10.7	4	52	132	11.5	3.19	74	.277	.290	-50	-59	95	96	.873	398	37	-2.7	-5.4	-4.7		-.2
TRO	75	3	0	695	840	10.9	13	47	210	11.5	2.80	89	.275	.286	-23	-22	100	110	.875	460	44	-4.4	-2.0	-2.9		-9.2
TOT	610	45	2	5797		9.6				10.4	2.50		.255	.271					.892	3131	384					

Runs
Jones-Bos	85
Hines-Pro	81
Wright-Pro	79
Kelly-Cin	78
Dickerson-Cin	73

Hits
Hines-Pro	146
O'Rourke-Pro	126
Kelly-Cin	120
Jones-Bos	112
D.White-Cin	110

Doubles
Eden-Cle	31
York-Pro	25
Hines-Pro	25
Dalrymple-Chi	25
Houck-Bos	24

Triples
Dickerson-Cin	14
Williamson-Chi	13
Kelly-Cin	12
O'Rourke-Bos	11

Home Runs
Jones-Bos	9
O'Rourke-Bos	6
Brouthers-Tro	4
Eden-Cle	3

Total Bases
Hines-Pro	197
Jones-Bos	181
Kelly-Cin	170
O'Rourke-Pro	166
O'Rourke-Bos	165

Runs Batted In
O'Rourke-Bos	62
Jones-Bos	62
Dickerson-Cin	57
McVey-Cin	55

Runs Produced
Jones-Bos	138
Hines-Pro	131
Dickerson-Cin	128
O'Rourke-Bos	125
Kelly-Cin	123

Bases On Balls
Jones-Bos	29
Williamson-Chi	24
York-Pro	19
Richardson-Buf	16
Barnes-Cin	16

Batting Average
Anson-Chi	.317
Hines-Pro	.357
O'Rourke-Pro	.348
Kelly-Cin	.348
O'Rourke-Bos	.341

On Base Percentage
O'Rourke-Pro	.371
Hines-Pro	.369
Jones-Bos	.367
Kelly-Cin	.363
O'Rourke-Bos	.357

Slugging Average
O'Rourke-Bos	.521
Jones-Bos	.510
Kelly-Cin	.493
Hines-Pro	.482
O'Rourke-Pro	.459

Production
O'Rourke-Bos	.877
Jones-Bos	.877
Kelly-Cin	.855
Hines-Pro	.851
O'Rourke-Pro	.829

Adjusted Production
Kelly-Cin	188
Jones-Bos	182
O'Rourke-Bos	181
Hines-Pro	181
O'Rourke-Pro	174

Batter Runs
Jones-Bos	33.1
Hines-Pro	32.9
Kelly-Cin	28.1
O'Rourke-Bos	28.0
O'Rourke-Pro	27.2

Adjusted Batter Runs
Hines-Pro	34.3
Kelly-Cin	32.1
Jones-Bos	31.2
O'Rourke-Bos	28.4
O'Rourke-Pro	26.4

Clutch Hitting Index
Gerhardt-Cin	150
McVey-Cin	143
Brown-Pro-Chi	137
Morrill-Bos	124
W.White-Cin	122

Runs Created
Hines-Pro	75
Jones-Bos	68
Kelly-Cin	63
O'Rourke-Pro	63
O'Rourke-Bos	60

Total Average
Jones-Bos	.864
O'Rourke-Bos	.828
Kelly-Cin	.791
Hines-Pro	.779
O'Rourke-Pro	.758

Stolen Bases

Stolen Base Average

Stolen Base Runs

Fielding Runs
Snyder-Bos	23.9
Wright-Pro	20.5
Shaffer-Chi	20.3
Evans-Tro	17.7
Fulmer-Buf	17.4

Total Player Rating
Kelly-Cin	3.9
Jones-Bos	3.5
Hines-Pro	3.3
Williamson-Chi	3.2
Wright-Pro	3.2

Wins
Ward-Pro	47
W.White-Cin	43
Bond-Bos	43
Galvin-Buf	37
Larkin-Chi	31

Win Percentage
Ward-Pro	.712
Bond-Bos	.694
Hankinson-Chi	.600
W.White-Cin	.581
Galvin-Buf	.578

Games
W.White-Cin	76
Ward-Pro	70
Galvin-Buf	66
Bond-Bos	64
McCormick-Cle	62

Complete Games
W.White-Cin	75
Galvin-Buf	65
McCormick-Cle	59
Bond-Bos	59
Ward-Pro	58

Shutouts
Bond-Bos	11
Galvin-Buf	6
McCormick-Syr	5
W.White-Cin	4
Larkin-Chi	4

Saves
Ward-Pro	1
Mathews-Pro	1

Innings Pitched
W.White-Cin	680.0
Galvin-Buf	593.0
Ward-Pro	587.0
Bond-Bos	555.1
McCormick-Cle	546.1

Fewest Hits/Game
McGunnigle-Buf	8.48
Ward-Pro	8.75
Bond-Bos	8.80
Galvin-Buf	8.88
W.White-Cin	8.95

Fewest BB/Game
Galvin-Buf	.39
Galvin-Buf	.47
Bradley-Tro	.48
Larkin-Chi	.53
Ward-Pro	.55

Strikeouts
Ward-Pro	239
W.White-Cin	232
McCormick-Cle	197
Bond-Bos	155
Larkin-Chi	142

Strikeouts/Game
McGunnigle-Buf	4.65
Mathews-Pro	4.29
Mitchell-Cle	4.16
Ward-Pro	3.66
McCormick-Cle	3.25

Ratio
Bond-Bos	9.19
Ward-Pro	9.31
Galvin-Buf	9.35
Larkin-Chi	9.54
McGunnigle-Buf	9.68

Earned Run Average
Bond-Bos	1.96
W.White-Cin	1.99
Ward-Pro	2.15
Salisbury-Tro	2.22
Galvin-Buf	2.28

Adjusted ERA
Bond-Bos	127
W.White-Cin	117
Galvin-Buf	115
Salisbury-Tro	112
Ward-Pro	110

Opponents' Batting Avg.
McGunnigle-Buf	.235
W.White-Cin	.238
Ward-Pro	.239
Larkin-Chi	.240
Galvin-Buf	.243

Opponents' On Base Pct.
Larkin-Chi	.250
Ward-Pro	.250
Galvin-Buf	.253
W.White-Cin	.256
Bond-Bos	.259

Starter Runs
W.White-Cin	38.6
Bond-Bos	33.0
Ward-Pro	22.8
Galvin-Buf	14.5
Goldsmith-Tro	6.5

Adjusted Starter Runs
Bond-Bos	32.3
W.White-Cin	26.2
Galvin-Buf	22.2
Ward-Pro	13.7
Larkin-Chi	7.4

Clutch Pitching Index
Salisbury-Tro	125
Mathews-Pro	122
Bond-Bos	117
McCormick-Cle	111
Mitchell-Cle	109

Relief Runs

Adjusted Relief Runs

Relief Ranking

Total Pitcher Index
Bond-Bos	3.8
Ward-Pro	2.9
Galvin-Buf	2.8
McCormick-Cle	.7
Goldsmith-Tro	.6

Total Baseball Ranking
Kelly-Cin	3.9
Bond-Bos	3.6
Jones-Bos	3.5
Hines-Pro	3.3
Williamson-Chi	3.2

February 12 The Boston club cuts the price of season tickets from $14 to $12 after the Red Stockings failed to win their third straight pennant last season.

February 25* Yale chooses not to join the American Collegiate Baseball Association because of professional players on other teams.

April 14 The new Cincinnati ballpark on Bank Street and Western Avenue (three blocks north of where Crosley Field will be located) is opened with an exhibition game between the Reds and the Washington Nationals. The park seats 3,490 and will serve professional teams in three leagues: NL in 1880, AA in 1882-83, and UA in 1884.

May 1 Opening Day in the NL. In Cincinnati, the Chicagos spoil the official opening of the Reds' new park by beating them, 4-3, with two runs in the bottom of the ninth. This is the first pro game ended in "sudden death," as the old rules required that the full inning be played out even if the team batting last was already ahead.

May 20 Chicago captain Cap Anson begins using hurlers Larry Corcoran and Fred Goldsmith in alternating games, thereby establishing the first "pitching rotation" ever.

June 2 Buffalo fines first baseman Oscar Walker $50 for breaking his temperance pledge.

June 10 Boston's Charley Jones, last year's home run king with nine, hits two home runs in one inning, becoming the first big leaguer to accomplish this feat.

Both come off Buffalo's Tom Poorman in the eighth inning of a 19-3 rout.

June 12 John Lee Richmond pitches the first perfect game in professional history, leading Worcester to a 1-0 victory over Cleveland. Right fielder Lon Knight saves the no-hitter by throwing out a batter at first base. Six days later, John Montgomery Ward pitches a perfect game in Providence against Buffalo, winning, 5-0, the second perfect game in NL history. The third will not be pitched until 1964, when Jim Bunning turns the trick.

July 8 Chicago wins its 21st consecutive decision, beating Providence, 5-4. This streak will be surpassed only once in major league history, by the New York Giants in 1916. The victory raises Chicago's won-lost record to 35-3, far ahead of second-place Providence's 21-16 mark.

August 28 Cincinnati commits nine errors in the fourth inning and 16 in the game as the Reds are trounced by Troy, 13-2. Second baseman Charlie Smith makes four errors on his way to an NL record 89 errors by a second baseman in one season.

September 2 The first night baseball is played in Nantasket Beach, Massachusetts, between teams from two Boston department stores, Jordan Marsh and R. H. White. The *Boston Post* reports the next day that "A clear, pure, bright light was produced, very strong and yet very pleasant to the sight" by the 12 carbon-

arc electric lamps. The game ends in a 16-16 tie.

September 8* The Polo Grounds in New York at 110th Street between Fifth and Sixth Avenues is leased by the new Metropolitan club. The grounds, which have been used for polo matches, will be converted into the first commercial baseball park to be built on Manhattan Island. It opens three weeks later with a 4-2 Mets victory over the NA champion Nationals.

September 29* The Polo Grounds is opened with a 4-2 victory by the non-league Mets over the NA champion Nationals. The crowd of around 2,500 is the largest for a ball game in the New York area in several years.

September 30 Chicago wins its final game to finish the season with a 67-17 record, establishing an NL record for winning percentage (.798), although winning percentage will not be used officially in the league until 1884. Providence is second, 15 games behind.

December 9 The NL adopts several new rules, including: moving the pitcher's box back five feet so that its front line is 50 feet from the back point of home plate; reducing the number of called balls for a walk, from eight to seven; eliminating substitutions (except in the case of illness or injury), the old rule having allowed subs in the first inning but not thereafter; prohibiting all pinch runners (this rule will be ignored many times).

BOSTON		BUFFALO		CHICAGO		CINCINNATI		CLEVELAND		PROVIDENCE		TROY		WORCESTER	
M	H.Wright	M	S.Crane	M	C.Anson	M	J.Clapp	M	J.McCormick	M	M.McGeary	M	B.Ferguson	M	F.Bancroft
1B	C.Foley	1B	D.Esterbrook	1B	C.Anson	1B	J.Reilly	1B	B.Phillips	M	M.Ward	1B	E.Cogswell	1B	C.Sullivan
2B	J.Burdock	2B	D.Force	2B	J.Quest	2B	P.Smith	2B	F.Dunlap	M	M.Dorgan	2B	B.Ferguson	2B	G.Creamer
SS	E.Sutton	SS	M.Moynahan	SS	T.Burns	SS	L.Say	SS	J.Glasscock	1B	J.Start	SS	E.Caskin	SS	A.Irwin
3B	J.Morrill	3B	H.Richardson	3B	N.Williamson	3B	H.Carpenter	3B	F.Hankinson	2B	J.Farrell	3B	R.Connor	3B	A.Whitney
LF	C.Jones	LF	J.Hornung	LF	A.Dalrymple	LF	M.Mansell	LF	N.Hanlon	SS	J.Peters	LF	P.Gillespie	LF	G.Wood
CF	Jo.O'Rourke	CF	B.Crowley	CF	G.Gore	CF	B.Purcell	CF	P.Hotaling	3B	G.Bradley	CF	J.Cassidy	CF	H.Stovey
RF	Ja.O'Rourke	RF	E.Stearns	RF	K.Kelly	RF	J.Manning	RF	O.Shaffer	LF	T.York	RF	J.Evans	RF	L.Knight
C	P.Powers	C	J.Rowe	C	S.Flint	C	J.Clapp	C	D.Kennedy	CF	P.Hines	C	B.Holbert	C	C.Bennett
										RF	M.Dorgan				
S	J.Richmond	1O	O.Walker	O	T.Beals	O	D.White	3	M.McGeary	C	E.Gross	1	B.Tobin	C	D.Bushong
C	S.Trott	SO	A.Latham	/O	T.Poorman	S3	A.Leonard	C	B.Gilligan			O	B.Dickerson	OP	F.Corey
O	S.Houck	O	D.Driscoll			OC	C.Reilley	/O	A.Hall	O	S.Houck	/C	B.Ewing	O	B.Dickerson
C	J.Bergh	S	D.Mack	P	L.Corcoran	O	J.Sommer	/O	H.Wheeler	3	M.McGeary	/C	B.Harbidge	/O	J.Dorgan
/O	S.Dignan	2	C.Fulmer	P	F.Goldsmith	O	H.Wheeler					/1	D.Brouthers	/3	J.Ellick
/O	D.O'Leary	2	S.Crane			/S	S.Wright					/C	J.Straub	/1	B.Tobin
/C	D.Sullivan	/O	C.Radbourn	/P	C.Guth	/3	A.Booth					/C	M.Lawlor	/O	S.Dignan
/S	G.Wright	/C	T.Kearns									/C	F.Haley	/O	B.Geer
/O	J.Leary	/C	J.Keenan			P	W.White					/O	D.Higham	/O	B.McGunnigle
												/C	C.Ahearn		
P	T.Bond	P	P.Galvin					P	J.McCormick	P	J.Ward	/C	F.Briody	P	L.Richmond
P	C.Foley	P	S.Wiedman					P	G.Gardner			P	M.Welch	/P	T.Nichols
		P	T.Poorman									P	T.Keefe		
		/P	B.McGunnigle									/P	T.Larkin		
												/P	F.Mountain		

TEAM	G	W	L	PCT	GB	R	OR	AB	H	2B	3B	HR	BB	SO	AVG	OBP	SLG	PRO	PRO+	BR	/A	PF	CHI	RC	SB	CS	SBA	SBR
CHI	86	67	17	.798		538	317	3135	876	164	39	4	104	217	.279	.303	.360	.663	119	81	52	106	109	350				
PRO	87	52	32	.619	15	419	299	3196	793	114	34	0	89	186	.248	.268	.313	.581	101	-6	7	97	102	275				
CLE	85	47	37	.560	20	387	337	3002	726	130	52	7	76	237	.242	.261	.327	.588	102	-1	7	98	99	262				
TRO	83	41	42	.494	25.5	392	438	3007	755	114	37	5	120	260	.251	.280	.319	.599	100	15	-6	105	95	275				
WOR	85	40	43	.482	26.5	412	370	3024	699	129	52	8	81	278	.231	.251	.316	.567	86	-21	-54	109	110	246				
BOS	86	40	44	.476	27	416	456	3080	779	134	41	20	105	221	.253	.278	.343	.621	115	34	48	97	95	300				
BUF	85	24	58	.293	42	331	502	2962	669	104	37	3	90	327	.226	.249	.289	.538	82	-48	-54	102	97	218				
CIN	83	21	59	.263	44	296	472	2895	649	91	36	7	75	267	.224	.244	.288	.532	82	-54	-50	99	91	208				
TOT	340					3191		24301	5946	980	328	62	740	1993	.245	.267	.320	.587										

TEAM	CG	SH	SV	IP	H	H/G	HR	BB	SO	RAT	ERA	ERA+	OAV	OOB	PR	/A	PF	CPI	FA	E	DP	FW	PW	BW	SBW	DIF
CHI	80	8	3	775	622	7.2	8	129	367	8.7	1.93	126	.209	.242	38	43	102	83	.913	329	41	2.3	4.2	5.1		13.4
PRO	75	13	6	799	663	7.5	7	51	286	8.0	1.64	134	.215	.228	65	49	93	87	.910	357	53	1.1	4.8	.7		3.5
CLE	83	7	1	759²	685	8.1	4	98	289	9.3	1.90	124	.228	.253	40	39	99	101	.910	330	52	2.0	3.8	.7		-1.5
TRO	81	4	0	738	760	9.3	8	112	169	10.6	2.74	92	.255	.282	-30	-18	106	100	.900	366	58	-.3	-1.7	-.6		2.2
WOR	68	7	5	762²	709	8.4	13	97	297	9.5	2.27	115	.233	.257	9	28	109	94	.906	355	49	.7	2.7	-5.2		.3
BOS	70	4	0	744²	840	10.2	2	86	187	11.2	3.08	74	.276	.296	-59	-67	96	102	.901	367	54	.3	-6.5	4.7		-.5
BUF	72	6	1	739	879	10.7	10	78	186	11.7	3.09	79	.279	.297	-59	-52	104	108	.891	408	55	-2.1	-5.1	-5.2		-4.6
CIN	79	3	0	713¹	785	9.9	10	88	208	11.0	2.44	102	.259	.280	-5	5	105	116	.877	437	49	-4.1	.5	-4.9		-10.6
TOT	608	52	12	6031¹		8.9				10.0	2.37		.245	.267					.901	2949	411					

Runs
Dalrymple-Chi 91
Stovey-Wor 76
Kelly-Chi 72
J.O'Rourke-Bos 71
Gore-Chi 70

Hits
Dalrymple-Chi 126
Anson-Chi 120
Gore-Chi 116
Hines-Pro 115
Connor-Tro 113

Doubles
Dunlap-Cle 27
Dalrymple-Chi 25
Anson-Chi 24
Gore-Chi 23
J.O'Rourke-Bos 22

Triples
Stovey-Wor 14
Dalrymple-Chi 12
J.O'Rourke-Bos ... 11
Hornung-Buf 11
Phillips-Cle 10

Home Runs
Stovey-Wor 6
J.O'Rourke-Bos ... 6
Jones-Bos 5
Dunlap-Cle 4

Total Bases
Dalrymple-Chi 175
Stovey-Wor 161
J.O'Rourke-Bos ... 160
Dunlap-Cle 160
Connor-Tro 156

Runs Batted In
Anson-Chi 74
Kelly-Chi 60
Gore-Chi 47
Connor-Tro 47
J.O'Rourke-Bos 45

Runs Produced
Kelly-Chi 131
Dalrymple-Chi 127
Anson-Chi 127
Gore-Chi 115
J.O'Rourke-Bos ... 110

Bases On Balls
Ferguson-Tro 24
J.O'Rourke-Bos ... 21
Gore-Chi 21
Clapp-Cin 21
Crowley-Buf 19

Batting Average
Gore-Chi .... .360
Anson-Chi .... .337
Connor-Tro .... .332
Dalrymple-Chi ..... .330
Burns-Chi .... .309

On Base Percentage
Gore-Chi .... .399
Anson-Chi .... .362
Connor-Tro .... .357
Dalrymple-Chi ... .335
Burns-Chi .... .333

Slugging Average
Gore-Chi .... .463
Connor-Tro .... .459
Dalrymple-Chi ..... .458
Stovey-Wor .... .454
J.O'Rourke-Bos ... .441

Production
Gore-Chi .... .862
Connor-Tro .... .816
Dalrymple-Chi ..... .793
Anson-Chi .... .781
J.O'Rourke-Bos ... .756

Adjusted Production
Gore-Chi 180
Connor-Tro 166
Jones-Bos 159
J.O'Rourke-Bos ... 158
Dalrymple-Chi 156

Batter Runs
Gore-Chi 30.4
Connor-Tro 25.4
Dalrymple-Chi ... 24.5
Anson-Chi 22.9
J.O'Rourke-Bos ... 19.9

Adjusted Batter Runs
Gore-Chi 26.0
J.O'Rourke-Bos ... 22.2
Connor-Tro 21.8
Dalrymple-Chi 20.2
Hines-Pro 19.1

Clutch Hitting Index
Anson-Chi 178
Hotaling-Cle 147
Kelly-Chi 141
Richmond-Wor 131
Creamer-Wor 127

Runs Created
Gore-Chi 61
Dalrymple-Chi 60
Connor-Tro 57
Anson-Chi 55
J.O'Rourke-Bos ... 52

Total Average
Gore-Chi .... .825
Connor-Tro .... .744
Dalrymple-Chi .... .695
Anson-Chi .... .691
J.O'Rourke-Bos ... .688

Stolen Bases

Stolen Base Average

Stolen Base Runs

Fielding Runs
Irwin-Wor 31.2
Force-Buf 30.9
Bradley-Pro 19.2
Shaffer-Cle 17.2
Clapp-Cin 17.2

Total Player Rating
Irwin-Wor 3.4
Clapp-Cin 2.9
Gore-Chi 2.8
Dunlap-Cle 2.7
Hines-Pro 2.4

Wins
McCormick-Cle 45
Corcoran-Chi 43
Ward-Pro 39
Welch-Tro 34
Richmond-Wor 32

Win Percentage
Goldsmith-Chi .... .875
Corcoran-Chi ..... .754
Ward-Pro .... .619
McCormick-Cle .... .616
Welch-Tro .... .531

Games
Richmond-Wor ... 74
McCormick-Cle ... 74
Ward-Pro 70
Welch-Tro 65

Complete Games
McCormick-Cle ... 72
Welch-Tro 64
Ward-Pro 59
W.White-Cin 58

Shutouts
Ward-Pro 8
McCormick-Cle ... 7
Richmond-Wor 5
Galvin-Buf 5

Saves
Richmond-Wor 3
Corey-Wor 2
Corcoran-Chi 2

Innings Pitched
McCormick-Cle ..657.2
Ward-Pro 595.0
Richmond-Wor ...590.2
Welch-Tro 574.0
Corcoran-Chi ...536.1

Fewest Hits/Game
Keefe-Tro 5.83
Corcoran-Chi 6.78
Bradley-Pro 7.26
Ward-Pro 7.58
Corey-Wor 7.95

Fewest BB/Game
Bradley-Pro .... .28
Galvin-Buf .... .63
Ward-Pro .... .68
Wiedman-Buf ...... .71
Goldsmith-Chi .... .77

Strikeouts
Corcoran-Chi 268
McCormick-Cle ... 260
Richmond-Wor 243
Ward-Pro 230
W.White-Cin 161

Strikeouts/Game
Corcoran-Chi 4.50
Goldsmith-Chi ... 3.85
Richmond-Wor 3.70
McCormick-Cle ... 3.56
Ward-Pro 3.48

Ratio
Keefe-Tro 7.20
Bradley-Pro 7.53
Ward-Pro 8.26
Corcoran-Chi 8.44
Goldsmith-Chi ... 8.86

Earned Run Average
Keefe-Tro .... .86
Bradley-Pro 1.38
Ward-Pro 1.74
Goldsmith-Chi ... 1.75
McCormick-Cle ... 1.85

Adjusted ERA
Keefe-Tro 294
Bradley-Pro 160
Goldsmith-Chi ... 138
McCormick-Cle.... 127
Ward-Pro 127

Opponents' Batting Avg.
Keefe-Tro .... .178
Corcoran-Chi ..... .199
Bradley-Pro ...... .210
Ward-Pro .... .217
Corey-Wor .... .219

Opponents' On Base Pct.
Keefe-Tro .... .212
Bradley-Pro ...... .217
Ward-Pro .... .232
Corcoran-Chi ..... .236
Corey-Wor .... .239

Starter Runs
Ward-Pro 42.0
McCormick-Cle ... 38.5
Corcoran-Chi 25.5
Bradley-Pro 21.7
Keefe-Tro 17.7

Adjusted Starter Runs
McCormick-Cle ... 36.8
Ward-Pro 30.8
Richmond-Wor 29.5
Corcoran-Chi 28.3
W.White-Cin 19.6

Clutch Pitching Index
W.White-Cin 124
Bond-Bos 114
Poorman-Buf-Chi.. 112
Galvin-Buf 111
Goldsmith-Chi ... 109

Relief Runs

Adjusted Relief Runs

Relief Ranking

Total Pitcher Index
McCormick-Cle 4.0
Ward-Pro 3.4
Corcoran-Chi 3.1
Keefe-Tro 2.2
Goldsmith-Chi 1.9

Total Baseball Ranking
Ward-Pro 4.1
McCormick-Cle 3.7
Irwin-Wor 3.4
Bradley-Pro 3.4
Clapp-Cin 2.9

March 8 The NL meets and adopts an 84-game schedule. An enterprising newsman gets the various magnates to predict the winner in the coming pennant race; Chicago is the consensus choice with five votes.

April 11* The Eastern Association is organized to link independent clubs in a loose pennant race. The clubs include the Nationals, Mets, Atlantics, Athletics, New Yorks, Quicksteps (of New York), and New Bostons.

May 4 Boston pitcher Jim Whitney shuts out Providence, 4-0. The hardworking righthander will wind up leading the NL in both wins and losses (with a 31-33 record), a feat not repeated in the major leagues until Phil Niekro does it in 1979.

May 20 Chicago resorts to trickery to beat Boston 5-4. Mike Kelly scores the go-ahead run from second base on a groundout by cutting third base by some 30 feet.

June 20 A new Red Stocking team in Cincinnati takes the field for the first time. This club would be among the founders of the new league, the American Association, next year and would eventually become the NL Reds.

June 25 Chicago's George Gore steals seven bases as the Whites beat Providence, second five times and third twice. This record will be tied only once, by Billy Hamilton on August 31, 1894.

August 14 Statistics published in the *Chicago Tribune* put Dan Brouthers at the top of the batting list with a .390 average. Cap Anson is second with .377. Official figures at the end of the season will declare Anson batting champ with a .399 average, Brouthers finishing seventh at .318.

August 21* The Eclipse club refuses to allow a black man, catcher M. Fleetwood Walker, to play for the visiting Cleveland Whites in a game in Louisville, much to the disgust of many fans and sportswriters.

August 23 Boston left fielder Joe Hornung makes 10 putouts and one assist as the Reds beat Buffalo, 4–3. This one-game record of 11 chances accepted by a left fielder still stands.

September 10 In a game in Albany, Troy's Roger Connor hits the first grand slam in NL history. The blow comes off Worcester's Lee Richmond with two out in the bottom of the ninth inning and wins the game, 8-7.

September 25 Although the league has offered membership to the Mets and the Athletics and been turned down, it is announced that all eight teams from this year will be back in the NL next season, a first for the league.

September 30 The NL meeting adopts an "ironclad" contract that gives the club the right to fine a player for any conduct the club deems detrimental to its interest. Furthermore, the player assumes the responsibility for all risks of injury or illness and must pay for his own medical treatment.

October 8 Chris Von der Ahe, president of the corporation that runs Sportsman's Park in St. Louis, signs the members of the previously independent St. Louis Browns semiprofessional club, giving Von der Ahe control over the players for the first time, a key step toward the establishment of the club that will eventually become the four-time champion of the American Association.

October 10 Cincinnati baseball backers meet in Pittsburgh with H. Denny McKnight and issue a call to other independent club operators to meet Nov. 2 to form a major league independent of the NL. A few weeks later, he organizes a new Allegheny Baseball Club of Pittsburgh in anticipation of the proposed new league.

	BOSTON		BUFFALO		CHICAGO		CLEVELAND		DETROIT		PROVIDENCE		TROY		WORCESTER
M	H.Wright	M	J.O'Rourke	M	C.Anson	M	M.McGeary	M	F.Bancroft	M	J.Farrell	M	B.Ferguson	M	M.Dorgan
1B	J.Morrill	1B	D.Brouthers	1B	C.Anson	M	J.Clapp	1B	M.Powell	M	T.York	1B	R.Connor	M	H.Stovey
2B	J.Burdock	2B	D.Force	2B	J.Quest	1B	B.Phillips	2B	J.Gerhardt	1B	J.Start	2B	B.Ferguson	1B	H.Stovey
SS	R.Barnes	SS	J.Peters	SS	T.Burns	2B	F.Dunlap	SS	S.Houck	2B	J.Farrell	SS	E.Caskin	2B	G.Creamer
3B	E.Sutton	3B	J.O'Rourke	3B	N.Williamson	SS	J.Glasscock	3B	A.Whitney	SS	B.McClellan	3B	F.Hankinson	SS	A.Irwin
LF	J.Hornung	LF	B.Purcell	LF	A.Dalrymple	3B	G.Bradley	LF	G.Wood	3B	J.Denny	LF	P.Gillespie	3B	H.Carpenter
CF	B.Crowley	CF	H.Richardson	CF	G.Gore	LF	M.Moynahan	CF	N.Hanlon	LF	T.York	CF	J.Cassidy	LF	B.Dickerson
RF	F.Lewis	RF	C.Foley	RF	K.Kelly	CF	J.Remsen	RF	L.Knight	CF	P.Hines	RF	J.Evans	CF	P.Hotaling
C	P.Snyder	C	J.Rowe	C	S.Flint	RF	O.Shaffer	C	C.Bennett	RF	J.Ward	C	B.Ewing	RF	F.Corey
						C	J.Clapp			C	E.Gross			C	D.Bushong
C	P.Deasley	12	D.White	O	H.Nicol			1	L.Brown			C	B.Holbert		
O	J.Richmond	C	S.Sullivan	/3	A.Piercy	C	D.Kennedy	C	C.Reilley	CS	B.Gilligan			1O	M.Dorgan
O	B.Mathews	3	J.Morrissey			O	B.Taylor	/3	D.Troy	O	L.Brown	P	T.Keefe	S	C.Nelson
/S	G.Wright	/2	P.Smith	P	L.Corcoran	O	B.Purcell	/O	M.Dorgan	/S	H.Myers	P	M.Welch	/O	P.Smith
/1	P.Quinn	/O	E.Swartwood	P	F.Goldsmith	3	M.McGeary	/C	S.Trott					/O	B.Taylor
/S	S.Wright	/O	J.Manning			3	P.Smith	/3	W.Foley	P	C.Radbourn			/O	L.Pike
						/3	H.Doscher	/O	J.Leary	P	B.Mathews			/C	C.Reilley
P	J.Whitney	P	P.Galvin			/C	P.Powers	/S	E.Stearns					/C	P.Quinn
P	J.Fox	P	J.Lynch			/C	R.Kemmler	/O	D.O'Leary					/S	A.Stratton
								/S	G.Bradley					/O	M.Flaherty
/P	T.Bond					P	J.McCormick	/3	M.Moynahan						
						P	T.Nolan	/3	B.Taylor					P	L.Richmond
								/3	S.Wise					P	H.McCormick
								P	G.Derby						
								P	S.Wiedman						
								P	F.Mountain						
								/P	T.Mullane						
								/P	W.White						

TEAM	G	W	L	PCT	GB	R	OR	AB	H	2B	3B	HR	BB	SO	AVG	OBP	SLG	PRO	PRO+	BR	/A	PF	CHI	RC	SB	CS	SBA	SBR
CHI	84	56	28	.667		550	379	3114	918	157	36	12	140	224	.295	.325	.380	.705	119	85	60	105	105	394				
PRO	85	47	37	.560	9	447	426	3077	780	144	37	11	146	214	.253	.287	.335	.622	100	-4	3	98	104	304				
BUF	83	45	38	.542	10.5	440	447	3019	797	157	50	12	108	270	.264	.289	.361	.650	109	22	28	99	99	323				
DET	84	41	43	.488	15	439	429	2995	780	131	53	17	136	250	.260	.293	.357	.650	103	22	4	104	99	320				
TRO	85	39	45	.464	17	399	429	3046	754	124	31	5	140	240	.248	.281	.314	.595	86	-32	-53	105	100	275				
BOS	83	38	45	.458	17.5	349	410	2916	733	121	27	5	110	193	.251	.279	.317	.596	94	-31	-14	95	93	264				
CLE	85	36	48	.429	20	392	414	3117	796	120	39	7	132	224	.255	.286	.326	.612	100	-16	6	95	93	297				
WOR	83	32	50	.390	23	410	492	3093	781	114	31	7	121	169	.253	.281	.316	.597	86	-31	-54	106	102	281				
TOT	336					3426		24377	6339	1068	304	76	1033	1784	.260	.289	.338	.627										

TEAM	CG	SH	SV	IP	H	H/G	HR	BB	SO	RAT	ERA	ERA+	OAV	OOB	PR	/A	PF	CPI	FA	E	DP	FW	PW	BW	SBW	DIF
CHI	81	9	0	744²	722	8.7	14	122	228	10.2	2.43	113	.243	.273	29	26	99	97	.916	309	54	2.1	2.4	5.6		3.9
PRO	76	7	0	757²	756	9.0	5	138	264	10.6	2.40	111	.243	.275	32	22	96	94	.896	390	66	-2.0	2.1	.3		4.7
BUF	72	5	0	742¹	881	10.7	9	89	185	11.8	2.84	98	.281	.301	-5	-5	100	114	.892	408	48	-3.4	-.5	2.6		4.8
DET	83	10	0	744²	785	9.5	8	137	265	11.1	2.65	110	.257	.289	11	22	105	102	.906	338	80	.5	2.1	.4		-3.9
TRO	85	8	0	770	813	9.5	11	159	207	11.4	2.97	99	.265	.301	-17	-2	106	102	.917	311	70	2.2	-.2	-5.0		-.0
BOS	72	6	3	730²	763	9.4	9	143	199	11.2	2.71	98	.258	.292	5	-4	96	103	.909	325	54	1.0	-.4	-1.3		-2.8
CLE	82	2	0	760	737	8.7	9	126	240	10.2	2.68	98	.244	.274	8	-5	94	87	.904	348	68	.2	-.5	.6		-6.3
WOR	80	5	0	737¹	882	10.8	11	120	196	12.2	3.54	85	.288	.315	-63	-43	109	101	.903	353	50	-.5	-4.0	-5.0		.6
TOT	631	52	3	5987¹		9.5				11.1	2.77		.260	.289					.905	2782	490					

Runs		Hits		Doubles		Triples		Home Runs		Total Bases	
Gore-Chi	86	Anson-Chi	137	Kelly-Chi	27	Rowe-Buf	11	Brouthers-Buf	8	Anson-Chi	175
Kelly-Chi	84	Dalrymple-Chi	117	Hines-Pro	27	Phillips-Cle	10	Bennett-Det	7	Dunlap-Cle	156
Dalrymple-Chi	72	Dickerson-Wor	116	Stovey-Wor	25			Farrell-Pro	5	Kelly-Chi	153
O'Rourke-Buf	71			Dunlap-Cle	25			Burns-Chi	4	Dalrymple-Chi	150
Farrell-Pro	69			White-Buf	24					Dickerson-Wor	149

Runs Batted In		Runs Produced		Bases On Balls		Batting Average		On Base Percentage		Slugging Average	
Anson-Chi	82	Anson-Chi	148	Clapp-Cle	35	Anson-Chi	.399	Anson-Chi	.442	Brouthers-Buf	.541
Bennett-Det	64	Kelly-Chi	137	York-Pro	29	Powell-Det	.338	York-Pro	.362	Anson-Chi	.510
Kelly-Chi	55	Gore-Chi	129	Ferguson-Tro	29	Rowe-Buf	.333	Brouthers-Buf	.361	Rowe-Buf	.480
		Knight-Det	118	Farrell-Pro	29	Start-Pro	.328	Dunlap-Cle	.358	Bennett-Det	.478
		Richardson-Buf	113			Dunlap-Cle	.325	Gore-Chi	.354	Dunlap-Cle	.444

Production		Adjusted Production		Batter Runs		Adjusted Batter Runs		Clutch Hitting Index		Runs Created	
Anson-Chi	.952	Anson-Chi	189	Anson-Chi	38.9	Anson-Chi	34.7	Knight-Det	164	Anson-Chi	79
Brouthers-Buf	.902	Brouthers-Buf	182	Brouthers-Buf	24.1	Brouthers-Buf	25.0	Anson-Chi	145	Dunlap-Cle	57
Bennett-Det	.819	Dunlap-Cle	159	Dunlap-Cle	20.0	Dunlap-Cle	23.8	Ward-Pro	143	Kelly-Chi	55
Dunlap-Cle	.802	York-Pro	150	Bennett-Det	18.3	York-Pro	18.9	Radbourn-Pro	135	Brouthers-Buf	54
York-Pro	.790	Bennett-Det	149	Kelly-Chi	18.0	O'Rourke-Buf	16.0	White-Buf	128	Dalrymple-Chi	54

Total Average		Stolen Bases		Stolen Base Average		Stolen Base Runs		Fielding Runs		Total Player Rating	
Anson-Chi	.976							Ewing-Tro	25.3	Bennett-Det	3.3
Brouthers-Buf	.891							Richardson-Buf	24.6	Anson-Chi	3.1
Bennett-Det	.770							Force-Buf	24.3	Richardson-Buf	3.1
York-Pro	.745							Williamson-Chi	22.2	Dunlap-Cle	3.0
Dunlap-Cle	.734							Bennett-Det	18.3	Ewing-Tro	2.2

Wins		Win Percentage		Games		Complete Games		Shutouts		Saves	
Whitney-Bos	31	Radbourn-Pro	.694	Whitney-Bos	66	Whitney-Bos	57	Derby-Det	9	Mathews-Pro-Bos	2
Corcoran-Chi	31	Corcoran-Chi	.689	McCormick-Cle	59	McCormick-Cle	57	Whitney-Bos	6	Morrill-Bos	1
Derby-Det	29	Goldsmith-Chi	.649	Galvin-Buf	56	Derby-Det	55	Goldsmith-Chi	5		
Galvin-Buf	28	Welch-Tro	.538	Derby-Det	56	Richmond-Wor	50	Galvin-Buf	5		
McCormick-Cle	26	Galvin-Buf	.538	Richmond-Wor	53	Galvin-Buf	48				

Innings Pitched		Fewest Hits/Game		Fewest BB/Game		Strikeouts		Strikeouts/Game		Ratio	
Whitney-Bos	552.1	McCormick-Cle	8.28	Galvin-Buf	.87	Derby-Det	212	Derby-Det	3.86	Wiedman-Det	9.39
McCormick-Cle	526.0	Wiedman-Det	8.45	Wiedman-Det	.94	McCormick-Cle	178	Corcoran-Chi	3.40	McCormick-Cle	9.72
Derby-Det	494.2	Radbourn-Pro	8.55	Goldsmith-Chi	1.20	Whitney-Bos	162	Ward-Pro	3.25	Goldsmith-Chi	10.15
Galvin-Buf	474.0	Corcoran-Chi	8.62	Richmond-Wor	1.32	Richmond-Wor	156	Radbourn-Pro	3.24	Radbourn-Pro	10.32
Richmond-Wor	462.1	Ward-Pro	8.89	McCormick-Cle	1.44	Corcoran-Chi	150	McCormick-Cle	3.05	Ward-Pro	10.34

Earned Run Average		Adjusted ERA		Opponents' Batting Avg.		Opponents' On Base Pct.		Starter Runs		Adjusted Starter Runs	
Wiedman-Det	1.80	Wiedman-Det	162	Radbourn-Pro	.235	Wiedman-Det	.258	Derby-Det	31.5	Derby-Det	39.3
Ward-Pro	2.13	Derby-Det	132	McCormick-Cle	.235	McCormick-Cle	.265	Ward-Pro	23.7	Galvin-Buf	21.3
Derby-Det	2.20	Ward-Pro	125	Wiedman-Det	.238	Radbourn-Pro	.270	Galvin-Buf	21.1	Ward-Pro	19.4
Corcoran-Chi	2.31	Corcoran-Chi	118	Corcoran-Chi	.242	Goldsmith-Chi	.271	Corcoran-Chi	20.3	Corcoran-Chi	18.7
Galvin-Buf	2.37	Galvin-Buf	117	Ward-Pro	.242	Ward-Pro	.271	McCormick-Cle	19.2	Wiedman-Det	14.3

Clutch Pitching Index		Relief Runs		Adjusted Relief Runs		Relief Ranking		Total Pitcher Index		Total Baseball Ranking	
Galvin-Buf	123							Derby-Det	3.0	Bennett-Det	3.3
Derby-Det	112							Galvin-Buf	2.6	Anson-Chi	3.1
Wiedman-Det	109							Ward-Pro	2.5	Richardson-Buf	3.1
Fox-Bos	108							Whitney-Bos	1.9	Dunlap-Cle	3.0
Lynch-Buf	106							Corcoran-Chi	1.4	Derby-Det	2.8

January 7 The NL will continue the practice of using different color patterns on uniforms for the different positions. Third basemen will wear gray and white uniforms, as the blue and white uniforms originally sought were "impossible to obtain."

January 20* The Kentucky Legislature modifies a recently passed law which inadvertently prohibited the playing of baseball games in the commonwealth.

February 4 NL players are now responsible for carrying their own bats and uniforms on road trips. They are also required to purchase and keep clean two complete uniforms, including the white linen ties to be worn on the field at all times.

February 25 Providence players and their opponents will be expected to parade down the streets of Providence in full uniform, accompanied by a brass band, on game days in order to encourage attendance.

May 5 Adrian "Cap" Anson is called out for walking back to his base after a foul ball, instead of running, as the rule specifies. This rule will be amended at the end of the season.

May 13 NL players are told that next season they will not be required to wear the uniforms known as "clown costumes," with different color combinations for each fielding position.

June 5 Boston defeats Detroit, 10–2. According to the *Chicago Tribune*, this is the first time a team scoring in double figures does so entirely with earned runs.

June 6 William "Blondie" Purcell of Buffalo is fined $10 for slicing open a soggy baseball. He did this to compel the umpire to put a fresh ball in play so his pitcher Pud Galvin might be able to throw a curve.

July 24 Chicago sets a NL record for runs by beating Cleveland, 35–4. Seven Chicago players get four or more hits and six score four or more runs. The record will last until June 29, 1897, when Chicago will run up 36 runs against Louisville.

August 17 In what is considered one of the greatest games in the century, Providence beats Detroit 1-0 on an 18th-inning home run by right fielder Charles Radbourn. This game will serve as the longest shutout in major league history until Sept. 1, 1967, when San Francisco blanks Cincinnati, 1-0, in 20 innings.

September 20 Chicago's Larry Corcoran pitches the second no-hitter of his career by shutting out Worcester, 5–0.

September 22 In a special NL meeting Troy and Worcester are kicked out of the league, to be replaced by teams from Philadelphia and New York. When the expelled clubs threaten to boycott the rest of the season, Chicago and Providence agree to play a best-of-nine series after the season to determine the league championship.

September 25 The NL Worcester Brown Stockings come up with a baseball innovation—the doubleheader. It is the first instance of two games for the price of one admission: all previous doubleheaders called for two separate admissions. The last place Brown Stockings will end their third and final season in Worcester by drawing a scant 25 and 18 fans for games against Troy on Sept. 28-29.

October 6 In the first postseason matchup between AA and NL champions, Cincinnati (AA) shuts out Chicago (NL), 4–0. The next day Chicago returns the favor by blanking Cincinnati, 2–0. At this point Cincinnati, under pressure from the AA, reluctantly cancels the series to avoid expulsion from the league.

December 6 At the NL meeting, Troy and Worcester are officially replaced by New York and Philadelphia. Starting in 1883, pitchers will be charged with an error after a walk, balk, wild pitch, or hit by pitch. Catchers will be charged with an error after a passed ball.

	BOSTON		BUFFALO		CHICAGO		CLEVELAND		DETROIT		PROVIDENCE		TROY		WORCESTER
M	J.Morrill	M	J.O'Rourke	M	C.Anson	M	J.McCormick	M	F.Bancroft	M	H.Wright	M	B.Ferguson	M	F.Brown
1B	J.Morrill	1B	D.Brouthers	1B	C.Anson	M	F.Dunlap	1B	M.Powell	1B	J.Start	1B	J.Smith	M	T.Bond
2B	J.Burdock	2B	H.Richardson	2B	T.Burns	1B	B.Phillips	2B	D.Troy	2B	J.Farrell	2B	B.Ferguson	2B	J.Chapman
SS	S.Wise	SS	D.Force	SS	K.Kelly	2B	F.Dunlap	SS	M.McGeary	SS	G.Wright	SS	F.Pfeffer	1B	H.Stovey
3B	E.Sutton	3B	D.White	3B	N.Williamson	SS	J.Glasscock	3B	J.Farrell	3B	J.Denny	3B	B.Ewing	2B	G.Creamer
LF	J.Hornung	LF	B.Purcell	LF	A.Dalrymple	3B	M.Muldoon	LF	G.Wood	LF	T.York	LF	P.Gillespie	SS	A.Irwin
CF	P.Hotaling	CF	J.O'Rourke	CF	G.Gore	LF	D.Esterbrook	CF	N.Hanlon	CF	P.Hines	CF	R.Connor	3B	F.Mann
RF	E.Rowen	RF	C.Foley	RF	H.Nicol	CF	J.Richmond	RF	L.Knight	RF	J.Ward	RF	C.Roseman	LF	J.Clinton
C	P.Deasley	C	J.Rowe	C	S.Flint	RF	O.Shaffer	C	C.Bennett	C	B.Gilligan	C	B.Holbert	CF	J.Hayes
						C	F.Briody							RF	J.Evans
/O	C.Buffinton	C	T.Dolan	2	J.Quest			C	S.Trott	C	S.Nava	O	B.Harbidge	C	D.Bushong
/O	H.McClure			/1	M.Scott	3	H.Doscher	3	A.Whitney	S	T.Manning	O3	J.Cassidy		
		P	P.Galvin			C	J.Kelly	2	T.Forster	O	C.Carroll	OP	J.Egan	SP	F.Corey
P	J.Whitney	P	H.Daily	P	F.Goldsmith	O	D.Rowe	S	W.Kinzie	S	A.Whitney	/O	J.Holdsworth	O	T.O'Brien
P	B.Mathews			P	L.Corcoran	O	J.Tilley	/3	B.Casey	/S	D.Troy			1	J.Smith
		/P	J.Burke			/O	J.Willigrod	S	Y.Robinson	/C	C.Reilley	P	T.Keefe	S	F.McLaughlin
						/O	B.McGunnigle	/2	T.Kearns	/O	C.Sweeney	P	M.Welch	1	E.Cogswell
						/O	J.Dwyer	/2	H.Luff					/O	T.Bond
						/C	D.Kennedy	/3	J.Morrissey	P	C.Radbourn			/O	D.O'Leary
								/S	J.Willigrod					/3	J.Halpin
						P	J.McCormick							/3	E.Merrill
						P	G.Bradley	P	S.Wiedman					/1	J.Irwin
								P	G.Derby						
														P	L.Richmond
														P	F.Mountain
														/P	J.Clarkson

TEAM	G	W	L	PCT	GB	R	OR	AB	H	2B	3B	HR	BB	SO	AVG	OBP	SLG	PRO	PRO+	BR	/A	PF	CHI	RC	SB	CS	SBA	SBR
CHI	84	55	29	.655		604	353	3225	892	209	54	15	142	262	.277	.307	.389	.696	119	82	56	105	108	395				
PRO	84	52	32	.619	3	463	356	3104	776	121	53	11	102	255	.250	.274	.334	.608	96	-16	-15	100	105	291				
BUF	84	45	39	.536	10	500	461	3128	858	146	47	18	116	228	.274	.300	.368	.668	113	50	41	102	98	355				
BOS	85	45	39	.536	10	472	414	3118	823	114	50	15	134	244	.264	.294	.347	.641	107	23	22	100	97	326				
CLE	84	42	40	.512	12	402	411	3009	716	139	40	20	122	261	.238	.268	.331	.599	96	-24	-10	97	95	273				
DET	86	42	41	.506	12.5	407	488	3144	724	117	44	19	122	308	.230	.259	.314	.573	84	-53	-52	100	99	262				
TRO	85	35	48	.422	19.5	430	522	3057	747	116	59	12	109	298	.244	.270	.333	.603	99	-20	1	95	100	282				
WOR	84	18	66	.214	37	379	652	2984	689	109	57	16	113	303	.231	.259	.322	.581	85	-43	-53	102	95	255				
TOT	338					3657		24769	6225	1071	404	126	960	2159	.251	.279	.342	.622										

TEAM	CG	SH	SV	IP	H	H/G	HR	BB	SO	RAT	ERA	ERA+	OAV	OOB	PR	/A	PF	CPI	FA	E	DP	FW	PW	BW	SBW	DIF
CHI	83	7	0	763²	667	7.9	13	102	279	9.1	2.22	129	.221	.246	57	51	99	87	.898	376	54	.1	4.6	5.1		3.1
PRO	80	10	1	752	690	8.3	12	87	273	9.3	2.27	123	.228	.250	51	47	97	94	.901	371	67	.4	4.3	-1.4		6.7
BUF	79	3	0	737	778	9.5	16	114	287	10.9	3.25	90	.254	.280	-30	-30	101	89	.910	315	42	3.3	-2.7	3.7		-1.3
BOS	81	4	0	749	738	8.9	10	77	352	9.8	2.80	102	.239	.258	7	4	99	83	.910	314	37	3.6	.4	2.0		-2.9
CLE	81	4	0	751²	743	8.9	22	132	232	10.5	2.75	101	.249	.280	11	1	97	106	.905	358	71	1.1	.0	-.9		.7
DET	82	7	0	793	808	9.2	19	129	354	10.1	2.98	98	.248	.277	-9	-8	101	94	.893	396	44	-.4	-.7	-4.7		6.4
TRO	81	6	0	757	837	10.0	13	168	189	11.9	3.08	91	.268	.305	-16	-24	98	113	.887	432	70	-2.5	-2.2	.0		-1.9
WOR	75	0	0	738¹	964	11.8	21	151	195	13.6	3.75	83	.294	.325	-71	-54	107	115	.878	468	66	-4.6	-4.9	-4.8		-9.7
TOT	642	41	1	6041²		9.3				10.7	2.89		.251	.279					.897	3030	451					

Runs		Hits		Doubles		Triples		Home Runs		Total Bases	
Gore-Chi	99	Brouthers-Buf	129	Kelly-Chi	37	Connor-Tro	18	Wood-Det	7	Brouthers-Buf	192
Dalrymple-Chi	96	Anson-Chi	126	Anson-Chi	29	Wood-Det	12	Muldoon-Cle	6	Connor-Tro	185
Stovey-Wor	90			Hines-Pro	28	Corey-Wor	12	Brouthers-Buf	6	Hines-Pro	177
Kelly-Chi	81			Williamson-Chi	27					Anson-Chi	174
Purcell-Buf	79			Glasscock-Cle	27					Dalrymple-Chi	167

Runs Batted In		Runs Produced		Bases On Balls		Batting Average		On Base Percentage		Slugging Average	
Anson-Chi	83	Anson-Chi	151	Gore-Chi	29	Brouthers-Buf	.368	Brouthers-Buf	.403	Brouthers-Buf	.547
Brouthers-Buf	63	Gore-Chi	147	Williamson-Chi	27	Anson-Chi	.362	Anson-Chi	.397	Connor-Tro	.530
Williamson-Chi	60	Kelly-Chi	135	Shaffer-Cle	27	Connor-Tro	.330	Whitney-Bos	.382	Whitney-Bos	.510
Richardson-Buf	57	Dalrymple-Chi	131	Hanlon-Det	26	Start-Pro	.329	Gore-Chi	.369	Anson-Chi	.500
Kelly-Chi	55	Brouthers-Buf	128			Whitney-Bos	.323	Connor-Tro	.354	Hines-Pro	.467

Production		Adjusted Production		Batter Runs		Adjusted Batter Runs		Clutch Hitting Index		Runs Created	
Brouthers-Buf	.950	Brouthers-Buf	198	Brouthers-Buf	39.1	Brouthers-Buf	37.5	Pfeffer-Tro	147	Brouthers-Buf	79
Anson-Chi	.897	Connor-Tro	188	Anson-Chi	32.7	Connor-Tro	33.6	Holbert-Tro	146	Anson-Chi	71
Whitney-Bos	.892	Whitney-Bos	183	Connor-Tro	29.7	Anson-Chi	28.9	Anson-Chi	143	Connor-Tro	67
Connor-Tro	.884	Anson-Chi	177	Whitney-Bos	23.7	Whitney-Bos	23.5	Rowen-Bos	129	Hines-Pro	59
Hines-Pro	.793	Hines-Pro	151	Gore-Chi	22.2	Hines-Pro	20.7	Hayes-Wor	128	Gore-Chi	59

Total Average		Stolen Bases	Stolen Base Average	Stolen Base Runs	Fielding Runs		Total Player Rating	
Brouthers-Buf	.959				Glasscock-Cle	24.0	Glasscock-Cle	4.1
Whitney-Bos	.894				A.Irwin-Wor	20.5	Connor-Tro	2.9
Anson-Chi	.874				Evans-Wor	19.8	Williamson-Chi	2.6
Connor-Tro	.846				Dunlap-Cle	17.6	Brouthers-Buf	2.6
Gore-Chi	.736				Williamson-Chi	16.2	Dunlap-Cle	2.6

Wins		Win Percentage		Games		Complete Games		Shutouts		Saves	
McCormick-Cle	36	Corcoran-Chi	.692	McCormick-Cle	68	McCormick-Cle	65	Radbourn-Pro	6	Ward-Pro	1
Radbourn-Pro	33	Radbourn-Pro	.623	Radbourn-Pro	55	Radbourn-Pro	51	Welch-Tro	5		
Goldsmith-Chi	28	Goldsmith-Chi	.622	Galvin-Buf	52	Galvin-Buf	48				
Galvin-Buf	28	Ward-Pro	.613	Whitney-Bos	49	Whitney-Bos	46				
Corcoran-Chi	27	Mathews-Bos	.559	Richmond-Wor	48	Goldsmith-Chi	45				

Innings Pitched		Fewest Hits/Game		Fewest BB/Game		Strikeouts		Strikeouts/Game		Ratio	
McCormick-Cle	595.2	Corcoran-Chi	7.11	Mathews-Bos	.69	Radbourn-Pro	201	Mathews-Bos	4.83	Corcoran-Chi	8.70
Radbourn-Pro	474.0	Radbourn-Pro	8.15	Galvin-Buf	.81	McCormick-Cle	200	Derby-Det	4.52	Radbourn-Pro	9.11
Galvin-Buf	445.1	McCormick-Cle	8.31	Goldsmith-Chi	.84	Derby-Det	182	Corcoran-Chi	4.30	Goldsmith-Chi	9.22
Whitney-Bos	420.0	Goldsmith-Chi	8.38	Wiedman-Det	.85	Whitney-Bos	180	Daily-Buf	4.08	Wiedman-Det	9.42
		Ward-Pro	8.45	Whitney-Bos	.88	Corcoran-Chi	170	Whitney-Bos	3.86	Mathews-Bos	9.47

Earned Run Average		Adjusted ERA		Opponents' Batting Avg.		Opponents' On Base Pct.		Starter Runs		Adjusted Starter Runs	
Corcoran-Chi	1.95	Corcoran-Chi	147	Corcoran-Chi	.200	Corcoran-Chi	.234	Radbourn-Pro	42.0	Radbourn-Pro	37.6
Radbourn-Pro	2.09	Radbourn-Pro	134	Radbourn-Pro	.226	Mathews-Bos	.246	Corcoran-Chi	37.0	Corcoran-Chi	35.9
McCormick-Cle	2.37	Goldsmith-Chi	118	Mathews-Bos	.232	Radbourn-Pro	.246	McCormick-Cle	34.0	McCormick-Cle	27.5
Goldsmith-Chi	2.42	McCormick-Cle	118	Ward-Pro	.232	Wiedman-Det	.253	Goldsmith-Chi	20.8	Goldsmith-Chi	19.5
Keefe-Tro	2.50	Keefe-Tro	113	Daily-Buf	.234	Goldsmith-Chi	.254	Keefe-Tro	16.2	Wiedman-Det	13.5

Clutch Pitching Index		Relief Runs	Adjusted Relief Runs	Relief Ranking	Total Pitcher Index		Total Baseball Ranking	
Egan-Tro	120				Radbourn-Pro	3.4	Glasscock-Cle	4.1
Richmond-Wor	116				Corcoran-Chi	3.1	Radbourn-Pro	3.3
F.Mountain-Wor-Wor	115				Whitney-Bos	3.1	Corcoran-Chi	3.1
Welch-Tro	113				Keefe-Tro	2.2	Whitney-Bos	3.1
Corey-Wor	112				McCormick-Cle	2.0	Connor-Tro	2.9

March 11 In retaliation for the "theft" of Sam Wise and Dasher Troy by the NL, the American Association creates a loophole that allows all players either expelled or blacklisted by the NL to join AA clubs after appealing to a special commission.

May 2 The American Association plays its first game, as visiting Pittsburgh beats Cincinnati, 10-9. The other teams are Baltimore, Louisville, Philadelphia, and St. Louis. Pittsburgh will play its games at Exposition Park, which was later used for games in the Union Association, National League, and Federal League.

July 18 Louisville hurler Tony Mullane pitches both right-handed and left-handed in a game against Baltimore, the first time the feat is performed in the major leagues. Starting in the fourth inning he pitches left-handed whenever Baltimore's lefty hitters are at bat. In addition to continuing to pitch right-handed to right-handed hitters. It works until the ninth when, with two outs, Charlie Householder hits his only homer of the year to beat Mullane, 9-8. A "dandy" whose impeccable grooming and well-waxed mustache earned for him the nickname of "The Count," Tony Mullane won 285 major league games, and the handsome pitcher was equally adept at pitching woo: his drawing power among females is credited with initiating the practice of Ladies Day.

September 5 Baltimore plays the first four innings of its game against Pittsburgh without its uniforms, which have been delayed at the Baltimore train station. Allegheny wins the game, 3-1.

September 11 Tony Mullane pitches a no-hitter over Cincinnati, 2-0. The next day Mullane does not allow a hit until the seventh inning, and wins, 10-4.

October 14 Columbus, which will join the AA in 1883, is officially incorporated with $5,000 in capital stock.

October 28 The Athletics reveal that in their first AA season they reaped a $22,000 profit, more than any NL team earned. This helps convince the NL that the AA is a viable league.

November 18 The case of the Allegheny Club versus Charles Bennett is won by Bennett. Prior to the 1882 season Allegheny (Pittsburgh) signed Bennett to a $100 agreement which stated that he would sign an 1883 contract with Allegheny after the season. Instead, Bennett re-signed with Detroit. This case will later have bearing on the fight over the reserve rule during the Players' League War of 1889-90.

December 9* James H. Dudley, manager of a top black club in Richmond, Virginia, initiates discussion concerning the formation of a black league with teams from New York, Philadelphia, Pittsburgh, Cincinnati, Baltimore, Washington, D.C.

December 14 At its first annual convention, the AA establishes the first permanent staff of umpires in major league history. Previously, the NL and AA umpires were local men hired on game day by the home club.

	BALTIMORE		CINCINNATi		LOUISVILLE		PHILADELPHIA		PITTSBURGH		ST.LOUIS
M	H.Myers	M	P.Snyder	M	D.Mack	M	J.Latham	M	A.Pratt	M	N.Cuthbert
1B	C.Householder	1B	E.Stearns	1B	G.Hecker	1B	J.Latham	1B	C.Lane	1B	C.Comiskey
2B	G.Pierce	2B	B.McPhee	2B	P.Browning	2B	C.Stricker	2B	G.Strief	2B	B.Smiley
SS	H.Myers	SS	C.Fulmer	SS	D.Mack	SS	L.Say	SS	J.Peters	SS	B.Gleason
3B	J.Shetzline	3B	H.Carpenter	3B	B.Schenck	3B	F.Mann	3B	J.Battin	3B	J.Gleason
LF	C.Waitt	LF	J.Sommer	LF	L.Maskrey	LF	J.Birchall	LF	M.Mansell	LF	N.Cuthbert
CF	M.Cline	CF	J.Macullar	CF	J.Reccius	CF	J.Mansell	CF	E.Swartwood	CF	O.Walker
RF	T.Brown	RF	H.Wheeler	RF	J.Wolf	RF	B.Blakiston	RF	J.Leary	RF	G.Seward
C	E.Whiting	C	P.Snyder	C	D.Sullivan	C	J.O'Brien	C	B.Taylor	C	S.Sullivan
3O	H.Jacoby	1	H.Luff	C	J.Strick	CO	J.Dorgan	O	C.Morton	O	H.McCaffery
2	B.Smiley	C	P.Powers	/2	G.Pierce	S	J.Say	C	R.Kemmler	CO	E.Fusselback
/O	N.Scharf	/C	R.Kemmler	/C	J.Crotty	O	J.Richmond	C	J.Keenan	O	E.Brown
O	F.Burt	/O	T.Thompson	/O	P.Reccius	3	P.Smith	O	B.Morgan	/2	C.Morton
/O	B.Jones	/1	B.Tierney	/O	C.Bohn	/O	B.Kienzle	1	J.Goodman	/C	J.Crotty
/3	H.East			/S	P.Smith	/C	J.Straub	/O	R.McKelvy	/2	F.Decker
/2	T.Evers	P	W.White	/2	A.Booth	/O	B.Greenwood	/O	R.Wylie	/2	J.Shoupe
/3	A.Booth	P	H.McCormick	/O	J.Dyler	/O	B.Farrell			/O	B.Mitchell
/O	J.Russ			/O	H.Maskrey	/C	T.Arundel	P	H.Salisbury		
/O	L.Smith			/2	H.McCaffery			P	D.Driscoll	P	J.McGinnis
				/3	J.Say	P	S.Weaver	P	H.Arundel	P	J.Schappert
P	D.Landis			/O	E.Merrill	P	B.Sweeney			P	B.Dorr
P	T.Nichols					P	F.Mountain	/P	M.Critchley		
P	E.Geis			P	T.Mullane			/P	J.Seymour	/P	M.Critchley
						/P	D.Landis			/P	J.Doyle
/P	J.Leary					/P	C.Reynolds			/P	E.Hogan
/P	B.Wise					/P	G.Snyder				
						/P	E.Halbriter				

TEAM	G	W	L	PCT	GB	R	OR	AB	H	2B	3B	HR	BB	SO	AVG	OBP	SLG	PRO	PRO+	BR	/A	PF	CHI	RC	SB	CS	SBA	SBR
CIN	80	55	25	.688		489	268	3007	795	95	47	5	102	204	.264	.289	.332	.621	107	38	12	106	104	295				
PHI	75	41	34	.547	11.5	406	389	2707	660	89	21	5	125	164	.244	.277	.298	.575	88	-4	-50	112	104	229				
LOU	80	42	38	.525	13	443	352	2806	728	110	28	9	128	193	.259	.292	.328	.620	120	37	62	95	99	275				
PIT	79	39	39	.500	15	428	418	2904	730	110	49	8	90	183	.251	.274	.348	.622	118	35	56	95	95	284				
STL	80	37	43	.463	18	399	496	2865	663	87	41	11	112	226	.231	.260	.302	.562	90	-19	-34	104	101	231				
BAL	74	19	54	.260	32.5	273	515	2583	535	60	24	4	72	215	.207	.229	.254	.483	72	-87	-66	92	97	153				
TOT	234					2438		16872	4111	551	220	52	629	1185	.244	.271	.312	.582										

TEAM	CG	SH	SV	IP	H	H/G	HR	BB	SO	RAT	ERA	ERA+	OAV	OOB	PR	/A	PF	CPI	FA	E	DP	FW	PW	BW	SBW	DIF
CIN	77	11	0	721¹	609	7.6	7	125	165	9.2	1.65	160	.214	.247	83	79	98	119	.907	332	41	3.7	7.3	1.1		2.9
PHI	72	2	0	663	682	9.3	13	99	190	10.6	2.97	100	.249	.275	-21	0	111	97	.895	361	36	1.2	.0	-4.6		6.9
LOU	73	6	0	693¹	637	8.3	6	112	240	9.7	2.03	122	.229	.259	51	34	92	113	.893	385	57	1.3	3.1	5.7		-8.1
PIT	77	2	0	696²	694	9.0	4	82	252	10.0	2.79	93	.243	.264	-8	-14	97	90	.889	397	40	.5	-1.3	5.1		-4.3
STL	75	3	1	688¹	729	9.5	7	103	225	10.9	2.92	96	.254	.280	-18	-9	105	101	.875	446	41	-1.6	-.8	-3.1		2.5
BAL	64	1	0	646¹	760	10.6	15	108	113	12.1	3.88	71	.275	.302	-86	-82	102	94	.859	490	41	-5.0	-7.5	-6.1		1.1
TOT	438	25	1	4109		9.0				10.4	2.68		.244	.271					.886	2411	256					

Runs		Hits		Doubles		Triples		Home Runs		Total Bases	
Swartwood-Pit	86	Carpenter-Cin	120	Swartwood-Pit	18	Mansell-Pit	16	Walker-StL	7	Swartwood-Pit	159
Sommer-Cin	82	Browning-Lou	109	Mansell-Pit	18	Taylor-Pit	13	Browning-Lou	5	Mansell-Pit	152
Carpenter-Cin	78	Swartwood-Pit	107	Browning-Lou	17	Wheeler-Cin	11	Swartwood-Pit	4	Carpenter-Cin	148
Browning-Lou	67	Sommer-Cin	102	Taylor-Pit	16	Swartwood-Pit	11			Browning-Lou	147
Birchall-Phi	65	B.Gleason-StL	100	Cuthbert-StL	16	Wolf-Lou	8			Taylor-Pit	135

Runs Batted In		Runs Produced		Bases On Balls		Batting Average		On Base Percentage		Slugging Average	
		Carpenter-Cin	144	J.Gleason-StL	27	Browning-Lou	.378	Browning-Lou	.430	Browning-Lou	.510
		Sommer-Cin	110	Browning-Lou	26	Carpenter-Cin	.342	Swartwood-Pit	.370	Swartwood-Pit	.489
		Comiskey-StL	102	Sommer-Cin	24	Swartwood-Pit	.329	Carpenter-Cin	.360	Taylor-Pit	.452
		Snyder-Cin	98	J.Reccius-Lou	23	O'Brien-Phi	.303	O'Brien-Phi	.339	Mansell-Pit	.438
		Birchall-Phi	92	Swartwood-Pit	21	Wolf-Lou	.299	Sommer-Cin	.333	Carpenter-Cin	.422

Production		Adjusted Production		Batter Runs		Adjusted Batter Runs		Clutch Hitting Index		Runs Created	
Browning-Lou	.940	Browning-Lou	228	Browning-Lou	35.3	Browning-Lou	39.7			Browning-Lou	65
Swartwood-Pit	.859	Swartwood-Pit	197	Swartwood-Pit	29.3	Swartwood-Pit	33.0			Swartwood-Pit	60
Carpenter-Cin	.782	Taylor-Pit	157	Carpenter-Cin	22.0	Carpenter-Cin	18.1			Carpenter-Cin	55
O'Brien-Phi	.758	Carpenter-Cin	154	Taylor-Pit	14.5	Mansell-Pit	17.4			Mansell-Pit	45
Taylor-Pit	.749	Mansell-Pit	150	Mansell-Pit	14.5	Taylor-Pit	17.1			Sommer-Cin	44

Total Average		Stolen Bases		Stolen Base Average		Stolen Base Runs		Fielding Runs		Total Player Rating	
Browning-Lou	.966							Stricker-Phi	22.5	Browning-Lou	4.7
Swartwood-Pit	.826							Snyder-Cin	19.4	Snyder-Cin	2.3
Carpenter-Cin	.684							White-Cin	12.0	Swartwood-Pit	2.2
O'Brien-Phi	.679							Browning-Lou	11.8	O'Brien-Phi	1.9
Taylor-Pit	.660							O'Brien-Phi	11.4	Mansell-Pit	1.8

Wins		Win Percentage		Games		Complete Games		Shutouts		Saves	
White-Cin	40	White-Cin	.769	Mullane-Lou	55	White-Cin	52	White-Cin	8	Fusselback-StL	1
Mullane-Lou	30	Weaver-Phi	.634	White-Cin	54	Mullane-Lou	51	Mullane-Lou	5		
Weaver-Phi	26	McGinnis-StL	.581	McGinnis-StL	45	McGinnis-StL	43	McGinnis-StL	3		
McGinnis-StL	25	Mullane-Lou	.556	Landis-Phi-Bal	44	Weaver-Phi	41	McCormick-Cin	3		
Salisbury-Pit	20	Salisbury-Pit	.526	Weaver-Phi	42	Salisbury-Pit	38	Weaver-Phi	2		

Innings Pitched		Fewest Hits/Game		Fewest BB/Game		Strikeouts		Strikeouts/Game		Ratio	
White-Cin	480.0	Hecker-Lou	6.49	Hecker-Lou	.43	Mullane-Lou	170	Salisbury-Pit	3.63	Hecker-Lou	6.92
Mullane-Lou	460.1	McCormick-Cin	7.25	Driscoll-Pit	.54	Salisbury-Pit	135	Arundel-Pit	3.53	Driscoll-Pit	7.79
McGinnis-StL	388.1	Driscoll-Pit	7.25	Weaver-Phi	.85	McGinnis-StL	134	Mullane-Lou	3.32	McCormick-Cin	8.97
Weaver-Phi	371.0	White-Cin	7.71	Salisbury-Pit	.99	White-Cin	122	McGinnis-StL	3.11	White-Cin	9.04
Landis-Phi-Bal	358.0	Geis-Bal	7.90	Landis-Phi-Bal	1.18	Weaver-Phi	104	J.Reccius-Lou	2.94	Salisbury-Pit	9.46

Earned Run Average		Adjusted ERA		Opponents' Batting Avg.		Opponents' On Base Pct.		Starter Runs		Adjusted Starter Runs	
Driscoll-Pit	1.21	Driscoll-Pit	216	Hecker-Lou	.188	Hecker-Lou	.199	White-Cin	61.1	White-Cin	58.7
Hecker-Lou	1.30	Hecker-Lou	191	McCormick-Cin	.206	Driscoll-Pit	.218	Mullane-Lou	41.2	Driscoll-Pit	31.2
McCormick-Cin	1.52	McCormick-Cin	174	Driscoll-Pit	.206	McCormick-Cin	.243	Driscoll-Pit	32.9	Mullane-Lou	30.7
White-Cin	1.54	White-Cin	172	White-Cin	.216	White-Cin	.244	McCormick-Cin	28.5	McCormick-Cin	27.4
Mullane-Lou	1.88	Mullane-Lou	132	Geis-Bal	.220	Salisbury-Pit	.253	Hecker-Lou	16.0	Hecker-Lou	13.6

Clutch Pitching Index		Relief Runs		Adjusted Relief Runs		Relief Ranking		Total Pitcher Index		Total Baseball Ranking	
White-Cin	124							White-Cin	7.3	White-Cin	7.2
McCormick-Cin	124							Mullane-Lou	5.1	Mullane-Lou	5.0
Mullane-Lou	120							Driscoll-Pit	2.4	Browning-Lou	4.7
J.Reccius-Lou	119							McCormick-Cin	2.1	Driscoll-Pit	2.4
Driscoll-Pit	113							Hecker-Lou	2.1	Snyder-Cin	2.3

February 17 At a meeting between the AA and the NL, the Tripartite Agreement (or the National Agreement) is drafted. In it the leagues, along with the Northwestern League, agree to respect each other's contracts, ending a brief period of player raids. Also, the reserve rule is amended to allow each team to reserve 11 players, an increase of six. The National Agreement will usher in a period of peaceful coexistence, lasting until the Players' League war of 1890.

March 31* The Olympic Town-Ball Club of Philadelphia, the nation's oldest ballclub, celebrates its 50th anniversary.

April 3 The Cleveland club visits the White House, where President Chester A. Arthur greets them by telling them that "Good ballplayers make good citizens."

April 15 The first weekly issue of *Sporting Life,* edited by Francis Richter, is published in Philadelphia. This outstanding magazine will last until 1917.

May 3 John Montgomery Ward becomes the first pitcher in history to hit two home runs in a game, giving him a 10-9 victory over Boston.

May 5 In the first game in Chicago's spectacular new ballpark, featuring 41 uniformed attendants, Detroit scores with two out in the bottom of the ninth to win, 3-2.

May 22 Future evangelist Billy Sunday, playing for the Chicago White Stockings has a miserable major league debut, going 0-for-4 with four strikeouts.

May 28* The first of two games between Fort Wayne and Indianapolis is played under electric lights.

June 9 Philadelphia (NL) receives permission to charge 25 cents for admission, instead of 50 cents, to allow them to compete with their popular cross-town rivals, the AA-leading Athletics. Philadelphia's attendance quadruples for the rest of the season.

June 16 The New York Gothams introduce the concept of "Ladies Day," which will become a baseball staple for nearly 100 years. Ladies, escorted or not, are admitted free. New York whips the Cleveland Spiders, 5-2.

July 28* In the first recorded game in Hawaii, the Honolulu Club wins over the Oceanic Club, 14-13.

August 21 In the most decisive shutout in major league history, Philadelphia routs Providence, 28-0.

September 6 Chicago concludes an extraordinarily successful series against Detroit with a 26–6 win. Chicago tallies six doubles in one inning, a record that won't be topped until Boston hits seven on Aug. 25, 1936. Chicago sets a major league record by scoring 18 runs in the seventh inning.

September 12 At a meeting in Pittsburgh, the Union Association is formed. The UA states its intention to ignore the reserve rule.

September 25* The Union League, later known as the Eastern League (and distinct from the Union Association) is officially formed in New York.

September 27 Boston beats Cleveland, 4-1, to officially clinch the NL title.

October 10 Jim Devlin, a former star pitcher for the Louisville Grays (who was expelled from baseball in 1877 for his role in throwing a series of games at the request of gamblers), dies in Philadelphia. Before his death he served as a policeman.

BOSTON		BUFFALO		CHICAGO		CLEVELAND		DETROIT		NEW YORK		PHILADELPHIA		PROVIDENCE	
M	J.Burdock	M	J.O'Rourke	M	C.Anson	M	F.Bancroft	M	J.Chapman	M	J.Clapp	M	B.Ferguson	M	H.Wright
M	J.Morrill	1B	D.Brouthers	1B	C.Anson	1B	B.Phillips	1B	M.Powell	1B	R.Connor	M	B.Purcell	1B	J.Start
1B	J.Morrill	2B	H.Richardson	2B	F.Pfeffer	2B	F.Dunlap	2B	S.Trott	2B	D.Troy	1B	S.Farrar	2B	J.Farrell
2B	J.Burdock	SS	D.Force	SS	T.Burns	SS	J.Glasscock	SS	S.Houck	SS	E.Caskin	2B	B.Ferguson	SS	A.Irwin
SS	S.Wise	3B	D.White	3B	N.Williamson	3B	M.Muldoon	3B	J.Farrell	3B	F.Hankinson	SS	B.McClellan	3B	J.Denny
3B	E.Sutton	LF	J.O'Rourke	LF	A.Dalrymple	LF	T.York	LF	G.Wood	LF	P.Gillespie	3B	F.Warner	LF	C.Carroll
LF	J.Hornung	CF	J.Lillie	CF	G.Gore	CF	P.Hotaling	CF	N.Hanlon	CF	J.Ward	LF	B.Purcell	CF	P.Hines
CF	E.Smith	RF	O.Shaffer	RF	K.Kelly	RF	J.Evans	RF	S.Wiedman	RF	M.Dorgan	CF	B.Harbidge	RF	J.Cassidy
RF	P.Radford	C	J.Rowe	C	S.Flint	C	D.Bushong	C	C.Bennett	C	B.Ewing	RF	J.Manning	C	B.Gilligan
C	M.Hines											C	E.Gross		
		O	D.Eggler	O	B.Sunday	C	F.Briody	OP	D.Burns	CO	J.Humphries			OP	L.Richmond
OP	C.Buffinton	O	C.Foley			O	B.Crowley	2	J.Quest	C	J.Clapp	CO	F.Ringo	C	S.Nava
C	M.Hackett	/O	D.Kennedy	P	L.Corcoran	/S	G.Bradley	O	T.Mansell	O	G.Pierce	O	F.Lewis	/S	J.Mulvey
1	L.Brown	/C	D.Darling	P	F.Goldsmith	/O	C.Cady	/O	B.Guiney	O	D.Cramer	O	J.Neagle	/1	E.Smith
		/O	T.Suck			/C	C.Broughton			/O	D.Orr	O	C.Doyle		
P	J.Whitney					/O	L.Hunter	P	S.Wiedman			/S	J.Pirie	P	C.Radbourn
		P	P.Galvin	P	H.Daily			P	D.Shaw	P	M.Welch	/2	A.Benedict	P	C.Sweeney
		P	G.Derby	P	J.McCormick			P	J.Jones	P	T.O'Neill	/3	J.Mulvey		
				P	W.Sawyer							/C	A.Wolstenholme		
		/P	E.Cushman					/P	G.Radbourn	/P	M.Allen	/O	B.Gallagher		
		/P	A.Hagan					/P	F.McIntyre			/3	C.Kelly		
		/P	J.Burke									/3	P.Ward		
												/3	B.Gladman		
												/O	J.Kelly		
												/O	C.Waitt		
												/S	C.White		
												P	J.Coleman		
												P	A.Hagan		
												/P	C.Hilsey		
												/P	H.Henderson		
												/P	E.Smith		
												/P	A.Breitenstein		

TEAM	G	W	L	PCT	GB	R	OR	AB	H	2B	3B	HR	BB	SO	AVG	OBP	SLG	PRO	PRO+	BR	/A	PF	CHI	RC	SB	CS	SBA	SBR
BOS	98	63	35	.643		669	456	3657	1010	209	86	34	123	423	.276	.300	.408	.708	114	68	53	102	104	459				
CHI	98	59	39	.602	4	679	540	3658	1000	277	61	13	129	399	.273	.298	.393	.691	106	49	13	106	109	439				
PRO	98	58	40	.592	5	636	436	3685	1001	189	59	21	149	309	.272	.300	.372	.672	104	29	13	103	104	422				
CLE	100	55	42	.567	7.5	476	443	3457	852	184	38	8	139	374	.246	.276	.329	.605	88	-53	-47	99	97	321				
BUF	98	52	45	.536	10.5	614	576	3729	1058	184	59	8	147	342	.284	.311	.371	.682	108	44	30	102	97	441				
NY	98	46	50	.479	16	530	577	3524	900	139	69	24	127	297	.255	.281	.354	.635	96	-18	-12	99	99	360				
DET	101	40	58	.408	23	524	650	3726	931	164	48	13	166	378	.250	.282	.330	.612	93	-46	-21	95	96	355				
PHI	99	17	81	.173	46	437	887	3576	859	181	48	3	141	355	.240	.269	.320	.589	90	-74	-32	91	89	316				
TOT	395					4565		29012	7611	1527	468	124	1121	2877	.262	.290	.360	.650										

TEAM	CG	SH	SV	IP	H	H/G	HR	BB	SO	RAT	ERA	ERA+	OAV	OOB	PR	/A	PF	CPI	FA	E	DP	FW	PW	BW	SBW	DIF
BOS	89	6	3	860	853	8.9	11	90	538	9.9	2.55	121	.245	.264	56	52	99	96	.901	409	58	3.1	4.5	4.6		1.7
CHI	91	5	1	862	942	9.8	21	123	299	11.1	2.78	115	.260	.284	34	37	102	109	.879	543	76	-3.5	3.2	1.1		9.1
PRO	88	4	1	871	827	8.5	12	111	376	9.7	2.37	130	.238	.262	75	68	100	99	.903	419	75	2.7	5.9	1.1		-.7
CLE	92	5	2	879	818	8.4	7	217	402	10.6	2.22	142	.237	.282	89	92	100	118	.909	389	69	4.6	8.0	-4.1		-2.0
BUF	90	5	2	859¹	971	10.2	12	101	362	11.2	3.32	96	.268	.288	-17	-8	101	97	.896	445	52	1.4	-.7	2.6		.2
NY	87	5	0	866	907	9.4	19	170	323	11.2	2.94	105	.253	.287	19	11	99	101	.889	468	52	.2	1.0	-1.0		-2.1
DET	89	5	2	894¹	1026	10.3	22	184	324	12.2	3.58	87	.270	.303	-44	-49	99	98	.893	470	77	.9	-4.3	-1.8		-3.7
PHI	91	3	0	864²	1267	13.2	20	125	253	14.5	5.34	58	.318	.338	-212	-216	98	92	.858	639	62	-8.0	-18.9	-2.8		-2.4
TOT	717	38	11	6956¹		9.8				11.3	3.14		.262	.290					.891	3782	521					

Runs
Hornung-Bos 107
Gore-Chi 105
O'Rourke-Buf 102
Sutton-Bos 101
Hines-Pro 94

Hits
Brouthers-Buf 159
Connor-NY 146
O'Rourke-Buf 143
Sutton-Bos 134
Wood-Det 133

Doubles
Williamson-Chi 49
Brouthers-Buf 41
Burns-Chi 37
Anson-Chi 36

Triples
Brouthers-Buf 17
Morrill-Bos 16
Sutton-Bos 15
Connor-NY 15

Home Runs
Ewing-NY 10
Hornung-Bos 8
Denny-Pro 8
Ward-NY 7
Morrill-Bos 6

Total Bases
Brouthers-Buf 243
Morrill-Bos 212
Connor-NY 207
Sutton-Bos 201
Hornung-Bos 199

Runs Batted In
Brouthers-Buf 97
Burdock-Bos 88
Sutton-Bos 73
Morrill-Bos 68
Anson-Chi 68

Runs Produced
Brouthers-Buf 179
Sutton-Bos 171
Hornung-Bos 165
Burdock-Bos 163
Gore-Chi 155

Bases On Balls
York-Cle 37
Hanlon-Det 34
Powell-Det 28
Shaffer-Buf 27
Gore-Chi 27

Batting Average
Brouthers-Buf ..... .374
Connor-NY ..... .357
Gore-Chi ..... .334
Burdock-Bos ..... .330
O'Rourke-Buf ..... .328

On Base Percentage
Brouthers-Buf ..... .397
Connor-NY ..... .394
Gore-Chi ..... .377
Dunlap-Cle ..... .361
Burdock-Bos ..... .353

Slugging Average
Brouthers-Buf ..... .572
Morrill-Bos ..... .525
Connor-NY ..... .506
Sutton-Bos ..... .486
Ewing-NY ..... .481

Production
Brouthers-Buf ..... .969
Connor-NY ..... .900
Morrill-Bos ..... .868
Gore-Chi ..... .849
Sutton-Bos ..... .836

Adjusted Production
Brouthers-Buf 186
Connor-NY 173
Morrill-Bos 155
Bennett-Det 155
Gore-Chi 148

Batter Runs
Brouthers-Buf 44.4
Connor-NY 34.6
Morrill-Bos 27.6
Gore-Chi 26.5
Sutton-Bos 24.4

Adjusted Batter Runs
Brouthers-Buf 41.9
Connor-NY 35.7
Morrill-Bos 25.4
Bennett-Det 25.0
Wood-Det 22.9

Clutch Hitting Index
Start-Pro 140
Burdock-Bos 135
Kelly-Chi 131
Sutton-Bos 131
Anson-Chi 124

Runs Created
Brouthers-Buf 99
Connor-NY 84
Morrill-Bos 75
Sutton-Bos 72
Gore-Chi 72

Total Average
Brouthers-Buf ..... .974
Connor-NY ..... .882
Morrill-Bos ..... .825
Gore-Chi ..... .812
Bennett-Det ..... .783

Stolen Bases

Stolen Base Average

Stolen Base Runs

Fielding Runs
Farrell-Pro 24.9
Shaffer-Buf 20.0
Ward-NY 19.3
Richardson-Buf 18.7
Williamson-Chi 17.8

Total Player Rating
Farrell-Pro 3.3
Richardson-Buf 3.1
Brouthers-Buf 2.9
Gore-Chi 2.7
Dunlap-Cle 2.7

Wins
Radbourn-Pro 48
Galvin-Buf 46
Whitney-Bos 37
Corcoran-Chi 34
McCormick-Cle 28

Win Percentage
McCormick-Cle ..... .700
Radbourn-Pro ..... .658
Buffinton-Bos ..... .641
Whitney-Bos ..... .638
Corcoran-Chi ..... .630

Games
Radbourn-Pro 76
Galvin-Buf 76
Coleman-Phi 65
Whitney-Bos 62
Corcoran-Chi 56

Complete Games
Galvin-Buf 72
Radbourn-Pro 66
Coleman-Phi 59
Whitney-Bos 54
Corcoran-Chi 51

Shutouts
Galvin-Buf 5
Welch-NY 4
Radbourn-Pro 4
Daily-Cle 4
Buffinton-Bos 4

Saves
Wiedman-Det 2
Whitney-Bos 2

Innings Pitched
Galvin-Buf 656.1
Radbourn-Pro 632.1
Coleman-Phi 538.1
Whitney-Bos 514.0
Corcoran-Chi 473.2

Fewest Hits/Game
Sawyer-Cle 7.60
Radbourn-Pro 8.01
McCormick-Cle 8.32
Daily-Cle 8.56
Whitney-Bos 8.61

Fewest BB/Game
Whitney-Bos ..... .61
Galvin-Buf ..... .69
Radbourn-Pro ..... .80
Coleman-Phi ..... .80
Goldsmith-Chi ..... .92

Strikeouts
Whitney-Bos 345
Radbourn-Pro 315
Galvin-Buf 279
Corcoran-Chi 216
Buffinton-Bos 188

Strikeouts/Game
Whitney-Bos 6.04
Buffinton-Bos 5.08
Sawyer-Cle 4.85
Radbourn-Pro 4.48
Corcoran-Chi 4.10

Ratio
Radbourn-Pro 8.81
Whitney-Bos 9.23
Galvin-Buf 9.96
McCormick-Cle 10.03
Ward-NY 10.04

Earned Run Average
McCormick-Cle 1.84
Radbourn-Pro 2.05
Whitney-Bos 2.24
Sawyer-Cle 2.36
Daily-Cle 2.42

Adjusted ERA
McCormick-Cle 171
Radbourn-Pro 150
Whitney-Bos 138
Sawyer-Cle 133
Daily-Cle 130

Opponents' Batting Avg.
Sawyer-Cle ..... .217
Radbourn-Pro ..... .227
McCormick-Cle ..... .233
Sweeney-Pro ..... .237
Whitney-Bos ..... .238

Opponents' On Base Pct.
Radbourn-Pro ..... .244
Whitney-Bos ..... .251
Galvin-Buf ..... .265
Ward-NY ..... .267
McCormick-Cle ..... .268

Starter Runs
Radbourn-Pro 76.4
Whitney-Bos 51.2
McCormick-Cle 49.2
Corcoran-Chi 34.1
Galvin-Buf 30.8

Adjusted Starter Runs
Radbourn-Pro 72.7
McCormick-Cle 49.7
Whitney-Bos 49.0
Corcoran-Chi 36.8
Galvin-Buf 33.5

Clutch Pitching Index
McCormick-Cle 125
Shaw-Det 121
Daily-Cle 119
O'Neill-NY 118
Goldsmith-Chi 113

Relief Runs

Adjusted Relief Runs

Relief Ranking

Total Pitcher Index
Radbourn-Pro 8.4
Whitney-Bos 6.0
McCormick-Cle 5.4
Corcoran-Chi 3.3
Galvin-Buf 2.6

Total Baseball Ranking
Radbourn-Pro 8.1
Whitney-Bos 6.1
McCormick-Cle 5.3
Farrell-Pro 3.3
Ward-NY 3.1

January 13 Both of the New York major league clubs will play games simultaneously at the Polo Grounds. Their fields will be separated by an eight-foot fence.

January 31* A Baltimore fan loses a suit against Baltimore player Andrew Burns, who, while batting, accidentally let his bat slip from his hands, hitting the spectator. The judge rules fans had been warned to keep a safe distance from the field.

March 14* In a Northwestern League meeting, Peoria moves to ban blacks in order to prevent Toledo from playing star catcher Moses Fleetwood Walker. After an "exciting discussion" the motion is withdrawn and Walker is allowed to play.

May 28 Heavyweight boxing champion John L. Sullivan pitches the Mets to a 20–15 victory in an exhibition game. For his efforts Sullivan pockets half of the proceeds—$1,595. On November 4 Sullivan will pitch another game.

June 13 The Allegheny field is partially underwater following a series of floods in Pittsburgh. Columbus scores in every inning to overcome the water-logged home club by a count of 25-10.

July 4 Tim Keefe of New York wins both ends of a doubleheader against Columbus, 9–3, and, 1–0, allowing a total of three hits.

July 6 Cincinnati thrashes Baltimore, 23–0, setting a major league record for the most decisive shutout. The record lasts for 46 days.

August 20 After the Eclipse-Allegheny game, Allegheny players Billy Taylor, Mike Mansell, and George Creamer are each fined $100 and suspended indefinitely for drunkenness.

September 4 Columbus crushes Baltimore, 21-4, behind Tom Brown, who goes 6-for-7 with five runs and four extra-base hits.

September 6 The Athletics cling to their lead in the AA by defeating second-place St. Louis for the third consecutive game. Over 45,000 fans attend the series.

September 12 Cincinnati mauls Allegheny, 27-5. Hick Carpenter and Long John Reilly each get six hits, while Reilly also scores six runs and hits for the cycle.

September 19 Cincinnati first baseman Long John Reilly again hits for the cycle against Philadelphia.

September 28 After losing two straight games to the Eclipse, the Athletics rally in the 10th inning for a 7-6 win to clinch the AA championship.

November 22 New York owner John B. Day proposes a resolution to prohibit a team from signing a player who has broken the reserve clause in his contract. This resolution, eventually adopted by both the AA and the NL, effectively changes the reserve rule from a device designed to protect owners from their own greediness to a vindictive weapon to be used against uncooperative players.

November 24 The AA agrees to expand to 12 teams by admitting Brooklyn, Washington, Indianapolis and Toledo.

December 15* In Louisville a "first-class colored team" is formed. The team, later known as the Falls Cities, becomes one of the nation's best black teams. It joins the National Colored Base Ball League (NCBBL) in 1887, but apparently disbands shortly after the collapse of the NCBBL in the first week of its season.

BALTIMORE		CINCINNATI		COLUMBUS		LOUISVILLE		NEW YORK		PHILADELPHIA		PITTSBURGH		ST.LOUIS	
M	B.Barnie	M	P.Snyder	M	H.Phillips	M	J.Gerhardt	M	J.Mutrie	M	L.Knight	M	A.Pratt	M	T.Sullivan
1B	E.Stearns	1B	J.Reilly	1B	J.Field	1B	J.Latham	1B	S.Brady	1B	H.Stovey	M	O.Butler	M	C.Comiskey
2B	T.Manning	2B	B.McPhee	2B	P.Smith	2B	J.Gerhardt	2B	S.Crane	2B	C.Stricker	M	J.Battin	1B	C.Comiskey
SS	L.Say	SS	C.Fulmer	SS	J.Richmond	SS	J.Leary	SS	C.Nelson	SS	M.Moynahan	1B	E.Swartwood	2B	G.Strief
3B	J.McCormick	3B	H.Carpenter	3B	B.Kuehne	3B	J.Gleason	3B	D.Esterbrook	3B	G.Bradley	2B	G.Creamer	SS	B.Gleason
LF	J.Clinton	LF	J.Sommer	LF	H.Wheeler	LF	P.Browning	LF	E.Kennedy	LF	J.Birchall	3B	J.Battin	3B	A.Latham
CF	D.Eggler	CF	C.Jones	CF	F.Mann	CF	L.Maskrey	CF	J.O'Rourke	CF	B.Blakiston	LF	M.Mansell	LF	T.Dolan
RF	D.Rowe	RF	P.Corkhill	RF	T.Brown	RF	J.Wolf	RF	C.Roseman	RF	L.Knight	CF	B.Dickerson	CF	F.Lewis
C	J.Kelly	C	P.Snyder	C	R.Kemmler	C	E.Whiting	C	B.Holbert	C	J.O'Brien	RF	B.Taylor	RF	H.Nicol
												C	J.Hayes	C	P.Deasley
O	G.Gardner	CO	P.Powers	C1	J.Straub	C	D.Sullivan	C	C.Reipschlager	3P	F.Corey			O	T.Mansell
2	T.O'Brien	C	B.Traffley	/2	G.Pierce	SO	T.McLaughlin	/1	D.Orr	C	E.Rowen	S	F.McLaughlin	2	J.Quest
CO	P.Baker	O	J.Macullar	/1	B.Schwartz	O	J.Reccius			O	B.Crowley	S	B.Morgan	O	N.Cuthbert
C	R.Sweeney	/O	P.Weihe			1	L.Brown	P	T.Keefe	/S	A.Hubbard	/C	W.Blogg	/O	J.Gleason
2	B.Reid			P	F.Mountain	/1	H.Luff	P	J.Lynch	/O	C.Mason	/S	J.Peters	/C	S.Sullivan
/O	B.Gallagher	P	W.White	P	E.Dundon	/O	G.Winkelman					/1	H.Oberbeck	/O	T.Loftus
C	B.Barnie	P	R.Deagle	P	J.Valentine	/O	W.Prince			P	B.Mathews			/O	H.McCaffery
/C	C.Broughton	P	H.McCormick			/O	J.Jones			P	J.Jones	P	D.Driscoll	/O	H.Oberbeck
/S	G.Baker			/P	P.Fries	/O	P.Reccius			P	J.Bakely	P	B.Barr	/O	J.Ewing
/S	N.Scharf	/P	B.Mountjoy	/P	F.McIntyre							P	J.Neagle	/O	J.Gorman
/2	J.Leary					P	G.Hecker								
/S	B.Farrell					P	S.Weaver					/P	T.Nolan	P	T.Mullane
/O	B.Loughlin											/P	N.Baker	P	J.McGinnis
/C	C.Ingraham													/P	C.Hodnett
/C	D.Oldfield														
/O	D.Allison														
P	H.Henderson														
P	B.Emslie														
P	J.Fox														
/P	J.Neagle														
/P	J.Devine														

TEAM	G	W	L	PCT	GB	R	OR	AB	H	2B	3B	HR	BB	SO	AVG	OBP	SLG	PRO	PRO+	BR	/A	PF	CHI	RC	SB	CS	SBA	SBR
PHI	98	66	32	.673	—	720	547	3712	974	149	50	20	200	268	.262	.300	.346	.646	103	45	-5	108	114	395				
STL	98	65	33	.663	1	549	409	3495	891	118	46	7	124	240	.255	.280	.321	.601	91	-14	-44	106	104	323				
CIN	98	61	37	.622	5	662	413	3669	961	122	74	34	139	261	.262	.289	.363	.652	106	46	12	106	108	395				
NY	97	54	42	.563	11	498	405	3534	883	111	58	6	142	259	.250	.279	.319	.598	91	-17	-40	104	93	322				
LOU	98	52	45	.536	13.5	564	562	3553	892	114	64	14	141	304	.251	.280	.331	.611	107	-3	38	93	103	337				
COL	97	32	65	.330	33.5	476	659	3553	854	101	79	15	134	409	.240	.268	.326	.594	102	-25	17	92	90	318				
PIT	98	31	67	.316	35	525	728	3607	892	120	58	13	164	345	.247	.280	.324	.604	102	-10	-15	95	95	335				
BAL	96	28	68	.292	37	471	742	3532	870	125	49	5	164	331	.246	.280	.314	.594	91	-21	-37	103	89	318				
TOT	390					4465		28655	7217	960	478	114	1208	2417	.252	.282	.331	.613										

TEAM	CG	SH	SV	IP	H	H/G	HR	BB	SO	RAT	ERA	ERA+	OAV	OOB	PR	/A	PF	CPI	FA	E	DP	FW	PW	BW	SBW	DIF
PHI	92	1	0	873	921	9.5	22	95	347	10.5	2.88	121	.254	.273	41	57	105	113	.865	584	40	-4.1	5.0	-.4		16.5
STL	93	9	1	879¹	729	7.5	7	150	325	9.0	2.23	156	.211	.244	104	122	106	97	.909	388	62	4.5	10.7	-3.9		4.6
CIN	96	8	0	866²	766	8.0	17	168	215	9.7	2.26	143	.222	.258	100	94	98	114	.905	383	57	4.7	8.3	1.1		-2.0
NY	97	6	0	874	751	7.7	12	123	490	9.0	2.90	115	.218	.244	38	41	101	78	.905	391	45	4.1	3.6	-3.5		1.8
LOU	96	7	0	873²	987	10.2	7	110	269	11.3	3.50	85	.267	.288	-20	-50	91	101	.886	478	67	.6	-4.4	3.3		4.0
COL	90	4	0	840¹	980	10.5	16	211	222	12.8	3.96	78	.274	.314	-62	-83	93	105	.874	535	69	-2.1	-7.3	1.5		-8.5
PIT	82	1	1	867²	1140	11.8	21	151	271	13.4	4.62	69	.298	.325	-127	-137	97	102	.884	504	55	-.6	-12.1	1.3		-6.7
BAL	86	1	0	844²	943	10.0	12	190	290	12.1	4.08	85	.265	.303	-74	-58	105	93	.855	624	44	-6.3	-5.1	-3.3		-5.4
TOT	732	37	2	6919¹		9.4				10.9	3.30		.252	.282					.885	3887	439					

Runs		Hits		Doubles		Triples		Home Runs		Total Bases	
Stovey-Phi	110	Swartwood-Pit	147	Stovey-Phi	31	Smith-Col	17	Stovey-Phi	14	Stovey-Phi	213
Reilly-Cin	103	Reilly-Cin	136	Swartwood-Pit	24	Reilly-Cin	14	Jones-Cin	10	Reilly-Cin	212
Carpenter-Cin	99	Carpenter-Cin	130	Knight-Phi	23	Kuehne-Col	14	Reilly-Cin	9	Swartwood-Pit	196
Knight-Phi	98	Stovey-Phi	128	Hayes-Pit	23	Mansell-Pit	13	Fulmer-Col	5	Jones-Cin	184
		Nelson-NY	127			Mann-Col	13	Brown-Col	5	B.Gleason-StL	167

Runs Batted In		Runs Produced		Bases On Balls		Batting Average		On Base Percentage		Slugging Average	
		Reilly-Cin	173	Stearns-Bal	34	Swartwood-Pit	.357	Swartwood-Pit	.394	Stovey-Phi	.506
		Stovey-Phi	162	Nelson-NY	31	Browning-Lou	.338	Browning-Lou	.378	Reilly-Cin	.485
		Moynahan-Phi	156	Moynahan-Phi	31	Clinton-Bal	.313	Moynahan-Phi	.360	Swartwood-Pit	.476
		Jones-Cin	154	J.Gleason-StL-Lou	29	Rowe-Bal	.313	Clinton-Bal	.357	Jones-Cin	.471
		Knight-Phi	150			Reilly-Cin	.311	Nelson-NY	.353	Browning-Lou	.464

Production		Adjusted Production		Batter Runs		Adjusted Batter Runs		Clutch Hitting Index		Runs Created	
Swartwood-Pit	.869	Swartwood-Pit	187	Swartwood-Pit	35.5	Swartwood-Pit	40.2			Swartwood-Pit	79
Stovey-Phi	.852	Browning-Lou	183	Stovey-Phi	32.4	Browning-Lou	33.8			Stovey-Phi	76
Browning-Lou	.842	Stovey-Phi	158	Browning-Lou	27.4	Stovey-Phi	24.7			Reilly-Cin	71
Reilly-Cin	.810	Reilly-Cin	149	Reilly-Cin	26.1	Reilly-Cin	21.0			Browning-Lou	64
Jones-Cin	.799	Jones-Cin	146	Jones-Cin	22.8	Jones-Cin	18.2			Jones-Cin	62

Total Average		Stolen Bases		Stolen Base Average		Stolen Base Runs		Fielding Runs		Total Player Rating	
Swartwood-Pit	.834							Holbert-NY	34.4	Richmond-Col	3.5
Stovey-Phi	.819							Battin-Pit	28.9	Smith-Col	3.1
Browning-Lou	.797							Richmond-Col	25.5	Swartwood-Pit	3.1
Jones-Cin	.739							Latham-StL	21.8	Gerhardt-Lou	2.4
Reilly-Cin	.734							Gerhardt-Lou	20.3	Browning-Lou	2.3

Wins		Win Percentage		Games		Complete Games		Shutouts		Saves	
White-Cin	43	Mullane-StL	.700	Keefe-NY	68	Keefe-NY	68	White-Cin	6	Mullane-StL	1
Keefe-NY	41	Mathews-Phi	.698	White-Cin	65	White-Cin	64	McGinnis-StL	6	Barr-Pit	1
Mullane-StL	35	Bradley-Phi	.696	Mountain-Col	59	Mountain-Col	57	Keefe-NY	5		
Mathews-Phi	30	White-Cin	.662	Mullane-StL	53	Hecker-Lou	51	Weaver-Lou	4		
		McGinnis-StL	.636	Hecker-Lou	53	Mullane-StL	49	Mountain-Col	4		

Innings Pitched		Fewest Hits/Game		Fewest BB/Game		Strikeouts		Strikeouts/Game		Ratio	
Keefe-NY	619.0	Keefe-NY	7.10	Mathews-Phi	.73	Keefe-NY	359	Keefe-NY	5.22	Keefe-NY	8.67
White-Cin	577.0	Mullane-StL	7.27	Weaver-Lou	.79	Mathews-Phi	203	Mathews-Phi	4.80	Mullane-StL	8.71
Mountain-Col	503.0	White-Cin	7.38	Lynch-NY	.88	Mullane-StL	191	Lynch-NY	4.20	White-Cin	9.00
Hecker-Lou	469.0	McGinnis-StL	7.64	Bradley-Phi	.92	Hecker-Lou	164	Mullane-StL	3.73	McGinnis-StL	9.27
Mullane-StL	460.2	Deagle-Cin	8.27	Driscoll-Pit	1.04	Mountain-Col	159	Henderson-Bal	3.64	Bradley-Phi	9.95

Earned Run Average		Adjusted ERA		Opponents' Batting Avg.		Opponents' On Base Pct.		Starter Runs		Adjusted Starter Runs	
White-Cin	2.09	Mullane-StL	159	Keefe-NY	.203	Keefe-NY	.237	White-Cin	77.4	White-Cin	73.8
Mullane-StL	2.19	White-Cin	155	Mullane-StL	.207	Mullane-StL	.238	Keefe-NY	60.8	Mullane-StL	66.1
Deagle-Cin	2.31	McGinnis-StL	149	White-Cin	.209	White-Cin	.244	Mullane-StL	56.8	Keefe-NY	63.5
McGinnis-StL	2.33	Mathews-Phi	141	McGinnis-StL	.215	McGinnis-StL	.249	McGinnis-StL	41.2	McGinnis-StL	48.9
Keefe-NY	2.41	Deagle-Cin	140	Deagle-Cin	.229	Bradley-Phi	.263	Mathews-Phi	35.6	Mathews-Phi	42.8

Clutch Pitching Index		Relief Runs		Adjusted Relief Runs		Relief Ranking		Total Pitcher Index		Total Baseball Ranking	
Mathews-Phi	127							White-Cin	6.6	White-Cin	6.6
Corey-Phi	124							Keefe-NY	6.6	Keefe-NY	6.6
McCormick-Cin	123							Mullane-StL	6.2	Mullane-StL	5.9
Valentine-Col	122							McGinnis-StL	4.2	McGinnis-StL	4.0
Deagle-Cin	117							Mathews-Phi	3.2	Richmond-Col	3.5

January 4* The newly organized Union League changes its name to Eastern League to avoid confusion with the new Union Association. The EL continues today as the AAA International League.

January 4 Larry Corcoran, who had signed with Chicago of the outlaw UA, breaks his contract to re-sign with his old club, Chicago's NL White Stockings.

March 4 The NL, meeting in Buffalo, reduces the number of balls required for a walk from seven to six. Club owners also agree to provide separate team benches to minimize fraternizing among opposing players during games.

March 6 High winds in New York destroy much of the fence and blow off part of the Polo Grounds grandstand roof, depositing it a block away.

May 14 Pitcher Charles Radbourn gets five hits—the same number he allows Detroit—to spur a 25–3 rout, the most decisive victory in the NL this year. Detroit contributes to its own demise by committing 18 errors, including five by right fielder Fred Wood, whose major league career will total only 13 games.

May 16 When a foul tip from a Detroit batter sticks in the mask of Boston catcher Mike Hines, umpire Van Court calls the batter out on a foul catch. NL Secretary Nick Young will later instruct league umpires not to rule an out in such cases.

May 29 Taking advantage of a ground rule change which scores balls hit over the close right field Chicago fence as home runs (instead of doubles), five players hit homers in the White Stockings' home opener against Detroit. Chicago will hit 142 during the 112-game season (more than 90 percent of them at home) to set a record that will be broken by the 1927 New York Yankees.

May 30 In the afternoon game of Chicago's doubleheader with Detroit, White Stocking Ned Williamson doubles and hits a major league record three home runs as Chicago overwhelms the Wolverines, 12–2. Williamson's homers are his first of 27 (25 at home), which will set a major league season record not broken until Babe Ruth hits 29 in 1919.

June 7 Charlie Sweeney of Providence strikes out 19 Boston Red Stockings to establish a major league record for a nine-inning game. It will be tied one month later but not broken until Roger Clemens fans 20 on April 29, 1986. Providence's 2–1 win moves it into first place, but Boston will take the next four from the Grays to regain the lead.

June 27 Chicago ace Larry Corcoran ends the Providence Grays' 10-game winning streak with the NL's first no-hitter of the season. The 6–0 win is Corcoran's third major league no-hitter.

July 22 Providence star Charles Sweeney is suspended without pay after he refuses to move from the mound to right field in the ninth inning with a safe lead over Philadelphia. Sweeney quits the Grays and jumps to St. Louis (UA), for whom he wins 24 games for a season's total of 41. As a result, Charles Radbourn is forced to pitch almost every game for the rest of the year. Sweeney's stubbornness has an immediate effect as substitute pitcher Joseph "Cyclone" Miller surrenders eight runs and gives the Athletics a 10–6 win.

August 28 Mickey Welch, who will win 39 games in 1884 and 307 in just 13 years, sets the all-time major league record by fanning the first nine Philadelphia batters he faces.

October 22 The weekly *Sporting Life* announces—just one day before the start of the event—that the two pennant winners have agreed to meet in a three-game series Oct. 23–25 at New York's Polo Grounds to decide "the championship of America."

October 25 Hoss Radbourn of Providence wins his third straight over the AA Mets to sweep the three-games series to capture the first World Series.

November 20 The NL agrees to allow overhand pitching, but rules that pitchers must keep both feet on the ground throughout their pitching motion in order to reduce the velocity of their pitches. They still must throw the ball at the height requested by the batter.

BOSTON	BUFFALO	CHICAGO	CLEVELAND	DETROIT	NEW YORK	PHILADELPHIA	PROVIDENCE
M J.Morrill 1B J.Morrill 2B J.Burdock SS S.Wise 3B E.Sutton LF J.Hornung CF J.Manning RF B.Crowley C M.Hackett C M.Hines O B.Annis C T.Gunning /O G.Moriarity /C M.Barrett P C.Buffinton P J.Whitney /P J.Connor /P D.Davis	M J.O'Rourke 1B D.Brouthers 2B H.Richardson SS D.Force 3B D.White LF J.O'Rourke CF D.Eggler RF J.Lillie C J.Rowe CO G.Myers 2 C.Collins /O E.Coughlin /O B.Ely P P.Galvin P B.Serad /P A.Hagan	M C.Anson 1B C.Anson 2B F.Pfeffer SS T.Burns 3B N.Williamson LF A.Dalrymple CF G.Gore RF K.Kelly C S.Flint O B.Sunday S W.Kinzie /O J.Brown /C S.Sutcliffe P L.Corcoran P F.Goldsmith P J.Clarkson /P T.Lee /P G.Crosby /P J.Hibbard /P F.Andrus /P M.Corcoran /P T.Lynch	M C.Hackett 1B B.Phillips 2B G.Smith SS J.Glasscock 3B M.Muldoon LF W.Murphy CF P.Hotaling RF J.Evans C D.Bushong OP S.Moffett C F.Briody 2S G.Pinkney O E.Burch 2 J.Ardner /2 M.Moynahan /O G.Whiteley /C J.Moore /O G.Strief /2 G.Fisher /O P.Gilman /O B.Smith P J.Harkins P J.McCormick /P J.Henry	M J.Chapman 1B M.Scott 2B B.Geis SS F.Meinke 3B J.Farrell LF G.Wood CF N.Hanlon RF S.Wiedman C C.Bennett 2O H.Jones SO H.Buker S F.Cox C E.Gastfield 2 T.Kearns /C F.Wood /C C.Zimmer /S E.Santry /O W.Prince /S F.Jones /O J.Weber /C B.Guiney C W.Walker /O D.Beatle /C D.Lowe P D.Shaw P C.Getzien P F.Brill	M J.Price M M.Ward 1B A.McKinnon 2B R.Connor SS E.Caskin 3B F.Hankinson LF P.Gillespie RF J.Ward C M.Dorgan RF/C B.Ewing OS D.Richardson C J.Humphries /C S.Griffin O Loughran /C C.Manlove /C H.Oxley P M.Welch P E.Begley /P J.Brown	M H.Wright 1B S.Farrar 2B E.Andrews SS B.McClellan 3B J.Mulvey LF B.Purcell CF J.Fogarty RF J.Manning C J.Crowley OP J.Coleman C F.Ringo /C T.Lynch O J.Remsen O B.Hoover /C J.Clements /C T.Cusick /C J.Kappel /C G.Vadeboncoeur /C P.Cook /C M.DePangher /C L.Hardie /C B.Conway /C H.Allen /C E.Sixsmith P C.Ferguson P B.Vinton P J.McElroy /P J.Knight /P C.Murphy /P S.Morton /P C.Miller /P S.Pyle	M F.Bancroft 1B J.Start 2B J.Farrell SS A.Irwin 3B J.Denny LF C.Carroll CF P.Hines RF P.Radford C B.Gilligan C S.Nava 3 C.Bassett /C M.Murray P C.Radbourn P C.Sweeney P E.Conley /P C.Miller /P H.Arundel /P J.Cattanach

TEAM	G	W	L	PCT	GB	R	OR	AB	H	2B	3B	HR	BB	SO	AVG	OBP	SLG	PRO	PRO+	BR	/A	PF	CHI	RC	SB	CS	SBA	SBR
PRO	114	84	28	.750		665	388	4093	987	153	43	21	300	469	.241	.293	.315	.608	97	-18	-2	98	107	387				
BOS	116	73	38	.658	10.5	684	468	4189	1063	179	60	36	207	660	.254	.289	.351	.640	105	17	20	100	104	435				
BUF	115	64	47	.577	19.5	700	626	4197	1099	163	69	39	215	458	.262	.298	.361	.659	106	46	23	103	102	463				
NY	116	62	50	.554	22	693	623	4124	1053	149	67	23	249	492	.255	.298	.341	.639	102	20	4	102	105	429				
CHI	113	62	50	.554	22	834	647	4182	1176	162	50	142	264	469	.281	.324	.446	.770	133	201	133	100	98	619				
PHI	113	39	73	.348	45	549	824	3998	934	149	39	14	209	512	.234	.272	.301	.573	88	-72	-47	95	101	335				
CLE	113	35	77	.313	49	458	716	3934	934	147	49	16	170	576	.237	.269	.312	.581	83	-63	-81	103	86	338				
DET	114	28	84	.250	56	445	736	3970	825	114	47	31	207	699	.208	.247	.284	.531	74	-132	-104	94	93	285				
TOT	457					5028		32687	8071	1216	424	322	1821	4335	.247	.287	.340	.626										

TEAM	CG	SH	SV	IP	H	H/G	HR	BB	SO	RAT	ERA	ERA+	OAV	OOB	PR	/A	PF	CPI	FA	E	DP	FW	PW	BW	SBW	DIF
PRO	107	16	2	1036¹	825	7.2	26	172	639	8.7	1.61	176	.209	.242	158	141	95	110	.918	398	50	5.1	12.6	-.2		10.4
BOS	109	14	2	1037	932	8.1	30	135	742	9.3	2.47	117	.226	.250	58	49	97	84	.922	384	46	6.3	4.4	1.8		5.0
BUF	108	14	1	1001	1041	9.4	46	189	534	11.1	2.95	107	.254	.286	3	21	106	105	.905	462	71	1.9	1.9	2.1		2.6
NY	111	4	0	1014	1011	9.0	28	326	567	11.9	3.12	95	.245	.300	-16	-19	100	98	.895	514	69	-.6	-1.7	.4		8.0
CHI	106	9	0	997¹	1028	9.3	83	231	472	11.4	3.03	103	.250	.290	-6	11	105	112	.886	595	107	-5.6	1.0	11.9		-1.2
PHI	103	3	1	981	1090	10.0	38	254	411	12.3	3.93	76	.261	.304	-103	-106	100	87	.888	536	67	-2.5	-9.5	-4.2		-.8
CLE	107	7	0	994²	1046	9.5	35	269	482	11.9	3.43	92	.256	.302	-50	-32	106	97	.897	512	75	-1.2	-2.9	-7.2		-9.7
DET	109	3	0	984²	1097	10.0	36	245	488	12.3	3.38	86	.262	.302	-44	-54	97	100	.886	550	62	-3.0	-4.8	-9.3		-10.9
TOT	863	70	6	8046		9.0				11.1	2.98		.247	.287					.899	3951	547					

Runs		Hits		Doubles		Triples		Home Runs		Total Bases	
Kelly-Chi	120	Sutton-Bos	162	Hines-Pro	36	Ewing-NY	20	Williamson-Chi	27	Dalrymple-Chi	263
O'Rourke-Buf	119	O'Rourke-Buf	162	O'Rourke-Buf	33	Brouthers-Buf	15	Pfeffer-Chi	25	Anson-Chi	258
Hornung-Bos	119	Dalrymple-Chi	161	Anson-Chi	30	Rowe-Buf	14	Dalrymple-Chi	22	Pfeffer-Chi	240
Dalrymple-Chi	111	Kelly-Chi	160	Manning-Phi	29	Phillips-Cle	12	Anson-Chi	21	Kelly-Chi	237
Anson-Chi	108	Anson-Chi	159			McKinnon-NY	12	Brouthers-Buf	14	Williamson-Chi	231

Runs Batted In		Runs Produced		Bases On Balls		Batting Average		On Base Percentage		Slugging Average	
Anson-Chi	102	Kelly-Chi	202	Gore-Chi	61	O'Rourke-Buf	.347	Kelly-Chi	.414	Brouthers-Buf	.563
Pfeffer-Chi	101	Anson-Chi	189	Kelly-Chi	46	Kelly-Chi	.354	Gore-Chi	.404	Williamson-Chi	.554
Kelly-Chi	95	Pfeffer-Chi	181	Hines-Pro	44	Sutton-Bos	.346	O'Rourke-Buf	.392	Anson-Chi	.543
Williamson-Chi	84	O'Rourke-Buf	177	Williamson-Chi	42	Anson-Chi	.335	Sutton-Bos	.384	Kelly-Chi	.524
Connor-NY	82	Connor-NY	176			Brouthers-Buf	.327	Brouthers-Buf	.378	Pfeffer-Chi	.514

Production		Adjusted Production		Batter Runs		Adjusted Batter Runs		Clutch Hitting Index		Runs Created	
Brouthers-Buf	.941	Brouthers-Buf	186	Kelly-Chi	48.8	Kelly-Chi	39.2	Connor-NY	148	Kelly-Chi	100
Kelly-Chi	.938	Kelly-Chi	178	Anson-Chi	44.6	Brouthers-Buf	37.8	Radbourn-Pro	132	Anson-Chi	99
Anson-Chi	.916	Anson-Chi	170	Brouthers-Buf	41.2	Anson-Chi	35.2	Caskin-NY	132	O'Rourke-Buf	90
Williamson-Chi	.898	O'Rourke-Buf	167	O'Rourke-Buf	38.8	O'Rourke-Buf	35.0	Kelly-Chi	131	Dalrymple-Chi	88
O'Rourke-Buf	.872	Williamson-Chi	164	Williamson-Chi	36.7	Sutton-Bos	33.8	Dorgan-NY	124	Brouthers-Buf	87

Total Average		Stolen Bases	Stolen Base Average	Stolen Base Runs	Fielding Runs		Total Player Rating	
Kelly-Chi	.969				Pfeffer-Chi	45.5	Pfeffer-Chi	6.1
Brouthers-Buf	.959				Williamson-Chi	23.8	Williamson-Chi	4.7
Anson-Chi	.908				Gilligan-Pro	17.2	Kelly-Chi	3.1
Williamson-Chi	.907				Lillie-Buf	16.0	Sutton-Bos	2.7
O'Rourke-Buf	.849				Hanlon-Det	13.3	Hines-Pro	2.6

Wins		Win Percentage		Games		Complete Games		Shutouts		Saves	
Radbourn-Pro	59	Radbourn-Pro	.831	Radbourn-Pro	75	Radbourn-Pro	73	Galvin-Buf	12	Morrill-Bos	2
Buffinton-Bos	48	Buffinton-Bos	.750	Galvin-Buf	72	Galvin-Buf	71	Radbourn-Pro	11	Sweeney-Pro	1
Galvin-Buf	46	Sweeney-Pro	.680	Buffinton-Bos	67	Buffinton-Bos	63	Buffinton-Bos	8	Radbourn-Pro	1
Welch-NY	39	Galvin-Buf	.676	Welch-NY	65	Welch-NY	62	L.Corcoran-Chi	7	O'Rourke-Buf	1
L.Corcoran-Chi	35	Welch-NY	.650	L.Corcoran-Chi	60	L.Corcoran-Chi	57	Whitney-Bos	6	Ferguson-Phi	1

Innings Pitched		Fewest Hits/Game		Fewest BB/Game		Strikeouts		Strikeouts/Game		Ratio	
Radbourn-Pro	678.2	Sweeney-Pro	6.23	Whitney-Bos	.72	Radbourn-Pro	441	Clarkson-Chi	7.78	Sweeney-Pro	7.41
Galvin-Buf	636.1	Radbourn-Pro	7.00	Galvin-Buf	.89	Buffinton-Bos	417	Whitney-Bos	7.23	Whitney-Bos	8.01
Buffinton-Bos	587.0	Clarkson-Chi	7.17	Buffinton-Bos	1.17	Galvin-Buf	369	Getzien-Det	6.54	Radbourn-Pro	8.30
Welch-NY	557.1	Getzien-Det	7.21	Sweeney-Pro	1.18	Welch-NY	345	Buffinton-Bos	6.39	Getzien-Det	8.74
L.Corcoran-Chi	516.2	Whitney-Bos	7.29	Coleman-Phi	1.28	L.Corcoran-Chi	272	Sweeney-Pro	5.90	Galvin-Buf	8.90

Earned Run Average		Adjusted ERA		Opponents' Batting Avg.		Opponents' On Base Pct.		Starter Runs		Adjusted Starter Runs	
Radbourn-Pro	1.38	Radbourn-Pro	204	Sweeney-Pro	.187	Sweeney-Pro	.215	Radbourn-Pro	120.5	Radbourn-Pro	108.6
Sweeney-Pro	1.55	Sweeney-Pro	182	Getzien-Det	.204	Whitney-Bos	.223	Galvin-Buf	69.5	Galvin-Buf	81.5
Getzien-Det	1.95	Galvin-Buf	158	Radbourn-Pro	.205	Radbourn-Pro	.234	Buffinton-Bos	54.2	Buffinton-Bos	48.2
Galvin-Buf	1.99	Getzien-Det	148	Whitney-Bos	.207	Getzien-Det	.237	Sweeney-Pro	35.1	L.Corcoran-Chi	41.7
Whitney-Bos	2.09	Clarkson-Chi	147	Clarkson-Chi	.208	Buffinton-Bos	.244	Whitney-Bos	33.2	Sweeney-Pro	31.2

Clutch Pitching Index		Relief Runs	Adjusted Relief Runs	Relief Ranking	Total Pitcher Index		Total Baseball Ranking	
Radbourn-Pro	117				Radbourn-Pro	9.8	Radbourn-Pro	9.5
Meinke-Det	116				Galvin-Buf	6.8	Galvin-Buf	6.8
L.Corcoran-Chi	113				Buffinton-Bos	5.7	Pfeffer-Chi	6.1
Moffett-Cle	110				L.Corcoran-Chi	4.6	Buffinton-Bos	5.2
Welch-NY	107				Whitney-Bos	4.0	Williamson-Chi	4.7

May 1 Moses Fleetwood Walker becomes the first black in the major leagues when he plays for the Toledo club in the American Association. He goes 0-for-3 in his major league debut, allowing two passed balls and committing four errors, as his team bows to Louisville, 5-1. He will do better in 41 subsequent games before injuries force Toledo to release him in late September. Only one other black player—Fleet's brother Welday—appears in a major league uniform until Jackie Robinson in 1947.

May 1 One person is killed and several others injured when a section of bleachers collapses following Cincinnati's Opening Day loss to Columbus.

May 10 Washington catcher Alex Gard-ner's first major league game is also his last, as he allows 12 passed balls, a major league record that still stands. Washington loses the game to the New York Mets, 11–3.

May 24 Against Pittsburgh, Philadelphia Athletics pitcher Al Atkinson hits the leadoff batter, Ed Swartwood, who steals second base, takes third base on a putout, and scores on a passed ball. But Atkinson sets down the next 27 Alleghenies for a near-perfect, no-hit 10–1 win.

June 13 Baltimore management surrounds the playing field with a barbed wire fence to restrain the crowd. Baltimore fans had surged onto the field and manhandled the umpire following a 13-inning tie with Louisville the day before.

July 4 Louisville ace Guy Hecker defeats Brooklyn in a morning game (5–4) and again in the afternoon (8–2) en route to a season total of 52 wins, an AA record.

October 30 Financially troubled despite finishing second to New York in the AA, the Columbus club decides to sell its players to Allegheny of Pittsburgh (AA)—for $6,000—and go out of business.

December 11 The AA votes to keep its ban on overhand pitching and to continue to allow fouls caught on one bounce to count as outs. It does abolish the tradition of team captains flipping for the honor of batting first. Now the home team will automatically bat first.

BALTIMORE		BROOKLYN		CINCINNATI		COLUMBUS		INDIANAPOLIS		LOUISVILLE		NEW YORK	
M	B.Barnie	M	G.Taylor	M	W.White	M	G.Schmelz	M	J.Gifford	M	M.Walsh	M	J.Mutrie
1B	E.Stearns	1B	C.Householder	M	P.Snyder	1B	J.Field	M	B.Watkins	1B	J.Latham	1B	D.Orr
2B	T.Manning	2B	B.Greenwood	1B	J.Reilly	2B	P.Smith	1B	J.Kerins	2B	J.Gerhardt	2B	D.Troy
SS	J.Macullar	SS	B.Geer	2B	B.McPhee	SS	J.Richmond	2B	E.Merrill	SS	T.McLaughlin	SS	C.Nelson
3B	J.Sommer	3B	F.Warner	SS	J.Peoples	3B	B.Kuehne	SS	M.Phillips	3B	P.Browning	3B	D.Esterbrook
LF	T.York	LF	I.Benners	3B	H.Carpenter	LF	J.Cahill	3B	P.Callahan	LF	L.Maskrey	LF	E.Kennedy
CF	J.Clinton	CF	J.Remsen	LF	T.Mansell	CF	F.Mann	LF	J.Peltz	CF	M.Cline	CF	C.Roseman
RF	G.Gardner	RF	J.Cassidy	CF	C.Jones	RF	T.Brown	CF	J.Morrison	RF	J.Wolf	RF	S.Brady
C	S.Trott	C	J.Corcoran	RF	P.Corkhill	C	R.Kemmler	RF	P.Weihe	C	D.Sullivan	C	B.Holbert
				C	P.Snyder			C	J.Keenan				
C	B.Traffley	O1	O.Walker			CO	F.Carroll			3P	P.Reccius	C	C.Reipschlager
O	D.Casey	13	J.Knowles	O	B.West	OP	E.Dundon	O	J.Dorgan	C	E.Whiting	/O	G.Pierce
O2	O.Burns	23	C.Jones	C	P.Powers	O	T.Mansell	2	C.Collins	/1	W.Andrews	/C	T.Murphy
O	B.Dickerson	OC	T.Wilson	S	F.Fennelly			3	J.Donnelly	/O	B.Dickerson	/C	H.Oxley
/3	J.Ake	C	J.Farrow	S	C.Fulmer	P	E.Morris	3	B.Watkins	/O	L.Stockwell		
/1	P.Burns	C	J.Hayes	/O	J.Woulfe	P	F.Mountain	O	J.Sneed	/C	B.Hunter	P	J.Lynch
/C	J.Roxburgh	/C	J.Dorgan	/O	F.Berkelbach			OC	T.Thompson			P	T.Keefe
				/C	G.Miller	/P	T.Sullivan	C	C.Robinson	P	G.Hecker		
P	B.Emslie	P	A.Terry	/O	I.Reeder	/P	A.Bauers	/O	G.Moriarity	P	D.Driscoll	/P	B.Becannon
P	H.Henderson	P	S.Kimber	/O	J.Parsons			/O	B.Butler	P	R.Deagle		
		P	J.Conway					/O	M.Locke				
/P	F.Goldsmith			P	W.White			/C	J.Tray				
/P	J.McLaughlin			P	B.Mountjoy			/1	B.Blakiston				
				P	G.Shallix			/O	J.Holdsworth				
								/C	H.Decker				
				/P	R.Deagle			/C	M.Barrett				
								/1	C.Levis				

PHILADELPHIA		PITTSBURGH		RICHMOND		ST.LOUIS		/O	F.Monroe	TOLEDO		WASHINGTON	
M	L.Knight	M	D.McKnight	M	F.Moses	M	J.Williams	/C	G.Mundinger	M	C.Morton	M	H.Hollingshead
1B	H.Stovey	M	B.Ferguson	1B	J.Powell	M	C.Comiskey	/O	C.Reising	1B	C.Lane	M	Bickerson
2B	C.Stricker	M	J.Battin	2B	T.Larkin	1B	C.Comiskey	/C	H.Weber	2B	S.Barkley	1B	W.Prince
SS	S.Houck	M	G.Creamer	SS	B.Schenck	2B	J.Quest	/O	P.Fries	SS	J.Miller	2B	T.Hawkes
3B	F.Corey	M	H.Phillips	3B	B.Nash	SS	B.Gleason			3B	E.Brown	SS	F.Fennelly
LF	J.Birchall	1B	J.Knowles	LF	E.Glenn	3B	A.Latham	P	L.McKeon	LF	F.Olin	3B	B.Gladman
CF	H.Larkin	2B	G.Creamer	CF	D.Johnston	LF	T.O'Neill	P	B.Barr	CF	C.Welch	LF	B.Morgan
RF	L.Knight	SS	B.White	RF	M.Mansell	CF	F.Lewis	P	J.Aydelott	RF	T.Poorman	CF	H.Mullin
C	J.Milligan	3B	J.Battin	C	J.Hanna	RF	H.Nicol	P	A.McCauley	C	F.Walker	RF	E.Trumbull
		LF	D.Miller			C	P.Deasley					C	J.Humphries
C	J.O'Brien	CF	L.Taylor	CO	M.Quinton			/P	M.MacArthur	13	J.Moffett		
O	B.Blakiston	RF	E.Swartwood	O	W.Goldsby	O	G.Strief	/P	T.Bond	C	D.McGuire	2	E.Yewell
O	J.Coleman	C	E.Colgan	/C	B.Dugan	C	T.Dolan			3	G.Meister	2O	F.Olin
O	M.Mansell			/C	B.Morgan	OP	B.Caruthers			3O	C.Morton	C	J.Hanna
/O	C.Hilsey	3O	J.McDonald	/1	A.Swan	O	C.Krehmeyer			1	T.McSorley	O	E.Smith
/C	F.Siffell	S	T.Forster	/O	W.Williams	O	J.Lavin			O	J.Tilley	O	J.Kiley
/C	E.Rowen	C	J.Hayes	/S	E.Ford	/O	W.Goldsby			C	T.Arundel	O	T.Farley
/C	E.Foster	O	C.Eden			/O	H.Wheeler			C	S.Bullas	1	S.King
/C	F.Ringo	1	J.Faatz	P	P.Meegan	/2	W.Kinzie			/O	E.Miller	/O	J.Beach
/O	M.Moynahan	O	M.Mansell	P	E.Dugan	/O	A.Struve			/O	W.Walker	/O	W.Goldsby
		3	A.Whitney			/2	C.Fulmer					/O	W.Murphy
P	B.Mathews	O	B.Reid	/P	W.Curry	/C	N.Alexander			P	T.Mullane	/1	A.Swan
P	B.Taylor	O	C.Doyle	/P	T.Firth	/C	J.McCauley			P	H.O'Day	/O	Jones
P	A.Atkinson	O	J.Woulfe									/O	Wills
		O	C.Lauer			P	J.McGinnis			/P	E.Kent	/O	L.Drake
/P	P.Smith	/2	J.Quest			P	D.Foutz					/C	A.Gardner
		/O	B.Ferguson			P	D.Davis						
		S	J.Dee									P	B.Barr
		/C	F.Smith									P	J.Hamill
		/1	C.Hautz										
		/S	G.Alberts										
		/S	J.Peters										
		/3	J.Gray										
		P	F.Sullivan										
		P	J.Neagle										
		/P	J.Fox										
		/P	B.Nelson										
		/P	F.Beck										
		/P	J.Gorman										
		/P	P.Smith										

TEAM	G	W	L	PCT	GB	R	OR	AB	H	2B	3B	HR	BB	SO	AVG	OBP	SLG	PRO	PRO+	BR	/A	PF	CHI	RC	SB	CS	SBA	SBR
NY	112	75	32	.701		734	**423**	4012	1052	155	64	22	203	**315**	.262	**.304**	.349	.653	120	70	87	98	109	436				
COL	110	69	39	.639	6.5	585	459	3759	901	107	96	46	196	629	.240	.288	.351	.639	121	47	97	92	95	390				
LOU	110	68	40	.630	7.5	573	425	3957	1004	152	69	17	146	408	.254	.286	.340	.626	112	29	57	96	93	395				
STL	110	67	40	.626	8	658	539	3952	987	151	60	11	172	339	.250	.288	.327	.615	100	16	-5	104	109	381				
CIN	112	68	41	.624	8	**754**	512	4090	1037	109	96	36	154	429	.254	.289	.354	.643	108	53	21	105	**114**	429				
BAL	108	63	43	.594	11.5	636	515	3845	896	133	84	32	**211**	545	.233	.284	.336	.620	101	25	1	104	105	377				
PHI	108	61	46	.570	14	700	546	3959	**1057**	**167**	**100**	26	153	434	**.267**	.301	.379	**.680**	117	**100**	56	106	102	**463**				
TOL	110	46	58	.442	27.5	463	571	3712	859	153	48	8	157	545	.231	.268	.305	.573	87	-39	-57	104	90	310				
BRO	109	40	64	.385	33.5	476	644	3763	845	112	47	16	179	417	.225	.263	.292	.555	83	-61	-64	101	95	296				
RIC	46	12	30	.286	30.5	194	294	1469	326	40	33	7	53	282	.222	.261	.308	.569	89	-18	-16	99	97	121				
PIT	110	30	78	.278	45.5	406	725	3689	777	105	50	2	143	411	.211	.248	.268	.516	71	-109	-116	102	92	251				
IND	110	29	78	.271	46	462	755	3813	890	129	62	20	125	561	.233	.262	.315	.577	93	-38	-24	97	88	323				
WAS	63	12	51	.190	41	248	481	2166	434	61	24	6	100	377	.200	.241	.259	.500	75	-75	-47	88	100	139				
TOT	659					6889		46186	11065	1574	833	243	1992	5672	.240	.278	.326	.604										

TEAM	CG	SH	SV	IP	H	H/G	HR	BB	SO	RAT	ERA	ERA+	OAV	OOB	PR	/A	PF	CPI	FA	E	DP	FW	PW	BW	SBW	DIF
NY	110	9	0	985	**802**	7.3	15	115	628	**8.6**	2.46	127	**.209**	.237	86	72	96	89	.907	441	42	2.3	6.6	7.9		4.6
COL	102	8	1	962¹	815	7.6	22	150	526	9.5	2.68	113	.217	.256	60	36	93	98	.908	433	74	2.3	3.3	**8.9**		.5
LOU	101	6	0	989²	836	7.6	**9**	**97**	470	8.8	**2.17**	**142**	.216	.241	**118**	**100**	95	106	**.912**	**426**	**84**	2.6	**9.1**	5.2		-2.9
STL	99	8	0	987	881	8.0	16	172	477	10.0	2.67	122	.226	.266	63	63	100	106	.900	490	65	-.2	5.8	-.5		8.4
CIN	**111**	**11**	0	983²	956	8.7	27	181	308	11.1	3.33	100	.243	.290	-10	-1	103	106	.909	430	82	**2.8**	-.0	1.9		8.9
BAL	105	8	1	955²	869	8.2	16	219	**635**	10.5	2.71	128	.224	.271	56	79	107	**107**	.899	461	61	.7	7.2	.0		2.0
PHI	105	5	0	948²	920	8.7	16	127	530	10.3	3.42	99	.237	.269	-18	-4	104	89	.901	457	63	.9	-.4	5.1		1.9
TOL	103	9	1	946	885	8.4	12	169	501	10.5	3.06	111	.233	.275	19	35	105	99	.900	469	67	.7	3.2	-5.2		-4.7
BRO	105	6	0	948²	996	9.4	20	163	378	11.2	3.79	87	.254	.288	-58	-51	102	94	.889	520	68	-1.6	-4.7	-5.8		.2
RIC	45	1	0	370¹	402	9.8	14	52	167	11.4	4.52	73	.257	.288	-53	-50	102	83	.874	239	27	-1.5	-4.6	-1.5		-1.4
PIT	108	4	0	943¹	1059	10.1	25	216	338	12.7	4.35	77	.265	.312	-116	-104	104	96	.889	523	71	-1.6	-9.5	-10.6		-2.3
IND	107	2	0	937²	1001	9.6	30	199	479	11.8	4.20	78	.255	.295	-100	-97	101	90	.889	515	45	-1.2	-8.9	-2.2		-12.2
WAS	62	3	0	543²	643	10.6	21	110	235	12.8	4.01	76	.273	.311	-46	-59	93	109	.858	400	40	-5.3	-5.4	-4.3		-4.6
TOT	1263	80	3	11501²		8.7				10.6	3.24		.240	.278					.897	5804	789					

Runs		Hits		Doubles		Triples		Home Runs		Total Bases	
Stovey-Phi	124	Orr-NY	162	Barkley-Tol	39	Stovey-Phi	23	Reilly-Cin	11	Reilly-Cin	247
Jones-Cin	117	Reilly-Cin	152	Browning-Lou	33	Reilly-Cin	19	Stovey-Phi	10	Orr-NY	247
Latham-StL	115	Esterbrook-NY	150	Orr-NY	32	Mann-Col	18	Orr-NY	9	Stovey-Phi	244
Reilly-Cin	114	Browning-Lou	150	Esterbrook-NY	29	Peltz-Ind	17	Mann-Col	7	Jones-Cin	222
Nelson-NY	114	Jones-Cin	148	Lewis-StL	25	Jones-Cin	17	Jones-Cin	7	Browning-Lou	211

Runs Batted In		Runs Produced		Bases On Balls		Batting Average		On Base Percentage		Slugging Average	
		Stovey-Phi	197	Nelson-NY	74	Orr-NY	.354	Jones-Cin	.376	Reilly-Cin	.551
		Reilly-Cin	194	Geer-Bro	38	Reilly-Cin	.339	Nelson-NY	.375	Stovey-Phi	.545
		Orr-NY	185	Jones-Cin	37	Browning-Lou	.336	Stovey-Phi	.368	Orr-NY	.539
		Jones-Cin	181	Macullar-Bal	36	Stovey-Phi	.326	Fennelly-Was-Cin	.367	Fennelly-Was-Cin	.480
		McPhee-Cin	166	Richmond-Col	35	Lewis-StL	.323	Reilly-Cin	.366	Browning-Lou	.472

Production		Adjusted Production		Batter Runs		Adjusted Batter Runs		Clutch Hitting Index		Runs Created	
Reilly-Cin	.918	Orr-NY	195	Stovey-Phi	44.8	Orr-NY	44.9			Reilly-Cin	93
Stovey-Phi	.913	Reilly-Cin	186	Reilly-Cin	44.6	Reilly-Cin	39.4			Stovey-Phi	92
Orr-NY	.901	Fennelly-Was-Cin	186	Orr-NY	42.1	Stovey-Phi	37.8			Orr-NY	92
Fennelly-Was-Cin	.847	Stovey-Phi	182	Jones-Cin	39.0	Fennelly-Was-Cin	36.6			Jones-Cin	85
Jones-Cin	.846	Browning-Lou	176	Browning-Lou	31.6	Browning-Lou	36.1			Browning-Lou	77

Total Average		Stolen Bases		Stolen Base Average		Stolen Base Runs		Fielding Runs		Total Player Rating	
Stovey-Phi	.907							Latham-StL	39.5	Barkley-Tol	4.4
Reilly-Cin	.899							Smith-Col	29.1	Latham-StL	4.2
Orr-NY	.855							Snyder-Cin	27.4	Fennelly-Was-Cin	4.0
Jones-Cin	.830							Gerhardt-Lou	27.3	Smith-Col	3.9
Fennelly-Was-Cin	.824							Barkley-Tol	24.6	Esterbrook-NY	3.4

Wins		Win Percentage		Games		Complete Games		Shutouts		Saves	
Hecker-Lou	52	Morris-Col	.723	Hecker-Lou	75	Hecker-Lou	72	White-Cin	7	O'Day-Tol	1
Lynch-NY	37	Hecker-Lou	.722	Mullane-Tol	67	Mullane-Tol	64	Mullane-Tol	7	Mountain-Col	1
Keefe-NY	37	Foutz-StL	.714	McKeon-Ind	61	McKeon-Ind	59	Hecker-Lou	6	O.Burns-Bal	1
Mullane-Tol	36	Lynch-NY	.712	Keefe-NY	58	Keefe-NY	56				
		Keefe-NY	.685	Terry-Bro	56	Terry-Bro	54				

Innings Pitched		Fewest Hits/Game		Fewest BB/Game		Strikeouts		Strikeouts/Game		Ratio	
Hecker-Lou	670.2	Morris-Col	7.02	Driscoll-Lou	.62	Hecker-Lou	385	Henderson-Bal	7.09	Hecker-Lou	8.02
Mullane-Tol	567.0	Hecker-Lou	7.06	Hecker-Lou	.75	Henderson-Bal	346	Davis-StL	6.49	Morris-Col	8.36
McKeon-Ind	512.0	Keefe-NY	7.08	Lynch-NY	.76	Keefe-NY	334	Morris-Col	6.33	Lynch-NY	8.56
Lynch-NY	496.0	Mountain-Col	7.21	E.Dugan-Ric	.81	Mullane-Tol	325	Keefe-NY	6.22	Keefe-NY	8.68
Keefe-NY	483.0	Foutz-StL	7.27	McGinnis-StL	.89	McKeon-Ind	308	Mathews-Phi	5.98	Foutz-StL	9.23

Earned Run Average		Adjusted ERA		Opponents' Batting Avg.		Opponents' On Base Pct.		Starter Runs		Adjusted Starter Runs	
Hecker-Lou	1.80	Hecker-Lou	171	Keefe-NY	.204	Hecker-Lou	.226	Hecker-Lou	107.6	Hecker-Lou	95.6
Foutz-StL	2.18	Foutz-StL	149	Hecker-Lou	.204	Morris-Col	.234	Keefe-NY	53.0	Mullane-Tol	55.7
Morris-Col	2.18	Morris-Col	139	Morris-Col	.204	Lynch-NY	.236	Morris-Col	50.8	Keefe-NY	46.2
Keefe-NY	2.25	Keefe-NY	138	Mountain-Col	.209	Keefe-NY	.239	Mullane-Tol	45.3	Henderson-Bal	40.9
Mountain-Col	2.45	Mullane-Tol	135	Foutz-StL	.212	Foutz-StL	.255	Mountain-Col	31.9	Morris-Col	40.3

Clutch Pitching Index		Relief Runs		Adjusted Relief Runs		Relief Ranking		Total Pitcher Index		Total Baseball Ranking	
Comiskey-StL	127							Hecker-Lou	12.6	Hecker-Lou	12.5
Foutz-StL	122							Mullane-Tol	7.7	Mullane-Tol	7.7
Davis-StL	120							Keefe-NY	5.5	Keefe-NY	5.6
O'Neill-StL	118							Henderson-Bal	4.4	Barkley-Tol	4.4
White-Cin	116							Morris-Col	4.2	Henderson-Bal	4.3

February 9 The grounds of Cincinnati's UA club are flooded under 20 feet of water from the Ohio River. It will cost $3,000 to rebuild the fallen pavilions and fences and restore the field.

March 17 The UA is very busy. The league admits a Boston club organized by George Wright to bring the number of teams to eight, expands its schedule to 112 games, decides to stick with the seven-ball walk rule, and adopts the percentage system to determine the champion. The season also gets started, as Bill Sweeney pitches Baltimore to a 7-3 win over Washington.

May 10 Altoona wins its first major league game after 11 straight losses, 9-4, over Boston. They will win only five more times before disbanding at the end of May.

May 24 After 20 consecutive wins St. Louis finally falls, 8-1 to Boston. The Maroons will finish the season with an .832 percentage.

May 31 The Altoona club disbands, the first casualty of the UA, and is replaced by a new club formed in Kansas City.

July 5 After a 17-2 loss at Cincinnati, Philadelphia Athletics (AA) pitcher Al Atkinson deserts his club for Chicago (UA)—the first player to break his contract and join the UA.

July 19 Boston's Fred "Dupee" Shaw holds pennant-bound St. Louis to one hit while fanning 18 batters, but loses the game, 1-0, when batter Bill Gleason gets all the way to second base on a dropped third strike and scores on a wild pitch. In his outings of July 16, 19, and 21, Shaw will amass 48 strikeouts, a major league record for three consecutive games.

September 15 In their final home game, against the Kansas City Unions, the last place Wilmington Quick Steps have exactly zero fans in the stands at game time. Manager Joe Simmons decides to forfeit the game rather than play. Wilmington then disbands, and, four days later, Pittsburg disbands as well.

September 16 Jim McCormick picks off four Boston Unions in an 8-4 Cincinnati victory, one of McCormick's 21 UA wins. Earlier in the season he won 19 games for Cleveland (NL). He will lead the UA in winning percentage and in ERA.

September 19 The UA decides to drop Pittsburgh and Wilmington and replace them with Milwaukee and Omaha. The latter club will last only eight days before St. Paul picks up the banner anew.

October 5 St. Louis pitchers Charlie Sweeney and Henry Boyle stop St. Paul without a hit or walk, striking out nine men, before rain halts play after five innings. But the Maroons lose the game when two St. Louis errors allow the game's only run. The Sweeney-Boyle performance caps what is still the premier major league season for no-hitters: 12 in all, including one of 10 innings and seven nine-inning games.

October 9 Fred Dunlap's 13th homer helps his St. Louis Maroons bury the Washington Nationals, 11-1. The second baseman will add the homer championship to his UA titles in batting, slugging, on base percentage, hits, doubles, and total bases, the most dominant season by any nonpitcher of the century. He also leads all UA second basemen in fielding average, putouts, assists, double plays, and total chances per game.

December 18 Only five clubs attend the "annual" meeting, one by proxy. The UA will die early in 1885.

ALTOONA		BALTIMORE		BOSTON		CINCINNATI		CHI-PITT		KANSAS CITY	
M	E.Curtis	M	B.Henderson	M	T.Murnane	M	D.O'Leary	M	E.Hengle	M	H.Wheeler
1B	F.Harris	1B	C.Levis	1B	T.Murnane	M	S.Crane	1B	J.Schoeneck	M	M.Porter
2B	C.Dougherty	2B	D.Phelan	2B	T.O'Brien	1B	M.Powell	2B	M.Hengle	M	T.Sullivan
SS	G.Smith	SS	L.Say	SS	W.Hackett	2B	S.Crane	SS	S.Matthias	1B	J.Sweeney
3B	H.Koons	3B	Y.Robinson	3B	J.Irwin	SS	J.Jones	3B	W.Foley	2B	C.Berry
LF	J.Murphy	LF	E.Seery	LF	K.Butler	3B	C.Barber	LF	C.Householder	SS	C.Cross
CF	F.Shaffer	CF	N.Cuthbert	CF	M.Slattery	LF	L.Sylvester	CF	H.Wheeler	3B	P.Sullivan
RF	J.Brown	RF	B.Graham	RF	E.Crane	CF	B.Harbidge	RF	J.Ellick	LF	F.Wyman
C	J.Moore	C	E.Fusselback	C	L.Brown	RF	B.Hawes	C	B.Krieg	CF	B.McLaughlin
						C	J.Kelly			RF	F.Shaffer
P	J.Murphy	CO	R.Sweeney	O	T.McCarthy			O2	C.Briggs	C	K.Baldwin
		O	H.Oberbeck	C	J.McKeever	OP	D.Burns	CS	T.Suck		
		O	J.O'Brien			S	J.Glasscock	O	G.Gardner	OP	B.Black
		O	H.Wheeler	P	J.Burke	1	M.McQuery	C	E.Gross	1	J.Gorman
		1	J.Schoeneck	P	D.Shaw	O	D.O'Leary	2	C.McGarr	2O	F.McLaughlin
				P	T.Bond	3	E.Cleveland	3	J.Battin	1O	J.Cudworth
		P	B.Sweeney			C	B.Schwartz	2	F.McLaughlin	3	H.Oberbeck
		P	T.Lee	/P	F.Tenney	C	F.Briody			OP	P.Veach
		P	A.Atkinson	/P	C.Daniels	C	J.Crotty	P	H.Daily	OC	H.Decker
						S	F.McLaughlin	P	A.Atkinson	S	L.Say
		/P	P.Smith					P	J.Horan	C	N.Alexander
		/P	J.Ryan			P	G.Bradley			O	H.Wheeler
						P	J.McCormick	/P	C.Cady	O	J.Strauss
								/P	F.Foreman		
										P	E.Hickman
										/P	J.Bakely
										/P	D.Blaisdell
										/P	D.Crothers
										/P	B.Hutchison

MILWAUKEE		PHILADELPHIA		ST.LOUIS		ST.PAUL		WASHINGTON		WILMINGTON	
M	T.Loftus	M	F.Malone	M	T.Sullivan	M	A.Thompson	M	M.Scanlon	M	J.Simmons
1B	T.Griffin	1B	J.McGuinness	M	F.Dunlap	1B	S.Dunn	1B	P.Joy	1B	R.Snyder
2B	A.Myers	2B	E.Peak	1B	J.Quinn	2B	M.Hengle	2B	T.Evers	2B	C.Bastian
SS	T.Sexton	SS	H.Easterday	2B	F.Dunlap	SS	J.Werrick	SS	J.Halpin	SS	H.Myers
3B	T.Morrissey	3B	J.McCormick	SS	M.Whitehead	3B	B.O'Brien	3B	J.McCormick	3B	J.Say
LF	S.Behel	LF	B.Hoover	3B	J.Gleason	LF	J.Tilley	LF	H.Moore	LF	T.Lynch
CF	L.Baldwin	CF	B.Kienzle	LF	H.Boyle	CF	B.Barnes	CF	P.Baker	CF	G.Fisher
RF	E.Hogan	RF	J.Flynn	CF	D.Rowe	RF	S.Carroll	RF	B.Wise	RF	J.Munce
C	C.Broughton	C	T.Gillen	RF	O.Shaffer	C	C.Ganzel	C	C.Fulmer	C	T.Cusick
				C	G.Baker						
P	H.Porter	OC	J.Clements			P	J.Brown	OP	A.Powell	P	J.Murphy
P	E.Cushman	O	H.Luff	CO	J.Brennan	P	L.Galvin	CO	J.Gunson	P	T.Nolan
				O	B.Dickerson			S	J.Deasley	P	D.Casey
		P	J.Bakely	C	T.Dolan			O	F.Tenney	P	J.Bakely
		P	S.Weaver					CO	E.McKenna		
		P	Fisher	P	C.Sweeney			3	T.Larkin		
				P	B.Taylor			OP	M.Lockwood		
		/P	B.Gallagher	P	P.Werden						
				P	C.Hodnett			P	B.Wise		
								P	A.Voss		
				/P	J.Cattanach			P	C.Gagus		
								/P	H.Daily		

TEAM	G	W	L	PCT	GB	R	OR	AB	H	2B	3B	HR	BB	SO	AVG	OBP	SLG	PRO	PRO+	BR	/A	PF	CHI	RC	SB	CS	SBA	SBR
STL	114	94	19	.832		887	429	4285	1251	259	41	32	181	542	.292	.321	.394	.715	113	-33	-56	104	103	555				
MIL	12	8	4	.667	35.5	53	34	395	88	25	0	0	20	70	.223	.260	.286	.546	124	-27	-21	54	91	30				
CIN	105	69	36	.657	21	703	466	3786	1027	118	63	26	147	482	.271	.298	.356	.654	92	-111	-150	108	102	413				
BAL	106	58	47	.552	32	662	627	3883	952	150	26	17	144	652	.245	.272	.310	.582	71	-215	-259	110	109	336				
BOS	111	58	51	.532	34	636	558	3940	928	168	32	19	128	787	.236	.260	.309	.569	74	-242	-236	98	107	324				
CP	93	41	50	.451	42	438	482	3212	742	127	26	10	119	505	.231	.258	.296	.554	69	-211	-209	99	93	252				
WAS	114	47	65	.420	46.5	572	679	3926	931	120	26	4	118	558	.237	.259	.284	.543	68	-271	-260	97	102	296				
PHI	67	21	46	.313	50	414	545	2518	618	108	35	7	103	405	.245	.275	.324	.599	89	-125	-105	93	101	230				
STP	9	2	6	.250	39.5	24	57	272	49	13	1	0	7	47	.180	.201	.235	.436	61	-30	-36	54	84	13				
ALT	25	6	19	.240	44	90	216	899	223	30	6	2	22	130	.248	.266	.301	.567	72	-55	-56	101	67	74				
KC	82	16	63	.203	61	311	669	2802	557	104	15	6	123	529	.199	.232	.253	.485	55	-255	-235	87	88	169				
WIL	18	2	16	.111	44.5	35	114	521	91	8	8	2	22	123	.175	.208	.232	.440	33	-56	-57	103	61	26				
TOT	428					4825		30439	7457	1230	279	125	1134	4830	.245	.272	.316	.588										

TEAM	CG	SH	SV	IP	H	H/G	HR	BB	SO	RAT	ERA	ERA+	OAV	OOB	PR	/A	PF	CPI	FA	E	DP	FW	PW	BW	SBW	DIF
STL	104	8	6	993	838	7.6	9	110	550	8.6	1.96	122	.214	.235	53	47	98	106	.888	554	79	3.7	4.1	-4.9		34.6
MIL	12	3	0	104	49	4.2	1	13	139	5.4	2.25	59	.132	.161	2	-11	54	12	.892	53	4	.6	-1.0	-1.8		4.2
CIN	95	11	1	914¹	831	8.2	17	90	503	9.1	2.38	107	.226	.245	6	18	105	102	.882	532	45	2.5	1.6	-13.1		25.5
BAL	92	4	0	946²	1002	9.5	24	177	628	11.2	3.01	89	.254	.286	-61	-36	110	115	.872	616	53	-.8	-3.2	-22.7		32.1
BOS	100	5	1	953¹	885	8.4	17	110	753	9.4	2.70	88	.231	.252	-28	-35	98	95	.868	633	39	-.3	-3.1	-20.7		27.6
CP	86	6	0	803²	743	8.3	12	137	679	9.9	2.72	90	.230	.261	-25	-26	100	98	.882	459	38	2.7	-2.3	-18.3		13.3
WAS	94	5	0	953²	992	9.4	16	168	684	10.9	3.44	70	.251	.282	-106	-110	98	95	.869	625	55	.7	-9.6	-22.8		22.7
PHI	64	1	0	593¹	726	11.0	7	105	310	12.6	4.63	50	.283	.311	-144	-152	95	89	.841	501	36	-5.2	-13.3	-9.2		15.2
STP	7	1	0	71	72	9.1	1	27	44	12.5	3.17	42	.248	.312	-6	-15	54	117	.872	47	6	.2	-1.3	-3.2		2.3
ALT	20	0	0	219²	292	12.0	3	52	93	14.1	4.67	57	.300	.335	-55	-49	109	104	.862	156	4	-.6	-4.3	-4.9		3.3
KC	70	0	0	702²	862	11.0	14	127	334	12.7	4.07	55	.283	.312	-128	-144	92	104	.861	520	51	-2.5	-12.6	-20.6		12.1
WIL	15	0	0	142	165	10.5	4	18	113	11.6	3.04	87	.273	.294	-10	-6	109	126	.860	104	10	-.1	-.5	-5.0		-1.4
TOT	759	44	8	7397¹		9.1				10.5	3.05		.245	.272					.872	4800	420					

Runs		Hits		Doubles		Triples		Home Runs		Total Bases	
Dunlap-StL	160	Dunlap-StL	185	Shaffer-StL	40	Burns-Cin	12	Dunlap-StL	13	Dunlap-StL	279
Shaffer-StL	130	Shaffer-StL	168	Dunlap-StL	39	Rowe-StL	11	Crane-Bos	12	Shaffer-StL	234
Seery-Bal-KC	115	Moore-Was	155	Rowe-StL	32	Shaffer-StL	10	Levis-Bal-Was	6	Rowe-StL	208
Robinson-Bal	101	Seery-Bal-KC	146	O'Brien-Bos	31					Crane-Bos	193
Rowe-StL	95	Rowe-StL	142	Gleason-StL	30					Seery-Bal-KC	192

Runs Batted In		Runs Produced		Bases On Balls		Batting Average		On Base Percentage		Slugging Average	
Dunlap-StL	147	Dunlap-StL	147	Robinson-Bal	37	Dunlap-StL	.412	Dunlap-StL	.448	Dunlap-StL	.621
Shaffer-StL	128	Shaffer-StL	128	Shaffer-StL	30	Taylor-StL	.366	Shaffer-StL	.398	Taylor-StL	.548
Seery-Bal-KC	113	Seery-Bal-KC	113	Dunlap-StL	29	Dickerson-StL	.365	Hoover-Phi	.390	Shaffer-StL	.501
Robinson-Bal	99	Robinson-Bal	99	Harbidge-Cin	25	Hoover-Phi	.364	Moore-Was	.363	Hoover-Phi	.495
Rowe-StL	91	Rowe-StL	91	Gleason-StL	23	Shaffer-StL	.360	Gleason-StL	.361	Burns-Cin	.457

Production		Adjusted Production		Batter Runs		Adjusted Batter Runs		Clutch Hitting Index		Runs Created	
Dunlap-StL	1.069	Dunlap-StL	213	Dunlap-StL	53.4	Dunlap-StL	49.1			Dunlap-StL	128
Shaffer-StL	.899	Hoover-Phi	180	Shaffer-StL	27.6	Shaffer-StL	24.0			Shaffer-StL	96
Hoover-Phi	.885	Shaffer-StL	165	Glasscock-Cin	16.9	Hoover-Phi	18.8			Moore-Was	71
Gleason-StL	.802	Moore-Was	139	Hoover-Phi	14.4	Glasscock-Cin	13.5			Seery-Bal-KC	67
Moore-Was	.777	Gleason-StL	137	Taylor-StL	12.6	Taylor-StL	11.2			Rowe-StL	65

Total Average		Stolen Bases		Stolen Base Average		Stolen Base Runs		Fielding Runs		Total Player Rating	
Dunlap-StL	1.167							Dunlap-StL	30.5	Dunlap-StL	6.9
Shaffer-StL	.883							Fusselback-Bal	19.3	Shaffer-StL	1.7
Hoover-Phi	.846							Baker-StL	16.3	Briody-Cin	1.5
Gleason-StL	.738							Robinson-Bal	16.1	Hoover-Phi	1.5
Moore-Was	.686							Krieg-CP	14.9	Glasscock-Cin	1.3

Wins		Win Percentage		Games		Complete Games		Shutouts		Saves	
B.Sweeney-Bal	40	McCormick-Cin	.875	B.Sweeney-Bal	62	B.Sweeney-Bal	58	McCormick-Cin	7	Taylor-StL	4
Daily-CP-Was	28	Taylor-StL	.862	Daily-CP-Was	58	Daily-CP-Was	58	Daily-CP-Was	5	Sylvester-Cin	1
Taylor-StL	25	Boyle-StL	.833	Wise-Was	50	Bakely-Phi-Wil-KC	43	Shaw-Bos	5	Dunlap-StL	1
Bradley-Cin	25	Sweeney-StL	.774	Bakely-Phi-Wil-KC	46	Bradley-Cin	36	Wise-Was	4	Brown-Bos	1
Sweeney-StL	24	B.Sweeney-Bal	.656	Bradley-Cin	41	Shaw-Bos	35	B.Sweeney-Bal	4	Boyle-StL	1

Innings Pitched		Fewest Hits/Game		Fewest BB/Game		Strikeouts		Strikeouts/Game		Ratio	
B.Sweeney-Bal	538.0	McCormick-Cin	6.47	Sweeney-StL	.43	Daily-CP-Was	483	Shaw-Bos	8.81	McCormick-Cin	7.07
Daily-CP-Was	500.2	Shaw-Bos	6.47	McCormick-Cin	.60	B.Sweeney-Bal	374	Daily-CP-Was	8.68	Sweeney-StL	7.31
Bakely-Phi-Wil-KC	394.2	Sweeney-StL	6.87	Boyle-StL	.60	Shaw-Bos	309	Gagus-Was	7.92	Shaw-Bos	7.53
Wise-Was	364.1	Boyle-StL	7.08	Bradley-Cin	.61	Wise-Was	268	Robinson-Bal	7.32	Boyle-StL	7.68
Bradley-Cin	342.0	Werden-StL	7.20	Murphy-Wil-Alt	.62	Burke-Bos	255	Burke-Bos	7.13	Werden-StL	8.60

Earned Run Average		Adjusted ERA		Opponents' Batting Avg.		Opponents' On Base Pct.		Starter Runs		Adjusted Starter Runs	
McCormick-Cin	1.54	McCormick-Cin	166	McCormick-Cin	.188	McCormick-Cin	.202	Shaw-Bos	23.5	McCormick-Cin	23.7
Taylor-StL	1.68	Taylor-StL	143	Shaw-Bos	.188	Sweeney-StL	.207	Taylor-StL	22.2	Shaw-Bos	21.3
Boyle-StL	1.74	Boyle-StL	137	Sweeney-StL	.197	Shaw-Bos	.212	McCormick-Cin	20.9	Taylor-StL	20.9
Shaw-Bos	1.77	Shaw-Bos	134	Boyle-StL	.202	Boyle-StL	.215	Sweeney-StL	18.4	Sweeney-StL	17.0
Sweeney-StL	1.83	Sweeney-StL	131	Werden-StL	.205	Werden-StL	.235	Boyle-StL	11.6	Boyle-StL	10.8

Clutch Pitching Index		Relief Runs		Adjusted Relief Runs		Relief Ranking		Total Pitcher Index		Total Baseball Ranking	
Hodnett-StL	140							Taylor-StL	2.8	Dunlap-StL	6.7
Robinson-Bal	132							Sweeney-StL	2.4	Taylor-StL	3.2
Taylor-StL	129							McCormick-Cin	1.8	Sweeney-StL	2.4
B.Sweeney-Bal	111							Shaw-Bos	1.5	McCormick-Cin	1.8
Murphy-Wil-Alt	110							Boyle-StL	.8	Shaffer-StL	1.7

January 6 Millionaire Henry V. Lucas, creator of the failed Union Association, purchases the Cleveland club and eventually fills the vacancy in the NL with his own St. Louis Maroons.

January 10 At an NL meeting, St. Louis is admitted to the league, Cleveland's registration is formally accepted, and Detroit has its request to remain in the NL granted, leaving only one opening for the season.

February 22 Boston pitcher Charlie Buffinton invents a baseball "roller skate" that gives pitchers greater impetus and swing in their delivery while still allowing them to keep both feet on the ground.

March 15 A lower court in New York decides that playing baseball on Sunday is a crime. This decision will be overturned, but it will be appealed.

May 2 In the NY Giants' opener, Mickey Welch throws a one-hitter against Boston for his first of 44 wins. He and Tim Keefe will combine for 76 victories this year, second in history only to the Grays' Hoss Radbourn and Charlie Sweeney, who won 77 between them in 1884.

June 6 The first game played at Chicago's new West Side Park proves victorious for the White Stockings, as they beat St. Louis, 9–2. Hugh "One-Arm" Daily makes his debut as a Maroon before more than 10,000 spectators.

July 11 Chicago releases injured pitcher Larry Corcoran. After averaging 34 wins the last five seasons, Corcoran wins only seven games in 1885.

August 1 The largest paying crowd to date gathers at the Polo Grounds; 13,427 fans watch the Giants defeat the Chicago White Stockings, 7–6.

August 27 Providence lays off former batting champ Paul Hines and accuses him of intentionally playing poorly to receive his release. His .358 in 1878 led the NL.

September 9 The Grays end their 13-game losing streak with a 3-1 win over the Phillies. This will be the last major league game ever played in Providence.

October 7 The last NL game ever played in Buffalo's Olympic Park attracts 12 fans as Providence takes two from the Bisons, 4–0, and 6–1. Grays pitcher Dupee Shaw goes the distance in both victories (each five innings), throwing a no-hitter in the first game.

October 14 The White Stockings (NL) and Browns (AA) engage in a "World's Championship" series. The winner of the seven-game series is to receive a $1,000 prize. Darkness ends Game 1 after eight innings, a 5–5 stalemate.

October 22 John Ward and several teammates secretly form the Brotherhood of Professional Base Ball Players. The Brotherhood is strengthened by fights against salary restrictions and abuses of the reserve clause. It will become a force to reckoned with by the end of the decade.

October 24 The St. Louis Browns defeat Chicago, 13-4 in the seventh and last game in their series. The AA Browns and NL White Stockings agree to throw out Game 2 of the series before the start of the seventh game. Each club wins three, loses three and has a tie; each club receives $500.

November 28 National League officials buy the Providence franchise and players for $6,000.

December 18 The Washington Nationals are admitted to the NL, in place of Providence.

BOSTON		BUFFALO		CHICAGO		DETROIT		NEW YORK		PHILADELPHIA		PROVIDENCE		ST.LOUIS	
M	J.Morrill	M	J.Galvin	M	C.Anson	M	C.Morton	M	J.Mutrie	M	H.Wright	M	F.Bancroft	M	F.Dunlap
1B	J.Morrill	M	J.Chapman	1B	C.Anson	M	B.Watkins	1B	R.Connor	1B	S.Farrar	1B	J.Start	M	A.McKinnon
2B	J.Burdock	1B	D.Brouthers	2B	F.Pfeffer	1B	M.McQuery	2B	J.Gerhardt	2B	A.Myers	2B	J.Farrell	M	F.Dunlap
SS	S.Wise	2B	D.Force	SS	T.Burns	2B	S.Crane	SS	J.Ward	SS	C.Bastian	SS	A.Irwin	1B	A.McKinnon
3B	E.Sutton	SS	J.Rowe	3B	N.Williamson	SS	M.Phillips	3B	D.Esterbrook	3B	J.Mulvey	3B	J.Denny	2B	F.Dunlap
LF	T.McCarthy	3B	D.White	LF	A.Dalrymple	3B	J.Donnelly	LF	P.Gillespie	LF	E.Andrews	LF	C.Carroll	SS	J.Glasscock
CF	J.Manning	LF	B.Crowley	CF	G.Gore	LF	G.Wood	CF	J.O'Rourke	CF	J.Fogarty	CF	P.Hines	3B	E.Caskin
RF	T.Poorman	CF	H.Richardson	RF	K.Kelly	CF	N.Hanlon	RF	M.Dorgan	RF	J.Manning	RF	P.Radford	LF	E.Seery
C	T.Gunning	RF	J.Lillie	C	S.Flint	RF	S.Thompson	C	B.Ewing	C	J.Clements	C	B.Gilligan	CF	E.Lewis
		C	G.Myers			C	C.Bennett							RF	O.Shaffer
O	G.Whiteley			O	B.Sunday			C	P.Deasley	C	T.Cusick	2S	C.Bassett	C	F.Briody
C	P.Dealy	S1	E.Stearns	S	S.Sutcliffe	2S	J.Quest	O3	D.Richardson	C	C.Ganzel	C	C.Daily		
2S	W.Hackett	C	J.McCauley	/S	J.Ryan	O	J.Dorgan			O	T.Lynch	O	L.Knight	OP	C.Sweeney
C	M.Hackett	O	E.Crane	/C	J.McCauley	1	M.Scott	P	M.Welch	/2	J.Hiland	S	T.Manning	O3	J.Quinn
O	D.Johnston	O	S.Carroll	/O	W.Williams	C	D.McGuire	P	T.Keefe			/3	D.Lyons	C	G.Baker
O	J.Hornung	/3	G.Hatfield	/C	E.Gastfield	3	C.Morton			P	E.Daily	/3	W.Andrus	O	D.Rowe
3	B.Nash	/2	M.Hengle	/O	B.Krieg	S	J.Manning	/P	L.Corcoran	P	C.Ferguson	/C	M.Hines	O	D.Burns
O	B.Purcell	/O	D.Eggler			/C	F.Ringo			P	B.Vinton	/O	E.Crane	C	S.Sutcliffe
O	M.Hines	/O	J.Staples	P	J.Clarkson	S	C.Collins							/O	R.Sweeney
/C	P.Tate	/O	B.Dickerson	P	J.McCormick	S	J.Halpin			/P	T.Nolan	P	C.Radbourn	/O	J.Brennan
/O	B.Collver	/2	D.Driscoll	P	T.Kennedy	/O	G.Moriarity					P	D.Shaw	/C	T.Dolan
		/2	D.Phelan			/C	J.Moore							/O	J.Fogarty
P	J.Whitney	/S	J.McDonald	/P	L.Corcoran	/S	N.Kellogg					/P	J.McCormick	/3	J.Gleason
P	C.Buffinton	/2	C.Ritter			/2	G.Bryant					/P	C.Hallstrom	/3	T.McSorley
P	D.Davis	/C	F.Wood			/3	F.Olin					/P	E.Smith	/3	B.Alvord
						/C	E.Gastfield					/P	J.Foley	/3	D.Phelan
						/O	F.Meinke					/P	S.Kimber	/C	C.Krehmeyer
/P	B.Stemmeyer	P	P.Galvin									/P	B.Stellberger		
		P	B.Serad			P	S.Wiedman					/P	J.Ward	P	H.Boyle
		P	P.Conway			P	C.Getzien					/P	E.Seward	P	J.Kirby
		P	P.Wood			P	L.Baldwin							P	H.Daily
						P	D.Casey							P	J.Healy
		/P	J.Connor												
		/P	Fisher											/P	Palmer

TEAM	G	W	L	PCT	GB	R	OR	AB	H	2B	3B	HR	BB	SO	AVG	OBP	SLG	PRO	PRO+	BR	/A	PF	CHI	RC	SB	CS	SBA	SBR
CHI	113	87	25	.777		834	470	4093	1079	184	75	54	340	429	.264	.320	.385	.705	115	143	36	115	113	517				
NY	112	85	27	.759	2	691	370	4029	1085	150	82	16	221	312	.269	.307	.359	.666	122	82	91	99	106	456				
PHI	111	56	54	.509	30	513	511	3893	891	156	35	20	220	401	.229	.270	.302	.572	91	-45	-35	98	102	326				
PRO	110	53	57	.482	33	442	531	3727	820	114	30	6	265	430	.220	.272	.272	.544	83	-74	-56	96	96	282				
BOS	113	46	66	.411	41	528	589	3950	915	144	53	22	190	522	.232	.267	.312	.579	94	-41	-23	96	103	337				
DET	108	41	67	.380	44	514	582	3773	917	149	66	25	216	451	.243	.284	.337	.621	105	17	16	100	93	371				
BUF	112	38	74	.339	49	495	761	3900	980	149	50	23	179	380	.251	.284	.333	.617	100	11	-8	103	89	378				
STL	111	36	72	.333	49	390	593	3758	829	121	21	8	214	412	.221	.263	.270	.533	81	-92	-64	94	89	273				
TOT	445					4407		31123	7516	1167	412	174	1845	3337	.241	.284	.322	.606										

TEAM	CG	SH	SV	IP	H	H/G	HR	BB	SO	RAT	ERA	ERA+	OAV	OOB	PR	/A	PF	CPI	FA	E	DP	FW	PW	BW	SBW	DIF
CHI	108	14	4	1015²	868	7.7	37	202	458	9.5	2.23	136	.221	.259	66	89	108	102	.903	496	80	-2.4	8.4	3.4		21.6
NY	109	16	1	994	758	6.9	11	265	516	9.3	1.72	155	.205	.258	121	106	95	114	.929	331	85	6.0	10.0	8.6		4.5
PHI	108	10	0	976	860	7.9	18	218	378	9.9	2.39	117	.224	.266	46	41	99	96	.905	447	66	-.3	3.9	-3.3		.7
PRO	108	8	0	960²	912	8.5	18	235	371	10.7	2.71	98	.235	.278	12	-7	94	96	.903	459	70	-1.1	-.7	-5.3		5.0
BOS	111	10	0	981	1045	9.6	26	188	480	11.3	3.03	89	.261	.294	-23	-38	95	107	.901	478	79	-1.5	-3.6	-2.2		-2.8
DET	105	6	1	954¹	966	9.1	18	224	475	11.2	2.88	99	.249	.290	-6	-2	101	104	.901	463	61	-1.7	-.2	1.5		-12.6
BUF	107	4	1	956	1175	11.1	31	234	320	13.3	4.29	69	.289	.328	-157	-140	106	99	.901	464	65	-.9	-13.2	-.8		-3.1
STL	107	4	0	965¹	935	8.7	15	278	337	11.3	3.37	82	.245	.296	-59	-68	97	89	.916	398	67	2.3	-6.4	-6.0		-7.9
TOT	863	72	7	7803		8.7				10.8	2.82		.241	.284					.908	3536	573					

Runs
Kelly-Chi 124
O'Rourke-NY 119
Gore-Chi 115
Dalrymple-Chi 109
Connor-NY 102

Hits
Connor-NY 169
Brouthers-Buf 146
Anson-Chi 144
Sutton-Bos 143
O'Rourke-NY 143

Doubles
Anson-Chi 35
Brouthers-Buf 32
Rowe-Buf 28
Dalrymple-Chi 27
Mulvey-Phi 25

Triples
O'Rourke-NY 16
Connor-NY 15
Gore-Chi 13
Bennett-Det 13

Home Runs
Dalrymple-Chi 11
Kelly-Chi 9

Total Bases
Connor-NY 225
Brouthers-Buf 221
Dalrymple-Chi 219
Anson-Chi 214
O'Rourke-NY 211

Runs Batted In
Anson-Chi 108
Kelly-Chi 75
Pfeffer-Chi 73
Burns-Chi 71

Runs Produced
Anson-Chi 201
Kelly-Chi 190
Gore-Chi 167
Connor-NY 166
Dalrymple-Chi 159

Bases On Balls
Williamson-Chi 75
Gore-Chi 68
Morrill-Bos 64
Connor-NY 51

Batting Average
Connor-NY 371
Brouthers-Buf 359
Dorgan-NY 326
Richardson-Buf ...319
Gore-Chi 313

On Base Percentage
Connor-NY .... .435
Brouthers-Buf .... .408
Gore-Chi .... .405
Hanlon-Det .... .372
Anson-Chi .... .357

Slugging Average
Brouthers-Buf 543
Connor-NY 495
Ewing-NY 471
Anson-Chi 461
Richardson-Buf ...458

Production
Brouthers-Buf 951
Connor-NY 929
Gore-Chi 858
Anson-Chi 819
Bennett-Det 812

Adjusted Production
Connor-NY 203
Brouthers-Buf 199
Bennett-Det 161
Ewing-NY 159
O'Rourke-NY 158

Batter Runs
Connor-NY 51.7
Brouthers-Buf ... 46.8
Gore-Chi 40.6
Anson-Chi 31.7
O'Rourke-NY 29.5

Adjusted Batter Runs
Connor-NY 53.3
Brouthers-Buf ... 43.2
O'Rourke-NY 30.9
Gore-Chi 25.2
Sutton-Bos 24.5

Clutch Hitting Index
White-Buf 146
Williamson-Chi ... 146
Anson-Chi 145
Gerhardt-NY 139
Pfeffer-Chi 136

Runs Created
Connor-NY 100
Brouthers-Buf 92
Gore-Chi 83
Anson-Chi 78
O'Rourke-NY 77

Total Average
Brouthers-Buf 977
Connor-NY 965
Gore-Chi 884
Bennett-Det 808
Anson-Chi 775

Stolen Bases

Stolen Base Average

Stolen Base Runs

Fielding Runs
Dunlap-StL 25.8
Pfeffer-Chi 25.4
Fogarty-Phi 24.8
Glasscock-StL ... 19.4
Richardson-Buf .. 13.1

Total Player Rating
Connor-NY 4.0
Dunlap-StL 4.0
Richardson-Buf ... 3.4
Ewing-NY 3.2
Glasscock-StL 3.1

Wins
Clarkson-Chi 53
Welch-NY 44
Keefe-NY 32
Radbourn-Pro 28

Win Percentage
Welch-NY .... .800
Clarkson-Chi ..... .768
McCormick-Pro-Chi .. .750
Keefe-NY .... .711
Radbourn-Pro .... .571

Games
Clarkson-Chi 70
Welch-NY 56
Whitney-Bos 51
Buffinton-Bos 51
Daily-Phi 50

Complete Games
Clarkson-Chi 68
Welch-NY 55
Whitney-Bos 50

Shutouts
Clarkson-Chi 10
Welch-NY 7
Keefe-NY 7
Shaw-Pro 6
Buffinton-Bos 6

Saves
Williamson-Chi 2
Pfeffer-Chi 2
Welch-NY 1
Galvin-Buf 1
Baldwin-Det 1

Innings Pitched
Clarkson-Chi 623.0
Welch-NY 492.0
Radbourn-Pro ... 445.2
Whitney-Bos 441.1
Daily-Phi 440.0

Fewest Hits/Game
Keefe-NY 6.75
Welch-NY 6.80
Baldwin-Det 6.88
Clarkson-Chi 7.18
Daily-Phi 7.57

Fewest BB/Game
Whitney-Bos ...... .75
Galvin-Buf 1.17
Clarkson-Chi 1.40
Baldwin-Det 1.41
C.Sweeney-StL ... 1.64

Strikeouts
Clarkson-Chi 308
Welch-NY 258
Buffinton-Bos 242
Keefe-NY 227
Whitney-Bos 200

Strikeouts/Game
Baldwin-Det 6.78
Keefe-NY 5.11
Buffinton-Bos ... 5.01
Welch-NY 4.72
Clarkson-Chi 4.45

Ratio
Baldwin-Det 8.28
Clarkson-Chi 8.58
Keefe-NY 9.05
Welch-NY 9.20
Daily-Phi 9.41

Earned Run Average
Keefe-NY 1.58
Welch-NY 1.66
Clarkson-Chi 1.85
Baldwin-Det 1.86
Radbourn-Pro 2.20

Adjusted ERA
Keefe-NY 169
Clarkson-Chi 164
Welch-NY 160
Baldwin-Det 153
Daily-Phi 126

Opponents' Batting Avg.
Baldwin-Det 197
Welch-NY 203
Keefe-NY 203
Clarkson-Chi 208
Shaw-Pro 209

Opponents' On Base Pct.
Baldwin-Det 228
Clarkson-Chi 239
Shaw-Pro 254
Keefe-NY 255
Daily-Phi 256

Starter Runs
Clarkson-Chi 67.0
Welch-NY 63.0
Keefe-NY 55.2
Radbourn-Pro 30.5
Daily-Phi 29.7

Adjusted Starter Runs
Clarkson-Chi 82.0
Welch-NY 54.7
Keefe-NY 48.4
Daily-Phi 28.2
Ferguson-Phi 25.4

Clutch Pitching Index
Keefe-NY 121
Getzien-Det 118
Radbourn-Pro 116
Welch-NY 112
Whitney-Bos 111

Relief Runs

Adjusted Relief Runs

Relief Ranking

Total Pitcher Index
Clarkson-Chi 8.9
Welch-NY 5.0
Keefe-NY 4.7
Ferguson-Phi 4.3
Radbourn-Pro 3.5

Total Baseball Ranking
Clarkson-Chi 8.8
Welch-NY 5.0
Keefe-NY 4.7
Ferguson-Phi 4.5
Connor-NY 4.0

January 20 The AA is reorganized, with clubs from St. Louis, Cincinnati, Pittsburgh, Brooklyn, Louisville, New York, Philadelphia and Baltimore.

February 12* The Western League is officially formed, with Indianapolis, Kansas City, Cleveland, Milwaukee, Toledo, and Omaha as the original clubs. It will last until June 23.

April 3 The Metropolitans release Tim Keefe and Thomas "Dude" Esterbrook; both players later sign with the NY Giants.

June 7 The AA wipes out all restrictions on pitchers using an overhand delivery.

June 17 Brooklyn's John "Phenomenal" Smith loses his AA debut to St. Louis by a score of 18-5. Every run against the brash left-hander is unearned due to 14 Brooklyn errors. Smith, who gave himself his nickname, brings it on himself. When he arrived in Brooklyn, he said he didn't need his teammates to win. The intentional misplays lead to

fines for each player, but Smith will be released to ensure team harmony.

July 4* An exhibition between two "old-time" teams is played at the Polo Grounds. The Old Mutual Nine (with pitcher Rynie Wolters) beats the Old Eckford club (with outfielder Dave Eggler and first baseman Andy Allison) by a score of 25-17.

July 18 The Browns lose to the Athletics in St. Louis, snapping their 27-game consecutive-win streak at home, still a major league record.

August 2 Allegheny pitcher Ed "Cannonball" Morris strikes out 15 Colonels, but still loses, 4–1. Morris will lead the league in complete games (63), innings pitched (581), and strikeouts (298) this year.

August 8 All games are canceled in New York City today because of General Ulysses S. Grant's funeral.

September 28 Harry Stovey hits his AA-leading 13th homer off Pittsburgh's John Hofford. This is also Stovey's 51st

career homer, which is the current major league record.

October 1* The first black professional team is organized by Frank P. Thompson. The team is called the Athletics but will shortly become known as the Cuban Giants.

October 15 Game 2 of the championship series is forfeited to Chicago. In the top of the sixth inning, Browns manager Charlie Comiskey calls his men off the field to protest a ruling made by umpire Sullivan. The series played in four cities (also played in New York and St. Louis). Chicago takes a 3–2 series lead by beating the Browns, 9–2.

October 17 At a joint meeting in New York between both leagues, a salary maximum of $2,000 and a minimum of $1,000 is set for the upcoming season.

December 8 At a meeting in Philadelphia, the AA decides to remove the Metropolitan club and admit the National club of Washington. The Mets will be readmitted by court order.

BALTIMORE		BROOKLYN		CINCINNATI		LOUISVILLE	
M	B.Barnie	M	C.Hackett	M	O.Caylor	M	J.Hart
1B	E.Stearns	M	C.Byrne	1B	J.Reilly	1B	J.Kerins
2B	T.Manning	1B	B.Phillips	2B	B.McPhee	2B	T.McLaughlin
SS	J.Macullar	2B	G.Pinkney	SS	F.Fennelly	SS	J.Miller
3B	M.Muldoon	SS	G.Smith	3B	H.Carpenter	3B	P.Reccius
LF	J.Sommer	3B	B.McClellan	LF	C.Jones	LF	L.Maskrey
CF	D.Casey	LF	E.Swartwood	CF	J.Clinton	CF	P.Browning
RF	O.Burns	RF	H.Hotaling	RF	P.Corkhill	RF	J.Wolf
C	B.Traffley	RF	J.Cassidy	C	P.Snyder	C	J.Crotty
		C	J.Hayes				
OC	E.Greer	OP	A.Terry	C	J.Keenan	C	A.Cross
2	G.Gardner	C	J.Peoples	C	K.Baldwin	S	B.Geer
1	J.Field	O	J.McTamany	C	P.Powers	C	D.Sullivan
S	S.Trott	C	B.Krieg	/C	J.Peoples	C	M.Murray
O	T.York	C	C.Robinson	P	W.White	2	R.Mack
O	J.Evans	/C	F.Bell	P	L.McKeon	/C	C.Krehmeyer
2	H.Jacoby	/C	D.Oldfield	P	B.Mountjoy	/O	M.Cline
/C	P.Powers	/1	G.McVey	P	G.Pechiney	/O	J.Strauss
/1	T.O'Brien	/C	M.Hines	P	G.Shallix	P	G.Hecker
/C	G.Derby	/3	B.Schenck	/P	H.McCaffery	P	N.Baker
/C	S.Nava	P	H.Porter			P	A.Mays
/2	G.Mappes	P	J.Harkins			P	T.Ramsey
/O	J.Visner	/P	P.Smith			/P	J.Connor
/O	O.Walker						
/1	C.Levis						
/O	J.Tener						
/2	S.McDermott						
P	H.Henderson						
P	B.Emslie						
P	J.Henry						
/P	B.Mountjoy						
/P	J.Brown						
/P	F.Foreman						
/P	S.Wetzel						

NEW YORK		PHILADELPHIA		PITTSBURGH		ST.LOUIS	
M	J.Gifford	M	H.Stovey	M	H.Phillips	M	C.Comiskey
1B	D.Orr	1B	H.Stovey	1B	J.Field	1B	C.Comiskey
2B	T.Forster	2B	C.Stricker	2B	P.Smith	2B	S.Barkley
SS	C.Nelson	SS	S.Houck	SS	A.Whitney	SS	B.Gleason
3B	P.Hankinson	3B	F.Corey	3B	B.Kuehne	3B	A.Latham
LF	E.Kennedy	LF	B.Purcell	LF	C.Eden	LF	Y.Robinson
CF	C.Roseman	CF	H.Larkin	CF	F.Mann	CF	C.Welch
RF	S.Brady	RF	J.Coleman	RF	T.Brown	RF	H.Nicol
C	C.Reipschlager	C	J.Milligan	C	F.Carroll	C	D.Bushong
CO	B.Holbert	C	J.O'Brien	1	M.Scott	O	T.O'Neill
2	D.Troy	3S	G.Strief	C	D.Miller	C	D.Sullivan
C	C.Broughton	O	L.Knight	SO	J.Richmond	/C	M.Drissel
/2	J.Reilly	1	M.Powell	C	R.Kemmler	/C	C.Broughton
/2	D.Pierson	/C	M.Quinton	/S	M.Phillips	P	B.Caruthers
/3	Jones	/C	E.Fusselback	/C	F.Ringo	P	D.Foutz
P	J.Lynch	/O	B.Hughes	P	E.Morris	P	J.McGinnis
P	E.Cushman	/C	F.Siffell	P	P.Meegan		
P	D.Crothers	/O	O.Shaffer	P	H.O'Day		
P	E.Begley	P	T.Lovett	P	P.Galvin		
P	B.Becannon	P	E.Knouff	/P	F.Mountain		
		P	E.Cushman	/P	J.Hofford		
		/P	B.Vinton				
		/P	B.Taylor				
		/P	B.Emslie				
		/P	J.Conway				
		/P	P.Smith				

TEAM	G	W	L	PCT	GB	R	OR	AB	H	2B	3B	HR	BB	SO	AVG	OBP	SLG	PRO	PRO+	BR	/A	PF	CHI	RC	SB	CS	SBA	SBR
STL	112	79	33	.705		677	**461**	3972	979	132	57	17	234	282	.246	.297	.321	.618	96	1	-27	105	**109**	388				
CIN	112	63	49	.563	16	642	575	4050	1046	108	77	26	153	420	.258	.294	.342	.636	103	18	6	102	101	417				
PIT	111	56	55	.505	22.5	547	539	3975	955	123	79	5	189	537	.240	.282	.315	.597	94	-32	-24	99	94	362				
PHI	113	55	57	.491	24	764	691	4142	1099	169	76	30	223	410	.265	.310	.365	.675	111	77	34	106	106	480				
LOU	112	53	59	.473	26	564	598	3969	986	126	83	19	152	448	.248	.281	.336	.617	99	-11	-10	100	95	384				
BRO	112	53	59	.473	26	624	650	3943	966	121	65	14	238	324	.245	.295	.319	.614	97	-4	-8	101	92	381				
NY	108	44	64	.407	33	526	688	3731	921	123	57	21	217	428	.247	.295	.327	.622	110	4	50	92	90	369				
BAL	110	41	68	.376	36.5	541	683	3820	837	124	59	17	279	529	.219	.280	.296	.576	87	-53	-45	99	99	324				
TOT	445					4885		31602	7789	1026	553	149	1685	3378	.246	.292	.328	.620										

TEAM	CG	SH	SV	IP	H	H/G	HR	BB	SO	RAT	ERA	ERA+	OAV	OOB	PR	/A	PF	CPI	FA	E	DP	FW	PW	BW	SBW	DIF
STL	**111**	11	0	1002	**879**	7.9	12	**168**	378	9.8	**2.44**	134	**.228**	.268	89	91	101	106	**.920**	381	64	3.0	8.2	-2.4		14.2
CIN	102	7	1	999¹	998	9.0	24	250	330	11.9	3.26	100	.253	.309	-2	-1	100	**112**	.911	423	**86**	.8	-.0	.5		5.8
PIT	104	8	0	1011	918	8.2	14	201	454	10.3	2.92	110	.232	.275	36	32	99	95	.912	422	77	.6	2.9	-2.2		-.9
PHI	105	5	0	1003¹	1038	9.3	11	212	**506**	11.6	3.23	106	.234	.298	2	23	106	104	.901	483	79	-2.2	2.1	3.1		-4.0
LOU	109	3	1	1002	927	8.3	13	217	462	10.6	2.68	120	.232	.278	63	60	99	104	.905	460	75	-1.2	5.4	-.9		-6.3
BRO	110	3	1	991²	955	8.7	27	211	436	10.8	3.46	95	.240	.283	-24	-19	102	89	.910	434	56	.2	-1.7	-.7		-.8
NY	103	2	0	937	1015	9.7	36	204	408	11.9	4.15	71	.262	.303	-94	-125	91	91	.901	452	62	-1.6	-11.3	4.5		-1.7
BAL	103	2	4	971	1059	9.8	12	222	395	12.3	3.90	83	.269	.316	-71	-71	100	100	.910	418	71	.6	-6.4	-4.1		-3.7
TOT	847	41	7	7917¹		8.9				11.1	3.24		.246	.292					.909	3473	570					

Runs		Hits		Doubles		Triples		Home Runs		Total Bases	
Stovey-Phi	130	Browning-Lou	174	Larkin-Phi	37	Orr-NY	21	Stovey-Phi	13	Browning-Lou	255
Larkin-Phi	114	Jones-Cin	157	Browning-Lou	34	Kuehne-Pit	19	Fennelly-Cin	10	Orr-NY	241
Jones-Cin	108	Stovey-Phi	153	Orr-NY	29	Wolf-Lou	17	Browning-Lou	9	Larkin-Phi	238
Nelson-NY	98	Orr-NY	152	Stovey-Phi	27	Jones-Cin	17	Larkin-Phi	8	Stovey-Phi	237
Browning-Lou	98	Larkin-Phi	149			Fennelly-Cin	17	Orr-NY	6	Jones-Cin	225

Runs Batted In		Runs Produced		Bases On Balls		Batting Average		On Base Percentage		Slugging Average	
Fennelly-Cin	89	Larkin-Phi	194	Nelson-NY	61	Browning-Lou	.362	Browning-Lou	.393	Orr-NY	.543
Larkin-Phi	88	Stovey-Phi	192	Macullar-Bal	49	Orr-NY	.342	Larkin-Phi	.372	Browning-Lou	.530
Orr-NY	77	Browning-Lou	162	Hotaling-Bro	49	Larkin-Phi	.329	Stovey-Phi	.371	Larkin-Phi	.525
Stovey-Phi	75	Fennelly-Cin	161	Stovey-Phi	39	Jones-Cin	.322	Brown-Pit	.366	Stovey-Phi	.488
Browning-Lou	73	Welch-StL	150			Stovey-Phi	.315	Phillips-Bro	.364	Jones-Cin	.462

Production		Adjusted Production		Batter Runs		Adjusted Batter Runs		Clutch Hitting Index		Runs Created	
Browning-Lou	.923	Orr-NY	197	Browning-Lou	47.0	Browning-Lou	47.3	Nicol-StL	131	Browning-Lou	103
Orr-NY	.901	Browning-Lou	190	Larkin-Phi	40.3	Orr-NY	46.6	Swartwood-Bro	131	Larkin-Phi	91
Larkin-Phi	.897	Larkin-Phi	171	Orr-NY	38.1	Larkin-Phi	33.8	Houck-Phi	125	Stovey-Phi	90
Stovey-Phi	.858	Stovey-Phi	160	Stovey-Phi	37.9	Stovey-Phi	31.2	Fennelly-Cin	125	Orr-NY	88
Jones-Cin	.824	Jones-Cin	156	Jones-Cin	31.5	Jones-Cin	29.5	Gleason-StL	123	Jones-Cin	83

Total Average		Stolen Bases	Stolen Base Average	Stolen Base Runs	Fielding Runs		Total Player Rating	
Browning-Lou	.912				G.Smith-Bro	39.9	Browning-Lou	4.3
Larkin-Phi	.885				Smith-Pit	33.2	Larkin-Phi	3.8
Orr-NY	.863				Houck-Phi	21.8	G.Smith-Bro	3.7
Stovey-Phi	.841				Hankinson-NY	18.0	Jones-Cin	3.4
Jones-Cin	.773				Corkhill-Cin	17.1	Smith-Pit	3.2

Wins		Win Percentage		Games		Complete Games		Shutouts		Saves	
Caruthers-StL	40	Caruthers-StL	.755	Morris-Pit	63	Morris-Pit	63	Morris-Pit	7	Burns-Bal	3
Morris-Pit	39	Foutz-StL	.702	Henderson-Bal	61	Henderson-Bal	59	Caruthers-StL	6	Terry-Bro	1
Porter-Bro	33	Mathews-Phi	.638	Porter-Bro	54	Porter-Bro	53	McGinnis-StL	3	Sommer-Bal	1
Foutz-StL	33	Morris-Pit	.619	Hecker-Lou	53	Caruthers-StL	53			Reccius-Lou	1
		Porter-Bro	.611	Caruthers-StL	53	Hecker-Lou	51			Corkhill-Cin	1

Innings Pitched		Fewest Hits/Game		Fewest BB/Game		Strikeouts		Strikeouts/Game		Ratio	
Morris-Pit	581.0	Morris-Pit	7.11	Lynch-NY	1.00	Morris-Pit	298	Mathews-Phi	6.09	Morris-Pit	8.89
Henderson-Bal	539.1	Mays-Lou	7.74	Hecker-Lou	1.01	Mathews-Phi	286	Cushman-Phi-NY	5.50	Caruthers-StL	9.44
Caruthers-StL	482.1	Foutz-StL	7.75	Caruthers-StL	1.06	Henderson-Bal	263	Morris-Pit	4.62	Hecker-Lou	9.86
Porter-Bro	481.2	McGinnis-StL	7.87	Mathews-Phi	1.21	Hecker-Lou	209	Henderson-Bal	4.39	McGinnis-StL	9.88
Hecker-Lou	480.0	Porter-Bro	7.98	McGinnis-StL	1.53	Porter-Bro	197	Harkins-Bro	4.33	Mathews-Phi	10.04

Earned Run Average		Adjusted ERA		Opponents' Batting Avg.		Opponents' On Base Pct.		Starter Runs		Adjusted Starter Runs	
Caruthers-StL	2.07	Caruthers-StL	158	Morris-Pit	.208	Morris-Pit	.247	Caruthers-StL	62.9	Caruthers-StL	64.1
Hecker-Lou	2.17	Hecker-Lou	148	Mays-Lou	.219	Caruthers-StL	.260	Morris-Pit	57.4	Hecker-Lou	55.8
Morris-Pit	2.35	Mathews-Phi	141	Porter-Bro	.223	Hecker-Lou	.265	Hecker-Lou	57.0	Morris-Pit	55.6
Mathews-Phi	2.43	Morris-Pit	137	McGinnis-StL	.225	Cushman-Phi-NY	.266	Mathews-Phi	38.2	Mathews-Phi	47.2
Foutz-StL	2.63	Foutz-StL	124	Foutz-StL	.227	Mathews-Phi	.267	Foutz-StL	28.0	Foutz-StL	29.0

Clutch Pitching Index		Relief Runs	Adjusted Relief Runs	Relief Ranking	Total Pitcher Index		Total Baseball Ranking	
Knight-Phi	283				Hecker-Lou	6.6	Caruthers-StL	6.5
Hecker-Lou	121				Caruthers-StL	6.6	Hecker-Lou	6.3
Caruthers-StL	118				Morris-Pit	4.5	Morris-Pit	4.5
Mountjoy-Cin-Bal	111				Foutz-StL	3.8	Browning-Lou	4.3
Foutz-StL	107				Mathews-Phi	3.8	Larkin-Phi	3.8

January 16 Washington is admitted to the NL, bringing the membership up to seven teams.

February 9 Kansas City is admitted to the NL on a one-year trial basis.

March 4 The NL adopts the stolen base and the 4-foot by 7-foot pitcher's box.

March 18* The New York State League admits Buffalo, Toronto, and Hamilton. The inclusion of the Canadian teams causes the league to change its name to the International League.

April 29 Opening Day for the NL. The *New York World* carries woodcuts of live action photographs taken by a "detective" camera, perhaps the first "live" pictures of baseball ever taken.

May 31 The first major league crowd of over 20,000 pays to see the afternoon game in New York versus Detroit. The Giants had snapped the Wolverines' 15-game winning streak in the morning game, but Detroit wins the nightcap before 20,632.

June 12 Detroit hits seven homers in one game. This record is broken by the Yankees on June 28, 1939.

June 26* Black left-hander George Stovey makes his pitching debut with Jersey City of the Eastern League after being purchased from the Cuban Giants, the pioneer all-black touring team.

July 3* Behind the pitching of Amos Alonzo Stagg, who will make his mark as a football coach, Yale beats Harvard in the deciding game of the college championship.

August 18 St. Louis Maroons owner Henry Lucas quits baseball, announcing that the club has cost him $27,000 in 3 years.

September 11 Connie Mack makes his major league debut with Washington, catching flawlessly and contributing a single as the Senators beat the Phillies, 4-3.

September 30 Spalding accepts Von der Ahe's challenge for a "World Series" and proposes a best-of-nine series with the winning club getting the total gross gate receipts. St. Louis will accept the winner-take-all provision, but the series will be best-of-seven.

October 8 Detroit's Lady Baldwin beats Philadelphia, 11-0, in eight innings for his 42nd win of the season—the all-time record for a southpaw and one more than rival left-hander Ed Morris of Pittsburgh. The game marks the eighth time in 1886 that Baldwin has beaten the Phillies, including five shutouts. No one else shut out Philadelphia all season.

October 18 The World Championship Series opens in Chicago, with the White Stockings beating the Browns, 6–0, behind John Clarkson's five-hitter.

November 16 The AA and NL Joint Rules Committee announces the new rules code, which includes four strikes for an out, five balls for a walk, and establishes a 55½-foot pitching distance.

November 18 The NL meets and admits Pittsburgh, which had been looking to leave the AA since last spring.

	BOSTON		CHICAGO		DETROIT		KANSAS CITY		NEW YORK		PHILADELPHIA		ST.LOUIS		WASHINGTON
M	J.Morrill	M	C.Anson	M	B.Watkins	M	D.Rowe	M	J.Mutrie	M	H.Wright	M	G.Schmelz	M	M.Scanlon
1B	S.Wise	1B	C.Anson	1B	D.Brouthers	1B	M.McQuery	1B	R.Connor	1B	S.Farrar	1B	A.McKinnon	M	J.Gaffney
2B	J.Burdock	2B	F.Pfeffer	2B	F.Dunlap	2B	A.Myers	2B	J.Gerhardt	2B	C.Bastian	2B	F.Dunlap	1B	P.Baker
SS	J.Morrill	SS	N.Williamson	SS	J.Rowe	SS	C.Bassett	SS	J.Ward	SS	A.Irwin	SS	J.Glasscock	2B	J.Farrell
3B	B.Nash	3B	T.Burns	3B	D.White	3B	J.Donnelly	3B	D.Esterbrook	3B	J.Mulvey	3B	J.Denny	SS	D.Force
LF	J.Hornung	LF	A.Dalrymple	LF	H.Richardson	LF	J.Lillie	LF	P.Gillespie	LF	G.Wood	LF	E.Seery	3B	J.Knowles
CF	D.Johnston	CF	G.Gore	CF	N.Hanlon	CF	D.Rowe	CF	D.Richardson	CF	E.Andrews	CF	J.McGeachy	LF	C.Carroll
RF	T.Poorman	RF	K.Kelly	RF	S.Thompson	RF	P.Radford	RF	M.Dorgan	RF	J.Fogarty	RF	J.Cahill	CF	P.Hines
C	C.Daily	C	S.Flint	C	C.Bennett	C	F.Briody	C	B.Ewing	C	D.McGuire	C	G.Myers	RF	E.Crane
														C	B.Gilligan
OS	E.Sutton	O	J.Ryan	C	C.Ganzel	CO	M.Hackett	OC	J.O'Rourke	OP	E.Daily	O2	J.Quinn	S	S.Houck
1P	C.Buffinton	O	B.Sunday	2	S.Crane	OP	P.Conway	CO	P.Deasley	C	J.Clements	C	F.Graves	3	B.Gladman
C	P.Tate	C	G.Moolic	O	J.Manning	C	F.Ringo	/O	B.Finley	C	T.Cusick	2	S.Crane	1	J.Start
C	T.Gunning	C	L.Hardie	C	H.Decker	/C	D.Dugdale	/C	G.Begley	2	J.Farrell	C	T.Dolan	1	B.Krieg
C	P.Dealy			/O	J.McGeachy	/C	G.Baker	/S	E.Caskin	/O	T.McCarthy	/C	G.Mappes	O	G.Shoch
/2	M.Allen			/S	B.Shindle			/O	L.Corcoran	/C	C.Ganzel	/O	R.Connolly	CO	J.Hayes
		P	J.Clarkson	/C	T.Gillen	P	S.Wiedman	/O	J.Devine			/O	L.Pelouze	O	L.Corcoran
P	C.Radbourn	P	J.McCormick			P	J.Whitney			P	C.Ferguson	P	J.Healy	C	D.Oldfield
P	B.Stemmeyer	P	J.Flynn					P	T.Keefe	P	D.Casey	P	J.Kirby	C	C.Mack
		P	L.Baldwin			/P	S.King	P	M.Welch			P	H.Boyle	/C	H.Decker
/P	C.Parsons	P	C.Getzien			/P	L.McKeon			/P	C.Titcomb	P	C.Sweeney	/C	E.Whiting
		P	P.Conway					/P	J.Devlin	/P	J.Strike	P		/O	W.Goldsby
		P	B.Smith									/P	J.Murphy	/3	J.McGlone
		/P	P.Smith									/P	A.Bauers	/C	T.Kinslow
		/P	L.Twitchell									/P	J.Reardon	/S	J.Gallagher
														/O	G.Winkelman
														/O	Joyce
														P	D.Shaw
														P	B.Barr
														P	T.Madigan
														P	F.Gilmore
														/P	H.Daily
														/P	H.O'Day
														/P	G.Keefe
														/P	J.Henry
														/P	E.Fuller
														/P	J.Fox
														/P	B.Wise
														/P	J.Yingling

TEAM	G	W	L	PCT	GB	R	OR	AB	H	2B	3B	HR	BB	SO	AVG	OBP	SLG	PRO	PRO+	BR	/A	PF	CHI	RC	SB	CS	SBA	SBR
CHI	126	90	34	.726		900	555	4378	1223	198	87	53	460	513	.279	.348	.401	.749	115	176	48	115	104	701	213			
DET	126	87	36	.707	2.5	829	538	4501	1260	176	81	53	374	426	.280	.335	.390	.725	122	137	113	103	100	670	194			
NY	124	75	44	.630	12.5	692	558	4298	1156	175	68	21	237	410	.269	.307	.356	.663	106	29	22	101	102	531	155			
PHI	119	71	43	.623	14	621	498	4072	976	145	66	26	282	516	.240	.289	.327	.616	91	-37	-42	101	106	461	226			
BOS	118	56	61	.479	30.5	657	661	4180	1085	151	59	24	250	537	.260	.301	.341	.642	104	0	23	96	104	489	156			
STL	126	43	79	.352	46	547	712	4250	1001	183	46	30	235	656	.236	.276	.321	.597	92	-71	-35	94	94	430	156			
KC	126	30	91	.248	58.5	494	872	4236	967	177	48	19	269	608	.228	.274	.306	.580	76	-92	-128	106	90	392	96			
WAS	125	28	92	.233	60	445	791	4082	856	135	51	23	265	582	.210	.258	.285	.543	73	-143	-116	94	93	345	143			
TOT	495					5185		33997	8524	1340	506	249	2372	4248	.251	.300	.342	.641						1339				

TEAM	CG	SH	SV	IP	H	H/G	HR	BB	SO	RAT	ERA	ERA+	OAV	OOB	PR	/A	PF	CPI	FA	E	DP	FW	PW	BW	SBW	DIF
CHI	116	8	3	1097²	988	8.1	49	262	647	10.2	2.54	142	.232	.277	91	131	110	111	.912	475	82	-1.8	11.9	4.4		13.5
DET	122	8	0	1103²	995	8.1	20	270	592	10.3	2.85	115	.231	.276	53	52	100	90	.928	373	82	3.8	4.7	10.2		6.8
NY	119	3	1	1062	1029	8.7	23	280	588	11.1	2.86	111	.247	.294	50	26	97	104	.927	359	70	4.2	2.4	2.0		7.0
PHI	110	10	2	1045²	923	7.9	29	264	540	10.2	2.45	134	.224	.271	97	94	100	101	.921	393	46	1.4	8.5	-3.8		7.9
BOS	116	3	0	1029	1049	9.2	33	298	511	11.8	3.24	98	.252	.302	5	-7	97	104	.905	465	63	-2.7	-.6	2.1		-1.2
STL	118	6	0	1077¹	1050	8.8	34	392	501	12.0	3.24	99	.246	.309	5	-7	105	92	.914	452	92	-.5	-.6	-3.2		-13.7
KC	117	4	0	1066²	1345	11.3	27	246	442	13.4	4.84	77	.295	.331	-184	-132	114	90	.910	482	79	-2.1	-12.0	-11.6		-4.8
WAS	115	4	0	1041	1147	9.9	34	379	500	13.2	4.30	76	.271	.331	-117	-124	99	95	.910	458	69	-1.0	-11.2	-10.5		-9.2
TOT	933	46	6	8523		9.0				11.5	3.29		.251	.300					.916	3457	583					

Runs
Kelly-Chi 155
Gore-Chi 150
Brouthers-Det 139
Richardson-Det ... 125
Anson-Chi 117

Hits
Richardson-Det 189
Anson-Chi 187
Brouthers-Det 181
Kelly-Chi 175
Connor-NY 172

Doubles
Brouthers-Det 40
Anson-Chi 35
Kelly-Chi 32
Hines-Was 30

Triples
Connor-NY 20
Wood-Phi 15
Brouthers-Det 15
Thompson-Det 13

Home Runs
Richardson-Det 11
Brouthers-Det 11
Anson-Chi 10
Hines-Was 9
Denny-StL 9

Total Bases
Brouthers-Det ... 284
Anson-Chi 274
Richardson-Det ... 271
Connor-NY 262
Kelly-Chi 241

Runs Batted In
Anson-Chi 147
Pfeffer-Chi 95
Thompson-Det 89
Rowe-Det 87
Ward-NY 81

Runs Produced
Anson-Chi 254
Kelly-Chi 230
Gore-Chi 207
Brouthers-Det 200
Thompson-Det 182

Bases On Balls
Gore-Chi......... 102
Kelly-Chi 83
Williamson-Chi 80
Brouthers-Det 66
Radford-KC 58

Batting Average
Kelly-Chi 388
Anson-Chi 371
Brouthers-Det 370
Connor-NY 355
Richardson-Det ...351

On Base Percentage
Kelly-Chi 483
Brouthers-Det 445
Gore-Chi 434
Anson-Chi 433
Connor-NY 405

Slugging Average
Brouthers-Det 581
Anson-Chi 544
Connor-NY 540
Kelly-Chi 534
Richardson-Det ...504

Production
Brouthers-Det 1.026
Kelly-Chi 1.018
Anson-Chi.........977
Connor-NY 945
Richardson-Det ...906

Adjusted Production
Brouthers-Det 204
Connor-NY 183
Kelly-Chi 182
Anson-Chi 170
Richardson-Det 169

Batter Runs
Brouthers-Det 65.9
Kelly-Chi 64.3
Anson-Chi 58.3
Connor-NY 48.7
Richardson-Det ... 47.4

Adjusted Batter Runs
Brouthers-Det 61.7
Connor-NY 47.5
Kelly-Chi 44.3
Richardson-Det ...43.7
Anson-Chi 38.5

Clutch Hitting Index
Anson-Chi 158
Ward-NY 153
Pfeffer-Chi 141
Dorgan-NY 139
Gillespie-NY 138

Runs Created
Kelly-Chi 146
Brouthers-Det 139
Anson-Chi 134
Richardson-Det ... 129
Connor-NY 116

Total Average
Kelly-Chi 1.366
Brouthers-Det ...1.205
Anson-Chi 1.129
Gore-Chi 1.042
Richardson-Det ..1.029

Stolen Bases
Andrews-Phi 56
Kelly-Chi 53
Hanlon-Det 50
Richardson-Det 42
Radford-KC 39

Stolen Base Average

Stolen Base Runs

Fielding Runs
Knowles-Was 27.7
Denny-StL 22.7
Dunlap-StL-Det ... 19.3
Johnston-Bos 16.6
Glasscock-StL.... 13.8

Total Player Rating
Richardson-Det 4.8
Kelly-Chi 4.5
Glasscock-StL 4.2
Connor-NY 3.9
Brouthers-Det 3.5

Wins
Keefe-NY 42
Baldwin-Det 42
Clarkson-Chi 36
Welch-NY 33
McCormick-Chi 31

Win Percentage
Flynn-Chi .... .793
Ferguson-Phi ..... .769
Baldwin-Det ...... .764
McCormick-Chi ... .738
Getzien-Det ...... .732

Games
Keefe-NY 64
Welch-NY 59
Radbourn-Bos 58
Baldwin-Det 56
Clarkson-Chi 55

Complete Games
Keefe-NY 62
Radbourn-Bos 57
Welch-NY 56
Baldwin-Det 55
Clarkson-Chi 50

Shutouts
Baldwin-Det........7
Ferguson-Phi 4
Casey-Phi 4

Saves
Ferguson-Phi 2
Williamson-Chi 1
Ryan-Chi 1
Flynn-Chi 1
Devlin-NY 1

Innings Pitched
Keefe-NY 535.0
Radbourn-Bos ...509.1
Welch-NY 500.0
Baldwin-Det 487.0
Clarkson-Chi 466.2

Fewest Hits/Game
Baldwin-Det 6.86
Ferguson-Phi 7.21
Flynn-Chi 7.25
Stemmeyer-Bos ... 7.74
Boyle-StL 7.84

Fewest BB/Game
Whitney-KC 1.26
Ferguson-Phi 1.57
Clarkson-Chi 1.66
Keefe-NY 1.72
Baldwin-Det 1.85

Strikeouts
Baldwin-Det 323
Clarkson-Chi 313
Keefe-NY 297
Welch-NY 272
Stemmeyer-Bos ... 239

Strikeouts/Game
Stemmeyer-Bos ... 6.17
Clarkson-Chi 6.04
Baldwin-Det 5.97
Healy-StL 5.42
Flynn-Chi 5.11

Ratio
Baldwin-Det 8.70
Ferguson-Phi 8.78
Flynn-Chi 9.46
Clarkson-Chi 9.74
Keefe-NY 9.77

Earned Run Average
Boyle-StL 1.76
Ferguson-Phi 1.98
Baldwin-Det 2.24
Flynn-Chi 2.24
Clarkson-Chi 2.41

Adjusted ERA
Boyle-StL 182
Ferguson-Phi 166
Flynn-Chi 161
Clarkson-Chi 150
Baldwin-Det 147

Opponents' Batting Avg.
Baldwin-Det ...... .202
Ferguson-Phi ..... .210
Flynn-Chi .... .210
Stemmeyer-Bos ... .218
Boyle-StL .... .220

Opponents' On Base Pct.
Baldwin-Det ...... .243
Ferguson-Phi 244
Flynn-Chi 257
Boyle-StL .... .261
Clarkson-Chi 264

Starter Runs
Ferguson-Phi 57.5
Baldwin-Det 56.9
Clarkson-Chi 45.4
Keefe-NY 43.4
Casey-Phi 35.8

Adjusted Starter Runs
Clarkson-Chi 62.7
Ferguson-Phi 57.1
Baldwin-Det 57.1
Flynn-Chi 39.3
Keefe-NY 37.5

Clutch Pitching Index
Boyle-StL 127
McCormick-Chi ... 126
Welch-NY 121
Kirby-StL 112
Radbourn-Bos 108

Relief Runs

Adjusted Relief Runs

Relief Ranking

Total Pitcher Index
Ferguson-Phi 6.5
Clarkson-Chi 6.5
Baldwin-Det....... 6.1
Flynn-Chi 4.1
Boyle-StL......... 3.9

Total Baseball Ranking
Ferguson-Phi 6.4
Clarkson-Chi 6.3
Baldwin-Det 6.0
Kelly-Chi 4.5
Richardson-Det 4.5

February 5* The patent dispute between Thayer & Wright and A. G. Spalding & Brothers goes to court in Chicago. Thayer is the Harvard player who claimed to have invented the catcher's mask, while George Wright and Spalding are former teammates on the champion Boston Red Stockings. In the eventual settlement, Thayer's claims will be upheld, and he will receive a royalty on masks subsequently sold by Spalding's company.

March 17 *The Sporting News,* the weekly that will become "The Baseball Paper of the World," publishes its first issue.

April 22 The Mets' lavish new park on Staten Island is opened with a loss to the Athletics 7–6. Later this summer, cranks (fans) will be able to look at New York Harbor from the St. George grandstand and see the Statue of Liberty being assembled.

May 14 Charles Comiskey of the Browns prevents a double play by running full tilt into Reds second baseman Bid McPhee, enabling the Browns to win

2–1. The Cincinnati fans are irate, but the umpire allows the play. The Browns are gradually making "breaking up the double play" an accepted part of the game.

June 16* On Opening Day in the Southern League of Colored Base Ballists, the Eclipse of Memphis beats the home Unions of New Orleans, 3-1. The SLCBB, the first black professional sports league, will collapse in August.

July 7 Five of the top seven spots in the AA batting race belong to pitchers, according to *Sporting Life.*

August 15 Louisville's Guy Hecker scores seven runs in a game, establishing a major league record. In addition, he hits three home runs, all inside the park, to tie the existing record.

August 22 Just as he reaches the ball on a long hit by Chicken Wolf, Reds center fielder Abner Powell's pants are grabbed by a stray dog. Wolf circles the bases with the homer that wins the game for Louisville, 5–3, in 11 innings.

August 24 Baltimore's Matt Kilroy fans 16 Athletics, his high in a season in

which he will set the all-time major league record with 513 strikeouts.

October 23 The St. Louis Browns win the world championship by beating Chicago 4–3 in 10 innings. Pitching his fourth game in six days, Clarkson holds St. Louis hitless for six innings as Chicago builds a 3–0 lead. The Browns tie the game in the eighth, and Curt Welch scores the "$15,000" run on a wild pitch in the tenth. St. Louis wins the entire gate receipts from the series ($13,920), with each of 12 players getting about $580.

November 11 The Executive Council of the Brotherhood of Professional Base Ball Players, formed the previous year, meets and chooses officers. John M. Ward is re-elected president, Dan Brouthers vice president, and Tim Keefe secretary-treasurer.

November 22 The AA admits Cleveland four days after Pittsburgh fled the league to join the NL.

December 15 The AA approves the new clause that allows a club to reserve a player for as long as it wants, not just for next year's contract.

	BALTIMORE		BROOKLYN		CINCINNATI		LOUISVILLE		NEW YORK		PHILADELPHIA		PITTSBURGH		ST.LOUIS
M	B.Barnie	M	C.Byrne	M	O.Caylor	M	J.Hart	M	J.Gifford	M	L.Simmons	M	H.Phillips	M	C.Comiskey
1B	M.Scott	1B	B.Phillips	1B	J.Reilly	1B	J.Kerins	M	B.Ferguson	M	B.Sharsig	1B	O.Schomberg	1B	C.Comiskey
2B	M.Muldoon	2B	B.McClellan	2B	B.McPhee	2B	R.Mack	1B	D.Orr	1B	H.Stovey	2B	S.Barkley	2B	Y.Robinson
SS	J.Macullar	SS	G.Smith	SS	F.Fennelly	SS	B.White	2B	T.Forster	2B	L.Bierbauer	SS	P.Smith	SS	B.Gleason
3B	J.Davis	3B	G.Pinkney	3B	H.Carpenter	3B	J.Werrick	SS	C.Nelson	SS	C.McGarr	3B	A.Whitney	3B	A.Latham
LF	J.Sommer	LF	E.Burch	LF	C.Jones	LF	J.Strauss	3B	F.Hankinson	3B	J.Gleason	LF	E.Glenn	LF	T.O'Neill
CF	P.O'Connell	CF	J.McTamany	CF	F.Lewis	CF	P.Browning	LF	C.Roseman	LF	H.Larkin	CF	F.Mann	CF	C.Welch
RF	J.Manning	RF	E.Swartwood	RF	P.Corkhill	RF	J.Wolf	CF	S.Behel	CF	E.Greer	RF	T.Brown	RF	H.Nicol
C	C.Fulmer	C	J.Peoples	C	K.Baldwin	C	A.Cross	RF	S.Brady	RF	J.Coleman	C	F.Carroll	C	D.Bushong
								C	C.Reipschlager	C	W.Robinson				
23	J.Farrell	CO	B.Clark	C1	P.Snyder	1C	P.Cook	O3	B.Kuehne	C	R.Kemmler				
S	S.Houck	C	D.Oldfield	C	J.Keenan	O	L.Sylvester	S2	T.McLaughlin	C3	J.O'Brien	CO	D.Miller	/S	T.McSorley
O	B.Hoover	/O	J.Strauss	O	L.Maskrey	O	H.Collins	OC	J.Donahue	C1	J.Milligan	/1	F.Ringo	/C	L.Harding
C	T.Dolan	C	J.McCauley	O	A.Powell	/O	L.Maskrey	2	J.Meister	S	J.Quest	1	F.Mountain		
O	B.Purcell	/O	E.Kennedy	O	L.Sylvester	/O	P.Reccius	C	B.Holbert	3	D.Lyons	O	J.Coleman	P	D.Foutz
C	B.Traffley	/O	P.Schriver	/O	L.Marr	/1	J.Heinzman	2O	E.Foster	O	O.Shaffer	/C	T.Quinn	P	B.Caruthers
O	J.Clinton			/O	L.Richmond	/O	J.Neale	C	J.Crotty	S	G.Bradley	/C	D.Sullivan	P	N.Hudson
O	L.Sowders	P	H.Porter	/C	J.Boyle	/O	T.Terrell	/C	C.Zimmer	/S	J.Irwin			P	J.McGinnis
/O	E.Greer	P	J.Harkins	/C	F.Vaughn	/O	C.Murphy	/3	P.Connell	O	J.Hyndman	P	E.Morris		
/C	B.Conway	P	A.Terry					/O	H.Brooks	/S	C.Kelly	P	P.Galvin	/P	J.Murphy
/C	N.Bligh	P	H.Henderson	P	T.Mullane	P	T.Ramsey					P	J.Handiboe		
/O	B.Barnie	P	S.Toole	P	G.Pechiney	P	G.Hecker	P	J.Lynch	P	A.Atkinson				
/S	S.Nava			P	L.McKeon			P	A.Mays	P	B.Mathews	/P	J.Hofford		
/C	T.Hellman					/P	T.Sullivan	P	E.Cushman	P	B.Hart	/P	B.Bishop		
/O	Zay			P	E.Smith	/P	B.Ely			P	T.Kennedy				
				/P	J.Murphy	/P	T.Kennedy	/P	J.Shaffer	P	C.Miller				
P	M.Kilroy			/P	W.White	/P	E.Chamberlain								
P	J.McGinnis			/P	B.Irwin										
P	H.Henderson			/P	D.Bickham					/P	J.Aydelott				
				/P	Smith					/P	S.Weaver				
/P	D.Conway			/P	C.Stephens					/P	R.Smith				
/P	B.Taylor			/P	J.Reardon					/P	J.Brown				
/P	A.Powell									/P	E.Clark				
/P	E.Knouff									/P	C.Gessner				
/P	F.Houseman														

TEAM	G	W	L	PCT	GB	R	OR	AB	H	2B	3B	HR	BB	SO	AVG	OBP	SLG	PRO	PRO+	BR	/A	PF	CHI	RC	SB	CS	SBA	SBR
STL	139	93	46	.669		944	592	5009	1365	206	85	20	400	425	.273	.333	.360	.693	116	114	71	105	102	729	336			
PIT	140	80	57	.584	12	810	647	4854	1171	186	96	16	478	713	.241	.314	.329	.643	106	31	35	100	97	598	260			
BRO	141	76	61	.555	16	832	832	5053	1261	196	80	16	433	523	.250	.311	.330	.641	103	22	14	101	99	610	248			
LOU	138	66	70	.485	25.5	833	805	4921	1294	182	88	20	410	558	.263	.323	.348	.671	108	74	24	106	95	634	202			
CIN	141	65	73	.471	27.5	883	865	4915	1225	145	95	45	374	633	.249	.311	.345	.656	106	45	18	103	105	599	185			
PHI	139	63	72	.467	28	772	942	4856	1142	192	82	21	378	697	.235	.296	.321	.617	95	-22	-30	101	101	560	284			
NY	137	53	82	.393	38	628	766	4683	1047	108	72	18	330	578	.224	.279	.289	.568	85	-101	-73	96	96	422	120			
BAL	139	48	83	.366	41	625	878	4639	945	124	51	8	379	603	.204	.269	.258	.527	70	-163	-148	98	106	404	269			
TOT	557					6327		38930	9450	1339	649	164	3182	4730	.243	.305	.323	.628						1904				

TEAM	CG	SH	SV	IP	H	H/G	HR	BB	SO	RAT	ERA	ERA+	OAV	OOB	PR	/A	PF	CPI	FA	E	DP	FW	PW	BW	DIF
STL	134	14	2	1229¹	1087	8.0	13	329	583	10.6	2.49	138	.227	.281	130	128	100	113	.915	494	96	3.3	11.2	6.2	2.7
PIT	137	15	1	1226	1130	8.3	10	299	515	10.7	2.83	120	.235	.285	84	74	98	104	.917	487	90	3.9	6.5	3.1	-1.9
BRO	138	6	0	1234²	1202	8.8	17	464	540	12.4	3.42	102	.243	.312	3	9	101	104	.900	610	87	-2.2	.8	1.2	7.7
LOU	131	5	2	1209²	1109	8.3	16	432	720	11.7	3.07	118	.230	.297	51	75	106	101	.901	593	89	-2.0	6.6	2.1	-8.7
CIN	129	3	0	1247²	1267	9.1	25	481	495	13.0	4.18	84	.255	.327	-103	-94	102	95	.905	582	122	-.8	-8.3	1.6	3.4
PHI	134	4	0	1218¹	1308	9.7	35	388	513	13.0	3.97	88	.259	.319	-72	-66	102	100	.894	637	99	-4.0	-5.8	-2.6	7.9
NY	134	5	0	1186¹	1148	8.7	23	386	559	11.8	3.50	97	.243	.304	-8	-14	99	98	.907	544	81	.3	-1.2	-6.4	-7.2
BAL	134	5	0	1206²	1197	8.9	25	403	805	12.3	4.08	84	.244	.308	-85	-90	99	87	.910	523	59	1.8	-7.9	-13.0	1.6
TOT	1071	57	5	9759		8.7				11.9	3.44		.243	.305					.906	4470	723				

Runs
Latham-StL	152
McPhee-Cin	139
Larkin-Phi	133
McClellan-Bro	131
Pinkney-Bro	119

Hits
Orr-NY	193
O'Neill-StL	190
Larkin-Phi	180
Latham-StL	174
Phillips-Bro	160

Doubles
Larkin-Phi	36
McClellan-Bro	33
Welch-StL	31
Barkley-Pit	31
Browning-Lou	29

Triples
Orr-NY	31
Coleman-Phi-Pit	17
Kuehne-Pit	17
Fennelly-Cin	17
Larkin-Phi	16

Home Runs
McPhee-Cin	8
Stovey-Phi	7
Orr-NY	7

Total Bases
Orr-NY	301
O'Neill-StL	255
Larkin-Phi	254
Welch-StL	221
McPhee-Cin	221

Runs Batted In
O'Neill-StL	107
Corkhill-Cin	97
Welch-StL	95
Orr-NY	91
Reilly-Cin	79

Runs Produced
O'Neill-StL	210
Welch-StL	207
Larkin-Phi	205
McPhee-Cin	201

Bases On Balls
Swartwood-Bro	70
Pinkney-Bro	70
Mack-Lou	68
Kerins-Lou	66

Batting Average
Hecker-Lou	.341
Browning-Lou	.340
Orr-NY	.338
Caruthers-StL	.334
O'Neill-StL	.328

On Base Percentage
Larkin-Phi	.390
Browning-Lou	.389
O'Neill-StL	.385
Stovey-Phi	.377
Swartwood-Bro	.377

Slugging Average
Orr-NY	.527
Caruthers-StL	.527
Larkin-Phi	.450
Hecker-Lou	.446
Browning-Lou	.441

Production
Orr-NY	.890
Larkin-Phi	.839
Browning-Lou	.830
O'Neill-StL	.826
Stovey-Phi	.817

Adjusted Production
Orr-NY	186
Larkin-Phi	161
Stovey-Phi	154
O'Neill-StL	151
Browning-Lou	151

Batter Runs
Orr-NY	45.9
Caruthers-StL	41.4
Larkin-Phi	41.3
O'Neill-StL	38.6
Stovey-Phi	32.1

Adjusted Batter Runs
Orr-NY	51.9
Larkin-Phi	39.9
Caruthers-StL	36.8
O'Neill-StL	32.4
Stovey-Phi	31.0

Clutch Hitting Index
Corkhill-Cin	151
Carpenter-Cin	142
Coleman-Phi-Pit	129
O'Brien-Phi	128
O'Neill-StL	124

Runs Created
Orr-NY	118
Larkin-Phi	114
Stovey-Phi	109
O'Neill-StL	104
Latham-StL	104

Total Average
Stovey-Phi	1.009
Larkin-Phi	.914
Robinson-StL	.903
Orr-NY	.897
Browning-Lou	.873

Stolen Bases
Stovey-Phi	68
Latham-StL	60
Welch-StL	59
Robinson-StL	51
McClellan-Bro	43

Stolen Base Average

Stolen Base Runs

Fielding Runs
Kerins-Lou	39.0
McPhee-Cin	30.5
Hankinson-NY	25.4
Smith-Pit	21.0
Peoples-Bro	18.5

Total Player Rating
Kerins-Lou	4.6
McPhee-Cin	4.6
Larkin-Phi	3.6
Carroll-Pit	3.6
O'Neill-StL	3.2

Wins
Morris-Pit	41
Foutz-StL	41
Ramsey-Lou	38
Mullane-Cin	33
Caruthers-StL	30

Win Percentage
Foutz-StL	.719
Caruthers-StL	.682
Morris-Pit	.672
Hudson-StL	.615
Atkinson-Phi	.595

Games
Kilroy-Bal	68
Ramsey-Lou	67
Morris-Pit	64
Mullane-Cin	63
Foutz-StL	59

Complete Games
Ramsey-Lou	66
Kilroy-Bal	66
Morris-Pit	63
Mullane-Cin	55
Foutz-StL	55

Shutouts
Morris-Pit	12
Foutz-StL	11
Terry-Bro	5
Kilroy-Bal	5
Ramsey-Lou	3

Saves
Morris-Pit	1
Hudson-StL	1
Foutz-StL	1
Ely-Lou	1

Innings Pitched
Ramsey-Lou	588.2
Kilroy-Bal	583.0
Morris-Pit	555.1
Mullane-Cin	529.2
Foutz-StL	504.0

Fewest Hits/Game
Ramsey-Lou	6.83
Kilroy-Bal	7.35
Morris-Pit	7.37
Foutz-StL	7.46
Caruthers-StL	7.51

Fewest BB/Game
Galvin-Pit	1.55
Morris-Pit	1.91
Caruthers-StL	2.00
McGinnis-StL-Bal	2.27
Atkinson-Phi	2.29

Strikeouts
Kilroy-Bal	513
Ramsey-Lou	499
Morris-Pit	326
Foutz-StL	283
Mullane-Cin	250

Strikeouts/Game
Kilroy-Bal	7.92
Ramsey-Lou	7.63
Morris-Pit	5.28
Miller-Phi	5.25
Terry-Bro	5.06

Ratio
Morris-Pit	9.40
Caruthers-StL	9.67
Ramsey-Lou	10.18
Foutz-StL	10.21
Cushman-NY	10.45

Earned Run Average
Foutz-StL	2.11
Caruthers-StL	2.32
Ramsey-Lou	2.45
Morris-Pit	2.45
Galvin-Pit	2.67

Adjusted ERA
Foutz-StL	163
Ramsey-Lou	148
Caruthers-StL	148
Morris-Pit	138
Hecker-Lou	127

Opponents' Batting Avg.
Ramsey-Lou	.198
Kilroy-Bal	.210
Morris-Pit	.214
Foutz-StL	.216
Caruthers-StL	.217

Opponents' On Base Pct.
Morris-Pit	.258
Caruthers-StL	.263
Ramsey-Lou	.269
Foutz-StL	.274
Kilroy-Bal	.274

Starter Runs
Foutz-StL	74.8
Ramsey-Lou	65.2
Morris-Pit	61.4
Caruthers-StL	48.2
Galvin-Pit	37.3

Adjusted Starter Runs
Ramsey-Lou	77.6
Foutz-StL	74.2
Morris-Pit	57.6
Caruthers-StL	47.7
Hecker-Lou	35.8

Clutch Pitching Index
Galvin-Pit	130
McGinnis-StL-Bal	127
Foutz-StL	122
Miller-Phi	119
Mays-NY	107

Relief Runs

Adjusted Relief Runs

Relief Ranking

Total Pitcher Index
Foutz-StL	8.1
Caruthers-StL	6.8
Ramsey-Lou	6.5
Hecker-Lou	5.2
Morris-Pit	4.4

Total Baseball Ranking
Foutz-StL	8.1
Caruthers-StL	7.9
Ramsey-Lou	6.5
Hecker-Lou	5.2
Kerins-Lou	4.6

February 16 Chicago announces the sale of Mike "King" Kelly to Boston for $10,000, more than twice the amount ever paid for a player before. With the contract and bonus, Kelly is dubbed a "$15,000 Beauty."

March 8 The NL franchise in St. Louis is sold to a group from Indianapolis for $12,000, including players. The Maroons will now become the Hoosiers.

March 9 The Kansas City Cowboys go out of business with the sale of their players to the league for $6,000. The club's spot in the league has already been taken by Pittsburgh.

March 13 After a week of conditioning in Macon, Ga., the Detroit team begins a six-week spring exhibition tour through the South and Midwest.

April 30 The Phillies open their new $80,000 wooden ballpark on Huntingdon Avenue and Broad Street, later known as the Baker Bowl, with a 19-10 win over New York. After a fire in 1894, the park is the first to be rebuilt using steel and concrete. The Phils will remain on this site until 1938.

May 6* The National Colored League, patterned after the NL, opens with a game in Pittsburgh, the Gorhams beating the Keystones, 11–8, before a crowd of 1,200. Because of rainouts and small crowds the league, which has been recognized by the National Agreement as a legitimate minor league, will fold on May 16 after only 13 games.

May 7 Sam Thompson of Detroit becomes the first major leaguer to hit two bases-loaded triples in one game.

May 20* Nearly two weeks after defeating the Falls Citys in their NCBBL opener in Louisville, the Boston Resolutes finally leave for home after earning enough money for train fare by working as waiters. Their departure, and the circumstances surrounding it, sounds the death knell for the second professional baseball league organized by African-Americans.

May 30 Chicago walks to a 12–11 victory in a morning holiday game in New York. Giants pitcher Bill George walks 16 batters to establish a major league mark. He walked 13 against Indianapolis on May 15 and would hand out another 13 passes against them on June 15.

June 5 Today's *Chicago Tribune* publishes NL batting figures through May 31 that show Fred Carroll (.476), Sam Thompson (.454), and Paul Hines (.438) leading the league. Walks are being counted as hits this year.

June 19 Cap Anson refuses to allow his NL champion White Sox to play against Newark's George Stovey, an outstanding black pitcher in the International League.

June 20* The International League passes a ban on black players. Although not strictly enforced this season, this action spells the end of the IL as a haven for black ballplayers.

October 10 The World Series opens in St. Louis with the Browns beating the Detroits, 6–1. Bob Caruthers holds the Wolverines to five hits and has three hits himself.

October 13 The best-of-15 World Series begins its tour of the other cities with a game in Pittsburgh, Detroit winning, 8–0, behind the two-hit pitching of Lady Baldwin.

October 27 The Brotherhood of Professional Base Ball Players holds a meeting and club representatives pledge not to sign standard contracts until negotiations are held concerning the wording of those documents.

November 16 The Joint Rules Committee does away with the four-strike rule and with the scoring of walks as hits. Five balls for a walk remains the rule.

November 17 The National League officially recognizes the Brotherhood of Professional Base Ball Players at a meeting with a committee of three players: Dan Brouthers, Ned Hanlon and John Ward.

November 18 The National League adopts a new contract that spells out reserve provisions for the first time. The NL refuses to accept the players' demand that the salary be written out on all contracts, however.

December 2* The International League disbands. Syracuse, Toronto, Hamilton, and Buffalo split off to form the International Association, while Newark, Jersey City, Wilkes-Barre, and Scranton become the nucleus of the Central League.

BOSTON		CHICAGO		DETROIT		INDIANAPOLIS		NEW YORK		PHILADELPHIA		PITTSBURGH		WASHINGTON	
M	K.Kelly	M	C.Anson	M	B.Watkins	M	W.Burnham	M	J.Mutrie	M	H.Wright	M	H.Phillips	M	J.Gaffney
M	J.Morrill	1B	C.Anson	M	F.Thomas	M	F.Thomas	1B	R.Connor	1B	S.Farrar	1B	S.Barkley	1B	B.O'Brien
1B	J.Morrill	2B	F.Pfeffer	2B	F.Dunlap	M	H.Fogel	2B	D.Richardson	2B	B.McLaughlin	2B	P.Smith	2B	A.Myers
2B	J.Burdock	SS	N.Williamson	SS	J.Rowe	1B	O.Schomberg	SS	J.Ward	SS	A.Irwin	SS	B.Kuehne	SS	J.Farrell
SS	S.Wise	3B	T.Burns	3B	D.White	2B	C.Bassett	3B	B.Ewing	3B	J.Mulvey	3B	A.Whitney	3B	J.Donnelly
3B	B.Nash	LF	M.Sullivan	LF	H.Richardson	SS	J.Glasscock	LF	P.Gillespie	LF	G.Wood	LF	A.Dalrymple	LF	C.Carroll
LF	J.Hornung	CF	J.Ryan	CF	N.Hanlon	3B	J.Denny	CF	G.Gore	CF	E.Andrews	CF	T.Brown	CF	P.Hines
CF	D.Johnston	RF	B.Sunday	RF	S.Thompson	LF	E.Seery	RF	M.Tiernan	RF	J.Fogarty	RF	J.Coleman	RF	E.Daily
RF	K.Kelly	C	T.Daly	C	C.Ganzel	CF	J.McGeachy	C	W.Brown	C	J.Clements	C	D.Miller	C	C.Mack
C	P.Tate					RF	J.Cahill								
		C	S.Flint	OP	L.Twitchell	C	G.Myers	C3	J.O'Rourke	2S	C.Bastian	OC	F.Carroll	O	G.Shoch
SO	E.Sutton	OP	G.Van Haltren	C	C.Bennett			O	M.Dorgan	C	D.McGuire	1	A.McKinnon	CS	P.Dealy
OS	B.Wheelock	OC	D.Darling	C	F.Briody	C	T.Arundel	C	P.Deasley	O	E.Daily	O	E.Beecher	1	B.Krieg
C	C.Daily	O	B.Pettit	3	B.Shindle	3	M.Hackett	C	J.Rainey	C	T.Gunning	OC	J.Fields	C	B.Gilligan
C	T.O'Rourke	3	P.Tebeau	O	J.Manning	O	T.Brown	C	P.Murphy	/O	T.McCarthy			/S	J.Irwin
		/2	E.Geiss			O	M.Polhemus	/3	G.Hatfield	/O	A.Maul	P	P.Galvin	/S	S.Crane
P	C.Radbourn	/O	J.Flynn	P	C.Getzien	O	G.Gardner	B.Becannon	/C	T.Cusick	P	J.McCormick	/2	J.O'Brien
P	K.Madden			P	L.Baldwin	O	B.Johnson	/2	R.Carey	/O	H.Lyons	P	E.Morris	/C	B.Wright
P	D.Conway	P	J.Clarkson	P	S.Wiedman	1	H.Jackson	/3	J.Gerhardt						
P	B.Stemmeyer	P	M.Baldwin	P	P.Conway	/O	L.Corcoran	/3	C.Nelson	P	D.Casey	/P	B.Bishop	P	J.Whitney
						/O	J.Sowders			P	C.Buffinton			P	H.O'Day
		/P	S.Pyle	/P	H.Gruber			P	T.Keefe	P	C.Ferguson			P	F.Gilmore
		/P	C.Sprague	/P	E.Beatin	P	J.Healy	P	M.Welch	/P	J.Devlin			P	D.Shaw
				/P	B.Burke	P	H.Boyle	P	B.George						
						P	L.Shreve							/P	G.Keefe
								/P	C.Titcomb						
						/P	D.Leitner	/P	M.Mattimore						
						/P	J.Kirby	/P	B.Swabach						
						/P	H.Morrison	/P	J.Roach						
						/P	S.Moffett	/P	S.Wiedman						
						/P	Fast								

TEAM	G	W	L	PCT	GB	R	OR	AB	H	2B	3B	HR	BB	SO	AVG	OBP	SLG	PRO	PRO+	BR	/A	PF	CHI	RC	SB	CS	SBA	SBR
DET	127	79	45	.637		969	714	4689	1404	213	126	55	352	258	.299	.353	.434	.787	118	134	104	103	103	833	267			
PHI	128	75	48	.610	3.5	901	702	4630	1269	213	89	47	385	346	.274	.337	.389	.726	99	35	-13	106	94	744	355			
CHI	127	71	50	.587	6.5	813	716	4350	1177	178	98	80	407	400	.271	.336	.412	.748	98	62	-44	113	99	748	382			
NY	129	68	55	.553	10.5	816	723	4516	1259	167	93	48	361	326	.279	.339	.389	.728	111	37	76	95	100	753	415			
BOS	127	61	60	.504	16.5	831	792	4531	1255	185	94	53	340	392	.277	.333	.394	.727	106	32	31	100	102	736	373			
PIT	125	55	69	.444	24	621	750	4414	1141	183	78	20	319	381	.258	.314	.349	.663	94	-69	-27	94	90	567	221			
WAS	126	46	76	.377	32	601	818	4314	1039	149	63	47	269	339	.241	.292	.337	.629	82	-126	-95	95	99	535	334			
IND	127	37	89	.294	43	628	965	4368	1080	162	70	33	300	379	.247	.302	.339	.641	85	-105	-82	96	97	562	334			
TOT	508					6180		35812	9624	1450	711	383	2733	2821	.269	.326	.381	.707						2681				

TEAM	CG	SH	SV	IP	H	H/G	HR	BB	SO	RAT	ERA	ERA+	OAV	OOB	PR	/A	PF	CPI	FA	E	DP	FW	PW	BW	SBW	DIF
DET	122	3	1	1116¹	1172	9.4	52	344	337	12.5	3.95	102	.264	.322	12	-3	99	97	.925	394	92	3.3	-.3	8.8		5.1
PHI	119	7	1	1132²	1173	9.3	48	305	435	12.0	3.47	121	.259	.311	72	89	104	104	.912	471	76	-.4	7.5	-1.1		7.5
CHI	117	4	3	1126	1156	9.2	55	338	510	12.4	3.46	129	.257	.317	73	120	110	108	.914	472	99	-.6	10.2	-3.7		4.7
NY	123	5	1	1113²	1096	8.9	27	373	415	12.2	3.57	105	.250	.314	59	18	93	96	.920	431	83	1.8	1.5	6.4		-3.3
BOS	123	4	1	1100²	1226	10.0	55	396	254	13.6	4.41	91	.273	.338	-44	-46	100	94	.905	522	94	-3.1	-3.9	2.6		4.9
PIT	123	4	0	1108²	1287	10.4	39	246	248	12.7	4.12	94	.281	.322	-9	-32	95	99	.921	425	70	1.4	-2.7	-2.3		-3.4
WAS	124	3	0	1090¹	1216	10.0	47	299	396	12.9	4.19	96	.272	.323	-18	-21	100	96	.909	483	77	-1.4	-1.8	-8.1		-3.8
IND	118	4	1	1088	1289	10.7	60	431	245	14.6	5.24	79	.284	.352	-145	-139	102	92	.912	479	105	-1.0	-11.8	-6.9		-6.3
TOT	969	34	8	8876¹		9.7				12.8	4.05		.269	.326					.915	3677	696					

Runs
Brouthers-Det 153
Rowe-Det 135
Richardson-Det ... 131
Kelly-Bos 120

Hits
Thompson-Det ... 203
Ward-NY 184
Richardson-Det ... 178
Rowe-Det 171
Brouthers-Det 169

Doubles
Brouthers-Det 36
Kelly-Bos 34
Denny-Ind 34
Anson-Chi 33

Triples
Thompson-Det 23
Connor-NY 22
Johnston-Bos 20
Brouthers-Det 20
Wood-Phi 19

Home Runs
B.O'Brien-Was 19
Connor-NY 17
Pfeffer-Chi 16
Wood-Phi 14

Total Bases
Thompson-Det 311
Brouthers-Det 281
Richardson-Det ... 263
Denny-Ind 256
Connor-NY 255

Runs Batted In
Thompson-Det 166
Connor-NY 104
Anson-Chi 102
Brouthers-Det ... 101
Denny-Ind 97

Runs Produced
Thompson-Det 273
Brouthers-Det ... 242
Rowe-Det 225
Richardson-Det ... 217
Anson-Chi 202

Bases On Balls
Fogarty-Phi 82
Connor-NY 75
Williamson-Chi.... 73
Seery-Ind 71
Brouthers-Det 71

Batting Average
Anson-Chi.........347
Thompson-Det 372
Brouthers-Det 338
Ward-NY 338
Wise-Bos 334

On Base Percentage
Brouthers-Det .... .426
Anson-Chi .... .422
Thompson-Det .... .416
Schomberg-Ind ... .397
Kelly-Bos .... .393

Slugging Average
Thompson-Det 571
Brouthers-Det 562
Connor-NY 541
Wise-Bos 522
Anson-Chi 517

Production
Brouthers-Det 988
Thompson-Det 987
Anson-Chi.........939
Connor-NY 933
Wise-Bos 913

Adjusted Production
Brouthers-Det 167
Thompson-Det 166
Connor-NY 164
Carroll-Pit 152
Wise-Bos.........151

Batter Runs
Thompson-Det ... 51.2
Brouthers-Det ... 50.5
Anson-Chi 39.3
Connor-NY 37.1
Wise-Bos 31.7

Adjusted Batter Runs
Thompson-Det ...46.6
Brouthers-Det 46.0
Connor-NY 43.1
Wise-Bos 31.6
Carroll-Pit 30.1

Clutch Hitting Index
Thompson-Det 149
O'Rourke-NY 143
Nash-Bos 129
Rowe-Det 125
Schomberg-Ind 122

Runs Created
Thompson-Det 142
Brouthers-Det ... 138
Kelly-Bos 129
Ward-NY 125
Connor-NY 120

Total Average
Brouthers-Det ...1.184
Kelly-Bos 1.146
Connor-NY 1.131
Thompson-Det ...1.094
Fogarty-Phi......1.085

Stolen Bases
Ward-NY 111
Fogarty-Phi 102
Kelly-Bos 84
Hanlon-Det 69
Glasscock-Ind 62

Stolen Base Average

Stolen Base Runs

Fielding Runs
Glasscock-Ind 35.0
Fogarty-Phi 31.7
Ward-NY 29.8
Johnston-Bos 25.3
Pfeffer-Chi 24.6

Total Player Rating
Thompson-Det 4.3
Denny-Ind......... 4.0
Ward-NY 3.9
Glasscock-Ind 3.5
Fogarty-Phi....... 3.3

Wins
Clarkson-Chi 38
Keefe-NY 35
Getzien-Det 29
Galvin-Pit 28
Casey-Phi 28

Win Percentage
Getzien-Det ...... .690
Ferguson-Phi..... .688
Casey-Phi .... .683
Keefe-NY .... .648
Clarkson-Chi ..... .644

Games
Clarkson-Chi 60
Keefe-NY 56
Radbourn-Bos 50
Galvin-Pit 49
Whitney-Was 47

Complete Games
Clarkson-Chi 56
Keefe-NY 54
Radbourn-Bos 48
Galvin-Pit 47
Whitney-Was 46

Shutouts
Casey-Phi 4
Madden-Bos 3
Healy-Ind 3
Galvin-Pit 3

Saves
VanHaltren-Chi...... 1
Twitchell-Det 1
Tiernan-NY 1
Stemmeyer-Bos 1
Pettit-Chi 1
Ferguson-Phi 1
Fast -Ind 1
Baldwin-Chi 1

Innings Pitched
Clarkson-Chi 523.0
Keefe-NY 476.2
Galvin-Pit 440.2
Radbourn-Bos ...425.0
Whitney-Was 404.2

Fewest Hits/Game
Keefe-NY 8.08
Conway-Det 8.14
Casey-Phi 8.69
Welch-NY 8.82
Clarkson-Chi 8.83

Fewest BB/Game
Whitney-Was 93
Galvin-Pit 1.37
Ferguson-Phi 1.42
Clarkson-Chi 1.58
Boyle-Ind 1.89

Strikeouts
Clarkson-Chi...... 237
Keefe-NY 189
Baldwin-Chi 164
Buffinton-Phi..... 160
Whitney-Was 146

Strikeouts/Game
Baldwin-Chi...... 4.42
Gilmore-Was 4.37
Buffinton-Phi 4.33
VanHaltren-Chi 4.25
Clarkson-Chi 4.08

Ratio
Keefe-NY 10.33
Clarkson-Chi 10.55
Ferguson-Phi 10.75
Whitney-Was 10.85
Welch-NY 11.32

Earned Run Average
Casey-Phi 2.86
Conway-Det 2.90
Ferguson-Phi 3.00
Clarkson-Chi 3.08
Keefe-NY 3.12

Adjusted ERA
Casey-Phi 147
Clarkson-Chi 145
Ferguson-Phi..... 140
Conway-Det 139
Baldwin-Chi....... 131

Opponents' Batting Avg.
Keefe-NY .... .230
Conway-Det ..... .235
Casey-Phi........ .246
Clarkson-Chi ..... .246
Baldwin-Chi ...... .248

Opponents' On Base Pct.
Keefe-NY .... .276
Clarkson-Chi ..... .281
Whitney-Was 284
Ferguson-Phi 289
Galvin-Pit 299

Starter Runs
Clarkson-Chi 56.1
Casey-Phi 51.5
Keefe-NY 49.3
Galvin-Pit 37.1
Whitney-Was 36.9

Adjusted Starter Runs
Clarkson-Chi 80.1
Casey-Phi 58.3
Ferguson-Phi 39.9
Baldwin-Chi 39.5
Whitney-Was 36.4

Clutch Pitching Index
VanHaltren-Chi ... 123
Casey-Phi 117
Baldwin-Chi 114
Ferguson-Phi 108
Madden-Bos 105

Relief Runs

Adjusted Relief Runs

Relief Ranking

Total Pitcher Index
Clarkson-Chi 8.3
Ferguson-Phi 4.7
Whitney-Was 4.7
Keefe-NY 3.8
Casey-Phi 3.7

Total Baseball Ranking
Clarkson-Chi 8.1
Ferguson-Phi 4.7
Whitney-Was 4.5
Thompson-Det 4.3
Denny-Ind........ 4.0

April 16 Two rookies, Mike Griffin of the Baltimore Orioles and George "White Wings" Tebeau of Cincinnati, hit home runs in their first major league at bats on Opening Day. They are the first of many to accomplish this.

April 21 Pop Snyder, the only catcher from the National Association still behind the plate, allows Louisville to steal 10 bases in just three innings before being replaced by Jim Toy. The Colonels beat the Cleveland "Babies", 14–7.

April 22 Tony Mullane pitches a regular-season game in Missouri for the first time since 1883. The Missouri injunction obtained against him by the St. Louis Unions in 1884 having finally been resolved, Tony leads the Reds to a 5–2 victory over the Browns.

May 1 Charlie Comiskey triples and homers to lead the Browns to a 14–13 victory over Cleveland. St. Louis scores 74 runs in a four-game sweep and is on its way to becoming the first team to score over 1,000 runs in a season.

June 9 Mets right fielder John "Candy" Nelson sets a major league record by starting three double plays, two on throws to home and one to start an infield rundown. Outfielders Jack McCarthy (April 26, 1905) and Ira Flagstead (April 19, 1926) will equal this feat.

June 13 Sportswriter O. P. Caylor takes over as manager of the Mets. Caylor had managed Cincinnati in 1885 and 1886 while writing for the *Cincinnati Enquirer,* now he is with the *New York Tribune* and managing again.

June 16 Before a riotous Baltimore club, Curt Welch of the Browns topples Orioles second baseman Bill Greenwood to prevent a double play and is promptly arrested for assault by a policeman on duty at the park. He will be fined $4.50 by a local judge.

July 4 Dave Foutz of the Browns has a banner day at the plate, driving in nine runs with two homers and five hits in the afternoon game of a doubleheader against the Mets after having hit a homer in the morning game. St. Louis wins both, 15–2, and 20–3.

July 22 Master Fred Chapman, age 14, pitches for Philadelphia against Cleveland in a 9-0 forfeited game. This is his only major league appearance.

August 12 At the Mets' grounds on Staten Island, Athletics batter Gus Weyhing hits an apparent triple that Mets right fielder Eddie Hogan kicks onto the stage of the play, "The Fall of Babylon." Since the ground rules at the park call for a double on hits into the theatrical set, the umpire orders Weyhing back to second. After a futile argument, the Athletics leave and forfeit the game.

August 17 Managing from the press table costs Ollie Caylor and the Mets a game. With a Baltimore runner on third base in the bottom of the 10th inning, manager Caylor yells last-second instructions to catcher Bill Holbert. Just as Holbert turns around to look at the press stand, Al Mays begins his delivery. When Mays sees Holbert turned away, however, he stops, committing a balk that sends the winning run across the plate for the Orioles.

August 29 Denny Lyons of Philadelphia (AA) is held hitless for the first time since May 23 to end a 52-game hitting streak. In two of those games, however, Lyons's only hits were actually bases on balls, scored as hits this year.

October 1 Matt Kilroy pitches and wins both games of a doubleheader to close the home season at Oriole Park. The fastballer would finish the season with a 46-20 record, the major league season record for a lefthander.

October 8 The Metropolitan franchise and player contracts are sold to AA rival Brooklyn for $15,000.

December 12* A baseball reporters association is organized. It pledges to work to standardize scoring practices, especially in the gray area of stolen bases.

BALTIMORE		BROOKLYN		CINCINNATI		CLEVELAND		LOUISVILLE		NEW YORK		PHILADELPHIA		ST.LOUIS	
M	B.Barnie	M	C.Byrne	M	G.Schmelz	M	J.Williams	M	J.Kelly	M	B.Ferguson	M	F.Bancroft	M	C.Comiskey
1B	T.Tucker	1B	B.Phillips	1B	J.Reilly	1B	J.Toy	1B	J.Kerins	M	D.Orr	M	C.Mason	1B	C.Comiskey
2B	B.Greenwood	2B	B.McClellan	2B	B.McPhee	2B	C.Stricker	2B	R.Mack	M	O.Caylor	1B	J.Milligan	2B	Y.Robinson
SS	O.Burns	SS	G.Smith	SS	F.Fennelly	SS	E.McKean	SS	B.White	1B	D.Orr	2B	L.Bierbauer	SS	B.Gleason
3B	J.Davis	3B	G.Pinkney	3B	H.Carpenter	3B	P.Reccius	3B	J.Werrick	2B	J.Gerhardt	SS	M.McGarr	3B	A.Latham
LF	J.Sommer	LF	E.Greer	LF	G.Tebeau	LF	F.Mann	LF	H.Collins	SS	P.Radford	3B	D.Lyons	LF	T.O'Neill
CF	M.Griffin	CF	J.McTamany	CF	P.Corkhill	CF	P.Hotaling	CF	P.Browning	3B	F.Hankinson	LF	H.Larkin	CF	C.Welch
RF	B.Purcell	RF	E.Swartwood	RF	H.Nicol	RF	M.Allen	RF	J.Wolf	LF	D.O'Brien	CF	H.Stovey	RF	B.Caruthers
C	S.Trott	C	J.Peoples	C	K.Baldwin	C	P.Snyder	C	P.Cook	CF	C.Jones	RF	T.Poorman	C	J.Boyle
										RF	C.Roseman	C	W.Robinson		
C	C.Fulmer	OP	A.Terry	C1	J.Keenan	C1	C.Reipschlager	1P	G.Hecker	C	B.Holbert			OP	D.Foutz
CO	L.Daniels	O	E.Burch	O	C.Jones	O	S.Carroll	CO	L.Cross			O	F.Mann	C	D.Bushong
/O	J.Hayes	C	B.Clark	/3	H.Kappel	10	C.Sweeney	O	P.Reccius	OS	C.Nelson	C	G.Townsend	O	L.Sylvester
		C	J.O'Brien	/O	J.O'Connor	3	J.McGlone	/C	A.Cross	C	J.Donahue	1	E.Flanagan	/O	E.Knouff
		S	B.Otterson			3	J.Say	/O	D.Hemp	O2	J.Meister	O	C.Roseman	/2	H.Lyons
P	M.Kilroy	/O	C.Roseman	P	E.Smith	O	J.Munyan			1	T.O'Brien	/O	E.Greer	/C	M.Goodfellow
P	P.Smith			P	T.Mullane	C	C.Zimmer	P	T.Ramsey	O	E.Hogan	/C	J.Roxburgh		
		P	H.Porter	P	B.Serad	3	E.Herr	P	E.Chamberlain	C	P.Sommers			P	S.King
/P	E.Knouff	P	J.Harkins			/3	E.Flynn			/1	D.Esterbrook	P	E.Seward		
/P	L.Shreve	P	S.Toole	/P	J.McGinnis	/O	H.Simon	/P	J.Neale	2	J.Knowles	P	G.Weyhing	/P	N.Hudson
/P	B.Gardner	/P	H.Henderson	/P	M.Shea	/S	F.Scheibeck	/P	P.Veach	S	C.Cross	P	A.Atkinson	/P	J.Murphy
/P	B.Keating			/P	M.Watson					/O	J.Morrison				
		/P	B.Cunningham	/P	W.Widner	P	B.Crowell			S	S.Houck	/P	B.Mathews		
						P	M.Morrison			/1	C.Ryan	/P	B.Hart		
						P	H.Daily			/O	F.O'Neill	/P	C.Titcomb		
						P	B.Gilks			/O	C.Hall	/O	B.Taylor		
						P	G.Pechiney			/C	T.Kinslow	/P	F.Chapman		
										/C	H.Collins	/P	B.Casey		
						/P	J.Kirby			/O	L.Pike				
										P	A.Mays				
										P	E.Cushman				
										P	J.Lynch				
										P	J.Shaffer				
										P	S.Wiedman				
										/P	B.Fagan				
										/P	C.Parsons				
										/P	G.McMullen				

TEAM	G	W	L	PCT	GB	R	OR	AB	H	2B	3B	HR	BB	SO	AVG	OBP	SLG	PRO	PRO+	BR	/A	PF	CHI	RC	SB	CS	SBA	SBR
STL	138	95	40	.704		1131	761	5048	1550	261	78	39	442	340	.307	.371	.413	.784	111	151	37	111	103	1012	581			
CIN	136	81	54	.600	14	892	745	4797	1285	179	102	37	382	366	.268	.329	.371	.700	97	-11	-31	102	102	778	527			
BAL	141	77	58	.570	18	975	861	4825	1337	202	100	31	469	334	.277	.349	.380	.729	114	50	106	94	102	852	545			
LOU	139	76	60	.559	19.5	956	854	4916	1420	194	98	27	436	356	.289	.352	.385	.737	107	61	42	102	98	850	466			
PHI	137	64	69	.481	30	893	890	4954	1370	231	84	29	321	388	.277	.327	.375	.702	99	-13	-14	100	100	782	476			
BRO	138	60	74	.448	34.5	904	918	4913	1281	200	82	25	456	365	.261	.330	.350	.680	92	-40	-51	101	103	720	409			
NY	138	44	89	.331	50	754	1093	4820	1197	193	66	21	439	463	.248	.318	.329	.647	88	-98	-63	96	94	615	305			
CLE	133	39	92	.298	54	729	1112	4649	1170	178	77	14	375	463	.252	.314	.332	.646	87	-99	-77	97	96	611	355			
TOT	550					7234		38922	10610	1638	687	223	3320	3075	.273	.337	.367	.704						3664				

TEAM	CG	SH	SV	IP	H	H/G	HR	BB	SO	RAT	ERA	ERA+	OAV	OOB	PR	/A	PF	CPI	FA	E	DP	FW	PW	BW	SBW	DIF
STL	132	6	2	1199¹	1254	9.4	19	323	334	12.2	3.77	120	.258	.311	69	100	106	94	.916	481	86	3.6	8.1	3.0		12.8
CIN	129	11	1	1182²	1202	9.1	28	396	330	12.6	3.58	121	.257	.322	93	99	101	107	.916	484	106	3.0	8.0	-2.5		5.0
BAL	132	8	0	1220	1288	9.5	16	418	470	13.0	3.87	106	.262	.326	58	30	95	100	.907	549	66	.8	2.4	8.6		-2.3
LOU	133	3	1	1205²	1274	9.5	31	357	544	12.5	3.82	115	.260	.316	63	75	102	98	.903	574	83	-.9	6.1	3.4		-.6
PHI	131	5	1	1186¹	1227	9.3	29	433	417	13.1	4.59	93	.259	.331	-39	-41	100	88	.907	528	95	1.0	-3.3	-1.1		.9
BRO	132	3	3	1185¹	1348	10.2	27	454	332	14.0	4.47	96	.281	.348	-24	-24	100	103	.905	562	88	-.5	-1.9	-4.1		-.4
NY	132	1	0	1180¹	1545	11.8	39	406	316	15.3	5.28	90	.308	.365	-130	-138	99	102	.894	632	102	-4.0	-11.2	-5.1		-2.2
CLE	127	2	1	1136	1472	11.7	34	533	332	16.4	4.99	87	.308	.384	-88	-84	101	115	.898	576	97	-2.2	-6.8	-6.2		-11.3
TOT	1048	39	9	9495²		10.1				13.6	4.29		.273	.337					.906	4386	723					

Runs		Hits		Doubles		Triples		Home Runs		Total Bases	
O'Neill-StL	167	O'Neill-StL	225	O'Neill-StL	52	Poorman-Phi	19	O'Neill-StL	14	O'Neill-StL	357
Latham-StL	163	Browning-Lou	220	Lyons-Phi	43	O'Neill-StL	19	Reilly-Cin	10	Browning-Lou	299
Griffin-Bal	142	Lyons-Phi	209	Reilly-Cin	35	McPhee-Cin	19	Burns-Bal	9	Lyons-Phi	298
Poorman-Phi	140	Latham-StL	198	Latham-StL	35	Kerins-Lou	19			Burns-Bal	286
Comiskey-StL	139	Burns-Bal	188	Browning-Lou	35	Davis-Bal	19			Reilly-Cin	263
						Burns-Bal	19				

Runs Batted In		Runs Produced		Bases On Balls		Batting Average		On Base Percentage		Slugging Average	
O'Neill-StL	123	O'Neill-StL	276	Radford-NY	106	O'Neill-StL	.435	O'Neill-StL	.490	O'Neill-StL	.691
Browning-Lou	118	Browning-Lou	251	Robinson-StL	92	Browning-Lou	.402	Browning-Lou	.464	Caruthers-StL	.547
Davis-Bal	109	Latham-StL	244	Nicol-Cin	86	Orr-NY	.368	Caruthers-StL	.463	Browning-Lou	.547
Welch-StL	108	Comiskey-StL	238	Mack-Lou	83	Lyons-Phi	.367	Robinson-StL	.445	Lyons-Phi	.523
Foutz-StL	108	Griffin-Bal	233	Fennelly-Cin	82	Caruthers-StL	.357	Lyons-Phi	.421	Burns-Bal	.519

Production		Adjusted Production		Batter Runs		Adjusted Batter Runs		Clutch Hitting Index		Runs Created	
O'Neill-StL	1.180	O'Neill-StL	205	O'Neill-StL	86.4	O'Neill-StL	67.9	Purcell-Bal	140	O'Neill-StL	194
Browning-Lou	1.011	Browning-Lou	178	Browning-Lou	60.9	Browning-Lou	57.6	Hotaling-Cle	128	Browning-Lou	191
Caruthers-StL	1.010	Burns-Bal	169	Lyons-Phi	46.7	Burns-Bal	52.5	Greenwood-Bal	127	Lyons-Phi	160
Lyons-Phi	.943	Caruthers-StL	164	Burns-Bal	43.7	Lyons-Phi	46.5	Welch-StL	127	Burns-Bal	146
Burns-Bal	.933	Lyons-Phi	162	Caruthers-StL	42.9	Caruthers-StL	30.9	Wolf-Lou	126	Latham-StL	146

Total Average		Stolen Bases		Stolen Base Average		Stolen Base Runs		Fielding Runs		Total Player Rating	
O'Neill-StL	1.514	Nicol-Cin	138					Smith-Bro	32.0	O'Neill-StL	4.7
Browning-Lou	1.422	Latham-StL	129					McPhee-Cin	26.2	Browning-Lou	4.2
Caruthers-StL	1.368	Comiskey-StL	117					Kerins-Lou	24.8	Lyons-Phi	3.5
Robinson-StL	1.197	Browning-Lou	103					White-Lou	21.5	McPhee-Cin	3.0
Lyons-Phi	1.175	McPhee-Cin	95					Welch-StL	19.4	Burns-Bal	2.8

Wins		Win Percentage		Games		Complete Games		Shutouts		Saves	
Kilroy-Bal	46	Caruthers-StL	.763	Kilroy-Bal	69	Kilroy-Bal	66	Mullane-Cin	6	Terry-Bro	3
Ramsey-Lou	37	King-StL	.727	Ramsey-Lou	65	Ramsey-Lou	61	Kilroy-Bal	6		
Smith-Cin	34	Kilroy-Bal	.708	Smith-Bal	58	Smith-Bal	54	Smith-Cin	3		
King-StL	32	Foutz-StL	.676	Weyhing-Phi	55	Weyhing-Phi	53	Seward-Phi	3		
Mullane-Cin	31	Smith-Cin	.667	Seward-Phi	55	Seward-Phi	52				

Innings Pitched		Fewest Hits/Game		Fewest BB/Game		Strikeouts		Strikeouts/Game		Ratio	
Kilroy-Bal	589.1	Smith-Cin	8.05	Hecker-Lou	1.58	Ramsey-Lou	355	Ramsey-Lou	5.70	Smith-Cin	10.76
Ramsey-Lou	561.0	Seward-Phi	8.51	Caruthers-StL	1.61	Kilroy-Bal	217	Morrison-Cle	4.49	Caruthers-StL	10.93
Smith-Bal	491.1	Toole-Bro	8.63	Lynch-NY	1.73	Smith-Bal	206	Terry-Bro	3.91	Kilroy-Bal	11.64
Seward-Phi	470.2	Ramsey-Lou	8.73	Foutz-StL	2.39	Weyhing-Phi	193	Smith-Bal	3.77	Seward-Phi	11.65
Weyhing-Phi	466.1	Caruthers-StL	8.89	Kilroy-Bal	2.40	Smith-Cin	176	Weyhing-Phi	3.72	Ramsey-Lou	11.66

Earned Run Average		Adjusted ERA		Opponents' Batting Avg.		Opponents' On Base Pct.		Starter Runs		Adjusted Starter Runs	
Smith-Cin	2.94	Smith-Cin	148	Smith-Cin	.230	Smith-Cin	.286	Kilroy-Bal	80.0	Smith-Cin	69.6
Kilroy-Bal	3.07	Caruthers-StL	137	Ramsey-Lou	.242	Caruthers-StL	.287	Smith-Cin	67.3	Kilroy-Bal	67.0
Mullane-Cin	3.24	Mullane-Cin	134	Seward-Phi	.244	Ramsey-Lou	.299	Ramsey-Lou	53.5	Ramsey-Lou	59.3
Caruthers-StL	3.30	Kilroy-Bal	133	Caruthers-StL	.247	Kilroy-Bal	.306	Mullane-Cin	48.5	Mullane-Cin	50.7
Ramsey-Lou	3.43	Ramsey-Lou	128	Kilroy-Bal	.253	Foutz-StL	.306	Caruthers-StL	37.6	Caruthers-StL	46.7

Clutch Pitching Index		Relief Runs		Adjusted Relief Runs		Relief Ranking		Total Pitcher Index		Total Baseball Ranking	
Daily-Cle	140							Kilroy-Bal	7.3	Caruthers-StL	7.7
Crowell-Cle	122							Caruthers-StL	6.2	Kilroy-Bal	7.1
Morrison-Cle	121							Smith-Cin	6.0	Smith-Cin	5.9
Mullane-Cin	119							Mullane-Cin	4.5	O'Neill-StL	4.7
Chamberlain-Lou	117							Ramsey-Lou	3.5	Mullane-Cin	4.3

February 2 Indianapolis announces that the roof of its new grandstand will hold 42 private boxes, to be sold to season subscribers only: the first sky boxes.

March 2 The NL meets in New York and abolishes all discounts from the 50-cent minimum admission price.

April 1* The Texas League plays its first game, Houston winning at home, 3–1, over Galveston before 3,000 fans.

April 3 Chicago pitching star John Clarkson is sold to Boston for $10,000. With last year's deal for King Kelly, the Beaneaters have acquired a "$20,000 Battery" from the White Stockings.

May 1 After holding out for a $4,000 salary, Tim Keefe wins his 1888 debut for the Giants, beating Boston, 6–1.

May 3 In New York, George Gore goes to left field to start the game, but box-seat holders scream for Mike Slattery, and captain Buck Ewing makes the change.

May 22 Future Hall of Fame slugger Ed Delahanty makes his major league debut with the Phillies, going hitless and making two errors at second base. His contract had been purchased from Wheeling in the Tri-State League for $2,000.

May 25 Boston opens its new Grand Pavilion, an elaborate double-decked structure, better known as South End Grounds. Though the Pavilion seats 2,800, a jam-packed crowd of 12,000 see the Beaneaters lose their home opener to the Phillies, 4–1.

June 20 Future Hall of Famer first baseman Jake Beckley makes his major league debut with Pittsburgh, with a double, triple, and stolen base.

June 30 With permission from the NL, the Phillies reduce admission to 25 cents. Twelve thousand fans turn out to see a one-hit 7–0 victory over Boston by Charlie Buffinton. After an average of 1,123 admissions at the 50-cent rate, attendance at Huntingdon Street Baseball Grounds will now jump to an average of 4,010.

July 28 Jimmy Ryan hits two triples, two singles, and a homer and pitches seven innings in relief to lead Chicago to a 21–17 decision over Detroit, dropping Detroit into a first-place tie with the Giants. The Colts (Cubs) trail by 2½ games.

August 14 Tim Keefe's winning streak is stopped at 19 games when Gus Krock and the Colts beat the Giants, 4–2, before a crowd of 10,240 at New York.

September 6 Indianapolis tries its second experimental night game (the first was August 22) but the natural-gas illumination is inadequate, and the idea is dropped.

September 12 New York forfeits a game in Chicago when Buck Ewing is injured and cannot continue. With no uniformed substitutes available, the Giants simply leave the field in the fifth.

September 15 Ed Morris of Pittsburgh pitches his fourth consecutive shutout, a record that will be unsurpassed in the NL until 1968. Morris' gems include 1-0 and 2-0 victories over the Phillies, a seven-inning 2-0 win over the Senators, and today's 1-0 win over the Giants.

October 1 When Indianapolis scores three runs in the top of the eighth inning to take a 4–2 lead at Washington, Senators catcher Connie Mack suddenly complains of a sore finger. The ensuing delay lasts until darkness and forces the game's end, the score reverting to a seven-inning 2–1 Washington victory.

October 16 The 10-game World Series opens in New York with the Giants and Tim Keefe edging the Browns and Silver King, 2–1. Each hurler allows only three hits.

October 25 The Giants clinch New York's first world championship six games to two by trouncing the Browns, 11-3. Tim Keefe gets his fourth win of the series.

November 20 The Joint Rules Committee reduces the number of balls for a walk from five to four, establishing the four balls/three strikes count that remains in effect more than a century later.

November 22 The NL adopts a salary classification plan that puts all players into five categories with a standard salary for each ranging from $1,500 to $2,500.

BOSTON	CHICAGO	DETROIT	INDIANAPOLIS	NEW YORK	PHILADELPHIA	PITTSBURGH	WASHINGTON
M J.Morrill	M C.Anson	M B.Watkins	M H.Spence	M J.Mutrie	M H.Wright	M H.Phillips	M W.Hewett
1B J.Morrill	1B C.Anson	M B.Leadley	1B D.Esterbrook	1B R.Connor	1B S.Farrar	1B J.Beckley	M T.Sullivan
2B J.Quinn	2B F.Pfeffer	1B D.Brouthers	2B C.Bassett	2B D.Richardson	2B C.Bastian	2B F.Dunlap	2B A.Myers
SS S.Wise	SS N.Williamson	2B H.Richardson	SS J.Glasscock	SS J.Ward	SS A.Irwin	SS P.Smith	SS G.Shoch
3B B.Nash	3B T.Burns	SS J.Rowe	3B J.Denny	3B A.Whitney	3B J.Mulvey	3B B.Kuehne	3B J.Donnelly
LF J.Hornung	LF M.Sullivan	3B D.White	LF E.Seery	LF J.O'Rourke	LF G.Wood	LF A.Dalrymple	LF W.Wilmot
CF D.Johnston	CF J.Ryan	LF L.Twitchell	CF P.Hines	CF M.Slattery	CF E.Andrews	CF B.Sunday	CF D.Hoy
RF T.Brown	RF H.Duffy	CF N.Hanlon	RF J.McGeachy	RF M.Tiernan	RF J.Fogarty	RF J.Coleman	RF E.Daily
C K.Kelly	C T.Daly	RF C.Campau	C D.Buckley	C B.Ewing	C J.Clements	C D.Miller	C C.Mack
		C C.Bennett					
S I.Ray	OP G.Van Haltren		C3 G.Myers	O G.Gore	2O E.Delahanty	CO F.Carroll	S S.Fuller
C P.Tate	CO D.Farrell	2C C.Ganzel	C C.Daily	O E.Foster	C P.Schriver	1O A.Maul	P P.Deasley
3 E.Sutton	O B.Pettit	SC S.Sutcliffe	1 J.Schoeneck	C P.Murphy	C B.Hallman	OC J.Fields	S3 J.Irwin
2 B.Klusman	O S.Flint	O T.Scheffler	O1 O.Schomberg	3S G.Hatfield	C D.McGuire	3 E.Cleveland	C T.Arundel
2 J.Burdock	C D.Darling	2 P.Nicholson		C W.Brown	/3 W.Wagenhorst	3 P.McShannic	/3 P.Sweeney
C T.O'Rourke	P G.Krock	C J.Wells	P H.Boyle	/O B.George	/2 J.Grim	/O S.Nichol	C M.Murray
O E.Glenn	P M.Baldwin	/C D.McGuire	P J.Healy	/3 E.Cleveland	/2 C.Childs	/O C.Carroll	/O P.Werden
2 B.Higgins	P J.Tener	/2 S.LaRoque	P L.Shreve	P T.Keefe	G.Gardner	/O H.Yaik	/S G.Gardner
/O M.Hines	P G.Borchers	/C B.Gilligan	P B.Burdick	P M.Welch	P C.Buffinton	/C B.Farmer	/C J.Banning
/C P.Sommers	/P A.Gumbert	/C C.Broughton	/P S.Moffett	P C.Titcomb	P D.Casey	P E.Morris	P H.O'Day
/O N.Wise	/P F.Dwyer	/S F.Scheibeck		P E.Crane	P B.Sanders	P P.Galvin	P J.Whitney
P J.Clarkson	/P T.Brynan	P C.Getzien		/P S.Wiedman	P K.Gleason	P H.Staley	P W.Widner
P B.Sowders	/P D.Clarke	P P.Conway			/P J.Tyng	/P H.Henderson	P G.Keefe
P C.Radbourn	P W.Mains	P H.Gruber				/P P.Knell	P F.Gilmore
P K.Madden		P E.Beatin					/P D.Shaw
/P D.Conway		/P L.Baldwin					/P G.Haddock
							/P J.Greening

TEAM	G	W	L	PCT	GB	R	OR	AB	H	2B	3B	HR	BB	SO	AVG	OBP	SLG	PRO	PRO+	BR	/A	PF	CHI	RC	SB	CS	SBA	SBR
NY	138	84	47	.641		659	479	4747	1149	130	76	55	270	456	.242	.287	.336	.623	105	21	29	99	102	562	314			
CHI	136	77	58	.570	9	734	659	4616	1201	147	95	77	290	563	.260	.308	.383	.691	118	127	74	107	99	649	287			
PHI	132	69	61	.531	14.5	535	509	4528	1021	151	46	16	268	485	.225	.276	.290	.566	82	-63	-91	105	100	441	246			
BOS	137	70	64	.522	15.5	669	619	4834	1183	167	89	56	282	524	.245	.291	.351	.642	108	51	39	102	97	593	293			
DET	134	68	63	.519	16	721	629	4849	1275	177	72	51	307	396	.263	.313	.361	.674	121	110	111	100	96	623	193			
PIT	139	66	68	.493	19.5	534	580	4713	1070	150	49	14	194	583	.227	.264	.289	.553	89	-93	-54	92	103	446	287			
IND	136	50	85	.370	36	603	731	4623	1100	180	33	34	236	492	.238	.281	.313	.594	93	-24	-35	102	103	518	350			
WAS	136	48	86	.358	37.5	482	731	4546	944	98	49	30	246	499	.208	.255	.271	.526	77	-129	-103	94	103	408	331			
TOT	544					4937		37456	8943	1200	509	333	2093	3998	.239	.285	.325	.609						2301				

TEAM	CG	SH	SV	IP	H	H/G	HR	BB	SO	RAT	ERA	ERA+	OAV	OOB	PR	/A	PF	CPI	FA	E	DP	FW	PW	BW	SBW	DIF
NY	133	20	1	1208	907	6.8	27	307	726	9.3	1.96	139	.199	.255	117	103	96	95	.924	432	76	1.2	10.1	2.9		4.3
CHI	123	13	1	1186¹	1139	8.6	63	308	588	11.4	2.96	102	.246	.301	-17	6	106	112	.927	417	112	1.7	.6	7.3		-.0
PHI	125	16	3	1167	1072	8.3	26	196	519	10.0	2.38	124	.236	.271	58	69	104	103	.923	424	70	.6	6.8	-9.0		5.6
BOS	134	7	0	1225¹	1104	8.1	36	269	484	10.4	2.61	109	.232	.280	30	27	100	100	.917	494	91	-2.2	2.7	3.8		-1.3
DET	130	10	1	1199	1115	8.4	44	183	522	10.0	2.74	100	.234	.266	12	-2	97	90	.919	463	83	-1.1	-.2	10.9		-7.1
PIT	135	13	0	1203¹	1190	8.9	23	223	367	10.8	2.67	99	.249	.287	22	-4	94	107	.927	416	88	2.3	-.4	-5.3		2.5
IND	132	6	0	1187²	1260	9.5	64	308	388	12.2	3.81	77	.263	.313	-129	-117	104	98	.921	449	84	-.0	-11.5	-3.4		-2.5
WAS	133	6	0	1179¹	1157	8.8	50	298	406	11.5	3.54	79	.248	.300	-93	-104	98	91	.912	494	69	-2.4	-10.2	-10.1		3.8
TOT	1045	91	6	9556		8.4				10.7	2.83		.239	.285					.921	3589	673					

Runs		Hits		Doubles		Triples		Home Runs		Total Bases	
Brouthers-Det	118	Ryan-Chi	182	Ryan-Chi	33	Johnston-Bos	18	Ryan-Chi	16	Ryan-Chi	283
Ryan-Chi	115	Anson-Chi	177	Brouthers-Det	33	Connor-NY	17	Connor-NY	14	Johnston-Bos	276
Johnston-Bos	102	Johnston-Bos	173	Johnston-Bos	31	Nash-Bos	15	Johnston-Bos	12	Anson-Chi	257
Anson-Chi	101	Brouthers-Det	160	Denny-Ind	27	Ewing-NY	15	Denny-Ind	12	Brouthers-Det	242
Connor-NY	98	White-Det	157	Hines-Ind	26			Anson-Chi	12	Connor-NY	231

Runs Batted In		Runs Produced		Bases On Balls		Batting Average		On Base Percentage		Slugging Average	
Anson-Chi	84	Brouthers-Det	175	Connor-NY	73	Anson-Chi	.344	Anson-Chi	.400	Ryan-Chi	.515
Nash-Bos	75	Anson-Chi	173	Hoy-Was	69	Ryan-Chi	.332	Brouthers-Det	.399	Anson-Chi	.499
Rowe-Det	74	Ryan-Chi	163	Brouthers-Det	68	Kelly-Bos	.318	Connor-NY	.389	Connor-NY	.480
Williamson-Chi	73	Johnston-Bos	158	Williamson-Chi	65	Brouthers-Det	.307	Ryan-Chi	.377	Kelly-Bos	.480
		Connor-NY	155	Seery-Ind	64	Ewing-NY	.306	Hoy-Was	.374	Johnston-Bos	.472

Production		Adjusted Production		Batter Runs		Adjusted Batter Runs		Clutch Hitting Index		Runs Created	
Anson-Chi	.899	Connor-NY	178	Ryan-Chi	49.4	Brouthers-Det	46.8	Rowe-Det	153	Ryan-Chi	133
Ryan-Chi	.892	Brouthers-Det	174	Anson-Chi	49.3	Connor-NY	45.0	Burns-Chi	150	Anson-Chi	117
Connor-NY	.869	Anson-Chi	173	Brouthers-Det	46.6	Anson-Chi	41.0	Bassett-Ind	126	Brouthers-Det	113
Brouthers-Det	.862	Ryan-Chi	170	Connor-NY	43.7	Ryan-Chi	40.8	Wood-Phi	122	Connor-NY	103
Kelly-Bos	.848	Kelly-Bos	166	Kelly-Bos	33.4	Kelly-Bos	31.8	Nash-Bos	121	Kelly-Bos	101

Total Average		Stolen Bases		Stolen Base Average		Stolen Base Runs		Fielding Runs		Total Player Rating	
Ryan-Chi	1.044	Hoy-Was	82					Pfeffer-Chi	38.3	Nash-Bos	4.9
Kelly-Bos	1.007	Seery-Ind	80					Nash-Bos	25.6	Pfeffer-Chi	4.4
Anson-Chi	.985	Sunday-Pit	71					Denny-Ind	24.5	Ewing-NY	3.9
Brouthers-Det	.983	Pfeffer-Chi	64					Burns-Chi	17.1	Ryan-Chi	3.8
Connor-NY	.982	Ryan-Chi	60					Sunday-Pit	16.6	Anson-Chi	3.6

Wins		Win Percentage		Games		Complete Games		Shutouts		Saves	
Keefe-NY	35	Keefe-NY	.745	Morris-Pit	55	Morris-Pit	54	Sanders-Phi	8	Wood-Phi	2
Clarkson-Bos	33	Conway-Det	.682	Clarkson-Bos	54	Clarkson-Bos	53	Keefe-NY	8	VanHaltren-Chi	1
Conway-Det	30	Sanders-Phi	.655	Keefe-NY	51	Galvin-Pit	49	Galvin-Pit	6	Tyng-Phi	1
Morris-Pit	29	Krock-Chi	.641	Galvin-Pit	50	Keefe-NY	48	Buffinton-Phi	6	Twitchell-Det	1
Buffinton-Phi	28	Clarkson-Bos	.623	Welch-NY	47	Welch-NY	47			Crane-NY	1

Innings Pitched		Fewest Hits/Game		Fewest BB/Game		Strikeouts		Strikeouts/Game		Ratio	
Clarkson-Bos	483.1	Keefe-NY	6.57	Sanders-Phi	1.08	Keefe-NY	335	Keefe-NY	6.94	Keefe-NY	8.68
Morris-Pit	480.0	Titcomb-NY	6.81	Galvin-Pit	1.09	Clarkson-Bos	223	Titcomb-NY	5.89	Buffinton-Phi	8.70
Galvin-Pit	437.1	Welch-NY	6.94	Krock-Chi	1.19	Getzien-Det	202	Baldwin-Chi	5.63	Conway-Det	8.86
Keefe-NY	434.1	Conway-Det	7.25	Getzien-Det	1.20	Buffinton-Phi	199	VanHaltren-Chi	5.09	Sanders-Phi	9.02
Welch-NY	425.1	Buffinton-Phi	7.28	Madden-Bos	1.31	O'Day-Was	186	Getzien-Det	4.50	Gruber-Det	9.04

Earned Run Average		Adjusted ERA		Opponents' Batting Avg.		Opponents' On Base Pct.		Starter Runs		Adjusted Starter Runs	
Keefe-NY	1.74	Keefe-NY	156	Keefe-NY	.196	Conway-Det	.243	Keefe-NY	52.6	Keefe-NY	47.3
Sanders-Phi	1.90	Sanders-Phi	156	Titcomb-NY	.201	Keefe-NY	.243	Welch-NY	42.8	Buffinton-Phi	46.2
Buffinton-Phi	1.91	Buffinton-Phi	154	Welch-NY	.207	Buffinton-Phi	.244	Buffinton-Phi	40.9	Welch-NY	37.6
Welch-NY	1.93	Welch-NY	141	Conway-Det	.208	Gruber-Det	.249	Sanders-Phi	28.6	Sanders-Phi	32.2
Sowders-Bos	2.07	Sowders-Bos	137	Buffinton-Phi	.213	Titcomb-NY	.253	Morris-Pit	28.0	Sowders-Bos	26.7

Clutch Pitching Index		Relief Runs		Adjusted Relief Runs		Relief Ranking		Total Pitcher Index		Total Baseball Ranking	
Baldwin-Chi	137							Buffinton-Phi	5.8	Buffinton-Phi	5.7
Gleason-Phi	125							Sanders-Phi	4.2	Nash-Bos	4.9
Burdick-Ind	116							Keefe-NY	4.2	Pfeffer-Chi	4.4
Sowders-Bos	113							Conway-Det	3.9	Keefe-NY	4.1
Morris-Pit	112							Welch-NY	3.3	Ryan-Chi	4.0

April 18 On Opening Day in the AA, umpire John Gaffney makes news by standing behind the pitcher with men on base.

May 6 "Long John" Reilly hits two homers, giving him four in Cincinnati's four-game series versus Kansas City. Reilly will finish the season with an AA-leading 13 homers.

May 10 The Athletics play their first official Sunday home game at Gloucester, N.J., or so they think. The league secretary will later rule the game illegally rescheduled and throw it out of official records.

May 30 The Brooklyn Bridegrooms, so called because many players married over the winter, move into first place by winning two games from previous leader Cincinnati.

June 3 Casey at the Bat by Ernest Lawrence Thayer is published in the *San Francisco Examiner*. The poem will not become popular until later in the year, when actor DeWolf Hopper recites it.

June 18 Two AA umpires work the Cleveland-Athletic game. The two-umpire system had worked well in last fall's postseason series, but this is believed to be a regular-season first.

June 22 Lou Bierbauer of the Athletics establishes the record for second basemen by making 12 putouts in a nine-inning game. This record will not be tied until Aug. 30, 1966.

July 5 The AA meets in St. Louis and refuses to allow its clubs to reduce admission prices from 50 cents to 25 cents. It also adopts a system of double substitute umpires in case the assigned umpire fails to show up for a game, one substitute player from each club sharing the duties.

July 20 St. Louis regains the lead by beating Kansas City, 18–5. The Browns will stay in first place the rest of the season.

August 2 Claiming illness, Brooklyn captain Dave Orr misses the practice session. But later in the day he is spotted at Coney Island, and owner Charles Byrne removes him as captain.

August 3 Kansas City rookie Billy Hamilton, recently purchased from Worcester, steals his first base in the major leagues. Before returning to the mi-

nors in 1902, "Sliding Billy" will amass 912 stolen bases, a record broken by Lou Brock in 1979.

August 7 At a stormy session in Philadelphia, owners finally vote to allow 25-cent admission again but drop the percentage system of paying visitors and replace it with a $130-per-game guarantee.

August 20 St. Louis nudges past Brooklyn, 1–0, on brilliant baserunning by Arlie Latham. He opens the game with a single, steals second base, and scores from second on an infield out. Silver King wins the pitchers' duel against Mickey Hughes.

October 9 The St. Louis Browns end the season with a 95-40 record. The mark is two better than the Browns' 1886 mark and it will not be topped until the adoption of the 154-game schedule.

December 5 Columbus is admitted to replace Cleveland.

December 6 The AA votes against adopting the NL's salary classification system, to the surprise of the press and the delight of the Brotherhood.

	BALTIMORE		BROOKLYN		CINCINNATI		CLEVELAND		KANSAS CITY		LOUISVILLE		PHILADELPHIA		ST.LOUIS
M	B.Barnie	M	B.McGunnigle	M	G.Schmelz	M	J.Williams	M	D.Rowe	M	J.Kelly	M	B.Sharsig		C.Comiskey
1B	T.Tucker	1B	D.Orr	1B	J.Reilly	M	T.Loftus	M	S.Barkley	M	M.Davidson	1B	H.Larkin	1B	C.Comiskey
2B	B.Greenwood	2B	J.Burdock	2B	B.McPhee	1B	J.Faatz	M	B.Watkins	M	J.Kerins	2B	L.Bierbauer	2B	Y.Robinson
SS	J.Farrell	SS	G.Smith	SS	F.Fennelly	2B	C.Stricker	1B	B.Phillips	M	M.Davidson	SS	B.Gleason	SS	B.White
3B	B.Shindle	3B	G.Pinkney	3B	H.Carpenter	SS	E.McKean	2B	S.Barkley	1B	S.Smith	3B	D.Lyons	3B	A.Latham
LF	O.Burns	LF	D.O'Brien	LF	G.Tebeau	3B	G.Alberts	SS	H.Easterday	2B	R.Mack	LF	H.Stovey	LF	T.O'Neill
CF	M.Griffin	CF	P.Radford	CF	P.Corkhill	LF	B.Gilks	3B	J.Davis	SS	B.White	CF	C.Welch	CF	H.Lyons
RF	B.Purcell	RF	D.Foutz	RF	H.Nicol	CF	P.Hotaling	LF	M.Cline	3B	J.Werrick	RF	T.Poorman	RF	T.McCarthy
C	C.Fulmer	C	D.Bushong	C	J.Keenan	RF	E.Hogan	CF	J.McTamany	LF	H.Collins	C	W.Robinson	C	J.Boyle
						C	C.Zimmer	RF	B.Hamilton	CF	P.Browning				
OS	J.Sommer	OP	B.Caruthers	C	K.Baldwin			C	J.Donahue	RF	J.Wolf	C	G.Townsend	C	J.Milligan
CO	J.O'Brien	2O	B.McClellan	S2	H.Kappel	O	M.Goodfellow			C	P.Cook	O3	M.Sullivan	SO	E.Herr
O	W.Goldsby	SO	O.Burns	O	J.O'Connor	C	P.Snyder	OC	L.Daniels			C	T.Gunning	2	C.McGarr
C	B.Cantz	C	B.Clark	/C	N.Bligh	3	J.McGlone	2	F.Hankinson	OC	J.Kerins	O	B.Purcell	C	T.Dolan
C	S.Trott	C	J.Peoples			O	D.McGuire	M	M.Allen	OP	S.Stratton	S	F.Fennelly		
/O	J.Peltz	O	P.Corkhill	P	L.Viau	O	B.McClellan	O	D.Rowe	1P	G.Hecker	/C	B.Farmer	P	S.King
/S	G.Bradley	C	B.Holbert	P	T.Mullane	3	D.Van Zant	OC	J.Brennan	/C	F.Vaughn	/C	F.Zinn	P	N.Hudson
		O	E.Silch	P	E.Smith			O	J.Burns	CO	L.Cross	/C	W.Gibson	P	E.Chamberlain
P	B.Cunningham	2	H.Collins			P	J.Bakely	O	R.Ehret	3	H.Raymond			P	J.Devlin
P	Ma.Kilroy			/P	J.Weyhing	P	D.O'Brien	S	F.Briody	S	P.Tomney	P	E.Seward	P	E.Knouff
P	P.Smith	P	M.Hughes	/P	B.Serad	P	B.Crowell	O	C.Jones	O	F.Weaver	P	G.Weyhing		
		P	A.Terry					/C	C.Hoover	1	W.Andrews	P	M.Mattimore	/P	J.Freeman
/P	S.Shaw	P	A.Mays					/O	E.Glenn	1	D.Esterbrook				
/P	G.Walker					/P	G.Proeser			/3	P.Reccius	/P	B.Blair		
/P	P.Whitaker					/P	E.Keas	P	H.Porter	/O	H.Burnett	/P	P.Smith		
/P	Mi.Kilroy					/P	M.Morrison	P	T.Sullivan	/O	E.Fusselback	/P	B.Gamble		
/P	J.Harkins					/P	D.Oberlander	P	B.Fagan	/O	Long				
						/P	B.Stemmeyer	P	F.Hoffman						
						/P	E.Knouff	P	S.Toole	P	T.Ramsey				
										P	E.Chamberlain				
								/P	J.Kirby	P	J.Ewing				
								/P	F.Hafner						
										/P	B.Crowell				

TEAM	G	W	L	PCT	GB	R	OR	AB	H	2B	3B	HR	BB	SO	AVG	OBP	SLG	PRO	PRO+	BR	/A	PF	CHI	RC	SB	CS	SBA	SBR
STL	137	92	43	.681		789	501	4755	1189	149	47	36	410	521	.250	.316	.324	.640	98	54	-30	111	102	651	468			
BRO	143	88	52	.629	6.5	758	584	4871	1177	172	70	25	353	439	.242	.300	.321	.621	103	17	19	100	101	584	334			
PHI	136	81	52	.609	10	827	594	4828	1209	183	89	31	303	473	.250	.305	.344	.649	113	60	65	99	106	656	434			
CIN	137	80	54	.597	11.5	745	628	4801	1161	132	82	32	345	555	.242	.301	.323	.624	99	21	-18	105	100	623	469			
BAL	137	57	80	.416	36	653	779	4656	1068	162	70	19	298	479	.229	.284	.306	.590	96	-37	-19	97	99	511	326			
CLE	135	50	82	.379	40.5	651	839	4603	1076	128	59	12	315	559	.234	.294	.295	.589	96	-32	-13	97	99	516	353			
LOU	139	48	87	.356	44	689	870	4881	1177	183	67	14	322	604	.241	.297	.315	.612	102	1	16	98	94	565	318			
KC	132	43	89	.326	47.5	579	896	4588	1000	142	61	19	288	604	.218	.273	.288	.561	78	-84	-122	106	97	441	257			
TOT	548					5691		37983	9057	1251	545	188	2634	4234	.238	.297	.315	.612						2959				

TEAM	CG	SH	SV	IP	H	H/G	HR	BB	SO	RAT	ERA	ERA+	OAV	OOB	PR	/A	PF	CPI	FA	E	DP	FW	PW	BW	SBW	DIF
STL	132	12	0	1212²	939	7.0	19	225	517	9.1	2.09	156	.206	.254	130	156	107	96	.924	430	73	3.4	14.4	-2.8		9.4
BRO	138	9	0	1286¹	1059	7.4	15	285	577	9.7	2.33	128	.217	.266	104	92	97	97	.918	502	88	.6	8.5	1.8		7.2
PHI	133	13	0	1208²	988	7.4	14	324	596	10.4	2.41	124	.216	.279	87	76	98	102	.919	475	73	.7	7.0	6.0		.8
CIN	132	10	2	1237²	1103	8.0	19	310	539	10.8	2.73	116	.230	.288	46	60	104	102	.923	456	100	2.0	5.5	-1.7		7.2
BAL	130	3	0	1200¹	1162	8.7	23	419	525	12.5	3.78	79	.245	.318	-96	-108	97	93	.920	461	88	1.7	-10.0	-1.8		-1.5
CLE	131	6	1	1171	1235	9.5	38	389	500	12.9	3.72	83	.261	.324	-86	-82	101	105	.915	488	87	-.2	-7.6	-1.2		-7.0
LOU	133	6	0	1231¹	1264	9.2	28	281	599	11.7	3.25	95	.256	.304	-26	-24	100	105	.900	609	75	-6.2	-2.2	1.5		-12.5
KC	128	4	0	1157²	1306	10.2	32	401	381	13.8	4.29	80	.275	.340	-159	-112	112	101	.914	507	95	-1.9	-10.3	-11.3		.5
TOT	1057	63	3	9705²		8.4				11.3	3.06		.238	.297					.917	3928	679					

Runs
Pinkney-Bro 134
Collins-Lou-Bro ... 133
Stovey-Phi 127
Welch-Phi 125
Latham-StL 119

Hits
O'Neill-StL 177
Reilly-Cin 169
McKean-Cle 164
Collins-Lou-Bro ... 162
Corkhill-Cin-Bro ... 160

Doubles
Collins-Lou-Bro ... 31
Wolf-Lou 28
Reilly-Cin 28
Larkin-Phi 28

Triples
Stovey-Phi 20
Burns-Bal-Bro 15
McKean-Cle 15
Reilly-Cin 14
Foutz-Bro 13

Home Runs
Reilly-Cin 13
Stovey-Phi 9
Larkin-Phi 7

Total Bases
Reilly-Cin 264
Stovey-Phi 244
O'Neill-StL 236
McKean-Cle 233
Burns-Bal-Bro 230

Runs Batted In
Reilly-Cin 103
Larkin-Phi 101
Foutz-Bro 99
O'Neill-StL 98
Corkhill-Cin-Bro ... 93

Runs Produced
Reilly-Cin 202
O'Neill-StL 189
Foutz-Bro 187
Larkin-Phi 186
Welch-Phi 185

Bases On Balls
Robinson-StL 116
Fennelly-Cin-Phi ... 72
Nicol-Cin 67
McTamany-KC 67
Pinkney-Bro 66

Batting Average
O'Neill-StL ...... .335
Reilly-Cin .... .321
Browning-Lou ..... .313
Collins-Lou-Bro ... .307
Orr-Bro .... .305

On Base Percentage
Robinson-StL ..... .400
O'Neill-StL ...... .390
Browning-Lou ..... .380
Collins-Lou-Bro ... .373
Stovey-Phi .... .365

Slugging Average
Reilly-Cin .... .501
Stovey-Phi .... .460
O'Neill-StL ...... .446
Browning-Lou ..... .436
Burns-Bal-Bro .... .435

Production
Reilly-Cin .... .864
O'Neill-StL .... .836
Stovey-Phi .... .825
Browning-Lou ..... .816
Collins-Lou-Bro ... .796

Adjusted Production
Reilly-Cin 167
Stovey-Phi 165
Browning-Lou 164
Collins-Lou-Bro ... 158
Burns-Bal-Bro 152

Batter Runs
Reilly-Cin 41.7
O'Neill-StL 39.7
Stovey-Phi 37.8
Collins-Lou-Bro ... 32.6
Burns-Bal-Bro 27.7

Adjusted Batter Runs
Stovey-Phi 38.6
Reilly-Cin 35.5
Collins-Lou-Bro ... 34.8
Burns-Bal-Bro 29.5
McKean-Cle 28.5

Clutch Hitting Index
Hotaling-Cle 153
Foutz-Bro 135
Lyons-Phi 133
Gleason-Phi 132
Smith-Bro 130

Runs Created
Reilly-Cin 129
Stovey-Phi 124
Collins-Lou-Bro ... 112
Welch-Phi 106
O'Neill-StL 105

Total Average
Reilly-Cin 1.064
Stovey-Phi 1.048
Collins-Lou-Bro ... .956
Robinson-StL ..... .934
Browning-Lou ..... .928

Stolen Bases
Latham-StL 109
Nicol-Cin 103
Welch-Phi 95
McCarthy-StL 93
Stovey-Phi 87

Fielding Runs
Shindle-Bal 36.8
McPhee-Cin 31.3
Davis-KC 29.8
McCarthy-StL 29.8
Easterday-KC 26.4

Total Player Rating
Collins-Lou-Bro ... 4.0
Stovey-Phi 3.5
McPhee-Cin 3.3
Davis-KC 3.0
McKean-Cle 3.0

Wins
King-StL 45
Seward-Phi 35
Caruthers-Bro 29
Weyhing-Phi 28
Viau-Cin 27

Win Percentage
Hudson-StL .... .714
Chamberlain-Lou-SL ... .694
King-StL .... .682
Caruthers-Bro .... .659
Viau-Cin .... .659

Games
King-StL 66
Bakely-Cle 61
Seward-Phi 57
Porter-KC 55
Cunningham-Bal ... 51

Complete Games
King-StL 64
Bakely-Cle 60
Seward-Phi 57
Porter-KC 53
Cunningham-Bal ... 50

Shutouts
Seward-Phi 6
King-StL 6
Smith-Cin 5
Hudson-StL 5

Saves
Mullane-Cin 1
Gilks-Cle 1

Innings Pitched
King-StL 585.2
Bakely-Cle 532.2
Seward-Phi 518.2
Porter-KC 474.0
Cunningham-Bal ... 453.1

Fewest Hits/Game
Terry-Bro 6.69
King-StL 6.72
Seward-Phi 6.73
Chamberlain-Lou-SL ... 6.95
Hughes-Bro 6.97

Fewest BB/Game
King-StL 1.17
Caruthers-Bro 1.22
Hudson-StL 1.59
Ewing-Lou 1.60
Hecker-Lou 1.73

Strikeouts
Seward-Phi 272
King-StL 258
Ramsey-Lou 228
Bakely-Cle 212
Weyhing-Phi 204

Strikeouts/Game
Terry-Bro 6.37
Ramsey-Lou 5.99
Chamberlain-Lou-SL ... 5.14
Smith-Bal-Phi 4.90
Seward-Phi 4.72

Ratio
King-StL 8.34
Caruthers-Bro 9.19
Seward-Phi 9.32
Foutz-Bro 9.51
Hughes-Bro 9.55

Earned Run Average
King-StL 1.64
Seward-Phi 2.01
Terry-Bro 2.03
Hughes-Bro 2.13
Chamberlain-Lou-SL ... 2.19

Adjusted ERA
King-StL 198
Seward-Phi 148
Terry-Bro 147
Chamberlain-Lou-SL ... 143
Hughes-Bro 140

Opponents' Batting Avg.
Terry-Bro .... .200
King-StL .... .200
Seward-Phi .... .201
Chamberlain-Lou-SL ... .206
Hughes-Bro ...... .206

Opponents' On Base Pct.
King-StL .... .237
Caruthers-Bro .... .255
Seward-Phi .... .258
Foutz-Bro .... .262
Hughes-Bro ...... .262

Starter Runs
King-StL 92.0
Seward-Phi 60.2
Hughes-Bro 37.3
Weyhing-Phi 36.3
Chamberlain-Lou-SL ... 29.7

Adjusted Starter Runs
King-StL 104.9
Seward-Phi 56.0
Hughes-Bro 34.1
Weyhing-Phi 33.0
Chamberlain-Lou-SL ... 32.4

Clutch Pitching Index
Sullivan-KC 115
Hecker-Lou 112
Terry-Bro 110
Ramsey-Lou 106
Bakely-Cle 106

Relief Runs

Adjusted Relief Runs

Relief Ranking

Total Pitcher Index
King-StL 11.4
Seward-Phi 4.9
Weyhing-Phi 3.7
Caruthers-Bro 3.5
Chamberlain-Lou-SL ... 3.1

Total Baseball Ranking
King-StL 11.3
Seward-Phi 4.8
Collins-Lou-Bro ... 4.0
Weyhing-Phi 3.6
Caruthers-Bro 3.6

January 22 Facing over $30,000 in debts, the Indianapolis team goes bankrupt and surrenders its franchise to the NL. A new Indianapolis group, headed by John T. Brush is later granted an NL franchise.

February 8 In New York City, workers are dismantling fences at the Polo Grounds to cut a street through the property, leaving the Giants without a home for the coming season.

March 22* The All America team beats Chicago 7–6 in England's Old Trafford Cricket Stadium. The *Manchester Guardian* said the "general verdict of the more than 1,000 spectators was that the American game was 'slow' and 'wanting in variety.'"

April 15* Invited to the White House after their world tour, the Chicago and All-America squads meet with new President Benjamin Harrison. Harrison proves to be quite a baseball fan and would attend many Washington games during his term in office.

April 24 The New York Giants open their season in Jersey City's Oakland Park, losing to Boston 8–7 before a crowd of 3,042. After just one more game in Jersey City, the Giants are forced to relocate at the Mets' old grounds in Staten Island. A rule currently in effect mandates that teams must play in the state in which their franchise is located.

April 29 The New York Giants play and win their first game, 4-2, at St. George Grounds on Staten Island. This picturesque park, home of the AA Mets in 1886 and 1887, houses the Giants and a production of the play "Nero". The right fielder is obliged to play out on top of the stage platform, necessitating the use of rubber-soled shoes in wet weather.

May 19 Washington center fielder William "Dummy" Hoy throws out three Indianapolis runners at home plate, setting a major league record. Hoy also has a single, two doubles, and a stolen base, but the Senators still lose, 8–3.

July 8 The New York Giants finally open the new Polo Grounds at 155th Street and 8th Avenue with a 7–5 victory over Pittsburgh. In 25 games in exile on Staten Island and in Jersey City, the Giants drew 57,000 fans. In 38 games in their new Manhattan home, they will draw 144,000.

July 14 A. G. Spalding's plan for classifying minor leagues is printed across the nation. It calls for strict salary and draft-price limits according to the class of the leagues, features that will serve as the basis for a century to come.

July 26 Cleveland loses, 8–4, despite a fluke homer by Jay Faatz, who hits a ball that ricochets off the foot of Pittsburgh third baseman Jim White and goes into the stands, giving Faatz time to circle the bases.

August 15 Cleveland's Larry Twitchell has a 6-for-6 day at the plate with a single, double, three triples, and a homer. The five extra-base hits tie a record set in 1885. Twitchell also pitches to two batters in the third inning before returning to the outfield. Cleveland wins, 19–8, over Boston, and becomes the first team in NL history to score in all nine innings in a single game.

September 10 New York Giants pitcher Mickey Welch strikes out as the first pinch hitter in major league history.

October 4 Both contenders win again, setting up the final day with New York in front of Boston by percentage points .656 to .654. Each team has the option of playing one or two games tomorrow, so New York manager Jim Mutrie travels to Pittsburgh to watch the Boston game. If the Beaneaters play an extra game, he is ready to wire to Cleveland, where the Giants are playing, so that the Giants can also play an additional one.

October 5 New York wins the pennant on the final day by beating Cleveland, 5–3, while Boston loses in Pittsburgh, 6–1, making doubleheaders unnecessary.

October 18 The best-of-11 World Series between Brooklyn and New York opens at the Polo Grounds with the Bridegrooms winning, 12–10, in eight innings.

October 29 The Giants win their second consecutive World Series by earning their sixth victory in nine games. After spotting Brooklyn two runs in the first, the Giants rally to win, 3-2, behind O'Day's pitching.

	BOSTON		CHICAGO		CLEVELAND		INDIANAPOLIS		NEW YORK		PHILADELPHIA		PITTSBURGH		WASHINGTON
M	J.Hart	M	C.Anson	M	T.Loftus	M	F.Bancroft	M	J.Mutrie	M	H.Wright	M	H.Phillips	M	J.Morrill
1B	D.Brouthers	1B	C.Anson	1B	J.Faatz	M	J.Glasscock	1B	R.Connor	1B	S.Farrar	M	F.Dunlap	M	A.Irwin
2B	H.Richardson	2B	F.Pfeffer	2B	C.Stricker	1B	P.Hines	2B	D.Richardson	2B	A.Myers	M	N.Hanlon	1B	J.Carney
SS	J.Quinn	SS	N.Williamson	SS	E.McKean	2B	C.Bassett	SS	J.Ward	SS	B.Hallman	1B	J.Beckley	2B	S.Wise
3B	B.Nash	3B	T.Burns	3B	P.Tebeau	SS	J.Glasscock	3B	A.Whitney	3B	J.Mulvey	2B	F.Dunlap	SS	A.Irwin
LF	T.Brown	LF	G.Van Haltren	LF	L.Twitchell	3B	J.Denny	LF	J.O'Rourke	LF	G.Wood	SS	J.Rowe	3B	J.Irwin
CF	D.Johnston	CF	J.Ryan	CF	J.McAleer	LF	E.Seery	CF	G.Gore	CF	J.Fogarty	3B	B.Kuehne	LF	W.Wilmot
RF	K.Kelly	RF	H.Duffy	RF	P.Radford	CF	M.Sullivan	RF	M.Tiernan	RF	S.Thompson	LF	A.Maul	CF	D.Hoy
C	C.Bennett	C	D.Farrell	C	C.Zimmer	RF	J.McGeachy	C	B.Ewing	C	J.Clements	CF	N.Hanlon	RF	E.Beecher
						C	D.Buckley					RF	B.Sunday	C	T.Daly
CO	C.Ganzel	S	C.Bastian	OS	B.Gilks			C	W.Brown	O2	E.Delahanty	C	D.Miller		
S	P.Smith	C	D.Darling	C	S.Sutcliffe	C	C.Daily	S	G.Hatfield	C	P.Schriver			CO	C.Mack
/S	I.Ray	C	S.Flint	C	P.Snyder	O	E.Andrews	O	M.Slattery	S	A.Irwin	CO	F.Carroll	3	P.Sweeney
/O	J.Hurley	C	P.Sommers			OC	G.Myers	/C	P.Murphy	/O	E.Andrews	OC	J.Fields	2	A.Myers
				P	D.O'Brien	C	P.Sommers	/O	H.Lyons	/2	H.Decker	S	P.Smith	1	J.Morrill
P	J.Clarkson	P	B.Hutchison	P	E.Beatin	1	J.Schoeneck	B.George	/2	P.Ward	3	D.White	CS	S.Clark
P	C.Radbourn	P	J.Tener	P	J.Bakely	/C	P.Weckbecker	/O	E.Foster			/C	C.Lauer	O	G.Shoch
P	K.Madden	P	F.Dwyer	P	H.Gruber					P	C.Buffinton			/C	H.Ebright
		P	A.Gumbert			P	H.Boyle	P	M.Welch	P	B.Sanders	P	H.Staley	/C	J.Riddle
/P	B.Daley			/P	C.Sprague	P	C.Getzien	P	T.Keefe	P	K.Gleason	P	P.Galvin	/3	J.Donnelly
/P	B.Sowders	/P	G.Krock			P	A.Rusie	P	E.Crane	P	D.Casey	P	E.Morris	/1	B.O'Brien
		/P	J.Healy					P	H.O'Day					/2	A.McCoy
		/P	B.Bishop			/P	J.Whitney			/P	D.Anderson	P	B.Sowders	/O	H.Clarke
						P	B.Burdick	/P	C.Titcomb	/P	B.Day	/P	B.Garfield	/C	J.Banning
						/P	J.Fee			/P	P.Wood	/P	P.Conway		
						/P	G.Krock					/P	A.Beam	P	A.Ferson
						P	L.Shreve					/P	A.Dunning	P	G.Haddock
						/P	V.Anderson					/P	A.Jones	P	G.Keefe
						/P	J.Fanning					/P	A.Krumm	P	H.O'Day
														P	J.Healy
														/P	G.Krock
														/P	M.Sullivan
														/P	J.Thornton

TEAM	G	W	L	PCT	GB	R	OR	AB	H	2B	3B	HR	BB	SO	AVG	OBP	SLG	PRO	PRO+	BR	/A	PF	CHI	RC	SB	CS	SBA	SBR
NY	131	83	43	.659		935	708	4671	1319	208	77	52	538	386	.282	.360	.393	.753	117	108	106	100	105	785	292			
BOS	133	83	45	.648	1	826	626	4628	1251	196	54	42	471	450	.270	.343	.363	.706	98	26	-22	106	104	707	331			
CHI	136	67	65	.508	19	867	814	4849	1274	184	66	79	518	516	.263	.338	.377	.715	101	36	-6	105	103	716	243			
PHI	130	63	64	.496	20.5	742	748	4695	1248	215	52	44	393	353	.266	.327	.362	.689	91	-12	-78	109	98	660	269			
PIT	134	61	71	.462	25	726	801	4748	1202	209	65	42	420	467	.253	.320	.351	.671	94	-44	-26	90	99	622	231			
CLE	136	61	72	.459	25.5	656	720	4673	1167	131	59	25	429	417	.250	.318	.319	.637	86	-93	-80	98	97	563	237			
IND	135	59	75	.440	28	819	894	4879	1356	228	35	62	377	447	.278	.335	.377	.712	103	27	11	102	100	719	252			
WAS	127	41	83	.331	41	632	892	4395	1105	151	57	25	466	456	.251	.329	.329	.658	96	-49	-7	94	92	566	232			
TOT	531					6203		37538	9922	1522	465	371	3612	3492	.264	.334	.359	.693							2087			

TEAM	CG	SH	SV	IP	H	H/G	HR	BB	SO	RAT	ERA	ERA+	OAV	OOB	PR	/A	PF	CPI	FA	E	DP	FW	PW	BW	SBW	DIF
NY	118	6	3	1151	1073	8.4	38	523	558	12.9	3.47	114	.241	.327	71	56	98	102	.919	437	90	-.3	4.9	9.2		6.3
BOS	121	10	4	1166	1152	8.9	41	413	497	12.4	3.36	124	.250	.317	86	106	104	105	.926	413	105	1.2	9.2	-1.9		10.5
CHI	123	6	2	1237	1313	9.6	71	408	434	12.8	3.73	112	.262	.323	41	64	104	106	.923	463	91	-.8	5.5	-.5		-3.2
PHI	106	4	2	1153¹	1288	10.1	33	428	443	13.6	4.00	109	.275	.339	3	42	108	103	.915	466	92	-2.0	3.6	-6.8		4.6
PIT	125	5	1	1130²	1296	10.3	42	374	345	13.5	4.51	83	.272	.329	-60	-78	93	92	.931	385	94	2.8	-6.8	2.3		-3.3
CLE	132	6	1	1191²	1182	8.9	36	519	435	13.2	3.66	110	.251	.332	48	47	100	102	.936	365	108	4.2	4.1	-6.9		-6.8
IND	109	3	2	1174¹	1365	10.5	73	420	408	14.0	4.85	86	.282	.344	-108	-88	104	95	.926	420	102	1.2	-7.6	1.0		-2.5
WAS	113	1	0	1103	1261	10.3	37	527	388	14.9	4.68	85	.279	.359	-80	-90	98	99	.904	519	91	-5.2	-7.8	-.6		-7.4
TOT	947	41	15	9307		9.6				13.4	4.02		.264	.334					.923	3468	773					

Runs
Tiernan-NY 147
Duffy-Chi 144
Ryan-Chi 140
Gore-NY 132
Glasscock-Ind 128

Hits
Glasscock-Ind 205
Brouthers-Bos 181
Ryan-Chi 177
Duffy-Chi 172
VanHaltren-Chi ... 168

Doubles
Kelly-Bos 41
Glasscock-Ind 40
Thompson-Phi 36
O'Rourke-NY 36
Richardson-Bos 33

Triples
Wilmot-Was 19
Fogarty-Phi 17
Connor-NY 17
Tiernan-NY 14
Ryan-Chi 14

Home Runs
Thompson-Phi 20
Denny-Ind 18
Ryan-Chi 17
Connor-NY 13
Duffy-Chi 12

Total Bases
Ryan-Chi 287
Glasscock-Ind 272
Thompson-Phi 262
Connor-NY 262
Tiernan-NY 248

Runs Batted In
Connor-NY 130
Brouthers-Bos 118
Anson-Chi 117
Denny-Ind 112
Thompson-Phi 111

Runs Produced
Connor-NY 234
Duffy-Chi 221
Brouthers-Bos 216
Tiernan-NY 210
Anson-Chi 210

Bases On Balls
Tiernan-NY 96
Connor-NY 93
Radford-Cle 91
Anson-Chi 86
Carroll-Pit 85

Batting Average
Brouthers-Bos .... .373
Glasscock-Ind .... .352
Tiernan-NY .... .335
Carroll-Pit ...... .330
Ewing-NY .... .327

On Base Percentage
Carroll-Pit ...... .486
Brouthers-Bos .... .462
Tiernan-NY .... .447
Connor-NY .... .426
Gore-NY .... .416

Slugging Average
Connor-NY .... .528
Brouthers-Bos .... .507
Ryan-Chi .... .498
Tiernan-NY .... .497
Thompson-Phi ..... .492

Production
Carroll-Pit ...... .970
Brouthers-Bos .... .969
Connor-NY .... .955
Tiernan-NY .... .944
Ryan-Chi .... .886

Adjusted Production
Carroll-Pit 190
Connor-NY 166
Tiernan-NY 163
Brouthers-Bos 161
Wilmot-Was 146

Batter Runs
Brouthers-Bos 49.6
Tiernan-NY 47.0
Connor-NY 46.1
Carroll-Pit 37.9
Ryan-Chi 35.3

Adjusted Batter Runs
Carroll-Pit 47.9
Tiernan-NY 46.8
Connor-NY 45.8
Brouthers-Bos 41.7
Ryan-Chi 28.7

Clutch Hitting Index
Anson-Chi 140
Dunlap-Pit 133
Twitchell-Cle 133
Whitney-NY 133
Brouthers-Bos 132

Runs Created
Ryan-Chi 132
Glasscock-Ind 132
Tiernan-NY 129
Brouthers-Bos 127
Connor-NY 124

Total Average
Carroll-Pit 1.263
Tiernan-NY 1.151
Brouthers-Bos 1.145
Connor-NY 1.115
Ryan-Chi 1.023

Stolen Bases
Fogarty-Phi 99
Kelly-Bos 68
Brown-Bos 63
Ward-NY 62
Glasscock-Ind 57

Stolen Base Average

Stolen Base Runs

Fielding Runs
Glasscock-Ind 35.5
Fogarty-Phi 19.4
Pfeffer-Chi 19.3
Ewing-NY 15.5
Wilmot-Was 14.5

Total Player Rating
Glasscock-Ind 5.9
Ewing-NY 3.8
Tiernan-NY 3.5
Carroll-Pit 3.2
Wilmot-Was 3.2

Wins
Clarkson-Bos 49
Keefe-NY 28
Buffinton-Phi 28
Welch-NY 27
Galvin-Pit 23

Win Percentage
Clarkson-Bos ..... .721
Welch-NY .... .692
Keefe-NY .... .683
Radbourn-Bos ..... .645
Buffinton-Phi .... .636

Games
Clarkson-Bos 73
Staley-Pit 49
Keefe-NY 47
Buffinton-Phi 47
Boyle-Ind 46

Complete Games
Clarkson-Bos 68
Staley-Pit 46
Welch-NY 39
O'Brien-Cle 39
Keefe-NY 39

Shutouts
Clarkson-Bos 8
Galvin-Pit 4

Saves
Sowders-Bos-Pit 2
Welch-NY 2
Bishop-Chi 2

Innings Pitched
Clarkson-Bos 620.0
Staley-Pit 420.0
Buffinton-Phi ... 380.0
Boyle-Ind 378.2
Welch-NY 375.0

Fewest Hits/Game
Keefe-NY 7.89
Welch-NY 8.16
Clarkson-Bos 8.55
Crane-NY 8.65
Hutchison-Chi 8.66

Fewest BB/Game
Galvin-Pit 2.06
Boyle-Ind 2.26
Radbourn-Bos 2.34
Dwyer-Chi 2.35
Sanders-Phi 2.47

Strikeouts
Clarkson-Bos 284
Keefe-NY 225
Staley-Pit 159
Buffinton-Phi 153
Getzien-Ind 139

Strikeouts/Game
Keefe-NY 5.56
Crane-NY 5.09
Rusie-Ind 4.36
Healy-Was-Chi 4.35
Clarkson-Bos 4.12

Ratio
Clarkson-Bos 11.74
Radbourn-Bos 11.76
Staley-Pit 11.94
Welch-NY 11.98
Keefe-NY 12.07

Earned Run Average
Clarkson-Bos 2.73
Bakely-Cle 2.96
Welch-NY 3.02
Buffinton-Phi 3.24
Keefe-NY 3.31

Adjusted ERA
Clarkson-Bos 153
Bakely-Cle 136
Buffinton-Phi 134
Welch-NY 131
Sanders-Phi 123

Opponents' Batting Avg.
Keefe-NY .... .228
Welch-NY .... .234
Clarkson-Bos ..... .243
Crane-NY .... .245
Hutchison-Chi .... .245

Opponents' On Base Pct.
Clarkson-Bos ..... .305
Radbourn-Bos ..... .306
Staley-Pit .... .309
Welch-NY .... .310
Keefe-NY .... .311

Starter Runs
Clarkson-Bos 89.2
Welch-NY 41.7
Bakely-Cle 36.1
Buffinton-Phi ... 32.9
Keefe-NY 28.7

Adjusted Starter Runs
Clarkson-Bos 99.4
Buffinton-Phi ... 47.0
Welch-NY 38.5
Bakely-Cle 36.5
Sanders-Phi 31.3

Clutch Pitching Index
Casey-Phi 118
Clarkson-Bos 116
Bakely-Cle 113
Sanders-Phi 113
Crane-NY 112

Relief Runs

Adjusted Relief Runs

Relief Ranking

Total Pitcher Index
Clarkson-Bos 10.1
Buffinton-Phi 4.3
Bakely-Cle 3.4
Sanders-Phi 3.0
Welch-NY 2.8

Total Baseball Ranking
Clarkson-Bos 10.1
Glasscock-Ind 5.9
Buffinton-Phi 4.3
Ewing-NY 3.8
Tiernan-NY 3.5

April 9 Pete Browning signs with Louisville for $1,600. Browning also delivers a signed pledge of abstinence sworn out before a local judge.

May 19 Fire destroys most of the stand at Brooklyn's Washington Park while the Bridegrooms are on a road trip.

May 20 The Kansas City Cowboys, after choosing to bat first, score at least one run in every inning against Brooklyn, winning 18–12. The Cowboys become the second team in AA history to score in all nine innings, Columbus having done so on June 14, 1883.

May 30 Brooklyn draws the largest crowd in AA history, 22,122, for the Bridegrooms' afternoon game against the Browns. An additional 8,462 saw the opener as the two teams split the pair.

June 13 After the Colonels lose for the 19th straight time, Louisville owner-manager Mordecai Davidson tells the players he will fine them $25 if they lose the next game.

June 15 Only six Louisville players show up for the game in Baltimore, the others sit out in protest against owner Davidson, who owes back pay and is now threatening them with fines.

June 22 Louisville's losing streak reaches 26 in a row, the all-time major league record, when the Colonels lose two heartbreakers to St. Louis, 7–6, and 3–2 in 10 innings.

June 23 The Colonels finally win, defeating St. Louis, 7–3.

September 7 The most controversial game in AA history is held in Brooklyn. The Browns hold a 4-2 lead in the ninth and claim it is too dark to continue, but the lighted candles in front of their bench make umpire Fred Goldsmith determined to finish the game no matter what. Several St. Louis players are hit with bottles as they leave the grounds. The Browns will forfeit their game the next day because they fear for their safety.

September 23 An emergency meeting of the American Association Board of Directors reverses the St. Louis forfeit of September 7, the game being ruled as a 4–2 Browns victory, although the forfeit of September 8 still stands.

October 6 Brooklyn wins its last home game, 9–0, over the Athletics in six innings before a crowd of 2,488, bringing the Bridegrooms' home attendance for the season to 353,690, a major league record.

October 9 Charlie Reilly hits two home runs in his major league debut with Columbus to lead the Babies to a 10–6 victory over the Athletics. Only Bob Nieman (in 1951) and Bert Campaneris (in 1964) will match this feat.

November 14 Disgusted by the conduct of the Association and especially the perceived dominance of St. Louis president Von der Ahe, Brooklyn president Charles Byrne and Cincinnati owner Aaron Stern withdraw from the AA and join the NL. The next day, Kansas City also drops out of the AA.

December 16 The Players League is officially formed with Colonel E.A. McAlpin of New York as president. The league will not allow player transfers without the player's consent, excess profits will be split between the capitalists and the players, while prize money will be awarded to teams in order of finish.

December 18 The Brotherhood, a players' group, begins preliminary work on the organization of the Players' League and expels members who have signed NL contracts, including Jack Glasscock, John Clarkson, Kid Gleason, and George Miller. Among those expelled, Jake Beckley, Joe Mulvey, and Ed Delahanty would eventually jump back to the Players League and would be reinstated.

BALTIMORE		BROOKLYN		CINCINNATI		COLUMBUS		KANSAS CITY		LOUISVILLE		PHILADELPHIA		ST.LOUIS	
M	B.Barnie	M	B.McGunnigle	M	G.Schmelz	M	A.Buckenberger	M	B.Watkins	M	D.Esterbrook	M	B.Sharsig	M	C.Comiskey
1B	T.Tucker	1B	D.Foutz	1B	J.Reilly	1B	D.Orr	1B	E.Stearns	M	C.Wolf	1B	H.Larkin	1B	C.Comiskey
2B	R.Mack	2B	H.Collins	2B	B.McPhee	2B	B.Greenwood	2B	S.Barkley	M	D.Shannon	2B	L.Bierbauer	2B	Y.Robinson
SS	J.Farrell	SS	G.Smith	SS	O.Beard	SS	H.Easterday	SS	H.Long	M	J.Chapman	SS	F.Fennelly	SS	S.Fuller
3B	B.Shindle	3B	G.Pinkney	3B	H.Carpenter	3B	L.Marr	3B	J.Davis	1B	G.Hecker	3B	D.Lyons	3B	A.Latham
LF	J.Hornung	LF	D.O'Brien	LF	G.Tebeau	LF	E.Daily	LF	J.Manning	2B	D.Shannon	LF	H.Stovey	LF	T.O'Neill
CF	M.Griffin	CF	P.Corkhill	CF	B.Holliday	CF	J.McTamany	CF	J.Burns	SS	P.Tomney	CF	C.Welch	CF	C.Duffee
RF	J.Sommer	RF	O.Burns	RF	H.Nicol	RF	S.Johnson	RF	B.Hamilton	3B	H.Raymond	RF	B.Purcell	RF	T.McCarthy
C	P.Tate	C	J.Visner	C	J.Keenan	C	J.O'Connor	C	C.Hoover	LF	P.Browning	C	W.Robinson	C	J.Boyle
										CF	F.Weaver				
C	T.Quinn	C	B.Clark	C	K.Baldwin	S3	H.Kappel	CO	J.Donahue	RF	J.Wolf	C	L.Cross	C	J.Milligan
S	W.Holland	C	D.Bushong	OC	B.Earle	C	J.Peoples	O3	J.Pickett	C	P.Cook	C	J.Brennan	/3	P.Sweeney
S	I.Ray	C	C.Reynolds			C	N.Bligh	3	B.Alvord			O	M.Mattimore	/O	T.Gettinger
O	J.Dowie			P	J.Duryea	2	J.Crooks	O	J.Gunson	CO	F.Vaughn	/C	T.Gunning	/O	J.Gill
C	B.Cantz	P	B.Caruthers	P	L.Viau	/C	J.Doyle	3	C.McGarr	OP	S.Stratton	/3	B.Graham	/S	J.Davis
O	C.Fulmer	P	A.Terry	P	T.Mullane	/C	R.Kemmler	O	M.Mattimore	O	J.Galligan	/C	B.Collins	/C	J.Bellman
/1	J.Kerins	P	T.Lovett	P	E.Smith	/3	C.Reilly	/2	R.Bittman	O	F.Carl			/C	D.Meek
/S	D.Miller	P	M.Hughes			/O	B.George	/O	C.Bell	1	E.Flanagan	P	G.Weyhing		
/O	G.Wood			/P	C.Petty	/C	S.McCaffrey	/O	S.Ladew	/O	J.Ryan	P	E.Seward	P	S.King
/S	C.McGarr			/P	T.Conovar			/C	C.Reynolds	S	B.Gleason	P	S.McMahon	P	E.Chamberlain
						P	M.Baldwin			/1	D.Esterbrook			P	J.Stivetts
P	M.Kilroy					P	W.Widner	P	P.Swartzel	/O	J.Kerins	/P	G.Bausewine		
P	F.Foreman					P	H.Gastright	P	J.Conway	/O	H.Scherer	/P	P.Smith	/P	J.Devlin
P	B.Cunningham					P	A.Mays	P	J.Sowders	/O	C.Fisher	/P	J.Coleman	/P	N.Hudson
								P	J.McCarty	/O	M.Gaule	/P	E.Knouff	/P	T.Ramsey
/P	G.Goetz					/P	J.Easton	P	T.Sullivan	/O	H.Smith				
/P	P.Whitaker					/P	J.Weyhing			/O	J.Traffley				
								/P	H.Porter			P	R.Ehret		
								/P	F.Pears			P	J.Ewing		
								/P	J.Bates			P	T.Ramsey		
												P	M.McDermott		
												/P	B.Robinson		
												/P	E.Springer		

TEAM	G	W	L	PCT	GB	R	OR	AB	H	2B	3B	HR	BB	SO	AVG	OBP	SLG	PRO	PRO+	BR	/A	PF	CHI	RC	SB	CS	SBA	SBR
BRO	140	93	44	.679		995	706	4815	1265	188	79	47	550	401	.263	.344	.364	.708	106	43	40	100	111	756	389			
STL	141	90	45	.667	2	957	680	4939	1312	211	64	58	493	477	.266	.339	.370	.709	94	38	-79	113	106	751	336			
PHI	138	75	58	.564	16	880	787	4868	1339	239	65	43	534	496	.275	.354	.377	.731	114	85	97	99	93	758	252			
CIN	141	76	63	.547	18	897	769	4844	1307	197	96	52	452	511	.270	.340	.382	.722	107	57	30	103	100	806	462			
BAL	139	70	65	.519	22	791	795	4756	1209	155	68	20	418	536	.254	.325	.328	.653	88	-56	-69	102	103	624	311			
COL	140	60	78	.435	33.5	779	924	4816	1247	171	95	36	507	609	.259	.335	.356	.691	106	8	51	95	91	693	304			
KC	139	55	82	.401	38	852	1031	4947	1256	162	76	18	430	626	.254	.322	.328	.650	84	-66	-112	106	108	692	472			
LOU	140	27	111	.196	66.5	632	1091	4955	1249	170	75	22	320	521	.252	.303	.330	.633	86	-109	-95	98	87	571	203			
TOT	559					6783		38940	10184	1493	618	296	3704	4177	.262	.333	.354	.687						2729				

TEAM	CG	SH	SV	IP	H	H/G	HR	BB	SO	RAT	ERA	ERA+	OAV	OOB	PR	/A	PF	CPI	FA	E	DP	FW	PW	BW	SBW	DIF
BRO	120	10	1	1212²	1205	8.9	33	400	471	12.2	3.61	103	.251	.315	31	14	97	93	.928	421	92	4.6	1.2	3.4		15.4
STL	121	7	3	1237²	1166	8.5	39	413	617	11.9	3.00	141	.242	.309	116	167	110	106	.925	438	100	3.8	14.1	-6.7		11.2
PHI	130	9	1	1199¹	1200	9.0	35	509	479	13.4	3.53	107	.253	.335	42	33	98	107	.920	465	120	1.7	2.8	8.2		-4.2
CIN	114	3	8	1243	1270	9.2	35	475	562	13.0	3.50	111	.257	.328	47	54	102	105	.926	440	121	3.7	4.6	2.5		-4.3
BAL	128	10	1	1192	1168	8.8	27	424	540	12.6	3.56	111	.249	.322	38	49	103	97	.907	536	104	-2.1	4.1	-5.8		6.3
COL	114	9	4	1199	1274	9.6	33	551	610	14.1	4.39	82	.264	.346	-73	-103	94	93	.915	497	92	.3	-8.7	4.3		-4.9
KC	128	0	2	1204¹	1373	10.3	51	457	447	14.1	4.36	88	.278	.347	-69	-25	109	101	.899	611	109	-6.3	-2.1	-9.5		4.3
LOU	127	2	1	1226¹	1529	11.2	43	475	451	15.1	4.81	80	.297	.362	-132	-133	100	101	.906	584	117	-4.5	-11.3	-8.0		-18.2
TOT	982	50	21	9714¹		9.4				13.3	3.84		.262	.333					.916	3992	855					

Runs
Stovey-Phi	152
Griffin-Bal	152
O'Brien-Bro	146
Hamilton-KC	144
Collins-Bro	139

Hits
Tucker-Bal	196
Orr-Col	183
Holliday-Cin	181
O'Neill-StL	179
Shindle-Bal	178

Doubles
Welch-Phi	39
Stovey-Phi	38
Lyons-Phi	36
O'Neill-StL	33
Long-KC	32

Triples
Marr-Col	15
Griffin-Bal	14
Beard-Cin	14

Home Runs
Stovey-Phi	19
Holliday-Cin	19
Duffee-StL	16
Milligan-StL	12

Total Bases
Stovey-Phi	292
Holliday-Cin	280
Tucker-Bal	255
O'Neill-StL	255
Orr-Col	250

Runs Batted In
Stovey-Phi	119
Foutz-Bro	113
O'Neill-StL	110
Bierbauer-Phi	105
Holliday-Cin	104

Runs Produced
Stovey-Phi	252
Foutz-Bro	225
O'Neill-StL	224
O'Brien-Bro	221
Hamilton-KC	218

Bases On Balls
Robinson-StL	118
McTamany-Col	116
Griffin-Bal	91
Marr-Col	87
Hamilton-KC	87

Batting Average
Tucker-Bal	.372
O'Neill-StL	.335
Lyons-Phi	.329
Orr-Col	.327
Holliday-Cin	.321

On Base Percentage
Tucker-Bal	.450
Larkin-Phi	.428
Lyons-Phi	.426
O'Neill-StL	.419
Hamilton-KC	.413

Slugging Average
Stovey-Phi	.525
Holliday-Cin	.497
Tucker-Bal	.484
O'Neill-StL	.478
Lyons-Phi	.469

Production
Tucker-Bal	.934
Stovey-Phi	.918
O'Neill-StL	.897
Lyons-Phi	.895
Holliday-Cin	.869

Adjusted Production
Tucker-Bal	163
Stovey-Phi	162
Lyons-Phi	157
Larkin-Phi	145
Holliday-Cin	142

Batter Runs
Tucker-Bal	48.2
Stovey-Phi	42.6
O'Neill-StL	39.9
Lyons-Phi	39.3
Larkin-Phi	34.2

Adjusted Batter Runs
Tucker-Bal	45.8
Stovey-Phi	44.5
Lyons-Phi	41.0
Larkin-Phi	35.9
Marr-Col	34.2

Clutch Hitting Index
Mack-Phi	147
Foutz-Bro	145
Johnson-Col	128
Hornung-Bal	127
Collins-Bro	126

Runs Created
Tucker-Bal	147
Stovey-Phi	143
Hamilton-KC	136
O'Brien-Bro	129
Holliday-Cin	124

Total Average
Tucker-Bal	1.187
Hamilton-KC	1.134
Stovey-Phi	1.125
O'Brien-Bro	1.020
O'Neill-StL	1.014

Stolen Bases
Hamilton-KC	111
O'Brien-Bro	91
Long-KC	89
Nicol-Cin	80
Latham-StL	69

Stolen Base Average

Stolen Base Runs

Fielding Runs
McPhee-Cin	41.1
Bierbauer-Phi	36.6
Long-KC	32.2
Tomney-Lou	26.7
Shindle-Bal	20.3

Total Player Rating
Stovey-Phi	4.9
Bierbauer-Phi	4.5
Lyons-Phi	4.5
Marr-Col	4.1
McPhee-Cin	4.0

Wins
Caruthers-Bro	40
King-StL	35
Duryea-Cin	32
Chamberlain-StL	32
Weyhing-Phi	30

Win Percentage
Caruthers-Bro	.784
King-StL	.686
Chamberlain-StL	.681
Lovett-Bro	.630
Duryea-Cin	.627

Games
Baldwin-Col	63
Kilroy-Bal	59
King-StL	56
Caruthers-Bro	56
Weyhing-Phi	54

Complete Games
Kilroy-Bal	55
Baldwin-Col	54
Weyhing-Phi	50
King-StL	47
Caruthers-Bro	46

Shutouts
Caruthers-Bro	7
Baldwin-Col	6
Kilroy-Bal	5
Foreman-Bal	5
Weyhing-Phi	4

Saves
Mullane-Cin	5

Innings Pitched
Baldwin-Col	513.2
Kilroy-Bal	480.2
King-StL	458.0
Weyhing-Phi	449.0
Caruthers-Bro	445.0

Fewest Hits/Game
Stivetts-StL	7.18
Weyhing-Phi	7.66
Terry-Bro	7.87
Foreman-Bal	7.91
Baldwin-Col	8.02

Fewest BB/Game
Caruthers-Bro	2.10
Conway-KC	2.42
King-StL	2.46
Lovett-Bro	2.55
Swartzel-KC	2.57

Strikeouts
Baldwin-Col	368
Kilroy-Bal	217
Weyhing-Phi	213
Chamberlain-StL	202
King-StL	188

Strikeouts/Game
Stivetts-StL	6.71
Baldwin-Col	6.45
Terry-Bro	5.13
Sowders-KC	5.06
Gastright-Col	4.65

Ratio
Stivetts-StL	10.61
Caruthers-Bro	11.35
Duryea-Cin	11.56
Foreman-Bal	11.76
Conway-KC	11.77

Earned Run Average
Stivetts-StL	2.25
Duryea-Cin	2.56
Kilroy-Bal	2.85
Weyhing-Phi	2.95
Chamberlain-StL	2.97

Adjusted ERA
Stivetts-StL	187
Duryea-Cin	152
Chamberlain-StL	142
Kilroy-Bal	138
King-StL	134

Opponents' Batting Avg.
Stivetts-StL	.212
Weyhing-Phi	.223
Terry-Bro	.228
Foreman-Bal	.229
Baldwin-Col	.231

Opponents' On Base Pct.
Stivetts-StL	.285
Caruthers-Bro	.299
Duryea-Cin	.303
Foreman-Bal	.306
Conway-KC	.306

Starter Runs
Duryea-Cin	57.3
Kilroy-Bal	53.3
Weyhing-Phi	44.8
Chamberlain-StL	41.1
King-StL	35.6

Adjusted Starter Runs
Duryea-Cin	59.8
Chamberlain-StL	58.7
Kilroy-Bal	58.4
King-StL	54.8
Stivetts-StL	41.9

Clutch Pitching Index
Mullane-Cin	119
Duryea-Cin	116
Kilroy-Bal	114
Hughes-Bro	110
Weyhing-Phi	109

Relief Runs

Adjusted Relief Runs

Relief Ranking

Total Pitcher Index
Kilroy-Bal	6.9
Duryea-Cin	6.7
Chamberlain-StL	4.7
King-StL	4.5
Caruthers-Bro	4.2

Total Baseball Ranking
Kilroy-Bal	6.9
Duryea-Cin	6.6
Stovey-Phi	4.9
Chamberlain-StL	4.7
Bierbauer-Phi	4.5

February 1 The NL Schedule Committee meets in Pittsburgh and decides on a schedule, but for security reasons does not release it. Pittsburgh NL president Nimick comments that "if I had my way, I would duplicate all the home games of the Brotherhood clubs." Hence the reason for security.

February 17 New York NL officials fail in an effort to woo star player and Brotherhood officer Buck Ewing to rejoin the Giants. Although he has rejected an offer reported at $33,000 for three years, Ewing is later accused by some players of spying for the NL.

March 6 The NL releases a schedule with 10 teams, including the Brooklyn and Cincinnati franchises formerly in the AA. Since the NL is expected to trim back down to eight teams, the release of this schedule is seen as a ruse to throw off the PL.

April 19 The NL's biggest Opening Day crowd, 6,311 at Chicago, watches 30-year-old righthander Wild Bill Hutchison beat Cincinnati, 5–4, the first of his 42 wins and 65 complete games out of 66 starts. He'll work 603 innings and relieve five times.

May 1 The 577 consecutive-game streak of third baseman George Pinckney of Brooklyn (NL) comes to an end after he is spiked in a game in Boston, which is later rained out. He has played every inning of the 577 games, a record that would last until surpassed by Cal Ripken, Jr. of Baltimore in 1985.

May 12 A scoreless pitching duel between future Hall of Famers Amos Rusie and Charles "Kid" Nichols is broken up by a tape-measure homer by New York outfielder Mike Tiernan in the 13th inning.

May 23 New York and Pittsburgh combine for an NL-record 17 stolen bases in a single game.

June 6 Harry Wright, manager of Philadelphia, is now said to be able to see while wearing colored glasses. A serious illness five days earlier had blinded him temporarily, making him the only blind manager in major league history.

July 15 New York Giants owner John B. Day tells other NL owners he must have $80,000 or sell out to the Players League. Spalding, Anson, Brush, and others come to the rescue to prevent New York's withdrawal from the league.

August 16 It's a bad day for Pittsburgh's Bill Phillips as he becomes the only pitcher in major league history to give up two grand slams in one inning. Tommy Burns and Malachi Kittredge each hit one in the fifth inning en route to an 18-5 victory at Chicago's West Side Park.

October 9 Cincinnati owner Aaron Stern sells to PL owners for $40,000. Committees from the three leagues meet to begin negotiations toward a settlement of the war. PL owners from Cleveland, Brooklyn, and New York seek consolidation with the NL. A truce, during which all contracts will be respected, is agreed upon. It is left to owners in each city to arrange their own deals.

December 29 After the New York and Pittsburgh PL clubs combine with their NL rivals, Spalding buys out Chicago's PL backer Addison for $18,000, some of which goes to pay off unpaid salaries and reimburse players half of their investments. Spalding gets the club's grandstand, equipment, and player contracts.

BOSTON	BROOKLYN	CHICAGO	CINCINNATI	CLEVELAND	NEW YORK	PHILADELPHIA	PITTSBURGH
M F.Selee	M B.McGunnigle	M C.Anson	M T.Loftus	M G.Schmelz	M J.Mutrie	M H.Wright	M G.Hecker
1B T.Tucker	1B D.Foutz	1B C.Anson	1B J.Reilly	1B B.Leadley	1B L.Whistler	M J.Clements	1B B.Hecker
2B P.Smith	2B H.Collins	2B B.Glenalvin	2B B.McPhee	1B P.Veach	2B C.Bassett	M A.Reach	2B S.LaRoque
SS H.Long	SS G.Smith	SS J.Cooney	SS O.Beard	2B J.Ardner	SS J.Glasscock	M B.Allen	SS E.Sales
3B C.McGarr	3B T.Burns	3B G.Pinkney	3B L.Marr	SS E.McKean	M J.Denny	M W.Wright	3B D.Miller
LF M.Sullivan	LF A.Terry	LF C.Carroll	LF J.Knight	3B W.Smalley	LF J.Hornung	1B A.McCauley	LF J.Kelty
CF P.Hines	CF D.O'Brien	CF W.Wilmot	CF B.Holliday	LF B.Gilks	CF M.Tiernan	2B A.Myers	CF B.Sunday
RF S.Brodie	RF O.Burns	RF J.Andrews	RF H.Nicol	CF G.Davis	RF J.Burkett	SS B.Allen	RF T.Berger
C C.Bennett	C T.Daly	C M.Kittridge	C J.Harrington	RF V.Dailey	C D.Buckley	3B E.Mayer	C H.Decker
				C C.Zimmer		LF B.Hamilton	
SO B.Lowe	OP B.Caruthers	O2 H.Earl	OP T.Mullane		CO A.Clarke	CF E.Burke	CO B.Wilson
CO L.Hardie	O P.Corkhill	C T.Nagle	C J.Keenan	1 J.Virtue	1 D.Esterbrook	RF S.Thompson	3 F.Roat
CO C.Ganzel	C B.Clark	2 P.O'Brien	3 A.Latham	O1 T.Dowse	O J.Henry	C J.Clements	O F.Osborne
O P.Donovan	O P.Donovan	C E.Foster	C K.Baldwin	O B.West	O P.Murphy		O M.Jordan
/O A.Schellhase	C D.Bushong	/O J.Stenzel	/S B.Clingman	2 B.Delaney	2 S.Howe	C1 P.Schriver	O E.Burke
	/C G.Stallings	/2 E.Hutchinson		O R.Wright	C G.McMillan	O B.Grey	10 P.Hines
P K.Nichols		/C C.Lauer	P B.Rhines	2 P.Lyons	/O E.Daily	O B.Sunday	2 S.Crane
P J.Clarkson	P T.Lovett	/O D.Lytle	P J.Duryea	/O J.Sommer	/1 S.Crane	/1 H.Decker	O D.Hemp
P C.Getzien		/C M.Honan	P F.Foreman	/C P.Sommers	/1 M.Scanlan	/1 F.Motz	2 F.Dunlap
	/P M.Hughes	/2 P.Wright	P L.Viau	/O L.Stockwell			/2 D.Lytle
/P J.Taber	/P L.Baldwin				/C T.O'Rourke	P K.Gleason	/3 H.Youngman
/P A.Lawson		P B.Hutchison	/P J.Dolan	P E.Beatin		P T.Vickery	/O C.Heard
/P T.Von Fricken		P P.Luby		P J.Wadsworth	P A.Rusie	P P.Smith	/1 P.Veach
		P E.Stein		P C.Young	P M.Welch		/O J.Coleman
		P M.Sullivan		P E.Lincoln	P J.Sharrott	/P D.Esper	/2 H.Gilbert
		P R.Coughlin		P L.Viau		/P B.Day	/S J.Gilbert
					/P B.Murphy	/P D.Anderson	/O F.McGinn
		/P R.Gibson		/P B.Garfield		/P J.McFetridge	/O P.Routcliffe
		/P F.Demarais		/P E.Smith		/P S.Bowman	/S R.Gray
		/P E.Eiteljorge		/P C.Parsons		/P J.Coleman	/O F.Truax
		/P O.France					/S E.Clements
							P K.Baker
							P D.Anderson
							P B.Sowders
							P C.Schmit
							P B.Phillips
							P B.Gumbert
							/P S.Bowman
							/P B.Day
							/P P.Smith
							/P C.Gray
							/P H.Jones
							/P P.Daniels
							/P D.Esper
							/P R.Gibson
							/P A.Lawson
							/P G.Ziegler
							/P J.Heyner

TEAM	G	W	L	PCT	GB	R	OR	AB	H	2B	3B	HR	BB	SO	AVG	OBP	SLG	PRO	PRO+	BR	/A	PF	CHI	RC	SB	CS	SBA	SBR
BRO	129	86	43	.667		884	620	4419	1166	184	75	43	517	361	.264	.346	.369	.715	113	74	71	100	112	702	349			
CHI	139	84	53	.613	6	847	692	4891	1271	147	60	67	516	514	.260	.336	.356	.692	102	37	4	104	103	713	329			
PHI	133	78	54	.591	9.5	823	707	4707	1267	220	78	23	522	403	.269	.350	.364	.714	110	79	58	103	98	735	335			
CIN	134	77	55	.583	10.5	753	633	4644	1203	150	120	27	433	377	.259	.329	.360	.689	106	25	29	100	99	670	312			
BOS	134	76	57	.571	12	763	593	4722	1220	175	62	31	530	515	.258	.342	.341	.683	96	30	-33	108	96	665	285			
NY	135	63	68	.481	24	713	698	4832	1250	208	89	25	350	479	.259	.315	.354	.669	99	-16	-17	100	97	647	289			
CLE	136	44	88	.333	43.5	630	832	4633	1073	132	59	21	497	474	.232	.312	.299	.611	84	-96	-84	98	97	491	152			
PIT	138	23	113	.169	66.5	597	1235	4739	1088	160	43	20	408	458	.230	.300	.294	.594	87	-134	-65	88	97	492	208			
TOT	539					6010		37587	9538	1376	586	257	3773	3581	.254	.329	.342	.671						2259				

TEAM	CG	SH	SV	IP	H	H/G	HR	BB	SO	RAT	ERA	ERA+	OAV	OOB	PR	/A	PF	CPI	FA	E	DP	FW	PW	BW	SBW	DIF
BRO	115	6	2	1145	1102	8.7	27	401	403	12.2	3.06	112	.246	.315	64	47	96	104	.940	320	92	4.5	4.2	6.3		6.5
CHI	126	6	3	1237¹	1103	8.0	41	481	504	11.9	3.24	113	.234	.311	44	50	103	93	.940	344	89	4.9	4.4	.4		5.8
PHI	122	9	2	1194²	1210	9.1	22	486	507	13.2	3.32	110	.255	.331	32	43	102	107	.929	398	122	.4	3.8	5.2		2.6
CIN	124	9	1	1190²	1097	8.3	41	407	488	11.8	2.79	127	.238	.307	102	100	100	109	.932	382	106	1.6	8.9	2.6		-2.1
BOS	132	13	1	1187	1132	8.6	27	354	506	11.5	2.93	128	.245	.303	83	104	105	101	.935	359	77	3.0	9.2	-2.9		.2
NY	115	6	1	1177	1029	7.9	14	607	612	13.0	3.06	114	.230	.331	66	52	98	104	.921	449	104	-2.3	4.6	-1.5		-3.3
CLE	129	2	0	1184¹	1322	10.0	33	462	306	14.0	4.13	86	.273	.342	-75	-70	100	99	.930	405	108	.6	-6.2	-7.5		-8.9
PIT	119	3	0	1176¹	1520	11.6	52	573	381	16.6	5.97	55	.304	.384	-315	-350	92	91	.897	607	94	-11.5	-31.1	-5.8		3.3
TOT	982	54	10	9492¹		9.0				13.0	3.56		.254	.329					.928	3264	792					

Runs		Hits		Doubles		Triples		Home Runs		Total Bases	
Collins-Bro	148	Thompson-Phi	172	Thompson-Phi	41	Reilly-Cin	26	Wilmot-Chi	13	Tiernan-NY	274
Carroll-Chi	134	Glasscock-NY	172	Glasscock-NY	32	McPhee-Cin	22	Tiernan-NY	13	Reilly-Cin	261
Hamilton-Phi	133	Tiernan-NY	168	Collins-Bro	32	Tiernan-NY	21	Burns-Bro	13	Thompson-Phi	243
Tiernan-NY	132	Reilly-Cin	166	Myers-Phi	29	Beard-Cin	15	Long-Bos	8	Wilmot-Chi	239
McPhee-Cin	125	Carroll-Chi	166	O'Brien-Bro	28					Glasscock-NY	225

Runs Batted In		Runs Produced		Bases On Balls		Batting Average		On Base Percentage		Slugging Average	
Burns-Bro	128	Burns-Bro	217	Anson-Chi	113	Glasscock-NY	.336	Anson-Chi	.443	Tiernan-NY	.495
Anson-Chi	107	Thompson-Phi	214	McKean-Cle	87	Hamilton-Phi	.325	Hamilton-Phi	.430	Clements-Phi	.472
Thompson-Phi	102	Collins-Bro	214	Allen-Phi	87	Clements-Phi	.315	Pinkney-Bro	.411	Reilly-Cin	.472
Wilmot-Chi	99	Wilmot-Chi	200	Collins-Bro	85	O'Brien-Bro	.314	McKean-Cle	.401	Burns-Bro	.464
Foutz-Bro	98	Foutz-Bro	199	Hamilton-Phi	83	Thompson-Phi	.313	Glasscock-NY	.395	Burkett-NY	.461

Production		Adjusted Production		Batter Runs		Adjusted Batter Runs		Clutch Hitting Index		Runs Created	
Tiernan-NY	.880	Tiernan-NY	156	Tiernan-NY	37.9	Tiernan-NY	37.7	Burns-Bro	150	Hamilton-Phi	132
Clements-Phi	.864	Clements-Phi	148	Anson-Chi	37.6	Anson-Chi	32.6	Anson-Chi	145	Tiernan-NY	130
Anson-Chi	.844	Pinkney-Bro	145	Hamilton-Phi	31.7	McKean-Cle	31.2	Myers-Phi	140	Wilmot-Chi	114
Pinkney-Bro	.842	Glasscock-NY	143	Pinkney-Bro	30.8	Pinkney-Bro	30.4	Hines-Pit-Bos	138	Glasscock-NY	113
Glasscock-NY	.834	McKean-Cle	141	McKean-Cle	28.9	Hamilton-Phi	28.8	Bassett-NY	129	Collins-Bro	111

Total Average		Stolen Bases		Stolen Base Average		Stolen Base Runs		Fielding Runs		Total Player Rating	
Hamilton-Phi	1.170	Hamilton-Phi	102					Allen-Phi	38.6	Glasscock-NY	4.9
Tiernan-NY	1.047	Collins-Bro	85					McPhee-Cin	30.0	McPhee-Cin	4.5
Pinkney-Bro	1.015	Sunday-Pit-Phi	84					Glasscock-NY	22.0	Allen-Phi	4.0
Anson-Chi	1.009	Wilmot-Chi	76					Smalley-Cle	16.6	Clements-Phi	2.9
Collins-Bro	1.005	Tiernan-NY	56					Carroll-Chi	14.5	Collins-Bro	2.7

Wins		Win Percentage		Games		Complete Games		Shutouts		Saves	
Hutchison-Chi	42	Lovett-Bro	.732	Hutchison-Chi	71	Hutchison-Chi	65	Nichols-Bos	7	Hutchison-Chi	2
Gleason-Phi	38	Gleason-Phi	.691	Rusie-NY	67	Rusie-NY	56	Rhines-Cin	6	Gleason-Phi	2
Lovett-Bro	30	Luby-Chi	.690	Gleason-Phi	60	Gleason-Phi	54	Gleason-Phi	6	Foutz-Bro	2
Rusie-NY	29	Caruthers-Bro	.676	Beatin-Cle	54	Beatin-Cle	53	Hutchison-Chi	5		
Rhines-Cin	28	Hutchison-Chi	.627	Nichols-Bos	48	Nichols-Bos	47				

Innings Pitched		Fewest Hits/Game		Fewest BB/Game		Strikeouts		Strikeouts/Game		Ratio	
Hutchison-Chi	603.0	Rusie-NY	7.15	Young-Cle	1.83	Rusie-NY	341	Rusie-NY	5.59	Rhines-Cin	10.43
Rusie-NY	548.2	Mullane-Cin	7.54	Duryea-Cin	1.97	Hutchison-Chi	289	Nichols-Bos	4.71	Nichols-Bos	10.55
Gleason-Phi	506.0	Hutchison-Chi	7.54	Getzien-Bos	2.11	Nichols-Bos	222	Terry-Bro	4.50	Hutchison-Chi	10.70
Beatin-Cle	474.1	Rhines-Cin	7.56	Nichols-Bos	2.38	Gleason-Phi	222	Hutchison-Chi	4.31	Getzien-Bos	10.98
Nichols-Bos	424.0	Luby-Chi	7.60	Rhines-Cin	2.53	Terry-Bro	185	Sharrott-NY	4.11	Duryea-Cin	11.10

Earned Run Average		Adjusted ERA		Opponents' Batting Avg.		Opponents' On Base Pct.		Starter Runs		Adjusted Starter Runs	
Rhines-Cin	1.95	Rhines-Cin	182	Rusie-NY	.212	Rhines-Cin	.282	Rhines-Cin	71.8	Nichols-Bos	71.3
Nichols-Bos	2.23	Nichols-Bos	168	Mullane-Cin	.221	Nichols-Bos	.284	Nichols-Bos	62.8	Rhines-Cin	71.3
Mullane-Cin	2.24	Mullane-Cin	159	Hutchison-Chi	.221	Hutchison-Chi	.287	Rusie-NY	61.1	Hutchison-Chi	63.6
Rusie-NY	2.56	Gleason-Phi	139	Rhines-Cin	.221	Getzien-Bos	.292	Hutchison-Chi	57.6	Gleason-Phi	57.0
Gleason-Phi	2.63	Rusie-NY	137	Luby-Chi	.222	Duryea-Cin	.295	Gleason-Phi	52.2	Rusie-NY	57.0

Clutch Pitching Index		Relief Runs		Adjusted Relief Runs		Relief Ranking		Total Pitcher Index		Total Baseball Ranking	
Mullane-Cin	131							Rusie-NY	6.9	Rusie-NY	6.7
Vickery-Phi	120							Nichols-Bos	6.7	Nichols-Bos	6.6
Rhines-Cin	118							Rhines-Cin	6.5	Rhines-Cin	6.5
Gleason-Phi	112							Hutchison-Chi	5.9	Hutchison-Chi	5.9
Nichols-Bos	110							Gleason-Phi	4.6	Glasscook-NY	4.9

April 22 Philadelphia and Syracuse combine for an AA record 19 stolen bases in one game.

April 27 St. Louis pitcher Jack Stivetts strikes out the first seven Columbus batters he faces. He finishes the game with 12 K's.

May 25 After a Louisville-Syracuse game played in Three Rivers, New York, part of the grandstand collapses, throwing 50 or more people to the ground. No deaths are reported, but many are injured.

June 10 St. Louis pitcher Jack Stivetts hits two homers in a game. He later duplicates this effort on Aug. 6, 1891, and on June 12, 1896, making him the first pitcher to achieve this feat three times. The only two pitchers to match this achievement are Wes Ferrell (who had five such games) and Don Newcombe.

July 20 After Rochester beats Columbus in a Sunday game 8–3 at Windsor Beach, both teams are arrested.

July 27 Brooklyn's AA club holds a 13-8 lead over Columbus in the eighth inning at Long Island Grounds in a Sunday game when they run out of baseballs and are forced to forfeit. Brooklyn will only win 26 of 100 games and will disband on Aug. 25.

September 17 Philadelphia (AA) is out of money and disbands. The team releases several players and sells the others, including Wilbert Robinson, Curt Welch and Sadie McMahon. The team will reorganize, but lose the remaining 22 games on the schedule.

November 22 At the AA annual meeting in Lousiville, Philadelphia is expelled for violating the league's constitution. A new team in Philadelphia is admitted, plus entries from Boston, Washington and Chicago to replace Syracuse, Toledo and Rochester.

BALTIMORE		BROOKLYN		COLUMBUS		LOUISVILLE		PHILADELPHIA	
M	B.Barnie	M	J.Kennedy	M	A.Buckenberger	M	J.Chapman	M	B.Sharsig	/O	J.McBride
1B	T.Power	1B	B.O'Brien	M	G.Schmelz	1B	H.Taylor	1B	J.O'Brien	/O	B.Stafford
2B	R.Mack	2B	J.Gerhardt	M	J.Sullivan	2B	T.Shinnick	2B	T.Shaffer	/S	B.Collins
SS	I.Ray	SS	C.Nelson	1B	M.Lehane	SS	P.Tomney	SS	B.Conroy	/C	Macey
3B	P.Gilbert	3B	J.Davis	2B	J.Crooks	3B	H.Raymond	3B	D.Lyons	/O	H.Sweigert
LF	J.Sommer	LF	H.Simon	SS	H.Easterday	LF	C.Hamburg	LF	B.Purcell		
CF	D.Long	CF	J.Peltz	3B	C.Reilly	CF	F.Weaver	CF	C.Welch	P	S.McMahon
RF	B.Johnson	RF	E.Daily	LF	S.Johnson	RF	J.Wolf	RF	O.Shaffer	P	E.Green
C	G.Townsend	C	J.Toy	CF	J.McTamany	C	J.Ryan	C	W.Robinson	P	E.Seward
				RF	J.Sneed					P	D.Esper
C	P.Tate	CO	F.Bowes	C	J.O'Connor	C	P.Weckbecker	OS	J.Kappel		
O	C.Welch	C3	H.Pitz			C	N.Bligh	SO	G.Carman	P	C.Stecher
C	W.Robinson	S	F.Fennelly	CS	J.Doyle	/1	D.Phelan	C	K.Baldwin	/P	E.O'Neil
O	J.McGuckin	3	F.Siefke	S	B.Wheelock	/1	D.O'Connor	CO	J.Riddle	/P	M.Hughes
/3	B.Hill	3	P.O'Connell	O	S.Nichol	/S	H.Easterday	O	J.Daly	/P	J.Whitney
		/O	H.Church	/C	N.Bligh	/1	C.Roseman	1	A.Knox	/P	B.Price
P	L.German			/O	J.Munyan	/S	P.Sweeney	S	H.Easterday	/P	H.Stine
P	S.McMahon	P	C.McCullough					/2	P.Sweeney	/P	H.Helmbold
P	M.O'Rourke	P	M.Mattimore	P	H.Gastright	P	S.Stratton	3	A.Sauters	/P	J.Sterling
P	M.Morrison	P	B.Murphy	P	F.Knauss	P	R.Ehret	/O	C.Snyder	/P	Lackey
				P	J.Easton	P	G.Meakim	/O	E.Pabst		
/P	N.Baker	/P	S.Toole	P	E.Chamberlain	P	H.Goodall	/C	B.Cantz		
		/P	T.Ford	P	W.Widner	P	E.Daily	/3	H.Meyers		
		/P	J.Powers					/O	G.Crawford		
		/P	G.Williams	/P	A.Mays	/P	M.Jones	/S	D.Fitzgerald		
		/P	J.Lynch	/P	T.Ford			/O	P.Hasney		
								/2	S.Campbell		

ROCHESTER		ST.LOUIS		SYRACUSE		TOLEDO	
M	P.Powers	M	T.McCarthy	M	G.Frazer	M	C.Morton
1B	T.O'Brien	M	J.Kerins	M	W.Fessenden	1B	P.Werden
2B	B.Greenwood	M	C.Roseman	M	G.Frazer	2B	P.Nicholson
SS	M.Phillips	M	C.Campau	1B	M.McQuery	SS	F.Scheibeck
3B	J.Knowles	M	T.McCarthy	2B	C.Childs	3B	B.Alvord
LF	H.Lyons	M	J.Gerhardt	SS	B.McLaughlin	LF	B.Van Dyke
CF	S.Griffin	1B	E.Cartwright	3B	Ti.O'Rourke	CF	G.Tebeau
RF	T.Scheffler	2B	B.Higgins	LF	B.Ely	RF	E.Swartwood
C	D.McGuire	SS	S.Fuller	CF	R.Wright	C	H.Sage
		3B	C.Duffee	RF	P.Friel		
CS	D.McKeough	LF	C.Campau	C	G.Briggs	OP	C.Sprague
SC	J.Grim	CF	C.Roseman			C	E.Rogers
1	J.Field	RF	T.McCarthy	C	To.O'Rourke	C1	T.Welch
S	L.Smith	C	J.Munyan	O	H.Simon	O	J.Peltz
O	D.Burke			O	M.Dorgan	/O	J.Sneed
/O	P.Reccius	O	T.Gettinger	3	J.Battin	/C	F.Ritter
		23	P.Sweeney	C	H.Pitz		
P	B.Barr	23	J.Gerhardt	C	P.Dealy	P	J.Healy
P	W.Calihan	C	J.Wells	O	G.Proeser	P	E.Cushman
P	C.Titcomb	O	D.Miller	/O	D.Hemp	P	F.Smith
P	B.Miller	C	B.Earle	/O	J.Leighton		
		3	J.Davis	/C	D.Burke	/P	E.O'Neil
P	J.Fitzgerald	2	B.Klusman	/O	J.Peltz	/P	D.Abbott
/P	H.Blauvelt	1	J.Kerins	/C	L.Graff	/P	B.Doty
		1	P.Hartnett	/2	B.Higgins		
		C	M.Trost				
		3	J.Donnelly	P	D.Casey		
		/2	E.Herr	P	J.Keefe		
		/1	J.Kane	P	M.Morrison		
		/C	D.Meek	P	E.Mars		
		/S	G.Creely				
		/O	E.Pabst	/P	B.Sullivan		
		/3	J.Burke	/P	C.McCullough		
		/C	J.Adams	/P	T.Lyons		
		/2	F.Millard	/P	E.Lincoln		
				/P	F.Keffer		
		P	J.Stivetts				
		P	T.Ramsey				
		P	B.Hart				
		P	B.Whitrock				
		P	J.Neale				
		/P	E.Chamberlain				
		/P	G.Nicol				

TEAM	G	W	L	PCT	GB	R	OR	AB	H	2B	3B	HR	BB	SO	AVG	OBP	SLG	PRO	PRO+	BR	/A	PF	CHI	RC	SB	CS	SBA	SBR
LOU	136	88	44	.667		819	588	4687	1310	156	65	15	410	460	.279	.344	.350	.694	113	53	72	98	101	699	341			
COL	140	79	55	.590	10	831	617	4741	1225	159	77	16	545	557	.258	.341	.335	.676	112	29	85	93	103	677	353			
STL	139	78	58	.574	12	870	736	4800	1308	178	73	48	474	490	.273	.350	.370	.720	103	100	-23	114	98	746	307			
TOL	134	68	64	.515	20	739	689	4575	1152	152	108	24	486	558	.252	.333	.348	.681	103	31	9	103	94	687	421			
ROC	133	63	63	.500	22	709	711	4553	1088	131	64	31	446	538	.239	.315	.316	.631	98	-53	-2	93	103	564	310			
BAL	38	15	19	.441	24	182	192	1213	278	34	16	2	125	152	.229	.316	.289	.605	79	-23	-31	105	103	146	101			
SYR	128	55	72	.433	30.5	698	831	4469	1158	151	59	14	457	482	.259	.333	.329	.662	112	1	77	90	96	600	292			
PHI	132	54	78	.409	34	702	945	4490	1057	181	51	24	475	540	.235	.320	.314	.634	94	-41	-25	98	100	564	305			
BRO	100	26	73	.263	45.5	492	733	3475	769	116	47	13	328	456	.221	.294	.293	.587	80	-98	-82	97	106	362	182			
TOT	540					6042		37003	9345	1258	560	187	3746	4233	.253	.330	.332	.662							2612			

TEAM	CG	SH	SV	IP	H	H/G	HR	BB	SO	RAT	ERA	ERA+	OAV	OOB	PR	/A	PF	CPI	FA	E	DP	FW	PW	BW	SBW	DIF
LOU	114	13	7	1206	1120	8.4	18	293	587	10.9	2.57	149	.239	.291	173	169	100	117	.934	380	79	2.8	14.9	6.3		-2.0
COL	120	14	3	1214²	976	7.2	20	471	624	11.2	2.99	120	.214	.297	118	80	93	95	.932	396	101	2.6	7.0	7.5		-5.1
STL	118	4	1	1195¹	1127	8.5	38	447	733	12.3	3.67	117	.242	.316	25	82	112	98	.916	478	93	-1.8	7.2	-2.0		6.6
TOL	122	4	2	1159¹	1122	8.7	23	429	533	12.6	3.56	111	.247	.321	39	49	102	102	.925	419	75	.4	4.3	.8		-3.5
ROC	122	5	2	1161²	1115	8.6	19	530	477	13.2	3.56	100	.246	.331	39	-2	92	106	.926	416	95	.4	-.2	-.2		-.0
BAL	36	1	0	315¹	307	8.8	3	123	134	13.0	4.00	101	.248	.328	-5	2	105	92	.928	109	21	.6	.2	-2.7		-.0
SYR	115	5	0	1089²	1158	9.6	28	518	454	14.4	4.98	71	.265	.351	-135	-176	91	89	.925	391	90	.9	-15.5	6.8		-.7
PHI	119	3	2	1132	1405	11.2	17	514	461	15.8	5.22	73	.296	.373	-171	-176	99	99	.918	452	93	-1.6	-15.5	-2.2		7.3
BRO	96	0	0	879	1011	10.4	21	421	230	15.2	4.71	83	.281	.365	-83	-81	101	104	.909	404	92	-4.4	-7.1	-7.2		-4.8
TOT	962	49	17	9353		9.0				13.1	3.86		.253	.330					.923	3445	739					

Runs		Hits		Doubles		Triples		Home Runs		Total Bases	
McTamany-Col	140	Wolf-Lou	197	Childs-Syr	33	Werden-Tol	20	Campau-StL	9	Wolf-Lou	260
McCarthy-StL	137	McCarthy-StL	192	Wolf-Lou	29	Johnson-Col	18	Cartwright-StL	8	McCarthy-StL	256
Fuller-StL	118	Johnson-Col	186	Lyons-Phi	29	Alvord-Tol	16	Stivetts-StL	7	Johnson-Col	248
Sneed-Tol-Col	117	Childs-Syr	170			Sneed-Tol-Col	15	Lyons-Phi	7	Childs-Syr	237
Welch-Phi-Bal	116	Taylor-Lou	169							Werden-Tol	227

Runs Batted In		Runs Produced		Bases On Balls		Batting Average		On Base Percentage		Slugging Average	
Johnson-Col	113	Johnson-Col	218	McTamany-Col	112	Wolf-Lou	.363	Lyons-Phi	.461	Lyons-Phi	.531
Wolf-Lou	98	McCarthy-StL	200	Crooks-Col	96	Lyons-Phi	.354	Swartwood-Tol	.444	Campau-StL	.513
Childs-Syr	89	Childs-Syr	196	Swartwood-Tol	80	McCarthy-StL	.350	Childs-Syr	.434	Childs-Syr	.481
Knowles-Roc	84	Wolf-Lou	194	Werden-Tol	78	Johnson-Col	.346	McCarthy-StL	.430	Wolf-Lou	.479
Shinnick-Lou	82	McTamany-Col	187	Scheffler-Roc	78	Childs-Syr	.345	Wright-Syr	.428	McCarthy-StL	.467

Production		Adjusted Production		Batter Runs		Adjusted Batter Runs		Clutch Hitting Index		Runs Created	
Lyons-Phi	.992	Lyons-Phi	197	McCarthy-StL	45.6	Childs-Syr	58.5	Crooks-Col	148	McCarthy-StL	150
Childs-Syr	.915	Childs-Syr	189	Childs-Syr	44.7	Wolf-Lou	46.3	Knowles-Roc	141	Wolf-Lou	132
Wolf-Lou	.900	Wolf-Lou	169	Wolf-Lou	43.3	Johnson-Col	46.0	O'Brien-Phi	139	Childs-Syr	130
McCarthy-StL	.898	Johnson-Col	168	Lyons-Phi	41.4	Lyons-Phi	43.7	Johnson-Col	136	Johnson-Col	122
Swartwood-Tol	.887	Swartwood-Tol	157	Swartwood-Tol	40.6	Swartwood-Tol	37.2	Shinnick-Lou	132	Werden-Tol	118

Total Average		Stolen Bases		Stolen Base Average		Stolen Base Runs		Fielding Runs		Total Player Rating	
Lyons-Phi	1.224	McCarthy-StL	83					Gerhardt-Bro-StL	41.5	Childs-Syr	6.7
McCarthy-StL	1.169	Scheffler-Roc	77					Reilly-Col	28.2	Lyons-Phi	4.8
Childs-Syr	1.149	VanDyke-Tol	73					Ely-Syr	19.3	O'Connor-Col	3.7
Swartwood-Tol	1.141	Welch-Phi-Bal	72					Tomney-Lou	17.6	Wolf-Lou	3.6
Werden-Tol	1.074							Welch-Phi-Bal	15.7	Swartwood-Tol	3.5

Wins		Win Percentage		Games		Complete Games		Shutouts		Saves	
McMahon-Phi-Bal	36	Stratton-Lou	.708	McMahon-Phi-Bal	60	McMahon-Phi-Bal	55	Chamberlain-SL-Col	6	Goodall-Lou	4
Stratton-Lou	34	Chamberlain-SL-Col	.682	Barr-Roc	57	Barr-Roc	52	Stratton-Lou	4	Knauss-Col	2
Gastright-Col	30	Gastright-Col	.682	Stivetts-StL	54	Stratton-Lou	44	Gastright-Col	4	Ehret-Lou	2
Barr-Roc	28	Ehret-Lou	.641	Stratton-Lou	50	Healy-Tol	44	Ehret-Lou	4		
Stivetts-StL	27	McMahon-Phi-Bal	.632	Gastright-Col	48						

Innings Pitched		Fewest Hits/Game		Fewest BB/Game		Strikeouts		Strikeouts/Game		Ratio	
McMahon-Phi-Bal	509.0	Knauss-Col	6.73	Stratton-Lou	1.27	McMahon-Phi-Bal	291	Ramsey-StL	6.63	Stratton-Lou	9.86
Barr-Roc	493.1	Gastright-Col	7.00	Ehret-Lou	1.98	Stivetts-StL	289	Stivetts-StL	6.20	Gastright-Col	10.43
Stratton-Lou	431.0	Easton-Col	7.50	Ramsey-StL	2.63	Ramsey-StL	257	Meakim-Lou	5.77	Knauss-Col	10.87
Stivetts-StL	419.1	Chamberlain-SL-Col	7.50	Smith-Tol	2.83	Healy-Tol	225	Chamberlain-SL-Col	5.49	Healy-Tol	11.04
Gastright-Col	401.1	Healy-Tol	7.54	McMahon-Phi-Bal	2.94	Barr-Roc	209	Healy-Tol	5.21	Ehret-Lou	11.21

Earned Run Average		Adjusted ERA		Opponents' Batting Avg.		Opponents' On Base Pct.		Starter Runs		Adjusted Starter Runs	
Stratton-Lou	2.36	Stratton-Lou	163	Knauss-Col	.202	Stratton-Lou	.270	Stratton-Lou	72.0	Stratton-Lou	71.1
Ehret-Lou	2.53	Ehret-Lou	152	Gastright-Col	.208	Gastright-Col	.282	Ehret-Lou	53.1	Ehret-Lou	52.3
Knauss-Col	2.81	Healy-Tol	136	Easton-Col	.220	Knauss-Col	.290	Healy-Tol	42.0	Healy-Tol	45.5
Chamberlain-SL-Col	2.83	Meakim-Lou	132	Chamberlain-SL-Col	.220	Healy-Tol	.293	Gastright-Col	41.3	Stivetts-StL	36.7
Healy-Tol	2.89	Chamberlain-SL-Col	131	Healy-Tol	.221	Ehret-Lou	.296	Barr-Roc	33.8	McMahon-Phi-Bal	33.8

Clutch Pitching Index		Relief Runs	Adjusted Relief Runs	Relief Ranking	Total Pitcher Index		Total Baseball Ranking	
Ehret-Lou	126				Stratton-Lou	8.9	Stratton-Lou	8.9
Titcomb-Roc	121				Stivetts-StL	4.9	Childs-Syr	6.7
Daily-Bro-Lou	113				Healy-Tol	4.7	Stivetts-StL	5.0
Stratton-Lou	110				Ehret-Lou	4.3	Lyons-Phi	4.8
Chamberlain-SL-Col	110				McMahon-Phi-Bal	4.0	Healy-Tol	4.6

January 16 Samuel Gompers, president of the American Federation of Labor, and three other labor leaders pledge support for the PL at a league meeting in Philadelphia.

January 28 In the first of many lawsuits filed against PL players by their former teams, the judge refuses to grant an injunction against John Ward, president of the Brotherhood. His decision, echoed frequently by other judges, states that the "want of fairness and mutuality" in the standard NL contract, specifically the clauses relating to the reserve rule, "[is] apparent."

March 27* The application of an all-black club made up of ex–Cuban Giants is rejected by the Inter-State League.

May 8 Cleveland's Willie McGill hurls a complete-game 14-5 victory over Buffalo in a Players League game at age 16, the youngest ever to perform this feat.

May 31 New York players George Gore, Buck Ewing, and Roger Connor hit consecutive homers in the eighth inning against Cincinnati. This feat will not be matched until May 10, 1894.

June 1* Professional baseball is born in England as four teams—Derby, Preston, Stoke, and Birmingham—form a league. Four Americans are imported to provide instruction.

June 2 Ed Delahanty of Cleveland goes 6-for-6 with five runs as his club crashes Chicago 20–7.

June 21 Charles "Silver" King of Chicago pitches an eight-inning no-hitter, but loses to Brooklyn, 1–0. Chicago bats first, and King does not pitch the last of the ninth.

July 23 Harry Stovey of Boston's PL club becomes the first major league player to reach 100 career home runs.

September 14 When Buffalo (PL) captain Jay Faatz disagrees with management, Connie Mack becomes captain of the team. This unofficially marks the start of Connie Mack's managing career that spans more than half a century.

October 9 Cincinnati (NL) owner Aaron Stern sells his team to PL owners for $40,000 (Giants owner John B. Day had threatened the same action in July, but received help from other owners to prevent it). Committees from the three leagues begin negotiations towards a settlement of the war. PL owners from New York, Cleveland and Brooklyn seek consolidation with the NL. A truce, during which all contracts will be respected, is agreed upon. It is up to owners in each city to arrange their own deals.

October 17* The AA and NL refuse to permit the Players League champion to take part in a World Series. Interest in the postseason meeting of league champions is lukewarm as Brooklyn wins a 9-0 opener over Louisville behind Adonis Terry (26-16). After breaking even in seven games, with one tie, the teams abandon the series.

October 20 Upset over PL backers seeking deals without consulting them, the Brotherhood meets and votes to add a players' committee to the three league committees for the next meeting. John M. Ward, Ned Hanlon, and Arthur Irwin are elected. Ward makes a long, spirited plea for the players' participation. Al Spalding, eager to split the backers and players, argues against him. The original three league committees vote 2–1 against the players' involvement. Each PL backer is now out to make his own deal and the league is dead.

	BOSTON		BROOKLYN		BUFFALO		CHICAGO		CLEVELAND		NEW YORK		PHILADELPHIA		PITTSBURGH
M	K.Kelly	M	M.Ward	M	J.Rowe	M	C.Comiskey	M	T.Larkin	M	B.Ewing	M	J.Fogarty	M	N.Hanlon
1B	D.Brouthers	1B	D.Orr	M	J.Faatz	1B	C.Comiskey	M	P.Tebeau	1B	R.Connor	M	C.Buffinton	1B	J.Beckley
2B	J.Quinn	2B	L.Bierbauer	2B	J.Rowe	2B	F.Pfeffer	1B	H.Larkin	2B	D.Shannon	1B	S.Farrar	2B	Y.Robinson
SS	A.Irwin	SS	J.Ward	1B	D.White	SS	C.Bastian	2B	C.Stricker	SS	D.Richardson	2B	J.Pickett	SS	T.Corcoran
3B	B.Nash	3B	B.Joyce	2B	S.Wise	3B	N.Williamson	SS	E.Delahanty	3B	A.Whitney	SS	B.Shindle	3B	B.Kuehne
LF	H.Richardson	LF	E.Seery	SS	J.Rowe	LF	T.O'Neill	3B	P.Tebeau	LF	G.Gore	3B	J.Mulvey	LF	J.Fields
CF	T.Brown	CF	E.Andrews	3B	J.Irwin	CF	J.Ryan	LF	P.Browning	CF	M.Slattery	LF	G.Wood	CF	N.Hanlon
RF	H.Stovey	RF	J.McGeachy	LF	E.Beecher	RF	H.Duffy	CF	J.McAleer	RF	J.O'Rourke	CF	M.Griffin	RF	J.Visner
C	M.Murphy	C	T.Kinslow	CF	D.Hoy	C	D.Farrell	RF	P.Radford	C	B.Ewing	RF	J.Fogarty	C	F.Carroll
				RF	J.Halligan			C	S.Sutcliffe			C	J.Milligan		
CS	K.Kelly	OP	G.Van Haltren	C	C.Mack	C3	J.Boyle			O	D.Johnston			C	T.Quinn
C	P.Swett	C1	P.Cook			1S	D.Darling	C3	J.Brennan	3S	G.Hatfield	OC	B.Hallman	/C	J.Hurley
/O	D.Johnston	C	C.Daily	OC	S.Clark	3	A.Latham	O	L.Twitchell	CO	W.Brown	CO	L.Cross	/2	R.Gray
/S	J.Morrill	O	A.Sunday	OP	L.Twitchell	S	F.Shugart	O	J.Carney	CO	F.Vaughn	2	D.Shannon		
		/O	J.Hayes	O	J.Rainey			C	P.Snyder	/2	F.Dunlap			P	H.Staley
P	C.Radbourn			1	J.Faatz	P	M.Baldwin	/C	N.Stynes			P	B.Sanders	P	A.Maul
P	A.Gumbert	P	G.Weyhing	1	J.Carney	P	S.King	/O	Budd	P	E.Crane	P	P.Knell	P	P.Galvin
P	B.Daley	P	J.Sowders	/O	Lewis	P	C.Bartson			P	H.O'Day	P	C.Buffinton	P	E.Morris
P	M.Kilroy	P	C.Murphy	/O	J.Gillespie			P	H.Gruber	P	J.Ewing	P	B.Husted	P	J.Tener
		P	G.Hemming			P	F.Dwyer	P	J.Bakely	P	T.Keefe	P	B.Cunningham		
P	K.Madden			P	G.Haddock			P	D.O'Brien					/P	F.Doe
				P	B.Cunningham			P	W.McGill						
				P	G.Keefe										
				P	G.Stafford			/P	G.Hemming						
								/P	C.Dewald						
				P	A.Ferson			/P	B.Gleason						
				/P	L.Baldwin										
				/P	J.Buckley										
				/P	G.Krock										
				/P	B.Duzen										
				/P	D.Cotter										
				/P	F.Doe										

TEAM	G	W	L	PCT	GB	R	OR	AB	H	2B	3B	HR	BB	SO	AVG	OBP	SLG	PRO	PRO+	BR	/A	PF	CHI	RC	SB	CS	SBA	SBR
BOS	130	81	48	.628		992	767	4626	1306	**223**	76	54	**652**	435	.282	**.376**	.398	**.774**	105	**90**	24	107	100	**869**	**412**			
BRO	133	76	56	.576	6.5	964	893	4887	1352	186	93	34	502	369	.277	.349	.374	.723	92	-13	-68	105	106	751	272			
NY	132	74	57	.565	8	**1018**	875	4913	**1393**	204	97	66	486	364	.284	.352	**.405**	.757	98	40	-44	109	106	800	231			
CHI	138	75	62	.547	10	886	770	4968	1311	200	95	31	492	410	.264	.335	.361	.696	87	-65	-101	104	102	712	276			
PHI	132	68	63	.519	14	941	855	4855	1350	187	**113**	49	431	**321**	.278	.343	.393	.736	100	2	-19	102	104	743	203			
PIT	128	60	68	.469	20.5	835	892	4577	1192	168	**113**	35	569	375	.260	.349	.369	.718	106	-15	56	92	97	694	249			
CLE	131	55	75	.423	26.5	849	1027	4804	1370	213	94	27	509	345	**.285**	.360	.386	.746	114	30	**107**	92	91	749	180			
BUF	134	36	96	.273	46.5	793	1199	4795	1249	180	64	20	541	367	.260	.347	.337	.684	96	-68	2	92	93	632	160			
TOT	529					7278		38425	10523	1561	745	316	4182	2986	.274	.351	.378	.729						1983				

TEAM	CG	SH	SV	IP	H	H/G	HR	BB	SO	RAT	ERA	ERA+	OAV	OOB	PR	/A	PF	CPI	FA	E	DP	FW	PW	BW	SBW	DIF
BOS	105	6	4	1137¹	1291	10.2	49	467	345	14.3	3.79	116	.274	.346	55	76	104	111	.918	460	109	1.7	6.1	1.9		6.8
BRO	111	4	**7**	1184	1334	10.1	**26**	570	377	14.9	3.95	113	.273	.356	37	65	105	106	.909	531	114	-1.8	5.2	-5.4		12.0
NY	111	3	6	1172¹	**1216**	9.3	37	569	449	14.1	4.17	109	.257	.343	8	47	107	92	**.921**	450	94	**2.8**	3.8	-3.5		5.5
CHI	124	5	2	1219¹	1238	**9.1**	27	503	**460**	13.2	**3.39**	**128**	.252	.327	**114**	**128**	103	100	.918	492	107	1.6	**10.2**	-8.1		2.7
PHI	118	4	2	1154¹	1292	10.1	33	495	361	14.4	4.05	105	.271	.347	22	27	101	100	.910	510	118	-.7	2.2	-1.5		2.6
PIT	121	**7**	0	1116²	1267	10.2	32	**334**	318	**13.2**	4.22	93	.274	.328	2	-39	92	89	.907	512	80	-1.7	-3.1	4.5		-3.6
CLE	115	1	0	1143²	1386	10.9	45	571	325	15.8	4.23	94	.287	.369	0	-33	94	**114**	.907	533	103	-2.3	-2.6	**8.5**		-13.6
BUF	**125**	2	0	1141	1499	11.8	67	673	351	17.5	6.11	67	.304	.393	-239	-257	97	93	.914	491	116	.8	-20.5	.2		-10.5
TOT	930	32	21	9268²		10.2				14.7	4.23		.274	.351					.913	3979	841					

Runs
Duffy-Chi 161
Brown-Bos 146
Stovey-Bos 142
Ward-Bro 134
Connor-NY 133

Hits
Duffy-Chi 191
Shindle-Phi 189
Ward-Bro 188
Browning-Cle 184
Richardson-Bos . . . 181

Doubles
Browning-Cle 40
Beckley-Pit 38
O'Rourke-NY 37
Duffy-Chi 36
Brouthers-Bos 36

Triples
Visner-Pit 22
Beckley-Pit 22
Shindle-Phi 21
Fields-Pit 20
Joyce-Bro 18

Home Runs
Connor-NY 14
Richardson-Bos . . . 13
Stovey-Bos 12
Shindle-Phi 10
Gore-NY 10

Total Bases
Shindle-Phi 282
Duffy-Chi 280
Beckley-Pit 276
Richardson-Bos . . . 274
Connor-NY 265

Runs Batted In
Richardson-Bos . . . 146
Orr-Bro 124
Beckley-Pit 120
O'Rourke-NY 115
Larkin-Cle 112

Runs Produced
Richardson-Bos . . . 259
Duffy-Chi 236
Connor-NY 222
Bierbauer-Bro 220
Beckley-Pit 220

Bases On Balls
Joyce-Bro 123
Robinson-Pit 101
Brouthers-Bos 99
Hoy-Buf 94

Batting Average
Browning-Cle 373
Orr-Bro 371
O'Rourke-NY 360
Connor-NY 349
Ryan-Chi 340

On Base Percentage
Brouthers-Bos 466
Browning-Cle 459
Connor-NY 450
Robinson-Pit 434
Gore-NY 432

Slugging Average
Connor-NY 548
B.Ewing-NY 545
Beckley-Pit 535
Orr-Bro 534
Browning-Cle 517

Production
Connor-NY 998
Browning-Cle 976
Orr-Bro 948
Gore-NY 931
O'Rourke-NY 925

Adjusted Production
Browning-Cle 175
Beckley-Pit 156
Larkin-Cle 153
Connor-NY 152
Orr-Bro 144

Batter Runs
Connor-NY 47.6
Browning-Cle 45.2
Brouthers-Bos 38.2
Orr-Bro 32.3
Larkin-Cle 30.2

Adjusted Batter Runs
Browning-Cle 57.1
Larkin-Cle 41.0
Beckley-Pit 38.7
Connor-NY 35.2
Brouthers-Bos 29.2

Clutch Hitting Index
Richardson-Bos . . . 128
Orr-Bro 128
Brouthers-Bos 125
Wise-Buf 119
Larkin-Cle 118

Runs Created
Duffy-Chi 141
Browning-Cle 136
Stovey-Bos 135
Connor-NY 132
Shindle-Phi 127

Total Average
Stovey-Bos 1.217
Connor-NY 1.194
Browning-Cle 1.191
Brouthers-Bos 1.149
Gore-NY 1.129

Stolen Bases
Stovey-Bos 97
Brown-Bos 79
Duffy-Chi 78
Hanlon-Pit 65
Ward-Bro 63

Stolen Base Average

Stolen Base Runs

Fielding Runs
Farrell-Chi 26.5
Richardson-NY . . . 25.3
Bierbauer-Bro 24.8
Pfeffer-Chi 24.1
Ward-Bro 21.3

Total Player Rating
Browning-Cle 4.5
Connor-NY 3.1
B.Ewing-NY 3.0
Ward-Bro 2.9
Shindle-Phi 2.6

Wins
Baldwin-Chi 33
Weyhing-Bro 30
King-Chi 30
Radbourn-Bos 27
Gumbert-Bos 23

Win Percentage
Daley-Bos 720
Radbourn-Bos 692
Knell-Phi 667
Gumbert-Bos 657
Weyhing-Bro 652

Games
Baldwin-Chi 58
King-Chi 56
Weyhing-Bro 49
Gruber-Cle 48
Staley-Pit 46

Complete Games
Baldwin-Chi 53
King-Chi 48
Staley-Pit 44
Gruber-Cle 39
Weyhing-Bro 38

Shutouts
King-Chi 4
Weyhing-Bro 3
Staley-Pit 3

Saves
Hemming-Cle-Bro . . . 3
O'Day-NY 3

Innings Pitched
Baldwin-Chi 492.0
King-Chi 461.0
Weyhing-Bro 390.0
Staley-Pit 387.2
Gruber-Cle 383.1

Fewest Hits/Game
King-Chi 8.20
Crane-NY 8.80
Keefe-NY 8.84
Hemming-Cle-Bro 8.88
Knell-Phi 9.01

Fewest BB/Game
Staley-Pit 1.72
Sanders-Phi 1.79
Galvin-Pit 2.03
Morris-Pit 2.18
Radbourn-Bos . . . 2.62

Strikeouts
Baldwin-Chi 206
King-Chi 185
Weyhing-Bro 177
Staley-Pit 145
J.Ewing-NY 145

Strikeouts/Game
J.Ewing-NY 4.88
Daley-Bos 4.21
Weyhing-Bro 4.08
McGill-Cle 4.02
Haddock-Buf 3.81

Ratio
Staley-Pit 11.07
King-Chi 11.67
Radbourn-Bos . . . 12.15
Keefe-NY 12.66
Sanders-Phi 12.75

Earned Run Average
King-Chi 2.69
Staley-Pit 3.23
Radbourn-Bos . . . 3.31
Baldwin-Chi 3.35
Keefe-NY 3.38

Adjusted ERA
King-Chi 161
Keefe-NY 134
Radbourn-Bos . . . 133
Baldwin-Chi 130
Weyhing-Bro 124

Opponents' Batting Avg.
King-Chi 232
Crane-NY 245
Keefe-NY 246
Hemming-Cle-Bro .247
Knell-Phi 250

Opponents' On Base Pct.
Staley-Pit 290
King-Chi 301
Radbourn-Bos 310
Keefe-NY 318
Sanders-Phi 320

Starter Runs
King-Chi 78.6
Baldwin-Chi 48.2
Staley-Pit 43.2
Radbourn-Bos . . . 35.2
Weyhing-Bro 27.2

Adjusted Starter Runs
King-Chi 84.2
Baldwin-Chi 54.2
Radbourn-Bos . . . 41.4
Weyhing-Bro 37.0
Keefe-NY 29.5

Clutch Pitching Index
O'Brien-Cle 127
Daley-Bos 124
McGill-Cle 117
Kilroy-Bos 114
Gruber-Cle 114

Relief Runs

Adjusted Relief Runs

Relief Ranking

Total Pitcher Index
King-Chi 7.1
Baldwin-Chi 4.8
Radbourn-Bos . . . 3.7
Staley-Pit 2.5
Sanders-Phi 2.4

Total Baseball Ranking
King-Chi 7.1
Baldwin-Chi 4.8
Browning-Cle 4.5
Radbourn-Bos . . . 3.5
Connor-NY 3.1

January 14 The NL votes to allow the AA to place a team in Boston, despite the vehement opposition of the owners of the Boston NL club.

January 16 The NL, AA, and Western Association sign a new National Agreement calling for the creation of a three-man Board of Control to settle disputes between clubs and leagues.

February 6 The New York Giants' salary list is leaked to the press. It shows a total player payroll of $54,600 with Buck Ewing's $5,500 salary topping the scale.

February 14 The National Board of Control "reluctantly"awards three disputed players (Lou Bierbauer, Harry Stovey, and Connie Mack) to the NL clubs that signed them despite the prior claims of the AA.

April 3 The Cleveland Spiders beat Pittsburgh, 6-3, in St. Augustine in the first spring training game ever played in Florida between two major league teams.

April 27 The Bridegrooms play their home opener at Eastern Park in the East New York section of Brooklyn. The park was used by the PL club in 1890, and the NL club will occupy it for seven years. It is located near a complex of streetcar and suburban railroad lines, forcing fans to "dodge trolleys" to get to the gates. This spawns the name "Trolley Dodgers" or "Dodgers" for the ball club.

May 1 Cleveland opens new League Park at 66th and Lexington with Cy Young pitching the Spiders to a 12-3 victory over the Reds before a crowd of about 9,500.

June 13 A new major league attendance record is set as 22,289 jam the Polo Grounds to see the Giants nip the Colts, 8–7.

July 25 An over-the-fence drive by Cliff Carroll caps a four-run rally in the bottom of the ninth to give the Chicago Colts a 15–14 victory in Cleveland. Although the ground rules at this park call for a homer on balls hit over all outfield fences, the winning run scores from second base, so Carroll gets credit for only a double.

August 25 The Boston NL club shocks the baseball world by announcing the signing of King Kelly away from the rival Boston AA club, thereby wrecking peace talks between the leagues. Kelly signs through the 1892 season for a total of $25,000, a figure that will not be topped by any player until the Federal League war of 1914 and 1915.

September 4 "Old Man" Cap Anson shows up for today's game wearing a wig and a long white beard, much to the delight of the Chicago crowd. Anson wears this costume throughout the game, which his Colts win over the Beaneaters, 5-3, stretching Chicago's lead to seven games over Boston.

September 18 Billy Hamilton steals four bases to pace the Phillies to an 11-6 decision over the Cincinnati Reds. Hamilton will finish the season with a league-leading 115 steals, breaking the 100 mark for the third year in a row.

October 1 Boston clinches the NL pennant with its 17th consecutive victory, 6–1, in Philadelphia, while Chicago is losing to Cincinnati by the same score.

November 11 The NL meets and dismisses the charges of collusion and game throwing against the eastern clubs brought by Chicago, thereby formally giving Boston the pennant. The league also plans its strategy for conquering the Association by consolidating the four strongest AA clubs into a 12-team league for next year.

December 17 The NL gains four new teams from the folding AA (St. Louis, Louisville, Washington, and Baltimore) and conducts other business as well. The NL allows Sunday games for the first time but will retain its 50-cent minimum admission price.

	BOSTON		BROOKLYN		CHICAGO		CINCINNATI		CLEVELAND		NEW YORK		PHILADELPHIA		PITTSBURGH
M	F.Selee	M	M.Ward	M	C.Anson	M	T.Loftus	M	B.Leadley	M	J.Mutrie	M	H.Wright	M	N.Hanlon
1B	T.Tucker	1B	D.Foutz	1B	C.Anson	1B	J.Reilly	M	P.Tebeau	1B	R.Connor	1B	W.Brown	M	B.McGunnigle
2B	J.Quinn	2B	H.Collins	2B	F.Pfeffer	2B	B.McPhee	1B	J.Virtue	2B	D.Richardson	2B	A.Myers	1B	J.Beckley
SS	H.Long	SS	J.Ward	SS	J.Cooney	SS	G.Smith	2B	C.Childs	SS	J.Glasscock	SS	B.Allen	2B	L.Bierbauer
3B	B.Nash	3B	G.Pinkney	3B	B.Dahlen	3B	A.Latham	SS	E.McKean	3B	C.Bassett	3B	B.Shindle	SS	F.Shugart
LF	B.Lowe	LF	D.O'Brien	LF	W.Wilmot	LF	P.Browning	3B	P.Tebeau	LF	J.O'Rourke	LF	B.Hamilton	3B	C.Reilly
CF	S.Brodie	CF	M.Griffin	CF	J.Ryan	CF	B.Holliday	LF	J.McAleer	CF	G.Gore	CF	E.Delahanty	LF	P.Browning
RF	H.Stovey	RF	O.Burns	RF	C.Carroll	RF	L.Marr	CF	G.Davis	RF	M.Tiernan	RF	S.Thompson	CF	N.Hanlon
C	C.Bennett	C	T.Kinslow	C	M.Kittridge	C	J.Harrington	RF	S.Johnson	C	D.Buckley	C	J.Clements	RF	F.Carroll
								C	C.Zimmer					C	C.Mack
CO	C.Ganzel	C	C.Daily	3	T.Burns	1C	J.Keenan			SO	L.Whistler	3O	E.Mayer		
O	M.Sullivan	C1	T.Daly	C	P.Schriver	O	J.Halligan	CO	J.Doyle	C	A.Clarke	CO	B.Grey	CS	D.Miller
C	K.Kelly	2	J.O'Brien	C	B.Bowman	O	M.Slattery	O	J.Burkett	C	B.Burrell	1	J.Denny	O	A.Maul
O	J.Kelley	S	B.Ely	C	B.Merritt	O	E.Curtis	3	J.Denny	/2	B.Ewing	/C	J.Fields	O	P.Corkhill
/O	G.Rooks	/2	J.Burdock	/C	T.Nagle	C	B.Clark	O	J.Shearon	/3	J.Denny	/C	L.Graulich	O	D.Lally
/C	F.Lake	/O	D.Esterbrook	/O	E.Foster	/O	P.Corkhill	3	B.Alvord			/O	J.Donohue	C2	T.Berger
				/C	M.Honan	/O	F.Foreman	O	E.Seward	P	A.Rusie	/S	H.Morelock	C	J.Fields
								/O	M.Sullivan	P	J.Ewing	/O	W.Plock	/3	J.Newell
P	J.Clarkson	P	T.Lovett			P	B.Hutchison	/O	B.Collins	P	M.Welch	/S	C.Bastian	/O	P.Ward
P	K.Nichols	P	B.Caruthers	P	A.Gumbert	P	B.Rhines	/O	J.Daly					/S	E.Spurney
P	H.Staley	P	G.Hemming	P	P.Luby	P	C.Radbourn			P	J.Sharrott	P	K.Gleason	/3	S.LaRoque
P	C.Getzien	P	A.Terry	P	E.Stein	P	E.Crane	P	C.Young	/P	R.Coughlin	P	D.Esper		
		P	B.Inks					P	H.Gruber	/P	T.Keefe	P	J.Thornton	P	M.Baldwin
/P	J.Kiley			P	T.Vickery	P	J.Duryea	P	L.Viau	/P	D.Clarkson			P	S.King
/P	C.Ryan			/P	G.Nicol	/P	C.Stephens			/P	B.Barr	P	T.Keefe	/P	P.Galvin
/P	T.Brynan							/P	E.Beatin	/P	M.Sullivan	P	B.Kling		
/P	J.Sullivan							/P	F.Knauss	/P	J.Taylor	/P	E.Cassian	/P	H.Staley
								/P	C.Getzien	/P	A.Dunning	/P	P.Smith	/P	S.Stratton
								/P	H.Killeen			/P	J.Schultze		
												/P	M.Kilroy		
												/P	J.Gormley		
												/P	P.Saylor		

TEAM	G	W	L	PCT	GB	R	OR	AB	H	2B	3B	HR	BB	SO	AVG	OBP	SLG	PRO	PRO+	BR	/A	PF	CHI	RC	SB	CS	SBA	SBR
BOS	140	87	51	.630		847	658	4956	1264	181	81	53	533	537	.255	.337	.356	.693	97	52	-47	112	101	710	289			
CHI	137	82	53	.607	3.5	832	730	4873	1231	159	88	60	526	457	.253	.332	.358	.690	107	41	42	100	102	674	238			
NY	136	71	61	.538	13	754	711	4833	1271	189	72	46	438	394	.263	.329	.360	.689	111	34	66	96	96	663	224			
PHI	138	68	69	.496	18.5	756	773	4929	1244	180	51	21	482	412	.252	.326	.322	.648	92	-27	-46	103	101	609	232			
CLE	141	65	74	.468	22.5	835	888	5074	1295	183	88	22	519	464	.255	.330	.339	.669	97	7	-26	104	104	663	242			
BRO	137	61	76	.445	25.5	765	820	4748	1233	200	69	23	435	435	.260	.330	.345	.675	103	16	21	99	101	669	337			
CIN	138	56	81	.409	30.5	646	790	4791	1158	148	90	40	414	439	.242	.308	.335	.643	92	-49	-54	101	93	584	244			
PIT	137	55	80	.407	30.5	679	744	4794	1148	148	71	29	427	503	.239	.308	.318	.626	90	-73	-56	98	101	547	205			
TOT	552					6114		38998	9844	1388	610	294	3804	3641	.252	.325	.342	.667						2011				

TEAM	CG	SH	SV	IP	H	H/G	HR	BB	SO	RAT	ERA	ERA+	OAV	OOB	PR	/A	PF	CPI	FA	E	DP	FW	PW	BW	SBW	DIF
BOS	126	9	6	1241²	1223	8.9	51	364	525	11.8	2.76	132	.248	.305	80	122	109	109	.938	358	96	4.7	10.9	-4.2		6.6
CHI	114	6	3	1220²	1207	8.9	53	475	477	12.7	3.47	96	.249	.322	-17	-21	100	96	.932	397	119	1.5	-1.9	3.8		11.1
NY	117	11	3	1204	1098	8.2	26	593	651	13.1	2.99	107	.234	.327	47	28	96	104	.933	384	104	2.2	2.5	5.9		-5.5
PHI	105	3	5	1229¹	1279	9.4	29	507	342	13.4	3.73	91	.259	.333	-53	-46	102	94	.925	443	108	-1.3	-4.1	-4.1		9.0
CLE	118	1	3	1244	1371	9.9	24	466	400	13.6	3.50	99	.270	.336	-22	-7	103	105	.920	485	86	-3.5	-.6	-2.3		1.9
BRO	121	8	3	1204²	1272	9.5	40	459	407	13.4	3.86	86	.261	.332	-68	-75	99	93	.924	432	73	-.8	-6.7	1.9		-1.9
CIN	125	6	1	1218²	1234	9.1	40	465	393	13.0	3.55	95	.253	.326	-28	-25	101	96	.931	409	101	.9	-2.2	-4.8		-6.4
PIT	122	7	2	1197²	1160	8.7	31	465	446	12.7	2.89	114	.245	.320	61	51	98	109	.917	475	76	-3.6	4.6	-5.0		-8.4
TOT	948	51	26	9760²		9.1				12.9	3.34		.252	.325					.928	3383	763					

Runs		Hits		Doubles		Triples		Home Runs		Total Bases	
Hamilton-Phi	141	Hamilton-Phi	179	Griffin-Bro	36	Stovey-Bos	20	Tiernan-NY	16	Stovey-Bos	271
Long-Bos	129	McKean-Cle	170	Davis-Cle	35	Beckley-Pit	19	Stovey-Bos	16	Tiernan-NY	268
Childs-Cle	120	Tiernan-NY	166	Stovey-Bos	31	McPhee-Cin	16	Wilmot-Chi	11	Long-Bos	235
Latham-Cin	119	Davis-Cle	165	Tiernan-NY	30	Ryan-Chi	15			Davis-Cle	233
Stovey-Bos	118	O'Rourke-NY	164			Virtue-Cle	14			Beckley-Pit	232

Runs Batted In		Runs Produced		Bases On Balls		Batting Average		On Base Percentage		Slugging Average	
Anson-Chi	120	Davis-Cle	201	Hamilton-Phi	102	Hamilton-Phi	.340	Hamilton-Phi	.453	Stovey-Bos	.498
Stovey-Bos	95	Childs-Cle	201	Childs-Cle	97	Holliday-Cin	.319	Connor-NY	.399	Tiernan-NY	.494
O'Rourke-NY	95	Hamilton-Phi	199	Connor-NY	83	Browning-Pit-Cin	.317	Childs-Cle	.395	Holliday-Cin	.473
Nash-Bos	95	Connor-NY	199	Long-Bos	80	Clements-Phi	.310	Browning-Pit-Cin	.395	Connor-NY	.449
Connor-NY	94	Stovey-Bos	197			Tiernan-NY	.306	Tiernan-NY	.388	Ryan-Chi	.434

Production		Adjusted Production		Batter Runs		Adjusted Batter Runs		Clutch Hitting Index		Runs Created	
Tiernan-NY	.882	Tiernan-NY	163	Hamilton-Phi	44.1	Tiernan-NY	43.0	Anson-Chi	130	Hamilton-Phi	155
Hamilton-Phi	.874	Connor-NY	153	Tiernan-NY	37.8	Hamilton-Phi	40.8	Delahanty-Phi	126	Tiernan-NY	128
Stovey-Bos	.871	Hamilton-Phi	151	Stovey-Bos	35.2	Connor-NY	35.3	Brodie-Bos	119	Stovey-Bos	125
Holliday-Cin	.848	Holliday-Cin	145	Connor-NY	30.7	Holliday-Cin	23.7	Zimmer-Cle	119	Long-Bos	114
Connor-NY	.848	Browning-Pit-Cin	139	Holliday-Cin	24.4	Browning-Pit-Cin	22.0	Allen-Phi	119	Latham-Cin	112

Total Average		Stolen Bases		Stolen Base Average	Stolen Base Runs	Fielding Runs		Total Player Rating	
Hamilton-Phi	1.270	Hamilton-Phi	111			Richardson-NY	49.1	Richardson-NY	4.5
Tiernan-NY	1.045	Latham-Cin	87			Griffin-Bro	25.7	Latham-Cin	3.7
Stovey-Bos	1.043	Griffin-Bro	65			Pfeffer-Cin	25.0	Hamilton-Phi	3.7
Latham-Cin	.974	Long-Bos	60			McPhee-Cin	23.3	Pfeffer-Chi	3.2
Connor-NY	.968					Latham-Cin	20.4	McPhee-Cin	3.1

Wins		Win Percentage		Games		Complete Games		Shutouts		Saves	
Hutchison-Chi	44	J.Ewing-NY	.724	Hutchison-Chi	66	Hutchison-Chi	56	Rusie-NY	6	Nichols-Bos	3
Rusie-NY	33	Hutchison-Chi	.698	Rusie-NY	61	Rusie-NY	52	Nichols-Bos	5	Clarkson-Bos	3
Clarkson-Bos	33	Staley-Pit-Bos	.649	Young-Cle	55	Baldwin-Pit	48	J.Ewing-NY	5	Young-Cle	2
Nichols-Bos	30	Nichols-Bos	.638	Clarkson-Bos	55	Clarkson-Bos	47	Hutchison-Chi	4	Thornton-Phi	2
Young-Cle	27	Clarkson-Bos	.635			Nichols-Bos	45				

Innings Pitched		Fewest Hits/Game		Fewest BB/Game		Strikeouts		Strikeouts/Game		Ratio	
Hutchison-Chi	561.0	Rusie-NY	7.03	Nichols-Bos	2.18	Rusie-NY	337	Rusie-NY	6.06	Staley-Pit-Bos	11.08
Rusie-NY	500.1	Baldwin-Pit	7.92	Staley-Pit-Bos	2.22	Hutchison-Chi	261	Nichols-Bos	5.08	Hutchison-Chi	11.12
Clarkson-Bos	460.2	J.Ewing-NY	7.92	Galvin-Pit	2.26	Nichols-Bos	240	J.Ewing-NY	4.61	Nichols-Bos	11.28
Baldwin-Pit	437.2	Hutchison-Chi	8.15	Radbourn-Cin	2.56	Baldwin-Pit	197	Hutchison-Chi	4.19	J.Ewing-NY	11.80
Mullane-Cin	426.1	Mullane-Cin	8.23	Hutchison-Chi	2.86	King-Pit	160	Baldwin-Pit	4.05	Clarkson-Bos	11.80

Earned Run Average		Adjusted ERA		Opponents' Batting Avg.		Opponents' On Base Pct.		Starter Runs		Adjusted Starter Runs	
J.Ewing-NY	2.27	Nichols-Bos	153	Rusie-NY	.207	Staley-Pit-Bos	.292	Nichols-Bos	45.1	Nichols-Bos	59.6
Nichols-Bos	2.39	J.Ewing-NY	141	Baldwin-Pit	.228	Hutchison-Chi	.293	Rusie-NY	43.9	Clarkson-Bos	43.9
Rusie-NY	2.55	Staley-Pit-Bos	138	J.Ewing-NY	.228	Nichols-Bos	.296	Hutchison-Chi	33.5	Rusie-NY	35.7
Staley-Pit-Bos	2.58	Clarkson-Bos	131	Hutchison-Chi	.233	J.Ewing-NY	.305	J.Ewing-NY	32.1	Staley-Pit-Bos	35.5
Baldwin-Pit	2.76	Rusie-NY	125	Mullane-Cin	.234	Clarkson-Bos	.305	Baldwin-Pit	28.6	Hutchison-Chi	32.4

Clutch Pitching Index		Relief Runs	Adjusted Relief Runs	Relief Ranking	Total Pitcher Index		Total Baseball Ranking	
Viau-Cle	117				Nichols-Bos	5.8	Nichols-Bos	5.8
Nichols-Bos	116				Clarkson-Bos	4.8	Clarkson-Bos	4.7
Caruthers-Bro	116				Rusie-NY	3.7	Richardson-NY	4.5
Galvin-Pit	112				Staley-Pit-Bos	3.1	Latham-Cin	3.7
J.Ewing-NY	111				Hutchison-Chi	2.7	Hamilton-Phi	3.7

February 17 The AA meets and indignantly unseats President Thurman, then withdraws from the National Agreement. This means "war," and the AA's first move is to switch its franchise from Chicago to Cincinnati to compete with the NL in the Queen City.

August 17 The AA franchise in Cincinnati folds. Milwaukee of the Western Association is elected to take its place, a move that dooms that minor league. The Brewers sign four of the Kellys and several players from other WA clubs. "The King of Ballplayers," Mike Kelly, joins the Boston Reds and is appointed captain.

October 2 In the first-ever major league game in Minnesota, the Milwaukee Brewers beat the Columbus Buckeyes 5–0 in Minneapolis's Athletic Park.

October 4 Browns rookie Ted Breitenstein gets his first start on the final day of the season and hurls a no-hitter versus Louisville. He wins 8–0 while walking one and facing the minimum 27 batters.

December 17 Four AA clubs (St. Louis, Louisville, Washington, and Baltimore) join with the NL eight in a 12-club league formally styled "The National League and American Association of Professional Base Ball Clubs." The other four AA clubs are bought out for about $130,000.

BALTIMORE		BOSTON		CINCINNATI		COLUMBUS		LOUISVILLE	
M	B.Barnie	M	A.Irwin	M	K.Kelly	M	G.Schmelz	M	J.Chapman
1B	P.Werden	1B	D.Brouthers	1B	J.Carney	1B	M.Lehane	1B	H.Taylor
2B	S.Wise	2B	C.Stricker	2B	Y.Robinson	2B	J.Crooks	2B	T.Shinnick
SS	G.Van Haltren	SS	P.Radford	SS	J.Canavan	SS	B.Wheelock	SS	H.Jennings
3B	P.Gilbert	3B	D.Farrell	3B	A.Whitney	3B	B.Kuehne	3B	O.Beard
LF	B.Johnson	LF	H.Richardson	LF	E.Andrews	LF	C.Duffee	LF	P.Donovan
CF	C.Welch	CF	T.Brown	CF	D.Johnston	CF	J.McTamany	CF	F.Weaver
RF	I.Ray	RF	H.Duffy	RF	E.Seery	RF	J.Sneed	RF	J.Wolf
C	W.Robinson	C	M.Murphy	C	K.Kelly	C	J.Donahue	C	J.Ryan
C	G.Townsend	3	B.Joyce	C	F.Vaughn	OC	J.O'Connor	CS	T.Cahill
S	J.McGraw	O	J.McGeachy	C	J.Hurley	O	L.Twitchell	3	B.Kuehne
S2	J.Walsh	O	J.Irwin	O	L.Marr	C	T.Dowse	C1	P.Cook
O	L.Hardie	/S	A.Irwin	/2	B.Clingman	3	T.O'Rourke	O	M.Cline
/S	J.O'Connell	/C	K.Kelly	/2	C.Bastian	3	J.Donnelly	S	H.Raymond
P	S.McMahon	/C	T.Cotter	/2	J.Burke	3	E.Cleveland	3	J.Irwin
P	B.Cunningham	/O	T.Dowd					2	S.LaRoque
P	K.Madden	/C	T.Donahue	P	F.Dwyer	P	P.Knell	/O	J.Long
P	J.Healy	/C	F.Quinlan	P	E.Crane	P	H.Gastright	/C	A.Schellhase
		/C	M.Flynn	P	W.Mains	P	J.Dolan	/3	P.Fox
/P	J.Bakely	P	G.Haddock	P	W.McGill	P	J.Easton	/2	J.Gerhardt
		P	C.Buffinton					/2	P.Pettee
		P	D.O'Brien	/P	M.Kilroy	/P	J.Leiper	/C	G.Briggs
		P	B.Daley	/P	C.Bell	/P	D.Clarke	/2	J.Wentz
				/P	K.Keenan	/P	J.Sullivan	/1	J.Darragh
				/P	W.Widner	/P	B.Lyston	/3	N.Reeder
		/P	C.Griffith	/P	J.Slagle	/P	E.Clark		
		/P	J.Fitzgerald					P	J.Fitzgerald
		/P	K.Madden					P	J.Meekin
								P	R.Ehret
								P	S.Stratton
								P	J.Doran
								P	E.Daily
								P	C.Bell
								/P	G.Boone

MILWAUKEE		PHILADELPHIA		ST.LOUIS		WASHINGTON	
M	C.Cushman	M	B.Sharsig	M	C.Comiskey	M	S.Trott
1B	J.Carney	M	G.Wood	1B	C.Comiskey	M	P.Snyder
2B	J.Canavan	1B	H.Larkin	2B	B.Eagan	M	D.Shannon
SS	G.Shoch	2B	B.Hallman	SS	S.Fuller	M	S.Griffin
3B	G.Alberts	SS	T.Corcoran	3B	D.Lyons	1B	M.McQuery
LF	A.Dalrymple	3B	J.Mulvey	LF	T.O'Neill	2B	T.Dowd
CF	E.Burke	LF	G.Wood	CF	D.Hoy	SS	G.Hatfield
RF	H.Earl	CF	P.Corkhill	RF	T.McCarthy	3B	B.Alvord
C	F.Vaughn	RF	L.Cross	C	J.Boyle	LF	E.Beecher
		C	J.Milligan			CF	P.Hines
C3	J.Grim			CO	J.Munyan	RF	L.Murphy
/2	B.Pettit	O	J.McTamany	C	D.Darling	C	D.McGuire
/O	T.Letcher	O	J.McGeachy	/O	J.Visner		
		OP	B.Sanders	/C	P.Cook	1	A.McCauley
P	G.Davies	O	E.Beecher	/3	J.Ricks	OC	S.Sutcliffe
P	F.Killen	C	D.McKeough	/2	P.McSweeney	C	P.Lohman
P	F.Dwyer	/S	B.Clymer	/2	M.McQuaid	O	E.Curtis
		/O	P.Friel	/3	A.Whitney	2	P.Smith
/P	J.Hughey	/O	B.Matthews	/2	Y.Robinson	O	J.Burns
/P	W.Mains			/C	B.Zies	O	E.Daily
		P	G.Weyhing	/3	H.Fuller	O	P.Donovan
		P	E.Chamberlain	/C	J.Schultz	S	S.Griffin
		P	W.Calihan			O	J.Visner
				P	J.Stivetts	S	D.Shannon
		/P	S.Bowman	P	W.McGill	O	M.Slattery
		/P	G.Meakim	P	C.Griffith	3	J.Davis
		/P	M.Sullivan	P	J.Neale	S	T.McLaughlin
				P	G.Rettger	/3	W.Smalley
						/1	P.Snyder
				/P	J.Easton	/2	F.Dunlap
				/P	H.Burrell	/C	T.Hart
				/P	T.Breitenstein	/C	M.Murray
				/P	J.Duryea		
						P	K.Carsey
						P	F.Foreman
						P	J.Bakely
						/P	E.Eiteljorge
						/P	E.Cassian
						/P	B.Freeman
						/P	B.Miller
						/P	G.Keefe
						/P	M.Duke
						/P	B.Quarles
						/P	J.Mace

TEAM	G	W	L	PCT	GB	R	OR	AB	H	2B	3B	HR	BB	SO	AVG	OBP	SLG	PRO	PRO+	BR	/A	PF	CHI	RC	SB	CS	SBA	SBR
BOS	139	93	42	.689		1028	675	4889	1341	163	100	52	651	499	.274	.367	.380	.747	121	127	142	99	106	868	447			
STL	141	86	52	.623	8.5	976	753	5005	1330	169	51	58	625	440	.266	.357	.355	.712	95	65	-72	115	106	753	283			
MIL	36	21	15	.583	22.5	227	156	1271	332	58	15	13	107	114	.261	.333	.361	.694	86	3	-40	120	106	173	47			
BAL	139	71	64	.526	22	850	798	4771	1217	142	99	30	551	553	.255	.346	.345	.691	102	22	13	101	101	705	342			
PHI	143	73	66	.525	22	817	794	5039	1301	182	123	55	447	548	.258	.328	.376	.704	103	23	-3	103	95	686	149			
COL	138	61	76	.445	33	702	777	4697	1113	154	61	20	529	530	.237	.319	.308	.627	89	-93	-54	94	101	565	280			
CIN	102	43	57	.430	32.5	549	643	3574	838	105	58	28	428	385	.234	.322	.320	.642	81	-52	-101	109	99	432	164			
LOU	141	55	84	.396	40	713	890	4833	1247	130	69	17	443	473	.258	.329	.324	.653	93	-52	-42	99	95	606	219			
WAS	139	44	91	.326	49	691	1067	4715	1183	147	84	19	468	485	.251	.330	.330	.658	97	-43	-9	96	93	597	219			
TOT	559					6553		38794	9902	1250	660	292	4249	4027	.255	.338	.344	.682						2161				

TEAM	CG	SH	SV	IP	H	H/G	HR	BB	SO	RAT	ERA	ERA+	OAV	OOB	PR	/A	PF	CPI	FA	E	DP	FW	PW	BW	SBW	DIF
BOS	108	9	7	1219²	1158	8.5	42	497	524	12.6	3.03	115	.242	.321	94	62	94	109	.934	392	115	4.0	5.3	12.2		4.0
STL	103	8	5	1222²	1106	8.1	50	576	621	12.9	3.27	129	.234	.325	61	126	113	102	.920	468	91	-.2	10.9	-6.2		12.5
MIL	35	3	0	309²	291	8.5	6	120	137	12.2	2.50	176	.241	.314	42	65	118	122	.922	116	20	.2	5.6	-3.4		.7
BAL	118	6	2	1217	1238	9.2	33	472	408	13.1	3.43	109	.255	.329	39	40	100	103	.915	503	103	-2.6	3.4	1.1		1.6
PHI	135	3	0	1233²	1274	9.3	35	520	533	13.6	4.01	95	.258	.338	-40	-27	103	93	.933	389	109	4.9	-2.3	-.3		1.2
COL	118	6	0	1213¹	1141	8.5	29	588	502	13.5	3.75	92	.241	.336	-4	-39	93	93	.935	379	126	4.5	-3.4	-4.7		-4.0
CIN	86	2	1	902	921	9.2	20	446	331	14.2	3.43	120	.256	.347	29	68	111	112	.913	389	68	-3.1	5.9	-8.7		-1.1
LOU	128	9	1	1226	1353	9.9	33	464	485	13.8	4.27	85	.271	.341	-75	-85	98	92	.922	458	113	.4	-7.3	-3.6		-4.0
WAS	123	2	2	1181	1420	10.8	44	566	486	15.9	4.83	77	.288	.374	-146	-144	101	101	.900	589	95	-7.7	-12.4	-.8		-2.6
TOT	954	48	18	9725		9.2				13.6	3.72		.255	.338					.922	3683	840					

Runs		Hits		Doubles		Triples		Home Runs		Total Bases	
Brown-Bos	177	Brown-Bos	189	Milligan-Phi	35	Brown-Bos	21	Farrell-Bos	12	Brown-Bos	276
VanHaltren-Bal	136	VanHaltren-Bal	180	Brown-Bos	30	Brouthers-Bos	19	Milligan-Phi	11	VanHaltren-Bal	251
Hoy-StL	136	Duffy-Bos	180	O'Neill-StL	28	Canavan-Cin-Mil	18	Lyons-StL	11	Brouthers-Bos	249
Duffy-Bos	134	McCarthy-StL	179	Duffee-Col	28	Werden-Bal	18			Duffy-Bos	243
McCarthy-StL	127	Brouthers-Bos	170	Larkin-Phi	27					McCarthy-StL	236

Runs Batted In		Runs Produced		Bases On Balls		Batting Average		On Base Percentage		Slugging Average	
Farrell-Bos	110	Brown-Bos	244	Hoy-StL	119	Brouthers-Bos	.350	Brouthers-Bos	.471	Brouthers-Bos	.512
Duffy-Bos	110	Duffy-Bos	235	Crooks-Col	103	Duffy-Bos	.336	Lyons-StL	.445	Milligan-Phi	.505
Brouthers-Bos	109	Brouthers-Bos	221	McTamany-Col-Phi	101	Brown-Bos	.321	Hoy-StL	.424	Farrell-Bos	.474
Milligan-Phi	106	McCarthy-StL	214	Radford-Bos	96	O'Neill-StL	.321	Seery-Cin	.423	Brown-Bos	.469
Werden-Bal	104	VanHaltren-Bal	210	Johnson-Bal	89	VanHaltren-Bal	.318	Duffy-Bos	.408	Cross-Phi	.458

Production		Adjusted Production		Batter Runs		Adjusted Batter Runs		Clutch Hitting Index		Runs Created	
Brouthers-Bos	.983	Brouthers-Bos	184	Brouthers-Bos	57.0	Brouthers-Bos	59.2	Sneed-Col	132	Brown-Bos	155
Milligan-Phi	.903	Milligan-Phi	153	Lyons-StL	39.2	Brown-Bos	37.2	Comiskey-StL	128	Duffy-Bos	137
Lyons-StL	.900	Brown-Bos	150	Brown-Bos	35.2	Duffy-Bos	34.0	Duffy-Bos	128	Brouthers-Bos	135
Brown-Bos	.865	Duffy-Bos	149	Milligan-Phi	33.3	Milligan-Phi	30.0	Ray-Bal	128	VanHaltren-Bal	133
Duffy-Bos	.861	Farrell-Bos	147	Duffy-Bos	32.1	Joyce-Bos	28.9	Radford-Bos	127	Hoy-StL	114

Total Average		Stolen Bases		Stolen Base Average		Stolen Base Runs		Fielding Runs		Total Player Rating	
Brouthers-Bos	1.237	Brown-Bos	106					Stricker-Bos	24.2	Farrell-Bos	4.4
Brown-Bos	1.140	Duffy-Bos	85					Radford-Bos	19.9	Brouthers-Bos	3.8
Duffy-Bos	1.104	VanHaltren-Bal	75					Crooks-Col	19.6	Crooks-Col	3.3
VanHaltren-Bal	1.039	Hoy-StL	59					Eagan-StL	19.5	Milligan-Phi	3.1
Lyons-StL	1.036	Radford-Bos	55					Farrell-Bos	19.0	Radford-Bos	2.9

Wins		Win Percentage		Games		Complete Games		Shutouts		Saves	
McMahon-Bal	35	Buffinton-Bos	.763	Stivetts-StL	64	McMahon-Bal	53	McMahon-Bal	5	O'Brien-Bos	2
Haddock-Bos	34	Haddock-Bos	.756	McMahon-Bal	61	Weyhing-Phi	51	Knell-Col	5	Daley-Bos	2
Stivetts-StL	33	Weyhing-Phi	.608	Knell-Col	58	Knell-Col	47	Haddock-Bos	5		
Weyhing-Phi	31	Stivetts-StL	.600	Carsey-Was	54	Carsey-Was	46				
Buffinton-Bos	29	McMahon-Bal	.593	Weyhing-Phi	52	Chamberlain-Phi	44				

Innings Pitched		Fewest Hits/Game		Fewest BB/Game		Strikeouts		Strikeouts/Game		Ratio	
McMahon-Bal	503.0	Knell-Col	7.07	Stratton-Lou	1.78	Stivetts-StL	259	Meekin-Lou	5.68	Buffinton-Bos	10.64
Knell-Col	462.0	Stivetts-StL	7.30	Sanders-Phi	2.30	Knell-Col	228	Stivetts-StL	5.30	Haddock-Bos	11.40
Weyhing-Phi	450.0	Buffinton-Bos	7.50	McMahon-Bal	2.67	Weyhing-Phi	219	McGill-Cin-StL	4.96	McMahon-Bal	11.79
Stivetts-StL	440.0	Crane-Cin	7.78	Ehret-Lou	2.85	McMahon-Bal	219	Daley-Bos	4.83	Weyhing-Phi	12.40
Carsey-Was	415.0	Haddock-Bos	7.82	Griffith-StL-Bos	2.90	Chamberlain-Phi	204	Chamberlain-Phi	4.53	Stivetts-StL	12.42

Earned Run Average		Adjusted ERA		Opponents' Batting Avg.		Opponents' On Base Pct.		Starter Runs		Adjusted Starter Runs	
Crane-Cin	2.45	Crane-Cin	168	Knell-Col	.209	Buffinton-Bos	.285	Haddock-Bos	51.9	Stivetts-StL	65.5
Haddock-Bos	2.49	Stivetts-StL	147	Stivetts-StL	.215	Haddock-Bos	.299	McMahon-Bal	50.9	McMahon-Bal	51.7
Buffinton-Bos	2.55	Haddock-Bos	140	Buffinton-Bos	.219	McMahon-Bal	.306	Buffinton-Bos	47.3	Crane-Cin	46.3
McMahon-Bal	2.81	Buffinton-Bos	137	Crane-Cin	.225	Weyhing-Phi	.317	Stivetts-StL	41.8	Haddock-Bos	42.0
Stivetts-StL	2.86	Mains-Cin-Mil	134	Haddock-Bos	.226	Stivetts-StL	.317	Knell-Col	40.9	Buffinton-Bos	37.8

Clutch Pitching Index		Relief Runs		Adjusted Relief Runs		Relief Ranking		Total Pitcher Index		Total Baseball Ranking	
Daley-Bos	134							Stivetts-StL	7.7	Stivetts-StL	7.5
Crane-Cin	128							Haddock-Bos	5.3	Haddock-Bos	5.0
O'Brien-Bos	123							McMahon-Bal	5.0	McMahon-Bal	4.9
Mains-Cin-Mil	122							Buffinton-Bos	3.6	Farrell-Bos	4.4
Foreman-Was	113							Crane-Cin	3.5	Brouthers-Bos	3.8

January 9 "Slide, Kelly, Slide," by George Gaskin, makes the pop music charts, the first baseball song to do so.

March 1 The first meeting of the united NL and AA takes place in New York. Only four teams from the collapsed American Association are invited to join the NL, which will expand to 12 teams with a 154-game schedule split into two championship series.

April 17 The first Sunday game in NL history features the hometown Cincinnati Reds defeating the St. Louis Browns 5-1. Bid McPhee contributes a home run.

April 30* Dr. S. B. Talcott, superintendent of the State Lunatic Asylum in New York, declares in the *New York Clipper* that "I believe that baseball is a homeopathic cure for lunacy. It is a kind of craze in itself, and gives the lunatics a new kind of crazing to relieve them of the malady which afflicts their minds."

June 6 President Benjamin Harrison watches Washington go down to a 7-4 defeat to Cincinnati in 11 innings. It marks the first visit to a major league game by a U.S. president.

June 10 Orioles catcher Wilbert Robinson goes 7-for-7 and bats in 11 runs, as Baltimore defeats the St. Louis Browns, 25-7.

June 30 Tony Mullane of Cincinnati and Ad Gumbert of Chicago pitch 20 innings in a 7–7 standoff. It is the longest major league game played in the 19th century.

July 11 Boston, having clinched the first-half championship, plays an unusual game at Chicago with team members, led by King Kelly, dressed in outlandish costumes and wearing beards.

August 18 In the course of a 13-4 win over Baltimore, Browns left fielder Cliff Carroll attempts to field a ground ball, but he misjudges it, and the ball becomes lodged in his shirt pocket. Before he can extricate it the Orioles batter makes it to third base. St. Louis owner Chris Von der Ahe is so outraged that he fines Carroll $50 and suspends him without pay for the rest of the season. Carroll appeals the fine and the suspension at the end of the season but is turned down.

October 15 Charles "Bumpus" Jones of Cincinnati, making his major league debut, pitches a no-hit game over Pittsburgh, winning, 7–1. Jones, who won 16 games in a row in the minors, will have a tough time the following season when the pitching distance is increased. He will go 1-4 with a 10.93 ERA and never pitch in the majors again.

October 17 To settle the championship of baseball's first split season, Boston, the first-half winner, starts a five-game series with Cleveland, the second-half champ. Jack Stivetts and Cy Young battle to an 11-inning scoreless tie.

November 17 NL magnates conclude a four-day meeting in Chicago where they agree to shorten the 1893 schedule to 132 games and drop the double championship concept.

	BALTIMORE		BOSTON		BROOKLYN		CHICAGO		CINCINNATI		CLEVELAND
M	G.Van Haltren	M	F.Selee	M	M.Ward	M	C.Anson	M	C.Comiskey	M	P.Tebeau
M	J.Waltz	1B	T.Tucker	1B	D.Brouthers	1B	C.Anson	1B	C.Comiskey	1B	J.Virtue
M	N.Hanlon	2B	J.Quinn	2B	J.Ward	2B	J.Canavan	2B	B.McPhee	2B	C.Childs
1B	S.Sutcliffe	SS	H.Long	SS	T.Corcoran	SS	B.Dahlen	SS	G.Smith	SS	E.McKean
2B	C.Stricker	3B	B.Nash	3B	B.Joyce	3B	J.Parrott	3B	A.Latham	3B	G.Davis
SS	T.O'Rourke	LF	B.Lowe	LF	D.O'Brien	LF	W.Wilmot	LF	T.O'Neill	LF	J.Burkett
3B	B.Shindle	CF	H.Duffy	CF	M.Griffin	CF	J.Ryan	CF	P.Browning	CF	J.McAleer
LF	H.Stovey	RF	T.McCarthy	RF	O.Burns	RF	S.Dungan	RF	B.Holliday	RF	J.O'Connor
CF	C.Welch	C	K.Kelly	C	C.Daily	C	P.Schriver	C	M.Murphy	C	C.Zimmer
RF	G.Van Haltren										
C	W.Robinson	C	C.Ganzel	3O	T.Daly	O2	G.Decker	C1	F.Vaughn	3	P.Tebeau
		O	H.Stovey	C	T.Kinslow	S	J.Cooney	SO	F.Genins	O	J.Doyle
CO	J.Gunson	C	C.Bennett	OP	D.Foutz	C	M.Kittridge	O	G.Wood		
SO	G.Shoch			O	H.Collins	O	C.Newman	O	J.Halligan	P	C.Young
O2	J.McGraw	P	K.Nichols					O	C.Welch	P	N.Cuppy
1	L.Whistler	P	J.Stivetts	P	G.Haddock	P	B.Hutchison	C	J.Harrington	P	J.Clarkson
O	P.Ward	P	H.Staley	P	E.Stein	P	A.Gumbert	P	E.Chamberlain	P	G.Davies
O1	J.Halligan	P	J.Clarkson	P	B.Hart	P	P.Luby	P	T.Mullane		
2	J.Pickett			P	B.Kennedy			P	F.Dwyer	/P	G.Rettger
O	G.Wood					/P	H.DeMiller	P	M.Sullivan		
				/P	B.Inks						
P	S.McMahon							P	B.Rhines		
P	G.Cobb							/P	J.Duryea		
P	T.Vickery							/P	D.Daub		
P	C.Buffinton							/P	W.McGill		
/P	J.Healy										
/P	C.Schmit										
/P	B.Stephens										

	LOUISVILLE		NEW YORK		PHILADELPHIA		PITTSBURGH		ST.LOUIS		WASHINGTON
M	J.Chapman	M	P.Powers	M	H.Wright	M	A.Buckenberger	M	J.Glasscock	M	B.Barnie
M	F.Pfeffer	1B	B.Ewing	1B	R.Connor	M	T.Burns	M	C.Stricker	M	A.Irwin
1B	L.Whistler	2B	E.Burke	2B	B.Hallman	M	A.Buckenberger	M	J.Crooks	M	D.Richardson
2B	F.Pfeffer	SS	S.Fuller	SS	B.Allen	1B	J.Beckley	M	G.Gore	1B	H.Larkin
SS	H.Jennings	3B	D.Lyons	3B	C.Reilly	2B	L.Bierbauer	M	B.Caruthers	2B	T.Dowd
3B	B.Kuehne	LF	J.O'Rourke	LF	B.Hamilton	SS	F.Shugart	1B	P.Werden	SS	D.Richardson
LF	F.Weaver	CF	H.Lyons	CF	E.Delahanty	3B	D.Farrell	2B	J.Crooks	3B	Y.Robinson
CF	T.Brown	RF	M.Tiernan	RF	S.Thompson	LF	E.Smith	SS	J.Glasscock	LF	C.Duffee
RF	H.Taylor	C	J.Boyle	C	J.Clements	CF	D.Miller	3B	G.Pinkney	CF	D.Hoy
C	J.Grim					RF	P.Donovan	LF	C.Carroll	RF	P.Radford
		2C	J.Doyle	3C	L.Cross	C	C.Mack	CF	S.Brodie	C	D.McGuire
3	C.Bassett	2O	H.Richardson	3	J.Mulvey			RF	B.Caruthers		
C	B.Merritt	O	G.Gore			O	P.Corkhill	C	D.Buckley	C1	J.Milligan
O	E.Seery	1	J.McMahon	P	G.Weyhing	O	J.Kelley			O	L.Twitchell
C1	T.Dowse	2	C.Bassett	P	K.Carsey			O	G.Moriarity	O	P.Donovan
O	P.Browning	OC	J.Fields	P	T.Keefe	P	M.Baldwin	3	L.Camp	S	T.Berger
				P	D.Esper	P	R.Ehret	2	C.Stricker		
P	S.Stratton	P	A.Rusie			P	A.Terry	C	B.Moran	P	F.Killen
P	B.Sanders	P	S.King	P	P.Knell	P	P.Galvin	O	G.Gore	P	B.Abbey
P	F.Clausen	P	E.Crane	/P	J.Taylor					P	B.Knell
P	J.Meekin					/P	B.Gumbert	P	K.Gleason	P	J.Duryea
P	A.Jones					/P	F.Woodcock	P	T.Breitenstein	P	J.Meekin
						/P	K.Camp	P	P.Hawley		
P	L.Viau					/P	D.Esper	P	C.Getzien	P	H.Gastright
/P	G.Hemming							P	B.Hawke	P	F.Foreman
/P	J.Fitzgerald									/P	J.Dolan
/P	J.Healy							P	P.Galvin	/P	A.Jones
								P	F.Dwyer	/P	M.Kilroy
								/P	J.Easton	/P	B.Inks

TEAM	G	W	L	PCT	GB	R	OR	AB	H	2B	3B	HR	BB	SO	AVG	OBP	SLG	PRO	PRO+	BR	/A	PF	CHI	RC	SB	CS	SBA	SBR
BOS	152	102	48	.680		862	649	5301	1324	203	51	34	526	492	.250	.325	.327	.652	93	18	-55	109	108	689	338			
CLE	153	93	56	.624	8.5	855	613	5412	1375	196	96	26	552	536	.254	.328	.340	.668	103	48	14	104	101	694	225			
BRO	158	95	59	.617	9	935	733	5485	1439	183	105	30	629	506	.262	.344	.350	.694	120	109	144	96	101	822	409			
PHI	155	87	66	.569	16.5	860	690	5413	1420	225	95	50	528	515	.262	.334	.367	.701	118	107	110	100	95	753	216			
CIN	155	82	68	.547	20	766	731	5349	1288	155	75	44	503	474	.241	.311	.322	.633	98	-23	-12	99	101	635	270			
PIT	155	80	73	.523	23.5	802	796	5469	1288	143	108	38	435	453	.236	.297	.322	.619	92	-59	-62	100	110	604	222			
CHI	147	70	76	.479	30	635	735	5063	1188	149	92	26	427	482	.235	.299	.316	.615	90	-60	-67	101	94	561	233			
NY	153	71	80	.470	31.5	811	826	5291	1326	173	85	39	510	474	.251	.320	.338	.658	106	25	38	98	101	686	301			
LOU	154	63	89	.414	40	649	804	5334	1208	133	61	18	443	508	.226	.290	.284	.574	85	-135	-85	92	102	533	275			
WAS	153	58	93	.384	44.5	731	869	5204	1245	149	78	37	529	553	.239	.314	.319	.633	100	-18	4	97	98	624	276			
STL	155	56	94	.373	46	703	922	5259	1187	138	53	45	607	491	.226	.312	.298	.610	95	-55	-19	95	96	568	209			
BAL	152	46	101	.313	54.5	779	1020	5296	1342	160	111	30	499	480	.253	.325	.343	.668	104	44	22	103	95	680	227			
TOT	921					9388		63876	15630	2007	1010	417	6178	5964	.245	.317	.327	.644						3201				

TEAM	CG	SH	SV	IP	H	H/G	HR	BB	SO	RAT	ERA	ERA+	OAV	OOB	PR	/A	PF	CPI	FA	E	DP	FW	PW	BW	SBW	DIF
BOS	142	15	1	1336	1156	7.8	41	460	514	11.1	2.86	123	.224	.292	64	96	107	93	.929	454	127	.5	8.9	-5.1		22.7
CLE	140	11	2	1336	1178	7.9	28	413	472	10.9	2.41	140	.228	.289	130	143	103	107	.935	407	95	3.4	13.2	1.3		.6
BRO	132	12	5	1405²	1285	8.2	26	600	597	12.4	3.25	97	.234	.315	6	-14	96	95	.940	398	98	4.8	-1.3	13.3		1.2
PHI	131	10	5	1379	1297	8.5	24	492	502	12.0	2.93	111	.239	.309	54	47	99	103	.939	393	128	4.5	4.4	10.2		-8.6
CIN	130	8	2	1377¹	1327	8.7	39	535	437	12.5	3.17	103	.243	.317	18	15	99	104	.939	402	140	4.0	1.4	-1.1		2.7
PIT	130	3	1	1347¹	1300	8.7	28	537	455	12.7	3.10	106	.244	.320	28	27	100	106	.927	483	113	-.7	2.5	-5.7		7.4
CHI	133	6	1	1298	1269	8.8	35	424	518	12.0	3.16	105	.244	.308	18	22	101	100	.932	424	85	1.3	2.0	-6.2		-.2
NY	139	5	1	1322²	1165	7.9	32	635	650	12.6	3.29	98	.227	.318	-1	-11	98	94	.912	565	97	-5.8	-1.0	3.5		-1.2
LOU	147	9	0	1346	1358	9.1	26	447	430	12.3	3.34	92	.252	.313	-8	-41	93	97	.928	471	133	-.2	-3.8	-7.9		-1.2
WAS	129	5	3	1315¹	1293	8.8	40	556	479	13.1	3.46	94	.247	.327	-26	-32	99	102	.916	547	122	-4.8	-3.0	.4		-10.1
STL	139	4	1	1344²	1466	9.8	47	543	478	13.8	4.20	76	.267	.339	-137	-151	97	96	.929	452	100	1.1	-14.0	-1.1		-4.4
BAL	131	2	2	1298²	1537	10.7	51	536	437	14.7	4.28	80	.284	.353	-144	-124	104	106	.910	584	100	-7.1	-11.5	2.0		-10.9
TOT	1623	90	24	16106²		8.7				12.5	3.28		.245	.317					.928	5580	1338					

Split Season: First-half Winner BOS (52-22); Second-half Winner CLE (53-23)

Runs		Hits		Doubles		Triples		Home Runs		Total Bases	
Childs-Cle	136	Brouthers-Bro	197	Connor-Phi	37	Delahanty-Phi	21	Holliday-Cin	13	Brouthers-Bro	282
Hamilton-Phi	132	Thompson-Phi	186	Long-Bos	33	Virtue-Cle	20	Connor-Phi	12	Holliday-Cin	270
Duffy-Bos	125	Duffy-Bos	184	Delahanty-Phi	30	Brouthers-Bro	20	Ryan-Chi	10	Thompson-Phi	263
Connor-Phi	123	Hamilton-Phi	183	Brouthers-Bro	30	Dahlen-Chi	19	Beckley-Pit	10	Connor-Phi	261
Brouthers-Bro	121	Long-Bos	181	Zimmer-Cle	29	Beckley-Pit	19	Thompson-Phi	9	Duffy-Bos	251

Runs Batted In		Runs Produced		Bases On Balls		Batting Average		On Base Percentage		Slugging Average	
Brouthers-Bro	124	Brouthers-Bro	240	Crooks-StL	136	Brouthers-Bro	.335	Childs-Cle	.443	Delahanty-Phi	.495
Thompson-Phi	104	Thompson-Phi	204	Childs-Cle	117	Hamilton-Phi	.330	Brouthers-Bro	.432	Brouthers-Bro	.480
Larkin-Was	96	Duffy-Bos	201	Connor-Phi	116	Childs-Cle	.317	Hamilton-Phi	.423	Ewing-NY	.473
Burns-Bro	96	Holliday-Cin	192	McCarthy-Bos	93	Burns-Bro	.315	Connor-Phi	.420	Connor-Phi	.463
Beckley-Pit	96					Ewing-NY	.310	Crooks-StL	.400	Burns-Bro	.454

Production		Adjusted Production		Batter Runs		Adjusted Batter Runs		Clutch Hitting Index		Runs Created	
Brouthers-Bro	.911	Brouthers-Bro	182	Brouthers-Bro	56.9	Brouthers-Bro	62.5	McKean-Cle	165	Brouthers-Bro	138
Connor-Phi	.883	Connor-Phi	167	Connor-Phi	50.6	Connor-Phi	51.0	Pfeffer-Lou	142	Hamilton-Phi	123
Delahanty-Phi	.855	Burns-Bro	163	Childs-Cle	45.5	Burns-Bro	41.8	Nash-Bos	135	Connor-Phi	122
Burns-Bro	.849	Delahanty-Phi	158	Hamilton-Phi	39.0	Childs-Cle	40.1	Larkin-Was	131	VanHaltren-Bal-Pit	117
Childs-Cle	.841	Hamilton-Phi	153	Burns-Bro	37.3	Hamilton-Phi	39.3	Brouthers-Bro	128	Holliday-Cin	114

Total Average		Stolen Bases		Stolen Base Average		Stolen Base Runs		Fielding Runs		Total Player Rating	
Brouthers-Bro	1.056	Ward-Bro	88					D.Richardson-Was	57.6	Brouthers-Bro	6.1
Connor-Phi	1.018	Brown-Lou	78					Shindle-Bal	35.5	Dahlen-Chi	4.6
Hamilton-Phi	1.005	Latham-Cin	66					Bierbauer-Pit	31.7	McPhee-Cin	4.5
Childs-Cle	.982	Hoy-Was	60					McPhee-Cin	25.3	Hamilton-Phi	4.3
Burns-Bro	.943	Dahlen-Chi	60					Dahlen-Chi	25.2	D.Richardson-Was	4.0

Wins		Win Percentage		Games		Complete Games		Shutouts		Saves	
Young-Cle	36	Young-Cle	.750	Hutchison-Chi	75	Hutchison-Chi	67	Young-Cle	9	Weyhing-Phi	3
Hutchison-Chi	36	Terry-Bal-Pit	.692	Rusie-NY	65	Rusie-NY	59	Weyhing-Phi	6	Duryea-Cin-Was	2
Stivetts-Bos	35	Haddock-Bro	.690	Killen-Was	60	Nichols-Bos	49	Stein-Bro	6		
Nichols-Bos	35	Staley-Bos	.688	Weyhing-Phi	59	Young-Cle	48				
				Baldwin-Pit	56						

Innings Pitched		Fewest Hits/Game		Fewest BB/Game		Strikeouts		Strikeouts/Game		Ratio	
Hutchison-Chi	622.0	Mullane-Cin	6.77	Stratton-Lou	1.79	Hutchison-Chi	312	Kennedy-Bro	5.09	Young-Cle	9.77
Rusie-NY	541.0	Rusie-NY	6.82	Dwyer-StL-Cin	1.98	Rusie-NY	304	Rusie-NY	5.06	Nichols-Bos	10.63
Weyhing-Phi	469.2	Terry-Bal-Pit	6.94	Sanders-Lou	2.08	Weyhing-Phi	202	Stein-Bro	4.53	Stratton-Lou	10.77
Killen-Was	459.2	Young-Cle	7.21	Young-Cle	2.34	Nichols-Bos	192	Hutchison-Chi	4.51	Keefe-Phi	10.83
		Duryea-Cin-Was	7.25	Ehret-Pit	2.36	Stein-Bro	190	Crane-NY	4.30	Mullane-Cin	11.01

Earned Run Average		Adjusted ERA		Opponents' Batting Avg.		Opponents' On Base Pct.		Starter Runs		Adjusted Starter Runs	
Young-Cle	1.93	Young-Cle	176	Mullane-Cin	.201	Young-Cle	.266	Young-Cle	68.3	Young-Cle	73.4
Keefe-Phi	2.36	J.Clarkson-Bos-Cle	139	Rusie-NY	.202	Nichols-Bos	.283	Hutchison-Chi	36.0	J.Clarkson-Bos-Cle	41.3
J.Clarkson-Bos-Cle	2.48	Keefe-Phi	138	Terry-Bal-Pit	.205	Stratton-Lou	.286	J.Clarkson-Bos-Cle	35.0	Hutchison-Chi	38.5
Cuppy-Cle	2.51	Cuppy-Cle	135	Young-Cle	.211	Keefe-Phi	.287	Weyhing-Phi	32.4	Cuppy-Cle	36.5
Terry-Bal-Pit	2.57	Davies-Cle	131	Duryea-Cin-Was	.212	Mullane-Cin	.290	Keefe-Phi	32.3	Nichols-Bos	33.6

Clutch Pitching Index		Relief Runs		Adjusted Relief Runs		Relief Ranking		Total Pitcher Index		Total Baseball Ranking	
Sullivan-Cin	136							Young-Cle	6.6	Young-Cle	6.6
Galvin-Pit-StL	122							Hutchison-Chi	4.6	Brouthers-Bro	6.1
Vickery-Bal	116							Cuppy-Cle	3.8	Dahlen-Chi	4.6
McMahon-Bal	115							Stivetts-Bos	3.7	McPhee-Cin	4.5
Luby-Chi	115							J.Clarkson-Bos-Cle	3.3	Hutchison-Chi	4.5

January 14* The Cuban Giants, perhaps the nation's best black baseball team, announce their desire to join the proposed Middle States League. Their application is rejected.

February 4* The first recorded version of *"Casey at the Bat,"* as recited by Russell Hunting, hits the charts. DeWolf Hopper's more famous version will not be released until October 1906.

March 7 In arguably the most significant rule change in major league history, the NL eliminates the pitching box and adds a pitcher's rubber five feet behind the previous back line of the box, establishing the modern pitching distance of 60 feet six inches. In addition, bats flattened on one side to facilitate bunting are banned.

May 19 Held scoreless for the first eight innings, both Brooklyn and the Boston Beaneaters score three runs in the ninth to send the game into extra innings. Boston's Billy Nash hits the ball over the left field fence in the bottom of the ninth, but he stays on third base "to bother the pitcher." The tactic works, as Nash does

score. Both teams score one run in the 10th—Boston scoring on another Nash blow over the left field fence, which he runs out this time. Boston finally claims the game after a 12-inning struggle, 5–4.

June 14 George Davis becomes the first player in major league history to hit a home run and a triple in the same inning as his Giants overcome the Chicago Colts, 11-10. Davis' feat will not be matched until 1926, when the Detroit Tigers' Bob Fothergill turns the trick.

July 7 Louisville officials, frustrated by their inability to sell alcohol or play Sunday baseball in their new ballpark—located in the suburb of Parkland, whose laws proscribe such activities—get permission from the Kentucky Legislature to annex the land on which the ballpark is located without the consent of Parkland residents. Alcohol sales and Sunday baseball commence almost immediately.

August 7 Facing a left-handed Brooklyn pitcher, New York first baseman Roger Connor bats right-handed for the first time in his career and slugs two homers and a single in a 10–3 win.

September 28 After moving into the lead with three runs in the top of the ninth, Philadelphia players allow themselves to be retired quickly in order to finish the game before it is called on account of darkness. However, Cleveland foils their plans by scoring four runs in the bottom of the ninth to win, 11–10.

September 30 It's a good day for Joe Quinn. In pregame ceremonies, the Cardinals second baseman is honored by *The Sporting News* as the most popular baseball player in America, and receives a gold watch. He then collects eight hits in the doubleheader against Boston, the first player to accomplish that feat.

October 14 Baseball legend Harry Wright suggests that umpires keep the ball-strike count a secret until the at bat is concluded. He feels this rule change will increase offense.

November 21* Ban Johnson is named president, secretary, and treasurer of the recently reorganized Western League. Under Johnson's leadership the Western League will prosper.

BALTIMORE		BOSTON		BROOKLYN		CHICAGO		CINCINNATI		CLEVELAND	
M	N.Hanlon	M	F.Selee	M	D.Foutz	M	C.Anson	M	C.Comiskey	M	P.Tebeau
1B	H.Taylor	1B	T.Tucker	1B	D.Brouthers	1B	C.Anson	1B	C.Comiskey	1B	J.Virtue
2B	H.Reitz	2B	B.Lowe	2B	D.Richardson	2B	B.Lange	2B	B.McPhee	2B	C.Childs
SS	J.McGraw	SS	H.Long	SS	T.Corcoran	SS	B.Dahlen	SS	G.Smith	SS	E.McKean
3B	B.Shindle	3B	B.Nash	3B	T.Daly	3B	J.Parrott	3B	A.Latham	3B	C.McGarr
LF	J.Long	LF	T.McCarthy	LF	D.Foutz	LF	W.Wilmot	LF	J.Canavan	LF	J.Burkett
CF	J.Kelley	CF	H.Duffy	CF	M.Griffin	CF	J.Ryan	CF	B.Holliday	CF	J.McAleer
RF	G.Treadway	RF	C.Carroll	RF	O.Burns	RF	S.Dungan	RF	J.McCarthy	RF	B.Ewing
C	W.Robinson	C	C.Bennett	C	T.Kinslow	C	M.Kittridge	C	F.Vaughn	C	C.Zimmer
C1	B.Clarke	CO	C.Ganzel	O3	G.Shoch	O1	G.Decker	C	M.Murphy	CO	J.O'Connor
O	T.O'Rourke	C	B.Merritt	C	C.Daily	C	P.Schriver	1	F.Motz	13	P.Tebeau
1	J.Milligan			O	H.Stovey	3O	L.Camp	O	P.Ward	C	J.Gunson
O	S.Brodie	P	K.Nichols	3	G.Hatfield	S	C.Irwin	O	G.Henry		
O	B.Gilks	P	J.Stivetts	3	W.Keeler	2	B.Glenalvin			P	C.Young
		P	H.Staley					P	F.Dwyer	P	J.Clarkson
P	S.McMahon	P	H.Gastright	P	B.Kennedy	P	B.Hutchison	P	E.Chamberlain	P	N.Cuppy
P	T.Mullane	/P	B.Quarles	P	E.Stein	P	W.McGill	P	M.Sullivan	P	C.Hastings
P	B.Hawke			P	G.Haddock	P	H.Mauck	P	T.Parrott		
P	E.McNabb			P	D.Daub			P	T.Mullane	/P	T.Williams
P	K.Baker			P	T.Lovett	P	F.Clausen			/P	C.Fisher
						P	G.McGinnis	P	S.King	/P	J.Scheible
/P	C.Schmit			P	G.Sharrott	/P	B.Abbey	/P	G.Darby	/P	G.Davies
/P	J.Wadsworth					/P	F.Donnelly	/P	B.Jones		
						/P	T.Parrott	/P	L.Cross		
						/P	C.Griffith				
						/P	S.Shaw				

LOUISVILLE		NEW YORK		PHILADELPHIA		PITTSBURGH		ST.LOUIS		WASHINGTON	
M	B.Barnie	M	M.Ward	M	H.Wright	M	A.Buckenberger	M	B.Watkins	M	J.O'Rourke
1B	W.Brown	1B	R.Connor	1B	J.Boyle	1B	J.Beckley	1B	P.Werden	1B	H.Larkin
2B	F.Pfeffer	2B	J.Ward	2B	B.Hallman	2B	L.Bierbauer	2B	J.Quinn	2B	S.Wise
SS	T.O'Rourke	SS	S.Fuller	SS	B.Allen	SS	J.Glasscock	SS	J.Glasscock	SS	J.Sullivan
3B	G.Pinkney	3B	G.Davis	3B	C.Reilly	3B	D.Lyons	3B	J.Crooks	3B	J.Mulvey
LF	P.Browning	LF	E.Burke	LF	E.Delahanty	LF	E.Smith	LF	C.Frank	LF	J.O'Rourke
CF	T.Brown	CF	G.Stafford	CF	B.Hamilton	CF	G.Van Haltren	CF	S.Brodie	CF	D.Hoy
RF	F.Weaver	RF	M.Tiernan	RF	S.Thompson	RF	P.Donovan	RF	T.Dowd	RF	P.Radford
C	J.Grim	C	J.Doyle	C	J.Clements	C	D.Miller	C	H.Peitz	C	D.Farrell
O	L.Twitchell	O	H.Lyons	C3	L.Cross	OC	J.Stenzel	OS	F.Shugart	C1	D.McGuire
S	J.Denny	C	J.Milligan	O	T.Turner	S	F.Shugart	S	B.Ely	2O	C.Stricker
S	H.Jennings	C	P.Wilson	OP	J.Sharrott	C	J.Mack	C	J.Gunson	O	C.Abbey
		C	K.Kelly			C	B.Earle	O	J.Bannon		
P	G.Hemming			P	G.Weyhing	C	J.Sugden	OC	D.Cooley	P	D.Esper
P	S.Stratton	P	A.Rusie	P	K.Carsey			O	S.Griffin	P	A.Maul
P	B.Rhodes	P	M.Baldwin	P	T.Keefe	P	F.Killen			P	J.Meekin
P	J.Menefee	P	L.German	P	J.Taylor	P	R.Ehret	P	T.Breitenstein	P	J.Duryea
						P	A.Terry	P	K.Gleason		
/P	B.Whitrock	P	E.Crane	P	T.Vickery	P	A.Gumbert	P	P.Hawley	P	O.Stocksdale
/P	M.Kilroy	/P	C.Petty	/P	G.McGinnis			P	D.Clarkson	/P	B.Stephens
/P	F.Clausen	/P	S.King			/P	H.Gastright				
/P	B.Rhines	/P	G.Davies			/P	T.Colcolough	/P	J.Dolan		
		/P	C.Schmit								

TEAM	G	W	L	PCT	GB	R	OR	AB	H	2B	3B	HR	BB	SO	AVG	OBP	SLG	PRO	PRO+	BR	/A	PF	CHI	RC	SB	CS	SBA	SBR
BOS	131	86	43	.667		1008	795	4678	1358	178	50	65	561	292	.290	.372	.391	.763	99	54	-18	108	111	790	243			
PIT	131	81	48	.628	5	970	766	4834	1447	176	127	37	537	274	.299	.377	.411	.788	116	96	115	98	99	848	210			
CLE	129	73	55	.570	12.5	976	839	4747	1425	222	98	32	532	229	.300	.374	.408	.782	106	84	28	106	103	841	252			
PHI	133	72	57	.558	14	1011	841	5151	1553	246	90	80	468	335	.301	.368	.431	.799	117	108	111	100	98	912	202			
NY	136	68	64	.515	19.5	941	845	4858	1424	182	101	61	504	281	.293	.366	.410	.776	111	69	66	100	99	860	299			
CIN	131	65	63	.508	20.5	759	814	4617	1195	161	65	29	532	256	.259	.342	.341	.683	84	-88	-106	102	101	634	238			
BRO	130	65	63	.508	20.5	775	845	4511	1200	173	83	45	473	296	.266	.341	.371	.712	97	-46	-11	95	101	659	213			
BAL	130	60	70	.462	26.5	820	893	4651	1281	164	86	27	539	323	.275	.359	.365	.724	95	-12	-25	102	98	711	233			
CHI	128	56	71	.441	29	829	874	4664	1299	186	93	32	465	242	.279	.348	.379	.727	99	-20	-8	99	102	722	255			
STL	135	57	75	.432	30.5	745	829	4879	1288	152	46	10	524	251	.264	.343	.341	.684	86	-89	-91	100	94	674	250			
LOU	126	50	75	.400	34	759	942	4566	1185	177	73	19	485	306	.260	.338	.343	.681	92	-94	-37	92	104	612	203			
WAS	130	40	89	.310	46	722	1032	4742	1258	180	83	23	523	237	.265	.346	.353	.699	92	-62	-40	97	90	648	154			
TOT	785					10315		56898	15913	2197	1047	460	6143	3342	.280	.356	.379	.736						2752				

TEAM	CG	SH	SV	IP	H	H/G	HR	BB	SO	RAT	ERA	ERA+	OAV	OOB	PR	/A	PF	CPI	FA	E	DP	FW	PW	BW	SBW	DIF
BOS	114	2	2	1163²	1314	10.2	66	402	253	13.6	4.43	111	.277	.339	30	64	106	100	.936	353	118	1.8	5.2	-1.5		16.0
PIT	104	8	2	1167	1232	9.5	29	504	280	13.8	4.08	112	.263	.342	75	60	98	101	.938	347	112	2.1	4.9	9.4		.0
CLE	110	2	2	1140¹	1361	10.7	35	356	242	13.8	4.20	116	.288	.342	59	86	105	106	.929	395	92	-.9	7.1	2.3		.6
PHI	107	4	2	1189	1357	10.3	30	521	283	14.8	4.68	98	.279	.357	-2	-14	98	98	.944	318	121	4.1	-1.1	9.1		-4.5
NY	111	6	4	1211¹	1271	9.4	36	581	395	14.2	4.29	108	.262	.347	49	48	100	99	.927	432	95	-1.8	3.9	5.4		-5.5
CIN	97	4	5	1172	1305	10.0	38	549	258	14.8	4.55	105	.274	.357	15	30	103	101	.943	321	138	3.6	2.5	-8.7		3.7
BRO	109	3	3	1154	1262	9.8	41	547	297	14.4	4.55	97	.270	.352	15	-16	95	98	.930	385	88	-.2	-1.3	-.9		3.4
BAL	104	1	2	1123²	1325	10.6	29	534	275	15.2	4.97	95	.285	.364	-39	-30	102	97	.929	384	95	-.1	-2.5	-2.0		-.4
CHI	101	4	5	1117¹	1278	10.3	26	553	273	15.3	4.81	96	.279	.365	-18	-24	99	99	.922	421	92	-2.5	-2.0	-.7		-2.3
STL	114	3	4	1207	1292	9.6	38	542	301	14.1	4.06	116	.266	.346	80	88	101	105	.930	398	110	-.0	7.2	-7.5		-8.7
LOU	113	4	1	1080	1431	11.9	38	479	190	16.3	5.90	74	.310	.380	-149	-181	94	94	.937	330	111	2.2	-14.8	-3.0		3.1
WAS	110	2	0	1139	1485	11.7	54	574	292	16.7	5.56	83	.306	.387	-114	-120	97	103	.912	497	96	-6.5	-9.8	-3.3		-4.9
TOT	1294	43	32	13864¹		10.3				14.7	4.66		.280	.356					.931	4581	1268					

Runs	Hits	Doubles	Triples	Home Runs	Total Bases
Long-Bos 149	Thompson-Phi 222	Thompson-Phi 37	Werden-StL 29	Delahanty-Phi 19	Delahanty-Phi 347
Duffy-Bos 147	Delahanty-Phi 219	Delahanty-Phi 35	Davis-NY 27	Clements-Phi 17	Thompson-Phi 318
Delahanty-Phi 145	Duffy-Bos 203	Tebeau-Cle 32	McKean-Cle 24	Tiernan-NY 14	Davis-NY 304
Childs-Cle 145	Davis-NY 195	Beckley-Pit 32	Smith-Pit 23	Lowe-Bos 14	Smith-Pit 272
Burkett-Cle 145	Ward-NY 193		Beckley-Pit 19		

Runs Batted In	Runs Produced	Bases On Balls	Batting Average	On Base Percentage	Slugging Average
Delahanty-Phi 146	Delahanty-Phi 272	Crooks-StL 121	Duffy-Bos .363	Hamilton-Phi .490	Delahanty-Phi .583
McKean-Cle 133	Duffy-Bos 259	Childs-Cle 120	Hamilton-Phi .380	Childs-Cle .463	Davis-NY .554
Thompson-Phi 126	Thompson-Phi 245	Radford-Was 104	Thompson-Phi .370	Burkett-Cle .459	Thompson-Phi .530
Nash-Bos 123	Ewing-Cle 233	McGraw-Bal 101	Delahanty-Phi .368	McGraw-Bal .454	Smith-Pit .525
Ewing-Cle 122	McKean-Cle 232	Burkett-Cle 98	Davis-NY .355	Smith-Pit .435	Hamilton-Phi .524

Production	Adjusted Production	Batter Runs	Adjusted Batter Runs	Clutch Hitting Index	Runs Created
Hamilton-Phi 1.014	Hamilton-Phi 170	Delahanty-Phi 52.7	Delahanty-Phi 53.2	Anson-Chi 148	Delahanty-Phi 167
Delahanty-Phi 1.007	Delahanty-Phi 167	Burkett-Cle 43.6	Smith-Pit 44.0	Vaughn-Cin 147	Thompson-Phi 146
Davis-NY .964	Smith-Pit 158	Thompson-Phi 43.3	Thompson-Phi 43.8	McKean-Cle 135	Davis-NY 143
Smith-Pit .960	Davis-NY 155	Smith-Pit 41.4	Hamilton-Phi 40.2	Glasscock-StL-Pit 132	Burkett-Cle 137
Thompson-Phi .954	Thompson-Phi 153	Davis-NY 40.0	Davis-NY 39.6	O'Rourke-Was 129	Smith-Pit 133

Total Average	Stolen Bases	Stolen Base Average	Stolen Base Runs	Fielding Runs	Total Player Rating
Hamilton-Phi 1.386	T.Brown-Lou 66			McPhee-Cin 34.0	Delahanty-Phi 6.3
Burkett-Cle 1.186	Dowd-StL 59			Delahanty-Phi 30.8	McPhee-Cin 3.5
Delahanty-Phi 1.173	Latham-Cin 57			T.Brown-Lou 27.1	Davis-NY 3.4
Smith-Pit 1.121	Burke-NY 54			G.Smith-Cin 19.5	Smith-Pit 3.3
Davis-NY 1.107	Brodie-StL-Bal 49			Allen-Phi 18.4	Hamilton-Phi 3.3

Wins	Win Percentage	Games	Complete Games	Shutouts	Saves
Killen-Pit 36	Gastright-Pit-Bos .750	Rusie-NY 56	Rusie-NY 50	Rusie-NY 4	Mullane-Cin-Bal 2
Young-Cle 34	Killen-Pit .720	Killen-Pit 55	Nichols-Bos 43	Ehret-Pit 4	Baldwin-Pit-NY 2
Nichols-Bos 34	Nichols-Bos .708	Young-Cle 53	Young-Cle 42		Dwyer-Cin 2
Rusie-NY 33	Young-Cle .680	Nichols-Bos 52	Kennedy-Bro 40		Donnelly-Chi 2
Kennedy-Bro 25	Staley-Bos .643	Mullane-Cin-Bal 49			Colcolough-Pit 2

Innings Pitched	Fewest Hits/Game	Fewest BB/Game	Strikeouts	Strikeouts/Game	Ratio
Rusie-NY 482.0	Rusie-NY 8.42	Young-Cle 2.19	Rusie-NY 208	Rusie-NY 3.88	Young-Cle 11.82
Nichols-Bos 425.0	Breitenstein-StL 8.44	Nichols-Bos 2.50	Kennedy-Bro 107	Meekin-Was 3.34	Nichols-Bos 11.84
Young-Cle 422.2	Killen-Pit 8.70	Cuppy-Cle 2.77	Young-Cle 102	Hawley-StL 2.89	Killen-Pit 12.06
Killen-Pit 415.0	Kennedy-Bro 8.84	Staley-Bos 2.77	Breitenstein-StL 102	Keefe-Phi 2.83	Breitenstein-StL 12.30
	Stein-Bro 8.87	Stratton-Lou 2.86	Weyhing-Phi 101	Terry-Pit 2.75	Stein-Bro 12.70

Earned Run Average	Adjusted ERA	Opponents' Batting Avg.	Opponents' On Base Pct.	Starter Runs	Adjusted Starter Runs
Breitenstein-StL 3.18	Breitenstein-StL 149	Rusie-NY .240	Young-Cle .308	Rusie-NY 76.6	Rusie-NY 76.1
Rusie-NY 3.23	Young-Cle 145	Breitenstein-StL .241	Nichols-Bos .308	Breitenstein-StL 63.2	Young-Cle 71.2
Young-Cle 3.36	Rusie-NY 144	Killen-Pit .246	Killen-Pit .312	Young-Cle 60.9	Nichols-Bos 66.9
Ehret-Pit 3.44	Nichols-Bos 140	Kennedy-Bro .249	Breitenstein-StL .316	Nichols-Bos 54.1	Breitenstein-StL 65.9
Clarkson-StL 3.48	Clarkson-StL 136	Stein-Bro .250	Stein-Bro .323	Killen-Pit 46.9	Killen-Pit 41.8

Clutch Pitching Index	Relief Runs	Adjusted Relief Runs	Relief Ranking	Total Pitcher Index	Total Baseball Ranking
Esper-Was 120				Rusie-NY 7.2	Rusie-NY 7.2
Clarkson-StL 117				Young-Cle 6.4	Young-Cle 6.4
McNabb-Bal 113				Breitenstein-StL 5.5	Delahanty-Phi 6.3
Cuppy-Cle 111				Nichols-Bos 5.5	Breitenstein-StL 5.5
Rusie-NY 111				Killen-Pit 5.2	Nichols-Bos 5.4

January 9 Boston's veteran catcher Charlie Bennett loses both legs in a horrible train accident. In 1900, Detroit, his prior team, will rename its ballpark Bennett Park, the site of Tiger Stadium.

February 26 In a series of rule changes designed to help pitchers, foul bunts will now be called strikes, and the infield fly rule is instituted.

March 14* U.S. Immigration Inspector De Barry will ask the Treasury Department if baseball is a "recognized profession" in order to determine if Buffalo has violated the alien contract labor law by signing two Canadians. Before De Barry gets a reply, Buffalo decides to play only Americans.

May 15 In the aftermath of a fierce fight between Baltimore's John McGraw and Boston's Tommy Tucker in the third inning, a devastating fire starts in the right field stands at Boston's South End Grounds. The fire destroys $70,000 worth of equipment as well as the park, the only truly double-decked grandstand Boston would ever have.

May 30 Boston second baseman Bobby Lowe hits homers in four consecutive at bats, including two in the third inning, to lead his team to a 20–11 conquest of Cincinnati and a sweep of the double-header. Lowe also adds a single to total 17 bases for the game, a record tied but not beaten until Joe Adcock in 1954. In the two games Lowe's teammate Herman Long sets a major league record by scoring nine runs, which has since been tied only once.

June 30 Future Hall of Famer Fred Clarke sets a record by going 5-for-5 in his first major league game.

July 20 Cincinnati benefits from bottom-of-the-10th-inning home runs by Harry "Farmer" Vaughn and George "Germany" Smith, the latter with two outs, to squeak past Pittsburgh, 7-6. Pirate outfielder Elmer Smith, who is allowed to retrieve the game-winning hit in the left field bleachers according to Cincinnati ground rules, is prevented from doing so by overzealous Reds fans, one of whom even draws a revolver on him.

August 6 Fire again strikes the major leagues as sparks from a plumber's torch starts a blaze that destroys the grandstand at Philadelphia's Huntingdon Grounds, better known as Baker Bowl. It will be rebuilt with concrete and steel.

August 7 Boston's Jimmy "Foxy Grandpa" Bannon becomes the first player to hit grand slams in consecutive games. Bannon's feat will not be matched until Sept. 24, 1901.

August 14 Taking advantage of the unusually small University of Pennsylvania field, visiting Louisville tags six homers, including two by Tom Brown, to beat Philadelphia, 13–7.

August 24 Chicago catcher William "Pop" Schriver becomes the first ballplayer to catch a ball dropped from the top of the Washington Monument. Later in the day the Colts top Washington, 10-5, and Schriver is 2-for-2.

September 30 Losing to Cincinnati 16–1 in the bottom of the sixth, Cleveland stages a furious comeback, including an 11-run outburst in the seventh, to conclude the season with a 16–16 tie.

October 8 New York whips NL regular season champion Baltimore, 16–3, to sweep the best-of-seven Temple Cup postseason series.

November 8 Mike "King" Kelly dies of pneumonia in Boston.

December 15 Veteran manager John Chapman expresses his support of a proposed rule change forbidding all but catchers and first basemen from wearing gloves. Chapman remarks that "as it is now, inferior players with big gloves can get into the game and force good men out."

BALTIMORE		BOSTON		BROOKLYN		CHICAGO		CINCINNATI		CLEVELAND	
M	N.Hanlon	M	F.Selee	M	D.Foutz	M	C.Anson	M	C.Comiskey	M	P.Tebeau
1B	D.Brouthers	1B	T.Tucker	1B	D.Foutz	1B	C.Anson	1B	C.Comiskey	1B	P.Tebeau
2B	H.Reitz	2B	B.Lowe	2B	T.Daly	2B	J.Parrott	2B	B.McPhee	2B	C.Childs
SS	H.Jennings	SS	H.Long	SS	T.Corcoran	SS	B.Dahlen	SS	G.Smith	SS	E.McKean
3B	J.McGraw	3B	B.Nash	3B	B.Shindle	3B	C.Irwin	3B	A.Latham	3B	C.McGarr
LF	J.Kelley	LF	T.McCarthy	LF	G.Treadway	LF	W.Wilmot	LF	B.Holliday	LF	J.Burkett
CF	S.Brodie	CF	H.Duffy	CF	M.Griffin	CF	B.Lange	CF	D.Hoy	CF	J.McAleer
RF	W.Keeler	RF	J.Bannon	RF	O.Burns	RF	J.Ryan	RF	J.Canavan	RF	H.Blake
C	W.Robinson	C	C.Ganzel	C	T.Kinslow	C	P.Schriver	C	M.Murphy	C	C.Zimmer
2	F.Bonner	C	J.Ryan	1C	C.LaChance	1O	G.Decker	C1	F.Vaughn	CO	J.O'Connor
C	B.Clarke	S	F.Connaughton	O3	G.Shoch	C	M.Kittridge	O1	J.McCarthy	O	B.Ewing
		C	F.Tenney	C	C.Daily			C	B.Merritt	O1	G.Tebeau
P	S.McMahon	O	J.Anderson			P	B.Hutchison	1	F.Motz	O	J.Virtue
P	B.Hawke					P	C.Griffith				
P	K.Gleason	P	K.Nichols	P	B.Kennedy	P	W.McGill	P	F.Dwyer	P	C.Young
P	B.Inks	P	J.Stivetts	P	E.Stein	P	A.Terry	P	T.Parrott	P	N.Cuppy
P	T.Mullane	P	H.Staley	P	D.Daub	P	S.Stratton	P	E.Chamberlain	P	J.Clarkson
		P	T.Lovett	P	H.Gastright			P	C.Fisher	P	M.Sullivan
P	D.Esper	P	G.Hodson			P	B.Abbey	P	B.Whitrock	/P	F.Griffith
/P	S.Brown			P	C.Lucid	/P	K.Camp	/P	L.Cross	/P	T.Mullane
/P	G.Hemming			/P	F.Underwood			/P	H.Fournier	/P	C.Petty
								/P	J.Tannehill	/P	B.Wallace

LOUISVILLE		NEW YORK		PHILADELPHIA		PITTSBURGH		ST.LOUIS		WASHINGTON	
M	B.Barnie	M	M.Ward	M	A.Irwin	M	A.Buckenberger	M	G.Miller	M	G.Schmelz
1B	L.Lutenberg	1B	J.Doyle	1B	J.Boyle	M	C.Mack	1B	R.Connor	1B	E.Cartwright
2B	F.Pfeffer	2B	J.Ward	2B	B.Hallman	1B	J.Beckley	2B	J.Quinn	2B	P.Ward
SS	D.Richardson	SS	S.Fuller	SS	J.Sullivan	2B	L.Bierbauer	SS	B.Ely	SS	F.Scheibeck
3B	J.Denny	3B	G.Davis	3B	L.Cross	SS	J.Glasscock	3B	H.Peitz	3B	B.Joyce
LF	F.Clarke	LF	E.Burke	LF	E.Delahanty	3B	D.Lyons	LF	C.Frank	LF	K.Selbach
CF	T.Brown	CF	G.Van Haltren	CF	B.Hamilton	LF	E.Smith	CF	F.Shugart	CF	C.Abbey
RF	O.Smith	RF	M.Tiernan	RF	S.Thompson	CF	J.Stenzel	RF	T.Dowd	RF	B.Hassamaer
C	J.Grim	C	D.Farrell	C	J.Clements	RF	P.Donovan	C	D.Miller	C	D.McGuire
						C	C.Mack				
OC	F.Weaver	SO	Y.Murphy	O	T.Turner	3	F.Hartman	O3	D.Cooley	S2	P.Radford
1O	T.O'Rourke	C1	P.Wilson	C1	M.Grady	C	A.Twineham	C	A.Twineham	O	G.Tebeau
O	L.Twitchell	1	R.Connor	C	D.Buckley	C	J.Sugden	O	M.Hogan	C	D.Dugdale
3	P.Flaherty			S	B.Allen	CS	F.Weaver	C	D.Buckley	/2	J.Sullivan
3	P.Gilbert	P	A.Rusie	3	C.Reilly	C	B.Merritt	3	T.O'Rourke		
O	G.Nicol	P	J.Meekin			S	F.Scheibeck			P	W.Mercer
C	B.Earle	P	H.Westervelt	P	J.Taylor			P	T.Breitenstein	P	A.Maul
		P	L.German	P	K.Carsey	P	R.Ehret	P	P.Hawley	P	M.Sullivan
P	G.Hemming	P	D.Clarke	P	G.Weyhing	P	A.Gumbert	P	D.Clarkson	P	O.Stocksdale
P	P.Knell			P	G.Harper	P	F.Killen			P	D.Esper
P	J.Menefee					P	T.Colcolough	/P	K.Gleason		
P	J.Wadsworth	P	G.Haddock	P	J.Menefee	P	J.Menefee	/P	E.Mason	P	C.Petty
		/P	N.Callahan							/P	G.Haddock
/P	B.Inks	/P	J.Johnson	/P	G.Nicol	/P	G.Nicol			/P	J.Malarkey
/P	S.Stratton	/P	J.Fanning	/P	J.Easton						
/P	M.Kilroy	/P	A.Lukens								

TEAM	G	W	L	PCT	GB	R	OR	AB	H	2B	3B	HR	BB	SO	AVG	OBP	SLG	PRO	PRO+	BR	/A	PF	CHI	RC	SB	CS	SBA	SBR
BAL	129	89	39	.695		1171	819	4799	1647	271	**150**	33	516	**200**	.343	**.418**	.483	**.901**	116	**173**	122	104	99	**1146**	324			
NY	137	88	44	.667	3	940	**789**	4806	1446	197	96	43	476	217	.301	.368	.409	.777	92	-68	-61	99	104	869	319			
BOS	133	83	49	.629	8	**1220**	1002	5011	1658	**272**	94	103	535	261	.331	.401	**.484**	.885	108	135	44	108	**106**	1102	241			
PHI	129	71	57	.555	18	1143	966	4967	**1732**	252	131	40	496	245	**.349**	.414	.476	.890	**122**	156	**187**	97	97	1132	273			
BRO	134	70	61	.534	20.5	1021	1007	4816	1507	228	130	42	466	294	.313	.378	.440	.818	109	5	75	93	104	941	282			
CLE	130	68	61	.527	21.5	932	896	4764	1442	241	90	37	471	301	.303	.368	.414	.782	89	-57	-92	104	103	837	220			
PIT	132	65	65	.500	25	955	972	4676	1458	222	124	48	434	208	.312	.379	.443	.822	103	11	21	99	98	921	256			
CHI	135	57	75	.432	34	1041	1066	4960	1555	265	86	65	496	298	.314	.380	.441	.821	97	12	-43	105	102	987	**327**			
STL	133	56	76	.424	35	771	953	4610	1320	171	113	54	442	289	.286	.354	.408	.762	87	-100	-100	100	92	763	190			
CIN	132	55	75	.423	35	910	1085	4671	1374	224	67	61	508	252	.294	.368	.410	.778	88	-62	-96	104	102	812	215			
WAS	132	45	87	.341	46	882	1122	4581	1317	218	118	59	**617**	375	.287	.381	.425	.806	101	-7	24	97	92	864	249			
LOU	130	36	94	.277	54	692	1001	4482	1206	173	88	42	350	364	.269	.330	.375	.705	78	-199	-152	93	99	652	217			
TOT	793					11678		57143	17662	2734	1287	627	5807	3304	.309	.379	.435	.814						3113				

TEAM	CG	SH	SV	IP	H	H/G	HR	BB	SO	RAT	ERA	ERA+	OAV	OOB	PR	/A	PF	CPI	FA	E	DP	FW	PW	BW	SBW	DIF
BAL	97	1	**11**	1116¹	1371	11.1	**31**	472	275	15.2	5.00	109	.299	.371	39	55	103	98	**.944**	293	105	**5.6**	4.2	9.4		5.8
NY	111	5	5	1212	**1292**	9.6	37	539	395	13.8	**3.83**	137	**.271**	**.349**	200	187	99	107	.924	443	101	-1.6	**14.3**	-4.7		13.9
BOS	108	3	2	1166	1529	11.8	89	**411**	262	15.3	5.41	105	.314	.372	-12	33	107	101	.925	415	120	-.7	2.5	3.4		11.8
PHI	102	3	4	1125²	1482	11.8	62	469	262	16.1	5.63	90	.314	.384	-39	-68	96	99	.935	338	111	3.0	-5.2	**14.3**		-5.2
BRO	105	3	5	1162¹	1447	11.2	41	555	285	16.0	5.51	90	.302	.382	-25	-75	93	95	.928	390	85	.9	-5.8	5.8		3.6
CLE	106	**6**	1	1124¹	1390	11.1	54	435	254	14.9	4.97	110	.301	.366	43	59	103	100	.935	344	107	2.9	4.5	-7.1		3.2
PIT	106	2	0	1164²	1552	12.0	39	457	304	15.8	5.60	93	.317	.380	-37	-50	98	96	.936	354	106	2.6	-3.8	1.6		-.4
CHI	**117**	0	0	1148	1561	12.2	43	557	281	17.1	5.68	99	.322	.398	-47	-11	106	103	.918	452	113	-2.4	-.8	-3.3		-2.4
STL	114	2	0	1161	1418	11.0	48	500	319	15.2	5.29	102	.299	.371	4	14	102	94	.923	426	109	-1.3	1.1	-7.7		-2.1
CIN	110	4	3	1147¹	1585	12.4	85	491	219	16.7	5.99	93	.325	.393	-85	-56	104	101	.925	423	119	-1.3	-4.3	-7.4		2.9
WAS	101	0	4	1107	1573	12.8	59	446	190	16.9	5.51	95	.331	.396	-24	-32	99	**110**	.908	499	81	-5.6	-2.5	1.8		-14.8
LOU	113	2	1	1096²	1462	12.0	39	475	258	16.3	5.45	93	.317	.386	-16	-44	96	101	.920	428	**130**	-1.9	-3.4	-11.7		-12.1
TOT	1290	31	36	13731¹		11.6				15.8	5.32		.309	.379					.927	4805	1287					

Runs		Hits		Doubles		Triples		Home Runs		Total Bases	
Hamilton-Phi	192	Duffy-Bos	237	Duffy-Bos	51	Reitz-Bal	31	Duffy-Bos	18	Duffy-Bos	374
Kelley-Bal	165	Hamilton-Phi	220	Kelley-Bal	48	Thompson-Phi	27	Lowe-Bos	17	Lowe-Bos	319
Keeler-Bal	165	Keeler-Bal	219	Wilmot-Chi	45	Treadway-Bro	26	Joyce-Was	17	Kelley-Bal	305
Duffy-Bos	160	Lowe-Bos	212			Connor-NY-StL	25	Dahlen-Chi	15	Keeler-Bal	305
Lowe-Bos	158	Brodie-Bal	210			Brouthers-Bal	23			Stenzel-Pit	303

Runs Batted In		Runs Produced		Bases On Balls		Batting Average		On Base Percentage		Slugging Average	
Duffy-Bos	145	Duffy-Bos	287	Hamilton-Phi	126	Duffy-Bos	.440	Hamilton-Phi	.523	Duffy-Bos	.694
Thompson-Phi	141	Hamilton-Phi	275	Kelley-Bal	107	Turner-Phi	.416	Kelley-Bal	.502	Thompson-Phi	.686
E.Delahanty-Phi	131	E.Delahanty-Phi	274	Childs-Cle	107	Thompson-Phi	.407	Duffy-Bos	.502	Joyce-Was	.648
Wilmot-Chi	130	Kelley-Bal	270	Nash-Bos	91	E.Delahanty-Phi	.407	Joyce-Was	.496	Kelley-Bal	.602
		Wilmot-Chi	259	McGraw-Bal	91	Hamilton-Phi	.404	E.Delahanty-Phi	.478	E.Delahanty-Phi	.585

Production		Adjusted Production		Batter Runs		Adjusted Batter Runs		Clutch Hitting Index		Runs Created	
Duffy-Bos	1.196	Joyce-Was	180	Duffy-Bos	75.7	Hamilton-Phi	64.7	Robinson-Bal	141	Duffy-Bos	217
Thompson-Phi	1.145	Thompson-Phi	177	Kelley-Bal	60.2	Duffy-Bos	61.4	Wilmot-Chi	132	Hamilton-Phi	207
Joyce-Was	1.143	Duffy-Bos	172	Hamilton-Phi	59.9	Thompson-Phi	52.9	McGraw-Bal	122	Kelley-Bal	182
Kelley-Bal	1.104	E.Delahanty-Phi	159	Thompson-Phi	49.3	Kelley-Bal	52.6	Bierbauer-Pit	121	Stenzel-Pit	165
E.Delahanty-Phi	1.063	Kelley-Bal	158	Joyce-Was	47.1	Joyce-Was	51.3	Reitz-Bal	118	Thompson-Phi	152

Total Average		Stolen Bases		Stolen Base Average	Stolen Base Runs	Fielding Runs		Total Player Rating	
Duffy-Bos	1.619	Hamilton-Phi	98			Jennings-Bal	33.1	Dahlen-Chi	4.8
Hamilton-Phi	1.605	McGraw-Bal	78			Dahlen-Chi	31.6	E.Delahanty-Phi	4.7
Joyce-Was	1.528	Wilmot-Chi	74			McPhee-Cin	31.2	Hamilton-Phi	4.6
Kelley-Bal	1.503	T.Brown-Lou	66			Farrell-NY	29.4	Duffy-Bos	4.3
Thompson-Phi	1.409	Lange-Chi	65			Reitz-Bal	26.9	Joyce-Was	3.7

Wins		Win Percentage		Games		Complete Games		Shutouts		Saves	
Rusie-NY	36	Meekin-NY	.786	Breitenstein-StL	56	Breitenstein-StL	46	Rusie-NY	3	Mullane-Bal-Cle	4
Meekin-NY	33	McMahon-Bal	.758	Rusie-NY	54	Rusie-NY	45	Nichols-Bos	3	Mercer-Was	3
Nichols-Bos	32	Rusie-NY	.735	Hawley-StL	53	Young-Cle	44	Cuppy-Cle	3	Hawke-Bal	3
Breitenstein-StL	27	Nichols-Bos	.711	Young-Cle	52	Nichols-Bos	40				
				Meekin-NY	52	Meekin-NY	40				

Innings Pitched		Fewest Hits/Game		Fewest BB/Game		Strikeouts		Strikeouts/Game		Ratio	
Breitenstein-StL	447.1	Rusie-NY	8.64	Young-Cle	2.33	Rusie-NY	195	Rusie-NY	3.95	Rusie-NY	12.79
Rusie-NY	444.0	Meekin-NY	8.89	Menefee-Lou-Pit	2.48	Breitenstein-StL	140	Hawke-Bal	2.97	Meekin-NY	12.89
Meekin-NY	409.0	Stein-Bro	9.98	Gleason-StL-Bal	2.54	Meekin-NY	133	Wadsworth-Lou	2.97	Clarkson-Cle	13.08
Young-Cle	408.2	Breitenstein-StL	10.00	Staley-Bos	2.63	Hawley-StL	120	Meekin-NY	2.93	Young-Cle	13.19
Nichols-Bos	407.0	Clarkson-Cle	10.33	Nichols-Bos	2.68	Nichols-Bos	113	Chamberlain-Cin	2.89	Nichols-Bos	13.67

Earned Run Average		Adjusted ERA		Opponents' Batting Avg.		Opponents' On Base Pct.		Starter Runs		Adjusted Starter Runs	
Rusie-NY	2.78	Rusie-NY	189	Rusie-NY	.250	Rusie-NY	.331	Rusie-NY	125.3	Rusie-NY	121.3
Meekin-NY	3.70	Meekin-NY	142	Meekin-NY	.256	Meekin-NY	.333	Meekin-NY	73.6	Meekin-NY	70.0
Mercer-Was	3.85	Young-Cle	138	Stein-Bro	.278	Clarkson-Cle	.336	Young-Cle	62.4	Young-Cle	68.7
Young-Cle	3.94	Mercer-Was	137	Breitenstein-StL	.279	Young-Cle	.338	Mercer-Was	55.4	Mercer-Was	53.2
Taylor-Phi	4.08	McMahon-Bal	129	Clarkson-Cle	.285	Nichols-Bos	.346	Taylor-Phi	41.0	Nichols-Bos	41.5

Clutch Pitching Index		Relief Runs	Adjusted Relief Runs	Relief Ranking	Total Pitcher Index		Total Baseball Ranking	
Mercer-Was	134				Rusie-NY	11.0	Rusie-NY	11.0
Rusie-NY	125				Young-Cle	5.6	Young-Cle	5.6
Terry-Pit-Chi	121				Meekin-NY	5.5	Meekin-NY	5.5
Hemming-Lou-Bal	112				Mercer-Was	5.0	Mercer-Was	5.0
Killen-Pit	111				Taylor-Phi	3.7	Dahlen-Chi	4.8

February 2 *The New York Clipper* and the *Cincinnati Times-Star* both express disapproval of the proposal of putting numbers on uniforms as a means of identifying individual players. The *Times-Star* advocates a return to the use of "distinctive colors in club uniforms," or the practice of assigning to each position a specific color pattern, first enacted in 1882.

February 9 New York owner Andrew Freedman institutes reserved grandstand seats to attract businessmen.

March 16 John Brush, owner of the Cincinnati Reds and the Indianapolis team of the Western League, transfers six Reds to his minor league team. This sort of exchange becomes increasingly common in the 1890s as owners of more than one team shuttle their players between their teams throughout each season in an attempt to stock their most profitable team of the moment.

April 12 In a rare matchup between a major league team and a black team, Cincinnati beats the Page Fence Giants for the second consecutive day.

April 19* Holy Cross defeats Brown University, 13–4, in a game between two of the top college teams. The Crusaders have five future major league players in their lineup, while the losers have two. Louis Sockalexis plays left field for the victors and has six stolen bases.

May 23 The Louisville Colonels drop a game to Brooklyn because they run out of baseballs. The home team is responsible for supplying balls, but the game begins with just three on hand, two of them practice balls borrowed from Brooklyn. By the third inning, the balls are worn out and a messenger sent for new ones does not come back in time. Louisville is forced to forfeit.

May 29 Jake Beckley hits a three-run homer to give Pittsburgh an 8–6 win over Washington. Under the rules of the era, which do not allow a team batting in the bottom of the last inning to win by more than one run, Beckley should be credited only with a triple. Apparently the rule is not strictly enforced.

June 3 Roger Connor becomes the major leagues' all-time home run leader, passing Harry Stovey with his fourth round-tripper of the season, and the 122nd of his career. This historic home run drives in St. Louis's only two runs in a 5-2 loss to Brooklyn.

June 15* Future novelist Zane Grey makes his minor league debut playing left field for Findlay, Ohio, against Wheeling (Tri-State League). The Pennsylvania University athlete, playing under the name Zane, fails to get a hit, but walks and scores on a grand slam by brother Romer "Reddy" Grey.

August 3* The Capital Colored All-Americans set sail for England with a team of players from Western League clubs.

August 12* Heavyweight boxing champion Jim Corbett, a good ballplayer and a great gate attraction, plays first base for the Scranton team in an Eastern League victory over Buffalo. Corbett collects two singles and knocks in two runs. His brother Joe, who will become a major league pitcher, plays shortstop.

October 8 Cleveland takes the Temple Cup by beating the Baltimore Orioles for the fourth time in five games. The lack of respect accorded the Cup is reflected in the "very cold reception" Cleveland receives after returning from Baltimore the following day.

November 15 Cap Anson makes his stage debut in "A Runaway Colt." Aside from forgetting a few lines Anson does quite well.

BALTIMORE		BOSTON		BROOKLYN		CHICAGO		CINCINNATI		CLEVELAND	
M	N.Hanlon	M	F.Selee	M	D.Foutz	M	C.Anson	M	B.Ewing	M	P.Tebeau
1B	S.Carey	1B	T.Tucker	1B	C.LaChance	1B	C.Anson	1B	B.Ewing	1B	P.Tebeau
2B	K.Gleason	2B	B.Lowe	2B	T.Daly	2B	A.Stewart	2B	B.McPhee	2B	C.Childs
SS	H.Jennings	SS	H.Long	SS	T.Corcoran	SS	B.Dahlen	SS	G.Smith	SS	E.McKean
3B	J.McGraw	3B	B.Nash	3B	B.Shindle	3B	B.Everitt	3B	A.Latham	3B	C.McGarr
LF	J.Kelley	LF	T.McCarthy	LF	J.Anderson	LF	W.Wilmot	LF	D.Hoy	LF	J.Burkett
CF	S.Brodie	CF	H.Duffy	CF	M.Griffin	CF	B.Lange	CF	G.Hogriever	CF	J.McAleer
RF	W.Keeler	RF	J.Bannon	RF	G.Treadway	RF	J.Ryan	RF	D.Miller	RF	H.Blake
C	W.Robinson	C	C.Ganzel	C	J.Grim	C	T.Donahue	C	F.Vaughn	C	C.Zimmer
23	H.Reitz	C	J.Ryan	O2	G.Shoch	O1	G.Decker	O	E.Burke	C1	J.O'Connor
C	B.Clarke	OC	F.Tenney	C	C.Daily	C	M.Kittridge	32	B.Grey	O1	G.Tebeau
		2	J.Harrington	O	D.Foutz	2	H.Truby	O	B.Holliday	3	E.Gremminger
P	B.Hoffer			O	O.Burns			C	M.Murphy		
P	G.Hemming	P	K.Nichols			P	C.Griffith	C	B.Merritt	P	C.Young
P	D.Esper	P	J.Stivetts	P	B.Kennedy	P	A.Terry			P	N.Cuppy
P	D.Clarkson	P	C.Dolan	P	E.Stein	P	B.Hutchison	P	F.Dwyer	P	B.Wallace
P	S.McMahon	P	J.Sullivan	P	A.Gumbert			P	B.Rhines	P	P.Knell
				P	D.Daub			P	T.Parrott		
		/P	F.Sexton	P	C.Lucid	/P	D.Parker	P	F.Foreman	/P	Z.Wilson
		/P	Z.Wilson			/P	D.Friend	P	B.Phillips	/P	M.Sullivan
		/P	O.Stocksdale	/P	B.Abbey	/P	W.Thornton				
						/P	S.Stratton				

LOUISVILLE		NEW YORK		PHILADELPHIA		PITTSBURGH		ST.LOUIS		WASHINGTON	
M	J.McCloskey	M	G.Davis	M	A.Irwin	M	C.Mack	M	A.Buckenberger	M	G.Schmelz
1B	H.Spies	M	J.Doyle	1B	J.Boyle	1B	J.Beckley	M	C.Von Der Ahe	1B	E.Cartwright
2B	J.O'Brien	M	H.Watkins	2B	B.Hallman	2B	L.Bierbauer	M	J.Quinn	2B	J.Crooks
SS	F.Shugart	1B	J.Doyle	SS	J.Sullivan	SS	M.Cross	M	L.Phelan	SS	F.Scheibeck
3B	J.Collins	2B	G.Stafford	3B	L.Cross	3B	B.Clingman	1B	R.Connor	3B	B.Joyce
LF	F.Clarke	SS	S.Fuller	LF	E.Delahanty	LF	E.Smith	2B	J.Quinn	LF	K.Selbach
CF	J.Wright	3B	G.Davis	CF	B.Hamilton	CF	J.Stenzel	SS	B.Ely	CF	C.Abbey
RF	T.Gettinger	LF	E.Burke	RF	S.Thompson	RF	P.Donovan	3B	D.Miller	RF	B.Hassamaer
C	J.Warner	CF	G.Van Haltren	C	J.Clements	C	B.Merritt	LF	D.Cooley	C	D.McGuire
		RF	M.Tiernan					CF	T.Brown		
O3	W.Preston	C	D.Farrell	O	T.Turner	O3	F.Genins	RF	T.Dowd	OP	J.Boyd
O	D.Holmes			S3	C.Reilly	C	J.Sugden	C	H.Peitz	O	T.Brown
C1	T.Welch	C1	P.Wilson	C	M.Grady	S	B.Stuart			S	J.Glasscock
O	T.McCreery	O	Y.Murphy	C	D.Buckley	C	T.Kinslow	O1	B.Sheehan	S	D.Coogan
1	D.Brouthers	O1	T.Bannon					3	D.Lyons		
1	B.Hassamaer	O	B.Burns	P	K.Carsey	P	P.Hawley	C	J.Otten	P	W.Mercer
O	D.Sweeney	C	P.Schriver	P	J.Taylor	P	B.Hart	3	I.Samuls	P	V.Anderson
S	J.Glasscock	1	W.Clark	P	W.McGill	P	B.Foreman			P	O.Stocksdale
/S	A.McGann			P	A.Orth	P	F.Killen	P	T.Breitenstein	P	A.Maul
		P	A.Rusie			P	J.Gardner	P	R.Ehret	P	J.Malarkey
P	B.Cunningham	P	D.Clarke	P	C.Lucid			P	H.Staley		
P	G.Weyhing	P	J.Meekin	P	T.Smith	P	S.Moran	P	B.Kissinger	/P	J.Gilroy
P	M.McDermott	P	L.German	/P	H.Lampe	/P	T.Colcolough	P	D.McDougal	/P	A.Boswell
P	B.Inks			P	E.Beam	/P	H.Jordan			/P	J.Corbett
		/P	A.Boswell	P	G.Hodson			/P	D.Clarkson	/P	D.McJames
P	P.Luby	/P	E.Doheny	/P	D.White					/P	C.Molesworth
P	P.Knell										
/P	D.McFarlan										

TEAM	G	W	L	PCT	GB	R	OR	AB	H	2B	3B	HR	BB	SO	AVG	OBP	SLG	PRO	PRO+	BR	/A	PF	CHI	RC	SB	CS	SBA	SBR
BAL	132	87	43	.669		1009	646	4725	1530	235	89	25	355	243	.324	.384	.427	.811	110	92	65	103	104	930	310			
CLE	131	84	46	.646	3	917	720	4658	1423	194	67	29	472	361	.305	.375	.395	.770	97	26	-26	106	102	790	187			
PHI	133	78	53	.595	9.5	1068	957	5037	1664	272	73	61	463	262	.330	.394	.450	.844	122	161	157	100	97	1040	276			
CHI	133	72	58	.554	15	866	854	4708	1401	171	85	55	422	344	.298	.361	.405	.766	95	6	-49	106	99	810	260			
BRO	133	71	60	.542	16.5	867	834	4717	1330	189	77	39	397	183	.282	.346	.379	.725	99	-66	-2	92	108	707	183			
BOS	132	71	60	.542	16.5	907	826	4715	1369	197	57	54	500	236	.290	.365	.391	.756	92	-4	-73	108	102	778	199			
PIT	134	71	61	.538	17	811	787	4645	1349	190	89	26	376	299	.290	.352	.386	.738	99	-41	3	95	99	753	257			
CIN	132	66	64	.508	21	903	854	4684	1395	235	105	36	414	249	.298	.359	.416	.775	99	18	-18	104	103	844	326			
NY	132	66	65	.504	21.5	852	834	4605	1324	191	90	32	454	292	.288	.355	.389	.744	98	-29	-9	98	104	763	292			
WAS	132	43	85	.336	43	837	1048	4577	1314	207	101	55	518	396	.287	.366	.412	.778	105	31	-8	99	94	805	237			
STL	135	39	92	.298	48.5	747	1032	4781	1344	155	88	38	384	279	.281	.338	.374	.712	88	-94	-84	99	96	699	205			
LOU	133	35	96	.267	52.5	698	1090	4724	1320	171	73	34	346	323	.279	.339	.368	.707	92	-100	-52	94	92	665	156			
TOT	796					10482		56576	16763	2407	994	484	5101	3602	.296	.361	.400	.761							2888			

TEAM	CG	SH	SV	IP	H	H/G	HR	BB	SO	RAT	ERA	ERA+	OAV	OOB	PR	/A	PF	CPI	FA	E	DP	FW	PW	BW	SBW	DIF
BAL	104	10	4	1134¹	1216	9.6	31	430	244	13.4	3.80	125	.271	.340	123	118	100	105	.946	288	108	5.4	9.6	5.3		1.8
CLE	108	6	3	1143²	1272	10.0	33	346	326	13.0	3.91	127	.278	.333	110	135	104	101	.936	348	77	1.8	10.9	-2.1		8.3
PHI	106	2	7	1161	1467	11.4	36	485	330	15.6	5.47	88	.304	.375	-89	-88	100	94	.933	369	93	1.0	-7.1	12.7		5.9
CHI	119	3	1	1150²	1422	11.1	38	432	297	15.0	4.67	109	.300	.366	14	52	106	105	.928	401	113	-.8	4.2	-4.0		7.6
BRO	103	5	6	1150²	1360	10.6	41	395	216	14.1	4.94	89	.290	.351	-21	-71	92	91	.941	325	96	3.5	-5.8	-.2		8.0
BOS	116	4	4	1175¹	1364	10.4	56	363	370	13.6	4.27	119	.286	.343	66	107	107	103	.934	364	104	1.1	8.7	-5.9		1.6
PIT	106	4	6	1171²	1263	9.7	17	500	382	14.2	4.05	112	.272	.353	95	60	95	102	.930	392	95	-.1	4.9	.2		.0
CIN	97	2	6	1147¹	1451	11.4	39	362	245	14.7	4.81	103	.304	.361	-4	19	104	101	.931	377	112	.4	1.5	-1.5		.5
NY	115	6	1	1147¹	1359	10.7	34	415	409	14.3	4.51	103	.291	.354	34	16	97	100	.922	438	106	-3.0	1.3	-.7		3.0
WAS	99	0	5	1101²	1507	12.3	55	465	258	16.7	5.28	91	.321	.391	-61	-60	100	110	.917	447	96	-3.5	-4.9	3.5		-16.1
STL	105	1	1	1152¹	1562	12.2	64	439	280	16.5	5.76	84	.319	.381	-126	-120	101	98	.930	380	94	.7	-9.7	-6.8		-10.7
LOU	104	3	1	1117¹	1520	12.2	40	470	245	16.5	5.90	78	.320	.389	-139	-158	97	96	.913	477	104	-5.1	-12.8	-4.2		-8.4
TOT	1282	46	45	13753¹		11.0				14.7	4.78		.296	.361					.930	4606	1198					

Runs		Hits		Doubles		Triples		Home Runs		Total Bases	
Hamilton-Phi	166	Burkett-Cle	225	Delahanty-Phi	49	Selbach-Was	22	Thompson-Phi	18	Thompson-Phi	352
Keeler-Bal	162	Keeler-Bal	213	Thompson-Phi	45	Tiernan-NY	21	Joyce-Was	17	Delahanty-Phi	296
Jennings-Bal	159	Thompson-Phi	211	Jennings-Bal	41	Thompson-Phi	21	Clements-Phi	13	Burkett-Cle	288
Burkett-Cle	153	Jennings-Bal	204	Stenzel-Pit	38	Cooley-StL	20	Delahanty-Phi	11	McKean-Cle	283
Delahanty-Phi	149	Hamilton-Phi	201	Griffin-Bro	38					Kelley-Bal	283

Runs Batted In		Runs Produced		Bases On Balls		Batting Average		On Base Percentage		Slugging Average	
Thompson-Phi	165	Jennings-Bal	280	Joyce-Was	96	Burkett-Cle	.409	Delahanty-Phi	.500	Thompson-Phi	.654
Kelley-Bal	134	Thompson-Phi	278	Hamilton-Phi	96	Delahanty-Phi	.404	Hamilton-Phi	.490	Delahanty-Phi	.617
Brodie-Bal	134	Kelley-Bal	272	Griffin-Bro	93	Clements-Phi	.394	Burkett-Cle	.486	Clements-Phi	.612
Jennings-Bal	125	Delahanty-Phi	244	Delahanty-Phi	86	Thompson-Phi	.392	McGraw-Bal	.459	Lange-Chi	.575
McKean-Cle	119	McKean-Cle	242	Kelley-Bal	77	Lange-Chi	.389	Lange-Chi	.456	Kelley-Bal	.546

Production		Adjusted Production		Batter Runs		Adjusted Batter Runs		Clutch Hitting Index		Runs Created	
Delahanty-Phi	1.117	Delahanty-Phi	186	Delahanty-Phi	66.4	Delahanty-Phi	65.8	Childs-Cle	141	Hamilton-Phi	178
Thompson-Phi	1.085	Thompson-Phi	177	Thompson-Phi	56.9	Thompson-Phi	56.3	Brodie-Bal	140	Delahanty-Phi	176
Lange-Chi	1.032	Stenzel-Pit	162	Burkett-Cle	54.2	Stenzel-Pit	49.7	Kelley-Bal	130	Thompson-Phi	167
Burkett-Cle	1.009	Lange-Chi	155	Hamilton-Phi	49.6	Hamilton-Phi	49.0	Cross-Phi	128	Burkett-Cle	165
Kelley-Bal	1.003	Hamilton-Phi	154	Kelley-Bal	47.3	Burkett-Cle	45.1	Jennings-Bal	124	Lange-Chi	160

Total Average		Stolen Bases		Stolen Base Average	Stolen Base Runs	Fielding Runs		Total Player Rating	
Delahanty-Phi	1.517	Hamilton-Phi	97			Jennings-Bal	35.7	Jennings-Bal	6.0
Hamilton-Phi	1.443	Lange-Chi	67			Dahlen-Chi	35.6	Thompson-Phi	4.7
Lange-Chi	1.373	McGraw-Bal	61			Fuller-NY	34.0	Delahanty-Phi	4.7
Kelley-Bal	1.289	Kelley-Bal	54			Cross-Phi	33.5	Griffin-Bro	3.6
Thompson-Phi	1.269					Collins-Bos-Lou	18.9	Kelley-Bal	3.5

Wins		Win Percentage		Games		Complete Games		Shutouts		Saves	
Young-Cle	35	Hoffer-Bal	.838	Hawley-Pit	56	Breitenstein-StL	46	Young-Cle	4	Parrott-Cin	3
Hoffer-Bal	31	Young-Cle	.778	Breitenstein-StL	54	Hawley-Pit	44	Rusie-NY	4	Nichols-Bos	3
Hawley-Pit	31	Rhines-Cin	.655	Rusie-NY	49	Rusie-NY	42	McMahon-Bal	4	Beam-Phi	3
						Nichols-Bos	42	Hoffer-Bal	4		
						Griffith-Chi	39	Hawley-Pit	4		

Innings Pitched		Fewest Hits/Game		Fewest BB/Game		Strikeouts		Strikeouts/Game		Ratio	
Hawley-Pit	444.1	Foreman-Pit	8.44	Young-Cle	1.83	Rusie-NY	201	Rusie-NY	4.60	Young-Cle	10.86
Breitenstein-StL	429.2	Hoffer-Bal	8.48	Clarke-NY	1.92	Hawley-Pit	142	McGill-Chi	4.32	Maul-Was	11.68
Rusie-NY	393.1	Rusie-NY	8.79	Nichols-Bos	2.04	Nichols-Bos	140	Foreman-Pit	3.48	Nichols-Bos	12.04
Nichols-Bos	379.2	Young-Cle	8.84	Staley-StL	2.21	Breitenstein-StL	127	Stivetts-Bos	3.43	Hawley-Pit	12.23
Young-Cle	369.2	Maul-Was	9.02	Taylor-Phi	2.23	Young-Cle	121	Nichols-Bos	3.32	Cuppy-Cle	12.42

Earned Run Average		Adjusted ERA		Opponents' Batting Avg.		Opponents' On Base Pct.		Starter Runs		Adjusted Starter Runs	
Maul-Was	2.45	Maul-Was	195	Foreman-Pit	.245	Young-Cle	.294	Hawley-Pit	78.8	Nichols-Bos	71.0
McMahon-Bal	2.94	Young-Cle	153	Hoffer-Bal	.246	Maul-Was	.309	Young-Cle	62.2	Young-Cle	70.6
Hawley-Pit	3.18	Nichols-Bos	149	Rusie-NY	.252	Nichols-Bos	.316	Nichols-Bos	57.5	Hawley-Pit	65.8
Hoffer-Bal	3.21	Hoffer-Bal	148	Young-Cle	.253	Hawley-Pit	.320	Hoffer-Bal	54.6	Cuppy-Cle	56.4
Foreman-Pit	3.22	Hawley-Pit	142	Maul-Was	.257	Cuppy-Cle	.323	Cuppy-Cle	48.3	Hoffer-Bal	53.8

Clutch Pitching Index		Relief Runs	Adjusted Relief Runs	Relief Ranking	Total Pitcher Index		Total Baseball Ranking	
Maul-Was	137				Hawley-Pit	7.4	Hawley-Pit	7.4
Mercer-Was	126				Young-Cle	7.0	Young-Cle	7.0
Clarke-NY	119				Cuppy-Cle	5.8	Jennings-Bal	6.0
Foreman-Cin	116				Nichols-Bos	5.7	Cuppy-Cle	5.8
Griffith-Chi	115				Griffith-Chi	4.5	Nichols-Bos	5.7

January 18 John Ward, who hasn't played or managed for the last two seasons, objects to being reserved by New York. At the NL meeting in February his appeal is upheld, and Ward becomes a free agent.

February 1 NL umpires oppose the proposed rule giving them the authority to eject "obstreperous players." They claim that the imposition of fines is a more effective form of discipline.

March 15 The Louisville infield is being rebuilt with base lines of blue clay. In addition, blue semicircles will radiate out from first base and third base, joining at second base to form, along with the bottom half of the diamond—a heart.

March 24 The NL adopts changes in the National Agreement. The minor leagues are divided into six classifications based on population, and new draft fees are instituted. The NL forbids players from deliberately soiling baseballs, declares that "a ball cutting the corners of the home plate, and being requisite height, must be called a strike," and empowers umpires to eject players.

April 7 Louisville's Pete Cassidy be-comes the first baseball player in history to be X-rayed, as a splinter of bone is removed from his wrist.

April 16 The 12-team NL season opens, with no franchise changes from last year. The largest Opening Day crowd of the century, 24,500, sees the opener in Philadelphia. Veteran Cincinnati Reds second baseman Bid McPhee opens the season sporting a glove for the first time and survives several weeks of good-natured ribbing by opponents. He is the last player to convert to wearing a mitt.

May 8 In the top of the ninth inning, Philadelphia's Billy Nash starts to argue with the umpire over a called strike but stays in the batter's box. Quick-witted pitcher Clark Griffith throws a pitch in the midst of the argument which nicks Nash's bat, resulting in a double play. His quick thinking helps the Chicago Colts take a 5-3 victory.

September 7 On Labor Day, Baltimore wins a rare tripleheader from Louisville 4-3, 9-1, and 12-1, the last game in eight innings.

September 19 Kid Nichols wins his 30th game for the sixth straight year in Boston's 3-1 victory over Brooklyn.

September 26 Jesse Burkett gets three hits for Cleveland in the final game of the season to finish at .410, becoming the first major leaguer to hit .400 in consecutive seasons, a feat later duplicated by Ty Cobb and Rogers Hornsby.

October 4* The Cuban Giants defeat the Chicago Unions, 11-9, and claim the title of black champions of America.

October 8 Following another rainout, the Orioles defeat Cleveland, 5-0, to win the Temple Cup in a four-game sweep. The Cup games are poorly attended, while the rowdy behavior of both teams does nothing to enhance the stature of the troubled series.

October 11 The annual league meeting gets underway in Chicago. Brooklyn owner Ferdinand H. Abell proposes to make all players free agents between Jan. 1 and March 1 and allow all teams to bid on them, subject to a salary limit. The plan is ignored.

November 13 The NL votes to award British-born journalist Henry Chadwick $50 per month for life in recognition of his past services to the game.

BALTIMORE		BOSTON		BROOKLYN		CHICAGO		CINCINNATI		CLEVELAND	
M	N.Hanlon	M	F.Selee	M	D.Foutz	M	C.Anson	M	B.Ewing	M	P.Tebeau
1B	J.Doyle	1B	T.Tucker	1B	C.LaChance	1B	C.Anson	1B	B.Ewing	1B	P.Tebeau
2B	H.Reitz	2B	B.Lowe	2B	T.Daly	2B	F.Pfeffer	2B	B.McPhee	2B	C.Childs
SS	H.Jennings	SS	H.Long	SS	T.Corcoran	SS	B.Dahlen	SS	G.Smith	SS	E.McKean
3B	J.Donnelly	3B	J.Collins	3B	B.Shindle	3B	B.Everitt	3B	C.Irwin	3B	C.McGarr
LF	J.Kelley	LF	H.Duffy	LF	T.McCarthy	LF	G.Decker	LF	E.Burke	LF	J.Burkett
CF	S.Brodie	CF	B.Hamilton	CF	M.Griffin	CF	B.Lange	CF	D.Hoy	CF	J.McAleer
RF	W.Keeler	RF	J.Bannon	RF	F.Jones	RF	J.Ryan	RF	D.Miller	RF	H.Blake
C	W.Robinson	C	M.Bergen	C	J.Grim	C	M.Kittridge	C	H.Peitz	C	C.Zimmer
C1	B.Clarke	OC	F.Tenney	O1	J.Anderson	1C	T.Donahue	1C	F.Vaughn	C1	J.O'Connor
/2	J.Quinn	3	J.Harrington	2O	G.Shoch	3	B.McCormick	2C	B.Grey	OP	B.Wallace
3	J.McGraw	C	C.Ganzel	C	B.Burrell	2	H.Truby	O	B.Holliday	O	J.Shearon
		2	D.McGann			O	G.Flynn				
P	B.Hoffer			P	B.Kennedy			P	F.Dwyer	P	C.Young
P	A.Pond	P	K.Nichols	P	H.Payne	P	C.Griffith	P	R.Ehret	P	N.Cuppy
P	G.Hemming	P	J.Stivetts	P	D.Daub	P	D.Friend	P	F.Foreman	P	Z.Wilson
P	S.McMahon	P	J.Sullivan	P	A.Abbey	P	A.Terry	P	C.Fisher		
P	D.Esper	P	F.Klobedanz	P	E.Stein	P	B.Briggs	P	B.Rhines	/P	D.Gear
/P	D.Clarkson	P	W.Mains	P	G.Harper	/P	D.Parker	/P	B.Foreman		
/P	J.Corbett	/P	T.Lewis	/P	A.Gumbert	/P	M.McFarland	/P	B.Inks		
/P	J.Nops	/P	C.Dolan			/P	W.Thornton				
		/P	B.Banks								

LOUISVILLE		NEW YORK		PHILADELPHIA		PITTSBURGH		ST.LOUIS		WASHINGTON	
M	J.McCloskey	M	A.Irwin	M	B.Nash	M	C.Mack	M	H.Diddlebock	M	G.Schmelz
M	B.McGunnigle	M	B.Joyce	1B	D.Brouthers	1B	J.Beckley	M	A.Latham	1B	E.Cartwright
1B	J.Rogers	1B	W.Clark	2B	B.Hallman	2B	D.Padden	M	C.Von Der Ahe	2B	J.O'Brien
2B	J.O'Brien	2B	K.Gleason	SS	B.Hulen	SS	B.Ely	M	R.Connor	SS	G.DeMontreville
SS	J.Dolan	SS	F.Connaughton	3B	B.Nash	3B	D.Lyons	M	T.Dowd	3B	B.Joyce
3B	B.Clingman	3B	G.Davis	LF	E.Delahanty	LF	E.Smith	1B	R.Connor	LF	K.Selbach
LF	F.Clarke	LF	G.Stafford	CF	D.Cooley	CF	J.Stenzel	2B	T.Dowd	CF	T.Brown
CF	C.Dexter	CF	G.Van Haltren	RF	S.Thompson	RF	P.Donovan	SS	M.Cross	RF	B.Lush
RF	T.McCreery	RF	M.Tiernan	C	M.Grady	C	J.Sugden	3B	B.Myers	C	D.McGuire
C	D.Miller	C	P.Wilson					LF	J.Sullivan		
				3S	L.Cross	C	B.Merritt	CF	T.Parrott	O	C.Abbey
1S	P.Cassidy	O1	H.Davis	O	J.Sullivan	2	L.Bierbauer	RF	K.Douglass	3	J.Rogers
O	O.Pickering	CS	D.Farrell	C	J.Clements	1O	H.Davis	C	E.McFarland	3	H.Smith
O	D.Holmes	1	J.Beckley	1	N.Lajoie	1	C.Mack			C3	D.Farrell
2	J.Crooks	3	B.Joyce	C1	J.Boyle			O	T.Turner	2	J.Crooks
S	F.Shannon	S	S.Fuller	O	S.Mertes	P	F.Killen	2	J.Quinn	C	P.McCauley
O	H.McFarland	C	D.Zearfoss			P	P.Hawley	C	M.Murphy		
C	J.Warner			P	J.Taylor	P	J.Hughey	O	D.Cooley	P	W.Mercer
1	B.Hassamaer	P	D.Clarke	P	A.Orth	P	C.Hastings	O	T.Niland	P	D.McJames
S	F.Eustace	P	J.Meekin	P	K.Carsey					P	L.German
2	A.Johnson	P	M.Sullivan	P	H.Keener	/P	B.Foreman	P	T.Breitenstein	P	S.King
		P	E.Doheny	P	W.McGill	/P	E.Horton	P	B.Hart		
P	C.Fraser							P	R.Donahue	/P	A.Maul
P	B.Hill	P	C.Seymour	P	A.Gumbert			P	B.Kissinger	/P	E.Norton
P	B.Cunningham	/P	S.Campfield	/P	C.Lucid					/P	J.Boyd
P	A.Herman			/P	G.Wheeler					/P	C.Flynn
P	M.McDermott										
P	T.Smith										
/P	G.Weyhing										

TEAM	G	W	L	PCT	GB	R	OR	AB	H	2B	3B	HR	BB	SO	AVG	OBP	SLG	PRO	PRO+	BR	/A	PF	CHI	RC	SB	CS	SBA	SBR
BAL	132	90	39	.698		995	662	4719	1548	207	100	23	386	201	.328	.393	.429	.822	120	151	137	101	103	1003	441			
CLE	135	80	48	.625	9.5	840	650	4856	1463	207	72	28	436	316	.301	.363	.391	.754	97	26	-23	106	98	785	175			
CIN	128	77	50	.606	12	783	620	4360	1283	204	73	20	382	226	.294	.357	.388	.745	95	7	-43	107	103	761	350			
BOS	132	74	57	.565	17	860	761	4717	1416	175	74	36	414	274	.300	.363	.392	.755	98	26	-23	106	102	791	241			
CHI	132	71	57	.555	18.5	815	799	4582	1311	182	97	34	409	290	.286	.349	.390	.739	95	-7	-37	104	105	769	332			
PIT	131	66	63	.512	24	787	741	4701	1371	169	94	27	387	286	.292	.353	.385	.738	103	-7	25	96	98	746	217			
NY	133	64	67	.489	27	829	821	4661	1383	159	87	40	439	271	.297	.364	.394	.758	108	32	55	97	99	795	274			
PHI	130	62	68	.477	28.5	890	891	4680	1382	234	84	49	438	297	.295	.363	.413	.776	110	58	68	99	103	801	191			
WAS	133	58	73	.443	33	818	920	4639	1328	179	79	45	516	365	.286	.365	.388	.753	103	29	30	100	97	783	258			
BRO	133	58	73	.443	33	692	764	4548	1292	174	87	28	344	269	.284	.340	.379	.719	100	-45	-4	94	95	680	198			
STL	131	40	90	.308	50.5	593	929	4520	1162	134	78	37	332	300	.257	.313	.346	.659	81	-149	-125	96	96	572	185			
LOU	134	38	93	.290	53	653	997	4588	1197	142	80	37	371	427	.261	.322	.351	.673	85	-123	-98	96	100	603	195			
TOT	792					9555		55571	16136	2166	1005	404	4854	3522	.290	.354	.387	.741						3057				

TEAM	CG	SH	SV	IP	H	H/G	HR	BB	SO	RAT	ERA	ERA+	OAV	OOB	PR	/A	PF	CPI	FA	E	DP	FW	PW	BW	SBW	DIF
BAL	115	9	1	1168¹	1281	9.9	22	339	302	12.7	3.67	116	.277	.331	89	77	98	100	.945	296	114	2.6	6.5	11.6		4.7
CLE	113	9	5	1195²	1363	10.3	27	280	336	12.6	3.46	131	.285	.329	119	141	104	109	.949	288	117	3.6	12.0	-2.0		2.4
CIN	105	12	4	1108	1240	10.1	27	310	219	13.0	3.67	125	.281	.335	84	114	106	105	.951	252	107	4.7	9.7	-3.6		2.8
BOS	110	6	3	1155²	1254	9.8	57	397	277	13.1	3.78	120	.275	.337	74	97	104	106	.934	368	94	-1.7	8.2	-2.0		3.9
CHI	118	2	1	1161	1302	10.1	30	467	353	14.3	4.41	103	.282	.358	-7	15	104	97	.934	366	115	-1.6	1.3	-3.1		10.4
PIT	108	8	1	1159¹	1286	10.0	18	439	362	13.9	4.30	98	.280	.351	7	-15	99	94	.941	317	103	1.2	-1.3	2.1		-.6
NY	104	1	2	1136²	1303	10.3	33	403	312	14.0	4.54	92	.286	.352	-24	-45	96	94	.933	365	90	-1.3	-3.8	4.7		-1.0
PHI	107	3	2	1117	1473	11.9	39	387	243	15.4	5.20	83	.316	.375	-104	-112	99	99	.941	313	112	1.3	-9.5	5.8		-.6
WAS	106	2	3	1136²	1435	11.4	24	435	292	15.2	4.61	95	.306	.372	-32	-28	101	105	.927	398	99	-3.3	-2.4	2.5		-4.3
BRO	97	3	1	1144	1353	10.6	39	400	259	14.1	4.25	97	.292	.354	14	-17	95	104	.945	297	104	2.7	-1.4	-.3		-8.5
STL	115	1	1	1130²	1448	11.5	40	456	279	15.5	5.33	82	.309	.376	-122	-124	100	95	.936	345	73	-.5	-10.5	-10.6		-3.4
LOU	108	1	4	1148²	1398	11.0	48	541	288	15.9	5.12	84	.298	.381	-98	-103	99	99	.916	475	110	-7.8	-8.7	-8.3		-2.6
TOT	1306	57	28	13761²		10.6				14.1	4.36		.290	.354					.938	4080	1238					

Runs
Burkett-Cle	160
Keeler-Bal	153
Hamilton-Bos	152
Kelley-Bal	148
Dahlen-Chi	137

Hits
Burkett-Cle	240
Keeler-Bal	210
Jennings-Bal	209
Delahanty-Phi	198
VanHaltren-NY	197

Doubles
Delahanty-Phi	44
Miller-Cin	38
Kelley-Bal	31
Dahlen-Chi	30

Triples
VanHaltren-NY	21
McCreery-Lou	21
Kelley-Bal	19
Dahlen-Chi	19
Clarke-Lou	18

Home Runs
Joyce-Was-NY	13
Delahanty-Phi	13
Thompson-Phi	12
Connor-StL	11

Total Bases
Burkett-Cle	317
Delahanty-Phi	315
Kelley-Bal	282
VanHaltren-NY	272
Keeler-Bal	270

Runs Batted In
Delahanty-Phi	126
Jennings-Bal	121
Duffy-Bos	113
McKean-Cle	112

Runs Produced
Jennings-Bal	246
Delahanty-Phi	244
Kelley-Bal	240
Keeler-Bal	231
Burkett-Cle	226

Bases On Balls
Hamilton-Bos	110
Joyce-Was-NY	101
Childs-Cle	100
Kelley-Bal	91
Tiernan-NY	77

Batting Average
Burkett-Cle	.410
Jennings-Bal	.401
Delahanty-Phi	.397
Keeler-Bal	.386
Tiernan-NY	.369

On Base Percentage
Hamilton-Bos	.477
Jennings-Bal	.472
Delahanty-Phi	.472
Joyce-Was-NY	.470
Kelley-Bal	.469

Slugging Average
Delahanty-Phi	.631
Dahlen-Chi	.553
McCreery-Lou	.546
Kelley-Bal	.543
Burkett-Cle	.541

Production
Delahanty-Phi	1.103
Kelley-Bal	1.013
Burkett-Cle	1.002
Dahlen-Chi	.990
Joyce-Was-NY	.988

Adjusted Production
Delahanty-Phi	192
Kelley-Bal	164
Joyce-Was-NY	162
Tiernan-NY	159
E.Smith-Pit	158

Batter Runs
Delahanty-Phi	64.7
Kelley-Bal	54.6
Burkett-Cle	54.5
Joyce-Was-NY	48.4
Hamilton-Bos	44.8

Adjusted Batter Runs
Delahanty-Phi	66.6
Kelley-Bal	52.5
Joyce-Was-NY	50.0
Tiernan-NY	47.8
Burkett-Cle	45.9

Clutch Hitting Index
Reitz-Bal	151
Duffy-Bos	148
Anson-Chi	141
Doyle-Bal	140
Cross-Phi	139

Runs Created
Kelley-Bal	178
Delahanty-Phi	170
Burkett-Cle	166
Hamilton-Bos	160
Jennings-Bal	158

Total Average
Kelley-Bal	1.430
Delahanty-Phi	1.405
Hamilton-Bos	1.316
Joyce-Was-NY	1.306
Jennings-Bal	1.263

Stolen Bases
Kelley-Bal	87
Lange-Chi	84
Hamilton-Bos	83
Miller-Cin	76
Doyle-Bal	73

Stolen Base Average

Stolen Base Runs

Fielding Runs
Childs-Cle	42.4
Jennings-Bal	34.2
Dahlen-Chi	24.5
Clingman-Lou	23.7
Corcoran-Bro	23.5

Total Player Rating
Jennings-Bal	6.7
Childs-Cle	6.6
Delahanty-Phi	6.0
Dahlen-Chi	5.5
Joyce-Was-NY	4.0

Wins
Nichols-Bos	30
Killen-Pit	30
Young-Cle	28
Meekin-NY	26

Win Percentage
Hoffer-Bal	.781
Hemming-Bal	.714
Dwyer-Cin	.686
Nichols-Bos	.682
Griffith-Chi	.676

Games
Killen-Pit	52
Young-Cle	51
Nichols-Bos	49
Hawley-Pit	49
Clarke-NY	48

Complete Games
Killen-Pit	44
Young-Cle	42
Mercer-Was	38

Shutouts
Young-Cle	5
Killen-Pit	5

Saves
Young-Cle	3
Hill-Lou	2
Fisher-Cin	2

Innings Pitched
Killen-Pit	432.1
Young-Cle	414.1
Hawley-Pit	378.0
Nichols-Bos	372.1
Mercer-Was	366.1

Fewest Hits/Game
Rhines-Cin	8.06
Hawley-Pit	9.10
Sullivan-NY	9.13
Friend-Chi	9.23
Hoffer-Bal	9.23

Fewest BB/Game
Young-Cle	1.35
Clarke-NY	1.54
Dwyer-Cin	1.87
Cuppy-Cle	1.89
Griffith-Chi	1.98

Strikeouts
Young-Cle	140
Hawley-Pit	137
Killen-Pit	134
Breitenstein-StL	114
Meekin-NY	110

Strikeouts/Game
Briggs-Chi	3.90
Pond-Bal	3.36
McJames-Was	3.31
Hawley-Pit	3.26
Young-Cle	3.04

Ratio
Rhines-Cin	11.64
Cuppy-Cle	11.82
Young-Cle	11.95
Nichols-Bos	11.97
Esper-Bal	12.08

Earned Run Average
Rhines-Cin	2.45
Nichols-Bos	2.83
Cuppy-Cle	3.12
Dwyer-Cin	3.15
Young-Cle	3.24

Adjusted ERA
Rhines-Cin	188
Nichols-Bos	160
Dwyer-Cin	146
Cuppy-Cle	145
Young-Cle	140

Opponents' Batting Avg.
Rhines-Cin	.238
Hawley-Pit	.261
Sullivan-NY	.261
Friend-Chi	.264
Hoffer-Bal	.264

Opponents' On Base Pct.
Rhines-Cin	.311
Cuppy-Cle	.314
Young-Cle	.317
Nichols-Bos	.317
Esper-Bal	.319

Starter Runs
Nichols-Bos	63.2
Young-Cle	51.5
Cuppy-Cle	49.3
Killen-Pit	45.3
Dwyer-Cin	38.7

Adjusted Starter Runs
Nichols-Bos	70.6
Young-Cle	59.6
Cuppy-Cle	56.2
Dwyer-Cin	46.7
Killen-Pit	37.5

Clutch Pitching Index
Nichols-Bos	122
Wallace-Cle	120
Payne-Bro	116
Dwyer-Cin	115
Rhines-Cin	114

Relief Runs

Adjusted Relief Runs

Relief Ranking

Total Pitcher Index
Nichols-Bos	6.6
Young-Cle	6.4
Cuppy-Cle	5.8
Dwyer-Cin	4.7
Killen-Pit	4.2

Total Baseball Ranking
Jennings-Bal	6.7
Childs-Cle	6.6
Nichols-Bos	6.5
Young-Cle	6.4
Delahanty-Phi	6.0

March 9 Cleveland signs Holy Cross star Louis Sockalexis to a contract. Sockalexis, a full-blooded Penobscot Indian, soon earns the admiration of Spiders fans with his phenomenal all-around skills. Before long, baseball fans start referring to the Cleveland team as the "Indians." Although Sockalexis will only play parts of three seasons due to acute alcoholism, the nickname will be revived in 1915 and become the club's official name.

March 27 Cleveland president Frank DeHaas Robison proposes that NL teams chip in to pay the 1896 salary of New York star Amos Rusie, who had refused to play due to a contract dispute. Robison and other NL officials want to avoid Rusie's lawsuit, in which he seeks free agency. Although New York president Andrew Freeman vehemently opposes the NL plan, the $3,000 payment is made and Rusie rejoins the Giants.

April 22 Willie Keeler's single and double in the Orioles' first game begins a streak of safe hits in 44 consecutive games.

May 11 Charles "Duke" Farrell, Washington catcher, sets a major league record by throwing out eight Orioles trying to steal second base, but the Senators lose anyway, 6-3.

May 23 A "shoot the chutes" waterslide opens at Sportsman's Park, St. Louis. With the Browns in last place, owner Von der Ahe is trying to draw customers with a variety of amusement park attractions.

May 31 Using mechanical dummies, "an electrical baseball machine" reproduces the Louisville doubleheader on stage at Philadelphia's McCauley Theater, which has been fitted out like a ballpark. Messages transmitted from the field are translated by "skillful manipulation" of the machine's keyboard into a reenactment.

June 29 Chicago scores in every inning to demolish Louisville, 36-7, to set the NL record for runs scored.

July 16* A game is played under electric lights at Clyde Park in San Antonio, Texas. Dallas wins the exhibition, 10–5.

July 18 Cap Anson makes his career 3,000th hit, a fourth-inning single, as Clark Griffith and the Colts defeat Baltimore, 6-3. The feat fails, however, to make the Chicago papers. Included in Cap's 3,000 hit total are 60 walks, officially counted as hits in 1887. In the eighth inning of the game, Orioles third baseman John McGraw twice steps in front of pitches from Chicago's Clark Griffith, and, each time, umpire Jim McDonald refuses to award first base to the cantankerous McGraw.

July 31 Brooklyn pitcher Bill Kennedy becomes so upset at umpire Hank O'Day that he throws a ball at him. The ball misses O'Day, who has his back turned, allowing George Davis to score the winning run for the Giants.

October 11 Baltimore wins the Temple Cup and $310 for each player by defeating Boston, 9-3. W. C. Temple of Pittsburgh, whose trophy has been contested for the last four baseball seasons, is extremely dissatisfied with this year's contest and later asks that the Cup be returned to him.

November 13 At the NL meetings, President Young announces that the Temple Cup Series has been discontinued, and adds that there will be two umpires per game next year.

	BALTIMORE		BOSTON		BROOKLYN		CHICAGO		CINCINNATI		CLEVELAND
M	N.Hanlon	M	F.Selee	M	B.Barnie	M	C.Anson	M	B.Ewing	M	P.Tebeau
1B	J.Doyle	1B	F.Tenney	1B	C.LaChance	1B	C.Anson	1B	J.Beckley	1B	P.Tebeau
2B	H.Reitz	2B	B.Lowe	2B	G.Shoch	2B	J.Connor	2B	B.McPhee	2B	C.Childs
SS	H.Jennings	SS	H.Long	SS	G.Smith	SS	B.Dahlen	SS	C.Ritchey	SS	E.McKean
3B	J.McGraw	3B	J.Collins	3B	B.Shindle	3B	B.Everitt	3B	C.Irwin	3B	B.Wallace
LF	J.Kelley	LF	H.Duffy	LF	J.Anderson	LF	G.Decker	LF	E.Burke	LF	J.Burkett
CF	J.Stenzel	CF	B.Hamilton	CF	M.Griffin	CF	B.Lange	CF	D.Hoy	CF	J.O'Connor
RF	W.Keeler	RF	C.Stahl	RF	F.Jones	RF	J.Ryan	RF	D.Miller	RF	C.Sockalexis
C	B.Clarke	C	M.Bergen	C	J.Grim	C	M.Kittridge	C	H.Peitz	C	C.Zimmer
3S	J.Quinn	OP	J.Stivetts	2	J.Canavan	2P	N.Callahan	S2	T.Corcoran	O	O.Pickering
C	W.Robinson	S	B.Allen	CO	A.Smith	3S	B.McCormick	1C	F.Vaughn	C	L.Criger
1O	T.O'Brien	C	C.Ganzel	C	B.Burrell	OP	W.Thornton	O	B.Holliday	O	S.McAllister
C	F.Bowerman	CO	G.Yeager			C	T.Donahue	O	P.Schriver	O	H.Blake
		C	F.Lake			2	F.Pfeffer			O	J.McAleer
P	J.Corbett			P	B.Kennedy			P	T.Breitenstein		
P	B.Hoffer	P	K.Nichols	P	J.Dunn	P	C.Griffith	P	B.Rhines	P	C.Young
P	A.Pond	P	F.Klobedanz	P	C.Fisher	P	D.Friend	P	F.Dwyer	P	Z.Wilson
P	J.Nops	P	T.Lewis	P	D.Daub	P	B.Briggs	P	R.Ehret	P	J.Powell
		P	J.Sullivan			P	R.Denzer	P	B.Dammann	P	N.Cuppy
P	D.Amole			/P	S.McMahon					/P	M.McDermott
/P	G.Blackburn					/P	J.Korwan			/P	H.Clarke
										/P	C.Brown

	LOUISVILLE		NEW YORK		PHILADELPHIA		PITTSBURGH		ST.LOUIS		WASHINGTON
M	J.Rogers	M	B.Joyce	M	G.Stallings	M	P.Donovan	M	T.Dowd	M	G.Schmelz
M	F.Clarke	1B	W.Clark	1B	N.Lajoie	1B	W.Davis	M	H.Nicol	M	T.Brown
1B	P.Werden	2B	K.Gleason	2B	L.Cross	2B	D.Padden	M	B.Hallman	1B	T.Tucker
2B	J.Rogers	SS	G.Davis	SS	S.Gillen	SS	B.Ely	M	C.Von Der Ahe	2B	J.O'Brien
SS	G.Stafford	3B	B.Joyce	3B	B.Nash	3B	J.Hoffmeister	1B	M.Grady	SS	G.DeMontreville
3B	B.Clingman	LF	D.Holmes	LF	E.Delahanty	LF	E.Smith	2B	B.Hallman	3B	C.Reilly
LF	F.Clarke	CF	G.Van Haltren	CF	D.Cooley	CF	S.Brodie	SS	M.Cross	LF	K.Selbach
CF	O.Pickering	RF	M.Tiernan	RF	T.Dowd	RF	P.Donovan	3B	F.Hartman	CF	T.Brown
RF	T.McCreery	C	J.Warner	C	J.Boyle	C	J.Sugden	LF	D.Lally	RF	C.Abbey
C	B.Wilson							CF	D.Harley	C	D.McGuire
		O	T.McCreery	O2	P.Geier	C	B.Merritt	RF	T.Turner		
OC	C.Dexter	C1	P.Wilson	C	J.Clements	OP	J.Tannehill	C	K.Douglass	OS	Z.Wrigley
O	H.Wagner	3	J.Donnelly	S	F.Shugart	3	J.Donnelly			C	D.Farrell
2S	A.Johnson	/3	C.Gettig	C	E.McFarland	1	D.Lyons	2O	J.Houseman	O	J.Gettman
S2	J.Dolan	1	J.Beckley	2	B.Hallman	1	J.Rothfuss	C	M.Murphy	1	E.Cartwright
O	D.Nance					O	T.Leahy	O	T.Dowd		
2	H.Smith	P	J.Taylor	P	J.Taylor			C	E.McFarland	P	W.Mercer
		P	A.Rusie	P	A.Orth	C	B.Merritt	1	R.Connor	P	D.McJames
P	C.Fraser	P	J.Meekin	P	J.Fifield	OP	J.Tannehill			P	C.Swaim
P	B.Cunningham	P	C.Seymour	P	G.Wheeler	P	F.Killen	P	R.Donahue	P	S.King
P	B.Hill	P	M.Sullivan			P	P.Hawley	P	B.Hart	P	L.German
P	B.Magee	P	E.Doheny			P	J.Hughey	P	K.Carsey		
				/P	D.Dunkle	P	C.Hastings	P	W.Sudhoff	/P	R.Bresnahan
/P	G.Hemming	/P	D.Clarke	/P	Y.Johnson	P	J.Gardner			/P	E.Norton
/P	R.Evans			/P	K.Carsey			/P	D.Esper		
/P	D.Clarke			/P	B.Becker			/P	P.Coleman		
/P	P.Dowling							/P	C.Lucid		
/P	A.Herman							/P	B.Hutchison		
/P	B.Miller							/P	M.McDermott		
								/P	J.Grimes		

TEAM	G	W	L	PCT	GB	R	OR	AB	H	2B	3B	HR	BB	SO	AVG	OBP	SLG	PRO	PRO+	BR	/A	PF	CHI	RC	SB	CS	SBA	SBR
BOS	135	93	39	.705		1025	665	4937	1574	230	83	45	423	262	.319	.378	.426	.804	110	117	59	106	108	919	233			
BAL	136	90	40	.692	2	964	674	4872	1584	243	66	19	437	256	.325	.394	.414	.808	118	138	138	100	100	984	401			
NY	137	83	48	.634	9.5	895	695	4844	1449	188	84	31	404	327	.299	.361	.392	.753	106	25	48	97	107	829	328			
CIN	134	76	56	.576	17	763	705	4524	1311	219	69	22	380	218	.290	.353	.383	.736	93	-6	-56	107	100	715	194			
CLE	132	69	62	.527	23.5	773	680	4604	1374	192	85	16	435	344	.298	.364	.389	.753	98	25	-18	105	96	747	181			
WAS	135	61	71	.462	32	781	793	4636	1376	194	77	36	374	348	.297	.357	.395	.752	104	18	22	100	98	755	208			
BRO	136	61	71	.462	32	802	845	4810	1343	202	72	24	351	255	.279	.336	.366	.702	95	-74	-34	95	110	684	187			
PIT	135	60	71	.458	32.5	676	835	4590	1266	140	108	25	359	334	.276	.337	.370	.707	95	-61	-34	96	95	657	170			
CHI	138	59	73	.447	34	832	894	4803	1356	189	76	38	430	317	.282	.347	.386	.733	94	-16	-46	104	105	766	264			
PHI	134	55	77	.417	38	752	792	4756	1392	213	83	40	399	299	.293	.353	.398	.751	106	13	34	97	93	754	163			
LOU	134	52	78	.400	40	669	859	4520	1197	160	70	40	370	453	.265	.329	.358	.687	89	-94	-71	97	100	624	195			
STL	132	29	102	.221	63.5	588	1083	4642	1277	149	67	31	354	314	.275	.336	.356	.692	89	-84	-70	98	85	639	172			
TOT	809					9520		56538	16499	2319	964	367	4716	3727	.292	.354	.386	.741							2696			

TEAM	CG	SH	SV	IP	H	H/G	HR	BB	SO	RAT	ERA	ERA+	OAV	OOB	PR	/A	PF	CPI	FA	E	DP	FW	PW	BW	SBW	DIF
BOS	115	8	7	1194¹	1273	9.6	39	393	329	12.9	3.65	122	.271	.333	87	107	104	102	.951	272	80	3.9	9.2	5.1		8.8
BAL	118	3	0	1197²	1296	9.7	18	382	361	13.2	3.55	117	.274	.338	100	81	97	104	.951	277	110	3.8	6.9	11.8		2.4
NY	118	8	3	1187¹	1214	9.2	26	486	456	13.4	3.47	120	.263	.342	110	89	96	106	.930	397	109	-3.3	7.6	4.1		9.1
CIN	100	4	2	1156²	1375	10.7	18	329	270	13.7	4.09	111	.294	.347	29	58	106	101	.948	273	100	3.7	5.0	-4.8		6.1
CLE	111	6	0	1119¹	1297	10.4	32	289	277	13.1	3.95	114	.288	.337	45	67	104	100	.950	261	74	4.2	5.7	-1.5		-4.9
WAS	102	7	6	1148	1383	10.8	27	400	348	14.6	4.01	108	.296	.362	37	40	101	112	.933	369	103	-1.9	3.4	1.9		-8.4
BRO	114	4	2	1194²	1417	10.7	34	410	256	14.2	4.60	89	.293	.355	-39	-68	95	94	.936	364	99	-1.5	-5.8	-2.9		5.2
PIT	112	2	2	1153¹	1397	10.9	22	318	342	13.9	4.67	89	.297	.350	-47	-66	97	91	.936	346	70	-.5	-5.7	-2.9		3.6
CHI	131	2	1	1197	1485	11.2	30	433	361	14.9	4.53	98	.303	.367	-30	-104	104	103	.932	393	111	-2.9	-1.0	-3.9		.9
PHI	115	4	2	1155¹	1415	11.0	28	364	253	14.0	4.60	91	.300	.356	-38	-53	97	96	.944	296	72	2.3	-4.5	2.9		-11.7
LOU	114	2	0	1138	1363	10.8	39	459	267	15.1	4.42	96	.295	.369	-14	-22	99	106	.929	395	84	-3.6	-1.9	-6.1		-1.4
STL	109	1	1	1127¹	1584	12.6	54	453	207	16.8	6.21	71	.329	.395	-239	-228	102	93	.933	375	84	-2.7	-19.5	-6.0		-8.2
TOT	1359	51	26	13969		10.6				14.1	4.31		.292	.354					.939	4018	1096					

Runs
Hamilton-Bos	152
Keeler-Bal	145
Griffin-Bro	136
Jones-Bro	134
Jennings-Bal	133

Hits
Keeler-Bal	239
F.Clarke-Lou	202
Delahanty-Phi	200
Burkett-Cle	198
Lajoie-Phi	197

Doubles
Stenzel-Bal	43
Lajoie-Phi	40
Delahanty-Phi	40
Wallace-Cle	33
Ryan-Chi	33

Triples
Davis-Pit	28
Lajoie-Phi	23
Wallace-Cle	21
Keeler-Bal	19

Home Runs
Duffy-Bos	11
Davis-NY	10
Lajoie-Phi	9
Beckley-NY-Cin	8

Total Bases
Lajoie-Phi	310
Keeler-Bal	304
Delahanty-Phi	285
F.Clarke-Lou	276
Duffy-Bos	265

Runs Batted In
Davis-NY	136
Collins-Bos	132
Duffy-Bos	129
Lajoie-Phi	127
Kelley-Bal	118

Runs Produced
Duffy-Bos	248
Davis-NY	238
Collins-Bos	229
Kelley-Bal	226

Bases On Balls
Hamilton-Bos	105
McGraw-Bal	99
Griffin-Bro	81
Selbach-Was	80
Joyce-NY	78

Batting Average
Keeler-Bal	.424
F.Clarke-Lou	.390
Burkett-Cle	.383
Delahanty-Phi	.377
Kelley-Bal	.362

On Base Percentage
McGraw-Bal	.471
Burkett-Cle	.468
Keeler-Bal	.464
Jennings-Bal	.463
F.Clarke-Lou	.462

Slugging Average
Lajoie-Phi	.569
Keeler-Bal	.539
Delahanty-Phi	.538
F.Clarke-Lou	.533
Davis-NY	.509

Production
Keeler-Bal	1.003
F.Clarke-Lou	.994
Delahanty-Phi	.981
Lajoie-Phi	.960
Burkett-Cle	.944

Adjusted Production
F.Clarke-Lou	168
Keeler-Bal	164
Delahanty-Phi	162
Lajoie-Phi	156
Kelley-Bal	147

Batter Runs
Keeler-Bal	52.1
F.Clarke-Lou	48.5
Delahanty-Phi	45.1
Burkett-Cle	42.0
Kelley-Bal	37.2

Adjusted Batter Runs
F.Clarke-Lou	53.2
Keeler-Bal	52.1
Delahanty-Phi	48.6
Lajoie-Phi	39.3
Kelley-Bal	37.2

Clutch Hitting Index
Gleason-NY	139
Shindle-Bro	138
Collins-Bos	133
Reitz-Bal	131
Tenney-Bos	128

Runs Created
Keeler-Bal	176
F.Clarke-Lou	158
Delahanty-Phi	142
Davis-NY	138
Stenzel-Bal	136

Total Average
F.Clarke-Lou	1.272
Keeler-Bal	1.262
Jennings-Bal	1.251
Hamilton-Bos	1.162
Kelley-Bal	1.143

Stolen Bases
Lange-Chi	73
Stenzel-Bal	69
Hamilton-Bos	66
Davis-NY	65
Keeler-Bal	64

Fielding Runs
Clingman-Lou	28.6
Cross-StL	27.8
Jennings-Bal	27.1
Davis-NY	21.7
Reitz-Bal	21.5

Total Player Rating
Jennings-Bal	5.4
Davis-NY	4.8
F.Clarke-Lou	4.2
Delahanty-Phi	4.0
Collins-Bos	3.5

Wins
Nichols-Bos	31
Rusie-NY	28
Klobedanz-Bos	26
Corbett-Bal	24
Breitenstein-Cin	23

Win Percentage
Klobedanz-Bos	.788
Nops-Bal	.769
Corbett-Bal	.750
Nichols-Bos	.738
Rusie-NY	.737

Games
Mercer-Was	47
Young-Cle	46
Nichols-Bos	46
Donahue-StL	46

Complete Games
Killen-Pit	38
Griffith-Chi	38
Donahue-StL	38
Nichols-Bos	37
Kennedy-Bro	36

Shutouts
Mercer-Was	3
McJames-Was	3

Saves
Nichols-Bos	3
Mercer-Was	3

Innings Pitched
Nichols-Bos	368.0
Donahue-StL	348.0
Griffith-Chi	343.2
Kennedy-Bro	343.1
Mercer-Was	342.0

Fewest Hits/Game
Seymour-NY	8.23
Rusie-NY	8.77
Nichols-Bos	8.85
Hill-Lou	9.45
Corbett-Bal	9.49

Fewest BB/Game
Young-Cle	1.31
Tannehill-Pit	1.52
Nichols-Bos	1.66
Cuppy-Cle	1.70
Killen-Pit	2.03

Strikeouts
McJames-Was	156
Seymour-NY	149
Corbett-Bal	149
Rusie-NY	135
Nichols-Bos	127

Strikeouts/Game
Seymour-NY	4.83
McJames-Was	4.34
Corbett-Bal	4.28
Rusie-NY	3.77
Nichols-Bos	3.11

Ratio
Nichols-Bos	10.59
Rusie-NY	11.48
Cuppy-Cle	11.80
Young-Cle	12.04
Nops-Bal	12.07

Earned Run Average
Rusie-NY	2.54
Nichols-Bos	2.64
Nops-Bal	2.81
Corbett-Bal	3.11
Powell-Cle	3.16

Adjusted ERA
Nichols-Bos	169
Rusie-NY	163
Nops-Bal	148
Powell-Cle	142
Cuppy-Cle	140

Opponents' Batting Avg.
Seymour-NY	.242
Rusie-NY	.254
Nichols-Bos	.256
Hill-Lou	.268
Corbett-Bal	.269

Opponents' On Base Pct.
Nichols-Bos	.291
Rusie-NY	.308
Cuppy-Cle	.314
Young-Cle	.318
Nops-Bal	.319

Starter Runs
Nichols-Bos	68.1
Rusie-NY	63.3
Mercer-Was	42.7
Corbett-Bal	41.8
Nops-Bal	36.6

Adjusted Starter Runs
Nichols-Bos	74.6
Rusie-NY	57.7
Mercer-Was	43.8
Corbett-Bal	36.8
Powell-Cle	33.2

Clutch Pitching Index
Mercer-Was	132
Nops-Bal	120
Corbett-Bal	117
Rusie-NY	117
McJames-Was	117

Total Pitcher Index
Nichols-Bos	7.3
Rusie-NY	6.1
Mercer-Was	5.0
Corbett-Bal	3.1
Breitenstein-Cin	3.1

Total Baseball Ranking
Nichols-Bos	7.3
Rusie-NY	6.1
Jennings-Bal	5.4
Mercer-Was	5.0
Davis-NY	4.8

January 31 Cap Anson is fired after 19 years as player-manager of Chicago. Strong-minded Cap, with a record of 1,288 victories and five pennants, was enormously popular in Chicago. Former infielder Tom Burns takes over for Chicago, who are now called the Orphans.

April 2* Famed heavyweight boxer Jim Corbett, whose brother Joe pitches for Baltimore, claims he made $17,000 last year by playing in well-advertised minor league games for a sizable cut of the gate.

April 16 The league urges official scorers to award hits, rather than automatic errors, on hard-hit balls that handcuff infielders; to be scrupulous in awarding assists to all players handling balls in rundowns; and to cease awarding hits to batters on fielder's-choice plays.

April 21 Phillies pitcher Bill Duggleby hits a bases-full home run in his first major league at bat against Cy Seymour, an event never duplicated. The Phillies win the game handily, 13-4.

April 22 Two no-hitters are pitched on the same day. Baltimore's Jim Hughes beats Boston in his second major league start, and Cincinnati's Ted Breitenstein no-hits Pittsburgh.

May 11 With the bases full and one out, Orioles right fielder Tommy O'Brien muffs Bobby Lowe's short fly, recovers the ball, runs in, tags Jimmy Collins at second base, and steps on the bag to force Chick Stahl and complete an unassisted double play.

June 10 A hard week for managers: Tom Brown is replaced at Washington by "Dirty Jack" Doyle, Billy Barnie is fired by ninth-place Brooklyn. Barnie's successor, center field Mike Griffin, resigns after four games; President Charlie Ebbets fills in. "Scrappy Bill" Joyce is dropped by the New York Giants in favor of Cap Anson, who takes over on June 11.

June 13* Former pitcher Charles Sweeney, recently released from San Quentin penitentiary where he served time for manslaughter, officiates in the San Francisco–San Jose game as a California League umpire.

July 5* With the agreement of Atlantic League president Ed Barrow, Lizzie (Stroud) Arlington pitches an inning for Reading against Allentown. The lady hurler gives up two hits but no runs in the first appearance of a woman in Organized Baseball.

July 7 Criticized for being unable "to handle men in the up-to-day style," Cap Anson resigns as Giants manager with a 9-13 record. Bill Joyce is reappointed on the same day.

August 26 Cleveland plays its final home game of the season and only their fourth in Cleveland since July 9. With 83 of their final 87 games on the road, the team has earned nicknames such as the Nomads, Exiles, Misfits, and Wanderers.

BALTIMORE		BOSTON		BROOKLYN		CHICAGO		CINCINNATI		CLEVELAND	
M	N.Hanlon	M	F.Selee	M	B.Barnie	M	T.Burns	M	B.Ewing	M	P.Tebeau
1B	D.McGann	1B	F.Tenney	M	M.Griffin	1B	B.Everitt	1B	J.Beckley	1B	P.Tebeau
2B	G.DeMontreville	2B	B.Lowe	M	C.Ebbets	2B	J.Connor	2B	B.McPhee	2B	C.Childs
SS	H.Jennings	SS	H.Long	1B	C.LaChance	SS	B.Dahlen	SS	T.Corcoran	SS	E.McKean
3B	J.McGraw	3B	J.Collins	2B	B.Hallman	3B	B.McCormick	3B	C.Irwin	3B	B.Wallace
LF	D.Holmes	LF	H.Duffy	SS	G.Magoon	LF	J.Ryan	LF	E.Smith	LF	J.Burkett
CF	J.Kelley	CF	B.Hamilton	3B	B.Shindle	CF	B.Lange	CF	A.McBride	CF	J.McAleer
RF	W.Keeler	RF	C.Stahl	LF	J.Sheckard	RF	S.Mertes	RF	D.Miller	RF	H.Blake
C	W.Robinson	C	M.Bergen	CF	M.Griffin	C	T.Donahue	C	H.Peitz	C	L.Criger
				RF	F.Jones						
C1	B.Clarke	C1	G.Yeager	C	J.Ryan	OP	W.Thornton	2O	H.Steinfeldt	1C	J.O'Connor
O	J.Stenzel	O	G.Stafford			O	D.Green	1C	F.Vaughn	O	E.Heidrick
S	S.Brodie	O1	J.Stivetts	1	T.Tucker	OP	F.Isbell	C	B.Wood	O	C.Sockalexis
3S	A.Ball			OC	A.Smith	CO	F.Chance	O	B.Holliday	C	C.Zimmer
O	T.O'Brien	P	K.Nichols	C	J.Grim			O	H.McFarland		
		P	T.Lewis	/O	J.Anderson	P	C.Griffith			P	C.Young
P	D.McJames	P	V.Willis	2	T.Daly	P	N.Callahan	P	P.Hawley	P	J.Powell
P	J.Hughes	P	F.Klobedanz			P	W.Woods	P	T.Breitenstein	P	Z.Wilson
P	A.Maul			P	B.Kennedy	P	M.Kilroy	P	B.Hill	P	N.Cuppy
P	J.Nops			P	J.Dunn			P	F.Dwyer		
P	F.Kitson			P	J.Yeager	/P	J.Taylor	P	B.Dammann	/P	C.Jones
				P	R.Miller	/P	B.Briggs			/P	S.McAllister
/P	B.Hoffer			P	K.McKenna	/P	B.Phyle			/P	C.Fraser
/P	A.Pond					/P	D.Friend			/P	F.Bates
				/P	E.Stein					/P	G.Kelb
				/P	H.Howell						
				/P	W.Gaston						

LOUISVILLE		NEW YORK		PHILADELPHIA		PITTSBURGH		ST.LOUIS		WASHINGTON	
M	F.Clarke	M	B.Joyce	M	G.Stallings	M	B.Watkins	M	T.Hurst	M	T.Brown
1B	H.Wagner	M	C.Anson	M	B.Shettsline	1B	W.Clark	1B	G.Decker	M	J.Doyle
2B	H.Smith	M	B.Joyce	1B	K.Douglass	2B	D.Padden	2B	J.Crooks	M	D.McGuire
SS	C.Ritchey	1B	B.Joyce	2B	N.Lajoie	SS	B.Ely	SS	G.Smith	M	A.Irwin
3B	B.Clingman	2B	K.Gleason	SS	M.Cross	3B	B.Grey	3B	L.Cross	1B	J.Doyle
LF	F.Clarke	SS	G.Davis	3B	B.Lauder	LF	J.McCarthy	LF	D.Harley	2B	H.Reitz
CF	D.Hoy	3B	F.Hartman	LF	E.Delahanty	CF	T.O'Brien	CF	J.Stenzel	SS	Z.Wrigley
RF	C.Dexter	LF	M.Tiernan	CF	D.Cooley	RF	P.Donovan	RF	T.Dowd	3B	J.Smith
C	M.Kittridge	CF	G.Van Haltren	RF	E.Flick	C	P.Schriver	C	J.Clements	LF	K.Selbach
		RF	J.Doyle	C	E.McFarland					CF	J.Anderson
		C	J.Warner			C	F.Bowerman	2S	J.Quinn	RF	J.Gettman
2O	G.Stafford			3	E.Abbaticchio	1	H.Davis	CO	J.Sugden	C	D.McGuire
1	G.Decker			C	M.Murphy	O	T.McCreery	1	T.Tucker		
1	H.Davis	CO	M.Grady	3	B.Nash	O	S.Brodie	SO	S.Sullivan	C1	D.Farrell
C	B.Wilson	OP	C.Gettig	O	S.Thompson	2	B.Eagan	S	R.Hall	3O	B.Wagner
C	D.Powers	O	W.Wilmot					O	T.Turner	3	D.Casey
O	D.Nance	O	T.McCreery					O	D.Holmes	3	B.Myers
O	T.Hartsel	O3	P.Foster	P	W.Piatt	P	J.Tannehill			O	B.Freeman
C	C.Snyder			P	R.Donahue	P	B.Rhines			OP	B.Donovan
		P	C.Seymour	P	A.Orth	P	J.Gardner	P	J.Taylor	1	C.Carr
P	B.Cunningham	P	J.Meekin	P	J.Fifield	P	F.Killen	P	W.Sudhoff		
P	B.Magee	P	A.Rusie	P	G.Wheeler	P	C.Hastings	P	J.Hughey	P	G.Weyhing
P	P.Dowling	P	E.Doheny					P	K.Carsey	P	W.Mercer
P	C.Fraser			P	D.Dunkle	P	B.Hart			P	B.Dinneen
		/P	B.Carrick	/P	B.Duggleby	/P	S.Leever	P	D.Esper	P	F.Killen
P	R.Ehret			/P	E.Murphy	/P	B.Hoffer	P	P.Daniels	P	C.Swaim
P	N.Altrock					/P	J.Cronin	/P	G.Gillpatrick		
						/P	Z.Rosebraugh	/P	H.Maupin	/P	R.Evans
										/P	D.Amole
										/P	K.Baker
										/P	P.Williams

TEAM	G	W	L	PCT	GB	R	OR	AB	H	2B	3B	HR	BB	SO	AVG	OBP	SLG	PRO	PRO+	BR	/A	PF	CHI	RC	SB	CS	SBA	SBR
BOS	152	102	47	.685		872	614	5276	1531	190	55	53	405	303	.290	.344	.377	.721	106	72	28	105	104	780	172			
BAL	154	96	53	.644	6	933	623	5242	1584	154	77	12	519	316	.302	.382	.368	.750	118	157	140	102	99	864	250			
CIN	157	92	60	.605	11.5	831	740	5334	1448	207	101	19	455	300	.271	.335	.359	.694	97	24	-31	107	103	732	165			
CHI	152	85	65	.567	17.5	828	679	5219	1431	175	84	18	476	394	.274	.343	.350	.693	104	29	31	100	104	735	220			
CLE	156	81	68	.544	21	730	683	5246	1379	162	56	18	545	306	.263	.338	.325	.663	96	-23	-13	99	97	641	93			
PHI	150	78	71	.523	24	823	784	5118	1431	238	81	33	472	382	.280	.348	.377	.725	118	84	120	96	98	769	182			
NY	157	77	73	.513	25.5	837	800	5349	1422	190	86	34	428	372	.266	.328	.353	.681	103	-5	19	97	109	714	214			
PIT	152	72	76	.486	29.5	634	694	5087	1313	140	88	14	393	343	.258	.313	.328	.641	90	-78	-65	98	96	589	107			
LOU	154	70	81	.464	33	728	833	5193	1389	150	71	32	375	429	.267	.325	.342	.667	98	-31	-19	98	101	687	235			
BRO	149	54	91	.372	46	638	811	5126	1314	156	66	17	328	314	.256	.309	.322	.631	85	-98	-95	100	101	577	130			
WAS	155	51	101	.336	52.5	704	939	5257	1423	177	80	36	370	386	.271	.327	.355	.682	100	-5	-3	100	94	703	197			
STL	154	39	111	.260	63.5	571	929	5214	1290	149	55	13	383	402	.247	.309	.305	.614	78	-127	-142	102	91	552	104			
TOT	921					9129		62661	16955	2088	900	299	5092	4247	.271	.334	.347	.681							2069			

TEAM	CG	SH	SV	IP	H	H/G	HR	BB	SO	RAT	ERA	ERA+	OAV	OOB	PR	/A	PF	CPI	FA	E	DP	FW	PW	BW	SBW	DIF
BOS	127	9	8	1340	1186	8.0	37	470	432	11.6	2.98	124	.236	.310	93	105	102	97	.950	310	102	3.1	9.8	2.6		12.0
BAL	138	12	0	1323	1236	8.4	17	400	422	11.5	2.90	123	.246	.310	104	98	99	99	.947	326	105	2.5	9.2	13.1		-3.2
CIN	131	10	2	1385¹	1484	9.6	16	449	294	13.0	3.50	110	.272	.336	17	51	106	103	.950	325	128	2.9	4.8	-2.9		11.2
CHI	137	13	0	1342²	1357	9.1	17	364	323	12.1	2.83	126	.261	.319	115	111	99	113	.936	412	149	-2.9	10.4	2.9		-.4
CLE	142	9	0	1334	1429	9.6	26	309	339	12.1	3.20	113	.272	.320	59	60	100	105	.952	301	95	4.2	5.6	-1.2		-2.1
PHI	129	10	0	1288¹	1440	10.1	23	399	325	13.4	3.72	92	.281	.342	-17	-42	95	104	.937	379	102	-1.2	-3.9	11.2		-2.6
NY	141	9	1	1353²	1359	9.0	21	587	558	13.5	3.44	101	.260	.344	25	4	96	106	.932	447	113	-4.2	.4	1.8		4.0
PIT	131	10	3	1323²	1400	9.5	14	346	330	12.3	3.41	104	.270	.323	29	21	99	98	.946	340	105	1.4	2.0	-6.1		.8
LOU	137	4	0	1334	1457	9.8	33	470	271	13.6	4.24	84	.276	.346	-95	-101	99	93	.939	382	114	-.8	-9.4	-1.8		6.5
BRO	134	1	0	1298²	1446	10.0	34	476	294	13.7	4.01	89	.280	.348	-59	-63	99	100	.947	334	125	1.3	-5.9	-8.9		-5.0
WAS	129	0	1	1307	1577	10.9	29	450	371	14.5	4.52	81	.297	.360	-134	-127	102	98	.929	443	119	-4.2	-11.9	-.3		-8.6
STL	133	0	2	1324¹	1584	10.8	32	372	288	13.9	4.53	83	.295	.350	-137	-111	105	93	.939	388	97	-1.2	-10.4	-13.3		-11.2
TOT	1609	87	17	15954²		9.6				12.9	3.60		.271	.334					.942	4387	1354					

Runs		Hits		Doubles		Triples		Home Runs		Total Bases	
McGraw-Bal	143	Keeler-Bal	216	Lajoie-Phi	43	Anderson-Br-Ws-Br	22	Collins-Bos	15	Collins-Bos	286
Jennings-Bal	135	Burkett-Cle	213	Delahanty-Phi	36	VanHaltren-NY	16	Wagner-Lou	10	Lajoie-Phi	280
VanHaltren-NY	129	VanHaltren-NY	204	Dahlen-Chi	35	Hoy-Lou	16	Joyce-NY	10	VanHaltren-NY	270
Keeler-Bal	126	Lajoie-Phi	197	Collins-Bos	35			Anderson-Br-Ws-Br	9	Anderson-Br-Ws-Br	257
Cooley-Phi	123			Anderson-Br-Ws-Br	33			McKean-Cle	9	Cooley-Phi	256

Runs Batted In		Runs Produced		Bases On Balls		Batting Average		On Base Percentage		Slugging Average	
Lajoie-Phi	127	Lajoie-Phi	234	McGraw-Bal	112	Keeler-Bal	.385	Hamilton-Bos	.480	Anderson-Br-Ws-Br	.494
Collins-Bos	111	Jennings-Bal	221	Joyce-NY	88	Hamilton-Bos	.369	McGraw-Bal	.475	Collins-Bos	.479
Kelley-Bal	110	Delahanty-Phi	203	Hamilton-Bos	87	McGraw-Bal	.342	Jennings-Bal	.454	Lajoie-Phi	.461
Duffy-Bos	108	Collins-Bos	203	Flick-Phi	86	Smith-Cin	.342	Flick-Phi	.430	Delahanty-Phi	.454
McGann-Bal	106	McGann-Bal	200	Jennings-Bal	78	Burkett-Cle	.341	Delahanty-Phi	.426	Hamilton-Bos	.453

Production		Adjusted Production		Batter Runs		Adjusted Batter Runs		Clutch Hitting Index		Runs Created	
Hamilton-Bos	.933	Hamilton-Bos	159	McGraw-Bal	45.1	Delahanty-Phi	45.6	Kelley-Bal	145	Delahanty-Phi	135
Delahanty-Phi	.880	Delahanty-Phi	159	Jennings-Bal	44.2	McGraw-Bal	42.8	Grey-Pit	137	McGraw-Bal	121
Flick-Phi	.878	Flick-Phi	158	Hamilton-Bos	43.4	Jennings-Bal	41.9	Davis-NY	136	Hamilton-Bos	120
Jennings-Bal	.876	Jennings-Bal	149	Delahanty-Phi	40.2	Flick-Phi	39.9	Connor-Chi	136	Jennings-Bal	119
McGraw-Bal	.871	McGraw-Bal	148	Flick-Phi	35.2	Hamilton-Bos	37.7	Hartman-NY	135	Ryan-Chi	119

Total Average		Stolen Bases		Stolen Base Average	Stolen Base Runs	Fielding Runs		Total Player Rating	
Hamilton-Bos	1.262	Delahanty-Phi	58			Davis-NY	34.6	Dahlen-Chi	4.6
McGraw-Bal	1.115	Hamilton-Bos	54			Dahlen-Chi	25.5	Jennings-Bal	4.5
Delahanty-Phi	1.082	DeMontreville-Bal	49			Gleason-NY	20.5	Davis-NY	4.4
Jennings-Bal	1.050	Dexter-Lou	44			Selbach-Was	19.9	Collins-Bos	3.8
Flick-Phi	1.035	McGraw-Bal	43			Cross-StL	18.4	Delahanty-Phi	3.7

Wins		Win Percentage		Games		Complete Games		Shutouts		Saves	
Nichols-Bos	31	Lewis-Bos	.765	Taylor-StL	50	Taylor-StL	42	Powell-Cle	6	Nichols-Bos	4
Cunningham-Lou	28	Maul-Bal	.741	Nichols-Bos	50	Cunningham-Lou	41	Piatt-Phi	6	Tannehill-Pit	2
McJames-Bal	27	Nichols-Bos	.721	Young-Cle	46	Young-Cle	40	Tannehill-Pit	5	Lewis-Bos	2
Hawley-Cin	27	Hawley-Cin	.711			Nichols-Bos	40	Nichols-Bos	5	Hickman-Bos	2
Lewis-Bos	26	Griffith-Chi	.706			McJames-Bal	40	Hughes-Bal	5	Dammann-Cin	2

Innings Pitched		Fewest Hits/Game		Fewest BB/Game		Strikeouts		Strikeouts/Game		Ratio	
Taylor-StL	397.1	Nichols-Bos	7.33	Young-Cle	.98	Seymour-NY	239	Seymour-NY	6.03	Nichols-Bos	9.63
Nichols-Bos	388.0	Willis-Bos	7.64	Dwyer-Cin	1.58	McJames-Bal	178	Willis-Bos	4.63	Maul-Bal	9.76
Young-Cle	377.2	Lewis-Bos	7.67	Cunningham-Lou	1.62	Willis-Bos	160	McJames-Bal	4.28	Young-Cle	10.41
McJames-Bal	374.0	Maul-Bal	7.77	Tannehill-Pit	1.74	Nichols-Bos	138	Doheny-NY	4.06	Griffith-Chi	10.75
Cunningham-Lou	362.0	McJames-Bal	7.87	Griffith-Chi	1.77	Piatt-Phi	121	Piatt-Phi	3.56	McJames-Bal	10.88

Earned Run Average		Adjusted ERA		Opponents' Batting Avg.		Opponents' On Base Pct.		Starter Runs		Adjusted Starter Runs	
Griffith-Chi	1.88	Griffith-Chi	190	Nichols-Bos	.221	Nichols-Bos	.272	Nichols-Bos	63.3	Nichols-Bos	67.1
Maul-Bal	2.10	Nichols-Bos	173	Willis-Bos	.229	Maul-Bal	.275	Griffith-Chi	62.4	Griffith-Chi	61.5
Nichols-Bos	2.13	Maul-Bal	170	Lewis-Bos	.229	Young-Cle	.288	McJames-Bal	51.7	McJames-Bal	50.5
McJames-Bal	2.36	McJames-Bal	152	Maul-Bal	.232	Griffith-Chi	.294	Young-Cle	45.2	Young-Cle	45.6
Callahan-Chi	2.46	Callahan-Chi	145	McJames-Bal	.234	McJames-Bal	.297	Maul-Bal	39.9	Maul-Bal	39.2

Clutch Pitching Index		Relief Runs	Adjusted Relief Runs	Relief Ranking	Total Pitcher Index		Total Baseball Ranking	
Griffith-Chi	135				Nichols-Bos	6.9	Nichols-Bos	6.9
Orth-Phi	120				Griffith-Chi	5.8	Griffith-Chi	5.8
Dammann-Cin	118				Young-Cle	5.3	Young-Cle	5.3
Doheny-NY	117				McJames-Bal	4.3	Dahlen-Chi	4.6
Callahan-Chi	116				Callahan-Chi	3.9	Jennings-Bal	4.5

February 7 Under a joint ownership arrangement, several Baltimore players are shifted to Brooklyn, and that club transfers several to the Orioles. Manager Ned Hanlon takes Willie Keeler, Joe Kelley, Hughie Jennings, and others with him while John McGraw and Wilbert Robinson remain in Baltimore. The powerful new Brooklyn team is nicknamed the Superbas.

April 3 The Robison brothers, owners of the Cleveland franchise, gain control of the St. Louis franchise as well, and redistribute players. St. Louis, which finished 12th in 1898, is enhanced with Cy Young, Jesse Burkett, Bobby Wallace, and manager-first baseman Patsy Tebeau. Cleveland is greatly weakened by the transfers. The new St. Louis owners change the name of Sportsman's Park to League Park and the color of the team socks from brown to red.

April 30 A new major league attendance record is set at Chicago as 27,000 fans watch Nixey Callahan shut out St. Louis, 4–0. The crowd spills into the field causing any hit into the crowd to count for only one base.

July 1 Cleveland, which has averaged under 200 fans a game at home, splits a twin bill with Boston and decides to spend the rest of the season on the road. The club's record is 12-49. They will play just seven more home games and finish the year with a total attendance of 6,088, the lowest in major league history.

September 4 The Superbas, already famous for their late rallies, stage "Brooklyn Finishes" in two different boroughs, winning the morning game in Brooklyn with two in the ninth, and then taking the afternoon game in Manhattan with four in the eighth.

September 18 After losing 24 games in a row, Cleveland defeats Washington, 5-4. The Spiders will go on to lose their next 16 games. They wind up with a record of 20-134.

October 11* The Western League holds its annual meeting in Chicago and changes its name to the American Baseball League. The AL considers putting clubs in Cleveland and Chicago.

December 8 Louisville president Barney Dreyfuss transfers to Pittsburgh (of which he is part owner) his top stars, including player-manager Fred Clarke, Hans Wagner, Tommy Leach, and Deacon Phillippe. Louisville is a likely candidate in the reduction of NL franchises from 12 to eight.

December 15 The NL rules Brooklyn's purchase of Zeke Wrigley in September is illegal and nullifies the 16 games he played for Brooklyn. But Brooklyn still wins the pennant.

BALTIMORE		BOSTON		BROOKLYN		CHICAGO		CINCINNATI		CLEVELAND	
M	J.McGraw	M	F.Selee	M	N.Hanlon	M	T.Burns	M	B.Ewing	M	L.Cross
1B	C.LaChance	1B	F.Tenney	1B	D.McGann	1B	B.Everitt	1B	J.Beckley	M	J.Quinn
2B	G.DeMontreville	2B	B.Lowe	2B	T.Daly	2B	B.McCormick	2B	B.McPhee	1B	T.Tucker
SS	B.Keister	SS	H.Long	SS	B.Dahlen	SS	G.DeMontreville	SS	T.Corcoran	2B	J.Quinn
3B	J.McGraw	3B	J.Collins	3B	D.Casey	3B	H.Wolverton	3B	C.Irwin	SS	H.Lochhead
LF	D.Holmes	LF	H.Duffy	LF	J.Kelley	LF	J.Ryan	LF	E.Smith	3B	S.Sullivan
CF	S.Brodie	CF	B.Hamilton	CF	F.Jones	CF	S.Mertes	CF	K.Selbach	LF	D.Harley
RF	J.Sheckard	RF	C.Stahl	RF	W.Keeler	RF	D.Green	RF	D.Miller	CF	T.Dowd
C	W.Robinson	C	M.Bergen	C	D.Farrell	C	T.Donahue	C	H.Peitz	RF	S.McAllister
										C	J.Sugden
O3	D.Fultz	C	B.Clarke	O1	J.Anderson	O1	B.Lange	32	H.Steinfeldt		
S	G.Magoon	O	G.Stafford	S	H.Jennings	23	J.Connor	O	A.McBride	O	C.Hemphill
1C	P.Crisham	O	C.Frisbee	C	D.McGuire	C	F.Chance	C	B.Wood	3	L.Cross
2	J.O'Brien	C	B.Sullivan	C	A.Smith	S	G.Magoon	S3	K.Elberfeld	C	O.Schreckengost
C	A.Smith					3	B.Bradley	O	S.Crawford	1C	J.Duncan
3	C.Harris	P	V.Willis	P	J.Dunn			1	F.Vaughn	C	C.Zimmer
		P	K.Nichols	P	J.Hughes	P	J.Taylor	O	J.Barrett		
P	J.McGinnity	P	T.Lewis	P	B.Kennedy	P	C.Griffith	O	S.Seybold	P	J.Hughey
P	F.Kitson	P	J.Meekin	P	D.McJames	P	N.Callahan			P	C.Knepper
P	J.Nops	P	F.Killen			P	N.Garvin	P	N.Hahn	P	F.Bates
P	H.Howell			/P	A.Maul			P	P.Hawley	P	C.Schmit
		P	H.Bailey	/P	B.Donovan	P	B.Phyle	P	B.Phillips	P	H.Colliflower
		P	C.Hickman			/P	D.Cogan	P	T.Breitenstein		
/P	B.Hill	/P	F.Klobedanz			/P	J.Katoll	P	J.Taylor	P	W.Sudhoff
/P	K.McKenna	/P	O.Streit							P	K.Carsey
/P	R.Miller							/P	E.Frisk	P	B.Hill
								/P	B.Dammann	/P	J.Harper
								/P	J.Cronin	/P	H.Maupin
								/P	F.Dwyer		

LOUISVILLE		NEW YORK		PHILADELPHIA		PITTSBURGH		ST.LOUIS		WASHINGTON	
M	F.Clarke	M	J.Day	M	B.Shettsline	M	B.Watkins	M	P.Tebeau	M	A.Irwin
1B	M.Kelley	M	F.Hoey	1B	D.Cooley	M	P.Donovan	1B	P.Tebeau	1B	D.McGann
2B	C.Ritchey	1B	J.Doyle	2B	N.Lajoie	1B	W.Clark	2B	C.Childs	2B	F.Bonner
SS	B.Clingman	2B	K.Gleason	SS	M.Cross	2B	J.O'Brien	SS	B.Wallace	SS	D.Padden
3B	T.Leach	SS	G.Davis	3B	B.Lauder	SS	B.Ely	3B	L.Cross	3B	C.Atherton
LF	F.Clarke	3B	B.Hartman	LF	E.Delahanty	3B	J.Williams	LF	J.Burkett	LF	J.O'Brien
CF	D.Hoy	LF	T.O'Brien	CF	R.Thomas	LF	J.McCarthy	CF	H.Blake	CF	J.Slagle
RF	C.Dexter	CF	G.Van Haltren	RF	E.Flick	CF	G.Beaumont	RF	E.Heidrick	RF	B.Freeman
C	C.Zimmer	RF	P.Foster	C	E.McFarland	RF	P.Donovan	C	L.Criger	C	D.McGuire
		C	J.Warner			C	F.Bowerman				
3O	H.Wagner			O1	P.Chiles			C1	J.O'Connor	3P	W.Mercer
C	D.Powers	C1	P.Wilson	C	K.Douglass	O	T.McCreery	S1	E.McKean	O1	S.Barry
1	G.Decker	C3	M.Grady	2	J.Dolan	C	P.Schriver	/1	O.Schreckengost	1	P.Cassidy
C	M.Kittridge	O	M.Tiernan	1	B.Goeckel	2	H.Reitz	O1	M.Donlin	C	M.Kittridge
1	D.Wills	O	T.Fleming			1	P.Dillon	O	J.Stenzel	2S	G.Stafford
O	T.Hartsel	S	S.Hardesty	P	W.Piatt	2S	A.Madison			S	F.Scheibeck
O	F.Ketchum	O	P.Woodruff	P	R.Donahue			P	J.Powell	C	M.Roach
				P	C.Fraser	P	S.Leever	P	C.Young	S	B.Hulen
P	B.Cunningham	P	B.Carrick	P	A.Orth	P	J.Tannehill	P	W.Sudhoff	1	H.Davis
P	D.Phillippe	P	C.Seymour	P	B.Bernhard	P	T.Sparks	P	N.Cuppy	O	J.Gettman
P	P.Dowling	P	E.Doheny			P	B.Hoffer				
P	W.Woods	P	J.Meekin	P	J.Fifield	P	J.Chesbro	P	C.Jones	P	G.Weyhing
		P	C.Gettig	/P	B.Magee			P	P.McBride	P	B.Dinneen
P	R.Waddell			/P	G.Wheeler	/P	C.Gray	/P	Z.Wilson	P	D.McFarlan
P	B.Magee	P	T.Colcolough			/P	B.Rhines	/P	T.Thomas		
/P	P.Flaherty					/P	J.Gardner	/P	J.Sutthoff	P	K.Baker
/P	H.Wilhelm					/P	H.Payne			/P	R.Evans
										/P	J.Fifield
										/P	B.Magee
										/P	K.Carsey
										/P	D.Dunkle

TEAM	G	W	L	PCT	GB	R	OR	AB	H	2B	3B	HR	BB	SO	AVG	OBP	SLG	PRO	PRO+	BR	/A	PF	CHI	RC	SB	CS	SBA	SBR
BRO	150	101	47	.682		892	658	4937	1436	178	97	27	477	263	.291	**.368**	.383	.751	110	87	68	102	103	824	271			
BOS	153	95	57	.625	8	858	**645**	5290	1517	178	90	39	431	269	.287	.345	.377	.722	94	21	-59	110	103	787	185			
PHI	154	94	58	.618	9	**916**	743	5353	**1613**	241	83	31	441	341	**.301**	.363	**.395**	.758	**118**	96	128	97	99	**879**	212			
BAL	152	86	62	.581	15	827	691	5073	1509	204	71	17	448	383	.297	.365	.376	.741	104	68	24	105	97	861	**364**			
STL	155	84	67	.556	18.5	819	739	5304	1514	172	88	**47**	468	262	.285	.347	.378	.725	102	28	5	102	97	801	210			
CIN	156	83	67	.553	19	856	770	5225	1439	194	105	13	**485**	295	.275	.345	.360	.705	97	-5	-20	102	**106**	762	228			
PIT	154	76	73	.510	25.5	834	765	5450	1574	196	**121**	29	384	345	.289	.343	.384	.727	105	26	29	100	97	815	179			
CHI	152	75	73	.507	26	812	763	5148	1428	173	82	27	406	342	.277	.338	.359	.697	99	-26	-5	97	105	743	247			
LOU	155	75	77	.493	28	827	775	5307	1484	192	68	40	436	375	.280	.343	.364	.707	99	-3	-2	100	101	781	233			
NY	152	60	90	.400	42	734	863	5092	1431	161	65	23	387	360	.281	.337	.352	.689	97	-39	-13	97	100	708	234			
WAS	155	54	98	.355	49	743	983	5256	1429	162	87	**47**	350	341	.272	.328	.363	.691	91	-45	-37	99	99	710	176			
CLE	154	20	134	.130	84	529	1252	5279	1333	142	50	12	289	280	.253	.299	.305	.604	76	-209	-168	93	92	541	127			
TOT	921					9647		62714	17707	2193	1007	350	4972	3856	.282	.343	.366	.710							2666			

TEAM	CG	SH	SV	IP	H	H/G	HR	BB	SO	RAT	ERA	ERA+	OAV	OOB	PR	/A	PF	CPI	FA	E	DP	FW	PW	BW	SBW	DIF
BRO	121	9	**9**	1269[1]	1320	9.4	32	463	331	13.0	**3.25**	120	.268	.337	85	92	102	**111**	.948	314	125	2.9	8.3	6.2		9.6
BOS	138	13	4	1348	**1273**	8.5	44	432	385	11.8	3.26	**127**	**.250**	**.317**	88	**133**	108	95	**.952**	303	124	**4.0**	**12.1**	-5.3		8.3
PHI	129	**15**	2	1333[1]	1398	9.4	17	370	281	12.5	3.47	106	.270	.328	56	30	96	97	.940	379	110	-.4	2.7	**11.6**		4.0
BAL	132	10	4	1304[1]	1403	9.7	**13**	349	294	12.6	3.31	119	.275	.330	78	93	103	103	.949	308	96	3.5	8.4	2.2		-2.1
STL	134	7	1	1340[2]	1476	9.9	41	**321**	331	12.4	3.36	118	.280	.327	73	91	103	107	.939	397	117	-1.3	8.2	.8		.7
CIN	130	8	5	1361	1484	9.8	26	370	360	12.8	3.70	106	.278	.333	23	32	102	97	.947	339	111	2.3	2.9	-1.8		4.6
PIT	117	9	4	1364	1464	9.7	27	437	334	13.0	3.60	106	.274	.337	38	32	99	101	.945	361	98	.7	2.9	2.6		-4.7
CHI	**147**	8	1	1331[1]	1433	9.7	20	330	313	12.5	3.37	111	.275	.328	71	55	97	102	.935	428	**145**	-3.5	5.0	-.5		-.0
LOU	134	5	2	1351[2]	1509	10.0	33	323	287	12.6	3.45	112	.282	.331	60	60	100	106	.939	394	101	-1.1	5.4	-.2		-5.2
NY	138	4	0	1278[1]	1454	10.2	19	628	**397**	15.3	4.29	87	.286	.375	-63	-78	97	103	.932	433	140	-3.8	-7.1	-1.2		-3.0
WAS	131	3	0	1300[1]	1649	11.4	35	422	328	14.9	4.93	79	.309	.368	-157	-149	102	95	.935	403	99	-1.6	-13.5	-3.4		-3.5
CLE	138	0	0	1264	1844	13.1	43	527	215	17.7	6.37	58	.340	.409	-353	-378	96	94	.937	388	121	-.9	-34.3	-15.2		-6.6
TOT	1589	91	32	15846[1]		10.1				13.4	3.85		.282	.343					.942	4447	1387					

Runs		Hits		Doubles		Triples		Home Runs		Total Bases	
McGraw-Bal	140	Delahanty-Phi	238	Delahanty-Phi	55	Williams-Pit	27	Freeman-Was	25	Delahanty-Phi	338
Keeler-Bro	140	Burkett-StL	221	Wagner-Lou	43	Freeman-Was	25	Wallace-StL	12	Freeman-Was	331
Thomas-Phi	137	Williams-Pit	219	Holmes-Bal	31	Stahl-Bos	19	Williams-Pit	9	Williams-Pit	328
Delahanty-Phi	135	Keeler-Bro	216	Long-Bos	30	Tenney-Bos	17	Mertes-Chi	9	Stahl-Bos	284
Williams-Pit	126	Tenney-Bos	209	Duffy-Bos	29	McCarthy-Pit	17	Delahanty-Phi	9	Wagner-Lou	282

Runs Batted In		Runs Produced		Bases On Balls		Batting Average		On Base Percentage		Slugging Average	
Delahanty-Phi	137	Delahanty-Phi	263	McGraw-Bal	124	Delahanty-Phi	.410	McGraw-Bal	.547	Delahanty-Phi	.582
Freeman-Was	122	Williams-Pit	233	Thomas-Phi	115	Burkett-StL	.396	Delahanty-Phi	.464	Freeman-Was	.563
Williams-Pit	116	Wagner-Lou	204	VanHaltren-NY	74	McGraw-Bal	.391	Burkett-StL	.463	Williams-Pit	.532
Wagner-Lou	113	Freeman-Was	204	Childs-StL	74	Keeler-Bro	.379	Thomas-Phi	.457	Burkett-StL	.500
Wallace-StL	108					Williams-Pit	.355	Stahl-Bos	.426	Wagner-Lou	.494

Production		Adjusted Production		Batter Runs		Adjusted Batter Runs		Clutch Hitting Index		Runs Created	
Delahanty-Phi	1.046	Delahanty-Phi	193	Delahanty-Phi	67.9	Delahanty-Phi	73.5	Brodie-Bal	139	Delahanty-Phi	175
McGraw-Bal	.994	McGraw-Bal	165	McGraw-Bal	56.8	McGraw-Bal	50.2	Long-Bos	131	Williams-Pit	152
Burkett-StL	.963	Burkett-StL	160	Burkett-StL	51.6	Williams-Pit	49.5	Magoon-Bal-Chi	129	Burkett-StL	145
Williams-Pit	.949	Williams-Pit	160	Williams-Pit	49.0	Burkett-StL	48.4	Lauder-Phi	128	McGraw-Bal	141
Freeman-Was	.925	Freeman-Was	154	Stahl-Bos	42.2	Freeman-Was	37.6	Corcoran-Cin	128	Stahl-Bos	139

Total Average		Stolen Bases		Stolen Base Average		Stolen Base Runs		Fielding Runs		Total Player Rating	
McGraw-Bal	1.601	Sheckard-Bal	77					G.Davis-NY	46.3	G.Davis-NY	6.2
Delahanty-Phi	1.245	McGraw-Bal	73					Wallace-StL	38.8	Delahanty-Phi	5.6
Burkett-StL	1.107	Heidrick-StL	55					Cross-Cle-StL	32.7	Wallace-StL	5.3
Williams-Pit	1.055	Holmes-Bal	50					Gleason-NY	25.7	Williams-Pit	5.2
Stahl-Bos	1.051	Clarke-Lou	49					Collins-Bos	20.9	Lajoie-Phi	4.9

Wins		Win Percentage		Games		Complete Games		Shutouts		Saves	
McGinnity-Bal	28	Hughes-Bro	.824	Leever-Pit	51	Young-StL	40	Willis-Bos	5	Leever-Pit	3
Hughes-Bro	28	Willis-Bos	.771	Powell-StL	48	Powell-StL	40				
Willis-Bos	27	Hahn-Cin	.742	McGinnity-Bal	48	Carrick-NY	40				
Young-StL	26	Donahue-Phi	.724	Young-StL	44	Taylor-Chi	39				
Tannehill-Pit	24	Kennedy-Bro	.710	Carrick-NY	44	McGinnity-Bal	38				

Innings Pitched		Fewest Hits/Game		Fewest BB/Game		Strikeouts		Strikeouts/Game		Ratio	
Leever-Pit	379.0	Willis-Bos	7.28	Young-StL	1.07	Hahn-Cin	145	Seymour-NY	4.76	Young-StL	10.19
Powell-StL	373.0	Hughes-Bro	7.71	Cuppy-StL	1.36	Seymour-NY	142	Hahn-Cin	4.22	Hahn-Cin	10.43
Young-StL	369.1	Hahn-Cin	8.16	Tannehill-Pit	1.47	Leever-Pit	121	Doheny-NY	3.90	Nichols-Bos	10.85
McGinnity-Bal	366.1	Seymour-NY	8.28	Kitson-Bal	1.79	Willis-Bos	120	McJames-Bro	3.43	Willis-Bos	11.14
Carrick-NY	361.2	Leever-Pit	8.38	Woods-Lou	1.79	Doheny-NY	115	Willis-Bos	3.15	Kitson-Bal	11.15

Earned Run Average		Adjusted ERA		Opponents' Batting Avg.		Opponents' On Base Pct.		Starter Runs		Adjusted Starter Runs	
Willis-Bos	2.50	Willis-Bos	166	Willis-Bos	.222	Young-StL	.285	Young-StL	52.0	Willis-Bos	63.1
Young-StL	2.58	Young-StL	154	Hughes-Bro	.232	Hahn-Cin	.290	Willis-Bos	51.6	Young-StL	57.2
McGinnity-Bal	2.68	McGinnity-Bal	148	Hahn-Cin	.242	Nichols-Bos	.298	McGinnity-Bal	47.7	McGinnity-Bal	52.1
Hahn-Cin	2.68	Hahn-Cin	146	Seymour-NY	.245	Willis-Bos	.303	Hahn-Cin	40.2	Nichols-Bos	44.5
Hughes-Bro	2.68	Hughes-Bro	146	Leever-Pit	.247	Kitson-Bal	.304	Kitson-Bal	39.2	Kitson-Bal	43.1

Clutch Pitching Index		Relief Runs		Adjusted Relief Runs		Relief Ranking		Total Pitcher Index		Total Baseball Ranking	
Kennedy-Bro	130							Young-StL	6.2	G.Davis-NY	6.2
Tannehill-Pit	124							Willis-Bos	5.3	Young-StL	6.2
Dowling-Lou	121							McGinnity-Bal	5.0	Delahanty-Phi	5.6
Callahan-Chi	121							Tannehill-Pit	4.8	Willis-Bos	5.3
Woods-Lou	118							Hughes-Bro	4.7	Wallace-StL	5.3

January 24 The NL Reduction Committee has a secret meeting in Cleveland, supposedly to discuss dropping Louisville, Baltimore, Washington, and Cleveland from the league roster.

February 17 Mary Hamilton Von Derbeck becomes owner of the Detroit AL franchise and Bennett Park in lieu of unpaid alimony. However, her ex-husband George Von Derbeck files the required bond with a Michigan court to cover the due alimony, regains ownership of the club, and sells it to Tiger manager George Stallings on March 6.

March 8 In New York, the NL meets and votes to go with eight teams. The league pays the Baltimore owners $30,000 for their franchise, with Ebbets and Hanlon reserving the right to sell the players. Cleveland, Louisville, and Washington receive $10,000 each, and Louisville owner Barney Dreyfuss sends most of his players to his Pittsburgh team. The circuit will remain the same for 53 years, until the Boston Braves move to Milwaukee in 1953.

March 16 At an AL meeting in Chicago Ban Johnson announces that an AL team will be placed in the Windy City, ensuring the stability of the league. Other franchises are in Kansas City, Minneapolis, Milwaukee, Indianapolis, Detroit, Cleveland, and Buffalo. In an agreement with Chicago NL officials the AL club will be situated on the south side of the city and will be permitted to use the nickname "White Stockings," formerly used by the NL team. However, the White Stockings will not be able to use the word "Chicago" in their official name.

April 30* Brothers Joe, Jim, and Tom Delahanty, playing their third year together with Allentown, open the Atlantic League season by banging out a family total of 11 hits good for 20 bases.

May 28 A fire in Cincinnati nearly destroys the grandstand. The new grandstand will not be built until 1902, and the Reds are forced to play on the road for a month.

June 9 A forerunner of today's players' union is organized in New York. Three delegates from each NL team launch the Players Protective Association (PPA) and elect Chief Zimmer president. Their goal is to negotiate contracts and rules changes.

July 7 Boston hurler Kid Nichols notches his 300th career victory, beating Chicago, 11-4. The win comes two months before his 31st birthday, making him the youngest ever to reach that magic figure.

July 17 At Brooklyn's Washington Park, the Superbas tie the score against the Giants in the fifth. With two men on base, New York captain George Davis takes out pitcher Ed Doheny and brings in rookie Christy Mathewson, just brought up from Norfolk. He hits three batters, walks two, and gives up six runs in a 13-7 loss.

September 17 Reds shortstop Tommy Corcoran, coaching at third in a game at Philadelphia, uncovers a wire in the coaching box that leads across the outfield to the Phils' locker room, where reserve catcher Morgan Murphy is reading the opposing catcher's signs and relaying them to the Phils' coach using a buzzer hidden in the dirt.

October 13 Ban Johnson promises to put the following provisions in all player contracts in the AL: no suspensions for more than 10 days; clubs to pay doctor bills for injuries occurring during a game; if a club abandons the league, its players become free agents after 10 days; no farming or selling without the player's written consent; no reserve clause for more than three years or for less salary than the current year; and binding arbitration for disputes.

October 15 The *Pittsburgh Chronicle-Telegraph* World Title series between first-place Brooklyn and second-place Pittsburgh begins with a 5-2 win for Joe McGinnity over Rube Waddell. The Superbas win the series, the Cup given by the newspaper, and half the gate receipts. For his efforts, which include a league-leading 29 wins and 347 innings pitched for Brooklyn, McGinnity is given permanent possession of the trophy and a $100 bonus.

November 14 The NL rejects the AL as an equal, declaring it an outlaw league outside of the National Agreement, thus inaugurating a state of war.

December 15 Amos Rusie, a holdout for two years, is traded to the Reds by the Giants for Christy Mathewson. (Mathewson made an unspectacular debut for the Giants in 1900, but upon returning to minor-league Norfolk, he was claimed by Cincinnati.) Though only 30, Rusie, a future Hall of Fame pitcher, will not add to the 245 wins he collected in nine seasons. Appearing in just three games in 1901, he will finish with an 0-1 record. Mathewson will set the NL record for career wins.

	BOSTON		BROOKLYN		CHICAGO		CINCINNATI		NEW YORK		PHILADELPHIA		PITTSBURGH		ST.LOUIS
M	F.Selee	M	N.Hanlon	M	T.Loftus	M	B.Allen	M	B.Ewing	M	B.Shettsline	M	F.Clarke	M	P.Tebeau
1B	F.Tenney	1B	H.Jennings	1B	J.Ganzel	1B	J.Beckley	M	G.Davis	1B	E.Delahanty	1B	D.Cooley	M	L.Heilbroner
2B	B.Lowe	2B	T.Daly	2B	C.Childs	2B	J.Quinn	1B	J.Doyle	2B	N.Lajoie	2B	C.Ritchey	1B	D.McGann
SS	H.Long	SS	B.Dahlen	SS	B.McCormick	SS	T.Corcoran	2B	K.Gleason	SS	M.Cross	SS	B.Ely	2B	B.Keister
3B	J.Collins	3B	L.Cross	3B	B.Bradley	3B	H.Steinfeldt	SS	G.Davis	3B	H.Wolverton	3B	J.Williams	SS	B.Wallace
LF	C.Stahl	LF	J.Sheckard	LF	J.McCarthy	LF	S.Crawford	3B	C.Hickman	LF	J.Slagle	LF	F.Clarke	3B	J.McGraw
CF	B.Hamilton	CF	F.Jones	CF	D.Green	CF	J.Barrett	LF	K.Selbach	CF	R.Thomas	CF	G.Beaumont	LF	J.Burkett
RF	B.Freeman	RF	W.Keeler	RF	J.Ryan	RF	A.McBride	CF	G.Van Haltren	RF	E.Flick	RF	H.Wagner	CF	E.Heidrick
C	B.Clarke	C	D.Farrell	C	T.Donahue	C	H.Peitz	RF	E.Smith	C	E.McFarland	C	C.Zimmer	RF	P.Donovan
								C	F.Bowerman					C	L.Criger
OS	S.Barry	O1	J.Kelley	O1	S.Mertes	3S	C.Irwin	32	J.Dolan	1O	T.O'Brien	O1	M.Donlin
C	B.Sullivan	C	D.McGuire	S	B.Clingman	C	M.Kahoe	C1	K.Douglass	3	T.Leach	C	W.Robinson
O	H.Duffy	2S	G.DeMontreville	C3	F.Chance	C3	B.Wood	12	J.Warner	C	J.O'Connor	O3	P.Dillard
C	J.Clements	/3	A.Smith	CO	C.Dexter	O	P.Geier	C	P.Chiles	O	T.McCreery	2	J.Quinn
/C	J.Connor	/C	F.Steelman	3	S.Strang	O	E.Smith	2	M.Murphy	/3	P.Schriver	3	L.Cross
		/3	D.Casey	1	B.Everitt	O	T.Hartsel	O	C.Bernard	/1	P.Dillon		
P	B.Dinneen			C	J.Kling	/O	D.Harley	/O	C.Frisbee	/3	C.Ziegler	/C	T.Latimer	C	J.O'Connor
P	V.Willis	P	J.McGinnity	O	C.Dolan	/S	B.Allen	/S	T.Sheehan			/C	J.Donahue	/C	F.Buelow
P	K.Nichols	P	B.Kennedy	/C	A.Nichols					P	A.Orth	/O	E.Poole	/S	P.Tebeau
P	T.Lewis	P	F.Kitson	/O	S.Dungan			P	B.Carrick	P	R.Donahue			/C	H.Stanton
P	T.Pittinger	P	H.Howell	/3	H.Wolverton			P	P.Hawley	P	C.Fraser	P	D.Phillippe		
				/C	R.Bresnahan			P	W.Mercer	P	B.Bernhard	P	J.Tannehill		
P	N.Cuppy	/P	J.Nops	P	B.Phillips	P	E.Scott	P	W.Piatt	P	S.Leever	P	C.Young
/P	H.Bailey	P	J.Dunn	P	N.Callahan	P	T.Breitenstein					P	J.Chesbro	P	C.Jones
/P	R.Chambers	/P	G.Weyhing	P	C.Griffith					D.Taylor	P	J.Dunn	P	R.Waddell	P	J.Powell
		/P	B.Donovan	P	N.Garvin	/P	A.Stimmel	P	C.Seymour	/P	A.Maul			P	W.Sudhoff
		/P	J.Yeager	P	J.Taylor			/P	C.Mathewson	/P	B.Conn	/P	P.Flaherty	P	J.Hughey
				P	J.Menefee			/P	D.Cogan	/P	W.McLaughlin	/P	J.Meekin		
												/P	B.Husting	/P	G.Weyhing
				/P	B.Cunningham							/P	W.Woods	/P	T.Thomas
				/P	F.Killen									/P	J.Harper
				/P	T.Hughes										
				/P	M.Eason										
				/P	E.Harvey										

TEAM	G	W	L	PCT	GB	R	OR	AB	H	2B	3B	HR	BB	SO	AVG	OBP	SLG	PRO	PRO+	BR	/A	PF	CHI	RC	SB	CS	SBA	SBR
BRO	142	82	54	.603		816	722	4860	1423	199	81	26	421	272	.293	.359	.383	.742	104	72	23	106	100	795	274			
PIT	140	79	60	.568	4.5	733	612	4817	1312	185	100	26	327	321	.272	.327	.368	.695	96	-25	-30	101	105	666	174			
PHI	141	75	63	.543	8	810	792	4969	1439	187	82	29	440	374	.290	.356	.378	.734	109	58	65	99	99	774	205			
BOS	142	66	72	.478	17	778	739	4952	1403	163	68	48	395	278	.283	.342	.373	.715	92	16	-78	112	102	724	182			
STL	142	65	75	.464	19	744	748	4877	1420	141	81	36	406	318	.291	.356	.375	.731	108	52	58	99	94	766	243			
CHI	146	65	75	.464	19	635	751	4907	1276	202	51	33	343	383	.260	.317	.342	.659	90	-87	-63	96	97	622	189			
CIN	144	62	77	.446	21.5	703	745	5026	1335	178	83	33	333	408	.266	.318	.354	.672	92	-71	-54	98	103	651	183			
NY	141	60	78	.435	23	713	823	4724	1317	177	61	23	369	343	.279	.338	.357	.695	102	-16	16	95	102	676	236			
TOT	569					5932		39132	10925	1432	607	254	3034	2697	.279	.339	.366	.705						1686				

TEAM	CG	SH	SV	IP	H	H/G	HR	BB	SO	RAT	ERA	ERA+	OAV	OOB	PR	/A	PF	CPI	FA	E	DP	FW	PW	BW	SBW	DIF
BRO	104	8	4	1225²	1370	10.1	30	405	300	13.6	3.89	99	.282	.346	-27	-8	104	99	.948	303	102	2.6	-.7	2.1		10.1
PIT	114	11	1	1229	1232	9.0	24	295	415	11.7	3.06	119	.261	.313	87	77	98	97	.945	322	106	1.1	7.0	-2.7		4.1
PHI	116	7	3	1248²	1506	10.9	29	402	284	14.2	4.12	88	.298	.357	-59	-71	98	103	.945	330	125	.8	-6.5	5.9		5.8
BOS	116	8	2	1240¹	1263	9.2	59	463	340	12.9	3.72	111	.264	.335	-4	55	112	97	.953	273	86	4.4	5.0	-7.1		-5.3
STL	117	12	0	1217¹	1373	10.2	37	299	325	12.7	3.75	97	.281	.331	-7	-16	98	97	.943	331	73	.8	-1.5	5.3		-9.7
CHI	137	9	1	1271	1375	9.7	21	324	357	12.6	3.23	112	.276	.330	66	52	98	106	.933	418	98	-3.9	4.8	-5.8		-.0
CIN	118	9	1	1274²	1383	9.8	28	404	399	13.0	3.83	96	.276	.338	-20	-24	99	94	.945	341	120	.5	-2.2	-4.9		-.9
NY	113	4	0	1207¹	1423	10.6	26	442	277	14.6	3.96	91	.293	.363	-35	-47	98	108	.928	439	124	-6.0	-4.3	1.5		-.2
TOT	935	68	12	9914		9.9				13.2	3.69		.279	.339					.942	2757	834					

Runs		Hits		Doubles		Triples		Home Runs		Total Bases	
Thomas-Phi	132	Keeler-Bro	204	Wagner-Pit	45	Wagner-Pit	22	Long-Bos	12	Wagner-Pit	302
Slagle-Phi	115	Burkett-StL	203	Lajoie-Phi	33	Kelley-Bro	17	Flick-Phi	11	Flick-Phi	297
VanHaltren-NY	114	Wagner-Pit	201	Flick-Phi	32	Hickman-NY	17	Donlin-StL	10	Burkett-StL	265
Barrett-Cin	114	Flick-Phi	200	Delahanty-Phi	32	Stahl-Bos	16	Hickman-NY	9	Keeler-Bro	253
Wagner-Pit	107	Beckley-Cin	190	VanHaltren-NY	30	Flick-Phi	16	Sullivan-Bos	8	Beckley-Cin	242

Runs Batted In		Runs Produced		Bases On Balls		Batting Average		On Base Percentage		Slugging Average	
Flick-Phi	110	Flick-Phi	205	Thomas-Phi	115	Wagner-Pit	.381	McGraw-StL	.505	Wagner-Pit	.573
Delahanty-Phi	109	Wagner-Pit	203	Hamilton-Bos	107	Flick-Phi	.367	Thomas-Phi	.451	Flick-Phi	.545
Wagner-Pit	100	Collins-Bos	193	McGraw-StL	85	Burkett-StL	.363	Hamilton-Bos	.449	Lajoie-Phi	.510
Collins-Bos	95	Beckley-Cin	190	Dahlen-Bro	73	Keeler-Bro	.362	Flick-Phi	.441	Kelley-Bro	.485
Beckley-Cin	94	Delahanty-Phi	189			McGraw-StL	.344	Wagner-Pit	.434	Hickman-NY	.482

Production		Adjusted Production		Batter Runs		Adjusted Batter Runs		Clutch Hitting Index		Runs Created	
Wagner-Pit	1.007	Wagner-Pit	175	Flick-Phi	53.5	Flick-Phi	54.7	Delahanty-Phi	143	Wagner-Pit	152
Flick-Phi	.986	Flick-Phi	172	Wagner-Pit	53.2	Wagner-Pit	52.3	Cross-Phi	142	Flick-Phi	151
McGraw-StL	.921	McGraw-StL	157	Burkett-StL	39.0	Burkett-StL	40.0	Jennings-Bro	138	Burkett-StL	133
Burkett-StL	.904	Selbach-NY	151	McGraw-StL	36.0	Selbach-NY	39.8	Lowe-Bos	122	Keeler-Bro	123
Selbach-NY	.885	Burkett-StL	150	Selbach-NY	34.3	McGraw-StL	36.8	Collins-Bos	119	Selbach-NY	121

Total Average		Stolen Bases		Stolen Base Average	Stolen Base Runs	Fielding Runs		Total Player Rating	
McGraw-StL	1.260	VanHaltren-NY	45			Steinfeldt-Cin	35.6	Lajoie-Phi	5.0
Wagner-Pit	1.193	Donovan-StL	45			Lajoie-Phi	29.5	Davis-NY	4.6
Flick-Phi	1.171	Barrett-Cin	44			Davis-NY	29.3	Flick-Phi	4.3
Selbach-NY	1.029	Keeler-Bro	41			Dahlen-Bro	19.8	Selbach-NY	3.5
Burkett-StL	1.017					Bradley-Chi	16.8	Wagner-Pit	3.3

Wins		Win Percentage		Games		Complete Games		Shutouts		Saves	
McGinnity-Bro	28	McGinnity-Bro	.778	Carrick-NY	45	Hawley-NY	34	Young-StL	4	Kitson-Bro	4
Tannehill-Pit	20	Tannehill-Pit	.769	McGinnity-Bro	44	Dinneen-Bos	33	Nichols-Bos	4	Bernhard-Phi	2
Philippe-Pit	20	Fraser-Phi	.625	Scott-Cin	42			Hahn-Cin	4		
Kennedy-Bro	20	Phillippe-Pit	.606	Kennedy-Bro	42			Griffith-Chi	4		
Dinneen-Bos	20	Kennedy-Bro	.606								

Innings Pitched		Fewest Hits/Game		Fewest BB/Game		Strikeouts		Strikeouts/Game		Ratio	
McGinnity-Bro	343.0	Waddell-Pit	7.59	Young-StL	1.01	Hahn-Cin	132	Waddell-Pit	5.61	Phillippe-Pit	10.42
Carrick-NY	341.2	Garvin-Chi	8.22	Phillippe-Pit	1.35	Waddell-Pit	130	Garvin-Chi	3.91	Waddell-Pit	10.52
Hawley-NY	329.1	Nichols-Bos	8.36	Tannehill-Pit	1.65	Young-StL	115	Hahn-Cin	3.82	Young-StL	10.53
Young-StL	321.1	Dinneen-Bos	8.53	Griffith-Chi	1.85	Garvin-Chi	107	Newton-Cin	3.38	Garvin-Chi	11.18
Dinneen-Bos	320.2	Phillippe-Pit	8.84	Leever-Pit	1.86	Dinneen-Bos	107	Leever-Pit	3.25	Leever-Pit	11.30

Earned Run Average		Adjusted ERA		Opponents' Batting Avg.		Opponents' On Base Pct.		Starter Runs		Adjusted Starter Runs	
Waddell-Pit	2.37	Waddell-Pit	153	Waddell-Pit	.229	Phillippe-Pit	.289	Garvin-Chi	35.1	Dinneen-Bos	35.9
Garvin-Chi	2.41	Garvin-Chi	149	Garvin-Chi	.243	Waddell-Pit	.291	Waddell-Pit	30.7	McGinnity-Bro	34.2
Taylor-Chi	2.55	Taylor-Chi	141	Nichols-Bos	.246	Young-StL	.291	McGinnity-Bro	28.8	Garvin-Chi	32.6
Leever-Pit	2.71	Nichols-Bos	134	Dinneen-Bos	.250	Garvin-Chi	.304	Taylor-Chi	28.3	Waddell-Pit	29.1
Sudhoff-StL	2.76	Leever-Pit	134	Phillippe-Pit	.257	Leever-Pit	.306	Phillippe-Pit	26.5	Nichols-Bos	27.0

Clutch Pitching Index		Relief Runs	Adjusted Relief Runs	Relief Ranking	Total Pitcher Index		Total Baseball Ranking	
Fraser-Phi	131				Dinneen-Bos	3.6	Lajoie-Phi	5.0
Taylor-Chi	119				Garvin-Chi	3.1	Davis-NY	4.6
McGinnity-Bro	118				Taylor-Chi	2.7	Flick-Phi	4.3
Carrick-NY	115				Tannehill-Pit	2.7	Dinneen-Bos	3.6
Donahue-Phi	113				Nichols-Bos	2.6	Selbach-NY	3.5

February 8 News leaks out that Napoleon Lajoie, the Phillies second baseman and leading NL hitter, has jumped to the new Philadelphia AL club, along with pitchers Chick Fraser and Bill Bernhard.

February 27 The NL Rules Committee decrees that all fouls are to count as strikes, except after two strikes. To cut the cost of balls fouled and unrecovered, the committee urges that "batsmen who foul off good strikes are to be disciplined." Other new rules: a ball will be called if the pitcher does not throw to a ready and waiting batter within 20 seconds, or, when a batter is hit by a pitch.

March 2 Jimmy Collins, Connie Mack's choice for the all-time best third baseman, leaves the Boston NL club to manage the AL's new Boston Somersets. The Beaneaters also lose outfielder Hugh Duffy, who will manage Milwaukee (AL), and catcher Billy Sullivan, who signs with the Chicago White Stockings.

March 28 Phillies owner John Rogers files for an injunction prohibiting Nap Lajoie, Bill Bernhard, and Chick Fraser from playing for any other team—the most serious legal test of the reserve clause to date.

April 8 Amos Rusie, the "Hoosier Thunderbolt," makes his first start for the Cincinnati Reds after a two-year layoff and is bombed, 14–3. After two more appearances, he goes back to digging ditches, having won 245 games.

April 26 After six postponements, the Giants finally get the season going. New York defeats the Brooklyn Superbas, 5-3. It is Christy Mathewson's first of an NL-record 373 career victories.

May 21 Giants fractious owner Andrew Freedman accuses umpire Billy Nash of incompetence and bars him from the Polo Grounds. One Pirate and one Giant are forced to officiate.

May 30 An NL record crowd of 28,500 sees St. Louis beat the Giants, 6–5, in 10 innings in the afternoon game of a split holiday doubleheader at New York.

June 9 Overflow crowds ringing the outfields of small parks is a frequent occurrence. At Cincinnati on this Sunday afternoon, the first-place Giants lead, 15–4, after six innings before 17,000 fans. Ground-rule doubles multiply, and 19 more runs score in the next 2½ innings. When the crowd edges onto the infield, with the Giants leading, 25–13, umpire Bob Emslie forfeits the game to New York. The game registers a record 31 hits and 13 doubles. Only one Giant will return to the team in 1902: five will go to the AL, and three will retire.

June 18 The Boston NL club lowers its admission price of 50 cents to the AL's 25 cents. The Somersets will still draw 200,000 more than the NL team.

June 20 Pittsburgh's Honus Wagner steals home twice in a single game, as Jack Chesbro blanks the Giants, 7–0.

July 15 Christy Mathewson (22 years old) of the Giants pitches a no-hitter, blanking St. Louis, 5–0, at League Park. Matty saves his own no-hitter in the sixth when an Otto Krueger hit caroms off first baseman John Ganzel's glove to Mathewson, who throws back to first base for a 3–1–3 putout.

August 4 Cincinnati and Pittsburgh players are clocked while running from home plate to first base. The fastest time for the 90-foot sprint is three seconds flat, by Pirates outfielder Ginger Beaumont.

August 6* The National Association of Professional Baseball Leagues is formed to help the minor leagues protect their interests.

September 19 All games are canceled out of respect for the funeral of President William McKinley, who died September 14 from gunshot wounds.

September 24 Jimmy Sheckard hits grand slams in two consecutive games, as Brooklyn beats Cincinnati, 16–2, the day after a 25–6 win.

	BOSTON		BROOKLYN		CHICAGO		CINCINNATI		NEW YORK		PHILADELPHIA		PITTSBURGH		ST.LOUIS
M	F.Selee	M	N.Hanlon	M	T.Loftus	M	B.McPhee	M	G.Davis	M	B.Shettsline	M	F.Clarke	M	P.Donovan
1B	F.Tenney	1B	J.Kelley	1B	J.Doyle	1B	J.Beckley	1B	J.Ganzel	1B	H.Jennings	1B	K.Bransfield	1B	D.McGann
2B	G.DeMontreville	2B	T.Daly	2B	C.Childs	2B	H.Steinfeldt	2B	R.Nelson	2B	B.Hallman	2B	C.Ritchey	2B	D.Padden
SS	H.Long	SS	B.Dahlen	SS	B.McCormick	SS	G.Magoon	SS	G.Davis	SS	M.Cross	SS	B.Ely	SS	B.Wallace
3B	B.Lowe	3B	C.Irwin	3B	F.Raymer	3B	C.Irwin	3B	S.Strang	3B	H.Wolverton	3B	T.Leach	3B	O.Krueger
LF	D.Cooley	LF	J.Sheckard	LF	T.Hartsel	LF	D.Harley	LF	K.Selbach	LF	E.Delahanty	LF	F.Clarke	LF	J.Burkett
CF	B.Hamilton	CF	T.McCreery	CF	D.Green	CF	J.Dobbs	CF	G.Van Haltren	CF	R.Thomas	CF	G.Beaumont	CF	E.Heidrick
RF	J.Slagle	RF	W.Keeler	RF	F.Chance	RF	S.Crawford	RF	A.McBride	RF	E.Flick	RF	L.Davis	RF	P.Donovan
C	M.Kittridge	C	D.McGuire	C	J.Kling	C	B.Bergen	C	J.Warner	C	E.McFarland	C	C.Zimmer	C	J.Ryan
O	F.Crolius	C1	D.Farrell	13	C.Dexter	C2	H.Peitz	OS	G.Hickman	23	S.Barry	SO	H.Wagner	CO	A.Nichols
C1	P.Moran	C	C.Dolan	C	M.Kahoe	2	B.Fox	C	F.Bowerman	C	J.Slagle	C	J.O'Connor	C1	P.Schriver
O	F.Murphy	3	F.Gatins	2	P.Childs	O	H.Bay	2O	F.Murphy	C	K.Douglass	C	G.Yeager	2	P.Childs
O	F.Gammons	O	L.Davis	C	C.Dolan	O	A.McBride	O	J.Jones	C	F.Jacklitsch	3	J.Burke	1	B.Richardson
O	J.Rickert	/S	J.Gochnauer	OP	J.Menefee	S	T.Corcoran	2	A.Smith	J	J.Dolan	/S	L.Carr	O	M.Heydon
O	E.Smith	/C	H.Hearne	3	J.Delahanty	2	P.O'Brien	O	C.Bernard	/O	G.Browne	/3	J.Smith		
O	P.Carney	/C	F.Steelman	C	B.Gannon	/C	J.Hurley	3	C.Buelow	/2	B.Conn	/S	T.Eagan	P	J.Powell
O	S.Barry			3	E.Hickey	/3	E.Haberer	2	J.Miller			/3	T.Turner	P	J.Harper
/O	B.Lush	P	B.Donovan	/3	L.Hoffman	/3	C.Heileman	/2	H.Smith	P	R.Donahue	/O	E.Smith	P	W.Sudhoff
/O	G.Grossart	P	F.Kitson	/O	H.Croft	/C	M.Kahoe	/2	D.Murphy	P	B.Duggleby	/C	J.Donahue	P	E.Murphy
/O	F.Brown	P	J.Hughes	/2	G.Schaefer	/C	C.Krause	/C	J.Wall	P	A.Orth				
/3	J.Hinton	P	D.Newton							P	D.White	P	D.Phillippe	P	C.Jones
		P	D.McJames	P	T.Hughes	P	N.Hahn	P	D.Taylor	P	H.Townsend	P	J.Chesbro	/P	M.O'Neill
P	K.Nichols			P	J.Taylor	P	B.Phillips	P	C.Mathewson			P	J.Tannehill	/P	S.Yerkes
P	B.Dinneen	P	B.Kennedy	P	R.Waddell	P	D.Newton	P	B.Phyle	/P	J.Dunn	P	S.Leever	/P	T.Breitenstein
P	V.Willis	/P	G.McCann	P	M.Eason	P	A.Stimmel							/P	B.Magee
P	T.Pittinger	/P	G.Wright					P	E.Doheny			PO	E.Poole	/P	C.Fisher
		/P	K.Carsey	/P	B.Cunningham	P	J.Sutthoff	P	R.Denzer			P	E.Doheny	/P	B.Wicker
/P	B.Lawson			/P	C.Ferguson	/P	B.McFadden	/P	B.Magee			/S	S.Wiltse	/P	F.Burns
						/P	W.Guese	/P	A.Maul			/P	G.Merritt		
						/P	C.Case	/P	D.Leitner			/P	R.Waddell		
						/P	L.Swormstedt	/P	D.Deegan						
						/P	A.Rusie	/P	W.Mills						
						/P	D.Scott	/P	I.Van Zandt						
						/P	C.Heismann	/P	J.Livingstone						
						/P	G.Weyhing	/P	L.Hesterfer						
						/P	D.Parker	/P	C.Fisher						
								/P	H.Felix						

TEAM	G	W	L	PCT	GB	R	OR	AB	H	2B	3B	HR	BB	SO	AVG	OBP	SLG	PRO	PRO+	BR	/A	PF	CHI	RC	SB	CS	SBA	SBR
PIT	140	90	49	.647		776	**534**	4913	1407	182	92	29	386	493	.286	**.345**	.379	**.724**	113	99	76	103	102	743	203			
PHI	140	83	57	.593	7.5	668	543	4793	1275	194	58	24	**430**	549	.266	.334	.346	.680	101	29	15	102	98	652	199			
BRO	137	79	57	.581	9.5	744	600	4879	1399	**206**	93	32	312	**449**	**.287**	.335	**.387**	.722	112	86	66	103	102	718	178			
STL	142	76	64	.543	14.5	792	689	5039	**1430**	187	**94**	**39**	314	540	.284	.337	.381	.718	**120**	87	**125**	95	**104**	**744**	190			
BOS	140	69	69	.500	20.5	531	556	4746	1180	135	36	28	303	519	.249	.298	.310	.608	75	-104	-153	109	101	515	158			
CHI	140	53	86	.381	37	578	699	4844	1250	153	61	18	314	532	.258	.310	.326	.636	94	-57	-35	96	99	575	**204**			
NY	141	52	85	.380	37	544	755	4839	1225	167	46	19	303	575	.253	.303	.318	.621	89	-83	-62	96	98	529	133			
CIN	142	52	87	.374	38	561	818	4914	1232	173	70	38	323	584	.251	.303	.338	.641	97	-56	-17	93	94	570	137			
TOT	561					5194		38967	10398	1397	550	227	2685	4241	.267	.321	.348	.669						1402				

TEAM	CG	SH	SV	IP	H	H/G	HR	BB	SO	RAT	ERA	ERA+	OAV	OOB	PR	/A	PF	CPI	FA	E	DP	FW	PW	BW	SBW	DIF
PIT	119	**15**	4	1244²	1198	8.7	20	**244**	505	10.9	2.58	126	.252	**.297**	**102**	94	98	104	.950	287	97	1.2	9.2	7.4		2.6
PHI	125	**15**	2	1246²	1221	8.8	19	259	480	11.0	2.87	119	.255	.300	63	73	102	97	**.954**	262	65	**2.7**	7.2	1.5		1.7
BRO	111	7	**5**	1213²	1244	9.2	**18**	435	583	12.8	3.14	107	.264	.333	24	27	101	**109**	.950	281	99	1.2	2.6	6.5		.7
STL	118	5	**5**	1269²	1333	9.4	39	332	445	12.2	3.68	86	.268	.321	-51	-71	96	93	.949	305	**108**	.4	-7.0	**12.3**		.3
BOS	128	11	0	1263	**1196**	**8.5**	29	349	558	11.3	2.90	125	**.249**	.305	59	**99**	109	98	.952	282	89	1.5	**9.7**	-15.0		3.8
CHI	**131**	2	0	1241²	1348	9.8	27	324	**586**	12.5	3.33	97	.275	.327	-2	-14	97	105	.943	336	87	-1.8	-1.4	-3.4		-9.9
NY	118	11	1	1232	1389	10.1	24	377	542	13.4	3.87	85	.283	.342	-75	-78	100	99	.941	348	81	-2.3	-7.6	-6.1		-.4
CIN	126	4	0	1265²	1469	10.4	51	365	542	13.5	4.17	77	.289	.345	-120	-138	96	99	.940	355	102	-2.6	-13.5	-1.7		.3
TOT	976	70	17	9977		9.4				12.2	3.32		.267	.321					.947	2456	728					

Runs		Hits		Doubles		Triples		Home Runs		Total Bases	
Burkett-StL	142	Burkett-StL	226	Delahanty-Phi	38	Sheckard-Bro	19	Crawford-Cin	16	Burkett-StL	306
Keeler-Bro	123	Keeler-Bro	202	Daly-Bro	38	Flick-Phi	17	Sheckard-Bro	11	Sheckard-Bro	296
Beaumont-Pit	120	Sheckard-Bro	196	Wagner-Pit	37			Burkett-StL	10	Delahanty-Phi	286
Clarke-Pit	118	Wagner-Pit	194	Beckley-Cin	36					Wagner-Pit	271
Sheckard-Bro	116	Delahanty-Phi	192	Wallace-StL	34						

Runs Batted In		Runs Produced		Bases On Balls		Batting Average		On Base Percentage		Slugging Average	
Wagner-Pit	126	Wagner-Pit	221	Thomas-Phi	100	Burkett-StL	.376	Burkett-StL	.440	Sheckard-Bro	.534
Delahanty-Phi	108	Sheckard-Bro	209	Hartsel-Chi	74	Delahanty-Phi	.354	Thomas-Phi	.437	Delahanty-Phi	.528
Sheckard-Bro	104	Burkett-StL	207	Davis-Bro-Pit	66	Sheckard-Bro	.354	Delahanty-Phi	.427	Crawford-Cin	.524
Crawford-Cin	104	Delahanty-Phi	206	Delahanty-Phi	65	Wagner-Pit	.353	Wagner-Pit	.417	Burkett-StL	.509
		Flick-Phi	192	Hamilton-Bos	64	Keeler-Bro	.339	Hartsel-Chi	.414	Flick-Phi	.500

Production		Adjusted Production		Batter Runs		Adjusted Batter Runs		Clutch Hitting Index		Runs Created	
Delahanty-Phi	.955	Burkett-StL	184	Burkett-StL	58.7	Burkett-StL	65.9	Ganzel-NY	139	Burkett-StL	151
Burkett-StL	.949	Delahanty-Phi	173	Delahanty-Phi	53.3	Delahanty-Phi	50.7	Dexter-Chi	136	Sheckard-Bro	139
Sheckard-Bro	.944	Crawford-Cin	172	Sheckard-Bro	49.8	Hartsel-Chi	47.2	Wagner-Pit	133	Delahanty-Phi	139
Wagner-Pit	.911	Sheckard-Bro	168	Wagner-Pit	44.9	Sheckard-Bro	46.5	Long-Bos	133	Wagner-Pit	138
Crawford-Cin	.903	Hartsel-Chi	163	Hartsel-Chi	42.6	Crawford-Cin	44.2	Krueger-StL	128	Hartsel-Chi	130

Total Average		Stolen Bases		Stolen Base Average		Stolen Base Runs		Fielding Runs		Total Player Rating	
Delahanty-Phi	1.097	Wagner-Pit	49					Wallace-StL	29.6	Wallace-StL	6.2
Burkett-StL	1.072	Hartsel-Chi	41					Davis-NY	23.1	Burkett-StL	5.2
Wagner-Pit	1.070	Strang-NY	40					Flick-Phi	14.9	Wagner-Pit	5.1
Sheckard-Bro	1.070	Harley-Cin	37					Dahlen-Bro	13.7	Davis-NY	4.9
Hartsel-Chi	1.027	Beaumont-Pit	36					Kittridge-Bos	12.0	Sheckard-Bro	4.3

Wins		Win Percentage		Games		Complete Games		Shutouts		Saves	
Donovan-Bro	25	Chesbro-Pit	.677	Taylor-NY	45	Hahn-Cin	41	Willis-Bos	6	Powell-StL	3
Harper-StL	23	Phillippe-Pit	.647	Powell-StL	45	Taylor-NY	37	Orth-Phi	6	Donovan-Bro	3
Phillippe-Pit	22	Tannehill-Pit	.643	Donovan-Bro	45	Mathewson-NY	36	Chesbro-Pit	6	Sudhoff-StL	2
Hahn-Cin	22	Harper-StL	.639	Hahn-Cin	42	Donovan-Bro	36			Phillippe-Pit	2
Chesbro-Pit	21	Kitson-Bro	.633	Mathewson-NY	40					Kitson-Bro	2

Innings Pitched		Fewest Hits/Game		Fewest BB/Game		Strikeouts		Strikeouts/Game		Ratio	
Hahn-Cin	375.1	Townsend-Phi	7.39	Orth-Phi	1.02	Hahn-Cin	239	Hughes-Chi	6.57	Orth-Phi	9.27
Taylor-NY	353.1	Mathewson-NY	7.71	Phillippe-Pit	1.16	Donovan-Bro	226	Waddell-Pit-Chi	6.16	Phillippe-Pit	9.79
Donovan-Bro	351.0	Willis-Bos	7.72	Tannehill-Pit	1.28	Hughes-Chi	225	Mathewson-NY	5.92	Tannehill-Pit	10.20
Powell-StL	338.1	Orth-Phi	7.99	Duggleby-Phi	1.30	Mathewson-NY	221	Donovan-Bro	5.79	Chesbro-Pit	10.23
Mathewson-NY	336.0	Chesbro-Pit	8.17	Powell-StL	1.33	Waddell-Pit-Chi	172	Hahn-Cin	5.73	Willis-Bos	10.35

Earned Run Average		Adjusted ERA		Opponents' Batting Avg.		Opponents' On Base Pct.		Starter Runs		Adjusted Starter Runs	
Tannehill-Pit	2.18	Willis-Bos	153	Townsend-Phi	.223	Orth-Phi	.264	Phillippe-Pit	36.2	Willis-Bos	42.6
Phillippe-Pit	2.22	Tannehill-Pit	150	Mathewson-NY	.230	Phillippe-Pit	.275	Mathewson-NY	34.0	Orth-Phi	35.3
Orth-Phi	2.27	Orth-Phi	150	Willis-Bos	.231	Tannehill-Pit	.284	Orth-Phi	32.9	Phillippe-Pit	34.4
Willis-Bos	2.36	Phillippe-Pit	147	Orth-Phi	.237	Chesbro-Pit	.284	Willis-Bos	32.7	Mathewson-NY	33.3
Chesbro-Pit	2.38	Chesbro-Pit	137	Chesbro-Pit	.241	Willis-Bos	.286	Tannehill-Pit	32.1	Tannehill-Pit	30.5

Clutch Pitching Index		Relief Runs		Adjusted Relief Runs		Relief Ranking		Total Pitcher Index		Total Baseball Ranking	
Kitson-Bro	122							Orth-Phi	4.8	Wallace-StL	6.2
Taylor-Chi	116							Willis-Bos	4.6	Burkett-StL	5.2
Hughes-Bro	114							Phillippe-Pit	4.4	Wagner-Pit	5.1
Taylor-NY	113							Mathewson-NY	4.1	Davis-NY	4.9
Donahue-Phi	109							Tannehill-Pit	3.2	Willis-Bos	4.6

January 4 The Baltimore AL club incorporates, with John McGraw as manager and part owner.

January 22 Connie Mack, Philadelphia A's manager/general manager, signs a 10-year lease on grounds at 29th and Columbia to be called Columbia Park. A contract is set for construction of single-deck stands to hold 7,500.

January 28 The AL formally organizes. The Baltimore Orioles, Philadelphia Athletics, and Boston Somersets are admitted to join the Washington Senators, Cleveland Blues, Detroit Tigers, Milwaukee Brewers, and Chicago White Stockings. Three of the original clubs—Indianapolis, Minneapolis, and Buffalo—are dropped. League power aggregates in president Ban Johnson as trustee for all ballpark leases and majority stockholdings, and with authority to buy out franchises. Player limit is 14 per team; schedule will be 140 games.

March 11 The *Cincinnati Enquirer* reports that Baltimore manager John McGraw has signed a Cherokee Indian named Tokohoma. It is really black second baseman Charlie Grant, who McGraw is trying to pass off as an Indian, but the ruse does not work.

April 3 Connie Mack accuses Christy Mathewson of reneging on a Philadelphia contact signed in January. The young pitcher had accepted advance money from Mack, but jumped back to the Giants in March. Mack considers going to court, but eventually accepts the loss of the pitcher.

April 24 Chicago hosts the first game of the new AL. Roy Patterson's first of 20 wins in 1901, an 8-2 win over the Cleveland Blues, puts the White Stockings on their way to winning the AL's first pennant.

April 25 Detroit scores the greatest Opening Day rally in its AL debut. Trailing, 13-4, in the bottom of the ninth, the Tigers score 10 runs for a 14-13 victory over the Milwaukee Brewers.

April 29 Admiral George Dewey and other prominent guests watch Washington defeat Baltimore, 5–2, in the AL opener in the nation's capital.

May 8 In their long-delayed AL home opener, Boston defeats Philadelphia, 12-4, behind Cy Young, who has jumped from the St. Louis NL team. He will lead the AL with his 1.62 ERA and 33 wins, 41.8 percent of his team's 79 victories. This post-1900 record will stand until Steve Carlton wins 45.8 percent of the Phils' 59 wins in 1972.

May 17 The Philadelphia Common Pleas Court rejects the Phillies' suit against Napoleon Lajoie, Chick Fraser, and Bill Bernhard. The decision is appealed to the State Supreme Court, but the trio remains with the Athletics all season. Lajoie will hit .422, while Fraser wins 22 and Bernhard 17 for the fourth-place Athletics.

May 23 Philadelphia's Nap Lajoie is intentionally walked with the bases loaded by the White Stockings.

May 27 Third baseman Jimmy Burke of Milwaukee makes four errors in one inning, a record tied by Cleveland's Ray Chapman in 1914 and the Cubs' Len Merullo in 1942.

August 10 The Washington Senators' Dale Gear gives up an AL record 41 total bases in losing, 13–0, to the Athletics. The 23 hits include four doubles, four triples, and two homers. Philadelphia A's pitcher Lewis "Snake" Wiltse has two doubles and two triples, becoming only the third hurler to collect four extra-base hits in a game.

September 3 Baltimore pitcher Joe McGinnity hurls two complete games against Milwaukee, winning, 10–0, and losing, 6–1.

November 5 Sportsman's Park in St. Louis is leased for five years by Ban Johnson and Charles Comiskey for an AL team; two weeks later the Milwaukee franchise is officially transferred.

	BALTIMORE		BOSTON		CHICAGO		CLEVELAND		DETROIT		MILWAUKEE		PHILADELPHIA		WASHINGTON
M	J.McGraw	M	J.Collins	M	C.Griffith	M	J.McAleer	M	G.Stallings	M	H.Duffy	M	C.Mack	M	J.Manning
1B	B.Hart	1B	B.Freeman	1B	F.Isbell	1B	C.LaChance	1B	P.Dillon	1B	J.Anderson	1B	H.Davis	1B	M.Grady
2B	J.Williams	2B	H.Ferris	2B	S.Mertes	2B	E.Beck	2B	K.Gleason	2B	B.Gilbert	2B	N.Lajoie	2B	J.Farrell
SS	B.Keister	SS	F.Parent	SS	F.Shugart	SS	F.Scheibeck	SS	K.Elberfeld	SS	W.Conroy	SS	J.Dolan	SS	B.Clingman
3B	J.McGraw	3B	J.Collins	3B	F.Hartman	3B	B.Bradley	3B	D.Casey	3B	J.Burke	3B	L.Cross	3B	B.Coughlin
LF	J.Jackson	LF	T.Dowd	LF	H.McFarland	LF	J.McCarthy	LF	D.Nance	LF	B.Hallman	LF	M.McIntyre	LF	P.Foster
CF	S.Brodie	CF	C.Stahl	CF	D.Hoy	CF	O.Pickering	CF	J.Barrett	CF	H.Duffy	CF	D.Fultz	CF	I.Waldron
RF	S.Seymour	RF	C.Hemphill	RF	F.Jones	RF	J.O'Brien	RF	D.Holmes	RF	I.Waldron	RF	S.Seybold	RF	S.Dungan
C	R.Bresnahan	C	O.Schreckengost	C	B.Sullivan	C	B.Wood	C	F.Buelow	C	B.Maloney	C	D.Powers	C	B.Clarke
O1	M.Donlin	C	L.Criger	C	J.Sugden	O	E.Harvey	C1	S.McAllister	3O	B.Friel	O	P.Geier	2	J.Quinn
3S	J.Dunn	O	C.Jones	S3	J.Burke	C	G.Yeager	C	A.Shaw	O	G.Hogriever	O	J.Hayden	OP	D.Gear
C	W.Robinson	/1	L.McLean	/O	P.Foster	C	J.Connor	1	D.Crockett	C1	J.Donahue	S	B.Ely	1	B.Everitt
1	F.Foutz	/C	J.Slattery	/2	D.Brain	O	F.Genins	/S	H.Lochhead	C	J.Connor	CO	F.Steelman	O	J.O'Brien
/1	G.Rohe	/3	H.Gleason			S	D.Shay			C	T.Leahy	/S	H.Lochhead	/O	C.Luskey
/O	C.Snodgrass			P	R.Patterson	O	T.Donovan	P	R.Miller	O	E.Bruyette	/C	H.Smith	/1	T.Jordan
/C	T.Latimer	P	C.Young	P	C.Griffith	S	J.McGuire	P	E.Siever	O	D.Jones	/C	M.Murphy	/O	B.Harrison
/1	S.Jordan	P	T.Lewis	P	N.Callahan	/S	B.Hallman	P	J.Cronin	S	G.Bone	/O	F.Ketchum		
		P	G.Winter	P	J.Katoll	/2	T.Eagan	P	J.Yeager	/O	P.Geier	/O	T.Leahy	P	B.Carrick
P	J.McGinnity	P	F.Mitchell	P	E.Harvey	/O	J.McAleer			/S	G.McBride	/O	B.Lindemann	P	W.Lee
P	H.Howell	P	N.Cuppy			/O	F.Cross	P	E.Frisk	/C	J.Butler	/1	C.Carr	P	C.Patten
P	F.Foreman			/P	J.Skopec	/O	E.Cermak	/P	F.Owen	/O	L.Gertenrich	/3	B.Lauder	P	W.Mercer
P	J.Nops	/P	W.Kellum	/P	W.Piatt	/O	S.Gallagher	/P	E.High			/2	B.McKinney		
		/P	G.Prentiss	/P	J.McAleese	/S	R.Hall			P	B.Reidy				
/P	C.Schmit	/P	B.Beville	/P	F.Dupee	/O	H.Hogan			P	N.Garvin	P	C.Fraser		
/P	B.Karns	/P	F.Foreman			/C	P.Livingston			P	B.Husting	P	E.Plank		
/P	S.Yerkes	/P	J.Volz							P	T.Sparks	P	B.Bernhard		
		/P	F.Morrissey			P	P.Dowling			P	P.Hawley	P	S.Wiltse		
						P	E.Moore					P	W.Piatt		
						P	B.Hart	P	P.Dowling						
						P	E.Scott					/P	B.Milligan		
						P	J.Bracken					/P	B.Baker		
												/P	J.McPherson		
						P	B.Hoffer					/P	D.Leitner		
						P	H.McNeal					/P	P.Loos		
						/P	B.Cristall								
						/P	D.Braggins								
						/P	G.Weyhing								
						/P	B.Baker								

TEAM	G	W	L	PCT	GB	R	OR	AB	H	2B	3B	HR	BB	SO	AVG	OBP	SLG	PRO	PRO+	BR	/A	PF	CHI	RC	SB	CS	SBA	SBR
CHI	137	83	53	.610		819	631	4725	1303	173	89	32	475	337	.276	.350	.370	.720	108	41	62	97	103	744	280			
BOS	138	79	57	.581	4	759	608	4866	1353	183	104	37	331	282	.278	.330	.381	.711	104	9	23	98	101	693	157			
DET	136	74	61	.548	8.5	741	694	4676	1303	180	80	29	380	346	.279	.340	.370	.710	98	15	-19	105	99	690	204			
PHI	137	74	62	.544	9	805	761	4882	1409	239	87	35	301	344	.289	.337	.395	.732	103	42	8	104	103	734	173			
BAL	135	68	65	.511	13.5	760	750	4589	1348	179	111	24	369	377	.294	.353	.397	.750	108	80	45	104	96	746	207			
WAS	138	61	72	.459	20.5	682	771	4772	1282	191	83	33	356	340	.269	.326	.364	.690	97	-24	-13	99	96	633	127			
CLE	138	54	82	.397	29	667	831	4833	1311	197	68	12	243	326	.271	.313	.348	.661	92	-82	-56	96	104	588	125			
MIL	139	48	89	.350	35.5	641	828	4795	1250	192	66	26	325	384	.261	.314	.345	.659	91	-81	-49	95	98	602	176			
TOT	549					5874		38138	10559	1534	688	228	2780	2736	.277	.333	.371	.704						1449				

TEAM	CG	SH	SV	IP	H	H/G	HR	BB	SO	RAT	ERA	ERA+	OAV	OOB	PR	/A	PF	CPI	FA	E	DP	FW	PW	BW	SBW	DIF
CHI	110	11	2	1218[1]	1250	9.2	27	312	394	11.9	2.98	117	.263	.315	93	68	95	106	.941	345	100	.9	6.1	5.6		2.4
BOS	123	7	1	1217	1178	8.7	33	294	396	11.2	3.04	116	.251	.301	84	66	96	93	.943	337	104	1.6	6.0	2.1		1.4
DET	118	8	2	1188[2]	1328	10.1	22	313	307	12.8	3.30	116	.280	.330	48	71	105	109	.930	410	127	-3.3	6.4	-1.7		5.1
PHI	124	6	1	1200[2]	1346	10.1	20	374	350	13.3	4.00	94	.280	.339	-45	-32	103	94	.942	337	93	1.4	-2.9	.7		6.8
BAL	115	4	3	1158	1313	10.2	21	344	271	13.3	3.73	104	.282	.338	-9	17	106	101	.926	401	76	-2.9	1.5	4.1		-1.2
WAS	118	8	2	1183	1396	10.6	51	284	308	13.3	4.09	89	.291	.339	-57	-58	100	100	.943	323	97	2.4	-5.2	-1.2		-1.5
CLE	122	7	4	1182[1]	1365	10.4	22	464	334	14.5	4.12	86	.286	.358	-60	-75	97	102	.942	399	99	2.1	-6.8	-5.1		-4.2
MIL	107	3	4	1218	1383	10.2	32	395	376	13.6	4.06	89	.283	.344	-53	-63	98	98	.934	393	106	-1.8	-5.7	-4.4		-8.6
TOT	937	54	19	9566		9.9				13.0	3.66		.277	.333					.938	2875	802					

Runs		Hits		Doubles		Triples		Home Runs		Total Bases	
Lajoie-Phi	145	Lajoie-Phi	232	Lajoie-Phi	48	Williams-Bal	21	Lajoie-Phi	14	Lajoie-Phi	350
Jones-Chi	120	Anderson-Mil	190	Anderson-Mil	46	Keister-Bal	21	Freeman-Bos	12	Collins-Bos	279
Williams-Bal	113	Collins-Bos	187	Collins-Bos	42	Mertes-Chi	17	Grady-Was	9	Anderson-Mil	274
Hoy-Chi	112	Waldron-Mil-Was	186	Farrell-Was	32	Stahl-Bos	16			Freeman-Bos	255
Barrett-Det	110	Dungan-Was	179			Collins-Bos	16			Williams-Bal	248

Runs Batted In		Runs Produced		Bases On Balls		Batting Average		On Base Percentage		Slugging Average	
Lajoie-Phi	125	Lajoie-Phi	256	Hoy-Chi	86	Lajoie-Phi	.426	Lajoie-Phi	.463	Lajoie-Phi	.643
Freeman-Bos	114	Williams-Bal	202	Jones-Chi	84	Donlin-Bal	.340	Jones-Chi	.412	Freeman-Bos	.520
Anderson-Mil	99	Collins-Bos	196	Barrett-Det	76	Freeman-Bos	.339	Donlin-Bal	.409	Seybold-Phi	.503
Mertes-Chi	98	Freeman-Bos	190	McFarland-Chi	75	Seybold-Phi	.334	Hoy-Chi	.407	Williams-Bal	.495
Williams-Bal	96	Mertes-Chi	187	McGraw-Bal	61	Collins-Bos	.332	Freeman-Bos	.400	Collins-Bos	.495

Production		Adjusted Production		Batter Runs		Adjusted Batter Runs		Clutch Hitting Index		Runs Created	
Lajoie-Phi	1.106	Lajoie-Phi	196	Lajoie-Phi	74.1	Lajoie-Phi	67.4	Burke-Mil-Chi	140	Lajoie-Phi	179
Freeman-Bos	.920	Freeman-Bos	157	Freeman-Bos	34.9	Freeman-Bos	36.9	Mertes-Chi	134	Collins-Bos	116
Seybold-Phi	.901	Seybold-Phi	142	McGraw-Bal	31.1	Collins-Bos	30.3	Keister-Bal	122	Anderson-Mil	114
Donlin-Bal	.883	Collins-Bos	142	Donlin-Bal	29.5	McGraw-Bal	27.9	Hartman-Chi	120	Freeman-Bos	112
Williams-Bal	.883	Donlin-Bal	138	Williams-Bal	29.3	Anderson-Mil	26.3	Seymour-Bal	117	Donlin-Bal	109

Total Average		Stolen Bases		Stolen Base Average		Stolen Base Runs		Fielding Runs		Total Player Rating	
Lajoie-Phi	1.327	Isbell-Chi	52					Lajoie-Phi	28.7	Lajoie-Phi	8.9
Donlin-Bal	1.000	Mertes-Chi	46					Elberfeld-Det	22.0	Elberfeld-Det	4.2
Freeman-Bos	.994	Seymour-Bal	38					Conroy-Was	19.4	Collins-Bos	4.0
Seybold-Phi	.963	Jones-Chi	38					Clingman-Was	17.8	Freeman-Bos	2.7
Williams-Bal	.956							Farrell-Was	16.6	Anderson-Mil	2.6

Wins		Win Percentage		Games		Complete Games		Shutouts		Saves	
Young-Bos	33	Griffith-Chi	.774	McGinnity-Bal	48	McGinnity-Bal	39	Young-Bos	5	Hoffer-Cle	3
McGinnity-Bal	26	Young-Bos	.767	Dowling-Mil-Cle	43	Young-Bos	38	Griffith-Chi	5	Garvin-Mil	2
Griffith-Chi	24	Callahan-Chi	.652	Young-Bos	43	Miller-Det	35	Patterson-Chi	4		
Miller-Det	23	Patten-Was	.643	Carrick-Was	42	Fraser-Phi	35	Patten-Was	4		
Fraser-Phi	22	Miller-Det	.639	Patterson-Chi	41	Carrick-Was	34	Moore-Cle	4		

Innings Pitched		Fewest Hits/Game		Fewest BB/Game		Strikeouts		Strikeouts/Game		Ratio	
McGinnity-Bal	382.0	Young-Bos	7.85	Young-Bos	.90	Young-Bos	158	Garvin-Mil	4.27	Young-Bos	8.92
Young-Bos	371.1	Callahan-Chi	8.15	Gear-Was	1.21	Patterson-Chi	127	Patten-Was	3.86	Callahan-Chi	10.62
Miller-Det	332.0	Moore-Cle	8.38	Lee-Was	1.55	Dowling-Mil-Cle	124	Young-Bos	3.83	Griffith-Chi	11.10
Fraser-Phi	331.0	Lewis-Bos	8.51	Griffith-Chi	1.69	Garvin-Mil	122	Patterson-Chi	3.66	Lewis-Bos	11.32
Carrick-Was	324.0	Winter-Bos	8.74	Cronin-Det	1.72	Fraser-Phi	110	Dowling-Mil-Cle	3.65	Winter-Bos	11.35

Earned Run Average		Adjusted ERA		Opponents' Batting Avg.		Opponents' On Base Pct.		Starter Runs		Adjusted Starter Runs	
Young-Bos	1.62	Young-Bos	217	Young-Bos	.232	Young-Bos	.256	Young-Bos	84.1	Young-Bos	78.5
Callahan-Chi	2.42	Yeager-Det	147	Callahan-Chi	.239	Callahan-Chi	.290	Callahan-Chi	29.6	Miller-Det	32.8
Yeager-Det	2.61	Callahan-Chi	143	Moore-Cle	.244	Griffith-Chi	.300	Griffith-Chi	29.5	Yeager-Det	27.3
Griffith-Chi	2.67	Griffith-Chi	130	Lewis-Bos	.247	Lewis-Bos	.304	Miller-Det	26.1	Callahan-Chi	25.2
Winter-Bos	2.80	Miller-Det	130	Winter-Bos	.252	Winter-Bos	.304	Yeager-Det	23.2	Griffith-Chi	24.1

Clutch Pitching Index		Relief Runs		Adjusted Relief Runs		Relief Ranking		Total Pitcher Index		Total Baseball Ranking	
Katoll-Chi	126							Young-Bos	8.3	Lajoie-Phi	8.9
Yeager-Det	121							Callahan-Chi	3.9	Young-Bos	8.3
Siever-Det	116							Griffith-Chi	3.7	Elberfeld-Det	4.2
Sparks-Mil	116							Yeager-Det	3.5	Collins-Bos	4.0
Young-Bos	113							Miller-Det	3.5	Callahan-Chi	3.9

January 30* Dashing Tony Mullane, the first player to have jumped the reserve rule by signing with the St. Louis Unions of the Union Association in 1883, signs a contract with Toledo, of the new American Association (AAA).

February 20 Nick Young remains as NL president when A. G. Spalding bows out of the battle, but the league will have no effective leadership until 1903.

April 21 The Pennsylvania Supreme Court, reversing a lower court's decision, grants a permanent injunction (effective only in Pennsylvania) barring jumpers Nap Lajoie, Chick Fraser, and Bill Bernhard from playing for the A's, or any team but the Phillies.

April 23 St. Louis Cardinals owner Frank DeHaas Robison offers to put up $10,000 that the Pirates will not repeat as NL champions. Pittsburgh players accept the challenge with a matching pool, and go on to win the pennant by 27½ games.

April 27 Cubs rookie right-handed pitcher Jim St. Vrain, sent up to pinch hit left-handed, grounds to Pittsburgh shortstop Honus Wagner. The confused St. Vrain runs toward third base as the astonished Wagner throws him out. Pittsburgh wins, 2–0.

May 7 The Cubs' Jack Taylor beats Christy Mathewson, 4–0, at Chicago. Cubs manager Frank Selee comments that the distance from the pitcher's mound to the plate looks short. Horace Fogel, the Giants manager, measures the distance and finds the lane is 15 inches short. The subsequent New York protest is upheld, and two games are ordered replayed.

May 16 Two deaf mutes face each other for the first time when William "Dummy" Hoy leads off for the Reds against Luther "Dummy" Taylor of the Giants. The Reds win, 5-3, with a five-run rally in the ninth. Hoy goes 2-for-4.

June 3 The Cardinals' Mike O'Neill, a pitcher and one of four major league brothers, hits the first pinch grand slam ever, against Boston Beaneater Togie Pittinger. It is an inside-the-park homer at Boston and scores his brother Jack.

June 15* Corsicana (Texas League) beats Texarkana, 51–3, as Nig Clarke hits eight homers. The team's 53 hits include 21 homers, mostly over a short outfield fence.

July 8 John McGraw negotiates his release from Baltimore and signs to manage the New York Giants, although he'd secretly signed a contract several days earlier. McGraw also conspires to swing the sale of Orioles to the NL teams that helped him. McGraw enables the Orioles to release Dan McGann, Roger Bresnahan, Joe McGinnity, and Jack Cronin to sign with the Giants. Joe Kelley and Cy Seymour go the Reds.

July 14 Little Tommy Leach of Pittsburgh, never considered a longball threat, hits two homers over the fence at Boston. He will close out the season with only six, but it's enough to give him sole leadership of the NL, which totals only 99. Leach's leading number is the lowest since Paul Hines hit four in a 60-game schedule in 1878.

September 1 Tinker, Evers, and Chance appear together in the Chicago Cubs lineup for the first time, but not in the positions that will earn them immortality. Johnny Evers, a New York State League rookie, starts at shortstop, with Joe Tinker at third, Frank Chance at first, and Bobby Lowe at second.

October 4 When Pirates owner Barney Dreyfuss demands a game be played despite a rain-soaked field, Cincinnati plays most of its team out of their normal positions. pitcher Rube Vickers, catching, sets a modern major league record with six passed balls. Pittsburgh wins, 11–2, but Dreyfuss refunds fans' money, and the Reds return their share of the gate for the sorry, and soggy, showing.

December 12 Harry Pulliam is elected president of the NL.

BOSTON		BROOKLYN		CHICAGO		CINCINNATI		NEW YORK		PHILADELPHIA		PITTSBURGH		ST.LOUIS	
M	A.Buckenberger	M	N.Hanlon	M	F.Selee	M	B.McPhee	M	H.Fogel	M	B.Shettsline	M	F.Clarke	M	P.Donovan
1B	F.Tenney	1B	T.McCreery	1B	F.Chance	M	F.Bancroft	M	H.Smith	1B	H.Jennings	1B	K.Bransfield	1B	R.Brashear
2B	G.DeMontreville	2B	T.Flood	2B	B.Lowe	M	J.Kelley	M	J.McGraw	2B	P.Childs	2B	C.Ritchey	2B	J.Farrell
SS	H.Long	SS	B.Dahlen	SS	J.Tinker	1B	J.Beckley	1B	D.McGann	SS	R.Hulswitt	SS	W.Conroy	SS	O.Krueger
3B	E.Gremminger	3B	C.Irwin	3B	G.Schaefer	2B	H.Peitz	2B	H.Smith	3B	B.Hallman	3B	T.Leach	3B	F.Hartman
LF	D.Cooley	LF	J.Sheckard	LF	J.Slagle	SS	T.Corcoran	SS	J.Bean	LF	G.Browne	LF	F.Clarke	LF	G.Barclay
CF	B.Lush	CF	C.Dolan	CF	J.Dobbs	3B	H.Steinfeldt	3B	B.Lauder	CF	R.Thomas	CF	G.Beaumont	CF	H.Smoot
RF	P.Carney	RF	W.Keeler	RF	D.Jones	LF	J.Dobbs	LF	J.Jones	RF	S.Barry	RF	H.Wagner	RF	P.Donovan
C	M.Kittridge	C	H.Hearne	C	J.Kling	CF	D.Hoy	CF	S.Brodie	C	R.Dooin	C	H.Smith	C	J.Ryan
						RF	S.Crawford	RF	J.Dunn						
C	P.Moran	C1	D.Farrell	31	C.Dexter	C	B.Bergen	C	F.Bowerman	1C	K.Douglass	O	L.Davis	1C	A.Nichols
S2	C.Dexter	32	E.Wheeler	OP	J.Menefee					O2	H.Krug	2O	J.Burke	C	J.O'Neill
O	E.Courtney	C	L.Ritter	O	D.Miller	O	C.Seymour	O	G.Browne	3	H.Wolverton	C	J.O'Connor	3	J.Calhoun
/O	F.Brown	C	G.Hildebrand	O	B.Congalton	2	E.Beck	1	J.Doyle	C	F.Jacklitsch	C	C.Zimmer	C	A.Weaver
		O	R.Ward	O1	A.Williams	2	G.Magoon	OC	R.Bresnahan	3	P.Greene	O	J.Sebring	/1	D.Hazleton
P	V.Willis	/C	T.Latimer	1	H.O'Hagen	O2	J.Kelley	O	J.Jackson	/O	B.Thomas	C	E.Phelps	/S	R.Kling
P	T.Pittinger	/C	J.Wall	2	J.Evers	O	M.Donlin	C	G.Yeager	C	T.Fleming	/O	F.Crolius	/S	O.Williams
P	M.Eason	/C	N.Fuller	O	J.Murray	O	B.Maloney	S	J.McGraw	/O	B.Clay	/O	G.Merritt	/3	J.Murphy
P	J.Malarkey	/C	P.Deisel	1	D.Clark	2	J.Morrissey	O	G.Van Haltren	/C	N.Shea	/O	B.Miller		
				/O	L.Schlafly	/O	H.Bay	/O	H.O'Hagen	/O	J.Berry	/C	L.Fohl	P	M.O'Neill
/P	D.Hale	P	B.Donovan	/O	M.Lynch			/O	R.Clark	/O	E.Watkins	/C	M.Hopkins	P	S.Yerkes
/P	B.Dresser	P	F.Kitson	/S	M.Jacobs	P	N.Hahn	S	H.Wagner	H	F.Mahar			P	E.Murphy
/P	F.Klobedanz	P	D.Newton	/C	M.Kahoe	P	B.Phillips	/O	J.Delahanty	R	T.Maher	P	J.Chesbro	P	B.Wicker
/P	R.Long	P	J.Hughes	/2	S.Strang	P	H.Thielman	/O	J.Hendricks			P	D.Phillippe	P	C.Currie
/P	S.Curran	P	R.Evans	/C	P.Lamer	P	E.Poole	/O	J.Wall	P	D.White	P	J.Tannehill	P	A.Pearson
				/S	E.Glenn	P	B.Ewing	/O	J.McDonald	P	B.Duggleby	P	S.Leever	/P	B.Popp
		/P	J.McMakin	/O	J.Hendricks	P	C.Currie	/O	J.Robinson	P	H.Iburg	P	E.Doheny	/P	W.Dunham
		/P	G.McCann	/O	C.Pedroes	/P	C.Heismann	/O	L.Washburn	P	C.Fraser			/P	J.Hackett
		/P	N.Garvin	/O	S.Kennedy	/P	A.Stimmel	/C	J.O'Neill	/P	B.Magee	/P	H.Cushman	/P	C.McFarland
		/P	L.Winham	/O	R.Hildebrand	/P	R.Vickers	/O	J.Callahan	P	C.Vorhees	/P	W.McLaughlin	/P	J.Adams
				/O	J.Hughes	/P	L.Swormstedt	/O	C.Hartley	P	H.Felix	/P	E.Poole		
				P	J.Taylor	/P	B.Hooker	P	C.Mathewson	/P	B.McFadden				
				P	P.Williams	/P	M.Glendon	P	D.Taylor	/P	J.Whiting				
				P	C.Lundgren			P	R.Evans	P	B.Wolfe				
				P	B.Rhoads			P	J.McGinnity	/P	B.Salisbury				
				P	J.St.Vrain			P	T.Sparks	P	H.Fox				
				/P	F.Morrissey			P	J.Cronin						
				/P	A.Hardy			P	R.Miller						
				/P	J.Gardner			/P	B.Kennedy						
				/P	M.Eason			/P	B.Blewett						
				/P	F.Glade			/P	J.Burke						
								/P	H.Thielman						
								/P	B.Magee						

TEAM	G	W	L	PCT	GB	R	OR	AB	H	2B	3B	HR	BB	SO	AVG	OBP	SLG	PRO	PRO+	BR	/A	PF	CHI	RC	SB	CS	SBA	SBR
PIT	142	103	36	.741		775	440	4926	1410	189	95	18	372	446	.286	.344	.374	.718	123	152	126	104	105	743	222			
BRO	141	75	63	.543	27.5	564	519	4845	1242	147	49	19	319	489	.256	.311	.319	.630	99	-4	-8	101	100	553	145			
BOS	142	73	64	.533	29	572	516	4728	1178	142	39	14	398	481	.249	.313	.305	.618	95	-16	-21	101	104	540	189			
CIN	141	70	70	.500	33.5	633	566	4908	1383	188	77	18	297	465	.282	.328	.362	.690	109	95	33	110	95	654	131			
CHI	141	68	69	.496	34	530	501	4802	1200	131	40	6	353	565	.250	.307	.298	.605	95	-41	-26	97	100	539	222			
STL	140	56	78	.418	44.5	517	695	4751	1226	116	37	10	273	438	.258	.306	.304	.610	97	-37	-16	96	101	516	158			
PHI	138	56	81	.409	46	484	649	4615	1139	110	43	5	356	481	.247	.305	.293	.598	90	-50	-50	100	98	473	108			
NY	139	48	88	.353	53.5	401	590	4571	1088	147	34	8	252	530	.238	.283	.290	.573	83	-98	-95	99	93	452	187			
TOT	562					4476		38146	9866	1170	414	98	2620	3895	.259	.313	.319	.631						1362				

TEAM	CG	SH	SV	IP	H	H/G	HR	BB	SO	RAT	ERA	ERA+	OAV	OOB	PR	/A	PF	CPI	FA	E	DP	FW	PW	BW	SBW	DIF
PIT	131	21	3	1264²	1142	8.1	4	250	564	10.3	2.30	119	.241	.288	67	61	98	94	.958	247	87	3.4	6.4	13.3		10.4
BRO	131	14	3	1256	1113	8.0	10	363	536	10.8	2.69	102	.238	.298	12	9	99	86	.952	275	79	1.5	.9	-.8		4.4
BOS	124	14	4	1259²	1233	8.8	16	372	523	11.8	2.61	108	.257	.316	24	29	102	109	.959	240	90	3.8	3.1	-2.2		-.2
CIN	130	9	1	1239	1228	8.9	15	352	430	11.9	2.67	112	.259	.318	14	43	108	108	.945	322	118	-1.4	4.5	3.5		-6.6
CHI	132	17	2	1275¹	1235	8.7	9	279	437	11.0	2.21	122	.254	.301	81	69	97	114	.946	327	111	-1.7	7.3	-2.7		-3.4
STL	112	7	4	1227¹	1399	10.3	16	338	400	13.0	3.47	79	.287	.338	-95	-101	99	102	.944	336	107	-2.4	-10.7	-1.7		3.7
PHI	118	8	3	1211	1323	9.8	12	334	504	12.7	3.50	80	.278	.333	-97	-93	101	95	.946	305	81	-.7	-9.8	-5.3		3.3
NY	118	11	1	1226¹	1193	8.8	16	332	501	11.6	2.82	99	.255	.312	-5	-3	101	98	.943	330	104	-2.1	-.3	-10.0		-7.5
TOT	996	101	21	9959²		8.9				11.6	2.78		.259	.313					.949	2382	777					

Runs		Hits		Doubles		Triples		Home Runs		Total Bases	
Wagner-Pit	105	Beaumont-Pit	193	Wagner-Pit	30	Leach-Pit	22	Leach-Pit	6	Crawford-Cin	256
Clarke-Pit	103	Keeler-Bro	186	Clarke-Pit	27	Crawford-Cin	22	Beckley-Cin	5	Wagner-Pit	247
Beaumont-Pit	100	Crawford-Cin	185	Cooley-Bos	26	Wagner-Pit	16	Sheckard-Bro	4	Beckley-Cin	227
Leach-Pit	97	Wagner-Pit	176	Dahlen-Bro	25	Clarke-Pit	14	McCreery-Bro	4	Beaumont-Pit	226
Crawford-Cin	92	Beckley-Cin	175	Beckley-Cin	23	Gremminger-Bos	12			Leach-Pit	219

Runs Batted In		Runs Produced		Bases On Balls		Batting Average		On Base Percentage		Slugging Average	
Wagner-Pit	91	Wagner-Pit	193	R.Thomas-Phi	107	Beaumont-Pit	.357	R.Thomas-Phi	.414	Wagner-Pit	.463
Leach-Pit	85	Leach-Pit	176	Lush-Bos	76	Crawford-Cin	.333	Tenney-Bos	.409	Crawford-Cin	.461
Crawford-Cin	78	Crawford-Cin	167	Tenney-Bos	73	Keeler-Bro	.333	Beaumont-Pit	.404	Clarke-Pit	.449
Dahlen-Bro	74	Beaumont-Pit	167	Sheckard-Bro	57	Wagner-Pit	.330	Clarke-Pit	.401	Beckley-Cin	.427
		Clarke-Pit	154			Beckley-Cin	.330	Wagner-Pit	.394	Leach-Pit	.426

Production		Adjusted Production		Batter Runs		Adjusted Batter Runs		Clutch Hitting Index		Runs Created	
Wagner-Pit	.857	Wagner-Pit	159	Wagner-Pit	39.9	Wagner-Pit	36.3	Hartman-StL	160	Wagner-Pit	118
Clarke-Pit	.850	Clarke-Pit	156	Crawford-Cin	38.6	Clarke-Pit	31.7	Bransfield-Pit	133	Beaumont-Pit	109
Crawford-Cin	.848	Beaumont-Pit	148	Clarke-Pit	34.9	Beaumont-Pit	30.7	Ritchey-Pit	124	Crawford-Cin	108
Beaumont-Pit	.822	Crawford-Cin	147	Beaumont-Pit	34.1	Crawford-Cin	29.1	McCreery-Bro	124	Clarke-Pit	97
Beckley-Cin	.804	Tenney-Bos	141	Beckley-Cin	28.7	Tenney-Bos	27.8	Wagner-Pit	123	Beckley-Cin	94

Total Average		Stolen Bases		Stolen Base Average	Stolen Base Runs	Fielding Runs		Total Player Rating	
Wagner-Pit	.966	Wagner-Pit	42			Farrell-StL	33.5	Wagner-Pit	4.4
Clarke-Pit	.955	Slagle-Chi	40			Lowe-Chi	26.0	Tenney-Bos	3.9
Beaumont-Pit	.868	Donovan-StL	34			H.Long-Bos	22.9	Farrell-StL	3.3
Crawford-Cin	.865	Beaumont-Pit	33			Steinfeldt-Cin	21.8	Leach-Pit	3.3
Tenney-Bos	.845	Smith-NY	32			Leach-Pit	12.7	Crawford-Cin	2.5

Wins		Win Percentage		Games		Complete Games		Shutouts		Saves	
Chesbro-Pit	28	Chesbro-Pit	.824	Willis-Bos	51	Willis-Bos	45	Mathewson-NY	8	Willis-Bos	3
Willis-Bos	27	Doheny-Pit	.800	Pittinger-Bos	46	Pittinger-Bos	36	Chesbro-Pit	8	M.O'Neill-StL	2
Pittinger-Bos	27	Tannehill-Pit	.769	Yerkes-StL	39	Hahn-Cin	35	Taylor-Chi	7	Newton-Bro	2
Taylor-Chi	23	Phillippe-Pit	.690			White-Phi	34	Pittinger-Bos	7	Leever-Pit	2
Hahn-Cin	23	Leever-Pit	.682			Taylor-Chi	33	Hahn-Cin	6		

Innings Pitched		Fewest Hits/Game		Fewest BB/Game		Strikeouts		Strikeouts/Game		Ratio	
Willis-Bos	410.0	Newton-Bro	7.08	Phillippe-Pit	.86	Willis-Bos	225	White-Phi	5.44	Taylor-Chi	8.98
Pittinger-Bos	389.1	McGinnity-NY	7.18	Tannehill-Pit	.97	White-Phi	185	Mathewson-NY	5.17	Tannehill-Pit	9.27
Taylor-Chi	324.2	Taylor-Chi	7.51	Menefee-Chi	1.19	Pittinger-Bos	174	Donovan-Bro	5.14	McGinnity-NY	9.59
Hahn-Cin	321.0	Donovan-Bro	7.56	Taylor-Chi	1.19	Donovan-Bro	170	Willis-Bos	4.94	Hahn-Cin	9.70
White-Phi	306.0	Chesbro-Pit	7.61	Leever-Pit	1.26	Mathewson-NY	159	Wicker-StL	4.61	Phillippe-Pit	9.76

Earned Run Average		Adjusted ERA		Opponents' Batting Avg.		Opponents' On Base Pct.		Starter Runs		Adjusted Starter Runs	
Taylor-Chi	1.33	Taylor-Chi	203	Newton-Bro	.217	Taylor-Chi	.260	Taylor-Chi	52.2	Taylor-Chi	49.3
Hahn-Cin	1.77	Hahn-Cin	169	McGinnity-NY	.219	Tannehill-Pit	.266	Hahn-Cin	36.1	Hahn-Cin	43.7
Tannehill-Pit	1.95	Poole-Pit-Cin	142	Taylor-Chi	.227	McGinnity-NY	.273	Willis-Bos	26.5	Willis-Bos	28.4
Lundgren-Chi	1.97	Tannehill-Pit	140	Donovan-Bro	.228	Hahn-Cin	.275	Phillippe-Pit	22.0	Mathewson-NY	21.2
Phillippe-Pit	2.05	Lundgren-Chi	137	Chesbro-Pit	.229	Phillippe-Pit	.276	Tannehill-Pit	21.3	Phillippe-Pit	20.6

Clutch Pitching Index		Relief Runs	Adjusted Relief Runs	Relief Ranking	Total Pitcher Index		Total Baseball Ranking	
Lundgren-Chi	144				Taylor-Chi	6.3	Taylor-Chi	6.0
Poole-Pit-Cin	140				Hahn-Cin	4.6	Hahn-Cin	4.5
Eason-Chi-Bos	136				Tannehill-Pit	3.1	Wagner-Pit	4.4
Taylor-NY	126				Willis-Bos	3.1	Tenney-Bos	3.9
Taylor-Chi	122				Phillips-Cin	3.1	Farrell-StL	3.3

January 4 Bill Dinneen, winner of 36 games for the Beaneaters (NL) in the past two years, signs with the rival Boston Somersets (AL), for whom he will win 20 or more in each of the next three years.

April 26 In his major league debut, Cleveland's Addie Joss hurls a one-hitter against the Browns to win, 3–0. The only hit is a scratch single by Jesse Burkett.

May 23 Cleveland financier Charles Somers, who is also the president of the Boston club, meets with Lajoie in Philadelphia and guarantees him a four-year contract at $7,000 per year no matter what the legal outcome of his case. Lajoie had played one game for the A's, then sat in the stands for two months. Even after joining Cleveland, for the rest of the season Lajoie stayed clear of Pennsylvania, where an injunction remained in force. In 1903 Cleveland fans will vote to rename the club the Naps in honor of Lajoie.

May 24 Bill Bradley, Cleveland third baseman, is the AL's first player to hit a home run in each of four consecutive games, a record not matched until Babe Ruth does it June 25, 1918.

June 10 Bobby Wallace, slick-fielding St. Louis shortstop, handles an AL record 17 chances in a nine-inning game while losing 5–4 to Boston.

June 11 Connie Mack signs Rube Waddell, who was pitching in the Pacific Coast League. He will go 24-7 for the remainder of 1902 for Philadelphia to finish second in the league in wins behind Cy Young's 32 for Boston.

June 30 Cleveland is the first AL team to hit three consecutive home runs in one inning as Napoleon Lajoie, Charles "Piano Legs" Hickman, and Bill Bradley connect in the first inning off St. Louis. Two days later, Ed Delahanty, Bill Coughlin, and William "Boileryard" Clarke will duplicate the feat for Washington against the White Stockings.

July 13 In the sixth inning of a game with the Tigers, Harry Davis of the A's attempts a double steal with Dave Fultz, who is on third base. But Davis does not draw a throw as he goes into second base. On the next pitch he "steals" first base. The next time he steals second base he does draw a throw and Fultz scores from third base. This double steal maneuver will be attempted in later years by Fred Tenney (July 31, 1908), and Germany Schaefer (Sept. 4, 1908).

July 17 Left with only five players available to play, the Orioles forfeit a game to St. Louis and their franchise to the league, which borrows players from other teams and operates the club for the balance of the season.

August 18* The first unassisted triple play ever in a professional game is executed by first base Hal O'Hagan, of the Rochester Broncos (IL) against Jersey City.

August 25 Ban Johnson announces the AL's intention to have a New York team in 1903, with Clark Griffith as manager.

September 28 The AL season ends with the Athletics five games in front of the St. Louis Browns. Philadelphia's Socks Seybold hits 16 homers for the highest total to lead the AL until Babe Ruth's 29 in 1919.

December 9 The AL announces the purchase of grounds for a ballpark in New York, and the next day the NL declares its readiness to make peace.

BALTIMORE	BOSTON	CHICAGO	CLEVELAND	DETROIT	PHILADELPHIA	ST.LOUIS	WASHINGTON
M J.McGraw	M J.Collins	M C.Griffith	M B.Armour	M F.Dwyer	M C.Mack	M J.McAleer	M T.Loftus
M W.Robinson	1B C.LaChance	1B F.Isbell	1B C.Hickman	1B P.Dillon	1B H.Davis	1B J.Anderson	1B S.Carey
1B D.McGann	2B H.Ferris	2B T.Daly	2B N.Lajoie	2B K.Gleason	2B D.Murphy	2B D.Padden	2B J.Doyle
2B J.Williams	SS F.Parent	SS G.Davis	SS J.Gochnauer	SS K.Elberfeld	SS M.Cross	SS B.Wallace	SS B.Ely
SS B.Gilbert	3B J.Collins	3B S.Strang	3B B.Bradley	3B D.Casey	3B L.Cross	3B B.McCormick	3B B.Coughlin
3B R.Bresnahan	LF P.Dougherty	LF S.Mertes	LF J.McCarthy	LF D.Harley	LF T.Hartsel	LF J.Burkett	LF E.Delahanty
LF K.Selbach	CF C.Stahl	CF F.Jones	CF H.Bay	CF J.Barrett	CF D.Fultz	CF E.Heidrick	CF J.Ryan
CF H.McFarland	RF B.Freeman	RF D.Green	RF E.Flick	RF D.Holmes	RF S.Seybold	RF C.Hemphill	RF W.Lee
RF C.Seymour	C L.Criger	C B.Sullivan	C H.Bemis	C D.McGuire	C O.Schreck't	C J.Sugden	C B.Clarke
C W.Robinson							
	3O H.Gleason	C E.McFarland	O O.Pickering	/1 S.McAllister	C D.Powers	O2 B.Friel	O2 B.Keister
O H.Arndt	C J.Warner	/O H.McFarland	C1 B.Wood	C F.Buelow	2 L.Castro	C M.Kahoe	3 H.Wolverton
O J.Kelley	O C.Hickman	/C E.Hughes	2 F.Bonner	1 E.Beck	2 F.Bonner	O B.Maloney	C L.Drill
1 T.Jones	/2 G.Wilson		2S J.Thoney	O P.LePine	/C F.Steelman	C J.Donahue	/O J.Stanley
C A.Smith		P N.Callahan	O C.Hemphill	O H.Arndt	/2 N.Lajoie	O D.Jones	/2 J.Atz
3 J.Mathison	P C.Young	P R.Patterson	1 O.Schreck't	/2 J.O'Connell		/O J.McAleer	/C T.Donahue
3 A.Oyler	P B.Dinneen	P W.Piatt	O E.Harvey	/O L.Post			
3 J.McGraw	P G.Winter	P C.Griffith	/1 H.O'Hagen	/O L.Schiappa'e	P E.Plank	P J.Powell	P A.Orth
C G.Yeager	P T.Sparks	P N.Garvin	/2 P.Graham		P R.Waddell	P R.Donahue	P C.Patten
1 B.Mellor			/C G.Starnagle	P W.Mercer	P B.Husting	P J.Harper	P B.Carrick
/O J.Sheckard	/P T.Hughes	/P J.Durham		P G.Mullin	P S.Wiltse	P W.Sudhoff	P H.Townsend
/2 S.McAllister	/P G.Prentiss	/P D.Leitner	P E.Moore	P E.Siever	P F.Mitchell	P B.Reidy	
/3 J.Thoney	/P D.Adkins	/P S.McMackin	P A.Joss	P R.Miller			
/C L.Drill	/P D.Williams	/P J.Katoll	P B.Bernhard	P J.Yeager	P H.Wilson		
/1 P.Dillon	/P N.Altrock		P G.Wright			/P C.Shields	
/3 E.Courtney	/P P.Deininger			P A.McCarthy	/P A.Coakley	/P H.Kane	
/O S.Jordan	/P B.Husting		/P O.Streit	/P R.Kisinger	/P B.Duggleby		
H C.Burns	/P F.Mitchell		/P O.Hess	/P W.Egan	/P E.Kenna		/P C.Vorhees
			/P G.Dorner	/P J.Cronin	/P B.Bernhard		
P J.McGinnity			/P J.Lundbom	/P S.McMackin	/P O.Porter		
P H.Howell			/P D.Taylor	/P J.Terry	/P T.Quinn		
P S.Wiltse			/P C.Smith	/P E.Fisher	/P T.Walker		
P C.Shields			/P D.Varney				
P J.Katoll			/P D.Leitner				
			/P L.Polchow				
P I.Butler			/P E.Walker				
P T.Hughes			/P G.Clark				
P J.Cronin			/P C.Vasbinder				
/P E.Ross							
/P F.Foreman							
/P C.Heismann							
/P D.Hale							
/P B.Lawson							
/P G.Prentiss							

TEAM	G	W	L	PCT	GB	R	OR	AB	H	2B	3B	HR	BB	SO	AVG	OBP	SLG	PRO	PRO+	BR	/A	PF	CHI	RC	SB	CS	SBA	SBR
PHI	137	83	53	.610		775	636	4762	1369	235	67	38	343	293	.287	.340	.389	.729	104	50	20	104	107	729	201			
STL	140	78	58	.574	5	619	607	4736	1254	208	61	29	373	327	.265	.323	.353	.676	94	-38	-29	99	97	612	137			
BOS	138	77	60	.562	6.5	664	600	4875	1356	195	95	42	275	375	.278	.322	.383	.705	98	0	-19	103	98	671	132			
CHI	138	74	60	.552	8	675	602	4654	1248	170	50	14	411	381	.268	.332	.335	.667	95	-43	-15	96	107	641	265			
CLE	137	69	67	.507	14	686	667	4840	1401	248	68	33	308	356	.289	.336	.389	.725	111	41	70	96	95	712	140			
WAS	138	61	75	.449	22	707	790	4734	1338	261	66	47	329	296	.283	.335	.395	.730	107	48	42	101	99	694	121			
DET	137	52	83	.385	30.5	566	657	4644	1167	141	55	22	359	287	.251	.312	.320	.632	79	-109	-120	102	103	527	130			
BAL	141	50	88	.362	34	715	848	4760	1318	202	107	33	417	429	.277	.342	.385	.727	103	51	19	104	97	723	189			
TOT	553					5407		38005	10451	1660	569	258	2815	2744	.275	.331	.369	.700						1315				

TEAM	CG	SH	SV	IP	H	H/G	HR	BB	SO	RAT	ERA	ERA+	OAV	OOB	PR	/A	PF	CPI	FA	E	DP	FW	PW	BW	SBW	DIF
PHI	114	5	2	1216¹	1292	9.6	33	368	455	12.7	3.29	111	.273	.334	39	51	103	110	.953	270	75	1.4	4.8	1.9		6.9
STL	120	7	2	1244	1273	9.2	36	343	348	12.0	3.34	106	.266	.321	32	26	99	99	.953	274	122	1.5	2.5	-2.8		8.7
BOS	123	6	1	1238	1217	8.8	27	326	431	11.5	3.02	118	.258	.311	75	75	100	99	.955	263	101	2.0	7.1	-1.8		1.2
CHI	116	11	0	1221²	1269	9.3	30	331	346	12.1	3.41	99	.269	.323	22	-5	95	98	.955	257	125	2.3	-.5	-1.4		6.6
CLE	116	16	3	1204¹	1199	9.0	26	411	361	12.4	3.28	105	.260	.327	39	21	96	101	.950	287	96	.3	2.0	6.6		-8.0
WAS	130	2	1	1207²	1403	10.5	56	312	300	13.2	4.36	85	.291	.341	-106	-88	104	94	.945	316	70	-1.3	-8.3	4.0		-1.3
DET	116	9	3	1190²	1267	9.6	20	370	245	12.7	3.56	102	.274	.333	1	10	102	99	.943	332	111	-2.5	.9	-11.4		-2.6
BAL	119	3	1	1210¹	1531	11.4	30	354	258	14.3	4.33	87	.309	.360	-102	-77	106	104	.938	357	109	-3.5	-7.3	1.8		-10.0
TOT	954	59	13	9733		9.7				12.6	3.57		.275	.331					.949	2356	809					

Runs		Hits		Doubles		Triples		Home Runs		Total Bases	
Hartsel-Phi	109	Hickman-Bos-Cle	193	Delahanty-Was	43	Williams-Bal	21	Seybold-Phi	16	Hickman-Bos-Cle	288
Fultz-Phi	109	L.Cross-Phi	191	Davis-Phi	43	Freeman-Bos	19	Hickman-Bos-Cle	11	Freeman-Bos	283
Strang-Chi	108	Bradley-Cle	187	L.Cross-Phi	39	Ferris-Bos	14	Freeman-Bos	11	Bradley-Cle	283
Bradley-Cle	104	Delahanty-Was	178	Bradley-Cle	39	Delahanty-Was	14	Bradley-Cle	11	Delahanty-Was	279
Delahanty-Was	103	Freeman-Bos	174	Freeman-Bos	38	Hickman-Bos-Cle	13	Delahanty-Was	10	Seybold-Phi	264

Runs Batted In		Runs Produced		Bases On Balls		Batting Average		On Base Percentage		Slugging Average	
Freeman-Bos	121	L.Cross-Phi	198	Hartsel-Phi	87	Lajoie-Phi-Cle	.378	Delahanty-Was	.453	Delahanty-Was	.590
Hickman-Bos-Cle	110	Delahanty-Was	186	Strang-Chi	76	Delahanty-Was	.376	Dougherty-Bos	.407	Lajoie-Phi-Cle	.565
L.Cross-Phi	108	Freeman-Bos	185	Barrett-Det	74	Hickman-Bos-Cle	.361	Barrett-Det	.397	Hickman-Bos-Cle	.539
Seybold-Phi	97	Davis-Phi	175	Burkett-StL	71	Dougherty-Bos	.342	Selbach-Bal	.393	Bradley-Cle	.515
		Hickman-Bos-Cle	173	Davis-Chi	65	L.Cross-Phi	.342	Jones-Chi	.390	Seybold-Phi	.506

Production		Adjusted Production		Batter Runs		Adjusted Batter Runs		Clutch Hitting Index		Runs Created	
Delahanty-Was	1.043	Delahanty-Was	186	Delahanty-Was	57.0	Delahanty-Was	56.0	Davis-Chi	136	Delahanty-Was	137
Hickman-Bos-Cle	.926	Hickman-Bos-Cle	159	Hickman-Bos-Cle	36.3	Hickman-Bos-Cle	39.1	L.Cross-Phi	131	Hickman-Bos-Cle	118
Bradley-Cle	.890	Bradley-Cle	151	Lajoie-Phi-Cle	32.5	Lajoie-Phi-Cle	35.7	Anderson-StL	131	Bradley-Cle	114
Seybold-Phi	.881	Seybold-Phi	137	Bradley-Cle	30.7	Bradley-Cle	35.1	Elberfeld-Det	130	Freeman-Bos	109
Williams-Bal	.861	Freeman-Bos	131	Seybold-Phi	28.5	Seybold-Phi	24.2	Mertes-Chi	129	L.Cross-Phi	105

Total Average		Stolen Bases		Stolen Base Average	Stolen Base Runs	Fielding Runs		Total Player Rating	
Delahanty-Was	1.224	Hartsel-Phi	47			Ferris-Bos	26.5	Lajoie-Phi-Cle	6.2
Hickman-Bos-Cle	.935	Mertes-Chi	46			Schreck-Cle-Phi	20.9	Delahanty-Was	4.7
Bradley-Cle	.895	Fultz-Phi	44			Padden-StL	18.2	Bradley-Cle	4.4
Seybold-Phi	.894					Jones-Chi	12.5	Hickman-Bos-Cle	2.7
Hartsel-Phi	.893					Coughlin-Was	11.8	Schreck-Cle-Phi	2.7

Wins		Win Percentage		Games		Complete Games		Shutouts		Saves	
Young-Bos	32	Bernhard-Phi-Cle	.783	Young-Bos	45	Young-Bos	41	Joss-Cle	5	Powell-StL	2
Waddell-Phi	24	Waddell-Phi	.774	Powell-StL	42	Dinneen-Bos	39	Siever-Det	4		
Powell-StL	22	Young-Bos	.744	Dinneen-Bos	42	Powell-StL	36	Moore-Cle	4		
R.Donahue-StL	22	R.Donahue-StL	.667	Wiltse-Phi-Bal	38	Orth-Was	36	Mercer-Det	4		
Dinneen-Bos	21	Griffith-Chi	.625	Orth-Was	38						

Innings Pitched		Fewest Hits/Game		Fewest BB/Game		Strikeouts		Strikeouts/Game		Ratio	
Young-Bos	384.2	Bernhard-Phi-Cle	7.01	Orth-Was	1.11	Waddell-Phi	210	Waddell-Phi	6.84	Bernhard-Phi-Cle	8.68
Dinneen-Bos	371.1	Waddell-Phi	7.30	Young-Bos	1.24	Young-Bos	160	Powell-StL	3.76	Siever-Det	9.56
Powell-StL	328.1	Joss-Cle	7.52	Bernhard-Phi-Cle	1.47	Powell-StL	137	Young-Bos	3.74	Waddell-Phi	9.71
Orth-Was	324.0	Siever-Det	7.93	Siever-Det	1.53	Dinneen-Bos	136	Joss-Cle	3.54	Young-Bos	9.73
R.Donahue-StL	316.1	Winter-Bos	7.97	Plank-Phi	1.83	Plank-Phi	107	Piatt-Chi	3.51	Joss-Cle	10.46

Earned Run Average		Adjusted ERA		Opponents' Batting Avg.		Opponents' On Base Pct.		Starter Runs		Adjusted Starter Runs	
Siever-Det	1.91	Siever-Det	191	Bernhard-Phi-Cle	.216	Bernhard-Phi-Cle	.254	Young-Bos	60.6	Young-Bos	60.6
Waddell-Phi	2.05	Waddell-Phi	179	Waddell-Phi	.223	Siever-Det	.273	Waddell-Phi	46.6	Waddell-Phi	49.5
Bernhard-Phi-Cle	2.15	Young-Bos	166	Joss-Cle	.228	Waddell-Phi	.276	Bernhard-Phi-Cle	35.7	Siever-Det	36.2
Young-Bos	2.15	Bernhard-Phi-Cle	160	Siever-Det	.237	Young-Bos	.276	Siever-Det	34.7	Bernhard-Phi-Cle	32.6
Garvin-Chi	2.21	Garvin-Chi	153	Winter-Bos	.238	Joss-Cle	.291	R.Donahue-StL	28.5	R.Donahue-StL	26.9

Clutch Pitching Index		Relief Runs	Adjusted Relief Runs	Relief Ranking	Total Pitcher Index		Total Baseball Ranking	
Garvin-Chi	129				Waddell-Phi	5.9	Lajoie-Phi-Cle	6.2
Shields-Bal-StL	123				Young-Bos	5.8	Waddell-Phi	5.9
Husting-Bos-Phi	120				Bernhard-Phi-Cle	2.9	Young-Bos	5.8
Moore-Cle	119				Siever-Det	2.6	Delahanty-Was	4.7
Sudhoff-StL	110				Garvin-Chi	2.4	Bradley-Cle	4.4

January 9 At Cincinnati peace talks, the NL proposes a consolidated 12-team league, which the AL rejects. An agreement is reached to coexist peacefully if the AL promises to stay out of Pittsburgh. In the awarding of disputed contracts, the most hotly contested case is that of Sam Crawford, Reds outfielder who batted .333 and led the NL with 23 triples in 1902. The future Hall of Famer, signed by both Detroit and the Reds, is awarded to the Tigers, having signed with them first.

February 28 A syndicate headed by Pittsburgh owner Barney Dreyfuss and James Potter buys the Philadelphia Phillies from John Rogers and A. J. Reach for $170,000. It will be another seven years before ownership interest in more than one team is prohibited.

March 7 In the first trade under the peace treaty, the Giants send their 1902 part-time manager Heinie Smith to Detroit for second baseman Kid Gleason, who is immediately moved to the Phils where he will end a 20-year playing career.

May 6 The Pirates' Deacon Phillippe, en route to 25 wins, lets one get away when the Cubs score nine in the ninth for an 11–4 triumph.

May 16 A record 31,500 at the Polo Grounds see the first-place Giants beat Pittsburgh.

June 9 The Phils score, breaking the Pirates' record run of six straight shutouts and 56 scoreless innings. The Giants were blanked twice, Boston three times, and the Phils once during the run.

June 25 Boston Beaneater Wiley Piatt loses two complete games in one day, falling to Pittsburgh, 1-0 and 5-3.

July 2 Pitcher Jack Doscher, making his debut with the Chicago Cubs, becomes the first son of a former major league player to also play in the major leagues. Father Herm was a third baseman with Troy, Chicago, and Cleveland before the turn of the century.

August 8 The Giants "Iron Man" Joe McGinnity pitches one of three doubleheaders he will win this month, beating Brooklyn, 6-1, and 4-3; he also steals home in the second game. On Aug. 1, he won two from Boston, 4-1 and 5-2. On Aug. 31, he will beat the Phillies twice. He has now done double work five times, including two losses on each of the two occasions at Baltimore in 1901. The combination of his 434 innings pitched and 31 wins, with Christy Mathewson's 366 innings pitched and 30 wins, will make them the century's most productive one-season duo.

September 11* A new National Agreement signed by the National Association of minor league clubs officially organizes professional baseball under one comprehensive set of rules.

October 1 The first modern World Series game, also called "Championship of the United States," is played at Boston's Huntington Avenue Grounds before 16,242. Deacon Phillippe pitches Pittsburgh to a 7-3 win over Cy Young. Pittsburgh right fielder Jimmy Sebring hits the first home run. Third baseman Tommy Leach hits two triples for the Pirates and winds up with four, a Series record.

October 6 Pitching on only one day's rest Deacon Phillippe beats Boston for the third time to give Pittsburgh a 3-1 World Series lead. Phillippe survives three ninth-inning runs for a 5-4 win.

October 13 Pittsburgh's Deacon Phillippe pitches his fifth complete game of the Series, losing to Bill Dinneen, 3-0. Only 7,455, the smallest crowd of the Series, see Boston win the championship. Deacon's five decisions and 44 innings pitched are still World Series records.

October 15 With Pirates owner Dreyfuss putting his club's $6,699.56 gate receipts into the players' pool, the 16 Pirates receive $1,316 each, more than the victorious Boston players' $1,182. Deacon Phillippe receives a bonus and 10 shares of stock in the Pirates for his heroic efforts.

BOSTON	BROOKLYN	CHICAGO	CINCINNATI	NEW YORK	PHILADELPHIA	PITTSBURGH	ST.LOUIS
M A.Buckenberger	M N.Hanlon	M F.Selee	M J.Kelley	M J.McGraw	M C.Zimmer	M F.Clarke	M P.Donovan
1B F.Tenney	1B J.Doyle	1B F.Chance	1B J.Beckley	1B D.McGann	1B K.Douglass	1B K.Bransfield	1B J.Hackett
2B E.Abbaticchio	2B T.Flood	2B J.Evers	2B T.Daly	2B B.Gilbert	2B K.Gleason	2B C.Ritchey	2B J.Farrell
SS H.Aubrey	SS B.Dahlen	SS J.Tinker	SS T.Corcoran	SS C.Babb	SS R.Hulswitt	SS H.Wagner	SS D.Brain
3B E.Gremminger	3B S.Strang	3B D.Casey	3B H.Steinfeldt	3B B.Lauder	3B H.Wolverton	3B T.Leach	3B J.Burke
LF D.Cooley	LF J.Sheckard	LF J.Slagle	LF M.Donlin	LF S.Mertes	LF S.Barry	LF F.Clarke	LF G.Barclay
CF C.Dexter	CF J.Dobbs	CF D.Jones	CF C.Seymour	CF R.Bresnahan	CF R.Thomas	CF G.Beaumont	CF H.Smoot
RF P.Carney	RF J.McCredie	RF D.Harley	RF C.Dolan	RF G.Browne	RF B.Keister	RF J.Sebring	RF P.Donovan
C P.Moran	C L.Ritter	C J.Kling	C H.Peitz	C J.Warner	C F.Roth	C E.Phelps	C J.O'Neill
O J.Stanley	23 D.Jordan	S O.Williams	OS J.Kelley	O G.Van Haltren	O J.Titus	SO O.Krueger	C1 J.Ryan
2S	C F.Jacklitsch	2 B.Lowe	C B.Bergen	23 J.Dunn	23 B.Hallman	C H.Smith	OP J.Dunleavy
C M.Kittridge	O D.Gessler	2 J.McCarthy	2 G.Magoon	C F.Bowerman	C R.Dooin	C A.Weaver	S O.Williams
O T.McCreery	O T.McCreery	C T.Raub	2 J.Morrissey	/S G.Davis	C C.Zimmer	/O G.Merritt	1 A.Nichols
P T.Pittinger	C H.Hearne	/O J.Cook	3 C.DeArmond	/2 J.McGraw	2 R.Brashear	/S J.Marshall	S L.DeMontreville
P V.Willis	O E.Householder	/1 B.Hanlon	/O P.Cregan	P J.McGinnity	/3 J.Walsh	/O G.Curtis	C A.Weaver
P J.Malarkey	/O H.Thielman	/3 G.Moriarty	/C L.Fohl	P C.Mathewson	H D.Rudolph	/C F.Carisch	/2 H.Berte
P W.Piatt	/O H.Jennings	/C L.McLean	/C E.Haberer	P D.Taylor	P B.Duggleby	/3 H.Lobert	/C J.Coveney
P P.Williams	/C F.McManus	P J.Taylor	/O D.Kerwin	P J.Cronin	P C.Fraser	/O E.Diehl	/1 L.Ury
	/2 M.Broderick	P J.Weimer	/O H.Wood	P R.Miller	P T.Sparks	/O L.Gertenrich	P C.McFarland
	/C E.Hug	P B.Wicker	/C P.Deisel	/P R.Ames	P F.Mitchell	/O R.Grey	P M.Brown
	P O.Jones	P C.Lundgren	P N.Hahn	/P B.Bartley	P J.McFetridge	/O S.Hofman	P C.Currie
	P H.Schmidt	P J.Menefee	P B.Ewing		/P F.Burchell	P D.Phillippe	P M.O'Neill
	P N.Garvin	/P C.Currie	P J.Sutthoff		/P L.Washburn	P S.Leever	P B.Rhoads
	P R.Evans	/P A.Hardy	P E.Poole		/P W.McLaughlin	P E.Doheny	P E.Murphy
	P B.Reidy	/P P.Graham	P J.Harper		/P P.Williams	P B.Kennedy	/P W.Sanders
	/P G.Thatcher	/P P.Williams	P B.Phillips			P K.Wilhelm	/P C.Moran
	/P R.Vickers	/P J.Doscher	/P R.Reagan			P B.Veil	/P H.Betts
	/P J.Doscher		/P J.Wiggs			P C.Falkenberg	/P P.Hynes
	/P B.Pounds		/P B.Hooker			/P G.Thompson	/P J.Lovett
						/P L.Winham	/P B.Wicker
						/P J.Pfiester	/P S.Yerkes
						/P D.Scanlan	/P L.Milton
						/P L.Moren	/P E.Taylor

TEAM	G	W	L	PCT	GB	R	OR	AB	H	2B	3B	HR	BB	SO	AVG	OBP	SLG	PRO	PRO+	BR	/A	PF	CHI	RC	SB	CS	SBA	SBR
PIT	141	91	49	.650		793	613	4988	1429	208	110	34	364		.286	.341	.393	.734	113	89	65	103	101	758	172			
NY	142	84	55	.604	6.5	729	567	4741	1290	181	49	20	379		.272	.338	.344	.682	97	9	-17	104	106	678	264			
CHI	139	82	56	.594	8	695	599	4733	1300	191	62	9	422		.275	.340	.347	.687	105	19	38	97	101	678	259			
CIN	141	74	65	.532	16.5	765	656	4857	1399	228	92	28	403		.288	.346	.390	.736	104	95	10	111	99	735	144			
BRO	139	70	66	.515	19	667	682	4534	1201	177	56	15	522		.265	.348	.339	.687	105	27	47	97	97	661	273			
BOS	140	58	80	.420	32	578	699	4682	1145	176	47	25	398		.245	.312	.318	.630	90	-83	-60	96	100	540	159			
PHI	139	49	86	.363	39.5	617	738	4781	1283	186	62	12	338		.268	.322	.341	.663	98	-33	-12	97	97	596	120			
STL	139	43	94	.314	46.5	505	795	4689	1176	138	65	8	277		.251	.297	.313	.610	83	-124	-108	97	98	511	171			
TOT	560					5349		38005	10223	1485	543	151	3103	3767	.269	.331	.349	.679							1562			

TEAM	CG	SH	SV	IP	H	H/G	HR	BB	SO	RAT	ERA	ERA+	OAV	OOB	PR	/A	PF	CPI	FA	E	DP	FW	PW	BW	SBW	DIF
PIT	117	16	5	1251¹	1215	8.7	9	384	454	11.8	2.91	111	.255	.316	48	44	99	95	.951	295	100	1.6	4.2	6.2		8.9
NY	115	8	8	1262²	1257	9.0	20	371	628	11.9	2.95	113	.258	.316	43	56	102	98	.951	287	87	2.3	5.4	-1.6		8.5
CHI	117	6	6	1240¹	1182	8.6	14	354	451	11.4	2.77	113	.250	.307	67	46	96	93	.942	338	78	-1.6	4.4	3.6		6.5
CIN	126	11	1	1230	1277	9.3	14	378	480	12.6	3.07	116	.268	.331	26	65	109	105	.946	312	84	.4	6.2	1.0		-3.1
BRO	118	11	4	1221¹	1276	9.4	18	377	438	12.7	3.44	92	.275	.339	-25	-38	98	100	.951	284	98	2.0	-3.6	4.5		-.9
BOS	125	8	1	1228²	1310	9.6	30	460	516	13.4	3.34	96	.278	.348	-11	-21	98	112	.939	361	89	-3.0	-2.0	-5.8		-.2
PHI	126	5	3	1212¹	1347	10.0	21	425	381	13.6	3.96	82	.285	.352	-95	-97	100	97	.947	300	76	1.0	-9.3	-1.2		-9.0
STL	111	4	2	1212¹	1353	10.0	25	430	419	13.6	3.67	89	.284	.350	-55	-56	100	104	.940	354	111	-2.7	-5.4	-10.4		-7.1
TOT	955	69	30	9859		9.3				12.6	3.26		.269	.331					.946	2531	723					

Runs
Beaumont-Pit 137
Donlin-Cin 110
Browne-NY 105
Slagle-Chi 104
Strang-Bro 101

Hits
Beaumont-Pit 209
Seymour-Cin 191
Browne-NY 185
Wagner-Pit 182
Donlin-Cin 174

Doubles
Steinfeldt-Cin 32
Mertes-NY 32
Clarke-Pit 32

Triples
Wagner-Pit 19
Donlin-Cin 18
Leach-Pit 17

Home Runs
Sheckard-Bro 9

Total Bases
Beaumont-Pit 272
Seymour-Cin 267
Wagner-Pit 265
Donlin-Cin 256
Sheckard-Bro 245

Runs Batted In
Mertes-NY 104
Wagner-Pit 101
Doyle-Bro 91
Leach-Pit 87
Steinfeldt-Cin 83

Runs Produced
Beaumont-Pit 198
Mertes-NY 197
Wagner-Pit 193
Leach-Pit 177
Doyle-Bro 175

Bases On Balls
Thomas-Phi 107
Dahlen-Bro 82
Slagle-Chi 81
Chance-Chi 78

Batting Average
Wagner-Pit ..... .355
Clarke-Pit ..... .351
Donlin-Cin ..... .351
Bresnahan-NY ..... .350
Seymour-Cin ..... .342

On Base Percentage
Thomas-Phi ..... .453
Bresnahan-NY ..... .443
Chance-Chi ..... .439
Sheckard-Bro ..... .423
Donlin-Cin ..... .420

Slugging Average
Clarke-Pit ..... .532
Wagner-Pit ..... .518
Donlin-Cin ..... .516
Bresnahan-NY ..... .493
Steinfeldt-Cin ..... .481

Production
Clarke-Pit ..... .946
Donlin-Cin ..... .936
Bresnahan-NY ..... .936
Wagner-Pit ..... .931
Sheckard-Bro ..... .899

Adjusted Production
Clarke-Pit 164
Sheckard-Bro 160
Bresnahan-NY 160
Wagner-Pit 160
Chance-Chi 155

Batter Runs
Donlin-Cin 42.6
Wagner-Pit 42.1
Sheckard-Bro 39.8
Bresnahan-NY 37.8
Clarke-Pit 37.3

Adjusted Batter Runs
Sheckard-Bro 43.3
Wagner-Pit 38.6
Chance-Chi 36.8
Clarke-Pit 34.3
Bresnahan-NY 34.1

Clutch Hitting Index
Corcoran-Cin 141
Doyle-Bro 131
Mertes-NY 123
Chance-Chi 118
Dobbs-Chi-Bro 118

Runs Created
Sheckard-Bro 137
Wagner-Pit 133
Donlin-Cin 122
Beaumont-Pit 119
Chance-Chi 118

Total Average
Chance-Chi 1.175
Bresnahan-NY 1.144
Sheckard-Bro 1.142
Wagner-Pit 1.097
Clarke-Pit 1.061

Stolen Bases
Sheckard-Bro 67
Chance-Chi 67
Wagner-Pit 46
Strang-Bro 46
Mertes-NY 45

Stolen Base Average

Stolen Base Runs

Fielding Runs
Farrell-StL 28.1
Wagner-Pit 24.6
Sheckard-Bro 23.4
Moran-Bos 19.3
Ritchey-Pit 19.0

Total Player Rating
Wagner-Pit 6.3
Sheckard-Bro 5.5
Thomas-Phi 3.8
Moran-Bos 3.5
Tenney-Bos 3.1

Wins
McGinnity-NY 31
Mathewson-NY 30
Phillippe-Pit 25
Leever-Pit 25

Win Percentage
Leever-Pit ..... .781
Phillippe-Pit ..... .735
Weimer-Chi ..... .714
Mathewson-NY ..... .698
Wicker-StL-Chi ..... .690

Games
McGinnity-NY 55
Mathewson-NY 45
Pittinger-Bos 44
Schmidt-Bro 40

Complete Games
McGinnity-NY 44
Mathewson-NY 37
Pittinger-Bos 35
Hahn-Cin 34
Taylor-Chi 33

Shutouts
Leever-Pit 7
Schmidt-Bro 5
Hahn-Cin 5
Phillippe-Pit 4
Jones-Bro 4

Saves
Miller-NY 3
Lundgren-Chi 3

Innings Pitched
McGinnity-NY 434.0
Mathewson-NY 366.1
Pittinger-Bos 351.2
Jones-Bro 324.1
Taylor-Chi 312.1

Fewest Hits/Game
Weimer-Chi 7.69
Mathewson-NY 7.89
Taylor-Chi 7.98
Leever-Pit 8.07
McGinnity-NY 8.11

Fewest BB/Game
Phillippe-Pit ..... .90
Hahn-Cin 1.43
Taylor-Chi 1.64
McFarland-StL 1.89
Leever-Pit 1.90

Strikeouts
Mathewson-NY 267
McGinnity-NY 171
Garvin-Bro 154
Pittinger-Bos 140
Weimer-Chi 128

Strikeouts/Game
Mathewson-NY 6.56
Piatt-Bos 4.97
Garvin-Bro 4.65
Weimer-Chi 4.09
Willis-Bos 4.05

Ratio
Phillippe-Pit 9.39
Taylor-Chi 9.77
Leever-Pit 10.13
Mathewson-NY 10.59
Hahn-Cin 10.70

Earned Run Average
Leever-Pit 2.06
Mathewson-NY 2.26
Weimer-Chi 2.30
Phillippe-Pit 2.43
McGinnity-NY 2.43

Adjusted ERA
Leever-Pit 157
Mathewson-NY 148
Hahn-Cin 141
McGinnity-NY 138
Weimer-Chi 136

Opponents' Batting Avg.
Weimer-Chi ..... .225
Mathewson-NY ..... .231
Taylor-Chi ..... .235
McGinnity-NY ..... .236
Leever-Pit ..... .238

Opponents' On Base Pct.
Phillippe-Pit ..... .263
Taylor-Chi ..... .273
Leever-Pit ..... .282
Mathewson-NY ..... .287
McGinnity-NY ..... .291

Starter Runs
Mathewson-NY 40.7
McGinnity-NY 40.2
Leever-Pit 38.0
Weimer-Chi 30.2
Taylor-Chi 28.2

Adjusted Starter Runs
McGinnity-NY 44.0
Mathewson-NY 43.9
Leever-Pit 37.0
Hahn-Cin 33.8
Weimer-Chi 26.0

Clutch Pitching Index
Brown-StL 153
Pittinger-Bos 126
Malarkey-Bos 115
Piatt-Bos 115
Poole-Cin 113

Relief Runs

Adjusted Relief Runs

Relief Ranking

Total Pitcher Index
Mathewson-NY 5.3
McGinnity-NY 4.0
Leever-Pit 3.4
Hahn-Cin 3.2
Taylor-Chi 2.9

Total Baseball Ranking
Wagner-Pit 6.3
Sheckard-Bro 5.5
Mathewson-NY 5.3
McGinnity-NY 4.0
Thomas-Phi 3.8

January 9 Despite attempts by John Brush and Andrew Freedman to use their political influence to prevent the AL from finding suitable grounds in New York, Ban Johnson, aided by baseball writer Joe Vila, finds backers. He also finds a ballpark site at 165th Street and Broadway. Frank Farrell and Bill Devery pay $18,000 for the Baltimore franchise and will build a wooden grandstand seating 15,000 on the highest point of Manhattan. The team, logically, will be called the Highlanders.

January 12 Detroit pitcher Win Mercer, winner of 15 games in 1902, commits suicide by inhaling gas in San Francisco's Occidental Hotel. Mercer had recently been named Tigers manager.

April 14 Ed Delahanty, one of five major league brothers, and the greatest natural hitter of his time, rejoins the Washington Nationals in accordance with the peace terms. A three-year contract with the Giants at $8,000 a year, signed during the winter, is canceled. The Nationals reimburse the Giants for the $3,000 advanced to Big Ed.

April 30 Hilltop Park, the new AL park, opens in New York with an estimated crowd of 16,000 watching the home team beat Washington, 6-2.

May 17 With Sunday baseball banned in Cleveland, the Blues (Indians) and Highlanders (Yankees) play at Columbus, Ohio. Cleveland's Addie Joss defeats Clark Griffith, 9–2.

June 26 Veteran shortstop George Davis, who played for the White Stockings in 1902 and was awarded to them as part of the peace treaty, gets the approval of NL president Harry Pulliam to play for the Giants. After Davis plays in four games for the Giants, Chicago's owner Charles Comiskey gets an injunction preventing Davis from playing. On July 20, the NL directors vote that Davis cannot play for any team except the White Stockings. Davis sits out the rest of the season, rejoins Chicago in 1904, and finishes a 20-year career with them in 1909.

July 2 Seeing that fellow former American Leaguer George Davis is playing for the Giants, Ed Delahanty decides to jump to New York, too. Leaving the AL Washington team in Detroit, he boards an eastbound train. He is put off the train for rowdy, and possibly drunken, behavior. When he tries to walk across the railroad bridge over the Niagara River, he falls to his death.

July 17* Dan McClelland of the Cuban X-Giants spins the first perfect game in black baseball history, blanking the Penn Park Athletic Club of York, Pennsylvania, 5–0.

August 4 Nap Lajoie is so furious that umpire Tommy Connolly has put an old black ball into play that he hurls the ball over the grandstand. His act results in Cleveland forfeiting the game to Detroit.

August 17 Ban Johnson orders betting suppressed at all AL parks, a noble but futile gesture.

September 3 Jesse Stovall of Cleveland pitches an 11-inning shutout in his major league debut. The 1-0 win over Detroit is the longest shutout ever in a debut.

September 17 The Boston Pilgrims clinch the AL pennant, beating Cleveland, 14-3.

October 13 Bill Dinneen beats the Pirates, 3–0, to make Boston the first world champions.

December 18 Ban Johnson is reelected AL president and given a raise to $10,000.

	BOSTON		CHICAGO		CLEVELAND		DETROIT		NEW YORK		PHILADELPHIA		ST.LOUIS		WASHINGTON
M	J.Collins	M	J.Callahan	M	B.Armour	M	E.Barrow	M	C.Griffith	M	C.Mack	M	J.McAleer	M	T.Loftus
1B	C.LaChance	1B	F.Isbell	1B	C.Hickman	1B	C.Carr	1B	J.Ganzel	1B	H.Davis	1B	J.Anderson	1B	B.Clarke
2B	H.Ferris	2B	G.Magoon	2B	N.Lajoie	2B	H.Smith	2B	J.Williams	2B	D.Murphy	2B	B.Friel	2B	B.McCormick
SS	F.Parent	SS	L.Tannehill	SS	J.Gochnauer	SS	S.McAllister	SS	K.Elberfeld	SS	M.Cross	SS	B.Wallace	SS	C.Moran
3B	J.Collins	3B	N.Callahan	3B	B.Bradley	3B	J.Yeager	3B	W.Conroy	3B	L.Cross	3B	H.Hill	3B	B.Coughlin
LF	P.Dougherty	LF	D.Holmes	LF	J.McCarthy	LF	B.Lush	LF	L.Davis	LF	T.Hartsel	LF	J.Burkett	LF	K.Selbach
CF	C.Stahl	CF	F.Jones	CF	H.Bay	CF	J.Barrett	CF	H.McFarland	CF	O.Pickering	CF	E.Heidrick	CF	J.Ryan
RF	B.Freeman	RF	D.Green	RF	E.Flick	RF	S.Crawford	RF	W.Keeler	RF	S.Seybold	RF	C.Hemphill	RF	W.Lee
C	L.Criger	C	J.Slattery	C	H.Bemis	C	D.McGuire	C	M.Beville	C	O.Schreck't	C	M.Kahoe	C	M.Kittridge
O3	J.O'Brien	O	B.Hallman	O	F.Abbott	S2	H.Long	O	D.Fultz	O	D.Hoffman	C	J.Sugden	2O	R.Robinson
C	J.Stahl	C	E.McFarland	O	J.Thoney	C	F.Buelow	C	J.O'Connor	C	D.Powers	23	B.McCormick	1	S.Carey
C	D.Farrell	2	T.Daly	2	B.Clingman	S	K.Elberfeld	S	H.Long	/2	B.Daly	O	J.Martin	O	E.Delahanty
C	A.Smith	1	B.Sullivan	/O	J.Hardy	O	D.Gessler	S	J.O'Connor	C	J.Kalahan	2	D.Padden	C	L.Drill
/3	H.Gleason	1	C.Dolan	/1	J.Slattery	3	E.Courtney	/C	P.McCauley	/3	E.Hilley	O	P.Swander	23	J.Martin
H	G.Stone	3	P.Clark	/O	H.Iott	2	J.Burns	/C	J.Zalusky			2	B.Bowcock	O	J.Hendricks
				H	H.Hill	/S	J.Murphy	/3	P.Greene	P	E.Plank	/C	O.Shannon	O	D.Holmes
P	C.Young	P	D.White			/S	S.Nicholls	/1	T.Jordan	P	R.Waddell	/2	C.Gouzzie	2	G.DeMontreville
P	B.Dinneen	P	P.Flaherty	P	A.Joss	/3	P.Greene	/1	F.Holmes	P	C.Bender			S	C.Osteen
P	T.Hughes	P	R.Patterson	P	E.Moore					P	W.Henley	P	J.Powell		
P	N.Gibson	P	F.Owen	P	B.Bernhard	P	G.Mullin	P	J.Chesbro			P	W.Sudhoff	P	C.Patten
P	G.Winter			P	R.Donahue	P	B.Donovan	P	J.Tannehill	/P	A.Coakley	P	E.Siever	P	A.Orth
		P	D.Dunkle	P	G.Wright	P	F.Kitson	P	C.Griffith	/P	J.Fairbank	P	R.Donahue	P	H.Wilson
/P	N.Altrock	P	N.Altrock			P	R.Kisinger	P	H.Howell	/P	C.McGeehan			P	H.Townsend
				P	G.Dorner			P	B.Wolfe	/P	T.Quinn	/P	G.Wright	P	D.Dunkle
				/P	E.Killian	P	J.Deering	/P	J.Deering	/P	E.Pinnance	/P	R.Evans		
				/P	J.Stovall	/P	M.Eason	/P	J.Deering				B.Pelty		
				/P	B.Rhoads	/P	J.Skopec	/P	S.Wiltse			/P	B.Reidy		
				/P	A.Pearson	/P	H.Kane	/P	A.Puttmann			/P	J.Terry		
				/P	M.Glendon	/P	A.Jones	/P	D.Adkins			/P	C.Morgan		
				/P	E.Walker			/P	E.Bliss						
				/P	B.Pounds			/P	E.Quick						

TEAM	G	W	L	PCT	GB	R	OR	AB	H	2B	3B	HR	BB	SO	AVG	OBP	SLG	PRO	PRO+	BR	/A	PF	CHI	RC	SB	CS	SBA	SBR
BOS	141	91	47	.659		708	504	4919	1336	222	113	48	262	561	.272	.313	.392	.705	111	91	55	105	103	680	141			
PHI	137	75	60	.556	14.5	597	519	4673	1236	227	68	32	268	513	.264	.309	.363	.672	102	36	9	105	100	598	157			
CLE	140	77	63	.550	15	639	579	4773	1265	231	95	31	259	595	.265	.308	.373	.681	112	51	62	98	102	634	175			
NY	136	72	62	.537	17	579	573	4565	1136	193	62	18	332	465	.249	.309	.330	.639	92	-6	-41	106	104	544	160			
DET	137	65	71	.478	25	567	539	4582	1229	162	91	12	292	526	.268	.318	.351	.669	110	39	56	97	94	587	128			
STL	139	65	74	.468	26.5	500	525	4639	1133	166	68	12	271	539	.244	.290	.317	.607	90	-66	-53	97	102	480	101			
CHI	138	60	77	.438	30.5	516	613	4670	1152	176	49	14	325	537	.247	.301	.314	.615	94	-46	-23	96	98	526	180			
WAS	140	43	94	.314	47.5	437	691	4613	1066	172	72	17	257	463	.231	.277	.311	.588	80	-98	-107	102	96	454	131			
TOT	554					4543		37434	9553	1549	618	184	2266	4199	.255	.303	.344	.648						1173				

TEAM	CG	SH	SV	IP	H	H/G	HR	BB	SO	RAT	ERA	ERA+	OAV	OOB	PR	/A	PF	CPI	FA	E	DP	FW	PW	BW	SBW	DIF
BOS	123	20	4	1255	1142	8.2	23	269	579	10.4	2.57	118	.242	.288	55	64	102	100	.959	239	86	2.3	6.6	5.7		7.4
PHI	112	10	1	1207	1124	8.4	20	315	728	11.3	2.98	103	.246	.305	-2	10	103	97	.960	217	66	3.2	1.0	.9		2.4
CLE	125	20	1	1243²	1161	8.4	16	271	521	10.6	2.73	105	.247	.293	32	17	96	97	.946	322	99	-3.2	1.8	6.4		2.0
NY	111	7	2	1201¹	1171	8.8	19	245	463	10.9	3.08	101	.255	.299	-16	5	105	93	.953	264	87	.0	.5	-4.3		8.7
DET	123	15	2	1196	1169	8.8	19	336	554	11.5	2.75	106	.256	.310	28	20	98	111	.950	281	82	-.9	2.1	5.8		-10.0
STL	124	12	3	1222¹	1220	9.0	26	237	511	11.0	2.77	105	.260	.300	26	19	98	108	.953	268	94	.2	2.0	-5.5		-1.1
CHI	114	9	4	1235	1233	9.0	23	287	391	11.5	3.02	93	.260	.309	-8	-29	95	103	.949	297	85	-1.8	-3.0	-2.4		-1.3
WAS	122	6	3	1223²	1333	9.8	38	306	452	12.4	3.82	82	.277	.325	-116	-94	106	96	.954	260	86	.8	-9.8	-11.1		-5.4
TOT	954	99	20	9784		8.8				11.2	2.96		.255	.303					.953	2148	685					

Runs
Dougherty-Bos 107
Bradley-Cle 101
Keeler-NY 95
Barrett-Det 95
Bay-Cle 94

Hits
Dougherty-Bos 195
Crawford-Det 184
Parent-Bos 170
Bay-Cle 169
Bradley-Cle 168

Doubles
Seybold-Phi 45
Lajoie-Cle 41
Freeman-Bos 39
Bradley-Cle 36
Anderson-StL 34

Triples
Crawford-Det 25
Bradley-Cle 22
Freeman-Bos 20
Parent-Bos 17
Collins-Bos 17

Home Runs
Freeman-Bos 13
Hickman-Cle 12
Ferris-Bos 9
Seybold-Phi 8

Total Bases
Freeman-Bos 281
Crawford-Det 269
Bradley-Cle 266
Lajoie-Cle 251
Dougherty-Bos 250

Runs Batted In
Freeman-Bos 104
Hickman-Cle 97
Lajoie-Cle 93
L.Cross-Phi 90
Crawford-Det 89

Runs Produced
Lajoie-Cle 176
Crawford-Det 173
Freeman-Bos 165
Bradley-Cle 163
Dougherty-Bos 162

Bases On Balls
Barrett-Det 74
Lush-Det 70
Pickering-Phi 53
Burkett-StL 52
Flick-Cle 51

Batting Average
Lajoie-Cle .... .344
Crawford-Det ...... .335
Dougherty-Bos ..... .331
Barrett-Det .... .315
Bradley-Cle .... .313

On Base Percentage
Barrett-Det .... .407
Hartsel-Phi .... .391
Lajoie-Cle .... .379
Lush-Det .... .379
Green-Chi .... .375

Slugging Average
Lajoie-Cle .... .518
Bradley-Cle .... .496
Freeman-Bos .... .496
Crawford-Det ...... .489
Hartsel-Phi .... .477

Production
Lajoie-Cle .... .896
Hartsel-Phi .... .868
Crawford-Det ...... .855
Bradley-Cle .... .844
Freeman-Bos .... .823

Adjusted Production
Lajoie-Cle 170
Crawford-Det 159
Bradley-Cle 154
Hartsel-Phi 152
Green-Chi 146

Batter Runs
Lajoie-Cle 37.6
Crawford-Det 34.5
Bradley-Cle 30.8
Barrett-Det 29.6
Hartsel-Phi 28.0

Adjusted Batter Runs
Lajoie-Cle 39.3
Crawford-Det 37.5
Bradley-Cle 32.6
Barrett-Det 32.5
Green-Chi 29.0

Clutch Hitting Index
Gochnauer-Cle 155
L.Cross-Phi 144
Carr-Det 135
Williams-NY 130
Anderson-StL 129

Runs Created
Dougherty-Bos 111
Crawford-Det 110
Lajoie-Cle 107
Bradley-Cle 104
Barrett-Det 98

Total Average
Lajoie-Cle .... .940
Hartsel-Phi .... .934
Barrett-Det .... .873
Crawford-Det ..... .858
Bradley-Cle .... .856

Stolen Bases
Bay-Cle 45
Pickering-Phi 40
Holmes-Was-Chi ... 35
Dougherty-Bos 35
Conroy-NY 33

Stolen Base Average

Stolen Base Runs

Fielding Runs
Lajoie-Cle 40.1
Criger-Bos 22.8
Schreckengost-Phi 18.2
Wallace-StL 17.9
Williams-NY 15.6

Total Player Rating
Lajoie-Cle 8.4
Bradley-Cle 4.7
Crawford-Det 3.3
Elberfeld-Det-NY ... 3.2
Barrett-Det 3.2

Wins
Young-Bos 28
Plank-Phi 23

Win Percentage
Young-Bos .... .757
Hughes-Bos .... .741
Moore-Cle .... .679
Dinneen-Bos ...... .618
Plank-Phi .... .590

Games
Plank-Phi 43
Mullin-Det 41
Young-Bos 40
Flaherty-Chi 40
Chesbro-NY 40

Complete Games
Young-Bos 34
Waddell-Phi 34
Donovan-Det 34

Shutouts
Young-Bos 7
Mullin-Det 6
Dinneen-Bos 6
Sudhoff-StL 5
Hughes-Bos 5

Saves
Young-Bos 2
Powell-StL 2
Orth-Was 2
Mullin-Det 2
Dinneen-Bos 2

Innings Pitched
Young-Bos 341.2
Plank-Phi 336.0
Chesbro-NY 324.2
Waddell-Phi 324.0
Mullin-Det 320.2

Fewest Hits/Game
Moore-Cle 7.12
Donovan-Det 7.24
Joss-Cle 7.36
Waddell-Phi 7.61
Dinneen-Bos 7.68

Fewest BB/Game
Young-Bos .... .97
Bernhard-Cle 1.14
Donahue-StL-Cle .. 1.14
Joss-Cle 1.17
Tannehill-NY 1.28

Strikeouts
Waddell-Phi 302
Donovan-Det 187
Young-Bos 176
Plank-Phi 176
Mullin-Det 170

Strikeouts/Game
Waddell-Phi 8.39
Donovan-Det 5.48
Moore-Cle 5.38
Powell-StL 4.97
Mullin-Det 4.77

Ratio
Joss-Cle 8.82
Young-Bos 8.96
Bernhard-Cle 9.34
Moore-Cle 9.56
Dinneen-Bos 9.78

Earned Run Average
Moore-Cle 1.74
Young-Bos 2.08
Bernhard-Cle 2.12
White-Chi 2.13
Joss-Cle 2.19

Adjusted ERA
Moore-Cle 164
Young-Bos 146
Bernhard-Cle 135
Dinneen-Bos 134
White-Chi 132

Opponents' Batting Avg.
Moore-Cle .... .217
Donovan-Det ...... .220
Joss-Cle .... .223
Waddell-Phi ...... .229
Dinneen-Bos ..... .230

Opponents' On Base Pct.
Joss-Cle .... .256
Young-Bos .... .259
Bernhard-Cle ..... .267
Moore-Cle .... .271
Dinneen-Bos ...... .276

Starter Runs
Moore-Cle 33.5
Young-Bos 33.4
White-Chi 27.7
Mullin-Det 25.5
Joss-Cle 24.4

Adjusted Starter Runs
Young-Bos 36.1
Moore-Cle 30.5
Dinneen-Bos 25.8
Plank-Phi 24.9
Mullin-Det 23.6

Clutch Pitching Index
Kitson-Det 127
Mullin-Det 121
Donahue-StL-Cle .. 119
Plank-Phi 116
Hughes-Bos 112

Relief Runs

Adjusted Relief Runs

Relief Ranking

Total Pitcher Index
Young-Bos 4.9
Mullin-Det 4.1
White-Chi 3.3
Sudhoff-StL 2.7
Joss-Cle 2.7

Total Baseball Ranking
Lajoie-Cle 8.4
Young-Bos 4.9
Bradley-Cle 4.7
Mullin-Det 4.1
Crawford-Det 3.3

February 1 The Cards purchase veteran first baseman Jack Beckley from the Cincinnati Reds. The future Hall of Famer will have four decreasingly productive years in St. Louis before retiring.

April 17 The Brooklyn Superbas play their first Sunday game at home, beating Boston, 9-1. To circumvent Sunday Blue Laws, no admission is charged, but fans are required to buy scorecards to enter the grandstand and box seats.

May 14 Cubs outfielder Jack McCarthy sprains an ankle by stepping on an umpire's broom at home plate. NL president Pulliam orders arbiters henceforward to use pocket-size whisk brooms for housekeeping at home. The AL will comply next year.

May 27 The Giants' Dan McGann steals five bases in one game, a feat not duplicated in the NL until Aug. 24, 1974, by Davey Lopes.

May 30 Frank Chance of the Cubs is hit with pitches three times in the first game of a doubleheader. He loses consciousness on one occasion and continues to play when he comes to. He is hit twice in the second game by Win Kellum for a record five times in one day. The Reds and Cubs split the holiday twinbill.

June 11 Bob Wicker pitches 9⅓ hitless innings for the Cubs before losing to the Giants in the 12th, 1-0.

June 16 Christy Mathewson beats the Cardinals to start a 24-game winning streak against them that will not end until 1908.

July 5 The Giants' 18-game winning streak ends when the Phillies prevail, 6-5 in 10 innings. The Giants' record is now 53-18, effectively ending the NL race. By Sept. 1, they will lead the Cubs by 15 games. John McGraw and John T. Brush say they have no intention of playing a postseason series with the AL champions. "When we clinch the NL pennant, we'll be champions of the only real major league," says McGraw.

September 15 Giants rookie George "Hooks" Wiltse wins his 12th straight game, setting a major league mark for consecutive games won at the start of a career. It will be tied by relief hurler Clarence "Butch" Metzger in 1976.

September 22 In the final game of his 19-year career as an outfielder/catcher, future Hall of Famer Jim O'Rourke, 52, is the Giants backstop in their 7–5 defeat of the Cincinnati Reds. It is O'Rourke's first major league game since 1893, and he singles and scores a run.

October 3 Christy Mathewson of the Giants strikes out a record 16 Cards in a 3-1 Giants victory, which lasts one hour and 15 minutes.

October 10 The Giants' .262 will lead the NL in team batting, 31 points below the 1900 leaders. Team batting averages have dropped since then, mainly due to: the foul-strike rule adopted in 1901; and the introduction of the spitball and other doctored pitches in 1903.

BOSTON	BROOKLYN	CHICAGO	CINCINNATI	NEW YORK	PHILADELPHIA	PITTSBURGH	ST.LOUIS
M A.Buckenberger	M N.Hanlon	M F.Selee	M J.Kelley	M J.McGraw	M H.Duffy	M F.Clarke	M K.Nichols
1B F.Tenney	1B P.Dillon	1B F.Chance	1B J.Kelley	1B D.McGann	1B J.Doyle	1B K.Bransfield	1B J.Beckley
2B F.Raymer	2B D.Jordan	2B J.Evers	2B M.Huggins	2B B.Gilbert	2B K.Gleason	2B C.Ritchey	2B J.Farrell
SS E.Abbaticchio	SS C.Babb	SS J.Tinker	SS T.Corcoran	SS B.Dahlen	SS R.Hulswitt	SS H.Wagner	SS D.Shay
3B J.Delahanty	3B M.McCormick	3B D.Casey	3B H.Steinfeldt	3B A.Devlin	3B H.Wolverton	3B T.Leach	3B J.Burke
LF D.Cooley	LF J.Sheckard	LF J.Slagle	LF F.Odwell	LF S.Mertes	LF J.Titus	LF F.Clarke	LF G.Barclay
CF P.Geier	CF J.Dobbs	CF J.McCarthy	CF C.Seymour	CF R.Bresnahan	CF R.Thomas	CF G.Beaumont	CF H.Smoot
RF R.Cannell	RF H.Lumley	RF D.Jones	RF F.Dolan	RF G.Browne	RF S.Magee	RF J.Sebring	RF S.Shannon
C T.Needham	C B.Bergen	C J.Kling	C A.Schlei	C J.Warner	C R.Dooin	C E.Phelps	C M.Grady
C3 P.Moran	O D.Gessler	O1 O.Williams	32 S.Woodruff	1O F.Bowerman	1O J.Lush	OS O.Krueger	S3 D.Brain
O P.Carney	23 S.Strang	C J.O'Neill	C1 H.Peitz	O M.McCormick	C F.Roth	O M.McCormick	O J.Dunleavy
O G.Barclay	C L.Ritter	O H.McChesney	O M.Donlin	3S J.Dunn	S3 S.Donahue	C H.Smith	O H.Hill
2 B.Lauterborn	3 E.Batch	C F.Schulte	O J.Sebring	3S M.Donlin	O B.Hall	C1 F.Carisch	C L.McLean
C D.Marshall	1 F.Jacklitsch	/O A.Smith	C G.Street	O D.Marshall	O S.Barry	O J.Gilbert	C D.Zearfoss
/O K.O'Hara	/1 J.Doyle	/O S.Hofman	/C P.O'Neill	/2 J.McGraw	O H.Duffy	O H.Cassady	C B.Byers
/O J.Stanley	/2 C.Loudenslager	/3 G.Moriarty	P N.Hahn	/1 D.Brouthers	O D.Van Buren	O B.Smith	/2 S.Murch
/O J.White	H D.Van Buren	/O I.Van Zandt	P J.Harper	/C J.O'Rourke	/O D.Marshall	/O E.Diehl	C J.Butler
/C G.McAuliffe	P O.Jones	/O B.Carney	P W.Kellum	P J.McGinnity	/3 J.Purnell	/C J.Archer	/2 S.Donahue
/S A.Sullivan	P J.Cronin	/C F.Holmes	P T.Walker	P C.Mathewson	/1 K.Douglass	/C J.Rafter	/C C.Swindells
P V.Willis	P N.Garvin	/O D.Rudolph	P B.Ewing	/2 D.Taylor	H.Long	/S T.Fleming	P J.Taylor
P T.Pittinger	P E.Poole	/C T.Stanton	P J.Sutthoff	P H.Wiltse	B.Rementer	H B.Lowe	P K.Nichols
P K.Wilhelm	P D.Scanlan	P J.Weimer	/P C.Elliott	P R.Ames	P C.Fraser	P S.Leever	P C.McFarland
P T.Fisher	/P F.Mitchell	P B.Briggs		/P B.Milligan	P B.Duggleby	P P.Flaherty	P M.O'Neill
P E.McNichol	/P D.Reisling	P C.Lundgren		/P C.Elliott	P T.Sparks	P M.Lynch	P J.Corbett
/P J.Stewart	/P B.Reidy	P B.Wicker			P J.Sutthoff	P D.Phillippe	/P J.McGinley
	/P B.Durham	P M.Brown			P J.McPherson	P C.Case	/P W.Sanders
	G.Thatcher	P F.Corridon			P F.Mitchell	P R.Miller	
	/P J.Koukalik	/P E.Groth			P F.Corridon	/P C.Robitaille	
	/P J.Doscher				/P R.Caldwell	P H.Camnitz	
					/P J.Brackenridge	P W.Lee	
					/P T.Barry	/P D.Scanlan	
						/P J.Pfiester	
						/P B.Veil	
						/P L.Moren	

TEAM	G	W	L	PCT	GB	R	OR	AB	H	2B	3B	HR	BB	SO	AVG	OBP	SLG	PRO	PRO+	BR	/A	PF	CHI	RC	SB	CS	SBA	SBR
NY	158	106	47	.693		744	476	5150	1347	202	65	31	434		.262	.328	.344	.672	109	87	57	104	104	712	283			
CHI	156	93	60	.608	13	599	517	5210	1294	157	62	22	298		.248	.295	.315	.610	94	-38	-39	100	104	582	227			
CIN	157	88	65	.575	18	695	547	5231	1332	189	92	21	399		.255	.313	.338	.651	98	42	-17	109	104	642	179			
PIT	156	87	66	.569	19	675	592	5160	1333	164	102	15	391		.258	.316	.338	.654	105	48	30	103	102	639	178			
STL	155	75	79	.487	31.5	602	595	5104	1292	175	66	24	343		.253	.306	.327	.633	106	7	34	96	96	602	199			
BRO	154	56	97	.366	50	497	614	4917	1142	159	53	15	411		.232	.297	.295	.592	91	-57	-44	98	93	521	205			
BOS	155	55	98	.359	51	491	749	5135	1217	153	50	24	316		.237	.287	.300	.587	90	-78	-59	96	94	508	143			
PHI	155	52	100	.342	53.5	571	784	5103	1268	170	54	23	377		.248	.305	.316	.621	102	-11	10	96	96	570	159			
TOT	623					4874		41010	10225	1369	544	175	2969	4277	.249	.306	.322	.628							1573			

TEAM	CG	SH	SV	IP	H	H/G	HR	BB	SO	RAT	ERA	ERA+	OAV	OOB	PR	/A	PF	CPI	FA	E	DP	FW	PW	BW	SBW	DIF
NY	127	21	15	1396²	1151	7.4	36	349	707	9.9	2.17	125	.222	.276	86	83	100	93	.956	294	93	2.3	8.8	6.0		12.4
CHI	139	18	6	1383²	1150	7.5	16	402	618	10.3	2.30	115	.224	.285	65	53	97	90	.954	298	89	1.8	5.6	-4.1		13.2
CIN	142	12	2	1392²	1256	8.1	13	343	502	10.7	2.34	125	.241	.295	60	88	107	102	.954	301	81	1.7	9.3	-1.8		2.3
PIT	133	15	1	1348¹	1273	8.5	13	379	455	11.4	2.89	95	.248	.306	-24	-24	100	92	.955	291	93	2.2	-2.5	3.2		7.6
STL	146	7	2	1368	1286	8.5	23	319	529	10.8	2.64	102	.239	.286	13	5	99	85	.952	307	83	1.1	.5	3.6		-7.2
BRO	135	12	2	1337¹	1281	8.6	27	414	453	11.8	2.70	101	.255	.319	4	4	100	112	.945	343	87	-1.4	.4	-4.7		-14.9
BOS	136	13	0	1348¹	1405	9.4	25	500	544	13.1	3.43	80	.272	.343	-105	-105	101	105	.945	353	91	-1.9	-11.1	-6.2		-2.3
PHI	131	10	2	1339¹	1418	9.5	22	425	469	12.9	3.39	79	.270	.332	-99	-110	98	100	.937	403	93	-5.1	-11.6	1.1		-8.3
TOT	1089	108	30	10914¹		8.4				11.3	2.73		.249	.306					.950	2590	710					

Runs		Hits		Doubles		Triples		Home Runs		Total Bases	
Browne-NY	99	Beaumont-Pit	185	Wagner-Pit	44	Lumley-Bro	18	Lumley-Bro	9	Wagner-Pit	255
Wagner-Pit	97	Beckley-StL	179	Mertes-NY	28	Wagner-Pit	14	Brain-StL	7	Lumley-Bro	247
Beaumont-Pit	97	Wagner-Pit	171	Delahanty-Bos	27	Tinker-Chi	13			Seymour-Cin	233
Huggins-Cin	96	Browne-NY	169	Seymour-Cin	26	Seymour-Cin	13			Beaumont-Pit	230
		Seymour-Cin	166	Dahlen-NY	26	Kelley-Cin	13			Beckley-StL	222

Runs Batted In		Runs Produced		Bases On Balls		Batting Average		On Base Percentage		Slugging Average	
Dahlen-NY	80	Wagner-Pit	168	Thomas-Phi	102	Wagner-Pit	.349	Wagner-Pit	.423	Wagner-Pit	.520
Mertes-NY	78	Mertes-NY	157	Huggins-Cin	88	Donlin-Cin-NY	.329	Thomas-Phi	.416	Grady-StL	.474
Lumley-Bro	78	Lumley-Bro	148	Devlin-NY	62	Beckley-StL	.325	Chance-Chi	.382	Donlin-Cin-NY	.457
Wagner-Pit	75	Dahlen-NY	148	Wagner-Pit	59	Grady-StL	.313	Huggins-Cin	.377	Seymour-Cin	.439
Corcoran-Cin	74	Beaumont-Pit	148	Ritchey-Pit	59	Seymour-Cin	.313	Beckley-StL	.375	Chance-Chi	.430

Production		Adjusted Production		Batter Runs		Adjusted Batter Runs		Clutch Hitting Index		Runs Created	
Wagner-Pit	.944	Wagner-Pit	186	Wagner-Pit	52.7	Wagner-Pit	49.7	Devlin-NY	154	Wagner-Pit	134
Chance-Chi	.812	Chance-Chi	150	Thomas-Phi	28.4	Thomas-Phi	31.8	Dahlen-NY	146	Lumley-Bro	95
Seymour-Cin	.790	Beckley-StL	147	Chance-Chi	27.2	Beckley-StL	29.8	Corcoran-Cin	137	Beckley-StL	94
Beckley-StL	.778	Thomas-Phi	141	Beckley-StL	25.7	Chance-Chi	27.2	Bransfield-Pit	132	Chance-Chi	93
Thomas-Phi	.761	Lumley-Bro	137	Seymour-Cin	24.9	Grady-StL	25.7	Gilbert-NY	128	Mertes-NY	93

Total Average		Stolen Bases		Stolen Base Average	Stolen Base Runs	Fielding Runs		Total Player Rating	
Wagner-Pit	1.163	Wagner-Pit	53			Leach-Pit	35.8	Wagner-Pit	4.8
Chance-Chi	.926	Mertes-NY	47			Evers-Chi	31.3	Leach-Pit	4.1
Thomas-Phi	.869	Dahlen-NY	47			Dahlen-NY	27.6	Thomas-Phi	4.0
Mertes-NY	.813	McGann-NY	42			Tinker-StL	19.3	Chance-Chi	3.7
McGann-NY	.802	Chance-Chi	42			Farrell-StL	16.3	Dahlen-NY	3.3

Wins		Win Percentage		Games		Complete Games		Shutouts		Saves	
McGinnity-NY	35	McGinnity-NY	.814	McGinnity-NY	51	Willis-Bos	39	McGinnity-NY	9	McGinnity-NY	5
Mathewson-NY	33	Mathewson-NY	.733	Mathewson-NY	48	Taylor-StL	39	Harper-Cin	6	Wiltse-NY	3
Harper-Cin	23	Harper-Cin	.719	Jones-Bro	46	McGinnity-NY	38			Briggs-Chi	3
Taylor-NY	21	Flaherty-Pit	.679	Willis-Bos	43	Jones-Bro	38			Ames-NY	3
Nichols-StL	21			Fraser-Phi	42						

Innings Pitched		Fewest Hits/Game		Fewest BB/Game		Strikeouts		Strikeouts/Game		Ratio	
McGinnity-NY	408.0	Brown-Chi	6.57	Hahn-Cin	1.06	Mathewson-NY	212	Wiltse-NY	5.74	Brown-Chi	8.94
Jones-Bro	377.0	Weimer-Chi	6.71	Phillippe-Pit	1.40	Willis-Bos	196	Mathewson-NY	5.19	McGinnity-NY	8.96
Mathewson-NY	367.2	McGinnity-NY	6.77	Nichols-StL	1.42	Weimer-Chi	177	Weimer-Chi	5.19	Hahn-Cin	9.07
Taylor-StL	352.0	Garvin-Bro	6.99	Kellum-Cin	1.84	Pittinger-Bos	146	Willis-Bos	5.04	Nichols-StL	9.17
Willis-Bos	350.0	Taylor-NY	7.02	McFarland-StL	1.87	McGinnity-NY	144	Phillippe-Pit	4.43	Mathewson-NY	9.50

Earned Run Average		Adjusted ERA		Opponents' Batting Avg.		Opponents' On Base Pct.		Starter Runs		Adjusted Starter Runs	
McGinnity-NY	1.61	McGinnity-NY	169	Brown-Chi	.199	Brown-Chi	.253	McGinnity-NY	50.6	McGinnity-NY	50.1
Garvin-Bro	1.68	Garvin-Bro	162	Weimer-Chi	.204	Nichols-StL	.256	Mathewson-NY	28.4	Hahn-Cin	28.5
Brown-Chi	1.86	Brown-Chi	142	McGinnity-NY	.206	McGinnity-NY	.256	Weimer-Chi	28.0	Mathewson-NY	28.0
Weimer-Chi	1.91	Hahn-Cin	142	Taylor-NY	.214	Hahn-Cin	.262	Nichols-StL	25.0	Weimer-Chi	25.6
Nichols-StL	2.02	Weimer-Chi	139	Garvin-Bro	.218	Mathewson-NY	.270	Hahn-Cin	22.2	Nichols-StL	23.6

Clutch Pitching Index		Relief Runs	Adjusted Relief Runs	Relief Ranking	Total Pitcher Index		Total Baseball Ranking	
Garvin-Bro	153				McGinnity-NY	5.6	McGinnity-NY	5.6
O'Neill-StL	131				Mathewson-NY	4.7	Wagner-Pit	4.8
Briggs-Chi	128				Flaherty-Pit	3.4	Mathewson-NY	4.7
Jones-Bro	117				Hahn-Cin	3.3	Leach-Pit	4.1
Mitchell-Phi-Bro	116				Weimer-Chi	2.9	Thomas-Phi	4.0

January 4 The Highlanders announce plans to play on Sundays at Ridgewood Park on Long Island, but the Brooklyn club objects.

January 22 William H. Yawkey, the 28-year-old heir to a lumber and mining fortune, buys the Detroit Tigers from S.F. Angus for $50,000. New money and Frank Navin's shrewd management will bring three straight pennants to the franchise within a few years.

April 21* Ty Cobb makes his professional debut for Augusta (South Atlantic League), hitting a double and a home run in an 8-7 loss to Columbus.

May 5 Boston Pilgrim Cy Young pitches the second of three no-hitters, a 3–0 perfect game against the Philadelphia Athletics and Rube Waddell. Eventually Young will go on to complete 24 straight hitless innings, still the record, and 45 shutout innings in a row, a record broken by Jack Coombs's 53 in 1910, Walter Johnson's 56 in 1913, and later by Don Drysdale and Orel Hershiser. For Waddell it is one of 18 losses, the most of his career, against 25 wins. He will strike out 349, a record until Sandy Koufax fans 382 in 1965.

July 4 Jack Chesbro, the New York Highlanders spitballer, wins his 14th in a row, an AL record until Walter Johnson wins 16 straight in 1912.

August 6 Prompt action by Boston Pilgrims players Bill Dinneen, Norwood Gibson, Freddy Parent, and Hobe Ferris prevents a tragedy in a Cleveland hotel. Returning to their rooms following the game, the four are confronted by a fire sweeping through the fifth floor. They extinguish the blaze and are cited as heroes.

August 6 Left-hander Nick Altrock of the White Sox (their new nickname), en route to the first of three 20-win seasons, handles 13 fielding chances—the modern major league record for pitchers—in an 8-1 victory over the Athletics. He will finish the year with 49 putouts, an AL record for pitchers.

August 10 Jack Chesbro is knocked out by the White Sox after pitching 30 complete games in a row. For the year he will win 41 games, pitching 48 complete games out of 51 starts for the Highlanders. All are post-1900 records.

August 17 Jesse Tannehill, a left-hander who will win 20 games or more six times, pitches a no-hitter for Boston against the White Sox.

August 24 Willie Keeler collects two homers against the St. Louis Browns—both inside the park—in a 9-1 win at New York.

September 3* Syracuse (Eastern League) beats Scranton three times in a tripleheader.

September 30 White Sox left-hander Guy "Doc" White pitches his fifth shutout in 18 days, defeating New York. Of his seven shutouts for the year, six come in September. His scoreless streak will end at 45 innings on Oct. 2, when the New York Highlanders score in the first inning.

October 7 George Stovall of Cleveland hits his first homer, and it comes off his older brother Jesse, pitching for Detroit in his last game. It marks the first time one brother gives up a homer to another, a feat which will be duplicated by the Ferrells in 1933 and the Niekros in 1976.

October 10 A doubleheader split will give Boston the AL pennant over the Highlanders. With the score 2–2 in the top of the ninth and a man on third base, Chesbro has a spitball get away from him for a wild pitch, and Boston's winning run scores. New York wins the second game, but Boston triumphs to earn its second consecutive pennant by 1½ games. The Pilgrim pitchers achieve 148 complete games—an AL record—as George Winter goes the route in the nightcap, a 1–0 loss. Both leagues set marks for total complete games: AL 1,098, NL 1,089.

October 28 After a fourth-place finish, the Cleveland Blues release Bill Armour and name Nap Lajoie manager. Eventually, they will rename the team the Naps in his honor.

	BOSTON		CHICAGO		CLEVELAND		DETROIT		NEW YORK		PHILADELPHIA		ST.LOUIS		WASHINGTON
M	J.Collins	M	J.Callahan	M	B.Armour	M	E.Barrow	M	C.Griffith	M	C.Mack	M	J.McAleer	M	M.Kittridge
1B	C.LaChance	M	F.Jones	1B	C.Hickman	M	B.Lowe	1B	J.Ganzel	1B	H.Davis	1B	T.Jones	M	P.Donovan
2B	H.Ferris	1B	J.Donahue	2B	N.Lajoie	1B	C.Carr	2B	J.Williams	2B	D.Murphy	2B	D.Padden	1B	J.Stahl
SS	F.Parent	2B	G.Dundon	SS	T.Turner	2B	B.Lowe	SS	K.Elberfeld	SS	M.Cross	SS	B.Wallace	2B	B.McCormick
3B	J.Collins	SS	G.Davis	3B	B.Bradley	SS	C.O'Leary	3B	W.Conroy	3B	L.Cross	3B	C.Moran	SS	J.Cassidy
LF	K.Selbach	3B	L.Tannehill	LF	B.Lush	3B	E.Gremminger	LF	P.Dougherty	LF	T.Hartsel	LF	J.Burkett	3B	H.Hill
CF	C.Stahl	LF	N.Callahan	CF	H.Bay	LF	M.McIntyre	CF	J.Anderson	CF	O.Pickering	CF	E.Heidrick	LF	F.Huelsman
RF	B.Freeman	CF	F.Jones	RF	E.Flick	CF	J.Barrett	RF	W.Keeler	RF	S.Seybold	RF	C.Hemphill	CF	B.O'Neill
C	L.Criger	RF	D.Green	C	H.Bemis	RF	S.Crawford	C	D.McGuire	C	O.Schreck't	C	J.Sugden	RF	P.Donovan
		C	B.Sullivan			C	L.Drill							C	M.Kittridge
C	D.Farrell			1	G.Stovall			O	D.Fultz	O	D.Hoffman	O	P.Hynes		
O	P.Dougherty	12	F.Isbell	O	F.Abbott	S3	R.Robinson	C	R.Kleinow	C	D.Powers	C	M.Kahoe	C1	B.Clarke
/O	B.O'Neill	O	D.Holmes	1	C.Carr	3	B.Coughlin	3O	J.Thoney	C1	P.Noonan	3	H.Hill	3	B.Coughlin
C	T.Doran	C	E.McFarland	C	F.Buelow	C	B.Wood	3	C.Osteen	/1	J.Mullin	S3	H.Gleason	S	C.Moran
/2	B.Unglaub		C.Jones	1	B.Schwartz	C1	M.Beville	/1	M.Beville	O	L.Bruce	O	F.Huelsman	O	K.Selbach
		/C	M.Heydon	O	C.Rossman	1	C.Hickman	/3	B.Unglaub			C	J.O'Connor	CO	L.Drill
P	C.Young	/O	F.Huelsman	O	R.Vinson	C	F.Buelow	/O	O.Collins	P	R.Waddell	/2	G.DeMontreville	P	J.Mullin
P	B.Dinneen	/C	C.Berry	/C	H.Ostdiek	/O	F.Huelsman	/C	F.McManus	P	E.Plank	/O	A.Bader	OP	A.Orth
P	J.Tannehill			/S	M.Donovan	/2	J.Burns	/O	E.Bliss	P	W.Henley	H	P.Swander	P	J.Thoney
P	N.Gibson	P	F.Owen			/C	F.McManus			P	C.Bender	H	H.Vahrenhorst	2	R.Nill
P	G.Winter	P	N.Altrock	P	B.Bernhard			P	J.Chesbro					1	L.Herring
		P	D.White	P	R.Donahue	P	G.Mullin	P	J.Powell	/P	A.Coakley	P	B.Pelty	/O	I.Hoffman
		P	F.Smith	P	E.Moore	P	E.Killian	P	A.Orth	/P	F.Applegate	P	H.Howell		
		P	R.Patterson	P	A.Joss	P	B.Donovan	P	T.Hughes	/P	J.Fairbank	P	F.Glade	P	C.Patten
				P	B.Rhoads	P	F.Kitson	P	C.Griffith	/P	J.Barthold	P	W.Sudhoff	P	H.Townsend
P	E.Walsh			P	J.Stovall			P		E.Siever	P	B.Jacobson
		/P	P.Flaherty	PO	O.Hess			P	W.Clarkson			P		P	B.Wolfe
		/P	E.Stricklett	/P	J.Hickey	/P	C.Jaeger	/P	A.Puttmann			/P	C.Morgan	P	T.Hughes
		/P	T.Dougherty			/P	B.Raymond	/P	B.Wolfe			/P	G.Wright		
						/P	C.Ferry	/P	N.Garvin					P	D.Dunkle
														/P	D.Mason
														/P	H.Wilson

TEAM	G	W	L	PCT	GB	R	OR	AB	H	2B	3B	HR	BB	SO	AVG	OBP	SLG	PRO	PRO+	BR	/A	PF	CHI	RC	SB	CS	SBA	SBR
BOS	157	95	59	.617		608	466	5231	1294	194	105	26	347	570	.247	.301	.340	.641	102	42	8	106	101	597	101			
NY	155	92	59	.609	1.5	598	526	5220	1354	195	91	27	312	548	.259	.308	.347	.655	107	69	40	105	96	640	163			
CHI	156	89	65	.578	6	600	482	5027	1217	193	68	14	373	586	.242	.300	.316	.616	104	4	26	96	109	578	216			
CLE	154	86	65	.570	7.5	647	482	5152	1340	225	90	27	307	714	.260	.308	.354	.662	116	78	84	99	103	650	178			
PHI	155	81	70	.536	12.5	557	503	5088	1266	197	77	31	313	605	.249	.298	.336	.634	101	28	-1	105	98	579	137			
STL	156	65	87	.428	29	481	604	5291	1266	153	53	10	332	609	.239	.291	.294	.585	96	-52	-20	94	94	526	150			
DET	162	62	90	.408	32	505	627	5321	1231	154	69	11	344	635	.231	.282	.292	.574	90	-75	-60	97	102	502	112			
WAS	157	38	113	.252	55.5	437	743	5149	1170	171	57	10	283	759	.227	.275	.288	.563	84	-94	-87	98	97	475	150			
TOT	626					4433		41479	10138	1482	610	156	2611	5026	.244	.295	.321	.616						1207				

TEAM	CG	SH	SV	IP	H	H/G	HR	BB	SO	RAT	ERA	ERA+	OAV	OOB	PR	/A	PF	CPI	FA	E	DP	FW	PW	BW	SBW	DIF
BOS	148	21	1	1406	1208	7.7	31	233	612	9.4	2.12	126	.233	.270	75	86	103	101	.962	242	83	1.6	9.6	.9		5.9
NY	123	15	1	1380²	1180	7.7	29	311	684	10.0	2.57	106	.232	.282	4	22	104	90	.958	275	90	-.8	2.5	4.5		10.4
CHI	134	26	3	1380	1161	7.6	13	303	550	9.8	2.30	107	.229	.279	45	23	95	93	.964	238	95	1.7	2.6	2.9		4.8
CLE	141	20	0	1356²	1273	8.4	10	285	627	10.6	2.22	114	.249	.294	56	47	98	116	.959	255	86	.4	5.3	9.4		-4.5
PHI	136	26	0	1361¹	1149	7.6	13	366	887	10.4	2.35	114	.230	.291	38	50	103	100	.959	250	67	.8	5.6	-.1		-.8
STL	135	13	1	1410	1335	8.5	25	333	577	11.0	2.83	88	.251	.303	-36	-55	96	100	.960	267	78	-.2	-6.1	-2.2		-2.4
DET	143	15	2	1430	1345	8.5	16	433	556	11.6	2.77	92	.250	.314	-27	-35	98	106	.959	273	92	.0	-3.9	-6.7		-3.5
WAS	137	7	4	1359²	1487	9.8	19	347	533	12.5	3.62	73	.279	.330	-155	-145	102	99	.951	314	97	-3.1	-16.2	-9.7		-8.4
TOT	1097	143	12	11084¹		8.2				10.7	2.60		.244	.295					.959	2114	688					

Runs
Dougherty-Bos-NY ... 113
Flick-Cle ... 97
Bradley-Cle ... 94
Lajoie-Cle ... 92

Hits
Lajoie-Cle ... 208
Keeler-NY ... 186
Bradley-Cle ... 183
Dougherty-Bos-NY ... 181
Flick-Cle ... 177

Doubles
Lajoie-Cle ... 49
Collins-Bos ... 33
Bradley-Cle ... 32

Triples
Stahl-Bos ... 19
Freeman-Bos ... 19
Cassidy-Was ... 19
Murphy-Phi ... 17
Flick-Cle ... 17

Home Runs
Davis-Phi ... 10
Murphy-Phi ... 7
Freeman-Bos ... 7

Total Bases
Lajoie-Cle ... 305
Flick-Cle ... 260
Freeman-Bos ... 246
Bradley-Cle ... 246

Runs Batted In
Lajoie-Cle ... 102
Freeman-Bos ... 84
Bradley-Cle ... 83
Anderson-NY ... 82

Runs Produced
Lajoie-Cle ... 188
Bradley-Cle ... 172
Parent-Bos ... 156
Collins-Bos ... 149
Murphy-Phi ... 148

Bases On Balls
Barrett-Det ... 79
Burkett-StL ... 78
Hartsel-Phi ... 75
Selbach-Was-Bos ... 72
Lush-Cle ... 72

Batting Average
Lajoie-Cle ... .376
Keeler-NY ... .343
Davis-Phi ... .309
Flick-Cle ... .306
Bradley-Cle ... .300

On Base Percentage
Lajoie-Cle ... .413
Keeler-NY ... .390
Flick-Cle ... .371
Stahl-Bos ... .366
Burkett-StL ... .363

Slugging Average
Lajoie-Cle ... .552
Davis-Phi ... .490
Flick-Cle ... .449
Murphy-Phi ... .440
Hickman-Cle-Det ... .437

Production
Lajoie-Cle ... .965
Flick-Cle ... .820
Keeler-NY ... .799
Stahl-Bos ... .782
Murphy-Phi ... .760

Adjusted Production
Lajoie-Cle ... 205
Flick-Cle ... 160
Keeler-NY ... 146
Stahl-Bos ... 139
Hickman-Cle-Det ... 137

Batter Runs
Lajoie-Cle ... 62.4
Flick-Cle ... 38.7
Keeler-NY ... 32.7
Stahl-Bos ... 32.7
Davis-Phi ... 27.5

Adjusted Batter Runs
Lajoie-Cle ... 63.5
Flick-Cle ... 39.6
Keeler-NY ... 28.5
Stahl-Bos ... 27.3
Burkett-StL ... 24.4

Clutch Hitting Index
Callahan-Chi ... 132
Wallace-StL ... 130
Bradley-Cle ... 129
Tannehill-Chi ... 129
Anderson-NY ... 124

Runs Created
Lajoie-Cle ... 142
Flick-Cle ... 115
Keeler-NY ... 100
Stahl-Bos ... 99
Bradley-Cle ... 95

Total Average
Lajoie-Cle ... 1.070
Flick-Cle ... .891
Keeler-NY ... .798
Stahl-Bos ... .782
Murphy-Phi ... .741

Stolen Bases
Flick-Cle ... 38
Bay-Cle ... 38
Heidrick-StL ... 35
Davis-Chi ... 32
Conroy-NY ... 30

Fielding Runs
Tannehill-Chi ... 27.8
Davis-Chi ... 16.8
Williams-NY ... 16.8
Carr-Det-Cle ... 15.8
Elberfeld-NY ... 15.3

Total Player Rating
Lajoie-Cle ... 7.2
Flick-Cle ... 4.5
Murphy-Phi ... 3.9
Bradley-Cle ... 3.9
Davis-Chi ... 3.4

Wins
Chesbro-NY ... 41
Young-Bos ... 26
Plank-Phi ... 26
Waddell-Phi ... 25

Win Percentage
Chesbro-NY ... .774
Tannehill-Bos ... .656
Smith-Chi ... .640
Bernhard-Cle ... .639
Dinneen-Bos ... .622

Games
Chesbro-NY ... 55
Powell-NY ... 47
Waddell-Phi ... 46
Patten-Was ... 45
Mullin-Det ... 45

Complete Games
Chesbro-NY ... 48
Mullin-Det ... 42
Young-Bos ... 40
Waddell-Phi ... 39
Powell-NY ... 38

Shutouts
Young-Bos ... 10
Waddell-Phi ... 8
White-Chi ... 7
Plank-Phi ... 7
Mullin-Det ... 7

Saves
Patten-Was ... 3

Innings Pitched
Chesbro-NY ... 454.2
Powell-NY ... 390.1
Waddell-Phi ... 383.0
Mullin-Det ... 382.1
Young-Bos ... 380.0

Fewest Hits/Game
Chesbro-NY ... 6.69
Owen-Chi ... 6.94
Smith-Chi ... 6.98
Gibson-Bos ... 7.12
Waddell-Phi ... 7.21

Fewest BB/Game
Young-Bos ... .69
Tannehill-Bos ... 1.05
Patterson-Chi ... 1.31
Joss-Cle ... 1.40
Altrock-Chi ... 1.41

Strikeouts
Waddell-Phi ... 349
Chesbro-NY ... 239
Powell-NY ... 202
Plank-Phi ... 201
Young-Bos ... 200

Strikeouts/Game
Waddell-Phi ... 8.20
Bender-Phi ... 6.58
Moore-Cle ... 5.49
Plank-Phi ... 5.06
Glade-StL ... 4.86

Ratio
Young-Bos ... 8.53
Chesbro-NY ... 8.57
Owen-Chi ... 9.00
Joss-Cle ... 9.22
Dinneen-Bos ... 9.33

Earned Run Average
Joss-Cle ... 1.59
Waddell-Phi ... 1.62
Hess-Cle ... 1.67
White-Chi ... 1.78
Chesbro-NY ... 1.82

Adjusted ERA
Waddell-Phi ... 165
Joss-Cle ... 159
Chesbro-NY ... 149
White-Chi ... 138
Young-Bos ... 136

Opponents' Batting Avg.
Chesbro-NY ... .208
Owen-Chi ... .214
Smith-Chi ... .215
Gibson-Bos ... .219
Waddell-Phi ... .221

Opponents' On Base Pct.
Young-Bos ... .251
Chesbro-NY ... .252
Owen-Chi ... .261
Joss-Cle ... .266
Dinneen-Bos ... .268

Starter Runs
Waddell-Phi ... 41.5
Chesbro-NY ... 39.2
Young-Bos ... 26.6
Owen-Chi ... 22.9
Joss-Cle ... 21.5

Adjusted Starter Runs
Chesbro-NY ... 45.0
Waddell-Phi ... 44.9
Young-Bos ... 29.8
Plank-Phi ... 20.3
Joss-Cle ... 20.2

Clutch Pitching Index
White-Chi ... 153
Siever-StL ... 134
Bernhard-Cle ... 130
Waddell-Phi ... 126
Donahue-Cle ... 118

Relief Runs

Adjusted Relief Runs

Relief Ranking

Total Pitcher Index
Chesbro-NY ... 6.9
Waddell-Phi ... 4.9
Owen-Chi ... 3.5
Mullin-Det ... 3.2
Young-Bos ... 3.1

Total Baseball Ranking
Lajoie-Cle ... 7.2
Chesbro-NY ... 6.9
Waddell-Phi ... 4.9
Flick-Cle ... 4.5
Murphy-Phi ... 3.9

January 14 Giants owner John T. Brush, who refused to play the AL pennant winners in 1904, proposes rules governing future World Series.

February 25 While most clubs go south or stay close to home, the Cubs go to Santa Monica, Cal., for spring training, foreshadowing their eventual move to Catalina Island.

April 10* A New York magistrate rules Sunday baseball legal, but the battle will continue in the courts.

April 14 Boston's Kaiser Wilhelm loses to the Giants, 10-1, in the opener at the Polo Grounds before 40,000. He will finish the year 4-22, one of four Beaneaters who will lose 20 or more this year. The other three are Irv Young, Vic Willis, and Chick Fraser.

April 26 Jack McCarthy becomes the second outfielder to complete three double plays in one game when he throws out three Pirates at home, preserving the 2–1 Chicago Cubs victory.

April 30 Over 30,000 attend a Sunday game between the Giants and Superbas in Brooklyn. To get around the law, fans make "contributions" for admission.

May 17* Waseda University of Tokyo defeats Los Angeles High School, 5–3, in the first game of an American tour. It is the first baseball game ever played by Japanese outside Japan. Waseda starts a powerhouse tradition at Japan's Big Six universities that continues today.

May 19 Banished yesterday for abusive behavior, John McGraw roams the Polo Grounds before today's game with the Pirates, shouting insults at Barney Dreyfuss. McGraw accuses him of controlling the NL umpires through league president Harry Pulliam and welshing on gambling debts. McGraw is again ejected during the game. Eight days later, Pulliam levies a $150 fine and a 15-day suspension. Dreyfuss demands an NL hearing. McGraw files for an injunction against the fine and suspension, which the judge eventually grants. On June 1, the NL board meets in Boston and clears McGraw of the Dreyfuss charges, then censures Dreyfuss for engaging in a public altercation with McGraw.

May 30 Both leagues post record attendance figures for the Memorial Day holiday. Thanks to morning-afternoon doubleheaders, 67,806 see seven NL games.

June 13 For eight innings, Christy Mathewson and the Cubs' Mordecai "Three Finger" Brown match no-hitters. The Giants get two hits in the ninth to win 1-0, and preserve Matty's second no-hitter.

July 31 Charles P. Taft, owner of the *Cincinnati Times-Star* and brother of a future president, finances Charles W. Murphy's purchase of the Chicago Cubs for $125,000.

August 1 The Giants win their 12th in a row, and eleventh straight against Cincinnati, 10–5. The Pirates will end the streak at 13 on Aug. 3, but the Giants will win the pennant easily, nine games ahead of Pittsburgh.

August 8 Pittsburgh second baseman Dave Brain, who hit three triples in a game for St. Louis against Pittsburgh on May 29, repeats the performance for Pittsburgh against Boston. He is the only player to perform the feat twice in one season.

September 14 Joe Tinker and Johnny Evers engage in a fistfight on the field during an exhibition game in Washington, Indiana, because Evers took a taxi to the park, leaving his teammates in the hotel lobby. The pair will not speak to each other again for 33 years.

October 7 Beaneaters first baseman Fred Tenney has one assist in the season's final game, giving him an NL record of 152. The mark will be topped by Sid Bream of Pittsburgh, with 166 in 1986.

October 9 At Philadelphia, the Giants' Christy Mathewson outpitches 26-game-winner Eddie Plank 3-0 in the first game of the all-shutout Series.

October 14 Christy Mathewson pitches his third shutout in six days, giving up six hits to Bender's five. The Giants win, 2-0. The A's .161 team batting average is the lowest ever for a World Series; the teams' combined .185 is also the lowest. Each winning share is worth $1,142. The A's receive $382 each, but the club owners donate their share of the gate, raising the players' checks to $832.22.

December 15 After losing a record 29 games this year, veteran righthander Vic Willis is traded by seventh-place Boston NL to Pittsburgh for three players.

BOSTON

Pos	Player
M	F.Tenney
1B	F.Tenney
2B	F.Raymer
SS	E.Abbaticchio
3B	H.Wolverton
LF	J.Delahanty
CF	R.Cannell
RF	C.Dolan
C	P.Moran
C	T.Needham
32	B.Lauterborn
O	B.Sharpe
O	G.Barclay
/3	A.Strobel
/C	G.Street
/S	D.Murphy
/C	B.McCarthy
P	I.Young
P	V.Willis
P	C.Fraser
P	K.Wilhelm
/P	D.Harley
/P	J.Volz
/P	F.Hershey

BROOKLYN

Pos	Player
M	N.Hanlon
1B	D.Gessler
2B	C.Malay
SS	P.Lewis
3B	E.Batch
LF	J.Sheckard
CF	J.Dobbs
RF	H.Lumley
C	L.Ritter
C	B.Bergen
S1	C.Babb
O	B.Hall
2	R.Owens
2	J.Hummel
/1	E.MacGamwell
/1	A.Yale
P	H.McIntire
P	D.Scanlan
P	E.Stricklett
P	M.Eason
P	O.Jones
P	B.Briggs
P	F.Mitchell
P	J.Doscher
/P	D.Reisling

CHICAGO

Pos	Player
M	F.Selee
M	F.Chance
1B	F.Chance
2B	J.Evers
SS	J.Tinker
3B	D.Casey
LF	F.Schulte
CF	J.Slagle
RF	B.Maloney
C	J.Kling
2	S.Hofman
C	J.O'Neill
O	J.McCarthy
1	S.Barry
1	H.Lobert
P	E.Reulbach
P	J.Weimer
P	M.Brown
P	B.Wicker
P	C.Lundgren
P	B.Briggs
P	B.Pfeffer
P	N.Hahn
/P	R.Vowinkel
/P	O.Johns
/P	E.Baker

CINCINNATI

Pos	Player
M	J.Kelley
1B	S.Barry
2B	M.Huggins
SS	T.Corcoran
3B	H.Steinfeldt
LF	J.Kelley
CF	C.Seymour
RF	F.Odwell
C	A.Schlei
3O	A.Bridwell
O	J.Sebring
C	E.Phelps
/C	G.Street
1	C.Dolan
1	C.Blankenship
O	J.Siegle
O	B.Hinchman
/3	M.Mowrey
P	O.Overall
P	B.Ewing
P	C.Chech
P	J.Harper
P	T.Walker

NEW YORK

Pos	Player
M	J.McGraw
1B	D.McGann
2B	B.Gilbert
SS	B.Dahlen
3B	A.Devlin
LF	S.Mertes
CF	M.Donlin
RF	G.Browne
C	R.Bresnahan
C1	F.Bowerman
2O	S.Strang
1C	B.Clarke
/3	O.Neal
/O	B.Hall
/O	M.Graham
/O	J.McGraw
P	C.Mathewson
P	J.McGinnity
P	R.Ames
P	D.Taylor
P	H.Wiltse
P	C.Elliott

PHILADELPHIA

Pos	Player
M	H.Duffy
1B	K.Bransfield
2B	K.Gleason
SS	M.Doolan
3B	E.Courtney
LF	S.Magee
CF	R.Thomas
RF	J.Titus
C	R.Dooin
C	F.Abbott
S	O.Krueger
C	M.Kahoe
/O	H.Duffy
/C	R.Munson
/O	J.Lush
P	T.Pittinger
P	B.Duggleby
P	T.Sparks
P	F.Corridon
P	K.Nichols
P	J.Sutthoff
/P	R.Caldwell
/P	H.Kane
/P	K.Brady
/P	B.Washer

PITTSBURGH

Pos	Player
M	F.Clarke
1B	D.Howard
2B	C.Ritchey
SS	H.Wagner
3B	D.Brain
LF	F.Clarke
CF	G.Beaumont
RF	O.Clymer
C	H.Peitz
O3	T.Leach
1	B.Clancy
C	G.Gibson
O	B.Ganley
1P	H.Hillebrand
C	F.Carisch
3	G.McBride
/O	J.Wallace
/O	S.Flanagan
/3	O.Knabe
/C	H.Smith
P	D.Phillippe
P	S.Leever
P	C.Case
P	M.Lynch
P	P.Flaherty
P	C.Robitaille
/P	L.Leifield
/P	E.Kinsella
/P	G.Moore

ST.LOUIS

Pos	Player
M	K.Nichols
M	J.Burke
M	S.Robison
1B	J.Beckley
2B	H.Arndt
SS	G.McBride
3B	J.Burke
LF	S.Shannon
CF	H.Smoot
RF	J.Dunleavy
C	M.Grady
2S	D.Shay
O2	J.Clarke
S	D.Brain
C	J.Warner
C	T.Leahy
3	A.Hoelskoetter
O	R.DeGroff
O	D.Zearfoss
O	J.Himes
/2	J.Farrell
/2	S.Murch
/C	G.Shea
P	J.Taylor
P	C.McFarland
P	J.Thielman
P	B.Brown
P	W.Egan
P	W.Kellum
/P	K.Nichols
/P	S.McDougal
/P	B.Campbell
/P	J.McGinley

TEAM	G	W	L	PCT	GB	R	OR	AB	H	2B	3B	HR	BB	SO	AVG	OBP	SLG	PRO	PRO+	BR	/A	PF	CHI	RC	SB	CS	SBA	SBR
NY	155	105	48	.686		780	505	5094	1392	191	88	39	517		.273	.351	.368	.719	119	143	126	102	99	796	291			
PIT	155	96	57	.627	9	692	570	5213	1385	190	91	22	382		.266	.320	.350	.670	104	38	21	103	102	683	202			
CHI	155	92	61	.601	13	667	442	5108	1249	157	82	12	448		.245	.313	.314	.627	90	-30	-54	104	109	625	267			
PHI	155	83	69	.546	21.5	708	602	5243	1362	187	82	16	406		.260	.318	.336	.654	106	13	38	96	107	655	180			
CIN	155	79	74	.516	26	735	698	5205	1401	160	101	27	434		.269	.332	.354	.686	101	74	-3	111	102	710	181			
STL	154	58	96	.377	47.5	535	734	5066	1254	140	85	20	391		.248	.307	.321	.628	97	-36	-18	97	92	576	162			
BOS	156	51	103	.331	54.5	468	733	5190	1217	148	52	17	302		.234	.284	.293	.577	80	-135	-124	98	96	491	132			
BRO	155	48	104	.316	56.5	506	807	5100	1255	154	60	29	327		.246	.297	.317	.614	97	-66	-25	93	91	564	186			
TOT	620					5091		41219	10515	1327	641	182	3207	4462	.255	.315	.332	.647						1601				

TEAM	CG	SH	SV	IP	H	H/G	HR	BB	SO	RAT	ERA	ERA+	OAV	OOB	PR	/A	PF	CPI	FA	E	DP	FW	PW	BW	SBW	DIF
NY	117	18	15	1370	1160	7.6	25	364	760	10.2	2.39	122	.229	.284	91	80	98	92	.960	258	93	2.3	8.3	13.1		4.8
PIT	113	12	6	1382²	1270	8.3	12	389	512	11.2	2.86	104	.248	.308	20	16	100	95	.961	255	112	2.5	1.7	2.2		13.2
CHI	133	23	2	1407¹	1135	7.3	14	385	627	10.0	2.04	146	.224	.286	149	144	99	105	.962	248	99	2.9	15.0	-5.6		3.2
PHI	119	12	5	1398²	1303	8.4	21	411	516	11.5	2.81	104	.252	.316	28	12	97	104	.957	275	99	1.2	1.2	4.0		.6
CIN	119	10	2	1365²	1409	9.3	22	439	547	12.5	3.01	109	.272	.335	-3	41	110	116	.953	310	122	-1.0	4.3	-.3		-.4
STL	135	10	2	1347²	1431	9.6	28	367	411	12.3	3.59	92	.276	.329	-89	-93	99	97	.957	274	83	1.2	-9.7	-1.9		-8.6
BOS	139	14	0	1383	1390	9.0	36	433	533	12.1	3.52	88	.265	.326	-81	-68	103	95	.951	325	89	-1.8	-7.1	-12.9		-4.2
BRO	125	7	3	1347	1416	9.5	24	476	556	13.1	3.76	77	.274	.343	-114	-132	96	98	.937	408	101	-7.2	-13.7	-2.6		-4.5
TOT	1000106	35		11002		8.6				11.6	2.99		.255	.315					.954	2353	798					

Runs		Hits		Doubles		Triples		Home Runs		Total Bases	
Donlin-NY	124	Seymour-Cin	219	Seymour-Cin	40	Seymour-Cin	21	Odwell-Cin	9	Seymour-Cin	325
Thomas-Phi	118	Donlin-NY	216	Titus-Phi	36	Mertes-NY	17	Seymour-Cin	8	Donlin-NY	300
Huggins-Cin	117	Wagner-Pit	199	Wagner-Pit	32	Magee-Phi	17	Lumley-Bro	7	Wagner-Pit	277
Wagner-Pit	114	Barry-Chi-Cin	182	Donlin-NY	31	Smoot-StL	16	Donlin-NY	7	Magee-Phi	253
		Magee-Phi	180	Ritchey-Pit	29	Donlin-NY	16	Dahlen-NY	7	Titus-Phi	239

Runs Batted In		Runs Produced		Bases On Balls		Batting Average		On Base Percentage		Slugging Average	
Seymour-Cin	121	Wagner-Pit	209	Huggins-Cin	103	Seymour-Cin	.377	Chance-Chi	.450	Seymour-Cin	.559
Mertes-NY	108	Seymour-Cin	208	Slagle-Chi	97	Wagner-Pit	.363	Seymour-Cin	.429	Wagner-Pit	.505
Wagner-Pit	101	Donlin-NY	197	Thomas-Phi	93	Donlin-NY	.356	Wagner-Pit	.427	Donlin-NY	.495
Magee-Phi	98	Magee-Phi	193	Chance-Chi	78	Beaumont-Pit	.328	Thomas-Phi	.417	Titus-Phi	.436
Titus-Phi	89	Titus-Phi	186	Titus-Phi	69	Thomas-Phi	.317	Donlin-NY	.413	Grady-StL	.434

Production		Adjusted Production		Batter Runs		Adjusted Batter Runs		Clutch Hitting Index		Runs Created	
Seymour-Cin	.988	Seymour-Cin	175	Seymour-Cin	64.8	Seymour-Cin	50.8	Mertes-NY	139	Seymour-Cin	153
Wagner-Pit	.932	Wagner-Pit	173	Wagner-Pit	52.3	Wagner-Pit	49.3	Dahlen-NY	136	Wagner-Pit	147
Donlin-NY	.908	Donlin-NY	166	Donlin-NY	51.3	Donlin-NY	48.7	Wolverton-Bos	132	Donlin-NY	142
Chance-Chi	.883	Chance-Chi	157	Chance-Chi	37.2	Titus-Phi	38.6	Corcoran-Cin	131	Magee-Phi	111
Titus-Phi	.834	Titus-Phi	154	Titus-Phi	34.7	Chance-Chi	33.7	Courtney-Phi	131	Mertes-NY	103

Total Average		Stolen Bases		Stolen Base Average	Stolen Base Runs	Fielding Runs		Total Player Rating	
Wagner-Pit	1.132	Maloney-Chi	59			Huggins-Cin	36.2	Wagner-Pit	7.3
Chance-Chi	1.131	Devlin-NY	59			Gilbert-NY	25.4	Seymour-Cin	5.7
Seymour-Cin	1.102	Wagner-Pit	57			Tenney-Bos	22.2	Huggins-Cin	4.5
Donlin-NY	1.003	Mertes-NY	52			Wagner-Pit	20.3	Thomas-Phi	4.5
McGann-NY	.898	Magee-Phi	48			Dahlen-NY	19.8	Titus-Phi	4.1

Wins		Win Percentage		Games		Complete Games		Shutouts		Saves	
Mathewson-NY	31	Leever-Pit	.800	Pittinger-Phi	46	Young-Bos	41	Mathewson-NY	8	Elliott-NY	6
Pittinger-Phi	23	Mathewson-NY	.775	McGinnity-NY	46	Willis-Bos	36	Young-Bos	7	Wiltse-NY	4
Ames-NY	22	Ames-NY	.733	Young-Bos	43	Fraser-Bos	35	Reulbach-Chi	5	McGinnity-NY	3
McGinnity-NY	21	Wiltse-NY	.714	Mathewson-NY	43	Taylor-StL	34	Phillippe-Pit	5		
		Lynch-Pit	.680	Overall-Cin	42			Briggs-Chi	5		

Innings Pitched		Fewest Hits/Game		Fewest BB/Game		Strikeouts		Strikeouts/Game		Ratio	
Young-Bos	378.0	Reulbach-Chi	6.42	Phillippe-Pit	1.55	Mathewson-NY	206	Ames-NY	6.78	Mathewson-NY	8.42
Willis-Bos	342.0	Mathewson-NY	6.70	Brown-Chi	1.59	Ames-NY	198	Wiltse-NY	5.48	Reulbach-Chi	9.23
Mathewson-NY	338.2	Lundgren-Chi	7.02	Young-Bos	1.69	Overall-Cin	173	Mathewson-NY	5.47	Phillippe-Pit	9.45
Pittinger-Phi	337.1	Wicker-Chi	7.03	Mathewson-NY	1.70	Ewing-Cin	164	Overall-Cin	4.90	Wicker-Chi	9.46
Fraser-Bos	334.1	Wiltse-NY	7.22	McGinnity-NY	1.99	Young-Bos	156	Scanlan-Bro	4.87	Brown-Chi	9.54

Earned Run Average		Adjusted ERA		Opponents' Batting Avg.		Opponents' On Base Pct.		Starter Runs		Adjusted Starter Runs	
Mathewson-NY	1.28	Mathewson-NY	229	Reulbach-Chi	.201	Mathewson-NY	.245	Mathewson-NY	64.6	Mathewson-NY	61.9
Reulbach-Chi	1.42	Reulbach-Chi	209	Mathewson-NY	.205	Reulbach-Chi	.266	Reulbach-Chi	50.9	Reulbach-Chi	50.3
Wicker-Chi	2.02	Wicker-Chi	147	Wiltse-NY	.219	Brown-Chi	.271	Phillippe-Pit	24.7	Ewing-Cin	27.1
Briggs-Chi	2.14	Briggs-Chi	139	Lundgren-Chi	.220	Phillippe-Pit	.274	Sparks-Phi	23.3	Phillippe-Pit	24.7
Brown-Chi	2.17	Brown-Chi	137	Wicker-Chi	.221	Wicker-Chi	.276	Brown-Chi	22.8	Brown-Chi	22.2

Clutch Pitching Index		Relief Runs	Adjusted Relief Runs	Relief Ranking	Total Pitcher Index		Total Baseball Ranking	
Chech-Cin	133				Mathewson-NY	9.6	Mathewson-NY	9.6
Duggleby-Phi	126				Reulbach-Chi	4.8	Wagner-Pit	7.3
Overall-Cin	119				Ewing-Cin	2.7	Seymour-Cin	5.7
Briggs-Chi	119				Brown-Chi	2.4	Reulbach-Chi	4.8
Case-Pit	115				Wiltse-NY	2.4	Huggins-Cin	4.5

February 2* Hugh Jennings, now managing Baltimore in the Eastern League, is admitted to the Maryland bar after completing law studies at Cornell. Two weeks later Yankees outfielder Dave Fultz, a Columbia graduate, passes the New York bar exam. In 1912 he will organize and lead the Players' Fraternity.

February 7 In Lynn, Mass., Rube Waddell prevents a fire by carrying a burning stove out of a store and throwing it into a snowbank. Three days later he flees nearby Peabody to escape charges of assaulting and injuring his wife's parents.

March 29 A committee of Washington writers votes for "Nationals" as the AL team nickname, but "Senators" continues as the general favorite.

April 12 The Washington owners offer the players a $1,000 bonus if they finish higher than eighth and $500 for each position higher. They finish seventh, 11 games ahead of St. Louis.

April 22 Having failed to give out rain checks the day before when a storm stopped the game, the Highlanders open the gates for free admission, and 30,000 people jam the park for the clash with Washington.

April 30* At Evansville, Indiana, future major league umpire Cy Rigler begins the practice of raising his right arm to indicate strikes, so that friends in the bleachers can distinguish calls.

May 30 Both leagues post record attendance figures for the Memorial Day holiday. Thanks to morning-afternoon doubleheaders, 80,963 attend eight AL games.

July 1 White Sox pitcher Frank Owen narrowly misses becoming the first man to pitch a doubleheader shutout as the Browns score one run off him in the two games.

July 4 In the afternoon game of a doubleheader, Philadelphia's Rube Waddell bests Cy Young in a 20-inning marathon, as the Athletics down Boston, 4-2. Philadelphia catcher Ossie Schreckengost works 28 innings in one day, a major league record.

August 9* Mistaking her husband for a burglar, Ty Cobb's mother shoots and kills him. The Georgia Peach will make his major league debut with the Tigers three weeks later.

August 30 Ty Cobb makes his major league debut, doubling off Jack Chesbro, as Detroit defeats New York, 5–3. The two-bagger is the first of his 4,189 hits, a record topped by Pete Rose in 1985.

September 16 The Highlanders find themselves a little short on infielders so right fielder Willie Keeler, who is left-handed, plays second base in both games of a twin bill.

September 20 Chicago President Charles Comiskey orders a houseboat built for the express purpose of transporting and housing the team during spring training.

September 28 In a game that helps decide the pennant, the A's beat the White Sox, 3–2, as Topsy Hartsel scores from second base with the winning run in the seventh inning. Harry Davis's RBI single to short left hits Hartsel's mitt, which the left fielder had left in the outfield when he came off the field. The A's take the series, two games to one, and will finish two games ahead of Chicago.

October 2 The Washington outfield has no putouts or assists in a 3-2 win over Chicago.

October 5 Athletics pitcher Chief Bender has three hits, including a triple with three on, in an 8–0 victory over Washington. He then relieves Andy Coakley in the second game and wins 9–7. Overall, he has two wins, six hits, and eight RBIs for the day.

BOSTON	CHICAGO	CLEVELAND	DETROIT	NEW YORK	PHILADELPHIA	ST.LOUIS	WASHINGTON
M J.Collins	M F.Jones	M N.Lajoie	M B.Armour	M C.Griffith	M C.Mack	M J.McAleer	M J.Stahl
1B M.Grimshaw	1B J.Donahue	M B.Bradley	1B C.Lindsay	1B H.Chase	1B H.Davis	1B T.Jones	1B J.Stahl
2B H.Ferris	2B G.Dundon	M N.Lajoie	2B G.Schaefer	2B J.Williams	2B D.Murphy	2B I.Rockenfield	2B C.Hickman
SS F.Parent	SS G.Davis	1B C.Carr	SS C.O'Leary	SS K.Elberfeld	SS J.Knight	SS B.Wallace	SS J.Cassidy
3B J.Collins	3B L.Tannehill	2B N.Lajoie	3B B.Coughlin	3B J.Yeager	3B L.Cross	3B H.Gleason	3B H.Hill
LF J.Burkett	LF N.Callahan	SS T.Turner	LF M.McIntyre	LF P.Dougherty	LF T.Hartsel	LF G.Stone	LF F.Huelsman
CF C.Stahl	CF F.Jones	3B B.Bradley	CF D.Cooley	CF D.Fultz	CF D.Hoffman	CF B.Koehler	CF C.Jones
RF K.Selbach	RF D.Green	LF J.Jackson	RF S.Crawford	RF W.Keeler	RF S.Seybold	RF E.Frisk	RF J.Anderson
C L.Criger	C B.Sullivan	CF H.Bay	C L.Drill	C R.Kleinow	C O.Schreck't	C J.Sugden	C M.Heydon
1O B.Freeman	2O F.Isbell	RF E.Flick	O1 C.Hickman	3O W.Conroy	S M.Cross	O I.Van Zandt	32 R.Nill
3 B.Unglaub	O D.Holmes	C F.Buelow	O3 B.Lowe	C D.McGuire	O B.Lord	C T.Spencer	O P.Knoll
C C.Armbruster	C E.McFarland	12 G.Stovall	O T.Cobb	O E.Hahn	C D.Powers	C F.Roth	C M.Kittridge
C A.McGovern	23 G.Rohe	C H.Bemis	C J.Warner	O J.Anderson	C H.Barton	2 C.Starr	2 J.Mullin
/O J.Godwin	/C H.Hart	OP O.Hess	C T.Doran	2 F.LaPorte	P E.Plank	C A.Weaver	O J.Stanley
1 C.LaChance	P F.Owen	2 N.Kahl	O J.Barrett	3 J.Cockman	P R.Waddell	2 C.Moran	/O H.Cassady
/O P.Rising	P N.Altrock	O R.Vinson	C J.Sullivan	/1 D.Powers	P A.Coakley	2 D.Padden	/O C.Rothgeb
/C D.Farrell	P F.Smith	/C N.Clarke	O B.Wood	/S R.Oldring	P C.Bender	/C C.Gibson	/O H.Tate
/C T.Doran	P D.White	O B.Congalton	/C N.Clarke	/1 P.Delahanty	P W.Henley	/C B.Rickey	/O D.Sullivan
/C F.Owens	P E.Walsh	2 J.Barbeau	P G.Mullin	/C J.Connor	/P J.Dygert	P H.Howell	/O S.Shaughnessy
P C.Young	P R.Patterson	/C H.Wakefield	P E.Killian	/1 F.Curtis	/P J.Myers	P F.Glade	P C.Patten
P J.Tannehill		/2 E.Grant	P B.Donovan	/1 J.Doyle		P B.Pelty	P T.Hughes
P G.Winter		/3 E.Leber	P F.Kitson	/C F.Jacklitsch		P W.Sudhoff	P H.Townsend
P B.Dinneen		P A.Joss	/P G.Disch	/C J.McCarthy		P J.Buchanan	P B.Wolfe
P N.Gibson		P E.Moore	/P J.Wiggs	R C.Fallon		P C.Morgan	P B.Jacobson
/P E.Barry		P B.Rhoads	/P G.Ford	P A.Orth		/P H.Ables	P C.Falkenberg
/P E.Hughes		P B.Bernhard	/P E.Cicotte	P J.Chesbro		/P J.Powell	P R.Adams
/P H.Olmsted		P R.Donahue	/P J.Eubank	P B.Hogg			/P H.Hardy
/P J.Harris		/P H.West	/P C.Jackson	P J.Powell			/P M.Manuel
		/P J.Halla	/P F.Thomas	P C.Griffith			
		/P C.Ferry	/P W.Justis	P A.Puttmann			
			/P A.Bruckmiller	P D.Newton			
				/P W.Clarkson			
				/P L.LeRoy			
				/P W.Good			
				/P A.Goodwin			

TEAM	G	W	L	PCT	GB	R	OR	AB	H	2B	3B	HR	BB	SO	AVG	OBP	SLG	PRO	PRO+	BR	/A	PF	CHI	RC	SB	CS	SBA	SBR
PHI	152	92	56	.622		623	492	5146	1310	256	51	24	376	644	.255	.310	.338	.648	109	60	49	102	98	632	190			
CHI	158	92	60	.605	2	612	451	5114	1213	200	55	11	439	613	.237	.305	.304	.609	103	0	24	96	104	577	194			
DET	154	79	74	.516	15.5	512	602	4971	1209	190	54	13	375	583	.243	.302	.311	.613	99	1	-3	101	92	540	129			
BOS	153	78	74	.513	16	579	564	5049	1179	165	69	29	486	553	.234	.305	.311	.616	100	14	8	101	99	550	131			
CLE	155	76	78	.494	19	567	587	5166	1318	211	72	18	286	712	.255	.301	.334	.635	106	33	25	101	94	608	188			
NY	152	71	78	.477	21.5	586	622	4957	1228	163	61	23	360	537	.248	.307	.319	.626	93	26	-40	111	101	580	200			
WAS	154	64	87	.424	29.5	559	623	5015	1121	193	68	22	298	824	.224	.274	.302	.576	92	-70	-51	96	115	492	169			
STL	156	54	99	.353	40.5	511	608	5204	1205	153	49	16	362	639	.232	.288	.289	.577	93	-64	-37	95	99	502	130			
TOT	617					4549		40622	9783	1531	479	156	2982	5105	.241	.299	.314	.613						1331				

TEAM	CG	SH	SV	IP	H	H/G	HR	BB	SO	RAT	ERA	ERA+	OAV	OOB	PR	/A	PF	CPI	FA	E	DP	FW	PW	BW	SBW	DIF
PHI	117	19	0	1383¹	1137	7.4	21	409	895	10.5	2.19	121	.227	.294	70	68	100	110	.957	265	64	.3	7.5	5.4		4.8
CHI	131	15	0	1427	1163	7.3	11	329	613	9.6	1.99	124	.226	.277	105	72	93	105	.968	217	95	4.2	7.9	2.6		1.3
DET	124	17	1	1348	1226	8.2	11	474	578	11.7	2.83	96	.246	.318	-27	-19	103	104	.957	267	80	.4	-2.1	-.3		4.5
BOS	124	14	1	1356¹	1198	7.9	33	292	652	10.2	2.84	95	.238	.286	-29	-21	102	88	.953	296	75	-1.6	-2.3	.9		5.1
CLE	140	16	0	1363¹	1251	8.3	23	334	555	10.9	2.85	92	.245	.299	-30	-31	99	96	.963	233	84	2.8	-3.4	2.7		-3.1
NY	88	16	4	1353²	1235	8.2	26	396	642	11.1	2.93	100	.246	.307	-42	-2	111	97	.952	293	88	-1.6	-.2	-4.4		2.7
WAS	118	12	1	1362¹	1250	8.3	12	385	539	11.2	2.87	92	.247	.308	-33	-35	100	98	.951	318	76	-3.0	-3.8	-5.6		.9
STL	134	10	2	1384²	1245	8.1	19	389	633	11.0	2.74	93	.243	.304	-14	-33	96	100	.955	296	78	-1.3	-3.6	-4.1		-13.5
TOT	976	119	9	10978²		8.0				10.8	2.65		.241	.299					.957	2185	640					

Runs
Davis-Phi	93
Jones-Chi	91
Bay-Cle	90
Hartsel-Phi	88
Keeler-NY	81

Hits
Stone-StL	187
Davis-Phi	173
Crawford-Det	171
Keeler-NY	169
Bay-Cle	166

Doubles
Davis-Phi	47
Crawford-Det	38
Hickman-Det-Was	37
Seybold-Phi	37

Triples
Flick-Cle	18
Ferris-Bos	16
Turner-Cle	14
Stone-StL	13
Burkett-Bos	13

Home Runs
Davis-Phi	8
Stone-StL	7

Total Bases
Stone-StL	259
Davis-Phi	256
Crawford-Det	247
Hickman-Det-Was	232
Flick-Cle	231

Runs Batted In
Davis-Phi	83
L.Cross-Phi	77
Donahue-Chi	76
Crawford-Det	75
Turner-Cle	72

Runs Produced
Davis-Phi	168
Donahue-Chi	146
L.Cross-Phi	146
Crawford-Det	142
Murphy-Phi	136

Bases On Balls
Hartsel-Phi	121
Jones-Chi	73
Selbach-Bos	67
Burkett-Bos	67
Davis-Chi	60

Batting Average
Flick-Cle	.308
Keeler-NY	.302
Bay-Cle	.301
Crawford-Det	.297
Isbell-Chi	.296

On Base Percentage
Hartsel-Phi	.409
Flick-Cle	.383
Keeler-NY	.357
Crawford-Det	.357
Selbach-Bos	.355

Slugging Average
Flick-Cle	.462
Isbell-Chi	.440
Crawford-Det	.430
Davis-Phi	.422
Stone-StL	.410

Production
Flick-Cle	.845
Crawford-Det	.786
Stone-StL	.756
Davis-Phi	.756
Hartsel-Phi	.755

Adjusted Production
Flick-Cle	165
Crawford-Det	148
Stone-StL	147
Hartsel-Phi	138
Davis-Phi	137

Batter Runs
Flick-Cle	38.6
Hartsel-Phi	32.9
Crawford-Det	31.0
Stone-StL	26.9
Davis-Phi	24.9

Adjusted Batter Runs
Flick-Cle	37.3
Stone-StL	32.1
Hartsel-Phi	31.2
Crawford-Det	30.3
Davis-Phi	23.4

Clutch Hitting Index
Gleason-StL	134
Donahue-Chi	131
L.Cross-Phi	128
Fultz-NY	121
Collins-Bos	116

Runs Created
Flick-Cle	106
Stone-StL	102
Davis-Phi	101
Crawford-Det	99
Hartsel-Phi	96

Total Average
Flick-Cle	.945
Hartsel-Phi	.885
Crawford-Det	.797
Davis-Phi	.776
Stone-StL	.751

Stolen Bases
Hoffman-Phi	46
Fultz-NY	44
Stahl-Was	41
Hartsel-Phi	37

Stolen Base Average

Stolen Base Runs

Fielding Runs
Cassidy-Was	33.9
Tannehill-Chi	28.1
Wallace-StL	19.8
Davis-Chi	16.7
McIntyre-Det	16.5

Total Player Rating
Davis-Chi	4.1
Crawford-Det	3.9
Wallace-StL	3.9
Flick-Cle	3.4
Stone-StL	2.9

Wins
Waddell-Phi	27
Plank-Phi	24
Killian-Det	23
Altrock-Chi	23
Tannehill-Bos	22

Win Percentage
Waddell-Phi	.730
Tannehill-Bos	.710
Coakley-Phi	.692
Plank-Phi	.667
Altrock-Chi	.657

Games
Waddell-Phi	46
Mullin-Det	44
Patten-Was	42
Owen-Chi	42

Complete Games
Plank-Phi	35
Mullin-Det	35
Howell-StL	35
Killian-Det	33
Owen-Chi	32

Shutouts
Killian-Det	8
Waddell-Phi	7
Tannehill-Bos	6
Orth-NY	6
Hughes-Was	6

Saves
Buchanan-StL	2

Innings Pitched
Mullin-Det	347.2
Plank-Phi	346.2
Owen-Chi	334.0
Waddell-Phi	328.2
Howell-StL	323.0

Fewest Hits/Game
Waddell-Phi	6.33
Smith-Chi	6.63
Young-Bos	6.96
Howell-StL	7.02
White-Chi	7.05

Fewest BB/Game
Young-Bos	.84
Joss-Cle	1.45
Owen-Chi	1.51
Bernhard-Cle	1.76
Altrock-Chi	1.80

Strikeouts
Waddell-Phi	287
Young-Bos	210
Plank-Phi	210
Howell-StL	198
Smith-Chi	171

Strikeouts/Game
Waddell-Phi	7.86
Young-Bos	5.89
Bender-Phi	5.58
Howell-StL	5.52
Hogg-NY	5.49

Ratio
Young-Bos	8.03
Waddell-Phi	9.06
Owen-Chi	9.19
White-Chi	9.37
Joss-Cle	9.53

Earned Run Average
Waddell-Phi	1.48
White-Chi	1.76
Young-Bos	1.82
Coakley-Phi	1.84
Altrock-Chi	1.88

Adjusted ERA
Waddell-Phi	179
Young-Bos	147
Coakley-Phi	144
White-Chi	140
Chesbro-NY	133

Opponents' Batting Avg.
Waddell-Phi	.200
Smith-Chi	.208
Young-Bos	.216
Howell-StL	.217
White-Chi	.218

Opponents' On Base Pct.
Young-Bos	.241
Waddell-Phi	.264
Owen-Chi	.267
White-Chi	.270
Joss-Cle	.274

Starter Runs
Waddell-Phi	42.7
Young-Bos	29.3
Altrock-Chi	26.9
White-Chi	25.6
Howell-StL	24.0

Adjusted Starter Runs
Waddell-Phi	42.8
Young-Bos	30.9
Chesbro-NY	24.6
Coakley-Phi	23.1
Altrock-Chi	20.3

Clutch Pitching Index
Coakley-Phi	142
Altrock-Chi	118
Waddell-Phi	116
Townsend-Was	115
Mullin-Det	113

Relief Runs

Adjusted Relief Runs

Relief Ranking

Total Pitcher Index
Howell-StL	4.9
Waddell-Phi	4.9
Young-Bos	3.3
Chesbro-NY	3.0
Altrock-Chi	2.8

Total Baseball Ranking
Waddell-Phi	4.9
Howell-StL	4.8
Davis-Chi	4.1
Crawford-Det	3.9
Wallace-StL	3.9

January 12 The owners of the Boston Beaneaters reject a $250,000 offer for the team, which is destined to finish last again.

March 6 Rookie owner Charles W. Murphy puts the last pieces of a Cubs dynasty in place, trading rookie infielder Hans Lobert and lefthander Jake Weimer to the Cincinnati Reds for third baseman Harry Steinfeldt. Not a heavy hitter, Steinfeldt completes the Tinker-Evers-Chance infield with more than adequate defense.

April 12 Boston outfielder Johnny Bates hits a homer in his first major league at bat, connecting in the second inning against the Brooklyn Superbas.

April 22 A new rule puts the umpire in sole charge of all game balls. The home team manager previously had some say as to when a new ball was introduced.

April 28 It's the only time two player-managers steal home on the same day, though not in the same game. Cubs pilot Frank Chance steals in the ninth to give Chicago a 1–0 win over the Reds, and Fred Clarke matches him in the Pirates' 10–1 win over the St. Louis Cardinals.

June 1 Women appear at the Polo Grounds ticket windows for the first time. New ticket-selling machines are also introduced.

June 9 A 19-game losing streak ends for the Boston Beaneaters with a 6–3 win over the Cardinals.

June 17 In another test of Sunday baseball in Brooklyn, the police arrest Superbas president Charles Ebbets and manager Ned Hanlon, the visiting Reds' manager Joe Kelley, and starting pitcher Mal Eason. The case is dismissed as no admission was charged, and the law does not apply to "voluntary contributions."

June 19 NL directors pass a resolution urging all clubs to provide dressing rooms for visiting teams. Even those that do, however, offer such primitive facilities that most teams on the road continue to dress at their hotels.

August 13 The Cubs' Jack Taylor is knocked out by Brooklyn in the third inning, ending a string of 187 complete games and 15 relief appearances in which he finished each game. The record run began on June 20, 1901. In 10 years he will fail to finish only eight of his 286 starts.

September 1 With the regular umpires sick from food poisoning, Cub pitcher Carl Lundgren and Cardinal catcher Pete Noonan umpire. The Cubs win 8-1 for the 14th win in a row at the West Side Grounds.

September 3* The Philadelphia Giants win the Negro Championship Cup on Labor Day in Philadelphia before 10,000 fans, black baseball's largest crowd to date. Andrew "Rube" Foster pitches them to a 3-2 victory over the Cuban X-Giants, who have John Henry Lloyd in the lineup.

September 26 Rookie outfielder John Cameron of Boston, after one relief appearance, gets a starting assignment against the Cardinals. Leadoff batter Tom O'Hara beats out an infield single. Al Burch's line drive hits Cameron in the head, and caroms back on a fly to catcher Jack O'Neill, who throws to Fred Tenney at first base, doubling off O'Hara. Cameron retires with one assist and a headache in his last major league game.

October 4 The Cubs score their record 116th win of the year, beating the Pirates, 4-0, in Pittsburgh. The win gives them a 60-15 road record, an .800 percentage mark that has never been equaled.

October 5 The Giants give Christy Mathewson's brother Henry a starting chance against Boston. He establishes a modern NL record by walking 14, hits one batter, and completes the 7-1 loss for the only major league decision of his career.

October 9 Snow flies at the Cubs' West Side Park as the first one-city World Series opens with the Cubs heavy favorites over the AL's "Hitless Wonders." Neither West Side Park nor the Sox's South Side Park can accommodate the crowds, so the *Chicago Tribune* recreates the games on mechanical boards displayed at theaters. White Sox starter Nick Altrock and Cubs starter Mordecai "Three Finger" Brown give up four hits each, but Cubs errors produce two unearned runs for a 2-1 White Sox victory.

October 12 It's Three Finger Brown's turn to throw a two-hit shutout, besting Altrock 1-0 and evening the Series.

	BOSTON		BROOKLYN		CHICAGO		CINCINNATI		NEW YORK		PHILADELPHIA		PITTSBURGH		ST.LOUIS
M	F.Tenney	M	P.Donovan	M	F.Chance	M	N.Hanlon	M	J.McGraw	M	H.Duffy	M	F.Clarke	M	J.McCloskey
1B	F.Tenney	1B	T.Jordan	1B	F.Chance	1B	S.Deal	1B	D.McGann	1B	K.Bransfield	1B	J.Nealon	1B	J.Beckley
2B	A.Strobel	2B	W.Alperman	2B	J.Evers	2B	M.Huggins	2B	B.Gilbert	2B	K.Gleason	2B	C.Ritchey	2B	P.Bennett
SS	A.Bridwell	SS	P.Lewis	SS	J.Tinker	SS	T.Corcoran	SS	B.Dahlen	SS	M.Doolan	SS	H.Wagner	SS	G.McBride
3B	D.Brain	3B	D.Casey	3B	H.Steinfeldt	3B	J.Delahanty	3B	A.Devlin	3B	E.Courtney	3B	T.Sheehan	3B	H.Arndt
LF	D.Howard	LF	J.McCarthy	LF	J.Sheckard	LF	J.Kelley	LF	S.Shannon	LF	S.Magee	LF	F.Clarke	LF	S.Shannon
CF	J.Bates	CF	B.Maloney	CF	J.Slagle	CF	C.Seymour	CF	C.Seymour	CF	R.Thomas	CF	G.Beaumont	CF	H.Smoot
RF	C.Dolan	RF	H.Lumley	RF	F.Schulte	RF	F.Jude	RF	G.Browne	RF	J.Titus	RF	B.Ganley	RF	A.Burch
C	T.Needham	C	B.Bergen	C	J.Kling	C	A.Schlei	C	R.Bresnahan	C	R.Dooin	C	G.Gibson	C	M.Grady
CO	S.Brown	2O	J.Hummel	1O	P.Moran	1O	S.Barry	C1	F.Bowerman	32	P.Sentell	3O	T.Leach	3S	A.Hoelskoetter
C	J.O'Neill	C	L.Ritter	O1	S.Hofman	3S	H.Lobert	2O	S.Strang	C	J.Donovan	OS	D.Meier	O1	S.Barry
O	G.Good	O	E.Batch	O	D.Gessler	O	H.Smoot	O	S.Mertes	3	J.Ward	C	H.Peitz	O	S.Mertes
O	J.Cameron	/1	D.Gessler	/1	P.Noonan	O	F.Odwell	O	M.Donlin	/C	C.Crist	C	E.Phelps	S	F.Crawford
S	F.Connaughton	/O	P.Donovan	H	B.Smith	C	P.Livingston	OC	D.Marshall	/C	H.Huston	O	B.Hallman	O	R.Murray
/O	C.Spencer	/O	P.Reardon	/C	T.Walsh	1	C.Carr	/S	J.Hannifin	H	H.Duffy	O	O.Clymer	C1	P.Noonan
/O	T.Madden	/C	J.Butler			O	J.Siegle	H	A.Smith			/2	B.Abstein	C	D.Marshall
/O	E.Diehl					O	B.Hinchman	/O	F.Burke			/C	F.Carisch	O	J.Marshall
/S	J.Schulte	P	E.Stricklett	P	M.Brown	3	M.Mowrey	3	M.Fitzgerald	P	T.Sparks	/3	A.Storke	C	T.Raub
		P	D.Scanlan	P	J.Pfiester	C	E.Phelps	/C	J.McGraw	P	J.Lush	/C	H.Smith	3	B.Phyle
P	I.Young	P	H.McIntire	P	E.Reulbach	C	L.McLean			P	B.Duggleby	P	V.Willis	S	T.O'Hara
P	V.Lindaman	P	M.Eason	P	C.Lundgren	/O	J.Barrett	P	J.McGinnity		L.Richie	P	S.Leever	C	J.McCarthy
P	B.Pfeffer	P	J.Pastorius	P	J.Taylor	/3	E.Tiemeyer	P	C.Mathewson	P	T.Pittinger	P	L.Leifield	S	E.Holly
P	G.Dorner					/C	O.Stanage	P	H.Wiltse			P	D.Phillippe	/C	D.Holmes
		/P	J.Whiting	P	O.Overall			P	D.Taylor	/P	W.Moser	P	M.Lynch	/3	E.Zimmerman
/P	R.Witherup	/P	J.Doscher	P	B.Wicker	P	J.Weimer	P	R.Ames	/P	J.McCloskey			/C	J.Slattery
/P	J.Moroney	/P	C.McFarland	P	F.Beebe	P	B.Ewing	RP	G.Ferguson	/P	H.Kane			/O	R.DeGroff
/P	B.McCarthy	/P	H.Knolls	/P	J.Harper	P	C.Fraser				C.Roy				
						P	B.Wicker	/P	H.Mathewson	/P	K.Nichols	/P	H.Hillebrand		
						P	C.Hall					/P	C.McFarland		
				P	O.Overall							/P	E.Karger	P	B.Brown
					C.Chech							/P	K.Brady	P	E.Karger
				/P	B.Essick							/P	C.Case	P	F.Beebe
				/P	J.Harper							/P	H.Camnitz	P	J.Taylor
				/P	C.Druhot							/P	L.Manske	P	C.Druhot
				/P	L.Hafford							/P	B.Maxwell		
				/P	G.Dorner							/P	I.McIlveen		
				/P	D.Mason									P	G.Thompson
														P	W.Egan
														/P	S.McGlynn
														/P	I.Higginbotham
														/P	C.Rhodes
														/P	C.McFarland
														/P	A.Fromme
														/P	A.Puttmann
														/P	J.Thielman
														/P	B.Adams

TEAM	G	W	L	PCT	GB	R	OR	AB	H	2B	3B	HR	BB	SO	AVG	OBP	SLG	PRO	PRO+	BR	/A	PF	CHI	RC	SB	CS	SBA	SBR
CHI	155	116	36	.763		705	381	5018	1316	181	71	20	448		.262	.328	.339	.667	109	83	46	106	109	695	283			
NY	153	96	56	.632	20	625	510	4768	1217	162	53	15	563		.255	.343	.321	.664	112	92	78	102	98	659	288			
PIT	154	93	60	.608	23.5	623	470	5030	1313	164	67	12	424		.261	.324	.327	.651	105	55	28	104	102	625	162			
PHI	154	71	82	.464	45.5	528	564	4911	1183	197	47	12	432		.241	.307	.307	.614	98	-10	-11	100	99	550	180			
BRO	153	66	86	.434	50	496	625	4897	1156	141	68	25	388		.236	.297	.308	.605	103	-31	8	92	98	532	175			
CIN	155	64	87	.424	51.5	533	582	5025	1198	140	71	16	395		.238	.301	.304	.605	91	-28	-51	104	101	545	170			
STL	154	52	98	.347	63	470	607	5075	1195	137	69	10	361		.235	.291	.296	.587	93	-66	-46	96	97	498	110			
BOS	152	49	102	.325	66.5	408	649	4925	1115	136	43	16	356		.226	.286	.281	.567	85	-96	-84	97	93	449	95			
TOT	615					4388		39649	9693	1258	489	126	3367	4537	.244	.310	.310	.620						1463				

TEAM	CG	SH	SV	IP	H	H/G	HR	BB	SO	RAT	ERA	ERA+	OAV	OOB	PR	/A	PF	CPI	FA	E	DP	FW	PW	BW	SBW	DIF
CHI	125	30	10	1388¹	1018	6.6	12	446	702	9.8	1.75	150	.207	.280	135	135	100	100	.969	194	100	4.5	15.0	5.1		15.3
NY	105	19	18	1334¹	1207	8.1	13	394	639	11.0	2.49	105	.241	.300	20	15	99	96	.963	233	84	1.8	1.7	8.7		7.9
PIT	116	27	2	1358	1234	8.2	13	309	532	10.5	2.21	120	.245	.294	62	70	102	107	.964	228	109	2.2	7.8	3.1		3.4
PHI	108	21	5	1354¹	1201	8.0	18	436	500	11.3	2.58	101	.235	.304	7	0	99	94	.956	271	83	-.6	.0	-1.2		-3.7
BRO	119	22	11	1348²	1255	8.4	15	453	476	11.7	3.13	80	.249	.316	-76	-93	96	88	.955	283	73	-1.5	-10.3	.9		1.0
CIN	126	12	5	1369²	1248	8.2	14	470	567	11.6	2.69	102	.250	.320	-10	6	105	105	.959	262	97	.0	.7	-5.7		-6.6
STL	118	4	2	1354	1246	8.3	17	479	559	11.9	3.04	86	.246	.318	-63	-65	100	91	.957	272	92	-.7	-7.2	-5.1		-10.0
BOS	137	10	0	1334¹	1291	8.7	24	436	562	12.0	3.14	85	.261	.328	-76	-70	102	100	.947	337	102	-5.2	-7.8	-9.3		-4.2
TOT	954	145	53	10841²		8.1				11.2	2.62		.244	.310					.959	2080	740					

Runs
Wagner-Pit 103
Chance-Chi 103
Sheckard-Chi 90
Nealon-Pit 82

Hits
Steinfeldt-Chi 176
Wagner-Pit 175
Seymour-Cin-NY ... 165
Magee-Phi 159
Huggins-Cin 159

Doubles
Wagner-Pit 38
Magee-Phi 36
Bransfield-Phi 28
Steinfeldt-Chi 27
Sheckard-Chi 27

Triples
Schulte-Chi........ 13
Clarke-Pit 13
Nealon-Pit 12
Lumley-Bro 12

Home Runs
Jordan-Bro 12
Lumley-Bro 9
Seymour-Cin-NY 8
Schulte-Chi 7

Total Bases
Wagner-Pit 237
Steinfeldt-Chi 232
Lumley-Bro 231
Magee-Phi 229
Schulte-Chi 223

Runs Batted In
Steinfeldt-Chi 83
Nealon-Pit........ 83
Seymour-Cin-NY ... 80
Jordan-Bro 78

Runs Produced
Wagner-Pit 172
Chance-Chi 171
Nealon-Pit 162
Steinfeldt-Chi 161
Seymour-Cin-NY ... 142

Bases On Balls
Thomas-Phi 107
Bresnahan-NY 81
Titus-Phi 78
Dahlen-NY 76
Devlin-NY 74

Batting Average
Wagner-Pit 339
Steinfeldt-Chi ..... .327
Lumley-Bro ...... .324
Strang-NY 319
Chance-Chi .... .319

On Base Percentage
Bresnahan-NY ..... .419
Chance-Chi ...... .419
Wagner-Pit .... .416
Devlin-NY .... .396
Steinfeldt-Chi ..... .395

Slugging Average
Lumley-Bro........477
Wagner-Pit ...... .459
Strang-NY .... .435
Steinfeldt-Chi ..... .430
Chance-Chi ...... .430

Production
Wagner-Pit .... .875
Lumley-Bro........864
Chance-Chi .... .849
Steinfeldt-Chi ..... .825
Devlin-NY .... .786

Adjusted Production
Lumley-Bro 184
Wagner-Pit 166
Chance-Chi 156
Jordan-Bro 153
Steinfeldt-Chi 149

Batter Runs
Wagner-Pit 44.7
Chance-Chi 39.1
Lumley-Bro 37.2
Steinfeldt-Chi 36.1
Devlin-NY 29.1

Adjusted Batter Runs
Lumley-Bro 44.6
Wagner-Pit 40.2
Chance-Chi 33.6
Steinfeldt-Chi 30.6
Devlin-NY 27.2

Clutch Hitting Index
Tinker-Chi 138
Nealon-Pit 134
Ritchey-Pit 128
Kelley-Cin 126
Shannon-StL-NY... 125

Runs Created
Wagner-Pit 124
Chance-Chi 114
Steinfeldt-Chi 109
Lumley-Bro 107
Magee-Phi 102

Total Average
Chance-Chi 1.062
Wagner-Pit 1.050
Lumley-Bro .... .963
Devlin-NY .... .940
Bresnahan-NY .... .911

Stolen Bases
Chance-Chi 57
Magee-Phi......... 55
Devlin-NY 54
Wagner-Pit 53
Evers-Chi........ 49

Stolen Base Average

Stolen Base Runs

Fielding Runs
Devlin-NY 28.0
Brain-Bos........ 25.7
Wagner-Pit....... 23.8
Gilbert-NY 22.6
Huggins-Cin 21.5

Total Player Rating
Wagner-Pit 7.3
Devlin-NY 6.5
Lumley-Bro 4.3
Huggins-Cin 4.0
Bresnahan-NY 3.9

Wins
McGinnity-NY 27
Brown-Chi 26
Willis-Pit 23
Mathewson-NY 22
Leever-Pit 22

Win Percentage
Reulbach-Chi .... .826
Brown-Chi .... .813
Leever-Pit .... .759
Lundgren-Chi .... .739
Pfiester-Chi ...... .714

Games
McGinnity-NY 45
Young-Bos 43
Sparks-Phi 42
Duggleby-Phi 42

Complete Games
Young-Bos 37
Pfeffer-Bos 33

Shutouts
Brown-Chi 9
Leifield-Pit 8

Saves
Ferguson-NY 7
Wiltse-NY 6
Stricklett-Bro 5

Innings Pitched
Young-Bos 358.1
McGinnity-NY ...339.2
Willis-Pit 322.0
Sparks-Phi 316.2
Lindaman-Bos ...307.1

Fewest Hits/Game
Reulbach-Chi 5.33
Pfiester-Chi 6.21
Brown-Chi 6.43
Beebe-Chi-StL ... 6.67
Lundgren-Chi ... 6.93

Fewest BB/Game
Phillippe-Pit 1.07
Leever-Pit 1.66
Sparks-Phi 1.76
Ewing-Cin 1.88
McGinnity-NY 1.88

Strikeouts
Beebe-Chi-StL ... 171
Pfeffer-Bos 158
Ames-NY 156
Pfiester-Chi 153

Strikeouts/Game
Ames-NY 6.90
Beebe-Chi-StL ... 6.67
Pfiester-Chi 5.49
Overall-Cin-Chi ... 5.05
Lush-Phi 4.84

Ratio
Brown-Chi 8.53
Pfiester-Chi 8.94
Sparks-Phi 8.98
Reulbach-Chi 9.66
Ewing-Cin........ 9.70

Earned Run Average
Brown-Chi 1.04
Pfiester-Chi 1.51
Reulbach-Chi 1.65
Willis-Pit 1.73
Leifield-Pit 1.87

Adjusted ERA
Brown-Chi 253
Pfiester-Chi 174
Reulbach-Chi 159
Willis-Pit 154
Leifield-Pit 143

Opponents' Batting Avg.
Reulbach-Chi ..... .175
Pfiester-Chi ...... .194
Brown-Chi .... .202
Beebe-Chi-StL .... .209
Sparks-Phi .... .211

Opponents' On Base Pct.
Brown-Chi 252
Sparks-Phi 257
Pfiester-Chi 258
Phillippe-Pit 276
Reulbach-Chi 278

Starter Runs
Brown-Chi 48.9
Willis-Pit 31.9
Pfiester-Chi 31.1
Reulbach-Chi 23.6
Leifield-Pit 21.6

Adjusted Starter Runs
Brown-Chi 49.0
Willis-Pit 33.3
Pfiester-Chi 31.3
Reulbach-Chi 23.7
Leifield-Pit 22.7

Clutch Pitching Index
Willis-Pit 139
Lindaman-Bos ... 126
Brown-Chi 122
Leifield-Pit 120
Lush-Phi 114

Relief Runs
Ferguson-NY 3

Adjusted Relief Runs
Ferguson-NY 1

Relief Ranking
Ferguson-NY 0

Total Pitcher Index
Brown-Chi 6.8
Willis-Pit 4.5
Taylor-StL-Chi 2.9
Weimer-Cin 2.9
Reulbach-Chi 2.8

Total Baseball Ranking
Wagner-Pit 7.3
Brown-Chi 6.8
Devlin-NY 6.5
Willis-Pit 4.5
Lumley-Bro 4.3

May 8 With the A's shorthanded because of injuries, Connie Mack puts pitcher Alvin "Chief" Bender in left field in the sixth inning in a game against the Boston Pilgrims. Bender hits two home runs, both inside the park.

May 17 Ty Cobb's bunt single spoils Rube Waddell's no-hit bid. The Philadelphia A's win, 5–0.

May 25 Jesse Tannehill snaps the Boston Pilgrims' 20-game losing streak with a 3-0 win over the White Sox. Both Boston teams will finish last, while both Chicago teams finish first. It's the first time two cities have had two winners and two cellar-dwellers, and it won't happen again until 1921, when New York has the winners and Philadelphia the cellar-dwellers.

July 5 Jack Coombs, the A's rookie righthander from Colby College, makes his major league debut, blanking Washington, 3–0, for the Athletics.

August 2 While the Athletics, crippled by injuries, falter, Doc White launches the White Sox on a 19-game winning streak (longest in AL history) with a 3-0 win over Boston. The streak, interrupted only by a 0-0 tie with New York, catapults Chicago from fourth place to first in 10 days.

August 3 Tom Hughes of the Washington Nationals and Fred Glade of the St. Louis Browns enter the 10th inning with a scoreless tie. Hughes hits a home run for a 1-0 victory, the first pitcher to win a 1-0 extra-inning game with his own home run.

August 18 "Wee Willie" Keeler is struck out for only the second time this season, both times by spitballer Ed Walsh of the White Sox.

August 30 After pitching a shutout in his major league debut, right-hander Slow Joe Doyle of the Highlanders becomes the first player to start out with two shutouts when he beats the Nationals, 5–0. Of his 23 lifetime victories, seven will be shutouts. He is nicknamed "Slow" because of his time-consuming pace on the mound.

August 31 Beset by injuries, the Tigers call 46-year-old Sam Thompson out of retirement; he drives in two runs in a 5–1 win over the Browns. Thompson last played in the majors in 1898. He appears in eight games and bats .226.

September 1 The Highlanders win their sixth game in three days from Washington, sweeping their third straight doubleheader for an AL record. Three days later, they'll move into first place, sweeping Boston, 7-0, and 1-0, for their fifth straight doubleheader sweep, a major league record.

September 1 The AL's longest game on record takes place in Boston. Rookie Jack Coombs and 24-year-old Joe Harris go the route in a 24-inning struggle, ending with a 4–1 Athletics victory after four hours and 47 minutes. Philadelphia's Coombs strikes out 18 and gives up 14 hits. The Pilgrims' Harris fans 14 and yields 16 hits.

September 17 Playing as "Sullivan" to conserve his college eligibility, Columbia University junior Eddie Collins makes his debut at shortstop with the Athletics. He gets one hit off Ed Walsh and strikes out twice. Collins will play 25 years in the major league, bat .333, and become a member of the Hall of Fame.

September 26 The Athletics finally score after being shut out for a major league record 48 consecutive innings, dating back to Sept. 22. Harry Davis breaks the long drought with a two-run double against Cleveland, but the A's still lose, 5–3.

October 1 Hugh Jennings resigns as Baltimore manager to take over at Detroit for 1907. Infusing the Tigers with aggressive Baltimore spirit, he will win pennants the next three years, and stay at the helm for 14.

October 14 The Sox jump on Three Finger Brown for seven runs in the first two innings, and coast behind Doc White to a 7–1 Series-ending victory. The Cubs' losers' share is $439.50, the lowest ever. The unlikely hero is reserve third baseman George Rohe, who delivers key hits for the "Hitless Wonders."

BOSTON		CHICAGO		CLEVELAND		DETROIT		NEW YORK		PHILADELPHIA		ST.LOUIS		WASHINGTON	
M	J.Collins	M	F.Jones	M	N.Lajoie	M	B.Armour	M	C.Griffith	M	C.Mack	M	J.McAleer	M	J.Stahl
M	C.Stahl	1B	J.Donahue	1B	C.Rossman	1B	C.Lindsay	1B	H.Chase	1B	H.Davis	1B	T.Jones	1B	J.Stahl
1B	M.Grimshaw	2B	F.Isbell	2B	N.Lajoie	2B	G.Schaefer	2B	J.Williams	2B	D.Murphy	2B	P.O'Brien	2B	L.Schlafly
2B	H.Ferris	SS	G.Davis	SS	T.Turner	SS	C.O'Leary	SS	K.Elberfeld	SS	M.Cross	SS	B.Wallace	SS	D.Altizer
SS	F.Parent	3B	L.Tannehill	3B	B.Bradley	3B	B.Coughlin	3B	F.LaPorte	3B	J.Knight	3B	R.Hartzell	3B	L.Cross
3B	R.Morgan	LF	E.Hahn	LF	J.Jackson	LF	M.McIntyre	LF	W.Conroy	LF	T.Hartsel	LF	G.Stone	LF	J.Anderson
LF	J.Hoey	CF	F.Jones	CF	E.Flick	CF	T.Cobb	CF	D.Hoffman	CF	B.Lord	CF	C.Hemphill	CF	C.Jones
CF	C.Stahl	RF	B.O'Neill	RF	B.Congalton	RF	S.Crawford	RF	W.Keeler	RF	S.Seybold	RF	H.Niles	RF	C.Hickman
RF	J.Hayden	C	B.Sullivan	C	H.Bemis	C	B.Schmidt	C	R.Kleinow	C	O.Schreckengost	C	B.Rickey	C	H.Wakefield
C	C.Armbruster	O	P.Dougherty	13	G.Stovall	O	D.Jones	O	F.Delahanty	O	H.Armbruster	C	T.Spencer	S2	R.Nill
O1	B.Freeman	3	G.Rohe	O	H.Bay	CO	F.Payne	3O	G.Moriarty	C	D.Powers	O	B.Koehler	O	J.Stanley
O	K.Selbach	2S	G.Dundon	O	N.Clarke	C	J.Warner	C	D.McGuire	3	R.Oldring	C	J.O'Connor	C	M.Heydon
3S	J.Godwin	C	F.Roth	3	J.Barbeau	S2	B.Lowe	S2	J.Yeager	3	A.Brouthers	2	I.Rockenfield	C	J.Warner
3	J.Collins	O	F.Hemphill	O	B.Caffyn	/O	S.Thompson	/O	I.Thomas	2	D.Shean	1	L.Nordyke	/O	M.Kittridge
C	B.Peterson	C	H.Hart	C	F.Buelow	/2	F.Scheibeck	O	P.Dougherty		S.Nicholls	P	H.Howell	/S	O.Williams
C	B.Carrigan	C	B.Towne	/O	J.Birmingham	/3	G.Hetling	/O	E.Hahn	C	B.Berry	P	F.Glade	/3	W.Shannabrook
C	C.Graham	/O	R.Vinson	/C	M.Kittridge	P	G.Mullin	P	A.Orth	C	J.Byrnes	P	B.Pelty	H	P.Duff
2	C.Chadbourne	/C	E.McFarland	/2	B.Shipke	P	R.Donahue	P	J.Chesbro	/O	D.Hoffman	P	J.Powell	P	C.Falkenberg
/2	H.Wagner	/S	L.Quillen	P	O.Hess	P	E.Siever	P	B.Hogg	/3	E.Lennox	P	E.Smith	P	C.Patten
/C	L.Criger	P	F.Owen	P	B.Rhoads	P	B.Donovan	P	W.Clarkson	/S	E.Collins	P	B.Jacobson	P	C.Smith
/C	T.Doran	P	N.Altrock	P	A.Joss	P	E.Killian	P	D.Newton	H	W.Fetzer			P	T.Hughes
P	C.Young	P	E.Walsh	P	B.Bernhard	P	J.Eubank	P	C.Griffith	H	J.Hannifin			P	F.Kitson
P	J.Harris	P	D.White	P	H.Townsend	/P	E.Willett	/P	S.Doyle	P	R.Waddell			/P	C.Goodwin
P	B.Dinneen	P	R.Patterson	P	H.Eells	/P	J.Wiggs	P	L.LeRoy	P	C.Bender			/P	H.Hardy
P	G.Winter	P	F.Smith	/P	E.Moore	/P	J.Rowan	P	N.Hahn	P	J.Dygert			/P	W.Sudhoff
P	J.Tannehill	/P	L.Fiene	/P	G.Liebhardt			/P	T.Hughes	P	E.Plank			/P	B.Wolfe
P	R.Glaze							/P	C.Barger	P	J.Coombs			/P	B.Edmondson
/P	F.Oberlin									P	A.Coakley			/P	W.Wilson
/P	E.Barry									/P	M.Cunningham			/P	C.Starkel
/P	L.Swormstedt									/P	H.Schumann				
/P	N.Gibson									/P	B.Bartley				
/P	E.Hughes									/P	J.Holmes				
/P	R.Kroh														

TEAM	G	W	L	PCT	GB	R	OR	AB	H	2B	3B	HR	BB	SO	AVG	OBP	SLG	PRO	PRO+	BR	/A	PF	CHI	RC	SB	CS	SBA	SBR
CHI	154	93	58	.616		570	460	4925	1133	152	52	7	453		.230	.301	.286	.587	91	-47	-33	97	110	531	214			
NY	155	90	61	.596	3	644	543	5095	1354	166	77	17	331		.266	.316	.339	.655	101	58	-5	110	103	644	192			
CLE	157	89	64	.582	5	663	482	5425	1514	240	73	12	330		.279	.325	.357	.682	121	111	121	99	93	735	203			
PHI	149	78	67	.538	12	561	543	4883	1206	213	49	32	385		.247	.308	.330	.638	102	30	12	103	97	581	165			
STL	154	76	73	.510	16	558	498	5030	1244	145	60	22	366		.247	.304	.312	.616	102	-6	18	96	101	579	221			
DET	151	71	78	.477	21	518	599	4930	1195	154	64	10	333		.242	.295	.306	.601	91	-37	-51	103	102	539	206			
WAS	151	55	95	.367	37.5	518	664	4956	1180	144	65	26	306		.238	.289	.309	.598	97	-44	-20	95	103	539	233			
BOS	155	49	105	.318	45.5	463	706	5168	1223	160	75	13	298		.237	.284	.304	.588	89	-66	-65	100	93	503	99			
TOT	613					4495		40412	10049	1374	515	137	2802	4561	.249	.303	.318	.621						1533				

TEAM	CG	SH	SV	IP	H	H/G	HR	BB	SO	RAT	ERA	ERA+	OAV	OOB	PR	/A	PF	CPI	FA	E	DP	FW	PW	BW	SBW	DIF
CHI	117	32	3	1375¹	1212	7.9	11	255	543	9.8	2.13	119	.239	.280	85	63	94	103	.963	243	80	1.8	6.9	-3.6		12.4
NY	99	18	5	1357²	1236	8.2	21	351	605	10.8	2.78	107	.246	.301	-13	28	110	95	.957	272	69	.1	3.1	-.5		11.9
CLE	133	27	4	1412²	1197	7.6	16	365	530	10.3	2.09	125	.232	.289	94	85	97	110	.967	217	111	3.8	9.3	13.3		-14.0
PHI	107	19	4	1322	1135	7.7	9	425	749	11.0	2.60	105	.236	.305	13	17	101	98	.956	267	86	-.2	1.9	1.3		2.5
STL	133	17	5	1357²	1132	7.5	14	314	558	10.0	2.23	116	.230	.284	70	54	96	98	.954	290	80	-1.1	5.9	2.0		-5.3
DET	128	7	4	1334¹	1398	9.4	14	389	469	12.4	3.06	90	.272	.330	-55	-43	103	111	.959	260	86	.4	-4.7	-5.6		6.4
WAS	115	13	1	1322²	1331	9.1	15	451	558	12.4	3.25	81	.265	.331	-83	-91	98	102	.955	279	78	-.8	-10.0	-2.2		-7.0
BOS	124	6	6	1382	1360	8.9	37	285	549	11.0	3.41	81	.262	.306	-111	-106	102	87	.949	335	84	-3.9	-11.7	-7.1		-5.3
TOT	956	139	32	10864¹		8.3				11.0	2.69		.249	.303					.958	2163	674					

Runs		Hits		Doubles		Triples		Home Runs		Total Bases	
Flick-Cle	98	Lajoie-Cle	214	Lajoie-Cle	48	Flick-Cle	22	Davis-Phi	12	Stone-StL	291
Keeler-NY	96	Stone-StL	208	Davis-Phi	42	Stone-StL	20	Hickman-Was	9	Lajoie-Cle	280
Hartsel-Phi	96	Flick-Cle	194	Flick-Cle	34	Crawford-Det	16	Stone-StL	6	Flick-Cle	275
Davis-Phi	94	Chase-NY	193	Murphy-Phi	28	Ferris-Bos	13	Seybold-Phi	5	Davis-Phi	253
Stone-StL	91	Keeler-NY	180	Turner-Cle	27					Chase-NY	236

Runs Batted In		Runs Produced		Bases On Balls		Batting Average		On Base Percentage		Slugging Average	
Davis-Phi	96	Lajoie-Cle	179	Hartsel-Phi	88	Stone-StL	.358	Stone-StL	.417	Stone-StL	.501
Lajoie-Cle	91	Davis-Phi	178	Jones-Chi	83	Lajoie-Cle	.355	Lajoie-Cle	.392	Lajoie-Cle	.465
Davis-Chi	80	Chase-NY	160	E.Hahn-NY-Chi	72	Chase-NY	.323	Flick-Cle	.372	Davis-Phi	.459
Williams-NY	77	Flick-Cle	159	Wallace-StL	58	Congalton-Cle	.320	Hartsel-Phi	.363	Flick-Cle	.441
Chase-NY	76	Stone-StL	156	McIntyre-Det	56	Seybold-Phi	.316	Davis-Phi	.355	Hickman-Was	.421

Production		Adjusted Production		Batter Runs		Adjusted Batter Runs		Clutch Hitting Index		Runs Created	
Stone-StL	.918	Stone-StL	195	Stone-StL	57.8	Stone-StL	63.2	Davis-Phi	154	Stone-StL	141
Lajoie-Cle	.857	Lajoie-Cle	170	Lajoie-Cle	44.9	Lajoie-Cle	46.4	Coughlin-Det	134	Lajoie-Cle	122
Davis-Phi	.815	Flick-Cle	156	Flick-Cle	38.4	Flick-Cle	39.9	Stahl-Was	133	Flick-Cle	121
Flick-Cle	.813	Davis-Phi	150	Davis-Phi	33.1	Davis-Phi	30.2	Wallace-StL	131	Davis-Phi	101
Crawford-Det	.747	Hickman-Was	135	Seybold-Phi	21.1	Hemphill-StL	19.7	Williams-NY	130	Chase-NY	95

Total Average		Stolen Bases		Stolen Base Average	Stolen Base Runs	Fielding Runs		Total Player Rating	
Stone-StL	1.032	Flick-Cle	39			Tannehill-Chi	39.3	Lajoie-Cle	8.4
Flick-Cle	.872	Anderson-Was	39			Lajoie-Cle	30.9	Stone-StL	5.9
Lajoie-Cle	.866	Isbell-Chi	37			Turner-Cle	22.6	Turner-Cle	4.6
Davis-Phi	.846	Altizer-Was	37			Schlafly-Was	14.8	Schlafly-Was	2.9
Hartsel-Phi	.753	Donahue-Chi	36			McIntyre-Det	11.9	Davis-Chi	2.8

Wins		Win Percentage		Games		Complete Games		Shutouts		Saves	
Orth-NY	27	Plank-Phi	.760	Chesbro-NY	49	Orth-NY	36	Walsh-Chi	10	Hess-Cle	3
Chesbro-NY	23	White-Chi	.750	Orth-NY	45	Mullin-Det	35	Joss-Cle	9	Bender-Phi	3
Rhoads-Cle	22	Joss-Cle	.700	Waddell-Phi	43	Hess-Cle	33	Waddell-Phi	8		
Owen-Chi	22	Rhoads-Cle	.688	Hess-Cle	43	Rhoads-Cle	31				
		Owen-Chi	.629	Owen-Chi	42						

Innings Pitched		Fewest Hits/Game		Fewest BB/Game		Strikeouts		Strikeouts/Game		Ratio	
Orth-NY	338.2	Pelty-StL	6.53	Young-Bos	.78	Waddell-Phi	196	Waddell-Phi	6.47	White-Chi	8.33
Hess-Cle	333.2	White-Chi	6.57	Altrock-Chi	1.31	Falkenberg-Was	178	Bender-Phi	6.00	Joss-Cle	8.49
Mullin-Det	330.0	Walsh-Chi	6.95	Joss-Cle	1.37	Walsh-Chi	171	Walsh-Chi	5.53	Walsh-Chi	9.05
Chesbro-NY	325.0	Joss-Cle	7.02	White-Chi	1.56	Hess-Cle	167	Falkenberg-Was	5.36	Pelty-StL	9.18
Rhoads-Cle	315.0	Powell-StL	7.23	Jacobson-StL	1.57	Bender-Phi	159	Powell-StL	4.87	Powell-StL	9.55

Earned Run Average		Adjusted ERA		Opponents' Batting Avg.		Opponents' On Base Pct.		Starter Runs		Adjusted Starter Runs	
White-Chi	1.52	White-Chi	167	Pelty-StL	.206	White-Chi	.249	Pelty-StL	31.9	Hess-Cle	29.0
Pelty-StL	1.59	Pelty-StL	163	White-Chi	.207	Joss-Cle	.252	Hess-Cle	31.7	Pelty-StL	28.8
Joss-Cle	1.72	Joss-Cle	152	Walsh-Chi	.217	Walsh-Chi	.265	Rhoads-Cle	31.1	Rhoads-Cle	28.6
Powell-StL	1.77	Powell-StL	146	Joss-Cle	.218	Pelty-StL	.267	Joss-Cle	30.3	Joss-Cle	28.0
Rhoads-Cle	1.80	Rhoads-Cle	145	Powell-StL	.223	Powell-StL	.275	White-Chi	28.6	White-Chi	24.9

Clutch Pitching Index		Relief Runs	Adjusted Relief Runs	Relief Ranking	Total Pitcher Index		Total Baseball Ranking	
Rhoads-Cle	126				Orth-NY	3.7	Lajoie-Cle	8.4
Siever-Det	125				Joss-Cle	3.7	Stone-StL	5.9
Hess-Cle	124				White-Chi	3.6	Turner-Cle	4.6
Smith-Was	121				Pelty-StL	3.3	Orth-NY	3.9
Donahue-Det	121				Hess-Cle	3.3	Joss-Cle	3.7

January 10 John McGraw stops a runaway team of horses in Los Angeles, saving two young women from injury.

January 28 In an effort to reduce playing-date conflicts between their leagues, presidents Pulliam and Johnson meet to plan schedules. Conflicting dates are reduced to 27.

March 4 A judgment of $52,000 is awarded to the Baltimore club from Brooklyn. When Baltimore left the NL in 1903, Brooklyn agreed to pay $40,000 for the franchise but never did. The award includes interest.

April 11 On a cold day in New York, the Giants open against the Phillies before 16,000. A late snowstorm has been cleared, but there are large piles of snow surrounding the field. Frank Corridon is in the eighth inning of a shutout for the Giants when fans, who have been pelting the players with snowballs, begin jumping from the stands and running around the outfield. There are no police on duty at the park, so umpire Bill Klem forfeits the game, 9-0 to the Phils.

April 11 New York catcher Roger Bresnahan appears wearing shin guards for the first time in a major league game,

although the Phils' Red Dooin had worn papier-mache guards under his stockings in 1906 while catching and at bat. It will be a few years before detachable guards are adopted by all catchers.

June 19 Miller Huggins, diminutive second baseman of the Reds, leads off a home game against New York with a homer off Christy Mathewson. The rare occurrence (he hits only nine in his career) astonishes the home town fans, and they celebrate by presenting him with a pair of shoes, a gold watch, a five-pound box of chocolates, a scarf pin, and a Morris chair.

July 8 Bombarded by pop bottles in Brooklyn, irate Cubs manager Frank Chance throws one back into the stands where it cuts a boy's leg. Chance is mobbed and leaves the park in an armored car with a police escort after the Cubs' 5-0 victory.

July 23* The Austin Senators (Texas League) steal 23 bases and beat San Antonio, 44-0.

July 30 Cincinnati manager Ned Hanlon, whose managing days began in 1889 at Pittsburgh, announces this will be his last season. His record includes five pen-

nants—four at Baltimore, one at Brooklyn.

August 11 In the second game of a doubleheader, shortened to seven innings by prior agreement, St. Louis Cardinals hurler Ed Karger pitches a perfect game, 4-0, against Boston.

September 1 Cubs pitcher Ed Reulbach, who will be 17-4 with a 1.69 ERA, goes into the ninth with a 2-0 lead over the Cardinals at Chicago. He gives up eight straight hits, seven runs, and loses the game.

September 30 Cardinals first baseman Ed Konetchy steals home twice in St. Louis' game against Boston. St. Louis sets a major league one-game record with three steals of home as Joe Delahanty also scores with a swipe of home in the eighth.

October 12 Three Finger Brown shuts out the Tigers, 2-0, to give Chicago a world championship. Each side has seven hits, but the Cubs steal four bases, giving them a total of 18 for the five-game series. The Cubs' staff has an ERA for the Series of 0.75, and the Tigers' big guns, Ty Cobb and Sam Crawford, score only one run apiece.

	BOSTON		BROOKLYN		CHICAGO		CINCINNATI		NEW YORK		PHILADELPHIA		PITTSBURGH		ST.LOUIS
M	F.Tenney	M	P.Donovan	M	F.Chance	M	N.Hanlon	M	J.McGraw	M	B.Murray	M	F.Clarke	M	J.McCloskey
1B	F.Tenney	1B	T.Jordan	1B	F.Chance	1B	J.Ganzel	1B	D.McGann	1B	K.Bransfield	1B	J.Nealon	1B	E.Konetchy
2B	C.Ritchey	2B	W.Alperman	2B	J.Evers	2B	M.Huggins	2B	L.Doyle	2B	O.Knabe	2B	E.Abbaticchio	2B	P.Bennett
SS	A.Bridwell	SS	P.Lewis	SS	J.Tinker	SS	H.Lobert	SS	B.Dahlen	SS	M.Doolan	SS	H.Wagner	SS	E.Holly
3B	D.Brain	3B	D.Casey	3B	H.Steinfeldt	3B	M.Mowrey	3B	A.Devlin	3B	E.Courtney	3B	A.Storke	3B	B.Byrne
LF	N.Randall	LF	E.Batch	LF	J.Sheckard	LF	F.Odwell	LF	S.Shannon	LF	S.Magee	LF	F.Clarke	LF	R.Murray
CF	G.Beaumont	CF	B.Maloney	CF	J.Slagle	CF	A.Kruger	CF	C.Seymour	CF	R.Thomas	CF	T.Leach	CF	J.Burnett
RF	J.Bates	RF	H.Lumley	RF	F.Schulte	RF	M.Mitchell	RF	G.Browne	RF	J.Titus	RF	G.Anderson	RF	S.Barry
C	T.Needham	C	L.Ritter	C	J.Kling	C	L.McLean	C	R.Bresnahan	C	R.Dooin	O	G.Gibson	C	D.Marshall
C	S.Brown	2O	J.Hummel	OS	S.Hofman	C1	F.Bowerman	3	E.Grant	O	B.Hallman	21	A.Hoelskoetter
3S	B.Sweeney	C	B.Bergen	C	P.Moran	O3	J.Kane	O2	S.Strang	C	F.Jacklitsch	3S	T.Sheehan	C	P.Noonan
O	D.Howard	O	A.Burch	1	D.Howard	C	A.Schlei	2	T.Corcoran	O	F.Osborn	C	E.Phelps	O	J.Kelly
O	F.Burke	O	J.McCarthy	O	N.Randall	O	D.Paskert	13	J.Hannifin	2	K.Gleason	1	H.Swacina	O	T.O'Hara
O	I.Hoffman	C	J.Butler	/C	M.Kahoe	/O	M.O'Neill	2	D.Shay	/S	P.Sentell	O	O.Clymer	O	A.Burch
C	J.Ball	/C	J.Hurley	/S	B.Sweeney	/O	C.Autry	1	F.Merkle			O	D.Moeller	1	J.Beckley
/C	J.Orndorff	/O	E.McLane	/2	H.Zimmerman	/C	H.Wolter	/C	M.Fitzgerald	P	F.Corridon	C	H.Smith	O	H.Wolter
/C	J.Knotts	/O	P.Donovan	/C	J.Hardy	/C	B.McCarthy	/C	H.Curtis	P	T.Sparks	/3	B.McKechnie	O	B.Hopkins
/S	O.Westerberg					/C	P.Lamer	/1	M.Pfyl	P	L.Moren	/O	H.Maggert	/1	H.Arndt
/C	T.Asmussen	P	N.Rucker	P	O.Overall	H	E.Tiemeyer	/O	H.Wade	P	B.Brown	/C	B.Kelsey	O	A.Shaw
/1	B.Brush	P	G.Bell	P	M.Brown					P	L.Richie	/S	M.Campbell	/S	F.Crawford
		P	E.Stricklett	P	C.Lundgren	P	B.Ewing	P	C.Mathewson					/O	J.Delahanty
P	G.Dorner	P	J.Pastorius	P	J.Pfiester	P	A.Coakley	P	J.McGinnity	P	T.Pittinger	P	V.Willis	/1	J.Baxter
P	V.Lindaman	P	H.McIntire	P	E.Reulbach	P	J.Weimer	P	R.Ames	/P	J.Lush	P	L.Leifield		
P	I.Young			P	C.Fraser	P	R.Hitt	P	H.Wiltse	/P	G.McQuillan	P	S.Leever	P	S.McGlynn
P	P.Flaherty	P	D.Scanlan	P	J.Taylor	P	D.Mason	P	D.Taylor	/P	B.Duggleby	P	D.Phillippe	P	E.Karger
P	B.Pfeffer	/P	W.Henley	/P	K.Durbin					/P	H.Coveleski	P	H.Camnitz	P	F.Beebe
		/P	J.Whiting			P	F.Smith	P	M.Lynch	/P	J.McCloskey			P	A.Fromme
P	J.Boultes					P	C.Hall	P	G.Ferguson			/P	N.Maddox	P	J.Lush
/P	S.Frock					/P	B.Spade	/P	R.Beecher			/P	B.Duggleby		
/P	F.Barberich					/P	B.Essick	/P	H.Mathewson			/P	M.Lynch	/P	B.Raymond
/P	R.Dessau					/P	B.Campbell					/P	B.Adams	/P	B.Brown
/P	E.Lindemann					/P	C.Minahan					/P	B.Otey	/P	C.Shields
						/P	F.Leary					/P	K.Brady	/P	C.Druhot
												/P	H.Wolter		
												/P	C.Walsh		

TEAM	G	W	L	PCT	GB	R	OR	AB	H	2B	3B	HR	BB	SO	AVG	OBP	SLG	PRO	PRO+	BR	/A	PF	CHI	RC	SB	CS	SBA	SBR
CHI	155	107	45	.704		574	390	4892	1224	162	48	13	435		.250	.318	.311	.629	98	25	-10	106	104	596	235			
PIT	157	91	63	.591	17	634	510	4957	1261	133	78	19	469		.254	.325	.324	.649	109	62	54	101	106	645	264			
PHI	149	83	64	.565	21.5	512	476	4725	1113	162	65	12	424		.236	.304	.305	.609	99	-11	-4	99	104	514	154			
NY	155	82	71	.536	25.5	574	510	4874	1222	160	48	23	516		.251	.331	.317	.648	107	68	49	103	96	617	205			
BRO	153	65	83	.439	40	446	522	4895	1135	142	63	18	336		.232	.287	.298	.585	98	-62	-26	92	98	488	121			
CIN	156	66	87	.431	41.5	526	519	4966	1226	126	90	15	372		.247	.304	.318	.622	98	3	-19	104	99	564	158			
BOS	152	58	90	.392	47	502	652	5020	1222	142	61	22	413		.243	.308	.309	.617	100	2	4	100	94	545	118			
STL	155	52	101	.340	55.5	419	608	5008	1163	121	51	19	312		.232	.283	.288	.571	88	-87	-73	97	97	474	125			
TOT	616					4187		39337	9566	1148	504	141	3277	4217	.243	.308	.309	.616							1380			

TEAM	CG	SH	SV	IP	H	H/G	HR	BB	SO	RAT	ERA	ERA+	OAV	OOB	PR	/A	PF	CPI	FA	E	DP	FW	PW	BW	SBW	DIF
CHI	114	32	8	1373¹	1054	6.9	11	402	586	9.8	1.73	144	.216	.281	112	115	101	101	.967	211	110	3.1	13.1	-1.1		16.0
PIT	111	24	5	1363	1207	8.0	12	368	497	10.7	2.30	106	.241	.299	25	19	99	99	.959	256	75	.2	2.2	6.1		5.5
PHI	110	21	4	1299¹	1095	7.6	13	422	499	10.9	2.43	99	.233	.304	5	-3	98	94	.957	256	104	-.7	-.3	-.5		11.0
NY	109	22	13	1371	1219	8.0	25	369	655	10.7	2.45	101	.238	.294	2	1	100	90	.963	232	75	1.6	.1	5.6		-1.8
BRO	125	20	1	1356¹	1218	8.1	16	463	479	11.4	2.38	98	.249	.319	12	-9	95	113	.959	262	94	-.7	-1.0	-3.0		-4.4
CIN	118	10	2	1351¹	1223	8.1	16	444	481	11.5	2.41	107	.251	.322	8	25	105	114	.963	227	118	2.1	2.8	-2.2		-13.3
BOS	121	9	2	1338²	1324	8.9	28	458	426	12.4	3.33	76	.268	.339	-129	-119	103	98	.961	249	128	.1	-13.5	.5		-3.1
STL	127	19	2	1365²	1212	8.0	20	500	594	11.6	2.70	93	.243	.318	-35	-32	101	97	.948	340	105	-5.8	-3.6	-8.3		-6.8
TOT	935	157	37	10818²		7.9				11.1	2.46		.243	.308					.960	2033	809					

Runs		Hits		Doubles		Triples		Home Runs		Total Bases	
Shannon-NY	104	Beaumont-Bos	187	Wagner-Pit	38	Ganzel-Cin	16	Brain-Bos	10	Wagner-Pit	264
Leach-Pit	102	Wagner-Pit	180	Magee-Phi	28	Alperman-Bro	16	Lumley-Bro	9	Beaumont-Bos	246
Wagner-Pit	98	Leach-Pit	166	Steinfeldt-Chi	25	Wagner-Pit	14	Murray-StL	7	Magee-Phi	229
Clarke-Pit	97	Magee-Phi	165	Seymour-NY	25	Beaumont-Bos	14	Wagner-Pit	6	Leach-Pit	221
Tenney-Bos	83	Mitchell-Cin	163	Brain-Bos	24	Clarke-Pit	13	Browne-NY	5	Brain-Bos	214

Runs Batted In		Runs Produced		Bases On Balls		Batting Average		On Base Percentage		Slugging Average	
Magee-Phi	85	Wagner-Pit	174	Thomas-Phi	83	Wagner-Pit	.350	Wagner-Pit	.408	Wagner-Pit	.513
Wagner-Pit	82	Magee-Phi	156	Huggins-Cin	83	Magee-Phi	.328	Magee-Phi	.396	Magee-Phi	.455
Abbaticchio-Pit	82	Clarke-Pit	154	Tenney-Bos	82	Beaumont-Bos	.322	Clarke-Pit	.383	Lumley-Bro	.425
Seymour-NY	75	Abbaticchio-Pit	143	Shannon-NY	82	Leach-Pit	.303	Devlin-NY	.376	Beaumont-Bos	.424
Steinfeldt-Chi	70	Leach-Pit	141	Anderson-Pit	80	Seymour-NY	.294	Thomas-Phi	.374	Brain-Bos	.420

Production		Adjusted Production		Batter Runs		Adjusted Batter Runs		Clutch Hitting Index		Runs Created	
Wagner-Pit	.921	Wagner-Pit	186	Wagner-Pit	50.5	Wagner-Pit	49.1	Abbaticchio-Pit	166	Wagner-Pit	137
Magee-Phi	.852	Magee-Phi	169	Magee-Phi	38.4	Magee-Phi	39.8	Seymour-NY	130	Magee-Phi	113
Beaumont-Bos	.790	Beaumont-Bos	148	Beaumont-Bos	29.5	Beaumont-Bos	29.8	Steinfeldt-Chi	130	Beaumont-Bos	103
Clarke-Pit	.772	Lumley-Bro	144	Clarke-Pit	26.5	Clarke-Pit	25.4	Devlin-NY	126	Leach-Pit	98
Leach-Pit	.756	Jordan-Bro	141	Leach-Pit	21.4	Jordan-Bro	25.3	Magee-Phi	121	Clarke-Pit	93

Total Average		Stolen Bases		Stolen Base Average		Stolen Base Runs		Fielding Runs		Total Player Rating	
Wagner-Pit	1.122	Wagner-Pit	61					Evers-Chi	27.7	Wagner-Pit	6.3
Magee-Phi	.982	Magee-Phi	46					Brain-Bos	24.8	Brain-Bos	5.0
Clarke-Pit	.865	Evers-Chi	46					Mitchell-Cin	22.2	Magee-Phi	4.6
Leach-Pit	.801	Leach-Pit	43					Byrne-StL	22.1	Beaumont-Bos	3.2
Beaumont-Bos	.791	Devlin-NY	38					Tinker-Chi	15.7	Mitchell-Cin	3.2

Wins		Win Percentage		Games		Complete Games		Shutouts		Saves	
Mathewson-NY	24	Reulbach-Chi	.810	McGinnity-NY	47	McGlynn-StL	33	Overall-Chi	8	McGinnity-NY	4
Overall-Chi	23	Brown-Chi	.769	McGlynn-StL	45	Ewing-Cin	32	Mathewson-NY	8	Overall-Chi	3
Sparks-Phi	22	Overall-Chi	.767	Mathewson-NY	41	Mathewson-NY	31	Lundgren-Chi	7	Brown-Chi	3
Willis-Pit	21	Sparks-Phi	.733	Ewing-Cin	41	Karger-StL	29				
		Lundgren-Chi	.720			Willis-Pit	27				

Innings Pitched		Fewest Hits/Game		Fewest BB/Game		Strikeouts		Strikeouts/Game		Ratio	
McGlynn-StL	352.1	Lundgren-Chi	5.65	Phillippe-Pit	1.51	Mathewson-NY	178	Ames-NY	5.63	Mathewson-NY	8.71
Ewing-Cin	332.2	Pfiester-Chi	6.60	Mathewson-NY	1.51	Ewing-Cin	147	Beebe-StL	5.32	Brown-Chi	8.73
Mathewson-NY	315.0	Overall-Chi	6.74	Brown-Chi	1.55	Ames-NY	146	Mathewson-NY	5.09	Pfiester-Chi	9.05
Karger-StL	314.0	Camnitz-Pit	6.75	McGinnity-NY	1.68	Overall-Chi	141	Overall-Chi	4.73	Overall-Chi	9.42
McGinnity-NY	310.1	Reulbach-Chi	6.89	Sparks-Phi	1.73	Beebe-StL	141	Reulbach-Chi	4.50	Sparks-Phi	9.48

Earned Run Average		Adjusted ERA		Opponents' Batting Avg.		Opponents' On Base Pct.		Starter Runs		Adjusted Starter Runs	
Pfiester-Chi	1.15	Pfiester-Chi	215	Lundgren-Chi	.185	Mathewson-NY	.247	Lundgren-Chi	29.7	Ewing-Cin	31.6
Lundgren-Chi	1.17	Lundgren-Chi	212	Pfiester-Chi	.207	Brown-Chi	.262	Pfiester-Chi	28.4	Lundgren-Chi	30.2
Brown-Chi	1.39	Brown-Chi	179	Overall-Chi	.208	Pfiester-Chi	.263	Brown-Chi	27.8	Pfiester-Chi	28.9
Leever-Pit	1.66	Ewing-Cin	149	Camnitz-Pit	.211	Overall-Chi	.268	Ewing-Cin	27.1	Brown-Chi	28.4
Overall-Chi	1.68	Overall-Chi	148	Mathewson-NY	.212	Karger-StL	.270	Overall-Chi	23.5	Overall-Chi	24.1

Clutch Pitching Index		Relief Runs		Adjusted Relief Runs		Relief Ranking		Total Pitcher Index		Total Baseball Ranking	
Coakley-Cin	133							Brown-Chi	4.0	Wagner-Pit	6.3
Pastorius-Bro	129							Lundgren-Chi	3.6	Brain-Bos	5.0
Brown-StL-Phi	126							Overall-Chi	3.5	Magee-Phi	4.6
McIntire-Bro	125							Pfiester-Chi	3.1	Brown-Chi	3.9
Leifield-Pit	122							Ewing-Cin	2.9	Lundgren-Chi	3.6

March 28 Boston outfielder Chick Stahl, who replaced Jimmy Collins as manager of the newly renamed Red Sox at the end of the 1906 season, commits suicide at spring training. After breakfast he returned to his room and drank four ounces of carbolic acid. He left a note: "Boys, I just couldn't help it. You drove me to it." Cy Young starts the season as manager, but there will be three others during the year.

April 15 The Cleveland club takes out a $100,000 policy to insure its players against injury in railroad accidents.

April 19 Ed Walsh has his sinker working as he fields 11 assists and two putouts during a 1–0 win over the Browns. His total of 13 chances ties the mark Nick Altrock set in 1904.

May 14 The flagpole at the White Sox ballpark, South Side Park, breaks during the pennant-raising ceremonies celebrating the 1906 championship.

June 13 The Boston Red Sox play an exhibition game at Providence, raising $3,140.50 for Chick Stahl's widow.

June 28 Washington steals a record 13 bases off catcher Branch Rickey in the Nationals' 16-5 win over New York. Rickey will spend the rest of the season in the outfield or at first base for the Highlanders.

July 16 Ed Walsh sets another fielding record for pitchers, handling 12 assists and three putouts in a 13-inning game.

August 2 Walter Johnson, 19, debuts with Washington and loses, 3-2, to Detroit. The first hit off him is a bunt single by Ty Cobb.

August 15 Chief Bender wins his 11th straight for the Athletics 4–2 over Cleveland, to tighten the race with the Tigers.

September 4 For his 32nd birthday tomorrow, Cleveland fans give manager Nap Lajoie a wagonload of gifts, including a live black sheep. Addie Joss pitches a one-hitter against Detroit.

September 30 An overflow crowd lines the outfield at Philadelphia's Columbia Park for the showdown doubleheader between the A's and Tigers, who are neck-and-neck in the pennant race. In the first game, the home team gets off to a 7-1 lead against 25-game winner Bill Donovan. But Rube Waddell, who relieves in the second, fails to hold the lead. A two-run home run by Ty Cobb ties it 8-8 in the ninth. Both teams score once in the 11th; an umpire's ruling costs Philadelphia the game in the 14th. Harry Davis hits a long fly into the crowd in left center field, ordinarily a ground rule double. As Tigers center fielder Sam Crawford goes to the crowd's edge, a policeman stands up and moves, either to interfere or to get out of the way. Home plate umpire Silk O'Loughlin says there is no interference, then reverses his ruling when base umpire Tom Connolly offers a different opinion. When play resumes, the Athletics' Danny Murphy hits a long single that would have scored Davis. The game is called because of darkness in the 17th, a 9-9 tie. The second game is never played. The Tigers, in first place, leave for Washington where they will win four. They will finish 1½ games in front.

October 2 Ty Cobb's 200th hit earns him a $500 bonus; he will wind up with 212 hits for the year.

October 8 With two out in the bottom of the ninth and the Tigers leading the Cubs, 3-2, Chicago pinch hitter Del Howard strikes out, but Detroit catcher Charlie "Boss" Schmidt drops the third strike, and the tying run scores. The game will eventually be called because of darkness, a 12-inning 3-3 tie.

	BOSTON		CHICAGO		CLEVELAND		DETROIT		NEW YORK		PHILADELPHIA		ST.LOUIS		WASHINGTON
M	C.Young	M	F.Jones	M	N.Lajoie	M	H.Jennings	M	C.Griffith	M	C.Mack	M	J.McAleer	M	J.Cantillon
M	G.Huff	1B	J.Donahue	1B	G.Stovall	1B	C.Rossman	1B	H.Chase	1B	H.Davis	1B	T.Jones	1B	J.Anderson
M	B.Unglaub	2B	F.Isbell	1B	N.Lajoie	2B	R.Downs	2B	J.Williams	2B	D.Murphy	2B	H.Niles	2B	J.Delahanty
M	D.McGuire	SS	G.Davis	2B	T.Turner	SS	C.O'Leary	SS	K.Elberfeld	SS	S.Nicholls	SS	B.Wallace	SS	D.Altizer
1B	B.Unglaub	3B	G.Rohe	3B	B.Bradley	3B	B.Coughlin	3B	G.Moriarty	3B	J.Collins	3B	J.Yeager	3B	B.Shipke
2B	H.Ferris	LF	P.Dougherty	LF	B.Hinchman	LF	D.Jones	LF	W.Conroy	LF	T.Hartsel	LF	G.Stone	LF	O.Clymer
SS	H.Wagner	CF	F.Jones	CF	J.Birmingham	CF	S.Crawford	CF	D.Hoffman	CF	R.Oldring	CF	C.Hemphill	CF	C.Jones
3B	J.Knight	RF	E.Hahn	RF	E.Flick	RF	T.Cobb	RF	W.Keeler	RF	S.Seybold	RF	O.Pickering	RF	B.Ganley
LF	J.Barrett	C	B.Sullivan	C	N.Clarke	C	B.Schmidt	C	R.Kleinow	C	O.Schreckengost	C	T.Spencer	C	J.Warner
CF	D.Sullivan														
RF	B.Congalton	3	L.Quillen	C	H.Bemis	2S	G.Schaefer	3O	F.LaPorte	S	M.Cross	32	R.Hartzell	2O	R.Nill
C	L.Criger	C	E.McFarland	23	P.O'Brien	C	F.Payne	S	I.Thomas	O	B.Lord	C	J.Stephens	1O	C.Hickman
		3	L.Tannehill	O	H.Bay	O	M.McIntyre	OC	B.Rickey	3	D.Powers	3	J.Delahanty	C	C.Milan
OS	F.Parent	C	H.Hart	1	P.Lister	C	J.Archer	O	R.Bell	3	J.Knight	C	J.O'Connor	C	M.Heydon
C	A.Shaw	O	M.Welday	O	F.Delahanty	3	B.Lowe	S	N.Ball	/S	E.Collins	C	F.Buelow	3	L.Cross
1O	M.Grimshaw	/O	C.Hickman	2	H.Hinchman	/C	T.Erwin	/C	W.Blair	/C	C.Berry	2	K.Butler	2S	N.Perrine
3	J.Collins	/3	J.Atz	/3	R.Nill	/2	H.Jennings	/3	B.Louden			H	E.Frisk	S	T.Smith
O	J.Hoey	/C	C.Armbruster	C	H.Wakefield	/O	R.Killefer	/C	D.McGuire	P	E.Plank	R	J.McAleer	3S	P.O'Brien
C	C.Armbruster			/O	B.Congalton					P	R.Waddell			C	C.Blankenship
O	C.Chadbourne	P	E.Walsh			P	G.Mullin	P	A.Orth	P	J.Dygert	P	H.Howell	2	L.Schlafly
3	H.Lord	P	F.Smith	P	A.Joss	P	E.Killian	P	J.Chesbro	P	C.Bender	P	B.Pelty	O	B.Kay
/O	T.Speaker	P	D.White	P	G.Liebhardt	P	E.Siever	P	S.Doyle	P	J.Coombs	P	J.Powell	C	B.Block
/C	B.Peterson	P	N.Altrock	P	B.Rhoads	P	B.Donovan	P	B.Hogg			P	F.Glade	C	M.Kahoe
/O	B.Freeman	P	R.Patterson	P	J.Thielman			P	D.Newton	P	B.Bartley	P	B.Dinneen	/C	O.Shannon
/O	G.Whiteman					P	J.Eubank			P	R.Vickers				
H	D.McGuire	P	F.Owen	P	O.Hess	P	E.Willett	P	E.Moore	/P	C.Fritz	/P	B.Jacobson	P	C.Smith
		/P	L.Fiene	P	W.Clarkson	P	E.Jones	P	F.Kitson	/P	G.Craig	P	C.Morgan	P	C.Patten
P	C.Young			P	H.Berger	/P	H.Malloy	P	B.Keefe	P	S.Hope	P	B.Bailey	P	C.Falkenberg
P	G.Winter			/P	B.Bernhard			P	T.Neuer			/P	B.McGill	P	T.Hughes
P	R.Glaze			/P	E.Moore			/P	L.Brockett					P	W.Johnson
P	T.Pruiett							/P	T.Hughes						
P	J.Tannehill							/P	R.Tift					P	O.Graham
								/P	W.Clarkson					P	H.Gehring
P	C.Morgan							/P	R.Castleton					P	F.Oberlin
P	J.Harris							/P	R.Manning					/P	F.Kitson
P	F.Oberlin							/P	C.Griffith					/P	S.Lanford
/P	R.Kroh							/P	C.Barger					/P	J.McDonald
/P	B.Dinneen													/P	B.Durham
/P	E.Barry													/P	S.Edmonston
/P	E.Steele													/P	D.Tonkin
/P	F.Burchell														
/P	B.Jacobson														

TEAM	G	W	L	PCT	GB	R	OR	AB	H	2B	3B	HR	BB	SO	AVG	OBP	SLG	PRO	PRO+	BR	/A	PF	CHI	RC	SB	CS	SBA	SBR
DET	153	92	58	.613		694	532	5204	1383	179	75	11	315		.266	.313	.335	.648	108	63	40	104	110	641	192			
PHI	150	88	57	.607	1.5	582	511	5010	1276	220	44	22	384		.255	.311	.329	.640	106	51	36	102	96	592	137			
CHI	157	87	64	.576	5.5	588	474	5070	1205	149	33	5	421		.238	.302	.283	.585	95	-37	-19	97	111	523	175			
CLE	158	85	67	.559	8	530	525	5068	1221	182	68	11	335		.241	.295	.310	.605	97	-12	-16	101	97	555	193			
NY	152	70	78	.473	21	605	665	5044	1258	150	67	15	304		.249	.299	.315	.614	93	1	-44	110	110	565	206			
STL	155	69	83	.454	24	542	555	5224	1324	154	63	10	370		.253	.308	.313	.621	96	18	20	100	91	580	144			
BOS	155	59	90	.396	32.5	464	558	5235	1224	154	48	18	305		.234	.281	.292	.573	89	-76	-72	99	94	493	125			
WAS	154	49	102	.325	43.5	506	691	5112	1243	134	57	12	390		.243	.304	.299	.603	105	-9	34	92	91	563	223			
TOT	617					4511		40967	10134	1322	455	104	2824	4479	.247	.302	.309	.611							1395			

TEAM	CG	SH	SV	IP	H	H/G	HR	BB	SO	RAT	ERA	ERA+	OAV	OOB	PR	/A	PF	CPI	FA	E	DP	FW	PW	BW	SBW	DIF
DET	120	15	7	1370²	1281	8.4	8	380	512	11.2	2.33	112	.251	.309	32	40	102	114	.959	260	79	1.0	4.4	4.4		7.2
PHI	106	27	6	1354²	1106	7.3	13	378	789	10.3	2.35	111	.226	.290	29	38	102	91	.958	263	67	.4	4.2	4.0		7.0
CHI	112	17	9	1406¹	1279	8.2	13	305	604	10.3	2.22	108	.245	.290	50	26	94	105	.966	233	101	3.4	2.9	-2.1		7.4
CLE	127	20	5	1392²	1253	8.1	8	362	513	10.8	2.26	111	.244	.300	43	36	99	108	.960	264	137	1.3	4.0	-1.8		5.5
NY	93	10	5	1333²	1327	9.0	13	428	511	12.2	3.03	92	.262	.325	-73	-35	110	92	.947	334	79	-4.4	-3.9	-4.9		9.1
STL	129	15	9	1381¹	1254	8.2	17	352	463	10.8	2.61	96	.245	.300	-10	-16	99	96	.959	266	97	.8	-1.8	2.2		-8.2
BOS	100	17	7	1414	1222	7.8	22	337	517	10.2	2.45	105	.236	.288	14	18	101	92	.959	274	100	.2	2.0	-8.0		-9.8
WAS	106	12	5	1351¹	1383	9.2	10	344	570	11.8	3.11	78	.268	.320	-86	-106	95	97	.951	310	69	-2.4	-11.7	3.8		-16.1
TOT	893	133	53	11004²		8.3				10.9	2.54		.247	.302					.958	2204	729					

Runs		Hits		Doubles		Triples		Home Runs		Total Bases	
Crawford-Det	102	Cobb-Det	212	Davis-Phi	35	Flick-Cle	18	Davis-Phi	8	Cobb-Det	283
D.Jones-Det	101	Stone-StL	191	Crawford-Det	34	Crawford-Det	17	Seybold-Phi	5	Crawford-Det	268
Cobb-Det	97	Crawford-Det	188	Lajoie-Cle	30	Cobb-Det	14	Hoffman-NY	5	Stone-StL	238
Hartsel-Phi	93	Ganley-Was	167	J.Collins-Bos-Phi	29	Unglaub-Bos	13	Cobb-Det	5	Davis-Phi	230
Hahn-Chi	87	Flick-Cle	166	Seybold-Phi	29					Flick-Cle	226

Runs Batted In		Runs Produced		Bases On Balls		Batting Average		On Base Percentage		Slugging Average	
Cobb-Det	119	Cobb-Det	211	Hartsel-Phi	106	Cobb-Det	.350	Hartsel-Phi	.405	Cobb-Det	.468
Seybold-Phi	92	Crawford-Det	179	Hahn-Chi	84	Crawford-Det	.323	Stone-StL	.387	Crawford-Det	.460
Davis-Phi	87	Davis-Phi	163	Jones-Chi	67	Stone-StL	.320	Flick-Cle	.386	Flick-Cle	.412
Crawford-Det	81	Seybold-Phi	145	Flick-Cle	64	Flick-Cle	.302	Cobb-Det	.380	Stone-StL	.399
Wallace-StL	70	Donahue-Chi	143	D.Jones-Det	60	Nicholls-Phi	.302	Crawford-Det	.366	Davis-Phi	.395

Production		Adjusted Production		Batter Runs		Adjusted Batter Runs		Clutch Hitting Index		Runs Created	
Cobb-Det	.848	Cobb-Det	164	Cobb-Det	44.2	Cobb-Det	40.4	Seybold-Phi	150	Cobb-Det	130
Crawford-Det	.826	Crawford-Det	157	Crawford-Det	38.6	Stone-StL	35.7	Cobb-Det	143	Crawford-Det	108
Flick-Cle	.798	Flick-Cle	153	Flick-Cle	35.7	Crawford-Det	35.0	Donahue-Chi	134	Flick-Cle	107
Stone-StL	.787	Stone-StL	151	Stone-StL	35.4	Flick-Cle	34.9	Chase-NY	133	Stone-StL	105
Hartsel-Phi	.771	Hartsel-Phi	143	Hartsel-Phi	33.0	Hartsel-Phi	30.7	Wallace-StL	133	Hartsel-Phi	87

Total Average		Stolen Bases		Stolen Base Average		Stolen Base Runs		Fielding Runs		Total Player Rating	
Cobb-Det	.919	Cobb-Det	49					Lajoie-Cle	45.9	Lajoie-Cle	6.7
Flick-Cle	.893	Flick-Cle	41					Donahue-Chi	20.6	Cobb-Det	5.0
Hartsel-Phi	.855	Conroy-NY	41					Murphy-Phi	13.5	Crawford-Det	4.1
Crawford-Det	.825	Ganley-Was	40					Ferris-Bos	13.4	Flick-Cle	3.3
Stone-StL	.805	Altizer-Was	38					D.Jones-Det	13.2	Stone-StL	2.9

Wins		Win Percentage		Games		Complete Games		Shutouts		Saves	
White-Chi	27	Donovan-Det	.862	Walsh-Chi	56	Walsh-Chi	37	Plank-Phi	8	Dinneen-Bos-StL	4
Joss-Cle	27	Dygert-Phi	.724	White-Chi	46	Mullin-Det	35	Waddell-Phi	7	Walsh-Chi	4
Killian-Det	25	Joss-Cle	.711	Mullin-Det	46	Joss-Cle	34	Young-Bos	6	Hughes-Was	4
Donovan-Det	25	Smith-Chi	.697	Waddell-Phi	44	Young-Bos	33	White-Chi	6		
		White-Chi	.675			Plank-Phi	33	Joss-Cle	6		

Innings Pitched		Fewest Hits/Game		Fewest BB/Game		Strikeouts		Strikeouts/Game		Ratio	
Walsh-Chi	422.1	Dygert-Phi	6.88	White-Chi	1.18	Waddell-Phi	232	Waddell-Phi	7.33	Young-Bos	9.02
Mullin-Det	357.1	Winter-Bos	6.94	Altrock-Chi	1.31	Walsh-Chi	206	Dygert-Phi	5.19	Joss-Cle	9.04
Plank-Phi	343.2	Walsh-Chi	7.27	Young-Bos	1.34	Plank-Phi	183	Plank-Phi	4.79	Bender-Phi	9.11
Young-Bos	343.1	Howell-StL	7.34	Bender-Phi	1.40	Dygert-Phi	151	Bender-Phi	4.60	Winter-Bos	9.19
Joss-Cle	338.2	Donovan-Det	7.37	Joss-Cle	1.44	Young-Bos	147	Walsh-Chi	4.39	Walsh-Chi	9.29

Earned Run Average		Adjusted ERA		Opponents' Batting Avg.		Opponents' On Base Pct.		Starter Runs		Adjusted Starter Runs	
Walsh-Chi	1.60	Walsh-Chi	150	Dygert-Phi	.214	Young-Bos	.263	Walsh-Chi	44.2	Walsh-Chi	37.3
Killian-Det	1.78	Killian-Det	146	Winter-Bos	.216	Joss-Cle	.264	Killian-Det	26.6	Killian-Det	28.8
Joss-Cle	1.83	Joss-Cle	136	Walsh-Chi	.224	Bender-Phi	.265	Joss-Cle	26.6	Joss-Cle	25.2
Howell-StL	1.93	Howell-StL	130	Howell-StL	.225	Winter-Bos	.267	Howell-StL	21.3	Young-Bos	22.1
Young-Bos	1.99	Young-Bos	129	Donovan-Det	.226	Walsh-Chi	.269	Young-Bos	20.9	Howell-StL	20.2

Clutch Pitching Index		Relief Runs		Adjusted Relief Runs		Relief Ranking		Total Pitcher Index		Total Baseball Ranking	
Killian-Det	144							Walsh-Chi	6.4	Lajoie-Cle	6.7
Hogg-NY	125							Killian-Det	4.7	Walsh-Chi	6.4
Liebhardt-Cle	125							Howell-StL	3.7	Cobb-Det	5.0
Rhoads-Cle	119							Joss-Cle	3.4	Killian-Det	4.8
Walsh-Chi	112							Plank-Phi	1.9	Crawford-Det	4.1

March 16 Pittsburgh's Honus Wagner, 34, announces his retirement. An annual rite of spring, it will not keep him from playing in 151 games, more than in any of the past 10 years, and leading the league in hitting (for the sixth time), hits, total bases, doubles, triples, RBIs, and stolen bases. He will miss the Triple Crown by hitting two fewer homers than Tim Jordan's 12.

August 21 Nationals catcher Gabby Street stands at the base of the Washington Monument and catches the 13th ball dropped from the top, 555 feet up, duplicating the feat performed by Pop Schriver of the Chicago Colts on Aug. 24, 1894.

September 4 In a game whose significance will not be recognized until three weeks later, the Pirates and Cubs are tied 0-0 in the last of the 10th at Pittsburgh. With two outs and the bases loaded, Pittsburgh's Owen Wilson singles to center field, scoring Fred Clarke with the winning run. Warren Gill, on first base, does not get to second base but stops short, turns, and heads for the dugout, a common practice. The Cubs' Johnny Evers calls for the ball from Jimmy Slagle, touches second base, and claims the run does not count as Gill has been forced. The lone umpire, Hank O'Day, has left the field. When queried, he rules that Clarke had already scored, so the run counts. The Cubs protest to league president Pulliam, but are denied. This is the first time the Cubs try this tactic, but not the last.

September 23 Giants pitcher Mathewson and Cubs pitcher Three Finger Brown battle in the most controversial game ever played. The score is 1-1, with two outs in the last of the ninth. The Giants' Harry McCormick is on third base, and Fred Merkle (19, who is subbing for the sore-legged veteran Fred Tenney) on first. Al Bridwell singles, scoring McCormick. Halfway to second base, Merkle turns and heads for the clubhouse in center field. Johnny Evers secures a ball (Joe McGinnity swears *he* picked up the ball that was in play and threw it into the stands) and touches second as the crowd overruns the field. Umpire O'Day at first base claims he didn't see the play, but that evening he rules the run does not count, and the game ends with a tie score. (Years later, in an interview, Merkle will describe it this way: "When Bridwell shot that long single, I started across the grass for the clubhouse. Matty was near me. When Evers began shouting for the ball, he noticed something was wrong. Matty caught me by the arm and told me to wait a minute. We walked over toward second base, and Matty spoke to Emslie. 'How about this, Bob, is there any trouble with the score of the play?' 'It's all right,' said Emslie. 'You've got the game. I don't see anything wrong with the play.' Matty then took me by the arm and we walked to the clubhouse confident that we had won the game.")

September 24 NL president Henry Pulliam upholds O'Day's delayed decision and declares the game a tie, a decision nobody likes. The Cubs demand the game be forfeited to them as the crowd prevented play from continuing, although darkness would have soon ended it. Both teams appeal. Pulliam sees no inconsistency with the Sept. 4 incident and claims he has merely upheld his umpire on a question of fact in each case.

October 4 The Cubs and Pirates play their last game of the year before 30,247, the largest crowd ever at West Side Park. The Cubs win, 5-2. Then they await the results of the three Giants games with Boston. In downtown Pittsburgh, 50,000 people watch the progress of the Cubs game on temporary scoreboards. Fans fill New York's Polo Grounds to watch the action in the same way. Men with megaphones announce each pitch.

October 8 Later admitting he had nothing on the ball, Christy Mathewson loses to the Cubs, 4-2, in the playoff replay of the disputed September 23 game. Three Finger Brown, relieving Jack Pfiester in the first, gets the win. The Giants played to a record 910,000 in attendance for the year, a figure that will be unmatched until 1920.

October 10 In Game 1 of the World Series, a rematch between the Cubs and Tigers, Chicago's Ed Reulbach, coasting with a 5-1 lead, tires in the seventh, and the Tigers take a 6-5 lead into the last of the eighth. But the Cubs jump on reliever Ed Summers, a 24-game winner, for six straight hits and five runs in the ninth, and Three Finger Brown gets the win, 10-6.

October 14 Before the smallest crowd in modern World Series history—6,210—the Tigers are tamed on three hits by Overall, who fans 10 in a 2-0 win. The Cubs win the series in five games. Upset over seating arrangements at the World Series, baseball reporters form a professional group that will become the Baseball Writers Association of America.

	BOSTON		BROOKLYN		CHICAGO		CINCINNATI		NEW YORK		PHILADELPHIA		PITTSBURGH		ST.LOUIS
M	J.Kelley	M	P.Donovan	M	F.Chance	M	J.Ganzel	M	J.McGraw	M	B.Murray	M	F.Clarke	M	J.McCloskey
1B	D.McGann	1B	T.Jordan	1B	F.Chance	1B	J.Ganzel	1B	F.Tenney	1B	K.Bransfield	1B	H.Swacina	1B	E.Konetchy
2B	C.Ritchey	2B	H.Pattee	2B	J.Evers	2B	M.Huggins	2B	L.Doyle	2B	O.Knabe	2B	E.Abbaticchio	2B	B.Gilbert
SS	B.Dahlen	SS	P.Lewis	SS	J.Tinker	SS	R.Hulswitt	SS	A.Bridwell	SS	M.Doolan	SS	H.Wagner	SS	P.O'Rourke
3B	B.Sweeney	3B	T.Sheehan	3B	H.Steinfeldt	3B	H.Lobert	3B	A.Devlin	3B	E.Grant	3B	T.Leach	3B	B.Byrne
LF	J.Bates	LF	A.Burch	LF	J.Sheckard	LF	D.Paskert	LF	S.Shannon	LF	S.Magee	LF	F.Clarke	LF	J.Delahanty
CF	G.Beaumont	CF	B.Maloney	CF	J.Slagle	CF	J.Kane	CF	C.Seymour	CF	F.Osborn	CF	R.Thomas	CF	A.Shaw
RF	G.Browne	RF	H.Lumley	RF	F.Schulte	RF	M.Mitchell	RF	M.Donlin	RF	J.Titus	RF	C.Wilson	RF	R.Murray
C	F.Bowerman	C	B.Bergen	C	J.Kling	C	A.Schlei	C	R.Bresnahan	C	R.Dooin	C	G.Gibson	C	B.Ludwig
32	J.Hannifin	O2	J.Hummel	O1	S.Hofman	C1	L.McLean	O	M.McCormick	31	E.Courtney	1	A.Storke	2S	C.Charles
O1	J.Kelley	2	W.Alperman	O	D.Howard	3	M.Mowrey	2S	B.Herzog	C	F.Jacklitsch	1	J.Kane	O	S.Barry
C	P.Graham	SO	T.McMillan	C	P.Moran	O	B.Bescher	S	T.Needham	S	D.Shean	O	S.Shannon	O	A.Hoelskoetter
O	B.Becker	C	L.Ritter	2	H.Zimmerman	1	D.Hoblitzel	O	S.Barry	/O	W.Clement	O	D.Moeller	C	J.Bliss
C	H.Smith	O	T.Catterson	O	J.Hayden	O	D.Bayless	2	S.Strang	/O	R.Thomas	1	W.Gill	S3	O.Osteen
1	F.Stem	C	J.Dunn	O	K.Durbin	2	D.Egan	1	F.Merkle	/O	M.McCormick	O	B.Becker	S	T.Reilly
/O	H.Moran	C	A.Farmer	/C	D.Marshall	O	D.Brain	/2	D.Brain	/O	C.Johnson	C	E.Phelps	S	W.Morris
/C	J.Ball	/1	S.Murch	H	V.Campbell	O	T.Daley	/O	J.Devore	/2	K.Gleason	2	C.Starr	C	C.Moran
/S	W.Thomas					/O	B.Coulson	/C	F.Snodgrass	/O	P.Deininger	/C	P.O'Connor	O	W.Murdoch
		P	N.Rucker	P	M.Brown	H	B.McGilvray	/O	S.Evans			H	H.Shaw	/O	R.McLaurin
P	V.Lindaman	P	K.Wilhelm	P	E.Reulbach	/C	D.Pearce	/O	J.Hannifin	P	G.McQuillan	/C	J.Sullivan	/C	D.Marshall
P	P.Flaherty	P	H.McIntire	P	J.Pfiester			R	A.Wilson	P	T.Sparks	/O	C.Neighbors		
P	G.Dorner	P	J.Pastorius	P	O.Overall	P	B.Ewing			P	F.Corridon			P	B.Raymond
P	G.Ferguson	P	G.Bell	P	C.Fraser	P	B.Spade	P	C.Mathewson	P	L.Richie	P	V.Willis	P	J.Lush
P	T.McCarthy					P	A.Coakley	P	H.Wiltse	P	L.Moren	P	N.Maddox	P	F.Beebe
		P	J.Holmes	P	C.Lundgren	P	B.Campbell	P	D.Crandall			P	H.Camnitz	P	E.Karger
P	I.Young	/P	A.Kruger	/P	A.Coakley	P	J.Weimer	P	J.McGinnity	P	B.Foxen	P	L.Leifield	P	S.Sallee
P	J.Boultes	/P	P.Finlayson	/P	R.Kroh			P	D.Taylor	/P	H.Coveleski	P	S.Leever		
/P	T.Tuckey			/P	C.Spongberg	P	J.Dubuc			/P	H.Hoch			P	A.Fromme
P	B.Chappelle	/P	B.Mack			/P	J.Rowan	P	R.Ames	/P	E.Moore	P	I.Young	P	I.Higginbotham
/P	A.Mattern					/P	J.Doscher	/P	B.Malarkey	/P	B.Brown	/P	H.Young	P	S.McGlynn
/P	H.Young					/P	J.Volz	/P	R.Beecher			/P	C.Brandom	/P	C.Rhodes
/P	B.Pfeffer					/P	R.Savidge	/P	R.Marquard			/P	B.Vail	/P	O.Baldwin
/P	C.Maloney					/P	M.O'Toole	/P	B.Durham			/P	D.Phillippe	/P	F.Gaiser
						/P	B.Tozer					/P	T.McCarthy		
						/P	B.Sincock					/P	H.Hillebrand		
						/P	T.McCarthy								
						/P	C.Rhodes								

TEAM	G	W	L	PCT	GB	R	OR	AB	H	2B	3B	HR	BB	SO	AVG	OBP	SLG	PRO	PRO+	BR	/A	PF	CHI	RC	SB	CS	SBA	SBR
CHI	158	99	55	.643		624	461	5085	1267	**196**	56	19	418		.249	.311	.321	.632	105	49	25	104	**107**	584	**212**			
PIT	155	98	56	.636	1	585	469	5109	1263	162	**98**	25	420		.247	.309	.332	.641	112	63	63	100	99	582	186			
NY	157	98	56	.636	1	**652**	456	5006	**1339**	182	43	20	**494**		**.267**	**.342**	**.333**	**.675**	117	138	106	105	97	**646**	181			
PHI	155	83	71	.539	16	504	**445**	5012	1223	194	68	11	334		.244	.298	.316	.614	100	12	-6	103	96	535	200			
CIN	155	73	81	.474	26	489	544	4879	1108	129	77	14	372		.227	.288	.294	.582	95	-41	-28	97	105	474	196			
BOS	156	63	91	.409	36	537	622	5131	1228	137	43	17	414		.239	.303	.293	.596	99	-12	-4	98	104	501	134			
BRO	154	53	101	.344	46	377	516	4897	1044	110	60	**28**	323		.213	.266	.277	.543	82	-112	-97	96	98	391	113			
STL	154	49	105	.318	50	371	626	4959	1105	134	57	17	282		.223	.271	.283	.554	87	-96	-77	95	92	420	150			
TOT	622					4139		40078	9577	1244	502	151	3057	4180	.239	.299	.306	.605						1372				

TEAM	CG	SH	SV	IP	H	H/G	HR	BB	SO	RAT	ERA	ERA+	OAV	OOB	PR	/A	PF	CPI	FA	E	DP	FW	PW	BW	SBW	DIF
CHI	108	**29**	12	1433²	**1137**	7.1	20	437	**668**	10.1	2.14	109	**.221**	.287	33	30	100	93	**.969**	205	76	**3.7**	3.5	2.9		11.9
PIT	100	24	9	1402¹	1142	7.3	16	406	468	10.3	2.12	108	.223	.287	34	24	97	92	.964	226	74	1.9	2.8	7.3		9.0
NY	95	25	**18**	1411	1214	7.7	26	288	656	**9.8**	2.14	112	.233	**.277**	32	39	102	92	.962	250	79	.4	4.5	**12.3**		3.7
PHI	116	22	6	1393	1167	7.5	**8**	379	476	10.3	**2.10**	115	.234	.294	**38**	**46**	103	103	.963	238	75	1.0	**5.3**	-.7		.3
CIN	110	17	8	1384	1218	7.9	19	415	433	10.9	2.37	96	.243	.307	-4	-19	98	**104**	.959	255	72	-.2	-2.2	-3.3		1.6
BOS	92	14	1	1404²	1262	8.1	29	423	416	11.2	2.79	86	.245	.310	-70	-68	102	93	.962	253	**90**	.0	-7.9	-.5		-5.7
BRO	**118**	20	4	1369	1165	7.7	17	444	535	11.0	2.47	94	.235	.306	-18	-24	99	97	.961	247	66	.3	-2.8	-11.3		-10.2
STL	97	13	4	1368	1217	8.0	16	430	528	11.1	2.64	89	.232	.296	-44	-51	100	82	.946	348	68	-6.8	-5.9	-8.9		-6.3
TOT	836	164	62	11165²		7.7				10.6	2.35		.239	.299					.961	2022	600					

Runs		Hits		Doubles		Triples		Home Runs		Total Bases	
Tenney-NY	101	Wagner-Pit	201	Wagner-Pit	39	Wagner-Pit	19	Jordan-Bro	12	Wagner-Pit	308
Wagner-Pit	100	Donlin-NY	198	Magee-Phi	30	Lobert-Cin	18	Wagner-Pit	10	Donlin-NY	268
Leach-Pit	93	Murray-StL	167	Chance-Chi	27	Magee-Phi	16	Murray-StL	7	Murray-StL	237
Evers-Chi	83	Lobert-Cin	167	Knabe-Phi	26	Leach-Pit	16	Tinker-Chi	6	Lobert-Cin	232
Clarke-Pit	83	Bransfield-Phi	160	Donlin-NY	26			Donlin-NY	6	Leach-Pit	222

Runs Batted In		Runs Produced		Bases On Balls		Batting Average		On Base Percentage		Slugging Average	
Wagner-Pit	109	Wagner-Pit	199	Bresnahan-NY	83	Wagner-Pit	.354	Wagner-Pit	.415	Wagner-Pit	.542
Donlin-NY	106	Donlin-NY	171	Tenney-NY	72	Donlin-NY	.334	Evers-Chi	.402	Donlin-NY	.452
Seymour-NY	92	Tenney-NY	148	Evers-Chi	66	Doyle-NY	.308	Bresnahan-NY	.401	Magee-Phi	.417
Bransfield-Phi	71	Seymour-NY	147	Clarke-Pit	65	Bransfield-Phi	.304	Titus-Phi	.365	Lobert-Cin	.407
Tinker-Chi	68					Evers-Chi	.300	Donlin-NY	.364	Murray-StL	.400

Production		Adjusted Production		Batter Runs		Adjusted Batter Runs		Clutch Hitting Index		Runs Created	
Wagner-Pit	.957	Wagner-Pit	205	Wagner-Pit	65.2	Wagner-Pit	65.2	Seymour-NY	150	Wagner-Pit	148
Donlin-NY	.816	Donlin-NY	153	Donlin-NY	36.6	Donlin-NY	32.0	McGann-NY	133	Donlin-NY	108
Evers-Chi	.777	Lobert-Cin	145	Magee-Phi	27.3	Lobert-Cin	27.3	Abbaticchio-Pit	132	Lobert-Cin	97
Magee-Phi	.776	Magee-Phi	143	Bresnahan-NY	27.0	Magee-Phi	24.6	Donlin-NY	129	Murray-StL	92
Bresnahan-NY	.760	Evers-Chi	143	Evers-Chi	26.4	Murray-StL	24.3	Steinfeldt-Chi	129	Magee-Phi	90

Total Average		Stolen Bases		Stolen Base Average		Stolen Base Runs		Fielding Runs		Total Player Rating	
Wagner-Pit	1.144	Wagner-Pit	53					Dahlen-Bos	37.5	Wagner-Pit	7.0
Evers-Chi	.904	Murray-StL	48					Tinker-Chi	30.4	Tinker-Chi	4.8
Magee-Phi	.857	Lobert-Cin	47					Ritchey-Bos	15.6	Dahlen-Bos	4.2
Donlin-NY	.825	Magee-Phi	40					Devlin-NY	12.8	Ritchey-Bos	3.1
Bresnahan-NY	.820	Evers-Chi	36					Burch-Bro	12.6	Donlin-NY	3.0

Wins		Win Percentage		Games		Complete Games		Shutouts		Saves	
Mathewson-NY	37	Reulbach-Chi	.774	Mathewson-NY	56	Mathewson-NY	34	Mathewson-NY	11	McGinnity-NY	5
Brown-Chi	29	Mathewson-NY	.771	Raymond-StL	48	Wilhelm-Bro	33	Brown-Chi	9	Mathewson-NY	5
Reulbach-Chi	24	Brown-Chi	.763	McQuillan-Phi	48	McQuillan-Phi	32			Brown-Chi	5
		Maddox-Pit	.742	Reulbach-Chi	46	Wiltse-NY	30			Overall-Chi	4
		Leever-Pit	.682			Rucker-Bro	30			Ewing-Cin	3

Innings Pitched		Fewest Hits/Game		Fewest BB/Game		Strikeouts		Strikeouts/Game		Ratio	
Mathewson-NY	390.2	Brown-Chi	6.17	Mathewson-NY	.97	Mathewson-NY	259	Overall-Chi	6.68	Mathewson-NY	7.60
McQuillan-Phi	359.2	Raymond-StL	6.55	Brown-Chi	1.41	Rucker-Bro	199	Mathewson-NY	5.97	Brown-Chi	7.72
Rucker-Bro	333.1	Mathewson-NY	6.57	Sparks-Phi	1.74	Overall-Chi	167	Rucker-Bro	5.37	McQuillan-Phi	9.01
Wilhelm-Bro	332.0	McQuillan-Phi	6.58	Ewing-Cin	1.75	Raymond-StL	145	Camnitz-Pit	4.49	Willis-Pit	9.28
Wiltse-NY	330.0	Overall-Chi	6.60	Campbell-Cin	1.79	Reulbach-Chi	133	Ferguson-Bos	4.24	Ewing-Cin	9.47

Earned Run Average		Adjusted ERA		Opponents' Batting Avg.		Opponents' On Base Pct.		Starter Runs		Adjusted Starter Runs	
Mathewson-NY	1.43	Mathewson-NY	168	Beebe-StL	.193	Mathewson-NY	.225	Mathewson-NY	39.8	Mathewson-NY	42.1
Brown-Chi	1.47	Brown-Chi	159	Brown-Chi	.195	Brown-Chi	.232	McQuillan-Phi	32.7	McQuillan-Phi	35.2
McQuillan-Phi	1.53	McQuillan-Phi	158	Mathewson-NY	.200	Willis-Pit	.262	Brown-Chi	30.4	Brown-Chi	30.1
Camnitz-Pit	1.56	Camnitz-Pit	147	McQuillan-Phi	.207	McQuillan-Phi	.263	Camnitz-Pit	20.7	Camnitz-Pit	19.1
Coakley-Cin-Chi	1.78	Richie-Phi	132	Raymond-StL	.207	Beebe-StL	.267	Wilhelm-Bro	17.5	Wilhelm-Bro	16.8

Clutch Pitching Index		Relief Runs		Adjusted Relief Runs		Relief Ranking		Total Pitcher Index		Total Baseball Ranking	
Coakley-Cin-Chi	134							Mathewson-NY	7.3	Mathewson-NY	7.3
McGinnity-NY	134							Brown-Chi	4.1	Wagner-Pit	7.0
Richie-Phi	126							McQuillan-Phi	3.9	Tinker-Chi	4.8
Fraser-Chi	126							Raymond-StL	2.1	Dahlen-Bos	4.2
Rucker-Bro	118							Wilhelm-Bro	1.9	Brown-Chi	4.1

February 3 Chris Von der Ahe, flamboyant former owner of the Browns, files for bankruptcy, claiming $27,000 in debts, and $200 in assets.

February 27 The sacrifice fly rule is adopted. No time at bat is charged if a run scores after the catch of a fly ball. The rule will be repealed in 1931, then reinstated or changed several times before permanent acceptance in 1954.

April 2 After a two-year investigation, the Mills Commission, formed on the recommendation of Al Spalding and headed by the former NL president A. G. Mills, declares that baseball was invented by Abner Doubleday in Cooperstown, New York, in 1839. Overwhelming evidence to the contrary is ignored, but the designation makes James Fenimore Cooper's town the most likely site for a Hall of Fame and museum when these establishments are conceived some 30 years later.

April 20 "The Father of Baseball," Henry Chadwick, reporter, commentator, scorer, and indefatigable promoter of the game, dies in Brooklyn at age 85.

June 30 Cy Young's third career no-hitter is an 8-0 Boston win over New York. At 41 years and three months, he is the oldest pitcher to turn the no-hit trick. Nolan Ryan will beat him in 1990 with a no-hitter at the age of 43.

August 13 Cy Young Day is celebrated by 20,000 at Huntington Avenue Grounds in Boston. He pitches briefly against an All-Star team that includes Jack Chesbro, Hal Chase, and Willie Keeler. The game is interrupted several times for presentations to the great hurler.

August 20 Rube Waddell strikes out 17 Washington Nationals in 10 innings.

September 4 With a runner on third base, Detroit's Germany Schaefer attempts to draw a throw by stealing second base, but the Cleveland catcher, Nig Clarke, holds on to the ball. With runners on second and third, Schaefer takes off for first base and is credited with a stolen base. On the next pitch he takes off again for second base and arrives safely, this time drawing a throw and allowing Davy Jones to score from third. This is the second time in five weeks this prank has been run.

September 7 Nationals pitcher Walter Johnson shuts out the New York Highlanders for the third time in four days, 4–0. He will pitch 110 shutouts during his career, 20 more than runner-up Grover Alexander.

September 13* Lancaster (Ohio State League) pitcher Walt "Smoke" Justis hurls his fourth no-hitter of the season, defeating Marion, 3–0. Justis had no record in two major league appearances with Detroit in 1905.

October 2 In a great pitching duel, Ed Walsh is almost perfect, giving up four hits and striking out 15 in eight innings, but Cleveland's Addie Joss is completely perfect, setting down 27 straight White Sox for a 1-0 victory. The only run scores on a passed ball by Ossie Schreckengost. It is the high point of Joss's career. He will finish 24-12 with a 1.16 ERA.

October 5 Ed Walsh of the White Sox tops Detroit, 6-1, for his 40th victory and forces the AL pennant race to the final day. He also leads the league in games (66), innings pitched (464), strikeouts (269), complete games (42), saves (6), shutouts (11), and winning percentage (.727). His ERA is 1.42.

October 6 Having pitched in 13 of the last 16 games, Ed Walsh does not start the White Sox finale against Detroit. Doc White is hit hard in the 7-0 loss that gives the pennant to the Tigers.

October 6 Detroit outfielder Sam Crawford leads the AL with seven homers. Having led the NL with 16 in 1901, he becomes the first player to lead both leagues in that department.

BOSTON	CHICAGO	CLEVELAND	DETROIT	NEW YORK	PHILADELPHIA	ST. LOUIS	WASHINGTON
M D.McGuire	M F.Jones	M N.Lajoie	M H.Jennings	M C.Griffith	M C.Mack	M J.McAleer	M J.Cantillon
M F.Lake	1B J.Donahue	1B G.Stovall	1B C.Rossman	M K.Elberfeld	1B H.Davis	1B T.Jones	1B J.Freeman
1B J.Stahl	2B G.Davis	2B N.Lajoie	2B R.Downs	1B H.Chase	2B E.Collins	2B J.Williams	2B J.Delahanty
2B A.McConnell	SS F.Parent	SS G.Perring	SS G.Schaefer	2B H.Niles	SS S.Nicholls	SS B.Wallace	SS G.McBride
SS H.Wagner	3B L.Tannehill	3B B.Bradley	3B B.Coughlin	SS N.Ball	3B J.Collins	3B H.Ferris	3B B.Shipke
3B H.Lord	LF P.Dougherty	LF J.Clarke	LF M.McIntyre	3B W.Conroy	LF T.Hartsel	LF G.Stone	LF B.Ganley
LF J.Thoney	CF F.Jones	CF J.Birmingham	CF S.Crawford	LF J.Stahl	CF R.Oldring	CF D.Hoffman	CF C.Milan
CF D.Sullivan	RF E.Hahn	RF B.Hinchman	RF T.Cobb	CF C.Hemphill	RF D.Murphy	RF R.Hartzell	RF O.Pickering
RF D.Gessler	C B.Sullivan	C N.Clarke	C B.Schmidt	RF W.Keeler	C O.Schreckengost	C T.Spencer	C G.Street
C L.Criger	O J.Anderson	C H.Bemis	S C.O'Leary	C R.Kleinow	OP J.Coombs	O C.Jones	O2 O.Clymer
O G.Cravath	12 F.Isbell	OS T.Turner	O D.Jones	13 G.Moriarty	C D.Powers	O A.Schweitzer	32 B.Unglaub
1 B.Unglaub	2S J.Atz	O1 C.Hickman	C I.Thomas	C W.Blair	2S J.Barry	J.Stephens	23 D.Altizer
23 F.LaPorte	3 B.Purtell	O W.Good	2 R.Killefer	O I.McIlveen	O S.Seybold	O E.Heidrick	C J.Warner
C B.Carrigan	C A.Shaw	O D.Altizer	S D.Bush	2O F.LaPorte	O S.Smith	C D.Criss	O B.Edmondson
O T.Speaker	C A.Weaver	C E.Flick	C F.Payne	O F.Delahanty	3 F.Manush	C S.Smith	M.Kahoe
C P.Donahue	/C O.Schreckengost	/O R.Nill	/3 C.Perry	OS Q.O'Rourke	O H.Moran	/2 J.Yeager	P T.Hughes
O J.McHale	P E.Walsh	/C G.Land	P E.Summers	C J.Sweeney	2 S.Barr	P H.Howell	P W.Johnson
C E.McFarland	P F.Smith	/O D.Sullivan	P G.Mullin	2 B.Cree	C J.Lapp	P R.Waddell	P C.Smith
O J.Hoey	P D.White	/C H.Davidson	P B.Donovan	2 E.Gardner	O A.Strunk	P J.Powell	P B.Keeley
/2 H.Niles	P F.Owen	/1 D.McGuire	P E.Willett	S K.Elberfeld	/3 F.Baker	P B.Dinneen	P B.Burns
/O W.Carlisle	P N.Altrock	R H.Bay	P E.Killian	/3 M.Donovan	/O J.Fox	P B.Pelty	P E.Cates
/3 L.Gardner	P M.Manuel	P A.Joss	P E.Siever	P J.Chesbro	/O S.Shaughnessy	P B.Grahame	P C.Falkenberg
/O J.Barrett	/P L.Fiene	P B.Rhoads	/P G.Winter	P J.Lake	/O J.Jackson	P B.Bailey	P J.Tannehill
/C H.Ostdiek	/P A.Nelson	P G.Liebhardt	/P G.Suggs	P R.Manning	/C B.Blue		/P R.Witherup
H D.McGuire	/P F.Olmstead	P H.Berger	/P H.Malloy	P B.Hogg	/C B.Egan		/P C.Patten
P C.Young		P C.Chech		P A.Orth	P R.Vickers		/P H.Gehring
P E.Cicotte		P J.Thielman		P D.Newton	P E.Plank		
P C.Morgan		/P C.Falkenberg		P S.Doyle	P J.Dygert		
P F.Burchell		/P J.Ryan		/P P.Wilson	P C.Bender		
P G.Winter		/P B.Lattimore		/P J.Warhop	P B.Schlitzer		
P E.Steele		/P E.Foster		/P F.Glade	P N.Carter		
P F.Arellanes		/P O.Hess		/P H.Billiard	/P J.Flater		
P T.Pruiett		/P W.Clarkson		/P A.O'Connor	/P H.Krause		
P R.Glaze		/P J.Graney		/P H.Vaughn	/P A.Kellogg		
/P J.Wood					/P G.Salve		
/P K.Brady					/P B.Maxwell		
/P D.McMahon					/P E.Files		
/P J.Tannehill					/P D.Martin		
/P C.Patten							
/P C.Hartman							
/P J.Thielman							

TEAM	G	W	L	PCT	GB	R	OR	AB	H	2B	3B	HR	BB	SO	AVG	OBP	SLG	PRO	PRO+	BR	/A	PF	CHI	RC	SB	CS	SBA	SBR
DET	154	90	63	.588		647	547	5115	1347	199	86	19	320		.263	.312	.347	.659	115	102	75	104	102	604	165			
CLE	157	90	64	.584	0.5	568	457	5108	1221	188	58	18	364		.239	.297	.309	.606	103	14	12	100	102	528	177			
CHI	155	88	64	.579	1.5	537	470	5027	1127	145	41	3	463		.224	.298	.271	.569	91	-37	-29	98	105	479	209			
STL	156	83	69	.546	6.5	544	483	5151	1261	173	52	20	343		.245	.296	.310	.606	102	13	10	101	98	514	126			
BOS	155	75	79	.487	15.5	564	513	5048	1239	117	88	14	289		.245	.295	.312	.607	100	13	-2	103	104	513	167			
PHI	157	68	85	.444	22	486	562	5065	1131	183	50	21	368		.223	.281	.292	.573	86	-46	-79	107	100	450	116			
WAS	155	67	85	.441	22.5	479	539	5041	1186	132	74	8	368		.235	.293	.296	.589	106	-15	28	92	92	490	170			
NY	155	51	103	.331	39.5	459	713	5047	1190	142	50	13	288		.236	.283	.291	.574	91	-45	-50	101	96	478	231			
TOT	622					4284		40602	9702	1279	499	116	2803	4930	.239	.294	.304	.598						1361				

TEAM	CG	SH	SV	IP	H	H/G	HR	BB	SO	RAT	ERA	ERA+	OAV	OOB	PR	/A	PF	CPI	FA	E	DP	FW	PW	BW	SBW	DIF
DET	119	15	5	1374¹	1313	8.6	12	318	553	11.1	2.40	100	.255	.306	-3	2	101	113	.953	305	95	-2.1	.2	8.6		6.8
CLE	108	18	5	1424¹	1172	7.4	16	328	548	9.7	2.02	118	.229	.280	59	56	100	102	.962	257	95	1.6	6.4	1.4		3.7
CHI	107	23	10	1414	1165	7.4	11	284	623	9.4	2.22	104	.225	.269	26	13	97	82	.966	232	82	3.2	1.5	-3.3		10.7
STL	107	15	5	1397	1151	7.4	7	387	607	10.3	2.15	111	.230	.294	37	36	100	105	.964	237	97	2.7	4.1	1.1		-1.0
BOS	102	12	7	1380¹	1200	7.8	18	364	624	10.5	2.28	108	.238	.295	17	27	103	105	.955	297	71	-1.4	3.1	-.2		-3.4
PHI	102	23	4	1400¹	1194	7.7	10	410	741	10.6	2.56	100	.235	.299	-27	-4	107	92	.957	272	68	.6	-.5	-9.0		-4.1
WAS	106	15	7	1391²	1236	8.0	16	348	649	10.5	2.34	97	.241	.294	7	-12	96	102	.958	275	89	.1	-1.4	3.2		-10.9
NY	90	11	3	1366	1293	8.5	26	458	585	12.0	3.16	78	.252	.322	-117	-106	104	96	.947	337	78	-4.1	-12.1	-5.7		-4.1
TOT	841	132	46	11148		7.9				10.5	2.39		.239	.294					.958	2212	675					

Runs		Hits		Doubles		Triples		Home Runs		Total Bases	
McIntyre-Det	105	Cobb-Det	188	Cobb-Det	36	Cobb-Det	20	Crawford-Det	7	Cobb-Det	276
Crawford-Det	102	Crawford-Det	184	Rossman-Det	33	Stahl-NY-Bos	16	Hinchman-Cle	6	Crawford-Det	270
Schaefer-Det	96	McIntyre-Det	168	Crawford-Det	33	Crawford-Det	16	Niles-NY-Bos	5	Rossman-Det	219
Jones-Chi	92	Lajoie-Cle	168	Lajoie-Cle	32	Gessler-Bos	14	Stone-StL	5	McIntyre-Det	218
Stone-StL	89	Stone-StL	165	Stovall-Cle	29			Davis-Phi	5	Lajoie-Cle	218

Runs Batted In		Runs Produced		Bases On Balls		Batting Average		On Base Percentage		Slugging Average	
Cobb-Det	108	Cobb-Det	192	Hartsel-Phi	93	Cobb-Det	.324	Gessler-Bos	.394	Cobb-Det	.475
Crawford-Det	80	Crawford-Det	175	Jones-Chi	86	Crawford-Det	.311	McIntyre-Det	.392	Crawford-Det	.457
Lajoie-Cle	74	Lajoie-Cle	149	McIntyre-Det	83	Gessler-Bos	.308	Hemphill-NY	.374	Gessler-Bos	.423
Ferris-StL	74	Schaefer-Det	145	J.Clarke-Cle	76	Hemphill-NY	.297	Hartsel-Phi	.371	Rossman-Det	.418
Rossman-Det	71	Jones-Chi	141	Davis-Phi	61	McIntyre-Det	.295	Dougherty-Chi	.367	McIntyre-Det	.383

Production		Adjusted Production		Batter Runs		Adjusted Batter Runs		Clutch Hitting Index		Runs Created	
Cobb-Det	.842	Cobb-Det	166	Cobb-Det	43.8	Cobb-Det	39.6	Cobb-Det	141	Cobb-Det	114
Gessler-Bos	.817	Gessler-Bos	161	Crawford-Det	38.3	Crawford-Det	34.2	Wallace-StL	127	Crawford-Det	100
Crawford-Det	.812	Crawford-Det	157	McIntyre-Det	36.5	McIntyre-Det	32.3	Ferris-StL	125	McIntyre-Det	93
McIntyre-Det	.775	McIntyre-Det	146	Gessler-Bos	33.2	Gessler-Bos	31.0	Lajoie-Cle	124	Lajoie-Cle	83
Rossman-Det	.748	Rossman-Det	137	Lajoie-Cle	23.3	Lajoie-Cle	23.0	Jones-Chi	124	Hemphill-NY	83

Total Average		Stolen Bases		Stolen Base Average		Stolen Base Runs		Fielding Runs		Total Player Rating	
Cobb-Det	.903	Dougherty-Chi	47					Lajoie-Cle	49.4	Lajoie-Cle	7.8
Gessler-Bos	.880	Hemphill-NY	42					McBride-Was	32.0	McIntyre-Det	4.7
McIntyre-Det	.818	Schaefer-Det	40					Wagner-Bos	31.8	Cobb-Det	4.2
Hemphill-NY	.800	Cobb-Det	39					Wallace-StL	18.1	McBride-Was	3.4
Crawford-Det	.799	J.Clarke-Cle	37					Tannehill-Chi	17.8	Wallace-StL	3.1

Wins		Win Percentage		Games		Complete Games		Shutouts		Saves	
Walsh-Chi	40	Walsh-Chi	.727	Walsh-Chi	66	Walsh-Chi	42	Walsh-Chi	11	Walsh-Chi	6
Summers-Det	24	Donovan-Det	.720	Vickers-Phi	53	Young-Bos	30	Joss-Cle	9	Hughes-Was	4
Joss-Cle	24	Joss-Cle	.686	Chesbro-NY	45	Joss-Cle	29	Vickers-Phi	6	Waddell-StL	3
Young-Bos	21	Summers-Det	.667	Waddell-StL	43	Howell-StL	27	Johnson-Was	6		
Waddell-StL	19	Young-Bos	.656	Hughes-Was	43	Mullin-Det	26	Donovan-Det	6		

Innings Pitched		Fewest Hits/Game		Fewest BB/Game		Strikeouts		Strikeouts/Game		Ratio	
Walsh-Chi	464.0	Joss-Cle	6.42	Joss-Cle	.83	Waddell-StL	269	Waddell-StL	7.31	Joss-Cle	7.31
Joss-Cle	325.0	Smith-Chi	6.44	Burns-Was	.99	Waddell-StL	232	Dygert-Phi	6.18	Walsh-Chi	7.91
Howell-StL	324.1	Walsh-Chi	6.65	Walsh-Chi	1.09	Hughes-Was	165	Johnson-Was	5.62	Young-Bos	8.07
Vickers-Phi	317.0	Johnson-Was	6.81	Young-Bos	1.11	Dygert-Phi	164	Hughes-Was	5.37	Burns-Was	8.62
Summers-Det	301.0	Berger-Cle	6.86	Summers-Det	1.64	Johnson-Was	160	Donovan-Det	5.23	Smith-Chi	8.71

Earned Run Average		Adjusted ERA		Opponents' Batting Avg.		Opponents' On Base Pct.		Starter Runs		Adjusted Starter Runs	
Joss-Cle	1.16	Joss-Cle	205	Joss-Cle	.197	Joss-Cle	.218	Walsh-Chi	50.0	Walsh-Chi	46.0
Young-Bos	1.26	Young-Bos	194	Smith-Chi	.203	Walsh-Chi	.232	Joss-Cle	44.2	Joss-Cle	44.0
Walsh-Chi	1.42	Walsh-Chi	163	Walsh-Chi	.203	Young-Bos	.240	Young-Bos	37.3	Young-Bos	39.5
Summers-Det	1.64	Summers-Det	147	Johnson-Was	.211	Smith-Chi	.256	Summers-Det	24.8	Summers-Det	25.6
Johnson-Was	1.65	Johnson-Was	138	Young-Bos	.213	Burns-Was	.257	Johnson-Was	21.0	Rhoads-Cle	18.4

Clutch Pitching Index		Relief Runs		Adjusted Relief Runs		Relief Ranking		Total Pitcher Index		Total Baseball Ranking	
Summers-Det	142							Walsh-Chi	8.1	Walsh-Chi	8.1
Willett-Det	140							Joss-Cle	5.9	Lajoie-Cle	7.8
Rhoads-Cle	137							Young-Bos	4.1	Joss-Cle	5.9
Howell-StL	122							Rhoads-Cle	2.9	McIntyre-Det	4.7
Chech-Cle	119							Summers-Det	2.4	Cobb-Det	4.2

January 11 The National Commission approves owner Charles Murphy's payment of a $10,000 bonus to his Cubs for their 1908 World Series triumph.

February 4 John Clarkson, a 326-game winner dies at Belmont, Mass. at age 47.

February 17 The NL deprives umpires of the power to fine players and decrees that relief pitchers must retire at least one batter before being relieved.

February 27 Joe "Iron Man" McGinnity is released by the Giants. He will pitch in the minor leagues for another 13 years, winning 20 or more in six of them.

April 15 Before an Opening Day crowd of 30,000 at New York, Red Ames pitches a no-hitter for nine innings against the Brooklyn Superbas, ruins it with one out in the 10th, then loses the game, 3-0, in the 13th.

April 23 In the sixth inning of the Reds-Pirates game in Pittsburgh, Honus Wagner steps across the plate to the other batter's box as Reds pitcher Harry Gaspar delivers the ball. Umpire Bill Klem refuses to call him out. The Pirates win, 2–1, but Reds manager Clark Griffith protests. Acting NL president Heydler backs Klem. The league will override Heydler and Klem and order the game replayed Sept. 20. The Pirates will win, 4–3.

May 2 Honus Wagner steals his way around the bases in the first inning of a game against the Cubs. It is the fourth time he has performed this feat, an NL record.

May 11* Fred Toney, later to pitch in the only double no-hitter, throws a 17-inning no-hitter for Winchester (Blue Grass League), winning, 1–0. He fans 19 opponents and walks only one.

June 16* Jim Thorpe makes his baseball pitching debut for Rocky Mount (Eastern Carolina League) with a 4–2 win over Raleigh. It is this professional play which will cause him to lose the medals he won in the 1912 Olympics.

June 19 An exhibition night game featuring two amateur teams is played in the Reds' park before 3,000 spectators, including the Cincinnati and Philadelphia teams, which had played there earlier.

July 29 NL president Harry Pulliam, despondent over his inability to handle the problems and controversies of the league, dies of a self-inflicted pistol wound.

August 18 Giants player-coach Arlie Latham steals second base in the Giants' 14–1 win over the Phillies. At 49, he is the oldest major leaguer ever to steal a base.

August 31 The A. J. Reach Company is granted a patent for a cork-centered baseball, which will replace the hard rubber-cored one. This change will be particularly apparent in the NL in 1910-11.

October 8 The World Series pits the two leagues' top offensive stars, Honus Wagner and Ty Cobb, against each other. Pittsburgh manager Fred Clarke starts 27-year-old rookie righthander Babe Adams against Tigers pitcher George Mullin. There are only 11 hits in the game, but one is a home run by Clarke, and the Pirates win, 4-1.

October 16 Babe Adams comes through with a six-hit 8-0 win. It is his third complete-game victory and gives the Pirates their first world championship.

November 26 The Phils are sold for $350,000 to a group headed by sportswriter Horace Fogel. Because of his dual roles, Fogel will become the only executive barred from a league meeting.

BOSTON	BROOKLYN	CHICAGO	CINCINNATI	NEW YORK	PHILADELPHIA	PITTSBURGH	ST.LOUIS
M F.Bowerman	M H.Lumley	M F.Chance	M C.Griffith	M J.McGraw	M B.Murray	M F.Clarke	M R.Bresnahan
M H.Smith	1B T.Jordan	1B F.Chance	1B D.Hoblitzel	1B F.Tenney	1B K.Bransfield	1B B.Abstein	1B E.Konetchy
1B F.Stem	2B W.Alperman	2B J.Evers	2B D.Egan	2B L.Doyle	2B O.Knabe	2B D.Miller	2B C.Charles
2B D.Shean	SS T.McMillan	SS J.Tinker	SS T.Downey	SS A.Bridwell	SS M.Doolan	SS H.Wagner	SS R.Hulswitt
SS J.Coffey	3B E.Lennox	3B H.Steinfeldt	3B H.Lobert	3B A.Devlin	3B E.Grant	3B J.Barbeau	3B B.Byrne
3B B.Sweeney	LF W.Clement	LF J.Sheckard	LF B.Bescher	LF M.McCormick	LF S.Magee	LF F.Clarke	LF R.Ellis
LF R.Thomas	CF A.Burch	CF S.Hofman	CF R.Oakes	CF B.O'Hara	CF J.Bates	CF T.Leach	CF A.Shaw
CF G.Beaumont	RF H.Lumley	RF F.Schulte	RF M.Mitchell	RF R.Murray	RF J.Titus	RF C.Wilson	RF S.Evans
RF B.Becker	C B.Bergen	C J.Archer	C L.McLean	C A.Schlei	C R.Dooin	C G.Gibson	C E.Phelps
C P.Graham	12 J.Hummel	C P.Moran	O P.Paskert	O C.Seymour	O F.Osborn	3 B.Byrne	O2 J.Delahanty
O1 F.Beck	3O P.McElveen	1 D.Howard	23 M.Huggins	1 F.Merkle	2 J.Ward	13 A.Storke	C R.Bresnahan
O J.Bates	O J.Kustus	2S H.Zimmerman	C F.Roth	C C.Meyers	O P.Deininger	S E.Abbaticchio	3 J.Barbeau
2 C.Starr	C D.Marshall	O J.Stanley	3S M.Mowrey	O B.Herzog	S D.Shean	/O H.Hyatt	S A.Storke
1 C.Autry	OP G.Hunter	/O J.Kane	O W.Miller	S A.Fletcher	C D.Martel	O W.Miller	C J.Bliss
S B.Dahlen	O Z.Wheat	O G.Browne	O T.Clarke	32 T.Shafer	C F.Jacklitsch	/C M.Simon	O H.Murphy
3 G.Getz	O J.Sebring	1 F.Luderus	2 C.Charles	O F.Snodgrass	H W.Clement	/C P.O'Connor	C C.Osteen
C H.Smith	O R.Downey	/C T.Needham	/1 C.Autry	C A.Wilson	H C.Starr	R K.Durbin	2 B.Gilbert
C F.Bowerman	/C J.Dunn	/O B.Davidson	/S R.Ellar	O J.Devore	O B.Froelich	P V.Willis	/2 M.Mowrey
2 C.Ritchey	/S L.Meyer	P M.Brown	/S B.Moriarty	/2 A.Latham	/C E.McDonough	P Ho.Camnitz	O B.James
C B.Rariden	/O H.Myers	P O.Overall	/C E.Haberer	P C.Mathewson	P E.Moore	P N.Maddox	/S C.Enwright
C A.Shaw	/2 H.Redmond	P E.Reulbach	/O S.McCabe	P B.Raymond	P L.Moren	P L.Leifield	/S T.Reilly
/O H.Moran	/O T.Catterson	P J.Pfiester	/O D.Johnston	P H.Wiltse	P G.McQuillan	P D.Phillippe	/C C.Blank
/3 H.Siner	P N.Rucker	P R.Kroh	/O C.Patterson	P R.Ames	P F.Corridon	P Ha.Camnitz	P F.Beebe
/O E.Diehl	P G.Bell	P R.Hagerman	/C S.Pauxtis	P R.Marquard	P T.Sparks	P B.Adams	P J.Lush
/O B.Dam	P H.McIntire	P I.Higginbotham	/O D.Young	P D.Crandall	P H.Coveleski	P S.Leever	P S.Sallee
P A.Mattern	P K.Wilhelm	/P R.Brown	/3 C.Dolan	/P A.Klawitter	P B.Foxen	P C.Brandom	P B.Harmon
P G.Ferguson	P D.Scanlan	/P K.Cole	H K.Durbin	/P L.Drucke	P L.Richie	/P S.Frock	P L.Backman
P K.White	P J.Pastorius	/P C.Lundgren	/C M.Konnick	/P G.Daly	/P B.Brown	/P B.Powell	RP S.Melter
P L.Richie	/P E.Dent	/P P.Ragan	/3 E.Midkiff	/P B.Durham	/P F.Scanlan	/P G.Moore	P J.Raleigh
P B.Brown	/P E.Knetzer	/P R.Schwenck	/C D.Pearce	/P J.Weimer	/P B.Van Dyke	/P C.Wacker	P E.Higgins
P T.Tuckey	/P S.Fletcher	/P C.Fraser	P A.Fromme	/P R.Waller			P C.Rhodes
P C.Curtis	/P P.Finlayson	/P A.Coakley	P H.Gaspar				P F.More
P V.Lindaman			P J.Rowan				/P G.Lowdermilk
P F.More			P B.Ewing				/P I.Higginbotham
/P T.McCarthy			P B.Campbell				/P J.Bernard
/P B.Chappelle			P B.Spade				/P H.Sullivan
/P G.Dorner			P J.Dubuc				
/P C.Evans			/P E.Karger				
/P J.Boultes			/P T.Cantwell				
/P B.Cooney			/P R.Castleton				
			/P P.Ragan				
			/P J.Bushelman				
			/P C.Carmichael				
			/P C.Griffith				
			/P B.Chappelle				
			/P R.Savidge				

TEAM	G	W	L	PCT	GB	R	OR	AB	H	2B	3B	HR	BB	SO	AVG	OBP	SLG	PRO	PRO+	BR	/A	PF	CHI	RC	SB	CS	SBA	SBR
PIT	154	110	42	.724		**699**	447	5129	**1332**	218	92	25	479		**.260**	.327	**.353**	**.680**	109	**100**	44	108	103	**656**	185			
CHI	155	104	49	.680	6.5	635	**390**	4999	1227	203	60	20	420		.245	.308	.322	.630	100	7	-7	102	**112**	562	187			
NY	158	92	61	.601	18.5	623	546	5218	1327	173	68	**26**	530		.254	**.329**	.328	.657	109	70	60	102	95	640	234			
CIN	157	77	76	.503	33.5	606	599	5088	1273	159	72	22	478		.250	.319	.323	.642	107	35	40	99	100	618	**280**			
PHI	154	74	79	.484	36.5	516	518	5034	1228	185	53	12	369		.244	.303	.309	.612	95	-26	-30	101	96	534	185			
BRO	155	55	98	.359	55.5	444	627	5056	1157	176	59	16	330		.229	.279	.296	.575	87	-98	-82	96	98	456	141			
STL	154	54	98	.355	56	583	731	5108	1242	148	56	15	**568**		.243	.326	.303	.629	109	25	**62**	94	97	556	161			
BOS	155	45	108	.294	65.5	435	683	5017	1121	125	43	14	400		.223	.285	.274	.559	76	-117	-137	105	99	435	135			
TOT	621					4541		40649	9907	1387	503	150	3574	4437	.244	.310	.314	.624							1508			

TEAM	CG	SH	SV	IP	H	H/G	HR	BB	SO	RAT	ERA	ERA+	OAV	OOB	PR	/A	PF	CPI	FA	E	DP	FW	PW	BW	SBW	DIF
PIT	93	21	11	1401²	1174	7.5	12	**320**	490	9.9	2.07	131	.232	.284	81	100	105	97	**.964**	228	100	3.5	11.1	4.9		14.5
CHI	111	**32**	11	1399¹	**1094**	**7.0**	6	364	680	**9.6**	**1.75**	**145**	**.215**	**.272**	**131**	**124**	98	94	.962	244	95	2.6	**13.8**	-.8		11.9
NY	105	17	**15**	1440²	1248	7.8	28	397	**735**	10.5	2.27	112	.238	.295	51	42	98	102	.954	307	99	-1.1	4.7	6.7		5.3
CIN	91	10	8	1407	1233	7.9	**5**	510	477	11.4	2.52	103	.240	.314	11	9	100	100	.952	309	**120**	-1.4	1.0	4.4		-3.6
PHI	89	17	6	1391	1190	7.7	23	472	612	11.0	2.44	106	.235	.304	23	20	100	99	.962	241	97	2.7	2.2	-3.3		-4.1
BRO	**126**	18	3	1384¹	1277	8.3	31	528	594	12.1	3.10	83	.256	.333	-79	-82	100	102	.955	282	86	.2	-9.1	-9.1		-3.5
STL	84	5	4	1379²	1368	8.9	22	483	435	12.4	3.41	74	.263	.331	-126	-139	97	92	.950	322	90	-2.5	-15.4	6.9		-10.9
BOS	98	13	6	1370²	1329	8.7	23	543	414	12.6	3.20	88	.263	.339	-93	-60	109	**103**	.948	342	101	-3.7	-6.7	-15.2		-5.9
TOT	797	133	64	11174¹		8.0				11.2	2.59		.244	.310					.956	2275	788					

Runs		Hits		Doubles		Triples		Home Runs		Total Bases	
Leach-Pit	126	Doyle-NY	172	Wagner-Pit	39	Mitchell-Cin	17	Murray-NY	7	Wagner-Pit	242
Clarke-Pit	97	Grant-Phi	170	Magee-Phi	33	Magee-Phi	14	Leach-Pit	6	Doyle-NY	239
Byrne-StL-Pit	92	Wagner-Pit	168	D.Miller-Pit	31	Konetchy-StL	14	Doyle-NY	6	Konetchy-StL	228
Wagner-Pit	92	Konetchy-StL	165	Sheckard-Chi	29	D.Miller-Pit	13	Becker-Bos	6	Mitchell-Cin	225
		Burch-Bro	163	Leach-Pit	29			Wagner-Pit	5	D.Miller-Pit	222

Runs Batted In		Runs Produced		Bases On Balls		Batting Average		On Base Percentage		Slugging Average	
Wagner-Pit	100	Wagner-Pit	187	Clarke-Pit	80	Wagner-Pit	.339	Wagner-Pit	.420	Wagner-Pit	.489
Murray-NY	91	Mitchell-Cin	165	Byrne-StL-Pit	78	Mitchell-Cin	.310	Bridwell-NY	.386	Mitchell-Cin	.430
D.Miller-Pit	87	Konetchy-StL	164	Evers-Chi	73	Hoblitzel-Cin	.308	Clarke-Pit	.384	Doyle-NY	.419
Mitchell-Cin	86	Leach-Pit	163	Sheckard-Chi	72	Doyle-NY	.302	Mitchell-Cin	.378	Hoblitzel-Cin	.418
Konetchy-StL	80	Clarke-Pit	162	Bridwell-NY	67	Bridwell-NY	.294	Evers-Chi	.369	McCormick-NY	.402

Production		Adjusted Production		Batter Runs		Adjusted Batter Runs		Clutch Hitting Index		Runs Created	
Wagner-Pit	.909	Wagner-Pit	168	Wagner-Pit	48.1	Wagner-Pit	39.6	Murray-NY	130	Wagner-Pit	117
Mitchell-Cin	.808	Mitchell-Cin	152	Mitchell-Cin	30.4	Mitchell-Cin	31.1	Abstein-Pit	129	Mitchell-Cin	98
Hoblitzel-Cin	.782	Konetchy-StL	145	Doyle-NY	26.2	Konetchy-StL	30.6	Wagner-Pit	128	Doyle-NY	96
Doyle-NY	.779	Hoblitzel-Cin	144	Clarke-Pit	25.4	Hoblitzel-Cin	25.0	Lobert-Cin	125	Clarke-Pit	92
Konetchy-StL	.762	Doyle-NY	140	Konetchy-StL	24.9	Doyle-NY	24.9	D.Miller-Pit	124	Konetchy-StL	92

Total Average		Stolen Bases		Stolen Base Average		Stolen Base Runs		Fielding Runs		Total Player Rating	
Wagner-Pit	1.058	Bescher-Cin	54					Doolan-Phi	24.6	Wagner-Pit	5.2
Mitchell-Cin	.884	Murray-NY	48					Egan-Cin	24.1	Konetchy-StL	3.7
Clarke-Pit	.821	Egan-Cin	39					Byrne-StL-Pit	22.8	Devlin-NY	3.7
Doyle-NY	.809	Magee-Phi	38					Bergen-Bro	21.7	Mitchell-Cin	3.4
Konetchy-StL	.791	Burch-Bro	38					Tinker-Chi	19.7	Byrne-StL-Pit	2.9

Wins		Win Percentage		Games		Complete Games		Shutouts		Saves	
M.Brown-Chi	27	Mathewson-NY	.806	M.Brown-Chi	50	M.Brown-Chi	32	Overall-Chi	9	M.Brown-Chi	7
Mathewson-NY	25	H.Camnitz-Pit	.806	Mattern-Bos	47	Bell-Bro	29	Mathewson-NY	8	Crandall-NY	6
H.Camnitz-Pit	25	M.Brown-Chi	.750	Gaspar-Cin	44	Rucker-Bro	28	M.Brown-Chi	8		
Willis-Pit	22	Pfiester-Chi	.739	Beebe-StL	44	Mathewson-NY	26				
		Leifield-Pit	.704								

Innings Pitched		Fewest Hits/Game		Fewest BB/Game		Strikeouts		Strikeouts/Game		Ratio	
M.Brown-Chi	342.2	Mathewson-NY	6.28	Mathewson-NY	1.18	Overall-Chi	205	Overall-Chi	6.47	Mathewson-NY	7.45
Mattern-Bos	316.1	Fromme-Cin	6.28	M.Brown-Chi	1.39	Rucker-Bro	201	Rucker-Bro	5.85	M.Brown-Chi	8.04
Rucker-Bro	309.1	Overall-Chi	6.44	Wiltse-NY	1.70	Moore-Phi	173	Ames-NY	5.75	H.Camnitz-Pit	8.97
Moore-Phi	299.2	M.Brown-Chi	6.46	Maddox-Pit	1.73	M.Brown-Chi	172	Marquard-NY	5.67	Overall-Chi	9.22
Willis-Pit	289.2	H.Camnitz-Pit	6.58	McQuillan-Phi	1.96	Ames-NY	156	Moore-Phi	5.20	McQuillan-Phi	9.34

Earned Run Average		Adjusted ERA		Opponents' Batting Avg.		Opponents' On Base Pct.		Starter Runs		Adjusted Starter Runs	
Mathewson-NY	1.14	Mathewson-NY	223	Overall-Chi	.198	Mathewson-NY	.228	M.Brown-Chi	48.6	M.Brown-Chi	46.5
M.Brown-Chi	1.31	M.Brown-Chi	193	Mathewson-NY	.200	M.Brown-Chi	.239	Mathewson-NY	44.2	Mathewson-NY	43.0
Overall-Chi	1.42	Overall-Chi	178	Fromme-Cin	.201	Overall-Chi	.262	Overall-Chi	37.0	Overall-Chi	35.2
H.Camnitz-Pit	1.62	H.Camnitz-Pit	167	M.Brown-Chi	.202	H.Camnitz-Pit	.267	H.Camnitz-Pit	30.4	H.Camnitz-Pit	34.3
Kroh-Chi	1.65	Reulbach-Chi	142	Moore-Phi	.210	McQuillan-Phi	.271	Reulbach-Chi	23.6	Adams-Pit	23.2

Clutch Pitching Index		Relief Runs	Adjusted Relief Runs	Relief Ranking	Total Pitcher Index		Total Baseball Ranking	
Richie-Phi-Bos	126				Mathewson-NY	7.0	Mathewson-NY	7.0
Corridon-Phi	123				M.Brown-Chi	5.4	M.Brown-Chi	5.4
Sallee-StL	119				Overall-Chi	5.1	Wagner-Pit	5.2
Wilhelm-Bro	117				H.Camnitz-Pit	3.7	Overall-Chi	5.1
Marquard-NY	117				Fromme-Cin	3.1	Konetchy-StL	3.7

February 18 The Boston Red Sox trade Cy Young, who won 21 games at age 41 last season, to the Cleveland Naps for pitchers Charlie Chech and Jack Ryan, and $12,500.

April 8 While at spring training, Hal Chase of the Highlanders contracts smallpox. The entire team is vaccinated and quarantined while traveling north.

April 12 Philadelphia's Shibe Park, the first original steel-and-concrete major league park, is dedicated as a record crowd of 31,160 sees 18-year-old John "Stuffy" McInnis make his major league debut at shortstop for the home club. Eddie Plank pitches the A's to an 8-1 win over Boston.

April 18 The Tigers announce plans to build a new concrete and steel stadium, and the Pirates name their million-dollar ballpark Forbes Field in honor of the Revolutionary War general who founded Pittsburgh.

May 31* Pitchers Otto Burns of Decatur and Ed Clarke of Bloomington (Three I League) both go the distance in a 26-inning game won by Decatur, 2–1.

June 10 George Mullin's winning streak reaches 11 with a 2–1 win over New York. On the 15th, he will finally lose to the Athletics, 5–4.

June 19 Walter Johnson has a strange day beating the New York Highlanders, 7–4. He gives up just three hits, but is unusually wild, issuing seven walks, uncorking four wild pitches, and hitting one batter, while fanning 10.

July 2 The White Sox steal 12 bases in the course of a 15–3 win over St. Louis. Three are steals of home, including one by pitcher Ed Walsh in the sixth inning.

July 16 Detroit and Washington play the longest scoreless game in AL history— 18 innings. Ed Summers pitches the complete game, holding the Nationals to seven hits. The Nationals' 30-year-old rookie, Bill "Dolly" Gray, allows only one hit before leaving with an injury in the ninth.

July 19 Cleveland shortstop Neal Ball executes the majors' first unassisted triple play in the new century in the top of the second against the Red Sox. With Heinie Wagner on second base and Jake Stahl on first base, Amby McConnell hits a line drive to Ball, who steps on second base and tags Stahl coming down from first base.

July 31 For the second time in two years—the first was on May 21,1908— Bill Burns has a no-hitter broken up with two outs in the ninth, when Washington's Otis Clymer singles. Burns is the only pitcher to suffer this fate twice, until Dave Stieb of Toronto does on Sept. 24 and 30, 1988.

August 4 Umpire Tim Hurst instigates a riot by spitting at Athletics second baseman Eddie Collins, who had questioned a call. This incident eventually leads to Hurst's banishment from baseball two weeks later.

September 13 Ty Cobb clinches the AL home run title with his ninth round-tripper. It is an inside-the-park drive against the Browns. In fact, all his nine home runs this season are inside the park, including two in one game on July 15. He is the only player in this century to lead in home runs without hitting one out of the park.

September 18 Ty Cobb wins the Triple Crown with a .377 batting average, nine home runs, and 107 RBIs. He also leads the AL with 216 hits, 116 runs, and 296 total bases.

October 9 The Tigers win the second game of the World Series behind Bill Donovan, 7-2. Ty Cobb's steal of home highlights a three-run third. Detroit has been defenseless against stolen bases in the past three World Series, giving up 16 in five games to the Cubs in 1907, 15 in five games to the Cubs in 1908, and 18 in seven games to the Pirates this year, for a total of 49 in 17 games, the highest stolen base totals in all of World Series history.

October 14 George Mullin outlasts three Pirates pitchers for a 5-4 win that sends the Series to a seventh game in Detroit, making this the first World Series to go the limit.

	BOSTON		CHICAGO		CLEVELAND		DETROIT		NEW YORK		PHILADELPHIA		ST.LOUIS		WASHINGTON
M	F.Lake	M	B.Sullivan	M	N.Lajoie	M	H.Jennings	M	G.Stallings	M	C.Mack	M	J.McAleer	M	J.Cantillon
1B	J.Stahl	1B	F.Isbell	1B	G.Stovall	1B	C.Rossman	1B	H.Chase	1B	H.Davis	1B	T.Jones	1B	J.Donahue
2B	A.McConnell	2B	J.Atz	2B	N.Lajoie	2B	G.Schaefer	2B	F.LaPorte	2B	E.Collins	2B	J.Williams	2B	J.Delahanty
SS	H.Wagner	SS	F.Parent	SS	N.Ball	SS	D.Bush	SS	J.Knight	SS	J.Barry	SS	B.Wallace	SS	G.McBride
3B	H.Lord	3B	L.Tannehill	3B	B.Bradley	3B	G.Moriarty	3B	J.Austin	3B	F.Baker	3B	H.Ferris	3B	W.Conroy
LF	H.Niles	LF	P.Dougherty	LF	B.Hinchman	LF	M.McIntyre	LF	C.Engle	LF	T.Hartsel	LF	G.Stone	LF	J.Lelivelt
CF	T.Speaker	CF	D.Altizer	CF	J.Birmingham	CF	S.Crawford	CF	R.Demmitt	CF	R.Oldring	CF	D.Hoffman	CF	C.Milan
RF	D.Gessler	RF	E.Hahn	RF	W.Good	RF	T.Cobb	RF	W.Keeler	RF	D.Murphy	RF	R.Hartzell	RF	G.Browne
C	B.Carrigan	C	B.Sullivan	C	T.Easterly	C	B.Schmidt	C	R.Kleinow	C	I.Thomas	C	L.Criger	C	G.Street
O	H.Hooper	32	B.Purtell	3S	G.Perring	32	C.O'Leary	O	B.Cree	O	B.Ganley	1O	A.Griggs	1O	B.Unglaub
C	P.Donahue	OP	D.White	O	B.Lord	C	O.Stanage	S3	K.Elberfeld	O	H.Heitmuller	O	J.McAleese	O	O.Clymer
2S	C.French	C	F.Owens	O	E.Flick	O	D.Jones	O	C.Hemphill	C	P.Livingston	C	J.Stephens	2	G.Schaefer
1P	H.Wolter	O	W.Cole	1	T.Jones	C	J.Sweeney	S	S.Nicholls	O	A.Schweitzer	O	R.Killefer
C	T.Spencer	2S	T.Turner	2	J.Delahanty	C	W.Blair	C	J.Lapp	O	W.Devoy	3	B.Yohe
O	J.Thoney	C	N.Clarke	2	R.Killefer	2	E.Gardner	S	S.Barr	O	N.Crompton	O	B.Ganley
/3	L.Garden	O	M.Welday	C	H.Beckendorf	1	G.McConnell	S	S.McInnis	O	B.Shotton	C	C.Blankenship
/C	B.Madden	1	G.Davis	O	D.Reilley	/C	J.Casey	/2	A.Orth	/O	A.Strunk	/1	H.Patterson	1	J.Slattery
/O	P.Howard	O	G.Cravath	S	D.Stark	/1	D.Gainer	/2	N.Ball	/S	M.Rath	C	W.Smith	O	D.Gessler
/1	B.Danzig	2	B.Reilly	/3	M.Netzel	/1	H.Jennings	/2	J.Ward	/O	J.Jackson	O	B.Killefer	O	W.Miller
/S	S.Yerkes	/O	C.Barrows	/O	T.Raftery			/2	B.Vaughn	/C	E.Larkin	/O	C.Rossman	1	J.Freeman
		/1	J.Donahue	/C	B.Higgins			/1	E.Tiemeyer	/2	J.Curry			3	S.Kelly
P	F.Arellanes	/1	H.Patterson	/O	J.Clarke	P	G.Mullin	/S	J.Wanner	/C	D.Powers	P	J.Powell	/O	J.Tannehill
P	J.Wood			/O	W.Doane	P	E.Willett	H	I.McIlveen			P	R.Waddell	/C	J.Hardy
P	E.Cicotte	P	F.Smith	/C	G.Land	P	E.Summers			P	E.Plank	P	B.Pelty	/3	B.Shipke
P	C.Chech	P	J.Scott	/O	D.Sullivan	P	E.Killian	P	J.Warhop	P	C.Bender	P	B.Bailey	/C	M.Kahoe
		P	E.Walsh			P	B.Donovan	P	J.Lake	P	C.Morgan	P	B.Grahame	/O	O.Collins
P	E.Steele	P	B.Burns	P	C.Young	P	K.Speer	P	R.Manning	P	H.Krause			/1	T.Crooke
P	R.Collins	P	H.Berger	P	R.Works	P	L.Brockett	P	J.Coombs	P	B.Dinneen	/O	G.Cravath
P	B.Schlitzer	P	H.Suter	P	A.Joss	/P	G.Suggs	P	S.Doyle			P	D.Criss	/O	F.Hemphill
P	E.Karger	P	L.Fiene	P	C.Falkenberg	/P	B.Lelivelt			P	J.Dygert	P	H.Howell	/O	J.Sebring
P	C.Morgan	/P	F.Olmstead	P	B.Rhoads	/P	E.Lafitte	P	T.Hughes	R	R.Vickers	/C	C.Rose
P	J.Ryan	/P	F.Owen			/P	E.Jones	P	J.Quinn	/P	B.Schlitzer	P	E.Kusel	P	W.Johnson
P	C.Hall	/P	N.Altrock	P	G.Liebhardt			P	P.Wilson	/P	T.Atkins	/P	J.Gilligan	P	B.Groom
P	L.Pape			P	C.Sitton			/P	J.Chesbro	/P	J.Kull	/P	P.Stremmel	P	D.Gray
P	F.Burchell			/P	H.Ables			/P	D.Newton			/P	B.McCorry	P	C.Smith
/P	C.Smith			/P	L.Wright			/P	D.Carroll					P	T.Hughes
/P	W.Matthews			/P	J.Upp			/P	B.Schmidt						
/P	F.Anderson			/P	H.Otis			/P	R.Ford					P	R.Witherup
/P	J.Chesbro			/P	R.Booles									/O	D.Reisling
/P	C.Nourse			/P	W.Mitchell									/P	F.Oberlin
				/P	F.Winchell									/P	N.Altrock
														/P	D.Walker
														/P	B.Burns
														/P	B.Forman
														/P	J.Ohl
														/P	B.Keeley
														/P	J.Hovlik

TEAM	G	W	L	PCT	GB	R	OR	AB	H	2B	3B	HR	BB	SO	AVG	OBP	SLG	PRO	PRO+	BR	/A	PF	CHI	RC	SB	CS	SBA	SBR
DET	158	98	54	.645		666	493	5095	1360	209	58	19	397		.267	.325	.342	.667	113	98	70	104	103	660	280			
PHI	153	95	58	.621	3.5	605	408	4906	1257	186	88	21	403		.256	.321	.343	.664	115	91	79	102	97	613	205			
BOS	152	88	63	.583	9.5	597	550	4979	1307	151	69	20	348		.263	.321	.333	.654	112	73	60	102	99	599	215			
CHI	159	78	74	.513	20	492	463	5018	1109	145	56	4	441		.221	.291	.275	.566	89	-73	-53	96	104	474	211			
NY	153	74	77	.490	23.5	590	587	4981	1234	143	61	16	407		.248	.313	.311	.624	103	25	21	101	105	547	187			
CLE	155	71	82	.464	27.5	493	532	5048	1216	173	81	10	283		.241	.288	.313	.601	93	-28	-48	104	99	501	174			
STL	154	61	89	.407	36	441	575	4964	1151	116	45	10	331		.232	.287	.279	.566	91	-79	-48	93	100	436	136			
WAS	156	42	110	.276	56	380	656	4983	1113	149	41	9	321		.223	.276	.275	.551	84	-108	-89	95	91	420	136			
TOT	620					4264		39974	9747	1272	499	109	2931	4918	.244	.303	.309	.611						1544				

TEAM	CG	SH	SV	IP	H	H/G	HR	BB	SO	RAT	ERA	ERA+	OAV	OOB	PR	/A	PF	CPI	FA	E	DP	FW	PW	BW	SBW	DIF
DET	117	17	12	1420¹	1254	7.9	16	359	528	10.6	2.26	111	.238	.293	33	40	102	100	.959	276	87	.4	4.5	8.0		9.1
PHI	110	27	3	1378	1069	7.0	9	386	728	9.9	1.93	124	.217	.282	82	72	97	96	.961	245	92	1.8	8.2	9.0		-.5
BOS	75	11	15	1360¹	1214	8.0	18	384	555	10.9	2.59	96	.243	.303	-19	-16	101	96	.955	292	95	-1.3	-1.8	6.8		8.8
CHI	115	26	4	1430¹	1182	7.4	8	340	669	9.9	2.05	114	.229	.283	67	44	95	96	.964	246	101	2.4	5.0	-6.0		.6
NY	94	18	8	1350¹	1223	8.2	21	422	597	11.4	2.65	95	.248	.316	-26	-21	102	104	.948	330	94	-3.6	-2.4	2.4		2.1
CLE	110	15	3	1361	1212	8.0	9	348	568	10.6	2.40	106	.250	.307	11	21	103	107	.957	278	110	-.0	2.4	-5.5		-2.4
STL	105	21	4	1354²	1287	8.6	16	383	620	11.4	2.88	84	.261	.319	-61	-72	98	101	.958	267	107	.5	-8.2	-5.5		-.9
WAS	99	11	2	1374²	1288	8.4	12	424	653	11.6	3.04	80	.248	.312	-87	-96	98	87	.957	280	100	-.0	-10.9	-10.1		-12.9
TOT	825	146	51	11029²		7.9				10.8	2.47		.244	.303					.957	2214	786					

Runs		Hits		Doubles		Triples		Home Runs		Total Bases	
Cobb-Det	116	Cobb-Det	216	Crawford-Det	35	Baker-Phi	19	Cobb-Det	9	Cobb-Det	296
Bush-Det	114	Collins-Phi	198	Lajoie-Cle	33	Murphy-Phi	14	Speaker-Bos	7	Crawford-Det	266
Collins-Phi	104	Crawford-Det	185	Cobb-Det	33	Crawford-Det	14	Stahl-Bos	6	Collins-Phi	257
Lord-Bos	86	Speaker-Bos	168	Collins-Phi	30			Crawford-Det	6	Baker-Phi	242
Crawford-Det	83	Lord-Bos	166	Murphy-Phi	28			Murphy-Phi	5	Speaker-Bos	241

Runs Batted In		Runs Produced		Bases On Balls		Batting Average		On Base Percentage		Slugging Average	
Cobb-Det	107	Cobb-Det	214	Bush-Det	88	Cobb-Det	.377	Cobb-Det	.431	Cobb-Det	.517
Crawford-Det	97	Crawford-Det	174	Collins-Phi	62	Collins-Phi	.347	Collins-Phi	.416	Crawford-Det	.452
Baker-Phi	85	Collins-Phi	157	Demmitt-NY	55	Lajoie-Cle	.324	Bush-Det	.380	Collins-Phi	.450
Speaker-Bos	77	Baker-Phi	154	McIntyre-Det	54	Crawford-Det	.314	Lajoie-Cle	.378	Baker-Phi	.447
Davis-Phi	75	Bush-Det	147			Lord-Bos	.311	Stahl-Bos	.377	Speaker-Bos	.443

Production		Adjusted Production		Batter Runs		Adjusted Batter Runs		Clutch Hitting Index		Runs Created	
Cobb-Det	.947	Cobb-Det	190	Cobb-Det	63.3	Cobb-Det	57.9	Chase-NY	143	Cobb-Det	159
Collins-Phi	.866	Collins-Phi	170	Collins-Phi	49.1	Collins-Phi	46.9	Engle-NY	132	Collins-Phi	134
Crawford-Det	.817	Stahl-Bos	153	Crawford-Det	36.7	Crawford-Det	32.4	Crawford-Det	129	Crawford-Det	108
Stahl-Bos	.812	Crawford-Det	151	Speaker-Bos	31.5	Speaker-Bos	29.6	Cobb-Det	125	Speaker-Bos	99
Lajoie-Cle	.809	Speaker-Bos	151	Lajoie-Cle	28.8	Stahl-Bos	26.8	Davis-Phi	122	Baker-Phi	90

Total Average		Stolen Bases		Stolen Base Average	Stolen Base Runs	Fielding Runs		Total Player Rating	
Cobb-Det	1.193	Cobb-Det	76			Speaker-Bos	23.0	Cobb-Det	6.1
Collins-Phi	1.051	Collins-Phi	67			Lajoie-Cle	18.6	Collins-Phi	5.7
Stahl-Bos	.857	Bush-Det	53			Parent-Chi	16.6	Speaker-Bos	5.2
Speaker-Bos	.854	Lord-Bos	36			McConnell-Bos	14.5	Lajoie-Cle	4.6
Crawford-Det	.851	Dougherty-Chi	36			Wagner-Bos	14.0	Baker-Phi	2.5

Wins		Win Percentage		Games		Complete Games		Shutouts		Saves	
Mullin-Det	29	Mullin-Det	.784	Smith-Chi	51	Smith-Chi	37	Walsh-Chi	8	Arellanes-Bos	8
Smith-Chi	25	Krause-Phi	.692	Arellanes-Bos	45	Young-Cle	30	Smith-Chi	7	Powell-StL	3
Willett-Det	21	Bender-Phi	.692	Groom-Was	44	Mullin-Det	29	Krause-Phi	7		
		Summers-Det	.679	Willett-Det	41	Johnson-Was	27	Coombs-Phi	6		
		Willett-Det	.677			Morgan-Bos-Phi	26				

Innings Pitched		Fewest Hits/Game		Fewest BB/Game		Strikeouts		Strikeouts/Game		Ratio	
Smith-Chi	365.0	Morgan-Bos-Phi	6.26	Joss-Cle	1.15	Smith-Chi	177	Berger-Cle	5.90	Walsh-Chi	8.60
Mullin-Det	303.2	Krause-Phi	6.38	White-Chi	1.57	Johnson-Was	164	Krause-Phi	5.87	Joss-Cle	8.64
Johnson-Was	296.1	Walsh-Chi	6.49	Powell-StL	1.58	Berger-Cle	162	Bender-Phi	5.80	Smith-Chi	8.73
Young-Cle	294.1	Cicotte-Bos	6.61	Bender-Phi	1.62	Bender-Phi	161	Waddell-StL	5.76	Bender-Phi	8.86
Morgan-Bos-Phi	293.1	Wood-Bos	6.78	Summers-Det	1.66	Waddell-StL	141	Bailey-StL	5.16	Krause-Phi	9.00

Earned Run Average		Adjusted ERA		Opponents' Batting Avg.		Opponents' On Base Pct.		Starter Runs		Adjusted Starter Runs	
Krause-Phi	1.39	Krause-Phi	172	Morgan-Bos-Phi	.202	Walsh-Chi	.253	Walsh-Chi	27.2	Krause-Phi	23.8
Walsh-Chi	1.41	Walsh-Chi	166	Walsh-Chi	.203	Bender-Phi	.254	Smith-Chi	27.2	Walsh-Chi	23.8
Bender-Phi	1.66	Joss-Cle	149	Krause-Phi	.204	Joss-Cle	.255	Krause-Phi	25.5	Joss-Cle	22.8
Joss-Cle	1.71	Killian-Det	147	Wood-Bos	.209	Smith-Chi	.257	Bender-Phi	22.6	Smith-Chi	21.7
Killian-Det	1.71	Bender-Phi	145	Cicotte-Bos	.210	Krause-Phi	.266	Morgan-Bos-Phi	21.5	Bender-Phi	20.6

Clutch Pitching Index		Relief Runs	Adjusted Relief Runs	Relief Ranking	Total Pitcher Index		Total Baseball Ranking	
Burns-Was-Chi	142				Smith-Chi	4.6	Cobb-Det	6.1
Killian-Det	132				Walsh-Chi	4.4	Collins-Phi	5.7
Brockett-NY	132				Bender-Phi	2.9	Speaker-Bos	5.2
Waddell-StL	125				Lake-NY	2.7	Lajoie-Cle	4.6
Bailey-StL	117				Plank-Phi	2.7	Smith-Chi	4.6

March 25 Chalmers Auto Company of Detroit offers to award a new car to the batting champs of each league, and the National Commission accepts.

April 1 Johnny Kling, who played for a Chicago semipro team while holding out for the entire 1909 season, is reinstated, fined $700, and required to play for the Cubs at his 1908 salary of $4,500.

May 4 President Taft sees the Reds and the Cardinals at Robison Field in St. Louis. Reds pitchers will walk 16 in the ugly 12–3 loss, but Taft doesn't stick around. He leaves for Sportsman's Park in hopes of seeing some good baseball and is rewarded by a 3–3, 14-inning battle between the Browns' Joe Lake and the Naps' Cy Young that ends in darkness.

May 23 The Reds' Dode Paskert steals second, third, and home in the last inning against Boston.

May 26 The Pirates' Honus Wagner and John Miller narrowly escape death when their car crashes into the safety gates of a railroad crossing in Carnegie, Pa.

June 21 Brooklyn rookie Jack Dalton has five straight hits off Christy Mathewson. Dalton will finish 1910 hitting .227.

June 22 Congressman John K. Tener, former Chicago White Stockings and Pittsburgh Alleghenies pitcher, wins the Republican nomination for governor of Pennsylvania. He will be elected and will serve as president of the NL while governor.

August 3 St. Louis manager-catcher Roger Bresnahan pitches 3⅓ innings, giving up six hits and no runs against Brooklyn. He last pitched in 1901, and will end his career with a mark of 4–1 as a hurler.

August 13 In the most evenly matched game ever played, the Pirates and Superbas (Dodgers) each have eight runs, 13 hits, 38 at bats, five strikeouts, three walks, one hit batter, one passed ball, 13 assists, 27 putouts, two errors, and use two pitchers.

August 23 Fred Clarke makes a record four outfield assists for Pittsburgh against the Phils.

September 19* A game between Mobile and Atlanta (Southern Association) takes just 32 minutes to complete. The game is conducted as an experiment with batters swinging at every good pitch and little time taken between pitches. There are no strikeouts and one walk as Mobile wins, 2–1.

October 9* The Leland Giants begin a 16-game series in Havana, Cuba. The black team will play a series against the AL champion Detroit Tigers.

October 18 The Reds beat the Indians, 8–5, in the seventh game of the first Ohio championship series.

October 20 Cubs manager Frank Chance becomes the first player ejected from a World Series game. Umpire Tom Connolly tosses Chance for protesting a Danny Murphy home run that struck a sign over the right field bleachers in Chicago in decisive Game 5.

December 13 Former New York Giant Dan McGann, who ended his 13-year career in 1908, shoots himself in a Louisville hotel.

	BOSTON		BROOKLYN		CHICAGO		CINCINNATI		NEW YORK		PHILADELPHIA		PITTSBURGH		ST.LOUIS
M	F.Lake	M	B.Dahlen	M	F.Chance	M	C.Griffith	M	J.McGraw	M	R.Dooin	M	F.Clarke	M	R.Bresnahan
1B	B.Sharpe	1B	J.Daubert	1B	F.Chance	1B	D.Hoblitzel	1B	F.Merkle	1B	K.Bransfield	1B	J.Flynn	1B	E.Konetchy
2B	D.Shean	2B	J.Hummel	2B	J.Evers	2B	D.Egan	2B	L.Doyle	2B	O.Knabe	2B	D.Miller	2B	M.Huggins
SS	B.Sweeney	SS	T.Smith	SS	J.Tinker	SS	T.McMillan	SS	A.Bridwell	SS	M.Doolan	SS	H.Wagner	SS	A.Hauser
3B	B.Herzog	3B	E.Lennox	3B	H.Steinfeldt	3B	H.Lobert	3B	A.Devlin	3B	E.Grant	3B	B.Byrne	3B	M.Mowrey
LF	B.Collins	LF	Z.Wheat	LF	J.Sheckard	LF	B.Bescher	LF	J.Devore	LF	S.Magee	LF	F.Clarke	LF	R.Ellis
CF	F.Beck	CF	B.Davidson	CF	S.Hofman	CF	D.Paskert	CF	F.Snodgrass	CF	J.Bates	CF	T.Leach	CF	R.Oakes
RF	D.Miller	RF	J.Dalton	RF	F.Schulte	RF	M.Mitchell	RF	R.Murray	RF	J.Titus	RF	C.Wilson	RF	S.Evans
C	P.Graham	C	B.Bergen	C	L.McLean	C	C.Meyers	C	R.Dooin	C	G.Gibson	C	E.Phelps
S	E.Abbaticchio	O1	A.Burch	C1	J.Archer	S3	T.Downey	O	C.Seymour	2O	J.Walsh	O	V.Campbell	S	R.Bresnahan
C	H.Smith	3	P.McElveen	2S	H.Zimmerman	C	T.Clarke	O	B.Becker	C	P.Moran	2S	B.McKechnie	S	R.Hulswitt
32	G.Getz	C	T.Erwin	O	W.Miller	S2	A.Fletcher	1	J.Ward	1	H.Hyatt	O	Z.Zacher
C	B.Rariden	S	D.Stark	C	T.Needham	3	S.Woodruff	O	R.Thomas	O	M.Simon	S	F.Betcher
O	W.Good	O	B.Coulson	O	J.Kane	2	M.Corcoran	C	A.Wilson	1	F.Luderus	/1	J.Kading	O	O.Abbott
O	H.Moran	O	H.Smith	1	F.Luderus	/3	A.Phelan	/3	T.Shafer	C	F.Jacklitsch	/1	B.Sharpe	C	J.Bliss
3	J.Burg	S	T.McMillan	H	D.Miller	/O	S.McCabe	/1	H.Gowdy	/C	E.McDonough	/S	A.McCarthy	/3	J.Barbeau
/O	R.Sellers	C	O.Miller			/C	F.Roth	/O	W.Keeler	/O	J.Castle	/O	M.Carey	/O	B.O'Hara
1	D.Martel	/O	H.Lumley	P	M.Brown	/S	C.Charles	/O	E.Zacher	/C	H.Cheek	/C	P.O'Connor	/C	E.Lush
/O	B.Cooney	H	T.Jordan	P	K.Cole	/3	J.Doyle					/S	E.Abbaticchio	/C	B.Kelly
H	F.Liese	H	B.Dahlen	P	H.McIntire	/S	D.Altizer	P	C.Mathewson	P	E.Moore				
/C	R.Elliott	/O	G.Hunter	P	E.Reulbach	/3	R.Robinson	P	H.Wiltse	P	B.Ewing	P	H.Camnitz	P	B.Harmon
H	A.Kruger			P	O.Overall	/S	M.Konnick	P	L.Drucke	P	L.Moren	P	B.Adams	P	J.Lush
H	F.Lake	P	N.Rucker			H	G.Wheeler	P	D.Crandall	P	G.McQuillan	P	L.Leifield	P	V.Willis
/O	J.Riley	P	G.Bell	P	L.Richie	/O	N.Crompton	P	R.Ames	P	E.Stack	P	K.White	P	F.Corridon
		P	C.Barger	P	J.Pfiester	H	J.Burns					P	D.Phillippe	P	L.Backman
P	A.Mattern	P	D.Scanlan	P	B.Pfeffer	/S	B.Meinke	P	B.Raymond	P	L.Schettler				
P	B.Brown	P	E.Knetzer	/P	R.Kroh	R	C.Griffith	P	R.Marquard	P	B.Foxen	P	S.Leever	P	S.Sallee
P	S.Frock	RP	R.Dessau	/P	O.Weaver			P	W.Dickson	P	A.Brennan	P	N.Maddox	/P	B.Steele
P	C.Curtis			/P	A.Carson	P	H.Gaspar	/P	E.Hendricks	P	J.Moroney	P	B.Powell	/P	R.Golden
P	G.Ferguson	P	K.Wilhelm	/P	B.Foxen	P	G.Suggs	/P	D.Rudolph	/C	C.Girard	/P	J.Ferry	/P	B.Hearn
		/P	F.Miller			P	J.Rowan	/P	A.Klawitter	/P	G.Chalmers	/P	L.Webb	/P	E.Zmich
P	B.Burke	/P	S.Burk			P	F.Beebe			P	B.Slaughter	/P	E.Steele	/P	C.Alberts
P	J.Parson	/P	G.Crable			P	B.Burns			/P	T.Sparks	/P	G.Moore	/P	E.Rieger
P	C.Evans	/P	F.Schneiberg							/P	B.Humphries	/P	K.Dowd	/P	E.Higgins
/P	K.White					P	A.Fromme			/P	B.Culp	/P	S.Frock	/P	C.Pickett
/P	L.Richie					/P	H.Coveleski			/P	P.Flaherty	/P	J.Mercer	/P	J.Raleigh
/P	L.Tyler					P	R.Benton							/P	R.Geyer
/P	R.Good					/P	W.Anderson							/P	H.Patton
						/P	B.Spade							/P	B.Chambers
						/P	R.Castleton								
						/P	S.Doyle								
						/P	M.Walker								
						/P	T.Cantwell								
						/P	W.Slagle								

TEAM	G	W	L	PCT	GB	R	OR	AB	H	2B	3B	HR	BB	SO	AVG	OBP	SLG	PRO	PRO+	BR	/A	PF	CHI	RC	SB	CS	SBA	SBR
CHI	154	104	50	.675		712	499	4977	1333	219	84	34	542	501	.268	.344	.366	.710	114	81	87	99	101	696	173			
NY	155	91	63	.591	13	715	567	5061	1391	204	83	31	562	489	.275	.354	.366	.720	116	106	105	100	97	759	282			
PIT	154	86	67	.562	17.5	655	576	5125	1364	214	83	33	437	524	.266	.328	.360	.688	100	30	-8	106	100	655	148			
PHI	157	78	75	.510	25.5	674	639	5171	1319	223	71	22	506	559	.255	.327	.338	.665	97	-4	-25	103	106	641	199			
CIN	156	75	79	.487	29	620	684	5121	1326	150	79	23	529	515	.259	.332	.333	.665	105	0	28	96	98	669	310			
BRO	156	64	90	.416	40	497	623	5125	1174	166	73	25	434	706	.229	.294	.305	.599	82	-132	-117	97	101	506	151			
STL	153	63	90	.412	40.5	639	718	4912	1217	167	70	15	655	581	.248	.345	.319	.664	103	19	43	96	99	609	179			
BOS	157	53	100	.346	50.5	495	701	5123	1260	173	49	31	359	540	.246	.301	.317	.618	81	-99	-122	105	96	536	152			
TOT	621					5007		40615	10384	1516	592	214	4024	4415	.256	.328	.338	.666						1594				

TEAM	CG	SH	SV	IP	H	H/G	HR	BB	SO	RAT	ERA	ERA+	OAV	OOB	PR	/A	PF	CPI	FA	E	DP	FW	PW	BW	SBW	DIF
CHI	100	25	13	1378^2	1171	7.6	18	474	609	11.0	2.51	115	.235	.307	79	54	95	95	.963	230	110	2.1	5.7	9.2		10.1
NY	96	9	10	1391^2	1290	8.3	30	397	717	11.2	2.68	110	.250	.308	54	44	98	99	.955	291	117	-1.7	4.6	11.1		.0
PIT	73	13	12	1376	1254	8.2	20	392	479	11.1	2.83	109	.250	.311	29	38	102	93	.961	245	102	1.1	4.0	-.8		5.2
PHI	84	17	9	1411^1	1297	8.3	36	547	657	12.1	3.05	102	.253	.330	-5	9	103	101	.960	258	132	.6	.9	-2.6		2.6
CIN	86	16	11	1386^2	1334	8.7	27	528	497	12.5	3.08	94	.261	.338	-9	-29	96	105	.955	291	103	-1.6	-3.1	2.9		-.3
BRO	103	15	5	1420^1	1331	8.4	17	545	555	12.1	3.07	99	.259	.335	-7	-9	100	101	.964	235	125	2.0	-.9	-12.3		-1.7
STL	81	4	14	1337^1	1396	9.4	30	541	466	13.3	3.78	79	.275	.350	-112	-120	98	96	.959	261	109	.0	-12.6	4.5		-5.4
BOS	72	12	9	1390^1	1328	8.6	36	599	531	12.8	3.22	103	.265	.349	-30	14	110	110	.954	305	137	-2.4	1.5	-12.8		-9.8
TOT	695	111	83	11092^1		8.4				12.0	3.02		.256	.328					.959	2116	935					

Runs		Hits		Doubles		Triples		Home Runs		Total Bases	
Magee-Phi	110	Wagner-Pit	178	Byrne-Pit	43	Mitchell-Cin	18	Schulte-Chi	10	Magee-Phi	263
Huggins-StL	101	Byrne-Pit	178	Magee-Phi	39	Magee-Phi	17	Beck-Bos	10	Schulte-Chi	257
Byrne-Pit	101	Wheat-Bro	172	Wheat-Bro	36	Konetchy-StL	16	Doyle-NY	8	Byrne-Pit	251
Doyle-NY	97	Magee-Phi	172	Merkle-NY	35	Hofman-Chi	16	Daubert-Bro	8	Wheat-Bro	244
Bescher-Cin	95	Hoblitzel-Cin	170	Wagner-Pit	34					Wagner-Pit	240

Runs Batted In		Runs Produced		Bases On Balls		Batting Average		On Base Percentage		Slugging Average	
Magee-Phi	123	Magee-Phi	227	Huggins-StL	116	Magee-Phi	.331	Magee-Phi	.445	Magee-Phi	.507
Mitchell-Cin	88	Wagner-Pit	167	Evers-Chi	108	Campbell-Pit	.326	Snodgrass-NY	.440	Hofman-Chi	.461
Murray-NY	87	Hofman-Chi	166	Magee-Phi	94	Hofman-Chi	.325	Evers-Chi	.413	Schulte-Chi	.460
Hofman-Chi	86	Mitchell-Cin	162	Titus-Phi	93	Snodgrass-NY	.321	Hofman-Chi	.406	Merkle-NY	.441
Wagner-Pit	81	Konetchy-StL	162	Sheckard-Chi	83	Wagner-Pit	.320	Huggins-StL	.399	Campbell-Pit	.436

Production		Adjusted Production		Batter Runs		Adjusted Batter Runs		Clutch Hitting Index		Runs Created	
Magee-Phi	.952	Magee-Phi	172	Magee-Phi	54.9	Magee-Phi	50.9	Magee-Phi	139	Magee-Phi	139
Snodgrass-NY	.871	Snodgrass-NY	154	Hofman-Chi	32.4	Hofman-Chi	33.2	Evans-StL	135	Byrne-Pit	104
Hofman-Chi	.867	Hofman-Chi	154	Snodgrass-NY	31.9	Snodgrass-NY	31.8	Devlin-NY	132	Wagner-Pit	103
Konetchy-StL	.822	Konetchy-StL	145	Konetchy-StL	28.0	Konetchy-StL	31.5	Murray-NY	125	Hofman-Chi	102
Wagner-Pit	.822	Schulte-Chi	137	Wagner-Pit	27.9	Wagner-Pit	22.4	Steinfeldt-Chi	124	Doyle-NY	101

Total Average		Stolen Bases		Stolen Base Average		Stolen Base Runs		Fielding Runs		Total Player Rating	
Magee-Phi	1.205	Bescher-Cin	70					Shean-Bos	42.5	Konetchy-StL	4.1
Snodgrass-NY	1.071	Murray-NY	57					Doolan-Phi	20.7	Hofman-Chi	3.4
Hofman-Chi	.975	Paskert-Cin	51					Tinker-Chi	15.5	Wagner-Pit	3.2
Konetchy-StL	.884	Magee-Phi	49					Paskert-Cin	14.1	Mowrey-StL	3.2
Paskert-Cin	.884	Devore-NY	43					Knabe-Phi	13.9	Magee-Phi	3.2

Wins		Win Percentage		Games		Complete Games		Shutouts		Saves	
Mathewson-NY	27	Cole-Chi	.833	Mattern-Bos	51	Rucker-Bro	27	Rucker-Bro	6	Gaspar-Cin	7
Brown-Chi	25	Crandall-NY	.810	Gaspar-Cin	48	Mathewson-NY	27	Moore-Phi	6	Brown-Chi	7
Moore-Phi	22	Mathewson-NY	.750			Brown-Chi	27	Mattern-Bos	6	Crandall-NY	5
Suggs-Cin	20	Adams-Pit	.667			Bell-Bro	25	Brown-Chi	6	Richie-Bos-Chi	4
Cole-Chi	20	Brown-Chi	.641			Barger-Bro	25			Phillippe-Pit	4

Innings Pitched		Fewest Hits/Game		Fewest BB/Game		Strikeouts		Strikeouts/Game		Ratio	
Rucker-Bro	320.1	Cole-Chi	6.53	Suggs-Cin	1.62	Moore-Phi	185	Drucke-NY	6.31	Brown-Chi	9.87
Mathewson-NY	318.1	Scanlan-Bro	7.25	Mathewson-NY	1.70	Mathewson-NY	184	Frock-Pit-Bos	5.98	Mathewson-NY	10.04
Bell-Bro	310.0	Moore-Phi	7.25	Crandall-NY	1.86	Frock-Pit-Bos	171	Moore-Phi	5.88	Bell-Bro	10.25
Mattern-Bos	305.0	Drucke-NY	7.27	Brown-Chi	1.95	Drucke-NY	151	Mathewson-NY	5.20	Adams-Pit	10.40
Brown-Chi	295.1	Ames-NY	7.61	Wiltse-NY	1.99	Rucker-Bro	147	Ames-NY	4.44	Crandall-NY	10.44

Earned Run Average		Adjusted ERA		Opponents' Batting Avg.		Opponents' On Base Pct.		Starter Runs		Adjusted Starter Runs	
McQuillan-Phi	1.60	Cole-Chi	159	Cole-Chi	.211	Brown-Chi	.277	Mathewson-NY	40.0	Mathewson-NY	37.6
Cole-Chi	1.80	Mathewson-NY	156	Drucke-NY	.228	Mathewson-NY	.286	Brown-Chi	38.2	Brown-Chi	33.3
Brown-Chi	1.86	Brown-Chi	155	Moore-Phi	.228	Crandall-NY	.289	Cole-Chi	32.5	Cole-Chi	28.5
Mathewson-NY	1.89	Adams-Pit	138	Brown-Chi	.232	Adams-Pit	.291	McQuillan-Phi	24.2	McQuillan-Phi	25.8
Ames-NY	2.22	Ames-NY	133	Scanlan-Bro	.234	Bell-Bro	.296	Adams-Pit	21.3	Adams-Pit	23.1

Clutch Pitching Index		Relief Runs		Adjusted Relief Runs		Relief Ranking		Total Pitcher Index		Total Baseball Ranking	
Cole-Chi	136							Mathewson-NY	6.0	Mathewson-NY	6.0
Brown-Bos	122							Brown-Chi	4.9	Brown-Chi	4.9
Barger-Bro	122							Cole-Chi	3.0	Konetchy-StL	4.1
Mathewson-NY	117							Brown-Bos	2.5	Hofman-Chi	3.4
Curtis-Bos	116							McQuillan-Phi	2.4	Wagner-Pit	3.2

April 14 William Howard Taft becomes the first president to throw out the first ball at an Opening Day game in Washington. Walter Johnson catches it, then pitches the first of his 14 openers. An easy fly hit into the overflow crowd—a ground-rule double—mars his pitching gem, and he emerges with a 3-0 one-hitter.

May 12 The Athletics' Chief Bender pitches a 4–0 no-hitter against the Naps, missing a perfect game with one walk. Bender will be 23–5, one of only two 20-game-win seasons the future Hall of Famer will have in 15 years.

July 1 White Sox Park opens with a 2-0 loss to the Browns. The stadium, later called Comiskey Park, is baseball's biggest at the time and will cost $750,000. The stadium will be the oldest in baseball when it is closed in 1990, to be replaced by a structure called New Comiskey Park.

July 19 Cleveland's Cy Young, 43, wins his 500th game, 5-4, over Washington in 11 innings.

August 4 Athletics' Jack Coombs and Chicago's Ed Walsh duel 16 innings to a 0–0 tie. Coombs gives up just three hits in what he calls his best game. (Working with little rest, he wins 18 of 19 starts in July, August, and September, finishing 30–9 with a 1.30 ERA. His 13 shutouts are the AL record; in 12 other games he gives up just one run.)

August 27* Using 20 temporary 137,000 candlepower arc lights, two amateur teams play a night game at White Sox Park before 20,000. It's first AL night game will be played there in 1939.

September 5 Athletics pitcher Jack Coombs begins a streak of 53 shutout innings, topping Doc White's 45 of 1904. Three years later, Walter Johnson will top Coombs.

October 9 The battle for the AL batting title is decided on the final day, when Detroit's Ty Cobb edges Cleveland's Nap Lajoie .3850687 to .3840947. Neither man covers himself with glory. Lajoie goes 8-for-8 in a doubleheader with the Browns, accepting six "gift" hits on bunt singles which Browns rookie third baseman John "Red" Corriden is purposely stationed too deep to field. The prejudiced St. Louis scorer also credits popular Nap with a "hit" on the Brownie shortstop's wild throw to first base. Cobb, meanwhile, rather than risk lowering his average, sits out the last two games. Ban Johnson investigates and clears everyone concerned, enabling Cobb to win the third of nine straight batting crowns. The embarrassed Chalmers Auto Company awards cars to both Ty and Nap. In 1981 Pete Palmer and Paul MacFarlane uncover an error that, if corrected, would give the championship to Lajoie. The commissioner's committee votes unanimously to leave history unchanged.

October 17 With sore-armed Eddie Plank unavailable, Connie Mack will squeeze five complete games out of two pitchers in the World Series. Chief Bender's 4-1 three-hitter wins Game 1 for the Athletics at Philadelphia. Frank Baker's three hits drive in all the runs needed to beat the Cubs' Orval Overall.

October 18 Jack Coombs struggles for a 9-3 win, walking nine and giving up eight hits, but strands 14 Cubs. A six-run seventh off Three Finger Brown wins the game for the A's. Eddie Collins has two doubles and two stolen bases.

October 20 The A's dispose of Ed Reulbach in two innings, and Jack Coombs coasts on one day's rest, 12-5. He helps himself with three hits.

October 23 Three Finger Brown comes back to face Coombs, who takes a 2–1 lead into the seventh. The A's get to Brown for five runs in the eighth and post a 7–2 win to take the championship. The crowd of 27,374 is the Series largest. The A's .316 batting average is a World Series record.

BOSTON	CHICAGO	CLEVELAND	DETROIT	NEW YORK	PHILADELPHIA	ST.LOUIS	WASHINGTON
M P.Donovan	M H.Duffy	M D.McGuire	M H.Jennings	M G.Stallings	M C.Mack	M J.O'Connor	M J.McAleer
1B J.Stahl	1B C.Gandil	1B G.Stovall	1B T.Jones	M H.Chase	1B H.Davis	1B P.Newnam	1B B.Unglaub
2B L.Gardner	2B R.Zeider	2B N.Lajoie	2B J.Delahanty	1B H.Chase	2B E.Collins	2B F.Truesdale	2B R.Killefer
SS H.Wagner	SS L.Blackburne	SS T.Turner	SS D.Bush	2B F.LaPorte	SS J.Barry	SS B.Wallace	SS G.McBride
3B H.Lord	3B B.Purtell	3B B.Bradley	3B G.Moriarty	SS J.Knight	3B F.Baker	3B R.Hartzell	3B K.Elberfeld
LF D.Lewis	LF P.Dougherty	LF J.Graney	LF D.Jones	3B J.Austin	LF T.Hartsel	LF G.Stone	LF J.Lelivelt
CF T.Speaker	CF F.Parent	CF J.Birmingham	CF T.Cobb	LF B.Cree	CF R.Oldring	CF D.Hoffman	CF C.Milan
RF H.Hooper	RF S.Collins	RF B.Lord	RF S.Crawford	CF C.Hemphill	RF D.Murphy	RF A.Schweitzer	RF D.Gessler
C B.Carrigan	C F.Payne	C T.Easterly	C O.Stanage	RF H.Wolter	C J.Lapp	C J.Stephens	C G.Street
				C J.Sweeney			
32 C.Engle	S1 L.Tannehill	O H.Niles	O M.McIntyre	O B.Daniels	O B.Lord	O2 A.Griggs	3O W.Conroy
3 B.Purtell	O P.Meloan	O A.Kruger	2S C.O'Leary	2 E.Gardner	C I.Thomas	C B.Killefer	2O G.Schaefer
C R.Kleinow	2O C.French	C H.Bemis	C B.Schmidt	S R.Roach	P.Livingston	O H.Northen	C E.Ainsmith
1 H.Bradley	3 H.Lord	3 G.Perring	1 H.Simmons	C F.Mitchell	H.Heitmuller	1 D.Criss	C H.Beckendorf
O H.Niles	C B.Block	S N.Ball	3 C.Lathers	S E.Foster	S.McInnis	1 H.Abstein	C1 J.Henry
/2 C.French	C B.Sullivan	C G.Land	C J.Casey	C L.Criger	B.Houser	S3 R.Corriden	2 B.Cunningham
C B.Madden	1 C.Mullen	C J.Jackson	/2 J.Kirke	/C W.Blair	A.Strunk	O R.Fisher	O D.Ralston
2 A.McConnell	2 A.McConnell	O A.Thomason	/C H.Beckendorf	/O L.Channell	M.Rath	3 J.McDonald	/1 J.Somerlott
/S D.Lerchen	O G.Browne	O E.Flick	P G.Mullin	/O C.Engle	E.Mack	/1 B.Graham	/O G.Browne
/1 D.Moskiman	O D.Zwilling	3 M.Rath	P E.Willett	/C R.Kleinow	C.Derrick	C S.Allen	/1 T.Crooke
/O H.Myers	O F.Chouinard	1 E.Hohnhorst	P E.Summers	/C J.Walsh	P J.Coombs	/O R.Demmitt	/C J.Hardy
/C P.Donahue	O W.Cole	S C.Knaupp	P B.Donovan	H T.Madden	P C.Morgan	/S T.Mee	P W.Johnson
/O R.Pond	O E.Hahn	C N.Clarke	P S.Stroud	/O L.McClure	P E.Plank	/3 R.Jansen	P B.Groom
/S E.Hearn	O R.Kelly	S R.Peckinpaugh	P R.Works	P R.Ford	P C.Bender	/C J.Crisp	P D.Gray
P E.Cicotte	/O B.Messenger	O D.Callahan	P E.Killian	P J.Warhop	P H.Krause	/C J.O'Connor	P D.Walker
P R.Collins	/O C.Barrows	/C S.Smith	P H.Pernoll	P J.Quinn	P J.Dygert	P J.Lake	P D.Reisling
P J.Wood	/O R.Bowser	/C B.Adams	P F.Browning	P H.Vaughn	P T.Atkins	P B.Bailey	/P F.Oberlin
P C.Hall	P E.Walsh	/3 H.Bronkie	/P A.Loudell	P T.Hughes	/P L.Russell	P B.Pelty	/P B.Otey
P E.Karger	P D.White	/C P.Donahue	/P M.Peasley	P R.Fisher		P F.Ray	/P E.Moyer
P C.Smith	P J.Scott	/C D.McGuire	/P B.Lelivelt	P R.Manning		P J.Powell	/P D.Hinrichs
P F.Arellanes	P F.Olmstead	/O J.Rutherford	/P D.Skeels	P J.Frill		/P R.Nelson	/P J.Hovlik
/P B.Hunt	P I.Young	/S S.Nicholls		/P R.Caldwell		/P A.Malloy	/P B.Forman
/P F.Smith	P F.Lange	P C.Falkenberg		/P S.Doyle		/P R.Mitchell	
/P M.McHale	P F.Smith	P W.Mitchell				/P E.Kinsella	
/P C.Mahoney	/P C.Chouneau	P C.Young				/P M.Hall	
/P F.Barberich	/P B.Burns	P E.Koestner				/P B.Grahame	
/P L.LeRoy		P S.Harkness				/P J.Gilligan	
		P F.Link				/P B.Spade	
		P A.Joss				/P R.Waddell	
		P G.Kahler				/P P.Stremmel	
		P H.Fanwell				/P F.Link	
		P H.Berger				/P R.Boyd	
		/P F.Blanding				/P B.Crouch	
		/P B.DeMott				/P H.Howell	
		/P W.Doane					
		/P H.Kirsch					

TEAM	G	W	L	PCT	GB	R	OR	AB	H	2B	3B	HR	BB	SO	AVG	OBP	SLG	PRO	PRO+	BR	/A	PF	CHI	RC	SB	CS	SBA	SBR
PHI	155	102	48	.680		673	**441**	5154	**1373**	191	**105**	19	409		**.266**	.326	**.355**	**.681**	120	105	112	99	99	665	207			
NY	156	88	63	.583	14.5	626	557	5051	1254	164	75	20	**464**		.248	.320	.322	.642	101	44	9	106	102	614	**288**			
DET	155	86	68	.558	18	**679**	582	5039	1317	190	72	28	459		.261	**.329**	.344	.673	110	96	52	107	102	655	249			
BOS	158	81	72	.529	22.5	638	564	5204	1350	175	87	**43**	430		.259	.323	.351	.674	114	93	77	102	94	656	194			
CLE	161	71	81	.467	32	548	657	5390	1316	188	64	9	366		.244	.297	.308	.605	94	-38	-45	101	99	548	189			
CHI	156	68	85	.444	35.5	457	479	5024	1058	115	58	7	403		.211	.275	.261	.536	76	-150	-133	96	**112**	415	183			
WAS	157	66	85	.437	36.5	501	550	4989	1175	145	47	9	449		.236	.309	.289	.598	98	-32	-7	95	94	508	192			
STL	158	47	107	.305	57	451	743	5077	1105	131	60	12	415		.218	.281	.274	.555	84	-117	-90	94	102	438	169			
TOT	628					4573		40928	9948	1299	568	147	3395	5278	.243	.308	.313	.621						1671				

TEAM	CG	SH	SV	IP	H	H/G	HR	BB	SO	RAT	ERA	ERA+	OAV	OOB	PR	/A	PF	CPI	FA	E	DP	FW	PW	BW	SBW	DIF
PHI	**123**	**24**	5	1421²	**1103**	7.0	8	450	789	10.2	**1.79**	133	**.221**	.292	116	91	94	111	**.965**	230	117	3.8	10.1	12.4		.6
NY	110	14	**8**	1399	1238	8.0	16	**364**	654	10.7	2.61	102	.243	.300	-15	4	106	91	.956	285	95	.2	.4	1.0		10.8
DET	108	17	5	1380¹	1257	8.2	34	460	532	11.6	2.82	93	.248	.319	-47	-28	104	101	.956	288	79	-.0	-3.1	5.8		6.4
BOS	100	12	6	1430	1236	7.8	30	414	670	10.7	2.45	104	.235	.297	10	14	101	94	.954	309	80	-1.1	1.6	8.6		-4.5
CLE	92	13	5	1467	1392	8.5	10	488	617	11.9	2.88	90	.261	.330	-60	-50	103	104	.964	248	112	3.4	-5.6	-5.0		2.2
CHI	103	23	7	1421	1130	7.2	16	381	785	**9.8**	2.03	118	.222	**.281**	77	56	95	92	.954	314	100	-1.7	6.2	-14.8		1.8
WAS	119	19	3	1373¹	1215	8.0	19	375	674	10.8	2.46	101	.244	.304	8	5	99	101	.959	264	99	1.8	.6	-.8		-11.1
STL	101	9	3	1391	1356	8.8	14	532	557	12.6	3.09	80	.265	.341	-89	-95	98	106	.943	385	113	-6.3	-10.6	-10.0		-3.2
TOT	856	131	42	11283¹		7.9				11.0	2.52		.243	.308					.956	2323	795					

Runs
- Cobb-Det 106
- Lajoie-Cle 94
- Speaker-Bos 92
- Bush-Det 90
- Milan-Was 89

Hits
- Lajoie-Cle 227
- Cobb-Det 194
- Collins-Phi 188
- Speaker-Bos 183
- Crawford-Det 170

Doubles
- Lajoie-Cle 51
- Cobb-Det 35
- Lewis-Bos 29
- Murphy-Phi 28
- Oldring-Phi 27

Triples
- Crawford-Det 19
- Lord-Cle-Phi 18
- Murphy-Phi 18
- Stahl-Bos 16
- Cree-NY 16

Home Runs
- Stahl-Bos........ 10
- Lewis-Bos 8
- Cobb-Det 8
- Speaker-Bos 7
- Crawford-Det....... 5

Total Bases
- Lajoie-Cle 304
- Cobb-Det 279
- Speaker-Bos 252
- Crawford-Det 249
- Murphy-Phi 244

Runs Batted In
- Crawford-Det 120
- Cobb-Det 91
- Collins-Phi 81
- Stahl-Bos 77
- Lajoie-Cle 76

Runs Produced
- Crawford-Det 198
- Cobb-Det 189
- Lajoie-Cle 166
- Collins-Phi 159
- Baker-Phi 155

Bases On Balls
- Bush-Det 78
- Milan-Was 71
- Wolter-NY 66
- Cobb-Det 64

Batting Average
- Cobb-Det 384
- Lajoie-Cle 384
- Speaker-Bos 340
- Collins-Phi 324
- Knight-NY 312

On Base Percentage
- Cobb-Det .... .456
- Lajoie-Cle .... .445
- Speaker-Bos ...... .404
- Collins-Phi .... .382
- Milan-Was .... .379

Slugging Average
- Cobb-Det 551
- Lajoie-Cle 514
- Speaker-Bos 468
- Murphy-Phi 436
- Oldring-Phi 430

Production
- Cobb-Det 1.008
- Lajoie-Cle 960
- Speaker-Bos 873
- Collins-Phi 800
- Cree-NY 775

Adjusted Production
- Cobb-Det 202
- Lajoie-Cle 198
- Speaker-Bos 169
- Collins-Phi 152
- Murphy-Phi 143

Batter Runs
- Lajoie-Cle 68.2
- Cobb-Det 67.9
- Speaker-Bos 44.9
- Collins-Phi 33.4
- Murphy-Phi 23.6

Adjusted Batter Runs
- Lajoie-Cle 66.5
- Crawford-Det..... 59.7
- Speaker-Bos 42.4
- Collins-Phi 34.4
- Murphy-Phi 24.4

Clutch Hitting Index
- LaPorte-NY 154
- Crawford-Det..... 153
- Chase-NY 135
- Moriarty-Det 127
- McBride-Was 122

Runs Created
- Cobb-Det 156
- Lajoie-Cle 147
- Collins-Phi 123
- Speaker-Bos 115
- Crawford-Det 89

Total Average
- Cobb-Det 1.321
- Lajoie-Cle 1.085
- Speaker-Bos 972
- Collins-Phi 964
- Cree-NY 820

Stolen Bases
- Collins-Phi......... 81
- Cobb-Det 65
- Zeider-Chi 49
- Bush-Det 49
- Milan-Was 44

Stolen Base Average

Stolen Base Runs

Fielding Runs
- Collins-Phi 33.7
- McBride-Was 26.6
- Wallace-StL 21.9
- Speaker-Bos 15.1
- Lajoie-Cle 15.0

Total Player Rating
- Lajoie-Cle 8.5
- Collins-Phi 7.0
- Cobb-Det 6.7
- Speaker-Bos 5.5
- Wallace-StL 3.6

Wins
- Coombs-Phi 31
- Ford-NY 26
- Johnson-Was 25
- Bender-Phi 23
- Mullin-Det 21

Win Percentage
- Bender-Phi ...... .821
- Ford-NY .... .813
- Coombs-Phi ...... .775
- Donovan-Det ..... .708
- Mullin-Det .... .636

Games
- Walsh-Chi 45
- Johnson-Was 45
- Coombs-Phi 45
- Scott-Chi 41

Complete Games
- Johnson-Was 38
- Coombs-Phi 35
- Walsh-Chi 33
- Ford-NY 29
- Mullin-Det 27

Shutouts
- Coombs-Phi 13
- Johnson-Was 8
- Ford-NY 8
- Walsh-Chi 7

Saves
- Walsh-Chi 5
- Browning-Det....... 3

Innings Pitched
- Johnson-Was ... 370.0
- Walsh-Chi 369.2
- Coombs-Phi 353.0
- Ford-NY 299.2
- Morgan-Phi...... 290.2

Fewest Hits/Game
- Ford-NY 5.83
- Walsh-Chi 5.89
- Coombs-Phi 6.32
- Johnson-Was 6.37
- Bender-Phi 6.55

Fewest BB/Game
- Walsh-Chi 1.49
- Young-Cle 1.49
- Collins-Bos 1.51
- Bender-Phi 1.69
- Johnson-Was 1.85

Strikeouts
- Johnson-Was 313
- Walsh-Chi 258
- Coombs-Phi 224
- Ford-NY 209
- Bender-Phi 155

Strikeouts/Game
- Johnson-Was 7.61
- Wood-Bos 6.64
- Walsh-Chi 6.28
- Ford-NY 6.28
- Coombs-Phi 5.71

Ratio
- Walsh-Chi 7.47
- Ford-NY 8.17
- Johnson-Was 8.54
- Bender-Phi 8.60
- Collins-Bos 9.09

Earned Run Average
- Walsh-Chi 1.27
- Coombs-Phi 1.30
- Johnson-Was ...1.36
- Morgan-Phi 1.55
- Bender-Phi 1.58

Adjusted ERA
- Walsh-Chi 189
- Johnson-Was 183
- Coombs-Phi 182
- Ford-NY 161
- Collins-Bos 158

Opponents' Batting Avg.
- Walsh-Chi .... .187
- Ford-NY .... .188
- Coombs-Phi ...... .201
- Johnson-Was .... .205
- Hall-Bos .... .207

Opponents' On Base Pct.
- Walsh-Chi .... .226
- Ford-NY .... .245
- Bender-Phi ...... .255
- Johnson-Was .... .257
- Collins-Bos ...... .264

Starter Runs
- Walsh-Chi 51.4
- Coombs-Phi 47.7
- Johnson-Was 47.5
- Morgan-Phi 31.3
- Ford-NY 28.8

Adjusted Starter Runs
- Johnson-Was 46.3
- Walsh-Chi 46.3
- Coombs-Phi 42.0
- Ford-NY 33.4
- Morgan-Phi 26.6

Clutch Pitching Index
- Morgan-Phi 142
- Olmstead-Chi 142
- Vaughn-NY 122
- Wood-Bos 116
- Coombs-Phi 114

Relief Runs

Adjusted Relief Runs

Relief Ranking

Total Pitcher Index
- Walsh-Chi 7.1
- Johnson-Was 5.8
- Coombs-Phi 4.8
- Ford-NY 4.0
- Bender-Phi 3.8

Total Baseball Ranking
- Lajoie-Cle 8.5
- Walsh-Chi 7.1
- Collins-Phi 7.0
- Cobb-Det 6.7
- Johnson-Was 5.8

March 24 Matthew Stanley Robison, president of the Cardinals, dies unexpectedly. He leaves the club and the bulk of his estate to his niece, Mrs. Helene Hathaway Britton, who becomes the first female owner of a major league club.

April 4 The idea of selecting a Most Valuable Player is introduced. Hugh Chalmers, the automobile maker, offers a new car to the player in each league chosen MVP by a committee of baseball writers.

April 13 The night after the Giants' opener, the Polo Grounds grandstand and left field bleachers go up in flames. President Frank Farrell of the Highlanders invites the Giants to use the AL grounds; the offer is accepted, paving the way for the Giants' invitation for the AL team to use the Polo Grounds when the Hilltop Park lease expires after the 1912 season.

May 13 Fred Merkle has six RBIs as the Giants tee off on three St. Louis pitchers for 13 runs in the first inning, including a major league record 10 before a single out is recorded. John McGraw decides to save starter Mathewson for another day. Rube Marquard works the last eight innings and strikes out 14, setting a record for strikeouts by a reliever. The Giants win, 19-5.

June 3 Cubs right fielder Frank "Wildfire" Schulte's grand slam beats the Giants. Schulte will hit four this season, a record number at the time but Schulte's only grand slams in his 11-year career.

July 11 The Federal Express of the New York, New Haven, and Hartford Railroad, carrying the St. Louis Cardinals to Boston, plunges down an 18-foot embankment outside Bridgeport, Connecticut, killing 14 passengers. The team's Pullmans were originally just behind the baggage coaches near the front. When noise prevented the players from sleeping, manager Roger Bresnahan requested the car be changed. The day coach that replaced the players' car was crushed and splintered. The players help remove bodies and rescue the injured, then board a special train to Boston, where the day's game is postponed. The railroad pays each player $25 for his rescue work and for lost belongings.

July 22 The Pirates pay St. Paul of the American Association $22,500 for right-hander Marty O'Toole, the highest purchase price to date for a player. In 1912, O'Toole will be 15–17 and lead the NL with 159 walks. He will last only two more years.

September 7 Grover Cleveland Alexander (24 years old), winning a rookie record 28 games, pitches the Phils to a 1–0 win over Boston's 44-year-old Cy Young. Alexander's 31 complete games, 367 innings pitched, and seven shutouts lead the NL.

September 22 Cy Young, now with Boston's NL club, shuts out Pittsburgh, 1-0, for his final career victory, number 511. His farewell appearance in a major league game on Oct. 6 is a letdown, as he loses to Brooklyn, 13-3, in his 906th game.

October 5 The National Commission sells motion picture rights to the World Series for $3,500. When the players demand a share of it, the Commission cancels the deal.

October 14 The World Series begins with the Giants dressed in the same black uniforms they wore in their 1905 conquest of the Mackmen, and this Series starts as their last meeting ended: with a Christy Mathewson win. The largest crowd ever to watch a ballgame—38,281—is at the Polo Grounds. Gate receipts are $77,379.

December 14 Pirates owner Barney Dreyfuss proposes that each team in the World Series be required to turn over one-fourth of its share of the gate to the league, to be divided among the other teams. Until now, 10 percent of the gross went to the National Commission, 60 percent to the players, and the rest to the two pennant-winning clubs. The NL will pass the resolution and send it to the AL. It marks the beginning of changes that ultimately give players of the first four clubs a percentage of the World Series money.

BOSTON	BROOKLYN	CHICAGO	CINCINNATI	NEW YORK	PHILADELPHIA	PITTSBURGH	ST.LOUIS
M F.Tenney	M B.Dahlen	M F.Chance	M C.Griffith	M J.McGraw	M R.Dooin	M F.Clarke	M R.Bresnahan
1B F.Tenney	1B J.Daubert	1B V.Saier	1B D.Hoblitzel	1B F.Merkle	1B F.Luderus	1B N.Hunter	1B E.Konetchy
2B B.Sweeney	2B J.Hummel	2B H.Zimmerman	2B D.Egan	2B L.Doyle	2B O.Knabe	2B D.Miller	2B M.Huggins
SS B.Herzog	SS B.Tooley	SS J.Tinker	SS T.Downey	SS A.Bridwell	SS M.Doolan	SS H.Wagner	SS A.Hauser
3B S.Ingerton	3B E.Zimmerman	3B J.Doyle	3B E.Grant	3B A.Devlin	3B H.Lobert	3B B.Byrne	3B M.Mowrey
LF A.Kaiser	LF Z.Wheat	LF J.Sheckard	LF B.Bescher	LF J.Devore	LF S.Magee	LF F.Clarke	LF R.Ellis
CF M.Donlin	CF B.Davidson	CF S.Hofman	CF J.Bates	CF F.Snodgrass	CF D.Paskert	CF M.Carey	CF R.Oakes
RF D.Miller	RF B.Coulson	RF F.Schulte	RF M.Mitchell	RF R.Murray	RF F.Beck	RF C.Wilson	RF S.Evans
C J.Kling	C B.Bergen	C J.Archer	C L.McLean	C C.Meyers	C R.Dooin	C G.Gibson	C J.Bliss
C B.Rariden	C T.Erwin	23 J.Evers	C T.Clarke	S3 A.Fletcher	O2 J.Walsh	OS T.Leach	C R.Bresnahan
S A.Bridwell	S2 D.Stark	O W.Good	S3 J.Esmond	3 B.Herzog	O J.Titus	12 B.McKechnie	3S W.Smith
3 E.McDonald	O A.Burch	2S D.Shean	O A.Marsans	O B.Becker	C P.Moran	C M.Simon	O L.Magee
O W.Good	3 R.Smith	1 F.Chance	3 R.Almeida	C A.Wilson	C B.Madden	S2 A.McCarthy	O O.McIvor
S H.Spratt	O H.Northen	O A.Kaiser	O F.Beck	C A.Hartley	O H.Welchonce	O V.Campbell	O I.Wingo
O G.Jackson	O J.Daley	C J.Kling	S D.Altizer	/O G.Burns	C D.Cotter	1 J.Flynn	O D.Wilie
O J.Clarke	C O.Miller	C P.Graham	/O H.Severeid	/1 M.Donlin	/1 K.Bransfield	/C B.Kelly	/O J.Clark
1 H.Gowdy	O H.Myers	C T.Needham	/S M.Balenti	/1 G.Paulette	C T.Spencer	/2 D.McGeehan	/2 D.McGeehan
O P.Flaherty	S T.Smith	/1 K.Bransfield	R D.Mahoney	/1 H.Gowdy	O R.Thomas	/1 M.Keliher	/S E.Conwell
O J.Kirke	/2 P.McElveen	/O B.Collins	H H.Northen	H A.Schlei	/O C.Lehr	/O J.Dorsey	H M.Reed
C P.Graham	/O A.Humphrey	P M.Brown	P G.Suggs	P C.Mathewson	/C B.Killefer	H J.Shovlin	/O F.Gilhooley
1 B.Houser	/O L.LeJeune	P L.Richie	P H.Gaspar	P R.Marquard	/C R.Kleinow	P L.Leifield	P B.Harmon
3 A.Butler	/O G.Browne	P E.Reulbach	P B.Keefe	P R.Ames	/O P.Mayes	P B.Adams	P B.Steele
3 H.Steinfeldt	/C B.Higgins	P K.Cole	P A.Fromme	P D.Crandall	/C J.Quinn	P H.Camnitz	P S.Sallee
O B.Jones	/S B.Dahlen	P H.McIntire	P F.Smith	P H.Wiltse	R H.Miller	P E.Steele	P R.Golden
O B.Collins	P N.Rucker	RP R.Richter	P G.McQuillan	P B.Raymond	P P.Alexander	P C.Hendrix	P R.Geyer
/3 H.Young	P C.Barger	P F.Toney	P B.Humphries	P L.Drucke	P E.Moore	/P H.Gardner	P L.Lowdermilk
H B.Weeden	P E.Knetzer	/P O.Weaver	/P R.Benton	/P B.Maxwell	P G.Chalmers	/P M.O'Toole	P G.Woodburn
P B.Brown	P B.Schardt	/C C.Smith	/P R.Boyd	/P C.Faust	P B.Burns	/P J.Nagle	P G.Lowdermilk
P A.Mattern	P D.Scanlan	/P J.Pfiester	/P J.Compton	/P D.Rudolph	P E.Stack	/P H.Robinson	/P G.Dale
P L.Tyler	P G.Bell	/P C.Slapnicka	/P B.Burns		/P F.Beebe	/P D.Phillippe	/P J.Willis
P H.Perdue	P P.Ragan	/P B.Foxen	/P B.Schreiber		/P J.Rowan	/P K.White	/P E.Zmich
P O.Weaver	P S.Burk	/P L.Cheney	/P H.Juul		/P C.Curtis	/P E.Cottrell	/P J.McAdams
P B.Pfeffer	/P E.Dent	/P C.Curtis	/P J.Tannehill		/P B.Humphries	/P S.Smith	/P R.Radebaugh
P H.Griffin	/P E.Steele	/P E.Ovitz			/P T.Shultz		/P J.Reis
P C.Young	/P W.Miller	/P J.Rowan			/P B.Ewing		/P G.Zackert
P C.Curtis	/P J.Ryan	/P H.Griffin			/P A.Brennan		/P P.Standridge
/P E.Donnelly	/P R.Aitchison				/P B.Hall		/P B.Hearn
P B.McTigue					/P B.Stanley		/P H.Camnitz
/P B.Hogg					/P J.Smith		
/P J.Parson					/P T.Puckett		
/P G.Ferguson							
/P S.Frock							
/P F.Thompson							
/P B.Burke							

TEAM	G	W	L	PCT	GB	R	OR	AB	H	2B	3B	HR	BB	SO	AVG	OBP	SLG	PRO	PRO+	BR	/A	PF	CHI	RC	SB	CS	SBA	SBR
NY	154	99	54	.647		756	542	5006	1399	225	103	41	530	506	.279	.358	.390	.748	113	109	85	103	96	820	347			
CHI	157	92	62	.597	7.5	757	607	5130	1335	218	101	54	585	617	.260	.341	.374	.715	107	44	43	100	102	729	214			
PIT	155	85	69	.552	14.5	744	557	5137	1345	206	106	49	525	583	.262	.336	.372	.708	101	28	1	104	104	698	160			
PHI	153	79	73	.520	19.5	658	669	5044	1307	214	56	60	490	588	.259	.328	.359	.687	98	-11	-19	101	100	647	153			
STL	158	75	74	.503	22	671	745	5132	1295	199	86	26	592	650	.252	.337	.340	.677	99	-18	0	97	99	651	175			
CIN	159	70	83	.458	29	682	706	5291	1379	180	105	21	578	594	.261	.337	.346	.683	102	-10	15	96	97	716	289			
BRO	154	64	86	.427	33.5	539	659	5059	1198	151	71	28	425	683	.237	.301	.311	.612	80	-152	-131	96	106	528	184			
BOS	156	44	107	.291	54	699	1021	5308	1417	249	54	37	554	577	.267	.340	.355	.695	93	10	-48	108	98	696	169			
TOT	623					5506		41107	10675	1642	682	316	4279	4798	.260	.335	.356	.691						1691				

TEAM	CG	SH	SV	IP	H	H/G	HR	BB	SO	RAT	ERA	ERA+	OAV	OOB	PR	/A	PF	CPI	FA	E	DP	FW	PW	BW	SBW	DIF
NY	95	19	13	1368	1267	8.3	33	369	771	11.0	2.69	125	.246	.300	106	100	99	97	.959	256	86	.5	10.0	8.5		3.4
CHI	85	12	16	1411	1270	8.1	26	525	582	11.7	2.90	114	.245	.320	78	62	97	100	.960	260	114	.6	6.2	4.3		3.9
PIT	91	13	11	1380[1]	1249	8.1	36	375	605	10.8	2.84	121	.248	.306	85	87	101	97	.963	232	131	2.1	8.7	.1		-2.9
PHI	90	20	10	1373[1]	1285	8.4	43	598	697	12.7	3.30	104	.255	.340	14	19	101	104	.963	231	113	1.9	1.9	-1.9		1.1
STL	88	6	10	1402[1]	1296	8.3	39	701	561	13.2	3.68	91	.254	.350	-46	-52	99	97	.960	261	106	.6	-5.2	.0		5.1
CIN	77	4	12	1425	1410	8.9	36	476	557	12.3	3.26	101	.265	.332	21	5	97	103	.955	295	108	-1.4	.5	1.5		-7.1
BRO	81	13	10	1371[2]	1310	8.6	27	566	533	12.6	3.39	98	.263	.344	0	-12	98	103	.962	241	112	1.4	-1.2	-13.2		1.9
BOS	73	5	7	1374	1570	10.3	76	672	486	15.1	5.08	75	.296	.381	-258	-195	113	96	.947	347	110	-5.0	-19.6	-4.8		-2.1
TOT	680	92	89	11105[2]		8.6				12.4	3.39		.260	.335					.958	2123	880					

Runs		Hits		Doubles		Triples		Home Runs		Total Bases	
Sheckard-Chi	121	Miller-Bos	192	Konetchy-StL	38	Doyle-NY	25	Schulte-Chi	21	Schulte-Chi	308
Huggins-StL	106	Hoblitzel-Cin	180	Miller-Bos	36	Mitchell-Cin	22	Luderus-Phi	16	Doyle-NY	277
Bescher-Cin	106	Daubert-Bro	176	Wilson-Pit	34	Schulte-Chi	21	Magee-Phi	15	Luderus-Phi	260
Schulte-Chi	105	Schulte-Chi	173	Herzog-Bos-NY	33	Zimmerman-Chi	17	Doyle-NY	13	Hoblitzel-Cin	258
Doyle-NY	102	Luderus-Phi	166	Sweeney-Bos	33	Byrne-Pit	17			Wilson-Pit	257

Runs Batted In		Runs Produced		Bases On Balls		Batting Average		On Base Percentage		Slugging Average	
Wilson-Pit	107	Schulte-Chi	191	Sheckard-Chi	147	Wagner-Pit	.334	Sheckard-Chi	.434	Schulte-Chi	.534
Schulte-Chi	107	Konetchy-StL	172	Bates-Cin	103	Miller-Bos	.333	Wagner-Pit	.423	Doyle-NY	.527
Luderus-Phi	99	Wilson-Pit	167	Bescher-Cin	102	Meyers-NY	.332	Bates-Cin	.415	Wagner-Pit	.507
Magee-Phi	94	Wagner-Pit	167	Huggins-StL	96	Clarke-Pit	.324	Sweeney-Bos	.404	Clarke-Pit	.492
		Sheckard-Chi	167	Knabe-Phi	94	Fletcher-NY	.319	Doyle-NY	.397	Magee-Phi	.483

Production		Adjusted Production		Batter Runs		Adjusted Batter Runs		Clutch Hitting Index		Runs Created	
Wagner-Pit	.930	Schulte-Chi	155	Schulte-Chi	40.6	Schulte-Chi	40.3	Hofman-Chi	133	Schulte-Chi	127
Doyle-NY	.924	Wagner-Pit	154	Doyle-NY	39.3	Doyle-NY	35.9	Miller-Pit	128	Doyle-NY	124
Schulte-Chi	.918	Doyle-NY	153	Wagner-Pit	38.8	Wagner-Pit	35.0	Grant-Cin	126	Bescher-Cin	115
Magee-Phi	.849	Magee-Phi	135	Sheckard-Chi	31.7	Sheckard-Chi	31.5	Snodgrass-NY	124	Wagner-Pit	109
Wilson-Pit	.826	Konetchy-StL	132	Clarke-Pit	27.0	Bates-Cin	27.5	Wilson-Pit	117	Miller-Bos	107

Total Average		Stolen Bases		Stolen Base Average		Stolen Base Runs		Fielding Runs		Total Player Rating	
Doyle-NY	1.077	Bescher-Cin	81					Tinker-Chi	23.4	Wagner-Pit	4.5
Wagner-Pit	1.057	Devore-NY	61					Doolan-Phi	20.3	Sheckard-Chi	3.8
Schulte-Chi	1.015	Snodgrass-NY	51					Ingerton-Bos	18.2	Herzog-Bos-NY	3.2
Sheckard-Chi	1.003	Merkle-NY	49					Herzog-Bos-NY	17.8	Tinker-Chi	3.1
Bates-Cin	.943							Merkle-NY	15.3	Schulte-Chi	2.7

Wins		Win Percentage		Games		Complete Games		Shutouts		Saves	
Alexander-Phi	28	Marquard-NY	.774	Brown-Chi	53	Alexander-Phi	31	Alexander-Phi	7	Brown-Chi	13
Mathewson-NY	26	Crandall-NY	.750	Harmon-StL	51	Mathewson-NY	29	Adams-Pit	6	Crandall-NY	5
Marquard-NY	24	Cole-Chi	.720	Rucker-Bro	48	Harmon-StL	28				
Harmon-StL	23	Alexander-Phi	.683	Alexander-Phi	48	Leifield-Pit	26				
		Mathewson-NY	.667			Adams-Pit	24				

Innings Pitched		Fewest Hits/Game		Fewest BB/Game		Strikeouts		Strikeouts/Game		Ratio	
Alexander-Phi	367.0	Alexander-Phi	6.99	Mathewson-NY	1.11	Marquard-NY	237	Marquard-NY	7.68	Adams-Pit	9.30
Harmon-StL	348.0	Marquard-NY	7.16	Adams-Pit	1.29	Alexander-Phi	227	Alexander-Phi	5.57	Ames-NY	10.01
Leifield-Pit	318.0	Rucker-Bro	7.27	Steele-Pit-Bro	1.71	Rucker-Bro	190	Rucker-Bro	5.42	Mathewson-NY	10.03
Rucker-Bro	315.2	Ames-NY	7.46	Brown-Chi	1.83	Moore-Phi	174	Ames-NY	5.18	Steele-Pit-Bro	10.33
Moore-Phi	308.1	Harmon-StL	7.50	Wiltse-NY	1.87	Harmon-StL	144	Moore-Phi	5.08	Alexander-Phi	10.35

Earned Run Average		Adjusted ERA		Opponents' Batting Avg.		Opponents' On Base Pct.		Starter Runs		Adjusted Starter Runs	
Mathewson-NY	1.99	Mathewson-NY	168	Alexander-Phi	.219	Adams-Pit	.271	Mathewson-NY	47.7	Mathewson-NY	46.4
Richie-Chi	2.31	Adams-Pit	147	Marquard-NY	.219	Ames-NY	.277	Adams-Pit	34.5	Adams-Pit	35.5
Adams-Pit	2.33	Richie-Chi	143	Ames-NY	.223	Mathewson-NY	.283	Alexander-Phi	33.3	Alexander-Phi	34.9
Marquard-NY	2.50	Marquard-NY	134	Rucker-Bro	.226	Wiltse-NY	.292	Richie-Chi	30.3	Leifield-Pit	27.9
Alexander-Phi	2.57	Alexander-Phi	133	Keefe-Cin	.229	Alexander-Phi	.293	Marquard-NY	27.6	Richie-Chi	27.8

Clutch Pitching Index		Relief Runs		Adjusted Relief Runs		Relief Ranking		Total Pitcher Index		Total Baseball Ranking	
Moore-Phi	130	Richter-Chi	1.6	Richter-Chi	1.1	Richter-Chi	.8	Mathewson-NY	6.7	Mathewson-NY	6.7
Mathewson-NY	122							Alexander-Phi	3.6	Wagner-Pit	4.5
Richie-Chi	119							Adams-Pit	3.5	Sheckard-Chi	3.8
Leifield-Pit	117							Leifield-Pit	3.2	Alexander-Phi	3.6
Gaspar-Cin	115							Rucker-Bro	3.0	Adams-Pit	3.5

January 3 The National Commission adopts a rule that bars World Series winners from playing postseason exhibition games. This obscure rule will lead to a direct confrontation between Babe Ruth and Commissioner Kenesaw Mountain Landis in 1921.

January 14 Bobby Wallace, the era's outstanding AL shortstop, is named manager of the Browns. St. Louis will finish last, and he will be an infielder again by June 1912.

March 17 Plumbers at work on the drain pipes at Washington's ballpark start a fire that burns down the grandstand. Since the water has been shut off, firemen can do nothing. Stands will be rebuilt in time for the home opener.

April 17 Addie Joss' funeral is held at Toledo with Billy Sunday preaching the sermon. The funeral is the second largest in the city's history. His teammates insist on being there, forcing postponement of the season opener.

June 18 Down 13–1 after 5½ innings, the Tigers stage the biggest comeback in major league history to defeat Chicago by a score of 16–15.

July 4 In the morning game between Chicago and Detroit, Ed Walsh stops Ty Cobb's 40-game hitting streak, as the White Sox win 7-3. Cobb has batted .491 since the streak started on May 15.

July 19* While playing center field for Vernon (Pacific Coast League), Walter Carlisle executes an unassisted triple play in the sixth inning against Los Angeles. With men on first base and second base, he makes a spectacular diving catch of a short fly by batter Roy Akin, touches second base, and runs to first base to retire both runners.

October 10 The first game of the Ohio championship between Cleveland and the Reds is won by Cincinnati, 4–0. The next day the St. Louis city series begins, and two days later the Chicago series. These postseason matches are popular with fans and players.

October 11 The first MVPs are announced. Using a point system—eight for a first-place vote, seven for second, and so on—the eight voting writers give outfielder Ty Cobb the maximum 64 points. pitcher Ed Walsh is second, and second baseman Eddie Collins third. The NL winner is the Cubs outfielder Frank "Wildfire" Schulte. Christy Mathewson is second. Winners receive Chalmers automobiles.

October 16 The World Series resumes today, Monday, and the pitchers continue to dominate. Rube Marquard and Eddie Plank are in command of a 1-1 game when Philadelphia's Eddie Collins doubles in the last of the sixth and Frank Baker hits one over the right field fence for a 3-1 victory.

October 17 After criticizing his teammate Marquard's pitching to Frank Baker in his newspaper column, Christy Mathewson takes the mound for Game 3 against 29-game winner Jack Coombs. Matty takes a 1-0 lead into the ninth. With one out, Baker lines another drive over the right field fence to tie it. With that blow, he becomes "Home Run" Baker to future generations; the A's win, 3-2.

October 24 After six days of rain, New York takes a 2-0 first-inning lead. But aided by an overflow crowd in the outfield, the A's collect seven doubles among their 11 hits, pick up three in the third and one in the fourth while Bender shuts down the Giants, and the A's take a 3-1 lead in games.

October 26 Chief Bender cruises to his second victory, a four-hit 13-2 breeze, capped by a seven-run seventh inning to give the A's a championship. Overall, the Giants manage just 13 runs and a .175 batting average off Bender, Coombs, and Plank. Because of the NL's extended playing season, this is the latest ending ever for a World Series, until the "Earthquake Series" of 1989.

BOSTON	CHICAGO	CLEVELAND	DETROIT	NEW YORK	PHILADELPHIA	ST.LOUIS	WASHINGTON
M P.Donovan	M H.Duffy	M D.McGuire	M H.Jennings	M H.Chase	M C.Mack	M B.Wallace	M J.McAleer
1B C.Engle	1B S.Collins	M G.Stovall	1B J.Delahanty	1B H.Chase	1B S.McInnis	1B J.Black	1B G.Schaefer
2B H.Wagner	2B A.McConnell	1B G.Stovall	2B C.O'Leary	2B E.Gardner	2B E.Collins	2B F.LaPorte	2B B.Cunningham
SS S.Yerkes	SS L.Tannehill	2B N.Ball	SS D.Bush	SS J.Knight	SS J.Barry	SS B.Wallace	SS G.McBride
3B L.Gardner	3B H.Lord	SS I.Olson	3B G.Moriarty	3B R.Hartzell	3B F.Baker	3B J.Austin	3B W.Conroy
LF D.Lewis	LF N.Callahan	3B T.Turner	LF D.Jones	LF B.Cree	LF B.Lord	LF W.Hogan	LF T.Walker
CF T.Speaker	CF P.Bodie	LF J.Graney	CF T.Cobb	CF B.Daniels	CF R.Oldring	CF B.Shotton	CF C.Milan
RF H.Hooper	RF M.McIntyre	CF J.Birmingham	RF S.Crawford	RF H.Wolter	RF D.Murphy	RF A.Schweitzer	RF D.Gessler
C B.Carrigan	C B.Sullivan	RF J.Jackson	C O.Stanage	C W.Blair	C I.Thomas	C N.Clarke	C G.Street
		C G.Fisher					
1C R.Williams	1S R.Zeider	OC T.Easterly	O D.Drake	C J.Sweeney	O A.Strunk	C J.Stephens	23 K.Elberfeld
C L.Nunamaker	O P.Dougherty	12 N.Lajoie	1 D.Gainer	S2 O.Johnson	1 H.Davis	O P.Meloan	C1 J.Henry
O J.Riggert	C F.Payne	C S.Smith	2 P.Baumann	O C.Hemphill	C J.Lapp	S2 E.Hallinan	O J.Lelivelt
O O.Henriksen	S R.Corhan	O H.Butcher	O B.Schaller	3 C.Dolan	C C.Derrick	O P.Compton	3 E.Ainsmith
3 B.Purtell	O B.Block	C G.Land	/C B.Schmidt	2 C.Derrick	C P.Livingston	O J.Murray	3 R.Morgan
2 J.Lewis	1 C.Mullen	2 A.Griggs	/2 C.Lathers	C B.Williams	1 T.Hartsel	1 J.Kutina	O T.Long
1 H.Bradley	O C.Barrows	3 B.Lindsay	1 J.Ness	/S R.Roach	/O W.Hogan	1 D.Criss	1 J.Somerlott
1 H.Myers	/1 T.Jones	S C.Knaupp	C J.Casey	/O M.Fitzgerald	/O C.Emerson	C P.Krichell	/O W.Miller
/3 H.Janvrin	/2 F.Chouinard	/C S.O'Neill	/2 G.Tutwiler	/S S.Magner	/3 E.Mack	O D.Hoffman	/O C.Conway
/2 W.Lonergan	/C R.Kreitz	/3 J.Mills	/C S.Wilson	/O G.Zinn	P J.Coombs	1 D.Rowan	R B.Smith
H J.Thoney	/O B.Messenger	/C D.Callahan	P G.Mullin	/O J.Priest	P E.Plank	1 P.Newnam	P W.Johnson
/C B.Madden	/2 F.Parent	/3 T.Hendryx	P E.Willett	/O M.Handiboe	P C.Morgan	1 H.Myers	P B.Groom
/C R.Kleinow	/2 M.Berghammer	/3 H.Bronkie	P E.Summers	/O G.Elliott	P C.Bender	/O G.Williams	P T.Hughes
/1 H.Gunning	/C W.Mayer	/C B.Adams	P E.Lafitte	/O E.Wilkinson	P H.Krause	/2 A.Moulton	P D.Walker
/O I.Wilson	/O P.Meloan	P V.Gregg	P B.Donovan	/2 J.Curry	P D.Martin	/1 E.Gust	P D.Gray
/S S.Carlstrom	/O J.Johnston	P G.Krapp	P R.Works	/O B.Bailey	P D.Danforth	/C C.Southwick	P C.Becker
/C T.Tonneman	P E.Walsh	P W.Mitchell	P J.Lively	/C J.Walsh	/P L.Russell	/3 A.Clancy	P C.Cashion
/S J.Giannini	P J.Scott	P F.Blanding	P T.Covington	P R.Ford	/P E.Leonard	/1 J.Duggan	P F.Sherry
/1 T.Baker	P D.White	P G.Kahler	/P W.Taylor	P R.Caldwell	/P B.Brown	/H J.Crisp	P B.Otey
P J.Wood	P F.Lange	P C.Falkenberg	/P C.Mitchell	P J.Warhop	/P L.Long	R F.Truesdale	/P W.Herrell
P E.Cicotte	P F.Olmstead	P H.West	/P P.Cavet	P J.Quinn	/P H.Armstrong	P J.Lake	
P R.Collins	P J.Baker	P S.Harkness		P R.Fisher	/P A.Collamore	P J.Powell	
P L.Pape	P I.Young	/P B.James		P H.Vaughn		P B.Pelty	
P C.Hall	P J.Benz	/P C.Young		P L.Brockett		P E.Hamilton	
P E.Karger	P J.Hovlik	/P E.Yingling		/P R.Hoff		P R.Mitchell	
P J.Killilay	/P G.Mogridge	/P J.Baskette		/P A.Coakley		P L.George	
/P B.O'Brien		/P J.Swindell		/P H.Ables		P R.Nelson	
/P J.Nagle		/P P.Paige		/P E.Klepfer		/P E.Hawk	
/P W.Moser		/P B.Reisigl				/P B.Bailey	
/P C.Hageman		/P B.DeMott				/P M.Allison	
/P J.Bushelman						/P C.Brown	
/P M.McHale						/P E.Brown	
/P B.Thomas						/P G.Curry	
/P C.Smith						/P J.Pfeffer	
/P F.Smith						/P B.Harper	
						/P H.Gregory	
						/P J.Willis	
						/P W.Moser	

TEAM	G	W	L	PCT	GB	R	OR	AB	H	2B	3B	HR	BB	SO	AVG	OBP	SLG	PRO	PRO+	BR	/A	PF	CHI	RC	SB	CS	SBA	SBR
PHI	152	101	50	.669		861	601	5199	1540	237	93	35	424		.296	.357	.398	.755	119	108	123	98	104	821	226			
DET	154	89	65	.578	13.5	831	776	5294	1544	230	96	30	471		.292	.355	.388	.743	108	91	50	105	102	825	276			
CLE	156	80	73	.523	22	691	712	5321	1501	238	81	20	354		.282	.333	.369	.702	101	1	-7	101	97	716	209			
CHI	154	77	74	.510	24	719	624	5213	1401	179	92	20	385		.269	.325	.350	.675	97	-46	-25	97	108	659	201			
BOS	153	78	75	.510	24	680	643	5014	1379	203	66	35	506		.275	.350	.363	.713	106	35	40	99	91	710	190			
NY	153	76	76	.500	25.5	684	724	5052	1374	190	96	25	493		.272	.344	.362	.706	97	24	-23	107	94	724	269			
WAS	154	64	90	.416	38.5	625	766	5065	1308	159	54	16	466		.258	.330	.320	.650	89	-75	-63	98	100	607	215			
STL	152	45	107	.296	56.5	567	812	4996	1192	187	63	17	460		.239	.307	.311	.618	81	-142	-121	96	105	515	125			
TOT	614					5658		41154	11239	1623	641	198	3559	5093	.273	.338	.358	.696						1711				

TEAM	CG	SH	SV	IP	H	H/G	HR	BB	SO	RAT	ERA	ERA+	OAV	OOB	PR	/A	PF	CPI	FA	E	DP	FW	PW	BW	SBW	DIF
PHI	97	13	13	1375²	1343	8.8	17	487	739	12.5	3.01	105	.264	.338	50	21	94	106	.964	225	100	4.9	2.1	12.1		6.5
DET	108	8	3	1387²	1514	9.8	28	460	538	13.3	3.73	93	.283	.348	-60	-45	104	97	.951	318	78	-1.0	-4.4	4.9		12.5
CLE	93	6	6	1390²	1382	8.9	17	552	675	12.9	3.36	101	.267	.345	-3	7	102	100	.954	302	108	.3	.7	-.7		3.2
CHI	85	17	11	1386¹	1349	8.8	22	384	752	11.5	2.97	108	.255	.310	57	38	96	88	.961	252	98	3.4	3.7	-2.5		-3.1
BOS	87	10	8	1351²	1309	8.7	21	473	711	12.2	2.74	119	.262	.332	89	78	98	113	.949	323	93	-1.4	7.7	4.5		-9.3
NY	90	5	3	1360²	1404	9.3	26	406	667	12.3	3.54	101	.270	.329	-30	9	108	89	.949	328	99	-1.7	.9	-2.3		3.1
WAS	106	13	3	1353¹	1471	9.8	39	410	628	12.8	3.52	93	.277	.334	-27	-38	98	96	.953	305	90	-.1	-3.7	-6.2		-3.0
STL	92	8	1	1332¹	1465	9.9	28	463	383	13.4	3.86	87	.278	.342	-77	-73	101	90	.945	358	104	-3.8	-7.2	-11.9		-8.1
TOT	758	80	48	10938¹		9.2				12.6	3.34		.273	.338					.953	2411	770					

Runs		Hits		Doubles		Triples		Home Runs		Total Bases	
Cobb-Det	147	Cobb-Det	248	Cobb-Det	47	Cobb-Det	24	Baker-Phi	11	Cobb-Det	367
Jackson-Cle	126	Jackson-Cle	233	Jackson-Cle	45	Cree-NY	22	Speaker-Bos	8	Jackson-Cle	337
Bush-Det	126	Crawford-Det	217	Baker-Phi	42	Jackson-Cle	19	Cobb-Det	8	Crawford-Det	302
Milan-Was	109	Baker-Phi	198	Lord-Phi	37	Lord-Chi	18			Baker-Phi	301
Crawford-Det	109	Milan-Was	194	LaPorte-StL	37	Wolter-NY	15			Cree-NY	267

Runs Batted In		Runs Produced		Bases On Balls		Batting Average		On Base Percentage		Slugging Average	
Cobb-Det	127	Cobb-Det	266	Bush-Det	98	Cobb-Det	.420	Jackson-Cle	.468	Cobb-Det	.621
Crawford-Det	115	Crawford-Det	217	Milan-Was	74	Jackson-Cle	.408	Cobb-Det	.467	Jackson-Cle	.590
Baker-Phi	115	Jackson-Cle	202	Gessler-Was	74	Crawford-Det	.378	Collins-Phi	.451	Crawford-Det	.526
Bodie-Chi	97	Baker-Phi	200	Hooper-Bos	73	Collins-Phi	.365	Crawford-Det	.438	Cree-NY	.513
Delahanty-Det	94			Austin-StL	69	Cree-NY	.348	Speaker-Bos	.418	Baker-Phi	.508

Production		Adjusted Production		Batter Runs		Adjusted Batter Runs		Clutch Hitting Index		Runs Created	
Cobb-Det	1.088	Cobb-Det	193	Cobb-Det	78.4	Cobb-Det	70.7	Stovall-Cle	163	Cobb-Det	207
Jackson-Cle	1.058	Jackson-Cle	192	Jackson-Cle	71.8	Jackson-Cle	70.1	Gessler-Was	147	Jackson-Cle	175
Crawford-Det	.964	Collins-Phi	163	Crawford-Det	52.4	Crawford-Det	45.9	Hartzell-NY	131	Crawford-Det	147
Collins-Phi	.932	Crawford-Det	160	Collins-Phi	43.0	Collins-Phi	45.0	Barry-Phi	130	Cree-NY	129
Cree-NY	.928	Speaker-Bos	158	Cree-NY	39.9	Speaker-Bos	39.3	Moriarty-Det	128	Baker-Phi	127

Total Average		Stolen Bases		Stolen Base Average		Stolen Base Runs		Fielding Runs		Total Player Rating	
Cobb-Det	1.464	Cobb-Det	83					Tannehill-Chi	42.5	Cobb-Det	7.1
Jackson-Cle	1.308	Milan-Was	58					Gardner-Bos	23.6	Jackson-Cle	6.8
Collins-Phi	1.125	Cree-NY	48					McBride-Was	23.5	Collins-Phi	4.4
Crawford-Det	1.120	Callahan-Chi	45					Bush-Det	16.7	Speaker-Bos	3.7
Cree-NY	1.103	Lord-Chi	43					Austin-StL	16.3	Baker-Phi	3.6

Wins		Win Percentage		Games		Complete Games		Shutouts		Saves	
Coombs-Phi	28	Bender-Phi	.773	Walsh-Chi	56	Johnson-Was	36	Plank-Phi	6	Walsh-Chi	4
Walsh-Chi	27	Gregg-Cle	.767	Coombs-Phi	47	Walsh-Chi	33	Johnson-Was	6	Plank-Phi	4
Johnson-Was	25	Plank-Phi	.742	Wood-Bos	44	Ford-NY	26	Wood-Bos	5	Hall-Bos	4
		Coombs-Phi	.700	Caldwell-NY	41	Coombs-Phi	26	Walsh-Chi	5	Wood-Bos	3
		Morgan-Phi	.682					Gregg-Cle	5	Bender-Phi	3

Innings Pitched		Fewest Hits/Game		Fewest BB/Game		Strikeouts		Strikeouts/Game		Ratio	
Walsh-Chi	368.2	Gregg-Cle	6.33	White-Chi	1.47	Walsh-Chi	255	Wood-Bos	7.54	Gregg-Cle	9.86
Coombs-Phi	336.2	Wood-Bos	7.38	Lake-StL	1.67	Wood-Bos	231	Walsh-Chi	6.23	Walsh-Chi	9.91
Johnson-Was	322.1	Krapp-Cle	7.62	Walsh-Chi	1.76	Johnson-Was	207	Lange-Chi	5.79	Wood-Bos	10.22
Ford-NY	281.1	Morgan-Phi	7.82	Warhop-NY	1.89	Coombs-Phi	185	Johnson-Was	5.78	Johnson-Was	10.33
Wood-Bos	275.2	Scott-Chi	7.91	Powell-StL	1.91	Ford-NY	158	Kahler-Cle	5.66	Ford-NY	10.59

Earned Run Average		Adjusted ERA		Opponents' Batting Avg.		Opponents' On Base Pct.		Starter Runs		Adjusted Starter Runs	
Gregg-Cle	1.80	Gregg-Cle	189	Gregg-Cle	.205	Walsh-Chi	.280	Johnson-Was	51.6	Johnson-Was	49.4
Johnson-Was	1.90	Johnson-Was	173	Wood-Bos	.223	Johnson-Was	.283	Walsh-Chi	45.8	Gregg-Cle	43.6
Wood-Bos	2.02	Wood-Bos	162	Krapp-Cle	.232	Wood-Bos	.284	Gregg-Cle	41.8	Ford-NY	41.2
Plank-Phi	2.10	Ford-NY	158	Ford-NY	.237	Gregg-Cle	.286	Wood-Bos	40.3	Walsh-Chi	40.8
Bender-Phi	2.16	Plank-Phi	150	Johnson-Was	.238	Ford-NY	.291	Plank-Phi	35.2	Wood-Bos	38.2

Clutch Pitching Index		Relief Runs	Adjusted Relief Runs	Relief Ranking	Total Pitcher Index		Total Baseball Ranking	
Plank-Phi	133				Wood-Bos	6.5	Cobb-Det	7.1
Pape-Bos	130				Johnson-Was	6.4	Jackson-Cle	6.8
Cicotte-Bos	122				Walsh-Chi	6.2	Wood-Bos	6.5
Bender-Phi	117				Gregg-Cle	4.7	Johnson-Was	6.4
Willett-Det	111				Ford-NY	4.3	Walsh-Chi	6.2

January 2 Brooklyn Dodgers president Charles Ebbets announces he has purchased grounds to build a new concrete-and-steel stadium to seat 30,000. During the year he will ease his pinched financial condition by selling half the team to Ed and Steve McKeever.

April 11 On Opening Day in Brooklyn, fans storm Washington Park hours before the 4 p.m. starting time, causing a near riot. An estimated 30,000 people crowd into the outfield and along foul lines. The Giants hit a record 13 ground-rule doubles and are leading, 19–3, in the sixth when the game is called due to darkness.

April 12 The Tinker-Evers-Chance double play combination plays its final major league game together for the Cubs. Vic Saier will replace Frank Chance at first base.

May 1* George Sisler, a University of Michigan freshman, strikes out 20 in seven innings.

May 30* Three doubleheader sweeps: Chicago Green Sox over Richmond, Virginia Rebels; Cincinnati over Reading, Pennsylvania; and, Pittsburgh Filipinos over Cleveland end a short, futile season of the would-be major league competitor, the United States League. Poorly organized and financed, the league began play May 1 and collapsed largely through the failure of the New York franchise to attract fans. The Filipinos, so named because old Pittsburgh favorite Deacon Phillippe was manager, had the best record: 16–8. Players and fields were barely above semipro level, but these promoters will be heard from again with the advent of the Federal League.

June 13 Christy Mathewson wins his 300th game, 3-2, over the Cubs, in his 10th straight 20-win season.

July 3 The Giants Rube Marquard nips Nap Rucker, 2-1, to capture his 19th straight game this season. With two end-of-year wins in 1911, he has 21 in a row in regular season play.

July 23* Iron Man McGinnity is *still* pitching doubleheaders, winning a pair of games for Newark against Rochester (International League) at age 41.

September 17 Center fielder Casey Stengel breaks in with Brooklyn and has four singles, a walk, two stolen bases, and two RBIs in the 7-3 win over Pittsburgh.

October 6 Pirates outfielder Owen "Chief" Wilson hits his 36th triple, a major league season record that still stands.

October 9 Three errors by Giants shortstop Art Fletcher help put Christy Mathewson behind, 4–2, until the team rallies for three in the eighth when George "Duffy" Lewis muffs a fly ball by Fred Snodgrass. Boston ties it in the last of the eighth. The Giants push across a run in the tenth off reliever Charles "Sea Lion" Hall, but Tris Speaker blasts a triple to deep center. Apparently out at home trying to stretch it into a homer, he is safe when catcher Art Wilson, who has just entered the game, drops the throw for New York's fifth error. Darkness ends the game at 6–6 after 11 innings.

October 15 In Game 7 on a cold day in Boston, the Giants catch up with Joe Wood's smoke, teeing off for six runs on seven hits before the 32,694 fans have settled down. Jeff Tesreau wobbles to an 11-4 win and the World Series is tied at three all. (The first game was tied when called by darkness.) The only Boston bright spot is Tris Speaker's unassisted double play in the eighth, the only one completed by an outfielder in World Series play.

BOSTON		BROOKLYN		CHICAGO		CINCINNATI		NEW YORK		PHILADELPHIA		PITTSBURGH		ST.LOUIS	
M	J.Kling	M	B.Dahlen	M	F.Chance	M	H.O'Day	M	J.McGraw	M	R.Dooin	M	F.Clarke	M	R.Bresnahan
1B	B.Houser	1B	J.Daubert	1B	V.Saier	1B	D.Hoblitzel	1B	F.Merkle	1B	F.Luderus	1B	D.Miller	1B	E.Konetchy
2B	B.Sweeney	2B	G.Cutshaw	2B	J.Evers	2B	D.Egan	2B	L.Doyle	2B	O.Knabe	2B	A.McCarthy	2B	M.Huggins
SS	F.O'Rourke	SS	B.Tooley	SS	J.Tinker	SS	J.Esmond	SS	A.Fletcher	SS	M.Doolan	SS	H.Wagner	SS	A.Hauser
3B	E.McDonald	3B	R.Smith	3B	H.Zimmerman	3B	A.Phelan	3B	B.Herzog	3B	H.Lobert	3B	B.Byrne	3B	M.Mowrey
LF	G.Jackson	LF	Z.Wheat	LF	J.Sheckard	LF	B.Bescher	LF	F.Snodgrass	LF	S.Magee	LF	M.Carey	LF	L.Magee
CF	V.Campbell	CF	H.Moran	CF	T.Leach	CF	A.Marsans	CF	B.Becker	CF	D.Paskert	CF	C.Wilson	CF	R.Oakes
RF	J.Titus	RF	H.Northen	RF	F.Schulte	RF	M.Mitchell	RF	R.Murray	RF	G.Cravath	RF	M.Donlin	RF	S.Evans
C	J.Kling	C	O.Miller	C	J.Archer	C	L.McLean	C	C.Meyers	C	B.Killefer	C	G.Gibson	C	I.Wingo
1S	A.Devlin	2O	J.Hummel	O	W.Miller	S3	E.Grant	O	J.Devore	C	R.Dooin	2	A.Butler	O	R.Ellis
O3	J.Kirke	S	B.Fisher	O	S.Hofman	O	J.Bates	S3	T.Shafer	O	D.Miller	C	B.Kelly	3S	W.Smith
C	B.Rariden	O	J.Daley	C	T.Needham	C	T.Clarke	O	A.Wilson	3	T.Downey	O	M.Simon	C	J.Bliss
O	D.Miller	C	T.Erwin	3	E.Lennox	S	T.McDonald	O	G.Burns	O	J.Titus	O	E.Mensor	C	R.Bresnahan
S	A.Bridwell	C	E.Phelps	O	C.Williams	C	H.Severeid	2	H.Groh	23	J.Walsh	H	H.Hyatt	2	J.Galloway
C	H.Gowdy	3	E.Kirkpatrick	3	D.Cotter	C	P.Knisely	/O	M.McCormick	O	J.Dodge	O	T.Leach	O	F.Gilhooley
S	H.Spratt	O	C.Stengel	O	W.Good	3	R.Almeida	C	G.Hartley	3	P.Graham	3	B.McKechnie	O	D.Wilie
S	R.Maranville	/2	R.Downs	/S	T.Downey	/O	A.Kyle	/1	D.Robertson	3	C.Dolan	3	J.Viox	3	P.Whitted
/O	A.Kaiser	/S	D.Stark	/S	C.Moore	/C	E.Blackburn	P	C.Mathewson	C	P.Moran	O	S.Edington	/O	E.Miller
/2	J.Schultz	/C	B.Higgins	/1	F.Chance	P	B.Keefe	P	R.Marquard	/3	J.Boyle	O	S.Hofman	/O	T.Cather
/S	D.Shean	P	N.Rucker	/C	H.Chapman	P	R.Benton	P	J.Tesreau	/O	G.Mangus	/1	S.Gray	C	F.Snyder
/C	G.Whitehouse	P	P.Ragan	/C	M.Hechinger	P	A.Fromme	/2	R.Ames	/3	B.Brinker	/O	O.Nicholson	/3	R.Rolling
/C	M.Gonzalez	P	E.Yingling	/C	G.Yantz	P	B.Humphries	P	D.Crandall		G.Steinbrenner	/3	O.Dodd	/3	J.Kelleher
H	B.Jones	P	E.Stack	P	L.Cheney	/P	H.Gaspar	/2	J.Savage		G.Browne	/O	W.Rehg	/C	E.Burns
/3	A.Schwind	P	E.Knetzer	P	J.Lavender	/P	F.Harter	/C	H.Wiltse	/2	J.Savage	H	R.Bisland	H	J.Clark
P	L.Tyler	P	F.Allen	P	L.Richie	/P	D.Davis	/P	A.Demaree	/C	M.Loan	/1	E.Blackburn	/1	J.Mercer
P	O.Hess	P	C.Barger	P	E.Reulbach	/P	F.Smith	/P	L.Kirby	P	P.Alexander	R	R.Capron	/C	M.Murphy
P	H.Perdue	P	M.Kent	P	C.Smith	/P	H.McGraner	/P	L.Bader	P	T.Seaton	R	M.Keliher	P	S.Sallee
P	W.Dickson	P	C.Curtis	P	M.Brown	/P	J.Bagby	/P	T.Goulait	P	E.Moore	P	C.Hendrix	P	B.Harmon
P	E.Donnelly	/P	B.Schardt	P	L.Leifield	/P	F.Gregory	/P	L.Drucke	P	A.Brennan	P	H.Camnitz	P	B.Steele
P	B.Brown	/P	S.Burk	/P	H.McIntire	/P	J.Frill	/P	E.Shore	P	E.Rixey	P	M.O'Toole	P	R.Geyer
P	B.McTigue	/P	E.Dent	/P	J.Moroney	/P	G.Moore			RP	T.Shultz	P	H.Robinson	P	J.Willis
P	B.Hogg			/P	F.Toney	/P	S.Fletcher			P	G.Chalmers	P	B.Adams	RP	G.Woodburn
/P	R.Kroh			/P	K.Cole	/P	R.Works			P	C.Curtis	P	K.Cole	P	G.Dale
/P	A.Mattern			/P	G.Pearce	/P	G.Packard			P	H.Finneran	P	E.Warner	P	D.Griner
/P	S.White			/P	G.Lowdermilk	/P	B.Taylor			/P	E.Mayer	P	J.Ferry	P	S.Burk
/P	K.Brady			/P	L.Madden	/P	E.Donalds			/P	R.Nelson	/P	W.Cooper	/P	P.Perritt
/P	H.Griffin			/P	E.Cottrell	/P	H.Horsey			/P	H.Ritter	/P	L.Leifield	/P	P.Redding
/P	B.Brady			/P	J.Vernon	/P	B.Prough			/P	H.Wallace	/P	S.Smith	/P	L.Lowdermilk
				/P	R.Sommers	/P	C.Tompkins			/P	F.Nicholson	/P	H.Gardner	/P	W.Dell
				/P	B.Powell	/P	B.Cramer			/P	R.Marshall			/P	R.Howell
						/P	B.Doak							/P	B.Ewing
														/P	G.Zackert

TEAM	G	W	L	PCT	GB	R	OR	AB	H	2B	3B	HR	BB	SO	AVG	OBP	SLG	PRO	PRO+	BR	/A	PF	CHI	RC	SB	CS	SBA	SBR
NY	154	103	48	.682		823	571	5067	1451	231	89	47	514	497	.286	.360	.395	.755	110	89	65	103	104	830	319			
PIT	152	93	58	.616	10	751	565	5252	1493	222	129	39	420	514	.284	.340	.398	.738	110	44	56	98	99	767	177			
CHI	152	91	59	.607	11.5	756	668	5048	1398	245	90	43	560	615	.277	.354	.387	.741	109	62	64	100	98	750	164			
CIN	155	75	78	.490	29	656	722	5115	1310	183	89	21	479	492	.256	.323	.339	.662	90	-90	-72	97	107	639	248			
PHI	152	73	79	.480	30.5	670	688	5077	1354	244	68	43	464	615	.267	.340	.367	.699	91	-23	-68	107	99	671	159			
STL	153	63	90	.412	41	659	830	5092	1366	190	77	27	508	620	.268	.340	.352	.692	97	-27	-11	98	97	675	193			
BRO	153	58	95	.379	46	651	754	5141	1377	220	73	32	490	584	.268	.336	.358	.694	100	-28	-2	96	96	677	179			
BOS	155	52	101	.340	52	693	861	5361	1465	227	68	35	454	690	.273	.335	.361	.696	94	-28	-40	102	99	693	137			
TOT	613					5659		41153	11214	1762	683	287	3889	4627	.272	.340	.369	.710							1576			

TEAM	CG	SH	SV	IP	H	H/G	HR	BB	SO	RAT	ERA	ERA+	OAV	OOB	PR	/A	PF	CPI	FA	E	DP	FW	PW	BW	SBW	DIF
NY	93	8	15	1369²	1352	8.9	36	338	652	11.3	2.58	130	.259	.307	124	118	99	103	.956	280	123	-2.1	11.6	6.4		11.6
PIT	94	18	7	1385	1268	8.2	28	497	664	11.8	2.85	114	.251	.324	84	60	96	99	.972	169	125	6.0	5.9	5.5		.1
CHI	80	15	9	1358²	1307	8.7	33	493	554	12.2	3.42	97	.259	.331	-4	-19	98	89	.960	249	125	-.0	-1.9	6.3		11.6
CIN	86	13	10	1377²	1455	9.5	28	452	561	12.9	3.42	98	.279	.344	-4	-14	99	102	.960	249	102	.4	-1.4	-7.1		6.6
PHI	81	10	9	1355	1381	9.2	43	515	616	12.9	3.25	111	.272	.344	23	54	106	107	.963	231	98	1.3	5.3	-6.7		-3.0
STL	61	6	12	1353	1466	9.8	31	560	487	13.7	3.85	89	.286	.361	-68	-63	101	102	.957	274	113	-1.8	-6.2	-1.1		-4.5
BRO	71	10	8	1357	1399	9.3	45	510	553	12.9	3.64	92	.273	.343	-37	-49	98	96	.959	255	96	-.3	-4.8	-.2		-13.1
BOS	88	5	5	1390²	1544	10.0	43	521	542	13.6	4.17	86	.291	.359	-119	-98	105	95	.954	297	129	-3.2	-9.6	-3.9		-7.7
TOT	654	85	75	10946²		9.2				12.7	3.40		.272	.340					.960	2004	911					

Runs		Hits		Doubles		Triples		Home Runs		Total Bases	
Bescher-Cin	120	Zimmerman-Chi	207	Zimmerman-Chi	41	Wilson-Pit	36	Zimmerman-Chi	14	Zimmerman-Chi	318
Carey-Pit	114	Sweeney-Bos	204	Paskert-Phi	37	Wagner-Pit	20	Schulte-Chi	12	Wilson-Pit	299
Paskert-Phi	102	Campbell-Bos	185	Wagner-Pit	35	Murray-NY	20	Wilson-Pit	11	Wagner-Pit	277
Campbell-Bos	102	Doyle-NY	184	Miller-Pit	33	Daubert-Bro	16	Merkle-NY	11	Sweeney-Bos	264
		Wagner-Pit	181	Doyle-NY	33			Cravath-Phi	11	Doyle-NY	263

Runs Batted In		Runs Produced		Bases On Balls		Batting Average		On Base Percentage		Slugging Average	
Wagner-Pit	102	Wagner-Pit	186	Sheckard-Chi	122	Zimmerman-Chi	.372	Evers-Chi	.431	Zimmerman-Chi	.571
Sweeney-Bos	100	Sweeney-Bos	183	Paskert-Phi	91	Meyers-NY	.358	Huggins-StL	.422	Wilson-Pit	.513
Zimmerman-Chi	99	Zimmerman-Chi	180	Huggins-StL	87	Sweeney-Bos	.344	Paskert-Phi	.420	Wagner-Pit	.496
Wilson-Pit	95	Doyle-NY	178	Bescher-Cin	83	Evers-Chi	.341	Zimmerman-Chi	.418	Meyers-NY	.477
Murray-NY	92	Carey-Pit	175	Titus-Phi-Bos	82	Doyle-NY	.330	Sweeney-Bos	.416	Doyle-NY	.471

Production		Adjusted Production		Batter Runs		Adjusted Batter Runs		Clutch Hitting Index		Runs Created	
Zimmerman-Chi	.989	Zimmerman-Chi	169	Zimmerman-Chi	49.8	Zimmerman-Chi	50.2	Sweeney-Bos	138	Zimmerman-Chi	141
Wagner-Pit	.891	Wagner-Pit	145	Wagner-Pit	32.1	Wagner-Pit	33.8	Tinker-Chi	131	Sweeney-Bos	123
Evers-Chi	.873	Evers-Chi	139	Sweeney-Bos	30.9	Evers-Chi	29.4	Hoblitzel-Cin	124	Wagner-Pit	118
Doyle-NY	.864	Wilson-Pit	134	Evers-Chi	29.1	Sweeney-Bos	29.0	Murray-NY	119	Doyle-NY	116
Titus-Phi-Bos	.862	Konetchy-StL	134	Meyers-NY	28.2	Meyers-NY	25.8	Snodgrass-NY	114	Paskert-Phi	108

Total Average		Stolen Bases		Stolen Base Average	Stolen Base Runs	Fielding Runs		Total Player Rating	
Zimmerman-Chi	1.100	Bescher-Cin	67			Sweeney-Bos	26.9	Wagner-Pit	6.6
Wagner-Pit	.976	Carey-Pit	45			Tinker-Chi	24.7	Zimmerman-Chi	5.1
Paskert-Phi	.965	Snodgrass-NY	43			Wagner-Pit	22.9	Sweeney-Bos	5.0
Evers-Chi	.962	Murray-NY	38			Herzog-NY	19.2	Evers-Chi	3.1
Doyle-NY	.955					Fletcher-NY	15.8	Konetchy-StL	2.8

Wins		Win Percentage		Games		Complete Games		Shutouts		Saves	
Marquard-NY	26	Hendrix-Pit	.727	Benton-Cin	50	Cheney-Chi	28	Rucker-Bro	6	Sallee-StL	6
Cheney-Chi	26	Cheney-Chi	.722	Sallee-StL	48	Mathewson-NY	27	Suggs-Cin	5	Rucker-Bro	4
Hendrix-Pit	24	Tesreau-NY	.708	Alexander-Phi	46	Suggs-Cin	25	O'Toole-Pit	5	Reulbach-Chi	4
Mathewson-NY	23	Marquard-NY	.703	Rucker-Bro	45	Hendrix-Pit	25			Mathewson-NY	4
Camnitz-Pit	22	Richie-Chi	.667	Seaton-Phi	44	Alexander-Phi	25				

Innings Pitched		Fewest Hits/Game		Fewest BB/Game		Strikeouts		Strikeouts/Game		Ratio	
Alexander-Phi	310.1	Tesreau-NY	6.56	Mathewson-NY	.99	Alexander-Phi	195	Alexander-Phi	5.66	Robinson-Pit	9.57
Mathewson-NY	310.0	Robinson-Pit	7.51	Robinson-Pit	1.54	Hendrix-Pit	176	Hendrix-Pit	5.49	Mathewson-NY	10.07
Cheney-Chi	303.1	O'Toole-Pit	7.75	Suggs-Cin	1.66	Marquard-NY	175	Marquard-NY	5.35	Rucker-Bro	10.49
Suggs-Cin	303.0	Cheney-Chi	7.77	Ames-NY	1.76	Benton-Cin	162	Tyler-Bos	5.06	Tesreau-NY	10.85
Benton-Cin	302.0	Brown-Bos	7.81	Adams-Pit	1.85	Rucker-Bro	151	O'Toole-Pit	4.90	Adams-Pit	10.94

Earned Run Average		Adjusted ERA		Opponents' Batting Avg.		Opponents' On Base Pct.		Starter Runs		Adjusted Starter Runs	
Tesreau-NY	1.96	Tesreau-NY	172	Tesreau-NY	.204	Mathewson-NY	.281	Mathewson-NY	44.1	Mathewson-NY	43.0
Mathewson-NY	2.12	Mathewson-NY	159	Cheney-Chi	.234	Robinson-Pit	.284	Rucker-Bro	39.4	Tesreau-NY	37.9
Rucker-Bro	2.21	Rucker-Bro	151	Robinson-Pit	.237	Rucker-Bro	.298	Tesreau-NY	38.8	Rucker-Bro	37.4
Robinson-Pit	2.26	Rixey-Phi	145	Brown-Bos	.239	Tesreau-NY	.298	Marquard-NY	27.3	Alexander-Phi	27.7
Ames-NY	2.46	Robinson-Pit	144	O'Toole-Pit	.241	Adams-Pit	.303	Sallee-StL	26.0	Sallee-StL	26.6

Clutch Pitching Index		Relief Runs	Adjusted Relief Runs	Relief Ranking	Total Pitcher Index		Total Baseball Ranking	
Ames-NY	125				Rucker-Bro	5.2	Wagner-Pit	6.6
Geyer-StL	125				Mathewson-NY	5.2	Rucker-Bro	5.2
Benton-Cin	116				Hendrix-Pit	4.3	Mathewson-NY	5.2
Dickson-Bos	116				Tesreau-NY	3.3	Zimmerman-Chi	5.1
Yingling-Bro	114				Alexander-Phi	3.1	Sweeney-Bos	5.0

April 20 The Boston Red Sox open in the new Fenway Park with a 7-6 11-inning win over the New York Highlanders before 27,000.

April 20 Detroit opens remodeled Navin Park (now Tiger Stadium) and beats Cleveland, 6–5, in 11 innings before 24,384.

May 15 Ty Cobb charges into the stands in New York and attacks heckler Claude Lueker. Other fans and Tigers mix it up before order is restored. Ban Johnson suspends Cobb indefinitely for the incident.

May 18 The Tiger players protest Cobb's suspension and vote to strike. Faced with a $5,000 fine for failing to field a team, club owner Frank Navin orders manager Hugh Jennings to sign up some local amateurs. Aloysius Travers, Bill Leinhauser, Dan McGarvey, Billy Maharg (whose real name was Graham, "Maharg" reversed), Jim McGarr, Pat Meany, Jack Coffey, Hap Ward, and Ed Irvin put on Tiger uniforms. Two Detroit coaches, Joe Sugden, 41, and Jim McGuire, 48, complete the lineup. The Athletics win, 24–2, as Travers goes all the way for Detroit, giving up 26 hits and 24 runs in eight innings. Irvin hits two triples in three at bats and closes his major league career with a 2.000 slugging average. Only one ever plays another major league game: Maharg will bat once for the Phils in 1916. He will also be involved as a conspirator in the Black Sox scandal of 1919. The Tigers return to the field two days later.

July 15* A U.S. team defeats the Swedish Vesteras Club, 13–3, in a one-game Olympic exhibition in Stockholm, Sweden.

August 26 Walter Johnson's 16-game winning streak ends under rules that have since been changed. In the second game of a doubleheader against the Browns, he relieves Tom Hughes with one out and two on in the seventh inning of a 2-2 game. The two runners score and the Nationals lose 4-3. The two runs are charged to Johnson, not Hughes.

September 6 In one of the more dramatic matchups in history, Walter Johnson, who had won 16 straight games before losing, takes the mound in a doubleheader nightcap against Joe Wood, who is seeking his 14th straight win. Wood strikes out nine and beats the visiting Senators, 1–0.

September 7 Eddie Collins steals six bases in the Athletics' 9-7 defeat of Detroit, a post-1900 record that is still unsurpassed. Remarkably, on Sept. 22, Collins will repeat with six steals against the Browns.

October 16 In the World Series finale, in the last of the 10th, Boston pinch hitter Clyde Engle lifts a can of corn to center fielder Fred Snodgrass, who drops the ball. Snodgrass then makes a great catch of a long drive by Harry Hooper. Steve Yerkes walks, bringing up Tris Speaker, who pops a high foul along the first baseman line. Catcher John "Chief" Meyers chases it, but it drops a few feet from first baseman Fred Merkle, who could have taken it easily. Reprieved, Speaker then singles in the tying run and sends Yerkes to third. Larry Gardner hits a long fly that scores Yerkes with the winning run.

BOSTON	CHICAGO	CLEVELAND	DETROIT	NEW YORK	PHILADELPHIA	ST.LOUIS	WASHINGTON
M J.Stahl	M J.Callahan	M H.Davis	M H.Jennings	M H.Wolverton	M C.Mack	M B.Wallace	M C.Griffith
1B J.Stahl	1B R.Zeider	M J.Birmingham	1B G.Moriarty	1B H.Chase	1B S.McInnis	M G.Stovall	1B C.Gandil
2B S.Yerkes	2B M.Rath	1B A.Griggs	2B B.Louden	2B H.Simmons	2B E.Collins	1B G.Stovall	2B R.Morgan
SS H.Wagner	SS B.Weaver	2B N.Lajoie	SS D.Bush	SS J.Martin	SS J.Barry	2B D.Pratt	SS G.McBride
3B L.Gardner	3B H.Lord	SS R.Peckinpaugh	3B C.Deal	3B R.Hartzell	3B F.Baker	SS B.Wallace	3B E.Foster
LF D.Lewis	LF N.Callahan	3B T.Turner	LF D.Jones	LF B.Daniels	LF A.Strunk	3B J.Austin	LF H.Shanks
CF T.Speaker	CF P.Bodie	CF J.Birmingham	CF T.Cobb	CF D.Sterrett	CF R.Oldring	LF W.Hogan	CF C.Milan
RF H.Hooper	RF S.Collins	RF J.Jackson	RF S.Crawford	RF G.Zinn	RF B.Lord	CF B.Shotton	RF D.Moeller
C B.Carrigan	C W.Kuhn	C S.O'Neill	C O.Stanage	C J.Sweeney	C J.Lapp	RF G.Williams	C J.Henry
12 C.Engle	O W.Mattick	S3 I.Olson	O3 O.Vitt	O B.Cree	O H.Maggert	C J.Stephens	C E.Ainsmith
1 H.Bradley	C B.Block	O J.Graney	2O J.Delahanty	O E.Gardner	O E.Murphy	O P.Compton	O1 G.Schaefer
C H.Cady	1 B.Borton	C T.Easterly	1 D.Gainer	C D.Paddock	2O I.Thomas	2O F.LaPorte	C R.Williams
C L.Nunamaker	C B.Sullivan	1 D.Johnston	3 R.Corriden	O J.Lelivelt	1 B.Egan	1 J.Kutina	2 F.LaPorte
O O.Henriksen	O M.McIntyre	2 N.Ball	1 E.Onslow	S T.McMillan	C D.Murphy	C P.Krichell	O T.Walker
2 N.Ball	1 J.Fournier	C R.Chapman	O B.Veach	S G.Street	O J.Walsh	O H.Jantzen	2 J.Knight
/S M.Krug	C R.Schalk	O H.Butcher	C J.Onslow	3 E.Midkiff	S C.Derrick	S W.Alexander	1 J.Flynn
/C P.Thomas	C T.Easterly	O T.Hendryx	C B.Kocher	3 P.Maloney	/3 J.Mathes	E E.Hallinan	O B.Kenworthy
P J.Wood	S E.Johnson	O F.Carisch	C P.Baumann	H C.Dolan	/3 H.Fahey	S J.Daley	/2 B.Cunningham
P B.O'Brien	/O C.Barrows	O B.Hunter	3 H.Perry	/3 H.Wolverton	H C.Emerson	/1 E.Miller	/O R.Moran
P H.Bedient	/C W.Mayer	C B.Adams	/O R.McDermott	P B.Williams	P J.Coombs	/O B.Brief	/S R.Roach
P R.Collins	/1 M.Ens	1 E.Hohnhorst	/O A.Bashang	P C.Coleman	P E.Plank	/C F.Crossin	H J.Agler
P C.Hall	/O D.Berran	C P.Livingston	3 C.O'Leary	/O H.Wolter	P B.Brown	/O R.Brown	/1 T.Long
P L.Pape	/3 L.Tannehill	/S K.Nash	/O B.Leinhauser	S J.Dowd	P B.Houck	/C C.Snell	/3 J.Ryan
/P E.Cicotte	/2 K.Gleason	/O A.Hauger	/2 J.McGarr	/O K.Smith	P C.Bender	/O G.Aiton	R D.Howard
/P B.Van Dyke	H P.McLarry	/3 H.Bronkie	/S O.O'Mara	RP B.Otis	RP H.Pennock	H H.Smoyer	P W.Johnson
/P J.Bushelman	/S L.Blackburne	/3 J.Kibble	/1 J.Sugden	J.Little	P C.Morgan	/S D.Shanley	P B.Groom
/P D.Smith	H D.Paddock	/O H.Davis	/3 E.Irvin	P B.Kauff	/P R.Crabb	/C P.Ketter	P T.Hughes
/P C.Hageman	P P.Wolfe	/O H.Eibel	/O D.McGarvey	/C G.Fisher	P S.Coveleski	/S L.Criger	P C.Cashion
	P E.Walsh	/C L.Nagelsen	/C D.McGuire	/C H.Thompson	/C A.Danforth	/S C.Miller	P H.Vaughn
	P J.Benz	/O M.Meixell	/S P.Meaney	P R.Ford	/C L.Russell	H T.Tennant	P J.Engel
	P D.White	/3 H.Grubb	H H.Ward	J.Warhop	/P H.Barry	/C F.Walden	P D.Walker
	P F.Lange	P V.Gregg	/C H.Jennings	/P R.Caldwell	P J.Bush	P E.Hamilton	P B.Pelty
	P E.Cicotte	P F.Blanding	/3 B.Maharg	/P G.McConnell	/P H.Krause	P J.Powell	P P.Musser
	P R.Peters	P G.Kahler	/3 J.Smith	P J.Quinn	P R.Salmon	P G.Baumgardner	/P J.Akers
	P G.Mogridge	P W.Mitchell	P E.Willett	P R.Fisher	P M.Allison	P C.Brown	/P C.Becker
	/P J.Scott	P B.Steen	P J.Dubuc	/P H.Vaughn	P E.Brown	P R.Mitchell	/P J.Boehling
	/P W.Taylor	P J.Baskette	P G.Mullin	/P G.Davis	/P D.Martin	/P J.Lake	/P L.Schegg
	P P.Douglas	/P G.Krapp	P J.Lake	/P R.Keating	P S.Harrell	/P C.Weilman	/P B.Gallia
	/P W.Johnson	P L.George	P R.Works	/P T.Thompson		/P W.Adams	/P N.Altrock
	/P R.Jordan	P B.James	/P T.Covington	/P R.Hoff		/P B.Pelty	/P H.Herring
	/P R.Crabb	/P B.Brenner	/P B.Burns	/P A.Schulz		/P B.Napier	/P S.White
	P R.Bell	/P L.James	/P C.Wheatley	/P G.Shears		/P R.Nelson	/P C.Griffith
	/P H.Smith	/P E.Wolf	/P W.Jensen			/P B.Bailey	
	/P F.Delhi	/P H.Krause	/P G.Boehler			/P J.Frill	
	/P F.Lamline	/P R.Walker	/P H.Dauss			/P H.Spencer	
		/P J.Neher	/P E.Summers				
		/P M.Walker	/P H.Moran				
			/P B.Donovan				
			/P H.Pernoll				
			/P A.Travers				
			/P B.Troy				
			/P E.Lafitte				
			/P A.Remneas				
			/P P.McGehee				

TEAM	G	W	L	PCT	GB	R	OR	AB	H	2B	3B	HR	BB	SO	AVG	OBP	SLG	PRO	PRO+	BR	/A	PF	CHI	RC	SB	CS	SBA	SBR
BOS	154	105	47	.691		**799**	**544**	5071	1404	**269**	84	**29**	565		.277	**.355**	**.380**	**.735**	110	**104**	64	105	100	752	185			
WAS	154	91	61	.599	14	699	581	5075	1298	202	86	20	472		.256	.324	.341	.665	94	-32	-37	101	**108**	645	**274**			
PHI	153	90	62	.592	15	779	658	5111	**1442**	204	**108**	22	485		**.282**	.349	.377	.726	**117**	83	**111**	96	101	**763**	258			
CHI	158	78	76	.506	28	639	648	5182	1321	174	80	17	423		.255	.317	.329	.646	93	-68	-48	97	102	610	205			
CLE	155	75	78	.490	30.5	677	681	5132	1403	219	77	16	407		.273	.333	.353	.686	98	5	-16	103	98	671	194			
DET	154	69	84	.451	36.5	720	777	5143	1376	189	86	19	530		.268	.343	.349	.692	106	26	49	97	100	705	270			
STL	157	53	101	.344	53	552	764	5080	1262	166	71	19	449		.248	.315	.320	.635	90	-86	-65	96	94	565	176			
NY	153	50	102	.329	55	630	842	5092	1320	168	79	18	463		.259	.329	.334	.663	90	-31	-70	106	97	638	247			
TOT	619					5495		40886	10826	1591	671	156	3794	5157	.265	.333	.348	.681						1809				

TEAM	CG	SH	SV	IP	H	H/G	HR	BB	SO	RAT	ERA	ERA+	OAV	OOB	PR	/A	PF	CPI	FA	E	DP	FW	PW	BW	SBW	DIF
BOS	**108**	**18**	6	1362	1243	8.2	18	**385**	712	**11.0**	2.76	124	.248	**.306**	88	104	103	98	.957	267	88	2.4	10.4	6.4		9.8
WAS	98	11	7	1376²	**1219**	**8.0**	24	525	**828**	11.8	**2.69**	125	**.242**	.320	**99**	**105**	101	108	.954	297	92	.7	**10.5**	-3.7		7.6
PHI	95	11	9	1357	1273	8.4	**12**	518	601	12.3	3.32	93	.258	.336	2	-31	93	99	**.959**	**263**	115	**2.5**	-3.1	**11.1**		3.5
CHI	85	14	**16**	1413	1398	8.9	26	426	698	11.8	3.06	105	.264	.322	44	26	96	104	.956	291	102	1.5	2.6	-4.8		1.7
CLE	94	7	7	1352²	1367	9.1	15	523	622	12.9	3.30	104	.272	.346	6	21	103	**110**	.954	287	124	1.4	2.1	-1.6		-3.4
DET	107	7	5	1367¹	1438	9.5	16	521	512	13.3	3.77	87	.277	.350	-66	-71	98	100	.950	338	91	-1.7	-7.1	4.9		-3.6
STL	85	8	5	1369²	1433	9.4	17	442	547	12.7	3.71	90	.277	.341	-56	-55	100	97	.947	341	**127**	-1.6	-5.5	-6.5		-10.5
NY	105	5	3	1335	1448	9.8	28	436	637	13.0	4.13	88	.282	.344	-117	-71	108	92	.940	382	77	-4.4	-7.1	-7.0		-7.5
TOT	777	81	58	10933¹		8.9				12.3	3.34		.265	.333					.952	2466	816					

Runs		Hits		Doubles		Triples		Home Runs		Total Bases	
Collins-Phi	137	Jackson-Cle	226	Speaker-Bos	53	Jackson-Cle	26	Speaker-Bos	10	Jackson-Cle	331
Speaker-Bos	136	Cobb-Det	226	Jackson-Cle	44	Cobb-Det	23	Baker-Phi	10	Speaker-Bos	329
Jackson-Cle	121	Speaker-Bos	222	Baker-Phi	40	Crawford-Det	21	Cobb-Det	7	Cobb-Det	323
Cobb-Det	120	Baker-Phi	200	Lewis-Bos	36	Baker-Phi	21			Baker-Phi	312
Baker-Phi	116					Gardner-Bos	18			Crawford-Det	273

Runs Batted In		Runs Produced		Bases On Balls		Batting Average		On Base Percentage		Slugging Average	
Baker-Phi	130	Baker-Phi	236	Bush-Det	117	Cobb-Det	.409	Speaker-Bos	.464	Cobb-Det	.584
Lewis-Bos	109	Speaker-Bos	216	Collins-Phi	101	Jackson-Cle	.395	Jackson-Cle	.458	Jackson-Cle	.579
Crawford-Det	109	Jackson-Cle	208	Rath-Chi	95	Speaker-Bos	.383	Cobb-Det	.456	Speaker-Bos	.567
McInnis-Phi	101	Collins-Phi	201	Shotton-StL	86	Lajoie-Cle	.368	Collins-Phi	.450	Baker-Phi	.541
		Cobb-Det	196	Speaker-Bos	82	Collins-Phi	.348	Lajoie-Cle	.414	Crawford-Det	.470

Production		Adjusted Production		Batter Runs		Adjusted Batter Runs		Clutch Hitting Index		Runs Created	
Cobb-Det	1.040	Cobb-Det	203	Speaker-Bos	72.8	Cobb-Det	71.7	Lajoie-Cle	145	Speaker-Bos	175
Jackson-Cle	1.036	Jackson-Cle	190	Jackson-Cle	70.3	Jackson-Cle	65.8	Lewis-Bos	130	Cobb-Det	173
Speaker-Bos	1.031	Speaker-Bos	185	Cobb-Det	67.1	Speaker-Bos	65.3	Gandil-Was	125	Jackson-Cle	166
Baker-Phi	.945	Baker-Phi	176	Baker-Phi	49.2	Baker-Phi	53.8	Milan-Was	124	Baker-Phi	140
Collins-Phi	.885	Collins-Phi	159	Collins-Phi	43.7	Collins-Phi	48.2	McInnis-Phi	120	Collins-Phi	136

Total Average		Stolen Bases		Stolen Base Average		Stolen Base Runs		Fielding Runs		Total Player Rating	
Cobb-Det	1.321	Milan-Was	88					McBride-Was	31.1	Speaker-Bos	7.7
Speaker-Bos	1.310	Collins-Phi	63					Bush-Det	29.4	Jackson-Cle	6.9
Jackson-Cle	1.249	Cobb-Det	61					Louden-Det	22.8	Cobb-Det	6.4
Collins-Phi	1.130	Speaker-Bos	52					Speaker-Bos	21.6	Baker-Phi	6.3
Baker-Phi	1.082	Zeider-Chi	47					Rath-Chi	18.3	Collins-Phi	5.8

Wins		Win Percentage		Games		Complete Games		Shutouts		Saves	
Wood-Bos	34	Wood-Bos	.872	Walsh-Chi	62	Wood-Bos	35	Wood-Bos	10	Walsh-Chi	10
Johnson-Was	33	Plank-Phi	.813	Johnson-Was	50	Johnson-Was	34	Johnson-Was	7	Warhop-NY	3
Walsh-Chi	27	Johnson-Was	.733	Wood-Bos	43	Walsh-Chi	32	Walsh-Chi	6	Mogridge-Chi	3
Plank-Phi	26	Bedient-Bos	.690	Groom-Was	43	Ford-NY	30	Plank-Phi	5	Lange-Chi	3
Groom-Was	24	Coombs-Phi	.677	Benz-Chi	42			Collins-Bos	4	Dubuc-Det	3

Innings Pitched		Fewest Hits/Game		Fewest BB/Game		Strikeouts		Strikeouts/Game		Ratio	
Walsh-Chi	393.0	Johnson-Was	6.32	Bender-Phi	1.74	Johnson-Was	303	Johnson-Was	7.39	Johnson-Was	8.56
Johnson-Was	369.0	Wood-Bos	6.99	Johnson-Was	1.85	Wood-Bos	258	Wood-Bos	6.75	Wood-Bos	9.44
Wood-Bos	344.0	Houck-Phi	7.37	Collins-Bos	1.90	Walsh-Chi	254	Gregg-Cle	6.10	Walsh-Chi	9.78
Groom-Was	316.0	Walsh-Chi	7.60	Powell-StL	1.99	Gregg-Cle	184	Walsh-Chi	5.82	Bedient-Bos	10.29
Ford-NY	291.2	O'Brien-Bos	7.74	Warhop-NY	2.06	Groom-Was	179	Lange-Chi	5.23	Collins-Bos	10.66

Earned Run Average		Adjusted ERA		Opponents' Batting Avg.		Opponents' On Base Pct.		Starter Runs		Adjusted Starter Runs	
Johnson-Was	1.39	Johnson-Was	241	Johnson-Was	.196	Johnson-Was	.248	Johnson-Was	79.9	Johnson-Was	80.5
Wood-Bos	1.91	Wood-Bos	179	Wood-Bos	.216	Wood-Bos	.272	Wood-Bos	54.6	Wood-Bos	57.8
Walsh-Chi	2.15	Walsh-Chi	149	Walsh-Chi	.231	Walsh-Chi	.279	Walsh-Chi	51.8	Walsh-Chi	46.5
Plank-Phi	2.22	Plank-Phi	140	Houck-Phi	.234	Bedient-Bos	.288	Plank-Phi	32.3	O'Brien-Bos	25.8
Collins-Bos	2.53	Collins-Bos	135	Dubuc-Det	.235	Collins-Bos	.297	Groom-Was	25.2	Groom-Was	25.8

Clutch Pitching Index		Relief Runs		Adjusted Relief Runs		Relief Ranking		Total Pitcher Index		Total Baseball Ranking	
Hughes-Was	129							Johnson-Was	11.2	Johnson-Was	11.2
McConnell-NY	121							Wood-Bos	8.6	Wood-Bos	8.6
Cashion-Was	120							Walsh-Chi	6.6	Speaker-Bos	7.7
Kahler-Cle	120							Plank-Phi	3.2	Jackson-Cle	6.9
Plank-Phi	119							McConnell-NY	2.9	Walsh-Chi	6.6

February 1 Jim Thorpe signs with the New York Giants, but the Olympic medal winner will be more of a gate attraction than a threat at the plate.

March 8* The Federal League is organized as a six-team "outlaw" circuit and elects John T. Powers president. It will play 120 games at a level equivalent to the lower minor leagues, but will enhance its status considerably in 1914 to challenge the major leagues.

April 5 An exhibition game with the newly christened Yankees opens the equally new Ebbets Field; 25,000 are on hand to watch Nap Rucker beat the New Yorkers, 3–2. The first homer is hit by Brooklyn's Casey Stengel, who legs out an inside-the-park homer.

April 9 With league approval, the Dodgers play their opener—and first regular-season game at Ebbets Field—a day ahead of the rest of the league. Cold weather keeps the crowd down to about 12,000, and the Phils' Tom Seaton beats Nap Rucker, 1-0.

May 22 Ruling that a ballplayer on the field is a "public person," a New York judge throws out cases brought by New York and Boston players against a motion picture company that took movies of the 1912 World Series.

May 30 John McGraw joins Fred Clarke, Cap Anson, Frank Selee, and Connie Mack as managers who have won 1,000 games.

July 18 In blanking the Cards, 5–0, Christy Mathewson yields a base on balls, ending a record string of 68 innings pitched without a walk.

August 10 Honus Wagner is given a souvenir bat carved from a piece of wood taken from naval hero Oliver Perry's flagship *Niagara,* which was sunk in Lake Erie 100 years before.

September 14 Cubs hurler Larry Cheney hurls a 14-hit shutout against the Giants, defeating them, 7-0, while setting a major league record for most hits allowed in a whitewashing. Milt Gaston of Washington will duplicate the feat on July 10, 1928.

October 4 Despite the Dodgers' sixth-place finish, first baseman Jake Daubert earns a new Chalmers automobile as the NL MVP. Daubert led the NL at .350 and will repeat his batting title in 1914.

October 8 Christy Mathewson ties the World Series for the Giants, shutting the Athletics out for 10 innings to beat Eddie Plank, 3-0. Mathewson also knocks in the winning run with a double in the tenth.

October 12 John McGraw hosts a reunion for Hugh Jennings and the old Orioles. After a night of heavy drinking, he blames his longtime friend, business partner, and teammate Wilbert Robinson for too many coaching mistakes in the Series. Robbie replies that McGraw made more mistakes than anybody. McGraw fires him. Eyewitnesses say Robbie douses McGraw with a glass of beer and leaves. They won't speak to each other for 17 years. Six days later Robbie will begin a legendary 18 years as Brooklyn manager. The team will carry the nickname Robins, as well as Dodgers, during his tenure.

BOSTON	BROOKLYN	CHICAGO	CINCINNATI	NEW YORK	PHILADELPHIA	PITTSBURGH	ST.LOUIS
M G.Stallings	M B.Dahlen	M J.Evers	M J.Tinker	M J.McGraw	M R.Dooin	M F.Clarke	M M.Huggins
1B H.Myers	1B J.Daubert	1B V.Saier	1B D.Hoblitzel	1B F.Merkle	1B F.Luderus	1B D.Miller	1B E.Konetchy
2B B.Sweeney	2B G.Cutshaw	2B J.Evers	2B H.Groh	2B L.Doyle	2B O.Knabe	2B J.Viox	2B M.Huggins
SS R.Maranville	SS B.Fisher	SS A.Bridwell	SS J.Tinker	SS A.Fletcher	SS M.Doolan	SS H.Wagner	SS C.O'Leary
3B A.Devlin	3B R.Smith	3B H.Zimmerman	3B J.Dodge	3B B.Herzog	3B H.Lobert	3B B.Byrne	3B M.Mowrey
LF J.Connolly	LF Z.Wheat	LF M.Mitchell	LF B.Bescher	LF G.Burns	LF S.Magee	LF M.Carey	LF L.Magee
CF L.Mann	CF C.Stengel	CF T.Leach	CF A.Marsans	CF F.Snodgrass	CF D.Paskert	CF M.Mitchell	CF R.Oakes
RF J.Titus	RF H.Moran	RF F.Schulte	RF J.Bates	RF R.Murray	RF G.Cravath	RF C.Wilson	RF S.Evans
C B.Rariden	C O.Miller	C J.Archer	C T.Clarke	C C.Meyers	C B.Killefer	C M.Simon	C I.Wingo
32 F.Smith	OS J.Hummel	23 A.Phelan	O J.Devore	32 T.Shafer	C R.Dooin	2S A.Butler	OS P.Whitted
O B.Lord	C W.Fischer	O W.Miller	C J.Kling	O M.McCormick	O C.Dolan	O F.Kommers	O T.Cather
C B.Whaling	C B.Collins	2S R.Bresnahan	S2 M.Berghammer	OS A.Wilson	3 B.Byrne	O G.Gibson	C L.McLean
3 T.McDonald	S E.Kirkpatrick	O C.Williams	3 R.Almeida	O L.McLean	/O J.Devore	O S.Hofman	O J.Sheckard
O G.Zinn	O B.Meyer	O O.Clymer	O J.Sheckard	/O J.Thorpe	/1 D.Howley	O B.Kelly	C P.Hildebrand
O T.Griffith	/O L.Callahan	S R.Corriden	3 E.Grant	O C.Cooper	O E.Burns	/1 H.Hyatt	O F.Quinlan
1 B.Schmidt	C T.Erwin	O W.Good	O A.Wickland	/3 E.Grant	S3 J.Walsh	O E.Booe	/S A.Hauser
O C.Seymour	/C L.McCarty	O T.Needham	C E.Blackburn	C G.Hartley	C M.Reed	S3 A.McCarthy	C S.Roberts
O J.Kirke	/O A.Scheer	/O T.Stewart	/S T.McDonald	/S M.Stock	/O V.Duncan	C E.Mensor	/S Z.Beck
O O.Clymer	/C E.Phelps	/1 F.Mollwitz	/3 B.Niehoff	/3 H.Groh	C J.Dodge	C B.Coleman	/C F.Snyder
2 C.Deal	/C M.Hechinger	/O M.Allison	R K.Meister	R J.Evers	/O R.Capron	/O R.Wood	/S W.Callahan
C D.Brown	/S R.Mowe	/S C.Keating	/C H.Severeid	/O J.Merritt	H P.Moran	/O F.Clarke	/C C.Miller
/O J.Schultz	P P.Ragan	/C B.Hargrave	/2 B.Hobbs	P C.Mathewson	P T.Seaton	/S G.Britton	/C H.Peitz
/1 B.Calhoun	P N.Rucker	H M.Hechinger	P H.Chapman	P R.Marquard	P P.Alexander	/C J.Kafora	/S A.Cabrera
/O G.Jackson	P F.Allen	H P.Knisely	/C M.Stewart	P J.Tesreau	P A.Brennan	P B.Adams	H D.Crandall
/3 O.Dugey	P C.Curtis	R E.McDonald	P C.Johnson	P A.Demaree	P E.Mayer	P C.Hendrix	H J.Vann
/C R.DeVogt	P E.Yingling	P L.Cheney	P G.Suggs	P A.Fromme	P E.Rixey	P H.Robinson	H J.Whelan
/C H.Gowdy	P E.Reulbach	P J.Lavender	P G.Packard	RP D.Crandall	P G.Chalmers	P H.Camnitz	P S.Sallee
/O B.McKechnie	P E.Stack	P B.Humphries	P R.Ames	P H.Wiltse	P E.Moore	P M.O'Toole	P B.Harmon
/O W.Collins	P B.Wagner	P G.Pearce	P M.Brown	P R.Ames	/P H.Camnitz	P G.McQuillan	P D.Griner
/3 J.McCleskey	P M.Walker	P C.Smith	RP F.Harter	/P B.Hearn	/P R.Marshall	/P W.Cooper	P P.Perritt
H F.Mitchell	/P J.Pfeffer	P O.Overall	P R.Benton	/P R.Schauer	/P D.Imlay	/P W.Luhrsen	P B.Doak
/2 A.Bues	/P E.Brown	P L.Richie	/P A.Fromme	/P F.Schupp	/P R.Nelson	/P J.Conzelman	RP R.Geyer
R B.McTigue	/P M.Kent	/P H.Vaughn	/P J.Rowan		/P H.Finneran	/P B.Duffy	P S.Burk
/C W.Tragesser	/P B.Hall	/P E.Stack	/P C.Smith		/P J.Haislip	/P E.Eayrs	P B.Steele
P L.Tyler		/P E.Reulbach	/P E.Herbert		/P R.Hartranft	/P J.Scheneberg	/P H.Trekell
P D.Rudolph		/P F.Toney	/P R.Works			/P J.Ferry	/P B.Hopper
P O.Hess		/P E.Moore	/P D.Robertson			/P A.Mamaux	/P D.Niehaus
P H.Perdue		/P L.Leifield	/P A.Harrington				/P J.Willis
P B.James		/P D.Watson	/P H.Betts				/P B.Hunt
P W.Dickson		/P Z.Zabel	/P J.McManus				/P W.Marbet
/P J.Quinn			/P C.Morgan				/P P.Redding
P W.Noyes			/P R.Nelson				
/P P.Strand			/P H.McIntire				
/P L.Gervais			/P B.Powell				
/P B.Brown							
/P G.Cocreham							
/P G.Davis							

TEAM	G	W	L	PCT	GB	R	OR	AB	H	2B	3B	HR	BB	SO	AVG	OBP	SLG	PRO	PRO+	BR	/A	PF	CHI	RC	SB	CS	SBA	SBR
NY	156	101	51	.664		684	515	5218	1427	226	71	30	444	501	.273	.338	.361	.699	105	43	38	101	99	700	296			
PHI	159	88	63	.583	12.5	693	636	5400	1433	257	78	73	383	578	.265	.318	.382	.700	102	29	1	104	100	683	156			
CHI	155	88	65	.575	13.5	720	630	5022	1289	195	96	59	554	634	.257	.335	.369	.704	107	52	51	100	104	661	181			
PIT	155	78	71	.523	21.5	673	585	5252	1383	210	86	35	391	545	.263	.319	.356	.675	104	-13	15	96	106	629	181			
BOS	154	69	82	.457	31.5	641	690	5145	1318	191	60	32	488	640	.256	.326	.335	.661	93	-26	-38	102	103	603	177			
BRO	152	65	84	.436	34.5	595	613	5165	1394	193	86	39	361	555	.270	.321	.363	.684	98	4	-13	103	94	637	188			
CIN	156	64	89	.418	37.5	607	717	5132	1339	170	96	27	458	579	.261	.325	.347	.672	98	-10	-7	100	96	630	226			
STL	153	51	99	.340	49	528	755	4967	1229	152	72	15	451	573	.247	.316	.316	.632	88	-78	-70	99	97	534	171			
TOT	620					5141		41301	10812	1594	645	310	3530	4605	.262	.325	.354	.679						1576				

TEAM	CG	SH	SV	IP	H	H/G	HR	BB	SO	RAT	ERA	ERA+	OAV	OOB	PR	/A	PF	CPI	FA	E	DP	FW	PW	BW	SBW	DIF
NY	82	12	17	1422	1276	8.1	38	315	651	10.2	2.42	128	.243	.289	122	107	97	99	.961	254	107	-.6	11.1	4.0		10.5
PHI	77	20	11	1455¹	1407	8.7	40	512	667	12.1	3.15	106	.261	.330	7	27	104	103	.968	214	112	2.2	2.8	.1		7.4
CHI	89	12	15	1372¹	1330	8.7	39	478	556	12.1	3.13	101	.260	.328	9	6	99	103	.959	260	106	-1.1	.6	5.3		6.7
PIT	74	9	7	1400	1344	8.6	26	434	590	11.6	2.90	104	.260	.320	46	16	94	104	.964	226	94	1.1	1.7	1.6		-.8
BOS	105	13	3	1373¹	1343	8.8	37	419	597	11.8	3.19	103	.263	.324	1	12	103	100	.957	273	82	-2.0	1.2	-4.0		-1.8
BRO	71	9	7	1373	1287	8.4	33	439	548	11.6	3.13	105	.255	.321	11	23	103	97	.961	243	125	-.3	2.4	-1.4		-10.2
CIN	71	10	10	1380	1398	9.1	40	456	522	12.4	3.46	94	.273	.338	-40	-36	101	102	.961	251	104	-.4	-3.7	-.7		-7.6
STL	74	6	11	1351²	1426	9.1	57	477	465	13.0	4.23	76	.280	.348	-156	-152	101	92	.965	219	113	1.3	-15.8	-7.3		-2.2
TOT	643	91	81	11127²		8.7				11.9	3.20		.262	.325					.962	1940	843					

Runs		Hits		Doubles		Triples		Home Runs		Total Bases	
Leach-Chi	99	Cravath-Phi	179	Smith-Bro	40	Saier-Chi	21	Cravath-Phi	19	Cravath-Phi	298
Carey-Pit	99	Daubert-Bro	178	Burns-NY	37	Miller-Pit	20	Luderus-Phi	18	Luderus-Phi	254
Lobert-Phi	98	Burns-NY	173	Magee-Phi	36	Konetchy-StL	17	Saier-Chi	14	Saier-Chi	249
Saier-Chi	94	Lobert-Phi	172	Cravath-Phi	34	Wilson-Pit	14	Magee-Phi	11	Miller-Pit	243
Magee-Phi	92	Carey-Pit	172			Cravath-Phi	14	Wilson-Pit	10	Lobert-Phi	243

Runs Batted In		Runs Produced		Bases On Balls		Batting Average		On Base Percentage		Slugging Average	
Cravath-Phi	128	Cravath-Phi	187	Bescher-Cin	94	Daubert-Bro	.350	Huggins-StL	.432	Cravath-Phi	.568
Zimmerman-Chi	95	Saier-Chi	172	Huggins-StL	92	Cravath-Phi	.341	Cravath-Phi	.407	Becker-Cin-Phi	.502
Saier-Chi	92	Miller-Pit	158	Leach-Chi	77	Viox-Pit	.317	Daubert-Bro	.405	Zimmerman-Chi	.490
Miller-Pit	90	Zimmerman-Chi	155	Bridwell-Chi	74	Tinker-Cin	.317	Viox-Pit	.399	Saier-Chi	.480
Luderus-Phi	86	Magee-Phi	151			Becker-Cin-Phi	.316	Leach-Chi	.391	Magee-Phi	.479

Production		Adjusted Production		Batter Runs		Adjusted Batter Runs		Clutch Hitting Index		Runs Created	
Cravath-Phi	.974	Cravath-Phi	169	Cravath-Phi	50.5	Cravath-Phi	45.8	Zimmerman-Chi	132	Cravath-Phi	120
Zimmerman-Chi	.868	Zimmerman-Chi	147	Saier-Chi	27.5	Viox-Pit	28.8	Cutshaw-Bro	127	Saier-Chi	97
Saier-Chi	.850	Viox-Pit	142	Zimmerman-Chi	26.3	Saier-Chi	27.3	Cravath-Phi	123	Lobert-Phi	96
Magee-Phi	.848	Saier-Chi	141	Daubert-Bro	25.2	Zimmerman-Chi	26.1	Doyle-NY	119	Daubert-Bro	94
Daubert-Bro	.829	Magee-Phi	136	Viox-Pit	24.8	Daubert-Bro	22.9	Fletcher-NY	116	Carey-Pit	92

Total Average		Stolen Bases		Stolen Base Average		Stolen Base Runs		Fielding Runs		Total Player Rating	
Cravath-Phi	1.058	Carey-Pit	61					Evers-Chi	29.9	Tinker-Cin	3.9
Saier-Chi	.927	Myers-Bos	57					Paskert-Phi	17.7	Cravath-Phi	3.7
Zimmerman-Chi	.925	Lobert-Phi	41					Cutshaw-Bro	17.5	Evers-Chi	3.5
Magee-Phi	.905	Burns-NY	40					Tinker-Cin	17.3	Zimmerman-Chi	3.4
Leach-Chi	.895	Cutshaw-Bro	39					Doolan-Phi	17.2	Wagner-Pit	3.1

Wins		Win Percentage		Games		Complete Games		Shutouts		Saves	
Seaton-Phi	27	Humphries-Chi	.800	Cheney-Chi	54	Tyler-Bos	28	Alexander-Phi	9	Cheney-Chi	11
Mathewson-NY	25	Alexander-Phi	.733	Seaton-Phi	52	Mathewson-NY	25	Seaton-Phi	5	Crandall-NY	6
Marquard-NY	23	Marquard-NY	.697	Sallee-StL	50	Cheney-Chi	25			Brown-Cin	6
Tesreau-NY	22	Mathewson-NY	.694	Alexander-Phi	47	Adams-Pit	24			Sallee-StL	5
Alexander-Phi	22	Seaton-Phi	.692	Camnitz-Pit-Phi	45	Alexander-Phi	23				

Innings Pitched		Fewest Hits/Game		Fewest BB/Game		Strikeouts		Strikeouts/Game		Ratio	
Seaton-Phi	322.1	Tesreau-NY	7.09	Mathewson-NY	.62	Seaton-Phi	168	Tesreau-NY	5.33	Mathewson-NY	9.18
Adams-Pit	313.2	Seaton-Phi	7.32	Humphries-Chi	1.19	Tesreau-NY	167	Hendrix-Pit	5.15	Adams-Pit	9.18
Alexander-Phi	306.1	Allen-Bro	7.42	Adams-Pit	1.41	Alexander-Phi	159	Marquard-NY	4.72	Marquard-NY	9.38
Mathewson-NY	306.0	Pearce-Chi	7.55	Marquard-NY	1.53	Marquard-NY	151	Seaton-Phi	4.69	Humphries-Chi	9.70
Cheney-Chi	305.0	Tyler-Bos	7.59	Suggs-Cin	1.58	Adams-Pit	144	Alexander-Phi	4.67	Demaree-NY	9.87

Earned Run Average		Adjusted ERA		Opponents' Batting Avg.		Opponents' On Base Pct.		Starter Runs		Adjusted Starter Runs	
Mathewson-NY	2.06	Mathewson-NY	151	Tesreau-NY	.220	Mathewson-NY	.266	Mathewson-NY	38.7	Mathewson-NY	35.9
Adams-Pit	2.15	Tesreau-NY	143	Seaton-Phi	.226	Adams-Pit	.267	Adams-Pit	36.4	Adams-Pit	29.8
Tesreau-NY	2.17	Demaree-NY	141	Allen-Bro	.231	Marquard-NY	.273	Tesreau-NY	32.2	Tesreau-NY	29.5
Demaree-NY	2.21	Adams-Pit	140	Pearce-Chi	.234	Humphries-Chi	.277	Marquard-NY	22.3	Seaton-Phi	26.2
Pearce-Chi	2.31	Brennan-Phi	139	Tyler-Bos	.235	Demaree-NY	.286	Demaree-NY	21.9	Brennan-Phi	21.5

Clutch Pitching Index		Relief Runs		Adjusted Relief Runs		Relief Ranking		Total Pitcher Index		Total Baseball Ranking	
Brennan-Phi	128	Crandall-NY	3.7	Crandall-NY	2.8	Crandall-NY	2.4	Mathewson-NY	4.6	Mathewson-NY	4.6
Packard-Cin	127							Tesreau-NY	3.9	Tinker-Cin	3.9
Brown-Cin	119							Adams-Pit	3.7	Tesreau-NY	3.9
Ames-NY-Cin	119							Tyler-Bos	2.9	Adams-Pit	3.7
Pearce-Chi	112							Seaton-Phi	2.7	Cravath-Phi	3.7

January 8 Frank Chance inherits Hal Chase and the weakest lineup the New York Yankees will ever have when he signs to manage the team.

January 22 The Giants give the Yankees permission to use the Polo Grounds for the season only, as the lease on the Hilltop grounds has expired. The Yankees will remain as tenants through 1922.

March 4 The Yankees become the first team to train outside the U.S. when they travel to Bermuda for spring practice.

April 10 President Woodrow Wilson, who receives a gold pass from Ban Johnson, throws out the first ball at Washington's home opener. In their first official game as Yankees, New York loses to Walter Johnson, 2–1. After giving up an unearned run in the first, Johnson begins a string of shutout innings that will reach a record 56 before the St. Louis Browns score in the fourth inning on May 14.

May 6* Better organized and financed than other aspiring circuits, the Federal League opens quietly, with clubs in Chicago, Cleveland, Pittsburgh, Indianapolis, St. Louis, Kansas City, and Covington, Ky. No attempt is made to sign established major league players. Cy Young manages Cleveland, Deacon Phillippe manages Pittsburgh. After a six-week season, the pennant winner is Indianapolis.

August 13* Petersburg pitcher Harry Hedgpeth (Virginia League) blanks Richmond twice, by scores of 1–0 and 10–0, both in nine innings. He gives up only one hit in the opener, while hurling a no-hitter in the second game.

September 22 Herb Pennock, 19, aided by Eddie Plank, blanks the Tigers, 1–0, to clinch the AL pennant for the A's.

October 7 Rube Marquard gets the call for the Giants against Philadelphia's Chief Bender in Game 1 of the World Series. Bender yields 11 hits, but Frank Baker's home run and three RBIs pace a 6-4 win over the New Yorkers.

October 11 John McGraw and the Giants lose to the AL for the third straight World Series. In Game 5, Mathewson is good, but Plank is better; his two-hitter wins the 3-1 finale. Frank Baker at .450 and Eddie Collins at .421 lead a strong A's offense.

October 19* The Giants and White Sox, fortified with other players, start their world tour in Cincinnati. After a 31-game tour to Seattle, they will head for the Philippines, Australia, China, and Japan.

November 2* St. Louis Browns manager George Stovall is the first major league player to jump to the Federal League, signing to manage Kansas City. With glib salesman Jim Gilmore as its president, and backed by several millionaires, including oil magnate Harry Sinclair and Brooklyn baker Robert Ward, the Feds declare open war two weeks later by announcing they will not honor the major leagues' reserve clause. It will prove a long, costly struggle, similar to the AL's beginnings, but with more losers than winners.

BOSTON	CHICAGO	CLEVELAND	DETROIT	NEW YORK	PHILADELPHIA	ST.LOUIS	WASHINGTON
M J.Stahl	M J.Callahan	M J.Birmingham	M H.Jennings	M F.Chance	M C.Mack	M G.Stovall	M C.Griffith
M B.Carrigan	1B H.Chase	1B D.Johnston	1B D.Gainer	1B J.Knight	1B S.McInnis	M J.Austin	1B C.Gandil
1B C.Engle	2B M.Rath	2B N.Lajoie	2B O.Vitt	2B R.Hartzell	2B E.Collins	M B.Rickey	2B R.Morgan
2B S.Yerkes	SS B.Weaver	SS R.Chapman	SS D.Bush	SS R.Peckinpaugh	SS J.Barry	SS G.Stovall	SS G.McBride
SS H.Wagner	3B H.Lord	3B I.Olson	3B G.Moriarty	3B E.Midkiff	3B F.Baker	2B D.Pratt	3B E.Foster
3B L.Gardner	LF P.Bodie	LF J.Graney	LF B.Veach	LF B.Cree	LF R.Oldring	SS M.Balenti	LF H.Shanks
LF D.Lewis	CF W.Mattick	CF N.Leibold	CF T.Cobb	CF H.Wolter	CF J.Walsh	3B J.Austin	CF C.Milan
CF T.Speaker	RF S.Collins	RF J.Jackson	RF S.Crawford	RF B.Daniels	RF E.Murphy	LF J.Johnston	RF D.Moeller
RF H.Hooper	C R.Schalk	C S.O'Neill	C O.Stanage	C J.Sweeney	C J.Lapp	CF B.Shotton	C J.Henry
C B.Carrigan						RF G.Williams	
S3 H.Janvrin	2 J.Berger	32 T.Turner	2 P.Baumann	3 F.Maisel	O A.Strunk	C S.Agnew	32 F.LaPorte
O W.Rehg	O L.Chappell	O B.Ryan	23 B.Louden	S2 R.Zeider	C W.Schang		C E.Ainsmith
C H.Cady	1O J.Fournier	C F.Carisch	C R.McKee	1 H.Chase	C T.Daley	1 B.Brief	C R.Williams
C P.Thomas	C T.Easterly	O J.Birmingham	2 H.High	2 B.McKechnie	B B.Orr	S D.Lavan	2 G.Schaefer
C L.Nunamaker	O B.Schaller	C G.Land	C H.Rondeau	1 B.Borton	/O D.Murphy	S B.Wallace	O J.Gedeon
2 N.Ball	C B.Borton	3 R.Bates	3 R.Gibson	C D.Gossett	C I.Thomas	C W.Alexander	O J.Calvo
1 B.Mundy	O J.Beall	/O J.Lelivelt	1 E.Onslow	O F.Gilhooley	/1 H.Davis	C P.Compton	/O B.Spencer
/O O.Henriksen	C W.Kuhn	/S G.Dunlop	3 C.Deal	/S H.Williams	/S D.Lavan	C B.McAllester	/O M.Acosta
/C W.Snell	/S J.Breton	/2 L.Kopf	1 G.Tutwiler	/3 D.Cook	/3 H.Fritz	O T.Walker	/2 B.Morley
H J.Stahl	/O D.Jones	H J.Beall	1 W.Pipp	S C.Derrick	/O G.Brickley	1 S.Covington	/C J.Ryan
P D.Leonard	/3 R.Zeider	/C E.Krueger	2 L.Hennessey	O B.Holden	/2 P.Cruthers	S D.Walsh	P W.Johnson
P H.Bedient	/O E.Roush	/1 E.Edmonson	/O A.Platte	/1 D.Sterrett	/C W.McAvoy	S R.Bisland	P B.Groom
P R.Collins	/O N.Callahan	/C J.Billings	C J.Burns	C J.Smith	/C J.Giebel	/2 B.Wares	P J.Boehling
P J.Wood	/C T.Daly	/C J.Bassler	O P.Peploski	O G.Whiteman	/S M.Peffer	/O T.Sloan	P J.Engel
P E.Moseley	/3 D.Rader	H G.Young	/3 S.Partenheimer	/S B.Stumpf	P E.Plank	/O G.Maisel	P T.Hughes
P C.Hall	/C B.Meyer	H R.Peckinpaugh	/O R.Powell	/O J.Lelivelt	P C.Bender	/O E.Walker	/P G.Gallia
P B.O'Brien	P R.Russell	/O B.Southworth	P J.Dubuc	/1 F.Chance	P B.Brown	/O W.Meinert	/P G.Mullin
P R.Foster	P J.Scott	R J.Swindell	P E.Willett	/C B.Williams	P J.Bush	/3 F.Graff	/P D.Ayers
P F.Anderson	P E.Cicotte	P V.Gregg	P H.Dauss	/S R.Young	P B.Houck	/C F.Crossin	/P S.Love
/P P.Maloy	P J.Benz	P C.Falkenberg	P M.Hall	/S L.Boone	P B.Shawkey	/3 C.Flanagan	/P H.Harper
/P E.Chaney	P D.White	P W.Mitchell	P J.Lake	/C B.Reynolds	P W.Wyckoff	H L.Bonin	/P J.Shaw
	P E.Walsh	P F.Blanding	RP F.House	/O D.Costello	P H.Pennock	H G.Tomer	/P J.Bentley
	P F.Lange	P B.Steen	P C.Zamloch	/C H.Hanson	/P J.Taff	P G.Baumgardner	/P N.Altrock
	P P.Smith	P G.Kahler	P R.Comstock	P R.Fisher	/P E.Cottrell	P C.Weilman	/P C.Cashion
	/P B.O'Brien	P N.Cullop	/P G.Mullin	P R.Ford	/P C.Boardman	P R.Mitchell	/P M.Williams
	/P B.Lathrop	P L.James	/P A.Klawitter	P A.Schulz	/P P.Bohen	P E.Hamilton	/P J.Wilson
	/P F.Miller	P J.Baskette	/P L.Williams	P G.McConnell	/P J.Coombs	P W.Leverenz	/P T.Drohan
	/P B.Smith	P L.Brenton	/P A.Clauss	P R.Caldwell	/P D.Morey	P D.Stone	/P R.Dawson
	/P J.Scoggins	/P L.Dashner	P C.Grover	/P R.Keating		P M.Allison	/P C.Griffith
		/P L.Glavenich	P G.Boehler	P J.Warhop		/P W.Taylor	/P H.Hedgpeth
		/P D.Gregg	/P L.North	/P M.McHale		/P C.Brown	
			/P E.Renfer	/P E.Klepfer		/P H.Schwenk	
			/P H.Elder	/P G.Clark		/P W.Adams	
			/P C.Harding	/P C.Pieh		/P J.Powell	
			/P L.Lorenzen	/P J.Hanley		/P P.Schmidt	
				/P R.Hoff			

TEAM	G	W	L	PCT	GB	R	OR	AB	H	2B	3B	HR	BB	SO	AVG	OBP	SLG	PRO	PRO+	BR	/A	PF	CHI	RC	SB	CS	SBA	SBR
PHI	153	96	57	.627		794	592	5044	1412	223	80	33	534	547	.280	.356	.375	.731	124	135	152	98	105	732	221			
WAS	155	90	64	.584	6.5	596	561	5074	1281	156	81	19	440	595	.252	.317	.326	.643	92	-35	-47	102	105	585	287			
CLE	155	86	66	.566	9.5	633	536	5031	1349	206	74	16	420	557	.268	.331	.348	.679	102	29	11	103	99	630	191			
BOS	151	79	71	.527	15.5	631	610	4965	1334	220	101	17	466	534	.269	.336	.364	.700	109	66	49	103	95	652	189			
CHI	153	78	74	.513	17.5	488	498	4822	1139	157	66	24	389	550	.236	.299	.311	.610	85	-94	-89	99	100	487	156			
DET	153	66	87	.431	30	624	716	5064	1344	180	101	24	496	501	.265	.336	.355	.691	111	56	66	99	93	655	218			
NY	153	57	94	.377	38	529	668	4880	1157	155	45	8	534	617	.237	.320	.292	.612	85	-75	-77	100	101	505	203			
STL	155	57	96	.373	39	528	642	5031	1193	179	73	18	455	769	.237	.306	.312	.618	90	-80	-65	97	101	524	209			
TOT	614					4823		39911	10209	1476	621	159	3743	4670	.256	.325	.336	.661						1674				

TEAM	CG	SH	SV	IP	H	H/G	HR	BB	SO	RAT	ERA	ERA+	OAV	OOB	PR	/A	PF	CPI	FA	E	DP	FW	PW	BW	SBW	DIF
PHI	69	17	22	1351¹	1200	8.0	24	532	630	11.8	3.19	87	.229	.304	-39	-65	94	70	.966	212	108	3.2	-6.9	16.2		7.0
WAS	78	23	20	1396¹	1177	7.6	35	465	758	11.0	2.73	108	.225	.297	31	34	101	80	.960	261	122	.3	3.6	-5.0		14.1
CLE	93	18	5	1386²	1278	8.3	19	502	689	11.8	2.54	119	.249	.321	59	74	104	108	.962	242	124	1.5	7.9	1.2		-.6
BOS	83	12	10	1358¹	1323	8.8	6	442	710	11.9	2.94	100	.260	.323	-2	-3	100	96	.961	237	84	1.4	-.3	5.2		-2.3
CHI	84	17	8	1360¹	1190	7.9	10	438	602	11.0	2.33	125	.237	.302	91	89	100	97	.960	255	104	.5	9.5	-9.5		1.5
DET	90	4	7	1360	1359	9.0	13	504	468	12.6	3.38	86	.265	.336	-68	-71	100	94	.954	300	105	-2.4	-7.6	7.0		-7.6
NY	75	8	7	1344	1318	8.8	31	455	530	12.2	3.27	91	.260	.337	-51	-42	102	94	.954	293	94	-1.9	-4.5	-8.2		-3.9
STL	104	14	5	1382¹	1369	8.9	21	454	476	12.2	3.06	96	.266	.332	-20	-22	100	103	.954	301	125	-2.2	-1.3	-6.9		-8.0
TOT	676	113	84	10939¹		8.4				11.8	2.93		.256	.325					.959	2101	866					

Runs		Hits		Doubles		Triples		Home Runs		Total Bases	
Collins-Phi	125	Jackson-Cle	197	Jackson-Cle	39	Crawford-Det	23	Baker-Phi	12	Crawford-Det	298
Baker-Phi	116	Crawford-Det	193	Speaker-Bos	35	Speaker-Bos	22	Crawford-Det	9	Jackson-Cle	291
Jackson-Cle	109	Baker-Phi	190	Baker-Phi	34	Jackson-Cle	17	Bodie-Chi	8	Baker-Phi	278
Shotton-StL	105	Speaker-Bos	189	Crawford-Det	32	Williams-StL	16	Jackson-Cle	7	Speaker-Bos	277
E.Murphy-Phi	105	Collins-Phi	184			Cobb-Det	16			Collins-Phi	242

Runs Batted In		Runs Produced		Bases On Balls		Batting Average		On Base Percentage		Slugging Average	
Baker-Phi	117	Baker-Phi	221	Shotton-StL	99	Cobb-Det	.390	Cobb-Det	.467	Jackson-Cle	.551
McInnis-Phi	90	Collins-Phi	195	Collins-Phi	85	Jackson-Cle	.373	Jackson-Cle	.460	Cobb-Det	.535
Lewis-Bos	90	Jackson-Cle	173	Wolter-NY	80	Speaker-Bos	.363	Collins-Phi	.441	Speaker-Bos	.533
Pratt-StL	87	Oldring-Phi	167	Jackson-Cle	80	Collins-Phi	.345	Speaker-Bos	.441	Baker-Phi	.493
Barry-Phi	85	McInnis-Phi	165	Bush-Det	80	Baker-Phi	.337	Baker-Phi	.413	Crawford-Det	.489

Production		Adjusted Production		Batter Runs		Adjusted Batter Runs		Clutch Hitting Index		Runs Created	
Jackson-Cle	1.011	Cobb-Det	196	Jackson-Cle	65.5	Jackson-Cle	61.8	Barry-Phi	163	Jackson-Cle	140
Cobb-Det	1.002	Jackson-Cle	190	Speaker-Bos	55.9	Cobb-Det	53.4	Lewis-Bos	133	Speaker-Bos	136
Speaker-Bos	.974	Speaker-Bos	180	Cobb-Det	51.8	Speaker-Bos	52.9	Pratt-StL	127	Collins-Phi	126
Baker-Phi	.906	Baker-Phi	168	Baker-Phi	45.9	Baker-Phi	48.5	McInnis-Phi	122	Cobb-Det	124
Collins-Phi	.894	Collins-Phi	165	Collins-Phi	45.7	Collins-Phi	48.3	Turner-Cle	121	Baker-Phi	122

Total Average		Stolen Bases		Stolen Base Average	Stolen Base Runs	Fielding Runs		Total Player Rating	
Cobb-Det	1.310	Milan-Was	75			Weaver-Chi	33.6	Speaker-Bos	7.3
Jackson-Cle	1.215	Moeller-Was	62			Speaker-Bos	23.7	Collins-Phi	6.4
Speaker-Bos	1.193	Collins-Phi	55			Turner-Cle	16.3	Baker-Phi	6.1
Collins-Phi	1.111	Cobb-Det	51			Collins-Phi	15.6	Jackson-Cle	6.0
Baker-Phi	1.029	Speaker-Bos	46			Shotton-StL	12.8	Cobb-Det	5.3

Wins		Win Percentage		Games		Complete Games		Shutouts		Saves	
Johnson-Was	36	Johnson-Was	.837	Russell-Chi	52	Johnson-Was	29	Johnson-Was	11	Bender-Phi	13
Falkenberg-Cle	23	Bush-Phi	.714	Scott-Chi	48	Russell-Chi	26	Russell-Chi	8	Hughes-Was	6
Russell-Chi	22	Boehling-Was	.708	Johnson-Was	48	Scott-Chi	25	Plank-Phi	7	Bedient-Bos	5
Bender-Phi	21	Collins-Bos	.704	Bender-Phi	48			Falkenberg-Cle	6		
		Falkenberg-Cle	.697	V.Gregg-Cle	44						

Innings Pitched		Fewest Hits/Game		Fewest BB/Game		Strikeouts		Strikeouts/Game		Ratio	
Johnson-Was	346.0	Johnson-Was	6.03	Johnson-Was	.99	Johnson-Was	243	Johnson-Was	6.32	Johnson-Was	7.26
Russell-Chi	316.2	Mitchell-Cle	6.35	Collins-Bos	1.35	V.Gregg-Cle	166	Mitchell-Cle	5.85	Russell-Chi	9.55
Scott-Chi	312.1	Engel-Was	6.78	Mitchell-StL	1.72	Falkenberg-Cle	166	Plank-Phi	5.60	Scott-Chi	10.00
V.Gregg-Cle	285.2	Leverenz-StL	7.06	Plank-Phi	2.11	Scott-Chi	158	Falkenberg-Cle	5.41	Cicotte-Chi	10.07
Falkenberg-Cle	276.0	Russell-Chi	7.11	Weilman-StL	2.15	Groom-Was	156	Groom-Was	5.31	Plank-Phi	10.13

Earned Run Average		Adjusted ERA		Opponents' Batting Avg.		Opponents' On Base Pct.		Starter Runs		Adjusted Starter Runs	
Johnson-Was	1.14	Johnson-Was	258	Johnson-Was	.187	Johnson-Was	.217	Johnson-Was	68.6	Johnson-Was	69.4
Cicotte-Chi	1.58	Cicotte-Chi	185	Mitchell-Cle	.199	Russell-Chi	.273	Cicotte-Chi	40.2	Cicotte-Chi	40.0
Scott-Chi	1.90	Mitchell-Cle	159	Engel-Was	.207	Bender-Phi	.277	Russell-Chi	36.1	Russell-Chi	35.8
Russell-Chi	1.90	Scott-Chi	154	Houck-Phi	.214	Cicotte-Chi	.281	Scott-Chi	35.7	Scott-Chi	35.4
Mitchell-Cle	1.91	Russell-Chi	153	Russell-Chi	.219	Scott-Chi	.281	Mitchell-Cle	24.6	Mitchell-Cle	27.1

Clutch Pitching Index		Relief Runs	Adjusted Relief Runs	Relief Ranking	Total Pitcher Index		Total Baseball Ranking	
Blanding-Cle	141				Johnson-Was	10.9	Johnson-Was	10.9
V.Gregg-Cle	130				Cicotte-Chi	5.2	Speaker-Bos	7.3
Ford-NY	123				Russell-Chi	4.2	Collins-Phi	6.4
Baumgardner-StL	118				Scott-Chi	3.8	Baker-Phi	6.1
Cicotte-Chi	114				Boehling-Was	2.6	Jackson-Cle	6.0

February 1 The White Sox and Giants play a 3–3 tie in Cairo. The next day a triple play will be made in the shadow of the Pyramids.

February 3 A joint NL-AL rules committee decrees that: a runner touched or held by a coach while rounding third base is out; coaches may now assist other members of their team, not just base runners; the frequently violated rule requiring pitchers to stand behind the rubber until ready to pitch is rescinded; they may now stand on the rubber; base runners are now not permitted to run on an infield fly. A move to eliminate the intentional walk is defeated.

March 21 Charles W. Murphy sells the Cubs to Charles P. Taft of Cincinnati.

April 20 The 25-player limit is suspended in the AL and NL. With uncertainty over who has signed with what teams, it is almost impossible to know how many players may be on the roster at any one time.

July 17 Giants outfielder John "Red" Murray is knocked unconscious by lightning after catching a fly ball that ends a 21-inning victory over Pittsburgh. Murray is uninjured. Pittsburgh's Babe Adams pitches all 21 innings without yielding a single walk, the longest non-walk game in major league history.

September 7 The Braves and Giants play a morning-afternoon twinbill in Boston on Labor Day. To accommodate the crowds, the Braves move their home games to Fenway Park. The contenders draw 74,163 on the day.

September 23 After dropping their 19th straight in the first of two at Boston, the Reds break the longest losing streak in the club's history (and third longest in the NL) when Charles "King" Lear wins his only game of the year and only shutout ever, 3-0.

September 29 The Boston Braves, who were in last place in mid-July, clinch the pennant with a sensational second-half drive.

October 1 Phillies outfielder Gavvy Cravath hits homer No. 19 to lead the NL. He also leads NL outfielders with 34 assists in right field.

October 9 The Boston Braves go into the World Series as underdogs, despite their strong finish. Only one regular, left fielder Joe Connolly, hit .300. Their strengths are pitchers Dick Rudolph, George "Lefty" Tyler, and "Seattle Bill" James, second baseman Johnny Evers, who wins Chalmers' final MVP automobile, and shortstop Rabbit Maranville, their cleanup hitter. The Philadelphia A's Eddie Collins, with a .344 batting average, wins the Chalmers AL award with 63 of 64 possible points. The A's have seven pitchers with 10 or more wins, led by Chief Bender's 17–3. Bender's World Series magic is quickly dispelled as the Braves knock him out in the sixth. Rudolph coasts to a five-hit, 7–1 victory. Hank Gowdy has a single, double, and triple. Gowdy will hit a World Series record .545, and Evers, .438. Bender makes his last World Series appearance, finishing with a record 59 strikeouts.

October 13 The first World Series sweep in history belongs to the Boston Braves—the only World Series the franchise will ever win in Boston. Bob Shawkey and Herb Pennock allow just six hits, but one is a two-run single by Evers, as Rudolph wins, 3-1.

	BOSTON		BROOKLYN		CHICAGO		CINCINNATI		NEW YORK		PHILADELPHIA		PITTSBURGH		ST.LOUIS
M	G.Stallings	M	W.Robinson	M	H.O'Day	M	B.Herzog	M	J.McGraw	M	R.Dooin	M	F.Clarke	M	M.Huggins
1B	B.Schmidt	1B	J.Daubert	1B	V.Saier	1B	D.Hoblitzel	1B	F.Merkle	1B	F.Luderus	1B	E.Konetchy	1B	D.Miller
2B	J.Evers	2B	G.Cutshaw	2B	B.Sweeney	2B	H.Groh	2B	L.Doyle	2B	B.Byrne	2B	J.Viox	2B	M.Huggins
SS	R.Maranville	SS	D.Egan	SS	R.Corriden	SS	B.Herzog	SS	A.Fletcher	SS	J.Martin	SS	H.Wagner	SS	A.Butler
3B	C.Deal	3B	R.Smith	3B	H.Zimmerman	3B	B.Niehoff	3B	M.Stock	3B	H.Lobert	3B	M.Mowrey	3B	Z.Beck
LF	J.Connolly	LF	Z.Wheat	LF	F.Schulte	LF	G.Twombly	LF	G.Burns	LF	B.Becker	LF	M.Carey	LF	C.Dolan
CF	L.Mann	CF	J.Dalton	CF	T.Leach	CF	B.Daniels	CF	B.Bescher	CF	D.Paskert	CF	Jo.Kelly	CF	L.Magee
RF	L.Gilbert	RF	C.Stengel	RF	W.Good	RF	H.Moran	RF	F.Snodgrass	RF	G.Cravath	RF	M.Mitchell	RF	C.Wilson
C	H.Gowdy	C	L.McCarty	C	R.Bresnahan	C	T.Clarke	C	C.Meyers	C	B.Killefer	C	G.Gibson	C	F.Snyder
O2	P.Whitted	S	O.O'Mara	C	J.Archer	C	M.Gonzalez	3S	E.Grant	OS	S.Magee	O	Ji.Kelly	O	W.Cruise
3	R.Smith	O	H.Myers	O	J.Johnston	O	D.Miller	O	D.Robertson	2	H.Irelan	O	Z.Collins	C	I.Wingo
C	B.Whaling	3	G.Getz	/S	C.Derrick	O	J.Bates	C	L.McLean	C	E.Burns	32	A.McCarthy	1	L.Dressen
O	H.Moran	1O	J.Hummel	O	C.Williams	O	R.Killefer	O	R.Murray	C	R.Dooin	C	B.Coleman	O	T.Cather
O	T.Cather	C	O.Miller	O	P.Knisely	12	B.Kellogg	H	M.Donlin	S2	M.Reed	3	J.Leonard	O	J.Riggert
O	J.Devore	C	W.Fischer	S	B.Fisher	O	A.Marsans	/O	J.Thorpe	/O	J.Devore	O	E.Mensor	3	K.Nash
O	J.Murray	O	J.Riggert	/3	A.Phelan	S2	M.Berghammer	C	E.Johnson	/S	D.Murphy	/1	H.Hyatt	O	C.Miller
O2	O.Dugey	S	K.Elberfeld	3	A.Bues	1	P.Mollwitz	/C	S.Piez	/O	P.Hilly	O	D.Costello	/3	P.Whitted
3	J.Martin	/C	T.Erwin	C	B.Hargrave	3O	F.Von Kolnitz	/C	H.Smith	/1	F.Mollenkamp	S	W.Gerber	/2	B.Betzel
C	T.Griffith			S	C.Keating	1	T.Graham	/1	W.Holke	H	F.Fletcher	2	P.Siglin	/C	P.O'Connor
O	W.Collins	P	J.Pfeffer	/1	F.Mollwitz	3	J.Rawlings	/2	F.Brainerd	H	G.McAvoy	C	B.Schang	/C	J.Roche
/C	F.Tyler	P	E.Reulbach	/C	T.Needham	O	M.Uhler	/S	B.Dyer	/C	P.Moran	O	F.Scheeren	/S	R.Daringer
/1	C.Kraft	P	P.Ragan	/O	J.Bates	O	H.LaRoss	/S	D.Beatty			/S	I.McAuley		
/S	B.Martin	P	R.Aitchison	/C	E.Tyree	O	H.Lohr			P	P.Alexander	C	J.Kafora	P	P.Perritt
		P	F.Allen	H	M.Allison	C	T.Erwin	P	J.Tesreau	P	E.Mayer	/O	C.Berger	P	S.Sallee
P	D.Rudolph			/3	H.Bronkie	O	B.Holden	P	C.Mathewson	P	B.Tincup	/C	S.Smith	P	B.Doak
P	B.James	P	N.Rucker	H	T.Stewart	P	N.Glockson	P	R.Marquard	P	R.Marshall	H	F.Clarke	P	D.Griner
P	L.Tyler	P	C.Schmutz			/S	C.Derrick	P	A.Demaree	P	J.Oeschger	H	P.Falsey	P	H.Perdue
P	D.Crutcher	P	E.Brown	P	L.Cheney	/O	E.Kippert	P	A.Fromme			/C	P.Kilhullen		
		/P	J.Enzmann	P	H.Vaughn	/O	K.McLaughlin			P	E.Rixey	/C	B.Wagner	P	H.Robinson
P	O.Hess	/P	B.Steele	P	J.Lavender			P	H.Wiltse	P	S.Baumgartner	/C	S.Brenegan	P	C.Hageman
/P	G.Davis	/P	B.Wagner	P	B.Humphries	P	R.Ames	P	M.O'Toole	P	E.Matteson	H	R.Shafer	P	B.Steele
P	P.Strand			P	G.Pearce	P	R.Benton	/P	R.Schauer	P	E.Jacobs			/P	D.Niehaus
/P	H.Perdue			RP	C.Hageman	P	P.Douglas	/P	F.Schupp	/P	G.Chalmers	P	B.Adams	/P	S.Williams
P	G.Cocreham					P	E.Yingling	/P	H.Ritter			P	W.Cooper	P	B.Hopper
/P	T.Hughes			P	Z.Zabel	P	P.Schneider	/P	E.Erickson			P	G.McQuillan		
/P	D.Luque			P	C.Smith			/P	A.Huenke			P	B.Harmon		
/P	E.Cottrell			/P	E.Stack	P	K.Lear					P	J.Conzelman		
				/P	G.McConnell	P	D.Davenport								
				/P	E.Koestner	/P	P.Fittery					P	M.O'Toole		
						P	J.Rowan					P	E.Kantlehner		
						/P	E.Koestner					P	A.Mamaux		
						/P	K.Adams					/P	H.Kelly		
						/P	P.Fahrer					/P	P.Bohen		
						/P	B.Ingersoll					/P	D.McArthur		
						/P	C.Johnson								
						/P	P.Griffin								

TEAM	G	W	L	PCT	GB	R	OR	AB	H	2B	3B	HR	BB	SO	AVG	OBP	SLG	PRO	PRO+	BR	/A	PF	CHI	RC	SB	CS	SBA	SBR
BOS	158	94	59	.614		657	548	5206	1307	213	60	35	**502**	617	.251	.323	.335	.658	103	17	21	99	103	602	139			
NY	156	84	70	.545	10.5	**672**	576	5146	1363	**222**	59	30	447	479	.265	**.330**	.348	.678	112	53	**75**	99	103	644	**239**			
STL	157	81	72	.529	13	558	**540**	5046	1249	203	65	33	445	618	.248	.314	.333	.647	100	-9	-2	99	95	576	204			
CHI	156	78	76	.506	16.5	605	638	5050	1229	199	74	42	501	577	.243	.317	.337	.654	101	7	9	100	100	579	164			
BRO	154	75	79	.487	19.5	622	618	5152	**1386**	172	**90**	31	376	559	.269	.323	.355	.678	106	43	29	102	97	629	173			
PHI	154	74	80	.481	20.5	651	687	5110	1345	211	52	**62**	472	570	.263	.329	**.361**	**.690**	105	69	26	107	97	636	145			
PIT	158	69	85	.448	25.5	503	**540**	5145	1197	148	79	18	416	608	.233	.295	.303	.598	88	-101	-80	96	101	488	147			
CIN	157	60	94	.390	34.5	530	651	4991	1178	142	64	16	441	627	.236	.305	.300	.605	83	-79	-94	103	**105**	506	224			
TOT	625					4798		40846	10254	1510	543	267	3600	4655	.251	.317	.334	.651						1435				

TEAM	CG	SH	SV	IP	H	H/G	HR	BB	SO	RAT	ERA	ERA+	OAV	OOB	PR	/A	PF	CPI	FA	E	DP	FW	PW	BW	SBW	DIF
BOS	**104**	19	6	1421	1272	8.1	38	477	606	11.4	2.74	100	.249	.319	7	1	99	102	.963	246	**143**	1.8	.1	2.3		13.3
NY	88	**20**	9	1390²	1298	8.4	47	**367**	563	11.0	2.94	90	.253	**.306**	-25	-46	95	92	.961	254	119	1.1	-5.0	**8.1**		2.8
STL	84	16	12	1424²	1279	8.1	**26**	422	531	11.1	**2.38**	117	.250	.313	**64**	64	100	**112**	.964	239	109	2.2	**6.9**	-.2		-4.4
CHI	70	14	11	1389¹	**1169**	**7.6**	37	528	**651**	11.2	2.71	103	**.233**	.311	12	9	100	92	.951	310	87	-2.7	1.0	1.0		1.8
BRO	80	11	11	1368¹	1282	8.4	36	466	605	11.8	2.82	101	.255	.323	-5	7	103	101	.961	248	112	1.2	.8	3.1		-7.1
PHI	85	14	7	1379¹	1403	9.2	**26**	452	650	12.4	3.06	96	.270	.335	-42	-21	105	106	.950	324	81	-3.9	-2.3	2.8		.3
PIT	86	10	11	1405	1272	8.1	27	392	488	**10.9**	2.70	98	.249	.308	13	-9	95	95	**.966**	**223**	96	**3.4**	-1.0	-8.6		-1.8
CIN	74	15	**15**	1387¹	1259	8.2	30	489	607	11.7	2.94	100	.248	.320	-24	-5	105	95	.952	314	113	-2.9	-.3	-10.1		-3.7
TOT	671	119	82	11165²		8.2				11.4	2.78		.251	.317					.958	2158	860					

Runs		Hits		Doubles		Triples		Home Runs		Total Bases	
Burns-NY	100	Magee-Phi	171	Magee-Phi	39	Carey-Pit	17	Cravath-Phi	19	Magee-Phi	277
Magee-Phi	96	Wheat-Bro	170	Zimmerman-Chi	36	Zimmerman-Chi	12	Saier-Chi	18	Cravath-Phi	249
Daubert-Bro	89	Burns-NY	170	Burns-NY	35	Wilson-StL	12	Magee-Phi	15	Wheat-Bro	241
Saier-Chi	87	Zimmerman-Chi	167	Connolly-Bos	28	Cutshaw-Bro	12	Luderus-Phi	12	Zimmerman-Chi	239
Doyle-NY	87	Becker-Phi	167							Burns-NY	234

Runs Batted In		Runs Produced		Bases On Balls		Batting Average		On Base Percentage		Slugging Average	
Magee-Phi	103	Magee-Phi	184	Huggins-StL	105	Daubert-Bro	.329	Stengel-Bro	.404	Magee-Phi	.509
Cravath-Phi	100	Zimmerman-Chi	158	Saier-Chi	94	Becker-Phi	.325	Burns-NY	.403	Cravath-Phi	.499
Wheat-Bro	89	Cravath-Phi	157	Burns-NY	89	Dalton-Bro	.319	Cravath-Phi	.402	Connolly-Bos	.494
D.Miller-StL	88	Burns-NY	157	Evers-Bos	87	Wheat-Bro	.319	Huggins-StL	.396	Wheat-Bro	.452
Zimmerman-Chi	87	D.Miller-StL	151	Cravath-Phi	83	Stengel-Bro	.316	Dalton-Bro	.396	Becker-Phi	.446

Production		Adjusted Production		Batter Runs		Adjusted Batter Runs		Clutch Hitting Index		Runs Created	
Cravath-Phi	.901	Cravath-Phi	157	Cravath-Phi	42.7	Burns-NY	37.5	Fletcher-NY	129	Burns-NY	113
Magee-Phi	.890	Magee-Phi	154	Magee-Phi	40.7	Cravath-Phi	36.0	Maranville-Bos	127	Magee-Phi	110
Wheat-Bro	.830	Burns-NY	149	Burns-NY	34.0	Magee-Phi	34.0	Cutshaw-Bro	123	Cravath-Phi	103
Stengel-Bro	.829	Stengel-Bro	143	Connolly-Bos	31.0	Connolly-Bos	31.5	D.Miller-StL	122	Wheat-Bro	95
Burns-NY	.820	Wheat-Bro	143	Wheat-Bro	29.3	Wheat-Bro	27.3	Schmidt-Bos	121	Becker-Phi	87

Total Average		Stolen Bases		Stolen Base Average	Stolen Base Runs	Fielding Runs		Total Player Rating	
Burns-NY	.997	Burns-NY	62			Maranville-Bos	51.8	Maranville-Bos	5.9
Cravath-Phi	.997	Herzog-Cin	46			Herzog-Cin	30.6	Herzog-Cin	4.7
Magee-Phi	.965	Dolan-StL	42			Cutshaw-Bro	27.5	Magee-Phi	4.5
Stengel-Bro	.904	Carey-Pit	38			Smith-Bro-Bos	22.6	Smith-Bro-Bos	4.2
Wheat-Bro	.857					Wheat-Bro	18.2	Wheat-Bro	4.1

Wins		Win Percentage		Games		Complete Games		Shutouts		Saves	
Alexander-Phi	27	James-Bos	.788	Cheney-Chi	50	Alexander-Phi	32	Tesreau-NY	8	Sallee-StL	6
Tesreau-NY	26	Doak-StL	.760	Mayer-Phi	48	Rudolph-Bos	31	Doak-StL	7	Ames-Cin	6
Rudolph-Bos	26	Tesreau-NY	.722	Ames-Cin	47	James-Bos	30	Rudolph-Bos	6	Cheney-Chi	5
James-Bos	26	Rudolph-Bos	.722			Mathewson-NY	29	Cheney-Chi	6	Pfeffer-Bro	4
Mathewson-NY	24	Pfeffer-Bro	.657			Pfeffer-Bro	27	Alexander-Phi	6	McQuillan-Pit	4

Innings Pitched		Fewest Hits/Game		Fewest BB/Game		Strikeouts		Strikeouts/Game		Ratio	
Alexander-Phi	355.0	Tesreau-NY	6.65	Mathewson-NY	.66	Alexander-Phi	214	Alexander-Phi	5.43	Rudolph-Bos	9.45
Rudolph-Bos	336.1	Doak-StL	6.79	Adams-Pit	1.24	Tesreau-NY	189	Tesreau-NY	5.28	Adams-Pit	9.51
James-Bos	332.1	Cheney-Chi	6.91	Marquard-NY	1.58	Vaughn-Chi	165	Vaughn-Chi	5.06	Mathewson-NY	9.78
Tesreau-NY	322.1	Douglas-Cin	6.99	Rudolph-Bos	1.63	Cheney-Chi	157	L.Tyler-Bos	4.64	Doak-StL	10.09
Mayer-Phi	321.0	James-Bos	7.07	Alexander-Phi	1.93	James-Bos	156	Ragan-Bro	4.58	Pfeffer-Bro	10.34

Earned Run Average		Adjusted ERA		Opponents' Batting Avg.		Opponents' On Base Pct.		Starter Runs		Adjusted Starter Runs	
Doak-StL	1.72	Doak-StL	162	Tesreau-NY	.209	Adams-Pit	.276	James-Bos	32.8	James-Bos	31.6
James-Bos	1.90	James-Bos	145	Cheney-Chi	.215	Rudolph-Bos	.276	Doak-StL	30.2	Pfeffer-Bro	30.9
Pfeffer-Bro	1.97	Pfeffer-Bro	145	Doak-StL	.216	Mathewson-NY	.278	Pfeffer-Bro	28.5	Doak-StL	30.4
Vaughn-Chi	2.05	Vaughn-Chi	135	Vaughn-Chi	.222	Alexander-Phi	.290	Vaughn-Chi	23.9	Vaughn-Chi	23.6
Sallee-StL	2.10	Sallee-StL	133	Douglas-Cin	.223	Doak-StL	.290	Sallee-StL	21.4	Alexander-Phi	21.8

Clutch Pitching Index		Relief Runs	Adjusted Relief Runs	Relief Ranking	Total Pitcher Index		Total Baseball Ranking	
Cooper-Pit	126				James-Bos	3.6	Maranville-Bos	5.9
James-Bos	121				Alexander-Phi	3.3	Herzog-Cin	4.7
Crutcher-Bos	120				Doak-StL	3.2	Magee-Phi	4.5
Perritt-StL	116				Pfeffer-Bro	3.1	Smith-Bro-Bos	4.2
Sallee-StL	116				Sallee-StL	2.9	Wheat-Bro	4.1

January 6 The National Commission grants some demands of the Players' Fraternity: players will be notified in writing of their transfer or release and receive a copy of their contract; players with 10 years in the major league are eligible to become free agents; clubs will pay traveling expenses to spring training and furnish all uniforms; all parks will have a blank green wall behind the pitcher in center field.

April 1 Future Hall of Famer Rube Waddell, weakened by a heroic effort to help contain a winter flood in Kentucky, dies at 37 of tuberculosis in a San Antonio sanitarium. Waddell won 20 games for four straight years with the Athletics and struck out 349 batters in 1904, still an AL record for left-handers and the AL standard until Nolan Ryan eclipsed it in 1974.

April 22 At age 19, Babe Ruth's first professional game (as a pitcher) is a six-hit 6-0 win for Baltimore (International League) over Buffalo. The second batter he faces is Joe McCarthy, the manager he will play for 17 years later with New York.

May 14 Jim Scott of the White Sox pitches a no-hitter for nine innings, then loses to Washington, 1–0, in the 10th. It is the first of a record four no-hitters that White Sox rookie catcher Ray Schalk will catch in his 17 years with the team.

July 11 Babe Ruth breaks in with Boston, pitching a 4-3 win over Cleveland. In his first major league time at bat, Ruth strikes out. He will be 2-1 with Boston, spending most of the year at Providence (IL).

August 11 After missing six weeks, first with broken ribs, then a broken thumb, Ty Cobb signs a new three-year contract and returns to the lineup. Cobb will get into just 97 games, but he will win another batting crown at .368. Under existing rules his 345 at bats are enough to qualify.

August 31 Jack Fournier, first baseman of the White Sox, hits two homers off Walter Johnson, both inside the park. The second comes in the tenth to give Chicago a 4–3 victory. He will be the only player to hit two homers off the Big Train in one game until Aug. 13, 1926, when Lou Gehrig will connect twice.

September 12 Yankee shortstop Roger Peckinpaugh, 23, replaces Frank Chance and becomes the youngest major league manager of all time and the seventh in the club's 12-year existence.

September 27 Cleveland second baseman Nap Lajoie collects his 3,000th major league hit, as the Indians defeat the Yankees, 5-3.

November 1 Connie Mack begins cleaning house, asks waivers on Jack Coombs, Eddie Plank, and Chief Bender. Colby Jack goes to Brooklyn (NL). Plank and Bender escape Mack's maneuvering by jumping to the Federal League. Even though the A's won the pennant, Philadelphia fans did not support them, and the club lost $50,000.

December 8 After weeks of rumors, Connie Mack sells Eddie Collins, generally regarded as the game's finest position player, to the White Sox for $50,000. Collins signs a five-year contract worth $75,000 and gets $15,000 as a signing bonus. The deal breaks up the A's "$100,000 Infield" and raises conjecture that Mack will leave to manage the Yankees.

December 31 Ban Johnson's efforts to strengthen the New York Yankees succeed when he arranges the purchase of the team by Colonel Jacob Ruppert and Cap Huston for $460,000. The new owners will name longtime Detroit pitcher Bill Donovan as manager.

	BOSTON		CHICAGO		CLEVELAND		DETROIT		NEW YORK		PHILADELPHIA		ST.LOUIS		WASHINGTON
M	B.Carrigan	M	J.Callahan	M	J.Birmingham	M	H.Jennings	M	F.Chance	M	C.Mack	M	B.Rickey	M	C.Griffith
1B	D.Hoblitzel	1B	J.Fournier	1B	D.Johnston	1B	G.Burns	M	R.Peckinpaugh	1B	S.McInnis	1B	J.Leary	1B	C.Gandil
2B	S.Yerkes	2B	L.Blackburne	2B	N.Lajoie	2B	M.Kavanagh	1B	C.Mullen	2B	E.Collins	2B	D.Pratt	2B	R.Morgan
SS	E.Scott	SS	B.Weaver	SS	R.Chapman	SS	D.Bush	2B	L.Boone	SS	J.Barry	SS	D.Lavan	SS	G.McBride
3B	L.Gardner	3B	J.Breton	3B	T.Turner	3B	G.Moriarty	SS	R.Peckinpaugh	3B	F.Baker	3B	J.Austin	3B	E.Foster
LF	D.Lewis	LF	R.Demmitt	LF	J.Graney	LF	B.Veach	3B	F.Maisel	LF	R.Oldring	LF	T.Walker	LF	H.Shanks
CF	T.Speaker	CF	P.Bodie	CF	N.Leibold	CF	T.Cobb	LF	R.Hartzell	CF	A.Strunk	CF	B.Shotton	CF	C.Milan
RF	H.Hooper	RF	S.Collins	RF	J.Jackson	RF	S.Crawford	CF	B.Cree	RF	E.Murphy	RF	G.Williams	RF	D.Moeller
C	B.Carrigan	C	R.Schalk	C	S.O'Neill	C	O.Stanage	RF	D.Cook	C	W.Schang	C	S.Agnew	C	J.Henry
								C	J.Sweeney						
21	H.Janvrin	1	H.Chase	S2	I.Olson	23	O.Vitt	O	J.Walsh	S	B.Wares	O	M.Mitchell		
C	H.Cady	3	S.Alcock	O1	J.Kirke	O	H.High	C	L.Nunamaker	C	J.Lapp	31	I.Howard	C	R.Williams
O	W.Rehg	S2	J.Berger	O1	R.Wood	2	F.Truesdale	C	T.Daley	O	E.Walker	C	E.Ainsmith		
1	C.Engle	O	T.Daly	S	B.Wambsganss	3	B.Purtell	S	L.Kopf	S	F.Crossin	2	W.Smith		
C	P.Thomas	O	B.Roth	C	F.Carisch	C	D.Baker	1	H.Williams	C	C.Davies	S	B.Wallace	O	M.Acosta
O	O.Henriksen	C	W.Mayer	C	B.Egan	C	R.McKee	O	B.Holden	/O	S.Thompson	/1	E.Miller	/2	G.Schaefer
12	D.Gainer	3	H.Lord	C	J.Bassler	/2	P.Baumann	J.Walsh	/S	B.Orr	C	W.Rumler	/O	C.Pick
/2	B.Swanson	3	H.Baker	3	L.Pezold	/S	F.McMullin	C	D.Gossett	/C	W.McAvoy	/C	J.Jenkins	/O	J.Gedeon
/C	L.Nunamaker	C	W.Kuhn	O	J.Lelivelt	R	R.Demmitt	/C	J.Rogers	/2	P.Cruthers	/S	D.Walsh	/O	I.Meusel
/C	L.Pratt	/O	L.Chappell	S	R.Bisland	/1	D.Gainer	/1	A.Aragon	/1	E.Mack	/1	D.Kauffman	/S	D.Neff
/1	S.Wilson	/O	P.Wolfe	O	E.Smith			/O	C.Meara	/1	H.Davis	/O	B.Clemens	/C	T.Wilson
		/O	C.Coombs	3	W.Barbare	P	H.Coveleski	/C	B.Reynolds	/S	S.Crane	/C	G.Hale		
P	R.Collins	/2	C.Manda	O	J.Birmingham	P	H.Dauss	P	P.Schwert	/1	F.Moore	/O	T.Bowden	P	W.Johnson
P	D.Leonard	H	C.Kavanagh	/S	B.Hartford	P	J.Dubuc	/O	F.Gilhooly	/C	D.Sturgis	/C	J.Enzenroth	P	D.Ayers
P	R.Foster	P	I.Porter	/C	J.Billings	P	P.Cavet	/1	H.Kingman	/C	I.Thomas	/3	E.Hemingway	P	J.Shaw
P	H.Bedient	/O	H.Schreiber	/C	F.Mills	P	A.Main	/3	T.Coyne	/O	B.Messenger	P	J.Boehling
P	E.Shore	H	D.Brown	/S	G.Dunlop			/1	J.Harris	/1	B.Rochefort	H	B.Rickey	P	J.Bentley
		/C	B.Sullivan	/3	A.Cypert	P	M.Hall	/C	B.Schwarz	/O	B.Sweeney	/1	C.Bold	RP	H.Harper
P	J.Wood			/O	T.Ginn	P	R.Reynolds	/O	A.Burr			H	D.Schirick		
P	R.Johnson	P	J.Benz	H	T.Reilly	P	G.Boehler	/1	F.Chance	P	B.Shawkey			P	J.Engel
P	V.Gregg	P	E.Cicotte			/P	R.Oldham			P	J.Bush	P	E.Hamilton	/P	M.Williams
P	F.Coumbe	P	J.Scott	P	W.Mitchell	/P	J.Williams	P	J.Warhop	P	W.Wyckoff	P	C.Weilman	/P	B.Gallia
/P	B.Ruth	P	R.Faber	P	B.Steen	P	E.McCreery	P	R.Caldwell	P	E.Plank	P	B.James	/P	C.Cashion
/P	G.Cooper	P	R.Russell	P	R.Hagerman	/P	L.Williams	P	R.Keating	P	C.Bender	P	G.Baumgardner	/P	J.Stevens
/P	M.Zeiser	RP	B.Lathrop	P	G.Morton			P	R.Fisher			P	W.Leverenz	/P	N.Altrock
/P	E.Kelly			P	F.Blanding			P	M.McHale	P	H.Pennock			/P	F.Barron
		P	M.Wolfgang							P	R.Bressler	P	R.Mitchell	/P	C.Griffith
		/P	E.Walsh	P	A.Collamore			P	K.Cole	P	B.Brown	P	H.Hoch		
		P	H.Jasper	P	V.Gregg			P	B.Brown	/P	B.Houck	P	W.Taylor		
				P	A.Bowman			/P	C.Pieh	/P	W.Jensen	/P	E.Manning		
				P	F.Coumbe			/P	A.Schulz	/P	J.Coombs	/P	G.Baichley		
				P	L.James			/P	G.Cooper	/P	C.Boardman	/P	A.Sothoron		
				P	H.Dillinger					/P	F.Worden				
				/P	P.Carter										
				/P	A.Tedrow										
				/P	G.Kahler										
				/P	L.Bishop										
				/P	N.Cullop										
				/P	S.Jones										
				/P	G.Beck										
				/P	H.Benn										

TEAM	G	W	L	PCT	GB	R	OR	AB	H	2B	3B	HR	BB	SO	AVG	OBP	SLG	PRO	PRO+	BR	/A	PF	CHI	RC	SB	CS	SBA	SBR
PHI	158	99	53	.651		749	529	5126	1392	165	80	29	545	517	.272	.348	.352	.700	123	112	140	96	107	662	231	188	55	-44
BOS	159	91	62	.595	8.5	589	510	5117	1278	226	85	18	490	549	.250	.320	.338	.658	105	26	26	100	98	567	177	176	50	-53
WAS	158	81	73	.526	19	572	519	5108	1245	176	81	18	470	640	.244	.313	.320	.633	93	-17	-39	104	102	544	220	163	57	-32
DET	157	80	73	.523	19.5	615	618	5102	1318	195	84	25	557	537	.258	.336	.344	.680	109	76	56	103	93	630	211	154	58	-29
STL	159	71	82	.464	28.5	523	615	5101	1241	185	75	17	423	863	.243	.306	.319	.625	99	-38	-17	96	99	516	233	189	55	-44
NY	157	70	84	.455	30	537	550	4992	1144	149	52	12	577	711	.229	.315	.287	.602	88	-60	-58	100	105	484	251	191	57	-39
CHI	157	70	84	.455	30	487	560	5040	1205	161	71	19	408	609	.239	.302	.311	.613	92	-59	-52	99	96	497	167	152	52	-41
CLE	157	51	102	.333	48.5	538	709	5157	1262	178	70	10	450	685	.245	.310	.312	.622	90	-39	-60	104	100	517	167	157	52	-44
TOT	631					4610		40743	10085	1435	598	148	3920	5111	.248	.319	.323	.642							1657	1370	55	-325

TEAM	CG	SH	SV	IP	H	H/G	HR	BB	SO	RAT	ERA	ERA+	OAV	OOB	PR	/A	PF	CPI	FA	E	DP	FW	PW	BW	SBW	DIF
PHI	89	24	17	1404	1264	8.1	18	521	720	11.6	2.78	94	.249	.322	-6	-27	95	100	.966	213	116	3.5	-3.0	15.5	-.4	7.4
BOS	88	24	8	1427¹	1207	7.6	18	393	602	10.3	2.36	114	.236	.295	59	50	98	94	.963	242	99	1.8	5.5	2.9	-1.4	5.6
WAS	75	25	20	1420²	1170	7.4	20	520	784	11.0	2.54	111	.233	.311	31	41	103	97	.961	254	116	1.0	4.5	-4.3	1.0	1.8
DET	81	14	12	1412	1285	8.2	17	498	567	11.8	2.86	98	.249	.322	-19	-10	103	97	.958	286	101	-1.1	-1.1	6.2	1.3	-1.8
STL	81	15	11	1410²	1309	8.4	20	540	553	12.1	2.85	95	.251	.327	-17	-22	99	103	.952	317	114	-2.7	-2.4	-1.9	-.4	1.9
NY	98	9	5	1397¹	1277	8.2	30	390	563	10.9	2.81	98	.250	.308	-12	-10	101	94	.963	238	93	1.9	-1.1	-6.4	.2	-1.5
CHI	74	17	11	1398²	1207	7.8	15	401	660	10.5	2.48	108	.239	.298	40	30	98	92	.955	299	90	-1.9	3.3	-5.7	-.0	-2.7
CLE	69	9	3	1391²	1365	8.8	10	666	688	13.4	3.21	90	.267	.357	-74	-55	105	110	.953	300	119	-1.9	-6.1	-6.6	-.4	-10.5
TOT	655	137	87	11262¹		8.1				11.5	2.73		.248	.319					.959	2149	848					

Runs
Collins-Phi	122
Speaker-Bos	101
Murphy-Phi	101
Bush-Det	97

Hits
Speaker-Bos	193
Crawford-Det	183
Baker-Phi	182
McInnis-Phi	181
Collins-Phi	181

Doubles
Speaker-Bos	46
Lewis-Bos	37
Pratt-StL	34
Collins-Chi	34
Leary-StL	28

Triples
Crawford-Det	26
Gardner-Bos	19
Speaker-Bos	18
T.Walker-StL	16
Hooper-Bos	15

Home Runs
Baker-Phi	9
Crawford-Det	8
T.Walker-StL	6
Fournier-Chi	6

Total Bases
Speaker-Bos	287
Crawford-Det	281
Baker-Phi	252
Pratt-StL	240
Collins-Phi	238

Runs Batted In
Crawford-Det	104
McInnis-Phi	95
Speaker-Bos	90
Baker-Phi	89
Collins-Phi	85

Runs Produced
Collins-Phi	205
Speaker-Bos	187
Crawford-Det	170
McInnis-Phi	168
Baker-Phi	164

Bases On Balls
Bush-Det	112
Collins-Phi	97
Murphy-Phi	87
Speaker-Bos	77
Maisel-NY	76

Batting Average
Cobb-Det	.368
Collins-Phi	.344
Speaker-Bos	.338
Jackson-Cle	.338
Baker-Phi	.319

On Base Percentage
Collins-Phi	.452
Speaker-Bos	.423
Jackson-Cle	.399
Crawford-Det	.388
Baker-Phi	.380

Slugging Average
Cobb-Det	.513
Speaker-Bos	.503
Crawford-Det	.483
Jackson-Cle	.464
Collins-Phi	.452

Production
Speaker-Bos	.926
Collins-Phi	.904
Crawford-Det	.871
Jackson-Cle	.862
Baker-Phi	.822

Adjusted Production
Collins-Phi	179
Speaker-Bos	178
Crawford-Det	157
Baker-Phi	153
Jackson-Cle	153

Batter Runs
Speaker-Bos	54.9
Collins-Phi	51.6
Cobb-Det	42.3
Crawford-Det	42.1
Jackson-Cle	31.6

Adjusted Batter Runs
Collins-Phi	56.4
Speaker-Bos	54.9
Cobb-Det	39.7
Crawford-Det	38.7
Baker-Phi	35.0

Clutch Hitting Index
McInnis-Phi	147
Gandil-Was	138
Collins-Phi	127
Lewis-Bos	125
Crawford-Det	125

Runs Created
Speaker-Bos	124
Collins-Phi	120
Crawford-Det	113
Baker-Phi	95
Cobb-Det	89

Total Average
Collins-Phi	.984
Speaker-Bos	.943
Crawford-Det	.867
Jackson-Cle	.835
T.Walker-StL	.776

Stolen Bases
Maisel-NY	74
Collins-Phi	58
Speaker-Bos	42
Shotton-StL	40

Stolen Base Average
Maisel-NY	81.3
Sweeney-NY	76.0
Chapman-Cle	72.7
Moriarty-Det	69.4
Peckinpaugh-NY	69.1

Stolen Base Runs
Maisel-NY	12.0
Sweeney-NY	2.1
Kopf-Phi	1.8
Chapman-Cle	1.8

Fielding Runs
Bush-Det	33.5
Speaker-Bos	27.7
Gandil-Was	23.7
Boone-NY	22.7
Turner-Cle	21.3

Total Player Rating
Speaker-Bos	7.6
Collins-Phi	5.9
Bush-Det	5.0
Baker-Phi	4.7
T.Walker-StL	3.9

Wins
Johnson-Was	28
Coveleski-Det	22
Collins-Bos	20
Leonard-Bos	19

Win Percentage
Bender-Phi	.850
Leonard-Bos	.792
Plank-Phi	.682
Shawkey-Phi	.667
Caldwell-NY	.654

Games
Johnson-Was	51
Ayers-Was	49
Shaw-Was	48
Benz-Chi	48

Complete Games
Johnson-Was	33
Coveleski-Det	23
Dauss-Det	22
Caldwell-NY	22

Shutouts
Johnson-Was	9
Leonard-Bos	7
Bender-Phi	7
Collins-Bos	6

Saves
Shaw-Was	4
Mitchell-StL	4
Faber-Chi	4
Dauss-Det	4
Bentley-Was	4

Innings Pitched
Johnson-Was	371.2
Coveleski-Det	303.1
Hamilton-StL	302.1
Dauss-Det	302.0
Weilman-StL	299.0

Fewest Hits/Game
Leonard-Bos	5.57
Caldwell-NY	6.46
Shaw-Was	6.93
Johnson-Was	6.95
Foster-Bos	6.97

Fewest BB/Game
McHale-NY	1.55
Russell-Chi	1.77
Johnson-Was	1.79
Warhop-NY	1.83
Ayers-Was	1.83

Strikeouts
Johnson-Was	225
Mitchell-Cle	179
Leonard-Bos	176
Shaw-Was	164
Dauss-Det	150

Strikeouts/Game
Leonard-Bos	7.05
Mitchell-Cle	6.27
Shaw-Was	5.74
Johnson-Was	5.45
Bender-Phi	5.38

Ratio
Leonard-Bos	8.29
Caldwell-NY	8.79
Johnson-Was	9.01
Foster-Bos	9.48
Ayers-Was	9.60

Earned Run Average
Leonard-Bos	.96
Foster-Bos	1.70
Johnson-Was	1.72
Caldwell-NY	1.94
Shore-Bos	2.00

Adjusted ERA
Leonard-Bos	279
Johnson-Was	163
Foster-Bos	158
Caldwell-NY	142
Cicotte-Chi	131

Opponents' Batting Avg.
Leonard-Bos	.180
Caldwell-NY	.205
Shaw-Was	.216
Johnson-Was	.217
Foster-Bos	.218

Opponents' On Base Pct.
Leonard-Bos	.246
Caldwell-NY	.260
Johnson-Was	.265
Foster-Bos	.274
Benz-Chi	.282

Starter Runs
Leonard-Bos	44.3
Johnson-Was	41.9
Foster-Bos	24.3
Weilman-StL	21.8
Cicotte-Chi	20.8

Adjusted Starter Runs
Johnson-Was	45.0
Leonard-Bos	43.0
Foster-Bos	23.2
Weilman-StL	20.6
Caldwell-NY	19.2

Clutch Pitching Index
Hagerman-Cle	126
Steen-Cle	123
Shawkey-Phi	109
James-StL	106
Bender-Phi	106

Relief Runs

Adjusted Relief Runs

Relief Ranking

Total Pitcher Index
Johnson-Was	7.3
Leonard-Bos	4.6
Cicotte-Chi	2.7
Foster-Bos	2.6
Caldwell-NY	2.5

Total Baseball Ranking
Speaker-Bos	7.6
Johnson-Was	7.2
Collins-Phi	5.9
Bush-Det	5.0
Baker-Phi	4.7

January 17 A report out of Chicago has FL president Gilmore offering Ty Cobb a five-year $75,000 contract. Cobb had replied he had already signed with the Tigers and could not sign with the Feds.

April 13 After building eight new ballparks in three months, the Federal League opens with the Baltimore Terrapins knocking off Buffalo in front of 27,140. Jack Quinn gets the first of his 26 wins, second in the league to ex-Pirate Claude Hendrix of the Chicago Whales. The Whales will finish second and the Terrapins third to Indianapolis.

June 3 Pitcher George "Chief" Johnson jumps from Cincinnati to Kansas City (FL); a judge grants a permanent injunction against him playing for K.C., but he pitches for the Packers through 1915.

June 5* Pitcher John Cantley of Opelika (Georgia-Alabama League) slugs three grand slams and a single for 15 RBI in a game against Talladega, winning the contest, 19–1.

June 15 First baseman Hal Chase jumps from the White Sox to the FL's Buffalo franchise after giving White Sox owner Charles Comiskey 10 days notice of his intent to do so.

July 7 Suffering heavy losses from Federal League competition in Baltimore, the Orioles' (IL) owner Jack Dunn offers Babe Ruth (plus Ernie Shore and catcher Ben Egan) for $10,000 to old friend Connie Mack, who refuses, pleading poverty. Cincinnati, which has a working agreement giving them the choice of two players, takes outfielder George Twombley and shortstop Claud Derrick. Dunn finally peddles his threesome to new owner Joe Lannin of the Red Sox for a reported $25,000.

September 5* Pitching for Providence in the IL, 19-year-old Babe Ruth beats Toronto, 9–0, with a one-hitter, and hits his only minor league homer.

September 7 Floods severely damage the Kansas City Packers' (FL) ballpark, washing away fences and demolishing the clubhouse.

September 19 Ed Lafitte pitches a 6–2 no-hitter for the Brooklyn Tip-Tops (FL) over the Kansas City Packers. Wildness costs him the two runs. He will lead the FL with 127 walks.

October 6 The Chicago Whales lose to Kansas City while the Indianapolis Hoosiers beat St. Louis, giving Indianapolis a 1½ game pennant margin. Five .300 hitters, led by Benny Kauff's .370, pace the winners. Claude Hendrix of the Whales is the FL's top pitcher, 29–11.

December 4 Walter Johnson accepts an advance from the FL Chicago Whales. Clark Griffith threatens to take Johnson to court, claiming he has paid Johnson for the reserve option in his contract. Ban Johnson says Walter Johnson was on the market and is "damaged goods," worth getting rid of. Griffith travels to Coffeyville, Kan. to persuade his franchise player that the option clause is legal and binding. Whales manager Joe Tinker says he has signed Johnson for $16,000 and given him a $6,000 bonus. Two weeks later Griffith signs Johnson for three years at $12,500 per year and Johnson returns the bonus to the Feds.

December 7 Chief Bender signs a two-year deal with the Federal League; he will be assigned to Baltimore.

BALTIMORE		BROOKLYN		BUFFALO		CHICAGO		INDIANAPOLIS		KANSAS CITY		PITTSBURGH		ST.LOUIS	
M	O.Knabe	M	B.Bradley	M	L.Schlafly	M	J.Tinker	M	B.Phillips	M	G.Stovall	M	D.Gessler	M	M.Brown
1B	H.Swacina	1B	H.Myers	1B	J.Agler	1B	F.Beck	1B	C.Carr	1B	G.Stovall	M	R.Oakes	M	F.Jones
2B	O.Knabe	2B	S.Hofman	2B	T.Downey	2B	J.Farrell	2B	F.LaPorte	2B	B.Kenworthy	1B	H.Bradley	1B	H.Miller
SS	M.Doolan	SS	E.Gagnier	SS	B.Louden	SS	J.Tinker	SS	J.Esmond	SS	P.Goodwin	2B	J.Lewis	2B	D.Crandall
3B	J.Walsh	3B	T.Wisterzil	3B	F.Smith	3B	R.Zeider	3B	B.McKechnie	3B	G.Perring	SS	E.Holly	SS	A.Bridwell
LF	H.Simmons	LF	C.Cooper	LF	F.Delahanty	LF	M.Flack	LF	A.Scheer	LF	C.Chadbourne	3B	E.Lennox	3B	A.Boucher
CF	V.Duncan	CF	A.Shaw	CF	C.Hanford	CF	D.Zwilling	CF	V.Campbell	CF	A.Kruger	LF	D.Jones	LF	W.Miller
RF	B.Meyer	RF	S.Evans	RF	T.McDonald	RF	A.Wickland	RF	B.Kauff	RF	G.Gilmore	CF	R.Oakes	CF	D.Drake
C	F.Jacklitsch	C	G.Land	C	W.Blair	C	A.Wilson	C	B.Rariden	C	T.Easterly	RF	J.Savage	RF	J.Tobin
												C	C.Berry	C	M.Simon
O	G.Zinn	O	G.Anderson	1	H.Chase	3	H.Fritz	O	A.Kaiser	O	C.Coles			2S	J.Misse
O	J.Bates	S	A.Halt	O	E.Booe	O	A.Walsh	O	E.Roush	S	J.Rawlings	O2	T.McDonald	O	F.Kommers
3S	E.Kirkpatrick	2	J.Delahanty	O	D.Young	C	B.Block	23	C.Vandagrift	S3	C.Daringer	13	C.Rheam	C2	G.Hartley
C	H.Russell	C	F.Owens	2	L.Schlafly	S	J.Stanley	1	B.Dolan	O	J.Potts	O	F.Delahanty	O	L.Kirby
O	F.Kommers	O	D.Murphy	3	C.Engle	/C	C.Clemens	C	G.Textor	C	J.Enzenroth	S	S.Yerkes	C	H.Chapman
C	D.Kerr	1	A.Griggs	C	A.LaVigne	/O	B.Jackson	C	B.Warren	C	D.Brown	O	M.Menosky	2	J.Mathes
/O	J.McCandless	O	F.Chouinard	O	L.Bonin	/S	L.Kavanagh	/1	F.Rooney	/S	W.Tappan	C	S.Roberts	3	M.Cueto
/3	F.Lobert	C	A.Watson	C	N.Allen	/S	J.Smith	/O	E.Booe			O	R.Mattis	/2	A.Marsans
/C	M.Boucher	/3	R.Williams	C	B.Collins	H	J.Kading			P	G.Packard	C	D.Kerr	H	F.Jones
/O	F.Chouinard	H	B.Bradley	H	N.Pettigrew	H	S.Roberts	P	C.Falkenberg	P	N.Cullop	O	B.Coulson		
				/C	J.Snyder			P	E.Moseley	P	D.Stone	/2	F.Chouinard		
P	J.Quinn	P	T.Seaton	/S	D.Wertz	P	C.Hendrix	P	G.Kaiserling	P	B.Harris	/S	J.Scott	P	B.Groom
P	G.Suggs	P	E.Lafitte			P	M.Fiske	P	G.Mullin	P	P.Henning	/C	F.Madden	P	D.Davenport
P	K.Wilhelm	P	H.Finneran	P	F.Anderson	P	E.Lange	P	H.Billiard			H	M.Boucher	P	H.Keupper
P	F.Smith			P	G.Krapp	P	D.Watson			P	D.Adams			P	E.Willett
P	B.Bailey	P	B.Houck	P	R.Ford	P	M.Prendergast	/P	R.McConnaughey	P	C.Johnson	P	E.Knetzer	P	M.Brown
		P	D.Marion	P	E.Moore			/P	C.Whitehouse	/P	G.Hogan	P	H.Camnitz	RP	E.Herbert
P	S.Conley	P	R.Sommers	P	A.Schulz			/P	F.Harter	/P	D.Swan	P	W.Dickson		
P	D.Yount	P	B.Chappelle			P	T.McGuire	/P	E.Henderson			P	C.Barger	/P	D.Watson
/P	J.Ridgway	P	B.Maxwell			P	R.Johnson	/P	K.Keifer			P	M.Walker	/P	T.Welch
/P	V.Hughes	P	J.Bluejacket	P	H.Moran	P	A.Brennan	/P	F.Ostendorf						
/P	J.Allen	P	B.Smith	P	B.Smith	/P	D.Black	/P	C.Woods			P	G.LaClaire		
		/P	M.Brown	P	D.Woodman	/P	D.Sherman					P	W.Adams		
		P	R.Peters	/P	J.Houser							/P	E.Henderson		
		/P	H.Juul	/P	E.Porray							/P	F.Allen		
		/P	F.Wilson	/P	B.Schlitzer										
		/P	E.Chaney												
		/P	J.Vernon												
		P	J.McGraw												

TEAM	G	W	L	PCT	GB	R	OR	AB	H	2B	3B	HR	BB	SO	AVG	OBP	SLG	PRO	PRO+	BR	/A	PF	CHI	RC	SB	CS	SBA	SBR
IND	157	88	65	.575		762	622	5176	1474	230	90	33	470	668	.285	.349	.383	.732	95	-36	-103	111	100	765	273			
CHI	157	87	67	.565	1.5	621	517	5098	1314	227	50	52	520	645	.258	.331	.352	.683	98	-125	-95	94	94	634	171			
BAL	160	84	70	.545	4.5	645	628	5120	1374	222	67	32	487	589	.268	.337	.357	.694	92	-105	-122	103	94	652	152			
BUF	155	80	71	.530	7	620	602	5064	1264	177	74	37	430	761	.250	.311	.336	.647	80	-202	-211	102	109	574	228			
BRO	157	77	77	.500	11.5	662	677	5221	1402	225	85	42	404	665	.269	.326	.368	.694	96	-117	-113	99	99	669	220			
KC	154	67	84	.444	20	644	683	5127	1369	226	77	39	399	621	.267	.324	.364	.688	97	-127	-106	96	99	637	171			
PIT	154	64	86	.427	22.5	605	698	5114	1339	180	90	34	410	575	.262	.321	.352	.673	90	-152	-148	99	96	613	153			
STL	154	62	89	.411	25	565	697	5078	1254	193	65	26	503	662	.247	.319	.326	.645	77	-198	-222	105	96	554	113			
TOT	624					5124		40998	10790	1680	598	295	3623	5186	.263	.323	.355	.678						1481				

TEAM	CG	SH	SV	IP	H	H/G	HR	BB	SO	RAT	ERA	ERA+	OAV	OOB	PR	/A	PF	CPI	FA	E	DP	FW	PW	BW	SBW	DIF
IND	104	15	9	1397²	1352	8.7	29	476	664	12.1	3.06	102	.258	.325	-27	9	108	100	.956	289	113	-1.2	.9	-10.7		22.5
CHI	93	17	8	1420¹	1204	7.6	43	393	650	10.3	2.44	109	.233	.291	70	33	92	94	.962	249	114	1.1	3.4	-9.9		15.4
BAL	88	15	13	1392	1389	9.0	34	392	732	11.7	3.13	97	.268	.323	-38	-16	105	101	.960	263	105	.6	-1.7	-12.7		20.8
BUF	89	15	16	1387	1249	8.1	45	505	662	11.7	3.16	94	.245	.318	-42	-31	103	91	.962	242	109	1.3	-3.2	-21.9		28.4
BRO	91	11	9	1385¹	1375	8.9	31	559	636	12.9	3.33	86	.264	.341	-69	-71	100	102	.956	283	120	-.9	-7.4	-11.8		20.0
KC	82	10	12	1361	1387	9.2	37	445	600	12.4	3.41	82	.268	.331	-79	-95	96	98	.957	279	135	-.9	-9.9	-11.0		13.3
PIT	97	9	6	1370	1416	9.3	38	444	510	12.4	3.56	80	.273	.333	-103	-107	99	96	.960	253	92	.6	-11.1	-15.4		14.9
STL	97	9	6	1367²	1418	9.3	38	409	661	12.3	3.59	85	.267	.324	-107	-83	105	89	.957	273	94	-.6	-8.6	-23.1		18.8
TOT	741	101	79	11081		8.8				12.0	3.20		.263	.323					.959	2131	882					

Runs		Hits		Doubles		Triples		Home Runs		Total Bases	
Kauff-Ind	120	Kauff-Ind	211	Kauff-Ind	44	Evans-Bro	15	Zwilling-Chi	16	Kauff-Ind	305
McKechnie-Ind	107	Zwilling-Chi	185	Evans-Bro	41	Esmond-Ind	15	Kenworthy-KC	15	Zwilling-Chi	287
Duncan-Bal	99	Evans-Bro	179	Kenworthy-KC	40	Kenworthy-KC	14	Hanford-Buf	12	Kenworthy-KC	286
Kenworthy-KC	93	Oakes-Pit	178	Zwilling-Chi	38			Evans-Bro	12	Evans-Bro	286
Evans-Bro	93	Hanford-Buf	174							Hanford-Buf	264

Runs Batted In		Runs Produced		Bases On Balls		Batting Average		On Base Percentage		Slugging Average	
LaPorte-Ind	107	Kauff-Ind	207	Wickland-Chi	81	Kauff-Ind	.370	Kauff-Ind	.447	Evans-Bro	.556
Evans-Bro	96	LaPorte-Ind	189	Agler-Buf	77	Evans-Bro	.348	Evans-Bro	.416	Kauff-Ind	.534
Zwilling-Chi	95	Evans-Bro	177	Kauff-Ind	72	Easterly-KC	.335	Lennox-Pit	.414	Kenworthy-KC	.525
Kauff-Ind	95	Zwilling-Chi	170			Shaw-Bro	.324	Meyer-Bal	.395	Lennox-Pit	.493
Kenworthy-KC	91	Kenworthy-KC	169			Campbell-Ind	.318	Wilson-Chi	.394	Zwilling-Chi	.485

Production		Adjusted Production		Batter Runs		Adjusted Batter Runs		Clutch Hitting Index		Runs Created	
Kauff-Ind	.981	Evans-Bro	165	Kauff-Ind	47.0	Evans-Bro	38.0	LaPorte-Ind	151	Kauff-Ind	160
Evans-Bro	.973	Kauff-Ind	150	Evans-Bro	37.2	Kauff-Ind	34.5	Swacina-Bal	137	Evans-Bro	121
Lennox-Pit	.907	Kenworthy-KC	148	Lennox-Pit	23.2	Kenworthy-KC	25.0	Wisterzil-Bro	128	Kenworthy-KC	114
Kenworthy-KC	.896	Lennox-Pit	148	Kenworthy-KC	21.3	Lennox-Pit	23.9	Stovall-KC	128	Zwilling-Chi	106
Wilson-Chi	.860	Wilson-Chi	142	Wilson-Chi	15.3	Wilson-Chi	19.8	Carr-Ind	127	McKechnie-Ind	94

Total Average		Stolen Bases		Stolen Base Average		Stolen Base Runs		Fielding Runs		Total Player Rating	
Kauff-Ind	1.278	Kauff-Ind	75					Doolan-Bal	29.3	Wilson-Chi	4.6
Evans-Bro	1.087	McKechnie-Ind	47					McKechnie-Ind	22.9	Kenworthy-KC	4.5
Lennox-Pit	1.034	Myers-Bro	43					Kenworthy-KC	20.8	Kauff-Ind	4.4
Kenworthy-KC	.995	Chadbourne-KC	42					Rariden-Ind	20.1	Evans-Bro	2.9
Wilson-Chi	.939							Tinker-Chi	19.1	Yerkes-Pit	1.6

Wins		Win Percentage		Games		Complete Games		Shutouts		Saves	
Hendrix-Chi	29	Ford-Buf	.778	Hendrix-Chi	49	Hendrix-Chi	34	Falkenberg-Ind	9	Ford-Buf	6
Quinn-Bal	26	Hendrix-Chi	.744	Falkenberg-Ind	49	Falkenberg-Ind	33	Seaton-Bro	7	Wilhelm-Bal	5
Seaton-Bro	25	Quinn-Bal	.650	Wilhelm-Bal	47	Moseley-Ind	29	Suggs-Bal	6	Packard-KC	5
Falkenberg-Ind	25	Seaton-Bro	.641	Suggs-Bal	46	Quinn-Bal	27	Hendrix-Chi	6	Hendrix-Chi	5
Suggs-Bal	24	Suggs-Bal	.632	Quinn-Bal	46						

Innings Pitched		Fewest Hits/Game		Fewest BB/Game		Strikeouts		Strikeouts/Game		Ratio	
Falkenberg-Ind	377.1	Hendrix-Chi	6.51	Ford-Buf	1.49	Falkenberg-Ind	236	Davenport-StL	5.93	Hendrix-Chi	8.55
Hendrix-Chi	362.0	Ford-Buf	6.91	Suggs-Bal	1.61	Moseley-Ind	205	Moseley-Ind	5.83	Ford-Buf	8.66
Quinn-Bal	342.2	Krapp-Buf	7.05	Quinn-Bal	1.71	Hendrix-Chi	189	Falkenberg-Ind	5.63	Falkenberg-Ind	10.16
Suggs-Bal	319.1	Fiske-Chi	7.32	Hendrix-Chi	1.91	Seaton-Bro	172	Groom-StL	5.36	Fiske-Chi	10.32
Moseley-Ind	316.2	Watson-Chi-StL	7.34	Keupper-StL	2.07	Groom-StL	167	Seaton-Bro	5.11	Lange-Chi	10.42

Earned Run Average		Adjusted ERA		Opponents' Batting Avg.		Opponents' On Base Pct.		Starter Runs		Adjusted Starter Runs	
Johnson-Chi	1.57	Ford-Buf	163	Hendrix-Chi	.203	Hendrix-Chi	.251	Hendrix-Chi	48.0	Hendrix-Chi	38.7
Hendrix-Chi	1.69	Hendrix-Chi	157	Krapp-Buf	.210	Ford-Buf	.254	Ford-Buf	29.3	Falkenberg-Ind	37.7
Ford-Buf	1.82	Falkenberg-Ind	141	Ford-Buf	.214	Lange-Chi	.282	Falkenberg-Ind	27.9	Ford-Buf	31.3
Watson-Chi-StL	2.01	Watson-Chi-StL	137	Lange-Chi	.224	Falkenberg-Ind	.284	Watson-Chi-StL	22.1	Watson-Chi-StL	18.6
Falkenberg-Ind	2.22	Lange-Chi	119	Watson-Chi-StL	.230	Anderson-Buf	.297	Cullop-KC	17.8	Quinn-Bal	16.4

Clutch Pitching Index		Relief Runs		Adjusted Relief Runs		Relief Ranking		Total Pitcher Index		Total Baseball Ranking	
Mullin-Ind	128							Hendrix-Chi	5.4	Hendrix-Chi	5.4
Lafitte-Bro	122							Falkenberg-Ind	3.8	Wilson-Chi	4.6
Watson-Chi-StL	114							Ford-Buf	3.1	Kenworthy-KC	4.5
Kaiserling-Ind	109							Quinn-Bal	2.7	Kauff-Ind	4.4
Quinn-Bal	106							Krapp-Buf	1.8	Falkenberg-Ind	3.8

February 11* The International League tries to put a team in the Bronx, but Giants president Hempstead objects.

April 19 St. Louis Cardinals right-hander Lee Meadows makes his NL debut and becomes the first player to wear glasses regularly on the field since pitcher Will White in 1886.

April 29 Benny Kauff of the Brooklyn Brookfeds causes quite a stir when he jumps from the FL to the NL. Boston refuses to play New York if Kauff is in the lineup and the game is forfeited to New York. NL president John Tener, who was called from the ballpark by the other umpire, declares Kauff ineligible until reinstated and orders the game forfeited to Boston. The Braves win the exhibition game, 13-8, and that score stands up when Tener rules it an official game and cancels both forfeits. Kauff returns to Brooklyn and leads the FL with a .342 average. John McGraw will have to wait until 1916 to sign him.

June 9 The Phils move into first place, as Grover Cleveland Alexander holds the Cubs hitless until the seventh. Alexander will be 31–10 and lead the NL with a 1.55 ERA, 36 complete games, 376 innings, 241 strikeouts, and 12 shutouts.

June 17 George "Zip" Zabel comes out of the Cubs bullpen with two outs in the first and winds up with a 4-3, 19-inning win over Brooklyn in the longest relief job ever.

June 18 Former Giants mascot Charley "Victory" Faust, 34, dies of pulmonary tuberculosis while confined to the Western Hospital for the Insane in Washington State.

July 23* Jack Ness of Oakland (Pacific Coast League) has his 49-game hitting streak stopped. He bats .440 in the longest streak thus far in Organized Baseball.

July 29 At 41, Honus Wagner becomes the oldest player in this century to hit a grand slam, an inside-the-park job against Jeff Pfeffer of Brooklyn. The record will stand until Tony Perez hits a grand slam on May 13, 1985, one day short of his 43rd birthday.

August 8 Hank O'Day, who managed the Cubs in 1914, returns to umpiring.

August 18 The new Braves Field opens in Boston. An estimated 46,500 jam the park to see the Braves beat the Cards 3-1.

August 18* *Asahi Shimbun,* the Japanese newspaper, sponsors the first National High School baseball tournament. It is an instant success and will continue every August (except during World War II) to the present. It will often be called the Koshien Tournament, after the stadium near Osaka where the games will be played, starting in 1924.

September 8 Fred Clarke resigns as Pirates manager, having won four pennants in 19 years.

September 29 The Phils clinch their first pennant on Grover Alexander's fourth one-hitter and 12th shutout of the year, 5-0, over the defending champion Braves.

October 9 President Wilson becomes the first president to attend a World Series game, at Game 2 in Philadelphia. Boston's 19-game winner Rube Foster allows the Phils three hits and drives in the winning run to break a 1–1 tie in the ninth against Erskine Mayer.

	BOSTON		BROOKLYN		CHICAGO		CINCINNATI		NEW YORK		PHILADELPHIA		PITTSBURGH		ST.LOUIS
M	G.Stallings	M	W.Robinson	M	R.Bresnahan	M	B.Herzog	M	J.McGraw	M	P.Moran	M	F.Clarke	M	M.Huggins
1B	B.Schmidt	1B	J.Daubert	1B	V.Saier	1B	F.Mollwitz	1B	F.Merkle	1B	F.Luderus	1B	D.Johnston	1B	D.Miller
2B	J.Evers	2B	G.Cutshaw	2B	H.Zimmerman	2B	B.Rodgers	2B	L.Doyle	2B	B.Niehoff	2B	J.Viox	2B	M.Huggins
SS	R.Maranville	SS	O.O'Mara	SS	B.Fisher	SS	B.Herzog	SS	A.Fletcher	SS	D.Bancroft	SS	H.Wagner	SS	A.Butler
3B	R.Smith	3B	G.Getz	3B	A.Phelan	3B	H.Groh	3B	H.Lobert	3B	B.Byrne	3B	D.Baird	3B	B.Betzel
LF	J.Connolly	LF	Z.Wheat	LF	F.Schulte	LF	R.Killefer	LF	G.Burns	LF	B.Becker	LF	M.Carey	LF	B.Bescher
CF	S.Magee	CF	H.Myers	CF	C.Williams	CF	T.Leach	CF	F.Snodgrass	CF	P.Whitted	CF	Z.Collins	CF	C.Wilson
RF	H.Moran	RF	C.Stengel	RF	W.Good	RF	T.Griffith	RF	D.Robertson	RF	G.Cravath	RF	B.Hinchman	RF	T.Long
C	H.Gowdy	C	O.Miller	C	J.Archer	C	I.Wingo	C	C.Meyers	C	B.Killefer	C	G.Gibson	C	F.Snyder
2O	E.Fitzpatrick	C	L.McCarty	C	R.Bresnahan	13	T.Clarke	O	F.Brainerd	O	D.Paskert	3S	W.Gerber	O	C.Dolan
O2	D.Egan	3	J.Schultz	O	R.Murray	O	K.Williams	3	E.Grant	C	M.Stock	O	D.Costello	1O	H.Hyatt
C	B.Whaling	O1	J.Hummel	O	P.Knisely	23	I.Olson	O	R.Murray	C	E.Burns	C	B.Schang	3	Z.Beck
O	P.Compton	O	B.Zimmerman	21	P.McLarry	2S	J.Wagner	O	R.Dooin	O	B.Weiser	O	E.Barney	C	M.Gonzalez
O	L.Gilbert	O	A.Nixon	23	A.McCarthy	3	F.Von Kolnitz	O	M.Becker	2	O.Dugey	O	L.LeJeune	S	R.Hornsby
O	T.Cather	/S	I.Olson	S	E.Mulligan	O	G.Twombly	O	J.Thorpe	C	B.Adams	/2	A.McCarthy	/C	J.Roche
O	F.Snodgrass	/O	R.Smyth	/C	B.Hargrave	O	J.Beall	/1	G.Kelly			O	L.Murphy	S	R.Daringer
/O	Z.Collins	/C	M.Wheat	/S	C.Keating	C	R.Dooin	C	L.Wendell	P	P.Alexander	/S	I.McAuley	/C	H.Glenn
/O	J.Shannon	H	D.Egan	/2	J.Schultz			O	C.Babington	P	E.Mayer	/2	P.Siglin	/O	J.Smith
/C	W.Tragesser	/3	J.Karst			P	G.Dale	C	L.McLean	P	A.Demaree	/O	P.Duncan	/O	J.Brown
/C	E.Blackburn					P	P.Schneider	C	H.Smith	P	E.Rixey	P	B.Wagner		
/3	F.Low	P	J.Pfeffer	/3	R.Corriden	P	F.Toney	/O	M.Jacobson	P	G.Chalmers	/O	F.Scheeren	P	B.Doak
/2	R.Shannon	P	W.Dell	/C	B.O'Farrell	P	R.Benton	/C	B.Schang			/O	F.Clarke	P	S.Sallee
		P	J.Coombs			P	K.Lear	/3	B.Dyer	/P	G.McQuillan	H	H.Daubert	P	L.Meadows
P	D.Rudolph	P	S.Smith	P	H.Vaughn			/C	B.Kocher	H	S.Baumgartner	H	S.Smith	P	D.Griner
P	T.Hughes	P	E.Appleton	P	J.Lavender	P	L.McKenry	/3	H.Baker	P	B.Tincup			P	H.Robinson
P	P.Ragan			P	G.Pearce	P	R.Ames			/P	J.Oeschger	P	B.Harmon		
P	L.Tyler	P	N.Rucker	P	B.Humphries	/P	P.Douglas	P	J.Tesreau			P	A.Mamaux	P	H.Perdue
		P	P.Douglas	P	Z.Zabel	/P	L.George	P	P.Perritt			P	B.Adams	P	R.Ames
		/P	R.Aitchison			/P	C.Brown	P	C.Mathewson			P	W.Cooper	P	D.Niehaus
P	A.Nehf	/P	L.Cheney	P	L.Cheney	/P	R.Callahan	P	S.Stroud			P	E.Kantlehner	/P	C.Boardman
P	G.Davis	/P	R.Marquard	P	P.Standridge	/P	H.McCluskey	P	R.Marquard			RP	J.Conzelman	/P	F.Lamline
P	B.James	/P	L.Cadore	P	K.Adams	/P	G.Cochran	RP	H.Ritter						
/P	J.Barnes	/P	P.Ragan	/P	P.Douglas			RP	F.Schupp			P	G.McQuillan		
P	D.Crutcher	/P	D.Mails	/P	B.Hogg							/P	C.Hill		
/P	P.Strand	/P	C.Schmutz	/P	E.Schorr			P	R.Schauer			/P	H.Kelly		
/P	O.Hess	/P	E.Brown	/P	B.Wright			P	R.Benton			/P	P.Slattery		
/P	D.Luque							/P	F.Herbert			/P	D.Vance		
/P	G.Cocreham							/P	A.Fromme						
								/P	E.Palmero						

TEAM	G	W	L	PCT	GB	R	OR	AB	H	2B	3B	HR	BB	SO	AVG	OBP	SLG	PRO	PRO+	BR	/A	PF	CHI	RC	SB	CS	SBA	SBR
PHI	153	90	62	.592		589	463	4916	1216	202	39	58	460	600	.247	.316	.340	.656	104	31	25	101	101	550	121	113	52	-32
BOS	157	83	69	.546	7	582	545	5070	1219	231	57	17	549	620	.240	.321	.319	.640	105	15	42	96	98	554	121	98	55	-23
BRO	154	80	72	.526	10	536	560	5120	1268	165	75	14	313	496	.248	.295	.317	.612	89	-56	-65	102	107	496	131	126	51	-36
CHI	156	73	80	.477	17.5	570	620	5114	1246	212	66	53	393	639	.244	.303	.342	.645	102	4	3	100	100	555	166	124	57	-25
PIT	156	73	81	.474	18	557	520	5113	1259	197	91	24	419	656	.246	.309	.334	.643	102	8	16	99	97	563	182	111	62	-12
STL	157	72	81	.471	18.5	590	601	5106	1297	159	92	20	457	658	.254	.320	.333	.653	104	30	29	100	100	568	162	144	53	-38
CIN	160	71	83	.461	20	516	585	5231	1323	194	84	15	360	512	.253	.308	.331	.639	98	-5	-15	102	91	553	156	142	52	-38
NY	155	69	83	.454	21	582	628	5218	1312	195	68	24	315	547	.251	.300	.329	.629	103	-27	4	94	109	526	155	137	53	-36
TOT	624					4522		40888	10140	1555	572	225	3266	4728	.248	.309	.331	.640							1194	995	55	-239

TEAM	CG	SH	SV	IP	H	H/G	HR	BB	SO	RAT	ERA	ERA+	OAV	OOB	PR	/A	PF	CPI	FA	E	DP	FW	PW	BW	SBW	DIF
PHI	98	20	8	1374¹	1161	7.6	26	342	652	10.0	2.17	126	.234	.288	87	85	100	103	.966	216	99	.8	9.4	2.8	-.2	1.2
BOS	95	17	13	1405²	1257	8.0	23	366	630	10.7	2.57	100	.246	.302	27	1	94	100	.966	213	115	1.4	.1	4.7	.8	.0
BRO	87	16	8	1389²	1252	8.1	29	473	499	11.6	2.66	104	.245	.318	14	17	101	108	.963	238	96	-.5	1.9	-7.2	-.7	10.6
CHI	71	18	8	1399	1272	8.2	28	480	657	11.6	3.11	89	.247	.316	-57	-54	101	91	.958	268	94	-2.3	-6.0	.3	.5	4.0
PIT	91	18	11	1380	1229	8.0	21	384	544	10.8	2.60	105	.246	.304	23	19	99	100	.966	214	100	1.2	2.1	1.8	2.0	-11.1
STL	79	13	9	1400²	1320	8.5	30	402	538	11.3	2.89	96	.256	.314	-22	-17	101	101	.964	235	109	-.0	-1.9	3.2	-.9	-4.9
CIN	80	19	12	1432¹	1304	8.2	28	497	572	11.6	2.84	101	.250	.321	-15	2	104	104	.966	222	148	1.1	.2	-1.7	-.9	-4.8
NY	78	15	9	1385	1350	8.8	40	325	637	11.2	3.11	82	.260	.308	-57	-86	93	94	.960	256	119	-1.6	-9.6	.4	-.7	4.4
TOT	679	136	78	11166²		8.2				11.1	2.75		.248	.309					.964	1862	880					

Runs		Hits		Doubles		Triples		Home Runs		Total Bases	
Cravath-Phi	89	Doyle-NY	189	Doyle-NY	40	Long-StL	25	Cravath-Phi	24	Cravath-Phi	266
Doyle-NY	86	Griffith-Cin	179	Luderus-Phi	36	H.Wagner-Pit	17	Williams-Chi	13	Doyle-NY	261
Bancroft-Phi	85	Hinchman-Pit	177	Saier-Chi	35	Griffith-Cin	16	Schulte-Chi	12	Griffith-Cin	254
Burns-NY	83	Groh-Cin	170	Smith-Bos	34	Hinchman-Pit	14	Saier-Chi	11	Hinchman-Pit	253
O'Mara-Bro	77	Burns-NY	169	Magee-Bos	34	Burns-NY	14	Becker-Phi	11	H.Wagner-Pit	239

Runs Batted In		Runs Produced		Bases On Balls		Batting Average		On Base Percentage		Slugging Average	
Cravath-Phi	115	Cravath-Phi	180	Cravath-Phi	86	Doyle-NY	.320	Cravath-Phi	.393	Cravath-Phi	.510
Magee-Bos	87	Magee-Bos	157	Bancroft-Phi	77	Luderus-Phi	.315	Luderus-Phi	.376	Luderus-Phi	.457
Griffith-Cin	85	Doyle-NY	152	Viox-Pit	75	Griffith-Cin	.307	Daubert-Bro	.369	Long-StL	.446
H.Wagner-Pit	78	Hinchman-Pit	144	Huggins-StL	74	Hinchman-Pit	.307	Hinchman-Pit	.368	Saier-Chi	.445
Hinchman-Pit	77	Miller-StL	143	Smith-Bos	67	Daubert-Bro	.301	Doyle-NY	.358	Doyle-NY	.442

Production		Adjusted Production		Batter Runs		Adjusted Batter Runs		Clutch Hitting Index		Runs Created	
Cravath-Phi	.902	Cravath-Phi	170	Cravath-Phi	46.8	Cravath-Phi	45.6	Fletcher-NY	134	Cravath-Phi	105
Luderus-Phi	.833	Doyle-NY	150	Luderus-Phi	30.3	Doyle-NY	32.5	Magee-Bos	131	Doyle-NY	94
Hinchman-Pit	.807	Luderus-Phi	150	Hinchman-Pit	29.7	Hinchman-Pit	31.0	Miller-StL	128	Hinchman-Pit	94
Doyle-NY	.799	Hinchman-Pit	146	Doyle-NY	27.1	Luderus-Phi	29.3	Schmidt-Bos	125	Luderus-Phi	87
Saier-Chi	.795	Saier-Chi	140	Griffith-Cin	25.4	Griffith-Cin	23.8	Cutshaw-Bro	123	Griffith-Cin	85

Total Average		Stolen Bases		Stolen Base Average		Stolen Base Runs		Fielding Runs		Total Player Rating	
Cravath-Phi	.942	Carey-Pit	36	Bresnahan-Chi	86.4	Bresnahan-Chi	3.9	Fletcher-NY	34.1	Cravath-Phi	4.9
Saier-Chi	.819	Herzog-Cin	35	Saier-Chi	76.3	Saier-Chi	3.3	Herzog-Cin	30.9	Herzog-Cin	4.2
Luderus-Phi	.799	Saier-Chi	29	Baird-Pit	70.7	Costello-Pit	1.5	Maranville-Bos	20.9	Luderus-Phi	3.7
Hinchman-Pit	.741	Baird-Pit	29	Robertson-NY	68.8	Baird-Pit	1.5	Cutshaw-Bro	16.8	Snyder-StL	3.1
Doyle-NY	.714	Cutshaw-Bro	28	Herzog-Cin	68.6	Gerber-Pit	1.2	Magee-Bos	15.4	Fletcher-NY	3.0

Wins		Win Percentage		Games		Complete Games		Shutouts		Saves	
Alexander-Phi	31	Alexander-Phi	.756	Hughes-Bos	50	Alexander-Phi	36	Alexander-Phi	12	Hughes-Bos	9
Rudolph-Bos	22	Toney-Cin	.739	Dale-Cin	49	Rudolph-Bos	30	Tesreau-NY	8	Benton-Cin-NY	5
Mayer-Phi	21	Mamaux-Pit	.724	Alexander-Phi	49	Pfeffer-Bro	26	Mamaux-Pit	8	Lavender-Chi	4
Mamaux-Pit	21	Vaughn-Chi	.625	Schneider-Cin	48	Harmon-Pit	25	Toney-Cin	6	Cooper-Pit	4
Vaughn-Chi	20	Coombs-Bro	.600	Sallee-StL	46	Tesreau-NY	24	Pfeffer-Bro	6		

Innings Pitched		Fewest Hits/Game		Fewest BB/Game		Strikeouts		Strikeouts/Game		Ratio	
Alexander-Phi	376.1	Alexander-Phi	6.05	Mathewson-NY	.97	Alexander-Phi	241	Alexander-Phi	5.76	Alexander-Phi	7.82
Rudolph-Bos	341.1	Toney-Cin	6.47	Humphries-Chi	1.21	Tesreau-NY	176	Hughes-Bos	5.49	Hughes-Bos	8.89
Tesreau-NY	306.0	Mamaux-Pit	6.51	Adams-Pit	1.25	Hughes-Bos	171	Mamaux-Pit	5.44	Tesreau-NY	9.26
Dale-Cin	296.2	Hughes-Bos	6.68	Alexander-Phi	1.53	Mamaux-Pit	152	Douglas-Cin-Br-Chi	5.26	Toney-Cin	9.54
Pfeffer-Bro	291.2	Zabel-Chi	6.85	Rudolph-Bos	1.69	Vaughn-Chi	148	Tesreau-NY	5.18	Adams-Pit	9.73

Earned Run Average		Adjusted ERA		Opponents' Batting Avg.		Opponents' On Base Pct.		Starter Runs		Adjusted Starter Runs	
Alexander-Phi	1.22	Alexander-Phi	224	Alexander-Phi	.191	Alexander-Phi	.234	Alexander-Phi	63.8	Alexander-Phi	63.4
Toney-Cin	1.58	Toney-Cin	181	Toney-Cin	.207	Hughes-Bos	.265	Toney-Cin	28.9	Toney-Cin	31.6
Mamaux-Pit	2.04	Mamaux-Pit	134	Mamaux-Pit	.208	Tesreau-NY	.269	Pfeffer-Bro	21.0	Pfeffer-Bro	21.9
Pfeffer-Bro	2.10	Pfeffer-Bro	132	Hughes-Bos	.213	Toney-Cin	.278	Mamaux-Pit	19.8	Mamaux-Pit	19.2
Hughes-Bos	2.12	Hughes-Bos	122	Tesreau-NY	.215	Adams-Pit	.280	Hughes-Bos	19.5	Hughes-Bos	14.5

Clutch Pitching Index		Relief Runs		Adjusted Relief Runs		Relief Ranking		Total Pitcher Index		Total Baseball Ranking	
Humphries-Chi	139							Alexander-Phi	8.6	Alexander-Phi	8.6
Perritt-NY	122							Toney-Cin	3.1	Cravath-Phi	4.9
Schneider-Cin	121							Pfeffer-Bro	2.6	Herzog-Cin	4.2
Rixey-Phi	120							Mayer-Phi	2.2	Luderus-Phi	3.7
Stroud-NY	118							Schneider-Cin	2.0	Snyder-StL	3.1

January 5 Thirteen years after a Pennsylvania Supreme Court decision effectively banned him from playing for the Athletics, Nap Lajoie rejoins the team. With Lajoie out of Cleveland, a local newspaper runs a contest to rename the Naps. The winning nickname will be the Indians, after the late Lou Sockalexis, a Penobscot Indian who was a popular Cleveland player in the late 1890s.

January 9* The National Commission declares University of Michigan senior George Sisler a free agent after a two-year fight. After graduating, Sisler will sign with the St. Louis Browns, managed by his former college coach, Branch Rickey.

February 3 The AL bans the emery ball, a pitch introduced by Russ Ford in 1910.

April 14 The A's Herb Pennock comes within one out of pitching the first Opening Day no-hitter. A scratch single by Harry Hooper is the Red Sox' only hit in a 5-0 loss.

May 6 Babe Ruth hits his first major league home run off the Yankees' Jack Warhop in the third inning at New York's Polo Grounds. Ruth has two other hits but loses the game in the 13th.

June 18 Ty Cobb steals home twice in a game against Washington, on the front end of double and triple steals.

July 2 The A's sell Jack Barry for $8,000 to Boston. Five days later, they will sell Bob Shawkey to the Yankees for $18,000. Shawkey will win 168 games while wearing the Yankees' new pinstripes.

July 14 White Sox pitcher Red Faber steals three bases in the fourth inning against the A's. With the White Sox leading 4–2 in the fourth and rain threatening, the A's try to delay the game. Joe Bush purposely hits Faber with a pitch, and Faber, trying to speed up the game, tries to get thrown out by stealing. Little effort is made to retire him, and he scores Chicago's fifth run. His "steal" of home is the winning run, as rain never materializes, and Chicago wins, 6–4.

August 29 George Sisler pitches against Walter Johnson and wins, 2–1. He will be 4–4 for the Browns and 1–2 next year before moving permanently to first base.

September 22 Having loaned the Braves the use of their larger park in 1914, the Boston Red Sox request the use of the new, larger NL park for this year's World Series.

September 30 The Red Sox clinch the AL pennant by beating Detroit, giving them a 2½-game margin. The Tigers will win 100 games, the first time a runner-up has reached that mark.

October 13 The Phils get four runs early off George "Rube" Foster, but the Red Sox break a tie in the ninth for the third time; reliever Eppa Rixey gives up Harry Hooper's second home run of the game, and Boston wins the game, 5-4, and the Series four games to one.

	BOSTON		CHICAGO		CLEVELAND		DETROIT		NEW YORK		PHILADELPHIA		ST.LOUIS		WASHINGTON
M	B.Carrigan	M	P.Rowland	M	J.Birmingham	M	H.Jennings	M	B.Donovan	M	C.Mack	M	B.Rickey	M	C.Griffith
1B	D.Hoblitzel	1B	J.Fournier	M	L.Fohl	1B	G.Burns	1B	W.Pipp	1B	S.McInnis	1B	J.Leary	1B	C.Gandil
2B	H.Wagner	2B	E.Collins	1B	J.Kirke	2B	R.Young	2B	L.Boone	2B	N.Lajoie	2B	D.Pratt	2B	R.Morgan
SS	E.Scott	SS	B.Weaver	2B	B.Wambsganss	SS	D.Bush	SS	R.Peckinpaugh	SS	L.Kopf	SS	D.Lavan	SS	G.McBride
3B	L.Gardner	3B	L.Blackburne	SS	R.Chapman	3B	O.Vitt	3B	F.Maisel	3B	W.Schang	3B	J.Austin	3B	E.Foster
LF	D.Lewis	LF	S.Collins	3B	W.Barbare	LF	B.Veach	LF	R.Hartzell	LF	R.Oldring	LF	B.Shotton	LF	H.Shanks
CF	T.Speaker	CF	H.Felsch	LF	J.Graney	CF	T.Cobb	CF	H.High	CF	J.Walsh	CF	T.Walker	CF	C.Milan
RF	H.Hooper	RF	E.Murphy	CF	N.Leibold	RF	S.Crawford	RF	D.Cook	RF	A.Strunk	RF	D.Walsh	RF	D.Moeller
C	P.Thomas	C	R.Schalk	RF	E.Smith	C	O.Stanage	C	L.Nunamaker	C	J.Lapp	C	S.Agnew	C	J.Henry
				C	S.O'Neill										
S3	H.Janvrin	3O	B.Roth			12	M.Kavanagh	23	P.Baumann	O	E.Murphy	13	I.Howard	C1	R.Williams
2	J.Barry	O	J.Jackson	O1	J.Jackson	C	D.Baker	O	B.Cree	23	L.Malone	1O	G.Sisler	O	M.Acosta
C	H.Cady	1	B.Brief	23	T.Turner	C	R.McKee	C	J.Sweeney	S	J.Barry	C	H.Severeid	3O	T.Connolly
1	D.Gainer	O	F.Quinlan	O	B.Southworth	1	B.Jacobson	1	C.Mullen	O	W.McAvoy	1	D.Kauffman	C	E.Ainsmith
C	B.Carrigan	3	P.Johns	O	B.Roth	3	G.Moriarty	O	E.Miller	O	C.Davies	O	G.Williams	O	C.Jamieson
O	O.Henriksen	O	N.Leibold	O	D.Wilie	/2	F.Fuller	/2	W.Alexander	3	T.Healy	O	B.Jacobson	32	D.Neff
3	M.McNally	C	W.Mayer	C	B.Egan	/C	J.Peters	O	T.Hendryx	H	H.Damrau	O	E.Walker	O	T.Barber
/O	C.Shorten	C	T.Daly	3	J.Evans			O	S.Shelton	/O	E.Bankston	O	B.Lee	1	J.Judge
/C	R.Haley	3	J.Breton	2	J.Hammond	P	H.Coveleski	O	E.Barney	/O	S.Thompson	/C	M.Ruel	O	H.Rondeau
/2	B.Rodgers	/O	R.Demmitt	1	R.Wood	P	H.Dauss	/C	E.Krueger	/S	S.Seibold	O	B.Wallace	/O	M.Kopp
/O	W.Rehg	H	H.Baker	1	P.Shields	P	J.Dubuc	/C	P.Schwert	/S	S.Crane	/C	G.O'Brien	/2	C.Sawyer
		H	L.Chappell	2	B.Rodgers	P	B.Boland	/O	T.Daley	/C	C.Perkins	/O	P.Parker	O	S.Mayer
P	R.Foster	H	C.Jackson	O	J.Eschen			/O	G.Layden	/3	O.Conway	/1	R.Schmandt	O	H.Milan
P	E.Shore			/C	J.Billings	P	B.Steen	/O	F.Gilhooley	/S	B.Danner	/S	S.Dee	H	C.Pick
P	B.Ruth	P	R.Faber	/3	T.Hoffman	P	P.Cavet	/C	R.Walters	/3	S.McConnell	/3	B.Dalrymple		
P	D.Leonard	P	J.Scott	H	B.Paschal	P	B.James			/3	H.Bostick	O	W.Alexander	P	W.Johnson
P	J.Wood	P	J.Benz	/C	H.Haworth	P	R.Oldham	P	R.Caldwell	/2	R.Edwards	H	C.Burkam	P	B.Gallia
		P	R.Russell	H	L.Gooch	/P	G.Lowdermilk	P	R.Fisher	/3	A.Corcoran			P	J.Boehling
P	C.Mays	P	E.Cicotte			/P	G.Boehler	P	B.Brown	/C	B.Haeffner	P	C.Weilman	P	D.Ayers
P	R.Collins			P	G.Morton	/P	R.Reynolds	P	J.Warhop	/1	H.Davis	P	G.Lowdermilk	P	J.Shaw
P	V.Gregg	P	M.Wolfgang	P	W.Mitchell	/P	R.Ledbetter	P	C.Pieh	/3	F.Lear	P	E.Hamilton		
/P	H.Pennock	/P	E.Walsh	P	R.Hagerman					/C	I.Thomas	P	B.James	P	H.Harper
/P	R.Comstock	/P	H.Jasper	P	S.Jones			P	B.Shawkey			P	E.Koob	/P	G.Dumont
/P	G.Cooper	/P	E.Klepfer	P	R.Walker			P	R.Keating	P	W.Wyckoff	RP	P.Perryman	P	J.Engel
		/P	D.Davis	RP	O.Harstad			P	M.McHale	P	R.Bressler			/P	B.Hopper
		/P	W.Johnson					P	K.Cole	P	J.Bush	P	R.Hoff	/P	S.Rice
		P	F.Coumbe					/P	G.Mogridge	P	T.Sheehan	/P	T.McCabe	/P	J.Bentley
		P	A.Collamore					/P	B.Donovan	P	T.Knowlson	/P	H.Hoch	/P	N.Altrock
		P	L.Brenton					P	D.Vance			/P	T.Phillips		
		P	B.Steen					/P	A.Russell	P	B.Shawkey	/P	J.Park		
		P	E.Klepfer					/P	C.Markle	P	B.Davis	/P	G.Baumgardner		
		P	P.Carter					/P	E.Cottrell	P	C.Crowell	/P	R.Cook		
		/P	C.Garrett					/P	D.Tipple	P	J.Nabors	/P	J.Tillman		
		/P	H.Hill					/P	N.Brady	P	H.Pennock	/P	W.Leverenz		
		/P	A.Bowman							/P	D.Fillingim	/P	P.Sims		
										/P	J.Richardson	/P	A.Remneas		
										/P	H.Eccles	/P	A.Sothoron		
										/P	B.Morrisette	/P	C.East		
										/P	W.Ancker	/P	S.Perry		
										/P	H.Weaver	/P	R.McKay		
										/P	J.Sherman				
										/P	B.Haas				
										/P	J.Harper				
										/P	E.Myers				
										/P	C.Ray				
										/P	B.Pepper				
										/P	S.Pillion				
										/P	B.Meehan				
										/P	T.Turner				
										/P	B.Cone				

TEAM	G	W	L	PCT	GB	R	OR	AB	H	2B	3B	HR	BB	SO	AVG	OBP	SLG	PRO	PRO+	BR	/A	PF	CHI	RC	SB	CS	SBA	SBR
BOS	155	101	50	.669		669	499	5024	1308	202	76	14	527	**476**	.260	.336	.339	.675	110	46	67	97	100	611	118	117	50	-35
DET	156	100	54	.649	2.5	778	597	5128	1372	207	94	23	681	527	.268	.357	.358	.715	114	131	93	105	101	711	241	146	62	-15
CHI	155	93	61	.604	9.5	717	509	4914	1269	163	102	25	583	575	.258	.345	.348	.693	110	83	62	103	102	637	233	183	56	-40
WAS	155	85	68	.556	17	569	**491**	5029	1225	152	79	12	458	541	.244	.312	.312	.624	90	-52	-63	102	**103**	535	186	106	**64**	**-8**
NY	154	69	83	.454	32.5	584	588	4982	1162	167	50	31	570	669	.233	.317	.305	.622	91	-46	-45	100	**103**	523	198	133	60	-20
STL	159	63	91	.409	39.5	521	680	5112	1255	166	65	19	472	765	.246	.315	.315	.630	98	-44	-22	96	91	535	202	160	56	-35
CLE	154	57	95	.375	44.5	539	670	5034	1210	169	79	20	490	681	.240	.312	.317	.629	91	-43	-54	102	95	526	138	117	54	-29
PHI	154	43	109	.283	58.5	545	888	5081	1204	183	72	16	436	634	.237	.304	.311	.615	92	-74	-56	97	**103**	507	127	89	59	-15
TOT	621					4922		40304	10005	1409	617	160	4217	4868	.248	.325	.326	.651							1443	1051	58	-198

TEAM	CG	SH	SV	IP	H	H/G	HR	BB	SO	RAT	ERA	ERA+	OAV	OOB	PR	/A	PF	CPI	FA	E	DP	FW	PW	BW	SBW	DIF
BOS	81	19	15	1397	1164	**7.5**	18	446	634	10.7	2.39	116	**.231**	.300	84	59	95	97	.964	226	95	2.5	6.3	7.1	-1.1	10.8
DET	86	10	**19**	1413¹	1259	8.0	14	492	550	11.5	2.86	106	.243	.316	11	25	103	94	.961	258	107	.5	2.7	**9.9**	1.0	9.0
CHI	91	16	9	1401	1242	8.0	14	**350**	635	10.4	2.43	122	.241	**.294**	78	84	101	95	.965	222	95	2.7	8.9	6.6	-1.6	-.6
WAS	87	**21**	13	1393²	**1161**	**7.5**	12	455	**715**	10.7	**2.31**	**129**	.232	.302	**97**	**102**	101	102	.964	230	101	2.2	**10.8**	-6.7	**1.8**	.4
NY	**101**	12	2	1382²	1272	8.3	41	517	559	12.0	3.06	96	.254	.329	-20	-20	100	**104**	**.966**	217	118	**2.9**	-2.1	-4.8	.5	-3.5
STL	76	6	7	1403	1256	8.1	21	612	566	12.4	3.04	94	.249	.338	-17	-31	98	103	.949	336	**144**	-4.3	-3.3	-2.3	-1.1	-3.0
CLE	62	11	10	1372	1287	8.4	18	518	610	12.0	3.13	97	.256	.329	-30	-13	104	98	.957	280	82	-1.2	-1.4	-5.7	-.5	-10.2
PHI	78	6	2	1348¹	1358	9.1	22	827	588	15.0	4.29	68	.278	.388	-204	-206	100	102	.947	338	118	-5.0	-21.9	-5.9	1.0	-1.2
TOT	662	101	77	11111		8.1				11.8	2.93		.248	.325					.959	2107	860					

Runs		Hits		Doubles		Triples		Home Runs		Total Bases	
Cobb-Det	144	Cobb-Det	208	Veach-Det	40	Crawford-Det	19	Roth-Chi-Cle	7	Cobb-Det	274
E.Collins-Chi	118	Crawford-Det	183	Pratt-StL	31	Fournier-Chi	18	Oldring-Phi	6	Crawford-Det	264
Vitt-Det	116	Veach-Det	178	Lewis-Bos	31	Roth-Chi-Cle	17			Veach-Det	247
Speaker-Bos	108	Speaker-Bos	176	Crawford-Det	31	S.Collins-Chi	17			Pratt-StL	237
Chapman-Cle	101	Pratt-StL	175	Cobb-Det	31	Chapman-Cle	17			E.Collins-Chi	227

Runs Batted In		Runs Produced		Bases On Balls		Batting Average		On Base Percentage		Slugging Average	
Veach-Det	112	Cobb-Det	240	E.Collins-Chi	119	Cobb-Det	.369	Cobb-Det	.486	Fournier-Chi	.491
Crawford-Det	112	E.Collins-Chi	191	Shotton-StL	118	E.Collins-Chi	.332	E.Collins-Chi	.460	Cobb-Det	.487
Cobb-Det	99	Veach-Det	190	Cobb-Det	118	Fournier-Chi	.322	Fournier-Chi	.429	Kavanagh-Det	.452
S.Collins-Chi	85	Crawford-Det	189	Bush-Det	118	Speaker-Bos	.322	Speaker-Bos	.416	J.Jackson-Cle-Chi	.445
J.Jackson-Cle-Chi	81	Speaker-Bos	177	Hooper-Bos	89	McInnis-Phi	.314	Shotton-StL	.409	Roth-Chi-Cle	.438

Production		Adjusted Production		Batter Runs		Adjusted Batter Runs		Clutch Hitting Index		Runs Created	
Cobb-Det	.973	Cobb-Det	182	Cobb-Det	71.6	Cobb-Det	64.5	Crawford-Det	138	Cobb-Det	155
Fournier-Chi	.920	Fournier-Chi	170	E.Collins-Chi	51.9	E.Collins-Chi	48.2	Veach-Det	135	E.Collins-Chi	116
E.Collins-Chi	.896	E.Collins-Chi	163	Fournier-Chi	40.9	Speaker-Bos	38.3	Schalk-Chi	128	Crawford-Det	101
J.Jackson-Cle-Chi	.830	Speaker-Bos	152	Speaker-Bos	35.0	Fournier-Chi	38.1	Gardner-Bos	123	Speaker-Bos	97
Speaker-Bos	.827	J.Jackson-Cle-Chi	145	Veach-Det	32.3	Shotton-StL	31.3	S.Collins-Chi	120	Veach-Det	97

Total Average		Stolen Bases		Stolen Base Average		Stolen Base Runs		Fielding Runs		Total Player Rating	
Cobb-Det	1.170	Cobb-Det	96	Schang-Phi	85.7	Maisel-NY	8.1	Boone-NY	20.8	Cobb-Det	6.2
E.Collins-Chi	.971	Maisel-NY	51	Maisel-NY	81.0	Cobb-Det	6.0	T.Walker-StL	14.8	E.Collins-Chi	6.1
Fournier-Chi	.964	E.Collins-Chi	46	Foster-Was	76.9	Schang-Phi	3.6	Vitt-Det	14.4	Speaker-Bos	4.0
Speaker-Bos	.801	Shotton-StL	43	Moeller-Was	76.2	Moeller-Was	3.6	Lajoie-Phi	14.1	Fournier-Chi	3.5
Veach-Det	.771	C.Milan-Was	40	Roth-Chi-Cle	72.2	Williams-StL	2.7	Speaker-Bos	13.4	Chapman-Cle	3.4

Wins		Win Percentage		Games		Complete Games		Shutouts		Saves	
Johnson-Was	27	Wood-Bos	.750	Faber-Chi	50	Johnson-Was	35	Scott-Chi	7	Mays-Bos	7
Scott-Chi	24	Shore-Bos	.704	Coveleski-Det	50	Caldwell-NY	31	Johnson-Was	7		
Faber-Chi	24	Foster-Bos	.704	Scott-Chi	48	Dauss-Det	27	Morton-Cle	6		
Dauss-Det	24	Ruth-Bos	.692	Jones-Cle	48	Scott-Chi	23	Foster-Bos	5		
Coveleski-Det	22	Scott-Chi	.686			Dubuc-Det	22	Dubuc-Det	5		

Innings Pitched		Fewest Hits/Game		Fewest BB/Game		Strikeouts		Strikeouts/Game		Ratio	
Johnson-Was	336.2	Leonard-Bos	6.38	Johnson-Was	1.50	Johnson-Was	203	Leonard-Bos	5.69	Johnson-Was	8.90
Coveleski-Det	312.2	Ruth-Bos	6.86	Ayers-Was	1.62	Faber-Chi	182	Mitchell-Cle	5.68	Morton-Cle	9.41
Dauss-Det	309.2	Wood-Bos	6.86	Benz-Chi	1.62	Wyckoff-Phi	157	Faber-Chi	5.47	Wood-Bos	9.44
Caldwell-NY	305.0	Johnson-Was	6.90	Russell-Chi	1.84	Coveleski-Det	150	Johnson-Was	5.43	Ayers-Was	9.50
Faber-Chi	299.2	Morton-Cle	7.09	Cicotte-Chi	1.93	Mitchell-Cle	149	Lowdermilk-StL-Det	5.32	Benz-Chi	9.63

Earned Run Average		Adjusted ERA		Opponents' Batting Avg.		Opponents' On Base Pct.		Starter Runs		Adjusted Starter Runs	
Wood-Bos	1.49	Johnson-Was	191	Leonard-Bos	.208	Johnson-Was	.260	Johnson-Was	51.7	Johnson-Was	52.9
Johnson-Was	1.55	Wood-Bos	186	Ruth-Bos	.212	Morton-Cle	.268	Shore-Bos	35.5	Shore-Bos	31.1
Shore-Bos	1.64	Shore-Bos	169	Johnson-Was	.214	Wood-Bos	.275	Scott-Chi	29.5	Scott-Chi	30.9
Scott-Chi	2.03	Scott-Chi	146	Morton-Cle	.216	Benz-Chi	.276	Wood-Bos	25.2	Morton-Cle	24.1
Fisher-NY	2.11	Morton-Cle	142	Wood-Bos	.216	Ayers-Was	.276	Foster-Bos	23.2	Benz-Chi	22.7

Clutch Pitching Index		Relief Runs		Adjusted Relief Runs		Relief Ranking		Total Pitcher Index		Total Baseball Ranking	
Hamilton-StL	125							Johnson-Was	7.7	Johnson-Was	7.6
Shore-Bos	122							Wood-Bos	3.6	Cobb-Det	6.2
Foster-Bos	121							Shore-Bos	3.5	E.Collins-Chi	6.1
Fisher-NY	119							Scott-Chi	3.4	Speaker-Bos	4.0
Wood-Bos	118							Dauss-Det	3.2	Wood-Bos	3.6

January 2 The Cardinals try to prevent outfielder Lee Magee, 25, from playing for the Brooklyn Tip-Tops. Like most such suits, it will fail. Magee will play and manage in the Federal League.

January 5 The Federal League sues Organized Baseball, claiming that it is an illegal trust and asking that it be dissolved and all contracts voided. The case is filed in U.S. court in Chicago, before Judge Kenesaw Mountain Landis. He will stall his decision, and peace is declared at the end of the year. The league shifts players to beef up teams in key cities. Benny Kauff, the FL's answer to Ty Cobb, is moved from Indianapolis to Brooklyn.

January 24 In a retreat from the FL competition, the Baltimore Orioles of the International League move to Richmond, Va. With the demise of the FL, the Orioles will return to Baltimore.

April 24 Frank Allen, Pittsburgh lefty, pitches a 2–0 no-hitter against the St. Louis Terriers. Allen will win 23 for Pittsburgh, who will finish third just a half game back of the first-place Chicago Whales and the second-place Terriers.

August 22 Newark takes two from Pittsburgh and leads by one percentage point over Kansas City, with Pittsburgh third and Chicago fourth, only 1½ games separating the teams. The race is so close by season's end Newark will be fifth, six games out. There will be nine 20-game winners, led by George McConnell's 25-10 for the Whales, the only year McConnell wins more than eight games.

September 7 The St. Louis Terriers' Dave Davenport, strikeout leader of the FL, pitches a 3–0 no-hitter over the Whales, one of his 10 shutouts and 22 wins. St. Louis will play two more games than Chicago and split them, thus trailing the Whales at season's end by one percentage point. Chicago will be 86–66; St. Louis, 87–67, and the Pittsburgh Rebels, 86–67. A percentage difference of .004, it is the closest bunching of the top three teams in any major league race.

October 9 Federal League officials meet secretly with the National Commission at Philadelphia's Bellevue-Stratford Hotel.

October 19 Brookfed owner Robert Ward dies at his New Rochelle, N.Y., mansion. Ward's death increases pressure on the FL to make peace with Organized Baseball.

December 17 Baltimore FL officials unsuccessfully try to buy their way into the major leagues for $250,000. They then try to gain entrance into the IL but fail again.

December 22 Organized Baseball and the Federal League sign a peace treaty at Cincinnati, ending their two-year war. The Feds agree to go out of existence, but the major leagues pay an enormous price: $600,000 for distribution to FL owners; amalgamation of two Fed franchises, one each into NL and AL; recognition of Fed players' eligibility, and agreement to bid for them in a Fed-controlled auction. Baltimore gets short shrift and balks, but conferees, eager for settlement, defer its claims—a decision they will later repent.

BALTIMORE		BROOKLYN		BUFFALO		CHICAGO		KANSAS CITY		NEWARK		PITTSBURGH		ST.LOUIS	
M	O.Knabe	M	L.Magee	M	L.Schlafly	M	J.Tinker	M	G.Stovall	M	B.Phillips	M	R.Oakes	M	F.Jones
1B	H.Swacina	M	J.Ganzel	M	W.Blair	1B	F.Beck	1B	G.Stovall	M	B.McKechnie	1B	E.Konetchy	1B	B.Borton
2B	O.Knabe	1B	H.Myers	M	H.Lord	2B	R.Zeider	2B	B.Kenworthy	1B	E.Huhn	2B	S.Yerkes	2B	B.Vaughn
SS	M.Doolan	2B	L.Magee	1B	H.Chase	SS	J.Smith	SS	J.Rawlings	2B	F.LaPorte	SS	M.Berghammer	SS	E.Johnson
3B	J.Walsh	SS	Fd.Smith	2B	B.Louden	3B	H.Fritz	3B	G.Perring	SS	J.Esmond	3B	M.Mowrey	3B	C.Deal
LF	V.Duncan	3B	A.Halt	SS	R.Roach	LF	L.Mann	LF	A.Shaw	3B	B.McKechnie	LF	A.Wickland	LF	W.Miller
CF	J.McCandless	LF	C.Cooper	3B	H.Lord	CF	D.Zwilling	CF	C.Chadbourne	LF	A.Scheer	CF	R.Oakes	CF	D.Drake
RF	S.Evans	CF	B.Kauff	LF	B.Meyer	RF	M.Flack	RF	G.Gilmore	CF	E.Roush	RF	J.Kelly	RF	J.Tobin
C	F.Owens	RF	G.Anderson	CF	C.Engle	C	A.Wilson	C	T.Easterly	RF	V.Campbell	C	C.Berry	C	G.Hartley
O	G.Zinn	C	G.Land	RF	J.Dalton	C	W.Fischer	O	A.Kruger	C	B.Rariden	2S	J.Lewis	3	A.Kores
1	J.Agler	O	S.Evans	C	W.Blair	2	J.Farrell	S2	P.Goodwin	O1	G.Schaefer	C	P.O'Connor	C	H.Chapman
32	E.Kirkpatrick	C	M.Simon	O1	S.Hofman	O	C.Hanford	C	D.Brown	1	R.Mills	O	C.Rheam	O	L.Kirby
C	F.Jacklitsch	1	H.Bradley	23	T.Downey	/3	T.Wisterzil	3	B.Bradley	O	G.Whitehouse	O	H.Bradley	23	A.Bridwell
2	J.Gallagher	3	T.Wisterzil	O	T.McDonald	1	B.Jackson	/C	J.Enzenroth	3	T.Reed	/3	E.Lennox	O	A.Marsans
O	B.Meyer	2	T.Helfrich	C	N.Allen	S	M.Doolan	P	N.Cullop	3	L.Strands	O	D.Jones	/3	J.Walsh
S	J.Smith	C	J.Smith	S	F.Smith	O	A.Wickland	P	G.Packard	/1	H.Bradley	/O	F.Delahanty	/O	T.Wisterzil
20	H.Simmons	S	E.Gagnier	O	J.Agler	1	J.Weiss	P	C.Johnson	/C	G.Textor	S	E.Holly	/O	P.Compton
1	K.Crawford	C	L.Pratt	/C	A.Watson	S	J.Tinker	P	A.Main	/C	L.Pratt	/O	M.Menosky	/O	F.Jones
O	J.Hickman	/1	A.Griggs	/O	D.Young	S	A.Hauser	P	P.Henning	/C	B.Warren	/O	J.Savage	/1	H.Miller
C	H.Russell	2	D.Howard	/2	E.Gagnier	3	C.Pechous	P	D.Adams	P	E.Reulbach	/C	O.Kerlin	P	D.Davenport
/1	K.Kolseth	S	M.Reed	P	A.Schulz	/C	C.Clemens	/P	C.Blackburn	P	E.Moseley	P	F.Allen	P	D.Crandall
/3	W.Reinecker	/2	J.Delahanty	P	H.Bedient	P	G.McConnell	/P	J.Gingras	P	G.Kaiserling	P	E.Knetzer	P	E.Plank
/2	C.Eakle	/C	A.Watson	P	F.Anderson	P	C.Hendrix	/P	B.Harris	P	H.Moran	P	C.Rogge	P	B.Groom
/C	D.Kerr	/O	F.Kane	P	G.Krapp	P	M.Prendergast			P	C.Falkenberg	P	B.Hearn	P	D.Watson
/C	C.Maisel	/2	A.Tesch	P	R.Ford	P	M.Brown			P	T.Seaton	P	C.Barger	P	E.Willett
/3	E.Forsythe	/2	D.Murphy	RP	R.Marshall	P	D.Black			P	C.Brandom	P	W.Dickson	P	E.Herbert
H	C.Miller	/C	D.Wright	P	H.Ehmke	P	A.Brennan			P	C.Whitehouse	P	R.Comstock		
P	J.Quinn	/O	F.Chouinard	P	E.Lafitte	P	R.Johnson			/P	G.Mullin	P	G.LaClaire		
P	G.Suggs	P	H.Finneran	/P	D.Woodman	/P	B.Bailey			/P	H.Billiard	/P	H.Camnitz		
P	B.Bailey	P	D.Marion	/P	G.LaClaire	/P	H.Rasmussen			/P	F.Trautman	P	S.Burk		
P	C.Bender	P	T.Seaton	/P	B.Smith							/P	A.Braithwood		
P	R.Johnson	P	J.Bluejacket									/P	J.Miljus		
P	F.Smith	P	B.Upham												
P	S.Conley	P	E.Lafitte												
P	G.LaClaire	P	Fk.Smith												
/P	C.Young	P	F.Wilson												
/P	D.Black	P	M.Walker												
/P	L.Douglas	P	H.Wiltse												
/P	T.Vereker	/P	C.Falkenberg												
/P	K.Wilhelm	/P	B.Herring												

TEAM	G	W	L	PCT	GB	R	OR	AB	H	2B	3B	HR	BB	SO	AVG	OBP	SLG	PRO	PRO+	BR	/A	PF	CHI	RC	SB	CS	SBA	SBR
CHI	155	86	66	.566		640	538	5133	1320	185	77	50	444	590	.257	.320	.352	.672	101	-110	-81	94	102	650	161			
STL	159	87	67	.565		634	527	5145	1344	199	81	23	576	502	.261	.340	.345	.685	94	-71	-100	105	92	698	195			
PIT	156	86	67	.562	0.5	592	524	5040	1318	180	80	20	448	561	.262	.326	.341	.667	94	-110	-106	99	95	655	224			
KC	153	81	72	.529	5.5	547	551	4937	1206	200	66	28	368	503	.244	.303	.329	.632	87	-182	-166	96	103	559	144			
NEW	155	80	72	.526	6	585	562	5097	1283	210	80	17	448	550	.252	.315	.334	.649	93	-148	-122	94	99	618	184			
BUF	153	74	78	.487	12	574	634	5065	1261	193	68	40	420	587	.249	.309	.338	.647	85	-158	-167	102	102	594	184			
BRO	153	70	82	.461	16	647	673	5035	1348	205	75	36	473	654	.268	.336	.360	.696	103	-56	-52	99	97	704	249			
BAL	154	47	107	.305	40	550	760	5060	1235	196	53	36	470	641	.244	.313	.325	.638	82	-167	-180	103	97	578	128			
TOT	619					4769		40512	10315	1568	580	250	3637	4588	.255	.316	.340	.656							1469			

TEAM	CG	SH	SV	IP	H	H/G	HR	BB	SO	RAT	ERA	ERA+	OAV	OOB	PR	/A	PF	CPI	FA	E	DP	FW	PW	BW	SBW	DIF
CHI	97	21	10	1397²	1232	7.9	33	402	576	10.7	2.64	95	.240	.299	14	-21	92	95	.964	233	102	.4	-2.3	-8.7		20.6
STL	94	24	9	1426	1267	8.0	22	396	698	10.7	2.73	105	.243	.300	-1	22	105	92	.967	212	111	2.0	2.4	-10.8		16.4
PIT	88	16	12	1382¹	1273	8.3	37	441	517	11.4	2.79	97	.253	.317	-10	-13	99	107	.971	182	98	3.5	-1.4	-11.4		18.8
KC	95	16	11	1359	1210	8.0	29	390	526	10.8	2.82	93	.242	.301	-14	-30	96	91	.962	246	96	-.5	-3.2	-17.9		26.1
NEW	100	16	7	1406²	1308	8.4	15	453	581	11.6	2.60	98	.253	.319	19	-7	94	111	.963	239	124	.0	-.8	-13.1		17.8
BUF	79	14	11	1360	1271	8.4	35	553	594	12.3	3.38	83	.254	.331	-99	-88	103	95	.964	232	112	.3	-9.5	-18.0		25.2
BRO	78	10	16	1355²	1299	8.6	27	536	467	12.3	3.37	81	.258	.332	-96	-98	100	97	.955	290	103	-3.1	-10.5	-5.6		13.3
BAL	85	5	7	1360¹	1455	9.6	52	466	570	13.0	3.96	72	.284	.349	-186	-165	105	100	.957	273	140	-2.0	-17.8	-19.4		9.2
TOT	716	122	83	11047²		8.4				11.6	3.03		.255	.316					.963	1907	886					

Runs
Borton-StL 97
Berghammer-Pit 96
Evans-Bro-Bal 94
Tobin-StL 92
Kauff-Bro 92

Hits
Tobin-StL 184
Konetchy-Pit 181
Evans-Bro-Bal 171
Kauff-Bro 165
Chase-Buf 165

Doubles
Evans-Bro-Bal 34
Zwilling-Chi 32
Konetchy-Pit 31
Chase-Buf 31

Triples
Mann-Chi 19
Konetchy-Pit 18
Kelly-Pit 17
Gilmore-KC 15

Home Runs
Chase-Buf 17
Zwilling-Chi 13
Kauff-Bro 12
Konetchy-Pit 10
Walsh-Bal-StL 9

Total Bases
Konetchy-Pit 278
Chase-Buf 267
Tobin-StL 254
Kauff-Bro 246
Zwilling-Chi 242

Runs Batted In
Zwilling-Chi 94
Konetchy-Pit 93
Chase-Buf 89
Kauff-Bro 83
Borton-StL 83

Runs Produced
Borton-StL 177
Kauff-Bro 163
Konetchy-Pit 162
Evans-Bro-Bal 157
Chase-Buf 157

Bases On Balls
Borton-StL 92
Kauff-Bro 85
Berghammer-Pit ... 83
W.Miller-StL 79

Batting Average
Kauff-Bro .... .342
Fischer-Chi ...... .329
Magee-Bro .... .323
Konetchy-Pit ..... .314
Flack-Chi .... .314

On Base Percentage
Kauff-Bro .... .446
W.Miller-StL ..... .400
Borton-StL .... .395
Evans-Bro-Bal .... .392
Cooper-Bro .... .388

Slugging Average
Kauff-Bro .... .509
Konetchy-Pit ..... .483
Chase-Buf .... .471
Fischer-Chi ...... .449
Zwilling-Chi ..... .442

Production
Kauff-Bro .... .955
Konetchy-Pit ..... .846
Evans-Bro-Bal .... .818
Zwilling-Chi ..... .808
Mann-Chi .... .795

Adjusted Production
Kauff-Bro 170
Konetchy-Pit 138
Zwilling-Chi 135
Mann-Chi 131
Flack-Chi 129

Batter Runs
Kauff-Bro 41.3
Konetchy-Pit 17.5
Wilson-Chi 17.5
Evans-Bro-Bal 16.3
Crandall-StL 13.9

Adjusted Batter Runs
Kauff-Bro 42.1
Wilson-Chi 20.7
Konetchy-Pit 18.3
Zwilling-Chi 16.0
Evans-Bro-Bal 15.1

Clutch Hitting Index
Oakes-Pit 152
Engle-Buf 129
F.Smith-Buf-Bro .. 123
Borton-StL 122
Halt-Bro 118

Runs Created
Kauff-Bro 132
Konetchy-Pit 111
Tobin-StL 106
Zwilling-Chi 99
Evans-Bro-Bal 99

Total Average
Kauff-Bro 1.233
Konetchy-Pit ..... .884
Cooper-Bro .... .868
W.Miller-StL ..... .863
Zwilling-Chi ..... .857

Stolen Bases
Kauff-Bro 55
Mowrey-Pit 40
Kelly-Pit 38
Flack-Chi 37
Magee-Bro 34

Stolen Base Average

Stolen Base Runs

Fielding Runs
Doolan-Bal-Chi ... 33.0
Rariden-New 23.0
Cooper-Bro 18.3
Johnson-StL 17.7
Perring-KC 14.8

Total Player Rating
Kauff-Bro 5.3
Rariden-New 3.8
Cooper-Bro 2.4
Wilson-Chi 2.0
Zwilling-Chi 1.8

Wins
McConnell-Chi 25
Allen-Pit 23
Davenport-StL 22
Cullop-KC 22

Win Percentage
McConnell-Chi .... .714
Brown-Chi .... .680
Reulbach-New ..... .677
Cullop-KC .... .667
Plank-StL .... .656

Games
Davenport-StL 55
Bedient-Buf 53
Crandall-StL 51
Johnson-KC 46

Complete Games
Davenport-StL 30
Hendrix-Chi 26
Schulz-Buf 25
Allen-Pit 24

Shutouts
Davenport-StL 10
Plank-StL 6
Allen-Pit 6

Saves
Bedient-Buf 10
Barger-Pit 6
Wiltse-Bro 5
Upham-Bro 5

Innings Pitched
Davenport-StL 392.2
Crandall-StL 312.2
Schulz-Buf 309.2
McConnell-Chi 303.0
Cullop-KC 302.1

Fewest Hits/Game
Davenport-StL 6.88
Main-KC 7.08
Plank-StL 7.11
Brown-Chi 7.20
Anderson-Buf 7.20

Fewest BB/Game
Plank-StL 1.81
Bender-Bal 1.87
Hearn-Pit 1.90
Cullop-KC 1.99
Quinn-Bal 2.07

Strikeouts
Davenport-StL 229
Schulz-Buf 160
McConnell-Chi 151
Plank-StL 147

Strikeouts/Game
Anderson-Buf 5.33
Davenport-StL 5.25
Plank-StL 4.93
Bailey-Bal-Chi ... 4.91
Groom-StL 4.78

Ratio
Plank-StL 9.02
Davenport-StL 9.19
Brown-Chi 9.90
Anderson-Buf 10.01
Reulbach-New 10.17

Earned Run Average
Moseley-New 1.91
Plank-StL 2.08
Brown-Chi 2.09
McConnell-Chi 2.20
Davenport-StL 2.20

Adjusted ERA
Plank-StL 138
Moseley-New 134
Davenport-StL 131
Brown-Chi 120
Reulbach-New 115

Opponents' Batting Avg.
Davenport-StL .... .215
Plank-StL .... .218
Brown-Chi .... .220
Main-KC .... .222
Anderson-Buf ..... .222

Opponents' On Base Pct.
Plank-StL .... .262
Davenport-StL .... .268
Brown-Chi .... .279
Anderson-Buf ..... .285
Reulbach-New ..... .287

Starter Runs
Moseley-New 24.2
Davenport-StL 23.0
Plank-StL 19.3
McConnell-Chi 17.8
Brown-Chi 16.6

Adjusted Starter Runs
Davenport-StL 29.5
Plank-StL 23.7
Moseley-New 19.2
Brown-Chi 10.9
McConnell-Chi 10.5

Clutch Pitching Index
Moran-New 129
Kaiserling-New ... 127
Rogge-Pit 127
Moseley-New 122
Suggs-Bal 117

Relief Runs

Adjusted Relief Runs

Relief Ranking

Total Pitcher Index
Plank-StL 2.9
Crandall-StL 2.6
McConnell-Chi 2.0
Brown-Chi 2.0
Moseley-New 1.3

Total Baseball Ranking
Kauff-Bro 5.3
Rariden-New 3.8
Plank-StL 2.9
Crandall-StL 2.6
Cooper-Bro 2.4

January 5 Happy to be rid of fractious Cubs owner Charles W. Murphy, the NL allows Charles H. Weeghman, president of the Federal League Chicago Whales, to buy the Cubs for $500,000. The Cubs will play in the FL's recently-built stadium, which will later become known as Wrigley Field.

January 8 Profiting handsomely on his 1913 investment of $187,000, owner James E. Gaffney sells his Boston Braves for $500,000 to Harvard's famous football coach, Percy Haughton, and a banking associate.

January 17 John McGraw's Giants buy the Feds' top star, Benny Kauff, from the Brooklyn Tip-Tops; their best catcher, Bill Rariden, from the Newark Peps; and spitballer Fred Anderson, from the Buffalo Buffeds (aka the Blues), for about $65,000.

February 7 The Federal League's year-old suit charging antitrust violations by Organized Baseball is dismissed by mutual consent in U.S. District Court in Chicago by Judge Kenesaw M. Landis.

February 8 The NL votes down a proposal by Charlie Ebbets of Brooklyn to limit the number of 25-cent seats clubs can sell to 2,000. Boston has 10,000 such seats; St. Louis, 9,000, Philadelphia, 6,500, and Cincinnati, 4,000.

March 3* Jack Dunn, owner of the IL Orioles, buys the park built by the FL Baltimore Terrapins.

April 29 Innovative owner Charles Weeghman allows Cubs fans to keep balls hit into stands.

May 14 The Cardinals' rookie Rogers Hornsby hits his first homer. It is inside the park against the Brooklyn Dodgers at spacious Robison Field in St. Louis.

July 1 At age 42 years and four months, Honus Wagner is the oldest player to hit an inside-the-park home run. He connects for the Pirates in the fourth inning at Cincinnati.

September 4 To help draw a crowd, and because of their longtime rivalry, Christy Mathewson and Three Finger Brown close out their careers in the same game. Matty, now the manager of the Reds, wins, 10-8, in his only game not pitched in a Giants uniform. Mathewson and Brown have dueled 25 times since 1903, with Brown, now back with the Cubs, winning 12 and losing 10; Matty was 12-13.

September 7 The Giants beat Brooklyn's Nap Rucker, 4-1, to launch New York's record 26-game winning streak.

October 10 Charles Ebbets becomes the first owner to raise the price of World Series grandstand seats to $5—up from $3.

October 16 Brooklyn owner Ebbets rewards manager Wilbert Robinson with a $5,000 bonus even though the Dodgers lost the World Series.

December 2 Under pressure from the Players' Fraternity, the National Commission orders that injured players shall get full pay for the duration of their contracts. The injury clause previously let clubs suspend players after 15 days pay.

BOSTON

Pos	Player
M	G.Stallings
1B	E.Konetchy
2B	J.Evers
SS	R.Maranville
3B	R.Smith
LF	S.Magee
CF	F.Snodgrass
RF	J.Wilhoit
C	H.Gowdy
O	Z.Collins
2S	D.Egan
2O	E.Fitzpatrick
C	E.Blackburn
O	J.Connolly
O	P.Compton
C	W.Tragesser
O	L.Chappell
/O	F.Bailey
/C	A.Rico
/2	J.Mathes
P	D.Rudolph
P	L.Tyler
P	P.Ragan
P	J.Barnes
P	T.Hughes
P	A.Nehf
P	F.Allen
P	E.Reulbach
/P	E.Knetzer

BROOKLYN

Pos	Player
M	W.Robinson
1B	J.Daubert
2B	G.Cutshaw
SS	I.Olson
3B	M.Mowrey
LF	Z.Wheat
CF	H.Myers
RF	C.Stengel
C	C.Meyers
O	J.Johnston
C	O.Miller
S	O.O'Mara
C1	L.McCarty
3	G.Getz
1	F.Merkle
/O	J.Hickman
/2	R.Smyth
/O	H.Miller
/S	B.Fabrique
/O	A.Nixon
/C	M.Wheat
/C	A.Dede
P	J.Pfeffer
P	S.Smith
P	R.Marquard
P	J.Coombs
P	W.Dell
P	E.Appleton
/P	N.Rucker
P	D.Mails
/P	L.Cadore

CHICAGO

Pos	Player
M	J.Tinker
1B	V.Saier
2B	O.Knabe
SS	G.Wortman
3B	H.Zimmerman
LF	L.Mann
CF	C.Williams
RF	M.Flack
C	J.Archer
32	R.Zeider
O	F.Schulte
S	E.Mulligan
C	W.Fischer
O	J.Kelly
2	S.Yerkes
C	A.Wilson
2	A.McCarthy
1	F.Mollwitz
S	M.Doolan
3	C.Pechous
C	R.Elliott
O	D.Zwilling
/S	L.Doyle
/O	E.Smith
/C	N.Allen
/O	S.Hofman
/C	C.Clemens
/O	M.Jacobson
/S	J.Tinker
/3	C.Deal
/S	M.Shay
/3	H.Hunter
H	E.Sicking
/C	J.O'Connor
/C	B.O'Farrell
P	H.Vaughn
P	C.Hendrix
P	J.Lavender
P	G.McConnell
P	G.Packard
P	M.Prendergast
P	T.Seaton
P	M.Brown
/P	P.Carter
/P	S.Perry
/P	G.Pearce

CINCINNATI

Pos	Player
M	B.Herzog
1B	I.Wingo
M	C.Mathewson
1B	H.Chase
2B	B.Louden
SS	B.Herzog
3B	H.Groh
LF	G.Neale
CF	E.Roush
RF	T.Griffith
C	I.Wingo
O	R.Killefer
1	F.Mollwitz
C	T.Clarke
S	B.Fisher
3	B.McKechnie
C1	E.Huhn
S	F.Emmer
O	P.Smith
S	L.Kopf
O	K.Williams
O	J.Beall
/S	B.Hobbs
/O	G.Twombly
/S	B.Rodgers
P	F.Toney
P	P.Schneider
P	A.Schulz
P	C.Mitchell
P	E.Knetzer
P	E.Moseley
P	G.Dale
/P	L.McKenry
/P	C.Mathewson
/P	J.Bluejacket
/P	T.Twining

NEW YORK

Pos	Player
M	J.McGraw
1B	F.Merkle
2B	L.Doyle
SS	A.Fletcher
3B	B.McKechnie
LF	G.Burns
CF	B.Kauff
RF	D.Robertson
C	B.Rariden
23	B.Herzog
3	H.Zimmerman
O	W.Holke
O	G.Kelly
2	H.Lobert
O	E.Roush
C	L.McCarty
C	B.Kocher
C	M.Doolan
/3	H.Hunter
C	R.Dooin
/3	F.Brainerd
H	L.Wendell
H	R.Killefer
H	H.Stafford
/C	D.Kelleher
R	J.Rodriguez
P	F.Tesreau
P	P.Perritt
P	R.Benton
P	F.Anderson
P	F.Schupp
P	S.Sallee
P	C.Mathewson
/P	S.Stroud
P	R.Schauer
/P	G.Smith
/P	E.Palmero
/P	H.Ritter

PHILADELPHIA

Pos	Player
M	P.Moran
1B	F.Luderus
2B	B.Niehoff
SS	D.Bancroft
3B	M.Stock
LF	P.Whitted
CF	D.Paskert
RF	G.Cravath
C	B.Killefer
C	E.Burns
C	B.Byrne
O	W.Good
O	C.Cooper
O	O.Dugey
C	B.Adams
/O	B.Weiser
/O	B.Gandy
/O	B.Maharg
H	B.Tincup
P	P.Alexander
P	E.Rixey
P	A.Demaree
P	E.Mayer
P	C.Bender
P	G.McQuillan
P	G.Chalmers
P	J.Oeschger
/P	G.Fortune
H	S.Baumgartner
/P	E.Kantlehner

PITTSBURGH

Pos	Player
M	J.Callahan
1B	D.Johnston
2B	J.Farmer
SS	H.Wagner
3B	D.Baird
LF	F.Schulte
CF	M.Carey
RF	B.Hinchman
C	W.Schmidt
23	J.Schultz
3	H.Warner
2O	C.Bigbee
O	D.Costello
S	A.McCarthy
C	E.Barney
23	J.Viox
C	A.Wilson
C	W.Fischer
S	J.Smith
2	O.Knabe
C	G.Gibson
C	R.O'Brien
C	B.Wagner
/O	L.King
/O	P.Compton
/2	J.Altenburg
/S	F.Smykal
/S	I.McAuley
/2	P.Siglin
/2	B.Gleason
	W.Fisher
/1	N.Halliday
H	G.Madden
H	B.Batsch
P	A.Mamaux
P	W.Cooper
P	F.Miller
P	B.Harmon
P	E.Kantlehner
P	E.Jacobs
P	B.Adams
/P	B.Grimes
/P	P.Carpenter
/P	C.Hill
/P	J.Scott

ST.LOUIS

Pos	Player
M	M.Huggins
1B	D.Miller
2B	B.Betzel
SS	R.Corhan
3B	R.Hornsby
LF	B.Bescher
CF	J.Smith
RF	C.Wilson
C	M.Gonzalez
O	T.Long
C1	F.Snyder
3	Z.Beck
O	A.Butler
S	S.Bohne
C	T.Brottem
/2	S.Stewart
/2	M.Huggins
/O	W.Cruise
P	L.Meadows
P	R.Ames
P	B.Doak
P	B.Steele
P	H.Jasper
RP	S.Williams
P	M.Watson
P	S.Sallee
P	C.Hall
P	J.Lotz
/P	M.Currie
/P	D.Griner
/P	C.Warmoth

TEAM	G	W	L	PCT	GB	R	OR	AB	H	2B	3B	HR	BB	SO	AVG	OBP	SLG	PRO	PRO+	BR	/A	PF	CHI	RC	SB	CS	SBA	SBR
BRO	156	94	60	.610		585	471	5234	1366	195	80	28	355	550	.261	.313	.345	.658	105	46	30	103	99	645	187			
PHI	154	91	62	.595	2.5	581	489	4985	1244	223	53	42	399	571	.250	.310	.341	.651	102	34	14	104	104	593	149			
BOS	158	89	63	.586	4	542	453	5075	1181	166	73	22	437	646	.233	.299	.307	.606	96	-38	-16	96	108	535	141			
NY	155	86	66	.566	7	597	504	5152	1305	188	74	42	356	558	.253	.307	.343	.650	112	31	61	95	106	617	206			
CHI	156	67	86	.438	26.5	520	541	5179	1237	194	56	46	399	662	.239	.298	.325	.623	88	-18	-74	111	99	559	133			
PIT	157	65	89	.422	29	484	586	5181	1246	147	91	20	372	618	.240	.298	.316	.614	94	-32	-37	101	95	556	173			
STL	153	60	93	.392	33.5	476	629	5030	1223	155	74	25	335	651	.243	.295	.318	.613	95	-35	-32	99	99	535	182			
CIN	155	60	93	.392	33.5	505	617	5254	1336	187	88	14	362	573	.254	.307	.331	.638	105	13	26	98	91	596	157			
TOT	622					4290		41090	10138	1455	589	239	3015	4829	.247	.303	.328	.632						1328				

TEAM	CG	SH	SV	IP	H	H/G	HR	BB	SO	RAT	ERA	ERA+	OAV	OOB	PR	/A	PF	CPI	FA	E	DP	FW	PW	BW	SBW	DIF
BRO	96	22	9	1427^1	1201	7.6	24	372	634	10.2	2.12	126	.232	.289	78	86	102	103	.965	224	90	1.2	9.8	3.4		2.5
PHI	97	25	9	1382^1	1238	8.1	28	295	601	10.3	2.36	112	.244	.292	39	44	101	101	.963	234	119	.4	5.0	1.6		7.5
BOS	97	23	11	1415^2	1206	7.7	24	325	644	9.9	2.19	113	.235	.285	66	45	95	99	.967	212	124	2.1	5.1	-1.8		7.5
NY	88	22	12	1397^1	1267	8.2	41	310	638	10.4	2.60	93	.245	.293	2	-28	93	95	.966	217	108	1.5	-3.2	7.0		4.7
CHI	72	17	13	1416^2	1265	8.0	32	365	616	10.6	2.65	110	.244	.298	-6	39	111	94	.957	286	104	-2.6	4.5	-8.5		-2.9
PIT	88	11	7	1419^2	1277	8.1	24	443	596	11.1	2.76	97	.247	.311	-24	-14	103	97	.959	260	97	-.9	-1.6	-4.2		-5.3
STL	58	13	15	1355	1331	8.8	31	445	529	12.1	3.14	84	.265	.330	-80	-77	101	104	.957	278	124	-2.4	-8.8	-3.7		-1.7
CIN	86	7	6	1408	1356	8.7	35	461	569	11.9	3.10	84	.261	.326	-76	-82	99	102	.965	228	126	.9	-9.4	3.0		-11.0
TOT	682	140	82	11222		8.1				10.8	2.61		.247	.303					.963	1939	892					

Runs
Burns-NY 105
Carey-Pit 90
Robertson-NY 88
Groh-Cin 85
Paskert-Phi 82

Hits
Chase-Cin 184
Robertson-NY 180
Z.Wheat-Bro 177
Hinchman-Pit 175
Burns-NY 174

Doubles
Niehoff-Phi 42
Z.Wheat-Bro 32
Paskert-Phi 30

Triples
Hinchman-Pit 16
Roush-NY-Cin 15
Kauff-NY 15
Hornsby-StL 15

Home Runs
Williams-Chi 12
Robertson-NY 12
Cravath-Phi 11
Z.Wheat-Bro 9
Kauff-NY 9

Total Bases
Z.Wheat-Bro 262
Robertson-NY 250
Chase-Cin 249
Hinchman-Pit 237
Burns-NY 229

Runs Batted In
Zimmerman-Chi-NY 83
Chase-Cin 82
Hinchman-Pit 76
Kauff-NY 74
Z.Wheat-Bro 73

Runs Produced
Zimmerman-Chi-NY 153
Robertson-NY 145
Chase-Cin 144
Konetchy-Bos 143
Burns-NY 141

Bases On Balls
Groh-Cin 84
Saier-Chi 79
Bancroft-Phi 74
Kauff-NY 68
Cravath-Phi 64

Batting Average
Chase-Cin 339
Daubert-Bro 316
Hinchman-Pit 315
Hornsby-StL 313
Z.Wheat-Bro 312

On Base Percentage
Cravath-Phi 379
Hinchman-Pit 378
Williams-Chi 372
Daubert-Bro 371
Groh-Cin 370

Slugging Average
Z.Wheat-Bro 461
Chase-Cin 459
Williams-Chi 459
Hornsby-StL 444
Cravath-Phi 440

Production
Williams-Chi 831
Z.Wheat-Bro 828
Chase-Cin 822
Cravath-Phi 819
Hornsby-StL 814

Adjusted Production
Chase-Cin 155
Hornsby-StL 150
Z.Wheat-Bro 149
Cravath-Phi 146
Hinchman-Pit 146

Batter Runs
Z.Wheat-Bro 34.5
Hinchman-Pit 31.1
Chase-Cin 30.2
Cravath-Phi 28.7
Hornsby-StL 28.2

Adjusted Batter Runs
Chase-Cin 32.2
Z.Wheat-Bro 32.0
Hornsby-StL 30.3
Hinchman-Pit 28.7
Cravath-Phi 25.9

Clutch Hitting Index
Mowrey-Bro 145
Zimmerman-Chi-NY 134
Magee-Bos 133
Smith-Bos 121
Fletcher-NY 119

Runs Created
Z.Wheat-Bro 103
Hinchman-Pit 96
Chase-Cin 93
Hornsby-StL 88
Carey-Pit 87

Total Average
Williams-Chi 863
Cravath-Phi 857
Z.Wheat-Bro 844
Hornsby-StL 826
Hinchman-Pit 797

Stolen Bases
Carey-Pit 63
Kauff-NY 40
Bescher-StL 39
Burns-NY 37
Herzog-Cin-NY 34

Stolen Base Average
Carey-Pit 76.8
Bescher-StL 76.5
Daubert-Bro 75.0
Maranville-Bos 68.1
Chase-Cin 66.7

Stolen Base Runs
Carey-Pit 7.5
Bescher-StL 4.5
Daubert-Bro 2.1
Maranville-Bos 6

Fielding Runs
Carey-Pit 29.9
Betzel-StL 28.4
Bancroft-Phi 24.5
Maranville-Bos 21.5
Doyle-NY-Chi 20.0

Total Player Rating
Groh-Cin 5.4
Carey-Pit 4.7
Fletcher-NY 4.3
Doyle-NY-Chi 4.2
Z.Wheat-Bro 3.7

Wins
Alexander-Phi 33
Pfeffer-Bro 25
Rixey-Phi 22
Mamaux-Pit 21

Win Percentage
Hughes-Bos 842
Alexander-Phi 733
Pfeffer-Bro 694
Rixey-Phi 688
Benton-NY 667

Games
Meadows-StL 51
Alexander-Phi 48
Mamaux-Pit 45
Ames-StL 45

Complete Games
Alexander-Phi 38
Pfeffer-Bro 30
Rudolph-Bos 27
Mamaux-Pit 26
Demaree-Phi 25

Shutouts
Alexander-Phi 16
Tyler-Bos 6
Pfeffer-Bro 6

Saves
Ames-StL 8
Packard-Chi 5
Marquard-Bro 5
Hughes-Bos 5

Innings Pitched
Alexander-Phi ...389.0
Pfeffer-Bro 328.2
Rudolph-Bos 312.0
Mamaux-Pit 310.0
Toney-Cin 300.0

Fewest Hits/Game
Cheney-Bro 6.33
Hughes-Bos 6.76
Cooper-Pit 6.91
Miller-Pit 7.02
Ragan-Bos 7.07

Fewest BB/Game
Rudolph-Bos 1.10
Alexander-Phi 1.16
Demaree-Phi 1.52
Sallee-StL-NY 1.63
Marquard-Bro 1.67

Strikeouts
Alexander-Phi 167
Cheney-Bro 166
Mamaux-Pit 163
Toney-Cin 146
Vaughn-Chi 144

Strikeouts/Game
Cheney-Bro 5.91
Hughes-Bos 5.42
Hendrix-Chi 4.83
Mamaux-Pit 4.73
Marquard-Bro 4.70

Ratio
Rudolph-Bos 8.86
Alexander-Phi 8.86
Marquard-Bro 9.09
McConnell-Chi 9.30
Ragan-Bos 9.40

Earned Run Average
Alexander-Phi 1.55
Marquard-Bro 1.58
Rixey-Phi 1.85
Cooper-Pit 1.87
Pfeffer-Bro 1.92

Adjusted ERA
Alexander-Phi 171
Marquard-Bro 169
Cooper-Pit 144
Rixey-Phi 143
Pfeffer-Bro 140

Opponents' Batting Avg.
Cheney-Bro 198
Cooper-Pit 215
Hughes-Bos 215
Ragan-Bos 218
McConnell-Chi 223

Opponents' On Base Pct.
Rudolph-Bos 261
Alexander-Phi 262
Marquard-Bro 267
Ragan-Bos 270
McConnell-Chi 271

Starter Runs
Alexander-Phi 45.9
Schupp-NY 26.7
Pfeffer-Bro 25.4
Rixey-Phi 24.3
Marquard-Bro 23.5

Adjusted Starter Runs
Alexander-Phi 47.4
Pfeffer-Bro 27.7
Rixey-Phi 25.4
Marquard-Bro 24.9
Schupp-NY 23.8

Clutch Pitching Index
Dell-Bro 124
Sallee-StL-NY 117
Meadows-StL 116
Schulz-Cin 114
Alexander-Phi 114

Total Pitcher Index
Alexander-Phi 7.3
Pfeffer-Bro 3.6
Rixey-Phi 3.2
Tyler-Bos 2.5
Cheney-Bro 2.3

Total Baseball Ranking
Alexander-Phi 7.3
Groh-Cin 5.4
Carey-Pit 4.7
Fletcher-NY 4.3
Doyle-NY-Chi 4.2

January 4 The St. Louis Browns are the first of two major league franchises awarded to Federal League owners. Philip de Catesby Ball, ice manufacturing tycoon and principal stockholder of the Feds' St. Louis Terriers, pays a reported $525,000 for the Browns.

January 14 Lee Magee, player-manager of the Brooklyn Tip-Tops, is sold to the Yankees for about $25,000, and becomes the first Federal Leaguer welcomed back to Organized Baseball.

February 15 The Yankees buy Frank "Home Run" Baker from the Athletics for $37,500. He sat out the 1915 season.

April 12 On Opening Day, young Babe Ruth goes 8⅓ innings for a 2–1 win over the Athletics at Boston. A poor throw by Charlie Pick, A's third baseman, is the first of his 42 errors. This contributes to his overall .899 fielding average, a mark that Butch Hobson would equal in 1978.

April 15 White Sox catcher Ray Schalk steals twice against Detroit en route to a season total of 30, a record for catchers until 1982 when John Wathan swipes 36.

June 20 Clarence "Tilly" Walker's homer over the left field wall is the only homer the Red Sox will hit at Fenway this season. Boston shortstop Everett Scott starts a string of 1,307 consecutive games, all played at shortstop. He will complete the streak as a Yankee.

June 26 Cleveland players wear numbers on their sleeves in a game with the White Sox, marking the first time players are identified by numbers corresponding to those on the scorecard.

July 4 Joe Jackson goes 3-for-5 against the Athletics. In 30 games since May 31, he has gone 55-for-104, a .524 BA.

September 8 Switch hitter Wally Schang of the A's hits homers from both sides of the plate against the Yankees. Only a handful of people see the rare feat on a rainy day.

September 24 Marty Kavanagh, Indians utility man, hits the AL's first pinch-hit grand slam for Cleveland in a 5-3 win over the Red Sox. The ball rolls through a hole in the fence and cannot be retrieved in time for a play at the plate.

September 26 Washington manager Griffith excuses several regulars for the remaining games of the season so he can use some new players. Included is Walter Johnson, who has already won 25 games for the seventh-place club. In a league-leading 371 innings pitched, he did not give up a home run, an all-time record.

October 7 Despite a four-run Brooklyn rally in the ninth, the Red Sox defeat Rube Marquard, 6-5, to win Game 1 of the World Series at Braves Field. Ernie Shore gets the win, Carl Mays earns a save, and the Sox turn four double plays.

October 9 Babe Ruth outpitches Sherry Smith to win Game 2 of the World Series, 2-1, in the 14th inning. This is the start of 29⅔ scoreless World Series innings pitched by Ruth.

October 12 Boston's 4-1 win in Game 5 ends the Series. The Red Sox players earn $3,826; The Dodgers get $2,834 per man.

November 1 Harry H. Frazee, New York theater owner and producer, buys the Red Sox for $675,000.

BOSTON	CHICAGO	CLEVELAND	DETROIT	NEW YORK	PHILADELPHIA	ST.LOUIS	WASHINGTON
M B.Carrigan	M P.Rowland	M L.Fohl	M H.Jennings	M B.Donovan	M C.Mack	M F.Jones	M C.Griffith
1B D.Hoblitzel	1B J.Fournier	1B C.Gandil	1B G.Burns	1B W.Pipp	1B S.McInnis	1B G.Sisler	1B J.Judge
2B J.Barry	2B E.Collins	2B I.Howard	2B R.Young	2B J.Gedeon	2B N.Lajoie	2B D.Pratt	2B R.Morgan
SS E.Scott	SS Z.Terry	SS B.Wambsganss	SS D.Bush	SS R.Peckinpaugh	SS W.Witt	SS D.Lavan	SS G.McBride
3B L.Gardner	3B B.Weaver	3B T.Turner	3B O.Vitt	3B F.Baker	3B C.Pick	3B J.Austin	3B E.Foster
LF D.Lewis	LF J.Jackson	LF J.Graney	LF B.Veach	LF H.High	LF W.Schang	LF B.Shotton	LF H.Shanks
CF T.Walker	CF H.Felsch	CF T.Speaker	CF T.Cobb	CF L.Magee	CF A.Strunk	CF A.Marsans	CF C.Milan
RF H.Hooper	RF S.Collins	RF B.Roth	RF S.Crawford	RF F.Gilhooley	RF J.Walsh	RF W.Miller	RF D.Moeller
C P.Thomas	C R.Schalk	C S.O'Neill	C O.Stanage	C L.Nunamaker	C B.Meyer	C H.Severeid	C J.Henry
S2 H.Janvrin	1 J.Ness	S3 R.Chapman	O1 H.Heilmann	O3 P.Baumann	3 L.McElwee	S3 E.Johnson	1C W.Williams
C H.Cady	3 F.McMullin	O E.Smith	C D.Baker	3 R.Walters	O R.Oldring	C G.Hartley	O S.Rice
1 D.Gainer	O E.Murphy	3 J.Evans	3 M.Kavanagh	O F.Maisel	OS L.King	O J.Tobin	3 J.Leonard
23 M.McNally	C J.Lapp	C T.Daly	C R.McKee	O3 R.Oldring	2 O.Lawry	1 B.Borton	O E.Smith
O C.Shorten	O N.Leibold	O G.Harper	O G.Harper	C E.Miller	C V.Picinich	3 C.Deal	O H.Rondeau
O O.Henriksen	3 F.Von Kolnitz	/2 M.Kavanagh	21 T.Spencer	C C.Mullen	C R.Haley	/C W.Rumler	O C.Jamieson
C S.Agnew	C B.Lynn	C H.DeBerry	3S B.Dyer	2 L.Boone	2 R.Grover	C H.Chapman	C E.Ainsmith
C B.Carrigan	/S C.Wright	C J.Billings	/O J.Dalton	C W.Alexander	O B.Stellbauer	C1 B.Wallace	C1 P.Gharrity
/O J.Walsh	/1 Z.Hasbrook	/O D.Moeller	/2 F.Fuller	O R.Hartzell	O J.Brown	/O B.Lee	/O M.Menosky
/3 H.Wagner	/1 G.Moriarty	C B.Coleman	/3 B.Ellison	O T.Hendryx	O R.Mitterling	/C V.Clemons	O T.Barber
H R.Haley	H T.Jourdan	/3 C.Engle	/3 G.Maisel	/O S.Hofman	/3 H.Rowe	H G.Paulette	/2 C.Sawyer
P B.Ruth	H J.Fautsch	/C L.Guisto	/C B.Sullivan	/3 A.Aragon	/O R.Lanning	/C G.Hale	H M.Acosta
P D.Leonard	R R.Shook	/O M.Allison	P H.Coveleski	/O D.Cook	H B.Thrasher	H R.Kennedy	P W.Johnson
P C.Mays	P R.Russell	/2 A.Bergman	P H.Dauss	/O G.Schaefer	C M.Murphy	P D.Davenport	P B.Gallia
P E.Shore	P L.Williams	/O H.Lohr	P J.Dubuc	P B.Shawkey	/3 T.Healy	P C.Weilman	P H.Harper
P R.Foster	P R.Faber	P J.Bradley	P J.James	P G.Mogridge	C D.Carroll	P E.Plank	P D.Ayers
P V.Gregg	P E.Cicotte	H L.Chappell	P G.Cunningham	P R.Fisher	/O C.Grimm	P B.Groom	P J.Boehling
P S.Jones	P J.Scott	/2 J.Leonard	RP B.Boland	P A.Russell	/O S.Thompson	P E.Koob	P J.Shaw
/P H.Pennock	P J.Benz	R O.Welf	P W.Mitchell	P N.Cullop	/O B.Johnson	/P E.Hamilton	P G.Dumont
/P W.Wyckoff	P M.Wolfgang	P J.Bagby	/P H.Ehmke	RP S.Love	/O M.Divis	/P J.Park	/P C.Thomas
/P M.McHale	P D.Danforth	P S.Coveleski	/P E.Hamilton	R R.Caldwell	/S S.Crane	/P T.McCabe	/P M.Craft
	/P E.Walsh	P G.Morton	/P E.Erickson	H R.Keating	/S L.Malone	/P B.Fincher	/P M.Goodwin
		P E.Klepfer	/P G.Boehler	P U.Shocker	H H.Davis	/P G.Baumgardner	P J.Bentley
		P F.Coumbe	/P D.Jones	P C.Markle	P E.Myers	/P D.Crandall	
		P A.Gould	/P B.McTigue	/P J.Buckles	P J.Bush		
		P F.Beebe	/P G.Lowdermilk	/P M.Cantwell	P J.Nabors		
		P O.Lambeth	/P B.Donovan	/P B.Donovan	P T.Sheehan		
		P J.Boehling			P J.Johnson		
		P G.Lowdermilk			P M.Williams		
		P W.Mitchell			/P C.Crowell		
		/P P.Smith			/P G.Hesselbacher		
		/P K.Penner			/P R.Parnham		
		/P M.McHale			/P S.Seibold		
		/P R.Hagerman			/P W.Wyckoff		
		/P S.DesJardien			/P R.Bressler		
		/P R.Gunkel			/P C.Ray		
					/P H.Weaver		
					/P M.Driscoll		
					/P A.Lindstrom		
					/P B.Morrisette		
					/P W.Whittaker		
					/P J.Richardson		

TEAM	G	W	L	PCT	GB	R	OR	AB	H	2B	3B	HR	BB	SO	AVG	OBP	SLG	PRO	PRO+	BR	/A	PF	CHI	RC	SB	CS	SBA	SBR
BOS	156	91	63	.591		550	480	5018	1246	197	56	14	464	482	.248	.317	.318	.635	97	-20	-22	100	101	580	129			
CHI	155	89	65	.578	2	601	497	5081	1277	194	100	17	447	591	.251	.319	.339	.658	103	18	12	101	102	638	197			
DET	155	87	67	.565	4	670	595	5193	1371	202	96	17	545	529	.264	.337	.350	.687	109	78	55	104	101	700	190			
NY	156	80	74	.519	11	577	561	5198	1277	194	59	35	516	632	.246	.318	.326	.644	98	-4	-16	102	100	613	179			
STL	158	79	75	.513	12	588	545	5159	1262	181	50	14	627	640	.245	.331	.307	.638	103	2	30	95	99	620	234			
CLE	157	77	77	.500	14	630	602	5064	1264	233	66	16	522	605	.250	.324	.331	.655	97	17	-18	106	106	625	160			
WAS	159	76	77	.497	14.5	536	543	5114	1238	170	60	12	535	597	.242	.320	.306	.626	95	-30	-25	99	98	579	185			
PHI	154	36	117	.235	54.5	447	776	5010	1212	169	65	19	406	631	.242	.303	.313	.616	96	-61	-38	95	91	538	151			
TOT	625					4599		40837	10147	1540	552	144	4062	4707	.248	.321	.324	.645						1425				

TEAM	CG	SH	SV	IP	H	H/G	HR	BB	SO	RAT	ERA	ERA+	OAV	OOB	PR	/A	PF	CPI	FA	E	DP	FW	PW	BW	SBW	DIF
BOS	76	24	16	1410²	1221	7.8	10	463	584	11.0	2.48	112	.239	.307	55	44	98	99	.972	183	108	3.0	4.9	-2.4		8.5
CHI	73	20	15	1412¹	1189	7.6	14	405	644	10.3	2.36	117	.236	.296	72	61	98	96	.968	205	134	1.5	6.8	1.3		2.4
DET	81	8	13	1410	1254	8.0	12	578	531	12.1	2.97	96	.248	.333	-23	-18	101	100	.968	211	110	1.1	-2.0	6.1		4.8
NY	84	12	17	1428	1249	7.9	37	476	616	11.2	2.77	104	.244	.314	8	17	102	100	.967	219	119	.7	1.9	-1.8		2.2
STL	74	9	13	1443²	1292	8.1	15	478	505	11.3	2.58	106	.248	.316	39	26	97	105	.963	248	120	-.9	2.9	3.3		-3.3
CLE	65	9	16	1410	1383	8.8	16	467	537	12.0	2.90	103	.264	.328	-13	16	106	107	.965	232	130	.0	1.8	-2.0		.2
WAS	85	11	7	1430²	1271	8.0	14	490	706	11.3	2.67	104	.244	.314	25	17	99	99	.964	232	119	.2	1.9	-2.8		.2
PHI	94	11	3	1343²	1311	8.8	26	715	575	13.8	3.92	73	.267	.364	-163	-160	101	97	.951	314	126	-5.5	-17.7	-4.2		-13.1
TOT	632	104	100	11289		8.1				11.6	2.82		.248	.321					.965	1844	966					

Runs		Hits		Doubles		Triples		Home Runs		Total Bases	
Cobb-Det	113	Speaker-Cle	211	Speaker-Cle	41	Jackson-Chi	21	Pipp-NY	12	Jackson-Chi	293
Graney-Cle	106	Jackson-Chi	202	Graney-Cle	41	E.Collins-Chi	17	Baker-NY	10	Speaker-Cle	274
Speaker-Cle	102	Cobb-Det	201	Jackson-Chi	40	Witt-Phi	15	Schang-Phi	7	Cobb-Det	267
Shotton-StL	97	Sisler-StL	177	Pratt-StL	35	Veach-Det	15	Felsch-Chi	7	Veach-Det	245
Veach-Det	92	Shotton-StL	174	Veach-Det	33						

Runs Batted In		Runs Produced		Bases On Balls		Batting Average		On Base Percentage		Slugging Average	
Pratt-StL	103	Veach-Det	180	Shotton-StL	111	Speaker-Cle	.386	Speaker-Cle	.470	Speaker-Cle	.502
Pipp-NY	93	Speaker-Cle	179	Graney-Cle	102	Cobb-Det	.371	Cobb-Det	.452	Jackson-Chi	.495
Veach-Det	91	Cobb-Det	176	E.Collins-Chi	86	Jackson-Chi	.341	E.Collins-Chi	.405	Cobb-Det	.493
Speaker-Cle	79	Jackson-Chi	166	Speaker-Cle	82	Strunk-Phi	.316	Jackson-Chi	.393	Veach-Det	.433
Jackson-Chi	78	Pratt-StL	162	Hooper-Bos	80	Gardner-Bos	.308	Strunk-Phi	.393	Baker-NY	.428

Production		Adjusted Production		Batter Runs		Adjusted Batter Runs		Clutch Hitting Index		Runs Created	
Speaker-Cle	.972	Speaker-Cle	181	Speaker-Cle	64.6	Speaker-Cle	57.2	Pratt-StL	136	Cobb-Det	136
Cobb-Det	.944	Cobb-Det	177	Cobb-Det	57.5	Cobb-Det	53.4	Heilmann-Det	132	Speaker-Cle	132
Jackson-Chi	.888	Jackson-Chi	165	Jackson-Chi	44.9	Jackson-Chi	43.7	Marsans-StL	132	Jackson-Chi	119
Strunk-Phi	.814	Strunk-Phi	152	E.Collins-Chi	30.5	Strunk-Phi	34.7	Gandil-Cle	129	E.Collins-Chi	99
E.Collins-Chi	.802	E.Collins-Chi	139	Strunk-Phi	30.2	E.Collins-Chi	29.5	Burns-Det	127	Veach-Det	94

Total Average		Stolen Bases		Stolen Base Average		Stolen Base Runs		Fielding Runs		Total Player Rating	
Cobb-Det	1.071	Cobb-Det	68	Cobb-Det	73.9	Cobb-Det	6.0	Lavan-StL	34.2	Speaker-Cle	5.7
Speaker-Cle	1.017	Marsans-StL	46	Hooper-Bos	71.1	Hooper-Bos	1.5	Lajoie-Phi	30.4	Cobb-Det	5.4
Jackson-Chi	.876	Shotton-StL	41	Schalk-Chi	69.8	Schalk-Chi	1.2	Vitt-Det	27.6	Pratt-StL	4.2
E.Collins-Chi	.814	E.Collins-Chi	40	Roth-Cle	67.4	Roth-Cle	.3	Pratt-StL	22.4	Jackson-Chi	3.6
Graney-Cle	.761	Speaker-Cle	35	Shanks-Was	65.7			Milan-Was	16.5	Lavan-StL	3.4

Wins		Win Percentage		Games		Complete Games		Shutouts		Saves	
Johnson-Was	25	Cicotte-Chi	.682	Davenport-StL	59	Johnson-Was	36	Ruth-Bos	9	Shawkey-NY	8
Shawkey-NY	24	Ruth-Bos	.657	Russell-Chi	56	Myers-Phi	31	Bush-Phi	8	Russell-NY	6
Ruth-Bos	23	Coveleski-Det	.656	Shawkey-NY	53	Bush-Phi	25	Leonard-Bos	6	Leonard-Bos	6
Coveleski-Det	21	Faber-Chi	.654	Gallia-Was	49	Ruth-Bos	23	Russell-Chi	5	Cicotte-Chi	5
Dauss-Det	19	Shawkey-NY	.632			Coveleski-Det	22			Bagby-Cle	5

Innings Pitched		Fewest Hits/Game		Fewest BB/Game		Strikeouts		Strikeouts/Game		Ratio	
Johnson-Was	369.2	Ruth-Bos	6.40	Russell-Chi	1.43	Johnson-Was	228	Johnson-Was	5.55	Russell-Chi	8.51
Coveleski-Det	324.1	Shawkey-NY	6.64	Cullop-NY	1.72	Myers-Phi	182	Williams-Chi	5.54	Johnson-Was	9.28
Ruth-Bos	323.2	Cicotte-Chi	6.64	Coveleski-Det	1.75	Ruth-Bos	170	Russell-NY	5.46	Shawkey-NY	9.47
Myers-Phi	315.0	Bush-Phi	6.97	Shore-Bos	1.95	Bush-Phi	157	Harper-Was	5.37	Coveleski-Det	9.77
Davenport-StL	290.2	Russell-Chi	7.05	Johnson-Was	2.00	Harper-Was	149	Myers-Phi	5.20	Ruth-Bos	9.90

Earned Run Average		Adjusted ERA		Opponents' Batting Avg.		Opponents' On Base Pct.		Starter Runs		Adjusted Starter Runs	
Ruth-Bos	1.75	Ruth-Bos	158	Ruth-Bos	.201	Russell-Chi	.254	Ruth-Bos	38.6	Johnson-Was	36.5
Cicotte-Chi	1.78	Cicotte-Chi	155	Shawkey-NY	.209	Johnson-Was	.270	Johnson-Was	38.0	Ruth-Bos	36.4
Johnson-Was	1.90	Johnson-Was	147	Cicotte-Chi	.218	Shawkey-NY	.273	Coveleski-Det	30.8	Coveleski-Det	32.1
Coveleski-Det	1.97	Coveleski-Det	145	Bush-Phi	.219	Ruth-Bos	.280	Cicotte-Chi	21.7	Shawkey-NY	20.7
Faber-Chi	2.02	Cullop-NY	141	Johnson-Was	.220	Coveleski-Det	.282	Weilman-StL	20.6	Cicotte-Chi	20.3

Clutch Pitching Index		Relief Runs		Adjusted Relief Runs		Relief Ranking		Total Pitcher Index		Total Baseball Ranking	
Cicotte-Chi	117							Ruth-Bos	5.9	Ruth-Bos	5.9
Gallia-Was	117							Johnson-Was	5.1	Speaker-Cle	5.7
Mogridge-NY	113							Coveleski-Det	3.9	Cobb-Det	5.4
Fisher-NY	113							Mays-Bos	3.2	Johnson-Was	5.1
Weilman-StL	113							Shawkey-NY	2.9	Pratt-StL	4.2

April 10 The U.S. entry into World War I and a cold, wet spring put a damper on the start of the season; 48 NL games will be postponed in the first month. Half the major league clubs will show losses this year, and eight of the 20 existing minor leagues will fold before the season is over.

May 2 The Cubs' left-hander Hippo Vaughn and right-hander Fred Toney of the Reds toe the mound in Chicago for a one-of-a-kind game. The Reds put up an all right-handed batting order, benching Edd Roush, who will lead the NL with a .341 batting average. At the end of nine innings, both pitchers have no-hitters. With one out in the top of the 10th and men on second base and third base, Jim Thorpe hits a swinging bunt near the mound. Vaughn picks it up and throws home, but Art Wilson freezes; the ball hits his chest protector, and Larry Kopf slides in safe for the only run. Fred Toney sets the Cubs down in order and has the fourth 10-inning no-hitter to date. The run scored by the Reds is their first in 34 innings.

May 23 Grover Cleveland Alexander of the Philadelphia Phils allows the Cincinnati Reds only two hits, collects three himself, including a homer, and wins, 5-1.

June 1 Hank Gowdy of the Braves becomes the first major league player to enlist when he signs up in the Ohio National Guard. He will play until he reports for duty July 15.

June 8 After a game in Cincinnati, John McGraw takes a swing at umpire Bill "Lord" Byron as they are leaving the field, splitting Byron's lip. NL president John Tener fines McGraw $500 and suspends him for 16 days. McGraw sounds off to writer Sid Mercer about the general shortcomings of Tener and his umpires. When McGraw's quotes are published, he signs a statement denying he'd said what was printed. The Baseball Writers Association protests, forcing another NL meeting at which Tener finds McGraw guilty and fines him another $1,000. Mercer, a friend of McGraw's, quits the beat and never speaks to McGraw again.

July 1 Reds right-hander Fred Toney pitches a doubleheader, beating the Pirates, 4-1 and 5-1. He walks one and allows three hits in each game, the fewest hits allowed by any pitcher winning two games in one day.

July 1 The Robins (Dodgers) play their first Sunday game in Brooklyn, charging regular admission and beating the Phils, 3-2. Admission is charged for a pregame band concert and military drill exhibition before the game to benefit wartime charities. When the band concert ends, ticket sales stop to conform with the Sunday baseball laws.

August 21 Now with the Philadelphia Phils, Chief Bender, 34, pitches his third straight shutout, winning, 6–0, over the Cubs. In his last active season, Bender will turn in four shutouts and win eight with two losses and a 1.67 ERA.

September 3 Trying to keep the Phils in the race, Grover Cleveland Alexander does double duty, beating Brooklyn, 6–0 and 9–3. He will win 30 for the third straight year, with a league-leading 1.86 ERA.

October 4 Braves southpaw Art Nehf's 40-inning scoreless streak is ended by the Robins in the eighth inning as Brooklyn beats Boston, 5-1.

October 11 The Phils sell Grover Cleveland Alexander and "Reindeer Bill" Killefer to the Cubs for right-hander "Iron Mike" Prendergast, catcher William "Pickles" Dillhoefer, and $55,000.

BOSTON		BROOKLYN		CHICAGO		CINCINNATI		NEW YORK		PHILADELPHIA		PITTSBURGH		ST.LOUIS	
M	G.Stallings	M	W.Robinson	M	F.Mitchell	M	C.Mathewson	M	J.McGraw	M	P.Moran	M	J.Callahan	M	M.Huggins
1B	E.Konetchy	1B	J.Daubert	1B	F.Merkle	1B	H.Chase	1B	W.Holke	1B	F.Luderus	M	H.Wagner	1B	G.Paulette
2B	J.Rawlings	2B	G.Cutshaw	2B	L.Doyle	2B	D.Shean	2B	B.Herzog	2B	B.Niehoff	M	H.Bezdek	2B	D.Miller
SS	R.Maranville	SS	I.Olson	SS	C.Wortman	SS	L.Kopf	SS	A.Fletcher	SS	D.Bancroft	1B	H.Wagner	SS	R.Hornsby
3B	R.Smith	3B	M.Mowrey	3B	C.Deal	3B	H.Groh	3B	H.Zimmerman	3B	M.Stock	2B	J.Pitler	3B	D.Baird
LF	J.Kelly	LF	Z.Wheat	LF	L.Mann	LF	G.Neale	LF	G.Burns	LF	P.Whitted	SS	C.Ward	LF	W.Cruise
CF	R.Powell	CF	J.Hickman	CF	C.Williams	CF	E.Roush	CF	B.Kauff	CF	D.Paskert	3B	T.Boeckel	CF	J.Smith
RF	W.Rehg	RF	C.Stengel	RF	M.Flack	RF	T.Griffith	RF	D.Robertson	RF	G.Cravath	LF	C.Bigbee	RF	T.Long
C	W.Tragesser	C	O.Miller	C	A.Wilson	C	I.Wingo	C	B.Rariden	C	B.Killefer	CF	M.Carey	C	F.Snyder
												RF	L.King		
O	S.Magee	O1	J.Johnston	O	H.Wolter	O	J.Thorpe	C	L.McCarty	2	J.Evers	C	W.Fischer	2O	B.Betzel
O	J.Wilhoit	O1	H.Myers	S3	R.Zeider	O	M.Cueto	2	J.Smith	O	F.Schulte			C1	M.Gonzalez
2O	E.Fitzpatrick	3	F.O'Rourke	C	R.Elliott	O	S.Magee	C	G.Gibson	C	B.Adams	O1	B.Hinchman	3	F.Smith
C	H.Gowdy	C	C.Meyers	S	P.Kilduff	2S	B.McKechnie	2	P.Kilduff	O	O.Dugey	C	W.Schmidt	O	B.Bescher
O	F.Bailey	S	B.Fabrique	C	P.Dillhoefer	C	T.Clarke	O	J.Thorpe	S	P.McGaffigan	32	A.McCarthy	/C	R.Smyth
O	G.Twombly	C	E.Krueger	/3	C.Pechous	C	E.Huhn	3	H.Lobert	C	E.Burns	C1	B.Wagner	/C	P.Livingston
2	M.Massey	C	M.Wheat	O	M.Schick	/C	H.Smith	O	J.Wilhoit	O	C.Cooper	1	F.Mollwitz	/C	J.Brock
2	J.Evers	/3	R.Smyth	/O	T.Barber	/2	G.Getz	/O	R.Youngs	/S	H.Pearce	3	D.Baird	/3	T.DeFate
C	C.Meyers	/C	J.Snyder	/2	P.Driscoll			/3	E.Hemingway	/3	B.Byrne	S3	A.Debus	/3	B.Wallace
1	S.Covington	/1	F.Merkle	/1	V.Saier	P	F.Toney	/2	A.Baird			O	C.Jackson	/O	S.Stewart
/O	Z.Collins	/2	B.Leard	/1	R.Leslie	P	P.Schneider	O	R.Murray	P	P.Alexander	1	B.Brief	/S	I.McAuley
C	A.Rico	R	L.Malone	/C	B.O'Farrell	P	M.Regan	/1	J.Rodriguez	P	E.Rixey	O	F.Schulte	/O	J.Roche
/S	H.Schreiber			/O	W.Marriott	P	C.Mitchell	/C	E.Krueger	P	J.Oeschger	S	H.Caton		
/O	L.Chappell	P	J.Pfeffer	/O	H.Wolfe	P	H.Eller	/C	J.Onslow	P	E.Mayer	2	B.Gleason	P	B.Doak
/C	F.Jacklitsch	P	L.Cadore	/2	H.Hunter			/O	G.Kelly	P	J.Lavender	O	D.Flinn	P	L.Meadows
		P	R.Marquard	H	J.Archer	P	J.Ring					/1	R.Miller	P	R.Ames
P	J.Barnes	P	S.Smith	H	E.Blackburn	/P	D.Ruether	P	F.Schupp	P	C.Bender	/1	G.Kelly	P	M.Watson
P	D.Rudolph	P	L.Cheney			/P	E.Knetzer	P	S.Sallee	P	P.Fittery	/C	R.Smith	P	G.Packard
P	L.Tyler			P	H.Vaughn	/P	R.Sanders	P	P.Perritt			/O	J.Altenburg		
P	A.Nehf	P	J.Coombs	P	P.Douglas	/P	S.Perry	P	R.Benton			/2	B.Webb	P	O.Horstmann
P	P.Ragan	P	W.Dell	P	C.Hendrix	/P	R.Bressler	P	J.Tesreau			/C	F.Blackwell	P	M.Goodwin
		/P	J.Russell	P	A.Demaree	/P	J.Engel			P	F.Anderson	/O	J.Wilhoit	P	B.Steele
P	F.Allen	/P	J.Miljus	P	P.Carter	/P	H.Pillette			P	A.Demaree	/3	H.Warner	P	J.May
P	T.Hughes	/P	P.Wachtel	RP	M.Prendergast					P	G.Smith	/2	H.Wolfe	/P	L.North
/P	J.Scott	/P	R.Durning							P	J.Middleton	H	B.Shaw	/P	G.Pearce
/P	E.Reulbach			P	V.Aldridge					/P	A.Swigler	/3	A.Reilly	/P	B.Hitt
/P	E.Walsh			P	T.Seaton									/P	T.Murchison
/P	C.Crum			P	D.Ruether							P	W.Cooper		
				/P	H.Weaver							P	E.Jacobs		
				/P	R.Walker							P	F.Miller		
				/P	G.Packard							P	B.Grimes		
												P	B.Steele		
												P	H.Carlson		
												P	A.Mamaux		
												/P	B.Evans		
												/P	E.Ponder		

TEAM	G	W	L	PCT	GB	R	OR	AB	H	2B	3B	HR	BB	SO	AVG	OBP	SLG	PRO	PRO+	BR	/A	PF	CHI	RC	SB	CS	SBA	SBR
NY	158	98	56	.636		635	457	5211	1360	170	71	39	373	533	.261	.317	.343	.660	113	50	69	97	105	597	162			
PHI	154	87	65	.572	10	578	500	5084	1262	225	60	38	435	533	.248	.310	.339	.649	101	29	5	104	100	556	109			
STL	154	82	70	.539	15	531	567	5083	1271	159	93	26	359	652	.250	.303	.333	.636	104	2	17	97	98	542	159			
CIN	157	78	76	.506	20	601	611	5251	1385	196	100	26	312	477	.264	.309	.354	.663	114	48	73	96	101	596	153			
CHI	157	74	80	.481	24	552	567	5135	1229	194	67	17	415	599	.239	.299	.313	.612	86	-35	-76	108	107	511	127			
BOS	157	72	81	.471	25.5	536	552	5201	1280	169	75	22	427	587	.246	.309	.320	.629	105	-2	30	94	96	549	155			
BRO	156	70	81	.464	26.5	511	559	5251	1299	159	78	25	334	527	.247	.296	.322	.618	93	-32	-46	103	98	522	130			
PIT	157	51	103	.331	47	464	595	5169	1230	160	61	9	399	580	.238	.298	.298	.596	86	-61	-78	103	94	493	150			
TOT	625					4408		41385	10316	1432	605	202	3054	4488	.249	.305	.328	.633							1145			

TEAM	CG	SH	SV	IP	H	H/G	HR	BB	SO	RAT	ERA	ERA+	OAV	OOB	PR	/A	PF	CPI	FA	E	DP	FW	PW	BW	SBW	DIF
NY	92	18	14	1426²	1221	7.7	29	327	551	9.9	2.27	112	.234	.283	69	43	94	97	.968	208	122	1.8	4.9	7.8		6.5
PHI	102	22	5	1389	1258	8.2	25	325	616	10.5	2.46	114	.246	.295	38	53	104	102	.967	212	112	1.2	6.0	.6		3.2
STL	66	16	10	1392²	1257	8.1	29	421	502	11.1	3.03	89	.248	.311	-51	-55	99	92	.967	221	153	.6	-6.2	1.9		9.7
CIN	94	12	6	1397¹	1358	8.7	20	402	488	11.5	2.70	97	.260	.317	1	-15	97	110	.962	247	120	-.7	-1.7	8.3		-4.9
CHI	79	16	9	1404	1303	8.4	34	374	654	10.9	2.62	110	.253	.307	14	40	107	108	.959	267	121	-1.9	4.5	-8.6		3.0
BOS	105	22	3	1424²	1309	8.3	19	371	593	10.8	2.77	92	.251	.304	-10	-38	94	96	.966	224	122	.7	-4.3	3.4		-4.3
BRO	99	8	9	1421¹	1288	8.2	32	405	582	11.0	2.78	100	.247	.307	-12	0	103	98	.962	245	102	-.7	.0	-5.2		.4
PIT	84	17	6	1417²	1318	8.4	14	432	509	11.3	3.01	94	.253	.314	-48	-29	105	94	.961	251	119	-.9	-3.3	-8.8		-13.0
TOT	721	131	62	11273¹		8.2				10.9	2.70		.249	.305					.964	1875	971					

Runs		Hits		Doubles		Triples		Home Runs		Total Bases	
Burns-NY	103	Groh-Cin	182	Groh-Cin	39	Hornsby-StL	17	Robertson-NY	12	Hornsby-StL	253
Groh-Cin	91	Burns-NY	180	Merkle-Bro-Chi	31	Cravath-Phi	16	Cravath-Phi	12	Groh-Cin	246
Kauff-NY	89	Roush-Cin	178	Smith-Bos	31	Chase-Cin	15	Hornsby-StL	8	Burns-NY	246
Hornsby-StL	86	Zimmerman-NY	174	Cravath-Phi	29	Roush-Cin	14			Cravath-Phi	238
		Carey-Pit	174	Chase-Cin	28	Long-StL	14				

Runs Batted In		Runs Produced		Bases On Balls		Batting Average		On Base Percentage		Slugging Average	
Zimmerman-NY	102	Zimmerman-NY	158	Burns-NY	75	Roush-Cin	.341	Groh-Cin	.385	Hornsby-StL	.484
Chase-Cin	86	Chase-Cin	153	Groh-Cin	71	Hornsby-StL	.327	Hornsby-StL	.385	Cravath-Phi	.473
Cravath-Phi	83	Kauff-NY	152	Cravath-Phi	70	Z.Wheat-Bro	.312	Burns-NY	.380	Roush-Cin	.454
Stengel-Bro	73	Roush-Cin	145	Luderus-Phi	65	Kauff-NY	.308	Roush-Cin	.379	Z.Wheat-Bro	.423
Luderus-Phi	72	Hornsby-StL	144	Paskert-Phi	62	Groh-Cin	.304	Kauff-NY	.379	Burns-NY	.412

Production		Adjusted Production		Batter Runs		Adjusted Batter Runs		Clutch Hitting Index		Runs Created	
Hornsby-StL	.868	Hornsby-StL	170	Hornsby-StL	39.6	Hornsby-StL	42.3	Zimmerman-NY	146	Burns-NY	102
Cravath-Phi	.842	Roush-Cin	162	Cravath-Phi	34.7	Groh-Cin	37.7	Ward-Pit	133	Hornsby-StL	100
Roush-Cin	.833	Cravath-Phi	151	Groh-Cin	33.5	Roush-Cin	36.0	Luderus-Phi	132	Groh-Cin	96
Groh-Cin	.796	Groh-Cin	150	Roush-Cin	32.3	Burns-NY	35.4	Deal-Chi	130	Roush-Cin	94
Burns-NY	.792	Burns-NY	148	Burns-NY	32.2	Cravath-Phi	30.9	Chase-Cin	121	Carey-Pit	94

Total Average		Stolen Bases		Stolen Base Average		Stolen Base Runs		Fielding Runs		Total Player Rating	
Hornsby-StL	.906	Carey-Pit	46					Bancroft-Phi	27.9	Hornsby-StL	7.7
Cravath-Phi	.870	Burns-NY	40					Fletcher-NY	27.4	Groh-Cin	5.3
Burns-NY	.868	Kauff-NY	30					Carey-Pit	24.5	Fletcher-NY	4.1
Roush-Cin	.843	Maranville-Bos	27					Hornsby-StL	21.3	Carey-Pit	3.9
Groh-Cin	.815	Baird-Pit-StL	26					Miller-StL	18.6	Burns-NY	3.5

Wins		Win Percentage		Games		Complete Games		Shutouts		Saves	
Alexander-Phi	30	Schupp-NY	.750	Douglas-Chi	51	Alexander-Phi	34	Alexander-Phi	8	Sallee-NY	4
Toney-Cin	24	Sallee-NY	.720	Barnes-Bos	50	Toney-Cin	31	Toney-Cin	7		
Vaughn-Chi	23	Perritt-NY	.708	Schneider-Cin	46	Vaughn-Chi	27	Cooper-Pit	7		
Schupp-NY	21	Alexander-Phi	.698	Alexander-Phi	45	Barnes-Bos	27	Schupp-NY	6		
Schneider-Cin	20	Nehf-Bos	.680	Doak-StL	44	Schupp-NY	25				

Innings Pitched		Fewest Hits/Game		Fewest BB/Game		Strikeouts		Strikeouts/Game		Ratio	
Alexander-Phi	388.0	Schupp-NY	6.68	Alexander-Phi	1.30	Alexander-Phi	200	Vaughn-Chi	5.94	Anderson-NY	8.78
Toney-Cin	339.2	Anderson-NY	6.78	Sallee-NY	1.42	Vaughn-Chi	195	Schupp-NY	4.86	Schupp-NY	9.13
Schneider-Cin	333.2	Nehf-Bos	7.60	Nehf-Bos	1.50	Douglas-Chi	151	Alexander-Phi	4.64	Alexander-Phi	9.23
Cooper-Pit	297.2	Pfeffer-Bro	7.61	Barnes-Bos	1.53	Schupp-NY	147	Douglas-Chi	4.63	Nehf-Bos	9.26
Vaughn-Chi	295.2	Tyler-Bos	7.64	Douglas-Chi	1.53	Schneider-Cin	138	Marquard-Bro	4.53	Barnes-Bos	9.58

Earned Run Average		Adjusted ERA		Opponents' Batting Avg.		Opponents' On Base Pct.		Starter Runs		Adjusted Starter Runs	
Alexander-Phi	1.83	Anderson-NY	176	Schupp-NY	.209	Anderson-NY	.255	Alexander-Phi	37.5	Alexander-Phi	41.7
Anderson-NY	1.44	Alexander-Phi	153	Anderson-NY	.209	Schupp-NY	.265	Vaughn-Chi	22.8	Vaughn-Chi	28.8
Perritt-NY	1.88	Vaughn-Chi	144	Nehf-Bos	.231	Alexander-Phi	.266	Schupp-NY	22.7	Anderson-NY	19.8
Schupp-NY	1.95	Perritt-NY	135	Marquard-Bro	.232	Nehf-Bos	.268	Anderson-NY	22.7	Schneider-Cin	18.7
Vaughn-Chi	2.01	Schupp-NY	130	Pfeffer-Bro	.234	Barnes-Bos	.277	Schneider-Cin	22.2	Schupp-NY	17.9

Clutch Pitching Index		Relief Runs		Adjusted Relief Runs		Relief Ranking		Total Pitcher Index		Total Baseball Ranking	
Schneider-Cin	145							Alexander-Phi	5.9	Hornsby-StL	7.7
Vaughn-Chi	120							Vaughn-Chi	4.1	Alexander-Phi	5.9
Perritt-NY	118							Rixey-Phi	2.6	Groh-Cin	5.3
Hendrix-Chi	117							Schneider-Cin	1.8	Vaughn-Chi	4.1
Mayer-Phi	114							Anderson-NY	1.7	Fletcher-NY	4.1

February 24 "Smokey Joe" Wood, his arm dead at 26, is sold by the Red Sox to Cleveland for $15,000. He will become an outfielder after one last, losing start on the mound, and will play five more years.

April 10 The AL gets the U.S. Army to assign drill sergeants to each team for daily pregame drills. A final contest will be held for a $500 prize. The St. Louis Browns will take the money.

April 11 Babe Ruth beats the Yankees, pitching a three-hit 10–3 win for the Red Sox in the opener. By the end of May he will be 10-3 on the way to his best year (24–13) and a league-leading 35 complete games.

May 5 St. Louis Browns pitcher Ernie Koob pitches a 1–0 no-hitter over the White Sox. A tainted first-inning hit by Buck Weaver is changed to an error after much discussion with umpires and players. The following day, the writers' association will take a mail vote on a resolution that a scorer's decision cannot be reversed.

May 6 No-hitters are thrown on consecutive days, as the Browns' Bob Groom no-hits the White Sox, 3–0, in the second game of the doubleheader. This year, Groom will be the losingest pitcher in the AL for the third time. He lost a record-setting 19 straight games as a rookie with Washington in 1909.

June 23 In Boston, Babe Ruth starts against Washington. He walks leadoff man Eddie Foster, griping to plate umpire Brick Owens after each pitch. On ball four, Ruth plants a right to the umpire's jaw. He is ejected, and Ernie Shore relieves. Foster is caught stealing, and Shore retires all 26 men he faces in a 4-0 win, getting credit in the books for a perfect game. Ruth is not fined but draws a 10-day suspension.

August 19 Coaching third in a 1-1 game against Washington, Detroit's Ty Cobb gives Tiger base runner "Tioga George" Burns a shove when Burns stops at third on a long hit; Burns keeps going and scores the winning run for the Tigers. Clark Griffith protests, and Ban Johnson upholds him, as the rules now ban coaches from touching a runner. The game is replayed, and Washington wins, 2-0.

October 6 Happy Felsch's home run is the difference in Chicago, as Ed Cicotte beats the Giants' Slim Sallee, 2-1, in the Series opener.

October 7 In Game 2 New York's Ferdie Schupp doesn't get out of the second inning, and reliever Fred Anderson is bombed in a five-run fourth, as the 14 White Sox hits produce a 7-2 win for Red Faber. Faber's pitching is better than his baserunning; in the fifth inning, he tries to steal third, only to find teammate Buck Weaver occupying it.

October 15 After Red Faber and Rube Benton match three scoreless innings, Eddie Collins leads off the fourth and hits a grounder to Heinie Zimmerman at third base. Collins takes second when the throw goes past first baseman Walter Holke. Joe Jackson's fly to right field is dropped by Dave Robertson, and Collins goes to third. When Happy Felsch hits one back to the pitcher, Collins breaks for home. Benton throws to third to catch Collins, and catcher Bill Rariden comes up the line. But Collins keeps running and slides home safely with Zimmerman in pursuit. Zimmerman will be blamed for chasing the runner, but nobody was covering home plate for New York on the play. Faber wins his third game of the Series, 4-2.

October 26 Miller Huggins, who managed the Cardinals to a third-place finish, is signed to run the Yankees by owner Jake Ruppert. Co-owner Til Huston, who favored Wilbert Robinson for the job, has a falling out with partner Ruppert and will sell his half interest to Ruppert in 1923.

December 13 Connie Mack and the A's need money. He sells pitcher Joe Bush, catcher Wally Schang, and outfielder Amos Strunk to the Red Sox for sore–armed pitcher Vean Gregg, outfielder Merlin Kopp, catcher Chester "Pinch" Thomas, and $60,000.

BOSTON	CHICAGO	CLEVELAND	DETROIT	NEW YORK	PHILADELPHIA	ST.LOUIS	WASHINGTON
M J.Barry	M P.Rowland	M L.Fohl	M H.Jennings	M B.Donovan	M C.Mack	M F.Jones	M C.Griffith
1B D.Hoblitzel	1B C.Gandil	1B J.Harris	1B G.Burns	1B W.Pipp	1B S.McInnis	1B G.Sisler	1B J.Judge
2B J.Barry	2B E.Collins	2B B.Wambsganss	2B R.Young	2B F.Maisel	2B R.Grover	2B D.Pratt	2B R.Morgan
SS E.Scott	SS S.Risberg	SS R.Chapman	SS D.Bush	SS R.Peckinpaugh	SS W.Witt	SS D.Lavan	SS H.Shanks
3B L.Gardner	3B B.Weaver	3B J.Evans	3B O.Vitt	3B F.Baker	3B R.Bates	3B J.Austin	3B E.Foster
LF D.Lewis	LF J.Jackson	LF J.Graney	LF B.Veach	LF H.High	LF P.Bodie	LF B.Shotton	LF M.Menosky
CF T.Walker	CF H.Felsch	CF T.Speaker	CF T.Cobb	CF E.Miller	CF A.Strunk	CF B.Jacobson	CF C.Milan
RF H.Hooper	RF N.Leibold	RF B.Roth	RF H.Heilmann	RF T.Hendryx	RF C.Jamieson	RF T.Sloan	RF S.Rice
C S.Agnew	C R.Schalk	C S.O'Neill	C O.Stanage	C L.Nunamaker	C W.Schang	C H.Severeid	C E.Ainsmith
C P.Thomas	O S.Collins	1 L.Guisto	O T.Spencer	C L.Magee	C B.Meyer	O A.Marsans	31 J.Leonard
O J.Walsh	3 F.McMullin	32 T.Turner	O G.Harper	C R.Walters	S J.Dugan	S2 E.Johnson	1 P.Gharrity
1 D.Gainer	C B.Lynn	O E.Smith	1 S.Crawford	S F.Gilhooley	O B.Johnson	O E.Smith	S G.McBride
O C.Shorten	/O E.Murphy	O J.Billings	2 B.Jones	2 J.Gedeon	C R.Haley	3 L.Magee	S E.Smith
2S H.Janvrin	1 T.Jourdan	/3 I.Howard	S B.Dyer	2 P.Baumann	O B.Thrasher	/O W.Rumler	O S.Crane
3 M.McNally	O J.Jenkins	O M.Allison	C A.Yelle	/O A.Marsans	O L.Gooch	O W.Miller	S C.Milan
C H.Cady	/2 B.Byrne	/C H.DeBerry	/1 B.Ellison	C W.Alexander	2 O.Lawry	C G.Hale	O H.Milan
2 J.Cooney	H J.Fournier	/1 R.Miller	/O F.Nicholson	/O A.Aragon	3 E.Palmer	O R.Demmitt	/O C.Jamieson
H O.Henriksen	/2 Z.Hasbrook	/O M.Kavanagh	/O I.Flagstead	O B.Lamar	O R.Sharman	S W.Gerber	/2 B.Murray
/C W.Mayer	/S Z.Terry	/3 F.Eunick	/2 T.DeFate	S C.Fewster	S R.Shannon	/1 G.Paulette	
			H F.Walker	O S.Vick	/1 P.Griffin	/C G.Hartley	
P B.Ruth	P E.Cicotte	P J.Bagby		/S A.Ward	/C W.McAvoy	/2 B.Kenworthy	P W.Johnson
P D.Leonard	P R.Faber	P S.Coveleski	P H.Dauss	/O H.Camp	/C C.Perkins	/3 S.Moore	P J.Shaw
P C.Mays	P L.Williams	P E.Klepfer	P B.Boland	/C M.Ruel	/O G.Bailey	/S E.Murray	P B.Gallia
P E.Shore	P R.Russell	P G.Morton	P H.Ehmke		/C V.Picinich	H T.Richardson	P D.Ayers
P R.Foster	P D.Danforth	P F.Coumbe	P B.James	P B.Shawkey	/2 D.Bradshaw	/R P.Bigler	P G.Dumont
			P W.Mitchell	P R.Caldwell	/O P.French	/S O.Neu	
P H.Pennock	P J.Scott	P O.Lambeth		H G.Mogridge	H H.Davis		P H.Harper
P L.Bader	P J.Benz	P A.Gould	P G.Cunningham			P D.Davenport	/P M.Craft
/P S.Jones	/P M.Wolfgang	P J.Boehling	P D.Jones	P N.Cullop	P J.Bush	P A.Sothoron	/P D.Waldbauer
/P W.Wyckoff		/P R.Torkelson	P H.Coveleski	P U.Shocker	P R.Schauer	P B.Groom	
		/P J.Wood	/P J.Couch	P R.Fisher	P E.Myers	P E.Koob	
		/P P.Smith		P S.Love	P J.Johnson	P E.Plank	
		/P G.Dickerson		P A.Russell	P W.Noyes	P T.Rogers	
				/P E.Monroe	P S.Seibold	P E.Hamilton	
				/P B.McGraw	P C.Falkenberg	P R.Wright	
				/P N.Brady	P W.Anderson	P V.Molyneaux	
				/P B.Piercy	/P R.Naylor	P J.Park	
				/P H.Thormahlen	P W.Johnson	/P G.Lowdermilk	
				/P J.Enright	/P R.Parnham	P C.Weilman	
				/P W.Smallwood	P E.Bacon	/P S.Martin	
					P D.Keefe	/P T.McCabe	
					P R.Hill	/P K.Pennington	
					/P J.Nabors		

TEAM	G	W	L	PCT	GB	R	OR	AB	H	2B	3B	HR	BB	SO	AVG	OBP	SLG	PRO	PRO+	BR	/A	PF	CHI	RC	SB	CS	SBA	SBR
CHI	156	100	54	.649		656	464	5057	1281	152	81	18	522	479	.253	.329	.326	.655	103	36	23	102	108	607	219			
BOS	157	90	62	.592	9	555	454	5048	1243	198	64	14	466	473	.246	.314	.319	.633	100	-10	-4	99	99	550	105			
CLE	156	88	66	.571	12	584	543	4994	1224	218	64	13	549	596	.245	.324	.322	.646	96	21	-23	107	99	588	210			
DET	154	78	75	.510	21.5	639	577	5093	1317	204	77	25	483	476	.259	.328	.344	.672	111	61	64	100	102	615	163			
WAS	157	74	79	.484	25.5	543	566	5142	1238	173	70	4	500	574	.241	.313	.304	.617	95	-34	-28	99	101	531	166			
NY	155	71	82	.464	28.5	524	558	5136	1226	172	52	27	496	535	.239	.310	.308	.618	93	-34	-39	101	99	526	136			
STL	155	57	97	.370	43	510	687	5091	1250	183	63	15	405	540	.246	.305	.315	.620	98	-39	-20	96	99	523	157			
PHI	154	55	98	.359	44.5	529	691	5109	1296	177	62	17	435	519	.254	.316	.323	.639	101	-1	7	99	94	551	112			
TOT	622					4540		40670	10075	1477	533	133	3856	4192	.248	.318	.320	.638						1268				

TEAM	CG	SH	SV	IP	H	H/G	HR	BB	SO	RAT	ERA	ERA+	OAV	OOB	PR	/A	PF	CPI	FA	E	DP	FW	PW	BW	SBW	DIF
CHI	78	22	21	1424[1]	1236	7.8	10	413	517	10.6	2.16	123	.238	.298	79	76	100	102	.967	204	117	2.3	8.5	2.6		9.7
BOS	115	15	7	1421[1]	1197	7.6	12	413	509	10.5	2.20	117	.231	.295	73	60	97	95	.972	183	116	3.9	6.7	-.4		3.9
CLE	73	20	22	1412[2]	1270	8.1	17	438	451	11.1	2.52	112	.247	.310	22	48	106	101	.964	242	136	-.5	5.3	-2.6		8.7
DET	78	20	15	1396[1]	1209	7.8	12	504	516	11.4	2.56	103	.240	.316	16	13	99	99	.964	234	95	-.1	1.4	7.1		-6.9
WAS	84	21	10	1413	1217	7.8	12	537	637	11.4	2.75	95	.239	.316	-14	-19	99	91	.961	251	127	-1.0	-2.1	-3.1		3.7
NY	87	10	6	1411[1]	1280	8.2	28	427	571	11.1	2.66	101	.252	.314	0	3	101	102	.965	225	129	.6	.3	-4.3		-2.1
STL	66	12	12	1385[1]	1320	8.6	19	537	429	12.3	3.20	81	.257	.332	-83	-96	98	94	.957	281	139	-3.4	-10.7	-2.2		-3.7
PHI	80	8	8	1365[2]	1310	8.6	23	562	516	12.5	3.27	84	.261	.338	-92	-79	103	97	.961	251	106	-1.4	-8.8	.8		-12.1
TOT	661	128	101	11230		8.0				11.4	2.66		.248	.318					.964	1871	965					

Runs		Hits		Doubles		Triples		Home Runs		Total Bases	
Bush-Det	112	Cobb-Det	225	Cobb-Det	44	Cobb-Det	24	Pipp-NY	9	Cobb-Det	335
Cobb-Det	107	Sisler-StL	190	Speaker-Cle	42	Jackson-Chi	17	Veach-Det	8	Veach-Det	261
Chapman-Cle	98	Speaker-Cle	184	Veach-Det	31	Judge-Was	15	Bodie-Phi	7	Speaker-Cle	254
Jackson-Chi	91	Veach-Det	182	Sisler-StL	30	Chapman-Cle	13			Sisler-StL	244
E.Collins-Chi	91			Roth-Cle	30					Bodie-Phi	233

Runs Batted In		Runs Produced		Bases On Balls		Batting Average		On Base Percentage		Slugging Average	
Veach-Det	103	Cobb-Det	203	Graney-Cle	94	Cobb-Det	.383	Cobb-Det	.444	Cobb-Det	.570
Felsch-Chi	102	Veach-Det	174	E.Collins-Chi	89	Sisler-StL	.353	Speaker-Cle	.432	Speaker-Cle	.486
Cobb-Det	102	Felsch-Chi	171	Hooper-Bos	80	Speaker-Cle	.352	Veach-Det	.393	Veach-Det	.457
Heilmann-Det	86	Jackson-Chi	161	Bush-Det	80	Veach-Det	.319	Sisler-StL	.390	Sisler-StL	.453
Jackson-Chi	75	E.Collins-Chi	158	Leibold-Chi	74	Felsch-Chi	.308	E.Collins-Chi	.389	Jackson-Chi	.429

Production		Adjusted Production		Batter Runs		Adjusted Batter Runs		Clutch Hitting Index		Runs Created	
Cobb-Det	1.014	Cobb-Det	210	Cobb-Det	74.4	Cobb-Det	75.0	Schalk-Chi	135	Cobb-Det	164
Speaker-Cle	.918	Speaker-Cle	168	Speaker-Cle	51.2	Speaker-Cle	43.3	Bates-Phi	134	Speaker-Cle	118
Veach-Det	.850	Sisler-StL	163	Veach-Det	40.1	Veach-Det	40.5	Felsch-Chi	133	Veach-Det	108
Sisler-StL	.843	Veach-Det	160	Sisler-StL	34.0	Sisler-StL	37.4	Veach-Det	130	Chapman-Cle	105
Jackson-Chi	.805	Jackson-Chi	142	Jackson-Chi	28.8	Jackson-Chi	26.9	E.Collins-Chi	128	Sisler-StL	104

Total Average		Stolen Bases		Stolen Base Average	Stolen Base Runs	Fielding Runs		Total Player Rating	
Cobb-Det	1.253	Cobb-Det	55			Chapman-Cle	24.4	Cobb-Det	8.5
Speaker-Cle	1.056	E.Collins-Chi	53			Felsch-Chi	18.9	Chapman-Cle	5.4
Veach-Det	.905	Chapman-Cle	52			Wambsganss-Cle	15.3	Speaker-Cle	4.7
Sisler-StL	.900	Roth-Cle	51			Ainsmith-Was	14.9	Veach-Det	4.0
E.Collins-Chi	.873	Sisler-StL	37			Pratt-StL	14.8	Sisler-StL	4.0

Wins		Win Percentage		Games		Complete Games		Shutouts		Saves	
Cicotte-Chi	28	Russell-Chi	.750	Danforth-Chi	50	Ruth-Bos	35	Coveleski-Cle	9	Danforth-Chi	9
Ruth-Bos	24	Mays-Bos	.710	Cicotte-Chi	49	Johnson-Was	30	Johnson-Was	8	Bagby-Cle	7
Johnson-Was	23	Cicotte-Chi	.700	Bagby-Cle	49	Cicotte-Chi	29	Bagby-Cle	8	Boland-Det	6
Bagby-Cle	23	Williams-Chi	.680	Sothoron-StL	48	Mays-Bos	27	Cicotte-Chi	7	Coumbe-Cle	5
Mays-Bos	22	Ruth-Bos	.649								

Innings Pitched		Fewest Hits/Game		Fewest BB/Game		Strikeouts		Strikeouts/Game		Ratio	
Cicotte-Chi	346.2	Coveleski-Cle	6.09	Russell-Chi	1.52	Johnson-Was	188	Johnson-Was	5.19	Cicotte-Chi	8.28
Ruth-Bos	326.1	Cicotte-Chi	6.39	Mogridge-NY	1.79	Cicotte-Chi	150	Harper-Was	4.97	Coveleski-Cle	8.96
Johnson-Was	326.0	Ruth-Bos	6.73	Cicotte-Chi	1.82	Leonard-Bos	144	Bush-Phi	4.67	Johnson-Was	9.11
Bagby-Cle	320.2	Johnson-Was	6.85	Johnson-Was	1.88	Coveleski-Cle	133	Leonard-Bos	4.40	Russell-Chi	9.65
Coveleski-Cle	298.1	Mays-Bos	7.16	Bagby-Cle	2.05	Ruth-Bos	128	Danforth-Chi	4.11	Mays-Bos	9.90

Earned Run Average		Adjusted ERA		Opponents' Batting Avg.		Opponents' On Base Pct.		Starter Runs		Adjusted Starter Runs	
Cicotte-Chi	1.53	Cicotte-Chi	173	Coveleski-Cle	.194	Cicotte-Chi	.248	Cicotte-Chi	43.5	Cicotte-Chi	43.3
Mays-Bos	1.74	Coveleski-Cle	156	Cicotte-Chi	.203	Coveleski-Cle	.261	Mays-Bos	29.4	Coveleski-Cle	33.8
Coveleski-Cle	1.81	Mays-Bos	148	Ruth-Bos	.211	Johnson-Was	.263	Coveleski-Cle	28.2	Bagby-Cle	30.9
Faber-Chi	1.92	Bagby-Cle	144	Johnson-Was	.211	Russell-Chi	.279	Bagby-Cle	24.8	Mays-Bos	26.8
Russell-Chi	1.95	Faber-Chi	138	Mays-Bos	.221	Mays-Bos	.282	Ruth-Bos	23.5	Ruth-Bos	20.5

Clutch Pitching Index		Relief Runs	Adjusted Relief Runs	Relief Ranking	Total Pitcher Index		Total Baseball Ranking	
Faber-Chi	136				Cicotte-Chi	5.4	Cobb-Det	8.5
Ayers-Was	128				Mays-Bos	4.8	Chapman-Cle	5.4
James-Det	127				Ruth-Bos	4.8	Cicotte-Chi	5.4
Morton-Cle	117				Bagby-Cle	3.8	Mays-Bos	4.8
Mitchell-Det	116				Coveleski-Cle	3.1	Ruth-Bos	4.8

January 2 Brooklyn sends outfielder Casey Stengel and infielder George Cutshaw to Pittsburgh for pitcher Burleigh Grimes, pitcher Al Mamaux, and infielder Chuck Ward.

February 23 Barney Dreyfuss of the Rules Committee launches a campaign to ban the spitter. He will succeed after the 1920 season.

April 4* Determined not to be a wartime casualty, the International League reorganizes. The Richmond, Montreal, and Providence franchises are replaced by Binghamton, Jersey City, and Syracuse. Expenses are slashed, causing the resignation of president Ed Barrow, who will go on to greater glory with the Boston Red Sox. The IL will be the only minor league to play its full schedule.

June 17 The National Commission rules that pitcher Scott Perry, who has been winning games for the Athletics, belongs to the Boston Braves. Although he was purchased by the Braves from Atlanta in 1917, the deal was not completed. While on Atlanta's ineligible list, he was sold to Connie Mack. Aroused by Perry's AL success, the Braves enter their proper claim. Mack breaks precedent, goes outside Organized Baseball to civil court, and gets an injunction against Boston. The NL, having sat still for the loss of George Sisler, is furious; President John K. Tener resigns. John Heydler succeeds him and arranges a compromise solution: Mack pays Boston $2,500 and keeps Perry (henceforth a loser). The clubs' anger at player-allocation decisions will ultimately topple the National Commission, making way for Judge Kenesaw Mountain Landis.

August 9 Reds manager Christy Mathewson suspects Hal Chase of taking bribes to fix games, and suspends him "for indifferent play." Chase will be reinstated and will play for the Giants in 1919.

August 24 Players in the World Series are granted an extended exemption from military service. The National Commission gets official approval to play three days later from General Enoch Crowder, providing that 10 percent of the revenue goes to war charities.

August 27 Christy Mathewson resigns as Reds manager to accept a commission as a captain in the chemical warfare branch of the Army.

September 10 Hippo Vaughn comes back with two days of rest for the Cubs and blanks the Red Sox, 3–0, on five hits in Game 5. Players on both sides threaten to strike unless they are guaranteed $2,500 to the winners and $1,000 each for the losers. They back off, however, when told they will appear greedy while their countrymen are fighting a war. There are no fines, but no World Series rings or mementos are given out. Seventy-five years later, the oversight is rectified. Descendants of about two-thirds of the players receive medallions created by Balfour, in the style in which they would have been crafted 75 years earlier, at a Fenway Park ceremony.

December 10 National League secretary John Heydler is elected president of the league.

BOSTON

Pos	Player
M	G.Stallings
1B	E.Konetchy
2B	B.Herzog
SS	J.Rawlings
3B	R.Smith
LF	R.Massey
CF	R.Powell
RF	A.Wickland
C	A.Wilson
O	Jo.Kelly
O	Ji.Kelly
O	W.Rehg
S	Z.Terry
O	C.Chadbourne
C	J.Henry
2	J.Smith
C	B.Wagner
S	R.Maranville
/O	B.Murphy
/2	R.Conway
H	F.Bailey
H	S.Covington
H	T.Miller
/H	D.Bass
/C	W.Tragesser
P	A.Nehf
P	P.Ragan
P	D.Rudolph
P	B.Hearn
P	D.Fillingim
/P	L.George
P	H.Canavan
/P	J.Northrop
/P	D.Crandall
/P	B.Upham
/P	T.Hughes
/P	H.McQuillan
/P	C.Crum

BROOKLYN

Pos	Player
M	W.Robinson
1B	J.Daubert
2B	M.Doolan
SS	I.Olson
3B	O.O'Mara
LF	Z.Wheat
CF	H.Myers
RF	J.Johnston
C	O.Miller
O	J.Hickman
C	M.Wheat
2	R.Schmandt
C	E.Krueger
/O	C.Mitchell
/C	J.Archer
/2	F.O'Rourke
/O	A.Nixon
/O	C.Ward
/O	A.Bashang
/2	R.Sheridan
P	B.Grimes
P	R.Marquard
P	L.Cheney
P	J.Coombs
P	D.Robertson
/P	S.Martin
/P	G.Smith
/P	L.Cadore
/P	J.Pfeffer
/P	A.Mamaux
/P	R.Durning
/P	N.Plitt
/P	J.Hehl
/P	M.Herrmann
/P	J.Russell
/P	H.Heitmann

CHICAGO

Pos	Player
M	F.Mitchell
1B	F.Merkle
2B	R.Zeider
SS	C.Hollocher
3B	C.Deal
LF	L.Mann
CF	D.Paskert
RF	M.Flack
C	B.Killefer
O	T.Barber
1O	B.O'Farrell
2	P.Kilduff
2	C.Pick
2	B.McCabe
/2	C.Wortman
/C	R.Elliott
/C	T.Daly
H	F.Lear
/C	T.Clarke
P	H.Vaughn
P	L.Tyler
P	C.Hendrix
P	P.Douglas
P	P.Carter
/P	S.Martin
/P	R.Walker
/P	H.Weaver
/P	P.Alexander
/P	V.Aldridge
/P	B.Napier

CINCINNATI

Pos	Player
M	C.Mathewson
1B	H.Groh
1B	H.Chase
2B	L.Magee
SS	L.Blackburne
3B	H.Groh
LF	G.Neale
CF	E.Roush
RF	T.Griffith
C	I.Wingo
1O	S.Magee
O2	M.Cueto
C	N.Allen
C	H.Smith
/C	J.Archer
P	H.Eller
P	P.Schneider
P	J.Ring
P	F.Toney
P	R.Bressler
P	D.Luque
P	M.Regan
P	G.Smith
/P	R.Mitchell
/P	L.Jacobus
/P	S.Conley
/P	D.Ruether
/P	J.Haines

NEW YORK

Pos	Player
M	J.McGraw
1B	W.Holke
2B	L.Doyle
SS	A.Fletcher
3B	H.Zimmerman
LF	G.Burns
CF	B.Kauff
RF	R.Youngs
C	L.McCarty
C	B.Rariden
2	J.Wilhoit
O	E.Sicking
2	J.Rodriguez
O	J.Thorpe
O	P.Compton
1	J.Kirke
/2	B.Niehoff
/C	G.Gibson
P	P.Perritt
P	R.Causey
P	A.Demaree
P	S.Sallee
P	F.Toney
RP	D.Davis
P	J.Tesreau
/P	F.Anderson
/P	B.Steele
/P	J.Barnes
/P	F.Schupp
/P	G.Smith
/P	R.Benton
/P	J.Ogden
/P	G.Ross
/P	W.Hoyt

PHILADELPHIA

Pos	Player
M	P.Moran
1B	F.Luderus
2B	P.McGaffigan
SS	D.Bancroft
3B	M.Stock
LF	I.Meusel
CF	C.Williams
RF	G.Cravath
C	B.Adams
C	E.Burns
2	H.Pearce
2	M.Fitzgerald
2	E.Hemingway
P	P.Whitted
/C	P.Dillhoefer
/C	M.Devine
/O	T.Pickup
P	M.Prendergast
P	B.Hogg
P	J.Oeschger
P	E.Jacobs
P	M.Watson
P	E.Mayer
/P	A.Main
/P	B.Fortune
/P	B.Tincup
/P	F.Woodward

PITTSBURGH

Pos	Player
M	H.Bezdek
1B	F.Mollwitz
2B	G.Cutshaw
SS	H.Caton
3B	B.McKechnie
LF	C.Bigbee
CF	M.Carey
RF	B.Southworth
C	W.Schmidt
O	C.Stengel
O	L.King
1	B.Hinchman
S	L.Boone
S	R.Ellam
C	T.Leach
C	J.Archer
C	R.Smith
/C	F.Blackwell
/3	G.Getz
/2	J.Pitler
P	W.Cooper
P	F.Miller
P	R.Sanders
P	E.Mayer
P	B.Harmon
/P	R.Comstock
/P	E.Hamilton
/P	C.Slapnicka
/P	B.Steele
/P	C.Hill
/P	B.Adams
/P	E.Jacobs
/P	H.Carlson

ST. LOUIS

Pos	Player
M	J.Hendricks
1B	G.Paulette
2B	B.Fisher
SS	R.Hornsby
3B	D.Baird
LF	A.McHenry
CF	C.Heathcote
RF	W.Cruise
C	M.Gonzalez
3O	B.Betzel
O	J.Smith
1	C.Grimm
O	G.Anderson
O2	R.Smyth
C	F.Snyder
2S	B.Wallace
2	B.Niehoff
3	H.Bronkie
C	J.Brock
O	J.Beall
/O	M.Kavanagh
/2	D.Distel
/O	W.Mattick
/S	B.Larmore
/O	D.Wheeler
/1	T.Brottem
/O	T.Menze
P	B.Doak
P	R.Ames
P	B.Sherdel
P	G.Packard
P	L.Meadows
P	J.May
P	O.Tuero
/P	O.Horstmann
/P	R.Johnson
/P	E.Howard

TEAM	G	W	L	PCT	GB	R	OR	AB	H	2B	3B	HR	BB	SO	AVG	OBP	SLG	PRO	PRO+	BR	/A	PF	CHI	RC	SB	CS	SBA	SBR
CHI	131	84	45	.651		538	393	4325	1147	164	53	21	358	343	.265	.325	.342	.667	106	48	35	102	102	524	159			
NY	124	71	53	.573	10.5	480	415	4164	1081	150	53	13	271	365	.260	.310	.330	.640	103	1	10	98	107	451	130			
CIN	129	68	60	.531	15.5	530	496	4265	1185	165	84	15	304	303	.278	.330	.366	.696	120	86	96	98	96	545	128			
PIT	126	65	60	.520	17	466	412	4091	1016	107	72	15	371	285	.248	.315	.321	.636	96	1	-15	104	102	466	200			
BRO	126	57	69	.452	25.5	360	463	4212	1052	121	62	10	212	326	.250	.291	.315	.606	90	-53	-51	100	91	405	113			
PHI	125	55	68	.447	26	430	507	4192	1022	158	28	25	346	400	.244	.305	.313	.618	97	-29	-58	107	101	417	97			
BOS	124	53	71	.427	28.5	424	469	4162	1014	107	59	13	350	438	.244	.307	.307	.614	97	-32	-14	96	100	412	83			
STL	131	51	78	.395	33	454	527	4369	1066	147	64	27	329	461	.244	.301	.325	.626	99	-21	-5	97	100	450	119			
TOT	508					3682		33780	8583	1119	475	139	2541	2921	.254	.311	.328	.638						1029				

TEAM	CG	SH	SV	IP	H	H/G	HR	BB	SO	RAT	ERA	ERA+	OAV	OOB	PR	/A	PF	CPI	FA	E	DP	FW	PW	BW	SBW	DIF
CHI	92	23	8	1197	1050	7.9	13	296	472	10.3	2.18	128	.239	.291	77	80	101	104	.966	188	91	.5	8.9	3.9		6.2
NY	74	18	11	1111[2]	1002	8.1	20	228	330	10.1	2.64	100	.243	.287	15	-1	95	87	.971	152	78	2.1	-.1	1.1		5.9
CIN	84	14	6	1142[1]	1136	9.0	19	381	321	12.1	3.00	89	.268	.332	-30	-42	97	109	.964	192	127	.0	-4.7	10.7		-2.1
PIT	85	10	7	1140[1]	1005	7.9	13	299	367	10.5	2.48	116	.243	.300	36	51	104	99	.966	179	108	.6	5.7	-1.7		-2.1
BRO	85	17	2	1131[1]	1024	8.1	22	320	395	10.9	2.81	99	.248	.307	-6	-4	101	95	.963	193	74	-.3	-.4	-5.7		.4
PHI	78	10	6	1139[2]	1086	8.6	22	369	312	11.7	3.15	95	.258	.323	-49	-20	109	96	.961	211	91	-1.5	-2.2	-6.5		3.7
BOS	96	13	0	1117[1]	1111	8.9	14	277	340	11.4	2.90	93	.266	.316	-17	-27	97	102	.965	184	89	.0	-3.0	-1.6		-4.5
STL	72	3	5	1193	1148	8.7	16	352	361	11.6	2.96	91	.261	.321	-27	-34	98	101	.962	220	116	-1.5	-3.8	-.6		-7.6
TOT	666	108	45	9172[2]		8.4				11.1	2.76		.254	.311					.965	1519	774					

	Runs		Hits		Doubles		Triples		Home Runs		Total Bases
Groh-Cin	86	Hollocher-Chi	161	Groh-Cin	28	Daubert-Bro	15	Cravath-Phi	8	Hollocher-Chi	202
Burns-NY	80	Groh-Cin	158	Mann-Chi	27	Wickland-Bos	13	Williams-Phi	6	Roush-Cin	198
Flack-Chi	74	Roush-Cin	145	Cravath-Phi	27	S.Magee-Cin	13	Cruise-StL	6	Groh-Cin	195
Hollocher-Chi	72	Youngs-NY	143	Meusel-Phi	25	L.Magee-Cin	13			Mann-Chi	188
		Merkle-Chi	143	Merkle-Chi	25					Merkle-Chi	187

	Runs Batted In		Runs Produced		Bases On Balls		Batting Average		On Base Percentage		Slugging Average
S.Magee-Cin	76	Burns-NY	127	Carey-Pit	62	Z.Wheat-Bro	.335	Groh-Cin	.395	Roush-Cin	.455
Cutshaw-Pit	68	Paskert-Chi	125	Flack-Chi	56	Roush-Cin	.333	Hollocher-Chi	.379	Daubert-Bro	.429
Luderus-Phi	67	Mann-Chi	122	Groh-Cin	54	Groh-Cin	.320	R.Smith-Bos	.373	Hornsby-StL	.416
R.Smith-Bos	65	Groh-Cin	122	Cravath-Phi	54	Hollocher-Chi	.316	S.Magee-Cin	.370	S.Magee-Cin	.415
Merkle-Chi	65	S.Magee-Cin	120	Bancroft-Phi	54	Daubert-Bro	.308	Z.Wheat-Bro	.369	Wickland-Bos	.398

	Production		Adjusted Production		Batter Runs		Adjusted Batter Runs		Clutch Hitting Index		Runs Created
Roush-Cin	.823	Roush-Cin	153	Groh-Cin	26.4	Groh-Cin	27.9	S.Magee-Cin	158	Hollocher-Chi	85
Groh-Cin	.791	Groh-Cin	144	Roush-Cin	24.3	Roush-Cin	25.6	Konetchy-Bos	137	Roush-Cin	80
Daubert-Bro	.789	S.Magee-Cin	142	Hollocher-Chi	23.0	Hollocher-Chi	21.0	R.Smith-Bos	135	Groh-Cin	79
S.Magee-Cin	.785	Daubert-Bro	141	S.Magee-Cin	19.2	S.Magee-Cin	20.3	Z.Wheat-Bro	122	Carey-Pit	76
Hollocher-Chi	.775	Wickland-Bos	139	Daubert-Bro	18.2	Daubert-Bro	18.4	Paulette-StL	122	Burns-NY	74

	Total Average		Stolen Bases		Stolen Base Average		Stolen Base Runs		Fielding Runs		Total Player Rating
Roush-Cin	.848	Carey-Pit	58					Fletcher-NY	22.3	Groh-Cin	3.6
Carey-Pit	.844	Burns-NY	40					Carey-Pit	18.6	Hornsby-StL	3.6
Wickland-Bos	.812	Hollocher-Chi	26					Bancroft-Phi	17.9	Fisher-StL	3.5
Burns-NY	.809	Cutshaw-Pit	25					Schmidt-Pit	15.8	Roush-Cin	3.0
S.Magee-Cin	.804	Baird-StL	25					Myers-Bro	13.0	L.Magee-Cin	3.0

	Wins		Win Percentage		Games		Complete Games		Shutouts		Saves
Vaughn-Chi	22	Hendrix-Chi	.741	Grimes-Bro	40	Nehf-Bos	28	Vaughn-Chi	8	Toney-Cin-NY	3
Hendrix-Chi	20	Tyler-Chi	.704	Cooper-Pit	38	Vaughn-Chi	27	Grimes-Bro	7	Oeschger-Phi	3
Tyler-Chi	19	Mayer-Phi-Pit	.696	Eller-Cin	37	Cooper-Pit	26	Tyler-Chi	6	Cooper-Pit	3
Grimes-Bro	19	Vaughn-Chi	.688			Tyler-Chi	22	Perritt-NY	6	Anderson-NY	3
Cooper-Pit	19	Grimes-Bro	.679			Hendrix-Chi	21				

	Innings Pitched		Fewest Hits/Game		Fewest BB/Game		Strikeouts		Strikeouts/Game		Ratio
Vaughn-Chi	290.1	Vaughn-Chi	6.70	Sallee-NY	.82	Vaughn-Chi	148	Vaughn-Chi	4.59	Sallee-NY	9.14
Nehf-Bos	284.1	Grimes-Bro	7.01	Perritt-NY	1.47	Cooper-Pit	117	Cooper-Pit	3.85	Vaughn-Chi	9.27
				G.Smith-Cin-NY-Bro	1.50						
Cooper-Pit	273.1	Cooper-Pit	7.21	Toney-Cin-NY	1.54	Grimes-Bro	113	Grimes-Bro	3.77	Grimes-Bro	9.68
Grimes-Bro	269.2	Tyler-Chi	7.28	Demaree-NY	1.58	Tyler-Chi	102	Cheney-Bro	3.72	Cooper-Pit	9.68
Tyler-Chi	269.1	Jacobs-Pit-Phi	7.50			Nehf-Bos	96	May-StL	3.60	Tyler-Chi	9.69

	Earned Run Average		Adjusted ERA		Opponents' Batting Avg.		Opponents' On Base Pct.		Starter Runs		Adjusted Starter Runs
Vaughn-Chi	1.74	Vaughn-Chi	160	Vaughn-Chi	.208	Sallee-NY	.259	Vaughn-Chi	33.1	Vaughn-Chi	33.8
Tyler-Chi	2.00	Tyler-Chi	139	Grimes-Bro	.216	Vaughn-Chi	.266	Tyler-Chi	22.7	Cooper-Pit	23.3
Cooper-Pit	2.11	Cooper-Pit	136	Cooper-Pit	.223	Grimes-Bro	.276	Cooper-Pit	19.9	Tyler-Chi	23.3
Douglas-Chi	2.13	Douglas-Chi	131	Tyler-Chi	.226	Perritt-NY	.278	Grimes-Bro	18.8	Grimes-Bro	19.4
Grimes-Bro	2.14	Grimes-Bro	130	Jacobs-Pit-Phi	.233	Cooper-Pit	.279	Hamilton-Pit	11.6	Hamilton-Pit	12.2

	Clutch Pitching Index		Relief Runs		Adjusted Relief Runs		Relief Ranking		Total Pitcher Index		Total Baseball Ranking
Bressler-Cin	123							Vaughn-Chi	4.4	Vaughn-Chi	4.4
Mayer-Phi-Pit	117							Cooper-Pit	3.1	Groh-Cin	3.6
Schneider-Cin	113							Tyler-Chi	3.0	Hornsby-StL	3.6
Eller-Cin	112							Grimes-Bro	2.6	Fisher-StL	3.5
Demaree-NY	112							Hogg-Phi	2.0	Cooper-Pit	3.1

April 7* In the morning game of a doubleheader in Los Angeles, James "Doc" Crandall's no-hit bid against Salt Lake City (Pacific Coast League) is spoiled with two outs in the ninth by Crandall's brother Karl, but Los Angeles wins, 14–0.

April 15 The AL season opens with Babe Ruth pitching a four-hit 7–1 victory over the A's. Red Sox manager Ed Barrow will start Ruth's conversion to slugger by working him into 72 games as an outfielder-first baseman.

April 18 With two Tigers on base in the ninth, Cleveland center fielder Tris Speaker turns an unassisted double play. On April 29, he will do the same against Chicago, the fourth unassisted double play of his career, a record he will share with Cleveland teammate Elmer Smith.

May 14 Sunday baseball is made legal in Washington, D.C. District commissioners rescind the ban in view of the large increase in the city's wartime population and the need for recreation and amusement facilities. Five days later, the Senators beat Cleveland, 1-0, in 18 innings in the first Sunday game as more than 15,000 fans attend.

June 1 Losing, 5–4, against the Yankees, the White Sox load the bases in the ninth with no outs. Chick Gandil lines a shot to third baseman Frank Baker, who turns it into a game-ending triple play.

July 8 Babe Ruth's blast over the fence in Fenway scores Amos Strunk, as the Red Sox win, 1-0, over Cleveland. Nevertheless, prevailing rules reduce Babe's home run to a triple because the winning run scored ahead of the home run. Ruth will tie for the AL title with 11 homers, even though he plays just 95 games.

July 19 Washington catcher Eddie Ainsmith applies for deferment from the draft. Secretary of War Newton D. Baker rules that baseball is not an essential occupation and all players of draft age are subject to the "work-in-essential-industries-or-fight" rule. The ruling sends many players to work in shipyards and other defense industries, where they can play part-time or semipro. Ban Johnson says the AL will close down July 21, but the next day both leagues vote to continue. A week later, Baker exempts players from the rule until Sept. 1. Both leagues vote to cut the season short, and it ends on Labor Day, Sept. 2.

July 25 Walter Johnson gives up one hit (a triple by George Sisler) in the first 11 innings of a 15-inning, four-hit 1–0 win.

September 1 Ty Cobb pitches two innings against the Browns while the Browns' George Sisler pitches one scoreless inning. The Browns win, 6-2, as Sisler hits a double off Cobb.

September 5 In order to cut down on the use of trains, the first three games of the World Series are played in Chicago, the next three in Boston. The Cubs switch their home games to Comiskey Park with its larger seating capacity. Babe Ruth, having completed 13 scoreless innings in his first World Series two years ago, adds nine more in edging Hippo Vaughn, 1-0, in the opener. During the seventh-inning stretch, a military band plays "The Star Spangled Banner." From then on, it is played at every World Series game, every season opener, and whenever a band is present to play it, though it is not yet adopted as the national anthem. The custom of playing it before every game will begin during World War II, after the installation of public address systems.

September 11 The Red Sox win the World Series in Game 6 on Carl Mays's second victory, a 2-1 three-hitter. With two on and two out in the third, utility outfielder George Whiteman lines a hard drive to right field. Max Flack drops it, allowing the only runs off Lefty Tyler. Cubs pitchers compile a 1.04 ERA, while Boston's .186 batting average is the lowest ever for a World Series winner. The Red Sox will realize $1,102 each, the Cubs $671, the smallest winner's share ever earned.

BOSTON	CHICAGO	CLEVELAND	DETROIT	NEW YORK	PHILADELPHIA	ST.LOUIS	WASHINGTON
M E.Barrow	M P.Rowland	M L.Fohl	M H.Jennings	M M.Huggins	M C.Mack	M F.Jones	M C.Griffith
1B S.McInnis	1B C.Gandil	1B D.Johnston	1B H.Heilmann	1B W.Pipp	1B G.Burns	M J.Austin	1B J.Judge
2B D.Shean	2B E.Collins	2B B.Wambsganss	2B R.Young	2B D.Pratt	2B J.Dykes	M J.Burke	2B R.Morgan
SS E.Scott	SS B.Weaver	SS R.Chapman	SS D.Bush	SS R.Peckinpaugh	SS J.Dugan	1B G.Sisler	SS D.Lavan
3B F.Thomas	3B F.McMullin	3B J.Evans	3B O.Vitt	3B F.Baker	3B L.Gardner	2B J.Gedeon	3B E.Foster
LF G.Whiteman	LF N.Leibold	LF J.Wood	LF B.Veach	LF P.Bodie	LF M.Kopp	SS J.Austin	LF B.Shotton
CF A.Strunk	CF S.Collins	CF T.Speaker	CF T.Cobb	CF E.Miller	CF T.Walker	3B F.Maisel	CF C.Milan
RF H.Hooper	RF E.Murphy	RF B.Roth	RF G.Harper	RF F.Gilhooley	RF C.Jamieson	LF E.Smith	RF F.Schulte
C S.Agnew	C R.Schalk	C S.O'Neill	C A.Yelle	C T.Hannah	C W.McAvoy	CF J.Tobin	C E.Ainsmith
						RF R.Demmitt	
OP B.Ruth	S3 S.Risberg	32 T.Turner	3 B.Jones	C R.Walters	S2 R.Shannon	C L.Nunamaker	O2 H.Shanks
CO W.Schang	O H.Felsch	C J.Graney	C O.Stanage	O H.Hyatt	C C.Perkins		C V.Picinich
1 D.Hoblitzel	1 W.Good	1 E.Miller	1 F.Walker	O A.Marsans	O M.Acosta	O T.Hendryx	S W.McBride
3 G.Cochran	3 B.Pinelli	C P.Thomas	C T.Spencer	O B.Lamar	O R.Oldring	S W.Gerber	/O S.Rice
C W.Mayer	C O.Jacobs	1 R.Williams	1 L.Dressen	1 D.Fournier	C C.Davidson	C H.Severeid	/C J.Casey
3 J.Stansbury	3 J.Jackson	3 A.Halt	3 A.Griggs	O J.Hummel	/O J.Munch	1 P.Johns	H P.Gharrity
3 J.Coffey	O J.Mostil	2 B.Bescher	2 J.Coffey	S A.Ward	/O F.Fahey	S E.Johnson	M.Acosta
2 F.Truesdale	/C A.DeVormer	1 M.Kavanagh	1 M.Kavanagh	/O A.High	P S.Perry	C G.Hale	/C B.Berman
3 W.Barbare	/1 T.Jourdan	/3 G.Getz	/O B.Ellison	/1 Z.Beck	P V.Gregg	H K.Williams	
O H.Miller	/O B.Lynn	/O J.Farmer	/2 J.Curry	/C M.Ruel	P W.Adams		P W.Johnson
/2 H.Wagner	H P.Hardgrove	/O E.Onslow	H J.Cobb	/C P.O'Connor	P M.Watson	P A.Sothoron	P H.Harper
/S E.Gonzalez	/C K.Willson	/2 G.Schaefer	/1 H.Jennings	/O S.Vick	P E.Myers	P D.Davenport	P J.Shaw
H R.Bluhm		/C J.Billings		/2 C.Fewster		P T.Rogers	P D.Ayers
		/C J.Peters				P B.Gallia	
P C.Mays	P E.Cicotte		P H.Dauss	P G.Mogridge	P B.Geary	P R.Wright	P E.Matteson
P J.Bush	P F.Shellenback	P S.Coveleski	P B.Boland	P S.Love	P R.Johnson	RP B.Houck	/P E.Yingling
P S.Jones	P J.Benz	P J.Bagby	P R.Kallio	P R.Caldwell	/P W.Pierson	P U.Shocker	/P E.Hovlik
P D.Leonard	P D.Danforth	P G.Morton	P G.Cunningham	P A.Russell	/P R.Shea	P G.Lowdermilk	/P N.Altrock
	P R.Russell	P F.Coumbe	P B.James	P H.Finneran	/P V.Keen	P L.Leifield	/P G.Dumont
/P L.Bader	P L.Williams	P J.Enzmann	P E.Erickson	P H.Thormahlen	/P T.Zachary	/P B.Morris	/P R.Hansen
/P W.Kinney	/P R.Faber		P D.Jones	P R.Keating	/P C.Holmes	/P T.McCabe	M.Craft
/P J.Dubuc	/P J.Quinn	/P B.Groom	/P B.Bailey	P H.Robinson	/P L.Bauer		A.Brennan
/P V.Molyneaux	/P R.Mitchell	/P G.McQuillan	/P H.Coveleski	/P R.Sanders			/P G.Buckeye
/P D.McCabe	/P M.Wolfgang	/P O.Lambeth	/P H.Finneran	/P B.Shawkey			S.Rees
/P B.Pertica	/P E.Corey	/P A.Brennan	/P C.Hall	/P A.Ferguson			
/P W.Wyckoff		/P R.Wilkinson	/P B.Donovan	/P E.Monroe			
			/P H.Hall	/P D.Vance			
			/P W.Mitchell	/P W.Bernhardt			
			/P B.Dyer	/P B.McGraw			

TEAM	G	W	L	PCT	GB	R	OR	AB	H	2B	3B	HR	BB	SO	AVG	OBP	SLG	PRO	PRO+	BR	/A	PF	CHI	RC	SB	CS	SBA	SBR
BOS	126	75	51	.595		474	380	3982	990	159	54	15	406	324	.249	.322	.327	.649	103	5	13	98	105	455	110			
CLE	129	73	54	.575	2.5	504	447	4166	1084	176	67	9	491	386	.260	.344	.341	.685	102	68	17	110	93	537	165			
WAS	130	72	56	.563	4	461	412	4472	1144	156	49	4	376	361	.256	.318	.315	.633	98	-21	-13	98	99	479	137			
NY	126	60	63	.488	13.5	493	475	4224	1085	160	45	20	367	370	.257	.320	.330	.650	99	2	-8	102	106	469	88			
STL	123	58	64	.475	15	426	448	4019	1040	152	40	5	397	340	.259	.331	.320	.651	105	11	25	97	93	467	138			
CHI	124	57	67	.460	17	457	446	4132	1057	136	55	8	375	358	.256	.322	.321	.643	98	-5	-9	101	102	458	116			
DET	128	55	71	.437	20	476	557	4262	1063	141	56	13	452	380	.249	.325	.318	.643	103	-2	17	96	101	470	123			
PHI	130	52	76	.406	24	412	538	4278	1039	124	44	22	343	485	.243	.303	.308	.611	88	-59	-63	101	102	415	83			
TOT	508					3703		33535	8502	1204	410	96	3207	3004	.254	.323	.322	.646						960				

TEAM	CG	SH	SV	IP	H	H/G	HR	BB	SO	RAT	ERA	ERA+	OAV	OOB	PR	/A	PF	CPI	FA	E	DP	FW	PW	BW	SBW	DIF
BOS	105	26	2	1120	931	7.5	9	380	392	10.8	2.31	116	.231	.302	58	47	97	95	.971	152	89	2.5	5.2	1.5		2.8
CLE	78	5	13	1161	1126	8.7	9	343	364	11.5	2.64	114	.262	.319	18	46	108	105	.962	207	82	-.7	5.1	1.9		3.1
WAS	75	19	8	1228	1021	7.5	10	395	505	10.6	2.14	127	.231	.298	86	80	98	99	.960	226	95	-1.8	8.9	-1.5		2.3
NY	59	8	13	1157¹	1103	8.6	25	463	370	12.5	3.00	94	.261	.340	-30	-24	102	107	.970	161	137	1.9	-2.7	-.9		.2
STL	67	8	8	1111¹	993	8.0	11	402	346	11.5	2.75	99	.246	.319	2	-2	99	95	.963	190	86	-.2	-.2	2.8		-5.4
CHI	76	9	8	1126	1092	8.7	9	300	349	11.3	2.73	100	.261	.314	5	-3	99	97	.967	169	98	1.2	-.3	-1.0		-4.9
DET	74	8	7	1160²	1130	8.8	10	437	374	12.4	3.40	78	.263	.335	-81	-99	96	89	.960	212	77	-1.1	-11.0	1.9		2.2
PHI	80	13	9	1156	1106	8.6	12	486	277	12.7	3.22	91	.266	.348	-58	-39	106	103	.959	228	136	-1.9	-4.4	-7.0		1.3
TOT	614	96	68	9220¹		8.3				11.7	2.77		.254	.323					.964	1545	800					

Runs		Hits		Doubles		Triples		Home Runs		Total Bases	
Chapman-Cle	84	Burns-Phi	178	Speaker-Cle	33	T.Cobb-Det	14	Walker-Phi	11	Burns-Phi	236
T.Cobb-Det	83	T.Cobb-Det	161	Ruth-Bos	26	Veach-Det	13	Ruth-Bos	11	T.Cobb-Det	217
Hooper-Bos	81	Sisler-StL	154	Hooper-Bos	26	Hooper-Bos	13	Burns-Phi	6	Baker-NY	206
Bush-Det	74	Baker-NY	154	Baker-NY	24	Roth-Cle	12	Baker-NY	6	Speaker-Cle	205
Speaker-Cle	73	Speaker-Cle	150							Sisler-StL	199

Runs Batted In		Runs Produced		Bases On Balls		Batting Average		On Base Percentage		Slugging Average	
Veach-Det	78	T.Cobb-Det	144	Chapman-Cle	84	T.Cobb-Det	.382	T.Cobb-Det	.440	Ruth-Bos	.555
Burns-Phi	70	Veach-Det	134	Bush-Det	79	Burns-Phi	.352	E.Collins-Chi	.407	T.Cobb-Det	.515
Wood-Cle	66	Speaker-Cle	134	Hooper-Bos	75	Sisler-StL	.341	Speaker-Cle	.403	Burns-Phi	.467
Ruth-Bos	66	Burns-Phi	125	E.Collins-Chi	73	Speaker-Cle	.318	Sisler-StL	.400	Sisler-StL	.440
T.Cobb-Det	64	Hooper-Bos	124	Shotton-Was	67	Baker-NY	.306	Hooper-Bos	.391	Speaker-Cle	.435

Production		Adjusted Production		Batter Runs		Adjusted Batter Runs		Clutch Hitting Index		Runs Created	
T.Cobb-Det	.955	T.Cobb-Det	196	T.Cobb-Det	44.0	T.Cobb-Det	47.8	Veach-Det	140	T.Cobb-Det	105
Burns-Phi	.857	Sisler-StL	159	Ruth-Bos	34.8	Ruth-Bos	36.0	Demmitt-StL	137	Sisler-StL	92
Sisler-StL	.841	Burns-Phi	157	Burns-Phi	32.8	Burns-Phi	31.9	McInnis-Bos	136	Burns-Phi	91
Speaker-Cle	.839	Hooper-Bos	142	Speaker-Cle	31.3	Sisler-StL	31.3	Shanks-Was	133	Speaker-Cle	90
Hooper-Bos	.796	Speaker-Cle	140	Sisler-StL	28.8	Hooper-Bos	26.5	S.Collins-Chi	132	Hooper-Bos	82

Total Average		Stolen Bases		Stolen Base Average		Stolen Base Runs		Fielding Runs		Total Player Rating	
T.Cobb-Det	1.131	Sisler-StL	45					Peckinpaugh-NY	25.0	T.Cobb-Det	4.8
Sisler-StL	.970	Roth-Cle	35					Scott-Bos	17.5	Sisler-StL	3.8
Speaker-Cle	.931	T.Cobb-Det	34					Dugan-Phi	17.0	Burns-Phi	3.6
Roth-Cle	.929	Chapman-Cle	30					Gedeon-StL	15.8	Baker-NY	3.2
Hooper-Bos	.875	Speaker-Cle	27					S.Collins-Chi	14.1	Speaker-Cle	3.0

Wins		Win Percentage		Games		Complete Games		Shutouts		Saves	
Johnson-Was	23	Jones-Bos	.762	Mogridge-NY	45	Perry-Phi	30	Mays-Bos	8	Mogridge-NY	7
Coveleski-Cle	22	Johnson-Was	.639	Bagby-Cle	45	Mays-Bos	30	Johnson-Was	8	Bagby-Cle	6
Mays-Bos	21	Coveleski-Cle	.629	Perry-Phi	44	Johnson-Was	29	Bush-Bos	7	Russell-NY	4
Perry-Phi	20	Mays-Bos	.618	Shaw-Was	41	Bush-Bos	26	Jones-Bos	5	Geary-Phi	4
Bagby-Cle	17	Shaw-Was	.571	Ayers-Was	40	Coveleski-Cle	25				

Innings Pitched		Fewest Hits/Game		Fewest BB/Game		Strikeouts		Strikeouts/Game		Ratio	
Perry-Phi	332.1	Sothoron-StL	6.55	Cicotte-Chi	1.35	Johnson-Was	162	Morton-Cle	5.16	Johnson-Was	8.81
Johnson-Was	326.0	Johnson-Was	6.65	Mogridge-NY	1.62	Shaw-Was	129	Shaw-Was	4.81	Ruth-Bos	9.52
Coveleski-Cle	311.0	Harper-Was	6.71	Benz-Chi	1.64	Bush-Bos	125	Johnson-Was	4.47	Sothoron-StL	9.56
Mays-Bos	293.1	Ruth-Bos	6.76	Enzmann-Cle	1.91	Morton-Cle	123	Bush-Bos	4.13	Coveleski-Cle	9.87
Bush-Bos	272.2	Mays-Bos	7.06	Johnson-Was	1.93	Mays-Bos	114	Love-NY	3.74	Mays-Bos	9.88

Earned Run Average		Adjusted ERA		Opponents' Batting Avg.		Opponents' On Base Pct.		Starter Runs		Adjusted Starter Runs	
Johnson-Was	1.27	Johnson-Was	214	Sothoron-StL	.205	Johnson-Was	.260	Johnson-Was	54.4	Johnson-Was	52.6
Coveleski-Cle	1.82	Coveleski-Cle	164	Johnson-Was	.210	Sothoron-StL	.274	Coveleski-Cle	32.8	Coveleski-Cle	40.6
Sothoron-StL	1.94	Perry-Phi	148	Harper-Was	.212	Ruth-Bos	.277	Perry-Phi	29.4	Perry-Phi	35.1
Perry-Phi	1.98	Sothoron-StL	141	Ruth-Bos	.214	Coveleski-Cle	.279	Bush-Bos	20.0	Sothoron-StL	18.5
Bush-Bos	2.11	Mogridge-NY	129	Mays-Bos	.221	Mays-Bos	.284	Sothoron-StL	19.4	Bush-Bos	17.1

Clutch Pitching Index		Relief Runs		Adjusted Relief Runs		Relief Ranking		Total Pitcher Index		Total Baseball Ranking	
Perry-Phi	124	Houck-StL	3.1	Houck-StL	2.8	Houck-StL	2.3	Johnson-Was	7.6	Johnson-Was	7.6
Mogridge-NY	123							Coveleski-Cle	4.6	Ruth-Bos	5.6
Coumbe-Cle	119							Mays-Bos	4.1	T.Cobb-Det	4.8
Russell-NY	119							Perry-Phi	3.9	Coveleski-Cle	4.6
Shellenback-Chi	116							Bush-Bos	3.1	Mays-Bos	4.1

January 14 John McGraw, Charles A. Stoneham, and Tammany politician Judge Francis X. McQuade buy a controlling interest in the Giants from the John Brush estate.

January 30 When no word is received from manager Christy Mathewson, who is still in France, the Reds hire Pat Moran as manager.

February 1 After winning an out-of-court settlement of his suit against the Dodgers for the balance of his salary ($2,150) when the 1918 season ended a month early, former MVP Jake Daubert is traded to the Reds for outfielder Tommy Griffith.

February 5 Charges brought in 1918 by Reds owner Garry Herrmann and manager Christy Mathewson against Hal Chase for betting against his team and throwing games in collusion with gamblers are dismissed by NL president John Heydler. Heydler decides Chase's sometimes indifferent play was mostly due to "carelessness." Two weeks later John McGraw trades first baseman Walter Holke and catcher Bill Rariden to the Reds for Chase.

April 19 Pushed through the legislature by future New York City mayor Jimmy Walker, a bill legalizing Sunday baseball in the state is signed by Governor Al Smith.

April 23 Anticipating a poor season at the gate, the major leagues open a reduced 140-game season. Despite the lack of close races, attendance remains high all year, and every club will show a profit.

May 4 The Giants play their first legal Sunday game at home, before 35,000 fans, losing to the Phils, 4–3. More than 25,000 turn out in Brooklyn the same day.

May 25 Ever-popular Casey Stengel, now a Pirate, is good-naturedly applauded when he comes to bat in the seventh inning at Brooklyn, doffs his cap in response, and to everyone's delight releases an "irate but much relieved" sparrow he had hidden there.

June 15 A rain check dispute arises. Cincinnati rain checks read "not to be used after four and a half innings have been completed." But the game is called with the Reds at bat with one out in the bottom of the fifth and the game tied, 1–1. The Reds honor the rain checks, but the Braves demand their share of the gate ($2,600), as a legal game has been played, based on the wording of the rain check. In a compromise, the Braves accept $1,300, and the other six clubs agree to share the cost. In future all rain checks will read "not good after five innings."

September 2 The National Commission recommends a best-of-nine World Series. The lengthier World Series is seen as a sign of greed and is abandoned after three years.

September 16 Dutch Ruether beats the Giants, 4–3, to clinch the Reds' first pennant since American Association days.

October 1 Eddie Cicotte, a 29-game winner, is driven to cover in a five-run fourth in the Series opener. Reds outfielder Greasy Neale, the only man to play in a World Series, coach a football team in the Rose Bowl, and become a pro football Hall of Fame coach, has three hits and will top the Reds with .357 for the Series.

October 9 Lefty Williams gets one man out in the first before departing. The Reds lead, 4-0, and go on to give Hod Eller a 10-5 victory and the Reds the world title in eight games.

December 10 The NL proposes to ban the spitball's use by all new pitchers. The ban will be formally worked out by the Rules Committee in February.

	BOSTON		BROOKLYN		CHICAGO		CINCINNATI		NEW YORK		PHILADELPHIA		PITTSBURGH		ST.LOUIS
M	G.Stallings	M	W.Robinson	M	F.Mitchell	M	P.Moran	M	J.McGraw	M	J.Coombs	M	H.Bezdek	M	B.Rickey
1B	W.Holke	1B	E.Konetchy	1B	F.Merkle	1B	J.Daubert	1B	H.Chase	M	G.Cravath	1B	F.Mollwitz	1B	D.Miller
2B	B.Herzog	2B	J.Johnston	2B	C.Pick	2B	M.Rath	2B	L.Doyle	1B	F.Luderus	2B	G.Cutshaw	2B	M.Stock
SS	R.Maranville	SS	I.Olson	SS	C.Hollocher	SS	L.Kopf	SS	A.Fletcher	2B	G.Paulette	SS	Z.Terry	SS	D.Lavan
3B	T.Boeckel	3B	L.Malone	3B	C.Deal	3B	H.Groh	3B	H.Zimmerman	SS	D.Bancroft	3B	W.Barbare	3B	R.Hornsby
LF	W.Cruise	LF	Z.Wheat	LF	L.Mann	LF	R.Bressler	3B	G.Burns	3B	L.Blackburne	LF	B.Southworth	LF	A.McHenry
CF	J.Riggert	CF	H.Myers	CF	D.Paskert	CF	E.Roush	CF	B.Kauff	LF	I.Meusel	CF	C.Bigbee	CF	C.Heathcote
RF	R.Powell	RF	T.Griffith	RF	M.Flack	RF	G.Neale	RF	R.Youngs	CF	C.Williams	RF	C.Stengel	RF	J.Smith
C	H.Gowdy	C	E.Krueger	C	B.Killefer	C	I.Wingo	C	L.McCarty	RF	L.Callahan	C	W.Schmidt	C	V.Clemons
										C	B.Adams				
O3	R.Smith	2	L.Magee	OS	L.Magee	C	B.Rariden	23	F.Frisch			O	M.Carey	O	J.Schultz
2O	J.Rawlings	C	O.Miller	O	T.Barber	O	S.Magee	C	M.Gonzalez	O2	P.Whitted	1	V.Saier	O	B.Shotton
C	A.Wilson	3	C.Ward	2	B.Herzog	O	P.Duncan	1	G.Kelly	2S	H.Pearce	3	T.Boeckel	C	F.Snyder
O	J.Thorpe	21	R.Schmandt	C	B.O'Farrell	M	M.Cueto	C	F.Snyder	3	D.Baird	1	P.Whitted	1	G.Paulette
O	L.Mann	C	M.Wheat	O	D.Robertson	3	H.Schreiber	2	A.Baird	O	G.Cravath	C	C.Lee	O	P.Dillhoefer
2	C.Pick	O	J.Hickman	3	P.Kilduff	/3	J.Smith	S2	J.Statz	S2	E.Sicking	S3	H.Caton	1	F.Mollwitz
3	L.Blackburne	3	P.Kilduff	O	B.McCabe	C	N.Allen	C	E.Smith	C	W.Tragesser	O	F.Nicholson	/3	D.Baird
O	J.Kelly	3	D.Baird	/1	F.Lear	/O	C.See	O	L.King	C	H.Cady	C	F.Blackwell	/1	R.Leslie
O	D.Nutter	/O	H.Allen	C	T.Daly	/O	W.Rehg	/S	E.Sicking	O	B.LeBourveau	1	C.Grimm	/O	W.Cruise
O	D.Carroll	/3	O.O'Mara	/O	B.Friberg	/O	B.Zitzmann	/S	J.Cooney	C	N.Clarke	C	J.Sweeney	/2	H.Janvrin
C	W.Tragesser	/3	T.Fitzsimmons	/O	H.Reilly			/O	B.Kinsella	/S	D.Wallace	/O	B.Zitzmann	/2	B.Fisher
/O	L.Christenbury					P	H.Eller	/O	C.Bowen	/2	L.Raymond	/3	H.Warner	/1	S.Fishburn
/S	H.Ford	P	J.Pfeffer	P	H.Vaughn	P	D.Ruether	/O	J.Thorpe	/3	J.Cavanaugh			/S	W.Kimmick
C	M.O'Neil	P	L.Cadore	P	P.Alexander	P	S.Sallee	R	D.Robertson	/1	M.Pasquella	P	W.Cooper	H	M.Pasquella
/O	G.Bailey	P	A.Mamaux	P	C.Hendrix	P	J.Ring			H	B.Yeabsley	P	B.Adams		
H	T.Miller	P	B.Grimes	P	S.Martin	P	R.Fisher	P	J.Barnes			P	F.Miller	P	B.Doak
H	L.King	P	S.Smith	P	P.Douglas			P	R.Benton	P	G.Smith	P	E.Hamilton	P	M.Goodwin
/C	S.White					P	D.Luque	P	F.Toney	P	L.Meadows	P	H.Carlson	P	O.Tuero
		P	C.Mitchell	P	P.Carter	/P	R.Mitchell	P	J.Dubuc	P	E.Rixey			P	B.Sherdel
P	D.Rudolph	/P	R.Marquard	P	S.Bailey	/P	E.Gerner	P	R.Causey	P	B.Hogg	P	E.Mayer	P	J.May
P	D.Fillingim	/P	L.Cheney	/P	L.Tyler	/P	M.Regan			P	G.Packard	/P	E.Ponder		
P	A.Nehf	/P	L.Henion	/P	H.Weaver			P	A.Nehf			/P	B.Evans	P	L.Meadows
P	R.Keating			/P	J.Newkirk			/P	P.Douglas	P	E.Jacobs	/P	J.Wisner	P	E.Jacobs
P	A.Demaree							/P	F.Schupp	P	F.Woodward	/P	C.Hill	P	F.Woodward
								P	J.Winters	/P	L.Cheney			P	R.Ames
P	J.Scott							/P	P.Ragan	/P	M.Watson			P	F.Schupp
P	R.Causey							/P	R.Ryan	/P	J.Oeschger			/P	O.Horstmann
P	H.McQuillan							P	P.Perritt	/P	P.Murray			/P	B.Bolden
/P	J.Oeschger							/P	B.Hubbell	/P	M.Cantwell			P	R.Parker
P	J.Northrop							P	G.Smith	/P	R.Ames			/P	W.Koenigsmark
/P	L.Cheney							/P	C.Snover	/P	M.Prendergast			/P	A.Reinhart
/P	P.Ragan							/P	J.Oeschger	/P	L.Weinert				
/P	B.James							/P	J.Jones	/P	R.Faircloth				
								/P	B.Steele						
								/P	V.Barnes						

TEAM	G	W	L	PCT	GB	R	OR	AB	H	2B	3B	HR	BB	SO	AVG	OBP	SLG	PRO	PRO+	BR	/A	PF	CHI	RC	SB	CS	SBA	SBR
CIN	140	96	44	.686		577	401	4577	1204	135	83	20	405	368	.263	.327	.342	.669	110	43	57	97	104	552	143			
NY	140	87	53	.621	9	605	470	4664	1254	204	64	40	328	407	.269	.322	.366	.688	113	64	70	99	106	576	157			
CHI	140	75	65	.536	21	454	407	4581	1174	166	58	21	298	359	.256	.308	.332	.640	98	-14	-16	101	93	500	150			
PIT	139	71	68	.511	24.5	472	466	4538	1132	130	82	17	344	381	.249	.306	.325	.631	91	-25	-44	104	100	493	196			
BRO	141	69	71	.493	27	525	513	4844	1272	167	66	25	258	405	.263	.304	.340	.644	97	-13	-24	102	104	518	112			
BOS	140	57	82	.410	38.5	465	563	4746	1201	142	62	24	355	481	.253	.311	.324	.635	100	-17	4	96	92	509	145			
STL	138	54	83	.394	40.5	463	552	4588	1175	163	52	18	304	418	.256	.305	.326	.631	101	-28	1	94	99	485	148			
PHI	138	47	90	.343	47.5	510	699	4746	1191	208	50	42	323	469	.251	.303	.342	.645	92	-9	-45	107	101	506	114			
TOT	558					4071		37284	9603	1315	517	207	2615	3288	.258	.311	.337	.648						1165				

TEAM	CG	SH	SV	IP	H	H/G	HR	BB	SO	RAT	ERA	ERA+	OAV	OOB	PR	/A	PF	CPI	FA	E	DP	FW	PW	BW	SBW	DIF
CIN	89	23	9	1274	1104	7.8	21	298	407	10.0	2.23	124	.239	.288	96	75	95	104	.974	151	98	2.7	8.3	6.3		8.6
NY	72	11	13	1256	1153	8.3	34	305	340	10.6	2.70	104	.247	.296	29	14	96	96	.964	216	96	-1.0	1.6	7.8		8.7
CHI	80	21	5	1265	1127	8.0	14	294	495	10.3	2.21	130	.242	.291	98	93	99	106	.969	185	87	.7	10.3	-1.8		-4.3
PIT	91	17	4	1249	1113	8.0	23	263	391	10.2	2.88	105	.244	.290	4	19	104	84	.970	165	89	1.8	2.1	-4.9		2.5
BRO	98	12	1	1281	1256	8.8	21	292	476	11.1	2.73	109	.262	.309	25	33	102	106	.963	219	84	-1.1	3.7	-2.7		-.9
BOS	79	5	9	1270[1]	1313	9.3	29	337	374	11.8	3.17	90	.276	.327	-36	-45	98	107	.966	204	111	-.4	-5.0	.4		-7.6
STL	55	6	8	1217[1]	1146	8.8	25	415	414	11.9	3.23	86	.256	.326	-44	-60	96	97	.963	214	112	-1.1	-6.7	.1		-6.8
PHI	93	6	2	1252	1391	10.0	40	408	397	13.3	4.14	78	.294	.356	-171	-129	111	100	.963	218	112	-1.3	-14.3	-5.0		-.8
TOT	657	101	51	10064[2]		8.6				11.2	2.91		.258	.311					.967	1572	789					

Runs		Hits		Doubles		Triples		Home Runs		Total Bases	
Burns-NY	86	Olson-Bro	164	Youngs-NY	31	Southworth-Pit	14	Cravath-Phi	12	Myers-Bro	223
Groh-Cin	79	Hornsby-StL	163	Luderus-Phi	30	Myers-Bro	14	Kauff-NY	10	Hornsby-StL	220
Daubert-Cin	79	Roush-Cin	162	Burns-NY	30			Williams-Phi	9	Z.Wheat-Bro	219
Rath-Cin	77	Burns-NY	162	Kauff-NY	27			Hornsby-StL	8	Roush-Cin	217
				Meusel-Phi	26			Doyle-NY	7	Burns-NY	216

Runs Batted In		Runs Produced		Bases On Balls		Batting Average		On Base Percentage		Slugging Average	
Myers-Bro	73	Roush-Cin	140	Burns-NY	82	Roush-Cin	.321	Burns-NY	.396	Myers-Bro	.436
Roush-Cin	71	Groh-Cin	137	Rath-Cin	64	Hornsby-StL	.318	Groh-Cin	.392	Doyle-NY	.433
Hornsby-StL	71	Hornsby-StL	131	Groh-Cin	56	Youngs-NY	.311	Hornsby-StL	.384	Groh-Cin	.431
Kauff-NY	67			Luderus-Phi	54	Groh-Cin	.310	Youngs-NY	.384	Roush-Cin	.431
Groh-Cin	63			Boeckel-Pit-Bos	53	Stock-StL	.307	Roush-Cin	.380	Hornsby-StL	.430

Production		Adjusted Production		Batter Runs		Adjusted Batter Runs		Clutch Hitting Index		Runs Created	
Groh-Cin	.823	Hornsby-StL	154	Cravath-Phi	32.2	Hornsby-StL	33.8	Kopf-Cin	125	Burns-NY	96
Hornsby-StL	.814	Groh-Cin	151	Burns-NY	30.0	Burns-NY	31.1	Southworth-Pit	123	Roush-Cin	88
Roush-Cin	.811	Roush-Cin	147	Hornsby-StL	28.5	Groh-Cin	29.4	Zimmerman-NY	121	Hornsby-StL	87
Burns-NY	.801	Burns-NY	142	Groh-Cin	27.4	Roush-Cin	29.1	Roush-Cin	121	Youngs-NY	84
Youngs-NY	.799	Youngs-NY	142	Roush-Cin	26.9	Cravath-Phi	28.3	Merkle-Chi	120	Groh-Cin	81

Total Average		Stolen Bases		Stolen Base Average		Stolen Base Runs		Fielding Runs		Total Player Rating	
Burns-NY	.909	Burns-NY	40					Maranville-Bos	28.7	Maranville-Bos	4.7
Groh-Cin	.887	Cutshaw-Pit	36					Fletcher-NY	24.0	Hornsby-StL	4.5
Youngs-NY	.846	Bigbee-Pit	31					Bigbee-Pit	17.9	Stock-StL	4.3
Hornsby-StL	.837	Smith-StL	30					Killefer-Chi	17.4	Groh-Cin	3.5
Roush-Cin	.833							Stock-StL	16.8	Roush-Cin	3.3

Wins		Win Percentage		Games		Complete Games		Shutouts		Saves	
J.Barnes-NY	25	Ruether-Cin	.760	Tuero-StL	45	Cooper-Pit	27	Alexander-Chi	9	Tuero-StL	4
Vaughn-Chi	21	Sallee-Cin	.750	Meadows-StL-Phi	40	Pfeffer-Bro	26	Eller-Cin	7		
Sallee-Cin	21	J.Barnes-NY	.735	Vaughn-Chi	38	Vaughn-Chi	25	Adams-Pit	6		
		Eller-Cin	.679	Eller-Cin	38	Rudolph-Bos	24	Fisher-Cin	5		
		Adams-Pit	.630	J.Barnes-NY	38						

Innings Pitched		Fewest Hits/Game		Fewest BB/Game		Strikeouts		Strikeouts/Game		Ratio	
Vaughn-Chi	306.2	Alexander-Chi	6.89	Adams-Pit	.79	Vaughn-Chi	141	Eller-Cin	4.97	Adams-Pit	8.17
J.Barnes-NY	295.2	Cooper-Pit	7.19	Sallee-Cin	.79	Eller-Cin	137	Alexander-Chi	4.63	Alexander-Chi	8.35
Cooper-Pit	286.2	Ruether-Cin	7.23	J.Barnes-NY	1.07	Alexander-Chi	121	Meadows-StL-Phi	4.17	J.Barnes-NY	9.13
Rudolph-Bos	273.2	Carlson-Pit	7.28	Cadore-Bro	1.40	Meadows-StL-Phi	116	Vaughn-Chi	4.14	Fisher-Cin	9.29
Nehf-Bos-NY	270.2	Fisher-Cin	7.28	Alexander-Chi	1.46	Cooper-Pit	106	Grimes-Bro	4.07	Miller-Pit	9.33

Earned Run Average		Adjusted ERA		Opponents' Batting Avg.		Opponents' On Base Pct.		Starter Runs		Adjusted Starter Runs	
Alexander-Chi	1.72	Alexander-Chi	167	Alexander-Chi	.211	Adams-Pit	.241	Vaughn-Chi	38.1	Vaughn-Chi	37.0
Vaughn-Chi	1.79	Vaughn-Chi	161	Adams-Pit	.220	Alexander-Chi	.245	Alexander-Chi	31.0	Adams-Pit	30.3
Ruether-Cin	1.82	Ruether-Cin	152	Ruether-Cin	.223	J.Barnes-NY	.260	Ruether-Cin	29.4	Alexander-Chi	30.1
Toney-NY	1.84	Toney-NY	152	Cooper-Pit	.225	Fisher-Cin	.271	Adams-Pit	27.1	Ruether-Cin	25.7
Adams-Pit	1.98	Adams-Pit	152	Nehf-Bos-NY	.225	Miller-Pit	.272	Rudolph-Bos	22.5	Rudolph-Bos	20.8

Clutch Pitching Index		Relief Runs		Adjusted Relief Runs		Relief Ranking		Total Pitcher Index		Total Baseball Ranking	
Rudolph-Bos	141							Alexander-Chi	4.4	Maranville-Bos	4.7
Smith-Bro	141							Vaughn-Chi	4.2	Hornsby-StL	4.5
Martin-Chi	122							Ruether-Cin	3.1	Alexander-Chi	4.4
Jacobs-Phi-StL	122							Rudolph-Bos	2.9	Stock-StL	4.3
Toney-NY	120							Adams-Pit	2.7	Vaughn-Chi	4.2

March 1 Connie Mack makes one of his biggest player mistakes, trading third baseman Larry Gardner, outfielder Charlie Jamieson, and pitcher Elmer Myers to Cleveland for outfielder Robert "Braggo" Roth. Roth will be shipped on to Boston by midseason. Gardner will put in six more .300 years, and Jamieson will be a top leadoff man and .303 hitter for the next 14 years.

July 13 Submarine pitcher Carl Mays quits the mound after two innings at Chicago, blaming his teammates for lack of support afield. In defiance of Ban Johnson's order that no action be taken until Mays is returned to good standing, Boston owner Harry Frazee trades Mays to the Yankees for pitchers Bob McGraw, Allen Russell and $40,000. Johnson suspends Mays indefinitely and orders umpires not to let him pitch for New York. The Yankees get a court order restraining Johnson from interfering, further eroding Johnson's authority and standing. The AL directors will reinstate Mays. In retaliation, on Oct. 29 the National Commission will refuse to recognize the Yankees' third-place finish and will withhold the players' share of the pool. New York's owners will pay out of their own pockets.

August 14 Chicago White Sox center fielder Oscar "Happy" Felsch ties the major league record with four outfield assists in one game, but Boston beats the White Sox, 15-6.

August 20* Wichita outfielder Joe Wilhoit (Western League) fails to get a hit, ending a 69-game streak in which he collected 155 hits in 299 at bats for a .505 batting average. The previous record was 49 by Oakland's Jack Ness (Pacific Coast League) in 1915.

August 24 Cleveland pitcher Ray Caldwell is flattened by a bolt of lightning in his debut with the team. He recovers to get the final out of the game, and defeats Philadelphia, 2-1. Two weeks later he no-hits the Yankees.

September 20 Babe Ruth ties Ned Williamson's major league home run mark of 27 with a game-winner off Lefty Williams of the White Sox. Four days later he will hit No. 28 over the roof of the Polo Grounds.

October 1 Just before the start of the World Series, the highly favored White Sox became the betting underdogs. A year later the White Sox will become known as the Black Sox. Eight of them—pitchers Eddie Cicotte and Lefty Williams, outfielders Joe Jackson and Happy Felsch, first baseman Chick Gandil, shortstop Swede Risberg, third baseman Buck Weaver, and utility infielder Fred McMullin—will be barred from baseball for taking part in throwing the World Series.

October 7 Happy Felsch's error and two boots by Swede Risberg help put Dickie Kerr in the hole, 4-0, but Felsch, Weaver, and Jackson combine for seven hits as the Sox win, 5-4. Dutch Ruether doesn't survive the sixth; Jimmy Ring is the loser, as Kerr wins his second game.

October 8 Ed Cicotte pitches Game 7, and the Sox play like they mean it. Joe Jackson and Felsch drive in two each for a 4-1 win.

December 26 Although it will not be officially announced until January, the Yankees buy Babe Ruth from financially pressed Harry Frazee, paying $100,000 (one-fourth cash, plus $25,000 a year at 6 percent) plus guaranteeing a $300,000 loan with Fenway Park as collateral.

	BOSTON		CHICAGO		CLEVELAND		DETROIT		NEW YORK		PHILADELPHIA		ST.LOUIS		WASHINGTON
M	E.Barrow	M	K.Gleason	M	L.Fohl	M	H.Jennings	M	M.Huggins	M	C.Mack	M	J.Burke	M	C.Griffith
1B	S.McInnis	1B	C.Gandil	M	T.Speaker	1B	H.Heilmann	1B	W.Pipp	1B	G.Burns	1B	G.Sisler	1B	J.Judge
2B	R.Shannon	2B	E.Collins	1B	D.Johnston	2B	R.Young	2B	D.Pratt	2B	W.Witt	2B	J.Gedeon	2B	H.Janvrin
SS	E.Scott	SS	S.Risberg	2B	B.Wambsganss	SS	D.Bush	SS	R.Peckinpaugh	SS	J.Dugan	SS	W.Gerber	SS	H.Shanks
3B	O.Vitt	3B	B.Weaver	SS	R.Chapman	3B	B.Jones	3B	F.Baker	3B	F.Thomas	3B	J.Austin	3B	E.Foster
LF	B.Ruth	LF	J.Jackson	3B	L.Gardner	LF	B.Veach	LF	D.Lewis	LF	M.Kopp	LF	J.Tobin	LF	M.Menosky
CF	B.Roth	CF	H.Felsch	LF	J.Graney	CF	T.Cobb	CF	P.Bodie	CF	T.Walker	CF	B.Jacobson	CF	C.Milan
RF	H.Hooper	RF	N.Leibold	CF	T.Speaker	RF	I.Flagstead	RF	S.Vick	RF	A.Strunk	RF	E.Smith	RF	S.Rice
C	W.Schang	C	R.Schalk	RF	E.Smith	C	E.Ainsmith	C	M.Ruel	C	C.Perkins	C	H.Severeid	C	V.Picinich
				C	S.O'Neill										
O	A.Strunk	O	S.Collins			O	C.Shorten	OS	C.Fewster	O	B.Roth	O	K.Williams	CO	P.Gharrity
O	B.Lamar	3	F.McMullin	O	J.Wood	2O	B.Ellison	1O	T.Hannah	1O	D.Burrus	O	R.Demmitt	O	B.Murphy
C	R.Walters	C	B.Lynn	1	J.Harris	C	O.Stanage	O	A.Wickland	C	W.McAvoy	32	H.Bronkie	23	J.Leonard
1O	D.Gainer	/O	E.Murphy	S	H.Lunte	3S	B.Dyer	/1	A.Ward	2	R.Shannon	C	J.Billings	S	F.Ellerbe
O	F.Gilhooley	/C	J.Jenkins	C	L.Nunamaker	/C	A.Yelle	/O	G.Halas	S2	T.Turner	O	T.Sloan	S	S.Agnew
2	J.Barry	/3	H.McClellan	C	P.Thomas	R	S.Dowd	/O	B.Lamar	1	I.Griffin	C	W.Mayer	2	R.Grover
2	D.Shean			/S	J.Evans			/O	F.Gleich	S	C.Galloway	3	J.Schepner	S	G.McBride
S3	M.McNally	P	E.Cicotte			P	H.Dauss	/O	F.Hofmann	O	A.Wingo	/2	J.Shovlin	/2	B.Harris
/O	J.Wilhoit	P	L.Williams	P	S.Coveleski	P	H.Ehmke	H	F.Kane	2	R.Grover	/C	P.Collins	/S	I.Davis
/C	N.McNeil	P	D.Kerr	P	J.Bagby	P	B.Boland	H	C.Walker	O	F.Welch	/S	G.Robertson	/3	C.Davidson
		P	R.Faber	P	G.Morton	P	D.Leonard			2	J.Dykes			/3	D.Silva
P	S.Jones	P	G.Lowdermilk	P	E.Myers	P	D.Ayers	P	J.Quinn	/3	A.Ewoldt	P	A.Sothoron	/O	G.Twombly
P	H.Pennock	RP	D.Danforth	P	G.Uhle	RP	G.Cunningham	P	B.Shawkey	/O	C.High	P	B.Gallia	H	F.Kelliher
P	C.Mays			RP	T.Phillips			P	H.Thormahlen	/O	B.Allen	P	U.Shocker	/S	J.Baker
P	A.Russell	P	B.James			P	S.Love	P	G.Mogridge	/C	L.Styles	P	C.Weilman		
P	W.Hoyt	/P	F.Shellenback	P	H.Jasper	P	R.Kallio	P	C.Mays	/2	S.Dowd	P	D.Davenport	P	J.Shaw
		/P	E.Mayer	P	J.Enzmann	/P	E.Erickson			/C	J.Walker	RP	E.Koob	P	W.Johnson
P	R.Caldwell	/P	R.Wilkinson	/P	R.Caldwell	/P	W.Mitchell	P	E.Shore	/3	L.Groh	RP	R.Wright	P	H.Harper
P	B.James	/P	J.Sullivan	/P	F.Coumbe	/P	B.James	P	A.Russell					P	E.Erickson
P	G.Dumont	/P	W.Noyes	/P	T.Faeth			P	P.Schneider	P	R.Naylor	P	L.Leifield		
P	B.McGraw	/P	T.McGuire	/P	C.Jamieson			/P	L.Nelson	P	W.Kinney	/P	R.Mapel	P	T.Zachary
/P	P.Musser	/P	J.Benz	/P	E.Klepfer			/P	W.Smallwood	P	J.Johnson	/P	E.Vangilder	P	M.Craft
/P	J.Bush	/P	C.Robertson	/P	J.Engel			/P	B.McGraw	P	S.Perry	/P	B.Bayne	P	D.Ayers
/P	G.Winn	/P	P.Ragan					/P	L.O'Doul	P	T.Rogers	/P	G.Lowdermilk	P	H.Thompson
		/P	R.Russell									/P	H.Haid	P	E.Gill
										P	W.Noyes	/P	T.Rogers	/P	D.Robertson
										P	S.Seibold			/P	H.Courtney
										/P	B.Geary			/P	A.Schacht
										/P	J.Zinn			/P	C.Whitehouse
										/P	C.Eckert			/P	B.Snyder
										/P	D.Boone			/P	E.Hovlik
										/P	W.Anderson			/P	C.Fisher
										/P	R.Roberts			/P	R.Jordan
										/P	M.Watson			/P	N.Altrock
										/P	B.Grevell				
										/P	B.Hasty				
										/P	H.Thompson				
										/P	P.Martin				
										/P	D.Keefe				
										/P	M.Kircher				
										/P	W.Pierson				
										/P	W.Adams				
										/P	L.York				

TEAM	G	W	L	PCT	GB	R	OR	AB	H	2B	3B	HR	BB	SO	AVG	OBP	SLG	PRO	PRO+	BR	/A	PF	CHI	RC	SB	CS	SBA	SBR
CHI	140	88	52	.629		667	534	4675	1343	218	70	25	427	358	.287	.351	.380	.731	111	69	66	100	103	668	150			
CLE	139	84	55	.604	3.5	636	537	4565	1268	254	72	24	498	367	.278	.354	.381	.735	107	78	39	106	98	651	113			
NY	141	80	59	.576	7.5	578	506	4775	1275	193	49	45	386	479	.267	.326	.356	.682	96	-20	-24	101	104	575	101			
DET	140	80	60	.571	8	618	578	4665	1319	222	84	23	429	427	.283	.346	.381	.727	113	60	75	98	97	649	121			
STL	140	67	72	.482	20.5	533	567	4672	1234	187	73	31	391	443	.264	.326	.355	.681	95	-22	-36	103	97	560	74			
BOS	138	66	71	.482	20.5	564	552	4548	1188	181	49	33	471	411	.261	.336	.344	.680	103	-11	21	94	102	559	108			
WAS	142	56	84	.400	32	533	570	4757	1238	177	63	24	416	511	.260	.325	.339	.664	93	-47	-42	99	100	558	142			
PHI	140	36	104	.257	52	457	742	4730	1156	175	71	35	349	565	.244	.300	.334	.634	82	-108	-113	101	100	487	103			
TOT	560					4586		37387	10021	1607	531	240	3367	3561	.268	.333	.359	.692						912				

TEAM	CG	SH	SV	IP	H	H/G	HR	BB	SO	RAT	ERA	ERA+	OAV	OOB	PR	/A	PF	CPI	FA	E	DP	FW	PW	BW	SBW	DIF
CHI	88	14	3	1265²	1245	8.9	24	342	468	11.5	3.04	105	.262	.315	26	19	99	92	.969	176	116	1.6	2.0	6.9		7.5
CLE	80	10	10	1245	1242	9.0	19	362	432	11.8	2.94	114	.264	.321	39	53	104	98	.965	201	102	-.0	5.5	4.1		4.9
NY	85	14	7	1287	1143	8.0	47	433	500	11.3	2.82	113	.240	.309	58	53	99	92	.968	193	108	.7	5.5	-2.5		6.8
DET	85	10	4	1256	1254	9.0	35	436	428	12.4	3.30	97	.266	.333	-11	-14	99	98	.964	205	81	-.2	-1.5	7.8		3.8
STL	78	14	4	1256	1255	9.0	35	421	415	12.3	3.13	106	.263	.328	13	24	103	99	.963	215	98	-.8	2.5	-3.8		-.4
BOS	89	15	8	1224¹	1251	9.2	16	421	381	12.5	3.31	91	.275	.341	-12	-41	94	101	.975	140	118	3.8	-4.3	2.2		-4.2
WAS	68	13	10	1274¹	1237	8.7	20	451	536	12.2	3.01	106	.259	.328	30	28	99	99	.960	227	86	-1.4	2.9	-4.4		-11.1
PHI	72	1	3	1239¹	1371	10.0	44	503	417	13.8	4.26	80	.292	.364	-143	-118	106	96	.956	257	96	-3.5	-12.4	-11.8		-6.3
TOT	645	91	49	10047²		9.0				12.2	3.22		.268	.333					.965	1614	805					

Runs
- Ruth-Bos 103
- Sisler-StL 96
- Cobb-Det 92
- Weaver-Chi........ 89
- Peckinpaugh-NY ... 89

Hits
- Veach-Det 191
- Cobb-Det 191
- Jackson-Chi 181
- Sisler-StL 180
- Rice-Was 179

Doubles
- Veach-Det 45
- Speaker-Cle 38
- Cobb-Det 36
- O'Neill-Cle 35

Triples
- Veach-Det 17
- Sisler-StL 15
- Heilmann-Det 15
- Jackson-Chi 14
- Cobb-Det 13

Home Runs
- Ruth-Bos 29
- T.Walker-Phi 10
- Sisler-StL 10
- Baker-NY 10
- Smith-Cle 9

Total Bases
- Ruth-Bos 284
- Veach-Det 279
- Sisler-StL 271
- Jackson-Chi 261

Runs Batted In
- Ruth-Bos 114
- Veach-Det 101
- Jackson-Chi 96
- Heilmann-Det 93
- Lewis-NY 89

Runs Produced
- Ruth-Bos 188
- Veach-Det 185
- Sisler-StL 169
- Jackson-Chi 168
- E.Collins-Chi 163

Bases On Balls
- Graney-Cle 105
- Ruth-Bos 101
- Judge-Was 81
- Hooper-Bos 79
- Bush-Det 75

Batting Average
- Cobb-Det .... .384
- Veach-Det ..... .355
- Sisler-StL ..... .352
- Jackson-Chi ..... .351
- Flagstead-Det ..... .331

On Base Percentage
- Ruth-Bos .... .456
- Cobb-Det ..... .429
- Jackson-Chi ..... .422
- Leibold-Chi ..... .404
- E.Collins-Chi ..... .400

Slugging Average
- Ruth-Bos .... .657
- Sisler-StL ..... .530
- Veach-Det ..... .519
- Cobb-Det ..... .515
- Jackson-Chi ..... .506

Production
- Ruth-Bos 1.114
- Cobb-Det ..... .944
- Jackson-Chi ..... .928
- Sisler-StL ..... .921
- Veach-Det ..... .916

Adjusted Production
- Ruth-Bos 224
- Cobb-Det 168
- Veach-Det 160
- Jackson-Chi 159
- Sisler-StL 153

Batter Runs
- Ruth-Bos 66.5
- Jackson-Chi 41.7
- Cobb-Det 41.6
- Veach-Det 37.7
- Sisler-StL 35.8

Adjusted Batter Runs
- Ruth-Bos 74.0
- Cobb-Det 44.0
- Jackson-Chi 41.3
- Veach-Det 40.1
- Sisler-StL 33.4

Clutch Hitting Index
- E.Collins-Chi 143
- Lewis-NY 131
- Jones-Det 130
- Shanks-Was 123
- Gardner-Cle 123

Runs Created
- Ruth-Bos 128
- Cobb-Det 116
- Veach-Det 115
- Sisler-StL 112
- Jackson-Chi 111

Total Average
- Ruth-Bos 1.358
- Cobb-Det 1.056
- Sisler-StL 1.000
- Jackson-Chi ..... .997
- Veach-Det ..... .968

Stolen Bases
- E.Collins-Chi 33
- Sisler-StL 28
- Cobb-Det 28
- Rice-Was 26

Stolen Base Average

Stolen Base Runs

Fielding Runs
- Pratt-NY 28.0
- Peckinpaugh-NY ... 27.7
- Felsch-Chi 21.4
- Speaker-Cle 19.1
- Young-Det 17.3

Total Player Rating
- Ruth-Bos 6.3
- Peckinpaugh-NY ... 5.1
- Sisler-StL 4.3
- Veach-Det 4.3
- Pratt-NY 3.8

Wins
- Cicotte-Chi 29
- Coveleski-Cle 24
- Williams-Chi 23
- Dauss-Det 21

Win Percentage
- Cicotte-Chi ..... .806
- Dauss-Det ..... .700
- Williams-Chi ..... .676
- Pennock-Bos ..... .667
- Coveleski-Cle ..... .667

Games
- Shaw-Was 45
- Russell-NY-Bos 44
- Kinney-Phi 43
- Coveleski-Cle 43

Complete Games
- Cicotte-Chi 30
- Williams-Chi 27
- Johnson-Was 27
- Mays-Bos-NY 26
- Coveleski-Cle 24

Shutouts
- Johnson-Was 7

Saves
- Russell-NY-Bos 5
- Shawkey-NY 5
- Shaw-Was 5
- Coveleski-Cle 4

Innings Pitched
- Shaw-Was 306.2
- Cicotte-Chi 306.2
- Williams-Chi 297.0
- Johnson-Was 290.1
- Coveleski-Cle 286.0

Fewest Hits/Game
- Johnson-Was 7.28
- Thormahlen-NY ... 7.39
- Shawkey-NY 7.51
- Cicotte-Chi 7.51
- Mays-Bos-NY 7.68

Fewest BB/Game
- Cicotte-Chi 1.44
- Johnson-Was 1.58
- Bagby-Cle 1.64
- Williams-Chi 1.76
- Coveleski-Cle 1.89

Strikeouts
- Johnson-Was 147
- Shaw-Was 128
- Williams-Chi 125
- Shawkey-NY 122
- Coveleski-Cle 118

Strikeouts/Game
- Erickson-Det-Was . 5.52
- Russell-NY-Bos 4.80
- Johnson-Was 4.56
- Kinney-Phi 4.31
- Leonard-Det 4.22

Ratio
- Cicotte-Chi 9.01
- Johnson-Was 9.08
- Williams-Chi 10.12
- Thormahlen-NY ... 10.49
- Quinn-NY 10.59

Earned Run Average
- Johnson-Was 1.49
- Cicotte-Chi 1.82
- Weilman-StL 2.07
- Mays-Bos-NY 2.10
- Sothoron-StL 2.20

Adjusted ERA
- Johnson-Was 215
- Cicotte-Chi 175
- Weilman-StL 160
- Sothoron-StL 151
- Mays-Bos-NY 147

Opponents' Batting Avg.
- Johnson-Was ..... .219
- Cicotte-Chi ..... .228
- Thormahlen-NY ... .228
- Shawkey-NY ..... .231
- Mays-Bos-NY ..... .233

Opponents' On Base Pct.
- Johnson-Was ..... .259
- Cicotte-Chi ..... .261
- Williams-Chi ..... .289
- Morton-Cle ..... .293
- Quinn-NY ..... .295

Starter Runs
- Johnson-Was 56.0
- Cicotte-Chi 47.8
- Mays-Bos-NY 33.3
- Sothoron-StL 30.7
- Coveleski-Cle 19.4

Adjusted Starter Runs
- Johnson-Was 55.3
- Cicotte-Chi 46.3
- Sothoron-StL 33.4
- Mays-Bos-NY 29.4
- Coveleski-Cle 23.2

Clutch Pitching Index
- Weilman-StL 119
- Sothoron-StL 114
- Ehmke-Det 113
- Harper-Was 107
- Pennock-Bos 107

Relief Runs
- Phillips-Cle 1.7

Adjusted Relief Runs
- Phillips-Cle 2.4

Relief Ranking
- Phillips-Cle 2.0

Total Pitcher Index
- Johnson-Was 7.2
- Cicotte-Chi 5.2
- Mays-Bos-NY 3.8
- Coveleski-Cle 3.6
- Sothoron-StL 3.1

Total Baseball Ranking
- Ruth-Bos 7.9
- Johnson-Was 7.1
- Cicotte-Chi 5.2
- Peckinpaugh-NY ... 5.1
- Sisler-StL 4.3

January 12 A plan developed by Charles Ebbets many years ago is finally adopted: the annual drafting of players from the minor leagues will be done in inverse order to the teams' final standings.

February 9 The Joint Rules Committee bans all foreign substances or other alterations to the ball by pitchers, including saliva, resin, talcum powder, paraffin, and the shine and emery ball. A pitcher caught cheating will be suspended for 10 days. The NL allows each club to name all its spitball pitchers. No pitchers other than those designated will be permitted to use it, and none at all after 1920. Other rules changes: the adoption of writer Fred Lieb's proposal that a game-winning homer with men on base be counted as a homer even if its run is not needed to win the game. Also, the intentional walk is banned, and everything that happens in a protested game will go in the records.

April 20 Phils' manager Gavvy Cravath inserts himself as a pinch hitter and hits a three-run home run, his last, to beat the Giants 3-0.

May 1 In Boston, Brooklyn's Leon Cadore and the Braves' Joe Oeschger duel 26 innings to a 1-1 tie in the longest game ever played in the major leagues. The Dodgers lose to the Phils at home in 13 innings the next day, then return to Boston for a Monday game where they lose again in 19. For 58 innings work in three days, they are 0-2.

September 17 The Cards set a record by cracking out 12 consecutive hits in the fourth and fifth innings against the Braves. Ten of the hits occur in the fourth inning when St. Louis scores eight runs. The last two outs come as Milt Stock tries to stretch a single into a double, and Austin McHenry tries for an extra base on a double; both are thrown out. In the fifth inning, Doc Lavan opens with a double, and, Cliff Heathcote singles before a Redbird finally makes an out. St. Louis wins, 9-4.

October 2 The Pirates and Reds, battling to determine second and third place, play a tripleheader in Pittsburgh. Starting at noon, the Reds win the first two, 13-4 and 7-3, and the Pirates take the finale, 6-0.

October 6 When Wheeler Johnston pinch-hits for Cleveland in the ninth inning of Game 2, his brother Jimmy is playing third baseman for Brooklyn. They become the first brothers to take opposite sides in a World Series. Spitballer Burleigh Grimes (23-11) strands 10 Indians while the Robins chip away at Jim Bagby (31-12) for three single tallies and a 3-0 Series evener.

November 8 At a meeting to depose Ban Johnson, a new 12-team National League, made up of the dissenting 11 teams plus one of the five teams loyal to Johnson, is proposed and agreed to. John Heydler will be its president and Judge Kenesaw Mountain Landis the proposed chairman of the new commission. With no stomach for another war, four of the five AL clubs still backing Johnson agree to a joint meeting.

November 12 With Johnson barred from the meeting, the 16 major league clubs settle their differences. The 12-team-league idea is discarded, and the two leagues will continue with their old identities. The owners unanimously elect Kenesaw Mountain Landis chairman for seven years. Judge Landis accepts, but only as sole commissioner with final authority over the players and owners, while remaining a federal judge (with his $7,500 federal salary deducted from the baseball salary of $50,000). The agreement will be signed on Jan. 12, 1921, when he is to begin his duties.

December 6 A five-year-old lawsuit that awarded $264,000 damages to the Baltimore Federal League club on April 12, 1919, is reversed by a court of appeals, which upholds the reserve clause and holds that baseball is not interstate commerce nor subject to antitrust laws. The original suit was initiated because the Baltimore Feds were not included in the settlement of the Federal League war. They wanted a major league team in Baltimore and did not get it.

December 15 The NL reveals a most telling statistic, pointing out the changes in the game: the use of 27,924 baseballs during the season, an increase of 10,248 over 1919.

	BOSTON		BROOKLYN		CHICAGO		CINCINNATI		NEW YORK		PHILADELPHIA		PITTSBURGH		ST.LOUIS
M	G.Stallings	M	W.Robinson	M	F.Mitchell	M	P.Moran	M	J.McGraw	M	G.Cravath	M	M.Gibson	M	B.Rickey
1B	W.Holke	1B	E.Konetchy	1B	F.Merkle	1B	J.Daubert	1B	G.Kelly	1B	G.Paulette	1B	C.Grimm	1B	J.Fournier
2B	C.Pick	2B	P.Kilduff	2B	Z.Terry	2B	M.Rath	2B	L.Doyle	2B	J.Rawlings	2B	G.Cutshaw	2B	R.Hornsby
SS	R.Maranville	SS	I.Olson	SS	C.Hollocher	SS	L.Kopf	SS	D.Bancroft	SS	A.Fletcher	SS	H.Caton	SS	D.Lavan
3B	T.Boeckel	3B	J.Johnston	3B	C.Deal	3B	H.Groh	3B	F.Frisch	3B	R.Miller	3B	P.Whitted	3B	M.Stock
LF	L.Mann	LF	Z.Wheat	LF	D.Robertson	LF	P.Duncan	LF	G.Burns	LF	I.Meusel	LF	C.Bigbee	LF	A.McHenry
CF	R.Powell	CF	H.Myers	CF	D.Paskert	CF	E.Roush	CF	L.King	CF	C.Williams	CF	M.Carey	CF	J.Smith
RF	W.Cruise	RF	T.Griffith	RF	M.Flack	RF	G.Neale	RF	R.Youngs	RF	C.Stengel	RF	B.Southworth	RF	C.Heathcote
C	M.O'Neil	C	O.Miller	C	B.O'Farrell	C	I.Wingo	C	F.Snyder	C	M.Wheat	C	W.Schmidt	C	V.Clemons
2S	H.Ford	O	B.Neis	1O	T.Barber	S3	S.Crane	C	E.Smith	23	D.Miller	O	F.Nicholson	C	J.Schultz
O	J.Sullivan	C	E.Krueger	23	B.Herzog	2	E.Sicking	S	A.Fletcher	O	B.LeBourveau	S2	W.Barbare	S1	H.Janvrin
O	E.Eayrs	C	R.Elliott	C	B.Killefer	C	B.Rariden	3	B.Kauff	3	R.Wrightstone	C	B.Haeffner	C	P.Dillhoefer
C	H.Gowdy	S	C.Ward	O	B.Twombly	C	N.Allen	O	V.Spencer	3S	W.Tragesser	3S	B.McKechnie	S	B.Shotton
O	L.Christenbury	S	B.McCabe	2O	B.Friberg	O	C.See	32	E.Sicking	C	D.Bancroft	C	C.Lee	/O	M.Knode
/O	G.Bailey	1	R.Schmandt	C	T.Daly			3	F.Lear	C	F.Withrow	S	P.Traynor	/O	H.Mueller
/3	A.Wilson	O	B.Lamar	2	W.Marriott	P	J.Ring	2	R.Grimes	/O	G.Cravath	3	C.Barnhart	/C	L.McCarty
/1	R.Torphy	/O	W.Hood	/S	H.Leathers	/C	D.Ruether	/C	L.McCarty	/1	F.Luderus	2	C.Tierney	/C	G.Gilham
/2	J.Rawlings	/C	Z.Taylor	/3	S.Clarke	P	R.Bressler	O	J.Statz	R	W.Walsh	/O	H.Summa	/C	T.Griesenbeck
/1	T.Whelan	/3	D.Baird	H	B.McCabe	/P	H.Eller	/S	A.Lefevre			H	B.Hinchman	/C	B.Schindler
R	O.Dugey	/S	J.Sheehan			P	D.Luque	/O	C.Walker	P	E.Rixey	/C	N.Clarke	/O	E.Hock
		/S	R.Sheridan	P	P.Alexander	P	R.Fisher	/O	M.Gonzalez	P	G.Smith	H	W.Hood		
P	J.Oeschger			P	H.Vaughn			/C	A.Gaston	P	L.Meadows			P	J.Haines
P	J.Scott	P	B.Grimes	P	C.Hendrix	P	S.Sallee	/3	D.Baird	P	R.Causey	P	W.Cooper	P	B.Doak
P	D.Fillingim	P	L.Cadore	P	L.Tyler	/P	B.Napier	/O	E.Brown	P	B.Hubbell	P	B.Adams	P	F.Schupp
P	H.McQuillan	P	J.Pfeffer	P	S.Martin	P	R.Bressler	/O	P.Griffin			P	H.Carlson	P	B.Sherdel
		P	A.Mamaux			/P	L.Brenton	/O	B.Kinsella	P	H.Betts	P	E.Hamilton	P	M.Goodwin
P	D.Rudolph	P	R.Marquard	P	P.Carter	/P	F.Coumbe	P	M.Swartz	P	B.Gallia	P	E.Ponder		
/P	M.Watson			P	S.Bailey	/P	G.Lowe			P	J.Enzmann			P	L.North
P	B.Hearn	P	S.Smith	/P	V.Cheeves	/P	J.Theis	P	J.Barnes	P	J.Wisner			P	E.Jacobs
/P	A.Pierotti	P1	C.Mitchell	/C	C.Gaw			P	A.Nehf	/P	M.Cantwell	P	J.Wisner	/P	J.May
/P	L.Townsend	P	G.Mohart	/P	C.Jones			P	F.Toney	P	L.Weinert	P	J.Meador	/P	M.Kircher
/P	J.Jones	/P	J.Miljus	/P	J.Newkirk			P	P.Douglas	/P	J.Keenan	/P	J.Zinn	/P	G.Lyons
/P	I.Townsend			/P	J.Jaeger			P	R.Benton			/P	S.Blake	/P	H.Kime
				/P	T.Turner							/P	W.Glazner	/P	W.Schulz
								P	J.Winters			/P	J.Morrison	/P	G.Scott
								P	B.Hubbell					/P	B.Glenn
								/P	S.Sallee					/P	O.Tuero
								/P	P.Perritt						
								/P	R.Ryan						
								/P	V.Barnes						
								/P	T.Grubbs						
								/P	C.Davenport						

TEAM	G	W	L	PCT	GB	R	OR	AB	H	2B	3B	HR	BB	SO	AVG	OBP	SLG	PRO	PRO+	BR	/A	PF	CHI	RC	SB	CS	SBA	SBR
BRO	155	93	61	.604		660	528	5399	1493	205	28	99	359	391	.277	.324	.367	.691	100	19	-2	103	103	637	70	80	47	-27
NY	155	86	68	.558	7	682	543	5309	1427	210	76	46	432	545	.269	.327	.363	.690	104	23	30	99	107	628	131	113	54	-29
CIN	154	82	71	.536	10.5	639	569	5176	1432	169	76	18	382	367	.277	.332	.349	.681	102	11	0	99	104	602	158	128	55	-29
PIT	155	79	75	.513	14	530	552	5219	1342	162	90	16	374	405	.257	.310	.332	.642	86	-67	-84	103	99	544	181	117	61	-16
STL	155	75	79	.487	18	675	682	5495	1589	238	96	32	373	484	.289	.337	.385	.722	117	83	110		94	704	126	114	53	-31
CHI	154	75	79	.487	18	619	635	5117	1350	223	67	34	428	421	.264	.326	.354	.680	98	7	-5	102	101	589	115	129	47	-43
BOS	153	62	90	.408	30	523	670	5218	1358	168	86	23	385	488	.260	.315	.339	.654	97	-45	-21	96	93	557	88	98	47	-32
PHI	153	62	91	.405	30.5	565	714	5264	1385	229	54	64	283	531	.263	.305	.364	.669	93	-30	-57	105	99	577	100	83	55	-20
TOT	617					4893		42197	11376	1604	644	261	3016	3632	.270	.322	.357	.679							969	862	53	-227

TEAM	CG	SH	SV	IP	H	H/G	HR	BB	SO	RAT	ERA	ERA+	OAV	OOB	PR	/A	PF	CPI	FA	E	DP	FW	PW	BW	SBW	DIF
BRO	89	17	10	1427¹	1381	8.7	25	327	553	10.9	2.62	122	.259	.304	81	91	102	102	.966	226	118	-.2	9.7	-.2	.1	6.5
NY	86	18	9	1408²	1379	8.8	44	297	380	10.8	2.80	107	.261	.303	51	30	96	99	.969	210	137	.8	3.2	3.2	-.0	1.9
CIN	90	12	9	1391²	1327	8.6	26	393	435	11.3	2.90	105	.256	.313	36	22	97	97	.968	200	125	1.3	2.4	2.1	-.0	-.2
PIT	92	17	10	1415¹	1389	8.8	25	280	444	10.8	2.89	111	.261	.301	39	51	103	91	.971	186	119	2.2	5.5	-9.0	1.3	2.0
STL	72	9	12	1426²	1488	9.4	30	479	529	12.8	3.43	87	.277	.343	-47	-72	95	103	.961	256	136	-2.0	-7.7	11.8	-.3	-3.8
CHI	95	13	9	1388²	1459	9.5	37	382	508	12.1	3.27	98	.276	.328	-21	-10	102	102	.965	225	112	-.2	-1.1	-.5	-1.6	1.4
BOS	93	14	6	1386¹	1464	9.5	39	415	368	12.4	3.54	86	.280	.337	-62	-75	97	100	.964	239	125	-1.1	-8.0	-2.2	-.4	-2.2
PHI	77	8	11	1380²	1480	9.6	35	444	419	12.8	3.63	94	.284	.345	-76	-35	109	102	.964	232	135	-.7	-3.7	-6.1	.9	-4.8
TOT	694	108	76	11225¹		9.1				11.7	3.13		.270	.322					.966	1774	1007					

Runs		Hits		Doubles		Triples		Home Runs		Total Bases	
Burns-NY	115	Hornsby-StL	218	Hornsby-StL	44	Myers-Bro	22	Williams-Phi	15	Hornsby-StL	329
Bancroft-Phi-NY	102	Youngs-NY	204	Bancroft-Phi-NY	36	Hornsby-StL	20	Meusel-Phi	14	Williams-Phi	293
Daubert-Cin	97	Stock-StL	204	Williams-Phi	36	Roush-Cin	16	Kelly-NY	11	Youngs-NY	277
Hornsby-StL	96	Roush-Cin	196	Myers-Bro	36	Maranville-Bos	15	Robertson-Chi	10	Wheat-Bro	270
Youngs-NY	92	Williams-Phi	192	Burns-NY	35	Bigbee-Pit	15	McHenry-StL	10	Myers-Bro	269

Runs Batted In		Runs Produced		Bases On Balls		Batting Average		On Base Percentage		Slugging Average	
Kelly-NY	94	Hornsby-StL	181	Burns-NY	76	Hornsby-StL	.370	Hornsby-StL	.431	Hornsby-StL	.559
Hornsby-StL	94	Roush-Cin	167	Youngs-NY	75	Nicholson-Pit	.360	Youngs-NY	.427	Nicholson-Pit	.530
Roush-Cin	90	Youngs-NY	164	Paskert-Chi	64	Youngs-NY	.351	Roush-Cin	.386	Williams-Phi	.497
Duncan-Cin	83	Stock-StL	161	Hornsby-StL	60	Roush-Cin	.339	Wheat-Bro	.385	Youngs-NY	.477
Myers-Bro	80	Myers-Bro	159	Groh-Cin	60	Wheat-Bro	.328	Groh-Cin	.375	Meusel-Phi	.473

Production		Adjusted Production		Batter Runs		Adjusted Batter Runs		Clutch Hitting Index		Runs Created	
Hornsby-StL	.990	Hornsby-StL	190	Hornsby-StL	62.6	Hornsby-StL	67.6	Whitted-Pit	151	Hornsby-StL	138
Youngs-NY	.904	Youngs-NY	161	Youngs-NY	47.1	Youngs-NY	48.4	Kopf-Cin	147	Youngs-NY	118
Williams-Phi	.861	Roush-Cin	142	Williams-Phi	32.1	Roush-Cin	31.1	Duncan-Cin	131	Williams-Phi	103
Wheat-Bro	.848	Williams-Phi	139	Wheat-Bro	31.9	Wheat-Bro	28.8	Roush-Cin	126	Wheat-Bro	102
Roush-Cin	.839	Wheat-Bro	138	Roush-Cin	29.7	Williams-Phi	27.5	Kelly-NY	122	Roush-Cin	98

Total Average		Stolen Bases		Stolen Base Average		Stolen Base Runs		Fielding Runs		Total Player Rating	
Hornsby-StL	1.008	Carey-Pit	52	Carey-Pit	83.9	Carey-Pit	9.6	Bancroft-Phi-NY	39.0	Hornsby-StL	8.1
Youngs-NY	.896	Roush-Cin	36	Frisch-NY	75.6	Frisch-NY	3.6	Lavan-StL	16.2	Bancroft-Phi-NY	5.7
Williams-Phi	.817	Frisch-NY	34	Neale-Cin	70.7	Neale-Cin	1.5	Roush-Cin	15.7	Youngs-NY	3.6
Wheat-Bro	.801	Bigbee-Pit	31	Bigbee-Pit	67.4	Tragesser-Phi	1.2	Maranville-Bos	14.3	Roush-Cin	3.4
Roush-Cin	.784	Neale-Cin	29	Meusel-Phi	60.7	Gowdy-Bos	1.2	Neale-Cin	14.3	Hollocher-Chi	2.7

Wins		Win Percentage		Games		Complete Games		Shutouts		Saves	
Alexander-Chi	27	Grimes-Bro	.676	Haines-StL	47	Alexander-Chi	33	Adams-Pit	8	Sherdel-StL	6
Cooper-Pit	24	Alexander-Chi	.659	Douglas-NY	46	Cooper-Pit	28	Alexander-Chi	7	McQuillan-Bos	5
Grimes-Bro	23	Toney-NY	.656	Alexander-Chi	46	Rixey-Phi	25			Alexander-Chi	5
Toney-NY	21	Pfeffer-Bro	.640	Scott-Bos	44	Grimes-Bro	25			Hubbell-NY-Phi	4
Nehf-NY	21	Nehf-NY	.636	Cooper-Pit	44	Vaughn-Chi	24			Mamaux-Bro	4

Innings Pitched		Fewest Hits/Game		Fewest BB/Game		Strikeouts		Strikeouts/Game		Ratio	
Alexander-Chi	363.1	Luque-Cin	7.28	Adams-Pit	.62	Alexander-Chi	173	Mamaux-Bro	4.77	Adams-Pit	8.86
Cooper-Pit	327.0	Ruether-Cin	7.96	Cooper-Pit	1.43	Vaughn-Chi	131	Alexander-Chi	4.29	Alexander-Chi	10.03
Grimes-Bro	303.2	Grimes-Bro	8.03	Nehf-NY	1.44	Grimes-Bro	131	Schupp-StL	4.27	Luque-Cin	10.05
Haines-StL	301.2	Mamaux-Bro	8.12	Benton-NY	1.44	Haines-StL	120	Marquard-Bro	4.22	J.Barnes-NY	10.12
Vaughn-Chi	301.0	Adams-Pit	8.21	Marquard-Bro	1.66	Schupp-StL	119	Sherdel-StL	3.92	Grimes-Bro	10.14

Earned Run Average		Adjusted ERA		Opponents' Batting Avg.		Opponents' On Base Pct.		Starter Runs		Adjusted Starter Runs	
Alexander-Chi	1.91	Alexander-Chi	168	Luque-Cin	.225	Adams-Pit	.259	Alexander-Chi	49.5	Alexander-Chi	52.4
Adams-Pit	2.16	Adams-Pit	149	Grimes-Bro	.238	Grimes-Bro	.282	Grimes-Bro	30.7	Grimes-Bro	33.0
Grimes-Bro	2.22	Grimes-Bro	144	Adams-Pit	.244	Alexander-Chi	.285	Adams-Pit	28.5	Adams-Pit	30.9
Cooper-Pit	2.39	Cooper-Pit	134	Ponder-Pit	.246	Luque-Cin	.286	Cooper-Pit	26.8	Cooper-Pit	29.8
Ruether-Cin	2.47	Vaughn-Chi	126	Ruether-Cin	.247	Ponder-Pit	.286	Vaughn-Chi	19.8	Vaughn-Chi	22.2

Clutch Pitching Index		Relief Runs		Adjusted Relief Runs		Relief Ranking		Total Pitcher Index		Total Baseball Ranking	
Meadows-Phi	121							Alexander-Chi	7.1	Hornsby-StL	8.1
Alexander-Chi	120							Grimes-Bro	5.4	Alexander-Chi	7.1
Vaughn-Chi	119							Smith-Bro	4.0	Bancroft-Phi-NY	5.7
Fillingim-Bos	118							Cooper-Pit	3.2	Grimes-Bro	5.4
Benton-NY	115							Adams-Pit	2.8	Smith-Bro	4.0

February 13* The Negro National League (chartered as the National Association of Colored Professional Baseball Clubs) is organized at a meeting at the YMCA in Kansas City, MO.

May 1 Babe Ruth's first home run as a Yankee clears the roof of the Polo Grounds in a 6-0 win over the Red Sox.

May 14 The Giants inform the Yankees that after the season, their lease will not be renewed. No reason is given but the recent signing of Babe Ruth appears to be the main cause.

June 26* Lou Gehrig gets his first national mention when, as a high school junior for New York City's School of Commerce, he steals the show in a high school championship game against Lane Tech in Chicago. His grand slam in the eighth gives the New York team a 12–8 victory. Scouts sit with open mouths as the ball sails out of Cubs Park (later known as Wrigley Field).

July 1 Walter Johnson pitches a no-hitter, his first, against the Red Sox at Fenway. An error by Bucky Harris costs him a perfect game. The next day Johnson comes up with the first sore arm of his life and is useless for the rest of the year.

July 10 After banging out 11 straight hits, Tris Speaker is stopped by Tom Zachary of Washington. It's the record until Michael "Pinky" Higgins of the Red Sox racks up 12 in a row in 1938.

August 16 At the Polo Grounds Cleveland shortstop Ray Chapman, 29, is beaned by a Carl Mays pitch. A right-handed batter who crowds the plate, Chapman freezes and fails to get out of the way of the submarine delivery. He is carried from the field and dies the next day from a fractured skull.

August 20 The Red Sox-Indians game in Boston is postponed to allow the Cleveland players to attend Ray Chapman's funeral.

September 28 A Chicago grand jury indicts the eight Chicago players in the 1919 World Series scandal. Charles Comiskey immediately suspends them. With the heart of the team sidelined, Chicago will lose two out of their final three games and the Indians win the pennant by two games. Had the grand jury come out with its findings a week later, the White Sox might have won, causing the cancellation of the World Series and the voiding of their pennant. For Cleveland it is their first pennant in any league after 39 years of trying.

September 29 Babe Ruth hits homer No. 54 in Philadelphia as the Yankees win, 7–2. That is more than any other team total except the Phils. He is responsible for 241 of his team's 838 runs, even though he misses 12 games.

October 3 In the Browns' 16-7 win over Chicago, George Sisler gets his 257th hit of the season to set a major league record. He also hurls a scoreless ninth inning in relief.

October 10 In the bottom of the first of an event-filled game, Grimes gives up hits to Charlie Jamieson, Bill Wambsganss, and Tris Speaker. Outfielder Elmer Smith then hits the first grand slam in World Series history. In the third inning pitcher Jim Bagby comes up with two on and crashes another Grimes delivery for a three-run home run, the first ever by a pitcher in World Series play. Bagby is roughed for 13 hits, but he gets out of jams with the aid of three double plays and an unassisted triple play. In the fifth with Pete Kilduff on second base and Otto Miller on first base, relief pitcher Clarence Mitchell hits a line drive at shortstop Wambsganss, who steps on second base and tags the off-and-running Miller before he can retreat. Cleveland dominates, 8-1.

October 12 Stan Coveleski wins his third game of the Series, and the Indians wrap it up, as Brooklyn bats are silent again. Burleigh Grimes is nicked for single scores in the fourth, fifth, and seventh, for a 3-0 loss.

October 23 The Chicago grand jury indictment adds the names of former featherweight boxing champ Abe Attell, Hal Chase, and Bill Burns as go-betweens in the World Series scandal. Confessions, later repudiated, are signed by Ed Cicotte, Joe Jackson, Lefty Williams, and Happy Felsch.

December 17 The AL votes to allow pitchers who used the spitball in 1920 to continue using it as long as they are in the league. The NL will do the same. There will be 17 in all.

	BOSTON		CHICAGO		CLEVELAND		DETROIT		NEW YORK		PHILADELPHIA		ST.LOUIS		WASHINGTON
M	E.Barrow	M	K.Gleason	M	T.Speaker	M	H.Jennings	M	M.Huggins	M	C.Mack	M	J.Burke	M	C.Griffith
1B	S.McInnis	1B	S.Collins	1B	D.Johnston	1B	H.Heilmann	1B	W.Pipp	1B	I.Griffin	1B	G.Sisler	1B	J.Judge
2B	M.McNally	2B	E.Collins	2B	B.Wambsganss	2B	R.Young	2B	D.Pratt	2B	J.Dykes	2B	J.Gedeon	2B	B.Harris
SS	E.Scott	SS	S.Risberg	SS	R.Chapman	SS	D.Bush	SS	R.Peckinpaugh	SS	C.Galloway	SS	W.Gerber	SS	J.O'Neill
3B	E.Foster	3B	B.Weaver	3B	L.Gardner	3B	B.Pinelli	3B	A.Ward	3B	F.Thomas	3B	J.Austin	3B	F.Ellerbe
LF	M.Menosky	LF	J.Jackson	LF	C.Jamieson	LF	B.Veach	LF	D.Lewis	LF	T.Walker	LF	K.Williams	LF	C.Milan
CF	T.Hendryx	CF	H.Felsch	CF	T.Speaker	CF	T.Cobb	CF	P.Bodie	CF	F.Welch	CF	B.Jacobson	CF	S.Rice
RF	H.Hooper	RF	N.Leibold	RF	E.Smith	RF	C.Shorten	RF	B.Ruth	RF	A.Strunk	RF	J.Tobin	RF	B.Roth
C	R.Walters	C	R.Schalk	C	S.O'Neill	C	O.Stanage	C	M.Ruel	C	C.Perkins	C	H.Severeid	C	P.Gharrity
CO	W.Schang	O	A.Strunk	O	J.Evans	O3	I.Flagstead	3S	B.Meusel	3S	J.Dugan	3O	E.Smith	3O	H.Shanks
32	O.Vitt	1	T.Jourdan	O	J.Graney	3	B.Jones	C	T.Hannah	O2	W.Witt	C	J.Billings	S2	R.Shannon
2	C.Brady	3	F.McMullin	O	J.Wood	C	E.Ainsmith	O	S.Vick	OC	G.Myatt	3	F.Thompson	C	V.Picinich
O	G.Bailey	O	E.Murphy	S	H.Lunte	1	B.Ellison	O	F.Gleich	1	D.Burrus	/C	P.Collins	C	F.Brower
/O	H.Eibel	C	B.Lynn	S	J.Sewell	3	S.Hale	C	F.Hofmann	S	F.Walker	/O	L.Lamb	S	F.O'Rourke
/3	H.Hiller	/S	H.McClellan	1	G.Burns	C	C.Manion	/S	C.Fewster	S	R.Shannon	/O	D.Wetzel	/3	G.McBride
/O	B.Paschal	C	B.Falk	C	L.Nunamaker	C	C.Woodall	/2	J.Lucey	OP	L.Bigbee	/S	J.Shovlin	/1	R.Torres
/C	M.Devine	/C	B.Jonnard	/C	P.Thomas	3	C.Huber	/S	R.French	O	P.Johnson	/2	B.Mullen	O	J.Calvo
/O	H.Hunter					/S	D.Claire	H	T.Connelly	O	C.High	/3	M.McManus	/O	E.Johnson
/O	G.Orme	P	R.Faber	P	J.Bagby					O	G.Burns	/S	D.Lee	/S	D.Prothro
/C	E.Chaplin	P	E.Cicotte	P	S.Coveleski	P	H.Dauss	P	C.Mays	/C	L.Styles	/3	P.Speraw	/3	F.Thomas
/1	R.Grimes	P	L.Williams	P	R.Caldwell	P	H.Ehmke	S	B.Shawkey	S	E.McCann	H	J.Heving	/3	B.Hollahan
/O	J.Statz	P	D.Kerr	P	G.Morton	P	R.Oldham	P	J.Quinn	/C	J.Walker	/O	E.Pruess	/S	B.LaMotte
/C	P.Smith	P	R.Wilkinson			P	D.Ayers	P	R.Collins	/1	B.Kelly			H	E.Bowman
				P	G.Uhle	P	D.Leonard	P	H.Thormahlen	/C	E.Wingo	P	D.Davis	/2	A.Watt
P	S.Jones	P	G.Payne	P	E.Myers			H	T.Kearns	P	U.Shocker	R	J.Leonard
P	J.Bush	/P	S.Hodge	/P	D.Mails	P	F.Okrie	P	G.Mogridge			P	A.Sothoron		
P	H.Pennock	/P	S.Heath	P	B.Clark	/P	B.Morrisette	P	E.Shore	P	S.Perry	P	C.Weilman	P	T.Zachary
P	H.Harper	/P	J.Kiefer	P	D.Niehaus	P	J.Bogart	P	B.McGraw	P	R.Naylor	P	B.Burwell	P	E.Erickson
P	W.Hoyt	/P	G.Lowdermilk	P	T.Faeth	P	E.Alten	/P	L.O'Doul	P	S.Harriss			P	J.Shaw
				/P	J.Boehling	/P	A.Conkwright			P	E.Rommel	P	E.Vangilder	P	H.Courtney
P	A.Russell			/P	T.Murchison	/P	H.Baumgartner			P	H.Moore	P	B.Bayne	P	W.Johnson
P	E.Myers			/P	G.Ellison	/P	B.Boland					P	J.DeBerry		
P	B.Karr					/P	J.Glaiser			P	D.Keefe	/P	A.Lynch	P	A.Schacht
P	G.Fortune					/P	R.Crumpler			P	B.Hasty	/P	R.Richmond	P	J.Acosta
/P	H.Deviney					/P	M.Wilson			P	W.Kinney	/P	R.Sanders	P	B.Snyder
						/P	J.Coombs			/P	P.Martin	/P	H.Leverette	/P	H.Biemiller
						/P	R.Cox			/P	C.Eckert	/P	L.Leifield	/P	G.Bono
						/P	S.Love			/P	B.Knowlton	/P	G.Boehler	/P	L.Carlson
						/P	C.Fried			/P	J.Slappey	/P	B.Gallia	/P	J.Gleason
						/P	L.Vedder			/P	F.Heimach	/P	J.Scheneberg	/P	C.Fisher
										/P	B.Shanner			/P	D.Shirey
														/P	J.Conway
														/P	J.Engel

TEAM	G	W	L	PCT	GB	R	OR	AB	H	2B	3B	HR	BB	SO	AVG	OBP	SLG	PRO	PRO+	BR	/A	PF	CHI	RC	SB	CS	SBA	SBR
CLE	154	98	56	.636		857	642	5196	1574	300	95	35	576	379	.303	.376	.417	.793	113	125	98	103	98	827	73	93	44	-34
CHI	154	96	58	.623	2	794	665	5328	1574	263	98	37	471	355	.295	.357	.402	.759	107	49	49	100	100	769	109	96	53	-25
NY	154	95	59	.617	3	838	629	5176	1448	268	71	115	539	626	.280	.350	.426	.776	107	71	43	104	105	773	64	82	44	-30
STL	154	76	77	.497	21.5	797	766	5358	1651	279	83	50	427	339	.308	.363	.419	.782	110	93	68	103	95	822	121	79	61	-11
BOS	154	72	81	.471	25.5	650	698	5199	1397	216	71	22	533	429	.269	.342	.350	.692	93	-70	-41	96	97	637	98	111	47	-37
WAS	153	68	84	.447	29	723	802	5251	1526	233	81	36	433	543	.291	.351	.386	.737	104	7	27	97	98	718	160	114	58	-20
DET	155	61	93	.396	37	652	833	5215	1408	228	72	30	479	391	.270	.334	.359	.693	91	-80	-64	98	100	639	76	68	53	-18
PHI	156	48	106	.312	50	558	834	5256	1324	220	49	44	353	593	.252	.305	.338	.643	74	-188	-193	101	106	543	50	67	43	-25
TOT	617					5869		41979	11902	2007	620	369	3811	3655	.284	.347	.387	.734							751	710	51	-201

TEAM	CG	SH	SV	IP	H	H/G	HR	BB	SO	RAT	ERA	ERA+	OAV	OOB	PR	/A	PF	CPI	FA	E	DP	FW	PW	BW	SBW	DIF
CLE	94	11	7	1377	1448	9.5	31	401	466	12.3	3.41	111	.276	.331	57	58	100	98	.971	184	124	2.1	5.6	9.5	-.9	4.6
CHI	109	9	10	1386²	1467	9.5	45	405	438	12.3	3.59	105	.280	.335	31	24	99	98	.968	198	142	1.2	2.3	4.8	.0	10.7
NY	88	15	11	1368	1414	9.3	48	420	480	12.3	3.32	115	.270	.328	-38	75	101	99	.969	194	129	1.4	7.3	4.2	-.5	5.6
STL	84	9	14	1378²	1481	9.7	53	578	444	13.7	4.03	97	.283	.359	-38	-23	103	99	.963	233	119	-1.2	-2.2	6.6	1.4	-5.0
BOS	92	11	6	1395¹	1481	9.6	39	461	481	12.7	3.82	95	.279	.339	-5	-30	96	93	.972	183	131	2.2	-2.9	-4.0	-1.2	1.3
WAS	81	10	10	1367	1521	10.0	51	520	418	13.7	4.17	89	.288	.357	-58	-70	98	97	.963	232	95	-1.3	-6.8	2.6	.5	-3.1
DET	74	9	7	1385	1487	9.7	46	561	483	13.7	4.04	92	.284	.359	-38	-51	98	99	.964	230	95	-.9	-4.9	-6.2	.7	-4.6
PHI	79	6	2	1380¹	1612	10.5	56	461	423	13.8	3.93	102	.302	.362	-21	12	106	110	.959	266	125	-3.3	1.2	-18.7	.0	-8.1
TOT	701	80	67	11038		9.7				13.1	3.79		.284	.347					.966	1720	960					

Runs		Hits		Doubles		Triples		Home Runs		Total Bases	
Ruth-NY	158	Sisler-StL	257	Speaker-Cle	50	Jackson-Chi	20	Ruth-NY	54	Sisler-StL	399
Speaker-Cle	137	E.Collins-Chi	224	Sisler-StL	49	Sisler-StL	18	Sisler-StL	19	Ruth-NY	388
Sisler-StL	137	Jackson-Chi	218	Jackson-Chi	42	Hooper-Bos	17	T.Walker-Phi	17	Jackson-Chi	336
E.Collins-Chi	117	Jacobson-StL	216					Felsch-Chi	14	Speaker-Cle	310
		Speaker-Cle	214							Jacobson-StL	305

Runs Batted In		Runs Produced		Bases On Balls		Batting Average		On Base Percentage		Slugging Average	
Ruth-NY	137	Ruth-NY	241	Ruth-NY	148	Sisler-StL	.407	Ruth-NY	.530	Ruth-NY	.847
Sisler-StL	122	Sisler-StL	240	Speaker-Cle	97	Speaker-Cle	.388	Speaker-Cle	.483	Sisler-StL	.632
Jacobson-StL	122	Speaker-Cle	236	Hooper-Bos	88	Jackson-Chi	.382	Sisler-StL	.449	Jackson-Chi	.589
Jackson-Chi	121	Jackson-Chi	214	Young-Det	85	Ruth-NY	.376	Jackson-Chi	.444	Speaker-Cle	.562
Gardner-Cle	118	Jacobson-StL	210	Roth-Was	75	E.Collins-Chi	.372	E.Collins-Chi	.438	Felsch-Chi	.540

Production		Adjusted Production		Batter Runs		Adjusted Batter Runs		Clutch Hitting Index		Runs Created	
Ruth-NY	1.378	Ruth-NY	252	Ruth-NY	113.2	Ruth-NY	106.7	Gardner-Cle	144	Ruth-NY	211
Sisler-StL	1.082	Sisler-StL	179	Sisler-StL	73.2	Sisler-StL	68.5	Roth-Was	131	Sisler-StL	176
Speaker-Cle	1.045	Jackson-Chi	172	Speaker-Cle	65.7	Speaker-Cle	61.2	Smith-Cle	123	Speaker-Cle	152
Jackson-Chi	1.033	Speaker-Cle	171	Jackson-Chi	58.4	Jackson-Chi	58.4	Risberg-Chi	121	Jackson-Chi	145
E.Collins-Chi	.932	E.Collins-Chi	146	E.Collins-Chi	42.3	E.Collins-Chi	42.3	Pratt-NY	118	E.Collins-Chi	134

Total Average		Stolen Bases		Stolen Base Average		Stolen Base Runs		Fielding Runs		Total Player Rating	
Ruth-NY	1.797	Rice-Was	63	E.Collins-Chi	71.4	Sisler-StL	2.4	Perkins-Phi	22.8	Ruth-NY	8.6
Sisler-StL	1.207	Sisler-StL	42	Sisler-StL	71.2	Burns-Phi-Cle	1.5	Ward-NY	21.8	Sisler-StL	7.8
Speaker-Cle	1.165	Roth-Was	24	Williams-StL	69.2	E.Collins-Chi	1.2	Rice-Was	21.4	E.Collins-Chi	5.6
Jackson-Chi	1.088	Menosky-Bos	23	Rice-Was	67.7	Smith-StL	.9	Pinelli-Det	19.9	Speaker-Cle	5.2
E.Collins-Chi	.984	Tobin-StL	21	Roth-Was	66.7	Rice-Was	.9	Felsch-Chi	17.7	Jackson-Chi	4.1

Wins		Win Percentage		Games		Complete Games		Shutouts		Saves	
Bagby-Cle	31	Bagby-Cle	.721	Bagby-Cle	48	Bagby-Cle	30	Mays-NY	6	Shocker-StL	5
Mays-NY	26	Mays-NY	.703	Ayers-Det	46	Faber-Chi	28	Shocker-StL	5	Kerr-Chi	5
Coveleski-Cle	24	Kerr-Chi	.700	Mays-NY	45	Cicotte-Chi	28	Shawkey-NY	5	Burwell-StL	4
Faber-Chi	23	Cicotte-Chi	.677	Kerr-Chi	45	Mays-NY	26				
Williams-Chi	22			Zachary-Was	44	Coveleski-Cle	26				

Innings Pitched		Fewest Hits/Game		Fewest BB/Game		Strikeouts		Strikeouts/Game		Ratio	
Bagby-Cle	339.2	Coveleski-Cle	8.11	Quinn-NY	1.71	Coveleski-Cle	133	Ayers-Det	4.44	Coveleski-Cle	10.09
Faber-Chi	319.0	Shocker-StL	8.21	Coveleski-Cle	1.86	Williams-Chi	128	Shawkey-NY	4.24	Shocker-StL	10.92
Coveleski-Cle	315.0	Collins-NY	8.22	Bagby-Cle	2.09	Shawkey-NY	126	Harper-Bos	3.93	Rommel-Phi	10.99
Mays-NY	312.0	Shawkey-NY	8.27	Cicotte-Chi	2.20	Faber-Chi	108	Shocker-StL	3.92	Shawkey-NY	11.16
Cicotte-Chi	303.1	Davis-StL	8.35	Perry-Phi	2.22	Shocker-StL	107	Williams-Chi	3.85	Bagby-Cle	11.18

Earned Run Average		Adjusted ERA		Opponents' Batting Avg.		Opponents' On Base Pct.		Starter Runs		Adjusted Starter Runs	
Shawkey-NY	2.45	Shawkey-NY	155	Coveleski-Cle	.243	Coveleski-Cle	.285	Coveleski-Cle	45.6	Coveleski-Cle	45.7
Coveleski-Cle	2.49	Coveleski-Cle	153	Collins-NY	.247	Shocker-StL	.305	Shawkey-NY	39.6	Shawkey-NY	40.3
Shocker-StL	2.71	Shocker-StL	144	Shawkey-NY	.248	Shawkey-NY	.308	Bagby-Cle	33.9	Bagby-Cle	34.1
Rommel-Phi	2.85	Rommel-Phi	141	Shocker-StL	.248	Quinn-NY	.308	Shocker-StL	29.4	Shocker-StL	32.7
Bagby-Cle	2.89	Bagby-Cle	131	Ehmke-Det	.253	Rommel-Phi	.309	Faber-Chi	28.2	Faber-Chi	27.2

Clutch Pitching Index		Relief Runs		Adjusted Relief Runs		Relief Ranking		Total Pitcher Index		Total Baseball Ranking	
Naylor-Phi	130							Coveleski-Cle	5.9	Ruth-NY	8.5
Harper-Bos	128							Shawkey-NY	4.3	Sisler-StL	7.9
Davis-StL	117							Shocker-StL	4.0	Coveleski-Cle	5.9
Oldham-Det	116							Bagby-Cle	3.8	E.Collins-Chi	5.6
Perry-Phi	113							Mays-NY	3.7	Speaker-Cle	5.2

January 21 Judge Kenesaw Mountain Landis officially takes over as baseball's commissioner.

January 22 The Reds trade pitcher Jimmy Ring and outfielder Greasy Neale to the Phils for lefty Eppa Rixey, who led the NL with 22 losses in 1920. Rixey will pitch his way into the Hall of Fame over the next 13 years.

June 13 Umpires in both leagues begin the practice of rubbing mud into the balls before each game, using a special clay supplied by A's coach Lena Blackburne from his New Jersey farm.

July 1 Casey Stengel is traded from the last-place Phils to the second-place Giants, along with infielder Johnny Rawlings and pitcher Red Causey for infielder Goldie Rapp and outfielders Lance Richbourg and Lee King.

July 29 John McGraw buys outfielder Irish Meusel, who is hitting .353 but has been suspended by the Phillies for lackadaisical play. McGraw gives up three bench warmers and $30,000. The Giants take three from the Reds and go into the NL lead for the first time. They will fall back by seven games before coming on with a rush in September.

August 5 The first radio broadcast of a major league game is heard over KDKA in Pittsburgh. The Pirates-Phils game is announced by Harold Arlin. The Pirates score three runs in the eighth inning, beating the Phils, 8-5. Arlin is the grandfather of future San Diego Padre Steve Arlin.

August 24 The Pirates, in front by seven and a half games, drop a doubleheader to the Giants in New York before 35,000. Art Nehf wins the opener, 10–2, and Phil Douglas takes the nightcap, 7–0.

September 29 The Bucs drop a doubleheader to the Cardinals allowing the idle Giants to clinch the NL pennant, their seventh under manager John McGraw.

October 5 The World Series opener is broadcast on KDKA radio, with Grantland Rice announcing; it's the only game of the season's World Series to be aired.

October 13 In the best-of-nine World Series Waite Hoyt and Art Nehf come back for Game 8 with two days rest. With two on and two outs in the first, Giants first baseman George Kelly hits a grounder that goes through Yankees shortstop Roger Peckinpaugh, and a run scores. Not another Giant reaches third base the rest of the day. After Aaron Ward walks in the ninth, Frank "Home Run" Baker hits a drive toward right, but second baseman Johnny Rawlings spears it and throws him out while on the ground. Ward heads for third base and is gunned down by a throw from Kelly to Frisch to end the Series. The Giants are the first team to lose the first two games and come back to win the Series.

October 16 Judge Landis outlaws gentleman's agreements and cover-ups of players optioned to the minors without proper paperwork. He declares six players free agents, including Heinie Manush, who will ride a 17-year .330 batting average into the Hall of Fame in 1964.

	BOSTON		BROOKLYN		CHICAGO		CINCINNATI		NEW YORK		PHILADELPHIA		PITTSBURGH		ST.LOUIS
M	F.Mitchell	M	W.Robinson	M	J.Evers	M	P.Moran	M	J.McGraw	M	B.Donovan	M	M.Gibson	M	B.Rickey
1B	W.Holke	1B	R.Schmandt	M	B.Killefer	1B	J.Daubert	1B	G.Kelly	M	K.Wilhelm	1B	C.Grimm	1B	J.Fournier
2B	H.Ford	2B	P.Kilduff	1B	R.Grimes	2B	S.Bohne	2B	J.Rawlings	1B	E.Konetchy	2B	G.Cutshaw	2B	R.Hornsby
SS	W.Barbare	SS	I.Olson	2B	Z.Terry	SS	L.Kopf	SS	D.Bancroft	2B	J.Smith	SS	R.Maranville	SS	D.Lavan
3B	T.Boeckel	3B	J.Johnston	SS	C.Hollocher	3B	H.Groh	3B	F.Frisch	SS	F.Parkinson	3B	C.Barnhart	3B	M.Stock
LF	W.Cruise	LF	Z.Wheat	3B	C.Deal	LF	P.Duncan	LF	I.Meusel	3B	R.Wrightstone	LF	C.Bigbee	LF	A.McHenry
CF	R.Powell	CF	H.Myers	LF	T.Barber	CF	E.Roush	CF	G.Burns	LF	I.Meusel	CF	M.Carey	CF	L.Mann
RF	B.Southworth	RF	T.Griffith	CF	G.Maisel	RF	R.Bressler	RF	R.Youngs	CF	C.Williams	RF	P.Whitted	RF	J.Smith
C	M.O'Neil	C	O.Miller	RF	M.Flack	C	I.Wingo	C	F.Snyder	RF	B.LeBourveau	C	W.Schmidt	C	V.Clemons
				C	B.O'Farrell					C	F.Bruggy				
O	F.Nicholson	O	B.Neis			21	L.Fonseca	C	E.Smith			23	C.Tierney	O	J.Schultz
C	H.Gowdy	1	E.Konetchy	32	J.Kelleher	C	B.Hargrave	O	C.Walker	31	D.Miller	O	D.Robertson	O	H.Mueller
O	A.Nixon	O	E.Krueger	O	J.Sullivan	O	G.Neale	3	G.Rapp	1O	C.Lee	C	T.Brottem	O	P.Dillhoefer
2	L.Christenbury	C	Z.Taylor	O	B.Twombly	S	S.Crane	O	E.Brown	2	J.Rawlings	O	J.Mokan	O	C.Heathcote
C	F.Gibson	S2	H.Janvrin	C	T.Daly	O	C.See	O	L.King	O	L.King	C	B.Skiff	C	E.Ainsmith
H	J.Sullivan	O	W.Hood	C	B.Killefer	O	D.Paskert	O	B.Cunningham	S3	R.Miller	O	R.Rohwer	2	S.Toporcer
		S	C.Ward	/2	W.Marriott	/C	A.Douglass	3	P.Patterson	3	G.Rapp	O	J.Gooch	O	B.Shotton
P	J.Oeschger	/2	J.Sheehan	3	H.Warner	/O	D.Williams	/1	M.Gonzalez	C	J.Peters	/3	P.Traynor	/1	H.Janvrin
P	M.Watson	/O	E.Eayrs	/O	D.Robertson	/3	W.Kimmick	2	A.Gaston	/C	J.Monroe	/C	M.Wilson	/C	C.Niebergall
P	H.McQuillan	/O	B.Lamar	/O	R.Thomas	/O	K.Hogan	/O	C.Stengel	C	B.Henline	/O	K.Cuyler	/1	H.Hunter
P	D.Fillingim			S	C.Elliott			/2	J.Monroe	O	C.Walker	/C	B.Warwick	/O	H.Jones
P	J.Scott	P	B.Grimes	/2	J.Klugmann	P	D.Luque	/2	J.Berry	O	C.Stengel			/S	R.Ewing
		P	L.Cadore	/C	K.Wirts	P	E.Rixey	/2	H.Schreiber	O	G.Neale	P	W.Cooper	H	G.Gilham
P	G.Braxton	P	D.Ruether			P	R.Marquard	/O	J.Connolly	/S	D.Rader	P	W.Glazner	H	W.Irwin
P	C.Morgan	P	C.Mitchell	P	P.Alexander	P	P.Donohue	/3	W.Kopf	/C	M.Wheat	P	E.Hamilton	H	L.McCarty
/P	J.Cooney	P	S.Smith	P	S.Martin	RP	B.Napier	/2	B.Heine	/2	L.Richbourg	P	B.Adams		
/P	I.Townsend			P	B.Freeman			H	B.Henline			P	J.Morrison	P	J.Haines
/P	E.Eayrs	P	J.Miljus	P	V.Cheeves	P	F.Coumbe	/2	J.Mahady	P	J.Ring			P	B.Doak
/P	A.Pierotti	P	F.Schupp	P	L.York	P	C.Markle			P	G.Smith	P	J.Zinn	P	B.Pertica
/P	L.Townsend	P	A.Mamaux			P	L.Brenton	P	A.Nehf	P	B.Hubbell	P	H.Carlson	P	R.Walker
		/P	J.Pfeffer	P	H.Vaughn	/C	C.Rogge	P	J.Barnes	P	L.Meadows	/P	C.Yellowhorse	P	B.Sherdel
		/P	S.Bailey	P	P.Jones	P	H.Eller	P	F.Toney	P	J.Winters	/P	E.Ponder	RP	L.North
		/P	R.Gordinier	P	E.Ponder	P	B.Geary	P	P.Douglas			/P	L.Bigbee		
		/P	G.Mohart	P	L.Tyler	/P	L.Clarke	P	R.Ryan	P	H.Betts	/P	R.Wheeler	P	J.Pfeffer
				/P	V.Keen			RP	S.Sallee	P	D.Sedgwick	P	B.Hughes	P	B.Bailey
				/P	T.Kaufmann					P	S.Baumgartner	/P	D.Rader	P	T.Riviere
				/P	G.Stueland			P	R.Benton	/P	R.Causey	/P	P.Morrison	P	F.Schupp
				/P	O.Hanson			/P	R.Shea	P	J.Keenan			P	M.Goodwin
				/P	S.Bailey			/P	R.Causey	/P	L.Weinert			/P	J.May
				/P	O.Fuhr			/P	P.Perritt	/P	P.Behan			/P	M.Kircher
								/P	C.Jonnard	/P	K.Wilhelm				
								/P	W.Zink						

TEAM	G	W	L	PCT	GB	R	OR	AB	H	2B	3B	HR	BB	SO	AVG	OBP	SLG	PRO	PRO+	BR	/A	PF	CHI	RC	SB	CS	SBA	SBR
NY	153	94	59	.614		840	637	5278	1575	237	93	75	469	390	.298	.359	.421	.780	112	94	92	100	104	795	137	114	55	-27
PIT	154	90	63	.588	4	692	595	5379	1533	231	104	37	341	371	.285	.330	.387	.717	93	-37	-55	103	102	684	134	93	59	-16
STL	154	87	66	.569	7	809	681	5309	1635	260	88	83	382	452	.308	.358	.437	.795	118	114	131	98	98	816	94	94	50	-28
BOS	153	79	74	.516	15	721	697	5385	1561	209	100	61	377	470	.290	.339	.400	.739	107	6	46	95	100	718	94	100	48	-32
BRO	152	77	75	.507	16.5	667	681	5263	1476	209	85	59	325	400	.280	.325	.386	.711	90	-52	-75	104	104	655	91	73	55	-17
CIN	153	70	83	.458	24	618	649	5112	1421	221	94	20	375	308	.278	.333	.370	.703	96	-56	-27	95	98	623	117	120	49	-37
CHI	153	64	89	.418	30	668	773	5321	1553	234	56	37	343	374	.292	.339	.378	.717	95	-31	-32	100	99	671	70	97	42	-37
PHI	154	51	103	.331	43.5	617	919	5329	1512	238	50	88	294	615	.284	.324	.397	.721	89	-37	-89	108	94	668	66	80	45	-28
TOT	613					5632		42376	12266	1839	670	460	2906	3380	.289	.338	.397	.736							803	771	51	-222

TEAM	CG	SH	SV	IP	H	H/G	HR	BB	SO	RAT	ERA	ERA+	OAV	OOB	PR	/A	PF	CPI	FA	E	DP	FW	PW	BW	SBW	DIF
NY	71	9	18	1372¹	1497	9.8	79	295	357	11.9	3.55	103	.286	.326	34	16	97	102	.971	187	155	1.3	1.6	9.1	.0	5.5
PIT	88	10	10	1415²	1448	9.2	37	322	500	11.5	3.17	121	.271	.316	96	104	101	96	.973	172	129	2.3	10.3	-5.4	1.2	5.3
STL	70	10	16	1371²	1486	9.8	61	399	464	12.6	3.62	101	.282	.337	24	5	97	102	.965	219	130	-.6	.5	12.9	-.0	-2.3
BOS	74	11	12	1385	1488	9.7	54	420	382	12.6	3.90	94	.280	.337	-18	-38	97	93	.969	199	122	.5	-3.8	4.5	-.4	1.6
BRO	82	8	12	1363¹	1556	10.3	46	361	471	12.9	3.70	105	.293	.342	13	28	103	103	.964	232	142	-1.5	2.8	-7.4	1.1	6.1
CIN	83	7	9	1363	1500	9.9	37	305	408	12.0	3.46	103	.287	.328	48	17	95	100	.969	193	139	.9	1.7	-2.7	-.9	-5.5
CHI	73	7	7	1363	1605	10.6	67	409	441	13.6	4.39	87	.303	.357	-93	-88	101	99	.974	166	129	2.5	-8.7	-3.2	-.9	-2.3
PHI	82	5	8	1348²	1665	11.1	79	371	333	13.8	4.48	94	.308	.356	-105	-39	112	99	.955	295	127	-5.2	-3.9	-8.8	-.0	-8.1
TOT	623	67	92	10982²		10.0				12.6	3.78		.289	.338					.967	1663	1073					

Runs
Hornsby-StL 131
Frisch-NY 121
Bancroft-NY 121
Powell-Bos 114
Burns-NY 111

Hits
Hornsby-StL 235
Frisch-NY 211
C.Bigbee-Pit 204
Johnston-Bro 203

Doubles
Hornsby-StL 44
Kelly-NY 42
Johnston-Bro 41
Grimes-Chi 38
McHenry-StL 37

Triples
Powell-Bos 18
Hornsby-StL 18
Grimm-Pit 17
Frisch-NY 17
C.Bigbee-Pit 17

Home Runs
Kelly-NY 23
Hornsby-StL 21
Williams-Phi 18
McHenry-StL 17
Fournier-StL 16

Total Bases
Hornsby-StL 378
Kelly-NY 310
McHenry-StL 305
Meusel-Phi-NY 302
Frisch-NY 300

Runs Batted In
Hornsby-StL 126
Kelly-NY 122
Youngs-NY 102
McHenry-StL 102
Frisch-NY 100

Runs Produced
Hornsby-StL 236
Frisch-NY 213
Kelly-NY 194
Youngs-NY 189
Bancroft-NY 182

Bases On Balls
Burns-NY 80
Youngs-NY 71
Grimes-Chi 70
Carey-Pit 70
Bancroft-NY 66

Batting Average
Hornsby-StL 397
Roush-Cin .... .352
McHenry-StL ...... .350
Cruise-Bos .... .346
Fournier-StL ...... .343

On Base Percentage
Hornsby-StL ..... .458
Youngs-NY .... .411
Fournier-StL ...... .409
Grimes-Chi .... .406
Carey-Pit .... .395

Slugging Average
Hornsby-StL 639
McHenry-StL ...... .531
Kelly-NY .... .528
Meusel-Phi-NY .... .515
Mann-StL .... .512

Production
Hornsby-StL 1.097
McHenry-StL ...... .924
Fournier-StL ...... .914
Meusel-Phi-NY .... .895
Kelly-NY .... .884

Adjusted Production
Hornsby-StL 191
McHenry-StL 145
Fournier-StL 144
Kelly-NY 131
Youngs-NY 129

Batter Runs
Hornsby-StL 74.4
Fournier-StL 34.5
McHenry-StL 33.5
Meusel-Phi-NY ... 27.6
Frisch-NY 24.8

Adjusted Batter Runs
Hornsby-StL 77.7
Fournier-StL 36.9
McHenry-StL 35.8
Cruise-Bos 28.5
Roush-Cin 26.7

Clutch Hitting Index
Youngs-NY 142
Stock-StL 142
Lavan-StL 140
Barnhart-Pit 123
Konetchy-Bro-Phi . 115

Runs Created
Hornsby-StL 169
Frisch-NY 118
Fournier-StL 114
McHenry-StL 111
Meusel-Phi-NY 110

Total Average
Hornsby-StL 1.203
Frisch-NY .... .902
Fournier-StL ...... .882
Carey-Pit .... .868
Youngs-NY .... .860

Stolen Bases
Frisch-NY 49
Carey-Pit 37
Johnston-Bro 28
Bohne-Cin 26
Maranville-Pit ... 25

Stolen Base Average
Frisch-NY 79.0
Carey-Pit 75.5
Maisel-Chi 70.8
Maranville-Pit ... 67.6
Johnston-Bro 63.6

Stolen Base Runs
Frisch-NY 6.9
Carey-Pit 3.9
Stock-StL 1.5
Cutshaw-Pit 1.2

Fielding Runs
Lavan-StL 18.5
Bancroft-NY 17.4
Williams-Phi 16.3
C.Bigbee-Pit 16.2
Carey-Pit 16.1

Total Player Rating
Hornsby-StL 7.1
Bancroft-NY 4.8
Frisch-NY 4.3
Johnston-Bro 3.0
Kelly-NY 2.5

Wins
Grimes-Bro 22
Cooper-Pit 22
Oeschger-Bos 20
Nehf-NY 20
Rixey-Cin 19

Win Percentage
Doak-StL .... .714
Nehf-NY .... .667
Grimes-Bro .... .629
Barnes-NY .... .625
Toney-NY .... .621

Games
Scott-Bos 47
Oeschger-Bos 46
McQuillan-Bos 45
Watson-Bos 44
Fillingim-Bos 44

Complete Games
Grimes-Bro 30
Cooper-Pit 29
Luque-Cin 25

Shutouts
Oeschger-Bos 3
J.Morrison-Pit 3
Mitchell-Bro 3
Luque-Cin 3
Haines-StL 3
Fillingim-Bos 3
Douglas-NY 3
Alexander-Chi 3

Saves
North-StL 7
Barnes-NY 6
McQuillan-Bos 5

Innings Pitched
Cooper-Pit 327.0
Luque-Cin 304.0
Grimes-Bro 302.1
Rixey-Cin 301.0
Oeschger-Bos ...299.0

Fewest Hits/Game
Glazner-Pit 8.23
Adams-Pit 8.72
Oeschger-Bos 9.12
Pertica-StL 9.16
Nehf-NY 9.18

Fewest BB/Game
Adams-Pit 1.01
Alexander-Chi 1.18
Barnes-NY 1.53
Hubbell-Phi 1.55
Doak-StL 1.60

Strikeouts
Grimes-Bro 136
Cooper-Pit 134
Luque-Cin 102
McQuillan-Bos 94

Strikeouts/Game
Grimes-Bro 4.05
Cooper-Pit 3.69
Doak-StL 3.58
Martin-Chi 3.56
Glazner-Pit 3.38

Ratio
Adams-Pit 9.73
Glazner-Pit 10.92
Nehf-NY 11.15
Luque-Cin 11.34
Alexander-Chi ...11.43

Earned Run Average
Doak-StL 2.59
Adams-Pit 2.64
Glazner-Pit 2.77
Rixey-Cin 2.78
Grimes-Bro 2.83

Adjusted ERA
Adams-Pit 145
Doak-StL 142
Glazner-Pit 138
Grimes-Bro 137
Mitchell-Bro 134

Opponents' Batting Avg.
Glazner-Pit ...... .250
Adams-Pit .... .251
Pertica-StL ...... .267
Watson-Bos ...... .270
Nehf-NY .... .271

Opponents' On Base Pct.
Adams-Pit .... .272
Glazner-Pit ...... .306
Nehf-NY .... .311
Luque-Cin .... .312
Doak-StL .... .313

Starter Runs
Rixey-Cin 33.4
Grimes-Bro 32.0
Doak-StL 27.6
Glazner-Pit 26.3
Adams-Pit 20.2

Adjusted Starter Runs
Grimes-Bro 35.5
Glazner-Pit 27.6
Rixey-Cin 26.6
Doak-StL 24.9
Cooper-Pit 21.2

Clutch Pitching Index
Barnes-NY 124
Mitchell-Bro 118
Doak-StL 116
Rixey-Cin 113
Grimes-Bro 112

Relief Runs
North-StL 2.3
Sallee-NY 1.5

Adjusted Relief Runs
North-StL 1.1
Sallee-NY 2

Relief Ranking
North-StL 1.1
Sallee-NY 2

Total Pitcher Index
Grimes-Bro 4.5
Rixey-Cin 2.8
Mitchell-Bro 2.8
Adams-Pit 2.5
Doak-StL 2.2

Total Baseball Ranking
Hornsby-StL 7.1
Bancroft-NY 4.8
Grimes-Bro 4.5
Frisch-NY 4.3
Johnston-Bro 3.0

April 13 With former President Woodrow Wilson, new President Warren G. Harding, and Vice President Calvin Coolidge watching, the Senators lose their home opener, 6-3, to the Red Sox. Walter Johnson leaves after four innings, the first time he has failed to finish an opening game.

June 6* The Detroit Stars' Bill Gatewood pitches the first no-hitter in Negro League history, defeating the Cuban Stars, 4-0.

June 7* The only Organized Baseball game canceled because of a murder occurs at Kingsport, Tennessee (Appalachian League), when the body of a slain girl is found at the ballpark. To keep the trail fresh, for bloodhounds, police close the park and cancel the scheduled game against Knoxville.

July 12 Babe Ruth hits his 137th career home run, passing 19th century star Roger Connor's career record of 136.

August 2 A Chicago jury brings in a verdict of not guilty against the Black Sox. That night, jurors and defendants celebrate with a party in an Italian restaurant. Ignoring the verdict, Judge Landis bans all eight defendants from baseball for life.

August 19 Ty Cobb gets hit No. 3,000 off Boston pitcher Elmer Myers. At 34, he's the youngest ever to turn the trick.

September 5 Walter Johnson breaks Cy Young's career strikeout mark by fanning seven Yankees to run his total to 2,287.

October 1 White Sox catcher Ray Schalk makes a putout at first base. When the Indians' speedy Charlie Jamieson singles to right field, Schalk jogs toward first base in case Jamieson takes too wide a turn toward second, which he does. Schalk takes a throw from the outfielder and makes the putout. Schalk is the only catcher to make a putout at every base.

October 1 After clinching the pennant with a 5-3 win in the opener, the Yankees bring Babe Ruth in to pitch in relief in the nightcap. Ruth, with just one other pitching appearance all season, takes over in the eighth with New York in the lead, 6-0. He quickly allows the A's six runs to tie the score but then knuckles down to hold them scoreless through the eleventh when New York scores a run to win, 7-6. The stunt still costs Waite Hoyt a 20-win season.

October 5 In the first one-city World Series since 1906, the Polo Grounds will be the site for all nine games. Carl Mays (27-9) is at his best, needing 86 pitches to set the Giants down with five hits in this 3-0 Yankee win.

October 16 In defiance of a Judge Landis ban on World Series participants playing postseason exhibitions, Babe Ruth, Bob Meusel, and pitcher Bill Piercy launch a barnstorming tour in Buffalo. Five days later, they cut it short in Scranton. In the meantime Ruth openly challenges Landis to act. The judge does, fining the players their World Series shares—$3,362.26—and suspending them until May 20 of the following season.

	BOSTON		CHICAGO		CLEVELAND		DETROIT		NEW YORK		PHILADELPHIA		ST.LOUIS		WASHINGTON
M	H.Duffy	M	K.Gleason	M	T.Speaker	M	T.Cobb	M	M.Huggins	M	C.Mack	M	L.Fohl	M	G.McBride
1B	S.McInnis	1B	E.Sheely	1B	D.Johnston	1B	L.Blue	1B	W.Pipp	1B	J.Walker	1B	G.Sisler	1B	J.Judge
2B	D.Pratt	2B	E.Collins	2B	B.Wambsganss	2B	R.Young	2B	A.Ward	2B	J.Dykes	2B	M.McManus	2B	B.Harris
SS	E.Scott	SS	E.Johnson	SS	J.Sewell	SS	D.Bush	SS	R.Peckinpaugh	SS	C.Galloway	SS	W.Gerber	SS	F.O'Rourke
3B	E.Foster	3B	E.Mulligan	3B	L.Gardner	3B	B.Jones	3B	F.Baker	3B	J.Dugan	3B	F.Ellerbe	3B	H.Shanks
LF	M.Menosky	LF	B.Falk	LF	C.Jamieson	LF	B.Veach	LF	B.Ruth	LF	T.Walker	LF	K.Williams	LF	B.Miller
CF	N.Leibold	CF	A.Strunk	CF	T.Speaker	CF	T.Cobb	CF	E.Miller	CF	F.Welch	CF	B.Jacobson	CF	S.Rice
RF	S.Collins	RF	H.Hooper	RF	E.Smith	RF	H.Heilmann	RF	B.Meusel	RF	W.Witt	RF	J.Tobin	RF	C.Milan
C	M.Ruel	C	R.Schalk	C	S.O'Neill	C	J.Bassler	C	W.Schang	C	C.Perkins	C	H.Severeid	C	P.Gharrity
3	O.Vitt	O	J.Mostil	1	G.Burns	SO	I.Flagstead	32	M.McNally	1	D.Lee	S2	D.Lee	O	F.Brower
C	R.Walters	2S	H.McClellan	2	R.Stephenson	O	C.Shorten	O2	C.Fewster	S	E.McCann	3	L.Lamb	O	E.Smith
O	T.Hendryx	C	Y.Yaryan	O	J.Wood	23	J.Sargent	O	B.Roth	O	P.Johnson	O	D.Wetzel	C	V.Picinich
O	P.Pittinger	C	G.Lees	O	J.Evans	C	E.Ainsmith	O	P.Bodie	1	I.Griffin	O	P.Collins	O	D.Lewis
O	S.Vick	/O	F.Bratschi	C	L.Nunamaker	O	L.Woodall	O	C.Hawks	O	Z.Collins	3	E.Smith	S	D.Bush
/O	E.Neitzke	H	R.Ostergard	O	J.Graney	S	H.Merritt	C	F.Hofmann	C	G.Myatt	2	B.Gleason	O	G.Goslin
/O	J.Perrin	/3	E.Leifer	C	P.Thomas	/2	S.Barnes	C	A.DeVormer	S	F.Walker	S	J.Austin	S	B.LaMotte
/C	E.Chaplin	H	E.Murphy	C	G.Shinault	/C	C.Manion	/S	J.Mitchell	S	F.Callaway	C	J.Billings	H	F.Ellerbe
H	H.Hiller	H	F.Pratt	/C	L.Sewell	/S	J.Tavener	/O	T.Connelly	/S	B.Barrett	/2	J.Riley	/C	T.Brottem
				/O	T.Jeanes	H	S.Hale			C	B.Mallonee	/3	B.Mullen	/3	G.Foss
P	S.Jones	P	R.Faber	/1	L.Guisto	/O	G.Cunningham	P	C.Mays	/C	L.Styles	/2	L.Stuart	P	R.Torres
P	J.Bush	P	D.Kerr	/C	A.Wilson	/3	C.Huber	P	W.Hoyt	H	E.Yoter				
P	H.Pennock	P	R.Wilkinson					P	B.Shawkey	/S	D.Fulghum	P	U.Shocker	P	G.Mogridge
P	A.Russell	P	S.Hodge	P	S.Coveleski	P	D.Leonard	P	R.Collins	H	R.Shannon	P	D.Davis	P	W.Johnson
P	E.Myers	P	D.McWeeny	P	G.Uhle	P	H.Dauss	P	J.Quinn			P	E.Vangilder	P	T.Zachary
				P	D.Mails	P	R.Oldham			P	E.Rommel	P	R.Kolp	P	E.Erickson
P	B.Karr	P	J.Russell	P	J.Bagby	P	H.Ehmke	P	B.Piercy	P	S.Harriss	P	B.Bayne	P	H.Courtney
P	H.Thormahlen	P	D.Mulrenan	P	R.Caldwell	P	C.Holling	P	A.Ferguson	P	R.Moore	RP	B.Burwell	RP	A.Schacht
/P	C.Fullerton	P	L.Davenport					/P	H.Harper	P	B.Hasty				
/P	A.Sothoron	/P	C.Twombly	P	A.Sothoron	P	J.Middleton	P	T.Sheehan	P	D.Keefe	P	E.Palmero	P	J.Acosta
/P	S.Dodge	/P	J.Wieneke	P	G.Morton	P	B.Cole	/P	T.Rogers	RP	H.Freeman	/P	A.Sothoron	P	J.Shaw
		/P	S.Connally	P	T.Odenwald	P	S.Sutherland					/P	B.Boland	/P	F.Woodward
		/P	L.Thompson	/P	B.Clark	P	S.Parks			P	R.Naylor	/P	R.Richmond	/P	T.Phillips
		/P	B.Morris	/P	J.Petty	/P	P.Perritt			P	S.Perry	/P	N.Cullop	/P	R.Bird
		/P	H.Fenner	/P	B.Henderson	/P	L.Stewart			P	J.Sullivan	P	J.DeBerry	/P	N.Gaines
		/P	R.Pence			/P	D.Ayers			/P	L.Wolf	/P	B.Morris	/P	V.McIlree
		/P	J.Michaelson			/P	J.Walsh			/P	F.Heimach	/P	D.Henry	/P	R.Miller
		/P	C.Blackburn			/P	D.Boone			/P	B.Bishop	/P	G.Boehler		
										/P	A.Taylor				
										/P	R.Miner				

TEAM	G	W	L	PCT	GB	R	OR	AB	H	2B	3B	HR	BB	SO	AVG	OBP	SLG	PRO	PRO+	BR	/A	PF	CHI	RC	SB	CS	SBA	SBR
NY	153	98	55	.641		948	708	5249	1576	285	87	134	588	569	.300	.375	.464	.839	116	142	122	102	102	929	89	64	58	-12
CLE	154	94	60	.610	4.5	925	712	5383	1656	355	90	42	623	376	.308	.383	.430	.813	111	112	98	102	100	916	51	42	55	-10
STL	154	81	73	.526	17.5	835	845	5442	1655	246	106	67	413	407	.304	.357	.425	.782	98	28	-20	106	102	827	91	71	56	-15
WAS	154	80	73	.523	18	704	738	5294	1468	240	96	42	462	472	.277	.342	.383	.725	95	-80	-47	95	101	712	112	66	63	-6
BOS	154	75	79	.487	23.5	668	696	5206	1440	248	69	17	428	344	.277	.335	.361	.696	84	-133	-116	97	107	642	83	65	56	-14
DET	154	71	82	.464	27	883	852	5461	1724	268	100	58	582	376	.316	.385	.433	.818	115	120	129	99	94	921	95	89	52	-25
CHI	154	62	92	.403	36.5	683	858	5329	1509	242	82	35	445	474	.283	.343	.379	.722	90	-86	-77	99	99	695	94	93	50	-28
PHI	155	53	100	.346	45	657	894	5465	1497	256	64	82	424	565	.274	.331	.389	.720	88	-102	-105	101	96	710	69	56	55	-13
TOT	616					6303		42829	12525	2140	694	477	3965	3583	.292	.356	.408	.765							684	546	56	-122

TEAM	CG	SH	SV	IP	H	H/G	HR	BB	SO	RAT	ERA	ERA+	OAV	OOB	PR	/A	PF	CPI	FA	E	DP	FW	PW	BW	SBW	DIF
NY	92	8	15	1364	1461	9.6	51	470	481	13.1	3.82	111	.277	.342	70	62	99	99	.965	222	138	-.3	5.8	11.4	.3	4.3
CLE	81	11	14	1377	1534	10.0	43	431	475	13.0	3.90	109	.288	.344	58	55	100	100	.967	204	124	.8	5.1	9.2	.5	1.4
STL	77	9	9	1379	1541	10.1	71	556	477	13.9	4.61	97	.288	.360	-51	-22	105	94	.964	224	127	-.3	-2.1	-1.9	.0	8.2
WAS	80	10	10	1383²	1568	10.2	51	442	452	13.3	3.97	104	.291	.349	47	22	96	102	.963	235	153	-.9	2.1	-4.4	.9	5.9
BOS	88	9	5	1364¹	1521	10.0	53	452	446	13.3	3.98	106	.291	.352	45	37	99	104	.975	157	151	3.5	3.5	-10.8	.1	1.8
DET	73	4	16	1386¹	1634	10.6	71	495	452	14.2	4.40	97	.297	.361	-18	-20	100	102	.963	232	107	-.8	-1.9	12.1	-.9	-14.0
CHI	84	7	9	1365¹	1603	10.6	52	549	392	14.4	4.94	86	.303	.372	-99	-107	99	94	.969	200	155	1.0	-10.0	-7.2	-1.2	2.3
PHI	75	2	7	1400¹	1645	10.6	85	548	431	14.3	4.61	97	.300	.367	-52	-25	104	102	.958	274	144	-3.1	-2.3	-9.8	.2	-8.5
TOT	650	60	85	11020		10.2				13.7	4.28		.292	.356					.965	1748	1099					

Runs		Hits		Doubles		Triples		Home Runs		Total Bases	
Ruth-NY	177	Heilmann-Det	237	Speaker-Cle	52	Tobin-StL	18	Ruth-NY	59	Ruth-NY	457
Tobin-StL	132	Tobin-StL	236	Ruth-NY	44	Sisler-StL	18	Williams-StL	24	Heilmann-Det	365
Peckinpaugh-NY	128	Sisler-StL	216	Veach-Det	43	Shanks-Was	18	Meusel-NY	24	Meusel-NY	334
Sisler-StL	125	Jacobson-StL	211	Heilmann-Det	43			T.Walker-Phi	23	Tobin-StL	327
Cobb-Det	124	Veach-Det	207	Meusel-NY	40			Heilmann-Det	19	Sisler-StL	326

Runs Batted In		Runs Produced		Bases On Balls		Batting Average		On Base Percentage		Slugging Average	
Ruth-NY	171	Ruth-NY	289	Ruth-NY	144	Heilmann-Det	.394	Ruth-NY	.512	Ruth-NY	.846
Heilmann-Det	139	Heilmann-Det	234	Blue-Det	103	Cobb-Det	.389	Cobb-Det	.452	Heilmann-Det	.606
Meusel-NY	135	Veach-Det	222	Peckinpaugh-NY	84	Ruth-NY	.378	Heilmann-Det	.444	Cobb-Det	.596
Veach-Det	128	Gardner-Cle	218	J.Sewell-Cle	80	Sisler-StL	.371	Speaker-Cle	.439	Williams-StL	.561
Gardner-Cle	120	Sisler-StL	217	Schang-NY	78	Speaker-Cle	.362	Williams-StL	.429	Sisler-StL	.560

Production		Adjusted Production		Batter Runs		Adjusted Batter Runs		Clutch Hitting Index		Runs Created	
Ruth-NY	1.358	Ruth-NY	236	Ruth-NY	119.2	Ruth-NY	114.7	Gardner-Cle	141	Ruth-NY	238
Heilmann-Det	1.051	Heilmann-Det	167	Heilmann-Det	58.4	Heilmann-Det	59.9	Severeid-StL	127	Heilmann-Det	159
Cobb-Det	1.048	Cobb-Det	167	Cobb-Det	50.3	Cobb-Det	51.5	Pratt-Bos	124	Cobb-Det	134
Williams-StL	.990	Speaker-Cle	146	Williams-StL	42.5	Speaker-Cle	36.5	O'Rourke-Was	113	Sisler-StL	133
Speaker-Cle	.977	Williams-StL	142	Speaker-Cle	38.2	Williams-StL	35.2	Sheely-Chi	112	Williams-StL	130

Total Average		Stolen Bases		Stolen Base Average		Stolen Base Runs		Fielding Runs		Total Player Rating	
Ruth-NY	1.745	Sisler-StL	35	Judge-Was	77.8	Sisler-StL	3.9	Scott-Bos	38.1	Ruth-NY	9.4
Cobb-Det	1.132	Harris-Was	29	Harris-Was	76.3	Harris-Was	3.3	Collins-Chi	27.1	Cobb-Det	4.9
Heilmann-Det	1.121	Rice-Was	26	Sisler-StL	76.1	Judge-Was	2.7	Dykes-Phi	25.0	Collins-Chi	4.0
Speaker-Cle	1.040	Johnson-Chi	22	Meusel-NY	73.9	Welch-Phi	1.8	Ward-NY	18.8	Sisler-StL	3.6
Williams-StL	1.037	Cobb-Det	22	Rice-Was	68.4			Johnson-Chi	18.0	Speaker-Cle	3.3

Wins		Win Percentage		Games		Complete Games		Shutouts		Saves	
Shocker-StL	27	Mays-NY	.750	Mays-NY	49	Faber-Chi	32	Jones-Bos	5	Middleton-Det	7
Mays-NY	27	Shocker-StL	.692	Shocker-StL	47	Shocker-StL	30	Shocker-StL	4	Mays-NY	7
Faber-Chi	25	Bush-Bos	.640	Bayne-StL	47	Mays-NY	30	Mogridge-Was	4		
Jones-Bos	23	Coveleski-Cle	.639	Rommel-Phi	46	Coveleski-Cle	28	Faber-Chi	4		
Coveleski-Cle	23	Faber-Chi	.625								

Innings Pitched		Fewest Hits/Game		Fewest BB/Game		Strikeouts		Strikeouts/Game		Ratio	
Mays-NY	336.2	Faber-Chi	7.97	Hasty-Phi	2.01	Johnson-Was	143	Johnson-Was	4.88	Faber-Chi	10.53
Faber-Chi	330.2	Bush-Bos	8.63	Mays-NY	2.03	Shocker-StL	132	Shawkey-NY	4.63	Mays-NY	11.15
Shocker-StL	326.2	Mays-NY	8.88	Mogridge-Was	2.06	Shawkey-NY	126	Bayne-StL	4.50	Mogridge-Was	11.69
Coveleski-Cle	315.0	Shawkey-NY	9.00	Bagby-Cle	2.07	Faber-Chi	124	Leonard-Det	4.41	Shocker-StL	12.04
Kerr-Chi	308.2	Johnson-Was	9.03	Zachary-Was	2.12	Leonard-Det	120	Mails-Cle	4.03	Jones-Bos	12.11

Earned Run Average		Adjusted ERA		Opponents' Batting Avg.		Opponents' On Base Pct.		Starter Runs		Adjusted Starter Runs	
Faber-Chi	2.48	Faber-Chi	171	Faber-Chi	.242	Faber-Chi	.297	Faber-Chi	66.3	Faber-Chi	64.6
Mogridge-Was	3.00	Mays-NY	139	Mays-NY	.257	Mays-NY	.303	Mays-NY	46.2	Mays-NY	44.4
Mays-NY	3.05	Mogridge-Was	137	Bush-Bos	.260	Mogridge-Was	.313	Mogridge-Was	41.0	Hoyt-NY	35.8
Hoyt-NY	3.09	Hoyt-NY	137	Shawkey-NY	.263	Shocker-StL	.319	Hoyt-NY	37.3	Mogridge-Was	35.7
Jones-Bos	3.22	Jones-Bos	131	Johnson-Was	.263	Johnson-Was	.326	Jones-Bos	35.1	Shocker-StL	33.6

Clutch Pitching Index		Relief Runs	Adjusted Relief Runs	Relief Ranking	Total Pitcher Index		Total Baseball Ranking	
Russell-Bos	122				Faber-Chi	7.0	Ruth-NY	8.7
Zachary-Was	118				Mays-NY	5.8	Faber-Chi	7.0
Keefe-Phi	114				Shocker-StL	4.3	Mays-NY	5.8
Uhle-Cle	108				Jones-Bos	4.0	Cobb-Det	4.9
Sothoron-SL-Bs-Cle	108				Hoyt-NY	3.3	Shocker-StL	4.3

February 18 Judge Landis resigns his Federal judgeship, claiming the two jobs (judge and commissioner) take up too much time.

April 12 For the first time since 1900, there are no playing managers in the NL. Long considered an economic necessity, the dual role is no longer essential. It won't be until 1930 that the AL has all bench managers.

April 13 Dazzy Vance, 31, makes his Brooklyn debut and loses to the Giants' Phil Douglas, 4–3. In 1915 when Vance made one start for the Pirates, it was Douglas who beat him. Since then Vance has been in the minors. Despite his late start, the right-hander will win 197 games in 14 years and a place in the Hall of Fame in 1955.

April 29 The New York Giants hit four inside-the-park homers in one wind-swept game in spacious Braves Field in Boston. George Kelly hits two, and Ross Youngs and Dave Bancroft hit the others.

May 29 The U.S. Supreme Court rules baseball is not interstate commerce, and the Baltimore Feds lose their case. The request for a rehearing will be denied.

June 12 The Cards get 10 straight hits in the sixth to beat the Phils, 14–8, tying their own record of Sept. 17, 1920. One of the hits would have been a homer by shortstop George "Specs" Toporcer, the first non-pitcher to wear glasses. Unfortunately, Toporcer's first major league homer is negated when he passes base runner Doc Lavan, and he is credited with only a single.

July 7 Pirates outfielder Max Carey is the busiest man on the field in an 18-inning 9-8 loss to the Giants. He gets six hits, draws three walks, has three stolen bases, including one of home, and catches seven fly balls.

July 22 When the Cards go into first place by beating Boston while the Reds are downing the Giants, it marks the first time both St. Louis teams are ever in first place at the same time.

August 25 In one of the most poorly pitched major league games ever played, the Cubs edge the Phils, 26–23 in Chicago. There are 51 hits, 23 walks, and 10 errors. The Phils, have the bases loaded in the ninth when the game ends, making a total of 16 left on base; the Cubs leave nine. When the Cubs score 14 in the fourth to take a 25–6 lead, outfielder Marty Callaghan bats three times, getting two hits and striking out. Time of game: 3:01.

September 20 Rogers Hornsby is stopped by Burleigh Grimes of Brooklyn after hitting in 33 straight games.

September 25 The Giants beat St. Louis, 5-4, in 10 innings to clinch John McGraw's eighth pennant and the Giants' 10th in 41 years in the NL.

October 1 Rogers Hornsby's 3-for-5 on the last day puts him at .401, the first .400-hitter in the NL since Ed Delahanty in 1899. His NL-record 250 hits top Willie Keeler's 243 in 1897, and he wins the Triple Crown with 152 RBIs and 42 home runs.

October 4 For the first time, the entire World Series will be broadcast over the radio. Writer Grantland Rice does the announcing for station WJZ, Newark; it is relayed to WGY in Schenectady. For the first time since 1908, two repeaters meet in the World Series. In a return to the seven-game format, the Giants will win four games while scoring in only five innings. The Yankees' Joe Bush (26-7) leads Art Nehf (19-13) 2-0 when Irish Meusel's two-run single and Pep Young's sacrifice fly score three in the eighth to give the Giants a 3-2 win in Game 1.

October 5 Bob Shawkey (20-12) goes the route, with the Giants scoring three in the first and the Yanks getting single tallies in the first, fourth, and eighth. A near-riot erupts among the 36,514 fans when umpire George Hildebrand, acting on umpire Bill Klem's advice, calls the game, a 3-3 tie, due to darkness after 10 innings. The fans think there's light enough to continue. It takes a police escort to get Judge Landis out of the park and away from the unruly mob. That night he bends over backwards to negate the public's opinion that the game might have been called to provide an extra day's gate by donating the $120,554 receipts to charities. Half will go to New York charities, and half will go to disabled soldiers.

October 8 The Yanks score first, but the Giants score two in the third and three in the eighth to win the finale, 5-3, as Art Nehf hands Joe Bush his second loss, and the Giants win the Series.

	BOSTON		BROOKLYN		CHICAGO		CINCINNATI		NEW YORK		PHILADELPHIA		PITTSBURGH		ST.LOUIS
M	F.Mitchell	M	W.Robinson	M	B.Killefer	M	P.Moran	M	J.McGraw	M	K.Wilhelm	M	M.Gibson	M	B.Rickey
1B	W.Holke	1B	R.Schmandt	1B	R.Grimes	1B	J.Daubert	1B	G.Kelly	1B	R.Leslie	M	B.McKechnie	1B	J.Fournier
2B	L.Kopf	2B	J.Johnston	2B	Z.Terry	2B	S.Bohne	2B	F.Frisch	2B	F.Parkinson	1B	C.Grimm	2B	R.Hornsby
SS	H.Ford	SS	I.Olson	SS	C.Hollocher	SS	I.Caveney	SS	D.Bancroft	SS	A.Fletcher	2B	C.Tierney	SS	S.Toporcer
3B	T.Boeckel	3B	A.High	3B	M.Krug	3B	B.Pinelli	3B	H.Groh	3B	G.Rapp	SS	R.Maranville	3B	M.Stock
LF	A.Nixon	LF	Z.Wheat	LF	H.Miller	LF	P.Duncan	LF	I.Meusel	LF	C.Lee	3B	P.Traynor	LF	J.Schultz
CF	R.Powell	CF	H.Myers	CF	J.Statz	CF	G.Burns	CF	C.Stengel	CF	C.Williams	LF	C.Bigbee	CF	J.Smith
RF	W.Cruise	RF	T.Griffith	RF	B.Friberg	RF	G.Harper	RF	R.Youngs	RF	C.Walker	CF	M.Carey	RF	M.Flack
C	M.O'Neil	C	H.DeBerry	C	B.O'Farrell	C	B.Hargrave	C	F.Snyder	C	B.Henline	RF	R.Russell	C	E.Ainsmith
												C	J.Gooch		
23	W.Barbare	O	B.Griffith	O	C.Heathcote	2	L.Fonseca	2	J.Rawlings	3S	R.Wrightstone			S	D.Lavan
O	F.Nicholson	C	O.Miller	O1	T.Barber	C	I.Wingo	C	E.Smith	O	B.LeBourveau	3O	C.Barnhart	O	A.McHenry
C	H.Gowdy	1	C.Mitchell	3	J.Kelleher	O	E.Roush	O	B.Cunningham	O	J.Mokan	C	W.Schmidt	C	V.Clemons
C1	F.Gibson	C	B.Hungling	O	M.Callaghan	S	W.Kimmick	O	R.Shinners	C	J.Peters	2	J.Ens	O	H.Mueller
O	B.Southworth	S	C.Ward	O	G.Maisel	/1	R.Bressler	/O	D.Robertson	S2	J.Smith	O	R.Rohwer	1	J.Bottomley
O	L.Christenbury	O	B.Neis	C	G.Hartnett	O	G.Neale	/1	L.King	O	L.King	O	W.Mueller	O	L.Mann
O	B.Roser	2	H.Janvrin	C	K.Wirts	/C	R.Lutz	C	A.Gaston	/C	F.Withrow	O	J.Mokan	O	R.Blades
1	S.Henry	/1	S.Post	O	M.Flack			/2	F.Maguire	/2	R.Benton	O	J.Mattox	O	C.Heathcote
/S	G.Gallagher	/C	Z.Taylor	2	S.Adams			/O	M.Higbee			C	B.Jonnard	1O	D.Gainer
		/S	S.Crane	/O	H.Fitzgerald	P	E.Rixey	/S	T.Jackson	P	J.Ring	/2	S.Stewart	/O	B.Shotton
P	M.Watson	H	P.Whitted	/3	G.Grantham	P	J.Couch	/3	W.MacPhee	P	L.Meadows	/2	J.Hammond	P	H.McCurdy
P	F.Miller	R	W.Hood	/1	W.Golvin	P	D.Luque	H	I.Boone	P	G.Smith	/O	J.Miller	/C	E.Vick
P	R.Marquard			/2	J.Klugmann	P	P.Donohue	P	J.Berry	P	B.Hubbell	H	T.Lovelace	/S	H.Freigau
P	J.Oeschger	P	D.Ruether	H	B.Weis	P	C.Keck	R	C.Dolan	P	L.Weinert	H	T.McNamara		
P	H.McQuillan	P	B.Grimes	H	H.Cotter	RP	J.Gillespie					H	A.Merewether	P	J.Pfeffer
RP	T.McNamara	P	D.Vance			P	C.Markle	P	A.Nehf	P	J.Winters	R	K.Cuyler	P	B.Sherdel
RP	G.Braxton	P	L.Cadore			P	K.Schnell	P	J.Barnes	P	J.Singleton			P	J.Haines
		P	S.Smith	P	V.Aldridge	/P	J.Scott	P	R.Ryan	/P	P.Behan	P	W.Cooper	P	B.Doak
P	D.Fillingim	RP	A.Mamaux	P	P.Alexander			P	P.Douglas	P	L.Pinto	P	J.Morrison	P	B.Pertica
P	G.Lansing			P	T.Osborne			P	H.McQuillan	/P	H.Betts	P	W.Glazner	RP	L.North
/P	H.Hulihan	P	H.Shriver	P	V.Cheeves			RP	C.Jonnard	/P	S.Baumgartner	P	B.Adams	RP	C.Barfoot
/P	J.Cooney	P	A.Decatur	P	P.Jones			RP	R.Causey	/P	T.Sullivan		E.Hamilton		
/P	J.Genewich	/P	R.Gordinier					RP	V.Barnes			RP	C.Yellowhorse	/P	E.Sell
/P	D.Rudolph	/P	J.Murray	P	T.Kaufmann									P	B.Bailey
/P	J.Matthews	/P	P.Schreiber	P	G.Stueland									R	R.Walker
/P	A.Yeargin			/P	V.Keen			P	F.Toney			P	H.Carlson	P	E.Dyer
/P	C.Morgan			P	B.Freeman			P	J.Scott			/P	M.Brown	/P	M.Goodwin
				/P	F.Fussell			/P	C.Hill			/P	B.Hollingsworth	/P	J.Knight
				/P	E.Morris			P	R.Shea			/P	J.Zinn	/P	J.Stuart
				/P	S.Martin			/P	F.Johnson			/P	R.Wheeler	/P	S.Benton
				/P	U.Eubanks			/P	C.Blume						
								/P	M.Cvengros						

TEAM	G	W	L	PCT	GB	R	OR	AB	H	2B	3B	HR	BB	SO	AVG	OBP	SLG	PRO	PRO+	BR	/A	PF	CHI	RC	SB	CS	SBA	SBR
NY	156	93	61	.604		852	658	5454	1661	253	90	80	448	421	.305	.363	.428	.791	109	77	70	101	99	848	116	83	58	-15
CIN	156	86	68	.558	7	766	677	5282	1561	226	99	45	436	381	.296	.353	.401	.754	102	8	23	98	99	737	130	136	49	-43
STL	154	85	69	.552	8	863	819	5425	1634	280	88	107	447	425	.301	.357	.444	.801	118	91	132	95	99	860	73	63	54	-16
PIT	155	85	69	.552	8	865	736	5521	1698	239	110	52	423	326	.308	.360	.419	.779	106	56	46	101	102	848	145	59	71	8
CHI	156	80	74	.519	13	771	808	5335	1564	248	71	42	525	447	.293	.359	.390	.749	97	7	-8	102	98	752	97	108	47	-36
BRO	155	76	78	.494	17	743	754	5413	1569	235	76	56	339	318	.290	.335	.392	.727	94	-58	-52	99	105	709	79	60	57	-12
PHI	154	57	96	.373	35.5	738	920	5459	1537	268	55	116	450	611	.282	.341	.415	.756	92	-3	-77	110	95	771	48	60	44	-22
BOS	154	53	100	.346	39.5	596	822	5161	1355	162	73	32	387	451	.263	.317	.341	.658	78	-179	-155	96	106	566	67	65	51	-19
TOT	620					6194		43050	12579	1911	662	530	3455	3380	.292	.348	.404	.753							755	634	54	-154

TEAM	CG	SH	SV	IP	H	H/G	HR	BB	SO	RAT	ERA	ERA+	OAV	OOB	PR	/A	PF	CPI	FA	E	DP	FW	PW	BW	SBW	DIF
NY	76	7	15	1396¹	1454	9.4	71	393	388	12.0	3.45	116	.272	.324	100	83	98	99	.970	194	145	1.1	7.8	6.6	.4	.0
CIN	88	8	3	1385²	1481	9.6	49	326	357	11.9	3.53	113	.278	.322	87	69	97	95	.968	205	147	.4	6.5	2.2	-2.2	2.2
STL	60	8	12	1362²	1609	10.6	61	447	465	13.9	4.44	87	.299	.358	-52	-87	94	98	.961	239	122	-2.0	-8.2	12.5	.3	5.5
PIT	88	15	7	1387¹	1613	10.5	52	358	490	13.9	3.98	102	.296	.343	18	13	99	99	.970	187	126	1.5	1.2	4.3	2.6	-1.6
CHI	74	8	12	1397²	1579	10.2	77	475	402	13.6	4.34	97	.292	.356	-38	-24	102	99	.968	204	154	.5	-2.3	-.8	-1.6	7.1
BRO	82	12	8	1385²	1574	10.2	74	490	499	13.6	4.05	100	.293	.356	8	2	99	106	.967	208	139	.1	.2	-4.9	.7	2.9
PHI	73	6	5	1372	1692	11.1	89	460	394	14.4	4.64	101	.307	.365	-82	7	114	102	.965	225	152	-1.1	.7	-7.3	-.3	-11.5
BOS	63	7	6	1348	1565	10.4	57	489	360	13.9	4.37	91	.291	.361	-41	-57	98	100	.965	215	121	-.4	-5.4	-14.6	.0	-3.1
TOT	604	71	68	11035¹		10.2				13.3	4.10		.292	.348					.967	1677	1106					

Runs		Hits		Doubles		Triples		Home Runs		Total Bases	
Hornsby-StL	141	Hornsby-StL	250	Hornsby-StL	46	Daubert-Cin	22	Hornsby-StL	42	Hornsby-StL	450
Carey-Pit	140	Bigbee-Pit	215	Grimes-Chi	45	Meusel-NY	17	Williams-Phi	26	Meusel-NY	314
Smith-StL	117	Bancroft-NY	209	Duncan-Cin	44	Maranville-Pit	15	Lee-Phi	17	Wheat-Bro	302
Bancroft-NY	117	Carey-Pit	207	Bancroft-NY	41	Bigbee-Pit	15	Kelly-NY	17	Williams-Phi	300
Maranville-Pit	115	Daubert-Cin	205	Hollocher-Chi	37					Daubert-Cin	300

Runs Batted In		Runs Produced		Bases On Balls		Batting Average		On Base Percentage		Slugging Average	
Hornsby-StL	152	Hornsby-StL	251	Carey-Pit	80	Hornsby-StL	.401	Hornsby-StL	.459	Hornsby-StL	.722
Meusel-NY	132	Meusel-NY	216	O'Farrell-Chi	79	Grimes-Chi	.354	Grimes-Chi	.442	Grimes-Chi	.572
Wheat-Bro	112	Bigbee-Pit	207	Bancroft-NY	79	Miller-Chi	.352	O'Farrell-Chi	.439	Lee-Phi	.540
Kelly-NY	107	Carey-Pit	200	Burns-Cin	78	Bigbee-Pit	.350	Carey-Pit	.408	Tierney-Pit	.515
		Wheat-Bro	188	Grimes-Chi	75	Tierney-Pit	.345	Bigbee-Pit	.405	Williams-Phi	.514

Production		Adjusted Production		Batter Runs		Adjusted Batter Runs		Clutch Hitting Index		Runs Created	
Hornsby-StL	1.181	Hornsby-StL	210	Hornsby-StL	90.0	Hornsby-StL	98.7	Terry-Chi	125	Hornsby-StL	200
Grimes-Chi	1.014	Grimes-Chi	157	Grimes-Chi	47.1	Grimes-Chi	44.8	Harper-Cin	117	Carey-Pit	131
Williams-Phi	.905	Daubert-Cin	130	Williams-Phi	27.5	Daubert-Cin	26.8	Meusel-NY	116	Grimes-Chi	130
Miller-Chi	.899	Wheat-Bro	129	Walker-Phi	26.3	Wheat-Bro	25.2	Pinelli-Cin	115	Walker-Phi	118
Walker-Phi	.899	Miller-Chi	128	Daubert-Cin	24.7	Russell-Pit	23.4	Tierney-Pit	114	Bigbee-Pit	116

Total Average		Stolen Bases		Stolen Base Average		Stolen Base Runs		Fielding Runs		Total Player Rating	
Hornsby-StL	1.353	Carey-Pit	51	Carey-Pit	96.2	Carey-Pit	14.1	Parkinson-Phi	31.0	Hornsby-StL	8.5
Grimes-Chi	1.107	Frisch-NY	31	Traynor-Pit	85.0	Traynor-Pit	3.3	Bancroft-NY	21.9	Bancroft-NY	4.5
Carey-Pit	.995	Burns-Cin	30	Smith-StL	72.0	Kelly-NY	1.8	Pinelli-Cin	21.1	Carey-Pit	4.1
O'Farrell-Chi	.951	Maranville-Pit	24	Johnston-Bro	66.7	T.Griffith-Bro	1.5	Carey-Pit	18.5	O'Farrell-Chi	3.8
Walker-Phi	.918	Bigbee-Pit	24	Youngs-NY	65.4	Smith-StL	1.2	Bigbee-Pit	16.6	Grimes-Chi	3.3

Wins		Win Percentage		Games		Complete Games		Shutouts		Saves	
Rixey-Cin	25	Donohue-Cin	.667	North-StL	53	Cooper-Pit	27	Vance-Bro	5	Jonnard-NY	5
Cooper-Pit	23	Rixey-Cin	.658	Sherdel-StL	47	Ruether-Bro	26	Morrison-Pit	5	North-StL	4
Ruether-Bro	21	Couch-StL	.640	Ryan-NY	46	Rixey-Cin	26	Cooper-Pit	4		
Pfeffer-StL	19	Ruether-Bro	.636	Oeschger-Bos	46			Adams-Pit	4		
Nehf-NY	19	Cooper-Pit	.622	Morrison-Pit	45			Sherdel-StL	3		

Innings Pitched		Fewest Hits/Game		Fewest BB/Game		Strikeouts		Strikeouts/Game		Ratio	
Rixey-Cin	313.1	Douglas-NY	8.79	Adams-Pit	.79	Vance-Bro	134	Vance-Bro	4.91	Douglas-NY	11.02
Cooper-Pit	294.2	Osborne-Chi	8.95	Alexander-Chi	1.25	Cooper-Pit	129	Ring-Phi	4.19	Adams-Pit	11.03
Morrison-Pit	286.1	Ryan-NY	9.11	Rixey-Cin	1.29	Ring-Phi	116	Osborne-Chi	3.96	Rixey-Cin	11.09
Nehf-NY	268.1	Luque-Cin	9.17	Donohue-Cin	1.60	Morrison-Pit	104	Cooper-Pit	3.94	Donohue-Cin	11.34
Ruether-Bro	267.1	Vance-Bro	9.49	J.Barnes-NY	1.61	Grimes-Bro	99	Doak-StL	3.64	Luque-Cin	11.69

Earned Run Average		Adjusted ERA		Opponents' Batting Avg.		Opponents' On Base Pct.		Starter Runs		Adjusted Starter Runs	
Douglas-NY	2.63	Douglas-NY	152	Douglas-NY	.257	Douglas-NY	.302	Cooper-Pit	30.2	Cooper-Pit	29.4
Ryan-NY	3.01	Weinert-Phi	137	Luque-Cin	.268	Rixey-Cin	.303	Donohue-Cin	26.2	Douglas-NY	24.1
Donohue-Cin	3.12	Ryan-NY	133	Ryan-NY	.269	Adams-Pit	.307	Douglas-NY	25.8	Weinert-Phi	23.4
Cooper-Pit	3.18	Cooper-Pit	128	Osborne-Chi	.271	J.Barnes-NY	.311	Nehf-NY	24.2	Donohue-Cin	23.2
Nehf-NY	3.29	Donohue-Cin	128	Rixey-Cin	.275	Donohue-Cin	.312	Ryan-NY	23.3	Nehf-NY	21.3

Clutch Pitching Index		Relief Runs		Adjusted Relief Runs		Relief Ranking		Total Pitcher Index		Total Baseball Ranking	
Weinert-Phi	129	McNamara-Bos	13.2	McNamara-Bos	12.4	McNamara-Bos	11.0	Cooper-Pit	4.0	Hornsby-StL	8.5
Ryan-NY	116	Causey-NY	7.2	Causey-NY	6.4	Causey-NY	5.9	Ryan-NY	2.8	Bancroft-NY	4.5
Cooper-Pit	113	Braxton-Bos	5.4	Braxton-Bos	4.6	Mamaux-Bro	2.1	Meadows-Phi	2.6	Carey-Pit	4.1
Morrison-Pit	111	Mamaux-Bro	3.9	Mamaux-Bro	3.6	Braxton-Bos	1.9	Luque-Cin	2.6	Cooper-Pit	4.0
McQuillan-Bos-NY	110	V.Barnes-NY	3.5	V.Barnes-NY	3.0	Jonnard-NY	1.3	Nehf-NY	2.5	O'Farrell-Chi	3.8

January 10 The following round-robin deal benefits everyone: Roger Peckinpaugh goes from Boston to Washington; Joe Dugan, from the Athletics to Boston; and outfielder Bing Miller and pitcher Jose Acosta, from Washington to Philadelphia. Acosta will be sold to Chicago on Feb. 4.

April 18 Willie Kamm doubles in his debut for the White Sox in a 6–5 loss at Cleveland. The first $100,000 minor leaguer (bought from the San Francisco Seals), Kamm will later be voted by Chicago fans the all-time White Sox third baseman.

April 22 The Browns' Ken Williams hits three home runs against the White Sox, each time with George Sisler on base. Williams will take the home run and RBI titles and become the first 30-30 man, with 39 home runs and 37 stolen bases.

April 30 Johnny Mostil, fleet-footed White Sox center fielder, moves over to left and makes two outstanding catches to save Charlie Robertson's 2–0 perfect game over Detroit. It's the only game Mostil ever plays in left field.

May 5 The Giants evict their AL tenants as of the end of the year, so the Yankees sign a contract to build their own $750,000 stadium on a site they had held an option on since 1920.

May 15 In a game at New York, Ty Cobb beats out a grounder to shortstop Everett Scott. Veteran writer Fred Lieb scores it a hit in the box score he files with the Associated Press. But official scorer John Kieran of the *Times* gives an error to Scott. At the season's end, the AL official records, based on Associated Press box scores, list Cobb at .401. New York writers complain unsuccessfully, claiming it should be .399, based on the official scorer's stats.

May 20 Babe Ruth and Bob Meusel, suspended on Oct. 16, 1921, by Judge Landis, return to the New York lineup and go hitless. Ruth will hit his first home run of the year two days later.

July 17 Ty Cobb gets five hits in a game for the fourth time this year, setting an AL mark. His previous five-hit games were on May 7, July 7, and July 12.

July 22 The Yankees pick up third baseman Joe Dugan and one-time World Series hero Elmer Smith from Boston, giving up outfielder Elmer Miller, shortstop Chick Fewster, shortstop John Mitchell, and pitcher Lefty O'Doul. This deal leads to a rule barring non-waiver trades after June 15.

August 13 The New York Yankees' Everett Scott nears 1,000 consecutive games played, but it takes extra effort to keep the streak alive. After a train he is wrecked, he spends $40 to hire a car to get to Chicago in time for the game.

August 14 Lizzie Murphy plays first base for an AL all-star team in an exhibition game against the Boston Red Sox, making her the first female to play for a major league team.

September 18 George Sisler's 41-game hit streak is stopped by New York's Joe Bush, the same pitcher he'd started the streak against on July 27.

September 21 The AL reinstates the MVP award, last given in 1914, appointing a committee of one writer from each city, headed by I. E. Sanborn of the *Chicago Tribune*. The trophy goes to George Sisler. The NL will pick up the idea two years later.

September 30 The Yankees clinch their second pennant by beating Boston, 3-1, behind Waite Hoyt and Joe Bush.

December 13 Alarmed at the increase in home run hitting (1,054 in the major leagues, up from 936), some AL owners back a zoning system setting a minimum of 300 feet for a ball to be called a home run. The motion dies.

December 16 The Eastern Colored League (chartered as the Mutual Association of Eastern Colored Baseball Clubs) is formally organized. The league will complete five seasons before folding in midsummer of 1928.

BOSTON	CHICAGO	CLEVELAND	DETROIT	NEW YORK	PHILADELPHIA	ST.LOUIS	WASHINGTON
M H.Duffy	M K.Gleason	M T.Speaker	M T.Cobb	M M.Huggins	M C.Mack	M L.Fohl	M C.Milan
1B G.Burns	1B E.Sheely	1B S.McInnis	1B L.Blue	1B W.Pipp	1B J.Hauser	1B G.Sisler	1B J.Judge
2B D.Pratt	2B E.Collins	2B B.Wambsganss	2B G.Cutshaw	2B A.Ward	2B R.Young	2B M.McManus	2B B.Harris
SS J.Mitchell	SS E.Johnson	SS J.Sewell	SS T.Rigney	SS E.Scott	SS C.Galloway	SS W.Gerber	SS R.Peckinpaugh
3B J.Dugan	3B E.Mulligan	3B L.Gardner	3B B.Jones	3B J.Dugan	3B J.Dykes	3B F.Ellerbe	3B B.LaMotte
LF M.Menosky	LF B.Falk	LF C.Jamieson	LF B.Veach	LF B.Ruth	LF T.Walker	LF K.Williams	LF G.Goslin
CF N.Leibold	CF J.Mostil	CF T.Speaker	CF T.Cobb	CF W.Witt	CF B.Miller	CF B.Jacobson	CF S.Rice
RF S.Collins	RF H.Hooper	RF J.Wood	RF H.Heilmann	RF B.Meusel	RF F.Welch	RF J.Tobin	RF F.Brower
C M.Ruel	C R.Schalk	C S.O'Neill	C J.Bassler	C W.Schang	C C.Perkins	C H.Severeid	C P.Gharrity
O1 J.Harris	O A.Strunk	32 R.Stephenson	31 F.Haney	3 F.Baker	O B.McGowan	3 E.Foster	3O H.Shanks
O E.Smith	3 H.McClellan	2 J.Evans	2 D.Clark	O E.Miller	1 D.Johnston	O C.Shorten	C V.Picinich
S3 F.O'Rourke	C Y.Yaryan	C L.Sewell	O B.Fothergill	3 M.McNally	23 H.Scheer	C P.Collins	O E.Smith
3S P.Pittinger	H H.Bubser	1 L.Guisto	C L.Woodall	O C.Fewster	2 F.Callaway	H H.Bronkie	3 D.Bush
O E.Miller	/2 J.Evers	O P.McNulty	O I.Flagstead	C F.Hofmann	/3 F.Brazill	/3 J.Austin	O C.Milan
3 E.Foster	/C R.Graham	O J.Graney	C C.Manion	O N.McMillan	/C O.Fuhrman	/3 G.Robertson	3 O.Bluege
C R.Walters	/2 J.Long	O H.Summa	O C.Gagnon	O A.DeVormer	/3 F.McCue	/O C.Durst	C P.Lapan
3 C.Fewster	C A.Swentor	O J.Connolly	/O J.Mohardt	/O C.Skinner	/C J.Berger	/C J.Billings	/O G.McNamara
C E.Chaplin	/C E.Pence	C L.Nunamaker	P H.Ehmke	O E.Smith	P E.Rommel	P U.Shocker	/C R.Torres
S C.Maynard	P R.Faber	/2 J.Hammond	P H.Pillette	/S J.Mitchell	P S.Harriss	P E.Vangilder	P W.Johnson
/O D.Reichle	P C.Robertson	/O J.Rabbitt	P H.Dauss	P B.Shawkey	P B.Hasty	P D.Davis	P G.Mogridge
/C W.Lynch	P D.Leverett	/3 B.Doran	P R.Oldham	P W.Hoyt	P F.Heimach	P R.Kolp	P F.Francis
P J.Quinn	P S.Hodge	/3 I.Kahdot	P O.Olsen	P S.Jones	P R.Naylor	P R.Wright	P T.Zachary
P R.Collins	P T.Blankenship	/1 U.Clanton	P S.Johnson	P J.Bush	RP J.Sullivan	RP H.Pruett	P E.Erickson
P H.Pennock	P H.Courtney	/S C.Sorrells	P B.Cole	P C.Mays	RP C.Eckert	P B.Bayne	P J.Brillheart
P A.Ferguson	P F.Schupp	P G.Uhle	P L.Stoner	RP G.Murray	P C.Ogden	P D.Danforth	P T.Phillips
P B.Karr	/P F.Mack	P S.Coveleski	/P R.Moore	/P L.O'Doul	/P R.Moore	/P D.Henry	/P J.Gleason
RP C.Fullerton	/P L.Davenport	P G.Morton	/P C.Holling	/P C.Llewellyn	P R.Yarrison	/P H.Meine	/P C.Warmoth
P A.Russell	/P J.Acosta	P D.Mails	/P K.Holloway		/P O.Rettig		/P L.Turk
P B.Piercy	/P R.Wilkinson	P J.Bagby			/P G.Ketchum		/P H.Courtney
/P S.Dodge	H.Blankenship	RP J.Lindsey			/P R.Schillings		/P C.Youngblood
/P E.Myers	/P L.Duff	P J.Edwards			/P H.O'Neill		/P S.McGrew
	/P D.McWeeny	P D.Boone					/P F.Woodward
	/P J.Russell	P D.Keefe					
	/P D.McCabe	/P G.Winn					
	/P E.Bowles	/P A.Sothoron					
	/P E.Cox	/P D.Metivier					
		/P S.Smith					
		/P P.Bedgood					
		/P J.Middleton					
		/P J.Shaute					
		/P L.Drake					
		/P G.Edmondson					
		/P N.Pott					
		/P T.Odenwald					
		/P D.Hamann					
		/P T.Jeanes					

TEAM	G	W	L	PCT	GB	R	OR	AB	H	2B	3B	HR	BB	SO	AVG	OBP	SLG	PRO	PRO+	BR	/A	PF	CHI	RC	SB	CS	SBA	SBR
NY	154	94	60	.610		758	618	5245	1504	220	75	95	497	532	.287	.353	.412	.765	103	36	19	102	99	774	62	59	51	-17
STL	154	93	61	.604	1	867	643	5416	1693	291	94	98	473	381	.313	.372	.455	.827	117	157	125	104	96	923	136	76	64	-5
DET	155	79	75	.513	15	828	791	5360	1641	250	87	54	530	378	.306	.372	.415	.787	115	94	121	97	98	847	78	62	56	-14
CLE	155	78	76	.506	16	768	817	5293	1544	320	73	32	554	331	.292	.364	.398	.762	104	43	37	101	97	792	90	58	61	-8
CHI	155	77	77	.500	17	691	691	5267	1463	243	62	45	458	463	.278	.343	.373	.716	92	-52	-49	100	101	690	109	84	56	-18
WAS	154	69	85	.448	25	650	706	5201	1395	229	76	45	458	442	.268	.334	.367	.701	93	-84	-53	95	103	656	97	63	61	-9
PHI	155	65	89	.422	29	705	830	5211	1409	229	63	111	437	591	.270	.331	.402	.733	94	-36	-54	103	104	695	60	69	47	-23
BOS	154	61	93	.396	33	598	769	5288	1392	250	55	45	366	455	.263	.316	.357	.673	82	-149	-144	99	105	599	64	67	49	-21
TOT	618					5865		42281	12041	2032	585	525	3797	3573	.285	.348	.398	.746						696	538	56	-114

TEAM	CG	SH	SV	IP	H	H/G	HR	BB	SO	RAT	ERA	ERA+	OAV	OOB	PR	/A	PF	CPI	FA	E	DP	FW	PW	BW	SBW	DIF
NY	100	7	14	1393²	1402	9.1	73	423	458	11.9	3.39	118	.268	.325	99	91	99	101	.975	157	124	2.0	8.8	1.8	-.3	4.5
STL	79	8	22	1392	1412	9.1	71	419	534	12.1	3.38	122	.268	.327	101	115	103	103	.968	201	158	-.5	11.2	12.1	.9	-7.7
DET	67	7	15	1391	1554	10.1	62	473	461	13.7	4.27	91	.288	.354	-37	-64	96	97	.970	191	133	.2	-6.2	11.8	.0	-3.7
CLE	76	14	7	1383²	1605	10.4	58	464	489	13.7	4.59	87	.296	.356	-85	-92	99	93	.968	202	147	-.5	-8.9	3.6	.6	6.2
CHI	86	13	8	1403²	1472	9.4	57	529	484	13.0	3.94	103	.278	.346	15	15	101	98	.975	155	143	2.2	1.5	-4.8	-.4	1.4
WAS	84	13	10	1362¹	1485	9.8	49	500	422	13.4	3.81	101	.286	.354	33	5	96	107	.969	196	168	-.2	.5	-5.1	.5	-3.7
PHI	73	4	6	1362¹	1573	10.4	107	469	373	13.7	4.59	92	.297	.357	-85	-55	105	99	.966	215	118	-1.2	-5.3	-5.2	.8	.6
BOS	71	10	6	1373¹	1508	9.9	48	503	359	13.5	4.30	95	.287	.354	-41	-32	102	94	.965	224	145	-1.8	-3.1	-14.0	-.7	3.5
TOT	636	76	88	11062	1508	9.8				13.1	4.03		.285	.348					.969	1541	1136					

Runs	Hits	Doubles	Triples	Home Runs	Total Bases
Sisler-StL 134	Sisler-StL 246	Speaker-Cle 48	Sisler-StL 18	Williams-StL 39	Williams-StL 367
Blue-Det 131	Cobb-Det 211	Pratt-Bos 44	Jacobson-StL 16	Walker-Phi 37	Sisler-StL 348
Williams-StL 128	Tobin-StL 207	Sisler-StL 42	Cobb-Det 16	Ruth-NY 35	Walker-Phi 310
Tobin-StL 122	Veach-Det 202	Cobb-Det 42	Judge-Was 15	Miller-Phi 21	Cobb-Det 297
			Mostil-Chi 14	Heilmann-Det 21	Tobin-StL 296

Runs Batted In	Runs Produced	Bases On Balls	Batting Average	On Base Percentage	Slugging Average
Williams-StL 155	Williams-StL 244	Witt-NY 89	Sisler-StL 420	Speaker-Cle 474	Ruth-NY 672
Veach-Det 126	Sisler-StL 231	Ruth-NY 84	Cobb-Det 401	Sisler-StL 467	Williams-StL 627
McManus-StL 109	Veach-Det 213	Blue-Det 82	Speaker-Cle 378	Cobb-Det 462	Speaker-Cle 606
Sisler-StL 105	Cobb-Det 194	Speaker-Cle 77	Heilmann-Det 356	Ruth-NY 434	Heilmann-Det 598
Jacobson-StL 102	McManus-StL 186	Williams-StL 74	Miller-Phi 335	Heilmann-Det 432	Sisler-StL 594

Production	Adjusted Production	Batter Runs	Adjusted Batter Runs	Clutch Hitting Index	Runs Created
Ruth-NY 1.106	Ruth-NY 181	Sisler-StL 64.4	Sisler-StL 59.4	Veach-Det 143	Sisler-StL 162
Speaker-Cle 1.080	Speaker-Cle 178	Williams-StL 56.1	Cobb-Det 56.5	O'Neill-Cle 132	Williams-StL 149
Sisler-StL 1.061	Cobb-Det 172	Speaker-Cle 52.8	Speaker-Cle 52.0	Johnson-Chi 127	Cobb-Det 133
Williams-StL 1.040	Heilmann-Det 172	Cobb-Det 52.4	Williams-StL 51.3	Wood-Cle 126	Speaker-Cle 127
Heilmann-Det . . . 1.030	Sisler-StL 169	Ruth-NY 50.5	Ruth-NY 48.1	Gardner-Cle 125	Ruth-NY 120

Total Average	Stolen Bases	Stolen Base Average	Stolen Base Runs	Fielding Runs	Total Player Rating
Speaker-Cle 1.272	Sisler-StL 51	Jacobson-StL 76.0	Sisler-StL 3.9	Harris-Was 26.4	Sisler-StL 6.6
Ruth-NY 1.254	Williams-StL 37	Sisler-StL 72.9	Veach-Det 2.1	Peckinpaugh-Was . 20.4	Speaker-Cle 5.0
Sisler-StL 1.203	Harris-Was 25	Harris-Was 69.4	Jacobson-StL 2.1	Schalk-Chi 20.2	Williams-StL 4.4
Heilmann-Det . . . 1.135	Johnson-Chi 21	Rice-Was 69.0	Evans-Cle 2.1	Scott-NY 17.3	Cobb-Det 4.3
Williams-StL 1.131		Rigney-Det 68.0	Shanks-Was 1.8	Sisler-StL 12.1	Ruth-NY 3.7

Wins	Win Percentage	Games	Complete Games	Shutouts	Saves
Rommel-Phi 27	Bush-NY 788	Rommel-Phi 51	Faber-Chi 31	Uhle-Cle 5	Jones-NY 8
Bush-NY 26	Rommel-Phi 675	Uhle-Cle 50	Shocker-StL 29		Pruett-StL 7
Shocker-StL 24	Shawkey-NY 625	Shocker-StL 48	Uhle-Cle 23		Wright-StL 5
Uhle-Cle 22	Pillette-Det 613	Harriss-Phi 47	Johnson-Was 23		
Faber-Chi 21	Hoyt-NY 613				

Innings Pitched	Fewest Hits/Game	Fewest BB/Game	Strikeouts	Strikeouts/Game	Ratio
Faber-Chi 352.0	Davis-StL 8.36	Shocker-StL 1.47	Shocker-StL 149	Morton-Cle 4.53	Faber-Chi 10.82
Shocker-StL 348.0	Bush-NY 8.46	Vangilder-StL 1.76	Faber-Chi 148	Harriss-Phi 4.00	Shocker-StL 11.02
Shawkey-NY 299.2	Faber-Chi 8.54	Mays-NY 1.88	Shawkey-NY 130	Shawkey-NY 3.90	Rommel-Phi 11.08
Rommel-Phi 294.0	Shawkey-NY 8.59	Kolp-StL 1.91	Ehmke-Det 108	Shocker-StL 3.85	Vangilder-StL 11.09
Uhle-Cle 287.1	Wright-StL 8.65	Hasty-Phi 1.92	Johnson-Was 105	Faber-Chi 3.78	Quinn-Bos 11.43

Earned Run Average	Adjusted ERA	Opponents' Batting Avg.	Opponents' On Base Pct.	Starter Runs	Adjusted Starter Runs
Faber-Chi 2.81	Faber-Chi 144	Davis-StL 250	Faber-Chi 299	Faber-Chi 47.7	Faber-Chi 48.8
Pillette-Det 2.85	Wright-StL 141	Bush-NY 252	Shocker-StL 304	Shocker-StL 40.9	Shocker-StL 44.8
Shawkey-NY 2.91	Shocker-StL 139	Faber-Chi 252	Rommel-Phi 309	Shawkey-NY 37.2	Shawkey-NY 36.0
Wright-StL 2.92	Shawkey-NY 137	Shawkey-NY 256	Vangilder-StL 310	Pillette-Det 36.0	Rommel-Phi 31.5
Shocker-StL 2.97	Pillette-Det 136	Pillette-Det 258	Quinn-Bos 311	Johnson-Was 32.4	Pillette-Det 31.1

Clutch Pitching Index	Relief Runs	Adjusted Relief Runs	Relief Ranking	Total Pitcher Index	Total Baseball Ranking
Mogridge-Was 124	Murray-NY 4	Murray-NY 2	Murray-NY 1	Faber-Chi 4.9	Sisler-StL 6.6
Wright-StL 118				Shocker-StL 4.8	Speaker-Cle 5.0
Johnson-Was 114				Rommel-Phi 4.0	Faber-Chi 4.9
Pillette-Det 110				Vangilder-StL 3.4	Shocker-StL 4.8
Shawkey-NY 109				Pillette-Det 3.2	Williams-StL 4.4

February 11 Jack Fournier comes to the Brooklyn Robins in a trade that sends catcher Hy Myers to St. Louis. Fournier, a Cardinal first baseman for years, says he'll quit if he has to move, but he gives in and plays another five years. With 22 homers, Fournier will finish second in the NL.

February 20 Christy Mathewson becomes president of the Boston Braves after buying the club for $300,000 with New York attorney Judge Emil Fuchs and Bostonian James McDonough. The deal does not include Braves Field, which still belongs to James Gaffney.

March 6 The Cardinals announce that their players will wear numerals on their uniforms and number them according to the batting order.

April 30 Phils outfielder Fred "Cy" Williams starts an unprecedented slugging spree, going 2-for-4 in a 12–3 loss to the Braves. In 15 games in the Baker Bowl, he will accumulate 65 total bases on 11 singles, five doubles, 11 home runs, and 29 RBIs. He will lead the NL with 41 homers.

May 30 After playing before the NL's

biggest crowd (41,000) in the afternoon game of the holiday twin bill against Brooklyn, the Giants head west with a four-game lead over the Pirates. With five future Hall of Famers in the lineup and eight on the roster during the season, the Giants will be the first team to hold first place from opening to closing day in a given season.

August 17 The Giants' George Kelly homers in the third, fourth, and fifth against the Cubs. New York wins, 13–6. Kelly adds a single and double to run his total bases to 15 for the game.

September 15* Paul Strand, right fielder for Salt Lake City (PCL), makes his 290th hit, a pro baseball record. He will play in 194 games, make 325 hits, including 66 doubles, 13 triples, and 43 homers, for a .394 BA, with 180 runs and 187 RBIs. He also has 612 total chances in the outfield. Strand, 30, had come up to the Braves as a pitcher in 1913 and was 6-2 for the 1914 pennant winners, mostly in relief. The Athletics will pay a reported $100,000 (which Mack later says was really $40,000) for him, but he will hit just .167.

September 24 Bill Terry takes his first swings in a Giants uniform as a pinch hitter.

October 10 It's an all-New York World Series for the third time. In the first World Series game at Yankee Stadium, the home team takes a quick 3-0 lead, but Heinie Groh triples in two runs in a four-run third that drives Waite Hoyt (17-9) to cover. A 4-4 tie is broken in the top of the ninth by the Giants when Casey Stengel's blast rolls to the outfield wall. The sore-legged veteran hobbles around the bases to score the winning run against reliever Joe Bush (19-15) before 55,307 spectators. This is also the first World Series to be broadcast on a nationwide radio network. Graham McNamee is at the mike, aided by baseball writers taking turns.

December 6 While in Paris, John McGraw announces plans for a tour of Europe by the Giants and White Sox in 1924, as world interest in baseball grows. In Romania, Queen Marie will throw out the first ball to mark the game's debut in July.

	BOSTON		BROOKLYN		CHICAGO		CINCINNATI		NEW YORK		PHILADELPHIA		PITTSBURGH		ST.LOUIS
M	F.Mitchell	M	W.Robinson	M	B.Killefer	M	P.Moran	M	J.McGraw	M	A.Fletcher	M	B.McKechnie	M	B.Rickey
1B	S.McInnis	1B	J.Fournier	1B	R.Grimes	1B	J.Daubert	1B	G.Kelly	1B	W.Holke	1B	C.Grimm	1B	J.Bottomley
2B	H.Ford	2B	I.Olson	2B	G.Grantham	2B	S.Bohne	2B	F.Frisch	2B	C.Tierney	2B	J.Rawlings	2B	R.Hornsby
SS	B.Smith	SS	J.Johnston	SS	S.Adams	SS	I.Caveney	SS	D.Bancroft	SS	H.Sand	SS	R.Maranville	SS	H.Freigau
3B	T.Boeckel	3B	A.High	3B	B.Friberg	3B	B.Pinelli	3B	H.Groh	3B	R.Wrightstone	3B	P.Traynor	3B	M.Stock
LF	G.Felix	LF	Z.Wheat	LF	H.Miller	LF	P.Duncan	LF	I.Meusel	LF	J.Mokan	LF	C.Bigbee	LF	J.Smith
CF	R.Powell	CF	B.Neis	CF	J.Statz	CF	E.Roush	CF	B.Cunningham	CF	C.Williams	CF	M.Carey	CF	H.Myers
RF	B.Southworth	RF	T.Griffith	RF	C.Heathcote	RF	G.Burns	RF	R.Youngs	RF	C.Walker	RF	C.Barnhart	RF	M.Flack
C	M.O'Neil	C	Z.Taylor	C	B.O'Farrell	C	B.Hargrave	C	F.Snyder	C	B.Henline	C	W.Schmidt	C	E.Ainsmith
O	A.Nixon	O	G.Bailey	S	C.Hollocher	21	L.Fonseca	S3	T.Jackson	O1	C.Lee	O	R.Russell	O	R.Blades
C	E.Smith	O	B.Griffith	C1	G.Hartnett	C	I.Wingo	O	J.O'Connell	C	J.Wilson	C	J.Gooch	2S	S.Toporcer
2	J.Conlon	O	H.DeBerry	1S	J.Kelleher	O	G.Harper	2S	C.Stengel	2	F.Parkinson	2	C.Tierney	O	H.Mueller
S	L.Kopf	3	B.McCarren	1	A.Elliott	1	R.Bressler	C	H.Gowdy	3	G.Rapp	O	W.Mueller	C	H.McCurdy
O	B.Bagwell	S	M.Berg	O	M.Callaghan	2	W.Kimmick	O	A.Gaston	O	F.Leach	2	S.Adams	S	D.Lavan
2	A.Hermann	1	D.Schliebner	S	B.Fowler	S	B.Fowler	C	E.Smith	3	C.Lord	O	K.Cuyler	O	L.Mann
C	F.Gibson	S	R.French	/C	G.Sanberg	2	F.Maguire	3	A.Woehr	/C	J.Mattox	S	L.Bell		
C	H.Gowdy	C	C.Hargreaves	/O	B.Weis	/C	E.Pick	/O	R.Shinners	/2	L.Metz	/1	J.Ens	/O	E.Dyer
/O	W.Cruise	O	T.Barber	/S	P.Turgeon	H	L.Mann	/O	H.Wilson	/O	T.Dennehey	/S	E.Moore	/S	J.Flowers
/O	B.Emmerich	/3	B.Mullen	/C	K.Wirts	R	E.Hock	/O	M.Solomon	/C	M.O'Brien	/O	F.Luce	/C	C.Niebergall
/S	E.Padgett	/2	S.Stewart	/O	T.Murray			/1	B.Terry	/C	D.Parker	/1	E.Barnes	/O	T.Douthit
H	S.Henry	/C	E.Ainsmith	H	B.Barrett	P	D.Luque			/3	J.Bennett			/1	J.Hudgens
/C	D.Cousineau	/C	B.Hungling			P	E.Rixey	P	H.McQuillan			P	J.Morrison	/O	J.Schultz
				P	P.Alexander	P	P.Donohue	P	J.Scott	P	J.Ring	P	W.Cooper	/1	S.Walker
P	R.Marquard	P	B.Grimes	P	V.Aldridge	P	R.Benton	P	A.Nehf	P	W.Glazner	P	L.Meadows	/C	G.Kopshaw
P	J.Genewich	P	D.Vance	P	T.Kaufman	RP	C.Keck	P	J.Bentley	P	L.Weinert	P	B.Adams	/O	T.Stone
P	J.Barnes	P	D.Ruether	P	T.Osborne			P	R.Ryan	P	C.Mitchell	P	E.Hamilton	R	B.Shotton
P	J.Oeschger	P	L.Dickerman	P	V.Keen	P	B.Harris	RP	C.Jonnard	P	R.Head				
P	T.McNamara	P	D.Henry	RP	F.Fussell	P	J.Couch	RP	V.Barnes	RP	B.Hubbell	P	J.Bagby	P	J.Haines
RP	D.Fillingim	RP	A.Decatur			P	H.McQuaid					P	R.Steineder	P	B.Sherdel
				P	N.Dumovich	/P	G.Abrams	P	M.Watson	P	P.Behan	P	E.Kunz	P	F.Toney
P	L.Benton	P	G.Smith	P	V.Cheeves	/P	H.Gill	P	J.Barnes	P	H.Betts	/P	W.Glazner	P	B.Doak
PO	J.Cooney	/P	L.Cadore	/P	R.Wheeler	/P	K.Schnell	P	C.Blume	P	J.Winters	/P	G.Boehler	/P	J.Pfeffer
/P	F.Miller	/P	P.Schreiber	/P	G.Stueland			/P	D.Gearin	P	J.Couch	/P	H.Carlson	RP	L.North
P	M.Watson	/P	A.Mamaux	/P	P.Collins			/P	F.Johnson	/P	J.Bishop	/P	A.Stone		
/P	D.Rudolph	/P	H.Harper	/P	E.Stauffer			/P	W.Huntzinger	/P	L.Meadows			P	J.Stuart
/P	J.Batchelder	/P	H.Shriver	/P	G.Bush			/P	R.Lucas	/P	B.Jones			P	C.Barfoot
								/P	R.Walberg	/P	J.Grant			/P	E.Sell
										/P	P.Ragan			/P	F.Wigington
										/P	R.Miller			/P	B.Pertica
										/P	A.Gardiner				

TEAM	G	W	L	PCT	GB	R	OR	AB	H	2B	3B	HR	BB	SO	AVG	OBP	SLG	PRO	PRO+	BR	/A	PF	CHI	RC	SB	CS	SBA	SBR
NY	153	95	58	.621		854	679	5452	1610	248	76	85	487	406	.295	.356	.415	.771	110	72	83	99	103	816	106	70	60	-10
CIN	154	91	63	.591	4.5	708	629	5278	1506	237	95	45	439	367	.285	.344	.392	.736	102	-1	14	98	96	707	96	105	48	-34
PIT	154	87	67	.565	8.5	786	696	5405	1592	224	111	49	407	362	.295	.347	.404	.751	102	26	9	102	103	766	154	75	67	1
CHI	154	83	71	.539	12.5	756	704	5259	1516	243	52	90	455	485	.288	.348	.406	.754	104	33	32	100	99	735	181	143	56	-32
STL	154	79	74	.516	16	746	732	5526	1582	274	76	63	438	446	.286	.343	.398	.741	103	5	21	98	97	761	89	61	59	-10
BRO	155	76	78	.494	19.5	753	741	5476	1559	214	81	62	425	382	.285	.340	.387	.727	100	-20	1	97	102	730	71	50	59	-9
BOS	155	54	100	.351	41.5	636	798	5329	1455	213	58	32	429	404	.273	.331	.353	.684	90	-99	-73	96	99	625	57	80	42	-31
PHI	155	50	104	.325	45.5	748	1008	5491	1528	259	39	112	414	556	.278	.333	.401	.734	89	-15	-100	112	101	729	70	73	49	-23
TOT	617					5987		43216	12348	1912	588	538	3494	3408	.286	.343	.395	.737							824	657	56	-147

TEAM	CG	SH	SV	IP	H	H/G	HR	BB	SO	RAT	ERA	ERA+	OAV	OOB	PR	/A	PF	CPI	FA	E	DP	FW	PW	BW	SBW	DIF
NY	62	10	18	1378	1440	9.4	82	424	453	12.3	3.90	98	.271	.328	15	-13	96	93	.972	176	141	2.4	-1.3	8.0	.8	8.6
CIN	88	11	9	1391[1]	1465	9.5	28	359	450	12.0	3.21	120	.273	.322	121	99	97	101	.969	202	144	.9	9.5	1.3	-1.5	3.7
PIT	92	5	9	1376[1]	1513	9.9	53	402	414	12.7	3.87	103	.284	.337	19	19	100	98	.971	179	157	2.3	1.8	.9	1.9	3.2
CHI	80	8	11	1366[2]	1419	9.3	86	435	408	12.4	3.82	105	.269	.329	27	25	100	96	.967	208	144	.5	2.4	3.1	-1.3	1.3
STL	77	9	7	1398[1]	1539	9.9	70	456	398	13.1	3.87	101	.284	.344	20	5	98	104	.963	232	141	-.9	.5	2.0	.8	.0
BRO	94	8	5	1396[2]	1503	9.7	55	476	548	13.0	3.74	103	.277	.344	39	20	97	100	.955	293	137	-4.4	1.9	.0	.9	.5
BOS	54	13	7	1392[2]	1662	10.7	64	394	351	13.5	4.21	94	.302	.352	-34	-41	100	102	.964	230	157	-.7	-3.9	-7.0	-1.2	-10.1
PHI	68	3	8	1376[1]	1801	11.8	100	549	384	15.6	5.34	86	.322	.386	-205	-115	115	102	.966	217	172	.0	-11.1	-9.6	-.4	-6.0
TOT	615	67	74	11076[1]		10.0				13.1	3.99		.286	.343					.966	1737	1193					

Runs
Youngs-NY 121
Carey-Pit 120
Frisch-NY 116
Johnston-Bro 111
Statz-Chi 110

Hits
Frisch-NY 223
Statz-Chi 209
Traynor-Pit 208
Johnston-Bro 203
Youngs-NY 200

Doubles
Roush-Cin 41
Tierney-Pit-Phi . . . 36
Grantham-Chi 36
Bottomley-StL 34

Triples
Traynor-Pit 19
Carey-Pit 19
Roush-Cin 18
Southworth-Bos . . 16

Home Runs
Williams-Phi 41
Fournier-Bro 22
Miller-Chi 20
Meusel-NY 19
Hornsby-StL 17

Total Bases
Frisch-NY 311
Williams-Phi 308
Fournier-Bro 303
Traynor-Pit 301
Statz-Chi 288

Runs Batted In
Meusel-NY 125
Williams-Phi 114
Frisch-NY 111
Kelly-NY 103
Fournier-Bro 102

Runs Produced
Frisch-NY 215
Meusel-NY 208
Youngs-NY 205
Traynor-Pit 197
Carey-Pit 177

Bases On Balls
Burns-Cin 101
Sand-Phi 82
Youngs-NY 73
Carey-Pit 73
Grantham-Chi 71

Batting Average
Hornsby-StL 384
Wheat-Bro 375
Bottomley-StL 371
Fournier-Bro 351
Roush-Cin 351

On Base Percentage
Hornsby-StL 459
Bottomley-StL 425
Youngs-NY 412
Fournier-Bro 411
O'Farrell-Chi 408

Slugging Average
Hornsby-StL 627
Fournier-Bro 588
Williams-Phi 576
Barnhart-Pit 563
Bottomley-StL 535

Production
Hornsby-StL 1.086
Fournier-Bro 999
Bottomley-StL 960
Williams-Phi 947
Roush-Cin 938

Adjusted Production
Hornsby-StL 188
Fournier-Bro 165
Bottomley-StL . . . 155
Roush-Cin 149
Frisch-NY 133

Batter Runs
Hornsby-StL 52.1
Fournier-Bro 43.7
Bottomley-StL . . . 39.2
Roush-Cin 34.0
Williams-Phi 33.2

Adjusted Batter Runs
Hornsby-StL 54.4
Fournier-Bro 47.0
Bottomley-StL . . . 41.5
Roush-Cin 36.2
Frisch-NY 29.8

Clutch Hitting Index
Stock-StL 136
McInnis-Bos 124
Frisch-NY 123
Meusel-NY 117
Bigbee-Pit 114

Runs Created
Fournier-Bro 125
Frisch-NY 123
Hornsby-StL 120
Bottomley-StL . . . 117
Carey-Pit 117

Total Average
Hornsby-StL 1.194
Fournier-Bro 1.071
Bottomley-StL 976
Williams-Phi 966
Carey-Pit 928

Stolen Bases
Carey-Pit 51
Grantham-Chi 43
Smith-StL 32
Heathcote-Chi 32

Stolen Base Average
Carey-Pit 86.4
Smith-StL 74.4
Frisch-NY 70.7
Traynor-Pit 68.3
Heathcote-Chi . . . 65.3

Stolen Base Runs
Carey-Pit 10.5
Smith-StL 3.0
Rawlings-Pit 2.7

Fielding Runs
Bancroft-NY 21.3
Carey-Pit 19.7
Johnston-Bro 19.4
Statz-Chi 17.7
Tierney-Pit-Phi . . . 14.4

Total Player Rating
Fournier-Bro 4.3
Traynor-Pit 4.0
Carey-Pit 3.6
Bancroft-NY 3.6
Johnston-Bro 3.6

Wins
Luque-Cin 27
Morrison-Pit 25
Alexander-Chi 22
Grimes-Bro 21
Donohue-Cin 21

Win Percentage
Luque-Cin 771
Ryan-NY 762
Scott-NY 696
Morrison-Pit 658
Alexander-Chi 647

Games
Ryan-NY 45
Jonnard-NY 45
Oeschger-Bos 44
J.Barnes-NY-Bos . . 43
Genewich-Bos 43

Complete Games
Grimes-Bro 33
Luque-Cin 28
Morrison-Pit 27
Cooper-Pit 26
Alexander-Chi 26

Shutouts
Luque-Cin 6
J.Barnes-NY-Bos . . 5
McQuillan-NY 5

Saves
Jonnard-NY 5
Ryan-NY 4

Innings Pitched
Grimes-Bro 327.0
Luque-Cin 322.0
Rixey-Cin 309.0
Alexander-Chi 305.0
Ring-Phi 304.1

Fewest Hits/Game
Luque-Cin 7.80
Vance-Bro 8.44
Morrison-Pit 8.56
Keen-Chi 8.59
Aldridge-Chi 8.67

Fewest BB/Game
Alexander-Chi 89
B.Adams-Pit 1.42
Genewich-Bos 1.82
Rixey-Cin 1.89
Meadows-Phi-Pit . . 2.15

Strikeouts
Vance-Bro 197
Luque-Cin 151
Grimes-Bro 119
Morrison-Pit 114
Ring-Phi 112

Strikeouts/Game
Vance-Bro 6.32
Luque-Cin 4.22
Bentley-NY 3.93
Osborne-Chi 3.46
Morrison-Pit 3.40

Ratio
Alexander-Chi 9.97
Luque-Cin 10.40
Ryan-NY 11.31
Aldridge-Chi 11.49
McQuillan-NY 11.56

Earned Run Average
Luque-Cin 1.93
Rixey-Cin 2.80
Keen-Chi 3.00
Kaufmann-Chi 3.10
Haines-StL 3.11

Adjusted ERA
Luque-Cin 200
Rixey-Cin 138
Keen-Chi 133
Kaufmann-Chi 129
Alexander-Chi 125

Opponents' Batting Avg.
Luque-Cin 235
Vance-Bro 250
Aldridge-Chi 251
Morrison-Pit 253
Osborne-Chi 255

Opponents' On Base Pct.
Alexander-Chi 277
Luque-Cin 291
Aldridge-Chi 307
Ryan-NY 308
McQuillan-NY 315

Starter Runs
Luque-Cin 73.9
Rixey-Cin 41.1
Alexander-Chi 27.4
Haines-StL 26.1
Kaufmann-Chi 20.6

Adjusted Starter Runs
Luque-Cin 69.1
Rixey-Cin 36.5
Alexander-Chi 27.4
Ring-Phi 24.3
Haines-StL 23.2

Clutch Pitching Index
Kaufmann-Chi 118
Rixey-Cin 116
Genewich-Bos 116
Doak-StL 116
Luque-Cin 115

Relief Runs
Decatur-Bro 15.3
Jonnard-NY 7.6
Keck-Cin 2.6
V.Barnes-NY 5

Adjusted Relief Runs
Decatur-Bro 14.0
Jonnard-NY 5.7
Keck-Cin 1.3

Relief Ranking
Decatur-Bro 8.7
Jonnard-NY 4.4
Keck-Cin 1.3

Total Pitcher Index
Luque-Cin 7.4
Rixey-Cin 3.4
Alexander-Chi 3.2
Kaufmann-Chi 2.4
Haines-StL 2.4

Total Baseball Ranking
Luque-Cin 7.4
Fournier-Bro 4.3
Traynor-Pit 4.0
Carey-Pit 3.6
Bancroft-NY 3.6

April 3 Two "Black Sox" sue the White Sox. Swede Risberg and Happy Felsch seek $400,000 damages and $6,750 back salary for conspiracy and injury to reputation, but their suit will be unsuccessful.

April 18 The debut of Yankee Stadium is a huge success with an announced attendance of 74,217. Bob Shawkey, aided by Babe Ruth's three-run home run, beats Howard Ehmke and the Red Sox, 4-1.

May 13 Washington rookie Wally Warmoth strikes out Cleveland shortstop Joe Sewell twice. It's the first of only two times in his 14-year career that Sewell will fan twice in the same contest.

May 21 Formal transfer of T. L. Huston's interest in the Yankees to Jake Ruppert is completed for $1.5 million. Ten days later Ruppert buys two more sets of uniforms so his players can wear a clean outfit every day, an unprecedented move.

July 7 Cleveland scores in every inning against the Red Sox, but playing at home, the team does not bat in the ninth. In the eight innings, they run up a then AL-record 27 runs, including 13 in the sixth, for a 27-3 win. In three innings, Lefty O'Doul gives up 16 runs on 11 hits and eight walks. This is his last season as a major league pitcher, but he will return to the major leagues in 1928 as an outfielder.

July 11 Harry Frazee, owner of the Red Sox since 1916, sells out for over $1 million to a group of Ohio businessmen, who bring in veteran front office man Bob Quinn from St. Louis to run the club. Frazee's departure is welcomed by Boston fans who are fed up with the sale of Frazee's best players over the years.

August 11 Babe Ruth goes 3-for-8 for against the Tigers, while Harry Heilmann is 5-for-10 against the Yanks. The two are neck and neck at .390 for the year. After the game, AL president Ban Johnson rules that Ruth must give up his Sam Crawford bat, made for him by the future Hall of Famer. The bat is "four pieces of seasoned wood, carefully glued together." On Aug. 21, Johnson rules that only one-piece bats will be allowed, a rule that also affects Ken Williams, who is using a plugged bat.

September 11 After leadoff hitter Whitey Witt reaches first on a controversial single, Boston pitcher Howard Ehmke retires the next 27 batters for a 3-0 win. The Boston crowd exhorted the scorer Fred Lieb to reverse his call on the hard grounder that third baseman Howard Shanks booted, but the one hit stood. Ehmke has now given up just one hit in his last two games.

September 14 George Burns, first baseman for the Boston Red Sox, makes an unassisted triple play on a line drive hit by Cleveland's Frank Brower. He tags out Rube Lutzke and rushes to second base for the third out before Riggs Stephenson returns.

October 2 Harry Heilmann goes 2-for-2 to put his average over .400. He will sit for the rest of the season, except for a pinch single on the final day, and will win the batting title with a .403 average.

October 15 After Babe Ruth's first-inning home run, the Giants peck away at Herb Pennock for four runs and take a 4-1 lead into the eighth. With one out, Art Nehf loads the bases on two singles and a walk, then walks in a run. Reliever Rosy Ryan forces in another run with a walk to Joe Dugan. Ruth strikes out, but Bob Meusel raps a single that scores the go-ahead runs. Sam Jones holds off the Giants, and the Yankees have their first world championship.

October 19 Citing the unsavory characters associated with the sport, AL president Ban Johnson persuades AL owners to prohibit boxing matches in their parks. The NL declines to go along with it.

October 26 Frank Chance signs to manage the White Sox, replacing Kid Gleason, but Chase will resign Feb. 17, 1924, because of illness. Coach Johnny Evers, named acting manager, will fill the job the entire season.

December 10 Traveling to Chicago for the major league meetings, Wild Bill Donovan, New Haven manager, is killed in a train wreck. Donovan was a pitcher for Detroit and managed the Yankees and Phils. New Haven president George Weiss, future general manager of the Yankees and Mets, had swapped berths with Donovan and escapes with only a minor injury.

	BOSTON		CHICAGO		CLEVELAND		DETROIT		NEW YORK		PHILADELPHIA		ST.LOUIS		WASHINGTON
M	F.Chance	M	K.Gleason	M	T.Speaker	M	T.Cobb	M	M.Huggins	M	C.Mack	M	L.Fohl	M	D.Bush
1B	G.Burns	1B	E.Sheely	1B	F.Brower	1B	L.Blue	1B	W.Pipp	1B	J.Hauser	M	J.Austin	1B	J.Judge
2B	C.Fewster	2B	E.Collins	2B	B.Wambsganss	2B	F.Haney	2B	A.Ward	2B	J.Dykes	1B	D.Schliebner	2B	B.Harris
SS	J.Mitchell	SS	H.McClellan	SS	J.Sewell	SS	T.Rigney	SS	E.Scott	SS	C.Galloway	2B	M.McManus	SS	R.Peckinpaugh
3B	H.Shanks	3B	W.Kamm	3B	R.Lutzke	3B	B.Jones	3B	J.Dugan	3B	S.Hale	SS	W.Gerber	3B	O.Bluege
LF	J.Harris	LF	B.Falk	LF	C.Jamieson	LF	B.Veach	LF	B.Meusel	LF	B.Miller	3B	G.Robertson	LF	G.Goslin
CF	D.Reichle	CF	J.Mostil	CF	T.Speaker	CF	T.Cobb	CF	W.Witt	CF	W.Matthews	LF	K.Williams	CF	N.Leibold
RF	I.Flagstead	RF	H.Hooper	RF	H.Summa	RF	H.Heilmann	RF	B.Ruth	RF	F.Welch	CF	B.Jacobson	RF	S.Rice
C	V.Picinich	C	R.Schalk	C	S.O'Neill	C	J.Bassler	C	W.Schang	C	C.Perkins	RF	J.Tobin	C	M.Ruel
												C	H.Severeid		
O	S.Collins	O	R.Elsh	2	R.Stephenson	O	B.Fothergill	C	F.Hofmann	O	B.McGowan			O3	J.Evans
32	N.McMillan	O	B.Barrett	C	G.Myatt	O	H.Manush	O	E.Smith	2	H.Scheer	3	H.Ezzell	C1	P.Gharrity
C	A.DeVormer	O	M.Archdeacon	1	L.Guisto	21	D.Pratt	O	H.Hendrick	3	H.Riconda	C	P.Collins	O	R.Wade
O	M.Menosky	2	J.Happenny	O	J.Connolly	C	L.Woodall	C	B.Bengough	C	T.Walker	2	E.Foster	3	B.Conroy
2S	P.Pittinger	3	R.Graham	3	L.Gardner	O	G.Cutshaw	S	E.Johnson	C	F.Bruggy	O	C.Durst	/S	P.Hargrave
C	R.Walters	C	B.Crouse	1	R.Knode	S	J.Kerr	S	M.McNally	O	W.French	O	B.Whaley	3	B.Murray
/O	J.Donahue	O	A.Strunk	/C	L.Sewell	/C	C.Manion	/1	L.Gehrig	/C	C.Rowland	3	F.Ellerbe	/2	J.O'Neill
/2	F.Fuller	S	E.Johnson	/O	W.Shaner	/3	L.Burke	O	H.Haines	/O	J.Jones	/C	J.Billings	/O	S.Fisher
O	N.Leibold	/2	L.Rosenberg	/O	S.Clarke	H	I.Flagstead	/S	M.Gazella	/S	D.Wood	/O	H.Bennett	/3	D.Bush
/O	I.Boone	O	C.Dorman	/O	T.Gulley	/C	F.Carisch					H	H.Rice	/O	C.Smith
/O	C.Skinner	H	J.Cortazzo	/O	J.Gallagher			P	J.Bush	P	E.Rommel	/C	J.Schulte	/3	D.Prothro
		H	R.Snipes	R	K.Hogan			P	B.Shawkey	P	B.Hasty	H	B.Mizeur	/1	J.Riley
P	H.Ehmke	R	L.Taylor			P	H.Dauss	P	S.Jones	P	S.Harriss	H	S.Simon	H	P.Lapan
P	J.Quinn			P	G.Uhle	P	H.Pillette	P	W.Hoyt	P	F.Heimach	/M	J.Austin	H	J.Propst
P	A.Ferguson	P	C.Robertson	P	S.Coveleski	P	K.Holloway	P	H.Pennock	P	R.Naylor				
P	B.Piercy	P	R.Faber	P	J.Edwards	P	S.Johnson					P	E.Vangilder	P	W.Johnson
P	G.Murray	P	M.Cvengros	P	J.Shaute	P	B.Cole	P	C.Mays	P	R.Walberg	P	U.Shocker	P	G.Mogridge
RP	L.O'Doul	P	T.Blankenship	RP	D.Metivier	RP	R.Francis	/P	G.Pipgras	P	C.Ogden	P	D.Danforth	P	T.Zachary
		P	D.Leverett	P	G.Morton			/P	O.Roettger	P	D.Burns	P	R.Kolp	P	A.Russell
P	C.Fullerton			RP	D.Boone	P	R.Collins			/P	R.Meeker	RP	C.Root	P	P.Zahniser
P	L.Howe	P	S.Thurston			/P	O.Olsen			/P	W.Kinney				
/P	C.Blethen	/P	T.Lyons	P	S.Smith	/P	H.Moore			/P	A.Kellett			P	C.Warmoth
/P	C.Stimson	P	F.Mack	/P	P.Bedgood	/P	E.Wells			/P	C.Wolfe	H	H.Pruett	/P	B.Hollingsworth
/P	D.Black	/P	C.Gillenwater	/P	J.Sullivan	/P	R.Clarke			/P	H.Hulvey	P	R.Wright	P	F.Marberry
		/P	P.Castner	/P	L.Drake					/P	R.Kelly	P	B.Bayne	/P	M.Mitchell
		/P	S.Connally	/P	G.Edmondson					/P	H.O'Neill	P	G.Grant	/P	S.Friday
		/P	H.Blankenship	/P	J.Fry					/P	D.Ozmer	/P	S.Thurston	/P	J.Brillheart
		/P	L.Davenport	/P	D.Levsen							/P	J.Elliott	/P	D.Sedgwick
		/P	R.Proctor	/P	G.Winn									/P	S.McGrew
		/P	S.Embrey											/P	S.Potter
		/P	L.Cadore											/P	C.Roe
		/P	F.Woodward											/P	F.Schemanske
														/P	T.Wingfield

TEAM	G	W	L	PCT	GB	R	OR	AB	H	2B	3B	HR	BB	SO	AVG	OBP	SLG	PRO	PRO+	BR	/A	PF	CHI	RC	SB	CS	SBA	SBR
NY	152	98	54	.645		823	622	5347	1554	231	79	105	521	516	.291	.357	.422	.779	108	73	59	102	101	811	69	74	48	-24
DET	155	83	71	.539	16	831	741	5266	1579	270	69	41	596	385	.300	.377	.401	.778	113	91	108	98	98	827	87	62	58	-11
CLE	153	82	71	.536	16.5	888	746	5290	1594	301	75	59	633	384	.301	.381	.420	.801	117	135	137	100	100	868	79	79	50	-24
WAS	155	75	78	.490	23.5	720	747	5244	1436	224	98	42	532	448	.274	.346	.367	.713	98	-46	-11	95	104	693	102	68	60	-10
STL	154	74	78	.487	24	688	720	5298	1489	248	62	82	442	423	.281	.339	.398	.737	94	-15	-55	106	96	724	64	54	54	-13
PHI	153	69	83	.454	29	661	761	5196	1407	229	64	53	445	517	.271	.333	.370	.703	89	-74	-82	101	103	653	72	62	54	-16
CHI	156	69	85	.448	30	692	741	5246	1463	254	57	42	532	458	.279	.350	.373	.723	97	-26	-17	99	97	707	191	118	62	-14
BOS	154	61	91	.401	37	584	809	5181	1354	253	54	34	391	480	.261	.318	.351	.669	81	-143	-146	101	104	579	79	91	46	-31
TOT	616					5887		42068	11876	2010	553	442	4092	3611	.282	.351	.388	.739							743	608	55	-142

TEAM	CG	SH	SV	IP	H	H/G	HR	BB	SO	RAT	ERA	ERA+	OAV	OOB	PR	/A	PF	CPI	FA	E	DP	FW	PW	BW	SBW	DIF
NY	101	9	10	1380²	1365	8.9	68	491	506	12.3	3.62	109	.263	.330	55	49	99	96	.977	144	131	3.3	4.7	5.7	-.6	8.9
DET	61	9	12	1373²	1502	9.8	58	449	447	13.1	4.09	94	.283	.345	-16	-34	97	96	.968	200	103	.0	-3.3	10.4	.7	-1.9
CLE	77	10	11	1376	1517	9.9	36	465	407	13.2	3.91	101	.285	.346	11	4	100	97	.964	226	143	-1.7	.4	13.2	-.6	-5.9
WAS	71	8	16	1374¹	1527	10.0	56	563	474	14.0	3.98	95	.291	.364	0	-30	95	109	.966	216	182	-.9	-2.9	-1.1	.7	2.6
STL	83	10	10	1373¹	1430	9.4	59	528	488	13.2	3.93	106	.275	.348	9	37	105	98	.971	177	145	1.4	3.6	-5.3	.5	-2.1
PHI	65	7	12	1364²	1465	9.7	68	560	400	13.5	4.08	101	.280	.352	-15	1	103	99	.965	221	127	-1.4	.0	-7.9	.2	2.0
CHI	74	5	11	1397	1512	9.7	49	534	467	13.4	4.05	98	.283	.353	-10	-13	99	99	.971	184	138	1.1	-1.3	-1.6	.4	-6.6
BOS	77	3	11	1372	1534	10.1	48	520	412	13.9	4.20	98	.294	.366	-33	-15	103	104	.963	232	126	-2.0	-1.5	-14.1	-1.3	3.8
TOT	609	61	93	11011²		9.7				13.3	3.98		.282	.351					.968	1600	1095					

Runs		Hits		Doubles		Triples		Home Runs		Total Bases	
Ruth-NY	151	Jamieson-Cle	222	Speaker-Cle	59	Rice-Was	18	Ruth-NY	41	Ruth-NY	399
Speaker-Cle	133	Speaker-Cle	218	Burns-Bos	47	Goslin-Was	18	Williams-StL	29	Speaker-Cle	350
Jamieson-Cle	130	Heilmann-Det	211	Ruth-NY	45	Tobin-StL	15	Heilmann-Det	18	Williams-StL	346
Heilmann-Det	121	Ruth-NY	205	Heilmann-Det	44	Mostil-Chi	15	Speaker-Cle	17	Heilmann-Det	331
Rice-Was	117	Tobin-StL	202	J.Sewell-Cle	41			Hauser-Phi	17	Tobin-StL	303

Runs Batted In		Runs Produced		Bases On Balls		Batting Average		On Base Percentage		Slugging Average	
Ruth-NY	131	Speaker-Cle	246	Ruth-NY	170	Heilmann-Det	.403	Ruth-NY	.545	Ruth-NY	.764
Speaker-Cle	130	Ruth-NY	241	J.Sewell-Cle	98	Ruth-NY	.393	Heilmann-Det	.481	Heilmann-Det	.632
Heilmann-Det	115	Heilmann-Det	218	Blue-Det	96	Speaker-Cle	.380	Speaker-Cle	.469	Williams-StL	.623
J.Sewell-Cle	109	J.Sewell-Cle	204	Speaker-Cle	93	Collins-Chi	.360	J.Sewell-Cle	.456	Speaker-Cle	.610
Pipp-NY	108	Rice-Was	189	Collins-Chi	84	Williams-StL	.357	Collins-Chi	.455	Harris-Bos	.520

Production		Adjusted Production		Batter Runs		Adjusted Batter Runs		Clutch Hitting Index		Runs Created	
Ruth-NY	1.309	Ruth-NY	238	Ruth-NY	119.1	Ruth-NY	115.7	Pipp-NY	137	Ruth-NY	223
Heilmann-Det	1.113	Heilmann-Det	195	Speaker-Cle	70.9	Heilmann-Det	73.7	J.Sewell-Cle	123	Speaker-Cle	166
Speaker-Cle	1.079	Speaker-Cle	183	Heilmann-Det	70.7	Speaker-Cle	71.2	Bassler-Det	122	Heilmann-Det	160
Williams-StL	1.062	Williams-StL	168	Williams-StL	61.2	Williams-StL	53.5	Sheely-Chi	122	Williams-StL	148
J.Sewell-Cle	.935	J.Sewell-Cle	147	J.Sewell-Cle	42.8	J.Sewell-Cle	43.0	Meusel-NY	121	J.Sewell-Cle	128

Total Average		Stolen Bases		Stolen Base Average		Stolen Base Runs		Fielding Runs		Total Player Rating	
Ruth-NY	1.683	Collins-Chi	48	Mostil-Chi	71.9	Mostil-Chi	2.7	Peckinpaugh-Was	22.8	Ruth-NY	10.6
Heilmann-Det	1.288	Mostil-Chi	41	Rice-Was	71.4	Barrett-Chi	1.8	Mostil-Chi	21.8	Speaker-Cle	6.4
Speaker-Cle	1.222	Harris-Was	23	Elsh-Chi	66.7	Veach-Det	1.2	Harris-Was	19.4	Heilmann-Det	6.2
Williams-StL	1.144	Rice-Was	20	Collins-Chi	62.3	Rice-Was	1.2	Ruel-Was	18.5	J.Sewell-Cle	6.0
J.Sewell-Cle	1.025			Harris-Was	59.0	Pratt-Det	1.2	Flagstead-Det-Bos	18.5	Williams-StL	4.8

Wins		Win Percentage		Games		Complete Games		Shutouts		Saves	
Uhle-Cle	26	Pennock-NY	.760	Rommel-Phi	56	Uhle-Cle	29	Coveleski-Cle	5	Russell-Was	9
Jones-NY	21	Jones-NY	.724	Uhle-Cle	54	Ehmke-Bos	28	Vangilder-StL	4	Quinn-Bos	7
Dauss-Det	21	Hoyt-NY	.654	Russell-Was	52	Shocker-StL	24	Dauss-Det	4	Harriss-Phi	6
Shocker-StL	20	Shocker-StL	.625	Cole-Det	52	Dauss-Det	22				
Ehmke-Bos	20	Uhle-Cle	.619	Dauss-Det	50	Bush-NY	22				

Innings Pitched		Fewest Hits/Game		Fewest BB/Game		Strikeouts		Strikeouts/Game		Ratio	
Uhle-Cle	357.2	Shawkey-NY	8.07	Shocker-StL	1.59	Johnson-Was	130	Johnson-Det	4.75	Shocker-StL	11.16
Ehmke-Bos	316.2	Hoyt-NY	8.56	Coveleski-Cle	1.66	Shawkey-NY	125	Johnson-Was	4.48	Hoyt-NY	11.20
Dauss-Det	316.0	Bush-NY	8.59	Thurston-StL-Chi	1.75	Bush-NY	125	Shawkey-NY	4.35	Pennock-NY	11.52
Rommel-Phi	297.2	Russell-Was	8.78	Quinn-Bos	1.96	Ehmke-Bos	121	Bush-NY	4.08	Jones-NY	11.63
Vangilder-StL	282.1	Danforth-StL	8.79	Dauss-Det	2.22			Harriss-Phi	3.83	Coveleski-Cle	11.64

Earned Run Average		Adjusted ERA		Opponents' Batting Avg.		Opponents' On Base Pct.		Starter Runs		Adjusted Starter Runs	
Coveleski-Cle	2.76	Coveleski-Cle	143	Shawkey-NY	.246	Shocker-StL	.306	Coveleski-Cle	30.9	Vangilder-StL	34.8
Hoyt-NY	3.02	Vangilder-StL	136	Hoyt-NY	.253	Hoyt-NY	.307	Vangilder-StL	28.9	Coveleski-Cle	30.4
Russell-Was	3.03	Hoyt-NY	131	Jones-NY	.257	Faber-Chi	.311	Hoyt-NY	25.6	Rommel-Phi	27.8
Vangilder-StL	3.06	Thurston-StL-Chi	127	Faber-Chi	.259	Jones-NY	.312	Rommel-Phi	23.7	Hoyt-NY	24.4
Mogridge-Was	3.11	Rommel-Phi	126	Bush-NY	.260	Pennock-NY	.314	Pennock-NY	22.4	Shocker-StL	23.5

Clutch Pitching Index		Relief Runs		Adjusted Relief Runs		Relief Ranking		Total Pitcher Index		Total Baseball Ranking	
Thurston-StL-Chi	139							Rommel-Phi	4.0	Ruth-NY	10.6
Russell-Was	128							Vangilder-StL	3.4	Speaker-Cle	6.4
Mogridge-Was	122							Coveleski-Cle	2.9	Heilmann-Det	6.2
Vangilder-StL	121							Bush-NY	2.6	J.Sewell-Cle	6.0
Coveleski-Cle	121							Uhle-Cle	2.4	Williams-StL	4.8

February 12 The NL decides to go along with the AL in offering a $1,000 prize to the player named MVP by a committee of writers.

April 15 The Cards' Rogers Hornsby is the only batter who ever goes 2-for-5 on Opening Day and improves on his batting average the rest of the year. His .424 will be the highest major league batting average in the century.

July 8 The Phils play a 25-inning doubleheader at Cincinnati without making an error.

July 16 Giants first baseman George Kelly hits his seventh homer and becomes the first man to hit homers in six consecutive games. He will finish with 21 for the year.

September 4 Dazzy Vance chalks up his 12th straight win and 24th on the year; it's also the Dodgers' 12th straight win. Two days later, spitballer Bill Doak pitches the Dodgers into first place with a 1–0 win over Boston, Brooklyn's 15th win in a row.

September 7 The Giants bring a half-game lead into Ebbets Field. With the park already packed, some 7,000 fans batter down the left field exit gate with a telephone pole and break into the field. The Giants win, 8-7, despite three Dodgers runs in the ninth.

September 10 The Giants rip the Braves, 22-1, in the opener of a doubleheader at the Polo Grounds. Frankie Frisch goes 6-for-6 before grounding out.

September 16 Cards first baseman Jim Bottomley's three singles, double, and two home runs produce a major league record 12 RBIs in the St. Louis 17-3 win over Brooklyn.

September 20 Carl Mays wins his 20th for the Reds, 9-6, over the Phils, becoming the first pitcher to win 20 for three different teams in his career. (Grover Alexander's 21 wins for the Cards in 1927 makes him the second; Gaylord Perry will be the third in 1978.)

September 27 The Giants clinch their fourth straight pennant, beating the Phils 5-1, while Brooklyn is losing, 3-2, to Boston.

October 1 Another bribery scandal clouds the World Series. Judge Landis bans Giants outfielder Jimmy O'Connell and coach Albert "Cozy" Dolan from the Series after they admit an attempt to bribe Phils shortstop Heinie Sand to "go easy" in their season-ending series against the Giants. O'Connell implicates Frank Frisch, George Kelly, and Ross Youngs, who deny everything and are cleared by Landis. O'Connell is out of baseball at 23.

October 4 For the fourth straight year, the Giants are in the Fall Classic. At third base is Fred Lindstrom, at 18 years, 10 months, the youngest ever to play in a World Series to date. President Calvin Coolidge is among 35,760 who jam the

D.C. stands in Game 1. George Kelly drops a home run into the bleachers in the second, and Terry does the same in the fourth for a 2-0 New York lead. Art Nehf (14-4) gives up one in the sixth. In the last of the ninth, the Senators score to send the game into extra innings. The Giants net two runs in the 12th. In the last of the 12th, Washington scores one, but the rally falls a run short, and Walter Johnson (23-7) loses his World Series debut. Nehf becomes the fifth pitcher to get three hits in a World Series game, a feat that will not be repeated until Orel Hershiser does it in 1988.

October 27 The Cubs trade pitcher Vic Aldridge, first baseman George Grantham, and first baseman Al Niehaus to Pittsburgh for first baseman Charlie Grimm, shortstop Rabbit Maranville, and pitcher Wilbur Cooper. Grantham will hit .300 for six seasons with the Bucs, while Grimm will play 11 seasons with Chicago, eventually becoming player-manager. In 1925, Maranville will be named a player-manager as well.

December 10 The two leagues agree on a permanent rotation for World Series play proposed by Charles Ebbets: first two games at one league's park, next three at the other league's park, last two if needed back at the first league's park, with openers to alternate between leagues. Next year's World Series will commence at the NL city.

	BOSTON		BROOKLYN		CHICAGO		CINCINNATI		NEW YORK		PHILADELPHIA		PITTSBURGH		ST.LOUIS
M	D.Bancroft	M	W.Robinson	M	B.Killefer	M	J.Hendricks	M	J.McGraw	M	A.Fletcher	M	B.McKechnie	M	B.Rickey
1B	S.McInnis	1B	J.Fournier	1B	H.Cotter	1B	J.Daubert	M	H.Jennings	1B	W.Holke	1B	C.Grimm	1B	J.Bottomley
2B	C.Tierney	2B	A.High	2B	G.Grantham	2B	H.Critz	M	J.McGraw	2B	H.Ford	2B	R.Maranville	2B	R.Hornsby
SS	B.Smith	SS	J.Mitchell	SS	S.Adams	SS	I.Caveney	1B	G.Kelly	SS	H.Sand	SS	G.Wright	SS	J.Cooney
3B	E.Padgett	3B	M.Stock	3B	B.Friberg	3B	B.Pinelli	2B	F.Frisch	3B	R.Wrightstone	3B	P.Traynor	3B	H.Freigau
LF	B.Cunningham	LF	Z.Wheat	LF	D.Grigsby	LF	P.Duncan	SS	T.Jackson	LF	J.Mokan	LF	K.Cuyler	LF	R.Blades
CF	G.Felix	CF	E.Brown	CF	J.Statz	CF	E.Roush	3B	H.Groh	CF	C.Williams	CF	M.Carey	CF	W.Holm
RF	C.Stengel	RF	T.Griffith	RF	C.Heathcote	RF	C.Walker	LF	I.Meusel	RF	G.Harper	RF	C.Barnhart	RF	J.Smith
C	M.O'Neil	C	Z.Taylor	C	G.Hartnett	C	B.Hargrave	CF	H.Wilson	C	B.Henline	C	J.Gooch	C	M.Gonzalez
								RF	R.Youngs						
S	D.Bancroft	S3	J.Johnston	S	C.Hollocher	2S	S.Bohne	C	F.Snyder	O	J.Wilson	O	C.Bigbee	O1	H.Mueller
C1	F.Gibson	C	H.DeBerry	C	B.O'Farrell	1O	R.Bressler	O	B.Southworth	O	J.Schultz	O3	E.Moore	O	M.Flack
O	F.Wilson	O	B.Neis	1	R.Grimes	O	G.Burns	3S	F.Parkinson	C	W.Schmidt	3S	S.Toporcer
O	R.Powell	O	D.Loftus	O	O.Vogel	O	I.Wingo	3	A.Woehr	C	E.Smith	O	T.Douthit
O	H.Thomas	2	J.Klugmann	21	B.Barrett	S	B.Fowler	1	B.Terry	O	F.Henrich	O	W.Mueller	O3	H.Myers
O	L.Mann	O	G.Bailey	O	B.Weis	O	G.Harper	O	J.O'Connell	O	C.Walker	/C	C.Knox	O	C.Hafey
2	M.Shay	S	B.Jones	O	H.Miller	O	C.Shorten	23	F.Lindstrom	O	C.Lee	/1	J.Ens	S	T.Thevenow
C	E.Smith	/C	C.Hargreaves	/O	H.Fitzgerald	2	L.Fonseca	/C	G.Hartley	C	L.Wendell	/1	E.Barnes	C	C.Niebergall
O	E.Sperber	/S	I.Olson	/1	T.Kearns	C	G.Sanberg	/C	E.Ainsmith	/O	F.Leach	H	J.Rawlings	C	L.Bell
/3	H.Lane	/2	F.Johnston	1	A.Elliott	/O	E.Hock	/O	B.Crump	/S	L.Metz			C	V.Clemons
H	W.Cruise			/S	R.Michaels	/O	C.Lee			/O	S.Emery	P	W.Cooper	C	E.Vick
/C	E.Phillips	P	B.Grimes	/C	J.Churry	/2	J.Begley	P	V.Barnes	P	R.Kremer	/O	E.Clough
/C	D.Cousineau	P	D.Vance			/O	G.Neale	P	J.Bentley	P	J.Ring	P	J.Morrison	/O	J.Schultz
H	A.Hermann	P	D.Ruether	P	V.Aldridge	/O	E.Pick	P	H.McQuillan	P	H.Carlson	P	L.Meadows	/2	D.Lavan
H	J.Kelleher	P	B.Doak	P	V.Keen	/C	J.Blott	P	A.Nehf	P	B.Hubbell	P	E.Yde	/C	R.Shepardson
H	W.Lefler	P	A.Decatur	P	T.Kaufmann			P	W.Dean	P	C.Mitchell	RP	A.Stone	/O	J.Bratcher
				P	E.Jacobs	P	E.Rixey	RP	C.Jonnard	P	W.Glazner				
P	J.Barnes	P	T.Osborne	P	P.Alexander	P	C.Mays					P	J.Pfeffer	P	J.Haines
P	J.Genewich	P	R.Ehrhardt			P	P.Donohue	P	R.Ryan	P	H.Betts	/P	B.Adams	P	A.Sothoron
P	J.Cooney	P	D.Henry	P	S.Blake	P	D.Luque	P	M.Watson	P	J.Couch	/P	D.Lundgren	P	B.Sherdel
P	T.McNamara	P	J.Roberts	P	R.Wheeler	P	T.Sheehan	P	E.Maun	P	J.Oeschger	/P	D.Songer	P	J.Stuart
P	A.Yeargin	/P	L.Dickerman	P	G.Bush	RP	J.May	P	H.Baldwin	/P	R.Steineder	/P	R.Steineder	P	E.Dyer
		/P	R.Yarrison	P	G.Milstead			P	W.Huntzinger	P	B.Lewis	/P	B.May		
P	L.Benton	P	N.Greene	/P	R.Pierce	P	R.Benton	/P	D.Gearin	/P	J.Bishop	/P	F.Sale	P	L.Dickerman
P	R.Lucas	P	B.Hollingsworth	/P	H.Brett	/P	P.Dibut	/P	J.Oeschger	/P	L.Weinert			P	H.Bell
P	D.Stryker	/P	T.Wilson	/P	T.Osborne	/P	B.Harris	/P	L.Cadore	/P	E.Hamilton			P	J.Pfeffer
/P	R.Marquard	/P	T.Long					/P	K.Greenfield	/P	L.Pinto			P	J.Fowler
/P	L.North													/P	F.Rhem
/P	S.Graham													P	B.Doak
/P	J.Muich													/P	A.Delaney
/P	I.Kamp													P	L.Day
/P	J.Batchelder													/P	L.North
/P	D.Gearin													/P	V.Shields
														P	B.Vines
														/P	J.Berly

TEAM	G	W	L	PCT	GB	R	OR	AB	H	2B	3B	HR	BB	SO	AVG	OBP	SLG	PRO	PRO+	BR	/A	PF	CHI	RC	SB	CS	SBA	SBR
NY	154	93	60	.608		**857**	641	5445	**1634**	269	81	**95**	467	479	**.300**	**.358**	**.432**	**.790**	120	**124**	148	97	102	**849**	82	53	61	-7
BRO	154	92	62	.597	1.5	717	675	5339	1534	227	54	72	447	357	.287	.345	.391	.736	105	19	42	97	99	725	34	46	43	-17
PIT	153	90	63	.588	3	724	588	5288	1517	222	**122**	44	366	396	.287	.336	.400	.736	100	11	0	102	**103**	715	**181**	92	**66**	**-1**
CIN	153	83	70	.542	10	649	**579**	5301	1539	236	111	36	349	**334**	.290	.337	.397	.734	100	8	19	99	93	698	103	98	51	-28
CHI	154	81	72	.529	12	698	699	5134	1419	207	59	66	**469**	521	.276	.340	.378	.718	96	-10	-16	101	**103**	652	137	149	48	-48
STL	154	65	89	.422	28.5	740	750	5349	1552	**270**	87	67	382	418	.290	.341	.411	.752	108	42	55	98	100	740	86	86	50	-26
PHI	152	55	96	.364	37	676	849	5306	1459	256	56	94	382	452	.275	.328	.397	.725	88	-13	-96	112	99	687	57	67	46	-23
BOS	154	53	100	.346	40	520	800	5283	1355	194	52	25	354	451	.256	.306	.327	.633	77	-181	-160	96	**103**	532	74	68	52	-19
TOT	614					5581		42445	12009	1881	622	499	3216	3408	.283	.337	.392	.729							754	659	53	-169

TEAM	CG	SH	SV	IP	H	H/G	HR	BB	SO	RAT	ERA	ERA+	OAV	OOB	PR	/A	PF	CPI	FA	E	DP	FW	PW	BW	SBW	DIF
NY	71	4	21	1378²	1464	9.6	77	392	406	12.2	3.62	101	.274	.326	38	7	95	100	.971	186	160	.4	.7	**14.7**	1.4	-.7
BRO	**97**	10	5	1376¹	1432	9.4	58	403	**638**	12.2	3.64	103	.270	.326	35	16	97	96	.968	196	121	-.2	1.6	4.2	.4	9.0
PIT	85	**15**	5	1382	**1387**	**9.0**	42	323	364	**11.3**	3.27	117	**.267**	.313	92	88	99	97	.971	183	161	.5	8.7	.0	**2.0**	2.3
CIN	77	14	9	1378	1408	9.2	**30**	293	451	**11.3**	**3.12**	121	**.267**	.309	115	99	97	97	.966	217	142	-1.4	**9.8**	1.9	-.7	-3.1
CHI	85	4	6	1380²	1459	9.5	89	438	416	12.5	3.83	102	.275	.333	6	11	101	101	.966	218	153	-1.4	1.1	-1.6	-2.7	9.1
STL	79	7	6	1364²	1528	10.1	70	486	393	13.5	4.15	91	.290	.354	-43	-57	98	104	.969	188	162	.3	-5.7	5.5	-.5	-11.6
PHI	59	7	10	1354¹	1689	11.2	84	469	349	14.5	4.87	92	.313	.372	-151	-60	115	103	.972	175	**168**	.8	-6.0	-9.5	-.2	-5.7
BOS	66	10	4	1379¹	1607	10.5	49	402	364	13.3	4.46	86	.301	.353	-92	-100	99	99	**.973**	168	154	1.4	-9.9	-15.9	.2	.7
TOT	619	71	66	10994		9.8				12.6	3.87		.283	.337					.970	1531	1221					

Runs
Hornsby-StL 121
Frisch-NY 121
Carey-Pit......... 113
Youngs-NY 112
Williams-Phi 101

Hits
Hornsby-StL 227
Wheat-Bro 212
Frisch-NY 198
High-Bro 191
Fournier-Bro 188

Doubles
Hornsby-StL 43
Wheat-Bro 41
Kelly-NY 37

Triples
Roush-Cin 21
Maranville-Pit 20
Wright-Pit 18
Cuyler-Pit 16
Frisch-NY 15

Home Runs
Fournier-Bro 27
Hornsby-StL 25
Williams-Phi 24
Kelly-NY 21

Total Bases
Hornsby-StL 373
Wheat-Bro 311
Williams-Phi 308
Kelly-NY 303
Fournier-Bro 302

Runs Batted In
Kelly-NY 136
Fournier-Bro 116
Wright-Pit 111
Bottomley-StL 111
Meusel-NY 102

Runs Produced
Kelly-NY 206
Hornsby-StL 190
Wright-Pit 184
Bottomley-StL.... 184
Frisch-NY 183

Bases On Balls
Hornsby-StL 89
Fournier-Bro 83
Youngs-NY 77
Williams-Phi 67
Friberg-Chi 66

Batting Average
Hornsby-StL 424
Wheat-Bro 375
Youngs-NY 356
Cuyler-Pit 354
Roush-Cin 348

On Base Percentage
Hornsby-StL 507
Youngs-NY 441
Fournier-Bro 428
Wheat-Bro 428
Williams-Phi 403

Slugging Average
Hornsby-StL......696
Williams-Phi 552
Wheat-Bro 549
Cuyler-Pit 539
Fournier-Bro 536

Production
Hornsby-StL 1.203
Wheat-Bro 978
Fournier-Bro 965
Youngs-NY 962
Williams-Phi 955

Adjusted Production
Hornsby-StL 223
Wheat-Bro 165
Fournier-Bro 162
Youngs-NY 161
Cuyler-Pit 147

Batter Runs
Hornsby-StL 94.1
Wheat-Bro 48.2
Fournier-Bro 48.1
Youngs-NY 45.3
Williams-Phi 42.0

Adjusted Batter Runs
Hornsby-StL 97.2
Fournier-Bro 52.2
Wheat-Bro 52.1
Youngs-NY 48.6
Kelly-NY 32.3

Clutch Hitting Index
Friberg-Chi........ 141
Griffith-Bro 140
Meusel-NY 135
Wright-Pit 130
Pinelli-Cin 129

Runs Created
Hornsby-StL 186
Fournier-Bro 133
Wheat-Bro 132
Youngs-NY 123
Williams-Phi 121

Total Average
Hornsby-StL 1.424
Fournier-Bro 1.045
Youngs-NY 1.023
Wheat-Bro 1.014
Cuyler-Pit 990

Stolen Bases
Carey-Pit 49
Cuyler-Pit 32
Heathcote-Chi.... 26
Traynor-Pit........ 24
Smith-StL 24

Stolen Base Average
Carey-Pit 79.0
Cuyler-Pit 74.4
Frisch-NY 71.0
Critz-Cin 63.3
Smith-StL 60.0

Stolen Base Runs
Carey-Pit.......... 6.9
Cuyler-Pit 3.0
Hartnett-Chi 1.8

Fielding Runs
Pinelli-Cin 26.7
Frisch-NY 24.9
Statz-Chi 14.5
Ford-Phi 11.9
Wright-Pit 10.7

Total Player Rating
Hornsby-StL 8.5
Frisch-NY 5.4
Fournier-Bro 4.7
Wheat-Bro 4.5
Youngs-NY 3.6

Wins
Vance-Bro 28
Grimes-Bro 22
Mays-Cin 20
Cooper-Pit 20
Kremer-Pit 18

Win Percentage
Yde-Pit........... .842
Vance-Bro .... .824
Bentley-NY ...... .762
Mays-Cin .... .690
Kremer-Pit .... .643

Games
Morrison-Pit 41
Kremer-Pit 41
Keen-Chi 40
Sheehan-Cin 39

Complete Games
Vance-Bro 30
Grimes-Bro 30
Cooper-Pit 25
Barnes-Bos 21
Aldridge-Chi 20

Shutouts
Yde-Pit 4
Sothoron-StL...... 4
Rixey-Cin 4
Kremer-Pit 4
Cooper-Pit 4
Barnes-Bos 4

Saves
May-Cin 6
Ryan-NY 5
Jonnard-NY 5

Innings Pitched
Grimes-Bro 310.2
Vance-Bro 308.1
Cooper-Pit 268.2
Barnes-Bos 267.2
Kremer-Pit 259.1

Fewest Hits/Game
Vance-Bro 6.95
Yde-Pit.......... 7.93
Morrison-Pit 8.07
Doak-StL-Bro 8.14
Rixey-Cin 8.27

Fewest BB/Game
Benton-Cin....... 1.33
Alexander-Chi 1.33
Cooper-Pit 1.34
Mays-Cin 1.43
Donohue-Cin 1.46

Strikeouts
Vance-Bro 262
Grimes-Bro 135
Luque-Cin 86
Morrison-Pit 85
Kaufmann-Chi 79

Strikeouts/Game
Vance-Bro 7.65
Grimes-Bro 3.91
Nehf-NY 3.77
Luque-Cin 3.53
Kaufmann-Chi 3.41

Ratio
Vance-Bro 9.46
Rixey-Cin 10.12
Benton-Cin 10.73
Doak-StL-Bro 10.87
McQuillan-NY ... 10.96

Earned Run Average
Vance-Bro 2.16
McQuillan-NY ... 2.69
Rixey-Cin 2.76
Benton-Cin 2.77
Yde-Pit 2.83

Adjusted ERA
Vance-Bro 173
Rixey-Cin 137
McQuillan-NY ... 136
Benton-Cin 136
Yde-Pit.......... 136

Opponents' Batting Avg.
Vance-Bro .... .213
Yde-Pit .... .244
Morrison-Pit ..... .245
Rixey-Cin .... .246
Doak-StL-Bro .... .249

Opponents' On Base Pct.
Vance-Bro .... .269
Rixey-Cin .... .285
Benton-Cin ...... .297
Alexander-Chi .... .299
Nehf-NY .... .301

Starter Runs
Vance-Bro 58.4
Rixey-Cin 29.4
McQuillan-NY ... 24.0
Yde-Pit 22.3
Barnes-NY 20.5

Adjusted Starter Runs
Vance-Bro 54.3
Rixey-Cin 26.7
Yde-Pit 21.7
McQuillan-NY ... 19.9
Kremer-Pit 18.6

Clutch Pitching Index
Sherdel-StL 117
Sothoron-StL 115
Ring-Phi 113
McQuillan-NY 113
Aldridge-Chi 110

Relief Runs
Jonnard-NY 14.5
May-Cin 9.5
Stone-Pit 6.5

Adjusted Relief Runs
Jonnard-NY 12.5
May-Cin 8.4
Stone-Pit 6.3

Relief Ranking
Jonnard-NY 12.9
May-Cin 5.7
Stone-Pit..........5.3

Total Pitcher Index
Vance-Bro 5.7
Mays-Cin 3.4
Rixey-Cin 3.1
Cooper-Pit 2.5
Yde-Pit........... 2.3

Total Baseball Ranking
Hornsby-StL 8.5
Vance-Bro 5.7
Frisch-NY 5.4
Fournier-Bro 4.7
Wheat-Bro 4.5

February 10 Clark Griffith picks 27-year-old second baseman Bucky Harris to manage the Senators.

April 15 George Sisler returns after missing a full year due to impaired vision caused by severe sinusitis. He is 2-for-4 in the Browns' 7–3 win over the White Sox.

May 23 Walter Johnson strikes out 14 in a 4-0 one-hitter over the White Sox for his 103rd shutout. Johnson will have his best season in five years, going 23-7.

June 13 The first place Yankees come to Detroit with the Tigers close on their heels. New York leads, 10-6, in the top of the ninth. Bob Meusel takes a pitch in his back, hurls his bat at pitcher Bert Cole, and charges the mound. Players from both teams start swinging. Fans rush out of the stands, eager to mix it up with players, police, and each other. The fight goes on for nearly 30 minutes while umpire Billy Evans, unable to clear the field, forfeits the game to New York. Cole and Meusel are suspended for 10 days.

August 2 A's first basemann Joe Hauser sets an AL record when he hits three homers and a double for 14 total bases. It'll be broken by Ty Cobb's 16 total bases on May 5, 1925.

August 13 Howard Ehmke has the White Sox popping up all day in his 6-0 win. Only one assist is made by Boston.

August 25 Walter Johnson hurls a seven-inning rain-shortened no-hitter against the Browns, winning by a score of 2-0.

August 28 Despite Babe Ruth's two home runs, the Senators beat the Yankees, 11-6, and move into first place. The Yankees will tie them for two days in September, but otherwise the Senators stay on top till the end.

September 6 Urban Shocker of the Browns hurls two complete-game victories over the White Sox, winning each contest by a score of 6-2; he fans only one batter in the two games.

September 14 Walter Johnson is elected AL MVP with 55 points. White Sox second baseman Eddie Collins is second. He was runner-up to Ruth last year.

September 29 The Senators clinch the pennant in Boston, finishing two games in front of the Yankees.

October 10 President and Mrs. Coolidge and 31,665 others thrill to the second three-hour battle of the Series. Bucky Harris starts 23-year-old righthander Curly Ogden (9-8) against Virgil Barnes (16-10), then pulls him after he fans Fred Lindstrom and walks Frisch. In comes lefty George Mogridge (16-11). Bucky Harris lifts one into the temporary seats in left field for a 1-0 lead. In the sixth a single ties it at 1-1, and Harris brings in Firpo Marberry for his fourth appearance. A base hit and two costly errors give the Giants a 3-1 lead. In the eighth, pinch hitter Nemo Liebold doubles and catcher Muddy Ruel singles. A walk loads the bases and up comes Harris, who hits a hard bounder to third base that strikes a pebble and skips over Lindstrom's head and down the left field line as the tying runs score. With one out in the last of the 12th, Giants reliever Jack Bentley gets Muddy Ruel to pop up near home plate, but veteran catcher Hank Gowdy trips on his discarded mask, and the ball falls to the ground. Ruel then gets his second hit, a double. Walter Johnson, who came on to pitch in the ninth, reaches first base on shortstop Travis Jackson's error. Earl McNeely hits a grounder at Lindstrom, and again the ball takes a bounce over his head. Ruel tears home with the run that gives Washington its World Series championship.

October 20* Kansas City Monarchs manager Jose Mendez takes the mound to spin a three-hit, 5–0 shutout over the Hilldales to win the final game of the first Negro League World Series. Nip Winters had pitched the first three Hilldale wins.

December 11 Eddie Collins signs as player-manager of the White Sox.

	BOSTON		CHICAGO		CLEVELAND		DETROIT		NEW YORK		PHILADELPHIA		ST.LOUIS		WASHINGTON
M	L.Fohl	M	E.Collins	M	T.Speaker	M	T.Cobb	M	M.Huggins	M	C.Mack	M	G.Sisler	M	B.Harris
1B	J.Harris	M	E.Sheely	1B	G.Burns	1B	L.Blue	1B	W.Pipp	1B	J.Hauser	1B	G.Sisler	1B	J.Judge
2B	B.Wambsganss	M	E.Collins	2B	C.Fewster	2B	D.Pratt	2B	A.Ward	2B	M.Bishop	2B	M.McManus	2B	B.Harris
SS	D.Lee	M	B.Barrett	SS	J.Sewell	SS	T.Rigney	SS	E.Scott	SS	C.Galloway	SS	W.Gerber	SS	R.Peckinpaugh
3B	D.Clark	1B	W.Kamm	3B	R.Lutzke	3B	B.Jones	3B	J.Dugan	3B	H.Riconda	3B	G.Robertson	3B	O.Bluege
LF	B.Veach	2B	B.Falk	LF	C.Jamieson	LF	H.Manush	LF	B.Meusel	LF	B.Lamar	LF	K.Williams	LF	G.Goslin
CF	I.Flagstead	SS	J.Mostil	CF	T.Speaker	CF	T.Cobb	CF	W.Witt	CF	A.Simmons	CF	B.Jacobson	CF	N.Leibold
RF	I.Boone	3B	H.Hooper	RF	H.Summa	RF	H.Heilmann	RF	B.Ruth	RF	B.Miller	RF	J.Tobin	RF	S.Rice
C	S.O'Neill	LF	B.Crouse	C	G.Myatt	C	J.Bassler	C	W.Schang	C	C.Perkins	C	H.Severeid	C	M.Ruel
3S	H.Ezzell	RF			P.McNulty	3	F.Haney	O	F.Hofmann	23	J.Dykes	O	J.Evans	O	E.McNeely
O1	S.Collins	C			R.Stephenson	2	L.Burke	2	E.Johnson	O	F.Welch	23	N.McMillan	O	W.Matthews
S3	H.Shanks				L.Sewell	2	F.O'Rourke	2	H.Hendrick	3	S.Hale	O	H.Bennett	3	D.Prothro
C	V.Picinich	O	M.Archdeacon	3	F.Ellerbe	O	B.Fothergill	23	M.McNally	O	P.Strand	3	H.Rice	1	M.Shirley
C	J.Heving	C	R.Schalk	C	F.Brower	C	L.Woodall	O	E.Combs	O	F.Bruggy	3	F.Ellerbe	3	T.Taylor
1	P.Todt	C	R.Elsh	O	S.Clarke	O	A.Wingo	O	S.Horan	S	J.Chapman	C	T.Rego	C	B.Tate
O	D.Williams	S	R.French	C	R.Walters	/2	C.Gehringer	O	B.Bengough	/O	A.Strunk	C	P.Collins	O	S.Fisher
S	C.Geygan	S	R.Morehart	3	E.Yoter	/C	C.Manion	/1	L.Gehrig	C	C.Gibson	/3	S.Simon	/C	P.Hargrave
/O	J.Connolly	S	H.McClellan	/3	L.Gardner	/3	J.Kerr	/O	B.Paschal	H	E.Sherling	/O	V.Elmore	/O	L.Richbourg
		C	J.Grabowski	1	R.Knode			/2	M.Hillis	H	J.Green	/3	P.Burke	/2	R.Miller
P	H.Ehmke	/1	B.Clancy	/O	T.Gulley	P	E.Whitehill	/C	C.Autry			H	B.Mizeur	/O	C.Smith
P	A.Ferguson	P	I.Davis	/O	J.Wyatt	P	L.Stoner			P	E.Rommel			/O	B.Griffith
P	J.Quinn	/C	J.Burns	/2	F.Spurgeon	P	R.Collins	P	H.Pennock	P	F.Heimach	P	U.Shocker	/O	W.Lefler
P	C.Fullerton	/C	K.Wirts	H	K.Hogan	P	K.Holloway	P	J.Bush	S	S.Baumgartner	P	D.Danforth	/O	C.East
P	B.Piercy	/2	B.Black			P	H.Dauss	P	W.Hoyt	P	D.Burns	P	E.Wingard	/S	C.Gagnon
RP	G.Murray	S	W.Dashiell	P	J.Shaute			P	B.Shawkey	P	S.Gray	P	D.Davis		
		/S	F.Naleway	P	S.Smith	P	B.Cole	P	S.Jones	RP	B.Hasty	P	E.Vangilder	P	W.Johnson
P	B.Ross	/S	B.DeViveiros	P	S.Johnson	RP	M.Gaston			RP	H.Pruett	P	G.Mogridge
P	O.Fuhr	H	A.Strunk	P	G.Uhle	P	E.Wells			P	R.Meeker	RP	G.Grant	P	T.Zachary
RP	T.Wingfield			RP	D.Metivier	/P	D.Leonard	P	A.Mamaux	P	S.Harriss	RP	B.Bayne	P	F.Marberry
/P	R.Ruffing	P	S.Thurston			/P	H.Pillette	/P	W.Beall	P	R.Naylor			P	J.Martina
/P	H.Workman	P	T.Lyons	P	J.Edwards	/P	W.Ludolph	P	C.Markle	/P	C.Ogden	P	R.Kolp	RP	A.Russell
/P	L.Howe	P	R.Faber	P	L.Roy	/P	R.Clarke	/P	G.Pipgras	/P	R.Walberg	P	G.Lyons	RP	B.Speece
/P	C.Winters	P	S.Connally	/P	C.Yowell	/P	K.Jones	/P	B.Shields	/P	W.Pierson	/P	O.Voigt		
/P	L.Jamerson	P	T.Blankenship	/P	W.Clark			/P	O.Roettger			/P	B.Lasley	P	C.Ogden
/P	J.Woods			/P	B.Messenger							/P	E.Barnhart	P	P.Zahniser
/P	A.Kellett	P	M.Cvengros	/P	J.Dawson							/P	B.Beck	P	S.McGrew
		P	D.Leverett	/P	V.Cheeves									P	T.Wingfield
		P	C.Robertson	/P	D.Levsen									/P	N.Altrock
		P	L.Mangum	P	J.Miller										
		P	D.McWeeny	/P	G.Morton										
		/P	M.Steengrafe	/P	L.Drake										
		/P	B.Barnes	/P	G.Edmondson										
		/P	H.Foreman	/P	F.Wayenberg										
		/P	L.Davenport	/P	P.Fitzke										
		/P	J.Dobb	/P	J.Lindsey										
		/P	B.Lawrence	/P	B.Kuhn										
		/P	W.Schultz												

TEAM	G	W	L	PCT	GB	R	OR	AB	H	2B	3B	HR	BB	SO	AVG	OBP	SLG	PRO	PRO+	BR	/A	PF	CHI	RC	SB	CS	SBA	SBR
WAS	156	92	62	.597		755	613	5304	1558	255	88	22	513	392	.294	.361	.387	.748	101	-8	16	97	98	762	116	85	58	-16
NY	153	89	63	.586	2	798	667	5240	1516	248	86	98	478	420	.289	.352	.426	.778	106	29	31	100	102	789	69	67	51	-20
DET	156	86	68	.558	6	849	796	5389	1604	315	76	35	607	400	.298	.373	.404	.777	108	53	67	98	100	837	100	77	56	-16
STL	153	74	78	.487	17	769	809	5236	1543	266	62	67	465	349	.295	.356	.408	.764	96	9	-38	106	101	762	85	85	50	-26
PHI	152	71	81	.467	20	685	778	5184	1459	251	59	63	374	484	.281	.334	.389	.723	90	-77	-83	101	105	674	77	68	53	-18
CLE	153	67	86	.438	24.5	755	814	5332	1580	306	59	41	492	371	.296	.361	.399	.760	100	8	-2	101	97	784	85	57	60	-9
BOS	157	67	87	.435	25	737	806	5340	1481	302	63	30	603	417	.277	.356	.374	.730	94	-42	-43	100	99	741	78	61	56	-13
CHI	154	66	87	.431	25.5	793	858	5255	1512	254	58	41	604	421	.288	.365	.382	.747	101	-6	18	97	103	761	137	92	60	-14
TOT	617					6141		42280	12253	2197	551	397	4136	3254	.290	.358	.397	.755							747	592	56	-131

TEAM	CG	SH	SV	IP	H	H/G	HR	BB	SO	RAT	ERA	ERA+	OAV	OOB	PR	/A	PF	CPI	FA	E	DP	FW	PW	BW	SBW	DIF
WAS	74	13	25	1383	1329	8.6	34	505	469	12.2	3.34	121	.259	.330	136	106	95	99	.972	171	149	1.3	10.0	1.5	.0	2.1
NY	76	13	13	1359¹	1483	9.8	59	522	487	13.4	3.86	108	.284	.353	56	44	98	107	.974	156	131	2.0	4.2	2.9	-.3	4.2
DET	60	5	20	1394²	1586	10.2	55	467	441	13.6	4.19	98	.293	.354	5	-12	97	101	.971	187	142	.4	-1.1	6.3	.0	3.4
STL	65	11	7	1353¹	1511	10.0	68	517	386	13.8	4.57	99	.289	.358	-51	-9	107	95	.969	184	142	.3	-.8	-3.6	-.9	3.0
PHI	68	8	10	1345	1527	10.2	43	597	371	14.4	4.39	98	.292	.368	-24	-15	101	101	.971	180	157	.5	-1.4	-7.8	-.2	3.9
CLE	87	7	7	1349	1603	10.7	43	503	315	14.3	4.40	97	.300	.365	-25	-20	101	101	.967	205	130	-1.0	-1.9	-.2	.7	-7.1
BOS	73	8	16	1391¹	1563	10.1	43	523	414	13.9	4.35	100	.290	.359	-19	2	103	97	.967	210	126	-1.0	.2	-4.1	.3	-5.5
CHI	76	1	11	1370²	1635	10.7	52	512	360	14.3	4.74	87	.305	.368	-78	-95	97	98	.963	229	136	-2.4	-9.0	1.7	.2	-1.1
TOT	579	66	109	10946¹		10.1				13.7	4.23		.290	.358					.969	1522	1113					

Runs
Ruth-NY 143
Cobb-Det 115
Collins-Chi 108
Hooper-Chi 107
Heilmann-Det 107

Hits
Rice-Was 216
Jamieson-Cle 213
Cobb-Det 211
Ruth-NY 200
Goslin-Was 199

Doubles
J.Sewell-Cle 45
Heilmann-Det 45
Wambsganss-Bos .. 41
Jacobson-StL 41
Meusel-NY 40

Triples
Pipp-NY 19
Goslin-Was 17
Heilmann-Det 16
Rice-Was 14
Jacobson-StL 12

Home Runs
Ruth-NY 46
Hauser-Phi 27
Jacobson-StL 19
Williams-StL 18
Boone-Bos 13

Total Bases
Ruth-NY 391
Jacobson-StL 306
Heilmann-Det 304
Goslin-Was 299
Hauser-Phi 290

Runs Batted In
Goslin-Was 129
Ruth-NY 121
Meusel-NY 120
Hauser-Phi 115

Runs Produced
Ruth-NY 218
Goslin-Was 217
Heilmann-Det 211
J.Sewell-Cle 201
Meusel-NY 201

Bases On Balls
Ruth-NY 142
Rigney-Det 102
Sheely-Chi 95
Collins-Chi 89
Cobb-Det 85

Batting Average
Ruth-NY .... .378
Jamieson-Cle .... .359
Falk-Chi .... .352
Collins-Chi ...... .349
Bassler-Det ...... .346

On Base Percentage
Ruth-NY .... .513
Collins-Chi .... .441
Speaker-Cle ...... .432
Heilmann-Det ..... .428
Sheely-Chi .... .426

Slugging Average
Ruth-NY .... .739
Heilmann-Det ..... .533
Williams-StL ..... .533
Jacobson-StL ..... .528
Myatt-Cle .... .518

Production
Ruth-NY 1.252
Heilmann-Det .... .961
Williams-StL .... .958
Speaker-Cle ..... .943
Goslin-Was ...... .937

Adjusted Production
Ruth-NY 221
Heilmann-Det 149
Goslin-Was 145
Speaker-Cle 141
Williams-StL 137

Batter Runs
Ruth-NY 100.8
Heilmann-Det 40.4
Goslin-Was 35.6
Speaker-Cle 32.4
Collins-Chi 30.5

Adjusted Batter Runs
Ruth-NY 101.1
Heilmann-Det 42.4
Goslin-Was 39.3
Collins-Chi 34.1
Speaker-Cle 31.1

Clutch Hitting Index
Sheely-Chi 149
Kamm-Chi 138
Pratt-Det 138
Rigney-Det 137
Veach-Bos 131

Runs Created
Ruth-NY 205
Heilmann-Det 134
Goslin-Was 125
Cobb-Det 121
Collins-Chi 119

Total Average
Ruth-NY 1.558
Heilmann-Det ... 1.042
Williams-StL 1.039
Speaker-Cle ..... .988
Collins-Chi ...... .976

Stolen Bases
Collins-Chi 42
Meusel-NY 26
Rice-Was 24
Cobb-Det 23
Jamieson-Cle 21

Stolen Base Average
Collins-Chi 71.2
Harris-Was 66.7
Meusel-NY 65.0
Rice-Was 64.9
Williams-StL 64.5

Stolen Base Runs
Collins-Chi 2.4

Fielding Runs
J.Sewell-Cle 21.4
Lutzke-Cle 19.4
Dykes-Phi 15.9
Jacobson-StL 15.8
Wambsganss-Bos .. 14.4

Total Player Rating
Ruth-NY 8.5
J.Sewell-Cle 4.3
Heilmann-Det 3.9
Rigney-Det 3.4
Collins-Chi 2.9

Wins
Johnson-Was 23
Pennock-NY 21
Thurston-Chi 20
Shaute-Cle 20
Ehmke-Bos 19

Win Percentage
Johnson-Was .... .767
Pennock-NY ..... .700
Whitehill-Det .... .654
Zachary-Was .... .625

Games
Marberry-Was 50
Holloway-Det 49
Shaute-Cle 46
Hoyt-NY 46
Ehmke-Bos 45

Complete Games
Thurston-Chi 28
Ehmke-Bos 26
Pennock-NY 25
Shaute-Cle 21
Rommel-Phi 21

Shutouts
Johnson-Was 6
Davis-StL 5
Shocker-StL 4
Pennock-NY 4
Ehmke-Bos 4

Saves
Marberry-Was 15
Russell-Was 8
Quinn-Bos 7
Dauss-Det 6
Connally-Chi 6

Innings Pitched
Ehmke-Bos 315.0
Thurston-Chi ... 291.0
Pennock-NY 286.1
Shaute-Cle 283.0
Rommel-Phi 278.0

Fewest Hits/Game
Johnson-Was 7.55
Collins-Det 8.29
Marberry-Was ... 8.75
Zachary-Was 8.79
Wingard-StL 8.88

Fewest BB/Game
Smith-Cle 1.53
Thurston-Chi 1.86
Shocker-StL 1.90
Pennock-NY 2.01
Quinn-Bos 2.05

Strikeouts
Johnson-Was 158
Ehmke-Bos 119
Shawkey-NY 114
Pennock-NY 101
Shocker-StL 88

Strikeouts/Game
Johnson-Was 5.12
Shawkey-NY 4.94
Ehmke-Bos 3.40
Shocker-StL 3.22
Pennock-NY 3.17

Ratio
Johnson-Was ... 10.37
Collins-Det 11.08
Zachary-Was ... 11.28
Smith-Cle 11.48
Pennock-NY ... 11.54

Earned Run Average
Johnson-Was 2.72
Zachary-Was 2.75
Pennock-NY 2.83
Baumgartner-Phi .. 2.88
Smith-Cle 3.02

Adjusted ERA
Baumgartner-Phi .. 149
Johnson-Was 148
Pennock-NY 147
Zachary-Was 147
Smith-Cle 142

Opponents' Batting Avg.
Johnson-Was .... .224
Collins-Det ..... .249
Marberry-Was ... .262
Wingard-StL .... .262
Davis-StL ...... .263

Opponents' On Base Pct.
Johnson-Was .... .284
Collins-Det ..... .307
Smith-Cle ...... .312
Pennock-NY ..... .314
Zachary-Was .... .315

Starter Runs
Johnson-Was 46.5
Pennock-NY 44.6
Smith-Cle 33.4
Zachary-Was 33.2
Baumgartner-Phi . 27.1

Adjusted Starter Runs
Pennock-NY 42.3
Johnson-Was 40.5
Smith-Cle 34.5
Ehmke-Bos 31.9
Zachary-Was 28.9

Clutch Pitching Index
Baumgartner-Phi .. 132
Pennock-NY 117
Zachary-Was 113
Ferguson-Bos 113
Hoyt-NY 112

Relief Runs
Speece-Was 9.5

Adjusted Relief Runs
Speece-Was 8.4

Relief Ranking
Speece-Was 4.2

Total Pitcher Index
Johnson-Was 4.5
Pennock-NY 3.8
Zachary-Was 3.7
Bush-NY 3.4
Smith-Cle 3.4

Total Baseball Ranking
Ruth-NY 8.5
Johnson-Was 4.5
J.Sewell-Cle 4.3
Heilmann-Det 3.9
Pennock-NY 3.8

January 5 During the tour of Europe by the White Sox and Giants, the French Baseball Federation awards silver medals to John McGraw, Charlie Comiskey, and Hugh Jennings for their efforts to advance the game in France.

February 2 The NL inaugurates its Golden Jubilee Year by holding its spring meeting in the same room in New York's Broadway Central Hotel where the league was organized on February 2, 1876.

February 25 John McGraw arrives in Florida and is installed as president of a real estate development near Bradenton called Pennant Park. With streets named for early Giants heroes, and lots offered for $2,500 to $5,000, McGraw hires a fleet of salesmen and heads north. A year later, the boom will go bust, washed away by two hurricanes. McGraw will incur a loss of $100,000 after paying off close friends, players, and other investors.

April 14 In the first regular-season Cubs game to be broadcast on the radio, Quin Ryan announces the contest from the grandstand roof for WGN. Grover Cleveland Alexander wins for the Cubs, 8-2, over the Pirates and adds a single, double, and home run.

April 18 Charles Ebbets, Dodgers president, dies on the morning of the opener at Ebbets Field, won by New York, 7-1. No NL games will be played on the April 21, the day of his funeral. Ed McKeever, the new club president, will catch a cold that turns into pneumonia and he will die May 27.

May 7 Pirates shortstop Glenn Wright pulls a solo triple play at second base in the ninth, grabbing Jim Bottomley's liner, stepping on the bag before Johnny Cooney can get back, and tagging Hornsby coming down from first base to end the game. The Pirates win, 10–9, after scoring six runs in the eighth.

May 8 Every NL city will have a Golden Jubilee Day. The first, between two of the original teams left from the 1876 season, at Boston, sees former Boston players from 1876 on hand. The Braves beat Chicago, 5–2.

May 30 Rogers Hornsby is named manager of the Cardinals, replacing Branch Rickey, who remains as general manager. Hornsby will be the only player-manager to win the triple crown, which he does by topping .400 for the third time in four years, hitting .403 with 39 home runs and 143 RBIs. His .756 slugging average is still the NL's best.

September 23 Rogers Hornsby will win the MVP honor in the NL, rewriting the offensive record book while bringing the Cards home fourth. Other strong contenders are Kiki Cuyler, the Pirates top hitter at .357; the Giants' George Kelly; Pirates' shortstop Glenn Wright; Brooklyn's Dazzy Vance; and Dave Bancroft, who hit .319 and topped NL shortstops in fielding average while managing the fifth-place Braves.

October 7 Christy Mathewson dies of tuberculosis at Saranac Lake, New York, at the age of 45.

October 15 A steady downpour the day before has left the field a muddy mess for Game 7 of the World Series. It's a short day for Vic Aldridge: three walks and two hits, and he's out of there with one out in the first. Walter Johnson takes a 4-0 lead to the mound for Washington. The Bucs clobber him for 15 hits, good for 24 total bases. The Senators make the most of seven hits, scoring seven runs, including Roger Peckinpaugh's home run, the 12th of the Series, a World Series record. Johnson would have fared better but for two more errors by shortstop Peckinpaugh, the MVP's seventh and eighth, still the World Series record for any position. Ray Kremer picks up his second win with a four-inning relief effort, as the Senators lose, 9-7. The Series breaks all financial records, grossing almost $1.2 million. Winning shares are $5,332.72; losing shares are $3,734.60.

BOSTON		BROOKLYN		CHICAGO		CINCINNATI		NEW YORK		PHILADELPHIA		PITTSBURGH		ST.LOUIS	
M	D.Bancroft	M	W.Robinson	M	B.Killefer	M	J.Hendricks	M	J.McGraw	M	A.Fletcher	M	B.McKechnie	M	B.Rickey
1B	D.Burrus	1B	J.Fournier	M	W.Maranville	1B	W.Holke	1B	H.Jennings	1B	C.Hawks	1B	G.Grantham	1B	R.Hornsby
2B	D.Gautreau	2B	M.Stock	M	M.Gibson	2B	H.Critz	M	J.McGraw	2B	B.Friberg	2B	E.Moore	1B	J.Bottomley
SS	W.Marriott	SS	J.Mitchell	1B	C.Grimm	SS	I.Caveney	SS	B.Terry	SS	H.Sand	SS	G.Wright	2B	R.Hornsby
3B	W.Marriott	3B	J.Johnston	2B	S.Adams	3B	B.Pinelli	2B	G.Kelly	3B	C.Huber	3B	P.Traynor	SS	S.Toporcer
LF	D.Harris	LF	Z.Wheat	SS	R.Maranville	LF	B.Zitzmann	SS	T.Jackson	LF	G.Burns	LF	C.Barnhart	3B	L.Bell
CF	G.Felix	CF	E.Brown	3B	H.Freigau	CF	E.Roush	3B	F.Lindstrom	CF	G.Harper	CF	M.Carey	LF	R.Blades
RF	J.Welsh	RF	D.Cox	LF	A.Jahn	RF	C.Walker	LF	I.Meusel	RF	C.Williams	RF	K.Cuyler	CF	H.Mueller
C	F.Gibson	C	Z.Taylor	CF	M.Brooks	C	B.Hargrave	CF	B.Southworth	C	J.Wilson	C	E.Smith	RF	C.Hafey
				RF	C.Heathcote			RF	R.Youngs					C	B.O'Farrell
O	B.Neis	3	C.Tierney	C	G.Hartnett	C	F.Snyder	C	F.Snyder	21	L.Fonseca	C	J.Gooch	O	R.Shinners
2S	E.Padgett	S	H.Ford	O	T.Griffith	1O	R.Bressler	32	F.Frisch	O	F.Leach	1	S.McInnis	O	J.Smith
C	M.O'Neil	C	H.DeBerry	C	M.Gonzalez	O	E.Smith	C	H.Wilson	OS	R.Wrightstone	O	C.Bigbee	M	M.Flack
3	A.High	O	D.Loftus	O	B.Weis	3	C.Dressen	C	H.Gowdy	C	B.Henline	2	J.Rawlings	S2	J.Cooney
O	L.Mann	23	A.High	S3	P.Pittinger	S2	S.Bohne	C	G.Hartley	O	J.Mokan	1	A.Niehaus	S	T.Thevenow
S2	B.Smith	C	C.Hargreaves	C	I.Wingo	1	A.Niehaus	O	F.Walker	O	J.Schultz	S2	F.Thompson	O	W.Schmidt
C	O.Siemer	S	C.Corgan	3O	B.Friberg	C	I.Wingo	3	H.Groh	/C	L.Wendell	S	R.Spencer	O	T.Douthit
/2	H.Kibbie	/O	R.Hutson	O	J.Statz	C	E.Krueger	S	D.Farrell	/O	G.Durning	/1	J.Ens	C	M.Gonzalez
O	F.Wilson	/O	T.Griffith	/O	D.Grigsby	O	J.Schultz	C	M.Devine	/S	L.Metz	/O	M.Haas	O	W.Holm
/O	S.Hogan	H	B.Barrett	S	I.McAuley	/C	A.Douglass	/C	H.McMullen	/2	B.Meyer	P	L.Meadows	C	B.Warwick
/2	A.Hood	/O	J.Standaert	O	H.Miller	/C	F.Bruggy	/O	A.Moore	P	J.Ring	P	R.Kremer	/C	E.Vick
/2	R.Lucas	P	D.Vance	3	R.Michaels	/1	J.Hudgens	/O	B.Carter	P	H.Carlson	P	V.Aldridge	/S	H.Freigau
/2	H.Thomas	P	B.Grimes	/O	A.Metzler	/O	H.Myers	H	E.Webb	P	C.Mitchell	P	J.Morrison	H	H.Myers
/O	C.Stengel	P	R.Ehrhardt	/O	J.Munson	H	B.Fowler	/O	P.Koehler	P	A.Decatur	P	E.Yde	P	J.Haines
H	E.Sperber	P	T.Osborne	/2	B.Barrett	/O	O.Klee	P	J.Scott	P	J.Knight	RP	T.Sheehan	P	B.Sherdel
/C	D.Cousineau	P	J.Petty	/C	G.Staley	/C	T.Sullivan	P	V.Barnes	RP	H.Betts	P	B.Adams	P	F.Rhem
P	J.Cooney	RP	B.Hubbell	/C	B.O'Farrell	P	P.Donohue	P	K.Greenfield	RP	J.Couch	P	R.Oldham	P	A.Sothoron
P	J.Barnes	/P	B.McGraw	P	J.Churry	P	D.Luque	RP	J.Bentley	P	D.Ulrich	/P	B.Culloton	P	A.Reinhart
P	L.Benton	/P	H.Thormahlen	/O	C.Taylor	P	E.Rixey	P	A.Nehf	/P	C.Willoughby	/P	D.Songer	P	L.Dickerman
P	J.Genewich	P	L.Brown	/1	T.Kearns	P	R.Benton	RP	W.Huntzinger	/P	S.O'Neal	/P	L.Koupal	P	D.Mails
P	S.Graham	P	J.Oeschger	R	M.Kerr	P	J.May	P	W.Dean	/P	D.Fillingim			P	E.Dyer
RP	R.Marquard	P	G.Cantrell	P	P.Alexander	P	N.Brady	P	C.Mays	/P	R.Crumpler			P	J.Stuart
RP	I.Kamp	P	N.Greene	P	S.Blake	P	T.Sheehan	P	F.Fitzsimmons	/P	B.Vines			P	P.Day
P	R.Ryan	/P	J.Elliott	P	W.Cooper	/P	M.Goodwin	P	H.McQuillan	/P	B.Hubbell			/P	B.Hallahan
P	B.Vargus	/P	A.Rush	P	T.Kaufmann	/P	P.Dibut	P	J.Wisner					/P	E.Clough
/P	J.Batchelder	/P	A.Decatur	P	G.Bush			/C	C.Davies					/P	G.Paulsen
/P	B.Anderson	/P	J.Roberts	RP	V.Keen			/P	H.Baldwin						
/P	F.Edwards			P	P.Jones										
/P	T.McNamara			P	E.Jacobs										
/P	J.Ogrodowski			/P	G.Milstead										
				P	H.Brett										
				/P	J.Brown										
				/P	G.Stueland										
				/P	B.Osborn										

TEAM	G	W	L	PCT	GB	R	OR	AB	H	2B	3B	HR	BB	SO	AVG	OBP	SLG	PRO	PRO+	BR	/A	PF	CHI	RC	SB	CS	SBA	SBR
PIT	153	95	58	.621		912	715	5372	1651	316	105	78	499	363	.307	.369	.449	.818	108	116	55	107	101	909	159	63	72	10
NY	152	86	66	.566	8.5	736	702	5327	1507	239	61	114	411	494	.283	.337	.415	.752	101	-26	3	96	100	742	79	65	55	-15
CIN	153	80	73	.523	15	690	643	5233	1490	221	90	44	409	327	.285	.339	.387	.726	93	-66	-49	98	100	680	108	107	50	-32
STL	153	77	76	.503	18	828	764	5329	1592	292	80	109	446	414	.299	.356	.445	.801	108	72	53	102	98	846	70	51	58	-10
BOS	153	70	83	.458	25	708	802	5365	1567	260	70	41	405	380	.292	.345	.390	.735	102	-48	15	91	98	722	77	72	52	-20
PHI	153	68	85	.444	27	812	930	5412	1598	288	58	100	456	542	.295	.354	.425	.779	96	35	-37	109	99	814	48	59	45	-21
BRO	153	68	85	.444	27	786	866	5468	1617	250	80	64	437	383	.296	.351	.406	.757	102	-6	15	97	101	787	37	30	55	-7
CHI	154	68	86	.442	27.5	723	773	5353	1473	254	70	86	397	470	.275	.329	.397	.726	89	-77	-87	102	104	700	94	70	57	-14
TOT	612					6195		42859	12495	2120	614	636	3460	3373	.292	.348	.414	.762							672	517	57	-109

TEAM	CG	SH	SV	IP	H	H/G	HR	BB	SO	RAT	ERA	ERA+	OAV	OOB	PR	/A	PF	CPI	FA	E	DP	FW	PW	BW	SBW	DIF
PIT	77	2	13	1354²	1526	10.1	81	387	386	12.9	3.87	115	.287	.339	59	88	105	105	.964	224	171	-.9	8.2	5.1	2.2	3.8
NY	80	6	8	1354	1532	10.2	73	408	446	13.0	3.94	102	.289	.342	49	17	95	104	.968	199	129	.5	1.6	.3	-.1	7.8
CIN	92	11	12	1375¹	1447	9.5	35	324	437	11.8	3.38	110	.272	.317	135	110	96	95	.968	203	161	.3	10.3	-4.6	-1.7	-.8
STL	82	8	7	1335²	1480	10.0	86	470	428	13.4	4.36	99	.283	.347	-14	-7	101	96	.966	204	156	.3	-.7	5.0	.3	-4.4
BOS	77	5	4	1366²	1567	10.3	67	458	351	13.4	4.39	91	.291	.348	-19	-58	94	96	.964	221	145	-.7	-5.4	1.4	-.6	-1.2
PHI	69	8	9	1350²	1753	11.7	117	444	371	14.8	5.02	95	.315	.368	-114	-39	112	103	.966	211	147	-.1	-3.7	-3.5	-.7	-.6
BRO	82	4	4	1350²	1608	10.7	95	477	518	14.1	4.77	88	.301	.362	-76	-90	98	97	.966	210	130	-.0	-8.4	1.4	.6	-2.0
CHI	75	5	10	1370	1575	10.3	102	485	435	13.7	4.41	98	.292	.353	-21	-14	101	102	.969	198	161	.7	-1.3	-8.1	-.0	-.2
TOT	634	49	67	10857²		10.4				13.4	4.27		.292	.348					.966	1670	1200					

Runs		Hits		Doubles		Triples		Home Runs		Total Bases	
Cuyler-Pit	144	Bottomley-StL	227	Bottomley-StL	44	Cuyler-Pit	26	Hornsby-StL	39	Hornsby-StL	381
Hornsby-StL	133	Wheat-Bro	221	Cuyler-Pit	43	Walker-Cin	16	Hartnett-Chi	24	Cuyler-Pit	369
Wheat-Bro	125	Cuyler-Pit	220	Wheat-Bro	42	Roush-Cin	16	Fournier-Bro	22	Bottomley-StL	358
Traynor-Pit	114	Hornsby-StL	203	Hornsby-StL	41	Fournier-Bro	16	Meusel-NY	21	Wheat-Bro	333
Blades-StL	112	Stock-Bro	202	Burrus-Bos	41			Bottomley-StL	21	Fournier-Bro	310

Runs Batted In		Runs Produced		Bases On Balls		Batting Average		On Base Percentage		Slugging Average	
Hornsby-StL	143	Hornsby-StL	237	Fournier-Bro	86	Hornsby-StL	.403	Hornsby-StL	.489	Hornsby-StL	.756
Fournier-Bro	130	Cuyler-Pit	228	Hornsby-StL	83	Bottomley-StL	.367	Fournier-Bro	.446	Cuyler-Pit	.598
Bottomley-StL	128	Wheat-Bro	214	Moore-Pit	73	Wheat-Bro	.359	Blades-StL	.423	Wrightstone-Phi	.591
Wright-Pit	121	Traynor-Pit	214	Youngs-NY	66	Cuyler-Pit	.357	Cuyler-Pit	.423	Bottomley-StL	.578
Barnhart-Pit	114	Fournier-Bro	207	Carey-Pit	66	Fournier-Bro	.350	Carey-Pit	.418	Fournier-Bro	.569

Production		Adjusted Production		Batter Runs		Adjusted Batter Runs		Clutch Hitting Index		Runs Created	
Hornsby-StL	1.245	Hornsby-StL	208	Hornsby-StL	87.1	Hornsby-StL	83.3	Barnhart-Pit	146	Hornsby-StL	187
Cuyler-Pit	1.021	Fournier-Bro	162	Cuyler-Pit	53.1	Fournier-Bro	53.8	Traynor-Pit	117	Cuyler-Pit	158
Fournier-Bro	1.015	Cuyler-Pit	148	Fournier-Bro	50.1	Cuyler-Pit	43.5	Felix-Bos	115	Bottomley-StL	145
Bottomley-StL	.992	Bottomley-StL	147	Bottomley-StL	45.5	Bottomley-StL	42.4	E.Brown-Bro	114	Fournier-Bro	141
Blades-StL	.958	Wheat-Bro	143	Wheat-Bro	35.0	Wheat-Bro	38.3	Moore-Pit	112	Wheat-Bro	134

Total Average		Stolen Bases		Stolen Base Average		Stolen Base Runs		Fielding Runs		Total Player Rating	
Hornsby-StL	1.539	Carey-Pit	46	Smith-StL	90.9	Carey-Pit	7.2	Adams-Chi	28.1	Hornsby-StL	6.0
Cuyler-Pit	1.141	Cuyler-Pit	41	Carey-Pit	80.7	Smith-StL	4.8	Traynor-Pit	22.9	Fournier-Bro	4.2
Fournier-Bro	1.117	Adams-Chi	26	Cuyler-Pit	75.9	Cuyler-Pit	4.5	Critz-Cin	21.6	Cuyler-Pit	4.1
Bottomley-StL	1.025	Roush-Cin	22	Moore-Pit	73.1	Stock-Bro	1.8	Pinelli-Cin	20.8	Bancroft-Bos	3.8
Carey-Pit	1.011	Frisch-NY	21	Adams-Chi	68.4	Grantham-Pit	1.8	Kelly-NY	16.4	Traynor-Pit	3.5

Wins		Win Percentage		Games		Complete Games		Shutouts		Saves	
Vance-Bro	22	Sherdel-StL	.714	Morrison-Pit	44	Donohue-Cin	27	Vance-Bro	4	Morrison-Pit	4
Rixey-Cin	21	Vance-Bro	.710	Donohue-Cin	42	Vance-Bro	26	Luque-Cin	4	Bush-Chi	4
Donohue-Cin	21	Aldridge-Pit	.682	Bush-Chi	42	Rixey-Cin	22	Carlson-Phi	4		
Meadows-Pit	19	Kremer-Pit	.680	Osborne-Bro	41	Luque-Cin	22	Donohue-Cin	3		
		Rixey-Cin	.656	Ring-Phi	40	Ring-Phi	21				

Innings Pitched		Fewest Hits/Game		Fewest BB/Game		Strikeouts		Strikeouts/Game		Ratio	
Donohue-Cin	301.0	Luque-Cin	8.13	Alexander-Chi	1.11	Vance-Bro	221	Vance-Bro	7.50	Luque-Cin	10.61
Luque-Cin	291.0	Benton-Bos	8.35	Donohue-Cin	1.47	Luque-Cin	140	Luque-Cin	4.33	Donohue-Cin	10.79
Rixey-Cin	287.1	Vance-Bro	8.38	Rixey-Cin	1.47	Ring-Phi	93	Sothoron-StL	3.87	Vance-Bro	10.96
Ring-Phi	270.0	Aldridge-Pit	9.20	Cooney-Bos	1.83	Blake-Chi	93	Bush-Chi	3.76	Rixey-Cin	11.15
Vance-Bro	265.1	Donohue-Cin	9.27	Sherdel-StL	1.89	Aldridge-Pit	88	Aldridge-Pit	3.71	Alexander-Chi	11.52

Earned Run Average		Adjusted ERA		Opponents' Batting Avg.		Opponents' On Base Pct.		Starter Runs		Adjusted Starter Runs	
Luque-Cin	2.63	Luque-Cin	156	Luque-Cin	.239	Luque-Cin	.291	Luque-Cin	53.0	Luque-Cin	47.9
Rixey-Cin	2.88	Rixey-Cin	143	Benton-Bos	.249	Donohue-Cin	.299	Rixey-Cin	44.2	Rixey-Cin	39.2
Reinhart-StL	3.05	Sherdel-StL	139	Vance-Bro	.250	Vance-Bro	.304	Donohue-Cin	39.7	Donohue-Cin	34.4
Donohue-Cin	3.08	Donohue-Cin	133	Donohue-Cin	.268	Rixey-Cin	.307	Scott-NY	29.6	Sherdel-StL	27.0
Benton-Bos	3.09	Benton-Bos	130	Scott-NY	.269	Cooney-Bos	.312	Sherdel-StL	25.8	Alexander-Chi	24.4

Clutch Pitching Index		Relief Runs		Adjusted Relief Runs		Relief Ranking		Total Pitcher Index		Total Baseball Ranking	
Nehf-NY	122	Huntzinger-NY	5.5	Huntzinger-NY	3.9	Huntzinger-NY	3.2	Luque-Cin	6.1	Luque-Cin	6.1
Yde-Pit	117							Donohue-Cin	4.0	Hornsby-StL	6.0
Sherdel-StL	109							Rixey-Cin	3.6	Fournier-Bro	4.2
Rixey-Cin	108							Scott-NY	3.3	Cuyler-Pit	4.1
Morrison-Pit	107							Sherdel-StL	2.6	Donohue-Cin	4.0

February 10 At the AL meeting, a plan is adopted to alternate the site of future World Series openers by league rather than deciding it by a coin toss, with Games 1, 2, 6, and 7 in one park and 3, 4, 5 in the other, unless a ban on Sunday baseball interferes in one city.

April 14 Two future Hall of Famers make their major league debuts for the A's in the same game. Lefty Grove starts against Boston and leaves in the fourth after walking four and striking out nobody. He gives up five runs on six hits. In the eighth, Gordon "Mickey" Cochrane pinch-hits for catcher Cy Perkins, singles and stays in behind the plate while the A's go on to score nine runs in the last four innings to win, 9-8, in 10 innings.

May 1 The A's introduce another future Hall of Famer, 17-year-old catcher Jimmie Foxx, who pinch hits and singles against Washington.

May 5 Ty Cobb is 6-for-6, including three home runs, in Detroit's 14-8 win over the Browns.

May 5 Everett Scott is benched by New York manager Miller Huggins, ending his 1,307-game playing streak. Pee Wee Wanninger replaces him at shortstop.

June 1 Lou Gehrig begins a consecutive-game streak that will surpass Everett Scott's mark by pinch-hitting for Pee Wee Wanninger, the shortstop who replaced Scott in the Yankees lineup. The next day, first baseman Wally Pipp shows up with a headache, and Gehrig takes over.

June 3 White Sox manager Eddie Collins makes hit No. 3,000 versus Detroit.

August 15 Little Dickie Kerr, the southpaw who won two games for the White Sox in the 1919 World Series, makes his first major league appearance since 1921. He has been playing semipro ball rather than accept Charles Comiskey's salary offer. When he relieves Red Faber in the third inning against the Tigers, play is stopped while admirers present him with a floral horseshoe.

August 29 After a night on the town, Babe Ruth shows up late for batting practice. Miller Huggins suspends Ruth and slaps a $5,000 fine on him for disobeying orders on the field and team rules off the field. In the showdown between the Bambino and the tiny manager, Jake Ruppert backs up his manager. Ruth is forced to apologize before he's reinstated nine days later. The day after his return to the lineup, Ruth hits home run number 300.

September 23 Washington shortstop Roger Peckinpaugh, a .294 hitter, is named the AL MVP with 45 points; A's outfielder Al Simmons is second with 41 points.

October 4 Harry Heilmann gets six hits in Detroit's doubleheader win over the Browns to edge out teammate Cobb for the batting crown, .393 to .389. Ty Cobb bats over .300 for the 20th time.

October 7 Walter Johnson (20-7) opens the World Series in Pittsburgh. A fifth-inning home run by Pie Traynor is the only damaging blow, as Johnson fans 10 of the heavy-hitting Bucs for a 4-1 win over Lee Meadows (19-10). Sam Rice, Joe Harris, and Ossie Bluege, with two hits each, drive in the Senators' runs in Game 1.

October 10 For Game 3 it's clear but bitterly cold in Washington following a rainstorm that caused the game to be rescheduled. President Coolidge throws out the first ball. The Pirates hold a slim 3-2 lead after six. A walk and two singles score two in the eighth for Washington, and Firpo Marberry (8-6) closes it. Joe Harris has two hits for the third time; he'll lead the Senators with .440. Sam Rice makes a controversial game-saving play in the eighth, tumbling into the stands in the right corner to spear a long drive by Earl Smith. About 15 seconds later he emerges with the ball. Despite the Pirates' arguments that a fan might have given it to him, ump Cy Rigler calls Smith out. Questioned about it for the rest of his life, Rice leaves a letter, to be opened after his death (in 1974), in which he states: "At no time did I lose possession of the ball."

	BOSTON		CHICAGO		CLEVELAND		DETROIT		NEW YORK		PHILADELPHIA		ST.LOUIS		WASHINGTON
M	L.Fohl	M	E.Collins	M	T.Speaker	M	T.Cobb	M	M.Huggins	M	C.Mack	M	G.Sisler	M	B.Harris
1B	P.Todt	1B	E.Sheely	1B	G.Burns	1B	L.Blue	1B	L.Gehrig	1B	J.Poole	1B	G.Sisler	1B	J.Judge
2B	B.Wambsganss	2B	E.Collins	2B	C.Fewster	2B	F.O'Rourke	2B	A.Ward	2B	M.Bishop	2B	M.McManus	2B	B.Harris
SS	D.Lee	SS	I.Davis	SS	J.Sewell	SS	J.Tavener	SS	P.Wanninger	SS	C.Galloway	SS	B.LaMotte	SS	R.Peckinpaugh
3B	D.Prothro	3B	W.Kamm	3B	R.Lutzke	3B	F.Haney	3B	J.Dugan	3B	S.Hale	3B	G.Robertson	3B	O.Bluege
LF	R.Carlyle	LF	B.Falk	LF	C.Jamieson	LF	A.Wingo	LF	B.Meusel	LF	B.Lamar	LF	K.Williams	LF	G.Goslin
CF	I.Flagstead	CF	J.Mostil	CF	T.Speaker	CF	T.Cobb	CF	E.Combs	CF	A.Simmons	CF	B.Jacobson	CF	E.McNeely
RF	I.Boone	RF	H.Hooper	RF	P.McNulty	RF	H.Heilmann	RF	B.Ruth	RF	B.Miller	RF	H.Rice	RF	S.Rice
C	V.Picinich	C	R.Schalk	C	G.Myatt	C	J.Bassler	C	B.Bengough	C	M.Cochrane	C	L.Dixon	C	M.Ruel
O	T.Vache	2O	B.Barrett	32	F.Spurgeon	O	H.Manush	O	B.Paschal	32	J.Dykes	O	H.Bennett	1O	J.Harris
3	D.Williams	O	B.Crouse	O	C.Lee	O	B.Fothergill	1	W.Pipp	O	F.Welch	S	W.Gerber	O	H.Severeid
O	H.Ezzell	O	S.Harris	O	H.Summa	2	L.Burke	2S	E.Johnson	C	C.Perkins	C	P.Hargrave	S	E.Scott
2	B.Rogell	/S	J.Kane	C	L.Sewell	C	L.Woodall	C	W.Schang	O	W.French	O	J.Tobin	O	N.Leibold
C	J.Bischoff	C	R.Elsh	3	J.Hodapp	3	B.Jones	32	H.Shanks	1	R.Holt	O	J.Evans	2	S.Adams
C	J.Heving	C	J.Grabowski	1	R.Knode	S	T.Rigney	O	B.Veach	/O	B.Bagwell	C	H.Severeid	O	B.Veach
S	B.Connolly	/C	J.Bischoff	2	J.Klugmann	1	J.Neun	S	M.Koenig	/S	C.Husta	C	T.Rego	C	B.Tate
O	S.Rosenthal	/C	M.Archdeacon	O	R.Stephenson	3	J.Warner	O	S.O'Neill	/C	C.Berry	/3	J.Austin	/1	M.Shirley
O	T.Jenkins	H	B.Clancy	O	I.Eichrodt	/2	C.Gehringer	S	E.Scott	S	R.Smith			/3	M.McNally
S	J.Rothrock	/O	J.Mallonee	/1	H.Hendrick	/C	O.Stanage	O	W.Witt	/C	J.Foxx	P	M.Gaston	O	T.Jeanes
C	A.Stokes	/C	L.Tankersley	/C	R.Walters	H	A.Harrington	/C	R.Luebbe	/2	D.Gautreau	P	J.Bush	/3	S.Stewart
2	M.Herrera			/1	C.Tolson			/1	F.Merkle	/1	J.Keesey	P	E.Vangilder	O	W.Matthews
S	H.Welch	P	T.Lyons	/C	F.McCrea	P	E.Whitehill	/C	F.Hofmann	/S	C.Engle	P	D.Davis	/S	B.Myer
/S	T.Gross	P	R.Faber	/2	G.Bedford	P	H.Dauss	H	L.Durocher			P	J.Giard	/1	P.Hargrave
/1	J.Harris	P	T.Blankenship	/2	D.Ussat	P	K.Holloway	/3	H.Odom	P	E.Rommel			/1	F.McGee
/S	C.Geygan	P	S.Thurston			P	L.Stoner			P	S.Harriss	P	D.Danforth	H	R.Carlyle
/O	B.Veach	P	C.Robertson	P	S.Smith	P	R.Collins	P	H.Pennock	P	S.Gray	P	E.Wingard		
/O	S.Collins	RP	S.Connally	P	G.Uhle	RP	J.Doyle	P	S.Jones	P	L.Grove	P	E.Stauffer	P	S.Coveleski
				P	B.Karr			P	U.Shocker	P	R.Walberg	P	C.Falk	P	W.Johnson
P	H.Ehmke	P	M.Cvengros	P	J.Miller	P	E.Wells	P	W.Hoyt			P	G.Grant	P	D.Ruether
P	T.Wingfield	/P	J.Edwards	P	G.Buckeye	P	D.Leonard	P	B.Shawkey	P	S.Baumgartner	/P	G.Mogridge	P	T.Zachary
P	R.Ruffing	P	D.Kerr			P	O.Carroll	RP	H.Johnson	P	J.Quinn	/P	B.Springer	RP	F.Marberry
P	P.Zahniser	/P	L.Mangum	P	J.Shaute	P	B.Cole	RP	A.Ferguson	P	A.Stokes	/P	G.Blaeholder	RP	V.Gregg
P	J.Quinn	/P	F.Mack	P	B.Speece	P	S.Johnson			P	F.Heimach			RP	A.Russell
RP	B.Ross	/P	T.Riviere	P	B.Cole	/P	B.Moore	/P	B.Shields	/P	E.Andrews				
RP	O.Fuhr	/P	K.Ash	P	J.Edwards			/P	G.Braxton	/P	T.Glass			P	A.Ferguson
		/P	J.Freeze	P	C.Yowell			/P	W.Beall	/P	L.Willis			P	G.Mogridge
/P	R.Francis	/P	C.Bender	/P	D.Levsen			/P	J.Marquis					P	C.Ogden
/P	C.Fullerton			/P	R.Benge			/P	R.Francis					/P	W.Ballou
/P	R.Kallio			/P	L.Roy			/P	C.Caldwell					/P	H.Kelley
/P	A.Ferguson													/P	L.Thomas
/P	J.Kiefer													/P	J.Lyle
/P	J.Lucey													/P	S.Pumpelly
/P	H.Neubauer														
/P	B.Adams														

TEAM	G	W	L	PCT	GB	R	OR	AB	H	2B	3B	HR	BB	SO	AVG	OBP	SLG	PRO	PRO+	BR	/A	PF	CHI	RC	SB	CS	SBA	SBR
WAS	152	96	55	.636		829	670	5206	1577	251	71	56	533	427	.303	.373	.411	.784	106	39	56	98	100	815	135	92	59	-15
PHI	153	88	64	.579	8.5	831	713	5399	1659	298	79	76	453	432	.307	.364	.434	.798	101	54	-2	107	97	856	67	60	53	-16
STL	154	82	71	.536	15	900	906	5440	1620	304	68	110	498	375	.298	.360	.439	.799	103	52	8	105	105	859	85	78	52	-21
DET	156	81	73	.526	16.5	903	829	5371	1621	277	84	50	640	386	.302	.379	.413	.792	109	63	76	99	102	872	97	63	61	-9
CHI	154	79	75	.513	18.5	811	770	5224	1482	299	59	38	662	405	.284	.370	.385	.755	102	-7	36	95	101	782	131	87	60	-13
CLE	155	70	84	.455	27.5	782	817	5436	1613	285	58	52	520	379	.297	.361	.399	.760	97	-12	-18	101	98	795	90	77	54	-19
NY	156	69	85	.448	28.5	706	774	5353	1471	247	74	110	470	482	.275	.336	.410	.746	96	-61	-48	98	97	739	69	73	49	-23
BOS	152	47	105	.309	49.5	639	922	5166	1375	257	64	41	513	422	.266	.336	.364	.700	83	-131	-130	100	100	647	42	56	43	-21
TOT	616					6401		42595	12418	2218	557	533	4289	3308	.292	.360	.408	.768							716	586	55	-137

TEAM	CG	SH	SV	IP	H	H/G	HR	BB	SO	RAT	ERA	ERA+	OAV	OOB	PR	/A	PF	CPI	FA	E	DP	FW	PW	BW	SBW	DIF
WAS	69	10	21	1358¹	1434	9.5	49	543	463	13.3	3.70	114	.278	.351	105	79	96	107	.972	170	166	1.8	7.3	5.2	.2	6.0
PHI	61	8	18	1381²	1468	9.6	60	544	495	13.3	3.87	120	.276	.347	81	119	106	101	.966	211	148	-.6	11.0	-.2	.1	1.6
STL	67	7	10	1379²	1588	10.4	99	675	419	15.0	4.92	95	.298	.380	-80	-39	106	102	.964	226	164	-1.4	-3.6	.7	-.4	10.1
DET	66	2	18	1383²	1582	10.3	70	556	419	14.2	4.61	94	.296	.366	-32	-46	98	99	.972	173	143	1.9	-4.3	7.0	.8	-1.4
CHI	71	12	13	1385²	1579	10.3	69	489	374	13.6	4.29	97	.295	.356	17	-21	95	102	.968	200	162	.2	-1.9	3.3	.4	.0
CLE	93	6	9	1372¹	1604	10.5	41	493	345	14.0	4.94	98	.296	.359	-15	-9	101	95	.967	210	146	-.4	-1.8	-1.7	-.2	-4.0
NY	80	8	13	1387²	1560	10.1	78	505	492	13.6	4.33	98	.289	.353	10	-11	97	99	.974	160	150	2.7	-1.0	-4.4	-.5	-4.7
BOS	68	6	6	1326²	1615	11.0	67	510	310	14.7	4.97	92	.308	.374	-84	-62	103	98	.957	271	150	-4.2	-5.7	-12.0	-.4	-6.6
TOT	575	59	108	10975²		10.2				14.0	4.39		.292	.360					.968	1621	1229					

Runs		Hits		Doubles		Triples		Home Runs		Total Bases	
Mostil-Chi	135	Simmons-Phi	253	McManus-StL	44	Goslin-Was	20	Meusel-NY	33	Simmons-Phi	392
Simmons-Phi	122	Rice-Was	227	Simmons-Phi	43	Mostil-Chi	16	Williams-StL	25	Meusel-NY	338
Combs-NY	117	Heilmann-Det	225	Sheely-Chi	43	Sisler-StL	15	Ruth-NY	25	Goslin-Was	329
Goslin-Was	116	Sisler-StL	224	Burns-Cle	41			Simmons-Phi	24	Heilmann-Det	326
Rice-Was	111	J.Sewell-Cle	204					Gehrig-NY	20	Sisler-StL	311

Runs Batted In		Runs Produced		Bases On Balls		Batting Average		On Base Percentage		Slugging Average	
Meusel-NY	138	Simmons-Phi	227	Mostil-Chi	90	Heilmann-Det	.393	Speaker-Cle	.479	Williams-StL	.613
Heilmann-Det	134	Heilmann-Det	218	Kamm-Chi	90	Speaker-Cle	.389	Cobb-Det	.468	Simmons-Phi	.599
Simmons-Phi	129	Goslin-Was	211	Collins-Chi	87	Simmons-Phi	.387	Collins-Chi	.461	Cobb-Det	.598
Goslin-Was	113	Meusel-NY	206	Bishop-Phi	87	Cobb-Det	.378	Heilmann-Det	.457	Speaker-Cle	.578
Sheely-Chi	111	Rice-Was	197	Blue-Det	83	Wingo-Det	.370	Wingo-Det	.456	Heilmann-Det	.569

Production		Adjusted Production		Batter Runs		Adjusted Batter Runs		Clutch Hitting Index		Runs Created	
Cobb-Det	1.066	Cobb-Det	171	Heilmann-Det	52.5	Heilmann-Det	54.6	Galloway-Phi	149	Simmons-Phi	155
Speaker-Cle	1.057	Speaker-Cle	166	Simmons-Phi	51.4	Cobb-Det	47.0	Blue-Det	136	Heilmann-Det	149
Heilmann-Det	1.026	Heilmann-Det	161	Speaker-Cle	47.0	Speaker-Cle	46.1	Sheely-Chi	127	Goslin-Was	131
Simmons-Phi	1.018	Wingo-Det	151	Cobb-Det	45.3	Simmons-Phi	42.1	Collins-Chi	123	Speaker-Cle	123
Wingo-Det	.983	Simmons-Phi	146	Wingo-Det	35.3	Wingo-Det	36.8	B.Harris-Was	120	Cobb-Det	118

Total Average		Stolen Bases		Stolen Base Average		Stolen Base Runs		Fielding Runs		Total Player Rating	
Speaker-Cle	1.231	Mostil-Chi	43	Blue-Det	79.2	Goslin-Was	3.3	Flagstead-Bos	19.9	Speaker-Cle	4.5
Cobb-Det	1.206	Goslin-Was	27	Goslin-Was	77.1	Haney-Det	2.7	J.Sewell-Cle	16.3	J.Sewell-Cle	3.8
Heilmann-Det	1.113	Rice-Was	26	Collins-Chi	76.0	Blue-Det	2.7	O'Rourke-Det	14.6	Heilmann-Det	3.7
Wingo-Det	1.041			Rice-Was	70.3	Collins-Chi	2.1	Goslin-Was	13.6	Goslin-Was	3.7
Collins-Chi	1.028			Mostil-Chi	68.3	Peckinpaugh-Was	1.5	Ruel-Was	11.5	Cobb-Det	3.3

Wins		Win Percentage		Games		Complete Games		Shutouts		Saves	
Rommel-Phi	21	Coveleski-Was	.800	Marberry-Was	55	Smith-Cle	22	Lyons-Chi	5	Marberry-Was	15
Lyons-Chi	21	Johnson-Was	.741	Walberg-Phi	53	Ehmke-Bos	22	Gray-Phi	4	Doyle-Det	8
Johnson-Was	20	Ruether-Was	.720	Vangilder-StL	52	Pennock-NY	21	Giard-StL	4	Connally-Chi	8
Coveleski-Was	20	Blankenship-Chi	.680	Rommel-Phi	52	Lyons-Chi	19			Walberg-Phi	7
Harriss-Phi	19	Rommel-Phi	.677	Pennock-NY	47	Wingfield-Bos	18				

Innings Pitched		Fewest Hits/Game		Fewest BB/Game		Strikeouts		Strikeouts/Game		Ratio	
Pennock-NY	277.0	Blankenship-Chi	8.46	Smith-Cle	1.82	Grove-Phi	116	Grove-Phi	5.30	Pennock-NY	11.05
Lyons-Chi	262.2	Johnson-Was	8.53	Quinn-Bos-Phi	1.85	Johnson-Was	108	Johnson-Was	4.24	Blankenship-Chi	11.13
Rommel-Phi	261.0	Coveleski-Was	8.59	Shocker-NY	2.14	Harriss-Phi	95	Shawkey-NY	3.92	Coveleski-Was	11.39
Ehmke-Bos	260.2	Pennock-NY	8.68	Faber-Chi	2.23	Ehmke-Bos	95	Walberg-Phi	3.85	Gray-Phi	11.71
Wingfield-Bos	254.1	Gray-Phi	8.79	Pennock-NY	2.31	Jones-NY	92	Gray-Phi	3.54	Johnson-Was	11.87

Earned Run Average		Adjusted ERA		Opponents' Batting Avg.		Opponents' On Base Pct.		Starter Runs		Adjusted Starter Runs	
Coveleski-Was	2.84	Coveleski-Was	149	Johnson-Was	.250	Pennock-NY	.303	Pennock-NY	44.2	Pennock-NY	40.2
Pennock-NY	2.96	Pennock-NY	144	Blankenship-Chi	.253	Blankenship-Chi	.308	Coveleski-Was	41.7	Coveleski-Was	37.2
Blankenship-Chi	3.03	Gray-Phi	142	Pennock-NY	.254	Coveleski-Was	.312	Blankenship-Chi	35.3	Harriss-Phi	32.5
Johnson-Was	3.07	Johnson-Was	138	Coveleski-Was	.255	Johnson-Was	.317	Johnson-Was	33.8	Gray-Phi	31.2
Dauss-Det	3.16	Blankenship-Chi	137	Gray-Phi	.260	Gray-Phi	.319	Lyons-Chi	33.3	Johnson-Was	29.6

Clutch Pitching Index		Relief Runs		Adjusted Relief Runs		Relief Ranking		Total Pitcher Index		Total Baseball Ranking	
Dauss-Det	119	Marberry-Was	9.6	Marberry-Was	7.8	Marberry-Was	13.4	Johnson-Was	4.3	Speaker-Cle	4.5
Shocker-NY	114	Gregg-Was	2.3	Gregg-Was	.9	Gregg-Was	.5	Pennock-NY	3.6	Johnson-Was	4.3
Zachary-Was	113							Harriss-Phi	3.6	J.Sewell-Cle	3.8
Lyons-Chi	111							Rommel-Phi	3.3	Heilmann-Det	3.7
Shawkey-NY	110							Dauss-Det	3.0	Goslin-Was	3.7

January 30 The major league Rules Committee agrees that pitchers may have access to a resin bag. On Feb. 8 the AL will refuse to permit its use but changes its policy in April.

April 27 In the Giants' 9-8 win over the Phillies, 17-year-old Mel Ott makes his first appearance pinch-hitting for Jimmy Ring. He strikes out. Ott won't play regularly till 1927.

May 1* Satchel Paige, 19 years old, makes his debut in the Negro Southern League, pitching Chattanooga to a 5-4 win over Birmingham.

May 23 Hack Wilson becomes the first player to hit a ball off the Wrigley Field scoreboard, smacking a fifth-inning home run off the center field scoreboard to start a rout of the Braves. The Cubs score seven runs in the eighth inning to win, 14-8.

June 22 The Cardinals pick up 39-year-old Grover Cleveland Alexander on waivers from the Cubs to help in the pennant chase. He'll be 9-7 down the stretch.

July 22 The Reds pound four triples in the second inning, including two by Curt Walker, against the Braves, tying a major league record, and go on to win, 13-3. Walker's feat, the first since 1900, won't be repeated until Al Zarilla does it in 1946.

August 15 The Braves are at Ebbets Field with Brooklyn's Hank DeBerry on third base, Dazzy Vance on second base, and Chick Fewster on first base. Babe Herman drives the ball against the right field wall, and DeBerry scores. Vance holds up, then rounds third base headed for home. Fewster stops at third base. The right fielder throws home and traps Vance, who heads back to third base. Herman slides into third base as Fewster steps off. Herman is out for passing a base runner. Fewster, thinking he's out, too, walks off with Babe, and gets tagged out. Vance, still on third base, later admits it was his fault, but Herman, who doubles into a double play, gets the blame.

October 9 Grover Cleveland Alexander scatters eight hits in Game 6 while the Cards tee off on Bob Shawkey (8-6), Urban Shocker, and Myles Thomas for 10 runs and 13 hits in a 10-2 romp.

October 10 Only 38,093 show up at the Stadium for the deciding World Series contest. Grover Cleveland Alexander, possibly sleeping off a hangover in the bullpen, barely notices as Jess Haines takes a 3-2 lead over Waite Hoyt. Haines weakens in the last of the seventh; three walks put Earle Combs, Bob Meusel, and Lou Gehrig on base with two out and Tony Lazzeri at the plate. Hornsby waves in Alexander. On a 1-1 count Lazzeri hits a line drive into the left-field seats, a few feet to the foul side of the pole, then swings and misses for strike three. Alexander sets the Yanks down in order until Babe Ruth draws his 11th walk with two out in the ninth, and is thrown out trying to steal second base. The Cards have their first world championship.

December 5 Cardinals catcher Bob O'Farrell is named NL MVP. O'Farrell caught 146 games and batted .293. He polls 79 points. Reds second baseman Hughie Critz is runner-up with 60. Critz set a major league record with 588 assists, which will be topped by Frank Frisch with 643 in 1927.

December 20 Rogers Hornsby is traded from the Cardinals to the New York Giants for Frankie Frisch and pitcher Jimmy Ring.

	BOSTON		BROOKLYN		CHICAGO		CINCINNATI		NEW YORK		PHILADELPHIA		PITTSBURGH		ST.LOUIS
M	D.Bancroft	M	W.Robinson	M	J.McCarthy	M	J.Hendricks	M	J.McGraw	M	A.Fletcher	M	B.McKechnie	M	R.Hornsby
1B	D.Burrus	1B	B.Herman	1B	C.Grimm	1B	W.Pipp	1B	G.Kelly	1B	J.Bentley	1B	G.Grantham	1B	J.Bottomley
2B	D.Gautreau	2B	C.Fewster	2B	S.Adams	2B	H.Critz	2B	F.Frisch	2B	B.Friberg	2B	H.Rhyne	2B	R.Hornsby
SS	D.Bancroft	SS	J.Butler	SS	J.Cooney	SS	F.Emmer	SS	T.Jackson	SS	H.Sand	SS	G.Wright	SS	T.Thevenow
3B	A.High	3B	W.Marriott	3B	H.Freigau	3B	C.Dressen	3B	F.Lindstrom	3B	C.Huber	3B	P.Traynor	3B	L.Bell
LF	E.Brown	LF	Z.Wheat	LF	R.Stephenson	LF	C.Christensen	LF	I.Meusel	LF	J.Mokan	LF	K.Cuyler	LF	R.Blades
CF	J.Smith	CF	G.Felix	CF	H.Wilson	CF	E.Roush	CF	T.Tyson	CF	F.Leach	CF	M.Carey	CF	T.Douthit
RF	J.Welsh	RF	D.Cox	RF	C.Heathcote	RF	C.Walker	RF	R.Youngs	RF	C.Williams	RF	P.Waner	RF	B.Southworth
C	Z.Taylor	C	M.O'Neil	C	G.Hartnett	C	B.Hargrave	C	P.Florence	C	J.Wilson	C	E.Smith	C	B.O'Farrell
3S	E.Taylor	O	M.Jacobson	C	M.Gonzalez	O	R.Bressler	1O	B.Terry	C	B.Henline	C	J.Gooch	C	C.Hafey
O	F.Wilson	1	J.Fournier	O	P.Scott	C	V.Picinich	O	H.Mueller	O	A.Nixon	O	C.Barnhart	O	H.Mueller
2S	E.Moore	S2	R.Maranville	O	J.Kelly	3S	B.Pinelli	S	D.Farrell	13	R.Wrightstone	2	J.Rawlings	2	W.Holm
O	L.Mann	C	C.Hargreaves	O	J.Munson	S	H.Ford	C	F.Snyder	O	G.Harper	2	E.Moore	2	S.Toporcer
1P	J.Cooney	23	S.Bohne	2	C.Beck	O	B.Zitzmann	O	B.Southworth	1	R.Grimes	1	S.McInnis	2	J.Flowers
O	B.Neis	C	H.DeBerry	1	C.Tolson	S	S.Bohne	1	H.McMullen	1	D.Attreau	2	J.Cronin	O	E.Vick
C	O.Siemer	23	J.Standaert	S	R.Shannon	/1	J.Hudgens	O	A.Moore	3	B.Rice	O	C.Bigbee	/C	B.Warwick
3	J.Johnston	O	M.Carey	O	M.Brooks	/O	E.Allen	O	J.Johnston	O	D.Sothern	O	W.Mueller	H	J.Smith
C	F.Gibson	O	W.Witt	/S	H.Schreiber	/C	I.Wingo	O	M.Ott	C	B.Jonnard	O	F.Brickell		
/C	S.Hogan	/O	M.Clabaugh	/3	J.Graves	/S	E.Scott	2S	A.Cohen	/1	W.Kimmick	C	R.Spencer	P	F.Rhem
/3	H.Riconda	/2	S.Dowd	/C	J.Churry	/3	D.Prothro	/1	H.Groh	/3	E.Cotter	/O	E.Murphy	P	B.Sherdel
/C	S.Womack	/2	M.Stock	H	R.Michaels	/2	H.Carter	C	G.Hartley	/S	G.Stutz	/O	A.Comorosky	P	J.Haines
						H	C.Sukeforth	/O	B.Carter	/S	J.Buskey			P	V.Keen
P	L.Benton	P	J.Petty	P	C.Root			/C	J.Cummings	/1	L.Dunham	P	R.Kremer	P	P.Alexander
P	J.Genewich	P	B.Grimes	P	S.Blake	P	P.Donohue	/2	S.Slayback	/C	L.Wendell	P	L.Meadows	RP	S.Johnson
P	B.Smith	P	D.McWeeny	P	T.Kaufmann	P	C.Mays	/2	F.Thompson	/2	C.Keating	P	V.Aldridge		
P	J.Werts	P	B.McGraw	P	P.Jones	P	D.Luque	/O	M.Smith			P	E.Yde	P	A.Reinhart
P	G.Mogridge	P	D.Vance	P	G.Bush	P	E.Rixey	/C	J.Hamby	P	H.Carlson	P	D.Songer	P	H.Bell
		RP	R.Ehrhardt			P	J.May	H	J.Connell	P	W.Dean			P	B.Hallahan
P	B.Hearn			P	B.Osborn			H	P.Cote	P	C.Mitchell	P	J.Morrison	P	A.Sothoron
P	H.Goldsmith	P	J.Barnes	P	B.Piercy			/C	J.Boyle	P	C.Willoughby	P	J.Bush	/P	W.Huntzinger
P	S.Graham	P	G.Boehler	/P	W.Cooper			R.Lucas	P	D.Ulrich	P	R.Oldham	/P	E.Dyer
/P	F.Edwards	/P	L.Williams	P	G.Milstead	/P	R.Meeker			P	R.Pierce	/P	C.Hill	/P	E.Clough
/P	R.Ryan	/P	D.Stryker	/P	P.Alexander	/P	A.Nehf	P	J.Scott	RP	E.Baecht	P	B.Adams	/P	D.Mails
/P	B.Vargus	/P	R.Moss	P	W.Huntzinger	/P	P.Day	K.Greenfield			/P	T.Sheehan		
				/P	J.Welch	P	M.Holland	P	F.Fitzsimmons			/P	L.Koupal		
						/P	B.Springer	P	V.Barnes	P	J.Knight	/P	L.Nichols		
						/P	R.Meadows	P	J.Ring	P	E.Maun	/P	R.Mahaffey		
								RP	C.Davies	/P	L.Taber	/P	B.Culloton		
										/P	M.Kelly				
								P	H.McQuillan	/P	P.Rambo				
								/P	J.Wisner	/P	A.Decatur				
								/P	J.Poetz	/P	R.Yarnall				
								/P	T.McNamara						
								/P	J.Bentley						
								/P	A.Nehf						
								/P	N.Porter						
								/P	A.Smith						

TEAM	G	W	L	PCT	GB	R	OR	AB	H	2B	3B	HR	BB	SO	AVG	OBP	SLG	PRO	PRO+	BR	/A	PF	CHI	RC	SB	CS	SBA	SBR
STL	156	89	65	.578		817	678	5381	1541	259	82	90	478	518	.286	.348	.415	.763	107	76	46	104	102	770	83			
CIN	157	87	67	.565	2	747	651	5320	1541	242	120	35	454	333	.290	.349	.400	.749	110	52	72	97	97	738	51			
PIT	157	84	69	.549	4.5	769	689	5312	1514	243	106	44	434	350	.285	.343	.396	.739	99	28	-11	105	105	713	91			
CHI	155	82	72	.532	7	682	602	5229	1453	291	49	66	445	447	.278	.338	.390	.728	100	7	-2	101	96	685	85			
NY	151	74	77	.490	13.5	663	668	5167	1435	214	58	73	339	420	.278	.325	.384	.709	97	-36	-28	99	104	631	94			
BRO	155	71	82	.464	17.5	623	705	5130	1348	246	62	40	475	464	.263	.328	.358	.686	91	-65	-56	99	100	607	76			
BOS	153	66	86	.434	22	624	719	5216	1444	209	62	16	426	348	.277	.345	.390	.685	91	-66	-10	91	99	612	81			
PHI	152	58	93	.384	29.5	687	900	5254	1479	244	50	75	422	479	.281	.337	.390	.727	96	5	-31	105	98	683	47			
TOT	618					5612		42009	11755	1948	589	439	3473	3359	.280	.338	.386	.724						608				

TEAM	CG	SH	SV	IP	H	H/G	HR	BB	SO	RAT	ERA	ERA+	OAV	OOB	PR	/A	PF	CPI	FA	E	DP	FW	PW	BW	SBW	DIF
STL	90	10	6	1398²	1423	9.2	76	397	365	11.8	3.67	106	.269	.322	24	36	102	96	.969	198	141	.3	3.6	4.5		3.6
CIN	88	14	8	1408²	1449	9.3	40	324	424	11.5	3.42	108	.271	.316	64	42	97	95	.972	183	160	1.3	4.2	7.1		-2.6
PIT	83	12	18	1379¹	1422	9.3	50	455	387	12.5	3.67	107	.272	.334	24	42	103	99	.965	220	161	-.9	4.2	-1.1		5.3
CHI	77	13	14	1378¹	1407	9.2	39	486	508	12.6	3.26	118	.273	.340	87	89	101	113	.974	162	174	2.4	8.8	-.2		-6.0
NY	61	4	15	1341²	1370	9.2	70	427	419	12.2	3.77	100	.269	.328	8	-3	98	96	.970	186	150	.7	-.3	-2.8		.9
BRO	83	5	9	1361²	1440	9.5	50	472	517	12.8	3.82	100	.276	.339	1	0	100	98	.963	229	95	-1.5	.0	-5.5		1.6
BOS	60	9	9	1365¹	1536	10.1	46	455	408	13.4	4.01	88	.294	.354	-28	-71	93	105	.967	208	150	-.5	-7.0	-1.0		-1.5
PHI	68	5	5	1334¹	1699	11.5	68	454	331	14.7	5.03	82	.315	.371	-179	-133	108	98	.964	224	153	-1.5	-13.1	-3.1		.2
TOT	610	72	84	10968		9.6				12.7	3.82		.280	.338					.968	1610	1184					

Runs		Hits		Doubles		Triples		Home Runs		Total Bases	
Cuyler-Pit	113	Brown-Bos	201	Bottomley-StL	40	Waner-Pit	22	Wilson-Chi	21	Bottomley-StL	305
Waner-Pit	101	Cuyler-Pit	197	Roush-Cin	37	Walker-Cin	20	Bottomley-StL	19	L.Bell-StL	301
Southworth-NY-StL	99	Adams-Chi	193	Wilson-Chi	36	Traynor-Pit	17	Williams-Phi	18	Wilson-Chi	285
Sand-Phi	99	L.Bell-StL	189					L.Bell-StL	17	Waner-Pit	283
								Southworth-NY-StL	16	Cuyler-Pit	282

Runs Batted In		Runs Produced		Bases On Balls		Batting Average		On Base Percentage		Slugging Average	
Bottomley-StL	120	Bottomley-StL	199	Wilson-Chi	69	Hargrave-Cin	.353	Waner-Pit	.413	Williams-Phi	.568
Wilson-Chi	109	Cuyler-Pit	197	Waner-Pit	66	Christensen-Cin	.350	Blades-StL	.409	Wilson-Chi	.539
L.Bell-StL	100	Wilson-Chi	185	Sand-Phi	66	Smith-Pit	.346	Wilson-Chi	.406	Waner-Pit	.528
Southworth-NY-StL	99	Southworth-NY-StL	182	Bancroft-Bos	64	Williams-Phi	.345	Grantham-Pit	.400	Hargrave-Cin	.525
Pipp-Cin	99	Hornsby-StL	178	Blades-StL	62	Waner-Pit	.336	Bancroft-Bos	.399	L.Bell-StL	.518

Production		Adjusted Production		Batter Runs		Adjusted Batter Runs		Clutch Hitting Index		Runs Created	
Wilson-Chi	.944	Wilson-Chi	150	Waner-Pit	39.5	Wilson-Chi	37.9	Butler-Bro	125	Waner-Pit	115
Waner-Pit	.941	Waner-Pit	144	Wilson-Chi	39.2	Waner-Pit	33.6	Pipp-Cin	122	Wilson-Chi	115
L.Bell-StL	.901	Herman-Bro	136	L.Bell-StL	31.6	L.Bell-StL	27.4	Hornsby-StL	116	L.Bell-StL	112
Grantham-Pit	.890	L.Bell-StL	135	Williams-Phi	29.8	Williams-Phi	26.0	Thevenow-StL	116	Bottomley-StL	109
Herman-Bro	.875	Grantham-Pit	131	Bottomley-StL	25.2	Herman-Bro	23.7	Burrus-Bos	116	Cuyler-Pit	105

Total Average		Stolen Bases		Stolen Base Average		Stolen Base Runs		Fielding Runs		Total Player Rating	
Wilson-Chi	1.031	Cuyler-Pit	35					Critz-Cin	24.0	Waner-Pit	3.1
Waner-Pit	1.022	Adams-Chi	27					Friberg-Phi	22.4	Wilson-Chi	3.0
Grantham-Pit	.938	Frisch-NY	23					Cooney-Chi	19.4	Bancroft-Bos	2.7
Blades-StL	.938	Douthit-StL	23					Thevenow-StL	18.4	O'Farrell-StL	2.7
L.Bell-StL	.929	Youngs-NY	21					Douthit-StL	17.8	Jackson-NY	2.6

Wins		Win Percentage		Games		Complete Games		Shutouts		Saves	
Rhem-StL	20	Kremer-Pit	.769	Scott-NY	50	Mays-Cin	24	Donohue-Cin	5	Davies-NY	6
Meadows-Pit	20	Rhem-StL	.741	Willoughby-Phi	47	Petty-Bro	23	B.Smith-Bos	4	Scott-NY	5
Kremer-Pit	20	Meadows-Pit	.690	Donohue-Cin	47	Root-Chi	21	Blake-Chi	4	Kremer-Pit	5
Donohue-Cin	20	Mays-Cin	.613	Ulrich-Phi	45	Rhem-StL	20			Ehrhardt-Bro	4
Mays-Cin	19	Donohue-Cin	.588	May-Cin	45	Carlson-Phi	20				

Innings Pitched		Fewest Hits/Game		Fewest BB/Game		Strikeouts		Strikeouts/Game		Ratio	
										Alexander-Chi-StL	
Donohue-Cin	285.2	Petty-Bro	8.03	Donohue-Cin	1.23	Vance-Bro	140	Vance-Bro	7.46		10.06
Mays-Cin	281.0	Greenfield-NY	8.33	Alexander-Chi-StL	1.39	Root-Chi	127	May-Cin	5.53	Petty-Bro	10.71
Petty-Bro	275.2	Rhem-StL	8.41	Carlson-Phi	1.58	May-Cin	103	Jones-Chi	4.49	Kremer-Pit	10.74
Root-Chi	271.1	Jones-Chi	8.48	Mays-Cin	1.70	Benton-Bos	103	Blake-Chi	4.33	Donohue-Cin	10.90
Carlson-Phi	267.1	Bush-Chi	8.52	Lucas-Cin	1.75	Petty-Bro	101	Root-Chi	4.21	Mays-Cin	10.99

Earned Run Average		Adjusted ERA		Opponents' Batting Avg.		Opponents' On Base Pct.		Starter Runs		Adjusted Starter Runs	
Kremer-Pit	2.61	Kremer-Pit	151	Petty-Bro	.240	Alexander-Chi-StL	.281	Kremer-Pit	31.3	Kremer-Pit	34.1
Root-Chi	2.82	Root-Chi	136	Alexander-Chi-StL	.250	Petty-Bro	.296	Root-Chi	30.3	Root-Chi	30.9
Petty-Bro	2.84	Petty-Bro	134	Rhem-StL	.250	Kremer-Pit	.296	Petty-Bro	30.1	Petty-Bro	30.0
Bush-Chi	2.86	Bush-Chi	134	Greenfield-NY	.251	Donohue-Cin	.298	Fitzsimmons-NY	23.0	Carlson-Phi	27.0
Barnes-NY	2.87	Barnes-NY	131	Kremer-Pit	.252	Rhem-StL	.305	Mays-Cin	21.4	Fitzsimmons-NY	21.3

Clutch Pitching Index		Relief Runs		Adjusted Relief Runs		Relief Ranking		Total Pitcher Index		Total Baseball Ranking	
Jones-Chi	122	Hallahan-StL	1.1	Hallahan-StL	1.6	Hallahan-StL	1.3	Kremer-Pit	3.7	Kremer-Pit	3.7
Blake-Chi	119							Root-Chi	3.2	Root-Chi	3.2
Fitzsimmons-NY	118							Mays-Cin	3.1	Waner-Pit	3.1
Werts-Bos	117							Petty-Bro	2.7	Mays-Cin	3.1
Root-Chi	111							Carlson-Phi	2.6	Wilson-Chi	3.0

April 13 Walter Johnson takes on A's knuckleballer Eddie Rommel in baseball's greatest Opening-Day pitchers' duel, a 15-inning battle won by the Senators, 1–0. Johnson gives up six walks and fans 12.

June 8 In Detroit, Babe Ruth slugs a homer reported to carry 626 feet. The hit, off Tigers pitcher Lil Stoner, lands at the intersection of Cherry Street and Brooklyn Avenue, two blocks from Navin Field.

August 4 Star Stanford fullback Ernie Nevers pitches his first complete game for the St. Louis Browns, beating the A's, 3-1.

August 22 After three games with the Tigers are rained out at home, Connie Mack and Tom Shibe decide that Sunday baseball is entitled to be played. Armed with a court injunction preventing police from interfering, they play the first Sunday game ever seen in Philadelphia. A light rain holds the crowd to 10,000, but Lefty Grove sets down the White Sox, 3–2, without incident. A court later rules Sunday baseball still illegal; it will be 1934 before that law changes in Philadelphia.

August 28 Emil Levsen of the pitches the Indians to a 6–1, 5–1 sweep of the Red Sox, making him the last major league pitcher to throw two complete games in a day.

September 25 The Yankees take two games from the Browns to nail down the AL flag.

September 26 Browns coach Jimmie Austin, 46 years old, participates in the last game of the season against the Yankees. He contributes to the win by knocking in a run with a double and then stealing home; he's the oldest major leaguer to accomplish that feat.

October 2 Game 1 of the World Series before 61,658 at New York belongs to southpaws Herb Pennock (25-11) and Bill Sherdel (16-12). Two hits give the Cards a quick first-inning run. Sherdel issues three walks for a New York run without a hit. In the sixth, Babe Ruth slaps a single to left, moves to second base on a sacrifice, and scores on a Lou Gehrig single for a 2-1 win.

October 6 In Game 4, the Yankees tee off on Flint Rhem (20-7) and four other Cardinals hurlers for 10 runs and 14 hits, while Waite Hoyt (16-12) strands 10 Cardinals runners for a 10-5 win. Babe Ruth hits three home runs. Ruth's third clout, in the sixth, is the longest blast ever seen in St. Louis. It clears the park and goes through the window of an auto dealer across the street.

November 29 Tris Speaker resigns as Indians manager. Stories of a thrown game and betting on games by Ty Cobb and Speaker gain momentum when Judge Landis holds a secret hearing with the two stars and former pitcher-outfielder Smoky Joe Wood. The story and testimony will not be released until Dec. 21. Former Tiger pitcher Dutch Leonard wrote to Harry Heilmann that he had turned over letters written to him by Joe Wood and Ty Cobb to AL president Ban Johnson, implicating Wood and Cobb in betting on a Tigers-Cleveland game played in Detroit, Sept. 25, 1919. He charged that Cobb and Speaker conspired to let Detroit win to help them gain third-place money. At a secret meeting of AL directors, it was decided to let Cobb and Speaker resign with no publicity. But, as rumors spread, Judge Landis takes charge of the matter and holds the hearings, at which Leonard refuses to appear. Cobb and Wood admit to the letters and say Leonard is angry for having been released to the Pacific Coast League by Cobb. Speaker, not named in the letters, denies everything. Public sympathy is with the stars, but the matter will remain unresolved until January of next year.

BOSTON	CHICAGO	CLEVELAND	DETROIT	NEW YORK	PHILADELPHIA	ST.LOUIS	WASHINGTON
M L.Fohl	M E.Collins	M T.Speaker	M T.Cobb	M M.Huggins	M C.Mack	M G.Sisler	M B.Harris
1B P.Todt	1B E.Sheely	1B G.Burns	1B L.Blue	1B L.Gehrig	1B J.Poole	1B G.Sisler	1B J.Judge
2B B.Regan	2B E.Collins	2B F.Spurgeon	2B C.Gehringer	2B T.Lazzeri	2B M.Bishop	2B S.Melillo	2B B.Harris
SS T.Rigney	SS B.Hunnefield	SS J.Sewell	SS J.Tavener	SS M.Koenig	SS C.Galloway	SS W.Gerber	SS B.Myer
3B F.Haney	3B W.Kamm	3B R.Lutzke	3B J.Warner	3B J.Dugan	3B J.Dykes	3B M.McManus	3B O.Bluege
LF S.Rosenthal	LF B.Falk	LF C.Jamieson	LF B.Fothergill	LF B.Meusel	LF B.Lamar	LF K.Williams	LF E.McNeely
CF I.Flagstead	CF J.Mostil	CF T.Speaker	CF H.Manush	CF E.Combs	CF A.Simmons	CF H.Rice	CF G.Goslin
RF B.Jacobson	RF B.Barrett	RF H.Summa	RF H.Heilmann	RF B.Ruth	RF W.French	RF B.Miller	RF S.Rice
C A.Gaston	C R.Schalk	C L.Sewell	C C.Manion	C P.Collins	C M.Cochrane	C W.Schang	C M.Ruel
23 M.Herrera	C S.Harris	C G.Myatt	1 J.Neun	C P.Paschal	3 S.Hale	10 G.Robertson	S J.Harris
O J.Tobin	2 R.Morehart	O I.Eichrodt	32 F.O'Rourke	3S M.Gazella	1 J.Hauser	O P.Hargrave	S R.Peckinpaugh
O W.Shaner	S E.Scott	3 E.Padgett	C A.Wingo	C H.Severeid	O F.Welch	O H.Bennett	C B.Tate
O F.Bratschi	C B.Crouse	/O P.McNulty	O T.Cobb	O B.Bengough	O C.Perkins	O C.Durst	2 S.Stewart
O R.Carlyle	C J.Grabowski	/O C.Lee	O J.Bassler	O R.Carlyle	O B.Miller	O B.Jacobson	O D.Taylor
C J.Bischoff	S M.Berg	1 R.Knode	C L.Woodall	/2 A.Ward	A.Metzler	C L.Dixon	3 B.Reeves
O H.Fitzgerald	C H.McCurdy	2 G.Lacy	2 L.Burke	/2 S.Adams	B.Wambsganss	S B.LaMotte	C H.Severeid
C A.Stokes	1 B.Clancy	/C C.Autry	/3 B.Mullen	/C B.Skiff	O D.Barbee	/3 J.Austin	/O J.Tobin
O T.Jenkins	O T.Gulley	/3 J.Hodapp	/C R.Hayworth	H N.Cullop	S F.Sigafoos	O T.Jeanes	/C R.Ennis
/C B.Moore	/O P.Purdy			/1 F.Merkle	C J.Foxx	P T.Zachary	
/S J.Rothrock	/S P.Veltman	P G.Uhle	P E.Whitehill	H H.Barnes	/O T.Jenkins	P M.Gaston	
/3 C.Geygan		P D.Levsen	P S.Gibson	/O K.Davis	S C.Engle	P E.Vangilder	P W.Johnson
/3 B.Fowler	P T.Lyons	P J.Shaute	P E.Wells			P E.Wingard	P S.Coveleski
/S D.Lee	P T.Thomas	P S.Smith	P L.Stoner	P H.Pennock	P L.Grove	P W.Ballou	P D.Ruether
/S E.McCann	P T.Blankenship	P G.Buckeye	P K.Holloway	P U.Shocker	P E.Rommel		P A.Crowder
H S.Langford	P R.Faber			P W.Hoyt	P J.Quinn	P J.Giard	P C.Ogden
	P J.Edwards	P B.Karr	P H.Dauss	P S.Jones	P R.Walberg	P D.Davis	RP F.Marberry
P H.Wiltse		P J.Miller	P R.Collins	P M.Thomas	P S.Gray	P E.Nevers	RP B.Morrell
P T.Wingfield	P S.Thurston	/P W.Hudlin	P A.Johns	RP G.Braxton	RP J.Pate	P C.Falk	RP A.Ferguson
P P.Zahniser	P S.Connally	/P N.Lehr	P G.Smith			P C.Jonnard	
P R.Ruffing	P M.Steengrafe	/P R.Benge	P C.Barfoot	P B.Shawkey	P H.Ehmke	/P C.Robertson	P G.Murray
P T.Welzer	/P D.Leverett	/P B.Speece	/P R.Kneisch	P W.Beall	P S.Harriss	/P S.Bolen	P J.Bush
RP J.Russell	/P L.Cox		/P W.Cooper	P H.McQuaid	/P F.Heimach		/P D.Jones
	/P P.McBee		/P J.Doyle	/P D.Ruether	P L.Willis		/P E.Palmero
P S.Harriss				/P H.Johnson	P S.Baumgartner		/P H.Kelley
P F.Heimach							/P L.Thomas
P H.Ehmke							/P J.Uchrinscko
P D.Lundgren							/P B.Hadley
P J.Kiefer							/P F.Loftus
/P D.MacFayden							
/P H.Foreman							
/P B.Ross							
/P B.Clowers							
/P R.Sommers							

TEAM	G	W	L	PCT	GB	R	OR	AB	H	2B	3B	HR	BB	SO	AVG	OBP	SLG	PRO	PRO+	BR	/A	PF	CHI	RC	SB	CS	SBA	SBR
NY	155	91	63	.591		847	713	5221	1508	262	75	121	642	580	.289	.369	.437	.806	119	123	137	98	98	866	79	62	56	-14
CLE	154	88	66	.571	3	738	612	5293	1529	333	49	27	455	332	.289	.349	.386	.735	97	-17	-23	101	103	735	88	42	68	1
PHI	150	83	67	.553	6	677	570	5046	1359	259	65	61	523	452	.269	.341	.386	.724	90	-39	-77	106	101	682	56	45	55	-10
WAS	152	81	69	.540	8	802	761	5223	1525	244	97	43	555	369	.292	.364	.401	.765	109	48	68	98	103	779	117	91	56	-20
CHI	155	81	72	.529	9.5	730	665	5220	1508	314	60	32	556	381	.289	.361	.390	.751	106	24	51	96	96	761	123	78	61	-10
DET	157	79	75	.513	12	793	830	5315	1547	281	90	36	599	423	.291	.367	.398	.765	105	52	42	101	99	801	88	71	55	-16
STL	155	62	92	.403	29	682	845	5259	1449	253	78	72	437	472	.276	.335	.394	.729	92	-38	-70	105	100	700	64	66	49	-20
BOS	154	46	107	.301	44.5	562	835	5185	1325	249	54	32	465	454	.256	.321	.343	.664	82	-156	-138	97	101	588	52	48	52	-13
TOT	616					5831		41762	11750	2195	568	424	4232	3463	.281	.351	.392	.743							667	503	57	-102

TEAM	CG	SH	SV	IP	H	H/G	HR	BB	SO	RAT	ERA	ERA+	OAV	OOB	PR	/A	PF	CPI	FA	E	DP	FW	PW	BW	SBW	DIF
NY	63	4	20	1372¹	1442	9.5	56	478	486	12.8	3.86	100	.274	.337	24	-1	96	96	.966	210	117	-1.1	-.0	13.3	-.1	2.0
CLE	96	11	4	1374	1412	9.2	49	450	381	12.5	3.40	119	.271	.334	94	101	101	105	.972	173	153	1.1	9.8	-2.2	1.3	1.1
PHI	62	10	16	1346	1362	9.1	38	451	571	12.3	3.00	139	.268	.331	153	174	104	114	.972	171	131	.9	16.9	-7.5	.3	-2.5
WAS	65	5	26	1348¹	1489	9.9	45	566	418	14.0	4.34	89	.287	.361	-48	-71	96	98	.969	184	129	.2	-6.9	6.6	-.7	6.8
CHI	85	11	12	1380	1426	9.3	47	506	458	12.7	3.74	103	.271	.336	43	16	96	96	.973	165	122	1.6	1.6	4.9	.3	-3.9
DET	57	10	18	1394²	1570	10.1	58	555	469	14.0	4.41	92	.292	.363	-61	-54	101	99	.969	193	151	.0	-5.2	4.1	-.3	3.4
STL	64	5	9	1368	1549	10.2	86	654	337	14.7	4.66	92	.297	.379	-98	-59	107	105	.963	235	167	-2.6	-5.7	-6.8	-.7	.8
BOS	53	6	5	1362	1520	10.0	45	546	336	13.9	4.72	86	.294	.365	-107	-101	101	92	.970	193	143	-.2	-9.8	-13.4	-.0	-7.2
TOT	545	62	110	10945¹		9.7				13.3	4.02		.281	.351					.969	1524	1113					

Runs		Hits		Doubles		Triples		Home Runs		Total Bases	
Ruth-NY	139	Rice-Was	216	Burns-Cle	64	Gehrig-NY	20	Ruth-NY	47	Ruth-NY	365
Gehrig-NY	135	Burns-Cle	216	Simmons-Phi	53	Gehringer-Det	17	Simmons-Phi	19	Simmons-Phi	329
Mostil-Chi	120	Goslin-Was	201	Speaker-Cle	52	Mostil-Chi	15	Lazzeri-NY	18	Gehrig-NY	314
Combs-NY	113	Simmons-Phi	199	Jacobson-StL-Bos	51	Goslin-Was	15	Williams-StL	17	Goslin-Was	308
Goslin-Was	105	Mostil-Chi	197	Gehrig-NY	47			Goslin-Was	17	Burns-Cle	298

Runs Batted In		Runs Produced		Bases On Balls		Batting Average		On Base Percentage		Slugging Average	
Ruth-NY	146	Ruth-NY	238	Ruth-NY	144	Manush-Det	.378	Ruth-NY	.516	Ruth-NY	.737
Lazzeri-NY	114	Gehrig-NY	231	Bishop-Phi	116	Ruth-NY	.372	Heilmann-Det	.445	Simmons-Phi	.564
Burns-Cle	114	Burns-Cle	207	Rigney-Bos	108	Fothergill-Det	.367	Bishop-Phi	.431	Manush-Det	.564
Gehrig-NY	112	Goslin-Was	196	Gehrig-NY	105	Heilmann-Det	.367	Goslin-Was	.425	Gehrig-NY	.549
Simmons-Phi	109	Falk-Chi	186	Speaker-Cle	94	Burns-Cle	.358	Manush-Det	.421	Goslin-Was	.542

Production		Adjusted Production		Batter Runs		Adjusted Batter Runs		Clutch Hitting Index		Runs Created	
Ruth-NY	1.253	Ruth-NY	228	Ruth-NY	97.4	Ruth-NY	100.3	Judge-Was	134	Ruth-NY	196
Manush-Det	.985	Goslin-Was	155	Gehrig-NY	44.2	Gehrig-NY	46.2	Dugan-NY	131	Gehrig-NY	137
Heilmann-Det	.979	Gehrig-NY	154	Goslin-Was	42.3	Goslin-Was	45.3	Haney-Bos	127	Goslin-Was	131
Gehrig-NY	.969	Manush-Det	153	Heilmann-Det	41.7	Heilmann-Det	40.3	Myer-Was	121	Simmons-Phi	129
Goslin-Was	.967	Heilmann-Det	152	Manush-Det	38.2	Manush-Det	36.8	Lutzke-Cle	118	Mostil-Chi	122

Total Average		Stolen Bases		Stolen Base Average		Stolen Base Runs		Fielding Runs		Total Player Rating	
Ruth-NY	1.606	Mostil-Chi	35	McNeely-Was	75.0	Mostil-Chi	2.1	Dykes-Phi	26.4	Ruth-NY	8.4
Gehrig-NY	1.058	Rice-Was	24	Hunnefield-Chi	72.7	McNeely-Was	1.8	Rigney-Bos	19.6	Goslin-Was	4.9
Heilmann-Det	1.040	Hunnefield-Chi	24	Mostil-Chi	71.4	Hunnefield-Chi	1.8	Goslin-Was	18.5	Mostil-Chi	4.0
Manush-Det	1.029	McNeely-Was	18	J.Sewell-Cle	70.8	Simmons-Phi	1.5	Regan-Bos	17.4	Rigney-Bos	3.9
Goslin-Was	1.008	J.Sewell-Cle	17	Lazzeri-NY	69.6			Mostil-Chi	17.1	J.Sewell-Cle	3.3

Wins		Win Percentage		Games		Complete Games		Shutouts		Saves	
Uhle-Cle	27	Uhle-Cle	.711	Marberry-Was	64	Uhle-Cle	32	Wells-Det	4	Marberry-Was	22
Pennock-NY	23	Pennock-NY	.676	Pate-Phi	47	Lyons-Chi	24			Dauss-Det	9
Shocker-NY	19	Shocker-NY	.633	Grove-Phi	45	Johnson-Was	22			Pate-Phi	6
Lyons-Chi	18	Faber-Chi	.625	Thomas-Chi	44	Grove-Phi	20			Grove-Phi	6
		Hoyt-NY	.571			Pennock-NY	19			Jones-NY	5

Innings Pitched		Fewest Hits/Game		Fewest BB/Game		Strikeouts		Strikeouts/Game		Ratio	
Uhle-Cle	318.1	Grove-Phi	7.92	Pennock-NY	1.45	Grove-Phi	194	Grove-Phi	6.77	Pennock-NY	11.52
Lyons-Chi	283.2	Thomas-Chi	8.13	Smith-Cle	1.48	Uhle-Cle	159	Thomas-Chi	4.59	Rommel-Phi	11.55
Pennock-NY	266.1	Uhle-Cle	8.48	Quinn-Phi	1.98	Thomas-Chi	127	Uhle-Cle	4.50	Johnson-Was	11.64
Johnson-Was	260.2	Lyons-Chi	8.50	Rommel-Phi	2.22	Johnson-Was	125	Johnson-Was	4.32	Grove-Phi	11.65
Shocker-NY	258.1	Buckeye-Cle	8.69	Wingfield-Bos	2.36	Whitehill-Det	109	Whitehill-Det	3.89	Lyons-Chi	11.90

Earned Run Average		Adjusted ERA		Opponents' Batting Avg.		Opponents' On Base Pct.		Starter Runs		Adjusted Starter Runs	
Grove-Phi	2.51	Grove-Phi	166	Thomas-Chi	.244	Pennock-NY	.313	Grove-Phi	43.1	Grove-Phi	47.4
Uhle-Cle	2.83	Uhle-Cle	143	Grove-Phi	.244	Rommel-Phi	.314	Uhle-Cle	42.1	Uhle-Cle	43.4
Lyons-Chi	3.01	Rommel-Phi	135	Lyons-Chi	.252	Hoyt-NY	.316	Lyons-Chi	31.6	Lyons-Chi	26.7
Rommel-Phi	3.08	Buckeye-Cle	131	Uhle-Cle	.253	Johnson-Was	.317	Coveleski-Was	24.5	Rommel-Phi	26.4
Buckeye-Cle	3.10	Lyons-Chi	128	Levsen-Cle	.261	Shocker-NY	.318	Rommel-Phi	22.7	Walberg-Phi	22.9

Clutch Pitching Index		Relief Runs		Adjusted Relief Runs		Relief Ranking		Total Pitcher Index		Total Baseball Ranking	
Wingard-StL	128	Pate-Phi	16.4	Pate-Phi	18.3	Marberry-Was	21.2	Uhle-Cle	5.2	Ruth-NY	8.4
Zachary-StL	122	Marberry-Was	15.6	Marberry-Was	13.3	Pate-Phi	15.3	Grove-Phi	4.0	Uhle-Cle	5.2
Grove-Phi	119	Braxton-NY	10.1	Braxton-NY	8.8	Braxton-NY	7.7	Lyons-Chi	3.3	Goslin-Was	4.9
Coveleski-Was	117	Russell-Bos	4.7	Russell-Bos	5.3	Russell-Bos	2.4	Walberg-Phi	2.8	Grove-Phi	4.0
Buckeye-Cle	114							Zachary-StL	2.7	Mostil-Chi	4.0

January 9 In a three-way deal, pitcher Burleigh Grimes goes from Brooklyn to the Giants, catcher Walter "Butch" Henline goes from Philadelphia to Brooklyn, and Giants second baseman Fresco Thompson and pitcher Jack Scott wind up with the Phils.

January 31 NL president John Heydler rules that Rogers Hornsby cannot continue to hold stock in the Cardinals and play for the Giants.

February 9 The Giants send versatile George Kelly, along with cash, to the Reds for truculent holdout outfielder and former batting champ Edd Roush.

April 8 Four days before the season opens, recently traded Rogers Hornsby breaks the impasse caused by his trade, selling his stock in the Cardinals for $112,000. He receives $86,000 from Sam Breadon, $2,000 from each of the other seven NL clubs, and an extra $12,000 from the Giants.

May 14 During a game between the Phils and Cards, a section of right field at Baker Bowl collapses from the weight of the crowd and thousands of fans fall on those below. There are many injuries, but the one death that occurs is because of the crowd stampede, not the stands collapsing. Philadelphia was leading, 12–4, in the seventh when the tragedy occurs, and the game is called. The Phils' 12 remaining home games in May will be played at Shibe Park.

May 30 Shortstop Jimmy Cooney makes an unassisted triple play for the Cubs against Pittsburgh as he catches Paul Waner's line drive, steps on second base to retire Lloyd Waner, and tags Clyde Barnhart going back to first base.

June 18 It's Charles Lindbergh Day in St. Louis as the transatlantic flyer helps raise the Cardinals NL pennant before a 6–4 win over the Giants.

July 19 It's John McGraw Day at the Polo Grounds, in honor of his 25 years as Giants manager. The Cubs spoil the day with an 8–5 win.

July 27 Mel Ott, 18 years old, hits his first major league home run, an inside-the-park round-tripper. It is the only inside-the-park job of his 511 career homers.

September 4 Paul and Lloyd Waner hit homers for Pittsburgh in the same inning at Cincinnati's Redland Field, and both are "bounce home runs." Fair balls that bounce into the stands will be considered homers in the NL until 1930.

October 1 The Pirates clinch the NL flag, beating the Reds, 9-6. They will finish a game and a half ahead of the Cards and two in front of New York.

October 22 Future Hall of Famer Ross Youngs, one of John McGraw's favorite players, dies of Bright's disease at age 30, cutting short a brilliant 10-year career in which he batted .322. Youngs had been accompanied by a specialist as early as 1924, and after the illness had been identified, the Giants hired a nurse to travel with Youngs. He was bedridden in 1927, after appearing in just 95 games in 1926.

December 4 Pirates outfielder Paul Waner noses out Frank Frisch for NL MVP honors with 72 points to 66.

BOSTON	BROOKLYN	CHICAGO	CINCINNATI	NEW YORK	PHILADELPHIA	PITTSBURGH	ST.LOUIS
M D.Bancroft	M W.Robinson	M J.McCarthy	M J.Hendricks	M J.McGraw	M S.McInnis	M D.Bush	M B.O'Farrell
1B J.Fournier	1B B.Herman	1B C.Grimm	1B W.Pipp	1B R.Hornsby	1B R.Wrightstone	1B J.Harris	1B J.Bottomley
2B D.Gautreau	2B J.Partridge	2B C.Beck	2B H.Critz	2B B.Terry	2B F.Thompson	2B G.Grantham	2B F.Frisch
SS D.Bancroft	SS J.Butler	SS W.English	SS H.Ford	SS T.Jackson	SS H.Sand	SS G.Wright	SS H.Schuble
3B A.High	3B B.Barrett	3B S.Adams	3B C.Dressen	3B F.Lindstrom	3B B.Friberg	3B P.Traynor	3B L.Bell
LF E.Brown	LF G.Felix	LF R.Stephenson	LF R.Bressler	LF H.Mueller	LF D.Spalding	LF C.Barnhart	LF C.Hafey
CF J.Welsh	CF J.Statz	CF H.Wilson	CF E.Allen	CF E.Roush	CF F.Leach	CF L.Waner	CF T.Douthit
RF L.Richbourg	RF M.Carey	RF E.Webb	RF C.Walker	RF G.Harper	RF C.Williams	RF P.Waner	RF B.Southworth
C S.Hogan	C H.DeBerry	C G.Hartnett	C B.Hargrave	C Z.Taylor	C J.Wilson	C J.Gooch	C F.Snyder
S2 D.Farrell	O1 H.Hendrick	O C.Heathcote	O B.Zitzmann	S R.Reese	S J.Cooney	O K.Cuyler	O W.Holm
32 E.Moore	S J.Flowers	3 E.Pick	12 G.Kelly	O M.Ott	O J.Mokan	C E.Smith	3S S.Toporcer
1 D.Burrus	C B.Henline	O P.Scott	O C.Christensen	O T.Tyson	O A.Nixon	23 H.Rhyne	S T.Thevenow
O J.Smith	C C.Hargreaves	S J.Cooney	C V.Picinich	S D.Farrell	C B.Jonnard	C R.Spencer	O R.Blades
C F.Gibson	O I.Meusel	C M.Gonzalez	S P.Wanninger	C A.DeVormer	/O D.Attreau	O A.Comorosky	C B.O'Farrell
C L.Urban	O O.Tremper	3 H.Freigau	2 P.Pittinger	C J.Cummings	/O B.Hohman	3 H.Groh	O E.Orsatti
C Z.Taylor	2 C.Corgan	/1 C.Tolson	3 B.Pinelli	O L.Mann	C H.O'Donnell	/2 J.Cronin	/O D.Clark
2 H.Thomas	/3 W.Marriott	3 E.Yoter	O P.Purdy	C M.O'Neil	/S B.Deitrick	/O F.Brickell	/S R.Maranville
O L.Mann	/O M.Jacobson	/3 H.Wilke	C C.Sukeforth	/O T.Jeanes	/O S.McInnis	/2 E.Sicking	/C B.Schang
O E.Clark	/O O.Roettger	H F.Haney	/2 J.White	/O H.Thomas	P J.Scott	/O H.Layne	/O H.Peel
/O S.Graves	H C.Fewster	/C J.Churry	/1 R.Wolf	H B.Jordan	P A.Ferguson	/S D.Bartell	/O W.Roettger
/O D.McNamara	P D.Vance	H T.Sewell	P R.Lucas	/O J.Klinger	P D.Ulrich	P L.Meadows	P J.Haines
H J.Cooney	P J.Petty	P C.Root	P J.May	/C R.Smith	P H.Pruett	P C.Hill	P P.Alexander
P B.Smith	P J.Elliott	P S.Blake	P D.Luque	RP B.Grimes	P L.Sweetland	P V.Aldridge	P B.Sherdel
P K.Greenfield	P D.McWeeny	P G.Bush	P E.Rixey	P F.Fitzsimmons	RP C.Willoughby	P R.Kremer	P F.Rhem
P J.Genewich	P B.Doak	P H.Carlson	P P.Donohue	P V.Barnes	P C.Mitchell	RP J.Morrison	RP H.Bell
P J.Werts	RP R.Ehrhardt	P J.Brillheart	P R.Kolp	P L.Benton	P H.Carlson	RP M.Cvengros	P A.Reinhart
P C.Robertson	RP W.Clark	P P.Jones	P C.Mays	P D.Henry	/P T.Kaufmann	P J.Dawson	/P F.Frankhouse
RP G.Mogridge	P J.Barnes	P B.Osborn	P A.Nehf	RP D.Songer	/P R.Miller	P J.Miljus	/P C.Littlejohn
P F.Edwards	P N.Plitt	/P T.Kaufmann	/P P.Appleton	P B.Clarkson	/P A.Walsh	/P E.Yde	P V.Keen
P H.McQuillan	/P G.Cantrell	/P A.Nehf	/P J.Beckman	P H.McQuillan	/P E.Baecht	/P C.Nichols	P J.Ring
P H.Goldsmith	/P R.Moss	P L.Roy		/P B.Cantwell	/P S.O'Neal	/P R.Mahaffey	P S.Johnson
P L.Benton	/P B.McGraw	/P L.Weinert		/P K.Greenfield	/P W.Dean	/P J.Bush	/P E.Dyer
P A.Mills		/P H.Grampp		/P F.Thomas	/P L.Taber	/P D.Songer	/P T.Kaufmann
P G.Morrison		/P W.Dean		/P J.Bush		/P R.Peery	
/P B.Hearn		/P J.Welch		/P J.Bentley			
/P J.Knight				/P J.Faulkner			
/P D.Rudolph				/P N.Plitt			
				/P V.Cheeves			
				/P H.Boney			
				/P B.Walker			
				/P A.Johnson			
				/P M.Holland			
				/P N.Porter			

TEAM	G	W	L	PCT	GB	R	OR	AB	H	2B	3B	HR	BB	SO	AVG	OBP	SLG	PRO	PRO+	BR	/A	PF	CHI	RC	SB	CS	SBA	SBR
PIT	156	94	60	.610		817	659	5397	1648	258	78	54	437	355	.305	.361	.412	.773	106	99	42	107	99	791	65			
STL	153	92	61	.601	1.5	754	665	5207	1450	264	79	84	484	511	.278	.343	.408	.751	104	47	24	103	101	723	110			
NY	155	92	62	.597	2	817	720	5372	1594	251	62	109	461	462	.297	.356	.427	.783	116	113	115	100	98	805	73			
CHI	153	85	68	.556	8.5	750	661	5303	1505	266	63	74	481	492	.284	.346	.400	.746	106	43	41	100	99	730	65			
CIN	153	75	78	.490	18.5	643	653	5185	1439	222	77	29	402	332	.278	.332	.367	.699	96	-47	-27	97	100	628	62			
BRO	154	65	88	.425	28.5	541	619	5193	1314	195	74	39	368	494	.253	.306	.342	.648	79	-152	-154	100	102	539	106			
BOS	155	60	94	.390	34	651	771	5370	1498	216	61	37	346	363	.279	.326	.363	.689	98	-73	-24	92	103	626	100			
PHI	155	51	103	.331	43	678	903	5317	1487	216	46	57	434	421	.280	.337	.370	.707	94	-30	-39	101	100	660	68			
TOT	617					5651		42344	11935	1888	540	483	3413	3491	.282	.339	.386	.725						649				

TEAM	CG	SH	SV	IP	H	H/G	HR	BB	SO	RAT	ERA	ERA+	OAV	OOB	PR	/A	PF	CPI	FA	E	DP	FW	PW	BW	SBW	DIF
PIT	90	10	10	1385	1400	9.1	58	418	435	12.0	3.66	112	.267	.324	39	68	105	95	.969	187	130	.6	6.7	4.1		5.5
STL	89	14	11	1367¹	1416	9.3	72	363	394	11.8	3.57	110	.271	.320	52	57	101	99	.966	213	170	-1.0	5.6	2.4		8.5
NY	65	7	16	1381²	1520	9.9	77	453	442	13.0	3.97	97	.283	.341	-8	-17	98	102	.969	195	160	.1	-1.7	11.3		5.2
CHI	75	11	5	1385	1439	9.4	50	514	465	12.9	3.65	106	.273	.342	40	31	99	104	.971	181	152	.8	3.1	4.0		.6
CIN	87	12	12	1368	1472	9.7	36	316	407	11.9	3.54	107	.281	.325	57	36	97	100	.973	165	160	1.6	3.6	-2.7		-4.0
BRO	74	7	10	1375¹	1382	9.0	63	418	574	11.9	3.36	118	.265	.323	85	90	101	103	.963	229	117	-1.8	8.9	-15.2		-3.4
BOS	52	3	11	1390	1602	10.4	43	468	402	13.6	4.22	88	.296	.356	-48	-79	95	102	.963	231	130	-1.8	-7.8	-2.4		-5.0
PHI	81	5	6	1355¹	1710	11.4	84	462	377	14.7	5.36	77	.317	.374	-218	-187	106	96	.972	169	152	1.5	-18.5	-3.8		-5.2
TOT	613	69	81	11007²		9.8				12.7	3.91		.282	.339					.969	1570	1171					

Runs
L.Waner-Pit	133
Hornsby-NY	133
Wilson-Chi	119
P.Waner-Pit	114
Frisch-StL	112

Hits
P.Waner-Pit	237
L.Waner-Pit	223
Frisch-StL	208
Hornsby-NY	205
Stephenson-Chi	199

Doubles
Stephenson-Chi	46
P.Waner-Pit	42
Lindstrom-NY	36
Dressen-Cin	36
Brown-Bos	35

Triples
P.Waner-Pit	18
Bottomley-StL	15
Thompson-Phi	14
Terry-NY	13
Wilson-Chi	12

Home Runs
Wilson-Chi	30
Williams-Phi	30
Hornsby-NY	26
Terry-NY	20
Bottomley-StL	19

Total Bases
P.Waner-Pit	342
Hornsby-NY	333
Wilson-Chi	319
Terry-NY	307
Bottomley-StL	292

Runs Batted In
P.Waner-Pit	131
Wilson-Chi	129
Hornsby-NY	125
Bottomley-StL	124
Terry-NY	121

Runs Produced
P.Waner-Pit	236
Hornsby-NY	232
Wilson-Chi	218
Terry-NY	202
Bottomley-StL	200

Bases On Balls
Hornsby-NY	86
Harper-NY	84
Grantham-Pit	74
Bottomley-StL	74

Batting Average
P.Waner-Pit	.380
Hornsby-NY	.361
L.Waner-Pit	.355
Stephenson-Chi	.344
Traynor-Pit	.342

On Base Percentage
Hornsby-NY	.448
P.Waner-Pit	.437
Harper-NY	.435
Stephenson-Chi	.415
Harris-Pit	.402

Slugging Average
Hafey-StL	.590
Hornsby-NY	.586
Wilson-Chi	.579
P.Waner-Pit	.549
Terry-NY	.529

Production
Hornsby-NY	1.035
P.Waner-Pit	.986
Wilson-Chi	.980
Harper-NY	.930
Terry-NY	.907

Adjusted Production
Hornsby-NY	175
Wilson-Chi	159
P.Waner-Pit	152
Harper-NY	149
Stephenson-Chi	141

Batter Runs
Hornsby-NY	62.5
P.Waner-Pit	55.6
Wilson-Chi	45.7
Harper-NY	37.1
Stephenson-Chi	35.7

Adjusted Batter Runs
Hornsby-NY	62.8
P.Waner-Pit	46.1
Wilson-Chi	45.5
Harper-NY	37.3
Stephenson-Chi	35.5

Clutch Hitting Index
P.Waner-Pit	135
Wright-Pit	134
Bressler-Cin	133
Farrell-NY-Bos	131
Bottomley-StL	124

Runs Created
Hornsby-NY	148
P.Waner-Pit	145
Wilson-Chi	126
Stephenson-Chi	117
Bottomley-StL	112

Total Average
Hornsby-NY	1.190
Wilson-Chi	1.088
P.Waner-Pit	1.062
Harper-NY	1.037
Stephenson-Chi	.955

Stolen Bases
Frisch-StL	48
Carey-Bro	32
Hendrick-Bro	29
Adams-Chi	26
Richbourg-Bos	24

Stolen Base Average

Stolen Base Runs

Fielding Runs
Frisch-StL	48.6
Jackson-NY	27.9
Friberg-Phi	25.3
Beck-Chi	22.0
Statz-Bro	15.2

Total Player Rating
Frisch-StL	7.3
Hornsby-NY	6.9
Jackson-NY	5.4
P.Waner-Pit	4.2
Wilson-Chi	3.5

Wins
Root-Chi	26
Haines-StL	24
Hill-Pit	22
Alexander-StL	21

Win Percentage
Benton-Bos-NY	.708
Haines-StL	.706
Kremer-Pit	.704
Grimes-NY	.704
Alexander-StL	.677

Games
Scott-Phi	48
Root-Chi	48
Ehrhardt-Bro	46
Henry-NY	45
May-Cin	44

Complete Games
Vance-Bro	25
Meadows-Pit	25
Haines-StL	25
Hill-Pit	22
Alexander-StL	22

Shutouts
Haines-StL	6
Root-Chi	4
Lucas-Cin	4
Kremer-Pit	3

Saves
Sherdel-StL	6
Nehf-Cin-Chi	5
Mogridge-Bos	5
Henry-NY	4

Innings Pitched
Root-Chi	309.0
Haines-StL	300.2
Meadows-Pit	299.1
Hill-Pit	277.2
Vance-Bro	273.1

Fewest Hits/Game
Vance-Bro	7.97
Kremer-Pit	8.16
Haines-StL	8.17
Bush-Chi	8.24
Hill-Pit	8.43

Fewest BB/Game
Alexander-StL	1.28
Lucas-Cin	1.46
Donohue-Cin	1.51
Carlson-Phi-Chi	1.63
Henry-NY	1.70

Strikeouts
Vance-Bro	184
Root-Chi	145
May-Cin	121
Grimes-NY	102
Petty-Bro	101

Strikeouts/Game
Vance-Bro	6.06
Elliott-Bro	4.73
May-Cin	4.62
Pruett-Phi	4.35
Root-Chi	4.22

Ratio
Alexander-StL	10.07
Lucas-Cin	10.14
Kremer-Pit	10.27
Vance-Bro	10.44
Petty-Bro	10.60

Earned Run Average
Kremer-Pit	2.47
Alexander-StL	2.52
Vance-Bro	2.70
Haines-StL	2.72
Petty-Bro	2.98

Adjusted ERA
Kremer-Pit	166
Alexander-StL	157
Vance-Bro	147
Haines-StL	145
Petty-Bro	133

Opponents' Batting Avg.
Vance-Bro	.239
Kremer-Pit	.244
Haines-StL	.245
Hill-Pit	.249
Bush-Chi	.250

Opponents' On Base Pct.
Alexander-StL	.286
Lucas-Cin	.287
Kremer-Pit	.289
Vance-Bro	.291
Petty-Bro	.293

Starter Runs
Alexander-StL	41.5
Haines-StL	39.8
Vance-Bro	36.9
Kremer-Pit	36.3
Petty-Bro	28.1

Adjusted Starter Runs
Alexander-StL	42.5
Kremer-Pit	41.1
Haines-StL	40.8
Vance-Bro	38.2
Petty-Bro	29.4

Clutch Pitching Index
Blake-Chi	117
McWeeny-Bro	116
B.Smith-Bos	114
Donohue-Cin	111
Alexander-StL	109

Relief Runs
Clark-Bro	13.0
Ehrhardt-Bro	3.6
Cvengros-Pit	3.3
Songer-Pit-NY	1.9

Adjusted Relief Runs
Clark-Bro	13.4
Cvengros-Pit	4.5
Ehrhardt-Bro	4.1
Songer-Pit-NY	1.7
H.Bell-StL	1

Relief Ranking
Clark-Bro	15.5
Ehrhardt-Bro	4.0
Cvengros-Pit	2.4
Songer-Pit-NY	2.3
H.Bell-StL	0

Total Pitcher Index
Alexander-StL	5.2
Haines-StL	4.3
Kremer-Pit	4.3
Vance-Bro	3.8
Hill-Pit	3.2

Total Baseball Ranking
Frisch-StL	7.3
Hornsby-NY	6.9
Jackson-NY	5.4
Alexander-StL	5.2
Haines-StL	4.3

January 27 Citing accuser Dutch Leonard's refusal to appear at the hearings of Jan. 5, Judge Landis issues a lengthy decision clearing Ty Cobb and Tris Speaker of any wrongdoing and ordering them reinstated by their teams. Both are made free agents; Connie Mack will sign Cobb on Feb. 8; Speaker will sign with Washington on Jan. 31.

April 26 Forty-year-old Ty Cobb has three hits, drives in the winning run, and steals home in the seventh inning. He tops that off with a ninth-inning shoestring catch in shallow right field and then traps the runner off first for an unassisted double play to end the game as the A's win a 9–8 squeaker over Boston.

May 30* The Reading, Pa. team managed by Fred "Bonehead" Merkle, defeats Baltimore in the International League to break its 32-game losing streak.

May 31 Detroit first baseman Johnny Neun pulls the second unassisted triple play in two days. It happens in the ninth against Cleveland to end the game when Neun catches Homer Summa's line drive, touches Charlie Jamieson in the baseline and runs to second base where he tags the base Glenn Myatt has vacated. Detroit wins, 1–0.

June 11 For the ninth inning, the Philadelphia Athletics field a team of seven Hall of Famers. The outfield consists of Ty Cobb in right, Al Simmons in center and Zack Wheat in left. At first base is

Jimmie Foxx, at second is Eddie Collins, and Lefty Grove pitches in relief. Cy Perkins started as the catcher, but, when Mickey Cochrane pinch hit for him in the last inning, seven Cooperstown-bound players were in the lineup.

August 2 Washington celebrates Walter Johnson Day on the 20th anniversary of his joining the team. He receives $14,764.05, a silver service, and a Distinguished Service Cross made of gold with 20 diamonds. But the Tigers kayo him in a three-run ninth to win, 7–6.

August 16 Babe Ruth christens the newly constructed Comiskey Park grandstand roof by cranking a Tommy Thomas pitch over the addition.

September 13 Babe Ruth hits two (52), and the Yankees win a pair from Cleveland to clinch the AL pennant with a 98-41 record.

September 30 With the score 2-2 in the eighth, Mark Koenig triples and Ruth hits home run number 60 off Tom Zachary for a 4-2 win. In the ninth Walter Johnson makes his final appearance as a player. He pinch-hits for Zachary and flies out to Ruth.

October 5 Pittsburgh's Ray Kremer (19-8) opens Game 1 against Waite Hoyt (22-7). In the third, two walks and two Pirates errors help the Yankees to three runs and a 4-1 lead. Final: 5-4, New York.

October 7 The 60,695 on hand for Game 3 see the Yankees' Herb Pennock

(19-8) take an 8-0 lead and a perfect game into the eighth. He retires Glenn Wright, but Pie Traynor breaks the spell with a single, and Clyde Barnhart doubles him home. Pennock settles for a 3-hit 8-1 victory.

October 8 Down three games to none, the Pirates give the ball to their biggest winner, Carmen Hill (22-11). In the fifth, Ruth's second home run of the Series scores Earle Combs ahead of him for a 3-1 lead. The Pirates tie it in the seventh. In the last of the ninth, Combs walks, Mark Koenig beats out a bunt, and Ruth walks to fill the bases. Reliever Johnny Miljus strikes out Lou Gehrig and Bob Meusel. With two strikes on Tony Lazzeri, a wild pitch rolls far enough away for Combs to score the winning run.

October 11 Lou Gehrig, who established a new major league record with 175 RBIs, is named AL MVP. With 56 points, Gehrig wins over Harry Heilmann's 35 and Ted Lyons's 34. Ruth is not considered because former winners are not eligible.

December 11 The Browns sell George Sisler to Washington for $25,000.

December 13 Senators president Clark Griffith gains approval to have Washington open the AL season one day before the rest of the league, to celebrate a "National Day" with the U.S. president throwing out the first ball. The AL also installs Ernest S. Barnard as its president.

	BOSTON		CHICAGO		CLEVELAND		DETROIT		NEW YORK		PHILADELPHIA		ST.LOUIS		WASHINGTON
M	B.Carrigan	M	R.Schalk	M	J.McCallister	M	G.Moriarty	M	M.Huggins	M	C.Mack	M	D.Howley	M	B.Harris
1B	P.Todt	1B	B.Clancy	1B	G.Burns	1B	L.Blue	1B	L.Gehrig	1B	J.Dykes	1B	G.Sisler	1B	J.Judge
2B	B.Regan	2B	A.Ward	2B	L.Fonseca	2B	C.Gehringer	2B	T.Lazzeri	2B	M.Bishop	2B	S.Melillo	2B	B.Harris
SS	B.Myer	SS	B.Hunnefield	SS	J.Sewell	SS	J.Tavener	SS	M.Koenig	SS	J.Boley	SS	W.Gerber	SS	B.Reeves
3B	B.Rogell	3B	W.Kamm	3B	R.Lutzke	3B	J.Warner	3B	J.Dugan	3B	S.Hale	3B	F.O'Rourke	3B	O.Bluege
LF	W.Shaner	LF	B.Falk	LF	C.Jamieson	LF	B.Fothergill	LF	B.Meusel	LF	B.Lamar	LF	K.Williams	LF	G.Goslin
CF	I.Flagstead	CF	A.Metzler	CF	I.Eichrodt	CF	H.Manush	CF	E.Combs	CF	A.Simmons	CF	B.Miller	CF	T.Speaker
RF	J.Tobin	RF	B.Barrett	RF	H.Summa	RF	H.Heilmann	RF	B.Ruth	RF	T.Cobb	RF	H.Rice	RF	S.Rice
C	G.Hartley	C	H.McCurdy	C	L.Sewell	C	L.Woodall	C	P.Collins	C	M.Cochrane	C	W.Schang	C	M.Ruel
O	C.Carlyle	O	B.Crouse	O	J.Hodapp	S2	M.McManus	2	J.Grabowski	2	E.Collins	23	S.Adams	O	E.McNeely
S2	J.Rothrock	S	R.Peckinpaugh	2	F.Spurgeon	1	J.Neun	2	R.Morehart	O	W.French	O	H.Bennett	S	T.Rigney
C	F.Hofmann	1	E.Sheely	O	B.Jacobson	C	J.Bassler	O	C.Durst	O	Z.Wheat	C	S.O'Neill	C	B.Tate
31	R.Rollings	S	R.Flaskamper	O	B.Neis	O	A.Wingo	3	M.Gazella	S	C.Galloway	O	F.Schulte	2	S.Stewart
O	B.Jacobson	O	B.Neis	C	G.Myatt	O	A.Ruble	O	B.Bengough	C	C.Perkins	C	L.Dixon	O	S.West
3	F.Haney	2C	M.Berg	O	N.Cullop	C	M.Shea	O	B.Paschal	1	J.Foxx	S3	O.Miller	O	B.Myer
C	B.Moore	O	I.Boone	O	S.Langford	S	B.DeViveiros	3	J.Wera	1	J.Poole	/S	R.Kress	O	B.Ganzel
O	A.Tarbert	O	C.Reynolds	O	J.Gill	H	C.Manion			1	D.Branom	/1	G.Sturdy	S	G.Gillis
S	P.Wanninger	C	R.Schalk	O	C.Autry			P	W.Hoyt	/O	C.Bates			/S	J.Hayes
/O	F.Welch	/O	J.Mostil	O	P.McNulty	P	E.Whitehill	P	W.Moore	P	B.Jacobson	P	M.Gaston	/O	O.Tucker
/3	T.Rigney	/O	R.Moore	2	C.Lind	P	L.Stoner	P	H.Pennock	/O	R.Saunders	P	E.Vangilder	/O	N.Cullop
/S	M.Karow	/O	K.Willson	/3	D.Ussat	P	S.Gibson	P	U.Shocker	/3	J.Mellana	P	S.Jones	/1	E.Onslow
/2	E.Eggert	/3	J.Battle	/O	G.Gerken	P	K.Holloway	P	D.Ruether			P	E.Wingard	/C	J.Berger
/O	J.Freeman	/2	B.Way	/2	J.Burnett	P	R.Collins			P	L.Grove	L.Stewart		/O	R.Barnes
H	F.Bratschi	H	L.Blackburne	/2	E.Padgett	RP	G.Smith	P	G.Pipgras	P	R.Walberg			/C	M.O'Neil
								P	M.Thomas	P	J.Quinn	P	E.Nevers	H	L.Atkinson
P	H.Wiltse	P	T.Thomas	P	W.Hudlin	P	O.Carroll	P	B.Shawkey	P	H.Ehmke	P	W.Ballou	/2	B.Dear
P	S.Harriss	P	T.Lyons	P	J.Shaute	P	J.Billings	P	J.Giard	P	E.Rommel	P	T.Zachary		
P	T.Welzer	P	T.Blankenship	P	G.Buckeye	P	D.Hankins	/P	W.Beall	RP	J.Pate	P	A.Crowder	P	H.Lisenbee
P	D.MacFayden	P	S.Connally	P	J.Miller	P	E.Wells					/P	C.Falk	P	S.Thurston
P	R.Ruffing	P	R.Faber	P	G.Uhle	/P	J.Doyle			P	S.Gray	/P	J.Wright	P	B.Hadley
		RP	E.Jacobs			/P	R.Smith			P	J.Johnson	/P	B.Beck	P	W.Johnson
P	J.Russell	RP	B.Cole	P	D.Levsen	/P	J.Walkup			P	L.Willis	/P	S.Bolen	P	T.Zachary
P	D.Lundgren			P	B.Karr	/P	A.Johns			P	I.Powers	P	G.Blaeholder	RP	F.Marberry
P	T.Wingfield	P	C.Barnabe	P	G.Grant					P	G.Cantrell			RP	G.Braxton
/P	J.Wilson	/P	F.Stewart	P	S.Smith					/P	N.Baker			RP	B.Burke
/P	H.Bradley	/P	J.Brown	/P	J.Brown					/P	B.Wetzel				
/P	R.Sommers			/P	H.McKain					/P	C.Yerkes			P	A.Crowder
/P	F.Bennett			/P	W.Underhill									/P	G.Murray
/P	B.Cremins			/P	H.Collard									/P	D.Coffman
/P	F.Bushey			/P	W.Ferrell									/P	S.Coveleski
														/P	P.Hopkins
														/P	R.Judd
														/P	D.Jones
														/P	C.Van Alstyne

TEAM	G	W	L	PCT	GB	R	OR	AB	H	2B	3B	HR	BB	SO	AVG	OBP	SLG	PRO	PRO+	BR	/A	PF	CHI	RC	SB	CS	SBA	SBR
NY	155	110	44	.714		975	599	5347	1644	291	103	158	635	605	.307	.383	.489	.872	135	235	266	97	95	1016	90	64	58	-11
PHI	155	91	63	.591	19	841	726	5296	1606	281	70	56	551	326	.303	.372	.414	.786	103	79	32	106	99	839	101	63	62	-8
WAS	157	85	69	.552	25	782	730	5389	1549	268	87	29	498	359	.287	.351	.386	.737	97	-25	-16	99	104	758	133	52	72	9
DET	156	82	71	.536	27.5	845	805	5299	1533	282	100	51	587	420	.289	.363	.409	.772	105	47	35	101	103	813	139	73	66	-2
CHI	153	70	83	.458	39.5	662	708	5157	1433	285	61	36	493	389	.278	.344	.378	.722	94	-54	-37	98	95	685	89	75	54	-18
CLE	153	66	87	.431	43.5	668	766	5202	1471	321	52	26	381	366	.283	.337	.379	.716	90	-70	-75	101	100	669	65	72	47	-24
STL	155	59	94	.386	50.5	724	904	5220	1440	262	59	55	443	420	.276	.338	.380	.718	88	-68	-91	103	106	683	90	66	58	-13
BOS	154	51	103	.331	59	597	856	5207	1348	271	78	28	430	456	.259	.320	.357	.677	82	-149	-137	98	100	614	81	46	64	-3
TOT	619					6094		42117	12024	2261	610	439	4018	3341	.285	.352	.399	.751							788	511	61	-70

TEAM	CG	SH	SV	IP	H	H/G	HR	BB	SO	RAT	ERA	ERA+	OAV	OOB	PR	/A	PF	CPI	FA	E	DP	FW	PW	BW	SBW	DIF
NY	82	11	20	1389²	1403	9.1	42	409	431	11.9	3.20	120	.267	.323	145	100	93	104	.969	195	123	.7	9.5	25.3	-.2	-2.3
PHI	66	8	25	1384	1467	9.5	65	442	553	12.6	3.97	107	.278	.338	26	45	103	97	.970	190	124	1.0	4.3	3.0	.0	5.6
WAS	62	10	23	1402	1434	9.2	53	491	497	12.6	3.97	102	.269	.335	26	14	98	91	.969	195	125	.8	1.3	-1.5	1.7	5.7
DET	75	5	17	1387²	1542	10.0	52	577	421	14.0	4.14	102	.290	.364	0	9	102	106	.968	206	173	.1	.9	3.3	.6	.6
CHI	85	10	8	1367	1467	9.7	55	440	365	12.7	3.91	103	.283	.342	34	19	98	101	.971	178	131	1.6	1.8	-3.5	-.9	-5.5
CLE	72	5	8	1353¹	1542	10.3	37	508	366	13.9	4.27	98	.295	.361	-20	-11	102	102	.968	201	146	.2	-1.0	-7.1	-1.4	-1.0
STL	80	4	8	1353¹	1592	10.6	79	604	385	14.7	4.95	88	.304	.378	-122	-91	105	101	.960	248	166	-2.5	-8.6	-8.6	-.4	2.7
BOS	63	6	7	1366¹	1603	10.6	56	558	381	14.5	4.72	89	.305	.376	-88	-77	102	102	.964	228	167	-1.4	-7.3	-13.0	.5	-4.8
TOT	585	59	116	11003¹		9.9				13.4	4.14		.285	.352					.967	1641	1155					

Runs		Hits		Doubles		Triples		Home Runs		Total Bases	
Ruth-NY	158	Combs-NY	231	Gehrig-NY	52	Combs-NY	23	Ruth-NY	60	Gehrig-NY	447
Gehrig-NY	149	Gehrig-NY	218	Burns-Cle	51	Manush-Det	18	Gehrig-NY	47	Ruth-NY	417
Combs-NY	137	Sisler-StL	201	Heilmann-Det	50	Gehrig-NY	18	Lazzeri-NY	18	Combs-NY	331
Gehringer-Det	110	Heilmann-Det	201	J.Sewell-Cle	48	Goslin-Was	15	Williams-StL	17	Heilmann-Det	311
Heilmann-Det	106	Goslin-Was	194	Meusel-NY	47	Rice-Was	14	Simmons-Phi	15	Goslin-Was	300

Runs Batted In		Runs Produced		Bases On Balls		Batting Average		On Base Percentage		Slugging Average	
Gehrig-NY	175	Gehrig-NY	277	Ruth-NY	138	Heilmann-Det	.398	Ruth-NY	.487	Ruth-NY	.772
Ruth-NY	164	Ruth-NY	262	Gehrig-NY	109	Simmons-Phi	.392	Heilmann-Det	.475	Gehrig-NY	.765
Heilmann-Det	120	Heilmann-Det	212	Bishop-Phi	105	Gehrig-NY	.373	Gehrig-NY	.474	Simmons-Phi	.645
Goslin-Was	120	Goslin-Was	203	Heilmann-Det	72	Fothergill-Det	.359	Bishop-Phi	.442	Heilmann-Det	.616
Fothergill-Det	114	Fothergill-Det	198	Blue-Det	71	Cobb-Phi	.357	Cobb-Phi	.440	Williams-StL	.525

Production		Adjusted Production		Batter Runs		Adjusted Batter Runs		Clutch Hitting Index		Runs Created	
Ruth-NY	1.259	Ruth-NY	229	Gehrig-NY	100.8	Gehrig-NY	106.6	Fothergill-Det	119	Gehrig-NY	212
Gehrig-NY	1.240	Gehrig-NY	224	Ruth-NY	100.7	Ruth-NY	106.4	Goslin-Was	118	Ruth-NY	208
Heilmann-Det	1.091	Heilmann-Det	179	Heilmann-Det	62.3	Heilmann-Det	60.4	Sisler-StL	116	Heilmann-Det	150
Fothergill-Det	.929	Combs-NY	143	Simmons-Phi	44.1	Combs-NY	41.0	Harris-Was	115	Combs-NY	138
Williams-StL	.928	Fothergill-Det	138	Combs-NY	37.1	Simmons-Phi	38.5	J.Sewell-Cle	114	Goslin-Was	119

Total Average		Stolen Bases		Stolen Base Average		Stolen Base Runs		Fielding Runs		Total Player Rating	
Ruth-NY	1.571	Sisler-StL	27	Harris-Was	85.7	Sisler-StL	3.9	Gehringer-Det	19.8	Ruth-NY	9.2
Gehrig-NY	1.500	Meusel-NY	24	Sisler-StL	79.4	Harris-Was	3.6	Falk-Chi	18.2	Gehrig-NY	8.1
Heilmann-Det	1.265	Neun-Det	22	Goslin-Was	77.8	Goslin-Was	2.7	Metzler-Chi	15.7	Heilmann-Det	4.2
Williams-StL	.959	Lazzeri-NY	22	Rice-Was	76.0			Bluege-Was	15.0	Simmons-Phi	3.4
Combs-NY	.955	Cobb-Phi	22	Neun-Det	75.9			Koenig-NY	13.8	Combs-NY	3.2

Wins		Win Percentage		Games		Complete Games		Shutouts		Saves	
Lyons-Chi	22	Hoyt-NY	.759	Braxton-Was	58	Lyons-Chi	30	Lisenbee-Was	4	Moore-NY	13
Hoyt-NY	22	Shocker-NY	.750	Marberry-Was	56	Thomas-Chi	24			Braxton-Was	13
Grove-Phi	20	Moore-NY	.731	Grove-Phi	51	Hoyt-NY	23			Marberry-Was	9
		Pennock-NY	.704	Moore-NY	50	Gaston-StL	21			Grove-Phi	9
		Lisenbee-Was	.667	Walberg-Phi	46						

Innings Pitched		Fewest Hits/Game		Fewest BB/Game		Strikeouts		Strikeouts/Game		Ratio	
Thomas-Chi	307.2	Moore-NY	7.82	Quinn-Phi	1.65	Grove-Phi	174	Grove-Phi	5.97	Moore-NY	10.35
Lyons-Chi	307.2	Thomas-Chi	7.93	Shocker-NY	1.85	Walberg-Phi	136	Braxton-Was	5.56	Braxton-Was	10.37
Hudlin-Cle	264.2	Pipgras-NY	8.01	Hoyt-NY	1.90	Thomas-Chi	107	Walberg-Phi	4.91	Lyons-Chi	10.47
Grove-Phi	262.1	Hadley-Was	8.02	Braxton-Was	1.91	Lisenbee-Was	105	Pipgras-NY	4.38	Hoyt-NY	10.53
Hoyt-NY	256.1	Lisenbee-Was	8.22	Lyons-Chi	1.96	Braxton-Was	96	Ruffing-Bos	4.38	Thomas-Chi	10.71

Earned Run Average		Adjusted ERA		Opponents' Batting Avg.		Opponents' On Base Pct.		Starter Runs		Adjusted Starter Runs	
Moore-NY	2.28	Moore-NY	169	Moore-NY	.234	Moore-NY	.289	Lyons-Chi	44.4	Lyons-Chi	41.3
Hoyt-NY	2.63	Hoyt-NY	146	Thomas-Chi	.244	Braxton-Was	.289	Moore-NY	43.9	Moore-NY	37.1
Shocker-NY	2.84	Lyons-Chi	143	Hadley-Was	.244	Lyons-Chi	.292	Hoyt-NY	42.8	Thomas-Chi	36.3
Lyons-Chi	2.84	Hadley-Was	142	Lisenbee-Was	.245	Hoyt-NY	.294	Thomas-Chi	39.4	Hoyt-NY	34.7
Hadley-Was	2.85	Braxton-Was	137	Braxton-Was	.246	Thomas-Chi	.303	Shocker-NY	28.9	Grove-Phi	31.2

Clutch Pitching Index		Relief Runs		Adjusted Relief Runs		Relief Ranking		Total Pitcher Index		Total Baseball Ranking	
Ruether-NY	119	Braxton-Was	20.4	Braxton-Was	19.1	Braxton-Was	24.6	Lyons-Chi	5.1	Ruth-NY	9.2
Gibson-Det	119	Burke-Was	1.9	G.Smith-Det	2.3	G.Smith-Det	1.5	Moore-NY	4.8	Gehrig-NY	8.1
Pennock-NY	118	G.Smith-Det	1.8	Burke-Was	1.1	Burke-Was	.5	Hoyt-NY	3.5	Lyons-Chi	5.1
Zachary-StL-Was	115							Grove-Phi	3.3	Moore-NY	4.8
Stoner-Det	114							Thomas-Chi	2.9	Heilmann-Det	4.2

January 14 Alfred J. Reach, founder of the A. J. Reach sporting goods firm, dies at 87. He was one of the first to receive a salary when he signed as a catcher with the Philadelphia Athletics for $25 a week in 1865.

April 18 The Cubs set an NL Opening Day attendance record as a reported 46,000 jam Wrigley Field to see Cincinnati top the Cubs, 9–6. The two teams combine for 28 hits.

June 2 The Phillies defeat the Cardinals, 2–1, with all the runs scoring as the result of a record three pinch-hit homers.

June 25 The Giants' Fred Lindstrom strokes nine hits in a doubleheader against Philadelphia to tie the major league mark. The Giants sweep, 12-4 and 8-2.

July 12 Baseball's biggest battery is recorded, appropriately, with the New York Giants, as Garland "Gob" Buckeye, a 260-pound pro football lineman in the off-season, makes his NL pitching debut with 250-pound Frank "Shanty" Hogan behind the plate. In a more significant move, the Giants purchase 25-year-old lefty Carl Hubbell from Beaumont for an amount rumored to be the most ever paid for a Texas League player.

August 11 Carl Hubbell's first major league victory is a 4-0 shutout of the Phils. He'll be 10-6 down the stretch and will pitch 16 years with the Giants.

September 4 The Braves play a record nine consecutive doubleheaders between now and the 15th. They lose five of them in a row, including four to the Giants.

September 27 With the Giants just a half game behind the Cardinals, New York loses the first game of a doubleheader to the Cubs, 3–2. On a controversial play at the plate in the sixth inning, New York's Andy Reese bowled over catcher Gabby Hartnett who grabbed the runner to keep from falling. As Hartnett held him, Reese was tagged out by the Cubs third baseman, and the Giants bench erupted. The protest would be disallowed.

September 29 The Cardinals win the NL pennant with a 3-1 win at Boston while the Cubs are beating New York. The final margin is two games over the Giants, four over the Cubs.

November 3 Voters in Massachusetts approve Sunday baseball in Boston, provided that the ballpark is more than 1,000 feet from a church. This leaves Pennsylvania as the only state with no Sunday baseball in the major leagues.

December 2 Cardinals first baseman Jim Bottomley is voted NL MVP with 76 points to 70 for Giants third baseman Fred Lindstrom, whose .358 batting average was third behind Hornsby and Paul Waner.

December 11 At the NL meeting, president John Heydler proposes the designated hitter for pitchers to improve and speed up the game. He contends fans are tired of seeing weak-hitting pitchers come to bat. Nothing comes of Heydler's proposition.

December 17 At a joint meeting, a rule is changed that ends the practice of minor league teams selling star prospects to friendly major league clubs for high prices, then getting the players back, forcing another major league club to pay the reputed price for the player. Another change bans the signing of players under the age of 17.

BOSTON		BROOKLYN		CHICAGO		CINCINNATI		NEW YORK		PHILADELPHIA		PITTSBURGH		ST.LOUIS	
M	J.Slattery	M	W.Robinson	M	J.McCarthy	M	J.Hendricks	M	J.McGraw	M	B.Shotton	M	D.Bush	M	B.McKechnie
M	R.Hornsby	1B	D.Bissonette	1B	C.Grimm	1B	G.Kelly	1B	B.Terry	1B	D.Hurst	1B	G.Grantham	1B	J.Bottomley
1B	G.Sisler	2B	J.Flowers	2B	F.Maguire	2B	H.Critz	2B	A.Cohen	2B	F.Thompson	2B	S.Adams	2B	F.Frisch
2B	R.Hornsby	SS	D.Bancroft	SS	W.English	SS	H.Ford	SS	T.Jackson	SS	H.Sand	SS	G.Wright	SS	R.Maranville
SS	D.Farrell	3B	H.Hendrick	3B	C.Beck	3B	C.Dressen	3B	F.Lindstrom	3B	P.Whitney	3B	P.Traynor	3B	W.Holm
3B	L.Bell	LF	R.Bressler	LF	R.Stephenson	LF	B.Zitzmann	LF	L.O'Doul	LF	F.Leach	LF	F.Brickell	LF	C.Hafey
LF	E.Brown	CF	M.Carey	CF	H.Wilson	CF	E.Allen	CF	J.Welsh	CF	D.Sothern	CF	L.Waner	CF	T.Douthit
CF	J.Smith	RF	B.Herman	RF	K.Cuyler	RF	C.Walker	RF	M.Ott	RF	C.Williams	RF	P.Waner	RF	G.Harper
RF	L.Richbourg	C	H.DeBerry	C	G.Hartnett	C	V.Picinich	C	S.Hogan	C	W.Lerian	C	C.Hargreaves	C	J.Wilson
C	Z.Taylor														
O	E.Moore	23	H.Riconda	3	J.Butler	1	W.Pipp	O2	R.Reese	C	K.Klein	2S	D.Bartell	32	A.High
O	H.Mueller	O	T.Tyson	C	M.Gonzalez	O	M.Callaghan	O	E.Roush	C	S.Davis	O	C.Barnhart	O	W.Roettger
1	D.Burrus	O	J.Statz	O	E.Webb	O	P.Purdy	C	B.O'Farrell	C	J.Schulte	O	P.Scott	S	T.Thevenow
C	A.Spohrer	3	W.Gilbert	O	C.Heathcote	C	B.Hargrave	O	G.Harper	O	B.Deitrick	C	A.Comorosky	O	R.Blades
O	E.Clark	C	B.Henline	23	N.McMillan	O3	J.Stripp	/O	A.Jahn	S	B.Friberg	C	R.Hemsley	O	E.Orsatti
S2	H.Freigau	C	J.Gooch	1	J.Kelly	C	S.Sukeforth	/1	J.Cummings	O	B.Kelly	C	E.Smith	C	E.Smith
S	Ji.Cooney	O	J.Harris	H	J.Moore	S	P.Pittinger	/1	R.Wrightstone	O	R.Wrightstone	C	J.Gooch	C	B.O'Farrell
/2	D.Gautreau	2	J.Partridge	H	R.Jacobs	/2	J.White	C	P.Veltman	1	B.Kelly	/3	E.Mulligan	C	G.Mancuso
/O	D.Harris	C	C.Hargreaves	/3	E.Yoter			/C	A.Spohrer	C	J.Wilson	/2	M.Hillis	/1	S.Toporcer
C	L.Urban	3	H.Freigau	P	P.Malone	P	E.Rixey	H	R.Foley	O	A.Nixon	/1	J.Harris	/O	P.Martin
H	C.Fitzberger	/O	O.Tremper	P	S.Blake	P	D.Luque	H	C.Fullis	/O	H.MacDonald	/S	C.Jones	H	H.Williamson
/O	D.McNamara	/O	M.West	P	C.Root	P	R.Kolp	/C	B.Haeffner			/C	J.O'Connell	/C	S.Davis
/C	B.Cronin	/C	A.Lopez	P	G.Bush	P	R.Lucas	/O	J.Price	P	R.Benge	/1	B.Windle		
/C	E.Williams	P	D.Vance	P	A.Nehf	P	P.Donohue			P	J.Ring			P	B.Sherdel
		P	D.McWeeny	RP	H.Carlson	RP	P.Appleton			P	L.Sweetland	P	B.Grimes	P	P.Alexander
P	B.Smith	P	J.Petty					P	L.Benton	P	A.Ferguson	P	C.Hill	P	J.Haines
P	E.Brandt	P	W.Clark	P	P.Jones	P	J.May	P	F.Fitzsimmons	P	C.Willoughby	P	R.Kremer	P	F.Rhem
P	A.Delaney	P	J.Elliott	P	E.Holley	P	C.Mays	P	J.Genewich			P	F.Fussell	P	C.Mitchell
P	K.Greenfield	RP	R.Moss	P	L.Weinert	/P	K.Ash	P	C.Hubbell	P	A.Walsh	P	J.Dawson	RP	H.Haid
RP	F.Edwards	RP	R.Ehrhardt	/P	B.Tincup	/P	J.Edwards	P	V.Aldridge	P	B.McGraw				
				/P	J.Welch	/P	J.Beckman	P	J.Faulkner	P	R.Miller	P	E.Brame	P	S.Johnson
P	B.Cantwell	P	B.Doak			/P	S.Johnson	P	B.Walker	P	H.Pruett	P	J.Miljus	P	F.Frankhouse
P	Jo.Cooney	P	L.Koupal			/P	H.Pyle	P	D.Henry	P	J.Milligan	/P	L.Bartholomew	P	A.Reinhart
P	J.Genewich							P	V.Barnes	/P	E.Caldwell	/P	H.Blankenship	P	C.Littlejohn
P	V.Barnes							P	J.Scott	/P	E.Lennon	/P	B.Burwell	/P	T.Kaufmann
P	C.Robertson							P	T.Chaplin	/P	C.Mitchell	/P	L.Meadows		
P	B.Clarkson							/P	B.Cantwell	/P	J.Greene	/P	G.Spencer		
/P	B.Hollingsworth							/P	B.Clarkson	/P	M.Walker	/P	E.Tutwiler		
P	J.Werts							/P	G.Buckeye						
/P	B.Hearn							/P	L.Mangum						
/P	H.Goldsmith							/P	C.Nichols						
/P	A.Mills														
/P	C.Touchstone														
/P	E.Palmero														
/P	R.Boggs														
/P	G.Morrison														

TEAM	G	W	L	PCT	GB	R	OR	AB	H	2B	3B	HR	BB	SO	AVG	OBP	SLG	PRO	PRO+	BR	/A	PF	CHI	RC	SB	CS	SBA	SBR
STL	154	95	59	.617		807	636	5357	1505	292	70	113	568	438	.281	.353	.425	.778	108	73	58	102	99	802	82			
NY	155	93	61	.604	2	807	653	5459	1600	276	59	118	444	376	.293	.349	.430	.779	110	68	65	100	100	805	62			
CHI	154	91	63	.591	4	714	615	5260	1460	251	64	92	508	517	.278	.345	.402	.747	103	11	21	99	97	728	83			
PIT	152	85	67	.559	9	837	704	5371	1659	246	100	52	435	352	.309	.364	.421	.785	108	89	56	104	103	809	64			
CIN	153	78	74	.513	16	648	686	5184	1449	229	67	32	386	330	.280	.333	.368	.701	91	-76	-66	98	104	630	83			
BRO	155	77	76	.503	17.5	665	640	5243	1393	229	70	66	557	510	.266	.340	.374	.714	94	-46	-37	99	98	673	81			
BOS	153	50	103	.327	44.5	631	878	5228	1439	241	41	52	447	377	.275	.335	.367	.702	95	-70	-37	95	99	643	60			
PHI	152	43	109	.283	51	660	957	5234	1396	257	47	85	503	510	.267	.333	.382	.715	90	-49	-72	103	99	667	53			
TOT	614					5769		42336	11901	2021	518	610	3848	3410	.281	.344	.397	.741							568			

TEAM	CG	SH	SV	IP	H	H/G	HR	BB	SO	RAT	ERA	ERA+	OAV	OOB	PR	/A	PF	CPI	FA	E	DP	FW	PW	BW	SBW	DIF
STL	83	4	21	1415¹	1470	9.3	86	399	422	12.1	3.38	118	.270	.323	96	98	100	105	.974	160	134	1.3	9.6	5.7		1.4
NY	79	7	16	1394	1454	9.4	77	405	399	12.1	3.67	107	.273	.327	50	37	98	98	.972	178	175	.3	3.6	6.4		5.7
CHI	75	12	14	1380²	1383	9.0	56	508	531	12.5	3.40	113	.267	.336	91	69	96	105	.975	156	176	1.6	6.7	2.1		3.6
PIT	82	8	11	1354	1422	9.5	66	446	385	12.6	3.95	103	.274	.335	6	16	102	93	.967	201	123	-1.3	1.6	5.5		3.2
CIN	68	11	11	1371¹²	1516	9.9	58	410	355	12.7	3.94	100	.289	.342	8	2	99	100	.974	162	194	1.1	.2	-6.5		7.1
BRO	75	16	15	1396	1378	8.9	59	468	551	12.1	3.25	122	.261	.324	114	112	100	101	.965	217	113	-2.0	10.9	-3.6		-4.8
BOS	54	1	6	1360	1596	10.6	100	524	343	14.2	4.83	81	.298	.363	-127	-140	98	97	.969	193	141	-.7	-13.7	-3.6		-8.5
PHI	42	4	11	1352²	1658	11.0	108	675	404	15.8	5.56	77	.314	.396	-237	-199	107	100	.971	181	171	-.0	-19.5	-7.0		-6.4
TOT	558	63	105	11024¹		9.7				13.0	3.99		.281	.344					.971	1448	1227					

Runs		Hits		Doubles		Triples		Home Runs		Total Bases	
P.Waner-Pit	142	Lindstrom-NY	231	P.Waner-Pit	50	Bottomley-StL	20	Wilson-Chi	31	Bottomley-StL	362
Bottomley-StL	123	P.Waner-Pit	223	Hafey-StL	46	P.Waner-Pit	19	Bottomley-StL	31	Lindstrom-NY	330
L.Waner-Pit	121	L.Waner-Pit	221	Hornsby-Bos	42	L.Waner-Pit	14	Hafey-StL	27	P.Waner-Pit	329
Douthit-StL	111	Richbourg-Bos	206	Bottomley-StL	42	Bressler-Bro	13	Bissonette-Bro	25	Bissonette-Bro	319
Frisch-StL	107	Traynor-Pit	192	Lindstrom-NY	39	Bissonette-Bro	13	Hornsby-Bos	21	Hafey-StL	314

Runs Batted In		Runs Produced		Bases On Balls		Batting Average		On Base Percentage		Slugging Average	
Bottomley-StL	136	Bottomley-StL	228	Hornsby-Bos	107	Hornsby-Bos	.387	Hornsby-Bos	.498	Hornsby-Bos	.632
Traynor-Pit	124	P.Waner-Pit	222	Douthit-StL	84	P.Waner-Pit	.370	P.Waner-Pit	.446	Bottomley-StL	.628
Wilson-Chi	120	Traynor-Pit	212	Bressler-Bro	80	Lindstrom-NY	.358	Grantham-Pit	.408	Hafey-StL	.604
Hafey-StL	111	Lindstrom-NY	192	Wilson-Chi	77	Sisler-Bos	.340	Stephenson-Chi	.407	Wilson-Chi	.588
Lindstrom-NY	107	Hafey-StL	185	P.Waner-Pit	77	Herman-Bro	.340	Wilson-Chi	.404	P.Waner-Pit	.547

Production		Adjusted Production		Batter Runs		Adjusted Batter Runs		Clutch Hitting Index		Runs Created	
Hornsby-Bos	1.130	Hornsby-Bos	204	Hornsby-Bos	72.5	Hornsby-Bos	80.3	Traynor-Pit	147	Hornsby-Bos	154
Bottomley-StL	1.030	Bottomley-StL	163	P.Waner-Pit	53.4	Bottomley-StL	50.1	Walker-Cin	126	P.Waner-Pit	145
Wilson-Chi	.992	Wilson-Chi	159	Bottomley-StL	52.5	P.Waner-Pit	48.0	Whitney-Phi	124	Bottomley-StL	142
P.Waner-Pit	.992	Hafey-StL	152	Wilson-Chi	42.1	Wilson-Chi	43.7	Ford-Cin	123	Bissonette-Bro	125
Hafey-StL	.990	P.Waner-Pit	152	Hafey-StL	38.5	Bissonette-Bro	38.1	Wilson-Phi-StL	121	Wilson-Chi	122

Total Average		Stolen Bases		Stolen Base Average	Stolen Base Runs	Fielding Runs		Total Player Rating	
Hornsby-Bos	1.409	Cuyler-Chi	37			Maguire-Chi	50.5	Hornsby-Bos	5.8
Bottomley-StL	1.147	Frisch-StL	29			Jackson-NY	28.3	Lindstrom-NY	4.8
P.Waner-Pit	1.100	Walker-Cin	19			Douthit-StL	24.3	Jackson-NY	4.3
Wilson-Chi	1.090	Thompson-Phi	19			Lindstrom-NY	15.1	Hartnett-Chi	4.2
Hafey-StL	1.055					Ford-Cin	11.9	P.Waner-Pit	4.0

Wins		Win Percentage		Games		Complete Games		Shutouts		Saves	
Grimes-Pit	25	Benton-NY	.735	Grimes-Pit	48	Grimes-Pit	28	Vance-Bro	4	Sherdel-StL	5
Benton-NY	25	Haines-StL	.714	Kolp-Cin	44	Benton-NY	28	McWeeny-Bro	4	Haid-StL	5
Vance-Bro	22	Bush-Chi	.714	Rixey-Cin	43	Vance-Bro	24	Lucas-Cin	4	Carlson-Chi	4
Sherdel-StL	21	Fitzsimmons-NY	.690			Sherdel-StL	20	Grimes-Pit	4	Benton-NY	4
		Vance-Bro	.688			Haines-StL	20	Blake-Chi	4		

Innings Pitched		Fewest Hits/Game		Fewest BB/Game		Strikeouts		Strikeouts/Game		Ratio	
Grimes-Pit	330.2	Vance-Bro	7.26	Alexander-StL	1.37	Vance-Bro	200	Vance-Bro	6.42	Vance-Bro	9.79
Benton-NY	310.1	Blake-Chi	7.82	Sherdel-StL	2.03	Malone-Chi	155	Malone-Chi	5.57	Benton-NY	10.73
Rixey-Cin	291.1	Malone-Chi	7.83	Benton-NY	2.06	Root-Chi	122	Root-Chi	4.63	Grimes-Pit	10.81
Vance-Bro	280.1	McWeeny-Bro	8.04	Rixey-Cin	2.07	Grimes-Pit	97	Clark-Bro	3.93	Lucas-Cin	11.08
Fitzsimmons-NY	261.1	Root-Chi	8.13	Grimes-Pit	2.10	Benton-NY	90	Ring-Phi	3.75	Alexander-StL	11.12

Earned Run Average		Adjusted ERA		Opponents' Batting Avg.		Opponents' On Base Pct.		Starter Runs		Adjusted Starter Runs	
Vance-Bro	2.09	Vance-Bro	190	Vance-Bro	.221	Vance-Bro	.277	Vance-Bro	59.2	Vance-Bro	58.7
Blake-Chi	2.47	Blake-Chi	156	McWeeny-Bro	.235	Grimes-Pit	.297	Benton-NY	43.5	Benton-NY	40.7
Nehf-Chi	2.65	Clark-Bro	148	Malone-Chi	.236	Benton-NY	.300	Blake-Chi	40.6	Grimes-Pit	39.0
Clark-Bro	2.68	Nehf-Chi	145	Blake-Chi	.240	Sherdel-StL	.303	Grimes-Pit	36.5	Blake-Chi	36.8
Benton-NY	2.73	Benton-NY	143	Root-Chi	.242	Lucas-Cin	.304	Malone-Chi	32.1	Sherdel-StL	31.4

Clutch Pitching Index		Relief Runs	Adjusted Relief Runs	Relief Ranking	Total Pitcher Index		Total Baseball Ranking	
Nehf-Chi	133				Vance-Bro	7.0	Vance-Bro	7.0
Bush-Chi	117				Grimes-Pit	6.1	Grimes-Pit	6.1
Blake-Chi	115				Benton-NY	3.9	Hornsby-Bos	5.8
Kolp-Cin	114				Blake-Chi	3.8	Lindstrom-NY	4.8
Rhem-StL	114				Sherdel-StL	3.7	Jackson-NY	4.3

June 2 St. Mary's College football star Larry Bettencourt breaks in at third base with the Browns. A future member of the College Football Hall of Fame, Bettencourt was an All-American center who will later play for the Green Bay Packers. The $6,000 bonus he receives is a record for a rookie just out of school.

June 15 Ty Cobb, 41 years old, steals home for the 50th and final time in his 24-year career to extend his major league record. It comes in the eighth against the Indians.

July 14 At Boston, White Sox pitcher Ed Walsh, Jr. picks up his first win, topping the Red Sox, 11–4. Junior will only win 11 games to his father's 195: all 206 Walsh victories are for the White Sox.

July 22 Pitcher Red Faber of the White Sox comes up to bat in the eighth with two runners on base and the game with the Yankees tied, 4–4. He swings twice right-handed against righty Wilcy Moore and misses. He then switches to the left side and knocks in the winning runs with a single to center.

July 29 The Indians score eight in the first and nine in the second in a 24–6 win over the Yankees at home. Johnny Hodapp of the Indians becomes the first AL player to get two hits in an inning twice in a game. He strokes two singles in both the second and sixth innings of the game. The Yankees' lead shrinks from 11½ games to six in one week.

September 3 Ty Cobb makes the last of his 4,189 hits, the 724th double of his career, as a pinch hitter in the ninth inning of the first game at Washington. The hit is off Bump Hadley.

September 8 The Yankees sweep two from the A's, 3–0 and 7–3, to move back into first place to stay. The A's, in first place at the end of August, will run out of gas.

September 30 In Washington's 9-1 win over the Browns, Washington outfielder Leon "Goose" Goslin gets two hits for the third day in a row to edge Browns outfielder Heinie Manush .379 to .378 for his only batting title in his 18-year career. Nats' ace Sam Jones volunteered to pitch to stop Manush, while Blaeholder tried the same for St. Louis. Blaeholder got Goslin in his first two at bats, but Goose then hit a fifth inning home run.

October 4 The first World Series game is a swift execution before 61,425 at New York. Babe Ruth has a single and double and scores twice, once on Bob Meusel's fourth-inning home run, and Lou Gehrig is 2-for-4 with two RBIs off Bill Sherdel (21-10). Waite Hoyt (23-7) sets the Cards down with three hits, one a solo home run by Bottomley in the seventh, for a 4-1 win.

October 9 After a rainout, Waite Hoyt and Bill Sherdel are back on the mound for Game 4. After six innings, the Cards hold a 2-1 lead. With one out in the seventh, Babe Ruth hits a home run, his second of the game, and Lou Gehrig follows suit. When Bob Meusel singles, in comes Grover Cleveland Alexander to face Tony Lazzeri, a replay of their confrontation two years earlier. Lazzeri doubles this time and later scores the fourth run of the inning. In the eighth, Cedric Durst, subbing for Earle Combs, hits one out of the park, and Ruth follows with his third home run of the game. The final score is 7-3, and the Yanks sweep their second straight World Series. Ruth's World Series batting average of .625 is still unmatched; with Gehrig's .545 and a record nine RBIs, they also set individual and team offensive records for hits, home runs, total bases, and at bats in a game.

October 15 Walter Johnson signs a three-year contract to manage the Senators.

October 16 Mickey Cochrane wins AL MVP honors, edging Heinie Manush by two points. Neither Ruth nor Gehrig is eligible, having won before.

November 3 Voters in Cleveland approve a bond issue to build a giant municipal stadium near the lakefront to attract events for the 1932 Olympics.

November 19 The Indians send $50,000 and two players to San Francisco (PCL) for outfielder Earl Averill.

BOSTON		CHICAGO		CLEVELAND		DETROIT		NEW YORK		PHILADELPHIA		ST.LOUIS		WASHINGTON	
M	B.Carrigan	M	R.Schalk	M	R.Peckinpaugh	M	G.Moriarty	M	M.Huggins	M	C.Mack	M	D.Howley	M	B.Harris
1B	P.Todt	M	L.Blackburne	1B	L.Fonseca	1B	B.Sweeney	1B	L.Gehrig	1B	J.Hauser	1B	L.Blue	1B	J.Judge
2B	B.Regan	1B	B.Clancy	2B	C.Lind	2B	C.Gehringer	2B	T.Lazzeri	2B	M.Bishop	2B	O.Brannan	2B	B.Harris
SS	W.Gerber	2B	B.Hunnefield	SS	J.Sewell	SS	J.Tavener	SS	M.Koenig	SS	J.Boley	SS	R.Kress	SS	B.Reeves
3B	B.Myer	SS	B.Cissell	3B	J.Hodapp	3B	M.McManus	3B	J.Dugan	3B	S.Hale	3B	F.O'Rourke	3B	O.Bluege
LF	K.Williams	3B	W.Kamm	LF	C.Jamieson	LF	B.Fothergill	LF	B.Meusel	LF	A.Simmons	LF	H.Manush	LF	G.Goslin
CF	I.Flagstead	LF	B.Falk	CF	S.Langford	CF	H.Rice	CF	E.Combs	CF	B.Miller	CF	F.Schulte	CF	S.West
RF	D.Taitt	CF	J.Mostil	RF	H.Summa	RF	H.Heilmann	RF	B.Ruth	RF	T.Cobb	RF	E.McNeely	RF	S.Rice
C	F.Hofmann	RF	A.Metzler	C	L.Sewell	C	P.Hargrave	C	J.Grabowski	C	M.Cochrane	C	W.Schang	C	M.Ruel
S2	B.Rogell	C	B.Crouse	1O	E.Morgan	O	A.Wingo	2S	L.Durocher	31	J.Foxx	C	C.Manion	O	R.Barnes
O3	J.Rothrock	O	C.Reynolds	1	G.Burns	3	J.Warner	O	G.Robertson	O	M.Haas	O	B.McGowan	S	J.Cronin
C	C.Berry	2S	B.Redfern	O	L.Harvel	C	L.Woodall	C	B.Bengough	2S	J.Dykes	3	L.Bettencourt	2S	J.Tate
C	J.Heving	O2	B.Barrett	C	G.Myatt	S3	C.Galloway	O	P.Collins	O	T.Speaker	23	S.Melillo	C	B.Tate
O	G.Loepp	C	M.Berg	O	G.Gerken	O	P.Easterling	O	C.Durst	1P	O.Orwoll	/1	G.Sturdy	C	E.Kenna
/1	R.Rollings	1	A.Shires	O	R.Dorman	O	J.Stone	O	B.Paschal	O	W.French	C	S.O'Neill	S	G.Gillis
O	C.Sumner	C	H.McCurdy	C	C.Autry	1	J.Neun	3	M.Gazella	S	J.Hassler	/S	W.Gerber	/O	B.Ganzel
/O	D.Williams	O	G.Blackerby	S	E.Montague	C	M.Shea	/C	B.Dickey	/2	E.Collins	/3	B.Mullen	O	D.Spalding
/O	A.Tarbert	2	K.Swanson	O	O.Tucker	P	O.Carroll	/1	G.Burns	C	C.Perkins	/3	O.Sax	/3	H.Boss
/C	C.Asbjornson	O	R.Moore	O	B.Caldwell	P	E.Whitehill	P	G.Pipgras	P	L.Grove	/O	F.Bennett	/3	P.Ballenger
/S	F.Moncewicz	/3	J.Mann	/S	J.Goldman	P	V.Sorrell	P	W.Hoyt	P	R.Walberg	/C	I.Danning	/C	A.Bool
R	P.Hinson	/C	R.Schalk	/1	A.Van Camp	P	E.Vangilder	P	H.Pennock	P	J.Quinn	/O	F.Wilson	/3	E.Crowley
P	R.Ruffing	P	T.Thomas	/1	C.Bolton	P	L.Stoner	P	H.Johnson	P	E.Rommel	P	S.Gray	H	H.McMullen
P	E.Morris	P	T.Lyons	/S	J.Burnett	RP	G.Smith	P	A.Shealy	P	G.Earnshaw	P	A.Crowder	P	B.Hadley
P	J.Russell	P	G.Adkins	/3	A.Ward	P	S.Gibson	RP	W.Moore	P	H.Ehmke	P	J.Ogden	P	S.Jones
P	D.MacFayden	P	R.Faber	/3	A.Reinholz	P	K.Holloway	P	F.Heimach	P	J.Bush	P	G.Blaeholder	P	G.Braxton
P	S.Harriss	P	T.Blankenship	H	J.Gill	P	J.Billings	P	S.Coveleski	/P	B.Shores	P	L.Stewart	P	F.Marberry
RP	M.Settlemire	RP	S.Connally	H	F.Wilson	/P	P.Page	/P	T.Zachary	/P	J.Johnson	RP	D.Coffman	P	M.Gaston
RP	P.Simmons	P	G.Cox	P	J.Shaute	/P	C.Sullivan	P	M.Thomas	/P	C.Yerkes	RP	H.Wiltse	P	L.Brown
P	H.Bradley	P	E.Walsh	P	W.Hudlin			P	A.Campbell	/P	A.Daney	RP	E.Strelecki	P	T.Zachary
P	M.Griffin	/P	C.Barnabe	P	G.Uhle			P	R.Ryan			P	B.Beck	P	B.Burke
/P	C.Garrison	/P	B.Weiland	P	J.Miller			/P	U.Shocker			/P	E.Nevers	P	H.Lisenbee
/P	H.Wiltse	/P	J.Goodell	P	G.Grant							/P	J.Wright	/P	C.Van Alstyne
/P	S.Slayton	/P	R.Wilson	RP	B.Bayne									/P	J.Weaver
/P	J.Wilson	/P	R.Leopold	RP	M.Harder										
/P	F.Bennett	/P	A.Williamson	P	J.Miljus										
/P	J.Shea	/P	D.Dugan	P	D.Levsen										
				/P	G.Buckeye										
				P	W.Underhill										
				/P	W.Ferrell										
				/P	J.Brown										
				/P	C.Brown										
				/P	L.Barnhart										
				/P	J.Moore										
				/P	H.Collard										

TEAM	G	W	L	PCT	GB	R	OR	AB	H	2B	3B	HR	BB	SO	AVG	OBP	SLG	PRO	PRO+	BR	/A	PF	CHI	RC	SB	CS	SBA	SBR
NY	154	101	53	.656		894	685	5337	1578	269	79	133	562	544	.296	.365	.450	.815	124	146	175	97	100	888	51	51	50	-15
PHI	153	98	55	.641	2.5	829	615	5226	1540	323	75	89	533	442	.295	.363	.436	.799	112	115	92	103	97	843	59	48	55	-11
STL	154	82	72	.532	19	772	742	5217	1431	276	76	63	548	479	.274	.346	.393	.739	97	2	-21	103	104	736	76	43	64	-3
WAS	155	75	79	.487	26	718	705	5320	1510	277	93	40	481	390	.284	.346	.393	.739	101	1	6	99	97	743	110	59	65	-2
CHI	155	72	82	.468	29	656	725	5207	1405	231	77	24	469	488	.270	.334	.358	.692	88	-88	-79	99	102	641	139	82	63	-8
DET	154	68	86	.442	33	744	804	5292	1476	265	97	62	469	438	.279	.340	.401	.741	99	-2	-13	102	102	730	113	77	59	-12
CLE	155	62	92	.403	39	674	830	5386	1535	299	61	34	377	426	.285	.335	.382	.717	93	-49	-56	101	98	693	50	52	49	-16
BOS	154	57	96	.373	43.5	589	770	5132	1356	260	62	38	389	512	.264	.319	.361	.680	86	-119	-108	98	100	602	99	64	61	-9
TOT	617					5876		42117	11831	2200	620	483	3828	3719	.281	.344	.397	.741						697	476	59	-77	

TEAM	CG	SH	SV	IP	H	H/G	HR	BB	SO	RAT	ERA	ERA+	OAV	OOB	PR	/A	PF	CPI	FA	E	DP	FW	PW	BW	SBW	DIF
NY	82	13	21	1375[1]	1466	9.6	59	452	487	12.7	3.74	101	.276	.335	46	3	93	102	.968	194	136	-.0	.3	16.9	-.5	7.4
PHI	81	15	16	1367[2]	1349	8.9	66	424	607	11.8	3.36	119	.259	.318	103	97	99	99	.970	181	124	.6	9.4	8.9	-.1	2.7
STL	80	6	15	1374[1]	1487	9.7	93	454	456	12.8	4.17	101	.282	.340	-20	3	104	100	.969	189	146	.2	.4	-2.0	.6	5.9
WAS	77	15	10	1384	1420	9.2	40	466	462	12.5	3.88	103	.272	.335	25	19	99	94	.972	178	146	1.0	1.8	.6	.7	-6.1
CHI	88	6	11	1378	1518	9.9	66	501	418	13.4	3.98	102	.287	.352	8	8	100	108	.970	186	149	.5	.8	-7.6	.2	1.2
DET	65	5	16	1372	1481	9.7	58	567	451	13.7	4.32	95	.281	.355	-42	-34	102	97	.965	218	140	-1.5	-3.3	-1.3	-.2	-2.7
CLE	71	4	15	1378	1615	10.5	52	511	416	14.2	4.47	93	.303	.369	-66	-52	103	105	.965	221	187	-1.6	-5.0	-5.4	-.6	-2.4
BOS	70	5	9	1352	1492	9.9	49	452	407	13.2	4.39	93	.288	.349	-53	-44	102	94	.971	178	139	.9	-4.3	-10.4	.0	-5.8
TOT	614	69	113	10981[1]		9.7				13.0	4.04		.281	.344					.969	1545	1167					

Runs		Hits		Doubles		Triples		Home Runs		Total Bases	
Ruth-NY	163	Manush-StL	241	Manush-StL	47	Combs-NY	21	Ruth-NY	54	Ruth-NY	380
Gehrig-NY	139	Gehrig-NY	210	Gehrig-NY	47	Manush-StL	20	Gehrig-NY	27	Manush-StL	367
Combs-NY	118	Rice-Was	202	Meusel-NY	45	Gehringer-Det	16	Goslin-Was	17	Gehrig-NY	364
Blue-StL	116	Combs-NY	194	Schulte-StL	44			Hauser-Phi	16	Combs-NY	290
Gehringer-Det	108	Gehringer-Det	193	Lind-Cle	42			Simmons-Phi	15	Heilmann-Det	283

Runs Batted In		Runs Produced		Bases On Balls		Batting Average		On Base Percentage		Slugging Average	
Ruth-NY	142	Gehrig-NY	254	Ruth-NY	135	Goslin-Was	.379	Gehrig-NY	.467	Ruth-NY	.709
Gehrig-NY	142	Ruth-NY	251	Blue-StL	105	Manush-StL	.378	Ruth-NY	.461	Gehrig-NY	.648
Meusel-NY	113	Manush-StL	199	Bishop-Phi	97	Gehrig-NY	.374	Goslin-Was	.442	Goslin-Was	.614
Manush-StL	108	Blue-StL	182	Gehrig-NY	95	Simmons-Phi	.351	Bishop-Phi	.435	Manush-StL	.575
		Meusel-NY	179	Judge-Was	80	Lazzeri-NY	.332	Manush-StL	.414	Simmons-Phi	.558

Production		Adjusted Production		Batter Runs		Adjusted Batter Runs		Clutch Hitting Index		Runs Created	
Ruth-NY	1.170	Ruth-NY	210	Ruth-NY	83.9	Ruth-NY	89.4	Cissell-Chi	130	Ruth-NY	182
Gehrig-NY	1.115	Gehrig-NY	196	Gehrig-NY	76.0	Gehrig-NY	81.2	Meusel-NY	128	Gehrig-NY	169
Goslin-Was	1.056	Goslin-Was	176	Manush-StL	50.3	Goslin-Was	49.8	Judge-Was	123	Manush-StL	150
Manush-StL	.989	Manush-StL	153	Goslin-Was	49.0	Manush-StL	46.2	Hodapp-Cle	118	Goslin-Was	125
Simmons-Phi	.954	Simmons-Phi	144	Foxx-Phi	30.5	Foxx-Phi	28.1	Boley-Phi	117	Combs-NY	114

Total Average		Stolen Bases		Stolen Base Average		Stolen Base Runs		Fielding Runs		Total Player Rating	
Ruth-NY	1.405	Myer-Bos	30	Rice-Was	84.2	Rice-Was	3.0	Gerber-StL-Bos	32.0	Ruth-NY	7.0
Gehrig-NY	1.256	Mostil-Chi	23	Goslin-Was	84.2	Goslin-Was	3.0	J.Sewell-Cle	27.0	J.Sewell-Cle	5.4
Goslin-Was	1.203	Rice-Det	20	Judge-Was	80.0	Reynolds-Chi	2.7	Jamieson-Cle	19.9	Gehrig-NY	5.1
Manush-StL	1.040	Cissell-Chi	18	Manush-StL	77.3	Judge-Was	2.4	Mostil-Chi	17.8	Goslin-Was	4.5
Simmons-Phi	.951	Bluege-Was	18			Manush-StL	2.1	Schulte-StL	17.3	Manush-StL	3.8

Wins		Win Percentage		Games		Complete Games		Shutouts		Saves	
Pipgras-NY	24	Crowder-StL	.808	Marberry-Was	48	Ruffing-Bos	25	Pennock-NY	5	Hoyt-NY	8
Grove-Phi	24	Hoyt-NY	.767	Morris-Bos	47	Thomas-Chi	24	Quinn-Phi	4	Hudlin-Cle	7
Hoyt-NY	23	Grove-Phi	.750	Pipgras-NY	46	Grove-Phi	24	Pipgras-NY	4	Lyons-Chi	6
Crowder-StL	21	Pennock-NY	.739	Rommel-Phi	43	Pipgras-NY	22	Jones-Was	4	Braxton-Was	6
Gray-StL	20	Quinn-Phi	.720					Grove-Phi	4		

Innings Pitched		Fewest Hits/Game		Fewest BB/Game		Strikeouts		Strikeouts/Game		Ratio	
Pipgras-NY	300.2	Braxton-Was	7.30	Rommel-Phi	1.35	Grove-Phi	183	Earnshaw-Phi	6.65	Braxton-Was	9.32
Ruffing-Bos	289.1	Grove-Phi	7.84	Quinn-Phi	1.45	Pipgras-NY	139	Grove-Phi	6.29	Grove-Phi	10.08
Thomas-Chi	283.0	Earnshaw-Phi	8.13	Pennock-NY	1.71	Thomas-Chi	129	Johnson-NY	4.97	Rommel-Phi	10.62
Hoyt-NY	273.0	Jones-Was	8.37	Braxton-Was	1.81	Ruffing-Bos	118	Walberg-Phi	4.28	Pennock-NY	10.88
Gray-StL	262.2	Johnson-NY	8.50	Russell-Bos	1.83	Earnshaw-Phi	117	Whitehill-Det	4.26	Hoyt-NY	11.21

Earned Run Average		Adjusted ERA		Opponents' Batting Avg.		Opponents' On Base Pct.		Starter Runs		Adjusted Starter Runs	
Braxton-Was	2.51	Braxton-Was	159	Braxton-Was	.222	Braxton-Was	.267	Grove-Phi	42.4	Grove-Phi	41.5
Pennock-NY	2.56	Grove-Phi	155	Grove-Phi	.229	Grove-Phi	.277	Braxton-Was	37.0	Braxton-Was	36.2
Grove-Phi	2.58	Pennock-NY	147	Earnshaw-Phi	.240	Rommel-Phi	.295	Pennock-NY	34.7	Thomas-Chi	30.2
Jones-Was	2.84	Jones-Was	141	Johnson-NY	.250	Pennock-NY	.302	Thomas-Chi	30.0	Gray-StL	29.4
Quinn-Phi	2.90	Quinn-Phi	138	Jones-Was	.252	Thomas-Chi	.310	Jones-Was	29.8	Jones-Was	29.0

Clutch Pitching Index		Relief Runs		Adjusted Relief Runs		Relief Ranking		Total Pitcher Index		Total Baseball Ranking	
Miller-Cle	119			Simmons-Bos	5	Simmons-Bos	1	Grove-Phi	4.6	Ruth-NY	7.0
Quinn-Phi	119							Jones-Was	3.5	J.Sewell-Cle	5.4
Blankenship-Chi	114							Gray-StL	3.5	Gehrig-NY	5.1
Pennock-NY	113							Braxton-Was	3.5	Grove-Phi	4.6
Adkins-Chi	113							Thomas-Chi	3.3	Goslin-Was	4.5

January 1* Outfielder Jim Bell of Cienfuegos becomes the first man to connect for three homers in a game during professional league play in Cuba. Bell's feat occurs at Alda Park in a 15–11 victory over Club Havana.

April 16 The Cubs open at Wrigley Field before an estimated 50,000, the biggest Opening Day in club history and beat the Pirates, 3–1.

May 8 The Giants' Carl Hubbell pitches an 11–0 no-hitter against the Pirates, allowing just one walk. In the ninth, the first two batters reached on errors before Hubbell recorded a strikeout and started the game-ending double play. It's the first no-hitter by a left-hander since Hub Leonard in 1918.

May 18 Brooklyn and Philadelphia score a major league-record 50 runs in a doubleheader at the Baker Bowl. The Robins (Dodgers) win the opener, 20–16, and the Phils take the second game, 8–6. Highlights include Brooklyn's Johnny Fredericks tallying five runs in the opener, which combined with his three yesterday, gives him a major league record eight in two games. The Dodgers pull off a triple play to keep some scoring down.

June 19 In their second straight doubleheader, The Giants sweep the Phillies, winning 15–14, in 11 innings, and 12–6. Mel Ott has two homers and four doubles for the day, while Edd Roush goes 8-for-12. In tomorrow's 11–6 win over the Phils, Ott will have three RBIs, giving him 11 straight games with at least one ribbie. The 20-year-old will have 27 RBIs in the 11 games and will finish the season with 151, second in the NL.

July 5 The Giants are the first team to use a public address system in a big league park, for a game against the Pirates.

July 18 Trying to curb the hitters, NL president Heydler orders umpires to rub up new balls before each game to remove the gloss.

August 10 Grover Cleveland Alexander beats the Phils 7-1 for his 373rd and last NL victory. He pitches four scoreless relief innings for the Cardinals and wins the game, 11-9, in the 11th.

August 26 It's definitely the Cubs' year in the NL. In the eighth inning of a 5-5 tie with the Reds at Wrigley Field, Chicago's Norm McMillan hits a line drive down the left field line that Cincinnati left fielder Evar Swanson, shaded towards center, can't find. McMillan circles the bases as the Cubs take a four-run lead. Chicago relief pitcher Ken Penner picks up his jacket in the bullpen and finds the ball in his right sleeve.

September 27 Phils outfielder Chuck Klein hits homer No. 42, tying Mel Ott and equaling Hornsby's NL record. He'll hit one more to top the NL with 43.

October 5 Mel Ott of the Giants and Chuck Klein of the Phillies go into a season-ending doubleheader tied for the NL home run lead. In the opener, Ott gets a single, but Klein homers off Carl Hubbell to take the lead. Phillies pitchers proceed to walk Ott intentionally five straight times. The last walk comes with the bases loaded. Meanwhile, Lefty O'Doul gets six hits for Philadelphia in the twinbill for an NL-record 254 hits.

BOSTON	BROOKLYN	CHICAGO	CINCINNATI	NEW YORK	PHILADELPHIA	PITTSBURGH	ST.LOUIS
M J.Fuchs	M W.Robinson	M J.McCarthy	M J.Hendricks	M J.McGraw	M B.Shotton	M D.Bush	M B.Southworth
1B G.Sisler	1B D.Bissonette	1B C.Grimm	1B G.Kelly	1B B.Terry	1B D.Hurst	M J.Ens	M G.Street
2B F.Maguire	2B E.Moore	2B R.Hornsby	2B H.Critz	2B A.Cohen	2B F.Thompson	1B E.Sheely	M B.McKechnie
SS R.Maranville	SS D.Bancroft	SS W.English	SS H.Ford	SS T.Jackson	SS T.Thevenow	2B G.Grantham	1B J.Bottomley
3B L.Bell	3B W.Gilbert	3B N.McMillan	3B C.Dressen	3B F.Lindstrom	3B P.Whitney	SS D.Bartell	2B F.Frisch
LF G.Harper	LF R.Bressler	LF R.Stephenson	LF E.Swanson	LF F.Leach	LF L.O'Doul	3B P.Traynor	SS C.Gelbert
CF E.Clark	CF J.Frederick	CF H.Wilson	CF E.Allen	CF E.Roush	CF D.Sothern	LF A.Comorosky	3B A.High
RF L.Richbourg	RF B.Herman	RF K.Cuyler	RF C.Walker	RF M.Ott	RF C.Klein	CF L.Waner	LF C.Hafey
C A.Spohrer	C V.Picinich	C Z.Taylor	C J.Gooch	C S.Hogan	C W.Lerian	RF P.Waner	CF T.Douthit
						C C.Hargreaves	RF E.Orsatti
O J.Welsh	O1 H.Hendrick	O C.Heathcote	C C.Sukeforth	C B.O'Farrell	C S.Davis	C R.Hemsley	C J.Wilson
3 J.Dugan	C H.DeBerry	3S C.Beck	S P.Pittinger	O C.Fullis	SO B.Friberg	S2 S.Adams	O W.Roettger
2 B.James	2 B.Rhiel	C M.Gonzalez	3 J.Stripp	2 R.Reese	O H.Peel	S3 S.Clarke	C W.Holm
C Z.Taylor	2 J.Flowers	1 C.Tolson	O P.Purdy	32 D.Farrell	O C.Farrell	O F.Brickell	C E.Smith
O H.Mueller	S J.Warner	C E.Grace	O B.Zitzmann	O J.Welsh	O T.Sigman	S C.Jones	/3 J.Butler
C L.Legett	O N.Cullop	/3 F.Blair	C L.Dixon	/1 P.Crawford	C G.Susce	/O I.Flagstead	2 C.Selph
OP J.Cooney	/S G.Wright	C J.Schulte	/1 W.Shaner	O T.Kaufmann	O J.O'Rourke	/C B.Linton	E.Delker
O P.Voyles	/O M.Carey	O J.Moore	H E.Crabtree	/2 D.Marshall	/1 T.Lyons	/S H.Riconda	/O B.Southworth
O B.Boyle	/O M.West	/C G.Hartnett	/C H.McMullen	/1 J.Cummings	P C.Willoughby	/3 J.Stroner	C B.Jonnard
/O B.Dunlap	H J.Gooch	/C T.Angley	/C I.Wingo	/1 B.Jordan	P L.Sweetland	/C J.O'Connell	F.Haney
/3 G.Robertson	P W.Clark	/O D.Taylor	P R.Lucas	/C R.Schalk	P R.Benge	/S B.Sankey	P B.Sherdel
/O R.Barron	P D.Vance	P C.Root	P E.Rixey	/O S.Leslie	P P.Collins	/1 B.Windle	P S.Johnson
/O J.Smith	P C.Dudley	P G.Bush	P J.May	/C P.Veltman	RP H.Elliott	R M.Ingram	P J.Haines
/C H.Gowdy	P D.McWeeny	P P.Malone	P P.Donohue	P C.Hubbell	RP B.McGraw	P B.Grimes	P M.Mitchell
/3 H.Peploski	RP C.Moore	P S.Blake	P D.Luque	P L.Benton	RP S.Dailey	P E.Brame	P H.Haid
/C B.Cronin	RP W.Ballou	P A.Nehf	RP K.Ash	P B.Walker	P L.Roy	P R.Kremer	P F.Frankhouse
/2 D.Farrell	P J.Morrison	RP M.Cvengros	RP R.Ehrhardt	P C.Mays	P L.Koupal	P J.Petty	P P.Alexander
/C J.Cummings	P L.Koupal	P H.Carlson	P R.Kolp	P F.Fitzsimmons	P H.Smythe	P S.Swetonic	P B.Hallahan
/C P.Collins	/P J.Elliott	P C.Jonnard	/P M.Gudat	RP R.Judd	/P J.Greene	RP C.Hill	/P A.Grabowski
H A.Weston	/P J.Pattison	P T.Horne	/P B.Frey	P J.Genewich	/P A.Ferguson	P L.French	/P J.Lindsey
/2 J.Evers	/P K.Greenfield	/P B.Frey	/P D.Kemner	/P R.Parmelee	/P E.Miller	P H.Meine	/P M.Holland
P B.Smith	/P B.Newsom	/P K.Penner	/P S.Johnson	/P J.Tennant	/P J.Milligan	P F.Fussell	/P H.Bell
P S.Seibold	/P J.Bradshaw	/P B.Osborn	/P P.Zahniser		/P J.Holloway	/P J.Dawson	/P B.Doak
P P.Jones	/P L.Roy	/P H.Grampp				/P L.Chagnon	/P C.Hill
P E.Brandt	/P C.Blethen					/P R.Erickson	/P H.Goldsmith
P B.Cantwell	/P A.Ferguson					/P L.Meadows	
P D.Leverett							
P B.Cunningham							
P A.Delaney							
/P R.Peery							
P B.Hearn							
/P K.Greenfield							
/P B.Clarkson							
/P J.Werts							
/P C.Touchstone							

TEAM	G	W	L	PCT	GB	R	OR	AB	H	2B	3B	HR	BB	SO	AVG	OBP	SLG	PRO	PRO+	BR	/A	PF	CHI	RC	SB	CS	SBA	SBR
CHI	156	98	54	.645		982	758	5471	1655	310	46	139	589	567	.303	.373	.452	.825	111	92	90	100	104	916	103			
PIT	154	88	65	.575	10.5	904	780	5490	1663	285	116	60	503	335	.303	.364	.430	.794	101	28	7	102	104	850	94			
NY	152	84	67	.556	13.5	897	709	5388	1594	251	47	136	482	405	.296	.358	.436	.794	103	18	21	100	106	827	85			
STL	154	78	74	.513	20	831	806	5364	1569	310	84	100	490	455	.293	.354	.438	.792	101	12	4	101	100	819	72			
PHI	154	71	82	.464	27.5	897	1032	5484	1693	305	51	153	573	470	.309	.377	.467	.844	108	125	62	107	92	951	59			
BRO	153	70	83	.458	28.5	755	888	5273	1535	282	69	99	504	454	.291	.355	.427	.782	102	-1	15	98	93	792	80			
CIN	155	66	88	.429	33	686	760	5269	1478	258	79	34	412	347	.281	.336	.379	.715	87	-133	-102	95	103	664	134			
BOS	154	56	98	.364	43	657	876	5291	1481	252	77	33	408	432	.280	.335	.375	.710	85	-142	-116	96	99	659	65			
TOT	616					6609		43030	12668	2253	569	754	3961	3465	.294	.357	.426	.783							692			

TEAM	CG	SH	SV	IP	H	H/G	HR	BB	SO	RAT	ERA	ERA+	OAV	OOB	PR	/A	PF	CPI	FA	E	DP	FW	PW	BW	SBW	DIF
CHI	79	14	21	1398²	1542	9.9	77	537	548	13.5	4.16	111	.284	.350	86	70	98	104	.975	154	169	1.4	6.4	8.2		6.0
PIT	79	5	13	1379	1530	10.0	96	439	409	13.0	4.36	109	.284	.340	54	62	101	98	.970	181	136	-.2	5.6	.6		5.5
NY	68	9	13	1372	1536	10.1	102	387	431	12.7	3.97	115	.287	.337	113	93	97	109	.975	158	163	.9	8.5	1.9		-2.8
STL	83	6	8	1359²	1604	10.6	101	474	453	13.9	4.66	100	.297	.357	8	-1	99	102	.971	174	149	.2	-.0	.4		1.6
PHI	45	5	24	1348	1743	11.6	122	616	369	16.0	6.13	85	.319	.391	-212	-142	110	96	.969	191	153	-.8	-12.9	5.6		2.6
BRO	59	8	16	1358	1553	10.3	92	549	549	14.2	4.92	94	.290	.360	-32	-48	98	95	.968	192	113	-.9	-4.4	1.4		-2.6
CIN	75	5	8	1369¹	1558	10.2	61	413	347	13.1	4.41	103	.292	.345	46	22	97	97	.974	162	148	.9	2.0	-9.3		-4.6
BOS	78	4	12	1352²	1604	10.7	103	530	366	14.4	5.12	91	.302	.367	-62	-68	99	99	.967	204	146	-1.5	-6.2	-10.6		-2.7
TOT	566	56	115	10937¹		10.4				13.8	4.71		.294	.357					.971	1416	1177					

Runs		Hits		Doubles		Triples		Home Runs		Total Bases	
Hornsby-Chi	156	O'Doul-Phi	254	Frederick-Bro	52	L.Waner-Pit	20	Klein-Phi	43	Hornsby-Chi	409
O'Doul-Phi	152	L.Waner-Pit	234	Hornsby-Chi	47	P.Waner-Pit	15	Ott-NY	42	Klein-Phi	405
Ott-NY	138	Hornsby-Chi	229	Hafey-StL	47	Walker-Cin	15	Wilson-Chi	39	O'Doul-Phi	397
Wilson-Chi	135	Terry-NY	226	Klein-Phi	45	Whitney-Phi	14	Hornsby-Chi	39	Wilson-Chi	355
L.Waner-Pit	134	Klein-Phi	219	Kelly-Cin	45			O'Doul-Phi	32	Herman-Bro	348

Runs Batted In		Runs Produced		Bases On Balls		Batting Average		On Base Percentage		Slugging Average	
Wilson-Chi	159	Hornsby-Chi	266	Ott-NY	113	O'Doul-Phi	.398	O'Doul-Phi	.465	Hornsby-Chi	.679
Ott-NY	151	Wilson-Chi	255	Grantham-Pit	93	Herman-Bro	.381	Hornsby-Chi	.459	Klein-Phi	.657
Hornsby-Chi	149	Ott-NY	247	P.Waner-Pit	89	Hornsby-Chi	.380	Ott-NY	.449	Ott-NY	.635
Klein-Phi	145	O'Doul-Phi	242	Hornsby-Chi	87	Terry-NY	.372	Stephenson-Chi	.445	Hafey-StL	.632
Bottomley-StL	137	Klein-Phi	228	Walker-Cin	85	Stephenson-Chi	.362	Cuyler-Chi	.438	O'Doul-Phi	.622

Production		Adjusted Production		Batter Runs		Adjusted Batter Runs		Clutch Hitting Index		Runs Created	
Hornsby-Chi	1.139	Hornsby-Chi	178	Hornsby-Chi	74.1	Hornsby-Chi	73.8	Traynor-Pit	139	Hornsby-Chi	183
O'Doul-Phi	1.087	Ott-NY	166	O'Doul-Phi	68.5	Ott-NY	58.9	Sheely-Pit	137	O'Doul-Phi	180
Ott-NY	1.084	Herman-Bro	160	Ott-NY	58.4	O'Doul-Phi	57.8	Comorosky-Pit	133	Klein-Phi	158
Klein-Phi	1.065	O'Doul-Phi	157	Klein-Phi	53.3	Herman-Bro	52.4	Grimm-Chi	127	Ott-NY	157
Herman-Bro	1.047	Wilson-Chi	155	Herman-Bro	49.6	Wilson-Chi	48.7	Kelly-Cin	122	Wilson-Chi	148

Total Average		Stolen Bases		Stolen Base Average		Stolen Base Runs		Fielding Runs		Total Player Rating	
Hornsby-Chi	1.338	Cuyler-Chi	43					Whitney-Phi	21.3	Hornsby-Chi	7.2
Ott-NY	1.287	Swanson-Cin	33					Maranville-Bos	19.5	Ott-NY	5.2
O'Doul-Phi	1.247	Frisch-StL	24					Jackson-NY	19.2	O'Doul-Phi	4.7
Herman-Bro	1.205	Herman-Bro	21					L.Waner-Pit	15.7	Jackson-NY	4.1
Cuyler-Chi	1.181	Allen-Cin	21					English-Chi	15.4	Wilson-Chi	3.2

Wins		Win Percentage		Games		Complete Games		Shutouts		Saves	
Malone-Chi	22	Root-Chi	.760	Bush-Chi	50	Lucas-Cin	28	Malone-Chi	5	Morrison-Bro	8
Root-Chi	19	Bush-Chi	.720	Willoughby-Phi	49			Root-Chi	4	Bush-Chi	8
Lucas-Cin	19	Grimes-Pit	.708	Sweetland-Phi	43			Fitzsimmons-NY	4	Koupal-Bro-Phi	6
		Malone-Chi	.688	Root-Chi	43						
		Kremer-Pit	.643	Collins-Phi	43						

Innings Pitched		Fewest Hits/Game		Fewest BB/Game		Strikeouts		Strikeouts/Game		Ratio	
Clark-Bro	279.0	Lucas-Cin	8.90	Vance-Bro	1.83	Malone-Chi	166	Malone-Chi	5.60	Lucas-Cin	10.87
Root-Chi	272.0	Hubbell-NY	9.17	Lucas-Cin	1.93	Clark-Bro	140	Vance-Bro	4.90	Hubbell-NY	11.62
Bush-Chi	270.2	Kremer-Pit	9.18	Petty-Pit	2.05	Vance-Bro	126	Clark-Bro	4.52	Kremer-Pit	11.65
Lucas-Cin	270.0	Johnson-StL	9.18	Hubbell-NY	2.25	Root-Chi	124	May-Cin	4.16	Petty-Pit	11.67
Hubbell-NY	268.0	Bush-Chi	9.21	Clark-Bro	2.29	Hubbell-NY	106	Root-Chi	4.10	Vance-Bro	11.67

Earned Run Average		Adjusted ERA		Opponents' Batting Avg.		Opponents' On Base Pct.		Starter Runs		Adjusted Starter Runs	
Walker-NY	3.09	Grimes-Pit	152	Lucas-Cin	.257	Lucas-Cin	.297	Grimes-Pit	40.8	Grimes-Pit	42.2
Grimes-Pit	3.13	Walker-NY	148	Johnson-StL	.265	Hubbell-NY	.313	Root-Chi	37.4	Root-Chi	34.4
Root-Chi	3.47	Root-Chi	133	Hubbell-NY	.265	Clark-Bro	.316	Malone-Chi	33.8	Malone-Chi	30.8
Malone-Chi	3.57	Johnson-StL	129	Bush-Chi	.265	Vance-Bro	.316	Lucas-Cin	33.3	Walker-NY	29.4
Lucas-Cin	3.60	Malone-Chi	129	Grimes-Pit	.269	Petty-Pit	.317	Walker-NY	32.0	Lucas-Cin	28.8

Clutch Pitching Index		Relief Runs		Adjusted Relief Runs		Relief Ranking		Total Pitcher Index		Total Baseball Ranking	
Mitchell-StL	129	Hill-Pit-StL	2.9	Hill-Pit-StL	3.3	Hill-Pit-StL	2.0	Grimes-Pit	4.7	Hornsby-Chi	7.2
Walker-NY	129	Cvengros-Chi	.5					Lucas-Cin	4.0	Ott-NY	5.2
Sweetland-Phi	116							Malone-Chi	3.0	Grimes-Pit	4.7
Grimes-Pit	116							Clark-Bro	2.5	O'Doul-Phi	4.7
Malone-Chi	115							Root-Chi	2.4	Jackson-NY	4.1

January 22 The Yankees announce they'll put numbers on the backs of their uniforms, and become the first baseball team to start continuous use of the numbers. The first numbers are based on positions in the batting order; thus, Babe Ruth will wear number three and Lou Gehrig four. By 1931 all AL teams will use them; it will be 1933 before all NL players are numbered.

February 20 The Red Sox announce they will play Sunday games, allowed for the first time in Boston, at Braves Field because Fenway Park is located too close to a church.

April 16 Cleveland outfielder Earl Averill becomes the first AL player to hit a home run on his first major league time at bat when he blasts an 0-and-2 pitch off Detroit's Earl Whitehill in the Indians' 5-4, 11-inning victory.

April 17 Babe Ruth and actress Claire Hodgson are married at five a.m. to avoid crowds. The Yankee opener with the Red Sox is rained out. The next day, in his first at bat against Red Ruffing, the Babe will hit a homer. Rounding second base, he doffs his cap to Claire in the stands. Gehrig adds a homer in the sixth, and New York wins 7–3.

April 28 The Red Sox play the first Sunday game in Boston history, but they do it at Braves Field losing to the A's, 7–3. Protests from a nearby church are the reason for the shift from Fenway. The Braves, rained out of their scheduled Sunday game on April 21, will play their first Sunday home game on May 5.

May 6 The AL announces that it will discontinue the MVP award. The NL will abandon it after this year; in 1931 the Baseball Writers Association will pick it up and conduct the balloting.

July 6 After watching the Tigers belt eight homers on the second, third, and fourth, the Browns use the off day to erect a screen in front of the right field pavilion. The screen stretches 156 feet from the foul pole toward center field, 310 feet down the line from home. In the next day's game, Heinie Manush will hit three balls off the screen against the Yankees' Waite Hoyt, while Ruth will hit two off it in the series. This screen will remain in place into the 1940s, the only stadium with extended outfield seating where it is impossible to catch a home run ball.

August 14 It is Charlie Gehringer Day in Detroit, and the popular second baseman handles 10 chances in the field, hits three singles and a homer, and steals home in a 17–13 win over the Yankees.

August 17 The Yankees buy pitcher Lefty Gomez from San Francisco (PCL) for delivery in September 1930.

September 25 Three days after turning the team over to coach Art Fletcher, Yankees manager Miller Huggins dies from blood poisoning at New York's St. Vincent Hospital. He was 49. On the day of his funeral in Cincinnati, the AL will cancel all games.

October 8 Howard Ehmke (7-2), who has been scouting the Cubs for a week, is the Athletics' surprise starter in Game 1 of the World Series at Chicago. A crowd of 50,740 Cubs fans watches Ehmke strike out a World Series-record 13 that will stand until Brooklyn's Carl Erskine fans 14 Yankees in 1953. He holds the Cubs scoreless until the ninth for a 3-1 win. Charlie Root (19-6) yields just three hits, but one is a home run by Jimmie Foxx in the seventh.

October 12 At age 45, John Quinn (11-9) gets a start against Charlie Root. After giving up a home run to Charlie Grimm with a man on in the third, Quinn serves up four straight singles to open the sixth, and in comes Rube Walberg (18-11). The inning ends with the score 7-0. Trailing 8-0 in the seventh, the Athletics, in the greatest rally in World Series history, shake Chicago by scoring 10 runs for a 10-8 victory. The most damaging play is Hack Wilson's misjudgment of a fly from George "Mule" Haas's bat, which goes for a three-run, inside-the-park home run.

October 14 After the teams take Sunday off, a special train from Washington brings President and Mrs. Hoover to Shibe Park to see if Howard Ehmke can wind up the Series against Pat Malone. They match zeros for three innings, but, with two outs in the fourth, a walk and three hits give the Cubs a 2-0 lead. Malone stifles the A's with two hits, and the 2-0 lead holds up into the ninth. The Athletics rally and come up with three runs, the winning run scoring on a Bing Miller double, and take the Series, four games to one.

BOSTON		CHICAGO		CLEVELAND		DETROIT		NEW YORK		PHILADELPHIA		ST.LOUIS		WASHINGTON	
M	B.Carrigan	M	L.Blackburne	M	R.Peckinpaugh	M	B.Harris	M	M.Huggins	M	C.Mack	M	D.Howley	M	W.Johnson
1B	P.Todt	1B	A.Shires	1B	L.Fonseca	1B	D.Alexander	M	A.Fletcher	1B	J.Foxx	1B	L.Blue	1B	J.Judge
2B	B.Regan	2B	J.Kerr	2B	J.Hodapp	2B	C.Gehringer	1B	L.Gehrig	2B	M.Bishop	2B	S.Melillo	2B	B.Myer
SS	H.Rhyne	SS	B.Cissell	SS	J.Tavener	SS	H.Schuble	2B	T.Lazzeri	SS	J.Boley	SS	R.Kress	SS	J.Cronin
3B	B.Reeves	3B	W.Kamm	3B	J.Sewell	3B	M.McManus	SS	L.Durocher	3B	S.Hale	3B	F.O'Rourke	3B	J.Hayes
LF	R.Scarritt	LF	A.Metzler	LF	C.Jamieson	LF	R.Johnson	3B	G.Robertson	LF	A.Simmons	LF	H.Manush	LF	G.Goslin
CF	J.Rothrock	CF	D.Hoffman	CF	E.Averill	CF	H.Rice	LF	B.Meusel	CF	M.Haas	CF	F.Schulte	CF	S.West
RF	Bi.Barrett	RF	C.Reynolds	RF	B.Falk	RF	H.Heilmann	CF	E.Combs	RF	B.Miller	RF	B.McGowan	RF	S.Rice
C	C.Berry	C	M.Berg	C	L.Sewell	C	E.Phillips	RF	B.Ruth	C	M.Cochrane	C	W.Schang	C	B.Tate
								C	B.Dickey						
O	E.Bigelow	1	B.Clancy	O	E.Morgan	C	B.Fothergill			O	J.Dykes	O	E.McNeely	32	O.Bluege
S2	B.Narleski	O	J.Watwood	S	R.Gardner	C	P.Hargrave	S3	M.Koenig	O	H.Summa	C	R.Badgro	C	M.Ruel
3	Bo.Barrett	2	B.Hunnefield	2	C.Lind	C	M.Shea	3S	L.Lary	C	C.Perkins	C	R.Ferrell	O	R.Barnes
C	J.Heving	O	D.Taitt	O2	D.Porter	C	J.Stone	O	L.Durst	C	J.Cronin	C	C.Manion	O	R.Spencer
O	K.Williams	C	B.Crouse	O	G.Myatt	S	Y.Wuestling	O	S.Byrd	1	G.Burns	2	O.Brannan	1	H.Boss
C	A.Gaston	C	C.Autry	/1	J.Hauser	S	B.Akers	O	B.Paschal	/2	W.French	/S	E.Roetz	/1	C.Gooch
S2	W.Gerber	2	B.Redfern	S	J.Burnett	C	R.Hayworth	/2	B.Bengough	3	B.Morse	3	L.Dondero	O	I.Flagstead
2	G.Gillis	O	J.Mostil	O	G.Hartley	C	F.Sigafoos	C	J.Grabowski	/O	B.LeBourveau	/O	T.Jenkins	/O	S.Harris
O	D.Taitt	/2	F.Sigafoos	R	D.Jessee	S	N.Richardson	/O	A.Jorgens	/S	E.McNair	/3	J.Austin	/2	S.Stewart
O	I.Flagstead	H	B.Barrett			/2	B.Harris	H	J.Wera	H	E.Collins			/O	D.Land
/O	J.Cicero	H	K.Swanson	P	W.Hudlin	H	L.Woodall	/3	B.Harris	/O	D.Cramer	P	S.Gray	H	P.Gharrity
C	C.Asbjornson			P	W.Ferrell			R	L.Funk	/C	C.Mattox	P	A.Crowder	/O	N.Altrock
1	J.Standaert	P	T.Thomas	P	J.Miller	P	G.Uhle			/S	J.Hassler	P	G.Blaeholder		
/C	E.Connolly	P	T.Lyons	P	J.Shaute	P	E.Whitehill	P	G.Pipgras	/3	R.Miller	P	R.Collins	P	F.Marberry
/O	J.Ryan	P	R.Faber	P	J.Miljus	P	V.Sorrell	P	W.Hoyt			P	L.Stewart	P	B.Hadley
		P	H.McKain			P	O.Carroll	P	E.Wells	P	L.Grove	RP	C.Kimsey	P	G.Braxton
P	R.Ruffing	P	G.Adkins	P	K.Holloway	RP	A.Prudhomme	P	H.Pennock	RP	R.Walberg	RP	D.Coffman	P	L.Brown
P	M.Gaston			P	J.Zinn	RP	L.Stoner	P	R.Sherid	P	G.Earnshaw			P	S.Jones
P	J.Russell	P	E.Walsh	P	M.Shoffner			RP	W.Moore	P	J.Quinn	/P	J.Ogden		
P	D.MacFayden	P	D.Dugan	P	G.Grant	P	E.Yde			P	B.Shores	/P	E.Strelecki	P	B.Burke
P	E.Morris	P	B.Weiland	P	M.Harder	P	S.Graham	P	F.Heimach			/P	F.Stiely	P	M.Thomas
RP	E.Carroll	/P	T.Blankenship	/P	C.Brown	P	G.Smith	P	T.Zachary	P	E.Rommel	P	P.Hopkins	P	A.Liska
		/P	D.Henry	/P	J.Moore	/P	A.Herring	P	H.Johnson	P	H.Ehmke	/P	H.Cobb	/P	P.Hopkins
P	B.Bayne	P	S.Connally			/P	C.Hogsett	P	G.Rhodes	P	C.Yerkes	/P	O.Estrada	/P	W.Beall
P	R.Dobens	/P	J.Byrne			P	P.Page	/P	B.Nekola	P	O.Orwoll			/P	P.McCullough
P	E.Durham	/P	L.Blackburne			/P	W.Wyatt	/P	M.Thomas	P	B.Breckinridge			/P	D.Savidge
/P	H.Lisenbee					/P	J.Billings							/P	A.Campbell
/P	P.Simmons					/P	E.Vangilder							/P	E.Wineapple
/P	H.Bradley					/P	F.Barnes								

TEAM	G	W	L	PCT	GB	R	OR	AB	H	2B	3B	HR	BB	SO	AVG	OBP	SLG	PRO	PRO+	BR	/A	PF	CHI	RC	SB	CS	SBA	SBR
PHI	151	104	46	.693	–	901	615	5204	1539	288	76	122	543	440	.296	.365	.451	.816	111	113	81	104	102	875	61	38	62	-5
NY	154	88	66	.571	18	899	775	5379	1587	262	74	142	554	518	.295	.364	.450	.814	123	111	171	93	101	892	51	44	54	-11
CLE	152	81	71	.533	24	717	736	5187	1525	294	79	62	453	363	.294	.354	.417	.771	100	26	-2	104	92	763	75	85	47	-29
STL	154	79	73	.520	26	733	713	5174	1426	277	64	46	589	431	.276	.352	.381	.733	91	-33	-61	104	100	723	72	46	61	-6
WAS	153	71	81	.467	34	730	776	5237	1445	244	66	48	556	400	.276	.347	.375	.722	90	-56	-61	101	102	706	86	61	59	-11
DET	155	70	84	.455	36	926	928	5592	1671	339	97	110	521	496	.299	.360	.453	.813	114	110	106	100	100	914	95	72	57	-15
CHI	152	59	93	.388	46	627	792	5248	1406	240	74	37	425	436	.268	.325	.363	.688	83	-134	-127	99	102	633	109	65	63	-6
BOS	155	58	96	.377	48	605	803	5160	1377	285	69	28	413	494	.267	.325	.365	.690	85	-130	-115	98	99	616	85	80	52	-23
TOT	613					6138		42181	11976	2229	599	595	4054	3578	.284	.349	.407	.756							634	491	56	-104

TEAM	CG	SH	SV	IP	H	H/G	HR	BB	SO	RAT	ERA	ERA+	OAV	OOB	PR	/A	PF	CPI	FA	E	DP	FW	PW	BW	SBW	DIF
PHI	70	9	24	1357	1371	9.1	73	487	573	12.4	3.44	123	.264	.329	121	119	100	105	.975	146	117	2.6	11.2	7.6	.8	6.8
NY	64	12	18	1366²	1475	9.7	83	485	484	13.1	4.19	92	.278	.341	7	-52	91	96	.971	178	153	.8	-4.9	16.1	.2	-1.2
CLE	80	8	10	1352	1570	10.5	56	488	389	13.9	4.05	99	.295	.357	28	57	105	109	.968	198	162	-.6	5.4	-.2	-1.5	1.9
STL	83	15	10	1371	1469	9.6	100	462	415	12.8	4.08	108	.279	.340	25	51	104	102	.975	156	148	2.2	4.8	-5.8	.7	1.1
WAS	62	3	17	1354¹	1429	9.5	48	496	494	12.9	4.34	98	.276	.342	-15	-16	100	89	.968	195	156	-.3	-1.5	-5.8	.2	2.4
DET	82	5	9	1390¹	1641	10.6	73	646	467	15.0	4.96	86	.301	.377	-111	-105	101	100	.961	242	149	-3.0	-9.9	10.0	-.2	-3.9
CHI	78	5	7	1357²	1481	9.8	84	505	328	13.4	4.41	97	.284	.351	-26	-22	101	98	.970	188	153	.0	-2.1	-12.0	.7	-3.7
BOS	84	9	5	1366²	1537	10.1	78	496	416	13.6	4.43	96	.291	.355	-28	-25	101	100	.965	218	159	-1.6	-2.4	-10.8	-.9	-3.3
TOT	603	66	100	10916		9.9				13.4	4.24		.284	.349					.969	1521	1197					

Runs		Hits		Doubles		Triples		Home Runs		Total Bases	
Gehringer-Det	131	Gehringer-Det	215	Manush-StL	45	Gehringer-Det	19	Ruth-NY	46	Simmons-Phi	373
Johnson-Det	128	Alexander-Det	215	Johnson-Det	45	Scarritt-Bos	17	Gehrig-NY	35	Alexander-Det	363
Gehrig-NY	127	Simmons-Phi	212	Gehringer-Det	45	B.Miller-Phi	16	Simmons-Phi	34	Ruth-NY	348
Foxx-Phi	123	Fonseca-Cle	209	Fonseca-Cle	44			Foxx-Phi	33	Gehringer-Det	337
Ruth-NY	121	Manush-StL	204					Alexander-Det	25		

Runs Batted In		Runs Produced		Bases On Balls		Batting Average		On Base Percentage		Slugging Average	
Simmons-Phi	157	Simmons-Phi	237	Bishop-Phi	128	Fonseca-Cle	.369	Foxx-Phi	.463	Ruth-NY	.697
Ruth-NY	154	Ruth-NY	229	Blue-StL	126	Simmons-Phi	.365	Gehrig-NY	.431	Simmons-Phi	.642
Alexander-Det	137	Gehringer-Det	224	Gehrig-NY	122	Manush-StL	.355	Ruth-NY	.430	Foxx-Phi	.625
Gehrig-NY	126	Alexander-Det	222	Foxx-Phi	103	Lazzeri-NY	.354	Lazzeri-NY	.429	Gehrig-NY	.584
Heilmann-Det	120	Gehrig-NY	218	Cronin-Was	85	Foxx-Phi	.354	Fonseca-Cle	.427	Alexander-Det	.580

Production		Adjusted Production		Batter Runs		Adjusted Batter Runs		Clutch Hitting Index		Runs Created	
Ruth-NY	1.128	Ruth-NY	199	Foxx-Phi	63.1	Ruth-NY	71.2	West-Was	130	Foxx-Phi	154
Foxx-Phi	1.088	Foxx-Phi	171	Ruth-NY	61.9	Gehrig-NY	61.1	Heilmann-Det	129	Ruth-NY	150
Simmons-Phi	1.040	Gehrig-NY	170	Gehrig-NY	51.6	Foxx-Phi	58.0	Kress-StL	123	Gehrig-NY	146
Gehrig-NY	1.015	Lazzeri-NY	164	Simmons-Phi	50.3	Lazzeri-NY	52.4	Myer-Was	119	Simmons-Phi	145
Lazzeri-NY	.991	Simmons-Phi	158	Lazzeri-NY	43.9	Simmons-Phi	45.6	Falk-Cle	118	Alexander-Det	140

Total Average		Stolen Bases		Stolen Base Average		Stolen Base Runs		Fielding Runs		Total Player Rating	
Ruth-NY	1.288	Gehringer-Det	27	Gehringer-Det	75.0	Gehringer-Det	2.7	Durocher-NY	26.2	Ruth-NY	5.0
Foxx-Phi	1.261	Cissell-Chi	25	B.Miller-Phi	72.7	B.Miller-Phi	1.8	Kerr-Chi	24.0	Simmons-Phi	4.9
Gehrig-NY	1.151	B.Miller-Phi	24	Myer-Was	72.0	Myer-Was	1.2	Melillo-StL	22.5	Lazzeri-NY	4.8
Simmons-Phi	1.097	Rothrock-Bos	23	Reynolds-Chi	67.9	Goslin-Was	1.2	Simmons-Phi	17.3	Gehringer-Det	3.9
Lazzeri-NY	1.041	Johnson-Det	20	Rice-Was	66.7	Berg-Chi	.9	West-Was	15.0	Gehrig-NY	3.7

Wins		Win Percentage		Games		Complete Games		Shutouts		Saves	
Earnshaw-Phi	24	Grove-Phi	.769	Marberry-Was	49	Thomas-Chi	24	MacFayden-Bos	4	Marberry-Was	11
Ferrell-Cle	21	Earnshaw-Phi	.750	Uhle-Det	44	Uhle-Det	23	Gray-StL	4	Moore-NY	8
Grove-Phi	20	Ferrell-Cle	.677	Gray-StL	43	Gray-StL	23	Crowder-StL	4	Shores-Phi	7
Marberry-Was	19	Walberg-Phi	.621	Ferrell-Cle	43	Hudlin-Cle	22	Blaeholder-StL	4	Ferrell-Cle	5
		Marberry-Was	.613			Lyons-Chi	21				

Innings Pitched		Fewest Hits/Game		Fewest BB/Game		Strikeouts		Strikeouts/Game		Ratio	
Gray-StL	305.0	Earnshaw-Phi	8.23	Russell-Bos	1.58	Grove-Phi	170	Grove-Phi	5.56	Marberry-Was	11.07
Hudlin-Cle	280.1	Wells-NY	8.33	Pennock-NY	1.60	Earnshaw-Phi	149	Earnshaw-Phi	5.27	Thomas-Chi	11.44
Grove-Phi	275.1	Marberry-Was	8.38	Thomas-Chi	2.08	Pipgras-NY	125	Pipgras-NY	4.99	Grove-Phi	11.83
Walberg-Phi	267.2	Walberg-Phi	8.61	Uhle-Det	2.10	Marberry-Was	121	Hadley-Was	4.52	Walberg-Phi	11.94
Crowder-StL	266.2	McKain-Chi	9.00	Quinn-Phi	2.18			Marberry-Was	4.35	Faber-Chi	11.96

Earned Run Average		Adjusted ERA		Opponents' Batting Avg.		Opponents' On Base Pct.		Starter Runs		Adjusted Starter Runs	
Grove-Phi	2.81	Grove-Phi	150	Earnshaw-Phi	.241	Marberry-Was	.308	Grove-Phi	43.7	Grove-Phi	43.3
Marberry-Was	3.06	Marberry-Was	139	Wells-NY	.248	Thomas-Chi	.310	Marberry-Was	32.9	Hudlin-Cle	34.3
Thomas-Chi	3.19	Thomas-Chi	134	Marberry-Was	.252	Grove-Phi	.316	Thomas-Chi	30.3	Marberry-Was	32.8
Earnshaw-Phi	3.29	Hudlin-Cle	133	Walberg-Phi	.254	Hudlin-Cle	.318	Hudlin-Cle	28.1	Thomas-Chi	31.4
Hudlin-Cle	3.34	Earnshaw-Phi	129	Grove-Phi	.262	Walberg-Phi	.320	Earnshaw-Phi	27.0	Earnshaw-Phi	26.6

Clutch Pitching Index		Relief Runs		Adjusted Relief Runs	Relief Ranking	Total Pitcher Index		Total Baseball Ranking	
McKain-Chi	130	Moore-NY	.7			Hudlin-Cle	3.9	Ruth-NY	5.0
M.Gaston-Bos	116					Marberry-Was	3.8	Simmons-Phi	4.9
Shaute-Cle	116					Grove-Phi	3.5	Lazzeri-NY	4.8
Ferrell-Cle	116					Thomas-Chi	3.4	Gehringer-Det	3.9
Collins-StL	113					Ferrell-Cle	3.4	Hudlin-Cle	3.9

January 20 Commissioner Kenesaw Mountain Landis bans boxing for all players in baseball following the brief boxing career of Art Shires. "Whataman" Shires fought football players as well as baseball players, and his challenge to Hack Wilson purportedly prompts the ban.

April 28* The first night game in Organized Baseball—played with temporary lights—is played in the Class C Western Association with 1,000 fans on hand. Home team Independence loses to Muskogee, 13-3.

April 29 Suspicions that the ball is the liveliest ever increase as 123 runs are scored in seven major league games. (The NL will hit .303 as a whole this year, and the AL hits .288.)

May 2* Des Moines (Western League) defeats Wichita, 13-6, to open the first ballpark with permanently installed lights. The Demons' victory is the first night game to be broadcast nationally.

May 12 The wind is blowing out at Wrigley Field as Giants pitcher Larry Benton sets a modern major league record (since tied several times) by surrendering six home runs in a single game, but he still gets credit for the 14-12 victory. (Benton also hits a home run.)

June 3 Grover Cleveland Alexander is released by the Phillies after posting a 0-3 record. He ends his career thinking he has the NL record for most wins at 373, one more than Christy Mathewson. In 1946, a win disallowed in 1902 is restored to Mathewson's record, to leave the two pitchers in a tie.

August 26 Hack Wilson hits his 44th home run, breaking Chuck Klein's one-year-old NL record, as the Cubs defeat the Pirates, 7-5.

September 12 Brooklyn catcher Al Lopez drives one over the head of Cincinnati left fielder Bob Meusel, and the ball bounces into the bleachers at Ebbets Field. It will be the major leagues' last recorded bounce home run, as the NL rules after the season that such a hit will henceforth be a double. The AL had made the change after the 1929 season.

September 16 At Ebbets Field, the Cards (82–60) and Brooklyn (84–60) square off before 30,000. St. Louis pitcher Bill Hallahan retires the first 20 batters, before he fumbles a grounder. A single in the eighth spoils his no-hitter. The Cards finally score in the 10th and hold on for a 1–0 win. The victory gives the Cards first place by a percentage point over Brooklyn, losers for the first time in 11 games.

September 20 Hack Wilson records his 176th RBI, passing Lou Gehrig's 1927 major league record.

September 27 Hack Wilson clubs two home runs to finish with a still-standing NL record of 56. The Cubs win 13-8 over the Reds at Wrigley as Pat Malone wins his 20th of the year.

September 27 Wally Berger hits his 38th home run for the Braves, at Ebbets Field, as Boston tops Brooklyn 7-1. It was a record for all rookies at the time and still stands as an NL record, later tied by Frank Robinson.

September 28 The Cubs bring down the season's curtain as Wilson has his 189th and 190th RBIs in a 12-11 victory over the Reds. With Riggs Stephenson and Kiki Cuyler each driving in 100 runs, the Cubs have an all-100 RBI outfield. (The Boston outfield in 1894 also had the same credentials.)

September 28 Bill Terry goes hitless as the Giants edge the Dodgers for third place with a 10-inning win over the Phillies at the Polo Grounds. He finishes at .401, the last NL player to hit over .400. The Giants set a 20th century single season batting average record of .319. (The Phillies hit .349 in 1894.)

September 28 Dizzy Dean scatters three hits for a 3-1 victory in his major league debut. The 19-year-old rookie, fresh from the Texas League, pitches the final game of the season for the pennant-winning Cardinals.

December 13 The 15-year career of George Sisler ends as the Boston Braves release him. A lifetime .340 hitter who twice led the AL with averages above .400, Sisler will be among the first to be elected to the Baseball Hall of Fame when he is enshrined in 1939.

BOSTON		BROOKLYN		CHICAGO		CINCINNATI		NEW YORK		PHILADELPHIA		PITTSBURGH		ST. LOUIS	
M	B.McKechnie	M	W.Robinson	M	J.McCarthy	M	D.Howley	M	J.McGraw	M	B.Shotton	M	J.Ens	M	G.Street
1B	G.Sisler	1B	D.Bissonette	M	R.Hornsby	1B	J.Stripp	1B	B.Terry	1B	D.Hurst	1B	G.Suhr	1B	J.Bottomley
2B	F.Maguire	2B	N.Finn	1B	C.Grimm	2B	H.Ford	2B	H.Critz	2B	F.Thompson	2B	G.Grantham	2B	F.Frisch
SS	R.Maranville	SS	G.Wright	2B	F.Blair	SS	L.Durocher	SS	T.Jackson	SS	T.Thevenow	SS	D.Bartell	SS	C.Gelbert
3B	B.Chatham	3B	W.Gilbert	SS	W.English	3B	T.Cuccinello	3B	F.Lindstrom	3B	P.Whitney	3B	P.Traynor	3B	S.Adams
LF	W.Berger	LF	R.Bressler	3B	L.Bell	LF	C.Walker	LF	F.Leach	LF	L.O'Doul	LF	A.Comorosky	LF	C.Hafey
CF	J.Welsh	CF	J.Frederick	LF	R.Stephenson	CF	B.Meusel	CF	W.Roettger	CF	D.Sothern	CF	L.Waner	CF	T.Douthit
RF	L.Richbourg	RF	B.Herman	CF	H.Wilson	RF	H.Heilmann	RF	M.Ott	RF	C.Klein	RF	P.Waner	RF	G.Watkins
C	A.Spohrer	C	A.Lopez	RF	K.Cuyler	C	C.Sukeforth	C	S.Hogan	C	S.Davis	C	R.Hemsley	C	J.Wilson
				C	G.Hartnett										
O	E.Clark	2	J.Flowers	S2	C.Beck	O	E.Swanson	C	B.O'Farrell	2O	B.Friberg	O	F.Brickell	O	S.Fisher
1	F.Neun	2O	E.Moore	O	D.Taylor	C	J.Gooch	O	E.Allen	1	M.Sherlock	O	A.Bool	C	G.Mancuso
O3	R.Moore	O	H.Hendrick	1	G.Kelly	O	M.Callaghan	S2	D.Marshall	O	F.Brickell	3S	C.Engle	3	A.High
C	B.Cronin	O	I.Boone	O	C.Heathcote	21	P.Crawford	O3	R.Reese	C	T.Rensa	O	I.Flagstead	1O	E.Orsatti
32	R.Rollings	C	H.DeBerry	S	D.Farrell	1	G.Kelly	2	P.Crawford	O	H.McCurdy	O	J.Mosolf	O	R.Blades
3	G.Robertson	O	V.Picinich	2	R.Hornsby	2	H.Critz	/S	D.Bancroft	O	T.Sigman	O	D.Sothern	O	H.Peel
3	B.Rhiel	O	H.Lee	C	Z.Taylor	O	E.Allen	/O	C.Fullis	/O	C.Williams	/O	G.Dugas	/O	D.Farrell
/O	B.Dunlap	S	G.Slade	/1	C.Tolson	/O	N.Cullop	/O	J.Moore	/C	J.Spotts	C	C.Hargreaves	/O	G.Puccinelli
C	H.Gowdy	/3	J.Warner			3	C.Dressen	/O	H.Rosenberg			/S	B.Sankey	/C	E.Smith
/2	B.James					/C	L.Styles	/C	F.Healy			/2	S.Clarke	H	P.Martin
/O	B.Boyle	P	D.Vance	P	P.Malone	H	H.Riconda	H	S.Leslie	P	P.Collins	/S	H.Groskloss	P	B.Hallahan
R	O.Kahn	P	W.Clark	P	G.Bush	P	B.Frey	P	B.Walker	P	R.Benge	P	R.Kremer	P	S.Johnson
P	S.Seibold	P	D.Luque	P	C.Root	P	R.Lucas	P	C.Hubbell	P	L.Sweetland	P	L.French	/P	J.Haines
P	B.Smith	P	J.Elliott	P	S.Blake	P	L.Benton	P	F.Fitzsimmons	P	C.Willoughby	P	E.Brame	/P	B.Grimes
P	B.Cantwell	P	R.Phelps	P	B.Teachout	P	R.Kolp	RP	H.Pruett	P	H.Collard	P	G.Spencer	/P	F.Rhem
P	T.Zachary		R.Moss	RP	L.Nelson	P	E.Rixey	P	C.Mitchell	RP	H.Elliott	P	H.Meine	RP	H.Bell
P	E.Brandt	P	S.Thurston	P	B.Osborn	RP	S.Johnson	RP	J.Heving	P	H.Smythe	P	S.Swetonic	RP	J.Lindsey
RP	B.Cunningham	P	C.Dudley	/P	H.Carlson	RP	A.Campbell				S.Hansen	P	L.Chagnon	P	A.Grabowski
P	B.Sherdel	/P	J.Morrison	/P	J.Petty	P	J.May				C.Nichols	/P	S.Wood	P	B.Sherdel
P	F.Frankhouse	/P	F.Heimach	P	A.Shealy	P	K.Ash			P	B.Phillips	/P	J.Petty	/P	H.Haid
P	B.Grimes	/P	B.Newsom	P	M.Moss	/P	P.Donohue			P	L.Koupal	P	P.Jones	/P	F.Frankhouse
/P	K.Jones	/P	J.Faulkner	/P	B.McAfee	/P	D.McWeeny			/P	J.Milligan	P	R.Erickson	/P	C.Hill
/P	J.Cooney	/P	C.Moore	/P	L.Warneke	/P	O.Carroll			/P	P.Alexander	/P	L.Stoner	/P	T.Kaufmann
/P	B.Brown					/P	A.Eckert			P	B.Speece	/P	M.Lang	/P	D.Dean
						/P	B.Wysong					/P	A.Bednar	/P	C.Mitchell
												/P	B.Walter		

TEAM	G	W	L	PCT	GB	R	OR	AB	H	2B	3B	HR	BB	SO	AVG	OBP	SLG	PRO	PRO+	BR	/A	PF	CHI	RC	SB	CS	SBA	SBR
STL	154	92	62	.597		1004	784	5512	1732	373	89	104	479	496	.314	.372	.471	.843	105	72	40	103	104	944	72			
CHI	156	90	64	.584	2	998	870	5581	1722	305	72	171	588	635	.309	.378	.481	.859	111	110	103	101	98	1001	70			
NY	154	87	67	.565	5	959	814	5553	1769	264	83	143	422	382	.319	.369	.473	.842	110	67	87	98	101	941	59			
BRO	154	86	68	.558	6	871	738	5433	1654	303	73	122	440	541	.304	.364	.454	.818	103	21	32	99	97	881	53			
PIT	154	80	74	.519	12	891	928	5346	1622	285	119	86	494	449	.303	.365	.449	.814	101	15	12	100	101	862	76			
BOS	154	70	84	.455	22	693	835	5356	1503	246	78	66	332	397	.281	.326	.393	.719	81	-186	-164	97	105	669	69			
CIN	154	59	95	.383	33	665	857	5245	1475	265	67	74	445	489	.281	.339	.400	.739	87	-135	-100	95	94	703	48			
PHI	156	52	102	.338	40	944	1199	5667	1783	345	44	126	450	459	.315	.367	.458	.825	97	37	-31	107	100	929	34			
TOT	618					7025		43693	13260	2386	625	892	3691	3848	.303	.360	.448	.808						481				

TEAM	CG	SH	SV	IP	H	H/G	HR	BB	SO	RAT	ERA	ERA+	OAV	OOB	PR	/A	PF	CPI	FA	E	DP	FW	PW	BW	SBW	DIF
STL	63	5	21	1380²	1596	10.4	87	476	639	13.7	4.39	114	.294	.353	89	95	101	104	.970	183	176	.2	8.4	3.5		2.9
CHI	67	6	12	1403²	1642	10.5	111	528	601	14.1	4.80	102	.294	.357	26	14	98	99	.973	170	167	1.0	1.2	9.1		1.6
NY	64	6	19	1363¹	1546	10.2	117	439	522	13.3	4.61	103	.290	.348	54	18	95	99	.974	164	144	1.3	1.6	7.7		-.5
BRO	74	13	15	1372	1480	9.7	115	394	526	12.4	4.03	122	.278	.330	144	135	99	102	.972	174	167	.7	11.9	2.8		-6.4
PIT	80	7	13	1361¹	1730	11.4	128	438	393	14.5	5.24	95	.313	.367	-41	-40	100	101	.965	216	164	-1.8	-3.5	1.1		7.2
BOS	71	6	11	1361	1624	10.7	117	475	424	14.0	4.91	100	.302	.360	9	3	99	102	.971	178	167	.4	.3	-14.5		6.8
CIN	61	6	11	1335	1650	11.1	75	394	361	13.9	5.08	95	.310	.361	-15	-37	97	96	.973	161	164	1.4	-3.3	-8.8		-7.3
PHI	54	3	7	1372²	1993	13.1	142	543	384	16.8	6.71	81	.346	.405	-266	-189	110	99	.962	239	169	-3.0	-16.7	-2.7		-2.6
TOT	534	52	109	10949²		10.9				14.1	4.97		.303	.360					.970	1485	1318					

Runs		Hits		Doubles		Triples		Home Runs		Total Bases	
Klein-Phi	158	Terry-NY	254	Klein-Phi	59	Comorosky-Pit	23	Wilson-Chi	56	Klein-Phi	445
Cuyler-Chi	155	Klein-Phi	250	Cuyler-Chi	50	P.Waner-Pit	18	Klein-Phi	40	Wilson-Chi	423
English-Chi	152	Herman-Bro	241	Herman-Bro	48	English-Chi	17	Berger-Bos	38	Herman-Bro	416
Wilson-Chi	146	Lindstrom-NY	231	Comorosky-Pit	47	Cuyler-Chi	17	Hartnett-Chi	37	Terry-NY	392
Herman-Bro	143	Cuyler-Chi	228	Frisch-StL	46	Terry-NY	15	Herman-Bro	35	Cuyler-Chi	351

Runs Batted In		Runs Produced		Bases On Balls		Batting Average		On Base Percentage		Slugging Average	
Wilson-Chi	190	Klein-Phi	288	Wilson-Chi	105	Terry-NY	.401	Ott-NY	.458	Wilson-Chi	.723
Klein-Phi	170	Wilson-Chi	280	Ott-NY	103	Herman-Bro	.393	Herman-Bro	.455	Klein-Phi	.687
Cuyler-Chi	134	Cuyler-Chi	276	English-Chi	100	Klein-Phi	.386	Wilson-Chi	.454	Herman-Bro	.678
Herman-Bro	130	Terry-NY	245	Grantham-Pit	81	O'Doul-Phi	.383	O'Doul-Phi	.453	Hafey-StL	.652
Terry-NY	129	Herman-Bro	238	Suhr-Pit	80	Lindstrom-NY	.379	Terry-NY	.452	Hartnett-Chi	.630

Production		Adjusted Production		Batter Runs		Adjusted Batter Runs		Clutch Hitting Index		Runs Created	
Wilson-Chi	1.177	Wilson-Chi	177	Wilson-Chi	75.4	Wilson-Chi	74.2	Thevenow-Phi	138	Wilson-Chi	189
Herman-Bro	1.132	Herman-Bro	171	Herman-Bro	68.7	Herman-Bro	70.7	Traynor-Pit	133	Klein-Phi	186
Klein-Phi	1.123	Terry-NY	159	Klein-Phi	67.3	Terry-NY	61.0	Cuyler-Chi	129	Herman-Bro	183
Terry-NY	1.071	Klein-Phi	155	Terry-NY	57.6	Klein-Phi	55.3	Frisch-StL	126	Terry-NY	170
Hafey-StL	1.059	Ott-NY	152	O'Doul-Phi	46.9	Ott-NY	48.3	Whitney-Phi	120	Cuyler-Chi	148

Total Average		Stolen Bases		Stolen Base Average		Stolen Base Runs		Fielding Runs		Total Player Rating	
Wilson-Chi	1.411	Cuyler-Chi	37					Frisch-StL	27.5	Klein-Phi	5.8
Herman-Bro	1.351	P.Waner-Pit	18					Klein-Phi	23.0	Terry-NY	5.0
Klein-Phi	1.274	Herman-Bro	18					Whitney-Phi	20.3	Wilson-Chi	4.8
Ott-NY	1.224							Terry-NY	12.6	Lindstrom-NY	4.8
Terry-NY	1.208							Cuyler-Chi	12.2	Frisch-StL	4.4

Wins		Win Percentage		Games		Complete Games		Shutouts		Saves	
Malone-Chi	20	Fitzsimmons-NY	.731	Elliott-Phi	48	Malone-Chi	22	Vance-Bro	4	Bell-StL	8
Kremer-Pit	20	Malone-Chi	.690	Collins-Phi	47	Brame-Pit	22	Root-Chi	4	Heving-NY	6
Fitzsimmons-NY	19	Brame-Pit	.680	Bush-Chi	46	French-Pit	21	Hubbell-NY	3	Clark-Bro	6
		Kremer-Pit	.625	Pruett-NY	45	Vance-Bro	20	French-Pit	3		
		Hallahan-StL	.625	Malone-Chi	45	Seibold-Bos	20				

Innings Pitched		Fewest Hits/Game		Fewest BB/Game		Strikeouts		Strikeouts/Game		Ratio	
Kremer-Pit	276.0	Vance-Bro	8.39	Clark-Bro	1.71	Hallahan-StL	177	Hallahan-StL	6.71	Vance-Bro	10.47
French-Pit	274.2	Hallahan-StL	8.84	Kolp-Cin	1.82	Vance-Bro	173	Vance-Bro	6.02	Clark-Bro	11.11
Malone-Chi	271.2	Fitzsimmons-NY	9.23	Johnson-StL	1.82	Malone-Chi	142	Root-Chi	5.07	Kolp-Cin	11.44
Vance-Bro	258.2	Elliott-Bro	9.26	Lucas-Cin	1.88	Root-Chi	124	Malone-Chi	4.70	Fitzsimmons-NY	11.63
Seibold-Bos	251.0	Clark-Bro	9.41	Vance-Bro	1.91	Hubbell-NY	117	Johnson-StL	4.41	Johnson-StL	12.33

Earned Run Average		Adjusted ERA		Opponents' Batting Avg.		Opponents' On Base Pct.		Starter Runs		Adjusted Starter Runs	
Vance-Bro	2.61	Vance-Bro	188	Vance-Bro	.246	Vance-Bro	.289	Vance-Bro	67.9	Vance-Bro	66.2
Hubbell-NY	3.87	Elliott-Bro	124	Hallahan-StL	.260	Clark-Bro	.306	Malone-Chi	31.1	Malone-Chi	28.5
Walker-NY	3.93	Malone-Chi	124	Fitzsimmons-NY	.266	Fitzsimmons-NY	.314	Hubbell-NY	29.5	Hubbell-NY	23.1
Malone-Chi	3.94	Grimes-Bos-StL	123	Walker-NY	.268	Kolp-Cin	.314	Walker-NY	28.5	Seibold-Bos	22.7
Elliott-Bro	3.95	Hubbell-NY	122	Malone-Chi	.271	Hubbell-NY	.327	Seibold-Bos	23.7	Walker-NY	22.0

Clutch Pitching Index		Relief Runs		Adjusted Relief Runs		Relief Ranking		Total Pitcher Index		Total Baseball Ranking	
Grimes-Bos-StL	119	Bell-StL	13.7	Bell-StL	14.3	Bell-StL	10.0	Vance-Bro	6.6	Vance-Bro	6.6
Smith-Bos	117	Lindsey-StL	6.4	Lindsey-StL	6.9	Lindsey-StL	7.8	Malone-Chi	2.8	Klein-Phi	5.8
Haines-StL	109	Johnson-Cin	.3					Grimes-Bos-StL	2.6	Terry-NY	5.0
Vance-Bro	108							Fitzsimmons-NY	2.2	Wilson-Chi	4.8
Seibold-Bos	107							Walker-NY	2.1	Lindstrom-NY	4.8

February 12 Connie Mack is awarded the prestigious Edward W. Bok Prize given to the Philadelphian who has done the most for the city in the past year. Mack, the first sports figure to be so honored, led the Athletics to a world championship in 1929.

March 8 Babe Ruth signs a two-year contract for $160,000 with New York to become, at $80,000 per year, the highest paid player of all time. When it is pointed out he is earning more money than the President of the United States, Ruth observes: "I had a better year than he did." Yankees general manager Ed Barrow, assures posterity, "No one will ever be paid more than Ruth."

May 21 Babe Ruth hits three consecutive home runs in the first game of a doubleheader against the A's, then batting against Jack Quinn in the ninth, Ruth decides to hit right-handed. After two strikes, he switches to lefty but strikes out.

May 26 Joe Sewell strikes out twice facing left-hander Pat Caraway of the White Sox. It is the last time the Indians third baseman will fan this season, striking out only three times in 353 at bats.

July 25 The Athletics pull off triple steals twice in one game against the Indians. Al Simmons, Bing Miller, and Dib Williams are the thieves in the first inning, and Cochrane, Simmons, and Foxx steal together in the fourth. This is the only time in major league history this has occurred.

September 18 The Philadelphia Athletics win the AL pennant for the second year in a row, defeating the White Sox, 14-10.

September 28 Babe Ruth returns to the scene of his youthful fame, the pitcher's mound at Fenway Park. The Yankees slugger hurls a 9–3 complete game win over the Red Sox in the season finale. Lou Gehrig takes Ruth's spot in left field, ending his streak of 885 consecutive games at first base.

October 1 The World Series opens at Philadelphia's Shibe Park. The defending World Champion Athletics are held to five hits by Burleigh Grimes. Lefty Grove limits the Cards to a pair of runs, as the A's five hits include home runs by Mickey Cochrane and Al Simmons, two triples and a double, providing Philadelphia with a 5-2 victory.

October 8 George Earnshaw finishes off the Cardinals, 7-1, pitching shutout ball until the ninth inning. He is clearly the pitching star of the World Series with two wins and seven shutout innings of a game in which reliever Lefty Grove got the decision. Despite the "lively" ball and the many outstanding hitters on both sides, it is a pitching-dominated Series. The Cards bat only .200 as a team and the A's hit .197.

October 10 With no MVP award for the second year in a row, the Associated Press polls its members and names Washington shortstop Joe Cronin unofficial AL MVP. The Baseball Writers Association names Hack Wilson the MVP of the NL. The Cubs give Wilson a bonus of $1,000, the monetary reward which the MVP title had carried as an official league honor.

November 25 *The Sporting News,* also acting to fill the MVP void, announces its selection of New York Giants first baseman Bill Terry as the Most Valuable Player in the NL and Joe Cronin in the AL.

December 11 The BBWAA votes to continue the custom of selecting an MVP for each league. Beginning in 1931 the annual vote of the BBWAA will designate a player for this honor in each league. Previous MVP winners will be able to repeat under the new rules, something that was prohibited by the AL in the 1920s.

December 12 The Rules Committee of baseball issues a greatly revised code, reducing the number of rules by combining many. The sacrifice fly rule is abolished as is the rule awarding home runs when the ball bounces into the stands. This rule had already been in effect in the AL but not in the NL.

BOSTON	CHICAGO	CLEVELAND	DETROIT	NEW YORK	PHILADELPHIA	ST.LOUIS	WASHINGTON
M H.Wagner	M D.Bush	M R.Peckinpaugh	M B.Harris	M B.Shawkey	M C.Mack	M B.Killefer	M W.Johnson
1B P.Todt	1B J.Watwood	1B E.Morgan	1B D.Alexander	1B L.Gehrig	1B J.Foxx	1B L.Blue	1B J.Judge
2B B.Regan	2B B.Cissell	2B J.Hodapp	2B C.Gehringer	2B T.Lazzeri	2B M.Bishop	2B S.Melillo	2B B.Myer
SS H.Rhyne	SS G.Mulleavy	SS J.Goldman	SS M.Koenig	SS L.Lary	SS J.Boley	SS R.Kress	SS J.Cronin
3B O.Miller	3B W.Kamm	3B J.Sewell	3B M.McManus	3B B.Chapman	3B J.Dykes	3B F.O'Rourke	3B O.Bluege
LF R.Scarritt	LF S.Jolley	LF C.Jamieson	LF J.Stone	LF E.Combs	LF A.Simmons	LF G.Goslin	LF H.Manush
CF T.Oliver	CF R.Barnes	CF E.Averill	CF L.Funk	CF H.Rice	CF M.Haas	CF F.Schulte	CF S.West
RF E.Webb	RF C.Reynolds	RF D.Porter	RF R.Johnson	RF B.Ruth	RF B.Miller	RF T.Gullic	RF S.Rice
C C.Berry	C B.Tate	C L.Sewell	C R.Hayworth	C B.Dickey	C M.Cochrane	C R.Ferrell	C R.Spencer
O C.Durst	2S J.Kerr	O B.Seeds	S3 B.Akers	O S.Byrd	S3 E.McNair	O1 E.McNeely	O D.Harris
3S B.Reeves	1 B.Clancy	C G.Myatt	S3 B.Rogell	O D.Cooke	2S D.Williams	O R.Badgro	C M.Ruel
1 B.Sweeney	O B.Fothergill	O B.Falk	O B.Fothergill	2 J.Reese	C W.Schang	O A.Metzler	O G.Goslin
C J.Heving	1 A.Shires	S3 E.Montague	C P.Hargrave	C B.Hargrave	O D.Cramer	O H.Manush	2 J.Hayes
S R.Warstler	C B.Crouse	3S J.Burnett	O H.Rice	O B.Bengough	O H.Summa	3 S.Hale	O G.Loepp
S3 B.Narleski	3S I.Jeffries	1 I.Fonseca	O G.Desautels	S M.Koenig	O J.Moore	C C.Manion	1 A.Shires
/O J.Rothrock	3 B.Ryan	S C.Lind	O P.Easterling	S Y.Wuestling	S.Harris	/S J.Levey	1 J.Kuhel
C E.Connolly	O D.Harris	C J.Sprinz	O F.Doljack	C A.Jorgens	Cy.Perkins	C B.Hungling	3 J.McLeod
/O J.Cicero	S B.Hunnefield	/O J.Vosmik	O T.Hughes	/O C.Durst	/3 P.Higgins	J.Burns	/C P.Hargrave
/O B.Barrett	O A.Metzler	/3 R.Winegarner	C T.Rensa	/S B.Werber	/1 J.Keesey	/2 L.Storti	/C B.Tate
/O C.Small	S E.Smith	S R.Gardner	1 J.Shevlin	/O B.Karlon	H E.Collins	/C J.Crouch	/3 R.Treadaway
H J.Galvin	C C.Autry	/3 C.DeTore	/S J.Watson	P G.Pipgras	/S J.Hassler	H R.Barnes	/O B.Barrett
H T.Winsett	C M.Berg	/C G.Hartley	/S Y.Wuestling	P R.Ruffing	G.Earnshaw	/O T.Jenkins	/O J.Powell
	C J.Riddle		/C H.Wise	P R.Sherid	L.Grove		
P M.Gaston	P JW.Moore	P W.Ferrell	H H.Greenberg	P B.Shores	R.Walberg	P L.Stewart	P H.Boss
P D.MacFayden	/S L.Appling	P W.Hudlin		P H.Johnson	B.Shores	/1 D.Coffman	/1 P.Gharrity
P H.Lisenbee	/O B.Campbell	P C.Brown	P G.Uhle	P H.Pennock	R.Mahaffey	P G.Blaeholder	
P J.Russell	/C B.Henline	P M.Harder	RP V.Sorrell	RP L.McEvoy	RP J.Quinn	P R.Collins	P B.Hadley
P E.Durham	/C J.Klinger	P P.Appleton	P E.Whitehill			P S.Gray	P A.Crowder
RP G.Smith	/2 H.Willingham		P C.Hogsett	P E.Wells	E.Rommel	RP C.Kimsey	P L.Brown
	P J.Miller		P W.Hoyt	P L.Gomez	Ch.Perkins	RP H.Holshouser	P F.Marberry
P E.Morris	P T.Lyons	RP M.Shoffner	RP C.Sullivan	/P W.Hoyt	H.Ehmke		P S.Jones
P F.Bushey	P P.Caraway	P B.Bean		P K.Holloway	G.Liebhardt	P R.Stiles	
/P R.Ruffing	P T.Thomas	/P R.Lawson	P W.Wyatt	P O.Carroll	A.Mahon	P A.Crowder	P A.Liska
/P B.Shields	P R.Faber	/P K.Holloway	/P A.Herring	/P T.Zachary		/P F.Stiely	P B.Burke
/P B.Bayne	/P D.Henry	/P S.Gliatto	/P T.Bridges	/P F.Barnes			P M.Thomas
/P F.Mulroney	RP E.Walsh	/P L.Barnhart	/P G.Cantrell	/P B.Henderson			/P C.Fischer
/P B.Kline	RP H.McKain	/P J.Shaute	/P O.Carroll	/P S.Gibson			P G.Braxton
	P G.Braxton		P P.Page	/P F.Edwards			/P C.Moore
	/P JS.Moore		/P J.Samuels	/P G.Rhodes			/P H.Child
	P B.Weiland						
	/P T.Blankenship						
	/P B.Wehde						

TEAM	G	W	L	PCT	GB	R	OR	AB	H	2B	3B	HR	BB	SO	AVG	OBP	SLG	PRO	PRO+	BR	/A	PF	CHI	RC	SB	CS	SBA	SBR
PHI	154	102	52	.662		951	751	5345	1573	319	74	125	599	531	.294	.369	.452	.821	108	102	60	104	100	913	48	33	59	-5
WAS	154	94	60	.610	8	892	689	5370	1620	300	98	57	537	438	.302	.369	.426	.795	106	59	55	100	99	860	101	67	60	-10
NY	154	86	68	.558	16	1062	898	5448	1683	298	110	152	644	569	.309	.384	.488	.872	131	206	255	96	99	1035	91	60	60	-9
CLE	154	81	73	.526	21	890	915	5439	1654	358	59	72	490	461	.304	.364	.431	.795	102	54	20	104	99	863	51	47	52	-13
DET	154	75	79	.487	27	783	833	5297	1504	298	90	82	461	508	.284	.344	.421	.765	96	-18	-33	102	98	771	98	70	58	-13
STL	154	64	90	.416	38	751	886	5278	1415	289	67	75	497	550	.268	.333	.391	.724	85	-96	-121	103	104	696	93	71	57	-15
CHI	154	62	92	.403	40	729	884	5419	1496	256	90	63	389	479	.276	.328	.391	.719	89	-111	-87	97	102	706	74	40	65	-2
BOS	154	52	102	.338	50	612	814	5286	1393	257	68	47	358	552	.264	.313	.365	.678	79	-192	-169	96	100	608	42	35	55	-8
TOT	616					6670		42882	12338	2375	656	673	3975	4088	.288	.351	.421	.772							598	423	59	-74

TEAM	CG	SH	SV	IP	H	H/G	HR	BB	SO	RAT	ERA	ERA+	OAV	OOB	PR	/A	PF	CPI	FA	E	DP	FW	PW	BW	SBW	DIF
PHI	72	8	21	1371	1457	9.6	84	488	672	12.9	4.28	109	.274	.337	56	58	101	98	.975	145	121	3.0	5.2	5.4	.4	11.0
WAS	78	6	14	1369	1367	9.0	52	504	524	12.5	3.96	116	.264	.332	104	96	99	97	.974	157	150	2.3	8.7	5.0	-.0	1.1
NY	65	7	15	1367²	1566	10.3	93	524	572	13.9	4.88	88	.287	.352	-36	-90	93	96	.965	207	132	-.7	-8.1	23.1	.0	-5.2
CLE	68	5	14	1360	1663	11.0	85	528	442	14.6	4.88	99	.305	.368	-36	-9	104	107	.962	237	156	-2.5	-.8	1.8	-.3	5.9
DET	68	4	17	1351²	1507	10.0	86	570	574	14.0	4.70	102	.286	.359	-8	13	103	102	.967	192	156	.2	1.2	-3.0	-.3	-.0
STL	68	5	10	1371²	1639	10.8	124	449	470	13.9	5.07	96	.300	.356	-65	-31	105	101	.970	188	152	.4	-2.8	-10.9	-.5	.9
CHI	63	2	10	1361	1629	10.8	74	407	471	13.6	4.71	98	.300	.352	-10	-15	99	101	.962	235	136	-2.4	-1.4	-7.9	.7	-4.0
BOS	78	4	5	1360¹	1515	10.0	75	488	356	13.4	4.68	98	.286	.348	-6	-12	99	97	.968	196	161	-.0	-1.1	-15.3	.1	-8.7
TOT	560	41	106	10912¹		10.2				13.6	4.65		.288	.351					.968	1557	1164					

Runs
Simmons-Phi 152
Ruth-NY 150
Gehringer-Det 144
Gehrig-NY 143
Combs-NY 129

Hits
Hodapp-Cle 225
Gehrig-NY 220
Simmons-Phi ... 211
Rice-Was 207
Morgan-Cle 204

Doubles
Hodapp-Cle 51
Manush-StL-Was .. 49
Morgan-Cle 47
Gehringer-Det 47

Triples
Combs-NY 22
Reynolds-Chi 18
Gehrig-NY 17
Simmons-Phi 16

Home Runs
Ruth-NY 49
Gehrig-NY 41
Goslin-Was-StL 37
Foxx-Phi 37
Simmons-Phi 36

Total Bases
Gehrig-NY 419
Simmons-Phi 392
Ruth-NY 379
Foxx-Phi 358

Runs Batted In
Gehrig-NY 174
Simmons-Phi 165
Foxx-Phi 156
Ruth-NY 153
Goslin-Was-StL ... 138

Runs Produced
Simmons-Phi 281
Gehrig-NY 276
Ruth-NY 254
Foxx-Phi 246
Cronin-Was 240

Bases On Balls
Ruth-NY 136
Bishop-Phi 128
Gehrig-NY 101
Foxx-Phi 93
Blue-StL 81

Batting Average
Simmons-Phi 381
Gehrig-NY 379
Ruth-NY 359
Reynolds-Chi 359
Cochrane-Phi 357

On Base Percentage
Ruth-NY 493
Gehrig-NY 473
Foxx-Phi 429
Bishop-Phi 426
Combs-NY 424

Slugging Average
Ruth-NY 732
Gehrig-NY 721
Simmons-Phi 708
Foxx-Phi 637

Production
Ruth-NY 1.225
Gehrig-NY 1.194
Simmons-Phi 1.130
Foxx-Phi 1.066
Morgan-Cle 1.014

Adjusted Production
Ruth-NY 216
Gehrig-NY 207
Simmons-Phi 173
Foxx-Phi 159
Morgan-Cle 148

Batter Runs
Ruth-NY 89.5
Gehrig-NY 88.4
Simmons-Phi 64.2
Foxx-Phi 57.0
Morgan-Cle 46.3

Adjusted Batter Runs
Ruth-NY 97.9
Gehrig-NY 96.9
Simmons-Phi 57.8
Foxx-Phi 50.5
Morgan-Cle 41.1

Clutch Hitting Index
Rice-Det-NY 137
Lazzeri-NY 125
Dykes-Phi 113
Cronin-Was 112
Alexander-Det 112

Runs Created
Gehrig-NY 195
Ruth-NY 191
Simmons-Phi 163
Foxx-Phi 154
Morgan-Cle 144

Total Average
Ruth-NY 1.509
Gehrig-NY 1.389
Simmons-Phi 1.272
Foxx-Phi 1.184
Morgan-Cle 1.089

Stolen Bases
McManus-Det 23
Gehringer-Det 19
Goslin-Was-StL 17
Johnson-Det 17
Cronin-Was 17

Stolen Base Average
Reynolds-Chi 80.0
McManus-Det 74.2
Cissell-Chi 64.0
Johnson-Det 63.0
Cronin-Was 63.0

Stolen Base Runs
Lary-NY 3.0
Reynolds-Chi 2.4
McManus-Det 2.1

Fielding Runs
Melillo-StL 26.8
Cronin-Was 26.1
Goldman-Cle 20.7
Oliver-Bos 15.2
Kamm-Chi 14.9

Total Player Rating
Ruth-NY 7.3
Gehrig-NY 6.9
Cronin-Was 6.7
Simmons-Phi 4.9
Cochrane-Phi 4.0

Wins
Grove-Phi 28
Ferrell-Cle 25
Lyons-Chi 22
Earnshaw-Phi 22
Stewart-StL 20

Win Percentage
Grove-Phi 848
Marberry-Was 750
Jones-Was 682
Ferrell-Cle 658
Ruffing-Bos-NY ...652

Games
Grove-Phi 50
Earnshaw-Phi 49
Pipgras-NY 44
Johnson-NY 44
Ferrell-Cle 43

Complete Games
Lyons-Chi 29
Crowder-StL-Was .. 25
Ferrell-Cle 25
Stewart-StL 23
Grove-Phi 22

Shutouts
Pipgras-NY 3
Earnshaw-Phi 3
Brown-Cle 3

Saves
Grove-Phi 9
Braxton-Was-Chi 6
Quinn-Phi 6
Sullivan-Det 5
McKain-Chi 5

Innings Pitched
Lyons-Chi 297.2
Ferrell-Cle 296.2
Earnshaw-Phi 296.0
Grove-Phi 291.0
Crowder-StL-Was ..279.2

Fewest Hits/Game
Hadley-Was 8.37
Grove-Phi 8.44
Collins-StL 8.81
Crowder-StL-Was. 8.88
Gaston-Bos 8.97

Fewest BB/Game
Pennock-NY 1.15
Lyons-Chi 1.72
Grove-Phi 1.86
Russell-Bos 2.08
Brown-Cle 2.15

Strikeouts
Grove-Phi 209
Earnshaw-Phi 193
Hadley-Was 162
Ferrell-Cle 143
Ruffing-Bos-NY ... 131

Strikeouts/Game
Grove-Phi 6.46
Johnson-NY 5.90
Earnshaw-Phi 5.87
Hadley-Was 5.60
Ruffing-Bos-NY .. 5.32

Ratio
Grove-Phi 10.45
Stewart-StL 11.69
Lyons-Chi 11.79
Marberry-Was 11.82
Caraway-Chi 11.82

Earned Run Average
Grove-Phi 2.54
Ferrell-Cle 3.31
Stewart-StL 3.45
Uhle-Det 3.65
Hadley-Was 3.73

Adjusted ERA
Grove-Phi 184
Ferrell-Cle 146
Stewart-StL 141
Uhle-Det 131
Sorrell-Det 124

Opponents' Batting Avg.
Grove-Phi 247
Hadley-Was 247
Crowder-StL-Was .259
Collins-StL 259
Gaston-Bos 259

Opponents' On Base Pct.
Grove-Phi 288
Stewart-StL.......315
Lyons-Chi 319
Marberry-Was 321
Crowder-StL-Was ..321

Starter Runs
Grove-Phi 68.3
Ferrell-Cle 44.2
Stewart-StL 35.9
Lyons-Chi 28.7
Hadley-Was 26.4

Adjusted Starter Runs
Grove-Phi 69.0
Ferrell-Cle 50.0
Stewart-StL 42.7
Uhle-Det 30.4
Lyons-Chi 27.8

Clutch Pitching Index
Henry-Chi 122
Harder-Cle 115
Sorrell-Det 115
Hoyt-NY-Det 113
Ferrell-Cle 113

Relief Runs
Quinn-Phi 2.3

Adjusted Relief Runs
Quinn-Phi 2.5

Relief Ranking
Quinn-Phi 4.5

Total Pitcher Index
Grove-Phi 7.3
Ferrell-Cle 6.2
Stewart-StL 4.7
Lyons-Chi 4.1
Uhle-Det 3.2

Total Baseball Ranking
Ruth-NY 7.6
Grove-Phi 7.3
Gehrig-NY 6.9
Cronin-Was 6.7
Ferrell-Cle 6.2

January 5* Mrs. Lucille Thomas becomes the first woman to buy a professional baseball team, purchasing the Topeka franchise in the Western League.

June 27 The largest total crowd in Cubs history, 51,556, jams Wrigley Field to watch Kiki Cuyler crack a 10th inning home run to beat Brooklyn, 7–5. The attendance includes 19,748 paying customers, 1,332 pass holders and 30,476 Ladies Day fans.

July 12 The largest crowd in the history of Sportsman's Park in St. Louis, 45,715 (in a ballpark with 35,000 seats), creates a travesty and permanently distorts the record for doubles hit in a game. Easy fly balls drop for ground-rule doubles among the fans encroaching on the field. There are 32 doubles hit in two games, 11 in the first and 21 in the second, records both for the most doubles in one game and for a doubleheader.

August 20 Tony Freitas, who will win 342 minor league games, is let out of jail to pitch for Sacramento (PCL). He wins the game and then returns to finish a five-day sentence for speeding.

September 16 World Series tickets can now be printed as the St. Louis Cardinals repeat as NL champions. They beat the Phillies, 6-3, and prepare for a rematch of the 1930 World Series.

September 27 The most desperately contested battle for individual honors takes place in the race for the NL batting title. Chick Hafey, who reported late due to a contract dispute, goes into the final doubleheader with the Reds batting .353, four points over Bill Terry, last year's champ. Hafey gets only one hit in eight times at bat to drop to .349. Bill Terry's Giants are playing archenemy Brooklyn at Ebbets Field. Brooklyn, in their last game as the Robins, wins 12-3. Terry gets only one hit in four times at bat. The title goes to Hafey, who batted .3488 to Terry's .3486. Jim Bottomley, Hafey's Cardinal teammate, finishes at .3481.

October 2 The Cards even the World Series as "Wild Bill" Hallahan shuts out the A's, 2-0, despite seven walks and a wild pitch. Pepper Martin continues to steal the Series, scoring from second base on a base hit in the second inning and sliding home in a cloud of dust on a squeeze play in the eighth. He has two stolen bases, but the game almost gets away on a bonehead play by the usually savvy Cardinals catcher Jimmy Wilson. With two on base in the ninth, and two outs, pinch hitter Johnny Moore swings at a ball in the dirt and misses. Wilson needs only to throw the ball to the first baseman. Instead, he throws it to third, and everyone is safe. Fortunately for Wilson's reputation, Jim Bottomley makes a sensational catch, leaning into the box seats to get the final out on a pop foul by Max Bishop.

October 7 Connie Mack, who surprised everyone in 1929 by starting veteran Howard Ehmke in the World Series opener, tries the ploy with Waite Hoyt. Pitching in his seventh World Series, Hoyt falls victim to Pepper Martin, who homers and drives in four runs with three hits. Hallahan wins for the Cards 5-1.

October 10 Burleigh Grimes carries a 4-0 lead into the ninth inning of Game 7 before he weakens. The A's score twice and have two on with two outs, when Bill Hallahan rescues Grimes. Max Bishop flies to Pepper Martin for the final out as the Cardinals take the Series, four games to three.

October 20 Frankie Frisch, the Cardinals' fiery field leader, is named MVP of the NL. He led in stolen bases with 28, hit .313, and was chosen for his all-around excellence.

October 23 Brooklyn announces Wilbert Robinson is through as manager and the club will be called the Robins only in the past tense. Max Carey, a no-nonsense sort, will take over next year.

December 9 Baseball owners, fearful of the effects of the Depression, vote to cut squads from 25 players to 23. Both leagues will also stop awarding MVP trophies, and the NL continues to prohibit uniform numbers.

December 11 Despite two wins in the World Series, spitball veteran Burleigh Grimes is traded by the Cards to the Cubs for the fallen Hack Wilson.

BOSTON		BROOKLYN		CHICAGO		CINCINNATI		NEW YORK		PHILADELPHIA		PITTSBURGH		ST.LOUIS	
M	B.McKechnie	M	W.Robinson	M	R.Hornsby	M	D.Howley	M	J.McGraw	M	B.Shotton	M	J.Ens	M	G.Street
1B	E.Sheely	1B	D.Bissonette	1B	C.Grimm	1B	H.Hendrick	1B	B.Terry	1B	D.Hurst	1B	G.Suhr	1B	J.Bottomley
2B	F.Maguire	2B	N.Finn	2B	R.Hornsby	2B	T.Cuccinello	2B	B.Hunnefield	2B	L.Mallon	2B	G.Grantham	2B	F.Frisch
SS	R.Maranville	SS	G.Slade	SS	W.English	SS	L.Durocher	SS	T.Jackson	SS	D.Bartell	SS	T.Thevenow	SS	C.Gelbert
3B	B.Urbanski	3B	W.Gilbert	3B	L.Bell	3B	J.Stripp	3B	J.Vergez	3B	P.Whitney	3B	P.Traynor	3B	S.Adams
LF	R.Worthington	LF	L.O'Doul	LF	D.Taylor	LF	E.Roush	LF	F.Leach	LF	C.Klein	LF	A.Comorosky	LF	C.Hafey
CF	W.Berger	CF	J.Frederick	CF	H.Wilson	CF	T.Douthit	CF	E.Allen	CF	F.Brickell	CF	L.Waner	CF	P.Martin
RF	W.Schulmerich	RF	B.Herman	RF	K.Cuyler	RF	E.Crabtree	RF	M.Ott	RF	B.Arlett	RF	P.Waner	RF	W.Watkins
C	A.Spohrer	C	A.Lopez	C	G.Hartnett	C	C.Sukeforth	C	S.Hogan	C	S.Davis	C	E.Phillips	C	J.Wilson
O	L.Richbourg	S	G.Wright	32	B.Jurges	O	N.Cullop	O	F.Lindstrom	23	B.Friberg	O	W.Jensen	1	R.Collins
O3	R.Moore	C	E.Lombardi	O	R.Stephenson	O	C.Heathcote	O	C.Fullis	O	C.Koster	2	T.Piet	O	G.Mancuso
3	B.Dreesen	2S	F.Thompson	21	F.Blair	2	W.Roettger	2	H.Critz	2	D.Taitt	2	H.Groskloss	O	E.Orsatti
C	B.Cronin	O	R.Bressler	O	V.Barton	S	H.Ford	2S	D.Marshall	C	H.McCurdy	C	E.Grace	O	W.Roettger
1	J.Neun	C	V.Picinich	C	R.Hemsley	3	C.Beck	3	B.O'Farrell	C	H.Lee	S	B.Sankey	S2	J.Flowers
C	A.Bool	O	J.Flowers	O	J.Moore	C	C.Asbjornson	S	S.Leslie	S	B.Stevens	2	B.Regan	O	T.Douthit
3	C.Wilson	O	D.Sothern	2	B.Herman	C	L.Styles	/3	G.English	/S	H.Willingham	O	F.Bennett	32	A.High
O	E.Clark	/3	B.Reis	S	J.Adair	/3	F.Sigafoos	/O	J.Moore	C	T.Rensa	/O	J.Mosolf	O	R.Blades
/S	B.Chatham	/O	M.Rosenfeld	/O	M.Kreevich	/1	M.Heath	/C	F.Healy	/C	G.Connell	/C	R.Hemsley	C	M.Gonzalez
/3	B.Walters	H	I.Boone	/C	E.Grace	/3	C.Dressen					/C	H.Finney	/S	J.Benes
/3	B.Hunnefield	/S	J.Warner	/C	Z.Taylor	/O	G.Moore	P	F.Fitzsimmons	P	J.Elliott	H	P.McClanahan	/3	R.Cunningham
H	J.Scalzi	/O	A.Cohen			H	R.Fitzgerald	P	C.Hubbell	P	R.Benge	P	B.Steinecke	/3	E.Delker
H	P.Veltman	H	H.Hendrick	P	C.Root			P	B.Walker	P	P.Collins			/O	J.Hunt
				P	B.Smith	P	S.Johnson	P	C.Mitchell	P	C.Dudley			/C	G.Street
P	E.Brandt	P	W.Clark	P	P.Malone	P	R.Lucas	P	J.Berly	P	F.Watt	P	H.Meine		
P	T.Zachary	P	D.Vance	P	G.Bush	P	L.Benton					P	L.French	P	B.Hallahan
P	S.Seibold	P	R.Phelps	P	L.Sweetland	P	B.Frey	P	S.Johnson	P	S.Bolen	P	R.Kremer	P	B.Grimes
P	B.Cantwell	P	S.Thurston	RP	J.May	P	E.Rixey	P	B.Morrell	P	S.Blake	P	S.Spencer	P	P.Derringer
P	B.Sherdel	P	F.Heimach	RP	B.Teachout			P	R.Parmelee	RP	E.Fallenstein	P	E.Brame	P	F.Rhem
RP	H.Haid	RP	J.Quinn			P	O.Carroll	P	T.Chaplin	P	D.Schesler	RP	B.Osborn	P	S.Johnson
		RP	C.Moore	P	E.Baecht	P	R.Kolp	P	J.Heving	P	H.Elliott	/O	S.Wood	RP	J.Lindsey
P	B.Cunningham	RP	P.Day	P	L.Warneke	P	J.Ogden	/P	H.Schumacher	/P	L.Stoner	P	B.Harris	RP	A.Stout
P	F.Frankhouse	P	J.Shaute	P	S.Blake	P	E.Strelecki	/P	P.Donohue	/P	J.Milligan	/P	S.Swetonic	P	J.Haines
P	R.Moss	P	D.Luque	/P	J.Welch	P	B.Wysong	/P	E.Planeta	/P	B.Adams	/P	C.Willoughby	P	T.Kaufmann
P	B.McAfee	/P	V.Mungo			P	A.Eckert	/P	R.Lucas	/P	C.Nichols	/P	G.Grant	P	T.Kaufmann
/P	B.Brown	/P	P.Gallivan			/P	W.Hilcher			/P	B.Shields	/P	A.Bednar		
		/P	E.Mattingly							/P	H.Wiltse				
		/P	R.Moss												

TEAM	G	W	L	PCT	GB	R	OR	AB	H	2B	3B	HR	BB	SO	AVG	OBP	SLG	PRO	PRO+	BR	/A	PF	CHI	RC	SB	CS	SBA	SBR
STL	154	101	53	.656		815	614	5435	1554	353	74	60	432	475	.286	.342	.411	.753	105	61	31	104	107	787	114			
NY	153	87	65	.572	13	768	599	5372	1554	251	64	101	383	395	.289	.340	.416	.756	112	61	80	98	103	776	83			
CHI	156	84	70	.545	17	828	710	5451	1578	340	66	84	577	641	.289	.360	.422	.782	115	131	117	102	97	865	49			
BRO	153	79	73	.520	21	681	673	5309	1464	240	77	71	409	512	.276	.331	.390	.721	101	-3	2	99	101	705	45			
PIT	155	75	79	.487	26	636	691	5360	1425	243	70	41	493	454	.266	.330	.360	.690	93	-54	-48	99	98	667	59			
PHI	155	66	88	.429	35	684	828	5375	1502	299	52	81	437	492	.279	.336	.400	.736	96	27	-30	108	99	745	42			
BOS	156	64	90	.416	37	533	680	5296	1367	221	59	34	368	430	.258	.309	.341	.650	84	-137	-118	96	98	580	46			
CIN	154	58	96	.377	43	592	742	5343	1439	241	70	21	403	463	.269	.323	.352	.675	94	-85	-49	94	99	631	24			
TOT	618					5537		42941	11883	2188	532	493	3502	3862	.277	.334	.387	.721						462				

TEAM	CG	SH	SV	IP	H	H/G	HR	BB	SO	RAT	ERA	ERA+	OAV	OOB	PR	/A	PF	CPI	FA	E	DP	FW	PW	BW	SBW	DIF
STL	80	17	20	1384[2]	1470	9.6	65	449	626	12.6	3.45	114	.273	.332	63	74	102	110	.974	160	169	1.0	7.4	3.1		12.6
NY	90	17	12	1360[2]	1341	8.9	71	422	570	11.8	3.30	112	.255	.313	85	58	96	100	.974	159	126	1.0	5.8	8.0		-3.7
CHI	80	8	8	1385[2]	1448	9.4	54	524	541	13.0	3.97	97	.268	.337	-17	-19	100	94	.973	169	141	.6	-1.9	11.6		-3.3
BRO	64	9	18	1356	1520	10.1	56	351	546	12.5	3.84	99	.283	.329	3	-5	99	100	.969	187	154	-.7	-.5	.2		4.0
PIT	89	9	5	1390	1489	9.6	55	442	345	12.6	3.66	105	.274	.331	32	28	100	102	.968	194	167	-.9	2.8	-4.8		.9
PHI	60	6	16	1360[1]	1603	10.6	75	511	499	14.2	4.58	93	.293	.358	-108	-51	110	100	.966	210	149	-1.9	-5.1	-3.0		-1.1
BOS	78	12	9	1380[1]	1465	9.6	66	406	419	12.3	3.90	97	.272	.325	-5	-18	98	94	.973	170	141	.5	-1.8	-11.7		.0
CIN	70	7	6	1345	1545	10.3	51	399	317	13.1	4.22	89	.294	.346	-53	-72	97	101	.973	165	194	.7	-7.2	-4.9		-7.6
TOT	611	85	94	10962[2]		9.8				12.8	3.86		.277	.334					.971	1414	1241					

Runs
Terry-NY 121
Klein-Phi 121
English-Chi 117
Cuyler-Chi 110
Ott-NY 104

Hits
L.Waner-Pit 214
Terry-NY 213
English-Chi 202
Cuyler-Chi 202
Klein-Phi 200

Doubles
Adams-StL 46
Berger-Bos 44
Terry-NY 43
Herman-Bro 43
Bartell-Phi 43

Triples
Terry-NY 20
Herman-Bro 16
Traynor-Pit 15
Bissonette-Bro 14

Home Runs
Klein-Phi 31
Ott-NY 29
Berger-Bos 19
Herman-Bro 18
Arlett-Phi 18

Total Bases
Klein-Phi 347
Terry-NY 323
Herman-Bro 320
Berger-Bos 316
Cuyler-Chi 290

Runs Batted In
Klein-Phi 121
Ott-NY 115
Terry-NY 112
Traynor-Pit 103
Herman-Bro 97

Runs Produced
Terry-NY 224
Klein-Phi 211
Ott-NY 190
Cuyler-Chi 189
Traynor-Pit 182

Bases On Balls
Ott-NY 80
P.Waner-Pit 73
Cuyler-Chi 72
Grantham-Pit 71
English-Chi 68

Batting Average
Hafey-StL 349
Terry-NY 349
Bottomley-StL 348
Klein-Phi 337
O'Doul-Bro 336

On Base Percentage
Hafey-StL 404
Cuyler-Chi 404
P.Waner-Pit 404
Grantham-Pit 400
Klein-Phi 398

Slugging Average
Klein-Phi 584
Hornsby-Chi 574
Hafey-StL 569
Ott-NY 545
Arlett-Phi 538

Production
Klein-Phi 982
Hafey-StL 973
Ott-NY 937
Terry-NY 926
Berger-Bos 892

Adjusted Production
Ott-NY 153
Hafey-StL 153
Terry-NY 150
Klein-Phi 149
Berger-Bos 143

Batter Runs
Klein-Phi 48.9
Terry-NY 39.0
Hafey-StL 36.2
Ott-NY 35.0
Hornsby-Chi 33.5

Adjusted Batter Runs
Terry-NY 42.0
Klein-Phi 39.3
Ott-NY 37.6
Berger-Bos 35.6
Hafey-StL 32.6

Clutch Hitting Index
Sheely-Bos 150
Traynor-Pit 127
Frisch-StL 122
Gelbert-StL 122
Hendrick-Bro-Cin . . . 120

Runs Created
Klein-Phi 140
Terry-NY 130
Cuyler-Chi 122
Berger-Bos 122
Herman-Bro 118

Total Average
Hafey-StL 1.055
Klein-Phi 1.051
Ott-NY 1.031
Terry-NY 955
Cuyler-Chi 925

Stolen Bases
Frisch-StL 28
Herman-Bro 17
Martin-StL 16
Adams-StL 16
Watkins-StL 15

Stolen Base Average

Stolen Base Runs

Fielding Runs
L.Waner-Pit 18.3
Frisch-StL 16.3
P.Waner-Pit 14.6
Gelbert-StL 12.9
Hurst-Phi 11.4

Total Player Rating
Ott-NY 3.6
Terry-NY 3.6
Berger-Bos 3.5
Cuccinello-Cin 3.3
P.Waner-Pit 3.1

Wins
Meine-Pit 19
Hallahan-StL 19
J.Elliott-Phi 19

Win Percentage
Derringer-StL 692
Hallahan-StL 679
Bush-Chi 667
Grimes-StL 654

Games
J.Elliott-Phi 52
Johnson-Cin 42
Collins-Phi 42

Complete Games
Lucas-Cin 24
Brandt-Bos 23
Meine-Pit 22
Hubbell-NY 21
French-Pit 20

Shutouts
Walker-NY 6
Hubbell-NY 4
Fitzsimmons-NY 4
Derringer-StL 4

Saves
Quinn-Bro 15
Lindsey-StL 7
J.Elliott-Phi 5
Hallahan-StL 4
Collins-Phi 4

Innings Pitched
Meine-Pit 284.0
French-Pit 275.2
Johnson-Cin 262.1
Fitzsimmons-NY . . .253.2
Root-Chi 251.0

Fewest Hits/Game
Hubbell-NY 7.66
Walker-NY 7.97
Brandt-Bos 8.21
Fitzsimmons-NY 8.59
Root-Chi 8.61

Fewest BB/Game
Johnson-StL 1.40
Lucas-Cin 1.47
Cantwell-Bos 1.96
Clark-Bro 2.01
Zachary-Bos 2.08

Strikeouts
Hallahan-StL 159
Hubbell-NY 155
Vance-Bro 150
Derringer-StL 134
Root-Chi 131

Strikeouts/Game
Vance-Bro 6.17
Hallahan-StL 5.75
Derringer-StL 5.70
Hubbell-NY 5.63
Root-Chi 4.70

Ratio
Hubbell-NY 10.23
Walker-NY 10.49
Johnson-StL 10.50
Fitzsimmons-NY . . . 10.79
Brandt-Bos 11.12

Earned Run Average
Walker-NY 2.26
Hubbell-NY 2.65
Brandt-Bos 2.92
Meine-Pit 2.98
Johnson-StL 3.00

Adjusted ERA
Walker-NY 164
Hubbell-NY 139
Benge-Phi 134
Johnson-StL 131
Brandt-Bos 130

Opponents' Batting Avg.
Hubbell-NY 227
Walker-NY 231
Brandt-Bos 244
Fitzsimmons-NY 251
Root-Chi 252

Opponents' On Base Pct.
Hubbell-NY 282
Walker-NY 283
Johnson-StL 286
Fitzsimmons-NY 296
Cantwell-Bcs 301

Starter Runs
Walker-NY 42.7
Hubbell-NY 33.5
Meine-Pit 27.9
Brandt-Bos 26.3
Fitzsimmons-NY . . 22.9

Adjusted Starter Runs
Walker-NY 38.1
Benge-Phi 29.4
Hubbell-NY 28.7
Meine-Pit 27.3
Brandt-Bos 24.2

Clutch Pitching Index
Benton-Cin 125
Dudley-Phi 120
Grimes-StL 114
Hallahan-StL 113
Derringer-StL 112

Relief Runs
Lindsey-StL 9.1
Quinn-Bro 8.6
Moore-Bro 5

Adjusted Relief Runs
Lindsey-StL 9.6
Quinn-Bro 8.2
Moore-Bro 1

Relief Ranking
Quinn-Bro 14.7
Lindsey-StL 13.6
Moore-Bro 0

Total Pitcher Index
Fitzsimmons-NY . . . 3.7
Brandt-Bos 3.6
Benge-Phi 3.3
Hubbell-NY 3.1
Walker-NY 2.8

Total Baseball Ranking
Fitzsimmons-NY . . . 3.7
Ott-NY 3.6
Terry-NY 3.6
Brandt-Bos 3.6
Berger-Bos 3.5

February 21 The White Sox and Giants become the first major league teams to meet in a night game. They collect 23 hits in a 10-inning exhibition game played in Houston, at Buffs Stadium.

February 27 E. S. Barnard, recently reappointed AL president, dies at 57. He had succeeded Ban Johnson in 1927.

February 28 Ban Johnson dies after a long illness. He had created the AL and been its dynamic, dictatorial leader until subdued by the advent of Judge Landis, who took office as the first commissioner in January 1921.

April 26 With Lyn Lary on base for the Yankees, Lou Gehrig's drive into the stands at Washington bounces back and is caught by center fielder Harry Rice. According to the rules, this is a home run, but when Lary sees Rice catching the ball, he thinks it's the final out of the inning. Lary heads for the dugout after crossing third base while Gehrig circles the bases. He is called out and gets credit for a triple instead of a home run and loses two RBIs. As a result, Gehrig will end the season tied for the home run title with Babe Ruth.

April 29 Wes Ferrell pitches a 9–0 no-hit game for Cleveland against the St. Louis Browns. His brother, Rick, almost gets a hit for the Browns when he beats out a grounder that is ruled an error. Ferrell strikes out eight and bats in four runs with a home run and a double.

May 27 AL Secretary Will Harridge is elected to succeed E. S. Barnard as president of the league.

June 15 Cut-down day for major league rosters brings the retirement of Eddie Collins and Harry Heilmann. Collins becomes a coach for the A's. Heilmann will return briefly to the Reds in 1932.

August 21 Babe Ruth hits his 600th home run, off George Blaeholder of the Browns, as the Yankees win, 11–7. Lou Gehrig homers immediately after the Babe's historic blow. In their 10 years as teammates, they will homer in the same inning 19 times and in the same game 72 times.

August 23 Lefty Grove is frustrated in his effort to win a record-breaking 17th game in a row, as Johnny Moore misjudges a routine fly ball to allow the game's lone run. The volatile Grove is outraged that Al Simmons, the Athletics' regular outfielder, misses the game, which is won by Dick Coffman of the Browns, 1-0.

September 15 The Philadelphia Athletics clinch the pennant, beating Cleveland at home. Eddie Rommel, veteran knuckleball pitcher for the A's, is the winning hurler, as Connie Mack wins his third successive pennant. It is Mack's ninth, and last, AL championship.

September 17 On his 32nd birthday, outfielder Earl Webb of the Red Sox sets the still-standing major league record for two-base hits at 65. He will finish the season with 67.

September 19 Lefty Grove wins his 30th game, beating the White Sox, 2-1. He is the first to win 30 since Jim Bagby of Cleveland in 1920 and will be the last AL hurler to do so until Denny McLain in 1968.

September 20 Lou Gehrig drives in four runs to break his old RBI mark of 175, set in 1927. By the season's end he will have a total of 184.

September 24 A round-robin playoff among New York City's three major league teams, to raise money for the unemployed, concludes with Brooklyn losing to both the Giants and the Yankees at the Polo Grounds. A near capacity crowd turns out and adds $48,000 to bring the fund to $108,000. In field events held between games, Babe Ruth, normally a left-handed hitter, bats righty and wins the fungo hitting contest. Ruth's drive lands in deep center field, 421 feet away.

October 1 John "Pepper" Martin, an unheralded rookie, gets three hits, but the A's Lefty Grove coasts to an easy 6-2 victory in the World Series opener in St. Louis.

October 5 Because of a Pennsylvania law banning baseball on Sunday, an extra day is added as the Series moves to Philadelphia. Lefty Grove pitches the third game with three days rest. However, St. Louis' Burleigh Grimes, who had lost twice to Grove in 1930, has a no-hitter until the eighth inning and holds on for the 5-2 win. Pepper Martin continues to excite the crowds with two more hits, scoring twice.

October 6 The A's George Earnshaw evens the World Series with a 3-0 shutout, giving up two hits to the red-hot Martin. Jimmie Foxx hits a ball over the left field stands, judged one of the longest drives ever at Shibe Park.

October 9 With the Series back in St. Louis, Lefty Grove evens matters by containing Pepper Martin and winning easily, 8-1.

	BOSTON		CHICAGO		CLEVELAND		DETROIT		NEW YORK		PHILADELPHIA		ST.LOUIS		WASHINGTON
M	S.Collins	M	D.Bush	M	R.Peckinpaugh	M	B.Harris	M	J.McCarthy	M	C.Mack	M	B.Killefer	M	W.Johnson
1B	B.Sweeney	1B	L.Blue	1B	E.Morgan	1B	D.Alexander	1B	L.Gehrig	1B	J.Foxx	1B	J.Burns	1B	J.Kuhel
2B	R.Warstler	2B	J.Kerr	2B	J.Hodapp	2B	C.Gehringer	2B	T.Lazzeri	2B	M.Bishop	2B	S.Melillo	2B	B.Myer
SS	H.Rhyne	SS	B.Cissell	SS	E.Montague	SS	B.Rogell	SS	L.Lary	SS	D.Williams	SS	J.Levey	SS	J.Cronin
3B	O.Miller	3B	B.Sullivan	3B	W.Kamm	3B	M.McManus	3B	J.Sewell	3B	J.Dykes	3B	R.Kress	3B	O.Bluege
LF	J.Rothrock	LF	L.Fonseca	LF	J.Vosmik	LF	J.Stone	LF	B.Chapman	LF	A.Simmons	LF	G.Goslin	LF	H.Manush
CF	T.Oliver	CF	J.Watwood	CF	E.Averill	CF	H.Walker	CF	E.Combs	CF	M.Haas	CF	F.Schulte	CF	S.West
RF	E.Webb	RF	C.Reynolds	RF	D.Porter	RF	R.Johnson	RF	B.Ruth	RF	B.Miller	RF	T.Jenkins	RF	S.Rice
C	C.Berry	C	B.Tate	C	L.Sewell	C	R.Hayworth	C	B.Dickey	C	M.Cochrane	C	R.Ferrell	C	R.Spencer
32	U.Pickering	S	L.Appling	S2	J.Burnett	2S	M.Koenig	O	S.Byrd	32	E.McNair	3	L.Storti	O	D.Harris
O1	A.Van Camp	C	B.Fothergill	C	G.Myatt	S3	M.Owen	2	J.Reese	S	J.Boley	O	L.Bettencourt	O	H.Rice
C	E.Connolly	C	F.Grube	O	B.Falk	O	G.Walker	C	A.Jorgens	O	D.Cramer	C	B.Bengough	2	J.Hayes
2	B.Reeves	3	I.Jeffries	O	B.Seeds	O	F.Doljack	1	P.Todt	O	E.McNeely	O	R.Young	C	P.Hargrave
C	M.Ruel	O	M.Simons	1	L.Fonseca	3	N.Richardson	O	D.Cooke	O	J.Moore	3	E.Grimes	1	J.Judge
/O	T.Winsett	O	I.Eichrodt	32	O.Hale	C	J.Grabowski	O	M.Hoag	C	J.Heving	C	R.Young	C	C.Bolton
3	M.McManus	O	S.Jolley	S	B.Hunnefield	C	W.Schang	/O	D.Walker	C	J.Palmisano	/O	F.Waddey	/O	J.Gill
2	M.Olson	3	W.Kamm	S	J.Goldman	S	B.Akers	/S	R.Rolfe	O	L.Finney	/O	B.Stanton	/1	B.Jordan
2	O.Marquardt	O	B.Norman	3S	G.DeTore	S	L.Brower					/C	J.Crouch	/3	B.Andrus
O	G.Rye	/O	B.Campbell	1	B.Connatser	O	G.Quellich	O	L.Gomez	P	R.Walberg	/S	F.O'Rourke	H	B.Phelps
/O	R.Scarritt	/C	B.Henline	/O	C.Jamieson	O	M.Ruel	P	L.Ruffing	P	L.Grove	/O	N.Kloza	H	N.Altrock
/O	G.Stumpf	/C	H.Garrity	/C	M.Berg	/3	J.Dugan	P	H.Johnson	P	G.Earnshaw			P	L.Brown
/C	H.Storie			/C	J.Sprinz	/C	G.Desautels	P	H.Pennock	P	R.Mahaffey	P	L.Stewart	P	F.Marberry
/1	J.Smith	P	V.Frasier			/O	I.Shiver	P	G.Pipgras	P	E.Rommel	P	S.Gray	P	C.Fischer
/2	P.Creeden	P	T.Thomas	P	W.Ferrell	/2	B.Harris					P	G.Blaeholder	P	B.Hadley
/O	J.Lucas	P	P.Caraway	P	W.Hudlin			P	E.Wells	P	W.Hoyt	P	D.Coffman		
H	B.McWilliams	P	R.Faber	P	C.Brown	P	E.Whitehill	P	G.Rhodes	P	H.McDonald	P	R.Collins	P	S.Jones
R	B.Marshall	P	H.McKain	P	M.Harder	P	V.Sorrell	P	R.Sherid	/P	B.Shores	RP	C.Kimsey	P	B.Burke
		RP	J.Moore	RP	P.Appleton	P	G.Uhle	P	J.Weaver	/P	J.Peterson	RP	R.Stiles	/P	W.Tauscher
		RP	G.Braxton			P	T.Bridges	/P	I.Andrews	/P	L.Krausse			/P	M.Weaver
P	J.Russell			P	S.Connally	P	A.Herring	P	L.Weinert	/P	S.Carter	P	W.Hebert	/P	W.Masters
P	D.MacFayden			P	R.Lawson			/P	L.McEvoy			/P	B.Cooney	/P	A.Liska
P	W.Moore	P	T.Lyons	P	F.Thomas	P	C.Hogsett					P	G.Braxton		
H	H.Lisenbee	P	B.Weiland	P	J.Miller	P	C.Sullivan					/P	F.Stiely		
P	E.Durham	P	G.Bowler	P	M.Shoffner	P	W.Hoyt					/P	J.Doyle		
		/P	L.Garland	P	O.Hildebrand	/P	W.Wyatt								
P	E.Morris	/P	B.Wehde	/P	B.Bean	/P	O.Collier								
P	M.Gaston			/P	H.Craghead										
P	B.Kline			/P	P.Donohue										
P	J.Brillheart														
/P	J.McLaughlin														
/P	W.Murphy														

TEAM	G	W	L	PCT	GB	R	OR	AB	H	2B	3B	HR	BB	SO	AVG	OBP	SLG	PRO	PRO+	BR	/A	PF	CHI	RC	SB	CS	SBA	SBR
PHI	153	107	45	.704		858	626	5377	1544	311	64	118	528	543	.287	.355	.435	.790	107	93	40	106	98	843	25	23	52	-6
NY	155	94	59	.614	13.5	1067	760	5608	1667	277	78	155	748	554	.297	.383	.457	.840	135	220	280	94	100	1016	138	68	67	1
WAS	156	92	62	.597	16	843	691	5576	1588	308	93	49	481	459	.285	.345	.400	.745	100	8	4	101	103	774	72	64	53	-17
CLE	155	78	76	.506	30	885	833	5445	1612	321	69	71	555	433	.296	.363	.419	.782	105	91	41	106	100	840	63	60	51	-17
STL	154	63	91	.409	45	722	870	5374	1455	287	62	76	488	580	.271	.333	.390	.723	92	-40	-66	104	98	696	73	80	48	-26
BOS	153	62	90	.408	45	625	800	5379	1409	289	34	37	405	565	.262	.315	.349	.664	85	-154	-121	95	102	596	42	43	49	-13
DET	154	61	93	.396	47	651	836	5430	1456	292	69	43	480	468	.268	.330	.371	.701	87	-79	-103	103	93	675	117	75	61	-10
CHI	156	56	97	.366	51.5	704	939	5481	1423	238	69	27	483	445	.260	.323	.343	.666	86	-146	-108	94	108	632	94	39	71	5
TOT	618					6355		43670	12154	2323	538	576	4168	4047	.278	.344	.396	.740							624	452	58	-84

TEAM	CG	SH	SV	IP	H	H/G	HR	BB	SO	RAT	ERA	ERA+	OAV	OOB	PR	/A	PF	CPI	FA	E	DP	FW	PW	BW	SBW	DIF
PHI	97	12	16	1365¹	1342	8.8	73	457	574	11.9	3.47	130	.256	.316	138	155	103	105	.976	141	151	3.2	14.4	3.7	.4	9.3
NY	78	4	17	1410¹	1461	9.3	67	543	686	12.9	4.20	94	.263	.332	28	-37	91	94	.972	169	131	1.7	-3.4	26.1	1.1	-7.9
WAS	60	7	24	1394¹	1434	9.3	73	498	582	12.6	3.76	114	.264	.327	95	82	98	104	.976	142	148	3.3	7.6	.4	-.6	4.3
CLE	76	6	9	1354²	1577	10.5	64	561	470	14.4	4.63	100	.286	.355	-38	-2	106	100	.963	232	143	-2.0	-.2	3.8	-.6	.0
STL	65	4	10	1362	1623	10.7	84	444	436	13.8	4.76	97	.293	.348	-57	-18	106	99	.963	232	160	-2.1	-1.7	-6.1	-1.4	-2.6
BOS	61	5	10	1366²	1559	10.3	54	473	365	13.5	4.60	94	.285	.344	-33	-44	98	95	.970	188	127	.4	-4.1	-11.3	-.2	1.2
DET	86	5	6	1384¹	1549	10.1	79	597	511	14.1	4.59	100	.280	.355	-32	-1	105	102	.964	220	139	-1.4	-.0	-9.6	-.0	-5.0
CHI	54	6	10	1390¹	1613	10.4	82	588	421	14.5	5.04	85	.287	.358	-101	-122	97	96	.961	245	131	-2.7	-11.4	-10.1	1.4	2.2
TOT	577	49	102	11028		9.9				13.5	4.38	85	.278	.344					.968	1569	1130					

Runs	Hits	Doubles	Triples	Home Runs	Total Bases
Gehrig-NY 163	Gehrig-NY 211	Webb-Bos 67	Johnson-Det 19	Ruth-NY 46	Gehrig-NY 410
Ruth-NY 149	Averill-Cle 209	Alexander-Det 47	Gehrig-NY 15	Gehrig-NY 46	Ruth-NY 374
Averill-Cle 140	Simmons-Phi 200	Kress-StL 46	Blue-Chi 15	Averill-Cle 32	Averill-Cle 361
Combs-NY 120	Ruth-NY 199	Cronin-Was 44	Vosmik-Cle 14	Foxx-Phi 30	Simmons-Phi 329
Chapman-NY 120	Webb-Bos 196		Reynolds-Chi 14	Goslin-StL 24	Goslin-StL 328

Runs Batted In	Runs Produced	Bases On Balls	Batting Average	On Base Percentage	Slugging Average
Gehrig-NY 184	Gehrig-NY 301	Ruth-NY 128	Simmons-Phi ..... .390	Ruth-NY .... .495	Ruth-NY .... .700
Ruth-NY 163	Ruth-NY 266	Blue-Chi 127	Ruth-NY .... .373	Morgan-Cle .... .451	Gehrig-NY .... .662
Averill-Cle 143	Averill-Cle 251	Gehrig-NY 117	Morgan-Cle .... .351	Gehrig-NY .... .446	Simmons-Phi ..... .641
Simmons-Phi 128	Chapman-NY 225	Bishop-Phi 112	Cochrane-Phi ..... .349	Simmons-Phi ..... .444	Averill-Cle .... .576
Cronin-Was 126	Cronin-Was 217	Lary-NY 88	Gehrig-NY .... .341	Blue-Chi .... .430	Foxx-Phi .... .567

Production	Adjusted Production	Batter Runs	Adjusted Batter Runs	Clutch Hitting Index	Runs Created
Ruth-NY 1.195	Ruth-NY 223	Ruth-NY 91.5	Ruth-NY 101.8	Bluege-Was 126	Ruth-NY 192
Gehrig-NY 1.108	Gehrig-NY 199	Gehrig-NY 79.9	Gehrig-NY 90.0	Kamm-Chi-Cle 124	Gehrig-NY 185
Simmons-Phi 1.085	Simmons-Phi 172	Simmons-Phi 59.6	Simmons-Phi 51.6	Vosmik-Cle 119	Simmons-Phi 145
Averill-Cle .... .979	Webb-Bos 151	Averill-Cle 48.2	Webb-Bos 43.4	Lazzeri-NY 118	Averill-Cle 144
Cochrane-Phi ..... .976	Goslin-StL 147	Goslin-StL 44.7	Averill-Cle 40.5	Spencer-Was 118	Goslin-StL 137

Total Average	Stolen Bases	Stolen Base Average	Stolen Base Runs	Fielding Runs	Total Player Rating
Ruth-NY 1.487	Chapman-NY 61	Cissell-Chi 75.0	Chapman-NY 4.5	Melillo-StL 33.1	Ruth-NY 7.3
Gehrig-NY 1.267	Johnson-Det 33	Reynolds-Chi 73.9	H.Walker-Det 2.4	McManus-Det-Bos 21.1	Gehrig-NY 5.8
Simmons-Phi 1.199	Burns-StL 19	Chapman-NY 72.6	Blue-Chi 2.1	West-Was 21.0	Cronin-Was 4.6
Morgan-Cle 1.046	Lazzeri-NY 18	Lazzeri-NY 66.7	Cissell-Chi........ 1.8	Burns-StL 18.4	Simmons-Phi 4.6
Cochrane-Phi ... 1.033	Cissell-Chi 18	Bluege-Was 61.5		Rhyne-Bos 16.9	Cochrane-Phi 4.3

Wins	Win Percentage	Games	Complete Games	Shutouts	Saves
Grove-Phi 31	Grove-Phi .... .886	Hadley-Was 55	Grove-Phi 27	Grove-Phi 4	Moore-Bos 10
Ferrell-Cle 22	Marberry-Was ... .800	Moore-Bos 53	Ferrell-Cle 27	Earnshaw-Phi 3	Hadley-Was 8
Gomez-NY 21	Mahaffey-Phi .... .789	Caraway-Chi 51	Earnshaw-Phi 23		Marberry-Was 7
Earnshaw-Phi 21	Earnshaw-Phi ... .750	Frasier-Chi 46	Whitehill-Det 22		Kimsey-StL........ 7
Walberg-Phi 20	Gomez-NY .... .700	Fischer-Was 46	Stewart-StL 20		Earnshaw-Phi 6

Innings Pitched	Fewest Hits/Game	Fewest BB/Game	Strikeouts	Strikeouts/Game	Ratio
Walberg-Phi 291.0	Hadley-Was 7.26	Pennock-NY 1.43	Grove-Phi 175	Hadley-Was 6.21	Grove-Phi 9.73
Grove-Phi 288.2	Gomez-NY 7.63	Gray-StL.......... 1.88	Earnshaw-Phi 152	Gomez-NY 5.56	Earnshaw-Phi ... 10.64
Earnshaw-Phi ... 281.2	Grove-Phi 7.76	Grove-Phi 1.93	Gomez-NY 150	Bridges-Det 5.46	Gomez-NY 10.93
Ferrell-Cle 276.1	Johnson-NY 8.07	Brown-Cle 2.12	Ruffing-NY 132	Grove-Phi 5.46	Coffman-StL..... 11.27
Whitehill-Det 271.1	Earnshaw-Phi ... 8.15	Blaeholder-StL.... 2.23	Hadley-Was 124	Ruffing-NY 5.01	Uhle-Det 11.33

Earned Run Average	Adjusted ERA	Opponents' Batting Avg.	Opponents' On Base Pct.	Starter Runs	Adjusted Starter Runs
Grove-Phi 2.06	Grove-Phi 218	Hadley-Was ...... .218	Grove-Phi 271	Grove-Phi 74.5	Grove-Phi 78.1
Gomez-NY 2.67	Gomez-NY 149	Earnshaw-Phi .... .226	Earnshaw-Phi .... .288	Gomez-NY 46.2	Gomez-NY 35.1
Hadley-Was 3.06	Hadley-Was 140	Grove-Phi .... .229	Gomez-NY .... .295	Brown-Was 33.9	Brown-Was...... 31.3
Brown-Was 3.20	Brown-Was 134	Johnson-NY ...... .234	Coffman-StL ..... .298	Hadley-Was 26.4	Ferrell-Cle 26.9
Marberry-Was ... 3.45	Uhle-Det 131	Earnshaw-Phi .... .236	Uhle-Det .... .304	Marberry-Was ... 22.6	Earnshaw-Phi..... 25.6

Clutch Pitching Index	Relief Runs	Adjusted Relief Runs	Relief Ranking	Total Pitcher Index	Total Baseball Ranking
Grove-Phi 118	Kimsey-StL 2.6	Kimsey-StL........2.9	Kimsey-StL........2.9	Grove-Phi 8.7	Grove-Phi 8.7
Faber-Chi 116				Ferrell-Cle 5.2	Ruth-NY 7.3
Whitehill-Det 115				Gomez-NY 3.5	Gehrig-NY 5.8
Pennock-NY 110				Brown-Was 3.4	Ferrell-Cle 5.2
Brown-Was 110				Earnshaw-Phi 2.9	Cronin-Was 4.6

January 26 William K. Wrigley, owner of the Cubs since 1919, dies and is buried on Catalina Island. His only son, Philip K. Wrigley, inherits the Cubs and the minor league Los Angeles Angels.

May 11 Cardinals hurler "Wild" Bill Hallahan lives up to his name with three wild pitches in the 12th inning in a game that Brooklyn wins at St. Louis, 6–3. He ties the record set by Jake Weimer of the Cubs on May 10, 1903.

June 3 John McGraw, who came to New York in 1902, resigns as manager of the Giants and is replaced by Bill Terry, the team's star first baseman.

June 7 Pitcher John Quinn, at 48, becomes the oldest player to have an extra-base hit (a double) and bat in a run, as the Dodgers beat the Cubs, 9–2.

June 22 The NL, at a meeting of club presidents, finally approves players wearing numbers. The AL had started the practice in 1929.

July 6 Cubs shortstop Bill Jurges is shot twice in his Chicago hotel room by a spurned girlfriend, Violet Popovich Valli. In a scuffle for the gun, Jurges is hit in the shoulder and hand. Jurges fails to prosecute, and Valli will be signed to a 22-week contract to sing in local nightclubs and theaters. She is billed as "Violet (What I Did for Love) Valli—the Most Talked About Girl in Chicago."

August 13 Commissioner Kenesaw Mountain Landis clears Rogers Hornsby of charges of fraudulently "borrowing" money from Cubs players. The Chicago papers said Hornsby had obtained money from players, either loaned to him to bet on horse races, or to share in joint ventures. When Hornsby is fined, the players want refunds. Hornsby wants a lump payoff by the Cubs, who refuse. Landis holds several hearings, and as he doesn't punish anyone, it is taken as exoneration.

August 14 John Quinn becomes, at 49, the oldest pitcher to win a major league game. He relieves Van Mungo in the ninth with the game between Brooklyn and New York tied at 1–1. The Dodgers win in the 10th after Johnny Frederick hits a pinch-hit home run off Carl Hubbell in the ninth to tie the game. It is Frederick's fourth pinch-hit homer of the year, for a new major league record. He will have six by the season's end.

September 7 Pirates catcher Earl Grace makes a wild throw to end a streak of 110 consecutive errorless games. It is Grace's only error of the season for a still-standing NL record.

September 20 The Chicago Cubs clinch the NL pennant when Kiki Cuyler hits a triple with the bases loaded for a 5-2 win over Pittsburgh.

September 22 The Cubs announce World Series shares and snub former manager Rogers Hornsby. Late-season arrival Mark Koenig gets just a half share.

September 26 Chuck Klein closes the season with 38 home runs and 20 stolen bases and becomes the only player of the lively ball era (1920 and after) to lead his league in these two departments.

October 19 The BBWAA MVP awards are announced, with Jimmie Foxx winning in the AL and Chuck Klein in the NL.

December 15 A joint meeting of AL and NL owners approves the concept of "chain store" baseball, developed as the St. Louis Cardinals farm system, despite strenuous objections by Judge Landis.

	BOSTON		BROOKLYN		CHICAGO		CINCINNATI		NEW YORK		PHILADELPHIA		PITTSBURGH		ST.LOUIS
M	B.McKechnie	M	M.Carey	M	R.Hornsby	M	D.Howley	M	J.McGraw	M	B.Shotton	M	M.Gibson	M	G.Street
1B	A.Shires	1B	G.Kelly	M	C.Grimm	1B	H.Hendrick	M	B.Terry	1B	D.Hurst	1B	G.Suhr	1B	R.Collins
2B	R.Maranville	2B	T.Cuccinello	1B	C.Grimm	2B	G.Grantham	1B	B.Terry	2B	L.Mallon	2B	T.Piet	2B	J.Reese
SS	B.Urbanski	SS	G.Wright	2B	B.Herman	SS	L.Durocher	2B	H.Critz	SS	D.Bartell	SS	A.Vaughan	SS	C.Gelbert
3B	F.Knothe	3B	J.Stripp	SS	B.Jurges	3B	W.Gilbert	SS	D.Marshall	3B	P.Whitney	3B	P.Traynor	3B	J.Flowers
LF	R.Worthington	LF	L.O'Doul	3B	W.English	LF	W.Roettger	3B	J.Vergez	LF	H.Lee	LF	A.Comorosky	LF	E.Orsatti
CF	W.Berger	CF	D.Taylor	LF	R.Stephenson	CF	E.Crabtree	LF	J.Moore	CF	K.Davis	CF	L.Waner	CF	P.Martin
RF	W.Schulmerich	RF	H.Wilson	CF	J.Moore	RF	B.Herman	CF	F.Lindstrom	RF	C.Klein	RF	P.Waner	RF	G.Watkins
C	A.Spohrer	C	A.Lopez	RF	K.Cuyler	C	E.Lombardi	RF	M.Ott	C	S.Davis	C	E.Grace	C	G.Mancuso
				C	G.Hartnett			C	S.Hogan						
O3	R.Moore	O	J.Frederick			O	T.Douthit			2	B.Friberg	O	D.Barbee	23	F.Frisch
O	F.Leach	S3	G.Slade	3	S.Hack	S2	J.Morrissey	O	C.Fullis	C	H.McCurdy	S3	T.Thevenow	1	J.Bottomley
C	P.Hargrave	1	B.Clancy	O	R.Hemsley	O	C.Hafey	3S	G.English	O	R.Bressler	C	T.Padden	C	J.Wilson
1	B.Jordan	3	N.Finn	O	L.Richbourg	32	A.High	S	T.Jackson	C	A.Todd	O	G.Dugas	O	R.Blades
O	D.Holland	C	C.Sukeforth	O	V.Barton	C	C.Manion	O	L.Koenecke	O	F.Brickell	3	H.Finney	3	S.Adams
2S	H.Ford	C	V.Picinich	S	M.Koenig	1	M.Heath	O	E.Allen	2	E.Delker	O	B.Brenzel	O	J.Puccinelli
3	B.Akers	O	M.Rosenfeld	O	M.Gudat	C	C.Asbjornson	S	E.Moore	/1	C.Heathcote	/3	B.Brubaker	O	J.Medwick
3	B.Walters	/O	A.Cohen	O	R.Hornsby	/1	H.Heilmann	/1	S.Leslie	/2	G.Knothe	/S	H.Groskloss	C	C.Wilson
O	E.Clark	/O	I.Boone	O	F.Demaree	/1	J.Shevlin	C	B.O'Farrell	/O	R.Scarritt	/O	W.Jensen	3	H.Hendrick
C	J.Schulte	/1	B.Caldwell	C	Z.Taylor	H	C.Heathcote	C	F.Healy	H	D.Taitt			O	R.Pepper
H	O.Eckhardt	/C	P.Richards	/O	D.Taylor	R	O.Bluege	/S	A.McLarney	H	H.Willingham	P	L.French	2	E.Delker
		/1	D.Siebert	/1	H.Taylor			H	J.Tobin			P	B.Swift	/C	B.DeLancey
P	E.Brandt	/3	B.Reis			P	R.Lucas	H	P.Veltman	P	E.Holley	P	H.Meine	/3	R.Cunningham
P	H.Betts	H	F.Thompson	P	L.Warneke	P	S.Johnson			P	R.Benge	P	B.Harris	/O	J.Hunt
P	B.Brown			P	G.Bush	P	O.Carroll	P	C.Hubbell	P	S.Hansen	P	S.Swetonic	/O	R.Bressler
P	T.Zachary	P	W.Clark	P	P.Malone	P	L.Benton	P	F.Fitzsimmons	P	P.Collins	RP	E.Brame	/O	W.Holm
P	B.Cantwell	P	V.Mungo	P	C.Root	P	R.Kolp	P	B.Walker	P	F.Rhem			/C	M.Gonzalez
RP	F.Frankhouse	P	D.Vance	RP	J.May	RP	J.Ogden	P	J.Mooney			P	G.Spencer	/S	H.Ford
RP	B.Cunningham	P	F.Heimach					P	H.Bell	P	J.Elliott	P	L.Chagnon	/S	S.Webb
		P	S.Thurston			P	B.Frey	RP	D.Luque	P	H.Elliott	P	R.Kremer		
P	S.Seibold	RP	J.Quinn	P	B.Smith	P	E.Rixey	RP	S.Gibson	P	J.Berly	/P	H.Smith	P	D.Dean
P	H.Pruett	RP	C.Moore	P	B.Tinning	P	W.Hilcher			P	R.Grabowski			P	P.Derringer
/P	L.Mangum			/P	L.Herrmann	/P	B.Wysong	P	H.Schumacher	/P	A.Liska			P	T.Carleton
/P	B.Sherdel	P	J.Shaute	/P	C.Yerkes			P	W.Hoyt	P	C.Nichols			P	B.Hallahan
		P	R.Phelps	/P	E.Baecht			/P	C.Mitchell	P	C.Dudley			P	S.Johnson
		/P	W.Hoyt	/P	B.Newsom			/P	R.Parmelee	/P	S.Bolen			RP	J.Lindsey
		/P	F.Thomas							/P	B.Adams			RP	A.Stout
		/P	E.Pipgras												
		/P	A.Jones											P	J.Haines
														/P	F.Rhem
														/P	R.Starr
														/P	J.Winford
														/P	B.Sherdel
														/P	B.Frey
														/P	D.Terwilliger
														/P	B.Teachout

TEAM	G	W	L	PCT	GB	R	OR	AB	H	2B	3B	HR	BB	SO	AVG	OBP	SLG	PRO	PRO+	BR	/A	PF	CHI	RC	SB	CS	SBA	SBR
CHI	154	90	64	.584		720	633	5462	1519	296	60	69	398	514	.278	.330	.392	.722	101	0	7	99	101	728	48			
PIT	154	86	68	.558	4	701	711	5421	1543	274	90	48	358	385	.285	.333	.395	.728	103	9	22	98	99	729	71			
BRO	154	81	73	.526	9	752	747	5433	1538	296	59	110	388	574	.283	.334	.420	.754	110	55	71	98	99	778	61			
PHI	154	78	76	.506	12	844	796	5510	1608	330	67	122	446	547	.292	.348	.442	.790	105	132	32	112	98	870	71			
BOS	155	77	77	.500	13	649	655	5506	1460	262	53	63	347	496	.265	.311	.366	.677	90	-94	-71	96	105	643	36			
STL	156	72	82	.468	18	684	717	5458	1467	307	51	76	420	514	.269	.324	.385	.709	93	-27	-47	103	100	702	92			
NY	154	72	82	.468	18	755	706	5530	1527	263	54	116	348	391	.276	.322	.406	.728	103	1	16	98	107	735	31			
CIN	155	60	94	.390	30	575	715	5443	1429	265	68	47	436	436	.263	.320	.362	.682	92	-77	-56	97	91	654	35			
TOT	618					5680		43763	12091	2293	502	651	3141	3857	.276	.328	.396	.724						445				

TEAM	CG	SH	SV	IP	H	H/G	HR	BB	SO	RAT	ERA	ERA+	OAV	OOB	PR	/A	PF	CPI	FA	E	DP	FW	PW	BW	SBW	DIF
CHI	79	9	7	1401	1444	9.3	68	409	527	12.1	3.44	109	.264	.319	68	50	97	102	.973	173	146	.4	4.9	.7		7.0
PIT	71	12	12	1377	1472	9.6	86	338	377	11.9	3.75	102	.270	.314	20	10	98	96	.969	185	124	-.4	1.0	2.2		6.2
BRO	61	7	16	1379²	1538	10.0	72	403	497	12.8	4.27	89	.282	.334	-60	-68	98	94	.971	183	169	-.3	-6.7	7.0		4.0
PHI	59	4	17	1384	1589	10.3	107	450	459	13.5	4.47	99	.287	.344	-91	-114	100	100	.968	194	133	-.9	-.9	3.2		-.3
BOS	72	8	8	1414	1483	9.4	61	420	440	12.3	3.53	107	.272	.328	55	36	97	105	.976	152	145	1.7	3.6	-7.0		1.7
STL	70	13	9	1396	1533	9.9	76	455	681	13.0	3.97	99	.282	.340	-14	-6	101	104	.971	175	155	.4	-.6	-4.7		-.1
NY	57	3	16	1375¹	1533	10.0	112	387	506	12.7	3.83	97	.280	.330	8	-18	96	108	.969	191	143	-.7	-1.8	1.6		-4.1
CIN	83	6	6	1394²	1505	9.7	69	276	359	11.6	3.79	102	.274	.311	14	10	99	92	.971	178	129	.1	1.0	-5.5		-12.6
TOT	552	62	91	11121²		9.8				12.5	3.88		.276	.328					.971	1431	1144					

Runs
Klein-Phi 152
Terry-NY 124
O'Doul-Bro 120
Ott-NY 119
Bartell-Phi 118

Hits
Klein-Phi 226
Terry-NY 225
O'Doul-Bro 219
P.Waner-Pit 215
Herman-Chi 206

Doubles
P.Waner-Pit 62
Klein-Phi 50
Stephenson-Chi ... 49
Bartell-Phi 48

Triples
Herman-Cin 19
Suhr-Pit 16
Klein-Phi 15

Home Runs
Ott-NY 38
Klein-Phi 38
Terry-NY 28
Hurst-Phi 24
Wilson-Bro 23

Total Bases
Klein-Phi 420
Terry-NY 373
Ott-NY 340
O'Doul-Bro 330
P.Waner-Pit 321

Runs Batted In
Hurst-Phi 143
Klein-Phi 137
Whitney-Phi 124
Wilson-Bro 123
Ott-NY 123

Runs Produced
Klein-Phi 251
Hurst-Phi 228
Terry-NY 213
Whitney-Phi 204
Ott-NY 204

Bases On Balls
Ott-NY 100
Hurst-Phi 65
Bartell-Phi 64
Suhr-Pit 63

Batting Average
O'Doul-Bro .... .368
Terry-NY .... .350
Hurst-Phi .... .348
P.Waner-Pit ...... .341
Hurst-Phi .... .339

On Base Percentage
Ott-NY .... .424
O'Doul-Bro .... .423
Hurst-Phi .... .412
Klein-Phi .... .404
P.Waner-Pit ...... .397

Slugging Average
Klein-Phi .... .646
Ott-NY .... .601
Terry-NY .... .580
O'Doul-Bro .... .555
Hurst-Phi .... .547

Production
Klein-Phi 1.050
Ott-NY 1.025
O'Doul-Bro .... .978
Terry-NY .... .962
Hurst-Phi .... .959

Adjusted Production
Ott-NY 175
O'Doul-Bro 164
Klein-Phi 158
Terry-NY 158
Herman-Cin 152

Batter Runs
Klein-Phi 68.2
Ott-NY 59.8
O'Doul-Bro 51.2
Terry-NY 46.4
Hurst-Phi 46.2

Adjusted Batter Runs
Ott-NY 62.8
O'Doul-Bro 53.9
Klein-Phi 50.9
Terry-NY 49.1
Herman-Cin 41.8

Clutch Hitting Index
Wilson-Bro 132
Whitney-Phi 131
Hogan-NY 129
Cuyler-Chi 126
Hurst-Phi 124

Runs Created
Klein-Phi 171
Ott-NY 151
O'Doul-Bro 142
Terry-NY 142
Hurst-Phi 134

Total Average
Klein-Phi 1.182
Ott-NY 1.166
O'Doul-Bro 1.059
Hurst-Phi 1.042
Terry-NY .... .981

Stolen Bases
Klein-Phi 20
Piet-Pit 19
Watkins-StL 18
Frisch-StL 18
K.Davis-Phi 16

Stolen Base Average

Stolen Base Runs

Fielding Runs
Jurges-Chi 31.7
Cuccinello-Bro ... 19.0
Herman-Chi 16.8
Frisch-StL 16.4
Stripp-Bro 15.9

Total Player Rating
Ott-NY 5.3
Klein-Phi 4.9
Terry-NY 4.9
Herman-Cin 4.7
O'Doul-Bro 3.9

Wins
Warneke-Chi 22
Clark-Bro 20
Bush-Chi 19

Win Percentage
Warneke-Chi ...... .786
Bush-Chi .... .633
Rhem-StL-Phi ..... .625
Clark-Bro .... .625
Hubbell-NY .... .621

Games
French-Pit 47
Dean-StL 46
Carleton-StL 44
Collins-Phi 43

Complete Games
Lucas-Cin 28
Warneke-Chi 25
Hubbell-NY 22

Shutouts
Warneke-Chi 4
Swetonic-Pit 4
Dean-StL 4

Saves
Quinn-Bro 8
Benge-Phi 6
Luque-NY 5
Cantwell-Bos 5

Innings Pitched
Dean-StL 286.0
Hubbell-NY 284.0
Warneke-Chi 277.0
French-Pit 274.1
Clark-Bro 273.0

Fewest Hits/Game
Swetonic-Pit 7.41
Brown-Bos 7.90
Warneke-Chi 8.03
Hubbell-NY 8.24
Malone-Chi 8.43

Fewest BB/Game
Swift-Pit 1.09
Lucas-Cin 1.17
Hubbell-NY 1.27
Benton-Cin 1.35
Betts-Bos 1.42

Strikeouts
Dean-StL 191
Hubbell-NY 137
Malone-Chi 120
Carleton-StL 113
Brown-Bos 110

Strikeouts/Game
Dean-StL 6.01
Hallahan-StL 5.51
Vance-Bro 5.28
Carleton-StL 5.18
Brown-Bos 4.65

Ratio
Hubbell-NY 9.63
Swift-Pit 9.78
Lucas-Cin 9.92
Warneke-Chi 10.17
Swetonic-Pit 10.46

Earned Run Average
Warneke-Chi 2.37
Hubbell-NY 2.50
Betts-Bos 2.80
Swetonic-Pit 2.82
Lucas-Cin 2.94

Adjusted ERA
Warneke-Chi 159
Hubbell-NY 148
Swetonic-Pit 135
Betts-Bos 134
Lucas-Cin 131

Opponents' Batting Avg.
Swetonic-Pit ..... .221
Warneke-Chi ...... .237
Hubbell-NY .... .238
Brown-Bos .... .238
Malone-Chi .... .244

Opponents' On Base Pct.
Hubbell-NY .... .268
Swift-Pit .... .272
Lucas-Cin .... .274
Warneke-Chi ...... .283
Swetonic-Pit ..... .286

Starter Runs
Warneke-Chi 46.4
Hubbell-NY 43.4
Lucas-Cin 28.1
Betts-Bos 26.5
French-Pit 26.2

Adjusted Starter Runs
Warneke-Chi 42.9
Hubbell-NY 38.1
Lucas-Cin 27.4
French-Pit 24.2
Betts-Bos 23.6

Clutch Pitching Index
Bush-Chi 123
French-Pit 123
Zachary-Bos 117
Hallahan-StL 113
Derringer-StL 113

Relief Runs
Quinn-Bro 5.6
Frankhouse-Bos ... 3.8

Adjusted Relief Runs
Quinn-Bro 5.0
Frankhouse-Bos ... 2.4

Relief Ranking
Quinn-Bro 6.2
Frankhouse-Bos ... 2.0

Total Pitcher Index
Hubbell-NY 4.8
Lucas-Cin 4.4
Warneke-Chi 4.1
Cantwell-Bos 2.6
French-Pit 2.5

Total Baseball Ranking
Ott-NY 5.3
Klein-Phi 4.9
Terry-NY 4.9
Hubbell-NY 4.8
Herman-Cin 4.7

May 30 A plaque in memory of Miller Huggins, former Yankees manager, is dedicated at Yankee Stadium. It is the first of an array of monuments erected in the ballpark.

June 3 Lou Gehrig hits four consecutive home runs and narrowly misses a fifth in the Yankees-Athletics slugfest won by New York, 20-13. But the bigger headlines go to John McGraw, who resigns after 30 years as manager of the Giants and is replaced by Bill Terry.

June 20 Roger Cramer of the A's has six hits in consecutive times at bat in a nine-inning game. Cramer will do this again in 1935, the only AL player to repeat the feat.

June 23 Lou Gehrig plays his 1,103rd successive game in a New York uniform, equaling Joe Sewell's record with one team (Cleveland).

July 10 An extraordinary 18-inning game is won by the Athletics at Cleveland, 18–17. To save train fare for the single-date appearance, Connie Mack takes along just two pitchers. Lew Krausse, Sr. the A's starting pitcher, gives up four hits in the first inning and his replacement, Eddie Rommel pitches 17 innings in relief, giving up a record 29 hits, but still wins. Cleveland's Johnny Burnett sets a major league record by collecting nine hits in 11 at bats, while the A's Jimmie Foxx strokes six hits, including three home runs. Foxx totals 16 bases in the game, the third AL player to do it.

July 31 Cleveland plays its first game in new Municipal Stadium before a crowd in excess of 80,000 (paid attendance of 76,979), but Mel Harder loses to the A's Lefty Grove, 1–0, on Cochrane's RBI single.

August 21 Cleveland's Wes Ferrell becomes the century's first pitcher to win 20 or more games in each of his first four seasons, beating Washington, 11-5.

September 3 Jimmie Foxx of the A's poles his 50th and 51st home runs to become the third player to reach 50 in a season, joining Babe Ruth and Hack Wilson.

September 25 Jimmie Foxx hits his 58th home run in the last game of the season to finish two short of Ruth's 1927 record of 60.

September 28 In the opening game of the World Series, Lou Gehrig's home run leads the Yankees to a 12-6 win over the Cubs.

September 29 Lefty Gomez breezes to a 5-2 win over the Cubs, and Gehrig gets three hits for the Yankees' second victory.

October 1 The World Series moves to Chicago, and the Yankees continue to torment the Cubs. In the fifth inning, Babe Ruth waits until he has two strikes and then gestures to pitcher Charlie Root. He belts the next pitch into the center fielder bleachers. It is Ruth's second home run of the game, the "Called Shot." Gehrig also hammers out two round-trippers.

October 2 Tony Lazzeri hits two home runs, and the Yankees sweep the Series, beating the demoralized Chicago Cubs, 13-6.

BOSTON		CHICAGO		CLEVELAND		DETROIT		NEW YORK		PHILADELPHIA		ST.LOUIS		WASHINGTON	
M	S.Collins	M	L.Fonseca	M	R.Peckinpaugh	M	B.Harris	M	J.McCarthy	M	C.Mack	M	B.Killefer	M	W.Johnson
M	M.McManus	1B	L.Blue	1B	E.Morgan	1B	H.Davis	1B	L.Gehrig	1B	J.Foxx	1B	J.Burns	1B	J.Kuhel
1B	D.Alexander	2B	J.Hayes	2B	B.Cissell	2B	C.Gehringer	2B	T.Lazzeri	2B	M.Bishop	2B	S.Melillo	2B	B.Myer
2B	M.Olson	SS	L.Appling	SS	J.Burnett	SS	B.Rogell	SS	F.Crosetti	SS	E.McNair	SS	J.Levey	SS	J.Cronin
SS	R.Warstler	3B	C.Selph	3B	W.Kamm	3B	H.Schuble	3B	J.Sewell	3B	J.Dykes	3B	A.Scharein	3B	O.Bluege
3B	U.Pickering	LF	B.Fothergill	LF	J.Vosmik	LF	J.Stone	LF	B.Chapman	LF	A.Simmons	LF	G.Goslin	LF	H.Manush
LF	S.Jolley	CF	L.Funk	CF	G.Averill	CF	G.Walker	CF	E.Combs	CF	M.Haas	CF	F.Schulte	CF	S.West
CF	T.Oliver	RF	B.Seeds	RF	D.Porter	RF	E.Webb	RF	B.Ruth	RF	D.Cramer	RF	B.Campbell	RF	C.Reynolds
RF	R.Johnson	C	F.Grube	C	L.Sewell	C	R.Hayworth	C	B.Dickey	C	M.Cochrane	C	R.Ferrell	C	R.Spencer
C	B.Tate														
		OS	R.Kress	C	G.Myatt	31	B.Rhiel	O	S.Byrd	O	B.Miller	3	L.Storti	O	S.Rice
O1	J.Watwood	13	B.Sullivan	S3	E.Montague	O	J.White	S	L.Lary	2	D.Williams	C	B.Bengough	1	J.Judge
23	M.McManus	O	C.Berry	1	J.Connatser	O	R.Johnson	C	A.Jorgens	O	J.Heving	O	D.Garms	C	M.Berg
C	E.Connolly	O	J.Hodapp	/O	M.Powers	3	N.Richardson	2	D.Farrell	3	E.Coleman	3	E.Grimes	O	D.Harris
S	H.Rhyne	O	J.Rothrock	C	F.Pytlak	C	M.Ruel	O	M.Hoag	1	O.Roettger	O	T.Jenkins	2S	J.Kerr
O	E.Webb	3	C.English	/2	J.Hodapp	2	G.Desautels	/C	J.Saltzgaver	/C	E.Madjeski	3	R.Kress	C	H.Maple
O	G.Stumpf	O	E.Swanson	/O	C.Jamieson	O	B.Lawrence	/C	E.Phillips	S	J.Boley	/O	L.Bettencourt	/3	W.Kingdon
1	A.Van Camp	O	J.Watwood	/S	J.Boley	/O	F.Doljack	/C	J.Glenn	/O	J.Jones	/C	J.Schulte	/3	D.Musser
O	J.Rothrock	O	B.Norman	/O	B.Seeds	/1	D.Alexander	/2	R.Schalk	/S	A.Reiss	/O	S.Fisher	/S	J.McLeod
1	J.Reder	/S	B.Cissell	/S	B.Berger	/C	G.Susce	H	D.Cooke	H	E.Cihocki	/O	N.Kloza		
/2	A.Spognardi	O	S.Jolley									/3	J.McLaughlin		
C	C.Berry	/O	L.Fonseca	P	W.Ferrell	P	E.Whitehill	P	L.Gomez	P	L.Grove			P	M.Weaver
/C	H.Storie	/O	H.Anderson	P	C.Brown	P	V.Sorrell	P	R.Ruffing	P	R.Walberg	P	L.Stewart	P	L.Brown
H	O.Miller	/O	B.Campbell	P	M.Harder	P	W.Wyatt	P	G.Pipgras	P	G.Earnshaw	P	G.Blaeholder	P	F.Marberry
H	J.Lucas	/C	B.Tate	P	W.Hudlin	P	T.Bridges	P	J.Allen	P	R.Mahaffey	P	B.Hadley	P	T.Thomas
/C	H.Patterson	/O	M.Simons	P	O.Hildebrand	P	C.Hogsett	P	H.Pennock	P	T.Freitas	P	S.Gray		
		/2	G.Mulleavy					RP	J.Brown	RP	L.Krausse	P	W.Hebert	P	B.Burke
P	B.Weiland											RP	C.Kimsey	P	D.Coffman
P	E.Durham	P	T.Lyons	P	J.Russell	P	G.Uhle	P	D.MacFayden	P	E.Rommel			P	C.Fischer
P	B.Kline	P	S.Jones	P	S.Connally	P	B.Marrow	P	E.Wells	P	S.Cain	P	C.Fischer	/P	B.McAfee
P	I.Andrews	/P	M.Gaston	/P	R.Winegarner	P	I.Goldstein	/P	H.Johnson	/P	T.McKeithan	P	B.Cooney	/P	F.Ragland
RP	W.Moore	/P	M.Pearson	/P	M.Herring	P	A.Herring	P	I.Andrews	/P	J.Bowman	/P	D.Coffman	/P	B.Friedrichs
RP	J.Michaels	P	V.Frasier	/P	L.Moon	/P	R.Sewell	/P	W.Moore	/P	J.DeShong	/P	L.Polli	/P	B.Thomas
RP	L.Boerner	P	P.Gregory	/P	P.Appleton			P	G.Rhodes	/P	I.Stein			/P	E.Edelen
		RP	R.Faber					/P	C.Devens						
								/P	J.Murphy						
P	G.Rhodes	P	P.Caraway												
P	D.MacFayden	P	P.Daglia												
P	H.Lisenbee	P	T.Thomas												
P	J.Welch	P	B.Chamberlain												
P	P.Appleton	P	P.Gallivan												
P	J.Russell	/P	C.Biggs												
/P	E.Gallagher	/P	E.Walsh												
/P	G.McNaughton	/P	B.Hadley												
/P	P.Donohue	/P	A.Evans												
/P	R.Leheny	/P	C.Kimsey												
/P	J.McLaughlin	/P	H.McKain												
		/P	F.Kowalik												
		/P	A.Smith												
		/P	A.Wise												
		/P	G.Bowler												
		/P	L.Bartholomew												
		/P	C.Fieber												
		/P	J.Moore												
		/P	B.Poser												

TEAM	G	W	L	PCT	GB	R	OR	AB	H	2B	3B	HR	BB	SO	AVG	OBP	SLG	PRO	PRO+	BR	/A	PF	CHI	RC	SB	CS	SBA	SBR
NY	156	107	47	.695		1002	724	5477	1564	279	82	160	766	527	.286	.376	.454	.830	128	172	225	95	99	961	77	66	54	-17
PHI	154	94	60	.610	13	981	752	5537	1606	303	52	172	647	630	.290	.366	.457	.823	115	148	113	104	100	951	38	23	62	-2
WAS	154	93	61	.604	14	840	716	5515	1565	303	100	61	505	442	.284	.347	.408	.755	102	8	19	99	103	793	70	47	60	-7
CLE	153	87	65	.572	19	845	747	5412	1544	310	74	78	566	454	.285	.357	.413	.770	99	44	-11	107	99	811	52	54	49	-17
DET	153	76	75	.503	29.5	799	787	5409	1479	291	80	80	486	523	.273	.345	.401	.746	92	-35	-65	104	106	741	103	49	68	2
STL	154	63	91	.409	44	736	898	5449	1502	274	69	67	507	528	.276	.339	.388	.727	89	-45	-88	106	97	726	69	62	53	-17
CHI	152	49	102	.325	56.5	667	897	5336	1426	274	56	36	459	386	.267	.327	.360	.687	90	-122	-80	94	101	642	89	58	61	-8
BOS	154	43	111	.279	64	566	915	5295	1331	253	57	53	469	539	.251	.314	.351	.665	80	-171	-154	97	94	593	46	46	50	-14
TOT	615					6436		43430	12017	2287	570	707	4405	4029	.277	.346	.404	.750							544	405	57	-80

TEAM	CG	SH	SV	IP	H	H/G	HR	BB	SO	RAT	ERA	ERA+	OAV	OOB	PR	/A	PF	CPI	FA	E	DP	FW	PW	BW	SBW	DIF
NY	96	11	15	1408	1425	9.1	93	561	780	12.8	3.98	102	.260	.331	78	15	91	101	.969	188	124	.2	1.4	20.8	-.6	8.3
PHI	95	10	10	1386	1477	9.6	112	511	595	13.0	4.45	102	.271	.336	4	11	101	98	.979	124	142	3.8	1.0	10.4	.7	1.0
WAS	66	11	22	1383[1]	1463	9.5	73	526	437	13.0	4.16	104	.271	.337	49	24	96	100	.979	125	157	3.8	2.2	1.8	.3	8.0
CLE	94	6	8	1377[1]	1506	9.8	70	446	439	12.8	4.12	115	.273	.329	55	96	106	98	.969	191	129	-.2	8.9	-1.0	-.6	4.0
DET	67	9	17	1362[2]	1421	9.4	89	592	521	13.5	4.30	109	.269	.346	27	61	105	102	.969	187	154	.0	5.6	-6.0	1.1	-.3
STL	63	7	11	1376[2]	1592	10.4	103	574	496	14.3	5.01	97	.290	.359	-81	-24	108	100	.969	188	156	.0	-2.2	-8.1	-.6	-3.0
CHI	50	2	12	1348[2]	1551	10.4	88	580	379	14.4	4.82	90	.287	.359	-52	-75	97	101	.958	264	170	-4.6	-6.9	-7.4	.2	-7.8
BOS	42	3	7	1362	1574	10.4	79	612	365	14.6	5.02	90	.289	.364	-81	-79	100	99	.963	233	165	-2.6	-7.3	-14.2	-.4	-9.5
TOT	573	59	102	11004[2]		9.8				13.6	4.48		.277	.346					.969	1500	1197					

Runs		Hits		Doubles		Triples		Home Runs		Total Bases	
Foxx-Phi	151	Simmons-Phi	216	McNair-Phi	47	Cronin-Was	18	Foxx-Phi	58	Foxx-Phi	438
Simmons-Phi	144	Manush-Was	214	Gehringer-Det	44	Myer-Was	16	Ruth-NY	41	Gehrig-NY	370
Combs-NY	143	Foxx-Phi	213	Cronin-Was	43	Lazzeri-NY	16	Simmons-Phi	35	Simmons-Phi	367
Gehrig-NY	138	Gehrig-NY	208			Chapman-NY	15	Gehrig-NY	34	Averill-Cle	359
Manush-Was	121	Averill-Cle	198					Averill-Cle	32	Manush-Was	325

Runs Batted In		Runs Produced		Bases On Balls		Batting Average		On Base Percentage		Slugging Average	
Foxx-Phi	169	Foxx-Phi	262	Ruth-NY	130	Alexander-Det-Bos	.367	Ruth-NY	.489	Foxx-Phi	.749
Simmons-Phi	151	Simmons-Phi	260	Foxx-Phi	116	Foxx-Phi	.364	Foxx-Phi	.469	Ruth-NY	.661
Gehrig-NY	151	Gehrig-NY	255	Bishop-Phi	110	Gehrig-NY	.349	Gehrig-NY	.451	Gehrig-NY	.621
Ruth-NY	137	Manush-Was	223	Gehrig-NY	108	Manush-Was	.342	Bishop-Phi	.412	Averill-Cle	.569
Averill-Cle	124	Ruth-NY	216	Cochrane-Phi	100	Ruth-NY	.341	Cochrane-Phi	.412	Simmons-Phi	.548

Production		Adjusted Production		Batter Runs		Adjusted Batter Runs		Clutch Hitting Index		Runs Created	
Foxx-Phi	1.218	Ruth-NY	206	Foxx-Phi	96.7	Foxx-Phi	90.0	Dykes-Phi	124	Foxx-Phi	207
Ruth-NY	1.150	Foxx-Phi	203	Ruth-NY	71.2	Ruth-NY	79.2	Cronin-Was	121	Gehrig-NY	168
Gehrig-NY	1.072	Gehrig-NY	184	Gehrig-NY	68.6	Gehrig-NY	77.2	Kamm-Cle	119	Ruth-NY	157
Averill-Cle	.961	Lazzeri-NY	140	Averill-Cle	41.1	Alexander-Det-Bos	33.3	Lazzeri-NY	118	Averill-Cle	140
Cochrane-Phi	.921	Averill-Cle	137	Alexander-Det-Bos	31.8	Averill-Cle	32.5	Davis-Det	114	Simmons-Phi	134

Total Average		Stolen Bases		Stolen Base Average		Stolen Base Runs		Fielding Runs		Total Player Rating	
Foxx-Phi	1.451	Chapman-NY	38	Walker-Det	83.3	Walker-Det	5.4	Warstler-Bos	27.9	Foxx-Phi	6.5
Ruth-NY	1.432	Walker-Det	30	Johnson-Det-Bos	76.9	Johnson-Det-Bos	2.4	Vosmik-Cle	23.8	Ruth-NY	5.8
Gehrig-NY	1.188	Johnson-Det-Bos	20	Blue-Chi	73.9	Blue-Chi	1.5	West-Was	19.3	Gehrig-NY	4.9
Cochrane-Phi	1.000	Cissell-Chi-Cle	18	Chapman-NY	67.9			Appling-Chi	18.1	Cochrane-Phi	4.1
Averill-Cle	.991			Burns-StL	60.7			Kress-StL-Chi	12.8	Cronin-Was	3.9

Wins		Win Percentage		Games		Complete Games		Shutouts		Saves	
Crowder-Was	26	Allen-NY	.810	Marberry-Was	54	Grove-Phi	27	Grove-Phi	4	Marberry-Was	13
Grove-Phi	25	Gomez-NY	.774	Gray-StL	52	Ferrell-Cle	26	Bridges-Det	4	Moore-Bos-NY	8
Gomez-NY	24	Ruffing-NY	.720	Crowder-Was	50	Ruffing-NY	22			Hogsett-Det	7
Ferrell-Cle	23	Grove-Phi	.714							Grove-Phi	7
Weaver-Was	22	Weaver-Was	.688							Faber-Chi	6

Innings Pitched		Fewest Hits/Game		Fewest BB/Game		Strikeouts		Strikeouts/Game		Ratio	
Crowder-Was	327.0	Allen-NY	7.59	Brown-Cle	1.71	Ruffing-NY	190	Ruffing-NY	6.60	Grove-Phi	10.77
Grove-Phi	291.2	Ruffing-NY	7.61	Crowder-Was	2.12	Grove-Phi	188	Gomez-NY	5.97	Crowder-Was	10.90
Ferrell-Cle	287.2	Bridges-Det	7.79	Gray-StL	2.31	Gomez-NY	176	Grove-Phi	5.80	Allen-NY	11.39
Walberg-Phi	272.0	Grove-Phi	8.30	Harder-Cle	2.40	Hadley-Chi-StL	145	Hadley-Chi-StL	5.26	Ruffing-NY	11.71
Gomez-NY	265.1	Crowder-Was	8.78	Grove-Phi	2.44	Pipgras-NY	111	Allen-NY	5.11	Sorrell-Det	12.06

Earned Run Average		Adjusted ERA		Opponents' Batting Avg.		Opponents' On Base Pct.		Starter Runs		Adjusted Starter Runs	
Grove-Phi	2.84	Grove-Phi	159	Ruffing-NY	.226	Grove-Phi	.292	Grove-Phi	53.2	Grove-Phi	54.6
Ruffing-NY	3.09	Bridges-Det	140	Allen-NY	.228	Crowder-Was	.295	Crowder-Was	41.7	Crowder-Was	35.7
Lyons-Chi	3.28	Hogsett-Det	133	Bridges-Det	.233	Allen-NY	.306	Ruffing-NY	39.9	Ferrell-Cle	34.6
Crowder-Was	3.33	Lyons-Chi	132	Grove-Phi	.241	Ruffing-NY	.311	Lyons-Chi	30.8	Bridges-Det	30.0
Bridges-Det	3.36	Ruffing-NY	132	Crowder-Was	.252	Brown-Cle	.314	Ferrell-Cle	26.2	Ruffing-NY	28.3

Clutch Pitching Index		Relief Runs		Adjusted Relief Runs		Relief Ranking		Total Pitcher Index		Total Baseball Ranking	
Hogsett-Det	129	Faber-Chi	8.8	Kimsey-StL-Chi	9.5	Kimsey-StL-Chi	8.9	Grove-Phi	5.9	Foxx-Phi	6.5
Lyons-Chi	120	Kimsey-StL-Chi	6.5	Faber-Chi	7.0	Faber-Chi	8.6	Ferrell-Cle	4.3	Grove-Phi	5.9
Weiland-Bos	117							Ruffing-NY	3.5	Ruth-NY	5.8
Bridges-Det	116							Crowder-Was	3.5	Gehrig-NY	4.9
Gaston-Chi	115							Bridges-Det	3.2	Ferrell-Cle	4.3

January 7 Baseball Commissioner Kenesaw Mountain Landis voluntarily cuts his salary by 40 percent as a signal that all salaries are to be trimmed because of the Depression.

May 6 The Reds sign Jack Quinn just two months short of his 50th birthday. He will appear in 14 games in relief for Cincinnati before he finally calls it quits after 23 seasons and 247 wins.

May 14 With rain pelting down at Ebbets Field, Hack Wilson pounds a ninth-inning pinch grand slam, the first in Dodgers history, to beat the Phils' Ad Liska, 8–6.

July 2 Carl Hubbell pitches an entire 18-inning shutout for the Giants over the Cardinals to tie a record for the longest 1–0 game. In the first game of a doubleheader, Hubbell strikes out 12 and walks none, allowing only six hits in a duel with Tex Carleton, who goes the first 16 innings. Jess Haines relieves in the 17th and in the 18th gives up a single to Joe Moore, a sacrifice bunt to Gus Mancuso, and an intentional pass to Travis Jackson. Hubbell then forces at second, and a single by Hughie Critz ends it. In the second game of the day, played in semidarkness, Roy Parmelee wins 1–0 on a Johnny Vergez home run. The notoriously wild Giants' pitcher does not issue a walk and strikes out 13 to beat Dizzy Dean, who is pitching on one day's rest.

July 24 Frankie Frisch replaces Gabby Street as manager of the Cardinals.

July 30 Cardinals pitcher Dizzy Dean becomes the first player in the 20th century to record 17 strikeouts in a single game. He does it in the opener of a doubleheader against the Cubs. Cards catcher Jimmie Wilson records 18 putouts, another first in the 20th century.

August 1 Carl Hubbell breaks Ed Reulbach's 1908 NL record for consecutive scoreless innings, with 45⅓, although the Giants lose to Boston 3-1.

September 10* The first Negro League East-West All-Star Game is played at Comiskey Park. Willie Foster goes the distance in the West's 11-7 victory.

September 17 The Giants spoil Dizzy Dean Day at Sportsman's Park, 4–3, but the popular pitcher drives home in a new Buick, given to him by St. Louis fans.

September 19 Although they lose to St. Louis 12-3, the Giants clinch the pennant when runner-up Pittsburgh splits a pair in Philadelphia.

September 23 Paul Derringer loses his 27th game for the last-place Reds.

October 3 The Giants take the opener of the World Series at the Polo Grounds, as Carl Hubbell holds the Senators to five hits and three unearned runs. Washington unravels when Buddy Myer makes a record-tying three errors. Mel Ott is the hitting star, tying a World Series record by going 4-for-4.

October 6 Carl Hubbell wins for the second time, going 11 innings for the 2–1 victory in a pitching duel with Monte Weaver. Heinie Manush is thrown out of the game for brushing umpire Charlie Moran in the sixth inning. Travis Jackson beats out a surprise bunt to open the 11th inning, is sacrificed to second base on a close play, and scores on a single by Blondy Ryan.

October 7 The World Series comes to a close when Mel Ott homers in the 10th inning for a 4-3 Giants victory. Dolf Luque gets the win in relief.

October 12 Jimmie Foxx (AL) and Carl Hubbell (NL) are named MVPs by the baseball writers.

November 21 Chuck Klein, who won the Triple Crown with the Phillies, is sold to the Chicago Cubs for $125,000 and veterans Mark Koenig, Harvey Hendrick, and rookie Ted Kleinhans. Klein, the only player to be traded after a Triple Crown season, will have two solid years at Wrigley before returning to the Phils.

December 15 The major leagues agree on a uniform ball to be livelier than the NL ball of recent seasons, to match the AL balls. Owners also agree to ban Sunday doubleheaders until after June 15.

	BOSTON		BROOKLYN		CHICAGO		CINCINNATI		NEW YORK		PHILADELPHIA		PITTSBURGH		ST.LOUIS
M	B.McKechnie	M	M.Carey	M	C.Grimm	M	D.Bush	M	B.Terry	M	B.Shotton	M	M.Gibson	M	G.Street
1B	B.Jordan	1B	S.Leslie	1B	C.Grimm	1B	J.Bottomley	1B	B.Terry	1B	D.Hurst	1B	G.Suhr	1B	F.Frisch
2B	R.Maranville	2B	T.Cuccinello	2B	Bi.Herman	2B	J.Morrissey	2B	H.Critz	2B	J.Warner	2B	T.Piet	1B	R.Collins
SS	B.Urbanski	SS	G.Wright	SS	B.Jurges	SS	O.Bluege	SS	B.Ryan	SS	D.Bartell	SS	A.Vaughan	2B	F.Frisch
3B	P.Whitney	3B	J.Stripp	3B	W.English	3B	S.Adams	3B	J.Vergez	3B	J.McLeod	3B	P.Traynor	SS	L.Durocher
LF	H.Lee	LF	H.Wilson	LF	R.Stephenson	LF	J.Moore	LF	J.Moore	LF	W.Schulmerich	LF	L.Waner	3B	P.Martin
CF	W.Berger	CF	D.Taylor	CF	F.Demaree	CF	C.Hafey	CF	K.Davis	CF	C.Fullis	CF	F.Lindstrom	LF	J.Medwick
RF	R.Moore	RF	J.Frederick	RF	Ba.Herman	RF	H.Rice	RF	M.Ott	RF	C.Klein	RF	P.Waner	CF	E.Orsatti
C	S.Hogan	C	A.Lopez	C	G.Hartnett	C	E.Lombardi	C	G.Mancuso	C	S.Davis	C	E.Grace	RF	G.Watkins
														C	J.Wilson
O	J.Mowry	O	B.Boyle	O	K.Cuyler	21	G.Grantham	O	L.O'Doul	2	N.Finn	2	T.Thevenow		
C	A.Spohrer	S2	J.Jordan	3S	M.Koenig	O	W.Roettger	O	H.Peel	O	H.Lee	O	W.Jensen	O	E.Allen
3	F.Knothe	S2	J.Flowers	1	H.Hendrick	C	R.Hemsley	1	S.Leslie	C	A.Todd	O	A.Comorosky	12	P.Crawford
3	D.Gyselman	O	J.Hutcheson	C	G.Campbell	C	C.Manion	2	B.James	3	P.Whitney	C	H.Finney	C	B.O'Farrell
O	T.Thompson	O	L.O'Doul	O	J.Mosolf	S	L.Durocher	S3	T.Jackson	3	F.Knothe	C	T.Padden	2	R.Hornsby
O	W.Schulmerich	C	C.Outen	O	T.Douthit	3	A.High	C	P.Richards	2	M.Haslin	C	V.Picinich	S	G.Slade
C	P.Hargrave	S	L.Frey	3	S.Hack	2	T.Robello	3	C.Dressen	1	G.Dugas	/2	P.Young	O	G.Moore
O	R.Worthington	1	D.Bissonette	1	D.Camilli	/C	J.Crouch	/1	J.Malay	/C	H.McCurdy	/3	B.Brubaker	/C	B.Lewis
/O	D.Holland	1	J.Judge	C	Z.Taylor	R	T.Douthit	/O	P.Weintraub	2	E.Delker	H	R.Nonnenkamp	/O	E.Crabtree
/O	E.Clark	C	C.Sukeforth	/C	B.Phelps	/3	E.Hunter	/C	H.Leiber	/O	A.Cohen			/S	S.Adams
/S	H.Ford	2	B.Delmas					/C	H.Danning	/O	F.Brickell	P	L.French	P	R.Pepper
/2	A.Wright	/O	M.Rosenfeld	P	L.Warneke	P	P.Derringer			H	H.Willingham	P	B.Swift	/S	B.Whitehead
		/C	V.Picinich	P	G.Bush	P	R.Lucas	P	C.Hubbell			P	H.Meine	/C	J.Sprinz
P	E.Brandt	/1	L.Blue	P	C.Root	P	S.Johnson	P	H.Schumacher	P	E.Holley	P	S.Swetonic	/S	C.Wilson
P	B.Cantwell			P	P.Malone	P	L.Benton	P	F.Fitzsimmons	P	S.Hansen	P	H.Smith		
P	F.Frankhouse	P	B.Beck	P	B.Tinning	P	R.Kolp	P	R.Parmelee	J.Elliott	RP	L.Chagnon	P	D.Dean
P	H.Betts	P	V.Mungo					RP	H.Bell	C.Moore	RP	B.Harris	P	T.Carleton
P	T.Zachary	P	R.Benge	P	L.Nelson	P	B.Frey	RP	D.Luque	P	C.Collins			P	B.Hallahan
		P	O.Carroll	P	B.Grimes	P	E.Rixey	RP	G.Spencer	RP	A.Liska	P	W.Hoyt	P	B.Walker
P	L.Mangum	P	S.Thurston	P	R.Henshaw	P	B.Smith					/P	R.Birkofer	P	J.Haines
P	B.Smith	RP	J.Shaute	/P	L.Herrmann	P	A.Stout	P	W.Clark	F.Rhem	/P	R.Kremer	RP	S.Johnson
P	S.Seibold	RP	R.Ryan	/P	B.Richmond	P	J.Quinn	/P	B.Shores	F.Pearce	P	C.Dudley		
/P	E.Fallenstein			/P	C.Yerkes			/P	J.Salveson	P	J.Jackson			P	D.Vance
/P	R.Starr	P	W.Clark					/P	G.Uhle	P	J.Berly			P	J.Mooney
/O	B.Brown	P	D.Leonard					/P	R.Starr	P	R.Grabowski			/P	P.Derringer
		P	F.Heimach							P	F.Ragland			/P	B.Grimes
		/P	R.Lucas							/P	C.Pickrel			/P	J.Lindsey
										/P	C.Butler			/P	A.Stout

TEAM	G	W	L	PCT	GB	R	OR	AB	H	2B	3B	HR	BB	SO	AVG	OBP	SLG	PRO	PRO+	BR	/A	PF	CHI	RC	SB	CS	SBA	SBR
NY	156	91	61	.599		636	515	5461	1437	204	41	82	377	477	.263	.312	.361	.673	100	-14	-4	98	104	617	31			
PIT	154	87	67	.565	5	667	619	5429	1548	249	84	39	366	334	.285	.333	.383	.716	111	71	72	100	96	709	34			
CHI	154	86	68	.558	6	646	536	5255	1422	256	51	72	392	475	.271	.325	.380	.705	107	47	49	100	99	643	52			
BOS	156	83	71	.539	9	552	531	5243	1320	217	56	54	326	428	.252	.299	.345	.644	98	-70	-27	92	104	538	25			
STL	154	82	71	.536	9.5	687	609	5387	1486	256	61	57	391	528	.276	.329	.378	.707	103	53	18	105	102	676	99			
BRO	157	65	88	.425	26.5	617	695	5367	1413	224	51	62	397	453	.263	.316	.359	.675	103	-8	18	96	101	612	82			
PHI	152	60	92	.395	31	607	760	5261	1439	240	41	60	381	479	.274	.326	.369	.695	93	32	-49	113	95	642	55			
CIN	153	58	94	.382	33	496	643	5156	1267	208	37	34	349	354	.246	.298	.320	.618	83	-111	-104	99	103	487	30			
TOT	618					4908		42559	11332	1854	422	460	2979	3528	.266	.317	.362	.679						408				

TEAM	CG	SH	SV	IP	H	H/G	HR	BB	SO	RAT	ERA	ERA+	OAV	OOB	PR	/A	PF	CPI	FA	E	DP	FW	PW	BW	SBW	DIF
NY	75	23	15	1408²	1280	8.2	61	400	555	10.9	2.71	118	.242	.299	98	78	96	102	.973	178	156	-.5	8.3	-.4		7.6
PIT	70	16	12	1373¹	1417	9.3	54	313	401	11.5	3.27	101	.264	.308	10	7	99	95	.972	166	133	.2	.7	7.6		1.5
CHI	95	16	9	1362	1316	8.7	51	413	488	11.6	2.93	112	.254	.312	62	52	98	105	.973	168	163	.0	5.5	5.2		-1.7
BOS	85	15	16	1403	1391	8.9	54	355	383	11.3	2.96	103	.261	.309	58	14	92	105	.978	138	148	2.1	1.5	-2.9		5.2
STL	73	11	16	1382²	1391	9.1	55	452	635	12.1	3.37	103	.261	.321	-5	16	104	98	.973	162	119	.4	1.7	1.5		1.5
BRO	71	9	10	1386¹	1502	9.8	51	374	415	12.4	3.73	86	.275	.326	-60	-79	96	95	.971	177	120	-.3	-8.4	1.9		-4.7
PHI	52	10	13	1336²	1563	10.5	87	410	341	13.6	4.34	88	.293	.348	-150	-79	114	101	.970	183	156	-1.1	-8.4	-5.2		-1.4
CIN	74	13	8	1352	1470	9.8	47	257	310	11.6	3.42	99	.279	.314	-13	-5	102	99	.971	177	139	-.6	-.5	-11.0		-5.8
TOT	595	113	99	11004²		9.3				11.9	3.34		.266	.317					.973	1349	1134					

Runs
- Martin-StL 122
- P.Waner-Pit 101
- Klein-Phi 101
- Ott-NY 98
- Medwick-StL 92

Hits
- Klein-Phi 223
- Fullis-Phi 200
- P.Waner-Pit 191
- Traynor-Pit 190
- Martin-StL 189

Doubles
- Klein-Phi 44
- Medwick-StL 40
- Lindstrom-Pit 39
- P.Waner-Pit 38
- Berger-Bos 37

Triples
- Vaughan-Pit 19
- P.Waner-Pit 16
- Martin-StL 12
- B.Herman-Chi 12

Home Runs
- Klein-Phi 28
- Berger-Bos 27
- Ott-NY 23
- Medwick-StL 18

Total Bases
- Klein-Phi 365
- Berger-Bos 299
- Medwick-StL 296
- P.Waner-Pit 282
- Vaughan-Pit 274

Runs Batted In
- Klein-Phi 120
- Berger-Bos 106
- Ott-NY 103
- Medwick-StL 98
- Vaughan-Pit 97

Runs Produced
- Klein-Phi 193
- Ott-NY 178
- Vaughan-Pit 173
- Medwick-StL 172
- Martin-StL 171

Bases On Balls
- Ott-NY 75
- Suhr-Pit 72
- Martin-StL 67
- Vaughan-Pit 64
- P.Waner-Pit 60

Batting Average
- Klein-Phi .... .368
- Davis-Phi .... .349
- Stephenson-Chi .... .329
- Piet-Pit .... .323
- Terry-NY .... .322

On Base Percentage
- Klein-Phi .... .422
- Davis-Phi .... .395
- Vaughan-Pit .... .388
- Martin-StL .... .387
- Terry-NY .... .375

Slugging Average
- Klein-Phi .... .602
- Berger-Bos .... .566
- B.Herman-Chi ...... .502
- Medwick-StL .... .497
- Vaughan-Pit .... .478

Production
- Klein-Phi 1.025
- Berger-Bos .... .932
- Davis-Phi .... .867
- Vaughan-Pit .... .866
- B.Herman-Chi ...... .855

Adjusted Production
- Berger-Bos 177
- Klein-Phi 168
- Vaughan-Pit 146
- B.Herman-Chi 142
- Ott-NY 139

Batter Runs
- Klein-Phi 69.1
- Berger-Bos 40.5
- Vaughan-Pit 35.2
- Martin-StL 32.3
- Davis-Phi 29.8

Adjusted Batter Runs
- Klein-Phi 52.4
- Berger-Bos 49.0
- Vaughan-Pit 35.4
- Ott-NY 29.9
- P.Waner-Pit 28.9

Clutch Hitting Index
- Hartnett-Chi 120
- Traynor-Pit 119
- Rice-Chi 117
- Ott-NY 114
- Bottomley-Cin 111

Runs Created
- Klein-Phi 162
- Berger-Bos 113
- Vaughan-Pit 112
- Martin-StL 111
- P.Waner-Pit 109

Total Average
- Klein-Phi 1.132
- Berger-Bos .... .935
- Martin-StL .... .881
- Vaughan-Pit .... .861
- B.Herman-Chi ...... .827

Stolen Bases
- Martin-StL 26
- Fullis-Phi 18
- Frisch-StL 18
- Klein-Phi 15
- Orsatti-StL 14

Fielding Runs
- Critz-NY 46.5
- B.Herman-Chi 29.1
- Jurges-Chi 20.1
- Lopez-Bro 18.4
- Ryan-NY 17.4

Total Player Rating
- Klein-Phi 5.5
- Berger-Bos 4.7
- Vaughan-Pit 3.8
- B.Herman-Chi 3.5
- Martin-StL 3.5

Wins
- Hubbell-NY 23
- Dean-StL 20
- Cantwell-Bos 20
- Bush-Chi 20
- Schumacher-NY 19

Win Percentage
- Cantwell-Bos ...... .667
- Hubbell-NY .... .657
- Meine-Pit .... .652
- Bush-Chi .... .625
- Schumacher-NY ..... .613

Games
- Dean-StL 48
- French-Pit 47
- Liska-Phi 45
- Hubbell-NY 45
- Carleton-StL 44

Complete Games
- Warneke-Chi 26
- Dean-StL 26
- Brandt-Bos 23
- Hubbell-NY 22

Shutouts
- Hubbell-NY 10
- Schumacher-NY 7
- French-Pit 5

Saves
- Collins-Phi 6
- Hubbell-NY 5
- Harris-Pit 5
- Bell-NY 5

Innings Pitched
- Hubbell-NY 308.2
- Dean-StL 293.0
- French-Pit 291.1
- Brandt-Bos 287.2
- Warneke-Chi 287.1

Fewest Hits/Game
- Schumacher-NY 6.92
- Hubbell-NY 7.46
- Parmelee-NY 7.87
- Brandt-Bos 8.01
- Mungo-Bro 8.09

Fewest BB/Game
- Lucas-Cin .... .74
- Hubbell-NY 1.37
- Swift-Pit 1.48
- Hansen-Phi 1.60
- French-Pit 1.70

Strikeouts
- Dean-StL 199
- Hubbell-NY 156
- Carleton-StL 147
- Warneke-Chi 133
- Parmelee-NY 132

Strikeouts/Game
- Dean-StL 6.11
- Parmelee-NY 5.44
- Carleton-StL 4.78
- Hubbell-NY 4.55
- Warneke-Chi 4.17

Ratio
- Hubbell-NY 8.92
- Schumacher-NY 9.88
- Betts-Bos 10.41
- Swift-Pit 10.47
- Brandt-Bos 10.51

Earned Run Average
- Hubbell-NY 1.66
- Warneke-Chi 2.00
- Schumacher-NY 2.16
- Brandt-Bos 2.60
- Root-Chi 2.60

Adjusted ERA
- Hubbell-NY 193
- Warneke-Chi 163
- Schumacher-NY 149
- Root-Chi 126
- French-Pit 122

Opponents' Batting Avg.
- Schumacher-NY ..... .214
- Hubbell-NY .... .227
- Parmelee-NY .... .232
- Mungo-Bro .... .236
- Warneke-Chi .... .244

Opponents' On Base Pct.
- Hubbell-NY .... .260
- Schumacher-NY ..... .280
- Swift-Pit .... .285
- Betts-Bos .... .290
- Cantwell-Bos ...... .291

Starter Runs
- Hubbell-NY 57.4
- Warneke-Chi 42.5
- Schumacher-NY 33.9
- Brandt-Bos 23.6
- Cantwell-Bos 20.4

Adjusted Starter Runs
- Hubbell-NY 53.1
- Warneke-Chi 40.4
- Schumacher-NY 30.2
- French-Pit 19.3
- Root-Chi 18.0

Clutch Pitching Index
- Warneke-Chi 131
- Root-Chi 120
- Walker-StL 117
- Holley-Phi 115
- Hubbell-NY 112

Relief Runs
- Bell-NY 15.0
- Luque-NY 5.8
- Harris-Pit 7

Adjusted Relief Runs
- Bell-NY 13.6
- Luque-NY 4.6
- Harris-Pit 6

Relief Ranking
- Bell-NY 14.2
- Luque-NY 5.7
- Harris-Pit 9

Total Pitcher Index
- Hubbell-NY 7.5
- Warneke-Chi 6.2
- Schumacher-NY 4.2
- Brandt-Bos 2.7
- Bush-Chi 2.1

Total Baseball Ranking
- Hubbell-NY 7.5
- Warneke-Chi 6.2
- Klein-Phi 5.5
- Berger-Bos 4.7
- Schumacher-NY 4.2

February 25 Multimillionaire sportsman Tom Yawkey and former star player Eddie Collins buy the Boston Red Sox from Robert Quinn.

April 23 Lou Gehrig's consecutive-game streak is threatened when he is knocked unconscious by an Earl Whitehill pitch in the New York-Washington game. He recovers and finishes the game.

May 18 The first major league All-Star Game is announced for July 6 at Comiskey Park. It will be played as part of the Chicago World's Fair celebration and is sponsored by the *Chicago Tribune*.

June 8 Jimmie Foxx homers in his first three at bats, as the A's outscore the Yankees, 14–10. He had homered his last time up the previous day to give him four consecutive home runs.

June 9 Walter Johnson takes over as Cleveland manager.

June 14 Lou Gehrig's consecutive-game streak of 1,249 survives, even though he and manager Joe McCarthy are thrown out of a game.

July 6 Babe Ruth is the star of the first All-Star Game. His two-run home run at Comiskey Park is the deciding blow as the AL is a 4-2 winner over the NL. John McGraw comes out of retirement to manage the National Leaguers.

July 19 For the first time, brothers on opposite teams homer in the same game. Red Sox catcher Rick Ferrell hits his home run off brother Wes of Cleveland. Wes hits his off Hank Johnson in the third inning. He will wind up his career with 38 home runs (not all of them hit as a pitcher) in 548 games. Rick will hit only 28 in 1,884 games.

August 3 The Yankees are shut out by the A's and Lefty Grove, 7-0, their first scoreless game since Aug. 2, 1931. They had tallied in 308 games in a row, during which they scored 1,986 runs (6.5 per game) to 1,434 for the opposition.

August 14 Jimmie Foxx hits for the cycle and drives in nine runs to break the AL record, as the A's beat the Indians, 11–5. A record eight players will hit for the cycle this year.

August 22 William Veeck, president of the Chicago Cubs, urges a midsummer series of interleague games. He also proposes a split season. While some owners are in agreement on interleague play, Washington owner Clark Griffith is opposed. "We're not going for any Hippodrome stuff. The American League is a big league."

September 10* The first Negro League East-West All-Star Game is played at Comiskey Park. Willie Foster goes the distance in the West's 11-7 victory.

December 3 Connie Mack sells catcher Mickey Cochrane to Detroit for $100,000. Cochrane is named manager. Nine days later Mack sells Lefty Grove, Max Bishop, and George Walberg to the Boston Red Sox for $125,000. George Earnshaw goes to the White Sox for $20,000 and another player.

December 29 Yankees owner Jake Ruppert refuses to release Babe Ruth so he can become manager of the Cincinnati Reds.

	BOSTON		CHICAGO		CLEVELAND		DETROIT		NEW YORK		PHILADELPHIA		ST.LOUIS		WASHINGTON
M	M.McManus	M	L.Fonseca	M	R.Peckinpaugh	M	B.Harris	M	J.McCarthy	M	C.Mack	M	B.Killefer	M	J.Cronin
1B	D.Alexander	1B	R.Kress	M	B.Falk	M	D.Baker	1B	L.Gehrig	1B	J.Foxx	M	A.Sothoron	1B	J.Kuhel
2B	J.Hodapp	2B	J.Hayes	M	W.Johnson	1B	H.Greenberg	2B	T.Lazzeri	2B	M.Bishop	M	R.Hornsby	2B	B.Myer
SS	R.Warstler	SS	L.Appling	1B	H.Boss	2B	C.Gehringer	SS	F.Crosetti	SS	D.Williams	1B	J.Burns	SS	J.Cronin
3B	M.McManus	3B	J.Dykes	2B	O.Hale	SS	B.Rogell	3B	J.Sewell	3B	P.Higgins	2B	S.Melillo	3B	O.Bluege
LF	S.Jolley	LF	A.Simmons	SS	B.Knickerb'r	3B	M.Owen	LF	B.Chapman	LF	B.Johnson	SS	J.Levey	LF	H.Manush
CF	D.Cooke	CF	M.Haas	3B	W.Kamm	LF	G.Walker	CF	B.Combs	CF	D.Cramer	3B	A.Scharein	CF	F.Schulte
RF	R.Johnson	RF	E.Swanson	LF	J.Vosmik	CF	P.Fox	RF	B.Ruth	RF	E.Coleman	LF	C.Reynolds	RF	G.Goslin
C	R.Ferrell	C	F.Grube	CF	E.Averill	RF	J.Stone	C	B.Dickey	C	M.Cochrane	CF	S.West	C	L.Sewell
				RF	D.Porter	C	R.Hayworth					RF	B.Campbell		
S3	B.Werber	C	C.Berry	C	R.Spencer			O	D.Walker	S2	E.McNair	C	M.Shea	O	D.Harris
O	T.Oliver	1	B.Sullivan			O	J.White	3S	L.Lary	O	L.Finney			23	B.Boken
1O	B.Seeds	O1	E.Webb	2S	B.Cissell	1	H.Davis	O	S.Byrd	C	E.Madjeski	O3	T.Gullic	O	S.Rice
3	B.Walters	23	H.Rhyne	S2	J.Burnett	O	F.Doljack	S2	D.Farrell	O	B.Miller	32	L.Storti	C	M.Berg
1	J.Judge	1	L.Fonseca	C	F.Pytlak	3	H.Schuble	C	A.Jorgens	S	E.Cihocki	O	D.Garms	3	C.Travis
C	J.Gooch	/O	J.Stoneham	O	M.Galatzer	C	J.Pasek	/C	F.Hayes	C	R.Hemsley	2	J.Kerr
C	M.Shea	/O	M.Bocek	1	E.Morgan	C	G.Desautels	/C	J.Glenn	/O	J.Zapustas	C	R.Ferrell	/C	C.Bolton
2	F.Muller	/2	C.English	C	G.Myatt	/C	F.Reiber	/3	B.Werber			C	M.Ruel	H	N.Altrock
O	M.Almada	/O	L.Funk	O	J.Oulliber	/O	B.Rhiel			P	L.Grove	/C	J.Crouch	
/2	B.Friberg	H	M.Lovett	O	M.Powers	/O	E.Webb	P	R.Ruffing	P	S.Cain	H	R.Hornsby	P	A.Crowder
O	G.Stumpf			1	H.Trosky			P	L.Gomez	P	R.Walberg			P	E.Whitehill
/O	B.Fothergill	P	T.Lyons			P	F.Marberry	P	J.Allen	P	R.Mahaffey	P	B.Hadley	P	L.Stewart
/O	J.Watwood	P	S.Jones	P	M.Harder	P	V.Sorrell	P	R.Van Atta	P	G.Earnshaw	P	G.Blaeholder	P	M.Weaver
/O	T.Winsett	P	M.Gaston	P	O.Hildebrand	P	T.Bridges	P	D.MacFayden	RP	J.Peterson	P	E.Wells	P	T.Thomas
/C	L.Legett	P	E.Durham	P	W.Ferrell	P	C.Fischer	RP	H.Pennock			P	R.Stiles	RP	J.Russell
/2	M.Olson	P	J.Miller	P	C.Brown	P	S.Rowe	RP	W.Moore			RP	S.Gray	RP	B.Burke
R	G.Mulleavy	RP	J.Heving	P	W.Hudlin	RP	C.Hogsett			P	D.Barrett	RP	W.Hebert	RP	B.McAfee
		RP	R.Faber	RP	S.Connally	RP	A.Herring	P	R.Brennan	P	T.Freitas	RP	H.McDonald	
				RP	B.Bean			P	J.Brown	/P	J.Marcum			/P	A.McColl
P	G.Rhodes	P	P.Gregory			P	V.Frasier	P	C.Devens	/P	B.Dietrich	P	J.Knott	/P	E.Linke
P	B.Weiland	P	C.Kimsey	P	M.Pearson	P	E.Auker	/O	G.Uhle	/P	H.McDonald	/P	D.Coffman	/P	R.Prim
P	L.Brown	P	W.Wyatt	P	H.Craghead	/P	L.Hamlin	/P	G.Pipgras	/P	G.Claset	/P	L.Brown	/P	E.Chapman
P	H.Johnson	/P	L.Tietje	/P	T.Lee	P	W.Wyatt	/P	P.Appleton	/P	T.McKeithan	/P	G.Braxton	/P	B.Thomas
P	I.Andrews	P	V.Frasier			/P	R.Lawson			/P	H.Winston			/P	J.Campbell
RP	J.Welch	/P	H.Haid			/P	B.Nekola			/P	E.Roy				
RP	B.Kline	/P	I.Hutchinson			/P	G.Uhle								
		/P	G.Murray												
P	G.Pipgras														
/P	C.Fullerton														
/P	J.McLaughlin														
/P	M.Meola														

TEAM	G	W	L	PCT	GB	R	OR	AB	H	2B	3B	HR	BB	SO	AVG	OBP	SLG	PRO	PRO+	BR	/A	PF	CHI	RC	SB	CS	SBA	SBR
WAS	153	99	53	.651		850	665	5524	1586	281	86	60	539	395	.287	.353	.402	.755	107	47	56	99	102	798	65	50	57	-11
NY	152	91	59	.607	7	927	768	5274	1495	241	75	144	700	506	.283	.369	.440	.809	129	155	211	94	100	880	76	59	56	-13
PHI	152	79	72	.523	19.5	875	853	5330	1519	297	57	139	625	618	.285	.362	.440	.802	118	135	126	101	97	868	34	34	50	-10
CLE	151	75	76	.497	23.5	654	669	5240	1366	218	77	50	448	426	.261	.321	.360	.681	82	-103	-132	105	103	616	36	40	47	-13
DET	155	75	79	.487	25	722	733	5502	1479	283	78	57	475	523	.269	.329	.380	.709	92	-54	-68	102	101	698	68	50	58	-10
CHI	151	67	83	.447	31	683	814	5318	1448	231	53	43	538	416	.272	.342	.360	.702	96	-50	-20	96	96	674	43	46	48	-15
BOS	149	63	86	.423	34.5	700	758	5201	1407	294	56	50	525	464	.271	.339	.377	.716	97	-29	-22	99	98	687	58	37	61	-5
STL	153	55	96	.364	43.5	669	820	5285	1337	244	64	64	520	556	.253	.322	.360	.682	81	-102	-143	106	103	625	72	60	55	-14
TOT	608					6080		42674	11637	2089	546	607	4370	3904	.273	.342	.390	.732							452	376	55	-90

TEAM	CG	SH	SV	IP	H	H/G	HR	BB	SO	RAT	ERA	ERA+	OAV	OOB	PR	/A	PF	CPI	FA	E	DP	FW	PW	BW	SBW	DIF
WAS	68	5	26	1389²	1415	9.2	64	452	447	12.2	3.82	109	.263	.322	71	56	98	98	.979	131	149	2.6	5.3	5.3	.0	9.8
NY	70	8	22	1354²	1426	9.5	66	612	711	13.6	4.36	89	.267	.344	-13	-72	91	96	.972	165	122	.4	-6.8	20.0	-.2	2.6
PHI	69	6	14	1343²	1523	10.2	77	644	423	14.6	4.81	89	.283	.361	-79	-78	100	99	.966	203	121	-1.9	-7.4	11.9	.1	.8
CLE	74	12	7	1350	1382	9.2	60	465	437	12.4	3.71	120	.264	.325	86	111	104	102	.974	156	127	.9	10.5	-12.5	-.2	.8
DET	69	6	17	1398	1415	9.1	84	561	575	12.9	3.95	109	.263	.335	52	57	101	103	.971	178	167	-.2	5.4	-6.4	.1	-.9
CHI	53	8	13	1371¹	1505	9.9	85	519	423	13.5	4.45	95	.277	.343	-26	-32	99	99	.970	186	143	-1.0	-3.0	-1.9	-.4	-1.8
BOS	60	4	14	1327²	1396	9.5	75	591	467	13.5	4.35	101	.271	.348	-10	4	102	100	.966	204	133	-2.2	.4	-2.1	.6	-8.2
STL	55	7	10	1360²	1574	10.4	96	531	426	14.0	4.82	97	.289	.354	-82	-205	109	100	.976	149	162	1.5	-2.4	-13.5	-.3	-5.8
TOT	518	56	123	10895²		9.6				13.3	4.28		.273	.342					.972	1372	1124					

Runs
Gehrig-NY 138
Foxx-Phi 125
Manush-Was 115
Chapman-NY 112
Cramer-Phi 109

Hits
Manush-Was 221
Gehringer-Det 204
Foxx-Phi 204
Simmons-Chi 200
Gehrig-NY 198

Doubles
Cronin-Was 45
Johnson-Phi 44
Burns-StL 43
Rogell-Det 42
Gehringer-Det 42

Triples
Manush-Was 17
Combs-NY 16
Averill-Cle 16
Myer-Was 15
Reynolds-StL 14

Home Runs
Foxx-Phi 48
Ruth-NY 34
Gehrig-NY 32
Johnson-Phi 21
Lazzeri-NY 18

Total Bases
Foxx-Phi 403
Gehrig-NY 359
Manush-Was 302
Gehringer-Det 294
Simmons-Chi 291

Runs Batted In
Foxx-Phi 163
Gehrig-NY 139
Simmons-Chi 119
Cronin-Was 118
Kuhel-Was 107

Runs Produced
Gehrig-NY 245
Foxx-Phi 240
Manush-Was 205
Cronin-Was 202
Chapman-NY 201

Bases On Balls
Ruth-NY 114
Cochrane-Phi 106
Bishop-Phi 106
Foxx-Phi 96
Swanson-Chi 93

Batting Average
Foxx-Phi 356
Manush-Was ..... .336
Gehrig-NY ..... .334
Simmons-Chi ..... .331
Gehringer-Det ..... .325

On Base Percentage
Cochrane-Phi ..... .459
Foxx-Phi ..... .449
Bishop-Phi ..... .446
Ruth-NY .... .442
Gehrig-NY ..... .424

Slugging Average
Foxx-Phi 703
Gehrig-NY ..... .605
Ruth-NY ..... .582
Cochrane-Phi ..... .515
Johnson-Phi 505

Production
Foxx-Phi 1.153
Gehrig-NY 1.030
Ruth-NY 1.023
Cochrane-Phi 974
Johnson-Phi 892

Adjusted Production
Foxx-Phi 199
Gehrig-NY 181
Ruth-NY 180
Cochrane-Phi 156
Dickey-NY 138

Batter Runs
Foxx-Phi 82.7
Gehrig-NY 59.5
Ruth-NY 49.5
Cochrane-Phi 41.6
Johnson-Phi 26.8

Adjusted Batter Runs
Foxx-Phi 81.0
Gehrig-NY 68.5
Ruth-NY 57.1
Cochrane-Phi 40.5
Lazzeri-NY 27.7

Clutch Hitting Index
Cronin-Was 126
Melillo-StL 125
Ferrell-StL-Bos 124
Bluege-Was 123
Kress-Chi 121

Runs Created
Foxx-Phi 184
Gehrig-NY 151
Ruth-NY 124
Gehringer-Det 117
Manush-Was 111

Total Average
Foxx-Phi 1.348
Ruth-NY 1.172
Cochrane-Phi 1.118
Gehrig-NY 1.098
Johnson-Phi 940

Stolen Bases
Chapman-NY 27
Walker-Det 26
Swanson-Chi 19
Kuhel-Was 17

Stolen Base Average
Walker-Det 74.3
Kuhel-Was 68.0
Swanson-Chi 63.3
Chapman-NY 60.0

Stolen Base Runs
Walker-Det 2.4
Werber-NY-Bos 1.5
Stumpf-Bos 1.2

Fielding Runs
Melillo-StL 23.3
Rogell-Det 19.5
Schulte-Was 15.8
Simmons-Chi 14.3
Scharein-StL 14.0

Total Player Rating
Foxx-Phi 6.7
Gehrig-NY 4.3
Cronin-Was 4.0
Ruth-NY 3.8
Cochrane-Phi 3.7

Wins
Grove-Phi 24
Crowder-Was 24
Whitehill-Was 22

Win Percentage
Grove-Phi .... .750
Whitehill-Was ..... .733
Stewart-Was ..... .714
Allen-NY .... .682

Games
Crowder-Was 52
Russell-Was 50
Welch-Bos 47
Kline-Bos 46

Complete Games
Grove-Phi 21
Whitehill-Was 19
Hadley-StL 19
Ruffing-NY 18

Shutouts
Hildebrand-Cle 6
Gomez-NY 4
Blaeholder-StL 3

Saves
Russell-Was 13
Hogsett-Det 9
Moore-NY 8
Heving-Chi 6
Grove-Phi 6

Innings Pitched
Hadley-StL 316.2
Crowder-Was 299.1
Grove-Phi 275.1
Whitehill-Was 270.0
Blaeholder-StL 255.2

Fewest Hits/Game
Bridges-Det 7.42
Weiland-Bos 8.20
Allen-NY 8.33
Gomez-NY 8.36
Hildebrand-Cle 8.37

Fewest BB/Game
Brown-Cle 1.65
Marberry-Det 2.30
Stewart-Was 2.34
Harder-Cle 2.38
Blaeholder-StL 2.43

Strikeouts
Gomez-NY 163
Hadley-StL 149
Ruffing-NY 122
Bridges-Det 120
Allen-NY 119

Strikeouts/Game
Gomez-NY 6.25
Allen-NY 5.80
Ruffing-NY 4.67
Bridges-Det 4.64
Fischer-Det 4.58

Ratio
Marberry-Det 11.10
Stewart-Was 11.24
Harder-Cle 11.53
Brown-Cle 11.58
Weaver-Was 11.88

Earned Run Average
Pearson-Cle 2.33
Harder-Cle 2.95
Bridges-Det 3.09
Gomez-NY 3.18
Grove-Phi 3.20

Adjusted ERA
Harder-Cle 151
Bridges-Det 140
Grove-Phi 134
Marberry-Det 131
Brown-Cle 130

Opponents' Batting Avg.
Bridges-Det 226
Gomez-NY ..... .240
Allen-NY ..... .242
Weiland-Bos ..... .244
Hildebrand-Cle ..... .245

Opponents' On Base Pct.
Marberry-Det 302
Stewart-Was 304
Harder-Cle 309
Brown-Cle 310
Grove-Phi 316

Starter Runs
Harder-Cle 37.4
Grove-Phi 33.0
Bridges-Det 30.8
Pearson-Cle 29.4
Gomez-NY 28.6

Adjusted Starter Runs
Harder-Cle 41.9
Grove-Phi 33.1
Pearson-Cle 31.8
Bridges-Det 31.6
Marberry-Det 27.2

Clutch Pitching Index
Cain-Phi 125
Jones-Chi 124
Harder-Cle 115
Whitehill-Was 112
Grove-Phi 111

Relief Runs
Russell-Was 22.0
Heving-Chi 21.1
Faber-Chi 8.1
Burke-Was 7.4
Herring-Det 3.0

Adjusted Relief Runs
Russell-Was 20.6
Heving-Chi 20.6
Faber-Chi 7.7
Gray-StL 6.9
Burke-Was 6.7

Relief Ranking
Russell-Was 31.8
Heving-Chi 21.2
Gray-StL 6.7
Burke-Was 6.6
Faber-Chi 6.6

Total Pitcher Index
Harder-Cle 5.7
Bridges-Det 3.5
Russell-Was 3.4
Pearson-Cle 3.3
Grove-Phi 2.9

Total Baseball Ranking
Foxx-Phi 6.7
Harder-Cle 5.7
Gehrig-NY 4.3
Cronin-Was 4.0
Ruth-NY 3.8

February 25 John McGraw, in ill health since his retirement as Giants manager early in the 1932 season, dies at his home in New Rochelle, N.Y., at age 60. His last public appearance had been the 1933 All-Star Game as the NL manager.

April 17 At Ebbets Field, Casey Stengel makes his managerial debut, but his Dodgers lose, 8–7, to the Braves.

April 29 With Pennsylvania's Blue Law repealed, Pittsburgh becomes the last major league city to play a home game on a Sunday, beating the Reds, 9-5.

July 4 When Dodgers manager Casey Stengel comes out to the mound to remove pitcher Walter "Boom Boom" Beck from the game in Philadelphia's Baker Bowl, the frustrated Beck turns and fires the ball at the tin wall in right field. Dodgers outfielder Hack Wilson, not paying attention to the happenings, hears the ball, hurries to retrieve it, and fires a strike to second base.

July 10 The second annual All-Star Game produces Carl Hubbell's amazing feat of striking out five future Hall of Famers in a row. Off to a shaky start with two on base in the first inning, Hubbell uses his screwball to fan Ruth, Gehrig, and Foxx. He adds Al Simmons and Joe Cronin to start the second. After three scoreless innings he leaves with the NL ahead, 4-0. The AL rallies, scoring nine runs off Warneke, Mungo, and Dean, while Mel Harder pitches five shutout innings in relief of Red Ruffing to hold the lead. Frisch and Medwick hit home runs. Earl Averill's three RBIs are decisive for the AL 9-7 victory.

August 8 Wilbert Robinson dies in Atlanta. Beloved as "Uncle Robbie," the jovial and bemused manager of the Dodgers for 18 seasons, his 7-for-7 day with Baltimore still stands as a major league record, though it's been tied by several players since.

September 13 Commissioner Kenesaw Mountain Landis sells the World Series broadcast rights to the Ford Motor Company for $100,000. Previously no fee had been charged.

September 16 The largest turnout in Polo Grounds history, 62,573, suffers as the Deans take two from the Giants. Diz needs relief from Tex Carleton in the 5–3 opener, but Paul goes 11 innings for a 3–1 win. The Cardinals leave New York three and a half games behind the league-leading Giants.

October 3 Dizzy Dean wins the opening game of the World Series, 8-3, as Detroit manager Mickey Cochrane holds back his ace, Lynwood "Schoolboy" Rowe. Veteran Al Crowder is ineffective as the Cardinals romp. Joe Medwick homers in a 4-for-4 day while the Tigers make five errors.

October 9 Dizzy Dean makes good his boast that "me and Paul will win all four games." He humbles Detroit, 11-0, as the Tigers go to pieces. When Joe Medwick slides roughly into third base in the sixth inning, he tangles with Marv Owen. Irate Tigers fans in the temporary left field stands then launch a barrage of fruit at Medwick, halting the game. With the score at 9-0, Commissioner Landis removes Medwick from the game "for his own safety."

November 8 Ford Frick, NL publicity director, is named league president. He will eventually become commissioner.

December 11 The NL votes to permit night baseball, authorizing a maximum of seven games by any team installing lights. The AL does not grant permission for night games until 1937.

December 26* Matsutaro Shoriki, head of Yomiuri Newspapers, announces the official formation of Japan's first professional team, the Tokyo-based Yomiuri Giants. The team is made up of players signed to compete against the American all-star team. Professional league play, with six teams, does not begin until 1936.

BOSTON	BROOKLYN	CHICAGO	CINCINNATI	NEW YORK	PHILADELPHIA	PITTSBURGH	ST.LOUIS
M B.McKechnie	M C.Stengel	M C.Grimm	M B.O'Farrell	M B.Terry	M J.Wilson	M M.Gibson	M F.Frisch
1B B.Jordan	1B S.Leslie	1B C.Grimm	M B.Shotton	1B B.Terry	1B D.Camilli	M P.Traynor	1B R.Collins
2B M.McManus	2B T.Cuccinello	2B Bi.Herman	2B C.Dressen	2B H.Critz	2B L.Chiozza	1B G.Suhr	2B F.Frisch
SS B.Urbanski	SS L.Frey	SS B.Jurges	1B J.Bottomley	SS T.Jackson	SS D.Bartell	2B C.Lavagetto	SS L.Durocher
3B P.Whitney	3B J.Stripp	3B S.Hack	2B T.Piet	3B J.Vergez	3B B.Walters	SS A.Vaughan	3B P.Martin
LF H.Lee	LF D.Taylor	LF C.Klein	SS G.Slade	LF J.Moore	3B E.Allen	3B P.Traynor	LF J.Medwick
CF W.Berger	CF L.Koenecke	CF K.Cuyler	3B M.Koenig	CF G.Watkins	LF K.Davis	LF F.Lindstrom	CF E.Orsatti
RF T.Thompson	RF B.Boyle	RF Ba.Herman	LF H.Pool	RF M.Ott	RF J.Moore	CF L.Waner	RF J.Rothrock
C A.Spohrer	C A.Lopez	C G.Hartnett	CF A.Hafey	C G.Mancuso	C A.Todd	RF P.Waner	C S.Davis
			RF A.Comorosky			C E.Grace	
C S.Hogan	O J.Frederick	S3 W.English	C E.Lombardi	3S B.Ryan	C J.Wilson	23 T.Thevenow	2S B.Whitehead
O1 R.Moore	S2 J.Jordan	O T.Stainback	32 S.Adams	2 H.Leiber	2 I.Jeffries	O W.Jensen	C B.DeLancey
2 L.Mallon	2 H.Wilson	2 A.Galan	O W.Schulmerich	O L.O'Doul	32 M.Haslin	O T.Padden	O C.Fullis
O J.Mowry	O2 G.Chapman	1 D.Hurst	O B.O'Farrell	C H.Danning	1 D.Hurst	/3 W.Roettger	O B.Mills
O R.Worthington	2 J.Bucher	1 D.Camilli	O L.Blakely	O P.Richards	O H.Hendrick	C P.Veltman	/3 P.Crawford
3 D.Gyselman	C R.Berres	O R.Stephenson	2 A.Kampouris	O P.Weintraub	O C.Fullis	/2 P.Young	/O K.Davis
/S D.McGee	C C.Sukeforth	2 B.Phelps	/1 I.Shiver	3 G.Grantham	3 A.High	/3 H.Finney	/O G.Moore
/O J.Tyler	1 J.McCarthy	C B.O'Farrell	H C.Manion	O F.Thompson	O A.Ruble	P L.French	/C F.Healy
/1 E.Fletcher	/O N.Tremark	/C B.Tate	O J.Moore	P C.Hubbell	/O W.Schulmerich	P B.Swift	H L.Riggs
P E.Brandt	/C W.Millies	/1 P.Cavarretta	1 J.Shevlin	P H.Schumacher	1 B.Clancy	P R.Birkofer	H R.Worthington
P F.Frankhouse	/3 B.Hogg	P L.Warneke	/1 F.McCormick	P F.Fitzsimmons	/O E.Boland	P W.Hoyt	P D.Dean
P H.Betts	P V.Mungo	P B.Lee	H J.Flowers	P R.Parmelee	/3 M.Hopkins	P R.Lucas	P T.Carleton
P F.Rhem	P R.Benge	P G.Bush	/2 B.Marshall	/P J.Bowman	/O P.Oana	RP L.Chagnon	P P.Dean
P B.Cantwell	P D.Leonard	P P.Malone	/O T.Petoskey	RP A.Smith	/O H.Wilson	RP H.Smith	P B.Hallahan
P B.Smith	P J.Babich	P J.Weaver	/1 H.McCurdy	RP H.Bell	/C J.Holden	P H.Meine	P B.Walker
P L.Mangum	P T.Zachary	P B.Tinning	H T.Robello	P D.Luque	/O F.Frink	/P B.Grimes	RP J.Haines
P B.Brown	RP O.Carroll	P C.Root	P P.Derringer	P J.Salveson	P C.Davis	/P B.Harris	RP J.Mooney
P D.Barrett	RP B.Beck	P R.Joiner	P B.Frey	/P W.Clark	P P.Collins	/P E.Holley	P D.Vance
/P T.Zachary	P L.Munns	/P C.Wiedemeyer	/P Si.Johnson	/P S.Castleman	P S.Hansen	/P C.Blanton	/P F.Rhem
/P C.Pickrel	P A.Herring	/P D.Ward	/P T.Freitas		P S.Johnson	/P S.Struss	/P J.Lindsey
/P J.Elliott	P R.Lucas	/P L.Nelson	P A.Stout		P C.Moore	/P L.Johnson	/P J.Winford
	P W.Clark		RP D.Brennan		RP R.Grabowski		/P B.Grimes
	P C.Perkins		RP R.Kolp		RP G.Darrow		/P C.Heise
	/P H.Smythe		P T.Kleinhans		P E.Moore		
	/P P.Page		P L.Benton		P E.Holley		
			/P B.Richmond		/P F.Pearce		
			/P D.Vance		/P T.Kleinhans		
			/P J.Shaute		/P B.Lohrman		
			/P W.Wistert		/P J.Elliott		
			/P L.Grissom		/P C.Malis		
			/P Sy.Johnson				
			/P J.Lindsey				
			/P S.Edwards				
			/P J.Barnes				

TEAM	G	W	L	PCT	GB	R	OR	AB	H	2B	3B	HR	BB	SO	AVG	OBP	SLG	PRO	PRO+	BR	/A	PF	CHI	RC	SB	CS	SBA	SBR
STL	154	95	58	.621		**799**	656	5502	**1582**	294	75	104	392	535	**.288**	.337	**.425**	**.762**	102	63	12	107	101	796	**69**			
NY	153	93	60	.608	2	760	**583**	5396	1485	240	41	**126**	406	526	.275	.329	.405	.734	105	8	25	98	**105**	736	19			
CHI	152	86	65	.570	8	705	639	5347	1494	263	44	101	375	630	.279	.330	.402	.732	103	5	19	98	99	719	59			
BOS	152	78	73	.517	16	683	714	5370	1460	233	44	83	375	440	.272	.323	.378	.701	101	-52	-3	93	104	660	30			
PIT	151	74	76	.493	19.5	735	713	5361	1541	281	**77**	52	440	398	.287	.344	.398	.742	102	34	17	102	99	742	44			
BRO	153	71	81	.467	23.5	748	795	5427	1526	284	52	79	**548**	555	.281	.350	.396	.746	**112**	51	90	95	95	782	55			
PHI	149	56	93	.376	37	675	794	5218	1480	286	35	56	398	534	.284	.338	.384	.722	87	-3	-95	113	98	685	52			
CIN	152	52	99	.344	42	590	801	5361	1428	227	65	55	313	532	.266	.311	.364	.675	88	-105	-91	98	99	603	34			
TOT	608					5695		42982	11996	2108	433	656	3247	4150	.279	.333	.394	.727						362				

TEAM	CG	SH	SV	IP	H	H/G	HR	BB	SO	RAT	ERA	ERA+	OAV	OOB	PR	/A	PF	CPI	FA	E	DP	FW	PW	BW	SBW	DIF
STL	**78**	15	16	1386²	1463	9.5	77	411	**689**	12.4	3.69	115	.268	.323	58	83	104	101	.972	166	141	.3	8.1	1.2		8.9
NY	68	13	**30**	1370	**1384**	**9.1**	75	**351**	499	**11.5**	3.19	121	.260	.308	132	102	95	105	.972	179	141	-.5	**9.9**	2.4		4.6
CHI	73	11	9	1361¹	1432	9.5	80	417	633	12.3	3.76	103	.269	.325	46	18	95	101	**.977**	137	135	**1.9**	1.8	1.9		5.0
BOS	62	12	20	1359²	1512	10.0	78	405	462	12.8	4.11	93	.284	.331	-7	-44	94	97	.972	169	120	.0	-4.3	-.3		7.1
PIT	63	8	8	1329²	1523	10.3	78	354	487	12.9	4.20	98	.284	.332	-20	-13	101	98	.975	145	118	1.4	-1.3	1.7		-2.8
BRO	66	6	12	1354¹	1540	10.2	81	475	520	13.6	4.48	87	.285	.346	-63	-87	96	97	.970	180	141	-.6	-8.5	8.8		-4.7
PHI	52	8	15	1297	1501	10.4	126	437	416	13.6	4.76	99	.288	.347	-101	-4	116	99	.966	197	140	-1.8	-.4	-9.3		-7.0
CIN	51	3	19	1347²	1645	11.0	**61**	389	438	13.8	4.37	93	.299	.348	-46	-43	101	102	.970	181	136	-.7	-4.2	-8.9		-9.8
TOT	513	76	129	10806¹		10.0				12.9	4.06		.279	.333					.972	1354	1072					

Runs
P.Waner-Pit 122
Ott-NY 119
Collins-StL 116
Vaughan-Pit 115
Medwick-StL 110

Hits
P.Waner-Pit 217
Terry-NY 213
Collins-StL 200
Medwick-StL 198

Doubles
Cuyler-Chi 42
Allen-Phi 42
Vaughan-Pit 41
Medwick-StL 40
Collins-StL 40

Triples
Medwick-StL 18
P.Waner-Pit 16
Suhr-Pit 13
Collins-StL 12

Home Runs
Ott-NY 35
Collins-StL 35
Berger-Bos 34
Hartnett-Chi 22
Klein-Chi 20

Total Bases
Collins-StL 369
Ott-NY 344
Berger-Bos 336
Medwick-StL 328
P.Waner-Pit 323

Runs Batted In
Ott-NY 135
Collins-StL 128
Berger-Bos 121
Medwick-StL 106
Suhr-Pit 103

Runs Produced
Ott-NY 219
Collins-StL 209
P.Waner-Pit 198
Medwick-StL 198
Vaughan-Pit 197

Bases On Balls
Vaughan-Pit 94
Ott-NY 85
Koenecke-Bro 70
Leslie-Bro 69
P.Waner-Pit 68

Batting Average
P.Waner-Pit 362
Terry-NY 354
Cuyler-Chi 338
Vaughan-Pit 333
Collins-StL 333

On Base Percentage
Vaughan-Pit 431
P.Waner-Pit 429
Ott-NY 415
Terry-NY 414
Koenecke-Bro 411

Slugging Average
Collins-StL 615
Ott-NY 591
DeLancey-StL 565
Berger-Bos 546
P.Waner-Pit 539

Production
Collins-StL 1.008
Ott-NY 1.006
P.Waner-Pit 968
Vaughan-Pit 942
Koenecke-Bro 919

Adjusted Production
Ott-NY 170
Collins-StL 155
P.Waner-Pit 154
Koenecke-Bro 152
Berger-Bos 148

Batter Runs
Ott-NY 55.2
Collins-StL 53.3
P.Waner-Pit 50.2
Vaughan-Pit 44.3
Terry-NY 31.5

Adjusted Batter Runs
Ott-NY 58.5
P.Waner-Pit 47.2
Collins-StL 44.9
Vaughan-Pit 41.5
Berger-Bos 37.7

Clutch Hitting Index
Thevenow-Pit 133
Durocher-StL 132
Leslie-Bro 126
Jackson-NY 124
Cuccinello-Bro 124

Runs Created
Ott-NY 150
Collins-StL 148
P.Waner-Pit 142
Vaughan-Pit 135
Terry-NY 122

Total Average
Ott-NY 1.075
Collins-StL 1.046
Vaughan-Pit 1.043
P.Waner-Pit 1.010
Koenecke-Bro 981

Stolen Bases
Martin-StL 23
Cuyler-Chi 15
Bartell-Phi 13
Taylor-Bro 12

Stolen Base Average

Stolen Base Runs

Fielding Runs
Critz-NY 25.0
K.Davis-StL-Phi . . 17.8
B.Herman-Chi 15.6
Bartell-Phi 13.5
Hartnett-Chi 13.5

Total Player Rating
Vaughan-Pit 5.1
P.Waner-Pit 4.6
Ott-NY 4.1
Collins-StL 3.8
Hartnett-Chi 3.5

Wins
D.Dean-StL 30
Schumacher-NY . . . 23
Warneke-Chi 22
Hubbell-NY 21

Win Percentage
D.Dean-StL 811
Hoyt-Pit 714
Schumacher-NY 697
Warneke-Chi 688
Frankhouse-Bos 654

Games
C.Davis-Phi 51
Hansen-Phi 50
D.Dean-StL 50
Hubbell-NY 49
French-Pit 49

Complete Games
Hubbell-NY 25
D.Dean-StL 24
Warneke-Chi 23
Mungo-Bro 22
Brandt-Bos 20

Shutouts
D.Dean-StL 7
Hubbell-NY 5
P.Dean-StL 5
Lee-Chi 4

Saves
Hubbell-NY 8
Luque-NY 7
D.Dean-StL 7
Bell-NY 6

Innings Pitched
Mungo-Bro 315.1
Hubbell-NY 313.0
D.Dean-StL 311.2
Schumacher-NY . . 297.0
Warneke-Chi 291.1

Fewest Hits/Game
Parmelee-NY 7.90
Hubbell-NY 8.22
D.Dean-StL 8.32
Warneke-Chi 8.43
Mungo-Bro 8.56

Fewest BB/Game
Hubbell-NY 1.06
Freitas-Cin 1.47
Frey-Cin 1.54
Leonard-Bro 1.62
Fitzsimmons-NY . . 1.74

Strikeouts
D.Dean-StL 195
Mungo-Bro 184
P.Dean-StL 150
Warneke-Chi 143
Derringer-Cin 122

Strikeouts/Game
P.Waner-Pit 5.79
D.Dean-StL 5.63
Weaver-Chi 5.55
Mungo-Bro 5.25
Malone-Chi 5.23

Ratio
Hubbell-NY 9.35
Warneke-Chi 10.53
D.Dean-StL 10.66
Hoyt-Pit 10.81
Fitzsimmons-NY . 10.87

Earned Run Average
Hubbell-NY 2.30
D.Dean-StL 2.66
Hoyt-Pit 2.93
C.Davis-Phi 2.95
Fitzsimmons-NY . . . 3.04

Adjusted ERA
Hubbell-NY 168
C.Davis-Phi 160
D.Dean-StL 159
Hoyt-Pit 141
Walker-StL 135

Opponents' Batting Avg.
Parmelee-NY 238
Hubbell-NY 239
D.Dean-StL 241
Warneke-Chi 244
P.Dean-StL 248

Opponents' On Base Pct.
Hubbell-NY 263
Warneke-Chi 287
D.Dean-StL 289
P.Dean-StL 292
Hoyt-Pit 296

Starter Runs
Hubbell-NY 61.3
D.Dean-StL 48.7
C.Davis-Phi 33.8
Fitzsimmons-NY . . 29.8
Schumacher-NY . . 29.0

Adjusted Starter Runs
Hubbell-NY 54.5
D.Dean-StL 54.3
C.Davis-Phi 54.0
Hoyt-Pit 25.2
Fitzsimmons-NY . . 24.1

Clutch Pitching Index
Walker-StL 137
Leonard-Bro 121
C.Davis-Phi 120
Freitas-Cin 111
Frankhouse-Bos . . . 110

Relief Runs
Haines-StL 5.6
Bell-NY 2.4
Brennan-Cin 2.2

Adjusted Relief Runs
Haines-StL 7.2
Brennan-Cin 2.4
Bell-NY 1.2

Relief Ranking
Haines-StL 6.0
Brennan-Cin 2.1
Bell-NY 1.7

Total Pitcher Index
C.Davis-Phi 7.8
D.Dean-StL 6.4
Hubbell-NY 6.0
Fitzsimmons-NY . . 3.7
Schumacher-NY . . 3.5

Total Baseball Ranking
C.Davis-Phi 7.8
D.Dean-StL 6.4
Hubbell-NY 6.0
Vaughan-Pit 5.1
P.Waner-Pit 4.6

January 15 Babe Ruth accepts a cut of $17,000 and signs a contract for $35,000.

January 19 Judge Landis denies "Shoeless" Joe Jackson's appeal for reinstatement.

March 20 All-around athlete Mildred "Babe" Didrickson pitches the first inning for the Philadelphia Athletics in a spring training exhibition game against the Brooklyn Dodgers. She gives up one walk but no hits.

April 21 Moe Berg, little-used Senators catcher, plays his 117th consecutive errorless game, dating back to 1931, an AL record.

May 6 The Red Sox score 12 runs in the fourth inning, helped along by a record four consecutive triples hit by Carl Reynolds, Moose Solters, Rick Ferrell, and Bucky Walters to beat Detroit, 14–4. The record is five, set in the AL's inaugural year of 1901.

May 18 At Comiskey Park, Jimmie Foxx tees off against Ted Lyons and hits the first home run ever to land in the center field bleachers. Hank Greenberg will match Double X in 1938, then no one will reach the bleachers until Alex Johnson in 1970.

July 5 Lou Gehrig hits an inside-the-park grand slam, as the Yankees beat the Senators, 8–3. It is his fourth of the season and 17th overall, passing Babe Ruth's career total. Gehrig will eventually set a career record of 23 grand slams.

July 13 Babe Ruth hits his 700th home run to win the game at Detroit's Navin Field and put the Yankees back in first place. Lou Gehrig has a lumbago seizure and is helped off the field.

July 14 Lou Gehrig's consecutive-game string is extended by having him lead off, listed in the lineup as shortstop. He singles and leaves the game.

July 17 Babe Ruth draws his 2,000th base on balls at Cleveland. He will retire with a still untopped walk record of 2,056.

August 12 Making a farewell appearance in Boston, Babe Ruth draws a record 46,766 fans, with an estimated 20,000 turned away at Fenway Park where he began his career as a pitcher 20 years ago. Ruth singles and doubles in the first game, but the Yankees lose to Wes Ferrell, 6–4. Walks hold him to one official at bat in the second game, which the Yankees win, and he leaves the field to standing cheers in the eighth inning.

August 25 Schoolboy Rowe, Detroit's sensational rookie pitcher, defeats the Senators 4–2 for his 16th win in a row, tying the AL record held by Walter Johnson, Joe Wood, and Lefty Grove.

September 24 Idle Detroit wins the pennant, as the Red Sox beat the Yankees, 5-0, in the season's finale at Yankee Stadium. Ruth walks in the first inning, limps to first base, and leaves for a pinch runner in his last home game.

September 30 Coach Charley O'Leary scores a run as a pinch hitter for the Browns at age 52—the oldest major league player ever to do so.

November 3 Although Lou Gehrig wins the Triple Crown with 49 home runs, 165 RBIs, and a .363 BA, Mickey Cochrane, with two home runs, 76 RBIs, and a .320 batting average, is named AL MVP. Dizzy Dean, with a 30-7 record, is chosen as NL MVP.

BOSTON	CHICAGO	CLEVELAND	DETROIT	NEW YORK	PHILADELPHIA	ST.LOUIS	WASHINGTON
M B.Harris	M L.Fonseca	M W.Johnson	M M.Cochrane	M J.McCarthy	M C.Mack	M R.Hornsby	M J.Cronin
1B E.Morgan	M J.Dykes	1B H.Trosky	1B H.Greenberg	1B L.Gehrig	1B J.Foxx	1B J.Burns	1B J.Kuhel
2B B.Cissell	1B Z.Bonura	2B O.Hale	2B C.Gehringer	2B T.Lazzeri	2B R.Warstler	2B S.Melillo	2B B.Myer
SS L.Lary	2B J.Hayes	SS B.Knickerb'r	SS B.Rogell	SS F.Crosetti	SS E.McNair	SS A.Strange	SS J.Cronin
3B B.Werber	SS L.Appling	3B W.Kamm	3B M.Owen	3B J.Saltzgaver	3B P.Higgins	3B H.Clift	3B C.Travis
LF R.Johnson	3B J.Dykes	LF J.Vosmik	LF G.Goslin	LF M.Hoag	LF B.Johnson	LF R.Pepper	LF H.Manush
CF C.Reynolds	LF A.Simmons	CF E.Averill	CF J.White	CF B.Chapman	CF D.Cramer	CF S.West	CF F.Schulte
RF D.Porter	CF M.Haas	RF S.Rice	RF P.Fox	RF B.Ruth	RF E.Coleman	RF B.Campbell	RF J.Stone
C R.Ferrell	RF E.Swanson	C F.Pytlak	C M.Cochrane	C B.Dickey	C C.Berry	C R.Hemsley	C E.Phillips
	C E.Madjeski						
21 M.Bishop	2S B.Boken	3 J.Burnett	O G.Walker	O S.Byrd	O1 L.Finney	S2 O.Bejma	3S O.Bluege
O M.Solters	O J.Conlan	O M.Galatzer	C R.Hayworth	S3 R.Rolfe	C F.Hayes	O D.Garms	O D.Harris
O D.Cooke	3 M.Hopkins	O B.Seeds	O F.Doljack	O E.Combs	2 D.Williams	C F.Grube	1 P.Susko
O M.Almada	C M.Shea	O D.Holland	/3 F.Clifton	2 D.Heffner	O B.Miller	/O E.Clark	C L.Sewell
3 B.Walters	O F.Uhalt	O G.Myatt	/S H.Schuble	C A.Jorgens	/O J.McQuaig	/O G.Puccinelli	1O R.Kress
C G.Hinkle	S3 J.Chamberlain	C M.Berg	/C R.York	O G.Selkirk	/C C.Moss	/3 R.Hornsby	C B.Bolton
O S.Graham	O F.Bordagaray	2 E.Moore	C C.Perkins	/O D.Walker	/C E.Madjeski	/C G.Hartley	32 J.Kerr
C L.Legett	C M.Ruel	O B.Brenzel	H F.Reiber	/C Z.Taylor		H A.Scharein	C M.Berg
/2 A.Niemiec	O R.Radcliff	O D.Porter	H I.Wilson	/1 L.Lary	P J.Marcum	H C.O'Leary	O J.Gill
/1 J.Judge	O M.Bocek	/O K.Carson			P S.Cain		/O J.Powell
/S R.Kellett	3 M.Mauldin	/C B.Garbark	P T.Bridges	P L.Gomez	P B.Dietrich	P B.Newsom	/O F.Sington
/O B.Seeds	/O C.Uhlir	/C R.Spencer	P S.Rowe	P R.Ruffing	P J.Cascarella	P G.Blaeholder	/3 B.Boken
/2 F.Muller	/C G.Caithamer		P E.Auker	P J.Murphy	P A.Benton	P B.Hadley	/O G.Dugas
	/2 R.Kress	P M.Pearson	P F.Marberry	P J.Broaca		P D.Coffman	C E.Klumpp
P G.Rhodes	/C J.Pasek	P M.Harder	P V.Sorrell	P J.DeShong	P R.Mahaffey	P I.Andrews	
P J.Welch	/C B.Fehring	P O.Hildebrand	RP C.Hogsett		P B.Kline	RP E.Wells	P E.Whitehill
P F.Ostermueller		P W.Hudlin		P D.MacFayden	P G.Caster	RP B.McAfee	P M.Weaver
P W.Ferrell	P G.Earnshaw	P L.Brown	P C.Fischer	P R.Van Atta	P M.Flohr		P B.Burke
P H.Johnson	P T.Lyons	P C.Brown	/P L.Hamlin	P J.Allen	P H.Matuzak	/P J.Knott	P L.Stewart
RP H.Pennock	P M.Gaston		/P A.Crowder	P B.Grimes	P W.Wilshere	/P J.Weaver	P T.Thomas
P L.Grove	P S.Jones	/P T.Lee	/P V.Frasier	P G.Uhle	/P E.Lagger	/P L.Mills	RP J.Russell
P R.Walberg	P L.Tietje	P R.Winegarner	/P S.Larkin	/P H.Smythe	/P J.Wilson	/P J.Walkup	RP A.McColl
P B.Weiland	RP J.Heving	P B.Weiland		/P C.Devens	/P T.McKeithan		
P J.Mulligan	RP W.Wyatt	/P S.Connally		/P V.Tamulis	/P R.Vaughn		P A.Crowder
/P G.Hockette	P P.Gallivan	/P B.Perrin		/P F.Newkirk			/P E.Linke
/P S.Merena	P H.Kinzy	/P D.Galehouse					/P R.Diggs
/P G.Pipgras	/P V.Kennedy						/P S.Cohen
	/P H.Klaerner						/P R.Prim
	/P L.Stine						/P O.Armbrust
	/P M.Stratton						/P A.Benson
	/P J.Pomorski						/P B.Kline
							/P J.Milligan
							/P M.Filley

TEAM	G	W	L	PCT	GB	R	OR	AB	H	2B	3B	HR	BB	SO	AVG	OBP	SLG	PRO	PRO+	BR	/A	PF	CHI	RC	SB	CS	SBA	SBR
DET	154	101	53	.656		958	708	5475	1644	349	53	74	639	528	.300	.376	.424	.800	113	112	110	100	104	905	125	55	69	5
NY	154	94	60	.610	7	842	669	5368	1494	226	61	135	700	597	.278	.364	.419	.783	117	70	130	93	96	848	71	46	61	-6
CLE	154	85	69	.552	16	814	763	5396	1550	340	46	100	526	433	.287	.353	.423	.776	105	44	32	102	98	820	52	32	62	-4
BOS	153	76	76	.500	24	820	775	5339	1465	287	70	51	610	535	.274	.350	.383	.733	90	-28	-82	107	108	748	116	47	71	7
PHI	153	68	82	.453	31	764	838	5317	1491	236	50	144	491	584	.280	.343	.425	.768	108	20	49	96	97	785	57	35	62	-4
STL	154	67	85	.441	33	674	800	5288	1417	252	59	62	514	631	.268	.335	.373	.708	82	-84	-142	108	98	680	43	31	58	-6
WAS	155	66	86	.434	34	729	806	5448	1512	278	70	51	570	447	.278	.348	.382	.730	99	-35	-6	96	95	747	47	42	53	-11
CHI	153	53	99	.349	47	704	946	5301	1395	237	40	71	565	524	.263	.336	.363	.699	84	-97	-118	103	103	672	36	27	57	-5
TOT	615					6305		42932	11968	2205	449	688	4615	4279	.279	.351	.399	.750							547	315	63	-25

TEAM	CG	SH	SV	IP	H	H/G	HR	BB	SO	RAT	ERA	ERA+	OAV	OOB	PR	/A	PF	CPI	FA	E	DP	FW	PW	BW	SBW	DIF
DET	74	13	14	1370²	1467	9.6	86	488	640	12.9	4.06	108	.273	.335	67	50	98	102	.974	159	150	1.2	4.6	10.2	.8	7.2
NY	83	13	10	1382²	1349	8.8	71	542	656	12.4	3.76	108	.254	.324	114	48	90	97	.973	157	151	1.3	4.5	12.1	-.3	-.5
CLE	72	8	19	1367	1476	9.7	70	582	554	13.7	4.28	106	.275	.349	33	40	101	101	.972	172	164	.4	3.7	3.0	-.0	1.0
BOS	68	9	9	1361	1527	10.1	70	543	538	13.8	4.32	111	.283	.351	27	73	107	103	.969	188	141	-.5	6.8	7.4	.9	.4
PHI	68	8	8	1337	1429	9.6	84	693	480	14.4	5.01	87	.275	.363	-77	-94	97	94	.967	196	166	-1.0	-8.7	4.6	-.0	-1.8
STL	50	6	20	1350	1499	10.0	94	632	499	14.3	4.49	111	.283	.361	1	75	111	107	.969	187	160	-.4	7.0	-13.2	-.3	-2.1
WAS	61	4	12	1381¹	1622	10.6	74	503	412	13.9	4.68	92	.295	.355	-28	-55	96	101	.974	162	167	1.0	-5.1	-.6	-.7	-4.6
CHI	72	5	8	1355	1599	10.6	139	628	506	14.9	5.41	88	.292	.367	-137	-101	105	97	.966	207	126	-1.6	-9.4	-11.0	-.2	-.9
TOT	548	66	100	10904²		9.9				13.8	4.50		.279	.351					.970	1428	1225					

Runs		Hits		Doubles		Triples		Home Runs		Total Bases	
Gehringer-Det	134	Gehringer-Det	214	Greenberg-Det	63	Chapman-NY	13	Gehrig-NY	49	Gehrig-NY	409
Werber-Bos	129	Gehrig-NY	210	Gehringer-Det	50	Manush-Was	11	Foxx-Phi	44	Trosky-Cle	374
Gehrig-NY	128	Trosky-Cle	206	Averill-Cle	48			Trosky-Cle	35	Greenberg-Det	356
Averill-Cle	128	Cramer-Phi	202	Trosky-Cle	45			Johnson-Phi	34	Foxx-Phi	352
Foxx-Phi	120	Greenberg-Det	201	Hale-Cle	44			Averill-Cle	31	Averill-Cle	340

Runs Batted In		Runs Produced		Bases On Balls		Batting Average		On Base Percentage		Slugging Average	
Gehrig-NY	165	Gehringer-Det	250	Foxx-Phi	111	Gehrig-NY	.363	Gehrig-NY	.465	Gehrig-NY	.706
Trosky-Cle	142	Gehrig-NY	244	Gehrig-NY	109	Gehringer-Det	.356	Gehringer-Det	.450	Foxx-Phi	.653
Greenberg-Det	139	Greenberg-Det	231	Ruth-NY	103	Manush-Was	.349	Foxx-Phi	.449	Greenberg-Det	.600
Foxx-Phi	130	Trosky-Cle	224	Myer-Was	102	Simmons-Chi	.344	Cochrane-Det	.428	Trosky-Cle	.598
Gehringer-Det	127	Rogell-Det	211			Vosmik-Cle	.341	Myer-Was	.419	Averill-Cle	.569

Production		Adjusted Production		Batter Runs		Adjusted Batter Runs		Clutch Hitting Index		Runs Created	
Gehrig-NY	1.172	Gehrig-NY	213	Gehrig-NY	85.6	Gehrig-NY	98.0	Dykes-Chi	137	Gehrig-NY	195
Foxx-Phi	1.102	Foxx-Phi	188	Foxx-Phi	66.4	Foxx-Phi	72.1	Cronin-Was	131	Foxx-Phi	165
Greenberg-Det	1.005	Greenberg-Det	156	Gehringer-Det	47.8	Gehringer-Det	47.5	Pepper-StL	129	Averill-Cle	145
Trosky-Cle	.987	Trosky-Cle	149	Greenberg-Det	46.7	Greenberg-Det	46.4	Cochrane-Det	129	Trosky-Cle	145
Averill-Cle	.982	Averill-Cle	149	Averill-Cle	45.6	Averill-Cle	43.6	Rogell-Det	126	Gehringer-Det	144

Total Average		Stolen Bases		Stolen Base Average		Stolen Base Runs		Fielding Runs		Total Player Rating	
Gehrig-NY	1.401	Werber-Bos	40	White-Det	82.4	White-Det	4.8	Hale-Cle	25.7	Gehrig-NY	7.8
Foxx-Phi	1.310	White-Det	28	Werber-Bos	72.7	Werber-Bos	3.0	Hemsley-StL	23.3	Foxx-Phi	6.1
Averill-Cle	1.075	Chapman-NY	26	Fox-Det	71.4	Lazzeri-NY	2.7	Werber-Bos	20.3	Gehringer-Det	5.7
Greenberg-Det	1.071	Fox-Det	25	Walker-Det	69.0	Cronin-Was	2.4	Cronin-Was	18.4	Averill-Cle	4.2
Gehringer-Det	1.053	Walker-Det	20	Chapman-NY	61.9			Melillo-StL	18.1	Werber-Bos	4.1

Wins		Win Percentage		Games		Complete Games		Shutouts		Saves	
Gomez-NY	26	Gomez-NY	.839	Russell-Was	54	Gomez-NY	25	Harder-Cle	6	Russell-Was	7
Rowe-Det	24	Rowe-Det	.750	Newsom-StL	47	Bridges-Det	23	Gomez-NY	6	L.Brown-Cle	6
Bridges-Det	22	Marberry-Det	.750	Rowe-Det	45	Lyons-Chi	21	Ruffing-NY	5	Newsom-StL	5
Harder-Cle	20	Auker-Det	.682	Knott-StL	45	Rowe-Det	20	Dietrich-Phi	4		
Ruffing-NY	19	Bridges-Det	.667								

Innings Pitched		Fewest Hits/Game		Fewest BB/Game		Strikeouts		Strikeouts/Game		Ratio	
Gomez-NY	281.2	Gomez-NY	7.13	W.Ferrell-Bos	2.44	Gomez-NY	158	Ruffing-NY	5.23	Gomez-NY	10.19
Bridges-Det	275.0	Ruffing-NY	8.15	Auker-Det	2.46	Bridges-Det	151	Gomez-NY	5.05	Rowe-Det	11.54
Rowe-Det	266.0	Bridges-Det	8.15	Blaeholder-StL	2.61	Ruffing-NY	149	Rowe-Det	5.04	Bridges-Det	11.65
Newsom-StL	262.1	Burke-Was	8.30	Rowe-Det	2.74	Rowe-Det	149	Pearson-Cle	4.95	Murphy-NY	11.66
Ruffing-NY	256.1	Murphy-NY	8.36	Weaver-Was	2.77	Pearson-Cle	140	Bridges-Det	4.94	Harder-Cle	11.77

Earned Run Average		Adjusted ERA		Opponents' Batting Avg.		Opponents' On Base Pct.		Starter Runs		Adjusted Starter Runs	
Gomez-NY	2.33	Harder-Cle	174	Gomez-NY	.215	Gomez-NY	.282	Gomez-NY	67.7	Harder-Cle	55.0
Harder-Cle	2.61	Gomez-NY	174	Ruffing-NY	.236	Ruffing-NY	.310	Harder-Cle	53.6	Gomez-NY	54.2
Murphy-NY	3.12	Ostermueller-Bos	138	Bridges-Det	.241	Rowe-Det	.312	Murphy-NY	31.8	Ostermueller-Bos	29.0
Burke-Was	3.21	Burke-Was	134	Burke-Was	.245	Bridges-Det	.312	Rowe-Det	30.9	Newsom-StL	28.6
Auker-Det	3.42	W.Ferrell-Bos	132	Benton-Phi	.249	Harder-Cle	.316	Bridges-Det	25.4	Rowe-Det	27.7

Clutch Pitching Index		Relief Runs		Adjusted Relief Runs		Relief Ranking		Total Pitcher Index		Total Baseball Ranking	
Harder-Cle	127	Pennock-Bos	10.0	Pennock-Bos	12.1	Bean-Cle	4.1	Harder-Cle	6.4	Gehrig-NY	7.8
Auker-Det	123	McColl-Was	8.0	McColl-Was	5.7	Pennock-Bos	3.9	Gomez-NY	4.8	Harder-Cle	6.4
Ostermueller-Bos	116	Russell-Was	5.8	Bean-Cle	3.9	McColl-Was	3.3	Rowe-Det	4.0	Foxx-Phi	6.1
Murphy-NY	113	Bean-Cle	3.7	Russell-Was	2.6	Russell-Was	2.5	Newsom-StL	3.2	Gehringer-Det	5.7
Coffman-StL	109			Wells-StL	2.1	Wells-StL	1.7	Ostermueller-Bos	3.1	Gomez-NY	4.8

April 16 Babe Ruth, released by the Yankees to sign with the Boston Braves for $20,000 and a share in the team's profits, draws the largest Opening Day crowd, 25,000, in Braves' history in his NL debut. It includes a 430-foot home run off Carl Hubbell, as Boston beats New York, 4-2.

April 28 Trade unions direct their attention at the Cardinals, voting to boycott their games because team captain Leo Durocher made an anti-union statement in behalf of his wife's dress business. The ballpark is eventually picketed to protest non-union ushers, gate men, and vendors.

May 8 Reds backstop Ernie Lombardi equals the major league record with four doubles in consecutive innings, each off a different pitcher. The slow-footed Lombardi also has a "long single" in the 23-hit, 15–4 win over the Phillies.

May 9 The Braves' Rabbit Maranville sets a new record for NL service by appearing in his 23rd season. It is his first appearance since breaking his ankle in last year's spring training.

May 24 The Cincinnati Reds host the Philadelphia Phillies in the first major league night game, winning, 2-1. On the initiative of Larry MacPhail, President Franklin Delano Roosevelt throws the switch at the White House to turn on the lights. The Reds will play seven night games, one each against the other NL teams.

May 25 Babe Ruth has a last hurrah, hitting three home runs at Pittsburgh. The final one, the last of his 714 career home runs, is the first to clear the right field grandstand at Forbes Field and is measured at 600 feet. He will announce his retirement June 2.

May 30 The Memorial Day twin bill at the Polo Grounds breaks all NL attendance records when 63,943 see the Giants take a pair from the Dodgers.

July 31 The Reds oversell their night game, and 30,000 jam in for the match against the Cards. Kitty Burke, a female fan, slips under the ropes around the infield and grabs a bat. Paul Dean lobs a pitch and she grounds out. Cardinals manager Frankie Frisch demands it count as an at bat.

September 22 The Boston Braves lose their 110th game and will lose 115, the most since 1900 until the 1962 expansion New York Mets lose 120 in a 162-game schedule. The Braves' winning percentage is .248.

September 27 The Cubs clinch the NL pennant in the first game of a doubleheader with the Cardinals, 6-2, besting Dizzy Dean, as Bill Lee wins his 20th. By winning the second game, 5-3, the Cubs extend their win streak to 21 games.

October 23 Gabby Hartnett is selected by the BBWAA as the NL MVP, with Dizzy Dean the runner-up.

October 24 Judge Kenesaw Mountain Landis levies $200 fines on umpire George Moriarty, Cubs manager Charlie Grimm, and Chicago players Woody English, Billy Jurges, and Billy Herman for their conduct in the World Series against the Tigers.

November 26 The NL takes over the bankrupt, last-place Boston Braves franchise after several failed attempts to buy the club, ultimately accepting Bob Quinn, who had been general manager of the Brooklyn Dodgers, as president.

BOSTON		BROOKLYN		CHICAGO		CINCINNATI		NEW YORK		PHILADELPHIA		PITTSBURGH		ST.LOUIS	
M	B.McKechnie	M	C.Stengel	M	C.Grimm	M	C.Dressen	M	B.Terry	M	J.Wilson	M	P.Traynor	M	F.Frisch
1B	B.Jordan	1B	S.Leslie	1B	P.Cavarretta	1B	J.Bottomley	1B	B.Terry	1B	D.Camilli	1B	G.Suhr	1B	R.Collins
2B	L.Mallon	2B	T.Cuccinello	2B	B.Herman	2B	A.Kampouris	2B	M.Koenig	2B	L.Chiozza	2B	P.Young	2B	F.Frisch
SS	B.Urbanski	SS	L.Frey	SS	B.Jurges	SS	B.Myers	SS	D.Bartell	SS	M.Haslin	SS	A.Vaughan	SS	L.Durocher
3B	P.Whitney	3B	J.Stripp	3B	S.Hack	3B	L.Riggs	3B	T.Jackson	3B	J.Vergez	3B	T.Thevenow	3B	P.Martin
LF	H.Lee	LF	D.Taylor	LF	A.Galan	LF	B.Herman	LF	J.Moore	LF	G.Watkins	LF	W.Jensen	LF	J.Medwick
CF	W.Berger	CF	F.Bordagaray	CF	F.Demaree	CF	S.Byrd	CF	H.Leiber	CF	E.Allen	CF	L.Waner	CF	T.Moore
RF	T.Thompson	RF	B.Boyle	RF	C.Klein	RF	I.Goodman	RF	M.Ott	RF	J.Moore	RF	P.Waner	RF	J.Rothrock
C	A.Spohrer	C	A.Lopez	C	G.Hartnett	C	E.Lombardi	C	G.Mancuso	C	A.Todd	C	T.Padden	C	B.DeLancey
O1	R.Moore	23	J.Bucher	O3	F.Lindstrom	13	B.Sullivan	2	H.Critz	C	J.Wilson	23	C.Lavagetto	C	S.Davis
3S	J.Coscarart	2S	J.Jordan	C	K.O'Dea	2	K.Cuyler	S2	A.Cuccinello	S2	C.Gomez	C	E.Grace	2	B.Whitehead
C	S.Hogan	O	L.Koenecke	O	K.Cuyler	C	G.Campbell	S	H.Danning	S	B.Ryan	3	P.Traynor	O	E.Orsatti
1	E.Fletcher	C	B.Phelps	O	T.Stainback	1	G.Slade	1	W.Weintraub	O	E.Boland	O	B.Hafey	3S	C.Gelbert
O	J.Mowry	OP	B.Reis	3S	W.English	O	A.Comorosky	O	K.Davis	O	F.Lucas	O	B.Herman	/3	C.Wilson
C	R.Mueller	O	B.Mills	/C	W.Stephenson	C	H.Erickson	/C	G.Myatt	/C	J.Holden	/1	E.Browne	/O	L.King
O	B.Ruth	C	Z.Taylor	/1	C.Grimm	O	H.Pool	/C	P.Richards	/S	A.Bramhall	/3	B.Brubaker	/O	T.Winsett
2	R.Maranville	1	J.McCarthy	H	J.Gill	O	C.Hafey	H	J.Malay	/3	B.Jonnard	/C	A.Epps	/2	L.Judy
O	J.Tyler	O	J.Cooney			S	C.Chapman			/S	D.Chiozza	R	S.Swetonic	/C	B.O'Farrell
/2	E.Moriarty	/2	V.Sherlock	P	L.Warneke	/1	L.Scarsella	P	C.Hubbell					/C	S.Narron
/C	A.Doll	/O	N.Tremark	P	B.Lee	/O	T.Petoskey	P	H.Schumacher	P	C.Davis	P	C.Blanton	H	G.Moore
/C	B.Lewis	/3	F.Skaff	P	L.French	/O	T.Piet	P	R.Parmelee	P	O.Jorgens	P	B.Swift		
		/S	R.Dedeaux	P	C.Root	/O	L.Gamble	P	S.Castleman	P	S.Johnson	P	G.Bush	P	D.Dean
P	F.Frankhouse	/C	W.Ock	P	T.Carleton			P	A.Smith	P	J.Bivin	P	J.Weaver	P	P.Dean
P	B.Cantwell	/C	R.Onis	RP	F.Kowalik	P	P.Derringer	P	A.Stout	P	B.Walters	P	W.Hoyt	P	B.Walker
P	B.Smith					RP	A.Hollingsworth	RP	F.Gabler	P	P.Pezzullo			P	B.Hallahan
P	E.Brandt	P	V.Mungo	P	R.Henshaw	P	G.Schott	P	F.Fitzsimmons	RP	R.Prim	P	R.Birkofer	P	E.Heusser
P	H.Betts	P	W.Clark	P	H.Casey	P	T.Freitas	P	L.Chagnon	P	H.Mulcahy	P	R.Lucas		
RP	L.Benton	P	G.Earnshaw	/P	C.Bryant	P	S.Johnson	/P	H.Gumbert			P	M.Brown	P	J.Haines
		P	T.Zachary	/P	C.Shoun			/P	E.Moore	J.Bowman		/P	J.Salveson	P	P.Collins
P	D.MacFayden	P	J.Babich	/P	R.Joiner	P	D.Brennan	/P	D.Luque	E.Moore		/P	C.Passeau	P	R.Harrell
P	B.Brown	RP	L.Munns			P	B.Frey			/P	H.Kelleher	/P	H.Smith	/P	M.Ryba
P	F.Rhem	RP	D.Vance			P	L.Herrmann			/P	P.Collins	/P	W.Osborne	/P	N.Kleinke
/P	A.Blanche					P	E.Nelson			/P	F.Pearce			/P	J.Winford
/P	L.Mangum	P	D.Leonard			/P	D.MacFayden			/P	T.Thomas			/P	B.McGee
		P	R.Benge			/P	L.Grissom			/P	S.Hansen			/P	B.Tinning
		P	T.Baker			/P	W.Hilcher							/P	T.Kaufmann
		/P	H.Eisenstat											/P	A.Eckert
		/P	F.Lamanske											/P	M.Copeland
		/P	B.Logan											/P	D.Ward
		/P	B.Barr												
		/P	H.Green												

TEAM	G	W	L	PCT	GB	R	OR	AB	H	2B	3B	HR	BB	SO	AVG	OBP	SLG	PRO	PRO+	BR	/A	PF	CHI	RC	SB	CS	SBA	SBR
CHI	154	100	54	.649		847	597	5486	1581	303	62	88	464	471	.288	.347	.414	.761	110	81	76	101	102	812	66			
STL	154	96	58	.623	4	829	625	5457	1548	286	59	86	404	521	.284	.335	.405	.740	101	33	3	104	109	759	71			
NY	156	91	62	.595	8.5	770	675	5623	1608	248	56	123	392	479	.286	.336	.416	.752	110	54	68	98	96	797	32			
PIT	153	86	67	.562	13.5	743	647	5415	1543	255	90	66	457	437	.285	.343	.402	.745	103	49	24	103	96	758	30			
BRO	154	70	83	.458	29.5	711	767	5410	1496	235	62	59	430	520	.277	.333	.376	.709	99	-21	-6	98	101	691	60			
CIN	154	68	85	.444	31.5	646	772	5296	1403	244	68	73	392	547	.265	.319	.378	.697	96	-51	-31	97	99	658	72			
PHI	156	64	89	.418	35.5	685	871	5442	1466	249	32	92	392	661	.269	.322	.378	.700	85	-47	-116	110	101	681	52			
BOS	153	38	115	.248	61.5	575	852	5309	1396	233	33	75	353	436	.263	.311	.362	.673	93	-98	-50	92	95	596	20			
TOT	617					5806		43438	12041	2053	462	662	3284	4072	.277	.331	.391	.722							403			

TEAM	CG	SH	SV	IP	H	H/G	HR	BB	SO	RAT	ERA	ERA+	OAV	OOB	PR	/A	PF	CPI	FA	E	DP	FW	PW	BW	SBW	DIF
CHI	81	12	14	1394¹	1417	9.1	85	400	589	11.9	3.26	121	.263	.317	118	103	98	111	.970	186	163	.3	10.0	7.4		5.3
STL	73	10	18	1384²	1445	9.4	68	377	602	12.0	3.52	116	.267	.318	76	89	102	101	.972	164	133	1.6	8.6	.3		8.5
NY	76	10	11	1403²	1433	9.2	106	411	524	12.0	3.78	102	.262	.318	37	11	96	98	.972	174	129	1.1	1.1	6.6		5.7
PIT	76	15	11	1365²	1428	9.4	63	312	549	11.6	3.42	120	.307		91	103	102	98	.968	190	94	.0	10.0	2.3		-2.8
BRO	62	11	20	1358	1519	10.1	88	436	480	13.1	4.22	94	.281	.337	-31	-37	99	100	.969	188	146	.2	-3.6	-.6		-2.5
CIN	59	9	13	1356	1490	9.9	65	438	500	13.0	4.30	93	.278	.336	-43	-49	99	94	.966	204	139	-.7	-4.8	-3.0		.0
PHI	53	8	15	1374²	1652	10.8	106	505	475	14.4	4.76	95	.295	.358	-113	-35	113	102	.963	228	145	-2.0	-3.4	-11.3		4.1
BOS	54	6	5	1330	1645	11.1	81	404	355	14.0	4.93	77	.303	.354	-135	-169	94	96	.967	197	101	-.4	-16.4	-4.9		-16.8
TOT	534	81	107	10967		9.9				12.7	4.02		.277	.331					.968	1531	1050					

Runs
Galan-Chi 133
Medwick-StL 132
Martin-StL 121
Ott-NY 113
Herman-Chi 113

Hits
Herman-Chi 227
Medwick-StL 224

Doubles
Herman-Chi 57
Medwick-StL 46
Allen-Phi 46
Martin-StL 41
Galan-Chi 41

Triples
Goodman-Cin 18
L.Waner-Pit 14
Medwick-StL 13

Home Runs
Berger-Bos 34
Ott-NY 31
Camilli-Phi 25
Medwick-StL 23
R.Collins-StL 23

Total Bases
Medwick-StL 365
Ott-NY 329
Berger-Bos 323
Herman-Chi 317
Leiber-NY 314

Runs Batted In
Berger-Bos 130
Medwick-StL 126
R.Collins-StL 122
Ott-NY 114
Leiber-NY 107

Runs Produced
Medwick-StL 235
R.Collins-StL 208
Galan-Chi 200
Ott-NY 196
Leiber-NY 195

Bases On Balls
Vaughan-Pit 97
Galan-Chi 87
Ott-NY 82
Suhr-Pit 70
Frey-Bro 66

Batting Average
Vaughan-Pit .... .385
Medwick-StL .... .353
Hartnett-Chi .... .344
Lombardi-Cin .... .343
Herman-Chi .... .341

On Base Percentage
Vaughan-Pit .... .491
Ott-NY .... .407
Hack-Chi .... .406
Galan-Chi .... .399
P.Waner-Pit .... .392

Slugging Average
Vaughan-Pit .... .607
Medwick-StL .... .576
Ott-NY .... .555
Berger-Bos .... .548
Hartnett-Chi .... .545

Production
Vaughan-Pit 1.098
Medwick-StL .... .962
Ott-NY .... .962
R.Collins-StL .... .915
Berger-Bos .... .903

Adjusted Production
Vaughan-Pit 187
Ott-NY 159
Berger-Bos 151
Medwick-StL 149
Leiber-NY 143

Batter Runs
Vaughan-Pit 71.9
Ott-NY 47.6
Medwick-StL 46.0
R.Collins-StL 35.0
Leiber-NY 34.3

Adjusted Batter Runs
Vaughan-Pit 67.3
Ott-NY 50.0
Medwick-StL 41.0
Berger-Bos 38.7
Leiber-NY 36.4

Clutch Hitting Index
Leslie-Bro 135
Young-Pit 128
Durocher-StL 125
Jurges-Chi 121
Whitney-Bos 113

Runs Created
Vaughan-Pit 163
Ott-NY 144
Medwick-StL 139
Galan-Chi 133
R.Collins-StL 125

Total Average
Vaughan-Pit 1.317
Ott-NY 1.037
Medwick-StL .... .948
Galan-Chi .... .937
R.Collins-StL .... .930

Stolen Bases
Galan-Chi 22
Martin-StL 20
Bordagaray-Bro 18
Hack-Chi 14
Goodman-Cin 14

Stolen Base Average

Stolen Base Runs

Fielding Runs
Jurges-Chi 30.2
Herman-Chi 18.9
Allen-Phi 16.5
Hartnett-Chi 14.5
T.Moore-StL 13.8

Total Player Rating
Vaughan-Pit 6.1
Herman-Chi 5.4
Ott-NY 4.9
Hartnett-Chi 4.8
Berger-Bos 4.0

Wins
D.Dean-StL 28
Hubbell-NY 23
Derringer-Cin 22
Warneke-Chi 20
Lee-Chi 20

Win Percentage
Lee-Chi .... .769
Castleman-NY .... .714
D.Dean-StL .... .700
Schumacher-NY .... .679
Hubbell-NY .... .657

Games
Jorgens-Phi 53
D.Dean-StL 50
Bivin-Phi 47
Smith-Bos 46
P.Dean-StL 46

Complete Games
D.Dean-StL 29
Hubbell-NY 24
Blanton-Pit 23
Warneke-Chi 20
Derringer-Cin 20

Shutouts
Weaver-Pit 4
Mungo-Bro 4
French-Chi 4
Fitzsimmons-NY 4
Blanton-Pit 4

Saves
Leonard-Bro 8
Johnson-Phi 6
Hoyt-Pit 6

Innings Pitched
D.Dean-StL 325.1
Hubbell-NY 302.2
Derringer-Cin 276.2
P.Dean-StL 269.2

Fewest Hits/Game
Blanton-Pit 7.79
Schumacher-NY 8.08
Parmelee-NY 8.52
Swift-Pit 8.53
Hollingsworth-Cin 8.57

Fewest BB/Game
Clark-Bro 1.22
Hubbell-NY 1.46
Hoyt-Pit 1.48
Derringer-Cin 1.59
Johnson-Phi 1.60

Strikeouts
D.Dean-StL 190
Hubbell-NY 150
Mungo-Bro 143
P.Dean-StL 143
Blanton-Pit 142

Strikeouts/Game
Mungo-Bro 6.00
D.Dean-StL 5.26
Blanton-Pit 5.02
P.Dean-StL 4.77
Hollingsworth-Cin 4.62

Ratio
Blanton-Pit 9.80
Swift-Pit 10.21
Clark-Bro 10.61
Warneke-Chi 10.66
Schumacher-NY 10.66

Earned Run Average
Blanton-Pit 2.58
Swift-Pit 2.70
Schumacher-NY 2.89
French-Chi 2.96
Lee-Chi 2.96

Adjusted ERA
Blanton-Pit 159
Swift-Pit 152
D.Dean-StL 135
Schumacher-NY 133
French-Chi 133

Opponents' Batting Avg.
Blanton-Pit .... .229
Schumacher-NY .... .238
Hollingsworth-Cin .... .243
Swift-Pit .... .247
P.Dean-StL .... .249

Opponents' On Base Pct.
Blanton-Pit .... .272
Swift-Pit .... .282
Clark-Bro .... .289
Schumacher-NY .... .292
P.Dean-StL .... .292

Starter Runs
Blanton-Pit 40.6
D.Dean-StL 35.3
Schumacher-NY 32.8
Swift-Pit 29.9
Lee-Chi 29.5

Adjusted Starter Runs
Blanton-Pit 43.0
D.Dean-StL 38.2
Swift-Pit 31.9
Schumacher-NY 28.0
Lee-Chi 27.0

Clutch Pitching Index
French-Chi 126
Zachary-Bro 121
Walker-StL 116
Lee-Chi 111
Hallahan-StL 111

Relief Runs

Adjusted Relief Runs

Relief Ranking

Total Pitcher Index
Blanton-Pit 4.7
D.Dean-StL 4.3
Schumacher-NY 3.7
Swift-Pit 3.2
Warneke-Chi 3.0

Total Baseball Ranking
Vaughan-Pit 6.1
Herman-Chi 5.4
Ott-NY 4.9
Hartnett-Chi 4.8
Blanton-Pit 4.7

April 18 Detroit center fielder Jo Jo White ties an AL record with five walks.

May 15 Lou Gehrig steals home in a 4-0 Yankees win over the Tigers. It is his 15th and last steal of home, all of which were double steals.

May 21 Buck Newsom is sold by the Browns to the Senators for $40,000.

May 22* The Albany Senators (IL) sign Alabama Pitts, legendary athletic star and parolee from Sing Sing prison.

June 1 At Yankee Stadium, the Bombers hit a record six solo home runs in beating Boston, 7-2. Bill Dickey, who hits two, Frank Crosetti, Ben Chapman, George Selkirk, and Red Rolfe are the sluggers.

June 28 Earl Averill's consecutive-game streak ends at 673 for the Indians when he is injured in a pre-Fourth of July fireworks accident.

July 8 The AL continues its All-Star Game reign, winning the third event, at Cleveland's Municipal Stadium, 4-1. Jimmie Foxx is the hitting star with a homer and three RBIs.

July 31 Two AL pitchers each hit two homers in a game. Wes Ferrell clouts a couple against Buck Newsom of the Browns and knocks in four runs in a 6-4 win for Boston. Mel Harder hits two for Cleveland but loses 6-4 to the White Sox.

August 4 Walter Johnson resigns as Cleveland manager and is replaced by Steve O'Neill.

August 31 Vern Kennedy pitches the first AL no-hitter since 1931, and the first ever in Comiskey Park, blanking Cleveland, 5-0. He also is the batting star with a bases-loaded triple.

September 7 With no outs and the bases loaded, and the Indians leading, 5-3, in the ninth, Boston's Joe Cronin lines a drive off the head of Cleveland third baseman Odell Hale. The ball caroms to shortstop Bill Knickerbocker, who starts a triple play that ends the game.

September 20* The Pittsburgh Crawfords beat the New York Cubans to win the Negro National League Championship, 3-0, behind the pitching of Leroy Matlock and the extra base hits of Josh Gibson, James "Cool Papa" Bell, and Oscar Charleston.

September 21 The Detroit Tigers clinch the pennant with a double header win over the St. Louis Browns.

October 3 The Tigers even the World Series against the Cubs behind Tommy Bridges, 8-3, but lose Hank Greenberg who injures his wrist trying to score from first on a single.

October 7 The Tigers end the Series in six games behind Tommy Bridges' second complete game, 4-3. Goose Goslin's single, with two out in the bottom of the ninth, wins the game.

October 20 Hank Greenberg is named AL MVP by the BBWAA; Wes Ferrell is runner-up.

December 10 Jimmie Foxx, with Johnny Marcum, is sold by the A's to the Red Sox for $150,000; Al Simmons is sold by the White Sox to the Tigers for $75,000.

BOSTON	CHICAGO	CLEVELAND	DETROIT	NEW YORK	PHILADELPHIA	ST.LOUIS	WASHINGTON
M J.Cronin	M J.Dykes	M W.Johnson	M M.Cochrane	M J.McCarthy	M C.Mack	M R.Hornsby	M B.Harris
1B B.Dahlgren	1B Z.Bonura	M S.O'Neill	1B H.Greenberg	1B L.Gehrig	1B J.Foxx	1B J.Burns	1B J.Kuhel
2B S.Melillo	2B J.Hayes	1B H.Trosky	2B C.Gehringer	2B T.Lazzeri	2B R.Warstler	2B T.Carey	2B B.Myer
SS J.Cronin	SS L.Appling	2B B.Berger	SS B.Rogell	SS F.Crosetti	SS E.McNair	SS L.Lary	SS O.Bluege
3B B.Werber	3B J.Dykes	SS B.Knickerb'r	3B M.Owen	3B R.Rolfe	3B P.Higgins	3B H.Clift	3B C.Travis
LF R.Johnson	LF R.Radcliff	3B O.Hale	LF G.Goslin	LF J.Hill	LF B.Johnson	LF M.Solters	LF H.Manush
CF M.Almada	CF A.Simmons	LF J.Vosmik	CF J.White	CF B.Chapman	CF D.Cramer	CF S.West	CF J.Powell
RF D.Cooke	RF M.Haas	CF E.Averill	RF P.Fox	RF G.Selkirk	RF W.Moses	RF E.Coleman	RF J.Stone
C R.Ferrell	C L.Sewell	RF M.Galatzer	C M.Cochrane	C B.Dickey	C P.Richards	C R.Hemsley	C C.Bolton
32 D.Williams	O G.Washington	C E.Phillips	O G.Walker	O E.Combs	O1 L.Finney	O R.Pepper	S R.Kress
O C.Reynolds	23 T.Piet	O B.Campbell	C R.Hayworth	23 J.Saltzgaver	C C.Berry	O1 B.Bell	O F.Schulte
O B.Miller	3 M.Hopkins	2S R.Hughes	3 F.Clifton	O M.Hoag	S2 S.Newsome	3S J.Burnett	O D.Miles
21 M.Bishop	O J.Conlan	/O A.Wright	/O H.Walker	S B.Ryan	1 A.Hooks	2 O.Bejma	C S.Holbrook
C M.Berg	C M.Shea	C F.Pytlak	C C.Morgan	C A.Jorgens	/2 J.Peerson	S A.Strange	S L.Lary
O M.Solters	/O F.Tauby	C B.Brenzel	/C F.Reiber	/S N.Richardson	/C E.Coleman	C T.Heath	S A.Strange
/C G.Dickey	/2 G.Wright	C G.Myatt	/3 H.Schuble	/C J.Glenn	/C B.Patton	2 S.Melillo	3 B.Estalella
/O S.Graham	/3 M.Kreevich	/C K.Carson	/O H.Shelley	2 D.Heffner	/2 B.Williams	O S.Mazzera	C J.Redmond
/2 D.Farrell	/C F.Grube	/C G.Garbark	P S.Rowe	/O D.Walker	/1 J.Owens	/1 H.Mueller	/3 B.Lewis
/3 J.Kroner	R B.Hafey	/3 W.Kamm	P T.Bridges	P L.Gomez	/C B.Conroy	/1 R.Hornsby	C S.Starr
R L.Legett	P J.Whitehead	/C G.George	P A.Crowder	P R.Ruffing	/C C.Moss	/O D.Garms	/S J.Mihalic
P W.Ferrell	P V.Kennedy	P M.Harder	P E.Auker	P J.Broaca	P J.Marcum	/C H.Warnock	/O F.Sington
P L.Grove	P T.Lyons	P W.Hudlin	P J.Sullivan	P J.Allen	P B.Dietrich	/C F.Grube	/O R.Marion
P G.Rhodes	P S.Jones	P M.Pearson	RP C.Hogsett	P V.Tamulis	P G.Blaeholder	P I.Andrews	P E.Whitehill
P J.Welch	RP W.Wyatt	P O.Hildebrand	P V.Sorrell	RP J.Murphy	P W.Wilshere	P J.Knott	P B.Hadley
P R.Walberg	P R.Phelps	RP L.Brown	/P R.Lawson	RP J.DeShong	P R.Mahaffey	P J.Walkup	P B.Newsom
RP J.Wilson	P C.Fischer	RP R.Winegarner	/P C.Hatter	RP P.Malone	RP A.Benton	P R.Van Atta	P E.Linke
RP G.Hockette	P J.Salveson	RP C.Brown	/P F.Marberry	/P R.Van Atta	RP G.Caster	P S.Cain	RP J.Russell
P F.Ostermueller	/P M.Stratton	P L.Stewart	/P C.Fischer	P J.Brown	RP D.Lieber	P F.Thomas	RP L.Pettit
P H.Johnson	/P J.Vance	/P D.Galehouse			P C.Doyle	P D.Coffman	P B.Burke
P S.Bowers	/P G.Earnshaw	/P B.Bean			P G.Turbeville	/P B.Newsom	P H.Coppola
/P J.Cascarella	/P I.Chelini				/P J.Cascarella	/P E.Caldwell	P B.Bean
/P G.Pipgras	/P L.Stine				P S.Cain	P B.Weiland	/P J.Hayes
/P H.Vandenberg					/P W.Upchurch	P S.Hansen	/P D.Lanahan
/P W.Ripley					/P H.Fink	/P G.Blaeholder	/P P.Hensiek
					/P V.Eaves	P B.Poser	/P M.Weaver
					/P A.Veach		/P B.Rogers
					/P B.Ferrazzi		/P A.McLean
					/P E.Huckleberry		/P L.Stewart
					/P W.Martini		/P T.Thomas

TEAM	G	W	L	PCT	GB	R	OR	AB	H	2B	3B	HR	BB	SO	AVG	OBP	SLG	PRO	PRO+	BR	/A	PF	CHI	RC	SB	CS	SBA	SBR
DET	152	93	58	.616		919	665	5423	1573	301	83	106	627	456	.290	.366	.435	.801	116	95	126	97	104	885	70	45	61	-6
NY	149	89	60	.597	3	818	632	5214	1462	255	70	104	604	469	.280	.358	.416	.774	111	42	87	94	102	799	68	46	60	-7
CLE	156	82	71	.536	12	776	739	5534	1573	324	77	93	460	567	.284	.341	.421	.762	100	3	-11	102	99	796	63	54	54	-14
BOS	154	78	75	.510	16	718	732	5288	1458	281	63	69	609	470	.276	.353	.392	.745	92	-11	-62	107	94	757	91	59	61	-8
CHI	153	74	78	.487	19.5	738	750	5314	1460	262	42	74	580	405	.275	.348	.382	.730	92	-41	-59	103	101	733	46	28	62	-3
WAS	154	67	86	.438	27	823	903	5592	1591	255	95	32	596	406	.285	.357	.381	.738	99	-18	8	97	104	788	54	37	59	-6
STL	155	65	87	.428	28.5	718	930	5365	1446	291	51	73	593	561	.270	.344	.384	.728	90	-49	-83	105	98	735	45	25	64	-2
PHI	149	58	91	.389	34	710	869	5269	1470	243	44	112	475	602	.279	.341	.406	.747	99	-23	-17	99	98	738	43	35	55	-8
TOT	611					6220		42999	12033	2212	525	663	4544	3936	.280	.351	.402	.753							480	329	59	-53

TEAM	CG	SH	SV	IP	H	H/G	HR	BB	SO	RAT	ERA	ERA+	OAV	OOB	PR	/A	PF	CPI	FA	E	DP	FW	PW	BW	SBW	DIF
DET	87	16	11	1364	1440	9.5	78	522	584	13.1	3.82	109	.271	.339	96	53	94	107	.978	128	154	2.3	5.0	11.8	.0	-1.6
NY	76	12	13	1331	1276	8.6	91	516	594	12.2	3.60	112	.251	.321	126	66	91	101	.974	151	114	.8	6.2	8.1	-.0	-.6
CLE	67	12	21	1396	1527	9.8	68	457	498	12.9	4.15	108	.278	.335	47	55	101	97	.972	177	147	-.3	5.2	-1.0	-.7	2.3
BOS	82	6	11	1376	1520	9.9	67	520	470	13.5	4.05	117	.280	.346	62	106	107	105	.969	194	136	-1.4	9.9	-5.8	-.1	-1.1
CHI	80	8	8	1360²	1443	9.5	105	574	436	13.5	4.38	106	.272	.346	12	36	104	100	.976	146	133	1.3	3.4	-5.5	.3	-1.5
WAS	67	5	12	1378¹	1672	10.9	89	613	456	15.1	5.25	82	.302	.374	-122	-142	97	99	.972	171	186	-.0	-13.3	.7	.0	3.0
STL	42	4	15	1380¹	1667	10.9	92	641	435	15.2	5.26	91	.297	.371	-124	-72	108	97	.970	187	138	-.9	-6.7	-7.8	.4	4.0
PHI	58	7	10	1326¹	1486	10.1	73	704	469	15.0	5.12	89	.285	.372	-97	-84	102	96	.968	190	150	-1.4	-7.9	-1.6	-.1	-5.5
TOT	559	70	101	10913		9.9				13.8	4.46		.280	.351					.972	1344	1158					

Runs		Hits		Doubles		Triples		Home Runs		Total Bases	
Gehrig-NY	125	Vosmik-Cle	216	Vosmik-Cle	47	Vosmik-Cle	20	Greenberg-Det	36	Greenberg-Det	389
Gehringer-Det	123	Myer-Was	215	Greenberg-Det	46	Stone-Was	18	Foxx-Phi	36	Foxx-Phi	340
Greenberg-Det	121	Cramer-Phi	214	Solters-Bos-StL	45	Greenberg-Det	16	Gehrig-NY	30	Vosmik-Cle	333
Foxx-Phi	118	Greenberg-Det	203	Fox-Det	38	Cronin-Bos	14	Johnson-Phi	28	Solters-Bos-StL	314
Chapman-NY	118			Chapman-NY	38	Averill-Cle	13	Trosky-Cle	26	Gehrig-NY	312

Runs Batted In		Runs Produced		Bases On Balls		Batting Average		On Base Percentage		Slugging Average	
Greenberg-Det	170	Greenberg-Det	255	Gehrig-NY	132	Myer-Was	.349	Gehrig-NY	.466	Foxx-Phi	.636
Gehrig-NY	119	Gehrig-NY	214	Appling-Chi	122	Vosmik-Cle	.348	Foxx-Phi	.461	Greenberg-Det	.628
Foxx-Phi	115	Gehringer-Det	212	Foxx-Phi	114	Foxx-Phi	.346	Cochrane-Det	.452	Gehrig-NY	.583
Trosky-Cle	113	Myer-Was	210	Myer-Was	96	Cramer-Phi	.332	Myer-Was	.440	Vosmik-Cle	.537
Solters-Bos-StL	112	Foxx-Phi	197	Cochrane-Det	96	Gehringer-Det	.330	Appling-Chi	.437	Fox-Det	.513

Production		Adjusted Production		Batter Runs		Adjusted Batter Runs		Clutch Hitting Index		Runs Created	
Foxx-Phi	1.096	Foxx-Phi	182	Foxx-Phi	67.2	Gehrig-NY	70.1	Owen-Det	134	Foxx-Phi	163
Gehrig-NY	1.049	Gehrig-NY	180	Gehrig-NY	61.6	Foxx-Phi	68.4	Kuhel-Was	124	Greenberg-Det	161
Greenberg-Det	1.039	Greenberg-Det	171	Greenberg-Det	57.5	Greenberg-Det	62.7	Goslin-Det	124	Gehrig-NY	154
Vosmik-Cle	.946	Vosmik-Cle	140	Vosmik-Cle	38.3	Myer-Was	40.8	Powell-Was	124	Vosmik-Cle	137
Gehringer-Det	.911	Myer-Was	139	Myer-Was	36.5	Gehringer-Det	36.3	Myer-Was	122	Myer-Was	132

Total Average		Stolen Bases		Stolen Base Average		Stolen Base Runs		Fielding Runs		Total Player Rating	
Foxx-Phi	1.288	Werber-Bos	29	Lary-Was-StL	87.5	Lary-Was-StL	6.0	Appling-Chi	21.3	Foxx-Phi	5.7
Gehrig-NY	1.230	Lary-Was-StL	28	Werber-Bos	80.6	Werber-Bos	4.5	Travis-Was	21.3	Myer-Was	5.4
Greenberg-Det	1.138	Almada-Bos	20	Almada-Bos	69.0	Solters-Bos-StL	2.1	Solters-Bos-StL	18.6	Gehrig-NY	4.8
Cochrane-Det	1.000	White-Det	19	White-Det	65.5	Hughes-Cle	2.1	Melillo-StL-Bos	18.6	Greenberg-Det	4.7
Vosmik-Cle	.980	Chapman-NY	17	Chapman-NY	63.0			Werber-Bos	17.2	Gehringer-Det	4.7

Wins		Win Percentage		Games		Complete Games		Shutouts		Saves	
W.Ferrell-Bos	25	Auker-Det	.720	VanAtta-NY-StL	58	W.Ferrell-Bos	31	Rowe-Det	6	Knott-StL	7
Harder-Cle	22	Broaca-NY	.682	Walkup-StL	55	Grove-Bos	23	Harder-Cle	4		
Bridges-Det	21	Bridges-Det	.677	Andrews-StL	50	Bridges-Det	23	Bridges-Det	4		
Grove-Bos	20	Harder-Cle	.667	Thomas-StL	49	Rowe-Det	21				
Rowe-Det	19	Lyons-Chi	.652	Knott-StL	48						

Innings Pitched		Fewest Hits/Game		Fewest BB/Game		Strikeouts		Strikeouts/Game		Ratio	
W.Ferrell-Bos	322.1	Allen-NY	8.03	Harder-Cle	1.66	Bridges-Det	163	Allen-NY	6.09	Grove-Bos	11.11
Harder-Cle	287.1	Ruffing-NY	8.15	Grove-Bos	2.14	Rowe-Det	140	Bridges-Det	5.35	Rowe-Det	11.17
Whitehill-Was	279.1	Gomez-NY	8.16	Rowe-Det	2.22	Gomez-NY	138	Gomez-NY	5.05	Ruffing-NY	11.27
Rowe-Det	275.2	Whitehead-Chi	8.46	Andrews-StL	2.24	Grove-Bos	121	VanAtta-NY-StL	4.63	Allen-NY	11.37
Bridges-Det	274.1	Grove-Bos	8.87	Hudlin-Cle	2.37	Allen-NY	113	Rowe-Det	4.57	Gomez-NY	11.38

Earned Run Average		Adjusted ERA		Opponents' Batting Avg.		Opponents' On Base Pct.		Starter Runs		Adjusted Starter Runs	
Grove-Bos	2.70	Grove-Bos	176	Allen-NY	.238	Rowe-Det	.301	Grove-Bos	53.1	Grove-Bos	61.9
Lyons-Chi	3.02	Lyons-Chi	153	Ruffing-NY	.239	Grove-Bos	.302	Harder-Cle	37.2	W.Ferrell-Bos	43.9
Ruffing-NY	3.12	Harder-Cle	137	Gomez-NY	.242	Ruffing-NY	.303	Gomez-NY	34.8	Harder-Cle	38.8
Gomez-NY	3.18	Andrews-StL	135	Whitehead-Chi	.250	Allen-NY	.307	W.Ferrell-Bos	33.6	Lyons-Chi	33.9
Harder-Cle	3.29	W.Ferrell-Bos	135	Broaca-NY	.254	Harder-Cle	.307	Ruffing-NY	32.9	Andrews-StL	29.6

Clutch Pitching Index		Relief Runs		Adjusted Relief Runs		Relief Ranking		Total Pitcher Index		Total Baseball Ranking	
Lyons-Chi	124	L.Brown-Cle	11.4	L.Brown-Cle	12.1	L.Brown-Cle	14.2	W.Ferrell-Bos	7.2	W.Ferrell-Bos	7.2
Bridges-Det	113	Hogsett-Det	9.9	Hogsett-Det	6.8	Hogsett-Det	8.4	Grove-Bos	6.4	Grove-Bos	6.4
Auker-Det	112	DeShong-NY	9.2	DeShong-NY	6.0	DeShong-NY	4.5	Harder-Cle	4.4	Foxx-Phi	5.7
Grove-Bos	112	Murphy-NY	4.9	Wilson-Bos	3.7	Wilson-Bos	3.8	Lyons-Chi	3.6	Myer-Was	5.4
Tietje-Chi	110	Wilson-Bos	1.7					Ruffing-NY	3.5	Gehrig-NY	4.8

January 15 IRS figures for 1934 show Branch Rickey as the highest paid man in baseball at $49,470. Commissioner Landis had voluntarily taken a cut in 1933 from $65,000 to $40,000 because of the Depression.

January 30 The new owners of the Boston Braves ask newspapermen to pick a new nickname for the team from suggestions made by fans. They choose the Bees, but the name will not catch on. It will be scrapped after the 1940 season.

April 14 In a 12-7 loss to the Cubs, Cardinals rookie Eddie Morgan becomes the first player to pinch hit a home run in his first major league at bat. It is the only one he'll hit in a 39-game career.

July 7 The NL, having lost the first three All-Star Games, finally wins, 4-3, at Fenway Park. After Dizzy Dean and Carl Hubbell each pitch scoreless three-inning stints, Curt Davis is hammered by the AL, including Lou Gehrig's home run, but Lon Warneke shuts the door. Meanwhile, the NL is helped by Joe DiMaggio's error and Augie Galan's home run. The NL plays its starting lineup except for two late-inning pinch hitters.

July 10 Philadelphia's Chuck Klein hits four home runs in five at bats in a 10-inning game at Forbes Field. His final home run beats the Pirates, 9-6.

July 15 Cincinnati plays the first Ladies Night game, beating Brooklyn, 5-3.

July 21 Cardinals slugger Joe Medwick has 10 hits in succession to equal the NL record. He had seven hits in his last seven times at bat in a doubleheader on July 19, and he hit safely in his first three today before being stopped by the Giants' Carl Hubbell.

August 12 The largest crowd ever to watch a baseball game, estimated at between 90,000 and 125,000, sees a "demonstration game" as an event of the Olympics in Berlin. The world amateurs beat the U.S. amateurs, 6-5.

September 14 Pittsburgh's Paul Waner ties Rogers Hornsby's modern NL record, reaching 200 hits for the seventh time.

September 23 Carl Hubbell notches his 16th consecutive victory, his 26th of the year, beating the Phils, 5-4. He resumes the streak next year to reach a record 24 wins in a row.

September 24 The Giants clinch the pennant, winning, 2-1, in the 10th of the opening game of a doubleheader with the Boston Bees. Pitcher Hal Schumacher singles in the winning run.

September 25 Joe Medwick sets a still-standing NL record with his 64th double.

September 27 When Johnny Mize is thrown out in the seventh inning for arguing, Cardinals rookie first baseman Walt Alston subs. In his only major league game, the future Hall of Fame manager makes one error in two chances and is fanned by Lon Warneke in his only at bat.

September 30 In the World Series opener, Carl Hubbell scatters seven hits in a 6-1 win and limits the Yankees to just a solo home run by George Selkirk.

October 20 Carl Hubbell, 26-6, edges out Dizzy Dean, 24-13, for MVP honors in the NL.

BOSTON		BROOKLYN		CHICAGO		CINCINNATI		NEW YORK		PHILADELPHIA		PITTSBURGH		ST.LOUIS	
M	B.McKechnie	M	C.Stengel	M	C.Grimm	M	C.Dressen	M	B.Terry	M	J.Wilson	M	P.Traynor	M	F.Frisch
1B	B.Jordan	1B	B.Hassett	1B	P.Cavarretta	1B	L.Scarsella	1B	S.Leslie	1B	D.Camilli	1B	G.Suhr	1B	J.Mize
2B	T.Cuccinello	2B	J.Jordan	2B	B.Herman	2B	A.Kampouris	2B	B.Whitehead	2B	C.Gomez	2B	P.Young	2B	S.Martin
SS	B.Urbanski	SS	L.Frey	SS	B.Jurges	SS	B.Myers	SS	D.Bartell	SS	L.Norris	SS	A.Vaughan	SS	L.Durocher
3B	J.Coscarart	3B	J.Stripp	3B	S.Hack	3B	L.Riggs	3B	T.Jackson	3B	P.Whitney	3B	B.Brubaker	3B	C.Gelbert
LF	H.Lee	LF	G.Watkins	LF	E.Allen	LF	B.Herman	LF	J.Moore	LF	J.Moore	LF	W.Jensen	LF	J.Medwick
CF	W.Berger	CF	J.Cooney	CF	A.Galan	CF	K.Cuyler	CF	H.Leiber	CF	E.Sulik	CF	L.Waner	CF	T.Moore
RF	G.Moore	RF	F.Bordagaray	RF	F.Demaree	RF	I.Goodman	RF	M.Ott	RF	C.Klein	RF	P.Waner	RF	P.Martin
C	A.Lopez	C	R.Berres	C	G.Hartnett	C	E.Lombardi	C	G.Mancuso	C	E.Grace	C	T.Padden	C	S.Davis
O1	T.Thompson	32	J.Bucher	C	K.O'Dea	O2	C.Chapman	O	J.Ripple	O2	L.Chiozza	1	A.Todd	1	R.Collins
S	R.Warstler	C	B.Phelps	S3	W.English	S2	T.Thevenow	1	B.Terry	C	J.Wilson	O	F.Schulte	C	B.Ogrodowski
3	M.Haslin	O	E.Wilson	O	J.Gill	O	H.Walker	3	E.Mayo	C	B.Atwood	23	C.Lavagetto	23	F.Frisch
C	R.Mueller	S	B.Geraghty	1	C.Grimm	C	G.Campbell	C	H.Danning	O	E.Allen	O	B.Hafey	32	A.Garibaldi
C	B.Lewis	O	D.Taylor	O	C.Klein	O	S.Byrd	O	K.Davis	23	C.Sheerin	O	H.Finney	O	L.King
3	P.Whitney	O	F.Lindstrom	O	T.Stainback	1	G.McQuinn	S	M.Koenig	O	G.Watkins	/O	E.Browne	3	D.Gutteridge
H	E.Moriarty	/S	R.Moore	/S	G.Lillard	2	L.Handley	C	R.Spencer	2	M.Haslin	/O	J.Dickshot	C	C.Fullis
H	A.Pilney	C	T.Winsett	/C	W.Stephenson	/1	E.Joost	/1	J.McCarthy	O	M.Arnovich	P	B.Swift	/O	E.Morgan
/2	S.Larsen	C	S.Gautreaux	P	B.Lee	/S	E.Miller	3	J.Martin	3	J.Vergez	P	B.Blanton	/3	J.Vergez
P	D.MacFayden	O	O.Eckhardt	P	L.French	P	P.Derringer	/C	J.Sheehan	2	S.Sperry	P	J.Weaver	/O	L.Scoffic
P	T.Chaplin	/O	N.Tremark	P	L.Warneke	P	A.Hollingsworth	/2	C.English	/1	G.Corbett	P	R.Lucas	/S	P.Ankenman
P	J.Lanning	2	J.Radtke	P	T.Carleton	P	G.Schott	H	B.Young	/O	W.Bashore	P	M.Brown	/1	W.Alston
P	B.Reis	/S	J.Hudson	P	C.Davis	P	B.Hallahan	P	C.Hubbell	H	J.Holden	P	W.Hoyt	/3	H.Schuble
P	B.Smith	/O	D.Siebert	RP	C.Root	P	B.Frey	P	H.Schumacher	P	B.Walters	P	R.Birkofer	P	D.Dean
P	B.Cantwell	P	V.Mungo	RP	C.Bryant	RP	D.Brennan	P	A.Smith	P	C.Passeau	P	J.Tising	P	R.Parmelee
P	R.Benge	P	F.Frankhouse			P	P.Davis	P	F.Gabler	P	B.Bowman	P	G.Bush	P	J.Winford
P	G.Bush	P	E.Brandt			P	L.Stine	P	H.Gumbert	P	O.Jorgens	/P	J.Welch	P	J.Haines
P	R.Weir	P	M.Butcher			P	W.Hilcher	RP	D.Coffman	P	S.Johnson	/P	R.Bauers	RP	E.Heusser
/P	W.Osborne	/P	W.Clark			/P	L.Grissom	P	F.Fitzsimmons	RP	E.Moore			RP	G.Earnshaw
P	A.Blanche	RP	G.Jeffcoat			/P	E.Nelson	P	S.Castleman	P	F.Kowalik			P	P.Dean
/P	A.Murray	RP	T.Baker			/P	J.Mooty	/P	F.Marberry	P	P.Sivess			P	B.Walker
/P	F.Kowalik	P	G.Earnshaw			/P	T.Freitas			P	C.Davis			P	S.Johnson
/P	B.Brown	P	D.Leonard			/P	D.Moore			P	R.Benge			P	M.Ryba
/P	A.Doll	P	H.Winston			/P	W.Moore			P	H.Kelleher			/P	B.Hallahan
/P	J.McCloskey	/P	H.Eisenstat			/P	S.Johnson			P	H.Mulcahy			/P	F.Rhem
/P	J.Babich	/P	T.Zachary							/P	T.Zachary			/P	L.Munns
/P	K.Weafer									/P	E.Burkart			/P	C.Pippen
/P	G.Ford									/P	H.Harris			/P	B.McGee
										/P	L.Bertrand			/P	B.Cox
										/P	P.Pezzullo			/P	N.Potter

TEAM	G	W	L	PCT	GB	R	OR	AB	H	2B	3B	HR	BB	SO	AVG	OBP	SLG	PRO	PRO+	BR	/A	PF	CHI	RC	SB	CS	SBA	SBR
NY	154	92	62	.597		742	621	5449	1529	237	48	97	431	452	.281	.337	.395	.732	104	19	27	99	99	744	31			
STL	155	87	67	.565	5	795	794	5537	1554	332	60	88	442	577	.281	.336	.410	.746	106	40	43	100	103	772	69			
CHI	154	87	67	.565	5	755	603	5409	1545	275	36	76	491	462	.286	.349	.392	.741	104	44	27	102	97	757	68			
PIT	156	84	70	.545	8	804	718	5586	1596	283	80	60	517	502	.286	.349	.397	.746	105	56	38	102	100	798	37			
CIN	154	74	80	.481	18	722	760	5393	1476	224	73	82	410	584	.274	.329	.388	.717	106	-14	30	94	104	699	68			
BOS	157	71	83	.461	21	631	715	5478	1450	207	45	67	433	582	.265	.322	.356	.678	94	-86	-45	94	98	635	23			
BRO	156	67	87	.435	25	662	752	5574	1518	263	43	33	390	458	.272	.323	.353	.676	87	-92	-98	101	104	649	55			
PHI	154	54	100	.351	38	726	874	5465	1538	250	46	103	451	586	.281	.339	.401	.740	95	32	-44	110	96	757	50			
TOT	620					5837		43891	12206	2071	431	606	3565	4203	.278	.335	.386	.722							401			

TEAM	CG	SH	SV	IP	H	H/G	HR	BB	SO	RAT	ERA	ERA+	OAV	OOB	PR	/A	PF	CPI	FA	E	DP	FW	PW	BW	SBW	DIF
NY	60	12	22	1385²	1458	9.5	75	401	500	12.2	3.46	113	.273	.327	86	67	97	110	.974	168	164	1.1	6.5	2.6		4.7
STL	65	5	24	1398	1610	10.4	89	434	559	13.4	4.47	88	.289	.344	-71	-84	98	98	.974	156	134	1.9	-8.2	4.2		12.1
CHI	77	18	10	1382¹	1413	9.2	77	434	597	12.2	3.54	113	.265	.324	74	68	99	104	.976	146	156	2.4	6.6	2.6		-1.6
PIT	67	5	12	1395¹	1475	9.5	74	379	559	12.1	3.89	104	.269	.319	20	25	101	92	.967	199	113	-.5	2.4	3.7		1.4
CIN	50	6	23	1367¹	1576	10.4	51	418	459	13.3	4.22	91	.287	.341	-31	-61	95	97	.969	191	150	-.2	-6.0	2.9		.2
BOS	61	7	13	1413¹	1566	10.0	69	451	421	13.0	3.94	97	.281	.337	12	-18	95	103	.971	189	175	.1	-1.8	-4.4		.0
BRO	59	7	18	1403	1466	9.4	84	528	651	13.0	3.98	104	.266	.333	5	22	103	97	.966	208	107	-1.0	2.1	-9.6		-1.6
PHI	51	7	14	1365¹	1630	10.7	87	515	454	14.4	4.64	98	.292	.356	-95	-17	113	100	.959	252	144	-3.7	-1.7	-4.3		-13.4
TOT	490	67	136	11110¹		9.9				12.9	4.02		.278	.335					.969	1509	1143					

Runs
Vaughan-Pit 122
P.Martin-StL 121
Ott-NY 120
Medwick-StL 115
Suhr-Pit 111

Hits
Medwick-StL 223
P.Waner-Pit 218
Demaree-Chi 212
Herman-Chi 211
Moore-NY 205

Doubles
Medwick-StL 64
Herman-Chi 57
P.Waner-Pit 53
Moore-StL 39
Moore-Bos 38

Triples
Goodman-Cin 14
Medwick-StL 13
Camilli-Phi 13

Home Runs
Ott-NY 33
Camilli-Phi 28
Klein-Chi-Phi 25
Berger-Bos 25
Mize-StL 19

Total Bases
Medwick-StL 367
Ott-NY 314
Klein-Chi-Phi 308
Camilli-Phi 306
P.Waner-Pit 304

Runs Batted In
Medwick-StL 138
Ott-NY 135
Suhr-Pit 118
Klein-Chi-Phi 104

Runs Produced
Medwick-StL 235
Ott-NY 222
Suhr-Pit 218
P.Waner-Pit 196
Vaughan-Pit 191

Bases On Balls
Vaughan-Pit 118
Camilli-Phi 116
Ott-NY 111
Suhr-Pit 95
Hack-Chi 89

Batting Average
P.Waner-Pit 373
Phelps-Bro 367
Medwick-StL 351
Demaree-Chi 350
Vaughan-Pit 335

On Base Percentage
Vaughan-Pit 453
Ott-NY 448
P.Waner-Pit 446
Camilli-Phi 441
Suhr-Pit 410

Slugging Average
Ott-NY 588
Camilli-Phi 577
Mize-StL 577
Medwick-StL 577
P.Waner-Pit 520

Production
Ott-NY 1.036
Camilli-Phi 1.018
P.Waner-Pit 965
Medwick-StL 964
Vaughan-Pit 927

Adjusted Production
Ott-NY 179
Medwick-StL 157
Camilli-Phi 156
P.Waner-Pit 156
Vaughan-Pit 146

Batter Runs
Ott-NY 61.9
Camilli-Phi 58.0
P.Waner-Pit 51.4
Vaughan-Pit 47.3
Medwick-StL 46.9

Adjusted Batter Runs
Ott-NY 63.5
P.Waner-Pit 48.4
Medwick-StL 47.4
Camilli-Phi 44.9
Vaughan-Pit 44.3

Clutch Hitting Index
Brubaker-Pit 147
Young-Pit 131
Suhr-Pit 124
Herman-Chi 115
Whitney-Bos-Phi . . . 114

Runs Created
Ott-NY 153
Camilli-Phi 148
Medwick-StL 141
P.Waner-Pit 140
Vaughan-Pit 137

Total Average
Ott-NY 1.188
Camilli-Phi 1.162
Vaughan-Pit 1.034
P.Waner-Pit 1.016
Medwick-StL 956

Stolen Bases
P.Martin-StL 23
S.Martin-StL 17
Hack-Chi 17
Chiozza-Phi 17

Stolen Base Average

Stolen Base Runs

Fielding Runs
Bartell-NY 44.8
Whitehead-NY 29.2
Kampouris-Cin 28.0
Berres-Bro 23.0

Total Player Rating
Bartell-NY 5.7
Medwick-StL 5.3
Ott-NY 5.2
Herman-Chi 5.0
P.Waner-Pit 4.9

Wins
Hubbell-NY 26
D.Dean-StL 24
Derringer-Cin 19

Win Percentage
Hubbell-NY 813
Lucas-Pit 789
French-Chi 667
D.Dean-StL 649
Lee-Chi 621

Games
Derringer-Cin 51
D.Dean-StL 51
Passeau-Phi 49
Brown-Pit 47

Complete Games
D.Dean-StL 28
Hubbell-NY 25
Mungo-Bro 22
MacFayden-Bos 21
Lee-Chi 20

Shutouts
Warneke-Chi 4
Walters-Phi 4
Smith-NY 4
Lee-Chi 4
French-Chi 4
Carleton-Chi 4
Blanton-Pit 4

Saves
D.Dean-StL 11
Brennan-Cin 9
Smith-Bos 8
Johnson-Phi 7
Coffman-NY 7

Innings Pitched
D.Dean-StL 315.0
Mungo-Bro 311.2
Hubbell-NY 304.0
Derringer-Cin 282.1
MacFayden-Bos . . 266.2

Fewest Hits/Game
Hubbell-NY 7.85
Mungo-Bro 7.94
Lee-Chi 8.28
D.Dean-StL 8.86
Blanton-Pit 8.97

Fewest BB/Game
Lucas-Pit 1.33
Derringer-Cin 1.34
D.Dean-StL 1.51
Hubbell-NY 1.69
Gabler-NY 1.89

Strikeouts
Mungo-Bro 238
D.Dean-StL 195
Blanton-Pit 127
Hubbell-NY 123
Derringer-Cin 121

Strikeouts/Game
Mungo-Bro 6.87
D.Dean-StL 5.57
Blanton-Pit 4.85
Weaver-Pit 4.31
Warneke-Chi 4.23

Ratio
Hubbell-NY 9.68
D.Dean-StL 10.46
Lucas-Pit 10.61
Blanton-Pit 11.19
Davis-Phi-Chi 11.35

Earned Run Average
Hubbell-NY 2.31
MacFayden-Bos . . 2.87
Gabler-NY 3.12
D.Dean-StL 3.17
Lucas-Pit 3.18

Adjusted ERA
Hubbell-NY 169
MacFayden-Bos . . 134
Passeau-Phi 130
Lucas-Pit 128
Gabler-NY 125

Opponents' Batting Avg.
Mungo-Bro 234
Hubbell-NY 236
Lee-Chi 246
D.Dean-StL 253
Blanton-Pit 257

Opponents' On Base Pct.
Hubbell-NY 276
D.Dean-StL 285
Lucas-Pit 287
Blanton-Pit 301
Mungo-Bro 305

Starter Runs
Hubbell-NY 57.7
MacFayden-Bos . . 34.0
D.Dean-StL 29.6
Mungo-Bro 23.1
Lee-Chi 20.4

Adjusted Starter Runs
Hubbell-NY 53.5
MacFayden-Bos . . 28.5
Mungo-Bro 27.0
D.Dean-StL 26.9
Passeau-Phi 25.4

Clutch Pitching Index
Schumacher-NY . . 120
Gabler-NY 119
Chaplin-Bos 111
Smith-NY 110
Carleton-Chi 109

Relief Runs
Bryant-Chi 4.6
Coffman-NY 1.4

Adjusted Relief Runs
Bryant-Chi 4.4
Johnson-Phi 2.9

Relief Ranking
Johnson-Phi 3.2
Bryant-Chi 2.1

Total Pitcher Index
Hubbell-NY 5.5
Passeau-Phi 3.3
D.Dean-StL 2.8
Mungo-Bro 2.8
MacFayden-Bos . . 2.7

Total Baseball Ranking
Bartell-NY 5.7
Hubbell-NY 5.5
Medwick-StL 5.3
Ott-NY 5.2
Herman-Chi 5.0

February 2 The baseball writers vote for the first players to be named to the new Baseball Hall of Fame. Ty Cobb, Babe Ruth, Honus Wagner, Christy Mathewson, and Walter Johnson each receive the requisite 75 percent of ballots cast. Active players also are eligible in this first election, with Rogers Hornsby finishing ninth, Mickey Cochrane 10th, Lou Gehrig 15th, and Jimmie Foxx 19th. Tainted former star Hal Chase receives 11 votes for 25th place, and "Shoeless" Joe Jackson gets two votes to tie for 36th place.

April 29* Nagoya defeats Daitokyo, 8-5, in the first professional baseball game played in Japan.

May 3 Joe DiMaggio makes his regular-season debut with the Yankees and has three hits, one a triple, as New York routs St. Louis, 14-5.

May 24 Yankees second baseman Tony Lazzeri sets several slugging marks with two grand slams, a third home run, and a triple for 15 total bases in a 25-2 slaughter of the Athletics at Shibe Park. He has hit seven home runs in four games and six in three games. He also sets a new AL mark of 11 RBIs in one game.

June 19 Joe McCarthy is named to manage the AL All-Stars, rather than the high-strung Mickey Cochrane, who is very close to a nervous breakdown.

June 24 Joe DiMaggio ties three major league records in New York's 10-run fifth inning against the White Sox, hitting two home runs for eight total bases. With two doubles, he equals the modern record of four long hits in a game. New York wins, 18-11.

July 19 Bob Feller makes his major league debut in relief. He pitches the eighth inning at Washington, giving up no hits and fanning one.

August 21 Wes Ferrell, in a tantrum for what he considers shabby support, walks off the mound during a Yankees rally and is suspended and fined $1,000 by Boston manager Joe Cronin. It is the second time in five days he has walked off the mound, having done it in Boston last Sunday in a game against the Senators. Ferrell, furious when he hears about the fine, says he will not pay it. "They can suspend me or trade me, but they're not getting any dough from me." The Red Sox lift the suspension in four days and will trade Ferrell after the season.

August 23 Seventeen-year-old Bob Feller makes his first start and strikes out 15, one less than the AL record, as Cleveland beats St. Louis, 4-1. He'll break the AL mark and ties the major league standard on Sept. 13 with 17 strikeouts.

October 2 The Yankees score a still-standing World Series record 18 runs, as they demolish the Giants, 18-4.

October 6 The Yankees roll to a 13-5 Series-ending victory. Lefty Gomez is the winning pitcher. In the six games the Yankees score 43 runs to the Giants' 23.

October 16 Lou Gehrig, who hit 49 home runs, scored 167 runs, knocked in 152, and batted .354, is voted AL MVP by the BBWAA.

December 9 The AL approves night baseball for St. Louis. The NL adopts a new design for home plate. It will have beveled edges, the first change in 50 years. The AL adopts a rule stating that no batter can be batting champion unless he has 400 or more at bats.

BOSTON	CHICAGO	CLEVELAND	DETROIT	NEW YORK	PHILADELPHIA	ST.LOUIS	WASHINGTON
M J.Cronin	M J.Dykes	M S.O'Neill	M M.Cochrane	M J.McCarthy	M C.Mack	M R.Hornsby	M B.Harris
1B J.Foxx	1B Z.Bonura	1B H.Trosky	M D.Baker	1B L.Gehrig	1B L.Finney	1B J.Bottomley	1B J.Kuhel
2B S.Melillo	2B J.Hayes	2B R.Hughes	M M.Cochrane	2B T.Lazzeri	2B R.Warstler	2B T.Carey	2B O.Bluege
SS E.McNair	SS L.Appling	SS B.Knickerb'r	1B J.Burns	SS F.Crosetti	SS S.Newsome	SS L.Lary	SS C.Travis
3B B.Werber	3B J.Dykes	3B O.Hale	2B C.Gehringer	3B R.Rolfe	3B P.Higgins	3B H.Clift	3B B.Lewis
LF H.Manush	LF R.Radcliff	LF J.Vosmik	SS B.Rogell	LF J.DiMaggio	LF B.Johnson	LF M.Solters	LF J.Stone
CF D.Cramer	CF M.Kreevich	RF R.Weatherly	3B M.Owen	CF J.Powell	CF W.Moses	CF S.West	CF B.Chapman
RF D.Cooke	RF M.Haas	C B.Sullivan	LF G.Goslin	RF G.Selkirk	RF G.Puccinelli	RF B.Bell	RF C.Reynolds
C R.Ferrell	C L.Sewell	C F.Pytlak	CF A.Simmons	C B.Dickey	C F.Hayes	C R.Hemsley	C C.Bolton
O M.Almada	23 T.Piet	O B.Campbell	RF G.Walker	O M.Hoag	1 C.Dean	C T.Giuliani	S2 R.Kress
23 J.Kroner	O L.Rosenthal	O J.Gleeson	C R.Hayworth	O R.Johnson	2 A.Niemiec	2 O.Bejma	O J.Hill
S3 J.Cronin	C F.Grube	O M.Galatzer	O P.Fox	O B.Chapman	S3 R.Peters	O E.Coleman	O W.Millies
C M.Berg	O D.Walker	C G.George	C M.Cochrane	O J.Glenn	C C.Moss	O R.Pepper	O J.Powell
1 B.Dahlgren	O G.Washington	C B.Berger	C G.Myatt	3 J.Saltzgaver	/2 D.Culler	/2 J.Burns	2 B.Myer
O F.Gaffke	/3 J.Morrissey	C J.Becker	C F.Reiber	O A.Jorgens	/1 H.Luby	/1 R.Hornsby	O F.Sington
O B.Miller	C M.Shea	O J.Heath	O J.White	/3 D.Heffner	/S J.Peerson	P C.Hogsett	2 J.Mihalic
C G.Dickey	O G.Stumpf	P J.Allen	1 H.Greenberg	/O B.Seeds	/O E.Mailho	P J.Knott	C S.Hogan
P W.Ferrell	/1 L.Rock	P M.Harder	C B.Tebbetts	/O D.Walker	C C.Berry	P I.Andrews	O D.Miles
P L.Grove	P V.Kennedy	P O.Hildebrand	/S F.Clifton	P R.Ruffing	/O B.Nicholson	P E.Caldwell	H B.Estalella
P F.Ostermueller	P J.Whitehead	P D.Galehouse	/S S.Parker	P M.Pearson	/1 J.Oglesby	P T.Thomas	/C A.Sabo
P J.Marcum	P S.Cain	P L.Brown	/3 G.English	P J.Broaca	/C B.Conroy	RP R.Van Atta	/C C.Starr
P J.Wilson	P T.Lyons	RP W.Hudlin	P T.Bridges	P L.Gomez	P H.Kelley	RP R.Mahaffey	P B.Newsom
P R.Walberg	RP M.Stratton	P G.Blaeholder	P S.Rowe	P B.Hadley	P G.Rhodes	RP G.Liebhardt	P J.DeShong
RP J.Henry	P C.Brown	RP B.Feller	P E.Auker	P P.Malone	P B.Ross	P L.Tietje	P E.Whitehill
P J.Russell	RP R.Evans	/P A.Milnar	P V.Sorrell	P J.Murphy	P H.Fink	/P S.Jakucki	P P.Appleton
/P J.Welch	P I.Chelini	/P R.Winegarner	P R.Lawson	P J.Brown	RP R.Gumpert	/P H.Kimberlin	P J.Cascarella
/M J.Cascarella	P B.Dietrich	/P B.Zuber	RP C.Kimsey	P T.Kleinhans	P H.Lisenbee	/P M.Meola	RP J.Russell
/M M.Meola	P R.Phelps	/P G.Uhle	/P R.Phillips	/P K.Wicker	P B.Dietrich	/P S.Cain	P M.Weaver
/P T.Olson	P B.Shores	/P P.Kardow	P J.Sullivan	/P S.Sundra	P G.Turbeville	/P J.Walkup	P E.Linke
/P J.Poindexter	/P W.Wyatt		/P J.Wade		/P C.Doyle		P S.Cohen
/P S.Bowers	/P L.Tietje		/P A.Crowder		/P S.Flythe		/P H.Coppola
/P E.Dickman			/P C.Hogsett		/P F.Archer		/P F.Marberry
					/P W.Upchurch		/P J.Bokina
					/P P.Naktenis		/P B.Dietrich
					/P E.Smith		/P B.Phebus
					/P W.Wilshere		/P K.Chase
					/P R.Bullock		
					/P H.Matuzak		
					/P H.Johnson		
					/P D.Lieber		

TEAM	G	W	L	PCT	GB	R	OR	AB	H	2B	3B	HR	BB	SO	AVG	OBP	SLG	PRO	PRO+	BR	/A	PF	CHI	RC	SB	CS	SBA	SBR
NY	155	102	51	.667		1065	731	5591	1676	315	83	182	700	594	.300	.381	.483	.864	124	162	200	97	100	1056	77	40	66	-1
DET	154	83	71	.539	19.5	921	871	5464	1638	326	55	94	640	462	.300	.377	.431	.808	106	57	54	100	98	912	73	49	60	-8
CHI	153	81	70	.536	20	920	873	5466	1597	282	56	60	684	417	.292	.374	.397	.771	94	-9	-41	104	104	851	66	29	69	2
WAS	153	82	71	.536	20	889	799	5433	1601	293	84	62	576	398	.295	.365	.414	.779	105	-7	41	94	104	847	104	42	71	6
CLE	157	80	74	.519	22.5	921	862	5646	1715	357	82	123	514	470	.304	.364	.461	.825	109	70	62	101	96	948	66	53	55	-12
BOS	155	74	80	.481	28.5	775	764	5383	1485	288	62	86	584	465	.276	.349	.400	.749	86	-72	-117	106	98	773	55	44	56	-10
STL	155	57	95	.375	44.5	804	1064	5391	1502	299	66	79	625	627	.279	.356	.403	.759	91	-51	-74	103	99	804	62	20	76	7
PHI	154	53	100	.346	49	714	1045	5373	1443	240	60	72	524	590	.269	.336	.376	.712	84	-151	-137	98	102	694	59	43	58	-8
TOT	618					7009		43747	12657	2400	548	758	4847	4023	.289	.363	.421	.784							562	320	64	-23

TEAM	CG	SH	SV	IP	H	H/G	HR	BB	SO	RAT	ERA	ERA+	OAV	OOB	PR	/A	PF	CPI	FA	E	DP	FW	PW	BW	SBW	DIF
NY	77	6	21	1400¹	1474	9.5	84	663	624	13.8	4.17	112	.271	.351	135	75	92	108	.973	163	148	.8	6.6	17.7	.2	.3
DET	76	13	13	1360	1568	10.4	100	562	526	14.2	5.00	99	.289	.358	6	-7	98	100	.975	153	159	1.3	-.6	4.8	-.4	1.0
CHI	80	5	8	1365	1603	10.6	104	578	414	14.5	5.06	103	.293	.363	-4	21	103	102	.973	168	174	.4	1.9	-3.6	.4	6.5
WAS	78	8	14	1345²	1484	9.9	73	588	462	14.0	4.58	104	.279	.353	68	29	95	101	.970	182	163	-.4	2.6	3.6	.8	-1.1
CLE	74	6	12	1389¹	1604	10.4	73	607	619	14.5	4.83	104	.289	.362	32	32	100	102	.971	178	154	.0	2.8	5.5	-.8	-4.6
BOS	78	11	9	1372¹	1501	9.8	78	552	584	13.6	4.39	121	.277	.346	99	142	106	102	.972	165	139	.7	12.5	-10.3	-.6	-5.2
STL	54	3	13	1348¹	1776	11.9	115	609	399	16.2	6.24	86	.314	.385	-180	-130	107	95	.969	188	143	-.6	-11.5	-6.5	.9	-1.2
PHI	68	3	12	1352¹	1645	10.9	131	696	405	15.7	6.08	84	.300	.381	-156	-146	101	94	.965	209	152	-1.9	-12.9	-12.1	-.4	3.8
TOT	585	55	102	10933¹		10.4				14.6	5.04		.289	.363					.971	1406	1232					

Runs
Gehrig-NY 167
Clift-StL 145
Gehringer-Det 144
Crosetti-NY 137
Averill-Cle 136

Hits
Averill-Cle 232
Gehringer-Det 227
Trosky-Cle 216
Bell-StL 212
Radcliff-Chi 207

Doubles
Gehringer-Det 60
Walker-Det 55
Chapman-NY-Was ... 50
Hale-Cle 50

Triples
Rolfe-NY 15
DiMaggio-NY 15
Averill-Cle 15
B.Johnson-Phi 14

Home Runs
Gehrig-NY 49
Trosky-Cle 42
Foxx-Bos 41
DiMaggio-NY 29
Averill-Cle 28

Total Bases
Trosky-Cle 405
Gehrig-NY 403
Averill-Cle 385
Foxx-Bos 369
DiMaggio-NY 367

Runs Batted In
Trosky-Cle 162
Gehrig-NY 152
Foxx-Bos 143
Bonura-Chi 138
Solters-StL 134

Runs Produced
Gehrig-NY 270
Bonura-Chi 246
Gehringer-Det 245
Trosky-Cle 244
Averill-Cle 234

Bases On Balls
Gehrig-NY 130
Lary-StL 117
Clift-StL 115
Foxx-Bos 105
Lazzeri-NY 97

Batting Average
Appling-Chi ...... .388
Averill-Cle ...... .378
Dickey-NY .... .362
Gehringer-Det .... .354
Gehrig-NY .... .354

On Base Percentage
Gehrig-NY .... .478
Appling-Chi ...... .474
Foxx-Bos .... .440
Averill-Cle ...... .438
Gehringer-Det .... .431

Slugging Average
Gehrig-NY .... .696
Trosky-Cle .... .644
Foxx-Bos .... .631
Averill-Cle ...... .627
Dickey-NY .... .617

Production
Gehrig-NY 1.174
Foxx-Bos 1.071
Averill-Cle 1.065
Trosky-Cle 1.026
Gehringer-Det .... .987

Adjusted Production
Gehrig-NY 193
Averill-Cle 159
Foxx-Bos 153
Trosky-Cle 148
Stone-Was 145

Batter Runs
Gehrig-NY 82.2
Foxx-Bos 56.8
Averill-Cle 56.4
Gehringer-Det 43.0
Trosky-Cle 41.9

Adjusted Batter Runs
Gehrig-NY 88.8
Averill-Cle 55.2
Foxx-Bos 48.2
Gehringer-Det 42.6
Trosky-Cle 40.8

Clutch Hitting Index
Appling-Chi 132
Sewell-Chi 131
Bonura-Chi 127
Owen-Det 126
Vosmik-Cle 125

Runs Created
Gehrig-NY 199
Averill-Cle 168
Foxx-Bos 168
Gehringer-Det 157
Trosky-Cle 150

Total Average
Gehrig-NY 1.426
Foxx-Bos 1.238
Averill-Cle 1.171
Appling-Chi 1.088
Gehringer-Det ... 1.075

Stolen Bases
Lary-StL 37
Powell-Was-NY 26
Werber-Bos 23
Chapman-NY-Was ... 20
Hughes-Cle 20

Stolen Base Average
Lary-StL 80.4
Crosetti-NY 72.0
Powell-Was-NY 70.3
Chapman-NY-Was ... 69.0
Hughes-Cle 69.0

Stolen Base Runs
Lary-StL 5.7
Hill-Was 3.3
Stone-Was 2.4
Sewell-Chi 2.1

Fielding Runs
Hayes-Chi 17.1
Hale-Cle 16.5
Cramer-Bos 16.3
Gehringer-Det 15.7
Appling-Chi 15.2

Total Player Rating
Gehrig-NY 6.4
Gehringer-Det 6.1
Appling-Chi 5.1
Averill-Cle 3.9
Dickey-NY 3.8

Wins
Bridges-Det 23
Kennedy-Chi 21
Ruffing-NY 20
W.Ferrell-Bos 20
Allen-Cle 20

Win Percentage
Pearson-NY .... .731
Kennedy-Chi ...... .700
Bridges-Det ...... .676
Allen-Cle .... .667
Rowe-Det .... .655

Games
VanAtta-StL 52
Knott-StL 47

Complete Games
W.Ferrell-Bos 28
Bridges-Det 26
Ruffing-NY 25
Newsom-Was 24
Grove-Bos 22

Shutouts
Grove-Bos 6
Bridges-Det 5
Rowe-Det 4
Newsom-Was 4
Allen-Cle 4

Saves
Malone-NY 9
Knott-StL 6
Murphy-NY 5
Brown-Chi 5
Hildebrand-Cle ... 4

Innings Pitched
W.Ferrell-Bos ... 301.0
Bridges-Det 294.2
Newsom-Was 285.2
Kennedy-Chi 274.1
Ruffing-NY 271.0

Fewest Hits/Game
Pearson-NY 7.71
Grove-Bos 8.42
Allen-Cle 8.67
Gomez-NY 8.78
Bridges-Det 8.83

Fewest BB/Game
Lyons-Chi 2.23
Grove-Bos 2.31
Rowe-Det 2.35
Andrews-StL 2.35
Marcum-Bos 2.69

Strikeouts
Bridges-Det 175
Allen-Cle 165
Newsom-Was 156
Grove-Bos 130
Pearson-NY 118

Strikeouts/Game
Allen-Cle 6.11
Bridges-Det 5.35
Gomez-NY 5.01
Newsom-Was 4.91
Pearson-NY 4.76

Ratio
Grove-Bos 10.87
Rowe-Det 12.18
Ruffing-NY 12.19
Allen-Cle 12.30
Appleton-Was 12.45

Earned Run Average
Grove-Bos 2.81
Allen-Cle 3.44
Appleton-Was 3.53
Bridges-Det 3.60
Pearson-NY 3.71

Adjusted ERA
Grove-Bos 189
Allen-Cle 146
Bridges-Det 137
Appleton-Was 135
Kelley-Phi 132

Opponents' Batting Avg.
Pearson-NY .... .233
Grove-Bos .... .246
Gomez-NY .... .254
Appleton-Was ..... .254
Bridges-Det ...... .255

Opponents' On Base Pct.
Grove-Bos .... .297
Rowe-Det .... .321
Ruffing-NY .... .323
Appleton-Was ..... .324
Bridges-Det ...... .326

Starter Runs
Grove-Bos 62.8
Bridges-Det 46.9
Allen-Cle 43.0
Ruffing-NY 35.7
Appleton-Was 33.9

Adjusted Starter Runs
Grove-Bos 70.6
Bridges-Det 44.1
Allen-Cle 43.0
W.Ferrell-Bos 37.8
Kelley-Phi 32.4

Clutch Pitching Index
Hadley-NY 116
Kelley-Phi 115
Grove-Bos 115
Bridges-Det 109
Thomas-StL 107

Relief Runs
Lee-Cle 2.1
Gumpert-Phi 1.9
Kimsey-Det 1.1
Brown-Chi 5

Adjusted Relief Runs
Gumpert-Phi 2.3
Lee-Cle 2.1
Brown-Chi 1.9
Kimsey-Det 6

Relief Ranking
Brown-Chi 2.0
Lee-Cle 1.3
Gumpert-Phi 1.2
Kimsey-Det 6

Total Pitcher Index
Grove-Bos 7.0
W.Ferrell-Bos 4.5
Allen-Cle 4.5
Bridges-Det 4.4
Ruffing-NY 3.9

Total Baseball Ranking
Grove-Bos 7.0
Gehrig-NY 6.4
Gehringer-Det 6.1
Appling-Chi 5.1
W.Ferrell-Bos 4.5

March 20* Josh Gibson and Judy Johnson, two future Hall of Famers, are traded to the Homestead Grays for two journeymen players and $2,500. The transaction is called the biggest deal in Negro baseball history.

April 2 Dizzy Dean, Paul Dean, and Joe Medwick have a scuffle in a Tampa hotel lobby with *New York News* reporter Jack Miley and *Chicago Tribune* writer Irv Kupcinet.

April 22* Satchel Paige and Josh Gibson are among 18 black players who jump to the Dominican Republic league. Negro League owners regard this as desertion and plan to ban the players from the league. In May, Paige will be banned for life, but he'll be back.

April 23 Carl Hubbell's first start of the season is a three-hitter against the Boston Bees. For the Giants ace, it is his 17th straight win, dating back to July 17 of last year.

April 25 Giants rookie pitcher Cliff

Melton strikes out 13 in his first major league game but loses to the Boston Bees 3-1.

May 31 A Memorial Day crowd of 61,756, the second-largest crowd in Polo Grounds history, sees the Dodgers end Carl Hubbell's consecutive-game winning streak at 24 over two seasons. Brooklyn routs King Carl in the fourth inning and wins, 10-3.

June 5 Gus Suhr's NL record of 822 consecutive games, started on Sept. 11, 1931, ends when he attends his mother's funeral in San Francisco.

June 6 One of baseball's rarest feats takes place when Woody English of the Dodgers wins a suit by hitting the sign of clothier Abe Stark at the base of the Ebbets Field scoreboard.

June 27 Backed by two Mel Ott home runs, Carl Hubbell outpitches Dizzy Dean to give the Giants an 8–1 win over the Cards. This is the last time the two Hall of Famers will face each other; Hub-

bell has won eight of the 11 matches.

August 6 For the first time in the century, the first two batters in a game—Roy Johnson and Rabbit Warstler of the Boston Bees—lead off with home runs. They do it off Cubs pitcher Tex Carleton.

September 18 Pittsburgh outfielder Paul Waner records his eighth year of 200 or more hits.

September 29 New York rookie Cliff Melton wins his 20th game in the opening game of a doubleheader, but the Phillies beat the Giants in the second game, preventing New York from clinching the flag, which they do the following day.

October 9 Carl Hubbell staves off a Yankee sweep with a six-hit, 7-3 victory. The Giants score six runs in the second inning.

October 25 Casey Stengel signs to manage the Boston Bees.

November 9 St. Louis Cardinals Triple Crown winner Joe Medwick is named NL MVP by the BBWAA.

	BOSTON		BROOKLYN		CHICAGO		CINCINNATI		NEW YORK		PHILADELPHIA		PITTSBURGH		ST.LOUIS
M	B.McKechnie	M	B.Grimes	M	C.Grimm	M	C.Dressen	M	B.Terry	M	J.Wilson	M	P.Traynor	M	F.Frisch
1B	E.Fletcher	1B	B.Hassett	1B	R.Collins	1B	J.McCarthy	1B	D.Camilli	1B	G.Suhr	1B	J.Mize
2B	T.Cuccinello	2B	C.Lavagetto	2B	B.Herman	1B	B.Jordan	2B	B.Whitehead	2B	D.Young	2B	L.Handley	2B	J.Brown
SS	R.Warstler	SS	W.English	SS	B.Jurges	2B	A.Kampouris	SS	D.Bartell	SS	G.Scharein	SS	A.Vaughan	SS	L.Durocher
3B	G.English	3B	J.Stripp	3B	S.Hack	SS	B.Myers	3B	L.Chiozza	3B	P.Whitney	3B	B.Brubaker	3B	D.Gutteridge
LF	D.Garms	LF	T.Winsett	LF	A.Galan	3B	L.Riggs	LF	J.Moore	LF	M.Arnovich	LF	W.Jensen	LF	J.Medwick
CF	V.DiMaggio	CF	J.Cooney	CF	J.Marty	LF	K.Cuyler	CF	J.Ripple	CF	H.Martin	CF	L.Waner	CF	T.Moore
RF	G.Moore	RF	H.Manush	RF	F.Demaree	CF	C.Hafey	RF	M.Ott	RF	C.Klein	RF	P.Waner	RF	D.Padgett
C	A.Lopez	C	B.Phelps	C	G.Hartnett	RF	I.Goodman	C	H.Danning	C	B.Atwood	C	A.Todd	C	B.Ogrodowski
						C	E.Lombardi								
O	R.Johnson	O	G.Brack	O1	P.Cavarretta			C	G.Mancuso	O1	E.Browne	S3	P.Young	3O	F.Bordagaray
C	R.Mueller	23	J.Bucher	C	K.O'Dea	1O	L.Scarsella	O	W.Berger	O	J.Moore	O	J.Dickshot	O	P.Martin
3	E.Mayo	C	R.Spencer	S2	L.Frey	O	H.Walker	1	S.Leslie	23	L.Norris	C	T.Padden	C	M.Owen
O	W.Berger	S	L.Brown	O	T.Stainback	O	S.Davis	O	H.Leiber	C	E.Grace	/O	F.Schulte	2	S.Martin
O	B.Reis	3S	T.Malinosky	C	J.Bottarini	O	P.Weintraub	O	K.Davis	J.Wilson	/3	P.Traynor	/1	D.Siebert
S	T.Thevenow	O	G.Rosen	/O	C.Reynolds	3	J.Outlaw	S	B.Ryan	/C	W.Stephenson	/C	R.Berres	C	H.Bremer
/O	B.McGowan	O	E.Wilson	H	B.Garbark	O	K.Davis	/S	M.Haslin	/O	F.Tauby	/S	B.Schuster	/2	F.Frisch
H	B.Jordan	C	P.Chervinko	R	D.Meyer	S	C.Gelbert	/C	E.Madjeski	/O	H.Gorman			/O	R.Moore
/C	J.Riddle	/1	E.Morgan			1	F.McCormick	/O	P.Weintraub	/3	G.Corbett	P	C.Blanton		
H	B.Urbanski	O	G.Cisar	3	C.English	/3	B.Andrus	P	R.Bauers	P	B.Weiland
/C	L.Wasem	/1	J.Daniel	P	B.Lee	S	E.Miller	P	C.Hubbell	P	E.Brandt	P	L.Warneke
		S	J.Hudson	P	L.French	O	H.Craft	P	C.Melton	P	C.Passeau	P	B.Swift	P	D.Dean
P	L.Fette	/O	B.Haas	P	C.Root	C	G.Campbell	P	H.Schumacher	P	B.Walters	P	J.Bowman	P	S.Johnson
P	J.Turner	C	R.Moore	P	R.Parmelee	/O	P.Jorgensen	P	H.Gumbert	P	W.LaMaster	RP	M.Brown	P	M.Ryba
P	D.MacFayden	/3	N.Polly	RP	C.Shoun	/O	D.Mele	P	S.Castleman	P	H.Mulcahy			RP	R.Harrell
P	G.Bush	/O	A.Parks			/C	D.Moore	RP	A.Smith	P	S.Johnson	P	R.Lucas		
P	J.Lanning	/C	E.Klumpp	P	C.Bryant	/2	E.Joost	RP	D.Coffman	O	O.Jorgens	P	J.Weaver	P	J.Haines
RP	I.Hutchinson	H	S.Gautreaux	P	C.Davis	H	D.Dwyer			RP	H.Kelleher	P	J.Tobin	P	J.Winford
		/2	G.Fallon	/P	B.Logan	/C	G.Brittain	P	T.Baker			P	W.Hoyt	P	S.Blake
P	F.Gabler			/P	K.Higbe	H	A.Moser	/P	F.Fitzsimmons	/P	P.Sivess	/P	K.Heintzelman	/P	T.Sunkel
P	B.Smith	P	M.Butcher	/P	N.Kimball	/C	H.Chozen	/P	B.Lohrman	/P	E.Burkart			/P	H.Krist
/P	M.Shoffner	P	L.Hamlin					/P	D.Brennan	/P	B.Allen			/P	N.Kleinke
P	R.Weir	P	F.Frankhouse			P	L.Grissom	/P	J.Brown	/P	L.Crawford			/P	B.McGee
/P	V.Frasier	P	W.Hoyt			P	P.Derringer	/P	F.Gabler	/P	L.Pettit			/P	N.Andrews
		P	V.Mungo			P	P.Davis	/P	H.Vandenberg	/P	W.Masters			/P	A.White
		RP	G.Jeffcoat			P	A.Hollingsworth	/P	B.Cantwell	/P	B.Burke			/P	J.Chambers
						P	G.Schott							/P	P.Dean
		P	R.Henshaw												
		P	F.Fitzsimmons			P	J.Vander Meer								
		P	H.Eisenstat			P	B.Hallahan								
		P	J.Lindsey			P	J.Cascarella								
		P	R.Birkofer			P	W.Moore								
		P	B.Cantwell			P	J.Mooty								
		/P	B.Marrow			/P	T.Kleinhans								
		/P	T.Baker			P	D.Brennan								
		/P	J.Peterson			/P	J.Brown								
		/P	W.Clark			/P	P.Gehrman								
						/P	R.Barrett								

TEAM	G	W	L	PCT	GB	R	OR	AB	H	2B	3B	HR	BB	SO	AVG	OBP	SLG	PRO	PRO+	BR	/A	PF	CHI	RC	SB	CS	SBA	SBR
NY	152	95	57	.625		732	602	5329	1484	251	41	111	412	492	.278	.334	.403	.737	105	40	31	101	100	734	45			
CHI	154	93	61	.604	3	811	682	5349	1537	253	74	96	538	496	.287	.355	.416	.771	111	117	83	104	98	816	71			
PIT	154	86	68	.558	10	704	646	5433	1550	223	86	47	463	480	.285	.343	.384	.727	104	30	30	100	96	734	32			
STL	157	81	73	.526	15	789	733	5476	1543	264	67	94	385	569	.282	.331	.406	.737	104	36	21	102	107	744	78			
BOS	152	79	73	.520	16	579	556	5124	1265	200	41	63	485	707	.247	.314	.339	.653	91	-109	-59	91	102	565	45			
BRO	155	62	91	.405	33.5	616	772	5295	1401	258	53	37	469	583	.265	.327	.354	.681	90	-57	-67	102	97	629	69			
PHI	155	61	92	.399	34.5	724	869	5424	1482	258	37	103	478	640	.273	.334	.391	.725	95	21	-38	108	100	730	66			
CIN	155	56	98	.364	40	612	707	5230	1329	215	59	73	437	586	.254	.315	.360	.675	94	-78	-49	95	102	599	53			
TOT	617					5567		42660	11591	1922	458	624	3667	4553	.272	.332	.382	.714							459			

TEAM	CG	SH	SV	IP	H	H/G	HR	BB	SO	RAT	ERA	ERA+	OAV	OOB	PR	/A	PF	CPI	FA	E	DP	FW	PW	BW	SBW	DIF
NY	67	11	17	1361	1341	8.9	85	404	653	11.7	3.43	113	.258	.314	73	69	99	102	.974	159	143	.9	6.8	3.1		8.2
CHI	73	11	13	1381[1]	1434	9.3	91	502	596	12.8	3.97	102	.267	.332	-10	0	102	99	.975	151	141	1.5	.0	8.2		6.3
PIT	67	12	17	1366[1]	1398	9.2	71	428	643	12.2	3.56	108	.264	.321	53	45	99	101	.970	181	135	-.2	4.5	3.0		1.8
STL	81	10	4	1392	1546	10.0	95	448	571	13.0	3.98	100	.281	.337	-10	-1	102	105	.973	164	127	1.0	-.0	2.1		1.1
BOS	85	16	10	1359[1]	1344	8.9	60	372	387	11.4	3.22	111	.310	.310	105	55	92	103	.975	157	128	1.0	5.5	-5.9		2.4
BRO	63	5	8	1362[2]	1470	9.7	68	476	592	13.0	4.13	98	.274	.336	-33	-14	103	96	.964	217	127	-2.2	-1.4	-6.6		-4.3
PHI	59	6	15	1373[1]	1629	10.7	116	501	529	14.2	5.05	86	.297	.359	-174	-114	111	97	.970	184	157	-.3	-11.3	-3.8		-.1
CIN	64	10	18	1358[1]	1428	9.5	38	533	581	13.1	3.94	95	.270	.339	-4	-32	95	97	.966	208	139	-1.6	-3.2	-4.9		-11.3
TOT	559	81	102	10954[2]		9.5				12.7	3.91		.272	.332					.971	1421	1097					

Runs
Medwick-StL 111
Herman-Chi 106
Hack-Chi 106
Galan-Chi 104
Demaree-Chi 104

Hits
Medwick-StL 237
P.Waner-Pit 219
Mize-StL 204
Demaree-Chi 199
Herman-Chi 189

Doubles
Medwick-StL 56
Mize-StL 40
Bartell-NY 38
Phelps-Bro 37
Moore-NY 37

Triples
Vaughan-Pit 17
Suhr-Pit 14
Handley-Pit 12
Goodman-Cin 12
Herman-Chi 11

Home Runs
Ott-NY 31
Medwick-StL 31
Camilli-Phi 27
Mize-StL 25
Galan-Chi 18

Total Bases
Medwick-StL 406
Mize-StL 333
Demaree-Chi 298
Ott-NY 285
Camilli-Phi 279

Runs Batted In
Medwick-StL 154
Demaree-Chi 115
Mize-StL 113
Suhr-Pit 97
Ott-NY 95

Runs Produced
Medwick-StL 234
Demaree-Chi 202
Mize-StL 191
Hack-Chi 167
P.Waner-Pit 166

Bases On Balls
Ott-NY 102
Camilli-Phi 90
Suhr-Pit 83
Hack-Chi 83
Galan-Chi 79

Batting Average
Medwick-StL ...... .374
Mize-StL .... .364
Hartnett-Chi .... .354
P.Waner-Pit .... .354
Whitney-Phi ...... .341

On Base Percentage
Camilli-Phi ...... .446
Mize-StL .... .427
Medwick-StL ...... .414
P.Waner-Pit .... .413
Ott-NY .... .408

Slugging Average
Medwick-StL ...... .641
Mize-StL .... .595
Camilli-Phi ...... .587
Hartnett-Chi .... .548
Ott-NY .... .523

Production
Medwick-StL 1.056
Camilli-Phi 1.034
Mize-StL 1.021
Ott-NY .... .931
Herman-Chi ...... .875

Adjusted Production
Medwick-StL 179
Mize-StL 171
Camilli-Phi 165
Ott-NY 149
P.Waner-Pit 132

Batter Runs
Medwick-StL 68.8
Mize-StL 57.4
Camilli-Phi 54.9
Ott-NY 41.2
Hartnett-Chi 31.1

Adjusted Batter Runs
Medwick-StL 65.9
Mize-StL 54.9
Camilli-Phi 45.4
Ott-NY 39.8
P.Waner-Pit 29.8

Clutch Hitting Index
Scharein-Phi 136
Durocher-StL 133
Suhr-Pit 129
Jurges-Chi 124
Todd-Pit 120

Runs Created
Medwick-StL 170
Mize-StL 150
Camilli-Phi 137
Ott-NY 128
P.Waner-Pit 118

Total Average
Camilli-Phi 1.189
Medwick-StL 1.113
Mize-StL 1.097
Ott-NY 1.021
Vaughan-Pit .... .864

Stolen Bases
Galan-Chi 23
Hack-Chi 16

Stolen Base Average

Stolen Base Runs

Fielding Runs
Bartell-NY 37.5
Whitehead-NY 26.1
Riggs-Cin 19.5
Herman-Chi 18.6
Young-Pit 18.1

Total Player Rating
Medwick-StL 6.2
Bartell-NY 6.1
Herman-Chi 5.2
Ott-NY 3.7
Camilli-Phi 3.3

Wins
Hubbell-NY 22
Turner-Bos 20
Melton-NY 20
Fette-Bos 20
Warneke-StL 18

Win Percentage
Hubbell-NY .... .733
Melton-NY .... .690
Fette-Bos .... .667
Carleton-Chi .... .667
Turner-Bos ...... .645

Games
Mulcahy-Phi 56
Jorgens-Phi 52

Complete Games
Turner-Bos 24
Fette-Bos 23
Weiland-StL 21

Shutouts
Turner-Bos 5
Grissom-Cin 5
Fette-Bos 5

Saves
Melton-NY 7
Brown-Pit 7
Grissom-Cin 6
Root-Chi 5
Hollingsworth-Cin ... 5

Innings Pitched
Passeau-Phi 292.1
Lee-Chi 272.1
Weiland-StL 264.1
Hubbell-NY 261.2
Fette-Bos 259.0

Fewest Hits/Game
Mungo-Bro 7.60
Grissom-Cin 7.77
Melton-NY 7.84
Carleton-Chi 7.91
Turner-Bos 7.99

Fewest BB/Game
D.Dean-StL 1.51
Root-Chi 1.61
Hoyt-Pit-Bro 1.66
Turner-Bos 1.81
Castleman-NY 1.85

Strikeouts
Hubbell-NY 159
Grissom-Cin 149
Blanton-Pit 143
Melton-NY 142

Strikeouts/Game
Mungo-Bro 6.82
Grissom-Cin 6.00
Bauers-Pit 5.66
Henshaw-Bro 5.64
LaMaster-Phi 5.51

Ratio
Turner-Bos 9.82
Melton-NY 10.05
Castleman-NY ... 10.16
Root-Chi 10.53
D.Dean-StL 10.72

Earned Run Average
Turner-Bos 2.38
Melton-NY 2.61
D.Dean-StL 2.69
Bauers-Pit 2.88
Fette-Bos 2.88

Adjusted ERA
Turner-Bos 150
Melton-NY 149
D.Dean-StL 148
Mungo-Bro 139
Bauers-Pit 134

Opponents' Batting Avg.
Mungo-Bro ...... .229
Grissom-Cin .... .232
Melton-NY ...... .233
Turner-Bos ...... .235
Carleton-Chi .... .236

Opponents' On Base Pct.
Turner-Bos ...... .274
Melton-NY ...... .280
Castleman-NY .... .287
Root-Chi .... .290
D.Dean-StL ...... .291

Starter Runs
Turner-Bos 43.5
Melton-NY 35.8
Fette-Bos 29.5
MacFayden-Bos . 26.9
D.Dean-StL 26.7

Adjusted Starter Runs
Melton-NY 35.0
Turner-Bos 34.2
D.Dean-StL 28.2
Bauers-Pit 20.5
Mungo-Bro 20.1

Clutch Pitching Index
Johnson-StL 128
Brandt-Pit 124
Weiland-StL 115
Frankhouse-Bro ... 113
MacFayden-Bos ... 112

Relief Runs
Coffman-NY 7.8
Hutchinson-Bos ... 1.8

Adjusted Relief Runs
Coffman-NY 7.5

Relief Ranking
Coffman-NY 9.9

Total Pitcher Index
Turner-Bos 4.5
Melton-NY 3.9
Mungo-Bro 3.0
D.Dean-StL 3.0
Fette-Bos 2.5

Total Baseball Ranking
Medwick-StL 6.2
Bartell-NY 6.1
Herman-Chi 5.2
Turner-Bos 4.5
Melton-NY 3.9

January 19 Nap Lajoie, Tris Speaker, and Cy Young are voted into the Baseball Hall of Fame by the BBWAA.

May 25 After hitting a home run against the Yankees in his prior at bat, Mickey Cochrane suffers a skull fracture from a Bump Hadley pitch and will never return to active play.

June 1 White Sox hurler Bill Dietrich pitches an 8–0 no-hitter against the Browns. It is the third no-hitter Luke Sewell has caught, having previously been behind the plate for Wes Ferrell in 1931 and Vern Kennedy in 1935.

June 3 Josh Gibson is credited with a drive that hits just two feet below the rim of Yankee Stadium, about 580 feet from home plate. It is estimated that the ball would have traveled nearly 700 feet.

July 7 Lou Gehrig leads the AL All-Stars over the NL 8-3 with a home run, double, and four RBIs. President Roosevelt attends the game in Washington. Dizzy Dean's toe is fractured by a drive off the bat of Earl Averill. After the injury Dean is unable to pitch with the same delivery. He uses an unnatural motion, causing an arm injury from which he never recovers.

August 29 The A's set a new AL record in the opener of a doubleheader with the White Sox by scoring 12 runs in the first inning, six of which are driven in by Bob Johnson.

August 31 Detroit's rookie Rudy York sets a new record for home runs in a month, hitting his 17th and 18th to eclipse Babe Ruth's mark set in September 1927. He knocks in seven runs against Pete Appleton, as Detroit beats Washington, 12-3. (York's mark will stand until Sammy Sosa hits 20 home runs in June 1998.)

September 2 The first two batters in a game—the White Sox Boze Berger and Mike Kreevich—hit home runs, victimizing Boston's Johnny Marcum. This is the first time two AL batters have opened with home runs.

September 17 Cleveland's Johnny Allen wins his 12th straight without a loss, equaling Tom Zachary's 1929 record of 12-0.

September 19 Hank Greenberg's home run in Detroit's 8–1 win over New York is the first ever hit into the center field stands at Yankee Stadium.

September 23 The Yankees lose 9–5 but clinch the pennant when the Red Sox beat Detroit.

October 6 Carl Hubbell and Lefty Gomez duel in the opening game of the World Series, a rematch of last year's teams. The Yankees score seven runs in the sixth inning on five singles, three walks, and two errors. Tony Lazzeri homers in the bottom of the eighth to make the final score, 8-1.

October 10 Lefty Gomez wins again, and the Yankees wrap up the Series. Gomez himself knocks in the winning run in the 4-2 clincher. It is a record fifth World Series win, without a loss, for Gomez.

November 2 AL batting champ Charlie Gehringer is named MVP by the BBWAA.

	BOSTON		CHICAGO		CLEVELAND		DETROIT		NEW YORK		PHILADELPHIA		ST.LOUIS		WASHINGTON
M	J.Cronin	M	J.Dykes	M	S.O'Neill	M	M.Cochrane	M	J.McCarthy	M	C.Mack	M	R.Hornsby	M	B.Harris
1B	J.Foxx	1B	Z.Bonura	1B	H.Trosky	M	D.Baker	1B	L.Gehrig	M	E.Mack	1B	J.Bottomley	1B	J.Kuhel
2B	E.McNair	2B	J.Hayes	2B	J.Kroner	M	M.Cochrane	2B	T.Lazzeri	1B	C.Dean	1B	H.Davis	2B	B.Myer
SS	J.Cronin	SS	L.Appling	SS	L.Lary	M	D.Baker	SS	F.Crosetti	2B	R.Peters	2B	T.Carey	SS	C.Travis
3B	P.Higgins	3B	T.Piet	3B	O.Hale	M	C.Perkins	3B	R.Rolfe	SS	S.Newsome	SS	B.Knickerb'r	3B	B.Lewis
LF	B.Mills	LF	R.Radcliff	LF	M.Solters	1B	H.Greenberg	LF	J.Powell	3B	B.Werber	3B	H.Clift	LF	A.Simmons
CF	D.Cramer	CF	M.Kreevich	CF	E.Averill	2B	C.Gehringer	CF	J.DiMaggio	LF	B.Johnson	LF	J.Vosmik	CF	M.Almada
RF	B.Chapman	RF	D.Walker	RF	B.Campbell	SS	B.Rogell	RF	M.Hoag	CF	J.Hill	CF	S.West	RF	J.Stone
C	G.Desautels	C	L.Sewell	C	F.Pytlak	3B	M.Owen	C	B.Dickey	RF	W.Moses	RF	B.Bell	C	R.Ferrell
						LF	G.Walker			C	E.Brucker	C	R.Hemsley		
O	F.Gaffke	3	B.Berger	32	R.Hughes	CF	J.White	O	G.Selkirk					O	F.Sington
O	D.Dallessandro	1	M.Haas	C	B.Sullivan	RF	P.Fox	O	T.Henrich	1O	L.Finney	O	E.Allen	C	W.Millies
2	B.Doerr	3	M.Connors	O	R.Weatherly	C	R.York	2S	D.Heffner	O	J.Rothrock	C	B.Huffman	O	B.Chapman
C	M.Berg	O	L.Rosenthal	C	J.Heath			C	J.Glenn	C	F.Hayes	1	J.Bottomley	S	O.Bluege
O	M.Almada	13	J.Dykes	C	J.Becker	O	C.Laabs	O	R.Johnson	2	W.Ambler	2	R.Barkley	1	J.Wasdell
C	R.Ferrell	O	H.Steinbacher	/O	H.Alexander	O	G.Goslin	C	A.Jorgens	2	B.Cissell	2	N.Lipscomb	2	J.Mihalic
2	S.Melillo	C	M.Shea	/2	B.Monaco	C	B.Tebbetts	/1	J.Saltzgaver	1	G.Hasson	O	E.Silber	O	J.Hill
/C	J.Peacock	C	T.Rensa	/3	K.Keltner	H	M.Cochrane	H	B.Dahlgren	S	A.Parker	2	R.Hornsby	O	G.Case
R	S.Bowers			H	B.Sodd	C	R.Hayworth			C	B.Conroy	C	T.Giuliani	C	S.Hogan
R	B.Daughters	P	V.Kennedy			2	G.English	P	L.Gomez	2S	W.Huston	C	T.Heath	2	J.Bloodworth
		P	T.Lee	P	M.Harder	C	C.Bolton	P	R.Ruffing	/O	B.Barna	/C	S.Harshany	/C	J.Riddle
P	L.Grove	P	T.Lyons	P	D.Galehouse	S	C.Gelbert	P	B.Hadley	/O	D.Morris	H	M.Mazzera	/C	M.Gray
P	J.Wilson	P	J.Whitehead	P	W.Hudlin	/3	F.Clifton	P	M.Pearson	/O	E.Yount	/O	T.Cafego	/S	F.Trechock
P	B.Newsom	P	M.Stratton	P	J.Allen	/O	B.Herman	RP	J.Murphy	/C	H.Wagner			/C	H.Crompton
P	J.Marcum	RP	C.Brown	P	B.Feller			RP	F.Makosky			P	O.Hildebrand	/C	M.Guerra
P	A.McKain			RP	L.Brown	P	E.Auker			P	G.Caster	P	J.Knott	/2	J.Lynn
		P	B.Dietrich	RP	W.Wyatt	P	T.Bridges	P	P.Malone	P	H.Kelley	P	C.Hogsett	/C	A.Sabo
P	R.Walberg	P	J.Rigney	RP	J.Heving	P	R.Lawson	P	K.Wicker	P	E.Smith	P	J.Walkup		
P	F.Ostermueller	P	S.Cain			P	J.Wade	P	S.Chandler	P	B.Thomas	P	J.Bonetti	P	J.DeShong
P	W.Ferrell	/P	B.Cox	P	E.Whitehill	P	B.Poffenberger	P	I.Andrews	P	B.Ross			P	W.Ferrell
P	T.Olson	/P	I.Chelini	P	I.Andrews			/P	J.Broaca	RP	H.Fink	P	B.Trotter	P	M.Weaver
/P	J.Gonzales	/P	G.Gick	/P	K.Jungels	/P	J.Vance	RP	G.Turbeville	P	L.Koupal	P	P.Appleton
/P	J.Henry			/P	C.Fischer	P	G.Gill					P	R.Van Atta	P	E.Linke
/P	T.Thomas					P	S.Coffman			P	L.Nelson	P	S.Blake	RP	S.Cohen
						P	J.Russell			P	A.Williams	/P	T.Thomas		
						P	P.McLaughlin			P	R.Gumpert	/P	L.Tietje	P	K.Chase
						P	S.Rowe			/P	B.Kalfass	/P	E.Caldwell	P	C.Fischer
						/P	V.Sorrell			/P	F.Archer	/P	B.Strickland	P	B.Newsom
						/P	C.Hatter					/P	H.Kimberlin	/P	B.Phebus
						/P	B.Logan					/P	L.Mills	P	J.Krakauskas
												/P	E.Bildilli	P	J.Cascarella
												/P	G.Hennessey	P	B.Jacobs
												/P	E.Baecht	/P	J.Kohlman
												/P	B.Miller	/P	R.Anderson
												/P	B.Muncrief	/P	D.Lanahan

TEAM	G	W	L	PCT	GB	R	OR	AB	H	2B	3B	HR	BB	SO	AVG	OBP	SLG	PRO	PRO+	BR	/A	PF	CHI	RC	SB	CS	SBA	SBR
NY	157	102	52	.662		**979**	671	5487	1554	282	73	**174**	**709**	607	.283	.369	**.456**	**.825**	113	112	106	101	**103**	952	60	36	63	-4
DET	155	89	65	.578	13	935	841	5516	**1611**	309	62	150	656	711	**.292**	**.370**	.452	.822	111	106	85	102	100	947	89	45	66	0
CHI	154	86	68	.558	16	780	730	5277	1478	280	76	67	549	**447**	.280	.350	.400	.750	95	-38	-37	100	**103**	763	70	34	**67**	**1**
CLE	156	83	71	.539	19	817	768	5353	1499	304	76	103	570	551	.280	.352	.423	.775	100	4	-1	101	101	813	78	51	60	-7
BOS	154	80	72	.526	21	821	775	5354	1506	269	64	100	601	557	.281	.357	.411	.768	96	-1	-32	104	102	804	79	61	56	-13
WAS	158	73	80	.477	28.5	757	841	5578	1559	245	**84**	47	591	503	.279	.351	.379	.730	94	-74	-40	96	100	767	61	35	64	-3
PHI	154	54	97	.358	46.5	699	854	5228	1398	278	60	94	583	557	.267	.341	.397	.738	93	-63	-52	98	97	732	**95**	48	66	0
STL	156	46	108	.299	56	715	1023	5510	1573	**327**	44	71	514	510	.285	.348	.399	.747	93	-47	-52	101	93	780	30	27	53	-7
TOT	622					6503		43303	12178	2294	539	806	4773	4443	.281	.355	.415	.770							562	337	63	-34

TEAM	CG	SH	SV	IP	H	H/G	HR	BB	SO	RAT	ERA	ERA+	OAV	OOB	PR	/A	PF	CPI	FA	E	DP	FW	PW	BW	SBW	DIF
NY	**82**	15	21	1396	**1417**	9.1	92	**506**	652	12.5	**3.65**	122	**.261**	**.325**	151	124	96	103	.972	170	134	.2	**11.4**	**9.7**	.0	3.7
DET	70	6	11	1378	1521	9.9	102	635	485	14.2	4.87	96	.279	.357	-38	-30	101	95	**.976**	147	149	1.4	-2.8	7.8	.4	5.2
CHI	70	**15**	21	1351[1]	1435	9.6	115	532	533	13.2	4.17	110	.273	.341	68	65	100	**104**	.971	174	173	-.2	6.0	-3.4	**.5**	6.2
CLE	64	4	15	1364[2]	1529	10.1	**61**	566	630	14.0	4.39	105	.285	.356	35	33	100	102	.974	159	153	.8	3.0	-.0	-.3	2.5
BOS	74	6	14	1366	1518	10.0	92	597	**682**	14.0	4.48	106	.279	.352	21	41	103	100	.970	177	139	-.4	3.8	-2.9	-.8	4.4
WAS	75	5	14	1398[2]	1498	9.6	96	671	524	14.1	4.58	97	.275	.357	7	-23	96	99	.972	170	**181**	.3	-2.1	-3.7	.1	1.9
PHI	65	6	9	1335	1490	10.0	105	613	469	14.3	4.85	97	.281	.358	-35	-21	102	97	.967	198	150	-1.7	-1.9	-4.8	.4	-13.5
STL	55	2	8	1363	1768	11.7	143	653	468	16.2	6.00	80	.315	.390	-209	-178	105	100	.972	173	166	-.0	-16.3	-4.8	-.3	-9.6
TOT	555	59	113	10952[2]		10.0				14.1	4.62		.281	.355					.972	1368	1245					

Runs		Hits		Doubles		Triples		Home Runs		Total Bases	
DiMaggio-NY	151	Bell-StL	218	Bell-StL	51	Walker-Chi	16	DiMaggio-NY	46	DiMaggio-NY	418
Rolfe-NY	143	DiMaggio-NY	215	Greenberg-Det	49	Kreevich-Chi	16	Greenberg-Det	40	Greenberg-Det	397
Gehrig-NY	138	Walker-Det	213	Moses-Phi	48	Stone-Was	15	Gehrig-NY	37	Gehrig-NY	366
Greenberg-Det	137	Lewis-Was	210	Vosmik-StL	47	DiMaggio-NY	15	Foxx-Bos	36	Moses-Phi	357
Gehringer-Det	133	Gehringer-Det	209	Lary-Cle	46	Greenberg-Det	14	York-Det	35	Trosky-Cle	329

Runs Batted In		Runs Produced		Bases On Balls		Batting Average		On Base Percentage		Slugging Average	
Greenberg-Det	183	Greenberg-Det	280	Gehrig-NY	127	Gehringer-Det	.371	Gehrig-NY	.473	DiMaggio-NY	.673
DiMaggio-NY	167	DiMaggio-NY	272	Greenberg-Det	102	Gehrig-NY	.351	Gehringer-Det	.458	Greenberg-Det	.668
Gehrig-NY	159	Gehrig-NY	260	Foxx-Bos	99	DiMaggio-NY	.346	Greenberg-Det	.436	York-Det	.651
Dickey-NY	133	Gehringer-Det	215	Johnson-Phi	98	Bonura-Chi	.345	Johnson-Phi	.425	Gehrig-NY	.643
Trosky-Cle	128	Foxx-Bos	202	Clift-StL	98	Travis-Was	.344	Dickey-NY	.417	Bonura-Chi	.573

Production		Adjusted Production		Batter Runs		Adjusted Batter Runs		Clutch Hitting Index		Runs Created	
Gehrig-NY	1.116	Gehrig-NY	177	Gehrig-NY	73.3	Gehrig-NY	72.3	Hayes-Chi	152	Gehrig-NY	181
Greenberg-Det	1.105	Greenberg-Det	171	Greenberg-Det	67.2	Greenberg-Det	63.7	Higgins-Bos	127	Greenberg-Det	178
DiMaggio-NY	1.085	DiMaggio-NY	168	DiMaggio-NY	61.3	DiMaggio-NY	60.4	Myer-Was	125	DiMaggio-NY	173
Dickey-NY	.987	Johnson-Phi	147	Gehringer-Det	44.0	Gehringer-Det	41.1	Hale-Cle	117	Gehringer-Det	140
Bonura-Chi	.984	Bonura-Chi	146	Dickey-NY	37.5	Johnson-Phi	36.8	Werber-Phi	116	Clift-StL	134

Total Average		Stolen Bases		Stolen Base Average		Stolen Base Runs		Fielding Runs		Total Player Rating	
Gehrig-NY	1.339	Chapman-Was-Bos	35	Hill-Was-Phi	81.8	Chapman-Was-Bos	3.3	Clift-StL	41.0	Clift-StL	7.2
Greenberg-Det	1.277	Werber-Phi	35	Walker-Det	76.7	Hill-Was-Phi	3.0	Hale-Cle	25.9	DiMaggio-NY	6.0
DiMaggio-NY	1.207	Walker-Det	23	Pytlak-Cle	76.2	Werber-Phi	2.7	Hayes-Chi	20.5	Gehringer-Det	5.2
Gehringer-Det	1.089			Chapman-Was-Bos	74.5	Walker-Det	2.7	Appling-Chi	13.8	Dickey-NY	5.1
Johnson-Phi	1.083			Werber-Phi	72.9	Kreevich-Chi	2.4	Dickey-NY	12.3	Greenberg-Det	4.7

Wins		Win Percentage		Games		Complete Games		Shutouts		Saves	
Gomez-NY	21	Allen-Cle	.938	Brown-Chi	53	W.Ferrell-Bos-Was	26	Gomez-NY	6	Brown-Chi	18
Ruffing-NY	20	Stratton-Chi	.750	Wilson-Bos	51	Gomez-NY	25	Stratton-Chi	5	Murphy-NY	10
Lawson-Det	18	Ruffing-NY	.741	Newsom-Was-Bos	41	Ruffing-NY	22	Whitehead-Chi	4	Wilson-Bos	7
Grove-Bos	17	Lawson-Det	.720	Kelley-Phi	41	Grove-Bos	21	Ruffing-NY	4	Malone-NY	6
Auker-Det	17	Gomez-NY	.656	Heving-Cle	40	DeShong-Was	20	Appleton-Was	4		

Innings Pitched		Fewest Hits/Game		Fewest BB/Game		Strikeouts		Strikeouts/Game		Ratio	
W.Ferrell-Bos-Was	281.0	Gomez-NY	7.53	Stratton-Chi	2.02	Gomez-NY	194	Gomez-NY	6.27	Stratton-Chi	9.89
Gomez-NY	278.1	Stratton-Chi	7.76	Hudlin-Cle	2.20	Newsom-Was-Bos	166	Wilson-Bos	5.57	Gomez-NY	10.57
Newsom-Was-Bos	275.1	Smith-Phi	8.15	Marcum-Bos	2.30	Grove-Bos	153	Newsom-Was-Bos	5.43	Ruffing-NY	10.92
DeShong-Was	264.1	Allen-Cle	8.17	Ruffing-NY	2.39	Feller-Cle	150	Grove-Bos	5.26	Allen-Cle	11.55
Grove-Bos	262.0	Ruffing-NY	8.50	Lyons-Chi	2.39	Bridges-Det	138	Bridges-Det	5.06	Lee-Chi	11.87

Earned Run Average		Adjusted ERA		Opponents' Batting Avg.		Opponents' On Base Pct.		Starter Runs		Adjusted Starter Runs	
Gomez-NY	2.33	Stratton-Chi	191	Gomez-NY	.223	Stratton-Chi	.280	Gomez-NY	70.9	Gomez-NY	65.5
Stratton-Chi	2.40	Gomez-NY	191	Stratton-Chi	.234	Gomez-NY	.287	Ruffing-NY	46.6	Grove-Bos	50.2
Allen-Cle	2.55	Allen-Cle	181	Smith-Phi	.242	Ruffing-NY	.296	Grove-Bos	46.5	Ruffing-NY	41.6
Ruffing-NY	2.98	Grove-Bos	157	Allen-Cle	.244	Lee-Chi	.312	Stratton-Chi	40.6	Stratton-Chi	40.2
Grove-Bos	3.02	Ruffing-NY	149	Ruffing-NY	.247	Allen-Cle	.313	Allen-Cle	39.8	Allen-Cle	39.6

Clutch Pitching Index		Relief Runs		Adjusted Relief Runs		Relief Ranking		Total Pitcher Index		Total Baseball Ranking	
Allen-Cle	120	Brown-Chi	13.3	Brown-Chi	13.1	Brown-Chi	21.9	Gomez-NY	6.5	Clift-StL	7.2
Whitehead-Chi	119	Cohen-Was	9.2	Cohen-Was	8.1	Cohen-Was	9.2	Stratton-Chi	4.5	Gomez-NY	6.5
Knott-StL	112	Murphy-NY	5.5	Fink-Phi	5.9	Murphy-NY	5.3	Grove-Bos	4.0	DiMaggio-NY	6.0
Grove-Bos	111	Fink-Phi	5.1	Murphy-NY	3.3	Fink-Phi	2.2	Ruffing-NY	3.7	Gehringer-Det	5.2
Galehouse-Cle	110	Wyatt-Cle	1.5	Wyatt-Cle	1.4	Wyatt-Cle	.8	Auker-Det	2.9	Dickey-NY	5.1

January 18 Grover Cleveland Alexander is elected to the Baseball Hall of Fame, the only player to get the required 75 percent of the BBWAA votes.

March 23 Judge Landis frees 74 Cardinal minor leaguers, among them Pete Reiser, in yet another attempt to halt the farm system "cover-up." Dodger general manager Larry MacPhail makes a pact with Branch Rickey to take the unknown player and swap him back in the future, but Reiser's ability is too great to hide.

April 16 Dizzy Dean is sold by the Cardinals to the Chicago Cubs. The Cubs pay $200,000 and send pitcher Curt Davis and Clyde Shoun to St. Louis. The Cardinals also buy Tuck Stainback from the Cubs for $15,000.

April 19 In the top of the first inning at Philadelphia, Dodger Ernie Koy homers in his first major league at bat. In the bottom of the inning, leadoff man Emmett Mueller also hits a home run in his first time up in the major leagues.

May 5 Harold Kelleher of the Phillies faces 16 batters in the sixth inning, as the Cubs score 12 runs. Both marks are NL records off one hurler in a single inning. The Cubs win 21–2 with Joe Marty tallying four runs, four RBIs, and four hits. The loss goes to Wayne LeMaster who threw just three pitches to leadoff batter Stan Hack before leaving the game with an injury.

June 15 Johnny Vander Meer stuns baseball by pitching his second successive no-hitter, defeating the Dodgers, 6-0, as Brooklyn plays the first night game ever at Ebbets Field. In front of 38,748 fans, Vandy strikes out seven and walks eight, including three walks in the ninth. A force at home and a fly ball end the game. In a pregame event, Ernie Koy, with a 10-yard start, beats Olympic champion Jesse Owens in the 100-yard dash.

June 18 Babe Ruth is signed as a Dodgers coach for the rest of the season. He is in uniform for batting demonstrations the following day.

July 6 The NL wins the sixth All-Star Game 4–1, with the aid of fine pitching and four AL errors. Starter Johnny Vander Meer gets the win.

August 2 Larry MacPhail has official baseballs dyed dandelion yellow, and they are used in the first game of a doubleheader between the Dodgers and Cardinals at Ebbets Field. The Dodgers win 6-2, but Johnny Mize hits a Freddie Fitzsimmons knuckleball for the first "yellow" home run. The Dodgers will use up their yellow balls in three more games in 1939.

September 28 Cubs manager Gabby Hartnett hits the homer in the gloamin' against Mace Brown in the bottom of the ninth to break a 5-5 tie and put the Cubs in first place ahead of the Pirates. With two outs and none on base, the umpires intended to call the game because of darkness after Hartnett's turn at bat.

October 1 The Cubs clinch the pennant, beating the Cards in the second game of a twin bill while the Reds beat the Pirates.

November 1 League batting champ Ernie Lombardi is named MVP by the BBWAA. Chicago pitcher Bill Lee is runner-up.

BOSTON	BROOKLYN	CHICAGO	CINCINNATI	NEW YORK	PHILADELPHIA	PITTSBURGH	ST.LOUIS
M C.Stengel	M B.Grimes	M C.Grimm	M B.McKechnie	M B.Terry	M J.Wilson	M P.Traynor	M F.Frisch
1B E.Fletcher	1B D.Camilli	M G.Hartnett	1B F.McCormick	1B J.McCarthy	1B H.Lobert	1B G.Suhr	M M.Gonzalez
2B T.Cuccinello	2B J.Hudson	1B R.Collins	2B L.Frey	2B A.Kampouris	2B P.Weintraub	2B P.Young	1B J.Mize
SS R.Warstler	SS L.Durocher	2B B.Herman	SS B.Myers	SS D.Bartell	2B H.Mueller	SS A.Vaughan	2B S.Martin
3B J.Olympo	3B C.Lavagetto	SS B.Jurges	3B L.Riggs	3B M.Ott	SS D.Young	3B L.Handley	SS L.Myers
LF M.West	LF B.Hassett	3B S.Hack	LF W.Berger	LF J.Moore	3B P.Whitney	LF J.Rizzo	3B D.Gutteridge
CF V.DiMaggio	CF E.Koy	LF A.Galan	CF H.Craft	CF H.Leiber	LF M.Arnovich	CF L.Waner	LF J.Medwick
RF J.Cooney	RF G.Rosen	CF C.Reynolds	RF I.Goodman	RF J.Ripple	CF H.Martin	RF P.Waner	CF T.Moore
C R.Mueller	C B.Phelps	RF F.Demaree	C E.Lombardi	C H.Danning	RF C.Klein	C A.Todd	RF E.Slaughter
		C G.Hartnett			C B.Atwood		C M.Owen
O3 D.Garms	O K.Cuyler	O1 P.Cavarretta	O D.Cooke	O B.Seeds	S2 G.Scharein	O W.Jensen	2S J.Brown
C A.Lopez	C G.Campbell	C K.O'Dea	C W.Hershberger	2O L.Chiozza	31 B.Jordan	3 B.Brubaker	O1 D.Padgett
O G.Moore	C M.Shea	O J.Marty	S N.Richardson	S3 G.Myatt	O G.Brack	C R.Berres	O P.Martin
3 G.English	O T.Stainback	S T.Lazzeri	/O L.Gamble	C G.Mancuso	C S.Davis	O J.Dickshot	3 J.Stripp
O H.Maggert	2 P.Coscarart	C B.Garbark	2 A.Kampouris	1 S.Leslie	O T.Stainback	/2 T.Thevenow	O F.Bordagaray
S J.Hitchcock	3 W.English	/O C.Triplett	3 D.Lang	2 B.Cissell	1 G.Corbett	H H.Manush	C J.Bremer
C J.Riddle	O O.Hockett	O J.Asbell	C S.Davis	32 M.Haslin	1 E.Browne		2 J.Bucher
/O R.Johnson	O G.Brack	/S S.Mesner	/O K.Davis	/O W.Berger	C C.Clark	P R.Bauers	O H.Epps
/3 E.Mayo	O F.Sington	/S B.Mattick	/S J.Stein	/2 B.Ryan	/3 J.Stein	P J.Tobin	/S C.Crespi
/S J.Walsh	O H.Manush	P B.Lee	/O N.Bongiovanni	H L.Powers	/S E.Feinberg	P C.Blanton	/O T.Stainback
/O R.McLeod	S W.Williams	P C.Bryant	H B.Jordan	P C.Melton	/O A.Pitko	P B.Klinger	H D.Siebert
/C B.Sutcliffe	C R.Spencer	P L.French	H D.West	P H.Gumbert	/O R.Stoviak	P B.Swift	P B.Weiland
H B.Kahle	/S P.Rogers	P T.Carleton	R J.Outlaw	P H.Schumacher	A.Rebel	RP M.Brown	P B.McGee
/2 T.Kane	/O T.Winsett	P C.Root	P P.Derringer	/C C.Hubbell	J.Wilson	P E.Brandt	P L.Warneke
P J.Turner	C P.Chervinko	RP J.Russell	P J.Vander Meer	P B.Lohrman	H H.Gorman	P R.Lucas	P C.Davis
P L.Fette	/C G.George	P D.Dean	P B.Walters	RP D.Coffman	P H.Mulcahy	P J.Bowman	P R.Henshaw
P D.MacFayden	/C R.Hayworth	P V.Page	P P.Davis	P J.Brown	P C.Passeau	P R.Sewell	RP C.Shoun
P I.Hutchinson	/C R.Thomas	/P A.Epperly	P J.Weaver	P S.Castleman	P A.Hollingsworth	/P K.Heintzelman	RP R.Harrell
P M.Shoffner	H B.Haas	/P B.Logan	RP G.Schott	P J.Wittig	P M.Butcher		P M.Macon
P J.Lanning	P L.Hamlin	/P K.Higbe	RP J.Cascarella	/P H.Vandenberg	RP P.Sivess		P M.Lanier
P D.Errickson	P F.Fitzsimmons	/P N.Kimball	P W.Moore	/P T.Baker	RP A.Smith		/P P.Dean
PO B.Reis	P T.Pressnell		P L.Grissom	/P O.Georgy	P B.Hallahan		P M.Cooper
/P R.Weir	P V.Tamulis		/P A.Hollingsworth		P S.Johnson		P S.Johnson
/P T.Earley	P B.Posedel		/P R.Barrett		P B.Walters		P G.Bush
/P T.Reis	P V.Mungo		/P R.Benge		P W.LaMaster		P M.Ryba
/P A.Doll	P F.Frankhouse		/P T.Kleinhans		/P E.Burkart		/P P.Roe
/P H.Moran	P M.Butcher				/P H.Kelleher		/P H.Krist
/P A.Kenney	P L.Rogers				/P T.Lanning		
/P J.Niggeling	P B.Marrow				/P T.Reis		
/P M.Balas	/P W.Hoyt				/P E.Heusser		
/P F.Gabler	/P J.Gaddy						
	/P W.LaMaster						
	/P S.Nahem						
	/P J.Winford						
	/P D.Potter						

TEAM	G	W	L	PCT	GB	R	OR	AB	H	2B	3B	HR	BB	SO	AVG	OBP	SLG	PRO	PRO+	BR	/A	PF	CHI	RC	SB	CS	SBA	SBR
CHI	154	89	63	.586		713	598	5333	1435	242	70	65	522	476	.269	.338	.377	.715	100	25	6	103	101	689	49			
PIT	152	86	64	.573	2	707	630	5422	1511	265	66	66	485	485	.279	.340	.388	.728	106	48	43	101	96	727	47			
NY	152	83	67	.553	5	705	637	5255	1424	210	36	125	465	528	.271	.334	.396	.730	106	45	39	101	99	715	31			
CIN	151	82	68	.547	6	723	634	5391	1495	251	57	110	366	518	.277	.327	.406	.733	110	43	62	97	101	720	19			
BOS	153	77	75	.507	12	561	618	5250	1311	199	39	54	424	548	.250	.309	.333	.642	91	-119	-66	90	104	549	49			
STL	156	71	80	.470	17.5	725	721	5528	1542	288	74	91	412	492	.279	.331	.407	.738	103	56	14	106	97	752	55			
BRO	151	69	80	.463	18.5	704	710	5142	1322	225	79	61	611	615	.257	.338	.367	.705	98	13	-3	102	103	671	66			
PHI	151	45	105	.300	43	550	840	5192	1318	233	29	40	423	507	.254	.312	.333	.645	85	-111	-96	97	101	549	38			
TOT	610					5388		42513	11358	1913	450	611	3708	4093	.267	.329	.376	.705							354			

TEAM	CG	SH	SV	IP	H	H/G	HR	BB	SO	RAT	ERA	ERA+	OAV	OOB	PR	/A	PF	CPI	FA	E	DP	FW	PW	BW	SBW	DIF
CHI	67	16	18	1396²	1414	9.1	71	454	583	12.1	3.37	113	.262	.322	64	66	101	105	.978	135	151	2.3	6.6	.6		3.5
PIT	57	8	15	1379²	1406	9.2	71	432	557	12.2	3.46	109	.266	.324	49	50	100	106	.974	163	168	.5	5.0	4.3		1.2
NY	59	8	18	1349	1370	9.1	87	389	497	11.9	3.62	104	.261	.314	24	20	99	97	.973	168	147	.2	2.0	3.9		1.9
CIN	72	11	16	1362	1329	8.8	75	463	542	11.9	3.62	101	.254	.316	25	3	96	94	.971	172	133	-.1	.3	6.2		.6
BOS	83	15	12	1380	1375	9.0	66	465	413	12.2	3.40	101	.258	.322	58	3	91	103	.972	173	136	-.0	.3	-6.6		7.4
STL	58	10	16	1384²	1482	9.6	77	474	534	12.8	3.84	103	.272	.333	-9	17	104	102	.967	199	145	-1.4	1.7	1.4		-6.2
BRO	56	12	14	1332	1464	9.9	88	446	469	13.1	4.07	96	.278	.338	-42	-26	103	102	.973	157	148	.8	-2.6	-.3		-3.3
PHI	68	3	6	1329¹	1516	10.3	76	582	492	14.4	4.93	79	.285	.358	-169	-155	103	92	.966	201	135	-1.8	-15.6	-9.7		-2.9
TOT	520	83	115	10913¹		9.4				12.6	3.78		.267	.329					.972	1368	1163					

Runs
Ott-NY 116
Hack-Chi 109
Camilli-Bro 106
Goodman-Cin 103
Medwick-StL 100

Hits
McCormick-Cin . . . 209
Hack-Chi 195
L.Waner-Pit 194
Medwick-StL 190
Mize-StL 179

Doubles
Medwick-StL 47
McCormick-Cin . . . 40
Young-Pit 36
Martin-Phi 36

Triples
Mize-StL 16
Gutteridge-StL 15
Suhr-Pit 14
Riggs-Cin 13
Koy-Bro 13

Home Runs
Ott-NY 36
Goodman-Cin 30
Mize-StL 27
Camilli-Bro 24
Rizzo-Pit 23

Total Bases
Mize-StL 326
Medwick-StL 316
Ott-NY 307
Goodman-Cin 303
Rizzo-Pit 285

Runs Batted In
Medwick-StL 122
Ott-NY 116
Rizzo-Pit 111
McCormick-Cin . . . 106
Mize-StL 102

Runs Produced
Medwick-StL 201
Ott-NY 196
McCormick-Cin . . . 190
Rizzo-Pit 185
Camilli-Bro 182

Bases On Balls
Camilli-Bro 119
Ott-NY 118
Vaughan-Pit 104
Hack-Chi 94
Suhr-Pit 87

Batting Average
Lombardi-Cin 342
Mize-StL 337
McCormick-Cin 327
Medwick-StL 322
Vaughan-Pit 322

On Base Percentage
Ott-NY 442
Vaughan-Pit 433
Mize-StL 422
Hack-Chi 411
Suhr-Pit 394

Slugging Average
Mize-StL 614
Ott-NY 583
Medwick-StL 536
Goodman-Cin 533
Lombardi-Cin 524

Production
Mize-StL 1.036
Ott-NY 1.024
Lombardi-Cin 915
Medwick-StL 905
Goodman-Cin 901

Adjusted Production
Ott-NY 178
Mize-StL 172
Lombardi-Cin 154
Goodman-Cin 149
Vaughan-Pit 140

Batter Runs
Ott-NY 61.9
Mize-StL 59.2
Vaughan-Pit 36.4
Medwick-StL 34.4
Goodman-Cin 33.5

Adjusted Batter Runs
Ott-NY 60.8
Mize-StL 52.2
Goodman-Cin 36.4
Vaughan-Pit 35.6
Lombardi-Cin 34.4

Clutch Hitting Index
Durocher-Bro 140
McCormick-Cin . . . 134
Arnovich-Phi 128
Todd-Pit 127
Lavagetto-Bro 125

Runs Created
Ott-NY 149
Mize-StL 141
Hack-Chi 119
Goodman-Cin 116
Vaughan-Pit 115

Total Average
Ott-NY 1.164
Mize-StL 1.104
Camilli-Bro 964
Vaughan-Pit 960
Goodman-Cin 908

Stolen Bases
Hack-Chi 16
Lavagetto-Bro 15
Koy-Bro 15
Vaughan-Pit 14
Gutteridge-StL 14

Stolen Base Average

Stolen Base Runs

Fielding Runs
Young-Pit 31.8
Herman-Chi 24.8
Bartell-NY 22.4
Vaughan-Pit 18.3
Arnovich-Phi 16.7

Total Player Rating
Vaughan-Pit 6.4
Ott-NY 6.1
Lombardi-Cin 3.8
Goodman-Cin 3.7
Hack-Chi 3.6

Wins
Lee-Chi 22
Derringer-Cin 21
Bryant-Chi 19
Weiland-StL 16

Win Percentage
Lee-Chi 710
Bryant-Chi 633
Brown-Pit 625
VanderMeer-Cin 600
Derringer-Cin 600

Games
Coffman-NY 51
Brown-Pit 51
McGee-StL 47
Mulcahy-Phi 46

Complete Games
Derringer-Cin 26
Turner-Bos 22
Walters-Phi-Cin . . . 20
MacFayden-Bos . . . 19
Lee-Chi 19

Shutouts
Lee-Chi 9
MacFayden-Bos . . . 5
Warneke-StL 4
Derringer-Cin 4

Saves
Coffman-NY 12
Root-Chi 8
Hamlin-Bro 6
Errickson-Bos 6

Innings Pitched
Derringer-Cin 307.0
Lee-Chi 291.0
Bryant-Chi 270.1
Turner-Bos 268.0
Mulcahy-Phi 267.1

Fewest Hits/Game
VanderMeer-Cin . . 7.07
Bauers-Pit 7.67
Bryant-Chi 7.82
MacFayden-Bos . . 8.52
Klinger-Pit 8.59

Fewest BB/Game
Davis-StL 1.40
Derringer-Cin 1.44
Hubbell-NY 1.66
Root-Chi 1.68
Turner-Bos 1.81

Strikeouts
Bryant-Chi 135
Derringer-Cin 132
VanderMeer-Cin . . 125
Lee-Chi 121

Strikeouts/Game
Hubbell-NY 5.23
VanderMeer-Cin . . 4.99
Weiland-StL 4.61
Bryant-Chi 4.49

Ratio
Hubbell-NY 10.36
Derringer-Cin 10.67
Root-Chi 10.92
Turner-Bos 10.95
Lee-Chi 11.04

Earned Run Average
Lee-Chi 2.66
Root-Chi 2.86
Derringer-Cin 2.93
MacFayden-Bos . . .2.95
Klinger-Pit 2.99

Adjusted ERA
Lee-Chi 144
Root-Chi 134
Fitzsimmons-Bro . . 129
Klinger-Pit 127
Derringer-Cin 124

Opponents' Batting Avg.
VanderMeer-Cin . . .213
Bauers-Pit 233
Bryant-Chi 235
MacFayden-Bos . . .247
Schumacher-NY . . .248

Opponents' On Base Pct.
Hubbell-NY 285
Derringer-Cin 291
Root-Chi 294
Lohrman-NY 294
Schumacher-NY . . .299

Starter Runs
Lee-Chi 36.3
Derringer-Cin 29.1
Bryant-Chi 20.6
MacFayden-Bos . . 20.3
Bauers-Pit 19.2

Adjusted Starter Runs
Lee-Chi 37.6
Derringer-Cin 24.3
Bryant-Chi 21.8
Fitzsimmons-Bro . . 19.8
Bauers-Pit 19.4

Clutch Pitching Index
Lee-Chi 119
Pressnell-Bro 111
Blanton-Pit 111
Tamulis-Bro 110
Fette-Bos 110

Relief Runs
Brown-NY 19.8
Russell-Chi 5.0
Coffman-NY 3.8

Adjusted Relief Runs
Brown-NY 19.6
Russell-Chi 5.5
Coffman-NY 3.5

Relief Ranking
Brown-NY 18.1
Coffman-NY 4.3
Russell-Chi 3.7

Total Pitcher Index
Lee-Chi 4.0
Bryant-Chi 2.4
Derringer-Cin 2.4
Fitzsimmons-Bro . . 2.3
Bauers-Pit 2.1

Total Baseball Ranking
Vaughan-Pit 6.4
Ott-NY 6.1
Lee-Chi 4.0
Lombardi-Cin 3.8
Goodman-Cin 3.7

April 24 Goose Goslin's pinch-hit home run is the fifth of his career, for a new AL record, but the Yankees beat the Senators 4–3.

May 3 Robert "Lefty" Grove defeats the Tigers 4–3 in 10 innings for the first of a record 20 consecutive victories at his new home field, Fenway Park in Boston. He will not lose there until May 12, 1941.

May 30 The largest crowd in Yankee Stadium history, 83,533, sees Red Ruffing end Lefty Grove's eight-game winning streak in a 10–0 victory over the Red Sox. Six thousand fans are turned away, and 511 are given refunds because there is no place to sit. The Yankees also take the second game of the doubleheader, 5–4, in a game made famous for a fight between Yankee outfielder Jake Powell and Boston player-manager Joe Cronin.

June 16 Jimmie Foxx is walked a record six consecutive times by Browns pitchers, as the Red Sox win 12–8.

August 20 Lou Gehrig hits a first inning grand slam, the 23rd and last of his career for a still-standing record. It comes off Buck Ross of the A's.

August 24* Virgil Trucks strikes out his 418th batter—the highest season total in organized ball—for Andalusia in the Alabama-Florida League game.

August 27 Yankees pitcher Monte Pearson tosses a no-hitter in the second game of a doubleheader with Cleveland, winning his 10th straight game, 13–0. Joe DiMaggio knocks three triples in the first game of a doubleheader, an 8-7 win in New York. The Yankees, playing their sixth successive doubleheader, increase their AL lead to 12 games.

September 10 Jimmie Foxx of the Red Sox hits two home runs in a game for the ninth time this season, breaking a record held by Babe Ruth and Hack Wilson.

September 13 A special committee names Alexander Cartwright to Baseball's Hall of Fame for originating the sport's basic concepts. Henry Chadwick, inventor of the box score and the first baseball writer, is also honored.

October 2 Bob Feller sets a major league strikeout record by fanning 18 Tigers. At one point Feller has six straight strikeouts, yet loses 4-1 to Harry Eisenstat's four-hitter.

October 5 Bill Dickey ties a World Series record with four hits, as Red Ruffing pitches the Yankees to a 3-1 win in the Series opener at Wrigley Field.

October 9 The Yankees become the first team to win three successive World Championships, defeating the Cubs by a score of 8-3, as Red Ruffing wins his second game and the Yankees sweep.

November 2 Jimmie Foxx is voted MVP of the AL for the third time, with Yankees catcher Bill Dickey second in the voting.

November 6 The three DiMaggio brothers play together for the first time, making up an outfield for an all-star team in a West Coast charity game.

December 14 The major leagues agree on a standard ball. The NL grants Cincinnati its season opener a day before the rest of the league in recognition of baseball's 100th anniversary and the 1869 Red Stockings being the first professional team. The AL permits Cleveland and Philadelphia to play night games.

	BOSTON		CHICAGO		CLEVELAND		DETROIT		NEW YORK		PHILADELPHIA		ST.LOUIS		WASHINGTON
M	J.Cronin	M	J.Dykes	M	O.Vitt	M	M.Cochrane	M	J.McCarthy	M	C.Mack	M	G.Street	M	B.Harris
1B	J.Foxx	1B	J.Kuhel	1B	H.Trosky	M	D.Baker	1B	L.Gehrig	1B	L.Finney	M	S.Melillo	1B	Z.Bonura
2B	B.Doerr	2B	J.Hayes	2B	O.Hale	1B	H.Greenberg	2B	J.Gordon	2B	D.Lodigiani	1B	G.McQuinn	2B	B.Myer
SS	J.Cronin	SS	L.Appling	SS	L.Lary	2B	C.Gehringer	SS	F.Crosetti	SS	W.Ambler	2B	D.Heffner	SS	C.Travis
3B	P.Higgins	3B	M.Owen	SS	K.Keltner	SS	B.Rogell	3B	R.Rolfe	3B	B.Werber	SS	R.Kress	3B	B.Lewis
LF	J.Vosmik	LF	G.Walker	LF	J.Heath	3B	D.Ross	LF	G.Selkirk	LF	S.Chapman	3B	H.Clift	LF	A.Simmons
CF	D.Cramer	CF	M.Kreevich	CF	E.Averill	LF	D.Walker	CF	J.DiMaggio	CF	B.Johnson	LF	B.Mills	CF	S.West
RF	B.Chapman	RF	H.Steinbacher	RF	B.Campbell	CF	C.Morgan	RF	T.Henrich	RF	W.Moses	CF	M.Almada	RF	G.Case
C	G.Desautels	C	L.Sewell	C	F.Pytlak	RF	P.Fox	C	B.Dickey	C	F.Hayes	RF	B.Bell	C	R.Ferrell
						C	R.York					C	B.Sullivan		
C	J.Peacock	S2	B.Berger	O	R.Weatherly			O	M.Hoag	2	S.Sperry			O	T.Wright
O	R.Nonnenkamp	O1	R.Radcliff	C	R.Hemsley	3S	M.Christman	O	J.Powell	1	D.Siebert	O	M.Mazzera	O	J.Stone
S2	E.McNair	C	T.Rensa	O	M.Solters	O	C.Laabs	2	B.Knickerb'r	O	E.Brucker	C	T.Heath	O	M.Almada
3	J.Tabor	C	N.Schlueter	2	J.Kroner	O	J.White	C	J.Glenn	S	A.Parker	O	S.West	2S	O.Bluege
/C	M.Berg	O	L.Rosenthal	S	S.Webb	C	B.Tebbetts	/3	B.Dahlgren	O	H.Wagner	O	G.McQuillen	1	J.Wasdell
/O	F.Gaffke	2	J.Dykes	/C	H.Helf	3	T.Piet	/C	A.Jorgens	1	N.Etten	2	R.Hughes	C	T.Giuliani
		2	G.Meyer	/2	O.Grimes	O	R.Cullenbine			O	M.Haas	O	J.Grace	O	G.Goslin
P	J.Bagby	1	M.Connors	/S	T.Irwin	/C	R.Hayworth	P	R.Ruffing	1	G.Hasson	/O	E.Allen	/C	M.Livingston
P	J.Wilson	C	M.Tresh	/2	R.Mack	/2	B.McCoy	P	L.Gomez	S	S.Newsome	P	S.Harshany		
P	F.Ostermueller	/S	J.Gerlach	/O	C.Workman	H	G.Archie	P	M.Pearson	S	I.Bartling	/S	S.Gryska	P	D.Leonard
P	L.Grove	/1	T.Thompson	/3	L.Boudreau			P	S.Chandler	/O	B.Barna	/3	J.Lucadello	P	P.Appleton
P	E.Dickman	/2	J.Landrum	R	L.Russell	P	V.Kennedy	P	B.Hadley	/O	P.Easterling			P	K.Chase
RP	A.McKain	R	J.Martin			P	G.Gill	RP	J.Murphy	/S	R.Peters	P	B.Newsom	P	W.Ferrell
						P	E.Auker	RP	I.Andrews	/C	C.Berry	P	L.Mills	P	H.Kelley
P	J.Marcum	P	T.Lee	P	M.Harder	P	T.Bridges					P	O.Hildebrand	RP	C.Hogsett
P	J.Heving	P	T.Lyons	P	J.Allen	P	R.Lawson	P	S.Sundra	G.Caster	P	R.Van Atta		
P	B.Harris	P	M.Stratton	P	E.Whitehill	RP	S.Coffman	P	J.Beggs	P	B.Thomas	P	J.Walkup	P	M.Weaver
P	C.Wagner	P	J.Whitehead	P	W.Hudlin	RP	J.Wade	/P	W.Ferrell	P	L.Nelson	RP	E.Cole	P	J.DeShong
P	D.Midkiff	P	J.Rigney	RP	J.Humphries			/P	A.Donald	P	B.Ross	RP	B.Cox	P	J.Krakauskas
P	L.Rogers			RP	A.Milnar	P	H.Eisenstat	/P	J.Vance	E.Smith			/P	R.Monteagudo
/P	A.Baker	P	J.Knott			P	B.Poffenberger	/P	L.Stine		P	F.Johnson	/P	J.Kohlman
/P	T.Olson	P	F.Gabler	P	D.Galehouse	P	A.Benton	/P	K.Wicker	N.Potter	P	L.Tietje	/P	B.Phebus
/P	B.Lefebvre	/P	B.Dietrich	P	B.Zuber	/P	S.Rowe			A.Williams	P	E.Linke		
/P	B.Humphrey	P	H.Boyles	/P	K.Jungels	/P	B.Harris			D.Smith	/P	J.Knott		
		/P	S.Cain	/P	C.Smith	/P	J.Rogalski			C.Dean	P	J.Bonetti		
		/P	C.Brown	/P	J.Heving	/P	W.Davis			J.Reninger	/P	E.Bildilli		
		/P	G.Ford	/P	C.Suche					R.Gumpert	/P	V.Tamulis		
		/P	B.Cox							R.Buxton	/P	H.Kimberlin		
		/P	B.Uhl							H.Kelley	/P	B.Trotter		
		/P	G.Gick								/P	J.Weaver		
												/P	G.Liebhardt		

TEAM	G	W	L	PCT	GB	R	OR	AB	H	2B	3B	HR	BB	SO	AVG	OBP	SLG	PRO	PRO+	BR	/A	PF	CHI	RC	SB	CS	SBA	SBR
NY	157	99	53	.651		966	710	5410	1480	283	63	174	749	616	.274	.366	.446	.812	111	77	82	100	104	926	91	28	76	11
BOS	150	88	61	.591	9.5	902	751	5229	1566	298	56	98	650	463	.299	.378	.434	.812	105	87	46	105	100	881	55	51	52	-14
CLE	153	86	66	.566	13	847	782	5356	1506	300	89	113	550	605	.281	.350	.434	.784	104	9	26	98	102	832	83	36	70	3
DET	155	84	70	.545	16	862	795	5270	1434	219	52	137	693	581	.272	.359	.411	.770	94	0	-47	106	104	812	76	41	65	-2
WAS	152	75	76	.497	23.5	814	873	5474	1602	278	72	85	573	379	.293	.362	.416	.778	108	12	71	93	96	845	65	37	64	-3
CHI	149	65	83	.439	32	709	752	5199	1439	239	55	67	514	489	.277	.343	.383	.726	86	-91	-107	102	101	700	56	39	59	-7
STL	156	55	97	.362	44	755	962	5333	1498	273	36	92	590	528	.281	.355	.397	.752	95	-38	-36	100	96	774	51	40	56	-9
PHI	154	53	99	.349	46	726	956	5229	1410	243	62	98	605	590	.270	.348	.396	.744	95	-57	-37	97	97	741	65	53	55	-12
TOT	613					6581		42500	11935	2133	485	864	4924	4251	.281	.358	.415	.773							542	325	63	-32

TEAM	CG	SH	SV	IP	H	H/G	HR	BB	SO	RAT	ERA	ERA+	OAV	OOB	PR	/A	PF	CPI	FA	E	DP	FW	PW	BW	SBW	DIF
NY	91	11	13	1382	1436	9.4	85	566	567	13.1	3.91	116	.268	.339	134	95	95	106	.973	169	177	.5	8.6	7.4	1.4	5.2
BOS	67	10	15	1316¹	1472	10.1	102	528	484	13.8	4.46	111	.281	.349	48	70	103	103	.968	190	172	-1.1	6.3	4.2	-.9	5.1
CLE	68	5	17	1353	1416	9.4	100	681	717	14.1	4.60	101	.268	.355	29	7	97	99	.974	151	145	1.2	.6	2.3	.6	5.1
DET	75	3	11	1348¹	1532	10.2	110	608	435	14.4	4.79	104	.287	.361	1	32	104	103	.976	147	172	1.6	2.9	-4.2	.2	6.6
WAS	59	6	11	1360¹	1472	9.7	92	655	515	14.3	4.94	91	.276	.358	-22	-64	94	179	.970	180	179	-.5	-5.8	6.4	.0	-.8
CHI	83	5	9	1316¹	1449	9.9	101	550	432	13.8	4.36	112	.279	.350	62	78	102	106	.967	196	155	-1.6	7.0	-9.7	-.3	-4.6
STL	71	3	7	1344²	1584	10.6	132	737	632	15.7	5.80	86	.295	.382	-151	-124	104	96	.975	145	163	1.8	-11.2	-3.3	-.4	-7.9
PHI	56	4	12	1324	1573	10.7	142	599	473	14.9	5.48	88	.292	.365	-101	-95	101	96	.965	206	119	-1.8	-8.6	-3.3	-.7	-8.6
TOT	570	47	95	10745		10.0				14.3	4.79		.281	.358					.971	1384	1282					

Runs		Hits		Doubles		Triples		Home Runs		Total Bases	
Greenberg-Det	144	Vosmik-Bos	201	Cronin-Bos	51	Heath-Cle	18	Greenberg-Det	58	Foxx-Bos	398
Foxx-Bos	139	Cramer-Bos	198	McQuinn-StL	42	Averill-Cle	15	Foxx-Bos	50	Greenberg-Det	380
Gehringer-Det	133	Almada-Was-StL	197	Trosky-Cle	40	DiMaggio-NY	13	Clift-StL	34	DiMaggio-NY	348
Rolfe-NY	132	Foxx-Bos	197	Chapman-Bos	40			York-Det	33	Johnson-Phi	311
DiMaggio-NY	129	Rolfe-NY	196	Vosmik-Bos	37			DiMaggio-NY	32	Heath-Cle	302

Runs Batted In		Runs Produced		Bases On Balls		Batting Average		On Base Percentage		Slugging Average	
Foxx-Bos	175	Foxx-Bos	264	Greenberg-Det	119	Foxx-Bos	.349	Foxx-Bos	.462	Foxx-Bos	.704
Greenberg-Det	146	DiMaggio-NY	237	Foxx-Bos	119	Heath-Cle	.343	Myer-Was	.454	Greenberg-Det	.683
DiMaggio-NY	140	Greenberg-Det	232	Clift-StL	118	Chapman-Bos	.340	Greenberg-Det	.438	Heath-Cle	.602
York-Det	127	Gehringer-Det	220	Gehringer-Det	113	Myer-Was	.336	Averill-Cle	.429	DiMaggio-NY	.581
Clift-StL	118	Clift-StL	203	Gehrig-NY	107	Travis-Was	.335	Cronin-Bos	.428	York-Det	.579

Production		Adjusted Production		Batter Runs		Adjusted Batter Runs		Clutch Hitting Index		Runs Created	
Foxx-Bos	1.166	Foxx-Bos	180	Foxx-Bos	78.2	Foxx-Bos	70.4	Higgins-Bos	140	Foxx-Bos	189
Greenberg-Det	1.122	Greenberg-Det	167	Greenberg-Det	66.0	Greenberg-Det	57.1	Heffner-StL	138	Greenberg-Det	172
York-Det	.995	Heath-Cle	146	Clift-StL	37.7	Clift-StL	38.0	R.Ferrell-Was	116	DiMaggio-NY	136
Heath-Cle	.985	Dickey-NY	144	Cronin-Bos	34.8	Johnson-Phi	35.8	Doerr-Bos	116	Clift-StL	133
Dickey-NY	.981	Clift-StL	143	York-Det	33.9	Averill-Cle	33.9	Bonura-Was	111	Gehrig-NY	131

Total Average		Stolen Bases		Stolen Base Average		Stolen Base Runs		Fielding Runs		Total Player Rating	
Foxx-Bos	1.392	Crosetti-NY	27	Lary-Cle	79.3	Gehringer-Det	3.6	Gordon-NY	23.7	Foxx-Bos	5.2
Greenberg-Det	1.306	Lary-Cle	23	Fox-Det	69.6	Rolfe-NY	3.3	Crosetti-NY	17.6	Clift-StL	4.8
Clift-StL	1.104	Werber-Phi	19	Crosetti-NY	69.2	Lary-Cle	3.3	Clift-StL	14.0	Cronin-Bos	4.2
York-Det	1.104	Lewis-Was	17	Lewis-Was	65.4	Hale-Cle	1.8	Johnson-Phi	10.3	Greenberg-Det	4.0
Dickey-NY	1.083	Fox-Det	16	Werber-Phi	55.9			Cramer-Bos	8.7	Dickey-NY	3.7

Wins		Win Percentage		Games		Complete Games		Shutouts		Saves	
Ruffing-NY	21	Ruffing-NY	.750	Humphries-Cle	45	Newsom-StL	31	Gomez-NY	4	Murphy-NY	11
Newsom-StL	20	Pearson-NY	.696	Newsom-StL	44	Ruffing-NY	22	Wilson-Bos	3	McKain-Bos	6
Gomez-NY	18	Harder-Cle	.630	E.Smith-Phi	43	Gomez-NY	20	Ruffing-NY	3	Humphries-Cle	6
Harder-Cle	17	Stratton-Chi	.625	Bagby-Bos	43	Feller-Cle	20	Leonard-Was	3	Potter-Phi	5
Feller-Cle	17	Feller-Cle	.607	Appleton-Was	43	Caster-Phi	20			Appleton-Was	5

Innings Pitched		Fewest Hits/Game		Fewest BB/Game		Strikeouts		Strikeouts/Game		Ratio	
Newsom-StL	329.2	Feller-Cle	7.29	Leonard-Was	2.14	Feller-Cle	240	Feller-Cle	7.78	Leonard-Was	11.32
Caster-Phi	281.1	Allen-Cle	8.51	Harder-Cle	2.33	Newsom-StL	226	Newsom-StL	6.17	Ruffing-NY	11.94
Feller-Cle	277.2	Pearson-NY	8.82	Lyons-Chi	2.40	L.Mills-StL	134	L.Mills-StL	5.73	Stratton-Chi	12.03
Ruffing-NY	247.1	Rigney-Chi	8.84	Chandler-NY	2.46	Gomez-NY	129	Grove-Bos	5.44	Chandler-NY	12.14
Lee-Chi	245.1	Hadley-NY	8.87	Thomas-Phi	2.63	Ruffing-NY	127	Allen-Cle	5.04	Harder-Cle	12.15

Earned Run Average		Adjusted ERA		Opponents' Batting Avg.		Opponents' On Base Pct.		Starter Runs		Adjusted Starter Runs	
Grove-Bos	3.08	Grove-Bos	160	Feller-Cle	.220	Leonard-Was	.305	Ruffing-NY	40.6	Lee-Chi	38.4
Ruffing-NY	3.31	Lee-Chi	140	Allen-Cle	.246	Stratton-Chi	.315	Gomez-NY	38.2	Grove-Bos	33.7
Gomez-NY	3.35	Rigney-Chi	138	Hadley-NY	.254	Ruffing-NY	.317	Lee-Chi	35.6	Ruffing-NY	33.6
Leonard-Was	3.43	Ruffing-NY	137	Stratton-Chi	.255	Harder-Cle	.319	Leonard-Was	33.8	Gomez-NY	31.4
Lee-Chi	3.49	Gomez-NY	135	Rigney-Chi	.256	Grove-Bos	.319	Grove-Bos	31.1	Leonard-Was	27.0

Clutch Pitching Index		Relief Runs		Adjusted Relief Runs		Relief Ranking		Total Pitcher Index		Total Baseball Ranking	
Lyons-Chi	125	Murphy-NY	5.6	McKain-Bos	4.6	McKain-Bos	4.4	Ruffing-NY	4.0	Foxx-Bos	5.2
Gill-Det	119	McKain-Bos	3.0	Murphy-NY	3.0	Murphy-NY	3.8	Lee-Chi	3.8	Clift-StL	4.8
Grove-Bos	118							Gomez-NY	3.3	Cronin-Bos	4.2
Rigney-Chi	117							Leonard-Was	3.1	Greenberg-Det	4.0
Ruffing-NY	110							Grove-Bos	3.1	Ruffing-NY	4.0

January 24 George Sisler, Eddie Collins, and Willie Keeler are elected to the Baseball Hall of Fame by the BBWAA.

May 14 Making his first appearance since elbow surgery in August 1938, Carl Hubbell pitches New York to a 2–1 win over the Phillies. Catcher Ken O'Dea hits a 10th inning home run to win it for King Carl.

May 17* The first baseball game ever televised, Princeton against Columbia at Baker Field, Columbia's home field, is seen by a handful of viewers via W2XBS in New York City. Bill Stern announces, as Princeton wins 2-1 in 10 innings. The second game of the doubleheader is not televised. Reviewing the game the next day, the *New York Times* sniffs, "it is difficult to see how this sort of thing can catch the public fancy."

June 6 At the Polo Grounds, the Giants unload on the Reds with five home runs in the fourth inning. Harry Danning and Frank Demaree hit homers, and then, with two out, Burgess Whitehead, pitcher Frank Salvo and Joe Moore hit successive shots. Clouts by Mel Ott and another by Moore give New York seven home runs for the day, as they coast to a 17–3 win.

June 12 The greatest gathering of members and future inductees of the Baseball Hall of Fame assembles in Cooperstown, NY, for the dedication of the museum. A six-inning game at Doubleday Field presents lineups studded with players who will be elected in the future, as Babe Ruth, Ty Cobb, Honus Wagner, Walter Johnson, Grover Alexander, Nap Lajoie, George Sisler, Eddie Collins, Tris Speaker, Cy Young, and Connie Mack accept their plaques.

July 15 A disputed call on a flyball down the left field foul line at the Polo Grounds touches off a melee in which the Giants Billy Jurges and umpire George Magerkurth spit at each other. Both will be fined $150 and suspended for 10 days. NL President Ford Frick announces that two-foot screens are to be installed inside all foul poles to prevent future arguments. The AL eventually also adopts the rule.

August 13 The Giants hit three successive home runs in the fourth inning, with Joe Moore, Alex Kampouris, and pitcher Bill Lohrman connecting. The Giants add four more home runs in the game to beat the Phils, 11–2. Pitcher Bill Kersieck gives up six of the 11 runs, including all of the runs scored in the fourth.

August 16 The Giants suspend second baseman Burgess Whitehead, who will show up the next day in full uniform at Yankee Stadium and ask to work out. Yankee manager Joe McCarthy refuses. Whitehead rejoins the Giants a few days later, but he will be suspended again in mid-September after leaving the team.

August 26 The first major league baseball game is telecast from Ebbets Field as the Reds play the Dodgers in a doubleheader. Red Barber broadcasts the game over W2XBS. The Dodgers take the first game 6-2, and the Reds take the second 5-1.

September 21 The NL announces that for the first time in the twentieth century, games will be transferred from one city to another. The Dodgers' doubleheader in Philadelphia will be moved to Brooklyn in an effort to top one million paid attendance.

September 28 Cincinnati clinches the pennant with Paul Derringer defeating second-place St. Louis 5-3.

October 17 Bucky Walters is voted league MVP by the BBWAA, with Johnny Mize second.

	BOSTON		BROOKLYN		CHICAGO		CINCINNATI		NEW YORK		PHILADELPHIA		PITTSBURGH		ST.LOUIS
M	C.Stengel	M	L.Durocher	M	G.Hartnett	M	B.McKechnie	M	B.Terry	M	D.Prothro	M	P.Traynor	M	R.Blades
1B	B.Hassett	1B	D.Camilli	1B	R.Russell	1B	F.McCormick	1B	Z.Bonura	1B	G.Suhr	1B	E.Fletcher	1B	J.Mize
2B	T.Cuccinello	2B	P.Coscarart	2B	B.Herman	2B	L.Frey	2B	B.Whitehead	2B	R.Hughes	2B	P.Young	2B	S.Martin
SS	E.Miller	SS	L.Durocher	SS	D.Bartell	SS	B.Myers	SS	B.Jurges	SS	G.Scharein	SS	A.Vaughan	SS	J.Brown
3B	H.Majeski	3B	C.Lavagetto	3B	S.Hack	3B	B.Werber	3B	T.Hafey	3B	P.May	3B	L.Handley	3B	D.Gutteridge
LF	M.West	LF	E.Koy	LF	A.Galan	LF	W.Berger	LF	J.Moore	LF	M.Arnovich	LF	J.Rizzo	LF	J.Medwick
CF	J.Cooney	CF	D.Walker	CF	H.Leiber	CF	H.Craft	CF	F.Demaree	CF	H.Martin	CF	L.Waner	CF	T.Moore
RF	D.Garms	RF	G.Moore	RF	J.Gleeson	RF	I.Goodman	RF	M.Ott	RF	L.Scott	RF	P.Waner	RF	E.Slaughter
C	A.Lopez	C	B.Phelps	C	G.Hartnett	C	E.Lombardi	C	H.Danning	C	S.Davis	C	R.Mueller	C	M.Owen
O	A.Simmons	S2	J.Hudson	O	C.Reynolds	O	L.Gamble	O1	A.Kampouris	23	G.Brack	O3	P.Martin
S2	R.Warstler	C	A.Todd	O	G.Mancuso	O	W.Hershberger	23	B.Seeds	O	H.Mueller	O	C.Klein	O	D.Padgett
23	S.Sisti	O	A.Parks	O	B.Nicholson	3	N.Bongiovanni	O	L.Chiozza	O	J.Marty	O	F.Bell	S3	L.Myers
O	J.Outlaw	S	T.Stainback	S	B.Mattick	2	E.Joost	S2	J.Ripple	D.Young	C	R.Berres	O	L.King
C	P.Masi	O	G.Rosen	O	J.Marty	C	F.Bordagaray	C	K.O'Dea	1	J.Bolling	1	G.Suhr	S	L.Lary
1	E.Fletcher	1	M.Almada	3	P.Cavaretta	3	L.Riggs	1	J.McCarthy	C	W.Millies	O	B.Elliott	/2	C.Crespi
S	W.Wietelmann	O	J.Ripple	S	S.Mesner	/O	A.Simmons	1	B.Young	1	P.Whitney	O	M.Van Robays	/1	H.Franks
O	B.Rowell	C	F.Sington	C	B.Garbark	/O	D.West	3	G.Myatt	O	B.Bates	3	G.Susce	/C	H.Bremer
/O	R.Hodgin	2	T.Lazzeri			/O	V.DiMaggio	3	T.Lazzeri	C	B.Warren	2	F.Gustine	/2	B.Repass
/O	C.Ross	S	L.Lary	P	B.Lee	H	L.Scarsella	O	J.Dickshot	1	L.Powers	2	R.Juelich	/1	J.Hopp
C	S.Andrews	S	R.Hayworth	P	C.Passeau	/O	B.Hafey	2	A.Glossop	/O	B.Hafey	/C	J.Schultz	/S	E.Lake
/O	C.Clemens	/C	C.Hartje	P	L.French	/1	M.Galatzer	/S	S.Scalzi	/O	S.Benjamin	/O	W.Jensen	/S	J.Orengo
/2	O.Huber	/O	O.Hockett	P	C.Root	/S	N.Richardson	/C	R.Hayworth	C.Klein	/O	H.Manush	H	B.Adams
/S	R.Barkley	/O	L.Deal	P	V.Page	/C	J.Wilson			2	C.Letchas	H	E.Yount	R	J.Echols
/S	B.Schuster	R	G.Schott	RP	J.Russell			P	H.Gumbert	/2	J.Shilling				
H	O.Hill			RP	G.Lillard	P	B.Walters	P	C.Melton	C	D.Coble	P	B.Klinger	P	C.Davis
		P	L.Hamlin			P	P.Derringer	P	B.Lohrman	P	E.Feinberg	P	M.Brown	P	M.Cooper
P	B.Posedel	P	H.Casey	P	D.Dean	P	W.Moore	H.Schumacher	/1	L.Gabrielson	P	J.Bowman	P	B.Bowman
P	D.MacFayden	P	V.Tamulis	P	E.Whitehill	P	L.Grissom	P	C.Hubbell	/C	B.Atwood	P	R.Sewell	P	L.Warneke
P	J.Turner	P	T.Pressnell	/P	C.Bryant	P	J.Thompson	RP	J.Brown	/1	J.Watwood	P	J.Tobin	P	B.McGee
P	L.Fette	P	F.Fitzsimmons	/P	K.Higbe			RP	R.Lynn	/C	J.Kracher			RP	C.Shoun
P	M.Shoffner	RP	I.Hutchinson	/P	R.Harrell	P	J.Vander Meer					P	B.Swift		
		RP	R.Evans	/P	V.Olsen	P	J.Niggeling	P	M.Salvo	P	H.Mulcahy	P	M.Butcher	P	B.Weiland
P	J.Lanning					P	J.Shoffner	P	D.Coffman	P	K.Higbe	P	R.Bauers	P	T.Sunkel
P	D.Errickson	P	W.Wyatt			P	P.Davis	P	S.Castleman	P	B.Beck	P	C.Blanton	P	P.Dean
P	J.Sullivan	P	V.Mungo			P	H.Johnson	/P	J.Wittig	P	I.Pearson	P	K.Heintzelman	/P	M.Lanier
P	T.Earley	/P	B.Crouch			P	W.Livengood	/P	H.Vandenberg	P	S.Johnson	P	B.Clemensen	P	N.Andrews
P	F.Frankhouse	/P	A.Hollingsworth			/P	R.Barrett	/P	T.Gorman	RP	B.Kerksieck	/P	O.Swigart	/P	M.Dickson
/P	H.Moran	/P	C.Doyle			/P	P.Naktenis					/P	J.Gee	/P	F.Barrett
/P	G.Barnicle	/P	B.Poffenberger			/P	J.Weaver			P	M.Butcher	/P	P.Rambert	/P	K.Raffensberger
/P	J.Callahan	/P	G.Jeffcoat			/P	E.Riddle			P	R.Harrell				
/P	A.Veigel					/P	A.Jacobs			P	A.Hollingsworth				
/P	R.Weir									P	C.Passeau				
										P	J.Poindexter				
										/P	R.Bruner				
										/P	J.Henry				
										/P	G.Schott				
										/P	A.Smith				
										/P	E.Burkart				
										/P	B.Hoffman				

TEAM	G	W	L	PCT	GB	R	OR	AB	H	2B	3B	HR	BB	SO	AVG	OBP	SLG	PRO	PRO+	BR	/A	PF	CHI	RC	SB	CS	SBA	SBR
CIN	156	97	57	.630		767	595	5378	1493	269	60	98	500	538	.278	.343	.405	.748	106	51	47	101	102	759	46			
STL	155	92	61	.601	4.5	779	633	5447	1601	332	62	98	475	566	.294	.354	.432	.786	110	122	72	106	94	834	44			
BRO	157	84	69	.549	12.5	708	645	5350	1420	265	57	78	564	639	.265	.338	.380	.718	96	0	-25	104	102	697	59			
CHI	156	84	70	.545	13	724	678	5293	1407	263	62	91	523	553	.266	.336	.391	.727	99	10	-2	102	103	702	61			
NY	151	77	74	.510	18.5	703	685	5129	1395	211	38	116	498	499	.272	.340	.396	.736	103	28	22	101	101	683	26			
PIT	153	68	85	.444	28.5	666	721	5269	1453	261	60	63	477	420	.276	.338	.384	.722	102	4	15	98	97	687	44			
BOS	152	63	88	.417	32.5	572	659	5286	1395	199	39	56	366	494	.264	.314	.348	.662	91	-117	-78	93	104	575	41			
PHI	152	45	106	.298	50.5	553	856	5133	1341	232	40	49	421	486	.261	.318	.351	.669	89	-98	-82	97	99	570	47			
TOT	616					5472		42285	11505	2032	418	649	3824	4195	.272	.335	.386	.721						368				

TEAM	CG	SH	SV	IP	H	H/G	HR	BB	SO	RAT	ERA	ERA+	OAV	OOB	PR	/A	PF	CPI	FA	E	DP	FW	PW	BW	SBW	DIF
CIN	86	13	9	1403²	1340	8.6	81	499	637	12.0	3.27	117	.255	.322	101	87	98	107	.974	162	170	.6	8.7	4.7		6.0
STL	45	18	32	1384²	1377	9.0	76	498	603	12.3	3.59	115	.260	.326	50	80	105	100	.971	177	140	-.2	8.0	7.2		.5
BRO	69	9	13	1410¹	1431	9.1	93	399	528	11.9	3.64	110	.263	.317	43	60	103	97	.972	176	157	-.0	6.0	-2.5		4.0
CHI	72	8	13	1392¹	1504	9.7	74	430	584	12.6	3.80	104	.276	.331	18	21	101	101	.970	186	126	-.6	2.1	-.2		5.7
NY	55	6	20	1319	1412	9.6	86	477	505	13.1	4.07	96	.275	.340	-22	-20	100	100	.975	153	151	.8	-2.0	2.2		.5
PIT	53	10	15	1354	1537	10.2	70	423	464	13.2	4.15	92	.287	.342	-36	-49	98	100	.972	168	153	.1	-4.9	1.5		-5.2
BOS	68	11	15	1358¹	1400	9.3	63	513	430	12.8	3.71	101	.271	.339	31	-3	94	104	.971	181	178	-.6	-.3	-7.8		-3.8
PHI	67	3	12	1326²	1502	10.2	106	579	447	14.4	5.17	77	.289	.365	-185	-171	102	93	.970	171	136	-.0	-17.1	-8.2		-5.1
TOT	515	78	129	10949		9.5				12.8	3.92		.272	.335					.972	1374	1211					

Runs
Werber-Cin 115
Hack-Chi 112
Herman-Chi 111
Camilli-Bro 105

Hits
McCormick-Cin 209
Medwick-StL 201
Mize-StL 197
Slaughter-StL 193
Brown-StL 192

Doubles
Slaughter-StL 52
Medwick-StL 48
Mize-StL 44
McCormick-Cin 41

Triples
Herman-Chi 18
Goodman-Cin 16
Mize-StL 14
Camilli-Bro 12

Home Runs
Mize-StL 28
Ott-NY 27
Camilli-Bro 26
Leiber-Chi 24
Lombardi-Cin 20

Total Bases
Mize-StL 353
McCormick-Cin . . . 312
Medwick-StL 307
Camilli-Bro 296
Slaughter-StL 291

Runs Batted In
McCormick-Cin . . . 128
Medwick-StL . . . 117
Mize-StL 108
Camilli-Bro 104
Leiber-Chi 88

Runs Produced
McCormick-Cin 209
Medwick-StL 201
Mize-StL 184
Camilli-Bro 183
Herman-Chi 174

Bases On Balls
Camilli-Bro 110
Ott-NY 100
Mize-StL 92
Werber-Cin 91
Lavagetto-Bro 78

Batting Average
Mize-StL 349
McCormick-Cin 332
Medwick-StL 332
P.Waner-Pit 328
Arnovich-Phi 324

On Base Percentage
Ott-NY 449
Mize-StL 444
Camilli-Bro 409
Goodman-Cin 401
Arnovich-Phi 397

Slugging Average
Mize-StL 626
Ott-NY 581
Leiber-Chi 556
Camilli-Bro 524
Goodman-Cin 515

Production
Mize-StL 1.070
Ott-NY 1.030
Camilli-Bro 933
Goodman-Cin 916
Medwick-StL 886

Adjusted Production
Mize-StL 174
Ott-NY 173
Camilli-Bro 144
Goodman-Cin 144
West-Bos 139

Batter Runs
Mize-StL 68.7
Ott-NY 45.9
Camilli-Bro 41.8
Leiber-Chi 30.5
Goodman-Cin 29.8

Adjusted Batter Runs
Mize-StL 60.0
Ott-NY 45.1
Camilli-Bro 37.6
Goodman-Cin 29.4
Leiber-Chi 29.1

Clutch Hitting Index
May-Phi 120
Lavagetto-Bro 116
McCormick-Cin 116
R.Russell-Chi 116
Bonura-NY 113

Runs Created
Mize-StL 162
Camilli-Bro 128
Medwick-StL 114
Ott-NY 112
McCormick-Cin 110

Total Average
Mize-StL 1.194
Ott-NY 1.194
Camilli-Bro 995
Goodman-Cin 941
Frey-Cin 860

Stolen Bases
Handley-Pit 17
Hack-Chi 17
Werber-Cin 15
Lavagetto-Bro 14
Hassett-Bos 13

Stolen Base Average

Stolen Base Runs

Fielding Runs
Slaughter-StL 15.8
Frey-Cin 15.1
Arnovich-Phi 14.9
Jurges-NY 14.9
Werber-Cin 12.6

Total Player Rating
Frey-Cin 4.0
Mize-StL 3.9
Vaughan-Pit 3.9
Ott-NY 3.6
Goodman-Cin 3.1

Wins
Walters-Cin 27
Derringer-Cin 25
Davis-StL 22
Hamlin-Bro 20
Lee-Chi 19

Win Percentage
Derringer-Cin 781
Walters-Cin 711
French-Chi 652
Gumbert-NY 621
Hamlin-Bro 606

Games
Shoun-StL 53
Sewell-Pit 52
Bowman-StL 51
Davis-StL 49
Brown-Pit 47

Complete Games
Walters-Cin 31
Derringer-Cin 28
Lee-Chi 20
Hamlin-Bro 19
Posedel-Bos 18

Shutouts
Fette-Bos 6
Posedel-Bos 5
Derringer-Cin 5
McGee-StL 4

Saves
Shoun-StL 9
Bowman-StL 9
Davis-StL 7
Brown-NY 7
Brown-Pit 7

Innings Pitched
Walters-Cin 319.0
Derringer-Cin 301.0
Lee-Chi 282.1
Passeau-Phi-Chi . 274.1
Hamlin-Bro 269.2

Fewest Hits/Game
Walters-Cin 7.05
Bowman-StL 7.49
Moore-Cin 8.49
Hamlin-Bro 8.51
Hubbell-NY 8.77

Fewest BB/Game
Derringer-Cin 1.05
Hubbell-NY 1.40
Davis-StL 1.74
Hamlin-Bro 1.80
Root-Chi 1.83

Strikeouts
Passeau-Phi-Chi . . 137
Walters-Cin 137
Cooper-StL 130
Derringer-Cin 128
Lee-Chi 105

Strikeouts/Game
Cooper-StL 5.55
Tamulis-Bro 4.71
French-Chi 4.55
Passeau-Phi-Chi . . 4.49
Bowman-StL 4.15

Ratio
Hubbell-NY 10.29
Walters-Cin 10.30
Hamlin-Bro 10.31
Derringer-Cin 10.73
Bowman-StL 10.74

Earned Run Average
Walters-Cin 2.29
Bowman-StL 2.60
Hubbell-NY 2.75
Casey-Bro 2.93
Derringer-Cin 2.93

Adjusted ERA
Walters-Cin 168
Bowman-StL 158
Hubbell-NY 143
Casey-Bro 137
Derringer-Cin 131

Opponents' Batting Avg.
Walters-Cin 220
Bowman-StL 232
Hamlin-Bro 248
Hubbell-NY 249
Moore-Cin 254

Opponents' On Base Pct.
Hubbell-NY 280
Hamlin-Bro 285
Walters-Cin 291
Derringer-Cin 295
Bowman-StL 302

Starter Runs
Walters-Cin 57.8
Derringer-Cin 33.0
Casey-Bro 24.9
Bowman-StL 24.7
Thompson-Cin . . . 23.3

Adjusted Starter Runs
Walters-Cin 54.7
Derringer-Cin 30.1
Bowman-StL 28.4
Casey-Bro 27.7
Thompson-Cin . . . 21.8

Clutch Pitching Index
Brown-Pit 120
Shoffner-Bos-Cin . . 115
Casey-Bro 113
Cooper-StL 113
Moore-Cin 113

Relief Runs
J.Russell-Chi 1.9
Shoun-StL 1.8

Adjusted Relief Runs
Shoun-StL 4.1
J.Russell-Chi 2.0

Relief Ranking
Shoun-StL 2.2
J.Russell-Chi 2.1

Total Pitcher Index
Walters-Cin 8.5
Davis-StL 3.3
Casey-Bro 3.1
Bowman-StL 2.7
Derringer-Cin 2.7

Total Baseball Ranking
Walters-Cin 8.5
Frey-Cin 4.0
Mize-StL 3.9
Vaughan-Pit 3.9
Ott-NY 3.6

January 13 Yankee owner Colonel Jacob Ruppert dies. Ed Barrow will be elected president to succeed Colonel Ruppert on Jan. 17.

April 20 The Red Sox show off rookie Ted Williams in the opener in New York. After striking out twice, he collects a double off Red Ruffing, who wins 2-0. Gehrig goes hitless in the only game featuring the two great sluggers. Other notables in what will become a historic box score include Joe DiMaggio, Bill Dickey, Jimmie Foxx, Joe Cronin, Bobby Doerr, and Lefty Grove.

May 2 Lou Gehrig voluntarily benches himself "for the good of the team." His consecutive-game string stops at 2,130. Elsworth "Babe" Dahlgren, his replacement, has a home run and double as the Yankees rout Detroit 22-2.

May 16 The first AL night game is played at Shibe Park, with Cleveland beating the A's 8-3 in 10 innings.

June 21 The New York Yankees announce Lou Gehrig's retirement, based on the report that he has amyotrophic lateral sclerosis. The 36-year-old star will remain with the team as captain despite his illness.

June 28 The Yankees hit eight home runs in the first game of a doubleheader with the A's, and five more in the nightcap. Both are major league records, as is the 53 total bases in a doubleheader. Joe DiMaggio, Babe Dahlgren, and Joe Gordon each hit three home runs. The Yankees win the opener, 23–2, and take the nightcap, 10–0.

July 4 A tearful Lou Gehrig tells 61,808 fans at Yankee Stadium, "I consider myself the luckiest man on the face of the earth." Gehrig's uniform number 4 is retired. He is the first major league player so honored.

July 11 With another Yankee-dominated lineup, the AL defeats the NL 3–1 in the seventh All-Star Game, at Yankee Stadium. Cincinnati outfielder Ival Goodman fractures his shoulder diving for a ball.

September 16 The New York Yankees clinch their fourth successive pennant with a win over Detroit.

September 27 The hometown Chicago White Sox play the first "day-night" doubleheader against Cleveland, but lose both games, 5-2 and 7-5. Fans are charged separate admissions for each game.

October 4 The World Series, with the Yankees as heavy favorites, begins in New York. The pitching of Red Ruffing for New York and Paul Derringer for Cincinnati produces a tense, low-scoring duel that is tied 1-1 until the last of the ninth, when Yankees catcher Bill Dickey singles home the winning run.

October 8 In the 10th inning of Game 4, the Reds make three errors and watch in shock as the Yankees run wild. The inning is climaxed by Joe DiMaggio's slide across the plate left unguarded by Ernie Lombardi, who was stunned by a kick in the groin from the preceding runner, Charlie Keller. The Yankees sweep the Reds and win their fourth straight world championship.

October 24 The league MVP is Joe DiMaggio, with Jimmie Foxx the runner-up, in the BBWAA poll.

December 7 Lou Gehrig, age 36, is elected to Baseball's Hall of Fame.

BOSTON	CHICAGO	CLEVELAND	DETROIT	NEW YORK	PHILADELPHIA	ST.LOUIS	WASHINGTON
M J.Cronin	M J.Dykes	M O.Vitt	M D.Baker	M J.McCarthy	M C.Mack	M F.Haney	M B.Harris
1B J.Foxx	1B J.Kuhel	1B H.Trosky	1B H.Greenberg	1B B.Dahlgren	M E.Mack	1B G.McQuinn	1B M.Vernon
2B B.Doerr	2B O.Bejma	2B O.Hale	2B C.Gehringer	2B J.Gordon	1B D.Siebert	2B J.Berardino	2B J.Bloodworth
SS J.Cronin	SS L.Appling	SS S.Webb	SS F.Croucher	SS F.Crosetti	2B J.Gantenbein	SS D.Heffner	SS C.Travis
3B J.Tabor	3B E.McNair	3B K.Keltner	3B P.Higgins	3B R.Rolfe	SS S.Newsome	3B H.Clift	3B B.Lewis
LF J.Vosmik	LF G.Walker	LF J.Heath	LF E.Averill	LF G.Selkirk	3B D.Lodigiani	LF J.Gallagher	LF T.Wright
CF D.Cramer	CF M.Kreevich	CF B.Chapman	CF B.McCosky	CF J.DiMaggio	LF B.Johnson	CF C.Laabs	CF S.West
RF T.Williams	RF L.Rosenthal	RF B.Campbell	RF P.Fox	RF C.Keller	CF S.Chapman	RF M.Hoag	RF G.Case
C J.Peacock	C M.Tresh	C R.Hemsley	C B.Tebbetts	C B.Dickey	RF W.Moses	C J.Glenn	C R.Ferrell
1O L.Finney	O1 R.Radcliff	21 O.Grimes	C1 R.York	O T.Henrich	C F.Hayes	OC B.Sullivan	O B.Estalella
C G.Desautels	2 J.Hayes	O R.Weatherly	2S B.McCoy	C B.Rosar	S2 W.Ambler	S M.Christman	2 B.Myer
2S T.Carey	3 M.Owen	S L.Boudreau	O R.Cullenbine	O J.Powell	O D.Miles	O J.Grace	O J.Welaj
O R.Nonnenkamp	O H.Steinbacher	O F.Pytlak	S3 B.Rogell	23 J.Gallagher	O B.Nagel	O S.Harshany	S3 C.Gelbert
C M.Berg	C K.Silvestri	2 R.Mack	S2 R.Kress	/1 L.Gehrig	C E.Brucker	O M.Almada	C T.Giuliani
S B.Berger	C N.Schlueter	O M.Solters	O D.Walker	/2 B.Knickerb'r	O E.Tipton	C M.Solters	1 J.Wasdell
H F.Gaffke	C T.Rensa	2 J.Shilling	O B.Bell	/C A.Jorgens	3 A.Brancato	C H.Spindel	1 B.Prichard
P L.Grove	/3 B.Kennedy	O E.Averill	/3 M.Christman	P R.Ruffing	S F.Chapman	O M.Mazzera	C J.Early
P J.Wilson	/3 J.Gerlach	C L.Sewell	/O L.Fleming	/O L.Gomez	P L.Finney	S T.Thompson	1 O.Bluege
P F.Ostermueller	/3 J.Dykes	/S L.Lary	/O C.Laabs	/O B.Hadley	P E.Collins	S S.Gryska	S H.Quick
P E.Auker	H T.Thompson	P B.Feller	/C M.Shea	P A.Donald	/S B.Lillard	S R.Kress	/2 E.Leip
P D.Galehouse	P T.Lee	P A.Milnar	/C D.Parsons	P M.Pearson	/O B.McNamara	/O B.Bell	/2 M.Aderholt
RP E.Dickman	P J.Rigney	P M.Harder	P B.Newsom	RP J.Murphy	/C H.Wagner	/2 J.Lucadello	/C A.Evans
RP J.Heving	P E.Smith	P J.Allen	P T.Bridges	P O.Hildebrand	/C H.O'Neill	/2 R.Hughes	/O E.Gedeon
RP J.Wade	P T.Lyons	P W.Hudlin	P S.Rowe	P S.Sundra	P L.Nelson	/S B.Neighbors	/O B.Loane
P J.Bagby	RP J.Knott	RP J.Dobson	P D.Trout	P M.Russo	P N.Potter	H E.Silber	/O A.Pitko
P W.Rich	RP C.Brown	P H.Eisenstat	P A.Benton	P S.Chandler	P B.Ross	P J.Kramer	P D.Leonard
/P C.Wagner	P B.Dietrich	P J.Broaca	RP B.Thomas	/P W.Ferrell	P B.Beckmann	P V.Kennedy	P K.Chase
/P B.Lefebvre	P J.Marcum	P B.Zuber	P A.McKain	/P M.Breuer	P G.Caster	P B.Trotter	P J.Krakauskas
/P M.Weaver	/P J.Whitehead	P J.Humphries	P F.Hutchinson		RP C.Dean	P R.Lawson	P J.Haynes
/P B.Sayles	/P V.Frasier	/P T.Drake	P S.Coffman		P C.Pippen	P L.Mills	P A.Carrasquel
	/P A.Herring	/P F.Stromme	P H.Eisenstat		P B.Joyce	RP J.Whitehead	RP P.Appleton
	/P V.Eaves	/P L.Sullivan	/P V.Kennedy		P R.Parmelee	P B.Harris	RP W.Masterson
	/P H.Boyles	/P M.Naymick	/P B.Harris		/P L.McCrabb	P G.Gill	P H.Kelley
	/P J.Dobernic		/P F.Giebell		/P S.Page	/P J.Marcum	/P J.DeShong
			/P C.Pippen		/P J.Reninger	P B.Newsom	/P E.Wynn
			/P J.Walkup		/P W.Masters	P H.Kimberlin	/P B.Thomas
			/P R.Lawson		/P E.Smith	/P E.Bildilli	/P D.Bass
			/P G.Gill		/P B.Thomas	/P J.Wade	/P B.Holland
			/P R.Lynn		/P J.Schelle	/P F.Johnson	/P L.Thuman
			/P H.Newhouser		/P D.Smith	/P L.Hanning	/P B.Jacobs
						/P B.Cox	/P M.Palagyi
						/P E.Pyle	
						/P R.Van Atta	
						/P E.Cole	
						/P B.Muncrief	
						/P J.Walkup	

TEAM	G	W	L	PCT	GB	R	OR	AB	H	2B	3B	HR	BB	SO	AVG	OBP	SLG	PRO	PRO+	BR	/A	PF	CHI	RC	SB	CS	SBA	SBR
NY	152	106	45	.702		967	556	5300	1521	259	55	166	701	543	.287	.374	.451	.825	119	134	149	98	102	923	72	37	66	-1
BOS	152	89	62	.589	17	890	795	5308	1543	287	57	124	591	505	.291	.363	.436	.799	106	78	45	104	101	831	42	44	49	-14
CLE	154	87	67	.565	20.5	797	700	5316	1490	291	79	85	581	574	.280	.350	.413	.763	105	4	32	97	100	775	72	46	61	-6
CHI	155	85	69	.552	22.5	755	737	5279	1451	220	56	64	579	502	.275	.349	.374	.723	89	-62	-81	103	103	708	113	61	65	-3
DET	155	81	73	.526	26.5	849	762	5326	1487	277	67	124	620	592	.279	.356	.426	.782	99	43	-21	108	100	821	88	38	70	4
WAS	153	65	87	.428	41.5	702	797	5334	1483	249	79	44	547	460	.278	.346	.379	.725	96	-62	-8	93	96	718	94	47	67	0
PHI	153	55	97	.362	51.5	711	1022	5309	1438	282	55	98	503	532	.271	.336	.400	.736	96	-55	-40	98	97	713	60	34	64	-2
STL	156	43	111	.279	64.5	733	1035	5422	1453	242	50	91	559	606	.268	.339	.381	.720	88	-79	-94	102	100	706	48	38	56	-8
TOT	615					6404		42594	11866	2107	498	796	4657	4314	.279	.352	.407	.759							589	345	63	-30

TEAM	CG	SH	SV	IP	H	H/G	HR	BB	SO	RAT	ERA	ERA+	OAV	OOB	PR	/A	PF	CPI	FA	E	DP	FW	PW	BW	SBW	DIF
NY	87	15	26	1348²	1208	8.1	85	567	565	11.9	3.31	132	.241	.319	196	157	94	107	.978	126	159	2.9	14.5	13.7	.3	-.8
BOS	52	4	20	1350²	1533	10.2	77	543	539	14.0	4.56	104	.287	.355	9	25	102	102	.970	180	147	.0	2.3	4.1	-.9	7.9
CLE	69	10	13	1364²	1394	9.2	75	602	614	13.3	4.08	108	.267	.344	81	49	95	103	.970	180	148	.2	4.5	2.9	-.2	2.5
CHI	62	5	21	1377	1470	9.6	99	454	535	12.7	4.31	110	.275	.333	48	65	102	98	.972	167	140	1.0	6.0	-7.5	.0	8.4
DET	64	8	16	1367¹	1430	9.4	104	574	633	13.3	4.29	114	.268	.341	50	91	106	100	.967	198	147	-.6	8.4	-1.9	.7	-2.5
WAS	72	4	10	1354²	1420	9.4	75	602	521	13.6	4.60	94	.271	.348	2	-39	94	94	.966	205	167	-1.1	-3.6	-.7	.3	-5.9
PHI	50	6	12	1342²	1687	11.3	148	579	397	15.3	5.79	81	.307	.375	-175	-162	102	99	.964	210	131	-1.4	-14.9	-3.7	.2	-1.2
STL	56	3	3	1371¹	1724	11.3	133	739	516	16.4	6.01	81	.310	.393	-212	-175	105	100	.968	199	144	-.6	-16.1	-8.7	-.4	-8.2
TOT	512	55	121	10877		9.8				13.8	4.62		.279	.352					.969	1465	1183					

Runs		Hits		Doubles		Triples		Home Runs		Total Bases	
Rolfe-NY	139	Rolfe-NY	213	Rolfe-NY	46	Lewis-Was	16	Foxx-Bos	35	Williams-Bos	344
Williams-Bos	131	McQuinn-StL	195	Williams-Bos	44	McCosky-Det	14	Greenberg-Det	33	Foxx-Bos	324
Foxx-Bos	130	Keltner-Cle	191	Greenberg-Det	42	McQuinn-StL	13	Williams-Bos	31	Rolfe-NY	321
McCosky-Det	120	McCosky-Det	190	McQuinn-StL	37	Campbell-Cle	13	DiMaggio-NY	30	McQuinn-StL	318
Johnson-Phi	115	Williams-Bos	185	Keltner-Cle	35			Gordon-NY	28	Greenberg-Det	311

Runs Batted In		Runs Produced		Bases On Balls		Batting Average		On Base Percentage		Slugging Average	
Williams-Bos	145	Williams-Bos	245	Clift-StL	111	DiMaggio-NY	.381	Foxx-Bos	.464	Foxx-Bos	.694
DiMaggio-NY	126	Johnson-Phi	206	Williams-Bos	107	Foxx-Bos	.360	Selkirk-NY	.452	DiMaggio-NY	.671
Johnson-Phi	114	Rolfe-NY	205	Appling-Chi	105	Johnson-Phi	.338	DiMaggio-NY	.448	Greenberg-Det	.622
Greenberg-Det	112	DiMaggio-NY	204	Selkirk-NY	103	Trosky-Cle	.335	Keller-NY	.447	Williams-Bos	.609
		Foxx-Bos	200	Johnson-Phi	99	Rolfe-NY	.329	Johnson-Phi	.440	Trosky-Cle	.589

Production		Adjusted Production		Batter Runs		Adjusted Batter Runs		Clutch Hitting Index		Runs Created	
Foxx-Bos	1.158	DiMaggio-NY	185	Foxx-Bos	66.1	Foxx-Bos	60.8	Wright-Was	129	Williams-Bos	157
DiMaggio-NY	1.119	Foxx-Bos	185	Williams-Bos	56.3	DiMaggio-NY	58.1	McNair-Chi	116	Foxx-Bos	150
Williams-Bos	1.045	Williams-Bos	158	DiMaggio-NY	56.0	Williams-Bos	50.9	Dahlgren-NY	116	DiMaggio-NY	139
Greenberg-Det	1.042	Trosky-Cle	157	Greenberg-Det	47.3	Johnson-Phi	48.5	Selkirk-NY	115	Johnson-Phi	138
Trosky-Cle	.994	Johnson-Phi	156	Johnson-Phi	45.7	Greenberg-Det	38.0	Higgins-Det	115	Greenberg-Det	136

Total Average		Stolen Bases		Stolen Base Average		Stolen Base Runs		Fielding Runs		Total Player Rating	
Foxx-Bos	1.304	Case-Was	51	McCosky-Det	83.3	Case-Was	5.1	Doerr-Bos	27.3	DiMaggio-NY	5.7
DiMaggio-NY	1.242	Kreevich-Chi	23	Kuhel-Chi	78.3	McCosky-Det	3.6	Kreevich-Chi	16.1	Foxx-Bos	4.9
Williams-Bos	1.161	Fox-Det	23	Chapman-Cle	75.0	Welaj-Was	2.7	Tebbetts-Det	14.5	Johnson-Phi	4.7
Greenberg-Det	1.152	McCosky-Det	20	Case-Was	75.0	Kuhel-Chi	2.4	Lewis-Was	13.6	Williams-Bos	4.3
Selkirk-NY	1.121			Walker-Chi	73.9	Henrich-NY	2.1	Clift-StL	12.0	Dickey-NY	3.9

Wins		Win Percentage		Games		Complete Games		Shutouts		Saves	
Feller-Cle	24	Grove-Bos	.789	Brown-Chi	61	Newsom-StL-Det	24	Ruffing-NY	5	Murphy-NY	19
Ruffing-NY	21	Ruffing-NY	.750	Dean-Phi	54	Feller-Cle	24	Feller-Cle	4	Brown-Chi	18
Newsom-StL-Det	20	Feller-Cle	.727	Dickman-Bos	48	Ruffing-NY	22	Newsom-StL-Det	3	Heving-Bos	7
Leonard-Was	20	Leonard-Was	.714	Heving-Bos	46	Leonard-Was	21			Dean-Phi	7
Bridges-Det	17	Bridges-Det	.708			Grove-Bos	17			Appleton-Was	6

Innings Pitched		Fewest Hits/Game		Fewest BB/Game		Strikeouts		Strikeouts/Game		Ratio	
Feller-Cle	296.2	Feller-Cle	6.89	Lyons-Chi	1.36	Feller-Cle	246	Feller-Cle	7.46	Lyons-Chi	9.85
Newsom-StL-Det	291.2	Hadley-NY	7.71	Leonard-Was	1.97	Newsom-StL-Det	192	Newsom-StL-Det	5.92	Ruffing-NY	11.11
Leonard-Was	269.1	Gomez-NY	7.86	Beckmann-Phi	2.38	Bridges-Det	129	Bridges-Det	5.86	Leonard-Was	11.26
Lee-Chi	235.0	Ruffing-NY	8.14	Lee-Chi	2.68	Rigney-Chi	119	Rigney-Chi	4.90	Grove-Bos	11.26
Ruffing-NY	233.1	Chase-Was	8.34	Grove-Bos	2.73	Chase-Was	118	Gomez-NY	4.64	Feller-Cle	11.29

Earned Run Average		Adjusted ERA		Opponents' Batting Avg.		Opponents' On Base Pct.		Starter Runs		Adjusted Starter Runs	
Grove-Bos	2.54	Grove-Bos	186	Feller-Cle	.210	Lyons-Chi	.276	Feller-Cle	58.3	Feller-Cle	51.1
Lyons-Chi	2.76	Lyons-Chi	171	Gomez-NY	.235	Ruffing-NY	.301	Grove-Bos	44.0	Grove-Bos	46.3
Feller-Cle	2.85	Feller-Cle	154	Hadley-NY	.237	Feller-Cle	.303	Ruffing-NY	43.8	Newsom-StL-Det	42.3
Ruffing-NY	2.93	Ruffing-NY	149	Ruffing-NY	.240	Bridges-Det	.304	Lyons-Chi	35.6	Lyons-Chi	37.8
Hadley-NY	2.98	Hadley-NY	146	Bridges-Det	.243	Leonard-Was	.305	Newsom-StL-Det	33.7	Ruffing-NY	36.9

Clutch Pitching Index		Relief Runs		Adjusted Relief Runs		Relief Ranking		Total Pitcher Index		Total Baseball Ranking	
Hadley-NY	132	Heving-Bos	10.9	Heving-Bos	12.2	Brown-Chi	21.7	Feller-Cle	5.6	DiMaggio-NY	5.7
Grove-Bos	126	Brown-Chi	9.7	Brown-Chi	11.2	Heving-Bos	16.1	Ruffing-NY	4.7	Feller-Cle	5.6
Trout-Det	116	Dickman-Bos	2.3	Dickman-Bos	3.7	Dickman-Bos	3.6	Lyons-Chi	4.3	Foxx-Bos	4.9
Harder-Cle	116	Murphy-NY	1.5					Grove-Bos	3.7	Johnson-Phi	4.7
Milnar-Cle	110	Appleton-Was	.7					Newsom-StL-Det	3.5	Ruffing-NY	4.7

May 8 The Waner brothers, Lloyd and Paul, lose their places in the Pittsburgh outfield when new manager Frank Frisch acquires Vince DiMaggio for Johnny Rizzo. Vince takes over center field, flanked by Maurice Van Robays and Bob Elliott, each playing their first full season.

May 24 The New York Giants rip the Boston Bees, 8–1, in the first night game at the Polo Grounds before 22,260. Harry Gumbert is the winner.

June 4 The Pirates rout the Boston Bees, 14–2, in the first night game at Pittsburgh's Forbes Field as 20,319 look on.

August 3 With Ernie Lombardi hurt, Reds catcher Willard Hershberger is hitting .309 after taking over. However, depressed in recent weeks, Hershberger commits suicide by slashing his throat in Boston's Copley Plaza Hotel. Hershberger blamed himself for calling wrong pitches in the 5-4 loss to New York on July 31. Leading 4-1, Bucky Walters retired the first two batters in the ninth and had two strikes on each of the next four batters. But Harry Danning and Burgess Whitehead each homered with a man on. Hershberger's father had also committed suicide, in 1928.

September 16 A rhubarb at Ebbets Field results in a suspension and fine for Dodger manager Leo Durocher for "inciting a riot." Perhaps better known from the game is the photo showing an obese Brooklyn fan astride George Magerkurth, pummeling the veteran umpire.

October 3 Jimmy Ripple's two-run home run in the third provides the winning margin as the Reds end the NL's 10-game World Series losing streak with a 5-3 win over the Detroit Tigers. Walters gives up only three hits, but he's lucky to escape a jittery first inning.

October 7 Back in Cincinnati, Bucky Walters evens the World Series for the Reds with a 4-0 shutout, scattering five Detroit hits. Walters also becomes the first pitcher in 14 years to hit a home run in the Series.

October 8 With only one day's rest, Louis "Bobo" Newsom comes back for the Tigers and nearly has enough to win Game 7. Detroit gets an unearned run off Paul Derringer in the third, and Newsom holds the Reds scoreless through six innings. In the seventh, however, Frank McCormick and Jimmy Ripple hit consecutive doubles, and Ripple later scores on Billy Myers's sacrifice fly. Derringer gives up seven hits in the first six innings but sets the Tigers down in order in the final three frames for the 2-1 win. Old Jimmy Wilson catches six of the seven games, hits .353, and has the only stolen base of the Series. The Reds' share is $5,803 and the Tigers get $3,532.

BOSTON	BROOKLYN	CHICAGO	CINCINNATI	NEW YORK	PHILADELPHIA	PITTSBURGH	ST.LOUIS
M C.Stengel	M L.Durocher	M G.Hartnett	M B.McKechnie	M B.Terry	M D.Prothro	M F.Frisch	M R.Blades
1B B.Hassett	1B D.Camilli	1B P.Cavarretta	1B F.McCormick	1B B.Young	1B A.Mahan	1B E.Fletcher	M M.Gonzalez
2B B.Rowell	2B P.Coscarart	2B B.Herman	2B L.Frey	2B T.Cuccinello	2B H.Schulte	2B F.Gustine	M B.Southworth
SS E.Miller	SS P.Reese	SS B.Mattick	SS B.Myers	SS M.Witek	SS B.Bragan	SS A.Vaughan	1B J.Mize
3B S.Sisti	3B C.Lavagetto	3B S.Hack	3B B.Werber	3B B.Whitehead	3B P.May	3B L.Handley	2B J.Orengo
LF C.Ross	LF J.Medwick	LF B.Nicholson	LF M.McCormick	LF J.Moore	LF J.Rizzo	LF M.Van Robays	SS M.Marion
CF J.Cooney	CF D.Walker	CF J.Gleeson	CF H.Craft	CF F.Demaree	CF J.Marty	CF V.DiMaggio	3B S.Martin
RF M.West	RF J.Vosmik	RF H.Leiber	RF I.Goodman	RF M.Ott	RF C.Klein	RF B.Elliott	LF E.Koy
C R.Berres	C B.Phelps	C A.Todd	C E.Lombardi	C H.Danning	C B.Warren	C S.Davis	CF T.Moore
O G.Moore	O1 J.Wasdell	S D.Dallessandro	S E.Joost	2O J.Rucker	2O H.Mueller	3O D.Garms	RF E.Slaughter
23 A.Glossop	3O P.Reiser	1 R.Russell	S M.Arnovich	C B.Jurges	S B.Atwood	O P.Waner	C M.Owen
C P.Masi	S2 J.Hudson	O A.Galan	O W.Hershberger	O1 B.Seeds	O1 M.Mazzera	C A.Lopez	23 J.Brown
3 T.Cuccinello	S L.Durocher	1 Z.Bonura	C J.Rizzo	O K.O'Dea	O D.Litwhiler	C L.Waner	C D.Padgett
C A.Lopez	C G.Mancuso	S2 R.Warstler	2 J.Ripple	2 J.Glossop	O M.Arnovich	2 P.Young	O P.Martin
1 L.Scarsella	O C.Gilbert	C R.Collins	3 L.Riggs	/1 J.McCarthy	3 H.Martin	3 B.Brubaker	O J.Medwick
2 R.Warstler	C H.Franks	C G.Hartnett	O B.Baker	/O B.Maynard	C W.Millies	C J.Schultz	O1 J.Hopp
2 W.Wietelmann	S J.Gallagher	O B.Rogell	O L.Gamble	/3 G.Stewart	C W.Berger	C E.Fernandes	3 D.Gutteridge
O M.Preibisch	/C R.Cullenbine	/C C.McCullough	C J.Wilson	S R.Tramback	G.Jumonville	C R.Berres	2 E.Lake
C S.Andrews	O E.Koy	/S B.Sturgeon	/C D.West	P H.Gumbert	D.Young	/O J.Rizzo	/O H.Walker
C S.Broskie	3 D.Ross	P C.Passeau	/O M.Dejan	/O H.Schumacher	/S N.Stewart	/2 E.Leip	/O C.Gillenwater
O B.Loane	/O G.Moore	P L.French	/O V.DiMaggio	P B.Lohrman	G.Suhr	H F.Bell	/C W.Cooper
/1 B.Gremp	/O J.Ripple	P B.Lee	H W.Berger	P C.Melton	G.Scharein	P R.Sewell	C B.DeLancey
/O D.Manno	/C T.Giuliani	P V.Olsen	P B.Walters	RP J.Brown	A.Monchak	P J.Bowman	/O H.Epps
/O C.Wilborn	P W.Wyatt	RP K.Raffensberger	P P.Derringer	RP R.Joiner	/S S.File	P M.Brown	/3 C.Crespi
H H.Majeski	P L.Hamlin	RP V.Page	RP J.Thompson	/2 P.Dean	P S.Benjamin	P K.Heintzelman	/O R.Jones
P D.Errickson	P V.Tamulis	P C.Root	P J.Turner	P R.Lynn	H E.Levy	RP B.Klinger	P L.Warneke
P B.Posedel	P H.Casey	P D.Dean	P W.Moore	/P B.Carpenter	/2 R.Hughes	RP D.Lanahan	P M.Cooper
P J.Sullivan	P T.Carleton	/P C.Bryant	RP J.Beggs	H.Vandenberg	P K.Higbe	RP D.MacFayden	P B.McGee
P M.Salvo	RP T.Pressnell	P J.Bonetti	RP M.Shoffner	/P W.Hudlin	P H.Mulcahy	P M.Butcher	P C.Shoun
P N.Strincevich	P C.Davis		RP J.Hutchings		/P I.Pearson	P J.Lanning	P B.Bowman
RP A.Javery	P F.Fitzsimmons		P J.Vander Meer		P Si.Johnson	P R.Bauers	RP J.Russell
RP A.Piechota	P L.Grissom		P E.Riddle		P B.Beck	/P O.Swigart	P M.Lanier
RP D.Coffman	P E.Head		/P L.Guise		P L.Smoll	/P D.Dietz	P C.Doyle
P J.Tobin	P N.Kimball		/P R.Barrett		P C.Blanton	/P P.Rambert	P I.Hutchinson
P G.Barnicle	/P V.Mungo				P C.Frye	/P R.Harrell	P C.Davis
/P L.Fette	/P W.Flowers				P Sy.Johnson		/P E.White
/P T.Earley	/P S.Rachunok				P L.Brown		/P N.Kimball
/P J.Callahan	/P C.Doyle				/P J.Podgajny		/P G.Lillard
/P F.LaManna	/P W.Ferrell				/P L.Hoerst		/P H.Brecheen
/P B.Swift	/P L.Fette				/P M.Wilson		/P M.Dickson
/P A.Williams	/P M.Macon				/P R.Bruner		/P B.Weiland
/P A.Johnson					/P P.Masterson		

TEAM	G	W	L	PCT	GB	R	OR	AB	H	2B	3B	HR	BB	SO	AVG	OBP	SLG	PRO	PRO+	BR	/A	PF	CHI	RC	SB	CS	SBA	SBR
CIN	155	100	53	.654		707	528	5372	1427	264	38	89	453	503	.266	.327	.379	.706	100	6	-1	101	103	672	72			
BRO	156	88	65	.575	12	697	621	5470	1421	256	70	93	522	570	.260	.327	.383	.710	96	15	-28	106	98	692	56			
STL	156	84	69	.549	16	747	699	5499	1514	266	61	119	479	610	.275	.336	.411	.747	106	83	39	106	96	764	97			
PIT	156	78	76	.506	22.5	809	783	5466	1511	276	68	76	553	494	.276	.346	.394	.740	112	84	90	99	104	757	69			
CHI	154	75	79	.487	25.5	681	636	5389	1441	272	48	86	482	566	.267	.331	.384	.715	106	25	39	98	97	691	63			
NY	152	72	80	.474	27.5	663	659	5324	1423	201	46	91	453	478	.267	.329	.374	.703	99	3	-2	101	98	653	45			
BOS	152	65	87	.428	34.5	623	745	5329	1366	219	50	59	402	581	.256	.311	.349	.660	93	-83	-51	95	108	581	48			
PHI	153	50	103	.327	50	494	750	5137	1225	180	35	75	435	527	.238	.300	.331	.631	83	-133	-113	96	96	512	25			
TOT	617					5421		42986	11328	1934	416	688	3779	4329	.264	.326	.376	.702							475			

TEAM	CG	SH	SV	IP	H	H/G	HR	BB	SO	RAT	ERA	ERA+	OAV	OOB	PR	/A	PF	CPI	FA	E	DP	FW	PW	BW	SBW	DIF
CIN	91	10	11	1407²	1263	8.1	73	445	557	11.0	3.05	124	.240	.302	125	115	98	102	.981	117	158	2.9	11.6	-.1		9.1
BRO	65	17	14	1433	1366	8.6	101	393	639	11.2	3.50	114	.248	.302	56	79	104	95	.970	183	110	-.3	8.0	-2.8		6.7
STL	71	10	14	1396	1457	9.4	83	488	550	12.7	3.83	104	.266	.329	3	24	104	102	.971	174	134	.1	2.4	3.9		1.0
PIT	49	8	24	1388²	1569	10.2	72	492	491	13.6	4.36	87	.283	.345	-79	-85	99	99	.966	217	161	-2.0	-8.6	9.1		2.5
CHI	69	12	14	1392	1418	9.2	74	430	564	12.1	3.54	106	.262	.319	47	32	97	103	.968	199	143	-1.2	3.2	3.9		-8.0
NY	57	11	18	1360¹	1383	9.1	110	473	606	12.4	3.79	102	.262	.325	9	-14	101	104	.977	139	132	1.6	1.4	-.2		-6.8
BOS	76	9	12	1359	1444	9.6	83	573	435	13.6	4.36	85	.274	.349	-77	-97	97	100	.970	184	169	-.6	-9.8	-5.2		4.6
PHI	66	5	8	1357	1429	9.5	92	475	485	12.8	4.40	89	.270	.333	-83	-75	101	93	.970	181	136	-.4	-7.6	-11.4		-7.1
TOT	544	82	115	11093²		9.2				12.4	3.85		.264	.326					.972	1394	1143					

Runs		Hits		Doubles		Triples		Home Runs		Total Bases	
Vaughan-Pit	113	F.McCormick-Cin	191	F.McCormick-Cin	44	Vaughan-Pit	15	Mize-StL	43	Mize-StL	368
Mize-StL	111	Hack-Chi	191	Vaughan-Pit	40	Ross-Bos	14	Nicholson-Chi	25	F.McCormick-Cin	298
Werber-Cin	105	Mize-StL	182	Gleeson-Chi	39	Slaughter-StL	13	Rizzo-Pit-Cin-Phi	24	Medwick-StL-Bro	280
Frey-Cin	102	Vaughan-Pit	178	Hack-Chi	38	Mize-StL	13	Camilli-Bro	23	Camilli-Bro	271
Hack-Chi	101	Medwick-StL-Bro	175	Walker-Bro	37	Camilli-Bro	13			Vaughan-Pit	269

Runs Batted In		Runs Produced		Bases On Balls		Batting Average		On Base Percentage		Slugging Average	
Mize-StL	137	Mize-StL	205	Fletcher-Pit	119	Garms-Pit	.355	Fletcher-Pit	.418	Mize-StL	.636
F.McCormick-Cin	127	Vaughan-Pit	201	Ott-NY	100	Davis-Pit	.326	Ott-NY	.407	Nicholson-Chi	.534
VanRobays-Pit	116	F.McCormick-Cin	201	Camilli-Bro	89	Lombardi-Cin	.319	Mize-StL	.404	Camilli-Bro	.529
Fletcher-Pit	104	VanRobays-Pit	187	Vaughan-Pit	88	Cooney-Bos	.318	Camilli-Bro	.397	DiMaggio-Cin-Pit	.519
Young-NY	101	Fletcher-Pit	182	Mize-StL	82	Hack-Chi	.317	Hack-Chi	.395	Slaughter-StL	.504

Production		Adjusted Production		Batter Runs		Adjusted Batter Runs		Clutch Hitting Index		Runs Created	
Mize-StL	1.039	Mize-StL	173	Mize-StL	63.9	Mize-StL	56.2	VanRobays-Pit	154	Mize-StL	152
Camilli-Bro	.926	Nicholson-Chi	148	Camilli-Bro	38.7	Fletcher-Pit	32.6	Fletcher-Pit	129	Camilli-Bro	114
Nicholson-Chi	.899	Camilli-Bro	144	Fletcher-Pit	31.8	Camilli-Bro	32.3	F.McCormick-Cin	121	Vaughan-Pit	113
Slaughter-StL	.874	Gleeson-Chi	139	Ott-NY	31.7	Ott-NY	30.8	Young-NY	115	Hack-Chi	112
Ott-NY	.864	Fletcher-Pit	137	Vaughan-Pit	28.8	Nicholson-Chi	30.5	Danning-NY	115	Ott-NY	107

Total Average		Stolen Bases		Stolen Base Average		Stolen Base Runs		Fielding Runs		Total Player Rating	
Mize-StL	1.135	Frey-Cin	22					Witek-NY	19.0	Vaughan-Pit	5.1
Camilli-Bro	1.005	Hack-Chi	21					Herman-Chi	18.9	Hack-Chi	4.5
Fletcher-Pit	.930	Moore-StL	18					Frey-Cin	18.2	Miller-Bos	3.5
Ott-NY	.915	Werber-Cin	16					Moore-StL	16.8	Mize-StL	3.4
Nicholson-Chi	.901	Reese-Bro	15					Miller-Bos	14.7	Frey-Cin	3.1

Wins		Win Percentage		Games		Complete Games		Shutouts		Saves	
Walters-Cin	22	Fitzsimmons-Bro	.889	Shoun-StL	54	Walters-Cin	29	Wyatt-Bro	5	Brown-NY	7
Passeau-Chi	20	Sewell-Pit	.762	Brown-Pit	48	Derringer-Cin	26	Salvo-Bos	5	Brown-Pit	7
Derringer-Cin	20	Walters-Cin	.688	Passeau-Chi	46	Mulcahy-Phi	21			Beggs-Cin	7
		Thompson-Cin	.640	Casey-Bro	44	Passeau-Chi	20			Shoun-StL	5
		Derringer-Cin	.625	Raffensberger-Chi	43	Higbe-Phi	20			Passeau-Chi	5

Innings Pitched		Fewest Hits/Game		Fewest BB/Game		Strikeouts		Strikeouts/Game		Ratio	
Walters-Cin	305.0	Walters-Cin	7.11	Derringer-Cin	1.46	Higbe-Phi	137	Melton-NY	4.91	Derringer-Cin	9.95
Derringer-Cin	296.2	Higbe-Phi	7.70	Turner-Cin	1.54	Wyatt-Bro	124	Schumacher-NY	4.88	Walters-Cin	9.97
Higbe-Phi	283.0	Thompson-Cin	7.87	Hamlin-Bro	1.68	Passeau-Chi	124	Wyatt-Bro	4.66	Passeau-Chi	10.33
Passeau-Chi	280.2	Casey-Bro	7.95	Davis-StL-Bro	1.79	Schumacher-NY	123	Hamlin-Bro	4.49	Turner-Cin	10.54
Mulcahy-Phi	280.0	Sullivan-Bos	7.97	Warneke-StL	1.82			Higbe-Phi	4.36	Tamulis-Bro	10.73

Earned Run Average		Adjusted ERA		Opponents' Batting Avg.		Opponents' On Base Pct.		Starter Runs		Adjusted Starter Runs	
Walters-Cin	2.48	Walters-Cin	153	Walters-Cin	.220	Derringer-Cin	.276	Walters-Cin	46.4	Walters-Cin	44.3
Passeau-Chi	2.50	Passeau-Chi	150	Higbe-Phi	.232	Passeau-Chi	.278	Passeau-Chi	42.0	Passeau-Chi	38.9
Sewell-Pit	2.80	Sewell-Pit	136	Thompson-Cin	.233	Walters-Cin	.283	Derringer-Cin	25.8	Derringer-Cin	23.8
Fitzsimmons-Bro	2.81	Turner-Cin	131	Passeau-Chi	.237	Tamulis-Bro	.288	Sewell-Pit	22.1	Warneke-StL	21.8
Turner-Cin	2.89	Hamlin-Bro	131	Casey-Bro	.237	Hamlin-Bro	.292	Turner-Cin	20.0	Sewell-Pit	21.3

Clutch Pitching Index		Relief Runs		Adjusted Relief Runs		Relief Ranking		Total Pitcher Index		Total Baseball Ranking	
Errickson-Bos	124	Beggs-Cin	15.8	Beggs-Cin	15.3	Beggs-Cin	30.0	Passeau-Chi	5.3	Passeau-Chi	5.3
Olsen-Chi	119	Russell-StL	8.9	Russell-StL	8.9	Russell-StL	10.8	Walters-Cin	4.7	Vaughan-Pit	5.1
Schumacher-NY	113	Raffensberger-Chi	6.0	Raffensberger-Chi	4.8	Raffensberger-Chi	6.2	Beggs-Cin	3.3	Walters-Cin	4.7
Turner-Cin	113	MacFayden-Pit	3.0	Brown-NY	2.9	Brown-NY	3.6	Sewell-Pit	2.7	Hack-Chi	4.5
Hamlin-Bro	111	Joiner-NY	2.7	Joiner-NY	2.9	Pressnell-Bro	3.6	Warneke-StL	2.6	Miller-Bos	3.5

January 14 Commissioner Kenesaw Landis gives free agency to 91 Detroit players and farmhands. Citing cover-ups of the movement of players within its organization, Landis hands freedom to Roy Cullenbine, Benny McCoy, Lloyd Dietz, and Steve Rachunok from the parent roster and orders $47,250 paid as compensation to 14 players. Johnny Sain is one of 23 players who will later make it to the major leagues. Landis' edict nullifies a deal which would have brought Wally Moses to the Tigers for Benny McCoy and George Coffman. McCoy is considered the plum of the 91 players, and several clubs bid for the second baseman. Connie Mack keeps Moses and signs McCoy for a $45,000 bonus and two-season contract at $10,000 a year.

April 16 Working in 47-degree weather, Bob Feller of the Cleveland Indians throws an Opening Day no-hitter against the Chicago White Sox winning, 1–0 at Comiskey Park. Rollie Hemsley has the only RBI, and Edgar Smith is the losing pitcher. It's the first Opening Day no-hitter since Leon "Red" Ames pitched one for the Giants in 1909.

May 14 Boston's Jimmie Foxx blasts a 10th inning home run off White Sox pitcher Johnny Rigney to give first-place Boston a 7-6 win. The ball goes over the left field roof and is considered the longest poke in the history of the original Comiskey Park .

May 24 The Cleveland Indians edge the St. Louis Browns, 3–2, in the first night game at Sportsman's Park in St. Louis, before 24,827. Bob Feller beats Eldon Auker and helps his cause by hitting a home run.

July 14 In the aftermath of the beanball wars, Spalding advertises a batting helmet with ear flaps in *The Sporting News*. Players express no interest, but next year Brooklyn will introduce a cap liner, which some batters start to use.

August 24 Ted Williams of the Boston Red Sox pitches the last two innings in a 12-1 loss to the Detroit Tigers. Williams allows three hits and one run but strikes out Tiger slugger Rudy York on three pitches.

September 24 George Caster of the Philadelphia Athletics allows six home runs against the Boston Red Sox, four of them coming in the sixth inning as Ted Williams, Jimmie Foxx, Joe Cronin, and Jim Tabor connect. Foxx's home run is his 500th. Boston wins 10–9 in 10 innings, then wins the second game, 3–2.

September 27 The Yankees, winners of eight straight games, have their pennant hopes dashed by the A's, 6-2 winners over New York. New York is out of the World Series for the first time since 1935 as the Tigers become champs.

October 2 The Series opens in Cincinnati, and the Reds lose 7-2, the tenth straight World Series loss for a NL team. The Tigers bunch five singles, a walk, and an error in the second off Paul Derringer to score five runs. Bruce Campbell adds a two-run home run, and Bobo Newsom rations eight hits and only one walk. Bobo's father, visiting from South Carolina, dies in a Cincinnati hotel the next morning.

October 6 Detroit regains the advantage with Bobo Newsom pitching even better than he had in the first game. Newsom's 8-0 whitewash is the first Detroit shutout in the World Series since 1909.

November 5 Former Washington hurler Walter Johnson, who won 417 games for the Senators, goes down in defeat as a Republican candidate for the U.S. House of Representatives from Maryland.

December 20 After nearly four decades with the team, Connie Mack acquires controlling interest in the Athletics from the Shibe family at the price of $42,000.

	BOSTON		CHICAGO		CLEVELAND		DETROIT		NEW YORK		PHILADELPHIA		ST.LOUIS		WASHINGTON
M	J.Cronin	M	J.Dykes	M	O.Vitt	M	D.Baker	M	J.McCarthy	M	C.Mack	M	F.Haney	M	B.Harris
1B	J.Foxx	1B	J.Kuhel	1B	H.Trosky	1B	R.York	1B	B.Dahlgren	1B	D.Siebert	1B	G.McQuinn	1B	Z.Bonura
2B	B.Doerr	2B	S.Webb	2B	R.Mack	2B	C.Gehringer	2B	J.Gordon	2B	B.McCoy	2B	D.Heffner	2B	J.Bloodworth
SS	J.Cronin	SS	L.Appling	SS	L.Boudreau	SS	D.Bartell	SS	F.Crosetti	SS	A.Brancato	SS	J.Berardino	SS	J.Pofahl
3B	J.Tabor	3B	B.Kennedy	3B	K.Keltner	3B	P.Higgins	3B	R.Rolfe	3B	A.Rubeling	3B	H.Clift	3B	C.Travis
LF	T.Williams	LF	M.Solters	LF	B.Chapman	LF	H.Greenberg	LF	G.Selkirk	LF	B.Johnson	LF	R.Radcliff	LF	G.Walker
CF	D.DiMaggio	CF	M.Kreevich	CF	R.Weatherly	CF	B.McCosky	CF	J.DiMaggio	CF	S.Chapman	CF	W.Judnich	CF	G.Case
RF	D.Cramer	RF	T.Wright	RF	B.Bell	RF	P.Fox	RF	C.Keller	RF	W.Moses	RF	R.Cullenbine	RF	B.Lewis
C	G.Desautels	C	M.Tresh	C	R.Hemsley	C	B.Tebbetts	C	B.Dickey	C	F.Hayes	C	B.Swift	C	R.Ferrell
O1	L.Finney	O	L.Rosenthal	O	J.Heath	O	B.Campbell	O	T.Henrich	O	D.Miles	O	C.Laabs	O	J.Welaj
C	J.Peacock	2	E.McNair	C	F.Pytlak	C	B.Sullivan	C	B.Rosar	S	B.Lillard	OC	J.Grace	2	B.Myer
3	C.Gelbert	C	T.Turner	/2	R.Peters	O	E.Averill	S3	B.Knickerb'r	3	J.Gantenbein	O	M.Hoag	C	J.Early
O	S.Spence	2	J.Hayes	O	S.Campbell	3S	R.Kress	O	B.Mills	O	A.Simmons	S	A.Strange	1	J.Sanford
S	T.Carey	2	D.Kolloway	/3	O.Hale	2	D.Meyer	/O	J.Powell	C	H.Wagner	C	G.Susce	1	S.West
/3	M.Owen	/C	K.Silvestri	/1	O.Grimes	S	F.Croucher	/O	M.Chartak	S	F.Chapman	O	J.Gallagher	S	C.Gelbert
C	J.Glenn	H	D.Short	/C	H.Helf	/O	T.Stainback			2	C.Davis	2	J.Lucadello	/1	J.Wasdell
/1	T.Lupien					2	S.Metha	P	R.Ruffing	C	E.Brucker	S	L.Lary	S	S.Robertson
H	R.Nonnenkamp	P	J.Rigney	P	B.Feller	/O	P.Mullin	P	M.Russo	/O	E.Valo	H	F.White	/C	A.Evans
		P	T.Lee	P	A.Milnar	H	F.Secory	P	S.Chandler	/S	J.Wallaesa	/C	S.Harshany	/1	M.Vernon
		P	E.Smith	P	M.Harder			P	M.Breuer	/O	E.Tipton			/O	J.Mallory
P	J.Bagby	P	T.Lyons	P	A.Smith	P	B.Newsom	P	A.Donald	H	D.Lodigiani	P	E.Auker	/C	D.Hahn
P	J.Wilson	P	J.Knott	P	J.Allen	P	T.Bridges	RP	J.Murphy	/C	B.Hancken	P	V.Kennedy	/2	M.Aderholt
P	L.Grove	RP	C.Brown	RP	J.Dobson	P	S.Rowe					P	B.Harris		
P	F.Ostermueller	RP	P.Appleton	RP	H.Eisenstat	P	J.Gorsica	P	M.Pearson	P	J.Babich	P	J.Niggeling	P	D.Leonard
P	H.Hash					P	H.Newhouser	P	T.Bonham	P	N.Potter	P	E.Bildilli	P	K.Chase
RP	E.Dickman	P	B.Dietrich	P	J.Humphries	RP	A.Benton	P	S.Sundra	P	G.Caster	RP	B.Trotter	P	S.Hudson
		/P	V.Eaves	P	M.Naymick	RP	T.Seats	P	S.Hadley	P	C.Dean	RP	S.Coffman	P	W.Masterson
P	D.Galehouse	/P	J.Hallett	/P	W.Hudlin	RP	A.McKain	/P	L.Gomez	P	B.Ross	RP	R.Lawson	P	J.Krakauskas
P	J.Heving	/P	E.Weiland	P	B.Zuber			P	O.Hildebrand	RP	E.Heusser			RP	J.Haynes
P	E.Johnson	/P	O.Grove	/P	N.Andrews	P	D.Trout	/P	L.Grissom			P	J.Kramer	RP	A.Carrasquel
P	M.Harris			/P	D.Howell	P	F.Hutchinson			P	B.Beckmann	P	L.Mills		
P	B.Fleming			/P	K.Jungels	P	C.Smith			P	P.Vaughan	P	J.Whitehead	P	R.Monteagudo
P	C.Wagner			/P	C.Dorsett	P	C.Pippen			P	H.Besse	P	B.Cox	/P	W.Hudlin
/P	B.Butland					/P	F.Giebell			/P	L.McCrabb	/P	W.Hudlin	/P	A.Hollingsworth
/P	Y.Terry					/P	L.Nelson			/P	P.Marchildon	/P	M.Newlin	/P	B.Jacobs
/P	A.Mustaikis					/P	B.Thomas			/P	C.Miles			/P	R.Anderson
/P	W.Rich					/P	D.Conger			/P	P.McLaughlin			/P	L.Thuman
						/P	B.Uhl							/P	G.Torres

TEAM	G	W	L	PCT	GB	R	OR	AB	H	2B	3B	HR	BB	SO	AVG	OBP	SLG	PRO	PRO+	BR	/A	PF	CHI	RC	SB	CS	SBA	SBR
DET	155	90	64	.584		**888**	717	5418	1549	**312**	65	134	664	556	.286	**.366**	.442	**.808**	105	**124**	38	110	97	**913**	66	39	63	-4
CLE	155	89	65	.578	1	710	**637**	5361	1422	287	61	101	519	597	.265	.332	.398	.730	98	-43	-22	97	99	724	53	36	60	-6
NY	155	88	66	.571	2	817	671	5286	1371	243	66	**155**	648	606	.259	.344	.418	.762	107	25	57	96	**103**	789	59	36	62	-4
CHI	155	82	72	.532	8	735	672	5386	1499	238	63	73	496	569	.278	.340	.387	.727	93	-41	-50	101	102	713	52	60	46	-20
BOS	154	82	72	.532	8	872	825	5481	**1566**	301	80	145	590	597	**.286**	.356	**.449**	.805	110	109	**73**	104	97	889	55	49	53	-13
STL	156	67	87	.435	23	757	882	5416	1423	278	58	118	556	642	.263	.333	.401	.734	94	-35	-50	102	**103**	744	51	40	56	-9
WAS	154	64	90	.416	26	665	811	5365	1453	266	67	52	468	**504**	.271	.331	.374	.705	95	-85	-42	97	100	690	**94**	40	**70**	4
PHI	154	54	100	.351	36	703	**932**	5304	1391	242	53	105	556	656	.262	.334	.387	.721	95	-53	-38	98	100	704	48	33	59	-5
TOT	619					6147		43017	11674	2167	513	883	4497	4727	.271	.342	.407	.750							478	333	59	-56

TEAM	CG	SH	SV	IP	H	H/G	HR	BB	SO	RAT	ERA	ERA+	OAV	OOB	PR	/A	PF	CPI	FA	E	DP	FW	PW	BW	SBW	DIF
DET	59	10	**23**	1375¹	1425	9.3	102	570	**752**	13.2	4.01	119	.266	.338	57	**114**	109	105	.968	194	116	-.7	**10.8**	3.6	.3	-1.0
CLE	72	**13**	22	1375	**1328**	8.7	86	512	686	12.2	**3.63**	116	.254	.324	115	89	96	102	**.975**	149	164	**1.7**	8.4	-2.1	.0	3.9
NY	76	10	14	1373	1389	9.1	119	511	559	12.6	3.89	104	.261	.328	76	22	92	104	**.975**	152	158	1.6	2.1	5.4	.3	1.7
CHI	**83**	10	18	1386²	1335	8.7	111	**480**	574	11.9	3.74	118	**.250**	.313	99	105	101	96	.969	185	125	-.2	9.9	-4.7	-1.2	1.2
BOS	51	4	16	1379¹	1568	10.2	124	625	613	14.5	4.89	92	.284	.359	-77	-60	103	101	.972	173	156	.4	-5.7	**6.9**	-.6	3.9
STL	64	4	9	1373¹	1592	10.4	113	646	439	14.8	5.12	89	.290	.367	-113	-82	105	100	.974	158	179	1.3	-7.7	-4.7	-.2	1.3
WAS	74	6	7	1350	1494	10.0	93	618	618	14.2	4.59	91	.281	.359	-31	-64	95	103	.968	194	166	-.7	-6.0	-4.0	**1.0**	-3.3
PHI	72	4	12	1345	1543	10.3	135	534	488	14.0	5.22	85	.283	.348	-125	-116	101	91	.960	238	131	-3.1	-11.0	-3.6	.2	-5.6
TOT	551	61	121	10958		9.6				13.4	4.38		.271	.342					.970	1443	1195					

Runs
Williams-Bos 134
Greenberg-Det 129
McCosky-Det 123
Gordon-NY 112
Kuhel-Chi 111

Hits
Radcliff-StL 200
McCosky-Det 200
Cramer-Bos 200
Appling-Chi 197
Wright-Chi 196

Doubles
Greenberg-Det 50
York-Det 46
Boudreau-Cle 46
Williams-Bos 43
Moses-Phi 41

Triples
McCosky-Det 19
Keller-NY 15
Finney-Bos 15
Williams-Bos 14
Appling-Chi 13

Home Runs
Greenberg-Det 41
Foxx-Bos 36
York-Det 33
Johnson-Phi 31
DiMaggio-NY 31

Total Bases
Greenberg-Det 384
York-Det 343
Williams-Bos 333
DiMaggio-NY 318
Gordon-NY 315

Runs Batted In
Greenberg-Det 150
York-Det 134
DiMaggio-NY 133
Foxx-Bos 119
Williams-Bos 113

Runs Produced
Greenberg-Det 238
Williams-Bos 224
York-Det 206
DiMaggio-NY 195
Cronin-Bos 191

Bases On Balls
Keller-NY 106
Clift-StL 104
Gehringer-Det 101
Foxx-Bos 101
Williams-Bos 96

Batting Average
DiMaggio-NY 352
Appling-Chi.......348
Williams-Bos 344
Radcliff-StL.......342
Greenberg-Det 340

On Base Percentage
Williams-Bos 442
Greenberg-Det 433
Gehringer-Det.....428
DiMaggio-NY 425
Appling-Chi.......420

Slugging Average
Greenberg-Det 670
DiMaggio-NY 626
Williams-Bos 594
York-Det..........583
Foxx-Bos.........581

Production
Greenberg-Det ...1.103
DiMaggio-NY 1.051
Williams-Bos 1.036
York-Det 993
Foxx-Bos 993

Adjusted Production
DiMaggio-NY 176
Greenberg-Det 166
Williams-Bos 159
Foxx-Bos 148
Keller-NY 142

Batter Runs
Greenberg-Det 68.8
Williams-Bos 57.2
DiMaggio-NY 50.8
York-Det 47.3
Foxx-Bos 42.6

Adjusted Batter Runs
DiMaggio-NY 55.9
Greenberg-Det 54.7
Williams-Bos 51.6
Foxx-Bos 37.8
York-Det 34.9

Clutch Hitting Index
Tresh-Chi 131
Boudreau-Cle 130
Walker-Was 117
Bell-Cle 114
Cronin-Bos 109

Runs Created
Greenberg-Det 171
Williams-Bos 154
York-Det 147
DiMaggio-NY 135
Foxx-Bos 124

Total Average
Greenberg-Det ...1.215
Williams-Bos 1.122
DiMaggio-NY 1.098
York-Det 1.050
Foxx-Bos 1.026

Stolen Bases
Case-Was 35
Walker-Was 21
Gordon-NY 18
Lewis-Was 15
Kreevich-Chi 15

Stolen Base Average
Walker-Was 84.0
Case-Was 77.8
Gordon-NY 69.2

Stolen Base Runs
Case-Was 4.5
Walker-Was 3.9
Gehringer-Det 3.0
Bartell-Det 2.4
Rosar-NY 1.5

Fielding Runs
Heffner-StL 19.1
Doerr-Bos 18.3
Tebbetts-Det 18.2
Travis-Was 15.7
Gordon-NY 14.0

Total Player Rating
DiMaggio-NY 4.5
Greenberg-Det 4.4
Williams-Bos 4.0
Gordon-NY 3.9
Doerr-Bos 3.6

Wins
Feller-Cle 27
Newsom-Det 21
Milnar-Cle 18
Hudson-Was 17

Win Percentage
Rowe-Det ...... .842
Newsom-Det .... .808
Feller-Cle ...... .711
Smith-Cle ...... .682
Milnar-Cle ...... .643

Games
Feller-Cle 43
Benton-Det 42
Wilson-Bos 41
Heusser-Phi 41
Dobson-Cle 40

Complete Games
Feller-Cle 31
Lee-Chi 24
Leonard-Was 23

Shutouts
Milnar-Cle 4
Lyons-Chi 4
Feller-Cle 4

Saves
Benton-Det 17
Brown-Chi 10
Murphy-NY 9

Innings Pitched
Feller-Cle 320.1
Leonard-Was ... 289.0
Rigney-Chi 280.2
Newsom-Det 264.0
Auker-StL 263.2

Fewest Hits/Game
Feller-Cle 6.88
Rigney-Chi 7.70
Smith-Chi 7.77
Bridges-Det 7.79
Newsom-Det 8.01

Fewest BB/Game
Lyons-Chi 1.79
Lee-Chi 2.21
Rowe-Det 2.29
Leonard-Was 2.43
Russo-NY 2.61

Strikeouts
Feller-Cle 261
Newsom-Det 164
Rigney-Chi 141
Bridges-Det 133
Chase-Was 129

Strikeouts/Game
Feller-Cle 7.33
Bridges-Det 6.06
Wilson-Bos 5.82
Newsom-Det 5.59
Smith-Chi 5.17

Ratio
Feller-Cle 10.34
Rigney-Chi 10.65
Lyons-Chi 10.87
Lee-Chi 11.09
Russo-NY 11.27

Earned Run Average
Feller-Cle 2.61
Newsom-Det 2.83
Rigney-Chi 3.11
Smith-Chi 3.21
Chase-Was 3.23

Adjusted ERA
Newsom-Det 168
Feller-Cle 161
Rigney-Chi 142
Bridges-Det 141
Smith-Chi 138

Opponents' Batting Avg.
Feller-Cle ...... .210
Smith-Chi ...... .228
Bridges-Det ..... .229
Rigney-Chi ..... .230
Newsom-Det .... .238

Opponents' On Base Pct.
Feller-Cle ...... .285
Lyons-Chi ...... .287
Rigney-Chi ..... .292
Lee-Chi .... .300
Russo-NY ...... .303

Starter Runs
Feller-Cle 63.0
Newsom-Det 45.6
Rigney-Chi 39.7
Chase-Was 33.4
Milnar-Cle 30.0

Adjusted Starter Runs
Feller-Cle 57.1
Newsom-Det 56.5
Rigney-Chi 40.9
Bridges-Det 30.5
Smith-Chi 27.9

Clutch Pitching Index
Chase-Was 134
Leonard-Was 122
Newsom-Det 119
Smith-Cle 117
Milnar-Cle 115

Relief Runs
Eisenstat-Cle 9.9
Trotter-StL 6.7
Brown-Chi 5.1
Murphy-NY 4.8

Adjusted Relief Runs
Trotter-StL 8.9
Eisenstat-Cle 8.6
Brown-Chi 5.4
Benton-Det 2.9
Murphy-NY 2.4

Relief Ranking
Trotter-StL 11.1
Brown-Chi 9.3
Benton-Det 6.7
Eisenstat-Cle 6.5
Murphy-NY 4.8

Total Pitcher Index
Feller-Cle 6.1
Newsom-Det 4.6
Rigney-Chi 4.2
Smith-Chi 2.9
Rowe-Det 2.9

Total Baseball Ranking
Feller-Cle 6.1
Newsom-Det 4.6
DiMaggio-NY 4.5
Greenberg-Det ... 4.4
Rigney-Chi 4.2

April 20 The Dodgers start to wear liners in their caps as a cautious response to the numerous beanball wars of 1940 that hospitalized Joe Medwick, Billy Jurges, and others. The liners are thin enough to be hardly noticeable, but most major league players continue to disdain the protection.

April 26 A baseball tradition is born at Wrigley Field. The Chicago ballpark is the first to install an organ, but the Cubs fall to the Cardinals, 6-2, in Roy Nelson's debut at the keyboard.

May 3 Hank Gornicki of the St. Louis Cardinals pitches a one-hitter in his big-league debut, beating the Philadelphia Phillies, 6-0. Stan Benjamin's single is the lone hit.

June 1 Mel Ott's two-run homer, the 400th of his career and his 1,500th RBI, gives the Giants a 3-2 win over the Reds.

June 6 The Giants use plastic batting helmets for the first time against the Pirates but lose a doubleheader to the Bucs, 5-4 and 4-3. In the nightcap, Pittsburgh pitcher Rip Sewell sets an NL record with 11 assists.

August 4 In the third inning, catcher Mickey Owens catches three foul flies, the first time in the major leagues that feat has been recorded. His Dodgers rally to whip the Giants, 11-6.

August 19 Pittsburgh Pirates manager Frankie Frisch is ejected by umpire Jocko Conlan from the second game of a doubleheader when he appears on the field with an umbrella to protest the rainy conditions at Brooklyn's Ebbets Field. The argument is later portrayed in an oil painting by artist Norman Rockwell.

August 30 The Cardinals' Lon Warneke no-hits the Cincinnati Reds, 2-0, with only three balls hit to the outfield. It is Warneke's 15th victory of the season and, with the Dodgers' doubleheader loss to the Giants, puts St. Louis in first place by two percentage points. The fifth place Giants beat Brooklyn, 4-3 and 5-1.

September 17 Stan Musial makes his major league debut, going 2-for-4 as the St. Louis Cardinals beat the Boston Braves. Musial, who started the season in the Western Association (Class C), will hit .426 in 12 games.

September 28 A jubilant crowd at Ebbets Field watches as the Dodgers beat the Phillies 6-1 to clinch the pennant. The crowd sets a new attendance record at 1,215,253.

October 5 With two out in the ninth inning, Dodger catcher Mickey Owen drops a third strike on Tommy Henrich, which would have given Brooklyn a 4-3 victory over New York and tied the Series at two games apiece. The Yankees then rally for a 7-4 win and clinch the next day behind pitcher Ernie "Tiny" Bonham.

December 2 The Giants name Mel Ott as player-manager replacing Bill Terry, who moves up to the general manager's spot.

BOSTON		BROOKLYN		CHICAGO		CINCINNATI		NEW YORK		PHILADELPHIA		PITTSBURGH		ST.LOUIS	
M	C.Stengel	M	L.Durocher	M	J.Wilson	M	B.McKechnie	M	B.Terry	M	D.Prothro	M	F.Frisch	M	B.Southworth
1B	B.Hassett	1B	D.Camilli	1B	B.Dahlgren	1B	F.McCormick	1B	B.Young	1B	N.Etten	1B	E.Fletcher	1B	J.Mize
2B	B.Rowell	2B	B.Herman	2B	L.Stringer	2B	L.Frey	2B	B.Whitehead	2B	D.Murtaugh	2B	F.Gustine	2B	C.Crespi
SS	E.Miller	SS	P.Reese	SS	B.Sturgeon	SS	E.Joost	SS	B.Jurges	SS	B.Bragan	SS	A.Vaughan	SS	M.Marion
3B	S.Sisti	3B	C.Lavagetto	3B	S.Hack	3B	B.Werber	3B	D.Bartell	3B	P.May	3B	L.Handley	3B	J.Brown
LF	M.West	LF	J.Medwick	LF	D.Dallessandro	LF	M.McCormick	LF	J.Moore	LF	D.Litwhiler	LF	M.Van Robays	LF	J.Hopp
CF	J.Cooney	CF	P.Reiser	CF	P.Cavarretta	CF	H.Craft	CF	J.Rucker	CF	J.Marty	CF	V.DiMaggio	CF	T.Moore
RF	G.Moore	RF	D.Walker	RF	B.Nicholson	RF	J.Gleeson	RF	M.Ott	RF	S.Benjamin	RF	B.Elliott	RF	E.Slaughter
C	R.Berres	C	M.Owen	C	C.McCullough	C	E.Lombardi	C	H.Danning	C	B.Warren	C	A.Lopez	C	G.Mancuso
O	P.Waner	O1	J.Wasdell	O	L.Novikoff	O	E.Koy	3	J.Orengo	C	M.Livingston	2	S.Martin	OC	D.Padgett
C	P.Masi	3	L.Riggs	O1	H.Leiber	C	D.West	O	E.Arnovich	C	J.Rizzo	S	A.Anderson	C	W.Cooper
2	S.Roberge	C	H.Franks	C	B.Scheffing	3	C.Aleno	C	G.Hartnett	2O	H.Mueller	3O	D.Garms	O	C.Triplett
1	B.Dahlgren	2	P.Coscarart	O	A.Galan	O	L.Waner	2	O.Hale	2S	H.Marnie	O	B.Stewart	O	E.Crabtree
O	F.Demaree	O	J.Vosmik	S2	J.Hudson	O	I.Goodman	2	M.Witek	O	C.Klein	C	S.Davis	S3	E.Lake
1	B.Gremp	2	A.Kampouris	O	C.Gilbert	C	J.Ripple	C	K.O'Dea	2	B.Nagel	C	B.Baker	3	S.Mesner
3	H.Majeski	S	L.Durocher	O	B.Olsen	O	E.Lukon	3	J.Davis	/O	J.Carlin	1	R.Collins	O	S.Musial
C	A.Montgomery	/O	P.Waner	C	G.George	S	B.Mattick	O	B.Barna	/O	P.Busby	S	B.Cox	C	E.Koy
O	L.Waner	C	B.Phelps	S	B.Myers	/O	H.Sauer	/1	J.McCarthy	/2	G.Jumonville	/C	V.Smith	/O	H.Walker
O	C.Ross	/O	A.Galan	2	B.Herman	/2	B.Zientara	O	F.Demaree	/C	W.Millies	/2	E.Leip	/O	E.Dusak
2	W.Wietlmann	/O	T.Tatum	/1	E.Waitkus	/3	P.Young	/O	S.Gordon	.		/O	C.Rikard	/O	W.Sessi
/O	D.Manno	/C	T.Giuliani	/S	L.Merullo	C	J.Riddle	/C	R.Blaemire	P	J.Podgajny	/O	L.Waner	/3	W.Kurowski
/2	J.Dudra	/C	G.Pfister	/1	R.Russell	/C	B.Baker	R	J.Aragon	P	T.Hughes	/C	J.Schultz	H	P.Young
/O	E.Averill			/O	F.Jelincich	H	E.Shokes			P	C.Blanton			/C	C.Marshall
/O	B.Bray	P	K.Higbe	H	A.Todd	/C	R.Lamanno	P	H.Schumacher	P	S.Johnson	P	R.Sewell		
/O	M.Preibisch	P	W.Wyatt					P	C.Melton	P	L.Grissom	P	M.Butcher	P	L.Warneke
		P	H.Casey	P	C.Passeau	P	B.Walters	P	C.Hubbell	RP	I.Pearson	P	K.Heintzelman	P	E.White
P	J.Tobin	P	C.Davis	P	V.Olsen	P	P.Derringer	RP	B.Lohrman	RP	L.Hoerst	P	J.Lanning	P	M.Cooper
P	M.Salvo	P	L.Hamlin	P	B.Lee	P	J.Vander Meer	RP	B.Carpenter	RP	B.Beck	P	B.Klinger	P	M.Lanier
P	A.Johnson			P	J.Mooty	P	E.Riddle	RP	B.Bowman					P	H.Gumbert
P	D.Errickson	P	F.Fitzsimmons	P	P.Erickson	RP	J.Turner	RP	A.Adams	P	R.Melton	P	D.Dietz	RP	C.Shoun
P	A.Javery	RP	J.Allen	RP	T.Pressnell	RP	W.Moore	RP	J.Brown	P	B.Crouch	P	L.Wilkie	RP	I.Hutchinson
RP	J.Hutchings	RP	N.Kimball	RP	V.Page	RP	J.Beggs			P	R.Bruner	P	J.Bowman		
RP	F.LaManna	P	M.Brown					P	B.McGee	P	B.Harman	P	J.Sullivan	P	H.Krist
		P	K.Wicker					/P	J.Wittig	/P	V.Tamulis	/P	R.Bauers	P	S.Nahem
P	T.Earley	P	T.Drake	P	L.French	P	J.Thompson	/P	H.Gumbert	/P	P.Masterson	/P	N.Strincevich	/P	H.Pollet
P	B.Posedel	P	B.Swift	P	C.Root	/P	R.Starr	/P	D.Koslo	/P	G.Lambert	/P	B.Clemensen	P	B.Crouch
P	J.Sullivan	P	V.Tamulis	P	V.Eaves	/P	M.Pearson	/P	H.Feldman	/P	D.Jones	/P	D.Lanahan	/P	B.McGee
/P	W.Ferrell	/P	L.French	/P	J.Schmitz	/P	J.Hutchings	/P	H.East			/P	B.Brandt	/P	J.Grodzicki
/P	G.Barnicle	/P	E.Albosta	P	K.Raffensberger	/P	B.Logan	/P	T.Sunkel			/P	J.Gee	/P	H.Gornicki
/P	N.Strincevich	/P	L.Grissom	/P	R.Meers			/P	B.Hadley			/P	D.Conger	/P	J.Beazley
/P	E.Carnett	/P	B.Chipman	/P	W.Lanfranconi			/P	R.Fischer			/P	M.Brown	/P	H.Lyons
/P	A.Piechota	/P	V.Mungo	/P	W.Quinn			/P	P.Dean						
				/P	E.Kush										
				/P	H.Gornicki										
				/P	D.Dean										

TEAM	G	W	L	PCT	GB	R	OR	AB	H	2B	3B	HR	BB	SO	AVG	OBP	SLG	PRO	PRO+	BR	/A	PF	CHI	RC	SB	CS	SBA	SBR
BRO	157	100	54	.649		800	581	5485	1494	286	69	101	600	535	.272	.347	.405	.752	113	128	93	104	98	792	36			
STL	155	97	56	.634	2.5	734	589	5457	1482	254	56	70	540	543	.272	.340	.377	.717	102	62	13	107	99	719	47			
CIN	154	88	66	.571	12	616	564	5218	1288	213	33	64	477	428	.247	.313	.337	.650	89	-72	-74	100	108	556	68			
PIT	156	81	73	.526	19	690	643	5297	1417	233	65	56	547	516	.268	.338	.368	.706	105	39	42	100	99	670	59			
NY	156	74	79	.484	25.5	667	706	5395	1401	248	35	95	504	518	.260	.326	.371	.697	101	15	1	102	98	659	36			
CHI	155	70	84	.455	30	666	670	5230	1323	239	25	99	559	670	.253	.327	.365	.692	105	9	33	96	101	642	39			
BOS	156	62	92	.403	38	592	720	5414	1357	231	38	48	471	608	.251	.312	.334	.646	92	-82	-58	96	103	568	61			
PHI	155	43	111	.279	57	501	793	5233	1277	188	38	64	451	596	.244	.307	.331	.638	89	-97	-77	96	93	528	65			
TOT	622					5266		42729	11039	1892	359	597	4149	4414	.258	.326	.361	.688						411				

TEAM	CG	SH	SV	IP	H	H/G	HR	BB	SO	RAT	ERA	ERA+	OAV	OOB	PR	/A	PF	CPI	FA	E	DP	FW	PW	BW	SBW	DIF
BRO	66	17	22	1421	1236	7.8	81	495	603	11.1	3.14	117	.233	.300	78	83	101	93	.974	162	125	.9	8.5	9.6		4.0
STL	64	15	20	1416[1]	1289	8.2	85	502	659	11.5	3.19	118	.242	.310	70	90	104	101	.973	172	146	.2	9.2	1.3		9.7
CIN	89	19	10	1386[2]	1300	8.4	61	510	627	11.9	3.17	114	.250	.319	72	66	99	106	.975	152	147	1.3	6.8	-7.6		10.6
PIT	71	8	12	1374[1]	1392	9.1	66	492	410	12.4	3.48	104	.260	.323	23	19	99	102	.968	196	130	-1.1	2.0	4.3		-1.1
NY	55	12	18	1391[1]	1455	9.4	90	539	566	13.0	3.94	94	.269	.337	-48	-39	102	102	.974	160	144	.9	-4.0	.1		.5
CHI	74	8	9	1364[2]	1431	9.4	60	449	548	12.5	3.72	94	.267	.327	-13	-32	97	98	.970	180	139	-.3	-3.3	3.4		-6.8
BOS	62	10	9	1385[2]	1440	9.4	75	554	446	13.2	3.95	90	.269	.341	-49	-58	98	102	.969	191	174	-.9	-6.0	-6.0		-2.2
PHI	35	4	9	1372[1]	1499	9.8	79	606	552	14.0	4.50	82	.279	.355	-132	-121	102	98	.969	187	147	-.7	-12.4	-7.9		-13.0
TOT	516	93	109	11112[2]		8.9				12.4	3.63		.258	.326					.972	1400	1152					

Runs		Hits		Doubles		Triples		Home Runs		Total Bases	
Reiser-Bro	117	Hack-Chi	186	Reiser-Bro	39	Reiser-Bro	17	Camilli-Bro	34	Reiser-Bro	299
Hack-Chi	111	Reiser-Bro	184	Mize-StL	39	Fletcher-Pit	13	Ott-NY	27	Camilli-Bro	294
Medwick-Bro	100	Litwhiler-Phi	180	Rucker-NY	38	Hopp-StL	11	Nicholson-Chi	26	Medwick-Bro	278
Rucker-NY	95	Rucker-NY	179	Dallessandro-Chi	36	Medwick-Bro	10	Young-NY	25	Litwhiler-Phi	275
Fletcher-Pit	95	Medwick-Bro	171			Elliott-Pit	10	Dahlgren-Bos-Chi	23	Young-NY	265

Runs Batted In		Runs Produced		Bases On Balls		Batting Average		On Base Percentage		Slugging Average	
Camilli-Bro	120	Reiser-Bro	179	Fletcher-Pit	118	Reiser-Bro	.343	Fletcher-Pit	.421	Reiser-Bro	.558
Young-NY	104	Camilli-Bro	178	Camilli-Bro	104	Cooney-Bos	.319	Hack-Chi	.417	Camilli-Bro	.556
Mize-StL	100	Medwick-Bro	170	Ott-NY	100	Medwick-Bro	.318	Camilli-Bro	.407	Mize-StL	.535
DiMaggio-Pit	100	Young-NY	169	Hack-Chi	99	Hack-Chi	.317	Reiser-Bro	.406	Medwick-Bro	.517
Nicholson-Chi	98	Fletcher-Pit	158			Mize-StL	.317	Mize-StL	.406	Slaughter-StL	.496

Production		Adjusted Production		Batter Runs		Adjusted Batter Runs		Clutch Hitting Index		Runs Created	
Reiser-Bro	.964	Reiser-Bro	163	Camilli-Bro	50.2	Camilli-Bro	45.1	Lavagetto-Bro	160	Camilli-Bro	128
Camilli-Bro	.962	Camilli-Bro	162	Reiser-Bro	48.0	Reiser-Bro	43.1	VanRobays-Pit	143	Reiser-Bro	124
Mize-StL	.941	Mize-StL	153	Mize-StL	40.2	Fletcher-Pit	38.6	Dallessandro-Chi	139	Ott-NY	115
Ott-NY	.898	Ott-NY	149	Ott-NY	38.7	Hack-Chi	37.9	Bragan-Phi	124	Hack-Chi	114
Slaughter-StL	.886	Fletcher-Pit	148	Fletcher-Pit	38.2	Ott-NY	36.5	Elliott-Pit	121	Fletcher-Pit	111

Total Average		Stolen Bases		Stolen Base Average	Stolen Base Runs	Fielding Runs		Total Player Rating	
Camilli-Bro	1.057	Murtaugh-Phi	18			May-Phi	25.2	Reiser-Bro	4.7
Reiser-Bro	1.006	Benjamin-Phi	17			Stringer-Chi	20.1	Camilli-Bro	3.7
Mize-StL	.991	Handley-Pit	16			Litwhiler-Phi	17.1	Fletcher-Pit	3.7
Ott-NY	.976	Frey-Cin	16			Werber-Cin	12.5	Ott-NY	3.3
Fletcher-Pit	.965	Hopp-StL	15			Miller-Bos	12.2	Litwhiler-Phi	3.2

Wins		Win Percentage		Games		Complete Games		Shutouts		Saves	
Wyatt-Bro	22	E.Riddle-Cin	.826	Higbe-Bro	48	Walters-Cin	27	Wyatt-Bro	7	Brown-NY	8
Higbe-Bro	22	Higbe-Bro	.710	Pearson-Phi	46	Wyatt-Bro	23	VanderMeer-Cin	6	Crouch-Phi-StL	7
Walters-Cin	19	White-StL	.708	Casey-Bro	45	Tobin-Bos	20	Walters-Cin	5	Casey-Bro	7
E.Riddle-Cin	19	Wyatt-Bro	.688	Hutchings-Cin-Bos	44	Passeau-Chi	20	Davis-Bro	5	Pearson-Phi	6
		Warneke-StL	.654	Johnson-Bos	43						

Innings Pitched		Fewest Hits/Game		Fewest BB/Game		Strikeouts		Strikeouts/Game		Ratio	
Walters-Cin	302.0	VanderMeer-Cin	6.84	Passeau-Chi	2.03	VanderMeer-Cin	202	VanderMeer-Cin	8.03	Wyatt-Bro	9.58
Higbe-Bro	298.0	Wyatt-Bro	6.96	Derringer-Cin	2.13	Wyatt-Bro	176	M.Cooper-StL	5.69	E.Riddle-Cin	10.14
Wyatt-Bro	288.1	White-StL	7.24	Lohrman-NY	2.26	Walters-Cin	129	Wyatt-Bro	5.49	White-StL	10.50
Sewell-Pit	249.0	Higbe-Bro	7.37	Tobin-Bos	2.27	Higbe-Bro	121	White-StL	5.01	Tobin-Bos	10.93
Warneke-StL	246.0	E.Riddle-Cin	7.48	Lee-Chi	2.31	M.Cooper-StL	118	Melton-NY	4.63	Sewell-Pit	11.28

Earned Run Average		Adjusted ERA		Opponents' Batting Avg.		Opponents' On Base Pct.		Starter Runs		Adjusted Starter Runs	
E.Riddle-Cin	2.24	E.Riddle-Cin	160	Wyatt-Bro	.212	Wyatt-Bro	.270	Wyatt-Bro	41.4	Wyatt-Bro	42.4
Wyatt-Bro	2.34	White-StL	157	VanderMeer-Cin	.214	E.Riddle-Cin	.282	E.Riddle-Cin	33.5	E.Riddle-Cin	32.6
White-StL	2.40	Wyatt-Bro	157	White-StL	.217	White-StL	.287	White-StL	28.8	White-StL	31.8
VanderMeer-Cin	2.82	VanderMeer-Cin	127	Higbe-Bro	.220	Sewell-Pit	.299	Walters-Cin	26.9	Walters-Cin	25.7
Walters-Cin	2.83	Walters-Cin	127	E.Riddle-Cin	.224	Tobin-Bos	.300	VanderMeer-Cin	20.4	VanderMeer-Cin	19.5

Clutch Pitching Index		Relief Runs		Adjusted Relief Runs		Relief Ranking		Total Pitcher Index		Total Baseball Ranking	
V.Olsen-Chi	120	Pressnell-Chi	4.3	Pressnell-Chi	3.3	Pressnell-Chi	3.5	Wyatt-Bro	5.3	Wyatt-Bro	5.3
Heintzelman-Pit	117	Brown-NY	2.0	Brown-NY	2.4	Brown-NY	3.0	E.Riddle-Cin	3.6	Reiser-Bro	4.7
Butcher-Pit	112	Pearson-Phi	.9	Pearson-Phi	1.9	Pearson-Phi	2.5	Walters-Cin	3.3	Camilli-Bro	3.7
Johnson-Bos	111	Sullivan-Bos-Pit	.0					White-StL	3.3	Fletcher-Pit	3.7
Walters-Cin	111							Gumbert-NY-StL	2.3	E.Riddle-Cin	3.6

May 6 Playing in his last game before induction into the Army, Hank Greenberg hits two home runs to lead Detroit to a 7-4 win over the Yankees. A few days later outfielder Joe Gallagher of the Dodgers is drafted, but no other regular major league player will be drafted during the season.

May 15 Joe DiMaggio gets a single in four at bats against Ed Smith of the Chicago White Sox to start his 56-game hitting streak.

May 25 Ted Williams raises his batting average over .400 for the first time during the season.

June 2 New York Yankees first baseman Lou Gehrig dies of amyotrophic lateral sclerosis at age 37 in New York. From that time on, the illness is known primarily as Lou Gehrig's Disease.

July 8 At the All-Star Game at Briggs Stadium, Ted Williams, hitting .405 at the break, homers off Chicago Cubs pitcher Claude Passeau with two out and two on in the ninth inning to give the AL a dramatic 7-5 victory. Williams's four RBIs are matched by NL shortstop Arky Vaughan, who hits home runs in the seventh and eighth.

July 17 In front of more than 60,000 fans at Cleveland, Joe DiMaggio's hitting streak is ended at 56 games. Indian pitchers Al Smith and Jim Bagby, plus sensational plays by third baseman Ken Keltner, stop the Yankee Clipper, but New York edges the Indians 6-5.

July 25 Forty-one-year-old Lefty Grove wins his 300th game as the Boston Red Sox defeat the Cleveland Indians 10-6 before a Fenway Ladies Day crowd of 16,000. Though he will make six more starts, this will be Grove's last career win.

August 1 Vernon "Lefty" Gomez of the New York Yankees pitches a 9–0 shutout over the St. Louis Browns despite walking 11 batters, the most ever issued in a shutout. Fifteen base runners are left stranded by the Browns.

August 3 Browns pitcher Johnny Niggling gets Joe DiMaggio in four at bats to stop Joe DiMaggio's streak of reaching base in 74 consecutive games.

September 28 Ted Williams collects four hits in five at bats in the 12-11 first-game victory in Philadelphia to bring his average to .404. He goes 2-for-3 in game two against rookie Fred Caligiuri, who beats Lefty Grove 7-1. Williams will finish the season with a .406 batting average.

September 29 Overshadowed by the .406 mark of Ted Williams and the hitting streak of Joe DiMaggio, Jeff Heath of the Indians hits over 20 doubles, triples, and home runs during the season. The Canadian muscleman will finish with 32 doubles, 20 triples, and 24 home runs. It will be 38 years before George Brett duplicates the feat in the AL.

October 1 Red Ruffing pitches the Yankees to a 3-2 win over the Dodgers at Yankee Stadium in the opening game of the World Series. Joe Gordon chips in with a home run and RBI single.

October 4 In the seventh inning of a scoreless tie, Yankees pitcher Marius Russo breaks pitcher Fred Fitzsimmons's knee with a line drive. The Yankees score two in the eighth off Hugh Casey to win, 2-1.

November 25 Lou Boudreau is named player-manager of the Cleveland Indians. At 24 years, four months, and eight days, Boudreau is the youngest manager appointed in this century. Scotland-born Jim McCormick managed Cleveland in 1879 at the age of 23.

November 27 Joe DiMaggio is named league MVP. His 56-game hitting streak edges out Ted Williams and his .406 batting average for the award (291 votes for DiMaggio and 254 for Williams).

	BOSTON		CHICAGO		CLEVELAND		DETROIT		NEW YORK		PHILADELPHIA		ST.LOUIS		WASHINGTON
M	J.Cronin	M	J.Dykes	M	R.Peckinpaugh	M	D.Baker	M	J.McCarthy	M	C.Mack	M	F.Haney	M	B.Harris
1B	J.Foxx	1B	J.Kuhel	1B	H.Trosky	1B	R.York	1B	J.Sturm	1B	D.Siebert	M	L.Sewell	1B	M.Vernon
2B	B.Doerr	2B	B.Knickerb'r	2B	R.Mack	2B	C.Gehringer	2B	J.Gordon	2B	B.McCoy	1B	G.McQuinn	2B	J.Bloodworth
SS	J.Cronin	SS	L.Appling	SS	L.Boudreau	SS	F.Croucher	SS	P.Rizzuto	SS	A.Brancato	2B	D.Heffner	SS	C.Travis
3B	J.Tabor	3B	D.Lodigiani	3B	K.Keltner	3B	P.Higgins	3B	R.Rolfe	3B	P.Suder	SS	J.Berardino	3B	G.Archie
LF	T.Williams	LF	M.Hoag	LF	G.Walker	LF	R.Radcliff	LF	C.Keller	LF	B.Johnson	3B	H.Clift	LF	G.Case
CF	D.DiMaggio	CF	M.Kreevich	CF	R.Weatherly	CF	B.McCosky	CF	J.DiMaggio	CF	S.Chapman	LF	R.Cullenbine	CF	D.Cramer
RF	L.Finney	RF	T.Wright	RF	J.Heath	RF	B.Campbell	RF	T.Henrich	RF	W.Moses	CF	W.Judnich	RF	B.Lewis
C	F.Pytlak	C	M.Tresh	C	R.Hemsley	C	B.Tebbetts	C	B.Dickey	C	F.Hayes	RF	C.Laabs	C	J.Early
												C	R.Ferrell		
O	P.Fox	2	D.Kolloway	O	S.Campbell	O	T.Stainback	C	B.Rosar	O	E.Collins	C	J.Grace	C	A.Evans
C	J.Peacock	3	B.Kennedy	12	O.Grimes	C	B.Sullivan	23	J.Priddy	O	D.Miles	O	J.Grace	O	B.Chapman
S2	S.Newsome	O	M.Solters	C	G.Desautels	O	P.Mullin	O	G.Selkirk	H	H.Wagner	2S	J.Lucadello	2	B.Myer
O	S.Spence	O	B.Chapman	O1	B.Bell	2	D.Meyer	S3	F.Crosetti	21	C.Davis	C	B.Swift	O	J.Welaj
/1	A.Flair	C	T.Turner	O	L.Rosenthal	S2	B.Perry	O	F.Bordagaray	S	F.Chapman	S	A.Strange	O	R.Ortiz
/3	O.Hale	2	S.Webb	O	H.Edwards	O	H.Greenberg	O	K.Silvestri	C	E.Valo	O	B.Estalella	S	J.Pofahl
/2	T.Carey	O	L.Rosenthal	S	R.Peters	O	N.Harris	H	J.Lindell	/3	D.Richmond	O	R.Radcliff	C	R.Ferrell
R	P.Campbell	C	G.Dickey	C	J.Hegan	3	E.McNair			/0	A.Simmons	C	F.Grube	3	H.Layne
		/1	J.Jones	/O	B.Frierson	/S	D.Bartell	P	M.Russo	/3	A.Rubeling	/1	G.Archie	/0	S.West
P	D.Newsome	/O	D.Philley	/1	L.Fleming	/S	M.Franklin	P	R.Ruffing	P	F.Mackiewicz	/0	G.McQuillen	/2	M.Aderholt
P	M.Harris	/O	D.Short	/1	V.Freiburger	/O	B.Patrick	P	S.Chandler	/O	E.Tipton	/1	C.Stevens	/C	C.Bolton
P	C.Wagner	H	S.Goletz	H	R.Howell	/O	D.Wakefield	P	A.Donald	/0	J.Leovich	/S	V.Stephens	/2	C.Letchas
P	L.Grove	C	C.Hajduk	/O	O.Hockett	/O	H.Evers	P	L.Gomez	H	R.Poole	H	M.Hoag	/1	J.Sanford
P	J.Dobson			/O	F.Gaffke	H	F.Hutchinson	RP	J.Murphy					/3	S.Robertson
		P	T.Lee	/3	B.Lemon			RP	C.Stanceu	P	P.Marchildon	P	E.Auker		
P	M.Ryba	P	E.Smith	H	C.Workman	P	B.Newsom	RP	N.Branch	J	J.Knott	P	B.Muncrief	P	D.Leonard
P	J.Wilson	P	J.Rigney	/S	J.Conway	P	H.Newhouser	P		P	L.McCrabb	P	D.Galehouse	P	S.Hudson
P	E.Johnson	P	T.Lyons	/C	G.Susce	P	J.Gorsica	P	M.Breuer	P	L.Harris	P	B.Harris	P	K.Chase
P	T.Hughson	P	B.Dietrich			P	A.Benton	P	T.Bonham	P	B.Beckmann	P	J.Niggeling	P	S.Sundra
P	B.Fleming			P	B.Feller	P	D.Trout	P	S.Peek			RP	J.Kramer	P	R.Anderson
/P	E.Dickman	P	B.Ross	P	A.Milnar	RP	B.Thomas	/P	G.Washburn	P	T.Ferrick	RP	B.Trotter	RP	A.Carrasquel
P	N.Potter	P	J.Hallett	P	A.Smith			P	B.Hadley			RP	B.Zuber
/P	O.Judd	P	J.Humphries	P	J.Bagby	P	T.Bridges	P	J.Babich	P	G.Caster	RP	W.Masterson
/P	H.Hash	/P	J.Haynes	RP	C.Brown	P	S.Rowe	P	C.Dean	P	J.Allen	
/P	W.Rich	P	P.Appleton	RP	J.Heving	P	A.McKain	F.Caligiuri	P	F.Ostermueller	P	V.Kennedy
		/P	O.Grove			P	F.Giebell	/P	D.Fowler	/P	V.Kennedy	/P	E.Wynn
				P	M.Harder	/P	H.Manders	N.Potter	/P	M.Newlin	/P	D.Mulligan
				/P	C.Dean	/P	L.Mueller	/P	P.Vaughan	/P	A.McKain	/P	D.MacFayden
				P	J.Krakauskas	/P	H.White	/P	H.Besse	/P	E.Bildilli	/P	H.Dean
				P	H.Eisenstat	/P	E.Cook	R.Wolff	/P	H.Iott	/P	R.Miller
				/P	S.Gromek	/P	V.Trucks	/P	R.Johnson		
				/P	K.Jungels			/P	T.Shirley		
				/P	C.Dorsett			/P	B.Ross		
				/P	R.Embree			P.Tobin		
				/P	N.Andrews					

TEAM	G	W	L	PCT	GB	R	OR	AB	H	2B	3B	HR	BB	SO	AVG	OBP	SLG	PRO	PRO+	BR	/A	PF	CHI	RC	SB	CS	SBA	SBR
NY	156	101	53	.656		830	631	5444	1464	243	60	151	616	565	.269	.346	.419	.765	111	64	75	99	103	822	51	33	61	-5
BOS	155	84	70	.545	17	865	750	5359	1517	304	55	124	683	567	.283	.366	.430	.796	115	136	115	102	98	872	67	51	57	-11
CHI	156	77	77	.500	24	638	649	5404	1376	245	47	47	510	476	.255	.322	.343	.665	84	-128	-120	99	106	612	91	53	63	-5
DET	155	75	79	.487	26	686	743	5370	1412	247	55	81	602	584	.263	.340	.375	.715	87	-27	-98	110	97	713	43	28	61	-4
CLE	155	75	79	.487	26	677	668	5283	1350	249	84	103	512	605	.256	.323	.393	.716	101	-40	-7	95	100	691	63	47	57	-9
WAS	156	70	84	.455	31	728	798	5521	1502	257	80	52	470	488	.272	.331	.376	.707	99	-53	-21	95	107	702	79	36	69	2
STL	157	70	84	.455	31	765	823	5408	1440	281	58	91	775	552	.266	.360	.390	.750	103	56	29	103	93	804	50	39	56	-8
PHI	154	64	90	.416	37	713	840	5336	1431	240	69	85	574	588	.268	.340	.387	.727	102	-7	11	98	99	711	27	36	43	-14
TOT	622					5902		43125	11492	2066	508	734	4742	4425	.266	.341	.389	.730							471	323	59	-53

TEAM	CG	SH	SV	IP	H	H/G	HR	BB	SO	RAT	ERA	ERA+	OAV	OOB	PR	/A	PF	CPI	FA	E	DP	FW	PW	BW	SBW	DIF
NY	75	13	26	1396[1]	1309	8.4	81	598	589	12.4	3.53	112	.248	.325	96	63	95	102	.973	165	196	.5	6.1	7.3	.2	10.0
BOS	70	8	11	1372	1453	9.5	88	611	574	13.7	4.19	100	.270	.347	-6	-3	101	102	.972	172	139	.0	-.3	11.1	-.4	-3.5
CHI	106	14	4	1416	1362	8.7	89	521	564	12.1	3.52	116	.252	.320	99	91	99	102	.971	180	145	-.3	8.8	-11.6	.2	3.0
DET	52	8	16	1381[2]	1399	9.1	80	645	697	13.4	4.18	109	.260	.341	-4	57	110	96	.969	186	129	-.7	5.5	-9.5	.2	2.5
CLE	68	10	19	1377	1366	8.9	71	660	617	13.4	3.90	101	.259	.344	39	7	95	103	.976	142	158	1.7	.7	-.7	-.2	-3.5
WAS	69	8	7	1389[1]	1524	9.9	69	603	544	13.9	4.35	93	.279	.353	-32	-48	98	101	.969	187	169	-.7	-4.7	-2.0	.8	-.4
STL	65	7	10	1389	1563	10.1	120	549	454	13.8	4.72	91	.283	.350	-88	-64	104	99	.975	151	156	1.3	-6.2	2.8	-.1	-4.8
PHI	64	3	18	1365[1]	1516	10.0	136	557	386	13.8	4.83	87	.279	.348	-104	-98	101	97	.967	200	150	-1.6	-9.5	1.1	-.7	-2.3
TOT	569	71	111	11086[2]		9.3				13.3	4.15		.266	.341					.972	1383	1242					

Runs		Hits		Doubles		Triples		Home Runs		Total Bases	
Williams-Bos	135	Travis-Was	218	Boudreau-Cle	45	Heath-Cle	20	Williams-Bos	37	DiMaggio-NY	348
DiMaggio-NY	122	Heath-Cle	199	DiMaggio-NY	43	Travis-Was	19	Keller-NY	33	Heath-Cle	343
DiMaggio-Bos	117	DiMaggio-NY	193	Judnich-StL	40	Keltner-Cle	13	Henrich-NY	31	Williams-Bos	335
Clift-StL	108	Appling-Chi	186	Travis-Was	39			DiMaggio-NY	30	Travis-Was	316
		Williams-Bos	185	Kuhel-Chi	39			York-Det	27	S.Chapman-Phi	300

Runs Batted In		Runs Produced		Bases On Balls		Batting Average		On Base Percentage		Slugging Average	
DiMaggio-NY	125	Williams-Bos	218	Williams-Bos	145	Williams-Bos	.406	Williams-Bos	.551	Williams-Bos	.735
Heath-Cle	123	DiMaggio-NY	217	Cullenbine-StL	121	Travis-Was	.359	Cullenbine-StL	.452	DiMaggio-NY	.643
Keller-NY	122	Travis-Was	200	Clift-StL	113	DiMaggio-NY	.357	DiMaggio-NY	.440	Heath-Cle	.586
Williams-Bos	120	Keller-NY	191	Keller-NY	102	Heath-Cle	.340	Keller-NY	.416	Keller-NY	.580
York-Det	111	Heath-Cle	188			Siebert-Phi	.334	Foxx-Bos	.412	S.Chapman-Phi	.543

Production		Adjusted Production		Batter Runs		Adjusted Batter Runs		Clutch Hitting Index		Runs Created	
Williams-Bos	1.286	Williams-Bos	232	Williams-Bos	102.0	Williams-Bos	97.9	Berardino-StL	152	Williams-Bos	202
DiMaggio-NY	1.083	DiMaggio-NY	186	DiMaggio-NY	64.3	DiMaggio-NY	66.3	Cullenbine-StL	126	DiMaggio-NY	162
Keller-NY	.996	Heath-Cle	165	Keller-NY	45.7	Heath-Cle	51.0	Tabor-Bos	125	Heath-Cle	138
Heath-Cle	.982	Keller-NY	163	Heath-Cle	44.8	Keller-NY	47.4	Foxx-Bos	116	Keller-NY	134
Travis-Was	.930	Travis-Was	152	Cullenbine-StL	38.3	Travis-Was	43.7	Wright-Chi	116	Travis-Was	131

Total Average		Stolen Bases		Stolen Base Average		Stolen Base Runs		Fielding Runs		Total Player Rating	
Williams-Bos	1.688	Case-Was	33	Kuhel-Chi	80.0	Case-Was	4.5	Bloodworth-Was	34.7	Williams-Bos	7.9
DiMaggio-NY	1.208	Kuhel-Chi	20	Case-Was	78.6	Kuhel-Chi	3.0	Keltner-Cle	22.5	DiMaggio-NY	6.4
Keller-NY	1.099	Heath-Cle	18	Kreevich-Chi	77.3	Kreevich-Chi	2.1	Rizzuto-NY	15.6	Travis-Was	5.3
Cullenbine-StL	1.023	Tabor-Bos	17	Tabor-Bos	65.4	Fox-Bos	1.5	Case-Was	15.2	Keller-NY	4.1
Heath-Cle	1.000	Kreevich-Chi	17	Heath-Cle	60.0			S.Chapman-Phi	14.4	Keltner-Cle	3.5

Wins		Win Percentage		Games		Complete Games		Shutouts		Saves	
Feller-Cle	25	Gomez-NY	.750	Feller-Cle	44	Lee-Chi	30	Feller-Cle	6	Murphy-NY	15
Lee-Chi	22	Ruffing-NY	.714	Newsom-Det	43	Feller-Cle	28	Leonard-Was	4	Ferrick-Phi	7
D.Newsome-Bos	19	Benton-Det	.714	Brown-Cle	41	Smith-Chi	21	Humphries-Chi	4	Benton-Det	7
Leonard-Was	18	Lee-Chi	.667	Ryba-Bos	40	Lyons-Chi	19	Chandler-NY	4	Ryba-Bos	6
		Feller-Cle	.658	Benton-Det	38	Leonard-Was	19				

Innings Pitched		Fewest Hits/Game		Fewest BB/Game		Strikeouts		Strikeouts/Game		Ratio	
Feller-Cle	343.0	Benton-Det	7.42	Lyons-Chi	1.78	Feller-Cle	260	Feller-Cle	6.82	Lee-Chi	10.61
Lee-Chi	300.1	Feller-Cle	7.45	Leonard-Was	1.90	Newsom-Det	175	Newsom-Det	6.29	Ruffing-NY	11.25
Smith-Chi	263.1	Lee-Chi	7.73	Muncrief-StL	2.23	Lee-Chi	130	Newhouser-Det	5.51	Benton-Det	11.30
Leonard-Was	256.0	Donald-NY	7.98	Ruffing-NY	2.62	Rigney-Chi	119	Harris-Bos	5.15	Chandler-NY	11.33
Newsom-Det	250.1	Chandler-NY	8.03	Lee-Chi	2.76			Rigney-Chi	4.52	Lyons-Chi	11.53

Earned Run Average		Adjusted ERA		Opponents' Batting Avg.		Opponents' On Base Pct.		Starter Runs		Adjusted Starter Runs	
Lee-Chi	2.37	Lee-Chi	173	Benton-Det	.221	Lee-Chi	.293	Lee-Chi	59.4	Lee-Chi	57.7
Benton-Det	2.97	Benton-Det	153	Feller-Cle	.226	Benton-Det	.302	Feller-Cle	38.1	Feller-Cle	30.2
Wagner-Bos	3.07	Wagner-Bos	136	Lee-Chi	.232	Ruffing-NY	.306	Smith-Chi	28.4	Benton-Det	27.6
Russo-NY	3.09	Smith-Chi	129	Donald-NY	.237	Chandler-NY	.307	Russo-NY	24.6	Smith-Chi	26.9
Feller-Cle	3.15	Harris-Bos	128	Chandler-NY	.239	Lyons-Chi	.308	Wagner-Bos	22.3	Wagner-Bos	22.8

Clutch Pitching Index		Relief Runs		Adjusted Relief Runs		Relief Ranking		Total Pitcher Index		Total Baseball Ranking	
Lee-Chi	122	Murphy-NY	18.6	Murphy-NY	16.8	Murphy-NY	28.8	Lee-Chi	6.6	Williams-Bos	7.9
Wagner-Bos	120	Heving-Cle	14.6	Heving-Cle	12.9	Heving-Cle	13.6	Smith-Chi	3.2	Lee-Chi	6.6
Gomez-NY	115	Carrasquel-Was	7.5	Carrasquel-Was	6.4	Carrasquel-Was	5.1	Feller-Cle	3.2	DiMaggio-NY	6.4
Marchildon-Phi	115	Brown-Cle	7.3	Brown-Cle	5.5	Brown-Cle	4.9	Benton-Det	3.1	Travis-Was	5.3
Smith-Chi	112			Thomas-Det	2.7	Thomas-Det	1.5	Murphy-NY	2.7	Keller-NY	4.1

January 4 Rogers Hornsby becomes the 14th player selected to the Hall of Fame, getting 78 percent of the vote.

January 15 The Cubs, who had signed contracts to install lights at Wrigley Field, drop their plans because of the military's need for the material.

February 5 In one of their best trades ever, the Braves get Tommy Holmes from the Yankees for Buddy Hassett and Gene Moore. Hassett will hit .284, then join the Navy, and will not make it back to the major leagues. The much-traveled Moore will never play for the Yanks. Holmes, who couldn't break into New York's outfield, will hit over .300 in 10 seasons with the Braves and win the MVP award in 1948.

May 8 At Ebbets Field, in the first twilight game in 24 years, the Dodgers top the Giants 7-6. Nearly $60,000 is raised for the Navy Relief Fund, as all the proceeds are donated. Everyone, including the ball players, pay their way into the park.

May 13 Pitcher Jim Tobin of the Boston Braves slams three successive home runs to beat the Chicago Cubs at Braves Field.

May 19 Paul Waner, now with the Boston Braves, joins Cap Anson and Honus Wagner as the only NL players with 3,000 hits, with a single off Rip Sewell of the Pittsburgh Pirates. Two days earlier,

Waner's grounder bounced off an infielder's glove and had been ruled a hit. Waner, who did not want his 3000th hit to be a tainted one, signaled to the scorekeeper that it was an error, and the ruling was changed.

May 31 Before 22,000 at Griffith Stadium, Satchel Paige pitches five innings to defeat the Dizzy Dean All-Stars 8-1. Judge Landis will prohibit a scheduled July 4 matchup because the first two games outdrew major league games.

September 13 Chicago Cubs shortstop Lennie Merullo ties the major league record four errors in the second inning of the nightcap against the Boston Braves. Merullo's son is born today and is named, appropriately, Boots. The Cubs win, 12–8, after losing the first game, 10–6.

September 24 Mort Cooper tosses his 10th shutout of the year to give the Cardinals a 6-0 victory over the Reds. His 22nd win of the year clinches at least a tie for the pennant.

September 26 Youngsters, admitted free for bringing scrap metal to aid the war effort, get restless and invade the field at the Polo Grounds in the eighth inning of the second game with the Giants leading, 5–2. Umpire Ziggy Sears forfeits the game, 9–0, to the Braves. Boston pitcher Warren Spahn is not

charged with a loss, although he was losing at the time of the forfeit. But he is given credit for a complete game, his only one in four appearances for the year.

September 27 On the last day of the season, the Cardinals, winners of nine games out of 10, have a 1½ game lead over the Dodgers, winner of seven straight. The Cardinals clinch the NL pennant by winning the first game of a doubleheader from the Cubs by a score of 9–2. Billy Southworth benches his regulars in the nightcap, but the Cards still win, 4–1, giving Johnny Beasley his 21st win of the year. Kirby Higbe wins for the Dodgers, 4–3, at Shibe Park. Brooklyn finishes with 104 victories, the most for a runner-up team since the 1909 Cubs won that many.

September 30 Down 7-0 to Red Ruffing in the World Series opener, the Cardinals rally for four ninth-inning runs. The Cards still lose 7-4, but they will win the next four games.

October 5 Whitey Kurowski's two-run home run in the ninth inning gives St. Louis a 4-2 World Series triumph and enables the Cardinals to upset the New York Yankees in five games.

November 1 After two decades in St. Louis, Branch Rickey splits with owner Sam Breadon and signs to become general manager at Brooklyn.

BOSTON		BROOKLYN		CHICAGO		CINCINNATI		NEW YORK		PHILADELPHIA		PITTSBURGH		ST.LOUIS	
M	C.Stengel	M	L.Durocher	M	J.Wilson	M	B.McKechnie	M	M.Ott	M	H.Lobert	M	F.Frisch	M	B.Southworth
1B	M.West	1B	D.Camilli	1B	P.Cavarretta	1B	F.McCormick	1B	J.Mize	1B	N.Etten	1B	E.Fletcher	1B	J.Hopp
2B	S.Sisti	2B	B.Herman	2B	L.Stringer	2B	L.Frey	2B	M.Witek	2B	A.Glossop	2B	F.Gustine	2B	C.Crespi
SS	E.Miller	SS	P.Reese	SS	L.Merullo	SS	E.Joost	SS	B.Jurges	SS	B.Bragan	SS	P.Coscarart	SS	M.Marion
3B	N.Fernandez	3B	A.Vaughan	3B	S.Hack	3B	B.Haas	3B	B.Werber	3B	P.May	3B	B.Elliott	3B	W.Kurowski
LF	C.Ross	LF	J.Medwick	LF	L.Novikoff	LF	E.Tipton	LF	B.Barna	LF	D.Litwhiler	LF	J.Wasdell	LF	S.Musial
CF	T.Holmes	CF	P.Reiser	CF	D.Dallessandro	CF	G.Walker	CF	W.Marshall	CF	E.Koy	CF	V.DiMaggio	CF	T.Moore
RF	P.Waner	RF	D.Walker	RF	B.Nicholson	RF	M.Marshall	RF	M.Ott	RF	R.Northey	RF	J.Barrett	RF	E.Slaughter
C	E.Lombardi	C	M.Owen	C	C.McCullough	C	R.Lamanno	C	H.Danning	C	B.Warren	C	A.Lopez	C	W.Cooper
C	C.Kluttz	O	J.Rizzo	12	R.Russell	O	I.Goodman	O1	B.Young	S3	D.Murtaugh	C	B.Phelps	23	J.Brown
1	B.Gremp	O	A.Galan	1	J.Foxx	O	M.McCormick	3S	D.Bartell	O	L.Waner	O	M.Van Robays	1	R.Sanders
O1	J.Cooney	3	L.Riggs	O	G.Gilbert	C	R.Hemsley	O3	B.Maynard	C	M.Livingston	O3	B.Stewart	C	K.O'Dea
O	F.Demaree	C	B.Sullivan	2S	B.Sturgeon	O	H.Craft	O1	H.Leiber	S	S.Benjamin	2	S.Martin	O	W.Walker
23	S.Roberge	O	F.Bordagaray	C	C.Hernandez	O	F.Kelleher	C	G.Mancuso	OP	E.Naylor	O	S.Burich	O	C.Triplett
32	T.Cuccinello	/2	A.Kampouris	S	B.Scheffing	S	D.Phillips	C	B.Berres	S	B.Burich	/O	C.Rikard	/O	E.Dusak
C	P.Masi	1	B.Dahlgren	O	P.Lowrey	O	D.West	2	C.Ryan	O	E.Freed	/O	F.Colman	S	B.Blattner
3	D.Detweiler	/C	C.Dapper	1	B.Dahlgren	O	C.Vollmer	/3	S.Gordon	H	H.Marnie	/O	J.Wyrostek	/C	G.Mancuso
S	W.Wietelmann	R	S.Rojek	/3	C.Block	C	A.Lakeman	/O	H.Moss	/1	E.Murphy	/S	H.Geary	/C	S.Narron
/O	F.McElyea			/O	M.Rickert	/3	J.Abreu	/C	C.Fox	H	C.Klein	/O	B.Baker	H	E.Crabtree
/S	M.Sandlock	P	K.Higbe	/C	P.Gillespie	/O	J.Gleeson			/3	B.Hodge	/O	J.Russell	/S	J.Cross
		P	W.Wyatt	/O	W.Platt	/1	H.Sauer	P	H.Schumacher	/C	B.Peterman	R	E.Leip		
		P	C.Davis	/C	M.Felderman	/3	C.Aleno	P	B.Carpenter	/C	B.Culp			P	M.Cooper
P	J.Tobin	P	L.French			/S	B.Mattick	P	B.Lohrman			P	R.Sewell	P	J.Beasley
P	A.Javery	P	E.Head	P	C.Passeau	/O	F.Secory	P	C.Hubbell	P	T.Hughes	P	B.Klinger	P	H.Gumbert
P	L.Tost	P	B.Lee	H	E.Koy			P	C.Melton	P	R.Melton	P	M.Butcher	P	M.Lanier
P	M.Salvo	RP	L.Webber	P	H.Bithorn			RP	A.Adams	P	S.Johnson	P	D.Dietz	P	E.White
P	T.Earley			P	V.Olsen	P	R.Starr			P	J.Podgajny	P	K.Heintzelman		
RP	J.Sain			P	B.Fleming	P	B.Walters	P	H.Feldman	P	L.Hoerst			P	M.Dickson
RP	B.Donovan	P	J.Allen			P	J.Vander Meer	P	B.McGee	RP	I.Pearson	P	J.Lanning	P	H.Krist
RP	D.Errickson	P	M.Macon			P	P.Derringer	P	D.Koslo	RP	S.Nahem	P	H.Gornicki	P	H.Pollet
		/P	B.Newsom	P	L.Warneke	P	E.Riddle	P	T.Sunkel	RP	B.Beck	P	L.Hamlin	P	L.Warneke
P	J.Hutchings	/P	S.Rowe	P	J.Schmitz	RP	J.Beggs	/P	V.Mungo			P	L.Wilkie	/P	B.Lohrman
P	L.Wallace	/P	N.Kimball	P	J.Mooty	RP	C.Shoun	/P	B.Voiselle	/P	C.Blanton	/P	J.Hallett	/P	W.Moore
/P	W.Spahn	/P	C.Kehn	P	P.Erickson			/P	H.East	/P	A.Lapihuska	/P	N.Strincevich	/P	B.Beckmann
/P	F.LaManna	/P	F.Fitzsimmons	P	T.Pressnell					/P	G.Hennessey	/P	B.Brandt	/P	C.Shoun
/P	A.Johnson	/P	B.Chipman	/P	H.Wyse	P	J.Thompson			/P	P.Masterson	P	K.Jungels		
/P	G.Diehl			P	D.Errickson	/P	E.Blackwell			/P	H.Flitcraft	/P	D.Conger		
/P	J.Hickey			/P	E.Hanyzewski	/P	J.Turner			/P	G.Lambert	/P	H.Shuman		
				/P	J.Flores	/P	W.Moore								
				/P	V.Eaves										
				/P	J.Berry										
				/P	E.Kush										
				/P	B.Bowman										

TEAM	G	W	L	PCT	GB	R	OR	AB	H	2B	3B	HR	BB	SO	AVG	OBP	SLG	PRO	PRO+	BR	/A	PF	CHI	RC	SB	CS	SBA	SBR
STL	156	106	48	.688		755	482	5421	1454	282	69	60	551	507	.268	.338	.379	.717	109	109	54	108	103	718	71			
BRO	155	104	50	.675	2	742	510	5285	1398	263	34	62	572	484	.265	.338	.362	.700	110	80	69	102	107	671	81			
NY	154	85	67	.559	20	675	600	5210	1323	162	35	109	558	511	.254	.330	.361	.691	108	59	56	101	102	627	39			
CIN	154	76	76	.500	29	527	545	5260	1216	198	39	66	483	549	.231	.299	.321	.620	88	-81	-80	100	102	519	42			
PIT	151	66	81	.449	36.5	585	631	5104	1250	173	49	54	537	536	.245	.320	.330	.650	95	-15	-29	103	102	556	41			
CHI	155	68	86	.442	38	591	665	5352	1360	224	41	75	509	607	.254	.321	.353	.674	108	23	47	96	93	619	63			
BOS	150	59	89	.399	44	515	645	5077	1216	210	19	68	474	507	.240	.307	.329	.636	94	-48	-37	98	97	520	49			
PHI	151	42	109	.278	62.5	394	706	5060	1174	168	37	44	392	488	.232	.289	.306	.595	84	-125	-103	95	89	451	37			
TOT	613					4784		41769	10391	1680	323	538	4076	4189	.249	.318	.343	.661						423				

TEAM	CG	SH	SV	IP	H	H/G	HR	BB	SO	RAT	ERA	ERA+	OAV	OOB	PR	/A	PF	CPI	FA	E	DP	FW	PW	BW	SBW	DIF
STL	70	18	15	1410[1]	1192	7.6	49	473	651	10.7	2.55	134	.228	.294	120	137	103	102	.972	169	137	-.1	14.7	5.8		8.6
BRO	67	16	24	1398[2]	1205	7.8	73	493	612	11.1	2.84	115	.231	.302	73	64	98	101	.977	138	150	1.7	6.9	7.4		11.1
NY	70	12	13	1370	1299	8.5	94	493	497	11.9	3.31	101	.250	.316	0	7	101	104	.977	138	128	1.6	.8	6.0		.6
CIN	80	12	8	1411[2]	1213	7.7	47	526	616	11.2	2.82	117	.230	.302	78	73	99	97	.971	177	158	-.7	7.8	-8.6		1.5
PIT	64	13	11	1351[1]	1376	9.2	62	435	426	12.1	3.58	94	.262	.320	-41	-30	102	97	.969	184	128	-1.3	-3.2	-3.1		.1
CHI	71	10	14	1400[2]	1447	9.3	70	525	507	12.8	3.60	89	.267	.334	-44	-62	97	105	.973	170	136	-.2	-6.7	5.0		-7.2
BOS	68	9	8	1334	1326	8.9	82	518	414	12.6	3.76	89	.260	.331	-66	-62	101	100	.976	142	138	1.1	-6.7	-4.0		-5.5
PHI	51	2	6	1341	1328	8.9	61	605	472	13.1	4.12	80	.260	.342	-120	-122	100	93	.968	194	147	-1.9	-13.1	-11.1		-7.4
TOT	541	92	99	11017[2]		8.5				11.9	3.31		.249	.318					.973	1312	1122					

Runs
Ott-NY 118
Slaughter-StL 100
Mize-NY 97
Hack-Chi 91

Hits
Slaughter-StL 188
Nicholson-Chi 173
Medwick-Bro 166
Hack-Chi 166
Elliott-Pit 166

Doubles
Marion-StL 38
Medwick-Bro 37
Hack-Chi 36
Herman-Bro 34
Reiser-Bro 33

Triples
Slaughter-StL 17
Nicholson-Chi 11
Musial-StL 10
Litwhiler-Phi 9

Home Runs
Ott-NY 30
Mize-NY 26
Camilli-Bro 26
Nicholson-Chi 21
West-Bos 16

Total Bases
Slaughter-StL 292
Mize-NY 282
Nicholson-Chi 280
Ott-NY 273
Camilli-Bro 247

Runs Batted In
Mize-NY 110
Camilli-Bro 109
Slaughter-StL 98
Medwick-Bro 96
Ott-NY 93

Runs Produced
Slaughter-StL 185
Ott-NY 181
Mize-NY 181
Camilli-Bro 172
Medwick-Bro 161

Bases On Balls
Ott-NY 109
Fletcher-Pit 105
Camilli-Bro 97
Hack-Chi 94
Slaughter-StL 88

Batting Average
Lombardi-Bos 330
Slaughter-StL 318
Musial-StL 315
Reiser-Bro 310
Mize-NY 305

On Base Percentage
Fletcher-Pit .... .417
Ott-NY .... .415
Slaughter-StL 412
Hack-Chi .... .402
Musial-StL .... .397

Slugging Average
Mize-NY 521
Ott-NY .... .497
Slaughter-StL 494
Musial-StL 490
Lombardi-Bos 482

Production
Ott-NY 912
Slaughter-StL 906
Mize-NY 901
Musial-StL 888
Nicholson-Chi 859

Adjusted Production
Ott-NY 165
Mize-NY 161
Nicholson-Chi 156
Slaughter-StL 153
Musial-StL 148

Batter Runs
Slaughter-StL 49.8
Ott-NY 49.3
Mize-NY 40.8
Nicholson-Chi 37.6
Musial-StL 35.0

Adjusted Batter Runs
Ott-NY 48.7
Nicholson-Chi 41.7
Slaughter-StL 41.1
Mize-NY 40.2
Hack-Chi 33.5

Clutch Hitting Index
Brown-StL 146
Medwick-Bro 143
Owen-Bro 120
Camilli-Bro 117
F.McCormick-Cin ..116

Runs Created
Slaughter-StL 128
Ott-NY 122
Nicholson-Chi 112
Mize-NY 110
Hack-Chi 100

Total Average
Ott-NY 990
Slaughter-StL 966
Musial-StL 926
Mize-NY 911
Camilli-Bro 888

Stolen Bases
Reiser-Bro 20
Reese-Bro 15
Fernandez-Bos 15
Merullo-Chi 14
Hopp-StL 14

Stolen Base Average

Stolen Base Runs

Fielding Runs
DiMaggio-Pit 19.8
Reese-Bro 17.4
May-Phi 17.2
Holmes-Bos 14.8
Fletcher-Pit 11.5

Total Player Rating
Nicholson-Chi 4.8
Ott-NY 4.2
Slaughter-StL 3.9
Fletcher-Pit 3.2
Mize-NY 3.0

Wins
M.Cooper-StL 22
Beazley-StL 21
Wyatt-Bro 19
Passeau-Chi 19
VanderMeer-Cin 18

Win Percentage
French-Bro .... .789
Beazley-StL 778
M.Cooper-StL 759
Wyatt-Bro 731
Davis-Bro........ .714

Games
Adams-NY 61
Casey-Bro 50
Podgajny-Phi 43
Beazley-StL 43

Complete Games
Tobin-Bos 28
Passeau-Chi 24
M.Cooper-StL 22
Walters-Cin 21
VanderMeer-Cin ... 21

Shutouts
M.Cooper-StL 10
Sewell-Pit 5
Javery-Bos 5
Davis-Bro.......... 5

Saves
Casey-Bro 13
Adams-NY 11
Beggs-Cin 8
Sain-Bos 6
Gumbert-StL 5

Innings Pitched
Tobin-Bos 287.2
M.Cooper-StL 278.2
Passeau-Chi 278.1
Starr-Cin 276.2
Javery-Bos 261.0

Fewest Hits/Game
M.Cooper-StL 6.69
VanderMeer-Cin .. 6.93
Higbe-Bro 7.31
Starr-Cin 7.42
Beazley-StL 7.57

Fewest BB/Game
Warneke-StL-Chi .. 1.79
Lohrman-StL-NY .. 1.85
Hubbell-NY 1.94
Derringer-Cin 2.11
M.Cooper-StL 2.20

Strikeouts
VanderMeer-Cin ... 186
M.Cooper-StL 152
Higbe-Bro 115
Walters-Cin 109
Melton-Phi 107

Strikeouts/Game
VanderMeer-Cin .. 6.86
Lanier-StL 5.20
M.Cooper-StL 4.91
Higbe-Bro 4.67
Melton-Phi 4.60

Ratio
M.Cooper-StL 9.04
Lohrman-StL-NY . 10.07
Davis-Bro........ 10.35
Warneke-StL-Chi . 10.39
Wyatt-Bro 10.56

Earned Run Average
M.Cooper-StL ... 1.78
Beazley-StL 2.13
Davis-Bro........ 2.36
VanderMeer-Cin .. 2.43
Lohrman-StL-NY .. 2.48

Adjusted ERA
M.Cooper-StL 193
Beazley-StL 161
Davis-Bro........ 138
Lohrman-StL-NY . 136
VanderMeer-Cin .. 135

Opponents' Batting Avg.
M.Cooper-StL .... .204
VanderMeer-Cin ...208
Higbe-Bro........223
Wyatt-Bro........225
Starr-Cin .... .226

Opponents' On Base Pct.
M.Cooper-StL 258
Lohrman-StL-NY ...281
Wyatt-Bro........286
Warneke-StL-Chi ..286
Davis-Bro........ .287

Starter Runs
M.Cooper-StL 47.6
Beazley-StL 28.3
French-Bro 24.4
VanderMeer-Cin .. 23.8
Davis-Bro........ 21.8

Adjusted Starter Runs
M.Cooper-StL 51.0
Beazley-StL 30.9
French-Bro 23.5
VanderMeer-Cin .. 23.0
Davis-Bro........ 20.6

Clutch Pitching Index
Bithorn-Chi 130
Passeau-Chi 121
Beazley-StL 114
Schumacher-NY .. 113
Carpenter-NY 112

Relief Runs
Adams-NY 14.4
Casey-Bro 13.2
Beggs-Cin 11.6
Shoun-StL-Cin ... 9.4
Webber-Bro 2.0

Adjusted Relief Runs
Adams-NY 14.8
Casey-Bro 12.6
Beggs-Cin 11.3
Shoun-StL-Cin ... 9.1
Webber-Bro 1.7

Relief Ranking
Adams-NY 20.9
Beggs-Cin 15.0
Casey-Bro.........12.4
Shoun-StL-Cin 4.4
Webber-Bro 1.6

Total Pitcher Index
M.Cooper-StL 5.0
Beazley-StL 4.0
French-Bro 3.4
Walters-Cin 3.0
VanderMeer-Cin .. 2.9

Total Baseball Ranking
M.Cooper-StL 5.0
Nicholson-Chi 4.8
Ott-NY 4.2
Beazley-StL 4.0
Slaughter-StL 3.9

January 6 Bob Feller, winner of 76 games for the Indians in three previous seasons, follows Hank Greenberg into the military. Feller, saying "I've always wanted to be on the winning side," enlists in the Navy and reports to Norfolk, Va., for duty.

January 15 President Roosevelt gives baseball the go-ahead to play despite World War II. In his famous "green light" letter FDR says, "I honestly think it would be best for the country to keep baseball going." He encourages more night baseball so that war workers may attend.

February 3 At a special meeting of owners to discuss wartime regulations, they decide to allow 14 night games for each club, with Washington allowed 21. Two All-Star Games will be played, one with a military All-Star team. Curfews are set for night games with no inning to start after 12:50 war time.

June 2 Red Sox star Ted Williams enlists as a Navy aviator. He will finish the season with his team as will many other players who enlist or await the draft. Among AL regulars of 1941 who are now in the service: Johnny Rigney, Joe Grace, John Berardino, Cecil Travis, Bob Feller, Pat Mullin, Buddy Lewis, Sam Chapman, and Johnny Sturm.

July 6 First-inning home runs by Lou Boudreau and Rudy York off Mort Cooper lead the AL to a 3–1 triumph over the NL in the All-Star Game at the Polo Grounds. Mickey Owen's pinch home run is the NL's only score. He does not hit a single homer during the regular schedule.

July 7 A military all-star team that includes Bob Feller, Cecil Travis, Sam Chapman, Benny McCoy, Johnny Sturm, and Frank Pytlak loses, 5–0, to AL stars in a game at Cleveland in front of more than 60,000 fans. Jim Bagby wins against his Indian teammate Feller. Military relief receives $160,000.

August 23 Walter Johnson pitching to Babe Ruth is the pregame attraction that draws 69,000 for the New York-Washington game at Yankee Stadium that provides $80,000 for Army-Navy relief. Ruth hits the fifth pitch into the right field stands.

September 14 The Yankees clinch the pennant against Cleveland 8-3. Ernie Bonham wins his 20th game, and DiMaggio strokes four hits.

September 14* Leon Day, pitching for the Homestead Grays in the Negro League World Series, fans 12 in beating Satchel Paige and the Kansas City Monarchs 4-1 in Game 4. The Monarchs protest, contending that Day and three other players were picked up from other teams. Day's win is disallowed, and the Monarchs sweep the four games.

September 30 Down 7–0 to Yankees hurler Red Ruffing in the Series opener, the Cardinals storm back for four ninth-inning runs. It's not enough to win, but it is a sign of things to come in the World Series.

October 1 Behind 3–0, the Yankees tie it up in the top of the eighth, but rookie Stan Musial singles in Enos Slaughter in the bottom of the inning to forge a 4–3 Cardinals victory to even the World Series.

November 3 Ted Williams is the Triple Crown winner in both leagues, but the writers select second baseman Joe Gordon by 21 votes as AL MVP. Gordon of the Yankees leads the league with 95 strikeouts, the most ground balls hit into double plays (22), and the most errors at his position (28). Pitcher Mort Cooper gets the MVP honor in the NL.

December 1 At major league meetings in Chicago, the owners decide that spring training in 1943 will be limited to locations north of the Potomac or Ohio rivers and east of the Mississippi.

BOSTON	CHICAGO	CLEVELAND	DETROIT	NEW YORK	PHILADELPHIA	ST.LOUIS	WASHINGTON
M J.Cronin	M J.Dykes	M L.Boudreau	M D.Baker	M J.McCarthy	M C.Mack	M L.Sewell	M B.Harris
1B T.Lupien	1B J.Kuhel	1B L.Fleming	1B R.York	1B B.Hassett	1B D.Siebert	1B G.McQuinn	1B M.Vernon
2B B.Doerr	2B D.Kolloway	2B R.Mack	2B J.Bloodworth	2B J.Gordon	2B B.Knickerb'r	2B D.Gutteridge	2B E.Clary
SS J.Pesky	SS L.Appling	SS L.Boudreau	SS B.Hitchcock	SS P.Rizzuto	SS P.Suder	SS V.Stephens	SS J.Sullivan
3B J.Tabor	3B B.Kennedy	3B K.Keltner	3B P.Higgins	3B F.Crosetti	3B B.Blair	3B H.Clift	3B B.Estalella
LF T.Williams	LF T.Wright	LF J.Heath	LF B.McCosky	LF C.Keller	LF B.Johnson	LF G.McQuillen	LF G.Case
CF D.DiMaggio	CF M.Hoag	CF R.Weatherly	CF D.Cramer	CF J.DiMaggio	CF M.Kreevich	CF W.Judnich	CF S.Spence
RF L.Finney	RF W.Moses	RF O.Hockett	RF N.Harris	RF T.Henrich	RF E.Valo	RF C.Laabs	RF B.Campbell
C B.Conroy	C M.Tresh	C O.Denning	C B.Tebbetts	C B.Dickey	C H.Wagner	C R.Ferrell	C J.Early
C J.Peacock	C T.Turner	O B.Mills	O3 D.Ross	3 R.Rolfe	O D.Miles	O T.Criscola	S2 J.Pofahl
O P.Fox	3 D.Lodigiani	C J.Hegan	C D.Parsons	2S B.Rosar	2S C.Davis	O M.Chartak	23 B.Repass
1 J.Foxx	O S.West	C G.Desautels	S M.Franklin	C J.Priddy	C B.Swift	C F.Hayes	O3 R.Cullenbine
32 S.Newsome	O G.Dickey	2 O.Grimes	O R.Radcliff	C R.Hemsley	O J.Wallaesa	C B.Swift	C A.Evans
3 J.Cronin	2 S.Webb	O F.Gaffke	O J.Lipon	S G.Selkirk	C E.McNair	/S J.Berardino	O M.Chartak
/O P.Campbell	O B.Mueller	S R.Peters	S E.McNair	O R.Cullenbine	/S F.Hayes	2 A.Strange	2 C.Gomez
/O A.Gilbert	S L.Wells	O H.Edwards	2 D.Meyer	1 E.Levy	/O E.Collins	/2 D.Heffner	2 F.Croucher
/2 T.Carey	/O V.Heim	/2 T.Sepkowski	/2 C.Gehringer	C E.Kearse	/C J.Castiglia	/C L.Sewell	/O R.Ortiz
P T.Hughson	3 J.Grant	/1 E.Robinson	C H.Riebe	/O T.Stainback	/C K.Richardson	H B.Dahlgren	/3 R.Hoffman
P C.Wagner	O B.Sketchley	/3 B.Lemon	/O B.Patrick	/O M.Chartak	/C F.Mackiewicz	H R.Hayworth	/3 S.Galle
P J.Dobson	/O T.Tucker	/C G.Susce	/C A.Unser	P T.Bonham	H G.Yankowski	P E.Auker	/O A.Kvasnak
P D.Newsome	/1 J.Jones	P J.Bagby	P A.Benton	P S.Chandler	/S L.Eschen	P J.Niggeling	/O G.Moore
P O.Judd	P J.Humphries	P M.Harder	P D.Trout	P R.Ruffing	/1 B.Konopka	P D.Galehouse	P S.Hudson
RP M.Brown	P E.Smith	P C.Dean	P H.White	P H.Borowy	/S D.Adkins	P A.Hollingsworth	P B.Newsom
P B.Butland	P T.Lyons	P A.Smith	P H.Newhouser	P M.Breuer	P P.Marchildon	RP B.Muncrief	P E.Wynn
P Y.Terry	P B.Dietrich	P A.Milnar	P T.Bridges	RP J.Murphy	P R.Wolff	RP G.Caster	P A.Carrasquel
P K.Chase	P B.Ross	RP T.Ferrick	RP R.Henshaw	RP J.Lindell	P L.Harris	P S.Sundra	P W.Masterson
P M.Ryba	RP J.Haynes	RP H.Eisenstat	RP J.Gorsica	P A.Donald	P R.Christopher	P S.Ferens	P B.Zuber
	P J.Wade	P V.Kennedy	P V.Trucks	P L.Gomez	P D.Fowler	/P F.Ostermueller	P R.Scarborough
	P T.Lee	P R.Embree	/C C.Fuchs	/P M.Russo	P H.Besse	/P B.Harris	P J.Wilson
	P O.Grove	P J.Heving	/P H.Manders	P N.Branch	P J.Knott	P P.Appleton	P B.Trotter
	/P J.Rigney	P S.Gromek	/P J.Wilson	/P J.Turner	P B.Harris	P F.Biscan	/P D.Leonard
	/P L.Perme	/P R.Poat	/P S.Rowe	/P M.Queen	P F.Caligiuri	P L.Hanning	P H.Cathey
	/P E.Weiland	/P C.Brown			P T.Shirley	/P E.Pyle	/P B.Kennedy
	/P P.Appleton	/P J.Krakauskas			/P B.Savage	/P J.Whitehead	/P S.Sundra
		/P A.Reynolds			/P B.Beckmann	/P B.Trotter	/P L.Bevil
		/P P.Center			/P J.Coleman		/P D.Adkins
		/P P.Calvert			/P L.McCrabb		/P P.McCullough
					/P T.Abernathy		
					/P S.Lowry		

TEAM	G	W	L	PCT	GB	R	OR	AB	H	2B	3B	HR	BB	SO	AVG	OBP	SLG	PRO	PRO+	BR	/A	PF	CHI	RC	SB	CS	SBA	SBR
NY	154	103	51	.669		801	507	5305	1429	223	57	108	591	556	.269	.346	.394	.740	118	104	120	98	104	759	69	33	68	1
BOS	152	93	59	.612	9	761	594	5248	1451	244	55	103	591	508	.276	.352	.403	.755	116	132	105	103	96	774	68	61	53	-16
STL	151	82	69	.543	19.5	730	637	5229	1354	239	62	98	609	607	.259	.338	.385	.723	109	68	57	102	101	703	37	38	49	-12
CLE	156	75	79	.487	28	590	659	5317	1344	223	58	50	500	544	.253	.320	.345	.665	100	-43	-7	94	96	596	69	74	48	-24
DET	156	73	81	.474	30	589	587	5327	1313	217	37	76	509	476	.246	.314	.344	.658	85	-57	-106	108	98	582	39	40	49	-12
CHI	148	66	82	.446	34	538	609	4949	1215	214	36	25	497	427	.246	.316	.318	.634	87	-87	-75	98	102	520	114	70	62	-8
WAS	151	62	89	.411	39.5	653	817	5295	1364	224	49	40	581	536	.258	.333	.341	.674	98	-14	-8	99	101	641	98	29	77	12
PHI	154	55	99	.357	48	549	801	5285	1315	213	46	33	440	490	.249	.309	.325	.634	86	-101	-98	99	101	536	44	45	49	-14
TOT	611					5211		41955	10785	1797	400	533	4318	4144	.257	.329	.357	.686							538	390	58	-73

TEAM	CG	SH	SV	IP	H	H/G	HR	BB	SO	RAT	ERA	ERA+	OAV	OOB	PR	/A	PF	CPI	FA	E	DP	FW	PW	BW	SBW	DIF
NY	88	18	17	1375	1259	8.2	71	431	558	11.2	2.91	118	.244	.304	115	82	94	108	.976	142	190	2.0	8.4	12.3	1.0	2.3
BOS	84	11	17	1358²	1260	8.3	65	553	500	12.1	3.44	108	.247	.322	32	43	102	99	.974	157	156	1.0	4.4	10.8	-.7	1.5
STL	68	12	13	1363	1387	9.2	63	505	488	12.7	3.59	103	.262	.330	10	17	101	103	.972	167	143	.4	1.7	5.8	-.3	-1.2
CLE	61	12	11	1402²	1353	8.7	61	560	448	12.4	3.59	96	.254	.327	10	-23	94	99	.974	163	175	1.0	-2.4	-.7	-1.5	1.6
DET	65	12	14	1399¹	1321	8.5	60	598	671	12.5	3.13	126	.248	.326	82	127	108	111	.969	194	142	-.8	13.0	-10.9	-.3	-5.1
CHI	86	8	8	1314¹	1304	8.9	74	473	432	12.3	3.58	100	.258	.325	11	3	98	102	.970	173	144	-.1	.3	-7.7	.1	-.6
WAS	68	12	11	1346²	1496	10.0	50	558	496	13.8	4.58	80	.279	.349	-139	-139	100	91	.962	222	133	-2.7	-14.2	-.8	2.2	2.1
PHI	67	5	9	1374¹	1404	9.2	89	639	546	13.5	4.45	85	.263	.344	-120	-120	102	103	.969	188	124	-.6	-10.4	-10.0	-.5	-.5
TOT	587	90	100	10934¹		8.9				12.6	3.66		.257	.329					.971	1406	1207					

Runs
Williams-Bos 141
DiMaggio-NY 123
DiMaggio-Bos 110
Clift-StL 108
Keller-NY 106

Hits
Pesky-Bos 205
Spence-Was 203
Williams-Bos 186
DiMaggio-NY 186
Keltner-Cle 179

Doubles
Kolloway-Chi 40
Clift-StL 39
Heath-Cle 37
DiMaggio-Bos 36

Triples
Spence-Was 15
Heath-Cle 13
DiMaggio-NY 13
McQuillen-StL 12

Home Runs
Williams-Bos 36
Laabs-StL 27
Keller-NY 26
York-Det 21
DiMaggio-NY 21

Total Bases
Williams-Bos 338
DiMaggio-NY 304
Keller-NY 279
Spence-Was 272
DiMaggio-Bos 272

Runs Batted In
Williams-Bos 137
DiMaggio-NY 114
Keller-NY 108
Gordon-NY 103
Doerr-Bos 102

Runs Produced
Williams-Bos 242
DiMaggio-NY 216
Keller-NY 188
Gordon-NY 173
Spence-Was 169

Bases On Balls
Williams-Bos 145
Keller-NY 114
Fleming-Cle 106
Clift-StL 106
Cullenbine-SL-W-NY 92

Batting Average
Williams-Bos 356
Pesky-Bos 331
Spence-Was 323
Gordon-NY 322
Case-Was 320

On Base Percentage
Williams-Bos ..... .499
Keller-NY ..... .417
Judnich-StL ..... .413
Fleming-Cle ..... .412
Gordon-NY ..... .409

Slugging Average
Williams-Bos ..... .648
Keller-NY ..... .513
Judnich-StL ..... .499
DiMaggio-NY ..... .498
Laabs-StL ..... .498

Production
Williams-Bos 1.147
Keller-NY 930
Judnich-StL 912
Gordon-NY 900
Laabs-StL 878

Adjusted Production
Williams-Bos 214
Keller-NY 164
Gordon-NY 156
Judnich-StL 153
DiMaggio-NY 148

Batter Runs
Williams-Bos 92.6
Keller-NY 46.9
Gordon-NY 38.6
Judnich-StL 35.4
DiMaggio-NY 34.5

Adjusted Batter Runs
Williams-Bos 87.0
Keller-NY 49.4
Gordon-NY 40.8
Fleming-Cle 38.3
DiMaggio-NY 36.8

Clutch Hitting Index
Lupien-Bos 124
Cullenbine-SL-W-NY .116
Vernon-Was 113
Siebert-Phi 113
Tabor-Bos 112

Runs Created
Williams-Bos 185
Keller-NY 131
DiMaggio-NY 120
Spence-Was 111
Gordon-NY 108

Total Average
Williams-Bos 1.394
Keller-NY 1.038
Judnich-StL 950
Gordon-NY 891
Laabs-StL 878

Stolen Bases
Case-Was 44
Vernon-Was 25
Rizzuto-NY 22
Kuhel-Chi 22

Stolen Base Average
Case-Was 88.0
Vernon-Was 80.6
Rizzuto-NY 78.6
Appling-Chi 77.3
Kuhel-Chi 71.0

Stolen Base Runs
Case-Was 9.6
Vernon-Was 3.9
Rizzuto-NY 3.0
Keller-NY 3.0
Appling-Chi 2.1

Fielding Runs
Rizzuto-NY 25.0
Pesky-Bos 17.7
DiMaggio-Bos 16.9
Keltner-Cle 15.6
York-Det 15.4

Total Player Rating
Williams-Bos 8.1
Gordon-NY 5.4
Keller-NY 4.4
Pesky-Bos 4.1
Rizzuto-NY 4.0

Wins
Hughson-Bos 22
Bonham-NY 21
Marchildon-Phi 17
Bagby-Cle 17
Chandler-NY 16

Win Percentage
Bonham-NY ..... .808
Borowy-NY ..... .789
Hughson-Bos ..... .786
Chandler-NY ..... .762
Bagby-Cle ..... .654

Games
Haynes-Chi 40
Caster-StL 39

Complete Games
Hughson-Bos 22
Bonham-NY 22
Lyons-Chi 20
Hudson-Was 19

Shutouts
Bonham-NY 6

Saves
Murphy-NY 11
Haynes-Chi 6
Brown-Bos 6
Newhouser-Det 5
Caster-StL 5

Innings Pitched
Hughson-Bos 281.0
Bagby-Cle 270.2
Auker-StL 249.0
Marchildon-Phi ..244.0
Hudson-Was 239.1

Fewest Hits/Game
Newhouser-Det ... 6.71
Niggeling-StL 7.55
Dobson-Bos 7.64
Trucks-Det 7.89
Chandler-NY 7.89

Fewest BB/Game
Bonham-NY ..... .96
Lyons-Chi 1.30
Ruffing-NY 1.91
Breuer-NY 2.03
Bagby-Cle 2.13

Strikeouts
Newsom-Was 113
Hughson-Bos 113
Marchildon-Phi 110
Benton-Det 110
Niggeling-StL 107

Strikeouts/Game
Newhouser-Det 5.05
Bridges-Det 5.02
Trucks-Det 4.88
Newsom-Was 4.76
Niggeling-StL 4.67

Ratio
Bonham-NY 8.92
Lyons-Chi 9.73
Ruffing-NY 10.55
Breuer-NY 10.68
Hughson-Bos 10.70

Earned Run Average
Lyons-Chi 2.10
Bonham-NY 2.27
Chandler-NY 2.38
Newhouser-Det ... 2.45
Borowy-NY 2.52

Adjusted ERA
Lyons-Chi 172
Newhouser-Det 161
Bonham-NY 152
Chandler-NY 145
Trucks-Det 144

Opponents' Batting Avg.
Newhouser-Det 207
Niggeling-StL 226
Dobson-Bos 231
Trucks-Det 231
Borowy-NY 233

Opponents' On Base Pct.
Bonham-NY 259
Lyons-Chi 275
Ruffing-NY 292
Breuer-NY 295
Hughson-Bos 296

Starter Runs
Bonham-NY 34.8
Hughson-Bos 33.2
Lyons-Chi 31.3
Chandler-NY 28.5
Humphries-Chi ... 24.8

Adjusted Starter Runs
Hughson-Bos 35.5
Newhouser-Det ... 30.6
Lyons-Chi 30.1
Bonham-NY 29.4
Benton-Det 26.5

Clutch Pitching Index
Chandler-NY 136
Lyons-Chi 131
Hollingsworth-StL ... 123
Humphries-Chi ... 121
Niggeling-StL 119

Relief Runs
Ferrick-Cle 15.0
Haynes-Chi 11.9
Caster-StL 7.5
Murphy-NY 1.6
Brown-Bos 1.5

Adjusted Relief Runs
Ferrick-Cle 13.2
Haynes-Chi 11.2
Caster-StL 7.9
Brown-Bos 5
Murphy-NY 2

Relief Ranking
Haynes-Chi 14.2
Caster-StL 10.0
Ferrick-Cle 8.4
Brown-Bos 4.0
Murphy-NY 5

Total Pitcher Index
Lyons-Chi 4.0
Newhouser-Det 4.0
Hughson-Bos 3.8
Chandler-NY 3.2
Humphries-Chi ... 2.7

Total Baseball Ranking
Williams-Bos 8.1
Gordon-NY 5.4
Keller-NY 4.4
Pesky-Bos 4.1
Lyons-Chi 4.0

February 9 The NL is looking for a buyer for the Phillies, whose owner, Gerry Nugent, has fallen in arrears on rent and bank loans. The league pays $10 a share for 4,685 out of 5,000 outstanding shares in club and sells the club nine days later to William D. Cox of New York.

February 20* Phil Wrigley and Branch Rickey charter the All-American Girls Softball League. The league will operate around the Chicago area and is formed as a backup in case the government shuts down major league baseball. The league will later change its name, switch to hardball with a pitching distance of 40 feet and bases 68 feet apart, and inspire the movie, *A League of Their Own.*

April 20 Braves manager Casey Stengel is struck by a taxi, fractures a leg, and will miss much of the season. The cab-driver is nominated Sportsman of the Year in Boston by a local newspaper, weary of Stengel's humor in the face of the Braves' pitiful record

May 30 The Cubs play 32 games before hitting a home run. Bill Nicholson finally hits the first Cubs blast of the year against the Braves in the club's 1,120th at bat of the season. Chicago's 53 home runs will be good for third in the NL.

June 1 Rip Sewell of the Pirates throws his dew-drop ball in a game. Sewell loops the ball 18 to 20 feet high on its way to the strike zone. Later it is called a blooper or "eephus" ball. The pitch is more than a gag, and Sewell is on his way to a 20-win season.

June 4 Mort Cooper of the St. Louis Cardinals pitches back-to-back one-hitters, beating the Brooklyn Dodgers on May 31 and the Philadelphia Phillies on June 4. Hits by Billy Herman on May 31 and by Jimmy Wasdell of the Phils deprive him of no-hitters.

July 18 Playing as if neither team wanted the win, the Giants and Phillies strand 30 baserunners, a major league record. New York wins, 10–6.

August 18 Carl Hubbell wins his 253rd and final game, all with the Giants, as he beats the Pirates 3-2. He will retire at the end of the year and take over the Giants' farm system.

September 18 The Cardinals clinch the NL pennant. St. Louis pitchers Howie Pollet, Max Lanier, and Mort Cooper will rank 1-2-3 in league ERA, and Al Brazle at 1.53 and Harry Brecheen at 2.27 are near the same level. Stan Musial, in his second season, hits .357 and has 220 hits, 347 total bases, 48 doubles, 20 triples.

October 6 Robert Cooper, father of pitcher Mort Cooper and catcher Walker Cooper, dies at his home in Independence, Missouri, but both players decide to play in the World Series. Mort goes on to beat the New York Yankees, 4-3, resurrecting memories of 1942 when the Yankees lost four straight after winning the opener. Marty Marion and Ray Sanders homer.

November 23 Commissioner Landis rules that Phils owner William D. Cox is permanently ineligible to hold office or be employed in baseball for having bet on his own team. The Carpenter family of Delaware will buy the Philadelphia club, and Bob Carpenter, age 28, will become president. The Phils, in an effort to change their image, will conduct a contest for a new name. The winning entry, the Blue Jays, submitted by a Mrs. John Crooks, will be the unpopular team name for 1944-45. It will be abandoned in 1946.

	BOSTON		BROOKLYN		CHICAGO		CINCINNATI		NEW YORK		PHILADELPHIA		PITTSBURGH		ST.LOUIS
M	B.Coleman	M	L.Durocher	M	J.Wilson	M	B.McKechnie	M	M.Ott	M	B.Harris	M	F.Frisch	M	B.Southworth
M	C.Stengel	1B	D.Camilli	1B	P.Cavarretta	1B	F.McCormick	1B	J.Orengo	M	F.Fitzsimmons	1B	E.Fletcher	1B	R.Sanders
1B	J.McCarthy	2B	B.Herman	2B	E.Stanky	2B	L.Frey	2B	M.Witek	1B	J.Wasdell	2B	P.Coscarart	2B	L.Klein
2B	C.Ryan	SS	A.Glossop	SS	L.Merullo	SS	E.Miller	SS	B.Jurges	2B	D.Murtaugh	SS	F.Gustine	SS	M.Marion
SS	W.Wietelmann	3B	A.Vaughan	3B	S.Hack	3B	S.Mesner	3B	D.Bartell	SS	G.Stewart	3B	B.Elliott	3B	W.Kurowski
3B	E.Joost	LF	D.Walker	LF	L.Novikoff	LF	E.Tipton	LF	J.Medwick	3B	P.May	LF	J.Russell	LF	D.Litwhiler
LF	B.Nieman	CF	A.Galan	CF	P.Lowrey	CF	G.Walker	CF	J.Rucker	LF	C.Triplett	CF	V.DiMaggio	CF	H.Walker
CF	T.Holmes	RF	P.Waner	RF	B.Nicholson	RF	M.Marshall	RF	M.Ott	CF	B.Adams	RF	J.Barrett	RF	S.Musial
RF	C.Workman	C	M.Owen	C	C.McCullough	C	R.Mueller	C	G.Mancuso	RF	R.Northey	C	A.Lopez	C	W.Cooper
C	P.Masi									C	M.Livingston				
		O3	F.Bordagaray	O	I.Goodman	O	E.Crabtree	31	S.Gordon			O	M.Van Robays	O3	D.Garms
O	C.Ross	O	L.Olmo	O	D.Dallessandro	13	B.Haas	C	E.Lombardi	13	B.Dahlgren	C	T.O'Brien	O1	J.Hopp
1	K.Farrell	C3	B.Bragan	C	C.Hernandez	O3	D.Clay	O3	B.Maynard	2S	R.Hamrick	C	B.Baker	C	K.O'Dea
C	C.Kluttz	1	H.Schultz	2	S.Martin	2	W.Williams	O	C.Mead	S	C.Brewster	2	A.Rubeling	2	J.Brown
C	H.Poland	O	J.Medwick	O	M.Livingston	C	A.Lakeman	1	N.Reyes	O	D.Litwhiler	S	H.Geary	O	F.Demaree
3	J.Burns	C	D.Moore	1	H.Becker	C	T.DePhillips	O	B.Barna	O	E.Naylor	O	J.Wyrostek	2	G.Fallon
3	H.Heltzel	O	G.Hermanski	O	A.Pafko	/O	M.McCormick	S	B.Kerr	C	D.Moore	O	F.Colman	/O	C.Triplett
/3	B.Brubaker	S	R.Barkley	O	E.Sauer	/O	C.Aleno	C	B.Berres	C	B.Finley	/S	T.Ordenana	/O	B.Adams
/3	T.Cuccinello	2	A.Kampouris	S	B.Schuster	/O	F.Kelleher	/C	J.Stephenson	C	A.Seminick	/C	H.Camelli	/C	S.Narron
/1	B.Etchison	/1	J.Cooney	C	A.Todd	/2	C.Brewster	/C	H.Poland	H	T.Padden	H	J.Wasdell		
H	C.Creeden	/S	B.Bartley	2	D.Johnson	/1	L.Goldstein	/O	V.Bradford	O	P.Busby			P	M.Cooper
H	S.Gentile	/2	A.Campanis	O	W.Platt	R	D.West			C	B.Culp	P	R.Sewell	P	M.Lanier
/2	B.Geraghty	/3	B.Hart	/3	P.Elko			P	C.Melton	/O	C.Klein	P	B.Klinger	P	H.Krist
		/S	L.Durocher	/O	J.Ostrowski	P	J.Vander Meer	P	J.Wittig	/S	G.DelSavio	P	M.Butcher	P	H.Brecheen
		/O	C.Gillenwater	P	C.Gilbert	P	E.Riddle	P	V.Mungo			P	W.Hebert	P	H.Gumbert
P	A.Javery	/3	J.Orengo	/C	B.Holm	P	B.Walters	P	R.Fischer	P	A.Gerheauser	P	H.Gornicki	RP	R.Munger
P	N.Andrews	/S	P.Ankenman	/C	M.Kreitner	P	R.Starr	P	K.Chase	P	J.Kraus	RP	B.Brandt		
P	R.Barrett	/3	G.Hodges			P	C.Shoun	RP	A.Adams	P	S.Rowe			P	H.Pollet
P	J.Tobin	H	H.Peck	P	C.Passeau	RP	J.Beggs	RP	B.Sayles	P	D.Barrett	P	X.Rescigno	P	M.Dickson
P	M.Salvo			P	H.Bithorn					P	S.Johnson	P	J.Gee	P	A.Brazle
RP	D.Odom	P	K.Higbe	P	P.Derringer	P	E.Heusser	P	H.Feldman	RP	N.Kimball	/P	J.Hallett	P	E.White
		P	W.Wyatt	P	H.Wyse	P	B.Lohrman					P	J.Podgajny	/P	B.Byerly
P	B.Cardoni	P	E.Head	P	E.Hanyzewski	/P	B.Malloy	P	C.Hubbell	P	C.Fuchs	P	J.Lanning		
P	D.MacFayden	P	C.Davis	RP	R.Prim	P	J.Niemes	P	K.Trinkle	P	J.Podgajny	P	H.Shuman		
/P	G.Jeffcoat	P	B.Newsom					P	J.Allen	P	B.Lee	/P	D.Dietz		
/P	B.Donovan	RP	L.Webber	P	L.Warneke			P	H.East	P	D.Conger	P	C.Cuccurullo		
/P	C.Lindquist			P	B.Lee			/P	B.Voiselle	/P	D.Dietz				
/P	J.Dagenhard			P	D.Barrett			/P	B.Coombs	/P	A.Karl				
/P	A.Stout	P	R.Melton	P	P.Erickson			/P	F.Seward	P	D.Matthewson				
/P	L.Tost	P	M.Macon	/P	J.Burrows			/P	T.Sunkel	P	G.Eyrich				
/P	G.Diehl	/P	R.Barney	P	B.Fleming					/P	B.Beck				
/P	R.Martin	/P	F.Fitzsimmons	P	W.Signer					/P	R.McKee				
/P	R.Talcott	P	J.Allen	/P	J.Signer					/P	K.Raffensberger				
		/P	B.Lohrman	/P	D.Alderson					/P	D.Donahue				
		/P	F.Ostermueller	/P	J.Mooty					/P	A.Lapihuska				
		/P	H.Gregg							/P	B.Webb				
		/P	B.Sayles							/P	M.Salvo				
		/P	N.Kimball												
		/P	C.Haughey												
		/P	B.Chipman												

TEAM	G	W	L	PCT	GB	R	OR	AB	H	2B	3B	HR	BB	SO	AVG	OBP	SLG	PRO	PRO+	BR	/A	PF	CHI	RC	SB	CS	SBA	SBR
STL	157	105	49	.682		679	475	5438	1515	259	72	70	428	438	.279	.333	.391	.724	110	92	61	104	95	720	40			
CIN	155	87	67	.565	18	608	543	5329	1362	229	47	43	445	476	.256	.315	.340	.655	96	-35	-27	99	106	581	49			
BRO	153	81	72	.529	23.5	716	674	5309	1444	263	35	39	580	422	.272	.346	.357	.703	110	70	69	100	104	675	58			
PIT	157	80	74	.519	25	669	605	5353	1401	240	73	42	573	566	.262	.335	.357	.692	103	45	22	103	100	657	64			
CHI	154	74	79	.484	30.5	632	600	5279	1380	207	56	52	574	522	.261	.336	.351	.687	107	38	48	99	97	641	53			
BOS	153	68	85	.444	36.5	465	612	5196	1213	202	36	39	469	609	.233	.299	.309	.608	82	-121	-114	99	98	491	56			
PHI	157	64	90	.416	41	571	676	5297	1321	186	36	66	499	556	.249	.316	.335	.651	98	-38	-15	96	100	565	29			
NY	156	55	98	.359	49.5	558	713	5290	1309	153	33	81	480	470	.247	.313	.335	.648	92	-48	-52	101	100	552	35			
TOT	621					4898		42491	10945	1739	388	432	4048	4059	.258	.324	.347	.672							384			

TEAM	CG	SH	SV	IP	H	H/G	HR	BB	SO	RAT	ERA	ERA+	OAV	OOB	PR	/A	PF	CPI	FA	E	DP	FW	PW	BW	SBW	DIF
STL	94	21	15	1427	1246	7.9	33	477	639	11.0	2.57	131	.237	.303	129	126	99	105	.976	151	183	.9	13.5	6.5		7.2
CIN	78	18	17	1404	1299	8.3	38	579	498	12.1	3.13	106	.251	.328	39	28	98	105	.980	125	193	2.2	3.0	-2.9		7.7
BRO	50	13	22	1369²	1326	8.7	59	637	588	13.1	3.88	86	.254	.338	-76	-80	99	93	.972	168	137	-.3	-8.5	7.4		6.0
PIT	74	11	12	1404	1424	9.1	44	422	396	11.9	3.08	113	.264	.319	47	60	103	107	.973	170	159	-.2	6.4	2.3		-5.5
CHI	67	13	14	1386	1379	9.0	53	394	513	11.6	3.31	101	.258	.311	11	3	99	95	.973	168	138	-.3	.3	5.1		-7.7
BOS	87	13	4	1397²	1361	8.8	66	441	409	11.8	3.25	105	.255	.314	20	25	101	100	.972	176	139	-.8	2.7	-12.2		1.8
PHI	66	10	14	1392²	1436	9.3	59	451	431	12.3	3.79	89	.267	.326	-62	-64	100	93	.969	189	143	-1.3	-6.8	-1.6		-3.3
NY	35	6	19	1394²	1474	9.5	80	626	588	13.7	4.08	84	.272	.350	-108	-99	102	101	.973	166	140	-.0	-10.6	-5.6		-5.3
TOT	551	105	117	11175²		8.8				12.2	3.38		.258	.324					.974	1313	1232					

Runs		Hits		Doubles		Triples		Home Runs		Total Bases	
Vaughan-Bro	112	Musial-StL	220	Musial-StL	48	Musial-StL	20	Nicholson-Chi	29	Musial-StL	347
Musial-StL	108	Witek-NY	195	Herman-Bro	41	Klein-StL	14	Ott-NY	18	Nicholson-Chi	323
Nicholson-Chi	95	Herman-Bro	193	DiMaggio-Pit	41	Lowrey-Chi	12	Northey-Phi	16	Elliott-Pit	258
Cavarretta-Chi	93	Nicholson-Chi	188	Vaughan-Bro	39	Elliott-Pit	12	Triplett-StL-Phi	15	Klein-StL	257
Stanky-Chi	92	Vaughan-Bro	186	Holmes-Bos	33			DiMaggio-Pit	15		

Runs Batted In		Runs Produced		Bases On Balls		Batting Average		On Base Percentage		Slugging Average	
Nicholson-Chi	128	Nicholson-Chi	194	Galan-Bro	103	Musial-StL	.357	Musial-StL	.425	Musial-StL	.562
Elliott-Pit	101	Musial-StL	176	Ott-NY	95	Herman-Bro	.330	Galan-Bro	.412	Nicholson-Chi	.531
Herman-Bro	100	Elliott-Pit	176	Fletcher-Pit	95	W.Cooper-StL	.318	Herman-Bro	.398	W.Cooper-StL	.463
DiMaggio-Pit	88	Herman-Bro	174	Stanky-Chi	92	Elliott-Pit	.315	Fletcher-Pit	.395	Elliott-Pit	.444
		Vaughan-Bro	173	Tipton-Cin	85	Witek-NY	.314	Tipton-Cin	.395	Triplett-StL-Phi	.439

Production		Adjusted Production		Batter Runs		Adjusted Batter Runs		Clutch Hitting Index		Runs Created	
Musial-StL	.988	Musial-StL	176	Musial-StL	65.5	Musial-StL	59.6	Miller-Cin	138	Musial-StL	147
Nicholson-Chi	.917	Nicholson-Chi	166	Nicholson-Chi	47.7	Nicholson-Chi	49.5	Herman-Bro	131	Nicholson-Chi	129
Elliott-Pit	.820	Tipton-Cin	138	Galan-Bro	28.5	Galan-Bro	28.3	Elliott-Pit	123	Herman-Bro	97
Tipton-Cin	.819	Galan-Bro	136	Herman-Bro	28.0	Herman-Bro	27.8	Wasdell-Pit-Phi	121	Vaughan-Bro	96
Galan-Bro	.818	Herman-Bro	135	Elliott-Pit	26.5	Tipton-Cin	27.1	Medwick-Bro-NY	117	Elliott-Pit	96

Total Average		Stolen Bases		Stolen Base Average		Stolen Base Runs		Fielding Runs		Total Player Rating	
Musial-StL	1.039	Vaughan-Bro	20					Miller-Cin	26.6	Musial-StL	6.4
Nicholson-Chi	.944	Lowrey-Chi	13					Marion-StL	25.3	Nicholson-Chi	4.9
Ott-NY	.895	Workman-Bos	12					Mueller-Cin	20.2	Galan-Bro	3.9
Galan-Bro	.876	Russell-Pit	12					Wietelmann-Bos	20.0	Mueller-Cin	3.8
Tipton-Cin	.825	Gustine-Pit	12					Galan-Bro	16.1	Witek-NY	3.3

Wins		Win Percentage		Games		Complete Games		Shutouts		Saves	
Sewell-Pit	21	M.Cooper-StL	.724	Adams-NY	70	Sewell-Pit	25	Bithorn-Chi	7	Webber-Bro	10
Riddle-Cin	21	Sewell-Pit	.700	Webber-Bro	54	Tobin-Bos	24	M.Cooper-StL	6	Adams-NY	9
M.Cooper-StL	21	Lanier-StL	.682	Head-Bro	47	M.Cooper-StL	24			Shoun-Cin	7
Bithorn-Chi	18	Riddle-Cin	.656	Shoun-Cin	45	Andrews-Bos	23			Head-Bro	6
Javery-Bos	17	Bithorn-Chi	.600	Mungo-NY	45					Beggs-Cin	6

Innings Pitched		Fewest Hits/Game		Fewest BB/Game		Strikeouts		Strikeouts/Game		Ratio	
Javery-Bos	303.0	Wyatt-Bro	6.92	Rowe-Phi	1.31	VanderMeer-Cin	174	VanderMeer-Cin	5.42	Wyatt-Bro	9.07
VanderMeer-Cin	289.0	VanderMeer-Cin	7.10	Wyse-Chi	1.96	M.Cooper-StL	141	Higbe-Bro	5.25	M.Cooper-StL	10.25
Andrews-Bos	283.2	M.Cooper-StL	7.49	Derringer-Chi	2.02	Javery-Bos	134	Lanier-StL	5.19	Rowe-Phi	10.31
M.Cooper-StL	274.0	Krist-StL	7.72	Davis-Phi	2.14	Lanier-StL	123	M.Cooper-StL	4.63	Andrews-Bos	10.60
Sewell-Pit	265.1	Barrett-Chi-Phi	7.94	Wyatt-Bro	2.14	Higbe-Bro	108	Head-Bro	4.40	Bithorn-Chi	10.60

Earned Run Average		Adjusted ERA		Opponents' Batting Avg.		Opponents' On Base Pct.		Starter Runs		Adjusted Starter Runs	
Pollet-StL	1.75	Lanier-StL	177	Wyatt-Bro	.207	Wyatt-Bro	.255	Lanier-StL	35.2	Lanier-StL	34.7
Lanier-StL	1.90	M.Cooper-StL	146	VanderMeer-Cin	.224	Rowe-Phi	.279	M.Cooper-StL	33.0	M.Cooper-StL	32.4
M.Cooper-StL	2.30	Sewell-Pit	137	M.Cooper-StL	.226	M.Cooper-StL	.286	Andrews-Bos	25.6	Sewell-Pit	27.5
Wyatt-Bro	2.49	Wyatt-Bro	135	Krist-StL	.233	Andrews-Bos	.291	Sewell-Pit	24.7	Andrews-Bos	26.6
Sewell-Pit	2.54	Butcher-Pit	134	Barrett-Chi-Phi	.237	Bithorn-Chi	.294	Riddle-Cin	21.9	Pollet-StL	21.2

Clutch Pitching Index		Relief Runs		Adjusted Relief Runs		Relief Ranking		Total Pitcher Index		Total Baseball Ranking	
Lanier-StL	151	Beggs-Cin	13.4	Beggs-Cin	12.5	Beggs-Cin	14.1	Sewell-Pit	4.0	Musial-StL	6.4
Butcher-Pit	122	Adams-NY	8.8	Adams-NY	9.7	Adams-NY	12.6	Tobin-Bos	3.5	Nicholson-Chi	4.9
Sewell-Pit	121	Prim-Chi	5.6	Prim-Chi	5.2	Prim-Chi	5.7	Lanier-StL	3.5	Sewell-Pit	4.0
Riddle-Cin	118	Brandt-Pit	1.6	Brandt-Pit	2.2	Brandt-Pit	1.7	Andrews-Bos	3.4	Galan-Bro	3.9
Tobin-Bos	113							M.Cooper-StL	3.2	Mueller-Cin	3.8

January 5 Teams agree to start the season later than usual and train in northern areas. Resorts, armories, and university facilities are chosen for training sites. The Dodgers train at Bear Mountain, New York; the Cards prepare at Cape Girardeau, Missouri; the Yankees get ready in Atlantic City.

February 24* The Texas League announces it will quit for the duration of the war. Only nine minor leagues will start the season, and advertisements for players appear in *The Sporting News*.

March 13 The major leagues approve an official ball, which will be made from reclaimed cork and balata in the interior, materials not needed in the war effort. Officials insist the ball will have the resiliency of the 1939 ball, but the players will express dismay that they cannot drive the new ball and point out the dearth of runs and homers in 1942 even with the old ball.

April 24 A spokesman for A. G. Spalding defends the wartime baseball, saying the 11 shutouts in the first 29 games are the result of the weather being "too wet and too cold." In time the new ball will prove to be just as lively as the old one." A few days later the company admits that the balls contain an inferior grade of rubber cement, which has hardened. The teams agree to use up their stock of balls left over from the 1942 season while a new supply of higher-quality balls is made.

June 17 Player-manager Joe Cronin of the Red Sox hits two three-run pinch home runs, one in each game of a doubleheader, as Boston beats the St. Louis Browns, 5–4, and loses, 8–7. He had hit a three-run pinch home run two nights before against the A's, three home runs in his last four at bats. He will pinch hit 42 times this year with 18 hits, including an AL record five pinch-hit homers.

July 13 The AL edges the NL 5-3 at Shibe Park in the first All-Star Game played under the lights. Bobby Doerr of the Red Sox is the hitting hero with a three-run home run off Mort Cooper in the second inning.

August 24 The Philadelphia Athletics drop their 20th game in a row, losing to Chicago, 6–5. This ties the league record. They dodge the bullet in the nightcap by scoring eight runs in the second inning to win, 8–1.

September 6 Pitcher Carl Scheib of the Philadelphia Athletics becomes the youngest player to appear in an AL game at age 16 years, 248 days. He gives up two hits in one-third of an inning, for the A's.

October 2 The Yankees take two from the Browns, 5–1 and 7–6, for their 14th sweep of a doubleheader, an AL mark. Arthur "Bud" Metheny hits a home run in the opener for the Yankees' 100th roundtripper of the season.

October 5 Many major league players have gone into the war, including several key Yankees and Cardinals players. Nevertheless, both these clubs are back in the Series. New York wins the opener at Yankee Stadium 4-2 behind Spurgeon "Spud" Chandler.

October 11 Bill Dickey's two-run home run off Mort Cooper in the sixth gives the Yanks the championship. Spud Chandler gives up 10 hits but strands 11 in the 2-0 victory. A full share is worth $6,139 to the New York players; the Cards get $4,321 each. The Series grosses $1.1 million at the gate, receives $100,000 for broadcast rights, and donates $308,000 to War Funds.

November 11 The MVPs for both leagues are named. Spud Chandler wins it in the AL; Stan Musial in the NL.

BOSTON	CHICAGO	CLEVELAND	DETROIT	NEW YORK	PHILADELPHIA	ST.LOUIS	WASHINGTON
M J.Cronin	M J.Dykes	M L.Boudreau	M S.O'Neill	M J.McCarthy	M C.Mack	M L.Sewell	M O.Bluege
1B T.Lupien	1B J.Kuhel	1B M.Rocco	1B R.York	1B N.Etten	1B D.Siebert	1B G.McQuinn	1B M.Vernon
2B B.Doerr	2B D.Kolloway	2B R.Mack	2B J.Bloodworth	2B J.Gordon	2B P.Suder	2B D.Gutteridge	2B J.Priddy
SS S.Newsome	SS L.Appling	SS L.Boudreau	SS J.Hoover	SS F.Crosetti	SS I.Hall	SS V.Stephens	SS J.Sullivan
3B J.Tabor	3B R.Hodgin	3B K.Keltner	3B P.Higgins	3B B.Johnson	3B E.Mayo	3B H.Clift	3B E.Clary
LF L.Culberson	LF G.Curtright	LF J.Heath	LF D.Wakefield	LF C.Keller	LF B.Estalella	LF C.Laabs	LF B.Johnson
CF C.Metkovich	CF T.Tucker	CF O.Hockett	CF D.Cramer	CF J.Lindell	CF J.White	CF M.Byrnes	CF S.Spence
RF P.Fox	RF W.Moses	RF R.Cullenbine	RF N.Harris	RF B.Metheny	RF J.Welaj	RF M.Chartak	RF G.Case
C R.Partee	C M.Tresh	C B.Rosar	C P.Richards	C B.Dickey	C H.Wagner	C F.Hayes	C J.Early
S E.Lake	2 S.Webb	OS H.Edwards	OS D.Ross	O R.Weatherly	O E.Valo	3S M.Christman	O G.Moore
O J.Lazor	3 J.Grant	3S R.Peters	23 J.Wood	S S.Stirnweiss	B.Swift	O A.Zarilla	32 A.Kampouris
O A.Simmons	C T.Turner	C G.Desautels	O R.Radcliff	2 T.Stainback	D.Heffner	C R.Ferrell	C T.Giuliani
O F.Garrison	32 D.Culler	1 O.Denning	C D.Parsons	C K.Sears	O J.Tyack	O M.Kreevich	O S.Powell
O D.Miles	3 T.Cuccinello	O P.Seerey	C A.Unser	O R.Hemsley	O J.Ripple	C J.Schultz	3 S.Robertson
C J.Peacock	C V.Castino	/O G.Woodling	O J.Outlaw	/S O.Grimes	O G.Staller	3 E.Clary	2 G.Myatt
O B.Barna	M S.Solters	/3 J.Grant	O C.Metro	H A.Robinson	O B.Burgo	O T.Criscola	/3 H.Clift
O T.McBride	/1 D.Hanski	/3 E.Turchin	H J.McHale	P S.Chandler	1 F.Skaff	S F.Baker	/S R.Roberts
C B.Conroy	/3 C.Michaels	/O F.Doljack	P D.Trout	P T.Bonham	2 J.Rullo	/O H.Epps	/O R.Marion
3 J.Cronin	H F.Kalin	/C J.McDonnell	P V.Trucks	P B.Wensloff	/O W.Wheaton	2 D.Heffner	1 E.Butka
C D.Doyle	P O.Grove	/C G.Susce	P H.Newhouser	P H.Borowy	/S E.Busch	R H.Schmulbach	/O R.Ortiz
P T.Hughson	P E.Smith	P J.Bagby	P T.Bridges	P A.Donald	/C T.Parisse	P D.Galehouse	/C T.Padden
P Y.Terry	P J.Humphries	P A.Smith	P H.White	RP J.Murphy	/O F.Mackiewicz	P S.Sundra	H R.Barbary
P J.Dobson	P B.Dietrich	P A.Reynolds	RP J.Gorsica	P B.Zuber	/O L.Flick	P B.Muncrief	P E.Wynn
P O.Judd	P B.Ross	P V.Kennedy	RP R.Henshaw	P M.Russo	/3 G.Kell	P N.Potter	P D.Leonard
P D.Newsome	RP G.Maltzberger	P M.Harder	P S.Overmire	H J.Turner	H V.Benson	P A.Hollingsworth	P M.Candini
RP M.Brown	RP B.Swift	RP J.Heving	P P.Oana	H T.Byrne	H B.Konopka	RP G.Caster	P M.Haefner
P M.Ryba	P T.Lee	RP M.Naymick	/P R.Gentry	/P M.Breuer	H E.Brucker	P J.Niggeling	P A.Carrasquel
P P.Woods	P J.Haynes	P J.Salveson	P J.Orrell		P J.Flores	P B.Newsom	P J.Mertz
P L.Lucier	P J.Wade	P C.Dean			P R.Wolff	P C.Fuchs	P R.Scarborough
P E.O'Neill	/P F.Speer	P R.Poat			P L.Harris	P F.Ostermueller	P E.Pyle
/P K.Chase		P P.Center			P D.Black	/P A.Milnar	/P J.Niggeling
P A.Karl		P A.Milnar			P O.Arntzen	/P P.Dean	/P B.Newsom
		/P E.Klieman			P R.Christopher	/P S.Peterson	/P B.Lefebvre
		/P P.Calvert			P L.Ciola	/P J.Kramer	/P D.Adkins
		/P S.Gromek			P E.Fagan	/P O.Miller	/P O.Scheetz
					/P B.Kuczynski	/P A.LaMacchia	/P O.Miller
					/P C.Scheib		/P L.Gomez
					/P C.Bowles		/P V.Curtis
					/P S.Lowry		/P L.Carpenter
					/P H.Besse		
					/P T.Abernathy		
					/P J.Burrows		
					/P J.Mains		
					/P N.Brown		
					/P T.Clyde		

TEAM	G	W	L	PCT	GB	R	OR	AB	H	2B	3B	HR	BB	SO	AVG	OBP	SLG	PRO	PRO+	BR	/A	PF	CHI	RC	SB	CS	SBA	SBR
NY	155	98	56	.636		669	542	5282	1350	218	59	100	624	562	.256	.337	.376	.713	114	97	92	101	95	683	46	60	43	-22
WAS	153	84	69	.549	13.5	666	595	5233	1328	245	50	47	605	579	.254	.336	.347	.683	110	45	69	96	103	656	142	55	72	10
CLE	153	82	71	.536	15.5	600	577	5269	1344	246	45	55	567	521	.255	.329	.350	.679	112	32	71	94	95	626	47	58	45	-21
CHI	155	82	72	.532	16	573	594	5254	1297	193	46	33	561	581	.247	.322	.320	.642	94	-33	-32	100	102	570	173	87	67	0
DET	155	78	76	.506	20	632	560	5364	1401	200	47	77	483	553	.261	.344	.359	.683	98	32	-17	108	99	620	40	43	48	-14
STL	153	72	80	.474	25	596	604	5175	1269	229	36	78	569	646	.245	.322	.349	.671	100	14	1	102	98	603	37	43	46	-15
BOS	155	68	84	.447	29	563	607	5392	1314	223	42	57	486	591	.244	.308	.332	.640	92	-48	-57	102	101	570	86	61	59	-11
PHI	155	49	105	.318	49	497	717	5244	1219	174	44	26	430	465	.232	.294	.297	.591	78	-137	-135	100	111	466	55	42	57	-9
TOT	617					4796		42213	10522	1728	369	473	4325	4498	.249	.322	.341	.663							626	449	58	-82

TEAM	CG	SH	SV	IP	H	H/G	HR	BB	SO	RAT	ERA	ERA+	OAV	OOB	PR	/A	PF	CPI	FA	E	DP	FW	PW	BW	SBW	DIF
NY	83	14	13	1415¹	1229	7.8	60	489	653	11.0	2.93	110	.234	.301	58	46	98	95	.974	160	166	.2	5.0	10.0	-1.3	7.1
WAS	61	16	21	1388	1293	8.4	48	540	495	12.0	3.18	101	.246	.318	17	3	97	99	.971	179	145	-1.0	.3	7.5	2.2	-1.5
CLE	64	14	20	1406¹	1234	7.9	52	606	585	11.9	3.15	99	.239	.322	23	-6	94	100	.975	157	183	.3	-.6	7.7	-1.2	-.7
CHI	70	12	19	1400¹	1352	8.7	54	501	476	12.1	3.20	104	.255	.324	15	21	101	105	.973	166	167	-.0	2.3	-3.5	1.1	5.2
DET	67	18	20	1411²	1226	7.8	51	549	706	11.4	3.00	117	.234	.308	46	81	107	95	.971	177	130	-.7	8.8	-1.8	-.4	-4.8
STL	64	10	14	1385	1397	9.1	74	488	572	12.4	3.41	97	.263	.327	-18	-13	101	106	.975	152	127	.6	-1.4	.1	-.5	-2.8
BOS	62	13	16	1426¹	1369	8.6	61	615	513	12.9	3.45	96	.265	.335	-25	-22	101	105	.976	153	119	.6	-2.4	-6.2	-.0	.0
PHI	73	5	13	1394	1421	9.2	73	536	503	12.9	4.05	84	.265	.336	-117	-101	103	94	.973	162	148	.1	-10.9	-14.6	.1	-2.7
TOT	544	102	136	11227		8.4				12.0	3.30		.249	.322					.973	1306	1245					

Runs		Hits		Doubles		Triples		Home Runs		Total Bases	
Case-Was	102	Wakefield-Det	200	Wakefield-Det	38	Moses-Chi	12	York-Det	34	York-Det	301
Keller-NY	97	Appling-Chi	192	Case-Was	36	Lindell-NY	11	Keller-NY	31	Wakefield-Det	275
Wakefield-Det	91	Cramer-Det	182	Gutteridge-StL	35	York-Det	11	Stephens-StL	22	Keller-NY	269
York-Det	90	Case-Was	180	Etten-NY	35	Keller-NY	11	Heath-Cle	18	Doerr-Bos	249
Vernon-Was	89					Spence-Was	10			Stephens-StL	247

Runs Batted In		Runs Produced		Bases On Balls		Batting Average		On Base Percentage		Slugging Average	
York-Det	118	York-Det	174	Keller-NY	106	Appling-Chi	.328	Appling-Chi	.419	York-Det	.527
Etten-NY	107	Etten-NY	171	Gordon-NY	98	Wakefield-Det	.316	Cullenbine-Cle	.407	Keller-NY	.525
Johnson-NY	94	Wakefield-Det	163	Cullenbine-Cle	96	Hodgin-Chi	.314	Keller-NY	.396	Stephens-StL	.482
Stephens-StL	91	Johnson-NY	159	Boudreau-Cle	90	Cramer-Det	.300	Boudreau-Cle	.388	Heath-Cle	.481
Spence-Was	88	Case-Was	153	Appling-Chi	90	Case-Was	.294	Curtright-Chi	.382	Wakefield-Det	.434

Production		Adjusted Production		Batter Runs		Adjusted Batter Runs		Clutch Hitting Index		Runs Created	
Keller-NY	.922	Keller-NY	167	Keller-NY	45.8	Keller-NY	45.0	Sullivan-Was	162	Keller-NY	116
York-Det	.893	Heath-Cle	157	York-Det	41.0	Appling-Chi	35.1	Johnson-NY	134	Appling-Chi	109
Heath-Cle	.850	York-Det	148	Appling-Chi	35.0	York-Det	33.0	Siebert-Phi	128	York-Det	108
Stephens-StL	.839	Cullenbine-Cle	146	Wakefield-Det	28.8	Cullenbine-Cle	32.9	Early-Was	125	Wakefield-Det	101
Appling-Chi	.825	Appling-Chi	142	Cullenbine-Cle	27.4	Heath-Cle	29.7	McQuinn-StL	125	Spence-Was	93

Total Average		Stolen Bases		Stolen Base Average		Stolen Base Runs		Fielding Runs		Total Player Rating	
Keller-NY	.979	Case-Was	61	Case-Was	81.3	Case-Was	9.9	Boudreau-Cle	28.4	Boudreau-Cle	6.7
York-Det	.871	Moses-Chi	56	Moses-Chi	80.0	Moses-Chi	8.4	Gordon-NY	25.7	Appling-Chi	6.0
Appling-Chi	.841	Tucker-Chi	29	Appling-Chi	77.1	Culberson-Bos	4.2	Clift-StL	18.3	Gordon-NY	5.4
Heath-Cle	.828	Appling-Chi	27	Vernon-Was	75.0	Appling-Chi	3.3	York-Det	17.6	York-Det	4.3
Cullenbine-Cle	.816	Vernon-Was	24	Fox-Bos	73.3	Vernon-Was	2.4	Bloodworth-Det	17.2	Keller-NY	4.3

Wins		Win Percentage		Games		Complete Games		Shutouts		Saves	
Trout-Det	20	Chandler-NY	.833	Brown-Bos	49	Hughson-Bos	20	Trout-Det	5	Maltzberger-Chi	14
Chandler-NY	20	Smith-Cle	.708	Trout-Det	44	Chandler-NY	20	Chandler-NY	5	Heving-Cle	9
Wynn-Was	18	Bonham-NY	.652	Wolff-Phi	41	Wensloff-NY	18	Hughson-Bos	4	Brown-Bos	9
Smith-Cle	17	Trout-Det	.625	Ryba-Bos	40	Trout-Det	18	Bonham-NY	4	Murphy-NY	8
Bagby-Cle	17	Grove-Chi	.625	Carrasquel-Was	39	Grove-Chi	18			Caster-StL	8

Innings Pitched		Fewest Hits/Game		Fewest BB/Game		Strikeouts		Strikeouts/Game		Ratio	
Bagby-Cle	273.0	Reynolds-Cle	6.34	Leonard-Was	1.88	Reynolds-Cle	151	Reynolds-Cle	6.84	Chandler-NY	9.07
Hughson-Bos	266.0	Niggeling-StL-Was	6.66	Chandler-NY	1.92	Newhouser-Det	144	Newhouser-Det	6.62	Trucks-Det	9.90
Wynn-Was	256.2	Haefner-Was	6.86	Bonham-NY	2.07	Chandler-NY	134	Bridges-Det	5.82	Bonham-NY	9.97
Chandler-NY	253.0	Chandler-NY	7.01	Muncrief-StL	2.11	Bridges-Det	124	Trucks-Det	5.24	Wensloff-NY	10.07
Trout-Det	246.2	Wensloff-NY	7.21	Trucks-Det	2.31	Trucks-Det	118	Chandler-NY	4.77	Niggeling-StL-Was	10.24

Earned Run Average		Adjusted ERA		Opponents' Batting Avg.		Opponents' On Base Pct.		Starter Runs		Adjusted Starter Runs	
Chandler-NY	1.64	Chandler-NY	197	Reynolds-Cle	.202	Chandler-NY	.261	Chandler-NY	46.6	Chandler-NY	44.4
Bonham-NY	2.27	Bridges-Det	147	Niggeling-StL-Was	.204	Trucks-Det	.276	Bonham-NY	25.6	Trout-Det	28.5
Haefner-Was	2.29	Trout-Det	142	Haefner-Was	.208	Wensloff-NY	.282	Trout-Det	22.3	Bridges-Det	24.0
Bridges-Det	2.39	Bonham-NY	141	Chandler-NY	.215	Bonham-NY	.282	Hughson-Bos	19.4	Bonham-NY	23.6
Trout-Det	2.48	Haefner-Was	140	Wensloff-NY	.219	Niggeling-StL-Was	.282	Bridges-Det	19.2	Hughson-Bos	19.9

Clutch Pitching Index		Relief Runs		Adjusted Relief Runs		Relief Ranking		Total Pitcher Index		Total Baseball Ranking	
Hughson-Bos	124	Brown-Bos	12.2	Brown-Bos	12.3	Caster-StL	19.2	Chandler-NY	5.7	Boudreau-Cle	6.7
Muncrief-StL	120	Caster-StL	10.0	Caster-StL	10.2	Brown-Bos	17.0	Trout-Det	4.7	Appling-Chi	6.0
Bonham-NY	116	Maltzberger-Chi	9.1	Maltzberger-Chi	9.6	Maltzberger-Chi	12.7	Bridges-Det	2.6	Chandler-NY	5.7
Galehouse-StL	115	Naymick-Cle	6.9	Naymick-Cle	5.6	Murphy-NY	12.6	Caster-StL	2.1	Gordon-NY	5.4
Candini-Was	115	Murphy-NY	5.9	Murphy-NY	5.3	Naymick-Cle	6.9	Bonham-NY	2.0	Trout-Det	4.7

January 27 Lou Perini, Guido Rugo, and Joseph Maney, known as "the Three Little Steamshovels," buy the Braves and oust Casey Stengel as manager.

February 2 The leagues meet at New York to discuss postwar action. They decide players with war service will be guaranteed 30 days of trial at pay and restrictions on their release or assignment. Military service will count as playing time.

April 27 Boston knuckleballer Jim Tobin hits a home run and no-hits the Brooklyn Dodgers, 2–0, before a midweek crowd of 1,984 at Braves Field. Tobin walks Paul Waner to lead off the game, then retires 26 consecutive batters before walking Waner again with two outs in the ninth inning

May 15 Reds reliever Clyde Shoun, making his first start of the season, throws a no-hitter to nip the Boston Braves, 1–0. Only 1,014 see the 32-year-old lefty top Jim Tobin, who had thrown one in April.

May 23 Wartime restrictions are eased, and the Polo Grounds is the scene of the first night game in New York City since 1941.

June 10 Pitcher Joe Nuxhall of the Cincinnati Reds becomes the youngest player in major league history. Nuxhall, only 15 years, 10 months old, pitches two-thirds of an inning in an 18-0 loss to the St. Louis Cardinals. He manages to give up five walks and two hits.

July 11 Phil Cavarretta of the Cubs sets an All-Star Game record by reaching base five successive times on a triple, single, and three walks in a 7-1 NL win.

August 3 Tommy Brown, just 16 years and eight months old, plays shortstop for Brooklyn in both games of a twin bill loss, 6-2 and 7-1, to the Cubs.

August 10 Red Barrett of the Boston Braves throws only 58 pitches and shuts out the Cincinnati Reds, 2–0. This is the major league record for fewest pitches in a nine-inning game. The game takes one hour, 15 minutes, the shortest night game ever.

September 21 The Cardinals finally clinch the NL flag with a 5-4 win over Boston. Twenty games ahead on September 1, the Cards then blew 15 of the next 20 games. They will finish with 105 victories and their third title under Billy Southworth, whose clubs win 316 games in three years.

October 9 Emil Verban drives in three runs as the Cardinals top the Browns 3-1 and win the Series in six games. Ted Wilks allows no one to reach base in 3⅔ innings of relief, fanning four pinch hitters. George McQuinn hits .438 for the Series. The winners get $4,626 each; the Browns take $2,743, the lowest player shares since 1933.

December 21 The league MVP award goes to fielding wizard Marty Marion, who tallies one more vote than Cubs slugger Bill Nicholson.

BOSTON		BROOKLYN		CHICAGO		CINCINNATI		NEW YORK		PHILADELPHIA		PITTSBURGH		ST.LOUIS	
M	B.Coleman	M	L.Durocher	M	J.Wilson	M	B.McKechnie	M	M.Ott	M	F.Fitzsimmons	M	F.Frisch	M	B.Southworth
1B	B.Etchison	1B	H.Schultz	M	R.Johnson	1B	F.McCormick	1B	P.Weintraub	1B	T.Lupien	1B	B.Dahlgren	1B	R.Sanders
2B	C.Ryan	2B	E.Stanky	M	C.Grimm	2B	W.Williams	2B	G.Hausmann	2B	M.Mullen	2B	P.Coscarart	2B	E.Verban
SS	W.Wietelmann	SS	B.Bragan	1B	P.Cavarretta	SS	E.Miller	SS	B.Kerr	SS	R.Hamrick	SS	F.Gustine	SS	M.Marion
3B	D.Phillips	3B	F.Bordagaray	2B	D.Johnson	3B	S.Mesner	3B	H.Luby	3B	G.Stewart	3B	B.Elliott	3B	W.Kurowski
LF	B.Nieman	LF	A.Galan	SS	L.Merullo	LF	E.Tipton	LF	J.Medwick	LF	J.Wasdell	LF	J.Russell	LF	D.Litwhiler
CF	T.Holmes	CF	G.Rosen	3B	S.Hack	CF	D.Clay	CF	J.Rucker	CF	B.Adams	CF	V.DiMaggio	CF	J.Hopp
RF	C.Workman	RF	D.Walker	LF	D.Dallessandro	RF	G.Walker	RF	M.Ott	RF	R.Northey	RF	J.Barrett	RF	S.Musial
C	P.Masi	C	M.Owen	CF	A.Pafko	C	R.Mueller	C	E.Lombardi	C	B.Finley	C	A.Lopez	C	W.Cooper
				RF	B.Nicholson										
1O	M.Macon	O2	L.Olmo	C	D.Williams	O	M.Marshall	13	N.Reyes	23	C.Letchas	O	F.Colman	C	K.O'Dea
C	C.Kluttz	S	T.Brown			O	T.Criscola	3S	B.Jurges	C	J.Peacock	O2	A.Rubeling	O	A.Bergamo
O	A.Wright	O	P.Waner	3S	R.Hughes	3	C.Aleno	C	G.Mancuso	3	T.Cieslak	S	F.Zak	O3	D.Garms
C	S.Hofferth	1	J.Bolling	S	B.Schuster	O	E.Crabtree	O	R.Treadway	O	C.Triplett	O	T.O'Brien	2S	G.Fallon
O	C.Ross	2	E.Basinski	O	I.Goodman	O	J.White	S	D.Gardella	O	G.Hamner	C	H.Camelli	O	P.Martin
2	F.Drews	2	B.Koch	O	L.Novikoff	/3	B.Fausett	O	B.Sloan	C	A.Seminick	S	S.Davis	/1	J.Antonelli
3	R.Gladu	3S	E.Miksis	C	B.Holm	C	J.Just	O	C.Mead	S	H.Heltzel	23	L.Handley	/C	B.Keely
3	W.Huston	S	B.Hart	C	M.Kreitner	/O	C.Ramos	O	S.Filipowicz	/C	M.Shea	/O	L.Waner		
2	S.Shemo	S3	G.English	S3	T.York	/C	L.Rice	C	R.Berres	/O	L.Riley	/O	A.Gionfriddo	P	M.Cooper
3	M.Sandlock	O	M.Aderholt	O	F.Secory	/2	J.Beeler	/2	R.Nichols	/O	C.Klein	/O	B.Rodgers	P	M.Lanier
/S	D.Culler	/O	R.Durrett	O	E.Sauer	H	A.Lakeman			/C	J.Antolick	/S	V.Barnhart	P	T.Wilks
/C	H.Poland	2	P.Ankenman	S	C.Brewster	/3	K.Wahl	P	B.Voiselle	/3	P.Caballero	/1	H.Sweeney	P	H.Brecheen
/O	C.Clemens	/2	L.Rochelli	C	R.Easterwood	R	M.Kosman	P	H.Feldman	/C	B.Culp			P	A.Jurisich
/2	B.Geraghty	/S	G.Mauch	/C	P.Gillespie	/C	J.Riddle	P	E.Pyle	H	N.Goulish	P	R.Sewell	RP	B.Donnelly
/2	P.Capri	/O	L.Waner	/2	E.Stanky			P	R.Fischer	H	T.Tyson	P	F.Ostermueller		
R	G.Patton	/C	R.Hayworth	P	P.Elko	P	B.Walters	RP	A.Adams			P	M.Butcher	P	R.Munger
		/C	S.Andrews	/3	J.Foxx	P	C.Shoun	RP	A.Hansen	P	K.Raffensberger	P	N.Strincevich	P	F.Schmidt
P	J.Tobin	/C	F.Dantonio	/O	J.Ostrowski	P	E.Heusser			P	C.Schanz	P	P.Roe	P	H.Gumbert
P	N.Andrews	/C	J.Cooney	/O	J.Stephenson	P	T.DeLa Cruz	P	J.Allen	P	D.Barrett	RP	X.Rescigno	/P	B.Byerly
P	A.Javery	H	C.Smyres	R	G.Mann	P	H.Gumbert	P	F.Seward	P	B.Lee			/P	B.Trotter
P	R.Barrett	/C	R.Jarvis					P	C.Melton	P	A.Gerheauser	P	C.Cuccurullo	/P	M.Naymick
P	I.Hutchinson			P	H.Wyse	P	T.DeLaCruz	P	J.Brewer	RP	A.Karl	P	R.Starr		
		P	H.Gregg	P	C.Passeau	P	A.Carter	P	L.Polli			/P	J.Gee		
P	B.Cardoni	P	C.Davis	P	P.Derringer	/P	J.Konstanty	/P	K.Brondell	P	V.Kennedy	/P	L.Gilmore		
P	J.Hutchings	P	R.Melton	P	B.Fleming	/P	E.Riddle	/P	B.Barthelson	P	C.Covington	/P	J.Vitelli		
P	S.Klopp	RP	L.Webber	P	B.Chipman	/P	B.Malloy	/P	J.Gee	P	D.Matthewson	/P	R.Wise		
/P	W.Rich					P	B.Katz	/P	W.Miller	P	H.Shuman				
/P	J.Hickey	P	C.McLish	P	H.Vandenberg	/P	B.Ferguson	/P	F.Rosso	P	B.Mussill				
/P	C.Lindquist	P	B.Chapman	P	P.Erickson	/P	J.Beggs	/P	W.Ockey	/P	D.Donahue				
/P	G.Woodend	P	T.Warren	P	R.Lynn	/P	H.Fox			/P	J.Fick				
/P	H.MacPherson	/P	E.Head	P	E.Hanyzewski	/P	B.Lohrman			/P	L.Lucier				
		P	A.Herring	P	D.Alderson	/P	J.Nuxhall			/P	R.McKee				
		P	R.Branca	/P	C.Gassaway	/P	K.Peterson			/P	C.Ripple				
		P	C.King	/P	M.Stewart	/P	J.Eisenhart			/P	A.Verdel				
		P	F.Ostermueller	/P	H.Miklos										
		/P	W.Wyatt	/P	J.Burrows										
		P	B.Chipman												
		P	T.Sunkel												
		/P	W.Flowers												
		/P	C.Fuchs												
		/P	J.Wells												
		/P	C.Zachary												
		/P	C.Crocker												
		/P	B.Lohrman												
		/P	C.Osgood												
		/P	J.Franklin												
		/P	F.Wurm												

TEAM	G	W	L	PCT	GB	R	OR	AB	H	2B	3B	HR	BB	SO	AVG	OBP	SLG	PRO	PRO+	BR	/A	PF	CHI	RC	SB	CS	SBA	SBR
STL	157	105	49	.682		772	490	5475	1507	274	59	100	544	473	.275	.344	.402	.746	114	110	96	102	98	775	37			
PIT	158	90	63	.588	14.5	744	662	5428	1441	248	80	70	573	616	.265	.338	.379	.717	104	58	27	104	102	707	87			
CIN	155	89	65	.578	16	573	537	5271	1340	229	31	51	423	391	.254	.313	.338	.651	92	-74	-53	96	101	558	51			
CHI	157	75	79	.487	30	702	669	5462	1425	236	46	71	520	521	.261	.328	.360	.688	101	-2	2	99	104	658	53			
NY	155	67	87	.435	38	682	773	5306	1398	191	47	93	512	480	.263	.331	.370	.701	103	22	24	100	100	656	39			
BOS	155	65	89	.422	40	593	674	5282	1299	250	39	79	456	509	.246	.308	.353	.661	88	-61	-85	104	101	586	37			
BRO	155	63	91	.409	42	690	832	5393	1450	255	51	56	486	451	.269	.331	.366	.697	104	16	28	98	101	664	45			
PHI	154	61	92	.399	43.5	539	658	5301	1331	199	42	55	470	500	.251	.316	.336	.652	92	-70	-51	97	92	571	32			
TOT	623					5295		42918	11191	1882	395	575	3984	3941	.261	.326	.363	.689							381			

TEAM	CG	SH	SV	IP	H	H/G	HR	BB	SO	RAT	ERA	ERA+	OAV	OOB	PR	/A	PF	CPI	FA	E	DP	FW	PW	BW	SBW	DIF
STL	89	26	12	1427	1228	7.7	55	468	637	10.8	2.67	132	.233	.298	148	134	98	103	.982	112	162	3.7	13.8	9.9		.7
PIT	77	10	19	1414[1]	1466	9.3	65	435	452	12.2	3.44	108	.265	.321	27	45	103	103	.970	191	122	-1.1	4.6	2.8		7.2
CIN	93	17	12	1398[1]	1292	8.3	60	390	369	10.9	2.97	117	.246	.300	99	80	97	99	.978	137	153	2.0	8.2	-5.4		7.2
CHI	70	11	13	1400[2]	1484	9.5	75	458	545	12.5	3.59	98	.274	.331	4	-8	98	108	.970	186	151	-.8	-.8	.2		-.5
NY	47	4	21	1363[2]	1413	9.3	116	587	499	13.4	4.29	85	.265	.342	-103	-94	102	98	.971	179	128	-.5	-9.6	2.5		-2.3
BOS	70	13	12	1388[1]	1430	9.3	80	527	454	12.8	3.67	104	.267	.335	-9	23	106	106	.971	182	160	-.7	2.4	-8.7		-4.9
BRO	50	4	13	1367[2]	1471	9.7	75	660	487	14.3	4.68	76	.274	.357	-162	-172	98	93	.966	197	112	-1.7	-17.7	2.9		2.4
PHI	66	11	6	1395[1]	1407	9.1	49	459	496	12.2	3.64	99	.261	.321	-4	-5	100	93	.972	177	138	-.5	-.5	-5.2		-9.3
TOT	562	96	108	11155[1]		9.0				12.4	3.61		.261	.326					.972	1361	1126					

Runs		Hits		Doubles		Triples		Home Runs		Total Bases	
Nicholson-Chi	116	Musial-StL	197	Musial-StL	51	Barrett-Pit	19	Nicholson-Chi	33	Nicholson-Chi	317
Musial-StL	112	Cavarretta-Chi	197	Galan-Bro	43	Elliott-Pit	16	Ott-NY	26	Musial-StL	312
Russell-Pit	109	Holmes-Bos	195	Holmes-Bos	42	Cavarretta-Chi	15	Northey-Phi	22	Holmes-Bos	288
Hopp-StL	106	Walker-Bro	191			Russell-Pit	14	McCormick-Cin	20	Walker-Bro	283
Cavarretta-Chi	106	Russell-Pit	181			Musial-StL	14	Kurowski-StL	20	Northey-Phi	283

Runs Batted In		Runs Produced		Bases On Balls		Batting Average		On Base Percentage		Slugging Average	
Nicholson-Chi	122	Nicholson-Chi	205	Galan-Bro	101	Walker-Bro	.357	Musial-StL	.440	Musial-StL	.549
Elliott-Pit	108	Musial-StL	194	Nicholson-Chi	93	Musial-StL	.347	Walker-Bro	.434	Nicholson-Chi	.545
Northey-Phi	104	Elliott-Pit	183	Ott-NY	90	Medwick-NY	.337	Galan-Bro	.426	Ott-NY	.544
Sanders-StL	102	Cavarretta-Chi	183	Musial-StL	90	Hopp-StL	.336	Ott-NY	.423	Walker-Bro	.529
McCormick-Cin	102			Barrett-Pit	86	Cavarretta-Chi	.321	Hopp-StL	.404	Weintraub-NY	.524

Production		Adjusted Production		Batter Runs		Adjusted Batter Runs		Clutch Hitting Index		Runs Created	
Musial-StL	.990	Musial-StL	174	Musial-StL	60.9	Musial-StL	58.5	Olmo-Bro	132	Musial-StL	145
Ott-NY	.967	Walker-Bro	173	Walker-Bro	51.2	Walker-Bro	53.4	Elliott-Pit	126	Nicholson-Chi	132
Walker-Bro	.963	Ott-NY	171	Nicholson-Chi	47.4	Galan-Bro	48.7	Dahlgren-Pit	119	Walker-Bro	128
Nicholson-Chi	.935	Nicholson-Chi	162	Galan-Bro	46.5	Nicholson-Chi	48.2	Schultz-Bro	118	Galan-Bro	123
Galan-Bro	.922	Galan-Bro	162	Ott-NY	40.4	Ott-NY	40.7	Medwick-NY	117	Russell-Pit	112

Total Average		Stolen Bases		Stolen Base Average		Stolen Base Runs		Fielding Runs		Total Player Rating	
Musial-StL	1.095	Barrett-Pit	28					Kerr-NY	16.8	Musial-StL	5.4
Ott-NY	1.087	Lupien-Phi	18					Luby-NY	16.4	Walker-Bro	4.4
Walker-Bro	1.034	Hughes-Chi	16					Williams-Cin	15.0	Nicholson-Chi	4.2
Nicholson-Chi	1.002	Hopp-StL	15					Pafko-Chi	14.7	Galan-Bro	4.0
Galan-Bro	.992	Kerr-NY	14					Russell-Pit	13.3	McCormick-Cin	3.7

Wins		Win Percentage		Games		Complete Games		Shutouts		Saves	
Walters-Cin	23	Wilks-StL	.810	Adams-NY	65	Tobin-Bos	28	M.Cooper-StL	7	Adams-NY	13
M.Cooper-StL	22	Brecheen-StL	.762	Webber-Bro	48	Walters-Cin	27	Walters-Cin	6	Schmidt-StL	5
Voiselle-NY	21	M.Cooper-StL	.759	Rescigno-Pit	48	Voiselle-NY	25	Tobin-Bos	5	Rescigno-Pit	5
Sewell-Pit	21	Walters-Cin	.742	Voiselle-NY	43	Sewell-Pit	24	Lanier-StL	5	Davis-Bro	4
Tobin-Bos	18	Sewell-Pit	.636	Tobin-Bos	43	M.Cooper-StL	22	Butcher-Pit	5	Cuccurullo-Pit	4

Innings Pitched		Fewest Hits/Game		Fewest BB/Game		Strikeouts		Strikeouts/Game		Ratio	
Voiselle-NY	312.2	Walters-Cin	7.36	Raffensberger-Phi	1.57	Voiselle-NY	161	Lanier-StL	5.66	Wilks-StL	9.66
Tobin-Bos	299.1	Wilks-StL	7.50	Strincevich-Pit	1.75	Lanier-StL	141	Javery-Bos	4.85	Heusser-Cin	9.72
Sewell-Pit	286.0	Lanier-StL	7.70	Davis-Bro	1.81	Javery-Bos	136	Raffensberger-Phi	4.73	De LaCruz-Cin	10.16
Walters-Cin	285.0	Heusser-Cin	7.71	Shoun-Cin	1.87	Raffensberger-Phi	136	Voiselle-NY	4.63	Walters-Cin	10.23
Raffensberger-Phi	258.2	Voiselle-NY	7.94	Derringer-Chi	1.95			Melton-Bro	4.37	M.Cooper-StL	10.41

Earned Run Average		Adjusted ERA		Opponents' Batting Avg.		Opponents' On Base Pct.		Starter Runs		Adjusted Starter Runs	
Heusser-Cin	2.38	Heusser-Cin	146	Walters-Cin	.219	Wilks-StL	.275	Walters-Cin	38.3	Walters-Cin	34.4
Walters-Cin	2.40	Walters-Cin	145	Wilks-StL	.227	Heusser-Cin	.275	M.Cooper-StL	32.2	M.Cooper-StL	29.8
M.Cooper-StL	2.46	M.Cooper-StL	143	Heusser-Cin	.231	Walters-Cin	.281	Munger-StL	30.5	Munger-StL	29.4
Wilks-StL	2.64	Wilks-StL	133	Voiselle-NY	.232	De LaCruz-Cin	.284	Heusser-Cin	26.3	Tobin-Bos	27.0
Lanier-StL	2.65	Lanier-StL	133	Lanier-StL	.234	Raffensberger-Phi	.285	Lanier-StL	24.0	Ostermueller-Br-Pt	23.9

Clutch Pitching Index		Relief Runs		Adjusted Relief Runs		Relief Ranking		Total Pitcher Index		Total Baseball Ranking	
Fleming-Chi	121	Karl-Phi	12.7	Karl-Phi	12.7	Karl-Phi	7.1	Walters-Cin	4.7	Musial-StL	5.4
Ostermueller-Br-Pt	120	Donnelly-StL	12.6	Donnelly-StL	11.9	Donnelly-StL	4.9	Tobin-Bos	4.7	Walters-Cin	4.7
Chipman-Bro-Chi	119							Munger-StL	3.6	Tobin-Bos	4.7
Wyse-Chi	113							M.Cooper-StL	3.0	Walker-Bro	4.4
Javery-Bos	111							Heusser-Cin	2.9	Nicholson-Chi	4.2

April 29 Jack Kramer pitches the Browns' to their AL record ninth straight win to start the season. The 3–1 win over the Indians gives the first place Browns a 3½ game lead.

May 1 George Myatt of the Washington Senators collects six hits in six at bats, as the Nats pound out 20 hits to beat Boston, 11–4.

May 10 Mel Harder wins his 200th career game as Cleveland defeats the Red Sox 5–4. He is the 50th to reach this mark.

June 6 All major league games are canceled as the country's focus is turned toward Europe while allied forces invade occupied France.

June 26 More than 50,000 pack the Polo Grounds to watch the Yankees, Dodgers, and Giants play each other in a six-inning contest to raise money for war bonds. Each team plays successive innings against the other two teams, then sits out an inning. The final score is Dodgers 5, Yankees 1, Giants 0.

July 20 The Browns' Nelson Potter becomes the first pitcher suspended for throwing spitballs. He is banished for 10 days for allegedly "putting an illegal substance on the ball." Potter will return to win 19 games for St. Louis.

September 15 Radio announcer Bill Stern reports on a scandal involving the Browns. A Chicago newspaper attributes the Browns' recent slump to the fact that the league wants a larger park for the World Series. Four days later Stern repudiates the story.

October 1 The Browns have their first sellout in 20 years as 37,815 pack Sportsman's Park. St. Louis clinches the flag on the final day of the season by sweeping the Yankees and winning 5-2 on a pair of two-run home runs by Chet Laabs.

October 4 The first all-St. Louis World Series, dubbed the "Streetcar Series," opens with the Browns as the visiting team, beating the Cardinals 2-1 on George McQuinn's home run. Denny Galehouse is the winning pitcher and Mort Cooper loses despite allowing just two hits. It is the first Series in which all games are played west of the Mississippi River and is played with no days off.

November 23 Five groups totaling 23 players, managers, umpires, and writers visit war theaters as part of the USO program. Included are Mel Ott, Emil "Dutch" Leonard, Frankie Frisch, William "Bucky" Walters, Harry Heilmann, Carl Hubbell, Freddie Fitzsimmons, Bill Summers, Beans Reardon, Johnny Lindell, George "Tuck" Stainback, Steve O'Neill, Leo Durocher, Joe Medwick, Nick Etten, Fred "Dixie" Walker, Paul Waner, and Truett "Rip" Sewell.

November 25 Kenesaw Mountain Landis, baseball's first commissioner, dies of a heart attack at age 78 in Chicago. The Commissioner had ruled over baseball since November 1920 in the wake of the Black Sox scandal, and wielded authority perhaps unparalleled in any other industry.

November 28 Hal Newhouser is named MVP in the AL, gathering four more votes than teammate Paul "Dizzy" Trout.

December 28 Former Washington third baseman John "Buddy" Lewis wins the Distinguished Flying Cross for precision flying over the Burma war theater.

BOSTON	CHICAGO	CLEVELAND	DETROIT	NEW YORK	PHILADELPHIA	ST.LOUIS	WASHINGTON
M J.Cronin	M J.Dykes	M L.Boudreau	M S.O'Neill	M J.McCarthy	M C.Mack	M L.Sewell	M O.Bluege
1B L.Finney	1B H.Trosky	1B M.Rocco	1B R.York	1B N.Etten	1B B.McGhee	1B G.McQuinn	1B J.Kuhel
2B B.Doerr	2B R.Schalk	2B R.Mack	2B E.Mayo	2B S.Stirnweiss	2B I.Hall	2B D.Gutteridge	2B G.Myatt
SS S.Newsome	SS S.Webb	SS L.Boudreau	SS J.Hoover	SS M.Milosevich	SS E.Busch	SS V.Stephens	SS J.Sullivan
3B J.Tabor	3B R.Hodgin	3B K.Keltner	3B P.Higgins	3B O.Grimes	3B G.Kell	3B M.Christman	3B G.Torres
LF B.Johnson	LF E.Carnett	LF P.Seerey	LF D.Wakefield	LF H.Martin	LF F.Garrison	LF M.Byrnes	LF G.Case
CF C.Metkovich	CF T.Tucker	CF O.Hockett	CF D.Cramer	CF J.Lindell	CF B.Estalella	CF M.Kreevich	CF S.Spence
RF P.Fox	RF W.Moses	RF R.Cullenbine	RF J.Outlaw	RF B.Metheny	RF J.White	RF G.Moore	RF R.Ortiz
C R.Partee	C M.Tresh	C B.Rosar	C P.Richards	C M.Garbark	C F.Hayes	C F.Mancuso	C R.Ferrell
O L.Culberson	O G.Curtright	2S R.Peters	O C.Hostetler	C R.Hemsley	1O D.Siebert	O A.Zarilla	O J.Powell
32 J.Bucher	3 G.Clarke	O M.Hoag	C B.Swift	3 D.Savage	C H.Epps	C R.Hayworth	M.Guerra
C H.Wagner	O J.Dickshot	P.O'Dea	O D.Ross	S F.Crosetti	2 J.Rullo	O C.Laabs	2 F.Vaughn
O T.McBride	3 T.Cuccinello	J.Heath	S3 J.Orengo	O E.Levy	2S B.Burgo	2S F.Baker	3 H.Layne
1 J.Cronin	C T.Turner	N.Schlueter	O C.Metro	R.Derry	1 J.Burns	1 M.Chartak	O E.Boland
S E.Lake	C V.Castino	2 J.Grant	/2 A.Unser	O L.Rosenthal	3 L.Rosenthal	O H.Epps	3 H.Clift
O F.Garrison	S C.Michaels	G.Susce	/2 D.Heffner	O T.Stainback	O C.Metro	O F.Demaree	1 E.Butka
C B.Conroy	C M.Hoag	J.McDonnell	/2 R.Borom	/O J.Cooney	/O L.Flick	3 E.Clary	/O R.Monteagudo
/O J.Lazor	C T.Jordan	R.Lyon	/S B.Floyd	B.Drescher	/S B.Wilkins	C T.Turner	O J.Vosmik
/C J.Peacock	/2 W.Metzig	/C H.Ruszkowski	H.Miller	H P.Waner	/C B.Garbark	/O T.Hafey	/C A.Evans
		/2 S.Biras	H J.McHale	/C R.Collins	H.Peck	/C J.Schultz	/3 E.Yost
P T.Hughson	P B.Dietrich	/C J.Devlin	/2 J.Sullivan	/O A.Simmons	/O B.Martin	/O B.Martin	/O G.Binks
P P.Woods	P O.Grove	P S.Gromek	P D.Trout	H B.Mills	H L.Schulte	P J.Kramer	/2 P.Gomez
P J.Bowman	P E.Lopat	P M.Harder	P H.Newhouser	P H.Borowy	T.Parisse	P N.Potter	/3 L.Suarez
P E.O'Neill	P J.Humphries	P A.Smith	P R.Gentry	P M.Dubiel	J.Pruett	P B.Muncrief	H R.Valdes
P M.Ryba	P J.Haynes	P E.Klieman	P S.Overmire	P T.Bonham	/C H.Wagner	P S.Jakucki	P D.Leonard
RP F.Barrett	RP G.Maltzberger	P A.Reynolds	P J.Gorsica	/C A.Donald	P R.Christopher	P D.Galehouse	P M.Haefner
P C.Hausmann	P T.Lee	RP J.Heving	RP B.Beck	B.Zuber	P B.Newsom	RP G.Caster	P E.Wynn
P Y.Terry	P B.Ross	RP R.Poat	P J.Mooty	J.Page	L.Hamlin	P A.Hollingsworth	P J.Niggeling
P R.Cecil	P J.Wade	RP P.Calvert	P J.Orrell	S.Roser	J.Flores	P T.Shirley	R.Wolff
/P C.Dreisewerd	/P D.Hanski	P J.Bagby	/P Z.Eaton	M.Queen	D.Black	P S.Zoldak	RP B.Lefebvre
/P O.Judd	/P F.Speer	P V.Kennedy	/P R.Henshaw	/P B.Bevens	J.Berry	P L.West	P A.Carrasquel
/P V.Johnson		P H.Kleine	/P B.Gillespie	A.Lyons	L.Harris	/P S.Sundra	P M.Candini
/P J.Wood		/P E.Henry	/P C.Hogsett	J.Johnson	W.Wheaton	/P W.Hudlin	P B.Ortiz
/P L.Lucier		/P M.Naymick		/P S.Chandler	C.Scheib		/P J.Thesenga
/P S.Partenheimer		/P B.Bonness			T.Abernathy		/P V.Curtis
		/P R.Embree			/P J.McGillen		/P S.Ullrich
							/P W.Holborow
							/P B.Zinser

TEAM	G	W	L	PCT	GB	R	OR	AB	H	2B	3B	HR	BB	SO	AVG	OBP	SLG	PRO	PRO+	BR	/A	PF	CHI	RC	SB	CS	SBA	SBR
STL	154	89	65	.578		684	587	5269	1328	223	45	72	531	604	.252	.323	.352	.675	94	-4	-40	106	**110**	629	44	33	57	-7
DET	156	88	66	.571	1	658	**581**	5344	1405	220	44	60	**532**	500	.263	.332	.354	.686	97	21	-15	106	100	641	61	55	53	-15
NY	154	83	71	.539	6	674	617	5331	1410	216	**74**	96	523	627	.264	.333	**.387**	**.720**	108	75	52	102	95	707	91	31	**75**	9
BOS	156	77	77	.500	12	**739**	676	5400	1456	**277**	56	69	522	505	**.270**	**.336**	.380	.716	112	73	82	99	103	**710**	60	40	60	-6
PHI	155	72	82	.468	17	525	594	5312	1364	169	47	36	422	490	.257	.314	.327	.641	90	-73	-65	99	96	547	42	32	57	-7
CLE	155	72	82	.468	17	643	677	5481	**1458**	270	50	70	512	593	.266	.331	.372	.703	111	46	72	96	93	684	48	42	53	-11
CHI	154	71	83	.461	18	543	662	5292	1307	210	55	23	439	**448**	.247	.307	.320	.627	86	-97	-90	99	104	533	66	47	58	-8
WAS	154	64	90	.416	25	592	664	5319	1386	186	42	33	470	477	.261	.324	.330	.654	97	-41	-15	96	101	594	**127**	59	68	3
TOT	619					5058		42748	11114	1771	413	459	3951	4244	.260	.325	.353	.678							539	339	61	-42

TEAM	CG	SH	SV	IP	H	H/G	HR	BB	SO	RAT	ERA	ERA+	OAV	OOB	PR	/A	PF	CPI	FA	E	DP	FW	PW	BW	SBW	DIF
STL	71	16	17	1397¹	1392	9.0	58	469	**581**	12.1	3.17	114	.259	.320	41	66	105	**105**	.972	171	142	.5	6.9	-4.2	-.2	9.0
DET	**87**	**20**	8	1400	1373	8.8	**39**	452	568	11.9	**3.09**	116	.257	.318	54	75	104	103	.970	190	184	-.5	**7.9**	-1.6	-1.0	6.2
NY	78	9	13	1390¹	1351	**8.7**	82	532	529	12.3	3.39	103	.257	.326	7	15	102	**105**	**.974**	**156**	170	**1.3**	1.6	5.5	**1.5**	-3.9
BOS	58	7	17	1394¹	1404	9.1	66	592	524	13.0	3.82	89	.263	.339	-60	-65	99	98	.972	171	154	.6	-6.8	8.6	-.0	-2.3
PHI	72	10	14	1397¹	1345	**8.7**	58	**390**	534	11.4	3.26	107	**.252**	**.307**	27	35	102	93	.971	176	127	.2	3.7	-6.8	-.2	-1.9
CLE	48	7	**18**	1419¹	1428	9.1	40	621	524	13.2	3.65	90	.265	.344	-35	-56	96	102	**.974**	165	**192**	.9	-5.9	7.6	-.6	-6.9
CHI	64	5	17	1390²	1411	9.1	68	420	481	12.0	3.58	96	.264	.320	-23	-23	100	97	.970	183	154	-.2	-2.4	-9.5	-.3	6.4
WAS	83	13	11	1381	1410	9.2	48	475	503	12.4	3.49	93	.264	.327	-10	-36	95	99	.964	218	156	-2.3	-3.8	-1.6	.9	-6.2
TOT	561	87	115	11170¹		9.0				12.3	3.43		.260	.325					.971	1430	1279					

Runs
Stirnweiss-NY 125
B.Johnson-Bos 106
Cullenbine-Cle 98
Doerr-Bos 95
Metkovich-Bos 94

Hits
Stirnweiss-NY 205
Boudreau-Cle 191
Spence-Was 187
Lindell-NY 178
Rocco-Cle 174

Doubles
Boudreau-Cle 45
Keltner-Cle 41
B.Johnson-Bos 40
Fox-Bos 37
Stirnweiss-NY 35

Triples
Stirnweiss-NY 16
Lindell-NY 16
Gutteridge-StL 11
Doerr-Bos 10

Home Runs
Etten-NY 22
Stephens-StL 20
York-Det 18
Spence-Was 18
Lindell-NY 18

Total Bases
Lindell-NY 297
Stirnweiss-NY 296
Spence-Was 288
B.Johnson-Bos 277

Runs Batted In
Stephens-StL 109
B.Johnson-Bos 106
Lindell-NY 103
Spence-Was 100
York-Det 98

Runs Produced
B.Johnson-Bos 195
Stephens-StL 180
Lindell-NY 176
Spence-Was 165
Cullenbine-Cle ... 162

Bases On Balls
Etten-NY 97
B.Johnson-Bos 95
Cullenbine-Cle 87
McQuinn-StL 85
Higgins-Det 81

Batting Average
Boudreau-Cle 327
Doerr-Bos 325
B.Johnson-Bos 324
Stirnweiss-NY 319
Spence-Was 316

On Base Percentage
B.Johnson-Bos 431
Boudreau-Cle 406
Doerr-Bos ...... .399
Etten-NY .... .399
Byrnes-StL ...... .396

Slugging Average
Doerr-Bos 528
B.Johnson-Bos 528
Lindell-NY ...... .500
Spence-Was 486

Production
B.Johnson-Bos 959
Doerr-Bos 927
Spence-Was 877
Etten-NY 865
Lindell-NY 851

Adjusted Production
B.Johnson-Bos 175
Doerr-Bos 166
Spence-Was 157
Boudreau-Cle 146
Etten-NY 142

Batter Runs
B.Johnson-Bos ... 52.9
Spence-Was 38.1
Doerr-Bos 38.0
Etten-NY 37.3
Wakefield-Det 36.7

Adjusted Batter Runs
B.Johnson-Bos ... 54.4
Spence-Was 43.1
Doerr-Bos 39.2
Boudreau-Cle 37.2
Etten-NY 33.7

Clutch Hitting Index
Christman-StL 134
Carnett-Chi 123
Mayo-Det 121
Torres-Was 115
Stephens-StL 112

Runs Created
Stirnweiss-NY 128
B.Johnson-Bos ... 124
Spence-Was 118
Etten-NY 114
Boudreau-Cle 112

Total Average
B.Johnson-Bos 987
Doerr-Bos 945
Stirnweiss-NY 910
Etten-NY 879
Spence-Was 856

Stolen Bases
Stirnweiss-NY 55
Case-Was 49
Myatt-Was 26
Moses-Chi 21
Gutteridge-StL 20

Stolen Base Average
Stirnweiss-NY 83.3
Moses-Chi 75.0
Case-Was 73.1
Myatt-Was 72.2
Gutteridge-StL ... 71.4

Stolen Base Runs
Stirnweiss-NY......9.9
Case-Was 3.9
Moses-Chi 2.1
Myatt-Was 1.8
Grimes-NY 1.8

Fielding Runs
Mayo-Det 29.4
Boudreau-Cle 25.8
Stirnweiss-NY 18.9
Spence-Was 18.6
Tucker-Chi 17.7

Total Player Rating
Boudreau-Cle 7.8
Stirnweiss-NY 7.1
Spence-Was 5.2
Doerr-Bos 5.2
B.Johnson-Bos ... 4.9

Wins
Newhouser-Det 29
Trout-Det 27
Potter-StL 19
Hughson-Bos 18

Win Percentage
Hughson-Bos 783
Newhouser-Det ...763
Potter-StL .... .731
Trout-Det 659
Borowy-NY ..... .586

Games
Heving-Cle 63
Berry-Phi 53
Trout-Det 49
Newhouser-Det 47
Klieman-Cle 47

Complete Games
Trout-Det 33
Newhouser-Det 25

Shutouts
Trout-Det 7
Newhouser-Det 6
Jakucki-StL 4

Saves
Maltzberger-Chi ... 12
Caster-StL 12
Berry-Phi 12
Heving-Cle 10
Barrett-Bos 8

Innings Pitched
Trout-Det 352.1
Newhouser-Det ... 312.1
Newsom-Phi 265.0
Kramer-StL 257.0
Borowy-NY 252.2

Fewest Hits/Game
Gromek-Cle 7.07
Niggeling-Was 7.17
Newhouser-Det 7.61
Hughson-Bos 7.61
Borowy-NY 7.98

Fewest BB/Game
Harris-Phi 1.34
Leonard-Was 1.45
Bonham-NY 1.73
Gorsica-Det 1.78
Hamlin-Phi 1.80

Strikeouts
Newhouser-Det ... 187
Trout-Det 144
Newsom-Phi 142
Kramer-StL 124
Niggeling-Was 121

Strikeouts/Game
Newhouser-Det ... 5.39
Niggeling-Was 5.29
Gromek-Cle 5.08
Hughson-Bos 4.96
Newsom-Phi 4.82

Ratio
Hughson-Bos 9.52
Trout-Det 10.24
Leonard-Was 10.28
Gromek-Cle 10.30
Newhouser-Det .. 10.58

Earned Run Average
Trout-Det 2.12
Newhouser-Det ... 2.22
Hughson-Bos 2.26
Niggeling-Was 2.32
Kramer-StL 2.49

Adjusted ERA
Trout-Det 168
Newhouser-Det 161
Hughson-Bos 151
Kramer-StL 145
Niggeling-Was 141

Opponents' Batting Avg.
Gromek-Cle ...... .219
Niggeling-Was .... .221
Hughson-Bos ..... .225
Newhouser-Det ... .230
Borowy-NY ...... .236

Opponents' On Base Pct.
Hughson-Bos 267
Leonard-Was 284
Trout-Det 284
Gromek-Cle 290
Newhouser-Det ...293

Starter Runs
Trout-Det 51.3
Newhouser-Det ... 42.1
Kramer-StL 27.0
Hughson-Bos 26.5
Niggeling-Was 25.5

Adjusted Starter Runs
Trout-Det 56.7
Newhouser-Det ... 46.8
Kramer-StL 31.8
Hughson-Bos 25.8
Borowy-NY 23.9

Clutch Pitching Index
Donald-NY 129
Woods-Bos 122
Smith-Cle 116
Haynes-Chi 116
Bonham-NY 115

Relief Runs
Heving-Cle 19.6
Berry-Phi 18.4
Caster-StL 8.9
Maltzberger-Chi ... 4.8

Adjusted Relief Runs
Berry-Phi 19.1
Heving-Cle 17.9
Caster-StL 10.4
Maltzberger-Chi ... 4.8

Relief Ranking
Berry-Phi 32.4
Heving-Cle 18.2
Caster-StL 17.3
Maltzberger-Chi 8.5

Total Pitcher Index
Trout-Det 9.1
Newhouser-Det ... 6.5
Kramer-StL 4.3
Berry-Phi 3.6
Hughson-Bos 3.0

Total Baseball Ranking
Trout-Det 9.1
Boudreau-Cle 7.8
Stirnweiss-NY 7.1
Newhouser-Det ... 6.5
Spence-Was 5.2

January 10 Baseball writers again fail to elect a new Hall of Famer. Frank Chance, Rube Waddell, and Ed Walsh come closest, but none gets the required three-fourths of the vote.

March 15 With wartime travel restrictions still in effect, the Dodgers open spring training at Bear Mountain, New York with 15 players in camp. Seven teams—the Browns, Tigers, Reds, Indians, Cubs, Pirates and White Sox—are training in Indiana, the most of any state. The Red Sox are at Tufts College while the Braves are prepping at the Choate School in Connecticut.

April 25 Baseball writers cannot seem to get any Hall of Fame candidates past the 75 percent requirement, but a committee selected to bring in some old-timers succeeds with these names: Jimmy Collins, Roger Bresnahan, Fred Clarke, Dan Brouthers, Ed Delahanty, Hugh Jennings, Mike Kelley, Jim O'Rourke, Wilbert Robinson and Hugh Duffy.

July 12 The Chicago Cubs stop Tommy Holmes' modern-day NL hitting streak at 37 games, beating the Boston Braves 6-1 behind Hank Wyse for their 11th victory in a row. Holmes hits .433 during the streak and will finish at .352, second in the league. His 9 strikeouts coupled with 28 home runs and 47 doubles is

unparalleled for making contact and hitting for average and power.

August 1 Mel Ott hits the 500th home run of his career. He will hit 10 more this season and one on Opening Day of 1946 to finish with 511. Of Ott's total, 324 will be hit in the Polo Grounds.

August 13 Branch Rickey becomes the principal stockholder of the Dodgers. He and associates Walter O'Malley and John Smith acquire the 50 percent interest of the Ebbets estate for a reported price of $750,000.

August 15 Commissioner Chandler sells World Series radio rights for $150,000 to Gillette. Ford had been the sponsor since 1934, paying $100,000 annually.

August 19 In game two of a doubleheader against the Reds, 37-year-old slugger Jimmie Foxx pitches the first seven innings for the Philadelphia Blue Jays. He leaves with a 4-1 lead, and Andy Karl saves Foxx's only major league decision. His ERA in 10 major league appearances is 1.52.

August 20 At the age of 17, shortstop Tommy Brown of the Brooklyn Dodgers is the youngest player to hit a major league home run. Brown homers off Pirates southpaw Preacher Roe.

September 29 The Cubs clinch the NL

flag on Hank Borowy's 4-3 win over Pittsburgh in the first game of a doubleheader. The final margin for Chicago is three games over the Cardinals. In 1945 the Chicago Cubs win 20 doubleheaders.

October 3 The Tigers and Cubs meet in the World Series for the fourth time. Hank Borowy pitches a six-hitter and Hal Newhouser is roughed up for eight runs in three innings; Cubs win, 9-0.

October 5 Claude Passeau of the Chicago Cubs pitches a one-hitter, beating the Detroit Tigers 3-0 in the third game of the World Series. Rudy York's second-inning single spoils Passeau's no-hit bid. Bill Nicholson drives in the first run to lead the way.

October 23 Branch Rickey announces the signing of Jackie Robinson by the Dodger organization and, one week later, signs him to Montreal (International League) for 1946.

November 15 The rules are revised for election of modern players to the Hall of Fame. A runoff election is formulated as a way to qualify more players for selection, but it fails to meet its objective as no one reaches the 75 percent requirement in the runoff. Frank Chance, Johnny Evers, Miller Huggins, and Ed Walsh come closest.

	BOSTON		BROOKLYN		CHICAGO		CINCINNATI		NEW YORK		PHILADELPHIA		PITTSBURGH		ST.LOUIS
M	B.Coleman	M	L.Durocher	M	C.Grimm	M	B.McKechnie	M	M.Ott	M	F.Fitzsimmons	M	F.Frisch	M	B.Southworth
M	D.Bissonette	1B	A.Galan	1B	P.Cavarretta	1B	F.McCormick	1B	P.Weintraub	M	B.Chapman	1B	B.Dahlgren	1B	R.Sanders
1B	V.Shupe	2B	E.Stanky	2B	D.Johnson	2B	W.Williams	2B	G.Hausmann	1B	J.Wasdell	2B	P.Coscarart	2B	E.Verban
2B	W.Wietelmann	SS	E.Basinski	SS	L.Merullo	SS	E.Miller	SS	B.Kerr	2B	T.Daniels	SS	F.Gustine	SS	M.Marion
SS	D.Culler	3B	F.Bordagaray	3B	S.Hack	3B	S.Mesner	3B	N.Reyes	SS	B.Mott	3B	B.Elliott	3B	W.Kurowski
3B	C.Workman	LF	L.Olmo	LF	P.Lowrey	LF	E.Tipton	LF	D.Gardella	3B	J.Antonelli	LF	J.Russell	LF	R.Schoendienst
LF	B.Nieman	CF	G.Rosen	CF	A.Pafko	CF	D.Clay	CF	J.Rucker	LF	C.Triplett	CF	A.Gionfriddo	CF	B.Adams
CF	C.Gillenwater	RF	D.Walker	RF	B.Nicholson	RF	A.Libke	RF	M.Ott	CF	V.DiMaggio	RF	J.Barrett	RF	J.Hopp
RF	T.Holmes	C	M.Sandlock	C	M.Livingston	C	A.Lakeman	RF	E.Lombardi	RF	V.Dinges	C	A.Lopez	C	K.O'Dea
C	P.Masi									C	A.Seminick				
		1	E.Stevens	S2	R.Hughes	O	G.Walker	O	R.Treadway			3	L.Handley	O	A.Bergamo
1	J.Mack	S	T.Brown	C	P.Gillespie	C	A.Unser	C	C.Kluttz	OP	R.Monteagudo	S	B.Salkeld	C	D.Rice
O1	J.Medwick	3	B.Hart	1	H.Becker	2S	K.Wahl	3	B.Jurges	OS	G.Crawford	S	V.Barnhart	3O	D.Garms
C	S.Hofferth	1	H.Schultz	C	D.Williams	O	D.Sipek	O	W.Lockman	13	J.Foxx	O	T.O'Brien	O	A.Rebel
2	F.Drews	C	F.Dantonio	C	L.Rice	O	H.Sauer	O	S.Filipowicz	O	G.Mancuso	1O	F.Colman	/S	L.Klein
23	E.Joost	O	J.Peacock	O	E.Sauer	S	W.Flager	1	M.Schemer	O	J.Powell	C	J.Saltzgaver	S	G.Fallon
O	B.Ramsey	C	M.Owen	O	F.Secory	C	J.Riddle	1	R.Zimmerman	S	W.Flager	C	S.Davis	O	D.Bartosch
32	T.Nelson	/O	M.Aderholt	S	B.Schuster	C	J.Just	O	J.Mallory	2	Ga.Hamner	S	F.Zak	S	P.Young
O	M.Aderholt	C	C.Sukeforth	/1	R.Otero	/O	E.Lukon	3	J.Medwick	N	N.Picciuto	/O	L.Waner	O	J.Mallory
C	C.Kluttz	C	S.Andrews	/3	J.Ostrowski	R	R.Medeiros	O	C.Mead	/C	H.Spindel	/C	H.Camelli	/C	W.Cooper
2	S.Shemo	/O	B.Herman	/2	C.Block			C	B.Berres	C	J.Peacock	R	B.Rodgers	/C	G.Crumling
/O	S.Wentzel	/O	R.Durrett	H	J.Moore	P	E.Heusser	/1	A.Gardella	2	E.Walczak	R	J.Vitelli	/3	J.Antonelli
/C	M.Ulisney	/1	J.Douglas	/O	L.Christopher	P	J.Bowman	/3	J.Hudson	O	B.Adams			/O	G.Crawford
/3	N.Wallen	/2	L.Durocher			P	B.Walters	/C	B.DeKoning	1	T.Lupien	P	P.Roe	/C	B.Keely
		/3	C.Corbitt	P	H.Wyse	P	H.Fox			O	B.Chapman	P	N.Strincevich		
P	J.Tobin	H	D.Lund	P	C.Passeau	P	V.Kennedy	P	B.Voiselle	S	Gr.Hamner	P	R.Sewell	P	R.Barrett
P	B.Logan	/C	R.Hayworth	P	P.Derringer	RP	H.Lisenbee	P	M.Feldman	S	S.Andrews	P	M.Butcher	P	K.Burkhart
P	J.Hutchings	/S	B.White	P	R.Prim			P	V.Mungo	/2	D.Hasenmayer	P	A.Gerheauser	P	B.Donnelly
P	N.Andrews	R	E.Palica	P	H.Borowy	P	F.Dasso	/O	J.Brewer	P	N.Goulish	RP	X.Rescigno	P	H.Brecheen
P	E.Wright			RP	B.Chipman	P	E.Harrist	P	S.Emmerich	/3	P.Caballero	RP	C.Cuccurullo	P	G.Dockins
RP	D.Hendrickson	P	H.Gregg			P	B.Beck	RP	A.Adams					RP	B.Byerly
		P	V.Lombardi	P	P.Erickson	P	A.Carter	RP	R.Fischer	P	D.Barrett	P	K.Gables	RP	A.Jurisich
P	B.Lee	P	C.Davis	P	H.Vandenberg	P	M.Modak			P	C.Schanz	P	F.Ostermueller		
P	M.Cooper	P	A.Herring	P+	M.Stewart	/P	J.Hetki	P	A.Hansen	P	C.Sproull	P	B.Beck	P	T.Wilks
P	A.Javery	P	T.Seats	/P	L.Warneke	P	E.Riddle	P	S.Maglie	P	D.Mauney	/P	R.Starr	P	J.Creel
P	T.Earley	RP	C.King	/P	R.Starr	P	M.Bosser	P	A.Zabala	RP	A.Karl	/P	J.Lanning	P	G.Gardner
/P	R.Barrett	RP	C.Buker	/P	J.Comellas	/P	H.Wehmeier	P	R.Harrell					/P	M.Lanier
/P	E.Singleton			/P	W.Signer	/P	G.Bush	/P	D.Fisher	P	O.Judd			/P	M.Cooper
P	I.Hutchinson	P	R.Branca	/P	E.Hanyzewski			/P	L.Bain	P	J.Kraus			/P	B.Crouch
/P	L.Wallace	P	L.Webber	/P	G.Hennessey			/P	R.Lee	P	B.Lee			/P	S.Partenheimer
/P	B.Whitcher	P	L.Pfund					/P	E.Pyle	P	W.Wyatt			/P	A.Lopatka
/P	H.Schacker	P	B.Chapman					/P	J.Phillips	P	I.Leon				
/P	E.Pyle	/P	O.Nitcholas					/P	J.Gee	P	V.Kennedy				
/P	L.Fette	/P	R.Hathaway							/P	H.Mulcahy				
/P	C.Cozart	/P	E.Rudolph							P	D.Coffman				
/P	J.Heving	/P	C.Crocker							/P	K.Raffensberger				
/P	B.Cardoni									/P	L.Scott				
										P	L.Lucier				
										/P	D.Grate				
										/P	C.Ripple				
										/P	M.Chetkovich				

TEAM	G	W	L	PCT	GB	R	OR	AB	H	2B	3B	HR	BB	SO	AVG	OBP	SLG	PRO	PRO+	BR	/A	PF	CHI	RC	SB	CS	SBA	SBR
CHI	155	98	56	.636		735	**532**	5298	1465	229	52	57	554	462	**.277**	**.349**	.372	.721	**109**	53	69	98	99	714	69			
STL	155	95	59	.617	3	756	583	5487	**1498**	256	44	64	515	488	.273	.338	.371	.709	102	25	7	102	**103**	716	55			
BRO	155	87	67	.565	11	**795**	724	5418	1468	257	**71**	57	**629**	434	.271	.349	.376	**.725**	109	66	72	99	102	**746**	75			
PIT	155	82	72	.532	16	753	686	5343	1425	**259**	56	72	590	480	.267	.342	.377	.719	102	45	16	104	102	701	81			
NY	154	78	74	.513	19	668	700	5350	1439	175	35	**114**	501	457	.269	.336	**.379**	.715	103	33	22	102	93	692	38			
BOS	154	67	85	.441	30	721	728	5441	1453	229	25	101	520	510	.267	.334	.374	.708	102	20	16	101	100	692	**82**			
CIN	154	61	93	.396	37	536	694	5283	1317	221	26	56	392	532	.249	.304	.333	.637	85	-122	-110	98	99	537	71			
PHI	154	46	108	.299	52	548	865	5203	1278	197	27	56	449	501	.246	.307	.326	.633	84	-122	-107	97	102	527	54			
TOT	618					5512		42823	11343	1823	336	577	4150	3864	.265	.333	.364	.696							525			

TEAM	CG	SH	SV	IP	H	H/G	HR	BB	SO	RAT	ERA	ERA+	OAV	OOB	PR	/A	PF	CPI	FA	E	DP	FW	PW	BW	SBW	DIF
CHI	**86**	15	14	1366[1]	1301	8.6	57	385	541	11.3	2.98	123	.249	.304	125	102	96	102	.980	121	124	3.4	10.2	6.9		.5
STL	77	**18**	9	1408[2]	1351	8.6	70	497	510	12.0	3.24	116	.253	.320	38	79	99	106	.977	137	150	2.4	7.9	.7		7.0
BRO	61	7	18	1392[1]	1357	8.8	74	586	**557**	12.8	3.70	101	.253	.331	15	7	99	98	.962	230	144	-3.2	.7	**7.2**		5.3
PIT	73	8	16	1387[1]	1477	9.6	61	455	518	12.7	3.76	105	.272	.331	6	27	104	100	.971	178	141	-.0	2.7	1.6		.8
NY	53	13	21	1374[2]	1401	9.2	85	528	530	12.8	4.06	96	.263	.332	-40	-23	103	95	.973	166	112	.6	-2.3	2.2		1.5
BOS	57	7	13	1391[2]	1474	9.5	99	557	404	13.3	4.04	95	.272	.342	-37	-32	101	104	.969	193	**160**	-1.1	-3.2	1.6		-6.3
CIN	77	11	6	1365[2]	1438	9.5	70	534	372	13.2	4.00	94	.271	.340	-31	-36	99	100	.976	146	138	1.8	-3.6	-11.0		-3.2
PHI	31	4	**26**	1352[2]	1544	10.3	61	608	432	14.5	4.64	83	.285	.360	-126	-123	101	97	.962	234	150	-3.5	-12.3	-10.7		-4.4
TOT	515	83	123	11039[1]		9.2				12.8	3.80		.265	.333					.971	1405	1119					

Runs		Hits		Doubles		Triples		Home Runs		Total Bases	
Stanky-Bro	128	Holmes-Bos	224	Holmes-Bos	47	Olmo-Bro	13	Holmes-Bos	28	Holmes-Bos	367
Rosen-Bro	126	Rosen-Bro	197	Walker-Bro	42	Pafko-Chi	12	Workman-NY	25	Adams-Phi-StL	279
Holmes-Bos	125	Hack-Chi	193	Galan-Bro	36	Rucker-NY	11	Adams-Phi-StL	22	Rosen-Bro	279
Galan-Bro	114	Clay-Cin	184	Elliott-Pit	36	Rosen-Bro	11	Ott-NY	21	Walker-Bro	266
Hack-Chi	110			Cavarretta-Chi	34	Cavarretta-Chi	10	Kurowski-StL	21	Kurowski-StL	261

Runs Batted In		Runs Produced		Bases On Balls		Batting Average		On Base Percentage		Slugging Average	
Walker-Bro	124	Walker-Bro	218	Stanky-Bro	148	Cavarretta-Chi	.355	Cavarretta-Chi	.449	Holmes-Bos	.577
Holmes-Bos	117	Holmes-Bos	214	Galan-Bro	114	Holmes-Bos	.352	Galan-Bro	.423	Kurowski-StL	.511
Pafko-Chi	110	Galan-Bro	197	Hack-Chi	99	Rosen-Bro	.325	Hack-Chi	.420	Cavarretta-Chi	.500
Olmo-Bro	110	Adams-Phi-StL	191	Nicholson-Chi	92	Hack-Chi	.323	Holmes-Bos	.420	Ott-NY	.499
Adams-Phi-StL	109	Rosen-Bro	189	Sanders-StL	83	Kurowski-StL	.323	Stanky-Bro	.417	Olmo-Bro	.462

Production		Adjusted Production		Batter Runs		Adjusted Batter Runs		Clutch Hitting Index		Runs Created	
Holmes-Bos	.997	Holmes-Bos	175	Holmes-Bos	62.9	Holmes-Bos	62.1	Walker-Bro	135	Holmes-Bos	156
Cavarretta-Chi	.949	Cavarretta-Chi	167	Cavarretta-Chi	46.4	Cavarretta-Chi	48.8	Elliott-Pit	135	Cavarretta-Chi	119
Ott-NY	.910	Ott-NY	150	Galan-Bro	36.8	Galan-Bro	37.7	Lowrey-Chi	129	Galan-Bro	116
Kurowski-StL	.894	Kurowski-StL	144	Ott-NY	33.4	Ott-NY	32.0	Cavarretta-Chi	126	Hack-Chi	111
Galan-Bro	.864	Galan-Bro	142	Kurowski-StL	30.7	Hack-Chi	31.7	Olmo-Bro	125	Rosen-Bro	110

Total Average		Stolen Bases		Stolen Base Average		Stolen Base Runs		Fielding Runs		Total Player Rating	
Holmes-Bos	1.078	Schoendienst-StL	26					Kerr-NY	28.3	Holmes-Bos	5.4
Cavarretta-Chi	1.037	Barrett-Pit	25					Gillenwater-Bos	23.8	Hack-Chi	5.2
Ott-NY	.959	Clay-Cin	19					Coscarart-Pit	21.1	Cavarretta-Chi	3.8
Galan-Bro	.936							Hack-Chi	18.0	Stanky-Bro	3.6
Kurowski-StL	.876							Walker-Bro	12.4	Kurowski-StL	3.3

Wins		Win Percentage		Games		Complete Games		Shutouts		Saves	
Barrett-Bos-StL	23	Brecheen-StL	.789	Karl-Phi	67	Barrett-Bos-StL	24	Passeau-Chi	5	Karl-Phi	15
Wyse-Chi	22	Burkhart-StL	.692	Adams-NY	65	Wyse-Chi	23	Voiselle-NY	4	Adams-NY	15
Gregg-Bro	18	Wyse-Chi	.688	Hutchings-Bos	57	Passeau-Chi	19	Heusser-Cin	4	Rescigno-Pit	9
Burkhart-StL	18	Barrett-Bos-StL	.657	Barrett-Bos-StL	45	Strincevich-Pit	18	Donnelly-StL	4		
Passeau-Chi	17	Passeau-Chi	.654	Fox-Cin	45	Heusser-Cin	18	Burkhart-StL	4		

Innings Pitched		Fewest Hits/Game		Fewest BB/Game		Strikeouts		Strikeouts/Game			
Barrett-Bos-StL	284.2	Prim-Chi	7.73	Prim-Chi	1.25	Roe-Pit	148	Roe-Pit	5.67	Prim-Chi	9.04
Wyse-Chi	278.1	Brecheen-StL	7.78	Barrett-Bos-StL	1.71	Gregg-Bro	139	Mungo-NY	4.97	Roe-Pit	10.53
Gregg-Bro	254.1	Gregg-Bro	7.82	Roe-Pit	1.76	Voiselle-NY	115	Gregg-Bro	4.92	Passeau-Chi	10.55
Roe-Pit	235.0	Mungo-NY	7.92	Wyse-Chi	1.78	Mungo-NY	101	Hutchings-Bos	4.82	Brecheen-StL	10.58
Voiselle-NY	232.1	Passeau-Chi	8.13	Strincevich-Pit	1.93	Hutchings-Bos	99	Prim-Chi	4.79	Wyse-Chi	10.74

Earned Run Average		Adjusted ERA		Opponents' Batting Avg.		Opponents' On Base Pct.		Starter Runs		Adjusted Starter Runs	
Borowy-Chi	2.13	Prim-Chi	152	Prim-Chi	.228	Prim-Chi	.256	Wyse-Chi	34.5	Passeau-Chi	30.1
Prim-Chi	2.40	Brecheen-StL	149	Gregg-Bro	.232	Passeau-Chi	.289	Passeau-Chi	33.8	Wyse-Chi	29.9
Passeau-Chi	2.46	Passeau-Chi	149	Brecheen-StL	.238	Barrett-Bos-StL	.295	Prim-Chi	25.8	Roe-Pit	28.0
Brecheen-StL	2.52	Walters-Cin	140	Mungo-NY	.238	Wyse-Chi	.296	Barrett-Bos-StL	25.2	Barrett-Bos-StL	23.7
Walters-Cin	2.68	Roe-Pit	137	Passeau-Chi	.238	Roe-Pit	.296	Roe-Pit	24.2	Prim-Chi	23.1

Clutch Pitching Index		Relief Runs		Adjusted Relief Runs		Relief Ranking		Total Pitcher Index		Total Baseball Ranking	
Butcher-Pit	124	Karl-Phi	16.3	Karl-Phi	16.9	Karl-Phi	16.6	Passeau-Chi	3.8	Holmes-Bos	5.4
Logan-Bos	124	Buker-Bro	4.9	Adams-NY	6.1	Adams-NY	11.5	Wyse-Chi	3.2	Hack-Chi	5.2
Walters-Cin	124	Adams-NY	4.7	Buker-Bro	4.4	Buker-Bro	4.7	Prim-Chi	3.0	Cavarretta-Chi	3.8
Lee-Phi-Bos	123	Chipman-Chi	2.4	Chipman-Chi	1.2	Chipman-Chi	1.4	Walters-Cin	2.9	Passeau-Chi	3.8
Wyse-Chi	117							Roe-Pit	2.8	Stanky-Bro	3.6

January 25 The Yankees are sold by the Ruppert estate to Larry MacPhail, Dan Topping, and Del Webb for $2.8 million. For that price the trio obtains 400 players, 266 of them in military service, Yankee Stadium, parks in Newark and Kansas City, and leases on other minor league ballparks. Jake Ruppert, who died in 1939, paid more than the new purchase price for the ground on which Yankee Stadium was built in 1923.

March 15 Bert Shepard, a one-legged veteran of the war, tries out as a pitcher for the Senators (and subsequently appears in a league game). The symbol of wartime baseball, outfielder Pete Gray of the Browns, will field and bat with only one arm.

May 13 David "Boo" Ferriss reaches 22 shutout innings before allowing a run versus the Tigers in a 6-2 Red Sox win. This sets an AL record for scoreless innings at the start of a major league career. Ferriss strikes out first baseman Rudy York four times.

May 20 In St. Louis, Pete Gray stars, as the Browns sweep the Yankees 10-1 and 5-2. Gray has two RBIs on three hits in the opener, and in the nightcap he scores the winning run and hauls in seven fly balls, three on spectacular catches.

July 1 The first of the superstars returns from the war. Hank Greenberg, gone for four years, homers in his first game following his release from the army. Charlie Gassaway of the Athletics gives up the blow before 47,700 in a Sunday game at Briggs Stadium. The Tigers win 9-5 to lead the Yankees by 3½ games with Chicago and Boston following.

July 10 The All-Star Game at Fenway Park is canceled because of travel restrictions. During the schedule break, seven interleague games are played for war charity. Plans for a USO-sponsored all-star game in Europe do not materialize, although the war in Germany is over, and fighting in the Pacific will be over in six weeks.

August 24 Cleveland ace Bob Feller returns from the Navy and attracts a crowd of 46,477, who watch him strike out 12 and yield only four hits in a 4-2 win over Detroit's Hal Newhouser. He will get nine starts during the remainder of the year, and his five wins will include a one-hitter and two four-hitters. With the war now over, fans are clamoring for entertainment, and it is clear Feller is still baseball's No. 1 ticket seller.

September 7 Joe Kuhel hits an inside-the-park home run, the only home run hit by a Senator all season at Washington's spacious Griffith Stadium. The Nats hit 26 on the road.

September 9 Dick Fowler of the Philadelphia Athletics returns from three years with the Canadian Army and pitches a no-hitter, walking four and beating the St. Louis Browns, 1-0, in the second game of a doubleheader. It is Fowler's first start since his return, his first major league shutout, and the first no-hitter by an Athletics pitcher since 1916.

September 30 Hank Greenberg's grand-slam home run in the ninth inning on the final day of the season beats the St. Louis Browns 6-3 and clinches the pennant for the Detroit Tigers. Virgil Trucks, discharged three days earlier from the Navy, is the starter, with Tigers ace Newhouser relieving in the fifth .

October 6 Tavern owner "Billy Goat" Sianis buys a box seat for his goat for the fourth game of the World Series and is escorted out of Wrigley Field. In retaliation Sianis casts a "goat curse" over the Cubs, dooming them never to win a World Series. The Tigers tie the series on Dizzy Trout's 5-hit 4-1 win. Detroit scores all its runs in the fourth, with Hank Greenberg, Roy Cullenbine, Paul Richards, and a forceout scoring the runners.

October 10 The Tigers tally five runs in the first inning and rout the Chicago Cubs 9-3 behind Hal Newhouser, who strikes out 10. Total receipts of $1.6 million set a World Series record.

	BOSTON		CHICAGO		CLEVELAND		DETROIT		NEW YORK		PHILADELPHIA		ST.LOUIS		WASHINGTON
M	J.Cronin	M	J.Dykes	M	L.Boudreau	M	S.O'Neill	M	J.McCarthy	M	C.Mack	M	L.Sewell	M	O.Bluege
1B	C.Metkovich	1B	K.Farrell	1B	M.Rocco	1B	R.York	1B	N.Etten	1B	D.Siebert	1B	G.McQuinn	1B	J.Kuhel
2B	S.Newsome	2B	R.Schalk	2B	D.Meyer	2B	E.Mayo	2B	S.Stirnweiss	2B	I.Hall	2B	D.Gutteridge	2B	G.Myatt
SS	E.Lake	SS	C.Michaels	SS	L.Boudreau	SS	S.Webb	SS	F.Crosetti	SS	E.Busch	SS	V.Stephens	SS	G.Torres
3B	J.Tobin	3B	T.Cuccinello	3B	D.Ross	3B	B.Maier	3B	O.Grimes	3B	G.Kell	3B	M.Christman	3B	H.Clift
LF	B.Johnson	LF	J.Dickshot	LF	J.Heath	LF	J.Outlaw	LF	H.Martin	LF	M.Smith	LF	M.Byrnes	LF	G.Case
CF	L.Culberson	CF	O.Hockett	CF	F.Mackiewicz	CF	D.Cramer	CF	T.Stainback	CF	B.Estalella	CF	M.Kreevich	CF	G.Binks
RF	J.Lazor	RF	W.Moses	RF	P.Seerey	RF	R.Cullenbine	RF	B.Metheny	RF	H.Peck	RF	G.Moore	RF	B.Lewis
C	B.Garbark	C	M.Tresh	C	F.Hayes	C	B.Swift	C	M.Garbark	C	B.Rosar	C	F.Mancuso	C	R.Ferrell
O1	T.McBride	O	G.Curtright	S3	A.Cihocki	O	H.Greenberg	O	R.Derry	O	B.McGhee	32	L.Schulte	2	F.Vaughn
2	B.Steiner	1	B.Nagel	O	P.O'Dea	C	P.Richards	O	C.Keller	O	C.Metro	O	P.Gray	O	M.Kreevich
O	P.Fox	32	F.Baker	O	L.Fleming	S	J.Hoover	C	A.Robinson	S	B.Wilkins	O1	L.Finney	C	A.Evans
3	T.LaForest	S2	D.Reynolds	O	M.Hoag	2	R.Borom	O	J.Lindell	O	G.George	O	B.Martin	3	H.Layne
1	D.Camilli	S	L.Appling	O	E.Carnett	/O	C.Hostetler	C	B.Drescher	C	F.Hayes	C	R.Hayworth	O	M.Guerra
3	J.Bucher	C	V.Castino	3S	E.Wheeler	/3	D.Ross	C	H.Crompton	O	E.Kish	O	C.Laabs	O	J.Zardon
C	B.Holm	/3	J.Orengo	C	J.McDonnell	/O	H.Walker	S	M.Milosevich	O	J.Burns	/C	J.Schultz	O	J.Powell
C	F.Walters	/O	B.Mueller	/O	H.Ruszkowski	/O	E.Mierkowicz	S	J.Buzas	O	L.Rosenthal	3	E.Clary	O	V.Ventura
C	R.Steiner			S	E.Weingartner	/1	J.McHale	3	D.Savage	S	A.Brancato			3	C.Travis
/C	F.Pytlak	P	T.Lee	/O	S.Benjamin	/C	H.Miller	H	P.Waner	/O	S.Chapman	P	N.Potter	O	D.Kimble
/O	L.Christopher	P	O.Grove	/C	R.Steiner	/C	M.Welch			/O	F.Garrison	P	J.Kramer	O	W.Chipple
/3	J.Cronin	P	E.Lopat	/1	P.Williams	H	R.Kerns	P	B.Bevens	/O	J.Cicero	P	S.Jakucki	/O	H.McFarland
/3	N.Polly	P	J.Humphries	/O	R.Cullenbine	H	C.McNabb	P	T.Bonham	/C	J.Astroth	P	T.Shirley		
H	L.Finney	P	B.Dietrich	/3	B.Rothel			P	A.Gettel	/C	J.Pruett	P	A.Hollingsworth	P	R.Wolff
		RP	J.Johnson	C	G.Desautels			P	M.Dubiel	/O	L.Drake	RP	S.Zoldak	P	M.Haefner
P	D.Ferriss							P	H.Borowy					P	M.Pieretti
P	J.Wilson	P	E.Caldwell	P	S.Gromek			P	D.Trout					P	D.Leonard
P	E.O'Neill	P	J.Haynes	P	A.Reynolds	P	A.Benton	RP	K.Holcombe	P	B.Newsom	P	B.Muncrief	P	J.Niggeling
P	C.Hausmann	P	F.Papish	P	J.Bagby	P	S.Overmire	RP	J.Turner	P	R.Christopher	P	L.West	RP	S.Ullrich
P	M.Ryba	P	B.Ross	P	A.Smith	P	L.Mueller			P	J.Flores	P	E.Jones		
RP	F.Barrett	/P	C.Touchstone	P	E.Klieman	RP	W.Wilson	P	B.Zuber	P	L.Knerr	/P	O.Miller		
				RP	P.Center	RP	G.Caster	P	J.Page	P	D.Black	/P	G.Caster	P	A.Carrasquel
				RP	J.Salveson			P	R.Ruffing	RP	J.Berry	/C	C.Fannin	P	W.Holborow
P	P.Woods					P	J.Tobin	/O	A.Donald			/P	A.LaMacchia	P	W.Masterson
P	R.Heflin					P	Z.Eaton	/P	S.Chandler	P	C.Gassaway	/P	P.Appleton	/P	P.Appleton
P	V.Johnson			P	M.Harder	P	J.Orrell	P	S.Roser	P	S.Gerkin	/P	D.Sanders	/P	A.Roche
P	O.Clark			/P	B.Feller	P	A.Houtteman	/P	P.Schreiber	/P	D.Fowler			/P	B.Shepard
P	Y.Terry			/P	R.Embree	/P	T.Bridges			/P	C.Bowles			/P	D.Stone
P	R.Cecil			P	E.Henry	/P	P.Oana			/P	P.Marchildon			/P	J.Cleary
/P	P.Cecil			/P	H.Kleine	/P	B.Pierce			/P	C.Scheib				
/P	J.Bowman			/P	P.Calvert	/P	V.Trucks			/P	B.Connelly				
/P	C.Dreisewerd					/P	P.McLaughlin			/P	W.Crowson				
/P	O.Judd														

TEAM	G	W	L	PCT	GB	R	OR	AB	H	2B	3B	HR	BB	SO	AVG	OBP	SLG	PRO	PRO+	BR	/A	PF	CHI	RC	SB	CS	SBA	SBR
DET	155	88	65	.575		633	565	5257	1345	227	47	77	517	533	.256	.324	.361	.685	98	20	-20	106	102	627	60	54	53	-14
WAS	156	87	67	.565	1.5	622	562	5326	1375	197	63	27	545	489	.258	.330	.334	.664	107	-8	43	92	103	612	110	65	63	-6
STL	154	81	70	.536	6	597	548	5227	1302	215	37	63	500	555	.249	.316	.341	.657	91	-29	-58	105	105	584	25	31	45	-11
NY	152	81	71	.533	6.5	676	606	5176	1343	189	61	93	618	567	.259	.343	.373	.716	108	90	58	105	97	698	64	43	60	-7
CLE	147	73	72	.503	11	557	548	4898	1249	216	48	65	505	505	.255	.325	.359	.685	109	23	48	96	95	588	19	31	38	-13
CHI	150	71	78	.477	15	596	633	5077	1330	204	55	22	470	467	.262	.326	.337	.663	101	-13	2	97	105	571	78	54	59	-9
BOS	157	71	83	.461	17.5	599	674	5367	1393	225	44	50	541	534	.260	.330	.346	.676	100	12	-2	102	96	634	72	50	59	-8
PHI	153	52	98	.347	34.5	494	638	5296	1297	201	37	33	449	463	.245	.306	.316	.622	86	-96	-94	100	98	523	25	45	36	-20
TOT	612					4774		41624	10634	1674	392	430	4145	4186	.255	.325	.346	.671							453	373	55	-88

TEAM	CG	SH	SV	IP	H	H/G	HR	BB	SO	RAT	ERA	ERA+	OAV	OOB	PR	/A	PF	CPI	FA	E	DP	FW	PW	BW	SBW	DIF
DET	78	19	16	1393²	1305	8.4	48	538	588	12.1	2.99	118	.250	.322	58	81	105	108	.975	158	173	.4	8.7	-2.1	-.3	4.9
WAS	82	19	11	1412¹	1307	8.3	42	440	550	11.2	2.92	106	.242	.301	69	28	92	93	.970	183	124	-1.0	3.0	4.6	.5	2.8
STL	91	10	8	1382²	1307	8.5	59	506	570	11.8	3.14	112	.249	.316	34	58	105	101	.976	143	123	1.2	6.2	-6.2	.0	4.3
NY	78	9	14	1355	1277	8.5	66	485	474	11.8	3.45	100	.250	.316	-13	1	103	93	.971	175	170	-.7	.1	6.2	.4	-1.0
CLE	76	14	12	1302¹	1269	8.8	39	501	497	12.4	3.31	98	.257	.328	8	-9	97	102	.977	126	149	1.7	-1.0	5.1	-.2	-5.2
CHI	84	13	13	1330²	1400	9.5	63	448	486	12.7	3.69	90	.270	.332	-49	-55	99	100	.970	180	139	-1.1	-5.9	.2	.2	3.1
BOS	71	15	13	1390²	1389	9.0	58	656	490	13.4	3.80	90	.264	.348	-67	-61	101	102	.973	169	198	-.1	-6.5	-2.1	.3	.5
PHI	65	11	8	1381	1380	9.0	55	571	531	12.9	3.62	95	.262	.337	-40	-29	102	101	.973	168	160	-.3	-3.1	-10.1	-1.0	-8.6
TOT	625	110	95	10948¹		8.7				12.3	3.36		.255	.325					.973	1302	1236					

Runs
Stirnweiss-NY 107
Stephens-StL 90
Cullenbine-Cle-Det ... 83

Hits
Stirnweiss-NY 195
Moses-Chi 168
Stephens-StL 165
Hall-Phi 161
Etten-NY 161

Doubles
Moses-Chi 35
Stirnweiss-NY 32
Binks-Was 32
McQuinn-StL 31

Triples
Stirnweiss-NY 22
Moses-Chi 15
Kuhel-Was 13
Dickshot-Chi 10
Peck-Phi 9

Home Runs
Stephens-StL 24
Cullenbine-Cle-Det 18
York-Det 18
Etten-NY 18
Heath-Cle 15

Total Bases
Stirnweiss-NY 301
Stephens-StL 270
Etten-NY 247
York-Det 246
Moses-Chi 239

Runs Batted In
Etten-NY 111
Cullenbine-Cle-Det 93
Stephens-StL 89
York-Det 87
Binks-Was 81

Runs Produced
Etten-NY 170
Stirnweiss-NY 161
Cullenbine-Cle-Det ... 158
Stephens-StL 155
Kuhel-Was 146

Bases On Balls
Cullenbine-Cle-Det .. 113
Lake-Bos 106
Grimes-NY 97
Etten-NY 90
Kuhel-Was 79

Batting Average
Stirnweiss-NY ..... .309
Cuccinello-Chi ..... .308
Dickshot-Chi ..... .302
Estalella-Phi ..... .299
Myatt-Was ..... .296

On Base Percentage
Lake-Bos ..... .412
Cullenbine-Cle-Det .. .402
Estalella-Phi ..... .399
Grimes-NY ..... .395
Etten-NY ..... .387

Slugging Average
Stirnweiss-NY ..... .476
Stephens-StL ..... .473
Cullenbine-Cle-Det ..... .444
Etten-NY ..... .437
Estalella-Phi ..... .435

Production
Stirnweiss-NY ..... .862
Cullenbine-Cle-Det ..... .846
Estalella-Phi ..... .834
Stephens-StL ..... .825
Etten-NY ..... .824

Adjusted Production
Stirnweiss-NY 143
Estalella-Phi 142
Kuhel-Was 137
Cullenbine-Cle-Det 137
Lake-Bos 136

Batter Runs
Stirnweiss-NY 39.1
Cullenbine-Cle-Det ... 35.1
Etten-NY 29.9
Heath-Cle 29.4
Lake-Bos 28.7

Adjusted Batter Runs
Stirnweiss-NY 34.0
Heath-Cle 32.6
Cullenbine-Cle-Det 29.2
Lake-Bos 26.7
Kuhel-Was 26.5

Clutch Hitting Index
Schalk-Chi 135
Michaels-Chi 132
Tresh-Chi 130
Etten-NY 121
Binks-Was 119

Runs Created
Stirnweiss-NY 121
Cullenbine-Cle-Det .. 106
Etten-NY 98
Stephens-StL 98
Moses-Chi 97

Total Average
Cullenbine-Cle-Det ..888
Stirnweiss-NY ..... .855
Lake-Bos ..... .849
Etten-NY ..... .794
Estalella-Phi ..... .789

Stolen Bases
Stirnweiss-NY 33
Myatt-Was 30
Case-Was 30
Metkovich-Bos 19
Dickshot-Chi 18

Stolen Base Average
Dickshot-Chi 85.7
Metkovich-Bos 76.0
Myatt-Was 73.2
Stirnweiss-NY 66.0
Case-Was 65.2

Stolen Base Runs
Dickshot-Chi 3.6
Myatt-Was 2.4
Metkovich-Bos 2.1
Crosetti-NY 1.5
Richards-Det 1.2

Fielding Runs
Hall-Phi 26.1
Stirnweiss-NY 25.5
Webb-Det 23.0
Newsome-Bos 22.2
Kell-Phi 21.7

Total Player Rating
Stirnweiss-NY 7.2
Lake-Bos 5.7
Cullenbine-Cle-Det ... 3.4
Mayo-Det 3.1
Newsome-Bos 2.9

Wins
Newhouser-Det 25
Ferriss-Bos 21
Wolff-Was 20
Gromek-Cle 19

Win Percentage
Newhouser-Det.... .735
Leonard-Was ..... .708
Gromek-Cle ..... .679
Ferriss-Bos ..... .677
Wolff-Was ..... .667

Games
Berry-Phi 52
Reynolds-Cle 44
Pieretti-Was 44
Trout-Det 41
Newhouser-Det 40

Complete Games
Newhouser-Det 29
Ferriss-Bos 26
Wolff-Was 21
Potter-StL 21
Gromek-Cle 21

Shutouts
Newhouser-Det 8
Ferriss-Bos 5
Benton-Det 5

Saves
Turner-NY 10
Berry-Phi 5

Innings Pitched
Newhouser-Det ..313.1
Ferriss-Bos 264.2
Newsom-Phi 257.1
Potter-StL 255.1
Gromek-Cle 251.0

Fewest Hits/Game
Newhouser-Det 6.86
Wolff-Was 7.20
Potter-StL 7.47
Lee-Chi 8.20
Niggeling-Was 8.20

Fewest BB/Game
Bonham-NY 1.10
Leonard-Was 1.46
Wolff-Was 1.91
Overmire-Det 2.33
Gromek-Cle 2.37

Strikeouts
Newhouser-Det 212
Potter-StL 129
Newsom-Phi 127
Reynolds-Cle 112

Strikeouts/Game
Newhouser-Det 6.09
Kramer-StL 4.62
Niggeling-Was 4.58
Potter-StL 4.55
Newsom-Phi 4.44

Ratio
Wolff-Was 9.14
Potter-StL 9.90
Newhouser-Det 10.02
Leonard-Was 10.21
Bonham-NY 10.41

Earned Run Average
Newhouser-Det ...1.81
Benton-Det 2.02
Wolff-Was 2.12
Leonard-Was 2.13
Lee-Chi 2.44

Adjusted ERA
Newhouser-Det 194
Benton-Det 174
Wolff-Was 146
Leonard-Was 146
Potter-StL 143

Opponents' Batting Avg.
Newhouser-Det ..... .211
Wolff-Was ..... .215
Potter-StL ..... .226
Niggeling-Was ..... .240
Benton-Det ..... .241

Opponents' On Base Pct.
Wolff-Was ..... .258
Potter-StL ..... .279
Leonard-Was ..... .279
Newhouser-Det ..... .281
Bonham-NY ..... .288

Starter Runs
Newhouser-Det ... 54.1
Wolff-Was 34.5
Leonard-Was 29.8
Benton-Det 28.7
Potter-StL 25.5

Adjusted Starter Runs
Newhouser-Det 59.4
Benton-Det 31.9
Potter-StL 29.8
Wolff-Was 27.2
Leonard-Was 23.5

Clutch Pitching Index
Benton-Det 139
Lee-Chi 121
Shirley-StL 116
Hollingsworth-StL .. 116
Ferriss-Bos 114

Relief Runs
Berry-Phi 14.7
Holcombe-NY 9.7
Barrett-Bos 7.2
Zoldak-StL 0

Adjusted Relief Runs
Berry-Phi 15.7
Holcombe-NY 10.3
Barrett-Bos 7.5
Zoldak-StL 1.2

Relief Ranking
Berry-Phi 17.6
Holcombe-NY 10.0
Barrett-Bos 6.1
Zoldak-StL 8

Total Pitcher Index
Newhouser-Det 7.8
Potter-StL 3.5
Ferriss-Bos 3.3
Benton-Det 3.2
Leonard-Was 2.8

Total Baseball Ranking
Newhouser-Det 7.8
Stirnweiss-NY 7.2
Lake-Bos 5.7
Potter-StL 3.5
Cullenbine-Cle-Det ... 3.4

January 12* The first professional league game is played in Venezuela, launching the newly constituted four-team Liga de Beisbol Profesional de Venezuela. The game is won by Magallanes 5-2.

February 19 Giants outfielder Danny Gardella becomes the first major leaguer to announce he is jumping to the "outlaw" Mexican League. His attempt to return to the major leagues a few years later will initiate a major court battle.

April 14 Manager Mel Ott of the Giants hits his 511th and final home run on Opening Day, an 8–4 home victory over the Phils. The next day Ott will injure his knee diving for a ball and will play only occasionally thereafter.

April 18 Jackie Robinson debuts as a second baseman for the Montreal Royals (International League) and becomes the first black player in Organized Baseball in this century. A home run and three singles versus Jersey City start the season in which he will win the league batting championship at .349.

April 24 Eleven former players—Joe Tinker, Johnny Evers, Frank Chance, Jess Burkett, Tom McCarthy, Rube Waddell, Eddie Plank, Ed Walsh, Jack Chesbro, Clark Griffith, and Joe McGinnity—are named to the Hall of Fame.

May 20 Claude Passeau of the Chicago Cubs makes his first error since September 21, 1941, ending his streak with an all-time fielding record for pitchers of 273 consecutive errorless chances.

May 30 In a play that anticipates a scene in "The Natural" by Brooklyn-native Bernard Malamud, the Braves' Carvel "Bama" Rowell smashes a home run in the second inning of the second game of a doubleheader at Ebbets Field. The ball shatters the Bulova clock high atop the right field scoreboard at 4:25 p.m., showering glass down on the Dodgers' right fielder Fred "Dixie" Walker. An hour later the clock stops.

July 22 Clubs approve a change to a 168-game schedule, but they will rescind the decision at another meeting Sept. 16. Television is first recognized, with clubs given rights to their own games. Players jumping to outlaw leagues will not be allowed to apply for reinstatement for five years.

August 8 The Dreyfuss family, owners of the Pittsburgh Pirates since 1900, sell the club to a group headed by Frank McKinney and John Galbreath. Singer Bing Crosby is among investors who pay $2.5 million for the Bucs.

October 3 The St. Louis Cardinals wallop the Brooklyn Dodgers 8-4 at Ebbets Field to win the NL playoffs 2-0 and advance to the World Series. Erv Dusak and Enos Slaughter lead the attack. Losing pitcher is Ralph Branca.

October 15 Enos Slaughter sprints all the way from first base and slides home with the winning run in the eighth inning on Harry Walker's double, as the Cardinals edge the Boston Red Sox 4-3, giving St. Louis the World Series four games to three. Harry Brecheen wins three games for the Cardinals. Billed as the duel between the two best hitters in baseball, the Series sees Stan Musial go 6-for-27 and Ted Williams 5-for-25.

November 22 The league names Stan Musial MVP.

BOSTON	BROOKLYN	CHICAGO	CINCINNATI	NEW YORK	PHILADELPHIA	PITTSBURGH	ST.LOUIS
M B.Southworth	M L.Durocher	M C.Grimm	M B.McKechnie	M M.Ott	M B.Chapman	M F.Frisch	M E.Dyer
1B R.Sanders	1B E.Stevens	1B E.Waitkus	M H.Gowdy	1B J.Mize	1B F.McCormick	M S.Davis	1B S.Musial
2B C.Ryan	2B E.Stanky	2B D.Johnson	1B H.Haas	2B B.Blattner	2B E.Verban	1B E.Fletcher	2B R.Schoendienst
SS D.Culler	SS P.Reese	SS B.Jurges	2B B.Adams	SS B.Kerr	SS S.Newsome	2B F.Gustine	SS M.Marion
3B N.Fernandez	3B C.Lavagetto	3B S.Hack	SS E.Miller	3B B.Rigney	3B J.Tabor	SS B.Cox	3B W.Kurowski
LF B.Rowell	LF P.Reiser	LF M.Rickert	3B G.Hatton	LF S.Gordon	LF D.Ennis	3B L.Handley	LF E.Dusak
CF C.Gillenwater	CF C.Furillo	CF P.Lowrey	LF E.Lukon	CF W.Marshall	CF J.Wyrostek	LF J.Russell	CF H.Walker
RF T.Holmes	RF D.Walker	RF P.Cavarretta	CF D.Clay	RF G.Rosen	RF R.Northey	CF R.Kiner	RF E.Slaughter
C P.Masi	C B.Edwards	C C.McCullough	RF A.Libke	C W.Cooper	C A.Seminick	RF B.Elliott	C J.Garagiola
			C R.Mueller			C A.Lopez	
1O J.Hopp	O3 A.Galan	O B.Nicholson	2O L.Frey	O J.Graham	S3 R.Hughes	S2 J.Brown	O T.Moore
21 B.Herman	O D.Whitman	S2 B.Sturgeon	23 B.Zientara	O J.Rucker	O C.Gilbert	O B.Salkeld	1O D.Sisler
O D.Litwhiler	1 H.Schultz	O A.Pafko	S C.Corbitt	1O B.Young	C R.Hemsley	O M.Van Robays	O B.Adams
3 S.Roberge	C F.Anderson	2 L.Stringer	C R.Lamanno	23 M.Witek	1 V.Dinges	C C.Workman	C D.Rice
O M.McCormick	32 B.Herman	C M.Livingston	C M.West	C E.Lombardi	S J.O'Neil	2 B.Whitehead	C C.Kluttz
C D.Padgett	32 B.Ramazzotti	3 J.Ostrowski	O B.Usher	O B.Warren	O J.Wasdell	C B.Baker	2 L.Klein
S W.Wietelmann	O G.Hermanski	S L.Merullo	1 E.Shokes	O M.Ott	/O L.Novikoff	O A.Gionfriddo	S J.Cross
C S.Hofferth	O J.Medwick	C B.Scheffing	O M.McCormick	3 B.Thomson	/2 K.Richardson	O H.Camelli	C K.O'Dea
O C.Workman	3 E.Miksis	1 D.Dallessandro	/C A.Lakeman	O J.Pike	/O V.DiMaggio	O J.Barrett	/O B.Endicott
O T.Neill	S S.Rojek	/O F.Secory	/O H.Moss	O V.DiMaggio	/2 D.Murtaugh	/O F.Colman	H W.Sessi
O J.Barrett	C M.Sandlock	/3 C.Block	/O C.Vollmer	/C M.Grasso	/2 C.Letchas	/C V.Smith	/2 N.Jones
C K.O'Dea	C D.Padgett	/O C.Gilbert	H L.Goldstein	/O G.Lawing	/C D.Moore	S F.Zak	/C D.Litwhiler
S A.Dark	/1 J.Graham	/3 H.Schenz	/O G.Lawing	/C J.Gladd	/3 D.Hasenmayer	/C R.Jarvis	/C D.Wilber
/1 J.McCarthy	/O J.Tepsic	/O A.Glossop	P J.Vander Meer	/2 D.Lajeskie	/S G.Hamner	/C B.Guintini	H E.Verban
/C H.Poland	/3 L.Riggs	H H.Becker	P E.Blackwell	/C C.Kluttz	/C H.Spindel	/S P.Coscarart	P H.Pollet
/C B.Brady	/O G.Rosen	H C.Garriott	/3 J.Beggs	/O B.Maynard	/3 B.Burich	H A.Anderson	P H.Brecheen
H D.Phillips	H E.Naylor	/C D.Williams	P E.Heusser	/O M.Arnovich	H G.Crawford	H V.Barnhart	P M.Dickson
H D.Detweiler	R J.Corriden	/C T.Pawelek	P B.Walters	H D.Bartell	P K.Raffensberger	P N.Strincevich	P A.Brazle
/1 M.West	R O.Davis	/O C.Maddern	P C.Shoun	H M.Schemer	P O.Judd	P K.Heintzelman	/P J.Beazley
/3 S.Sisti	P J.Hatten	P J.Schmitz	RP B.Malloy	P D.Koslo	P S.Rowe	P R.Sewell	RP T.Wilks
P J.Sain	P K.Higbe	RP H.Wyse	RP C.Lambert	P M.Kennedy	P C.Schanz	P E.Bahr	RP R.Barrett
P M.Cooper	P V.Lombardi	RP H.Borowy	P J.Hetki	P B.Voiselle	P T.Hughes	RP A.Gerheauser	/P K.Burkhart
P E.Wright	P H.Behrman	P P.Erickson	P H.Gumbert	RP K.Trinkle	P A.Karl	P J.Hallett	/P M.Lanier
P B.Lee	P H.Gregg	P E.Kush	RP N.Andrews	RP H.Schumacher	RP D.Mulligan	P K.Gables	P R.Munger
P S.Johnson	RP H.Casey	P C.Passeau	/P H.Fox	RP M.Budnick	P D.Mauney	P J.Lanning	/P F.Martin
RP L.Wallace	RP A.Herring	/P B.Chipman	/P G.Burpo	RP J.Thompson	P B.Donnelly	P P.Roe	/P F.Schmidt
P W.Spahn	RP R.Branca	P H.Bithorn	/P F.Dasso	P N.Andrews	P C.Stanceu	P E.Albosta	P H.Krist
/P J.Niggeling	P R.Melton	/P R.Bauers		P B.Joyce	P L.Hoerst	/P H.Gornicki	/P B.Donnelly
P F.Barrett	P E.Head	P B.Fleming		P J.Gee	P A.Jurisich	/P L.Howard	/P J.Grodzicki
P S.Roser	P R.Barney	P R.Prim		P W.Abernathy	/P H.Mulcahy	/P J.Walsh	
P E.Singleton	P L.Webber	P R.Meyer		P B.Carpenter	/P J.Humphries	/P A.Tate	
P B.Posedel	/P J.Roy	/P D.Lade		P R.Fischer	/P I.Pearson	/P L.Wilkie	
P E.White	/P H.Taylor	/P R.Adams		/P S.Jones	/P L.Possehl	/P J.Hopper	
P J.Konstanty	/P P.Minner	/P R.Meers		/P J.Kraus	/P D.Grate	/P B.Clemensen	
/P D.Mulligan	/P C.Davis	/P V.Olsen		/P M.Grissom	/P A.Lopatka		
/P J.Hutchings	/P G.Moulder	/P E.Hanyzewski		/P N.Andrews	/P E.Hodkey		
/P A.Javery	/P C.McLish	/P H.Manders		/P S.Emmerich	/P S.Johnson		
/P E.Reid		/P E.O'Neill		/P H.Feldman	/P D.Koecher		
/P A.Williams				/P R.Kress	/P C.Ripple		
				/P A.Adams	/P B.Chapman		
				/P J.Brewer	/P A.Milnar		
				/P J.Carden			

TEAM	G	W	L	PCT	GB	R	OR	AB	H	2B	3B	HR	BB	SO	AVG	OBP	SLG	PRO	PRO+	BR	/A	PF	CHI	RC	SB	CS	SBA	SBR
STL	156	98	58	.628		712	545	5372	1426	265	56	81	530	537	.265	.334	.381	.715	105	54	25	104	105	702	58			
BRO	157	96	60	.615	2	701	570	5285	1376	233	66	55	691	575	.260	.348	.361	.709	106	60	53	101	101	699	100			
CHI	155	82	71	.536	14.5	626	581	5298	1344	223	50	56	586	599	.254	.331	.346	.677	100	-9	3	98	102	622	43			
BOS	154	81	72	.529	15.5	630	592	5225	1377	238	48	44	558	468	.264	.337	.353	.690	101	16	8	101	100	641	60			
PHI	155	69	85	.448	28	560	705	5233	1351	209	40	80	417	590	.258	.315	.359	.674	100	-30	-14	97	99	598	41			
CIN	156	67	87	.435	30	523	570	5291	1262	206	33	65	493	604	.239	.307	.327	.634	88	-101	-82	96	102	546	82			
PIT	155	63	91	.409	34	552	668	5199	1300	202	52	60	592	555	.250	.328	.344	.672	95	-18	-33	103	93	602	48			
NY	154	61	93	.396	36	612	685	5191	1326	176	37	121	532	546	.255	.328	.374	.702	104	27	23	101	97	644	46			
TOT	621					4916		42094	10762	1752	382	562	4399	4474	.256	.329	.355	.684							478			

TEAM	CG	SH	SV	IP	H	H/G	HR	BB	SO	RAT	ERA	ERA+	OAV	OOB	PR	/A	PF	CPI	FA	E	DP	FW	PW	BW	SBW	DIF
STL	75	18	15	1397	1326	8.5	63	493	607	11.9	3.01	115	.254	.322	63	70	101	108	.980	124	167	2.1	7.4	2.7		7.8
BRO	52	14	28	1418	1280	8.1	58	671	647	12.5	3.05	111	.243	.331	58	52	99	107	.972	174	154	-.9	5.5	5.6		7.7
CHI	59	15	11	1393	1370	8.9	58	527	619	12.4	3.24	102	.256	.325	26	15	97	102	.976	146	119	.7	1.6	.3		2.9
BOS	73	10	12	1371	1291	8.5	76	478	566	11.7	3.35	102	.249	.314	10	13	101	93	.972	169	129	-.8	1.4	.8		3.0
PHI	55	11	23	1369	1442	9.5	73	542	490	13.3	3.99	86	.273	.344	-88	-85	101	98	.975	148	144	.6	-9.0	-1.5		1.9
CIN	69	17	11	1413[1]	1334	8.5	70	467	506	11.6	3.08	109	.252	.314	53	42	98	101	.975	155	192	.2	4.5	-8.7		-6.0
PIT	61	10	6	1370	1406	9.2	50	561	458	13.1	3.72	95	.269	.342	-46	-29	103	99	.970	184	127	-1.6	-3.1	-3.5		-5.8
NY	47	8	13	1353[1]	1313	8.7	114	660	581	13.2	3.92	88	.256	.343	-76	-71	101	100	.973	159	121	-.2	-7.5	2.4		-10.7
TOT	491	103	119	11084[2]		8.7				12.5	3.41		.256	.329					.974	1259	1153					

Runs
Musial-StL 124
Slaughter-StL 100
Stanky-Bro 98
Schoendienst-StL 94
Cavarretta-Chi 89

Hits
Musial-StL 228
Walker-Bro 184
Slaughter-StL 183
Holmes-Bos 176
Schoendienst-StL . . . 170

Doubles
Musial-StL 50
Holmes-Bos 35
Kurowski-StL 32
Herman-Bro-Bos . . . 31

Triples
Musial-StL 20
Reese-Bro 10
Cavarretta-Chi 10
Walker-Bro 9

Home Runs
Kiner-Pit 23
Mize-NY 22
Slaughter-StL 18
Ennis-Phi 17

Total Bases
Musial-StL 366
Slaughter-StL 283
Ennis-Phi 262
Walker-Bro 258
Holmes-Bos 241

Runs Batted In
Slaughter-StL 130
Walker-Bro 116
Musial-StL 103
Kurowski-StL 89
Kiner-Pit 81

Runs Produced
Slaughter-StL 212
Musial-StL 211
Walker-Bro 187
Cavarretta-Chi 159
Holmes-Bos 153

Bases On Balls
Stanky-Bro 137
Fletcher-Pit 111
Cavarretta-Chi 88
Reese-Bro 87
Hack-Chi 83

Batting Average
Musial-StL 365
Hopp-Bos 333
Walker-Bro 319
Ennis-Phi 313
Holmes-Bos 310

On Base Percentage
Stanky-Bro 436
Musial-StL 434
Cavarretta-Chi 401
Herman-Bro-Bos 395
Walker-Bro 391

Slugging Average
Musial-StL 587
Ennis-Phi 485
Slaughter-StL 465
Kurowski-StL 462
Walker-Bro 448

Production
Musial-StL 1.021
Kurowski-StL 853
Ennis-Phi 849
Walker-Bro 839
Slaughter-StL 838

Adjusted Production
Musial-StL 180
Ennis-Phi 144
Cavarretta-Chi 140
Walker-Bro 136
Kurowski-StL 136

Batter Runs
Musial-StL 70.9
Mize-NY 43.6
Kurowski-StL 29.1
Walker-Bro 28.9
Slaughter-StL 28.6

Adjusted Batter Runs
Musial-StL 64.8
Mize-NY 43.0
Cavarretta-Chi 29.5
Walker-Bro 27.9
Ennis-Phi 27.9

Clutch Hitting Index
Walker-Bro 138
Slaughter-StL 131
Elliott-Pit 127
Fletcher-Pit 123
Reiser-Bro 120

Runs Created
Musial-StL 164
Slaughter-StL 110
Walker-Bro 104
Mize-NY 100
Kurowski-StL 97

Total Average
Musial-StL 1.114
Stanky-Bro 890
Reiser-Bro 877
Kurowski-StL 855
Walker-Bro 848

Stolen Bases
Reiser-Bro 34
Haas-Cin 22
Hopp-Bos 21
Adams-Cin 16
Walker-Bro 14

Stolen Base Average

Stolen Base Runs

Fielding Runs
Marion-StL 18.8
Wyrostek-Phi 17.2
Ennis-Phi 13.6
Handley-Pit 13.2
Mueller-Cin 9.8

Total Player Rating
Musial-StL 5.7
Mize-NY 4.4
Ennis-Phi 3.7
Stanky-Bro 3.1
Kurowski-StL 2.9

Wins
Pollet-StL 21
Sain-Bos 20
Higbe-Bro 17
Dickson-StL 15
Brecheen-StL 15

Win Percentage
Dickson-StL 714
Higbe-Bro 680
Pollet-StL 677
Sain-Bos 588
Brecheen-StL 500

Games
Trinkle-NY 48
Dickson-StL 47
Behrman-Bro 47
Casey-Bro 46

Complete Games
Sain-Bos 24
Pollet-StL 22
Koslo-NY 17
Ostermueller-Pit . . . 16
Cooper-Bos 15

Shutouts
Brecheen-StL 5
Blackwell-Cin 5
VanderMeer-Cin . . . 4
Pollet-StL 4
Cooper-Bos 4

Saves
Raffensberger-Phi . . . 6
Pollet-StL 5
Karl-Phi 5
Herring-Bro 5
Casey-Bro 5

Innings Pitched
Pollet-StL 266.0
Koslo-NY 265.1
Sain-Bos 265.0
Brecheen-StL 231.1
Schmitz-Chi 224.1

Fewest Hits/Game
Kennedy-NY 7.38
Schmitz-Chi 7.38
Blackwell-Cin 7.41
Higbe-Bro 7.60
Sain-Bos 7.64

Fewest BB/Game
Cooper-Bos 1.76
Raffensberger-Phi . 1.79
Beggs-Cin 1.85
Heusser-Cin 2.09
Strincevich-Pit . . . 2.25

Strikeouts
Schmitz-Chi 135
Higbe-Bro 134
Sain-Bos 129
Koslo-NY 121
Brecheen-StL 117

Strikeouts/Game
Higbe-Bro 5.72
Schmitz-Chi 5.42
Blackwell-Cin 4.63
Brecheen-StL 4.55
Voiselle-NY 4.50

Ratio
Cooper-Bos 9.95
Beggs-Cin 10.18
Sain-Bos 10.66
Dickson-StL 10.74
Pollet-StL 10.79

Earned Run Average
Pollet-StL 2.10
Sain-Bos 2.21
Beggs-Cin 2.32
Blackwell-Cin 2.45
Brecheen-StL 2.49

Adjusted ERA
Pollet-StL 165
Sain-Bos 155
Beggs-Cin 144
Brecheen-StL 139
Blackwell-Cin 136

Opponents' Batting Avg.
Schmitz-Chi 221
Kennedy-NY 224
Blackwell-Cin 226
Higbe-Bro 229
Sain-Bos 230

Opponents' On Base Pct.
Cooper-Bos 276
Beggs-Cin 287
Sain-Bos 294
Dickson-StL 295
Pollet-StL 300

Starter Runs
Pollet-StL 38.9
Sain-Bos 35.5
Brecheen-StL 23.7
Beggs-Cin 23.1
Blackwell-Cin 20.7

Adjusted Starter Runs
Pollet-StL 40.1
Sain-Bos 36.0
Brecheen-StL 24.8
Beggs-Cin 21.6
Rowe-Phi 19.9

Clutch Pitching Index
Hatten-Bro 129
Pollet-StL 127
Beggs-Cin 124
Wyse-Chi 117
Ostermueller-Pit . . . 110

Relief Runs
Casey-Bro 15.8
Thompson-NY 14.8
Malloy-Cin 5.3
Budnick-NY 2.5
Herring-Bro 6

Adjusted Relief Runs
Casey-Bro 15.5
Thompson-NY 15.0
Malloy-Cin 4.8
Budnick-NY 2.8
Wilks-StL 5

Relief Ranking
Casey-Bro 24.1
Thompson-NY 23.7
Malloy-Cin 4.5
Budnick-NY 1.6
Wilks-StL 4

Total Pitcher Index
Sain-Bos 5.9
Pollet-StL 5.1
Brecheen-StL 3.1
Beggs-Cin 2.9
Casey-Bro 2.9

Total Baseball Ranking
Sain-Bos 5.9
Musial-StL 5.7
Pollet-StL 5.1
Mize-NY 4.4
Ennis-Phi 3.7

April 30 Dispelling the rumors that he had lost his fastball after nearly four years in the Navy, Bob Feller of the Cleveland Indians hurls his second no-hitter, beating the New York Yankees 1-0 on Frankie Hayes' home run in the ninth inning.

May 28 The Washington Senators edge the New York Yankees 2-1 before 49,917 fans in the first night game at Yankee Stadium.

June 21 A Federal judge rules that the Seattle club does not have to play returning serviceman Al Niemiec but it does have to pay him his $720 a month contract through the season. At midseason 143 players who had major league contracts when they went to war had been released or sent to the minors. Former major league players Van Mungo, Lou Finney, Alfred "Chubby" Dean, Nate Andrews, and Max Butcher all play in Class D leagues.

June 22 Bill Veeck heads a syndicate which purchases the Cleveland Indians, launching Veeck on a long career as a lively promoter. A minor but typical change is the regular posting of NL scores on the Cleveland scoreboard, a departure from the long-standing practice of both leagues.

July 8 A special meeting of clubs deals with Mexican League defections and attempts by players to gain new rights. Some of the results include: $5,000 minimum salary, $25-per-week training-camp expenses, a fixed period for spring training, 25 days for postseason barnstorming, maximum pay cut of 25 percent. A pension fund aimed at providing $100 a month for retired 10-year players will be funded by World Series rights and net proceeds from All-Star Games. Each league will have a player rep to baseball councils. The first player reps named are Yankees pitcher Johnny Murphy and Dodgers outfielder Fred "Dixie" Walker.

July 14 Player-manager Lou Boudreau of Cleveland hits four doubles and one home run, but Ted Williams wallops three home runs and drives in eight runs, as the Boston Red Sox top the Indians 11-10. Boudreau's five extra base hits is a major league record that Willie Stargell will tie August 1, 1970. In the second game, the famous Boudreau Shift is born. Boudreau shifts all his players, except the third baseman and left fielder, to the right side of the diamond in an effort to stop Williams. Ted grounds out and walks twice while ignoring the shift.

September 8 With the Red Sox running away with the AL race, attention closes in on Bob Feller's strikeout pace. He reaches 300 today, a number reached by Walter Johnson and Rube Waddell twice each. Can Feller beat Waddell's 346 of 1904? Boudreau finds plenty of innings for Feller to work as the season comes to an end, and statisticians discover an error in the August 24 box score that shorted the fireballer one strikeout against the A's. Counting that one, Feller ends with 348. Alas Waddell's old record of 346 was apparently based on the compilations of George Moreland, an early baseball historian. Researchers from *The Sporting News* later revise Waddell's total to 349.

October 6 The World Series opens with a Red Sox 3-2 win as Rudy York hits a 10th-inning home run off Howie Pollet. The Sox tie the game in the ninth when an easy grounder to Marty Marion takes a freak bounce and goes through his legs.

November 15 Ted Williams is picked as the league MVP.

BOSTON	CHICAGO	CLEVELAND	DETROIT	NEW YORK	PHILADELPHIA	ST.LOUIS	WASHINGTON
M J.Cronin	M J.Dykes	M L.Boudreau	M S.O'Neill	M J.McCarthy	M C.Mack	M L.Sewell	M O.Bluege
1B R.York	M T.Lyons	1B L.Fleming	1B H.Greenberg	M B.Dickey	1B G.McQuinn	M Z.Taylor	1B M.Vernon
2B B.Doerr	1B H.Trosky	2B D.Meyer	2B J.Bloodworth	M J.Neun	2B G.Handley	1B C.Stevens	2B J.Priddy
SS J.Pesky	2B D.Kolloway	SS L.Boudreau	SS E.Lake	1B N.Etten	SS P.Suder	2B J.Berardino	SS B.Hitchcock
3B R.Russell	SS L.Appling	3B K.Keltner	3B G.Kell	2B J.Gordon	3B H.Majeski	SS V.Stephens	3B C.Travis
LF T.Williams	3B D.Lodigiani	LF G.Case	LF D.Wakefield	SS P.Rizzuto	LF S.Chapman	3B M.Christman	LF J.Grace
CF D.DiMaggio	LF B.Kennedy	CF P.Seerey	CF H.Evers	3B S.Stirnweiss	CF B.McCosky	LF J.Heath	CF S.Spence
RF C.Metkovich	CF T.Tucker	RF H.Edwards	RF R.Cullenbine	LF K.Keller	RF E.Valo	CF W.Judnich	RF B.Lewis
C H.Wagner	RF T.Wright	C J.Hegan	C B.Tebbetts	CF J.DiMaggio	C B.Rosar	RF A.Zarilla	C A.Evans
3 P.Higgins	C M.Tresh	2S J.Conway	O3 J.Outlaw	RF T.Henrich	O T.Stainback	C F.Mancuso	32 S.Robertson
O L.Culberson	2S C.Michaels	O F.Mackiewicz	O P.Mullin	C A.Robinson	S J.Wallaesa	O C.Laabs	C J.Early
O W.Moses	O R.Hodgin	2 R.Mack	O D.Cramer	O1 J.Lindell	2 O.Grimes	3 B.Dillinger	S3 G.Torres
O T.McBride	O W.Platt	C F.Hayes	2 E.Mayo	2 B.Johnson	2 I.Hall	32 J.Lucadello	/3 J.Heath
C R.Partee	1 J.Kuhel	3 D.Ross	2 S.Webb	C B.Dickey	O R.Derry	C H.Helf	C G.Binks
3 E.Pellagrini	C F.Hayes	1 H.Becker	C P.Richards	1 S.Souchock	O H.Peck	O G.McQuillen	O G.Coan
/2 D.Gutteridge	O W.Moses	O G.Woodling	O A.Moore	S F.Crosetti	S G.Desautels	O J.Grace	C M.Guerra
3 E.Andres	3 L.Wells	1 M.Rocco	C B.Swift	C G.Niarhos	1 B.Konopka	1 B.Dahlgren	/3 G.Myatt
C E.McGah	1 J.Jones	C S.Lollar	O B.McCosky	/S O.Grimes	S J.Caulfield	1 J.Witte	/1 J.Sanford
/O J.Lazor	C G.Dickey	O D.Mitchell	3 P.Higgins	/S B.Brown	3 G.Kell	C J.Schultz	/3 E.Yost
/1 P.Campbell	O D.Philley	/S T.Jordan	/S J.Lipon	/C Y.Berra	3 D.Richmond	O P.Lehner	/1 J.Kuhel
/C F.Pytlak	O G.Curtright	/3 H.Moss	/O J.Groth	C K.Silvestri	/O F.Garrison	C L.Moss	/O R.Goolsby
/2 T.Carey	C E.Fernandes	/1 E.Robinson	H N.Harris	/O F.Colman	/C J.Astroth	/O L.Finney	P M.Haefner
/3 B.Steiner	/3 F.Baker	/O B.Mills	P H.Newhouser	/3 E.Bockman	/C G.Armstrong	/C K.Sears	P B.Newsom
/O A.Gilbert	/S F.Whitman	/S R.Peters	P D.Trout	/3 H.Majeski	/O V.Benson	/O G.Bradley	P D.Leonard
P T.Hughson	/C T.Jordan	P J.Price	P V.Trucks	/C B.Drescher	P P.Marchildon	/1 G.Archie	P R.Scarborough
P D.Ferriss	/O J.Smaza	P R.Weigel	P F.Hutchinson	H B.Metheny	P D.Fowler	/C B.Martin	P S.Hudson
P M.Harris	P E.Lopat	/3 T.Sepkowski	P A.Benton	H R.Weatherly	P B.Savage	/2 L.Schulte	RP M.Pieretti
P J.Dobson	P O.Grove	H B.Monaco	P S.Overmire	P S.Chandler	P J.Flores	P J.Kramer	P R.Wolff
P J.Bagby	P J.Haynes	/S C.Brewster	P G.Caster	P B.Bevens	P L.Knerr	P D.Galehouse	P E.Wynn
RP E.Johnson	P E.Smith	P B.Feller	P H.White	P J.Page	P L.Harris	P S.Zoldak	P W.Masterson
RP B.Klinger	P F.Papish	P R.Embree	P J.Gorsica	P R.Gumpert	P R.Christopher	P N.Potter	P B.Kennedy
RP C.Dreisewerd	RP E.Caldwell	P A.Reynolds	/P T.Bridges	P T.Bonham	P B.Newsom	P T.Shirley	/P J.Niggeling
P B.Zuber	RP R.Hamner	P S.Gromek	/P T.Gray	/P A.Gettel	P E.Fagan	RP S.Ferens	/P M.Candini
/P C.Wagner	RP A.Hollingsworth	RP B.Lemon	/P L.Kretlow	/P C.Marshall	/P H.Besse	RP E.Kinder	P V.Curtis
P M.Brown	P J.Rigney	RP J.Krakauskas	/P A.Houtteman	/P R.Ruffing	/P B.McCahan	P B.Muncrief	/P M.Wilson
/P B.Butland	P B.Dietrich	P M.Harder	/P H.Manders	/P J.Murphy	P L.Griffeth	P C.Fannin	/P J.Wade
/P R.Heflin	/P T.Lee	P C.Gassaway	/P R.Gentry	/P B.Wight	P J.Berry	P O.Miller	/P A.LaMacchia
/P M.Ryba	P T.Lyons	P D.Black		/P J.Wade	P J.Coleman	P T.Ferrick	
/P M.Deutsch	P G.Maltzberger	P J.Berry		/P M.Queen	P N.Brown	P F.Biscan	
/P J.Wilson	/P E.O'Neill	P P.Center		/P M.Russo	P J.Knott	P F.Sanford	
	/P L.Perme	/P T.Ferrick		/P V.Raschi	/P P.Cooper	/P C.Johnson	
		/P E.Klieman		/P F.Hiller	/P P.Vaughan	/P A.LaMacchia	
		/P V.Johnson		/P T.Byrne		/P A.Milnar	
		/P B.Kuzava		/P A.Lyons		/P A.Hollingsworth	
		/P R.Flanigan		/P K.Drews		/P S.Sundra	
		/P J.Podgajny		/P B.Zuber		/P R.Shore	
		/P L.Webber		/P C.Stanceu			
		/P R.McCabe		/P S.Roser			
				/P H.Karpel			

TEAM	G	W	L	PCT	GB	R	OR	AB	H	2B	3B	HR	BB	SO	AVG	OBP	SLG	PRO	PRO+	BR	/A	PF	CHI	RC	SB	CS	SBA	SBR
BOS	156	104	50	.675		792	594	5318	1441	268	50	109	687	661	.271	.356	.402	.758	113	136	92	106	101	790	45	36	56	-8
DET	155	92	62	.597	12	704	567	5318	1373	212	41	108	622	616	.258	.337	.374	.711	100	42	0	106	103	698	65	41	61	-5
NY	154	87	67	.565	17	684	547	5139	1275	208	50	136	627	706	.248	.334	.387	.721	107	55	46	101	101	695	48	35	58	-7
WAS	155	76	78	.494	28	608	706	5337	1388	260	63	60	511	641	.260	.327	.366	.693	106	1	39	94	96	653	51	50	50	-15
CHI	155	74	80	.481	30	562	595	5312	1364	206	44	37	501	600	.257	.323	.333	.656	94	-64	-43	96	100	579	78	64	55	-15
CLE	156	68	86	.442	36	537	638	5242	1285	233	56	79	506	697	.245	.313	.356	.669	99	-49	-12	94	94	596	57	49	54	-12
STL	156	66	88	.429	38	621	710	5373	1350	220	46	84	465	713	.251	.313	.356	.669	89	-53	-82	105	108	601	23	35	40	-14
PHI	155	49	105	.318	55	529	680	5200	1317	220	51	40	482	594	.253	.318	.338	.656	91	-68	-65	99	97	574	39	30	57	-6
TOT	621					5037		42239	10793	1827	401	653	4401	5228	.256	.328	.364	.692							406	340	54	-82

TEAM	CG	SH	SV	IP	H	H/G	HR	BB	SO	RAT	ERA	ERA+	OAV	OOB	PR	/A	PF	CPI	FA	E	DP	FW	PW	BW	SBW	DIF
BOS	79	15	20	1396²	1359	8.8	89	501	667	12.1	3.38	108	.254	.319	19	44	105	100	.977	139	163	1.5	4.6	9.6	.2	11.0
DET	94	18	15	1402	1277	8.2	97	497	896	11.5	3.22	114	.241	.307	45	68	104	95	.974	155	138	.5	7.1	.0	.6	6.9
NY	68	17	17	1361	1232	8.1	66	552	653	11.9	3.13	110	.243	.319	56	48	99	100	.975	150	174	.7	5.0	4.8	.3	-.9
WAS	71	8	10	1396¹	1459	9.4	81	547	537	13.1	3.74	89	.269	.339	-36	-61	96	103	.966	211	162	-2.8	-6.4	4.1	-.5	4.6
CHI	62	9	16	1392¹	1348	8.7	80	508	550	12.1	3.10	110	.255	.323	63	49	97	110	.972	175	170	-.7	5.1	-4.5	-.5	-2.4
CLE	63	16	13	1388²	1282	8.3	84	649	789	12.6	3.62	91	.245	.331	-17	-48	94	96	.975	147	147	1.0	-5.0	-1.3	-.2	-3.5
STL	63	13	12	1382¹	1465	9.5	73	573	574	13.3	3.95	94	.272	.343	-69	-34	107	99	.974	159	157	.3	-3.6	-8.6	-.4	1.3
PHI	61	10	5	1342²	1371	9.2	83	577	562	13.2	3.90	91	.264	.340	-59	-53	101	98	.971	167	141	-.2	-5.6	-6.8	.4	-15.8
TOT	561	106	108	11062		8.8				12.5	3.50		.256	.328					.973	1303	1252					

Runs
Williams-Bos 142
Pesky-Bos 115
Lake-Det 105
Keller-NY 98
Doerr-Bos 95

Hits
Pesky-Bos 208
Vernon-Was 207
Appling-Chi 180
Williams-Bos 176
Lewis-Was 170

Doubles
Vernon-Was 51
Spence-Was 50
Pesky-Bos 43
Williams-Bos 37
Doerr-Bos 34

Triples
Edwards-Cle 16
Lewis-Was 13
Kell-Phi-Det 10
Spence-Was 10
Keller-NY 10

Home Runs
Greenberg-Det 44
Williams-Bos 38
Keller-NY 30
Seerey-Cle 26
DiMaggio-NY 25

Total Bases
Williams-Bos 343
Greenberg-Det 316
Vernon-Was 298
Spence-Was 287
Keller-NY 287

Runs Batted In
Greenberg-Det ... 127
Williams-Bos 123
York-Bos 119
Doerr-Bos 116
Keller-NY 101

Runs Produced
Williams-Bos 227
Doerr-Bos 193
York-Bos 180
Greenberg-Det ... 174
Keller-NY 169

Bases On Balls
Williams-Bos 156
Keller-NY 113
Lake-Det 103
Cullenbine-Det ... 88
Henrich-NY 87

Batting Average
Vernon-Was 353
Williams-Bos 342
Pesky-Bos 335
Kell-Phi-Det 322
DiMaggio-Bos 316

On Base Percentage
Williams-Bos 497
Keller-NY 405
Vernon-Was 403
Pesky-Bos 401
DiMaggio-Bos 393

Slugging Average
Williams-Bos 667
Greenberg-Det 604
Keller-NY 533
DiMaggio-NY 511
Edwards-Cle 509

Production
Williams-Bos 1.164
Greenberg-Det 977
Keller-NY 938
Vernon-Was 910
DiMaggio-NY 878

Adjusted Production
Williams-Bos 211
Vernon-Was 163
Greenberg-Det 160
Keller-NY 158
Edwards-Cle 151

Batter Runs
Williams-Bos 94.2
Greenberg-Det ... 46.1
Keller-NY 45.9
Cullenbine-Det .. 42.2
Vernon-Was 40.3

Adjusted Batter Runs
Williams-Bos 85.2
Vernon-Was 46.9
Keller-NY 44.4
Greenberg-Det ... 39.6
Cullenbine-Det .. 37.0

Clutch Hitting Index
Travis-Was 136
York-Bos 135
Doerr-Bos 126
Henrich-NY 119
Heath-Was-StL 109

Runs Created
Williams-Bos 188
Keller-NY 127
Vernon-Was 120
Greenberg-Det 119
Pesky-Bos 111

Total Average
Williams-Bos 1.431
Greenberg-Det ...1.010
Keller-NY 1.005
Vernon-Was 873
DiMaggio-NY 862

Stolen Bases
Case-Cle 28
Stirnweiss-NY 18
Lake-Det 15

Stolen Base Average
Stirnweiss-NY 75.0
Case-Cle 71.8

Stolen Base Runs
Stirnweiss-NY 1.8
Dillinger-StL 1.8
Case-Cle 1.8
Philley-Chi 1.5
Evers-Det 1.5

Fielding Runs
Doerr-Bos 26.8
Gordon-NY 21.5
Boudreau-Cle 16.2
Rizzuto-NY 13.1
Pesky-Bos 12.0

Total Player Rating
Williams-Bos 7.9
Doerr-Bos 4.8
Pesky-Bos 4.2
Vernon-Was 3.6
Greenberg-Det 3.5

Wins
Newhouser-Det 26
Feller-Cle 26
Ferriss-Bos 25
Hughson-Bos 20
Chandler-NY 20

Win Percentage
Ferriss-Bos ...... .806
Newhouser-Det .... .743
Chandler-NY ...... .714
Harris-Bos .... .654
Hughson-Bos ...... .645

Games
Feller-Cle 48
Savage-Phi 40
Ferriss-Bos 40
Hughson-Bos 39
Caldwell-Chi 39

Complete Games
Feller-Cle 36
Newhouser-Det 29
Ferriss-Bos 26
Trout-Det 23
Hughson-Bos 21

Shutouts
Feller-Cle 10
Newhouser-Det 6
Hughson-Bos 6
Ferriss-Bos 6
Chandler-NY 6

Saves
Klinger-Bos 9
Caldwell-Chi 8
Murphy-NY 7
Ferrick-Cle-StL ... 6

Innings Pitched
Feller-Cle 371.1
Newhouser-Det 292.2
Hughson-Bos 278.0
Trout-Det 276.1
Ferriss-Bos 274.0

Fewest Hits/Game
Newhouser-Det ... 6.61
Feller-Cle 6.71
Chandler-NY 6.99
Embree-Cle 7.65
Bevens-NY 7.68

Fewest BB/Game
Hughson-Bos 1.65
Lopat-Chi 1.87
Leonard-Was 2.00
Flores-Phi 2.21
Ferriss-Bos 2.33

Strikeouts
Feller-Cle 348
Newhouser-Det 275
Hughson-Bos 172
Trucks-Det 161
Trout-Det 151

Strikeouts/Game
Newhouser-Det 8.46
Feller-Cle 8.43
Trucks-Det 6.12
Hutchinson-Det ... 6.00
Hughson-Bos 5.57

Ratio
Newhouser-Det 9.66
Hughson-Bos 9.87
Chandler-NY 10.18
Lopat-Chi 10.32
Feller-Cle 10.49

Earned Run Average
Newhouser-Det 1.94
Chandler-NY 2.10
Feller-Cle 2.18
Bevens-NY 2.23
Flores-Phi 2.32

Adjusted ERA
Newhouser-Det 189
Chandler-NY 164
Trout-Det 156
Bevens-NY 154
Flores-Phi 153

Opponents' Batting Avg.
Newhouser-Det .... .201
Feller-Cle .... .208
Chandler-NY ...... .218
Embree-Cle .... .227
Bevens-NY .... .232

Opponents' On Base Pct.
Newhouser-Det ... .269
Hughson-Bos ..... .274
Chandler-NY ..... .288
Lopat-Chi .... .288
Feller-Cle ...... .291

Starter Runs
Feller-Cle 54.5
Newhouser-Det ... 50.9
Chandler-NY 40.2
Trout-Det 35.6
Bevens-NY 35.2

Adjusted Starter Runs
Newhouser-Det ... 55.8
Feller-Cle 46.5
Trout-Det 40.2
Chandler-NY 38.7
Bevens-NY 33.7

Clutch Pitching Index
Grove-Chi 126
Flores-Phi 121
Trout-Det 119
Haynes-Chi 118
Bevens-NY 115

Relief Runs
Caldwell-Chi 14.3
Lemon-Cle 10.6
Klinger-Bos 7.2
Kinder-StL 1.7

Adjusted Relief Runs
Caldwell-Chi 13.4
Lemon-Cle 8.5
Klinger-Bos 8.2
Kinder-StL 3.9

Relief Ranking
Caldwell-Chi 25.2
Klinger-Bos 9.4
Lemon-Cle 7.6
Kinder-StL 2.5

Total Pitcher Index
Newhouser-Det ... 7.1
Trout-Det 5.3
Feller-Cle 4.9
Chandler-NY 4.8
Bevens-NY 3.0

Total Baseball Ranking
Williams-Bos 7.9
Newhouser-Det ... 7.1
Trout-Det 5.3
Feller-Cle 4.9
Chandler-NY 4.8

January 18 The Pirates buy first baseman Hank Greenberg from the Tigers for a reported $25,000 to $35,000. Greenberg led the AL in home runs with 44 in 1946.

April 1 Branch Rickey deflects pressure on Jackie Robinson by keeping him in Montreal, although it is clear the contending Dodgers can use the 1946 International League batting king.

April 9 Commissioner Happy Chandler suspends manager Leo Durocher of the Brooklyn Dodgers for the entire season for incidents detrimental to baseball.

April 15 Jackie Robinson goes hitless in three trips in his Brooklyn debut but handles 11 chances at first base, a new position for him, in a 5-3 win over the Braves. Coach Clyde Sukeforth, interim manager and the man credited with first scouting Robinson, guides the team to two wins before stepping down.

April 18 Dodger scout Burt Shotton is the surprise choice to replace Leo Durocher on the third day of the season.

May 8 A movement among Cardinal players to protest its first meeting with Jackie Robinson and the Dodgers is aborted by a clubhouse talk from owner Sam Breadon, according to a story by league president Ford Frick. Breadon denies the story.

June 22 Ewell Blackwell just misses pitching back-to-back no-hitters when Eddie Stanky of the Brooklyn Dodgers singles with one out in the ninth inning. Blackwell then gets Al Gionfriddo before Jackie Robinson bangs out a second single. Blackwell wins, 4-0, his ninth straight win to improve to 11-2. Stanky's hit ends Blackwell's hitless-inning skein at 19.

June 24 The Dodgers win 4-2 over the Pirates, as Jackie Robinson swipes home for the first of 19 times in his career.

July 30 The New York Giants edge the Cincinnati Reds 6-5 in 10 innings, ending Ewell Blackwell's winning streak at 16 games. All were complete games, and five were shutouts.

August 20 The Boston Braves hit a million in attendance for the first time.

August 21* The first Little League World Series tournament is held in Williamsport, Pennsylvania. The Maynard Midgets of Williamsport win the World Series 16-7.

September 12 Ralph Kiner hits his record eighth home run in four games to pass Johnny Mize in the home run race as Pittsburgh tops the Boston Braves 4-3.

September 17 Jackie Robinson is named Rookie of the Year by *The Sporting News* two weeks before the season is over. At year's end he has hit .297 and led the NL in stolen bases and sacrifices.

September 22 The Dodgers win the pennant while idle. The Cards lose to the Cubs to clinch the Dodgers' first title since 1941, this time with a 5-game margin.

September 29 Hitless the first four innings against Brooklyn's Ralph Branca, the Yankees score five runs in the fifth inning and win the World Series opener 5-3 before a record World Series crowd of 73,365 at Yankee Stadium.

October 2 The Dodgers squeak to a 9-8 win, jumping on Bobo Newsom and Vic Raschi in the second for six runs. Yogi Berra becomes the first player to hit a pinch home run in World Series history, against Brooklyn's Ralph Branca in the seventh inning.

October 3 Brooklyn pinch hitter Cookie Lavagetto doubles home two runs with two out in the bottom of the ninth to break up Floyd Bevens' no-hit bid and give the Dodgers a dramatic 3-2 victory over the Yankees in Game 4 at Ebbets Field.

October 5 Center fielder Al Gionfriddo's magnificent catch takes a home run away from Joe DiMaggio, which would have tied the sixth game of the World Series at Yankee Stadium. The Brooklyn Dodgers go on to win 8-6 before a record World Series crowd of 74,065.

	BOSTON		BROOKLYN		CHICAGO		CINCINNATI		NEW YORK		PHILADELPHIA		PITTSBURGH		ST.LOUIS
M	B.Southworth	M	C.Sukeforth	M	C.Grimm	M	J.Neun	M	M.Ott	M	B.Chapman	M	B.Herman	M	E.Dyer
1B	E.Torgeson	M	B.Shotton	1B	E.Waitkus	1B	B.Young	1B	J.Mize	1B	H.Schultz	M	B.Burwell	1B	S.Musial
2B	C.Ryan	1B	J.Robinson	2B	D.Johnson	2B	B.Zientara	2B	B.Rigney	2B	E.Verban	1B	H.Greenberg	2B	R.Schoendienst
SS	D.Culler	2B	E.Stanky	SS	L.Merullo	SS	E.Miller	SS	B.Kerr	SS	S.Newsome	2B	J.Bloodworth	SS	M.Marion
3B	B.Elliott	SS	P.Reese	3B	P.Lowrey	3B	G.Hatton	3B	J.Lohrke	3B	L.Handley	SS	B.Cox	3B	W.Kurowski
LF	B.Rowell	3B	S.Jorgensen	LF	P.Cavarretta	LF	A.Galan	LF	S.Gordon	LF	D.Ennis	3B	F.Gustine	LF	E.Slaughter
CF	J.Hopp	LF	P.Reiser	CF	A.Pafko	CF	B.Haas	CF	B.Thomson	CF	H.Walker	LF	R.Kiner	CF	T.Moore
RF	T.Holmes	CF	C.Furillo	RF	B.Nicholson	RF	F.Baumholtz	RF	W.Marshall	RF	J.Wyrostek	CF	J.Russell	RF	R.Northey
C	P.Masi	RF	D.Walker	C	B.Scheffing	C	R.Lamanno	C	W.Cooper	C	A.Seminick	RF	W.Westlake	C	D.Rice
		C	B.Edwards									C	D.Howell		
O	M.McCormick			3	S.Hack	2	B.Adams	O	G.Gearhart	3	J.Tabor			O	C.Diering
O	D.Litwhiler	O	G.Hermanski	C	C.McCullough	O	E.Lukon	2	M.Witek	S	R.LaPointe	O	C.Rikard	O	E.Dusak
1	F.McCormick	O3	A.Vaughan	S2	B.Sturgeon	O	R.Mueller	23	B.Blattner	O	B.Adams	C	C.Kluttz	C	J.Garagiola
S	N.Fernandez	2O	E.Miksis	O	C.Aberson	O	T.Tatum	C	E.Lombardi	1C	A.Lakeman	2	E.Basinski	O	J.Medwick
S	S.Sisti	O	D.Snider	O	M.Rickert	O	C.Vollmer	O	J.Lafata	C	D.Padgett	1	E.Fletcher	O	D.Wilber
C	H.Camelli	S	S.Rojek	O	D.Dallessandro	3	K.Wahl	/2	B.Rhawn	O	C.Gilbert	S2	W.Wietelmann	1	D.Sisler
/O	T.Neill	C	G.Hodges	2	R.Mack	/1	C.Kress	H	B.Young	S	J.Albright	O	G.Woodling	2	N.Jones
/2	D.Murtaugh	3	C.Lavagetto	/2	L.Frey	/O	B.Usher	/O	F.White	3	W.Jones	C	B.Salkeld	3S	J.Cross
H	B.Brady	O	A.Gionfriddo	S	B.Jurges	/C	H.Poland	/C	W.Westrum	O	R.Northey	C	B.Sullivan	H	W.Walker
		C	B.Bragan	/C	M.Livingston	/1	T.Kluszewski	/C	M.Livingston	1	N.Etten	S	P.Castiglione	S	B.Creger
P	W.Spahn	/3	T.Brown	/S	S.Madrid	H	A.Lakeman	/C	B.Warren	1	F.McCormick	2	B.Herman		
P	J.Sain	/O	D.Lund	/3	H.Schenz	/S	V.Stallcup	/C	S.Yvars	/O	J.Levan	C	R.Jarvis	P	M.Dickson
P	R.Barrett	/1	E.Stevens	/C	D.Williams			H	M.Ott	/C	H.Poland	/2	G.Mauch	P	R.Munger
P	B.Voiselle	/O	D.Whitman			P	E.Blackwell	H	W.Lockman	/2	P.Caballero	H	A.Gionfriddo	P	H.Brecheen
P	S.Johnson	/O	M.Rackley	P	J.Schmitz	P	J.Vander Meer			/S	G.Hamner			P	H.Pollet
RP	C.Shoun	/O	T.Tatum	P	D.Lade	P	K.Peterson	P	L.Jansen	H	L.Finney	P	K.Higbe	P	A.Brazle
RP	E.Wright	/1	H.Schultz	P	H.Borowy	P	B.Lively	P	D.Koslo	/C	R.Hemsley	P	F.Ostermueller	RP	K.Burkhart
RP	W.Lanfranconi			P	P.Erickson	P	B.Walters	P	M.Kennedy			P	T.Bonham	RP	T.Wilks
		P	R.Branca	P	H.Wyse	RP	J.Hetki	P	C.Hartung	P	D.Leonard	P	P.Roe		
P	M.Cooper	P	J.Hatten	RP	E.Kush	RP	H.Gumbert	RP	K.Trinkle	P	S.Rowe	P	R.Sewell	P	J.Hearn
P	A.Karl	P	V.Lombardi	RP	R.Meers			RP	J.Beggs	P	O.Judd	RP	N.Strincevich	P	G.Staley
/P	J.Beazley	P	H.Taylor			P	E.Erautt			P	K.Heintzelman	RP	E.Singleton	P	J.Grodzicki
P	G.Elliott	RP	H.Gregg	P	B.Chipman	P	K.Raffensberger	P	A.Hansen	P	T.Hughes			/P	K.Johnson
/P	R.Martin	RP	H.Behrman	P	C.Passeau	P	J.Beggs	RP	H.Iott	RP	F.Schmidt	P	J.Bagby	/P	F.Schmidt
/P	J.Lanning	RP	R.Barney	P	R.Meyer	P	E.Riddle	/C	R.Poat			P	E.Bahr		
/P	E.White			/P	R.Hamner	P	C.Shoun	P	S.Jones	P	B.Donnelly	P	M.Queen		
/P	M.Macon	P	C.King	P	B.Lee	/P	H.Perkowski	P	B.Voiselle	P	A.Jurisich	P	R.Wolff		
/P	D.Mulligan	P	H.Casey	/P	O.Miller	/P	C.Lambert	P	M.Cooper	P	C.Schanz	P	A.Lyons		
		P	E.Chandler	/P	B.Carpenter	/P	K.Polivka	P	J.Thompson	P	K.Raffensberger	P	H.Behrman		
		/P	K.Higbe	/P	F.Schmidt	/P	M.Schultz	P	B.Ayers	/P	D.Koecher	/P	S.Nagy		
		/P	P.Haugstad			/P	B.Malloy	/P	M.Budnick	/P	D.Mauney	/P	A.Herring		
		/P	D.Bankhead			/P	H.Wehmeier	/P	H.Andrews	/P	L.Hoerst	/P	H.Mulcahy		
		/P	J.Banta					/P	M.Picone	/P	C.Simmons	/P	K.Heintzelman		
		/P	G.Dockins					/P	B.Carpenter	/P	H.Spragins	/P	L.Howard		
		/P	R.Melton					/P	W.Abernathy	/P	L.Possehl	/P	C.McLish		
		/P	E.Palica									/P	L.Tost		
		/P	W.Ramsdell									/P	K.Gables		
		/P	J.Van Cuyk												

TEAM	G	W	L	PCT	GB	R	OR	AB	H	2B	3B	HR	BB	SO	AVG	OBP	SLG	PRO	PRO+	BR	/A	PF	CHI	RC	SB	CS	SBA	SBR
BRO	155	94	60	.610		774	668	5249	1428	241	50	83	732	561	.272	.364	.384	.748	102	62	32	104	98	781	88			
STL	156	89	65	.578	5	780	634	5422	1462	235	65	115	612	511	.270	.347	.401	.748	101	41	7	104	102	762	28			
BOS	154	86	68	.558	8	701	622	5253	1444	265	42	85	558	500	.275	.346	.390	.736	105	19	36	98	97	717	58			
NY	155	81	73	.526	13	830	761	5343	1446	220	48	221	494	568	.271	.335	.454	.789	114	95	90	101	104	809	29			
CIN	154	73	81	.474	21	681	755	5299	1372	242	43	95	539	530	.259	.330	.375	.705	95	-48	-43	99	103	672	46			
CHI	155	69	85	.448	25	567	722	5305	1373	231	48	71	471	578	.259	.321	.361	.682	91	-93	-69	96	94	620	22			
PIT	156	62	92	.403	32	744	817	5307	1385	216	44	156	607	687	.261	.340	.406	.746	102	31	10	103	100	738	30			
PHI	155	62	92	.403	32	589	687	5256	1354	210	52	60	464	594	.258	.321	.352	.673	88	-108	-87	96	101	597	60			
TOT	620						5666	42434	11264	1860	392	886	4477	4529	.265	.338	.390	.729							361			

TEAM	CG	SH	SV	IP	H	H/G	HR	BB	SO	RAT	ERA	ERA+	OAV	OOB	PR	/A	PF	CPI	FA	E	DP	FW	PW	BW	SBW	DIF
BRO	47	14	34	1375	1299	8.5	104	626	592	12.8	3.82	108	.251	.336	37	49	102	100	.978	129	169	.9	4.8	3.1		8.1
STL	65	12	20	1397²	1417	9.1	106	495	642	12.4	3.53	117	.266	.330	83	94	102	110	.979	128	169	1.1	9.2	.7		1.0
BOS	74	14	13	1362²	1342	8.9	93	453	494	11.9	3.62	108	.255	.316	67	41	96	95	.974	153	124	-.6	4.0	3.5		2.0
NY	58	6	14	1363¹	1428	9.4	122	590	553	13.4	4.44	92	.267	.342	-58	-56	100	94	.974	155	136	-.7	-5.5	8.9		1.3
CIN	54	13	13	1365¹	1442	9.5	102	589	633	13.5	4.41	93	.274	.349	-53	-46	101	98	.977	138	134	.3	-4.5	-4.2		4.4
CHI	46	8	15	1367	1449	9.5	106	618	571	13.7	4.04	98	.274	.353	4	-13	97	109	.975	150	159	-.4	-1.3	-6.8		.4
PIT	44	9	13	1374	1488	9.7	155	592	530	13.9	4.68	90	.278	.354	-95	-71	104	101	.975	149	131	-.2	-7.0	1.0		-8.8
PHI	70	8	14	1362	1399	9.2	98	513	514	12.8	3.96	101	.276	.346	15	7	99	108	.974	152	140	-.5	.7	-8.6		-6.7
TOT	458	84	136	10967¹		9.2				13.1	4.06		.265	.338					.976	1154	1162					

Runs		Hits		Doubles		Triples		Home Runs		Total Bases	
Mize-NY	137	Holmes-Bos	191	Miller-Cin	38	Walker-StL-Phi	16	Mize-NY	51	Kiner-Pit	361
Robinson-Bro	125	Walker-StL-Phi	186	B.Elliott-Bos	35	Slaughter-StL	13	Kiner-Pit	51	Mize-NY	360
Kiner-Pit	118	Musial-StL	183	Ryan-Bos	33	Musial-StL	13	Marshall-NY	36	Marshall-NY	310
Musial-StL	113	Gustine-Pit	183	Holmes-Bos	33	Schoendienst-StL	9	W.Cooper-NY	35	W.Cooper-NY	302
Kurowski-StL	108	Baumholtz-Cin	182	Baumholtz-Cin	32	Baumholtz-Cin	9	Thomson-NY	29	Musial-StL	296

Runs Batted In		Runs Produced		Bases On Balls		Batting Average		On Base Percentage		Slugging Average	
Mize-NY	138	Mize-NY	224	Reese-Bro	104	Walker-StL-Phi	.363	Galan-Cin	.449	Kiner-Pit	.639
Kiner-Pit	127	Kiner-Pit	194	Greenberg-Pit	104	B.Elliott-Bos	.317	Walker-StL-Phi	.436	Mize-NY	.614
W.Cooper-NY	122	Musial-StL	189	Stanky-Bro	103	Cavarretta-Chi	.314	Kurowski-StL	.420	W.Cooper-NY	.586
B.Elliott-Bos	113	Kurowski-StL	185	Kiner-Pit	98	Kiner-Pit	.313	Kiner-Pit	.417	Kurowski-StL	.544
Marshall-NY	107	B.Elliott-Bos	184	Walker-Bro	97	Musial-StL	.312	Walker-Bro	.415	Marshall-NY	.528

Production		Adjusted Production		Batter Runs		Adjusted Batter Runs		Clutch Hitting Index		Runs Created	
Kiner-Pit	1.055	Kiner-Pit	172	Kiner-Pit	61.4	Kiner-Pit	57.5	Marion-StL	128	Kiner-Pit	154
Mize-NY	.998	Mize-NY	160	Mize-NY	48.3	Mize-NY	47.5	Haas-Cin	125	Mize-NY	143
Kurowski-StL	.964	Walker-StL-Phi	150	Kurowski-StL	41.8	B.Elliott-Bos	39.5	Walker-Bro	125	B.Elliott-Bos	120
B.Elliott-Bos	.927	B.Elliott-Bos	148	B.Elliott-Bos	36.8	Walker-StL-Phi	38.8	Edwards-Bro	125	Kurowski-StL	118
W.Cooper-NY	.926	Kurowski-StL	148	Walker-StL-Phi	35.4	Kurowski-StL	36.8	Jorgensen-Bro	122	Musial-StL	118

Total Average		Stolen Bases		Stolen Base Average		Stolen Base Runs		Fielding Runs		Total Player Rating	
Kiner-Pit	1.155	Robinson-Bro	29					Marion-StL	20.1	Kiner-Pit	6.0
Mize-NY	1.060	Reiser-Bro	14					Verban-Phi	16.9	Mize-NY	4.9
Kurowski-StL	1.019	Walker-StL-Phi	13					Gustine-Pit	14.8	Walker-StL-Phi	4.2
Walker-StL-Phi	.979	Hopp-Bos	13					Kiner-Pit	13.2	B.Elliott-Bos	3.7
Torgeson-Bos	.973	Torgeson-Bos	11					Kerr-NY	12.1	Marshall-NY	2.9

Wins		Win Percentage		Games		Complete Games		Shutouts		Saves	
Blackwell-Cin	22	Jansen-NY	.808	Trinkle-NY	62	Blackwell-Cin	23	Spahn-Bos	7	Casey-Bro	18
Spahn-Bos	21	Munger-StL	.762	Higbe-Bro-Pit	50	Spahr-Bos	22	Munger-StL	6	Trinkle-NY	10
Sain-Bos	21	Blackwell-Cin	.733	Behrman-Bro-Pt-Bro	50	Sain-Bos	22	Blackwell-Cin	6	Gumbert-Cin	10
Jansen-NY	21	Hatten-Bro	.680	Kush-Chi	47	Jansen-NY	20	Dickson-StL	4	Behrman-Bro-Pt-Bro	8
Branca-Bro	21	Spahn-Bos	.677	Dickson-StL	47	Leonard-Phi	19	Branca-Bro	4		

Innings Pitched		Fewest Hits/Game		Fewest BB/Game		Strikeouts		Strikeouts/Game		Ratio	
Spahn-Bos	289.2	Taylor-Bro	7.22	Jansen-NY	2.07	Blackwell-Cin	193	Blackwell-Cin	6.36	Spahn-Bos	10.25
Branca-Bro	280.0	Blackwell-Cin	7.48	Rowe-Phi	2.07	Branca-Bro	148	Munger-StL	4.93	Blackwell-Cin	10.75
Blackwell-Cin	273.0	Spahn-Bos	7.61	Leonard-Phi	2.18	Sain-Bos	132	Branca-Bro	4.76	Leonard-Phi	10.84
Sain-Bos	266.0	Lombardi-Bro	8.04	Barrett-Bos	2.26	Spahn-Bos	123	Brazle-StL	4.55	Jansen-NY	10.85
Jansen-NY	248.0	Branca-Bro	8.07	Brazle-StL	2.57	Munger-StL	123	Sain-Bos	4.47	Barrett-Bos	10.89

Earned Run Average		Adjusted ERA		Opponents' Batting Avg.		Opponents' On Base Pct.		Starter Runs		Adjusted Starter Runs	
Spahn-Bos	2.33	Spahn-Bos	167	Taylor-Bro	.225	Spahn-Bos	.283	Spahn-Bos	55.7	Spahn-Bos	50.3
Blackwell-Cin	2.47	Blackwell-Cin	166	Spahn-Bos	.226	Barrett-Bos	.292	Blackwell-Cin	48.2	Blackwell-Cin	49.5
Branca-Bro	2.67	Branca-Bro	155	Blackwell-Cin	.234	Blackwell-Cin	.304	Branca-Bro	43.3	Branca-Bro	45.6
Leonard-Phi	2.68	Leonard-Phi	149	Branca-Bro	.240	Leonard-Phi	.306	Leonard-Phi	36.0	Leonard-Phi	34.6
Brazle-StL	2.84	Brazle-StL	146	Lombardi-Bro	.241	Jansen-NY	.306	Dickson-StL	25.5	Dickson-StL	27.4

Clutch Pitching Index		Relief Runs		Adjusted Relief Runs		Relief Ranking		Total Pitcher Index		Total Baseball Ranking	
Brazle-StL	139	Lanfranconi-Bos	7.9	Lanfranconi-Bos	6.7	Lanfranconi-Bos	7.8	Blackwell-Cin	5.2	Kiner-Pit	6.0
Leonard-Phi	123	Kush-Chi	7.1	Kush-Chi	5.9	Kush-Chi	7.2	Spahn-Bos	5.1	Blackwell-Cin	5.2
Branca-Bro	122	Trinkle-NY	3.3	Trinkle-NY	3.4	Gumbert-Cin	4.9	Branca-Bro	4.4	Spahn-Bos	5.1
Blackwell-Cin	115	Gumbert-Cin	1.8	Gumbert-Cin	2.2	Trinkle-NY	4.7	Leonard-Phi	4.3	Mize-NY	4.9
Jansen-NY	114	Casey-Bro	.6	Casey-Bro	1.2	Casey-Bro	2.6	Brazle-StL	3.4	Branca-Bro	4.4

January 20 Famed Negro League slugger Josh Gibson dies of a brain tumor at age 35.

January 21 A rule change that restricts voting to players after 1921 produces four new Hall of Famers: Carl Hubbell, Frank Frisch, Mickey Cochrane, and Lefty Grove. Pie Traynor misses selection by two votes.

March 1 In anticipation of the signing of the first black players, Bill Veeck, a resident of Phoenix, had set up a spring training camp there for the Cleveland Indians. Arizona was chosen because of its relatively tolerant racial climate.

May 1 For the first time Cleveland will play all its games at Municipal Stadium, abandoning League Park, where the club played most weekday games. Bill Veeck installs an inner fence to cut power alleys from 435 to 365 feet.

June 13 The Boston Red Sox beat the Chicago White Sox, 5-3, before 34,510 "first nighters" in the first night game at Fenway Park.

July 5 Larry Doby of the Cleveland Indians becomes the first black to play in the AL. He strikes out as a pinch hitter, as the Chicago White Sox edge the Indians 6-5. Tomorrow he will go 1-for-5 in his first full game at first base.

July 8 Clutch pinch hits by Luke Appling and Stan Spence lead the AL to a 2–1 win over the NL in the All-Star Game at Wrigley Field. Lynwood "Schoolboy" Rowe pinch hits for Johnny Sain, becoming the first player to appear for each side. Rowe pitched three innings for the AL in 1936.

September 15 Even though they're rained out, the Yankees clinch the pennant when the Red Sox lose. New York is 90-53 at the time.

September 28 On the season's last day, the Browns, desperate to attract fans, bring announcer Dizzy Dean in to pitch against the White Sox. He gives up only three hits in four innings and laces a clean single in his only at bat, but a pulled leg muscle forces his retirement. The White Sox score all their runs in the ninth to win 5-2. Even with Diz, the game draws fewer than 16,000, and the Browns finish the year with only 320,000 attendance, less than half that of 1946.

September 29 Joe McCarthy, who led the Yankees to nine pennants, is coaxed out of retirement and signs to manage the Red Sox. Joe Cronin will become general manager of Tom Yawkey's team.

October 1 New York's Allie Reynolds spaces nine hits and coasts to a 10–3 victory to give the Yankees a two games-to-none lead in the World Series. Tommy Henrich's solo home run in the fifth puts the game away for the Yankees.

October 6 The New York Yankees beat the Brooklyn Dodgers 5-2 to win the World Series in seven games. Relief pitcher Hugh Casey of the Dodgers appears in six games, winning two while notching an 0.87 ERA. Series heroes Bevens, Gionfriddo, and Lavagetto will never play another major league game.

October 7 Larry MacPhail resigns as Yankees general manager moments after the final game of the Series. Co-owners Dan Topping and Del Webb then buy out MacPhail's one-third interest in the club for $2 million. George Weiss will become general manager.

October 20 Radio rights for the World Series sell for $475,000 for three years. Every franchise but Pittsburgh has sold 1948 TV rights. The Giants get $400,000 for radio-TV rights from Chesterfield.

November 27 Setting off a storm of controversy, Joe DiMaggio is named American League MVP by a single point over Ted Williams. Williams, the Triple Crown winner, receives 201 points, and is completely left off a Boston writer's ballot. Even a 10th-place vote would have given Williams the needed two points; however, Williams is selected *The Sporting News* Player of the Year.

BOSTON	CHICAGO	CLEVELAND	DETROIT	NEW YORK	PHILADELPHIA	ST.LOUIS	WASHINGTON
M J.Cronin	M T.Lyons	M L.Boudreau	M S.O'Neill	M B.Harris	M C.Mack	M M.Ruel	M O.Bluege
1B J.Jones	1B R.York	1B E.Robinson	1B R.Cullenbine	1B G.McQuinn	1B F.Fain	1B W.Judnich	1B M.Vernon
2B B.Doerr	2B D.Kolloway	2B J.Gordon	2B E.Mayo	2B S.Stirnweiss	2B P.Suder	2B J.Berardino	2B J.Priddy
SS J.Pesky	SS L.Appling	SS L.Boudreau	SS E.Lake	SS P.Rizzuto	SS E.Joost	SS V.Stephens	SS M.Christman
3B S.Dente	3B F.Baker	3B K.Keltner	3B G.Kell	3B B.Johnson	3B H.Majeski	3B B.Dillinger	3B E.Yost
LF T.Williams	LF T.Wright	LF D.Mitchell	LF D.Wakefield	LF J.Lindell	LF B.McCosky	LF J.Heath	LF J.Grace
CF D.DiMaggio	CF D.Philley	CF C.Metkovich	CF H.Evers	CF J.DiMaggio	CF S.Chapman	CF P.Lehner	CF S.Spence
RF S.Mele	RF B.Kennedy	RF H.Edwards	RF P.Mullin	RF T.Henrich	RF E.Valo	RF A.Zarilla	RF B.Lewis
C B.Tebbetts	C M.Tresh	C J.Hegan	C B.Swift	C A.Robinson	C B.Rosar	C L.Moss	C A.Evans
O W.Moses	23 C.Michaels	1 L.Fleming	O V.Wertz	CO Y.Berra	O1 G.Binks	O R.Coleman	O3 S.Robertson
3S E.Pellagrini	O T.Tucker	O H.Peck	O H.Wagner	O C.Keller	C M.Guerra	23 B.Hitchcock	3S C.Travis
1 R.York	1 G.Dickey	O P.Seerey	3S D.Cramer	3S B.Brown	C J.Handley	C J.Early	O T.McBride
C R.Partee	SO J.Wallaesa	C A.Lopez	O J.Outlaw	1 R.Houk	1 D.Adams	1 J.Witte	S J.Sullivan
23 D.Gutteridge	O R.Hodgin	3 E.Bockman	1 J.McHale	O A.Clark	O A.Knickerbocker	O H.Thompson	C F.Mancuso
O L.Culberson	1 J.Jones	/2 L.Doby	2 S.Webb	1 J.Phillips	O M.Rutner	O Wi.Brown	O R.Ferrell
3 M.Combs	C J.Stephenson	C H.Ruszkowski	C B.Tebbetts	/C S.Lollar	3 C.Laabs	2 R.Peters	O G.Case
C H.Wagner	/O L.Christopher	/O J.Frazier	O E.Mierkowicz	/O F.Colman	H D.Richmond	H J.Schultz	O G.Coan
3 R.Russell	H J.Kuhel	/3 A.Rosen	/C H.Riebe	/2 L.Frey	/S P.Cooper	/S G.McQuillen	/2 E.Lyons
/C M.Batts	P E.Lopat	/O T.Sepkowski	/O J.Groth	/2 J.Lucadello	/1 P.Currin		/O J.Wooten
/C E.McGah	P F.Papish	/C F.Mackiewicz	R B.Steiner	/C K.Silvestri	/C H.Franks		/O G.Myatt
/C F.Hayes	P J.Haynes	H H.Becker		/2 F.Crosetti	H R.Poole		/O F.Mackiewicz
/3 S.Shofner	P O.Grove	H J.Wasdell		R R.Mack	/2 N.Fox		/2 C.Ermer
/O B.Goodman	P B.Gillespie	P B.Feller	P H.Newhouser	R T.Sepkowski	H T.Kirk		P W.Masterson
/O T.McBride	RP E.Harrist	P D.Black	P F.Hutchinson	P A.Reynolds	P P.Marchildon	P J.Kramer	P E.Wynn
/C T.Aulds	RP P.Gebrian	P B.Lemon	P D.Trout	P S.Shea	P D.Fowler	P E.Kinder	P M.Haefner
P J.Dobson	RP G.Maltzberger	P R.Embree	P V.Trucks	P B.Bevens	RP B.McCahan	P F.Sanford	P R.Scarborough
P D.Ferriss	P T.Lee	P A.Gettel	RP H.White	P S.Chandler	P J.Coleman	P B.Muncrief	P S.Hudson
P T.Hughson	P E.Caldwell	RP B.Stephens	RP J.Gorsica	P B.Newsom	P J.Flores	P S.Zoldak	RP M.Candini
P D.Galehouse	/P R.Ruffing	RP E.Klieman	P A.Benton	RP J.Page	P R.Christopher	RP G.Moulder	RP T.Ferrick
P E.Johnson	P J.Rigney	RP S.Gromek	P A.Houtteman	RP R.Gumpert	P B.Savage	P C.Fannin	RP S.Cary
RP J.Murphy	P E.Smith	P M.Harder	/P R.Gentry	P V.Raschi	P C.Scheib	P N.Potter	P B.Newsom
RP B.Zuber	/P H.Bithorn	P L.Willis		P K.Drews	/P B.Dietrich	P Wa.Brown	P M.Pieretti
P H.Dorish		/P B.Kuzava		P D.Johnson	/P L.Brissie	/P D.Galehouse	/P L.Knerr
P M.Harris		/P R.Wolff		P B.Wensloff		/P H.Iott	/P B.Kennedy
P M.Parnell		/P C.Dorsett		/P D.Starr		/P B.Swartz	/P H.Toenes
P B.Klinger		/P E.Groth		/P A.Lyons		/P D.Dean	/P L.Harris
/P T.Fine		/P L.Linde		/P B.Wight			/P B.Dozier
/P E.Smith		/P G.Bearden		/P M.Queen			
/P C.Deal				/P T.Byrne			
/P C.Stobbs				/P R.Ardizoia			
/P B.Butland							
/P A.Widmar							

TEAM	G	W	L	PCT	GB	R	OR	AB	H	2B	3B	HR	BB	SO	AVG	OBP	SLG	PRO	PRO+	BR	/A	PF	CHI	RC	SB	CS	SBA	SBR
NY	155	97	57	.630		794	568	5308	1439	230	72	115	610	581	.271	.349	.407	.756	117	110	118	99	104	780	27	23	54	-6
DET	158	85	69	.552	12	714	642	5276	1363	234	42	103	762	565	.258	.353	.377	.730	106	77	55	103	96	735	52	60	46	-20
BOS	157	83	71	.539	14	720	669	5322	1412	206	54	103	666	590	.265	.349	.382	.731	102	71	17	107	98	734	41	35	54	-9
CLE	157	80	74	.519	17	687	588	5367	1392	234	51	112	502	609	.259	.324	.385	.709	106	9	27	97	105	687	29	25	54	-6
PHI	156	78	76	.506	19	633	614	5198	1311	218	52	61	605	563	.252	.333	.349	.682	94	-24	-36	102	102	635	37	33	53	-9
CHI	155	70	84	.455	27	553	661	5274	1350	211	41	53	492	527	.256	.321	.342	.663	93	-69	-48	96	98	584	91	57	61	-7
WAS	154	64	90	.416	33	496	675	5112	1234	186	48	42	525	534	.241	.313	.321	.634	84	-118	-105	97	99	523	53	51	51	-15
STL	154	59	95	.383	38	564	744	5145	1238	189	52	90	583	664	.241	.320	.350	.670	90	-55	-66	102	98	596	69	49	58	-9
TOT	623					5161		42002	10739	1708	412	679	4745	4633	.256	.333	.364	.698							399	333	55	-80

TEAM	CG	SH	SV	IP	H	H/G	HR	BB	SO	RAT	ERA	ERA+	OAV	OOB	PR	/A	PF	CPI	FA	E	DP	FW	PW	BW	SBW	DIF
NY	73	14	21	1374¹	1221	8.0	95	628	691	12.2	3.39	104	.238	.323	48	22	95	100	.981	109	151	1.5	2.3	12.2	.4	3.6
DET	77	15	18	1398²	1382	8.9	79	531	648	12.4	3.57	106	.258	.326	21	31	102	100	.975	155	142	-1.0	3.2	5.7	-1.0	1.1
BOS	64	13	19	1391	1383	8.9	84	575	586	12.8	3.81	102	.261	.335	-16	12	105	100	.977	137	172	-.0	1.2	1.8	.1	2.9
CLE	55	13	29	1402¹	1244	8.0	94	628	590	12.2	3.44	101	.240	.325	41	7	94	100	.983	104	178	1.9	.7	2.8	.4	-2.8
PHI	70	12	15	1391	1291	8.4	85	597	493	12.3	3.51	109	.247	.326	30	46	103	99	.976	143	161	-.4	4.8	-3.7	.1	.3
CHI	47	11	27	1391	1384	9.0	76	603	522	13.0	3.64	100	.261	.339	11	3	99	105	.975	155	180	-1.2	.3	-5.0	.3	-1.5
WAS	67	15	12	1362	1408	9.3	63	579	551	12.2	3.97	94	.267	.342	-40	-37	101	98	.976	143	151	-.5	-3.8	-10.9	-.5	2.7
STL	50	7	13	1365	1426	9.4	103	604	552	13.4	4.33	90	.272	.348	-94	-68	105	98	.977	134	169	.0	-7.0	-6.8	.1	-4.2
TOT	503	100	154	11076		8.7				12.7	3.71		.256	.333					.977	1080	1304					

Runs
Williams-Bos 125
Henrich-NY 109
Pesky-Bos 106
Stirnweiss-NY 102
DiMaggio-NY 97

Hits
Pesky-Bos 207
Kell-Det 188
Williams-Bos 181
McCosky-Phi 179

Doubles
Boudreau-Cle 45
Williams-Bos 40
Henrich-NY 35
DiMaggio-NY 31

Triples
Henrich-NY 13
Vernon-Was 12
Philley-Chi 11

Home Runs
Williams-Bos 32
Gordon-Cle 29
Heath-StL 27
Cullenbine-Det 24
York-Bos-Chi 21

Total Bases
Williams-Bos 335
Gordon-Cle 279
DiMaggio-NY 279
Henrich-NY 267
Pesky-Bos 250

Runs Batted In
Williams-Bos 114
Henrich-NY 98
DiMaggio-NY 97
Jones-Chi-Bos 96

Runs Produced
Williams-Bos 207
Henrich-NY 191
DiMaggio-NY 174
Kell-Det 163
Doerr-Bos 157

Bases On Balls
Williams-Bos 162
Cullenbine-Det ... 137
Lake-Det 120
Joost-Phi 114
Fain-Phi 95

Batting Average
Williams-Bos ...... .343
McCosky-Phi ...... .328
Pesky-Bos ...... .324
Wright-Chi ...... .324
Kell-Det ...... .320

On Base Percentage
Williams-Bos ...... .499
Fain-Phi ...... .414
Cullenbine-Det .... .401
McCosky-Phi .... .395
McQuinn-NY ...... .395

Slugging Average
Williams-Bos ...... .634
DiMaggio-NY ...... .522
Gordon-Cle ...... .496
Henrich-NY ...... .485
Heath-StL ...... .485

Production
Williams-Bos 1.133
DiMaggio-NY 913
Henrich-NY 857
Heath-StL 850
Gordon-Cle 842

Adjusted Production
Williams-Bos 199
DiMaggio-NY 154
Henrich-NY 139
Gordon-Cle 136
Heath-StL 133

Batter Runs
Williams-Bos 91.1
DiMaggio-NY 36.5
Henrich-NY 26.4
Fain-Phi 24.7
Cullenbine-Det ... 23.8

Adjusted Batter Runs
Williams-Bos 79.3
DiMaggio-NY 37.5
Henrich-NY 27.4
McQuinn-NY 24.2
Gordon-Cle 23.8

Clutch Hitting Index
B.Johnson-NY 140
Kell-Det 121
Jones-Chi-Bos 119
Joost-Phi 118
Majeski-Phi 115

Runs Created
Williams-Bos 186
DiMaggio-NY 112
Henrich-NY 104
Pesky-Bos 103
McQuinn-NY 97

Total Average
Williams-Bos 1.391
DiMaggio-NY 918
Cullenbine-Det 898
Heath-StL 856
Henrich-NY 849

Stolen Bases
Dillinger-StL 34
Philley-Chi 21
Vernon-Was 12
Pesky-Bos 12

Stolen Base Average
Dillinger-StL 72.3
Philley-Chi 56.8

Stolen Base Runs
Dillinger-StL 2.4
Valo-Phi 1.5
Binks-Phi 1.2

Fielding Runs
Doerr-Bos 23.8
DiMaggio-Bos 19.0
Baker-Chi 18.3
Kell-Det 17.9
Boudreau-Cle 16.7

Total Player Rating
Williams-Bos 7.2
Boudreau-Cle 4.8
Doerr-Bos 3.3
Cullenbine-Det ... 3.3
Gordon-Cle 3.1

Wins
Feller-Cle 20
Reynolds-NY 19
Marchildon-Phi 19
Hutchinson-Det 18
Dobson-Bos 18

Win Percentage
Reynolds-NY ..... .704
Dobson-Bos ...... .692
Marchildon-Phi ... .679
Feller-Cle ...... .645
Hutchinson-Det ... .643

Games
Klieman-Cle 58
Page-NY 56
Johnson-Bos 45
Savage-Phi 44
Christopher-Phi 44

Complete Games
Newhouser-Det ... 24
Wynn-Was 22
Lopat-Chi 22
Marchildon-Phi ... 21
Feller-Cle 20

Shutouts
Feller-Cle 5
Reynolds-NY 4
Masterson-Was 4
Haefner-Was 4

Saves
Page-NY 17
Klieman-Cle 17
Christopher-Phi ... 12
Ferrick-Was 9

Innings Pitched
Feller-Cle 299.0
Newhouser-Det ... 285.0
Marchildon-Phi ... 276.2
Masterson-Was ... 253.0
Lopat-Chi 252.2

Fewest Hits/Game
Shea-NY 6.40
Feller-Cle 6.92
Marchildon-Phi ... 7.42
Embree-Cle 7.58
Masterson-Was ... 7.65

Fewest BB/Game
Galehouse-StL-Bos....
...... 2.48
Hutchinson-Det ... 2.50
Lopat-Chi 2.60
Muncrief-StL 2.60
Dobson-Bos 2.87

Strikeouts
Feller-Cle 196
Newhouser-Det ... 176
Masterson-Was ... 135
Reynolds-NY 129
Marchildon-Phi ... 128

Strikeouts/Game
Feller-Cle 5.90
Hughson-Bos 5.66
Newhouser-Det ... 5.56
Trucks-Det 5.38
Kinder-StL 5.09

Ratio
Feller-Cle 10.87
Dobson-Bos 10.90
Shea-NY 11.08
Masterson-Was ... 11.17
Hutchinson-Det ... 11.23

Earned Run Average
Haynes-Chi 2.42
Chandler-NY 2.46
Feller-Cle 2.68
Fowler-Phi 2.81
Lopat-Chi 2.81

Adjusted ERA
Haynes-Chi 151
Fowler-Phi 136
Dobson-Bos 132
Newhouser-Det ... 131
Feller-Cle 130

Opponents' Batting Avg.
Shea-NY ...... .200
Feller-Cle ...... .215
Marchildon-Phi ... .224
Reynolds-NY ..... .227
Embree-Cle ...... .233

Opponents' On Base Pct.
Dobson-Bos ...... .299
Feller-Cle ...... .300
Shea-NY ...... .303
Hutchinson-Det ... .304
Lopat-Chi ...... .307

Starter Runs
Feller-Cle 34.1
Newhouser-Det ... 26.3
Haynes-Chi 25.9
Lopat-Chi 25.0
Fowler-Phi 22.6

Adjusted Starter Runs
Newhouser-Det ... 28.3
Feller-Cle 26.7
Fowler-Phi 25.3
Haynes-Chi 24.9
Dobson-Bos 23.8

Clutch Pitching Index
Haynes-Chi 124
Fowler-Phi 119
Lopat-Chi 116
Ferriss-Bos 114
Newsom-Was-NY . 112

Relief Runs
Page-NY 19.2
Christopher-Phi ... 7.2
Klieman-Cle 6.9
Murphy-Bos 5.5
Ferrick-Was 3.7

Adjusted Relief Runs
Page-NY 16.5
Christopher-Phi ... 8.2
Murphy-Bos 6.6
Klieman-Cle 4.6
Ferrick-Was 3.8

Relief Ranking
Page-NY 27.6
Christopher-Phi ... 18.2
Klieman-Cle 6.0
Ferrick-Was 5.9
Maltzberger-Chi 1.6

Total Pitcher Index
Newhouser-Det ... 3.9
Hutchinson-Det ... 3.7
Feller-Cle 3.1
Page-NY 3.0
Haynes-Chi 2.9

Total Baseball Ranking
Williams-Bos 7.2
Boudreau-Cle 4.8
Newhouser-Det ... 3.9
Hutchinson-Det ... 3.7
Doerr-Bos 3.3

February 27 Herb Pennock and Pie Traynor are elected to the Hall of Fame. With 91 votes needed for selection, Pennock, who died a month before, gets 94, Traynor 93.

April 21 Leo Durocher, back at the helm of the Dodgers after a one-year suspension, uses 24 men in one game, a 9–5 loss to the Giants.

May 8 An infield single by Johnny Blatnik of the Phillies in the seventh prevents a perfect game by Harry Brecheen of the Cardinals. The Cards win, 5–0. Brecheen will become the NL ERA leader with 2.24 and the winning percentage leader on a 20-7 record.

June 18 The Pirates spoil Robin Roberts' debut, beating the Phils' rookie 2-0. Roberts was called up after a 9-1 start at Wilmington (Interstate League).

July 1 Brooklyn's Roy Campanella makes his debut, catching Ralph Branca. Campy doubles in his first at-bat and adds two singles, but the Giants win 6-4.

July 16 There are three managerial changes in one day. The Giants remove Mel Ott and replace him with Leo Durocher, who obtains his release from Brooklyn. The Dodgers bring back Burt Shotton, and Eddie Sawyer replaces Ben Chapman with the Phillies.

July 26 Leo Durocher makes his first appearance at Ebbets Field since taking over the Giants, and a turnaway crowd delights in the Dodgers' 13–4 win.

September 23 The Braves clinch the NL flag by defeating the Giants 3-2. Two days before the season is over they lose their best hitter, outfielder Jeff Heath, who breaks an ankle sliding home against Brooklyn.

October 3* Luke Easter's grand slam highlights the Homestead Grays' 19-hit assault on the Birmingham Black Barons in the fourth game of the final Negro League World Series; the Negro National League becomes a casualty of integration and folds during the winter.

October 6 In the World Series opener in Boston, Phil Masi is called safe at second base on a disputed call by umpire Bill Stewart on a pickoff attempt in the eighth. Masi then scores on a single by Tommy Holmes as Johnny Sain and the Boston Braves top the Cleveland Indians and Bob Feller, 1-0.

October 10 A six-run seventh inning knocks out Cleveland starter Bob Feller and two successors for the Braves' 11–5 victory to cut the World Series deficit to three games to two. Bob Elliott has two home runs. The World Series crowd is even larger than the day before, 86,288, and won't be exceeded until Game 3 in the Los Angeles Coliseum in the 1959 World Series (92,394).

October 11 In Boston, the Cleveland Indians nip the Braves 4-3 to take the World Series in six games. Rookie lefty Gene Bearden is the pitching hero in relief.

December 2 Stan Musial is picked MVP in the NL. Musial led the league in batting at .365, runs (135), RBI (131), and in doubles and triples. His 39 home runs were one short of Mize and Kiner.

	BOSTON		BROOKLYN		CHICAGO		CINCINNATI		NEW YORK		PHILADELPHIA		PITTSBURGH		ST.LOUIS
M	B.Southworth	M	L.Durocher	M	C.Grimm	M	J.Neun	M	M.Ott	M	B.Chapman	M	B.Meyer	M	E.Dyer
1B	E.Torgeson	M	R.Blades	1B	E.Waitkus	M	B.Walters	M	L.Durocher	M	D.Cooke	1B	E.Stevens	1B	N.Jones
2B	E.Stanky	M	B.Shotton	2B	H.Schenz	1B	T.Kluszewski	M	J.Mize	2B	E.Sawyer	2B	D.Murtaugh	2B	R.Schoendienst
SS	A.Dark	1B	G.Hodges	SS	R.Smalley	2B	B.Adams	2B	B.Rigney	1B	D.Sisler	SS	S.Rojek	SS	M.Marion
3B	B.Elliott	2B	J.Robinson	3B	A.Pafko	SS	V.Stallcup	SS	B.Kerr	2B	G.Hamner	3B	F.Gustine	3B	D.Lang
LF	J.Heath	SS	P.Reese	LF	P.Lowrey	3B	G.Hatton	3B	S.Gordon	SS	E.Miller	LF	R.Kiner	LF	E.Slaughter
CF	J.Russell	3B	B.Cox	CF	H.Jeffcoat	LF	H.Sauer	LF	B.Thomson	3B	P.Caballero	CF	W.Westlake	CF	T.Moore
RF	T.Holmes	LF	M.Rackley	RF	B.Nicholson	CF	J.Wyrostek	CF	W.Lockman	LF	J.Blatnik	RF	D.Walker	RF	S.Musial
C	P.Masi	CF	C.Furillo	C	B.Scheffing	RF	F.Baumholtz	RF	W.Marshall	CF	R.Ashburn	C	E.Fitz Gerald	C	D.Rice
		RF	G.Hermanski				R.Lamanno		W.Cooper	RF	D.Ennis				
O	M.McCormick	C	R.Campanella	1O	P.Cavarretta					C	A.Seminick	O1	J.Hopp	O2	E.Dusak
O	C.Conatser			2	E.Verban	O3	D.Litwhiler	32	J.Lohrke			C	C.Kluttz	O	R.Northey
2S	S.Sisti	CO	B.Edwards	C	C.Maddern	23	C.Corbitt	C	W.Westrum	31	B.Haas	3	E.Bockman	2S	R.LaPointe
C	B.Salkeld	23	E.Miksis	C	C.McCullough	2	B.Zientara	C	M.Livingston	O	H.Walker	1O	M.West	3	W.Kurowski
1	F.McCormick	O	D.Whitman	C	R.Walker	1	B.Young	O	L.Layton	3O	H.Rowell	O	T.Beard	C	B.Baker
2	C.Ryan	O	G.Shuba	2S	G.Mauch	C	D.Williams	O	D.Mueller	2	E.Verban	2	M.Basgall	1	Ba.Young
2	B.Sturgeon	O	D.Snider	S	D.Culler	O	A.Galan	/1	J.McCarthy	C	D.Padgett	C	J.Riddle	C	D.Wilber
/O	D.Litwhiler	1	P.Ward	/O	C.Aberson	1	H.Schultz	C	L.Frey	C	A.Lakeman	/S	G.Wilson	C	J.Garagiola
/O	M.Rickert	3	T.Brown	/S	J.Cross	C	R.Mueller	2	J.Conway	3	W.Jones	/S	P.Castiglione	/O	H.Rice
/C	P.Burris	O	P.Reiser	/2	D.Johnson	/O	S.Filipowicz	S	B.Rhawn	O	J.Mayo	H	D.Gutteridge	/3	E.Kazak
H	R.Sanders	O	A.Vaughan	/2	D.Lynch	/O	C.Vollmer	S	S.Yvars	/C	S.Lopata	/C	E.Turner	/O	J.Medwick
		3	S.Jorgensen	/O	C.Mauro	H	M.Rickert	/O	P.Milne	/1	H.Schultz			/O	C.Diering
P	J.Sain	O	D.Lund	H	C.Sawatski	H	H.Poland	/2	B.Blattner	/C	H.Wagner	P	B.Chesnes	/C	J.Bucha
P	W.Spahn	/2	G.Mauch					/O	H.Bamberger			P	E.Riddle	H	L.Miggins
P	B.Voiselle	/C	B.Bragan	P	J.Schmitz	P	J.Vander Meer	/1	J.Harshman	P	D.Leonard	P	V.Lombardi	/3	Bo.Young
P	V.Bickford	/3	B.Ramazzotti	P	R.Meyer	P	K.Raffensberger	H	J.Lafata	P	C.Simmons	P	T.Bonham	R	J.Cross
P	R.Barrett			P	D.McCall	P	H.Fox			P	M.Dubiel	P	F.Ostermueller		
RP	B.Hogue	P	R.Barney	P	B.Rush	P	H.Wehmeier	P	L.Jansen	P	S.Rowe	RP	K.Higbe	P	M.Dickson
RP	C.Shoun	P	R.Branca	P	H.Borowy	P	E.Blackwell	P	S.Jones	P	R.Roberts	RP	E.Singleton	P	H.Brecheen
		P	J.Hatten	RP	J.Dobernic	RP	H.Gumbert	RP	R.Poat	RP	E.Heusser	RP	M.Queen	P	H.Pollet
P	N.Potter	P	P.Roe	RP	E.Kush	RP	W.Cress	P	C.Hartung	P	S.Nahem			P	R.Munger
P	E.White	P	E.Palica	RP	B.Chipman			P	D.Koslo			P	R.Sewell	P	A.Brazle
P	J.Prendergast	RP	H.Behrman			P	K.Peterson	RP	A.Hansen	P	B.Donnelly	P	H.Gregg	RP	T.Wilks
/P	J.Beazley	RP	P.Minner	P	R.Hamner	RP	K.Burkhart	RP	K.Trinkle	P	K.Heintzelman	P	W.Main	RP	J.Hearn
/P	A.Lyons	RP	W.Ramsdell	P	C.Chambers	/P	B.Walters			P	C.Bicknell	/P	C.McLish	RP	G.Staley
/P	E.Wright			P	D.Lade	P	J.Blackburn	P	M.Kennedy	P	P.Erickson	/P	N.Strincevich		
/P	J.Antonelli	P	H.Taylor	/P	P.Erickson	P	T.Hughes	P	A.Konikowski	/P	N.Strincevich	/P	J.Walsh	P	K.Johnson
/P	G.Elliott	P	C.Erskine	/P	B.Wade	P	B.Lively	P	T.Lee	P	L.Possehl			P	K.Burkhart
/P	R.Martin	/P	H.Casey	/P	W.Hacker	/P	J.Hetki	/P	R.Webb	/P	O.Judd			P	A.Papai
		/P	C.King	/P	T.Jacobs	/P	E.Erautt	/P	B.Newsom	/P	J.Thompson			P	C.Beers
		/P	L.Sloat	/P	D.Carlsen	/P	K.Holcombe	/P	C.Dreisewerd	/P	J.Konstanty			/P	R.Yochim
		/P	J.Van Cuyk					/P	L.Lombardo	/P	D.Koecher				
		/P	J.Hall					/P	J.Hallett	/P	L.Grasmick				
		/P	J.Banta					/P	M.McGowan	/P	A.Porto				
		/P	P.Haugstad					/P	H.Andrews						
		/P	E.Sexauer					/P	P.Erickson						
								/P	J.Beggs						

TEAM	G	W	L	PCT	GB	R	OR	AB	H	2B	3B	HR	BB	SO	AVG	OBP	SLG	PRO	PRO+	BR	/A	PF	CHI	RC	SB	CS	SBA	SBR
BOS	154	91	62	.595		739	584	5297	1458	272	49	95	671	536	.275	.359	.399	.758	114	95	109	98	92	784	43			
STL	155	85	69	.552	6.5	742	646	5302	1396	238	58	105	594	521	.263	.340	.389	.729	98	31	-10	106	103	713	24			
BRO	155	84	70	.545	7.5	744	667	5328	1393	256	54	91	601	684	.261	.338	.381	.719	98	13	-11	103	105	709	114			
PIT	156	83	71	.539	8.5	706	699	5286	1388	191	54	108	580	578	.263	.338	.380	.718	99	10	-4	102	101	698	68			
NY	155	78	76	.506	13.5	780	704	5277	1352	210	49	164	599	648	.256	.334	.408	.742	106	46	42	101	106	731	51			
PHI	155	66	88	.429	25.5	591	729	5287	1367	227	39	91	440	598	.259	.318	.368	.686	94	-63	-52	98	97	625	68			
CIN	153	64	89	.418	27	588	752	5127	1266	221	37	104	478	586	.247	.313	.365	.678	92	-76	-56	97	101	587	42			
CHI	155	64	90	.416	27.5	597	706	5352	1402	225	44	87	443	578	.262	.322	.369	.691	97	-52	-27	96	95	641	39			
TOT	619					5487		42256	11022	1840	384	845	4406	4729	.261	.333	.383	.715							449			

TEAM	CG	SH	SV	IP	H	H/G	HR	BB	SO	RAT	ERA	ERA+	OAV	OOB	PR	/A	PF	CPI	FA	E	DP	FW	PW	BW	SBW	DIF
BOS	70	10	17	1389[1]	1354	8.8	93	430	579	11.6	3.37	114	.249	.306	89	71	97	96	.976	143	132	.7	7.1	10.9		-4.2
STL	60	13	18	1368	1392	9.2	103	476	625	12.4	3.91	105	.262	.324	7	28	103	97	.980	119	138	2.1	2.8	-1.0		4.1
BRO	52	9	22	1392[2]	1328	8.6	119	633	670	12.9	3.75	106	.253	.337	31	37	101	107	.973	161	151	-.2	3.7	-1.1		4.6
PIT	65	5	19	1371[2]	1373	9.0	120	564	543	12.9	4.15	98	.261	.335	-29	-12	103	98	.977	137	150	1.2	-1.2	-.4		6.4
NY	54	15	21	1373	1425	9.3	122	556	527	13.2	3.93	100	.269	.342	4	0	100	109	.974	156	134	.1	.0	4.2		-3.3
PHI	61	6	15	1362[1]	1385	9.1	95	556	550	13.0	4.08	97	.262	.335	-18	-20	100	97	.964	210	126	-2.8	-2.0	-5.2		-1.0
CIN	40	8	20	1343[1]	1410	9.4	104	572	599	13.4	4.47	87	.274	.344	-77	-85	99	95	.973	158	135	-.1	-8.5	-5.6		1.7
CHI	51	7	10	1355[1]	1355	9.0	89	619	636	13.2	4.00	97	.261	.342	-7	-15	99	101	.972	172	152	-.7	-1.5	-2.7		-8.1
TOT	453	73	142	10955[2]		9.1				12.8	3.95		.261	.333					.974	1256	1118					

Runs		Hits		Doubles		Triples		Home Runs		Total Bases	
Musial-StL	135	Musial-StL	230	Musial-StL	46	Musial-StL	18	Mize-NY	40	Musial-StL	429
Lockman-NY	117	Holmes-Bos	190	Ennis-Phi	40	Hopp-Pit	12	Kiner-Pit	40	Mize-NY	316
Mize-NY	110	Rojek-Pit	186	Dark-Bos	39	Slaughter-StL	11	Musial-StL	39	Ennis-Phi	309
Robinson-Bro	108	Slaughter-StL	176	Robinson-Bro	38	Waitkus-Chi	10	Sauer-Cin	35	Kiner-Pit	296
Kiner-Pit	104	Dark-Bos	175	Holmes-Bos	35	Lockman-NY	10			Pafko-Chi	283

Runs Batted In		Runs Produced		Bases On Balls		Batting Average		On Base Percentage		Slugging Average	
Musial-StL	131	Musial-StL	227	B.Elliott-Bos	131	Musial-StL	.376	Musial-StL	.450	Musial-StL	.702
Mize-NY	125	Mize-NY	195	Kiner-Pit	112	Ashburn-Phi	.333	B.Elliott-Bos	.423	Mize-NY	.564
Kiner-Pit	123	Kiner-Pit	187	Mize-NY	94	Holmes-Bos	.325	Ashburn-Phi	.410	Gordon-NY	.537
Gordon-NY	107	Robinson-Bro	181			Dark-Bos	.322	Slaughter-StL	.409	Kiner-Pit	.533
Pafko-Chi	101	Gordon-NY	177			Slaughter-StL	.321	Mize-NY	.395	Ennis-Phi	.525

Production		Adjusted Production		Batter Runs		Adjusted Batter Runs		Clutch Hitting Index		Runs Created	
Musial-StL	1.152	Musial-StL	196	Musial-StL	90.2	Musial-StL	80.8	Murtaugh-Pit	135	Musial-StL	191
Mize-NY	.959	Mize-NY	156	Mize-NY	44.6	Mize-NY	43.9	Jones-StL	129	Mize-NY	131
Gordon-NY	.927	Gordon-NY	148	Kiner-Pit	38.5	B.Elliott-Bos	39.8	Stallcup-Cin	128	Kiner-Pit	120
Kiner-Pit	.924	Kiner-Pit	145	B.Elliott-Bos	37.8	Kiner-Pit	36.2	Lowrey-Chi	123	B.Elliott-Bos	117
B.Elliott-Bos	.897	B.Elliott-Bos	145	Gordon-NY	35.1	Gordon-NY	34.4	Torgeson-Bos	118	Slaughter-StL	110

Total Average		Stolen Bases		Stolen Base Average		Stolen Base Runs		Fielding Runs		Total Player Rating	
Musial-StL	1.298	Ashburn-Phi	32					Ashburn-Phi	17.8	Musial-StL	6.3
Mize-NY	1.032	Reese-Bro	25					Pafko-Chi	12.8	Mize-NY	4.6
B.Elliott-Bos	.980	Rojek-Pit	24					Reese-Bro	10.3	Pafko-Chi	4.3
Kiner-Pit	.974	Robinson-Bro	22					Marion-StL	9.4	Kiner-Pit	3.4
Gordon-NY	.953	Torgeson-Bos	19					Gustine-Pit	9.0	B.Elliott-Bos	2.8

Wins		Win Percentage		Games		Complete Games		Shutouts		Saves	
Sain-Bos	24	Brecheen-StL	.741	Gumbert-Cin	61	Sain-Bos	28	Brecheen-StL	7	Gumbert-Cin	17
Brecheen-StL	20	Jones-NY	.667	Wilks-StL	57	Brecheen-StL	21	Sain-Bos	4	Wilks-StL	13
Schmitz-Chi	18	Sain-Bos	.615	Higbe-Pit	56	Schmitz-Chi	18	Raffensberger-Cin	4	Higbe-Pit	10
Jansen-NY	18	Jansen-NY	.600	Jones-NY	55	Spahn-Bos	16	Jansen-NY	4	Trinkle-NY	7
VanderMeer-Cin	17	Schmitz-Chi	.581	Dobernic-Chi	54	Leonard-Phi	16	Barney-Bro	4	Behrman-Bro	7

Innings Pitched		Fewest Hits/Game		Fewest BB/Game		Strikeouts		Strikeouts/Game		Ratio	
Sain-Bos	314.2	Schmitz-Chi	6.92	Roe-Bro	1.67	Brecheen-StL	149	Brecheen-StL	5.75	Brecheen-StL	9.41
Jansen-NY	277.0	Barney-Bro	7.04	Jansen-NY	1.75	Barney-Bro	138	Branca-Bro	5.09	Roe-Bro	9.68
Spahn-Bos	257.0	Brecheen-StL	7.44	Raffensberger-Cin	1.85	Sain-Bos	137	Barney-Bro	5.04	Schmitz-Chi	10.60
Dickson-StL	252.1	Branca-Bro	7.89	Brecheen-StL	1.89	Jansen-NY	126	Higbe-Pit	4.90	Sain-Bos	11.01
Barney-Bro	246.2	Roe-Bro	7.90	Leonard-Phi	2.15	Branca-Bro	122	Meyer-Chi	4.86	Spahn-Bos	11.03

Earned Run Average		Adjusted ERA		Opponents' Batting Avg.		Opponents' On Base Pct.		Starter Runs		Adjusted Starter Runs	
Brecheen-StL	2.24	Brecheen-StL	183	Schmitz-Chi	.215	Brecheen-StL	.265	Sain-Bos	47.3	Brecheen-StL	48.0
Leonard-Phi	2.51	Leonard-Phi	157	Barney-Bro	.217	Roe-Bro	.271	Brecheen-StL	44.5	Sain-Bos	43.0
Sain-Bos	2.60	Roe-Bro	152	Brecheen-StL	.222	Schmitz-Chi	.295	Leonard-Phi	36.2	Leonard-Phi	35.9
Roe-Bro	2.63	Schmitz-Chi	148	Branca-Bro	.232	Sain-Bos	.296	Schmitz-Chi	35.3	Schmitz-Chi	34.0
Schmitz-Chi	2.64	Sain-Bos	147	Roe-Bro	.233	Raffensberger-Cin	.296	Roe-Bro	26.1	Roe-Bro	26.8

Clutch Pitching Index		Relief Runs		Adjusted Relief Runs		Relief Ranking		Total Pitcher Index		Total Baseball Ranking	
Leonard-Phi	134	Wilks-StL	19.4	Wilks-StL	21.4	Wilks-StL	22.4	Brecheen-StL	5.5	Musial-StL	6.3
Jones-NY	126	Hansen-NY	10.9	Higbe-Pit	12.4	Higbe-Pit	12.4	Sain-Bos	5.3	Brecheen-StL	5.5
Hatten-Bro	124	Minner-Bro	10.5	Minner-Bro	10.8	Minner-Bro	11.3	Schmitz-Chi	4.6	Sain-Bos	5.3
Voiselle-Bos	120	Higbe-Pit	10.4	Hansen-NY	10.7	Gumbert-Cin	9.7	Leonard-Phi	4.6	Schmitz-Chi	4.6
Sain-Bos	115	Dobernic-Chi	7.6	Dobernic-Chi	7.2	Trinkle-NY	8.1	Roe-Bro	2.6	Leonard-Phi	4.6

April 16 The White Sox beat the Cubs 4-1 at Wrigley Field with Jack Brickhouse at the WGN-TV mike, the first telecast in Chicago history.

May 20 In a 13-4 Cleveland win, the Indians collect 18 bases on balls in a game with the Red Sox to tie the AL record.

May 27 Recently retired slugger Hank Greenberg buys an interest in the Cleveland club, becoming the Indians' second-largest stockholder.

June 13 The Yankees retire Babe Ruth's No. 3 in the Babe's final appearance at Yankee Stadium. After the ceremonies the Yankees beat the Indians, 5-3.

June 15 The Detroit Tigers beat the Philadelphia Athletics 4-1 before a crowd of 54,480 in the first night game at Briggs Stadium. The Tigers are the last AL team to install lights.

June 20 Cleveland draws 82,781 for a doubleheader, a major league record for a regular season game that will be broken by the same club in 1954. The Indians will attract 2.6 million for the season, surpassing the Yankees' record attendance of a yeaar earlier.

July 4 Ted Williams of the Red Sox faces three pitchers in the seventh inning, a first in league history as Boston scores 14 runs and beats the Philadelphia Athletics, 20-8. The 14 runs in one inning is also a record.

July 7 The Indians sign Satchel Paige, fabulous veteran Negro League pitcher. Although his signing is ridiculed as a Bill Veeck publicity stunt, the 42-year-old Paige will finish at 6-1.

July 18 Pat Seerey, chunky Sox outfielder, hits four home runs, his last in the 11th inning, to lead the Chicago White Sox to a 12-11 victory over the Athletics in Philadelphia. Seerey is the fifth major league player to accomplish the feat.

July 26 Babe Ruth makes his last public appearance, at the New York premiere of the film "The Babe Ruth Story." He will die three weeks later.

August 13 The promise of Paige on the mound brings 51,013 to Comiskey Park to see "Ol' Satch" pitch; he throws his first major league shutout as Cleveland wins 5-0.

August 16 Babe Ruth dies of throat cancer at age 53 in New York.

August 17 Tom Henrich hits his fourth grand slam of the season, off the Senators' Sid Hudson, to tie Ruth, Gehrig, and Rudy York for the AL record.

August 21 Aaron Robinson homers in the ninth off Bob Lemon to help the White Sox beat the Indians 3-2. The run breaks the 47-inning scoreless streak by Indians pitchers. Satchel Paige, Gene Bearden, Sam Zoldak, and Bob Lemon had shutouts during the streak.

September 22 Stan Musial collects his fifth hit in a game for the fifth time in one season, tying Ty Cobb's all-time record. Musial hits a home run, a double, and three singles against the Boston Braves.

September 24 The Yankees whip the Red Sox 9-6 while Cleveland loses at Detroit, 4-3. New York, Boston and Cleveland are now tied for first place in the AL with identical 91-56 records.

October 4 In a one-game playoff for the AL pennant at Fenway Park, the Cleveland Indians beat the Boston Red Sox 8-3 behind rookie knuckleballer Gene Bearden, who wins his 20th game.

November 30 Player-manager Lou Boudreau is selected the league MVP. Boudreau had almost been traded to the Browns earlier in the year, but protests by fans kept Lou in Cleveland. After the World Series win, owner Bill Veeck commented, "Sometimes the best trades are the ones you never make."

BOSTON	CHICAGO	CLEVELAND	DETROIT	NEW YORK	PHILADELPHIA	ST.LOUIS	WASHINGTON
M J.McCarthy	M T.Lyons	M L.Boudreau	M S.O'Neill	M B.Harris	M C.Mack	M Z.Taylor	M J.Kuhel
1B B.Goodman	1B T.Lupien	1B E.Robinson	1B G.Vico	1B G.McQuinn	1B F.Fain	1B C.Stevens	1B M.Vernon
2B B.Doerr	2B D.Kolloway	2B J.Gordon	2B E.Mayo	2B S.Stirnweiss	2B P.Suder	2B J.Priddy	2B A.Kozar
SS V.Stephens	SS C.Michaels	SS L.Boudreau	SS J.Lipon	SS P.Rizzuto	SS E.Joost	SS E.Pellagrini	SS M.Christman
3B J.Pesky	3B L.Appling	3B K.Keltner	3B G.Kell	3B B.Johnson	3B H.Majeski	3B B.Dillinger	3B E.Yost
LF T.Williams	LF P.Seerey	LF D.Mitchell	LF V.Wertz	LF J.Lindell	LF B.McCosky	LF W.Platt	LF G.Coan
CF D.DiMaggio	CF D.Philley	CF T.Tucker	CF H.Evers	CF J.DiMaggio	CF S.Chapman	CF P.Lehner	CF J.Wooten
RF S.Spence	RF T.Wright	RF L.Doby	RF P.Mullin	RF T.Henrich	RF E.Valo	RF A.Zarilla	RF B.Stewart
C B.Tebbetts	C A.Robinson	C J.Hegan	C B.Swift	C G.Niarhos	C B.Rosar	C L.Moss	C J.Early
O W.Moses	32 F.Baker	O A.Clark	O D.Wakefield	CO Y.Berra	O3 D.White	S S.Dente	C A.Evans
O S.Mele	O R.Hodgin	O1 W.Judnich	S2 N.Berry	3S B.Brown	O R.Coleman	O D.Kokos	O C.Gillenwater
23 B.Hitchcock	O R.Weigel	O H.Edwards	23 E.Lake	O C.Keller	1 M.Guerra	1 H.Arft	O T.McBride
C M.Batts	O B.Kennedy	21 J.Berardino	3O J.Outlaw	1 S.Souchock	C H.Franks	C R.Partee	O S.Robertson
1 J.Jones	C M.Tresh	C J.Tipton	C H.Wagner	O C.Mapes	/2 S.Webb	O D.Lund	S J.Sullivan
/2 L.Stringer	O J.Delsing	O Bo.Kennedy	1 P.Campbell	O H.Bauer	1 R.York	O P.Laydon	C S.Okrie
/C B.Martin	/S J.Wallaesa	/O H.Peck	C H.Riebe	O S.Lollar	O G.Binks	2S A.Anderson	S S.Meeks
H T.Wright	/O H.Adams	/P P.Seerey	C J.Ginsberg	C R.Houk	/S B.DeMars	H J.Schultz	O L.Culberson
H J.Ostrowski	/O J.Scala	O R.Boone	/O J.Groth	/2 F.Crosetti	/2 N.Fox	/O R.Coleman	/S A.Fleitas
H N.Sheridan	/S F.Whitman	/3 A.Rosen	/2 J.Bero	/C C.Silvera	/1 B.Wellman	/O K.Wood	/S J.Clark
		H R.Murray	/O E.Mierkowicz	H J.Collins	/C E.Brucker	/O G.Binks	/O L.Drake
			/O D.Cramer	H B.Stewart		/1 J.McCarthy	/O C.Vollmer
P J.Dobson	P B.Wight	P B.Lemon	H J.McHale	/1 J.Phillips	P P.Marchildon	H T.Jordan	H J.Difani
P M.Parnell	P J.Haynes	P B.Feller	P H.Newhouser	R L.Frey	P J.Coleman	P F.Sanford	P E.Wynn
P J.Kramer	P A.Gettel	P G.Bearden	P F.Hutchinson	P A.Reynolds	P D.Fowler	P C.Fannin	P W.Masterson
P E.Kinder	P M.Pieretti	P S.Gromek	P V.Trucks	P E.Lopat	P C.Scheib	P N.Garver	P R.Scarborough
P D.Galehouse	P R.Gumpert	P S.Zoldak	P D.Trout	P V.Raschi	P L.Brissie	P B.Kennedy	S S.Hudson
RP E.Johnson	RP H.Judson	RP E.Klieman	P A.Houtteman	P S.Shea	RP B.Harris	RP B.Stephens	P M.Haefner
RP F.Papish	RP F.Papish	RP R.Christopher	RP S.Overmire	P T.Byrne	P B.Savage	RP F.Biscan	P F.Thompson
P D.Ferriss	RP O.Grove	RP D.Black	RP B.Pierce	RP J.Page	RP B.McCahan	RP A.Widmar	RP M.Candini
P M.Harris	P G.Moulder	P S.Paige	P T.Gray	RP F.Hiller	P A.Kellner	P J.Ostrowski	RP T.Ferrick
/P M.McDermott	P B.Gillespie	P B.Muncrief	P A.Benton		/P N.Potter	P S.Zoldak	/P D.Welteroth
P T.Hughson	P I.Pearson	/P Bi.Kennedy	P H.White		/P W.Holborow	P K.Drews	/P E.Harrist
/P H.Dorish	P E.Caldwell	/P L.Linde	/P L.Kretlow		/P B.Dietrich	P R.Shore	/P D.Weik
/P E.Caldwell	P E.Harrist	/P A.Gettel	P R.Gentry			P B.Schwamb	/P M.Pieretti
/P C.Stobbs	P M.Rotblatt	/P M.Garcia				P A.Gerheauser	/P R.Garcia
/P C.Deal	/P F.Bradley	/P B.Wensloff				P C.Dreisewerd	/P C.Cooper
/P M.Palm	/P J.Goodwin	/P E.Groth				/P N.Potter	
/P W.McCall		/P L.Webber				/P J.Wilson	

TEAM	G	W	L	PCT	GB	R	OR	AB	H	2B	3B	HR	BB	SO	AVG	OBP	SLG	PRO	PRO+	BR	/A	PF	CHI	RC	SB	CS	SBA	SBR
CLE	156	97	58	.626		840	568	5446	1534	242	54	155	646	575	.282	.360	.431	.791	119	112	134	97	97	868	54	44	55	-10
BOS	155	96	59	.619	1	907	720	5363	1471	277	40	121	823	552	.274	.374	.409	.783	109	116	72	105	104	869	38	17	69	1
NY	154	94	60	.610	2.5	857	633	5324	1480	251	75	139	623	478	.278	.356	.432	.788	116	99	107	99	103	838	24	24	50	-7
PHI	154	84	70	.545	12.5	729	735	5181	1345	231	47	68	726	523	.260	.353	.362	.715	96	-20	-21	100	102	699	40	32	56	-7
DET	154	78	76	.506	18.5	700	726	5235	1396	219	58	78	671	504	.267	.353	.375	.728	96	0	-20	103	95	723	22	32	41	-13
STL	155	59	94	.386	37	671	849	5303	1438	251	62	63	578	572	.271	.345	.378	.723	96	-21	-39	103	95	711	63	44	59	-8
WAS	154	56	97	.366	40	578	796	5111	1245	203	75	31	568	572	.244	.322	.331	.653	81	-151	-135	97	105	566	76	48	61	-6
CHI	154	51	101	.336	44.5	559	814	5192	1303	172	39	55	595	528	.251	.329	.331	.660	84	-134	-115	97	97	588	46	47	49	-14
TOT	618					5841		42155	11212	1846	450	710	5230	4304	.266	.349	.382	.731							363	288	56	-64

TEAM	CG	SH	SV	IP	H	H/G	HR	BB	SO	RAT	ERA	ERA+	OAV	OOB	PR	/A	PF	CPI	FA	E	DP	FW	PW	BW	SBW	DIF
CLE	66	26	30	1409¹	1246	8.0	82	625	593	12.1	3.22	126	.239	.323	167	130	95	108	.982	114	183	1.4	12.6	13.0	-.2	-7.3
BOS	70	11	13	1379¹	1445	9.4	83	592	513	13.4	4.26	103	.270	.345	4	21	102	99	.981	116	174	1.2	2.0	7.0	.9	7.4
NY	62	16	24	1365²	1289	8.5	94	641	654	12.9	3.75	109	.250	.336	82	51	95	104	.979	120	161	.9	4.9	10.4	.0	.6
PHI	74	7	18	1368²	1456	9.6	86	638	486	13.9	4.43	97	.275	.355	-21	-20	100	101	.981	113	180	1.3	-1.9	-2.0	.0	9.6
DET	60	5	22	1377	1367	8.9	92	589	678	12.9	4.15	105	.259	.335	21	33	102	95	.974	155	143	-.9	3.2	-1.9	-.5	1.2
STL	35	4	20	1373¹	1513	9.9	103	737	531	14.9	5.01	91	.281	.371	-109	-69	106	99	.972	168	190	-1.6	-6.7	-3.8	.0	-5.4
WAS	42	4	22	1357¹	1439	9.5	81	734	446	14.6	4.65	93	.273	.364	-55	-47	101	99	.974	154	144	-.9	-4.6	-13.1	.2	-2.2
CHI	35	2	23	1345²	1454	9.7	89	673	403	14.4	4.89	87	.280	.365	-90	-94	99	97	.974	160	176	-1.2	-9.1	-11.1	-.6	-3.0
TOT	444	75	172	10976¹		9.2				13.6	4.29		.266	.349					.977	1100	1351					

Runs
Henrich-NY 138
DiMaggio-Bos 127
Williams-Bos 124
Pesky-Bos 124
Boudreau-Cle 116

Hits
Dillinger-StL 207
Mitchell-Cle 204
Boudreau-Cle 199
DiMaggio-NY 190
Williams-Bos 188

Doubles
Williams-Bos 44
Henrich-NY 42
Majeski-Phi 41
Priddy-StL 40
DiMaggio-Bos 40

Triples
Henrich-NY 14
Stewart-NY-Was 13
Yost-Was 11
Mullin-Det 11
DiMaggio-NY 11

Home Runs
DiMaggio-NY 39
Gordon-Cle 32
Keltner-Cle 31
Stephens-Bos 29
Doerr-Bos 27

Total Bases
DiMaggio-NY 355
Henrich-NY 326
Williams-Bos 313
Stephens-Bos 299
Boudreau-Cle 299

Runs Batted In
DiMaggio-NY 155
Stephens-Bos 137
Williams-Bos 127
Gordon-Cle 124
Majeski-Phi 120

Runs Produced
Williams-Bos 226
DiMaggio-NY 226
Stephens-Bos 222
Henrich-NY 213
DiMaggio-Bos 205

Bases On Balls
Williams-Bos 126
Joost-Phi 119
Fain-Phi 113
DiMaggio-Bos 101
Pesky-Bos 99

Batting Average
Williams-Bos ...... .369
Boudreau-Cle ...... .355
Mitchell-Cle ...... .336
Zarilla-StL .... .329
McCosky-Phi .... .326

On Base Percentage
Williams-Bos ...... .497
Boudreau-Cle ...... .453
Appling-Chi .... .423
Goodman-Bos .... .414
Fain-Phi .... .412

Slugging Average
Williams-Bos ...... .615
DiMaggio-NY .... .598
Henrich-NY .... .554
Boudreau-Cle ...... .534
Keltner-Cle .... .522

Production
Williams-Bos 1.112
DiMaggio-NY .... .994
Boudreau-Cle ...... .987
Henrich-NY .... .945
Keltner-Cle .... .917

Adjusted Production
Williams-Bos 185
Boudreau-Cle 166
DiMaggio-NY 164
Henrich-NY 151
Keltner-Cle 146

Batter Runs
Williams-Bos 75.7
Boudreau-Cle 52.7
DiMaggio-NY 48.6
Henrich-NY 38.9
Keltner-Cle 33.0

Adjusted Batter Runs
Williams-Bos 68.2
Boudreau-Cle 56.2
DiMaggio-NY 49.9
Henrich-NY 40.1
Keltner-Cle 36.0

Clutch Hitting Index
Platt-StL 126
Majeski-Phi 121
Goodman-Bos 120
Stephens-Bos 120
Tebbetts-Bos 119

Runs Created
Williams-Bos 172
Boudreau-Cle 143
DiMaggio-NY 140
Henrich-NY 130
Keltner-Cle 116

Total Average
Williams-Bos 1.347
Boudreau-Cle 1.058
DiMaggio-NY 1.012
Henrich-NY .... .955
Keltner-Cle ...... .918

Stolen Bases
Dillinger-StL 28
Coan-Was 23
Vernon-Was 15
Mitchell-Cle 13

Stolen Base Average
Coan-Was 71.9
Dillinger-StL 71.8

Stolen Base Runs
Robertson-Was 2.4
Tucker-Cle 2.1
DiMaggio-Bos 1.8
Dillinger-StL 1.8

Fielding Runs
Pellagrini-StL 24.0
Priddy-StL 23.5
Hegan-Cle 21.3
DiMaggio-Bos 15.8
Philley-Chi 15.1

Total Player Rating
Boudreau-Cle 6.9
Williams-Bos 5.8
Priddy-StL 4.4
DiMaggio-NY 4.3
Doerr-Bos 3.6

Wins
Newhouser-Det 21
Lemon-Cle 20
Bearden-Cle 20
Raschi-NY 19
Feller-Cle 19

Win Percentage
Kramer-Bos .... .783
Bearden-Cle ...... .741
Raschi-NY .... .704
Reynolds-NY ...... .696

Games
Page-NY 55
Widmar-StL 49
Biscan-StL 47
Thompson-Was 46

Complete Games
Lemon-Cle 20
Newhouser-Det ... 19
Raschi-NY 18
Feller-Cle 18

Shutouts
Lemon-Cle 10
Raschi-NY 6
Bearden-Cle 6
Dobson-Bos 5

Saves
Christopher-Cle ... 17
Page-NY 16
Houtteman-Det ... 10
Ferrick-Was 10
Judson-Chi 8

Innings Pitched
Lemon-Cle 293.2
Feller-Cle 280.1
Newhouser-Det .. 272.1
Dobson-Bos 245.1
Reynolds-NY 236.1

Fewest Hits/Game
Shea-NY 6.76
Lemon-Cle 7.08
Bearden-Cle 7.33
Scarborough-Was 8.06
Trucks-Det 8.08

Fewest BB/Game
Hutchinson-Det .. 1.95
Zoldak-StL-Cle .. 2.42
Lopat-NY 2.62
Kramer-Bos 2.81
Houtteman-Det .. 2.85

Strikeouts
Feller-Cle 164
Lemon-Cle 147
Newhouser-Det ... 143
Brissie-Phi 127
Raschi-NY 124

Strikeouts/Game
Brissie-Phi 5.89
Feller-Cle 5.27
Trucks-Det 5.23
Raschi-NY 5.01
Newhouser-Det ... 4.73

Ratio
Hutchinson-Det .. 11.08
Lemon-Cle 11.12
Raschi-NY 11.52
Newhouser-Det .. 11.53
Bearden-Cle 11.60

Earned Run Average
Bearden-Cle 2.43
Scarborough-Was . 2.82
Lemon-Cle 2.82
Newhouser-Det ... 3.01
Parnell-Bos 3.14

Adjusted ERA
Bearden-Cle 167
Scarborough-Was . 154
Newhouser-Det ... 145
Lemon-Cle 144
Parnell-Bos 140

Opponents' Batting Avg.
Shea-NY .... .208
Lemon-Cle .... .216
Bearden-Cle ...... .229
Scarborough-Was . .233
Trucks-Det ...... .240

Opponents' On Base Pct.
Hutchinson-Det ... .297
Lemon-Cle .... .302
Scarborough-Was . .307
Newhouser-Det ... .309
Raschi-NY .... .310

Starter Runs
Lemon-Cle 48.0
Bearden-Cle 47.5
Newhouser-Det ... 38.8
Scarborough-Was 30.3
Parnell-Bos 27.1

Adjusted Starter Runs
Bearden-Cle 41.6
Newhouser-Det ... 41.1
Lemon-Cle 40.4
Scarborough-Was . 31.5
Parnell-Bos 29.5

Clutch Pitching Index
Bearden-Cle 132
Garver-StL 129
Fowler-Phi 119
Lopat-NY 118
Reynolds-NY 117

Relief Runs
Klieman-Cle 15.0
Christopher-Cle .. 9.1
Thompson-Was 6.6
Hiller-NY 1.7
Harris-Phi 1.6

Adjusted Relief Runs
Klieman-Cle 12.9
Christopher-Cle .. 7.6
Thompson-Was 7.4
Harris-Phi 1.6
Ferrick-Was 1.6

Relief Ranking
Christopher-Cle .. 10.7
Klieman-Cle 8.8
Thompson-Was 8.6
Ferrick-Was 1.8
Harris-Phi 1.3

Total Pitcher Index
Lemon-Cle 6.8
Bearden-Cle 5.5
Newhouser-Det ... 4.9
Scarborough-Was . 3.8
Garver-StL 2.7

Total Baseball Ranking
Boudreau-Cle 6.9
Lemon-Cle 6.8
Williams-Bos 5.8
Bearden-Cle 5.5
Newhouser-Det ... 4.9

April 28 A New York fan charges Leo Durocher with assault after the Giants lose, 15–2, to Brooklyn. Commissioner Chandler suspends Durocher, but he is absolved on May 3. Chandler criticizes teams for lax security that allows fans on the field.

April 30 Rocky Nelson hits an "inside-the-glove" two-run home run in short left field to turn a ninth inning 3–1 Cubs' lead into a 4–3 Cardinals' victory. Cubs center fielder Andy Pafko's catch is ruled a trap by umpire Al Barlick, as Pafko races in, holding the ball high as runners circle the bases.

May 22 In his first major league start, Don Newcombe shuts out Cincinnati on five hits to win 3-0.

June 15 Eddie Waitkus of the Phillies is shot by 19-year-old Ruth Steinhagen at Chicago's Edgewater Beach Hotel. She will later be placed in a mental hospital. Waitkus battles for his life and will come back to play the following season.

July 8 Monte Irvin and Hank Thompson, brought up from Jersey City three days earlier, are the first blacks to play for the Giants. Thompson, who was also the first black to play for the St. Louis Browns in 1947, starts at second, and Irvin pinch hits in the eighth for Clint Hartung. When Thompson steps in against Don Newcombe, it is the first time in major league history that a black pitcher and a black hitter have faced off. The Dodgers win the game, 4–3.

July 18 Jackie Robinson testifies in front of the House Un-American Activities Committee, then, that night, scores twice, once on a steal of home, to lead the Dodgers past the Cubs, 3–0.

August 21 A barrage of bottles from the Philadelphia stands to protest a decision by umpire George Barr over a line drive trapped by Richie Ashburn results in the first forfeiture in the major leagues in seven years.

September 15 Pirates pitcher Ernie Bonham dies following an appendectomy and stomach surgery, just 18 days after his last pitching performance, an 8–2 win over the Phillies. Mrs. Bonham will receive the first benefits under the players pension plan, $90 a month for 10 years.

September 30 Ralph Kiner hits his 54th homer and 16th in September, as the Pirates beat Herm Wehmeier and the Reds 3-2.

October 2 One game back on the final day, the Cards win 13-5 over the Cubs and await the progress of the Dodgers against the Phils. The Phillies shell Don Newcombe and tie the game 7-7 in the sixth. The game goes overtime before the Dodgers get two in the 10th to win the pennant.

October 6 With a 1-0 game, Preacher Roe wins this one for Brooklyn to knot the Series. Gil Hodges' single drives in Jackie Robinson in the second for the winner.

November 18 NL batting leader (.342) Jackie Robinson is picked for the MVP award.

December 31 The 1940s ends as the only decade in Major League Baseball history in which no new stadiums are built. After Cleveland opened Municipal Stadium in 1932, no new ballpark will be opened until County Stadium in Milwaukee is unveiled in 1953.

	BOSTON		BROOKLYN		CHICAGO		CINCINNATI		NEW YORK		PHILADELPHIA		PITTSBURGH		ST. LOUIS
M	B.Southworth	M	B.Shotton	M	C.Grimm	M	B.Walters	M	L.Durocher	M	E.Sawyer	M	B.Meyer	M	E.Dyer
M	J.Cooney	1B	G.Hodges	M	F.Frisch	M	L.Sewell	1B	J.Mize	1B	D.Sisler	1B	J.Hopp	1B	N.Jones
1B	E.Fletcher	2B	J.Robinson	1B	H.Reich	1B	T.Kluszewski	2B	H.Thompson	2B	E.Miller	2B	M.Basgall	2B	R.Schoendienst
2B	E.Stanky	SS	P.Reese	2B	E.Verban	2B	J.Bloodworth	SS	B.Kerr	SS	G.Hamner	SS	S.Rojek	SS	M.Marion
SS	A.Dark	3B	B.Cox	SS	R.Smalley	SS	V.Stallcup	3B	S.Gordon	3B	W.Jones	3B	P.Castiglione	3B	E.Kazak
3B	B.Elliott	LF	G.Hermanski	3B	F.Gustine	3B	G.Hatton	LF	W.Lockman	LF	D.Ennis	LF	R.Kiner	LF	E.Slaughter
LF	M.Rickert	CF	D.Snider	LF	H.Sauer	LF	P.Lowrey	CF	B.Thomson	CF	R.Ashburn	CF	D.Restelli	CF	C.Diering
CF	J.Russell	RF	C.Furillo	CF	A.Pafko	CF	L.Merriman	RF	W.Marshall	RF	B.Nicholson	RF	W.Westlake	RF	S.Musial
RF	T.Holmes	C	R.Campanella	RF	H.Jeffcoat	RF	J.Wyrostek	C	W.Westrum	C	A.Seminick	C	C.McCullough	C	D.Rice
C	B.Salkeld			C	M.Owen	C	W.Cooper								
		/O	M.Rackley					S2	B.Rigney	O	S.Hollmig	2	D.Murtaugh	O	R.Northey
O2	S.Sisti	C	B.Edwards	1O	P.Cavarretta	23	B.Adams	23	J.Lohrke	S.Lopata	1	E.Stevens	3	T.Glaviano
C	D.Crandall	O	M.McCormick	3S	B.Ramazzotti	O	D.Litwhiler	C	R.Mueller	1	E.Waitkus	3	E.Bockman	1	R.Nelson
O	P.Reiser	3	S.Jorgensen	O	H.Edwards	O	H.Walker	C	W.Cooper	2	M.Goliat	O	T.Saffell	C	J.Garagiola
O	E.Sauer	3	E.Miksis	C	R.Walker	1	H.Howell	13	J.Lafata	23	B.Blattner	O	D.Walker	S	L.Klein
3S	C.Ryan	O	L.Olmo	O	F.Baumholtz	O	H.Sauer	13	B.Haas	2	P.Caballero	O	E.FitzGerald	O	H.Rice
O	J.Heath	O	T.Brown	O	H.Walker	C	R.Mueller	O	M.Irvin	O	J.Mayo	C	P.Masi	O	E.Sauer
C	P.Masi	2S	D.Whitman	C	G.Mauch	S2	C.Corbitt	/O	M.Livingston	/O	E.Sanicki	1	J.Phillips	2	S.Hemus
1	E.Torgeson	/O	C.Abrams	O	B.Scheffing	O	F.Baumholtz	/O	D.Mueller	/1	B.Glynn	/O	W.Judnich	C	B.Baker
C	M.Livingston	2	J.Hopp	2	W.Terwilliger	/2	S.Meeks	2	D.Williams	/O	J.Blatnik	/O	M.Rackley	/1	S.Bilko
/1	R.Sanders	/3	B.Ramazzotti	O	P.Lowrey	2	C.Kress	2	B.Hofman	/C	K.Silvestri	/1	L.Fleming	/3	W.Kurowski
/O	D.Thompson	H	C.Connors	C	R.Novotney	C	J.Pramesa	2	G.Hausmann	/C	H.Wagner	/1	T.Beard	/O	B.Howerton
/1	A.Lakeman	H	G.Shuba	/O	S.Burgess	/O	W.Post	/O	P.Milne	H	B.Haas	/3	B.Rhawn	/C	D.Wilber
H	S.Kuczek			3	B.Serena			/2	B.Rhawn			R	J.Cassini	H	R.Derry
		P	D.Newcombe	/3	H.Schenz	P	K.Raffensberger	/1	A.Galan	P	K.Heintzelman			R	E.Dusak
		P	P.Roe	/1	C.Maddern	/S	R.Rufer	P	R.Roberts	P	M.Dickson		
P	W.Spahn	P	J.Hatten	/O	C.Aberson	/C	S.Yvars	P	R.Meyer	P	B.Werle	P	H.Pollet
P	J.Sain	P	R.Branca	H	J.Kirby	P	H.Wehmeier	/C	H.Franks	P	H.Borowy	P	C.Chambers	P	H.Brecheen
P	V.Bickford	P	J.Banta			P	J.Vander Meer	/S	D.Culler	P	C.Simmons	P	B.Chesnes	P	A.Brazle
P	B.Voiselle	RP	E.Palica			P	B.Lively			RP	J.Konstanty	P	V.Lombardi	P	R.Munger
P	J.Antonelli	RP	P.Minner	P	J.Schmitz	RP	E.Erautt			RP	K.Trinkle	RP	R.Sewell	P	G.Staley
RP	N.Potter			P	B.Rush	RP	E.Blackwell	P	L.Jansen	P	S.Rowe			RP	T.Wilks
RP	B.Hall	P	R.Barney	P	D.Leonard	RP	K.Peterson	P	M.Kennedy			P	T.Bonham	
RP	B.Hogue	P	C.Erskine	P	M.Dubiel			P	D.Koslo			P	E.Riddle	P	M.Lanier
		P	M.Martin	P	D.Lade	P	F.Fanovich	P	S.Jones	P	C.Hartung	/P	J.Walsh	P	F.Martin
P	G.Elliott	/P	P.McGlothin	RP	B.Chipman	P	H.Gumbert	/P	J.Thompson	/P	J.Walsh	P	H.Casey	P	J.Hearn
P	R.Barrett	/P	B.Podbielan	RP	D.Adkins	/P	K.Burkhart	RP	K.Higbe	P	C.Bicknell	P	B.Muncrief	P	K.Johnson
/P	J.Beazley	/P	J.Van Cuyk	RP	B.Muncrief	/P	H.Perkowski	RP	H.Behrman	P	B.Miller	P	R.Poat	P	B.Reeder
/P	C.Shoun					P	J.Dobernic	RP	A.Hansen			P	H.Gumbert	/P	C.Boyer
				P	W.Hacker	/P	M.Howell					/P	H.Gregg	/P	R.Yochim
				P	E.Kush	/P	W.Cress	P	R.Webb			/P	K.Higbe	/P	K.Krieger
				/P	C.McLish			P	A.Zabala						
				/P	R.Hamner			/P	R.Bowman						
				/P	L.Sloat			/P	A.Tomasic						
				/P	J.Dobernic			/P	R.Poat						
				/P	M.Cooper										

TEAM	G	W	L	PCT	GB	R	OR	AB	H	2B	3B	HR	BB	SO	AVG	OBP	SLG	PRO	PRO+	BR	/A	PF	CHI	RC	SB	CS	SBA	SBR
BRO	156	97	57	.630		879	651	5400	1477	236	47	152	638	570	.274	.354	.419	.773	110	103	69	104	106	815	117			
STL	157	96	58	.623	1	766	616	5463	1513	281	54	102	569	482	.277	.348	.404	.752	103	61	25	100	98	777	17			
PHI	154	81	73	.526	16	662	668	5307	1349	232	55	122	528	670	.254	.325	.388	.713	100	-27	-9	97	99	674	27			
BOS	157	75	79	.487	22	706	719	5336	1376	246	33	103	684	656	.258	.345	.374	.719	105	6	45	95	97	710	28			
NY	156	73	81	.474	24	736	693	5308	1383	203	52	147	613	523	.261	.340	.401	.741	105	36	37	100	99	735	43			
PIT	154	71	83	.461	26	681	760	5214	1350	191	41	126	548	554	.259	.332	.384	.716	96	-14	-32	103	101	682	48			
CIN	156	62	92	.403	35	627	770	5469	1423	264	35	86	429	559	.260	.316	.368	.684	88	-84	-91	101	101	636	31			
CHI	154	61	93	.396	36	593	773	5214	1336	212	53	97	396	573	.256	.312	.373	.685	91	-83	-67	97	100	601	53			
TOT	622					5650		42711	11207	1865	370	935	4405	4587	.262	.334	.389	.723							364			

TEAM	CG	SH	SV	IP	H	H/G	HR	BB	SO	RAT	ERA	ERA+	OAV	OOB	PR	/A	PF	CPI	FA	E	DP	FW	PW	BW	SBW	DIF
BRO	62	15	17	1408²	1306	8.3	132	582	743	12.2	3.80	108	.246	.324	37	46	102	99	.980	122	162	1.5	4.6	6.8		7.1
STL	64	13	19	1407²	1356	8.7	87	507	606	12.1	3.44	121	.252	.319	94	113	103	101	.976	146	149	.3	11.2	2.5		5.1
PHI	58	12	15	1391²	1389	9.0	104	502	495	12.4	3.89	101	.268	.335	23	8	98	105	.974	156	141	-.5	.8	-.9		4.6
BOS	68	12	11	1400	1466	9.4	110	520	589	12.9	3.99	95	.268	.334	8	-32	94	102	.976	148	144	.1	-3.2	4.5		-3.4
NY	68	10	9	1374¹	1328	8.7	132	544	516	12.4	3.82	104	.249	.321	33	24	99	97	.973	161	134	-.6	2.4	3.7		-9.4
PIT	53	9	15	1356	1452	9.6	142	535	556	13.4	4.57	92	.274	.344	-79	-55	104	99	.978	132	173	.9	-5.5	-3.2		1.7
CIN	55	10	6	1401²	1423	9.1	124	640	538	13.4	4.34	96	.264	.345	-47	-24	100	99	.977	138	150	.6	-2.4	-9.0		-4.2
CHI	44	8	17	1357²	1487	9.9	104	575	544	13.8	4.50	100	.279	.351	-70	-71	100	100	.970	186	160	-2.1	-7.0	-6.6		-.2
TOT	472	89	109	11097²		9.1				12.8	4.04		.262	.334					.975	1189	1213					

Runs
Reese-Bro	132
Musial-StL	128
Robinson-Bro	122
Kiner-Pit	116
Schoendienst-StL	102

Hits
Musial-StL	207
Robinson-Bro	203
Thomson-NY	198
Slaughter-StL	191
Schoendienst-StL	190

Doubles
Musial-StL	41
Ennis-Phi	39
Robinson-Bro	38
Hatton-Cin	38

Triples
Slaughter-StL	13
Musial-StL	13
Robinson-Bro	12
Ennis-Phi	11
Ashburn-Phi	11

Home Runs
Kiner-Pit	54
Musial-StL	36
Sauer-Cin-Chi	31
Thomson-NY	27
Gordon-NY	26

Total Bases
Musial-StL	382
Kiner-Pit	361
Thomson-NY	332
Ennis-Phi	320
Robinson-Bro	313

Runs Batted In
Kiner-Pit	127
Robinson-Bro	124
Musial-StL	123
Hodges-Bro	115
Ennis-Phi	110

Runs Produced
Robinson-Bro	230
Musial-StL	215
Reese-Bro	189
Kiner-Pit	189
Hodges-Bro	186

Bases On Balls
Kiner-Pit	117
Reese-Bro	116
Stanky-Bos	113
Musial-StL	107
Gordon-NY	95

Batting Average
Robinson-Bro	.342
Musial-StL	.338
Slaughter-StL	.336
Furillo-Bro	.322
Kiner-Pit	.310

On Base Percentage
Musial-StL	.438
Robinson-Bro	.432
Kiner-Pit	.432
Slaughter-StL	.418
Stanky-Bos	.417

Slugging Average
Kiner-Pit	.658
Musial-StL	.624
Robinson-Bro	.528
Ennis-Phi	.525
Thomson-NY	.518

Production
Kiner-Pit	1.089
Musial-StL	1.062
Robinson-Bro	.960
Slaughter-StL	.929
Gordon-NY	.909

Adjusted Production
Kiner-Pit	183
Musial-StL	174
Robinson-Bro	150
Gordon-NY	142
Slaughter-StL	141

Batter Runs
Musial-StL	72.4
Kiner-Pit	70.0
Robinson-Bro	49.9
Slaughter-StL	40.1
Gordon-NY	31.6

Adjusted Batter Runs
Kiner-Pit	66.2
Musial-StL	65.3
Robinson-Bro	44.5
Slaughter-StL	34.8
Ennis-Phi	32.3

Clutch Hitting Index
Robinson-Bro	130
Marion-StL	117
Russell-Bos	116
Hodges-Bro	116
Cooper-NY-Cin	114

Runs Created
Musial-StL	173
Kiner-Pit	163
Robinson-Bro	135
Slaughter-StL	127
Ennis-Phi	118

Total Average
Kiner-Pit	1.247
Musial-StL	1.185
Robinson-Bro	1.078
Slaughter-StL	.971
Gordon-NY	.925

Stolen Bases
Robinson-Bro	37
Reese-Bro	26

Stolen Base Average

Stolen Base Runs

Fielding Runs
Ashburn-Phi	24.7
Schoendienst-StL	24.0
Thomson-NY	19.5
Marion-StL	16.6
Reich-Chi	14.1

Total Player Rating
Kiner-Pit	5.6
Robinson-Bro	4.9
Musial-StL	3.8
Thomson-NY	3.6
B.Elliott-Bos	3.5

Wins
Spahn-Bos	21
Pollet-StL	20
Raffensberger-Cin	18

Win Percentage
Roe-Bro	.714
Pollet-StL	.690
Newcombe-Bro	.680
Meyer-Phi	.680
Munger-StL	.652

Games
Wilks-StL	59
Konstanty-Phi	53
Palica-Bro	49
Banta-Bro	48
Muncrief-Pit-Chi	47

Complete Games
Spahn-Bos	25
Raffensberger-Cin	20
Newcombe-Bro	19
Pollet-StL	17
Jansen-NY	17

Shutouts
Raffensberger-Cin	5
Pollet-StL	5
Newcombe-Bro	5
Heintzelman-Phi	5

Saves
Wilks-StL	9
Potter-StL	7
Konstanty-Phi	7
Staley-StL	6
Palica-Bro	6

Innings Pitched
Spahn-Bos	302.1
Raffensberger-Cin	284.0
Jansen-NY	259.2
Heintzelman-Phi	250.0
Newcombe-Bro	244.1

Fewest Hits/Game
Staley-StL	8.09
Koslo-NY	8.19
Newcombe-Bro	8.21
Kennedy-NY	8.38
Meyer-Phi	8.41

Fewest BB/Game
Koslo-NY	1.83
Roe-Bro	1.86
Werle-Pit	2.08
Jansen-NY	2.15
Leonard-Chi	2.15

Strikeouts
Spahn-Bos	151
Newcombe-Bro	149
Jansen-NY	113
Roe-Bro	109
Branca-Bro	109

Strikeouts/Game
Newcombe-Bro	5.49
Branca-Bro	5.26
Chambers-Pit	4.72
Roe-Bro	4.61
Spahn-Bos	4.50

Ratio
Koslo-NY	10.02
Staley-StL	10.40
Roe-Bro	10.45
Newcombe-Bro	11.01
Spahn-Bos	11.07

Earned Run Average
Koslo-NY	2.50
Staley-StL	2.73
Pollet-StL	2.77
Roe-Bro	2.79
Heintzelman-Phi	3.02

Adjusted ERA
Koslo-NY	159
Staley-StL	152
Pollet-StL	150
Roe-Bro	147
Brazle-StL	131

Opponents' Batting Avg.
Staley-StL	.238
Koslo-NY	.239
Kennedy-NY	.242
Newcombe-Bro	.243
Spahn-Bos	.245

Opponents' On Base Pct.
Koslo-NY	.278
Staley-StL	.286
Roe-Bro	.293
Spahn-Bos	.299
Newcombe-Bro	.301

Starter Runs
Koslo-NY	36.2
Spahn-Bos	32.7
Pollet-StL	32.6
Roe-Bro	29.5
Heintzelman-Phi	28.2

Adjusted Starter Runs
Pollet-StL	35.7
Koslo-NY	34.8
Roe-Bro	30.9
Staley-StL	27.2
Heintzelman-Phi	25.5

Clutch Pitching Index
Roe-Bro	126
Heintzelman-Phi	123
Brazle-StL	121
Jones-NY	116
Dickson-Pit	113

Relief Runs
Erautt-Cin	8.6
Konstanty-Phi	8.5
Hogue-Bos	7.3
Palica-Bro	4.5
Wilks-StL	4.1

Adjusted Relief Runs
Erautt-Cin	10.3
Konstanty-Phi	7.5
Wilks-StL	5.7
Hogue-Bos	5.2
Palica-Bro	5.2

Relief Ranking
Erautt-Cin	12.6
Konstanty-Phi	11.0
Palica-Bro	8.9
Wilks-StL	6.6
Hogue-Bos	3.1

Total Pitcher Index
Pollet-StL	4.2
Koslo-NY	4.2
Staley-StL	3.5
Dickson-Pit	3.0
Newcombe-Bro	2.8

Total Baseball Ranking
Kiner-Pit	5.6
Robinson-Bro	4.9
Pollet-StL	4.2
Koslo-NY	4.2
Musial-StL	3.8

March 1 The Browns, owners of Sportsman's Park, move to evict the Cardinals in order to gain a rent increase.

April 19 At pregame ceremonies marking the season opener in Yankee Stadium, a granite monument to Babe Ruth is unveiled in center field. Plaques honoring Lou Gehrig and Miller Huggins are also presented.

May 5 Tigers second baseman Charlie Gehringer is picked for the Hall of Fame. Two days later, the Old-Timers Committee will select Kid Nichols and Three-Finger Brown.

May 6 Nine hitless innings in relief are thrown by A's rookie Bobby Shantz in a 13-inning, 5–4, Athletics win over the Tigers. Shantz gives up a run in the 13th, but old-timer Wally Moses saves him with a two-run home run.

May 27 The Indians start so badly, 12-17, that owner Bill Veeck arranges a "Second Opening Day."

July 12 The NL commits five errors, allowing the AL to record an 11-7 triumph in the All-Star Game at Ebbets Field. The contest marks the first appearance of black players—Jackie Robinson, Roy Campanella, and Don Newcombe in the NL lineup and Larry Doby among the AL stars.

August 6 Luke Appling appears as shortstop in his 2,154th game, surpassing Rabbit Maranville's major league mark. Appling will finish his career with 2,218.

September 26 Before 67,434 at Yankee Stadium, the Red Sox survive a rhubarb-filled, 7-6 win when Johnny Pesky scores on a disputed squeeze play. Leading by one game, the Sox move on to Washington for a three-game series before the last two games of the year with the Yankees.

October 2 The New York Yankees and the Boston Red Sox enter the final day of the season tied for first place. Nearly 70,000 pack Yankee Stadium to see the finale. Vic Raschi nurses a 1-0 lead into the eighth against Ellis Kinder before the Yankees score four against a tired Mel Parnell and an unlucky Tex Hughson. A Sox rally falls short, and the Yankees win the game and the pennant 5-3. Ted Williams is hitless in two official trips, while George Kell of the Tigers goes 2-for-3. Kell's final mark is .3429 and Williams's is .3427.

October 5 In the Series opener at the Stadium, the New York Yankees and Allie Reynolds beat the Brooklyn Dodgers 1-0 on Tommy Henrich's ninth-inning home run off Don Newcombe. Newcombe had struck out 11 and walked none before Henrich's blast.

October 9 The Yankees pound the Dodgers 10-6 to win the World Series in five games. Pinch hitter and third baseman Bobby Brown is the hitting hero, batting .500 and driving in five runs.

October 29 In arguably their best trade ever, the White Sox send catcher Joe Tipton, who hit .204 in his one season in Chicago, to the Athletics for young Nellie Fox.

November 21 Bill Veeck sells the Indians for $2.2 million to a local syndicate headed by Ellis Ryan. Hank Greenberg will be general manager.

November 25 Ted Williams, who lost the Triple Crown when his batting average was .0002 below that of George Kell, wins the MVP vote in a landslide. Phil Rizzuto and Joe Page finish second and third in the voting.

December 12 By a 7-1 vote, the AL rejects a proposal to bring back the legal spitball. The rules committee also alters the strike zone to the space between the armpits and the top of the knees.

BOSTON	CHICAGO	CLEVELAND	DETROIT	NEW YORK	PHILADELPHIA	ST.LOUIS	WASHINGTON
M J.McCarthy	M J.Onslow	M L.Boudreau	M R.Rolfe	M C.Stengel	M C.Mack	M Z.Taylor	M J.Kuhel
1B B.Goodman	1B C.Kress	1B M.Vernon	1B P.Campbell	1B T.Henrich	1B F.Fain	1B J.Graham	1B E.Robinson
2B B.Doerr	2B C.Michaels	2B J.Gordon	2B N.Berry	2B J.Coleman	2B P.Suder	2B J.Priddy	2B A.Kozar
SS V.Stephens	SS L.Appling	SS L.Boudreau	SS J.Lipon	SS P.Rizzuto	SS E.Joost	SS E.Pellagrini	SS S.Dente
3B J.Pesky	3B F.Baker	3B K.Keltner	3B G.Kell	3B B.Brown	3B H.Majeski	3B B.Dillinger	3B E.Yost
LF T.Williams	LF G.Zernial	LF D.Mitchell	LF H.Evers	LF G.Woodling	LF E.Valo	LF R.Sievers	LF B.Stewart
CF D.DiMaggio	CF C.Metkovich	CF L.Doby	CF J.Groth	CF C.Mapes	CF S.Chapman	CF S.Spence	CF C.Vollmer
RF A.Zarilla	RF D.Philley	RF B.Kennedy	RF V.Wertz	RF H.Bauer	RF W.Moses	RF D.Kokos	RF B.Lewis
C B.Tebbetts	C D.Wheeler	C J.Hegan	C A.Robinson	C Y.Berra	C M.Guerra	C S.Lollar	C C.Evans
C M.Batts	O1 S.Souchock	S R.Boone	21 D.Kolloway	31 B.Johnson	2 N.Fox	O1 P.Lehner	O G.Coan
1 B.Hitchcock	O H.Adams	O T.Tucker	S2 E.Lake	O J.DiMaggio	O D.White	C L.Moss	23 S.Robertson
O T.O'Brien	3 J.Tipton	3 J.Berardino	O P.Mullin	O J.Lindell	O T.Wright	O W.Platt	O1 S.Mele
O S.Mele	C E.Malone	O A.Clark	C B.Swift	C D.Kryhoski	C J.Astroth	S3 J.Sullivan	C J.Early
1 W.Dropo	O J.Ostrowski	O L.Easter	1 G.Vico	2 S.Stirnweiss	C B.Rosar	S A.Anderson	O R.Ortiz
/2 L.Stringer	1 G.Goldsberry	3 A.Rosen	O D.Wakefield	S3 B.Silvera	S3 T.Davis	O A.Zarilla	3 M.Christman
/3 M.Combs	O J.Scala	C M.Tresh	C H.Riebe	C C.Keller	O A.Galan	O G.Elder	O J.Simmons
/O S.Spence	O B.Bowers	/O H.Peck	H J.Outlaw	1 J.Phillips	/1 H.Biasatti	/2 O.Friend	C R.Weigel
H T.Wright	3 B.Rhawn	/O M.Minoso	H D.Lund	C J.Niarhos	O B.Estalella	/S A.Naples	H H.Keller
/C B.Martin	3 R.Krsnich	/O H.Edwards	R B.Mavis	/1 F.Mole	P A.Kellner	/O K.Wood	H H.Reich
P M.Parnell	O E.Rapp	/2 B.Avila	H E.Rapp	/O J.Delsing	P J.Coleman	H H.Arft	/2 J.Difani
P E.Kinder	S F.Hancock	/O M.Nielsen	P H.Newhouser	/1 J.Collins	P L.Brissie	H F.Pack	P S.Hudson
P J.Dobson	/O D.Lane	/O H.Reich	P V.Trucks	/C R.Houk	P D.Fowler	P N.Garver	P R.Scarborough
P C.Stobbs	/O B.Higdon	R F.Marsh	P A.Houtteman	H M.Witek	P C.Scheib	P B.Kennedy	P P.Calvert
P J.Kramer	/C G.Yankowski	P B.Lemon	P T.Gray	P V.Raschi	RP B.Harris	P C.Fannin	P M.Harris
RP T.Hughson	/S J.Baumer	P B.Feller	P F.Hutchinson	P E.Lopat	P B.Shantz	P A.Papai	P L.Hittle
RP E.Johnson	/3 D.Kolloway	P M.Garcia	RP D.Trout	P A.Reynolds	/P B.McCahan	P J.Ostrowski	RP J.Haynes
P M.McDermott	/O P.Seerey	P E.Wynn	P L.Kretlow	P T.Byrne	/P P.Marchildon	RP T.Ferrick	RP D.Welteroth
P M.Masterson	P B.Wight	P A.Benton	P M.Grissom	RP J.Page	/P J.Wilson	RP D.Starr	P D.Weik
/P M.Harris	P R.Gumpert	RP S.Paige	RP M.Stuart	RP S.Shea	/P C.Hausmann	P K.Drews	P M.Haefner
/P F.Quinn	P B.Pierce	RP F.Papish	RP S.Overmire	RP C.Marshall		P R.Embree	P W.Masterson
/P W.McCall	P B.Kuzava	RP S.Zoldak	/P H.White	P B.Porterfield		P R.Shore	P A.Gettel
/P H.Dorish	P H.Judson	P B.Bearden	/P S.Rogovin	P D.Pillette		/P R.Winegarner	/P J.Gonzalez
/P D.Ferriss	RP M.Pieretti	P S.Gromek		P R.Buxton		/P R.Raney	/P F.Thompson
/P J.Robinson	RP M.Surkont			/P H.Casey		/P B.Malloy	/P M.Candini
/P D.Galehouse	P M.Haefner			/P F.Hiller		/P B.Savage	/P B.Dozier
/P J.Wittig	P A.Gettel			/P W.Hood		/P E.Albrecht	/P J.Pearce
	P E.Klieman					/P I.Medlinger	/P E.Klieman
	P C.Shoun					/P J.Bilbrey	/P D.Sutherland
	/P B.Cain						
	/P J.Bruner						
	/P B.Evans						
	/P E.Groth						
	/P A.Carrasquel						
	/P F.Bradley						
	/P O.Grove						

TEAM	G	W	L	PCT	GB	R	OR	AB	H	2B	3B	HR	BB	SO	AVG	OBP	SLG	PRO	PRO+	BR	/A	PF	CHI	RC	SB	CS	SBA	SBR
NY	155	97	57	.630		829	637	5196	1396	215	60	115	731	539	.269	.362	.400	.762	108	58	58	100	106	790	58	30	66	-1
BOS	155	96	58	.623	1	896	667	5320	1500	272	36	131	835	510	.282	.381	.420	.801	111	147	83	107	100	890	43	25	63	-2
CLE	154	89	65	.578	8	675	574	5221	1358	194	58	112	601	534	.260	.339	.384	.723	99	-30	-16	98	99	696	44	40	52	-11
DET	155	87	67	.565	10	751	655	5259	1405	215	51	88	751	502	.267	.361	.378	.739	102	20	18	100	99	739	39	52	43	-20
PHI	154	81	73	.526	16	726	725	5123	1331	214	49	82	783	493	.260	.361	.369	.730	104	6	31	97	99	719	36	25	59	-4
CHI	154	63	91	.409	34	648	737	5204	1340	207	66	43	702	596	.257	.347	.347	.694	93	-66	-45	97	99	657	62	55	53	-14
STL	155	53	101	.344	44	667	913	5112	1301	213	30	117	631	700	.254	.339	.377	.716	92	-41	-69	104	101	670	38	39	49	-12
WAS	154	50	104	.325	47	584	868	5234	1330	207	41	81	593	495	.254	.333	.356	.689	90	-93	-80	98	95	640	46	33	58	-6
TOT	618					5776		41669	10961	1737	391	769	5627	4369	.263	.353	.379	.732							366	299	55	-70

TEAM	CG	SH	SV	IP	H	H/G	HR	BB	SO	RAT	ERA	ERA+	OAV	OOB	PR	/A	PF	CPI	FA	E	DP	FW	PW	BW	SBW	DIF
NY	59	12	36	1371¹	1231	8.1	98	812	671	13.6	3.69	110	.242	.351	77	54	96	107	.977	138	195	.0	5.3	5.6	.7	8.3
BOS	84	16	16	1377	1375	9.0	82	661	598	13.5	3.97	110	.262	.347	34	59	104	101	.980	120	207	1.1	5.7	8.1	.7	3.4
CLE	65	10	19	1383²	1275	8.3	82	611	594	12.4	3.36	119	.247	.329	129	98	95	104	.983	103	192	2.1	9.5	-1.6	-.2	2.2
DET	70	19	12	1393²	1338	8.6	102	628	631	12.8	3.77	110	.254	.335	66	60	99	100	.978	131	174	.4	5.8	1.8	-1.1	3.1
PHI	85	9	11	1365	1359	9.0	105	758	490	14.1	4.23	97	.263	.360	-5	-19	98	103	.976	140	217	-.1	-1.8	3.0	.5	2.5
CHI	57	10	17	1363¹	1362	9.0	108	693	502	13.7	4.30	97	.264	.353	-15	-19	99	99	.977	141	180	-.2	-1.8	-4.4	-.5	-7.0
STL	43	3	16	1341¹	1583	10.6	113	685	432	15.4	5.21	87	.294	.377	-151	-102	108	98	.971	166	154	-1.6	-9.9	-6.7	-.3	-5.4
WAS	44	9	9	1345²	1438	9.6	79	779	451	15.0	5.10	84	.276	.373	-134	-126	101	91	.973	161	168	-1.4	-12.3	-7.8	.3	-5.8
TOT	507	88	136	10941		9.0				13.8	4.20		.263	.353					.977	1100	1487					

Runs
Williams-Bos 150
Joost-Phi 128
DiMaggio-Bos 126
Stephens-Bos 113
Pesky-Bos 111

Hits
Mitchell-Cle 203
Williams-Bos 194
DiMaggio-Bos 186
Wertz-Det 185
Pesky-Bos 185

Doubles
Williams-Bos 39
Kell-Det 38
DiMaggio-Bos 34
Zarilla-StL-Bos 33
Stephens-Bos 31

Triples
Mitchell-Cle 23
Dillinger-StL 13
Valo-Phi 12

Home Runs
Williams-Bos 43
Stephens-Bos 39

Total Bases
Williams-Bos 368
Stephens-Bos 329
Wertz-Det 283
Mitchell-Cle 274
Doerr-Bos 269

Runs Batted In
Williams-Bos 159
Stephens-Bos 159
Wertz-Det 133
Doerr-Bos 109
Chapman-Phi 108

Runs Produced
Williams-Bos 266
Stephens-Bos 233
Wertz-Det 209
Joost-Phi 186
Doerr-Bos 182

Bases On Balls
Williams-Bos 162
Joost-Phi 149
Fain-Phi 136
Appling-Chi 121
Valo-Phi 119

Batting Average
Kell-Det ..... .343
Williams-Bos ..... .343
Dillinger-StL ..... .324
Mitchell-Cle ..... .317
Doerr-Bos ..... .309

On Base Percentage
Williams-Bos ..... .490
Appling-Chi ..... .439
Joost-Phi ..... .429
Kell-Det ..... .424
Michaels-Chi ..... .417

Slugging Average
Williams-Bos ..... .650
Stephens-Bos ..... .539
Henrich-NY ..... .526
Doerr-Bos ..... .497
Berra-NY ..... .480

Production
Williams-Bos 1.141
Henrich-NY ..... .942
Stephens-Bos ..... .930
Kell-Det ..... .892
Doerr-Bos ..... .890

Adjusted Production
Williams-Bos 187
Henrich-NY 148
Joost-Phi 138
Kell-Det 136
Stephens-Bos 135

Batter Runs
Williams-Bos 88.9
Stephens-Bos 36.9
Joost-Phi 31.9
DiMaggio-NY 31.7
Henrich-NY 29.7

Adjusted Batter Runs
Williams-Bos 76.6
Joost-Phi 35.8
DiMaggio-NY 31.7
Henrich-NY 29.7
Stephens-Bos 28.3

Clutch Hitting Index
Fain-Phi 143
Lipon-Det 124
Valo-Phi 124
Wertz-Det 121
Williams-Bos 120

Runs Created
Williams-Bos 193
Stephens-Bos 132
Joost-Phi 119
DiMaggio-Bos 110
Wertz-Det 110

Total Average
Williams-Bos 1.347
Henrich-NY 1.017
Joost-Phi ..... .995
Stephens-Bos ..... .947
Kell-Det ..... .877

Stolen Bases
Dillinger-StL 20
Rizzuto-NY 18
Valo-Phi 14
Philley-Chi 13

Stolen Base Average
Rizzuto-NY 75.0
Dillinger-StL 58.8

Stolen Base Runs
Tebbetts-Bos 1.8
Rizzuto-NY 1.8
Mapes-NY 1.8
Fain-Phi 1.8
Philley-Chi 1.5

Fielding Runs
Doerr-Bos 27.8
Pesky-Bos 21.4
Vernon-Cle 18.8
DiMaggio-Bos 14.3
Baker-Chi 11.8

Total Player Rating
Williams-Bos 6.7
Joost-Phi 5.2
Doerr-Bos 5.0
Stephens-Bos 4.1
Michaels-Chi 3.9

Wins
Parnell-Bos 25
Kinder-Bos 23
Lemon-Cle 22
Raschi-NY 21
Kellner-Phi 20

Win Percentage
Kinder-Bos ..... .793
Parnell-Bos ..... .781
Reynolds-NY ..... .739
Lemon-Cle ..... .688

Games
Page-NY 60
Welteroth-Was 52
Ferrick-StL 50
Kennedy-StL 48
Surkont-Chi 44

Complete Games
Parnell-Bos 27
Newhouser-Det 22
Lemon-Cle 22
Raschi-NY 21

Shutouts
Trucks-Det 6
Kinder-Bos 6
Garcia-Cle 5

Saves
Page-NY 27
Benton-Cle 10
Ferrick-StL 6
Paige-Cle 5

Innings Pitched
Parnell-Bos 295.1
Newhouser-Det 292.0
Lemon-Cle 279.2
Trucks-Det 275.0
Raschi-NY 274.2

Fewest Hits/Game
Byrne-NY 5.74
Lemon-Cle 6.79
Trucks-Det 6.84
Gray-Det 7.52
Pierce-Chi 7.60

Fewest BB/Game
Hutchinson-Det 2.48
Houtteman-Det 2.61
Lopat-NY 2.88
Garcia-Cle 3.07
Wynn-Cle 3.12

Strikeouts
Trucks-Det 153
Newhouser-Det 144
Lemon-Cle 138
Kinder-Bos 138
Byrne-NY 129

Strikeouts/Game
Byrne-NY 5.92
Trucks-Det 5.01
Pierce-Chi 4.98
Kinder-Bos 4.93
Garcia-Cle 4.82

Ratio
Hutchinson-Det 10.49
Trucks-Det 11.03
Garcia-Cle 11.07
Lemon-Cle 11.39
Gumpert-Chi 11.81

Earned Run Average
Garcia-Cle 2.36
Parnell-Bos 2.77
Trucks-Det 2.81
Hutchinson-Det 2.96
Lemon-Cle 2.99

Adjusted ERA
Garcia-Cle 169
Parnell-Bos 157
Trucks-Det 148
Hutchinson-Det 141
Lemon-Cle 133

Opponents' Batting Avg.
Byrne-NY ..... .183
Lemon-Cle ..... .211
Trucks-Det ..... .211
Gray-Det ..... .227
Pierce-Chi ..... .228

Opponents' On Base Pct.
Hutchinson-Det ..... .290
Trucks-Det ..... .301
Garcia-Cle ..... .308
Lemon-Cle ..... .309
Gumpert-Chi ..... .318

Starter Runs
Parnell-Bos 46.7
Trucks-Det 42.3
Lemon-Cle 37.4
Garcia-Cle 35.9
Benton-Cle 31.3

Adjusted Starter Runs
Parnell-Bos 52.1
Trucks-Det 41.1
Garcia-Cle 31.9
Lemon-Cle 31.0
Benton-Cle 28.2

Clutch Pitching Index
Garcia-Cle 123
Lopat-NY 122
Wight-Chi 118
Houtteman-Det 115
Kinder-Bos 114

Relief Runs
Page-NY 24.1
Paige-Cle 10.7
Papish-Cle 6.9
Ferrick-StL 3.7

Adjusted Relief Runs
Page-NY 21.8
Paige-Cle 8.8
Ferrick-StL 7.5
Papish-Cle 5.5
Starr-StL 1.9

Relief Ranking
Page-NY 40.3
Paige-Cle 11.7
Ferrick-StL 7.4
Starr-StL 1.7
Papish-Cle 1.0

Total Pitcher Index
Lemon-Cle 5.7
Parnell-Bos 5.5
Page-NY 3.8
Garcia-Cle 3.6
Hutchinson-Det 3.4

Total Baseball Ranking
Williams-Bos 6.7
Lemon-Cle 5.7
Parnell-Bos 5.5
Joost-Phi 5.2
Doerr-Bos 5.0

January 23 The Associated Press picks the "Miracle Braves" of 1914 as the greatest sports upset of the century.

April 18 The first Opening Day night game is played in St. Louis with the Cardinals defeating the Pirates 4-2.

July 4 Braves slugger Sid Gordon ties the major league season grand slam record with four when he hits one against the Phillies. Boston's 12–9 win in the second game of a twinbill means totals of 40 runs, 55 hits, and 90 total bases for the day.

July 11 Making a leaping, off-the-wall catch of a Ralph Kiner drive, Ted Williams fractures his left elbow in the All-Star game at Chicago. Remaining in the game, he puts the AL ahead, 3-2, with an RBI single. Kiner's ninth-inning home run evens up the game, and Red Schoendienst's blast in the 14th wins it for the NL.

July 26 Brooklyn beats the Cardinals 7-5 as the Dodgers' Jim Russell switch hits home runs, making him the first switch hitter in history to do it more than once.

August 16 Henry Thompson of the Giants hits two inside the park, against the Dodgers at the Polo Grounds. He's the first player to do this since Terry Moore hit two for the Cardinals at Forbes Field on this date in 1939.

August 19 The Gillette Safety Razor Co. pays $800,000 for TV rights to the World Series. Radio rights will add another $175,000 more.

September 26 Phils' relief ace Jim Konstanty makes his 71st appearance, a major league record, in the Phils' 8-7 win over the Braves in front of 1,987 Boston fans.

October 1 Dick Sisler's dramatic home run off Don Newcombe in the 10th clinches the pennant 4-1 for the Whiz Kids. It is the Phillies' first pennant in 35 years. In the play that sets the stage for Sisler's heroics, center fielder Richie Ashburn throws out Dodgers runner Cal Abrams at the plate in the bottom of the ninth.

October 3 Baseball rules that Phils lefty Curt Simmons cannot play in the World Series despite his being on furlough from the Army.

October 4 Relief ace Jim Konstanty of the Phils starts and loses to Vic Raschi and the Yankees in Philadelphia 1-0 in Game 1 of the World Series. Bobby Brown doubles and comes around on two long flies to score the lone run.

October 16 The Brooklyn Dodgers fail to renew Branch Rickey's contract as president.

November 2 The baseball writers select Phillies relief pitcher Jim Konstanty as the National League's MVP.

November 6 After his contract as Dodgers president is not renewed, Branch Rickey sells his 25 percent interest in the club for a reported $1.05 million and signs a five-year contract as executive vice president/general manager with the Pittsburgh Pirates.

November 9 The baseball writers name Sam Jethroe of the Boston Braves as the NL Rookie of the Year.

December 11 At the winter meeting, held in St. Petersburg, Fla. major league owners vote, 9-7, against renewing Commissioner Happy Chandler's contract for a new term, starting in 1951. The Cardinals' Fred Saigh led the opposition to Chandler, who had jeopardized the reserve clause and ordered investigations of the alleged gambling activities of several owners.

December 12 The owners vote to drop the four-year-old bonus and high school rule. This rule, passed to prevent the wealthy clubs from buying up all the talent, required that "bonus" players must stay on the major league roster after just one season in the minors.

BOSTON	BROOKLYN	CHICAGO	CINCINNATI	NEW YORK	PHILADELPHIA	PITTSBURGH	ST.LOUIS
M B.Southworth	M B.Shotton	M F.Frisch	M L.Sewell	M L.Durocher	M E.Sawyer	M B.Meyer	M E.Dyer
1B E.Torgeson	1B G.Hodges	1B P.Ward	1B T.Kluszewski	1B T.Gilbert	1B E.Waitkus	1B J.Hopp	1B R.Nelson
2B R.Hartsfield	2B J.Robinson	2B W.Terwilliger	2B C.Ryan	2B E.Stanky	2B M.Goliat	2B D.Murtaugh	2B R.Schoendienst
SS B.Kerr	SS P.Reese	SS R.Smalley	SS V.Stallcup	SS A.Dark	SS G.Hamner	SS S.Rojek	SS M.Marion
3B B.Elliott	3B B.Cox	3B B.Serena	3B G.Hatton	3B H.Thompson	3B W.Jones	3B N.Fernandez	3B T.Glaviano
LF S.Gordon	LF G.Hermanski	LF H.Sauer	LF J.Adcock	LF W.Lockman	LF D.Sisler	LF R.Kiner	LF S.Musial
CF S.Jethroe	CF D.Snider	CF A.Pafko	CF B.Usher	CF B.Thomson	CF R.Ashburn	CF W.Westlake	CF B.Howerton
RF T.Holmes	RF C.Furillo	RF B.Borkowski	RF J.Wyrostek	RF D.Mueller	RF D.Ennis	RF G.Bell	RF E.Slaughter
C W.Cooper	C R.Campanella	C M.Owen	C D.Howell	C W.Westrum	C A.Seminick	C C.McCullough	C D.Rice
O W.Marshall	O J.Russell	1 P.Cavarretta	23 B.Adams	1O M.Irvin	O D.Whitman	3S P.Castiglione	O C.Diering
C D.Crandall	3S B.Morgan	C R.Walker	O L.Merriman	23 B.Rigney	C S.Lopata	S3 D.O'Connell	3 E.Kazak
O L.Olmo	C B.Edwards	O C.Mauro	O P.Lowrey	O R.Weatherly	2 J.Bloodworth	3 B.Dillinger	S E.Miller
2 G.Mauch	O G.Shuba	O H.Jeffcoat	C J.Pramesa	C S.Calderone	1 B.Nicholson	1 J.Phillips	O H.Walker
S2 S.Sisti	O T.Brown	23 B.Ramazzotti	O D.Litwhiler	3 J.Lohrke	O J.Mayo	O T.Saffell	O H.Rice
O P.Reiser	2S E.Miksis	O R.Northey	S S.Meeks	/O J.Maguire	/2 P.Caballero	O T.Beard	O J.Lindell
2 C.Ryan	O C.Abrams	3 R.Jackson	O R.Northey	/3 S.Jorgensen	O K.Silvestri	C R.Mueller	C J.Garagiola
/O B.Addis	/1 W.Belardi	O H.Edwards	C W.Cooper	/1 J.Harshman	/O S.Hollmig	2 J.Berardino	/2 P.Lowrey
/C B.Burris	/C S.Lembo	C C.Sawatski	C B.Scheffing	/C S.Yvars	/O J.Blatnik	1 D.Coogan	C J.Bucha
/C W.Linden	/3 S.Jorgensen	/2 E.Verban	/2 J.Bloodworth	/C R.Mueller		23 H.Schenz	/1 S.Bilko
/2 E.Verban		/C B.Scheffing	/C H.Landrith	/S R.Rufer	P R.Roberts	C E.Turner	/1 N.Jones
	P D.Newcombe	/C H.Chiti	H T.Tappe	H M.McCormick	P C.Simmons	1 E.Stevens	/O J.Blatnik
P V.Bickford	P P.Roe		H M.Rackley	H P.Milne	P B.Miller	3 G.Strickland	/3 S.Hemus
P W.Spahn	P E.Palica	P B.Rush	/O J.Bolger	H M.Blaylock	P R.Meyer	/O M.Rickert	/1 D.Bollweg
P J.Sain	P R.Branca	P J.Schmitz		/1 N.Reyes	P B.Church	/C E.FitzGerald	/1 E.Mickelson
P B.Chipman	P D.Bankhead	P P.Minner	P E.Blackwell		RP J.Konstanty		H D.Gardella
RP B.Hogue		P F.Hiller	P K.Raffensberger	P L.Jansen		P C.Chambers	H E.Mierkowicz
RP J.Antonelli	P C.Erskine	P M.Dubiel	P H.Wehmeier	P S.Maglie	P K.Heintzelman	P M.Dickson	
RP B.Hall	P B.Podbielan	RP J.Vander Meer	P H.Fox	P S.Jones	P K.Johnson	P B.Werle	P H.Pollet
	P J.Hatten	RP D.Leonard	P W.Ramsdell	P D.Koslo	P M.Candini	P B.Macdonald	P M.Lanier
P N.Roy	P J.Banta	RP B.Voiselle	RP F.Smith	P J.Hearn	P B.Donnelly	P V.Law	P G.Staley
/P M.Surkont	P R.Barney		RP E.Erautt	RP J.Kramer	/P H.Borowy	RP V.Lombardi	P A.Brazle
P D.Donovan	P B.Loes	P D.Lade	RP J.Hetki	RP A.Hansen	/P P.Stuffel	RP J.Walsh	P H.Brecheen
/P M.Haefner	P B.Loes	P J.Klippstein		P M.Kennedy	/P J.Brittin	P M.Queen	RP F.Martin
P E.Johnson	/P A.Epperly	/P W.Hacker	P H.Perkowski	P C.Hartung	P J.Thompson	/P B.Chesnes	P R.Munger
/P D.Cole	/P J.Landrum	/P A.Varga	/P K.Peterson	P K.Higbe	/P S.Ridzik	P B.Pierro	P C.Boyer
/P M.Wall	/P W.Ramsdell		/P B.Byerly	P G.Spencer		P H.Borowy	P E.Dusak
/P B.Walters	/P J.Romano		/P J.Avrea			P W.Main	P T.Wilks
/P D.Manville	/P C.Labine					/P W.McCall	P A.Papai
	/P P.McGlothin					/P H.Gregg	/P T.Poholsky
	/P M.Mallette					/P F.Barrett	/P J.Hearn
						/P H.Gumbert	/P K.Johnson
						/P F.Papish	/P C.Deal

TEAM	G	W	L	PCT	GB	R	OR	AB	H	2B	3B	HR	BB	SO	AVG	OBP	SLG	PRO	PRO+	BR	/A	PF	CHI	RC	SB	CS	SBA	SBR
PHI	157	91	63	.591		722	624	5426	1440	225	55	125	535	569	.265	.334	.396	.730	100	-14	-2	98	101	714	33			
BRO	155	89	65	.578	2	847	724	5364	1461	247	46	194	607	632	.272	.349	.444	.793	113	107	90	102	101	833	77			
NY	154	86	68	.558	5	735	643	5238	1352	204	50	133	627	629	.258	.342	.392	.734	100	4	0	101	101	726	42			
BOS	156	83	71	.539	8	785	736	5363	1411	246	36	148	615	616	.263	.342	.405	.747	110	24	73	94	104	750	71			
STL	153	78	75	.510	12.5	693	670	5215	1353	255	50	102	606	604	.259	.339	.386	.725	93	-15	-49	105	99	696	23			
CIN	153	66	87	.431	24.5	654	734	5253	1366	257	27	99	504	497	.260	.327	.376	.703	91	-65	-67	100	102	643	37			
CHI	154	64	89	.418	26.5	643	772	5230	1298	224	47	161	479	767	.248	.315	.401	.716	95	-53	-45	99	100	658	46			
PIT	154	57	96	.373	33.5	681	857	5327	1404	227	59	138	564	693	.264	.338	.406	.744	99	13	-11	103	93	729	43			
TOT	618					5760		42416	11085	1885	370	1100	4537	5007	.261	.336	.401	.737							372			

TEAM	CG	SH	SV	IP	H	H/G	HR	BB	SO	RAT	ERA	ERA+	OAV	OOB	PR	/A	PF	CPI	FA	E	DP	FW	PW	BW	SBW	DIF
PHI	57	13	27	1406	1324	8.5	122	530	620	12.0	3.50	116	.250	.320	101	86	98	105	.975	151	155	.1	8.4	-.2		5.7
BRO	62	10	21	1389²	1397	9.0	163	591	772	13.0	4.28	96	.263	.339	-22	-29	99	102	.979	127	183	1.4	-2.8	8.8		4.7
NY	67	19	15	1375	1268	8.3	140	536	596	12.0	3.71	110	.246	.320	66	59	99	100	.977	137	181	.8	5.8	.0		2.5
BOS	88	7	10	1385¹	1411	9.2	129	554	615	13.0	4.14	93	.263	.336	0	-45	93	99	.970	182	146	-1.7	-4.4	7.1		4.9
STL	57	10	14	1356	1398	9.3	119	535	603	13.0	3.97	108	.268	.339	26	49	104	105	.978	130	172	1.1	4.8	-4.8		.4
CIN	67	7	13	1357²	1363	9.0	145	582	686	13.2	4.32	98	.259	.338	-26	-13	102	97	.976	140	132	.5	-1.3	-6.5		-3.2
CHI	55	9	19	1371¹	1452	9.5	130	593	559	13.6	4.28	98	.271	.347	-21	-11	101	103	.968	201	169	-2.8	-1.1	-4.4		-4.2
PIT	42	6	16	1368²	1472	9.7	152	616	556	13.9	4.96	88	.275	.353	-124	-88	106	95	.977	136	165	.8	-8.6	-1.1		-10.6
TOT	498	81	135	11009²		9.1				13.0	4.14		.261	.336					.975	1204	1303					

Runs
Torgeson-Bos 120
Stanky-NY 115
Kiner-Pit 112
Snider-Bro 109
Musial-StL 105

Hits
Snider-Bro 199
Musial-StL 192
Furillo-Bro 189
Ennis-Phi 185
Waitkus-Phi 182

Doubles
Schoendienst-StL .. 43
Musial-StL 41
Robinson-Bro 39
Kluszewski-Cin ... 37
Dark-NY 36

Triples
Ashburn-Phi 14
Bell-Pit 11
Snider-Bro 10
Smalley-Chi 9
Schoendienst-StL . 9

Home Runs
Kiner-Pit 47
Pafko-Chi 36
Sauer-Chi 32
Hodges-Bro 32

Total Bases
Snider-Bro 343
Musial-StL 331
Ennis-Phi 328
Kiner-Pit 323
Pafko-Chi 304

Runs Batted In
Ennis-Phi 126
Kiner-Pit 118
Hodges-Bro 113
Kluszewski-Cin .. 111
Musial-StL 109

Runs Produced
Furillo-Bro 187
Ennis-Phi 187
Musial-StL 186
Snider-Bro 185
Torgeson-Bos 184

Bases On Balls
Stanky-NY 144
Torgeson-Bos 119
Westrum-NY 92
Reese-Bro 91

Batting Average
Musial-StL ...... .346
Robinson-Bro .... .328
Snider-Bro ...... .321
Ennis-Phi .... .311
Kluszewski-Cin .. .307

On Base Percentage
Stanky-NY .... .460
Musial-StL ...... .437
Robinson-Bro .... .423
Glaviano-StL .... .421
Torgeson-Bos .... .412

Slugging Average
Musial-StL ...... .596
Pafko-Chi .... .591
Kiner-Pit .... .590
Gordon-Bos ...... .557
Snider-Bro ...... .553

Production
Musial-StL 1.034
Kiner-Pit .... .998
Pafko-Chi .... .989
Gordon-Bos ...... .960
Snider-Bro ...... .932

Adjusted Production
Musial-StL 161
Gordon-Bos 160
Pafko-Chi 158
Kiner-Pit 154
Elliott-Bos 143

Batter Runs
Musial-StL 57.3
Kiner-Pit 48.7
Pafko-Chi 41.5
Snider-Bro 35.6
Gordon-Bos 35.3

Adjusted Batter Runs
Musial-StL 50.9
Kiner-Pit 44.5
Pafko-Chi 42.8
Gordon-Bos 42.1
Torgeson-Bos 38.7

Clutch Hitting Index
D.Mueller-NY 138
Slaughter-StL ... 136
Westlake-Pit 115
Wyrostek-Cin 112
Thompson-NY 111

Runs Created
Musial-StL 149
Kiner-Pit 133
Snider-Bro 131
Pafko-Chi 124
Torgeson-Bos 121

Total Average
Musial-StL 1.139
Kiner-Pit 1.071
Pafko-Chi 1.057
Stanky-NY 1.013
Gordon-Bos 1.003

Stolen Bases
Jethroe-Bos 35
Reese-Bro 17
Snider-Bro 16
Torgeson-Bos 15
Ashburn-Phi 14

Stolen Base Average

Stolen Base Runs

Fielding Runs
Smalley-Chi 21.3
Cox-Bro 12.0
Ryan-Bos-Cin 11.6
Robinson-Bro 10.6
Westrum-NY 10.4

Total Player Rating
Robinson-Bro 4.7
Stanky-NY 4.1
Gordon-Bos 4.1
Pafko-Chi 3.5
Seminick-Phi 3.5

Wins
Spahn-Bos 21
Sain-Bos 20
Roberts-Phi 20

Win Percentage
Maglie-NY .... .818
Konstanty-Phi ... .696
Simmons-Phi ..... .680
Roberts-Phi ..... .645

Games
Konstanty-Phi ... 74
Dickson-Pit 51
Werle-Pit 48
Maglie-NY 47
Brazle-StL 46

Complete Games
Bickford-Bos 27
Spahn-Bos 25
Sain-Bos 25
Roberts-Phi 21
Jansen-NY 21

Shutouts
Hearn-StL-NY 5
Roberts-Phi 5
Maglie-NY 5
Jansen-NY 5

Saves
Konstanty-Phi ... 22
Werle-Pit 8
Hogue-Bos 7
Branca-Bro 7

Innings Pitched
Bickford-Bos 311.2
Roberts-Phi 304.1
Spahn-Bos 293.0
Sain-Bos 278.1
Jansen-NY 275.0

Fewest Hits/Game
Blackwell-Cin ... 7.00
Maglie-NY 7.38
Simmons-Phi 7.46
Spahn-Bos 7.62
Jansen-NY 7.79

Fewest BB/Game
Raffensberger-Cin . 1.51
Jansen-NY 1.80
Sain-Bos 2.26
Roberts-Phi 2.28
Roe-Bro 2.37

Strikeouts
Spahn-Bos 191
Blackwell-Cin ... 188
Jansen-NY 161
Simmons-Phi 146
Roberts-Phi 146

Strikeouts/Game
Blackwell-Cin ... 6.48
Simmons-Phi 6.12
Spahn-Bos 5.87
Palica-Bro 5.86
Jansen-NY 5.27

Ratio
Jansen-NY 9.62
Roberts-Phi 10.68
Brecheen-StL 10.97
Spahn-Bos 11.06
Simmons-Phi 11.24

Earned Run Average
Hearn-StL-NY 2.49
Maglie-NY 2.71
Blackwell-Cin ... 2.97
Jansen-NY 3.01
Roberts-Phi 3.02

Adjusted ERA
Maglie-NY 151
Blackwell-Cin ... 143
Lanier-StL 137
Jansen-NY 136
Roberts-Phi 134

Opponents' Batting Avg.
Blackwell-Cin ... .210
Simmons-Phi ..... .223
Maglie-NY .... .226
Spahn-Bos .... .227
Jansen-NY .... .232

Opponents' On Base Pct.
Jansen-NY .... .271
Roberts-Phi ..... .297
Brecheen-StL .... .298
Spahn-Bos .... .299
Blackwell-Cin ... .301

Starter Runs
Roberts-Phi 38.0
Jansen-NY 34.5
Blackwell-Cin ... 34.1
Maglie-NY 32.8
Spahn-Bos 31.8

Adjusted Starter Runs
Blackwell-Cin ... 36.7
Roberts-Phi 34.8
Jansen-NY 33.1
Maglie-NY 31.7
Pollet-StL 25.9

Clutch Pitching Index
Brazle-StL 125
Roe-Bro 118
Maglie-NY 116
Ramsdell-Bro-Cin . 115
Minner-Chi 113

Relief Runs
Konstanty-Phi ... 24.9
Kramer-NY 5.9
Leonard-Chi 3.1
VanderMeer-Chi .. 2.9
Smith-Cin 2.7

Adjusted Relief Runs
Konstanty-Phi ... 23.3
Kramer-NY 5.4
Smith-Cin 3.6
Leonard-Chi 3.5
VanderMeer-Chi .. 3.4

Relief Ranking
Konstanty-Phi ... 39.4
Kramer-NY 5.2
Smith-Cin 3.5
Leonard-Chi 3.2
VanderMeer-Chi .. 3.0

Total Pitcher Index
Blackwell-Cin ... 4.3
Jansen-NY 3.8
Konstanty-Phi ... 3.6
Maglie-NY 3.3
Spahn-Bos 3.1

Total Baseball Ranking
Robinson-Bro 4.7
Blackwell-Cin ... 4.3
Stanky-NY 4.1
Gordon-Bos 4.1
Jansen-NY 3.8

January 18 The Indians' Bob Feller, whose 1949 record was a lackluster 15-14, takes a $20,000 salary cut to $45,000 at his own suggestion.

February 7 Red Sox slugger Ted Williams becomes the highest paid player in history, by signing for $125,000.

April 18 President Harry Truman throws out two balls at the Washington opener—one left-handed and the other right-handed—then watches the Senators beat the A's 8-7.

May 26 The Athletics make some changes. Connie Mack's son, Earle, who had been assistant manager, assumes the duties of chief scout. Earle, who had hoped to succeed his father as manager, is replaced by Jimmie Dykes. Mickey Cochrane is named general manager.

June 2 St. Louis Browns pitcher Harry Dorish becomes the last AL pitcher to steal home, doing it on the front end of a double steal.

June 8 In the most lopsided score since 1900, the Boston Red Sox annihilate the St. Louis Browns at Fenway Park 29-4. Bobby Doerr has three home runs and eight RBIs; Walt Dropo, two home runs and seven RBIs, and Ted Williams, two home runs and five RBIs.

June 12 Major League Baseball names Connie Mack as the Honorary Manager of the All-Star Game.

June 21 Joe DiMaggio gets his 2,000th hit, a seventh-inning single off the Indians' Chick Pieretti, as the Yanks win, 8–2. DiMaggio joins Luke Appling and Wally Moses as the only active players with 2,000 or more hits.

July 2 Indians hurler Bob Feller wins his 200th major league game, 5–3, over Detroit in the second game of a doubleheader split.

July 3 With rookie Joe Collins not hitting and Tommy Henrich injured, Casey Stengel asks Joe DiMaggio to play first baseman in an experiment. In the 7-2 loss he handles 13 chances cleanly.

August 11 Hitting just .279, Yankee great Joe DiMaggio is benched for the first time in his career. He is languishing in a 4-for-38 slump.

August 28 Earle and Roy Mack, Connie's sons by his first marriage, purchase 54 percent interest in the Athletics from Connie Mack, Jr., their younger brother from a 2nd marriage. Earle, Roy and Connie Mack now own the club outright.

September 10 Joe DiMaggio becomes the first player to hit three home runs in one game at spacious Griffith Stadium, as the Yanks beat Washington 8-1.

September 15 For a record sixth time, Johnny Mize hits three home runs in one game, but the Yanks lose 9-7 at Detroit.

September 29 The idle Yankees clinch their second consecutive pennant under Casey Stengel, as Cleveland's Bob Lemon sets down Detroit 12-2 for his 23rd win.

October 2 Dom DiMaggio of the Red Sox is the league leader in steals with 15, the lowest league-leading figure ever.

October 7 Whitey Ford wins his first World Series game, 5-2 over Bob Miller at the Stadium. The four-game sweep gives the Yankees their 13th World Championship.

October 26 The Baseball Writers of America select Yankee shortstop Phil Rizzuto as the league MVP.

November 8 The Baseball Writers Association of America announces that slugging first baseman Walt Dropo of the Boston Red Sox is the Rookie of the Year in the AL. Dropo led the league in RBIs with 144.

November 9 The White Sox release Luke Appling, who has been with the Sox since 1930, so he can become the manager of the Memphis Chicks of the Southern Association.

November 10 After nine years at the helm, the Indians fire manager Lou Boudreau amid the howls of fan protest. Although Boudreau's overall winning percentage is a moderate .529, he won 92 games in a fourth-place finish, his best showing since his Tribe won 97 in the championship year of 1948. Al Lopez, who has piloted Minneapolis (AA) since 1948, takes over with a two-year contract.

	BOSTON		CHICAGO		CLEVELAND		DETROIT		NEW YORK		PHILADELPHIA		ST.LOUIS		WASHINGTON
M	J.McCarthy	M	J.Onslow	M	L.Boudreau	M	R.Rolfe	M	C.Stengel	M	C.Mack	M	Z.Taylor	M	B.Harris
M	S.O'Neill	M	R.Corriden	1B	L.Easter	1B	D.Kolloway	1B	J.Collins	1B	F.Fain	1B	D.Lenhardt	1B	M.Vernon
1B	W.Dropo	1B	E.Robinson	2B	J.Gordon	2B	J.Priddy	2B	J.Coleman	2B	B.Hitchcock	2B	O.Friend	2B	C.Michaels
2B	B.Doerr	2B	N.Fox	SS	R.Boone	SS	J.Lipon	SS	P.Rizzuto	SS	E.Joost	SS	T.Upton	SS	S.Dente
SS	V.Stephens	SS	C.Carrasquel	3B	A.Rosen	3B	G.Kell	3B	B.Johnson	3B	B.Dillinger	3B	B.Sommers	3B	E.Yost
3B	J.Pesky	3B	H.Majeski	LF	D.Mitchell	LF	H.Evers	LF	G.Woodling	LF	P.Lehner	LF	D.Kokos	LF	B.Stewart
LF	T.Williams	LF	G.Zernial	CF	L.Doby	CF	J.Groth	CF	J.DiMaggio	CF	S.Chapman	CF	R.Coleman	CF	I.Noren
CF	D.DiMaggio	CF	D.Philley	RF	B.Kennedy	RF	V.Wertz	RF	H.Bauer	RF	E.Valo	RF	K.Wood	RF	S.Mele
RF	A.Zarilla	RF	M.Rickert	C	J.Hegan	C	A.Robinson	C	Y.Berra	C	M.Guerra	C	S.Lollar	C	A.Evans
C	B.Tebbetts	C	P.Masi												
				S	L.Boudreau	1	D.Kryhoski	3	B.Brown	3S	K.Wahl	1	H.Arft	O	G.Coan
O3	B.Goodman	3	F.Baker	2	B.Avila	O	P.Mullin	O	C.Mapes	O	W.Moses	O3	R.Sievers	O	M.Grasso
C	M.Batts	O	M.McCormick	O	A.Clark	C	B.Swift	1	J.Mize	23	P.Suder	23	S.Stirnweiss	O	J.Ostrowski
O	C.Vollmer	2	C.Michaels	C	R.Murray	C	J.Ginsberg	C	T.Henrich	C	J.Tipton	C	L.Moss	1	E.Robinson
O	T.Wright	S1	L.Appling	O	T.Tucker	/O	C.Keller	O	J.Jensen	O	B.McCosky	J	J.Delsing	O2	S.Robertson
C	B.Rosar	1	G.Goldsberry	S	N.Berry	S	N.Berry	2	B.Martin	C	J.Astroth	S	B.DeMars	S	M.Combs
/O	T.O'Brien	O	H.Adams	/S	E.Lake	1	J.Hopp	/O	B.Wellman	3	L.Thomas	/P	R.Ortiz		
/3	K.Keltner	C	G.Niarhos	/1	H.Conyers	/C	F.House	C	J.Silvera	/O	R.Ortiz	/3	F.Gustine	2	A.Kozar
/3	L.Stringer	C	E.Malone	/2	J.Berardino	H	P.Campbell	/O	J.Lindell	/2	G.Markland			/C	H.Keller
/3	F.Hatfield	O	J.Scala					H	J.Delsing	/O	B.Guintini	P	N.Garver	O	L.Okrie
/O	C.Maxwell	/O	J.Ostrowski	P	B.Lemon	P	A.Houtteman	/C	R.Houk	/O	B.Rinker	P	A.Widmar	/1	F.Taylor
/O	J.Piersall	O	J.Busby	P	B.Feller	P	F.Hutchinson	/1	H.Workman	P	S.Overmire	/O	C.Vollmer
H	M.Combs	/C	J.Erautt	P	E.Wynn	P	H.Newhouser	/2	S.Stirnweiss	P	L.Brissie	P	D.Starr	/O	T.O'Brien
/C	B.Scherbarth	/2	A.Kozar	P	M.Garcia	P	D.Trout	H	D.Wakefield	P	A.Kellner	P	H.Dorish	H	G.Genovese
		/1	C.Kress	P	S.Gromek	P	T.Gray	R	G.Niarhos	P	B.Shantz	RP	C.Marshall		
P	M.Parnell	/O	E.McGhee	RP	H.White	RP	H.White			P	H.Wyse			P	S.Hudson
P	E.Kinder	/O	B.Wilson	RP	A.Benton	RP	P.Calvert	P	V.Raschi	P	B.Hooper	P	C.Fannin	P	B.Kuzava
P	J.Dobson	/3	J.Kirrene	RP	J.Flores			P	A.Reynolds	RP	C.Scheib	P	D.Johnson	P	C.Marrero
P	C.Stobbs	/C	B.Salkeld			/P	V.Trucks	P	E.Lopat			P	D.Pillette	P	S.Consuegra
P	M.McDermott			P	M.Pieretti	P	M.Stuart	P	T.Byrne	P	D.Fowler	/P	J.Ostrowski	P	J.Haynes
		P	B.Pierce	P	G.Bearden	P	S.Rogovin	P	F.Sanford	P	J.Coleman	P	T.Fine	RP	M.Harris
P	W.Masterson	P	B.Wight	P	D.Weik	P	H.Borowy	RP	T.Ferrick	/P	J.Murray	P	J.Bruner	RP	J.Pearce
P	W.Nixon	P	B.Cain	P	D.Rozek	/P	R.Herbert	/P	J.Page	P	J.Kucab	P	T.Ferrick		
P	A.Papai	P	R.Gumpert	/P	A.Aber	/P	B.Connelly			/P	M.Burtschy	/P	L.Kretlow	P	A.Sima
P	D.Littlefield	P	R.Scarborough					P	W.Ford	/P	H.Byrd	/P	S.Schacht	P	G.Bearden
P	C.Schanz	RP	H.Judson					P	J.Ostrowski	/P	E.Klieman	/P	E.Albrecht	/P	R.Scarborough
/P	J.McDonald	RP	L.Aloma					P	B.Porterfield	/P	L.McCrabb	/P	R.Bauers	/P	S.Nagy
/P	H.Taylor	RP	M.Haefner					/P	D.Johnson			/P	B.Kennedy	P	D.Weik
P	E.Johnson							/P	D.Pillette			/P	R.Raney	P	L.Hittle
/P	G.Mueller	P	K.Holcombe					/P	E.Nevel			/P	L.Sleater	P	E.Singleton
/P	J.Atkins	P	B.Kuzava					/P	D.Madison					/P	J.Moreno
/P	J.Suchecki	P	L.Kretlow					/P	L.Burdette					/P	C.Pascual
P	F.Quinn	/P	J.Bruner											/P	B.Ross
/P	D.Ferriss	/P	M.Rotblatt											/P	D.Welteroth
/P	B.Gillespie	/P	J.Perkovich											/P	R.Martinez
/P	P.Marchildon	/P	B.Connelly												
		/P	G.Keriazakos												
		/P	C.Cuellar												

TEAM	G	W	L	PCT	GB	R	OR	AB	H	2B	3B	HR	BB	SO	AVG	OBP	SLG	PRO	PRO+	BR	/A	PF	CHI	RC	SB	CS	SBA	SBR
NY	155	98	56	.636		914	691	5361	1511	234	70	159	687	463	.282	.367	.441	.808	116	92	118	97	104	902	41	28	59	-5
DET	157	95	59	.617	3	837	713	5381	1518	285	50	114	722	480	.282	.369	.417	.786	104	60	33	103	97	846	23	40	37	-17
BOS	154	94	60	.610	4	1027	804	5516	1665	287	61	161	719	582	.302	.385	.464	.849	112	185	90	91	103	1014	32	17	65	-1
CLE	155	92	62	.597	6	806	654	5263	1417	222	46	164	693	624	.269	.358	.422	.780	109	39	66	97	98	820	40	34	54	-8
WAS	155	67	87	.435	31	690	813	5251	1365	190	53	76	671	606	.260	.347	.360	.707	91	-93	-61	95	101	690	42	25	63	-2
CHI	156	60	94	.390	38	625	749	5260	1368	172	47	93	551	566	.260	.333	.364	.697	86	-125	-107	97	98	648	19	22	46	-8
STL	154	58	96	.377	40	684	916	5163	1269	235	43	106	690	744	.246	.337	.370	.707	84	-102	-127	104	103	667	39	40	49	-12
PHI	154	52	102	.338	46	670	913	5212	1361	204	53	100	685	493	.261	.349	.378	.727	94	-56	-42	98	94	708	42	25	63	-2
TOT	620					6253		42407	11474	1829	423	973	5418	4558	.271	.356	.402	.759							278	231	55	-55

TEAM	CG	SH	SV	IP	H	H/G	HR	BB	SO	RAT	ERA	ERA+	OAV	OOB	PR	/A	PF	CPI	FA	E	DP	FW	PW	BW	SBW	DIF
NY	66	12	31	1372²	1322	8.7	118	708	712	13.5	4.15	103	.255	.348	65	22	94	102	.980	119	188	1.3	2.1	11.0	.2	6.4
DET	72	9	20	1407¹	1444	9.2	141	553	576	13.0	4.12	114	.267	.339	71	88	102	105	.981	120	194	1.3	8.2	3.1	-.9	6.3
BOS	66	6	28	1362¹	1413	9.3	121	748	630	14.4	4.88	100	.270	.364	-46	3	107	97	.981	111	181	1.7	.3	8.4	.6	6.1
CLE	69	11	16	1378²	1289	8.4	120	647	674	12.8	3.75	115	.248	.333	126	88	95	103	.978	129	160	.7	8.2	6.2	-.1	-.0
WAS	59	7	18	1364²	1479	9.8	99	648	486	14.2	4.66	96	.278	.359	-12	-25	98	99	.972	167	181	-1.4	-2.3	-5.7	.5	-1.0
CHI	62	7	9	1365²	1370	9.0	107	734	566	14.0	4.41	102	.263	.356	26	12	98	100	.977	140	181	.2	1.1	-10.0	-.5	-8.2
STL	56	7	14	1365¹	1629	10.7	129	651	448	15.2	5.20	95	.295	.372	-94	-38	108	100	.967	196	155	-3.1	-3.6	-11.9	-.5	-.0
PHI	50	3	18	1346¹	1528	10.2	138	729	466	15.3	5.49	83	.287	.376	-136	-140	99	96	.974	155	208	-.8	-13.1	-3.9	.5	-7.7
TOT	500	62	154	10963		9.4				14.0	4.58		.271	.356					.976	1137	1448					

Runs		Hits		Doubles		Triples		Home Runs		Total Bases	
DiMaggio-Bos	131	Kell-Det	218	Kell-Det	56	Evers-Det	11	Rosen-Bos	37	Dropo-Bos	326
Stephens-Bos	125	Rizzuto-NY	200	Wertz-Det	37	Doerr-Bos	11	Dropo-Bos	34	Stephens-Bos	321
Rizzuto-NY	125	DiMaggio-Bos	193	Rizzuto-NY	36	DiMaggio-Bos	11	DiMaggio-NY	32	Berra-NY	318
Berra-NY	116	Berra-NY	192	Evers-Det	35			Stephens-Bos	30	Kell-Det	310
		Stephens-Bos	185	Stephens-Bos	34			Zernial-Chi	29	DiMaggio-NY	307

Runs Batted In		Runs Produced		Bases On Balls		Batting Average		On Base Percentage		Slugging Average	
Stephens-Bos	144	Stephens-Bos	239	Yost-Was	141	Goodman-Bos	.354	Doby-Cle	.442	DiMaggio-NY	.585
Dropo-Bos	144	Berra-NY	212	Fain-Phi	133	Kell-Det	.340	Yost-Was	.440	Dropo-Bos	.583
Berra-NY	124	Dropo-Bos	211	Pesky-Bos	104	DiMaggio-Bos	.328	Pesky-Bos	.437	Evers-Det	.551
Wertz-Det	123	Kell-Det	207	Joost-Phi	103	Doby-Cle	.326	Fain-Phi	.430	Doby-Cle	.545
DiMaggio-NY	122	DiMaggio-NY	204	Rosen-Cle	100	Zarilla-Bos	.325	Goodman-Bos	.427	Rosen-Cle	.543

Production		Adjusted Production		Batter Runs		Adjusted Batter Runs		Clutch Hitting Index		Runs Created	
Doby-Cle	.986	Doby-Cle	156	Doby-Cle	41.7	Doby-Cle	45.7	Vernon-Cle-Was	126	Doby-Cle	130
DiMaggio-NY	.979	DiMaggio-NY	152	Williams-Bos	40.9	DiMaggio-NY	38.8	Mele-Was	125	Wertz-Det	128
Dropo-Bos	.961	Rosen-Cle	146	DiMaggio-NY	35.4	Rosen-Cle	38.3	Noren-Was	116	DiMaggio-NY	125
Evers-Det	.959	Evers-Det	139	Rosen-Cle	34.3	Williams-Bos	32.1	Stephens-Bos	110	Berra-NY	125
Rosen-Cle	.948	Berra-NY	136	Evers-Det	33.5	Evers-Det	30.0	Fain-Phi	108	Rizzuto-NY	124

Total Average		Stolen Bases		Stolen Base Average		Stolen Base Runs		Fielding Runs		Total Player Rating	
Doby-Cle	1.073	DiMaggio-Bos	15			DiMaggio-NY	2.1	Priddy-Det	31.3	Rizzuto-NY	4.1
DiMaggio-NY	1.018	Valo-Phi	12			Vernon-Cle-Was	1.8	Hegan-Cle	24.2	Berra-NY	3.4
Wertz-Det	.978	Rizzuto-NY	12			Collins-NY	1.5	Pesky-Bos	21.5	DiMaggio-NY	3.1
Zarilla-Bos	.954	Coan-Was	10			Avila-Cle	1.5	Noren-Was	15.9	Rosen-Cle	3.1
Rosen-Cle	.953	Lipon-Det	9			Jensen-NY	1.2	Carrasquel-Chi	11.2	Doby-Cle	3.1

Wins		Win Percentage		Games		Complete Games		Shutouts		Saves	
B.Lemon-Cle	23	Raschi-NY	.724	Harris-Was	53	B.Lemon-Cle	22	Houtteman-Det	4	Harris-Was	15
Raschi-NY	21	Wynn-Cle	.692	Kinder-Bos	48	Garver-StL	22			Page-NY	13
Houtteman-Det	19	Lopat-NY	.692	Ferrick-StL-NY	46	Parnell-Bos	21			Ferrick-StL-NY	11
		Hutchinson-Det	.680	Judson-Chi	46	Houtteman-Det	21			Kinder-Bos	9
		B.Lemon-Cle	.676	Brissie-Phi	46					Brissie-Phi	8

Innings Pitched		Fewest Hits/Game		Fewest BB/Game		Strikeouts		Strikeouts/Game		Ratio	
B.Lemon-Cle	288.0	Wynn-Cle	6.99	Hutchinson-Det	1.86	B.Lemon-Cle	170	Wynn-Cle	6.02	Wynn-Cle	11.41
Houtteman-Det	274.2	Pierce-Chi	7.76	Lopat-NY	2.48	Reynolds-NY	160	Reynolds-NY	5.98	Lopat-NY	11.92
Garver-StL	260.0	Cain-Chi	8.02	Overmire-StL	2.52	Raschi-NY	155	Raschi-NY	5.44	Houtteman-Det	11.93
Raschi-NY	256.2	Reynolds-NY	8.04	Trout-Det	3.12	Wynn-Cle	143	B.Lemon-Cle	5.31	Raschi-NY	12.31
Parnell-Bos	249.0	Raschi-NY	8.14	Houtteman-Det	3.24	Feller-Cle	119	Byrne-NY	5.22	Feller-Cle	12.32

Earned Run Average		Adjusted ERA		Opponents' Batting Avg.		Opponents' On Base Pct.		Starter Runs		Adjusted Starter Runs	
Wynn-Cle	3.20	Garver-StL	146	Wynn-Cle	.212	Wynn-Cle	.305	Garver-StL	34.3	Garver-StL	45.0
Garver-StL	3.39	Parnell-Bos	136	Pierce-Chi	.228	Lopat-NY	.317	Wynn-Cle	32.7	Parnell-Bos	35.5
Feller-Cle	3.43	Wynn-Cle	135	Reynolds-NY	.242	Houtteman-Det	.322	Houtteman-Det	31.7	Houtteman-Det	35.1
Lopat-NY	3.47	Houtteman-Det	132	Raschi-NY	.243	Feller-Cle	.325	Feller-Cle	31.7	Wynn-Cle	26.8
Houtteman-Det	3.54	Feller-Cle	126	Cain-Chi	.244	Raschi-NY	.327	Lopat-NY	29.2	Feller-Cle	24.9

Clutch Pitching Index		Relief Runs		Adjusted Relief Runs		Relief Ranking		Total Pitcher Index		Total Baseball Ranking	
Garver-StL	119	Judson-Chi	8.0	Judson-Chi	6.8	Ferrick-StL-NY	13.0	Garver-StL	5.7	Garver-StL	5.7
Hudson-Was	113	Aloma-Chi	7.6	Aloma-Chi	6.9	Aloma-Chi	6.9	Parnell-Bos	3.9	Rizzuto-NY	4.1
B.Lemon-Cle	111	Benton-Cle	7.0	Ferrick-StL-NY	6.2	Benton-Cle	5.3	B.Lemon-Cle	3.7	Parnell-Bos	3.9
Houtteman-Det	110	Ferrick-StL-NY	7.0	Benton-Cle	5.3	Flores-Cle	4.2	Wynn-Cle	3.6	B.Lemon-Cle	3.7
Parnell-Bos	110	Flores-Cle	5.0	Flores-Cle	3.5	Judson-Chi	2.7	Houtteman-Det	3.5	Wynn-Cle	3.6

January 26 The baseball writers vote Mel Ott and Jimmie Foxx into the Hall of Fame.

April 17 In pregame ceremonies at Wrigley Field, Sam Snead tees off from home plate and hits a golf ball off the center field scoreboard, the only ball ever to reach the structure. The Cubs follow up in their home opener by beating the Reds 8–3.

May 25 Giants rookie Willie Mays, who was hitting .477 with Minneapolis, goes 0-for-5 in his major league debut against the Phils.

May 28 After going 0-for-12, Willie Mays connects for his first major league hit, a home run off Braves pitcher Warren Spahn. The Giants lose the game, 4–1.

July 10 Exploding for a record four home runs, the NL trounces the AL 8–3 at the annual All-Star Game at Briggs Stadium in Detroit. Pittsburgh slugger Ralph Kiner homers for the third year in a row.

July 20 In a move that will aid their pennant drive, the Giants put outfielder Bobby Thomson at third baseman to replace Hank Thompson, out with an injury. Thomson, who's been riding the bench since losing his starting job to the rookie Mays, will hit .357 for the rest of the season.

September 13 The Cards split a rare doubleheader with two different teams, defeating the Giants 6-4 in the first game in the afternoon and losing 2-0 to the Braves in the nightcap. It's the first time a team in the NL has played two different teams in the same day since the early years of the century.

September 20 The owners elect NL President Ford Frick as the third commissioner of baseball for a seven-year term at $65,000 per annum.

October 1 With both the Dodgers and Giants tied 96-58 at the end of the regular season, Brooklyn wins the coin toss and elects to play the first game of the play-offs at home. The next two games will be played at the Polo Grounds. In the league's first best-of-three playoff since 1946, Ralph Branca of the Dodgers loses to Jim Hearn and the Giants 3-1. Branca serves up home runs to Bobby Thomson and Monte Irvin in the first game ever to be telecast live coast-to-coast.

October 2 The Dodgers bounce back as rookie Clem Labine evens the playoff with a 10-0 win, besting the Giants' Sheldon Jones. Home runs are smashed by Jackie Robinson, Gil Hodges, Andy Pafko, and Rube Walker. Willie Mays grounds into three double plays.

October 3 The Giants' Bobby Thomson hits the most famous home run in history, off Ralph Branca. His "shot heard 'round the world" with two on and the Giants trailing 4-2 in the bottom of the ninth defeats Brooklyn 5-4 and sends the jubilant Giants into the World Series.

October 4 In the opening game of the World Series, Monte Irvin steals home in the first inning and collects four hits. The Giants defeat Allie Reynolds and the Yankees 5-1 with Dave Koslo going all the way at Yankee Stadium.

October 6 Back at the Polo Grounds, the Giants win, 6-2, as Whitey Lockman homers with two on in the fifth. The Giants score five in the inning after Eddie Stanky kicks the ball out of Phil Rizzuto's glove on a tag play at second baseman.

November 1 The NL votes Roy Campanella the league's MVP for what will be the first of three such awards.

Rosters

BOSTON

Pos	Player
M	B.Southworth
M	T.Holmes
1B	E.Torgeson
2B	R.Hartsfield
SS	B.Kerr
3B	B.Elliott
LF	S.Gordon
CF	S.Jethroe
RF	W.Marshall
C	W.Cooper
S2	S.Sisti
C	E.St.Claire
O	B.Addis
S	J.Logan
O	L.Marquez
C	R.Mueller
O	L.Olmo
/O	T.Holmes
S	G.Mauch
H	B.Thorpe
P	W.Spahn
P	M.Surkont
P	V.Bickford
P	J.Sain
P	C.Nichols
RP	D.Cole
RP	G.Estock
RP	B.Chipman
P	J.Wilson
P	P.Paine
/P	D.Donovan
/P	B.Hogue
/P	S.Schacht
/P	L.Burdette

BROOKLYN

Pos	Player
M	C.Dressen
1B	G.Hodges
2B	J.Robinson
SS	P.Reese
3B	B.Cox
LF	A.Pafko
CF	D.Snider
RF	C.Furillo
C	R.Campanella
O	C.Abrams
32	R.Bridges
O	D.Thompson
O	G.Hermanski
C	R.Walker
O	D.Williams
2	W.Terwilliger
/C	B.Edwards
H	H.Edwards
/O	T.Brown
O	J.Russell
/3	E.Miksis
/C	M.Livingston
H	W.Belardi
P	D.Newcombe
P	P.Roe
P	R.Branca
P	C.Erskine
RP	C.King
RP	B.Podbielan
RP	E.Palica
P	C.Labine
P	J.Schmitz
P	J.Hatten
P	P.Haugstad
/P	C.Van Cuyk
/P	D.Bankhead
/P	E.Mossor

CHICAGO

Pos	Player
M	F.Frisch
M	P.Cavarretta
1B	C.Connors
2B	E.Miksis
SS	R.Smalley
3B	R.Jackson
LF	H.Sauer
CF	H.Jeffcoat
RF	F.Baumholtz
C	S.Burgess
O	G.Hermanski
1	P.Cavarretta
2	W.Terwilliger
O	A.Pafko
1	D.Fondy
S	J.Cusick
S	B.Ramazzotti
C	B.Edwards
C	M.Owen
C	R.Walker
O	B.Borkowski
3	B.Serena
/C	H.Chiti
/O	C.Mauro
/1	F.Richards
P	B.Rush
P	P.Minner
P	C.McLish
P	F.Hiller
P	T.Lown
RP	D.Leonard
RP	M.Dubiel
P	B.Kelly
P	J.Klippstein
P	B.Schultz
P	J.Hatten
/P	J.Schmitz
/P	A.Varga
/P	W.Hacker

CINCINNATI

Pos	Player
M	L.Sewell
1B	T.Kluszewski
2B	C.Ryan
SS	V.Stallcup
3B	G.Hatton
LF	J.Adcock
CF	L.Merriman
RF	J.Wyrostek
C	D.Howell
32	B.Adams
O	B.Usher
C	J.Pramesa
S3	R.McMillan
2	H.Edwards
O	B.Scheffing
C	B.McCosky
/O	W.Post
/3	S.Meeks
/O	D.Litwhiler
/C	H.Landrith
H	T.Tappe
R	J.Bolger
P	K.Raffensberger
P	E.Blackwell
P	H.Fox
P	W.Ramsdell
RP	H.Wehmeier
RP	H.Perkowski
RP	F.Smith
RP	B.Byerly

NEW YORK

Pos	Player
M	L.Durocher
1B	W.Lockman
2B	E.Stanky
SS	A.Dark
3B	H.Thompson
LF	M.Irvin
CF	W.Mays
RF	D.Mueller
C	W.Westrum
O3	B.Thomson
C	R.Noble
3	B.Rigney
2	D.Williams
O	S.Jorgensen
2	C.Hartung
C	C.Yvars
3	J.Lohrke
/2	A.Wilson
/O	A.Maguire
H	E.Rapp
R	H.Schenz
P	S.Maglie
P	L.Jansen
P	J.Hearn
P	D.Koslo
RP	G.Spencer
P	S.Jones
RP	M.Kennedy
P	A.Corwin
P	A.Gettel
/P	R.Bowman
/P	J.Kramer
/P	A.Konikowski
P	G.Bamberger
/P	R.Hardy

PHILADELPHIA

Pos	Player
M	E.Sawyer
1B	E.Waitkus
2B	P.Caballero
SS	G.Hamner
3B	W.Jones
LF	D.Sisler
CF	R.Ashburn
RF	D.Ennis
C	A.Seminick
C	D.Wilber
C	E.Pellagrini
O2	T.Brown
C	B.Nicholson
2	M.Goliat
2	D.Young
/2	J.Bloodworth
/O	M.Clark
/O	D.Whitman
/O	K.Silvestri
/O	J.Mayo
/C	S.Lopata
O	E.Sanicki
	S.Hollmig
P	R.Roberts
P	B.Church
P	R.Meyer
P	J.Thompson
P	K.Heintzelman
RP	J.Konstanty
P	K.Johnson
P	A.Hansen
P	N.Jordan
P	B.Miller
P	M.Candini
P	K.Drews
RP	L.Cristante
RP	L.Possehl
/P	J.Brittin

PITTSBURGH

Pos	Player
M	B.Meyer
1B	J.Phillips
2B	D.Murtaugh
SS	G.Strickland
3B	P.Castiglione
LF	R.Kiner
CF	C.Metkovich
RF	G.Bell
C	C.McCullough
O	B.Howerton
C	J.Garagiola
1O	R.Nelson
3O	W.Westlake
2	M.Basgall
O	F.Thomas
O	P.Reiser
2	D.Cole
C	E.FitzGerald
O	T.Saffell
2	H.Schenz
2	J.Merson
O	T.Beard
3	D.Smith
3	B.Dillinger
O	E.Dusak
O	D.Restelli
/S	S.Rojek
/1	D.Long
2	J.Maguire
H	H.Fisher
P	M.Dickson
P	M.Queen
P	B.Friend
P	H.Pollet
P	V.Law
RP	B.Werle
RP	T.Wilks
RP	J.Walsh
P	C.Chambers
P	P.LaPalme
/P	D.Carlsen
P	B.Koski
/P	J.Muir
/P	L.Yochim
/P	C.Dempsey
/P	P.Pettit

ST.LOUIS

Pos	Player
M	M.Marion
1B	N.Jones
2B	R.Schoendienst
SS	S.Hemus
3B	B.Johnson
LF	S.Musial
CF	P.Lowrey
RF	E.Slaughter
C	D.Rice
O	W.Westlake
O	H.Rice
S	S.Rojek
O	T.Glaviano
C	B.Sarni
C	C.Diering
1	J.Bilko
C	J.Garagiola
O	B.Howerton
/3	V.Benson
2	D.Cole
3	D.Richmond
3	E.Kazak
/O	H.Walker
/1	R.Nelson
C	B.Scheffing
/1	D.Bollweg
/O	J.Van Noy
/O	L.Ciaffone
P	G.Staley
P	T.Poholsky
P	M.Lanier
P	H.Brecheen
P	C.Chambers
P	A.Brazle
RP	D.Bokelmann
P	R.Munger
P	J.Presko
P	C.Boyer
P	T.Wilks
/P	J.Collum
P	J.Crimian
/P	H.Pollet
/P	E.Dusak
/P	B.Habenicht
/P	K.Krieger
/P	D.Lewandowski

TEAM	G	W	L	PCT	GB		R	OR	AB	H	2B	3B	HR	BB	SO		AVG	OBP	SLG	PRO	PRO+		BR	/A	PF	CHI	RC		SB	CS	SBA	SBR
NY	157	98	59	.624			781	**641**	5360	1396	201	53	179	**671**	624		.260	.347	.418	.765	111		91	85	101	97	812		55	34	62	-4
BRO	158	97	60	.618	1		**855**	672	5492	**1511**	249	37	184	603	649		**.275**	**.352**	**.434**	**.786**	116		130	113	102	101	843		89	70	56	-15
STL	155	81	73	.526	15.5		683	671	5317	1404	230	57	95	569	492		.264	.339	.382	.721	99		7	3	101	97	705		30	30	50	-9
BOS	155	76	78	.494	20.5		723	662	5293	1385	234	37	130	565	617		.262	.336	.394	.730	111		20	70	93	102	719		63	28	69	2
PHI	154	73	81	.474	23.5		648	644	5332	1384	199	47	108	505	525		.260	.326	.375	.701	96		-38	-28	99	99	676		63	28	69	2
CIN	155	68	86	.442	28.5		559	667	5285	1309	215	33	88	415	577		.248	.304	.351	.655	81		-134	-142	102	104	562		44	40	52	-11
PIT	155	64	90	.416	32.5		689	845	5318	1372	218	56	137	557	615		.258	.331	.397	.728	99		11	-9	103	98	712		29	27	52	-8
CHI	155	62	92	.403	34.5		614	750	5307	1327	200	47	103	477	647		.250	.315	.364	.679	86		-86	-97	102	103	613		63	30	68	1
TOT	622						5552		42704	11088	1746	367	1024	4362	4746		.260	.331	.390	.721									453	293	61	-40

TEAM	CG	SH	SV	IP		H	H/G	HR	BB	SO	RAT		ERA	ERA+	OAV	OOB		PR	/A	PF	CPI		FA	E	DP		FW	PW	BW	SBW	DIF
NY	64	9	18	1412²		**1334**	8.5	148	482	625	11.7		3.48	113	.248	.313		75	69	99	104		.972	171	175		-1.0	**6.9**	8.5	.0	5.0
BRO	64	10	13	1423¹		1360	8.6	150	549	**693**	12.2		3.88	101	.253	.326		13	8	99	101		.979	129	**192**		**1.3**	.8	**11.3**	-1.0	6.1
STL	58	9	**23**	1387²		1391	9.0	119	568	546	12.8		3.95	100	.264	.338		1	2	100	103		**.980**	**125**	187		**1.3**	.2	.3	-.4	2.6
BOS	**73**	16	12	1389		1378	8.9	**96**	595	604	13.0		3.75	98	.259	.337		33	-11	93	104		.977	145	157		.3	-1.1	7.0	**.9**	-8.1
PHI	57	**19**	15	1384²		1373	8.9	110	497	570	12.3		3.81	101	.258	.324		23	6	97	98		.977	138	146		.6	.6	-2.8	.7	-3.1
CIN	55	14	**23**	1390²		1357	8.8	119	490	584	12.2		3.70	100	.255	.323		40	58	103	100		.977	140	141		.5	5.8	-14.2	-.6	-.5
PIT	40	9	22	1380¹		1479	9.6	157	609	580	13.8		4.79	88	.274	.350		-128	-88	107	97		.972	170	178		-1.1	-8.8	-.9	-.3	-1.9
CHI	48	10	10	1385²		1416	9.2	125	572	544	13.1		4.34	94	.265	.340		-58	-38	103	96		.971	181	161		-1.7	-3.8	-9.7	.6	-.4
TOT	459	96	136	11154			8.9				12.6		3.96		.260	.331							.975	1199	1337						

Runs		Hits		Doubles		Triples		Home Runs		Total Bases	
Musial-StL	124	Ashburn-Phi	221	Dark-NY	41	Musial-StL	12	Kiner-Pit	42	Musial-StL	355
Kiner-Pit	124	Musial-StL	205	Kluszewski-Cin	35	Bell-Pit	12	Hodges-Bro	40	Kiner-Pit	333
Hodges-Bro	118	Furillo-Bro	197	Robinson-Bro	33	Irvin-NY	11	Campanella-Bro	33	Hodges-Bro	307
Dark-NY	114	Dark-NY	196	Campanella-Bro	33	Jethroe-Bos	10	Thomson-NY	32	Campanella-Bro	298
Robinson-Bro	106	Robinson-Bro	185			Baumholtz-Chi	10	Musial-StL	32		

Runs Batted In		Runs Produced		Bases On Balls		Batting Average		On Base Percentage		Slugging Average	
Irvin-NY	121	Musial-StL	200	Kiner-Pit	137	Musial-StL	.355	Kiner-Pit	.452	Kiner-Pit	.627
Kiner-Pit	109	Kiner-Pit	191	Stanky-NY	127	Ashburn-Phi	.344	Musial-StL	.449	Musial-StL	.614
Gordon-Bos	109	Irvin-NY	191	Westrum-NY	104	Robinson-Bro	.338	Robinson-Bro	.429	Campanella-Bro	.590
Musial-StL	108	Hodges-Bro	181	Torgeson-Bos	102	Campanella-Bro	.325	Irvin-NY	.415	Thomson-NY	.562
Campanella-Bro	108	Gordon-Bos	176	Musial-StL	98	Irvin-NY	.312	Stanky-NY	.401	Hodges-Bro	.527

Production		Adjusted Production		Batter Runs		Adjusted Batter Runs		Clutch Hitting Index		Runs Created	
Kiner-Pit	1.079	Musial-StL	182	Kiner-Pit	70.8	Musial-StL	69.2	Slaughter-StL	136	Musial-StL	169
Musial-StL	1.063	Kiner-Pit	182	Musial-StL	70.1	Kiner-Pit	66.5	Reese-Bro	130	Kiner-Pit	165
Campanella-Bro	.983	Campanella-Bro	158	Robinson-Bro	45.8	Robinson-Bro	43.4	Irvin-NY	118	Robinson-Bro	133
Robinson-Bro	.957	Robinson-Bro	153	Campanella-Bro	41.7	Irvin-NY	39.7	Westlake-Pit-StL	112	Irvin-NY	127
Thomson-NY	.947	Thomson-NY	150	Irvin-NY	40.7	Campanella-Bro	39.6	Torgeson-Bos	109	Hodges-Bro	119

Total Average		Stolen Bases		Stolen Base Average		Stolen Base Runs		Fielding Runs		Total Player Rating	
Kiner-Pit	1.251	Jethroe-Bos	35	Jethroe-Bos	87.5	Jethroe-Bos	7.5	Ashburn-Phi	32.3	Robinson-Bro	6.8
Musial-StL	1.180	Ashburn-Phi	29	Ashburn-Phi	82.9	Ashburn-Phi	5.1	Robinson-Bro	16.5	Musial-StL	6.4
Robinson-Bro	1.034	Robinson-Bro	25	Robinson-Bro	75.8	Robinson-Bro	2.7	Furillo-Bro	16.1	Kiner-Pit	5.4
Irvin-NY	.985	Torgeson-Bos	20	Torgeson-Bos	64.5	Jackson-Chi	2.4	Schoendienst-StL	15.5	Campanella-Bro	5.2
Campanella-Bro	.978	Reese-Bro	20	Reese-Bro	58.8	Irvin-NY	2.4	Hemus-StL	13.4	Ashburn-Phi	5.2

Wins		Win Percentage		Games		Complete Games		Shutouts		Saves	
Maglie-NY	23	Roe-Bro	.880	Wilks-StL-Pit	65	Spahn-Bos	26	Spahn-Bos	7	Wilks-StL-Pit	13
Jansen-NY	23	Maglie-NY	.793	Werle-Pit	59	Roberts-Phi	22	Roberts-Phi	6	Smith-Cin	11
Spahn-Bos	22	Newcombe-Bro	.690	Konstanty-Phi	58	Maglie-NY	22	Raffensberger-Cin	5	Konstanty-Phi	9
Roe-Bro	22	Jansen-NY	.676	Spencer-NY	57	Roe-Bro	19			Brazle-StL	7
Roberts-Phi	21	Hearn-NY	.654	Brazle-StL	56	Dickson-Pit	19				

Innings Pitched		Fewest Hits/Game		Fewest BB/Game		Strikeouts		Strikeouts/Game		Ratio	
Roberts-Phi	315.0	Maglie-NY	7.67	Raffensberger-Cin	1.38	Spahn-Bos	164	Queen-Pit	6.58	Raffensberger-Cin	9.99
Spahn-Bos	310.2	Newcombe-Bro	7.78	Jansen-NY	1.81	Newcombe-Bro	164	Rush-Chi	5.49	Roberts-Phi	10.03
Maglie-NY	298.0	Blackwell-Cin	7.89	Roberts-Phi	1.83	Maglie-NY	146	Newcombe-Bro	5.43	Jansen-NY	10.11
Dickson-Pit	288.2	Branca-Bro	7.94	Roe-Bro	2.24	Jansen-NY	145	Branca-Bro	5.21	Maglie-NY	10.45
Jansen-NY	278.2	Queen-Pit	7.97	Sain-Bos	2.53	Rush-Chi	129	Spahn-Bos	4.75	Roe-Bro	10.86

Earned Run Average		Adjusted ERA		Opponents' Batting Avg.		Opponents' On Base Pct.		Starter Runs		Adjusted Starter Runs	
Nichols-Bos	2.88	Maglie-NY	134	Maglie-NY	.230	Roberts-Phi	.278	Maglie-NY	34.1	Maglie-NY	32.7
Maglie-NY	2.93	Roe-Bro	129	Newcombe-Bro	.230	Jansen-NY	.279	Spahn-Bos	33.7	Roberts-Phi	28.7
Spahn-Bos	2.98	Jansen-NY	129	Blackwell-Cin	.233	Raffensberger-Cin	.279	Roberts-Phi	32.6	Jansen-NY	27.2
Roberts-Phi	3.03	Nichols-Bos	127	Queen-Pit	.233	Maglie-NY	.289	Jansen-NY	28.6	Roe-Bro	25.3
Jansen-NY	3.04	Roberts-Phi	127	Branca-Bro	.237	Newcombe-Bro	.297	Roe-Bro	26.4	Spahn-Bos	23.8

Clutch Pitching Index		Relief Runs		Adjusted Relief Runs		Relief Ranking		Total Pitcher Index		Total Baseball Ranking	
Roe-Bro	122	Brazle-StL	14.9	Brazle-StL	15.0	Leonard-Chi	24.3	Roberts-Phi	3.4	Robinson-Bro	6.8
Sain-Bos	113	Kennedy-NY	12.9	Wilks-StL-Pit	14.7	Wilks-StL-Pit	14.8	Maglie-NY	2.9	Musial-StL	6.4
Nichols-Bos	112	Perkowski-Cin	12.9	Perkowski-Cin	14.2	Perkowski-Cin	11.6	Blackwell-Cin	2.9	Kiner-Pit	5.4
Minner-Chi	111	Wilks-StL-Pit	12.3	Leonard-Chi	13.1	Smith-Cin	11.2	Jansen-NY	2.9	Campanella-Bro	5.2
Bickford-Bos	108	Leonard-Chi	11.9	Kennedy-NY	12.6	Brazle-StL	11.1	Spahn-Bos	2.9	Ashburn-Phi	5.2

January 29 Baseball signs a six-year All-Star Game pact for TV-radio rights calling for $6 million.

February 9 The St. Louis Browns sign Satchel Paige, 45. He had been out of major league baseball since last pitching for the Indians in 1949.

February 21 The South Carolina House introduces a resolution urging that "Shoeless Joe" Jackson, who was banished from baseball because of his part in the Black Sox Scandal of 1919, be reinstated.

April 18 Mickey Mantle goes 1-for-4 in his first game as Eddie Lopat two-hits the Red Sox 6-1.

May 1 The Yankees' new phenom, Mickey Mantle, connects for his first major league home run, off Randy Gumpert of the White Sox. Minnie Minoso becomes the first black to play for the White Sox. He plays third base and, facing Vic Raschi in his first major league at bat, rips a home run to center field. The Yankees win 8–3.

July 1 Bob Feller pitches the third no-hitter of his career, tying the record of Cy Young and Larry Corcoran, as he beats Detroit's Bob Cain 2-1.

July 2 Bill Veeck gets the necessary 75 percent of outstanding stock on the last day of his option to buy the St. Louis Browns from Bill and Charlie DeWitt.

July 8 The feud between Joe DiMaggio and Casey Stengel reaches a head. After DiMag makes a misplay in the first inning, Stengel sends reserve Jackie Jensen out to center field to relieve the Yankee Clipper in the second.

August 19 Bill Veeck signs 3-foot-7-inch, Eddie Gaedel, who goes to bat wearing the number ⅛ in the first inning of the nightcap with the Tigers. Lefty Bob Cain walks him on four pitches. Jim Delsing then pinch runs for Gaedel. Two days later the major league commissioner bars Gaedel from appearing in any more games.

August 28 The Yankees make another late-season insurance measure, buying Johnny Sain from the Braves for $50,000 and a young pitcher named Lew Burdette.

September 28 Allie Reynolds pitches his second no-hitter of the season, defeating the Red Sox in Yankee Stadium 8-0. With two outs in the ninth, Ted Wil-liams hits a foul pop that catcher Yogi Berra drops. Williams then hits another foul fly that Berra grabs for the last out.

October 9 Gil McDougald becomes the first rookie to hit a grand slam in the World Series, as the Yankees win in a romp, 13-1.

October 10 Hank Bauer's bases-loaded triple propels the Yankees to a 4-3 win and their third straight championship.

November 8 Yogi Berra of the Yankees wins the first of his three MVP awards.

November 18 Former Cub first baseman and future star of "The Rifleman" Chuck Connors is the first player to oppose the major league draft. Currently the first baseman of the Los Angeles Angels (Pacific Coast League), Connors wants to stay in California, instead of going to whatever team might draft him for the major leagues. The PCL views his refusal in a positive manner, allowing them to ask higher prices for players than what the major league usually offers.

December 11 Joe DiMaggio officially retires as a member of the New York Yankees with 361 home runs and an average of .325 after 13 seasons.

	BOSTON		CHICAGO		CLEVELAND		DETROIT		NEW YORK		PHILADELPHIA		ST.LOUIS		WASHINGTON
M	S.O'Neill	M	P.Richards	M	A.Lopez	M	R.Rolfe	M	C.Stengel	M	J.Dykes	M	Z.Taylor	M	B.Harris
1B	W.Dropo	1B	E.Robinson	1B	L.Easter	1B	D.Kryhoski	1B	J.Collins	1B	F.Fain	1B	H.Arft	1B	M.Vernon
2B	B.Doerr	2B	N.Fox	2B	B.Avila	2B	J.Priddy	2B	J.Coleman	2B	P.Suder	2B	B.Young	2B	C.Michaels
SS	J.Pesky	SS	C.Carrasquel	SS	R.Boone	SS	J.Lipon	SS	P.Rizzuto	SS	E.Joost	SS	B.Jennings	SS	P.Runnels
3B	V.Stephens	3B	B.Dillinger	3B	A.Rosen	3B	G.Kell	3B	B.Brown	3B	H.Majeski	3B	F.Marsh	3B	E.Yost
LF	T.Williams	LF	M.Minoso	LF	D.Mitchell	LF	H.Evers	LF	G.Woodling	LF	G.Zernial	LF	R.Coleman	LF	G.Coan
CF	D.DiMaggio	CF	J.Busby	CF	L.Doby	CF	J.Groth	CF	J.DiMaggio	CF	D.Philley	CF	J.Delsing	CF	I.Noren
RF	C.Vollmer	RF	A.Zarilla	RF	B.Kennedy	RF	V.Wertz	RF	H.Bauer	RF	E.Valo	RF	K.Wood	RF	S.Mele
C	L.Moss	C	P.Masi	C	J.Hegan	C	J.Ginsberg	C	Y.Berra	C	J.Tipton	C	S.Lollar	C	M.Guerra
12	B.Goodman	O	B.Stewart	O	S.Chapman	O	P.Mullin	O	M.Mantle	1	L.Limmer	C	M.Batts	S2	S.Dente
S3	L.Boudreau	O	D.Lenhardt	O1	H.Simpson	1	D.Kolloway	32	G.McDougald	32	B.Hitchcock	O	C.Mapes	O	M.McCormick
C	B.Rosar	O	R.Coleman	O	B.Tebbetts	O	S.Souchock	1	J.Mize	C	J.Astroth	S	J.Bero	S2	M.Verble
3	F.Hatfield	C	G.Niarhos	2	S.Stirnweiss	S2	N.Berry	O	J.Jensen	O3	A.Clark	S	T.Upton	C	M.Grasso
O	C.Maxwell	3	F.Baker	O	B.McCosky	O	B.Swift	1	J.Hopp	2	L.Klein	O	J.Maguire	O	C.Kluttz
C	A.Robinson	C	B.Sheely	S	M.Combs	C	A.Robinson	2	B.Martin	O	W.Moses	3	J.Berardino	O	S.Robertson
O	T.Wright	S2	J.DeMaestri	/1	M.Minoso	/O	C.Keller	O	C.Mapes	C	R.Murray	1	D.Long	/O	F.Campos
C	M.Guerra	O	P.Lehner	/O	P.Lehner	C	F.House	C	C.Silvera	O	S.Chapman	O	D.Lenhardt	/O	D.Porter
C	M.Batts	/1	B.Haas	/O	C.Maddern	/O	R.Sullivan	3	B.Johnson	3	K.Wahl	O	E.Rapp	/C	F.Sacka
C	A.Evans	/3	H.Majeski	/O	A.Clark	/2	A.Federoff	/O	B.Cerv	/O	P.Lehner	1	B.Taylor	/1	F.Taylor
/2	M.Hoderlein	C	J.Erautt	/C	H.Naragon	H	D.Daugherty	/S	J.Brideweser	/O	B.McCosky	O	R.Sievers	/S	W.Miranda
/1	N.Zauchin	/O	D.Philley	H	M.Nielsen			/C	R.Houk	/2	T.Davis	O	P.Lehner	/C	L.Okrie
/O	B.DiPietro	/O	G.Zernial	H	L.Klein	P	T.Gray	/O	A.Wilson	/2	E.Samcoff	C	L.Moss	/1	R.Hawes
/S	A.Richter	/1	B.Boyd	/2	R.Murray	P	D.Trout	/C	C.Courtney			O	B.Nieman		
/C	S.White	/1	G.Goldsberry	H	T.Tucker	P	F.Hutchinson			P	A.Kellner	1	J.Lutz	P	C.Marrero
/O	K.Olson	/C	R.Wilson	R	D.Hansen	P	V.Trucks	P	V.Raschi	P	B.Shantz	/3	K.Wahl	P	S.Consuegra
		/C	S.Hairston			P	B.Cain	P	E.Lopat	P	B.Hooper	S	B.Thomas	P	D.Johnson
P	M.Parnell	H	R.Nelson	P	E.Wynn	RP	G.Bearden	P	A.Reynolds	P	C.Scheib	/3	J.Dyck	P	S.Hudson
P	R.Scarborough			P	B.Lemon	RP	H.White	P	T.Morgan	/O	M.Martin	/O	F.Saucier	P	B.Porterfield
P	M.McDermott	P	B.Pierce	P	M.Garcia			P	S.Shea	RP	J.Kucab	/2	M.Goliat	RP	M.Harris
P	C.Stobbs	P	S.Rogovin	P	B.Feller	RP	M.Stuart	RP	J.Ostrowski			/S	B.DeMars	RP	J.Haynes
P	W.Nixon	P	K.Holcombe	P	S.Gromek	P	H.Newhouser			P	S.Zoldak	/C	C.Kluttz		
RP	E.Kinder	P	J.Dobson	RP	L.Brissie	P	H.Borowy	P	B.Kuzava	P	D.Fowler	H	E.Gaedel	P	J.Moreno
RP	H.Taylor	P	R.Gumpert			/P	S.Rogovin	P	A.Schallock	P	J.Coleman			P	A.Sima
RP	W.Masterson	RP	L.Aloma	P	B.Chakales	/P	R.Herbert	P	S.Overmire	/P	M.Burtschy	P	N.Garver	/P	D.Starr
		RP	M.Rotblatt	P	G.Zuverink	/P	W.McLeland	P	J.Kramer	/P	H.Wyse	P	D.Pillette	/P	B.Kuzava
P	B.Wight			/P	D.Rozek	/P	E.Johnson	P	J.Sain	P	L.Brissie	P	T.Byrne	P	T.Ferrick
P	L.Kiely	P	L.Kretlow	/P	S.Jones	/P	D.Marlowe	P	F.Sanford	P	B.Harris	P	A.Widmar	P	F.Sanford
/P	B.Evans	P	H.Judson	/P	J.Fahr	/P	P.Calvert	/P	T.Byrne			RP	B.Mahoney	P	B.Ross
/P	H.Hisner	P	H.Dorish	/P	B.Harris			/P	T.Ferrick			RP	S.Paige	/P	A.Brown
/P	B.Flowers	/P	B.Cain	/P	J.Vander Meer			/P	B.Wiesler			RP	B.Kennedy	/P	H.Wyse
/P	P.Hinrichs	/P	R.Grimsley					/P	B.Hogue					/P	G.Bearden
		/P	D.Littlefield					/P	E.Nevel			P	J.Suchecki		
		/P	H.Brown					/P	B.Muncrief			P	J.McDonald		
		/P	B.Mahoney					/P	B.Porterfield			P	L.Sleater		
												P	D.Starr		
												/P	S.Overmire		
												P	B.Hogue		
												/P	F.Sanford		
												/P	D.Markell		
												/C	C.Fannin		
												/P	D.Johnson		
												/P	I.Medlinger		
												/P	B.Turley		
												/P	S.Schacht		
												/P	B.Herrera		

TEAM	G	W	L	PCT	GB	R	OR	AB	H	2B	3B	HR	BB	SO	AVG	OBP	SLG	PRO	PRO+	BR	/A	PF	CHI	RC	SB	CS	SBA	SBR
NY	154	98	56	.636		798	621	5194	1395	208	48	140	605	547	.269	.349	.408	.757	113	62	90	96	104	762	78	39	67	0
CLE	155	93	61	.604	5	696	594	5250	1346	208	35	140	606	632	.256	.336	.389	.725	106	0	40	94	98	710	52	35	60	-5
BOS	154	87	67	.565	11	804	725	5378	1428	233	32	127	756	594	.266	.358	.392	.750	98	64	-13	110	100	778	20	21	49	-7
CHI	155	81	73	.526	17	714	644	5378	1453	229	64	86	596	524	.270	.349	.385	.734	105	23	39	98	95	745	99	51	59	-12
DET	154	73	81	.474	25	685	741	5336	1413	231	35	104	568	525	.265	.338	.380	.718	99	-14	-17	100	98	697	37	34	52	-9
PHI	154	70	84	.455	28	736	745	5277	1381	262	43	102	677	565	.262	.349	.386	.735	101	29	13	102	98	745	47	36	57	-8
WAS	154	62	92	.403	36	672	764	5329	1399	242	45	54	560	515	.263	.336	.355	.691	93	-60	-48	98	103	648	45	38	54	-9
STL	154	52	102	.338	46	611	882	5219	1288	223	47	86	521	693	.247	.317	.357	.674	84	-102	-119	103	103	592	35	38	48	-12
TOT	617					5716		42361	11103	1836	349	839	4889	4595	.262	.342	.381	.723							413	311	57	-63

TEAM	CG	SH	SV	IP	H	H/G	HR	BB	SO	RAT	ERA	ERA+	OAV	OOB	PR	/A	PF	CPI	FA	E	DP	FW	PW	BW	SBW	DIF
NY	66	24	22	1367	1290	8.5	92	562	664	12.4	3.56	107	.250	.328	85	41	93	103	.975	144	190	.3	4.0	8.9	.8	7.0
CLE	76	10	19	1391¹	1287	8.3	86	577	642	12.2	3.38	112	.245	.323	114	63	92	103	.978	134	151	.9	6.2	3.9	.3	4.7
BOS	46	7	24	1399	1413	9.1	100	599	658	13.2	4.14	108	.264	.342	-2	50	108	100	.977	141	184	.5	4.9	-1.3	.0	5.8
CHI	74	11	14	1418¹	1353	8.6	109	549	572	12.2	3.50	115	.252	.323	97	84	98	105	.975	151	176	.0	8.3	3.8	-.4	-7.7
DET	51	8	17	1384	1385	9.0	102	602	597	13.2	4.29	97	.262	.342	-26	-18	101	96	.973	163	166	-.7	-1.8	-1.7	-.1	.2
PHI	52	7	22	1358	1421	9.4	109	569	437	13.4	4.47	96	.272	.347	-52	-29	104	98	.978	136	204	.8	-2.9	1.3	-.0	-6.2
WAS	58	6	13	1366¹	1429	9.4	110	630	475	13.7	4.49	91	.259	.348	-55	-59	99	97	.973	160	148	-.5	-5.8	-4.7	-.1	-3.8
STL	56	5	9	1370¹	1525	10.0	131	801	550	15.5	5.18	85	.282	.379	-160	-119	107	101	.971	172	179	-1.2	-11.7	-11.7	-.4	-.0
TOT	479	78	140	11054¹		9.0				13.2	4.12		.252	.342					.975	1201	1398					

Runs
DiMaggio-Bos 113
Minoso-Cle-Chi . . . 112
Yost-Was 109
Williams-Bos . . . 109
Joost-Phi 107

Hits
Kell-Det 191
Fox-Chi 189
DiMaggio-Bos 189
Minoso-Cle-Chi . . . 173
Williams-Bos 169

Doubles
Yost-Was 36
Mele-Was 36
Kell-Det 36

Triples
Minoso-Cle-Chi . . . 14
Coleman-StL-Chi . . . 12
Fox-Chi 12
Young-StL 9

Home Runs
Zernial-Chi-Phi 33
Williams-Bos 30
Robinson-Chi 29

Total Bases
Williams-Bos 295
Zernial-Chi-Phi . . . 292
Robinson-Chi 279
Berra-NY 269
DiMaggio-Bos 267

Runs Batted In
Zernial-Chi-Phi 129
Williams-Bos 126
Robinson-Chi 117
Easter-Cle 103
Rosen-Cle 102

Runs Produced
Williams-Bos 205
Zernial-Chi-Phi . . . 188
Minoso-Cle-Chi . . . 178
Robinson-Chi 173
DiMaggio-Bos 173

Bases On Balls
Williams-Bos 144
Yost-Was 126
Joost-Phi 106
Doby-Cle 101
Rosen-Cle 85

Batting Average
Fain-Phi 344
Minoso-Cle-Chi 326
Kell-Det 319
Williams-Bos 318
Fox-Chi 313

On Base Percentage
Williams-Bos 464
Fain-Phi 451
Doby-Cle 428
Yost-Was 423
Minoso-Cle-Chi 422

Slugging Average
Williams-Bos 556
Doby-Cle 512
Zernial-Chi-Phi 511
Wertz-Det 511
Minoso-Cle-Chi 500

Production
Williams-Bos 1.019
Doby-Cle 941
Minoso-Cle-Chi 922
Fain-Phi 921
Wertz-Det 894

Adjusted Production
Doby-Cle 163
Williams-Bos 159
Minoso-Cle-Chi . . . 152
Fain-Phi 146
Wertz-Det 140

Batter Runs
Williams-Bos 62.8
Minoso-Cle-Chi . . . 38.2
Doby-Cle 37.0
Fain-Phi 33.8
Joost-Phi 30.5

Adjusted Batter Runs
Williams-Bos 49.5
Doby-Cle 42.9
Minoso-Cle-Chi . . . 40.8
Yost-Was 32.2
Fain-Phi 31.8

Clutch Hitting Index
Mele-Was 136
Busby-Chi 127
Noren-Was 120
Zernial-Chi-Phi 118
DiMaggio-NY 113

Runs Created
Williams-Bos 152
Minoso-Cle-Chi . . . 120
Yost-Was 117
Joost-Phi 115
Doby-Cle 108

Total Average
Williams-Bos . . . 1.177
Doby-Cle 1.031
Minoso-Cle-Chi 987
Fain-Phi 959
Yost-Was 909

Stolen Bases
Minoso-Cle-Chi 31
Busby-Chi 26
Rizzuto-NY 18

Stolen Base Average
Rizzuto-NY 85.7
Minoso-Cle-Chi . . . 75.6
Busby-Chi 70.3

Stolen Base Runs
Rizzuto-NY 3.6
Minoso-Cle-Chi 3.3
Carrasquel-Chi 1.8

Fielding Runs
Coan-Was 22.0
Noren-Was 21.1
Stephens-Bos 14.1
Fain-Phi 12.6
Carrasquel-Chi . . . 12.5

Total Player Rating
Williams-Bos 4.5
Joost-Phi 3.9
Doby-Cle 3.6
Fain-Phi 3.6
Berra-NY 3.3

Wins
Feller-Cle 22
Raschi-NY 21
Lopat-NY 21

Win Percentage
Feller-Cle 733
Lopat-NY 700
Reynolds-NY 680
Raschi-NY 677
Shantz-Phi 643

Games
Kinder-Bos 63
Brissie-Phi-Cle 56
Garcia-Cle 47
Scheib-Phi 46

Complete Games
Garver-StL 24
Wynn-Cle 21
Lopat-NY 20
Pierce-Chi 18

Shutouts
Reynolds-NY 7
Raschi-NY 4
Lopat-NY 4
Feller-Cle 4

Saves
Kinder-Bos 14
Scheib-Phi 10
Brissie-Phi-Cle 9
Reynolds-NY 7
Garcia-Cle 6

Innings Pitched
Wynn-Cle 274.1
Lemon-Cle 263.1
Raschi-NY 258.1
Garcia-Cle 254.0
Feller-Cle 249.2

Fewest Hits/Game
Reynolds-NY 6.96
McDermott-Bos . . . 7.38
Wynn-Cle 7.45
Rogovin-Det-Chi . . 7.85
Lopat-NY 8.02

Fewest BB/Game
Hutchinson-Det . . . 1.29
Lopat-NY 2.72
Pierce-Chi 2.73
Hooper-Phi 2.90
Garcia-Cle 2.91

Strikeouts
Raschi-NY 164
Wynn-Cle 133
Lemon-Cle 132
Gray-Det 131
McDermott-Bos . . . 127

Strikeouts/Game
McDermott-Bos . . 6.65
Gray-Det 5.97
Raschi-NY 5.71
Reynolds-NY 5.13
Lemon-Cle 4.51

Ratio
Lopat-NY 10.85
Rogovin-Det-Chi . . 10.97
Wynn-Cle 11.06
Hutchinson-Det . . 11.13
Reynolds-NY 11.24

Earned Run Average
Rogovin-Det-Chi . . 2.78
Lopat-NY 2.91
Wynn-Cle 3.02
Pierce-Chi 3.03
Reynolds-NY 3.05

Adjusted ERA
Rogovin-Det-Chi . . 146
Parnell-Bos 137
McDermott-Bos . . . 133
Pierce-Chi 133
Lopat-NY 131

Opponents' Batting Avg.
Reynolds-NY 213
Wynn-Cle 225
McDermott-Bos . . .226
Rogovin-Det-Chi . . .235
Lopat-NY 239

Opponents' On Base Pct.
Lopat-NY 298
Rogovin-Det-Chi . . .301
Wynn-Cle 301
Hutchinson-Det . . .302
Reynolds-NY 304

Starter Runs
Wynn-Cle 33.6
Rogovin-Det-Chi . . 32.2
Lopat-NY 31.5
Pierce-Chi 29.1
Garcia-Cle 27.3

Adjusted Starter Runs
Rogovin-Det-Chi . . 30.5
Parnell-Bos 29.5
Pierce-Chi 26.7
Lopat-NY 23.8
Wynn-Cle 23.4

Clutch Pitching Index
Parnell-Bos 119
Pierce-Chi 113
Rogovin-Det-Chi . . 111
Feller-Cle 109
Raschi-NY 108

Relief Runs
Kinder-Bos 22.2
Aloma-Chi 17.7
Brissie-Phi-Cle . . . 7.5
Ostrowski-NY 6.7
Masterson-Bos . . . 5.2

Adjusted Relief Runs
Kinder-Bos 26.9
Aloma-Chi 17.1
Masterson-Bos . . . 7.4
Brissie-Phi-Cle . . . 3.6
Ostrowski-NY 3.6

Relief Ranking
Kinder-Bos 31.5
Aloma-Chi 15.0
Harris-Was 4.3
Masterson-Bos . . . 3.9
Ostrowski-NY 3.8

Total Pitcher Index
Parnell-Bos 4.1
Garver-StL 3.1
Lopat-NY 3.0
Pierce-Chi 2.9
Kinder-Bos 2.7

Total Baseball Ranking
Williams-Bos 4.5
Parnell-Bos 4.1
Joost-Phi 3.9
Doby-Cle 3.6
Fain-Phi 3.6

January 16 The U.S. Standardization Board clears the way for Stan Musial to get a salary increase to $85,000. Prior to this relaxation of the rules, there was a wage freeze in effect due to the Korean War.

January 31 Harry Heilmann with 203 votes and Paul Waner with 195 become the newest members of the Hall of Fame.

February 16 Hall of Famer Honus Wagner, 77, retires after 40 years as a major league player and coach. He receives a pension from the Pirates, with whom he spent most of those years.

April 15 In the last home opener in Braves Field in Boston, 4,694 fans watch Warren Spahn lose 3-2 to Brooklyn's Preacher Roe.

April 23 Future Hall of Famer Hoyt Wilhelm of the New York Giants wins his first major league game pitching five innings in relief in a 9-5 win. He homers in his first at bat against the Braves' Dick Hoover. It's Wilhelm's only major league home run in 1,070 games.

May 28 Willie Mays enters the army. Although Mays is hitting just .236, the Giants are 2½ games in first place. They will lose eight of their next 10 games.

May 31 Charlie Grimm succeeds Tommy Holmes as manager of the Boston Braves. Holmes will sign on with the Dodgers as a pinch hitter, but hit just .111.

June 14 The Braves get a split. Warren Spahn ties the NL record of Jim Whitney with 18 strikeouts but loses to the Cubs 3-1 in 15 innings; however, on the same day, Braves scout Dewey Griggs signs Henry Aaron to a Braves contract.

July 8 The NL defeats the AL, 3–2, behind the pitching of the Phils' Curt Simmons and the Cubs' Bob Rush at the All-Star Game in Philadelphia. The game is ended after five innings because of rain. Cub Hank Sauer's homer with Stan Musial aboard in the fourth proves to be the deciding run.

July 30 Baseball Commissioner Ford Frick sets a waiver rule to bar interleague deals until all clubs bid, with the club lowest in the league to get the first pick. He sets the price at $10,000. He also bars all other deals after July 31.

September 15 The Braves play their last game in Boston's Braves Field before moving to Milwaukee, losing to Brooklyn's Joe Black, 8-2. The crowd of 8,822 is the Braves' second largest of the season.

September 23 The Dodgers clinch the pennant, the first time in four years the league winner is not determined by the outcome of the last game.

September 29 Stan Musial makes his only major league pitching appearance. With his sixth batting title wrapped up, he takes the mound against the Cubs Frank Baumholtz, the runner-up in the batting race. Baumholtz, batting right-handed, reaches base on an error, and Harvey Haddix relieves Musial. The Cubs win, 3–0, behind Paul Minner.

October 1 In Game 1 of the World Series, the Dodgers defeat the Yankees 4-2 at Ebbets Field behind relief ace Joe Black, who started only two games during the season.

November 20 The writers name Cubs slugger Hank Sauer as the MVP. The Cubs finished in fifth place, despite Sauer's 37 home runs and 121 RBIs.

November 21 Dodgers pitcher Joe Black, who had a record of 15-4, is voted league Rookie of the Year.

BOSTON	BROOKLYN	CHICAGO	CINCINNATI	NEW YORK	PHILADELPHIA	PITTSBURGH	ST.LOUIS
M T.Holmes	M C.Dressen	M P.Cavarretta	M L.Sewell	M L.Durocher	M E.Sawyer	M B.Meyer	M E.Stanky
M C.Grimm	1B G.Hodges	1B D.Fondy	M E.Brucker	1B W.Lockman	1B S.O'Neill	1B T.Bartirome	1B D.Sisler
1B E.Torgeson	2B J.Robinson	2B E.Miksis	M R.Hornsby	2B D.Williams	1B E.Waitkus	2B J.Merson	2B R.Schoendienst
2B J.Dittmer	SS P.Reese	SS R.Smalley	1B T.Kluszewski	SS A.Dark	2B C.Ryan	SS D.Groat	SS S.Hemus
SS J.Logan	3B B.Cox	3B R.Jackson	2B G.Hatton	3B B.Thomson	SS G.Hamner	3B P.Castiglione	3B B.Johnson
3B E.Mathews	LF A.Pafko	LF H.Sauer	SS R.McMillan	LF B.Elliott	3B W.Jones	LF R.Kiner	LF P.Lowrey
LF S.Gordon	CF D.Snider	CF H.Jeffcoat	3B B.Adams	CF H.Thompson	LF D.Ennis	CF B.Del Greco	CF S.Musial
CF S.Jethroe	RF C.Furillo	RF F.Baumholtz	CF J.Adcock	RF D.Mueller	CF R.Ashburn	RF G.Bell	RF E.Slaughter
RF J.Daniels	C R.Campanella	C T.Atwell	C B.Borkowski	C W.Westrum	RF J.Wyrostek	C J.Garagiola	C D.Rice
C W.Cooper	O G.Shuba	O G.Hermanski	RF W.Marshall	O D.Rhodes	C S.Burgess	S2 C.Koshorek	O H.Rice
O B.Thorpe	3 B.Morgan	32 B.Serena	C A.Seminick	C S.Yvars	C S.Lopata	1O C.Metkovich	3 T.Glaviano
2O S.Sisti	C R.Walker	O B.Addis	O H.Edwards	O W.Mays	O M.Clark	2S G.Strickland	O L.Miggins
1 G.Crowe	O D.Williams	S2 T.Brown	O W.Westlake	O M.Irvin	O J.Mayo	2 C.McCullough	O E.Stanky
C P.Burris	2S R.Bridges	2 B.Ramazzotti	O C.Abrams	O G.Wilson	O B.Nicholson	3 S.Senerchia	2 W.Westlake
C E.St.Claire	O S.Amoros	C H.Chiti	C J.Rossi	/S B.Rigney	/S P.Caballero	O B.Davis	1 S.Bilko
2 J.Hartsfield	/1 R.Nelson	C B.Edwards	O J.Wyrostek	/1 C.Hartung	/1 N.Jones	O D.Hall	C L.Fusselman
S J.Cusick	/O T.Holmes	1 P.Cavarretta	2 E.Pellagrini	/C R.Katt	/S J.Lohrke	O L.Walls	S V.Benson
O W.Marshall	/C C.Abrams	C J.Pramesa	2 J.Temple	/2 C.Diering	/C T.Brown	C E.FitzGerald	S V.Stallcup
2 B.Reed	/C S.Lembo	/S L.Brinkopf	O J.Greengrass	H D.Spencer	H D.Wilber	3 D.Smith	/1 N.Hertweck
O P.Whisenant	P C.Erskine	/S B.Hardin	O W.Post	/O B.Howerton	P R.Roberts	2 J.Berardino	/C B.Sarni
/S B.Clarkson	P B.Loes	H R.Northey	C H.Landrith	/C R.Noble	P R.Meyer	O T.Beard	/S G.Mauch
/S B.Klaus	P B.Wade	H B.Usher	C D.Howell	H D.Wakefield	P K.Drews	O E.Dusak	/3 E.Kazak
P W.Spahn	P P.Roe	P B.Rush	/O D.Sisler	P J.Hearn	P C.Simmons	/O B.Howerton	H H.Gorman
P J.Wilson	P C.Van Cuyk	P J.Klippstein	/3 E.Kazak	P S.Maglie	P S.Ridzik	/O F.Thomas	P G.Staley
P M.Surkont	RP J.Black	P W.Hacker	/S V.Stallcup	RP L.Jansen	RP J.Konstanty	/P J.Mangan	P V.Mizell
P V.Bickford	P J.Rutherford	P P.Minner	P K.Raffensberger	RP D.Koslo	RP A.Hansen	/1 J.Phillips	P J.Presko
P L.Burdette	P C.Labine	P T.Lown	P H.Perkowski	P M.Lanier	P H.Fox	P M.Dickson	P C.Boyer
RP S.Jones	P R.Branca	RP B.Schultz	P H.Wehmeier	RP H.Wilhelm	/P K.Heintzelman	P H.Pollet	P B.Brecheen
P E.Johnson	C K.King	RP D.Leonard	P B.Church	RP M.Kennedy	/P L.Possehl	P B.Friend	RP A.Brazle
P V.Jester	/P J.Landrum	P B.Kelly	RP F.Hiller	/P G.Spencer	/P B.Miller	RP W.Main	RP E.Yuhas
P D.Cole	/P J.Schmitz	P W.Ramsdell	RP F.Smith	/P A.Corwin	/P K.Peterson	RP R.Kline	P C.Chambers
P B.Chipman	/P R.Moore	P J.Hatten	RP J.Nuxhall	/P H.Gregg	/P P.Stuffel	RP T.Wilks	P S.Miller
/P G.Conley	/P J.Hughes	P D.Manville	P E.Blackwell	/P B.Connelly	/P B.Church	RP P.LaPalme	/P H.Haddix
/P D.Donovan	/P K.Lehman	/P V.Fear	P B.Podbielan	/P M.Picone		P C.Hogue	/P B.Werle
/P B.Thiel	/P R.Negray	/P C.Howe	P B.Byerly	/P J.Harshman		P R.Necciai	/P W.Schmidt
/P D.Hoover	/P B.Podbielan	/P M.Dubiel	/P P.Haugstad	/P G.Bamberger		P J.Waugh	/P M.Clark
			/P N.Jordan	/P R.Bowman		P J.Muir	/P D.Bokelmann
			/P J.Schmitz			/P R.Munger	/P J.Crimian
			/P E.Blake			/P H.Fisher	/P B.Tiefenauer
						/P B.Bell	/P R.Munger
						/P D.Carlsen	/P J.Collum
						/P J.Suchecki	/P F.Hahn
						/P J.Dunn	
						/P B.Werle	
						/P E.Wolfe	
						/P M.Queen	

TEAM	G	W	L	PCT	GB	R	OR	AB	H	2B	3B	HR	BB	SO	AVG	OBP	SLG	PRO	PRO+	BR	/A	PF	CHI	RC	SB	CS	SBA	SBR
BRO	155	96	57	.627		775	603	5266	1380	199	32	153	663	699	.262	.348	.399	.747	113	107	98	101	100	754	90	49	65	-2
NY	154	92	62	.597	4.5	722	639	5229	1337	186	56	151	536	672	.256	.329	.399	.728	107	56	51	101	103	712	30	31	49	-10
STL	154	88	66	.571	8.5	677	630	5200	1386	247	54	97	537	479	.267	.340	.391	.731	110	68	67	100	95	708	33	32	51	-9
PHI	154	87	67	.565	9.5	657	552	5205	1353	237	45	93	540	534	.260	.332	.376	.708	104	26	33	99	98	671	60	41	59	-7
CHI	155	77	77	.500	19.5	628	631	5330	1408	223	45	107	422	712	.264	.321	.383	.704	101	5	-3	101	97	652	50	40	56	-9
CIN	154	69	85	.448	27.5	615	659	5234	1303	212	45	104	480	709	.249	.314	.366	.680	95	-36	-34	100	102	610	32	42	43	-16
BOS	155	64	89	.418	32	569	651	5221	1214	187	31	110	483	711	.233	.301	.343	.644	88	-102	-83	97	106	555	58	34	63	-3
PIT	155	42	112	.273	54.5	515	793	5193	1201	181	30	92	486	724	.231	.300	.331	.631	79	-125	-139	103	101	530	43	41	51	-12
TOT	618					5158		41878	10582	1672	338	907	4147	5240	.253	.323	.374	.697							396	310	56	-67

TEAM	CG	SH	SV	IP	H	H/G	HR	BB	SO	RAT	ERA	ERA+	OAV	OOB	PR	/A	PF	CPI	FA	E	DP	FW	PW	BW	SBW	DIF
BRO	45	11	24	1399¹	1295	8.3	121	544	773	12.0	3.53	103	.247	.321	31	17	98	103	.982	106	169	2.0	1.8	10.1	.7	4.9
NY	49	12	31	1371	1282	8.4	121	538	655	12.2	3.59	103	.248	.323	22	17	99	103	.974	158	175	-.8	1.8	5.3	-.2	8.9
STL	49	12	27	1361¹	1274	8.4	119	501	712	11.9	3.66	101	.247	.317	11	8	100	98	.977	141	159	.1	.8	6.9	-.0	3.2
PHI	80	17	16	1386²	1306	8.5	95	373	609	11.0	3.07	119	.249	.301	102	90	98	104	.975	150	145	-.4	9.3	3.4	.1	-2.5
CHI	59	15	15	1386¹	1265	8.2	101	534	661	11.9	3.58	107	.240	.314	23	41	103	94	.976	146	123	-.1	4.2	-.3	-.0	-3.8
CIN	56	11	12	1363¹	1377	9.1	111	517	579	12.8	4.01	94	.267	.338	-43	-36	101	103	.982	107	145	1.9	-3.7	-3.5	-.8	-1.9
BOS	63	11	13	1396	1388	8.9	106	525	687	12.5	3.78	96	.259	.329	-7	-26	97	102	.975	154	143	-.5	-2.7	-8.6	.6	-1.3
PIT	43	5	8	1363²	1395	9.2	133	615	564	13.4	4.65	86	.265	.345	-139	-99	107	94	.970	182	167	-2.0	-10.2	-14.4	-.4	-8.0
TOT	444	94	146	11027²		8.6				12.2	3.73		.253	.323					.976	1144	1226					

Runs		Hits		Doubles		Triples		Home Runs		Total Bases	
Musial-StL	105	Musial-StL	194	Musial-StL	42	Thomson-NY	14	Sauer-Chi	37	Musial-StL	311
Hemus-StL	105	Schoendienst-StL	188	Schoendienst-StL	40	Slaughter-StL	12	Kiner-Pit	37	Sauer-Chi	301
Robinson-Bro	104	Adams-Cin	180	McMillan-Cin	32	Kluszewski-Cin	11	Hodges-Bro	32	Thomson-NY	293
Lockman-NY	99	Dark-NY	177	Sauer-Chi	31	Ennis-Phi	10	Mathews-Bos	25	Ennis-Phi	281
Reese-Bro	94	Lockman-NY	176	Ashburn-Phi	31			Gordon-Bos	25	Snider-Bro	264

Runs Batted In		Runs Produced		Bases On Balls		Batting Average		On Base Percentage		Slugging Average	
Sauer-Chi	121	Ennis-Phi	177	Kiner-Pit	110	Musial-StL	.336	Robinson-Bro	.440	Musial-StL	.538
Thomson-NY	108	Musial-StL	175	Hodges-Bro	107	Baumholtz-Chi	.325	Musial-StL	.432	Sauer-Chi	.531
Ennis-Phi	107	Thomson-NY	173	Robinson-Bro	106	Kluszewski-Cin	.320	Hemus-StL	.392	Kluszewski-Cin	.509
Hodges-Bro	102	Sauer-Chi	173	Musial-StL	96	Robinson-Bro	.308	Hodges-Bro	.386	Kiner-Pit	.500
Slaughter-StL	101	Slaughter-StL	163	Hemus-StL	96	Snider-Bro	.303	Slaughter-StL	.386	Hodges-Bro	.500

Production		Adjusted Production		Batter Runs		Adjusted Batter Runs		Clutch Hitting Index		Runs Created	
Musial-StL	.970	Musial-StL	167	Musial-StL	55.7	Musial-StL	55.6	Slaughter-StL	138	Musial-StL	141
Robinson-Bro	.904	Robinson-Bro	149	Robinson-Bro	41.9	Robinson-Bro	40.7	Hatton-Cin	129	Robinson-Bro	116
Kluszewski-Cin	.892	Kluszewski-Cin	146	Sauer-Chi	32.8	Gordon-Bos	31.8	Campanella-Bro	128	Sauer-Chi	111
Sauer-Chi	.892	Gordon-Bos	144	Kiner-Pit	32.7	Sauer-Chi	31.5	Sauer-Chi	115	Kiner-Pit	111
Hodges-Bro	.886	Sauer-Chi	143	Hodges-Bro	32.4	Hodges-Bro	31.3	Wyrostek-Cin-Phi	112	Hodges-Bro	106

Total Average		Stolen Bases		Stolen Base Average		Stolen Base Runs		Fielding Runs		Total Player Rating	
Musial-StL	1.017	Reese-Bro	30	Reese-Bro	85.7	Reese-Bro	6.0	Schoendienst-StL	32.9	Robinson-Bro	5.6
Robinson-Bro	.995	Jethroe-Bos	28	Robinson-Bro	77.4	Robinson-Bro	3.0	Logan-Bos	17.6	Schoendienst-StL	4.9
Kiner-Pit	.955	Robinson-Bro	24	Jethroe-Bos	75.7	Jethroe-Bos	3.0	Sauer-Chi	16.6	Sauer-Chi	4.2
Hodges-Bro	.921	Ashburn-Phi	16	Ashburn-Phi	59.3	Davis-Pit	1.5	Ashburn-Phi	15.1	Musial-StL	4.2
Sauer-Chi	.886					Slaughter-StL	1.2	McMillan-Cin	10.6	Hemus-StL	3.8

Wins		Win Percentage		Games		Complete Games		Shutouts		Saves	
Roberts-Phi	28	Wilhelm-NY	.833	Wilhelm-NY	71	Roberts-Phi	30	Simmons-Phi	6	Brazle-StL	16
Maglie-NY	18	Roberts-Phi	.800	Black-Bro	56	Dickson-Pit	21	Raffensberger-Cin	6	Black-Bro	15
Staley-StL	17	Black-Bro	.789	Yuhas-StL	54	Spahn-Bos	19			Wilhelm-NY	11
Rush-Chi	17	Maglie-NY	.692	Smith-Cin	53	Raffensberger-Cin	18			Leonard-Chi	11
Raffensberger-Cin	17	Hacker-Chi	.625	Main-Pit	48	Rush-Chi	17				

Innings Pitched		Fewest Hits/Game		Fewest BB/Game		Strikeouts		Strikeouts/Game		Ratio	
Roberts-Phi	330.0	Hacker-Chi	7.01	Roberts-Phi	1.23	Spahn-Bos	183	Mizell-StL	6.92	Hacker-Chi	8.56
Spahn-Bos	290.0	Wilhelm-NY	7.17	Hacker-Chi	1.51	Rush-Chi	157	Simmons-Phi	6.30	Roberts-Phi	9.33
Dickson-Pit	277.2	Erskine-Bro	7.27	Raffensberger-Cin	1.64	Roberts-Phi	148	Wilhelm-NY	6.10	Erskine-Bro	10.45
Rush-Chi	250.1	Rush-Chi	7.37	Staley-StL	1.95	Mizell-StL	146	Wade-Bro	5.90	Rush-Chi	10.50
Raffensberger-Cin	247.0	Loes-Bro	7.40	Drews-Phi	2.05	Simmons-Phi	141	Erskine-Bro	5.70	Drews-Phi	10.59

Earned Run Average		Adjusted ERA		Opponents' Batting Avg.		Opponents' On Base Pct.		Starter Runs		Adjusted Starter Runs	
Wilhelm-NY	2.43	Wilhelm-NY	152	Hacker-Chi	.212	Hacker-Chi	.247	Roberts-Phi	41.8	Roberts-Phi	39.0
Hacker-Chi	2.58	Hacker-Chi	149	Rush-Chi	.216	Roberts-Phi	.263	Rush-Chi	28.8	Rush-Chi	32.1
Roberts-Phi	2.59	Rush-Chi	143	Wilhelm-NY	.220	Rush-Chi	.282	Drews-Phi	25.8	Raffensberger-Cin	26.6
Loes-Bro	2.69	Roberts-Phi	141	Erskine-Bro	.220	Erskine-Bro	.289	Raffensberger-Cin	25.4	Hacker-Chi	26.2
Rush-Chi	2.70	Loes-Bro	135	Loes-Bro	.224	Spahn-Bos	.291	Spahn-Bos	24.3	Drews-Phi	23.8

Clutch Pitching Index		Relief Runs		Adjusted Relief Runs		Relief Ranking		Total Pitcher Index		Total Baseball Ranking	
Roe-Bro	127	Black-Bro	25.0	Black-Bro	23.5	Black-Bro	33.9	Rush-Chi	5.0	Robinson-Bro	5.6
Church-Phi-Cin	119	Wilhelm-NY	23.1	Wilhelm-NY	22.5	Wilhelm-NY	26.4	Roberts-Phi	4.0	Rush-Chi	4.9
Wilhelm-NY	119	Brazle-StL	12.3	Leonard-Chi	12.5	Brazle-StL	20.9	Black-Bro	3.3	Schoendienst-StL	4.9
Raffensberger-Cin	117	Leonard-Chi	11.6	Brazle-StL	12.1	Yuhas-StL	15.4	Wilhelm-NY	2.9	Sauer-Chi	4.2
Maglie-NY	116	Yuhas-StL	11.2	Yuhas-StL	11.0	Leonard-Chi	11.4	Drews-Phi	2.8	Musial-StL	4.2

January 9 As the Korean War drags on, the Marines give notice that they will recall Ted Williams to active duty.

April 23 Bob Cain of the Browns and Bob Feller of the Indians' each pitch a one-hitter, with the Browns prevailing 1-0. It ties a major league record for the fewest hits by two teams in a game. Bobby Young hits a triple in the first inning and scores on an Al Rosen error, as the Browns move into first place. The Indians only hit is a single by Luke Easter. For Feller, it is the fourth time he's one-hit the Browns.

April 28 The St. Louis Browns lend two black minor league players, third baseman John Britton and pitcher Jim Newberry, to the Hankyu Braves of the Japanese Pacific League, making them the first team to send players outside of the United States Abe Saperstein, owner and coach of the world-famous Harlem Globetrotters, negotiates this special example in "lend-lease"for both sides.

April 30 Before 24,767 at Ted Williams Day at Fenway Park, the Red Sox slugger plays in his final game before going to Korea as a marine fighter pilot. In his last at bat, Williams hits a game-winning two-run home run against Detroit's Paul "Dizzy" Trout to give Boston a 5–3 win.

June 10 The St. Louis Browns fire manager Rogers Hornsby in Boston. The players present owner Bill Veeck with a trophy for freeing them from Rajah's tyranny. The stunt was actually the work of Veeck and team traveling secretary Bill Durney. The Browns name Marty Marion as their player-manager.

August 25 In a 1-0 win at Yankee Stadium, Virgil Trucks of the Detroit Tigers pitches his second no-hitter of the season. The no-hitter is in doubt for three innings when a play made by shortstop Johnny Pesky in the third inning is under debate. The official scorer, John Drebinger, records it as an error when Pesky has trouble getting a ball hit by Phil Rizzuto out of his glove. Dan Daniel of the *New York World Telegram* convinces Drebinger that it cannot be ruled an error because the ball was stuck in the fielder's glove, and Rizzuto is awarded a hit. In the sixth inning, Drebinger calls Pesky in the dugout from the press box, and the shortstop says that he should be given the error rather than Rizzuto the hit. The call is changed yet again, and Virgil Trucks' no-hitter is preserved.

September 7 Johnny Mize's pinch-hit grand slam gives the Yanks a 5–1 win at Washington. He has now homered in each one of the 15 major league parks, including Sportsman's Park in St. Louis while in each league.

September 25 Hal Newhouser of the Tigers wins his 200th game. It is his last win for Detroit, who will release him in early 1953.

September 26 The Yanks clinch their fourth straight pennant, an 11-inning 5-2 win at Philadelphia behind Ed Lopat and Johnny Sain.

October 6 At Ebbets Field, the Yankees even it up for the third time, as Raschi and Reynolds combine for a 3-2 win in Brooklyn. Right fielder Carl Furillo robs Johnny Mize of a home run in the ninth.

October 7 In Game 7 the Yankees take their fourth consecutive World Series championship, as Allie Reynolds, one of three relievers, defeats Joe Black 4-2. Billy Martin saves the day by snaring a two-out, bases-loaded infield pop off the bat of Jackie Robinson. Gil Hodges goes hitless again and is 0-for-21 in the Series.

November 12 The baseball writers name Philadelphia pitcher Bobby Shantz as the AL MVP. He was 24-7 for the 79-75 A's.

Each roster cell is shown as "position-code Player".

BOSTON	CHICAGO	CLEVELAND	DETROIT	NEW YORK	PHILADELPHIA	ST.LOUIS	WASHINGTON
M L.Boudreau	M P.Richards	M A.Lopez	M R.Rolfe	M C.Stengel	M J.Dykes	M R.Hornsby	M B.Harris
1B D.Gernert	1B E.Robinson	1B L.Easter	M F.Hutchinson	1B J.Collins	1B F.Fain	M M.Marion	1B M.Vernon
2B B.Goodman	2B N.Fox	2B B.Avila	1B W.Dropo	2B B.Martin	2B S.Kell	1B D.Kryhoski	2B F.Baker
SS J.Lipon	SS C.Carrasquel	SS R.Boone	2B J.Priddy	SS P.Rizzuto	SS E.Joost	2B B.Young	SS P.Runnels
3B G.Kell	3B H.Rodriguez	3B A.Rosen	SS N.Berry	3B G.McDougald	3B B.Hitchcock	SS J.DeMaestri	3B E.Yost
LF H.Evers	LF M.Minoso	LF D.Mitchell	3B F.Hatfield	LF G.Woodling	LF G.Zernial	3B J.Dyck	LF G.Coan
CF D.DiMaggio	CF R.Coleman	CF L.Doby	LF P.Mullin	CF M.Mantle	CF D.Philley	LF J.Delsing	CF J.Busby
RF F.Throneberry	RF S.Mele	RF H.Simpson	CF J.Groth	RF H.Bauer	RF E.Valo	CF J.Rivera	RF J.Jensen
C S.White	C S.Lollar	C J.Hegan	RF V.Wertz	C Y.Berra	C J.Astroth	RF B.Nieman	C M.Grasso
			C J.Ginsberg			C C.Courtney	
S3 V.Stephens	O B.Stewart	O J.Fridley	O3 S.Souchock	O1 I.Noren	2S P.Suder	/2 F.Marsh	O K.Wood
23 T.Lepcio	O J.Rivera	S M.Combs	2 A.Federoff	1 M.Mize	2 C.Michaels	1 G.Goldsberry	2 M.Hoderlein
O C.Vollmer	/S W.Miranda	S J.Tipton	O C.Mapes	3 B.Brown	O A.Clark	S M.Marion	O C.Kluttz
SO J.Piersall	S3 S.Dente	C B.Tebbetts	S2 J.Pesky	O B.Cerv	C R.Murray	3 C.Michaels	O F.Campos
C D.Wilber	O T.Wright	1 B.Glynn	C M.Batts	C B.Silvera	3 H.Majeski	O V.Wertz	O A.Wilson
1 W.Dropo	S A.Zarilla	S G.Strickland	1 D.Kolloway	2 J.Coleman	C K.Thomas	O A.Zarilla	2 C.Michaels
O D.Lenhardt	3 R.Krsnich	O B.McCosky	3 G.Kell	3 A.Carey	C J.Tipton	3 L.Thomas	O E.Rapp
3 J.Pesky	C B.Sheely	O W.Westlake	O D.Lenhardt	S J.Brideweser	/2 S.Robertson	O L.Moss	2 J.Snyder
O G.Schmees	P P.Masi	3 H.Majeski	S J.Lipon	1 J.Hopp	/3 H.Bevan	O J.Porter	O I.Noren
O A.Zarilla	O J.Busby	O P.Reiser	/3 J.Delsing	2 K.Segrist	/1 T.Hamilton	C D.Johnson	/O S.Mele
C G.Niarhos	C D.Johnson	C B.Kennedy	S H.Kuenn	/3 L.Babe	/S J.Littrell	O T.Wright	/2 F.Marsh
O G.Stephens	/3 L.Thomas	O D.Pope	C B.Swift	/O J.Jensen	P B.Shantz	O G.Schmees	/C G.Bradshaw
O A.Wilson	/O H.Edwards	/2 J.Berardino	O R.Sullivan	/C R.Houk	P A.Kellner	/O E.Rapp	C H.Keller
S M.Bolling	/C G.Wilson	/C Q.Trouppe	/O J.Hopp	H A.Wilson	P H.Byrd	O D.Lenhardt	/1 F.Taylor
3 F.Hatfield	/1 K.Landenberger	/3 S.Stirnweiss	/O B.Tuttle	/O C.Keller	P C.Scheib	O R.Coleman	/S T.Upton
O K.Wood	/S S.Esposito	/O G.Lerchen	/O D.Lund	P A.Reynolds	P B.Hooper	/1 R.Sievers	/O B.Varner
/1 C.Maxwell	/C R.Wilson	P B.Lemon	/1 B.Taylor	P V.Raschi	RP J.Kucab	1 H.Arft	R S.Robertson
/O T.Williams	H D.Nicholas	P M.Garcia	H C.Linhart	P E.Lopat	P S.Zoldak	/O J.Crawford	P B.Porterfield
/O P.Lehner	P B.Pierce	P E.Wynn	H H.Evers	P J.Sain	P D.Fowler	/S W.Miranda	P C.Marrero
/S L.Boudreau	P S.Rogovin	P B.Feller	R A.Garbowski	P B.Kuzava	P B.Newsom	/S S.Rojek	P S.Shea
/3 H.Bevan	P J.Dobson	P S.Gromek	P T.Gray	RP J.McDonald	P E.Wright	/2 M.Goliat	P W.Masterson
/C L.Okrie	P M.Grissom	RP L.Brissie	P A.Houtteman	RP B.Hogue	/P C.Bishop	P D.Pillette	P J.Moreno
P M.Parnell	P C.Stobbs	RP M.Harris	P V.Trucks	/P C.Bishop	P M.Martin	P T.Byrne	RP S.Consuegra
P M.McDermott	RP H.Dorish	P S.Jones	P H.Newhouser	/P T.Morgan	P M.Fricano	P B.Cain	P D.Johnson
P D.Trout	RP B.Kennedy	P D.Rozek	P B.Wight	/P B.Miller	P W.Kellner	/P G.Bearden	RP T.Ferrick
P S.Hudson	/P L.Kretlow	/P B.Chakales	RP H.White	/P T.Gorman	P T.Hoyle	P N.Garver	P R.Gumpert
P D.Brodowski	P H.Brown	/P T.Wilks	RP D.Littlefield	P J.Ostrowski	/P L.Matarazzo	RP D.Madison	P J.Haynes
RP I.Delock	P L.Aloma	/P B.Abernathie	P B.Hoeft	/P J.Scarborough		P S.Paige	P S.Hudson
RP R.Scarborough	/P K.Holcombe	/P G.Zuverink	P M.Stuart	/P H.Schaeffer		P E.Harrist	P L.Sleater
P W.Nixon	P H.Judson		P F.Hutchinson	/P E.Blackwell		/P D.Littlefield	/P M.Fornieles
P E.Kinder	/P H.Hudson		P D.Trout	/P J.Schmitz		P S.Overmire	P B.Newsom
P B.Henry	/P A.Widmar		P D.Madison	/P A.Schallock		P M.Stuart	/P R.Sanchez
P A.Benton			/P K.Johnson			P K.Holcombe	P M.Harris
P R.Brickner			/P D.Marlowe			P C.Fannin	P B.Stewart
P B.Wight			/P N.Garver			/P B.Hogue	H.Grossman
P R.Gumpert			/P B.Black			/P J.Hetki	
/P H.Freeman			/P W.McLeland			/P L.Sleater	
/P J.Atkins						/P H.Hudson	
/P H.Taylor						/P B.Mahoney	
/P W.Masterson						/P P.Taylor	

TEAM	G	W	L	PCT	GB	R	OR	AB	H	2B	3B	HR	BB	SO	AVG	OBP	SLG	PRO	PRO+	BR	/A	PF	CHI	RC	SB	CS	SBA	SBR
NY	154	95	59	.617		727	**557**	5294	**1411**	221	**56**	129	566	652	**.267**	.341	.403	**.744**	121	89	134	94	99	758	52	42	55	-10
CLE	155	93	61	.604	2	**763**	606	5330	1399	211	49	**148**	626	749	.262	.342	**.404**	**.746**	122	**95**	**144**	94	102	**759**	46	39	54	-10
CHI	156	81	73	.526	14	610	568	5316	1337	199	38	80	541	521	.252	.327	.348	.675	93	-35	-40	101	99	633	**61**	38	**62**	**-5**
PHI	155	79	75	.513	16	664	723	5163	1305	212	39	87	**683**	561	.253	**.343**	.359	.702	96	26	-16	106	99	659	52	43	55	-10
WAS	157	78	76	.506	17	598	608	5357	1282	225	44	50	580	607	.239	.317	.326	.643	88	-98	-79	97	**107**	572	48	37	56	-8
BOS	154	76	78	.494	19	668	658	5246	1338	**233**	34	113	542	739	.255	.328	.377	.705	96	14	-37	108	103	659	59	47	55	-11
STL	155	64	90	.416	31	604	733	5340	1340	225	46	84	540	720	.243	.322	.356	.678	92	-39	-56	103	99	631	30	34	47	-11
DET	156	50	104	.325	45	557	738	5258	1278	190	37	103	553	605	.243	.318	.352	.670	92	-52	-57	101	99	594	27	38	42	-15
TOT	621					5191		42317	10690	1716	339	794	4631	5154	.253	.330	.365	.695							375	318	54	-78

TEAM	CG	SH	SV	IP	H	H/G	HR	BB	SO	RAT	ERA	ERA+	OAV	OOB	PR	/A	PF	CPI	FA	E	DP	FW	PW	BW	SBW	DIF
NY	72	**21**	27	1381	**1240**	8.1	94	581	666	12.1	**3.14**	106	.243	.324	82	28	90	110	.979	127	**199**	.8	2.9	13.9	-.0	.5
CLE	**80**	19	18	1407	1278	8.2	94	556	671	11.9	3.32	101	.241	.316	55	4	91	99	.975	155	141	-.8	.4	**14.9**	-.0	1.5
CHI	53	15	**28**	1416^2	1251	**7.9**	86	578	774	**11.7**	3.25	112	**.238**	.316	66	62	99	98	**.980**	123	158	1.1	6.4	-4.2	**.5**	.1
PHI	73	11	16	1384^1	1402	9.1	113	**526**	562	12.8	4.15	95	.263	.333	-74	-30	108	94	.977	140	148	.0	-3.1	-1.7	-.0	6.7
WAS	75	10	15	1429^2	1405	8.8	**78**	577	574	12.7	3.37	105	.258	.332	48	29	97	108	.978	132	152	.6	3.0	-8.2	.2	5.4
BOS	53	7	24	1372^1	1332	8.7	107	623	624	13.1	3.80	104	.256	.340	-20	21	107	104	.976	145	181	-.3	2.2	-3.8	-.1	1.1
STL	48	6	18	1399	1388	8.9	111	598	581	13.0	4.12	95	.260	.339	-69	-32	107	97	.974	155	176	-.8	-3.3	-5.8	-.1	-2.9
DET	51	10	14	1388^1	1394	9.0	111	591	702	13.0	4.25	90	.262	.338	-89	-69	104	95	.975	152	145	-.6	-7.2	-5.9	-.5	-12.8
TOT	505	99	160	11178^1		8.6				12.5	3.67		.253	.330					.977	1129	1300					

Runs
- Doby-Cle 104
- Avila-Cle 102
- Rosen-Cle 101
- Berra-NY 97
- Minoso-Chi 96

Hits
- Fox-Chi 192
- Avila-Cle 179
- Robinson-Chi 176
- Fain-Phi 176

Doubles
- Fain-Phi 43
- Mantle-NY 37
- Vernon-Was 33
- Robinson-Chi 33

Triples
- Avila-Cle 11
- Simpson-Cle 10
- Rizzuto-NY 10
- Fox-Chi 10

Home Runs
- Doby-Cle 32
- Easter-Cle 31
- Berra-NY 30
- Dropo-Bos-Det 29
- Zernial-Phi 29

Total Bases
- Rosen-Cle 297
- Mantle-NY 291
- Dropo-Bos-Det 282
- Doby-Cle 281
- Robinson-Chi 277

Runs Batted In
- Rosen-Cle 105
- Robinson-Chi 104
- Doby-Cle 104
- Zernial-Phi 100
- Berra-NY 98

Runs Produced
- Rosen-Cle 178
- Doby-Cle 176
- Berra-NY 165
- Robinson-Chi 161
- Mantle-NY 158

Bases On Balls
- Yost-Was 129
- Joost-Phi 122
- Fain-Phi 105
- Valo-Phi 101
- Doby-Cle 90

Batting Average
- Fain-Phi .... .327
- Mitchell-Cle ...... .323
- Mantle-NY .... .311
- Kell-Det-Bos ...... .311
- Woodling-NY .... .309

On Base Percentage
- Fain-Phi .... .438
- Valo-Phi .... .432
- Mantle-NY .... .394
- Joost-Phi .... .388
- Rosen-Cle .... .387

Slugging Average
- Doby-Cle .... .541
- Mantle-NY .... .530
- Rosen-Cle .... .524
- Easter-Cle .... .513
- Wertz-Det-StL ..... .506

Production
- Mantle-NY .... .924
- Doby-Cle .... .924
- Rosen-Cle .... .911
- Wertz-Det-StL ..... .887
- Fain-Phi .... .867

Adjusted Production
- Doby-Cle 166
- Mantle-NY 166
- Rosen-Cle 162
- Easter-Cle 144
- Wertz-Det-StL 143

Batter Runs
- Mantle-NY 40.3
- Rosen-Cle 38.6
- Doby-Cle 37.9
- Fain-Phi 36.3
- Robinson-Chi 28.3

Adjusted Batter Runs
- Mantle-NY 46.9
- Rosen-Cle 45.8
- Doby-Cle 44.8
- Fain-Phi 29.8
- Woodling-NY 28.2

Clutch Hitting Index
- Runnels-Was 120
- Philley-Phi 116
- McDougald-NY 115
- Easter-Cle 110
- Joost-Phi 107

Runs Created
- Mantle-NY 123
- Doby-Cle 116
- Rosen-Cle 115
- Robinson-Chi 113
- Fain-Phi 107

Total Average
- Doby-Cle .... .974
- Mantle-NY .... .961
- Wertz-Det-StL ..... .912
- Rosen-Cle .... .900
- Valo-Phi .... .873

Stolen Bases
- Minoso-Chi 22
- Rivera-StL-Chi 21
- Jensen-NY-Was 18
- Rizzuto-NY 17
- Throneberry-Bos ... 16

Stolen Base Average
- Jensen-NY-Was 75.0
- Rizzuto-NY 73.9
- Rivera-StL-Chi 70.0
- Throneberry-Bos ... 69.6
- Minoso-Chi 57.9

Stolen Base Runs
- Jensen-NY-Was 1.8
- Rizzuto-NY 1.5
- Michaels-Ws-SL-Phi ... 1.2
- Porter-StL 1.2
- Goodman-Bos 1.2

Fielding Runs
- Goodman-Bos 20.1
- Rizzuto-NY 18.9
- Martin-NY 18.3
- Hatfield-Bos-Det ... 17.8
- Fain-Phi 16.0

Total Player Rating
- Doby-Cle 5.1
- Mantle-NY 4.6
- Fain-Phi 3.9
- Berra-NY 3.5
- Goodman-Bos 3.0

Wins
- Shantz-Phi 24
- Wynn-Cle 23
- Lemon-Cle 22
- Garcia-Cle 22
- Reynolds-NY 20

Win Percentage
- Shantz-Phi .... .774
- Raschi-NY .... .727
- Reynolds-NY .... .714
- Lemon-Cle .... .667
- Garcia-Cle .... .667

Games
- Kennedy-Chi 47
- Paige-StL 46
- Garcia-Cle 46
- Hooper-Phi 43

Complete Games
- Lemon-Cle 28
- Shantz-Phi 27
- Reynolds-NY 24
- Wynn-Cle 19
- Garcia-Cle 19

Shutouts
- Reynolds-NY 6
- Garcia-Cle 6
- Shantz-Phi 5
- Lemon-Cle 5

Saves
- Dorish-Chi 11
- Paige-StL 10
- Sain-NY 7

Innings Pitched
- Lemon-Cle 309.2
- Garcia-Cle 292.1
- Wynn-Cle 285.2
- Shantz-Phi 279.2
- Pierce-Chi 255.1

Fewest Hits/Game
- Lemon-Cle 6.86
- Raschi-NY 7.02
- Reynolds-NY 7.15
- Dobson-Chi 7.36
- Shantz-Phi 7.40

Fewest BB/Game
- Shantz-Phi 2.03
- Pillette-StL 2.41
- Marrero-Was 2.59
- Houtteman-Det 2.65
- Garcia-Cle 2.68

Strikeouts
- Reynolds-NY 160
- Wynn-Cle 153
- Shantz-Phi 152
- Pierce-Chi 144
- Garcia-Cle 143

Strikeouts/Game
- McDermott-Bos 6.50
- Reynolds-NY 5.89
- Trucks-Det 5.89
- Gray-Det 5.54
- Grissom-Chi 5.26

Ratio
- Shantz-Phi 9.56
- Dobson-Chi 10.05
- Lemon-Cle 10.09
- Pierce-Chi 10.43
- Raschi-NY 10.94

Earned Run Average
- Reynolds-NY 2.06
- Garcia-Cle 2.37
- Shantz-Phi 2.48
- Lemon-Cle 2.50
- Dobson-Chi 2.51

Adjusted ERA
- Reynolds-NY 161
- Shantz-Phi 160
- Dobson-Chi 145
- Pierce-Chi 142
- Garcia-Cle 141

Opponents' Batting Avg.
- Lemon-Cle .... .208
- Raschi-NY .... .216
- Reynolds-NY .... .218
- Dobson-Chi .... .222
- Shantz-Phi .... .225

Opponents' On Base Pct.
- Shantz-Phi .... .272
- Lemon-Cle .... .279
- Dobson-Chi .... .280
- Pierce-Chi .... .289
- Reynolds-NY .... .300

Starter Runs
- Reynolds-NY 43.8
- Garcia-Cle 42.4
- Lemon-Cle 40.4
- Shantz-Phi 37.2
- Pierce-Chi 31.3

Adjusted Starter Runs
- Shantz-Phi 46.0
- Reynolds-NY 34.2
- Garcia-Cle 31.6
- Pierce-Chi 30.5
- Lemon-Cle 29.1

Clutch Pitching Index
- Garcia-Cle 127
- Byrd-Phi 126
- Reynolds-NY 125
- Porterfield-Was ... 120
- Hudson-Was-Bos ... 117

Relief Runs
- Dorish-Chi 12.2
- Kennedy-Chi 6.9
- Consuegra-Was 5.1
- Brissie-Cle 1.8
- Littlefield-Det-SL ... 1.4

Adjusted Relief Runs
- Dorish-Chi 11.9
- Kennedy-Chi 6.7
- Consuegra-Was 4.1
- Littlefield-Det-SL ... 3.3
- White-Det 8

Relief Ranking
- Dorish-Chi 17.4
- Kennedy-Chi 4.4
- Consuegra-Was 3.6
- Littlefield-Det-SL ... 2.6
- White-Det 1.1

Total Pitcher Index
- Shantz-Phi 5.5
- Lemon-Cle 4.6
- Reynolds-NY 3.9
- Garcia-Cle 3.6
- Pierce-Chi 3.2

Total Baseball Ranking
- Shantz-Phi 5.5
- Doby-Cle 5.1
- Mantle-NY 4.6
- Lemon-Cle 4.6
- Fain-Phi 3.9

January 21 The Hall of Fame passes over Joe DiMaggio in his first year of eligibility and elects pitcher Dizzy Dean and outfielder Al Simmons to Cooperstown.

February 20 August A. Busch buys the Cardinals for $3.75 million and pledges not to move the team from St. Louis.

March 18 The Braves move to Milwaukee, the first franchise shift in baseball since 1903 when Baltimore moved to New York. The Braves had been in Boston for 77 years.

April 9 August Busch buys Sportsman's Park for $800,000 from Browns owner Bill Veeck. Busch gives a five-year lease to the Browns, turning the tables in a manner of speaking, since the Cardinals had been tenants of the Browns since 1920. Busch initially renames Sportsman's Park Budweiser Park, but, in response to protests about the commercialization of his ballpark, Busch renames Budweiser Park Busch Stadium. The following season his company comes out with a new beer, Busch Bavarian Beer.

April 14 In a 3–2 victory, Braves outfielder Billy Bruton hits the first major league home run in Milwaukee's County Stadium, in the 10th inning off Gerry Staley of the Cards. This is the first major league game for the home crowd since 1901, when the Milwaukee Brewers were charter members of the AL.

April 29 Joe Adcock becomes the first major league player to homer into the center fielder bleacher seats in the Polo Grounds, over 475 feet away. Lou Brock and Hank Aaron will match it in 1962. The Braves win the game 3-2 on a ninth-inning wild pitch by Hoyt Wilhelm.

May 25 Ralph Kiner becomes the 12th player to hit 300 home runs with a blast at Forbes Field against the Giants. He accomplishes the feat in less than eight seasons.

July 14 The NL wins its fourth All-Star Game in a row, 5–1 in Cincinnati's Crosley Field behind the stellar pitching of Robin Roberts and Warren Spahn. Cardinals outfielder Enos Slaughter gets two hits, scores twice, and robs Harvey Kuenn of an extra-base blow.

July 27 The veterans committee enshrines Chief Bender, Bobby Wallace, Harry Wright, executive Ed Barrow, and umpires Bill Klem and Tom Connolly into the Hall of Fame at Cooperstown.

August 23 Phil Paine, a former Boston Braves pitcher in military service with the U.S. Air Force in Japan, becomes the first ex-major league player to play in Japan, pitching in nine games for the Nishitetsu Lions.

September 6 Roy Campanella sets the major league mark for home runs by a catcher. His 38th tops the NL high of 37 hit by the Cubs' Gabby Hartnett in 1930. The next day, he sets the major league record for RBIs by a catcher when he smacks a three-run home run in a 6-3 Dodgers' win over the Phils, surpassing Yogi Berra's 124 set in 1950.

September 20 Ernie Banks of the Cubs hits his first major league home run, against Gerry Staley, but the Cards win 11-6.

September 22 The Dodgers tie the record for the most wins in a home park, beating Pittsburgh 5-4. They go an incredible 60-17 at Ebbets Field, tying the record of the St. Louis Cardinals in 1942. Only the 61 wins of the San Francisco Giants in 1962 in an 81-game home season will surpass this mark.

October 2 The World Series moves to Ebbets Field as Carl Erskine establishes a new Series strikeout record by fanning 14 Yanks, including Mickey Mantle and Joe Collins four times each. Roy Campanella breaks a 2-2 tie with a game-winning solo home run in the eighth for a 3-2 Brooklyn win.

November 24 The Dodgers sign the relatively unknown Walter Alston to a one-year pact as their manager for 1954.

	BROOKLYN		CHICAGO		CINCINNATI		MILWAUKEE		NEW YORK		PHILADELPHIA		PITTSBURGH		ST.LOUIS
M	C.Dressen	M	P.Cavarretta	M	R.Hornsby	M	C.Grimm	M	L.Durocher	M	S.O'Neill	M	F.Haney	M	E.Stanky
1B	G.Hodges	1B	D.Fondy	1B	B.Mills	1B	J.Adcock	1B	W.Lockman	1B	E.Torgeson	1B	P.Ward	1B	S.Bilko
2B	J.Gilliam	2B	E.Miksis	1B	T.Kluszewski	2B	J.Dittmer	2B	D.Williams	2B	G.Hamner	2B	J.O'Brien	2B	R.Schoendienst
SS	P.Reese	SS	R.Smalley	2B	R.Bridges	SS	J.Logan	SS	A.Dark	SS	T.Kazanski	SS	E.O'Brien	SS	S.Hemus
3B	B.Cox	3B	R.Jackson	SS	R.McMillan	3B	E.Mathews	3B	H.Thompson	3B	W.Jones	3B	D.O'Connell	3B	R.Jablonski
LF	D.Thompson	LF	R.Kiner	3B	B.Adams	LF	S.Gordon	LF	M.Irvin	LF	D.Ennis	LF	H.Rice	LF	S.Musial
CF	D.Snider	CF	F.Baumholtz	LF	J.Greengrass	CF	B.Bruton	CF	B.Thomson	CF	R.Ashburn	CF	F.Thomas	CF	R.Repulski
RF	C.Furillo	RF	H.Sauer	CF	G.Bell	RF	A.Pafko	RF	D.Mueller	RF	J.Wyrostek	RF	C.Abrams	RF	E.Slaughter
C	R.Campanella	C	C.McCullough	RF	W.Marshall	C	D.Crandall	C	W.Westrum	C	S.Burgess	C	M.Sandlock	C	D.Rice
				C	A.Seminick										
O3	J.Robinson	O	H.Jeffcoat			O	J.Pendleton	S3	D.Spencer	2	C.Ryan	S	D.Cole	O2	P.Lowrey
3S	B.Morgan	23	B.Serena	O	B.Borkowski	C	W.Cooper	32	B.Hofman	1	E.Waitkus	1O	P.Smith	O	H.Elliott
O	G.Shuba	C	J.Garagiola	21	G.Hatton	2	H.Hanebrink	O	D.Rhodes	C	S.Lopata	O	C.Bernier	S	S.Yvars
1	W.Belardi	S	T.Brown	O	H.Landrith	C	E.St.Claire	1	T.Gilbert	M	C.Clark	23	E.Pellagrini	3	P.Castiglione
C	R.Walker	O	C.Metkovich	2	J.Temple	/1	G.Crowe	C	R.Noble	32	T.Glaviano	3	P.Castiglione	1	D.Sisler
O	D.Williams	O	P.Ward	O	B.Marquis	O	B.Thorpe	C	S.Yvars	O	B.Nicholson	O	R.Kiner	S	D.Schofield
O	B.Antonello	O	T.Atwell	O	W.Post	2	S.Sisti	C	S.Calderone	/2	J.Lohrke	C	T.Atwell	C	F.Anderson
/O	C.Mauro	C	C.Sawatski	/C	F.Baldwin	H	B.Klaus	/O	R.Katt	/O	J.Mayo	C	V.Janowicz	/C	D.Rand
H	D.Howell	O	G.Hermanski	/O	G.Lerchen	/2	M.Roach	/3	B.Rigney	/O	S.Palys	C	J.Garagiola	/2	E.Stanky
H	D.Teed	2	B.Ramazzotti	/C	H.Foiles	/C	P.Burris	H	G.Wilson			O	G.Hermanski	O	G.Dunlap
		S	E.Banks	/O	J.Szekely					P	R.Roberts	O	F.Montemayor	C	L.Fusselman
P	C.Erskine	/O	B.Talbot	/C	E.Bailey	P	W.Spahn	P	R.Gomez	P	C.Simmons	S	D.Smith	H	H.Rice
P	R.Meyer	/2	G.Baker			P	L.Burdette	P	J.Hearn	P	K.Drews	/1	C.Metkovich	3	B.Johnson
P	B.Loes	H	P.Cavarretta	P	H.Perkowski	P	J.Antonelli	P	L.Jansen	P	J.Konstanty	/O	B.Davis	H	V.Benson
P	P.Roe	/O	B.Addis	P	B.Podbielan	P	M.Surkont	P	S.Maglie	P	B.Miller	/2	D.Hall	H	V.Stallcup
P	B.Milliken	/O	P.Schramka	P	K.Raffensberger	P	B.Buhl	P	D.Koslo	RP	S.Ridzik	C	E.FitzGerald	/1	F.Marolewski
RP	C.Labine			P	J.Nuxhall	RP	E.Johnson	RP	H.Wilhelm	RP	A.Hansen	/C	N.Koback	R	E.Phillips
RP	B.Wade	P	W.Hacker	P	F.Baczewski	RP	V.Bickford	RP	A.Corwin			/C	P.Naton		
RP	J.Hughes	P	P.Minner	RP	F.Smith					P	T.Kipper	/C	J.Shepard	P	H.Haddix
		P	J.Klippstein	RP	H.Wehmeier	P	D.Liddle	P	A.Worthington	P	K.Peterson	H	B.Addis	P	G.Staley
P	J.Podres	P	B.Rush	RP	C.King	P	J.Wilson	P	M.Grissom	/P	J.Lindell	H	C.Koshorek	P	V.Mizell
P	J.Black	P	T.Lown			P	D.Jolly	P	F.Hiller	/P	T.Qualters			P	J.Presko
/P	R.Branca	RP	D.Leonard	P	J.Collum	P	D.Cole	P	M.Kennedy	/P	P.Stuffel	P	M.Dickson	P	S.Miller
/P	R.Moore			P	B.Kelly	/P	J.Jay	/P	B.Connelly			P	J.Lindell	RP	A.Brazle
/P	G.Mickens	P	H.Pollet	P	B.Church	/P	V.Jester	/P	M.Lanier			P	P.LaPalme	RP	H.White
/P	E.Palica	P	B.Church	P	H.Judson			/P	G.Spencer			P	B.Friend	RP	C.Chambers
		P	D.Simpson	P	E.Nevel							P	B.Hall		
		P	J.Willis	/P	E.Erautt							RP	R.Face	P	M.Clark
		P	S.Jones	/P	B.Martin							RP	J.Hetki	P	E.Erautt
		P	B.Kelly	/P	E.Blake							RP	R.Bowman	/P	W.Schmidt
		/P	B.Schultz											/P	J.Faszholz
		/P	F.Baczewski									P	J.Waugh	/P	J.Collum
		/P	D.Elston									P	P.Pettit	/P	J.Romonosky
		/P	B.Moisan									/P	C.Hogue	/P	D.Bokelmann
												/P	B.Schultz	/P	E.Yuhas
												P	H.Pollet		
												/P	B.Macdonald		
												/P	W.Main		

TEAM	G	W	L	PCT	GB	R	OR	AB	H	2B	3B	HR	BB	SO	AVG	OBP	SLG	PRO	PRO+	BR	/A	PF	CHI	RC	SB	CS	SBA	SBR
BRO	155	105	49	.682		955	689	5373	1529	274	59	208	655	686	.285	.366	.474	.840	121	188	167	102	101	963	90	47	66	-1
MIL	157	92	62	.597	13	738	589	5349	1422	227	52	156	439	637	.266	.325	.415	.740	104	-22	22	94	104	727	46	27	63	-2
STL	157	83	71	.539	22	768	713	5397	1474	281	56	140	574	617	.273	.347	.424	.771	107	53	54	100	95	806	18	22	45	-8
PHI	156	83	71	.539	22	716	666	5290	1400	228	62	115	530	597	.265	.335	.396	.731	97	-25	-21	99	101	727	42	21	67	0
NY	155	70	84	.455	35	768	747	5362	1452	195	45	176	499	608	.271	.336	.422	.758	101	20	6	102	101	771	31	21	60	-3
CIN	155	68	86	.442	37	714	788	5343	1396	190	34	166	485	701	.261	.325	.403	.728	94	-42	-47	101	103	711	25	20	56	-5
CHI	155	65	89	.422	40	633	835	5272	1372	204	57	137	514	746	.260	.328	.399	.727	93	-41	-56	102	92	697	49	21	70	2
PIT	154	50	104	.325	55	622	887	5253	1297	178	49	99	524	715	.247	.319	.356	.675	82	-130	-126	99	103	614	41	39	51	-11
TOT	622					5914		42639	11342	1777	414	1197	4220	5307	.266	.335	.411	.747							342	218	61	-28

TEAM	CG	SH	SV	IP	H	H/G	HR	BB	SO	RAT	ERA	ERA+	OAV	OOB	PR	/A	PF	CPI	FA	E	DP	FW	PW	BW	SBW	DIF
BRO	51	11	29	1380²	1337	8.7	169	509	817	12.1	4.10	104	.253	.320	29	25	99	97	.980	118	161	1.7	2.4	16.1	.2	7.6
MIL	72	14	15	1387	1282	8.3	107	539	738	12.0	3.30	119	.245	.318	153	96	92	106	.976	143	169	.4	9.2	2.1	.1	3.1
STL	51	11	36	1386²	1406	9.1	139	533	732	12.9	4.23	101	.262	.333	9	5	99	98	.977	138	161	.7	.5	5.2	-.4	.0
PHI	76	13	15	1369²	1410	9.3	138	410	637	12.1	3.80	111	.265	.320	74	62	98	104	.975	147	161	.0	6.0	-2.0	.3	1.6
NY	46	10	20	1365²	1403	9.2	146	610	647	13.4	4.25	101	.264	.343	5	6	100	103	.975	151	151	-.2	.6	.6	.0	-8.0
CIN	47	7	15	1365	1484	9.8	179	488	506	13.2	4.64	94	.279	.343	-53	-43	102	102	.978	129	176	1.1	-4.1	-4.5	-.1	-1.2
CHI	38	3	22	1359	1491	9.9	151	554	623	13.8	4.79	93	.276	.347	-76	-51	104	97	.967	193	141	-2.5	-4.9	-5.4	.5	.3
PIT	49	4	10	1358	1529	10.1	168	577	607	14.1	5.22	86	.285	.356	-141	-113	104	96	.973	163	139	-.9	-10.9	-12.1	-.7	-2.4
TOT	430	73	162	10971²		9.3				12.9	4.29		.266	.335					.975	1182	1259					

Runs		Hits		Doubles		Triples		Home Runs		Total Bases	
Snider-Bro	132	Ashburn-Phi	205	Musial-StL	53	Gilliam-Bro	17	Mathews-Mil	47	Snider-Bro	370
Musial-StL	127	Musial-StL	200	Dark-NY	41	Bruton-Mil	14	Snider-Bro	42	Mathews-Mil	363
Dark-NY	126	Snider-Bro	198	Snider-Bro	38	Hemus-StL	11	Campanella-Bro	41	Musial-StL	361
Gilliam-Bro	125	Dark-NY	194	Furillo-Bro	38	Fondy-Chi	11	Kluszewski-Cin	40	Kluszewski-Cin	325
		Schoendienst-StL	193	Bell-Cin	37			Kiner-Pit-Chi	35	Bell-Cin	320

Runs Batted In		Runs Produced		Bases On Balls		Batting Average		On Base Percentage		Slugging Average	
Campanella-Bro	142	Snider-Bro	216	Musial-StL	105	Furillo-Bro	.344	Musial-StL	.437	Snider-Bro	.627
Mathews-Mil	135	Musial-StL	210	Kiner-Pit-Chi	100	Schoendienst-StL	.342	Robinson-Bro	.425	Mathews-Mil	.627
Snider-Bro	126	Campanella-Bro	204	Gilliam-Bro	100	Musial-StL	.337	Snider-Bro	.419	Campanella-Bro	.611
Ennis-Phi	125	Mathews-Mil	198	Mathews-Mil	99	Snider-Bro	.336	Irvin-NY	.406	Musial-StL	.609
Hodges-Bro	122			Hemus-StL	86	Mueller-NY	.333	Mathews-Mil	.406	Furillo-Bro	.580

Production		Adjusted Production		Batter Runs		Adjusted Batter Runs		Clutch Hitting Index		Runs Created	
Snider-Bro	1.046	Mathews-Mil	175	Musial-StL	62.7	Mathews-Mil	63.8	Slaughter-StL	142	Musial-StL	166
Musial-StL	1.046	Musial-StL	169	Snider-Bro	59.3	Musial-StL	62.9	Jablonski-StL	128	Snider-Bro	161
Mathews-Mil	1.033	Snider-Bro	165	Mathews-Mil	54.9	Snider-Bro	56.2	Robinson-Bro	125	Mathews-Mil	157
Campanella-Bro	1.006	Campanella-Bro	154	Campanella-Bro	42.9	Campanella-Bro	40.4	Ennis-Phi	121	Campanella-Bro	128
Furillo-Bro	.973	Furillo-Bro	146	Kluszewski-Cin	35.0	Kluszewski-Cin	34.2	Campanella-Bro	119	Kluszewski-Cin	126

Total Average		Stolen Bases		Stolen Base Average		Stolen Base Runs		Fielding Runs		Total Player Rating	
Musial-StL	1.143	Bruton-Mil	26	Robinson-Bro	81.0	Reese-Bro	3.0	Ashburn-Phi	25.7	Schoendienst-StL	5.8
Snider-Bro	1.134	Reese-Bro	22	Reese-Bro	78.6	Robinson-Bro	2.7	Schoendienst-StL	25.3	Mathews-Mil	5.8
Mathews-Mil	1.119	Gilliam-Bro	21	Bruton-Mil	70.3	Torgeson-Phi	1.5	Logan-Mil	20.6	Campanella-Bro	4.7
Campanella-Bro	1.048	Robinson-Bro	17	Snider-Bro	69.6	Miksis-Chi	1.5	Crandall-Mil	14.8	Snider-Bro	4.6
Robinson-Bro	.988	Snider-Bro	16	Gilliam-Bro	60.0	Jeffcoat-Chi	1.5	Bell-Cin	13.7	Musial-StL	4.4

Wins		Win Percentage		Games		Complete Games		Shutouts		Saves	
Spahn-Mil	23	Erskine-Bro	.769	Wilhelm-NY	68	Roberts-Phi	33	Haddix-StL	6	Brazle-StL	18
Roberts-Phi	23	Spahn-Mil	.767	Brazle-StL	60	Spahn-Mil	24	Spahn-Mil	5	Wilhelm-NY	15
Haddix-StL	20	Meyer-Bro	.750	Hetki-Pit	54	Simmons-Phi	19	Roberts-Phi	5	Hughes-Bro	9
Erskine-Bro	20	Burdette-Mil	.750	Smith-Cin	50	Haddix-StL	19	Simmons-Phi	4	Leonard-Chi	8
Staley-StL	18	Haddix-StL	.690			Erskine-Bro	16	Erskine-Bro	4	Burdette-Mil	8

Innings Pitched		Fewest Hits/Game		Fewest BB/Game		Strikeouts		Strikeouts/Game		Ratio	
Roberts-Phi	346.2	Spahn-Mil	7.15	Roberts-Phi	1.58	Roberts-Phi	198	Mizell-StL	6.94	Spahn-Mil	9.55
Spahn-Mil	265.2	Gomez-NY	7.32	Raffensberger-Cin	1.71	Erskine-Bro	187	Erskine-Bro	6.82	Roberts-Phi	10.05
Haddix-StL	253.0	Mizell-StL	7.74	Minner-Chi	1.79	Mizell-StL	173	Antonelli-Mil	6.72	Haddix-StL	10.42
Erskine-Bro	246.2	Erskine-Bro	7.77	Staley-StL	2.11	Haddix-StL	163	Klippstein-Chi	6.07	Simmons-Phi	11.19
Simmons-Phi	238.0	Haddix-StL	7.83	Hacker-Chi	2.19	Spahn-Mil	148	Haddix-StL	5.80	Erskine-Bro	11.35

Earned Run Average		Adjusted ERA		Opponents' Batting Avg.		Opponents' On Base Pct.		Starter Runs		Adjusted Starter Runs	
Spahn-Mil	2.10	Spahn-Mil	187	Spahn-Mil	.217	Spahn-Mil	.270	Spahn-Mil	64.5	Roberts-Phi	56.1
Roberts-Phi	2.75	Roberts-Phi	153	Gomez-NY	.218	Roberts-Phi	.276	Roberts-Phi	59.1	Spahn-Mil	53.8
Haddix-StL	3.06	Haddix-StL	139	Mizell-StL	.227	Haddix-StL	.287	Haddix-StL	34.5	Haddix-StL	33.6
Antonelli-Mil	3.18	Simmons-Phi	131	Erskine-Bro	.230	Hacker-Chi	.299	Simmons-Phi	28.3	Simmons-Phi	26.3
Simmons-Phi	3.21	Gomez-NY	126	Haddix-StL	.232	Simmons-Phi	.302	Buhl-Mil	22.5	Gomez-NY	20.2

Clutch Pitching Index		Relief Runs		Adjusted Relief Runs		Relief Ranking		Total Pitcher Index		Total Baseball Ranking	
Raffensberger-Cin	115	Wilhelm-NY	20.1	Wilhelm-NY	20.1	Labine-Bro	27.9	Spahn-Mil	6.6	Spahn-Mil	6.6
Dickson-Pit	112	Labine-Bro	18.5	Labine-Bro	18.2	Wilhelm-NY	23.4	Roberts-Phi	6.1	Roberts-Phi	6.1
Drews-Phi	112	Johnson-Mil	14.6	White-StL	12.0	White-StL	16.3	Haddix-StL	4.7	Schoendienst-StL	5.8
Burdette-Mil	110	White-StL	12.3	Johnson-Mil	11.3	Johnson-Mil	8.8	Labine-Bro	2.7	Mathews-Mil	5.8
Roe-Bro	108	Hughes-Bro	7.8	Hughes-Bro	7.6	Hughes-Bro	7.3	Simmons-Phi	2.4	Haddix-StL	4.7

January 8 The Cleveland Indians bar night games with the Browns due to St. Louis owner Bill Veeck's refusal to share receipts of the telecasts.

February 13 The Athletics change the name of Shibe Park to Connie Mack Stadium, in honor of their longtime owner and manager.

February 19 Ted Williams safely crashlands his damaged Panther jet after flying a combat mission in Korea.

April 17 Mickey Mantle hits the longest home run in Griffith Stadium history, a 565-foot shot off Chuck Stobbs of the Washington Senators. The Yanks win, 7-3.

May 6 Alva "Bobo" Holloman of the St. Louis Browns pitches a no-hitter in his first major league start, only the third rookie to do so, in a 6-0 win over the A's. Within three months he will be out of the major leagues for good, the winner of just three games.

June 15 Duane Pillette of the Browns ends the Yankee win streak at 18 and the Browns team record 14-game losing streak with a 3–1 victory over New York in Yankee Stadium. Johnny Mize becomes the 93rd player in baseball history to get 2,000 hits when he singles in the Yankee run in the fifth.

June 18 Red Sox rookie outfielder Gene Stephens becomes the only AL player to get three hits in the same inning, as Boston scores 17 in the seventh inning in a 23-3 romp over Detroit. The Red Sox send 23 to the plate in the seventh, getting 14 hits and six walks before third baseman George Kell flies out to end it.

August 6 Ted Williams is back in a Red Sox uniform after military duty in Korea. He will finish with 13 home runs and a .407 mark.

September 14 The Yanks clinch their fifth straight pennant with an 8-5 win over the Indians. Second baseman Billy Martin has four RBIs.

September 26 Billy Hunter becomes the last St. Louis Browns player to homer in a game. The Browns lose anyway, 6-3 to Chicago.

September 27 Washington's Mickey Vernon goes into the last game of the season still fighting for the batting title with Cleveland's Al Rosen. Near the end of the game Vernon is hitting .337 when word arrives that Rosen's game is over and Vernon is ahead by .0011 points. Instead of letting Vernon bat again, his teammates contrive to make an out to end the game.

September 27 The St. Louis Browns play both their last game in Sportsman's Park and the last game in the franchise's 52-year history, losing 2-1 to the Chicago White Sox in 10 innings for their 100th defeat of the season.

September 29 The AL adopts a constitutional amendment calling for expansion to 10 teams.

September 30 The Yanks defeat Brooklyn 9-5 in the first game of the World Series. Carl Erskine is ineffective, walking the first three batters, who score on a Hank Bauer triple. The Dodgers tie it up 5-5, but Clem Labine gets the loss in relief.

October 4 In Game 5, Mickey Mantle hits a grand slam off Russ Meyer, and the Yanks hold on to win 11-7.

October 5 The Yanks end the World Series in six as Billy Martin's 12th World Series hit, a record-breaking single to center in the bottom of the ninth, gives the Yankees their fifth championship in a row.

October 28 Red Barber resigns from the Dodger broadcast booth and takes a job with the rival New York Yankees.

November 17 The St. Louis Browns' name officially becomes the Baltimore Baseball Club Inc. The Baltimore franchise board officially changes its name to the "Orioles."

November 27 Indians third baseman Al Rosen is unanimously named the AL's MVP with a record 336 votes.

BOSTON	CHICAGO	CLEVELAND	DETROIT	NEW YORK	PHILADELPHIA	ST.LOUIS	WASHINGTON
M L.Boudreau	M P.Richards	M A.Lopez	M F.Hutchinson	M C.Stengel	M J.Dykes	M M.Marion	M B.Harris
1B D.Gernert	1B F.Fain	1B B.Glynn	1B W.Dropo	1B J.Collins	1B E.Robinson	1B D.Kryhoski	1B M.Vernon
2B B.Goodman	2B N.Fox	2B B.Avila	2B J.Pesky	2B B.Martin	2B C.Michaels	2B B.Young	2B W.Terwilliger
SS M.Bolling	SS C.Carrasquel	SS G.Strickland	SS H.Kuenn	SS P.Rizzuto	SS J.DeMaestri	SS B.Hunter	SS P.Runnels
3B G.Kell	3B B.Elliott	3B A.Rosen	3B R.Boone	3B G.McDougald	3B L.Babe	3B J.Dyck	3B E.Yost
LF H.Evers	LF M.Minoso	LF D.Mitchell	LF B.Nieman	LF G.Woodling	LF G.Zernial	LF D.Kokos	LF C.Vollmer
CF T.Umphlett	CF J.Rivera	CF L.Doby	CF J.Delsing	CF M.Mantle	CF E.McGhee	CF J.Groth	CF J.Busby
RF J.Piersall	RF S.Mele	RF B.Kennedy	RF D.Lund	RF H.Bauer	RF D.Philley	RF V.Wertz	RF J.Jensen
C S.White	C S.Lollar	C J.Hegan	C M.Batts	C Y.Berra	C J.Astroth	C C.Courtney	C E.Fitz Gerald
O G.Stephens	1O B.Boyd	O H.Simpson	32 F.Hatfield	O I.Noren	O P.Suder	C D.Lenhardt	C M.Grasso
32 F.Baker	C R.Wilson	O W.Westlake	1 D.Bollweg	32 P.Murray	1 R.Murray	1 R.Sievers	O G.Coan
2S T.Lepcio	O T.Wright	1 L.Easter	21 J.Priddy	O B.Renna	S E.Joost	C L.Moss	S J.Snyder
S J.Lipon	3 R.Krsnich	C A.Smith	C J.Bucha	1 J.Mize	O C.Mauro	3 V.Stephens	S Y.Davalillo
C D.Wilber	3 V.Stephens	S R.Boone	O P.Mullin	C C.Silvera	O E.Valo	3 B.Elliott	/O K.Thomas
O T.Williams	3S F.Marsh	C J.Ginsberg	2 O.Friend	3 A.Carey	O A.Clark	O H.Edwards	2 M.Hoderlein
O A.Zarilla	O B.Stewart	C J.Tipton	S R.Sullivan	/1 W.Miranda	/1 T.Hamilton	/O J.Pisoni	/O K.Wood
32 B.Consolo	3 C.Ryan	2 O.Friend	1 J.Ginsberg	/C G.Triandos	32 K.Thomas	/3 E.Mickelson	/C L.Peden
O K.Olson	C B.Sheely	2 H.Majeski	C J.Ginsberg	2 J.Coleman	/O N.Watlington	/3 J.Lipon	/O C.Mauro
G G.Niarhos	/O B.Wilson	O J.Lemon	3 B.Hitchcock	/3 R.Houk	/3 T.Giordano	H D.Upright	/S G.Verble
/2 J.Merson	/1 A.Clark	H B.McCosky	O A.Kaline	/O B.Cerv	H S.Wilhelm	/3 M.Marion	/C F.Sacka
H D.DiMaggio	/2 N.Berry	/C H.Foiles	/3 J.Baumgartner	/S J.Brideweser	/3 D.Kolloway	/S W.Miranda	/C B.Oldis
/S A.Richter	/S S.Dente	/C D.Aylward	/O F.Carswell	R A.Schult	P H.Byrd	/1 F.Kellert	H F.Campos
H C.Vollmer		R D.Weik	/C B.Swift	/S F.Verdi		/C B.Martin	/2 T.Roig
	P B.Pierce	P B.Lemon	/2 R.Bertoia		P A.Kellner		/3 F.Baker
P M.Parnell	P V.Trucks	P M.Garcia	H G.Freese	P W.Ford	P C.Bishop	P D.Larsen	/O B.Barnes
P M.McDermott	P M.Fornieles	P E.Wynn		P J.Sain	P B.Shantz	P D.Pillette	
P H.Brown	P S.Rogovin	P B.Feller	P B.Hoeft	P V.Raschi	RP M.Martin	P D.Littlefield	P B.Porterfield
P S.Hudson	P S.Consuegra	RP D.Hoskins	P N.Garver	P E.Lopat	P C.Scheib	P H.Brecheen	P W.Masterson
P W.Nixon	RP H.Dorish	RP B.Hooper	P T.Gray	P A.Reynolds	P J.Coleman	P B.Cain	P S.Shea
RP E.Kinder	RP G.Bearden		P S.Gromek	RP T.Gorman	P B.Newsom	RP S.Paige	P C.Stobbs
RP B.Flowers		P A.Houtteman	P R.Branca	RP R.Scarborough	/P B.Trice	RP M.Stuart	P C.Marrero
RP I.Delock	P J.Dobson	/P B.Chakales	RP D.Marlowe	P J.McDonald	P R.Monahan	RP M.Blyzka	RP S.Dixon
	P B.Keegan	/P B.Wight	RP R.Herbert	P B.Miller	P D.Rozek	P V.Trucks	RP A.Sima
P B.Henry	P C.Johnson	/P L.Brissie	RP D.Madison	/P S.Kraly	P W.Kellner	P L.Kretlow	RP J.Lane
P M.Grissom	P L.Aloma	/P S.Gromek	P A.Houtteman	/P A.Schallock	P B.Harrington	P B.Holloman	P J.Schmitz
P H.Freeman	/P L.Kretlow	/P D.Tomanek	P A.Aber	/P E.Blackwell	P J.Mackinson	P B.Turley	P J.Moreno
P F.Sullivan	/P T.Byrne	/P A.Aber	P B.Miller	/P J.Schmitz		P M.Lanier	/P T.Byrne
P B.Kennedy	/P E.Harrist	/P T.Wilks	P H.Erickson			P H.White	/P B.Stewart
/P B.Werle	/P H.Hudson		P B.Wight			/P B.Habenicht	/P J.Pearce
/P K.Holcombe			/P H.Newhouser				/P D.Stone
			P R.Scarborough				/P S.Consuegra
			/P E.Harrist				
			P D.Weik				
			/P M.Jordan				
			/P P.Foytack				
			/P F.Hutchinson				

TEAM	G	W	L	PCT	GB	R	OR	AB	H	2B	3B	HR	BB	SO	AVG	OBP	SLG	PRO	PRO+	BR	/A	PF	CHI	RC	SB	CS	SBA	SBR
NY	151	99	52	.656		**801**	547	5194	1420	226	52	139	**656**	644	**.273**	**.359**	**.417**	**.776**	120	113	**141**	97	100	**809**	34	44	44	-16
CLE	155	92	62	.597	8.5	770	627	5285	1426	201	29	**160**	609	683	.270	.349	.410	.759	114	77	98	97	100	780	33	29	53	-8
CHI	156	89	65	.578	11.5	716	592	5212	1345	226	53	74	601	**530**	.258	.341	.364	.705	93	-17	-37	103	106	666	**73**	55	57	-11
BOS	153	84	69	.549	16	656	632	5246	1385	255	37	101	496	601	.264	.332	.384	.716	94	-10	-45	105	98	683	33	45	42	-17
WAS	152	76	76	.500	23.5	687	614	5149	1354	230	53	69	596	604	.263	.343	.368	.711	100	-6	10	98	103	675	65	36	**64**	-2
DET	158	60	94	.390	40.5	695	923	5553	1479	259	44	108	506	603	.266	.331	.387	.718	100	-10	-2	99	99	716	30	35	46	-12
PHI	157	59	95	.383	41.5	632	799	5455	1398	205	38	116	498	602	.256	.321	.372	.693	89	-61	-85	104	100	658	41	24	63	-2
STL	154	54	100	.351	46.5	555	778	5264	1310	214	25	112	507	644	.249	.317	.363	.680	87	-83	-94	102	93	606	17	34	33	-15
TOT	618					5512		42358	11117	1816	331	879	4469	4911	.262	.336	.383	.720							326	302	52	-83

TEAM	CG	SH	SV	IP	H	H/G	HR	BB	SO	RAT	ERA	ERA+	OAV	OOB	PR	/A	PF	CPI	FA	E	DP	FW	PW	BW	SBW	DIF
NY	50	**18**	39	1358[1]	**1286**	8.5	94	500	604	12.1	3.20	115	.251	**.321**	120	74	92	110	.979	126	182	.3	7.4	**14.1**	-.6	2.2
CLE	**81**	11	15	1373	1311	8.6	**92**	519	586	12.2	3.64	103	.253	.325	53	16	94	99	.979	127	**197**	.4	1.6	9.8	.2	2.9
CHI	57	17	33	1403[2]	1299	**8.3**	113	583	**714**	12.2	3.41	118	**.246**	.324	91	95	101	105	**.980**	125	144	.6	9.5	-3.7	-.0	5.7
BOS	41	15	37	1373	1333	8.7	**92**	584	642	12.7	3.58	118	.254	.331	63	**96**	105	104	.975	148	173	-.9	**9.6**	-4.5	-.7	3.9
WAS	76	16	10	1344[2]	1313	8.8	112	**478**	515	12.2	3.66	106	.258	.324	50	35	98	103	.979	**120**	173	**.7**	3.5	1.0	**.8**	-6.0
DET	50	2	16	1415	1633	10.4	154	585	645	14.4	5.25	77	.291	.363	-198	-187	102	96	.978	135	149	.1	-18.7	-.2	-.2	2.0
PHI	51	7	11	1409	1475	9.4	121	594	566	13.6	4.67	92	.271	.349	-106	-60	107	93	.977	137	161	-.0	-6.0	-8.5	**.8**	-4.3
STL	28	10	24	1383[2]	1467	9.5	101	626	639	13.8	4.48	94	.273	.351	-74	-43	105	97	.974	152	165	-1.0	-4.3	-9.4	-.5	-7.8
TOT	434	96	185	11060[1]		9.0				12.9	3.99		.262	.336					.978	1070	1344					

Runs
Rosen-Cle	115
Yost-Was	107
Mantle-NY	105
Minoso-Chi	104
Vernon-Was	101

Hits
Kuenn-Det	209
Vernon-Was	205
Rosen-Cle	201
Philley-Phi	188
Busby-Was	183

Doubles
Vernon-Was	43
Kell-Bos	41
White-Bos	34
Kuenn-Det	33
Goodman-Bos	33

Triples
Rivera-Chi	16
Vernon-Was	11
Piersall-Bos	9
Philley-Phi	9

Home Runs
Rosen-Cle	43
Zernial-Phi	42
Doby-Cle	29
Berra-NY	27
Boone-Cle-Det	26

Total Bases
Rosen-Cle	367
Vernon-Was	315
Zernial-Phi	311
Philley-Phi	263
Berra-NY	263

Runs Batted In
Rosen-Cle	145
Vernon-Was	115
Boone-Cle-Det	114
Zernial-Phi	108
Berra-NY	108

Runs Produced
Rosen-Cle	217
Vernon-Was	201
Minoso-Chi	193
Boone-Cle-Det	182
Mantle-NY	176

Bases On Balls
Yost-Was	123
Fain-Chi	108
Doby-Cle	96
Gernert-Bos	88
Rosen-Cle	85

Batting Average
Vernon-Was	.337
Rosen-Cle	.336
Goodman-Bos	.313
Minoso-Chi	.313
Busby-Was	.312

On Base Percentage
Woodling-NY	.429
Rosen-Cle	.422
Minoso-Chi	.410
Fain-Chi	.405
Yost-Was	.403

Slugging Average
Rosen-Cle	.613
Zernial-Phi	.559
Berra-NY	.523
Boone-Cle-Det	.519
Vernon-Was	.518

Production
Rosen-Cle	1.034
Vernon-Was	.921
Zernial-Phi	.914
Boone-Cle-Det	.909
Woodling-NY	.898

Adjusted Production
Rosen-Cle	181
Vernon-Was	151
Woodling-NY	147
Boone-Cle-Det	146
Mantle-NY	145

Batter Runs
Rosen-Cle	63.3
Vernon-Was	39.7
Minoso-Chi	30.6
Boone-Cle-Det	30.5
Zernial-Phi	30.4

Adjusted Batter Runs
Rosen-Cle	67.2
Vernon-Was	42.5
Boone-Cle-Det	32.0
Mantle-NY	30.4
Woodling-NY	30.1

Clutch Hitting Index
Rizzuto-NY	128
Dropo-Det	122
Fox-Chi	120
Vernon-Was	119
Robinson-Phi	118

Runs Created
Rosen-Cle	155
Vernon-Was	127
Zernial-Phi	113
Boone-Cle-Det	106
Minoso-Chi	106

Total Average
Rosen-Cle	1.078
Mantle-NY	.943
Boone-Cle-Det	.925
Zernial-Phi	.917
Doby-Cle	.912

Stolen Bases
Minoso-Chi	25
Rivera-Chi	22
Jensen-Was	18
Philley-Phi	13
Busby-Was	13

Stolen Base Average
Jensen-Was	69.2
Minoso-Chi	61.0
Rivera-Chi	59.5

Stolen Base Runs
Michaels-Phi	2.1
Coan-Was	2.1
Zernial-Phi	1.2
Souchock-Det	.9
Philley-Phi	.9

Fielding Runs
Busby-Was	18.9
Groth-StL	17.1
Piersall-Bos	16.1
Strickland-Cle	15.6
Hunter-StL	14.6

Total Player Rating
Rosen-Cle	6.2
Zernial-Phi	3.5
Berra-NY	3.4
Boone-Cle-Det	3.2
Vernon-Was	3.1

Wins
Porterfield-Was	22
Parnell-Bos	21
B.Lemon-Cle	21
Trucks-StL-Chi	20

Win Percentage
Lopat-NY	.800
Ford-NY	.750
Parnell-Bos	.724
Porterfield-Was	.688

Games
Kinder-Bos	69
Stuart-StL	60
Martin-Phi	58
Paige-StL	57
Dorish-Chi	55

Complete Games
Porterfield-Was	24
B.Lemon-Cle	23
Garcia-Cle	21
Pierce-Chi	19
Trucks-StL-Chi	17

Shutouts
Porterfield-Was	9
Pierce-Chi	7
Trucks-StL-Chi	5
Parnell-Bos	5
B.Lemon-Cle	5

Saves
Kinder-Bos	27
Dorish-Chi	18
Reynolds-NY	13
Paige-StL	11
Sain-NY	9

Innings Pitched
B.Lemon-Cle	286.2
Garcia-Cle	271.2
Pierce-Chi	271.1
Trucks-StL-Chi	264.1
Porterfield-Was	255.0

Fewest Hits/Game
Pierce-Chi	7.16
McDermott-Bos	7.37
Raschi-NY	7.46
Masterson-Was	7.85
Trucks-StL-Chi	7.97

Fewest BB/Game
Lopat-NY	1.61
Sain-NY	2.14
A.Kellner-Phi	2.28
Porterfield-Was	2.58
Hoeft-Det	2.64

Strikeouts
Pierce-Chi	186
Trucks-StL-Chi	149
Wynn-Cle	138
Parnell-Bos	136
Garcia-Cle	134

Strikeouts/Game
Pierce-Chi	6.17
Gray-Det	5.88
Masterson-Was	5.14
Parnell-Bos	5.08
Trucks-StL-Chi	5.07

Ratio
Raschi-NY	10.24
Lopat-NY	10.35
Pierce-Chi	10.65
Porterfield-Was	11.19
Sain-NY	11.29

Earned Run Average
Lopat-NY	2.42
Pierce-Chi	2.72
Trucks-StL-Chi	2.93
Sain-NY	3.00
Ford-NY	3.00

Adjusted ERA
Lopat-NY	152
Pierce-Chi	148
McDermott-Bos	140
Trucks-StL-Chi	139
Parnell-Bos	137

Opponents' Batting Avg.
Pierce-Chi	.218
McDermott-Bos	.224
Raschi-NY	.224
Masterson-Was	.232
Trucks-StL-Chi	.238

Opponents' On Base Pct.
Raschi-NY	.283
Lopat-NY	.288
Pierce-Chi	.292
Masterson-Was	.304
Garcia-Cle	.307

Starter Runs
Pierce-Chi	38.4
Trucks-StL-Chi	31.3
Lopat-NY	31.2
Parnell-Bos	25.0
Ford-NY	22.9

Adjusted Starter Runs
Pierce-Chi	39.3
Trucks-StL-Chi	33.9
Parnell-Bos	30.6
McDermott-Bos	27.4
Lopat-NY	25.1

Clutch Pitching Index
Ford-NY	127
Lopat-NY	123
Sain-NY	118
B.Lemon-Cle	113
Parnell-Bos	112

Relief Runs
Kinder-Bos	25.5
Dorish-Chi	9.7
Kuzava-NY	7.0
Bearden-Chi	6.9
Paige-StL	6.1

Adjusted Relief Runs
Kinder-Bos	28.0
Dorish-Chi	10.1
Paige-StL	8.7
Bearden-Chi	7.1
Kuzava-NY	3.9

Relief Ranking
Kinder-Bos	53.6
Dorish-Chi	12.8
Paige-StL	9.9
Bearden-Chi	6.5
Kuzava-NY	4.5

Total Pitcher Index
Kinder-Bos	5.9
McDermott-Bos	4.4
Trucks-StL-Chi	3.8
Pierce-Chi	3.5
Parnell-Bos	3.4

Total Baseball Ranking
Rosen-Cle	6.2
Kinder-Bos	5.9
McDermott-Bos	4.4
Trucks-StL-Chi	3.8
Zernial-Phi	3.5

March 13 Newly acquired Brave Bobby Thomson breaks his ankle sliding into third base in an exhibition game with the Pirates, thus opening the way for Henry Aaron to start in the outfield.

March 29 Phil Cavarretta gives Cubs owner Phil Wrigley an honest assessment of the team's chances, and is fired for his "defeatist attitude," the first manager to be given the gate during spring training.

April 11 To make room for promising rookie outfielder Wally Moon, the Cardinals trade long-time great Enos Slaughter to the Yankees. In what turns out to be a good deal for both teams, the Cardinals get center fielder Bill Virdon, pitcher Mel Wright, and outfielder Emil Tellinger in return. Virdon will become the NL Rookie of the Year in 1955, and Slaughter will help the Yankees to win 103 games.

April 13 Back in center field after two years in the Army, Willie Mays of the Giants hits a two-run shot that beats Brooklyn, 4–3.

April 23 At Sportsman's Park, Henry Aaron hits the first of his 755 major league home runs, off Vic Raschi of St. Louis. The Braves win in 14 innings 7-5.

May 2 Stan Musial hits five home runs in a doubleheader split with the Giants in St. Louis. In attendance is 8-year-old Nate Colbert, who will be the only other player in history to accomplish this feat.

May 24 In a unique Birdie Tebbetts shift against the Cards' Stan Musial, the Redlegs enlist a "fourth" outfielder in place of regular shortstop Roy McMillan. This causes a box score irregularity because left-handed outfielder Nino Escalero is officially listed as a left-handed shortstop. After all that, Art Fowler strikes out Musial as the Reds win, 4–2.

June 12 Jim Wilson, 32, no-hits the Phillies, 2–0, before 28,218 in Milwaukee. Robin Roberts takes the loss, his first after nine straight wins over the Braves. It is Wilson's first start after pitching just 8⅓ innings of relief, giving up seven runs. Ironically, the Braves asked waivers on Wilson two weeks earlier, with no takers.

July 31 Using a borrowed bat, Dodger killer Joe Adcock hits four home runs and a double for 18 total bases in the Braves' 15–7 victory at Ebbets Field. The 18 total bases is a major league mark and, combined with the seven total bases from the day before, gives him a two-day tally of 25, which ties the record of Ty Cobb.

August 29 A disappointed crowd of 45,922 at Milwaukee's County Stadium sees the Dodgers take two from the Braves, 12–4 and 11–4. In game one, the Dodgers break a tie with a record eight runs in the 11th. The Braves establish a new NL attendance mark of 1,841,666 on their way to a season total of 2,131,388.

September 10 Attempting to handle Hoyt Wilhelm's knuckleball against the Redlegs, catcher Ray Katt of the Giants sets a major league record with four passed balls in the eighth inning.

September 26 In his second start, rookie Brooklyn lefty Karl Spooner shuts out Pittsburgh 1-0 on a Gil Hodges home run in the eighth inning. He fans 12 for a total of 27 strikeouts in his first two major league games, establishing a new record. The home run by Hodges gives him 42 for the season, tying him with Edwin "Duke" Snider for the most by a Dodger.

September 29 In Game 1 of the World Series, Willie Mays of the Giants makes one of the greatest catches in history when he races back to deep center field in the Polo Grounds to make an over-the-head catch of Indian Vic Wertz's 462-foot drive in the eighth with the score tied at 2-2. In the 10th inning, James "Dusty" Rhodes hits a pinch-hit, three-run, 260-foot home run off Bob Lemon to give the Giants a 5-2 victory.

October 2 In Game 4 the Giants sweep as they score four runs in the fifth to take a 7-0 lead over Cleveland. The final is 7-4 as Don Liddle defeats Bob Lemon.

December 11 With the Athletics poised to move to Kansas City, the Phillies purchase Connie Mack Stadium.

BROOKLYN	CHICAGO	CINCINNATI	MILWAUKEE	NEW YORK	PHILADELPHIA	PITTSBURGH	ST.LOUIS
M W.Alston	M S.Hack	M B.Tebbetts	M C.Grimm	M L.Durocher	M S.O'Neill	M F.Haney	M E.Stanky
1B G.Hodges	1B D.Fondy	1B T.Kluszewski	1B J.Adcock	1B W.Lockman	M T.Moore	1B B.Skinner	1B J.Cunningham
2B J.Gilliam	2B G.Baker	2B J.Temple	2B D.O'Connell	2B D.Williams	1B E.Torgeson	2B C.Roberts	2B R.Schoendienst
SS P.Reese	SS E.Banks	SS R.McMillan	SS J.Logan	SS A.Dark	2B G.Hamner	SS G.Allie	SS A.Grammas
3B D.Hoak	3B R.Jackson	3B B.Adams	3B E.Mathews	3B H.Thompson	SS B.Morgan	3B D.Cole	3B R.Jablonski
LF J.Robinson	LF R.Kiner	LF J.Greengrass	LF H.Aaron	LF M.Irvin	3B W.Jones	LF D.Hall	LF R.Repulski
CF D.Snider	CF B.Talbot	CF G.Bell	CF B.Bruton	CF W.Mays	LF D.Schell	CF F.Thomas	CF W.Moon
RF C.Furillo	RF H.Sauer	RF W.Post	RF A.Pafko	RF D.Mueller	CF R.Ashburn	RF S.Gordon	RF S.Musial
C R.Campanella	C J.Garagiola	C A.Seminick	C D.Crandall	C W.Westrum	RF D.Ennis	C T.Atwell	C B.Sarni
O S.Amoros	3 F.Baumholtz	3 C.Harmon	2 J.Dittmer	C R.Katt	C S.Burgess	O J.Lynch	S3 S.Hemus
32 B.Cox	C W.Cooper	C E.Bailey	O J.Pendleton	O D.Rhodes	C S.Lopata	1O P.Ward	1 T.Alston
C R.Walker	C E.Tappe	1O B.Borkowski	1O C.Metkovich	12 B.Hofman	O1 J.Wyrostek	C J.Shepard	O D.Rice
O W.Moryn	2 E.Miksis	O L.Merriman	32 B.Thomson	32 B.Gardner	O M.Clark	3 E.Pellagrini	O J.Frazier
O G.Shuba	1 S.Bilko	C H.Landrith	C C.White	/O B.Taylor	T T.Kazanski	O H.Rice	O P.Lowrey
O D.Williams	C M.McCullough	O N.Escalera	/S R.Smalley	C F.St.Claire	/3 F.Baker	3 V.Janowicz	S S.Yvars
S D.Zimmer	O H.Rice	S2 R.Bridges	C S.Calderone	/3 F.Castleman	/3 J.Command	O C.Abrams	/O T.Burgess
O D.Thompson	3 V.Morgan	/O J.Bolger	/1 M.Roach	/O H.Evers	H J.Lindell	/3 D.Smith	/1 S.Bilko
/C T.Thompson	3 B.Serena	H J.Hatton	/O B.Queen	/C J.Garagiola	/C G.Niarhos	/O J.Henley	S D.Schofield
/1 C.Kress	C J.Fanning	H J.Lipon	R S.Sisti	/O E.Rodin	/O S.Palys	/C J.Mangan	/3 P.Castiglione
H W.Belardi	O L.Marquez	H D.Murphy	P W.Spahn	/3 J.Amalfitano	H S.Jok	/C W.Cooper	P P.Haddix
P C.Erskine	/O D.Robertson	H C.Ryan	P L.Burdette	/2 R.Samford	/S M.Micelotta	/O N.Koback	P V.Raschi
P R.Meyer	H B.Edwards	P A.Fowler	P G.Conley	H H.Gentry	P R.Roberts	/O L.Marquez	P B.Lawrence
P J.Podres	/S C.Kitsos	P C.Valentine	P J.Wilson	B B.Lennon	P C.Simmons	/C B.Hall	P G.Staley
P B.Loes	P B.Rush	P J.Nuxhall	P C.Nichols	P J.Antonelli	P M.Dickson	/O S.Jethroe	P T.Poholsky
P D.Newcombe	P P.Minner	P B.Podbielan	RP D.Jolly	P R.Gomez	P B.Miller	P M.Surkont	RP A.Brazle
RP C.Labine	P W.Hacker	P F.Baczewski	RP E.Johnson	P S.Maglie	H B.Wehmeier	P B.Friend	RP J.Presko
RP J.Hughes	P J.Klippstein	RP H.Judson	RP R.Crone	P J.Hearn	RP S.Ridzik	P V.Law	RP C.Deal
RP E.Palica	P H.Pollet	RP F.Smith	P B.Buhl	P D.Liddle	RP J.Konstanty	P D.Littlefield	P G.Jones
P B.Milliken	RP J.Davis	RP J.Collum	P J.Jay	RP M.Grissom	R.Mrozinski	P B.Purkey	P R.Lint
P P.Roe	RP H.Jeffcoat	P H.Perkowski	P D.Koslo	RP H.Wilhelm	B.Greenwood	RP J.Hetki	P R.Beard
P B.Wade	RP B.Tremel	P K.Drews	P P.Paine	RP W.McCall	/P K.Drews	P J.Thies	P S.Miller
P P.Wojey	P D.Cole	P H.Wehmeier	/P C.Gorin	P L.Jansen	/P P.Penson	P P.LaPalme	P B.Wade
/P K.Spooner	P J.Brosnan	P M.Savransky		P A.Corwin	P T.Kipper	P G.O'Donnell	/P M.Wright
/P B.Darnell	P J.Willis	/P M.Picone		P A.Worthington		P L.Pepper	/P C.Scheib
/P T.Lasorda	/P J.Lane	/P K.Raffensberger		P M.Picone		P L.Yochim	/P H.White
/P J.Black	/P J.Pearce	/P G.Zuverink		P A.Konikowski		P C.Hogue	/P B.Greason
	/P B.Zick	/P C.Ross		/P G.Spencer		P J.Page	/P M.Luna
	/P B.Church			/P R.Monzant		/P N.King	
	/P A.Lary			/P J.Giel			
	/P J.Pyecha						

TEAM	G	W	L	PCT	GB	R	OR	AB	H	2B	3B	HR	BB	SO	AVG	OBP	SLG	PRO	PRO+	BR	/A	PF	CHI	RC	SB	CS	SBA	SBR
NY	154	97	57	.630		732	550	5245	1386	194	42	186	522	561	.264	.335	.424	.759	102	17	13	101	102	747	30	23	57	-5
BRO	154	92	62	.597	5	778	740	5251	1418	246	56	186	634	625	.270	.353	.444	.797	110	100	75	103	96	821	46	39	54	-10
MIL	154	89	65	.578	8	670	556	5261	1395	217	41	139	471	619	.265	.330	.401	.731	103	-33	10	94	101	697	54	31	64	-2
PHI	154	75	79	.487	22	659	644	5184	1384	243	58	102	604	620	.267	.345	.395	.740	99	-2	-1	100	95	707	30	27	53	-7
CIN	154	74	80	.481	23	729	763	5234	1369	221	46	147	557	645	.262	.336	.406	.742	96	-8	-27	103	105	726	47	30	61	-4
STL	154	72	82	.468	25	799	790	5405	1518	285	58	119	582	586	.281	.354	.421	.775	107	65	59	101	102	807	63	46	58	-9
CHI	154	64	90	.416	33	700	766	5359	1412	229	45	159	478	693	.263	.327	.412	.739	97	-21	-28	101	103	717	46	31	60	-5
PIT	154	53	101	.344	44	557	845	5088	1260	181	57	76	566	737	.248	.326	.350	.676	83	-119	-111	99	98	596	21	13	62	-2
TOT	616					5624		42027	11142	1816	403	1114	4414	5086	.265	.338	.407	.745							337	240	58	-43

TEAM	CG	SH	SV	IP	H	H/G	HR	BB	SO	RAT	ERA	ERA+	OAV	OOB	PR	/A	PF	CPI	FA	E	DP	FW	PW	BW	SBW	DIF
NY	45	19	33	1390	1258	8.1	113	613	692	12.3	3.09	130	.243	.328	151	145	99	113	.975	154	172	-.5	14.4	1.3	.0	4.9
BRO	39	8	36	1393²	1399	9.0	164	533	762	12.6	4.31	95	.261	.330	-36	-35	100	93	.978	129	138	.8	-3.5	7.4	-.5	10.7
MIL	63	13	21	1394²	1296	8.4	106	553	698	12.1	3.19	117	.250	.326	137	83	92	110	.981	116	171	1.5	8.2	1.0	.3	.9
PHI	78	14	12	1365¹	1329	8.8	133	450	570	11.8	3.59	112	.256	.318	73	68	99	100	.975	145	133	-.0	6.7	-.0	-.2	-8.4
CIN	34	8	27	1367¹	1491	9.8	169	547	537	13.6	4.50	93	.282	.354	-65	-47	103	105	.977	137	194	.4	-4.7	-2.7	.1	3.8
STL	40	11	18	1390¹	1484	9.6	170	535	680	13.4	4.50	91	.275	.345	-66	-60	101	100	.976	146	178	-.0	-5.9	5.8	-.4	-4.4
CHI	41	6	19	1374¹	1375	9.0	131	619	622	13.2	4.51	93	.264	.345	-66	-46	103	92	.974	154	164	-.5	-4.6	-2.8	.0	-5.2
PIT	37	4	15	1346	1510	10.1	128	564	525	14.0	4.92	85	.287	.359	-127	-109	103	95	.971	173	136	-1.6	-10.8	-11.0	.3	-1.0
TOT	377	83	181	11021²		9.1				12.9	4.07		.265	.338					.976	1154	1286					

Runs
Snider-Bro 120
Musial-StL 120
Mays-NY 119
Ashburn-Phi 111
Gilliam-Bro 107

Hits
Mueller-NY 212
Snider-Bro 199
Musial-StL 195
Mays-NY 195
Moon-StL 193

Doubles
Musial-StL 41
Snider-Bro 39
Repulski-StL 39
Hamner-Phi 39

Triples
Mays-NY 13
Hamner-Phi 11
Snider-Bro 10

Home Runs
Kluszewski-Cin 49
Hodges-Bro 42
Sauer-Chi 41
Mays-NY 41

Total Bases
Snider-Bro 378
Mays-NY 377
Kluszewski-Cin 368
Musial-StL 359
Hodges-Bro 335

Runs Batted In
Kluszewski-Cin 141
Snider-Bro 130
Hodges-Bro 130
Musial-StL 126
Ennis-Phi 119

Runs Produced
Musial-StL 211
Snider-Bro 210
Kluszewski-Cin 196
Hodges-Bro 194

Bases On Balls
Ashburn-Phi 125
Mathews-Mil 113
Musial-StL 103
Thompson-NY 90
Reese-Bro 90

Batting Average
Mays-NY .... .345
Mueller-NY .... .342
Snider-Bro .... .341
Musial-StL .... .330
Kluszewski-Cin ... .326

On Base Percentage
Ashburn-Phi ...... .442
Musial-StL .... .433
Mathews-Mil ...... .428
Snider-Bro .... .427
Mays-NY .... .415

Slugging Average
Mays-NY .... .667
Snider-Bro .... .647
Kluszewski-Cin ... .642
Musial-StL .... .607
Mathews-Mil ...... .603

Production
Mays-NY 1.083
Snider-Bro 1.074
Kluszewski-Cin .. 1.052
Musial-StL 1.040
Mathews-Mil 1.031

Adjusted Production
Mathews-Mil 177
Mays-NY 176
Snider-Bro 170
Musial-StL 166
Kluszewski-Cin 165

Batter Runs
Snider-Bro 64.6
Mays-NY 61.8
Musial-StL 60.7
Kluszewski-Cin ... 57.1
Mathews-Mil 48.6

Adjusted Batter Runs
Mays-NY 61.1
Snider-Bro 60.2
Musial-StL 59.6
Mathews-Mil 56.6
Kluszewski-Cin ... 53.4

Clutch Hitting Index
Ennis-Phi 132
Jablonski-StL 127
Post-Cin 126
Furillo-Bro 119
Bell-Cin 117

Runs Created
Snider-Bro 161
Mays-NY 155
Musial-StL 153
Kluszewski-Cin ... 151
Mathews-Mil 131

Total Average
Mathews-Mil 1.169
Mays-NY 1.158
Snider-Bro 1.156
Kluszewski-Cin .. 1.117
Musial-StL 1.087

Stolen Bases
Bruton-Mil 34
Temple-Cin 21
Fondy-Chi 20
Moon-StL 18
Ashburn-Phi 11

Stolen Base Average
Fondy-Chi 80.0
Temple-Cin 75.0
Bruton-Mil 72.3
Moon-StL 64.3

Stolen Base Runs
Fondy-Chi 3.0
Bruton-Mil 2.4
Temple-Cin 2.1
Torgeson-Phi 1.5

Fielding Runs
Schoendienst-StL . 32.9
Grammas-StL 29.8
Ashburn-Phi 17.2
Mays-NY 15.5
Logan-Mil 14.4

Total Player Rating
Mays-NY 6.7
Mathews-Mil 5.2
Schoendienst-StL ... 4.8
Snider-Bro 4.6
Musial-StL 4.6

Wins
Roberts-Phi 23
Spahn-Mil 21
Antonelli-NY 21
Haddix-StL 18
Erskine-Bro 18

Win Percentage
Antonelli-NY ..... .750
Lawrence-StL ..... .714
Gomez-NY .... .654
Spahn-Mil .... .636
Roberts-Phi ...... .605

Games
Hughes-Bro 60
Hetki-Pit 58
Brazle-StL 58
Wilhelm-NY 57
Grissom-NY 56

Complete Games
Roberts-Phi 29
Spahn-Mil 23
Simmons-Phi 21
Antonelli-NY 18

Shutouts
Antonelli-NY 6

Saves
Hughes-Bro 24
Smith-Cin 20
Grissom-NY 19
Jolly-Mil 10
Hetki-Pit 9

Innings Pitched
Roberts-Phi 336.2
Spahn-Mil 283.1
Erskine-Bro 260.1
Haddix-StL 259.2
Antonelli-NY 258.2

Fewest Hits/Game
Antonelli-NY 7.27
Roberts-Phi 7.73
Conley-Mil 7.92
Lawrence-StL 8.00
Wehmeier-Cin-Phi . 8.02

Fewest BB/Game
Roberts-Phi 1.50
Minner-Chi 2.06
Hacker-Chi 2.10
Burdette-Mil 2.34
Meyer-Bro 2.45

Strikeouts
Roberts-Phi 185
Haddix-StL 184
Erskine-Bro 166
Antonelli-NY 152
Spahn-Mil 136

Strikeouts/Game
Haddix-StL 6.38
Erskine-Bro 5.74
Littlefield-Pit .. 5.34
Antonelli-NY 5.29
Conley-Mil 5.23

Ratio
Roberts-Phi 9.36
Antonelli-NY 10.72
Burdette-Mil 10.97
Spahn-Mil 11.09
Hacker-Chi 11.23

Earned Run Average
Antonelli-NY 2.30
Burdette-Mil 2.76
Simmons-Phi 2.81
Gomez-NY 2.88
Conley-Mil 2.96

Adjusted ERA
Antonelli-NY 176
Simmons-Phi 144
Gomez-NY 140
Roberts-Phi 136
Burdette-Mil 135

Opponents' Batting Avg.
Antonelli-NY ..... .219
Roberts-Phi ...... .231
Simmons-Phi ...... .239
Littlefield-Pit .. .239
Wehmeier-Cin-Phi . .239

Opponents' On Base Pct.
Roberts-Phi ...... .267
Antonelli-NY ..... .293
Spahn-Mil .... .302
Burdette-Mil ..... .302
Hacker-Chi .... .304

Starter Runs
Antonelli-NY 51.0
Roberts-Phi 41.3
Simmons-Phi 35.5
Burdette-Mil 34.7
Gomez-NY 29.3

Adjusted Starter Runs
Antonelli-NY 50.0
Roberts-Phi 40.1
Simmons-Phi 34.6
Gomez-NY 28.4
Burdette-Mil 25.5

Clutch Pitching Index
Gomez-NY 130
Dickson-Phi 123
Fowler-Cin 116
Conley-Mil 116
Antonelli-NY 115

Relief Runs
Wilhelm-NY 24.4
Grissom-NY 23.4
Jolly-Mil 20.4
Johnson-Mil 13.9
Smith-Cin 12.7

Adjusted Relief Runs
Wilhelm-NY 23.9
Grissom-NY 22.9
Jolly-Mil 16.1
Smith-Cin 13.7
Johnson-Mil 10.1

Relief Ranking
Grissom-NY 36.6
Wilhelm-NY 34.3
Smith-Cin 27.5
Jolly-Mil 25.4
Hughes-Bro 15.6

Total Pitcher Index
Antonelli-NY 5.5
Grissom-NY 3.6
Roberts-Phi 3.6
Wilhelm-NY 3.4
Simmons-Phi 3.3

Total Baseball Ranking
Mays-NY 6.7
Antonelli-NY 5.5
Mathews-Mil 5.2
Schoendienst-StL .. 4.8
Snider-Bro 4.6

January 14 Joe DiMaggio marries Marilyn Monroe.

April 15 Clint Courtney of the Orioles hits the first home run in Memorial Stadium. Baltimore draws a record Opening Day crowd of 46,354 in a 3-1 win over the White Sox.

May 16 Ted Williams returns to action after breaking his collarbone and goes 8-for-9 with two home runs and seven RBIs in a doubleheader against the Tigers.

July 13 In the All-Star Game, the AL breaks the NL's four-game winning streak with an 11–9 win. Larry Doby's pinch home run in the eighth, followed by Nellie Fox's two-run single, ends the highest scoring All-Star Game to this date. The two teams combine for 31 hits, with the AL amassing 17. The Indians' Al Rosen has two home runs and drives in five runs.

July 30 Against Allie Reynolds, third baseman Bob Kennedy hits the first grand slam for the new Baltimore Orioles. The Orioles surpass the top season attendance the Browns had in their 52 years, as they draw 27,385 for the game, giving them 7,000 more than the 712,918 St. Louis drew in 1922.

August 12 Eddie Yost of the Senators draws his 100th walk for the fifth year in a row.

August 31 The Indians beat the Yanks, 6–1, to record their 26th win of the month, tying the 1931 A's.

September 12 A record crowd of 86,587 jams Cleveland's Memorial Stadium to see the Indians sweep a doubleheader from the Yanks, 4–1 and 3–2, behind Bob Lemon and Early Wynn.

September 18 The Indians clinch their third pennant in history and the first since 1948 with a 3–2 win over the Tigers.

September 25 Early Wynn two-hits the Tigers 11-1 for his league-leading 23rd win as the Indians notch their 111th victory, a new AL record eclipsing the 110 wins of the 1927 Yankees.

September 26 Art Ditmar of the Athletics defeats the Yanks, 8-6, in the last game the franchise will play in Philadelphia before moving to Kansas City. Yogi Berra plays his only game at third base, and Mickey Mantle plays shortstop in Casey Stengel's "power line-up."

October 28 The major league owners vote down the sale of the Athletics to a Philadelphia syndicate. A week later, Arnold Johnson buys a controlling interest in the Athletics from the Mack family for $3.5 million and moves the team to Kansas City.

November 18 In an enormous two-part trade begun on Nov. 14, the Yankees and Orioles exchange 17 players. Among those who change place is Don Larsen, who will pitch the only perfect game in World Series history for the Yankees in 1956.

	BALTIMORE		BOSTON		CHICAGO		CLEVELAND		DETROIT		NEW YORK		PHILADELPHIA		WASHINGTON
M	J.Dykes	M	L.Boudreau	M	P.Richards	M	A.Lopez	M	F.Hutchinson	M	C.Stengel	M	E.Joost	M	B.Harris
1B	E.Waitkus	1B	H.Agganis	M	M.Marion	1B	B.Glynn	1B	W.Dropo	1B	J.Collins	1B	L.Limmer	1B	M.Vernon
2B	B.Young	2B	T.Lepcio	1B	F.Fain	2B	B.Avila	2B	F.Bolling	2B	G.McDougald	2B	S.Jacobs	2B	W.Terwilliger
SS	B.Hunter	SS	M.Bolling	2B	N.Fox	SS	G.Strickland	SS	H.Kuenn	SS	P.Rizzuto	SS	J.DeMaestri	SS	P.Runnels
3B	V.Stephens	3B	G.Hatton	SS	C.Carrasquel	3B	A.Rosen	3B	R.Boone	3B	A.Carey	3B	J.Finigan	3B	E.Yost
LF	J.Fridley	LF	T.Williams	3B	C.Michaels	LF	A.Smith	LF	J.Delsing	LF	I.Noren	LF	G.Zernial	LF	R.Sievers
CF	C.Diering	CF	J.Jensen	LF	M.Minoso	CF	L.Doby	CF	B.Tuttle	CF	M.Mantle	CF	V.Power	CF	J.Busby
RF	C.Abrams	RF	J.Piersall	CF	J.Groth	RF	D.Philley	RF	A.Kaline	RF	H.Bauer	RF	B.Renna	RF	T.Umphlett
C	C.Courtney	C	S.White	RF	J.Rivera	C	J.Hegan	C	F.House	C	Y.Berra	C	J.Astroth	C	E.Fitz Gerald
				C	S.Lollar										
O	G.Coan	21	B.Goodman			1	V.Wertz	O	B.Nieman	2S	J.Coleman	1	D.Bollweg	O	T.Wright
3O	B.Kennedy	O	K.Olson	13	G.Kell	O	W.Westlake	O	W.Belardi	O	G.Woodling	O	E.Valo	2	J.Pesky
1	D.Kryhoski	S3	B.Consolo	C	M.Batts	3	R.Regalado	23	F.Hatfield	1	B.Skowron	O	B.Wilson	C	J.Tipton
O	S.Mele	1O	S.Mele	1	P.Cavarretta	S	S.Dente	C	R.Wilson	1	E.Robinson	23	P.Suder	S	J.Snyder
S2	J.Brideweser	C	C.Maxwell	23	C.Sawatski	C	H.Majeski	O	H.Evers	O	E.Slaughter	C	Bi.Shantz	O	J.Lemon
C	L.Moss	3	G.Kell	3	F.Marsh	O	D.Pope	O	D.Lund	S	W.Miranda	C	J.Robertson	C	C.Vollmer
O	V.Wertz	C	M.Owen	1	R.Jackson	C	H.Naragon	/O	S.Souchock	O	B.Cerv	O	J.Taylor	/S	M.Hoderlein
2	C.Garcia	O	D.Lenhardt	O	E.McGhee	/O	D.Mitchell	2	R.Bertoia	3	B.Brown	O	E.McGhee	/C	B.Oldis
C	R.Murray	C	D.Wilber	O	W.Marshall	H	L.Easter	/1	C.Kress	C	C.Silvera	/S	E.Joost	/O	C.Paula
O	J.Durham	/1	D.Gernert	O1	B.Boyd	/C	M.Grasso	O	C.King	/C	L.Berberet	/S	J.Littrell	/2	R.Dietzel
/1	F.Kellert	/3	F.Baker	O	B.Wilson	/1	R.Nelson	/C	M.Batts	/1	F.Leja			/2	H.Killebrew
/O	D.Lenhardt	/O	H.Evers	3	G.Hatton	/C	J.Ginsberg	H	J.Pesky	/S	W.Held	P	A.Portocarrero	/3	J.Levan
/O	D.Kokos	H	G.Morton	/3	J.Kirrene	H	J.Dyck	/C	A.Lakeman	H	R.Houk	P	A.Kellner	/S	S.Korcheck
/S	N.Berry			/C	R.Wilson	/O	B.Kennedy	/S	G.Bullard	/C	G.Triandos	P	M.Fricano		
		P	F.Sullivan	/O	B.Stewart			/C	W.Streuli			P	B.Trice	P	B.Porterfield
P	B.Turley	P	W.Nixon	/3	S.Jok	P	E.Wynn	P	S.Gromek	P	W.Ford	P	J.Gray	P	M.McDermott
P	J.Coleman	P	T.Brewer	R	B.Cain	P	M.Garcia	P	B.Grim	RP	S.Dixon	P	J.Schmitz
P	D.Larsen	P	L.Kiely	H	D.Nicholas	P	B.Lemon	P	N.Garver	P	E.Lopat	RP	M.Burtschy	P	C.Stobbs
P	D.Pillette	P	B.Henry			P	A.Houtteman	P	G.Zuverink	P	A.Reynolds	RP	A.Sima	P	D.Stone
P	L.Kretlow	RP	H.Brown	P	V.Trucks	P	B.Feller	P	B.Hoeft	P	T.Morgan			RP	C.Pascual
RP	B.Chakales	RP	E.Kinder	P	B.Keegan	RP	D.Mossi	P	A.Aber	RP	J.Sain	P	C.Bishop	RP	G.Keriazakos
RP	M.Blyzka	RP	S.Hudson	P	B.Pierce	RP	R.Narleski	RP	D.Marlowe			P	M.Martin	RP	B.Stewart
RP	H.Fox			P	J.Harshman	RP	H.Newhouser	RP	R.Herbert	P	H.Byrd	P	A.Ditmar		
		P	M.Parnell	P	S.Consuegra			RP	B.Miller	P	J.McDonald	/P	L.Wheat	P	S.Shea
P	M.Stuart	P	R.Kemmerer	RP	H.Dorish	P	B.Hooper			/P	T.Byrne	/P	O.Van Brabant	P	C.Marrero
/P	B.Kuzava	P	T.Clevenger	RP	M.Martin	P	D.Hoskins	P	T.Gray	/P	B.Kuzava	/P	B.Oster	P	S.Dixon
/P	B.O'Dell	P	T.Hurd			/P	B.Chakales	P	R.Branca	P	T.Gorman	/P	D.Romberger		
/P	D.Koslo	P	T.Herrin	P	D.Johnson	/O	J.Santiago	/P	D.Weik	/P	B.Wiesler	/P	Bo.Shantz		
/P	D.Littlefield	P	B.Werle	P	M.Fornieles	/O	D.Tomanek	/P	D.Donovan	/P	J.Konstanty	/P	B.Upton		
/P	V.Bickford	/P	J.Dobson	/P	D.Strahs			/P	F.Lary	/P	M.Stuart	/P	H.Raether		
/P	J.Heard			/P	A.Sima					/P	A.Schallock	/P	C.Scheib		
/P	R.Duren			/P	T.Flanigan					/P	R.Branca	/P	D.Rozek		
				/P	V.Valentinetti					/P	B.Miller				

TEAM	G	W	L	PCT	GB	R	OR	AB	H	2B	3B	HR	BB	SO	AVG	OBP	SLG	PRO	PRO+	BR	/A	PF	CHI	RC	SB	CS	SBA	SBR
CLE	156	111	43	.721		746	504	5222	1368	188	39	156	637	668	.262	.345	.403	.748	109	76	64	102	102	739	30	33	48	-11
NY	155	103	51	.669	8	805	563	5226	1400	215	59	133	650	632	.268	.351	.408	.759	118	101	128	97	106	768	34	41	45	-14
CHI	155	94	60	.610	17	711	521	5168	1382	203	47	94	604	536	.267	.350	.379	.729	103	51	27	103	101	700	98	58	63	-5
BOS	156	69	85	.448	42	700	728	5399	1436	244	41	123	654	660	.266	.348	.395	.743	99	73	-9	111	93	749	51	30	63	-3
DET	155	68	86	.442	43	584	664	5233	1351	215	41	90	492	603	.258	.324	.367	.691	97	-37	-26	98	97	609	48	44	52	-12
WAS	155	66	88	.429	45	632	680	5249	1292	188	69	81	610	719	.246	.328	.355	.683	98	-44	-11	95	104	631	37	21	64	-2
BAL	154	54	100	.351	57	483	668	5206	1309	195	49	52	468	634	.251	.316	.338	.654	92	-104	-65	93	91	553	30	31	49	-10
PHI	156	51	103	.331	60	542	875	5206	1228	191	41	94	504	677	.236	.307	.342	.649	84	-117	-119	100	105	553	30	29	51	-8
TOT	621					5203		41909	10766	1639	386	823	4619	5129	.257	.334	.373	.707							358	287	56	-65

TEAM	CG	SH	SV	IP	H	H/G	HR	BB	SO	RAT	ERA	ERA+	OAV	OOB	PR	/A	PF	CPI	FA	E	DP	FW	PW	BW	SBW	DIF
CLE	77	12	36	1419¹	1220	7.7	89	486	678	10.9	2.78	132	.232	.299	148	141	99	100	.979	128	148	.7	14.6	6.6	-.3	12.4
NY	51	16	37	1379¹	1284	8.4	86	552	655	12.2	3.26	105	.251	.328	71	27	92	107	.979	126	198	.8	2.8	13.2	-.6	9.8
CHI	60	23	33	1383	1255	8.2	94	517	701	11.6	3.05	122	.244	.314	103	105	100	105	.982	108	149	1.8	10.8	2.8	.3	1.2
BOS	41	10	22	1412¹	1434	9.1	118	612	707	13.3	4.01	102	.265	.344	-46	15	110	101	.972	176	163	-2.0	1.5	-.9	.5	-7.2
DET	58	13	13	1383	1375	8.9	138	506	603	12.5	3.81	97	.261	.330	-13	-17	99	103	.978	129	131	.6	-1.8	-2.7	-.4	-4.8
WAS	69	10	7	1383¹	1396	9.1	79	573	562	13.0	3.84	93	.265	.340	-18	-43	96	99	.977	137	172	.2	-4.4	-1.1	.6	-6.2
BAL	58	6	8	1373¹	1279	8.4	78	688	668	13.0	3.88	92	.250	.341	-24	-45	96	94	.975	147	152	-.4	-4.6	-6.7	-.2	-11.0
PHI	49	3	13	1371¹	1523	10.0	141	685	555	14.7	5.18	75	.285	.370	-222	-194	105	95	.972	169	163	-1.6	-20.0	-12.3	.0	7.9
TOT	463	93	169	11105		8.7				12.6	3.72		.257	.334					.977	1120	1276					

Runs		Hits		Doubles		Triples		Home Runs		Total Bases	
Mantle-NY	129	Kuenn-Det	201	Vernon-Was	33	Minoso-Chi	18	Doby-Cle	32	Minoso-Chi	304
Minoso-Chi	119	Fox-Chi	201	Smith-Cle	29	Runnels-Was	15	Williams-Bos	29	Vernon-Was	294
Avila-Cle	112	Avila-Cle	189	Minoso-Chi	29	Vernon-Was	14	Mantle-NY	27	Mantle-NY	285
Fox-Chi	111	Busby-Was	187			Mantle-NY	12	Jensen-Bos	25	Berra-NY	285
Carrasquel-Chi	106	Minoso-Chi	182			Tuttle-Det	11			Doby-Cle	279

Runs Batted In		Runs Produced		Bases On Balls		Batting Average		On Base Percentage		Slugging Average	
Doby-Cle	126	Minoso-Chi	216	Williams-Bos	136	Avila-Cle	.341	Williams-Bos	.516	Minoso-Chi	.535
Berra-NY	125	Mantle-NY	204	Yost-Was	131	Minoso-Chi	.320	Minoso-Chi	.416	Mantle-NY	.525
Jensen-Bos	117	Berra-NY	191	Mantle-NY	102	Noren-NY	.319	Rosen-Cle	.412	Rosen-Cle	.506
Minoso-Chi	116	Doby-Cle	188	Smith-Cle	88	Fox-Chi	.319	Mantle-NY	.411	Vernon-Was	.492
		Jensen-Bos	184			Berra-NY	.307	Yost-Was	.406	Berra-NY	.488

Production		Adjusted Production		Batter Runs		Adjusted Batter Runs		Clutch Hitting Index		Runs Created	
Williams-Bos	1.151	Williams-Bos	193	Williams-Bos	70.9	Williams-Bos	57.6	Berra-NY	123	Williams-Bos	139
Minoso-Chi	.951	Mantle-NY	160	Minoso-Chi	47.3	Mantle-NY	46.8	Minoso-Chi	122	Mantle-NY	127
Mantle-NY	.936	Minoso-Chi	154	Mantle-NY	42.8	Minoso-Chi	43.2	Rosen-Cle	118	Minoso-Chi	125
Rosen-Cle	.918	Rosen-Cle	148	Rosen-Cle	34.2	Rosen-Cle	32.6	Sievers-Was	117	Avila-Cle	109
Avila-Cle	.882	Noren-NY	140	Avila-Cle	31.5	Avila-Cle	29.8	Doby-Cle	116	Doby-Cle	108

Total Average		Stolen Bases		Stolen Base Average		Stolen Base Runs		Fielding Runs		Total Player Rating	
Williams-Bos	1.452	Jensen-Bos	22	Busby-Was	89.5	Busby-Was	3.9	Coleman-NY	17.9	Williams-Bos	5.0
Mantle-NY	1.013	Rivera-Chi	18	Jacobs-Phi	85.0	Jacobs-Phi	3.3	Carey-NY	16.7	Minoso-Chi	5.0
Minoso-Chi	.969	Minoso-Chi	18	Jensen-Bos	75.9	Jensen-Bos	2.4	Lepcio-Bos	16.1	Avila-Cle	4.7
Rosen-Cle	.959	Jacobs-Phi	17	Rivera-Chi	64.3	Cavarretta-Chi	1.2	Bolling-Bos	15.3	Mantle-NY	4.1
Doby-Cle	.862	Busby-Was	17	Fox-Chi	64.0			Minoso-Chi	13.4	Berra-NY	3.6

Wins		Win Percentage		Games		Complete Games		Shutouts		Saves	
Wynn-Cle	23	Consuegra-Chi	.842	Dixon-Was-Phi	54	Porterfield-Was	21	Trucks-Chi	5	Sain-NY	22
Lemon-Cle	23	Grim-NY	.769	Martin-Phi-Chi	48	Lemon-Cle	21	Garcia-Cle	5	Kinder-Bos	15
Grim-NY	20	Lemon-Cle	.767	Pascual-Was	48	Wynn-Cle	20			Narleski-Cle	13
Trucks-Chi	19	Garcia-Cle	.704	Kinder-Bos	48	Gromek-Det	17				
Garcia-Cle	19	Houtteman-Cle	.682								

Innings Pitched		Fewest Hits/Game		Fewest BB/Game		Strikeouts		Strikeouts/Game		Ratio	
Wynn-Cle	270.2	Turley-Bal	6.48	Lopat-NY	1.75	Turley-Bal	185	Pierce-Chi	7.06	Garcia-Cle	10.19
Trucks-Chi	264.2	Ford-NY	7.26	Gromek-Det	2.03	Wynn-Cle	155	Harshman-Chi	6.81	Wynn-Cle	10.24
Garcia-Cle	258.2	Wynn-Cle	7.48	Garver-Det	2.27	Trucks-Chi	152	Turley-Bal	6.73	Garver-Det	10.30
Lemon-Cle	258.1	Coleman-Bal	7.48	Garcia-Cle	2.47	Pierce-Chi	148	Hoeft-Det	5.86	Gromek-Det	10.86
Gromek-Det	252.2	Reynolds-NY	7.61	Zuverink-Det	2.75	Harshman-Chi	134	Reynolds-NY	5.72	Trucks-Chi	10.88

Earned Run Average		Adjusted ERA		Opponents' Batting Avg.		Opponents' On Base Pct.		Starter Runs		Adjusted Starter Runs	
Garcia-Cle	2.64	Garcia-Cle	139	Turley-Bal	.203	Garcia-Cle	.284	Garcia-Cle	31.0	Garcia-Cle	29.6
Lemon-Cle	2.72	Lemon-Cle	135	Wynn-Cle	.225	Wynn-Cle	.284	Wynn-Cle	30.0	Wynn-Cle	28.5
Wynn-Cle	2.73	Wynn-Cle	135	Ford-NY	.227	Garver-Det	.287	Lemon-Cle	28.9	Trucks-Chi	27.8
Gromek-Det	2.74	Gromek-Det	135	Trucks-Chi	.228	Gromek-Det	.297	Gromek-Det	27.5	Lemon-Cle	27.5
Trucks-Chi	2.79	Trucks-Chi	134	Garcia-Cle	.229	Trucks-Chi	.297	Trucks-Chi	27.5	Gromek-Det	26.7

Clutch Pitching Index		Relief Runs		Adjusted Relief Runs		Relief Ranking		Total Pitcher Index		Total Baseball Ranking	
Keegan-Chi	126	Mossi-Cle	18.5	Mossi-Cle	18.0	Mossi-Cle	15.2	Lemon-Cle	4.1	Williams-Bos	5.0
Gromek-Det	116	Narleski-Cle	14.8	Narleski-Cle	14.3	Narleski-Cle	13.4	Gromek-Det	3.4	Minoso-Chi	5.0
Houtteman-Cle	114	Dorish-Chi	12.1	Dorish-Chi	12.2	Dorish-Chi	11.6	Wynn-Cle	3.3	Avila-Cle	4.7
Lopat-NY	114	Miller-Det	9.8	Miller-Det	9.6	Kinder-Bos	9.7	Trucks-Chi	3.2	Lemon-Cle	4.1
Harshman-Chi	114	Sain-NY	4.9	Kinder-Bos	5.9	Sain-NY	4.9	Garcia-Cle	2.9	Mantle-NY	4.1

April 21 Brooklyn wins its 10th in a row, trouncing Robin Roberts of the Phils, 14–2. This sets a new major league record for consecutive wins to start a season, later topped by Atlanta and Oakland.

June 3 Stan Musial hits the 300th home run of his career, a three-run shot in the fifth-inning against Brooklyn's Johnny Podres. The Cards use a NL-record eight pitchers in a 12–5 loss.

June 8 The Dodgers option pitcher Tommy Lasorda to Montreal to make room on the roster for bonus baby Sandy Koufax, who has been on the injured list.

August 15 At Sportsman's Park in St. Louis, Braves pitcher Warren Spahn cracks a home run off Cardinals pitcher Mel Wright. It gives Spahn a home run in every National League park.

August 27 Dodgers bonus baby Sandy Koufax fans 14 Redlegs in a 7–0 win, as the two teams total 23 strikeouts.

September 5 Pitcher Don Newcombe wins his 20th game of the season 11-4 over the Phillies and hits his seventh homer of the season to set a new NL record for home runs by a pitcher.

September 8 Brooklyn clinches the pennant by beating the Braves 10-2 for their eighth straight win and break their own major league record for the earliest clinching, set in 1953.

September 19 Cubs slugger Ernie Banks hits his fifth grand slam of the season to set a new major league mark, but the Cubs lose 6-5 in 12 innings, to the Cardinals.

September 20 Giants slugger Willie Mays poles two home runs against the Pirates, giving him 50 for the year, making him only the seventh player in history to accomplish the feat.

September 25 Bobby Hofman of the Giants lines into a season-ending triple play against the Phillies in a 3–1 loss. The Giants win the opener, 5–2, as Willie Mays belts his 51st home run of the year.

October 2 Surprise Brooklyn rookie Roger Craig pitches six innings in World Series Game 1 for a 5–3 win. Two home runs by Duke Snider and one by Sandy Amoros in the first five innings prove too much for New York. Snider, who hit four home runs in the 1952 World Series, becomes the first player in history to do this more than once.

October 4 No more "wait till next year" as the Dodgers, behind the 2-0 pitching of Johnny Podres, brings the first World Series championship to Brooklyn in eight tries. Sixth-inning replacement Sandy Amoros races over to the wall in left field to one-hand an opposite-field bid for extra bases by Yogi Berra with the tying runs on. Amoros turns and fires to shortstop Pee Wee Reese who throws a bullet to Gil Hodges at first baseman for the double play on Yankee base runner Gil McDougald.

October 12 The Cardinals give manager Harry Walker his hat and replace him with Fred Hutchinson. With the departure of Walker, who pinch hit for the Cards during the season, the 1956 season will be the first one in NL history without a player-manager. The AL first went to all bench managers in 1930, then repeated in 1951.

October 25 Baseball great Branch Rickey steps down as general manager of the Pirates and moves into an advisory role with the Pirates. Joe L. Brown, son of actor Joe E. Brown, replaces him.

	BROOKLYN		CHICAGO		CINCINNATI		MILWAUKEE		NEW YORK		PHILADELPHIA		PITTSBURGH		ST.LOUIS
M	W.Alston	M	S.Hack	M	B.Tebbetts	M	C.Grimm	M	L.Durocher	M	M.Smith	M	F.Haney	M	E.Stanky
1B	G.Hodges	1B	D.Fondy	1B	T.Kluszewski	1B	G.Crowe	1B	G.Harris	1B	M.Blaylock	1B	D.Long	M	H.Walker
2B	J.Gilliam	2B	G.Baker	2B	J.Temple	2B	D.O'Connell	2B	W.Terwilliger	2B	B.Morgan	2B	J.O'Brien	1B	S.Musial
SS	P.Reese	SS	E.Banks	SS	R.McMillan	SS	J.Logan	SS	A.Dark	SS	R.Smalley	SS	D.Groat	2B	R.Schoendienst
3B	J.Robinson	3B	R.Jackson	3B	R.Bridges	3B	E.Mathews	3B	H.Thompson	3B	W.Jones	3B	Gn.Freese	SS	A.Grammas
LF	S.Amoros	LF	H.Sauer	LF	S.Palys	LF	B.Thomson	LF	W.Lockman	LF	D.Ennis	LF	J.Lynch	3B	K.Boyer
CF	D.Snider	CF	E.Miksis	CF	G.Bell	CF	B.Bruton	CF	W.Mays	CF	R.Ashburn	CF	F.Thomas	LF	R.Repulski
RF	C.Furillo	RF	J.King	RF	W.Post	RF	H.Aaron	RF	D.Mueller	RF	J.Greengrass	RF	R.Clemente	CF	B.Virdon
C	R.Campanella	C	H.Chiti	C	S.Burgess	C	D.Crandall	C	R.Katt	C	A.Seminick	C	J.Shepard	RF	W.Moon
														C	B.Sarni
3	D.Hoak	O	F.Baumholtz	3O	C.Harmon	O	C.Tanner	1C	B.Hofman	2S	G.Hamner	32	D.Cole	
2S	D.Zimmer	O	B.Speake	3O	R.Jablonski	1	J.Adcock	C1	D.Rhodes	O	S.Lopata	O	E.O'Brien	32	S.Hemus
C	R.Walker	O	J.Bolger	O	B.Thurman	O3	A.Pafko	2	D.Williams	O	G.Gorbous	C	T.Atwell	C	N.Burbrink
1	F.Kellert	O	L.Merriman	3	B.Adams	2	J.Dittmer	S3	B.Gardner	1	E.Torgeson	3	Gr.Freese	O	H.Elliott
/O	G.Shuba	C	W.Cooper	3	M.Smith	C	D.Rice	O	M.Irvin	1	E.Waitkus	1	P.Ward	O	P.Whisenant
C	D.Howell	C	C.McCullough	C	H.Landrith	C	C.White	3O	S.Gordon	O	P.Lowrey	O	R.Mejias	S	B.Stephenson
/O	B.Borkowski	O	T.Tappe	O	M.Batts	/S	J.Pendleton	C	W.Westrum	O	S.Palys	O	T.Saffell	O	J.Frazier
/O	W.Moryn	/O	G.Wade	O	S.Mele	/1	B.Taylor	/O	B.Taylor	/O	M.Clark	O	F.Montemayor	C	D.Rice
H	B.Hamric	/C	J.Fanning	C	E.Bailey	/C	B.Roselli	/2	F.Castleman	/C	S.Burgess	/C	H.Peterson	/2	D.Blasingame
		/3	O.Friend	O	J.Greengrass			/S	J.Amalfitano	/C	T.Kazanski	/3	S.Gordon	/O	W.Walker
P	D.Newcombe	/3	V.Morgan	O	B.Borkowski	P	W.Spahn	/O	G.Coan	/C	G.Niarhos	/2	C.Roberts	/C	D.Rand
P	C.Erskine	R	A.Lary	H	J.Brovia	P	L.Burdette	/C	M.Grasso	/3	F.Baker	/C	E.Smith	/1	T.Alston
P	J.Podres	/C	E.Tappe	/O	G.Gorbous	P	B.Buhl			H	J.Command	/C	N.Koback	/S	D.Schofield
P	B.Loes			/C	A.Seminick	P	G.Conley	P	J.Antonelli	/S	M.Micelotta	/O	J.Powers	
P	K.Spooner	P	S.Jones	/O	B.Hazle	P	C.Nichols	P	J.Hearn	/O	B.Bowman	/S	D.Smith	P	H.Haddix
RP	C.Labine	P	B.Rush	/O	A.Silvera	RP	E.Johnson	P	R.Gomez	H	D.Schell			P	L.Jackson
RP	E.Roebuck	P	W.Hacker			RP	D.Jolly	P	S.Maglie	/C	B.Burgess	P	V.Law	P	L.Arroyo
RP	D.Bessent	P	P.Minner	P	J.Nuxhall			P	D.Liddle	R	J.Easton	P	B.Friend	P	T.Poholsky
		P	J.Davis	P	A.Fowler	P	R.Crone	RP	H.Wilhelm	H	F.Van Dusen	P	M.Surkont	P	W.Schmidt
P	R.Craig	RP	H.Jeffcoat	P	J.Klippstein	P	H.Robinson	RP	W.McCall			P	R.Kline	RP	B.Lawrence
P	R.Meyer	RP	H.Pollet	P	J.Collum	P	P.Paine	RP	M.Grissom	P	R.Roberts	P	D.Littlefield	RP	P.LaPalme
P	J.Hughes	RP	D.Hillman	P	G.Staley	P	R.Vargas			P	M.Dickson			
P	S.Koufax			RP	R.Minarcin	P	J.Jay	P	R.Monzant	P	H.Wehmeier	P	R.Face	P	F.Wooldridge
/P	J.Black	P	H.Perkowski	RP	H.Freeman	/P	J.Edelman	P	P.Giel	P	C.Simmons	P	L.Donoso	P	G.Jones
/P	C.Templeton	P	J.Andre			/C	C.Gorin	P	A.Corwin	RP	J.Meyer	P	D.Hall	P	F.Smith
/P	T.Lasorda	P	B.Tremel	P	J.Black	/P	D.Koslo	/P	P.Burnside	RP	B.Miller	P	B.Purkey	P	M.Wright
		P	D.Kaiser	P	D.Gross			/P	G.Spencer			P	N.King	P	B.Tiefenauer
		/P	H.Cohen	P	B.Podbielan					P	S.Rogovin	P	B.Wade	P	B.Schultz
		/P	V.Amor	P	S.Ridzik					P	R.Negray	P	L.Pepper	/P	B.Flowers
		/P	B.Church	P	C.Valentine					P	T.Kipper	P	R.Bowman	P	H.Moford
		/P	B.Thorpe	/P	B.Hooper					P	R.Mrozinski	/P	A.Grunwald	/P	J.Mackinson
				/P	J.Lane					P	B.Kuzava	/P	P.Martin	/P	L.McDaniel
				/P	M.Fisher					/P	D.Cole	/P	F.Waters	/P	A.Gettel
				/P	J.Pearce					/P	L.Lovenguth	/P	J.Thies	/P	T.Jacobs
				/P	F.Baczewski					/P	S.Ridzik	/P	R.Swanson	/P	V.Raschi
										/P	J.Owens	/P	B.Bell	
										/P	J.Spring			
										/P	B.Greenwood			

TEAM	G	W	L	PCT	GB	R	OR	AB	H	2B	3B	HR	BB	SO	AVG	OBP	SLG	PRO	PRO+	BR	/A	PF	CHI	RC	SB	CS	SBA	SBR
BRO	154	98	55	.641		**857**	**650**	5193	1406	**230**	44	**201**	674	718	.271	.359	.448	.807	116	142	118	103	100	834	79	56	59	-10
MIL	154	85	69	.552	13.5	743	668	5277	1377	219	55	182	504	735	.261	.329	.427	.756	109	27	63	95	102	733	42	27	61	-4
NY	154	80	74	.519	18.5	702	673	5288	1377	173	34	169	497	**581**	.260	.328	.402	.730	98	-15	-16	100	102	699	38	22	**63**	**-2**
PHI	154	77	77	.500	21.5	675	666	5092	1300	214	50	132	652	673	.255	.343	.395	.738	103	14	27	98	95	692	44	32	58	-6
CIN	154	75	79	.487	23.5	761	684	5270	**1424**	216	28	181	556	657	.270	.344	.425	.769	103	63	19	106	99	773	51	36	59	-6
CHI	154	72	81	.471	26	626	713	5214	1287	187	55	164	408	806	.247	.305	.398	.705	91	-75	-73	100	**103**	623	37	35	51	-10
STL	154	68	86	.442	30.5	654	757	5266	1375	228	36	143	458	597	.261	.324	.400	.724	96	-30	-29	100	99	662	64	59	52	-16
PIT	154	60	94	.390	38.5	560	767	5173	1262	210	**60**	91	471	652	.244	.310	.361	.671	84	-127	-119	99	100	567	22	22	50	-7
TOT	616					5578		41773	10808	1677	362	1263	4240	5419	.259	.330	.407	.737							377	289	57	-60

TEAM	CG	SH	SV	IP	H	H/G	HR	BB	SO	RAT	ERA	ERA+	OAV	OOB	PR	/A	PF	CPI	FA	E	DP	FW	PW	BW	SBW	DIF
BRO	46	11	**37**	1378	1296	8.5	168	483	**773**	11.7	3.68	110	.248	.314	54	58	101	100	.978	133	156	.5	5.8	11.7	-.2	3.8
MIL	**61**	5	12	1383	1339	8.7	**138**	591	654	12.7	3.85	98	.256	.333	29	-14	93	102	.975	152	155	-.6	-1.4	6.3	.4	3.4
NY	52	6	14	1386²	1347	8.7	155	560	721	12.7	3.77	107	.257	.334	41	39	100	**107**	.976	142	165	.0	3.9	-1.6	**.5**	.2
PHI	58	11	21	1356²	**1291**	8.6	161	477	657	11.9	3.93	101	.251	.318	17	6	98	96	**.981**	110	117	**1.8**	.6	2.7	.2	-5.2
CIN	38	**12**	22	1363	1373	9.1	161	443	576	12.1	3.95	107	.264	.324	13	43	105	102	.977	139	169	.2	4.3	1.9	.2	-8.5
CHI	47	10	23	1378¹	1306	8.5	153	601	686	12.6	4.17	98	.251	.332	-21	-13	101	95	.975	147	147	-.3	-1.3	-7.2	-.2	4.6
STL	42	10	15	1376²	1376	9.0	185	549	730	12.9	4.56	89	.262	.337	-80	-77	101	95	.975	146	152	-.2	-7.6	-2.9	-.8	2.6
PIT	41	5	16	1362	1480	9.8	142	536	622	13.5	4.39	94	.281	.350	-54	-42	102	104	.972	166	**175**	-1.4	-4.2	-11.8	.0	.3
TOT	385	70	160	10984¹		8.9				12.5	4.04		.259	.330					.976	1135	1236					

Runs		Hits		Doubles		Triples		Home Runs		Total Bases	
Snider-Bro	126	Kluszewski-Cin	192	Logan-Mil	37	Mays-NY	13	Mays-NY	51	Mays-NY	382
Mays-NY	123	Aaron-Mil	189	Aaron-Mil	37	Long-Pit	13	Kluszewski-Cin	47	Kluszewski-Cin	358
Post-Cin	116	Bell-Cin	188	Snider-Bro	34	Bruton-Mil	12	Banks-Chi	44	Banks-Chi	355
Kluszewski-Cin	116	Post-Cin	186	Post-Cin	33	Clemente-Pit	11	Snider-Bro	42	Post-Cin	345
Gilliam-Bro	110			Ashburn-Phi	32			Mathews-Mil	41	Snider-Bro	338

Runs Batted In		Runs Produced		Bases On Balls		Batting Average		On Base Percentage		Slugging Average	
Snider-Bro	136	Snider-Bro	220	Mathews-Mil	109	Ashburn-Phi	.338	Ashburn-Phi	.449	Mays-NY	.659
Mays-NY	127	Mays-NY	199	Ashburn-Phi	105	Mays-NY	.319	Snider-Bro	.421	Snider-Bro	.628
Ennis-Phi	120	Post-Cin	185	Snider-Bro	104	Musial-StL	.319	Mathews-Mil	.417	Mathews-Mil	.601
Banks-Chi	117	Aaron-Mil	184	Thompson-NY	84	Campanella-Bro	.318	Musial-StL	.411	Banks-Chi	.596
Kluszewski-Cin	113	Kluszewski-Cin	182			Aaron-Mil	.314	Mays-NY	.404	Kluszewski-Cin	.585

Production		Adjusted Production		Batter Runs		Adjusted Batter Runs		Clutch Hitting Index		Runs Created	
Mays-NY	1.063	Mays-NY	176	Mays-NY	62.3	Mays-NY	62.0	Long-Pit	117	Mays-NY	157
Snider-Bro	1.050	Mathews-Mil	175	Snider-Bro	58.9	Mathews-Mil	56.3	Jones-Phi	117	Snider-Bro	145
Mathews-Mil	1.018	Snider-Bro	169	Mathews-Mil	50.0	Snider-Bro	55.2	Mueller-NY	116	Kluszewski-Cin	136
Campanella-Bro	.985	Musial-StL	156	Musial-StL	46.5	Musial-StL	46.6	Ennis-Phi	116	Musial-StL	131
Musial-StL	.977	Campanella-Bro	153	Kluszewski-Cin	44.9	Ashburn-Phi	38.8	Temple-Cin	115	Mathews-Mil	131

Total Average		Stolen Bases		Stolen Base Average		Stolen Base Runs		Fielding Runs		Total Player Rating	
Mays-NY	1.180	Bruton-Mil	25	Mays-NY	85.7	Mays-NY	4.8	Mays-NY	19.8	Mays-NY	7.7
Snider-Bro	1.147	Mays-NY	24	Temple-Cin	82.6	Temple-Cin	3.3	McMillan-Cin	16.6	Banks-Chi	5.3
Mathews-Mil	1.124	Boyer-StL	22	Bruton-Mil	69.4	Robinson-Bro	1.8	O'Connell-Mil	15.8	Mathews-Mil	4.9
Musial-StL	1.020	Temple-Cin	19	Boyer-StL	56.4	Blaylock-Phi	1.2	Groat-Pit	15.4	Snider-Bro	4.7
Campanella-Bro	1.000	Gilliam-Bro	15					Bruton-Mil	14.7	Ashburn-Phi	4.0

Wins		Win Percentage		Games		Complete Games		Shutouts		Saves	
Roberts-Phi	23	Newcombe-Bro	.800	Labine-Bro	60	Roberts-Phi	26	Nuxhall-Cin	5	Meyer-Phi	16
Newcombe-Bro	20	Roberts-Phi	.622	Wilhelm-NY	59	Newcombe-Bro	17	Jones-Chi	4	Roebuck-Bro	12
Spahn-Mil	17	Nuxhall-Cin	.586	LaPalme-StL	56	Spahn-Mil	16	Dickson-Phi	4	Labine-Bro	11
Nuxhall-Cin	17	Spahn-Mil	.548	Grissom-NY	55					Freeman-Cin	11
				Freeman-Cin	52					Grissom-NY	8

Innings Pitched		Fewest Hits/Game		Fewest BB/Game		Strikeouts		Strikeouts/Game		Ratio	
Roberts-Phi	305.0	Jones-Chi	6.52	Newcombe-Bro	1.46	Jones-Chi	198	Jones-Chi	7.37	Newcombe-Bro	10.05
Nuxhall-Cin	257.0	Buhl-Mil	7.50	Roberts-Phi	1.56	Roberts-Phi	160	Haddix-StL	6.49	Roberts-Phi	10.24
Spahn-Mil	245.2	Rush-Chi	7.85	Hacker-Chi	1.82	Haddix-StL	150	Podres-Bro	6.44	Friend-Pit	10.42
Jones-Chi	241.2	Antonelli-NY	7.88	Friend-Pit	2.34	Newcombe-Bro	143	Conley-Mil	6.09	Hacker-Chi	10.44
Antonelli-NY	235.1	Dickson-Phi	7.92	Spahn-Mil	2.38	Antonelli-NY	143	Newcombe-Bro	5.51	Rush-Chi	10.73

Earned Run Average		Adjusted ERA		Opponents' Batting Avg.		Opponents' On Base Pct.		Starter Runs		Adjusted Starter Runs	
Friend-Pit	2.83	Friend-Pit	145	Jones-Chi	.206	Roberts-Phi	.280	Friend-Pit	26.9	Friend-Pit	28.6
Newcombe-Bro	3.20	Newcombe-Bro	127	Buhl-Mil	.227	Newcombe-Bro	.280	Roberts-Phi	25.8	Roberts-Phi	23.5
Buhl-Mil	3.21	Nuxhall-Cin	122	Rush-Chi	.234	Hacker-Chi	.285	Newcombe-Bro	21.8	Newcombe-Bro	22.5
Spahn-Mil	3.26	Roberts-Phi	121	Antonelli-NY	.234	Friend-Pit	.294	Spahn-Mil	21.2	Nuxhall-Cin	21.9
Roberts-Phi	3.28	Antonelli-NY	121	Dickson-Phi	.238	Rush-Chi	.295	Antonelli-NY	18.6	Schmidt-StL	18.5

Clutch Pitching Index		Relief Runs		Adjusted Relief Runs		Relief Ranking		Total Pitcher Index		Total Baseball Ranking	
Minner-Chi	122	Freeman-Cin	19.1	Freeman-Cin	21.1	Freeman-Cin	28.5	Newcombe-Bro	4.2	Mays-NY	7.7
Spahn-Mil	114	Miller-Phi	16.2	Miller-Phi	15.5	Miller-Phi	19.1	Roberts-Phi	3.7	Banks-Chi	5.3
Jackson-StL	113	LaPalme-StL	13.1	LaPalme-StL	13.4	Jeffcoat-Chi	17.6	Friend-Pit	3.3	Mathews-Mil	4.9
Law-Pit	109	Labine-Bro	12.8	Labine-Bro	13.1	Labine-Bro	17.0	Freeman-Cin	3.1	Snider-Bro	4.7
Friend-Pit	109	Jeffcoat-Chi	12.2	Jeffcoat-Chi	12.7	Bessent-Bro	13.3	Antonelli-NY	2.6	Newcombe-Bro	4.2

April 12 After a big civic parade, the Athletics open their first season in Kansas City with a 6-2 win over the Tigers before 32,844.

April 14 Elston Howard becomes the first black to wear the Yankee uniform. He singles in his first at bat, against the Red Sox, as the Yanks win 8–4.

May 29 Larry Doby of the Indians hits the first major league home run over the outer wall in Kansas City, an estimated 500-foot clout. The Indians win 4–2.

June 24 Washington rookie infielder Harmon Killebrew hits his first home run in an 18-7 loss to the Detroit Tigers.

August 5 After playing 274 straight games at second base, Nellie Fox is given a day off by White Sox manager Marty Marion. Fox will come back the next day and play in 798 more consecutive games.

August 13 Larry Doby makes his first error in the outfield in 167 games, a new AL record.

September 7 Whitey Ford throws his second consecutive one-hitter, beating the A's 2-1. Jim Finigan hits a two-out single in the seventh for the Nats' only hit.

September 14 Herb Score of the Indians breaks Grover Cleveland Alexander's rookie record of 235 strikeouts. He finishes the season with 245.

September 17 Future Hall of Famer Brooks Robinson goes 2-4 in his first game as the O's top the Senators 3-1.

September 23 The Yanks clinch the pennant by beating the Red Sox 3-2.

September 25 Detroit outfielder Al Kaline becomes the youngest batting champ in history, as he takes the AL crown at age 20.

September 26 The Red Sox beat the Yankees, 8–1, as Ted Williams goes 1-for-2. Williams finishes the season at .356, well ahead of Kaline's .340, but does not have enough at bats to win the batting title. The same thing happened in 1954. Williams was walked 136 times in 1954 and 71 times (AL-leading 17 were intentional) this year. A rule change will be made to recognize plate appearances, not times at bat.

September 28 The Yanks win the first game of the World Series, as Whitey Ford beats Don Newcombe 6-5. In a controversial play with Frank Kellert at bat, Jackie Robinson steals home in the eighth to bring the Dodgers to within a run of a tie. Films later disclose that Robinson is out by a whisker, but Yogi Berra actually balked on the play, receiving Whitey Ford's pitch before Kellert could swing at it.

BALTIMORE	BOSTON	CHICAGO	CLEVELAND	DETROIT	KANSAS CITY	NEW YORK	WASHINGTON
M P.Richards	M P.Higgins	M M.Marion	M A.Lopez	M B.Harris	M L.Boudreau	M C.Stengel	M C.Dressen
1B G.Triandos	1B N.Zauchin	1B W.Dropo	1B V.Wertz	1B E.Torgeson	1B V.Power	1B B.Skowron	1B M.Vernon
2B F.Marsh	2B B.Goodman	2B N.Fox	2B B.Avila	2B F.Hatfield	2B J.Finigan	2B G.McDougald	2B P.Runnels
SS W.Miranda	SS B.Klaus	SS C.Carrasquel	SS G.Strickland	SS H.Kuenn	SS J.DeMaestri	SS B.Hunter	SS J.Valdivielso
3B W.Causey	3B G.Hatton	3B G.Kell	3B A.Rosen	3B R.Boone	3B H.Lopez	3B A.Carey	3B E.Yost
LF D.Philley	LF T.Williams	LF M.Minoso	LF R.Kiner	LF J.Delsing	LF G.Zernial	LF I.Noren	LF R.Sievers
CF C.Diering	CF J.Piersall	CF J.Busby	CF L.Doby	CF B.Tuttle	CF H.Simpson	CF M.Mantle	CF T.Umphlett
RF C.Abrams	RF J.Jensen	RF J.Rivera	RF A.Smith	RF A.Kaline	RF E.Slaughter	RF H.Bauer	RF C.Paula
C H.Smith	C S.White	C S.Lollar	C J.Hegan	C F.House	C J.Astroth	C Y.Berra	C E.Fitz Gerald
O D.Pope	O G.Stephens	O B.Nieman	O G.Woodling	O B.Phillips	O B.Renna	1O J.Collins	O E.Oravetz
O3 J.Dyck	O F.Throneberry	3O B.Kennedy	C H.Naragon	O R.Wilson	O B.Wilson	O E.Howard	C C.Courtney
32 B.Cox	3 T.Lepcio	3 J.Groth	1 F.Fain	2 H.Malmberg	1 E.Valo	1 E.Robinson	O J.Busby
2 B.Young	S2 E.Joost	1 R.Jackson	C H.Foiles	C F.Fain	C Bi.Shantz	S P.Rizzuto	O J.Groth
O H.Evers	1 H.Agganis	C L.Moss	S3 S.Dente	1 J.Phillips	2 P.Suder	S2 J.Coleman	S B.Kline
1 B.Hale	C P.Daley	S J.Brideweser	O D.Philley	O C.Maxwell	S3 Ct.Boyer	O B.Cerv	3 J.Delis
O G.Woodling	S O.Friend	3 V.Stephens	3 D.Pope	O R.Bertoia	S J.Littrell	2 B.Martin	2S J.Snyder
O G.Coan	/O S.Mele	S W.Marshall	1 J.Altobelli	/1 J.Porter	/2 J.Schypinski	/2 B.Richardson	3 H.Killebrew
3 J.Pyburn	/1 D.Gernert	C C.Courtney	/1 D.Mitchell	/O C.King	1 D.Kryhoski	H E.Slaughter	C B.Edwards
1 E.Waitkus	/3 F.Malzone	/1 B.Adams	/C H.Majeski	1 J.Small	H T.Saffell	/S T.Carroll	S T.Roig
O B.Kennedy	/2 B.Consolo	/3 B.Peterson	H B.Young	/2 W.Streuli	/2 S.Jacobs	/C L.Berberet	O J.Schoonmaker
2 D.Leppert	/C H.Sullivan	/O G.Coan	/S R.Regalado	/O W.Belardi	/O B.Stewart	/O D.Tettelbach	S K.Korcheck
C L.Moss	/S M.Bolling	O R.Northey	H W.Westlake	H B.Young	/O D.Plarski	/C J.Blanchard	/O J.Lemon
/3 H.Majeski	/C J.Pagliaroni	O E.McGhee	/O B.Harrell	/S R.Samford	/S A.George	/1 F.Leja	H J.Levan
/O T.Nelson	P F.Sullivan	/O P.Cavarretta	/O S.Locklin	/S S.Souchock	/1 D.Bollweg	/1 M.Throneberry	1 J.Becquer
C T.Gastall	P W.Nixon	/3 S.Esposito	/O R.Colavito	P F.Lary	/1 J.Robertson	P W.Ford	H T.Wright
/O W.Westlake	P G.Susce	/3 S.Jok	/2 S.Pawloski	P N.Garver	/3 H.Bevan	P B.Turley	/C B.Oldis
/3 B.Robinson	P I.Delock	/S E.White	/S K.Kuhn	P B.Hoeft	/C E.MacKenzie	P T.Byrne	P D.Stone
/O A.Dagres	RP L.Kiely	H L.Merriman	H H.Simpson	P S.Gromek	P A.Ditmar	P J.Kucks	P B.Porterfield
/3 K.Segrist	RP T.Hurd	R L.Powell	P E.Wynn	RP B.Birrer	P A.Kellner	P D.Larsen	P B.Schmitz
/3 V.Stephens	RP E.Kinder	P B.Pierce	P H.Score	RP A.Aber	P Bo.Shantz	RP J.Konstanty	P M.McDermott
H C.Maxwell	P B.Henry	P D.Donovan	P B.Lemon	RP P.Foytack	P A.Ceccarelli	RP T.Morgan	P C.Stobbs
/O R.Marquis	P M.Parnell	P J.Harshman	P M.Garcia	P D.Maas	RP A.Portocarrero	RP T.Sturdivant	RP P.Ramos
P J.Wilson	/P F.Baumann	P V.Trucks	P A.Houtteman	P J.Bunning	RP T.Gorman	P B.Grim	RP T.Abernathy
P E.Palica	P D.Brodowski	P D.Johnson	P R.Narleski	RP L.Cristante	RP B.Harrington	P E.Lopat	RP S.Shea
P R.Moore	/P R.Kemmerer	RP S.Consuegra	P G.Zuverink	P G.Zuverink	P V.Raschi	P R.Coleman	P C.Pascual
P B.Wight	/P H.Brown	RP D.Howell	RP S.Consuegra	P J.Coleman	P Cd.Boyer	/P J.Sain	P B.Chakales
RP A.Schallock	/P H.Freeman	RP M.Martin	RP D.Mossi	/P B.Miller	S R.Herbert	/P T.Gray	/P W.Clarke
RP D.Johnson	/P B.Smith	P H.Byrd	P B.Feller	/P D.Marlowe	/P J.Sain	/P A.Schallock	/P B.Stewart
RP H.Dorish	/P J.Trimble	P M.Fornieles	/P J.Santiago	/P B.Black	/P J.Gray	/P G.Staley	/P B.Currie
P G.Zuverink		P B.Keegan	P S.Maglie	/P V.Fletcher	/P L.Sleater		/P V.Gonzales
P S.Rogovin		P H.Dorish	P B.Wight	/P B.Wight	/P M.Kume		/P D.Hyde
P H.Byrd		/P B.Chakales	/P H.Aguirre	/P H.Aguirre	P M.Fricano		
P H.Brown		/P A.Papai	/P B.Daley	/P B.Froats	/P W.Craddock		
P J.McDonald		/P T.Gray	P T.Gray	/P B.Schultz	/P G.Keriazakos		
P E.Lopat			/P H.Newhouser		/P M.Burtschy		
P L.Kretlow					/P B.Trice		
/P D.Pillette					/P C.Bishop		
/P T.Gray					/P E.Blackwell		
/P J.Coleman					/P B.Spicer		
/P B.Kuzava					/P G.Cox		
/P D.Ferrarese					/P S.Dixon		
/P B.Alexander					/P O.Van Brabant		
/P B.Miller					/P L.Wheat		
/P C.Locke							
/P B.Harrison							

TEAM	G	W	L	PCT	GB	R	OR	AB	H	2B	3B	HR	BB	SO	AVG	OBP	SLG	PRO	PRO+	BR	/A	PF	CHI	RC	SB	CS	SBA	SBR
NY	154	96	58	.623		762	569	5161	1342	179	55	175	609	658	.260	.343	.418	.761	113	71	83	98	101	759	55	25	69	2
CLE	154	93	61	.604	3	698	601	5146	1325	195	31	148	723	715	.257	.353	.394	.747	104	60	32	104	93	741	28	24	54	-6
CHI	155	91	63	.591	5	725	557	5220	1401	204	36	116	567	595	.268	.347	.388	.735	101	31	11	103	101	712	69	45	61	-6
BOS	154	84	70	.545	12	755	652	5273	1392	241	39	137	707	733	.264	.354	.402	.756	101	77	7	109	97	773	43	17	72	3
DET	154	79	75	.513	17	775	658	5283	1407	211	38	130	641	583	.266	.348	.394	.742	108	46	63	98	104	736	41	22	65	-1
KC	155	63	91	.409	33	638	911	5335	1395	189	46	121	463	725	.261	.323	.382	.705	95	-40	-47	101	100	637	22	36	38	-15
BAL	156	57	97	.370	39	540	754	5257	1263	177	39	54	560	742	.240	.316	.320	.636	83	-159	-123	93	104	532	34	46	43	-17
WAS	154	53	101	.344	43	598	789	5142	1277	178	54	80	538	654	.248	.324	.351	.675	93	-86	-55	95	103	586	25	32	44	-12
TOT	618					5491		41817	10802	1574	338	961	4808	5405	.258	.339	.381	.720							317	247	56	-53

TEAM	CG	SH	SV	IP	H	H/G	HR	BB	SO	RAT	ERA	ERA+	OAV	OOB	PR	/A	PF	CPI	FA	E	DP	FW	PW	BW	SBW	DIF
NY	52	19	33	1372[1]	1163	7.6	108	688	731	12.3	3.23	116	.232	.328	111	78	95	107	.978	128	180	.5	7.8	8.3	.9	1.5
CLE	45	15	36	1386[1]	1285	8.3	111	558	877	12.1	3.39	118	.245	.320	88	92	101	101	.981	108	152	1.7	9.2	3.2	.0	1.9
CHI	55	20	23	1378	1301	8.5	111	497	720	11.9	3.37	117	.251	.319	90	89	100	103	.981	111	147	1.5	8.9	1.1	.0	2.4
BOS	44	9	34	1384[1]	1333	8.7	128	582	674	12.7	3.72	115	.253	.331	37	48	108	102	.977	136	140	.0	8.8	.7	1.0	-3.5
DET	66	16	12	1380[1]	1381	9.0	126	517	629	12.6	3.79	101	.261	.331	26	7	97	102	.976	139	159	-.2	.7	6.3	.6	-5.4
KC	29	9	22	1382	1486	9.7	175	707	572	14.6	5.35	78	.278	.367	-214	-181	105	94	.976	146	174	-.5	-18.1	-4.7	-.8	10.2
BAL	35	10	20	1388[2]	1403	9.1	103	625	595	13.4	4.21	91	.266	.348	-39	-61	96	98	.972	167	159	-1.7	-6.1	-12.3	-1.0	1.2
WAS	37	10	16	1354[2]	1450	9.6	99	634	607	14.2	4.62	83	.279	.362	-100	-119	97	98	.974	154	170	-1.0	-11.9	-5.5	-.5	-5.0
TOT	363	108	196	11026[2]		8.8				13.0	3.96		.258	.339					.977	1089	1281					

Runs		Hits		Doubles		Triples		Home Runs		Total Bases	
Smith-Cle	123	Kaline-Det	200	Kuenn-Det	38	Mantle-NY	11	Mantle-NY	37	Kaline-Det	321
Mantle-NY	121	Fox-Chi	198	Power-KC	34	Carey-NY	11	Zernial-KC	30	Mantle-NY	316
Kaline-Det	121	Power-KC	190	Goodman-Bos	31	Power-KC	10	Williams-Bos	28	Power-KC	301
Tuttle-Det	102	Kuenn-Det	190	White-Bos	30					Smith-Cle	287
Kuenn-Det	101	Smith-Cle	186	Finigan-KC	30					Jensen-Bos	275

Runs Batted In		Runs Produced		Bases On Balls		Batting Average		On Base Percentage		Slugging Average	
Jensen-Bos	116	Kaline-Det	196	Mantle-NY	113	Kaline-Det	.340	Mantle-NY	.433	Mantle-NY	.611
Boone-Det	116	Jensen-Bos	185	Goodman-Bos	99	Power-KC	.319	Kaline-Det	.425	Kaline-Det	.546
Berra-NY	108	Mantle-NY	183	Yost-Was	95	Kell-Chi	.312	Smith-Cle	.411	Zernial-KC	.508
Sievers-Was	106	Smith-Cle	178	Fain-Det-Cle	94	Fox-Chi	.311	Yost-Was	.410	Doby-Cle	.505
Kaline-Det	102	Tuttle-Det	166	Smith-Cle	93	Kuenn-Det	.306	Goodman-Bos	.397	Power-KC	.505

Production		Adjusted Production		Batter Runs		Adjusted Batter Runs		Clutch Hitting Index		Runs Created	
Mantle-NY	1.044	Mantle-NY	181	Williams-Bos	59.3	Mantle-NY	61.2	Kell-Chi	137	Mantle-NY	148
Kaline-Det	.971	Kaline-Det	163	Mantle-NY	59.0	Kaline-Det	53.2	Boone-Det	137	Kaline-Det	135
Smith-Cle	.884	Sievers-Was	136	Kaline-Det	50.2	Williams-Bos	50.1	Zauchin-Bos	114	Smith-Cle	128
Doby-Cle	.877	Vernon-Was	133	Smith-Cle	34.7	Smith-Cle	30.4	Jensen-Bos	111	Williams-Bos	118
Power-KC	.862	Smith-Cle	132	Valo-KC	24.8	Vernon-Was	25.2	Sievers-Was	111	Power-KC	103

Total Average		Stolen Bases		Stolen Base Average		Stolen Base Runs		Fielding Runs		Total Player Rating	
Mantle-NY	1.206	Rivera-Chi	25	Minoso-Chi	70.4	Torgeson-Det	2.7	Fox-Chi	26.9	Mantle-NY	6.3
Kaline-Det	.993	Minoso-Chi	19	Jensen-Bos	69.6	Busby-Was-Chi	1.8	McDougald-NY	19.4	Kaline-Det	5.0
Smith-Cle	.928	Jensen-Bos	16	Rivera-Chi	61.0	Mantle-NY	1.8	Miranda-Bal	19.0	Williams-Bos	4.4
Doby-Cle	.884	Busby-Was-Chi	12			Klaus-Bos	1.8	Lopez-KC	15.1	Fox-Chi	3.9
Jensen-Bos	.849	Smith-Cle	11					Tuttle-Det	14.9	McDougald-NY	3.5

Wins		Win Percentage		Games		Complete Games		Shutouts		Saves	
F.Sullivan-Bos	18	Byrne-NY	.762	Narleski-Cle	60	Ford-NY	18	Hoeft-Det	7	Narleski-Cle	19
Lemon-Cle	18	Ford-NY	.720	Mossi-Cle	57	Hoeft-Det	17	Wynn-Cle	6	Kinder-Bos	18
Ford-NY	18	Hoeft-Det	.696	Gorman-KC	57			Turley-NY	6	Gorman-KC	18
Wynn-Cle	17	Lemon-Cle	.643	Dorish-Chi-Bal	48			Pierce-Chi	6	Konstanty-NY	11
Turley-NY	17	Donovan-Chi	.625	Moore-Bal	46					Morgan-NY	10

Innings Pitched		Fewest Hits/Game		Fewest BB/Game		Strikeouts		Strikeouts/Game		Ratio	
F.Sullivan-Bos	260.0	Turley-NY	6.13	Gromek-Det	1.84	Score-Cle	245	Score-Cle	9.70	Pierce-Chi	10.02
Ford-NY	253.2	Score-Cle	6.26	Donovan-Chi	2.31	Turley-NY	210	Turley-NY	7.66	Ford-NY	10.71
Turley-NY	246.2	Ford-NY	6.67	Garcia-Cle	2.39	Pierce-Chi	157	Pierce-Chi	6.87	Hoeft-Det	10.96
Wilson-Bal	235.1	Pierce-Chi	7.09	Garver-Det	2.61	Ford-NY	137	Harshman-Chi	5.82	Wilson-Bal	11.13
Lary-Det	235.0	Harshman-Chi	7.23	Porterfield-Was	2.73	Hoeft-Det	133	Hoeft-Det	5.44	Wynn-Cle	11.35

Earned Run Average		Adjusted ERA		Opponents' Batting Avg.		Opponents' On Base Pct.		Starter Runs		Adjusted Starter Runs	
Pierce-Chi	1.97	Pierce-Chi	201	Turley-NY	.193	Pierce-Chi	.277	Pierce-Chi	45.5	Pierce-Chi	45.2
Ford-NY	2.63	F.Sullivan-Bos	148	Score-Cle	.194	Ford-NY	.297	Ford-NY	37.6	F.Sullivan-Bos	39.9
Wynn-Cle	2.82	Ford-NY	143	Ford-NY	.208	Hoeft-Det	.298	F.Sullivan-Bos	30.4	Ford-NY	31.5
Score-Cle	2.85	Wynn-Cle	142	Pierce-Chi	.213	Wilson-Bal	.300	Wynn-Cle	29.2	Wynn-Cle	29.9
F.Sullivan-Bos	2.91	Score-Cle	140	Harshman-Chi	.224	Wynn-Cle	.307	Score-Cle	28.1	Score-Cle	28.8

Clutch Pitching Index		Relief Runs		Adjusted Relief Runs		Relief Ranking		Total Pitcher Index		Total Baseball Ranking	
Pierce-Chi	119	Consuegra-Chi	18.6	Consuegra-Chi	18.4	Kinder-Bos	21.1	Pierce-Chi	5.3	Mantle-NY	6.3
Byrne-NY	119	Mossi-Cle	13.9	Kiely-Bos	14.9	Hurd-Bos	19.5	F.Sullivan-Bos	4.2	Pierce-Chi	5.3
F.Sullivan-Bos	115	Konstanty-NY	13.4	Mossi-Cle	14.2	Consuegra-Chi	16.7	Wynn-Cle	3.3	Kaline-Det	5.0
Lary-Det	115	Kiely-Bos	11.6	Konstanty-NY	11.6	Konstanty-NY	16.7	Ford-NY	3.1	Williams-Bos	4.4
Schmitz-Was	115	Dorish-Chi-Bal	10.4	Hurd-Bos	11.4	Mossi-Cle	14.5	Lary-Det	2.5	F.Sullivan-Bos	4.2

January 19 The City of Hoboken dedicates a plaque honoring the achievements of Alexander Cartwright in organizing early baseball at Elysian Field in the New Jersey city.

January 27 The New York Giants football team of the NFL switches its home games to Yankee Stadium, leading to speculation that the baseball team will soon vacate the Polo Grounds as well.

March 3 In an effort to keep the Giants in New York, Manhattan Borough President Hulan Jack makes plans for a new 110,000-seat stadium over the New York Central railroad tracks, on a 470,000-foot site stretching from 60th to 72nd streets on Manhattan's West Side. The $75 million estimated cost eventually dooms the project and will be a major factor in Horace Stoneham's decision to move to San Francisco.

April 28 Redlegs rookie left fielder Frank Robinson hits the first home run of his 586 lifetime blasts, off Cubs pitcher Paul Minner in Crosley Field. The Cubs lose the opener, 9–1. Cincinnati outfielder Wally Post hits four home runs in a doubleheader sweep for the Redlegs.

May 7 The future NL president, Bill White of the New York Giants, homers in his first time up in the major leagues. The Giants lose to St. Louis, 6–3.

May 19 Pirates slugger Dale Long hits a ninth-inning home run against the Cubs for the first of a string of eight home runs in eight games.

July 6 Ford Frick inaugurates the Cy Young Award, to honor the outstanding pitcher each year. The BBWAA will do the voting. Only one pitcher will be honored each year until 1967, when a pitcher in each league will be selected.

July 10 In the All-Star Game, Ken Boyer of the Cardinals makes three sparkling plays at third base and gets three hits as the NL defeats the AL, 7–3. Willie Mays, Mickey Mantle, Ted Williams, and Stan Musial all homer. Mays's pinch-hit two-run home run off Whitey Ford is his seventh straight hit against the Yankee lefty.

July 23 Joe Cronin and Hank Greenberg are officially inducted into the Hall of Fame at Cooperstown, NY.

July 25 Brooklyn's right fielder Carl Furillo is the first Dodger player to homer in Jersey City, as the Dodgers lose to the Reds 2-1 at Roosevelt Field.

September 11 Frank Robinson ties the NL record for home runs by a rookie with 38 in an 11-5 Redlegs win over New York.

September 30 Sandy Amoros and Duke Snider each hit two home runs against the Pirates, as the Dodgers win 8-6 to edge Milwaukee for the pennant on the last day of the season.

October 3 Sal Maglie and the Dodgers defeat the Yankees 6-3 in the first game of the World Series.

October 9 The Dodgers bounce back in Game 6. Clem Labine comes out of the bullpen to pitch a 1-0 victory in 10 innings. Enos Slaughter misjudges Jackie Robinson's line drive, and Jim Gilliam scores from second base.

November 21 Don Newcombe, who won the 1949 Rookie of the Year Award, wins the league MVP and the first-ever Cy Young Award.

December 1 Cincinnati slugger Frank Robinson is unanimously voted the league Rookie of the Year.

December 13 The Dodgers trade Jackie Robinson to the Giants for pitcher Dick Littlefield and $35,000. Robinson retires rather than accept the trade.

BROOKLYN	CHICAGO	CINCINNATI	MILWAUKEE	NEW YORK	PHILADELPHIA	PITTSBURGH	ST.LOUIS
M W.Alston	M S.Hack	M B.Tebbetts	M C.Grimm	M B.Rigney	M M.Smith	M B.Bragan	M F.Hutchinson
1B G.Hodges	1B D.Fondy	1B T.Kluszewski	M F.Haney	1B B.White	1B M.Blaylock	1B D.Long	1B S.Musial
2B J.Gilliam	2B G.Baker	2B J.Temple	1B J.Adcock	2B R.Schoendienst	2B T.Kazanski	2B B.Mazeroski	2B D.Blasingame
SS P.Reese	SS E.Banks	SS R.McMillan	2B D.O'Connell	SS D.Spencer	SS G.Hamner	SS D.Groat	SS A.Dark
3B R.Jackson	3B D.Hoak	3B R.Jablonski	SS J.Logan	3B F.Castleman	3B W.Jones	3B F.Thomas	3B K.Boyer
LF S.Amoros	LF M.Irvin	LF F.Robinson	3B E.Mathews	LF J.Brandt	LF D.Ennis	LF L.Walls	LF R.Repulski
CF D.Snider	CF P.Whisenant	CF G.Bell	LF B.Thomson	CF W.Mays	CF R.Ashburn	CF B.Virdon	CF B.Del Greco
RF C.Furillo	RF W.Moryn	RF W.Post	CF B.Bruton	RF D.Mueller	RF E.Valo	RF R.Clemente	RF W.Moon
C R.Campanella	C H.Landrith	C E.Bailey	RF H.Aaron	C B.Sarni	C S.Lopata	C J.Shepard	C H.Smith
			C D.Crandall				
32 J.Robinson	O J.King	C S.Burgess		O D.Rhodes	O1 J.Greengrass	O1 B.Skinner	O W.Lockman
C R.Walker	30 E.Miksis	1 G.Crowe	1 F.Torre	S A.Dark	S S.Hemus	C H.Foiles	C R.Katt
2 C.Neal	O S.Drake	3S A.Grammas	O D.Rice	30 H.Thompson	S R.Smalley	32 G.Freese	2 R.Schoendienst
1 R.Nelson	C H.Chiti	O B.Thurman	O W.Covington	O W.Lockman	A.Seminick	2 J.O'Brien	O H.Sauer
S C.Fernandez	1 F.Kellert	O S.Palys	2 J.Dittmer	S E.Bressoud	O F.Baumholtz	32 D.Cole	C B.Sarni
O G.Cimoli	S J.Kindall	3 R.Bridges	O A.Pafko	C W.Westrum	/O G.Gorbous	/O D.Kravitz	23 B.Morgan
/O D.Mitchell	/O C.McCullough	/O J.Frazier	/O C.Tanner	/O R.Katt	B.Morgan	2 C.Roberts	2 G.Hatton
/S D.Zimmer	/3 E.Winceniak	/1 J.Dyck	S F.Mantilla	/1 G.Wilson	E.Bouchee	S E.O'Brien	O B.Virdon
/C D.Howell	/O G.Wade	/O A.Schult	C T.Atwell	/C B.Hofman	/C J.Lonnett	2 S.Jacobs	C W.Cooper
H D.Williams	/C J.Fanning	/C B.Edwards	/O E.Hersh	O B.Lennon	O B.Bowman	/3 P.Ward	1 R.Nelson
/O D.Demeter	H O.Friend	/O C.Harmon	/S J.Pendleton	H G.Harris	H W.Westlake	O J.Powers	O C.Peete
H B.Aspromonte	/O R.Myers	/O B.Balcena	/C B.Roselli	/C J.Mangan	/C M.Burk	O B.DelGreco	O J.Brandt
	/C E.Tappe	H M.Batts		/2 W.Terwilliger		/O J.Lynch	/S D.Schofield
P D.Newcombe		H C.Flood	P W.Spahn	/3 O.Virgil	P R.Roberts	/C T.Atwell	/O J.Frazier
P R.Craig	P B.Rush	R J.Oldham	P L.Burdette	/O B.Taylor	P H.Haddix	/C B.Hall	O C.Harmon
P S.Maglie	P S.Jones	R A.Silvera	P B.Buhl	H G.Coan	P C.Simmons		/S A.Grammas
P C.Erskine	P W.Hacker		P R.Crone		P S.Rogovin	P B.Friend	H S.Hemus
P D.Drysdale	P D.Kaiser	P B.Lawrence	P G.Conley	P J.Antonelli	P S.Miller	P R.Kline	/1 J.Cunningham
RP C.Labine	P J.Brosnan	P J.Klippstein	RP B.Trowbridge	P R.Gomez	RP B.Miller	P V.Law	/1 T.Alston
RP E.Roebuck	RP J.Davis	P J.Nuxhall	RP E.Johnson	RP A.Worthington	RP J.Meyer	P R.Munger	
RP D.Bessent	RP T.Lown	P A.Fowler	P T.Phillips	P J.Hearn	RP R.Negray	RP R.Face	P V.Mizell
	RP V.Valentinetti	P H.Jeffcoat	P D.Jolly	P D.Littlefield	P J.Owens	RP N.King	P T.Poholsky
P S.Koufax	P R.Meyer	RP H.Freeman	RP L.Sleater	RP S.Ridzik	P M.Dickson	RP F.Waters	P M.Dickson
P K.Lehman	/P M.Drabowsky	RP T.Acker	RP R.Murff	RP H.Wilhelm	P D.Pillette	P D.Hall	P H.Wehmeier
/P C.Templeton	P P.Minner	RP J.Black	/P C.Nichols	RP M.Grissom	/P H.Wehmeier	P C.Naranjo	P W.Schmidt
/P J.Hughes	P J.Hughes	P D.Gross	/P H.Robinson	P J.Margoneri	/P J.Sanford	P L.Pepper	RP L.McDaniel
/P R.Branca	/P D.Hillman	P L.Jansen	/P P.Paine	/P W.McCall	/P A.LiPetri	P L.Arroyo	RP L.Jackson
/P B.Darnell	/P J.Briggs	P P.LaPalme		P D.Liddle	/P T.Farrell	P H.Pollet	RP J.Collum
/P B.Loes	/P G.Piktuzis	/P P.Scantlebury		/P M.Surkont	/P B.Ross	P D.Littlefield	P B.Blaylock
	/P B.Tremel	/P F.Smith		/P R.Monzant		/P J.McMahan	P J.Konstanty
		/P B.Kennedy		/P M.McCormick		/P R.Swanson	P E.Kinder
		/P R.Meyer		/P J.Constable		/P B.Garber	P D.Liddle
				/P R.Wright		/P B.Purkey	/P H.Haddix
						/P L.Donoso	/P B.Flowers
						/P M.Surkont	/P G.Jones
							/P D.Littlefield
							/P S.Miller
							/P M.Surkont
							/P P.LaPalme

TEAM	G	W	L	PCT	GB	R	OR	AB	H	2B	3B	HR	BB	SO	AVG	OBP	SLG	PRO	PRO+	BR	/A	PF	CHI	RC	SB	CS	SBA	SBR
BRO	154	93	61	.604		720	601	5098	1315	212	36	179	649	738	.258	.344	.419	.763	103	81	24	108	97	728	65	37	64	-3
MIL	155	92	62	.597	1	709	569	5207	1350	212	54	177	486	714	.259	.325	.423	.748	113	38	80	94	101	714	29	20	59	-3
CIN	155	91	63	.591	2	775	658	5291	1406	201	32	221	528	760	.266	.338	.441	.779	107	103	54	106	100	789	45	22	67	0
STL	156	76	78	.494	17	678	698	5378	1443	234	49	124	503	622	.268	.335	.399	.734	103	25	25	100	97	707	41	35	54	-9
PHI	154	71	83	.461	22	668	738	5204	1313	207	49	121	585	673	.252	.331	.461	.712	99	-12	0	98	103	658	45	23	66	0
NY	154	67	87	.435	26	540	650	5190	1268	192	45	145	402	659	.244	.301	.382	.683	89	-85	-81	99	97	586	67	34	66	0
PIT	157	66	88	.429	27	588	653	5221	1340	199	57	110	383	752	.257	.310	.380	.690	93	-70	-57	98	102	594	24	33	42	-13
CHI	157	60	94	.390	33	597	708	5260	1281	202	50	142	446	776	.244	.304	.382	.686	91	-79	-69	98	103	606	55	38	59	-6
TOT	621					5275		41849	10716	1659	372	1219	3982	5694	.256	.324	.401	.725							371	242	61	-34

TEAM	CG	SH	SV	IP	H	H/G	HR	BB	SO	RAT	ERA	ERA+	OAV	OOB	PR	/A	PF	CPI	FA	E	DP	FW	PW	BW	SBW	DIF
BRO	46	12	30	1368²	1251	8.2	171	441	772	11.3	3.57	111	.244	.307	31	60	105	97	.981	111	149	1.4	6.1	2.5	.1	5.9
MIL	64	12	27	1393¹	1295	8.4	133	467	639	11.5	3.11	111	.247	.311	102	54	92	107	.979	130	159	.3	5.5	8.2	.1	.8
CIN	47	4	29	1389	1406	9.1	141	458	653	12.3	3.85	103	.265	.327	-12	20	106	101	.981	113	147	1.3	2.0	5.5	.4	4.6
STL	41	12	30	1388²	1339	8.7	155	546	709	12.3	3.97	95	.257	.329	-30	-28	100	98	.978	134	172	.1	-2.9	2.6	-.5	-.3
PHI	57	4	15	1377¹	1407	9.2	172	437	750	12.2	4.20	89	.266	.325	-66	-73	99	95	.975	144	140	-.6	-7.5	.0	.4	1.6
NY	31	9	28	1378	1287	8.4	144	551	765	12.2	3.78	100	.250	.326	-1	1	100	98	.976	144	143	-.6	.1	-8.3	.4	-1.7
PIT	37	8	24	1376¹	1406	9.2	142	469	662	12.4	3.74	101	.267	.329	5	5	100	105	.973	162	140	-1.5	.5	-5.8	-.9	-3.3
CHI	37	6	17	1392	1325	8.6	161	613	744	12.7	3.96	95	.252	.334	-29	-29	100	100	.976	144	141	-.4	-3.0	-7.1	-.2	-6.4
TOT	360	67	200	11063¹		8.7				12.1	3.77		.256	.324					.977	1082	1191					

Runs
Robinson-Cin 122
Snider-Bro 112
Aaron-Mil 106
Mathews-Mil 103
Gilliam-Bro 102

Hits
Aaron-Mil 200
Ashburn-Phi 190
Virdon-StL-Pit ... 185
Musial-StL 184
Boyer-StL 182

Doubles
Aaron-Mil 34
Snider-Bro 33
Musial-StL 33
Lopata-Phi 33
Bell-Cin 31

Triples
Bruton-Mil 15
Aaron-Mil 14
Walls-Pit 11
Moon-StL 11
Virdon-StL-Pit ... 10

Home Runs
Snider-Bro 43
Robinson-Cin 38
Adcock-Mil 38
Mathews-Mil 37

Total Bases
Aaron-Mil 340
Snider-Bro 324
Mays-NY 322
Robinson-Cin 319
Musial-StL 310

Runs Batted In
Musial-StL 109
Adcock-Mil 103
Kluszewski-Cin ... 102
Snider-Bro 101
Boyer-StL 98

Runs Produced
Aaron-Mil 172
Snider-Bro 170
Musial-StL 169
Robinson-Cin 167
Boyer-StL 163

Bases On Balls
Snider-Bro 99
Gilliam-Bro 95
Jones-Phi 92
Mathews-Mil 91
Moon-StL 80

Batting Average
Aaron-Mil .... .328
Virdon-StL-Pit ... .319
Clemente-Pit ..... .311
Musial-StL .... .310
Boyer-StL .... .306

On Base Percentage
Snider-Bro .... .402
Gilliam-Bro ...... .400
Musial-StL .... .390
Moon-StL .... .390
Jones-Phi .... .387

Slugging Average
Snider-Bro .... .598
Adcock-Mil .... .597
Aaron-Mil .... .558
Robinson-Cin ..... .558
Mays-NY .... .557

Production
Snider-Bro 1.000
Robinson-Cin ..... .939
Adcock-Mil .... .936
Mays-NY .... .928
Aaron-Mil .... .927

Adjusted Production
Adcock-Mil 154
Aaron-Mil 154
Snider-Bro 152
Mays-NY 146
Mathews-Mil 146

Batter Runs
Snider-Bro 50.5
Robinson-Cin 39.1
Aaron-Mil 36.3
Musial-StL 36.3
Mays-NY 35.9

Adjusted Batter Runs
Aaron-Mil 43.1
Snider-Bro 41.1
Mays-NY 36.7
Musial-StL 36.3
Mathews-Mil 36.2

Clutch Hitting Index
McMillan-Cin 145
Thomson-Mil 123
Ennis-Phi 115
Jones-Phi 109
Long-Pit 109

Runs Created
Snider-Bro 128
Robinson-Cin 121
Musial-StL 119
Mays-NY 118
Aaron-Mil 115

Total Average
Snider-Bro 1.052
Mays-NY .... .972
Robinson-Cin ..... .960
Mathews-Mil ...... .946
Adcock-Mil .... .916

Stolen Bases
Mays-NY 40
Gilliam-Bro 21
White-NY 15
Temple-Cin 14
Reese-Bro 13

Stolen Base Average
Mays-NY 80.0
Gilliam-Bro 70.0

Stolen Base Runs
Mays-NY 6.0
Ashburn-Phi 2.4
Temple-Cin 1.8
Post-Cin 1.8
Mathews-Mil 1.8

Fielding Runs
McMillan-Cin 29.9
Ashburn-Phi 25.3
Blasingame-StL ... 21.9
Gilliam-Bro 17.7
Baker-Chi 17.2

Total Player Rating
Mays-NY 4.7
Aaron-Mil 4.4
McMillan-Cin 3.7
Gilliam-Bro 3.4
Musial-StL 3.3

Wins
Newcombe-Bro 27
Spahn-Mil 20
Antonelli-NY 20

Win Percentage
Newcombe-Bro ..... .794
Buhl-Mil .... .692
Lawrence-Cin ..... .655
Burdette-Mil ..... .655
Spahn-Mil .... .645

Games
Face-Pit 68
Wilhelm-NY 64
Freeman-Cin 64
Labine-Bro 62
Lown-Chi 61

Complete Games
Roberts-Phi 22
Spahn-Mil 20
Friend-Pit 19
Newcombe-Bro 18
Burdette-Mil 16

Shutouts
Burdette-Mil 6
Newcombe-Bro 5
Antonelli-NY 5
Friend-Pit 4

Saves
Labine-Bro 19
Freeman-Cin 18
Lown-Chi 13
Jackson-StL 9
Bessent-Bro 9

Innings Pitched
Friend-Pit 314.1
Roberts-Phi 297.1
Spahn-Mil 281.1
Newcombe-Bro 268.0
Kline-Pit 264.0

Fewest Hits/Game
Maglie-Bro 7.26
Newcombe-Bro 7.35
Jones-Chi 7.39
Mizell-StL 7.42
Craig-Bro 7.64

Fewest BB/Game
Roberts-Phi 1.21
Newcombe-Bro 1.54
Spahn-Mil 1.66
Fowler-Cin 1.77
Burdette-Mil 1.83

Strikeouts
Jones-Chi 176
Haddix-StL-Phi ... 170
Friend-Pit 166
Roberts-Phi 157
Mizell-StL 153

Strikeouts/Game
Jones-Chi 8.40
Haddix-StL-Phi ... 6.64
Mizell-StL 6.60
Nuxhall-Cin 5.38
Worthington-NY ... 5.16

Ratio
Newcombe-Bro 9.00
Spahn-Mil 9.73
Maglie-Bro 9.94
Burdette-Mil 10.15
Rush-Chi 10.18

Earned Run Average
Burdette-Mil 2.70
Spahn-Mil 2.78
Antonelli-NY 2.86
Maglie-Bro 2.87
Newcombe-Bro 3.06

Adjusted ERA
Maglie-Bro 138
Antonelli-NY 132
Newcombe-Bro 130
Burdette-Mil 128
Spahn-Mil 124

Opponents' Batting Avg.
Newcombe-Bro ..... .221
Jones-Chi .... .221
Mizell-StL .... .222
Maglie-Bro .... .222
Craig-Bro .... .231

Opponents' On Base Pct.
Newcombe-Bro ..... .257
Spahn-Mil .... .276
Maglie-Bro .... .281
Burdette-Mil ..... .282
Rush-Chi .... .282

Starter Runs
Spahn-Mil 30.9
Burdette-Mil 30.4
Antonelli-NY 26.3
Newcombe-Bro 21.3
Maglie-Bro 19.0

Adjusted Starter Runs
Newcombe-Bro 27.1
Antonelli-NY 26.6
Maglie-Bro 23.2
Burdette-Mil 21.6
Spahn-Mil 21.2

Clutch Pitching Index
Conley-Mil 127
Klippstein-Cin ... 111
Kline-Pit 110
Poholsky-StL 108
Jeffcoat-Cin 105

Relief Runs
Grissom-NY 19.8
Acker-Cin 13.1
Bessent-Bro 11.2
B.Miller-Phi 7.3
Labine-Bro 5.5

Adjusted Relief Runs
Grissom-NY 19.9
Acker-Cin 15.0
Bessent-Bro 13.0
Labine-Bro 8.0
Freeman-Cin 7.0

Relief Ranking
Freeman-Cin 13.7
Bessent-Bro 13.6
Labine-Bro 13.6
Acker-Cin 11.7
Grissom-NY 8.3

Total Pitcher Index
Newcombe-Bro 4.3
Antonelli-NY 3.6
Spahn-Mil 2.9
Burdette-Mil 2.6
Dickson-Phi-StL .. 2.2

Total Baseball Ranking
Mays-NY 4.7
Aaron-Mil 4.4
Newcombe-Bro 4.3
McMillan-Cin 3.7
Antonelli-NY 3.6

February 4 The AL plans to test the automatic intentional walk during spring training.

February 8 The legendary Connie Mack dies at age 93. He began his career with Washington in 1886 as a catcher. After managing the NL Pittsburgh club from 1894-96, he became a prominent figure in Ban Johnson's Western League and a founder of the AL and its Philadelphia franchise in 1901. In 50 years as the Athletics pilot he won nine pennants and five World Championships, but also finished last 17 times.

February 15 The Pirates and the Kansas City A's cancel an exhibition game in Birmingham, Ala., because of a local ordinance barring black players from playing against white players.

April 24 AL umpire Frank Umont is the first to wear glasses in a regular season game, between Detroit and Kansas City. The former NFL tackle (New York Giants) still presents an intimidating appearance to most players and fans.

May 18 Mickey Mantle homers from both sides of the plate for the third time in his career, eclipsing the mark of Jim Russell. The visiting New Yorkers nip Chicago, 8–7, in 10 innings.

May 30 Mickey Mantle hits one of the most memorable home runs in his career, in the second game of a doubleheader with the Washington Senators. He tags a pitch from Pedro Ramos that comes within 18 inches of leaving Yankee Stadium, something never accomplished by any major leaguer. The ball was still climbing when it caromed off the upper-stand facade, about 396 feet from home plate. Estimates are that the ball could have traveled more than 600 feet. It is Mantle's 20th home run of the season; no one else has ever hit 20 home runs before June.

August 7 The Boston Red Sox fine Ted Williams $5,000 for spitting at Boston fans, as the Red Sox edge the Yanks in 11 innings on Williams's bases-loaded walk. The spitting started after the crowd of 36,350 started booing the Splendid Splinter for muffing Mickey Mantle's windblown fly in the 11th.

September 18 Mickey Mantle hits his 50th home run, off Chicago's Billy Pierce, as New York wins 3-2 to clinch another pennant. Mantle will win the Triple Crown with a .353 batting average, 52 home runs, and 130 RBIs.

September 30 White Sox hurler Jim Derrington becomes the youngest pitcher since 1900 to start a game. He loses to Kansas City 7-6 at the age of 16 years and 10 months.

October 8 Series history is made by Don Larsen of the Yankees, who pitches a perfect game to defeat the Dodgers, 2-0, in Game 5. He requires only 97 pitches.

October 10 In Game 7 the Yankees win their first World Series championship in three years as Johnny Kucks sets down the Bums, 9-0. Yogi Berra hits a pair of two-run home runs and Bill Skowron hits a grand slam. Don Newcombe takes the loss, his fourth in Series competition.

December 18 Former Yankee shortstop Phil Rizzuto signs as a Yankee radio-TV announcer.

BALTIMORE	BOSTON	CHICAGO	CLEVELAND	DETROIT	KANSAS CITY	NEW YORK	WASHINGTON
M P.Richards	M P.Higgins	M M.Marion	M A.Lopez	M B.Harris	M L.Boudreau	M C.Stengel	M C.Dressen
1B B.Boyd	1B M.Vernon	1B W.Dropo	1B V.Wertz	1B E.Torgeson	1B V.Power	1B B.Skowron	1B P.Runnels
2B B.Gardner	2B B.Goodman	2B N.Fox	2B B.Avila	2B F.Bolling	2B J.Finigan	2B B.Martin	2B H.Plews
SS W.Miranda	SS D.Buddin	SS L.Aparicio	SS C.Carrasquel	SS H.Kuenn	SS J.DeMaestri	SS G.McDougald	SS J.Valdivielso
3B G.Kell	3B B.Klaus	3B F.Hatfield	3B A.Rosen	3B R.Boone	3B H.Lopez	3B A.Carey	3B E.Yost
LF B.Nieman	LF T.Williams	LF M.Minoso	LF A.Smith	LF C.Maxwell	LF L.Skizas	LF E.Howard	LF R.Sievers
CF D.Williams	CF J.Piersall	CF L.Doby	CF J.Busby	CF B.Tuttle	CF J.Groth	CF M.Mantle	CF W.Herzog
RF T.Francona	RF J.Jensen	RF J.Rivera	RF R.Colavito	RF A.Kaline	RF H.Simpson	RF H.Bauer	RF J.Lemon
C G.Triandos	C S.White	C S.Lollar	C J.Hegan	C F.House	C T.Thompson	C Y.Berra	C C.Courtney
C H.Smith	O1 D.Gernert	1O D.Philley	O G.Woodling	C R.Wilson	C G.Zernial	O1 J.Collins	C L.Berberet
1 B.Hale	O G.Stephens	3S S.Esposito	2S G.Strickland	1 J.Phillips	O A.Pilarcik	2S J.Coleman	O K.Olson
O J.Pyburn	23 T.Lepcio	C L.Moss	1O P.Ward	O3 B.Kennedy	O E.Slaughter	O N.Siebern	C E.FitzGerald
O D.Philley	C P.Daley	O B.Phillips	C H.Naragon	S2 J.Brideweser	C J.Ginsberg	O B.Cerv	S J.Snyder
O H.Evers	S3 M.Bolling	3 G.Kell	O S.Mele	1 W.Belardi	O E.Robinson	O E.Slaughter	O E.Oravetz
32 B.Adams	3 F.Malzone	1 R.Jackson	O E.Averill	O J.Small	C H.Smith	S B.Hunter	S L.Luttrell
O C.Diering	1 N.Zauchin	/O R.Northey	O D.Pope	2 R.Bertoia	2 C.Boyer	S J.Lumpe	2S T.Roig
3 W.Causey	O F.Throneberry	O J.Delsing	3 R.Regalado	S B.Hicks	S M.Baxes	1 E.Robinson	3 H.Killebrew
O J.Frazier	/2 G.Mauch	O B.Nieman	O J.Caffie	/C J.Porter	2 S.Jacobs	S P.Rizzuto	O C.Paula
O T.Nelson	2 B.Consolo	/3 B.Kennedy	/O D.Mitchell	/O J.Delsing	O R.Pless	O I.Noren	O J.Tettelbach
23 G.Hatton	H G.Hatton	S J.Brideweser	S K.Kuhn	/2 F.Hatfield	3 B.Renna	3 T.Carroll	H T.Wright
C T.Gastall	H M.Keough	/C E.Battey	/O S.Locklin	/O C.King	/O J.Pisoni	/O G.Wilson	
3 B.Robinson		/O C.Abrams	H H.Evers	/C C.Lau	/C J.Astroth	/C C.Silvera	P C.Stobbs
/C J.Ginsberg	P T.Brewer		/C H.Foiles	/C W.Streuli	/C E.Valo	/2 B.Richardson	P C.Pascual
/S F.Marsh	P F.Sullivan	P B.Pierce	R B.Young		/O D.Melton	H L.Skizas	P P.Ramos
/O J.Dyck	P W.Nixon	P D.Donovan		P F.Lary			P D.Stone
/O D.Pope	P D.Sisler	P J.Harshman	P E.Wynn	P P.Foytack	P A.Ditmar	P W.Ford	P B.Wiesler
	P M.Parnell	P J.Wilson	P B.Lemon	P B.Hoeft	P T.Gorman	P J.Kucks	RP H.Griggs
P R.Moore	RP I.Delock	P B.Keegan	P H.Score	P S.Gromek	P W.Burnette	P D.Larsen	RP B.Chakales
RP C.Johnson	RP T.Hurd	RP D.Howell	P M.Garcia	P V.Trucks	P L.Kretlow	P T.Sturdivant	RP C.Grob
P B.Wight			RP D.Mossi	RP D.Maas	P T.Herriage	P B.Turley	
P H.Brown	P B.Porterfield	P G.Staley	RP C.McLish	RP A.Aber	RP J.Crimian	RP T.Byrne	P B.Stewart
P E.Palica	P G.Susce	P P.LaPalme	RP R.Narleski	RP W.Masterson	RP B.Shantz	RP B.Grim	P B.Byerly
RP D.Ferrarese	P L.Kiely	P S.Consuegra			RP J.McMahan	RP T.Morgan	P T.Clevenger
RP G.Zuverink	/P F.Baumann	P E.Kinder	H.Aguirre	J.Bunning			/P T.Abernathy
RP B.Loes	P H.Dorish	P H.Pollet	P B.Feller	P B.Miller	P A.Kellner	P R.Coleman	/P E.Hernandez
	/P R.Minarcin	/P J.McDonald	P A.Houtteman	/P N.Garver	P T.Lasorda	P M.McDermott	/P D.Brodowski
P M.Fornieles	/P J.Schmitz	/P M.Martin	/P B.Daley	/P D.Marlowe	P M.Burtschy	/P R.Terry	
/P J.Wilson		/P M.Fornieles	/P S.Maglie	/P B.Black	P B.Harrington	/P J.Konstanty	
P J.Schmitz		/P C.Johnson		/P J.Brady	/P G.Cox	/P S.Dixon	
P H.Dorish		/P J.Derrington		/P G.Host	/P J.Santiago	/P J.Coates	
/P F.Besana		/P H.Byrd		/P H.Woodeshick	/P A.Ceccarelli	/P G.Staley	
/P C.Beamon		/P J.Dahlke		/P P.Wojey	/P G.Brunet		
/P S.Consuegra		/P B.Fischer			/P W.Craddock		
/P R.Moeller		/P D.Marlowe			/P A.Portocarrero		
/P B.O'Dell					/P C.Duser		
/P M.Held					/P B.Bradford		
/P B.Birrer					/P B.Spicer		
/P M.Martin							
/P B.Harrison							
/P G.Werley							
/P G.Sundin							

TEAM	G	W	L	PCT	GB	R	OR	AB	H	2B	3B	HR	BB	SO	AVG	OBP	SLG	PRO	PRO+	BR	/A	PF	CHI	RC	SB	CS	SBA	SBR
NY	154	97	57	.630		857	631	5312	1433	193	55	190	615	755	.270	.349	.434	.783	116	80	107	97	106	814	51	37	58	-7
CLE	155	88	66	.571	9	712	581	5148	1256	199	23	153	681	764	.244	.337	.381	.718	93	-35	-50	102	105	681	40	32	56	-7
CHI	154	85	69	.552	12	776	634	5286	1412	218	43	128	619	660	.267	.352	.397	.749	102	30	19	101	102	756	70	33	68	1
BOS	155	84	70	.545	13	780	751	5349	1473	261	45	139	727	687	.275	.365	.419	.784	101	100	-1	112	93	826	28	19	60	-3
DET	155	82	72	.532	15	789	699	5364	1494	209	50	150	644	618	.279	.359	.420	.779	111	84	82	100	97	816	43	26	62	-3
BAL	154	69	85	.448	28	571	705	5090	1242	198	34	91	563	725	.244	.322	.350	.672	90	-123	-80	92	101	572	39	42	48	-14
WAS	155	59	95	.383	38	652	924	5202	1302	198	62	112	690	877	.250	.343	.377	.720	96	-27	-26	100	94	681	37	34	52	-9
KC	154	52	102	.338	45	619	831	5256	1325	204	41	112	480	727	.252	.317	.370	.687	86	-108	-110	100	105	610	40	30	57	-6
TOT	618					5756		42007	10937	1680	353	1075	5019	5813	.260	.343	.394	.737							348	253	58	-47

TEAM	CG	SH	SV	IP	H	H/G	HR	BB	SO	RAT	ERA	ERA+	OAV	OOB	PR	/A	PF	CPI	FA	E	DP	FW	PW	BW	SBW	DIF
NY	50	10	35	1382	1285	8.4	114	652	732	12.9	3.63	107	.249	.337	82	37	93	105	.977	136	214	.6	3.6	10.5	-.1	5.4
CLE	67	17	24	1384	1233	8.0	116	564	845	11.9	3.32	127	.238	.316	129	136	101	100	.978	129	130	1.0	13.3	-4.9	-.1	1.7
CHI	65	11	13	1389	1351	8.8	118	524	722	12.3	3.73	110	.255	.325	67	58	99	99	.979	122	160	1.3	5.7	1.9	.7	-1.6
BOS	50	8	20	1398	1354	8.7	130	668	712	13.3	4.17	111	.254	.342	-1	71	111	96	.972	169	168	-1.2	7.0	-.0	.3	1.1
DET	62	10	15	1379	1389	9.1	140	655	788	13.6	4.06	101	.264	.351	15	9	99	108	.976	140	151	.4	.9	8.0	.3	-4.6
BAL	38	10	24	1360²	1362	9.0	99	547	715	12.8	4.20	93	.263	.337	-6	-42	94	93	.977	137	142	.5	-4.1	-7.8	-.8	4.2
WAS	36	1	18	1368²	1539	10.1	171	730	663	15.1	5.33	81	.287	.376	-179	-153	104	99	.972	171	173	-1.3	-15.0	-2.5	-.3	1.1
KC	30	3	18	1370¹	1424	9.4	187	679	636	14.1	4.86	89	.271	.359	-107	-81	100	101	.973	166	187	-1.1	-7.9	-10.8	.0	-5.2
TOT	398	70	167	11031²		8.9				13.2	4.16		.260	.343					.975	1170	1325					

Runs		Hits		Doubles		Triples		Home Runs		Total Bases	
Mantle-NY	132	Kuenn-Det	196	Piersall-Bos	40	Simpson-KC	11	Mantle-NY	52	Mantle-NY	376
Fox-Chi	109	Kaline-Det	194	Kuenn-Det	32	Minoso-Chi	11	Wertz-Cle	32	Kaline-Det	327
Minoso-Chi	106	Fox-Chi	192	Kaline-Det	32	Lemon-Was	11	Berra-NY	30	Jensen-Bos	287
		Mantle-NY	188			Jensen-Bos	11	Sievers-Was	29	Minoso-Chi	286
		Jensen-Bos	182					Maxwell-Det	28		

Runs Batted In		Runs Produced		Bases On Balls		Batting Average		On Base Percentage		Slugging Average	
Mantle-NY	130	Mantle-NY	210	Yost-Was	151	Mantle-NY	.353	Williams-Bos	.479	Mantle-NY	.705
Kaline-Det	128	Kaline-Det	197	Mantle-NY	112	Williams-Bos	.345	Mantle-NY	.467	Williams-Bos	.605
Wertz-Cle	106	Minoso-Chi	173	Williams-Bos	102	Kuenn-Det	.332	Nieman-Chi-Bal	.438	Maxwell-Det	.534
Simpson-KC	105	Kuenn-Det	172	Doby-Chi	102	Maxwell-Det	.326	Minoso-Chi	.430	Berra-NY	.534
Berra-NY	105	Berra-NY	168	Sievers-Was	100	Nieman-Chi-Bal	.320	Maxwell-Det	.420	Kaline-Det	.530

Production		Adjusted Production		Batter Runs		Adjusted Batter Runs		Clutch Hitting Index		Runs Created	
Mantle-NY	1.172	Mantle-NY	213	Mantle-NY	83.3	Mantle-NY	88.7	Kaline-Det	117	Mantle-NY	188
Williams-Bos	1.084	Williams-Bos	164	Williams-Bos	54.1	Minoso-Chi	41.5	Lollar-Chi	117	Minoso-Chi	130
Minoso-Chi	.954	Nieman-Chi-Bal	156	Minoso-Chi	43.2	Williams-Bos	40.9	Triandos-Bal	114	Kaline-Det	129
Maxwell-Det	.954	Maxwell-Det	150	Maxwell-Det	37.5	Nieman-Chi-Bal	38.8	Doby-Chi	113	Williams-Bos	121
Nieman-Chi-Bal	.934	Minoso-Chi	149	Kaline-Det	33.4	Maxwell-Det	37.3	Carey-NY	109	Maxwell-Det	118

Total Average		Stolen Bases		Stolen Base Average		Stolen Base Runs		Fielding Runs		Total Player Rating	
Mantle-NY	1.426	Aparicio-Chi	21	Aparicio-Chi	84.0	Aparicio-Chi	3.9	Piersall-Bos	17.6	Mantle-NY	8.7
Williams-Bos	1.255	Rivera-Chi	20	Avila-Cle	81.0	Avila-Cle	2.7	Kaline-Det	17.3	Kaline-Det	4.2
Minoso-Chi	1.031	Avila-Cle	17	Rivera-Chi	69.0	Mantle-NY	2.4	Hegan-Cle	15.6	Berra-NY	4.2
Maxwell-Det	1.015	Minoso-Chi	12					Buddin-Bos	13.9	Maxwell-Det	4.2
Nieman-Chi-Bal	.955							Maxwell-Det	13.1	Minoso-Chi	3.6

Wins		Win Percentage		Games		Complete Games		Shutouts		Saves	
Lary-Det	21	Ford-NY	.760	Zuverink-Bal	62	Pierce-Chi	21	Score-Cle	5	Zuverink-Bal	16
		Wynn-Cle	.690	Crimian-KC	54	Lemon-Cle	21			Mossi-Cle	11
		Score-Cle	.690	Gorman-KC	52	Lary-Det	20			Morgan-NY	11
		Pierce-Chi	.690	Mossi-Cle	48					Shantz-KC	9
		Brewer-Bos	.679	Delock-Bos	48					Delock-Bos	9

Innings Pitched		Fewest Hits/Game		Fewest BB/Game		Strikeouts		Strikeouts/Game		Ratio	
Lary-Det	294.0	Score-Cle	5.85	Stobbs-Was	2.03	Score-Cle	263	Score-Cle	9.49	Score-Cle	10.58
Wynn-Cle	277.2	Larsen-NY	6.66	Donovan-Chi	2.26	Pierce-Chi	192	Pascual-Was	7.73	Donovan-Chi	10.62
Pierce-Chi	276.1	Harshman-Chi	7.27	Kucks-NY	2.89	Foytack-Det	184	Foytack-Det	6.47	Wynn-Cle	10.66
Foytack-Det	256.0	Brewer-Bos	7.37	Wynn-Cle	2.95	Hoeft-Det	172	Pierce-Chi	6.25	Sturdivant-NY	10.80
Lemon-Cle	255.1	Foytack-Det	7.42	Sturdivant-NY	2.96	Lary-Det	165	Sturdivant-NY	6.25	Ford-NY	10.97

Earned Run Average		Adjusted ERA		Opponents' Batting Avg.		Opponents' On Base Pct.		Starter Runs		Adjusted Starter Runs	
Ford-NY	2.47	Score-Cle	166	Score-Cle	.186	Sturdivant-NY	.291	Score-Cle	45.2	Score-Cle	46.5
Score-Cle	2.53	Ford-NY	156	Larsen-NY	.204	Donovan-Chi	.292	Wynn-Cle	44.3	Wynn-Cle	45.7
Wynn-Cle	2.72	Wynn-Cle	154	Brewer-Bos	.220	Score-Cle	.292	Ford-NY	42.3	Ford-NY	35.0
Lemon-Cle	3.03	Lemon-Cle	139	Harshman-Chi	.221	Wynn-Cle	.294	Lary-Det	32.9	Lemon-Cle	33.3
Harshman-Chi	3.10	Sullivan-Bos	135	Sturdivant-NY	.224	Ford-NY	.303	Lemon-Cle	32.0	Sullivan-Bos	32.2

Clutch Pitching Index		Relief Runs		Adjusted Relief Runs		Relief Ranking		Total Pitcher Index		Total Baseball Ranking	
Lary-Det	117	Narleski-Cle	17.4	Narleski-Cle	17.7	Narleski-Cle	16.1	Lemon-Cle	5.2	Mantle-NY	8.7
Sullivan-Bos	116	Grim-NY	11.5	Grim-NY	9.1	Byerly-Was	9.6	Wynn-Cle	5.1	Lemon-Cle	5.2
Hoeft-Det	116	Byrne-NY	9.7	Byerly-Was	7.9	Delock-Bos	9.2	Score-Cle	4.8	Wynn-Cle	5.1
Ford-NY	114	Byerly-Was	6.9	Byrne-NY	6.1	Grim-NY	9.0	Ford-NY	4.5	Score-Cle	4.8
Stobbs-Was	114	Mossi-Cle	5.5	Mossi-Cle	6.0	Mossi-Cle	8.4	Brewer-Bos	4.1	Ford-NY	4.5

January 4 The Dodgers buy a 44-passenger twin-engine airplane for $775,000, which they will use to transport the club during the season. They are the first team to own their own plane.

April 18 New York Parks Commissioner Robert Moses proposes a 78-acre tract in Flushing Meadows as a site for a new NL stadium. The plan, submitted to Mayor Robert Wagner, includes a 50,000-seat stadium with a plastic dome, to be built by the Parks Department.

May 28 The NL approves the proposed moves of the Dodgers and the Giants to the West Coast, provided both clubs make their request before Oct. 1 and move at the same time.

June 12 Cardinal Stan Musial plays in his 823rd game for a new NL consecutive-game streak, beating Gus Suhr's record.

June 28 By stuffing the ballot box, Cincinnati fans elect eight Redlegs as starters in the All-Star Game. Over protests from Reds fans, Commissioner Ford Frick names Stan Musial, Willie Mays, and Hank Aaron to replace Reds Gus Bell, George Crowe, and Wally Post in the starting lineup.

August 1 Gil Hodges hits his 13th career grand slam, the last in the history of the Brooklyn Dodgers, to establish a new NL record.

August 17 Richie Ashburn, known for his ability to foul pitches off, hits spectator Alice Roth twice in the same at bat. The first one breaks her nose, and the second one hits her while she is being removed from her seat on a stretcher. Ironically, she is the wife of Earl Roth, the sports editor of the Philadelphia *Bulletin*.

September 3 Warren Spahn of the Braves hurls his 41st shutout, the most by a NL lefthander, as he beats Chicago 8-0.

September 16 The Los Angeles City Council approves a 300-acre site in Chavez Ravine for a Dodger stadium if the club will finance a public recreation area.

September 21 Gail Harris is the last player to hit a home run as a New York Giant. New York beats the Pirates 9-5 in the second game of a doubleheader and Ruben Gomez gains the last New York Giants' victory.

September 22 Duke Snider's 39th and 40th home runs are the last that will be hit at Ebbets Field. The Duke of Flatbush ties Ralph Kiner's NL mark of hitting at least 40 home runs in five consecutive seasons. Phillie Robin Roberts, who has a penchant for throwing gopher balls, is the loser, 7-3.

September 23 The Milwaukee Braves clinch the pennant by beating the Cardinals 4-2 on Hank Aaron's 11th-inning home run.

September 24 In the last game at Ebbets Field, 6,702 fans watch Dodgers lefty Danny McDevitt prevail over the Pirates, 2-0. Gil Hodges has the last RBI.

September 29 With 1895 manager Jack Doyle among the 11,606 looking on, the Giants lose their last game at the Polo Grounds, 9-1. Pirate pitcher Bob Friend defeats Johnny Antonelli.

October 6 With the score tied at 5-5, Eddie Mathews of the Braves evens the World Series at two games with a two-run home run in the bottom of the 10th.

October 9 With Warren Spahn stricken by the flu, Lew Burdette, pitching with two days rest, achieves his third complete game and second shutout to beat New York 5-0. The Braves win their first World Series championship since the "Miracle Braves" of 1914 beat Connie Mack's Athletics.

November 28 Warren Spahn of the Braves wins the Cy Young Award as major league Pitcher of the Year almost unanimously. White Sox pitcher Dick Donovan receives one vote.

	BROOKLYN		CHICAGO		CINCINNATI		MILWAUKEE		NEW YORK		PHILADELPHIA		PITTSBURGH		ST.LOUIS
M	W.Alston	M	B.Scheffing	M	B.Tebbetts	M	F.Haney	M	B.Rigney	M	M.Smith	M	B.Bragan	M	F.Hutchinson
1B	G.Hodges	1B	D.Long	1B	G.Crowe	1B	F.Torre	1B	W.Lockman	1B	E.Bouchee	M	D.Murtaugh	1B	S.Musial
2B	J.Gilliam	2B	B.Morgan	2B	J.Temple	2B	R.Schoendienst	2B	D.O'Connell	2B	G.Hamner	1B	D.Fondy	2B	D.Blasingame
SS	C.Neal	SS	J.Littrell	SS	R.McMillan	SS	J.Logan	SS	D.Spencer	SS	C.Fernandez	2B	B.Mazeroski	SS	A.Dark
3B	P.Reese	3B	E.Banks	3B	D.Hoak	3B	E.Mathews	3B	R.Jablonski	3B	W.Jones	SS	D.Groat	3B	E.Kasko
LF	G.Cimoli	LF	L.Walls	LF	F.Robinson	LF	W.Covington	LF	H.Sauer	LF	H.Anderson	3B	G.Freese	LF	W.Moon
CF	D.Snider	CF	B.Speake	CF	G.Bell	CF	B.Bruton	CF	W.Mays	CF	R.Ashburn	LF	B.Skinner	CF	K.Boyer
RF	C.Furillo	RF	W.Moryn	RF	W.Post	RF	H.Aaron	RF	D.Mueller	RF	R.Repulski	CF	B.Virdon	RF	D.Ennis
C	R.Campanella	C	C.Neeman	C	E.Bailey	C	D.Crandall	C	V.Thomas	C	S.Lopata	RF	R.Clemente	C	H.Smith
												C	H.Foiles		
O	S.Amoros	O	J.Bolger	C	S.Burgess	O	A.Pafko	3O	O.Virgil		B.Bowman			1O	J.Cunningham
3S	D.Zimmer	O	C.Tanner	O	B.Thurman	2	J.Adcock	2	R.Schoendienst	32	T.Kazanski	3S	G.Baker	C	H.Landrith
C	R.Walker	3	B.Adams	1	T.Kluszewski	2	D.O'Connell	1	G.Harris	C	J.Lonnett	1O	F.Thomas	O	BG.Smith
O	E.Valo	23	J.Kindall	O	J.Lynch	S2	F.Mantilla	O	B.Thomson	2	S.Hemus	O	P.Smith	C	W.Cooper
3	R.Jackson	O	B.Will	O	J.Taylor	O	B.Thomson	O	D.Rhodes	O	C.Harmon	O	R.Mejias	S	D.Schofield
C	J.Roseboro	2	C.Wise	S2	A.Grammas	C	D.Rice	C	R.Katt	S	R.Smalley	C	D.Rand	O	E.Miksis
/O	B.Kennedy	C	J.Fanning	O	P.Whisenant	O	B.Hazle	S3	E.Bressoud	1	M.Blaylock	C	H.Peterson	/O	J.King
/C	J.Pignatano	C	C.Silvera	/O	A.Schult	C	C.Sawatski	O	W.Westrum	H	R.Northey	/O	J.Pendleton	/O	I.Noren
/1	J.Gentile	1	D.Fondy	/C	D.Dotterer	1	N.Jones	S	A.Rodgers	/C	A.Seminick	C	D.Kravitz	/1	T.Alston
H	R.Miller	/S	E.Winceniak	/S	B.Henrich	O	C.Tanner	/3	F.Castleman	/O	D.Landrum	/O	J.Powers	/O	G.Green
		3	G.Baker	/3	C.Flood	O	J.DeMerit	H	B.Taylor	H	F.Baumholtz	/1	D.Long	/O	D.Lassetter
P	D.Drysdale	O	B.DelGreco	/2	R.Bridges	/2	B.Malkmus	H	B.Hofman	H	G.Gorbous	O	L.Walls	/O	C.Harmon
P	D.Newcombe	/3	J.Goryl	/S	B.Durnbaugh	2	D.Cole			/3	J.Kennedy	S	B.Pritchard		
P	J.Podres	O	F.Ernaga	H	D.Pavletich	P	H.Hanebrink	P	R.Gomez	/S	K.Hamlin			P	L.Jackson
P	D.McDevitt	/O	E.Haas			/2	M.Roach	P	J.Antonelli			P	B.Friend	P	L.McDaniel
P	R.Craig	/O	B.Lennon	P	B.Lawrence	/O	R.Shearer	P	C.Barclay	P	R.Roberts	P	B.Friend	P	S.Jones
RP	C.Labine	/C	G.Massa	P	H.Jeffcoat	/C	H.Taylor	P	S.Miller	P	J.Sanford	P	R.Kline	P	H.Wehmeier
RP	E.Roebuck	/1	E.Mickelson	P	J.Nuxhall			P	R.Crone	P	C.Simmons	P	B.Purkey	P	V.Mizell
		R	J.Woods	P	D.Gross	P	W.Spahn	RP	A.Worthington	P	H.Haddix	P	V.Law	RP	W.Schmidt
P	S.Koufax			P	J.Klippstein	P	L.Burdette	RP	M.Grissom	P	D.Cardwell	RP	L.Arroyo	RP	L.Merritt
P	S.Maglie	P	M.Drabowsky	RP	T.Acker	P	B.Buhl	RP	R.Monzant	RP	T.Farrell	RP	R.Face	RP	H.Wilhelm
P	C.Erskine	P	D.Drott	RP	A.Fowler	P	G.Conley			RP	J.Hearn	RP	R.Swanson		
P	D.Bessent	P	B.Rush	RP	H.Freeman	P	B.Trowbridge	RP	B.Miller					P	V.McDaniel
/P	R.Valdez	P	D.Elston			RP	T.Phillips					P	B.Smith	P	M.Dickson
/P	B.Harris	P	D.Hillman	P	R.Sanchez	RP	E.Johnson	P	M.McCormick	P	W.Hacker	P	N.King	P	B.Muffett
/P	K.Lehman	RP	J.Brosnan	P	W.Hacker	RP	D.McMahon	P	J.Constable	P	S.Morehead	P	W.Douglas	P	J.Davis
/P	J.Collum	RP	T.Lown	/P	V.Amor			P	S.Ridzik	P	J.Meyer	P	J.O'Brien	/P	M.Martin
/P	F.Kipp	RP	D.Littlefield	/P	B.Podbielan	P	J.Pizarro	/P	G.Jones	/P	S.Rogovin	/P	J.Trimble	/P	F.Barnes
/P	D.Elston			/P	B.Kennedy	P	R.Crone	P	J.Davis	/P	T.Qualters	/P	E.O'Brien	/P	Bo.Smith
		P	T.Poholsky	/P	J.Hook	P	D.Jolly	/P	M.Surkont			/P	D.Hall	/P	T.Cheney
		P	D.Kaiser	/P	C.Rabe	P	R.Murff	/P	S.Consuegra			/P	L.Pepper	/P	L.Lovenguth
		/P	B.Anderson	/P	D.Skaugstad	/P	P.Paine	/P	W.McCall			/P	C.Churn	/P	B.Miller
		/P	E.Singleton	/P	C.Osteen	/P	J.Jay					/P	B.Daniels	/P	B.Kuzava
		/P	V.Valentinetti									/P	B.Kuzava		
		/P	J.Collum									/P	G.Witt		
		P	E.Mayer												
		/P	J.Briggs												
		/P	G.Hobbie												

TEAM	G	W	L	PCT	GB	R	OR	AB	H	2B	3B	HR	BB	SO	AVG	OBP	SLG	PRO	PRO+	BR	/A	PF	CHI	RC	SB	CS	SBA	SBR
MIL	155	95	59	.617		772	613	5458	1469	221	62	199	461	729	.269	.329	.442	.771	121	82	138	93	101	787	35	16	69	1
STL	154	87	67	.565	8	737	666	5472	1497	235	43	132	493	672	.274	.336	.405	.741	103	36	22	102	102	731	58	44	57	-9
BRO	154	84	70	.545	11	690	591	5242	1325	188	38	147	550	848	.253	.328	.387	.715	89	-11	-75	110	104	664	60	34	64	-2
CIN	154	80	74	.519	15	747	781	5389	1452	251	33	187	546	752	.269	.341	.432	.773	106	97	42	107	95	794	51	36	59	-6
PHI	156	77	77	.500	18	623	656	5241	1311	213	44	117	534	758	.250	.325	.375	.700	97	-39	-19	97	99	635	57	26	69	2
NY	154	69	85	.448	26	643	701	5346	1349	171	54	157	447	669	.252	.313	.393	.706	95	-42	-40	100	103	646	64	38	63	-4
PIT	155	62	92	.403	33	586	696	5402	1447	231	60	92	374	733	.268	.318	.384	.702	97	-46	-27	97	93	649	46	35	57	-7
CHI	156	62	92	.403	33	628	722	5369	1312	223	31	147	461	989	.244	.307	.380	.687	91	-78	-68	98	105	623	28	25	53	-7
TOT	619					5426		42919	11162	1733	365	1178	3866	6150	.260	.325	.400	.724							399	254	61	-33

TEAM	CG	SH	SV	IP	H	H/G	HR	BB	SO	RAT	ERA	ERA+	OAV	OOB	PR	/A	PF	CPI	FA	E	DP	FW	PW	BW	SBW	DIF
MIL	60	9	24	1411	1347	8.6	124	570	693	12.3	3.47	101	.253	.327	64	4	90	107	.981	120	173	1.0	.4	14.0	.5	2.0
STL	46	11	29	1413¹	1385	8.8	140	506	778	12.2	3.78	105	.257	.324	16	29	102	100	.979	131	168	.4	2.9	2.2	-.5	5.0
BRO	44	18	29	1399	1285	8.3	144	456	891	11.4	3.35	124	.244	.307	82	127	107	101	.979	127	136	.6	12.9	-7.6	.2	.9
CIN	40	5	29	1395²	1486	9.6	179	429	707	12.7	4.62	89	.275	.334	-116	-79	106	95	.982	107	139	1.7	-8.0	4.3	-.2	5.3
PHI	54	9	23	1401²	1363	8.8	139	412	858	11.5	3.79	100	.254	.310	13	1	98	92	.976	136	117	.2	.1	-1.9	.6	1.0
NY	35	9	20	1398²	1436	9.2	150	471	701	12.5	4.01	98	.267	.330	-20	-12	101	101	.974	161	180	-1.3	-1.2	-4.1	.0	-1.4
PIT	47	9	15	1395	1463	9.4	158	421	663	12.3	3.88	98	.270	.325	0	-14	98	105	.972	170	143	-1.7	-1.4	-2.7	-.3	-8.8
CHI	30	5	26	1403¹	1397	9.0	144	601	859	13.0	4.13	94	.261	.339	-39	-40	100	100	.975	149	140	-.5	-4.1	-6.9	-.3	-3.2
TOT	356	75	195	11217²		9.0				12.2	3.88		.260	.325					.977	1101	1196					

Runs
Aaron-Mil 118
Banks-Chi 113
Mays-NY 112
Mathews-Mil 109
Blasingame-StL . . . 108

Hits
Schoendienst-NY-MI . 200
Aaron-Mil 198
Robinson-Cin 197
Mays-NY 195
Ashburn-Phi 186

Doubles
Hoak-Cin 39
Musial-StL 38
Bouchee-Phi 35
Banks-Chi 34
Moryn-Chi 33

Triples
Mays-NY 20
Virdon-Pit 11
Mathews-Mil 9
Bruton-Mil 9

Home Runs
Aaron-Mil 44
Banks-Chi 43
Snider-Bro 40
Mays-NY 35
Mathews-Mil 32

Total Bases
Aaron-Mil 369
Mays-NY 366
Banks-Chi 344
Robinson-Cin 323
Mathews-Mil 309

Runs Batted In
Aaron-Mil 132
Ennis-StL 105
Musial-StL 102
Banks-Chi 102
Hodges-Bro 98

Runs Produced
Aaron-Mil 206
Mays-NY 174
Banks-Chi 172
Mathews-Mil 171
Hodges-Bro 165

Bases On Balls
Temple-Cin 94
Ashburn-Phi 94
Mathews-Mil 90
Bouchee-Phi 84
Snider-Bro 77

Batting Average
Musial-StL 351
Mays-NY 333
Robinson-Cin 322
Aaron-Mil 322
Groat-Pit 315

On Base Percentage
Musial-StL 428
Mays-NY 411
Bouchee-Phi 396
Ashburn-Phi 392
Temple-Cin 391

Slugging Average
Mays-NY 626
Musial-StL 612
Aaron-Mil 600
Snider-Bro 587
Banks-Chi 579

Production
Musial-StL 1.040
Mays-NY 1.037
Aaron-Mil 979
Snider-Bro 957
Banks-Chi 942

Adjusted Production
Mays-NY 174
Musial-StL 172
Aaron-Mil 170
Mathews-Mil 157
Banks-Chi 150

Batter Runs
Mays-NY 60.5
Musial-StL 54.1
Aaron-Mil 48.3
Banks-Chi 38.6
Mathews-Mil 38.3

Adjusted Batter Runs
Mays-NY 61.0
Aaron-Mil 57.5
Musial-StL 51.8
Mathews-Mil 46.7
Banks-Chi 40.5

Clutch Hitting Index
McMillan-Cin 134
Ennis-StL 131
Hamner-Phi 115
Post-Cin 112
Hoak-Cin 112

Runs Created
Mays-NY 145
Aaron-Mil 136
Musial-StL 129
Mathews-Mil 126
Banks-Chi 123

Total Average
Musial-StL 1.103
Mays-NY 1.092
Aaron-Mil 988
Mathews-Mil 973
Snider-Bro 962

Stolen Bases
Mays-NY 38
Gilliam-Bro 26
Blasingame-StL . . . 21
Temple-Cin 19
Fernandez-Phi 18

Stolen Base Average
Temple-Cin 79.2
Fernandez-Phi 78.3
Gilliam-Bro 72.2
Blasingame-StL . . . 70.0
Mays-NY 66.7

Stolen Base Runs
Temple-Cin 2.7
Fernandez-Phi 2.4
Robinson-Cin 1.8
Gilliam-Bro 1.8

Fielding Runs
Ashburn-Phi 32.4
Blasingame-StL . . . 25.8
Logan-Mil 23.9
Robinson-Cin 18.7
Campanella-Bro . . . 16.0

Total Player Rating
Mays-NY 6.3
Aaron-Mil 5.0
Mathews-Mil 4.8
Musial-StL 4.5
Robinson-Cin 3.8

Wins
Spahn-Mil 21
Sanford-Phi 19
Buhl-Mil 18
Drysdale-Bro 17
Burdette-Mil 17

Win Percentage
Buhl-Mil 720
Sanford-Phi 704
Spahn-Mil 656
Drysdale-Bro 654
Burdette-Mil 654

Games
Lown-Chi 67
Face-Pit 59
Labine-Bro 58
Worthington-NY 55
Grissom-NY 55

Complete Games
Spahn-Mil 18
Friend-Pit 17
Gomez-NY 16
Sanford-Phi 15

Shutouts
Podres-Bro 6
Spahn-Mil 4
Newcombe-Bro 4
Drysdale-Bro 4

Saves
Labine-Bro 17
Grissom-NY 14
Lown-Chi 12
Wilhelm-StL 11

Innings Pitched
Friend-Pit 277.0
Spahn-Mil 271.0
Burdette-Mil 256.2
Lawrence-Cin 250.1
Roberts-Phi 249.2

Fewest Hits/Game
Sanford-Phi 7.38
Podres-Bro 7.71
Drott-Chi 7.86
Buhl-Mil 7.93
Worthington-NY . . 7.99

Fewest BB/Game
Newcombe-Bro . . . 1.49
Roberts-Phi 1.55
Law-Pit 1.67
Purkey-Pit 1.90
Jeffcoat-Cin 2.00

Strikeouts
Sanford-Phi 188
Drott-Chi 170
Drabowsky-Chi 170
Jones-StL 154
Drysdale-Bro 148

Strikeouts/Game
Jones-StL 7.59
Haddix-Phi 7.17
Sanford-Phi 7.15
Drott-Chi 6.68
Drabowsky-Chi 6.38

Ratio
Podres-Bro 9.78
Roberts-Phi 10.45
Newcombe-Bro . . 10.56
Spahn-Mil 10.66
Law-Pit 10.74

Earned Run Average
Podres-Bro 2.66
Drysdale-Bro 2.69
Spahn-Mil 2.69
Buhl-Mil 2.74
Law-Pit 2.87

Adjusted ERA
Podres-Bro 156
Drysdale-Bro 155
Law-Pit 132
Spahn-Mil 130
Buhl-Mil 128

Opponents' Batting Avg.
Sanford-Phi 221
Podres-Bro 230
Drott-Chi 234
Drysdale-Bro 236
Spahn-Mil 237

Opponents' On Base Pct.
Podres-Bro 274
Roberts-Phi 284
Newcombe-Bro 290
Law-Pit 291
Spahn-Mil 293

Starter Runs
Spahn-Mil 35.8
Drysdale-Bro 29.2
Buhl-Mil 27.4
Podres-Bro 26.5
Sanford-Phi 21.0

Adjusted Starter Runs
Drysdale-Bro 36.3
Podres-Bro 32.7
Spahn-Mil 24.3
Sanford-Phi 19.0
Buhl-Mil 18.2

Clutch Pitching Index
Buhl-Mil 135
Barclay-NY 117
Law-Pit 113
Spahn-Mil 109
Antonelli-NY 108

Relief Runs
Farrell-Phi 13.9
Roebuck-Bro 12.5
Grissom-NY 11.6
Face-Pit 8.4
Miller-Phi 8.0

Adjusted Relief Runs
Roebuck-Bro 15.6
Farrell-Phi 13.2
Grissom-NY 12.1
Labine-Bro 8.4
Miller-Phi 7.5

Relief Ranking
Farrell-Phi 20.7
Roebuck-Bro 17.5
Grissom-NY 15.2
Labine-Bro 11.8
Miller-Phi 9.5

Total Pitcher Index
Drysdale-Bro 4.7
Podres-Bro 3.5
Spahn-Mil 3.0
Roebuck-Bro 2.3
Farrell-Phi 2.2

Total Baseball Ranking
Mays-NY 6.3
Aaron-Mil 5.0
Mathews-Mil 4.8
Drysdale-Bro 4.7
Musial-StL 4.5

February 25 The U.S. Supreme Court decides 6-3 that baseball is the only professional sport exempt from antitrust laws. The issue arises when pro football seeks similar protection from the laws.

March 19 In what is believed to be the largest offer for a player ever made to date, the Indians reject a million-dollar offer for lefty Herb Score from Red Sox general manager Joe Cronin. Cleveland GM Hank Greenberg refuses, saying that the team is interested in building for the future, not in selling its best ballplayers.

May 7 Gil McDougald of the Yankees hits a wicked line-drive that strikes Cleveland's Herb Score in the right eye. Score is carried off the feld on a stretcher, with a broken nose and lacerations. Bob Lemon relieves and wins the game, 2–1. Score will return the following year, but his pitching will not be the same.

May 16 The Yankees celebrate Billy Martin's 29th birthday in a raucous fashion. An ensuing fight at Manhattan's Copacabana Club leads to $5,500 in fines and the eventual trade of Martin to Kansas City. Hank Bauer allegedly starts the fight by hitting a patron, although Bauer denies it. The Yanks fine Ford, Bauer, Berra, Mantle and Martin $1,000 each and Kucks $500.

May 22 The Red Sox tie an AL record by smashing four home runs in the sixth inning in an 11-0 win over Cleveland. Gene Mauch, Ted Williams, Dick Gernert, and Frank Malzone do the honors. Williams had set the record with Jimmie Foxx, Joe Cronin, and Jim Tabor in 1940.

June 13 For the second time this year, the Red Sox' Ted Williams hits three home runs in a game, a 9–2 win over the Indians. Williams is the first to do this in the AL.

June 28 Ray Moore blanks Cleveland 6–0 as the Orioles pitching staff hurls its fourth consecutive shutout, for a new league mark.

July 8 The owners decide to re-elect Commissioner Ford Frick to another seven-year term when his present contract is up in 1958.

July 9 At Sportsman's Park in St. Louis, the AL nips the NL, 6–5, in the 24th All-Star Game. Both teams score three in the ninth inning, but Minnie Minoso's running catch with the bases loaded chokes off the NL's last-half rally.

September 24 The Yankees clinch their 23rd pennant and eighth under Casey Stengel, as Kansas City tips the White Sox, 6-5.

October 2 Whitey Ford wins 3-1 over Warren Spahn in Game 1 of the Series at Yankee Stadium.

October 8 The Yankees stay alive as Hank Bauer homers off the foul pole in left field to give the Yankees a 3-2 win behind the four-hit pitching of Bob Turley. The World Series is even at three apiece.

November 22 Mickey Mantle edges Ted Williams 233 to 209 votes to win the league MVP. Williams, at 39 years of age, led the league in hitting with a .388 average, hit 38 home runs, and compiled a slugging average of .731. Red Sox owner Tom Yawkey brands the voting "incompetent and unqualified," noting that two Chicago writers listed Williams in the ninth and tenth places on their ballots.

	BALTIMORE		BOSTON		CHICAGO		CLEVELAND		DETROIT		KANSAS CITY		NEW YORK		WASHINGTON
M	P.Richards	M	P.Higgins	M	A.Lopez	M	K.Farrell	M	J.Tighe	M	L.Boudreau	M	C.Stengel	M	C.Dressen
1B	B.Boyd	1B	D.Gernert	1B	E.Torgeson	1B	V.Wertz	1B	R.Boone	M	H.Craft	1B	B.Skowron	M	C.Lavagetto
2B	B.Gardner	2B	T.Lepcio	2B	N.Fox	2B	B.Avila	2B	F.Bolling	1B	V.Power	2B	B.Richardson	1B	P.Runnels
SS	W.Miranda	SS	B.Klaus	SS	L.Aparicio	SS	C.Carrasquel	SS	H.Kuenn	2B	B.Hunter	SS	G.McDougald	2B	H.Plews
3B	G.Kell	3B	F.Malzone	3B	B.Phillips	3B	A.Smith	3B	R.Bertoia	SS	J.DeMaestri	3B	A.Carey	SS	R.Bridges
LF	B.Nieman	LF	T.Williams	LF	M.Minoso	LF	G.Woodling	LF	C.Maxwell	3B	H.Lopez	LF	E.Howard	3B	E.Yost
CF	J.Busby	CF	J.Piersall	CF	L.Doby	CF	R.Maris	CF	B.Tuttle	LF	G.Zernial	CF	M.Mantle	LF	R.Sievers
RF	A.Pilarcik	RF	J.Jensen	RF	J.Landis	RF	R.Colavito	RF	A.Kaline	CF	W.Held	RF	H.Bauer	CF	B.Usher
C	G.Triandos	C	S.White	C	S.Lollar	C	J.Hegan	C	F.House	RF	L.Skizas	C	Y.Berra	RF	J.Lemon
										C	H.Smith			C	L.Berberet
O	T.Francona	O	G.Stephens	3S	S.Esposito	3S	L.Raines	C	R.Wilson			OS	T.Kubek		
3	B.Goodman	1	M.Vernon	O1	J.Rivera	O3	D.Williams	3	J.Finigan	O	B.Cerv	O	E.Slaughter	1	J.Becquer
C	J.Ginsberg	2	G.Mauch	1	W.Dropo	2S	G.Strickland	1O	D.Philley	23	B.Martin	O1	H.Simpson	2S	M.Bolling
O3	D.Williams	S2	B.Consolo	C	E.Battey	C	R.Nixon	OC	J.Porter	C	T.Thompson	23	J.Coleman	1O	A.Schult
O	J.Durham	C	P.Daley	C	L.Moss	C	H.Naragon	O	J.Groth	1O	H.Simpson	1O	J.Collins	C	C.Courtney
S	J.Brideweser	1	N.Zauchin	3	F.Hatfield	C	D.Brown	S2	R.Samford	1	I.Noren	23	B.Martin	O	F.Throneberry
3	B.Robinson	2	K.Aspromonte	O	T.Beard	O	J.Caffie	1	E.Torgeson	2	M.Graff	3	J.Lumpe	C	E.FitzGerald
/1	B.Hale	/O	M.Keough	O	D.Philley	1	J.Altobelli	O	J.Small	O	B.Martyn	C	D.Johnson	S2	J.Snyder
O	C.Powis	H	B.Goodman	1	R.Jackson	O	J.Busby	/3	S.Boros	O	J.Pisoni	/O	Z.Bella	O	W.Herzog
O	J.Pyburn	H	M.Bolling	S	B.Harrell	/O	B.Osborne	O	J.Groth	/O	B.DelGreco	O	N.Chrisley
O	L.Green	/C	H.Sullivan	H	B.Kennedy	2	K.Kuhn	/O	B.Taylor	/2	C.Boyer	H	W.Held	S	L.Luttrell
/O	T.Nelson	H	F.Throneberry	R	L.Powell	/1	E.Robinson	/3	J.Dittmer					/3	H.Killebrew
/S	B.Peterson					/1	P.Ward	/O	K.Olson	P	N.Garver	P	T.Sturdivant	/O	J.Schoonmaker
/C	F.Zupo	P	F.Sullivan	P	B.Pierce	/O	B.Usher	/1	E.Robinson	P	T.Morgan	P	J.Kucks	/O	K.Olson
/2	W.Causey	P	T.Brewer	P	D.Donovan			/O	M.Clark	P	A.Kellner	P	B.Turley	/O	D.Tettelbach
H	E.Robinson	P	W.Nixon	P	J.Wilson	P	E.Wynn	H	J.Phillips	P	R.Terry	P	B.Shantz		
/C	T.Patton	P	M.Fornieles	P	J.Harshman	P	M.Garcia	/3	G.Thomas	P	J.Urban	P	D.Larsen	P	P.Ramos
H	E.Miksis	P	D.Sisler	P	B.Keegan	P	M.Dossi	/C	T.Yewcic	P	V.Trucks	RP	A.Ditmar	P	C.Stobbs
		RP	I.Delock	RP	G.Staley	P	R.Narleski			RP	W.Burnette	RP	T.Byrne	P	C.Pascual
P	C.Johnson			RP	D.Howell	P	C.McLish	P	J.Bunning	RP	M.McDermott	RP	B.Grim	P	R.Kemmerer
P	R.Moore	P	B.Porterfield			RP	B.Daley	P	F.Lary					RP	T.Clevenger
P	B.Loes	P	G.Susce	P	B.Fischer	RP	D.Tomanek	P	D.Maas	T	T.Gorman	P	W.Ford	P	B.Hyde
P	H.Brown	P	D.Stone	P	P.LaPalme	RP	S.Pitula	P	P.Foytack	P	A.Portocarrero	P	A.Cicotte	RP	B.Byerly
P	B.O'Dell	P	R.Minarcin	P	J.Derrington			P	B.Hoeft	P	R.Duren	/P	S.Maglie		
RP	G.Zuverink	P	B.Chakales	P	J.McDonald	P	B.Lemon	RP	L.Sleater	P	R.Coleman	/P	R.Terry	P	T.Abernathy
RP	K.Lehman	P	M.Wall	/P	B.Latman	/P	H.Score	RP	H.Byrd	P	G.Host			P	E.Hernandez
RP	A.Ceccarelli	/P	F.Baumann	/P	D.Rudolph	P	V.Valentinetti			P	G.Cox			/P	J.Heise
		/P	R.Meyer	/P	J.Hughes	P	H.Aguirre	P	D.Lee	/P	G.Brunet			/P	B.Chakales
P	B.Wight	/P	R.Kemmerer	/P	E.Kinder	/P	J.Gray	P	A.Aber	/P	H.Taylor			/P	B.Wiesler
P	M.Fornieles	/P	J.Spring	/P	S.McIlwain	/P	B.Alexander	P	S.Gromek	/P	A.Aber			/P	H.Griggs
P	J.Walker					/P	A.Houtteman	/P	J.Stump	/P	E.Blake			/P	J.Black
/P	D.Ferrarese					/P	H.Wilhelm	/P	J.Presko	/P	D.Hill			/P	D.Brodowski
/P	C.Beamon							/P	B.Shaw	/P	H.Raether			/P	R.Lumenti
/P	M.Pappas							/P	J.Crimian					/P	D.Minnick
/P	A.Houtteman							/P	J.Tsitouris					/P	G.Shifflett
/P	S.Consuegra							/P	C.Daniel					/P	D.Stone
/P	D.Trout							/P	P.Wojey						

TEAM	G	W	L	PCT	GB	R	OR	AB	H	2B	3B	HR	BB	SO	AVG	OBP	SLG	PRO	PRO+	BR	/A	PF	CHI	RC	SB	CS	SBA	SBR
NY	154	98	56	.636		723	534	5271	1412	200	54	145	562	709	.268	.341	.409	.750	113	76	88	98	99	729	49	38	56	-8
CHI	155	90	64	.584	8	707	566	5265	1369	208	41	106	633	745	.260	.347	.375	.722	103	40	36	101	100	708	109	51	68	2
BOS	154	82	72	.532	16	721	668	5267	1380	231	32	153	624	739	.262	.343	.405	.748	104	76	34	106	98	725	29	21	58	-4
DET	154	78	76	.506	20	614	614	5348	1376	224	37	116	504	643	.257	.324	.378	.702	96	-18	-35	103	96	644	36	47	43	-17
BAL	154	76	76	.500	21	597	588	5264	1326	191	39	87	504	699	.252	.321	.353	.674	96	-66	-30	94	101	600	57	35	62	-4
CLE	153	76	77	.497	21.5	682	722	5171	1304	199	26	140	591	786	.252	.332	.382	.714	102	10	17	99	103	661	40	47	46	-16
KC	154	59	94	.386	38.5	563	710	5170	1262	195	40	166	364	760	.244	.297	.394	.691	92	-60	-70	102	100	578	35	27	56	-6
WAS	154	55	99	.357	43	603	808	5231	1274	215	38	111	527	733	.244	.318	.363	.681	93	-56	-49	99	102	592	13	38	25	-19
TOT	616					5210		41987	10703	1663	307	1024	4309	5814	.255	.328	.382	.710							368	304	55	-72

TEAM	CG	SH	SV	IP	H	H/G	HR	BB	SO	RAT	ERA	ERA+	OAV	OOB	PR	/A	PF	CPI	FA	E	DP	FW	PW	BW	SBW	DIF
NY	41	13	42	1395[1]	1198	7.7	110	580	810	11.7	3.00	120	.234	.317	122	91	95	109	.980	123	183	.2	9.4	9.1	.1	2.2
CHI	59	16	27	1401[2]	1305	8.4	124	470	665	11.6	3.35	112	.248	.313	69	61	99	102	.982	107	169	1.1	6.3	3.7	1.1	.7
BOS	55	9	23	1376[2]	1391	9.1	116	498	692	12.6	3.88	103	.264	.331	-14	17	105	100	.976	149	179	-1.2	1.8	3.5	.5	.4
DET	52	9	21	1417[2]	1330	8.4	147	505	756	11.9	3.56	108	.250	.320	37	47	102	104	.980	121	151	.3	4.9	-3.6	-.8	.3
BAL	44	13	25	1408	1272	8.1	95	493	767	11.5	3.46	104	.243	.312	51	20	95	92	.981	112	159	.8	2.1	-3.1	.5	-.3
CLE	46	7	23	1380[2]	1381	9.0	130	618	807	13.3	4.06	96	.261	.343	-42	-53	98	101	.974	153	154	-1.4	-5.5	1.8	-.7	5.4
KC	26	6	19	1369[2]	1344	8.8	153	565	626	12.7	4.19	94	.260	.336	-61	-35	104	99	.979	125	162	.1	-3.6	-7.2	.3	-7.1
WAS	31	5	16	1377	1482	9.7	149	580	691	13.7	4.85	80	.278	.353	-162	-146	103	95	.979	128	159	-.0	-15.1	-5.1	-1.0	-.8
TOT	354	78	196	11126[2]		8.7				12.4	3.79		.255	.328					.979	1018	1316					

Runs
Mantle-NY 121
Fox-Chi 110
Piersall-Bos 103
Sievers-Was 99

Hits
Fox-Chi 196
Malzone-Bos 185
Minoso-Chi 176
Mantle-NY 173
Kuenn-Det 173

Doubles
Minoso-Chi 36
Gardner-Bal 36
Malzone-Bos 31
Kuenn-Det 30

Triples
Simpson-KC-NY 9
McDougald-NY 9
Bauer-NY 9
Fox-Chi 8
Boyd-Bal 8

Home Runs
Sievers-Was 42
Williams-Bos 38
Mantle-NY 34
Wertz-Cle 28
Zernial-KC 27

Total Bases
Sievers-Was 331
Mantle-NY 315
Williams-Bos 307
Kaline-Det 276
Malzone-Bos 271

Runs Batted In
Sievers-Was 114
Wertz-Cle 105
Minoso-Chi 103
Malzone-Bos 103
Jensen-Bos 103

Runs Produced
Minoso-Chi 187
Mantle-NY 181
Sievers-Was 171
Malzone-Bos 170
Fox-Chi 165

Bases On Balls
Mantle-NY 146
Williams-Bos 119
Smith-Cle 79
Minoso-Chi 79
Wertz-Cle 78

Batting Average
Williams-Bos 388
Mantle-NY 365
Woodling-Cle 321
Boyd-Bal 318
Fox-Chi 317

On Base Percentage
Williams-Bos ..... .528
Mantle-NY ..... .515
Minoso-Chi ..... .413
Woodling-Cle ..... .412
Fox-Chi ..... .404

Slugging Average
Williams-Bos 731
Mantle-NY 665
Sievers-Was 579
Woodling-Cle 521
Wertz-Cle 485

Production
Williams-Bos 1.259
Mantle-NY 1.179
Sievers-Was 968
Woodling-Cle 933
Minoso-Chi 867

Adjusted Production
Williams-Bos 227
Mantle-NY 223
Sievers-Was 163
Woodling-Cle 155
Minoso-Chi 136

Batter Runs
Williams-Bos 89.9
Mantle-NY 88.9
Sievers-Was 47.3
Woodling-Cle 33.0
Minoso-Chi 32.7

Adjusted Batter Runs
Mantle-NY 91.4
Williams-Bos 81.5
Sievers-Was 48.7
Woodling-Cle 33.9
Minoso-Chi 32.2

Clutch Hitting Index
Minoso-Chi 126
Doby-Chi 125
Skowron-NY 123
Malzone-Bos 117
Jensen-Bos 114

Runs Created
Mantle-NY 178
Williams-Bos 167
Sievers-Was 131
Fox-Chi 109
Minoso-Chi 106

Total Average
Williams-Bos 1.599
Mantle-NY 1.534
Sievers-Was 1.010
Woodling-Cle 944
Maxwell-Det 876

Stolen Bases
Aparicio-Chi 28
Rivera-Chi 18
Minoso-Chi 18
Mantle-NY 16

Stolen Base Average
Rivera-Chi 90.0
Mantle-NY 84.2
Aparicio-Chi 77.8
Minoso-Chi 54.5

Stolen Base Runs
Rivera-Chi 4.2
Aparicio-Chi 3.6
Mantle-NY 3.0
Landis-Chi 1.8
Martin-NY-KC 1.5

Fielding Runs
Bridges-Was 29.3
Fox-Chi 20.9
Berra-NY 15.6
Phillips-Chi 15.5
McDougald-NY 15.1

Total Player Rating
Mantle-NY 8.6
Williams-Bos 7.1
Fox-Chi 5.6
Sievers-Was 4.4
McDougald-NY 4.2

Wins
Pierce-Chi 20
Bunning-Det 20
Sturdivant-NY 16
Donovan-Chi 16
Brewer-Bos 16

Win Percentage
Sturdivant-NY ..... .727
Donovan-Chi ...... .727
Bunning-Det ...... .714
Wilson-Chi .... .652
Pierce-Chi .... .625

Games
Zuverink-Bal 56
Hyde-Was 52
Clevenger-Was 52
Delock-Bos 49
Trucks-KC 48

Complete Games
Pierce-Chi 16
Donovan-Chi 16
Brewer-Bos 15

Shutouts
Wilson-Chi 5
Turley-NY 4
Pierce-Chi 4

Saves
Grim-NY 19
Narleski-Cle 16
Delock-Bos 11
Zuverink-Bal 9
Clevenger-Was 8

Innings Pitched
Bunning-Det 267.1
Wynn-Cle 263.0
Pierce-Chi 257.0
Johnson-Bal 242.0
F.Sullivan-Bos 240.2

Fewest Hits/Game
Turley-NY 6.12
Bunning-Det 7.20
Foytack-Det 7.43
Sturdivant-NY 7.59
F.Sullivan-Bos 7.70

Fewest BB/Game
F.Sullivan-Bos 1.80
Donovan-Chi 1.84
Shantz-NY 2.08
Loes-Bal 2.14
Bunning-Det 2.42

Strikeouts
Wynn-Cle 184
Bunning-Det 182
Johnson-Bal 177
Pierce-Chi 171
Turley-NY 152

Strikeouts/Game
Turley-NY 7.76
Johnson-Bal 6.58
Wynn-Cle 6.30
Bunning-Det 6.13
Pierce-Chi 5.99

Ratio
F.Sullivan-Bos ... 9.76
Bunning-Det 10.00
Donovan-Chi 10.44
Johnson-Bal 10.45
Pierce-Chi 10.51

Earned Run Average
Shantz-NY 2.45
Sturdivant-NY 2.54
Bunning-Det 2.69
Turley-NY 2.71
F.Sullivan-Bos 2.73

Adjusted ERA
Shantz-NY 147
F.Sullivan-Bos 146
Bunning-Det 143
Sturdivant-NY 141
Donovan-Chi 135

Opponents' Batting Avg.
Turley-NY 194
Bunning-Det 218
Foytack-Det 226
F.Sullivan-Bos 230
Sturdivant-NY 232

Opponents' On Base Pct.
F.Sullivan-Bos 275
Bunning-Det 279
Pierce-Chi 287
Johnson-Bal 289
Donovan-Chi 293

Starter Runs
Bunning-Det 32.5
F.Sullivan-Bos ... 28.3
Sturdivant-NY 27.9
Shantz-NY 25.8
Donovan-Chi 24.9

Adjusted Starter Runs
Bunning-Det 34.5
F.Sullivan-Bos 33.6
Donovan-Chi 23.6
Sturdivant-NY 23.4
Shantz-NY 22.0

Clutch Pitching Index
Shantz-NY 131
Sturdivant-NY 121
Narleski-Cle 112
Kemmerer-Bos-Was ... 110
Donovan-Chi 108

Relief Runs
Staley-Chi 20.2
Zuverink-Bal 16.4
Trucks-KC 9.8
Grim-NY 9.3
Lehman-Bal 7.6

Adjusted Relief Runs
Staley-Chi 19.6
Zuverink-Bal 14.0
Trucks-KC 12.0
Byerly-Was 8.1
Grim-NY 7.7

Relief Ranking
Grim-NY 23.8
Zuverink-Bal 20.3
Trucks-KC 16.5
Staley-Chi 13.0
Byerly-Was 10.4

Total Pitcher Index
F.Sullivan-Bos 3.5
Bunning-Det 3.3
Shantz-NY 3.1
Grim-NY 2.6
Donovan-Chi 2.5

Total Baseball Ranking
Mantle-NY 8.6
Williams-Bos 7.1
Fox-Chi 5.6
Sievers-Was 4.4
McDougald-NY 4.2

January 29 Dodgers catcher Roy Campanella suffers a broken neck in an early morning auto accident on Long Island. His spinal column is nearly severed and his legs are permanently paralyzed.

April 7 The Dodgers erect a 42-foot screen in left field at the Los Angeles Coliseum to cut down on home runs, since it is only 250 feet down the line.

April 15 The San Francisco Giants defeat the Los Angeles Dodgers in the first major league game played at Seals Stadium, with Ruben Gomez pitching an 8-0 shutout. Giants shortstop Daryl Spencer hits the first home run. The Giants set an attendance record for Seals Stadium by drawing 23,192 fans.

April 18 Following a downtown parade in the morning, the Giants-Dodgers game in Los Angeles sets a NL single-game record with 78,682 fans in attendance, as the Dodgers prevail 6-5. Hank Sauer hits two home runs for the Giants, including the first at the Coliseum. After he scores what would have been the tying run in the ninth, Giant Jim Davenport is called out for failing to touch third.

May 13 With his pinch double in Wrigley Field off Moe Drabowsky, Stan Musial of the Cardinals becomes the eighth hitter in history to get 3,000 hits. The Cards win 5-3.

June 3 The "Dodger referendum" passes by a slim margin of 24,293 votes in Los Angeles. The proposition allows the city to sell 300 acres of Chavez Ravine to the Dodgers for their stadium. The NL president had stated that the Dodgers should vacate Los Angeles if the bill failed.

July 7 At the NL meeting, William Shea outlines plans for a $12 million stadium at Flushing Meadows, the eventual site of Shea Stadium.

August 20 Out of catchers, the Cubs put left-handed first baseman Dale Long behind the plate in the opener against the Pirates. He is the first lefty backstop since 1906. The Cubs lose 4-2, then win the nightcap 5-1 with Long back at first base.

September 13 The Braves' Warren Spahn becomes the first lefty to win 20 or more games nine times, as he beats St. Louis, 8-2. Eddie Plank and Lefty Grove each won 20 games eight times.

September 29 In a race that goes down to the last game, Philadelphia's Richie Ashburn wins the league batting title with a 3-for-4 day that raises him to .350, three percentage points ahead of Mays, despite Willie's three hits in the Giants' 7-2 win over St. Louis.

October 1 In the World Series, the Braves pick up where they left off the previous year, defeating the Yankees behind Warren Spahn 4-3 in 10 innings.

October 5 Milwaukee goes up three games to one with a 3-0 shutout by Warren Spahn, who allows just two hits.

November 25 The BBWAA names Chicago Cubs slugger Ernie Banks the 1958 MVP. Willie Mays is the runner-up.

December 10 The University of Pittsburgh agrees to buy Forbes Field from the Pirates and lease it to them for five years, or until a new municipal stadium is built.

CHICAGO	CINCINNATI	LOS ANGELES	MILWAUKEE	PHILADELPHIA	PITTSBURGH	SAN FRANCISCO	ST.LOUIS
M B.Scheffing	M B.Tebbetts	M W.Alston	M F.Haney	M M.Smith	M D.Murtaugh	M B.Rigney	M F.Hutchinson
1B D.Long	M J.Dykes	1B G.Hodges	1B F.Torre	1B E.Sawyer	1B T.Kluszewski	1B O.Cepeda	M S.Hack
2B T.Taylor	1B G.Crowe	2B C.Neal	2B R.Schoendienst	1B E.Bouchee	2B B.Mazeroski	2B D.O'Connell	1B S.Musial
SS E.Banks	2B J.Temple	SS D.Zimmer	SS J.Logan	2B S.Hemus	SS D.Groat	SS D.Spencer	2B D.Blasingame
3B A.Dark	SS R.McMillan	3B D.Gray	3B E.Mathews	SS C.Fernandez	3B F.Thomas	3B J.Davenport	SS E.Kasko
LF W.Moryn	3B D.Hoak	LF J.Gilliam	LF A.Pafko	3B W.Jones	LF B.Skinner	LF H.Sauer	3B K.Boyer
CF B.Thomson	LF F.Robinson	CF G.Cimoli	CF B.Bruton	LF H.Anderson	CF B.Virdon	CF W.Mays	LF D.Ennis
RF L.Walls	CF G.Bell	RF C.Furillo	RF H.Aaron	CF R.Ashburn	RF R.Clemente	RF W.Kirkland	CF C.Flood
C S.Taylor	RF J.Lynch	C J.Roseboro	C D.Crandall	RF W.Post	C H.Foiles	C B.Schmidt	RF W.Moon
	C E.Bailey			C S.Lopata			C H.Smith
32 J.Goryl		O D.Snider	1O J.Adcock		1 D.Stuart	3 R.Jablonski	
C C.Neeman	C S.Burgess	O1 N.Larker	O W.Covington	2S T.Kazanski	O R.Mejias	O L.Wagner	1O J.Cunningham
O J.Bolger	S3 A.Grammas	S3 P.Reese	O2 F.Mantilla	O R.Repulski	C B.Hall	O F.Alou	OC G.Green
O C.Tanner	O B.Thurman	C J.Pignatano	2 M.Roach	O1 D.Philley	C D.Kravitz	C V.Thomas	O I.Noren
1 B.Adams	O P.Whisenant	O D.Demeter	O H.Hanebrink	O B.Bowman	1 R.Stevens	2 E.Bressoud	S2 G.Freese
1O J.Marshall	1 W.Dropo	1 S.Bilko	C D.Rice	C C.Sawatski	J.Powers	O2 W.Lockman	C H.Landrith
O L.Jackson	1O D.Fondy	O E.Valo	2 C.Wise	32 G.Hamner	3 G.Baker	S B.Speake	S D.Schofield
C E.Tappe	O V.Pinson	S B.Lillis	O B.Hazle	O C.Essegian	/S D.Schofield	A.Rodgers	O BG.Smith
/C M.Thacker	1 S.Bilko	3 R.Jackson	/O E.Haas	31 P.Herrera	H.Bright	O J.King	S R.Amaro
/1 P.Smith	O3 E.Miksis	O R.Fairly	/C C.Sawatski	2 B.Young	/3 G.Freese	O J.Brandt	/S A.Dark
H F.Ernaga	/C D.Dotterer	R.Walker	/S J.Koppe	C J.Hegan	/C H.Peterson	O D.Taussig	C R.Katt
/O C.King	O D.Morejon	/1 J.Gentile	/O H.Taylor	J.Lonnett	H J.Pendleton	/1 B.White	/S L.Tate
/2 J.Kindall	/O C.Coles	/O F.Howard	/O J.DeMerit	/C J.Coker	P.Smith	/2 J.Finigan	/O E.Burton
H F.Johnson	/O J.Fridley	/O D.Miles	H B.Roselli	/S R.Smalley	J.O'Brien	/C N.Testa	/O J.Taylor
/O B.Will	/S B.Henrich	/3 E.Robinson		H M.Burk			/3 B.Valenzuela
H G.Gabler	/2 F.Hatfield	/O B.Wilson	P W.Spahn				/S J.O'Brien
H G.Massa			P L.Burdette	P R.Roberts	P B.Friend	P J.Antonelli	
H B.Morgan	P B.Purkey	P D.Drysdale	P B.Rush	P R.Semproch	P R.Kline	P R.Gomez	
	P H.Haddix	P J.Podres	P C.Willey	P J.Sanford	P V.Law	P S.Miller	P S.Jones
P T.Phillips	P B.Lawrence	P S.Koufax	P J.Pizarro	P C.Simmons	P G.Witt	P M.McCormick	P L.Jackson
P G.Hobbie	P J.Nuxhall	P S.Williams	RP G.Conley	P D.Cardwell	RP B.Porterfield	P R.Monzant	P V.Mizell
P D.Drott	P D.Newcombe	P C.Erskine	RP D.McMahon	RP T.Farrell	RP R.Face	RP A.Worthington	P J.Brosnan
P D.Hillman	RP H.Jeffcoat	RP C.Labine	RP B.Trowbridge	RP J.Meyer	D.Gross	RP M.Grissom	RP B.Mabe
P M.Drabowsky	RP W.Schmidt	RP F.Kipp		RP J.Hearn			RP B.Muffett
RP D.Elston		RP J.Klippstein	P J.Jay		P R.Blackburn	P P.Giel	RP P.Paine
RP B.Henry			P B.Buhl	P S.Morehead	P B.Smith	P G.Jones	RP B.Wight
	P T.Acker	P D.McDevitt	P H.Robinson	P B.Miller	/P B.Daniels	P R.Crone	
	A.Kellner	P E.Roebuck	P E.Johnson	P J.Gray	G.Perez	P D.Johnson	P L.McDaniel
P J.Briggs	P J.Klippstein	P B.Birrer	/P D.Littlefield	/P W.Hacker	/P D.Williams	/P C.Barclay	P S.Maglie
P B.Anderson	/P C.Rabe	P D.Newcombe		/P J.Anderson	/P E.O'Brien	/P P.Burnside	P C.Stobbs
/P J.Brosnan	/P O.Pena	/P R.Craig		/P D.Erickson		/P J.Constable	P N.Chittum
P M.Solis	P T.Lown	/P B.Giallombardo		/P B.Conley		/P D.Zanni	P M.Martin
P D.Nichols	/P H.Freeman	/P D.Bessent		/P J.Owens		/P J.Fitzgerald	/P F.Barnes
P G.Fodge	/P J.O'Toole	/P R.Mauriello		/P H.Mason		/P J.Shipley	/P Bi.Smith
/P J.Buzhardt	/P B.Wight	/P R.Negray		/P A.LiPetri			P P.Clark
P E.Mayer	/P L.Hayden	/P L.Sherry		/P T.Qualters			H H.Wehmeier
/P H.Freeman	/P J.Hook	/P J.Collum					V.McDaniel
/P F.Rodriguez	/P B.Kelly						/P T.Flanigan
/P E.Singleton	/P T.Wieand						
/P T.Lown							
/P D.Ellsworth							

TEAM	G	W	L	PCT	GB	R	OR	AB	H	2B	3B	HR	BB	SO	AVG	OBP	SLG	PRO	PRO+	BR	/A	PF	CHI	RC	SB	CS	SBA	SBR
MIL	154	92	62	.597		675	**541**	5225	1388	221	21	167	478	646	**.266**	.331	.412	.743	111	14	**72**	92	98	705	26	8	**76**	**3**
PIT	154	84	70	.545	8	662	607	5247	1386	229	**68**	134	396	753	.264	.319	.410	.729	101	-21	-4	97	103	669	30	15	67	0
SF	154	80	74	.519	12	**727**	698	5318	1399	**250**	42	170	531	817	.263	.334	.422	.756	107	37	54	98	100	**747**	64	29	69	2
CIN	154	76	78	.494	16	695	621	5273	1399	242	40	123	572	765	.258	.333	.389	.722	92	-19	-54	105	104	690	61	38	62	-5
STL	154	72	82	.468	20	619	704	5255	1371	216	39	111	533	**637**	.261	.331	.380	.711	90	-38	-63	104	97	638	44	43	51	-13
CHI	154	72	82	.468	20	709	725	5289	1402	207	49	**182**	487	853	.265	.332	**.426**	**.758**	108	**39**	50	98	99	737	39	23	63	-2
LA	154	71	83	.461	21	668	761	5173	1366	166	50	172	495	850	.251	.319	.402	.721	93	-32	-52	103	**106**	650	73	47	61	-6
PHI	154	69	85	.448	23	664	762	5363	**1424**	238	56	124	573	871	**.266**	**.341**	.400	.741	103	20	30	99	93	729	51	33	61	-5
TOT	616					5419		42143	11026	1769	365	1183	4065	6192	.262	.330	.405	.735							388	236	62	-25

TEAM	CG	SH	SV	IP	H	H/G	HR	BB	SO	RAT	ERA	ERA+	OAV	OOB	PR	/A	PF	CPI	FA	E	DP	FW	PW	BW	SBW	DIF
MIL	**72**	**16**	17	1376	**1261**	8.2	125	426	773	**11.2**	3.21	110	**.244**	.305	113	47	89	99	.980	120	152	.8	4.7	7.3	.6	1.5
PIT	43	10	**41**	1367	1344	8.8	**123**	470	679	12.1	3.56	109	.261	.325	59	46	98	105	.978	133	173	.1	4.6	-.4	.3	2.3
SF	38	7	25	1389[1]	1400	9.1	166	512	775	12.6	3.98	96	.263	.332	-4	-25	97	103	.975	152	156	-.9	-2.5	5.4	.5	.5
CIN	50	7	20	1385[1]	1422	9.2	148	**419**	705	12.1	3.73	111	.267	.324	34	**64**	105	**105**	**.983**	**100**	148	**1.9**	**6.5**	-5.4	-.2	-3.7
STL	45	6	25	1381[2]	1398	9.1	158	567	822	13.1	4.12	100	.264	.340	-25	2	105	102	.974	153	163	-.9	.2	-6.4	-1.0	3.1
CHI	27	5	24	1361	1322	8.7	146	619	805	13.1	4.22	93	.254	.338	-40	-46	99	94	.975	150	161	-.8	-4.6	5.0	.1	-4.7
LA	30	7	31	1368[1]	1399	9.2	173	606	**855**	13.4	4.47	92	.267	.347	-79	-57	104	100	.975	146	**198**	-.6	-5.5	-5.2	-.3	5.9
PHI	51	6	15	1397	1480	9.5	148	446	778	12.5	4.32	92	.272	.329	-58	-56	100	93	.978	129	136	.3	-5.6	3.0	-.2	-5.5
TOT	356	64	198	11025[2]		9.0				12.5	3.95		.262	.330					.977	1083	1287					

Runs		Hits		Doubles		Triples		Home Runs		Total Bases	
Mays-SF	121	Ashburn-Phi	215	Cepeda-SF	38	Ashburn-Phi	13	Banks-Chi	47	Banks-Chi	379
Banks-Chi	119	Mays-SF	208	Groat-Pit	36	Virdon-Pit	11	Thomas-Pit	35	Mays-SF	350
Aaron-Mil	109	Aaron-Mil	196	Musial-StL	35	Mays-SF	11	Robinson-Cin	31	Aaron-Mil	328
Boyer-StL	101	Banks-Chi	193	H.Anderson-Phi	34	Banks-Chi	11	Mathews-Mil	31	Cepeda-SF	309
Ashburn-Phi	98	Cepeda-SF	188	Aaron-Mil	34			Aaron-Mil	30	Thomas-Pit	297

Runs Batted In		Runs Produced		Bases On Balls		Batting Average		On Base Percentage		Slugging Average	
Banks-Chi	129	Banks-Chi	201	Ashburn-Phi	97	Ashburn-Phi	.350	Ashburn-Phi	.441	Banks-Chi	.614
Thomas-Pit	109	Mays-SF	188	Temple-Cin	91	Mays-SF	.347	Musial-StL	.426	Mays-SF	.583
H.Anderson-Phi	97	Aaron-Mil	174	Mathews-Mil	85	Musial-StL	.337	Mays-SF	.423	Aaron-Mil	.546
Mays-SF	96	Boyer-StL	168	Cunningham-StL	82	Aaron-Mil	.326	Temple-Cin	.406	Thomas-Pit	.528
Cepeda-SF	96	Thomas-Pit	163			Skinner-Pit	.321	Skinner-Pit	.390	Musial-StL	.528

Production		Adjusted Production		Batter Runs		Adjusted Batter Runs		Clutch Hitting Index		Runs Created	
Mays-SF	1.006	Mays-SF	167	Mays-SF	55.3	Mays-SF	58.4	H.Anderson-Phi	111	Mays-SF	152
Banks-Chi	.984	Banks-Chi	157	Banks-Chi	45.7	Banks-Chi	47.7	Fernandez-Phi	110	Banks-Chi	135
Musial-StL	.953	Aaron-Mil	157	Aaron-Mil	37.0	Aaron-Mil	46.9	Long-Chi	103	Ashburn-Phi	129
Aaron-Mil	.933	Musial-StL	145	Musial-StL	36.7	Ashburn-Phi	38.2	Spencer-SF	103	Aaron-Mil	121
H.Anderson-Phi	.900	H.Anderson-Phi	137	Ashburn-Phi	36.5	Musial-StL	32.8	Banks-Chi	103	Skinner-Pit	102

Total Average		Stolen Bases		Stolen Base Average		Stolen Base Runs		Fielding Runs		Total Player Rating	
Mays-SF	1.110	Mays-SF	31	Mays-SF	83.8	Mays-SF	5.7	Zimmer-LA	32.6	Mays-SF	7.2
Banks-Chi	.984	Ashburn-Phi	30	Blasingame-StL	80.0	Zimmer-LA	3.0	Clemente-Pit	25.2	Banks-Chi	5.7
Musial-StL	.970	T.Taylor-Chi	21	T.Taylor-Chi	77.8	Blasingame-StL	3.0	Boyer-StL	23.4	Ashburn-Phi	5.3
Ashburn-Phi	.929	Blasingame-StL	20	Ashburn-Phi	71.4	T.Taylor-Chi	2.7	Ashburn-Phi	22.1	Aaron-Mil	4.1
Aaron-Mil	.916	Gilliam-LA	18	Gilliam-LA	62.1	Robinson-Cin	2.4	Flood-StL	19.3	Boyer-StL	4.0

Wins		Win Percentage		Games		Complete Games		Shutouts		Saves	
Spahn-Mil	22	Spahn-Mil	.667	Elston-Chi	69	Spahn-Mil	23	Willey-Mil	4	Face-Pit	20
Friend-Pit	22	Burdette-Mil	.667	Klippstein-Cin-LA	57	Roberts-Phi	21	Witt-Pit	3	Labine-LA	14
Burdette-Mil	20	Friend-Pit	.611	Face-Pit	57	Burdette-Mil	19	Purkey-Cin	3	Farrell-Phi	11
Roberts-Phi	17	Purkey-Cin	.607	Hobbie-Chi	55	Purkey-Cin	17	Jay-Mil	3		
Purkey-Cin	17	Antonelli-SF	.552			Friend-Pit	16	Burdette-Mil	3		

Innings Pitched		Fewest Hits/Game		Fewest BB/Game		Strikeouts		Strikeouts/Game		Ratio	
Spahn-Mil	290.0	Jones-StL	7.34	Burdette-Mil	1.63	Jones-StL	225	Jones-StL	8.10	Spahn-Mil	10.40
Burdette-Mil	275.1	Koufax-LA	7.49	Roberts-Phi	1.70	Spahn-Mil	150	Koufax-LA	7.43	Miller-SF	10.43
Friend-Pit	274.0	Miller-SF	7.91	Law-Pit	1.73	Podres-LA	143	Drott-Chi	6.83	Roberts-Phi	10.78
Roberts-Phi	269.2	Spahn-Mil	7.98	Purkey-Cin	1.76	Antonelli-SF	143	Podres-LA	6.12	Burdette-Mil	10.92
		Brosnan-Chi-StL	7.99	Newcombe-LA-Cin	1.93	Friend-Pit	135	Miller-SF	5.88	Purkey-Cin	11.23

Earned Run Average		Adjusted ERA		Opponents' Batting Avg.		Opponents' On Base Pct.		Starter Runs		Adjusted Starter Runs	
Miller-SF	2.47	Miller-SF	154	Koufax-LA	.220	Miller-SF	.286	Burdette-Mil	31.9	Jones-StL	34.7
Jones-StL	2.88	Jones-StL	143	Jones-StL	.223	Spahn-Mil	.288	Miller-SF	29.9	Miller-SF	27.1
Burdette-Mil	2.91	Roberts-Phi	122	Miller-SF	.233	Roberts-Phi	.294	Jones-StL	29.8	Witt-Pit	26.5
Spahn-Mil	3.07	Brosnan-Chi-StL	121	Spahn-Mil	.237	Burdette-Mil	.301	Spahn-Mil	28.3	Roberts-Phi	21.6
Roberts-Phi	3.24	Burdette-Mil	121	Antonelli-SF	.239	Purkey-Cin	.306	Witt-Pit	27.5	Burdette-Mil	18.7

Clutch Pitching Index		Relief Runs		Adjusted Relief Runs		Relief Ranking		Total Pitcher Index		Total Baseball Ranking	
Haddix-Cin	116	Elston-Chi	11.6	Elston-Chi	11.2	Elston-Chi	20.3	Spahn-Mil	3.9	Mays-SF	7.2
Newcombe-LA-Cin	115	Face-Pit	9.9	Schmidt-Cin	9.9	Farrell-Phi	12.0	Burdette-Mil	3.1	Banks-Chi	5.7
Mizell-StL	114	Henry-Chi	9.7	Henry-Chi	9.4	Face-Pit	11.7	Jones-StL	2.9	Ashburn-Phi	5.3
Miller-SF	110	Schmidt-Cin	8.4	Face-Pit	9.1	Henry-Chi	10.9	Roberts-Phi	2.5	Aaron-Mil	4.1
Podres-LA	109	Porterfield-Pit	6.5	Farrell-Phi	6.4	Schmidt-Cin	10.3	Witt-Pit	2.5	Boyer-StL	4.0

January 15 In a deal worth over a million dollars, the Yankees announce that they will televise 140 games in the 1958 season. Six days later, the Phillies agree to televise 78 games into the New York City area.

January 30 Commissioner Ford Frick announces that players and coaches, rather than the fans, will vote for the All-Star teams this year.

February 6 Ted Williams signs with the Red Sox for $135,000, making him the highest paid player in major league history.

March 11 Starting this season, AL batters will be required to wear batting helmets.

April 23 In an ongoing dispute, a Chicago Court orders Mrs. Dorothy Comiskey Rigney to distribute stock from her mother's estate, so she can not effectively bar her brother Charles A. Comiskey from sitting on the White Sox Board.

April 30 Ted Williams becomes the tenth major league player to get 1,000 extra-base hits.

June 2 Brooks Robinson, in a 2-1 Orioles loss to the Washington Senators, hits into the first of his record four triple plays.

July 8 The AL edges the NL, 4–3, in the All-Star Game played at Baltimore's Memorial Stadium. The Yankees' Gil McDougald singles to score Boston's Frank Malzone with the deciding run. Billy O'Dell of Baltimore pitches perfect ball for three innings and gets the save in the first All-Star Game played without an extra-base hit.

August 27 Owner Clark Griffith says that the Senators will probably accept a good offer from Minneapolis/St. Paul, if one is made. President Dwight D. Eisenhower says that the Senators should improve the team and stay in Washington, D.C.

August 28 White Sox second baseman Nellie Fox sets a record for consecutive games without striking out (98).

September 14 The Yankees win their 24th pennant, and ninth under Casey Stengel. This ties Casey for first with Connie Mack for the most AL pennants won.

September 20 Orioles pitcher Hoyt Wilhelm, in a rare start, pitches a 1–0 no-hitter, the first in O's history, against Don Larsen of the Yankees. The Orioles acquired Wilhelm in August for the $20,000 waiver price. The win, Wilhelm's first major league complete game, improves his record to 3-10. The winning margin is Gus Triandos's 30th home run.

October 8 The Yankees win the World Series on Moose Skowron's three-run homer off Lew Burdette in the eighth that puts the game on ice 6-2.

November 12 The Yankees' Bob Turley wins the Cy Young Award, gathering five votes to four for last year's winner, Warren Spahn.

November 26 The AL MVP is Boston slugger Jackie Jensen, winning over New York's Bob Turley and Cleveland's Rocky Colavito.

BALTIMORE	BOSTON	CHICAGO	CLEVELAND	DETROIT	KANSAS CITY	NEW YORK	WASHINGTON
M P.Richards	M P.Higgins	M A.Lopez	M B.Bragan	M J.Tighe	M H.Craft	M C.Stengel	M C.Lavagetto
1B B.Boyd	1B D.Gernert	1B E.Torgeson	M J.Gordon	M B.Norman	1B V.Power	1B B.Skowron	1B N.Zauchin
2B B.Gardner	2B P.Runnels	2B N.Fox	1B M.Vernon	1B G.Harris	2B M.Baxes	2B G.McDougald	2B K.Aspromonte
SS W.Miranda	SS D.Buddin	SS L.Aparicio	2B B.Avila	2B F.Bolling	SS J.DeMaestri	SS T.Kubek	SS R.Bridges
3B B.Robinson	3B F.Malzone	3B B.Goodman	SS B.Hunter	SS B.Martin	3B H.Lopez	3B A.Carey	3B E.Yost
LF G.Woodling	LF T.Williams	LF J.Rivera	3B B.Harrell	3B R.Bertoia	LF B.Cerv	LF N.Siebern	LF R.Sievers
CF J.Busby	CF J.Piersall	CF J.Landis	LF M.Minoso	LF C.Maxwell	CF B.Tuttle	CF M.Mantle	CF A.Pearson
RF A.Pilarcik	RF J.Jensen	RF A.Smith	CF L.Doby	CF H.Kuenn	RF R.Maris	RF H.Bauer	RF J.Lemon
C G.Triandos	C S.White	C S.Lollar	RF R.Colavito	RF A.Kaline	C H.Chiti	C Y.Berra	C C.Courtney
			C R.Nixon	C R.Wilson			
S F.Castleman	O G.Stephens	3S S.Esposito	2S B.Moran	S C.Veal	O B.Martyn	CO E.Howard	O N.Chrisley
O B.Nieman	O L.Berberet	1 R.Boone	31 V.Power	3 O.Virgil	3C H.Smith	3 J.Lumpe	23 H.Plews
O3 D.Williams	2 T.Lepcio	C E.Battey	O G.Geiger	O J.Groth	13 P.Ward	23 B.Richardson	S2 O.Alvarez
1 J.Marshall	O M.Keough	O D.Mueller	O R.Maris	C J.Hegan	1O H.Simpson	1 M.Throneberry	1 J.Becquer
C J.Ginsberg	S B.Klaus	1 R.Jackson	C D.Brown	O G.Zernial	C F.House	C E.Slaughter	C E.FitzGerald
O L.Green	2S B.Consolo	31 J.Callison	S3 C.Carrasquel	O R.Boone	3S C.Carrasquel	O H.Simpson	O F.Throneberry
O J.Taylor	C P.Daley	OS W.Dropo	1 R.Boone	O T.Francona	O W.Held	/C D.Johnson	2 B.Malkmus
O W.Tasby	O B.Renna	/O J.McAnany	31 W.Ward	C C.Lau	O1 W.Herzog	O B.DelGreco	S K.Korcheck
/1 B.Hale	/2 K.Aspromonte	/O N.Cash	OS W.Held	/1 K.Hadley	S B.Hunter	/2 F.Brickell	O B.Allison
S J.Adair		/C J.Romano	3 R.Jackson	/O L.Skizas	/2 L.Klimchock		/3 H.Killebrew
S R.Hansen	P T.Brewer	O C.Lindstrom	O J.Porter	S M.Bolling	/O D.Melton	P B.Turley	/2 J.Schaive
/O C.Oertel	P F.Sullivan	H L.Moss	S E.Averill	/O B.Taylor	/O J.Small	P W.Ford	/2 J.Snyder
/O L.Burke	P I.Delock		3 C.Hardy	/C T.Thompson	/2 M.Graff	P A.Ditmar	/C L.Berberet
H B.Hamric	P D.Sisler		/1 V.Wertz	/O G.Alusik		P B.Shantz	/O W.Herzog
/S E.Miksis	P M.Fornieles		/O H.Naragon	/2 S.Boros	P R.Terry	P J.Kucks	
/C F.Zupo	RP M.Wall	P D.Donovan	/2 L.Raines	H B.Osborne	P N.Garver	RP R.Duren	P P.Ramos
	RP L.Kiely	P B.Pierce	/O R.Graber	P R.Herbert	P J.Urban	RP Z.Monroe	P R.Kemmerer
P J.Harshman	P B.Smith	P E.Wynn	/C J.Feller	P J.Urban	P B.Grim	P D.Larsen	P C.Pascual
P B.O'Dell	P T.Bowsfield	P J.Wilson	/O G.Thomas	P F.Lary	RP T.Gorman	P D.Maas	P H.Griggs
P A.Portocarrero	P B.Monbouquette	P R.Moore	P C.McLish	RP P.Foytack	RP D.Tomanek	P T.Sturdivant	P V.Valentinetti
P M.Pappas	P F.Baumann	RP G.Staley	P M.Grant	P J.Bunning	RP B.Daley	P V.Trucks	RP T.Clevenger
P C.Johnson	P W.Nixon	RP B.Shaw	P R.Narleski	RP P.Foytack	P M.Dickson	P S.Maglie	RP D.Hyde
RP G.Zuverink	P B.Byerly		P G.Bell	RP J.Bunning	P D.Maas	/P M.Dickson	/P M.Dickson
RP K.Lehman	/P A.Schroll	P B.Latman	P D.Ferrarese	P B.Hoeft	P W.Craddock	P B.Grim	P C.Stobbs
RP C.Beamon	/P D.Wilson	P T.Qualters	RP D.Mossi	P H.Moford	/P A.Kellner	/P J.James	/P J.Romonosky
P B.Loes	/P B.Porterfield	P T.Lown	RP H.Aguirre	RP T.Morgan	/P B.Davis		/P A.Cicotte
P H.Brown	/P J.Casale	P B.Fischer	RP T.Morgan		/P W.Burnette		P J.Constable
/P H.Wilhelm	/P G.Susce	P D.Rudolph	P H.Wilhelm	P G.Susce	/P V.Trucks		/P B.Byerly
/P J.Walker		P S.McIlwain	P H.Woodeshick	P A.Cicotte	/P H.Reed		/P B.Fischer
/P L.Sleater		/P H.Trosky	P D.Tomanek	P B.Fischer	/P G.Cox		/P R.Lumenti
/P R.Moeller		/P D.Howell	P H.Score	P B.Shaw	/P J.Tsitouris		/P B.Wiesler
		/P J.McDonald	P B.Kelly	/P H.Wehmeier	/P C.Duser		/P J.Spring
			P B.Lemon	/P V.Valentinetti	/P K.Johnson		/P J.Albanese
			P M.Martin	/P J.Presko			
			/P D.Brodowski	/P G.Spencer			
			/P C.Churn	/P L.Sleater			
			/P J.Constable	/P D.Lee			
			/P S.Ridzik	/P M.McDermott			
			/P M.Garcia				

TEAM	G	W	L	PCT	GB	R	OR	AB	H	2B	3B	HR	BB	SO	AVG	OBP	SLG	PRO	PRO+	BR	/A	PF	CHI	RC	SB	CS	SBA	SBR
NY	155	92	62	.597		759	577	5294	1418	212	39	164	537	822	.268	.338	.416	.754	117	88	115	96	102	746	48	32	60	-5
CHI	155	82	72	.532	10	634	615	5249	1348	191	42	101	518	669	.257	.329	.367	.696	99	-13	0	98	99	647	101	33	75	11
BOS	155	79	75	.513	13	697	691	5218	1335	229	30	155	638	820	.256	.340	.400	.740	102	70	21	107	96	708	29	22	57	-5
CLE	153	77	76	.503	14.5	694	635	5201	1340	210	31	161	494	819	.258	.327	.403	.730	109	38	55	98	102	677	50	49	51	-14
DET	154	77	77	.500	15	659	606	5194	1384	229	41	109	463	678	.266	.329	.389	.718	96	20	-28	107	100	657	48	32	60	-5
BAL	154	74	79	.484	17.5	521	575	5111	1233	195	19	108	483	731	.241	.310	.350	.660	92	-85	-56	95	96	546	33	35	49	-11
KC	156	73	81	.474	19	642	713	5261	1297	196	50	138	452	747	.247	.309	.381	.690	93	-40	-51	102	106	601	22	36	38	-15
WAS	156	61	93	.396	31	553	747	5156	1240	161	38	121	477	751	.240	.309	.357	.666	91	-78	-67	99	99	555	22	41	35	-18
TOT	619					5159		41684	10595	1623	290	1057	4062	6037	.254	.324	.383	.707							353	280	56	-62

TEAM	CG	SH	SV	IP	H	H/G	HR	BB	SO	RAT	ERA	ERA+	OAV	OOB	PR	/A	PF	CPI	FA	E	DP	FW	PW	BW	SBW	DIF
NY	53	21	33	1379	1201	7.8	116	557	796	11.8	3.22	110	.235	.315	85	48	94	103	.978	128	182	-.1	5.0	11.9	.3	-2.0
CHI	55	15	25	1389²	1296	8.4	152	515	751	11.8	3.61	101	.250	.320	25	5	97	104	.981	114	160	.7	.5	.0	1.9	1.9
BOS	44	5	28	1380	1396	9.1	121	521	695	12.7	3.92	102	.264	.334	-23	13	106	101	.976	145	172	-1.1	1.3	2.2	.3	-.7
CLE	51	2	20	1373¹	1283	8.4	123	604	766	12.5	3.73	98	.249	.331	6	-12	97	101	.974	152	171	-1.5	-1.2	5.7	-.6	-1.8
DET	59	8	19	1357¹	1294	8.6	133	437	797	11.6	3.59	112	.252	.316	26	67	107	101	.982	106	140	1.1	6.9	-2.9	.3	-5.4
BAL	55	15	28	1369²	1277	8.4	106	403	749	11.3	3.40	106	.249	.308	57	30	95	97	.980	114	159	.6	3.1	-5.8	-.3	-.1
KC	42	9	25	1398¹	1405	9.0	150	467	721	12.2	4.15	94	.262	.324	-59	-38	104	95	.979	125	166	.1	-3.9	-5.3	-.7	5.8
WAS	28	6	28	1376²	1443	9.4	156	558	762	13.3	4.53	84	.272	.344	-116	-110	101	98	.980	118	163	.5	-11.4	-6.9	-1.1	2.9
TOT	387	81	206	11024		8.6				12.2	3.77		.254	.324					.979	1002	1313					

Runs
Mantle-NY 127
Runnels-Bos 103
Power-KC-Cle 98
Minoso-Cle 94
Cerv-KC 93

Hits
Fox-Chi 187
Malzone-Bos 185
Power-KC-Cle 184
Runnels-Bos 183
Kuenn-Det 179

Doubles
Kuenn-Det 39
Power-KC-Cle 37
Kaline-Det 34
Runnels-Bos 32
Jensen-Bos 31

Triples
Power-KC-Cle 10
Tuttle-KC 9
Lemon-Was 9
Aparicio-Chi 9
Harris-Det 8

Home Runs
Mantle-NY 42
Colavito-Cle 41
Sievers-Was 39
Cerv-KC 38
Jensen-Bos 35

Total Bases
Mantle-NY 307
Cerv-KC 305
Colavito-Cle 303
Sievers-Was 299
Jensen-Bos 293

Runs Batted In
Jensen-Bos 122
Colavito-Cle 113
Sievers-Was 108
Cerv-KC 104
Mantle-NY 97

Runs Produced
Mantle-NY 182
Jensen-Bos 170
Power-KC-Cle 162
Cerv-KC 159

Bases On Balls
Mantle-NY 129
Jensen-Bos 99
Williams-Bos 98
Runnels-Bos 87
Colavito-Cle 84

Batting Average
Williams-Bos ..... .328
Runnels-Bos ...... .322
Kuenn-Det .... .319
Kaline-Det .... .313
Power-KC-Cle ..... .312

On Base Percentage
Williams-Bos ..... .462
Mantle-NY .... .445
Runnels-Bos ...... .418
Colavito-Cle ..... .407
Jensen-Bos .... .398

Slugging Average
Colavito-Cle ..... .620
Cerv-KC .... .592
Mantle-NY .... .592
Williams-Bos ..... .584
Sievers-Was ...... .544

Production
Williams-Bos 1.046
Mantle-NY 1.036
Colavito-Cle 1.027
Cerv-KC .... .964
Jensen-Bos .... .933

Adjusted Production
Mantle-NY 189
Colavito-Cle 183
Williams-Bos 174
Cerv-KC 158
Sievers-Was 148

Batter Runs
Mantle-NY 64.2
Williams-Bos 53.6
Colavito-Cle 52.8
Jensen-Bos 42.7
Cerv-KC 40.7

Adjusted Batter Runs
Mantle-NY 69.2
Colavito-Cle 55.7
Williams-Bos 46.3
Cerv-KC 38.8
Jensen-Bos 35.0

Clutch Hitting Index
Courtney-Was 131
Lollar-Chi 127
F.Bolling-Det 117
Harris-Det 116
Skowron-NY 116

Runs Created
Mantle-NY 147
Colavito-Cle 122
Jensen-Bos 120
Williams-Bos 112
Runnels-Bos 107

Total Average
Mantle-NY 1.208
Williams-Bos 1.163
Colavito-Cle 1.078
Jensen-Bos .... .980
Cerv-KC .... .947

Stolen Bases
Aparicio-Chi 29
Rivera-Chi 21
Landis-Chi 19
Mantle-NY 18
Minoso-Cle 14

Stolen Base Average
Rivera-Chi 87.5
Mantle-NY 85.7
Aparicio-Chi 82.9
Landis-Chi 73.1

Stolen Base Runs
Aparicio-Chi 5.1
Rivera-Chi 4.5
Mantle-NY 3.6
Wilson-Det 3.0

Fielding Runs
Kaline-Det 23.0
Kubek-NY 20.0
Cerv-KC 20.0
Malzone-Bos 16.6
Kuenn-Det 15.1

Total Player Rating
Mantle-NY 6.5
Cerv-KC 5.1
Colavito-Cle 5.0
Runnels-Bos 3.8
Kaline-Det 3.6

Wins
Turley-NY 21
Pierce-Chi 17
McLish-Cle 16
Lary-Det 16

Win Percentage
Turley-NY .... .750
McLish-Cle .... .667
Pierce-Chi .... .607
Portocarrero-Bal . .577
Foytack-Det ...... .536

Games
Clevenger-Was 55
Tomanek-Cle-KC ... 54
Hyde-Was 53
Wall-Bos 52

Complete Games
Turley-NY 19
Pierce-Chi 19
Lary-Det 19
Harshman-Bal 17

Shutouts
Ford-NY 7
Turley-NY 6
Wynn-Chi 4
Ramos-Was 4
Donovan-Chi 4

Saves
Duren-NY 20
Hyde-Was 18
Kiely-Bos 12
Wall-Bos 10

Innings Pitched
Lary-Det 260.1
Ramos-Was 259.1
Donovan-Chi 248.0
Turley-NY 245.1
Pierce-Chi 245.0

Fewest Hits/Game
Turley-NY 6.53
Bell-Cle 6.97
Ford-NY 7.14
Pierce-Chi 7.49
Portocarrero-Bal . 7.61

Fewest BB/Game
Donovan-Chi 1.92
O'Dell-Bal 2.07
Sullivan-Bos 2.21
Lary-Det 2.35
Pierce-Chi 2.42

Strikeouts
Wynn-Chi 179
Bunning-Det 177
Turley-NY 168
Harshman-Bal 161
Pascual-Was 146

Strikeouts/Game
Pascual-Was 7.41
Bunning-Det 7.25
Wynn-Chi 6.72
Turley-NY 6.16
Harshman-Bal 6.13

Ratio
Ford-NY 9.81
Pierce-Chi 9.96
Portocarrero-Bal . 10.25
O'Dell-Bal 10.41
Harshman-Bal 10.74

Earned Run Average
Ford-NY 2.01
Pierce-Chi 2.68
Harshman-Bal 2.89
Lary-Det 2.90
O'Dell-Bal 2.97

Adjusted ERA
Ford-NY 176
Lary-Det 139
Pierce-Chi 136
Harshman-Bal 124
McLish-Cle 122

Opponents' Batting Avg.
Turley-NY .... .206
Bell-Cle .... .213
Ford-NY .... .217
Pierce-Chi .... .227
Grant-Cle .... .228

Opponents' On Base Pct.
Ford-NY .... .276
Pierce-Chi .... .280
Portocarrero-Bal . .286
O'Dell-Bal .... .288
Harshman-Bal ..... .294

Starter Runs
Ford-NY 42.9
Pierce-Chi 29.6
Lary-Det 25.0
Harshman-Bal 23.0
Turley-NY 21.7

Adjusted Starter Runs
Ford-NY 37.1
Lary-Det 32.8
Pierce-Chi 26.0
Wilhelm-Cle-Bal .. 18.9
Harshman-Bal 18.4

Clutch Pitching Index
McLish-Cle 120
Ford-NY 117
Pierce-Chi 114
Lary-Det 113
Wilson-Chi 110

Relief Runs
Hyde-Was 23.1
Duren-NY 14.7
Kiely-Bos 6.9
Staley-Chi 5.7
Morgan-Det 4.2

Adjusted Relief Runs
Hyde-Was 23.7
Duren-NY 12.7
Kiely-Bos 9.1
Morgan-Det 6.1
Wall-Bos 4.9

Relief Ranking
Hyde-Was 36.2
Duren-NY 22.6
Kiely-Bos 10.1
Wall-Bos 7.5
Morgan-Det 6.4

Total Pitcher Index
Ford-NY 3.9
Hyde-Was 3.9
Lary-Det 3.6
Harshman-Bal 3.4
Pierce-Chi 2.8

Total Baseball Ranking
Mantle-NY 6.5
Cerv-KC 5.1
Colavito-Cle 5.0
Ford-NY 3.9
Hyde-Was 3.9

February 1 Slugging Dodgers outfielder Zack Wheat is unanimously elected to the Hall of Fame by the 11-member veterans committee.

May 7 The Los Angeles Coliseum is jammed by 93,103 on "Roy Campanella Night" for an exhibition game between the Dodgers and the New York Yankees. This is the largest crowd to see a game featuring major leagues.

May 26 In a singular performance, Harvey Haddix of the Pirates pitches a perfect game against Milwaukee for 12 innings, only to lose in the 13th. Felix Mantilla opens the last inning by reaching base on an error. A sacrifice and an intentional walk to Hank Aaron bring up Joe Adcock, who hits one out of the park in right-center field for an apparent 3-0 victory. Aaron pulls a "Merkle," leaving the field, and Adcock passes him on the basepaths. Both are called out as Mantilla scores. Lew Burdette goes all the way for his eighth win, scattering 12 hits.

June 30 In Chicago, two balls are in play at the same time. On a wild pitch from Bob Anderson, Stan Musial draws a walk. As the pitch gets by catcher Sammy Taylor, Musial tries for second base. In what can only be described as a reflex action, umpire Vic Delmore puts another ball in play by mistake. Taylor promptly throws the ball into center field. Third baseman Alvin Dark, who chased down the original ball, throws to shortstop Ernie Banks, who tags out a confused Musial. After a 10-minute conference, the umpires agree that Musial is out. Delmore will be fired because of the boner.

July 7 The NL defeats the AL, 5–4, in the All-Star Game at Forbes Field in Pittsburgh. Willie Mays knocks in Henry Aaron with the deciding run. Don Drysdale pitches perfect ball the first three innings.

July 30 In his major league debut, Willie McCovey goes 4-for-4 with two triples off Robin Roberts to lead the Giants to a 7-2 win over the Phils. McCovey was hitting .372 with 29 home runs at Phoenix when promoted.

August 18 Branch Rickey resigns as chairman of the Pirates to become president of the Continental League, which never plays a game.

August 31 Sandy Koufax breaks Dizzy Dean's NL mark and ties Bob Feller's major league record of 18 strikeouts in a game against the Giants as 82,974 fans watch.

September 27 The Braves and Dodgers finish in a tie (86-68), with the Giants a close third (83-71).

September 29 The Dodgers win Game two of the playoff 6-5, and take the NL pennant. Los Angeles overcomes a 5-2, ninth-inning deficit to tie the game; they win it in the 12th when Gil Hodges scores from second on Felix Mantilla's off-balance heave past first on a difficult chance on Carl Furillo's grounder.

October 8 The Los Angeles Dodgers win 9-3 to take the Series in Chicago, again behind Larry Sherry, in relief of Johnny Podres. Each Dodger receives a record $11,231 winning share. The White Sox get a record $7,275 for losing.

November 4 "Mr. Cub" Ernie Banks wins his second MVP award in a row on the strength of his 45 home runs and 143 RBIs. Eddie Mathews finishes second.

November 17 Giants slugger Willie McCovey is the NL Rookie of the Year. McCovey gets all 24 votes to make him the second Giant in a row to win the award unanimously.

CHICAGO	CINCINNATI	LOS ANGELES	MILWAUKEE	PHILADELPHIA	PITTSBURGH	SAN FRANCISCO	ST.LOUIS
M B.Scheffing	M M.Smith	M W.Alston	M F.Haney	M E.Sawyer	M D.Murtaugh	M B.Rigney	M S.Hemus
1B D.Long	M F.Hutchinson	1B G.Hodges	1B J.Adcock	1B E.Bouchee	1B D.Stuart	1B O.Cepeda	1B S.Musial
2B T.Taylor	1B F.Robinson	2B C.Neal	2B F.Mantilla	2B S.Anderson	2B B.Mazeroski	2B D.Spencer	2B D.Blasingame
SS E.Banks	2B J.Temple	SS D.Zimmer	SS J.Logan	SS J.Koppe	SS D.Groat	SS E.Bressoud	SS A.Grammas
3B A.Dark	SS E.Kasko	3B J.Gilliam	3B E.Mathews	3B G.Freese	3B D.Hoak	3B J.Davenport	3B K.Boyer
LF B.Thomson	3B W.Jones	LF W.Moon	LF W.Covington	LF H.Anderson	LF B.Skinner	LF J.Brandt	LF G.Cimoli
CF G.Altman	LF J.Lynch	CF D.Demeter	CF B.Bruton	CF R.Ashburn	CF B.Virdon	CF W.Mays	CF C.Flood
RF L.Walls	CF V.Pinson	RF D.Snider	RF H.Aaron	RF W.Post	RF R.Clemente	RF W.Kirkland	RF J.Cunningham
C S.Taylor	RF G.Bell	C J.Roseboro	C D.Crandall	C C.Sawatski	C S.Burgess	C H.Landrith	C H.Smith
	C E.Bailey						
1 J.Marshall		O R.Fairly	1 F.Torre	O1 D.Philley	O R.Mejias	O F.Alou	O1 B.White
O W.Moryn	3O F.Thomas	1O N.Larker	2 B.Avila	3 W.Jones	1 R.Nelson	S A.Rodgers	O G.Oliver
C3 E.Averill	S R.McMillan	S M.Wills	O A.Pafko	C V.Thomas	C D.Kravitz	1 W.McCovey	1 G.Crowe
O I.Noren	C D.Dotterer	O J.Pignatano	S L.Maye	S C.Fernandez	1 D.Schofield	S2 B.Schmidt	S2 W.Shannon
1O A.Schult	O3 J.Pendleton	O R.Repulski	2 J.O'Brien	1 H.Hanebrink	T.Kluzewski	O L.Wagner	3 R.Jablonski
C C.Neeman	1 W.Lockman	1 C.Furillo	1 M.Vernon	C J.Lonnett	C H.Foiles	3 D.O'Connell	OC G.Green
3 R.Jackson	O P.Whisenant	3 D.Gray	2 C.Wise	O B.Bowman	/O H.Bright	H D.Rhodes	O BG.Smith
2 J.Goryl	/O J.Powers	O B.Lillis	S S.Lopata	S G.Hamner	3 H.Simpson	3 J.Pagan	S D.Gray
O B.Williams	1 W.Dropo	O C.Essegian	/2 M.Roach	S S.Drake	C J.Christopher	C J.Hegan	S L.Tate
H L.Jackson	/3 C.Cook	3 J.Baxes	/C D.Rice	C J.Hegan	/S K.Hamlin	/O H.Sauer	/O C.Essegian
/O C.King	/O B.Gilbert	/O F.Howard	2 C.Cottier	/O J.Bolger	/1 R.Stevens	H B.Speake	C J.Porter
/1 B.Adams	/O D.Ennis	/O S.Drake	J.Pisoni	H J.Easton	/C H.Peterson	/C R.McCardell	C R.Katt
/3 D.Eaddy	H B.Thurman	H S.Amoros	/2 J.Morgan				/C T.McCarver
	/S B.Henrich	H N.Sherry	/O E.Slaughter	P R.Roberts	P V.Law	P J.Antonelli	O D.Carmel
P B.Anderson	R D.Pavletich	H T.Davis	/1 R.Boone	P J.Owens	P B.Friend	P S.Jones	/2 S.Hemus
P G.Hobbie			/O A.Spangler	P G.Conley	P H.Haddix	P M.McCormick	/O I.Noren
P D.Hillman	P D.Newcombe	P D.Drysdale	/O J.DeMerit	P D.Cardwell	P R.Kline	P J.Sanford	/O C.King
P M.Drabowsky	P B.Purkey	P J.Podres	/2 R.Schoendienst	P R.Semproch	RP B.Daniels	RP S.Miller	/O J.Durham
P A.Ceccarelli	P J.Nuxhall	P S.Koufax		RP J.Meyer	RP R.Face	RP A.Worthington	H C.O'Rourke
RP B.Henry	P J.O'Toole	P R.Craig	P W.Spahn	RP H.Robinson			
RP D.Elston	RP O.Pena	P D.McDevitt	P L.Burdette	RP T.Phillips	P G.Witt	P G.Jones	P L.Jackson
	RP B.Lawrence	RP C.Labine	P B.Buhl		P R.Blackburn	P E.Fisher	P V.Mizell
P J.Buzhardt	RP W.Schmidt	RP A.Fowler	P J.Jay	P R.Gomez	/P B.Porterfield	P J.Shipley	P E.Broglio
P E.Singleton			P J.Pizarro	P T.Farrell	P F.Green	P B.Byerly	P G.Blaylock
/P D.Drott	P J.Brosnan	P S.Williams	RP D.McMahon	/P C.Short	P D.Gross	/P D.Zanni	RP L.McDaniel
P S.Morehead	P J.Hook	P L.Sherry		/P J.Hearn	/P B.Smith	/P B.Muffett	RP M.Bridges
/P B.Johnson	P T.Acker	P J.Klippstein	P C.Willey	/P S.Morehead	/P A.Jackson	/P M.Renfroe	
/P T.Phillips	P B.Mabe	P C.Churn	P B.Rush	/P C.Simmons	/P D.Williams	/P C.Barclay	P B.Gibson
/P E.Donnelly	P H.Jeffcoat	P G.Snyder	P B.Trowbridge	/P E.Keegan	/P D.Hall		P B.Miller
/P J.Schaffernoth	P L.Arroyo	P C.Erskine	P B.Giggie	/P A.Schroll	/P P.Giel		P D.Ricketts
/P B.Porterfield	/P J.Bailey	/P F.Kipp	/P B.Hartman	/P F.Rodriguez	/P J.Umbricht		P A.Kellner
/P M.Martin	/P C.Osteen	/P B.Harris					P J.Brosnan
/P B.Smith	/P D.Rudolph						P D.Stone
	/P M.Cuellar						P B.Duliba
							P H.Nunn
							P H.Jeffcoat
							P T.Cheney
							/P J.Urban
							/P B.Blaylock
							/P Bi.Smith
							/P P.Clark
							/P T.Hughes
							/P M.Grissom

TEAM	G	W	L	PCT	GB	R	OR	AB	H	2B	3B	HR	BB	SO	AVG	OBP	SLG	PRO	PRO+	BR	/A	PF	CHI	RC	SB	CS	SBA	SBR
LA	156	88	68	.564		705	670	5282	1360	196	46	148	591	891	.257	.335	.396	.731	94	17	-34	107	99	706	84	51	62	-5
MIL	157	86	70	.551	2	724	623	5388	1426	216	36	177	488	765	.265	.329	.417	.746	115	32	93	92	100	729	41	14	75	4
SF	154	83	71	.539	4	705	613	5281	1377	239	35	167	473	875	.261	.324	.414	.738	105	16	32	98	101	711	81	34	70	4
PIT	155	78	76	.506	9	651	680	5369	1414	230	42	112	442	715	.263	.322	.384	.706	95	-39	-33	99	101	653	32	26	55	-6
CIN	154	74	80	.481	13	764	738	5288	1448	258	34	161	499	763	.274	.340	.427	.767	108	76	54	103	101	764	65	28	70	3
CHI	155	74	80	.481	13	673	688	5296	1321	209	44	163	498	911	.249	.319	.398	.717	98	-23	-16	99	102	673	32	19	63	-2
STL	154	71	83	.461	16	641	725	5317	1432	244	49	118	485	747	.269	.333	.400	.733	96	14	-30	106	92	699	65	53	55	-12
PHI	155	64	90	.416	23	599	725	5109	1237	196	38	113	498	858	.242	.314	.362	.676	86	-92	-101	102	105	574	39	46	46	-16
TOT	620					5462		42330	11015	1788	324	1159	3974	6525	.260	.327	.400	.727							439	271	62	-31

TEAM	CG	SH	SV	IP	H	H/G	HR	BB	SO	RAT	ERA	ERA+	OAV	OOB	PR	/A	PF	CPI	FA	E	DP	FW	PW	BW	SBW	DIF
LA	43	14	26	1411²	1317	8.4	157	614	1077	12.6	3.79	111	.247	.331	24	68	107	103	.981	114	154	1.5	6.8	-3.4	-.1	5.2
MIL	69	18	18	1400²	1406	9.0	128	429	775	11.9	3.51	101	.260	.317	68	5	90	104	.979	127	138	.8	.5	9.4	.8	-3.4
SF	52	12	23	1376¹	1279	8.4	139	500	873	11.8	3.47	110	.246	.316	74	52	97	103	.974	152	118	-.8	5.2	3.2	.8	-2.5
PIT	48	7	17	1393¹	1432	9.2	134	418	730	12.1	3.90	99	.267	.323	7	-5	98	100	.975	154	165	-.8	-.5	-3.3	-.2	5.9
CIN	44	7	26	1357¹	1460	9.7	162	456	690	12.9	4.31	94	.275	.337	-55	-39	103	102	.978	126	157	.7	-3.9	5.4	.7	-5.9
CHI	30	11	25	1391	1337	8.7	152	519	765	12.2	4.01	98	.254	.323	-10	-10	100	96	.977	140	142	-.0	-1.0	-1.6	.2	-.5
STL	36	8	21	1363	1427	9.4	137	564	846	13.3	4.34	98	.271	.344	-59	-15	100	100	.975	146	158	-.4	-1.5	-3.0	-.8	-.2
PHI	54	8	15	1354	1357	9.0	150	474	769	12.4	4.27	96	.261	.326	-49	-25	104	93	.973	154	132	-.8	-2.5	-10.2	-1.2	1.7
TOT	376	85	171	11047¹		9.0				12.4	3.95		.260	.327					.977	1113	1164					

Runs
Pinson-Cin 131
Mays-SF 125
Mathews-Mil 118
Aaron-Mil 116
Robinson-Cin 106

Hits
Aaron-Mil 223
Pinson-Cin 205
Cepeda-SF 192
Temple-Cin 186
Mathews-Mil 182

Doubles
Pinson-Cin 47
Aaron-Mil 46
Mays-SF 43
Cimoli-StL 40

Triples
Neal-LA 11
Moon-LA 11
White-StL 9
Pinson-Cin 9
Dark-Chi 9

Home Runs
Mathews-Mil 46
Banks-Chi 45
Aaron-Mil 39
Robinson-Cin 36
Mays-SF 34

Total Bases
Aaron-Mil 400
Mathews-Mil 352
Banks-Chi 351
Mays-SF 335
Pinson-Cin 330

Runs Batted In
Banks-Chi 143
Robinson-Cin 125
Aaron-Mil 123
Bell-Cin 115
Mathews-Mil 114

Runs Produced
Aaron-Mil 200
Robinson-Cin 195
Pinson-Cin 195
Mays-SF 195
Banks-Chi 195

Bases On Balls
Gilliam-LA 96
Cunningham-StL ... 88
Moon-LA 81
Mathews-Mil 80
Ashburn-Phi 79

Batting Average
Aaron-Mil 355
Cunningham-StL ...345
Cepeda-SF 317
Pinson-Cin 316
Mays-SF 313

On Base Percentage
Cunningham-StL ...456
Aaron-Mil 406
Robinson-Cin 397
Moon-LA 396
Mathews-Mil 391

Slugging Average
Aaron-Mil 636
Banks-Chi 596
Mathews-Mil 593
Robinson-Cin 583
Mays-SF 583

Production
Aaron-Mil 1.042
Mathews-Mil.....984
Robinson-Cin 980
Banks-Chi 975
Mays-SF 967

Adjusted Production
Aaron-Mil 188
Mathews-Mil 172
Mays-SF 157
Banks-Chi 156
Robinson-Cin ... 152

Batter Runs
Aaron-Mil 62.8
Mathews-Mil 48.4
Banks-Chi 44.4
Robinson-Cin 44.0
Mays-SF 42.6

Adjusted Batter Runs
Aaron-Mil 75.3
Mathews-Mil 59.4
Banks-Chi 45.8
Mays-SF 45.3
Robinson-Cin 40.7

Clutch Hitting Index
Bell-Cin 134
Post-Phi 128
Mazeroski-Pit ... 120
Bouchee-Phi 111
Cimoli-StL 111

Runs Created
Aaron-Mil 156
Mathews-Mil 143
Mays-SF 131
Banks-Chi 126
Pinson-Cin 124

Total Average
Aaron-Mil 1.089
Mathews-Mil.....1.041
Mays-SF 1.037
Robinson-Cin 1.015
Cunningham-StL ...978

Stolen Bases
Mays-SF 27
T.Taylor-Chi 23
Gilliam-LA 23
Cepeda-SF 23
Pinson-Cin 21

Stolen Base Average
Mays-SF 87.1
Pinson-Cin 77.8
Neal-LA 73.9
T.Taylor-Chi 71.9
Cepeda-SF 71.9

Stolen Base Runs
Mays-SF 5.7
Pinson-Cin 2.7
Temple-Cin 2.4
Aaron-Mil 2.4
Cimoli-StL 2.1

Fielding Runs
Virdon-Pit 23.5
Blasingame-StL... 20.5
Neal-LA 20.0
Pinson-Cin 19.7
H.Anderson-Phi... 18.3

Total Player Rating
Aaron-Mil 6.6
Banks-Chi 6.2
Mathews-Mil 6.2
Mays-SF 5.0
Pinson-Cin 3.9

Wins
Spahn-Mil 21
S.Jones-SF 21
Burdette-Mil 21
Antonelli-SF 19

Win Percentage
Face-Pit .... .947
Law-Pit .... .667
Antonelli-SF ...... .655
Buhl-Mil .... .625

Games
Henry-Chi 65
Elston-Chi 65
McDaniel-StL 62
McMahon-Mil 60
Miller-SF 59

Complete Games
Spahn-Mil 21
Law-Pit 20
Burdette-Mil 20
Roberts-Phi 19

Shutouts
Spahn-Mil 4
S.Jones-SF 4
Drysdale-LA 4
Craig-LA 4
Burdette-Mil 4
Buhl-Mil 4
Antonelli-SF 4

Saves
McMahon-Mil 15
McDaniel-StL 15
Elston-Chi 13
Henry-Chi 12

Innings Pitched
Spahn-Mil 292.0
Burdette-Mil 289.2
Antonelli-SF 282.0
S.Jones-SF 270.2
Drysdale-LA 270.2

Fewest Hits/Game
Haddix-Pit 7.58
S.Jones-SF 7.71
Hobbie-Chi 7.85
Drysdale-LA 7.88
Antonelli-SF 7.88

Fewest BB/Game
Newcombe-Cin 1.09
Burdette-Mil 1.18
Roberts-Phi 1.22
Purkey-Cin 1.78
Law-Pit 1.79

Strikeouts
Drysdale-LA 242
S.Jones-SF 209
Koufax-LA 173
Antonelli-SF 165
McCormick-SF 151

Strikeouts/Game
Drysdale-LA 8.05
S.Jones-SF 6.95
Podres-LA 6.69
Broglio-StL 6.60
McCormick-SF ... 6.02

Ratio
Haddix-Pit 9.63
Newcombe-Cin ... 10.05
Conley-Phi 10.15
Law-Pit 10.15
Antonelli-SF 10.40

Earned Run Average
S.Jones-SF 2.83
Miller-SF 2.84
Buhl-Mil 2.86
Spahn-Mil 2.96
Law-Pit 2.98

Adjusted ERA
Conley-Phi 137
S.Jones-SF 135
Miller-SF 134
Law-Pit 130
Jackson-StL 128

Opponents' Batting Avg.
S.Jones-SF ...... .228
Haddix-Pit .... .228
Antonelli-SF ..... .233
Drysdale-LA ..... .233
Conley-Phi ...... .235

Opponents' On Base Pct.
Haddix-Pit .... .273
Newcombe-Cin ... .280
Conley-Phi ...... .281
Law-Pit .... .282
Antonelli-SF ..... .286

Starter Runs
S.Jones-SF 33.7
Spahn-Mil 32.1
Craig-LA 32.0
Law-Pit 28.7
Antonelli-SF 26.7

Adjusted Starter Runs
Craig-LA 36.7
S.Jones-SF 29.6
Jackson-StL 26.6
Law-Pit 26.3
Drysdale-LA 23.1

Clutch Pitching Index
Miller-SF 134
Buhl-Mil 120
Spahn-Mil 105
Jackson-StL 104
S.Jones-SF 104

Relief Runs
Miller-SF 20.5
Henry-Chi 18.9
Face-Pit 12.9
McMahon-Mil 12.4
Elston-Chi 6.8

Adjusted Relief Runs
Henry-Chi 18.9
Miller-SF 18.0
Face-Pit 12.1
McMahon-Mil 8.7
Meyer-Phi 7.7

Relief Ranking
Henry-Chi 25.3
Face-Pit 25.1
Miller-SF 16.4
Elston-Chi 13.4
McDaniel-StL 12.5

Total Pitcher Index
Newcombe-Cin 3.5
S.Jones-SF 3.4
Craig-LA 3.2
Drysdale-LA 3.0
Spahn-Mil 2.8

Total Baseball Ranking
Aaron-Mil 6.6
Banks-Chi 6.2
Mathews-Mil 6.2
Mays-SF 5.0
Pinson-Cin 3.9

January 31 Joe Cronin, former Senators and Red Sox shortstop, becomes president of the AL.

March 10 Dorothy Comiskey Rigney, granddaughter of the Old Roman, sells her 54 percent ownership in the White Sox to Bill Veeck's syndicate for $2.7 million. Brother Chuck fails in his attempt to match or improve the bid. Comiskey control of the franchise ends after 60 years.

April 9 In the fifth inning against Washington, the Orioles become the first team in history to turn a triple play on Opening Day. Vice President Richard Nixon, a righthander, substitutes for President Dwight D. Eisenhower and watches the Senators win 9–2.

May 1 White Sox pitcher Early Wynn, 39, pitches a one-hitter for a 1–0 victory over Boston. He fans 14 and belts a home run in the eighth for the only run.

May 11 At Yankee Stadium, Yogi Berra's errorless streak of 148 games comes to an end when he blunders in a 7–6 loss to the Indians.

May 26 At Comiskey Park, a helicopter lands behind second base before a Sox-Indians game, and four midgets dressed as spacemen jump out. Capturing 5-foot-9-inch Nellie Fox and 5-foot-10-inch Luis Aparicio, the spacemen, led by Eddie Gaedel, present the two with ray guns.

June 10 Rocky Colavito hits four consecutive home runs in Baltimore's Memorial Stadium to lead the Indians to an 11-8 win. Colavito joins Lou Gehrig and Bobby Lowe as the only major league players to hit four consecutive four-baggers.

July 12 NBC uses outfield TV cameras with 80-inch lenses to show the catchers' signals during a Yankee-Red Sox game. Commissioner Ford Frick requests that they halt their use.

July 21 Pumpsie Green pinch runs for the Red Sox, who become the last major league team to field a black player. The next day Green goes 0-for-3 against Early Wynn.

August 3 For the first time, there are two All-Star Games in the same year. With the managers picking the starting lineup, the AL wins this second contest 5–3, as five home runs are hit at the Los Angeles Coliseum.

September 22 The "Go-Go" White Sox clinch their first pennant in 40 years with a 4-2 win over the second-place Indians. Early Wynn gets the win, with Gerry Staley saving the game in the ninth.

October 1 The Go-Go Sox change character at home and hammer the LA Dodgers 11-0 in the first game of the World Series, as Ted Kluszewski has two home runs and five RBIs.

October 6 White Sox hurler Dick Donovan keeps the Series alive with a splendid 1-0 win over the Dodgers. Sherm Lollar's double play grounder scores the only run. The attendance mark falls for the second day in a row, as 92,706 fans jam the Coliseum.

November 12 White Sox second baseman Nellie Fox wins the AL's MVP award. Teammates Luis Aparicio and Early Wynn finish second and third in the voting.

November 18 Outfielder Bob Allison of Washington is voted the AL Rookie of the Year. Cleveland's Jim Perry is a distant second.

December 11 The A's Arnold Johnson gives the New York Yankees an early Christmas present—Roger Maris. The Yankees acquire the slugger in a seven-player deal that sends pitcher Don Larsen, right fielder Hank Bauer, first baseman Marv Throneberry, and left fielder Norm Siebern to the Athletics.

BALTIMORE		BOSTON		CHICAGO		CLEVELAND		DETROIT		KANSAS CITY		NEW YORK		WASHINGTON	
M	P.Richards	M	P.Higgins	M	A.Lopez	M	J.Gordon	M	B.Norman	M	H.Craft	M	C.Stengel	M	C.Lavagetto
1B	B.Boyd	M	R.York	1B	E.Torgeson	1B	V.Power	M	J.Dykes	1B	K.Hadley	1B	B.Skowron	1B	R.Sievers
2B	B.Gardner	M	B.Jurges	2B	N.Fox	2B	B.Martin	1B	G.Harris	2B	W.Terwilliger	2B	B.Richardson	2B	R.Bertoia
SS	C.Carrasquel	1B	D.Gernert	SS	L.Aparicio	SS	W.Held	2B	F.Bolling	SS	J.DeMaestri	SS	T.Kubek	SS	B.Consolo
3B	B.Robinson	2B	P.Runnels	3B	B.Phillips	3B	G.Strickland	SS	R.Bridges	3B	D.Williams	3B	H.Lopez	3B	H.Killebrew
LF	G.Woodling	SS	D.Buddin	LF	A.Smith	LF	M.Minoso	3B	E.Yost	LF	B.Cerv	LF	N.Siebern	LF	J.Lemon
CF	W.Tasby	3B	F.Malzone	CF	J.Landis	CF	J.Piersall	LF	C.Maxwell	CF	B.Tuttle	CF	M.Mantle	CF	B.Allison
RF	A.Pilarcik	LF	G.Stephens	RF	J.Rivera	RF	R.Colavito	CF	A.Kaline	RF	R.Maris	RF	H.Bauer	RF	F.Throneberry
C	G.Triandos	CF	G.Geiger	C	S.Lollar	C	R.Nixon	RF	H.Kuenn	C	F.House	C	Y.Berra	C	H.Naragon
		RF	J.Jensen					C	L.Berberet						
S3	B.Klaus	C	S.White	3	B.Goodman	O1	T.Francona			2S	J.Lumpe	1C	E.Howard	1	J.Becquer
O	B.Nieman			23	J.McAnany	23	J.Baxes	C	R.Wilson	3C	H.Smith	2S	G.McDougald	S2	R.Samford
C	J.Ginsberg	O	M.Keough	C	J.Romano	C	D.Brown	S2	T.Lepcio	O	R.Snyder	1O	M.Throneberry	2S	K.Aspromonte
1	W.Dropo	1	V.Wertz	C	J.Callison	C	E.FitzGerald	1	R.Osborne	C	H.Chiti	S3	C.Boyer	O	L.Green
O	A.Pearson	1	T.Williams	1	N.Cash	2	R.Webster	2	G.Zernial	2	H.Lopez	3	A.Carey	C	J.Courtney
3	J.Finigan	2	P.Green	1	T.Kluszewski	S	G.Hamner	O	N.Chrisley	1	R.Boone	O	E.Slaughter	C	J.Porter
S3	W.Miranda	C	P.Daley	O	D.Ennis	O	C.Hardy	O	J.Groth	O	W.Herzog	C	J.Blanchard	O	A.Pearson
O	B.Shetrone	O	J.Busby	O	H.Simpson	O	C.Tanner	S	C.Veal	1	P.Ward	3	J.Lumpe	1	N.Zauchin
1	W.Lockman	2	B.Avila	3S	S.Esposito	3	G.Leek		L.Doby	O	Z.Bella	S	F.Brickell	C	E.FitzGerald
/1	B.Hale	S	J.Mahoney	C	E.Battey	C	H.Naragon	/3	S.Demeter		L.Klimchock		J.Pisoni	O	D.Dobbek
O	B.Avila	/O	B.Renna		L.Doby	/O	E.Valo	/C	R.Shoop	3	R.Jablonski	/O	K.Hunt	2	J.Schaive
2	J.Adair	/O	J.Mallett	/1	R.Boone	/3	W.Jones	/C	C.Lau	/3	J.Morgan	/O	G.Windhorn	S	Z.Versalles
O	J.Taylor	/S	B.Consolo	/2	R.Jackson	/2	B.Moran	H	O.Alvarez		H.Simpson			C	S.Korcheck
O	L.Green	/2	H.Plews	/O	L.Skizas	/1	G.Coleman			/S	T.Carroll			/2	H.Plews
/O	F.Valentine	/C	D.Gile	/O	J.Hicks	H	D.Dillard	P	J.Bunning	R	B.Martyn	P	W.Ford	S	J.Valdivielso
/2	L.Burke	/2	T.Lepcio	/3	J.Martin	H	J.Bolger	P	P.Foytack			P	A.Ditmar	R	B.Malkmus
/S	R.Hansen	/S	H.Sullivan	H	D.Mueller	/3	R.Jackson	P	D.Mossi		B.Daley	P	B.Turley	P	D.Maas
R	B.Saverine			/C	C.Carreon			P	F.Lary		N.Garver	P	R.Terry	P	C.Pascual
		P	T.Brewer			P	C.McLish	RP	R.Narleski	P	R.Herbert	RP	J.Coates	P	R.Ramos
P	H.Wilhelm	P	J.Casale	P	E.Wynn	P	G.Bell	RP	T.Morgan	P	J.Kucks	RP	B.Shantz	P	K.Kemmerer
P	M.Pappas	P	F.Sullivan	P	B.Shaw	P	M.Grant	RP	P.Burnside	P	B.Grim	RP	R.Duren	P	B.Fischer
P	B.O'Dell	P	B.Monbouquette	P	B.Pierce	P	H.Score			RP	B.Coleman			RP	T.Clevenger
P	J.Walker	P	I.Delock	P	D.Donovan	P	J.Perry	P	D.Sisler	RP	T.Sturdivant	P	D.Larsen	RP	H.Griggs
P	H.Brown	RP	M.Fornieles	P	B.Latman	RP	M.Garcia	P	J.Davie	RP	M.Dickson	P	E.Grba	RP	C.Stobbs
RP	B.Loes	RP	L.Kiely	RP	G.Staley			P	B.Schultz			P	J.Bronstad		
RP	E.Johnson			RP	T.Lown	P	B.Locke	/P	G.Susce		J.Tsitouris	P	G.Blaylock	P	H.Woodeshick
			F.Baumann			P	D.Ferrarese	/P	B.Smith	/P	R.Terry	/P	T.Sturdivant		D.Hyde
P	A.Portocarrero	/P	T.Wills	P	R.Moore	P	J.Harshman	/P	J.Stump	/P	R.Meyer	/P	G.Gabler	P	J.Romonosky
P	J.Fisher	P	M.Wall	P	R.Arias	P	A.Cicotte	P	B.Hoeft	/P	H.Reed	/P	J.Kucks	/P	J.Kralick
P	J.Harshman	P	A.Schroll	P	K.McBride	P	D.Brodowski	/P	H.Aguirre	P	D.Tomanek	/P	M.Freeman		V.Valentinetti
P	B.Hoeft	P	N.Chittum	P	J.Stanka	P	B.Smith	/P	J.Proctor	P	T.Gorman	/P	Z.Monroe	/P	J.Kaat
/P	W.Stock	/P	J.Harshman	/P	C.Raymond	/P	B.Bruce			/P	A.Grunwald			/P	R.Lumenti
/P	G.Zuverink	/P	E.Wilson	/P	D.Rudolph	/P	B.Podbielan			/P	K.Johnson			/P	T.McAvoy
/P	G.Bamberger	/P	B.Hoeft	/P	G.Peters	/P	H.Robinson			/P	M.Kutyna			/P	M.Wall
/P	R.Coleman	/P	T.Bowsfield			/P	J.Striker			/P	E.Killeen				
		/P	H.Moford							/P	G.Brunet				
		/P	D.Sisler							/P	M.Freeman				

TEAM	G	W	L	PCT	GB	R	OR	AB	H	2B	3B	HR	BB	SO	AVG	OBP	SLG	PRO	PRO+	BR	/A	PF	CHI	RC	SB	CS	SBA	SBR
CHI	156	94	60	.610		669	**588**	5297	1325	220	**46**	97	580	**634**	.250	.330	.364	.694	97	-20	-11	99	100	653	**113**	53	68	2
CLE	154	89	65	.578	5	**745**	646	5288	1390	216	25	**167**	433	721	**.263**	.323	**.408**	.731	110	32	**59**	96	**107**	682	33	36	48	-12
NY	155	79	75	.513	15	687	647	5379	**1397**	224	40	153	457	828	.260	.321	.402	.723	107	17	41	97	98	695	45	22	67	0
DET	154	76	78	.494	18	713	732	5211	1346	196	30	160	580	737	.258	**.338**	.400	**.738**	102	57	17	105	97	**720**	34	17	67	0
BOS	154	75	79	.487	19	726	696	5225	1335	**248**	28	125	**626**	810	.256	**.338**	.385	.723	99	36	3	105	101	697	68	25	**73**	5
BAL	155	74	80	.481	20	551	621	5208	1240	182	23	109	536	690	.238	.312	.345	.657	88	-96	-83	98	96	563	36	24	60	-4
KC	154	66	88	.429	28	681	760	5264	1383	231	43	117	442	780	.263	.328	.390	.718	100	16	4	102	99	669	34	24	59	-4
WAS	154	63	91	.409	31	619	701	5092	1205	173	32	163	517	881	.237	.310	.379	.689	94	-43	-40	100	101	594	51	34	60	-5
TOT	618					5391		41964	10621	1690	267	1091	4210	6081	.253	.325	.384	.709							414	235	64	-17

TEAM	CG	SH	SV	IP	H	H/G	HR	BB	SO	RAT	ERA	ERA+	OAV	OOB	PR	/A	PF	CPI	FA	E	DP	FW	PW	BW	SBW	DIF
CHI	44	13	**36**	1425¹	1297	8.2	129	525	761	11.7	**3.29**	114	.242	**.313**	91	74	97	106	**.979**	130	141	.6	**7.5**	-1.1	.4	9.6
CLE	58	7	23	1383²	**1230**	**8.0**	148	635	799	12.3	3.75	98	**.239**	.325	18	-10	95	101	.978	127	138	.7	-1.0	**6.0**	-1.0	7.3
NY	38	**15**	28	1399	1281	8.2	120	594	**836**	12.2	3.60	101	.244	.324	40	7	94	102	.978	131	160	.5	.7	4.2	.2	-3.6
DET	53	9	24	1360	1327	8.8	177	**432**	829	11.9	4.20	97	.254	.316	-52	-21	105	94	.978	**124**	131	**.9**	-2.1	1.7	.2	-1.7
BOS	38	9	25	1364	1386	9.1	135	589	724	13.2	4.17	97	.266	.343	-47	-17	105	104	.978	131	**167**	.5	-1.7	.3	**.7**	-1.8
BAL	45	**15**	30	1400¹	1290	8.3	**111**	476	735	**11.5**	3.56	106	.246	**.313**	47	35	98	96	.976	146	163	-.4	3.5	-8.4	-.2	2.4
KC	44	8	21	1360²	1452	9.6	148	492	703	13.2	4.35	92	.274	.341	-74	-52	104	102	.973	160	156	-1.2	-5.3	.4	-.2	-4.7
WAS	46	10	21	1360	1358	9.0	123	467	694	12.3	4.01	98	.259	.324	-23	-14	101	96	.973	162	140	-1.4	-1.4	-4.0	-.3	-6.9
TOT	366	86	208	11053		8.6				12.3	3.86		.253	.325					.977	1111	1196					

Runs
Yost-Det 115
Mantle-NY 104
Power-Cle 102
Jensen-Bos 101
Kuenn-Det 99

Hits
Kuenn-Det 198
Fox-Chi 191
Runnels-Bos 176
Power-Cle 172
Minoso-Cle 172

Doubles
Kuenn-Det 42
Malzone-Bos 34
Fox-Chi 34
Williams-KC 33
Runnels-Bos 33

Triples
Allison-Was 9
McDougald-NY 8

Home Runs
Killebrew-Was ... 42
Colavito-Cle 42
Lemon-Was 33
Maxwell-Det 31
Mantle-NY 31

Total Bases
Colavito-Cle 301
Killebrew-Was 282
Kuenn-Det 281
Mantle-NY 278
Allison-Was 275

Runs Batted In
Jensen-Bos 112
Colavito-Cle 111
Killebrew-Was 105
Lemon-Was 100
Maxwell-Det 95

Runs Produced
Jensen-Bos 185
Minoso-Cle 163
Malzone-Bos 163
Kuenn-Det 161
Killebrew-Was 161

Bases On Balls
Yost-Det 135
Runnels-Bos 95
Mantle-NY 93
Buddin-Bos 92
Killebrew-Was 90

Batting Average
Kuenn-Det .... .353
Kaline-Det .... .327
Runnels-Bos ...... .314
Fox-Chi .... .306
Minoso-Cle .... .302

On Base Percentage
Yost-Det .... .437
Runnels-Bos ...... .415
Kaline-Det .... .414
Woodling-Bal ..... .405
Kuenn-Det .... .405

Slugging Average
Killebrew-Was .... .530
Mantle-NY .... .514
Colavito-Cle ..... .512
Lemon-Was .... .510

Production
Kaline-Det .... .944
Kuenn-Det .... .906
Mantle-NY .... .905
Yost-Det .... .873
Killebrew-Was .... .873

Adjusted Production
Mantle-NY 152
Kaline-Det 149
Kuenn-Det 140
Woodling-Bal 139
Killebrew-Was 137

Batter Runs
Kaline-Det 41.6
Yost-Det 37.9
Francona-Cle 36.6
Kuenn-Det 36.2
Mantle-NY 36.0

Adjusted Batter Runs
Francona-Cle 40.0
Mantle-NY 39.8
Kaline-Det 35.8
Yost-Det 31.8
Kuenn-Det 30.6

Clutch Hitting Index
Strickland-Cle ... 125
Fox-Chi 121
Woodling-Bal 120
Jensen-Bos 115
Cerv-KC 115

Runs Created
Mantle-NY 117
Kuenn-Det 117
Yost-Det 115
Kaline-Det 114
Killebrew-Was 103

Total Average
Yost-Det .... .992
Mantle-NY .... .985
Kaline-Det .... .983
Kuenn-Det .... .903
Jensen-Bos .... .888

Stolen Bases
Aparicio-Chi 56
Mantle-NY 21
Landis-Chi 20
Jensen-Bos 20
Allison-Was 13

Stolen Base Average
Mantle-NY 87.5
Aparicio-Chi 81.2
Jensen-Bos 80.0
Landis-Chi 69.0

Stolen Base Runs
Aparicio-Chi 9.0
Mantle-NY 4.5
Jensen-Bos 3.0
Malzone-Bos 1.8
Yost-Det 1.5

Fielding Runs
Gardner-Det 30.5
Minoso-Cle 16.2
Landis-Chi 15.8
Jensen-Bos 15.1
Colavito-Cle 11.6

Total Player Rating
Mantle-NY 4.5
Kaline-Det 4.0
Jensen-Bos 3.4
Minoso-Cle 3.4
Runnels-Bos 3.3

Wins
Wynn-Chi 22
McLish-Cle 19
Shaw-Chi 18

Win Percentage
Shaw-Chi .... .750
McLish-Cle .... .704
Wynn-Chi .... .688
Mossi-Det .... .654

Games
Staley-Chi 67
Lown-Chi 60
Clevenger-Was 50
Shaw-Chi 47

Complete Games
Pascual-Was 17
Pappas-Bal 15
Mossi-Det 15
Wynn-Chi 14
Bunning-Det 14

Shutouts
Pascual-Was 6
Wynn-Chi 5
Pappas-Bal 4

Saves
Lown-Chi 15
Staley-Chi 14
Loes-Bal 14
Duren-NY 14
Fornieles-Bos 11

Innings Pitched
Wynn-Chi 255.2
Bunning-Det 249.2
Foytack-Det 240.1
Pascual-Was 238.2
McLish-Cle 235.1

Fewest Hits/Game
Score-Cle 6.89
Ditmar-NY 6.95
Wilhelm-Bal 7.09
Wynn-Chi 7.11
O'Dell-Bal 7.36

Fewest BB/Game
Brown-Bal 1.76
Lary-Det 1.86
Garver-KC 1.88
Mossi-Det 1.93
Ramos-Was 2.00

Strikeouts
Bunning-Det 201
Pascual-Was 185
Wynn-Chi 179
Score-Cle 147
Wilhelm-Bal 139

Strikeouts/Game
Score-Cle 8.23
Bunning-Det 7.25
Pascual-Was 6.98
Turley-NY 6.47
Wynn-Chi 6.30

Ratio
Ditmar-NY 9.62
Pascual-Was 10.33
Mossi-Det 10.34
O'Dell-Bal 10.43
Brown-Bal 10.48

Earned Run Average
Wilhelm-Bal 2.19
Pascual-Was 2.64
Shaw-Chi 2.69
Ditmar-NY 2.90
Walker-Bal 2.92

Adjusted ERA
Wilhelm-Bal 173
Pascual-Was 148
Shaw-Chi 140
Walker-Bal 130
O'Dell-Bal 129

Opponents' Batting Avg.
Score-Cle .... .210
Ditmar-NY .... .211
Wynn-Chi .... .216
O'Dell-Bal ...... .220
Wilhelm-Bal ..... .224

Opponents' On Base Pct.
Ditmar-NY .... .270
Pascual-Was ..... .284
O'Dell-Bal ...... .286
Mossi-Det .... .286
Brown-Bal .... .290

Starter Runs
Wilhelm-Bal 42.0
Pascual-Was 32.4
Shaw-Chi 30.0
Ditmar-NY 21.7
Perry-Cle 20.6

Adjusted Starter Runs
Wilhelm-Bal 40.0
Pascual-Was 33.8
Shaw-Chi 27.3
Daley-KC 20.2
O'Dell-Bal 18.8

Clutch Pitching Index
Wilhelm-Bal 132
Daley-KC 122
Ford-NY 119
Shaw-Chi 114
McLish-Cle 114

Relief Runs
Staley-Chi 20.9
Duren-NY 16.9
Shantz-NY 15.6
Coates-NY 11.0
Lown-Chi 10.0

Adjusted Relief Runs
Staley-Chi 19.6
Duren-NY 15.0
Shantz-NY 13.3
Stobbs-Was 9.4
Fornieles-Bos 9.0

Relief Ranking
Staley-Chi 25.0
Duren-NY 22.1
Shantz-NY 13.6
Lown-Chi 12.7
Fornieles-Bos ... 10.6

Total Pitcher Index
Pascual-Was 5.0
Wilhelm-Bal 3.7
Daley-KC 3.1
Perry-Cle 2.8
Ford-NY 2.8

Total Baseball Ranking
Pascual-Was 5.0
Mantle-NY 4.5
Kaline-Det 4.0
Wilhelm-Bal 3.7
Jensen-Bos 3.4

January 21 Stan Musial asks for, and receives, a pay cut from $100,000 to $80,000 a year. Musial says he was overpaid in 1957 and 1958, and his salary should be cut, based on his performance in 1959.

February 4 For the second straight year, the BBWAA voters fail to elect a new Hall of Fame member. Edd Roush gets 146 votes, but 202 are necessary for election. Sam Rice (143) and Eppa Rixey (142) are next in line.

February 18 Walter O'Malley, owner of the Dodgers, completes the purchase of the Chavez Ravine area in Los Angeles by paying $494,000 for property valued at $92,000.

February 20 Branch Rickey meets with officials of the proposed Western Carolinas League about pooling talent for Continental League clubs.

April 17 Eddie Mathews hits his 300th homer, off Robin Roberts, plus a double and triple, as Milwaukee beats Philadelphia 8-4. Only Jimmie Foxx hit his 300th at a younger age.

May 4 When the Cubs pluck Lou Boudreau out of the broadcast booth to replace Charlie Grimm (6-11) as manager, Jolly Cholly takes Lou's chair behind the mike.

June 26 Hoping to speed up the election process, the Hall of Fame changes its voting procedures. The new rules allow the Special Veterans Committee to vote annually, rather than every other year, and to induct up to two players a year. The BBWAA is authorized to hold a run-off election of the top 30 vote getters if no one is elected in the first ballot.

July 18 The NL votes to expand to 10 clubs if the Continental League does not join Organized Baseball. The new NL clubs would invade Continental League territories.

July 19 In his major league debut, Giant Juan Marichal pitches no-hit ball until Clay Dalrymple pinch-hit singles with two out in the seventh. Marichal winds up with 12 strikeouts and a one-hit 2-0 win against the Phillies. Marichal is the first NL pitcher since 1900 to debut with a one-hitter.

August 18 Facing just 27 batters, Lew Burdette pitches a 1-0 no-hitter against the Phillies. Tony Gonzalez, the only Phil to reach base, is hit by a Burdette pitch in the fifth inning but is then erased on a double play.

September 15 Willie Mays ties the modern major league record with three triples in a game against the Phillies. His three-bagger off Turk Farrell gives the Giants an 8-6 win in 11 innings. Mays also strokes a double and single.

September 16 Warren Spahn, 39 years old, notches his 11th 20-win season with a no-hitter against the Phillies, winning by a score of 4-0.

September 25 For the first time since 1927, the Pirates are headed for the World Series. A gigantic torchlight victory parade in Pittsburgh's Golden Triangle at midnight celebrates the pennant.

October 14 In a 9-9 tie, Bill Mazeroski leads off the last of the ninth and hits what is the most dramatic home run in Series history, off Ralph Terry, to give Pittsburgh a 10-9 win and the World Championship.

October 16 The NL votes to admit Houston and New York to the league, the first structural change since 1900.

November 3 Pittsburgh's Vern Law is voted Cy Young Award winner. He outpolls Warren Spahn 8-4.

November 16 NL batting champion Dick Groat is named league MVP, outpolling Pirate teammate Don Hoak 276-162.

December 21 Cubs owner P. K. Wrigley says Chicago will have no manager but will use a college of coaches instead.

CHICAGO

M C.Grimm · M L.Boudreau · 1B E.Bouchee · 2B J.Kindall · SS E.Banks · 3B R.Santo · LF R.Ashburn · CF G.Altman · RF B.Will · C M.Thacker · 1O F.Thomas · 23 D.Zimmer · C S.Taylor · O W.Moryn · C E.Tappe · C E.Averill · O A.Heist · 1 D.Gernert · 2 T.Taylor · O D.Murphy · O L.Johnson · C D.Rice · O B.Williams · C J.Hegan · /2 G.Hatton · /C D.Bertell · /3 S.Drake · /O A.Schult · /C C.Neeman · /1 I.Noren · /O N.Mathews · /2 J.McKnight · P G.Hobbie · P B.Anderson · P D.Ellsworth · P D.Cardwell · RP D.Elston · RP S.Morehead · RP M.Freeman · P D.Drott · P J.Schaffernoth · P M.Drabowsky · P B.Johnson · /P J.Brewer · /P M.Wright · /P A.Ceccarelli · /P D.Burwell · /P J.Goetz · /P A.Schroll

CINCINNATI

M F.Hutchinson · 1B F.Robinson · 2B B.Martin · SS R.McMillan · 3B E.Kasko · LF W.Post · CF V.Pinson · RF G.Bell · C E.Bailey · O J.Lynch · 1 G.Coleman · 3 C.Cook · 3 W.Jones · S L.Cardenas · 2 E.Chacon · O T.Gonzalez · O L.Walls · C D.Dotterer · 1 H.Anderson · C J.Azcue · /C F.House · /O J.Gaines · /1 W.Lockman · /1 R.Alvarez · H P.Whisenant · P B.Purkey · P J.Hook · P J.O'Toole · P C.McLish · RP J.Nuxhall · P J.Brosnan · RP B.Henry · P D.Newcombe · P J.Maloney · P C.Osteen · P B.Grim · P M.Bridges · /P R.Sanchez · /P O.Pena · /P B.Lawrence · /P T.Wieand · /P D.Richards

LOS ANGELES

M W.Alston · 1B N.Larker · 2B C.Neal · SS M.Wills · 3B J.Gilliam · LF W.Moon · CF T.Davis · RF F.Howard · C J.Roseboro · 13 G.Hodges · O D.Snider · O D.Demeter · C N.Sherry · O J.Pignatano · O W.Davis · O C.Essegian · S3 B.Lillis · 3 C.Smith · S B.Aspromonte · O R.Fairly · H I.Noren · /C D.Camilli · /O S.Amoros · /O C.Furillo · /O R.Repulski · P D.Drysdale · P J.Podres · P S.Williams · P S.Koufax · RP R.Craig · RP L.Sherry · RP E.Roebuck · RP D.McDevitt · E.Palmquist · /P E.Rakow · /P C.Labine · /P J.Golden · /P P.Ortega

MILWAUKEE

M C.Dressen · 1B J.Adcock · 2B C.Cottier · SS J.Logan · 3B E.Mathews · LF A.Spangler · CF B.Bruton · RF H.Aaron · C D.Crandall · O W.Covington · 2 R.Schoendienst · 2S F.Mantilla · O1 A.Dark · O2 M.Roach · O L.Maye · C C.Lau · 1 F.Torre · /O E.Haas · /1 R.Boone · S2 M.Krsnich · /C S.Lopata · /O L.Gabrielson · H J.Torre · 1 E.Bouchee · 3 L.Burdette · P W.Spahn · P B.Buhl · P C.Willey · P J.Jay · RP D.McMahon · RP G.Brunet · P R.Piche · P J.Pizarro · /P D.Nottebart · P B.Rush · P T.Fox · /P K.MacKenzie · /P B.Giggie

PHILADELPHIA

M E.Sawyer · M A.Cohen · M G.Mauch · 1B P.Herrera · 2B T.Taylor · SS R.Amaro · 3B A.Dark · LF B.Smith · CF B.Del Greco · RF K.Walters · C J.Coker · O T.Curry · O J.Callison · O T.Gonzalez · 3O L.Walls · S J.Koppe · C C.Neeman · C C.Dalrymple · 3S T.Lepcio · B.Malkmus · O1 H.Anderson · W.Post · 3 J.Morgan · 1 E.Bouchee · 3 L.Woods · /O D.Philley · /S B.Wine · P R.Roberts · P J.Buzhardt · P G.Conley · P R.Owens · P D.Green · RP C.Short · RP T.Farrell · RP R.Gomez · P A.Mahaffey · H.Robinson · /P D.Cardwell · /P J.Meyer · /P T.Phillips · /P A.Neiger · /P H.Mason · /P C.Simmons

PITTSBURGH

M D.Murtaugh · 1B D.Stuart · 2B B.Mazeroski · SS D.Groat · 3B D.Hoak · LF B.Skinner · CF B.Virdon · RF R.Clemente · C S.Burgess · O G.Cimoli · H.Smith · 1 R.Nelson · S2 D.Schofield · C J.Christopher · /3 G.Baker · C B.Oldis · M.Vernon · D.Barone · /C D.Kravitz · H H.Bright · /1 R.Stevens · R.Mejias · P B.Friend · V.Law · H.Haddix · V.Mizell · RP R.Face · RP J.Gibbon · RP F.Green · B.Daniels · P.Giel · C.Labine · G.Witt · /P E.Francis · /P D.Olivo · /P D.Gross

SAN FRANCISCO

M B.Rigney · M T.Sheehan · 1B W.McCovey · 2B D.Blasingame · SS E.Bressoud · 3B J.Davenport · LF F.Alou · CF W.Mays · RF W.Kirkland · C B.Schmidt · 32 J.Amalfitano · O1 O.Cepeda · S3 A.Rodgers · C H.Landrith · 1 J.Marshall · O D.Philley · 1 D.Long · S J.Pagan · /C N.Wilson · /O M.Alou · P M.McCormick · P Sa.Jones · P J.Sanford · P B.O'Dell · RP J.Antonelli · RP S.Miller · P J.Marichal · P G.Maranda · P B.Loes · P Sh.Jones · P B.Byerly · P J.Shipley · /P E.Fisher · /P D.Choate · /P R.Monzant

ST.LOUIS

M S.Hemus · 1B B.White · 2B J.Javier · SS D.Spencer · 3B K.Boyer · LF S.Musial · CF C.Flood · RF J.Cunningham · C H.Smith · S2 A.Grammas · O W.Moryn · O B.Nieman · C.Sawatski · O L.Wagner · /1 G.Crowe · C J.James · O J.Landrum · O J.Glenn · O E.Burton · 2 W.Shannon · /C T.McCarver · /C C.Cannizzaro · /S J.Gotay · /2 D.Gray · /3 E.Olivares · /1 D.Carmel · /O G.Kolb · /C D.Johnson · /C D.Rice · /2 B.Sadowski · /2 R.Bridges · /O D.Clemens · P L.Jackson · P E.Broglio · P R.Sadecki · P C.Simmons · P R.Kline · RP L.McDaniel · P B.Gibson · /P V.Mizell · P B.Miller · /P M.Duliba · P M.Bridges · P B.Grim · /P E.Bauta · F.Barnes · /P M.Nelson · /P C.Browning

TEAM	G	W	L	PCT	GB	R	OR	AB	H	2B	3B	HR	BB	SO	AVG	OBP	SLG	PRO	PRO+	BR	/A	PF	CHI	RC	SB	CS	SBA	SBR
PIT	155	95	59	.617		734	593	5406	1493	236	56	120	486	747	.276	.338	.407	.745	109	72	68	101	99	737	34	24	59	-4
MIL	154	88	66	.571	7	724	658	5263	1393	198	48	170	463	793	.265	.327	.417	.744	118	60	114	93	102	714	69	37	65	-2
STL	155	86	68	.558	9	639	616	5187	1317	213	48	138	501	792	.254	.323	.393	.716	94	13	-44	109	97	652	48	35	58	-7
LA	154	82	72	.532	13	662	593	5227	1333	216	38	126	529	837	.255	.327	.383	.710	94	6	-37	106	99	659	95	53	64	-3
SF	156	79	75	.513	16	671	631	5324	1357	220	62	130	467	846	.255	.319	.393	.712	106	1	41	94	102	663	86	45	66	-1
CIN	154	67	87	.435	28	640	692	5289	1324	230	40	140	512	858	.250	.320	.388	.708	98	-1	-12	102	97	661	73	37	66	0
CHI	156	60	94	.390	35	634	776	5311	1293	213	48	119	531	897	.243	.314	.369	.683	94	-48	-41	99	103	617	51	34	60	-5
PHI	154	59	95	.383	36	546	691	5169	1235	196	44	99	448	1054	.239	.304	.351	.655	85	-102	-103	100	102	546	45	48	48	-15
TOT	619					5250		42176	10745	1722	384	1042	3937	6824	.255	.322	.388	.710							501	313	62	-38

TEAM	CG	SH	SV	IP	H	H/G	HR	BB	SO	RAT	ERA	ERA+	OAV	OOB	PR	/A	PF	CPI	FA	E	DP	FW	PW	BW	SBW	DIF
PIT	47	11	33	1399²	1363	8.8	105	386	811	11.3	3.49	107	.257	.309	42	40	100	99	.979	128	163	.7	4.1	7.0	.0	6.1
MIL	55	13	28	1387¹	1327	8.6	130	518	807	12.2	3.76	91	.251	.322	0	-52	91	99	.976	141	137	-.0	-5.4	11.7	.3	4.4
STL	37	11	30	1371	1316	8.6	127	511	906	12.1	3.64	112	.253	.322	18	69	109	103	.976	141	152	.0	7.1	-4.5	-.2	6.6
LA	46	13	20	1398	1218	7.8	154	564	1122	11.7	3.40	117	.234	.312	56	89	106	103	.979	125	142	.9	9.2	-3.8	.2	-1.4
SF	55	16	26	1396	1288	8.3	107	512	897	11.8	3.44	101	.245	.315	50	6	93	99	.972	166	117	-1.3	.6	4.2	.4	-1.9
CIN	33	8	35	1390¹	1417	9.2	134	442	740	12.3	4.00	96	.267	.328	-37	-27	102	101	.979	125	155	.9	-2.8	-1.2	.5	-7.3
CHI	36	6	25	1402²	1393	8.9	152	565	805	12.8	4.35	87	.260	.335	-92	-89	100	96	.977	143	133	-.0	-9.2	-4.2	-.0	-3.6
PHI	45	6	16	1375¹	1423	9.3	133	439	736	12.3	4.01	97	.270	.328	-38	-20	103	101	.974	155	129	-.8	-2.1	-10.6	-1.1	-3.5
TOT	354	84	213	11120¹		8.7				12.1	3.76		.255	.322					.977	1124	1128					

Runs		Hits		Doubles		Triples		Home Runs		Total Bases	
Bruton-Mil	112	Mays-SF	190	Pinson-Cin	37	Bruton-Mil	13	Banks-Chi	41	Aaron-Mil	334
Mathews-Mil	108	Pinson-Cin	187	Cepeda-SF	36	Pinson-Cin	12	Aaron-Mil	40	Banks-Chi	331
Pinson-Cin	107	Groat-Pit	186	Skinner-Pit	33	Mays-SF	12	Mathews-Mil	39	Mays-SF	330
Mays-SF	107	Bruton-Mil	180	Robinson-Cin	33	Aaron-Mil	11	Boyer-StL	32	Boyer-StL	310
Aaron-Mil	102	Clemente-Pit	179	Banks-Chi	32			Robinson-Cin	31	Pinson-Cin	308

Runs Batted In		Runs Produced		Bases On Balls		Batting Average		On Base Percentage		Slugging Average	
Aaron-Mil	126	Mathews-Mil	193	Ashburn-Chi	116	Groat-Pit	.325	Ashburn-Chi	.416	Robinson-Cin	.595
Mathews-Mil	124	Aaron-Mil	188	Mathews-Mil	111	Larker-LA	.323	Robinson-Cin	.413	Aaron-Mil	.566
Banks-Chi	117	Mays-SF	181	Gilliam-LA	96	Mays-SF	.319	Mathews-Mil	.401	Boyer-StL	.562
Mays-SF	103	Banks-Chi	170	Robinson-Cin	82	Clemente-Pit	.314	Moon-LA	.387	Mays-SF	.555
Boyer-StL	97	Clemente-Pit	167	Spencer-StL	81	Boyer-StL	.304	Mays-SF	.386	Banks-Chi	.554

Production		Adjusted Production		Batter Runs		Adjusted Batter Runs		Clutch Hitting Index		Runs Created	
Robinson-Cin	1.007	Mathews-Mil	170	Robinson-Cin	47.8	Mathews-Mil	55.4	Larker-LA	149	Mathews-Mil	128
Mathews-Mil	.952	Robinson-Cin	169	Mathews-Mil	46.0	Mays-SF	50.7	Mathews-Mil	120	Mays-SF	124
Mays-SF	.941	Mays-SF	164	Mays-SF	43.5	Aaron-Mil	46.0	Bailey-Cin	120	Aaron-Mil	119
Boyer-StL	.934	Aaron-Mil	161	Boyer-StL	37.9	Robinson-Cin	46.0	Stuart-Pit	114	Banks-Chi	113
Aaron-Mil	.925	Banks-Chi	145	Aaron-Mil	37.4	Banks-Chi	35.6	Clemente-Pit	112	Robinson-Cin	113

Total Average		Stolen Bases		Stolen Base Average		Stolen Base Runs		Fielding Runs		Total Player Rating	
Robinson-Cin	1.069	Wills-LA	50	Javier-StL	82.6	Wills-LA	7.8	Mazeroski-Pit	25.4	Mays-SF	5.9
Mathews-Mil	1.029	Pinson-Cin	32	Wills-LA	80.6	Javier-StL	3.3	Wills-LA	20.5	Banks-Chi	5.8
Mays-SF	.953	T.Taylor-Chi-Phi	26	Ashburn-Chi	80.0	Blasingame-SF	3.0	Grammas-StL	19.8	Aaron-Mil	4.8
Aaron-Mil	.935	Mays-SF	25	Pinson-Cin	72.7	Pinson-Cin	2.4	Smith-StL	18.0	Robinson-Cin	4.5
Boyer-StL	.918	Bruton-Mil	22	Mays-SF	71.4	Ashburn-Chi	2.4	Mays-SF	13.7	Mathews-Mil	4.2

Wins		Win Percentage		Games		Complete Games		Shutouts		Saves	
Spahn-Mil	21	Broglio-StL	.700	Face-Pit	68	Spahn-Mil	18	Sanford-SF	6	McDaniel-StL	26
Broglio-StL	21	Law-Pit	.690	McDaniel-StL	65	Law-Pit	18	Drysdale-LA	5	Face-Pit	24
Law-Pit	20	Spahn-Mil	.677	Elston-Chi	60	Burdette-Mil	18			Henry-Cin	17
Burdette-Mil	19	Buhl-Mil	.640	Farrell-Phi	59	Hobbie-Chi	16			Brosnan-Cin	12
		Purkey-Cin	.607	Roebuck-LA	58	Friend-Pit	16				

Innings Pitched		Fewest Hits/Game		Fewest BB/Game		Strikeouts		Strikeouts/Game		Ratio	
Jackson-StL	282.0	Broglio-StL	6.84	Burdette-Mil	1.14	Drysdale-LA	246	Koufax-LA	10.13	Drysdale-LA	9.90
Friend-Pit	275.2	Koufax-LA	6.84	Roberts-Phi	1.29	Koufax-LA	197	Drysdale-LA	8.23	Friend-Pit	10.15
Burdette-Mil	275.2	Williams-LA	7.03	Law-Pit	1.33	S.Jones-SF	190	Williams-LA	7.60	Law-Pit	10.27
Law-Pit	271.2	Drysdale-LA	7.16	Friend-Pit	1.47	Broglio-StL	188	Broglio-StL	7.48	Burdette-Mil	10.35
Drysdale-LA	269.0	Buhl-Mil	7.62	Haddix-Pit	1.98	Friend-Pit	183	S.Jones-SF	7.31	Williams-LA	10.37

Earned Run Average		Adjusted ERA		Opponents' Batting Avg.		Opponents' On Base Pct.		Starter Runs		Adjusted Starter Runs	
McCormick-SF	2.70	Broglio-StL	149	Koufax-LA	.207	Drysdale-LA	.275	McCormick-SF	29.8	Broglio-StL	34.0
Broglio-StL	2.74	Drysdale-LA	140	Williams-LA	.210	Friend-Pit	.281	Drysdale-LA	27.5	Drysdale-LA	33.6
Drysdale-LA	2.84	Simmons-Phi-StL	134	Broglio-StL	.213	Williams-LA	.282	Broglio-StL	25.6	Friend-Pit	22.9
Williams-LA	3.00	Williams-LA	133	Drysdale-LA	.215	Law-Pit	.287	Friend-Pit	23.2	Williams-LA	22.4
Friend-Pit	3.00	Podres-LA	129	Buhl-Mil	.229	Burdette-Mil	.287	Law-Pit	20.6	Podres-LA	22.4

Clutch Pitching Index		Relief Runs		Adjusted Relief Runs		Relief Ranking		Total Pitcher Index		Total Baseball Ranking	
Simmons-Phi-StL	121	McDaniel-StL	21.6	McDaniel-StL	26.0	McDaniel-StL	45.2	McDaniel-StL	5.0	Mays-SF	5.9
Podres-LA	117	Brosnan-Cin	15.4	Brosnan-Cin	16.1	Farrell-Phi	22.2	Broglio-StL	4.8	Banks-Chi	5.8
O'Dell-SF	110	Roebuck-LA	12.8	Roebuck-LA	15.5	Face-Pit	20.3	Drysdale-LA	4.3	McDaniel-StL	5.0
Sadecki-StL	109	Farrell-Phi	12.2	Farrell-Phi	13.6	Brosnan-Cin	17.5	McCormick-SF	2.7	Aaron-Mil	4.8
Buhl-Mil	108	Face-Pit	10.9	Face-Pit	10.8	Roebuck-LA	15.5	Williams-LA	2.6	Broglio-StL	4.8

June 17 A two-run homer off Wynn Hawkins at Cleveland Municipal Stadium makes Ted Williams the fourth player in major league history to hit 500 homers. The Red Sox win, 3-1.

July 27 William Shea, chairman of Mayor Robert Wagner's New York baseball committee, announces the formation of the Continental League. The five founding cities are New York, Houston, Toronto, Denver, and Minneapolis/St. Paul.

August 3 Frank Lane trades managers with Detroit's GM Bill DeWitt. The Indians' Joe Gordon (49-46) is dealt to the Tigers for Jimmy Dykes (44-52). For one game, until the pair can change places, Jo-Jo White pilots the Indians and Billy Hitchcock guides the Tigers.

September 2 In the first game of a doubleheader, Ted Williams homers off Don Lee of the Senators. Williams had homered against Lee's father, Thornton, 20 years earlier.

September 26 In his final major league plate appearance, against Baltimore's Jack Fisher, Ted Williams picks out a 1-1 pitch and drives it 450 feet into the right-center field seats behind the Boston bullpen. It is Williams' 521st and last homer, putting him third on the all-time list. Williams' homer gives the seventh-place

Red Sox a 5-4 victory. Williams stays in the dugout, ignoring the crowd's cheers, but when he trots out to left field in the ninth, he is replaced immediately by Carroll Hardy. The Splendid Splinter retires as a standing crowd roars.

October 3 The Yankees head into the Series with a 15-game winning streak. New York's 193 homers are an AL record, three better than the 1956 Yanks.

October 5 In a portent of things to come, Bill Mazeroski's two-run fifth-inning homer off Jim Coates is the difference as Pittsburgh beats New York 6-4 in its first World Series win since 1925. Roy Face survives a two-run ninth-inning Elston Howard homer to preserve Vern Law's victory.

October 6 Mickey Mantle's two homers highlight New York's 16-3 victory at Forbes Field, evening the Series.

October 27 Trying to jump ahead of the NL, the AL admits Los Angeles and Washington to the league with plans to have the new clubs begin competition in 1961. Calvin Griffith is given permission to move the existing Washington Senators franchise to Minneapolis/St. Paul. League president Joe Cronin says the AL will play a 162-game schedule, with 18 games against each opponent.

November 2 Roger Maris nips Mickey Mantle for the AL's Most Valuable Player award, 225-222.

November 17 The new Washington franchise is awarded to Elwood Quesada, Washington native, head of the Federal Aviation Agency.

November 22 The AL proposes that both leagues expand to nine teams in 1961 and begin interleague play. It will delay entering the Los Angeles market if the NL agrees.

November 26 Twins is the appropriate new name chosen for the club transplanted from Washington to the Twin Cities of Minneapolis/St. Paul.

December 5 President Joe Cronin suggests that if the NL starts its new New York franchise in 1961, the AL will stay out of Los Angeles until 1962. The NL turned down the suggested compromise of November 22 because Houston will not be ready in 1961.

December 6 A group headed by movie star Gene Autry and former football star Bob Reynolds is awarded the new AL Los Angeles Angels. Fred Haney will be general manager.

December 20 Charlie Finley buys 52 percent of the A's from the late Arnold Johnson's estate.

	BALTIMORE		BOSTON		CHICAGO		CLEVELAND		DETROIT		KANSAS CITY		NEW YORK		WASHINGTON
M	P.Richards	M	B.Jurges	M	A.Lopez	M	J.Gordon	M	J.Dykes	M	B.Elliott	M	C.Stengel	M	C.Lavagetto
1B	J.Gentile	M	D.Baker	1B	R.Sievers	M	J.White	M	B.Hitchcock	1B	M.Throneberry	1B	B.Skowron	1B	G.Becquer
2B	M.Breeding	M	P.Higgins	2B	N.Fox	M	J.Dykes	M	J.Gordon	2B	J.Lumpe	2B	B.Richardson	2B	B.Gardner
SS	R.Hansen	1B	V.Wertz	SS	L.Aparicio	1B	V.Power	1B	N.Cash	SS	K.Hamlin	SS	T.Kubek	SS	J.Valdivielso
3B	B.Robinson	2B	P.Runnels	3B	G.Freese	2B	K.Aspromonte	2B	F.Bolling	3B	A.Carey	3B	C.Boyer	3B	R.Bertoia
LF	G.Woodling	SS	D.Buddin	LF	M.Minoso	SS	W.Held	SS	C.Fernandez	LF	N.Siebern	LF	H.Lopez	LF	J.Lemon
CF	J.Brandt	3B	F.Malzone	CF	J.Landis	3B	B.Phillips	3B	E.Yost	CF	B.Tuttle	CF	M.Mantle	CF	L.Green
RF	G.Stephens	LF	T.Williams	RF	A.Smith	LF	T.Francona	LF	C.Maxwell	RF	R.Snyder	RF	R.Maris	RF	B.Allison
C	G.Triandos	CF	W.Tasby	C	S.Lollar	CF	J.Piersall	CF	A.Kaline	C	P.Daley	C	E.Howard	C	E.Battey
		RF	L.Clinton			RF	H.Kuenn	RF	R.Colavito						
O	A.Pilarcik	C	R.Nixon	1	T.Kluszewski	C	J.Romano	C	L.Berberet	O	H.Bauer	CO	Y.Berra	S2	B.Consolo
1	W.Dropo			3S	S.Esposito					31	D.Williams	32	G.McDougald	O	D.Dobbek
O	J.Busby	2S	P.Green	3	B.Goodman	23	J.Temple	O	N.Chrisley	O	W.Herzog	O	B.Cerv	13	H.Killebrew
C	C.Courtney	O	G.Geiger	C	J.Ginsberg	S	M.DeLaHoz	1	S.Bilko	C	H.Chiti	C	J.Blanchard	O	F.Throneberry
O	D.Nicholson	O	C.Hardy	1	E.Torgeson	O	M.Keough	C	R.Wilson	C	D.Kravitz	1	K.Hadley	O	P.Whisenant
O	W.Tasby	O	R.Repulski	O	J.Hicks	O	W.Bond	3	O.Virgil	S2	B.Johnson	1	D.Long	C	H.Naragon
1	B.Boyd	C	H.Sullivan	O	F.Robinson	C	R.Wilson	C	H.Chiti	O	B.Cerv	2S	J.DeMaestri	D	D.Mincher
O	A.Pearson	O	B.Thomson	C	D.Brown	C	R.Nixon	2S	C.Wise	O	J.Delsing	O	K.Hunt	/O	E.Valo
2S	B.Klaus	O	G.Stephens	/3	J.Martin	/1	B.Hale	O	S.Amoros	/O	L.Posada	O	J.Pisoni	S	Z.Versalles
/O	D.Philley	O	M.Keough	/C	C.Carreon	C	H.Foiles	S	C.Veal	/O	R.Jablonski	/C	J.Gonder	/2	J.Schaive
C	J.Ginsberg	C	E.Sadowski	O	J.Rivera	3	J.Morgan	/2	H.Foiles	/2	C.Boak	/O	E.Valo	H	K.Aspromonte
/O	J.Powers	1	R.Boone	/C	E.Averill	S3	G.Strickland	1	D.Gernert	/1	J.McManus	/3	D.Johnson	H	J.Jacobs
/C	V.Thomas	C	J.Pagliaroni	/O	S.Johnson	/S	R.Bridges	/S	D.McAuliffe	/2	L.Klimchock	/3	A.Carey		
/O	R.Barker	C1	D.Gile	H	J.McAnany	/O	T.Cline	O	J.Groth	/2	H.Foiles	/C	Bi.Shantz	P	P.Ramos
/O	B.Thomson	/1	R.Jackson			/O	C.Tanner	/3	R.Bridges	/2	W.Terwilliger			P	D.Lee
/2	J.Adair	2	M.Coughtry	P	E.Wynn	O	C.Hardy	/1	G.Harris			P	A.Ditmar	P	P.Pascual
/O	G.Green	/2	R.Webster	P	B.Pierce	H	J.Powers	H	E.Lindbeck	P	R.Herbert	P	W.Ford	P	J.Kralick
/C	D.Rice	/O	J.Busby	P	B.Shaw	/O	D.Dillard			P	B.Daley	P	B.Turley	RP	T.Clevenger
R	B.Shetrone			P	F.Baumann	/O	P.Whisenant	P	F.Lary	P	D.Hall	P	R.Terry	RP	C.Stobbs
		P	B.Monbouquette	P	R.Kemmerer	/3	S.Demeter	P	J.Bunning	P	N.Garver	P	J.Coates	RP	H.Woodeshick
P	C.Estrada	P	T.Brewer	RP	G.Staley			P	B.Bruce	RP	J.Kucks	RP	D.Maas		
P	M.Pappas	P	F.Sullivan	RP	D.Donovan	P	J.Perry	P	D.Mossi	RP	K.Johnson	RP	Bo.Shantz	P	B.Fischer
P	J.Fisher	P	I.Delock	RP	T.Lown	P	M.Grant	P	P.Burnside	RP	M.Kutyna	RP	G.Gabler	P	R.Moore
P	S.Barber	P	B.Muffett			P	G.Bell	RP	H.Aguirre					P	J.Kaat
P	H.Brown	RP	M.Fornieles	P	H.Score	P	B.Latman	RP	D.Sisler	P	D.Larsen	P	E.Grba	P	R.Hernandez
RP	G.Jones	RP	T.Sturdivant	P	R.Moore	P	D.Stigman	RP	B.Fischer			P	B.Stafford	P	T.Morgan
		RP	T.Borland	P	M.Garcia	RP	J.Klippstein			P	B.Trowbridge	P	R.Duren	/P	R.Kemmerer
P	H.Wilhelm			/P	B.Rush	RP	D.Newcombe	P	P.Foytack	P	J.Tsitouris	P	B.Short	/P	T.Sadowski
P	J.Walker	P	J.Casale	/P	K.McBride			P	R.Regan	P	B.Davis	P	J.James	/P	D.Hyde
P	A.Portocarrero	P	E.Wilson	/P	A.Worthington	P	B.Locke	P	T.Morgan	P	L.Kiely	P	L.Arroyo	/P	T.Abernathy
P	W.Stock	P	D.Hillman	/P	D.Ferrarese	P	W.Hawkins	P	R.Semproch	/P	J.Briggs	/P	F.Kipp	/P	H.Maestri
P	B.Hoeft	P	T.Wills	/P	J.Striker	P	J.Harshman	P	C.Labine	/P	G.Brunet	P	H.Stowe		
/P	J.Anderson	P	T.Bowsfield	/P	G.Peters	P	T.Bowsfield	/P	G.Spencer	/P	D.Wickersham				
/P	R.Coleman	/P	C.Nichols			P	J.Briggs			P	R.Blemker				
/P	B.Mabe	/P	A.Worthington			/P	F.Funk	P	H.Reed						
		/P	N.Chittum			/P	C.Mathias								
		/P	A.Earley			/P	C.Thomas								
		/P	T.Stallard			/P	M.Lee								
						/P	B.Tiefenauer								
						/P	B.Grim								

TEAM	G	W	L	PCT	GB	R	OR	AB	H	2B	3B	HR	BB	SO	AVG	OBP	SLG	PRO	PRO+	BR	/A	PF	CHI	RC	SB	CS	SBA	SBR
NY	155	97	57	.630		746	627	5290	1377	215	40	193	537	818	.260	.332	.426	.758	117	63	105	94	100	747	37	23	62	-3
BAL	154	89	65	.578	8	682	606	5170	1307	206	33	123	596	801	.253	.334	.377	.711	99	-8	1	99	103	659	37	24	61	-3
CHI	154	87	67	.565	10	741	617	5191	1402	242	38	112	567	648	.270	.348	.396	.744	108	57	64	99	101	726	122	48	72	8
CLE	154	76	78	.494	21	667	693	5296	1415	218	20	127	444	573	.267	.328	.388	.716	102	-11	10	97	101	673	58	25	70	2
WAS	154	73	81	.474	24	672	696	5248	1283	205	43	147	584	883	.244	.326	.384	.710	99	-18	-11	99	101	656	52	43	55	-10
DET	154	71	83	.461	26	633	644	5202	1243	188	34	150	636	728	.239	.326	.375	.701	93	-32	-50	103	97	651	66	32	67	1
BOS	154	65	89	.422	32	658	775	5215	1359	234	32	124	570	798	.261	.336	.389	.725	99	16	-8	104	95	674	34	28	55	-7
KC	155	58	96	.377	39	615	756	5226	1303	212	34	110	513	744	.249	.318	.366	.684	90	-68	-72	101	103	598	16	11	59	-2
TOT	617					5414		41838	10689	1720	274	1086	4447	5993	.255	.331	.388	.718							422	234	64	-14

TEAM	CG	SH	SV	IP	H	H/G	HR	BB	SO	RAT	ERA	ERA+	OAV	OOB	PR	/A	PF	CPI	FA	E	DP	FW	PW	BW	SBW	DIF
NY	38	16	42	1398	1225	7.9	129	609	712	12.0	3.52	102	.238	.322	55	10	93	98	.979	129	162	.2	1.0	10.6	-.1	8.3
BAL	48	11	22	1375²	1222	8.0	117	552	785	11.8	3.52	108	.241	.320	54	44	98	98	.982	108	172	1.4	4.5	-.1		6.2
CHI	42	11	26	1381	1338	8.7	127	533	695	12.3	3.60	105	.258	.329	41	27	98	106	.982	109	175	1.4	2.7	6.5	1.0	-1.5
CLE	32	10	30	1382¹	1308	8.5	161	636	771	12.8	3.95	95	.252	.336	-12	-33	97	103	.978	128	165	.2	-3.3	1.0	.4	.8
WAS	34	10	35	1405¹	1392	8.9	130	538	775	12.6	3.77	103	.260	.331	16	18	100	103	.973	165	159	-2.1	1.8	-1.1	-.8	-1.7
DET	40	7	25	1405²	1336	8.6	141	474	824	11.9	3.64	109	.251	.317	37	50	102	99	.977	138	138	-.5	5.1	-5.1	.3	-5.8
BOS	34	6	23	1361	1440	9.5	127	580	767	13.6	4.62	87	.273	.349	-113	-88	104	94	.976	141	156	-.6	-8.9	-.8	-.5	-1.1
KC	44	4	14	1374	1428	9.4	160	525	664	13.1	4.38	91	.271	.342	-77	-60	103	100	.979	127	149	.3	-6.1	-7.3	-.0	-5.9
TOT	312	75	217	11083		8.7				12.5	3.87		.255	.331					.978	1045	1276					

Runs		Hits		Doubles		Triples		Home Runs		Total Bases	
Mantle-NY	119	Minoso-Chi	184	Francona-Cle	36	Fox-Chi	10	Mantle-NY	40	Mantle-NY	294
Maris-NY	98	Robinson-Bal	175	Skowron-NY	34	Robinson-Bal	9	Maris-NY	39	Maris-NY	290
Minoso-Chi	89	Fox-Chi	175	Minoso-Chi	32			Lemon-Was	38	Skowron-NY	284
Landis-Chi	89	Smith-Chi	169	Freese-Chi	32			Colavito-Det	35	Minoso-Chi	284
Sievers-Chi	87	Runnels-Bos	169					Killebrew-Was	31	Lemon-Was	268

Runs Batted In		Runs Produced		Bases On Balls		Batting Average		On Base Percentage		Slugging Average	
Maris-NY	112	Minoso-Chi	174	Yost-Det	125	Runnels-Bos	.320	Yost-Det	.416	Maris-NY	.581
Minoso-Chi	105	Mantle-NY	173	Mantle-NY	111	Smith-Chi	.315	Woodling-Bal	.403	Mantle-NY	.558
Wertz-Bos	103	Maris-NY	171	Allison-Was	92	Minoso-Chi	.311	Runnels-Bos	.403	Killebrew-Was	.534
Lemon-Was	100	Sievers-Chi	152	Woodling-Bal	84	Skowron-NY	.309	Mantle-NY	.402	Sievers-Chi	.534
Gentile-Bal	98	Robinson-Bal	148	Landis-Chi	80	Kuenn-Cle	.308	Sievers-Chi	.399	Skowron-NY	.528

Production		Adjusted Production		Batter Runs		Adjusted Batter Runs		Clutch Hitting Index		Runs Created	
Mantle-NY	.960	Mantle-NY	166	Mantle-NY	43.9	Mantle-NY	50.6	Wertz-Bos	149	Mantle-NY	125
Maris-NY	.955	Maris-NY	164	Williams-Bos	43.5	Maris-NY	42.3	Power-Cle	115	Maris-NY	111
Sievers-Chi	.933	Sievers-Chi	152	Maris-NY	36.5	Williams-Bos	40.4	Woodling-Bal	110	Minoso-Chi	104
Killebrew-Was	.911	Killebrew-Was	145	Sievers-Chi	32.1	Sievers-Chi	33.0	Fox-Chi	109	Lemon-Was	99
Skowron-NY	.884	Skowron-NY	144	Killebrew-Was	26.9	Skowron-NY	29.7	Minoso-Chi	109	Francona-Cle	96

Total Average		Stolen Bases		Stolen Base Average		Stolen Base Runs		Fielding Runs		Total Player Rating	
Mantle-NY	1.053	Aparicio-Chi	51	Aparicio-Chi	86.4	Aparicio-Chi	10.5	Aparicio-Chi	30.4	Mantle-NY	4.4
Maris-NY	.992	Landis-Chi	23	Kaline-Det	82.6	Landis-Chi	3.3	Boyer-NY	27.6	Maris-NY	3.8
Sievers-Chi	.960	Green-Was	21	Landis-Chi	79.3	Kaline-Det	3.3	Power-Cle	21.0	Aparicio-Chi	3.8
Killebrew-Was	.936	Kaline-Det	19	Piersall-Cle	78.3	Piersall-Cle	2.4	Tuttle-KC	17.1	Williams-Bos	3.3
Lemon-Was	.871	Piersall-Cle	18	Green-Was	72.4	Mantle-NY	2.4	Landis-Chi	12.9	Runnels-Bos	3.2

Wins		Win Percentage		Games		Complete Games		Shutouts		Saves	
Perry-Cle	18	Perry-Cle	.643	Fornieles-Bos	70	Lary-Det	15	Wynn-Chi	4	Klippstein-Cle	14
Estrada-Bal	18	Ditmar-NY	.625	Staley-Chi	64	Ramos-Was	14	Perry-Cle	4	Fornieles-Bos	14
B.Daley-KC	16	Estrada-Bal	.621	Clevenger-Was	53	Herbert-KC	14	Ford-NY	4	Moore-Chi-Was	13
		Pappas-Bal	.577	Moore-Chi-Was	51	Wynn-Chi	13			B.Shantz-NY	11
				Kutyna-KC	51	B.Daley-KC	13				

Innings Pitched		Fewest Hits/Game		Fewest BB/Game		Strikeouts		Strikeouts/Game		Ratio	
Lary-Det	274.1	Estrada-Bal	6.99	Brown-Bal	1.25	Bunning-Det	201	Bunning-Det	7.18	Brown-Bal	10.08
Ramos-Was	274.0	Turley-NY	7.17	Mossi-Det	1.82	Ramos-Was	160	Bell-Cle	6.34	Bunning-Det	10.43
Perry-Cle	261.1	Barber-Bal	7.33	Hall-KC	1.88	Wynn-Chi	158	Estrada-Bal	6.21	Baumann-Chi	10.83
Herbert-KC	252.2	Bunning-Det	7.75	Lary-Det	2.03	Lary-Det	149	Wynn-Chi	5.99	Mossi-Det	10.86
Bunning-Det	252.0	Ford-NY	7.85	Pierce-Chi	2.11	Estrada-Bal	144	Monbouquette-Bos	5.61	Ford-NY	10.93

Earned Run Average		Adjusted ERA		Opponents' Batting Avg.		Opponents' On Base Pct.		Starter Runs		Adjusted Starter Runs	
Baumann-Chi	2.67	Bunning-Det	142	Estrada-Bal	.218	Brown-Bal	.286	Bunning-Det	30.4	Bunning-Det	32.8
Bunning-Det	2.79	Baumann-Chi	141	Turley-NY	.222	Bunning-Det	.293	Baumann-Chi	24.7	Baumann-Chi	22.8
Brown-Bal	3.06	Brown-Bal	125	Barber-Bal	.226	Mossi-Det	.296	Ditmar-NY	18.0	Herbert-KC	19.7
Ditmar-NY	3.06	Herbert-KC	121	Ford-NY	.235	Ford-NY	.299	Ford-NY	16.9	Pascual-Was	14.5
Ford-NY	3.08	Barber-Bal	118	Bunning-Det	.236	Terry-NY	.300	Herbert-KC	16.7	Kralick-Was	14.2

Clutch Pitching Index		Relief Runs		Adjusted Relief Runs		Relief Ranking		Total Pitcher Index		Total Baseball Ranking	
Ditmar-NY	121	Staley-Chi	18.6	Staley-Chi	17.4	Staley-Chi	32.0	Staley-Chi	3.7	Mantle-NY	4.4
Perry-Cle	113	Fornieles-Bos	14.9	Fornieles-Bos	17.0	Fornieles-Bos	25.9	Fornieles-Bos	2.9	Maris-NY	3.8
Lee-Was	113	Sisler-Det	12.4	Sisler-Det	13.2	Sisler-Det	20.0	Bunning-Det	2.6	Aparicio-Chi	3.8
Baumann-Chi	113	Aguirre-Det	10.7	Aguirre-Det	11.6	Aguirre-Det	11.6	Herbert-KC	2.5	Staley-Chi	3.7
Herbert-KC	111	B.Shantz-NY	8.1	Stobbs-Was	7.5	Klippstein-Cle	11.2	Pascual-Was	2.2	Williams-Bos	3.3

January 31 Houston voters approve a bond to finance a luxury domed stadium, the final hurdle standing between the city and major league baseball.

February 9 Willie Mays signs for $85,000, currently the biggest contract in major league baseball.

March 14 George Weiss is lured from retirement to become president of the New York Mets.

March 24 The New York State Senate approves $55 million for a new baseball stadium at Flushing Meadows Park in Queens.

March 31 A Pacific Coast League proposal to use a designated batter for the pitcher is voted down 8-1 by the Professional Baseball Rules Committee. The committee also rules that every club must designate a manager within 30 minutes of game time, a move prompted by the Cubs' college of coaches.

April 23 Art Mahaffey fans a batter in each inning and 17 in all, a Phillies' record, while beating the Cubs, 6-0. The Phils won the first game, 1-0, behind Frank Sullivan.

April 28 Five days past his 40th birthday, Braves left-hander Warren Spahn becomes the second-oldest major league pitcher (after Cy Young) to hurl a no-hitter, blanking San Francisco, 1-0. Hank Aaron drives in the only run off loser Sam Jones. It is Spahn's 290th win and 52nd shutout.

April 30 Using Joey Amalfitano's bat, Willie Mays becomes the ninth player in major league history to enjoy a four-homer game. His eight RBIs pace the Giants to a 14-4 win at Milwaukee's County Stadium.

May 3 Another brilliant Warren Spahn performance is spoiled when left fielder Mel Roach's misplay costs the Milwaukee ace a second no-hitter in a row. He settles for a two-hitter in topping the Dodgers, 4-1.

June 23 With two home runs, Stan Musial passes Lou Gehrig on the all-time list for extra base hits.

July 7 Pittsburgh puts Vern Law on the retired list, on doctor's orders, to rest his sore right arm.

July 11 Strong winds dominate the first All-Star Game of 1961. A capacity crowd sees pitcher Stu Miller blown off the mound in the ninth inning at Candlestick Park. A balk is called, and it enables the AL to forge a 3-3 tie before losing 5-4 in 10 innings.

August 3 A 19-0 rout of St. Louis by Pittsburgh matches the most lopsided shutout in the century. The first had been achieved by the Cubs against the Giants on June 7, 1906.

August 16 Cincinnati takes the NL lead for good with a shutout sweep 6-0 and 8-0 at Los Angeles before 72,140, a record crowd for a NL doubleheader. Jim O'Toole and Bob Purkey are the winning pitchers.

September 26 Cincinnati clinches its first NL pennant since 1940. Home runs by Frank Robinson and Jerry Lynch give the Reds a 6-3 win at Chicago.

September 27 Sandy Koufax fans seven Phils in the course of a 2-1 win to set a NL record for strikeouts in a season: 269. This surpasses Christy Mathewson's 267 in 1903, which was accomplished in 367 innings pitched, as opposed to Koufax's 255.

October 2 Casey Stengel agrees to come out of retirement to manage the NL expansion New York Mets next year.

October 10 An expansion draft to stock the new NL clubs takes place in Cincinnati. Houston selections include Bobby Shantz, Ken Johnson, Dick Farrell, and Bob Lillis. New York takes Roger Craig, Gil Hodges, Don Zimmer, and Gus Bell among others.

November 22 Right fielder Frank Robinson is the first Reds player in 21 years to win the NL MVP, taking 219 of 224 possible votes.

CHICAGO		CINCINNATI		LOS ANGELES		MILWAUKEE		PHILADELPHIA		PITTSBURGH		SAN FRANCISCO		ST.LOUIS	
M	V.Himsl	M	F.Hutchinson	M	W.Alston	M	C.Dressen	M	G.Mauch	M	D.Murtaugh	M	A.Dark	M	S.Hemus
M	H.Craft	1B	G.Coleman	1B	G.Hodges	M	B.Tebbetts	1B	P.Herrera	1B	D.Stuart	1B	W.McCovey	M	J.Keane
M	V.Himsl	2B	D.Blasingame	2B	C.Neal	1B	J.Adcock	2B	T.Taylor	2B	B.Mazeroski	2B	J.Amalfitano	1B	B.White
M	E.Tappe	SS	E.Kasko	SS	M.Wills	2B	F.Bolling	SS	R.Amaro	SS	D.Groat	SS	J.Pagan	2B	J.Javier
M	H.Craft	3B	G.Freese	3B	J.Gilliam	SS	R.McMillan	3B	C.Smith	3B	D.Hoak	3B	J.Davenport	SS	A.Grammas
M	V.Himsl	LF	W.Post	LF	W.Moon	3B	E.Mathews	LF	J.Callison	LF	B.Skinner	LF	H.Kuenn	3B	K.Boyer
M	E.Tappe	CF	V.Pinson	CF	W.Davis	LF	F.Thomas	CF	T.Gonzalez	CF	B.Virdon	CF	W.Mays	LF	S.Musial
M	L.Klein	RF	F.Robinson	RF	T.Davis	CF	H.Aaron	RF	K.Walters	RF	R.Clemente	RF	F.Alou	CF	C.Flood
M	E.Tappe	C	J.Zimmerman	C	J.Roseboro	RF	L.Maye	C	C.Dalrymple	C	S.Burgess	C	E.Bailey	RF	C.James
1B	E.Bouchee					C	J.Torre							C	J.Schaffer
2B	D.Zimmer	O	G.Bell	O1	R.Fairly			2S	B.Malkmus	C	H.Smith	1O	O.Cepeda		
SS	E.Banks	O	J.Lynch	1	N.Larker	O	G.Cimoli	O1	D.Demeter	O	J.Christopher	2	C.Hiller	O1	J.Cunningham
3B	R.Santo	S	L.Cardenas	O	F.Howard	13	M.Jones	1	L.Walls	S	R.Nelson	O	M.Alou	O	D.Taussig
LF	B.Williams	O	J.Edwards	O	D.Snider	O	A.Spangler	O	B.Smith	O	D.Schofield	S	E.Bressoud	S2	B.Lillis
CF	A.Heist	2	E.Chacon	3	D.Spencer	S2	F.Mantilla	O	W.Covington	O	G.Cimoli	C	J.Orsino	C	C.Sawatski
RF	G.Altman	C	B.Schmidt	O	N.Sherry	C	C.Lau	O	B.DelGreco	O	W.Moryn	C	H.Landrith	O	C.Warwick
C	D.Bertell	1	D.Gernert	/3	B.Aspromonte	O	J.DeMerit	C	D.Johnson	C	D.Leppert	C	T.Haller	S	D.Spencer
		C	D.Johnson	O	G.Windhorn	C	S.White	3	B.Sadowski	/3	J.Logan	2S	E.Bowman	C	H.Smith
O	R.Ashburn	C	E.Bailey	O	D.Camilli	/1	B.Boyd	3	J.Woods	/O	D.Clendenon	/1	J.Marshall	2	R.Schoendienst
2S	J.Kindall	/2	J.Baumer	O	D.Demeter	/O	M.Roach	C	C.Coleman	/3	G.Baker	O	B.Farley	S	J.Buchek
C	S.Taylor	O	P.Whisenant	/3	C.Smith	/C	D.Crandall	/O	E.Valo	/C	B.Oldis	/C	B.Schmidt	C	T.McCarver
1S	A.Rodgers	/3	W.Jones	O	C.Warwick	/O	H.Taylor	/O	T.Curry	/O	R.Mejias	H	D.Blasingame	C	D.Landrum
O	B.Will	/3	C.Cook	3	B.Lillis	/O	W.Covington	2	G.Williams					C	G.Oliver
O	F.Thomas	H	H.Anderson	/1	T.Harkness	/S	J.Logan	C	C.Neeman	P	B.Friend	P	M.McCormick	S	J.Gotay
/1	M.Roach	H	H.Bevan			H	N.Chrisley	C	J.Coker	P	J.Gibbon	P	J.Sanford	/O	W.Moryn
C	M.Thacker	/O	J.Gaines	P	S.Koufax	H	B.Martin	C	A.Kenders	P	H.Haddix	P	J.Marichal	O	E.Olivares
C	C.Barragan			P	D.Drysdale	/C	P.Roof	/S	J.Koppe	P	E.Francis	P	S.Jones	/O	B.Nieman
/2	K.Hubbs			P	S.Williams					P	V.Mizell	P	B.Loes	/O	D.Clemens
/1	M.Morhardt	P	J.O'Toole	P	J.Podres	P	L.Burdette	P	A.Mahaffey	RP	C.Labine	RP	B.O'Dell	H	G.Crowe
/O	D.Murphy	P	B.Purkey	RP	R.Craig	P	W.Spahn	RP	R.Face	RP	S.Miller	/C	C.Cannizzaro
/O	L.Brock	P	K.Hunt	RP	L.Sherry	P	B.Buhl	P	F.Sullivan	RP	B.Shantz	RP	J.Duffalo		
/O	J.McAnany	P	J.Maloney	RP	R.Perranoski	P	C.Willey	P	D.Ferrarese					P	R.Sadecki
/O	N.Mathews	RP	J.Brosnan			P	D.Nottebart	P	D.Green	P	T.Sturdivant	P	D.LeMay	P	L.Jackson
H	G.Freese	RP	J.Hook	P	T.Farrell	RP	D.McMahon	RP	J.Baldschun	P	A.McBean	P	B.Bolin	P	B.Gibson
/O	S.Drake	RP	S.Jones	P	J.Golden			RP	K.Lehman	P	V.Law	P	E.Fisher	P	C.Simmons
				/P	P.Ortega	P	B.Hendley	P	C.Short	/P	A.Jackson	/P	D.Zanni	P	E.Broglio
P	D.Cardwell	P	K.Johnson	/P	E.Palmquist	P	T.Cloninger	P	C.Short	P	F.Green			RP	L.McDaniel
P	G.Hobbie	P	B.Henry	/P	E.Roebuck	P	M.Drabowsky	P	R.Roberts	/P	G.Witt			RP	A.Cicotte
P	D.Ellsworth	P	H.Nunn			P	R.Piche	P	J.Owens	/P	L.Foss			RP	B.Miller
P	J.Curtis	P	M.Bridges			P	C.Raymond	/P	P.Brown	/P	J.Umbricht				
RP	B.Anderson	/P	C.Osteen			P	S.Morehead	/P	T.Farrell	/P	T.Cheney			P	C.Anderson
RP	D.Drott					/P	J.Antonelli	/P	J.Meyer					P	M.McDermott
RP	D.Elston					/P	K.MacKenzie							/P	R.Washburn
						/P	G.Brunet							P	E.Bauta
						/P	C.Olivo							/P	B.Tiefenauer
P	J.Brewer														
P	B.Schultz														
P	J.Schaffernoth														
P	M.Wright														
/P	D.Burwell														

TEAM	G	W	L	PCT	GB	R	OR	AB	H	2B	3B	HR	BB	SO	AVG	OBP	SLG	PRO	PRO+	BR	/A	PF	CHI	RC	SB	CS	SBA	SBR
CIN	154	93	61	.604		710	653	5243	1414	247	35	158	423	761	.270	.328	.421	.749	102	19	10	101	101	713	70	33	68	1
LA	154	89	65	.578	4	735	697	5189	1358	193	40	157	596	796	.262	.340	.405	.745	95	29	-35	109	100	722	86	45	66	-1
SF	155	85	69	.552	8	773	655	5233	1379	219	32	183	506	764	.264	.332	.423	.755	109	35	62	96	106	719	79	54	59	-9
MIL	155	83	71	.539	10	712	656	5288	1365	199	34	188	534	880	.258	.330	.415	.745	110	19	63	94	98	714	70	43	62	-5
STL	155	80	74	.519	13	703	668	5307	1436	236	51	103	494	745	.271	.336	.393	.729	90	-3	-72	110	100	702	46	28	62	-3
PIT	154	75	79	.487	18	694	675	5311	1448	232	57	128	428	721	.273	.330	.410	.740	101	8	6	100	99	694	26	30	46	-10
CHI	156	64	90	.416	29	689	800	5344	1364	238	51	176	539	1027	.255	.327	.418	.745	101	16	7	101	95	726	35	25	58	-5
PHI	155	47	107	.305	46	584	796	5213	1265	185	50	103	475	928	.243	.311	.357	.668	84	-123	-115	99	102	577	56	30	65	-1
TOT	619					5600		42128	11029	1749	350	1196	3995	6622	.262	.329	.405	.735							468	288	62	-32

TEAM	CG	SH	SV	IP	H	H/G	HR	BB	SO	RAT	ERA	ERA+	OAV	OOB	PR	/A	PF	CPI	FA	E	DP	FW	PW	BW	SBW	DIF
CIN	46	12	40	1370	1300	8.5	147	500	829	12.0	3.78	107	.250	.320	38	43	101	98	.977	134	124	.7	4.3	1.0	.5	9.6
LA	40	10	35	1378[1]	1346	8.8	167	544	1105	12.7	4.04	101	.256	.331	-2	46	108	101	.975	144	162	.1	4.6	-3.5	.3	10.5
SF	39	9	30	1388	1306	8.5	152	502	924	11.9	3.77	101	.249	.318	40	6	95	98	.977	133	126	.8	.6	6.2	-.5	1.0
MIL	57	8	16	1391[1]	1357	8.8	153	493	652	12.1	3.89	96	.258	.324	21	-24	93	101	.982	111	152	2.0	-2.4	6.3	-.0	.2
STL	49	10	24	1368[2]	1334	8.8	136	570	823	12.7	3.74	118	.256	.333	44	100	109	106	.972	166	165	-1.1	9.9	-7.1	.1	1.2
PIT	34	9	29	1362	1442	9.5	121	400	759	12.3	3.92	102	.274	.328	17	10	99	102	.975	150	187	-.2	1.0	-.6	-.6	-2.8
CHI	34	6	25	1385	1492	9.7	165	465	755	12.9	4.48	93	.277	.338	-70	-47	104	99	.970	183	175	-2.0	-4.7	.7	-.0	-7.0
PHI	29	9	13	1383[1]	1452	9.4	155	521	775	13.1	4.61	88	.273	.342	-88	-82	101	96	.976	146	179	.0	-8.1	-11.4	.3	-10.8
TOT	328	73	212	11026[2]		9.0				12.5	4.03		.262	.329					.976	1167	1270					

Runs
Mays-SF 129
Robinson-Cin 117
Aaron-Mil 115
Boyer-StL 109

Hits
Pinson-Cin 208
Clemente-Pit 201
Aaron-Mil 197
Boyer-StL 194
Cepeda-SF 182

Doubles
Aaron-Mil 39
Pinson-Cin 34
Santo-Chi 32
Robinson-Cin 32
Mays-SF 32

Triples
Altman-Cin 12
White-StL 11
Callison-Phi 11
Boyer-StL 11

Home Runs
Cepeda-SF 46
Mays-SF 40
Robinson-Cin 37
Stuart-Pit 35
Adcock-Mil 35

Total Bases
Aaron-Mil 358
Cepeda-SF 356
Mays-SF 334
Robinson-Cin 333
Clemente-Pit 320

Runs Batted In
Cepeda-SF 142
Robinson-Cin 124
Mays-SF 123
Aaron-Mil 120
Stuart-Pit 117

Runs Produced
Mays-SF 212
Robinson-Cin 204
Cepeda-SF 201
Aaron-Mil 201
Boyer-StL 180

Bases On Balls
Mathews-Mil 93
Moon-LA 89
Mays-SF 81
Gilliam-LA 79

Batting Average
Clemente-Pit ..... .351
Pinson-Cin ..... .343
Boyer-StL ..... .329
Moon-LA ..... .328
Aaron-Mil ..... .327

On Base Percentage
Moon-LA ..... .438
Robinson-Cin ..... .411
Mathews-Mil ..... .405
Boyer-StL ..... .400
Mays-SF ..... .395

Slugging Average
Robinson-Cin ..... .611
Cepeda-SF ..... .609
Aaron-Mil ..... .594
Mays-SF ..... .584
Stuart-Pit ..... .581

Production
Robinson-Cin 1.022
Aaron-Mil ..... .979
Mays-SF ..... .979
Cepeda-SF ..... .972
Clemente-Pit ..... .951

Adjusted Production
Aaron-Mil 165
Robinson-Cin 164
Mays-SF 162
Cepeda-SF 158
Mathews-Mil 156

Batter Runs
Robinson-Cin 52.4
Aaron-Mil 46.0
Mays-SF 45.8
Cepeda-SF 40.7
Mathews-Mil 40.4

Adjusted Batter Runs
Aaron-Mil 53.8
Robinson-Cin 50.8
Mays-SF 50.4
Mathews-Mil 47.8
Cepeda-SF 45.1

Clutch Hitting Index
Moon-LA 113
McMillan-Mil 110
Davenport-SF 110
Adcock-Mil 105
Cepeda-SF 105

Runs Created
Robinson-Cin 137
Aaron-Mil 132
Mays-SF 130
Mathews-Mil 128
Boyer-StL 126

Total Average
Robinson-Cin 1.119
Mays-SF 1.017
Moon-LA 1.003
Aaron-Mil ..... .993
Mathews-Mil ..... .981

Stolen Bases
Wills-LA 35
Pinson-Cin 23
Robinson-Cin 22
Aaron-Mil 21
Mays-SF 18

Stolen Base Average
Robinson-Cin 88.0
Wills-LA 70.0
Aaron-Mil 70.0
Pinson-Cin 69.7
Mays-SF 66.7

Stolen Base Runs
Robinson-Cin 4.8
Maye-Mil 2.4
Williams-Chi 1.8
Wills-LA 1.5
Gonzalez-Phi 1.5

Fielding Runs
Mazeroski-Pit 30.5
Pinson-Cin 19.2
Malkmus-Phi 16.3
Clemente-Pit 14.4
Amaro-Phi 14.1

Total Player Rating
Aaron-Mil 5.6
Robinson-Cin 5.5
Mays-SF 5.0
Clemente-Pit 4.4
Mathews-Mil 4.2

Wins
Spahn-Mil 21
Jay-Cin 21
O'Toole-Cin 19

Win Percentage
Podres-LA ..... .783
O'Toole-Cin ..... .679
Jay-Cin ..... .677
Burdette-Mil ..... .621
Spahn-Mil ..... .618

Games
Baldschun-Phi 65
Miller-SF 63
Face-Pit 62
Elston-Chi 58
Anderson-Chi 57

Complete Games
Spahn-Mil 21
Koufax-LA 15
Jay-Cin 14
Burdette-Mil 14

Shutouts
Spahn-Mil 4
Jay-Cin 4

Saves
Miller-SF 17
Face-Pit 17
Henry-Cin 16
Brosnan-Cin 16
L.Sherry-LA 15

Innings Pitched
Burdette-Mil 272.1
Spahn-Mil 262.2
Cardwell-Chi 259.1
Koufax-LA 255.2
O'Toole-Cin 252.2

Fewest Hits/Game
Koufax-LA 7.46
Jay-Cin 7.90
Gibson-StL 7.92
Sadecki-StL 7.92
Spahn-Mil 8.09

Fewest BB/Game
Burdette-Mil 1.09
Friend-Pit 1.72
Purkey-Cin 1.86
Spahn-Mil 2.19
Ellsworth-Chi 2.31

Strikeouts
Koufax-LA 269
Williams-LA 205
Drysdale-LA 182
O'Toole-Cin 178
Gibson-StL 166

Strikeouts/Game
Koufax-LA 9.47
Williams-LA 7.84
Gibson-StL 7.07
Drysdale-LA 6.71
Gibbon-Pit 6.68

Ratio
Spahn-Mil 10.42
Burdette-Mil 10.94
Koufax-LA 10.95
Purkey-Cin 11.03
Jackson-StL 11.22

Earned Run Average
Spahn-Mil 3.02
O'Toole-Cin 3.10
Simmons-StL 3.13
McCormick-SF 3.20
Gibson-StL 3.24

Adjusted ERA
Simmons-StL 141
Gibson-StL 136
O'Toole-Cin 131
Spahn-Mil 124
Koufax-LA 123

Opponents' Batting Avg.
Koufax-LA ..... .222
Jay-Cin ..... .236
Sadecki-StL ..... .238
Gibson-StL ..... .239
O'Toole-Cin ..... .240

Opponents' On Base Pct.
Spahn-Mil ..... .293
Koufax-LA ..... .295
Burdette-Mil ..... .296
Purkey-Cin ..... .297
Jackson-StL ..... .303

Starter Runs
Spahn-Mil 29.7
O'Toole-Cin 26.2
McCormick-SF 23.0
Simmons-StL 19.6
Gibson-StL 18.7

Adjusted Starter Runs
Simmons-StL 27.6
Gibson-StL 27.3
O'Toole-Cin 27.1
Koufax-LA 23.3
Spahn-Mil 21.2

Clutch Pitching Index
Simmons-StL 122
Ellsworth-Chi 121
Podres-LA 116
McCormick-SF 115
Gibson-StL 114

Relief Runs
Miller-SF 18.6
Perranoski-LA 14.1
McMahon-Mil 12.2
Henry-Cin 10.9
Schultz-Chi 9.9

Adjusted Relief Runs
Perranoski-LA 17.2
Miller-SF 15.6
Henry-Cin 11.1
Schultz-Chi 11.0
McMahon-Mil 9.2

Relief Ranking
Miller-SF 26.8
Perranoski-LA 22.8
Schultz-Chi 21.8
Brosnan-Cin 18.5
Henry-Cin 13.1

Total Pitcher Index
Spahn-Mil 3.9
Gibson-StL 3.3
Miller-SF 3.1
Simmons-StL 3.0
O'Toole-Cin 2.7

Total Baseball Ranking
Aaron-Mil 5.6
Robinson-Cin 5.5
Mays-SF 5.0
Clemente-Pit 4.4
Mathews-Mil 4.2

January 29 Billy Hamilton and Max Carey are voted into the Hall of Fame by the Special Veterans Committee.

May 9 Jim Gentile becomes the fourth player to hit grand slams in consecutive at bats (Tony Lazzeri in 1936, Jim Tabor in 1939, Rudy York in 1946 also hit two grand slams, but not in consecutive innings) when he homers off Pedro Ramos in the first and Paul Giel in the second. His eight RBIs in consecutive innings set a record. Gentile also tacks on a sacrifice fly to give him nine RBIs in the 13-5 drubbing of the Twins.

May 12 Bill Monbouquette's 17 strikeouts for the Red Sox are a club record and the most yet by an AL pitcher in a night game. He beats Washington 2-1.

June 12 An ailing Bill Veeck sells his interest in the White Sox to Arthur Allyn. Allyn also buys Hank Greenberg's stock to acquire a controlling interest.

June 18 St. Louis Browns midget Eddie Gaedel dies of a heart attack following a mugging in Chicago. He was 36.

July 17 Following a year-long illness, Ty Cobb succumbs to cancer at age 74 at Emory University Hospital in Atlanta.

September 20 The Yankees' 155th game of 1961 (including a tie) is Roger Maris's last chance to beat the Babe, in compliance with Commissioner Ford Frick's statement that Maris must do it in the same number of games as Ruth. Maris's 59th homer of the year, off Jack Fisher, is short of the record, but helps New York beat Baltimore 4-2, clinching its 26th AL pennant.

September 22 Jim Gentile's fifth grand slam ties the major league single-season record in Baltimore's 8-6 win over Chicago. Each of Gentile's slams comes with Chuck Estrada pitching for the Orioles.

October 1 Maris's tortuous season-long race against Babe Ruth ends in a dramatic at bat against Boston's Tracy Stallard. Maris's classic left-handed swing sends homer No. 61 into the right field stands in "The House That Ruth Built." (Fan Sal Durante grabs the historic ball which he sells for $5,000.) New York's 1-0 win gives the Yanks 109 wins, one short of the club's 1927 record.

October 4 Whitey Ford's third straight World Series shutout, with home runs by Elston Howard and Bill Skowron, gives New York a 2-0 win in the opener against Cincinnati at Yankee Stadium.

October 9 Star reserves Johnny Blanchard and Hector Lopez spark a five-run first inning and 13-5 win for New York. Both hit home runs, and Lopez drives in five runs. Bud Daley's long relief effort wraps up the Series, as Ralph Houk becomes the third rookie pilot to guide a World Series winner.

October 31 A Federal judge rules that Birmingham, Ala., laws against integrated playing fields are illegal, eliminating the last barrier against integration in the Southern Association.

November 8 Whitey Ford is voted the Cy Young Award winner over Warren Spahn.

November 15 Roger Maris is voted AL MVP with 202 votes to 198 for Mickey Mantle and 157 for Jim Gentile.

November 26 The Rules Committee votes 8-1 against legalizing the spitball. Only NL supervisor of umpires Cal Hubbard votes in favor.

BALTIMORE		BOSTON		CHICAGO		CLEVELAND		DETROIT	
M	P.Richards	M	P.Higgins	M	A.Lopez	M	J.Dykes	M	B.Scheffing
M	L.Harris	1B	P.Runnels	1B	R.Sievers	M	M.Harder	1B	N.Cash
1B	J.Gentile	2B	C.Schilling	2B	N.Fox	1B	V.Power	2B	J.Wood
2B	J.Adair	SS	D.Buddin	SS	L.Aparicio	2B	J.Temple	SS	C.Fernandez
SS	R.Hansen	3B	F.Malzone	3B	A.Smith	SS	W.Held	3B	S.Boros
3B	B.Robinson	LF	C.Yastrzemski	LF	M.Minoso	3B	B.Phillips	LF	R.Colavito
LF	R.Snyder	CF	G.Geiger	CF	J.Landis	LF	T.Francona	CF	B.Bruton
CF	J.Brandt	RF	J.Jensen	RF	F.Robinson	CF	J.Piersall	RF	A.Kaline
RF	W.Herzog	C	J.Pagliaroni	C	S.Lollar	RF	W.Kirkland	C	D.Brown
C	G.Triandos					C	J.Romano		
		1	V.Wertz	13	J.Martin			S3	D.McAuliffe
O1	D.Williams	O	C.Hardy	C	C.Carreon	P	M.Grant	C	M.Roarke
2	M.Breeding	C	R.Nixon			P	G.Bell		
O	E.Robinson	S	P.Green	P	J.Pizarro	P	J.Perry	P	F.Lary
				P	F.Baumann	P	B.Latman	P	J.Bunning
P	S.Barber	P	B.Monbouquette	P	B.Pierce	P	W.Hawkins	P	D.Mossi
P	C.Estrada	P	G.Conley	P	C.McLish	RP	B.Locke	P	P.Foytack
P	J.Fisher	P	D.Schwall	P	R.Herbert	RP	F.Funk	P	P.Regan
P	M.Pappas	P	I.Delock	RP	T.Lown	RP	B.Allen	RP	T.Fox
P	H.Brown	P	T.Stallard	RP	R.Kemmerer			RP	H.Aguirre
RP	H.Wilhelm	RP	M.Fornieles	RP	D.Larsen	P	D.Stigman		
RP	W.Stock	RP	B.Muffett					P	R.Kline
		RP	D.Hillman	P	E.Wynn				
P	B.Hoeft			P	B.Shaw				
P	D.Hall	P	G.Cisco	P	W.Hacker				
		P	C.Nichols						
		P	A.Earley						

KANSAS CITY		LOS ANGELES		MINNESOTA		NEW YORK		WASHINGTON	
M	J.Gordon	M	B.Rigney	M	C.Lavagetto	M	R.Houk	M	M.Vernon
M	H.Bauer	1B	S.Bilko	M	S.Mele	1B	B.Skowron	1B	D.Long
1B	N.Siebern	2B	K.Aspromonte	M	C.Lavagetto	2B	B.Richardson	2B	C.Cottier
2B	J.Lumpe	SS	J.Koppe	M	S.Mele	SS	T.Kubek	SS	C.Veal
SS	D.Howser	3B	E.Yost	SS	T.Kubek	3B	C.Boyer	3B	D.O'Connell
3B	W.Causey	LF	L.Wagner	1B	H.Killebrew	LF	Y.Berra	LF	M.Keough
LF	L.Posada	CF	K.Hunt	2B	B.Martin	CF	M.Mantle	CF	W.Tasby
CF	B.Del Greco	RF	E.Pearson	SS	Z.Versalles	RF	R.Maris	RF	G.Woodling
RF	D.Johnson	C	E.Averill	3B	B.Tuttle	C	E.Howard	C	G.Green
C	H.Sullivan			LF	J.Lemon				
		1	T.Kluszewski	CF	L.Green	CO	J.Blanchard	O	J.King
C	J.Pignatano	O1	L.Thomas	RF	B.Allison	O	H.Lopez	O	C.Hinton
		O3	G.Thomas	C	E.Battey			3S	B.Klaus
		2S	R.Bridges			P	W.Ford	S	B.Johnson
P	J.Archer			P	P.Ramos	P	B.Stafford	C	P.Daley
P	N.Bass			P	C.Pascual	P	R.Terry		
P	J.Walker	P	K.McBride	P	J.Kralick	P	R.Sheldon	P	J.McClain
P	B.Shaw	P	E.Grba	P	J.Kaat	P	J.Coates	P	B.Daniels
P	J.Nuxhall	P	T.Bowsfield	P	D.Lee	RP	L.Arroyo	P	D.Donovan
RP	E.Rakow	P	R.Moeller	RP	B.Pleis			P	E.Hobaugh
RP	B.Kunkel	P	R.Kline	RP	R.Moore	P	B.Daley	P	P.Burnside
RP	A.Ditmar	RP	J.Donohue			P	B.Turley	RP	M.Kutyna
		RP	R.Duren	P	A.Schroll	P	A.Ditmar	RP	J.Klippstein
P	R.Herbert	RP	T.Morgan					RP	D.Sisler
P	B.Daley								
P	L.Krausse	P	A.Fowler					P	G.Gabler
		P	J.James					P	T.Sturdivant

TEAM	G	W	L	PCT	GB	R	OR	AB	H	2B	3B	HR	BB	SO	AVG	OBP	SLG	PRO	PRO+	BR	/A	PF	CHI	RC	SB	CS	SBA	SBR
NY	163	109	53	.673		827	612	5559	1461	194	40	**240**	543	785	.263	.332	**.442**	**.774**	118	82	**125**	95	101	811	28	18	61	-2
DET	163	101	61	.623	8	**841**	671	5561	1481	215	**53**	180	673	867	**.266**	**.349**	.421	.770	109	96	72	103	99	**835**	98	36	73	**8**
BAL	163	95	67	.586	14	691	**588**	5481	1393	227	36	149	581	902	.254	.328	.390	.718	102	-16	9	97	97	699	39	30	57	-6
CHI	163	86	76	.531	23	765	726	5556	1475	216	46	138	550	**612**	.265	.338	.395	.733	104	17	29	98	101	754	**100**	40	71	6
CLE	161	78	83	.484	30.5	737	752	5609	**1493**	257	39	150	492	720	**.266**	.328	.406	.734	105	9	29	97	99	743	34	11	**76**	4
BOS	163	76	86	.469	33	729	792	5508	1401	251	37	112	647	847	.254	.336	.374	.710	94	-22	-39	102	101	704	56	36	61	-5
MIN	161	70	90	.438	38	707	778	5417	1353	215	40	167	597	840	.250	.328	.397	.725	95	-5	-45	106	98	698	47	43	52	-12
LA	162	70	91	.435	38.5	744	784	5424	1331	218	22	189	**681**	1068	.245	.333	.398	.731	91	12	-72	111	99	734	37	28	57	-6
WAS	161	61	100	.379	47.5	618	776	5366	1307	217	44	119	558	917	.244	.317	.367	.684	90	-83	-74	99	98	625	81	47	63	-4
KC	162	61	100	.379	47.5	683	863	5423	1342	216	47	90	580	772	.247	.323	.354	.677	85	-90	-101	102	**107**	642	58	22	73	4
TOT	811					7342		54904	14037	2226	404	1534	5902	8330	.256	.331	.395	.726							578	311	65	-13

TEAM	CG	SH	SV	IP	H	H/G	HR	BB	SO	RAT	ERA	ERA+	OAV	OOB	PR	/A	PF	CPI	FA	E	DP	FW	PW	BW	SBW	DIF
NY	47	14	**39**	1451	1288	8.0	137	542	866	**11.5**	3.46	107	.239	.312	91	42	92	99	**.980**	124	180	1.6	4.2	**12.4**	-.0	9.9
DET	62	12	30	1459¹	1404	8.7	170	**469**	836	11.7	3.55	116	.252	.313	78	90	102	**106**	.976	146	147	.3	8.9	7.1	**.9**	2.7
BAL	54	21	33	1471¹	**1226**	**7.5**	**109**	617	926	**11.5**	**3.22**	**120**	**.227**	**.310**	132	103	96	97	**.980**	128	173	1.4	**10.2**	.9	-.5	2.0
CHI	39	3	33	1448²	1491	9.3	158	498	814	12.4	4.06	97	.268	.329	-5	-23	97	102	**.980**	128	138	1.4	-2.3	2.9	.7	2.3
CLE	35	12	23	1443¹	1426	8.9	178	599	801	12.8	4.15	95	.258	.334	-20	-34	98	102	.977	139	142	.6	-3.4	2.9	.5	-3.2
BOS	35	6	30	1442²	1472	9.2	167	679	831	13.5	4.29	97	.266	.348	-43	-12	104	105	.977	144	170	.4	-2.0	-3.9	-.4	.8
MIN	49	14	23	1432¹	1415	8.9	163	571	914	12.8	4.28	99	.256	.331	-41	-6	105	95	.972	174	150	-1.4	-.6	-4.5	-1.1	-2.5
LA	25	5	34	1438	1391	8.7	180	713	**973**	13.4	4.31	105	.254	.343	-46	32	112	101	.969	192	154	-2.4	3.2	-7.1	-.5	-3.6
WAS	39	8	21	1425	1405	8.9	131	586	666	12.8	4.23	95	.260	.336	-33	-34	100	96	.975	156	171	-.4	-3.4	-7.3	-.3	-8.2
KC	32	5	23	1415	1519	9.7	141	629	703	14.0	4.74	88	.275	.355	-113	-89	104	97	.972	175	160	-1.4	-8.8	-10.0	.5	.2
TOT	417	100	289	14426²		8.8				12.6	4.02		.256	.331					.976	1506	1585					

Runs		Hits		Doubles		Triples		Home Runs		Total Bases	
Maris-NY	132	Cash-Det	193	Kaline-Det	41	Wood-Det	14	Maris-NY	61	Maris-NY	366
Mantle-NY	132	B.Robinson-Bal	192	B.Robinson-Bal	38	Lumpe-KC	9	Mantle-NY	54	Cash-Det	354
Colavito-Det	129	Kaline-Det	190	Kubek-NY	38	Keough-Was	9	Killebrew-Min	46	Colavito-Det	353
Cash-Det	119	Francona-Cle	178	Siebern-KC	36			Gentile-Bal	46	Killebrew-Min	328
Kaline-Det	116	Richardson-NY	173	Power-Cle	34			Colavito-Det	45		

Runs Batted In		Runs Produced		Bases On Balls		Batting Average		On Base Percentage		Slugging Average	
Maris-NY	142	Colavito-Det	224	Mantle-NY	126	Cash-Det	.361	Cash-Det	.488	Mantle-NY	.687
Gentile-Bal	141	Maris-NY	213	Cash-Det	124	Kaline-Det	.324	Mantle-NY	.452	Cash-Det	.662
Colavito-Det	140	Cash-Det	210	Colavito-Det	113	Piersall-Cle	.322	Gentile-Bal	.428	Gentile-Bal	.646
Cash-Det	132	Mantle-NY	206	Killebrew-Min	107	Mantle-NY	.317	Pearson-LA	.422	Maris-NY	.620
Mantle-NY	128	Gentile-Bal	191	Allison-Min	103	Gentile-Bal	.302	Killebrew-Min	.409	Killebrew-Min	.606

Production		Adjusted Production		Batter Runs		Adjusted Batter Runs		Clutch Hitting Index		Runs Created	
Cash-Det	1.150	Mantle-NY	210	Cash-Det	86.1	Mantle-NY	84.4	Schilling-Bos	120	Cash-Det	178
Mantle-NY	1.138	Cash-Det	198	Mantle-NY	76.3	Cash-Det	81.5	Gentile-Bal	115	Mantle-NY	174
Gentile-Bal	1.074	Gentile-Bal	189	Gentile-Bal	59.1	Gentile-Bal	63.7	Malzone-Bos	115	Colavito-Det	141
Killebrew-Min	1.015	Maris-NY	170	Killebrew-Min	52.9	Maris-NY	56.5	Allison-Min	111	Gentile-Bal	138
Maris-NY	.997	Killebrew-Min	159	Colavito-Det	51.5	Colavito-Det	47.8	Siebern-KC	109	Maris-NY	138

Total Average		Stolen Bases		Stolen Base Average		Stolen Base Runs		Fielding Runs		Total Player Rating	
Mantle-NY	1.384	Aparicio-Chi	53	Hinton-Was	81.5	Aparicio-Chi	8.1	Boyer-NY	30.3	Mantle-NY	8.0
Cash-Det	1.358	Howser-KC	37	Howser-KC	80.4	Howser-KC	5.7	Landis-Chi	19.3	Cash-Det	7.1
Gentile-Bal	1.196	Wood-Det	30	Aparicio-Chi	80.3	Wood-Det	3.6	Power-Cle	18.1	Gentile-Bal	5.3
Killebrew-Min	1.098	Hinton-Was	22	Geiger-Bos	80.0	Kaline-Det	3.6	Cottier-Det-Was	16.9	Colavito-Det	4.7
Colavito-Det	1.051	Bruton-Det	22	Landis-Chi	79.2	Hinton-Was	3.6	Lumpe-KC	16.0	Howard-NY	4.2

Wins		Win Percentage		Games		Complete Games		Shutouts		Saves	
Ford-NY	25	Ford-NY	.862	Arroyo-NY	65	Lary-Det	22	Pascual-Min	8	Arroyo-NY	29
Lary-Det	23	Terry-NY	.842	Morgan-LA	59	Pascual-Min	15	Barber-Bal	8	Wilhelm-Bal	18
Barber-Bal	18	Arroyo-NY	.750	Lown-Chi	59	Barber-Bal	14	Pappas-Bal	4	Fornieles-Bos	15
Bunning-Det	17	Lary-Det	.719	Kunkel-KC	58			Lary-Det	4	Moore-Min	14
Terry-NY	16			Fornieles-Bos	57			Bunning-Det	4	Fox-Det	12

Innings Pitched		Fewest Hits/Game		Fewest BB/Game		Strikeouts		Strikeouts/Game		Ratio	
Ford-NY	283.0	Estrada-Bal	6.75	Mossi-Det	1.76	Pascual-Min	221	Pizarro-Chi	8.69	Donovan-Was	9.39
Lary-Det	275.1	Pappas-Bal	6.79	Brown-Bal	1.78	Ford-NY	209	Pascual-Min	7.88	Terry-NY	9.80
Bunning-Det	268.0	Barber-Bal	7.03	Donovan-Was	1.87	Bunning-Det	194	Estrada-Bal	6.79	Brown-Bal	10.10
Ramos-Min	264.1	Pascual-Min	7.31	Terry-NY	2.01	Pizarro-Chi	188	McBride-LA	6.70	Bunning-Det	10.48
Pascual-Min	252.1	Donovan-Was	7.36	McClain-Was	2.04	McBride-LA	180	Ford-NY	6.65	Lary-Det	10.59

Earned Run Average		Adjusted ERA		Opponents' Batting Avg.		Opponents' On Base Pct.		Starter Runs		Adjusted Starter Runs	
Donovan-Was	2.40	Donovan-Was	167	Estrada-Bal	.207	Donovan-Was	.269	Hoeft-Bal	30.7	Mossi-Det	30.5
Stafford-NY	2.68	Stafford-NY	139	Pappas-Bal	.208	Terry-NY	.277	Donovan-Was	30.4	Donovan-Was	30.3
Mossi-Det	2.96	Mossi-Det	139	Pascual-Min	.217	Bunning-Det	.285	Stafford-NY	29.2	Hoeft-Bal	28.0
Pappas-Bal	3.04	Archer-KC	131	Barber-Bal	.218	Brown-Bal	.286	Mossi-Det	28.5	Bunning-Det	27.1
Pizarro-Chi	3.05	Schwall-Bos	129	Donovan-Was	.224	Ford-NY	.292	Ford-NY	25.5	Lary-Det	26.5

Clutch Pitching Index		Relief Runs		Adjusted Relief Runs		Relief Ranking		Total Pitcher Index		Total Baseball Ranking	
Schwall-Bos	131	Arroyo-NY	24.2	Morgan-LA	21.9	Arroyo-NY	41.6	Arroyo-NY	4.3	Mantle-NY	8.0
Mossi-Det	119	Wilhelm-Bal	21.0	Arroyo-NY	20.2	Wilhelm-Bal	31.8	Lary-Det	3.7	Cash-Det	7.1
Shaw-Chi-KC	115	Morgan-LA	17.0	Wilhelm-Bal	18.9	Morgan-LA	26.9	Donovan-Was	3.7	Gentile-Bal	5.3
Monbouquette-Bos	115	Fox-Det	16.6	Fox-Det	17.1	Fox-Det	26.9	Wilhelm-Bal	3.2	Colavito-Det	4.7
McBride-LA	112	Lown-Chi	14.2	Lown-Chi	12.9	Lown-Chi	17.0	Fox-Det	2.8	Arroyo-NY	4.3

April 13 Just 12,447 Mets fans welcome the return of NL baseball to New York. Sherman Jones drops a 4-3 decision to the Pirates at the Polo Grounds.

April 24 Sandy Koufax ties the modern major league record he shares with Bob Feller by fanning 18 Cubs in nine innings. The Dodgers win, 10-2.

May 19 Stan Musial gets hit number 3,431, to break Honus Wagner's recognized NL record of 3,430 (since revised to 3,415), as St. Louis downs the Dodgers, 8-1. Musial's ninth-inning single comes off Ron Perranoski.

June 30 With the aid of 13 strikeouts, Sandy Koufax no-hits Bob Miller and the Mets, 5-0, in Los Angeles.

July 10 Roberto Clemente has three hits as the NL wins 3-1 in the first All-Star Game of 1962, at DC Stadium.

July 17 Sandy Koufax leaves after one inning of a 7-5 loss at Cincinnati. The 14-game winner has a circulatory problem in the index finger and palm of his pitching hand and will be sidelined until late September.

July 23 Bob Feller, Jackie Robinson, Bill McKechnie, and Edd Roush are inducted into the Baseball Hall of Fame.

July 25 Stan Musial becomes the NL's all-time leader in runs batted in with 1,862, driving in both of the Cardinal runs in a 5-2 loss to the Dodgers.

July 31 The NL rejects Commissioner Ford Frick's proposal for interleague play in 1963.

September 5 Ken Hubbs of the Cubs sets major league records at second base for consecutive games without an error (78) and consecutive chances accepted (418) without an error. His streak ends with a fourth-inning throwing error as Cincinnati beats Chicago 4-1.

September 18 Bob Aspromonte of the Colt .45s sets a NL record for third basemen with his 57th straight errorless game.

September 23 A 12-2 Dodger loss at St. Louis is enlivened by Maury Wills, who ties Ty Cobb's long-standing major league single-season record of 96 steals by swiping second base after singling in the third, and breaks it with a repeat performance in the seventh.

September 29 The Dodgers (101-59) send Don Drysdale against the Cardinals, but Ernie Broglio wins the pitching duel 2-0. The Dodgers lead by one game with one to play.

September 30 Willie Mays's 47th homer, an eighth-inning blast off Dick Farrell (10-20), gives the Giants a critical 2-1 win. They then stay in the clubhouse to hear results of the Dodger game. Gene Oliver's homer off Johnny Podres gives Curt Simmons and St. Louis a 1-0 win against the Dodgers and a three-game sweep at Chavez Ravine. The loss forces the fourth playoff in NL history.

October 3 A crowd of 45,693, giving the Dodgers a major league-record season attendance of 2,755,184, attends the deciding game of the NL season. In the seventh, Maury Wills collects his fourth single of the day, and his 103rd and 104th steals of the year. But the Giants score four in the ninth to win 6-4 and put themselves in the World Series.

November 23 Dodgers shortstop Maury Wills is named the NL's Most Valuable Player.

November 29 Major league officials and player representatives agree to return to a single All-Star Game in 1963. The players' pension fund will receive 95 percent of the one game's proceeds (not 60 percent of the two games).

CHICAGO		CINCINNATI		HOUSTON		LOS ANGELES		MILWAUKEE	
M	E.Tappe	M	F.Hutchinson	M	H.Craft	M	W.Alston	M	B.Tebbetts
M	L.Klein	1B	G.Coleman	1B	N.Larker	1B	R.Fairly	1B	J.Adcock
M	C.Metro	2B	D.Blasingame	2B	J.Amalfitano	2B	L.Burright	2B	F.Bolling
1B	E.Banks	SS	L.Cardenas	SS	B.Lillis	SS	M.Wills	SS	R.McMillan
2B	K.Hubbs	3B	E.Kasko	3B	B.Aspromonte	3B	J.Gilliam	3B	E.Mathews
SS	A.Rodgers	LF	W.Post	LF	A.Spangler	LF	T.Davis	LF	L.Maye
3B	R.Santo	CF	V.Pinson	CF	C.Warwick	CF	W.Davis	CF	H.Aaron
LF	B.Williams	RF	F.Robinson	RF	R.Mejias	RF	F.Howard	RF	M.Jones
CF	L.Brock	C	J.Edwards	C	H.Smith	C	J.Roseboro	C	D.Crandall
RF	G.Altman								
C	D.Bertell	O1	M.Keough	O	J.Pendleton	O1	W.Moon	1O	T.Aaron
		O	J.Lynch	C	M.Ranew			C	J.Torre
O	D.Landrum					P	D.Drysdale	O	G.Bell
		P	B.Purkey	P	T.Farrell	P	J.Podres	S2	A.Samuel
P	B.Buhl	P	J.Jay	P	K.Johnson	P	S.Williams		
P	D.Ellsworth	P	J.O'Toole	P	B.Bruce	P	S.Koufax	P	W.Spahn
P	D.Cardwell	P	J.Maloney	P	J.Golden	RP	E.Roebuck	P	B.Shaw
P	C.Koonce	RP	J.Klippstein	P	H.Woodeshick	RP	R.Perranoski	P	B.Hendley
P	G.Hobbie	RP	J.Brosnan	RP	B.Tiefenauer	RP	L.Sherry	P	L.Burdette
RP	B.Anderson	RP	T.Wills	RP	D.McMahon			P	T.Cloninger
RP	B.Schultz			RP	R.Kemmerer	P	J.Moeller	RP	J.Curtis
RP	D.Elston	P	M.Drabowsky			P	P.Richert	RP	C.Willey
		P	J.Nuxhall	P	D.Giusti	P	P.Ortega	RP	D.Nottebart
P	D.Gerard			P	J.Umbricht				
				P	G.Brunet			P	D.Lemaster
				P	D.Stone			P	R.Piche

NEW YORK		PHILADELPHIA		PITTSBURGH		SAN FRANCISCO		ST.LOUIS	
M	C.Stengel	M	G.Mauch	M	D.Murtaugh	M	A.Dark	M	J.Keane
1B	M.Throneberry	1B	R.Sievers	1B	D.Stuart	1B	O.Cepeda	1B	B.White
2B	C.Neal	2B	T.Taylor	2B	B.Mazeroski	2B	C.Hiller	2B	J.Javier
SS	E.Chacon	SS	B.Wine	SS	D.Groat	SS	J.Pagan	SS	J.Gotay
3B	F.Mantilla	3B	D.Demeter	3B	D.Hoak	3B	J.Davenport	3B	K.Boyer
LF	F.Thomas	LF	T.Savage	LF	B.Skinner	LF	H.Kuenn	LF	S.Musial
CF	J.Hickman	CF	T.Gonzalez	CF	B.Virdon	CF	W.Mays	CF	C.Flood
RF	R.Ashburn	RF	J.Callison	RF	R.Clemente	RF	F.Alou	RF	C.James
C	C.Cannizzaro	C	C.Dalrymple	C	S.Burgess	C	T.Haller	C	G.Oliver
O	J.Christopher	O	W.Covington	1O	D.Clendenon	C	E.Bailey	C	C.Sawatski
23	R.Kanehl	3S	B.Klaus			O1	W.McCovey		
		1	F.Torre	P	B.Friend			P	L.Jackson
P	R.Craig	S	R.Amaro	P	A.McBean	P	B.O'Dell	P	B.Gibson
P	A.Jackson			P	E.Francis	P	J.Sanford	P	E.Broglio
P	J.Hook	P	A.Mahaffey	P	H.Haddix	P	J.Marichal	P	R.Washburn
P	RL.Miller	P	J.Hamilton	P	V.Law	P	B.Pierce	P	C.Simmons
RP	C.Anderson	P	D.Bennett	RP	T.Sturdivant	P	M.McCormick	RP	L.McDaniel
RP	B.Moorhead	P	C.McLish	RP	R.Face	RP	S.Miller	RP	B.Shantz
RP	R.Daviault	P	C.Short	RP	D.Olivo	RP	B.Bolin	RP	D.Ferrarese
		RP	J.Baldschun			RP	D.Larsen		
P	RG.Miller	RP	P.Brown	P	J.Lamabe			P	R.Sadecki
P	K.MacKenzie	RP	B.Smith	P	J.Gibbon				
P	W.Hunter								
		P	D.Green						
		P	J.Owens						

TEAM	G	W	L	PCT	GB	R	OR	AB	H	2B	3B	HR	BB	SO	AVG	OBP	SLG	PRO	PRO+	BR	/A	PF	CHI	RC	SB	CS	SBA	SBR
SF	165	103	62	.624		878	690	5588	1552	235	32	204	523	822	.278	.344	.441	.785	119	123	138	98	102	838	73	50	59	-8
LA	165	102	63	.618	1	842	697	5628	1510	192	65	140	572	886	.268	.339	.400	.739	112	41	89	94	107	783	198	43	82	34
CIN	162	98	64	.605	3.5	802	685	5645	1523	252	40	167	498	903	.270	.333	.417	.750	104	54	29	103	102	779	66	39	63	-4
PIT	161	93	68	.578	8	706	626	5483	1468	240	65	108	432	836	.268	.323	.394	.717	99	-15	-16	100	102	682	50	39	56	-6
MIL	162	86	76	.531	15.5	730	665	5458	1376	204	38	181	581	975	.252	.328	.403	.731	105	16	36	97	99	720	57	27	68	1
STL	163	84	78	.519	17.5	774	664	5643	1528	221	31	137	515	846	.271	.337	.394	.731	94	22	-51	110	102	747	86	41	68	1
PHI	161	81	80	.503	20	705	759	5420	1410	199	39	142	531	923	.260	.332	.390	.722	103	4	26	97	98	705	79	42	65	-2
HOU	162	64	96	.400	36.5	592	717	5558	1370	170	47	105	493	806	.246	.312	.351	.663	91	-117	-72	93	97	605	42	30	58	-5
CHI	162	59	103	.364	42.5	632	827	5534	1398	196	56	126	504	1044	.253	.319	.377	.696	90	-53	-77	104	94	657	78	50	61	-7
NY	161	40	120	.250	60.5	617	948	5492	1318	166	40	139	616	991	.240	.320	.361	.681	88	-75	-86	102	94	640	59	48	55	-11
TOT	812					7278		55449	14453	2075	453	1449	5265	9032	.261	.329	.393	.722							788	409	66	-9

TEAM	CG	SH	SV	IP	H	H/G	HR	BB	SO	RAT	ERA	ERA+	OAV	OOB	PR	/A	PF	CPI	FA	E	DP	FW	PW	BW	SBW	DIF
SF	62	10	39	1461²	1399	8.6	148	503	886	11.9	3.79	100	.251	.316	24	0	96	95	.977	142	153	1.0	.0	13.8	-.7	6.5
LA	44	8	46	1488²	1386	8.4	115	588	1104	12.1	3.62	100	.245	.319	54	2	92	94	.970	193	144	-2.1	.2	8.9	3.5	9.0
CIN	51	13	35	1460²	1397	8.6	149	567	964	12.4	3.75	107	.254	.329	31	44	102	104	.977	145	144	.6	4.4	2.9	-.3	9.4
PIT	40	13	41	1432¹	1433	9.0	118	466	897	12.1	3.37	117	.262	.322	90	89	100	110	.976	152	177	.2	8.9	-1.6	-.7	5.8
MIL	59	10	24	1434²	1443	9.1	151	407	802	11.8	3.68	103	.262	.317	42	19	96	103	.980	124	154	1.9	1.9	3.6	.2	-2.6
STL	53	17	25	1463¹	1394	8.6	149	517	914	11.9	3.55	120	.252	.319	64	117	108	104	.979	132	170	1.5	11.7	-5.1	.2	-5.2
PHI	43	7	24	1426²	1469	9.3	155	574	863	13.2	4.28	90	.264	.343	-53	-65	98	102	.977	138	167	1.0	-6.5	2.6	-.1	3.5
HOU	34	9	19	1453²	1446	9.1	113	471	1047	12.1	3.83	98	.259	.321	19	-15	95	95	.973	173	149	-1.0	-1.5	-7.2	-.4	-5.9
CHI	29	4	26	1438¹	1509	9.4	159	601	783	13.5	4.54	91	.272	.348	-95	-62	105	99	.977	146	171	.6	-6.2	-7.7	-.6	-8.1
NY	43	4	10	1430	1577	9.9	192	571	772	13.8	5.04	83	.281	.352	-175	-137	106	96	.967	210	167	-3.3	-13.7	-8.6	-1.0	-13.4
TOT	458	95	289	14490		9.0				12.5	3.94		.261	.329					.975	1555	1596					

Runs		Hits		Doubles		Triples		Home Runs		Total Bases	
Robinson-Cin	134	T.Davis-LA	230	Robinson-Cin	51	Wills-LA	10	Mays-SF	49	Mays-SF	382
Wills-LA	130	Wills-LA	208	Mays-SF	36	Virdon-Pit	10	H.Aaron-Mil	45	Robinson-Cin	380
Mays-SF	130	Robinson-Cin	208	Groat-Pit	34	W.Davis-LA	10	Robinson-Cin	39	H.Aaron-Mil	366
H.Aaron-Mil	127	White-StL	199			Callison-Phi	10	Banks-Chi	37	T.Davis-LA	356
T.Davis-LA	120	Groat-Pit	199					Cepeda-SF	35	Cepeda-SF	324

Runs Batted In		Runs Produced		Bases On Balls		Batting Average		On Base Percentage		Slugging Average	
T.Davis-LA	153	T.Davis-LA	246	Mathews-Mil	101	T.Davis-LA	.346	Robinson-Cin	.424	Robinson-Cin	.624
Mays-SF	141	Robinson-Cin	231	Gilliam-LA	93	Robinson-Cin	.342	Musial-StL	.420	H.Aaron-Mil	.618
Robinson-Cin	136	Mays-SF	222	Ashburn-NY	81	Musial-StL	.330	Skinner-Pit	.397	Mays-SF	.615
H.Aaron-Mil	128	H.Aaron-Mil	210	Mays-SF	78	White-StL	.324	Altman-Chi	.394	Howard-LA	.560
Howard-LA	119					H.Aaron-Mil	.323	H.Aaron-Mil	.393	T.Davis-LA	.535

Production		Adjusted Production		Batter Runs		Adjusted Batter Runs		Clutch Hitting Index		Runs Created	
Robinson-Cin	1.048	Robinson-Cin	172	Robinson-Cin	66.6	Robinson-Cin	62.0	T.Davis-LA	125	Robinson-Cin	160
H.Aaron-Mil	1.012	H.Aaron-Mil	171	Mays-SF	54.1	H.Aaron-Mil	57.6	Howard-LA	122	Mays-SF	146
Mays-SF	1.001	Mays-SF	167	H.Aaron-Mil	54.0	Mays-SF	56.4	Musial-StL	112	H.Aaron-Mil	140
Musial-StL	.928	T.Davis-LA	151	T.Davis-LA	37.2	T.Davis-LA	44.7	Fairly-LA	112	T.Davis-LA	129
T.Davis-LA	.914	Howard-LA	149	Altman-Chi	31.5	Mathews-Mil	30.5	Santo-Chi	111	White-StL	114

Total Average		Stolen Bases		Stolen Base Average		Stolen Base Runs		Fielding Runs		Total Player Rating	
Robinson-Cin	1.125	Wills-LA	104	Mays-SF	90.0	Wills-LA	23.4	Mazeroski-Pit	41.1	Mays-SF	6.4
Mays-SF	1.060	W.Davis-LA	32	Wills-LA	88.9	W.Davis-LA	5.4	Callison-Phi	22.9	Robinson-Cin	6.0
H.Aaron-Mil	1.050	Pinson-Cin	26	W.Davis-LA	82.1	Mays-SF	4.2	Flood-StL	15.7	H.Aaron-Mil	5.5
Musial-StL	.957	Javier-StL	26	Clendenon-Pit	80.0	Pinson-Cin	3.0	Williams-Chi	15.5	Mazeroski-Pit	5.0
Skinner-Pit	.930	Taylor-Phi	20	Pinson-Cin	76.5			Kanehl-NY	14.5	Callison-Phi	3.9

Wins		Win Percentage		Games		Complete Games		Shutouts		Saves	
Drysdale-LA	25	Purkey-Cin	.821	Perranoski-LA	70	Spahn-Mil	22	Gibson-StL	5	Face-Pit	28
Sanford-SF	24	Sanford-SF	.774	Baldschun-Phi	67	O'Dell-SF	20	Friend-Pit	5	Perranoski-LA	20
Purkey-Cin	23	Drysdale-LA	.735	Roebuck-LA	64	Mahaffey-Phi	20			Miller-SF	19
Jay-Cin	21	Pierce-SF	.727	Face-Pit	63	Drysdale-LA	19			McDaniel-StL	14
		Shaw-Mil	.625	Olivo-Pit	62						

Innings Pitched		Fewest Hits/Game		Fewest BB/Game		Strikeouts		Strikeouts/Game		Ratio	
Drysdale-LA	314.1	Koufax-LA	6.54	Shaw-Mil	1.76	Drysdale-LA	232	Koufax-LA	10.55	Koufax-LA	9.42
Purkey-Cin	288.1	Gibson-StL	6.70	Friend-Pit	1.82	Koufax-LA	216	Johnson-Hou	8.13	Farrell-Hou	10.06
O'Dell-SF	280.2	Bennett-Phi	7.42	Spahn-Mil	1.84	Gibson-StL	208	Gibson-StL	8.01	Spahn-Mil	10.23
Mahaffey-Phi	274.0	Drysdale-LA	7.79	Pierce-SF	1.94	Farrell-Hou	203	Bennett-Phi	7.68	Pierce-SF	10.26
Jay-Cin	273.0	Broglio-StL	7.81	Purkey-Cin	2.00	O'Dell-SF	195	Farrell-Hou	7.56	Drysdale-LA	10.34

Earned Run Average		Adjusted ERA		Opponents' Batting Avg.		Opponents' On Base Pct.		Starter Runs		Adjusted Starter Runs	
Koufax-LA	2.54	Gibson-StL	150	Koufax-LA	.197	Koufax-LA	.261	Drysdale-LA	38.6	Purkey-Cin	38.9
Shaw-Mil	2.80	Purkey-Cin	143	Gibson-StL	.204	Farrell-Hou	.280	Purkey-Cin	36.3	Gibson-StL	36.8
Purkey-Cin	2.81	Koufax-LA	143	Bennett-Phi	.224	Drysdale-LA	.283	Koufax-LA	28.7	Broglio-StL	31.4
Drysdale-LA	2.83	Broglio-StL	142	Drysdale-LA	.230	Pierce-SF	.284	Shaw-Mil	28.5	Drysdale-LA	27.8
Gibson-StL	2.85	Shaw-Mil	136	Farrell-Hou	.233	Spahn-Mil	.287	Gibson-StL	28.3	Friend-Pit	25.4

Clutch Pitching Index		Relief Runs		Adjusted Relief Runs		Relief Ranking		Total Pitcher Index		Total Baseball Ranking	
Shaw-Mil	123	Face-Pit	20.8	Face-Pit	20.8	Face-Pit	45.2	Gibson-StL	5.0	Mays-SF	6.4
Friend-Pit	119	McMahon-Mil-Hou	19.9	Shantz-Hou-StL	18.9	McMahon-Mil-Hou	26.6	Face-Pit	4.5	Robinson-Cin	6.0
Broglio-StL	116	Shantz-Hou-StL	17.3	McMahon-Mil-Hou	18.1	Shantz-Hou-StL	23.9	Purkey-Cin	3.6	H.Aaron-Mil	5.5
McBean-Pit	114	Umbricht-Hou	14.3	Umbricht-Hou	12.8	Elston-Chi	23.9	Drysdale-LA	3.4	Gibson-StL	5.0
Koonce-Chi	111	Perranoski-LA	13.0	Elston-Chi	12.6	Baldschun-Phi	20.3	Spahn-Mil	3.1	Mazeroski-Pit	5.0

April 9 President John F. Kennedy throws out the first ball to open the baseball season at new District of Columbia Stadium. Despite rain, a record Washington crowd of 42,143 shows up to see Bennie Daniels stop Detroit with a five-hit, 4-1 win.

April 25 Harry Chiti is traded for himself. Cleveland sends catcher Harry Chiti to the Mets for a player to be named later, a deal completed June 15 when the Mets send Chiti back to Cleveland.

May 5 Angels rookie Bo Belinsky pitches a no-hitter against the Orioles, the organization from which the cocky lefty was drafted last year. Belinsky has nine strikeouts and beats Steve Barber, 2-0.

May 26 Al Kaline suffers a broken right collarbone while making a diving, game-saving catch to seal Detroit's 2-1 win against the Yankees. He will be out until June 23.

July 8 The Yankees complete a three-game sweep in Minnesota, winning 7-5, 6-3, and 9-8 to regain first place. They will remain there the rest of the way.

July 26 Pitcher Gene Conley and infielder Pumpsie Green of the Red Sox mysteriously disappear after a game with the Yankees. They leave the team bus in traffic to use a restroom and fail to return. Conley decides he wants to fly to Israel, and goes to the airport, but is refused a ticket because he does not have a visa.

August 13 Bert Campaneris of Daytona Beach (Florida State League) pitches ambidextrously in a relief appearance.

August 26 The Twins Jack Kralick no-hits the A's and wins 1-0 on Lenny Green's sacrifice fly off Bill Fischer. A walk to George Alusik with one out in the ninth puts the only runner on.

September 12 Washington's Tom Cheney sets a major league mark with 21 strikeouts in a 16-inning game at Baltimore. Bud Zipfel's 16th-inning homer off Dick Hall gives the Senators a 2-1 win.

September 25 Whitey Ford beats Washington 8-3, as the Yankees clinch the AL pennant. Ralph Houk becomes the fifth manager to capture pennants in each of his first two seasons.

October 4 At Candlestick Park, in Game 1 of the World Series, Roger Maris stakes Whitey Ford to a two-run lead with a first-inning, two-run double. Only

right fielder Felipe Alou's leaping effort keeps Maris's drive in the park. Whitey Ford's record consecutive-shutout-inning streak ends at 33⅔ innings when a surprise bunt by Jose Pagan brings Willie Mays home. Clete Boyer's seventh-inning homer gives the Yankees a 6-2 win, the last of a record 10 World Series victories for Ford.

October 16 New York scores the game's only run, as Tony Kubek grounds into a fifth-inning double play. In the ninth, with two outs and Matty Alou on first base, Willie Mays rips a double to right off Ralph Terry, but great fielding by Roger Maris keeps Alou from scoring. Willie McCovey then hits a screaming liner toward right, but second baseman Bobby Richardson gloves it, giving the Yankees a 1-0 win and a second straight World Series victory. Terry is named World Series MVP.

November 15 The White Sox release Early Wynn so that the 299-game winner will be free to deal with other clubs, and earn his 300th.

November 20 Mickey Mantle is named the AL Most Valuable Player for the third time.

BALTIMORE		BOSTON		CHICAGO		CLEVELAND		DETROIT	
M	B.Hitchcock	M	P.Higgins	M	A.Lopez	M	M.McGaha	M	B.Scheffing
1B	J.Gentile	1B	P.Runnels	1B	J.Cunningham	M	M.Harder	1B	N.Cash
2B	M.Breeding	2B	C.Schilling	2B	N.Fox	1B	T.Francona	2B	J.Wood
SS	J.Adair	SS	E.Bressoud	SS	L.Aparicio	2B	J.Kindall	SS	C.Fernandez
3B	B.Robinson	3B	F.Malzone	3B	A.Smith	SS	W.Held	3B	S.Boros
LF	B.Powell	LF	C.Yastrzemski	LF	F.Robinson	3B	B.Phillips	LF	R.Colavito
CF	J.Brandt	CF	G.Geiger	CF	J.Landis	LF	C.Essegian	CF	B.Bruton
RF	R.Snyder	RF	C.Hardy	RF	M.Hershberger	CF	T.Cline	RF	A.Kaline
C	G.Triandos	C	J.Pagliaroni	C	C.Carreon	RF	W.Kirkland	C	D.Brown
						C	J.Romano		
O	W.Herzog	O	L.Clinton	C	S.Lollar			23	D.McAuliffe
O	D.Nicholson	C	B.Tillman	O	C.Maxwell	O	A.Luplow		
2	J.Temple							P	J.Bunning
		P	G.Conley	P	R.Herbert	P	D.Donovan	P	H.Aguirre
P	C.Estrada	P	B.Monbouquette	P	J.Pizarro	P	P.Ramos	P	D.Mossi
P	M.Pappas	P	E.Wilson	P	E.Fisher	P	J.Perry	P	P.Regan
P	R.Roberts	P	D.Schwall	P	E.Wynn	P	B.Latman	P	P.Foytack
P	J.Fisher	RP	D.Radatz	P	J.Buzhardt	P	M.Grant	RP	S.Jones
P	S.Barber	RP	M.Fornieles	RP	D.Zanni	RP	G.Bell	RP	R.Kline
RP	D.Hall	RP	A.Earley	RP	T.Lown	RP	F.Funk	RP	R.Nischwitz
RP	B.Hoeft								
RP	H.Wilhelm	P	I.Delock	P	F.Baumann	P	S.McDowell	P	F.Lary
		P	G.Cisco	P	J.Horlen			P	T.Fox
P	H.Brown	P	H.Kolstad						
P	W.Stock	P	C.Nichols						

KANSAS CITY		LOS ANGELES		MINNESOTA		NEW YORK		WASHINGTON	
M	H.Bauer	M	B.Rigney	M	S.Mele	M	R.Houk	M	M.Vernon
1B	N.Siebern	1B	L.Thomas	1B	V.Power	1B	B.Skowron	1B	H.Bright
2B	J.Lumpe	2B	B.Moran	2B	B.Allen	2B	B.Richardson	2B	C.Cottier
SS	D.Howser	SS	J.Koppe	SS	Z.Versalles	SS	T.Tresh	SS	K.Hamlin
3B	E.Charles	3B	F.Torres	3B	R.Rollins	3B	C.Boyer	3B	B.Johnson
LF	M.Jimenez	LF	L.Wagner	LF	H.Killebrew	LF	H.Lopez	LF	C.Hinton
CF	B.Del Greco	CF	A.Pearson	CF	L.Green	CF	M.Mantle	CF	J.Piersall
RF	G.Cimoli	RF	G.Thomas	RF	B.Allison	RF	R.Maris	RF	J.King
C	H.Sullivan	C	B.Rodgers	C	E.Battey	C	E.Howard	C	K.Retzer
S3	W.Causey	P	D.Chance	O	B.Tuttle	OC	J.Blanchard	O	J.Hicks
O	J.Tartabull	P	B.Belinsky			CO	Y.Berra	C	B.Schmidt
C	J.Azcue	P	E.Grba	P	J.Kaat			32	D.O'Connell
O	G.Alusik	P	D.Lee	P	C.Pascual	P	R.Terry	O	D.Lock
		P	K.McBride	P	J.Kralick	P	W.Ford	3	J.Schaive
P	E.Rakow	RP	A.Fowler	P	D.Stigman	P	B.Stafford		
P	D.Pfister	RP	R.Duren	P	J.Bonikowski	P	J.Bouton	P	D.Stenhouse
P	J.Walker	RP	J.Spring	RP	L.Stange	P	R.Sheldon	P	D.Rudolph
P	B.Fischer			RP	G.Maranda	RP	J.Coates	P	T.Cheney
P	D.Segui	P	T.Bowsfield	RP	R.Moore	RP	B.Daley	P	B.Daniels
RP	J.Wyatt	P	B.Botz			RP	M.Bridges	P	C.Osteen
RP	D.McDevitt	P	T.Morgan	/P	D.Lee			RP	S.Hamilton
		P	D.Osinski			P	B.Turley	RP	M.Kutyna
								RP	E.Hobaugh
P	D.Wickersham								
P	O.Pena							P	P.Burnside
P	N.Bass							P	J.Hannan

TEAM	G	W	L	PCT	GB	R	OR	AB	H	2B	3B	HR	BB	SO	AVG	OBP	SLG	PRO	PRO+	BR	/A	PF	CHI	RC	SB	CS	SBA	SBR
NY	162	96	66	.593		817	680	5644	1509	240	29	199	584	842	.267	.339	.426	.765	116	87	113	97	99	816	42	29	59	-5
MIN	163	91	71	.562	5	798	713	5561	1445	215	39	185	649	823	.260	.340	.412	.752	104	67	38	104	100	789	33	20	62	-2
LA	162	86	76	.531	10	718	706	5499	1377	232	35	137	602	917	.250	.328	.380	.708	100	-23	-1	97	103	698	46	27	63	-2
DET	161	85	76	.528	10.5	758	692	5456	1352	191	36	209	651	894	.248	.332	.411	.743	102	41	14	104	100	757	69	21	77	8
CHI	162	85	77	.525	11	707	658	5514	1415	250	56	92	620	674	.257	.336	.372	.708	97	-13	-9	100	99	701	76	40	66	-1
CLE	162	80	82	.494	16	682	745	5484	1341	202	22	180	502	939	.245	.314	.388	.702	97	-46	-26	97	103	671	35	16	69	1
BAL	162	77	85	.475	19	652	680	5491	1363	225	34	156	516	931	.248	.316	.387	.703	101	-42	0	94	98	665	45	32	58	-6
BOS	160	76	84	.475	19	707	756	5530	1429	257	53	146	525	923	.258	.326	.403	.729	99	9	-14	103	98	716	39	33	54	-8
KC	162	72	90	.444	24	745	837	5576	1467	220	58	116	556	803	.263	.334	.386	.720	96	3	-31	105	102	738	76	21	78	10
WAS	162	60	101	.373	35.5	599	716	5484	1370	206	38	132	466	789	.250	.310	.373	.683	90	-82	-77	99	97	623	99	53	65	-2
TOT	809					7183		55239	14068	2238	400	1552	5671	8535	.255	.328	.394	.722							560	292	66	-7

TEAM	CG	SH	SV	IP	H	H/G	HR	BB	SO	RAT	ERA	ERA+	OAV	OOB	PR	/A	PF	CPI	FA	E	DP	FW	PW	BW	SBW	DIF
NY	33	10	42	1470[1]	1375	8.4	146	499	838	11.6	3.70	101	.247	.312	44	7	94	96	.979	131	151	.4	.7	11.4	-.4	3.0
MIN	53	11	27	1463[1]	1400	8.6	166	493	948	11.9	3.89	105	.253	.319	13	31	103	99	.980	129	173	.5	3.1	3.8	-.1	2.7
LA	23	15	47	1466	1412	8.7	118	616	858	12.8	3.70	104	.253	.332	45	27	97	104	.973	175	153	-2.2	2.7	-.1	-.1	4.7
DET	46	8	35	1443[2]	1452	9.1	169	503	873	12.4	3.81	107	.259	.323	26	42	103	105	.974	156	114	-1.1	4.2	1.4	.9	-.9
CHI	50	13	28	1451[2]	1380	8.6	123	537	821	12.0	3.73	105	.251	.320	38	28	98	97	.982	110	153	1.6	2.8	-.9	-.0	.6
CLE	45	12	31	1441	1410	8.8	174	594	780	12.7	4.14	94	.258	.334	-27	-43	98	102	.978	139	168	-.1	-4.3	-2.6	.2	5.9
BAL	32	8	33	1462[1]	1373	8.5	147	549	898	12.0	3.69	100	.249	.320	45	1	93	101	.980	122	152	.9	.1	.0	-.5	-4.4
BOS	34	12	40	1437[2]	1416	8.9	159	632	923	13.1	4.22	98	.258	.339	-40	-14	104	101	.979	131	152	.3	-1.4	-1.4	-.7	-.7
KC	32	4	33	1434	1450	9.1	199	655	825	13.5	4.79	88	.263	.346	-131	-91	106	97	.979	132	131	.3	-9.1	-3.1	1.1	1.7
WAS	38	11	13	1445	1400	8.7	151	593	771	12.5	4.04	100	.256	.331	-12	-1	102	100	.978	139	160	-.1	-.1	-7.7	-.1	-12.4
TOT	386	104	329	14515		8.7				12.4	3.97		.255	.328					.978	1364	1507					

Runs		Hits		Doubles		Triples		Home Runs		Total Bases	
Pearson-LA	115	Richardson-NY	209	Robinson-Chi	45	Cimoli-KC	15	Killebrew-Min	48	Colavito-Det	309
Siebern-KC	114	Lumpe-KC	193	Yastrzemski-Bos	43	Robinson-Chi	10	Cash-Det	39	B.Robinson-Bal	308
Allison-Min	102	B.Robinson-Bal	192	Bressoud-Bos	40	Lumpe-KC	10	Wagner-LA	37	Wagner-LA	306
Yastrzemski-Bos	99	Yastrzemski-Bos	191	Richardson-NY	38	Clinton-Bos	10	Colavito-Det	37	Yastrzemski-Bos	303
Richardson-NY	99	Robinson-Chi	187							Killebrew-Min	301

Runs Batted In		Runs Produced		Bases On Balls		Batting Average		On Base Percentage		Slugging Average	
Killebrew-Min	126	Siebern-KC	206	Mantle-NY	122	Runnels-Bos	.326	Mantle-NY	.488	Mantle-NY	.605
Siebern-KC	117	Robinson-Chi	187	Siebern-KC	110	Mantle-NY	.321	Siebern-KC	.416	Killebrew-Min	.545
Colavito-Det	112	Rollins-Min	176	Killebrew-Min	106	Robinson-Chi	.312	Cunningham-Chi	.415	Colavito-Det	.514
Robinson-Chi	109	Allison-Min	175	Cash-Det	104	Hinton-Was	.310	Runnels-Bos	.411	Cash-Det	.513
Wagner-LA	107	Yastrzemski-Bos	174	Cunningham-Chi	101	Siebern-KC	.308	Robinson-Chi	.387	Allison-Min	.511

Production		Adjusted Production		Batter Runs		Adjusted Batter Runs		Clutch Hitting Index		Runs Created	
Mantle-NY	1.093	Mantle-NY	198	Mantle-NY	57.3	Mantle-NY	61.0	Siebern-KC	125	Siebern-KC	129
Killebrew-Min	.914	Siebern-KC	138	Siebern-KC	41.1	Siebern-KC	35.4	Robinson-Chi	124	Mantle-NY	126
Siebern-KC	.911	Killebrew-Min	137	Killebrew-Min	33.1	Killebrew-Min	29.1	Rollins-Min	121	Colavito-Det	117
Cash-Det	.897	Cash-Det	134	Colavito-Det	31.4	Kaline-Det	27.8	Howard-NY	115	Killebrew-Min	113
Colavito-Det	.889	Colavito-Det	132	Kaline-Det	30.7	Colavito-Det	27.5	L.Thomas-LA	111	Robinson-Chi	113

Total Average		Stolen Bases		Stolen Base Average		Stolen Base Runs		Fielding Runs		Total Player Rating	
Mantle-NY	1.385	Aparicio-Chi	31	Howser-KC	90.5	Wood-Det	5.4	Boyer-NY	36.2	Mantle-NY	5.0
Siebern-KC	.956	Hinton-Was	28	Wood-Det	88.9	Howser-KC	4.5	Versalles-Min	31.6	Boyer-NY	4.0
Cash-Det	.950	Wood-Det	24	Charles-KC	83.3	Charles-KC	3.6	Bressoud-Bos	24.5	Bressoud-Bos	3.8
Killebrew-Min	.945	Charles-KC	20	Tartabull-KC	79.2	Tartabull-KC	2.7	Kindall-Cle	20.7	Colavito-Det	3.6
Allison-Min	.901			Hinton-Was	73.7	Mantle-NY	2.7	Cottier-Was	20.5	Kaline-Det	3.4

Wins		Win Percentage		Games		Complete Games		Shutouts		Saves	
Terry-NY	23	Herbert-Chi	.690	Radatz-Bos	62	Pascual-Min	18	Pascual-Min	5	Radatz-Bos	24
Pascual-Min	20	Ford-NY	.680	Wyatt-KC	59	Kaat-Min	16	Kaat-Min	5	Bridges-NY	18
Herbert-Chi	20	Donovan-Cle	.667			Donovan-Cle	16	Donovan-Cle	5	Fox-Det	16
Donovan-Cle	20	Aguirre-Det	.667			Terry-NY	14	Monbouquette-Bos	4	Wilhelm-Bal	15
Bunning-Det	19	Terry-NY	.657					McBride-LA	4	Bell-Cle	12

Innings Pitched		Fewest Hits/Game		Fewest BB/Game		Strikeouts		Strikeouts/Game		Ratio	
Terry-NY	298.2	Aguirre-Det	6.75	Donovan-Cle	1.69	Pascual-Min	206	Pizarro-Chi	7.66	Terry-NY	9.55
Kaat-Min	269.0	Cheney-Was	6.96	Terry-NY	1.72	Bunning-Det	184	Cheney-Was	7.63	Aguirre-Det	9.67
Bunning-Det	258.0	Belinsky-LA	7.16	Mossi-Det	1.80	Terry-NY	176	Pascual-Min	7.20	Pascual-Min	10.37
Pascual-Min	257.2	Wilson-Bos	7.67	Roberts-Bal	1.93	Pizarro-Chi	173	Belinsky-LA	6.97	Roberts-Bal	10.40
Ford-NY	257.2	Stenhouse-Was	7.72	Pascual-Min	2.06	Kaat-Min	173	Estrada-Bal	6.65	Fisher-Chi	10.59

Earned Run Average		Adjusted ERA		Opponents' Batting Avg.		Opponents' On Base Pct.		Starter Runs		Adjusted Starter Runs	
Aguirre-Det	2.21	Aguirre-Det	184	Aguirre-Det	.205	Aguirre-Det	.269	Aguirre-Det	42.3	Aguirre-Det	44.7
Roberts-Bal	2.78	Roberts-Bal	133	Cheney-Was	.213	Terry-NY	.270	Ford-NY	30.7	Kaat-Min	28.1
Ford-NY	2.90	Chance-LA	130	Belinsky-LA	.216	Pascual-Min	.286	Terry-NY	25.8	Ford-NY	24.3
Chance-LA	2.96	Kaat-Min	130	Terry-NY	.231	Roberts-Bal	.289	Roberts-Bal	25.4	Pascual-Min	22.0
Fisher-Chi	3.10	Ford-NY	129	Wilson-Bos	.231	Fisher-Chi	.293	Kaat-Min	24.7	Monbouquette-Bos	21.0

Clutch Pitching Index		Relief Runs		Adjusted Relief Runs		Relief Ranking		Total Pitcher Index		Total Baseball Ranking	
Chance-LA	114	Radatz-Bos	24.0	Radatz-Bos	26.2	Radatz-Bos	39.5	Kaat-Min	4.2	Mantle-NY	5.0
Roberts-Bal	111	Hall-Bal	22.2	Hall-Bal	18.7	Wilhelm-Bal	36.5	Wilhelm-Bal	3.8	Kaat-Min	4.2
Ramos-Cle	110	Wilhelm-Bal	21.0	Wilhelm-Bal	18.2	Hall-Bal	19.1	Radatz-Bos	3.7	Boyer-NY	4.0
Ford-NY	110	Fox-Det	14.6	Fox-Det	15.2	Fox-Det	18.7	Aguirre-Det	3.7	Bressoud-Bos	3.8
Perry-Cle	109	Fowler-LA	10.0	Fowler-LA	9.0	Bridges-NY	10.0	Pascual-Min	3.4	Wilhelm-Bal	3.8

April 11 Warren Spahn's Opening Day, 6-1 victory over the Mets is the 328th of his career. He thus moves ahead of yesteryear's great Eddie Plank as the all-time winningest lefthander. Except for Duke Snider's home run, no Met gets past second base.

April 13 After 11 hitless at bats, Cincinnati second baseman Pete Rose records his first major league hit, a triple off Pittsburgh's Bob Friend.

May 8 A Stan Musial home run against the Dodgers gives him 1,357 extra-base hits, surpassing Babe Ruth's major league record. He will get 20 more and permanent possession of second place lifetime. The Cards lose 11-5.

June 9 The Colt .45s beat the Giants, 3-0, in the major leagues' first Sunday night game. The exception is made because of Houston's oppressive daytime heat.

July 2 At 12:31 a.m. in San Francisco, Willie Mays's round-tripper off Warren Spahn in the bottom of the 16th gives Juan Marichal a 1-0 win, the NL's longest win ended by a home run.

July 9 Willie Mays is held to a single, but dominates a 5-3 NL win in the All-Star Game. He also walks, steals twice, scores twice, bats in a pair, and makes a great catch. This All-Star Game also marks Stan Musial's 24th appearance, a record.

July 19 With one out and a man on in the ninth, Roy Sievers hits his 300th career home run to give the Phils a 2-1 win over the Mets. Roger Craig is the victim, his 13th straight loss.

August 9 Roger Craig's NL record-tying 18-game losing streak ends thanks to Jim Hickman's ninth-inning grand slam off Lindy McDaniel. New York beats the Cubs 7-3.

September 8 Braves pitcher Warren Spahn ties Christy Mathewson with his 13th 20-win season by notching a 3-2 victory in Philadelphia. At 42, Spahn becomes the oldest 20-game winner.

September 10 Stan Musial hits a home run in his first at bat as a grandfather, and Bob Gibson (17-8) blanks the Cubs 8-0.

September 15 The Alou brothers—Felipe, Matty, and Jesus—appear in the San Francisco outfield for one inning of a 13-5 win against the Pirates. This necessitates the "benching" of Willie Mays.

October 2 In the World Series opener, Sandy Koufax fans the first five batters he faces en route to a World Series record 15. John Roseboro's three-run home run is the difference, as Los Angeles beats the Yankees 5-2 at New York.

October 5 Fans attending the first World Series game at Dodger Stadium see a pitching duel between Don Drysdale and Jim Bouton. A first-inning run is all Los Angeles needs to take a three games-to-none lead.

October 6 Sandy Koufax beats the Yanks again, 2-1, for a shocking World Series sweep for the Dodgers. Whitey Ford gives up only two hits, both by Frank Howard, who crashes a long home run in the fifth to start the Los Angeles scoring. The Bronx Bombers bat just .171 and score only four runs, the second lowest total in World Series history.

October 24 Sandy Koufax is the unanimous winner of the Cy Young Award.

October 30 Sandy Koufax wins again, outpolling Pittsburgh's Dick Groat 237 to 190 for the NL MVP award.

November 26 Cincinnati second baseman Pete Rose is a landslide winner of NL Rookie of the Year honors, taking 17 of 20 votes.

	CHICAGO		CINCINNATI		HOUSTON		LOS ANGELES		MILWAUKEE
M	B.Kennedy	M	F.Hutchinson	M	H.Craft	M	W.Alston	M	B.Bragan
1B	E.Banks	1B	G.Coleman	1B	R.Staub	1B	R.Fairly	1B	G.Oliver
2B	K.Hubbs	2B	P.Rose	2B	E.Fazio	2B	J.Gilliam	2B	F.Bolling
SS	A.Rodgers	SS	L.Cardenas	SS	B.Lillis	SS	M.Wills	SS	R.McMillan
3B	R.Santo	3B	G.Freese	3B	B.Aspromonte	3B	K.McMullen	3B	E.Mathews
LF	B.Williams	LF	F.Robinson	LF	A.Spangler	LF	T.Davis	LF	L.Maye
CF	E.Burton	CF	V.Pinson	CF	H.Goss	CF	W.Davis	CF	M.Jones
RF	L.Brock	RF	T.Harper	RF	C.Warwick	RF	F.Howard	RF	H.Aaron
C	B.Bertell	C	J.Edwards	C	J.Bateman	C	J.Roseboro	C	J.Torre
O	D.Landrum	P	J.Maloney	12	P.Runnels	O	W.Moon	S3	D.Menke
		P	J.O'Toole	23	J.Temple	S2	D.Tracewski	C	D.Crandall
P	D.Ellsworth	P	J.Nuxhall	OS	J.Wynn	1	B.Skowron		
L	L.Jackson	P	J.Tsitouris					P	W.Spahn
P	B.Buhl	P	J.Jay	P	K.Johnson	P	D.Drysdale	P	D.Lemaster
P	G.Hobbie	RP	A.Worthington	P	T.Farrell	P	S.Koufax	P	B.Hendley
P	P.Toth	RP	B.Henry	P	D.Nottebart	P	J.Podres	P	B.Shaw
RP	L.McDaniel			P	B.Bruce	P	B.Miller	P	T.Cloninger
RP	D.Elston	P	B.Purkey	P	H.Brown	RP	R.Perranoski	RP	H.Fischer
RP	J.Brewer			RP	H.Woodeshick	RP	L.Sherry	RP	C.Raymond
				RP	D.McMahon			RP	R.Piche
P	C.Koonce			RP	J.Umbricht	P	P.Richert		
								P	B.Sadowski
				P	D.Drott			P	L.Burdette
				P	C.Zachary				

	NEW YORK		PHILADELPHIA		PITTSBURGH		SAN FRANCISCO		ST.LOUIS
M	C.Stengel	M	G.Mauch	M	D.Murtaugh	M	A.Dark	M	J.Keane
1B	T.Harkness	1B	R.Sievers	1B	D.Clendenon	1B	O.Cepeda	1B	B.White
2B	R.Hunt	2B	T.Taylor	2B	B.Mazeroski	2B	C.Hiller	2B	J.Javier
SS	A.Moran	SS	B.Wine	SS	D.Schofield	SS	J.Pagan	SS	D.Groat
3B	C.Neal	3B	D.Hoak	3B	B.Bailey	3B	J.Davenport	3B	K.Boyer
LF	F.Thomas	LF	T.Gonzalez	LF	W.Stargell	LF	W.McCovey	LF	C.James
CF	J.Hickman	CF	D.Demeter	CF	B.Virdon	CF	W.Mays	CF	C.Flood
RF	D.Snider	RF	J.Callison	RF	R.Clemente	RF	F.Alou	RF	G.Altman
C	C.Coleman	C	C.Dalrymple	C	J.Pagliaroni	C	E.Bailey	C	T.McCarver
O3	R.Kanehl	S3	R.Amaro	C	S.Burgess	C	T.Haller	O	S.Musial
O1	E.Kranepool	O	W.Covington	O	J.Lynch	O3	H.Kuenn		
								P	B.Gibson
P	R.Craig	P	C.McLish	P	B.Friend	P	J.Marichal	P	E.Broglio
P	A.Jackson	P	R.Culp	P	D.Cardwell	P	J.Sanford	P	C.Simmons
P	C.Willey	P	C.Short	P	D.Schwall	P	B.O'Dell	P	R.Sadecki
P	G.Cisco	P	A.Mahaffey	P	J.Gibbon	P	J.Fisher	P	L.Burdette
P	T.Stallard	P	D.Green	RP	A.McBean	RP	B.Bolin	RP	R.Taylor
RP	L.Bearnarth	RP	J.Baldschun	RP	T.Sisk	RP	B.Pierce	RP	B.Shantz
RP	K.MacKenzie	RP	J.Klippstein	RP	E.Francis	RP	G.Perry	RP	E.Bauta
RP	D.Rowe	RP	R.Duren						
				P	B.Veale	P	J.Duffalo	P	R.Washburn
P	J.Hook	P	D.Bennett	P	V.Law	P	D.Larsen		
P	G.Powell	P	J.Boozer	P	R.Face				
				P	H.Haddix				

TEAM	G	W	L	PCT	GB	R	OR	AB	H	2B	3B	HR	BB	SO	AVG	OBP	SLG	PRO	PRO+	BR	/A	PF	CHI	RC	SB	CS	SBA	SBR
LA	163	99	63	.611		640	550	5428	1361	178	34	110	453	867	.251	.311	.357	.668	106	-3	39	93	105	596	124	70	64	-5
STL	162	93	69	.574	6	747	628	5678	1540	231	66	128	458	915	.271	.328	.403	.731	107	119	50	109	99	751	77	42	65	-2
SF	162	88	74	.543	11	725	641	5579	1442	206	35	197	441	889	.258	.318	.414	.732	118	111	119	99	98	712	55	49	53	-13
PHI	162	87	75	.537	12	642	578	5524	1390	228	54	126	403	955	.252	.308	.381	.689	106	28	36	99	99	640	56	39	59	-7
CIN	162	86	76	.531	13	648	594	5416	1333	225	44	122	474	960	.246	.312	.371	.683	100	25	6	103	101	630	92	58	61	-7
MIL	163	84	78	.519	15	677	603	5518	1345	204	39	139	525	954	.244	.314	.370	.684	105	30	37	99	100	643	75	52	59	-9
CHI	162	82	80	.506	17	570	578	5404	1286	205	44	127	439	1049	.238	.300	.363	.663	92	-21	-53	105	97	573	68	60	53	-16
PIT	162	74	88	.457	25	567	595	5536	1385	181	49	108	464	940	.250	.310	.359	.669	98	-2	-6	101	92	603	57	41	58	-8
HOU	162	66	96	.407	33	464	640	5384	1184	170	39	62	456	938	.220	.284	.301	.585	80	-159	-132	94	103	461	39	30	57	-6
NY	162	51	111	.315	48	501	774	5336	1168	156	35	96	457	1078	.219	.286	.315	.601	79	-129	-137	102	106	477	41	52	44	-19
TOT	811					6181		54803	13434	1984	439	1215	4560	9545	.245	.307	.364	.671							684	493	58	-91

TEAM	CG	SH	SV	IP	H	H/G	HR	BB	SO	RAT	ERA	ERA+	OAV	OOB	PR	/A	PF	CPI	FA	E	DP	FW	PW	BW	SBW	DIF
LA	51	24	29	1469²	1329	8.1	111	402	1095	10.8	2.85	106	.239	.294	71	27	92	103	.975	159	129	-.0	2.9	4.2	.4	10.4
STL	49	17	32	1463	1329	8.2	124	463	978	11.3	3.32	107	.241	.305	-5	37	108	97	.976	147	136	.6	4.0	5.4	.8	1.2
SF	46	9	30	1469	1380	8.5	126	464	954	11.5	3.35	96	.246	.307	-9	-24	97	99	.975	156	113	.1	-2.6	12.9	-.4	-3.0
PHI	45	12	31	1457¹	1262	7.8	113	553	1052	11.4	3.09	105	.235	.311	32	23	98	104	.978	142	147	.9	2.5	3.9	.2	-1.6
CIN	55	22	36	1439²	1307	8.2	117	425	1048	11.1	3.29	102	.242	.302	-1	8	102	96	.978	135	127	1.3	.9	.7	.2	1.9
MIL	56	18	25	1471²	1327	8.1	149	489	924	11.3	3.27	99	.241	.306	4	-8	98	103	.980	129	161	1.8	-.9	4.0	.0	-1.9
CHI	45	15	28	1457	1357	8.4	119	400	851	11.0	3.08	114	.249	.303	34	70	107	105	.976	155	172	.2	7.6	-5.8	-.8	-.3
PIT	34	16	33	1448	1350	8.4	99	457	900	11.5	3.10	107	.249	.313	31	33	100	107	.972	182	195	-1.4	3.6	-.7	.1	-8.6
HOU	36	16	20	1450¹	1341	8.3	95	378	937	10.9	3.44	92	.245	.298	-24	-46	96	87	.974	162	100	-.3	-5.0	-14.3	.3	4.2
NY	42	5	12	1427²	1452	9.2	162	529	806	12.8	4.12	85	.263	.332	-132	-101	106	100	.967	210	151	-3.1	-11.0	-14.9	-1.1	.0
TOT	459	154	276	14553¹		8.3				11.4	3.29		.245	.307					.975	1577	1431					

Runs		Hits		Doubles		Triples		Home Runs		Total Bases	
H.Aaron-Mil	121	Pinson-Cin	204	Groat-StL	43	Pinson-Cin	14	McCovey-SF	44	H.Aaron-Mil	370
Mays-SF	115	Groat-StL	201	Pinson-Cin	37	Gonzalez-Phi	12	H.Aaron-Mil	44	Mays-SF	347
Flood-StL	112	H.Aaron-Mil	201	Williams-Chi	36	Groat-StL	11	Mays-SF	38	Pinson-Cin	335
White-StL	106	White-StL	200	Gonzalez-Phi	36	Callison-Phi	11	Cepeda-SF	34	Cepeda-SF	326
McCovey-SF	103	Flood-StL	200	Callison-Phi	36	Brock-Chi	11	Howard-LA	28	White-StL	323

Runs Batted In		Runs Produced		Bases On Balls		Batting Average		On Base Percentage		Slugging Average	
H.Aaron-Mil	130	H.Aaron-Mil	207	Mathews-Mil	124	T.Davis-LA	.326	Mathews-Mil	.400	H.Aaron-Mil	.586
Boyer-StL	111	White-StL	188	Robinson-Cin	81	Clemente-Pit	.320	H.Aaron-Mil	.394	Mays-SF	.582
White-StL	109	Pinson-Cin	180	H.Aaron-Mil	78	Groat-StL	.319	Mays-SF	.384	McCovey-SF	.566
Pinson-Cin	106	Mays-SF	180	Boyer-StL	70	H.Aaron-Mil	.319	Robinson-Cin	.381	Cepeda-SF	.563
Mays-SF	103	Boyer-StL	173	Schofield-Pit	69	Cepeda-SF	.316	Groat-StL	.380	Pinson-Cin	.514

Production		Adjusted Production		Batter Runs		Adjusted Batter Runs		Clutch Hitting Index		Runs Created	
H.Aaron-Mil	.980	H.Aaron-Mil	180	H.Aaron-Mil	63.0	H.Aaron-Mil	64.5	Sievers-Phi	135	H.Aaron-Mil	149
Mays-SF	.966	Mays-SF	176	Mays-SF	55.8	Mays-SF	57.2	Fairly-LA	135	Mays-SF	131
Cepeda-SF	.930	Cepeda-SF	166	Cepeda-SF	45.4	Cepeda-SF	46.6	Robinson-Cin	126	White-StL	117
McCovey-SF	.916	McCovey-SF	161	McCovey-SF	41.1	McCovey-SF	42.2	Boyer-StL	120	Cepeda-SF	113
Pinson-Cin	.864	Mathews-Mil	147	Mathews-Mil	37.4	Mathews-Mil	38.6	Edwards-Cin	120	Pinson-Cin	113

Total Average		Stolen Bases		Stolen Base Average		Stolen Base Runs		Fielding Runs		Total Player Rating	
H.Aaron-Mil	1.063	Wills-LA	40	H.Aaron-Mil	86.1	H.Aaron-Mil	6.3	Mazeroski-Pit	56.7	Mays-SF	6.6
Mays-SF	.984	H.Aaron-Mil	31	Gilliam-LA	79.2	Pinson-Cin	3.3	Callison-Phi	22.7	H.Aaron-Mil	6.5
McCovey-SF	.911	Pinson-Cin	27	Pinson-Cin	77.1	Maye-Mil	3.0	Hubbs-Chi	20.1	Mazeroski-Pit	6.0
Cepeda-SF	.906	Robinson-Cin	26	Robinson-Cin	72.2	Harper-Cin	3.0	Flood-StL	19.5	Mathews-Mil	5.3
Mathews-Mil	.894	W.Davis-LA	25	Taylor-Phi	71.9	Gilliam-LA	2.7	Harkness-NY	16.4	Callison-Phi	4.8

Wins		Win Percentage		Games		Complete Games		Shutouts		Saves	
Marichal-SF	25	Perranoski-LA	.842	Perranoski-LA	69	Spahn-Mil	22	Koufax-LA	11	McDaniel-Chi	22
Koufax-LA	25	Koufax-LA	.833	Baldschun-Phi	65	Koufax-LA	20	Spahn-Mil	7	Perranoski-LA	21
Spahn-Mil	23	Spahn-Mil	.767	Bearnarth-NY	58	Ellsworth-Chi	19	Simmons-StL	6	Face-Pit	16
Maloney-Cin	23	Maloney-Cin	.767	Sisk-Pit	57	Marichal-SF	18	Maloney-Cin	6	Baldschun-Phi	16
Ellsworth-Chi	22	Marichal-SF	.758	McDaniel-Chi	57	Drysdale-LA	17			Henry-Cin	14

Innings Pitched		Fewest Hits/Game		Fewest BB/Game		Strikeouts		Strikeouts/Game		Ratio	
Marichal-SF	321.1	Koufax-LA	6.19	Friend-Pit	1.47	Koufax-LA	306	Maloney-Cin	9.53	Koufax-LA	7.96
Drysdale-LA	315.1	Culp-Phi	6.55	Farrell-Hou	1.56	Maloney-Cin	265	Koufax-LA	8.86	Farrell-Hou	8.81
Koufax-LA	311.0	Maloney-Cin	6.58	Nuxhall-Cin	1.62	Drysdale-LA	251	Culp-Phi	7.79	Marichal-SF	9.02
Ellsworth-Chi	290.2	Ellsworth-Chi	6.90	Drysdale-LA	1.63	Marichal-SF	248	Short-Phi	7.27	Ellsworth-Chi	9.29
Sanford-SF	284.1	Farrell-Hou	7.16	Koufax-LA	1.68	Gibson-StL	204	Lemaster-Mil	7.22	Friend-Pit	9.55

Earned Run Average		Adjusted ERA		Opponents' Batting Avg.		Opponents' On Base Pct.		Starter Runs		Adjusted Starter Runs	
Koufax-LA	1.88	Ellsworth-Chi	167	Koufax-LA	.189	Koufax-LA	.230	Koufax-LA	48.6	Ellsworth-Chi	45.3
Ellsworth-Chi	2.11	Koufax-LA	161	Maloney-Cin	.202	Marichal-SF	.256	Ellsworth-Chi	38.2	Koufax-LA	39.4
Friend-Pit	2.34	Simmons-StL	143	Culp-Phi	.206	Farrell-Hou	.256	Marichal-SF	31.4	Jackson-Chi	29.2
Marichal-SF	2.41	Friend-Pit	141	Ellsworth-Chi	.210	Ellsworth-Chi	.263	Friend-Pit	28.2	Friend-Pit	28.5
Simmons-StL	2.48	Jackson-Chi	137	Broglio-StL	.216	Friend-Pit	.269	Drysdale-LA	23.2	Marichal-SF	28.2

Clutch Pitching Index		Relief Runs		Adjusted Relief Runs		Relief Ranking		Total Pitcher Index		Total Baseball Ranking	
Schwall-Pit	118	Perranoski-LA	23.1	Veale-Pit	19.5	Perranoski-LA	32.7	Ellsworth-Chi	5.2	Mays-SF	6.6
Spahn-Mil	115	Veale-Pit	19.4	Perranoski-LA	19.3	Woodeshick-Hou	26.5	Jackson-Chi	4.1	H.Aaron-Mil	6.5
Short-Phi	111	Klippstein-Phi	16.9	Klippstein-Phi	16.2	Baldschun-Phi	20.6	Perranoski-LA	3.7	Mazeroski-Pit	6.0
Cardwell-Pit	110	Woodeshick-Hou	16.6	Woodeshick-Hou	14.9	Veale-Pit	17.5	Woodeshick-Hou	3.3	Mathews-Mil	5.3
Buhl-Chi	109	Baldschun-Phi	12.5	Baldschun-Phi	11.8	Klippstein-Phi	16.9	Spahn-Mil	3.2	Ellsworth-Chi	5.2

January 26 The Major League Rules Committee votes to expand the strike zone, restoring it to pre-1950 standards: from the top of the shoulders to the bottom of the knees.

January 27 The Hall of Fame Special Veterans Committee votes in Sam Rice, Eppa Rixey, Elmer Flick, and John Clarkson.

April 8 The Tigers claim young pitcher Denny McLain from the White Sox for the $25,000 waiver price.

June 23 A major league fielding record is set by Boston first baseman Dick Stuart as "Dr. Strangeglove" handles three first-inning grounders and tosses to pitcher Bob Heffner for putouts. Stuart's teammates and Fenway fans give him a standing ovation. Regardless, the Yankees beat the Sox, 8–0.

July 8 Reports of Charlie Finley's intention to move the Kansas City A's to Oakland surface during the All-Star break at Cleveland.

July 13 At Kansas City in the second game of a doubleheader, Cleveland's Early Wynn leaves with a lead after struggling through five innings. Four scoreless relief innings by Jerry Walker enable Wynn to score his 300th career victory 7-4.

August 21 Orioles shortstop Luis Aparicio becomes the first major league player since George Case in 1945 to reach 300 career steals.

September 6 Baseball historian Lee Allen says the Indians-Senators game is the 100,000th in major league history. Bennie Daniels celebrates by beating the Tribe 7-2.

September 13 Jim Bouton's 20th win, 2–0, at Minnesota, clinches the Yankees 28th pennant.

October 1 The season ends, and there are no full-schedule players in the AL for the first time since 1910. Brooks Robinson played in the most games, 161, missing only one. Ron Santo, Vada Pinson, and Bill White all play the full schedule in the NL.

October 12 In the first (and last) Hispanic American major league all-star game, the NL team beats the AL 5-2 at the Polo Grounds. The game features such names as Minnie Minoso, Tony Oliva, Roberto Clemente, Orlando Cepeda, Julian Javier, Felipe Alou, Luis Aparicio, and Zoilo Versalles. Vic Power receives a pregame award as the number-one Latin player. National League starter Juan Marichal strikes out six in four innings, though reliever Al McBean is the winner. Pinch hitter Manny Mota drives in two against loser Pedro Ramos.

October 24 Yogi Berra is appointed manager of the Yankees.

November 7 Catcher Elston Howard is named AL MVP. New York's Howard tops Detroit's Al Kaline 248 to 148.

December 2 The Major League Rules Committee bans oversized catcher's mitts, effective in 1965.

BALTIMORE		BOSTON		CHICAGO		CLEVELAND		DETROIT	
M	B.Hitchcock	M	J.Pesky	M	A.Lopez	M	B.Tebbetts	M	B.Scheffing
1B	J.Gentile	1B	D.Stuart	1B	T.McCraw	1B	F.Whitfield	M	C.Dressen
2B	J.Adair	2B	C.Schilling	2B	N.Fox	2B	W.Held	1B	N.Cash
SS	L.Aparicio	SS	E.Bressoud	SS	R.Hansen	SS	J.Kindall	2B	J.Wood
3B	B.Robinson	3B	F.Malzone	3B	P.Ward	3B	M.Alvis	SS	D.McAuliffe
LF	B.Powell	LF	C.Yastrzemski	LF	D.Nicholson	LF	T.Francona	3B	B.Phillips
CF	J.Brandt	CF	G.Geiger	CF	J.Landis	CF	V.Davalillo	LF	R.Colavito
RF	R.Snyder	RF	L.Clinton	RF	F.Robinson	RF	W.Kirkland	CF	B.Bruton
C	J.Orsino	C	B.Tillman	C	J.Martin	C	J.Azcue	RF	A.Kaline
								C	G.Triandos
O2	B.Saverine	O	R.Mejias	C	C.Carreon	1	J.Adcock		
O	A.Smith	C	R.Nixon	O	M.Hershberger	O	A.Luplow	C1	B.Freehan
2	B.Johnson			2S	A.Weis	C	J.Romano	32	D.Wert
		P	B.Monbouquette	1	J.Cunningham	S2	L.Brown		
P	S.Barber	P	E.Wilson					P	J.Bunning
P	R.Roberts	P	D.Morehead	P	G.Peters	P	M.Grant	P	H.Aguirre
P	M.Pappas	P	B.Heffner	P	R.Herbert	P	D.Donovan	P	P.Regan
P	M.McCormick	RP	J.Lamabe	P	J.Pizarro	P	J.Kralick	P	M.Lolich
P	D.McNally	RP	D.Radatz	P	J.Buzhardt	P	P.Ramos	P	D.Mossi
RP	S.Miller	RP	A.Earley	P	J.Horlen	P	B.Latman	RP	T.Fox
RP	D.Hall			RP	H.Wilhelm	RP	G.Bell	RP	B.Anderson
RP	W.Stock	P	W.Wood	RP	J.Brosnan	RP	J.Walker	RP	T.Sturdivant
		P	C.Nichols	RP	F.Baumann	RP	T.Abernathy		
								P	F.Lary
				P	E.Fisher	P	S.McDowell	P	B.Faul
				P	D.DeBusschere	P	B.Allen		
						P	E.Wynn		

KANSAS CITY		LOS ANGELES		MINNESOTA		NEW YORK		WASHINGTON	
M	E.Lopat	M	B.Rigney	M	S.Mele	M	R.Houk	M	M.Vernon
1B	N.Siebern	1B	L.Thomas	1B	V.Power	1B	J.Pepitone	M	E.Yost
2B	J.Lumpe	2B	B.Moran	2B	B.Allen	2B	B.Richardson	M	G.Hodges
SS	W.Causey	SS	J.Fregosi	SS	Z.Versalles	SS	T.Kubek	1B	B.Osborne
3B	E.Charles	3B	F.Torres	3B	R.Rollins	3B	C.Boyer	2B	C.Cottier
LF	B.Del Greco	LF	L.Wagner	LF	H.Killebrew	LF	H.Lopez	SS	E.Brinkman
CF	J.Tartabull	CF	A.Pearson	CF	J.Hall	CF	T.Tresh	3B	D.Zimmer
RF	G.Cimoli	RF	B.Perry	RF	B.Allison	RF	J.Reed	LF	C.Hinton
C	D.Edwards	C	B.Rodgers	C	E.Battey	C	E.Howard	CF	D.Lock
								RF	J.King
O	C.Essegian	1	C.Dees	O	L.Green	O	R.Maris	C	K.Retzer
1O	K.Harrelson			1	D.Mincher	O	J.Blanchard		
O	G.Alusik	P	K.McBride					O	M.Minoso
		P	D.Chance	P	C.Pascual	P	W.Ford	1	D.Phillips
P	D.Wickersham	P	D.Osinski	P	D.Stigman	P	R.Terry	2	D.Blasingame
P	O.Pena	P	D.Lee	P	J.Kaat	P	J.Bouton	C	D.Leppert
P	E.Rakow	RP	J.Navarro	P	J.Perry	P	A.Downing		
P	M.Drabowsky	RP	A.Fowler	P	L.Stange	P	S.Williams	P	C.Osteen
P	D.Segui	RP	P.Foytack	RP	B.Dailey	RP	H.Reniff	P	D.Rudolph
RP	T.Bowsfield			RP	B.Pleis	RP	S.Hamilton	P	B.Daniels
RP	B.Fischer	P	B.Turley	RP	G.Roggenburk			P	T.Cheney
RP	J.Wyatt	P	B.Belinsky			P	B.Stafford	P	J.Duckworth
		P	M.Nelson					RP	R.Kline
P	T.Sturdivant							RP	P.Burnside
								RP	E.Roebuck
								P	S.Ridzik
								P	D.Stenhouse
								P	J.Bronstad

TEAM	G	W	L	PCT	GB	R	OR	AB	H	2B	3B	HR	BB	SO	AVG	OBP	SLG	PRO	PRO+	BR	/A	PF	CHI	RC	SB	CS	SBA	SBR
NY	161	104	57	.646		714	547	5506	1387	197	35	188	434	808	.252	.310	.403	.713	106	27	33	99	105	686	42	26	62	-3
CHI	162	94	68	.580	10.5	683	544	5508	1379	208	40	114	571	896	.250	.325	.365	.690	101	4	15	98	101	675	64	28	70	2
MIN	161	91	70	.565	13	767	602	5531	1408	223	35	225	547	912	.255	.326	.430	.756	115	116	101	102	98	777	32	14	70	1
BAL	162	86	76	.531	18.5	644	621	5448	1359	207	32	146	469	940	.249	.312	.380	.692	103	-7	-17	96	100	645	97	34	74	9
DET	162	79	83	.488	25.5	700	703	5500	1388	195	36	148	592	908	.252	.329	.382	.711	102	43	19	103	98	699	73	32	70	3
CLE	162	79	83	.488	25.5	635	702	5496	1314	214	29	169	469	1102	.239	.304	.381	.685	98	-26	-20	99	100	634	59	36	62	-4
BOS	161	76	85	.472	28	666	704	5575	1403	247	34	171	475	954	.252	.313	.400	.713	102	31	9	103	96	684	27	16	63	-2
KC	162	73	89	.451	31.5	615	704	5495	1356	225	38	95	529	829	.247	.316	.353	.669	88	-41	-76	106	99	616	47	26	64	-2
LA	161	70	91	.435	34	597	660	5506	1378	208	38	95	448	916	.250	.312	.354	.666	98	-53	-18	94	99	608	43	30	59	-5
WAS	162	56	106	.346	48.5	578	812	5446	1237	190	35	138	497	963	.227	.295	.351	.646	86	-95	-93	100	104	569	68	28	71	4
TOT	808					6599		55011	13609	2114	352	1489	5031	9228	.247	.314	.380	.694							552	270	67	4

TEAM	CG	SH	SV	IP	H	H/G	HR	BB	SO	RAT	ERA	ERA+	OAV	OOB	PR	/A	PF	CPI	FA	E	DP	FW	PW	BW	SBW	DIF
NY	59	19	31	1449	1239	7.7	115	476	965	10.8	3.07	114	.232	.297	89	71	97	98	.982	110	162	1.4	7.5	3.5	-.4	11.5
CHI	49	21	39	1469	1311	8.0	100	440	932	10.9	2.97	118	.239	.299	107	87	97	102	.979	131	163	.3	9.1	1.6	.2	1.9
MIN	58	13	30	1446¹	1322	8.2	162	459	941	11.2	3.28	111	.242	.303	56	59	100	105	.976	144	140	-.5	6.2	10.6	.0	-5.8
BAL	35	8	43	1452	1353	8.4	137	507	913	11.7	3.45	101	.248	.316	29	3	96	104	.984	99	157	2.1	.3	1.8	.9	-.0
DET	42	7	28	1456¹	1407	8.7	195	477	930	11.9	3.90	96	.253	.317	-44	-25	103	102	.982	113	124	1.3	-2.6	2.0	-.3	-2.9
CLE	40	14	25	1469	1390	8.5	176	478	1018	11.6	3.79	95	.249	.311	-27	-28	100	98	.977	143	129	-.4	-2.9	-2.1	-.5	3.9
BOS	29	7	32	1449¹	1367	8.5	152	539	1009	12.0	3.97	95	.248	.318	-55	-30	104	93	.978	135	119	-.0	-3.2	.9	-.2	-2.0
KC	35	11	29	1458	1417	8.7	156	540	887	12.4	3.92	100	.256	.327	-47	-3	108	101	.980	127	131	.5	-.3	-8.0	-.2	.0
LA	30	13	31	1455¹	1317	8.1	120	578	889	12.0	3.52	97	.242	.320	17	-16	94	100	.974	163	155	-1.6	-1.7	-1.9	-.6	-4.8
WAS	29	8	25	1447	1486	9.2	176	537	744	12.8	4.42	84	.266	.334	-126	-114	102	98	.971	182	165	-2.6	-12.0	-9.8	.4	-1.0
TOT	406	121	313	14551²		8.4				11.7	3.63		.247	.314					.978	1347	1445					

Runs		Hits		Doubles		Triples		Home Runs		Total Bases	
Allison-Min	99	Yastrzemski-Bos	183	Yastrzemski-Bos	40	Versalles-Min	13	Killebrew-Min	45	Stuart-Bos	319
Pearson-LA	92	Ward-Chi	177	Ward-Chi	34	Hinton-Was	12	Stuart-Bos	42	Ward-Chi	289
Yastrzemski-Bos	91	Pearson-LA	176	Torres-LA	32	Fregosi-LA	12	Allison-Min	35	Killebrew-Min	286
Tresh-NY	91	Kaline-Det	172	Causey-KC	32	Cimoli-KC	11	Hall-Min	33	Kaline-Det	283
Colavito-Det	91	Fregosi-LA	170	Alvis-Cle	32			Howard-NY	28	Allison-Min	281

Runs Batted In		Runs Produced		Bases On Balls		Batting Average		On Base Percentage		Slugging Average	
Stuart-Bos	118	Kaline-Det	163	Yastrzemski-Bos	95	Yastrzemski-Bos	.321	Yastrzemski-Bos	.419	Killebrew-Min	.555
Kaline-Det	101	Colavito-Det	160	Pearson-LA	92	Kaline-Det	.312	Pearson-LA	.403	Allison-Min	.533
Killebrew-Min	96	Stuart-Bos	157	Allison-Min	90	Rollins-Min	.307	Cash-Det	.388	Howard-NY	.528
Colavito-Det	91	Allison-Min	155	Cash-Det	89	Pearson-LA	.304	Allison-Min	.381	Stuart-Bos	.521
Allison-Min	91	Siebern-KC	147	Colavito-Det	84	Ward-Chi	.295	Kaline-Det	.378	Hall-Min	.521

Production		Adjusted Production		Batter Runs		Adjusted Batter Runs		Clutch Hitting Index		Runs Created	
Allison-Min	.914	Allison-Min	150	Yastrzemski-Bos	42.0	Yastrzemski-Bos	38.4	Hansen-Chi	127	Yastrzemski-Bos	118
Killebrew-Min	.908	Killebrew-Min	147	Allison-Min	38.6	Allison-Min	36.6	Torres-LA	115	Allison-Min	113
Yastrzemski-Bos	.894	Yastrzemski-Bos	145	Kaline-Det	34.3	Killebrew-Min	31.6	Siebern-KC	114	Kaline-Det	105
Kaline-Det	.891	Kaline-Det	142	Killebrew-Min	33.5	Kaline-Det	30.9	L.Thomas-LA	112	Ward-Chi	104
Howard-NY	.871	Howard-NY	141	Cash-Det	28.7	Pearson-LA	29.8	Phillips-Det	112	Pearson-LA	100

Total Average		Stolen Bases		Stolen Base Average		Stolen Base Runs		Fielding Runs		Total Player Rating	
Allison-Min	.967	Aparicio-Bal	40	Tartabull-KC	94.1	Aparicio-Bal	8.4	Hansen-Chi	27.0	Yastrzemski-Bos	4.4
Yastrzemski-Bos	.916	Hinton-Was	25	Aparicio-Bal	87.0	Tartabull-KC	4.2	Boyer-NY	22.3	Allison-Min	4.2
Killebrew-Min	.907	Wood-Det	18	Wood-Det	78.3	Weis-Chi	3.9	Moran-LA	15.2	Hansen-Chi	3.6
Tresh-NY	.879	Snyder-Bal	18	Snyder-Bal	78.3	Richardson-NY	3.9	Lock-Was	14.8	Battey-Min	3.1
Cash-Det	.876	Pearson-LA	17	Hinton-Was	73.5	Smith-Bal	2.7	Geiger-Bos	13.7	Pearson-LA	2.9

Wins		Win Percentage		Games		Complete Games		Shutouts		Saves	
Ford-NY	24	Ford-NY	.774	S.Miller-Bal	71	Terry-NY	18	Herbert-Chi	7	S.Miller-Bal	27
Pascual-Min	21	Bouton-NY	.750	Radatz-Bos	66	Pascual-Min	18	Bouton-NY	6	Radatz-Bos	25
Bouton-NY	21	Radatz-Bos	.714	Dailey-Min	66	Stigman-Min	15			Wyatt-KC	21
Monbouquette-Bos	20	Peters-Chi	.704	Lamabe-Bos	65	Herbert-Chi	14			Wilhelm-Chi	21
Barber-Bal	20	Pascual-Min	.700	Wyatt-KC	63	Aguirre-Det	14			Dailey-Min	21

Innings Pitched		Fewest Hits/Game		Fewest BB/Game		Strikeouts		Strikeouts/Game		Ratio	
Ford-NY	269.1	Downing-NY	5.84	Donovan-Cle	1.22	Pascual-Min	202	Downing-NY	8.76	Terry-NY	9.71
Terry-NY	268.0	Bouton-NY	6.89	Terry-NY	1.31	Bunning-Det	196	Ramos-Cle	8.24	Roberts-Bal	9.78
Monbouquette-Bos	266.2	Drabowsky-KC	6.97	Herbert-Chi	1.40	Stigman-Min	193	Pascual-Min	7.32	Ramos-Cle	9.80
Barber-Bal	258.2	Morehead-Bos	7.06	Monbouquette-Bos	1.42	Peters-Chi	189	Stigman-Min	7.21	Peters-Chi	9.93
Roberts-Bal	251.1	McBride-LA	7.10	Roberts-Bal	1.43	Ford-NY	189	Bunning-Det	7.10	Downing-NY	9.94

Earned Run Average		Adjusted ERA		Opponents' Batting Avg.		Opponents' On Base Pct.		Starter Runs		Adjusted Starter Runs	
Peters-Chi	2.33	Peters-Chi	150	Downing-NY	.184	Roberts-Bal	.272	Peters-Chi	35.0	Pascual-Min	32.6
Pizarro-Chi	2.39	Pascual-Min	148	Morehead-Bos	.211	Terry-NY	.273	Pascual-Min	32.2	Peters-Chi	31.7
Pascual-Min	2.46	Pizarro-Chi	147	Bouton-NY	.212	Ramos-Cle	.273	Bouton-NY	30.6	Bouton-NY	27.3
Bouton-NY	2.53	Bouton-NY	139	Drabowsky-KC	.214	Downing-NY	.277	Pizarro-Chi	29.6	Pizarro-Chi	26.6
Downing-NY	2.56	Stange-Min	139	Peters-Chi	.216	Peters-Chi	.278	Ford-NY	26.6	Ford-NY	23.2

Clutch Pitching Index		Relief Runs		Adjusted Relief Runs		Relief Ranking		Total Pitcher Index		Total Baseball Ranking	
Barber-Bal	126	Radatz-Bos	24.4	Radatz-Bos	26.7	Radatz-Bos	49.4	Radatz-Bos	5.0	Radatz-Bos	5.0
Osteen-Was	120	Dailey-Min	19.8	Dailey-Min	20.0	S.Miller-Bal	24.3	Pascual-Min	4.6	Pascual-Min	4.6
Stange-Min	120	S.Miller-Bal	17.3	S.Miller-Bal	15.4	Dailey-Min	23.6	Peters-Chi	4.5	Peters-Chi	4.5
Segui-KC	115	Wilhelm-Chi	15.0	Wilhelm-Chi	13.1	Wilhelm-Chi	15.8	S.Miller-Bal	3.0	Yastrzemski-Bos	4.4
Pascual-Min	115	Fowler-LA	12.0	Lamabe-Bos	10.7	Kline-Was	14.1	Dailey-Min	3.0	Allison-Min	4.2

February 2 The Hall of Fame Special Veterans Committee tabs Red Faber, Burleigh Grimes, Tim Keefe, Heinie Manush, John Montgomery Ward, and Miller Huggins for induction, the biggest veterans class ever.

February 15 Cubs second baseman Ken Hubbs, 22, dies when his private plane crashes near Provo, Utah, while en route to Colton, Calif. As a rookie in 1962, Hubbs had played in 78 consecutive games without making an error.

May 31 After Juan Marichal's 5-3, first-game win, SF holds a 6-1 lead in the second until New York rallies for five to tie in the seventh. Eventually, with two out in the 23rd, pinch hitter Del Crandall delivers a run-scoring double off Galen Cisco, and the Giants prevail 8-6 after seven hours, 22 minutes—a record. Gaylord Perry pitches 10 scoreless innings to get the win. Thirty-two innings and an elapsed time of nine hours, 50 minutes are doubleheader records, as are 47 strikeouts. New York's 22 K's in the second game are the most by one club in an overtime contest.

June 4 Sandy Koufax becomes the fourth pitcher to hurl three no-hitters by blanking the NL-leading Phillies 3-0 at Connie Mack Stadium. Koufax strikes out 12 and walks one.

June 21 On Father's Day at Shea Stadium, Jim Bunning pitches the first perfect game (excluding Don Larsen's 1956 World Series effort and Harvey Haddix's 1959 overtime loss) since Charlie Robertson's on April 30, 1922. He is also the first to win no-hitters in both leagues and drives in two runs as Philadelphia beats the Mets 6-0. Gus Triandos becomes the first catcher to catch a no-hitter in each league.

September 1 Southpaw relief pitcher Masanori Murakami becomes the first major league player from Japan. He debuts in a 4-1 SF loss at New York. His first 11 innings will be scoreless ones.

September 26 The Braves and Phillies set the major league record by using 43 players in a nine-inning game. The Braves' 25 match the high mark for NL clubs. Eight of the 25 are pitchers, tying the league mark.

October 4 The Phils bomb the Reds, 10-0, as both teams finish one game behind St. Louis. They then sit in the visitor's clubhouse and hope that Galen Cisco (6-18) can stop the Cards. The Mets take a 3-2 lead into the fifth, but St. Louis scores three runs to take the lead. The Mets score once more but the Cards complete their scoring with three in the eighth to win 11-5. Bob Gibson wins in relief. For St. Louis, it is their first pennant since 1946.

October 7 Ailing Whitey Ford struggles as St. Louis wins the World Series opener 9-4 at Busch Stadium. Ray Sadecki and Barney Schultz combine for the win.

October 15 St. Louis takes an early lead in the deciding World Series Game 7. Lou Brock's fifth-inning home run triggers a second three-run frame and a 6-0 lead for Bob Gibson. Brothers Ken and Clete Boyer become the only brothers to homer in the same Series game, and the Cards win 7-5 to become World Champs.

November 7 With their home attendance below 800,000 for the past two seasons, the NL orders the Braves to stay in Milwaukee in 1965, but permits a move to Atlanta in 1966.

November 24 Third baseman Ken Boyer of the Cardinals is voted NL MVP, with 243 votes to 187 for Philadelphia outfielder Johnny Callison.

CHICAGO		CINCINNATI		HOUSTON		LOS ANGELES		MILWAUKEE	
M	B.Kennedy	M	F.Hutchinson	M	H.Craft	M	W.Alston	M	B.Bragan
1B	E.Banks	M	D.Sisler	M	L.Harris	1B	R.Fairly	1B	G.Oliver
2B	J.Amalfitano	M	F.Hutchinson	1B	W.Bond	2B	N.Oliver	2B	F.Bolling
SS	A.Rodgers	M	D.Sisler	2B	N.Fox	SS	M.Wills	SS	D.Menke
3B	R.Santo	1B	D.Johnson	SS	E.Kasko	3B	J.Gilliam	3B	E.Mathews
LF	B.Williams	2B	P.Rose	3B	B.Aspromonte	LF	T.Davis	LF	R.Carty
CF	B.Cowan	SS	L.Cardenas	LF	A.Spangler	CF	W.Davis	CF	L.Maye
RF	L.Gabrielson	3B	S.Boros	CF	M.White	RF	F.Howard	RF	H.Aaron
C	D.Bertell	LF	T.Harper	RF	J.Gaines	C	J.Roseboro	C	J.Torre
		CF	V.Pinson	C	J.Grote				
2S	J.Stewart	RF	F.Robinson			O1	W.Parker	O1	F.Alou
O	L.Brock	C	J.Edwards	2S	B.Lillis	23	D.Tracewski	O	T.Cline
				1O	R.Staub	3O	D.Griffith	C	E.Bailey
P	L.Jackson	O	M.Keough	C	J.Bateman				
P	D.Ellsworth	32	C.Ruiz	O	J.Wynn	P	D.Drysdale	P	T.Cloninger
P	B.Buhl					P	S.Koufax	P	D.Lemaster
P	L.Burdette	P	J.O'Toole	P	K.Johnson	P	P.Ortega	P	W.Spahn
P	E.Broglio	P	J.Maloney	P	B.Bruce	P	J.Moeller	P	H.Fischer
RP	L.McDaniel	P	B.Purkey	P	T.Farrell	RP	B.Miller	P	B.Sadowski
RP	D.Elston	P	J.Jay	P	D.Nottebart	RP	R.Perranoski	RP	B.Tiefenauer
RP	S.Slaughter	P	J.Tsitouris	P	H.Brown	RP	J.Brewer	RP	B.Hoeft
		RP	S.Ellis	RP	J.Owens			RP	C.Olivo
		RP	B.McCool	RP	C.Raymond	P	H.Reed		
		RP	B.Henry	RP	H.Woodeshick	P	L.Miller	P	W.Blasingame
		P	J.Nuxhall	P	D.Larsen				
				P	G.Jones				

NEW YORK		PHILADELPHIA		PITTSBURGH		SAN FRANCISCO		ST.LOUIS	
M	C.Stengel	M	G.Mauch	M	D.Murtaugh	M	A.Dark	M	J.Keane
1B	E.Kranepool	1B	J.Herrnstein	1B	D.Clendenon	1B	O.Cepeda	1B	B.White
2B	R.Hunt	2B	T.Taylor	2B	B.Mazeroski	2B	H.Lanier	2B	J.Javier
SS	R.McMillan	SS	B.Wine	SS	D.Schofield	SS	J.Pagan	SS	D.Groat
3B	C.Smith	3B	D.Allen	3B	B.Bailey	3B	J.Hart	3B	K.Boyer
LF	G.Altman	LF	W.Covington	LF	M.Mota	LF	H.Kuenn	LF	L.Brock
CF	J.Hickman	CF	T.Gonzalez	CF	B.Virdon	CF	W.Mays	CF	C.Flood
RF	J.Christopher	RF	J.Callison	RF	R.Clemente	RF	J.Alou	RF	M.Shannon
C	J.Gonder	C	C.Dalrymple	C	J.Pagliaroni	C	T.Haller	C	T.McCarver
2O	R.Kanehl	S1	R.Amaro	3	G.Freese	O	M.Alou	O	C.James
CO	H.Taylor	O2	C.Rojas	O	J.Lynch	S3	J.Davenport		
O	L.Elliot			O1	W.Stargell	O1	W.McCovey		
23	B.Klaus	P	J.Bunning	S	G.Alley	2	C.Hiller	P	B.Gibson
		P	C.Short					P	C.Simmons
P	J.Fisher	P	De.Bennett	P	B.Veale	P	J.Marichal	P	R.Sadecki
P	T.Stallard	P	A.Mahaffey	P	B.Friend	P	G.Perry	P	R.Craig
P	A.Jackson	P	R.Culp	P	V.Law	P	B.Bolin	RP	R.Taylor
P	G.Cisco	RP	J.Baldschun	P	J.Gibbon	P	B.Hendley	RP	M.Cuellar
RP	B.Wakefield	RP	E.Roebuck	RP	S.Blass	P	R.Herbel	RP	B.Schultz
RP	L.Bearnarth	RP	R.Wise	RP	A.McBean	RP	B.Shaw		
				RP	R.Face	RP	B.O'Dell	P	E.Broglio
P	D.Ribant	P	Da.Bennett	RP	T.Butters	RP	J.Duffalo	P	R.Washburn
P	F.Lary	P	J.Boozer						
				P	T.Sisk	P	J.Sanford		
				P	D.Schwall				

TEAM	G	W	L	PCT	GB	R	OR	AB	H	2B	3B	HR	BB	SO	AVG	OBP	SLG	PRO	PRO+	BR	/A	PF	CHI	RC	SB	CS	SBA	SBR
STL	162	93	69	.574		715	652	5625	**1531**	240	53	109	427	925	**.272**	.326	.392	.718	100	62	0	109	99	711	73	51	59	-9
PHI	162	92	70	.568	1	693	632	5493	1415	241	51	130	440	924	.258	.317	.391	.708	107	41	50	99	100	672	30	35	46	-12
CIN	163	92	70	.568	1	660	**566**	5561	1383	220	38	130	457	974	.249	.310	.372	.682	96	-10	-33	104	102	642	90	36	**71**	5
SF	162	90	72	.556	3	656	587	5535	1360	185	38	**165**	**505**	900	.246	.313	.382	.695	100	16	2	102	97	657	64	35	65	-2
MIL	162	88	74	.543	5	**803**	744	5591	1522	**274**	32	159	486	**825**	**.272**	**.335**	**.418**	**.753**	118	132	127	101	101	**764**	53	41	56	-9
PIT	162	80	82	.494	13	663	636	5566	1469	225	**54**	121	408	970	.264	.317	.389	.706	105	35	36	100	97	668	39	33	54	-8
LA	164	80	82	.494	13	614	572	5499	1375	180	39	79	438	893	.250	.308	.340	.648	96	-70	-28	93	105	581	**141**	60	70	**6**
CHI	162	76	86	.469	17	649	724	5545	1391	239	50	145	490	1041	.251	.316	.390	.706	101	37	9	104	94	679	70	49	59	-8
HOU	162	66	96	.407	27	495	628	5303	1214	162	41	70	381	872	.229	.287	.315	.602	81	-158	-132	94	**106**	469	40	48	45	-17
NY	163	53	109	.327	40	569	776	5566	1372	195	31	103	353	932	.246	.297	.348	.645	90	-84	-71	98	102	552	36	31	54	-8
TOT	812					6517		55284	14032	2161	427	1211	4394	9256	.254	.313	.374	.687							636	419	60	-61

TEAM	CG	SH	SV	IP	H	H/G	HR	BB	SO	RAT	ERA	ERA+	OAV	OOB	PR	/A	PF	CPI	FA	E	DP	FW	PW	BW	SBW	DIF
STL	47	10	38	1445¹	1405	8.7	133	410	877	11.5	3.43	111	.255	.310	17	60	108	104	.973	172	147	-.7	6.3	-.0	-.3	6.7
PHI	37	17	**41**	1461	1402	8.6	129	440	1009	11.7	3.36	103	.252	.313	28	17	98	**106**	.975	157	150	.0	1.8	5.3	-.6	4.5
CIN	54	14	35	1467	1306	8.0	112	436	**1122**	10.9	3.07	**118**	.238	.298	75	**88**	102	100	**.979**	**130**	137	**1.6**	**9.3**	-3.5	1.2	2.4
SF	48	17	30	1476¹	1348	8.2	118	480	1023	11.4	3.19	112	.241	.306	57	61	101	102	.975	159	136	-.0	6.4	.2	.4	1.9
MIL	45	14	19	1434²	1411	8.9	160	452	906	11.8	4.12	86	.257	.316	-92	-95	100	94	.977	143	139	.8	-10.0	13.4	-.3	3.1
PIT	42	14	29	1443²	1429	8.9	92	476	951	12.1	3.52	100	.260	.322	2	-2	99	103	.972	177	**179**	-1.0	-.2	3.8	-.2	-3.4
LA	47	**19**	27	1483²	**1289**	7.8	88	458	1062	10.8	**2.95**	110	**.232**	**.294**	96	47	92	95	.973	170	126	-.5	5.0	-3.0	**1.3**	-3.8
CHI	**58**	11	19	1445	1510	9.4	144	423	737	12.1	4.08	91	.270	.323	-87	-59	105	98	.975	162	147	-.2	-6.2	1.0	-.2	.7
HOU	30	9	31	1428	1421	9.0	105	353	852	11.4	3.41	100	.260	.309	20	1	97	102	.976	149	124	.5	.1	-13.9	-1.2	-.5
NY	40	10	15	1438²	1511	9.5	130	466	717	12.7	4.25	84	.272	.334	-115	-108	101	98	.974	167	154	-.4	-11.4	-7.5	-.2	-8.5
TOT	448	135	304	14523¹		8.7				11.6	3.54		.254	.313					.975	1586	1439					

Runs
Allen-Phi 125
Mays-SF 121
Brock-Chi-StL 111
Robinson-Cin 103
Aaron-Mil 103

Hits
Flood-StL 211
Clemente-Pit 211
Williams-Chi 201
Allen-Phi 201
Brock-Chi-StL 200

Doubles
Maye-Mil 44
Clemente-Pit 40
Williams-Chi 39
Robinson-Cin 38
Allen-Phi 38

Triples
Santo-Chi 13
Allen-Phi 13
Brock-Chi-StL 11
Pinson-Cin 11

Home Runs
Mays-SF 47
Williams-Chi 33
Hart-SF 31
Cepeda-SF 31
Callison-Phi 31

Total Bases
Allen-Phi 352
Mays-SF 351
Williams-Chi 343
Santo-Chi 334
Callison-Phi 322

Runs Batted In
Boyer-StL 119
Santo-Chi 114
Mays-SF 111
Torre-Mil 109
Callison-Phi 104

Runs Produced
Boyer-StL 195
Allen-Phi 187
Mays-SF 185
Santo-Chi 178
Torre-Mil 176

Bases On Balls
Santo-Chi 86
Mathews-Mil 85
Mays-SF 82
Robinson-Cin 79
Boyer-StL 70

Batting Average
Clemente-Pit 339
Carty-Mil 330
Aaron-Mil 328
Torre-Mil 321
Allen-Phi 318

On Base Percentage
Santo-Chi 401
Robinson-Cin 399
Aaron-Mil 394
Carty-Mil 391
Clemente-Pit 391

Slugging Average
Mays-SF 607
Santo-Chi 564
Allen-Phi 557
Carty-Mil 554
Robinson-Cin 548

Production
Mays-SF 992
Santo-Chi 966
Robinson-Cin 947
Carty-Mil 945
Allen-Phi 940

Adjusted Production
Mays-SF 171
Allen-Phi 163
Santo-Chi 162
Carty-Mil 162
Robinson-Cin 158

Batter Runs
Mays-SF 56.5
Santo-Chi 55.1
Allen-Phi 50.5
Robinson-Cin 49.5
Williams-Chi 42.5

Adjusted Batter Runs
Mays-SF 53.9
Allen-Phi 52.1
Santo-Chi 49.9
Robinson-Cin 45.3
Aaron-Mil 40.2

Clutch Hitting Index
Fairly-LA 142
Boyer-StL 117
T.Davis-LA 116
Torre-Mil 113
Javier-StL 111

Runs Created
Mays-SF 136
Santo-Chi 135
Allen-Phi 135
Robinson-Cin 127
Williams-Chi 125

Total Average
Mays-SF 1.059
Robinson-Cin ...1.012
Santo-Chi 998
Allen-Phi 944
Carty-Mil 920

Stolen Bases
Wills-LA 53
Brock-Chi-StL 43
W.Davis-LA 42
Harper-Cin 24
Robinson-Cin 23

Stolen Base Average
Harper-Cin 88.9
Aaron-Mil 84.6
Robinson-Cin 82.1
Mays-SF 79.2
W.Davis-LA 76.4

Stolen Base Runs
Wills-LA 5.7
Harper-Cin 5.4
W.Davis-LA 4.8
Aaron-Mil 4.2
Robinson-Cin 3.9

Fielding Runs
Mazeroski-Pit 33.9
W.Davis-LA 24.9
Edwards-Cin 22.6
Callison-Phi 19.4
Rodgers-Chi 19.4

Total Player Rating
Santo-Chi 6.5
Mays-SF 6.5
Allen-Phi 5.8
Aaron-Mil 5.1
Robinson-Cin 4.6

Wins
Jackson-Chi 24
Marichal-SF 21
Sadecki-StL 20

Win Percentage
Koufax-LA .... .792
Marichal-SF ...... .724
O'Toole-Cin ...... .708
Bunning-Phi ...... .704
Jackson-Chi ...... .686

Games
B.Miller-LA 74
Perranoski-LA 72
Baldschun-Phi 71
Taylor-StL 63
McDaniel-Chi 63

Complete Games
Marichal-SF 22
Drysdale-LA 21
Jackson-Chi 19
Gibson-StL 17
Ellsworth-Chi 16

Shutouts
Koufax-LA 7
Law-Pit 5
Fischer-Mil 5
Drysdale-LA 5
Bunning-Phi 5

Saves
Woodeshick-Hou 23
McBean-Pit 22
Baldschun-Phi 21
McDaniel-Chi 15

Innings Pitched
Drysdale-LA 321.1
Jackson-Chi 297.2
Gibson-StL 287.1
Bunning-Phi 284.1
Veale-Pit 279.2

Fewest Hits/Game
Koufax-LA 6.22
Drysdale-LA 6.78
Short-Phi 7.10
Veale-Pit 7.14
Maloney-Cin 7.29

Fewest BB/Game
Bunning-Phi 1.46
Bruce-Hou 1.47
Law-Pit 1.50
Marichal-SF 1.74
Jackson-Chi 1.75

Strikeouts
Veale-Pit 250
Gibson-StL 245
Drysdale-LA 237
Koufax-LA 223
Bunning-Phi 219

Strikeouts/Game
Koufax-LA 9.00
Maloney-Cin 8.92
Veale-Pit 8.05
Gibson-StL 7.67
Lemaster-Mil 7.53

Ratio
Koufax-LA 8.35
Drysdale-LA 8.96
Short-Phi 9.34
Bunning-Phi 9.75
Jackson-Chi 9.80

Earned Run Average
Koufax-LA 1.74
Drysdale-LA 2.18
Short-Phi 2.20
Marichal-SF 2.48
Bunning-Phi 2.63

Adjusted ERA
Koufax-LA 187
Short-Phi 157
Drysdale-LA 148
Marichal-SF 144
O'Toole-Cin 136

Opponents' Batting Avg.
Koufax-LA 191
Drysdale-LA 207
Veale-Pit 217
Short-Phi 217
Bolin-SF 220

Opponents' On Base Pct.
Koufax-LA 241
Drysdale-LA 256
Short-Phi 268
Jackson-Chi 273
Marichal-SF 273

Starter Runs
Drysdale-LA 48.2
Koufax-LA 44.6
Short-Phi 32.7
Marichal-SF 31.7
Bunning-Phi 28.7

Adjusted Starter Runs
Drysdale-LA 37.6
Koufax-LA 37.2
Marichal-SF 32.5
Short-Phi 31.0
Bunning-Phi 26.6

Clutch Pitching Index
Craig-StL 122
D.Bennett-Phi 119
Farrell-Hou 115
Tsitouris-Cin 115
Hendley-SF 110

Relief Runs
McBean-Pit 16.2
B.Miller-LA 14.1
Ellis-Cin 13.1
Roebuck-Phi 11.4
McCool-Cin 11.1

Adjusted Relief Runs
McBean-Pit 16.0
Ellis-Cin 14.1
McCool-Cin 11.9
Roebuck-Phi 10.8
B.Miller-LA 9.5

Relief Ranking
McBean-Pit 26.5
Ellis-Cin 17.1
McCool-Cin 15.2
Roebuck-Phi 13.8
Woodeshick-Hou ..11.0

Total Pitcher Index
Drysdale-LA 4.7
Koufax-LA 3.5
Short-Phi 3.5
Marichal-SF 3.4
McBean-Pit 3.3

Total Baseball Ranking
Santo-Chi 6.5
Mays-SF 6.5
Allen-Phi 5.8
Aaron-Mil 5.1
Drysdale-LA 4.7

January 15 Major League Baseball executives vote to hold a free-agent draft in New York City and also sign a new TV contract.

January 16 AL owners vote 9-1 against Charlie Finley's proposal to move the A's to Louisville. Finley is given an ultimatum to sign a lease in Kansas City or lose his franchise.

February 17 White Sox shortstop Luke Appling is voted into the Hall of Fame.

July 14 Oriole Bob Johnson's sixth straight hit as a pinch hitter sets an AL mark, but the Yankees win 4-3.

July 23 A's rookie Bert Campaneris sends Minnesota to defeat 4-3 with two homers in his major league debut. The 21-year-old Cuban joins Bob Nieman as the only player since 1900 with two home runs in his first major league game.

August 5 After weeks of negotiating, Ford Frick tells the league presidents and club owners he will not run for another term as commissioner.

August 12 Mickey Mantle homers from each side of the plate in the same game for the tenth and final time, a major league record, and New York beats Chicago 7-3 at Yankee Stadium.

August 14 Bo Belinsky is suspended by the Angels after attacking sportswriter Braven Dyer. Four days later Belinsky is assigned to Hawaii (Pacific Coast League), then suspended for the season when he refuses to report.

August 20 On the New York team bus following a 5–0 White Sox win, Phil Linz begins to play "Mary Had a Little Lamb" on his harmonica. Manager Yogi Berra orders Linz to stop, then slaps the instrument out of his hands when he continues playing. The incident is reported as indicating dissension on the club and Berra's lack of control, as well as the level of Linz's humor.

August 31 Ground is broken for Anaheim Stadium, future home of the Los Angeles (later California and Anaheim) Angels.

September 17 The Yankees whip the Angels, 6–2, to lock on to first place for good with a two-percentage-point lead over the idle White Sox and Orioles. Roger Maris and Mickey Mantle each have three hits. Mantle's include his 2,000th career hit and his 450th home run, his 31st of the year. The Yankees have won two in a row and will run their win streak to 11 games.

October 17 A World Series loss is enough reason for the Yankees to fire manager Yogi Berra (99-63).

November 18 Baltimore third baseman Brooks Robinson is voted AL MVP, outpolling Mickey Mantle 269 to 171.

December 4 Baseball approves a free agent draft. At their winter meetings in Houston, the minor league and major league organizations establish a system basically like that of professional football, which will take effect in January 1965 and be held every four months thereafter. Choices will be exercised by clubs in inverse order of their previous year's standing. Draftees must be included in their club's 40-man roster or be susceptible to claim at the waiver price the following season.

BALTIMORE		BOSTON		CHICAGO		CLEVELAND		DETROIT	
M	H.Bauer	M	J.Pesky	M	A.Lopez	M	G.Strickland	M	C.Dressen
1B	N.Siebern	M	.Herman	1B	T.McCraw	M	B.Tebbetts	1B	N.Cash
2B	J.Adair	1B	D.Stuart	2B	A.Weis	1B	B.Chance	2B	J.Lumpe
SS	L.Aparicio	2B	D.Jones	SS	R.Hansen	2B	L.Brown	SS	D.McAuliffe
3B	B.Robinson	SS	E.Bressoud	3B	P.Ward	SS	D.Howser	3B	D.Wert
LF	B.Powell	3B	F.Malzone	LF	F.Robinson	3B	M.Alvis	LF	G.Brown
CF	J.Brandt	LF	T.Conigliaro	CF	J.Landis	LF	L.Wagner	CF	G.Thomas
RF	S.Bowens	CF	C.Yastrzemski	RF	M.Hershberger	CF	V.Davalillo	RF	A.Kaline
C	D.Brown	RF	L.Thomas	C	J.Martin	RF	T.Francona	C	B.Freehan
		C	B.Tillman			C	J.Romano		
C	J.Orsino			23	D.Buford			O	B.Bruton
S1	B.Johnson	O2	F.Mantilla	O	D.Nicholson	2O	W.Held	O1	D.Demeter
				1	B.Skowron	1	F.Whitfield		
P	M.Pappas	P	B.Monbouquette			O2	C.Salmon	P	D.Wickersham
P	W.Bunker	P	E.Wilson	P	G.Peters	C	J.Azcue	P	M.Lolich
P	R.Roberts	P	J.Lamabe	P	J.Pizarro			P	H.Aguirre
P	D.McNally	P	D.Morehead	P	J.Horlen	P	J.Kralick	P	E.Rakow
P	S.Barber	RP	B.Heffner	P	J.Buzhardt	P	S.McDowell	P	P.Regan
RP	S.Miller	RP	D.Radatz	P	R.Herbert	P	D.Donovan	RP	F.Gladding
RP	H.Haddix	RP	B.Spanswick	RP	H.Wilhelm	P	S.Siebert	RP	L.Sherry
RP	D.Hall			RP	E.Fisher	P	P.Ramos	RP	T.Fox
		P	E.Connolly			RP	G.Bell		
P	C.Estrada	P	P.Charton	P	F.Talbot	RP	D.McMahon	P	D.McLain
P	D.Vineyard	P	A.Earley			RP	T.Abernathy	P	J.Sparma
						P	L.Tiant		
						P	T.John		
						P	L.Stange		
						P	M.Grant		

KANSAS CITY		LOS ANGELES		MINNESOTA		NEW YORK		WASHINGTON	
M	E.Lopat	M	B.Rigney	M	S.Mele	M	Y.Berra	M	G.Hodges
M	M.McGaha	1B	J.Adcock	1B	B.Allison	1B	J.Pepitone	1B	B.Skowron
1B	J.Gentile	2B	B.Knoop	2B	B.Allen	2B	B.Richardson	2B	D.Blasingame
2B	D.Green	SS	J.Fregosi	SS	Z.Versalles	SS	T.Kubek	SS	E.Brinkman
SS	W.Causey	3B	F.Torres	3B	R.Rollins	3B	C.Boyer	3B	J.Kennedy
3B	E.Charles	LF	W.Smith	LF	H.Killebrew	LF	T.Tresh	LF	C.Hinton
LF	J.Tartabull	CF	J.Piersall	CF	J.Hall	CF	M.Mantle	CF	D.Lock
CF	N.Mathews	RF	L.Clinton	RF	T.Oliva	RF	R.Maris	RF	J.King
RF	R.Colavito	C	B.Rodgers	C	E.Battey	C	E.Howard	C	M.Brumley
C	D.Edwards								
		O	A.Pearson	1	D.Mincher	S3	P.Linz	1	D.Phillips
O1	G.Alusik	31	T.Satriano	O	H.Lopez	O	F.Valentine		
SO	B.Campaneris	O	B.Perry	P	C.Pascual			3	D.Zimmer
C	B.Bryan	13	V.Power	P	J.Kaat	P	J.Bouton	P	C.Osteen
O	M.Jimenez	O	E.Kirkpatrick	P	D.Stigman	P	W.Ford	P	B.Narum
				P	M.Grant	P	A.Downing	P	B.Daniels
P	O.Pena	P	D.Chance	RP	G.Arrigo	P	R.Terry	P	A.Koch
P	D.Segui	P	F.Newman	RP	A.Worthington	P	R.Sheldon	RP	S.Ridzik
P	J.O'Donoghue	P	B.Latman	RP	J.Perry	RP	P.Mikkelsen	RP	J.Hannan
P	M.Drabowsky	P	B.Belinsky			RP	H.Reniff	RP	R.Kline
RP	J.Wyatt	P	K.McBride	P	J.Roland	RP	B.Stafford		
RP	T.Bowsfield	RP	B.Lee	P	L.Stange				
RP	W.Stock	RP	D.Osinski	P	B.Pleis	P	M.Stottlemyre	P	D.Stenhouse
		RP	D.Lee			P	S.Williams	P	D.Rudolph
P	J.Santiago					P	S.Hamilton	P	J.Duckworth
		P	B.Duliba						
		P	A.Gatewood						

TEAM	G	W	L	PCT	GB	R	OR	AB	H	2B	3B	HR	BB	SO	AVG	OBP	SLG	PRO	PRO+	BR	/A	PF	CHI	RC	SB	CS	SBA	SBR
NY	164	99	63	.611		730	577	5705	**1442**	208	35	162	520	976	.253	.319	.387	.706	100	13	2	102	**105**	705	54	18	**75**	5
CHI	162	98	64	.605	1	642	**501**	5491	1356	184	40	106	**562**	902	.247	.323	.353	.676	98	-32	-15	97	101	643	75	39	66	-1
BAL	163	97	65	.599	2	679	567	5463	1357	229	20	162	537	1019	.248	.319	.387	.706	102	14	17	100	101	671	78	38	67	1
DET	163	85	77	.525	14	699	678	5513	1394	199	**57**	157	517	912	.253	.321	.395	.716	103	35	25	102	100	707	60	27	69	2
LA	162	82	80	.506	17	544	551	5362	1297	186	27	102	472	920	.242	.306	.344	.650	97	-89	-36	102	99	552	49	39	56	-9
MIN	163	79	83	.488	20	**737**	678	5610	1413	227	46	**221**	553	1019	.252	**.324**	**.427**	**.751**	113	98	93	101	95	775	46	22	68	1
CLE	164	79	83	.488	20	689	693	5603	1386	208	22	164	500	1063	.247	.315	.380	.695	100	-8	-3	99	104	666	79	51	61	-7
BOS	162	72	90	.444	27	688	793	5513	1425	253	29	186	504	917	**.258**	**.324**	.416	.740	106	76	40	105	94	725	18	16	53	-4
WAS	162	62	100	.383	37	578	733	5396	1246	199	28	125	514	1124	.231	.301	.348	.649	86	-95	-92	100	**105**	566	47	30	61	-4
KC	163	57	105	.352	42	621	836	5524	1321	216	29	166	548	1104	.239	.313	.379	.692	95	-14	-33	103	96	645	34	20	63	-2
TOT	814					6607		55180	13637	2109	333	1551	5227	9956	.247	.316	.382	.698							540	300	64	-18

TEAM	CG	SH	SV	IP	H	H/G	HR	BB	SO	RAT	ERA	ERA+	OAV	OOB	PR	/A	PF	CPI	FA	E	DP	FW	PW	BW	SBW	DIF
NY	46	18	45	1506²	1312	7.8	129	504	989	11.0	3.15	115	.234	.300	79	78	100	97	.983	109	158	1.1	8.2	.2	.7	7.8
CHI	44	20	45	1467²	**1216**	**7.5**	124	**401**	955	**10.1**	**2.72**	127	**.226**	**.283**	**147**	119	95	100	.981	122	164	.2	**12.5**	-1.6	.0	5.7
BAL	44	17	41	1458²	1292	8.0	129	456	939	11.0	3.16	113	.239	.302	76	67	99	100	**.985**	95	159	**1.9**	7.0	1.8	.3	5.0
DET	35	11	35	1453	1343	8.3	164	536	993	12.0	3.84	95	.244	.317	-35	-29	101	95	.982	111	137	1.0	-3.0	2.6	.4	3.1
LA	30	**28**	41	1450²	1273	7.9	**100**	530	965	11.5	2.91	113	.236	.310	115	60	91	**107**	.978	138	168	-.7	6.3	-3.8	-.8	-.0
MIN	**47**	4	29	1477²	1361	8.3	181	545	1099	11.8	3.58	100	.243	.314	8	1	99	102	.977	145	131	-1.1	.1	**9.8**	.3	-11.1
CLE	37	16	37	1487²	1443	8.7	154	565	**1162**	12.3	3.75	96	.255	.326	-21	-25	99	103	.981	118	149	.6	-2.6	-.3	-.5	.9
BOS	21	9	38	1422	1464	9.3	178	571	1094	13.1	4.50	86	.266	.339	-138	-96	102	106	.977	138	123	-.7	-10.7	4.2	-.2	-1.5
WAS	27	5	26	1435¹	1417	8.9	172	505	794	12.2	3.98	93	.259	.324	-57	-45	102	100	.979	127	145	-.0	-4.7	-9.7	-.2	-4.3
KC	18	6	27	1455²	1516	9.4	220	614	966	13.5	4.71	81	.269	.346	-175	-144	105	101	.975	158	152	-1.9	-15.1	-3.5	-.0	-3.5
TOT	349	134	364	14615		8.4				11.8	3.63		.247	.316					.980	1261	1486					

Runs		Hits		Doubles		Triples		Home Runs		Total Bases	
Oliva-Min	109	Oliva-Min	217	Oliva-Min	43	Versalles-Min	10	Killebrew-Min	49	Oliva-Min	374
Howser-Cle	101	B.Robinson-Bal	194	Bressoud-Bos	41	Rollins-Min	10	Powell-Bal	39	B.Robinson-Bal	319
Killebrew-Min	95	Richardson-NY	181	B.Robinson-Bal	35	Yastrzemski-Bos	9	Mantle-NY	35	Killebrew-Min	316
Wagner-Cle	94	Howard-NY	172	Versalles-Min	33	Oliva-Min	9	Colavito-KC	34	Colavito-KC	298
Versalles-Min	94	Versalles-Min	171			Fregosi-LA	9	Stuart-Bos	33	Stuart-Bos	296

Runs Batted In		Runs Produced		Bases On Balls		Batting Average		On Base Percentage		Slugging Average	
B.Robinson-Bal	118	B.Robinson-Bal	172	Siebern-Bal	106	Oliva-Min	.323	Mantle-NY	.426	Powell-Bal	.606
Stuart-Bos	114	Oliva-Min	171	Mantle-NY	99	B.Robinson-Bal	.317	Allison-Min	.406	Mantle-NY	.591
Mantle-NY	111	Mantle-NY	168	Killebrew-Min	93	Howard-NY	.313	Powell-Bal	.400	Oliva-Min	.557
Killebrew-Min	111	Wagner-Cle	163	Allison-Min	92	Mantle-NY	.303	Robinson-Chi	.388	Allison-Min	.553
Colavito-KC	102			Causey-KC	88	Robinson-Chi	.301	Kaline-Det	.385	Killebrew-Min	.548

Production		Adjusted Production		Batter Runs		Adjusted Batter Runs		Clutch Hitting Index		Runs Created	
Mantle-NY	1.017	Mantle-NY	177	Mantle-NY	53.0	Mantle-NY	51.2	Rodgers-LA	125	Oliva-Min	132
Powell-Bal	1.007	Powell-Bal	176	Allison-Min	45.0	Powell-Bal	44.5	Boyer-NY	118	Killebrew-Min	122
Allison-Min	.959	Allison-Min	163	Powell-Bal	44.1	Allison-Min	44.2	Pepitone-NY	118	Mantle-NY	121
Killebrew-Min	.927	Killebrew-Min	153	Killebrew-Min	43.1	Killebrew-Min	42.3	Mantle-NY	117	Allison-Min	119
Oliva-Min	.918	Oliva-Min	150	Oliva-Min	43.0	Oliva-Min	42.2	Cash-Det	116	B.Robinson-Bal	115

Total Average		Stolen Bases		Stolen Base Average		Stolen Base Runs		Fielding Runs		Total Player Rating	
Mantle-NY	1.122	Aparicio-Bal	57	Aparicio-Bal	77.0	Aparicio-Bal	6.9	Knoop-LA	37.2	Powell-Bal	4.4
Powell-Bal	1.081	Weis-Chi	22	Weis-Chi	75.9	Tresh-NY	3.9	Yastrzemski-Bos	27.7	Fregosi-LA	4.4
Allison-Min	1.058	Davalillo-Cle	21	Howser-Cle	74.1	Wagner-Cle	3.0	Boyer-NY	19.3	Hansen-Chi	4.3
Killebrew-Min	.956	Howser-Cle	20	Hinton-Was	73.9	Weis-Chi	2.4	Green-KC	16.5	Oliva-Min	4.1
Oliva-Min	.894	Hinton-Was	17	Davalillo-Cle	65.6	Allison-Min	2.4	Brandt-Bal	16.1	Yastrzemski-Bos	3.9

Wins		Win Percentage		Games		Complete Games		Shutouts		Saves	
Peters-Chi	20	Bunker-Bal	.792	Wyatt-KC	81	Chance-LA	15	Chance-LA	11	Radatz-Bos	29
Chance-LA	20	Ford-NY	.739	Radatz-Bos	79	Pascual-Min	14	Ford-NY	8	Wilhelm-Chi	27
Wickersham-Det	19	Peters-Chi	.714	Wilhelm-Chi	73	Pappas-Bal	13	Pappas-Bal	7	Miller-Bal	23
Pizarro-Chi	19	Pappas-Bal	.696	McMahon-Cle	70	Osteen-Was	13	Lolich-Det	6	Wyatt-KC	20
Bunker-Bal	19	Chance-LA	.690	Miller-Bal	66	Kaat-Min	13	Monbouquette-Bos	5	B.Lee-LA	19

Innings Pitched		Fewest Hits/Game		Fewest BB/Game		Strikeouts		Strikeouts/Game		Ratio	
Chance-LA	278.1	Horlen-Chi	6.07	Monbouquette-Bos	1.54	Downing-NY	217	McDowell-Cle	9.19	Horlen-Chi	8.59
Peters-Chi	273.2	Chance-LA	6.27	Pappas-Bal	1.72	Pascual-Min	213	Downing-NY	8.00	Chance-LA	9.12
Bouton-NY	271.1	Bunker-Bal	6.77	Newman-LA	1.85	Chance-LA	207	Pena-KC	7.55	Pizarro-Chi	9.45
Pascual-Min	267.1	Peters-Chi	7.14	Bouton-NY	1.99	Peters-Chi	205	Stigman-Min	7.53	Bunker-Bal	9.50
Osteen-Was	257.0	Pizarro-Chi	7.27	Pizarro-Chi	2.07	Lolich-Det	192	Morehead-Bos	7.51	Bouton-NY	9.72

Earned Run Average		Adjusted ERA		Opponents' Batting Avg.		Opponents' On Base Pct.		Starter Runs		Adjusted Starter Runs	
Chance-LA	1.65	Chance-LA	199	Horlen-Chi	.190	Horlen-Chi	.250	Chance-LA	61.1	Chance-LA	50.6
Horlen-Chi	1.88	Horlen-Chi	184	Chance-LA	.195	Chance-LA	.261	Horlen-Chi	40.9	Ford-NY	40.5
Ford-NY	2.13	Ford-NY	170	Bunker-Bal	.207	Pizarro-Chi	.267	Ford-NY	40.6	Horlen-Chi	36.9
Peters-Chi	2.50	Peters-Chi	138	Peters-Chi	.219	Bunker-Bal	.269	Peters-Chi	34.2	Peters-Chi	29.1
Pizarro-Chi	2.56	Pizarro-Chi	135	Pizarro-Chi	.219	Bouton-NY	.273	Pizarro-Chi	28.3	Pizarro-Chi	23.7

Clutch Pitching Index		Relief Runs		Adjusted Relief Runs		Relief Ranking		Total Pitcher Index		Total Baseball Ranking	
McDowell-Cle	123	B.Lee-LA	32.2	Radatz-Bos	27.3	Radatz-Bos	49.2	Radatz-Bos	5.1	Radatz-Bos	5.1
Roberts-Bal	121	Wilhelm-Chi	23.9	B.Lee-LA	27.0	Wilhelm-Chi	39.6	Chance-LA	4.7	Chance-LA	4.7
Kralick-Cle	118	Radatz-Bos	23.2	Wilhelm-Chi	21.4	Worthington-Min	31.2	Horlen-Chi	4.2	Powell-Bal	4.4
Grant-Cle-Min	112	Worthington-Min	18.1	Stock-Bal-KC	18.6	Kline-Was	27.7	Wilhelm-Chi	4.2	Fregosi-LA	4.4
Peters-Chi	111	Hall-Bal	17.3	Worthington-Min	17.8	B.Lee-LA	27.0	Ford-NY	4.2	Hansen-Chi	4.3

January 31 Pud Galvin is chosen for Hall of Fame induction by the Special Veterans Committee.

March 17 Jackie Robinson is signed as a member of the ABC-TV baseball broadcast team, the first black to receive a network position broadcasting baseball.

April 9 President Lyndon B. Johnson joins 47,878 fans for the opening of Harris County Domed Stadium (the Astrodome). The Astros win an exhibition with the Yankees 2-1 in 12 innings. Mickey Mantle hits the first home run in the new park.

June 8 Arizona star sophomore Rick Monday, selected by the Athletics, is the first player chosen in the initial major league free-agent draft of high school, college, and sandlot players. Picking second, the Mets take pitcher Les Rohr. The Mets finally take Nolan Ryan in the 10th round.

June 14 No-hit pitching and 18 strikeouts, tying the NL extra-inning record, net Cincinnati's Jim Maloney a 0-0 tie with the last-place Mets through 10 innings. Johnny Lewis' 11th-inning home run gives New York and reliever Larry Bearnarth a 1-0 win.

August 19 Jim Maloney's second no-hit effort of 1965 is another 0-0 duel through nine innings, until Reds shortstop Leo Cardenas homers off the left field foul pole in the 10th at Wrigley Field. Maloney allows a record 10 walks and fans 12 in his 1-0 win.

August 20 Eddie Mathews hits his 28th home run as the Braves win 4-3 at Pittsburgh. The duo of Mathews and Hank Aaron, in the period 1954-1965, becomes the top home run tandem in major league history, passing the Babe Ruth-Lou Gehrig total of 772 home runs.

August 29 Willie Mays sets a NL record for homers in one month with his 17th of August, 41st overall, as San Francisco beats the Mets, 8-3.

August 30 Following his doctor's advice, Casey Stengel announces his retirement as manager of the Mets. He will head up Mets scouting in California. The 75-year-old Stengel has been in professional baseball since 1910.

September 9 A duel between Dodgers southpaw Sandy Koufax and Bob Hendley of the Cubs is perfect until Los Angeles left fielder Lou Johnson walks in the fifth. Following a sacrifice, Johnson steals third and scores on catcher Chris Krug's wild throw. Johnson later gets the game's only hit, a seventh-inning single. Koufax's fourth no-hitter in four years is a perfect game.

October 3 The Cubs tie a major league record with their third triple play of the season—first baseman Ernie Banks to shortstop Don Kessinger—but Pittsburgh wins, 6-3.

October 14 Working on two days' rest, Sandy Koufax pitches a three-hitter and blanks Minnesota, 2-0, giving the Dodgers a second world championship in three years. He is named World Series MVP.

November 3 Sandy Koufax is named Cy Young Award winner by a unanimous vote.

November 10 Willie Mays is named NL MVP, receiving 224 votes to 177 for Sandy Koufax.

	CHICAGO		CINCINNATI		HOUSTON		LOS ANGELES		MILWAUKEE
M	B.Kennedy	M	D.Sisler	M	L.Harris	M	W.Alston	M	B.Bragan
M	L.Klein	1B	T.Perez	1B	W.Bond	1B	W.Parker	1B	F.Alou
1B	E.Banks	2B	P.Rose	2B	J.Morgan	2B	J.Lefebvre	2B	F.Bolling
2B	G.Beckert	SS	L.Cardenas	SS	B.Lillis	SS	M.Wills	SS	W.Woodward
SS	D.Kessinger	3B	D.Johnson	3B	B.Aspromonte	3B	J.Kennedy	3B	E.Mathews
3B	R.Santo	LF	T.Harper	LF	J.Maye	LF	L.Johnson	LF	R.Carty
LF	D.Clemens	CF	V.Pinson	CF	J.Wynn	CF	W.Davis	CF	M.Jones
CF	D.Landrum	RF	F.Robinson	RF	R.Staub	RF	R.Fairly	RF	H.Aaron
RF	B.Williams	C	J.Edwards	C	R.Brand	C	J.Roseboro	C	J.Torre
C	V.Roznovsky								
		1	G.Coleman	O	J.Gaines	3O	J.Gilliam	C1	G.Oliver
OS	J.Stewart			1	J.Gentile			O	T.Cline
		P	S.Ellis	S	E.Kasko	P	S.Koufax		
P	L.Jackson	P	J.Maloney			P	D.Drysdale	P	T.Cloninger
P	D.Ellsworth	P	J.Jay	P	B.Bruce	P	C.Osteen	P	W.Blasingame
P	B.Buhl	P	J.Nuxhall	P	T.Farrell	P	J.Podres	P	K.Johnson
P	C.Koonce	P	J.Tsitouris	P	D.Nottebart	RP	R.Perranoski	P	D.Lemaster
RP	T.Abernathy	RP	B.McCool	P	L.Dierker	RP	B.Miller	P	B.Sadowski
RP	L.McDaniel	RP	T.Davidson	P	D.Giusti	RP	H.Reed	RP	B.O'Dell
RP	B.Humphreys	RP	R.Craig	RP	C.Raymond			RP	D.Osinski
				RP	J.Owens			RP	P.Niekro
P	B.Faul	P	J.O'Toole	RP	R.Taylor				
P	B.Hendley	P	G.Arrigo					P	H.Fischer
P	E.Broglio								
P	B.Hoeft			P	R.Roberts				
				P	M.Cuellar				
				/P	K.Johnson				

	NEW YORK		PHILADELPHIA		PITTSBURGH		SAN FRANCISCO		ST.LOUIS
M	C.Stengel	M	G.Mauch	M	H.Walker	M	H.Franks	M	R.Schoendienst
M	W.Westrum	1B	D.Stuart	1B	D.Clendenon	1B	W.McCovey	1B	B.White
1B	E.Kranepool	2B	T.Taylor	2B	B.Mazeroski	2B	H.Lanier	2B	J.Javier
2B	C.Hiller	SS	B.Wine	SS	G.Alley	SS	D.Schofield	SS	D.Groat
SS	R.McMillan	3B	D.Allen	3B	B.Bailey	3B	J.Hart	3B	K.Boyer
3B	C.Smith	LF	A.Johnson	LF	W.Stargell	LF	M.Alou	LF	L.Brock
LF	R.Swoboda	CF	T.Gonzalez	CF	B.Virdon	CF	W.Mays	CF	C.Flood
CF	J.Hickman	RF	J.Callison	RF	R.Clemente	RF	J.Alou	RF	M.Shannon
RF	J.Lewis	C	C.Dalrymple	C	J.Pagliaroni	C	T.Haller	C	T.McCarver
C	C.Cannizzaro								
		1S	R.Amaro	O	M.Mota	3S	J.Davenport	2O	P.Gagliano
O	J.Christopher	O	W.Covington			O	L.Gabrielson		
2S	B.Klaus	2O	C.Rojas	P	B.Veale			P	B.Gibson
		O	J.Briggs	P	D.Cardwell	P	J.Marichal	P	C.Simmons
P	J.Fisher			P	B.Friend	P	B.Shaw	P	T.Stallard
P	A.Jackson	P	C.Short	P	V.Law	P	G.Perry	P	R.Sadecki
P	W.Spahn	P	J.Bunning	P	J.Gibbon	P	R.Herbel	P	B.Purkey
P	G.Cisco	P	R.Culp	RP	A.McBean	P	B.Bolin	RP	N.Briles
RP	T.McGraw	P	R.Herbert	RP	T.Sisk	RP	F.Linzy	RP	H.Woodeshick
RP	T.Parsons	P	B.Belinsky	RP	D.Schwall	RP	M.Murakami	RP	D.Dennis
RP	G.Kroll	RP	G.Wagner						
		RP	J.Baldschun	P	W.Wood	P	J.Sanford	P	R.Washburn
P	L.Bearnarth	RP	E.Roebuck			P	W.Spahn		
P	F.Lary								
P	L.Miller	P	L.Burdette						
P	G.Richardson	P	A.Mahaffey						

TEAM	G	W	L	PCT	GB	R	OR	AB	H	2B	3B	HR	BB	SO	AVG	OBP	SLG	PRO	PRO+	BR	/A	PF	CHI	RC	SB	CS	SBA	SBR
LA	162	97	65	.599		608	**521**	5425	1329	193	32	78	492	891	.245	.314	.335	.649	96	-61	-22	93	103	593	**172**	77	69	**5**
SF	163	95	67	.586	2	682	593	5495	1384	169	43	159	476	**844**	.252	.315	.385	.700	101	24	6	103	101	649	47	27	64	-2
PIT	163	90	72	.556	7	675	580	5686	1506	217	57	111	419	1008	.265	.319	.382	.701	103	27	24	101	97	671	51	38	57	-8
CIN	162	89	73	.549	8	**825**	704	5658	**1544**	268	61	183	538	1003	**.273**	**.341**	**.439**	**.780**	118	188	129	107	95	**842**	82	40	67	1
MIL	162	86	76	.531	11	708	633	5542	1419	243	28	**196**	408	976	.256	.311	.416	.727	110	67	63	101	99	699	64	37	63	-3
PHI	162	85	76	.528	11.5	654	667	5528	1380	205	53	144	494	1091	.250	.315	.384	.699	105	24	36	98	96	665	46	32	59	-5
STL	162	80	81	.497	16.5	707	674	5579	1415	234	46	109	477	882	.254	.316	.371	.687	91	3	-59	109	**107**	659	100	52	66	-1
CHI	164	72	90	.444	25	635	723	5540	1316	202	33	134	532	948	.238	.309	.358	.667	92	-34	-49	102	101	613	65	47	58	-9
HOU	162	65	97	.401	32	569	711	5483	1299	188	42	97	502	877	.237	.306	.340	.646	96	-73	-33	93	98	574	90	37	**71**	5
NY	164	50	112	.309	47	495	752	5441	1202	203	27	107	392	1129	.221	.278	.327	.605	79	-164	-147	96	105	480	28	42	40	-17
TOT	813					6558		55377	13794	2122	422	1318	4730	9649	.249	.313	.374	.687							745	429	63	-34

TEAM	CG	SH	SV	IP	H	H/G	HR	BB	SO	RAT	ERA	ERA+	OAV	OOB	PR	/A	PF	CPI	FA	E	DP	FW	PW	BW	SBW	DIF
LA	**58**	**23**	34	1476	**1223**	7.5	127	425	1079	10.3	**2.81**	116	**.224**	**.284**	**119**	74	92	99	.979	134	135	.8	7.8	-2.3	**.9**	8.8
SF	42	17	**42**	1465[1]	1325	8.1	137	408	1060	10.9	3.20	112	.238	.295	55	65	102	98	.976	148	124	.0	6.9	.6	.1	6.3
PIT	49	17	27	1479	1324	8.1	**89**	469	882	11.2	3.01	**117**	.241	.306	87	**82**	99	103	.977	152	**189**	-.1	**8.7**	2.5	-.5	-1.6
CIN	43	9	34	1457[1]	1355	8.4	136	587	**1113**	12.3	3.88	96	.247	.325	-56	-22	106	96	**.981**	**117**	142	**1.8**	-2.3	**13.6**	.5	-5.6
MIL	43	4	38	1447[2]	1336	8.3	123	541	966	11.8	3.52	100	.246	.318	3	1	100	101	.978	140	145	.5	.1	6.7	.0	-2.3
PHI	50	18	21	1468[2]	1426	8.7	116	466	1071	12.0	3.53	98	.256	.320	2	-12	98	104	.975	157	153	-.5	-1.3	3.8	-.2	2.6
STL	40	11	35	1461[1]	1414	8.7	166	467	916	11.8	3.77	102	.255	.317	-37	12	109	102	.979	130	152	1.1	1.3	-6.2	.3	3.2
CHI	33	9	35	1472	1470	9.0	148	481	855	12.1	3.78	98	.260	.321	-39	-15	104	104	.974	171	166	-1.2	-1.6	-5.2	-.6	-.5
HOU	29	7	26	1461	1459	9.0	123	**388**	931	11.6	3.84	87	.260	.312	-49	-79	95	94	.974	166	130	-1.0	-8.3	-3.5	.9	-4.1
NY	29	11	14	1454[2]	1462	9.0	147	498	776	12.4	4.06	87	.262	.328	-84	-86	100	99	.974	171	153	-1.2	-9.1	-15.5	-1.4	-3.8
TOT	416	126	306	14643		8.5				11.6	3.54		.249	.313					.977	1486	1489					

Runs		Hits		Doubles		Triples		Home Runs		Total Bases	
Harper-Cin	126	Rose-Cin	209	H.Aaron-Mil	40	Callison-Phi	16	Mays-SF	52	Mays-SF	360
Mays-SF	118	Pinson-Cin	204	Williams-Chi	39	Clendenon-Pit	14	McCovey-SF	39	Williams-Chi	356
Rose-Cin	117	Williams-Chi	203	Rose-Cin	35	Clemente-Pit	14	Williams-Chi	34	Pinson-Cin	324
Williams-Chi	115	Clemente-Pit	194	Brock-StL	35	Allen-Phi	14	Santo-Chi	33	H.Aaron-Mil	319
		Flood-StL	191	Pinson-Cin	34	Morgan-Hou	12	Robinson-Cin	33	Johnson-Cin	317

Runs Batted In		Runs Produced		Bases On Balls		Batting Average		On Base Percentage		Slugging Average	
Johnson-Cin	130	Johnson-Cin	190	Morgan-Hou	97	Clemente-Pit	.329	Mays-SF	.399	Mays-SF	.645
Robinson-Cin	113	Williams-Chi	189	Santo-Chi	88	H.Aaron-Mil	.318	Robinson-Cin	.388	H.Aaron-Mil	.560
Mays-SF	112	Robinson-Cin	189	McCovey-SF	88	Mays-SF	.317	H.Aaron-Mil	.384	Williams-Chi	.552
Williams-Chi	108	Rose-Cin	187	Wynn-Hou	84	Williams-Chi	.315	McCovey-SF	.383	Robinson-Cin	.540
Stargell-Pit	107	Mays-SF	178	Harper-Cin	78	Rose-Cin	.312	Rose-Cin	.383	McCovey-SF	.539

Production		Adjusted Production		Batter Runs		Adjusted Batter Runs		Clutch Hitting Index		Runs Created	
Mays-SF	1.044	Mays-SF	184	Mays-SF	64.7	Mays-SF	61.2	Stargell-Pit	120	Mays-SF	143
H.Aaron-Mil	.943	H.Aaron-Mil	161	Williams-Chi	49.3	Williams-Chi	46.4	Johnson-Cin	118	Williams-Chi	132
Williams-Chi	.932	Williams-Chi	155	H.Aaron-Mil	45.9	H.Aaron-Mil	45.4	Boyer-StL	118	H.Aaron-Mil	122
Robinson-Cin	.928	McCovey-SF	152	Robinson-Cin	45.9	McCovey-SF	38.9	Stuart-Phi	118	Santo-Chi	121
McCovey-SF	.922	Robinson-Cin	148	McCovey-SF	41.8	Allen-Phi	38.4	Flood-StL	118	Robinson-Cin	120

Total Average		Stolen Bases		Stolen Base Average		Stolen Base Runs		Fielding Runs		Total Player Rating	
Mays-SF	1.114	Wills-LA	94	Wynn-Hou	91.5	Wynn-Hou	10.5	Alley-Pit	29.5	Mays-SF	7.3
H.Aaron-Mil	.980	Brock-StL	63	H.Aaron-Mil	85.7	Wills-LA	9.6	Mazeroski-Pit	25.6	Wynn-Hou	6.1
McCovey-SF	.945	Wynn-Hou	43	Harper-Cin	85.4	Harper-Cin	6.9	Wine-Phi	21.7	H.Aaron-Mil	5.5
Robinson-Cin	.938	Harper-Cin	35	Wills-LA	75.2	H.Aaron-Mil	4.8	Wills-LA	21.2	Santo-Chi	5.4
Williams-Chi	.935	W.Davis-LA	25	W.Davis-LA	73.5	Allen-Phi	3.3	Wynn-Hou	20.1	Williams-Chi	4.3

Wins		Win Percentage		Games		Complete Games		Shutouts		Saves	
Koufax-LA	26	Koufax-LA	.765	Abernathy-Chi	84	Koufax-LA	27	Marichal-SF	10	Abernathy-Chi	31
Cloninger-Mil	24	Maloney-Cin	.690	Woodeshick-Hou-StL	78	Marichal-SF	24	Koufax-LA	8	McCool-Cin	21
Drysdale-LA	23	Ellis-Cin	.688	McDaniel-Chi	71	Gibson-StL	20	Veale-Pit	7	Linzy-SF	21
Marichal-SF	22	Cloninger-Mil	.686	Baldschun-Phi	65	Drysdale-LA	20	Drysdale-LA	7		
Ellis-Cin	22	Bunning-Phi	.679			Cloninger-Mil	16	Bunning-Phi	7		

Innings Pitched		Fewest Hits/Game		Fewest BB/Game		Strikeouts		Strikeouts/Game		Ratio	
Koufax-LA	335.2	Koufax-LA	5.79	Marichal-SF	1.40	Koufax-LA	382	Koufax-LA	10.24	Koufax-LA	7.83
Drysdale-LA	308.1	Maloney-Cin	6.66	Law-Pit	1.45	Veale-Pit	276	Veale-Pit	9.34	Marichal-SF	8.35
Gibson-StL	299.0	Marichal-SF	6.83	Bruce-Hou	1.49	Gibson-StL	270	Maloney-Cin	8.60	Law-Pit	9.11
Short-Phi	297.1	Bolin-SF	6.90	Farrell-Hou	1.51	Bunning-Phi	268	Bunning-Phi	8.29	Bunning-Phi	10.11
Marichal-SF	295.1	Gibson-StL	7.31	Johnson-Hou-Mil	1.87	Maloney-Cin	244	Gibson-StL	8.13	Drysdale-LA	10.16

Earned Run Average		Adjusted ERA		Opponents' Batting Avg.		Opponents' On Base Pct.		Starter Runs		Adjusted Starter Runs	
Koufax-LA	2.04	Marichal-SF	169	Koufax-LA	.179	Koufax-LA	.228	Koufax-LA	56.0	Marichal-SF	48.1
Marichal-SF	2.13	Law-Pit	163	Marichal-SF	.205	Marichal-SF	.240	Marichal-SF	46.1	Koufax-LA	45.7
Law-Pit	2.15	Koufax-LA	160	Maloney-Cin	.206	Law-Pit	.264	Law-Pit	33.5	Maloney-Cin	34.3
Maloney-Cin	2.54	Maloney-Cin	148	Bolin-SF	.214	Drysdale-LA	.280	Bunning-Phi	30.4	Law-Pit	32.8
Bunning-Phi	2.60	Shaw-SF	136	Gibson-StL	.222	Shaw-SF	.280	Maloney-Cin	28.4	Bunning-Phi	27.8

Clutch Pitching Index		Relief Runs		Adjusted Relief Runs		Relief Ranking		Total Pitcher Index		Total Baseball Ranking	
Law-Pit	115	Linzy-SF	19.1	Linzy-SF	19.7	Linzy-SF	37.4	Marichal-SF	6.0	Mays-SF	7.3
Koonce-Chi	112	O'Dell-Mil	16.8	Abernathy-Chi	16.8	O'Dell-Mil	27.4	Koufax-LA	5.0	Wynn-Hou	6.1
Culp-Phi	108	McBean-Pit	15.8	O'Dell-Mil	16.6	Woodeshick-Hou-StL	23.5	Linzy-SF	4.9	Marichal-SF	6.0
Spahn-NY-SF	107	Perranoski-LA	15.2	McDaniel-Chi	15.7	McBean-Pit	20.2	Law-Pit	4.6	H.Aaron-Mil	5.5
Buhl-Chi	107	Abernathy-Chi	14.6	McBean-Pit	15.5	Abernathy-Chi	19.7	Maloney-Cin	4.6	Santo-Chi	5.4

June 15 Tigers pitcher Denny McLain makes a first-inning relief appearance and fans the first seven batters he faces, setting a major league record. He has 14 strikeouts in 6⅔ innings as Detroit rallies to beat Boston, 6–5. Bill Freehan posts a record-tying 19 putouts at catcher.

July 9 Senators left fielder Frank Howard ties a major league record with seven strikeouts in Washington's twin bill split with the Red Sox.

July 20 Mel Stottlemyre of the Yankees becomes the first pitcher to hit an inside-the-park grand slam since Deacon Phillippe did it for the Pirates in 1910. Stottlemyre's bases-loaded drive assures him a 6-3 victory over the Red Sox.

August 18 In a 3–2 Orioles' win over the Red Sox, Brooks Robinson hits into his third triple play against Boston, tying the record of George Sisler in 1921, '22, and '26.

September 3 Preparing a move to Anaheim, the Angels change their name from Los Angeles to California.

September 8 Bert Campaneris plays all nine positions against the Angels in a promotion to boost attendance at Kansas City. He leaves the game in the ninth after a collision with Angels catcher Ed Kirkpatrick. The Angels win it in the 13th inning 5-3.

September 16 An eventful day in Boston includes the firing of general manager Mike Higgins and a no-hitter by Dave Morehead. Boston beats Cleveland, 2–0. Morehead lost a no-hitter against Cleveland in 1963 on Fred Whitfield's bad-hop single in the eighth inning.

September 18 On Mickey Mantle Day at Yankee Stadium, 50,180 fans see Mantle play his 2,000th game.

September 25 Another Kansas City publicity stunt makes the great Satchel Paige baseball's oldest performer. At 59, Paige hurls the first three innings, garners one strikeout, and allows just one hit, to Carl Yastrzemski, in Paige's first major league appearance since 1953. The Red Sox jump on reliever Don Mossi for a 5-2 win.

September 26 Minnesota gains its first AL pennant by defeating Washington, 2–1. Jim Kaat (17-11) wins the clincher.

October 3 Knuckleballer Eddie Fisher of the White Sox sets an AL record with his 82nd appearance, one more than John Wyatt in 1964.

October 6 Minnesota's six-run third inning routs Dodger Don Drysdale and sparks an 8-2 Twins win in the first game of the World Series. Jim Grant gets the win.

October 13 Twins pitcher Jim "Mudcat" Grant does it all himself. He smacks a three-run home run and pitches a 5–1 win at Minnesota to knot the World Series with the Dodgers.

November 17 Retired Air Force Lieutenant-General William Eckert is unanimously elected commissioner of baseball. Ford Frick leaves office after 14 years.

November 18 Zoilo Versalles is named AL MVP. The Minnesota shortstop gets 275 votes to 174 for outfield teammate Tony Oliva.

November 22 Baltimore outfielder Curt Blefary edges Angels pitcher Marcelino Lopez for AL Rookie of the Year honors.

BALTIMORE		BOSTON		CALIFORNIA		CHICAGO		CLEVELAND	
M	H.Bauer	M	B.Herman	M	B.Rigney	M	A.Lopez	M	B.Tebbetts
1B	B.Powell	1B	L.Thomas	1B	V.Power	1B	B.Skowron	1B	F.Whitfield
2B	J.Adair	2B	F.Mantilla	2B	B.Knoop	2B	B.Buford	2B	P.Gonzalez
SS	L.Aparicio	SS	R.Petrocelli	SS	J.Fregosi	SS	R.Hansen	SS	L.Brown
3B	B.Robinson	3B	F.Malzone	3B	P.Schaal	3B	P.Ward	3B	M.Alvis
LF	C.Blefary	LF	C.Yastrzemski	LF	W.Smith	LF	D.Cater	LF	L.Wagner
CF	P.Blair	CF	L.Green	CF	J.Cardenal	CF	K.Berry	CF	V.Davalillo
RF	R.Snyder	RF	T.Conigliaro	RF	A.Pearson	RF	F.Robinson	RF	R.Colavito
C	D.Brown	C	B.Tillman	C	B.Rodgers	C	J.Martin	C	J.Azcue
1	N.Siebern	S	E.Bressoud	1	J.Adcock	1O	T.McCraw	O1	C.Hinton
1S	B.Johnson	3	D.Jones	O	L.Clinton	C	T.Romano	S2	D.Howser
O	J.Brandt	O	J.Gosger			2	A.Weis		
C	J.Orsino			P	F.Newman			P	S.McDowell
O	S.Bowens	P	E.Wilson	P	D.Chance	P	J.Horlen	P	L.Tiant
		P	B.Monbouquette	P	M.Lopez	P	J.Buzhardt	P	S.Siebert
P	M.Pappas	P	D.Morehead	P	G.Brunet	P	T.John	P	R.Terry
P	S.Barber	P	J.Lonborg	P	R.May	P	G.Peters	P	L.Stange
P	D.McNally	P	D.Bennett	P	B.Lee	P	B.Howard	RP	G.Bell
P	W.Bunker	RP	D.Radatz	RP	A.Gatewood	RP	E.Fisher	RP	J.Kralick
P	R.Roberts	RP	A.Earley			RP	H.Wilhelm	RP	D.McMahon
RP	S.Miller	RP	J.Ritchie			RP	B.Locker		
RP	D.Hall							P	F.Weaver
RP	D.Larsen	P	B.Duliba			P	J.Pizarro	P	S.Hargan
		P	J.Stephenson						
P	J.Miller								
P	J.Palmer								

DETROIT		KANSAS CITY		MINNESOTA		NEW YORK		WASHINGTON	
M	B.Swift	M	M.McGaha	M	S.Mele	M	J.Keane	M	G.Hodges
M	C.Dressen	M	H.Sullivan	1B	D.Mincher	1B	J.Pepitone	1B	D.Nen
1B	N.Cash	1B	K.Harrelson	2B	J.Kindall	2B	B.Richardson	2B	D.Blasingame
2B	J.Lumpe	2B	D.Green	SS	Z.Versalles	SS	T.Kubek	SS	E.Brinkman
SS	D.McAuliffe	SS	B.Campaneris	3B	R.Rollins	3B	C.Boyer	3B	K.McMullen
3B	D.Wert	3B	E.Charles	LF	B.Allison	LF	M.Mantle	LF	F.Howard
LF	W.Horton	LF	T.Reynolds	CF	J.Hall	CF	T.Tresh	CF	D.Lock
CF	D.Demeter	CF	J.Landis	RF	T.Oliva	RF	H.Lopez	RF	W.Held
RF	A.Kaline	RF	M.Hershberger	C	E.Battey	C	E.Howard	C	M.Brumley
C	B.Freehan	C	B.Bryan						
				13	H.Killebrew	1	R.Barker	2S	K.Hamlin
O	G.Brown	S2	W.Causey	O	S.Valdespino	S	P.Linz	O	J.King
O	J.Northrup	O	J.Tartabull			O	R.Repoz	O	W.Kirkland
		C	R.Lachemann	P	M.Grant			C3	D.Zimmer
P	M.Lolich			P	J.Kaat	P	M.Stottlemyre	1	J.Cunningham
P	D.McLain	P	F.Talbot	P	J.Perry	P	W.Ford		
P	H.Aguirre	P	R.Sheldon	P	C.Pascual	P	A.Downing	P	P.Richert
P	D.Wickersham	P	J.O'Donoghue	P	D.Boswell	P	J.Bouton	P	P.Ortega
P	J.Sparma	P	D.Segui	RP	A.Worthington	P	B.Stafford	P	B.Narum
RP	L.Sherry	P	C.Hunter	RP	J.Klippstein	RP	P.Ramos	P	M.McCormick
RP	T.Fox	RP	W.Stock	RP	D.Stigman	RP	H.Reniff	P	B.Daniels
RP	F.Gladding	RP	J.Wyatt			RP	P.Mikkelsen	RP	S.Ridzik
		RP	J.Dickson					RP	R.Kline
P	O.Pena			P	J.Merritt	P	J.Cullen	RP	F.Kreutzer
P	P.Regan	P	D.Mossi	P	M.Nelson	P	S.Hamilton		
		P	J.Aker	P	B.Pleis			P	H.Koplitz
								P	J.Duckworth
								P	M.Bridges

TEAM	G	W	L	PCT	GB	R	OR	AB	H	2B	3B	HR	BB	SO	AVG	OBP	SLG	PRO	PRO+	BR	/A	PF	CHI	RC	SB	CS	SBA	SBR
MIN	162	102	60	.630		**774**	600	5488	**1396**	257	42	150	554	969	**.254**	.327	.399	.726	**107**	84	**52**	104	**106**	**730**	92	33	**74**	8
CHI	162	95	67	.586	7	647	**555**	5509	1354	200	38	125	533	916	.246	.317	.364	.681	106	1	41	94	99	636	50	33	60	-5
BAL	162	94	68	.580	8	641	578	5450	1299	227	38	125	529	907	.238	.309	.363	.672	95	-21	-33	102	103	607	67	31	68	2
DET	162	89	73	.549	13	680	602	5368	1278	190	27	162	554	952	.238	.314	.374	.688	101	10	3	101	**106**	628	57	41	58	-8
CLE	162	87	75	.537	15	663	613	5469	1367	198	21	156	506	**857**	.250	.317	.379	.696	103	26	21	101	99	667	109	46	70	5
NY	162	77	85	.475	25	611	604	5470	1286	196	31	149	489	951	.235	.300	.364	.664	95	-42	-38	99	103	593	35	20	64	-2
CAL	162	75	87	.463	27	527	569	5354	1209	200	36	92	443	973	.239	.300	.341	.641	90	-81	-69	98	97	549	107	59	64	-3
WAS	162	70	92	.432	32	591	721	5374	1227	179	33	136	570	1125	.228	.306	.350	.656	94	-47	-38	99	101	586	30	19	61	-2
BOS	162	62	100	.383	40	669	791	5487	1378	244	40	**165**	**607**	964	.251	**.329**	**.400**	.729	107	95	51	106	90	715	47	24	66	0
KC	162	59	103	.364	43	585	755	5393	1294	186	**59**	110	521	1020	.240	.311	.358	.669	97	-25	-16	99	96	604	**110**	51	68	2
TOT	810					6388		54362	13158	2077	365	1370	5306	9634	.242	.313	.369	.682							704	357	66	-3

TEAM	CG	SH	SV	IP	H	H/G	HR	BB	SO	RAT	ERA	ERA+	OAV	OOB	PR	/A	PF	CPI	FA	E	DP	FW	PW	BW	SBW	DIF
MIN	32	12	45	1457[1]	1278	7.9	166	503	934	11.2	3.14	113	.235	.303	52	68	103	**107**	.973	172	158	-2.3	7.3	**5.5**	.9	9.6
CHI	21	14	**53**	1481[2]	1261	**7.7**	122	**460**	946	10.6	2.99	107	**.231**	**.294**	76	33	92	98	.980	127	156	.6	3.5	4.4	-.5	6.0
BAL	32	**15**	41	1477[2]	1268	**7.7**	120	510	939	11.0	**2.98**	116	.233	.302	**78**	80	100	104	.980	126	152	.6	**8.5**	-3.5	.2	7.1
DET	**45**	14	31	1455	1283	7.9	137	509	1069	11.4	3.35	104	.237	.308	17	20	101	99	**.981**	116	126	1.3	2.1	.3	-.8	5.1
CLE	41	13	41	1458[1]	**1254**	**7.7**	129	500	**1156**	11.0	3.30	106	.236	.300	26	30	101	94	**.981**	114	127	**1.4**	3.2	2.2	.6	-1.4
NY	41	11	31	1459[2]	1337	8.2	126	511	1001	11.6	3.28	104	.245	.313	29	20	98	104	.978	137	**166**	-.0	2.1	-4.1	-.2	-1.8
CAL	39	14	33	1441[2]	1259	7.9	**91**	563	847	11.5	3.17	107	.237	.313	46	37	98	100	**.981**	123	148	.8	3.9	-7.4	-.3	-3.1
WAS	21	8	40	1435[2]	1376	8.6	160	633	867	12.8	3.93	88	.254	.336	-75	-73	101	105	.977	143	148	-.4	-7.8	-4.1	-.2	1.5
BOS	33	9	25	1439[1]	1443	9.0	158	543	993	12.6	4.24	88	.260	.329	-125	-82	108	95	.974	162	129	-1.6	-8.7	5.4	.0	-14.1
KC	18	7	32	1433	1399	8.8	161	574	882	12.6	4.24	82	.256	.331	-124	-119	101	96	.977	139	142	-.2	-12.7	-1.7	.2	-7.6
TOT	323	117	372	14539[1]		8.1				11.6	3.46		.242	.313					.978	1359	1453					

Runs		Hits		Doubles		Triples		Home Runs		Total Bases	
Versalles-Min	126	Oliva-Min	185	Yastrzemski-Bos	45	Versalles-Min	12	Conigliaro-Bos	32	Versalles-Min	308
Oliva-Min	107	Versalles-Min	182	Versalles-Min	45	Campaneris-KC	12	Cash-Det	30	Tresh-NY	287
Tresh-NY	94	Colavito-Cle	170	Oliva-Min	40	Aparicio-Bal	10	Horton-Det	29	Oliva-Min	283
Buford-Chi	93	Tresh-NY	168	Tresh-NY	29	W.Smith-Cal	9	Wagner-Cle	28	Colavito-Cle	277
Colavito-Cle	92	Fregosi-Cal	167	Richardson-NY	28					Conigliaro-Bos	267

Runs Batted In		Runs Produced		Bases On Balls		Batting Average		On Base Percentage		Slugging Average	
Colavito-Cle	108	Oliva-Min	189	Colavito-Cle	93	Oliva-Min	.321	Yastrzemski-Bos	.398	Yastrzemski-Bos	.536
Horton-Det	104	Versalles-Min	184	Blefary-Bal	88	Yastrzemski-Bos	.312	Colavito-Cle	.387	Conigliaro-Bos	.512
Oliva-Min	98	Colavito-Cle	174	Mantilla-Bos	79	Davalillo-Cle	.301	Oliva-Min	.384	Cash-Det	.512
Mantilla-Bos	92	Hall-Min	147	Cash-Det	77	Robinson-Bal	.297	Blefary-Bal	.382	Wagner-Cle	.495
Whitfield-Cle	90	Horton-Det	144	Robinson-Chi	76	Wagner-Cle	.294	Mantilla-Bos	.377	Oliva-Min	.491

Production		Adjusted Production		Batter Runs		Adjusted Batter Runs		Clutch Hitting Index		Runs Created	
Yastrzemski-Bos	.935	Yastrzemski-Bos	154	Yastrzemski-Bos	41.6	Yastrzemski-Bos	35.6	Mantilla-Bos	126	Colavito-Cle	110
Cash-Det	.886	Cash-Det	147	Oliva-Min	35.3	Colavito-Cle	33.7	Horton-Det	120	Oliva-Min	109
Oliva-Min	.876	Wagner-Cle	143	Colavito-Cle	34.6	Oliva-Min	30.8	Powell-Bal	116	Yastrzemski-Bos	102
Wagner-Cle	.866	Oliva-Min	141	Cash-Det	31.0	Cash-Det	30.1	Allison-Min	116	Versalles-Min	102
Colavito-Cle	.855	Colavito-Cle	140	Wagner-Cle	29.6	Wagner-Cle	28.8	Adair-Min	115	Tresh-NY	101

Total Average		Stolen Bases		Stolen Base Average		Stolen Base Runs		Fielding Runs		Total Player Rating	
Yastrzemski-Bos	.931	Campaneris-KC	51	Hinton-Cle	85.0	Versalles-Min	5.1	Boyer-NY	25.9	Yastrzemski-Bos	3.6
Cash-Det	.894	Cardenal-Cal	37	Versalles-Min	84.4	Campaneris-KC	3.9	Hansen-Chi	16.7	Weis-Chi	3.4
Wagner-Cle	.882	Versalles-Min	27	Howser-Cle	81.0	Davalillo-Cle	3.6	Davalillo-Cle	14.7	Buford-Chi	3.3
Blefary-Bal	.876	Davalillo-Cle	26	Davalillo-Cle	78.8	Aparicio-Bal	3.6	Conigliaro-Bos	13.5	Oliva-Min	3.3
Oliva-Min	.863	Aparicio-Bal	26	Aparicio-Bal	78.8	Hinton-Cle	3.3	Knoop-Cal	12.8	Colavito-Cle	3.1

Wins		Win Percentage		Games		Complete Games		Shutouts		Saves	
Grant-Min	21	Grant-Min	.750	Fisher-Chi	82	Stottlemyre-NY	18	Grant-Min	6	Kline-Was	29
Stottlemyre-NY	20	McLain-Det	.727	Kline-Was	74	McDowell-Cle	14	Stottlemyre-NY	4	S.Miller-Bal	24
Kaat-Min	18	Stottlemyre-NY	.690	B.Lee-Cal	69	Grant-Min	14	McLain-Det	4	Fisher-Chi	24
McDowell-Cle	17	Fisher-Chi	.682	Dickson-KC	68	McLain-Det	13	Horlen-Chi	4	B.Lee-Cal	23
		Siebert-Cle	.667	S.Miller-Bal	67			Chance-Cal	4	Radatz-Bos	22

Innings Pitched		Fewest Hits/Game		Fewest BB/Game		Strikeouts		Strikeouts/Game		Ratio	
Stottlemyre-NY	291.0	McDowell-Cle	5.87	Terry-Cle	1.25	McDowell-Cle	325	McDowell-Cle	10.71	Fisher-Chi	8.87
McDowell-Cle	273.0	Fisher-Chi	6.42	Monbouquette-Bos	1.57	Lolich-Det	226	Siebert-Cle	9.11	Siebert-Cle	9.06
Grant-Min	270.1	Siebert-Cle	6.63	Horlen-Chi	1.60	McLain-Det	192	Lolich-Det	8.35	Terry-Cle	9.67
Kaat-Min	264.1	Richert-Was	6.77	Ford-NY	1.84	Siebert-Cle	191	McLain-Det	7.84	McLain-Det	9.72
Newman-Cal	260.2	Brunet-Cal	6.81	Grant-Min	2.03	Downing-NY	179	Morehead-Bos	7.61	Newman-Cal	10.01

Earned Run Average		Adjusted ERA		Opponents' Batting Avg.		Opponents' On Base Pct.		Starter Runs		Adjusted Starter Runs	
McDowell-Cle	2.18	McDowell-Cle	146	McDowell-Cle	.185	Siebert-Cle	.262	McDowell-Cle	38.9	McDowell-Cle	39.5
Fisher-Chi	2.40	Siebert-Cle	143	Fisher-Chi	.205	Fisher-Chi	.262	Stottlemyre-NY	26.8	Stottlemyre-NY	25.0
Siebert-Cle	2.43	Perry-Min	135	Siebert-Cle	.206	Terry-Cle	.269	Siebert-Cle	21.5	Siebert-Cle	21.9
Brunet-Cal	2.56	Richert-Was	134	Brunet-Cal	.209	McLain-Det	.273	Pappas-Bal	21.1	Kaat-Min	21.4
Richert-Was	2.60	Pappas-Bal	133	Richert-Was	.210	Pappas-Bal	.281	McLain-Det	20.7	Pappas-Bal	21.3

Clutch Pitching Index		Relief Runs		Adjusted Relief Runs		Relief Ranking		Total Pitcher Index		Total Baseball Ranking	
Kaat-Min	123	Wilhelm-Chi	26.3	Wilhelm-Chi	22.1	S.Miller-Bal	41.5	S.Miller-Bal	4.7	S.Miller-Bal	4.7
Perry-Min	117	B.Lee-Cal	22.5	B.Lee-Cal	21.6	B.Lee-Cal	31.1	McDowell-Cle	4.1	McDowell-Cle	4.1
Peters-Chi	113	S.Miller-Bal	20.9	S.Miller-Bal	21.0	Worthington-Min	30.8	Worthington-Min	3.6	Worthington-Min	3.6
Richert-Was	110	Fisher-Chi	19.5	Fisher-Chi	14.6	Wilhelm-Chi	25.3	Kaat-Min	3.5	Yastrzemski-Bos	3.6
Pappas-Bal	110	Hamilton-NY	13.4	Hamilton-NY	13.1	Fisher-Chi	21.7	B.Lee-Cal	3.4	Kaat-Min	3.5

March 8 The Hall of Fame Special Veterans Committee waives election rules and inducts Casey Stengel, recently retired manager of the Mets.

March 30 Sandy Koufax and Don Drysdale end their 32-day holdout, signing for $130,000 and $105,000 respectively.

April 3 Tom Seaver, University of Southern California pitcher, signs with the Mets for a reported $50,000 bonus. A selection of the Braves in the January free-agent draft, Seaver was signed by Atlanta's Richmond farm club a month later, after USC had begun its baseball schedule. The violation netted Richmond a $500 fine and forbade Atlanta from signing Seaver for three years. However, Seaver was also declared ineligible at the college level, so an unprecedented special draft is held. Three clubs willing to match Richmond's $40,000 contract—the Indians, Phillies, and Mets—participate. New York's name is drawn from a hat as the winner.

April 12 The Braves lose their first game in Atlanta, 3-2, to Pittsburgh in 13 innings, with 50,761 fans on hand.

April 24 Atlanta's 5–2 win at Atlanta-Fulton County Stadium in the first game of a doubleheader is an NL-record 18th straight home win against the Mets. "Home" for 17 of those wins, though, was actually Milwaukee.

May 4 Willie Mays hits a NL record 512th home run—topping another Giant, Mel Ott—and the Giants beat the Dodgers 6-1.

May 12 The Cardinals open new Busch Memorial Stadium with a 12-inning, 4-3 win over the Braves.

June 7 The New York Mets, picking first in the June free-agent draft, pass up Arizona State outfielder Reggie Jackson to select catcher Steve Chilcott. Chilcott will retire after six years in the minors and will be the first number-one pick never to play in the major leagues. The A's take Jackson with the second pick.

July 3 Pitcher Tony Cloninger hits two grand slams and drives in nine runs, as the Braves rout the Giants at Candlestick Park 17-3. Cloninger is the only NL player to hit two in a game, and his nine RBIs are a major league record for pitchers.

July 12 St. Louis hosts a hot midsummer All-Star classic. Maury Wills's 10th-inning single scores Tim McCarver, as the NL wins 2-1 in 105-degree heat. Brooks Robinson's three hits at the plate and eight chances in the field earn him the game MVP.

August 16 Willie Mays hits his 534th home run, matching Jimmie Foxx's record for righthanded batters, as Gaylord Perry beats the Cardinals 3-1.

September 29 Sandy Koufax pitches a four-hitter, beats the Cards 2-1, and becomes the first major league pitcher to achieve a third 300-strikeout season since Amos Rusie in 1890-92.

November 1 Sandy Koufax becomes the first three-time winner of the Cy Young Award. He is a unanimous winner for the second straight year. This is the last year that only one award is given for pitchers in both of the major leagues.

November 12 The Dodgers complete an 18-game tour of Japan with a 9-8-1 record, the most losses ever for a major league club touring the Far East.

November 16 Pirate outfielder Roberto Clemente is named MVP in the NL. He edges Koufax by 10 votes.

November 18 Sandy Koufax announces his retirement, due to increasing pain in his arthritic left elbow.

November 25 Cincinnati's Tommy Helms is voted NL Rookie of the Year.

ATLANTA		CHICAGO		CINCINNATI		HOUSTON		LOS ANGELES	
M	B.Bragan	M	L.Durocher	M	D.Heffner	M	G.Hatton	M	W.Alston
M	B.Hitchcock	1B	E.Banks	M	D.Bristol	1B	C.Harrison	1B	W.Parker
1B	F.Alou	2B	G.Beckert	1B	T.Perez	2B	J.Morgan	2B	J.Lefebvre
2B	W.Woodward	SS	D.Kessinger	2B	P.Rose	SS	S.Jackson	SS	M.Wills
SS	D.Menke	3B	R.Santo	SS	L.Cardenas	3B	B.Aspromonte	3B	J.Kennedy
3B	E.Mathews	LF	B.Browne	3B	T.Helms	LF	L.Maye	LF	L.Johnson
LF	R.Carty	CF	A.Phillips	LF	D.Johnson	CF	J.Wynn	CF	W.Davis
CF	M.Jones	RF	B.Williams	CF	V.Pinson	RF	R.Staub	RF	R.Fairly
RF	H.Aaron	C	R.Hundley	RF	T.Harper	C	J.Bateman	C	J.Roseboro
C	J.Torre			C	J.Edwards				
2	F.Bolling	O1	J.Boccabella			O	D.Nicholson	O	T.Davis
		P	D.Ellsworth	C1	D.Pavletich			3	J.Gilliam
P	T.Cloninger	P	K.Holtzman	O	A.Shamsky	P	M.Cuellar	P	S.Koufax
P	K.Johnson	P	F.Jenkins	1	G.Coleman	P	D.Giusti	P	D.Drysdale
P	D.Lemaster	P	B.Hands			P	L.Dierker	P	C.Osteen
RP	C.Carroll	RP	C.Koonce	P	J.Maloney	P	T.Farrell	P	D.Sutton
RP	C.Olivo	RP	B.Hendley	P	S.Ellis	P	B.Bruce	RP	P.Regan
RP	T.Abernathy			P	M.Pappas	RP	C.Raymond	RP	B.Miller
		P	C.Simmons	P	J.O'Toole	RP	R.Taylor	RP	R.Perranoski
P	D.Kelley	P	E.Broglio	P	J.Nuxhall	RP	J.Owens		
P	W.Blasingame	P	B.Faul	RP	D.Nottebart			P	J.Moeller
P	P.Jarvis			RP	B.McCool	P	B.Latman		
P	P.Niekro			RP	T.Davidson	P	R.Roberts		
						P	C.Zachary		
				P	J.Jay				
				P	J.Baldschun				

NEW YORK		PHILADELPHIA		PITTSBURGH		SAN FRANCISCO		ST.LOUIS	
M	W.Westrum	M	G.Mauch	M	H.Walker	M	H.Franks	M	R.Schoendienst
1B	E.Kranepool	1B	B.White	1B	D.Clendenon	1B	W.McCovey	1B	O.Cepeda
2B	R.Hunt	2B	C.Rojas	2B	B.Mazeroski	2B	H.Lanier	2B	J.Javier
SS	E.Bressoud	SS	D.Groat	SS	G.Alley	SS	T.Fuentes	SS	D.Maxvill
3B	K.Boyer	3B	D.Allen	3B	B.Bailey	3B	J.Hart	3B	C.Smith
LF	R.Swoboda	LF	T.Gonzalez	LF	W.Stargell	LF	J.Alou	LF	L.Brock
CF	C.Jones	CF	B.Briggs	CF	M.Alou	CF	W.Mays	CF	C.Flood
RF	A.Luplow	RF	J.Callison	RF	R.Clemente	RF	O.Brown	RF	M.Shannon
C	J.Grote	C	C.Dalrymple	C	J.Pagliaroni	C	T.Haller	C	T.McCarver
23	C.Hiller	23	T.Taylor	O	M.Mota	S3	J.Davenport	2S	J.Buchek
S	R.McMillan	C	B.Uecker	3S	J.Pagan	O	L.Gabrielson	3	P.Gagliano
P	J.Fisher	P	J.Bunning	P	B.Veale	P	J.Marichal	P	B.Gibson
P	D.Ribant	P	C.Short	P	W.Fryman	P	G.Perry	P	A.Jackson
P	B.Shaw	P	L.Jackson	P	V.Law	P	B.Bolin	P	R.Washburn
P	R.Gardner	P	B.Buhl	P	S.Blass	P	R.Herbel	P	N.Briles
RP	J.Hamilton	P	R.Culp	P	T.Sisk	P	R.Sadecki	P	L.Jaster
RP	D.Selma	RP	D.Knowles	RP	P.Mikkelsen	RP	L.McDaniel	RP	J.Hoerner
RP	B.Hepler	RP	R.Herbert	RP	A.McBean	RP	F.Linzy	RP	H.Woodeshick
				RP	B.O'Dell	RP	B.Priddy	RP	D.Dennis
P	B.Friend	P	R.Wise						
P	T.McGraw			P	D.Cardwell	P	J.Gibbon	/P	S.Carlton
P	L.Bearnarth			P	R.Face			P	T.Stallard

TEAM	G	W	L	PCT	GB	R	OR	AB	H	2B	3B	HR	BB	SO	AVG	OBP	SLG	PRO	PRO+	BR	/A	PF	CHI	RC	SB	CS	SBA	SBR
LA	162	95	67	.586		606	490	5471	1399	201	27	108	430	830	.256	.316	.362	.678	103	-37	12	92	98	615	94	64	59	-10
SF	161	93	68	.578	1.5	675	626	5539	1373	195	31	181	414	860	.248	.304	.392	.696	96	-14	-33	103	105	633	29	30	49	-9
PIT	162	92	70	.568	3	759	641	5676	1586	238	66	158	405	1011	.279	.331	.428	.759	116	117	116	100	96	779	64	60	52	-17
PHI	162	87	75	.537	8	696	640	5607	1448	224	49	117	510	969	.258	.323	.378	.701	101	12	11	100	101	683	56	42	57	-8
ATL	163	85	77	.525	10	782	683	5617	1476	220	32	207	512	913	.263	.329	.424	.753	113	106	94	102	100	775	59	47	56	-11
STL	162	83	79	.512	12	571	577	5480	1377	196	61	108	345	977	.251	.300	.368	.668	91	-66	-69	101	99	592	144	61	70	7
CIN	160	76	84	.475	18	692	702	5521	1434	232	33	149	394	877	.260	.311	.395	.706	94	7	-51	109	105	658	70	50	58	-9
HOU	163	72	90	.444	23	612	695	5511	1405	203	35	112	491	885	.255	.320	.365	.685	104	-19	25	93	94	640	90	47	66	-1
NY	161	66	95	.410	28.5	587	761	5371	1286	187	35	98	446	992	.239	.303	.342	.645	87	-99	-87	98	108	546	55	46	54	-11
CHI	162	59	103	.364	36	644	809	5592	1418	203	43	140	457	998	.254	.315	.380	.695	98	-6	-14	101	97	665	76	47	62	-5
TOT	809					6624		55385	14202	2099	412	1378	4404	9312	.256	.315	.384	.699							737	494	60	-75

TEAM	CG	SH	SV	IP	H	H/G	HR	BB	SO	RAT	ERA	ERA+	OAV	OOB	PR	/A	PF	CPI	FA	E	DP	FW	PW	BW	SBW	DIF
LA	52	20	35	1458	1287	7.9	84	356	1084	10.3	2.62	126	.237	.288	159	109	91	102	.979	133	128	.9	11.4	1.3	-.3	.7
SF	52	14	27	1476²	1370	8.3	140	359	973	10.7	3.24	113	.244	.294	61	71	102	96	.974	168	131	-1.2	7.4	-3.5	-.2	9.8
PIT	35	12	43	1463¹	1445	8.9	125	463	898	12.0	3.52	101	.261	.322	13	8	99	105	.978	141	215	.4	.8	12.2	-1.0	-1.4
PHI	52	15	23	1459¹	1439	8.9	137	412	928	11.8	3.57	101	.258	.316	6	4	100	102	.982	113	147	2.0	.4	1.2	-.0	2.5
ATL	37	10	36	1469¹	1430	8.8	129	485	884	11.9	3.68	99	.257	.319	-12	-7	101	98	.976	154	139	-.3	-.7	9.9	-.4	-4.5
STL	47	19	32	1459²	1345	8.3	130	448	892	11.3	3.11	115	.246	.307	80	77	100	107	.977	145	166	.2	8.1	-7.2	1.5	-.6
CIN	28	10	35	1436	1408	8.8	153	490	1043	12.2	4.08	96	.254	.324	-76	-28	108	94	.980	122	133	1.4	-2.9	-5.3	-.2	3.0
HOU	34	13	26	1443²	1468	9.2	130	391	929	11.8	3.76	91	.262	.314	-24	-54	95	96	.972	174	126	-1.4	-5.7	2.6	.7	-5.3
NY	37	9	22	1427	1497	9.4	166	521	773	12.9	4.17	87	.272	.339	-89	-85	101	104	.975	159	171	-.6	-8.9	-9.1	-.4	4.5
CHI	28	6	24	1458	1513	9.3	184	479	908	12.5	4.33	85	.268	.328	-118	-106	102	97	.974	166	132	-1.0	-11.1	-1.5	.3	-8.7
TOT	402	128	303	14551¹		8.8				11.7	3.61		.256	.315					.977	1475	1488					

Runs
Alou-Atl	122
Aaron-Atl	117
Allen-Phi	112
Clemente-Pit	105
Williams-Chi	100

Hits
Alou-Atl	218
Rose-Cin	205
Clemente-Pit	202
Beckert-Chi	188

Doubles
Callison-Phi	40
Rose-Cin	38
Pinson-Cin	35
Alou-Atl	32

Triples
McCarver-StL	13
Brock-StL	12
Clemente-Pit	11

Home Runs
Aaron-Atl	44
Allen-Phi	40
Mays-SF	37
Torre-Atl	36
McCovey-SF	36

Total Bases
Alou-Atl	355
Clemente-Pit	342
Allen-Phi	331
Aaron-Atl	325
Mays-SF	307

Runs Batted In
Aaron-Atl	127
Clemente-Pit	119
Allen-Phi	110
White-Phi	103
Mays-SF	103

Runs Produced
Aaron-Atl	200
Clemente-Pit	195
Allen-Phi	182
White-Phi	166

Bases On Balls
Santo-Chi	95
Morgan-Hou	89
McCovey-SF	76
Aaron-Atl	76
Menke-Atl	71

Batting Average
Alou-Pit	.342
Alou-Atl	.327
Carty-Atl	.326
Allen-Phi	.317
Clemente-Pit	.317

On Base Percentage
Santo-Chi	.417
Morgan-Hou	.412
Allen-Phi	.398
Carty-Atl	.396
McCovey-SF	.394

Slugging Average
Allen-Phi	.632
McCovey-SF	.586
Stargell-Pit	.581
Torre-Atl	.560
Mays-SF	.556

Production
Allen-Phi	1.030
McCovey-SF	.979
Stargell-Pit	.965
Santo-Chi	.955
Torre-Atl	.945

Adjusted Production
Allen-Phi	181
Stargell-Pit	164
McCovey-SF	163
Santo-Chi	161
Torre-Atl	157

Batter Runs
Allen-Phi	56.8
Santo-Chi	51.2
McCovey-SF	46.9
Torre-Atl	43.0
Stargell-Pit	41.1

Adjusted Batter Runs
Allen-Phi	56.7
Santo-Chi	49.7
McCovey-SF	43.8
Torre-Atl	41.4
Stargell-Pit	41.0

Clutch Hitting Index
White-Phi	125
Beckert-Chi	117
Clemente-Pit	117
Woodward-Atl	117
Staub-Hou	116

Runs Created
Allen-Phi	131
Santo-Chi	127
Alou-Atl	123
McCovey-SF	119
Clemente-Pit	119

Total Average
Allen-Phi	1.088
McCovey-SF	1.039
Santo-Chi	.988
Stargell-Pit	.980
Mays-SF	.941

Stolen Bases
Brock-StL	74
Jackson-Hou	49
Wills-LA	38
Phillips-Phi-Chi	32
Harper-Cin	29

Stolen Base Average
Aaron-Atl	87.5
Brock-StL	80.4
Jackson-Hou	77.8
Harper-Cin	74.4
White-Phi	72.7

Stolen Base Runs
Brock-StL	11.4
Jackson-Hou	6.3
Aaron-Atl	4.5
Harper-Cin	2.7

Fielding Runs
Mazeroski-Pit	40.8
Santo-Chi	28.8
Lanier-SF	28.2
Maxvill-StL	23.8
Clemente-Pit	15.4

Total Player Rating
Santo-Chi	7.5
Clemente-Pit	4.6
Allen-Phi	4.5
Mazeroski-Pit	4.5
Aaron-Atl	4.3

Wins
Koufax-LA	27
Marichal-SF	25
Perry-SF	21
Gibson-StL	21
Short-Phi	20

Win Percentage
Marichal-SF	.806
Koufax-LA	.750
Perry-SF	.724
Short-Phi	.667
Maloney-Cin	.667

Games
Carroll-Phi	73
Mikkelsen-Pit	71
Knowles-Phi	69
Regan-LA	65
McDaniel-SF	64

Complete Games
Koufax-LA	27
Marichal-SF	25
Gibson-StL	20
Short-Phi	19
Bunning-Phi	16

Shutouts
L.Jackson-Chi-Phi	5
Maloney-Cin	5
Koufax-LA	5
Jaster-StL	5
Gibson-StL	5
Bunning-Phi	5

Saves
Regan-LA	21
McCool-Cin	18
Face-Pit	18
Raymond-Hou	16
Linzy-SF	16

Innings Pitched
Koufax-LA	323.0
Bunning-Phi	314.0
Marichal-SF	307.1
Gibson-StL	280.1
Drysdale-LA	273.2

Fewest Hits/Game
Marichal-SF	6.68
Koufax-LA	6.72
Gibson-StL	6.74
Maloney-Cin	6.97
Bolin-SF	6.98

Fewest BB/Game
Marichal-SF	1.05
Law-Pit	1.22
Perry-SF	1.41
Drysdale-LA	1.48
Bunning-Phi	1.58

Strikeouts
Koufax-LA	317
Bunning-Phi	252
Veale-Pit	229
Gibson-StL	225
Marichal-SF	222

Strikeouts/Game
Koufax-LA	8.83
Maloney-Cin	8.65
Sutton-LA	8.34
Veale-Pit	7.68
Jenkins-Phi-Chi	7.32

Ratio
Marichal-SF	7.88
Koufax-LA	8.86
Gibson-StL	9.41
Bunning-Phi	9.57
Cuellar-Hou	9.70

Earned Run Average
Koufax-LA	1.73
Cuellar-Hou	2.22
Marichal-SF	2.23
Bunning-Phi	2.41
Gibson-StL	2.44

Adjusted ERA
Koufax-LA	191
Marichal-SF	165
Cuellar-Hou	154
Bunning-Phi	149
Gibson-StL	147

Opponents' Batting Avg.
Marichal-SF	.202
Koufax-LA	.205
Gibson-StL	.207
Bolin-SF	.211
Maloney-Cin	.214

Opponents' On Base Pct.
Marichal-SF	.230
Koufax-LA	.253
Gibson-StL	.267
Bunning-Phi	.270
Cuellar-Hou	.274

Starter Runs
Koufax-LA	67.4
Marichal-SF	47.2
Bunning-Phi	41.8
Gibson-StL	36.3
Cuellar-Hou	35.1

Adjusted Starter Runs
Koufax-LA	56.3
Marichal-SF	49.2
Bunning-Phi	41.4
Gibson-StL	35.8
Cuellar-Hou	30.5

Clutch Pitching Index
Jackson-StL	117
L.Jackson-Chi-Phi	110
Ellsworth-Chi	108
Johnson-Atl	108
Osteen-LA	107

Relief Runs
Regan-LA	25.8
Carroll-Atl	19.8
Hoerner-StL	17.5
McCool-Cin	13.2
Woodeshick-StL	13.2

Adjusted Relief Runs
Regan-LA	21.7
Carroll-Atl	20.4
Hoerner-StL	17.3
McCool-Cin	16.7
McDaniel-SF	13.6

Relief Ranking
Regan-LA	33.9
McCool-Cin	29.2
Carroll-Atl	22.5
Hoerner-StL	19.0
McDaniel-SF	16.6

Total Pitcher Index
Marichal-SF	5.8
Koufax-LA	5.4
Gibson-StL	4.4
Jackson-StL	4.2
Bunning-Phi	4.1

Total Baseball Ranking
Santo-Chi	7.5
Marichal-SF	5.8
Koufax-LA	5.4
Clemente-Pit	4.6
Allen-Phi	4.5

January 20 The BBWAA voters elect Ted Williams to the Hall of Fame. Williams receives 282 of a possible 302 votes.

March 5 Player representatives elect Marvin Miller, assistant to the president of the United Steelworkers, as executive director of the Major Leagues Players' Association.

April 11 A crowd of 44,468, including Vice President Hubert Humphrey, attends a historic opener at Washington. Emmett Ashford becomes the major league's first black umpire in Cleveland's 5-2 win against the Senators.

April 19 In the first regular season game at Anaheim Stadium, California drops a 3-1 decision to the White Sox before 31,660 fans. Rick Reichardt hits the Angels' first regular-season home run in the new facility.

April 28 Cleveland ties the Brooklyn Dodgers' record with its 10th straight win since Opening Day. Wilfred "Sonny" Siebert defeats the Angels, 2–1. Cleveland will finally lose tomorrow, 4-1, to Gary Peters and the White Sox.

May 8 Orioles right fielder Frank Robinson hits the first ball ever hit completely out of Baltimore's Memorial Stadium, a 451-foot shot, ending Luis Tiant's scoreless-innings streak at 27. Baltimore wins, 8-3, and ties Cleveland for first place.

June 9 Minnesota rocks Kansas City with the first five-home run inning in AL history. Rich Rollins, Zoilo Versalles, Tony Oliva, Don Mincher, and Harmon Killebrew connect in the seventh inning to give the Twins a 9-4 victory.

June 10 Sonny Siebert pitches a no-hitter against the Senators. Leon Wagner homers off loser Phil Ortega, as first-place Cleveland wins 2-0.

September 17 Cleveland pitchers set an AL record by fanning 19 batters in the first nine innings of a 10-inning 6-2 win at Detroit.

September 22 The Orioles beat the A's 6–1 to clinch their first AL pennant. Frank Robinson, who drives in two runs in the clincher, will end the year as the Triple Crown winner, the first to achieve the feat since Mickey Mantle in 1956. He

finishes with a batting average of .316, 49 home runs, and 122 RBIs.

October 5 With first-inning homers by Frank Robinson and Brooks Robinson and 11 strikeouts from relief pitcher Moe Drabowsky, the Orioles win Game 1 of the World Series, 5-2.

October 9 Dave McNally wraps up Baltimore's brilliant pitching display, and a World Championship, with a four-hit, 1-0 win. Frank Robinson's home run off Don Drysdale gives Baltimore a surprising sweep of the defending champion Dodgers. The 33 consecutive scoreless innings pitched by Baltimore are a World Series record.

November 8 Frank Robinson of the Orioles is the unanimous choice as AL MVP. He is the only player to win the award in both leagues.

November 23 Chicago outfielder Tommie Agee is voted AL Rookie of the Year, gathering 16 of the 18 votes. Kansas City pitcher Jim Nash gets the other two. Agee had been brought up briefly the past four seasons before finding a permanent spot this year.

BALTIMORE		BOSTON		CALIFORNIA		CHICAGO		CLEVELAND	
M	H.Bauer	M	B.Herman	M	B.Rigney	M	E.Stanky	M	B.Tebbetts
1B	B.Powell	M	P.Runnels	1B	N.Siebern	1B	T.McCraw	M	G.Strickland
2B	D.Johnson	1B	G.Scott	2B	B.Knoop	2B	A.Weis	1B	F.Whitfield
SS	L.Aparicio	2B	G.Smith	SS	J.Fregosi	SS	L.Elia	2B	P.Gonzalez
3B	B.Robinson	SS	R.Petrocelli	3B	P.Schaal	3B	D.Buford	SS	L.Brown
LF	C.Blefary	3B	J.Foy	LF	R.Reichardt	LF	K.Berry	3B	M.Alvis
CF	P.Blair	LF	C.Yastrzemski	CF	J.Cardenal	CF	T.Agee	LF	L.Wagner
RF	F.Robinson	CF	D.Demeter	RF	E.Kirkpatrick	RF	F.Robinson	CF	V.Davalillo
C	A.Etchebarren	RF	T.Conigliaro	C	B.Rodgers	C	J.Romano	RF	R.Colavito
		C	M.Ryan					C	J.Azcue
O	R.Snyder			C1	T.Satriano	S2	J.Adair		
O	S.Bowens	2	D.Jones	O	J.Johnstone	1	B.Skowron	O	C.Hinton
P	D.McNally	C	B.Tillman	1	J.Adcock	O3	P.Ward	S2	C.Salmon
P	J.Palmer	P	J.Lonborg	P	D.Chance	P	T.John	P	G.Bell
E.Watt	P	J.Santiago	P	G.Brunet	P	J.Horlen	P	S.Siebert
W.Bunker	P	B.Brandon	P	M.Lopez	P	G.Peters	P	S.McDowell
P	S.Barber	P	L.Stange	P	F.Newman	P	J.Buzhardt	P	S.Hargan
RP	M.Drabowsky	P	E.Wilson	RP	J.Sanford	P	B.Howard	P	L.Tiant
RP	S.Miller	RP	D.Stigman	RP	B.Lee	RP	B.Locker	RP	J.Kralick
RP	E.Fisher	RP	D.McMahon	RP	M.Rojas	RP	D.Higgins	RP	D.Radatz
		RP	J.Wyatt			RP	J.Pizarro	RP	B.Allen
P	J.Miller			P	C.Wright				
P	G.Brabender	P	R.Sheldon	P	L.Burdette	P	J.Lamabe	P	J.O'Donoghue
P	D.Hall	P	D.Bennett	P	J.McGlothlin	P	H.Wilhelm	P	T.Kelley
P	F.Bertaina	P	D.Osinski						
		P	J.Stephenson						

DETROIT		KANSAS CITY		MINNESOTA		NEW YORK		WASHINGTON	
M	C.Dressen	M	A.Dark	M	S.Mele	M	J.Keane	M	G.Hodges
M	B.Swift	1B	K.Harrelson	1B	D.Mincher	M	R.Houk	1B	D.Nen
M	F.Skaff	2B	D.Green	2B	B.Allen	1B	J.Pepitone	2B	B.Saverine
1B	N.Cash	SS	B.Campaneris	SS	Z.Versalles	2B	B.Richardson	SS	E.Brinkman
2B	J.Lumpe	3B	E.Charles	3B	H.Killebrew	SS	H.Clarke	3B	K.McMullen
SS	D.McAuliffe	LF	L.Stahl	LF	J.Hall	3B	C.Boyer	LF	F.Howard
3B	D.Wert	CF	J.Nossek	CF	T.Uhlaender	LF	T.Tresh	CF	D.Lock
LF	W.Horton	RF	M.Hershberger	RF	T.Oliva	CF	M.Mantle	RF	F.Valentine
CF	A.Kaline	C	P.Roof	C	E.Battey	RF	R.Maris	C	P.Casanova
RF	J.Northrup					C	E.Howard		
C	B.Freehan	13	D.Cater	2S	C.Tovar			O	J.King
		O1	R.Repoz	3	R.Rollins	O	R.White	O	W.Kirkland
2	J.Wood	O	J.Gosger					1	K.Harrelson
O	M.Stanley			P	J.Kaat	P	M.Stottlemyre	2	D.Blasingame
S	R.Oyler	P	L.Krausse	P	M.Grant	P	F.Peterson		
		P	C.Hunter	P	J.Perry	P	A.Downing	P	P.Richert
P	D.McLain	P	J.Nash	P	D.Boswell	P	F.Talbot	P	M.McCormick
P	M.Lolich	P	P.Lindblad	P	J.Merritt	P	J.Bouton	P	P.Ortega
P	E.Wilson	RP	J.Aker	RP	A.Worthington	RP	H.Reniff	P	J.Hannan
P	D.Wickersham	RP	K.Sanders	RP	P.Cimino	RP	P.Ramos	RP	C.Cox
P	J.Podres			RP	D.Siebler	RP	S.Hamilton	RP	B.Humphreys
RP	O.Pena	P	B.Odom					RP	R.Kline
RP	L.Sherry	P	C.Dobson	P	C.Pascual	P	D.Womack		
RP	F.Gladding	P	R.Sheldon			P	W.Ford	P	D.Lines
		P	F.Talbot					P	D.Segui
P	H.Aguirre	P	R.Terry					P	B.Moore
P	B.Monbouquette								
P	J.Sparma								

TEAM	G	W	L	PCT	GB	R	OR	AB	H	2B	3B	HR	BB	SO	AVG	OBP	SLG	PRO	PRO+	BR	/A	PF	CHI	RC	SB	CS	SBA	SBR
BAL	160	97	63	.606		755	601	5529	1426	243	35	175	514	926	.258	.325	.409	.734	119	114	126	98	100	727	55	43	56	-9
MIN	162	89	73	.549	9	663	581	5390	1341	219	33	144	513	844	.249	.319	.382	.701	101	49	6	106	98	643	67	42	61	-5
DET	162	88	74	.543	10	719	698	5507	1383	224	45	179	551	987	.251	.323	.406	.729	112	102	85	102	96	714	41	34	55	-8
CHI	163	83	79	.512	15	574	517	5348	1235	193	40	87	476	872	.231	.299	.331	.630	93	-83	-47	93	106	539	153	78	66	-1
CLE	162	81	81	.500	17	574	586	5474	1300	156	25	155	450	914	.237	.299	.360	.659	95	-38	-38	100	97	579	53	41	56	-9
CAL	162	80	82	.494	18	604	643	5360	1244	179	54	122	525	1062	.232	.305	.354	.659	98	-29	-13	97	101	582	80	54	60	-8
KC	160	74	86	.463	23	564	648	5328	1259	212	56	70	421	982	.236	.295	.337	.632	90	-84	-67	97	107	535	132	50	73	10
WAS	159	71	88	.447	25.5	557	659	5318	1245	185	40	126	450	1069	.234	.296	.355	.651	94	-50	-44	99	99	548	53	37	59	-6
BOS	162	72	90	.444	26	655	731	5498	1318	228	44	145	542	1020	.240	.312	.376	.688	93	24	-44	110	98	640	35	24	59	-4
NY	160	70	89	.440	26.5	611	612	5330	1254	182	36	162	485	817	.235	.302	.374	.676	104	-5	18	96	100	598	49	29	63	-3
TOT	806					6276		54082	13005	2021	408	1365	4927	9493	.240	.308	.369	.676							718	432	62	-44

TEAM	CG	SH	SV	IP	H	H/G	HR	BB	SO	RAT	ERA	ERA+	OAV	OOB	PR	/A	PF	CPI	FA	E	DP	FW	PW	BW	SBW	DIF
BAL	23	13	51	1466^{1}	1267	7.8	127	514	1070	11.1	3.32	100	.233	.303	19	2	97	97	.981	115	142	1.3	.2	13.5	-.5	2.4
MIN	52	11	28	1438^{2}	1246	7.8	139	392	1015	10.4	3.13	115	.232	.287	48	74	105	97	.977	139	118	.0	8.0	.6	-.0	-.6
DET	36	11	38	1454^{1}	1356	8.4	185	520	1026	11.9	3.85	90	.247	.317	-67	-60	101	102	.980	120	142	1.1	-6.4	9.1	-.4	3.6
CHI	38	22	34	1475^{1}	1229	7.5	101	403	896	10.2	2.68	118	.226	.283	123	80	92	100	.976	159	149	-1.1	8.6	-5.1	.4	-.8
CLE	49	15	28	1467^{1}	1260	7.7	129	489	1111	10.9	3.23	107	.232	.299	34	35	100	98	.978	138	132	.0	3.8	-4.1	-.5	.7
CAL	31	12	40	1457^{1}	1364	8.4	136	511	836	11.8	3.56	94	.251	.320	-21	-33	98	105	.979	136	186	.2	-3.5	-1.4	-.4	4.1
KC	19	11	47	1435	1281	8.0	106	630	854	12.2	3.56	96	.241	.326	-19	-25	99	101	.977	139	154	-.0	-2.7	-7.2	1.5	2.4
WAS	25	6	35	1419	1282	8.1	154	448	866	11.1	3.70	93	.242	.304	-42	-39	101	95	.977	142	139	-.3	-4.2	-4.7	-.2	.9
BOS	32	10	31	1463^{2}	1402	8.6	164	577	977	12.4	3.92	97	.253	.327	-78	-18	111	103	.975	155	153	-.9	-1.9	-4.7	.0	-1.5
NY	29	7	32	1415^{2}	1318	8.4	124	443	842	11.3	3.41	97	.248	.308	3	-14	97	102	.977	142	142	-.3	-1.5	1.9	.1	-9.8
TOT	334	118	364	14492^{2}		8.1				11.3	3.44		.240	.308					.978	1385	1457					

Runs
F.Robinson-Bal ... 122
Oliva-Min ... 99
Cash-Det ... 98
Agee-Chi ... 98

Hits
Oliva-Min ... 191
F.Robinson-Bal ... 182
Aparicio-Bal ... 182
Agee-Chi ... 172
Cash-Det ... 168

Doubles
Yastrzemski-Bos ... 39
B.Robinson-Bal ... 35
F.Robinson-Bal ... 34
Oliva-Min ... 32
Fregosi-Cal ... 32

Triples
Knoop-Cal ... 11
Campaneris-KC ... 10
Brinkman-Was ... 9

Home Runs
F.Robinson-Bal ... 49
Killebrew-Min ... 39
Powell-Bal ... 34
Cash-Det ... 32
Pepitone-NY ... 31

Total Bases
F.Robinson-Bal ... 367
Oliva-Min ... 312
Killebrew-Min ... 306
Cash-Det ... 288
Agee-Chi ... 281

Runs Batted In
F.Robinson-Bal ... 122
Killebrew-Min ... 110
Powell-Bal ... 109
B.Robinson-Bal ... 100
Horton-Det ... 100

Runs Produced
F.Robinson-Bal ... 195
B.Robinson-Bal ... 168
Agee-Chi ... 162
Oliva-Min ... 161
Killebrew-Min ... 160

Bases On Balls
Killebrew-Min ... 103
Foy-Bos ... 91
F.Robinson-Bal ... 87
Tresh-NY ... 86
Yastrzemski-Bos ... 84

Batting Average
F.Robinson-Bal ... .316
Oliva-Min ... .307
Kaline-Det ... .288
Powell-Bal ... .287
Killebrew-Min ... .281

On Base Percentage
F.Robinson-Bal ... .415
Kaline-Det ... .396
Killebrew-Min ... .393
McAuliffe-Det ... .375
Powell-Bal ... .374

Slugging Average
F.Robinson-Bal ... .637
Killebrew-Min ... .538
Kaline-Det ... .534
Powell-Bal ... .532
McAuliffe-Det ... .509

Production
F.Robinson-Bal ... 1.052
Killebrew-Min ... .931
Kaline-Det ... .931
Powell-Bal ... .905
McAuliffe-Det ... .884

Adjusted Production
F.Robinson-Bal ... 200
Kaline-Det ... 161
Powell-Bal ... 159
Killebrew-Min ... 155
McAuliffe-Det ... 148

Batter Runs
F.Robinson-Bal ... 73.6
Killebrew-Min ... 49.9
Kaline-Det ... 42.1
Powell-Bal ... 36.3
Oliva-Min ... 33.2

Adjusted Batter Runs
F.Robinson-Bal ... 75.9
Killebrew-Min ... 42.4
Kaline-Det ... 39.8
Powell-Bal ... 37.8
Mantle-NY ... 31.4

Clutch Hitting Index
Powell-Bal ... 119
Horton-Det ... 119
Green-KC ... 116
Hershberger-KC ... 115
D.Johnson-Bal ... 113

Runs Created
F.Robinson-Bal ... 146
Killebrew-Min ... 122
Oliva-Min ... 106
Kaline-Det ... 105
Cash-Det ... 101

Total Average
F.Robinson-Bal ... 1.104
Kaline-Det ... .969
Killebrew-Min ... .967
Powell-Bal ... .898
McAuliffe-Det ... .877

Stolen Bases
Campaneris-KC ... 52
Buford-Chi ... 51
Agee-Chi ... 44
Aparicio-Bal ... 25
Cardenal-Cal ... 24

Stolen Base Average
Campaneris-KC ... 83.9
Tartabull-KC-Bos ... 82.6
Tovar-Min ... 72.7
Agee-Chi ... 71.0
Buford-Chi ... 69.9

Stolen Base Runs
Campaneris-KC ... 9.6
Tartabull-KC-Bos ... 3.3
Salmon-Cle ... 2.4
Agee-Chi ... 2.4

Fielding Runs
Weis-Chi ... 36.9
Tresh-NY ... 27.7
Boyer-NY ... 19.9
Yastrzemski-Bos ... 16.6
Knoop-Cal ... 16.5

Total Player Rating
F.Robinson-Bal ... 6.7
Tresh-NY ... 4.1
Fregosi-Cal ... 3.9
Kaline-Det ... 3.9
Oliva-Min ... 3.5

Wins
Kaat-Min ... 25
McLain-Det ... 20
Wilson-Bos-Det ... 18
Siebert-Cle ... 16
Palmer-Bal ... 15

Win Percentage
Siebert-Cle ... .667
Kaat-Min ... .658
Wilson-Bos-Det ... .621
Palmer-Bal ... .600
McLain-Det ... .588

Games
Fisher-Chi-Bal ... 67
Cox-Was ... 66
Aker-KC ... 66
Worthington-Min ... 65
Kline-Was ... 63

Complete Games
Kaat-Min ... 19
McLain-Det ... 14
Wilson-Bos-Det ... 13
Bell-Cle ... 12

Shutouts
Tiant-Cle ... 5
McDowell-Cle ... 5
John-Chi ... 5

Saves
Aker-KC ... 32
Kline-Was ... 23
Sherry-Det ... 20
Fisher-Chi-Bal ... 19
S.Miller-Bal ... 18

Innings Pitched
Kaat-Min ... 304.2
McLain-Det ... 264.1
Wilson-Bos-Det ... 264.0
Chance-Cal ... 259.2
Bell-Cle ... 254.1

Fewest Hits/Game
McDowell-Cle ... 6.02
Boswell-Min ... 6.38
Peters-Chi ... 6.86
McLain-Det ... 6.98
Chance-Cal ... 7.14

Fewest BB/Game
Kaat-Min ... 1.62
Peterson-NY ... 1.67
Grant-Min ... 1.77
Peters-Chi ... 1.98
Hargan-Cle ... 2.11

Strikeouts
McDowell-Cle ... 225
Kaat-Min ... 205
Wilson-Bos-Det ... 200
Richert-Was ... 195
Bell-Cle ... 194

Strikeouts/Game
McDowell-Cle ... 10.42
Boswell-Min ... 9.19
Lolich-Det ... 7.64
Richert-Was ... 7.14
Bell-Cle ... 6.87

Ratio
Peters-Chi ... 8.97
Kaat-Min ... 9.72
Richert-Was ... 9.74
Siebert-Cle ... 9.75
Ortega-Was ... 9.85

Earned Run Average
Peters-Chi ... 1.98
Horlen-Chi ... 2.43
Hargan-Cle ... 2.48
Perry-Min ... 2.54
John-Chi ... 2.62

Adjusted ERA
Peters-Chi ... 160
Perry-Min ... 142
Hargan-Cle ... 138
Kaat-Min ... 131
Horlen-Chi ... 130

Opponents' Batting Avg.
McDowell-Cle ... .188
Boswell-Min ... .197
Peters-Chi ... .212
McLain-Det ... .214
Richert-Was ... .215

Opponents' On Base Pct.
Peters-Chi ... .261
Richert-Was ... .271
Kaat-Min ... .271
Ortega-Was ... .276
Siebert-Cle ... .278

Starter Runs
Peters-Chi ... 33.1
Horlen-Chi ... 23.5
Kaat-Min ... 23.3
Hargan-Cle ... 20.3
John-Chi ... 20.1

Adjusted Starter Runs
Kaat-Min ... 28.8
Peters-Chi ... 27.1
Perry-Min ... 21.7
Hargan-Cle ... 20.4
Nash-KC ... 18.9

Clutch Pitching Index
McNally-Bal ... 118
Horlen-Chi ... 114
Brunet-Cal ... 114
Perry-Min ... 113
Hargan-Cle ... 110

Relief Runs
Aker-KC ... 18.1
Wilhelm-Chi ... 16.0
S.Miller-Bal ... 12.1
Fisher-Chi-Bal ... 10.8
Lines-Was ... 10.7

Adjusted Relief Runs
Aker-KC ... 17.7
Wilhelm-Chi ... 13.7
Worthington-Min ... 11.5
S.Miller-Bal ... 11.1
Lines-Was ... 10.9

Relief Ranking
Aker-KC ... 26.8
McMahon-Cle-Bos ... 20.5
S.Miller-Bal ... 18.4
Kline-Was ... 16.1
Worthington-Min ... 14.2

Total Pitcher Index
Kaat-Min ... 4.1
Peters-Chi ... 3.9
Wilson-Bos-Det ... 3.3
Aker-KC ... 3.2
Perry-Min ... 2.4

Total Baseball Ranking
F.Robinson-Bal ... 6.7
Tresh-NY ... 4.1
Kaat-Min ... 4.1
Fregosi-Cal ... 3.9
Peters-Chi ... 3.9

January 29 Branch Rickey and Lloyd Waner are elected to the Baseball Hall of Fame by a unanimous vote of the Special Veterans Committee.

February 16 Red Ruffing is selected for the Hall of Fame through a special runoff election, since nobody received the required 75 percent vote in January.

May 10 In the eighth inning against Jim Bunning of the Phillies, Hank Aaron drives a ball to deep center field and scores ahead of the relay. It will be the only inside-the-park home run among his 755.

June 4 Curt Flood's record string of 568 straight chances without an error ends when he drops a fly ball during a 4-3 win over the Cubs at St. Louis. The Cardinals center fielder had played a NL-record 227 straight games without an error beginning Sept. 3, 1965.

July 12 Reds third baseman Tony Perez ends the longest All-Star Game (15 innings, three hours and 41 minutes) with a home run off Catfish Hunter. Homers by NL third baseman Richie Allen and AL third baseman Brooks Robinson account for the other runs in a 2-1 NL triumph.

July 14 Eddie Mathews becomes the seventh member of the 500-home run club, connecting off loser Juan Marichal as the Astros beat the Giants 8-6.

October 1 Pittsburgh right fielder Roberto Clemente ends his season with a flourish, winning his fourth batting title with a .357 average by going 2-for-5 with a triple and his 23rd home run, as the Pirates wallop the Astros 10-3.

October 4 Cardinals left fielder Lou Brock has four hits, two stolen bases, and scores twice, as St. Louis edges Boston 2-1 to open the World Series at Fenway Park. Bob Gibson has 10 strikeouts and outduels Jose Santiago, whose home run is Boston's only score.

October 8 Bob Gibson is overpowering again in a five-hit 6-0 win in Game 4.

Roger Maris and Tim McCarver each drive in two runs for St. Louis.

October 9 Roger Maris homers for the Cardinals in the ninth, but Jim Lonborg's 3-1 win sends the World Series back to Boston.

October 12 The Cardinals earn their second world championship of the decade with a 7-2 victory. Bob Gibson notches his third World Series win with a three-hitter, 10 strikeouts, and a fifth-inning home run. Lou Brock steals three bases for a record seven thefts in a seven-game World Series.

October 31 San Francisco's Mike McCormick is the NL Cy Young Award winner, as pitchers are honored in each league for the first time.

November 7 Orlando Cepeda of the Cards is the first unanimous selection as NL MVP.

November 20 Mets pitcher Tom Seaver (16-12) is named NL Rookie of the Year.

ATLANTA		CHICAGO		CINCINNATI		HOUSTON		LOS ANGELES	
M	B.Hitchcock	M	L.Durocher	M	D.Bristol	M	G.Hatton	M	W.Alston
M	K.Silvestri	1B	E.Banks	1B	L.May	1B	E.Mathews	1B	W.Parker
1B	F.Alou	2B	G.Beckert	2B	T.Helms	2B	J.Morgan	2B	R.Hunt
2B	W.Woodward	SS	D.Kessinger	SS	L.Cardenas	SS	S.Jackson	SS	G.Michael
SS	D.Menke	3B	R.Santo	3B	T.Perez	3B	B.Aspromonte	3B	J.Lefebvre
3B	C.Boyer	LF	B.Williams	LF	P.Rose	LF	R.Davis	LF	L.Johnson
LF	R.Carty	CF	A.Phillips	CF	V.Pinson	CF	J.Wynn	CF	W.Davis
CF	M.Jones	RF	T.Savage	RF	T.Harper	RF	R.Staub	RF	R.Fairly
RF	H.Aaron	C	R.Hundley	C	J.Edwards	C	J.Bateman	C	J.Roseboro
C	J.Torre								
		P	F.Jenkins	13	D.Johnson	2S	J.Gotay	3O	B.Bailey
1	T.Francona	P	R.Nye	23	C.Ruiz	C	R.Brand	O	A.Ferrara
		P	J.Niekro	C	D.Pavletich			O	L.Gabrielson
P	D.Lemaster	P	R.Culp			P	M.Cuellar	2S	N.Oliver
P	K.Johnson	P	B.Hands	P	G.Nolan	P	D.Giusti	S	D.Schofield
P	P.Niekro	RP	C.Hartenstein	P	M.Pappas	P	D.Wilson		
P	P.Jarvis	RP	B.Stoneman	P	M.Queen	P	B.Belinsky	P	C.Osteen
RP	D.Kelley	RP	C.Koonce	P	J.Maloney	P	L.Dierker	P	D.Drysdale
RP	C.Carroll			P	S.Ellis	RP	B.Latman	P	D.Sutton
RP	J.Ritchie	P	K.Holtzman	RP	T.Abernathy	RP	C.Sembera	P	B.Singer
		P	C.Simmons	RP	D.Nottebart	RP	D.Eilers	P	J.Brewer
P	T.Cloninger			RP	G.Arrigo			RP	R.Perranoski
P	R.Hernandez					P	W.Blasingame	RP	P.Regan
				P	B.McCool	P	D.Schneider	RP	B.Miller
				P	B.Lee	P	B.Von Hoff		

NEW YORK		PHILADELPHIA		PITTSBURGH		SAN FRANCISCO		ST.LOUIS	
M	W.Westrum	M	G.Mauch	M	H.Walker	M	H.Franks	M	R.Schoendienst
M	S.Parker	1B	B.White	M	D.Murtaugh	1B	W.McCovey	1B	O.Cepeda
1B	E.Kranepool	2B	C.Rojas	1B	D.Clendenon	2B	T.Fuentes	2B	J.Javier
2B	J.Buchek	SS	B.Wine	2B	B.Mazeroski	SS	H.Lanier	SS	D.Maxvill
SS	B.Harrelson	3B	D.Allen	SS	G.Alley	3B	J.Hart	3B	M.Shannon
3B	E.Charles	LF	T.Gonzalez	3B	M.Wills	LF	J.Alou	LF	L.Brock
LF	T.Davis	CF	J.Briggs	LF	W.Stargell	CF	W.Mays	CF	C.Flood
CF	C.Jones	RF	J.Callison	CF	M.Alou	RF	O.Brown	RF	R.Maris
RF	R.Swoboda	C	C.Dalrymple	RF	R.Clemente	C	T.Haller	C	T.McCarver
C	J.Grote			C	J.May				
		O	D.Lock			3S	J.Davenport	O1	B.Tolan
O	T.Reynolds	SO	G.Sutherland	O	M.Mota			23	P.Gagliano
21	B.Johnson	13	T.Taylor	3O	J.Pagan	P	G.Perry		
		C	G.Oliver			P	M.McCormick	P	D.Hughes
P	T.Seaver			P	T.Sisk	P	J.Marichal	P	S.Carlton
P	J.Fisher	P	J.Bunning	P	B.Veale	P	R.Sadecki	P	R.Washburn
P	D.Cardwell	P	L.Jackson	P	D.Ribant	P	R.Herbel	P	B.Gibson
P	B.Shaw	P	C.Short	P	S.Blass	RP	F.Linzy	P	N.Briles
RP	D.Selma	P	R.Wise	P	W.Fryman	RP	J.Gibbon	RP	A.Jackson
RP	R.Taylor	P	D.Ellsworth	RP	A.McBean	RP	L.McDaniel	RP	R.Willis
RP	D.Shaw	RP	T.Farrell	RP	J.Pizarro			RP	J.Hoerner
		RP	D.Hall	RP	R.Face	P	B.Bolin		
P	D.Frisella	RP	G.Jackson					P	L.Jaster
P	B.Hendley			P	V.Law				
P	B.Denehy	P	J.Boozer	P	B.O'Dell				
				P	P.Mikkelsen				

TEAM	G	W	L	PCT	GB	R	OR	AB	H	2B	3B	HR	BB	SO	AVG	OBP	SLG	PRO	PRO+	BR	/A	PF	CHI	RC	SB	CS	SBA	SBR
STL	161	101	60	.627		695	557	5566	1462	225	40	115	443	919	.263	.322	.379	.701	109	52	61	99	103	676	102	54	65	-2
SF	162	91	71	.562	10.5	652	551	5524	1354	201	39	140	520	978	.245	.315	.372	.687	104	24	33	99	100	641	22	30	42	-11
CHI	162	87	74	.540	14	702	624	5463	1373	211	49	128	509	912	.251	.319	.378	.697	101	44	13	105	105	654	63	50	56	-11
CIN	162	87	75	.537	14.5	604	563	5519	1366	251	54	109	372	969	.248	.299	.372	.671	88	-20	-88	111	102	592	92	63	59	-10
PHI	162	82	80	.506	19.5	612	581	5401	1306	221	47	109	545	1033	.242	.314	.357	.671	98	-1	-7	101	99	604	79	62	56	-14
PIT	163	81	81	.500	20.5	679	693	5724	1585	193	62	91	387	914	.277	.327	.380	.707	108	63	60	101	97	693	79	37	68	2
ATL	162	77	85	.475	24.5	631	640	5450	1307	191	29	158	512	947	.240	.309	.372	.681	102	10	19	99	100	615	55	45	55	-11
LA	162	73	89	.451	28.5	519	595	5456	1285	203	38	82	485	881	.236	.303	.332	.635	97	-74	-30	92	95	541	56	47	54	-11
HOU	162	69	93	.426	32.5	626	742	5506	1372	259	46	93	537	934	.249	.319	.364	.683	107	20	42	97	97	640	88	38	70	4
NY	162	61	101	.377	40.5	498	672	5417	1288	178	23	83	362	981	.238	.290	.325	.615	83	-118	-110	98	103	500	58	44	57	-9
TOT	810					6218		55026	13698	2133	427	1102	4672	9468	.249	.312	.363	.675							694	470	60	-74

TEAM	CG	SH	SV	IP	H	H/G	HR	BB	SO	RAT	ERA	ERA+	OAV	OOB	PR	/A	PF	CPI	FA	E	DP	FW	PW	BW	SBW	DIF
STL	44	17	45	1465	1313	8.1	97	431	956	10.9	3.05	108	.239	.299	54	39	97	98	.978	140	127	.0	4.2	6.6	.6	9.1
SF	64	17	25	1474¹	1283	7.8	113	453	990	10.8	2.92	113	.234	.296	75	61	97	101	.979	134	149	.4	6.6	3.6	-.4	-.2
CHI	47	7	28	1457	1352	8.4	142	463	888	11.4	3.48	102	.246	.308	-17	10	105	99	.981	121	143	1.1	1.1	1.4	-.4	3.3
CIN	34	18	39	1468	1328	8.1	101	498	1065	11.5	3.05	111	.241	.309	54	115	111	104	.980	121	124	1.1	12.5	-9.5	-.3	2.2
PHI	46	17	23	1453²	1372	8.5	86	403	967	11.2	3.10	110	.250	.306	44	50	101	102	.978	137	174	.2	5.4	-.8	-.7	-3.2
PIT	35	5	35	1458¹	1439	8.9	108	561	820	12.5	3.74	90	.261	.332	-59	-61	100	103	.978	141	186	.0	-6.6	6.5	1.0	-.9
ATL	35	5	32	1454	1377	8.5	118	449	862	11.6	3.47	96	.251	.313	-16	-24	98	100	.978	138	148	.2	-2.6	2.1	-.4	-3.2
LA	41	17	24	1473	1421	8.7	93	393	967	11.3	3.21	96	.254	.308	27	-19	92	102	.975	160	144	-1.1	-2.1	-3.2	-.4	-1.2
HOU	35	8	21	1445²	1444	9.0	120	485	1060	12.3	4.03	82	.260	.324	-105	-115	98	93	.974	159	120	-1.0	-12.5	4.5	1.2	-4.3
NY	36	10	19	1433²	1369	8.6	124	536	893	12.1	3.73	91	.253	.323	-56	-54	100	99	.975	157	147	-.9	-5.8	-11.9	-.2	-1.1
TOT	417	121	291	14582²		8.5				11.6	3.38		.249	.312					.978	1408	1462					

Runs		Hits		Doubles		Triples		Home Runs		Total Bases	
Brock-StL	113	Clemente-Pit	209	Staub-Hou	44	Pinson-Cin	13	Aaron-Atl	39	Aaron-Atl	344
Aaron-Atl	113	Brock-StL	206	Cepeda-StL	37	Williams-Chi	12	Wynn-Hou	37	Brock-StL	325
Santo-Chi	107	Pinson-Cin	187	Aaron-Atl	37	Brock-StL	12	Santo-Chi	31	Clemente-Pit	324
Clemente-Pit	103	Wills-Pit	186			Morgan-Hou	11	McCovey-SF	31	Williams-Chi	305
Wynn-Hou	102	Alou-Pit	186					Hart-SF	29	Santo-Chi	300

Runs Batted In		Runs Produced		Bases On Balls		Batting Average		On Base Percentage		Slugging Average	
Cepeda-StL	111	Clemente-Pit	190	Santo-Chi	96	Clemente-Pit	.357	Allen-Phi	.404	Aaron-Atl	.573
Clemente-Pit	110	Aaron-Atl	183	Morgan-Hou	81	Gonzalez-Phi	.339	Cepeda-StL	.403	Allen-Phi	.566
Aaron-Atl	109	Cepeda-StL	177	Phillips-Chi	80	Alou-Pit	.338	Staub-Hou	.402	Clemente-Pit	.554
Wynn-Hou	107	Santo-Chi	174	Hart-SF	77	Flood-StL	.335	Clemente-Pit	.402	McCovey-SF	.535
Perez-Cin	102	Wynn-Hou	172	Allen-Phi	75	Staub-Hou	.333	Santo-Chi	.401	Cepeda-StL	.524

Production		Adjusted Production		Batter Runs		Adjusted Batter Runs		Clutch Hitting Index		Runs Created	
Allen-Phi	.970	Allen-Phi	173	Clemente-Pit	52.1	Aaron-Atl	51.8	Shannon-StL	141	Clemente-Pit	126
Clemente-Pit	.956	Clemente-Pit	170	Aaron-Atl	50.1	Clemente-Pit	51.6	Lanier-SF	125	Aaron-Atl	126
Aaron-Atl	.946	Aaron-Atl	169	Santo-Chi	47.9	Cepeda-StL	48.8	Maxvill-StL	120	Santo-Chi	120
Cepeda-StL	.927	Cepeda-StL	166	Cepeda-StL	47.3	Allen-Phi	45.1	Fairly-LA	118	Cepeda-StL	118
McCovey-SF	.916	McCovey-SF	162	Allen-Phi	46.1	Santo-Chi	42.5	Boyer-Atl	117	Hart-SF	111

Total Average		Stolen Bases		Stolen Base Average		Stolen Base Runs		Fielding Runs		Total Player Rating	
Allen-Phi	1.054	Brock-StL	52	Morgan-Hou	85.3	Morgan-Hou	5.7	Santo-Chi	30.6	Santo-Chi	7.3
Aaron-Atl	.965	Wills-Pit	29	Wynn-Hou	80.0	Brock-StL	4.8	Lanier-SF	28.9	Aaron-Atl	6.1
Clemente-Pit	.959	Morgan-Hou	29	Allen-Phi	80.0	Pinson-Cin	3.0	Wine-Phi	28.9	Clemente-Pit	5.8
Cepeda-StL	.950	Pinson-Cin	26	Davis-LA	76.9	Allen-Phi	3.0	Fuentes-SF	24.5	Cepeda-StL	4.4
McCovey-SF	.941	Phillips-Chi	24	Pinson-Cin	76.5	Wills-Pit	2.7	Mazeroski-Pit	16.7	Allen-Phi	4.4

Wins		Win Percentage		Games		Complete Games		Shutouts		Saves	
McCormick-SF	22	Hughes-StL	.727	Perranoski-LA	70	Jenkins-Chi	20	Bunning-Phi	6	Abernathy-Cin	28
Jenkins-Chi	20	McCormick-SF	.688	Abernathy-Cin	70	Seaver-NY	18	Osteen-LA	5	Linzy-SF	17
Osteen-LA	17	Veale-Pit	.667	Willis-StL	65	Perry-SF	18	Nolan-Cin	5	Face-Pit	17
Bunning-Phi	17	Jenkins-Chi	.606	Face-Pit	61	Marichal-SF	18	McCormick-SF	5	Perranoski-LA	16
		Jarvis-Atl	.600					L.Jackson-Phi	4	Hoerner-StL	15

Innings Pitched		Fewest Hits/Game		Fewest BB/Game		Strikeouts		Strikeouts/Game		Ratio	
Bunning-Phi	302.1	Hughes-StL	6.64	Pappas-Cin	1.57	Bunning-Phi	253	Nolan-Cin	8.18	Hughes-StL	8.78
Perry-SF	293.0	Wilson-Hou	6.90	Osteen-LA	1.62	Jenkins-Chi	236	Veale-Pit	7.94	Bunning-Phi	9.73
Jenkins-Chi	289.1	Perry-SF	7.10	Johnson-Atl	1.63	Perry-SF	230	Carlton-StL	7.83	Queen-Cin	9.80
Osteen-LA	288.1	Queen-Cin	7.13	Niekro-Chi	1.70	Nolan-Cin	206	Wilson-Hou	7.78	Perry-SF	9.80
Drysdale-LA	282.0	Niekro-Atl	7.13	L.Jackson-Phi	1.86	Cuellar-Hou	203	Gibson-StL	7.55	Niekro-Atl	9.83

Earned Run Average		Adjusted ERA		Opponents' Batting Avg.		Opponents' On Base Pct.		Starter Runs		Adjusted Starter Runs	
Niekro-Atl	1.87	Niekro-Atl	178	Hughes-StL	.203	Hughes-StL	.252	Bunning-Phi	36.4	Bunning-Phi	37.5
Bunning-Phi	2.29	Bunning-Phi	149	Wilson-Hou	.209	Bunning-Phi	.273	Niekro-Atl	34.6	Niekro-Atl	33.4
Short-Phi	2.39	Nolan-Cin	145	Perry-SF	.214	Queen-Cin	.273	Perry-SF	24.9	Nolan-Cin	29.5
Nolan-Cin	2.58	Short-Phi	142	Queen-Cin	.215	Perry-SF	.274	Short-Phi	21.8	Jenkins-Chi	24.0
Perry-SF	2.61	Queen-Cin	136	Bunning-Phi	.217	Jenkins-Chi	.277	Nolan-Cin	20.0	Short-Phi	22.5

Clutch Pitching Index		Relief Runs		Adjusted Relief Runs		Relief Ranking		Total Pitcher Index		Total Baseball Ranking	
Ellis-Cin	123	Abernathy-Cin	24.9	Abernathy-Cin	29.3	Abernathy-Cin	39.7	Abernathy-Cin	4.5	Santo-Chi	7.3
Niekro-Atl	121	Linzy-SF	19.9	Linzy-SF	19.0	Linzy-SF	32.5	Bunning-Phi	4.1	Aaron-Atl	6.1
Seaver-NY	114	Nottebart-Cin	12.8	Nottebart-Cin	16.1	Hall-Phi	24.2	Linzy-SF	3.9	Clemente-Pit	5.8
Marichal-SF	114	McBean-Pit	12.1	Farrell-Hou-Phi	12.1	Farrell-Hou-Phi	20.0	Niekro-Atl	3.8	Abernathy-Cin	4.5
Short-Phi	114	Farrell-Hou-Phi	11.9	McBean-Pit	12.0	Face-Pit	15.3	Jenkins-Chi	3.1	Cepeda-StL	4.4

March 3 The White Sox are given permission to use a semi-designated hitter in training camp. With home club permission, clubs will be allowed to use a designated pinch hitter twice in the same game.

April 14 Red Sox rookie Billy Rohr debuts at Yankee Stadium. He startles everyone by taking a no-hitter to the ninth inning, but Elston Howard lines a 3-2 pitch for a single to right-center with two outs. Carl Yastrzemski had kept the no-hitter alive with a spectacular grab of a Tom Tresh drive to deep left field to open the ninth. The Red Sox go on to win, 3-0. Rohr will pitch only one more game for Boston before returning to the minors.

May 14 Mickey Mantle becomes the sixth member of the 500-home run club in New York's 6-5 win against Baltimore. Mantle connects batting left-handed off Stu Miller.

June 7 The last-place Yankees have the first pick in the free-agent draft and use it to take Ron Blomberg.

July 25 Race riots in Detroit force postponement of a Tigers-Orioles game. Games scheduled the next two days are shifted to Baltimore.

August 6 Against Chicago, Brooks Robinson of the Orioles hits into the fourth triple play of his career for a major league mark.

August 18 A baseball tragedy occurs when Tony Conigliaro of the Red Sox is beaned by the Angels' Jack Hamilton. Hit on the left cheekbone, just below the eye socket, Conigliaro will miss the rest of 1967 and all of 1968. He was hitting .267 with 20 homers and 67 RBIs in 95 games.

August 26 Dean Chance pitches a 2-1 no-hitter, and the Twins sweep Cleveland to take the AL lead. The victory gives Chance a 17-9 record and lowers his ERA to 2.42.

October 1 Boston clinches the AL pennant with a 5-3 win over Minnesota, Jim Lonborg besting Dean Chance. Carl Yastrzemski goes 4-for-4 and has 10 hits in his final 13 at bats to win the Triple Crown (.326, 44, 121). Detroit, which could tie for the lead with a sweep, beats California in the opener, 6-4. They then drop the second game, 8-5, despite sending eight pitchers to the mound. The four teams combined for a 6-12 record over the final week, while Boston wins the pennant with a .568 winning percentage, the lowest in league history.

October 11 A World Series record three home runs in one inning—consecutively, by Carl Yastrzemski, Reggie Smith, and Rico Petrocelli—power Boston to an 8-4 win that evens the Series at three games each.

November 3 Boston's Jim Lonborg is named American League Cy Young Award winner.

November 15 Boston's Carl Yastrzemski is the overwhelming selection as AL MVP.

November 22 Minnesota second baseman Rod Carew (.292) is the runaway choice for AL Rookie of the Year.

BALTIMORE		BOSTON		CALIFORNIA		CHICAGO		CLEVELAND	
M	H.Bauer	M	D.Williams	M	B.Rigney	M	E.Stanky	M	J.Adcock
1B	B.Powell	1B	G.Scott	1B	D.Mincher	1B	T.McCraw	1B	T.Horton
2B	D.Johnson	2B	M.Andrews	2B	B.Knoop	2B	W.Causey	2B	P.Gonzalez
SS	L.Aparicio	SS	R.Petrocelli	SS	J.Fregosi	SS	R.Hansen	SS	L.Brown
3B	B.Robinson	3B	J.Foy	3B	P.Schaal	3B	D.Buford	3B	M.Alvis
LF	C.Blefary	LF	C.Yastrzemski	LF	R.Reichardt	LF	P.Ward	LF	L.Wagner
CF	P.Blair	CF	R.Smith	CF	J.Cardenal	CF	T.Agee	CF	V.Davalillo
RF	F.Robinson	RF	T.Conigliaro	RF	J.Hall	RF	K.Berry	RF	C.Hinton
C	A.Etchebarren	C	M.Ryan	C	B.Rodgers	C	J.Martin	C	J.Azcue
O	R.Snyder	O	J.Tartabull	O	J.Johnstone	O	W.Williams	O	L.Maye
		3S	J.Adair	O	B.Morton			1	F.Whitfield
P	T.Phoebus			3C	T.Satriano	P	G.Peters	C	D.Sims
P	P.Richert	P	J.Lonborg			P	J.Horlen	2	V.Fuller
P	B.Dillman	P	L.Stange	P	G.Brunet	P	T.John	O1	C.Salmon
P	D.McNally	P	G.Bell	P	J.McGlothlin	P	B.Howard		
P	J.Hardin	P	B.Brandon	P	R.Clark	RP	B.Locker	P	S.McDowell
RP	E.Watt	RP	J.Santiago	P	J.Hamilton	RP	W.Wood	P	S.Hargan
RP	M.Drabowsky	RP	J.Wyatt	RP	M.Rojas	RP	D.McMahon	P	L.Tiant
RP	E.Fisher	RP	D.Osinski	RP	B.Kelso			P	S.Siebert
				RP	P.Cimino	P	J.Buzhardt	P	J.O'Donoghue
P	G.Brabender	P	D.Bennett			P	H.Wilhelm	RP	O.Pena
P	W.Bunker			P	C.Wright	P	J.O'Toole	RP	G.Culver
P	S.Miller			P	J.Coates			RP	S.Bailey
P	S.Barber								
								P	S.Williams
								/P	G.Bell
								P	B.Allen

DETROIT		KANSAS CITY		MINNESOTA		NEW YORK		WASHINGTON	
M	M.Smith	M	A.Dark	M	S.Mele	M	R.Houk	M	G.Hodges
1B	N.Cash	M	L.Appling	M	C.Ermer	1B	M.Mantle	1B	M.Epstein
2B	D.McAuliffe	1B	R.Webster	1B	H.Killebrew	2B	H.Clarke	2B	B.Allen
SS	R.Oyler	2B	J.Donaldson	2B	R.Carew	SS	R.Amaro	SS	E.Brinkman
3B	D.Wert	SS	B.Campaneris	SS	Z.Versalles	3B	C.Smith	3B	K.McMullen
LF	J.Northrup	3B	D.Green	3B	R.Rollins	LF	T.Tresh	LF	F.Howard
CF	M.Stanley	LF	J.Gosger	LF	B.Allison	CF	J.Pepitone	CF	F.Valentine
RF	A.Kaline	CF	R.Monday	CF	T.Uhlaender	RF	S.Whitaker	RF	C.Peterson
C	B.Freehan	RF	M.Hershberger	RF	T.Oliva	C	J.Gibbs	C	P.Casanova
		C	P.Roof	C	J.Zimmerman				
O	W.Horton					O	B.Robinson	O	H.Allen
		3O	D.Cater	O3	C.Tovar	O3	R.White	S2	T.Cullen
P	E.Wilson							1	D.Nen
P	D.McLain	P	C.Hunter	P	D.Chance	P	M.Stottlemyre	2S	B.Saverine
P	J.Sparma	P	J.Nash	P	J.Kaat	P	A.Downing	O	E.Stroud
P	M.Lolich	P	C.Dobson	P	J.Merritt	P	F.Peterson		
RP	D.Wickersham	P	L.Krausse	P	D.Boswell	P	F.Talbot	P	P.Ortega
RP	F.Gladding	P	B.Odom	P	J.Perry	P	B.Monbouquette	P	C.Pascual
RP	J.Hiller	RP	P.Lindblad	RP	A.Worthington	RP	T.Tillotson	P	B.Moore
		RP	T.Pierce	RP	R.Kline	RP	D.Womack	P	J.Coleman
		RP	J.Aker			RP	J.Verbanic	P	F.Bertaina
P	J.Podres			P	M.Grant			RP	D.Knowles
P	M.Marshall							RP	B.Priddy
		P	D.Segui			P	S.Barber	RP	B.Humphreys
						P	S.Hamilton	P	D.Lines
								P	C.Cox
								P	D.Baldwin
								P	P.Richert
								/P	D.Bosman

TEAM	G	W	L	PCT	GB	R	OR	AB	H	2B	3B	HR	BB	SO	AVG	OBP	SLG	PRO	PRO+	BR	/A	PF	CHI	RC	SB	CS	SBA	SBR
BOS	162	92	70	.568		722	614	5471	1394	216	39	158	522	1020	.255	.323	.395	.718	109	118	60	108	100	694	68	59	54	-15
MIN	164	91	71	.562	1	671	590	5458	1309	216	48	131	512	976	.240	.310	.369	.679	99	44	-8	108	104	625	55	37	60	-6
DET	163	91	71	.562	1	633	587	5410	1315	192	36	152	626	994	.243	.310	.376	.703	111	100	81	103	96	681	37	21	64	-2
CHI	162	89	73	.549	3	531	491	5383	1209	181	34	89	480	849	.225	.293	.320	.613	90	-80	-61	96	104	504	124	82	60	-12
CAL	161	84	77	.522	7.5	567	587	5307	1265	170	37	114	453	1021	.238	.302	.349	.651	102	-12	10	96	99	553	40	36	53	-10
WAS	161	76	85	.472	15.5	550	637	5441	1211	168	25	115	472	1037	.223	.289	.326	.615	92	-81	-61	96	107	512	53	37	59	-6
BAL	161	76	85	.472	15.5	654	592	5456	1312	215	44	138	531	1002	.240	.313	.372	.685	110	54	59	99	99	639	54	37	59	-6
CLE	162	75	87	.463	17	559	613	5461	1282	213	35	131	413	984	.235	.295	.359	.654	98	-15	-20	101	96	563	53	65	45	-23
NY	163	72	90	.444	20	522	621	5443	1225	166	17	100	532	1043	.225	.298	.317	.615	91	-74	-54	96	98	522	63	37	63	-3
KC	161	62	99	.385	29.5	533	660	5349	1244	212	50	69	452	1019	.233	.297	.330	.627	94	-54	-37	97	100	539	132	59	69	4
TOT	810					5992		54179	12766	1949	365	1197	4993	9945	.236	.305	.351	.656							679	470	59	-78

TEAM	CG	SH	SV	IP	H	H/G	HR	BB	SO	RAT	ERA	ERA+	OAV	OOB	PR	/A	PF	CPI	FA	E	DP	FW	PW	BW	SBW	DIF
BOS	41	9	44	1459¹	1307	8.1	142	477	1010	11.3	3.36	104	.239	.306	-21	20	108	101	.977	142	142	-.6	2.2	6.6	-.8	3.6
MIN	58	18	24	1461	1336	8.2	115	396	1089	10.9	3.14	110	.243	.298	15	53	107	101	.978	132	123	.1	5.9	-.9	.2	4.7
DET	46	17	40	1443²	1230	7.7	151	472	1038	10.8	3.32	98	.230	.297	-14	-9	101	97	.978	132	126	.0	-1.0	8.9	.6	1.3
CHI	36	24	39	1490¹	1197	7.2	87	465	927	10.4	2.45	127	.219	.288	129	108	96	106	.979	138	149	-.3	11.9	-6.7	-.5	3.6
CAL	19	14	46	1430¹	1246	7.8	118	525	892	11.4	3.19	98	.237	.311	6	-8	97	105	.982	111	135	1.3	-.9	1.1	-.2	2.2
WAS	24	14	39	1473¹	1334	8.1	113	495	878	11.4	3.38	93	.242	.309	-25	-36	98	98	.978	144	167	-.8	-4.0	-6.7	.2	6.8
BAL	29	17	36	1457¹	1218	7.5	116	566	1034	11.2	3.32	95	.228	.305	-15	-27	98	95	.980	124	144	.5	-3.0	6.5	.2	-8.7
CLE	49	14	27	1477²	1258	7.7	120	559	1189	11.3	3.25	101	.231	.307	-3	3	101	99	.981	116	138	1.0	.3	-2.2	-1.7	-3.5
NY	37	16	27	1480²	1375	8.4	110	480	898	11.5	3.24	97	.249	.313	-2	-19	97	106	.976	154	144	-1.3	-2.1	-6.0	.5	-.2
KC	26	10	34	1428	1265	8.0	125	558	990	11.7	3.68	87	.238	.315	-71	-79	99	94	.978	132	120	-.0	-8.7	-4.1	1.3	-7.0
TOT	365	153	356	14601²		7.9				11.2	3.23		.236	.305					.979	1325	1388					

Runs
Yastrzemski-Bos .. 112
Killebrew-Min 105
Tovar-Min 98
Kaline-Det 94
McAuliffe-Det 92

Hits
Yastrzemski-Bos ... 189
Tovar-Min 173
Scott-Bos 171
Fregosi-Cal 171
B.Robinson-Bal.... 164

Doubles
Oliva-Min 34
Tovar-Min 32
Yastrzemski-Bos .. 31
D.Johnson-Bal ... 30
Campaneris-KC 29

Triples
Blair-Bal 12
Buford-Chi 9

Home Runs
Yastrzemski-Bos 44
Killebrew-Min 44
Howard-Was 36
F.Robinson-Bal 30

Total Bases
Yastrzemski-Bos .. 360
Killebrew-Min 305
F.Robinson-Bal ... 276
B.Robinson-Bal ... 265
Howard-Was 265

Runs Batted In
Yastrzemski-Bos ... 121
Killebrew-Min 113
F.Robinson-Bal ... 94
Howard-Was 89
Oliva-Min 83

Runs Produced
Yastrzemski-Bos ... 189
Killebrew-Min 174
F.Robinson-Bal ... 147
Kaline-Det 147
B.Robinson-Bal.... 143

Bases On Balls
Killebrew-Min 131
Mantle-NY 107
McAuliffe-Det ... 105
Yastrzemski-Bos .. 91
Kaline-Det 83

Batting Average
Yastrzemski-Bos ...326
F.Robinson-Bal ...311
Kaline-Det 308
Scott-Bos 303
Blair-Bal 293

On Base Percentage
Yastrzemski-Bos ...421
Kaline-Det 415
Killebrew-Min 413
F.Robinson-Bal ...408
Mantle-NY 394

Slugging Average
Yastrzemski-Bos ..622
F.Robinson-Bal ...576
Killebrew-Min 558
Kaline-Det........541
Howard-Was 511

Production
Yastrzemski-Bos .1.043
F.Robinson-Bal ...984
Killebrew-Min 970
Kaline-Det 957
Mincher-Cal 855

Adjusted Production
Yastrzemski-Bos ... 189
F.Robinson-Bal ... 189
Kaline-Det 176
Killebrew-Min 170
Mincher-Cal 156

Batter Runs
Yastrzemski-Bos .. 76.4
Killebrew-Min 62.3
F.Robinson-Bal ... 53.3
Kaline-Det 48.4
Scott-Bos 33.8

Adjusted Batter Runs
Yastrzemski-Bos .. 65.3
F.Robinson-Bal ...54.2
Killebrew-Min 52.2
Kaline-Det 45.7
Mincher-Cal 34.6

Clutch Hitting Index
Hershberger-KC ...124
D.Johnson-Bal ...113
Hansen-Chi 111
Northrup-Det 109
Versalles-Min 108

Runs Created
Yastrzemski-Bos .. 155
Killebrew-Min 131
F.Robinson-Bal ... 113
Kaline-Det 104
Scott-Bos 97

Total Average
Yastrzemski-Bos .1.134
Killebrew-Min 1.058
F.Robinson-Bal ...1.029
Kaline-Det 1.009
Mantle-NY 874

Stolen Bases
Campaneris-KC 55
Buford-Chi 34
Agee-Chi 28
McCraw-Chi 24
Clarke-NY 21

Stolen Base Average
Valentine-Was 85.0
Clarke-NY 84.0
Aparicio-Chi 78.3
Campaneris-KC ... 77.5
Agee-Chi 73.7

Stolen Base Runs
Campaneris-KC 6.9
Clarke-NY 3.9
Valentine-Was......3.3

Fielding Runs
B.Robinson-Bal ... 30.8
Blair-Bal 20.9
Smith-Bos 16.5
Monday-KC 15.2
Clarke-NY 15.2

Total Player Rating
Yastrzemski-Bos ... 7.3
Kaline-Det......... 5.2
B.Robinson-Bal 5.0
F.Robinson-Bal 4.8
Blair-Bal 4.1

Wins
Wilson-Det 22
Lonborg-Bos 22
Chance-Min 20
Horlen-Chi 19
McLain-Det 17

Win Percentage
Horlen-Chi 731
Lonborg-Bos 710
Wilson-Det 667
Sparma-Det 640
Peters-Chi 593

Games
Locker-Chi 77
Rojas-Cal 72
Kelso-Cal 69
Womack-NY....... 65
McMahon-Bos-Chi . 63

Complete Games
Chance-Min 18
Lonborg-Bos....... 15
Hargan-Cle 15

Shutouts
McGlothlin-Cal 6
Lolich-Det 6
John-Chi 6
Horlen-Chi 6
Hargan-Cle 6

Saves
Rojas-Cal 27
Wyatt-Bos 20
Locker-Chi 20
Womack-NY 18
Worthington-Min ... 16

Innings Pitched
Chance-Min 283.2
Lonborg-Bos ... 273.1
Wilson-Det 264.0
Kaat-Min 263.1
Peters-Chi 260.0

Fewest Hits/Game
Peters-Ch 6.47
Boswell-Min 6.55
Horlen-Ch 6.56
Siebert-Cle 6.60
Downing-NY 7.05

Fewest BB/Game
Merritt-Min 1.19
Kaat-Min 1.44
Stange-Bos 1.59
Horlen-Ch 2.02
Peterson-NY 2.13

Strikeouts
Lonborg-Bos 246
McDowell-Cle 236
Chance-Min 220
Tiant-Cle 219
Peters-Chi 215

Strikeouts/Game
Tiant-Cle 9.22
McDowell-Cle 8.99
Boswell-Min...... 8.25
Lonborg-Bos 8.10
Phoebus-Bal 7.75

Ratio
Horlen-Chi 8.72
Merritt-Min 9.21
Siebert-Cle 9.52
John-Chi 9.84
Peters-Chi 10.00

Earned Run Average
Horlen-Chi 2.06
Peters-Chi 2.28
Siebert-Cle 2.38
John-Chi 2.47
Merritt-Min 2.53

Adjusted ERA
Horlen-Chi 151
Siebert-Cle 137
Merritt-Min 137
Peters-Chi 136
Chance-Min 127

Opponents' Batting Avg.
Peters-Chi 199
Boswell-Min 202
Siebert-Cle 202
Horlen-Chi 203
Downing-NY 217

Opponents' On Base Pct.
Horlen-Chi 253
Merritt-Min 262
Siebert-Cle 268
John-Chi 277
Peters-Chi 277

Starter Runs
Horlen-Chi 33.6
Peters-Chi 27.3
Merritt-Min 17.7
Siebert-Cle 17.5
Chance-Min 15.8

Adjusted Starter Runs
Horlen-Chi 30.0
Peters-Chi 23.7
Merritt-Min 23.5
Chance-Min 23.0
Siebert-Cle 18.3

Clutch Pitching Index
Clark-Cal 121
Stottlemyre-NY ... 117
Kaat-Min 108
Tiant-Cle 107
Stange-Bos 105

Relief Runs
Wilhelm-Chi 18.9
Drabowsky-Bal ... 17.2
Locker-Chi 15.7
McMahon-Bos-Chi .. 15.2
Baldwin-Was 11.6

Adjusted Relief Runs
Wilhelm-Chi 17.7
Drabowsky-Bal ... 16.4
McMahon-Bos-Chi .. 14.5
Locker-Chi 14.0
Baldwin-Was 11.1

Relief Ranking
Wilhelm-Chi 24.6
Drabowsky-Bal ...22.8
Wyatt-Bos 19.0
Rojas-Cal 17.0
Locker-Chi 16.7

Total Pitcher Index
Peters-Chi 3.7
Horlen-Chi 3.5
Drabowsky-Bal ... 2.9
Wilhelm-Chi 2.6
Chance-Min 2.4

Total Baseball Ranking
Yastrzemski-Bos ... 7.3
Kaline-Det......... 5.2
B.Robinson-Bal ... 5.0
F.Robinson-Bal 4.8
Blair-Bal 4.1

January 23 Joe Medwick is voted into the Baseball Hall of Fame.

January 28 Goose Goslin and Kiki Cuyler are admitted to the Hall of Fame by unanimous vote of the Special Veterans Committee.

April 15 Three records are smashed when the Astros score an unearned run in the 24th inning to squeeze by the Mets 1-0. It is the longest NL game played to completion, in terms of innings, the longest major league night game, and the first 23 innings are the longest major league scoreless game. The game ties the AL's longest complete game: A's 4, Red Sox 1, in 24 frames, on Sept. 1, 1906.

June 8 Don Drysdale works four scoreless innings against Philadelphia before finally allowing a run, after 58⅔ shutout innings, on Howie Bedell's sacrifice fly. Drysdale breaks the major league record of 56 consecutive scoreless innings set by Walter Johnson in 1913.

July 1 A first inning wild pitch breaks Bob Gibson's streak of 47⅔ innings of scoreless pitching as the Cards beat the Dodgers in Los Angeles 8-1.

July 9 Appropriately, pitching dominates the All-Star Game. Willie Mays tallies an unearned run in the first inning against AL starter Luis Tiant to complete the scoring for the day—the first All-Star Game to end 1-0. Don Drysdale, Juan Marichal, Steve Carlton, Tom Seaver, Ron Reed, and Jerry Koosman hold the AL to three hits.

July 14 Houston's Don Wilson fans 18 batters, tying the major league record set by Bob Feller. He also ties the major league record with eight strikeouts in a row. For all his efforts, Wilson is not the winner.

September 17 Gaylord Perry hurls a no-hitter at Candlestick, as the Giants edge the Cards and Bob Gibson 1-0. Perry evens his record at 14-14.

September 18 Sixteen hours after Perry's feat, Ray Washburn of the Cards makes major league history by hurling a second consecutive no-hitter in one park. Run-scoring hits by Mike Shannon and Curt Flood down the Giants 2-0.

September 27 A 1-0 win and 11 strikeouts against the Astros enable Cardinal Bob Gibson to lower his ERA to 1.12, a new NL season mark. His phenomenal campaign includes 28 complete games, 268 strikeouts, and 13 shutouts.

October 2 For the first time, two soon-to-be-named MVPs oppose each other. St. Louis' Bob Gibson records a World Series-record 17 strikeouts and a 4-0 win over Denny McLain. Detroit manager Mayo Smith moves Gold Glove center fielder Mickey Stanley to shortstop, improving his offense by opening a spot for Al Kaline.

October 14 In the NL expansion draft, the Expos choose 30 players, including Maury Wills, Jim Grant, Donn Clendenon, and Manny Mota. San Diego's 30 selections include Dave Giusti, Nate Colbert, Zoilo Versalles, Al McBean, and Clarence Gaston.

November 13 Bob Gibson edges Pete Rose to win the NL MVP award.

November 22 Reds catcher Johnny Bench is named NL Rookie of the Year, getting 10½ votes to edge out NY's Jerry Koosman, who had 9½.

	ATLANTA		CHICAGO		CINCINNATI		HOUSTON		LOS ANGELES
M	L.Harris	M	L.Durocher	M	D.Bristol	M	G.Hatton	M	W.Alston
1B	D.Johnson	1B	E.Banks	1B	L.May	M	H.Walker	1B	W.Parker
2B	F.Millan	2B	G.Beckert	2B	T.Helms	1B	R.Staub	2B	P.Popovich
SS	S.Jackson	SS	D.Kessinger	SS	L.Cardenas	2B	D.Menke	SS	Z.Versalles
3B	C.Boyer	3B	R.Santo	3B	T.Perez	SS	H.Torres	3B	B.Bailey
LF	M.Lum	LF	B.Williams	LF	A.Johnson	3B	D.Rader	LF	L.Gabrielson
CF	F.Alou	CF	A.Phillips	CF	V.Pinson	LF	J.Wynn	CF	W.Davis
RF	H.Aaron	RF	J.Hickman	RF	P.Rose	CF	R.Davis	RF	R.Fairly
C	J.Torre	C	R.Hundley	C	J.Bench	RF	N.Miller	C	T.Haller
						C	J.Bateman		
O1	T.Francona	O	L.Johnson	O	M.Jones			O	J.Fairey
S3	M.Martinez					3O	B.Aspromonte	23	J.Lefebvre
O1	T.Aaron	P	F.Jenkins	P	G.Culver	O	L.Thomas	31	K.Boyer
C	B.Tillman	P	B.Hands	P	J.Maloney				
		P	K.Holtzman	P	G.Arrigo	P	D.Giusti	P	B.Singer
P	P.Niekro	P	J.Niekro	P	G.Nolan	P	L.Dierker	P	C.Osteen
P	P.Jarvis	P	R.Nye	RP	T.Abernathy	P	D.Lemaster	P	D.Drysdale
P	R.Reed	RP	P.Regan	RP	C.Carroll	P	D.Wilson	P	D.Sutton
P	K.Johnson	RP	J.Lamabe	RP	B.Lee	P	M.Cuellar	P	M.Kekich
P	M.Pappas					RP	J.Buzhardt	RP	M.Grant
RP	C.Upshaw			P	T.Cloninger	RP	J.Ray	RP	J.Brewer
RP	J.Britton			P	M.Pappas	RP	T.Dukes	RP	J.Billingham
RP	C.Raymond			P	J.Ritchie				
				P	B.Kelso			P	J.Purdin
P	D.Kelley			P	B.McCool				
P	G.Stone								

	NEW YORK		PHILADELPHIA		PITTSBURGH		SAN FRANCISCO		ST.LOUIS
M	G.Hodges	M	G.Mauch	M	L.Shepard	M	H.Franks	M	R.Schoendienst
1B	E.Kranepool	M	G.Myatt	1B	D.Clendenon	1B	W.McCovey	1B	O.Cepeda
2B	P.Linz	M	B.Skinner	2B	B.Mazeroski	2B	R.Hunt	2B	J.Javier
SS	B.Harrelson	1B	B.White	SS	G.Alley	SS	H.Lanier	SS	D.Maxvill
3B	E.Charles	2B	C.Rojas	3B	M.Wills	3B	J.Davenport	3B	M.Shannon
LF	C.Jones	SS	R.Pena	LF	W.Stargell	LF	J.Alou	LF	L.Brock
CF	T.Agee	3B	T.Taylor	CF	M.Alou	CF	W.Mays	CF	C.Flood
RF	R.Swoboda	LF	D.Allen	RF	R.Clemente	RF	B.Bonds	RF	R.Maris
C	J.Grote	CF	T.Gonzalez	C	J.May	C	D.Dietz	C	T.McCarver
		RF	J.Callison						
O1	A.Shamsky	C	M.Ryan	O	M.Mota	O1	T.Cline	O	B.Tolan
2	K.Boswell			S	F.Patek	3O	J.Hart	C	J.Edwards
S2	A.Weis	O1	J.Briggs			C1	J.Hiatt		
C1	J.Martin	O	D.Lock	P	B.Veale			P	B.Gibson
		C	C.Dalrymple	P	S.Blass	P	J.Marichal	P	N.Briles
P	T.Seaver			P	A.McBean	P	G.Perry	P	S.Carlton
P	J.Koosman	P	C.Short	P	B.Moose	P	R.Sadecki	P	R.Washburn
P	D.Cardwell	P	L.Jackson	P	J.Bunning	P	M.McCormick	P	L.Jaster
P	D.Selma	P	W.Fryman	RP	R.Kline	P	B.Bolin	RP	R.Willis
P	N.Ryan	P	R.Wise	RP	T.Sisk	RP	F.Linzy	RP	D.Hughes
RP	C.Koonce	P	J.James	RP	L.Walker			RP	M.Nelson
RP	R.Taylor	RP	T.Farrell						
RP	D.Frisella	RP	G.Wagner	P	D.Ellis				
		RP	J.Boozer	P	R.Face				
P	A.Jackson								
P	J.McAndrew	P	J.Johnson						
		P	G.Jackson						

TEAM	G	W	L	PCT	GB	R	OR	AB	H	2B	3B	HR	BB	SO	AVG	OBP	SLG	PRO	PRO+	BR	/A	PF	CHI	RC	SB	CS	SBA	SBR
STL	162	97	65	.599		583	472	5561	1383	227	48	73	378	897	.249	.300	.346	.646	102	2	9	99	104	581	110	45	71	6
SF	163	88	74	.543	9	599	529	5441	1301	162	33	108	508	904	.239	.310	.341	.651	103	20	21	100	103	577	50	37	57	-7
CHI	163	84	78	.519	13	612	611	5458	1319	203	43	130	415	854	.242	.300	.366	.666	100	36	-4	107	104	593	41	30	58	-6
CIN	163	83	79	.512	14	690	673	5767	1573	281	36	106	379	938	.273	.322	.389	.711	114	130	85	106	98	688	59	55	52	-15
ATL	163	81	81	.500	16	514	549	5552	1399	179	31	80	414	782	.252	.308	.339	.647	101	9	7	100	90	564	83	44	65	-2
PIT	163	80	82	.494	17	583	532	5569	1404	180	44	80	422	953	.252	.309	.343	.652	105	19	28	99	100	580	130	59	69	4
PHI	162	76	86	.469	21	543	615	5372	1253	178	30	100	462	1003	.233	.297	.333	.630	96	-24	-24	100	104	527	58	51	53	-13
LA	162	76	86	.469	21	470	509	5354	1234	202	36	67	439	980	.230	.291	.319	.610	97	-61	-25	92	97	501	57	43	57	-9
NY	163	73	89	.451	24	473	499	5503	1252	178	30	81	379	1203	.228	.283	.315	.598	86	-91	-93	101	102	486	72	45	62	-5
HOU	162	72	90	.444	25	510	588	5336	1233	205	28	66	479	988	.231	.300	.317	.617	94	-41	-31	98	100	505	44	51	46	-17
TOT	813					5577		54913	13351	1995	359	891	4275	9502	.243	.302	.341	.643							704	460	60	-65

TEAM	CG	SH	SV	IP	H	H/G	HR	BB	SO	RAT	ERA	ERA+	OAV	OOB	PR	/A	PF	CPI	FA	E	DP	FW	PW	BW	SBW	DIF
STL	63	30	32	1479[1]	1282	7.8	82	375	971	10.3	2.49	116	.234	.286	82	67	97	105	.978	140	135	-.0	7.7	1.0	1.4	5.9
SF	77	20	16	1469	1302	8.0	86	344	942	10.2	2.71	109	.236	.283	45	38	99	96	.975	162	125	-1.3	4.4	2.4	-.0	1.6
CHI	46	12	32	1453[2]	1399	8.7	138	392	894	11.3	3.41	93	.254	.306	-69	-40	106	100	.981	119	149	1.2	-4.6	-.5	.0	6.8
CIN	24	16	38	1490	1399	8.4	114	573	963	12.2	3.56	89	.250	.324	-96	-66	106	100	.978	144	144	-.2	-7.6	9.8	-1.0	1.0
ATL	44	16	29	1474[2]	1326	8.1	87	362	871	10.5	2.92	103	.241	.292	11	13	100	96	.980	125	139	.9	1.5	.8	.5	-3.7
PIT	42	19	30	1487	1322	8.0	73	485	897	11.2	2.74	107	.240	.306	40	31	98	107	.979	139	162	.0	3.6	3.2	1.2	-9.0
PHI	42	12	27	1448[1]	1416	8.8	91	421	935	11.1	3.36	89	.257	.315	-61	-57	101	100	.980	127	163	.7	-6.5	-2.8	-.7	4.3
LA	38	23	31	1448[2]	1293	8.0	65	414	994	10.8	2.69	103	.241	.300	48	12	93	104	.977	144	144	-.3	-4.6	-2.9	-.3	-2.9
NY	45	25	32	1483[1]	1250	7.6	87	430	1014	10.5	2.72	111	.230	.292	43	49	101	98	.979	133	142	.4	5.6	-10.7	.2	-3.5
HOU	50	12	23	1446[2]	1362	8.5	68	479	1021	11.7	3.26	91	.249	.313	-44	-49	99	96	.975	156	129	-1.0	-5.6	-3.6	-1.2	2.4
TOT	471	185	290	14681		8.2				11.0	2.99		.243	.302					.978	1389	1432					

Runs		Hits		Doubles		Triples		Home Runs		Total Bases	
Beckert-Chi	98	Rose-Cin	210	Brock-StL	46	Brock-StL	14	McCovey-SF	36	Williams-Chi	321
Rose-Cin	94	Alou-Atl	210	Rose-Cin	42	Clemente-Pit	12	Allen-Phi	33	H.Aaron-Atl	302
Perez-Cin	93	Beckert-Chi	189	Bench-Cin	40	Davis-LA	10	Banks-Chi	32	Rose-Cin	294
Brock-StL	92	A.Johnson-Cin	188	Staub-Hou	37	Allen-Phi	9	Williams-Chi	30	Alou-Atl	290
Williams-Chi	91	Flood-StL	186	Alou-Atl	37	Williams-Chi	8	H.Aaron-Atl	29	McCovey-SF	285

Runs Batted In		Runs Produced		Bases On Balls		Batting Average		On Base Percentage		Slugging Average	
McCovey-SF	105	Perez-Cin	167	Santo-Chi	96	Rose-Cin	.335	Rose-Cin	.394	McCovey-SF	.545
Williams-Chi	98	Williams-Chi	159	Wynn-Hou	90	Alou-Pit	.332	McCovey-SF	.383	Allen-Phi	.520
Santo-Chi	98	Santo-Chi	158	Hunt-SF	78	Alou-Atl	.317	Wynn-Hou	.378	Williams-Chi	.500
Perez-Cin	92	McCovey-SF	150	Allen-Phi	74	A.Johnson-Cin	.312	Mays-SF	.376	H.Aaron-Atl	.498
Allen-Phi	90	Allen-Phi	144	Staub-Hou	73	Flood-StL	.301	Staub-Hou	.376	Mays-SF	.488

Production		Adjusted Production		Batter Runs		Adjusted Batter Runs		Clutch Hitting Index		Runs Created	
McCovey-SF	.928	McCovey-SF	176	McCovey-SF	48.8	McCovey-SF	48.9	Hundley-Chi	134	Rose-Cin	113
Allen-Phi	.876	Allen-Phi	160	Rose-Cin	44.5	Wynn-Hou	40.4	Staub-Hou	123	McCovey-SF	110
Mays-SF	.864	Mays-SF	158	H.Aaron-Atl	39.0	H.Aaron-Atl	38.7	Clendenon-Pit	122	Williams-Chi	107
Rose-Cin	.863	Wynn-Hou	158	Wynn-Hou	38.4	Allen-Phi	38.0	Santo-Chi	117	H.Aaron-Atl	104
H.Aaron-Atl	.855	H.Aaron-Atl	154	Allen-Phi	38.0	Rose-Cin	37.8	Swoboda-NY	117	Alou-Atl	103

Total Average		Stolen Bases		Stolen Base Average		Stolen Base Runs		Fielding Runs		Total Player Rating	
McCovey-SF	.953	Brock-StL	62	H.Aaron-Atl	84.8	Brock-StL	11.4	Mazeroski-Pit	25.7	H.Aaron-Atl	5.5
Allen-Phi	.869	Wills-Pit	52	Brock-StL	83.8	H.Aaron-Atl	5.4	Alley-Pit	25.6	McCovey-SF	4.6
Mays-SF	.853	Davis-LA	36	Taylor-Phi	81.5	Davis-LA	4.8	Kessinger-Chi	17.9	Wynn-Hou	4.5
H.Aaron-Atl	.852	H.Aaron-Atl	28	Davis-LA	78.3	Taylor-Phi	3.6	Flood-StL	17.5	Santo-Chi	4.0
Wynn-Hou	.826	Jones-NY	23			Wills-Pit	3.0	Santo-Chi	17.3	Clemente-Pit	3.9

Wins		Win Percentage		Games		Complete Games		Shutouts		Saves	
Marichal-SF	26	Blass-Pit	.750	Abernathy-Cin	78	Marichal-SF	30	Gibson-StL	13	Regan-LA-Chi	25
Gibson-StL	22	Marichal-SF	.743	Regan-LA-Chi	73	Gibson-StL	28	Drysdale-LA	8	Carroll-Atl-Cin	17
Jenkins-Chi	20	Gibson-StL	.710	Carroll-Atl-Cin	68	Jenkins-Chi	20	Koosman-NY	7	Hoerner-StL	17
		Briles-StL	.633	Taylor-NY	58	Perry-SF	19	Blass-Pit	7	Brewer-LA	14
				Linzy-SF	57	Koosman-NY	17				

Innings Pitched		Fewest Hits/Game		Fewest BB/Game		Strikeouts		Strikeouts/Game		Ratio	
Marichal-SF	326.0	Gibson-StL	5.85	Hands-Chi	1.25	Gibson-StL	268	Singer-LA	7.97	Gibson-StL	7.89
Jenkins-Chi	308.0	Bolin-SF	6.52	Marichal-SF	1.27	Jenkins-Chi	260	Gibson-StL	7.92	Jarvis-Atl	8.93
Gibson-StL	304.2	Veale-Pit	6.86	Seaver-NY	1.56	Singer-LA	227	Maloney-Cin	7.87	Bolin-SF	9.07
Perry-SF	291.0	Jarvis-Atl	7.10	Pappas-Cin-Atl	1.57	Marichal-SF	218	Jenkins-Chi	7.60	Seaver-NY	9.08
Seaver-NY	277.2	Moose-Pit	7.14	Niekro-Atl	1.58	Sadecki-SF	206	Wilson-Hou	7.55	Hands-Chi	9.15

Earned Run Average		Adjusted ERA		Opponents' Batting Avg.		Opponents' On Base Pct.		Starter Runs		Adjusted Starter Runs	
Gibson-StL	1.12	Gibson-StL	258	Gibson-StL	.184	Gibson-StL	.233	Gibson-StL	63.1	Gibson-StL	60.0
Bolin-SF	1.99	Bolin-SF	148	Bolin-SF	.200	Jarvis-Atl	.255	Koosman-NY	26.5	Koosman-NY	27.5
Veale-Pit	2.05	Koosman-NY	145	Veale-Pit	.211	Bolin-SF	.258	Veale-Pit	25.4	Seaver-NY	25.2
Koosman-NY	2.08	Veale-Pit	142	Jarvis-Atl	.214	Seaver-NY	.262	Seaver-NY	24.1	Veale-Pit	23.8
Blass-Pit	2.12	Blass-Pit	138	Moose-Pit	.218	Hands-Chi	.264	Drysdale-LA	22.3	Blass-Pit	19.6

Clutch Pitching Index		Relief Runs		Adjusted Relief Runs		Relief Ranking		Total Pitcher Index		Total Baseball Ranking	
Blass-Pit	125	Kline-Pit	16.4	Kline-Pit	15.6	Kline-Pit	23.4	Gibson-StL	7.3	Gibson-StL	7.3
Briles-StL	124	Regan-LA-Chi	10.7	Regan-LA-Chi	13.0	Regan-LA-Chi	20.1	Seaver-NY	3.1	H.Aaron-Atl	5.5
Koosman-NY	123	Linzy-SF	9.4	Abernathy-Cin	10.3	Linzy-SF	17.0	Koosman-NY	3.0	McCovey-SF	4.6
Lemaster-Hou	122	Grant-LA	9.4	Linzy-SF	9.0	Abernathy-Cin	13.9	Marichal-SF	2.7	Wynn-Hou	4.5
Drysdale-LA	117	Abernathy-Cin	7.7	Carroll-Atl-Cin	7.2	Upshaw-Atl	9.6	Kline-Pit	2.4	Santo-Chi	4.0

March 21 Royals is chosen as the name of the new Kansas City AL franchise.

March 31 The name for Seattle's AL club is the Pilots.

May 9 Oakland's Jim "Catfish" Hunter pitches a perfect game against the Twins, winning 3-0. The 22-year-old right-hander hurls the first AL regular season perfecto in 46 years. He strikes out 11 and drives in all three A's runs.

May 15 The first AL game played in Milwaukee since 1901 is a 4-2 California win against Chicago before 23,403 fans. This is the first of nine games the White Sox will play in Milwaukee in 1968.

May 18 Frank Howard ties the AL record with a home run in his sixth consecutive game to lead Washington to an 8-4 win over Detroit. For Detroit, Al Kaline belts a pinch home run off Steve Jones. For Kaline, it is his 307th home run, surpassing Hank Greenberg's 306 in a Tiger uniform.

July 3 Luis Tiant registers 19 strikeouts in 10 innings, as Cleveland beats Minnesota 1-0.

July 24 Hoyt Wilhelm's 907th game breaks Cy Young's record for major league pitching appearances, but he loses a 2-1 decision to Oakland.

September 14 Denny McLain becomes the first 30-game winner since Dizzy Dean in 1934, as the Tigers beat the A's 5-4. Denny gives up six hits and strikes out 10.

September 17 Detroit clinches the AL pennant with a 2-1 win over the Yankees.

September 19 Denny McLain's 31st win is overshadowed by Mickey Mantle's 535th home run. McLain says he purposely fed a belt-high fastball to the aging slugger. The home run gives Mantle undisputed hold of third place on the all-time home run list.

September 22 Cesar Tovar becomes the second player to play every position in a game. Minnesota's all-purpose star leads the Twins to a 2-1 win over the Oakland A's. Bert Campaneris of the Kansas City A's was the first to pull off this stunt in 1965.

September 29 Carl Yastrzemski maintains a .3005 batting average, to win his second straight batting crown with the lowest championship average ever. Yaz is the AL's only .300 hitter: Oakland's Danny Cater is second with .290.

September 29 White Sox relief pitcher

Wilbur Wood ends his season with a 7-6 win at California and a major league record 88 appearances.

October 9 Denny McLain returns to form, scattering nine singles, as Detroit evens the World Series with a 10-run third inning and 13-1 win at St. Louis in Game 6.

October 10 Mickey Lolich bests Bob Gibson and brings Detroit its first World Series championship since 1945. The hefty lefty hurls a five-hitter, giving Detroit a 4-1 win.

October 15 Roger Nelson is the initial choice of the Royals in the AL expansion draft. Don Mincher is the Pilots' first choice. Other Seattle selections include Tommy Harper, Tommy Davis, Gary Bell, and Lou Piniella. Kansas City chooses Wally Bunker, Moe Drabowsky, Hoyt Wilhelm, and Joe Foy.

November 1 Denny McLain is the unanimous AL winner of the Cy Young Award.

November 5 Denny McLain is the unanimous choice as AL MVP.

November 19 Yankees pitcher Stan Bahnsen, who was 17-12, is named AL Rookie of the Year.

BALTIMORE		BOSTON		CALIFORNIA		CHICAGO		CLEVELAND	
M	H.Bauer	M	D.Williams	M	B.Rigney	M	E.Stanky	M	A.Dark
M	E.Weaver	1B	G.Scott	1B	D.Mincher	M	L.Moss	1B	T.Horton
1B	B.Powell	2B	M.Andrews	2B	B.Knoop	M	L.Moss	2B	V.Fuller
2B	D.Johnson	SS	R.Petrocelli	SS	J.Fregosi	M	A.Lopez	SS	L.Brown
SS	M.Belanger	3B	J.Foy	3B	A.Rodriguez	M	A.Lopez	3B	M.Alvis
3B	B.Robinson	LF	C.Yastrzemski	LF	R.Reichardt	1B	T.McCraw	LF	L.Maye
LF	C.Blefary	CF	R.Smith	CF	V.Davalillo	2B	S.Alomar	CF	J.Cardenal
CF	P.Blair	RF	K.Harrelson	RF	R.Repoz	SS	L.Aparicio	RF	T.Harper
RF	F.Robinson	C	R.Gibson	C	B.Rodgers	3B	P.Ward	C	J.Azcue
C	A.Etchebarren					LF	T.Davis		
		12	D.Jones	1O	C.Hinton	CF	K.Berry	23	C.Salmon
O2	D.Buford	S2	J.Adair	C2	T.Satriano	RF	B.Bradford	C1	D.Sims
O	C.Motton	C	E.Howard	3	P.Schaal	C	D.Josephson	O	R.Snyder
								O	L.Johnson
P	D.McNally	P	R.Culp	P	G.Brunet	P	J.Horlen	P	S.McDowell
P	J.Hardin	P	G.Bell	P	J.McGlothlin	P	J.Fisher	P	L.Tiant
P	T.Phoebus	P	D.Ellsworth	P	S.Ellis	P	T.John	P	S.Siebert
P	D.Leonhard	P	J.Santiago	P	C.Wright	P	G.Peters	P	S.Williams
P	G.Brabender	P	J.Lonborg	P	T.Murphy	P	C.Carlos	P	S.Hargan
RP	E.Watt	RP	L.Stange	RP	M.Pattin	RP	W.Wood	RP	E.Fisher
RP	P.Richert	RP	S.Lyle	RP	A.Messersmith	RP	H.Wilhelm	RP	M.Paul
RP	M.Drabowsky	RP	B.Landis	RP	T.Burgmeier	RP	B.Locker	RP	V.Romo
P	W.Bunker	P	J.Pizarro	P	R.Clark	P	B.Priddy		
P	R.Nelson	P	G.Waslewski	P	M.Rojas				
		P	J.Stephenson						
		P	D.Morehead						

DETROIT		MINNESOTA		NEW YORK		OAKLAND		WASHINGTON	
M	M.Smith	M	C.Ermer	M	R.Houk	M	B.Kennedy	M	J.Lemon
1B	N.Cash	1B	R.Reese	1B	M.Mantle	1B	D.Cater	1B	M.Epstein
2B	D.McAuliffe	2B	R.Carew	2B	H.Clarke	2B	J.Donaldson	2B	B.Allen
SS	R.Oyler	SS	J.Hernandez	SS	T.Tresh	SS	B.Campaneris	SS	R.Hansen
3B	D.Wert	3B	C.Tovar	3B	B.Cox	3B	S.Bando	3B	K.McMullen
LF	W.Horton	LF	B.Allison	LF	R.White	LF	M.Hershberger	LF	F.Howard
CF	M.Stanley	CF	T.Uhlaender	CF	B.Robinson	CF	R.Monday	CF	D.Unser
RF	J.Northrup	RF	T.Oliva	RF	A.Kosco	RF	R.Jackson	RF	E.Stroud
C	B.Freehan	C	J.Roseboro	C	J.Gibbs	C	D.Duncan	C	P.Casanova
O1	A.Kaline	3S	R.Clark	O1	J.Pepitone	2	D.Green	O	C.Peterson
S2	T.Matchick	13	H.Killebrew						
S3	D.Tracewski	23	F.Quilici	P	M.Stottlemyre	P	C.Hunter	P	J.Coleman
		3	R.Rollins	P	S.Bahnsen	P	B.Odom	P	C.Pascual
P	D.McLain			P	F.Peterson	P	J.Nash	P	J.Hannan
P	E.Wilson	P	D.Chance	P	S.Barber	P	C.Dobson	P	D.Bosman
P	M.Lolich	P	J.Merritt	P	F.Talbot	P	L.Krausse	P	F.Bertaina
P	J.Sparma	P	J.Kaat	RP	J.Verbanic	RP	D.Segui	RP	D.Higgins
P	J.Hiller	P	D.Boswell	RP	D.Womack	RP	J.Aker	RP	B.Humphreys
RP	P.Dobson	P	J.Perry	RP	L.McDaniel	RP	E.Sprague		
RP	D.Patterson	RP	R.Perranoski					P	B.Moore
		RP	A.Worthington	P	B.Monbouquette	P	P.Lindblad	P	P.Ortega
		RP	B.Miller	P	A.Downing				
				P	S.Hamilton				
		P	J.Roland						

TEAM	G	W	L	PCT	GB	R	OR	AB	H	2B	3B	HR	BB	SO	AVG	OBP	SLG	PRO	PRO+	BR	/A	PF	CHI	RC	SB	CS	SBA	SBR
DET	164	103	59	.636		**671**	492	5490	1292	190	39	**185**	521	964	.235	.309	**.385**	**.694**	114	**102**	82	103	100	**646**	26	32	45	-11
BAL	162	91	71	.562	12	579	497	5275	1187	**215**	28	133	570	1019	.225	.306	.352	.658	106	41	40	100	97	585	78	32	**71**	4
CLE	162	86	75	.534	16.5	516	504	5416	1266	210	36	75	427	858	.234	.294	.327	.621	96	-34	-26	99	100	525	115	61	65	-2
BOS	162	86	76	.531	17	614	611	5303	1253	207	17	125	**582**	974	.236	**.316**	.352	.668	102	62	21	107	99	590	76	62	55	-14
NY	164	83	79	.512	20	536	531	5310	1137	154	34	109	566	958	.214	.293	.318	.611	95	-46	-30	97	**106**	507	90	50	64	-3
OAK	163	82	80	.506	21	569	544	5406	**1300**	192	40	94	472	1022	**.240**	.306	.343	.649	108	19	47	95	99	580	**147**	61	71	8
MIN	162	79	83	.488	24	562	546	5373	1274	207	**41**	105	445	966	.237	.301	.350	.651	99	20	-8	105	99	564	98	54	64	-3
CAL	162	67	95	.414	36	498	615	5331	1209	170	33	83	447	1080	.227	.293	.318	.611	96	-51	-33	96	100	498	62	50	55	-11
CHI	162	67	95	.414	36	463	527	5405	1233	169	33	71	397	**840**	.228	.286	.311	.597	86	-82	-87	101	99	480	90	50	64	-3
WAS	161	65	96	.404	37.5	524	665	5400	1208	160	37	124	454	960	.224	.289	.336	.625	99	-31	-14	97	101	518	29	19	60	-3
TOT	812					5532		53709	12359	1874	338	1104	4881	9641	.230	.299	.339	.639						811	471	63	-39	

TEAM	CG	SH	SV	IP	H	H/G	HR	BB	SO	RAT	ERA	ERA+	OAV	OOB	PR	/A	PF	CPI	FA	E	DP	FW	PW	BW	SBW	DIF
DET	**59**	19	29	1489²	1180	7.1	129	486	1115	10.3	2.71	111	.217	**.285**	44	49	101	100	**.983**	105	133	2.0	5.6	9.4	-.8	5.8
BAL	53	16	31	1451¹	1111	6.9	101	502	1044	**10.3**	2.66	110	.212	.287	51	43	98	96	.981	120	131	1.0	4.9	4.6	.9	-1.5
CLE	48	**23**	32	1464¹	**1087**	6.7	98	540	**1157**	10.3	2.66	111	.206	.286	**53**	49	99	93	.979	127	130	.6	**5.6**	-3.0	.2	2.0
BOS	55	17	31	1447	1303	8.1	115	523	972	11.7	3.33	95	.241	.313	-57	-28	106	100	.979	128	147	.6	-3.2	2.4	-1.2	6.4
NY	45	14	27	1467¹	1308	8.0	99	424	831	10.8	2.79	104	.240	.298	31	18	97	108	.979	139	142	.0	2.1	-3.4	.1	3.3
OAK	45	18	29	1455²	1220	7.5	124	505	997	10.9	2.94	96	.227	.297	6	-20	95	101	.977	145	136	-.4	-2.3	5.4	**1.4**	-3.1
MIN	46	14	29	1433¹	1224	7.7	**92**	**414**	996	10.5	2.89	107	.229	.290	13	31	104	94	.973	130	117	-2.0	3.6	-.9	.1	-2.8
CAL	29	11	31	1437	1234	7.7	131	519	869	11.2	3.43	85	.233	.306	-72	-83	98	94	.977	140	**156**	-.2	-9.5	-3.8	-.8	.3
CHI	20	11	**40**	1468	1290	7.9	97	451	834	11.1	2.75	110	.236	.303	38	46	102	**110**	.977	151	152	-.8	5.3	-10.0	.1	-8.6
WAS	26	11	28	1439²	1402	8.8	118	517	826	12.3	3.64	80	.258	.327	-106	-116	98	104	.976	148	144	-.7	-13.3	-1.6	.1	.0
TOT	426	154	307	14553¹		7.6				10.9	2.98		.230	.299					.978	1373	1388					

Runs		Hits		Doubles		Triples		Home Runs		Total Bases	
McAuliffe-Det	95	Campaneris-Oak	177	Smith-Bos	37	Fregosi-Cal	13	F.Howard-Was	44	F.Howard-Was	330
Yastrzemski-Bos	90	Tovar-Min	167	B.Robinson-Bal	36	McCraw-Chi	12	Horton-Det	36	Horton-Det	278
White-NY	89	F.Howard-Was	164	Yastrzemski-Bos	32	Stroud-Was	11	Harrelson-Bos	35	Harrelson-Bos	277
Tovar-Min	89	Aparicio-Chi	164	Tovar-Min	31	McAuliffe-Det	10	Jackson-Oak	29	Yastrzemski-Bos	267
Stanley-Det	88	Yastrzemski-Bos	162			Campaneris-Oak	9			Northrup-Det	259

Runs Batted In		Runs Produced		Bases On Balls		Batting Average		On Base Percentage		Slugging Average	
Harrelson-Bos	109	Harrelson-Bos	153	Yastrzemski-Bos	119	Yastrzemski-Bos	.301	Yastrzemski-Bos	.429	F.Howard-Was	.552
F.Howard-Was	106	Northrup-Det	145	Mantle-NY	106	Cater-Oak	.290	F.Robinson-Bal	.391	Horton-Det	.543
Northrup-Det	90	Yastrzemski-Bos	141	Foy-Bos	84	Oliva-Min	.289	Mantle-NY	.387	Harrelson-Bos	.518
Powell-Bal	85	F.Howard-Was	141	McAuliffe-Det	82	Horton-Det	.285	Monday-Oak	.373	Yastrzemski-Bos	.495
Horton-Det	85	Stanley-Det	137	Andrews-Bos	81	Uhlaender-Min	.283	Andrews-Bos	.369	Oliva-Min	.477

Production		Adjusted Production		Batter Runs		Adjusted Batter Runs		Clutch Hitting Index		Runs Created	
Yastrzemski-Bos	.924	F.Howard-Was	172	Yastrzemski-Bos	57.5	Yastrzemski-Bos	49.9	Foy-Bos	118	Yastrzemski-Bos	121
Horton-Det	.900	Yastrzemski-Bos	168	F.Howard-Was	45.1	F.Howard-Was	48.5	Cater-Oak	116	F.Howard-Was	110
F.Howard-Was	.892	Horton-Det	165	Horton-Det	41.1	Horton-Det	38.3	Powell-Bal	113	Horton-Det	95
Harrelson-Bos	.877	Harrelson-Bos	153	Harrelson-Bos	40.2	Harrelson-Bos	34.0	Tresh-NY	111	Harrelson-Bos	94
Oliva-Min	.837	F.Robinson-Bal	153	Freehan-Det	32.7	Freehan-Det	30.0	Harrelson-Bos	111	Freehan-Det	94

Total Average		Stolen Bases		Stolen Base Average		Stolen Base Runs		Fielding Runs		Total Player Rating	
Yastrzemski-Bos	1.000	Campaneris-Oak	62	McCraw-Chi	80.0	Campaneris-Oak	5.4	Clarke-NY	29.5	Yastrzemski-Bos	6.6
F.Howard-Was	.872	Cardenal-Cle	40	Nelson-Cle	76.7	McCraw-Chi	3.0	Aparicio-Chi	24.7	Freehan-Det	4.8
Horton-Det	.867	Tovar-Min	35	Foy-Bos	76.5	Foy-Bos	3.0	Unser-Was	18.8	F.Howard-Was	4.6
F.Robinson-Bal	.865	Buford-Bal	27	Clarke-NY	74.1	Tovar-Min	2.7	Yastrzemski-Bos	17.3	Campaneris-Oak	3.8
Harrelson-Bos	.835	Foy-Bos	26	Campaneris-Oak	73.8	Nelson-Cle	2.7	B.Robinson-Bal	16.6	Aparicio-Chi	3.7

Wins		Win Percentage		Games		Complete Games		Shutouts		Saves	
McLain-Det	31	McLain-Det	.838	Wood-Chi	88	McLain-Det	28	Tiant-Cle	9	Worthington-Min	18
McNally-Bal	22	Culp-Bos	.727	Wilhelm-Chi	72	Tiant-Cle	19			Wood-Chi	16
Tiant-Cle	21	Tiant-Cle	.700	Locker-Chi	70	Stottlemyre-NY	19			Higgins-Was	13
Stottlemyre-NY	21	Ellsworth-Bos	.696	Perranoski-Min	66	McNally-Bal	18				
Hardin-Bal	18	McNally-Bal	.688			Hardin-Bal	16				

Innings Pitched		Fewest Hits/Game		Fewest BB/Game		Strikeouts		Strikeouts/Game		Ratio	
McLain-Det	336.0	Tiant-Cle	5.30	Peterson-NY	1.23	McDowell-Cle	283	McDowell-Cle	9.47	McNally-Bal	7.91
Chance-Min	292.0	McNally-Bal	5.77	McLain-Det	1.69	McLain-Det	280	Tiant-Cle	9.20	Tiant-Cle	7.98
Stottlemyre-NY	278.2	McDowell-Cle	6.06	Ellsworth-Bos	1.70	Tiant-Cle	264	Lolich-Det	8.06	McLain-Det	8.30
McNally-Bal	273.0	Siebert-Cle	6.33	Kaat-Min	1.73	Chance-Min	234	Culp-Bos	7.90	Chance-Min	9.15
McDowell-Cle	269.0	McLain-Det	6.46	McNally-Bal	1.81	McNally-Bal	202	McLain-Det	7.50	Peterson-NY	9.32

Earned Run Average		Adjusted ERA		Opponents' Batting Avg.		Opponents' On Base Pct.		Starter Runs		Adjusted Starter Runs	
Tiant-Cle	1.60	Tiant-Cle	185	Tiant-Cle	.168	Tiant-Cle	.233	Tiant-Cle	39.5	McLain-Det	39.3
McDowell-Cle	1.81	McDowell-Cle	164	McNally-Bal	.182	McNally-Bal	.234	McLain-Det	38.2	Tiant-Cle	38.9
McNally-Bal	1.95	McLain-Det	154	McDowell-Cle	.189	McLain-Det	.243	McDowell-Cle	35.0	McDowell-Cle	34.4
McLain-Det	1.96	John-Chi	153	Siebert-Cle	.198	Chance-Min	.261	McNally-Bal	31.4	McNally-Bal	29.7
John-Chi	1.98	McNally-Bal	150	McLain-Det	.200	Nash-Oak	.270	Bahnsen-NY	27.5	Bahnsen-NY	25.2

Clutch Pitching Index		Relief Runs		Adjusted Relief Runs		Relief Ranking		Total Pitcher Index		Total Baseball Ranking	
Horlen-Chi	133	Wood-Chi	19.6	Wood-Chi	20.5	Wood-Chi	33.6	McLain-Det	4.9	Yastrzemski-Bos	6.6
John-Chi	119	Wilhelm-Chi	13.0	Wilhelm-Chi	13.5	Romo-Cle	14.7	Tiant-Cle	4.2	McLain-Det	4.9
Fisher-Chi	116	Romo-Cle	12.6	Romo-Cle	12.4	Wilhelm-Chi	14.3	McDowell-Cle	4.0	Freehan-Det	4.8
McDowell-Cle	113	McMahon-Chi-Det	9.0	McMahon-Chi-Det	9.4	Drabowsky-Bal	9.9	McNally-Bal	3.9	F.Howard-Was	4.6
Bahnsen-NY	111	Drabowsky-Bal	7.3	Locker-Chi	7.4	Locker-Chi	8.5	Wood-Chi	3.9	Tiant-Cle	4.2

January 21 Stan Musial and Roy Campanella are voted into the Hall of Fame by BBWAA members.

February 2 Stan Coveleski and Waite Hoyt are voted into the Hall of Fame by the Veterans Committee.

February 4 Attorney Bowie Kuhn is a compromise choice for commissioner and is elected on a temporary basis.

June 29 On Billy Williams Day in Chicago, the Cubs outfielder passes Stan Musial's NL record for consecutive games played (896).

July 9 With one out in the ninth, Chicago's Jimmy Qualls bloops a single to left-center field, the only blemish on Tom Seaver's 4-0, near-perfect win before a record crowd (59,083) at Shea Stadium.

July 23 Willie McCovey hits two homers as the NL beats the AL, 9-3, for its seventh straight All-Star Game win. Mel Stottlemyre starts for the AL when Denny McLain is late arriving from a dental appointment.

August 11 Don Drysdale retires because of damage to his right shoulder. Drysdale is the last Brooklyn Dodger active with the Los Angeles Dodgers.

August 13 Commissioner Bowie Kuhn is elected for a seven-year term.

September 13 Bobby Bonds becomes the fourth 30-homer, 30-steal player in major league history. His 32nd steal, on Aug. 13, erased Willie Mays' San Francisco record of 31.

September 15 Steve Carlton of the Cardinals fans a major league-record 19 batters and still loses. Ron Swoboda hits a pair of two-run home runs, and New York beats St. Louis 4-3.

September 22 Willie Mays joins Babe Ruth in the 600-homer club, while batting for rookie George Foster. Bobby Bonds sets a major league record with his 176th strikeout, as San Francisco beats San Diego, 4-2.

October 6 New York rallies twice and wins the first National League Championship Series. Tommie Agee, Ken Boswell, and Wayne Garrett hit homers in a 7-4 win.

October 15 A memorable World Series game pits Tom Seaver against Mike Cuellar. Right fielder Ron Swoboda's dive at Brooks Robinson's sinking liner with runners at first base and third in the ninth results in a brilliant catch, even though Frank Robinson tags and scores the tying run. In the 10th, pinch-hitter J. C. Martin, running illegally inside the first base line, is hit on the wrist by pitcher Pete Richert's errant throw, enabling pinch-runner Rod Gaspar to score from second as the Mets win, 2-1.

October 16 In Game 5 Cleon Jones, awarded first base when shoe polish on the ball proves he was hit by a pitch, scores on Donn Clendenon's home run. Al Weis' home run an inning later ties the game. Ron Swoboda's double and two Baltimore errors in the eighth give New York a 5-3 win and the Series. Jerry Koosman completes the Mets achievement with a five-hitter.

October 29 Tom Seaver is voted the NL Cy Young Award.

November 20 San Francisco's Willie McCovey edges Tom Seaver as NL MVP.

November 28 Second baseman Ted Sizemore becomes the seventh Dodger to win NL Rookie honors.

	ATLANTA		CHICAGO		CINCINNATI		HOUSTON		LOS ANGELES		MONTREAL
M	L.Harris	M	L.Durocher	M	D.Bristol	M	H.Walker	M	W.Alston	M	G.Mauch
1B	O.Cepeda	1B	E.Banks	1B	L.May	1B	C.Blefary	1B	W.Parker	1B	B.Bailey
2B	F.Millan	2B	G.Beckert	2B	T.Helms	2B	J.Morgan	2B	T.Sizemore	2B	G.Sutherland
SS	S.Jackson	SS	D.Kessinger	SS	W.Woodward	SS	D.Menke	SS	M.Wills	SS	B.Wine
3B	C.Boyer	3B	R.Santo	3B	T.Perez	3B	D.Rader	3B	B.Sudakis	3B	C.Laboy
LF	T.Gonzalez	LF	B.Williams	LF	A.Johnson	LF	J.Alou	LF	W.Crawford	LF	M.Jones
CF	F.Alou	CF	D.Young	CF	B.Tolan	CF	J.Wynn	CF	W.Davis	CF	A.Phillips
RF	H.Aaron	RF	J.Hickman	RF	P.Rose	RF	N.Miller	RF	A.Kosco	RF	R.Staub
C	B.Didier	C	R.Hundley	C	J.Bench	C	J.Edwards	C	T.Haller	C	R.Brand
O	R.Carty	O1	W.Smith	O2	J.Stewart	P	L.Dierker	O	B.Russell	O1	T.Cline
O	M.Lum	O	A.Spangler	S	D.Chaney	P	D.Lemaster	O	M.Mota	1O	R.Fairly
S	G.Garrido					P	D.Wilson	32	J.Lefebvre	C	J.Bateman
		P	F.Jenkins	P	J.Merritt	P	T.Griffin				
P	P.Niekro	P	B.Hands	P	T.Cloninger	RP	J.Ray	P	C.Osteen	P	B.Stoneman
P	R.Reed	P	K.Holtzman	P	J.Maloney	RP	J.Billingham	P	B.Singer	P	J.Robertson
P	P.Jarvis	P	D.Selma	P	J.Fisher	RP	F.Gladding	P	D.Sutton	P	M.Wegener
P	G.Stone	RP	P.Regan	P	G.Nolan			P	A.Foster	P	G.Waslewski
P	M.Pappas	RP	T.Abernathy	RP	C.Carroll	P	W.Blasingame	RP	J.Brewer	P	H.Reed
RP	C.Upshaw	RP	R.Nye	RP	W.Granger	P	D.Womack	RP	P.Mikkelsen	RP	D.McGinn
RP	G.Neibauer			RP	P.Ramos			RP	J.Moeller	RP	D.Shaw
RP	C.Raymond									RP	R.Face
				P	G.Culver			P	D.Drysdale		
P	J.Britton			P	G.Arrigo			/P	J.Bunning	P	S.Renko
										P	L.Jaster
										P	M.Grant

	NEW YORK		PHILADELPHIA		PITTSBURGH		SAN DIEGO		SAN FRANCISCO		ST.LOUIS
M	G.Hodges	M	B.Skinner	M	L.Shepard	M	P.Gomez	M	C.King	M	R.Schoendienst
1B	E.Kranepool	M	G.Myatt	M	A.Grammas	1B	N.Colbert	1B	W.McCovey	1B	J.Torre
2B	K.Boswell	1B	D.Allen	1B	A.Oliver	2B	J.Arcia	2B	R.Hunt	2B	J.Javier
SS	B.Harrelson	2B	C.Rojas	2B	B.Mazeroski	SS	T.Dean	SS	H.Lanier	SS	D.Maxvill
3B	W.Garrett	SS	D.Money	SS	F.Patek	3B	E.Spiezio	3B	J.Davenport	3B	M.Shannon
LF	C.Jones	3B	T.Taylor	3B	R.Hebner	LF	A.Ferrara	LF	K.Henderson	LF	L.Brock
CF	T.Agee	LF	J.Briggs	LF	W.Stargell	CF	C.Gaston	CF	W.Mays	CF	C.Flood
RF	R.Swoboda	CF	L.Hisle	CF	M.Alou	RF	O.Brown	RF	B.Bonds	RF	V.Pinson
C	J.Grote	RF	J.Callison	RF	R.Clemente	C	C.Cannizzaro	C	D.Dietz	C	T.McCarver
		C	M.Ryan	C	M.Sanguillen						
O	R.Gaspar					O	I.Murrell	1O	B.Burda	P	B.Gibson
O	A.Shamsky	O3	D.Johnson	3O	J.Pagan	S2	R.Pena	O	D.Marshall	P	S.Carlton
S2	A.Weis	31	R.Joseph	O1	C.Taylor	2	J.Sipin	23	D.Mason	P	N.Briles
32	B.Pfeil	O	R.Stone	2S	G.Alley	32	V.Kelly	O	J.Hart	P	R.Washburn
1	D.Clendenon	S2	T.Harmon							P	C.Taylor
P	T.Seaver	P	G.Jackson	P	B.Veale	P	C.Kirby	P	G.Perry	RP	M.Grant
P	J.Koosman	P	W.Fryman	P	D.Ellis	P	J.Niekro	P	J.Marichal	RP	J.Hoerner
P	G.Gentry	P	R.Wise	P	S.Blass	P	A.Santorini	P	M.McCormick		
P	D.Cardwell	P	J.Johnson	P	B.Moose	P	D.Kelley	P	B.Bolin	P	M.Torrez
P	J.McAndrew	P	B.Champion	RP	C.Hartenstein	RP	T.Sisk	P	R.Sadecki	P	D.Giusti
RP	T.McGraw	RP	J.Boozer	RP	B.Dal Canton	RP	G.Ross	RP	F.Linzy		
RP	C.Koonce	RP	T.Farrell	RP	J.Gibbon	RP	F.Reberger	RP	R.Herbel		
RP	R.Taylor	RP	A.Raffo			P	J.Baldschun	P	R.Bryant		
		P	L.Walker			P	J.Podres				
P	N.Ryan	P	L.Palmer			P	B.McCool				
P	J.DiLauro	P	B.Wilson								

TEAM	G	W	L	PCT	GB	R	OR	AB	H	2B	3B	HR	BB	SO	AVG	OBP	SLG	PRO	PRO+	BR	/A	PF	CHI	RC	SB	CS	SBA	SBR
EAST																												
NY	162	100	62	.617		632	541	5427	1311	184	41	109	527	1089	.242	.313	.351	.664	91	-52	-65	102	**105**	601	66	43	61	-6
CHI	163	92	70	.568	8	720	611	5530	1400	215	40	142	559	928	.253	.326	.384	.710	94	37	-53	113	102	693	30	32	48	-10
PIT	162	88	74	.543	12	725	652	5626	1557	220	**52**	119	454	944	**.277**	.336	.398	.734	115	84	**100**	98	97	742	74	34	**69**	2
STL	162	87	75	.537	13	595	**540**	5536	1403	**228**	44	90	503	876	.253	.318	.359	.677	96	-25	-27	100	94	632	87	49	64	-3
PHI	162	63	99	.389	37	645	745	5408	1304	227	35	137	549	1130	.241	.314	.372	.686	102	-12	5	97	101	629	73	49	60	-8
MON	162	52	110	.321	48	582	791	5419	1300	227	33	125	529	962	.240	.312	.359	.671	94	-40	-42	100	96	596	52	52	50	-16
WEST																												
ATL	162	93	69	.574		691	631	5460	1411	195	22	141	485	**665**	.258	.323	.380	.703	104	20	18	100	103	655	59	48	55	-11
SF	162	90	72	.556	3	713	636	5474	1325	187	28	136	711	1054	.242	.336	.361	.697	104	32	45	98	100	690	71	32	**69**	2
CIN	163	89	73	.549	4	798	768	5634	**1558**	224	42	**171**	474	1042	**.277**	.338	.422	.760	114	**133**	92	105	99	**791**	79	56	59	-10
LA	162	85	77	.525	8	645	561	5532	1405	185	**52**	97	484	823	.254	.316	.359	.675	103	-31	13	93	103	626	80	51	61	-7
HOU	162	81	81	.500	12	676	668	5348	1284	204	40	104	499	972	.240	.332	.352	.684	101	7	20	98	101	649	**101**	58	64	-5
SD	162	52	110	.321	41	468	746	5357	1203	180	42	99	423	1143	.225	.286	.329	.615	81	-153	-134	96	98	491	45	44	51	-13
TOT	973					7890		65751	16461	2455	471	1470	6397	11628	.250	.321	.369	.690							817	548	60	-84

TEAM	CG	SH	SV	IP	H	H/G	HR	BB	SO	RAT	ERA	ERA+	OAV	OOB	PR	/A	PF	CPI	FA	E	DP	FW	PW	BW	SBW	DIF
EAST																										
NY	51	**28**	35	1468¹	**1217**	7.5	119	517	1012	**10.8**	2.99	122	**.227**	.298	99	109	102	99	.980	122	146	1.4	11.4	-6.8	.1	12.9
CHI	58	22	27	1454¹	1366	8.5	118	475	1017	11.6	3.34	120	.248	.311	41	110	112	101	.979	136	149	.6	**11.5**	-5.6	-.3	4.7
PIT	39	9	33	1445²	1348	8.4	**96**	553	1124	12.1	3.61	97	.248	.322	-3	-20	97	95	.975	155	169	-.5	-2.1	**10.5**	.9	-1.9
STL	63	12	26	1460¹	1289	7.9	99	511	1004	11.3	**2.94**	121	.237	.307	**106**	102	99	**105**	.978	138	144	.5	10.7	-2.8	.4	-2.8
PHI	47	14	21	1434	1494	9.4	134	570	921	13.2	4.14	86	.270	.342	-88	-96	99	102	.978	137	157	.5	-10.1	.5	-.1	-8.9
MON	26	8	21	1426	1429	9.0	145	702	973	13.8	4.33	85	.263	.353	-117	-104	102	102	.971	184	**179**	-2.1	-10.9	-4.4	-.9	-10.6
WEST																										
ATL	38	7	42	1445	1334	8.3	144	438	893	11.2	3.53	102	.245	.304	11	13	100	95	**.981**	115	114	**1.8**	1.4	1.9	-.4	7.4
SF	**71**	15	17	1473²	1381	8.4	120	461	906	11.5	3.26	108	.248	.309	55	40	97	102	.974	169	155	-1.3	4.2	4.7	**.9**	.4
CIN	23	11	**44**	1465	1478	9.1	149	611	818	13.2	4.11	92	.262	.340	-84	-57	105	102	.974	167	158	-1.1	-6.0	9.7	-.3	5.8
LA	47	20	31	1457	1324	8.2	122	**420**	975	11.0	3.08	108	.242	.301	83	39	93	102	.980	126	130	1.2	4.1	1.4	.0	-2.6
HOU	52	11	34	1435²	1347	8.4	111	547	**1221**	12.1	3.60	98	.247	.319	-1	-9	99	96	.975	153	136	-.4	-.9	2.1	.2	-1.0
SD	16	9	25	1422¹	1454	9.2	113	592	764	13.2	4.24	83	.267	.343	-102	-111	98	97	.975	156	140	-.5	-11.7	-14.1	-.6	-2.2
TOT	531	166	356	17387¹		8.5				12.1	3.59		.250	.321					.977	1758	1777					

Runs		Hits		Doubles		Triples		Home Runs		Total Bases	
Rose-Cin	120	Alou-Pit	231	Alou-Pit	41	Clemente-Pit	12	McCovey-SF	45	H.Aaron-Atl	332
Bonds-SF	120	Rose-Cin	218	Kessinger-Chi	38	Rose-Cin	11	H.Aaron-Atl	44	Perez-Cin	331
Wynn-Hou	113	Brock-StL	195	Williams-Chi	33	Williams-Chi	10	May-Cin	38	McCovey-SF	322
Kessinger-Chi	109	Tolan-Cin	194	Rose-Cin	33	Tolan-Cin	10	Perez-Cin	37	Rose-Cin	321
Alou-Pit	105	Williams-Chi	188	Brock-StL	33	Brock-StL	10	Wynn-Hou	33	May-Cin	321

Runs Batted In		Runs Produced		Bases On Balls		Batting Average		On Base Percentage		Slugging Average	
McCovey-SF	126	Santo-Chi	191	Wynn-Hou	148	Rose-Cin	.348	McCovey-SF	.458	McCovey-SF	.656
Santo-Chi	123	Perez-Cin	188	McCovey-SF	121	Clemente-Pit	.345	Wynn-Hou	.440	H.Aaron-Atl	.607
Perez-Cin	122	Rose-Cin	186	Staub-Mon	110	Jones-NY	.340	Rose-Cin	.432	Allen-Phi	.573
May-Cin	110	McCovey-SF	182	Morgan-Hou	110	Alou-Pit	.331	Staub-Mon	.427	Stargell-Pit	.556
Banks-Chi	106	Bonds-SF	178	Santo-Chi	96	McCovey-SF	.320	Jones-NY	.424	Clemente-Pit	.544

Production		Adjusted Production		Batter Runs		Adjusted Batter Runs		Clutch Hitting Index		Runs Created	
McCovey-SF	1.114	McCovey-SF	212	McCovey-SF	76.1	McCovey-SF	78.7	Menke-Hou	134	McCovey-SF	151
H.Aaron-Atl	1.005	H.Aaron-Atl	177	H.Aaron-Atl	56.3	H.Aaron-Atl	55.9	Rader-Hou	132	Rose-Cin	138
Clemente-Pit	.958	Clemente-Pit	170	Rose-Cin	56.0	Wynn-Hou	53.4	Banks-Chi	132	Staub-Mon	128
Staub-Mon	.953	Wynn-Hou	168	Staub-Mon	52.6	Staub-Mon	52.2	Santo-Chi	122	H.Aaron-Atl	128
Allen-Phi	.952	Allen-Phi	168	Wynn-Hou	51.0	Rose-Cin	49.3	D.Johnson-Phi	121	Wynn-Hou	126

Total Average		Stolen Bases		Stolen Base Average		Stolen Base Runs		Fielding Runs		Total Player Rating	
McCovey-SF	1.296	Brock-StL	53	Bonds-SF	91.8	Bonds-SF	11.1	Lanier-SF	28.6	McCovey-SF	6.3
Wynn-Hou	1.118	Morgan-Hou	49	Brock-StL	79.1	Brock-StL	7.5	Kessinger-Chi	24.6	Wynn-Hou	6.0
H.Aaron-Atl	1.032	Bonds-SF	45	Morgan-Hou	77.8	Morgan-Hou	6.3	Maxvill-StL	21.1	H.Aaron-Atl	5.2
Staub-Mon	1.018	Wills-Mon-LA	40	Wynn-Hou	76.7	Wynn-Hou	2.7	Grote-NY	19.3	Staub-Mon	5.0
Allen-Phi	.988	Tolan-Cin	26	Alou-Pit	73.3	Millan-Atl	2.4	Money-Phi	17.3	Clemente-Pit	4.9

Wins		Win Percentage		Games		Complete Games		Shutouts		Saves	
Seaver-NY	25	Seaver-NY	.781	Granger-Cin	90	Gibson-StL	28	Marichal-SF	8	Gladding-Hou	29
Niekro-Atl	23	Marichal-SF	.656	McGinn-Mon	74	Marichal-SF	27	Osteen-LA	7	Upshaw-Atl	27
Marichal-SF	21	Merritt-Cin	.654	Regan-Chi	71	Perry-SF	26	Jenkins-Chi	7	Granger-Cin	27
Jenkins-Chi	21	Koosman-NY	.654	Carroll-Cin	71	Jenkins-Chi	23	Koosman-NY	6	Brewer-LA	20
		Reed-Atl	.643	Reberger-SD	67	Niekro-Atl	21	Holtzman-Chi	6	Regan-Chi	17

Innings Pitched		Fewest Hits/Game		Fewest BB/Game		Strikeouts		Strikeouts/Game		Ratio	
Perry-SF	325.1	Seaver-NY	6.65	Marichal-SF	1.62	Jenkins-Chi	273	Griffin-Hou	9.56	Marichal-SF	9.13
Osteen-LA	321.0	Maloney-Cin	6.80	Niekro-Atl	1.80	Gibson-StL	269	Wilson-Hou	9.40	Dierker-Hou	9.23
Singer-LA	315.2	Singer-LA	6.96	Jenkins-Chi	2.05	Singer-LA	247	Moose-Pit	8.74	Singer-LA	9.35
Gibson-StL	314.0	Koosman-NY	6.98	Niekro-Chi-SD	2.07	Wilson-Hou	235	Selma-SD-Chi	8.54	Niekro-Atl	9.40
Jenkins-Chi	311.1	Carlton-StL	7.05	Osteen-LA	2.07	Perry-SF	233	Veale-Pit	8.49	Seaver-NY	9.58

Earned Run Average		Adjusted ERA		Opponents' Batting Avg.		Opponents' On Base Pct.		Starter Runs		Adjusted Starter Runs	
Marichal-SF	2.10	Marichal-SF	166	Seaver-NY	.207	Dierker-Hou	.262	Marichal-SF	49.6	Hands-Chi	51.1
Carlton-StL	2.17	Seaver-NY	166	Maloney-Cin	.208	Marichal-SF	.263	Gibson-StL	49.3	Gibson-StL	48.6
Gibson-StL	2.18	Carlton-StL	165	Singer-LA	.210	Singer-LA	.263	Singer-LA	44.0	Marichal-SF	46.5
Seaver-NY	2.21	Gibson-StL	164	Dierker-Hou	.214	Niekro-Atl	.264	Dierker-Hou	42.9	Seaver-NY	44.0
Koosman-NY	2.28	Hands-Chi	162	Carlton-StL	.216	Seaver-NY	.273	Seaver-NY	42.1	Dierker-Hou	41.1

Clutch Pitching Index		Relief Runs		Adjusted Relief Runs		Relief Ranking		Total Pitcher Index		Total Baseball Ranking	
Carlton-StL	122	McGraw-NY	15.1	McGraw-NY	15.7	McGraw-NY	21.2	Gibson-StL	6.0	McCovey-SF	6.3
Perry-SF	117	Granger-Cin	12.8	Granger-Cin	15.5	Granger-Cin	20.9	Seaver-NY	5.6	Gibson-StL	6.0
Veale-Pit	114	Brewer-LA	10.3	DiLauro-NY	8.8	Taylor-NY	15.1	Hands-Chi	5.5	Wynn-Hou	6.0
Robertson-Mon	113	Gibbon-SF-Pit	9.5	Gibbon-SF-Pit	8.7	Brewer-LA	14.0	Marichal-SF	5.4	Seaver-NY	5.6
Hands-Chi	111	DiLauro-NY	8.4	Upshaw-Atl	8.2	Gibbon-SF-Pit	13.9	Carlton-StL	4.9	Hands-Chi	5.5

March 1 Mickey Mantle retires.

April 7 At RFK Stadium, 45,000 fans, including President Richard Nixon, look on as Ted Williams makes his managerial debut for the Senators. The Yanks spoil it, winning 8-4.

April 8 Expansion teams Kansas City Royals, Montreal Expos, San Diego Padres, and Seattle Pilots make things look easy by winning their first regular season games.

April 8 After a long recovery following a 1967 beaning, Tony Conigliaro starts his first game for Boston. His dramatic two-run tenth-inning home run gives the Red Sox a brief lead, and his 12th-inning run wins it.

April 27 Harmon Killebrew hits his 400th home run, and the Twins take first place in the AL West by beating Chicago 4-3.

June 7 The Washington Senators name Jeff Burroughs the No. 1 pick in the June free-agent draft. The Astros choose J. R. Richard as the second pick.

July 16 Rod Carew steals home for the seventh time, as the AL West-leading Twins sweep the White Sox. Carew ties Pete Reiser's record for steals of home in a season.

July 21 A gala All-Star Game banquet in Washington is one of baseball's great events. An all-time team and all-time living team is announced. Babe Ruth is selected Greatest All-Time Player, and Joe DiMaggio Greatest Living Player.

July 22 For the first time, the All-Star Game is postponed due to rain.

August 13 Baltimore's Jim Palmer leaves no doubt about his comeback with an 8-0 no-hitter against Oakland. Reggie Jackson, leading the AL with 42 home runs, walks three times, as the A's drop two games behind the Twins in the West. Palmer, now 11-2, pushes the O's lead to a comfortable 14½ games.

September 29 Rico Petrocelli blasts his 40th home run, a season record for shortstops, as Boston wins 8-5 over Washington. Petrocelli is hitting .301 with only 14 errors in the field.

October 2 The Pilots play what will be their last game in Seattle in a 3-1 loss to Oakland. A crowd of 5,473 fans show up to pay their respects.

October 4 The first League Championship Series begin in Atlanta and Baltimore. New York survives homers by Hank Aaron and Tony Gonzalez off Tom Seaver and scores five runs off Phil Niekro in the eighth to coast 9-5. Paul Blair's 12th-inning squeeze bunt gives the Orioles a 4-3 win over Minnesota.

October 6 Baltimore wins the first ALCS as Paul Blair delivers five hits and Don Buford has four in an 11-2 win at Minnesota.

October 11 Don Buford's leadoff home run starts a 4-1 Baltimore win over New York to open the World Series. Mike Cuellar bests Tom Seaver.

November 6 Denny McLain and Mike Cuellar finish dead even in AL Cy Young Award voting.

November 12 Minnesota's Harmon Killebrew is voted AL MVP honors.

November 25 Kansas City's Lou Piniella is voted AL Rookie of the Year.

BALTIMORE		BOSTON		CALIFORNIA		CHICAGO		CLEVELAND		DETROIT	
M	E.Weaver	M	D.Williams	M	B.Rigney	M	A.Lopez	M	A.Dark	M	M.Smith
1B	B.Powell	M	E.Popowski	M	L.Phillips	1B	G.Hopkins	1B	T.Horton	1B	N.Cash
2B	D.Johnson	1B	D.Jones	1B	J.Spencer	2B	B.Knoop	2B	V.Fuller	2B	D.McAuliffe
SS	M.Belanger	2B	M.Andrews	2B	S.Alomar	SS	L.Aparicio	SS	L.Brown	SS	T.Tresh
3B	B.Robinson	SS	R.Petrocelli	SS	J.Fregosi	3B	B.Melton	3B	M.Alvis	3B	D.Wert
LF	D.Buford	3B	G.Scott	3B	A.Rodriguez	LF	C.May	LF	R.Snyder	LF	W.Horton
CF	P.Blair	LF	C.Yastrzemski	LF	R.Reichardt	CF	K.Berry	CF	J.Cardenal	CF	J.Northrup
RF	F.Robinson	CF	R.Smith	CF	J.Johnstone	RF	W.Williams	RF	K.Harrelson	RF	A.Kaline
C	E.Hendricks	RF	T.Conigliaro	RF	B.Voss	C	E.Herrmann	C	D.Sims	C	B.Freehan
		C	R.Gibson	C	J.Azcue						
C	A.Etchebarren							O	R.Scheinblum	OS	M.Stanley
		O	J.Lahoud	O1	R.Repoz	13	P.Ward	32	L.Klimchock	23	T.Matchick
		3S	S.O'Brien			O	B.Bradford	23	Z.Versalles		
P	M.Cuellar	2S	D.Schofield			1O	T.McCraw	S	E.Leon	P	D.McLain
P	D.McNally			P	A.Messersmith					P	M.Lolich
P	T.Phoebus			P	T.Murphy						
P	J.Palmer	P	R.Culp	P	J.McGlothlin	P	J.Horlen	P	S.McDowell	P	E.Wilson
P	J.Hardin	P	M.Nagy	P	R.May	P	T.John	P	L.Tiant	P	M.Kilkenny
RP	D.Leonhard	P	S.Siebert	P	G.Brunet	P	G.Peters	P	S.Hargan	RP	P.Dobson
RP	E.Watt	P	J.Lonborg	RP	E.Fisher	P	B.Wynne	P	D.Ellsworth	RP	J.Hiller
RP	M.Lopez	P	L.Stange	RP	K.Tatum	RP	W.Wood	RP	S.Williams	RP	T.Timmermann
		RP	V.Romo	RP	H.Wilhelm	RP	D.Osinski	RP	M.Paul		
P	D.Hall	RP	S.Lyle			RP	C.Carlos	RP	J.Pizarro	P	J.Sparma
P	P.Richert	RP	B.Landis	P	C.Wright			P	R.Law		
						P	P.Edmondson				
		P	R.Jarvis			P	J.Nyman				
		P	B.Lee								

KANSAS CITY		MINNESOTA		NEW YORK		OAKLAND		SEATTLE		WASHINGTON	
M	J.Gordon	M	B.Martin	M	R.Houk	M	H.Bauer	M	J.Schultz	M	T.Williams
1B	M.Fiore	1B	R.Reese	1B	J.Pepitone	M	J.McNamara	1B	D.Mincher	1B	M.Epstein
2B	J.Adair	2B	R.Carew	2B	H.Clarke	1B	D.Cater	2B	J.Donaldson	2B	B.Allen
SS	J.Hernandez	SS	L.Cardenas	SS	G.Michael	2B	D.Green	SS	R.Oyler	SS	E.Brinkman
3B	J.Foy	3B	H.Killebrew	3B	J.Kenney	SS	B.Campaneris	3B	T.Harper	3B	K.McMullen
LF	L.Piniella	LF	T.Uhlaender	LF	R.White	3B	S.Bando	LF	T.Davis	LF	F.Howard
CF	B.Oliver	CF	C.Tovar	CF	R.Woods	LF	T.Reynolds	CF	W.Comer	CF	D.Unser
RF	P.Kelly	RF	T.Oliva	RF	B.Murcer	CF	R.Monday	RF	S.Hovley	RF	H.Allen
C	E.Rodriguez	C	J.Roseboro	C	J.Gibbs	RF	R.Jackson	C	J.McNertney	C	P.Casanova
						C	P.Roof				
O	E.Kirkpatrick	32	F.Quilici	CO	F.Fernandez			O1	M.Hegan	O	B.Alyea
1	C.Harrison	O3	G.Nettles	O	B.Robinson	S2	T.Kubiak	32	G.Gil	2	T.Cullen
C	B.Martinez			O	J.Hall	O	J.Tartabull			O	E.Stroud
3	P.Schaal	P	J.Perry					P	G.Brabender	O	L.Maye
		P	D.Boswell					P	M.Pattin		
P	W.Bunker	P	J.Kaat	P	M.Stottlemyre	P	C.Hunter	P	F.Talbot	P	J.Coleman
P	D.Drago	P	T.Hall	P	F.Peterson	P	C.Dobson	RP	D.Segui	P	D.Bosman
P	B.Butler	RP	R.Perranoski	P	S.Bahnsen	P	B.Odom	RP	J.Gelnar	P	C.Cox
P	R.Nelson	RP	B.Miller	P	B.Burbach	P	L.Krausse	RP	J.Bouton	P	J.Hannan
P	J.Rooker	RP	D.Woodson	P	A.Downing	P	J.Nash			P	B.Moore
RP	M.Drabowsky			RP	L.McDaniel	RP	R.Fingers			RP	J.Shellenback
RP	T.Burgmeier	P	D.Chance	RP	J.Aker	RP	J.Roland	P	M.Marshall	RP	D.Higgins
RP	D.Wickersham	P	A.Worthington	RP	S.Hamilton	RP	P.Lindblad	P	S.Barber	RP	D.Knowles
								P	B.Locker		
				P	M.Kekich	P	G.Lauzerique	P	J.O'Donoghue		
P	M.Hedlund							P	G.Brunet	P	B.Humphreys
								P	G.Bell	P	D.Baldwin
										P	C.Pascual

TEAM	G	W	L	PCT	GB	R	OR	AB	H	2B	3B	HR	BB	SO	AVG	OBP	SLG	PRO	PRO+	BR	/A	PF	CHI	RC	SB	CS	SBA	SBR
EAST																												
BAL	162	109	53	.673		779	**517**	5518	1465	234	29	175	634	**806**	.265	**.346**	.414	**.760**	118	**135**	**128**	101	96	791	82	45	65	-2
DET	162	90	72	.556	19	701	601	5441	1316	188	29	182	578	922	.242	.318	.387	.705	99	17	-12	104	104	674	35	28	56	-6
BOS	162	87	75	.537	22	743	736	5494	1381	234	37	**197**	658	923	.251	.335	**.415**	.750	110	110	69	105	95	761	41	47	47	-16
WAS	162	86	76	.531	23	694	644	5447	1365	171	40	148	630	900	.251	.332	.378	.710	111	38	75	95	99	675	52	40	57	-8
NY	162	80	81	.497	28.5	562	587	5308	1247	210	**44**	94	565	840	.235	.310	.344	.654	92	-74	-53	96	99	572	119	74	62	-9
CLE	161	62	99	.385	46.5	573	717	5365	1272	173	24	119	535	906	.237	.309	.345	.654	86	-77	-96	103	101	568	85	37	70	3
WEST																												
MIN	162	97	65	.599		**790**	618	5677	**1520**	246	32	163	599	906	**.268**	.342	.408	.750	114	118	101	102	98	**794**	115	70	62	-8
OAK	162	88	74	.543	9	740	678	5614	1400	210	28	148	617	953	.249	.330	.376	.706	109	32	63	96	103	712	100	39	72	7
CAL	163	71	91	.438	26	528	652	5316	1221	151	29	88	516	929	.230	.302	.319	.621	84	-137	-112	95	**105**	518	54	39	58	-7
KC	163	69	93	.426	28	586	688	5462	1311	179	32	98	522	901	.240	.311	.338	.649	87	-84	-87	101	102	577	129	70	65	-3
CHI	162	68	94	.420	29	625	723	5450	1346	210	27	112	552	844	.247	.322	.357	.679	92	-25	-56	105	98	638	54	22	71	3
SEA	163	64	98	.395	33	639	799	5444	1276	179	27	125	626	1015	.234	.317	.346	.663	94	-53	-43	98	104	622	**167**	59	**74**	15
TOT	973					7960		65536	16120	2385	378	1649	7032	10845	.246	.323	.369	.693							1033	570	64	-32

TEAM	CG	SH	SV	IP	H	H/G	HR	BB	SO	RAT	ERA	ERA+	OAV	OOB	PR	/A	PF	CPI	FA	E	DP	FW	PW	BW	SBW	DIF
EAST																										
BAL	50	20	36	1473²	**1194**	7.3	117	498	897	10.5	2.83	126	.223	.291	130	121	98	97	.984	101	145	2.2	12.7	13.4	-.0	-.4
DET	**55**	20	28	1455¹	1250	7.7	128	586	**1032**	11.6	3.31	113	.232	.312	50	67	103	98	.979	130	130	.5	7.0	-1.3	-.3	3.0
BOS	30	7	41	1466²	1423	8.7	155	685	935	13.2	3.92	97	.254	.343	-49	-19	105	106	.975	157	**178**	-1.0	-2.0	7.2	-1.4	3.2
WAS	28	10	41	1447¹	1310	8.1	135	656	835	12.4	3.49	99	.244	.330	22	-4	96	107	.978	140	159	-.0	-.4	7.9	-.6	-1.8
NY	53	13	20	1440²	1258	7.9	118	522	801	11.2	3.23	108	.236	.306	63	40	96	97	.979	131	158	.5	4.2	-5.6	-.7	1.0
CLE	35	7	22	1437	1330	8.3	134	681	1000	12.9	3.94	96	.248	.338	-51	-27	104	99	.976	145	153	-.4	-2.8	-10.1	.6	-5.8
WEST																										
MIN	41	8	**43**	1497²	1388	8.3	119	524	906	11.7	3.24	113	.246	.315	64	69	101	104	.977	150	177	-.6	7.2	10.6	-.6	-.7
OAK	42	14	36	1480²	1356	8.2	163	586	887	12.0	3.71	93	.245	.322	-15	-45	95	100	.979	136	162	.2	-4.7	6.6	1.0	3.9
CAL	25	9	39	1438¹	1294	8.1	126	517	885	11.7	3.54	98	.242	.315	13	-9	96	96	.978	136	164	.2	-.9	-11.7	-.5	2.9
KC	42	10	25	1464²	1357	8.3	136	560	894	11.9	3.72	94	.246	.319	-15	-5	102	96	.975	157	114	-1.0	-.5	-9.1	-.0	-1.4
CHI	29	10	25	1437²	1470	9.2	146	564	810	12.9	4.21	92	.267	.339	-93	-56	107	99	.981	122	163	1.0	-5.9	-5.9	.6	-2.8
SEA	21	6	33	1463²	1490	9.2	172	653	963	13.5	4.35	84	.264	.345	-118	-116	100	101	.974	167	149	-1.5	-12.2	-4.5	1.9	-.6
TOT	451	134	389	17503¹		8.3				12.1	3.62		.246	.323					.978	1672	1852					

Runs
Jackson-Oak ... 123
F.Robinson-Bal ... 111
Howard-Was ... 111
Killebrew-Min ... 106
Bando-Oak ... 106

Hits
Oliva-Min ... 197
Clarke-NY ... 183
Blair-Bal ... 178
Howard-Was ... 175
Horton-Cle ... 174

Doubles
Oliva-Min ... 39
Jackson-Oak ... 36
Johnson-Bal ... 34
Petrocelli-Bos ... 32
Blair-Bal ... 32

Triples
Unser-Was ... 8
Smith-Bos ... 7
Clarke-NY ... 7

Home Runs
Killebrew-Min ... 49
Howard-Was ... 48
Jackson-Oak ... 47
Yastrzemski-Bos ... 40
Petrocelli-Bos ... 40

Total Bases
Howard-Was ... 340
Jackson-Oak ... 334
Killebrew-Min ... 324
Oliva-Min ... 316
Petrocelli-Bos ... 315

Runs Batted In
Killebrew-Min ... 140
Powell-Bal ... 121
Jackson-Oak ... 118
Bando-Oak ... 113

Runs Produced
Killebrew-Min ... 197
Jackson-Oak ... 194
Bando-Oak ... 188
F.Robinson-Bal ... 179

Bases On Balls
Killebrew-Min ... 145
Jackson-Oak ... 114
Bando-Oak ... 111
Howard-Was ... 102
Yastrzemski-Bos ... 101

Batting Average
Carew-Min ... .332
Smith-Bos ... .309
Oliva-Min ... .309
F.Robinson-Bal ... .308
Powell-Bal ... .304

On Base Percentage
Killebrew-Min ... .430
F.Robinson-Bal ... .417
Jackson-Oak ... .410
Petrocelli-Bos ... .407
Howard-Was ... .403

Slugging Average
Jackson-Oak ... .608
Petrocelli-Bos ... .589
Killebrew-Min ... .584
Howard-Was ... .574
Powell-Bal ... .559

Production
Jackson-Oak ... 1.019
Killebrew-Min ... 1.014
Petrocelli-Bos ... .996
Howard-Was ... .978
F.Robinson-Bal ... .957

Adjusted Production
Jackson-Oak ... 190
Howard-Was ... 180
Killebrew-Min ... 177
Petrocelli-Bos ... 167
F.Robinson-Bal ... 164

Batter Runs
Killebrew-Min ... 65.6
Jackson-Oak ... 62.0
Howard-Was ... 56.8
Petrocelli-Bos ... 54.8
F.Robinson-Bal ... 49.9

Adjusted Batter Runs
Jackson-Oak ... 67.9
Howard-Was ... 63.8
Killebrew-Min ... 62.6
F.Robinson-Bal ... 48.8
Petrocelli-Bos ... 48.4

Clutch Hitting Index
White-NY ... 128
Cater-Oak ... 120
Bando-Oak ... 118
Foy-KC ... 116
T.Conigliaro-Bos ... 113

Runs Created
Killebrew-Min ... 146
Jackson-Oak ... 144
Howard-Was ... 132
Petrocelli-Bos ... 129
F.Robinson-Bal ... 126

Total Average
Killebrew-Min ... 1.143
Jackson-Oak ... 1.139
Petrocelli-Bos ... 1.048
F.Robinson-Bal ... 1.026
Howard-Was ... 1.004

Stolen Bases
Harper-Sea ... 73
Campaneris-Oak ... 62
Tovar-Min ... 45
Kelly-KC ... 40
Foy-KC ... 37

Stolen Base Average
Campaneris-Oak ... 88.6
Alomar-Chi-Cal ... 87.0
Cardenal-Cle ... 85.7
Aparicio-Chi ... 85.7
Davis-Sea ... 82.6

Stolen Base Runs
Campaneris-Oak ... 13.8
Harper-Sea ... 11.1
Cardenal-Cle ... 7.2
Tovar-Min ... 6.3
Aparicio-Chi ... 4.8

Fielding Runs
Cardenas-Min ... 33.5
Aparicio-Chi ... 29.3
Blair-Bal ... 24.8
Knoop-Cal-Chi ... 24.5
Quilici-Min ... 24.2

Total Player Rating
Petrocelli-Bos ... 6.9
Jackson-Oak ... 6.6
Cardenas-Min ... 5.6
Aparicio-Chi ... 5.1
F.Robinson-Bal ... 4.2

Wins
McLain-Det ... 24
Cuellar-Bal ... 23

Win Percentage
Palmer-Bal ... .800
Perry-Min ... .769
McNally-Bal ... .741
McLain-Det ... .727
Odom-Oak ... .714

Games
Wood-Chi ... 76
Perranoski-Min ... 75
Lyle-Bos ... 71
Locker-Chi-Sea ... 68
Segui-Sea ... 66

Complete Games
Stottlemyre-NY ... 24
McLain-Det ... 23
McDowell-Cle ... 18
Cuellar-Bal ... 18
Peterson-NY ... 16

Shutouts
McLain-Det ... 9
Palmer-Bal ... 6
Cuellar-Bal ... 5

Saves
Perranoski-Min ... 31
K.Tatum-Cal ... 22
Lyle-Bos ... 17
Watt-Bal ... 16
Higgins-Was ... 16

Innings Pitched
McLain-Det ... 325.0
Stottlemyre-NY ... 303.0
Cuellar-Bal ... 290.2
McDowell-Cle ... 285.0
Lolich-Det ... 280.2

Fewest Hits/Game
Messersmith-Cal ... 6.08
Palmer-Bal ... 6.51
Cuellar-Bal ... 6.60
Lolich-Det ... 6.86
Odom-Oak ... 6.96

Fewest BB/Game
Peterson-NY ... 1.42
Bosman-Was ... 1.82
McLain-Det ... 1.86
Perry-Min ... 2.27
Cuellar-Bal ... 2.45

Strikeouts
McDowell-Cle ... 279
Lolich-Det ... 271
Messersmith-Cal ... 211
Boswell-Min ... 190

Strikeouts/Game
McDowell-Cle ... 8.81
Lolich-Det ... 8.69
Messersmith-Cal ... 7.60
Butler-KC ... 7.25
Williams-Cle ... 7.01

Ratio
Peterson-NY ... 9.07
Cuellar-Bal ... 9.07
Bosman-Was ... 9.19
Palmer-Bal ... 9.75
Messersmith-Cal ... 9.86

Earned Run Average
Bosman-Was ... 2.19
Palmer-Bal ... 2.34
Cuellar-Bal ... 2.38
Messersmith-Cal ... 2.52
Peterson-NY ... 2.55

Adjusted ERA
Bosman-Was ... 158
Palmer-Bal ... 153
Cuellar-Bal ... 150
Messersmith-Cal ... 138
Peterson-NY ... 136

Opponents' Batting Avg.
Messersmith-Cal ... .190
Palmer-Bal ... .200
Cuellar-Bal ... .204
Lolich-Det ... .210
McDowell-Cle ... .213

Opponents' On Base Pct.
Cuellar-Bal ... .261
Bosman-Was ... .262
Peterson-NY ... .263
Palmer-Bal ... .272
Messersmith-Cal ... .276

Starter Runs
Cuellar-Bal ... 40.0
Peterson-NY ... 32.5
Bosman-Was ... 30.7
Messersmith-Cal ... 30.6
McLain-Det ... 29.8

Adjusted Starter Runs
Cuellar-Bal ... 38.1
McLain-Det ... 33.7
Peterson-NY ... 28.1
Bosman-Was ... 27.3
Messersmith-Cal ... 26.8

Clutch Pitching Index
Cox-Was ... 128
Nagy-Bos ... 119
Tiant-Cle ... 118
John-Chi ... 114
Wilson-Det ... 112

Relief Runs
K.Tatum-Cal ... 21.7
Perranoski-Min ... 20.2
Watt-Bal ... 15.6
Roland-Oak ... 13.7
Knowles-Was ... 12.9

Adjusted Relief Runs
Perranoski-Min ... 20.6
K.Tatum-Cal ... 20.4
Watt-Bal ... 15.1
Lyle-Bos ... 14.4
Hall-Bal ... 12.0

Relief Ranking
Perranoski-Min ... 41.3
K.Tatum-Cal ... 30.9
Watt-Bal ... 21.1
Wood-Chi ... 21.0
Lyle-Bos ... 19.2

Total Pitcher Index
Perranoski-Min ... 4.4
Cuellar-Bal ... 4.1
Stottlemyre-NY ... 3.8
K.Tatum-Cal ... 3.8
Peterson-NY ... 3.7

Total Baseball Ranking
Petrocelli-Bos ... 6.9
Jackson-Oak ... 6.6
Cardenas-Min ... 5.6
Aparicio-Chi ... 5.1
Perranoski-Min ... 4.4

January 16 Curt Flood, Cardinals Gold Glove outfielder, files a civil lawsuit challenging Major League Baseball's reserve clause, a suit that will have historic implications. Flood refused to report to the Phillies after he was traded by the Cardinals three months ago, contending the baseball rule violates Federal anti-trust laws.

April 22 Tom Seaver strikes out 19 Padres, including the last 10 in succession in winning 2-1 for the Mets. Seaver's 19 strikeouts tie the major league record (since broken), but his 10 straight K's still stands.

May 10 While losing 6-5 to St. Louis, the Braves' Hoyt Wilhelm becomes the first pitcher ever to appear in 1,000 games.

May 12 Ernie Banks becomes the eighth member of the 500 homer club, connecting off Pat Jarvis during a 4-3 Cub win over the Braves.

May 17 During a 7-6 Atlanta loss to Cincinnati in the second game of a doubleheader, Hank Aaron collects his 3,000th career hit. The ninth man to amass 3,000 hits, Aaron is the first to also have 500 homers.

May 30 All-Star voting is returned to the fans, as computerized punch-card ballots appear in stores and ballparks coast to coast. Since 1958 the All-Star squads had been selected by managers, coaches, and players.

July 14 The NL wins its eighth straight All-Star Game, a thrilling 12-inning 5-4 victory in Cincinnati. Pete Rose crashes into Cleveland catcher Ray Fosse to score the winning run.

July 18 During a 10-1 win over Montreal, the Giants' Willie Mays singles off Mike Wegener. It is career hit No. 3,000 for Mays.

August 11 Jim Bunning notches his 100th NL victory, a 6-5 Phillies win over the Astros. Bunning is the first pitcher since Cy Young to win 100 games in each league.

August 12 Curt Flood loses his $4.1 million antitrust suit against baseball, as Federal Judge Irving Ben Cooper upholds the legality of the sport's reserve clause. Cooper does recommend changes in the reserve system, to be achieved through negotiation between players and owners. Less than six years later, this recommendation would become a reality.

September 3 After an NL record 1,117 consecutive games, Billy Williams asks to sit one out.

October 1 The Angels' Alex Johnson grounds out and then hits two singles in the final game of the season to edge Boston's Carl Yastrzemski for the AL batting title, .3290 to .3286. Johnson leaves the game after his second hit.

October 4 Major league umpires return after a one-day walkout in quest of higher wages. Minor league umps had been pressed into service for the opening LCS games the day before. There had been rumors of a strike for several days as negotiations between the umpires and Major League Baseball had reached an impasse.

November 3 Bob Gibson wins the NL Cy Young Award by a 118-51 margin over Giant Gaylord Perry. Gibson posted a 23-7 record for the Cardinals.

November 18 Johnny Bench wins the NL MVP Award with 326 points, 108 more than the Cubs' Billy Williams. Bench had 45 homers, 148 RBIs, and a .293 average for the Reds.

ATLANTA

Pos	Player
M	L.Harris
1B	O.Cepeda
2B	F.Millan
SS	S.Jackson
3B	C.Boyer
LF	R.Carty
CF	T.Gonzalez
RF	H.Aaron
C	B.Tillman
S2	G.Garrido
O	M.Lum
C	H.King
P	P.Jarvis
P	P.Niekro
P	J.Nash
P	G.Stone
P	R.Reed
RP	H.Wilhelm
RP	B.Priddy
P	M.McQueen

CHICAGO

Pos	Player
M	L.Durocher
1B	E.Banks
2B	G.Beckert
SS	D.Kessinger
3B	R.Santo
LF	B.Williams
CF	J.Hickman
RF	J.Callison
C	R.Hundley
O	C.James
O1	J.Pepitone
P	F.Jenkins
P	K.Holtzman
P	B.Hands
P	M.Pappas
P	J.Decker
RP	P.Regan
RP	J.Colborn

CINCINNATI

Pos	Player
M	S.Anderson
1B	L.May
2B	T.Helms
SS	D.Concepcion
3B	T.Perez
LF	B.Carbo
CF	B.Tolan
RF	P.Rose
C	J.Bench
O2	J.Stewart
S3	W.Woodward
P	G.Nolan
P	J.Merritt
P	J.McGlothlin
P	W.Simpson
P	T.Cloninger
RP	C.Carroll
RP	W.Granger
RP	D.Gullett
P	R.Washburn

HOUSTON

Pos	Player
M	H.Walker
1B	B.Watson
2B	J.Morgan
SS	D.Menke
3B	D.Rader
LF	J.Wynn
CF	C.Cedeno
RF	J.Alou
C	J.Edwards
1O	J.Pepitone
O	N.Miller
O	T.Davis
P	L.Dierker
P	J.Billingham
P	D.Wilson
P	D.Lemaster
P	T.Griffin
RP	J.Ray
RP	R.Cook
RP	J.Bouton
P	W.Blasingame
P	F.Gladding

LOS ANGELES

Pos	Player
M	W.Alston
1B	W.Parker
2B	T.Sizemore
SS	M.Wills
3B	B.Grabarkewitz
LF	M.Mota
CF	W.Davis
RF	W.Crawford
C	T.Haller
23	J.Lefebvre
O	B.Russell
C3	B.Sudakis
O	A.Kosco
P	D.Sutton
P	C.Osteen
P	A.Foster
P	J.Moeller
P	S.Vance
RP	J.Brewer
RP	F.Norman
RP	P.Mikkelsen
P	B.Singer
P	R.Lamb
P	J.Pena

MONTREAL

Pos	Player
M	G.Mauch
1B	R.Fairly
2B	G.Sutherland
SS	B.Wine
3B	C.Laboy
LF	M.Jones
CF	A.Phillips
RF	R.Staub
C	J.Bateman
3O	B.Bailey
2	M.Staehle
O1	J.Gosger
O	J.Fairey
P	C.Morton
P	S.Renko
P	B.Stoneman
P	M.Wegener
RP	D.McGinn
RP	H.Reed
RP	C.Raymond
P	J.Strohmayer
P	M.Marshall

NEW YORK

Pos	Player
M	G.Hodges
1B	D.Clendenon
2B	K.Boswell
SS	B.Harrelson
3B	J.Foy
LF	C.Jones
CF	T.Agee
RF	R.Swoboda
C	J.Grote
32	W.Garrett
O1	A.Shamsky
P	T.Seaver
P	J.Koosman
P	G.Gentry
P	J.McAndrew
P	R.Sadecki
RP	T.McGraw
RP	R.Taylor
RP	D.Frisella
P	N.Ryan

PHILADELPHIA

Pos	Player
M	F.Lucchesi
1B	D.Johnson
2B	D.Doyle
SS	L.Bowa
3B	D.Money
LF	J.Briggs
CF	L.Hisle
RF	R.Stone
C	M.Ryan
O	B.Browne
23	T.Taylor
O	O.Gamble
P	R.Wise
P	J.Bunning
P	C.Short
P	G.Jackson
P	B.Lersch
RP	D.Selma
RP	L.Palmer
RP	B.Wilson
P	W.Fryman
P	J.Hoerner

PITTSBURGH

Pos	Player
M	D.Murtaugh
1B	B.Robertson
2B	B.Mazeroski
SS	G.Alley
3B	R.Hebner
LF	W.Stargell
CF	M.Alou
RF	R.Clemente
C	M.Sanguillen
O1	A.Oliver
S	F.Patek
3	J.Pagan
2	D.Cash
P	B.Veale
P	D.Ellis
P	S.Blass
RP	B.Moose
RP	L.Walker
RP	D.Giusti
RP	B.Dal Canton
P	J.Nelson

SAN DIEGO

Pos	Player
M	P.Gomez
1B	N.Colbert
2B	D.Campbell
SS	J.Arcia
3B	E.Spiezio
LF	A.Ferrara
CF	C.Gaston
RF	O.Brown
C	C.Cannizzaro
O	I.Murrell
S3	S.Huntz
P	P.Dobson
P	C.Kirby
P	D.Coombs
P	D.Roberts
P	M.Corkins
RP	R.Herbel
RP	T.Dukes
RP	G.Ross
P	A.Santorini
P	E.Wilson
P	R.Willis

SAN FRANCISCO

Pos	Player
M	C.King
M	C.Fox
1B	W.McCovey
2B	R.Hunt
SS	H.Lanier
3B	A.Gallagher
LF	K.Henderson
CF	W.Mays
RF	B.Bonds
C	D.Dietz
2S	T.Fuentes
3O	J.Hart
P	G.Perry
P	J.Marichal
P	R.Robertson
P	F.Reberger
RP	R.Bryant
RP	D.McMahon
RP	Je.Johnson
P	S.Pitlock
P	M.McCormick
P	Ja.Johnson

ST.LOUIS

Pos	Player
M	R.Schoendienst
1B	J.Hague
2B	J.Javier
SS	D.Maxvill
3B	J.Torre
LF	L.Brock
CF	J.Cardenal
RF	L.Lee
C	T.Simmons
13	D.Allen
O	V.Davalillo
O1	Ca.Taylor
P	B.Gibson
P	S.Carlton
P	M.Torrez
P	J.Reuss
P	N.Briles
RP	Ch.Taylor
RP	F.Linzy
RP	S.Campisi
P	G.Culver

TEAM	G	W	L	PCT	GB	R	OR	AB	H	2B	3B	HR	BB	SO	AVG	OBP	SLG	PRO	PRO+	BR	/A	PF	CHI	RC	SB	CS	SBA	SBR
EAST																												
PIT	162	89	73	.549		729	664	5637	**1522**	235	**70**	130	444	871	**.270**	.328	.406	.734	105	12	28	98	99	740	66	34	66	-1
CHI	162	84	78	.519	5	806	679	5491	1424	228	44	179	607	844	.259	.335	.415	.750	95	49	-44	112	**104**	773	39	16	71	2
NY	162	83	79	.512	6	695	**630**	5443	1358	211	42	120	684	1062	.249	.336	.370	.706	96	-23	-24	100	98	689	118	54	69	3
STL	162	76	86	.469	13	744	747	5689	1497	218	51	113	569	961	.263	.333	.379	.712	95	-20	-35	102	103	719	117	47	71	7
PHI	161	73	88	.453	15.5	594	730	5456	1299	224	58	101	519	1066	.238	.307	.356	.663	85	-125	-109	97	101	582	72	64	53	-17
MON	162	73	89	.451	16	687	807	5411	1284	211	35	136	659	972	.237	.324	.365	.689	91	-62	-61	100	103	658	65	45	59	-8
WEST																												
CIN	162	102	60	.630		775	681	5540	1498	253	45	**191**	547	984	**.270**	.339	**.436**	**.775**	113	94	92	100	94	814	115	52	69	3
LA	161	87	74	.540	14.5	749	684	5606	1515	233	67	87	541	841	**.270**	.337	.382	.719	104	-4	28	96	102	730	**138**	57	71	7
SF	162	86	76	.531	16	**831**	826	5578	1460	**257**	35	165	**729**	1005	.262	**.353**	.409	.762	112	92	102	99	98	**821**	83	27	**75**	9
HOU	162	79	83	.488	23	744	763	5574	1446	250	47	129	598	911	.259	.334	.391	.725	104	5	36	96	100	728	114	41	74	**10**
ATL	162	76	86	.469	26	736	772	5546	1495	215	24	160	522	**736**	**.270**	.337	.404	.741	99	32	-13	106	97	742	58	34	63	-3
SD	162	63	99	.389	39	681	788	5494	1353	208	36	172	500	1164	.246	.314	.391	.705	98	-49	-22	96	102	669	60	45	57	-9
TOT	971					8771		66465	17151	2743	554	1683	6919	11417	.258	.332	.392	.724							1045	516	67	4

TEAM	CG	SH	SV	IP	H	H/G	HR	BB	SO	RAT	ERA	ERA+	OAV	OOB	PR	/A	PF	CPI	FA	E	DP	FW	PW	BW	SBW	DIF
EAST																										
PIT	36	13	43	1453^2	1386	8.6	106	625	990	12.7	3.70	106	.255	.336	56	33	96	**106**	.979	137	**195**	.3	3.3	2.8	-.1	1.8
CHI	**59**	9	25	1435	1402	8.8	143	**475**	1000	11.9	3.76	**120**	.256	.318	46	18	111	101	.978	137	146	.3	**11.8**	-4.4	.2	-4.8
NY	47	10	32	1459^2	**1260**	**7.8**	135	575	**1064**	11.5	3.45	117	**.233**	.310	97	93	99	98	.979	124	136	1.0	9.3	-2.4	.3	-6.2
STL	51	11	20	1475^2	1483	9.0	102	632	960	13.0	4.06	101	.263	.340	-2	10	102	100	.977	150	159	-.4	1.0	-3.5	.7	-2.8
PHI	24	8	36	1461	1483	9.1	132	538	1047	12.7	4.17	96	.265	.333	-20	-29	99	98	**.981**	114	134	**1.5**	-2.9	-10.9	-1.7	6.5
MON	29	10	32	1438^2	1434	9.0	162	716	914	13.8	4.50	91	.261	.351	-73	-63	102	101	.977	141	193	.0	-6.3	-6.1	-.8	5.1
WEST																										
CIN	32	15	**60**	1444^2	1370	8.5	118	592	843	12.4	3.69	109	.251	.327	57	55	100	102	.976	151	173	-.5	5.5	9.2	.3	6.6
LA	37	**17**	42	1458^2	1394	8.6	164	496	880	11.9	3.82	100	.256	.316	37	2	95	99	.978	135	135	.4	.2	2.8	.7	2.5
SF	50	7	30	1457^2	1514	9.3	156	604	931	13.3	4.50	88	.267	.341	-74	-86	98	98	.973	170	153	-1.5	-8.6	**10.2**	.9	4.1
HOU	36	6	35	1456	1491	9.2	131	577	942	13.0	4.23	92	.265	.338	-30	-58	96	99	.978	140	144	.1	-5.8	3.6	**1.0**	-.9
ATL	45	9	24	1430^2	1451	9.1	185	478	960	12.3	4.33	92	.261	.322	-45	-6	106	96	.977	141	118	.0	-.6	-1.3	-.3	-2.9
SD	24	9	32	1440^1	1483	9.3	149	611	886	13.3	4.36	91	.267	.344	-50	-61	98	102	.975	158	159	-.9	-6.1	-2.2	-.9	-7.9
TOT	470	124	411	17411^2		8.9				12.6	4.05		.258	.332					.977	1698	1845					

Runs		Hits		Doubles		Triples		Home Runs		Total Bases	
Williams-Chi	137	Williams-Chi	205	Parker-LA	47	Davis-LA	16	Bench-Cin	45	Williams-Chi	373
Bonds-SF	134	Rose-Cin	205	McCovey-SF	39	Kessinger-Chi	14	Williams-Chi	42	Bench-Cin	355
Rose-Cin	120	Torre-StL	203	Rose-Cin	37	Clemente-Pit	10	Perez-Cin	40	Perez-Cin	346
Brock-StL	114	Brock-StL	202	Dietz-SF	36	Bonds-SF	10	McCovey-SF	39	Bonds-SF	334
Tolan-Cin	112	Alou-Pit	201	Bonds-SF	36					Gaston-SD	317

Runs Batted In		Runs Produced		Bases On Balls		Batting Average		On Base Percentage		Slugging Average	
Bench-Cin	148	Williams-Chi	224	McCovey-SF	137	Carty-Atl	.366	Carty-Atl	.456	McCovey-SF	.612
Williams-Chi	129	Bench-Cin	200	Staub-Mon	112	Torre-StL	.325	McCovey-SF	.446	Perez-Cin	.589
Perez-Cin	129	Perez-Cin	196	Dietz-SF	109	Sanguillen-Pit	.325	Dietz-SF	.430	Bench-Cin	.587
McCovey-SF	126	Bonds-SF	186	Wynn-Hou	106	Williams-Chi	.322	Hickman-Chi	.421	Williams-Chi	.586
H.Aaron-Atl	118			Morgan-Hou	102	Parker-LA	.319	Perez-Cin	.405	Carty-Atl	.584

Production		Adjusted Production		Batter Runs		Adjusted Batter Runs		Clutch Hitting Index		Runs Created	
McCovey-SF	1.058	McCovey-SF	183	McCovey-SF	62.0	McCovey-SF	63.6	Parker-LA	126	Williams-Chi	147
Carty-Atl	1.040	Carty-Atl	167	Carty-Atl	54.4	Perez-Cin	51.7	Dietz-SF	122	McCovey-SF	140
Hickman-Chi	1.003	Perez-Cin	162	Perez-Cin	52.1	Carty-Atl	47.5	Wine-Mon	118	Perez-Cin	140
Perez-Cin	.994	Dietz-SF	154	Williams-Chi	51.1	Dietz-SF	42.2	Santo-Chi	117	Bonds-SF	134
Williams-Chi	.979	Hickman-Chi	148	Hickman-Chi	49.5	Carbo-Cin	40.2	Davis-LA	115	Hickman-Chi	129

Total Average		Stolen Bases		Stolen Base Average		Stolen Base Runs		Fielding Runs		Total Player Rating	
McCovey-SF	1.214	Tolan-Cin	57	Henderson-SF	87.0	Bonds-SF	8.4	Maxvill-StL	37.5	McCovey-SF	6.2
Carty-Atl	1.102	Brock-StL	51	Harrelson-NY	85.2	Brock-StL	6.3	Alley-Pit	33.7	Bench-Cin	4.5
Hickman-Chi	1.080	Bonds-SF	48	Wynn-Hou	82.8	Tolan-Cin	5.1	Mazeroski-Pit	23.9	Perez-Cin	4.3
Perez-Cin	1.045	Morgan-Hou	42	Bonds-SF	82.8	Morgan-Hou	4.8	Rader-Hou	23.8	Wynn-Hou	4.2
Williams-Chi	1.018	Davis-LA	38	Cedeno-Hou	81.0	Harrelson-NY	4.5	Wine-Mon	19.7	Carty-Atl	4.2

Wins		Win Percentage		Games		Complete Games		Shutouts		Saves	
Perry-SF	23	Gibson-StL	.767	Herbel-SD-NY	76	Jenkins-Chi	24	Perry-SF	5	Granger-Cin	35
Gibson-StL	23	Nolan-Cin	.720	Selma-Phi	73	Perry-SF	23	Sutton-LA	4	Giusti-Pit	26
Jenkins-Chi	22	Walker-Pit	.714	Linzy-SF-StL	67	Gibson-StL	23	Osteen-LA	4	Brewer-LA	24
Merritt-Cin	20	Perry-SF	.639	Granger-Cin	67	Seaver-NY	19	Morton-Mon	4	Raymond-Mon	23
		Merritt-Cin	.625	Giusti-Pit	66	Dierker-Hou	17	Ellis-Pit	4	Selma-Phi	22

Innings Pitched		Fewest Hits/Game		Fewest BB/Game		Strikeouts		Strikeouts/Game		Ratio	
Perry-SF	328.2	Simpson-Cin	6.39	Jenkins-Chi	1.73	Seaver-NY	283	Seaver-NY	8.76	Jenkins-Chi	9.55
Jenkins-Chi	313.0	Seaver-NY	7.12	Marichal-SF	1.78	Jenkins-Chi	274	Gibson-StL	8.39	Seaver-NY	9.82
Gibson-StL	294.0	Walker-Pit	7.12	Osteen-LA	1.81	Gibson-StL	274	Veale-Pit	7.93	McAndrew-NY	10.06
Seaver-NY	290.2	Gentry-NY	7.41	McAndrew-NY	1.86	Perry-SF	214	Jenkins-Chi	7.88	Perry-SF	10.52
Holtzman-Chi	287.2	Jenkins-Chi	7.62	Merritt-Cin	2.04	Holtzman-Chi	202	Stoneman-Mon	7.63	Gibson-StL	10.84

Earned Run Average		Adjusted ERA		Opponents' Batting Avg.		Opponents' On Base Pct.		Starter Runs		Adjusted Starter Runs	
Seaver-NY	2.82	Seaver-NY	143	Simpson-Cin	.198	Jenkins-Chi	.265	Seaver-NY	39.7	Seaver-NY	38.9
Simpson-Cin	3.02	Simpson-Cin	134	Seaver-NY	.214	Seaver-NY	.273	Perry-SF	30.7	Jenkins-Chi	38.5
Walker-Pit	3.04	Pappas-Atl-Chi	133	Walker-Pit	.219	McAndrew-NY	.281	Gibson-StL	30.2	Holtzman-Chi	35.8
Gibson-StL	3.12	Holtzman-Chi	133	Jenkins-Chi	.224	Perry-SF	.290	Jenkins-Chi	22.7	Gibson-StL	32.4
Koosman-NY	3.14	Jenkins-Chi	133	Gentry-NY	.224	Gibson-StL	.296	Nolan-Cin	21.7	Perry-SF	28.1

Clutch Pitching Index		Relief Runs		Adjusted Relief Runs		Relief Ranking		Total Pitcher Index		Total Baseball Ranking	
Ellis-Pit	119	Selma-Phi	19.4	Selma-Phi	18.5	Selma-Phi	27.6	Seaver-NY	4.5	McCovey-SF	6.2
Morton-Mon	118	Carroll-Cin	16.9	Carroll-Cin	16.8	Granger-Cin	26.5	Gibson-StL	4.2	Seaver-NY	4.5
Coombs-SD	113	Gullett-Cin	13.9	C.Taylor-StL	13.8	Carroll-Cin	24.3	Jenkins-Chi	4.0	Bench-Cin	4.5
Pappas-Atl-Chi	109	Granger-Cin	13.1	Gullett-Cin	13.8	Hoerner-Pit	21.5	Holtzman-Chi	3.4	Perez-Cin	4.3
Dobson-SD	108	C.Taylor-StL	12.9	Granger-Cin	12.9	McMahon-SF	18.8	Selma-Phi	3.0	Gibson-StL	4.2

January 20 Lou Boudreau reaches the Hall of Fame, receiving 232 votes in the BBWAA election. Ralph Kiner finishes with 167, 58 votes short.

February 1 The Hall of Fame Special Committee on Veterans selects Ford Frick, Earle Combs, and Jesse Haines for enshrinement.

April 1 The Milwaukee Brewers Baseball Club, headed by Bud Selig, purchases the Seattle Pilots for $10,800,000.

April 7 Major League Baseball returns to Wisconsin as the Brewers play their first game in Milwaukee, losing to California 12-0 before a crowd of 37,237.

April 13 Oakland uses gold-colored bases during the club's home opener. The Rules Committee subsequently bans this innovation.

June 21 Detroit's Cesar Gutierrez goes 7-for-7 to tie a record set in 1892, in a 12-inning 9-8 win over Cleveland. Mickey Stanley's homer wins it for the Tigers. Gutierrez will collect just seven hits in all of 1971, and 128 hits for his career.

July 1 The return of Denny McLain following his suspension is witnessed by a gathering of 53,863 fans and 71 writers. He is knocked out of the box in the sixth inning, but the Tigers rally to beat the Yankees in the 11th 6-5.

July 2 Detroit's Joe Niekro no-hits the Yankees until Horace Clarke singles in the ninth inning. The Tigers win 5-0. This is the third time in a month that Clarke has broken up a no-hitter, having spoiled bids by Kansas City's Jim Rooker (June 4) and Boston's Sonny Siebert (June 19).

June 3 In pregame ceremonies, California's Clyde Wright is inducted into the National Association of Intercollegiate Athletics (NAIA) Hall of Fame for his pitching while at Carson-Newman College. He then hurls a 4-0 no-hitter against Oakland.

September 21 The A's Vida Blue no-hits the Twins, 6-0, becoming the youngest pitcher to perform the feat since Paul Dean, 36 years ago to the day. The only base runner is Harmon Killebrew, who walks in the fourth. An Oakland crowd of only 4,284 watches Blue's second major league start.

October 10 Baltimore overcomes a 3-0 deficit to beat the Reds, 4-3, in the World Series opener at Riverfront Stadium as Boog Powell, Ellie Hendricks, and Brooks Robinson contribute homers.

October 15 For the third time the Orioles overcome a 3-0 deficit to bury the Reds, 9-3, and win the world championship four games to one. Brooks Robinson, the "human vacuum cleaner," easily wins the Series MVP award.

November 6 Minnesota's Jim Perry wins the AL Cy Young Award in a close race. Perry, who won 24 games during the season, receives 55 points to edge out Dave McNally (47), Sam McDowell (45), and Mike Cuellar (44).

November 11 Boog Powell, who batted .297 with 35 homers and 114 RBIs for Baltimore, is named AL MVP.

November 25 Yankee catcher Thurman Munson receives 23 of 24 votes in being named AL Rookie of the Year.

BALTIMORE		BOSTON		CALIFORNIA		CHICAGO		CLEVELAND		DETROIT	
M	E.Weaver	M	E.Kasko	M	L.Phillips	M	D.Gutteridge	M	A.Dark	M	M.Smith
1B	B.Powell	1B	C.Yastrzemski	1B	J.Spencer	M	B.Adair	1B	T.Horton	1B	N.Cash
2B	D.Johnson	2B	M.Andrews	2B	S.Alomar	M	C.Tanner	2B	E.Leon	2B	D.McAuliffe
SS	M.Belanger	SS	R.Petrocelli	SS	J.Fregosi	1B	G.Hopkins	SS	J.Heidemann	SS	C.Gutierrez
3B	B.Robinson	3B	G.Scott	3B	K.McMullen	2B	B.Knoop	3B	G.Nettles	3B	D.Wert
LF	D.Buford	LF	B.Conigliaro	LF	A.Johnson	SS	L.Aparicio	LF	R.Foster	LF	W.Horton
CF	P.Blair	CF	R.Smith	CF	J.Johnstone	3B	B.Melton	CF	T.Uhlaender	CF	M.Stanley
RF	F.Robinson	RF	T.Conigliaro	RF	R.Repoz	LF	C.May	RF	V.Pinson	RF	J.Northrup
C	E.Hendricks	C	J.Moses	C	J.Azcue	CF	K.Berry	C	R.Fosse	C	B.Freehan
O	M.Rettenmund					RF	W.Williams				
C	A.Etchebarren	P	R.Culp	C	T.Egan	C	E.Herrmann	1O	C.Hinton	O1	A.Kaline
		P	S.Siebert			1O	T.McCraw	CO	D.Sims	3O	E.Maddox
P	J.Palmer	P	G.Peters	P	C.Wright	32	S.O'Brien	P	S.McDowell	P	M.Lolich
P	M.Cuellar	P	K.Brett	P	T.Murphy	C	D.Josephson	P	R.Hand	P	J.Niekro
P	D.McNally	P	M.Nagy	P	R.May			P	D.Chance	P	L.Cain
P	J.Hardin	RP	V.Romo	P	A.Messersmith	P	T.John	P	S.Hargan	P	M.Kilkenny
P	T.Phoebus	RP	S.Lyle	RP	E.Fisher	P	J.Janeski	RP	D.Higgins	P	E.Wilson
RP	M.Lopez	P	C.Koonce	RP	K.Tatum	P	J.Horlen	RP	M.Paul	RP	J.Hiller
RP	D.Hall			RP	G.Garrett	RP	W.Wood	RP	P.Hennigan	RP	T.Timmermann
RP	E.Watt					RP	J.Crider			RP	D.Patterson
				P	T.Bradley	RP	D.Murphy	P	S.Dunning		
P	P.Richert			P	M.Queen			P	B.Moore	P	D.McLain
				P	D.LaRoche	P	B.Johnson	P	R.Austin	P	F.Scherman
						P	B.Moore	P	F.Lasher		
						P	B.Miller				
						P	F.Weaver				

KANSAS CITY		MILWAUKEE		MINNESOTA		NEW YORK		OAKLAND		WASHINGTON	
M	C.Metro	M	D.Bristol	M	B.Rigney	M	R.Houk	M	J.McNamara	M	T.Williams
M	B.Lemon	1B	M.Hegan	1B	R.Reese	1B	D.Cater	1B	D.Mincher	1B	M.Epstein
1B	B.Oliver	2B	T.Kubiak	2B	D.Thompson	2B	H.Clarke	2B	D.Green	2B	T.Cullen
2B	C.Rojas	SS	R.Pena	SS	L.Cardenas	SS	G.Michael	SS	B.Campaneris	SS	E.Brinkman
SS	J.Hernandez	3B	T.Harper	3B	H.Killebrew	3B	J.Kenney	3B	S.Bando	3B	A.Rodriguez
3B	P.Schaal	LF	D.Walton	LF	J.Holt	LF	R.White	LF	F.Alou	LF	F.Howard
LF	L.Piniella	CF	D.May	CF	C.Tovar	CF	B.Murcer	CF	R.Monday	CF	E.Stroud
CF	A.Otis	RF	R.Snyder	RF	T.Oliva	RF	C.Blefary	RF	R.Jackson	RF	D.Unser
RF	P.Kelly	C	P.Roof	C	G.Mitterwald	C	T.Munson	C	F.Fernandez	C	P.Casanova
C	E.Kirkpatrick	C1	J.McNertney	23	F.Quilici	1	J.Ellis	O1	J.Rudi	23	B.Allen
		O	T.Savage	O	B.Alyea	O	R.Woods	C	D.Duncan	O	R.Reichardt
S2	R.Severson	O	B.Burda					O	T.Davis	O	L.Maye
C	E.Rodriguez			P	J.Perry	P	M.Stottlemyre				
		P	M.Pattin	P	J.Kaat	P	F.Peterson	P	C.Dobson	P	D.Bosman
P	D.Drago	P	L.Krausse	P	B.Blyleven	P	S.Bahnsen	P	C.Hunter	P	J.Coleman
P	B.Johnson	P	S.Lockwood	P	B.Zepp	P	S.Kline	P	D.Segui	P	C.Cox
P	J.Rooker	P	B.Bolin	RP	T.Hall	P	M.Kekich	P	B.Odom	P	J.Hannan
P	B.Butler	P	G.Brabender	RP	S.Williams	RP	L.McDaniel	P	R.Fingers	P	G.Brunet
P	D.Morehead	RP	K.Sanders	RP	R.Perranoski	RP	R.Klimkowski	RP	M.Grant	RP	D.Knowles
RP	A.Fitzmorris	RP	J.Gelnar			RP	J.Aker	RP	P.Lindblad	RP	J.Grzenda
RP	T.Burgmeier			P	L.Tiant			RP	M.Lachemann	RP	H.Pina
RP	T.Abernathy	P	A.Downing	P	D.Boswell	P	J.Cumberland				
		P	J.Morris			P	G.Waslewski				
P	W.Bunker							P	B.Locker	P	J.Shellenback
P	K.Wright									P	J.Brown
										P	D.Such

TEAM	G	W	L	PCT	GB	R	OR	AB	H	2B	3B	HR	BB	SO	AVG	OBP	SLG	PRO	PRO+	BR	/A	PF	CHI	RC	SB	CS	SBA	SBR
EAST																												
BAL	162	108	54	.667		**792**	**574**	5545	1424	213	25	179	**717**	952	.257	**.346**	.401	.747	**112**	101	**92**	101	99	**795**	84	39	68	2
NY	163	93	69	.574	15	680	612	5492	1381	208	**41**	111	588	**808**	.251	.327	.365	.692	102	-18	16	95	103	662	105	61	63	-5
BOS	162	87	75	.537	21	786	722	5535	**1450**	**252**	28	**203**	594	855	**.262**	.338	**.428**	**.766**	109	**119**	63	107	98	786	50	48	51	-14
DET	162	79	83	.488	29	666	731	5377	1282	207	38	148	656	825	.238	.325	.374	.699	98	-4	-9	101	99	658	29	30	49	-9
CLE	162	76	86	.469	32	649	675	5463	1358	197	23	183	503	909	.249	.316	.394	.710	96	3	-30	105	97	670	25	36	41	-14
WAS	162	70	92	.432	38	626	689	5460	1302	184	28	138	635	989	.238	.323	.358	.681	99	-36	-5	95	97	638	72	42	63	-4
WEST																												
MIN	162	98	64	.605		744	605	5483	1438	230	**41**	153	501	905	**.262**	.329	.403	.732	107	50	40	101	103	709	57	52	52	-14
OAK	162	89	73	.549	9	678	593	5376	1338	208	24	171	584	977	.249	.327	.392	.719	108	28	53	96	98	689	**131**	68	66	-2
CAL	162	86	76	.531	12	631	630	5532	1391	197	40	114	447	922	.251	.311	.363	.674	95	-64	-43	97	104	622	69	27	**72**	**5**
MIL	163	65	97	.401	33	613	751	5395	1305	202	24	126	592	985	.242	.321	.358	.679	92	-42	-46	101	97	618	91	73	55	-17
KC	162	65	97	.401	33	611	705	5503	1341	202	**41**	97	514	958	.244	.311	.348	.659	88	-88	-87	100	**105**	593	97	53	65	-3
CHI	162	56	106	.346	42	633	822	5514	1394	192	20	123	477	872	.253	.317	.362	.679	90	-50	-74	104	102	627	53	33	62	-4
TOT	973					8109		65675	16404	2492	373	1746	6808	10957	.250	.324	.379	.703							863	562	61	-78

TEAM	CG	SH	SV	IP	H	H/G	HR	BB	SO	RAT	ERA	ERA+	OAV	OOB	PR	/A	PF	CPI	FA	E	DP	FW	PW	BW	SBW	DIF
EAST																										
BAL	**60**	12	31	1478^2	1317	8.0	139	469	941	**11.0**	**3.15**	**116**	.240	**.302**	**93**	**82**	98	102	.981	117	148	**1.1**	**8.5**	**9.5**	.9	7.0
NY	36	6	49	1471^2	1386	8.5	**130**	**451**	777	11.4	3.24	108	.249	.308	77	45	95	**103**	.980	130	146	.4	4.7	1.7	.2	5.1
BOS	38	8	44	1446^1	1391	8.7	156	594	1003	12.6	3.87	102	.251	.329	-25	14	107	100	.974	156	131	-1.2	1.5	6.5	-.8	-.0
DET	33	9	39	1447^1	1443	9.0	153	623	1045	13.1	4.09	91	.260	.338	-61	-59	100	100	.978	133	142	.2	-6.1	-.9	-.3	5.2
CLE	34	8	35	1451^1	1333	8.3	163	689	**1076**	12.8	3.91	101	.247	.337	-31	8	107	**103**	.979	133	168	.2	.8	-3.1	-.8	-2.1
WAS	20	11	40	1457^2	1375	8.5	139	611	823	12.4	3.80	94	.252	.330	-13	-39	96	100	**.982**	**116**	173	**1.1**	-4.0	-.5	.3	-7.8
WEST																										
MIN	26	12	**58**	1448^1	1329	8.3	**130**	486	940	11.5	3.23	115	.244	.310	78	79	100	**103**	.980	123	130	.7	8.2	4.1	-.8	4.7
OAK	33	**15**	40	1442^2	**1253**	**7.8**	134	542	858	11.4	3.30	107	**.234**	.308	66	38	95	98	.977	141	152	-.3	3.9	5.5	.5	-1.6
CAL	21	10	49	1462^1	1280	7.9	154	559	922	11.6	3.48	104	.237	.313	37	21	97	99	.980	127	169	.5	2.2	-4.5	**1.2**	5.6
MIL	31	2	27	1446^2	1397	8.7	146	587	895	12.6	4.21	90	.255	.332	-79	-67	102	93	.978	136	142	.0	-6.9	-4.8	-1.1	-3.2
KC	30	11	25	1463^2	1346	8.3	138	641	915	12.4	3.78	99	.247	.331	-11	-7	101	99	.976	152	162	-.9	-.7	-9.0	.4	-5.7
CHI	20	6	30	1430^1	1554	9.8	164	556	762	13.6	4.54	86	.280	.350	-132	-103	105	101	.975	165	**187**	-1.7	-10.7	-7.7	.3	-5.2
TOT	382	110	467	17447		8.5				12.2	3.71		.250	.324					.978	1629	1850					

Runs
Yastrzemski-Bos .. 125
Tovar-Min 120
White-NY 109
Smith-Bos 109
Harper-Mil 104

Hits
Oliva-Min 204
Johnson-Cal 202
Tovar-Min 195
Yastrzemski-Bos ... 186
White-NY 180

Doubles
Tovar-Min 36
Otis-KC 36
Oliva-Min 36
Harper-Mil 35
Cardenas-Min 34

Triples
Tovar-Min 13
Stanley-Det 11
Otis-KC 9

Home Runs
Howard-Was 44
Killebrew-Min 41
Yastrzemski-Bos 40
T.Conigliaro-Bos 36
Powell-Bal 35

Total Bases
Yastrzemski-Bos .. 335
Oliva-Min 323
Harper-Mil 315
Howard-Was 309
Powell-Bal 289

Runs Batted In
Howard-Was 126
T.Conigliaro-Bos .. 116
Powell-Bal 114
Killebrew-Min 113
Oliva-Min 107

Runs Produced
Yastrzemski-Bos ... 187
White-NY 181
Oliva-Min 180
Howard-Was 172
T.Conigliaro-Bos .. 169

Bases On Balls
Howard-Was 132
Yastrzemski-Bos ... 128
Killebrew-Min 128
Bando-Oak 118
Buford-Bal 109

Batting Average
Johnson-Cal ...... .329
Yastrzemski-Bos ... .329
Oliva-Min .... .325
Aparicio-Chi ...... .313
F.Robinson-Bal .... .306

On Base Percentage
Yastrzemski-Bos ... .453
Howard-Was ...... .420
Powell-Bal .... .417
Killebrew-Min .... .416
Buford-Bal .... .409

Slugging Average
Yastrzemski-Bos .. .592
Powell-Bal .... .549
Killebrew-Min .... .546
Howard-Was ...... .546
Harper-Mil .... .522

Production
Yastrzemski-Bos . 1.045
Powell-Bal .... .967
Howard-Was ...... .966
Killebrew-Min ..... .962
F.Robinson-Bal .... .922

Adjusted Production
Yastrzemski-Bos ... 174
Howard-Was 173
Powell-Bal 163
Killebrew-Min 161
F.Robinson-Bal 151

Batter Runs
Yastrzemski-Bos .. 71.7
Howard-Was 54.1
Killebrew-Min 49.5
Powell-Bal 49.2
Harper-Mil 37.5

Adjusted Batter Runs
Yastrzemski-Bos ... 61.7
Howard-Was 60.5
Powell-Bal 47.9
Killebrew-Min 47.8
White-NY 38.2

Clutch Hitting Index
Piniella-KC 128
Cater-NY 117
McMullen-Was-Cal . 116
Howard-Was 116
Belanger-Bal 115

Runs Created
Yastrzemski-Bos .. 157
Howard-Was 130
Powell-Bal 123
Harper-Mil 122
Killebrew-Min 116

Total Average
Yastrzemski-Bos . 1.170
Powell-Bal 1.034
Howard-Was 1.026
Killebrew-Min ... 1.000
F.Robinson-Bal .... .944

Stolen Bases
Campaneris-Oak ... 42
Harper-Mil 38
Alomar-Cal 35
Kelly-KC 34
Otis-KC 33

Stolen Base Average
Otis-KC 94.3
Johnson-Cal 89.5
Campaneris-Oak .. 80.8
Stroud-Was 78.4
Kenney-NY 76.9

Stolen Base Runs
Otis-KC 8.7
Campaneris-Oak ... 6.6
Stroud-Was 3.9
Johnson-Cal 3.9
Alomar-Cal 3.3

Fielding Runs
Knoop-Chi 35.1
Brinkman-Was 31.1
Nettles-Cle 27.8
Cullen-Was 26.5
Mitterwald-Min ... 24.3

Total Player Rating
Yastrzemski-Bos ... 5.2
Aparicio-Chi 4.6
Oliva-Min 4.3
Fregosi-Cal 4.2
Howard-Was 4.2

Wins
Perry-Min 24
McNally-Bal 24
Cuellar-Bal 24
Wright-Cal 22

Win Percentage
Cuellar-Bal ...... .750
McNally-Bal ...... .727
Perry-Min .... .667
Palmer-Bal .... .667
Siebert-Bos ...... .652

Games
Wood-Chi 77
Grant-Oak 72
Knowles-Was 71
Williams-Min 68

Complete Games
Cuellar-Bal 21
McDowell-Cle 19
Palmer-Bal 17
McNally-Bal 16
Culp-Bos 15

Shutouts
Palmer-Bal 5
Dobson-Oak 5
Peters-Bos 4
Perry-Min 4
Cuellar-Bal 4

Saves
Perranoski-Min 34
McDaniel-NY 29
Timmermann-Det ... 27
Knowles-Was 27
Grant-Oak 24

Innings Pitched
Palmer-Bal 305.0
McDowell-Cle 305.0
Cuellar-Bal 297.2
McNally-Bal 296.0
Perry-Min 278.2

Fewest Hits/Game
Messersmith-Cal . 6.66
McDowell-Cle 6.96
Segui-Oak 7.22
Johnson-KC 7.49
Culp-Bos 7.56

Fewest BB/Game
Peterson-NY 1.38
Perry-Min 1.84
Cox-Was 2.06
Cuellar-Bal 2.09
Horlen-Chi 2.14

Strikeouts
McDowell-Cle 304
Lolich-Det 230
Johnson-KC 206
Palmer-Bal 199
Culp-Bos 197

Strikeouts/Game
McDowell-Cle 8.97
Johnson-KC 8.66
Cain-Det 7.77
Lolich-Det 7.59
Messersmith-Cal .. 7.49

Ratio
Peterson-NY 10.03
Cuellar-Bal 10.37
Perry-Min 10.46
Blyleven-Min 10.54
Messersmith-Cal . 10.54

Earned Run Average
Segui-Oak 2.56
Palmer-Bal 2.71
Wright-Cal 2.83
Peterson-NY 2.90
McDowell-Cle 2.92

Adjusted ERA
Segui-Oak 139
McDowell-Cle 136
Palmer-Bal 134
Culp-Bos 130
Wright-Cal 128

Opponents' Batting Avg.
Messersmith-Cal .. .205
McDowell-Cle .... .213
Segui-Oak .... .222
Culp-Bos .... .224
Johnson-KC ..... .228

Opponents' On Base Pct.
Peterson-NY ..... .280
Cuellar-Bal ...... .286
Perry-Min .... .287
Blyleven-Min ..... .289
Messersmith-Cal .. .290

Starter Runs
Palmer-Bal 33.9
McDowell-Cle 26.9
Wright-Cal 25.6
Peterson-NY 23.4
Perry-Min 21.0

Adjusted Starter Runs
McDowell-Cle 35.2
Palmer-Bal 31.6
Culp-Bos 25.6
Wright-Cal 22.7
Perry-Min 21.2

Clutch Pitching Index
Stottlemyre-NY ... 113
Kaat-Min 112
Bahnsen-NY 109
Segui-Oak 108
Wright-Cal 107

Relief Runs
Grant-Oak 25.9
Knowles-Was 22.2
Williams-Min 21.8
McDaniel-NY 21.1
Sanders-Mil 20.1

Adjusted Relief Runs
Grant-Oak 23.5
Williams-Min 21.9
Sanders-Mil 20.9
Hall-Min 20.2
Knowles-Was 20.1

Relief Ranking
Knowles-Was 32.8
McDaniel-NY 30.0
Wood-Chi 28.6
Perranoski-Min ... 28.5
Williams-Min 24.5

Total Pitcher Index
Knowles-Was 3.5
Perry-Min 3.3
McDaniel-NY 3.3
Wood-Chi 3.2
McDowell-Cle 3.0

Total Baseball Ranking
Yastrzemski-Bos ... 5.2
Aparicio-Chi 4.6
Oliva-Min 4.3
Fregosi-Cal 4.2
Howard-Was 4.2

January 21 The BBWAA fails to elect anyone in the annual Hall of Fame election. With 270 votes required, the nearest finishers are Yogi Berra (242) and Early Wynn (240).

January 31 The Hall of Fame Special Veterans Committee selects seven men for enshrinement: former players Jake Beckley, Joe Kelley, Harry Hooper, Rube Marquard, Chick Hafey, Dave Bancroft, and executive George Weiss.

February 9 Satchel Paige is nominated for the Hall of Fame. The Hall's new Special Committee on the Negro Leagues will formally select Paige for induction on June 10.

April 10 The Phillies debut in new $49.5 million Veterans Stadium, beating Montreal, 4-1. Don Money connects for the park's first homer.

April 27 Hank Aaron becomes the third member of the 600-home run club, but one of the other two members—the Giants' Willie Mays—hits a 10th-inning single to beat Aaron's Braves.

May 28 Clete Boyer, involved in a dispute with Braves owner Paul Richards and manager Lum Harris over alleged mismanagement, gets his release and retires. Boyer had hit safely in the last nine games of his career, including five home runs and 14 RBIs.

May 30 Willie Mays hits his 638th career home run for the Giants, adding his NL record 1,950th run scored in the process. Stan Musial had been the record holder with 1,949 runs.

June 3 Cub southpaw Ken Holtzman tosses the second no-hitter of his career, victimizing the Reds 1-0. Holtzman scores the only run, in the third inning.

June 6 Willie Mays strokes a 12th-inning home run off Joe Hoerner of the Phillies in the second game of a doubleheader. It is his 22nd—and last—career extra-inning belt, a major league record.

June 23 Phillie Rick Wise no-hits the Reds 4-0 and hits two home runs to drive in all the runs in the game.

August 14 Before 30,678 Pittsburgh fans, Cardinals ace Bob Gibson, 35, hurls the first no-hitter of his career, an 11-0 shellacking of the Pirates. The Cards make it easy for Gibson by scoring five runs in the top of the first inning.

September 5 Astros pitcher J. R. Richard makes his major league debut, striking out 15 Giants in a 5-3 win.

September 29 In the sixth inning of the Expos' 6–5 win over the Cubs, Ron Hunt is hit by a Milt Pappas pitch. It is the 50th time Hunt has been plunked in 1971, setting a major league record.

October 6 The Pirates outslug the Giants 9-5 to win the NLCS three games to one, as Richie Hebner's bat takes Pittsburgh into the World Series. Hebner has three hits and three RBIs, including a homer.

October 14 Nelson Briles hurls a two-hit shutout and Bob Robertson slugs his sixth postseason homer as the Pirates win the fifth game 4-0 and take a 3-2 Series advantage. Roberto Clemente hits safely in his 12th straight Series game.

October 17 Steve Blass hurls a four-hitter and Clemente homers as the Pirates win Game 7 of the World Series, 2-1, becoming World Champions for the first time since 1960.

November 10 Joe Torre, who hit 24 homers for the Cardinals and led the NL in RBIs (137) and batting (.363), wins the MVP Award.

November 24 Earl Williams, who belted 33 home runs and knocked in 87 runs for the Braves, wins the NL Rookie of the Year honors. Williams gets 18 of 24 votes, with the others going to Willie Montanez of the Phillies.

December 1 The Cubs release Ernie Banks and sign him as a coach.

	ATLANTA		CHICAGO		CINCINNATI		HOUSTON		LOS ANGELES		MONTREAL
M	L.Harris	M	L.Durocher	M	S.Anderson	M	H.Walker	M	W.Alston	M	G.Mauch
1B	H.Aaron	1B	J.Pepitone	1B	L.May	1B	D.Menke	1B	W.Parker	1B	R.Fairly
2B	F.Millan	2B	G.Beckert	2B	T.Helms	2B	J.Morgan	2B	J.Lefebvre	2B	R.Hunt
SS	M.Perez	SS	D.Kessinger	SS	D.Concepcion	SS	R.Metzger	SS	M.Wills	SS	B.Wine
3B	D.Evans	3B	R.Santo	3B	T.Perez	3B	D.Rader	3B	S.Garvey	3B	B.Bailey
LF	R.Garr	LF	B.Williams	LF	H.McRae	LF	J.Alou	LF	D.Allen	LF	J.Fairey
CF	S.Jackson	CF	B.Davis	CF	G.Foster	CF	C.Cedeno	CF	W.Davis	CF	B.Day
RF	M.Lum	RF	J.Callison	RF	P.Rose	RF	J.Wynn	RF	B.Buckner	RF	R.Staub
C	E.Williams	C	C.Cannizzaro	C	J.Bench	C	J.Edwards	C	D.Sims	C	J.Bateman
1	O.Cepeda	O1	J.Hickman	O	B.Carbo	O1	B.Watson	O	W.Crawford	2S	G.Sutherland
		23	P.Popovich	S3	W.Woodward			S3	B.Valentine		
P	P.Niekro					P	D.Wilson	O	M.Mota	P	B.Stoneman
P	R.Reed	P	F.Jenkins	P	G.Nolan	P	J.Billingham	2O	B.Russell	P	S.Renko
P	G.Stone	P	M.Pappas	P	D.Gullett	P	K.Forsch	C	T.Haller	P	C.Morton
P	P.Jarvis	P	B.Hands	P	J.McGlothlin	P	L.Dierker			P	E.McAnally
P	T.Kelley	P	K.Holtzman	P	R.Grimsley	P	W.Blasingame	P	D.Sutton	P	J.Strohmayer
RP	C.Upshaw	P	J.Pizarro	P	W.Simpson	RP	J.Ray	P	A.Downing	RP	M.Marshall
RP	S.Barber	RP	P.Regan	RP	W.Granger	RP	G.Culver	P	C.Osteen	RP	D.McGinn
RP	B.Priddy	RP	B.Bonham	RP	C.Carroll	RP	D.Lemaster	P	B.Singer	RP	H.Reed
				RP	J.Gibbon			RP	J.Brewer		
P	J.Nash					P	F.Gladding	RP	P.Mikkelsen	P	C.Raymond
P	M.McQueen	P	J.Merritt					RP	J.Moeller		
P	R.Herbel	P	T.Cloninger								
								P	D.Alexander		

	NEW YORK		PHILADELPHIA		PITTSBURGH		SAN DIEGO		SAN FRANCISCO		ST.LOUIS
M	G.Hodges	M	F.Lucchesi	M	D.Murtaugh	M	P.Gomez	M	C.Fox	M	R.Schoendienst
1B	E.Kranepool	1B	D.Johnson	1B	B.Robertson	1B	N.Colbert	1B	W.McCovey	1B	J.Hague
2B	K.Boswell	2B	D.Doyle	2B	D.Cash	2B	D.Mason	2B	T.Fuentes	2B	J.Sizemore
SS	B.Harrelson	SS	L.Bowa	SS	G.Alley	SS	E.Hernandez	SS	C.Speier	SS	D.Maxvill
3B	B.Aspromonte	3B	J.Vukovich	3B	R.Hebner	3B	E.Spiezio	3B	A.Gallagher	3B	J.Torre
LF	C.Jones	LF	O.Gamble	LF	W.Stargell	LF	L.Stahl	LF	K.Henderson	LF	L.Brock
CF	T.Agee	CF	W.Montanez	CF	A.Oliver	CF	C.Gaston	CF	W.Mays	CF	M.Alou
RF	K.Singleton	RF	R.Freed	RF	R.Clemente	RF	O.Brown	RF	B.Bonds	RF	J.Cardenal
C	J.Grote	C	T.McCarver	C	M.Sanguillen	C	B.Barton	C	D.Dietz	C	T.Simmons
23	T.Foli	3O	D.Money	O	G.Clines	23	D.Campbell	32	H.Lanier	O	J.Cruz
O	D.Hahn	2	T.Harmon	O1	V.Davalillo	O	I.Murrell			2	J.Javier
O	D.Marshall			S	J.Hernandez	O	L.Lee	P	G.Perry		
1	D.Clendenon	P	R.Wise					P	J.Marichal	P	S.Carlton
3	W.Garrett	P	B.Lersch	P	S.Blass	P	D.Roberts	P	J.Cumberland	P	B.Gibson
		P	C.Short	P	D.Ellis	P	C.Kirby	P	R.Bryant	P	R.Cleveland
P	T.Seaver	P	K.Reynolds	P	B.Johnson	P	S.Arlin	P	S.Stone	P	J.Reuss
P	G.Gentry	P	W.Fryman	P	L.Walker	P	T.Phoebus	RP	J.Johnson	RP	C.Taylor
P	J.Koosman	RP	B.Champion	P	B.Moose	P	F.Norman	RP	D.McMahon	RP	M.Drabowsky
P	R.Sadecki	RP	B.Brandon	RP	D.Giusti	RP	A.Severinsen	RP	R.Robertson	RP	F.Linzy
P	N.Ryan	RP	J.Hoerner	RP	M.Grant	RP	B.Miller				
RP	T.McGraw					RP	D.Kelley	P	D.Carrithers	P	C.Zachary
RP	D.Frisella	P	J.Bunning	P	N.Briles					P	D.Shaw
RP	C.Williams	P	B.Wilson	P	B.Kison	P	D.Coombs			P	A.Santorini
P	J.McAndrew										
P	R.Taylor										

TEAM	G	W	L	PCT	GB	R	OR	AB	H	2B	3B	HR	BB	SO	AVG	OBP	SLG	PRO	PRO+	BR	/A	PF	CHI	RC	SB	CS	SBA	SBR
EAST																												
PIT	162	97	65	.599		**788**	599	5674	**1555**	223	**61**	154	469	919	.274	.333	.416	**.749**	119	121	**125**	100	103	776	65	31	68	1
STL	163	90	72	.556	7	739	699	5610	1542	225	54	95	543	757	**.275**	**.342**	.385	.727	108	91	62	104	100	736	**124**	53	70	5
NY	162	83	79	.512	14	588	**550**	5477	1365	203	29	98	547	958	.249	.321	.351	.672	98	-20	-11	99	95	614	89	43	67	1
CHI	162	83	79	.512	14	637	648	5438	1401	202	34	128	527	772	.258	.327	.378	.705	93	41	-56	115	95	663	44	32	58	-6
MON	162	71	90	.441	25.5	622	729	5335	1312	197	29	88	543	800	.246	.325	.343	.668	96	-20	-22	100	102	598	51	43	54	-11
PHI	162	67	95	.414	30	558	688	5538	1289	209	35	123	499	1031	.233	.300	.350	.650	90	-74	-73	100	99	586	63	39	62	-5
WEST																												
SF	162	90	72	.556		706	644	5461	1348	224	36	140	**654**	1042	.247	.331	.378	.709	109	57	68	98	101	699	101	36	**74**	9
LA	162	89	73	.549	1	663	587	5523	1469	213	38	95	489	755	.266	.328	.370	.698	111	28	68	94	100	661	76	40	66	-1
ATL	162	82	80	.506	8	643	699	5575	1434	192	30	153	434	**747**	.257	.314	.385	.699	98	18	-23	106	98	658	57	46	55	-11
HOU	162	79	83	.488	11	585	567	5492	1319	**230**	52	71	478	888	.240	.304	.340	.644	90	-81	-67	97	**107**	573	101	51	66	0
CIN	162	79	83	.488	11	586	581	5414	1306	203	28	138	438	907	.241	.301	.366	.667	96	-45	-33	98	103	580	59	33	64	-2
SD	161	61	100	.379	28.5	486	610	5366	1250	184	31	96	438	966	.233	.294	.332	.626	89	-117	-84	93	98	513	70	45	61	-6
TOT	972					7601		65903	16590	2505	457	1379	6059	10542	.252	.318	.366	.685							900	492	65	-25

TEAM	CG	SH	SV	IP	H	H/G	HR	BB	SO	RAT	ERA	ERA+	OAV	OOB	PR	/A	PF	CPI	FA	E	DP	FW	PW	BW	SBW	DIF
EAST																										
PIT	43	15	**48**	1461	1426	8.8	108	470	813	11.9	3.31	102	.257	.318	26	12	98	105	.979	133	164	.0	1.3	**13.4**	.3	.9
STL	56	14	22	1467	1482	9.1	104	576	911	12.9	3.85	93	.263	.336	-63	-41	104	99	.978	142	155	-.4	-4.4	6.6	.8	6.4
NY	42	13	22	1466[1]	**1227**	**7.5**	100	529	**1157**	11.0	**2.99**	114	**.227**	**.300**	78	68	98	94	.981	114	135	1.2	**7.3**	-1.2	.3	-5.6
CHI	75	17	13	1444	1458	9.1	132	411	900	11.8	3.61	109	.262	.316	-23	52	114	101	.980	126	150	.5	5.6	-6.0	-.4	2.4
MON	49	8	25	1434[1]	1418	8.9	133	658	829	13.2	4.12	86	.260	.344	-104	-94	102	100	.976	150	164	-.9	-10.1	-2.4	-1.0	4.3
PHI	31	10	25	1470[2]	1396	8.5	132	525	838	12.0	3.71	95	.254	.323	-41	-31	102	98	.981	122	158	.7	-3.3	-7.8	-.3	-3.3
WEST																										
SF	45	14	30	1454[2]	1324	8.2	128	471	831	11.3	3.32	102	.242	.306	24	13	98	97	.972	179	153	-2.6	1.4	7.3	**1.2**	1.7
LA	48	**18**	33	1449[2]	1363	8.5	110	**399**	853	11.1	3.23	100	.250	.304	37	-1	93	98	.979	131	159	.2	-.1	7.3	.1	.5
ATL	40	11	31	1474[2]	1529	9.3	152	485	823	12.5	3.75	99	.269	.330	-46	-6	107	**108**	.977	146	**180**	-.7	-.6	-2.5	-1.0	5.7
HOU	43	10	25	1471[1]	1318	8.1	**75**	475	914	11.3	3.13	107	.241	.309	55	38	97	95	.983	106	152	1.6	4.1	-7.2	.2	-.8
CIN	27	11	38	1444	1298	8.1	112	501	750	11.4	3.35	100	.243	.311	18	0	97	97	**.984**	**103**	174	**1.8**	.0	-3.5	.0	-.3
SD	47	10	17	1438	1351	8.5	93	559	923	12.1	3.22	102	.249	.249	39	12	95	106	.974	161	144	-1.6	1.3	-9.0	-.4	-9.8
TOT	546	151	329	17475[2]		8.5				11.9	3.47		.252	.318					.979	1613	1888					

Runs
Brock-StL 126
Bonds-SF 110
Stargell-Pit 104
Garr-Atl 101
Torre-StL 97

Hits
Torre-StL 230
Garr-Atl 219
Brock-StL 200
Davis-LA 198

Doubles
Cedeno-Hou 40
Brock-StL 37
Torre-StL 34
Staub-Mon 34
Davis-LA 33

Triples
Morgan-Hou 11
Metzger-Hou 11
Davis-LA 10
Gaston-SD 9

Home Runs
Stargell-Pit 48
H.Aaron-Atl 47
May-Cin 39
Johnson-Phi 34

Total Bases
Torre-StL 352
H.Aaron-Atl 331
Stargell-Pit 321
Bonds-SF 317
Williams-Chi 300

Runs Batted In
Torre-StL 137
Stargell-Pit 125
H.Aaron-Atl 118
Bonds-SF 102
Montanez-Phi 99

Runs Produced
Torre-StL 210
Stargell-Pit 181
Brock-StL 180
Bonds-SF 179
Staub-Mon 172

Bases On Balls
Mays-SF 112
Dietz-SF 97
Bailey-Mon 97
Allen-LA 93
Morgan-Hou 88

Batting Average
Torre-StL .... .363
Garr-Atl .... .343
Beckert-Chi .... .342
Clemente-Pit ..... .341
H.Aaron-Atl ...... .327

On Base Percentage
Mays-SF .... .429
Torre-StL .... .424
H.Aaron-Atl ...... .414
Hunt-Mon .... .403
Stargell-Pit .... .401

Slugging Average
H.Aaron-Atl ...... .669
Stargell-Pit ...... .628
Torre-StL .... .555
May-Cin .... .532
Bonds-SF .... .512

Production
H.Aaron-Atl 1.082
Stargell-Pit 1.029
Torre-StL .... .979
Mays-SF .... .911
Williams-Chi ...... .889

Adjusted Production
H.Aaron-Atl 190
Stargell-Pit 188
Torre-StL 169
Mays-SF 160
Allen-LA 154

Batter Runs
H.Aaron-Atl 65.2
Torre-StL 62.5
Stargell-Pit 58.7
Williams-Chi 39.4
Staub-Mon 38.5

Adjusted Batter Runs
Stargell-Pit 59.3
H.Aaron-Atl 57.7
Torre-StL 57.3
Allen-LA 41.1
Mays-SF 39.1

Clutch Hitting Index
Fairly-Mon 129
Sanguillen-Pit 125
Bailey-Mon 123
Watson-Hou 121
Simmons-StL 120

Runs Created
Torre-StL 145
H.Aaron-Atl 137
Stargell-Pit 131
Bonds-SF 115
Brock-StL 114

Total Average
H.Aaron-Atl 1.178
Stargell-Pit 1.117
Mays-SF 1.067
Torre-StL .... .998
Bonds-SF .... .876

Stolen Bases
Brock-StL 64
Morgan-Hou 40
Garr-Atl 30

Stolen Base Average
Mays-SF 88.5
Henderson-SF 85.7
Morgan-Hou 83.3
Agee-NY 82.4
Hernandez-SD 80.8

Stolen Base Runs
Brock-StL 7.8
Morgan-Hou 7.2
Mays-SF 5.1
Agee-NY 4.8
Harrelson-NY 4.2

Fielding Runs
Maxvill-StL 29.2
Garr-Atl 16.2
Robertson-Pit 15.2
Helms-Cin 14.4
Barton-SD 14.0

Total Player Rating
Stargell-Pit 5.8
H.Aaron-Atl 4.2
Torre-StL 4.1
Staub-Mon 3.6
Mays-SF 3.6

Wins
Jenkins-Chi 24
Seaver-NY 20
Downing-LA 20
Carlton-StL 20
Ellis-Pit 19

Win Percentage
Gullett-Cin .... .727
Downing-LA ...... .690
Carlton-StL .... .690
Ellis-Pit .... .679
Seaver-NY .... .667

Games
Granger-Cin 70
J.Johnson-SF 67
Marshall-Mon 66
McMahon-SF 61
Carroll-Cin 61

Complete Games
Jenkins-Chi 30
Seaver-NY 21
Stoneman-Mon ... 20
Gibson-StL 20

Shutouts
Pappas-Chi 5
Gibson-StL 5
Downing-LA 5
Blass-Pit 5

Saves
Giusti-Pit 30
Marshall-Mon 23
Brewer-LA 22
J.Johnson-SF 18
Upshaw-Atl 17

Innings Pitched
Jenkins-Chi 325.0
Stoneman-Mon ... 294.2
Seaver-NY 286.1
Perry-SF 280.0
Marichal-SF 279.0

Fewest Hits/Game
Wilson-Hou 6.55
Seaver-NY 6.60
Kirby-SD 7.17
Gentry-NY 7.39
Stoneman-Mon ... 7.42

Fewest BB/Game
Jenkins-Chi 1.02
Marichal-SF 1.81
Stone-Atl 1.82
Hands-Chi 1.86
Sutton-LA 1.87

Strikeouts
Seaver-NY 289
Jenkins-Chi 263
Stoneman-Mon ... 251
Kirby-SD 231
Sutton-LA 194

Strikeouts/Game
Seaver-NY 9.08
Kirby-SD 7.78
Stoneman-Mon ... 7.67
Jenkins-Chi 7.28
Gentry-NY 6.86

Ratio
Seaver-NY 8.64
Wilson-Hou 9.44
Jenkins-Chi 9.58
Marichal-SF 9.77
Sutton-LA 9.87

Earned Run Average
Seaver-NY 1.76
Roberts-SD 2.10
Wilson-Hou 2.45
Forsch-Hou 2.53
Sutton-LA 2.54

Adjusted ERA
Seaver-NY 194
Roberts-SD 157
Jenkins-Chi 142
Wilson-Hou 137
Forsch-Hou 133

Opponents' Batting Avg.
Wilson-Hou ...... .202
Seaver-NY .... .206
Kirby-SD .... .216
Cumberland-SF ... .223
Gentry-NY .... .224

Opponents' On Base Pct.
Seaver-NY .... .253
Wilson-Hou ...... .268
Jenkins-Chi .... .271
Marichal-SF ...... .274
Nolan-Cin .... .275

Starter Runs
Seaver-NY 54.3
Roberts-SD 40.9
Wilson-Hou 30.2
Sutton-LA 27.2
Jenkins-Chi 25.2

Adjusted Starter Runs
Seaver-NY 52.4
Jenkins-Chi 42.1
Roberts-SD 35.8
Wilson-Hou 27.2
Niekro-Atl 21.8

Clutch Pitching Index
Roberts-SD 120
Downing-LA 115
Short-Phi 115
Johnson-Pit 112
Wise-Phi 112

Relief Runs
McGraw-NY 21.7
Miller-Chi-SD-Pit . 20.0
Frisella-NY 14.9
Ray-Hou 14.6
Brewer-LA 14.3

Adjusted Relief Runs
McGraw-NY 21.0
Miller-Chi-SD-Pit . 18.9
Frisella-NY 14.3
Ray-Hou 13.5
Hoerner-Phi 12.6

Relief Ranking
McGraw-NY 29.0
Miller-Chi-SD-Pit . 26.7
Frisella-NY 22.7
Brewer-LA 22.3
Ray-Hou 18.4

Total Pitcher Index
Seaver-NY 6.5
Jenkins-Chi 6.4
Roberts-SD 4.6
Wise-Phi 3.4
McGraw-NY 3.4

Total Baseball Ranking
Seaver-NY 6.5
Jenkins-Chi 6.4
Stargell-Pit 5.8
Roberts-SD 4.6
H.Aaron-Atl 4.2

January 11 Tigers pitcher John Hiller, age 27, suffers a heart attack. He will miss the season before making a remarkable comeback.

April 27 Curt Flood jumps the Senators after 13 games and departs for Denmark, ending his playing career. He will continue his antitrust suit, which will eventually reach the Supreme Court.

June 21 Indians slugger Ken Harrelson announces his retirement from baseball to join the pro golf tour.

June 26 Last year's AL batting king Alex Johnson is suspended by the Angels following a series of incidents (including five benchings and 29 fines) resulting from his failure to hustle.

July 13 In an All-Star Game featuring homers by Johnny Bench, Hank Aaron, Roberto Clemente, Reggie Jackson, Frank Robinson, and Harmon Killebrew, the AL triumphs at Detroit 6-4. It is the league's only All-Star win between 1962 and 1983. Jackson's homer goes 520 feet.

August 10 Harmon Killebrew becomes the 10th player to amass 500 homers, and adds his 501st, but the Orioles beat the Twins, 5-4.

August 10 Sixteen baseball researchers at Cooperstown form the Society for American Baseball Research (SABR), with founder L. Robert Davids as president.

September 26 Jim Palmer becomes the fourth member of the Orioles pitching staff to notch his 20th victory. Only one other team in major league history—the 1920 White Sox—boasted four 20-game winners.

September 28 Arbitrator Lewis Gill rules that Alex Johnson was "emotionally incapacitated" during events leading to his June suspension, and that he should be treated the same as a physically disabled player. Johnson wins nearly $30,000 in back salary from the Angels.

September 28 Baltimore achieves 108 wins for the season with doubleheader victories at Boston 10-2 and 5-4. The Orioles become only the third team to win 100 games in three straight seasons.

September 30 The Senators, in their final game in Washington, hold a 7-5 lead over the Yankees with two outs in the

ninth. Fans then swarm onto the field, causing the game to be forfeited.

October 5 The Orioles overcome two Reggie Jackson home runs to complete a sweep of Oakland in the ALCS with a 5-3 victory.

October 9 The Orioles win Game 1 of the World Series over the Pirates 5-3 behind Dave McNally's three-hitter and Merv Rettenmund's three-run homer.

October 11 Brooks Robinson ties a Series record by reaching base five straight times on three hits and two walks as Baltimore rolls over Pittsburgh 11-3 to take a 2-0 Series advantage.

October 26 Vida Blue wins the AL Cy Young Award. Blue was 24-8 for the A's, posting 301 strikeouts, eight shutouts, and a 1.82 ERA. Ferguson Jenkins won the Cy Young Award in the NL.

November 10 Vida Blue adds the AL MVP to his list of awards.

December 10 The Angels trade shortstop Jim Fregosi to the Mets for four players, including outfielder Leroy Stanton and pitcher Nolan Ryan. This will rank as probably the Angels' best trade (and as one of the worst by the Mets).

	BALTIMORE		BOSTON		CALIFORNIA		CHICAGO		CLEVELAND		DETROIT
M	E.Weaver	M	E.Kasko	M	L.Phillips	M	C.Tanner	M	A.Dark	M	B.Martin
1B	B.Powell	1B	G.Scott	1B	J.Spencer	1B	C.May	M	J.Lipon	1B	N.Cash
2B	D.Johnson	2B	D.Griffin	2B	S.Alomar	2B	M.Andrews	1B	C.Chambliss	2B	D.McAuliffe
SS	M.Belanger	SS	L.Aparicio	SS	J.Fregosi	SS	L.Alvarado	2B	E.Leon	SS	E.Brinkman
3B	B.Robinson	3B	R.Petrocelli	3B	K.McMullen	3B	B.Melton	SS	J.Heidemann	3B	A.Rodriguez
LF	D.Buford	LF	C.Yastrzemski	LF	T.Gonzalez	LF	R.Reichardt	3B	G.Nettles	LF	W.Horton
CF	P.Blair	CF	B.Conigliaro	CF	K.Berry	CF	J.Johnstone	LF	T.Uhlaender	CF	M.Stanley
RF	M.Rettenmund	RF	R.Smith	RF	R.Repoz	RF	W.Williams	CF	V.Pinson	RF	A.Kaline
C	E.Hendricks	C	D.Josephson	C	J.Stephenson	C	E.Herrmann	RF	R.Foster	C	B.Freehan
								C	R.Fosse		
O1	F.Robinson	O	J.Lahoud	O	M.Rivers	2O	R.McKinney			O1	J.Northrup
C	A.Etchebarren	2S	J.Kennedy	O	T.Conigliaro	SO	L.Richard	P	S.McDowell		
		C	B.Montgomery	S	S.O'Brien	C	T.Egan	P	S.Dunning	P	M.Lolich
P	M.Cuellar			O	A.Johnson	O	P.Kelly	P	A.Foster	P	J.Coleman
P	J.Palmer	P	R.Culp					P	R.Lamb	P	L.Cain
P	P.Dobson	P	S.Siebert	P	C.Wright	P	W.Wood	P	S.Hargan	P	J.Niekro
P	D.McNally	P	G.Peters	P	A.Messersmith	P	T.Bradley	RP	V.Colbert	RP	F.Scherman
RP	G.Jackson	P	J.Lonborg	P	T.Murphy	P	T.John	RP	P.Hennigan	RP	D.Chance
		RP	B.Lee	P	R.May	P	B.Johnson	RP	E.Farmer	RP	M.Kilkenny
P	D.Leonhard	RP	B.Bolin	RP	E.Fisher	P	J.Horlen				
		RP	K.Brett	RP	L.Allen	RP	S.Kealey	P	M.Paul	P	T.Timmermann
				RP	D.LaRoche	RP	V.Romo	P	R.Hand		
		P	L.Tiant			RP	T.Forster	P	S.Mingori		
		P	R.Moret	P	M.Queen						
		P	K.Tatum								
		P	S.Lyle								

	KANSAS CITY		MILWAUKEE		MINNESOTA		NEW YORK		OAKLAND		WASHINGTON
M	B.Lemon	M	D.Bristol	M	B.Rigney	M	R.Houk	M	D.Williams	M	T.Williams
1B	G.Hopkins	1B	J.Briggs	1B	R.Reese	1B	D.Cater	1B	M.Epstein	1B	D.Mincher
2B	C.Rojas	2B	R.Theobald	2B	R.Carew	2B	H.Clarke	2B	D.Green	2B	T.Cullen
SS	F.Patek	SS	R.Auerbach	SS	L.Cardenas	SS	G.Michael	SS	B.Campaneris	SS	T.Harrah
3B	P.Schaal	3B	T.Matchick	3B	S.Braun	3B	J.Kenney	3B	S.Bando	3B	D.Nelson
LF	L.Piniella	LF	T.Harper	LF	C.Tovar	LF	R.White	LF	J.Rudi	LF	F.Howard
CF	A.Otis	CF	D.May	CF	J.Holt	CF	B.Murcer	CF	R.Monday	CF	E.Maddox
RF	J.Keough	RF	B.Voss	RF	T.Oliva	RF	F.Alou	RF	R.Jackson	RF	D.Unser
C	J.May	C	E.Rodriguez	C	G.Mitterwald	C	T.Munson	C	D.Duncan	C	P.Casanova
OC	E.Kirkpatrick	O1	A.Kosco	13	H.Killebrew	1	J.Ellis	O	A.Mangual	23	A.Allen
1O	B.Oliver	13	R.Pena			C	J.Gibbs	1O	T.Davis	CO	D.Billings
		2S	T.Kubiak	P	B.Blyleven					O1	T.McCraw
P	D.Drago			P	J.Perry	P	F.Peterson	P	V.Blue	2	L.Randle
P	M.Hedlund	P	M.Pattin	P	J.Kaat	P	M.Stottlemyre	P	C.Hunter		
P	P.Splittorff	P	B.Parsons	RP	R.Corbin	P	S.Bahnsen	P	C.Dobson	P	D.Bosman
P	B.Dal Canton	P	S.Lockwood	RP	T.Hall	P	S.Kline	P	D.Segui	P	D.McLain
P	A.Fitzmorris	P	L.Krausse	RP	S.Williams	P	M.Kekich	P	B.Odom	P	P.Broberg
RP	J.York	P	J.Slaton			RP	L.McDaniel	P	R.Fingers	P	B.Gogolewski
RP	T.Burgmeier	RP	K.Sanders	P	S.Luebber	RP	J.Aker	RP	B.Locker	P	J.Shellenback
RP	T.Abernathy	RP	J.Morris					RP	D.Knowles	RP	C.Cox
		RP	M.Lopez							RP	P.Lindblad
P	K.Wright									RP	D.Riddleberger
P	J.Rooker										
										P	J.Grzenda
										P	M.Thompson
										P	J.Janeski
										P	H.Pina

TEAM	G	W	L	PCT	GB	R	OR	AB	H	2B	3B	HR	BB	SO	AVG	OBP	SLG	PRO	PRO+	BR	/A	PF	CHI	RC	SB	CS	SBA	SBR
EAST																												
BAL	158	101	57	.639		**742**	**530**	5303	1382	207	25	158	**672**	844	**.261**	**.349**	.398	**.747**	120	133	140	99	97	750	66	38	63	-3
DET	162	91	71	.562	12	701	645	5502	1399	214	38	**179**	540	854	.254	.327	**.405**	.732	110	88	60	104	97	715	35	43	45	-15
BOS	162	85	77	.525	18	691	667	5401	1360	**246**	28	161	552	871	.252	.325	.397	.722	104	68	19	107	100	686	51	34	60	-5
NY	162	82	80	.506	21	648	641	5413	1377	195	**43**	97	581	**717**	.254	.331	.360	.691	109	22	62	94	99	643	75	55	58	-11
WAS	159	63	96	.396	38.5	537	660	5290	1219	189	30	86	575	956	.230	.309	.326	.635	91	-86	-56	94	102	538	68	45	60	-7
CLE	162	60	102	.370	43	543	747	5467	1303	200	20	109	467	868	.238	.302	.342	.644	81	-83	-133	109	101	558	57	37	61	-5
WEST																												
OAK	161	101	60	.627		691	564	5494	1383	195	25	160	542	1018	.252	.323	.384	.707	109	42	56	98	102	681	80	53	60	-8
KC	161	85	76	.528	16	603	566	5295	1323	225	40	80	490	819	.250	.316	.353	.669	97	-28	-23	99	**104**	594	**130**	46	**74**	**11**
CHI	162	79	83	.488	22.5	617	597	5382	1346	185	30	138	562	870	.250	.327	.373	.700	102	33	13	103	94	661	83	65	56	-14
CAL	162	76	86	.469	25.5	511	576	5495	1271	213	18	96	441	827	.231	.292	.329	.621	88	-131	-96	93	**104**	518	72	34	68	1
MIN	160	74	86	.463	26.5	654	670	5414	**1406**	197	31	116	512	846	.260	.326	.372	.698	101	28	8	103	101	641	66	44	60	-7
MIL	161	69	92	.429	32	534	609	5185	1188	160	23	104	543	924	.229	.306	.329	.635	87	-88	-82	99	103	534	82	53	61	-7
TOT	966					7472		64641	15957	2426	351	1484	6477	10414	.247	.320	.364	.684							865	547	61	-69

TEAM	CG	SH	SV	IP	H	H/G	HR	BB	SO	RAT	ERA	ERA+	OAV	OOB	PR	/A	PF	CPI	FA	E	DP	FW	PW	BW	SBW	DIF
EAST																										
BAL	71	15	22	1415¹	1257	8.0	125	**416**	793	10.8	**2.99**	112	.239	**.297**	74	57	97	101	.981	112	148	.7	6.1	**15.1**	.3	-.2
DET	53	11	32	1468¹	1355	8.3	126	609	**1000**	12.3	3.63	99	.247	.327	-28	-7	104	99	**.983**	106	156	**1.2**	-.8	6.5	-1.0	4.1
BOS	44	11	35	1443	1424	8.9	136	535	871	12.5	3.80	97	.259	.329	-55	-18	107	100	.981	116	149	.6	-1.9	2.0	.0	3.2
NY	67	15	12	1452	1382	8.6	126	423	707	11.3	3.43	94	.252	.308	4	-33	93	97	.981	125	159	.1	-3.5	6.7	-.6	-1.7
WAS	30	10	26	1418²	1376	8.7	132	554	762	12.5	3.70	89	.258	.333	-37	-62	96	105	.977	141	170	-1.0	-6.7	-6.0	-.1	-2.7
CLE	21	7	32	1440	1352	8.4	154	770	937	13.6	4.28	89	.252	.351	-130	-72	111	99	.981	116	159	.6	-7.7	-14.3	.0	.3
WEST																										
OAK	57	18	36	1469¹	**1229**	**7.5**	131	501	999	10.8	3.05	109	**.228**	.298	67	46	96	97	.981	117	157	.5	4.9	6.0	-.2	9.2
KC	34	14	**44**	1420¹	1301	8.2	**84**	501	775	11.6	3.25	106	.247	.316	33	28	99	98	.979	132	**178**	-.4	3.0	-2.5	**1.8**	2.5
CHI	46	19	32	1450¹	1348	8.4	100	468	976	11.4	3.12	**115**	.247	.309	55	75	104	101	.975	160	128	-1.9	**8.1**	1.4	-.9	-8.6
CAL	39	11	32	1481	1246	7.6	101	607	904	11.5	3.10	104	.230	.312	60	23	94	98	.980	131	159	-.2	2.5	-10.3	.7	2.4
MIN	43	9	25	1416²	1384	8.8	139	529	895	12.4	3.81	93	.257	.328	-55	-41	103	100	.980	118	134	.4	-4.4	.9	-.1	-2.7
MIL	32	**23**	32	1416¹	1303	8.4	130	569	795	12.1	3.38	103	.247	.324	13	14	100	**106**	.977	138	152	-.7	1.5	-8.8	-.1	-3.3
TOT	537	164	360	17291¹		8.3				11.9	3.46		.247	.320					.980	1512	1849					

Runs
- Buford-Bal ... 99
- Tovar-Min ... 94
- Murcer-NY ... 94
- Carew-Min ... 88
- Jackson-Oak ... 87

Hits
- Tovar-Min ... 204
- Alomar-Cal ... 179
- Carew-Min ... 177
- Smith-Bos ... 175
- Murcer-NY ... 175

Doubles
- Smith-Bos ... 33
- Schaal-KC ... 31
- Rodriguez-Det ... 30
- Oliva-Min ... 30

Triples
- Patek-KC ... 11
- Carew-Min ... 10
- Blair-Bal ... 8

Home Runs
- Melton-Chi ... 33
- Jackson-Oak ... 32
- Cash-Det ... 32
- Smith-Bos ... 30

Total Bases
- Smith-Bos ... 302
- Jackson-Oak ... 288
- Murcer-NY ... 287
- Melton-Chi ... 267
- Oliva-Min ... 266

Runs Batted In
- Killebrew-Min ... 119
- F.Robinson-Bal ... 99
- Smith-Bos ... 96
- Murcer-NY ... 94
- Bando-Oak ... 94

Runs Produced
- Murcer-NY ... 163
- F.Robinson-Bal ... 153
- Killebrew-Min ... 152
- White-NY ... 151
- Smith-Bos ... 151

Bases On Balls
- Killebrew-Min ... 114
- Yastrzemski-Bos ... 106
- Schaal-KC ... 103
- Petrocelli-Bos ... 91
- Murcer-NY ... 91

Batting Average
- Oliva-Min ... .337
- Murcer-NY ... .331
- Rettenmund-Bal ... .318
- Tovar-Min ... .311
- Carew-Min ... .307

On Base Percentage
- Murcer-NY ... .429
- Rettenmund-Bal ... .424
- Kaline-Det ... .421
- Buford-Bal ... .415
- White-NY ... .399

Slugging Average
- Oliva-Min ... .546
- Murcer-NY ... .543
- Cash-Det ... .531
- F.Robinson-Bal ... .510
- Jackson-Oak ... .508

Production
- Murcer-NY ... .972
- Oliva-Min ... .918
- Cash-Det ... .905
- F.Robinson-Bal ... .900
- Buford-Bal ... .891

Adjusted Production
- Murcer-NY ... 185
- White-NY ... 155
- F.Robinson-Bal ... 154
- Buford-Bal ... 153
- Oliva-Min ... 152

Batter Runs
- Murcer-NY ... 53.7
- Rettenmund-Bal ... 34.8
- Buford-Bal ... 34.5
- White-NY ... 33.7
- Oliva-Min ... 33.6

Adjusted Batter Runs
- Murcer-NY ... 61.1
- White-NY ... 39.8
- Rettenmund-Bal ... 35.7
- Buford-Bal ... 35.3
- F.Robinson-Bal ... 33.8

Clutch Hitting Index
- Killebrew-Min ... 140
- Powell-Bal ... 137
- Alou-Oak-NY ... 123
- F.Robinson-Bal ... 121
- May-Chi ... 120

Runs Created
- Murcer-NY ... 126
- Smith-Bos ... 106
- Jackson-Oak ... 103
- White-NY ... 103
- Rettenmund-Bal ... 99

Total Average
- Murcer-NY ... 1.035
- Buford-Bal ... .970
- Cash-Det ... .933
- F.Robinson-Bal ... .905
- Rettenmund-Bal ... .904

Stolen Bases
- Otis-KC ... 52
- Patek-KC ... 49
- Alomar-Cal ... 39
- Campaneris-Oak ... 34

Stolen Base Average
- Harper-Mil ... 89.3
- Otis-KC ... 86.7
- Campaneris-Oak ... 82.9
- Pinson-Cle ... 80.6
- Alomar-Cal ... 79.6

Stolen Base Runs
- Otis-KC ... 10.8
- Patek-KC ... 6.3
- Campaneris-Oak ... 6.0
- Harper-Mil ... 5.7
- Alomar-Cal ... 5.7

Fielding Runs
- Nettles-Cle ... 42.3
- Melton-Chi ... 27.0
- Alomar-Cal ... 21.4
- Cullen-Was ... 20.5
- Otis-KC ... 19.8

Total Player Rating
- Murcer-NY ... 5.5
- Nettles-Cle ... 5.3
- Melton-Chi ... 5.1
- White-NY ... 4.5
- Otis-KC ... 4.2

Wins
- Lolich-Det ... 25
- Blue-Oak ... 24
- Wood-Chi ... 22
- McNally-Bal ... 21
- Hunter-Oak ... 21

Win Percentage
- McNally-Bal ... .808
- Dobson-Oak ... .750
- Blue-Oak ... .750
- Dobson-Bal ... .714

Games
- Sanders-Mil ... 83
- Scherman-Det ... 69
- Burgmeier-KC ... 67
- Abernathy-KC ... 63

Complete Games
- Lolich-Det ... 29
- Blue-Oak ... 24
- Wood-Chi ... 22
- Cuellar-Bal ... 21
- Palmer-Bal ... 20

Shutouts
- Blue-Oak ... 8
- Wood-Chi ... 7
- Stottlemyre-NY ... 7
- Bradley-Chi ... 6

Saves
- Sanders-Mil ... 31
- Abernathy-KC ... 23
- Scherman-Det ... 20
- Fingers-Oak ... 17
- Burgmeier-KC ... 17

Innings Pitched
- Lolich-Det ... 376.0
- Wood-Chi ... 334.0
- Blue-Oak ... 312.0
- Cuellar-Bal ... 292.1
- Coleman-Det ... 286.0

Fewest Hits/Game
- Blue-Oak ... 6.03
- McDowell-Cle ... 6.71
- May-Cal ... 6.91
- Messersmith-Cal ... 7.29
- Wright-Cal ... 7.32

Fewest BB/Game
- Peterson-NY ... 1.38
- Kline-NY ... 1.50
- Kaat-Min ... 1.62
- Wood-Chi ... 1.67
- Drago-KC ... 1.72

Strikeouts
- Lolich-Det ... 308
- Blue-Oak ... 301
- Coleman-Det ... 236
- Blyleven-Min ... 224
- Wood-Chi ... 210

Strikeouts/Game
- Blue-Oak ... 8.68
- McDowell-Cle ... 8.05
- Johnson-Chi ... 7.74
- Coleman-Det ... 7.43
- Lolich-Det ... 7.37

Ratio
- Blue-Oak ... 8.68
- Wood-Chi ... 9.19
- Kline-NY ... 9.84
- Dobson-Bal ... 9.98
- McNally-Bal ... 10.07

Earned Run Average
- Blue-Oak ... 1.82
- Wood-Chi ... 1.91
- Palmer-Bal ... 2.68
- Hedlund-KC ... 2.71
- Blyleven-Min ... 2.81

Adjusted ERA
- Wood-Chi ... 188
- Blue-Oak ... 183
- Siebert-Bos ... 127
- Hedlund-KC ... 126
- Blyleven-Min ... 126

Opponents' Batting Avg.
- Blue-Oak ... .189
- McDowell-Cle ... .207
- May-Cal ... .213
- Messersmith-Cal ... .218
- Palmer-Bal ... .221

Opponents' On Base Pct.
- Blue-Oak ... .252
- Wood-Chi ... .264
- Kline-NY ... .276
- Dobson-Bal ... .279
- Hunter-Oak ... .282

Starter Runs
- Wood-Chi ... 57.5
- Blue-Oak ... 57.0
- Palmer-Bal ... 24.5
- Lolich-Det ... 22.6
- Blyleven-Min ... 20.0

Adjusted Starter Runs
- Wood-Chi ... 62.2
- Blue-Oak ... 52.6
- Lolich-Det ... 28.0
- Blyleven-Min ... 22.8
- Palmer-Bal ... 21.0

Clutch Pitching Index
- Drago-KC ... 119
- Krausse-Mil ... 118
- Johnson-Chi ... 117
- Bosman-Was ... 112
- Wood-Chi ... 112

Relief Runs
- Sanders-Mil ... 23.4
- Burgmeier-KC ... 17.0
- Mingori-Cle ... 12.8
- Queen-Cal ... 12.3
- Grzenda-Was ... 12.0

Adjusted Relief Runs
- Sanders-Mil ... 23.5
- Burgmeier-KC ... 16.7
- Mingori-Cle ... 15.1
- Scherman-Det ... 11.1
- Lee-Bos ... 10.9

Relief Ranking
- Sanders-Mil ... 41.6
- Burgmeier-KC ... 34.4
- Scherman-Det ... 19.4
- Abernathy-KC ... 13.8
- Grzenda-Was ... 11.4

Total Pitcher Index
- Wood-Chi ... 6.6
- Blue-Oak ... 4.9
- Sanders-Mil ... 4.7
- Burgmeier-KC ... 4.4
- Siebert-Bos ... 3.5

Total Baseball Ranking
- Wood-Chi ... 6.6
- Murcer-NY ... 5.5
- Nettles-Cle ... 5.3
- Melton-Chi ... 5.1
- Blue-Oak ... 4.9

January 13 Former umpire, now housewife Bernice Gera wins her suit against baseball, initiated on March 15, 1971. Mrs. Gera is slated to umpire in the New York-Pennsylvania League starting in June.

April 2 Mets manager Gil Hodges dies of a heart attack at West Palm Beach, Florida, two days shy of his 48th birthday. Yogi Berra is named manager.

April 6 For the first time in history, the major league season fails to open due to a general player strike. The strike, announced April 1, will erase 86 games from major league schedules.

April 13 The end of the baseball strike is announced, with an abbreviated schedule to start two days later.

April 16 In Chicago, 22-year-old rookie Burt Hooton of the Cubs no-hits the Phillies, 4-0. It is Hooton's fourth major league game over two seasons and he has allowed just eight hits in 30 innings. Throwing his knuckle curve, Hooton walks seven and fans seven.

May 11 The Giants trade future Hall of Famer Willie Mays to the Mets for minor league pitcher Charlie Williams and cash.

June 18 By a 5-3 vote, the U.S. Supreme Court confirms lower court rulings in the Curt Flood case, upholding baseball's exemption from antitrust laws and the legitimacy of its reserve clause. Its decision is narrowly construed, however, and leaves the way open for legislation or collective bargaining to undercut the reserve system. By the year's end, owners will agree to salary arbitration.

August 1 Nate Colbert ties one major league record with five home runs, and sets another with 13 RBIs, as the Padres take a doubleheader from the Braves, 9–0 and 11–7.

August 29 During a 3-0 win over St. Louis, San Francisco's Jim Barr retires the first 20 batters to face him. Six days earlier, Barr had gotten out the last 21 men to face him. This gives Barr a major league record of 41 consecutive batsmen retired.

September 2 Milt Pappas of the Cubs hurls a no-hit game in beating the Padres 8-0. Pappas has a perfect game until pinch hitter Larry Stahl walks with two outs in the ninth inning. Pappas and catcher Randy Hundley both said of the pitches to Stahl, "They were so close I don't know how Stahl could take them, but they were balls."

September 30 During a 5-0 win over the Mets, the Pirates' Roberto Clemente doubles off Jon Matlack in the fourth inning for his 3,000th—and final—career hit in regular-season play.

October 2 Bill Stoneman of Montreal pitches his second no-hitter, beating the Mets 7-0.

October 11 The Pirates lead the Reds 3-2 in the bottom of the ninth inning of the final game of the NLCS. Johnny Bench homers to tie the game, and two singles and a Bob Moose wild pitch later, the Reds are NL champs.

October 24 Hall of Famer Jackie Robinson dies of heart disease at age 53.

November 2 Steve Carlton caps off a remarkable season with a unanimous NL Cy Young Award.

November 22 Reds catcher Johnny Bench wins the NL MVP.

December 10 The major leagues adopt the save as an official statistic.

December 31 A plane carrying Roberto Clemente to Nicaragua on a mercy mission for earthquake victims crashes into the Atlantic Ocean. Clemente, who batted .317 with exactly 3,000 hits in 18 seasons with the Pirates, is presumed dead at age 38.

ATLANTA		CHICAGO		CINCINNATI		HOUSTON		LOS ANGELES		MONTREAL	
M	L.Harris	M	L.Durocher	M	S.Anderson	M	H.Walker	M	W.Alston	M	G.Mauch
M	E.Mathews	M	W.Lockman	1B	T.Perez	M	S.Parker	1B	W.Parker	1B	M.Jorgensen
1B	H.Aaron	1B	J.Hickman	2B	J.Morgan	M	L.Durocher	2B	L.Lacy	2B	R.Hunt
2B	F.Millan	2B	G.Beckert	SS	D.Concepcion	1B	L.May	SS	B.Russell	SS	T.Foli
SS	M.Perez	SS	D.Kessinger	3B	D.Menke	2B	T.Helms	3B	S.Garvey	3B	B.Bailey
3B	D.Evans	3B	R.Santo	LF	P.Rose	SS	R.Metzger	LF	M.Mota	LF	K.Singleton
LF	R.Carty	LF	B.Williams	CF	B.Tolan	3B	D.Rader	CF	W.Davis	CF	B.Day
CF	D.Baker	CF	R.Monday	RF	C.Geronimo	LF	B.Watson	RF	F.Robinson	RF	C.Mashore
RF	R.Garr	RF	J.Cardenal	C	J.Bench	CF	C.Cedeno	C	C.Cannizzaro	C	J.Boccabella
C	E.Williams	C	R.Hundley	P	J.Billingham	RF	J.Wynn	O1	B.Buckner	O1	R.Fairly
O	M.Lum	31	C.Fanzone	P	R.Grimsley	C	J.Edwards	O	W.Crawford	O	R.Woods
P	P.Niekro	1	J.Pepitone	P	G.Nolan	P	D.Wilson	23	B.Valentine	CO	T.McCarver
P	R.Reed	P	F.Jenkins	P	J.McGlothlin	P	L.Dierker			C	T.Humphrey
P	R.Schueler	P	B.Hooton	P	D.Gullett	P	D.Roberts	P	D.Sutton		
P	T.Kelley	P	M.Pappas	RP	T.Hall	P	J.Reuss	P	C.Osteen	P	B.Stoneman
P	G.Stone	P	B.Hands	RP	P.Borbon	P	K.Forsch	P	A.Downing	P	M.Torrez
RP	P.Jarvis	P	R.Reuschel	RP	C.Carroll	RP	G.Culver	P	T.John	P	C.Morton
RP	C.Upshaw	RP	T.Phoebus			RP	T.Griffin	P	B.Singer	P	E.McAnally
		RP	J.Aker	P	W.Simpson	RP	J.Ray	RP	J.Brewer	P	B.Moore
P	J.Hardin	RP	D.McGinn	P	E.Sprague			RP	P.Mikkelsen	RP	M.Marshall
P	M.McQueen							RP	P.Richert	RP	J.Strohmayer
P	D.McLain	P	J.Pizarro							RP	T.Walker
		P	B.Bonham								
										P	S.Renko

NEW YORK		PHILADELPHIA		PITTSBURGH		SAN DIEGO		SAN FRANCISCO		ST.LOUIS	
M	Y.Berra	M	F.Lucchesi	M	B.Virdon	M	P.Gomez	M	C.Fox	M	R.Schoendienst
1B	E.Kranepool	M	P.Owens	1B	W.Stargell	M	D.Zimmer	1B	W.McCovey	1B	M.Alou
2B	K.Boswell	1B	T.Hutton	2B	D.Cash	1B	N.Colbert	2B	T.Fuentes	2B	T.Sizemore
SS	B.Harrelson	2B	D.Doyle	SS	G.Alley	2B	D.Thomas	SS	C.Speier	SS	D.Maxvill
3B	J.Fregosi	SS	L.Bowa	3B	R.Hebner	SS	E.Hernandez	3B	A.Gallagher	3B	J.Torre
LF	J.Milner	3B	D.Money	LF	V.Davalillo	3B	D.Roberts	LF	K.Henderson	LF	L.Brock
CF	T.Agee	LF	G.Luzinski	CF	A.Oliver	LF	L.Lee	CF	G.Maddox	CF	J.Cruz
RF	R.Staub	CF	W.Montanez	RF	R.Clemente	CF	J.Jeter	RF	B.Bonds	RF	L.Melendez
C	D.Dyer	RF	B.Robinson	C	M.Sanguillen	RF	C.Gaston	C	D.Rader	C	T.Simmons
32	W.Garrett	C	J.Bateman	O	G.Clines	C	F.Kendall	31	D.Kingman	O	B.Carbo
2S	T.Martinez	1	D.Johnson	1O	B.Robertson	O	J.Morales			S2	E.Crosby
O1	C.Jones	2S	T.Harmon	2O	R.Stennett	O	L.Stahl	P	R.Bryant	P	B.Gibson
C	J.Grote					23	G.Jestadt	P	J.Barr	P	R.Wise
		P	S.Carlton	P	S.Blass	P	S.Arlin	P	J.Marichal	P	R.Cleveland
P	T.Seaver	P	K.Reynolds	P	B.Moose	P	C.Kirby	P	S.McDowell	P	A.Santorini
P	J.Matlack	P	B.Champion	P	N.Briles	P	F.Norman	P	S.Stone	P	S.Spinks
P	G.Gentry	P	W.Fryman	P	D.Ellis	RP	M.Caldwell	RP	J.Johnson	RP	D.Segui
P	J.Koosman	RP	W.Twitchell	P	B.Kison	P	B.Greif	RP	R.Moffitt		
P	J.McAndrew	RP	B.Brandon	RP	D.Giusti	RP	M.Corkins	RP	D.McMahon		
RP	T.McGraw	RP	B.Lersch	RP	R.Hernandez	RP	G.Ross				
RP	R.Sadecki	P	D.Selma	RP	B.Miller	RP	E.Acosta	P	F.Reberger		
RP	D.Frisella			P	B.Johnson			P	D.Carrithers		
				P	L.Walker			P	J.Willoughby		
P	B.Capra										

TEAM	G	W	L	PCT	GB	R	OR	AB	H	2B	3B	HR	BB	SO	AVG	OBP	SLG	PRO	PRO+	BR	/A	PF	CHI	RC	SB	CS	SBA	SBR
EAST																												
PIT	155	96	59	.619		691	**512**	5490	**1505**	**251**	**47**	110	404	871	**.274**	.327	**.397**	**.724**	114	74	89	98	100	**701**	49	30	62	-3
CHI	156	85	70	.548	11	685	567	5247	1346	206	40	133	565	815	.257	.332	.387	.719	100	74	2	111	100	670	69	47	59	-8
NY	156	83	73	.532	13.5	528	578	5135	1154	175	31	105	589	990	.225	.309	.332	.641	91	-68	-54	97	99	530	41	41	50	-12
STL	156	75	81	.481	21.5	568	600	5326	1383	214	42	70	437	793	.260	.319	.355	.674	99	-14	-6	99	96	591	104	48	68	2
MON	156	70	86	.449	26.5	513	609	5156	1205	156	22	91	474	828	.234	.304	.325	.629	84	-92	-101	102	102	513	68	66	51	-19
PHI	156	59	97	.378	37.5	503	635	5248	1240	200	36	98	487	930	.236	.304	.344	.648	88	-65	-78	103	94	545	42	50	46	-17
WEST																												
CIN	154	95	59	.617		707	557	5241	1317	214	44	124	**606**	914	.251	**.333**	.380	.713	**116**	67	**107**	94	104	676	**140**	63	69	4
HOU	153	84	69	.549	10.5	**708**	636	5267	1359	233	38	134	524	907	.258	.329	.393	.722	114	**75**	89	98	103	686	111	56	66	0
LA	155	85	70	.548	10.5	584	527	5270	1349	178	39	98	480	786	.256	.321	.360	.681	102	1	16	98	96	610	82	39	68	1
ATL	155	70	84	.455	25	628	730	5278	1363	186	17	144	532	**770**	.258	.330	.382	.712	100	60	-1	109	94	661	47	35	57	-7
SF	155	69	86	.445	26.5	662	649	5245	1281	211	36	**150**	480	964	.244	.311	.384	.695	102	17	8	101	**107**	630	123	45	**73**	**10**
SD	153	58	95	.379	36.5	488	665	5213	1181	168	38	102	407	976	.227	.284	.332	.616	87	-130	-98	93	106	489	78	46	63	-4
TOT	930					7265		63116	15683	2392	430	1359	5985	10544	.248	.317	.365	.682							954	566	63	-53

TEAM	CG	SH	SV	IP	H	H/G	HR	BB	SO	RAT	ERA	ERA+	OAV	OOB	PR	/A	PF	CPI	FA	E	DP	FW	PW	BW	SBW	DIF
EAST																										
PIT	39	15	48	1414^1	1282	8.2	90	433	838	11.1	2.81	118	.243	.304	102	81	96	**108**	.978	136	**171**	-.0	8.7	9.6	.2	.1
CHI	54	19	32	1398^2	1329	8.6	112	**421**	824	11.5	3.22	118	.251	.311	37	**92**	110	105	.979	132	148	.2	**9.9**	.2	-.4	-2.4
NY	32	12	41	1414^2	1263	8.0	118	486	**1059**	11.3	3.26	103	.240	.308	30	15	97	99	.980	116	122	1.1	1.6	-5.8	-.8	8.9
STL	**64**	13	13	1399^2	1290	8.3	87	531	912	11.8	3.42	99	.247	.319	5	-3	99	97	.977	141	146	-.3	-.3	-.6	.7	-2.4
MON	39	11	23	1401^1	1281	8.2	103	579	888	12.1	3.59	99	.245	.323	-21	-6	103	97	.978	134	141	.0	-.6	-10.9	-1.6	5.0
PHI	43	13	15	1400	1318	8.5	117	536	927	12.1	3.66	98	.251	.324	-33	-11	104	99	.981	116	142	1.1	-1.2	-8.4	-1.3	-9.2
WEST																										
CIN	25	15	**60**	1412^2	1313	8.4	129	435	806	11.3	3.21	100	.247	.307	38	0	93	104	**.982**	**110**	143	**1.3**	.0	**11.5**	.9	4.3
HOU	38	14	31	1385^1	1340	8.7	114	498	971	12.2	3.77	89	.256	.325	-48	-62	97	98	.980	116	151	.9	-6.7	9.6	.5	3.2
LA	50	**23**	29	1403	**1196**	**7.7**	**83**	429	856	**10.6**	**2.78**	**120**	**.230**	**.292**	**104**	85	97	96	.974	162	145	-1.5	9.1	1.7	.6	-2.5
ATL	40	4	27	1377	1412	9.2	155	512	732	12.7	4.27	89	.266	.333	-126	-74	110	97	.974	156	130	-1.1	-8.0	-.1	-.3	2.5
SF	44	8	23	1386^1	1309	8.5	130	507	771	12.0	3.69	94	.250	.320	-37	-32	101	98	.974	156	121	-1.1	-3.4	.9	**1.6**	-6.3
SD	39	17	19	1403^2	1350	8.7	121	618	960	12.9	3.78	87	.255	.337	-50	-76	95	103	.976	144	146	-.6	-8.2	-10.5	.0	.7
TOT	507	164	361	16796^2		8.4				11.8	3.45		.248	.317					.978	1619	1706					

Runs
Morgan-Cin 122
Bonds-SF 118
Wynn-Hou 117
Rose-Cin 107
Cedeno-Hou 103

Hits
Rose-Cin 198
Brock-StL 193
Williams-Chi 191
Simmons-StL 180
Garr-Atl 180

Doubles
Montanez-Phi 39
Cedeno-Hou 39
Simmons-StL 36
Williams-Chi 34

Triples
Bowa-Phi 13
Rose-Cin 11
Sanguillen-Pit 8
Cedeno-Hou 8
Brock-StL 8

Home Runs
Bench-Cin 40
Colbert-SD 38
Williams-Chi 37
Aaron-Atl 34
Stargell-Pit 33

Total Bases
Williams-Chi 348
Cedeno-Hou 300
Bench-Cin 291
May-Hou 290
Colbert-SD 286

Runs Batted In
Bench-Cin 125
Williams-Chi 122
Stargell-Pit 112
Colbert-SD 111
May-Hou 98

Runs Produced
Wynn-Hou 183
Williams-Chi 180
Morgan-Cin 179
Bonds-SF 172
Bench-Cin 172

Bases On Balls
Morgan-Cin 115
Wynn-Hou 103
Bench-Cin 100
Aaron-Atl 92
Evans-Atl 90

Batting Average
Williams-Chi .333
Garr-Atl .325
Baker-Atl .321
Cedeno-Hou .320
Watson-Hou .312

On Base Percentage
Morgan-Cin .419
Williams-Chi .403
Santo-Chi .397
Aaron-Atl .391
Wynn-Hou .391

Slugging Average
Williams-Chi .606
Stargell-Pit .558
Bench-Cin .541
Cedeno-Hou .537
Aaron-Atl .514

Production
Williams-Chi 1.010
Stargell-Pit .935
Bench-Cin .927
Cedeno-Hou .924
Aaron-Atl .906

Adjusted Production
Bench-Cin 171
Stargell-Pit 166
Williams-Chi 166
Cedeno-Hou 163
Hebner-Pit 155

Batter Runs
Williams-Chi 61.1
Bench-Cin 44.0
Cedeno-Hou 42.9
Stargell-Pit 39.6
Morgan-Cin 37.2

Adjusted Batter Runs
Bench-Cin 50.6
Williams-Chi 48.2
Cedeno-Hou 45.2
Morgan-Cin 43.5
Stargell-Pit 41.7

Clutch Hitting Index
Parker-LA 140
Tolan-Cin 131
Helms-Hou 120
Sanguillen-Pit 119
Oliver-Pit 117

Runs Created
Williams-Chi 137
Morgan-Cin 117
Cedeno-Hou 115
Bench-Cin 110
Rose-Cin 109

Total Average
Williams-Chi 1.050
Morgan-Cin .973
Cedeno-Hou .959
Stargell-Pit .958
Aaron-Atl .945

Stolen Bases
Brock-StL 63
Morgan-Cin 58
Cedeno-Hou 55
Bonds-SF 44
Tolan-Cin 42

Stolen Base Average
Hernandez-SD 88.9
Bonds-SF 88.0
Davis-LA 87.0
Brock-StL 77.8
Morgan-Cin 77.3

Stolen Base Runs
Bonds-SF 9.6
Brock-StL 8.1
Morgan-Cin 7.2
Hernandez-SD 5.4
Davis-LA 4.2

Fielding Runs
Helms-Hou 26.5
Money-Phi 20.3
Rader-Hou 18.0
Rose-Cin 16.1
Russell-LA 15.0

Total Player Rating
Cedeno-Hou 5.6
Morgan-Cin 5.5
Bench-Cin 5.1
Rose-Cin 4.3
Williams-Chi 4.1

Wins
Carlton-Phi 27
Seaver-NY 21
Osteen-LA 20
Jenkins-Chi 20

Win Percentage
Nolan-Cin .750
Carlton-Phi .730
Pappas-Chi .708
Blass-Pit .704
Ellis-Pit .682

Games
Marshall-Mon 65
Carroll-Cin 65
Borbon-Cin 62
Ross-SD 60

Complete Games
Carlton-Phi 30
Jenkins-Chi 23
Gibson-StL 23
Wise-StL 20
Sutton-LA 18

Shutouts
Sutton-LA 9
Carlton-Phi 8
Norman-SD 6
Jenkins-Chi 5
Dierker-Hou 5

Saves
Carroll-Cin 37
McGraw-NY 27
Giusti-Pit 22
Marshall-Mon 18

Innings Pitched
Carlton-Phi 346.1
Jenkins-Chi 289.1
Niekro-Atl 282.1
Gibson-StL 278.0
Sutton-LA 272.2

Fewest Hits/Game
Sutton-LA 6.14
Carlton-Phi 6.68
Gibson-StL 7.32
Seaver-NY 7.39
Bryant-SF 7.40

Fewest BB/Game
Pappas-Chi 1.34
Nolan-Cin 1.53
Niekro-Atl 1.69
Ellis-Pit 1.82
Moose-Pit 1.87

Strikeouts
Carlton-Phi 310
Seaver-NY 249
Gibson-StL 208
Sutton-LA 207
Jenkins-Chi 184

Strikeouts/Game
Seaver-NY 8.55
Reuss-Hou 8.16
Koosman-NY 8.12
Carlton-Phi 8.06
Norman-SD 7.10

Ratio
Sutton-LA 8.35
Carlton-Phi 8.97
Nolan-Cin 9.10
McAndrew-NY 9.86
Niekro-Atl 9.95

Earned Run Average
Carlton-Phi 1.97
Nolan-Cin 1.99
Sutton-LA 2.08
Matlack-NY 2.32
Gibson-StL 2.46

Adjusted ERA
Carlton-Phi 182
Nolan-Cin 161
Sutton-LA 160
Matlack-NY 145
Gibson-StL 138

Opponents' Batting Avg.
Sutton-LA .189
Carlton-Phi .206
Gibson-StL .224
Seaver-NY .224
Bryant-SF .224

Opponents' On Base Pct.
Sutton-LA .240
Carlton-Phi .259
Nolan-Cin .262
Niekro-Atl .275
McAndrew-NY .278

Starter Runs
Carlton-Phi 56.9
Sutton-LA 41.6
Gibson-StL 30.7
Matlack-NY 30.6
Nolan-Cin 28.5

Adjusted Starter Runs
Carlton-Phi 62.2
Sutton-LA 38.0
Gibson-StL 29.1
Matlack-NY 28.1
Hooton-Chi 24.4

Clutch Pitching Index
Blass-Pit 131
Nolan-Cin 115
Hooton-Chi 115
Matlack-NY 115
Downing-LA 115

Relief Runs
Marshall-Mon 21.5
McGraw-NY 20.7
Brewer-LA 19.1
R.Hernandez-Pit 13.9
Carroll-Cin 12.8

Adjusted Relief Runs
Marshall-Mon 22.8
McGraw-NY 19.6
Brewer-LA 18.0
R.Hernandez-Pit 12.8
Giusti-Pit 11.6

Relief Ranking
Marshall-Mon 46.8
Brewer-LA 39.8
McGraw-NY 34.5
Giusti-Pit 23.0
Carroll-Cin 18.5

Total Pitcher Index
Carlton-Phi 7.4
Marshall-Mon 5.3
Brewer-LA 4.5
Gibson-StL 4.2
Sutton-LA 3.9

Total Baseball Ranking
Carlton-Phi 7.4
Cedeno-Hou 5.6
Morgan-Cin 5.5
Marshall-Mon 5.3
Bench-Cin 5.1

January 19 The BBWAA elects Sandy Koufax (344 votes), Yogi Berra (339), and Early Wynn (301) to the Hall of Fame. Koufax makes it in his first try and, at 36, is the youngest honoree in history.

February 2 The Special Veterans Committee selects Lefty Gomez, Ross Youngs, and William Harridge for the Hall of Fame.

February 8 Commissioner Bowie Kuhn announces the Hall of Fame selection of Josh Gibson and Buck Leonard by the Special Committee on the Negro Leagues.

May 13 The Brewers score in the top of the 22nd to win 4-3, then lose to the Twins 4-3 in 15 innings. The two games take nine hours and 23 minutes to complete and sets an AL record for consecutive innings played in two days.

July 14 In a major league first, the plate umpire and the catcher in a game are brothers. Bill Haller is the ump and Tom Haller is the Tigers catcher during a game with the Royals. Kansas City wins 1-0.

August 5 During a 4-3 win over Cleveland, Detroit shortstop Ed Brinkman commits an error, thus ending his major league-record streak of 72 games and 331 total chances without a miscue.

August 23 Chicago's Dick Allen becomes the fourth major league player (Jimmie Foxx, Hank Greenberg, and Alex Johnson are the others) to hit a ball into the center field bleachers in Comiskey Park when he connects off New York's Lindy McDaniel.

October 2 After a pinch RBI single, White Sox reliever Terry Forster steals second. Forster, later described by David Letterman as "a fat tub of goo," is the last AL pitcher to steal a base.

October 3 Roric Harrison homers as Baltimore beats Cleveland 4-3 in the second game of a doubleheader. With the DH rule on the horizon, it will be the last homer hit by an AL pitcher until interleague play in 1997.

October 4 Ted Williams manages his final game as the Rangers lose to the Royals, 4-0. Williams will be replaced by Whitey Herzog.

October 12 Oakland takes the AL flag with a 2-1 win in the fifth game of the ALCS. The A's Reggie Jackson steals home, but pulls a hamstring in the process, sidelining him for the Series.

October 14 Catcher Gene Tenace becomes the first player ever to homer in each of his first two World Series at bats, leading the A's to a 3-2 opening-game win over the Reds.

October 18 With runners at second base and third base and a 3-2 count, the A's fake an intentional walk and strike out Johnny Bench looking. The Reds still win Game 3 by a 1-0 score.

October 22 The A's win their first world championship in 42 years with a 3-2 victory in Game 7.

October 31 Gaylord Perry wins the AL Cy Young award by a 64-58 margin over Chicago's Wilbur Wood. Perry won 24 games for the fifth-place Indians.

November 15 The White Sox' Dick Allen wins the AL MVP Award by an overwhelming margin.

November 21 Boston's Carlton Fisk is the unanimous choice for league Rookie of the Year, the first time this has happened.

December 10 The AL votes unanimously to adopt the designated-hitter rule for a three-year experiment. In the December 1975 meeting the league will vote to permanently adopt the DH. The NL declines to go along.

	BALTIMORE		BOSTON		CALIFORNIA		CHICAGO		CLEVELAND		DETROIT
M	E.Weaver	M	E.Kasko	M	D.Rice	M	C.Tanner	M	K.Aspromonte	M	B.Martin
1B	B.Powell	1B	D.Cater	1B	B.Oliver	1B	D.Allen	1B	C.Chambliss	1B	N.Cash
2B	D.Johnson	2B	D.Griffin	2B	S.Alomar	2B	M.Andrews	2B	J.Brohamer	2B	D.McAuliffe
SS	M.Belanger	SS	L.Aparicio	SS	L.Cardenas	SS	R.Morales	SS	F.Duffy	SS	E.Brinkman
3B	B.Robinson	3B	R.Petrocelli	3B	K.McMullen	3B	E.Spiezio	3B	G.Nettles	3B	A.Rodriguez
LF	D.Buford	LF	C.Yastrzemski	LF	V.Pinson	LF	C.May	LF	A.Johnson	LF	W.Horton
CF	P.Blair	CF	T.Harper	CF	K.Berry	CF	J.Johnstone	CF	D.Unser	CF	M.Stanley
RF	M.Rettenmund	RF	R.Smith	RF	L.Stanton	RF	P.Kelly	RF	B.Bell	RF	J.Northrup
C	J.Oates	C	C.Fisk	C	A.Kusnyer	C	E.Herrmann	C	R.Fosse	C	B.Freehan
O	D.Baylor	O	B.Oglivie	1O	J.Spencer	S2	L.Alvarado	O1	T.McCraw	O	G.Brown
O1	T.Crowley	2S	J.Kennedy			O	R.Reichardt	2S	E.Leon	O1	A.Kaline
S2	B.Grich			P	N.Ryan	3	B.Melton			2	T.Taylor
		P	M.Pattin	P	C.Wright			P	G.Perry		
P	J.Palmer	P	S.Siebert	P	R.May			P	D.Tidrow	P	M.Lolich
P	P.Dobson	P	L.Tiant	P	A.Messersmith	P	W.Wood	P	M.Wilcox	P	J.Coleman
P	M.Cuellar	P	J.Curtis	P	R.Clark	P	T.Bradley	P	R.Lamb	P	T.Timmermann
P	D.McNally	P	L.McGlothen	RP	L.Allen	P	S.Bahnsen	P	S.Dunning	P	W.Fryman
P	D.Alexander	RP	G.Peters	RP	E.Fisher	P	D.Lemonds	RP	P.Hennigan	RP	C.Seelbach
RP	R.Harrison	RP	B.Lee	RP	S.Barber	RP	T.Forster	RP	E.Farmer	RP	F.Scherman
		RP	L.Krausse			RP	R.Gossage	RP	M.Kilkenny	RP	J.Niekro
						RP	S.Kealey				
		P	R.Culp					P	V.Colbert	P	B.Slayback
						P	V.Romo	P	S.Mingori		
								P	D.Riddleberger		

	KANSAS CITY		MILWAUKEE		MINNESOTA		NEW YORK		OAKLAND		TEXAS
M	B.Lemon	M	D.Bristol	M	B.Rigney	M	R.Houk	M	D.Williams	M	T.Williams
1B	J.Mayberry	M	R.McMillan	M	F.Quilici	1B	R.Blomberg	1B	M.Epstein	1B	F.Howard
2B	C.Rojas	M	D.Crandall	1B	H.Killebrew	2B	H.Clarke	2B	T.Cullen	2B	L.Randle
SS	F.Patek	1B	G.Scott	2B	R.Carew	SS	G.Michael	SS	B.Campaneris	SS	T.Harrah
3B	P.Schaal	2B	R.Theobald	SS	D.Thompson	3B	C.Sanchez	3B	S.Bando	3B	D.Nelson
LF	L.Piniella	SS	R.Auerbach	3B	E.Soderholm	LF	R.White	LF	J.Rudi	LF	L.Biittner
CF	A.Otis	3B	M.Ferraro	LF	S.Brye	CF	B.Murcer	CF	R.Jackson	CF	J.Lovitto
RF	R.Scheinblum	LF	J.Briggs	CF	B.Darwin	RF	J.Callison	RF	A.Mangual	RF	T.Ford
C	E.Kirkpatrick	CF	D.May	RF	C.Tovar	C	T.Munson	C	D.Duncan	C	D.Billings
		RF	J.Lahoud	C	P.Roof			1	M.Hegan		
O	S.Hovley	C	E.Rodriguez			1O	F.Alou	C	G.Tenace	O	E.Maddox
				32	S.Braun	32	B.Allen				
P	D.Drago	23	B.Heise	O	J.Nettles			P	C.Hunter	P	P.Broberg
P	P.Splittorff			1O	R.Reese	P	M.Stottlemyre	P	K.Holtzman	P	D.Bosman
P	R.Nelson	P	J.Lonborg			P	F.Peterson	P	B.Odom	P	R.Hand
P	B.Dal Canton	P	B.Parsons	P	B.Blyleven	P	S.Kline	P	V.Blue	P	M.Paul
P	M.Hedlund	P	S.Lockwood	P	D.Woodson	P	M.Kekich	P	D.Hamilton	P	B.Gogolewski
RP	A.Fitzmorris	P	J.Colborn	P	J.Perry	P	R.Gardner	RP	R.Fingers	RP	P.Lindblad
RP	T.Abernathy	P	K.Brett	P	R.Corbin	RP	S.Lyle	RP	J.Horlen	RP	J.Panther
RP	T.Burgmeier	RP	K.Sanders	P	J.Kaat	RP	L.McDaniel	RP	B.Locker	RP	H.Pina
		RP	E.Stephenson	RP	D.LaRoche	RP	F.Beene				
		RP	F.Linzy	RP	W.Granger					P	D.Stanhouse
P	J.Rooker							P	D.Knowles	P	C.Cox
P	T.Murphy	P	G.Ryerson	P	D.Goltz					P	J.Shellenback
/P	M.Montgomery	P	J.Bell								

TEAM	G	W	L	PCT	GB	R	OR	AB	H	2B	3B	HR	BB	SO	AVG	OBP	SLG	PRO	PRO+	BR	/A	PF	CHI	RC	SB	CS	SBA	SBR
EAST																												
DET	156	86	70	.551		558	514	5099	1206	179	32	122	483	793	.237	.306	.356	.662	100	18	0	103	101	549	17	21	45	-8
BOS	155	85	70	.548	0.5	640	620	5208	1289	229	34	124	522	858	.248	.320	.376	.696	108	83	49	106	102	634	66	30	69	2
BAL	154	80	74	.519	5	519	430	5028	1153	193	29	100	507	935	.229	.304	.339	.643	96	-12	-25	103	100	523	78	41	66	-1
NY	155	79	76	.510	6.5	557	527	5168	1288	201	24	103	491	689	.249	.318	.357	.675	111	45	65	97	95	588	71	42	63	-4
CLE	156	72	84	.462	14	472	519	5207	1220	187	18	91	420	762	.234	.295	.330	.625	89	-54	-70	103	98	495	49	53	48	-17
MIL	156	65	91	.417	21	493	595	5124	1204	167	22	88	472	868	.235	.303	.328	.631	96	-35	-26	98	99	495	64	57	53	-15
WEST																												
OAK	155	93	62	.600		604	457	5200	1248	195	29	134	463	886	.240	.308	.366	.674	113	37	45	95	104	584	87	64	64	-3
CHI	154	87	67	.565	5.5	566	538	5083	1208	170	28	108	511	991	.238	.311	.346	.657	100	14	3	102	103	550	100	52	66	-1
MIN	154	77	77	.500	15.5	537	535	5234	1277	182	31	93	478	905	.244	.311	.344	.655	96	9	-18	105	97	554	53	41	56	-9
KC	154	76	78	.494	16.5	580	545	5167	1317	220	26	78	534	711	.255	.329	.353	.682	111	65	68	100	95	601	85	44	66	-1
CAL	155	75	80	.484	18	454	533	5165	1249	171	26	78	358	850	.242	.294	.330	.624	98	-55	-28	94	97	487	57	37	61	-5
TEX	154	54	100	.351	38.5	461	628	5029	1092	166	17	56	503	926	.217	.292	.290	.582	83	-115	-97	96	111	438	126	73	63	-6
TOT	929					6441		61712	14751	2260	316	1175	5742	10174	.239	.308	.343	.651							853	539	61	-68

TEAM	CG	SH	SV	IP	H	H/G	HR	BB	SO	RAT	ERA	ERA+	OAV	OOB	PR	/A	PF	CPI	FA	E	DP	FW	PW	BW	SBW	DIF
EAST																										
DET	46	11	33	1388.1	1212	7.9	101	465	952	11.2	2.96	106	.236	.306	15	28	103	102	.984	96	137	1.9	3.2	.0	-.3	3.2
BOS	48	20	25	1382.2	1309	8.5	101	512	918	12.1	3.47	93	.251	.323	-63	-39	105	100	.978	130	141	-.0	-4.4	5.6	.9	5.6
BAL	62	20	21	1371.1	1116	7.3	85	395	788	10.0	2.53	121	.224	.283	81	82	100	97	.983	100	150	1.6	9.3	-2.8	.5	-5.6
NY	35	19	39	1373.1	1306	8.6	87	419	625	11.5	3.05	97	.252	.312	2	-15	96	105	.978	134	179	-.3	-1.7	7.4	.2	-4.1
CLE	47	13	24	1410	1232	7.9	123	534	846	11.5	2.92	110	.237	.313	23	47	105	112	.981	116	157	.8	5.3	-8.0	-1.3	-2.9
MIL	37	14	32	1391.2	1289	8.3	116	486	740	11.7	3.45	88	.247	.315	-61	-65	99	97	.977	139	145	-.5	-7.4	-3.0	-1.1	-1.0
WEST																										
OAK	42	23	43	1417.2	1170	7.4	96	418	862	10.2	2.58	110	.226	.286	76	42	93	99	.979	130	146	-.0	4.8	7.6	.3	2.9
CHI	36	14	42	1385.1	1269	8.2	94	431	936	11.2	3.12	100	.245	.307	-9	1	102	99	.977	135	136	-.4	.1	.3	.5	9.4
MIN	37	17	34	1399.1	1188	7.6	105	444	838	10.7	2.84	113	.230	.296	35	58	105	99	.974	159	133	-1.8	6.6	-2.0	-.4	-2.4
KC	44	16	29	1381.1	1293	8.4	85	405	801	11.3	3.24	94	.251	.309	-27	-32	99	97	.981	116	164	.7	-3.6	7.7	.5	-6.3
CAL	57	18	16	1377.2	1109	7.2	90	620	1000	11.5	3.06	95	.222	.312	0	-23	95	96	.981	114	135	.8	-2.6	-3.2	.0	2.4
TEX	11	8	34	1374.2	1258	8.2	92	613	868	12.6	3.53	85	.246	.332	-71	-79	98	99	.972	166	147	-2.2	-9.0	-11.0	-.0	-.8
TOT	502	193	372	16653.2		8.0				11.3	3.06		.239	.308					.979	1535	1770					

Runs		Hits		Doubles		Triples		Home Runs		Total Bases	
Murcer-NY	102	Rudi-Oak	181	Piniella-KC	33	Rudi-Oak	9	D.Allen-Chi	37	Murcer-NY	314
Rudi-Oak	94	Piniella-KC	179	Rudi-Oak	32	Fisk-Bos	9	Murcer-NY	33	D.Allen-Chi	305
Harper-Bos	92	Murcer-NY	171	Murcer-NY	30	Blair-Bal	8	Killebrew-Min	26	Rudi-Oak	288
D.Allen-Chi	90	Carew-Min	170	White-NY	29	Murcer-NY	7	Epstein-Oak	26	Mayberry-KC	255
Tovar-Min	86	May-Chi	161	Harper-Bos	29	Kelly-Chi	7			Piniella-KC	253

Runs Batted In		Runs Produced		Bases On Balls		Batting Average		On Base Percentage		Slugging Average	
D.Allen-Chi	113	D.Allen-Chi	166	White-NY	99	Carew-Min	.318	D.Allen-Chi	.422	D.Allen-Chi	.603
Mayberry-KC	100	Murcer-NY	165	D.Allen-Chi	99	Piniella-KC	.312	May-Chi	.408	Fisk-Bos	.538
Murcer-NY	96	Rudi-Oak	150	Killebrew-Min	94	D.Allen-Chi	.308	Mayberry-KC	.396	Murcer-NY	.537
Scott-Mil	88	Mayberry-KC	140	May-Chi	79	May-Chi	.308	White-NY	.385	Mayberry-KC	.507
Powell-Bal	81					Rudi-Oak	.305	Scheinblum-KC	.385	Epstein-Oak	.490

Production		Adjusted Production		Batter Runs		Adjusted Batter Runs		Clutch Hitting Index		Runs Created	
D.Allen-Chi	1.025	D.Allen-Chi	199	D.Allen-Chi	66.1	D.Allen-Chi	63.6	Billings-Tex	138	D.Allen-Chi	131
Fisk-Bos	.909	Murcer-NY	171	Murcer-NY	44.9	Murcer-NY	48.6	Rojas-KC	123	Murcer-NY	114
Mayberry-KC	.903	Mayberry-KC	168	Mayberry-KC	43.0	Mayberry-KC	43.5	Scheinblum-KC	123	Mayberry-KC	101
Murcer-NY	.900	Epstein-Oak	166	Fisk-Bos	37.1	Epstein-Oak	37.6	Petrocelli-Bos	122	May-Chi	96
Epstein-Oak	.868	Fisk-Bos	159	May-Chi	36.7	Rudi-Oak	35.8	Bando-Oak	121	Rudi-Oak	95

Total Average		Stolen Bases		Stolen Base Average		Stolen Base Runs		Fielding Runs		Total Player Rating	
D.Allen-Chi	1.121	Campaneris-Oak	52	Baylor-Bal	92.3	Campaneris-Oak	7.2	Patek-KC	29.5	Murcer-NY	5.5
Mayberry-KC	.910	Nelson-Tex	51	Patek-KC	82.5	Baylor-Bal	6.0	Rodriguez-Det	24.0	D.Allen-Chi	5.4
Fisk-Bos	.908	Patek-KC	33	Scott-Mil	80.0	Patek-KC	5.7	Michael-NY	23.7	Fisk-Bos	4.4
Murcer-NY	.888	Kelly-Chi	32	Campaneris-Oak	78.8	Nelson-Tex	5.1	Belanger-Bal	20.8	Patek-KC	3.8
Epstein-Oak	.885	Otis-KC	28	Harper-Bos	78.1	Kelly-Chi	4.2	May-Mil	14.9	White-NY	3.4

Wins		Win Percentage		Games		Complete Games		Shutouts		Saves	
Wood-Chi	24	Hunter-Oak	.750	Lindblad-Tex	66	Perry-Cle	29	Ryan-Cal	9	Lyle-NY	35
Perry-Cle	24	Tiant-Bos	.714	Fingers-Oak	65	Lolich-Det	23	Wood-Chi	8	Forster-Chi	29
Lolich-Det	22	Odom-Oak	.714	Granger-Min	63	Wood-Chi	20	Stottlemyre-NY	7	Fingers-Oak	21
		Palmer-Bal	.677			Ryan-Cal	20			Granger-Min	19
		Kline-NY	.640			Palmer-Bal	18			Sanders-Mil	17

Innings Pitched		Fewest Hits/Game		Fewest BB/Game		Strikeouts		Strikeouts/Game		Ratio	
Wood-Chi	376.2	Ryan-Cal	5.26	Peterson-NY	1.58	Ryan-Cal	329	Ryan-Cal	10.43	Nelson-KC	7.89
Perry-Cle	342.2	Hunter-Oak	6.09	Nelson-KC	1.61	Lolich-Det	250	Messersmith-Cal	7.53	Hunter-Oak	8.32
Lolich-Det	327.1	Nelson-KC	6.23	Kline-NY	1.68	Perry-Cle	234	May-Cal	7.41	Perry-Cle	9.11
Hunter-Oak	295.1	Tiant-Bos	6.44	Holtzman-Oak	1.76	Blyleven-Min	228	Bradley-Chi	7.23	Palmer-Bal	9.51
Blyleven-Min	287.1	Messersmith-Cal	6.63	Wood-Chi	1.77	Coleman-Det	222	Blyleven-Min	7.14	Wood-Chi	9.70

Earned Run Average		Adjusted ERA		Opponents' Batting Avg.		Opponents' On Base Pct.		Starter Runs		Adjusted Starter Runs	
Tiant-Bos	1.91	Tiant-Bos	168	Ryan-Cal	.171	Nelson-KC	.236	Perry-Cle	43.5	Perry-Cle	49.5
Perry-Cle	1.92	Perry-Cle	168	Hunter-Oak	.189	Hunter-Oak	.242	Hunter-Oak	33.4	Palmer-Bal	30.7
Hunter-Oak	2.04	Palmer-Bal	149	Nelson-KC	.196	Perry-Cle	.261	Palmer-Bal	30.3	Hunter-Oak	26.3
Palmer-Bal	2.07	Nelson-KC	146	Tiant-Bos	.202	Palmer-Bal	.269	Ryan-Cal	24.6	Tiant-Bos	25.9
Nelson-KC	2.08	Hunter-Oak	139	Perry-Cle	.205	Tiant-Bos	.277	Wood-Chi	23.1	Wood-Chi	25.8

Clutch Pitching Index		Relief Runs		Adjusted Relief Runs		Relief Ranking		Total Pitcher Index		Total Baseball Ranking	
Paul-Tex	128	Lyle-NY	13.6	Lyle-NY	12.3	Lyle-NY	23.3	Perry-Cle	7.0	Perry-Cle	7.0
Odom-Oak	124	Knowles-Oak	12.3	Bell-Mil	12.3	Forster-Chi	16.0	Palmer-Bal	4.2	Murcer-NY	5.5
Wilcox-Cle	119	Bell-Mil	11.0	Knowles-Oak	10.7	Knowles-Oak	12.9	Wood-Chi	3.1	D.Allen-Chi	5.4
Lonborg-Mil	112	Forster-Chi	9.0	Forster-Chi	9.7	Abernathy-KC	11.0	Tiant-Bos	3.0	Fisk-Bos	4.4
Lolich-Det	111	Abernathy-KC	8.8	Abernathy-KC	8.6	Fingers-Oak	8.5	Lyle-NY	2.7	Palmer-Bal	4.2

January 24 Warren Spahn is elected to the Hall of Fame in his first try, receiving 316 of 380 votes.

January 28 The Hall of Fame Special Veterans Committee selects players Mickey Welch and George Kelly, plus umpire Billy Evans, for enshrinement.

February 1 Commissioner Bowie Kuhn announces the selection of Monte Irvin for the Hall of Fame by the Special Committee on the Negro Leagues.

February 25 A new three-year Basic Agreement is reached between players and owners, and spring training is slated to start March 1. Among the provisions of the agreement are a $15,000 minimum salary, salary arbitration, and the "10 and five" trade rule, which permits a player with 10 years in the major league, the last five of which are with his current team, to veto any trade involving him.

March 20 In a special election held by the BBWAA, the late Roberto Clemente receives 393 of 424 votes to earn entry in the Hall of Fame. The Hall's Board of Directors had earlier waived the five-year-wait rule for Clemente. His number 21 will be retired in Pittsburgh 17 days later.

May 8 For the second time in his career,

Pirate Willie Stargell poles one out of Dodger Stadium. His blast off Andy Messersmith hits the right field pavilion roof 470 feet away. His first such homer, a 506-foot shot, came off Alan Foster on Aug. 5, 1969. No other player until Mike Piazza in 1997 would hit one out of the stadium.

June 20 Bobby Bonds leads off with a homer, but the Giants lose 7-5 to the Reds. It is Bonds's 22nd leadoff homer, breaking Lou Brock's NL record.

June 23 Phillies pitcher Ken Brett beats the Expos, 7–2, and hits a home run for a major league-record fourth consecutive game. He hit home runs on June 9, 13, and 18: he will total 10 for his career.

July 21 Hank Aaron hits a Ken Brett fastball for a two-run home run during the Braves' 8–4 loss to the Phillies. It is the 700th career homer for Aaron, only the second player to reach that milestone.

August 6 Roberto Clemente and Warren Spahn head the list of new inductees at Cooperstown. Clemente is the first Latin-born player to achieve membership at Cooperstown.

August 17 Willie Mays hits the 660th— and last—home run of his major league

career off Don Gullett of Cincinnati.

October 10 Tom Seaver hurls the Mets into the World Series with a 7-2 victory over the Reds. New York has 13 hits in the contest.

October 14 The Mets win Game 2, 10-7, scoring four runs in an 11th inning, featuring the last major league hit by Willie Mays and two errors by Oakland second base Mike Andrews. Andrews is subsequently put on the "disabled list" by Oakland owner Charles Finley,

October 31 Tom Seaver wins the NL Cy Young Award, the first time the honor has gone to a player with fewer than 20 wins. Seaver was 19-10 and led the league in ERA (2.08) and strikeouts (251).

November 21 Pete Rose wins the NL MVP in a controversial vote, edging out Willie Stargell. Rose led the league with 230 hits and won his third batting crown with a .338 mark. Stargell led with 44 homers, 119 RBIs, and a .646 slugging average while batting .299.

November 27 Gary Matthews receives 11 of 24 nominations for the league Rookie of the Year Award. The Giants outfielder batted .300 in 145 games.

	ATLANTA		CHICAGO		CINCINNATI		HOUSTON		LOS ANGELES		MONTREAL
M	E.Mathews	M	W.Lockman	M	S.Anderson	M	L.Durocher	M	W.Alston	M	G.Mauch
1B	M.Lum	1B	J.Hickman	1B	T.Perez	1B	L.May	1B	B.Buckner	1B	M.Jorgensen
2B	D.Johnson	2B	G.Beckert	2B	J.Morgan	2B	T.Helms	2B	D.Lopes	2B	R.Hunt
SS	M.Perez	SS	D.Kessinger	SS	D.Concepcion	SS	R.Metzger	SS	B.Russell	SS	T.Foli
3B	D.Evans	3B	R.Santo	3B	D.Menke	3B	D.Rader	3B	R.Cey	3B	B.Bailey
LF	H.Aaron	LF	B.Williams	LF	P.Rose	LF	B.Watson	LF	M.Mota	LF	R.Fairly
CF	D.Baker	CF	R.Monday	CF	C.Geronimo	CF	C.Cedeno	CF	W.Davis	CF	R.Woods
RF	R.Garr	RF	J.Cardenal	RF	B.Tolan	RF	J.Wynn	RF	W.Crawford	RF	K.Singleton
C	J.Oates	C	R.Hundley	C	J.Bench	C	S.Jutze	C	J.Ferguson	C	J.Boccabella
OS	S.Jackson	O	G.Hiser	S2	D.Chaney	C	J.Edwards	1O	S.Garvey	1	H.Breeden
C	P.Casanova	2	P.Popovich	31	D.Driessen	O	T.Agee			O	B.Day
								P	D.Sutton	S2	P.Frias
P	C.Morton	P	F.Jenkins	P	J.Billingham	P	J.Reuss	P	A.Messersmith		
P	P.Niekro	P	B.Hooton	P	R.Grimsley	P	D.Roberts	P	C.Osteen	P	S.Renko
P	R.Schueler	P	R.Reuschel	P	D.Gullett	P	D.Wilson	P	T.John	P	M.Torrez
P	R.Harrison	P	M.Pappas	P	F.Norman	P	K.Forsch	P	A.Downing	P	B.Moore
P	R.Reed	P	B.Bonham	RP	P.Borbon	P	T.Griffin	RP	C.Hough	P	E.McAnally
RP	T.House	RP	B.Locker	RP	T.Hall	RP	J.Crawford	RP	J.Brewer	P	M.Rogers
		RP	R.Burris	RP	C.Carroll	RP	J.Ray	RP	D.Rau	RP	M.Marshall
P	G.Gentry	RP	J.Aker			RP	J.York			RP	T.Walker
P	P.Dobson			P	J.McGlothlin			P	P.Richert		
		P	L.Gura	P	R.Nelson	P	J.Richard			P	B.Stoneman
		P	D.LaRoche								

	NEW YORK		PHILADELPHIA		PITTSBURGH		SAN DIEGO		SAN FRANCISCO		ST.LOUIS
M	Y.Berra	M	D.Ozark	M	B.Virdon	M	D.Zimmer	M	C.Fox	M	R.Schoendienst
1B	J.Milner	1B	W.Montanez	M	D.Murtaugh	1B	N.Colbert	1B	W.McCovey	1B	J.Torre
2B	F.Millan	2B	D.Doyle	1B	B.Robertson	2B	R.Morales	2B	T.Fuentes	2B	T.Sizemore
SS	B.Harrelson	SS	L.Bowa	2B	D.Cash	SS	D.Thomas	SS	C.Speier	SS	M.Tyson
3B	W.Garrett	3B	M.Schmidt	SS	D.Maxvill	3B	D.Roberts	3B	E.Goodson	3B	K.Reitz
LF	C.Jones	LF	G.Luzinski	3B	R.Hebner	LF	L.Lee	LF	G.Matthews	LF	L.Brock
CF	D.Hahn	CF	D.Unser	LF	W.Stargell	CF	J.Grubb	CF	G.Maddox	CF	L.Melendez
RF	R.Staub	RF	B.Robinson	CF	A.Oliver	RF	C.Gaston	RF	B.Bonds	RF	J.Cruz
C	J.Grote	C	B.Boone	RF	R.Zisk	C	F.Kendall	C	D.Rader	C	T.Simmons
				C	M.Sanguillen						
1O	E.Kranepool	1	T.Hutton			O	J.Morales	31	D.Kingman	O	B.Carbo
SO	T.Martinez	3O	C.Tovar	O	G.Clines	S	E.Hernandez	1O	G.Thomasson	1C	T.McCarver
O1	W.Mays			C	M.May	32	D.Hilton				
		P	S.Carlton	2S	R.Stennett	O1	I.Murrell	P	R.Bryant	P	R.Wise
P	T.Seaver	P	W.Twitchell					P	J.Barr	P	R.Cleveland
P	J.Koosman	P	K.Brett	P	N.Briles	P	B.Greif	P	T.Bradley	P	A.Foster
P	J.Matlack	P	J.Lonborg	P	B.Moose	P	C.Kirby	P	J.Marichal	P	B.Gibson
P	G.Stone	P	D.Ruthven	P	D.Ellis	P	S.Arlin	P	J.Willoughby	RP	D.Segui
P	R.Sadecki	RP	B.Lersch	P	J.Rooker	P	R.Troedson	RP	E.Sosa	RP	R.Folkers
RP	T.McGraw	RP	M.Scarce	P	L.Walker	P	R.Jones	RP	R.Moffitt	RP	O.Pena
RP	H.Parker	RP	B.Brandon	RP	D.Giusti	RP	M.Caldwell	RP	D.Carrithers		
		RP	B.Johnson	RP	M.Corkins						
		RP	R.Hernandez	RP	V.Romo					P	T.Murphy
P	J.McAndrew	P	S.Blass	P	G.Ross					P	A.Hrabosky
				P	F.Norman						

TEAM	G	W	L	PCT	GB	R	OR	AB	H	2B	3B	HR	BB	SO	AVG	OBP	SLG	PRO	PRO+	BR	/A	PF	CHI	RC	SB	CS	SBA	SBR
EAST																												
NY	161	82	79	.509		608	588	5457	1345	198	24	85	540	805	.246	.317	.338	.655	89	-81	-72	98	104	583	27	22	55	-5
STL	162	81	81	.500	1.5	643	603	5478	1418	240	35	75	531	796	.259	.328	.357	.685	96	-24	-22	100	100	635	100	46	68	2
PIT	162	80	82	.494	2.5	704	693	5608	1465	257	44	154	432	842	.261	.317	.405	.722	109	30	48	97	101	697	23	30	43	-11
MON	162	79	83	.488	3.5	668	702	5369	1345	190	23	125	695	777	.251	.341	.364	.705	98	30	5	104	94	672	77	68	53	-18
CHI	161	77	84	.478	5	614	655	5363	1322	201	21	117	575	855	.247	.322	.357	.679	88	-35	-81	107	99	605	65	58	53	-15
PHI	162	71	91	.438	11.5	642	717	5546	1381	218	29	134	476	979	.249	.312	.371	.683	93	-40	-56	103	102	641	51	47	52	-13
WEST																												
CIN	162	99	63	.611		741	621	5505	1398	232	34	137	639	947	.254	.335	.383	.718	111	43	81	95	102	724	148	55	73	11
LA	162	95	66	.590	3.5	675	565	5604	1473	219	29	110	497	795	.263	.326	.371	.697	104	-5	25	96	100	676	109	50	69	3
SF	162	88	74	.543	11	739	702	5537	1452	212	52	161	590	913	.262	.337	.407	.744	108	87	56	104	96	765	112	52	68	2
HOU	162	82	80	.506	17	681	672	5532	1391	216	35	134	469	962	.251	.314	.376	.690	97	-28	-26	100	107	639	92	48	66	-1
ATL	162	76	85	.472	22.5	799	774	5631	1497	219	34	206	608	870	.266	.341	.427	.768	111	134	73	108	97	826	84	40	68	1
SD	162	60	102	.370	39	548	770	5457	1330	198	26	112	401	966	.244	.298	.351	.649	92	-110	-67	92	102	566	88	36	71	5
TOT	971					8062		66087	16817	2600	386	1550	6453	10507	.254	.324	.376	.700							976	552	64	-38

TEAM	CG	SH	SV	IP	H	H/G	HR	BB	SO	RAT	ERA	ERA+	OAV	OOB	PR	/A	PF	CPI	FA	E	DP	FW	PW	BW	SBW	DIF
EAST																										
NY	47	15	40	1465	1345	8.3	127	490	1027	11.4	3.26	111	.245	.309	65	58	99	101	.980	126	140	1.1	6.0	-7.5	-.2	2.0
STL	42	14	36	1460²	1366	8.4	105	486	867	11.6	3.25	112	.248	.312	66	63	100	100	.975	159	149	-.7	6.6	-2.3	.5	-4.1
PIT	26	11	44	1450²	1426	8.8	110	564	839	12.6	3.73	94	.258	.331	-12	-35	96	100	.976	151	156	-.3	-3.6	5.0	-.8	-1.3
MON	26	6	38	1451²	1356	8.4	128	681	866	12.8	3.71	103	.250	.337	-9	16	104	103	.974	163	156	-.9	1.7	.5	-1.5	-1.7
CHI	27	13	40	1437²	1471	9.2	128	438	885	12.1	3.66	108	.267	.325	1	46	108	104	.975	157	155	-.7	4.8	-8.4	-1.2	2.0
PHI	49	11	22	1447¹	1435	8.9	131	632	919	13.1	3.99	95	.263	.343	-53	-31	104	103	.979	134	179	.7	-3.2	-5.8	-1.0	-.6
WEST																										
CIN	39	17	43	1473	1389	8.5	135	518	801	11.8	3.40	100	.252	.319	42	0	93	105	.982	115	162	1.8	.0	8.4	1.5	6.3
LA	45	15	38	1491	1270	7.7	129	461	961	10.6	3.00	115	.231	.294	109	72	94	97	.981	125	166	1.2	7.5	2.6	.6	2.5
SF	33	8	44	1452¹	1442	8.9	145	485	787	12.1	3.79	101	.251	.320	-21	-4	104	97	.974	163	138	-.9	.4	5.8	.5	1.2
HOU	45	14	26	1460²	1389	8.6	111	575	907	12.3	3.75	97	.252	.325	-14	-19	99	95	.981	116	140	1.7	-2.0	-2.7	.2	3.7
ATL	34	9	35	1462	1467	9.0	144	575	803	12.7	4.25	93	.263	.335	-95	-51	107	95	.974	166	142	-1.1	-5.3	7.6	.4	-6.1
SD	34	10	23	1430	1461	9.2	157	548	845	12.8	4.16	83	.267	.336	-79	-110	95	100	.973	170	152	-1.3	-11.5	-7.0	.9	-2.1
TOT	447	143	429	17482		8.7				12.2	3.66		.254	.324					.977	1745	1835					

Runs		Hits		Doubles		Triples		Home Runs		Total Bases	
Bonds-SF	131	Rose-Cin	230	Stargell-Pit	43	Metzger-Hou	14	Stargell-Pit	44	Bonds-SF	341
Morgan-Cin	116	Garr-Atl	200	Oliver-Pit	38	Matthews-SF	10	Johnson-Atl	43	Stargell-Pit	337
Rose-Cin	115	Brock-StL	193	Staub-NY	36	Maddox-SF	10	Evans-Atl	41	Evans-Atl	331
Evans-StL	114	Simmons-StL	192	Simmons-StL	36	Davis-LA	9	Aaron-Atl	40	Johnson-Atl	305
Brock-StL	110	Oliver-Pit	191	Rose-Cin	36			Bonds-SF	39	Oliver-Pit	303

Runs Batted In		Runs Produced		Bases On Balls		Batting Average		On Base Percentage		Slugging Average	
Stargell-Pit	119	Bonds-SF	188	Evans-Atl	124	Rose-Cin	.338	Singleton-Mon	.429	Stargell-Pit	.646
May-Hou	105	Stargell-Pit	181	Singleton-Mon	123	Cedeno-Hou	.320	Fairly-Mon	.422	Evans-Atl	.556
Evans-Atl	104	Singleton-Mon	180	Morgan-Cin	111	Maddox-SF	.319	Morgan-Cin	.408	Johnson-Atl	.546
Bench-Cin	104	Baker-Atl	179	McCovey-SF	105	Perez-Cin	.314	Evans-Atl	.407	Cedeno-Hou	.537
Singleton-Mon	103	Evans-Atl	177	Monday-Chi	92	Watson-Hou	.312	Watson-Hou	.405	Bonds-SF	.530

Production		Adjusted Production		Batter Runs		Adjusted Batter Runs		Clutch Hitting Index		Runs Created	
Stargell-Pit	1.041	Stargell-Pit	189	Stargell-Pit	57.8	Stargell-Pit	61.0	Cey-LA	126	Evans-Atl	143
Evans-Atl	.964	Perez-Cin	162	Evans-Atl	54.8	Morgan-Cin	47.8	Sizemore-StL	123	Stargell-Pit	136
Perez-Cin	.923	Morgan-Cin	157	Aaron-Atl	45.5	Perez-Cin	47.2	Bench-Cin	121	Bonds-SF	130
Johnson-Atl	.917	Evans-Atl	153	Singleton-Mon	44.8	Evans-Atl	45.0	Speier-SF	119	Morgan-Cin	128
Cedeno-Hou	.914	Cedeno-Hou	151	Morgan-Cin	41.6	Singleton-Mon	40.6	Tolan-Cin	116	Rose-Cin	119

Total Average		Stolen Bases		Stolen Base Average		Stolen Base Runs		Fielding Runs		Total Player Rating	
Stargell-Pit	1.129	Brock-StL	70	Baker-Atl	88.9	Morgan-Cin	11.1	Schmidt-Phi	21.2	Stargell-Pit	6.3
Evans-Atl	1.048	Morgan-Cin	67	Morgan-Cin	81.7	Brock-StL	9.0	Kessinger-Chi	17.0	Morgan-Cin	6.1
Morgan-Cin	1.034	Cedeno-Hou	56	Concepcion-Cin	81.5	Cedeno-Hou	7.8	Unser-Phi	16.7	Cedeno-Hou	5.3
Cedeno-Hou	.949	Bonds-SF	43	Cedeno-Hou	78.9	Baker-Atl	5.4	Rose-Cin	16.7	Evans-Atl	5.2
Johnson-Atl	.947	Lopes-LA	36	Brock-StL	77.8	Garr-Atl	3.9	Cey-LA	16.2	Rose-Cin	4.6

Wins		Win Percentage		Games		Complete Games		Shutouts		Saves	
Bryant-SF	24	John-LA	.696	Marshall-Mon	92	Seaver-NY	18	Billingham-Cin	7	Marshall-Mon	31
Seaver-NY	19	Gullett-Cin	.692	Borbon-Cin	80	Carlton-Phi	18	Roberts-Hou	6	McGraw-NY	25
Billingham-Cin	19	Bryant-SF	.667	Sosa-SF	71	Billingham-Cin	16	Wise-StL	5	Giusti-Pit	20
Sutton-LA	18	Seaver-NY	.655	Giusti-Pit	67			Twitchell-Phi	5	Brewer-LA	20
Gullett-Cin	18	Billingham-Cin	.655	Segui-StL	65						

Innings Pitched		Fewest Hits/Game		Fewest BB/Game		Strikeouts		Strikeouts/Game		Ratio	
Carlton-Phi	293.1	Seaver-NY	6.80	Marichal-SF	1.61	Seaver-NY	251	Seaver-NY	7.79	Seaver-NY	8.91
Billingham-Cin	293.1	Sutton-LA	6.88	Jenkins-Chi	1.89	Carlton-Phi	223	Moore-Mon	7.71	Sutton-LA	9.02
Seaver-NY	290.0	Twitchell-Phi	6.93	Barr-SF	1.91	Matlack-NY	205	Matlack-NY	7.62	Messersmith-LA	10.06
Reuss-Hou	279.1	Wilson-Hou	7.03	Sutton-LA	1.97	Sutton-LA	200	Sutton-LA	7.02	Gibson-StL	10.11
Jenkins-Chi	271.0	Messersmith-LA	7.07	Seaver-NY	1.99			Carlton-Phi	6.84	Rooker-Pit	10.41

Earned Run Average		Adjusted ERA		Opponents' Batting Avg.		Opponents' On Base Pct.		Starter Runs		Adjusted Starter Runs	
Seaver-NY	2.08	Seaver-NY	174	Seaver-NY	.206	Seaver-NY	.254	Seaver-NY	51.0	Seaver-NY	49.5
Sutton-LA	2.42	Twitchell-Phi	152	Sutton-LA	.209	Sutton-LA	.258	Sutton-LA	35.3	Rogers-Mon	33.8
Twitchell-Phi	2.50	Marshall-Mon	143	Wilson-Hou	.213	Messersmith-LA	.279	Rogers-Mon	31.5	Twitchell-Phi	32.2
Marshall-Mon	2.66	Sutton-LA	142	Messersmith-LA	.214	Gibson-StL	.284	Twitchell-Phi	28.8	Sutton-LA	28.9
Messersmith-LA	2.70	Renko-Mon	136	Renko-Mon	.218	Briles-Pit	.288	Messersmith-LA	26.6	Renko-Mon	27.8

Clutch Pitching Index		Relief Runs		Adjusted Relief Runs		Relief Ranking		Total Pitcher Index		Total Baseball Ranking	
Marshall-Mon	134	Borbon-Cin	20.2	Marshall-Mon	22.9	Marshall-Mon	36.8	Seaver-NY	5.4	Stargell-Pit	6.3
Roberts-Hou	122	Marshall-Mon	19.8	Locker-Chi	16.6	Locker-Chi	28.2	Marshall-Mon	4.4	Morgan-Cin	6.1
Twitchell-Phi	121	Giusti-Pit	14.1	Borbon-Cin	16.6	Borbon-Cin	22.7	Rogers-Mon	4.1	Seaver-NY	5.4
Grimsley-Cin	116	Moffitt-SF	13.8	Moffitt-SF	15.6	Giusti-Pit	17.8	Renko-Mon	3.6	Cedeno-Hou	5.3
Moose-Pit	113	Locker-Chi	13.3	Giusti-Pit	12.6	Scarce-Phi	16.1	Locker-Chi	3.1	Evans-Atl	5.2

January 3 A group of investors, headed by shipbuilder George Steinbrenner, purchases the New York Yankees from CBS for $10 million.

April 6 Yankee Ron Blomberg, facing Boston's Luis Tiant, becomes the first official designated hitter in the major league. Blomberg walks with the bases loaded and winds up 1-for-3 in the 15-5 loss to the Red Sox.

April 27 In 50-degree Detroit weather, Royals rookie Steve Busby no-hits the Tigers 3-0. It is the first Royals no-hitter, and Busby is the first no-hit game pitcher not to bat.

May 15 California's Nolan Ryan strikes out 12 and hurls his first career no-hitter in beating Kansas City 3-0.

June 7 The Rangers make Texas high school pitcher David Clyde the No. 1 pick in the free-agent draft. He will make his major league debut later this month. Dave Winfield, the No. 4 pick, will go straight to the major leagues. Winfield was also taken in the NBA and NFL drafts. John Stearns is taken second by the Phillies, and the Brewers, picking third, take Robin Yount.

June 27 David Clyde, 18 and fresh out of Houston's Westchester High School, makes his eagerly awaited debut with the Rangers, before 35,698, the largest Rangers' crowd of the year. Clyde goes five innings and is the winner, 4-3.

July 15 Before 41,411 in Detroit, Angel Nolan Ryan hurls his second no-hitter of the season in taming the Tigers, 6-0. Ryan fans 17 batters.

July 20 Chicago's Wilbur Wood starts and loses both games of a doubleheader with the Yankees, 12-2 and 7-0.

July 30 The Rangers Jim Bibby no-hits first-place Oakland, 6-0. Bibby, who came to Texas in a June 6 trade with the Cardinals, strikes out 13 batters.

August 1 Thurman Munson and Carlton Fisk brawl at Fenway. With a 2-2 score in the top of the ninth, Munson, attempting to score from third on a missed bunt, crashes into Fisk and they both come up swinging. Boston wins 3-2 in the bottom of the inning.

September 19 The Angels down the Rangers 6-2 and 9-4 at Arlington Stadium. Frank Robinson homers in the 32nd different park of his major league career—a record.

September 27 Nolan Ryan fans 16 in 11 innings, beating the Twins 5-4. The final strikeout victim, Rich Reese, is 383 of the season for Ryan, enabling him to surpass the major league record set by Sandy Koufax in 1965.

October 21 Oakland wins the world championship for the second straight year as Bert Campaneris and MVP Reggie Jackson homer in the 5-2, seventh-game victory.

November 14 Reggie Jackson wins the league MVP Award unanimously. The Oakland star led the league in runs (99), homers (32), RBI (117), and slugging (.531). Jim Palmer is named the league Cy Young winner.

BALTIMORE	BOSTON	CALIFORNIA	CHICAGO	CLEVELAND	DETROIT
M E.Weaver	M E.Kasko	M B.Winkles	M C.Tanner	M K.Aspromonte	M B.Martin
1B B.Powell	M E.Popowski	1B M.Epstein	1B T.Muser	1B C.Chambliss	M J.Schultz
2B B.Grich	1B C.Yastrzemski	2B S.Alomar	2B J.Orta	2B J.Brohamer	1B N.Cash
SS M.Belanger	2B D.Griffin	SS R.Meoli	SS E.Leon	SS F.Duffy	2B D.McAuliffe
3B B.Robinson	SS L.Aparicio	3B A.Gallagher	3B B.Melton	3B B.Bell	SS E.Brinkman
LF D.Baylor	3B R.Petrocelli	LF V.Pinson	LF C.May	LF C.Spikes	3B A.Rodriguez
CF P.Blair	LF T.Harper	CF K.Berry	CF J.Jeter	CF G.Hendrick	LF W.Horton
RF R.Coggins	CF R.Miller	RF L.Stanton	RF P.Kelly	RF R.Torres	CF M.Stanley
C E.Williams	RF D.Evans	C J.Torborg	C E.Herrmann	C D.Duncan	RF J.Northrup
DH T.Davis	C C.Fisk	DH F.Robinson	DH K.Henderson	DH O.Gamble	C B.Freehan
	DH O.Cepeda				DH G.Brown
O A.Bumbry		O1 T.McCraw	1 D.Allen	CD J.Ellis	
O M.Rettenmund	O R.Smith	3O B.Oliver	O1 J.Hairston	O2 J.Lowenstein	O1 A.Kaline
	S2 M.Guerrero	O R.Scheinblum	2S L.Alvarado	OD W.Williams	2 T.Taylor
P J.Palmer					C D.Sims
P M.Cuellar	P B.Lee	P N.Ryan	P W.Wood	P G.Perry	D F.Howard
P D.McNally	P L.Tiant	P B.Singer	P S.Bahnsen	P D.Tidrow	
P D.Alexander	P J.Curtis	P C.Wright	P S.Stone	P M.Wilcox	P M.Lolich
P J.Jefferson	P M.Pattin	P R.May	P T.Forster	P T.Timmermann	P J.Coleman
RP B.Reynolds	P R.Moret	RP S.Barber	P E.Fisher	P B.Strom	P J.Perry
RP G.Jackson	RP B.Bolin	RP D.Sells	RP C.Acosta	RP T.Hilgendorf	P W.Fryman
RP E.Watt			RP R.Gossage	RP R.Lamb	RP J.Hiller
	P D.Pole	P R.Hand		RP J.Johnson	RP F.Scherman
	P R.Culp	P D.Lange	P B.Johnson		RP L.LaGrow
				P D.Bosman	
				P M.Kekich	P M.Strahler

KANSAS CITY	MILWAUKEE	MINNESOTA	NEW YORK	OAKLAND	TEXAS
M J.McKeon	M D.Crandall	M F.Quilici	M R.Houk	M D.Williams	M W.Herzog
1B J.Mayberry	1B G.Scott	1B J.Lis	1B F.Alou	1B G.Tenace	M D.Wilber
2B C.Rojas	2B P.Garcia	2B R.Carew	2B H.Clarke	2B D.Green	M B.Martin
SS F.Patek	SS T.Johnson	SS D.Thompson	SS G.Michael	SS B.Campaneris	1B J.Spencer
3B P.Schaal	3B D.Money	3B S.Braun	3B G.Nettles	3B S.Bando	2B D.Nelson
LF L.Piniella	LF J.Briggs	LF J.Holt	LF R.White	LF J.Rudi	SS J.Mason
CF A.Otis	CF D.May	CF L.Hisle	CF B.Murcer	CF B.North	3B T.Harrah
RF E.Kirkpatrick	RF B.Coluccio	RF B.Darwin	RF M.Alou	RF R.Jackson	LF R.Carty
C F.Healy	C D.Porter	C G.Mitterwald	C T.Munson	C R.Fosse	CF V.Harris
DH H.McRae	DH O.Brown	DH T.Oliva	DH J.Hart	DH D.Johnson	RF J.Burroughs
					C K.Suarez
32 K.Bevacqua	CD El.Rodriguez	S3 J.Terrell	D1 R.Blomberg	2S T.Kubiak	DH A.Johnson
OD S.Hovley	DO J.Lahoud	O S.Brye			O E.Maddox
		1 H.Killebrew			C D.Billings
P P.Splittorff	P J.Colborn	P B.Blyleven	P M.Stottlemyre	P K.Holtzman	O1 L.Biittner
P S.Busby	P J.Slaton	P J.Kaat	P D.Medich	P V.Blue	31 B.Sudakis
P D.Drago	P J.Bell	P J.Decker	P F.Peterson	P C.Hunter	
P G.Garber	P S.Lockwood	P B.Hands	P L.McDaniel	P B.Odom	P J.Bibby
P B.Dal Canton	P B.Champion	P D.Woodson	P P.Dobson	RP R.Fingers	P J.Merritt
RP D.Bird	RP Ed.Rodriguez	RP R.Corbin	RP S.Lyle	RP D.Knowles	P S.Siebert
RP S.Mingori	RP C.Short	RP E.Bane	P S.McDowell	RP H.Pina	P P.Broberg
	RP F.Linzy	RP B.Campbell	P F.Beene		RP B.Gogolewski
P A.Fitzmorris			P S.Kline	P P.Lindblad	RP M.Paul
P K.Wright	P B.Parsons	P D.Goltz		P D.Hamilton	RP J.Brown
P W.Simpson		P D.Fife			P S.Dunning
					P D.Clyde
					P D.Stanhouse
					P C.Hudson
					P S.Foucault

TEAM	G	W	L	PCT	GB	R	OR	AB	H	2B	3B	HR	BB	SO	AVG	OBP	SLG	PRO	PRO+	BR	/A	PF	CHI	RC	SB	CS	SBA	SBR
EAST																												
BAL	162	97	65	.599		754	**561**	5537	1474	229	48	119	**648**	752	.266	**.348**	.389	.737	108	61	67	99	98	**765**	146	64	70	5
BOS	162	89	73	.549	8	738	647	5513	1472	235	30	147	581	799	.267	.340	**.401**	**.741**	102	58	14	106	98	751	114	45	**72**	7
DET	162	85	77	.525	12	642	674	5508	1400	213	32	157	509	721	.254	.322	.390	.712	94	-9	-54	107	95	674	28	30	48	-10
NY	162	80	82	.494	17	641	610	5492	1435	212	17	131	489	**680**	.261	.324	.378	.702	101	-25	-2	97	98	655	47	43	52	-12
MIL	162	74	88	.457	23	708	731	5526	1399	229	40	145	563	977	.253	.327	.388	.715	103	2	17	98	101	702	110	66	63	-7
CLE	162	71	91	.438	26	680	826	5592	1429	205	29	**158**	471	793	.256	.317	.387	.704	95	-27	-38	102	103	666	60	68	47	-23
WEST																												
OAK	162	94	68	.580		**758**	615	5507	1431	216	28	147	595	919	.260	.336	.389	.725	**110**	28	66	95	**104**	730	128	57	69	4
KC	162	88	74	.543	6	755	752	5508	1440	239	40	114	644	696	.261	.342	.381	.723	96	31	-25	108	103	720	105	69	60	-10
MIN	162	81	81	.500	13	738	692	5625	**1521**	**240**	44	120	588	722	**.270**	.344	.393	.737	103	56	26	104	97	756	87	46	65	-2
CAL	162	79	83	.488	15	629	657	5505	1395	183	29	93	509	816	.253	.320	.348	.668	95	-84	-38	92	**104**	609	59	47	56	-11
CHI	162	77	85	.475	17	652	705	5475	1400	228	38	111	537	952	.256	.326	.372	.698	93	-28	-50	103	99	647	83	73	53	-19
TEX	162	57	105	.352	37	619	844	5488	1397	195	29	110	503	791	.255	.320	.361	.681	95	-63	-37	96	100	629	91	53	63	-5
TOT	972					8314		66276	17193	2624	404	1552	6647	9851	.259	.331	.381	.712							1058	661	62	-79

TEAM	CG	SH	SV	IP	H	H/G	HR	BB	SO	RAT	ERA	ERA+	OAV	OOB	PR	/A	PF	CPI	FA	E	DP	FW	PW	BW	SBW	DIF
EAST																										
BAL	67	14	26	1461²	**1297**	8.0	124	475	715	**11.0**	3.07	122	.240	.303	122	**108**	98	102	.981	119	184	1.3	**11.0**	6.9	1.2	-4.4
BOS	67	10	33	1440¹	1417	8.9	158	499	808	12.2	3.65	110	.259	.325	27	59	105	**106**	.979	127	162	.8	6.0	1.4	**1.4**	-1.7
DET	39	11	**46**	1447²	1468	9.1	154	493	911	12.4	3.90	105	.265	.328	-13	30	107	101	**.982**	112	144	**1.7**	3.1	-5.5	-.3	5.1
NY	47	16	39	1427²	1379	8.7	109	**457**	708	11.7	3.34	110	.254	.315	75	51	96	102	.976	156	172	-.8	5.2	-.2	-.6	-4.7
MIL	50	11	28	1454	1476	9.1	119	623	671	13.2	3.98	94	.265	.342	-27	-36	99	101	.977	145	167	-.2	-3.7	1.7	-.0	-4.8
CLE	55	9	21	1464²	1532	9.4	172	602	883	13.4	4.58	85	.271	.345	-125	-108	103	96	.978	139	174	.2	-11.0	-3.9	-1.7	6.5
WEST																										
OAK	46	16	41	1457¹	1311	8.1	143	494	797	11.3	3.29	108	.241	.308	86	42	93	100	.978	137	170	.3	4.3	6.8	1.1	.6
KC	40	7	41	1449¹	1521	9.4	114	617	790	13.5	4.19	98	.273	.349	-60	-13	108	100	.974	162	**192**	-1.4	-1.3	-2.6	-.3	12.7
MIN	48	**18**	34	1451²	1443	8.9	115	519	879	12.4	3.77	105	.259	.327	7	30	104	97	.978	139	147	.2	3.1	2.7	.5	-6.4
CAL	**72**	13	19	1456¹	1351	8.3	104	614	**1010**	12.4	3.53	100	.246	.326	46	3	93	98	.975	156	153	-.8	.3	-3.9	-.5	2.8
CHI	48	15	35	1456	1484	9.2	110	574	848	13.0	3.86	102	.266	.338	-8	15	104	101	.977	144	165	-.1	1.5	-5.1	-1.3	1.0
TEX	35	10	27	1430	1514	9.5	130	680	831	14.1	4.64	88	.273	.357	-131	-146	98	96	.974	161	164	-1.1	-14.9	-3.8	.2	-4.4
TOT	614	150	390	17396²		8.9				12.5	3.82		.259	.331					.977	1702	1994					

Runs		Hits		Doubles		Triples		Home Runs		Total Bases	
Jackson-Oak	99	Carew-Min	203	Garcia-Mil	32	Carew-Min	11	Jackson-Oak	32	Scott-Mil	295
Scott-Mil	98	May-Mil	189	Bando-Oak	32	Bumbry-Bal	11	Robinson-Cal	30	May-Mil	295
North-Oak	98	Murcer-NY	187	Scott-Mil	30	Orta-Chi	10	Burroughs-Tex	30	Bando-Oak	295
Carew-Min	98	Scott-Mil	185	Chambliss-Cle	30	Coggins-Bal	9	Bando-Oak	29	Murcer-NY	286
Bando-Oak	97	Johnson-Tex	179	Carew-Min	30	Coluccio-Mil	8			Jackson-Oak	286

Runs Batted In		Runs Produced		Bases On Balls		Batting Average		On Base Percentage		Slugging Average	
Jackson-Oak	117	Jackson-Oak	184	Mayberry-KC	122	Carew-Min	.350	Mayberry-KC	.420	Jackson-Oak	.531
Scott-Mil	107	Scott-Mil	181	Grich-Bal	107	Scott-Mil	.306	Carew-Min	.415	Bando-Oak	.498
Mayberry-KC	100	Bando-Oak	166	Yastrzemski-Bos	105	Davis-Bal	.306	Yastrzemski-Bos	.411	Robinson-Cal	.489
Bando-Oak	98	May-Mil	164	Tenace-Oak	101	Murcer-NY	.304	Tenace-Oak	.391	Scott-Mil	.488
Robinson-Cal	97	Mayberry-KC	161	Briggs-Mil	87	May-Mil	.303	Jackson-Oak	.387	Munson-NY	.487

Production		Adjusted Production		Batter Runs		Adjusted Batter Runs		Clutch Hitting Index		Runs Created	
Jackson-Oak	.918	Jackson-Oak	165	Mayberry-KC	41.0	Jackson-Oak	46.4	Davis-Bal	134	Bando-Oak	113
Mayberry-KC	.898	Robinson-Cal	153	Jackson-Oak	40.5	Bando-Oak	41.5	Robinson-Bal	124	Carew-Min	113
Carew-Min	.885	Bando-Oak	153	Carew-Min	38.9	Robinson-Cal	38.1	Piniella-KC	123	Mayberry-KC	113
Bando-Oak	.876	Scott-Mil	144	Yastrzemski-Bos	36.8	Carew-Min	34.5	Johnson-Oak	122	Jackson-Oak	112
Yastrzemski-Bos	.874	Carew-Min	143	Bando-Oak	35.5	Scott-Mil	33.9	May-Chi	119	Scott-Mil	106

Total Average		Stolen Bases		Stolen Base Average		Stolen Base Runs		Fielding Runs		Total Player Rating	
Mayberry-KC	.995	Harper-Bos	54	Rojas-KC	81.8	Harper-Bos	7.8	Patek-KC	35.3	Carew-Min	5.3
Jackson-Oak	.953	North-Oak	53	Money-Mil	81.5	Campaneris-Oak	4.2	Nettles-NY	26.0	Grich-Bal	4.7
Carew-Min	.885	Nelson-Tex	43	Harper-Bos	79.4	Baylor-Bal	4.2	Bell-Cle	24.3	Jackson-Oak	4.6
Yastrzemski-Bos	.879	Carew-Min	41	Baylor-Bal	78.0	North-Oak	3.9	North-Oak	23.6	Munson-NY	3.8
Bando-Oak	.876	Patek-KC	36	Campaneris-Oak	77.3	Money-Mil	3.6	Grich-Bal	21.0	Robinson-Cal	3.8

Wins		Win Percentage		Games		Complete Games		Shutouts		Saves	
Wood-Chi	24	Hunter-Oak	.808	Hiller-Det	65	Perry-Cle	29	Blyleven-Min	9	Hiller-Det	38
Coleman-Det	23	Palmer-Bal	.710	Fingers-Oak	62	Ryan-Cal	26	Perry-Cle	7	Lyle-NY	27
Palmer-Bal	22	Blue-Oak	.690	Bird-KC	54	Blyleven-Min	25	Palmer-Bal	6	Fingers-Oak	22
		Splittorff-KC	.645	Knowles-Oak	52	Tiant-Bos	23			Bird-KC	20
		Colborn-Mil	.625			Colborn-Mil	22			Acosta-Chi	18

Innings Pitched		Fewest Hits/Game		Fewest BB/Game		Strikeouts		Strikeouts/Game		Ratio	
Wood-Chi	359.1	Bibby-Tex	6.04	Kaat-Min-Chi	1.73	Ryan-Cal	383	Ryan-Cal	10.57	Tiant-Bos	9.99
Perry-Cle	344.0	Ryan-Cal	6.57	Blyleven-Min	1.86	Blyleven-Min	258	Bibby-Tex	7.74	Hunter-Oak	10.25
Ryan-Cal	326.0	Palmer-Bal	6.83	Holtzman-Oak	2.00	Singer-Cal	241	Blyleven-Min	7.14	Blyleven-Min	10.30
Blyleven-Min	325.0	Tiant-Bos	7.18	Wood-Chi	2.28	Perry-Cle	238	Stone-Chi	7.04	Palmer-Bal	10.36
Singer-Cal	315.2	Blue-Oak	7.30	Lolich-Det	2.30	Lolich-Det	214	Singer-Cal	6.87	Holtzman-Oak	10.44

Earned Run Average		Adjusted ERA		Opponents' Batting Avg.		Opponents' On Base Pct.		Starter Runs		Adjusted Starter Runs	
Palmer-Bal	2.40	Blyleven-Min	157	Bibby-Tex	.192	Tiant-Bos	.281	Blyleven-Min	46.8	Blyleven-Min	51.9
Blyleven-Min	2.52	Palmer-Bal	156	Ryan-Cal	.203	Hunter-Oak	.284	Palmer-Bal	46.6	Palmer-Bal	43.9
Lee-Bos	2.75	Lee-Bos	146	Palmer-Bal	.211	Blyleven-Min	.287	Ryan-Cal	34.2	Lee-Bos	40.1
Ryan-Cal	2.87	Medich-NY	124	Tiant-Bos	.219	Holtzman-Oak	.287	Lee-Bos	33.7	Ryan-Cal	24.4
Medich-NY	2.95	Ryan-Cal	123	Blue-Oak	.224	Palmer-Bal	.289	Holtzman-Oak	28.1	Perry-Cle	20.8

Clutch Pitching Index		Relief Runs		Adjusted Relief Runs		Relief Ranking		Total Pitcher Index		Total Baseball Ranking	
Lee-Bos	119	Hiller-Det	33.1	Hiller-Det	36.9	Hiller-Det	64.9	Hiller-Det	6.7	Hiller-Det	6.7
Forster-Chi	116	Fingers-Oak	26.7	Fingers-Oak	22.9	Acosta-Chi	35.4	Blyleven-Min	5.7	Blyleven-Min	5.7
Curtis-Bos	113	Reynolds-Bal	23.1	Reynolds-Bal	22.0	Fingers-Oak	33.3	Palmer-Bal	4.5	Carew-Min	5.3
Drago-KC	112	Acosta-Chi	17.1	Acosta-Chi	18.6	Reynolds-Bal	25.4	Lee-Bos	4.0	Grich-Bal	4.7
Bahnsen-Chi	112	Jackson-Bal	17.1	Jackson-Bal	16.3	Lyle-NY	23.8	Acosta-Chi	3.6	Jackson-Oak	4.6

January 25 Ray Kroc, fast-food entrepreneur (McDonald's), buys the Padres for $12 million.

April 4 In his first swing of the season, Hank Aaron hits a three-run home run off Jack Billingham, but the Braves lose to the Reds, 7–6. It is home run 714 for Aaron to tie him with Babe Ruth as the top slugger of all time.

April 8 In the fourth inning of the Braves home opener against the Dodgers, Henry Aaron parks an Al Downing pitch in the left-center field stands for career homer 715, breaking Babe Ruth's once unapproachable record.

May 27 The Pirates' Ken Brett no-hits the Padres until the ninth inning, settling for a two-hit 6-0 shutout.

June 10 During a 12-0 win over the Astros, Phillies rookie third baseman Mike Schmidt hits a ball off the public address speaker hanging from the Astrodome roof, 117 feet up and 300 feet from the plate. Schmidt must settle for a titanic single.

July 3 Pitching in his major league record 13th consecutive game for the Dodgers, Mike Marshall saves Tommy John's 4–1 win over the Reds in the first game of a doubleheader.

July 17 Cardinals pitching great Bob Gibson fans the Reds' Cesar Geronimo to become the second hurler to strike out 3,000 batters. Geronimo will become Nolan Ryan's 3,000th K victim six years later.

July 23 The NL triumphs in the All-Star Game at Pittsburgh, winning 7-2. Write-in choice Dodger first baseman Steve Garvey is the game's MVP.

August 12 Nolan Ryan strikes out 19 as the Angels top the Red Sox 4-2.

September 3 John Montefusco makes his major league debut, homers in his first official time at bat, and pitches nine innings of relief for the Giants to earn a 9–5 victory over the Dodgers.

September 10 The Cardinals lose to the Phillies, 8-2, but Lou Brock breaks Maury Wills's major league record by stealing his 104th and 105th bases of the season. It also gives him 740 career sto-len bases, breaking Max Carey's National League record of 738.

October 2 During a 13–0 win over Reds, Hank Aaron homers off Rawly Eastwick. It is Aaron's 733rd career clout and comes in his last NL at bat.

October 9 Los Angeles advances to the World Series with a 12-1 win over the Bucs as Don Sutton wins his second NLCS game and 11th in a row.

November 2 The Braves trade Hank Aaron to the Brewers for outfielder Dave May and a minor league pitcher to be named later. Aaron will finish his major league career in Milwaukee, where he started it in 1954.

November 6 The Dodgers' Mike Marshall becomes the first relief pitcher to win the Cy Young Award, setting major league records with 106 appearances and 208 innings in relief.

November 13 The Dodgers' Steve Garvey wins the NL MVP Award.

November 27 Cardinals outfielder Bake McBride wins the NL Rookie of the Year Award.

ATLANTA		CHICAGO		CINCINNATI		HOUSTON		LOS ANGELES		MONTREAL	
M	E.Mathews	M	W.Lockman	M	S.Anderson	M	P.Gomez	M	W.Alston	M	G.Mauch
M	C.King	M	J.Marshall	1B	T.Perez	1B	L.May	1B	S.Garvey	1B	M.Jorgensen
1B	D.Johnson	1B	A.Thornton	2B	J.Morgan	2B	T.Helms	2B	D.Lopes	2B	J.Cox
2B	M.Perez	2B	V.Harris	SS	D.Concepcion	SS	R.Metzger	SS	B.Russell	SS	T.Foli
SS	C.Robinson	SS	D.Kessinger	3B	D.Driessen	3B	D.Rader	3B	R.Cey	3B	R.Hunt
3B	D.Evans	3B	B.Madlock	LF	P.Rose	LF	B.Watson	LF	B.Buckner	LF	B.Bailey
LF	H.Aaron	LF	J.Morales	CF	C.Geronimo	CF	C.Cedeno	CF	J.Wynn	CF	W.Davis
CF	D.Baker	CF	R.Monday	RF	G.Foster	RF	G.Gross	RF	W.Crawford	RF	K.Singleton
RF	R.Garr	RF	J.Cardenal	C	J.Bench	C	M.May	C	S.Yeager	C	B.Foote
C	J.Oates	C	S.Swisher								
				32	D.Chaney	O	B.Gallagher	CO	J.Ferguson	1O	R.Fairly
O	R.Office	1O	B.Williams	O	K.Griffey	2	L.Milbourne			2S	L.Lintz
1O	M.Lum	C	G.Mitterwald	O	M.Rettenmund			P	A.Messersmith		
C	V.Correll					P	L.Dierker	P	D.Sutton	P	S.Rogers
		P	B.Bonham	P	D.Gullett	P	T.Griffin	P	D.Rau	P	S.Renko
P	P.Niekro	P	R.Reuschel	P	C.Kirby	P	D.Wilson	P	T.John	P	M.Torrez
P	C.Morton	P	B.Hooton	P	J.Billingham	P	D.Roberts	P	A.Downing	P	D.Blair
P	B.Capra	P	S.Stone	P	F.Norman	C	C.Osteen	RP	M.Marshall	P	M.McAnally
P	R.Reed	RP	K.Frailing	RP	P.Borbon	RP	K.Forsch	RP	C.Hough	RP	C.Taylor
P	R.Harrison	RP	D.LaRoche	RP	C.Carroll	RP	M.Cosgrove			RP	T.Walker
RP	T.House	RP	J.Todd	RP	T.Hall	RP	F.Scherman	P	G.Zahn	RP	J.Montague
RP	M.Leon										
RP	L.Krausse	P	O.Zamora	P	R.Nelson	P	J.Richard			P	D.Murray
		P	R.Burris	P	T.Carroll					P	D.Carrithers
		P	T.Dettore							P	D.DeMola

NEW YORK		PHILADELPHIA		PITTSBURGH		SAN DIEGO		SAN FRANCISCO		ST.LOUIS	
M	Y.Berra	M	D.Ozark	M	D.Murtaugh	M	J.McNamara	M	C.Fox	M	R.Schoendienst
1B	J.Milner	1B	W.Montanez	1B	B.Robertson	1B	W.McCovey	M	W.Westrum	1B	J.Torre
2B	F.Millan	2B	D.Cash	2B	R.Stennett	2B	D.Thomas	1B	D.Kingman	2B	T.Sizemore
SS	B.Harrelson	SS	L.Bowa	SS	F.Taveras	SS	E.Hernandez	2B	T.Fuentes	SS	M.Tyson
3B	W.Garrett	3B	M.Schmidt	3B	R.Hebner	3B	D.Roberts	SS	C.Speier	3B	K.Reitz
LF	C.Jones	LF	G.Luzinski	LF	W.Stargell	LF	D.Winfield	3B	S.Ontiveros	LF	L.Brock
CF	D.Hahn	CF	D.Unser	CF	A.Oliver	CF	J.Grubb	LF	G.Matthews	CF	B.McBride
RF	D.Staub	RF	M.Anderson	RF	R.Zisk	RF	B.Tolan	CF	G.Maddox	RF	R.Smith
C	J.Grote	C	B.Boone	C	M.Sanguillen	C	F.Kendall	RF	B.Bonds	C	T.Simmons
								C	D.Rader		
S3	T.Martinez	O	B.Robinson	O	G.Clines	1O	N.Colbert			O	J.Cruz
O	D.Schneck	1O	T.Hutton	1O	E.Kirkpatrick	O	C.Gaston	1	E.Goodson		
23	K.Boswell	O	J.Johnstone	O	D.Parker	32	D.Hilton	32	M.Phillips	P	B.Gibson
O1	E.Kranepool							O1	G.Thomasson	P	L.McGlothen
		P	S.Carlton	P	J.Rooker	P	B.Greif			P	J.Curtis
P	J.Matlack	P	J.Lonborg	P	J.Reuss	P	D.Freisleben	P	J.Barr	P	A.Foster
P	J.Koosman	P	D.Ruthven	P	K.Brett	P	R.Jones	P	J.D'Acquisto	P	S.Siebert
P	T.Seaver	P	R.Schueler	P	D.Ellis	P	D.Spillner	P	M.Caldwell	RP	R.Folkers
P	H.Parker	P	W.Twitchell	P	B.Kison	RP	L.Hardy	P	T.Bradley	RP	A.Hrabosky
P	R.Sadecki	RP	M.Scarce	RP	D.Giusti	RP	V.Romo	P	R.Bryant	RP	M.Garman
RP	B.Apodaca	RP	G.Garber	RP	R.Hernandez	RP	D.Tomlin	RP	R.Moffitt		
RP	T.McGraw			RP	J.Morlan			RP	E.Sosa	P	B.Forsch
RP	B.Miller					P	L.Palmer	RP	C.Williams		
				P	L.Demery	P	S.Arlin				
P	G.Stone					P	M.Corkins	P	E.Halicki		

TEAM	G	W	L	PCT	GB	R	OR	AB	H	2B	3B	HR	BB	SO	AVG	OBP	SLG	PRO	PRO+	BR	/A	PF	CHI	RC	SB	CS	SBA	SBR
EAST																												
PIT	162	88	74	.543		751	657	5702	**1560**	238	46	114	514	828	**.274**	.338	.391	.729	114	66	94	96	100	745	55	31	64	-2
STL	161	86	75	.534	1.5	677	643	5620	1492	216	46	83	531	752	.265	.334	.365	.699	102	9	15	99	98	687	**172**	62	74	**14**
PHI	162	80	82	.494	8	676	701	5494	1434	233	**50**	95	469	822	.261	.322	.373	.695	96	-7	-34	104	**104**	658	115	58	66	0
MON	161	79	82	.491	8.5	662	657	5343	1355	201	29	86	652	812	.254	.338	.350	.688	93	2	-35	106	99	657	124	49	72	8
NY	162	71	91	.438	17	572	646	5468	1286	183	22	96	597	**735**	.235	.314	.329	.643	86	-99	-89	98	100	571	43	23	65	-1
CHI	162	66	96	.407	22	669	826	5574	1397	221	42	110	621	857	.251	.329	.365	.694	96	-1	-29	104	98	668	78	73	52	-20
WEST																												
LA	162	102	60	.630		**798**	**561**	5557	1511	231	34	**139**	597	820	.272	**.346**	**.401**	**.747**	**120**	103	135	96	102	774	149	75	67	0
CIN	163	98	64	.605	4	776	631	5535	1437	**271**	35	135	**693**	940	.260	.345	.394	.739	115	95	107	99	99	**776**	146	49	**75**	14
ATL	163	88	74	.543	14	661	563	5533	1375	202	37	120	571	772	.249	.321	.363	.684	93	-23	-51	104	101	649	72	44	62	-5
HOU	162	81	81	.500	21	653	632	5489	1441	222	41	110	471	864	.263	.324	.378	.702	107	6	35	96	98	663	108	65	62	-7
SF	162	72	90	.444	30	634	723	5482	1380	228	38	93	548	869	.252	.323	.358	.681	92	-28	-58	105	100	642	107	51	68	2
SD	162	60	102	.370	42	541	830	5415	1239	196	27	99	564	900	.229	.304	.330	.634	87	-122	-99	96	101	555	85	45	65	-2
TOT	972					8070		66212	16907	2642	447	1280	6828	9971	.255	.328	.367	.695							1254	625	67	1

TEAM	CG	SH	SV	IP	H	H/G	HR	BB	SO	RAT	ERA	ERA+	OAV	OOB	PR	/A	PF	CPI	FA	E	DP	FW	PW	BW	SBW	DIF
EAST																										
PIT	**51**	9	17	1466	1428	8.8	93	543	721	12.3	3.49	99	.256	.326	21	-7	95	100	.975	162	154	-.5	-.7	9.8	-.2	-1.4
STL	37	13	20	1473¹	1399	8.5	97	616	794	12.5	3.48	103	.254	.331	22	15	99	**104**	.977	147	**192**	.4	1.6	1.6	**1.4**	.6
PHI	46	4	19	1447¹	1394	8.7	111	682	892	13.1	3.91	97	.257	.343	-47	-22	104	101	.976	148	168	.4	-2.3	-3.5	-.0	4.5
MON	35	8	**27**	1429	1340	8.4	99	544	822	12.0	3.60	107	.249	.321	3	38	106	94	.976	153	157	.0	4.0	-3.6	.8	-2.6
NY	46	15	14	1470¹	1433	8.8	99	504	908	12.0	3.42	104	.257	.322	33	24	99	102	.975	158	150	-.2	2.5	-9.3	-.1	-2.9
CHI	23	6	26	1466¹	1593	9.8	122	576	895	13.6	4.28	89	.277	.347	-108	-76	105	100	.969	199	141	-2.6	-7.9	-3.0	-2.1	.7
WEST																										
LA	33	19	23	1465¹	**1272**	**7.8**	112	**464**	943	**10.8**	2.97	114	**.233**	**.296**	**105**	70	94	96	.975	157	122	-.2	7.3	**14.1**	-.0	-.2
CIN	34	11	27	1466¹	1364	8.4	126	536	875	11.8	3.41	102	.247	.316	33	12	96	100	.979	134	151	1.2	1.2	11.1	**1.4**	1.9
ATL	46	**21**	22	1474¹	1343	8.2	97	488	772	11.3	3.05	**124**	.244	.309	93	**119**	104	102	.979	132	161	1.3	**12.4**	-5.3	-.5	-.9
HOU	36	18	18	1450²	1396	8.7	**84**	601	738	12.6	3.46	100	.255	.333	25	-0	96	104	**.982**	113	161	**2.4**	.0	3.6	-.7	-5.3
SF	27	11	25	1439	1409	8.8	116	559	756	12.5	3.78	101	.257	.328	-26	3	105	97	.972	175	153	-1.2	.3	-6.0	.2	-2.2
SD	25	7	19	1445²	1536	9.6	124	715	855	14.3	4.58	78	.275	.362	-155	-165	98	99	.973	170	126	-.9	-17.2	-10.3	-.2	7.6
TOT	439	142	257	17493²		8.7				12.4	3.62		.255	.328					.976	1848	1836					

Runs		Hits		Doubles		Triples		Home Runs		Total Bases	
Rose-Cin	110	Garr-Atl	214	Rose-Cin	45	Garr-Atl	17	Schmidt-Phi	36	Bench-Cin	315
Schmidt-Phi	108	Cash-Phi	206	Oliver-Pit	38	Oliver-Pit	12	Bench-Cin	33	Schmidt-Phi	310
Bench-Cin	108	Garvey-LA	200	Bench-Cin	38	Cash-Phi	11	Wynn-LA	32	Garr-Atl	305
Morgan-Cin	107	Oliver-Pit	198	Stargell-Pit	37	Metzger-Hou	10	Perez-Cin	28	Garvey-LA	301
Brock-StL	105	Stennett-Pit	196			Bowa-Phi	10	Cedeno-Hou	26	Oliver-Pit	293

Runs Batted In		Runs Produced		Bases On Balls		Batting Average		On Base Percentage		Slugging Average	
Bench-Cin	129	Bench-Cin	204	Evans-Atl	126	Garr-Atl	.353	Morgan-Cin	.430	Schmidt-Phi	.546
Schmidt-Phi	116	Schmidt-Phi	188	Morgan-Cin	120	Oliver-Pit	.321	Stargell-Pit	.409	Stargell-Pit	.537
Garvey-LA	111	Garvey-LA	185	Wynn-LA	108	Gross-Hou	.314	Bailey-Mon	.400	Smith-StL	.528
Wynn-LA	108	Wynn-LA	180	Schmidt-Phi	106	Buckner-LA	.314	Schmidt-Phi	.398	Bench-Cin	.507
Simmons-StL	103	Cedeno-Hou	171	Rose-Cin	106	Madlock-Chi	.313	Smith-StL	.394	Garr-Atl	.503

Production		Adjusted Production		Batter Runs		Adjusted Batter Runs		Clutch Hitting Index		Runs Created	
Stargell-Pit	.947	Stargell-Pit	169	Schmidt-Phi	48.3	Stargell-Pit	48.5	Sizemore-StL	128	Schmidt-Phi	130
Schmidt-Phi	.944	Morgan-Cin	160	Morgan-Cin	45.2	Morgan-Cin	46.9	Singleton-Mon	123	Morgan-Cin	125
Morgan-Cin	.924	Smith-StL	158	Stargell-Pit	44.4	Schmidt-Phi	43.4	Montanez-Phi	121	Stargell-Pit	115
Smith-StL	.922	Schmidt-Phi	156	Smith-StL	38.5	Wynn-LA	40.8	Cey-LA	120	Bench-Cin	114
Wynn-LA	.891	Wynn-LA	154	Wynn-LA	36.4	Smith-StL	39.4	Zisk-Pit	119	Garr-Atl	113

Total Average		Stolen Bases		Stolen Base Average		Stolen Base Runs		Fielding Runs		Total Player Rating	
Morgan-Cin	1.108	Brock-StL	118	Lintz-Mon	87.7	Brock-StL	15.6	Cash-Phi	29.1	Schmidt-Phi	6.9
Schmidt-Phi	1.017	Lopes-LA	59	Concepcion-Cin	87.2	Lintz-Mon	10.8	Schmidt-Phi	26.3	Morgan-Cin	5.2
Stargell-Pit	.997	Morgan-Cin	58	Morgan-Cin	82.9	Morgan-Cin	10.2	Cedeno-Hou	20.9	Stargell-Pit	4.5
Smith-StL	.920	Cedeno-Hou	57	Bonds-SF	78.8	Concepcion-Cin	8.7	Foli-Mon	19.4	Wynn-LA	4.3
Wynn-LA	.915	Lintz-Mon	50	Hernandez-SD	78.7			Rose-Cin	17.6	Concepcion-Cin	4.3

Wins		Win Percentage		Games		Complete Games		Shutouts		Saves	
P.Niekro-Atl	20	Messersmith-LA	.769	Marshall-LA	106	P.Niekro-Atl	18	Matlack-NY	7	Marshall-LA	21
Messersmith-LA	20	Sutton-LA	.679	Hardy-SD	76	Carlton-Phi	17	P.Niekro-Atl	6	Moffitt-SF	15
Sutton-LA	19	Capra-Atl	.667	Borbon-Cin	73	Lonborg-Phi	16			Borbon-Cin	14
Billingham-Cin	19	Torrez-Mon	.652	Forsch-Hou	70	Rooker-Pit	15			Giusti-Pit	12
		Billingham-Cin	.633	Sosa-SF	68						

Innings Pitched		Fewest Hits/Game		Fewest BB/Game		Strikeouts		Strikeouts/Game		Ratio	
P.Niekro-Atl	302.1	Capra-Atl	6.76	Barr-SF	1.76	Carlton-Phi	240	Seaver-NY	7.67	Messersmith-LA	9.97
Messersmith-LA	292.1	Messersmith-LA	6.99	Reed-Atl	1.98	Messersmith-LA	221	Carlton-Phi	7.42	P.Niekro-Atl	10.21
Carlton-Phi	291.0	P.Niekro-Atl	7.41	Ellis-Pit	2.09	Seaver-NY	201	Bonham-Chi	7.08	Barr-SF	10.21
Lonborg-Phi	283.0	Gullett-Cin	7.44	Lonborg-Phi	2.23	P.Niekro-Atl	195	D'Acquisto-SF	6.99	Matlack-NY	10.24
Sutton-LA	276.0	Wilson-Hou	7.48	Marshall-LA	2.42	Matlack-NY	195	Norman-Cin	6.81	Reed-Atl	10.35

Earned Run Average		Adjusted ERA		Opponents' Batting Avg.		Opponents' On Base Pct.		Starter Runs		Adjusted Starter Runs	
Capra-Atl	2.28	Capra-Atl	166	Capra-Atl	.208	Messersmith-LA	.278	P.Niekro-Atl	41.5	P.Niekro-Atl	46.9
P.Niekro-Atl	2.38	P.Niekro-Atl	159	Messersmith-LA	.212	Matlack-NY	.285	Matlack-NY	35.6	Capra-Atl	36.1
Matlack-NY	2.41	Matlack-NY	148	Gullett-Cin	.222	P.Niekro-Atl	.286	Messersmith-LA	33.5	Matlack-NY	34.0
Marshall-LA	2.42	Marshall-LA	141	P.Niekro-Atl	.225	Reed-Atl	.286	Capra-Atl	32.2	Barr-SF	28.1
Messersmith-LA	2.59	Barr-SF	139	Matlack-NY	.226	Capra-Atl	.287	Rooker-Pit	24.6	Messersmith-LA	26.4

Clutch Pitching Index		Relief Runs		Adjusted Relief Runs		Relief Ranking		Total Pitcher Index		Total Baseball Ranking	
Caldwell-SF	117	Marshall-LA	27.7	Marshall-LA	22.7	Marshall-LA	31.6	P.Niekro-Atl	5.2	Schmidt-Phi	6.9
Morton-Atl	117	Murray-Mon	20.0	Murray-Mon	21.7	C.Carroll-Cin	24.8	Capra-Atl	3.7	P.Niekro-Atl	5.2
Marshall-LA	116	House-Atl	19.3	House-Atl	21.1	House-Atl	19.9	Marshall-LA	3.5	Morgan-Cin	5.2
Schueler-Phi	113	Taylor-Mon	17.3	Taylor-Mon	19.9	Taylor-Mon	17.9	Messersmith-LA	3.4	Stargell-Pit	4.5
McGlothen-StL	112	C.Carroll-Cin	16.5	C.Carroll-Cin	15.0	Leon-Atl	13.4	Rooker-Pit	3.2	Wynn-LA	4.3

January 1 Lee MacPhail takes over as AL president, succeeding Joe Cronin, who retires.

January 16 The BBWAA elects former Yankee teammates Mickey Mantle and Whitey Ford to the Hall of Fame. Mantle becomes only the seventh player to make it in his first try.

January 28 The Hall of Fame Special Veterans Committee selects Sam Thompson, Jim Bottomley, and umpire Jocko Conlan.

February 11 Forty-eight major league players invoke the new arbitration procedure established to settle contract differences. The first is pitcher Dick Woodson (seeking a contract for $29,000) and his team, the Twins (offering $23,000), who present their respective cases to Detroit lawyer and labor arbitrator Harry H. Platt. He must decide on one of the monetary amounts presented. Woodson wins.

February 13 Speedster James "Cool Papa" Bell is named for Hall of Fame honors by the Special Committee on the Negro Leagues.

July 19 Cleveland's Dick Bosman no-hits Oakland, 4-0. He has no one but himself to blame for not picking up a rare perfect game. His throwing error in the fourth puts the only A's runner on base.

September 24 Al Kaline doubles off Dave McNally for his 3,000th career hit, as the Tigers beat the Orioles, 5-4.

October 3 Frank Robinson becomes the first black manager in the major leagues, as the Indians name him to replace Ken Aspromonte for the 1975 season.

October 9 The A's get just one hit, but draw 11 walks in beating the Orioles 2-1 to take the pennant in four games.

October 12 Oakland slugging star Reggie Jackson connects for a homer off Andy Messersmith to start the scoring, and pitcher Ken Holtzman scores the second run in the fifth on a suicide squeeze. The A's win the World Series opener 3-2 as the Dodgers strand 12 base runners.

October 13 Hall of Fame outfielder Sam Rice dies at Rossmor, Maryland, at age 84, leaving a letter—opened at Cooperstown—confirming his controversial catch in the 1925 World Series.

October 17 Vida Blue and Don Sutton are tied 2-2 going into the bottom of the sixth when Mike Marshall relieves and retires the side. In the seventh, a shower of debris halts the game for 15 minutes. When play is resumed, Joe Rudi hits Marshall's first pitch for a homer to give the A's a third 3-2 win, clinching a third straight world championship.

October 30 Catfish Hunter is named the league Cy Young Award winner. He led the league with 25 wins and a 2.49 ERA.

November 20 Jeff Burroughs, the Texas outfielder who batted .301 with 25 homers and a league-leading 118 RBIs, wins the league MVP Award.

November 26 Catfish Hunter meets with Charlie Finley in the American Arbitration Association office in New York City for a hearing to determine the validity of Hunter's breach-of-contract claim. Hunter contends that Finley failed to pay $50,000, half of Hunter's salary, to a life insurance fund. The case will go to arbitration. On Dec. 13 Hunter wins his claim against Finley and is declared a free agent by arbitrator Peter Seitz.

December 31 The Yankees sign Catfish Hunter to a five-year contract worth a reported $3.75 million. This is triple the salary of any other major league player.

BALTIMORE		BOSTON		CALIFORNIA		CHICAGO		CLEVELAND		DETROIT	
M	E.Weaver	M	D.Johnson	M	B.Winkles	M	C.Tanner	M	K.Aspromonte	M	R.Houk
1B	B.Powell	1B	C.Yastrzemski	M	W.Herzog	1B	D.Allen	1B	J.Ellis	1B	B.Freehan
2B	B.Grich	2B	D.Griffin	M	D.Williams	2B	J.Orta	2B	J.Brohamer	2B	G.Sutherland
SS	M.Belanger	SS	M.Guerrero	1B	J.Doherty	SS	B.Dent	SS	F.Duffy	SS	E.Brinkman
3B	B.Robinson	3B	R.Petrocelli	2B	D.Doyle	3B	B.Melton	3B	B.Bell	3B	A.Rodriguez
LF	D.Baylor	LF	B.Carbo	SS	D.Chalk	LF	C.May	LF	J.Lowenstein	LF	W.Horton
CF	P.Blair	CF	J.Beniquez	3B	P.Schaal	CF	K.Henderson	CF	G.Hendrick	CF	M.Stanley
RF	R.Coggins	RF	D.Evans	LF	J.Lahoud	RF	B.Sharp	RF	C.Spikes	RF	J.Northrup
C	E.Williams	C	B.Montgomery	CF	M.Rivers	C	E.Herrmann	C	D.Duncan	C	J.Moses
DH	T.Davis	DH	T.Harper	RF	L.Stanton	DH	P.Kelly	DH	O.Gamble	DH	A.Kaline
				C	E.Rodriguez						
O	A.Bumbry	S2	R.Burleson	DH	F.Robinson	CO	B.Downing	O	R.Torres	O	R.LeFlore
		O	R.Miller			1D	T.Muser	O	L.Lee	O1	B.Oglivie
P	R.Grimsley	1D	C.Cooper	13	B.Oliver	D2	R.Santo				
P	M.Cuellar	23	D.McAuliffe	OS	B.Valentine			P	G.Perry	P	M.Lolich
P	D.McNally					P	W.Wood	P	J.Perry	P	J.Coleman
P	J.Palmer	P	L.Tiant	P	N.Ryan	P	J.Kaat	P	F.Peterson	P	L.LaGrow
P	D.Alexander	P	B.Lee	P	F.Tanana	P	S.Bahnsen	P	D.Bosman	P	W.Fryman
RP	B.Reynolds	P	R.Cleveland	P	A.Hassler	P	B.Johnson	RP	T.Buskey	RP	J.Hiller
RP	G.Jackson	P	D.Drago	P	D.Lange	RP	T.Forster	RP	F.Beene	RP	J.Ray
RP	J.Jefferson	P	R.Moret	P	B.Singer	RP	S.Pitlock	RP	M.Wilcox		
		RP	D.Segui	RP	S.Lockwood	RP	R.Gossage			P	L.Walker
P	W.Garland							P	B.Johnson	P	D.Lemanczyk
P	D.Hood	P	J.Marichal	P	E.Figueroa			P	S.Kline	P	B.Slayback
				P	B.Stoneman						

KANSAS CITY		MILWAUKEE		MINNESOTA		NEW YORK		OAKLAND		TEXAS	
M	J.McKeon	M	D.Crandall	M	F.Quilici	M	B.Virdon	M	A.Dark	M	B.Martin
1B	J.Mayberry	1B	G.Scott	1B	C.Kusick	1B	C.Chambliss	1B	G.Tenace	1B	M.Hargrove
2B	C.Rojas	2B	P.Garcia	2B	R.Carew	2B	S.Alomar	2B	D.Green	2B	D.Nelson
SS	F.Patek	SS	R.Yount	SS	D.Thompson	SS	J.Mason	SS	B.Campaneris	SS	T.Harrah
3B	G.Brett	3B	D.Money	3B	E.Soderholm	3B	G.Nettles	3B	S.Bando	3B	L.Randle
LF	J.Wohlford	LF	J.Briggs	LF	L.Hisle	LF	L.Piniella	LF	J.Rudi	LF	C.Tovar
CF	A.Otis	CF	B.Coluccio	CF	S.Brye	CF	E.Maddox	CF	B.North	CF	J.Lovitto
RF	V.Pinson	RF	D.May	RF	B.Darwin	RF	B.Murcer	RF	R.Jackson	RF	J.Burroughs
C	F.Healy	C	D.Porter	C	G.Borgmann	C	T.Munson	C	L.Haney	C	J.Sundberg
DH	H.McRae	DH	B.Mitchell	DH	T.Oliva	DH	R.Blomberg	DH	J.Alou	DH	J.Spencer
O	A.Cowens	OD	K.Berry	O3	S.Braun	OD	R.White	2S	T.Kubiak	OD	A.Johnson
2S	F.White	S2	T.Johnson	D1	H.Killebrew	D1	B.Sudakis	OD	A.Mangual	DO	T.Grieve
1D	T.Solaita	C	C.Moore	S2	J.Terrell			DO	C.Washington	13	J.Fregosi
						P	P.Dobson	C	R.Fosse		
P	S.Busby	P	J.Slaton	P	B.Blyleven	P	D.Medich			P	F.Jenkins
P	P.Splittorff	P	C.Wright	P	J.Decker	P	D.Tidrow	P	C.Hunter	P	J.Bibby
P	A.Fitzmorris	P	J.Colborn	P	D.Goltz	P	R.May	P	V.Blue	P	J.Brown
P	B.Dal Canton	P	K.Kobel	P	V.Albury	P	M.Stottlemyre	P	K.Holtzman	P	S.Hargan
P	M.Pattin	P	B.Champion	P	B.Hands	RP	S.Lyle	P	D.Hamilton	P	D.Clyde
RP	L.McDaniel	RP	T.Murphy	RP	B.Campbell	RP	C.Upshaw	P	G.Abbott	RP	S.Foucault
RP	D.Bird	RP	E.Rodriguez	RP	T.Burgmeier	RP	M.Wallace	RP	R.Fingers		
RP	S.Mingori	RP	B.Travers					RP	P.Lindblad		
				P	R.Corbin	/P	L.Gura	RP	B.Odom		
P	N.Briles	P	E.Sprague	P	B.Butler						
								P	D.Knowles		

TEAM	G	W	L	PCT	GB	R	OR	AB	H	2B	3B	HR	BB	SO	AVG	OBP	SLG	PRO	PRO+	BR	/A	PF	CHI	RC	SB	CS	SBA	SBR
EAST																												
BAL	162	91	71	.562		659	612	5535	1418	226	27	116	509	770	.256	.325	.370	.695	103	-2	19	97	98	671	145	58	**71**	9
NY	162	89	73	.549	2	671	623	5524	1451	220	30	101	515	**690**	.263	.328	.368	.696	102	1	12	98	100	666	53	35	60	-5
BOS	162	84	78	.519	7	**696**	661	5499	1449	**236**	31	109	**569**	811	.264	.336	.377	.713	98	39	-11	107	98	699	104	58	64	-4
CLE	162	77	85	.475	14	662	694	5474	1395	201	19	131	432	756	.255	.312	.370	.682	97	-36	-30	99	**108**	610	79	68	54	-17
MIL	162	76	86	.469	15	647	660	5472	1335	228	**49**	120	500	909	.244	.310	.369	.679	96	-41	-37	99	105	622	106	75	59	-13
DET	162	72	90	.444	19	620	768	5568	1375	200	35	131	436	784	.247	.304	.366	.670	89	-64	-85	104	104	607	67	38	64	-3
WEST																												
OAK	162	90	72	.556		689	**551**	5331	1315	205	37	132	568	876	.247	.324	.373	.697	107	1	44	94	105	648	**164**	93	64	-7
TEX	161	84	76	.525	5	690	698	5449	1482	198	39	99	508	710	**.272**	**.338**	.377	.715	108	42	**60**	98	98	677	113	80	59	-14
MIN	163	82	80	.506	8	673	669	5632	**1530**	190	37	111	520	791	**.272**	**.338**	.378	.716	103	44	21	103	93	**707**	74	45	62	-5
CHI	163	80	80	.500	9	684	721	5577	1492	225	23	**135**	519	858	.268	.333	**.389**	**.722**	104	49	32	102	99	701	64	53	55	-13
KC	162	77	85	.475	13	667	662	5582	1448	232	42	89	550	768	.259	.329	.364	.693	94	-2	-40	106	99	668	146	76	66	-2
CAL	163	68	94	.420	22	618	657	5401	1372	203	31	95	509	801	.254	.323	.356	.679	101	-30	6	94	99	615	119	79	60	-12
TOT	973					7976		66044	17062	2564	400	1369	6135	9524	.258	.325	.371	.697							1234	758	62	-85

TEAM	CG	SH	SV	IP	H	H/G	HR	BB	SO	RAT	ERA	ERA+	OAV	OOB	PR	/A	PF	CPI	FA	E	DP	FW	PW	BW	SBW	DIF
EAST																										
BAL	57	**16**	25	1474	1393	8.5	101	480	701	11.6	3.27	105	.253	.316	56	29	95	102	**.980**	128	174	1.0	3.0	2.0	**1.7**	2.3
NY	53	13	24	1455^1	1402	8.7	104	528	829	12.1	3.31	106	.256	.325	50	35	97	**107**	.977	142	158	.2	3.7	1.3	.2	2.7
BOS	**71**	12	18	1455^1	1462	9.0	126	463	751	12.1	3.72	103	.262	.323	-16	20	106	99	.977	145	156	.0	2.1	-1.2	.3	1.7
CLE	45	9	27	1445^2	1419	8.8	138	479	650	12.0	3.80	95	.260	.323	-30	-31	100	98	.977	146	157	-.0	-3.2	-3.1	-1.0	3.4
MIL	43	11	24	1457^2	1476	9.1	126	493	621	12.3	3.76	96	.266	.329	-23	-23	100	102	**.980**	127	168	**1.1**	-2.4	-3.9	-.6	.8
DET	54	7	15	1455^2	1443	8.9	148	621	869	13.0	4.16	91	.262	.341	-88	-58	105	99	.975	158	155	-.7	-6.1	-8.9	.4	6.2
WEST																										
OAK	49	12	28	1439^2	**1322**	8.3	90	430	755	11.1	**2.95**	112	**.246**	.305	107	59	92	103	.977	141	154	.3	**6.2**	4.6	.0	-2.0
TEX	62	**16**	12	1433^2	1423	8.9	126	449	871	12.0	3.82	93	.260	.321	-33	-41	99	95	.974	163	164	-1.1	-4.3	**6.3**	-.7	3.8
MIN	43	11	**29**	1455^1	1436	8.9	115	513	934	12.3	3.64	102	.260	.327	-4	-13	103	101	.976	151	144	-.3	1.4	2.2	.2	-2.5
CHI	55	11	**29**	1471^2	1470	9.0	103	548	826	12.7	3.94	95	.263	.334	-52	-34	103	96	.977	147	**188**	-.0	-3.6	3.3	-.6	.9
KC	54	13	17	1471^2	1477	9.0	91	482	731	12.2	3.51	109	.263	.325	17	50	106	101	.976	152	166	-.4	5.2	-4.2	.5	-5.2
CAL	64	13	12	1439	1339	8.4	101	649	**986**	12.7	3.52	98	.248	.334	15	-14	95	102	.976	147	150	-.0	-1.5	.6	-.5	-11.6
TOT	650	144	260	17448^2		8.8				12.2	3.62		.258	.325					.977	1747	1954					

Runs
Yastrzemski-Bos ... 93
Grich-Bal ... 92
Jackson-Oak ... 90
Otis-KC ... 87
Carew-Min ... 86

Hits
Carew-Min ... 218
Davis-Bal ... 181
Money-Mil ... 178
K.Henderson-Chi ... 176
Rudi-Oak ... 174

Doubles
Rudi-Oak ... 39
Scott-Mil ... 36
McRae-KC ... 36
K.Henderson-Chi ... 35
Burroughs-Tex ... 33

Triples
Rivers-Cal ... 11
Otis-KC ... 9

Home Runs
D.Allen-Chi ... 32
Jackson-Oak ... 29
Tenace-Oak ... 26
Darwin-Min ... 25
Burroughs-Tex ... 25

Total Bases
Rudi-Oak ... 287
K.Henderson-Chi ... 281
Burroughs-Tex ... 279
Carew-Min ... 267

Runs Batted In
Burroughs-Tex ... 118
Bando-Oak ... 103
Rudi-Oak ... 99
K.Henderson-Chi ... 95
Darwin-Min ... 94

Runs Produced
Burroughs-Tex ... 177
Bando-Oak ... 165
Yastrzemski-Bos ... 157
Grich-Bal ... 155
Jackson-Oak ... 154

Bases On Balls
Tenace-Oak ... 110
Yastrzemski-Bos ... 104
Burroughs-Tex ... 91
Grich-Bal ... 90

Batting Average
Carew-Min ... .364
Orta-Chi ... .316
McRae-KC ... .310
Piniella-NY ... .305
Maddox-NY ... .303

On Base Percentage
Carew-Min ... .435
Yastrzemski-Bos ... .421
Burroughs-Tex ... .405
Maddox-NY ... .397
Jackson-Oak ... .396

Slugging Average
D.Allen-Chi ... .563
Jackson-Oak ... .514
Burroughs-Tex ... .504
Rudi-Oak ... .484
McRae-KC ... .475

Production
D.Allen-Chi ... .942
Jackson-Oak ... .910
Burroughs-Tex ... .908
Carew-Min ... .880
Yastrzemski-Bos ... .866

Adjusted Production
Jackson-Oak ... 171
Burroughs-Tex ... 164
D.Allen-Chi ... 164
Carew-Min ... 149
Robinson-Cal-Cle ... 143

Batter Runs
Burroughs-Tex ... 45.3
Carew-Min ... 44.7
Jackson-Oak ... 41.0
D.Allen-Chi ... 39.3
Yastrzemski-Bos ... 38.1

Adjusted Batter Runs
Burroughs-Tex ... 48.2
Jackson-Oak ... 48.1
Carew-Min ... 40.9
D.Allen-Chi ... 37.0
Grich-Bal ... 31.3

Clutch Hitting Index
Murcer-NY ... 134
Bando-Oak ... 132
Burroughs-Tex ... 131
Petrocelli-Bos ... 119
Evans-Bos ... 115

Runs Created
Carew-Min ... 118
Burroughs-Tex ... 113
Jackson-Oak ... 109
Yastrzemski-Bos ... 102
K.Henderson-Chi ... 100

Total Average
Jackson-Oak ... .992
D.Allen-Chi ... .953
Burroughs-Tex ... .919
Yastrzemski-Bos ... .900
Carew-Min ... .879

Stolen Bases
North-Oak ... 54
Carew-Min ... 38
Lowenstein-Cle ... 36
Campaneris-Oak ... 34
Patek-KC ... 33

Stolen Base Average
Jackson-Oak ... 83.3
Coggins-Bal ... 81.3
Pinson-KC ... 80.8
Otis-KC ... 78.3
Money-Mil ... 76.0

Stolen Base Runs
Jackson-Oak ... 4.5
Coggins-Bal ... 4.2
Pinson-KC ... 3.3
Miller-Bos ... 2.7
Blair-Bal ... 2.7

Fielding Runs
Terrell-Min ... 23.3
Rodriguez-Det ... 21.6
Robinson-Bal ... 20.5
North-Oak ... 18.4
Doyle-Cal ... 16.4

Total Player Rating
Carew-Min ... 6.0
Jackson-Oak ... 5.6
Grich-Bal ... 4.8
Burroughs-Tex ... 3.3
Robinson-Bal ... 3.2

Wins
Jenkins-Tex ... 25
Hunter-Oak ... 25

Win Percentage
Cuellar-Bal ... .688
Jenkins-Tex ... .676
Hunter-Oak ... .676
Tiant-Bos ... .629

Games
Fingers-Oak ... 76
Murphy-Mil ... 70
Foucault-Tex ... 69
Lyle-NY ... 66
Campbell-Min ... 63

Complete Games
Jenkins-Tex ... 29
G.Perry-Cle ... 28
Lolich-Det ... 27
Ryan-Cal ... 26
Tiant-Bos ... 25

Shutouts
Tiant-Bos ... 7
Jenkins-Tex ... 6
Hunter-Oak ... 6
Cuellar-Bal ... 5
Bibby-Tex ... 5

Saves
Forster-Chi ... 24
Murphy-Mil ... 20
Campbell-Min ... 19
Buskey-NY-Cle ... 18
Fingers-Oak ... 18

Innings Pitched
Ryan-Cal ... 332.2
Jenkins-Tex ... 328.1
G.Perry-Cle ... 322.1
Wood-Chi ... 320.1
Hunter-Oak ... 318.1

Fewest Hits/Game
Ryan-Cal ... 5.98
G.Perry-Cle ... 6.42
DalCanton-KC ... 6.93
Hassler-Cal ... 7.33
Hunter-Oak ... 7.58

Fewest BB/Game
Jenkins-Tex ... 1.23
Hunter-Oak ... 1.30
Holtzman-Oak ... 1.80
Kaat-Chi ... 2.04
Wright-Mil ... 2.09

Strikeouts
Ryan-Cal ... 367
Blyleven-Min ... 249
Jenkins-Tex ... 225
G.Perry-Cle ... 216
Lolich-Det ... 202

Strikeouts/Game
Ryan-Cal ... 9.93
Blyleven-Min ... 7.98
Jenkins-Tex ... 6.17
Busby-KC ... 6.10
G.Perry-Cle ... 6.03

Ratio
Hunter-Oak ... 8.99
Jenkins-Tex ... 9.29
G.Perry-Cle ... 9.35
Grimsley-Bal ... 10.53
Blyleven-Min ... 10.57

Earned Run Average
Hunter-Oak ... 2.49
G.Perry-Cle ... 2.51
Hassler-Cal ... 2.61
Blyleven-Min ... 2.66
Fitzmorris-KC ... 2.79

Adjusted ERA
G.Perry-Cle ... 144
Blyleven-Min ... 140
Fitzmorris-KC ... 137
Hunter-Oak ... 133
Hassler-Cal ... 132

Opponents' Batting Avg.
Ryan-Cal ... .190
G.Perry-Cle ... .204
DalCanton-KC ... .211
Hassler-Cal ... .225
Hunter-Oak ... .229

Opponents' On Base Pct.
Hunter-Oak ... .260
Jenkins-Tex ... .264
G.Perry-Cle ... .272
Blyleven-Min ... .292
Tiant-Bos ... .293

Starter Runs
Hunter-Oak ... 39.9
G.Perry-Cle ... 39.6
Blyleven-Min ... 29.9
Jenkins-Tex ... 29.0
Ryan-Cal ... 26.7

Adjusted Starter Runs
G.Perry-Cle ... 39.4
Blyleven-Min ... 33.3
Tiant-Bos ... 31.9
Hunter-Oak ... 29.3
Jenkins-Tex ... 27.0

Clutch Pitching Index
Goltz-Min ... 124
Hassler-Cal ... 121
Lee-Bos ... 119
Fitzmorris-KC ... 116
Tanana-Cal ... 113

Relief Runs
Lyle-NY ... 24.8
Murphy-Mil ... 23.4
Foucault-Tex ... 22.0
Lindblad-Oak ... 17.5
Hiller-Det ... 16.3

Adjusted Relief Runs
Lyle-NY ... 23.6
Murphy-Mil ... 23.4
Foucault-Tex ... 21.1
Hiller-Det ... 19.4
Campbell-Min ... 14.8

Relief Ranking
Murphy-Mil ... 42.9
Hiller-Det ... 39.8
Lyle-NY ... 29.4
Foucault-Tex ... 26.4
Campbell-Min ... 21.9

Total Pitcher Index
Murphy-Mil ... 4.9
G.Perry-Cle ... 4.4
Blyleven-Min ... 4.0
Hiller-Det ... 3.9
Lyle-NY ... 3.0

Total Baseball Ranking
Carew-Min ... 6.0
Jackson-Oak ... 5.6
Murphy-Mil ... 4.9
Grich-Bal ... 4.8
G.Perry-Cle ... 4.4

January 23 Ralph Kiner earns Hall of Fame membership by a single vote.

February 3 Billy Herman, Earl Averill, and Bucky Harris are selected for the Hall of Fame by the Special Veterans Committee.

February 10 The Special Committee on the Negro Leagues picks William "Judy" Johnson for the Hall of Fame.

May 4 The Giants beat the Astros 8-6 in the first game of a doubleheader at Candlestick. In the second inning, Houston's Bob Watson scores what is calculated as Major League Baseball's one-millionth run of all time (the Philadelphia Nationals' Wes Fisler scored the first run on April 22, 1876).

August 9 Davey Lopes steals his 32nd consecutive base for the Dodgers without being caught in a 2-0 win over the Mets. This breaks the major league record set by Max Carey in 1922.

August 21 Pitching brothers Rick and Paul Reuschel combine to hurl the Cubs to a 7-0 victory over the Dodgers—the first time brothers have collaborated on a shutout.

September 1 Mets ace Tom Seaver shuts out the Pirates 3-0 and reaches 200 strikeouts for a major league record eighth straight season.

September 7 The Reds clinch the NL West flag with an 8-4 win over the Giants. It is the earliest clinching date in league history.

September 16 Pirates second baseman Rennie Stennett ties Wilbert Robinson's major league record, set June 10, 1892, by going 7-for-7 in a nine-inning game.

October 7 Pittsburgh's John Candelaria strikes out 14 Reds, but is knocked out of the box by Pete Rose's eighth-inning homer. The Reds complete their sweep of the NLCS with a 5-3 win.

October 14 In a game featuring six homers, three by each team, the Reds prevail 6-5 in the tenth inning. The game is marred by a controversial play involving Cincinnati's Ed Armbrister and Boston's Carlton Fisk. Armbrister lays down a sacrifice bunt in the tenth and seemingly hesitates breaking out of the batter's box; Fisk's subsequent throwing error leads to the Reds' winning run. The Sox claim interference, to no avail.

October 22 The Sox take a 3-0 lead but the Reds rally to tie it in the seventh. Jim Willoughby is relieved by Jim Burton and Joe Morgan's single wins the deciding game, 4-3. Rose is named the World Series MVP.

November 12 The Mets' Tom Seaver wins his third Cy Young Award. He led the NL with 22 wins, notched 243 strikeouts, and had a 2.38 ERA.

November 19 By the most overwhelming margin ever, the Reds' Joe Morgan is named NL MVP. Morgan batted .327, with 67 stolen bases, and a league-leading 132 walks.

ATLANTA		CHICAGO		CINCINNATI		HOUSTON		LOS ANGELES		MONTREAL	
M	C.King	M	J.Marshall	M	S.Anderson	M	P.Gomez	M	W.Alston	M	G.Mauch
M	C.Ryan	1B	A.Thornton	1B	T.Perez	M	B.Virdon	1B	S.Garvey	1B	M.Jorgensen
1B	E.Williams	2B	M.Trillo	2B	J.Morgan	1B	B.Watson	2B	D.Lopes	2B	P.Mackanin
2B	M.Perez	SS	D.Kessinger	SS	D.Concepcion	2B	R.Andrews	SS	B.Russell	SS	T.Foli
SS	L.Blanks	3B	B.Madlock	3B	P.Rose	SS	R.Metzger	3B	R.Cey	3B	L.Parrish
3B	D.Evans	LF	J.Cardenal	LF	G.Foster	3B	D.Rader	LF	B.Buckner	LF	L.Biittner
LF	R.Garr	CF	R.Monday	CF	C.Geronimo	LF	W.Howard	CF	J.Wynn	CF	P.Mangual
CF	R.Office	RF	J.Morales	RF	K.Griffey	CF	C.Cedeno	RF	W.Crawford	RF	G.Carter
RF	D.Baker	C	S.Swisher	C	J.Bench	RF	G.Gross	C	S.Yeager	C	B.Foote
C	V.Correll					C	M.May				
		1O	P.LaCock	1O	D.Driessen			2O	L.Lacy	O	B.Bailey
1O	M.Lum	C1	G.Mitterwald			O1	E.Cabell	O	J.Hale		
O	D.May					O	J.Cruz	CO	J.Ferguson	P	S.Rogers
23	R.Gilbreath	P	R.Burris	P	G.Nolan	1C	C.Johnson			P	S.Renko
		P	R.Reuschel	P	J.Billingham			P	A.Messersmith	P	D.Warthen
P	C.Morton	P	B.Bonham	P	F.Norman			P	D.Rau	P	D.Blair
P	P.Niekro	P	S.Stone	P	D.Gullett	P	L.Dierker	P	D.Sutton	P	W.Fryman
RP	M.Leon	RP	D.Knowles	P	P.Darcy	P	J.Richard	P	B.Hooton	RP	D.Murray
RP	T.House	RP	T.Dettore	RP	P.Borbon	P	D.Roberts	P	R.Rhoden	RP	D.DeMola
RP	M.Beard	RP	O.Zamora	RP	C.Carroll	P	D.Konieczny	RP	M.Marshall	RP	F.Scherman
				RP	W.McEnaney	P	K.Forsch	RP	C.Hough		
P	B.Capra	P	G.Zahn			RP	J.Niekro			P	D.Carrithers
P	R.Reed	P	K.Frailing	P	C.Kirby	RP	J.Crawford	P	A.Downing	P	D.McNally
P	J.Easterly			P	R.Eastwick	RP	W.Granger			P	C.Taylor
P	B.DalCanton										
P	R.Sadecki					P	T.Griffin				
P	E.Sosa					P	M.Cosgrove				
P	B.Odom										
P	R.Harrison										
P	M.Thompson										

NEW YORK		PHILADELPHIA		PITTSBURGH		SAN DIEGO		SAN FRANCISCO		ST.LOUIS	
M	Y.Berra	M	D.Ozark	M	D.Murtaugh	M	J.McNamara	M	W.Westrum	M	R.Schoendienst
M	R.McMillan	1B	D.Allen	1B	W.Stargell	1B	W.McCovey	1B	W.Montanez	1B	R.Smith
1B	E.Kranepool	2B	D.Cash	2B	R.Stennett	2B	T.Fuentes	2B	D.Thomas	2B	T.Sizemore
2B	F.Millan	SS	L.Bowa	SS	F.Taveras	SS	E.Hernandez	SS	C.Speier	SS	M.Tyson
SS	M.Phillips	3B	M.Schmidt	3B	R.Hebner	3B	T.Kubiak	3B	S.Ontiveros	3B	K.Reitz
3B	W.Garrett	LF	G.Luzinski	LF	R.Zisk	LF	B.Tolan	LF	G.Matthews	LF	L.Brock
LF	D.Kingman	CF	G.Maddox	CF	A.Oliver	CF	J.Grubb	CF	V.Joshua	CF	B.McBride
CF	D.Unser	RF	M.Anderson	RF	D.Parker	RF	D.Winfield	RF	B.Murcer	RF	W.Davis
RF	R.Staub	C	B.Boone	C	M.Sanguillen	C	F.Kendall	C	D.Rader	C	T.Simmons
C	J.Grote										
		1O	T.Hutton	O	B.Robinson	13	M.Ivie	32	B.Miller	1O	R.Fairly
31	J.Torre	O	J.Johnstone			O	G.Locklear	O1	G.Thomasson	O	L.Melendez
O1	J.Milner	C	J.Oates	P	J.Reuss	S3	H.Torres			
O	G.Clines			P	J.Rooker			P	J.Montefusco	P	L.McGlothen
		P	S.Carlton	P	B.Kison	P	R.Jones	P	J.Barr	P	B.Forsch
P	T.Seaver	P	T.Underwood	P	D.Ellis	P	J.McIntosh	P	P.Falcone	P	R.Reed
P	J.Koosman	P	L.Christenson	P	J.Candelaria	P	D.Freisleben	P	M.Caldwell	P	J.Curtis
P	J.Matlack	P	J.Lonborg	RP	L.Demery	P	D.Spillner	P	E.Halicki	P	J.Denny
P	R.Tate	P	W.Twitchell	RP	D.Giusti	P	R.Folkers	RP	C.Williams	RP	A.Hrabosky
P	H.Webb	RP	G.Garber	RP	B.Moose	RP	D.Frisella	RP	G.Lavelle	RP	M.Garman
RP	R.Baldwin	RP	T.McGraw			RP	D.Tomlin	RP	R.Moffitt		
RP	B.Apodaca	RP	T.Hilgendorf	P	K.Brett	RP	B.Greif			P	B.Gibson
RP	T.Hall			P	R.Hernandez			P	D.Heaverlo	P	E.Rasmussen
		P	R.Schueler	P	K.Tekulve	P	B.Strom			
P	G.Stone			P	J.Johnson						

TEAM	G	W	L	PCT	GB	R	OR	AB	H	2B	3B	HR	BB	SO	AVG	OBP	SLG	PRO	PRO+	BR	/A	PF	CHI	RC	SB	CS	SBA	SBR
EAST																												
PIT	161	92	69	.571		712	565	5489	1444	255	47	**138**	468	832	.263	.325	.402	.727	109	44	50	99	102	709	49	28	64	-2
PHI	162	86	76	.531	6.5	735	694	5592	1506	**283**	42	125	610	960	.269	.344	.402	.746	109	98	67	104	94	785	126	57	69	4
NY	162	82	80	.506	10.5	646	625	5587	1430	217	34	101	501	805	.256	.321	.361	.682	100	-36	-7	95	102	639	32	26	55	-6
STL	163	82	80	.506	10.5	662	689	5597	1527	239	46	81	444	649	**.273**	.329	.375	.704	99	7	-17	104	99	649	116	49	70	5
MON	162	75	87	.463	17.5	601	690	5518	1346	216	31	98	579	954	.244	.319	.348	.667	87	-63	-89	104	99	623	108	58	65	-2
CHI	162	75	87	.463	17.5	712	827	5470	1419	229	41	95	650	802	.259	.341	.368	.709	99	33	2	104	100	702	67	55	55	-13
WEST																												
CIN	162	108	54	.667		**840**	586	5581	1515	278	37	124	**691**	916	.271	**.355**	.401	**.756**	114	128	113	102	103	**829**	168	36	82	29
LA	162	88	74	.543	20	648	**534**	5453	1355	217	31	118	611	825	.248	.328	.365	.693	103	-10	18	96	98	667	138	52	73	10
SF	161	80	81	.497	27.5	659	671	5447	1412	235	45	84	604	775	.259	.336	.365	.701	97	11	-17	104	98	673	99	47	68	2
SD	162	71	91	.438	37	552	683	5429	1324	215	22	78	506	754	.244	.313	.335	.648	92	-100	-66	94	99	571	85	50	63	-5
ATL	161	67	94	.416	40.5	583	739	5424	1323	179	28	107	543	759	.244	.315	.346	.661	86	-75	-96	104	101	587	55	38	59	-6
HOU	162	64	97	.398	43.5	664	711	5515	1401	218	**54**	84	523	762	.254	.322	.359	.681	102	-36	9	93	**106**	643	133	62	68	3
TOT	971					8014		66102	17002	2781	458	1233	6730	9793	.257	.329	.369	.698							1176	558	68	18

TEAM	CG	SH	SV	IP	H	H/G	HR	BB	SO	RAT	ERA	ERA+	OAV	OOB	PR	/A	PF	CPI	FA	E	DP	FW	PW	BW	SBW	DIF
EAST																										
PIT	43	14	31	1437[1]	1302	8.2	**79**	551	768	11.7	3.01	118	.243	.315	98	85	98	103	.976	151	147	.2	**8.9**	5.2	-.4	-2.4
PHI	33	11	30	1455	1353	8.4	111	546	897	11.9	3.82	98	.249	.320	-33	-15	103	89	.976	152	156	.2	-1.6	7.0	.3	-.9
NY	40	14	31	1466	1344	8.3	99	580	**989**	12.0	3.39	102	.246	.321	38	10	95	98	.976	151	144	.3	1.0	-.7	-.8	1.2
STL	33	13	36	1454[2]	1452	9.0	98	571	824	12.7	3.57	105	.260	.331	8	30	104	102	.973	171	140	-.8	3.1	-1.8	.4	.0
MON	30	12	25	1480	1448	8.8	102	665	831	13.1	3.72	103	.259	.341	-17	17	106	103	.973	180	**179**	-1.3	1.8	-9.3	-.4	3.2
CHI	27	8	33	1444[1]	1587	9.9	130	551	850	13.6	4.49	86	.281	.349	-140	-105	106	98	.972	179	152	-1.3	-11.0	.2	-1.5	7.6
WEST																										
CIN	22	8	50	1459	1422	8.8	112	487	663	12.0	3.37	107	.257	.321	41	36	99	105	**.984**	102	173	**3.0**	3.8	**11.8**	**2.9**	5.6
LA	51	18	21	1469[2]	**1215**	7.4	104	448	894	10.4	**2.92**	116	**.225**	**.287**	114	78	94	88	.979	127	106	1.6	8.1	1.9	.9	-5.5
SF	37	9	24	1432[2]	1406	8.8	92	612	856	12.9	3.74	102	.259	.339	-19	-10	105	101	.976	146	164	.5	1.0	-1.8	.0	-.3
SD	40	12	20	1463[1]	1494	9.2	99	521	713	12.5	3.48	100	.266	.331	23	-1	96	**107**	.971	188	163	-1.8	-.1	-6.9	-.7	-.5
ATL	32	4	24	1430	1543	9.7	101	519	669	13.3	3.91	96	.278	.344	-47	-23	104	105	.972	175	147	-1.1	-2.4	-10.0	-.8	.8
HOU	39	6	25	1458[1]	1436	8.9	106	679	839	13.3	4.04	83	.262	.347	-67	-108	93	99	.979	137	166	1.1	-11.3	.9	.2	-7.4
TOT	427	129	350	17450[1]		8.8				12.4	3.62		.257	.329					.976	1859	1837					

Runs		Hits		Doubles		Triples		Home Runs		Total Bases	
Rose-Cin	112	Cash-Phi	213	Rose-Cin	47	Garr-Atl	11	Schmidt-Phi	38	Luzinski-Phi	322
Cash-Phi	111	Rose-Cin	210	Cash-Phi	40	Parker-Pit	10	Kingman-NY	36	Garvey-LA	314
Lopes-LA	108	Garvey-LA	210	Oliver-Pit	39	Kessinger-Chi	10	Luzinski-Phi	34	Parker-Pit	302
Morgan-Cin	107	Simmons-StL	193	Bench-Cin	39	Joshua-SF	10	Bench-Cin	28	Schmidt-Phi	294
Thomas-SF	99	Millan-NY	191	Garvey-LA	38	Gross-Hou	10			Rose-Cin	286

Runs Batted In		Runs Produced		Bases On Balls		Batting Average		On Base Percentage		Slugging Average	
Luzinski-Phi	120	Morgan-Cin	184	Morgan-Cin	132	Madlock-Chi	.354	Morgan-Cin	.471	Parker-Pit	.541
Bench-Cin	110	Staub-NY	179	Wynn-LA	110	Simmons-StL	.332	Wynn-LA	.407	Luzinski-Phi	.540
Perez-Cin	109	Rose-Cin	179	Evans-Atl	105	Sanguillen-Pit	.328	Rose-Cin	.407	Schmidt-Phi	.523
Staub-NY	105	Luzinski-Phi	171	Schmidt-Phi	101	Morgan-Cin	.327	Madlock-Chi	.406	Bench-Cin	.519
		Bench-Cin	165			Watson-Hou	.324	Murcer-SF	.404	Foster-Cin	.518

Production		Adjusted Production		Batter Runs		Adjusted Batter Runs		Clutch Hitting Index		Runs Created	
Morgan-Cin	.979	Morgan-Cin	168	Morgan-Cin	57.1	Morgan-Cin	54.9	Perez-Cin	133	Morgan-Cin	145
Luzinski-Phi	.939	Luzinski-Phi	152	Luzinski-Phi	47.5	Luzinski-Phi	42.6	Morales-Chi	133	Luzinski-Phi	128
Parker-Pit	.899	Watson-Hou	152	Simmons-StL	35.7	Parker-Pit	32.5	Trillo-Chi	132	Rose-Cin	120
Stargell-Pit	.894	Parker-Pit	148	Thornton-Chi	35.4	Simmons-StL	32.1	Montanez-Phi-SF	127	Schmidt-Phi	113
Schmidt-Phi	.890	Stargell-Pit	147	Schmidt-Phi	33.7	Thornton-Chi	31.7	Murcer-SF	123	Simmons-StL	108

Total Average		Stolen Bases		Stolen Base Average		Stolen Base Runs		Fielding Runs		Total Player Rating	
Morgan-Cin	1.279	Lopes-LA	77	Morgan-Cin	87.0	Lopes-LA	15.9	Schmidt-Phi	24.0	Morgan-Cin	7.1
Luzinski-Phi	.956	Morgan-Cin	67	Lopes-LA	86.5	Morgan-Cin	14.1	Evans-Atl	23.4	Schmidt-Phi	5.7
Schmidt-Phi	.943	Brock-StL	56	Maddox-SF-Phi	86.2	Brock-StL	7.2	Maddox-SF-Phi	21.0	Bench-Cin	3.9
Bench-Cin	.901	Cedeno-Hou	50	Winfield-SD	85.2	Concepcion-Cin	6.3	Mackanin-Mon	18.2	Parker-Pit	3.7
Stargell-Pit	.895	Cardenal-Chi	34	Concepcion-Cin	84.6	Maddox-SF-Phi	5.1	Trillo-Chi	16.0	Evans-Atl	3.5

Wins		Win Percentage		Games		Complete Games		Shutouts		Saves	
Seaver-NY	22	Gullett-Cin	.789	Garber-Phi	71	Messersmith-LA	19	Messersmith-LA	7	Hrabosky-StL	22
Jones-SD	20	Seaver-NY	.710	McEnaney-Cin	70	Jones-SD	18	Reuss-Pit	6	Eastwick-Cin	22
Messersmith-LA	19	Hooton-Chi-LA	.667	Tomlin-SD	67	Seaver-NY	15	Jones-SD	6	Giusti-Pit	17
Hooton-Chi-LA	18	Murray-Mon	.652	Borbon-Cin	67	Reuss-Pit	15	Seaver-NY	5	McEnaney-Cin	15
Reuss-Pit	18			Garman-StL	66					Knowles-Chi	15

Innings Pitched		Fewest Hits/Game		Fewest BB/Game		Strikeouts		Strikeouts/Game		Ratio	
Messersmith-LA	321.2	Messersmith-LA	6.83	Nolan-Cin	1.24	Seaver-NY	243	Montefusco-SF	7.94	Jones-SD	9.41
Jones-SD	285.0	Seaver-NY	6.97	Jones-SD	1.77	Montefusco-SF	215	Richard-Hou	7.80	Sutton-LA	9.45
Seaver-NY	280.1	Warthen-Mon	6.98	Reed-Atl-StL	1.91	Messersmith-LA	213	Seaver-NY	7.80	Messersmith-LA	9.65
Morton-Atl	277.2	Sutton-LA	7.15	Rau-LA	2.13	Carlton-Phi	192	Warthen-Mon	6.87	Hooton-Chi-LA	9.89
Niekro-Atl	275.2	Hooton-Chi-LA	7.29	Barr-SF	2.14	Richard-Hou	176	Carlton-Phi	6.77	Nolan-Cin	9.91

Earned Run Average		Adjusted ERA		Opponents' Batting Avg.		Opponents' On Base Pct.		Starter Runs		Adjusted Starter Runs	
Jones-SD	2.24	Jones-SD	155	Messersmith-LA	.213	Sutton-LA	.264	Messersmith-LA	47.4	Messersmith-LA	39.5
Messersmith-LA	2.29	Messersmith-LA	148	Sutton-LA	.213	Jones-SD	.271	Jones-SD	43.7	Jones-SD	39.0
Seaver-NY	2.38	Seaver-NY	145	Seaver-NY	.214	Hooton-Chi-LA	.276	Seaver-NY	38.8	Seaver-NY	33.5
Reuss-Pit	2.54	Reuss-Pit	139	Warthen-Mon	.217	Messersmith-LA	.276	Reuss-Pit	28.5	Reuss-Pit	26.4
Forsch-StL	2.86	Montefusco-SF	132	Hooton-Chi-LA	.219	Nolan-Cin	.278	Sutton-LA	21.3	Montefusco-SF	24.8

Clutch Pitching Index		Relief Runs		Adjusted Relief Runs		Relief Ranking		Total Pitcher Index		Total Baseball Ranking	
Reuss-Pit	122	Hrabosky-StL	21.2	Hrabosky-StL	22.6	Hrabosky-StL	44.9	Jones-SD	4.9	Morgan-Cin	7.1
Niekro-Atl	122	Apodaca-NY	20.1	Apodaca-NY	18.5	Apodaca-NY	20.1	Hrabosky-StL	4.8	Schmidt-Phi	5.7
Blair-Mon	114	Hilgendorf-Phi	15.9	Hilgendorf-Phi	17.1	Garman-StL	18.4	Seaver-NY	4.3	Jones-SD	4.9
Koosman-NY	113	McEnaney-Cin	11.6	Garman-StL	12.0	Hilgendorf-Phi	15.9	Messersmith-LA	4.1	Hrabosky-StL	4.8
Barr-SF	110	Garman-StL	10.8	McEnaney-Cin	11.3	McGraw-Phi	13.9	Reuss-Pit	3.7	Seaver-NY	4.3

April 8 Frank Robinson, making his debut as the Indians player-manager, homers in his first at bat (as a DH) during a 5-3 win over the Yankees. It is Robby's eighth Opening Day homer, setting a major league record.

April 11 In Milwaukee, 48,160 fans brave 37 degree weather to welcome home Hank Aaron. Hank drives in a run as the Brewers whip the Indians 6-2.

June 6 Nolan Ryan's bid for a second no-hitter in a row is foiled by Hank Aaron's single in the sixth inning. Ryan gives up one other hit in overpowering the Brewers 6-0.

September 28 In a major league first, four pitchers share in a no-hitter, as the A's shut down the Angels 5-0. Vida Blue, Glenn Abbott, Paul Lindblad, and Rollie Fingers are the unique quartet.

October 7 The Red Sox match Cincin-nati with a 5-3 win and three-game sweep over Oakland.

October 11 Boston's Luis Tiant shuts down the Big Red Machine and scores the first run as the Red Sox win the opening game of the World Series 6-0.

October 21 Fred Lynn's three-run first-inning homer is matched by teammate Bernie Carbo's pinch homer in the eighth to tie the game at 6-all. The Sox then fill the bases with no outs in the ninth but fail to bring in a run. But Boston evens the Series again with a 7-6 victory, won by Carlton Fisk's dramatic 12th-inning home run.

November 4 The Orioles Jim Palmer wins his second Cy Young Award, after pacing the league in wins (23), shutouts (10), and ERA (2.09).

November 10 The Royals release slug-ger Harmon Killebrew, ending a 22-year career marked by 573 homers, good for fifth on the all-time list.

November 26 Fred Lynn, already named Rookie of the Year, becomes the first novice to win MVP honors, taking the AL award. Lynn batted .331 with 21 homers, 105 RBI, and league-leading figures in runs (103), doubles (47), and slugging (.566).

December 23 Arbitrator Peter Seitz announces a landmark decision in favor of the Players' Association, making pitchers Andy Messersmith and Dave McNally free agents. Seitz is immediately fired by John Gaherin, chairman of the owners' Player Relations Committee. McNally, who retired June 8, will not return to the major leagues, finishing with a 184-119 career record.

BALTIMORE		BOSTON		CALIFORNIA		CHICAGO		CLEVELAND		DETROIT	
M	E.Weaver	M	D.Johnson	M	D.Williams	M	C.Tanner	M	F.Robinson	M	R.Houk
1B	L.May	1B	C.Yastrzemski	1B	B.Bochte	1B	C.May	1B	B.Powell	1B	J.Pierce
2B	B.Grich	2B	D.Griffin	2B	J.Remy	2B	J.Orta	2B	D.Kuiper	2B	G.Sutherland
SS	M.Belanger	SS	R.Burleson	SS	M.Miley	SS	B.Dent	SS	F.Duffy	SS	T.Veryzer
3B	B.Robinson	3B	R.Petrocelli	3B	D.Chalk	3B	B.Melton	3B	B.Bell	3B	A.Rodriguez
LF	D.Baylor	LF	B.Carbo	LF	M.Nettles	LF	N.Nyman	LF	O.Gamble	LF	B.Oglivie
CF	P.Blair	CF	F.Lynn	CF	M.Rivers	CF	K.Henderson	CF	R.Manning	CF	R.LeFlore
RF	K.Singleton	RF	D.Evans	RF	L.Stanton	RF	P.Kelly	RF	G.Hendrick	RF	L.Roberts
C	D.Duncan	C	C.Fisk	C	E.Rodriguez	C	B.Downing	C	A.Ashby	C	B.Freehan
DH	T.Davis	DH	J.Rice	DH	T.Harper	DH	D.Johnson	DH	R.Carty	DH	W.Horton
DO	A.Bumbry	D1	C.Cooper	OD	D.Collins	23	B.Stein	O	C.Spikes	O1	D.Meyer
C	E.Hendricks	2	D.Doyle			O	J.Hairston	C	J.Ellis		
		OD	J.Beniquez	P	F.Tanana			OD	J.Lowenstein	P	M.Lolich
P	J.Palmer			P	E.Figueroa	P	J.Kaat	2	J.Brohamer	P	J.Coleman
P	M.Torrez	P	L.Tiant	P	N.Ryan	P	W.Wood			P	V.Ruhle
P	M.Cuellar	P	B.Lee	P	B.Singer	P	C.Osteen	P	D.Eckersley	P	L.LaGrow
P	R.Grimsley	P	R.Wise	P	A.Hassler	P	J.Jefferson	P	F.Peterson	P	R.Bare
P	D.Alexander	P	R.Cleveland	RP	D.Kirkwood	RP	R.Gossage	P	D.Hood	RP	J.Hiller
RP	G.Jackson	P	R.Moret	RP	M.Scott	RP	D.Hamilton	P	R.Harrison		
		RP	D.Drago			RP	O.Osborn	P	G.Perry	P	T.Walker
P	W.Garland	RP	D.Segui	P	D.Lange			RP	D.LaRoche	P	D.Lemanczyk
P	P.Mitchell	RP	J.Burton			P	S.Bahnsen	RP	T.Buskey	P	F.Arroyo
						P	B.Gogolewski	RP	J.Brown		
		P	D.Pole					P	J.Bibby		
								P	E.Raich		
								P	J.Kern		
								P	R.Waits		

KANSAS CITY		MILWAUKEE		MINNESOTA		NEW YORK		OAKLAND		TEXAS	
M	J.McKeon	M	D.Crandall	M	F.Quilici	M	B.Virdon	M	A.Dark	M	B.Martin
M	W.Herzog	M	H.Kuenn	1B	C.Kusick	M	B.Martin	1B	J.Rudi	M	F.Lucchesi
1B	J.Mayberry	1B	G.Scott	2B	R.Carew	1B	C.Chambliss	2B	P.Garner	1B	J.Spencer
2B	C.Rojas	2B	P.Garcia	SS	D.Thompson	2B	S.Alomar	SS	B.Campaneris	2B	L.Randle
SS	F.Patek	SS	R.Yount	3B	E.Soderholm	SS	J.Mason	3B	S.Bando	SS	T.Harrah
3B	G.Brett	3B	D.Money	LF	S.Braun	3B	G.Nettles	LF	C.Washington	3B	R.Howell
LF	H.McRae	LF	B.Sharp	CF	D.Ford	LF	R.White	CF	B.North	LF	M.Hargrove
CF	A.Otis	CF	G.Thomas	RF	L.Bostock	CF	E.Maddox	RF	R.Jackson	CF	D.Moates
RF	A.Cowens	RF	S.Lezcano	C	G.Borgmann	RF	B.Bonds	C	G.Tenace	RF	J.Burroughs
C	B.Martinez	C	D.Porter	DH	T.Oliva	C	T.Munson	DH	B.Williams	C	J.Sundberg
DH	H.Killebrew	DH	H.Aaron			DH	E.Herrmann			DH	C.Tovar
				S2	J.Terrell			1	J.Holt		
O	V.Pinson	32	K.Bevacqua	1O	J.Briggs	S2	F.Stanley			OD	T.Grieve
2S	F.White	CO	C.Moore	OD	L.Hisle			P	V.Blue	S2	R.Smalley
O	J.Wohlford	OD	B.Mitchell	O	S.Brye	P	C.Hunter	P	K.Holtzman		
D1	T.Solaita	O1	M.Hegan			P	D.Medich	P	D.Bosman	P	F.Jenkins
						P	R.May	P	G.Abbott	P	S.Hargan
P	S.Busby	P	P.Broberg	P	B.Blyleven	P	P.Dobson	P	S.Bahnsen	P	G.Perry
P	A.Fitzmorris	P	J.Slaton	P	J.Hughes	P	L.Gura	RP	R.Fingers	P	B.Hands
P	D.Leonard	P	J.Colborn	P	D.Goltz	RP	S.Lyle	RP	J.Todd	RP	J.Umbarger
P	M.Pattin	P	B.Travers	P	V.Albury	RP	D.Tidrow	RP	P.Lindblad	RP	S.Foucault
P	P.Splittorff	P	T.Hausman	RP	B.Campbell					RP	S.Thomas
RP	D.Bird	RP	E.Rodriguez	RP	T.Burgmeier			P	J.Perry		
RP	L.McDaniel	RP	T.Murphy	P	R.Corbin			P	S.Siebert	P	C.Wright
RP	S.Mingori			P	B.Butler					P	J.Brown
		P	B.Champion							P	J.Bibby
P	N.Briles	P	B.Castro							P	S.Perzanowski
		P	E.Sprague								

TEAM	G	W	L	PCT	GB	R	OR	AB	H	2B	3B	HR	BB	SO	AVG	OBP	SLG	PRO	PRO+	BR	/A	PF	CHI	RC	SB	CS	SBA	SBR
EAST																												
BOS	160	95	65	.594		**796**	709	5448	**1500**	**284**	44	134	565	741	**.275**	**.347**	**.417**	**.764**	106	**108**	41	109	99	**776**	66	58	53	-15
BAL	159	90	69	.566	4.5	682	**553**	5474	1382	224	33	124	580	834	.252	.328	.373	.701	105	-14	30	94	100	680	104	55	65	-2
NY	160	83	77	.519	12	681	588	5415	1430	230	39	110	486	710	.264	.328	.382	.710	102	-3	8	98	101	665	102	59	63	-5
CLE	159	79	80	.497	15.5	688	703	5404	1409	201	25	153	525	**667**	.261	.329	.392	.721	103	17	18	100	99	672	106	89	54	-22
MIL	162	68	94	.420	28	675	792	5378	1343	242	34	146	553	922	.250	.323	.389	.712	100	-2	-5	101	99	663	65	64	50	-19
DET	159	57	102	.358	37.5	570	786	5366	1338	171	39	125	383	872	.249	.303	.366	.669	84	-94	-119	104	101	573	63	57	53	-15
WEST																												
OAK	162	98	64	.605		758	606	5415	1376	220	33	151	609	846	.254	.335	.391	.726	**107**	34	**51**	98	104	725	183	82	**69**	6
KC	162	91	71	.562	7	710	649	5491	1431	263	**58**	118	591	675	.261	.336	.394	.730	103	40	21	103	96	736	155	75	67	2
TEX	162	79	83	.488	19	714	733	5599	1431	208	17	134	**613**	863	.256	.332	.371	.703	99	-10	-4	99	102	693	102	62	62	-7
MIN	159	76	83	.478	20.5	724	736	5514	1497	215	28	121	563	746	.271	.343	.386	.729	105	46	36	101	97	732	81	48	63	-5
CHI	161	75	86	.466	22.5	655	703	5490	1400	209	38	94	611	800	.255	.334	.358	.692	95	-24	-33	101	97	659	101	54	65	-2
CAL	161	72	89	.447	25.5	628	723	5377	1324	195	41	55	593	811	.246	.324	.328	.652	91	-99	-58	93	**106**	596	220	108	67	1
TOT	963					8281		65371	16861	2662	429	1465	6672	9487	.258	.330	.379	.709							1348	811	62	-82

TEAM	CG	SH	SV	IP	H	H/G	HR	BB	SO	RAT	ERA	ERA+	OAV	OOB	PR	/A	PF	CPI	FA	E	DP	FW	PW	BW	SBW	DIF
EAST																										
BOS	62	11	31	1436[2]	1463	9.2	145	**490**	720	12.4	3.98	102	.265	.327	-33	14	108	99	.977	139	142	.9	1.4	4.2	-.8	9.3
BAL	**70**	**19**	21	1451	1285	8.0	110	500	717	**11.1**	**3.17**	111	.242	.308	**98**	55	93	100	**.983**	**107**	**175**	**2.6**	5.6	3.1	.5	-1.3
NY	**70**	11	20	1424	1325	8.4	104	502	809	11.7	3.29	112	.249	.317	78	**62**	97	103	.978	135	148	1.1	**6.3**	.8	.2	-5.4
CLE	37	6	33	1435[1]	1395	8.7	136	599	800	12.7	3.84	98	.258	.335	-10	-10	100	103	.978	134	156	1.1	-1.0	1.8	-1.5	-.9
MIL	36	10	34	1431[2]	1496	9.4	133	624	643	13.7	4.34	88	.271	.351	-89	-81	101	100	.971	180	162	-1.4	-8.3	-.5	-1.2	-1.6
DET	52	10	17	1396	1496	9.6	137	533	787	13.3	4.27	94	.275	.343	-77	-40	106	100	.972	173	141	-1.1	-4.1	-12.2	-.8	-4.3
WEST																										
OAK	36	10	**44**	1448	**1267**	7.9	102	523	784	11.4	3.27	111	**.236**	.308	82	58	96	94	.977	143	140	.7	5.9	**5.2**	**1.3**	3.8
KC	52	11	25	1456[2]	1422	8.8	108	498	815	12.0	3.47	111	.258	.322	50	**62**	102	102	.976	155	151	.0	**6.3**	2.1	.9	.6
TEX	60	16	17	1465[2]	1456	8.9	123	518	792	12.4	3.86	97	.261	.329	-14	-17	99	98	.971	191	173	-2.0	-1.7	-.4	-.0	2.1
MIN	57	7	22	1423	1381	8.7	137	617	846	12.9	4.05	94	.257	.337	-43	-35	101	98	.973	170	147	-.9	-3.6	3.7	.2	-2.8
CHI	34	7	39	1452[1]	1489	9.2	107	655	799	13.5	3.93	99	.268	.349	-24	-9	103	**105**	.978	140	155	.9	-.9	-3.4	.5	-2.6
CAL	59	**19**	16	1453[1]	1386	8.8	123	613	**975**	12.6	3.89	97	.261	.333	-18	-55	94	97	.971	184	164	-1.6	-5.6	-5.9	.8	3.9
TOT	625	137	319	17273[2]		8.8				12.5	3.78		.258	.330					.975	1851	1854					

Runs		Hits		Doubles		Triples		Home Runs		Total Bases	
Lynn-Bos	103	Brett-KC	195	Lynn-Bos	47	Rivers-Cal	13	Scott-Mil	36	Scott-Mil	318
Mayberry-KC	95	Carew-Min	192	Jackson-Oak	39	Brett-KC	13	Jackson-Oak	36	Mayberry-KC	303
Bonds-NY	93	Munson-NY	190	McRae-KC	38	Orta-Chi	10	Mayberry-KC	34	Jackson-Oak	303
Rice-Bos	92	C.Washington-Oak	182	Mayberry-KC	38	Cowens-KC	8	Bonds-NY	32	Lynn-Bos	299
				Chambliss-NY	38					Brett-KC	289

Runs Batted In		Runs Produced		Bases On Balls		Batting Average		On Base Percentage		Slugging Average	
Scott-Mil	109	Lynn-Bos	187	Mayberry-KC	119	Carew-Min	.359	Carew-Min	.428	Lynn-Bos	.566
Mayberry-KC	106	Munson-NY	173	Singleton-Bal	118	Lynn-Bos	.331	Mayberry-KC	.419	Mayberry-KC	.547
Lynn-Bos	105	Rice-Bos	172	Grich-Bal	107	Munson-NY	.318	Singleton-Bal	.418	Powell-Cle	.524
Jackson-Oak	104	Mayberry-KC	167	Tenace-Oak	106	Rice-Bos	.309	Harrah-Tex	.406	Scott-Mil	.515
		Brett-KC	162	Harrah-Tex	98	C.Washington-Oak	.308	Lynn-Bos	.405	Bonds-NY	.512

Production		Adjusted Production		Batter Runs		Adjusted Batter Runs		Clutch Hitting Index		Runs Created	
Lynn-Bos	.971	Mayberry-KC	167	Mayberry-KC	56.0	Mayberry-KC	52.6	Stanton-Cal	135	Mayberry-KC	135
Mayberry-KC	.966	Carew-Min	159	Lynn-Bos	49.4	Singleton-Bal	49.2	Robinson-Cal	130	Lynn-Bos	120
Carew-Min	.926	Lynn-Bos	158	Carew-Min	44.4	Carew-Min	42.9	Munson-NY	122	Singleton-Bal	118
Powell-Cle	.906	Singleton-Bal	156	Singleton-Bal	41.3	Lynn-Bos	39.7	Duffy-Cle	116	Carew-Min	118
Bonds-NY	.891	Powell-Cle	154	Bonds-NY	35.4	Bonds-NY	37.2	Bando-Oak	115	Harrah-Tex	105

Total Average		Stolen Bases		Stolen Base Average		Stolen Base Runs		Fielding Runs		Total Player Rating	
Mayberry-KC	1.059	Rivers-Cal	70	Hisle-Min	85.0	Rivers-Cal	12.6	Belanger-Bal	28.0	Harrah-Tex	6.2
Lynn-Bos	1.000	C.Washington-Oak	40	Bumbry-Bal	84.2	Patek-KC	5.4	Dent-Chi	27.2	Grich-Bal	5.8
Carew-Min	.986	Otis-KC	39	Rivers-Cal	83.3	Otis-KC	5.1	Grich-Bal	24.0	Carew-Min	5.7
Tenace-Oak	.919	Carew-Min	35	Alomar-NY	82.4	Carew-Min	5.1	Rodriguez-Det	20.7	Lynn-Bos	4.7
Harrah-Tex	.914	Remy-Cal	34	Patek-KC	82.1	Alomar-NY	4.8	North-Oak	19.6	Mayberry-KC	4.6

Wins		Win Percentage		Games		Complete Games		Shutouts		Saves	
Palmer-Bal	23	Torrez-Bal	.690	Fingers-Oak	75	Hunter-NY	30	Palmer-Bal	10	Gossage-Chi	26
Hunter-NY	23	Leonard-KC	.682	Lindblad-Oak	68	G.Perry-Cle-Tex	25	Hunter-NY	7	Fingers-Oak	24
Blue-Oak	22	Palmer-Bal	.676	Gossage-Chi	62	Palmer-Bal	25			Murphy-Mil	20
Torrez-Bal	20	Blue-Oak	.667	LaRoche-Cle	61	Jenkins-Tex	22			LaRoche-Cle	17
Kaat-Chi	20	Lee-Bos	.654	Foucault-Tex	59	Blyleven-Min	20			Drago-Bos	15

Innings Pitched		Fewest Hits/Game		Fewest BB/Game		Strikeouts		Strikeouts/Game		Ratio	
Hunter-NY	328.0	Hunter-NY	6.80	Jenkins-Tex	1.87	Tanana-Cal	269	Tanana-Cal	9.41	Hunter-NY	9.22
Palmer-Bal	323.0	Ryan-Cal	6.91	G.Perry-Cle-Tex	2.06	G.Perry-Cle-Tex	233	Ryan-Cal	8.45	Palmer-Bal	9.33
G.Perry-Cle-Tex	305.2	Palmer-Bal	7.05	Grimsley-Bal	2.15	Blyleven-Min	233	Blyleven-Min	7.61	Blyleven-Min	10.02
Kaat-Chi	303.2	Eckersley-Cle	7.09	Palmer-Bal	2.23	Palmer-Bal	193	Eckersley-Cle	7.33	Tanana-Cal	10.18
Wood-Chi	291.1	Blyleven-Min	7.15	Hunter-NY	2.28	Blue-Oak	189	G.Perry-Cle-Tex	6.86	G.Perry-Cle-Tex	10.33

Earned Run Average		Adjusted ERA		Opponents' Batting Avg.		Opponents' On Base Pct.		Starter Runs		Adjusted Starter Runs	
Palmer-Bal	2.09	Palmer-Bal	168	Hunter-NY	.208	Hunter-NY	.263	Palmer-Bal	60.6	Palmer-Bal	51.0
Hunter-NY	2.58	Eckersley-Cle	145	Ryan-Cal	.213	Palmer-Bal	.267	Hunter-NY	43.7	Hunter-NY	40.1
Eckersley-Cle	2.60	Hunter-NY	143	Eckersley-Cle	.215	Blyleven-Min	.283	Tanana-Cal	33.0	Tanana-Cal	26.4
Tanana-Cal	2.62	Tanana-Cal	135	Palmer-Bal	.216	G.Perry-Cle-Tex	.284	Eckersley-Cle	24.4	Kaat-Chi	25.7
Figueroa-Cal	2.91	Blyleven-Min	127	Blyleven-Min	.219	Tanana-Cal	.288	Blyleven-Min	23.7	Blyleven-Min	25.1

Clutch Pitching Index		Relief Runs		Adjusted Relief Runs		Relief Ranking		Total Pitcher Index		Total Baseball Ranking	
Kaat-Chi	119	Gossage-Chi	30.5	Gossage-Chi	32.0	Gossage-Chi	47.7	Palmer-Bal	6.1	Harrah-Tex	6.2
Eckersley-Cle	116	Todd-Oak	20.2	Todd-Oak	18.2	LaRoche-Cle	19.5	Gossage-Chi	5.2	Palmer-Bal	6.1
Torrez-Bal	111	LaRoche-Cle	14.6	LaRoche-Cle	14.6	Todd-Oak	18.8	Hunter-NY	3.9	Grich-Bal	5.8
Osteen-Chi	110	Lindblad-Oak	14.4	Lindblad-Oak	14.5	Hiller-Det	15.7	Tanana-Cal	3.3	Carew-Min	5.7
Hargan-Tex	108	Hiller-Det	12.7	Lindblad-Oak	12.3	Fingers-Oak	14.1	Busby-KC	2.6	Gossage-Chi	5.2

January 14 Ted Turner completes the purchase of 100 percent of the Atlanta Braves.

April 25 Cubs outfielder Rick Monday snatches an American flag from two fans who are about to set it on fire in the outfield during a game at Dodger Stadium. The Dodgers win 5-4 in 10 innings. The next day, the Illinois legislature unanimously approves May 4 as Rick Monday Day.

May 29 The only homer Joe Niekro hits in his 22-year career comes at the expense of brother Phil.

June 15 The scheduled game at the Astrodome is canceled when heavy rains make it difficult for the visiting team and umpires to get through flooded streets to the stadium.

June 22 Randy Jones pitches the Padres to a 4-2 win over the Giants, and ties Christy Mathewson's 63-year-old NL record by going 68 innings without a base on balls. He receives a standing ovation from the home crowd after striking out Darrell Evans to end the seventh. His streak ends when he walks Marc Hill leading off the eighth. It is Jones' 13th win of the year.

September 29 The Dodgers' Walter Alston, after 23 years and 2,040 victories, steps down as manager. Third base coach Tommy Lasorda is promoted to the post.

October 3 The Cubs' Bill Madlock wrests the NL crown from the Reds' Ken Griffey by collecting four singles in an 11-1 win over the Braves. The hits raise Madlock from .333 to .339, one point ahead of the idle Griffey, who belatedly joins the Reds' 8-2 win over the Expos and goes 0-for-2, dipping his average to .336.

October 12 The Reds score seven times in the final three innings to secure a 7-6 win and complete a sweep of the NLCS. Johnny Bench and George Foster hit successive homers to start the rally.

October 16 Don Gullett and Pedro Borbon combine on a five-hitter, as the Reds win Game 1 of the World Series 5-1 over the Yankees. Three hits by Tony Perez, the first World Series designated hitter, and a Joe Morgan homer supply the offense.

October 21 The Reds take a 3-0 lead against Ed Figueroa, but the Yankees close it to 3-2. A four-run splurge in the ninth, topped by Johnny Bench's second homer of the game, ices Cincinnati's 7-2 win and a four-game sweep of the Yankees. World Series MVP Johnny Bench has two homers and five RBIs, and demolishes the Yankees with .533 hitting. The Reds become the first team ever to go through an entire League Championship Series and World Series without a defeat.

November 2 Padres ace Randy Jones beats out Met Jerry Koosman for the NL Cy Young Award. Jones led the league with 315 innings, and posted a 22-14 record for the fifth-place Padres.

November 24 The Reds' Joe Morgan outscores teammate George Foster to win his second straight NL MVP Award. Morgan led with a .576 slugging average, and hit .320, scored 113 runs, knocked in 111, and stole 60 bases.

ATLANTA		CHICAGO		CINCINNATI		HOUSTON		LOS ANGELES		MONTREAL	
M	D.Bristol	M	J.Marshall	M	S.Anderson	M	B.Virdon	M	W.Alston	M	K.Kuehl
1B	W.Montanez	1B	P.LaCock	1B	T.Perez	1B	B.Watson	M	T.Lasorda	M	C.Fox
2B	R.Gilbreath	2B	M.Trillo	2B	J.Morgan	2B	R.Andrews	1B	S.Garvey	1B	M.Jorgensen
SS	D.Chaney	SS	M.Kelleher	SS	D.Concepcion	SS	R.Metzger	2B	D.Lopes	2B	P.Mackanin
3B	J.Royster	3B	B.Madlock	3B	P.Rose	3B	E.Cabell	SS	B.Russell	SS	T.Foli
LF	J.Wynn	LF	J.Cardenal	LF	G.Foster	LF	J.Cruz	3B	R.Cey	3B	L.Parrish
CF	R.Office	CF	R.Monday	CF	C.Geronimo	CF	C.Cedeno	LF	B.Buckner	LF	D.Unser
RF	K.Henderson	RF	J.Morales	RF	K.Griffey	RF	G.Gross	CF	D.Baker	CF	J.White
C	V.Correll	C	S.Swisher	C	J.Bench	C	E.Herrmann	RF	R.Smith	RF	E.Valentine
								C	S.Yeager	C	B.Foote
O	D.May	C1	G.Mitterwald	1O	D.Driessen	CO	C.Johnson				
O1	T.Paciorek	O	J.Wallis	23	D.Flynn	O	L.Roberts	2	T.Sizemore	1C	J.Morales
		S	D.Rosello							CO	G.Carter
P	P.Niekro			P	G.Nolan	P	J.Richard	P	D.Sutton	O	P.Mangual
P	D.Ruthven	P	R.Reuschel	P	P.Zachry	P	L.Dierker	P	D.Rau		
P	A.Messersmith	P	R.Burris	P	F.Norman	P	J.Andujar	P	B.Hooton	P	S.Rogers
P	C.Morton	P	B.Bonham	P	J.Billingham	P	J.Niekro	P	T.John	P	W.Fryman
P	F.LaCorte	P	S.Renko	P	S.Alcala	RP	K.Forsch	P	R.Rhoden	P	D.Stanhouse
RP	R.Moret	RP	P.Reuschel	RP	P.Borbon	RP	G.Pentz	RP	C.Hough	P	D.Carrithers
RP	A.Devine	RP	B.Sutter	RP	R.Eastwick	RP	G.Rondon	RP	M.Marshall	RP	D.Murray
RP	B.Dal Canton	RP	J.Coleman	RP	W.McEnaney			RP	S.Wall	RP	S.Dunning
						P	D.Larson			RP	C.Lang
P	P.Torrealba	P	M.Garman	P	D.Gullett	P	M.Cosgrove				
		P	S.Stone			P	B.McLaughlin			P	D.Warthen
		P	D.Knowles			P	J.Sambito			P	C.Kirby
		P	O.Zamora							P	J.Kerrigan

NEW YORK		PHILADELPHIA		PITTSBURGH		SAN DIEGO		SAN FRANCISCO		ST.LOUIS	
M	J.Frazier	M	D.Ozark	M	D.Murtaugh	M	J.McNamara	M	B.Rigney	M	R.Schoendienst
1B	E.Kranepool	1B	D.Allen	1B	W.Stargell	1B	M.Ivie	1B	D.Evans	1B	K.Hernandez
2B	F.Millan	2B	D.Cash	2B	R.Stennett	2B	T.Fuentes	2B	M.Perez	2B	M.Tyson
SS	B.Harrelson	SS	L.Bowa	SS	F.Taveras	SS	E.Hernandez	SS	C.Speier	SS	D.Kessinger
3B	R.Staiger	3B	M.Schmidt	3B	R.Hebner	3B	D.Rader	3B	K.Reitz	3B	H.Cruz
LF	J.Milner	LF	G.Luzinski	LF	R.Zisk	LF	J.Grubb	LF	G.Matthews	LF	L.Brock
CF	D.Unser	CF	G.Maddox	CF	A.Oliver	CF	W.Davis	CF	L.Herndon	CF	J.Mumphrey
RF	D.Kingman	RF	J.Johnstone	RF	D.Parker	RF	D.Winfield	RF	B.Murcer	RF	W.Crawford
C	J.Grote	C	B.Boone	C	M.Sanguillen	C	F.Kendall	C	D.Rader	C	T.Simmons
1	J.Torre	O	J.Martin	O3	B.Robinson	O	J.Turner	O1	G.Thomasson	2O	V.Harris
O	B.Boisclair	1O	B.Tolan			S	H.Torres	2	D.Thomas	O	B.McBride
S2	M.Phillips	O	O.Brown	P	J.Candelaria	32	T.Kubiak	1	W.Montanez	S	G.Templeton
32	W.Garrett			P	J.Reuss	1	W.McCovey				
		P	S.Carlton	P	J.Rooker			P	J.Montefusco	P	P.Falcone
P	T.Seaver	P	J.Kaat	P	B.Kison	P	R.Jones	P	J.Barr	P	J.Denny
P	J.Matlack	P	J.Lonborg	P	D.Medich	P	B.Strom	P	E.Halicki	P	L.McGlothen
P	J.Koosman	P	L.Christenson	RP	K.Tekulve	P	D.Freisleben	P	R.Dressler	P	B.Forsch
P	M.Lolich	P	T.Underwood	RP	B.Moose	P	D.Spillner	P	J.D'Acquisto	P	E.Rasmussen
P	C.Swan	RP	R.Reed	RP	D.Giusti	RP	B.Metzger	RP	G.Lavelle	RP	A.Hrabosky
RP	S.Lockwood	RP	T.McGraw			RP	D.Tomlin	RP	M.Caldwell	RP	M.Wallace
RP	B.Apodaca	RP	G.Garber	P	L.Demery	RP	R.Folkers	RP	R.Moffitt	RP	B.Greif
		P	W.Twitchell			P	A.Foster	P	C.Williams	P	J.Curtis
		P	R.Schueler			P	R.Sawyer	P	D.Heaverlo		
						P	T.Griffin				

TEAM	G	W	L	PCT	GB	R	OR	AB	H	2B	3B	HR	BB	SO	AVG	OBP	SLG	PRO	PRO+	BR	/A	PF	CHI	RC	SB	CS	SBA	SBR
EAST																												
PHI	162	101	61	.623		770	557	5528	1505	259	45	110	542	793	.272	.342	.395	.737	112	106	83	103	101	746	127	70	64	-4
PIT	162	92	70	.568	9	708	630	5604	1499	249	56	110	433	807	.267	.323	.391	.714	107	50	44	101	102	700	130	45	74	12
NY	162	86	76	.531	15	615	**538**	5415	1334	198	34	102	561	797	.246	.320	.352	.672	103	-19	17	94	99	608	66	58	53	-15
CHI	162	75	87	.463	26	611	728	5519	1386	216	24	105	490	834	.251	.316	.356	.672	89	-27	-83	109	99	605	74	74	50	-22
STL	162	72	90	.444	29	629	671	5516	1432	243	57	63	512	860	.260	.325	.359	.684	99	1	-5	101	97	644	123	55	69	4
MON	162	55	107	.340	46	531	734	5428	1275	224	32	94	433	841	.235	.293	.340	.633	82	-109	-131	104	102	539	86	44	66	-1
WEST																												
CIN	162	102	60	.630		**857**	633	5702	**1599**	271	63	141	681	902	.280	.360	.424	.784	126	214	193	102	95	**907**	210	57	79	29
LA	162	92	70	.568	10	608	543	5472	1371	200	34	91	486	744	.251	.315	.349	.664	96	-39	-28	98	101	604	144	55	72	10
HOU	162	80	82	.494	22	625	657	5464	1401	195	50	66	530	719	.256	.325	.347	.672	107	-20	36	91	101	622	150	57	72	11
SF	162	74	88	.457	28	595	686	5452	1340	211	37	85	518	778	.246	.314	.345	.659	90	-48	-66	103	100	591	88	55	62	-7
SD	162	73	89	.451	29	570	662	5369	1327	216	37	64	488	716	.247	.313	.337	.650	98	-65	-19	92	100	570	92	46	67	0
ATL	162	70	92	.432	32	620	700	5345	1309	170	30	82	589	811	.245	.322	.334	.656	87	-44	-82	106	**104**	579	74	61	55	-14
TOT	972					7739		65814	16778	2652	499	1113	6263	9602	.255	.323	.361	.684							1364	677	67	3

TEAM	CG	SH	SV	IP	H	H/G	HR	BB	SO	RAT	ERA	ERA+	OAV	OOB	PR	/A	PF	CPI	FA	E	DP	FW	PW	BW	SBW	DIF
EAST																										
PHI	34	9	44	1459	1377	8.5	98	397	918	11.1	3.08	**115**	.250	.303	69	76	101	102	.981	115	148	1.7	**8.1**	8.8	-.5	1.8
PIT	45	12	35	1466[1]	1402	8.6	95	460	762	11.5	3.36	104	.253	.313	22	20	100	99	.975	163	142	-1.0	2.1	4.7	1.2	4.0
NY	53	18	25	1449	**1248**	7.8	97	419	**1025**	10.5	2.94	112	**.233**	.292	91	57	94	95	.979	131	116	.8	6.1	1.8	-1.6	-2.1
CHI	27	12	33	1471[1]	1511	9.2	123	490	850	12.4	3.93	98	.268	.330	-71	-12	110	100	.978	140	145	.3	-1.3	-8.8	-2.4	6.2
STL	35	15	26	1453[2]	1416	8.8	91	581	731	12.5	3.60	98	.258	.332	-16	-11	101	100	.973	174	163	-1.7	-1.2	-.5	.4	-6.0
MON	26	10	21	1440	1442	9.0	89	659	783	13.4	3.99	93	.266	.350	-79	-44	106	102	.976	155	**179**	-.6	-4.7	-13.9	-.1	-6.7
WEST																										
CIN	33	12	**45**	1471	1436	8.8	100	491	790	11.9	3.51	100	.258	.321	-1	0	100	101	**.984**	102	157	2.5	.0	20.5	3.1	-5.0
LA	47	17	28	1470[2]	1330	8.1	97	479	747	11.2	3.02	112	.243	.307	79	60	97	104	.980	128	154	1.0	6.4	-3.0	1.0	5.6
HOU	42	17	29	1444[1]	1349	8.4	82	662	780	12.7	3.56	90	.250	.335	-9	-59	91	101	.978	140	155	.3	-6.3	3.8	1.1	.0
SF	27	**18**	31	1461[2]	1464	9.0	**68**	518	746	12.3	3.53	103	.263	.328	-4	16	104	100	.971	186	153	-2.4	1.7	-7.0	-.8	1.4
SD	47	11	18	1432[1]	1368	8.6	87	543	652	12.1	3.65	90	.253	.323	-24	-61	93	95	.978	141	148	.2	-6.5	-2.0	-.0	.3
ATL	33	13	27	1438	1435	9.0	86	564	818	12.8	3.86	98	.261	.335	-58	-12	108	97	.973	167	151	-1.3	-1.3	-8.7	-1.5	1.8
TOT	449	164	362	17457[1]		8.6				12.0	3.50		.255	.323					.977	1742	1811					

Runs
Rose-Cin 130
Morgan-Cin 113
Schmidt-Phi 112
Griffey-Cin 111
Monday-Chi 107

Hits
Rose-Cin 215
Montanez-SF-Atl . 206
Garvey-LA 200
Buckner-LA 193

Doubles
Rose-Cin 42
Johnstone-Phi 38
Maddox-Phi 37
Garvey-LA 37

Triples
Cash-Phi 12
Geronimo-Cin 11
Parker-Pit 10
W.Davis-SD 10

Home Runs
Schmidt-Phi 38
Kingman-NY 37
Monday-Chi 32
Foster-Cin 29
Morgan-Cin 27

Total Bases
Schmidt-Phi 306
Rose-Cin 299
Foster-Cin 298
Garvey-LA 284

Runs Batted In
Foster-Cin 121
Morgan-Cin 111
Schmidt-Phi 107
Watson-Hou 102
Luzinski-Phi 95

Runs Produced
Morgan-Cin 197
Rose-Cin 183
Schmidt-Phi 181
Griffey-Cin 179
Foster-Cin 178

Bases On Balls
Wynn-Atl 127
Morgan-Cin 114
Schmidt-Phi 100
Cey-LA 89
Rose-Cin 86

Batting Average
Madlock-Chi ..... .339
Griffey-Cin ...... .336
Maddox-Phi ...... .330
Rose-Cin .... .323
Morgan-Cin ...... .320

On Base Percentage
Morgan-Cin ...... .453
Madlock-Chi ..... .415
Rose-Cin .... .406
Griffey-Cin ...... .403
Cey-LA .... .389

Slugging Average
Morgan-Cin ...... .576
Foster-Cin .... .530
Schmidt-Phi ..... .524
Monday-Chi ..... .507
Kingman-NY ..... .506

Production
Morgan-Cin 1.029
Madlock-Chi ..... .915
Schmidt-Phi ..... .904
Foster-Cin .... .899
Rose-Cin .... .855

Adjusted Production
Morgan-Cin 186
Watson-Hou 151
Schmidt-Phi 150
Foster-Cin 149
Madlock-Chi 146

Batter Runs
Morgan-Cin 61.4
Schmidt-Phi 42.7
Madlock-Chi 40.6
Rose-Cin 39.6
Foster-Cin 36.7

Adjusted Batter Runs
Morgan-Cin 58.4
Schmidt-Phi 39.2
Watson-Hou 38.3
Rose-Cin 36.8
Foster-Cin 34.3

Clutch Hitting Index
Cruz-StL 119
Brock-StL 117
Milner-NY 117
Bench-Cin 116
Reitz-SF 116

Runs Created
Morgan-Cin 144
Rose-Cin 123
Schmidt-Phi 121
Foster-Cin 111
Griffey-Cin 109

Total Average
Morgan-Cin 1.319
Schmidt-Phi ..... .944
Foster-Cin .... .911
Madlock-Chi ..... .882
Griffey-Cin ...... .876

Stolen Bases
Lopes-LA 63
Morgan-Cin 60
Taveras-Pit 58
Cedeno-Hou 58
Brock-StL 56

Stolen Base Average
Morgan-Cin 87.0
Lopes-LA 86.3
Foster-Cin 85.0
Taveras-Pit 84.1
Geronimo-Cin ... 81.5

Stolen Base Runs
Lopes-LA 12.9
Morgan-Cin 12.6
Taveras-Pit 10.8
Cedeno-Hou 8.4
Cabell-Hou 5.7

Fielding Runs
Schmidt-Phi 24.7
Maddox-Phi 24.3
Trillo-Chi 18.3
Stennett-Pit 17.4
Royster-Atl 16.6

Total Player Rating
Schmidt-Phi 6.4
Morgan-Cin 5.8
Maddox-Phi 4.5
Cedeno-Hou 4.4
Concepcion-Cin .. 4.1

Wins
Jones-SD 22
Sutton-LA 21
Koosman-NY 21
Richard-Hou 20
Carlton-Phi 20

Win Percentage
Carlton-Phi ...... .741
Candelaria-Pit .... .696
Sutton-LA .... .677
Koosman-NY .... .677
Rooker-Pit .... .652

Games
Murray-Mon 81
Metzger-SD 77
Hough-LA 77
Eastwick-Cin 71
Borbon-Cin 69

Complete Games
Jones-SD 25
Koosman-NY 17
Matlack-NY 16
Sutton-LA 15
Richard-Hou 14

Shutouts
Montefusco-SF ... 6
Matlack-NY 6
Seaver-NY 5
Jones-SD 5

Saves
Eastwick-Cin 26
Lockwood-NY 19
Forsch-Hou 19
Hough-LA 18
Metzger-SD 16

Innings Pitched
Jones-SD 315.1
Richard-Hou 291.0
Seaver-NY 271.0
Niekro-Atl 270.2
Sutton-LA 267.2

Fewest Hits/Game
Richard-Hou 6.84
Seaver-NY 7.01
Candelaria-Pit 7.08
Messersmith-Atl .. 7.21
Falcone-StL 7.34

Fewest BB/Game
Nolan-Cin 1.02
Kaat-Phi 1.27
Jones-SD 1.43
Matlack-NY 1.96
Lonborg-Phi 2.03

Strikeouts
Seaver-NY 235
Richard-Hou 214
Koosman-NY 200
Carlton-Phi 195
Niekro-Atl 173

Strikeouts/Game
Seaver-NY 7.80
Koosman-NY 7.28
Carlton-Phi 6.95
Richard-Hou 6.62
Zachry-Cin 6.31

Ratio
Jones-SD 9.36
Candelaria-Pit 9.61
Seaver-NY 9.70
Nolan-Cin 9.78
Koosman-NY 9.90

Earned Run Average
Denny-StL 2.52
Rau-LA 2.57
Seaver-NY 2.59
Koosman-NY 2.69
Zachry-Cin 2.74

Adjusted ERA
Denny-StL 140
Rau-LA 132
Zachry-Cin 128
Montefusco-SF ... 128
Seaver-NY 127

Opponents' Batting Avg.
Richard-Hou ..... .212
Seaver-NY .... .213
Candelaria-Pit .... .216
Messersmith-Atl .. .219
Falcone-StL ...... .222

Opponents' On Base Pct.
Jones-SD .... .267
Candelaria-Pit .... .273
Seaver-NY .... .273
Nolan-Cin .... .276
Koosman-NY .... .279

Starter Runs
Seaver-NY 27.4
Jones-SD 26.7
Richard-Hou 24.2
Rau-LA 23.9
Denny-StL 22.5

Adjusted Starter Runs
Denny-StL 23.3
Montefusco-SF ... 22.1
Seaver-NY 21.2
Rau-LA 20.8
Burris-Chi 20.8

Clutch Pitching Index
Rau-LA 139
Denny-StL 129
Burris-Chi 118
Christenson-Phi ... 112
Fryman-Mon 112

Relief Runs
Hough-LA 20.5
Eastwick-Cin 16.9
Reed-Phi 14.8
Moffitt-SF 14.1
Forsch-Hou 13.8

Adjusted Relief Runs
Hough-LA 18.6
Eastwick-Cin 16.9
Moffitt-SF 15.5
Reed-Phi 15.4
Twitchell-Phi 12.3

Relief Ranking
Eastwick-Cin 31.8
Hough-LA 28.8
Moffitt-SF 21.0
Reed-Phi 20.1
Lavelle-SF 17.8

Total Pitcher Index
Hough-LA 3.3
Eastwick-Cin 3.1
Barr-SF 2.8
Denny-StL 2.7
Rau-LA 2.6

Total Baseball Ranking
Schmidt-Phi 6.4
Morgan-Cin 5.8
Maddox-Phi 4.5
Cedeno-Hou 4.4
Concepcion-Cin .. 4.1

January 22 Pitchers Robin Roberts and Bob Lemon are voted into the Hall of Fame.

February 2 The Special Veterans Committee selects old-time players Roger Connor and Fred Lindstrom, and umpire Cal Hubbard, for Cooperstown. Hubbard becomes the first man elected to both the Pro Football and Baseball Halls of Fame.

February 9 Oscar Charleston is selected for the Hall of Fame by the Special Committee on the Negro Leagues.

April 15 Newly remodeled Yankee Stadium is jammed with 52,613 fans for Opening Day ceremonies. The 1923 Yankee team is honored, and Bob Shawkey, winner of the 1923 Stadium opener, throws out the first ball.

May 13 The Royals beat the White Sox 13-2 as George Brett sets a major league record by collecting three hits for the sixth consecutive game, breaking Rod Carew's record.

July 20 Hank Aaron hits the 755th, and last, homer of his career, connecting off Dick Drago of the California Angels.

July 28 Blue Moon Odom and Francisco Barrios combine on a no-hitter as the White Sox top the A's, 2-1. Odom walks nine in five innings and is lifted after throwing a ball in the sixth. For Odom (2-0), this is his last major league victory.

September 11 Minnie Minoso comes to bat for the White Sox after a 12-year hiatus. He goes hitless in his three at bats against Frank Tanana, but his appearance makes him one of a handful of major league players to play in four decades. His at bat in 1980 will match him with Nick Altrock as a five-decade player.

October 3 George Brett edges Royals teammate Hal McRae for the AL batting title, .333 to .332, when his blooper drops in front of Twins outfielder Steve Brye and skips over his head for an inside-the-park homer.

October 14 In the final ALCS game, the Yankees take the early lead only to see the Royals even it up on Brett's three-run homer in the eighth. Chris Chambliss then connects on a dramatic ninth-inning homer off relief ace Mark Littell to win the game 7-6 and the pennant for the Yankees. By the time Chambliss reaches second base, he is surrounded by screaming fans who escort him around the bases. After he reaches the dugout he returns with a police escort to make sure he touches third base and home.

November 4 The first mass market free-agent re-entry draft is held at New York's Plaza Hotel. Among those available are Reggie Jackson, Joe Rudi, Don Gullett, Bill Campbell, Gene Tenace, Rollie Fingers, Don Baylor, Bobby Grich, and Willie McCovey.

November 5 New AL franchises in Seattle and Toronto fill up their rosters by selecting 30 players apiece from unprotected players on other AL rosters. Outfielder Ruppert Jones (Seattle) and infielder-outfielder Bob Bailor (Toronto) are the first choices.

November 5 Baltimore's Jim Palmer easily outpoints Detroit's sensational rookie Mark Fidrych to win the AL Cy Young Award.

	BALTIMORE		BOSTON		CALIFORNIA		CHICAGO		CLEVELAND		DETROIT
M	E.Weaver	M	D.Johnson	M	D.Williams	M	P.Richards	M	F.Robinson	M	R.Houk
1B	T.Muser	M	D.Zimmer	M	N.Sherry	1B	J.Spencer	1B	B.Powell	1B	J.Thompson
2B	B.Grich	1B	C.Yastrzemski	1B	B.Bochte	2B	J.Brohamer	2B	D.Kuiper	2B	P.Garcia
SS	M.Belanger	2B	D.Doyle	2B	J.Remy	SS	B.Dent	SS	F.Duffy	SS	T.Veryzer
3B	D.DeCinces	SS	R.Burleson	SS	D.Chalk	3B	K.Bell	3B	B.Bell	3B	A.Rodriguez
LF	K.Singleton	3B	B.Hobson	3B	R.Jackson	LF	J.Orta	LF	G.Hendrick	LF	A.Johnson
CF	P.Blair	LF	J.Rice	LF	L.Stanton	CF	C.Lemon	CF	R.Manning	CF	R.LeFlore
RF	R.Jackson	CF	F.Lynn	CF	R.Torres	RF	R.Garr	RF	C.Spikes	RF	R.Staub
C	D.Duncan	RF	D.Evans	RF	B.Bonds	C	B.Downing	C	A.Ashby	C	B.Kimm
DH	L.May	C	C.Fisk	C	A.Etchebarren	DH	P.Kelly	DH	R.Carty	DH	W.Horton
		DH	C.Cooper	DH	T.Davis						
OD	A.Bumbry					23	B.Stein	S2	L.Blanks	O1	D.Meyer
DO	A.Mora	O	R.Miller	OD	D.Collins	D1	L.Johnson	C	R.Fosse	O	B.Oglivie
3	B.Robinson	3	R.Petrocelli	D1	B.Melton			OD	J.Lowenstein	C	B.Freehan
				2S	M.Guerrero	P	R.Gossage			2S	C.Scrivener
P	J.Palmer	P	L.Tiant	1O	D.Briggs	P	B.Johnson	P	P.Dobson	O1	M.Stanley
P	W.Garland	P	R.Wise	1	T.Solaita	P	K.Brett	P	D.Eckersley		
P	R.May	P	F.Jenkins			P	F.Barrios	P	J.Brown	P	D.Roberts
P	R.Grimsley	P	R.Cleveland	P	F.Tanana	P	T.Forster	P	J.Bibby	P	M.Fidrych
P	M.Cuellar	P	D.Pole	P	N.Ryan	RP	D.Hamilton	P	R.Waits	P	V.Ruhle
RP	D.Miller	RP	J.Willoughby	P	G.Ross	RP	C.Carroll	RP	J.Kern	P	R.Bare
		RP	T.Murphy	P	P.Hartzell			RP	S.Thomas	P	J.Crawford
P	K.Holtzman			P	D.Kirkwood	P	P.Vuckovich	RP	D.LaRoche	RP	J.Hiller
P	M.Flanagan	P	R.Jones	RP	D.Drago	P	J.Jefferson			RP	S.Grilli
P	D.Alexander	P	B.Lee			/P	W.Wood	P	T.Buskey		
				P	S.Monge	P	C.Knapp	P	D.Hood	P	B.Laxton
						/P	K.Kravec			P	D.Lemanczyk
										P	J.Coleman

	KANSAS CITY		MILWAUKEE		MINNESOTA		NEW YORK		OAKLAND		TEXAS
M	W.Herzog	M	A.Grammas	M	G.Mauch	M	B.Martin	M	C.Tanner	M	F.Lucchesi
1B	J.Mayberry	1B	G.Scott	1B	R.Carew	1B	C.Chambliss	1B	G.Tenace	1B	M.Hargrove
2B	F.White	2B	T.Johnson	2B	B.Randall	2B	W.Randolph	2B	P.Garner	2B	L.Randle
SS	F.Patek	SS	R.Yount	SS	R.Smalley	SS	F.Stanley	SS	B.Campaneris	SS	T.Harrah
3B	G.Brett	3B	D.Money	3B	M.Cubbage	3B	G.Nettles	3B	S.Bando	3B	R.Howell
LF	T.Poquette	LF	S.Lezcano	LF	L.Hisle	LF	R.White	LF	J.Rudi	LF	G.Clines
CF	A.Otis	CF	V.Joshua	CF	L.Bostock	CF	M.Rivers	CF	B.North	CF	J.Beniquez
RF	A.Cowens	RF	G.Thomas	RF	D.Ford	RF	O.Gamble	RF	C.Washington	RF	J.Burroughs
C	B.Martinez	C	D.Porter	C	B.Wynegar	C	T.Munson	C	L.Haney	C	J.Sundberg
DH	H.McRae	DH	H.Aaron	DH	C.Kusick	DH	C.May	DH	B.Williams	DH	T.Grieve
O	J.Wohlford	CO	C.Moore	DO	S.Braun	OD	L.Piniella	O1	D.Baylor	P	G.Perry
C	B.Stinson	DO	M.Hegan	O	S.Brye	S	J.Mason	31	K.McMullen	P	N.Briles
										P	B.Blyleven
P	D.Leonard	P	J.Slaton	P	D.Goltz	P	C.Hunter	P	V.Blue	P	J.Umbarger
P	A.Fitzmorris	P	B.Travers	P	J.Hughes	P	E.Figueroa	P	M.Torrez	P	S.Hargan
P	D.Bird	P	J.Colborn	P	B.Singer	P	D.Ellis	P	S.Bahnsen	RP	S.Foucault
P	P.Splittorff	P	J.Augustine	P	S.Luebber	P	K.Holtzman	P	P.Mitchell	RP	M.Bacsik
P	M.Pattin	P	E.Rodriguez	P	P.Redfern	P	D.Alexander	P	D.Bosman	RP	J.Terpko
RP	M.Littell	RP	B.Castro	RP	B.Campbell	RP	S.Lyle	RP	R.Fingers		
RP	S.Mingori	RP	D.Frisella	RP	T.Burgmeier	RP	D.Tidrow	RP	P.Lindblad	P	T.Boggs
				RP	V.Albury	RP	G.Jackson	RP	J.Todd	P	S.Barr
P	A.Hassler	P	P.Broberg							P	B.Singer
P	S.Busby			P	B.Blyleven	P	R.May	P	M.Norris		
P	L.Gura			P	E.Bane			P	G.Abbott		
				P	J.Decker						

TEAM	G	W	L	PCT	GB	R	OR	AB	H	2B	3B	HR	BB	SO	AVG	OBP	SLG	PRO	PRO+	BR	/A	PF	CHI	RC	SB	CS	SBA	SBR
EAST																												
NY	159	97	62	.610		730	**575**	5555	1496	231	36	120	470	**616**	.269	.330	.389	.719	111	64	**71**	99	103	723	163	65	71	10
BAL	162	88	74	.543	10.5	619	598	5457	1326	213	28	119	519	883	.243	.311	.358	.669	102	-33	5	94	102	612	150	61	71	8
BOS	162	83	79	.512	15.5	716	660	5511	1448	257	53	**134**	500	832	.263	.327	**.402**	**.729**	101	**80**	-8	112	98	709	95	70	58	-14
CLE	159	81	78	.509	16	615	615	5412	1423	189	38	85	479	631	.263	.324	.359	.683	101	-2	5	99	97	611	75	69	52	-19
DET	161	74	87	.460	24	609	709	5441	1401	207	38	101	450	730	.257	.318	.365	.683	96	-7	-31	104	97	611	107	59	64	-3
MIL	161	66	95	.410	32	570	655	5396	1326	170	38	88	511	909	.246	.314	.340	.654	93	-57	-46	98	98	575	62	61	50	-18
WEST																												
KC	162	90	72	.556		713	611	5540	1490	259	**57**	65	484	650	.269	.331	.371	.702	104	37	32	101	103	687	218	106	67	2
OAK	161	87	74	.540	2.5	686	598	5353	1319	208	33	113	**592**	818	.246	.327	.361	.688	105	13	40	96	**105**	663	**341**	**123**	**73**	**29**
MIN	162	85	77	.525	5	**743**	704	5574	**1526**	222	51	81	550	714	**.274**	**.343**	.375	.718	108	78	63	102	100	**727**	146	75	66	-1
TEX	162	76	86	.469	14	616	652	5555	1390	213	26	80	568	809	.250	.323	.341	.664	93	-32	-45	102	98	616	87	45	66	-1
CAL	162	76	86	.469	14	550	631	5385	1265	210	23	63	534	812	.235	.309	.318	.627	86	-105	-72	94	102	531	126	80	61	-10
CHI	161	64	97	.398	25.5	586	745	5532	1410	209	46	73	471	739	.255	.317	.349	.666	94	-36	-40	101	96	622	120	53	69	4
TOT	967					7753		65711	16820	2588	467	1122	6128	9143	.256	.323	.361	.684							1690	867	66	-13

TEAM	CG	SH	SV	IP	H	H/G	HR	BB	SO	RAT	ERA	ERA+	OAV	OOB	PR	/A	PF	CPI	FA	E	DP	FW	PW	BW	SBW	DIF
EAST																										
NY	62	15	37	1455	**1300**	8.0	97	448	674	10.9	3.19	107	**.241**	**.301**	53	36	97	95	.980	126	141	.9	3.8	**7.5**	1.2	4.1
BAL	59	16	23	1468²	1396	8.6	**80**	489	678	11.7	3.32	99	.255	.318	33	-7	93	101	**.982**	118	157	**1.5**	-.7	.5	1.0	4.8
BOS	49	13	27	1458	1495	9.2	109	**409**	673	12.0	3.52	111	.267	.320	-1	62	111	104	.978	141	148	.2	6.6	-.8	-1.4	-2.5
CLE	30	**17**	**46**	1432	1361	8.6	80	533	928	12.1	3.47	101	.255	.326	8	3	99	101	.980	121	159	1.2	.3	.5	-1.9	1.4
DET	55	12	20	1431¹	1426	9.0	101	550	738	12.6	3.87	96	.263	.334	-56	-25	105	99	.974	168	161	-1.4	-2.7	-3.3	-.2	1.1
MIL	45	10	27	1435¹	1406	8.8	99	567	677	12.6	3.64	96	.260	.334	-20	-24	99	104	.975	152	160	-.5	-2.5	-4.9	-1.8	-4.8
WEST																										
KC	41	12	35	1472¹	1356	8.3	83	493	735	11.5	3.21	109	.247	.312	51	48	100	99	.978	139	147	.3	5.1	3.4	.3	-.1
OAK	39	15	29	1459¹	1412	8.7	96	415	711	11.5	3.26	103	.255	.310	42	16	95	101	.977	144	130	-.0	1.7	4.2	**3.2**	-2.6
MIN	29	11	23	1459	1421	8.8	89	610	762	12.8	3.69	97	.259	.337	-29	-20	102	102	.973	172	**182**	-1.6	-2.1	6.7	.0	1.0
TEX	63	15	15	1472¹	1464	9.0	106	461	773	12.0	3.45	104	.262	.322	10	21	102	**105**	.976	156	142	-.7	2.2	-4.8	-.0	-1.8
CAL	**64**	15	17	1477¹	1323	8.1	95	553	**992**	11.7	3.36	99	**.241**	.315	26	-5	95	96	.977	150	139	-.3	-.5	-7.6	-.9	4.5
CHI	54	10	22	1448	1460	9.1	87	600	802	13.0	4.25	84	.266	.342	-118	-111	101	92	.979	130	155	.7	-11.8	-4.2	.5	-1.8
TOT	590	161	321	17468¹		8.7				12.0	3.52		.256	.323					.977	1717	1821					

Runs		Hits		Doubles		Triples		Home Runs		Total Bases	
White-NY	104	Brett-KC	215	Otis-KC	40	Brett-KC	14	Nettles-NY	32	Brett-KC	298
Carew-Min	97	Carew-Min	200	McRae-KC	34	Garner-Oak	12	R.Jackson-Bal	27	Chambliss-NY	283
Rivers-NY	95	Chambliss-NY	188	Evans-Bos	34	Carew-Min	12	Bando-Oak	27	Rice-Bos	280
Brett-KC	94	Munson-NY	186	Carty-Cle	34	Poquette-KC	10			Carew-Min	280
		Rivers-NY	184	Brett-KC	34	Bostock-Min	9			Nettles-NY	277

Runs Batted In		Runs Produced		Bases On Balls		Batting Average		On Base Percentage		Slugging Average	
L.May-Bal	109	Carew-Min	178	Hargrove-Tex	97	Brett-KC	.333	McRae-KC	.412	R.Jackson-Bal	.502
Munson-NY	105	Munson-NY	167	Harrah-Tex	91	McRae-KC	.332	Hargrove-Tex	.401	Rice-Bos	.482
Yastrzemski-Bos	102	Hisle-Min	163	Grich-Bal	86	Carew-Min	.331	Carew-Min	.398	Nettles-NY	.475
		Otis-KC	161	White-NY	83	Bostock-Min	.323	Staub-Det	.392	Lynn-Bos	.467
				Staub-Det	83	LeFlore-Det	.316	Carty-Cle	.384	Carew-Min	.463

Production		Adjusted Production		Batter Runs		Adjusted Batter Runs		Clutch Hitting Index		Runs Created	
McRae-KC	.873	R.Jackson-Bal	158	Carew-Min	40.0	McRae-KC	38.1	Mayberry-KC	137	Brett-KC	114
Carew-Min	.861	McRae-KC	154	McRae-KC	38.8	Carew-Min	37.7	Rudi-Oak	131	Carew-Min	111
R.Jackson-Bal	.855	Tenace-Oak	150	Brett-KC	36.2	Brett-KC	35.4	L.May-Bal	127	McRae-KC	101
Brett-KC	.843	Carew-Min	149	Staub-Det	33.2	R.Jackson-Bal	34.3	Yastrzemski-Bos	124	Staub-Det	99
Lynn-Bos	.842	Brett-KC	145	Carty-Cle	29.8	Carty-Cle	30.8	Hisle-Min	124	White-NY	98

Total Average		Stolen Bases		Stolen Base Average		Stolen Base Runs		Fielding Runs		Total Player Rating	
McRae-KC	.862	North-Oak	75	Rivers-NY	86.0	Campaneris-Oak	9.0	White-NY	21.1	Nettles-NY	4.1
R.Jackson-Bal	.857	LeFlore-Det	58	Campaneris-Oak	81.8	Rivers-NY	8.7	Kuiper-Cle	20.0	Brett-KC	4.0
Tenace-Oak	.855	Campaneris-Oak	54	Baylor-Oak	81.3	Baylor-Oak	8.4	Beniquez-Tex	19.5	Grich-Bal	3.9
Carew-Min	.854	Baylor-Oak	52	Bumbry-Bal	80.8	Bumbry-Bal	6.6	Brohamer-Chi	18.0	R.Jackson-Bal	3.7
Brett-KC	.797	Patek-KC	51	R.Jackson-Bal	80.0	Patek-KC	6.3	Nettles-NY	17.2	Belanger-Bal	3.6

Wins		Win Percentage		Games		Complete Games		Shutouts		Saves	
Palmer-Bal	22	Campbell-Min	773	Campbell-Min	78	Fidrych-Det	24	Ryan-Cal	7	Lyle-NY	23
Tiant-Bos	21	Garland-Bal	741	Fingers-Oak	70	Tanana-Cal	23	Blyleven-Min-Tex	6	LaRoche-Cle	21
Garland-Bal	20	Ellis-NY	680	Lindblad-Oak	65	Palmer-Bal	23	Palmer-Bal	6	Fingers-Oak	20
		Fidrych-Det	679	Lyle-NY	64			Blue-Oak	6	Campbell-Min	20
				LaRoche-Cle	61					Littell-KC	16

Innings Pitched		Fewest Hits/Game		Fewest BB/Game		Strikeouts		Strikeouts/Game		Ratio	
Palmer-Bal	315.0	Ryan-Cal	6.11	Bird-KC	1.41	Ryan-Cal	327	Ryan-Cal	10.35	Tanana-Cal	9.18
Hunter-NY	298.2	Tanana-Cal	6.62	Jenkins-Bos	1.85	Tanana-Cal	261	Eckersley-Cle	9.03	Fidrych-Det	9.81
Blue-Oak	298.1	Eckersley-Cle	7.00	Perry-Tex	1.87	Blyleven-Min-Tex	219	Tanana-Cal	8.15	Palmer-Bal	9.91
Blyleven-Min-Tex	297.2	Palmer-Bal	7.29	Blue-Oak	1.90	Eckersley-Cle	200	Blyleven-Min-Tex	6.62	Blue-Oak	10.02
Slaton-Mil	292.2	Brett-NY-Chi	7.67	Fidrych-Det	1.91	Hunter-NY	173	Campbell-Min	6.17	Perry-Tex	10.21

Earned Run Average		Adjusted ERA		Opponents' Batting Avg.		Opponents' On Base Pct.		Starter Runs		Adjusted Starter Runs	
Fidrych-Det	2.34	Fidrych-Det	159	Ryan-Cal	.195	Tanana-Cal	.261	Blue-Oak	38.6	Fidrych-Det	38.1
Blue-Oak	2.35	Blue-Oak	142	Tanana-Cal	.203	Fidrych-Det	.279	Palmer-Bal	35.1	Blue-Oak	33.1
Tanana-Cal	2.43	Tanana-Cal	137	Eckersley-Cle	.214	Blue-Oak	.280	Tanana-Cal	34.7	Tanana-Cal	28.5
Torrez-Oak	2.50	Torrez-Oak	134	Palmer-Bal	.224	Palmer-Bal	.282	Fidrych-Det	32.8	Palmer-Bal	26.5
Palmer-Bal	2.51	Palmer-Bal	130	Brett-NY-Chi	.233	Bird-KC	.283	Torrez-Oak	30.1	Tiant-Bos	26.2

Clutch Pitching Index		Relief Runs		Adjusted Relief Runs		Relief Ranking		Total Pitcher Index		Total Baseball Ranking	
Hartzell-Cal	124	Littell-KC	16.7	Hiller-Det	17.9	Hiller-Det	30.9	Fidrych-Det	5.0	Fidrych-Det	5.0
Travers-Mil	120	Fingers-Oak	15.6	Littell-KC	16.4	Fingers-Oak	25.5	Palmer-Bal	3.6	Nettles-NY	4.1
Umbarger-Tex	118	Hiller-Det	15.3	Kern-Cle	14.6	Lyle-NY	24.0	Hiller-Det	3.3	Brett-KC	4.0
Garland-Bal	116	Kern-Cle	15.0	Thomas-Cle	14.0	Kern-Cle	23.2	Tanana-Cal	3.2	Grich-Bal	3.9
Torrez-Oak	115	Lyle-NY	14.5	Burgmeier-Min	13.8	Littell-KC	22.8	Blue-Oak	3.1	R.Jackson-Bal	3.7

January 2 Commissioner Bowie Kuhn suspends Braves owner Ted Turner for one year as a result of tampering charges in the Gary Matthews free-agency signing, but the Braves are permitted to keep the outfielder.

January 19 The BBWAA elects Ernie Banks to the Hall of Fame in his first year of eligibility.

January 31 The Special Veterans Committee selects Joe Sewell, Amos Rusie, and Al Lopez for the Hall of Fame.

February 3 The Hall of Fame's Special Committee on the Negro Leagues picks Martin Dihigo and John Lloyd for induction. The committee then dissolves, its functions being taken over by the Veterans Committee.

May 11 With the Braves mired in a 16-game losing streak, owner Ted Turner takes over as field manager. After the Braves lose again 2-1, Turner is relieved of his new job by NL president Chub Feeney. A league rule prohibits a manager from owning part of his club.

June 15 The Mets trade ace pitcher Tom Seaver to the Reds. In return they get pitcher Pat Zachry, infielder Doug Flynn, and minor leaguers Steve Henderson and Dan Norman. The Mets also trade slugger Dave Kingman to the Padres for utility player Bobby Valentine and a minor league pitcher.

July 19 At Yankee Stadium, the NL scores four times in the opening inning off Jim Palmer, en route to a 7-5 All-Star Game victory. Don Sutton, hurling three scoreless innings, is named MVP.

August 29 The Cardinals' Lou Brock steals second base in a 4-3 loss to the Padres. It is career steal 893 for Brock, breaking Ty Cobb's modern record.

September 3* Sadaharu Oh hits the 756th homer of his career to surpass Hank Aaron's total and make him the most prolific homer hitter in professional baseball history.

October 2 Dusty Baker homers in his final at bat of the season. It is Baker's 30th homer of the year, enabling him to join teammates Steve Garvey (33), Reggie Smith (32), and Ron Cey (30) in making the Dodgers the first team ever to boast four 30-homer hitters in one season.

October 7 Down 5-3 with two outs in the ninth inning, the Dodgers catch lightning in a bottle. Pinch hitter Vic Davalillo beats out a two-strike drag bunt, and pinch hitter Manny Mota follows with a long double. Los Angeles pulls out a 6-5 victory over the Phillies to win the NLCS.

November 2 The Phillies' Steve Carlton tops Tommy John of the Dodgers to win his second Cy Young Award. Carlton led the NL with 23 wins, losing 10, and posting a 2.64 ERA.

November 9 The Reds' George Foster wins the NL MVP Award.

November 22 Montreal's Andre Dawson wins the NL Rookie of the Year Award by one vote over New York's Steve Henderson.

	ATLANTA		CHICAGO		CINCINNATI		HOUSTON		LOS ANGELES		MONTREAL
M	D.Bristol	M	H.Franks	M	S.Anderson	M	B.Virdon	M	T.Lasorda	M	D.Williams
M	T.Turner	1B	B.Buckner	1B	D.Driessen	1B	B.Watson	1B	S.Garvey	1B	T.Perez
M	V.Benson	2B	M.Trillo	2B	J.Morgan	2B	A.Howe	2B	D.Lopes	2B	D.Cash
M	D.Bristol	SS	I.DeJesus	SS	D.Concepcion	SS	R.Metzger	SS	B.Russell	SS	C.Speier
1B	W.Montanez	3B	S.Ontiveros	3B	P.Rose	3B	E.Cabell	3B	R.Cey	3B	L.Parrish
2B	R.Gilbreath	LF	J.Cardenal	LF	G.Foster	LF	T.Puhl	LF	D.Baker	LF	W.Cromartie
SS	P.Rockett	CF	J.Morales	CF	C.Geronimo	CF	C.Cedeno	CF	R.Monday	CF	A.Dawson
3B	J.Moore	RF	B.Murcer	RF	K.Griffey	RF	J.Cruz	RF	R.Smith	RF	E.Valentine
LF	G.Matthews	C	G.Mitterwald	C	J.Bench	C	J.Ferguson	C	S.Yeager	C	G.Carter
CF	R.Office										
RF	J.Burroughs	1O	L.Biittner	P	F.Norman	S2	J.Gonzalez	P	D.Sutton	O1	D.Unser
C	B.Pocoroba	O	G.Gross	P	T.Seaver			P	B.Hooton		
		O	G.Clines	P	J.Billingham	P	J.Richard	P	T.John	P	S.Rogers
O3	B.Bonnell	C	S.Swisher	P	P.Moskau	P	M.Lemongello	P	R.Rhoden	P	J.Brown
3S	J.Royster			P	D.Capilla	P	J.Niekro	P	D.Rau	P	D.Stanhouse
S2	D.Chaney	P	R.Reuschel	RP	P.Borbon	P	J.Andujar	RP	C.Hough	P	W.Twitchell
		P	R.Burris	RP	D.Murray	P	F.Bannister	RP	E.Sosa	P	S.Bahnsen
P	P.Niekro	P	B.Bonham			RP	J.Sambito	RP	M.Garman	RP	J.Kerrigan
P	D.Ruthven	P	M.Krukow	P	W.Fryman	RP	G.Pentz			RP	W.McEnaney
P	B.Capra	RP	W.Hernandez	P	P.Zachry	RP	K.Forsch			RP	B.Atkinson
P	A.Messersmith	RP	B.Sutter	P	M.Soto						
RP	D.Campbell	RP	P.Reuschel			P	D.Larson			P	S.Alcala
RP	M.Leon					P	B.McLaughlin				
RP	R.Camp	P	D.Roberts								
P	E.Solomon	P	S.Renko								
P	D.Collins										
P	P.Hanna										
P	J.Easterly										

	NEW YORK		PHILADELPHIA		PITTSBURGH		SAN DIEGO		SAN FRANCISCO		ST.LOUIS
M	J.Frazier	M	D.Ozark	M	C.Tanner	M	J.McNamara	M	J.Altobelli	M	V.Rapp
M	J.Torre	1B	R.Hebner	1B	B.Robinson	M	B.Skinner	1B	W.McCovey	1B	K.Hernandez
1B	J.Milner	2B	T.Sizemore	2B	R.Stennett	M	A.Dark	2B	R.Andrews	2B	M.Tyson
2B	F.Millan	SS	L.Bowa	SS	F.Taveras	1B	M.Ivie	SS	T.Foli	SS	G.Templeton
SS	B.Harrelson	3B	M.Schmidt	3B	P.Garner	2B	M.Champion	3B	B.Madlock	3B	K.Reitz
3B	L.Randle	LF	G.Luzinski	LF	A.Oliver	SS	B.Almon	LF	G.Thomasson	LF	L.Brock
LF	S.Henderson	CF	G.Maddox	CF	O.Moreno	3B	T.Ashford	CF	D.Thomas	CF	J.Mumphrey
CF	L.Mazzilli	RF	J.Johnstone	RF	D.Parker	LF	G.Richards	RF	J.Clark	RF	H.Cruz
RF	M.Vail	C	B.Boone	C	D.Dyer	CF	G.Hendrick	C	M.Hill	C	T.Simmons
C	J.Stearns					RF	D.Winfield				
		1	T.Hutton	C	E.Ott	C	G.Tenace	O1	D.Evans	O	T.Scott
O1	E.Kranepool	O	J.Martin					O	T.Whitfield		
O	B.Boisclair	O	B.McBride	P	J.Candelaria	O	M.Rettenmund			P	E.Rasmussen
S2	D.Flynn			P	J.Reuss	O	J.Turner	P	E.Halicki	P	B.Forsch
O1	D.Kingman			P	J.Rooker			P	J.Barr	P	J.Denny
		P	S.Carlton	P	B.Kison	P	B.Shirley	P	B.Knepper	P	J.Urrea
		P	L.Christenson	RP	R.Gossage	P	B.Owchinko	P	J.Montefusco	RP	B.Metzger
P	J.Koosman	P	R.Lerch	RP	K.Tekulve	RP	T.Griffin	RP	C.Williams	RP	C.Carroll
P	N.Espinosa	P	J.Kaat	RP	G.Jackson	P	R.Jones	RP	G.Lavelle	RP	A.Hrabosky
P	J.Matlack	P	J.Lonborg			P	D.Freisleben	RP	D.Heaverlo		
P	C.Swan	RP	R.Reed			RP	R.Fingers				
P	P.Zachry	RP	G.Garber	P	L.Demery	RP	D.Spillner	P	R.Moffitt	P	T.Underwood
RP	S.Lockwood	RP	T.McGraw	P	T.Forster	RP	R.Sawyer	P	L.McGlothen	P	B.Schultz
RP	B.Myrick							P	J.Curtis	P	R.Eastwick
RP	B.Apodaca	P	W.Brusstar			P	D.Tomlin				
						P	D.Wehrmeister				
P	T.Seaver										
P	J.Todd										
P	R.Baldwin										

TEAM	G	W	L	PCT	GB	R	OR	AB	H	2B	3B	HR	BB	SO	AVG	OBP	SLG	PRO	PRO+	BR	/A	PF	CHI	RC	SB	CS	SBA	SBR
EAST																												
PHI	162	101	61	.623		847	668	5546	1548	266	56	186	573	806	.279	.351	.448	.799	114	143	105	104	98	865	135	68	67	0
PIT	162	96	66	.593	5	734	665	5662	1550	278	57	133	474	878	.274	.334	.413	.747	102	37	17	103	98	776	260	120	68	6
STL	162	83	79	.512	18	737	688	5527	1490	252	56	96	489	823	.270	.332	.388	.720	100	-13	-1	98	107	690	134	112	54	-27
CHI	162	81	81	.500	20	692	739	5604	1489	271	37	111	534	796	.266	.333	.387	.720	88	-11	-90	111	98	709	64	45	59	-8
MON	162	75	87	.463	26	665	736	5675	1474	294	50	138	478	877	.260	.320	.402	.722	101	-20	0	97	95	715	88	50	64	-4
NY	162	64	98	.395	37	587	663	5410	1319	227	30	88	529	887	.244	.315	.346	.661	87	-125	-99	95	103	577	98	81	55	-19
WEST																												
LA	162	98	64	.605		769	582	5589	1484	223	28	191	588	896	.266	.338	.418	.756	109	58	62	100	98	794	114	62	65	-3
CIN	162	88	74	.543	10	802	725	5524	1513	269	42	181	600	911	.274	.348	.436	.784	113	115	100	102	97	847	170	64	73	13
HOU	162	81	81	.500	17	680	650	5530	1405	263	60	114	515	839	.254	.322	.385	.707	104	-41	-18	91	102	697	187	72	72	13
SF	162	75	87	.463	23	673	711	5497	1392	227	41	134	568	842	.253	.326	.383	.709	95	-35	-32	100	100	683	90	59	60	-8
SD	162	69	93	.426	29	692	834	5602	1397	245	49	120	602	1057	.249	.325	.375	.700	104	-49	21	90	102	700	133	57	70	6
ATL	162	61	101	.377	37	678	895	5534	1404	218	20	139	537	876	.254	.322	.376	.698	82	-58	-136	112	104	660	82	53	61	-7
TOT	972					8556		66700	17465	3033	526	1631	6487	10488	.262	.330	.396	.727							1555	843	65	-39

TEAM	CG	SH	SV	IP	H	H/G	HR	BB	SO	RAT	ERA	ERA+	OAV	OOB	PR	/A	PF	CPI	FA	E	DP	FW	PW	BW	SBW	DIF
EAST																										
PHI	31	7	47	1455²	1451	9.0	134	482	856	12.1	3.71	108	.263	.325	32	47	102	103	.981	120	168	1.3	4.8	10.6	.3	3.0
PIT	25	15	39	1481²	1406	8.5	149	485	890	11.6	3.61	110	.252	.314	50	62	102	99	.977	145	137	-.0	6.3	1.7	.9	6.1
STL	26	10	31	1446	1420	8.8	139	532	768	12.3	3.81	101	.260	.329	16	6	98	102	.978	139	174	.3	.6	-.1	-2.4	3.6
CHI	16	10	44	1468	1500	9.2	128	489	942	12.3	4.01	109	.266	.327	-16	61	112	96	.977	153	147	-.5	6.2	-9.1	-.5	3.9
MON	31	11	33	1481	1426	8.7	135	579	856	12.3	4.01	95	.255	.327	-17	-34	97	94	.980	129	128	.8	-3.4	.0	-.0	-3.3
NY	27	12	28	1433²	1378	8.7	118	490	911	11.9	3.77	99	.254	.319	22	-6	96	94	.978	134	132	.5	-.6	-10.0	-1.6	-5.3
WEST																										
LA	34	13	39	1475¹	1393	8.5	119	438	930	11.3	3.22	119	.251	.309	113	99	98	104	.981	124	160	1.1	10.0	6.3	.0	-.4
CIN	33	12	32	1437¹	1469	9.2	156	544	868	12.8	4.21	93	.267	.337	-49	-46	101	100	.984	95	154	2.7	-4.7	10.1	1.6	-2.8
HOU	37	11	28	1465²	1384	8.5	110	546	871	12.0	3.54	101	.251	.321	61	5	91	99	.978	142	136	.0	.5	1.8	1.6	-4.1
SF	27	10	33	1459	1501	9.3	114	529	854	12.7	3.75	104	.267	.333	26	26	100	104	.972	179	136	-2.0	2.6	-3.2	-.5	-2.9
SD	6	5	44	1466¹	1556	9.6	160	673	827	13.8	4.43	80	.276	.355	-85	-146	91	105	.971	189	142	-2.5	-14.8	2.1	.9	2.2
ATL	28	5	31	1445¹	1581	9.8	169	701	915	14.5	4.85	92	.279	.363	-151	-65	114	101	.972	175	127	-1.7	-6.6	-13.8	-.4	2.5
TOT	321	121	429	17515		9.0				12.5	3.91		.262	.330					.977	1724	1741					

Runs		Hits		Doubles		Triples		Home Runs		Total Bases	
Foster-Cin	124	Parker-Pit	215	Parker-Pit	44	Templeton-StL	18	Foster-Cin	52	Foster-Cin	388
Griffey-Cin	117	Rose-Cin	204	Cash-Mon	42	Schmidt-Phi	11	Burroughs-Atl	41	Parker-Pit	338
Schmidt-Phi	114	Templeton-StL	200	Hernandez-StL	41	Richards-SD	11	Luzinski-Phi	39	Luzinski-Phi	329
Morgan-Cin	113	Foster-Cin	197	Cromartie-Mon	41	Almon-SD	11	Schmidt-Phi	38	Garvey-LA	322
Parker-Pit	107	Garvey-LA	192					Garvey-LA	33	Schmidt-Phi	312

Runs Batted In		Runs Produced		Bases On Balls		Batting Average		On Base Percentage		Slugging Average	
Foster-Cin	149	Foster-Cin	221	Tenace-SD	125	Parker-Pit	.338	Smith-LA	.432	Foster-Cin	.631
Luzinski-Phi	130	Luzinski-Phi	190	Morgan-Cin	117	Templeton-StL	.322	Morgan-Cin	.420	Luzinski-Phi	.594
Garvey-LA	115	Schmidt-Phi	177	Smith-LA	104	Foster-Cin	.320	Tenace-SD	.417	Smith-LA	.576
Burroughs-Atl	114	Parker-Pit	174	Schmidt-Phi	104	Griffey-Cin	.318	Simmons-StL	.410	Schmidt-Phi	.574
		Garvey-LA	173	Cey-LA	93	Simmons-StL	.318	Parker-Pit	.399	Bench-Cin	.540

Production		Adjusted Production		Batter Runs		Adjusted Batter Runs		Clutch Hitting Index		Runs Created	
Foster-Cin	1.017	Smith-LA	168	Foster-Cin	56.0	Foster-Cin	53.6	Watson-Hou	121	Foster-Cin	144
Smith-LA	1.008	Foster-Cin	165	Smith-LA	50.3	Smith-LA	50.9	Cey-LA	116	Luzinski-Phi	132
Luzinski-Phi	.993	Luzinski-Phi	155	Luzinski-Phi	48.6	Luzinski-Phi	43.3	Bench-Cin	114	Parker-Pit	130
Schmidt-Phi	.972	Schmidt-Phi	151	Schmidt-Phi	45.8	Schmidt-Phi	40.5	Robinson-Pit	114	Schmidt-Phi	129
Parker-Pit	.929	Hendrick-SD	148	Parker-Pit	42.0	Parker-Pit	38.7	Evans-SF	114	Smith-LA	129

Total Average		Stolen Bases		Stolen Base Average		Stolen Base Runs		Fielding Runs		Total Player Rating	
Smith-LA	1.121	Taveras-Pit	70	Bowa-Phi	91.4	Taveras-Pit	10.2	DeJesus-Chi	35.8	Schmidt-Phi	6.7
Morgan-Cin	1.054	Cedeno-Hou	61	McBride-StL-Phi	83.7	Cedeno-Hou	9.9	Parker-Pit	32.5	Foster-Cin	6.1
Schmidt-Phi	1.046	Richards-SD	56	Morgan-Cin	83.1	Richards-SD	9.6	Trillo-Chi	30.1	Parker-Pit	5.8
Luzinski-Phi	1.043	Moreno-Pit	53	Richards-SD	82.4	Morgan-Cin	8.7	Schmidt-Phi	28.8	Hendrick-SD	3.8
Foster-Cin	1.039	Morgan-Cin	49	Cedeno-Hou	81.3	Bowa-Phi	7.8	Tyson-StL	22.0	Smith-LA	3.7

Wins		Win Percentage		Games		Complete Games		Shutouts		Saves	
Carlton-Phi	23	Candelaria-Pit	.800	Fingers-SD	78	Niekro-Atl	20	Seaver-NY-Cin	7	Fingers-SD	35
Seaver-NY-Cin	21	Seaver-NY-Cin	.778	Tomlin-SD	76	Seaver-NY-Cin	19	Rogers-Mon	4	Sutter-Chi	31
		Christenson-Phi	.760	Spillner-SD	76	Rogers-Mon	17	R.Reuschel-Chi	4	Gossage-Pit	26
		John-LA	.741	Metzger-SD-StL	75	Carlton-Phi	17			Hough-LA	22
		Forsch-StL	.741			Richard-Hou	13				

Innings Pitched		Fewest Hits/Game		Fewest BB/Game		Strikeouts		Strikeouts/Game		Ratio	
Niekro-Atl	330.1	Seaver-NY-Cin	6.85	Candelaria-Pit	1.95	Niekro-Atl	262	Koosman-NY	7.62	Seaver-NY-Cin	9.13
Rogers-Mon	301.2	Richard-Hou	7.15	John-LA	2.04	Richard-Hou	214	Richard-Hou	7.21	Candelaria-Pit	9.72
Carlton-Phi	283.0	Carlton-Phi	7.28	Rau-LA	2.08	Rogers-Mon	206	Niekro-Atl	7.14	Hooton-LA	9.95
Richard-Hou	267.0	Hooton-LA	7.41	Barr-SF	2.15	Carlton-Phi	198	Seaver-NY-Cin	6.75	Carlton-Phi	10.24
Seaver-NY-Cin	261.1	Candelaria-Pit	7.69	Lemongello-Hou	2.18	Seaver-NY-Cin	196	Matlack-NY	6.55	Sutton-LA	10.45

Earned Run Average		Adjusted ERA		Opponents' Batting Avg.		Opponents' On Base Pct.		Starter Runs		Adjusted Starter Runs	
Candelaria-Pit	2.34	Candelaria-Pit	170	Seaver-NY-Cin	.209	Seaver-NY-Cin	.260	Candelaria-Pit	40.2	R.Reuschel-Chi	44.8
Seaver-NY-Cin	2.58	R.Reuschel-Chi	157	Richard-Hou	.218	Candelaria-Pit	.276	Carlton-Phi	39.9	Carlton-Phi	42.7
Hooton-LA	2.62	Carlton-Phi	151	Carlton-Phi	.223	Hooton-LA	.281	Seaver-NY-Cin	38.5	Candelaria-Pit	42.1
Carlton-Phi	2.64	Seaver-NY-Cin	149	Hooton-LA	.225	Carlton-Phi	.287	Hooton-LA	32.0	Seaver-NY-Cin	37.0
John-LA	2.78	Hooton-LA	146	Koosman-NY	.232	Sutton-LA	.291	R.Reuschel-Chi	31.4	Hooton-LA	29.9

Clutch Pitching Index		Relief Runs		Adjusted Relief Runs		Relief Ranking		Total Pitcher Index		Total Baseball Ranking	
Candelaria-Pit	126	Gossage-Pit	33.8	Sutter-Chi	36.3	Gossage-Pit	61.1	Gossage-Pit	6.4	Schmidt-Phi	6.7
John-LA	120	Sutter-Chi	30.6	Gossage-Pit	34.9	Sutter-Chi	51.8	Carlton-Phi	6.0	Gossage-Pit	6.2
Rooker-Pit	118	Lavelle-SF	24.4	Lavelle-SF	24.4	Lavelle-SF	34.4	R.Reuschel-Chi	5.8	Foster-Cin	6.1
Lemongello-Hou	116	Garber-Phi	17.9	Garber-Phi	18.9	Garber-Phi	30.2	Sutter-Chi	5.6	Carlton-Phi	6.0
Rau-LA	114	Reed-Phi	16.0	Reed-Phi	17.2	W.Hernandez-Chi	21.6	Candelaria-Pit	4.7	R.Reuschel-Chi	5.8

January 4 Mary Shane is hired by the Chicago White Sox as the first woman TV play-by-play announcer.

March 21 Mark Fidrych, the 1976 Rookie of the Year, rips the cartilage in his left knee and will undergo surgery ten days later. The injury will effectively end the fabled career of the Bird.

March 28 The Rangers' Lenny Randle, angry for having been benched during spring training, attacks 50-year-old manager Frank Lucchesi, sending him to the hospital with a shattered cheekbone. Lucchesi helped precipitate the incident by calling the good-natured Randle "a punk." Randle's days in Texas are numbered.

April 6 The Seattle Mariners make their debut, losing to Frank Tanana and the Angels, 7–0.

April 7 Al Woods hits a pinch home run in his first major league at bat and the Toronto Blue Jays make a successful debut in a 9-5 win over the White Sox at Exhibition Stadium.

May 14 Jim Colborn hurls a no-hit game as Kansas City beats Texas, 6–0.

May 30 Twenty-two-year-old Dennis Eckersley fires a no-hitter as the Indians top the Angels, 1-0.

June 7 The White Sox select Harold Baines with the No. 1 pick in the draft. Bill Veeck had first seen Baines play Little League ball and had followed his career.

June 8 Nolan Ryan notches his fourth career 19-strikeout game, hurling the first 10 innings of a game against Toronto.

July 4 The Red Sox wallop a major league-record eight home runs, including seven solo shots, in beating Toronto, 9–6, at Fenway. Four home runs come in the eighth inning.

July 24 Seattle's John Montague pitches 6⅓ innings of perfect relief against California, giving him 33 consecutive batsmen retired over two games to tie the AL record.

September 9 In the second game of a doubleheader at Fenway Park in Boston, Tigers rookies Lou Whitaker and Alan Trammell debut together. They will hold down the second base and shortstop jobs in Detroit for a record 19 years.

September 16 Seattle beats Kansas City 4–1 to end the Royals' winning streak at 16 games—the longest in the majors in 24 years.

September 18 Boston's Ted Cox goes 4-for-4 in his first major league game, a 10–4 win over the Orioles to spoil Brooks Robinson Night in Baltimore. Cox will get two more hits the following day against the Yankees, setting a major league record for consecutive hits at the start of a career.

October 9 For the second year in succession, the Yanks score in the ninth inning of the fifth game to beat the Royals in the ALCS. Mickey Rivers gets the game-winning hit.

October 11 The Yankees win the opening game of the World Series 4-3 in 12 innings as Willie Randolph doubles and scores the winning run on a single by Paul Blair.

October 18 Reggie Jackson becomes "Mr. October." Three homers in three swings lead the Yankees to an 8-4, Series-clinching victory.

BALTIMORE	BOSTON	CALIFORNIA	CHICAGO	CLEVELAND	DETROIT	KANSAS CITY
M E.Weaver	M D.Zimmer	M N.Sherry	M B.Lemon	M F.Robinson	M R.Houk	M W.Herzog
1B L.May	1B G.Scott	M D.Garcia	1B J.Spencer	M J.Torborg	1B J.Thompson	1B J.Mayberry
2B B.Smith	2B D.Doyle	1B T.Solaita	2B J.Orta	1B A.Thornton	2B T.Fuentes	2B F.White
SS M.Belanger	SS R.Burleson	2B J.Remy	SS A.Bannister	2B D.Kuiper	SS T.Veryzer	SS F.Patek
3B D.DeCinces	3B B.Hobson	SS R.Mulliniks	3B E.Soderholm	SS F.Duffy	3B A.Rodriguez	3B G.Brett
LF P.Kelly	LF C.Yastrzemski	3B D.Chalk	LF R.Garr	3B B.Bell	LF S.Kemp	LF T.Poquette
CF A.Bumbry	CF F.Lynn	LF J.Rudi	CF C.Lemon	LF B.Bochte	CF R.LeFlore	CF A.Otis
RF K.Singleton	RF R.Miller	CF G.Flores	RF R.Zisk	CF J.Norris	RF B.Oglivie	RF A.Cowens
C R.Dempsey	C C.Fisk	RF B.Bonds	C J.Essian	RF P.Dade	C M.May	C D.Porter
DH E.Murray	DH J.Rice	C T.Humphrey	DH O.Gamble	C F.Kendall	DH R.Staub	DH H.McRae
	DH D.Baylor			DH R.Carty		
1O T.Muser	O D.Evans		D1 L.Johnson		3 P.Mankowski	O J.Zdeb
2 R.Dauer	O B.Carbo	13 R.Jackson		S3 L.Blanks	O M.Stanley	1D P.LaCock
O A.Mora		SD M.Guerrero	O R.Manning			
C D.Skaggs	P F.Jenkins	O T.Bosley	P S.Stone	C R.Fosse	P D.Rozema	P D.Leonard
	P R.Cleveland		P K.Kravec	O R.Pruitt	P F.Arroyo	P J.Colborn
P J.Palmer	P L.Tiant	P N.Ryan	P C.Knapp		P B.Sykes	P P.Splittorff
P R.May	P B.Stanley	P F.Tanana	P W.Wood	P W.Garland	P D.Roberts	P A.Hassler
P M.Flanagan	P R.Wise	P P.Hartzell	RP L.LaGrow	P D.Eckersley	P J.Crawford	P M.Pattin
P R.Grimsley	RP B.Campbell	P K.Brett	RP D.Hamilton	P J.Bibby	RP J.Hiller	RP D.Bird
P D.Martinez	RP J.Willoughby	P W.Simpson		P R.Waits	RP S.Foucault	RP L.Gura
RP T.Martinez		RP D.Miller	P B.Johnson	P A.Fitzmorris	RP S.Grilli	RP M.Littell
	P B.Lee	RP D.LaRoche	P K.Brett	RP D.Hood		
P S.McGregor	P M.Paxton	RP M.Barlow	/P S.Renko	RP J.Kern	P M.Wilcox	P S.Mingori
	P D.Aase				P M.Fidrych	
	P G.Ross		P P.Dobson		P V.Ruhle	

MILWAUKEE	MINNESOTA	NEW YORK	OAKLAND	SEATTLE	TEXAS	TORONTO
M A.Grammas	M G.Mauch	M B.Martin	M J.McKeon	M D.Johnson	M F.Lucchesi	M R.Hartsfield
1B C.Cooper	1B R.Carew	1B C.Chambliss	M B.Winkles	1B D.Meyer	M E.Stanky	1B D.Ault
2B D.Money	2B B.Randall	2B W.Randolph	1B D.Allen	2B J.Baez	M C.Ryan	2B S.Staggs
SS R.Yount	SS R.Smalley	SS B.Dent	2B M.Perez	SS C.Reynolds	M B.Hunter	SS H.Torres
3B S.Bando	3B M.Cubbage	3B G.Nettles	SS R.Picciolo	3B B.Stein	1B M.Hargrove	3B R.Howell
LF J.Wohlford	LF L.Hisle	LF R.White	3B W.Gross	LF S.Braun	2B B.Wills	LF A.Woods
CF V.Joshua	CF L.Bostock	CF M.Rivers	LF M.Page	CF Ru.Jones	SS B.Campaneris	CF B.Bailor
RF S.Lezcano	RF D.Ford	RF R.Jackson	CF T.Armas	RF L.Stanton	3B T.Harrah	RF O.Velez
C C.Moore	C B.Wynegar	C T.Munson	RF J.Tyrone	C B.Stinson	LF C.Washington	C A.Ashby
DH J.Quirk	DH C.Kusick	DH C.May	C J.Newman	DH J.Bernhardt	CF J.Beniquez	DH R.Fairly
			DH M.Sanguillen		RF D.May	
O S.Brye	DO R.Chiles	OD L.Piniella		OD D.Collins	C J.Sundberg	OD S.Ewing
	DO G.Adams		2S R.Scott	O C.Lopez	DH W.Horton	3D D.Rader
P J.Slaton	32 J.Terrell	DC E.Williams		2S L.Milbourne		23 D.McKay
P J.Augustine		1O M.Jorgensen			O K.Henderson	O J.Scott
P M.Haas	P D.Goltz	P E.Figueroa	P V.Blue	P G.Abbott	OD T.Grieve	O G.Woods
P E.Rodriguez	P P.Thormodsgard	P M.Torrez	P R.Langford	P J.Montague		
P L.Sorensen	P G.Zahn	P R.Guidry	P D.Medich	P D.Pole	P G.Perry	P D.Lemanczyk
RP S.Hinds	P P.Redfern	P D.Gullett	RP J.Coleman	RP E.Romo	P D.Alexander	P J.Garvin
RP B.McClure	RP T.Johnson	P D.Tidrow	RP B.Lacey	RP D.Segui	P B.Blyleven	P J.Jefferson
RP B.Castro	RP R.Schueler	RP S.Lyle		RP M.Kekich	P D.Ellis	RP P.Vuckovich
	RP T.Burgmeier	RP K.Clay	RP P.Torrealba		P N.Briles	RP M.Willis
		P C.Hunter			RP A.Devine	P J.Johnson
		K.Holtzman		P T.House	RP D.Knowles	
P B.Travers			P D.Bair	P G.Wheelock	RP P.Lindblad	
P M.Caldwell	P D.Johnson		P M.Norris	P B.Laxton		P J.Byrd
P G.Beare			P D.Giusti	P D.Pagan		P J.Clancy
				P S.Thomas	P R.Moret	P B.Singer
						P T.Murphy

TEAM	G	W	L	PCT	GB	R	OR	AB	H	2B	3B	HR	BB	SO	AVG	OBP	SLG	PRO	PRO+	BR	/A	PF	CHI	RC	SB	CS	SBA	SBR
EAST																												
NY	162	100	62	.617		831	**651**	5605	1576	267	47	184	533	681	.281	.347	.444	.791	**115**	104	**113**	99	98	853	93	57	62	-6
BAL	161	97	64	.602	2.5	719	653	5494	1433	231	25	148	560	945	.261	.332	.393	.725	103	-23	21	94	102	711	90	51	64	-4
BOS	161	97	64	.602	2.5	859	712	5510	1551	258	56	**213**	528	905	.281	.349	**.465**	**.814**	107	**144**	43	112	98	**875**	66	47	58	-8
DET	162	74	88	.457	26	714	751	5604	1480	228	45	166	452	764	.264	.321	.410	.731	93	-25	-62	105	101	717	60	46	57	-10
CLE	161	71	90	.441	28.5	676	739	5491	1476	221	46	100	531	688	.269	.337	.380	.717	98	-31	-9	97	96	682	87	87	50	-26
MIL	162	67	95	.414	33	639	765	5517	1425	255	46	125	443	862	.258	.316	.389	.705	91	-73	-72	100	99	660	85	67	56	-15
TOR	161	54	107	.335	45.5	605	822	5418	1367	230	41	100	449	819	.252	.318	.365	.683	85	-106	-115	112	99	610	65	55	54	-14
WEST																												
KC	162	102	60	.630		822	**651**	5594	1549	**299**	**77**	146	522	687	.277	.343	.436	.779	110	82	75	101	100	835	170	87	**66**	**-1**
TEX	162	94	68	.580	8	767	657	5541	1497	265	39	135	**596**	904	.270	.345	.405	.750	103	34	26	101	98	780	154	85	64	-5
CHI	162	90	72	.556	12	844	771	5633	1568	254	52	192	559	**666**	.278	.347	.444	.791	114	107	109	100	99	858	42	44	49	-14
MIN	161	84	77	.522	17.5	**867**	776	5639	**1588**	273	60	123	563	754	**.282**	**.351**	.417	.768	110	71	83	99	105	827	105	65	62	-8
CAL	162	74	88	.457	28	675	695	5410	1380	233	40	131	542	880	.255	.327	.386	.713	97	-47	-20	96	100	681	159	89	64	-6
SEA	162	64	98	.395	38	624	855	5460	1398	218	33	133	426	769	.256	.314	.381	.695	89	-91	-85	99	100	643	110	67	62	-7
OAK	161	63	98	.391	38.5	605	749	5358	1284	176	37	117	516	910	.240	.311	.352	.663	81	-145	-137	99	**107**	589	**176**	89	**66**	**-1**
TOT	1131					10247		77274	20572	3408	644	2013	7270	11234	.266	.333	.405	.738							1462	936	61	-123

TEAM	CG	SH	SV	IP	H	H/G	HR	BB	SO	RAT	ERA	ERA+	OAV	OOB	PR	/A	PF	CPI	FA	E	DP	FW	PW	BW	SBW	DIF
EAST																										
NY	52	16	34	1449¹	1395	8.7	139	486	758	11.8	3.61	109	.254	.318	73	54	97	101	.979	132	151	.6	5.4	**11.2**	.3	1.5
BAL	**65**	11	23	1451	1414	8.8	124	494	737	12.0	3.74	101	.260	.325	51	8	93	101	**.983**	106	**189**	**2.0**	.8	2.1	.5	11.1
BOS	40	13	40	1428	1555	9.8	158	**378**	758	12.3	4.11	109	.278	.327	-8	60	111	102	.978	133	162	.5	6.0	4.3	.0	5.7
DET	44	3	23	1457	1526	9.4	162	470	784	12.5	4.13	104	.271	.329	-11	26	106	100	.978	142	153	.0	2.6	-6.2	-.1	-3.3
CLE	45	8	30	1452¹	1441	8.9	136	550	876	12.5	4.10	96	.261	.331	-6	-25	97	96	.979	130	145	.7	-2.5	-.9	-1.7	-5.1
MIL	38	6	25	1431	1461	9.2	136	566	719	13.0	4.32	94	.268	.341	-42	-40	100	97	.978	139	165	.2	-4.0	-7.2	-.6	-2.5
TOR	40	3	20	1428¹	1538	9.7	152	623	771	13.7	4.57	92	.278	.354	-81	-59	103	101	.974	164	133	-1.2	-5.9	-11.4	-.5	-7.4
WEST																										
KC	41	15	**42**	1460²	**1377**	8.5	110	499	850	11.8	**3.52**	**115**	.251	.318	88	84	99	98	.978	137	145	.3	**8.3**	7.5	**.8**	4.1
TEX	49	**17**	31	1472¹	1412	8.6	134	471	864	**11.7**	3.56	114	.255	**.317**	81	84	101	101	.982	117	156	1.5	**8.3**	2.6	.4	.2
CHI	34	3	40	1444²	1557	9.7	136	516	842	13.2	4.25	96	.277	.342	-31	-27	101	101	.974	159	125	-.9	-2.7	10.8	-.5	2.3
MIN	35	4	25	1442	1546	9.6	151	507	737	13.1	4.36	91	.278	.342	-48	-60	98	101	.978	143	184	-.0	-6.0	8.2	.0	1.2
CAL	53	13	26	1437²	1383	8.7	136	572	**965**	12.5	3.72	105	.256	.336	54	31	96	**105**	.976	147	137	-.2	3.1	-2.0	.3	-8.1
SEA	18	1	31	1433	1508	9.5	194	578	785	13.5	4.83	85	.272	.347	-123	-114	101	96	.976	147	162	-.2	-11.3	-8.4	.2	2.8
OAK	32	4	26	1436²	1459	9.1	145	560	788	12.8	4.04	100	.265	.336	3	-3	99	102	.970	190	136	-2.7	-.3	-13.6	.8	-1.6
TOT	586	117	416	20224		9.2				12.6	4.06		.266	.333					.977	1986	2143					

Runs		Hits		Doubles		Triples		Home Runs		Total Bases	
Carew-Min	128	Carew-Min	239	McRae-KC	54	Carew-Min	16	Rice-Bos	39	Rice-Bos	382
Fisk-Bos	106	LeFlore-Det	212	Jackson-NY	39	Rice-Bos	15	Nettles-NY	37	Carew-Min	351
Brett-KC	105	Rice-Bos	206	Lemon-Chi	38	Cowens-KC	14	Bonds-Cal	37	McRae-KC	330
		Bostock-Min	199	Carew-Min	38	Brett-KC	13	Scott-Bos	33	Cowens-KC	318
		Burleson-Bos	194			Bostock-Min	12	Jackson-NY	32	LeFlore-Det	310

Runs Batted In		Runs Produced		Bases On Balls		Batting Average		On Base Percentage		Slugging Average	
Hisle-Min	119	Carew-Min	214	Harrah-Tex	109	Carew-Min	.388	Carew-Min	.452	Rice-Bos	.593
Bonds-Cal	115	Cowens-KC	187	Singleton-Bal	107	Bostock-Min	.336	Singleton-Bal	.442	Carew-Min	.570
Rice-Bos	114	Hisle-Min	186	Hargrove-Tex	103	Singleton-Bal	.328	Hargrove-Tex	.424	Jackson-NY	.550
Hobson-Bos	112	Fisk-Bos	182	Gross-Oak	86	Rivers-NY	.326	Fisk-Bos	.408	Hisle-Min	.533
Cowens-KC	112	Bonds-Cal	181	Mayberry-KC	83	LeFlore-Det	.325	Page-Oak	.407	Brett-KC	.532

Production		Adjusted Production		Batter Runs		Adjusted Batter Runs		Clutch Hitting Index		Runs Created	
Carew-Min	1.022	Carew-Min	179	Carew-Min	67.0	Carew-Min	69.3	Wynegar-Min	130	Carew-Min	160
Rice-Bos	.972	Singleton-Bal	168	Rice-Bos	51.4	Singleton-Bal	56.5	Doyle-Bos	128	Rice-Bos	136
Singleton-Bal	.949	Page-Oak	153	Singleton-Bal	48.5	Page-Oak	39.0	Sundberg-Tex	128	Singleton-Bal	124
Fisk-Bos	.929	Jackson-NY	151	Fisk-Bos	39.9	Bostock-Min	37.6	Carty-Cle	123	McRae-KC	119
Page-Oak	.928	Thornton-Cle	149	Hargrove-Tex	37.8	Jackson-NY	36.8	Staub-Det	116	Page-Oak	117

Total Average		Stolen Bases		Stolen Base Average		Stolen Base Runs		Fielding Runs		Total Player Rating	
Carew-Min	1.093	Patek-KC	53	Page-Oak	89.4	Page-Oak	9.6	Lemon-Chi	34.9	Carew-Min	6.3
Page-Oak	1.064	Page-Oak	42	Jackson-NY	85.0	Patek-KC	8.1	Sundberg-Tex	22.9	Singleton-Bal	4.9
Singleton-Bal	1.011	Remy-Cal	41	Harrah-Tex	84.4	Harrah-Tex	5.1	R.Jones-Sea	22.0	Page-Oak	4.9
Jackson-NY	.997	Bonds-Cal	41	White-KC	82.1	White-KC	3.9	Belanger-Bal	20.7	Brett-KC	4.4
Harrah-Tex	.964	LeFlore-Det	39	Patek-KC	80.3			Smalley-Min	18.7	Lemon-Chi	4.0

Wins		Win Percentage		Games		Complete Games		Shutouts		Saves	
Palmer-Bal	20	Splittorff-KC	.727	Lyle-NY	72	Ryan-Cal	22	Tanana-Cal	7	Campbell-Bos	31
Leonard-KC	20	T.Johnson-Min	.696	T.Johnson-Min	71	Palmer-Bal	22	Leonard-KC	5	Lyle-NY	26
Goltz-Min	20	Guidry-NY	.696	Campbell-Bos	69	Leonard-KC	21	Guidry-NY	5	LaGrow-Chi	25
Ryan-Cal	19	Rozema-Det	.682	McClure-Mil	68	Garland-Cle	21	Blyleven-Tex	5	Kern-Cle	18
				LaGrow-Chi	66	Tanana-Cal	20			LaRoche-Cle-Cal	17

Innings Pitched		Fewest Hits/Game		Fewest BB/Game		Strikeouts		Strikeouts/Game		Ratio	
Palmer-Bal	319.0	Ryan-Cal	5.96	Rozema-Det	1.40	Ryan-Cal	341	Ryan-Cal	10.26	Blyleven-Tex	9.86
Goltz-Min	303.0	Blyleven-Tex	6.94	Jenkins-Bos	1.68	Leonard-KC	244	Tanana-Cal	7.65	Eckersley-Cle	10.01
Ryan-Cal	299.0	Palmer-Bal	7.42	Hartzell-Cal	1.81	Tanana-Cal	205	Guidry-NY	7.52	Guidry-NY	10.21
Leonard-KC	292.2	Guidry-NY	7.43	Eckersley-Cle	1.96	Palmer-Bal	193	Leonard-KC	7.50	Tanana-Cal	10.22
Garland-Cle	282.2	Tanana-Cal	7.50	Cleveland-Bos	2.03	Eckersley-Cle	191	Blyleven-Tex	6.98	Leonard-KC	10.24

Earned Run Average		Adjusted ERA		Opponents' Batting Avg.		Opponents' On Base Pct.		Starter Runs		Adjusted Starter Runs	
Tanana-Cal	2.54	Tanana-Cal	154	Ryan-Cal	.193	Eckersley-Cle	.278	Ryan-Cal	42.8	Ryan-Cal	38.0
Blyleven-Tex	2.72	Blyleven-Tex	150	Blyleven-Tex	.214	Blyleven-Tex	.279	Palmer-Bal	40.8	Tanana-Cal	36.9
Ryan-Cal	2.77	Ryan-Cal	141	Guidry-NY	.224	Guidry-NY	.284	Tanana-Cal	40.8	Blyleven-Tex	35.3
Guidry-NY	2.82	Guidry-NY	140	Tanana-Cal	.227	Leonard-KC	.285	Blyleven-Tex	34.8	Leonard-KC	32.2
Palmer-Bal	2.91	Rozema-Det	139	Leonard-KC	.227	Tanana-Cal	.286	Leonard-KC	33.0	Palmer-Bal	31.3

Clutch Pitching Index		Relief Runs		Adjusted Relief Runs		Relief Ranking		Total Pitcher Index		Total Baseball Ranking	
Slaton-Mil	118	Lyle-NY	28.8	Lyle-NY	27.0	Campbell-Bos	45.6	Lyle-NY	4.4	Carew-Min	6.3
Rozema-Det	116	Torrealba-Oak	18.6	Campbell-Bos	23.8	Lyle-NY	43.4	Ryan-Cal	4.2	Singleton-Bal	4.9
Grimsley-Bal	110	LaGrow-Chi	17.5	Torrealba-Oak	18.1	Romo-Sea	28.1	Campbell-Bos	3.9	Page-Oak	4.9
Splittorff-KC	108	Campbell-Bos	17.1	LaGrow-Chi	17.8	LaGrow-Chi	26.3	Blyleven-Tex	3.8	Brett-KC	4.4
Tanana-Cal	106	Coleman-Oak	15.6	Romo-Sea	16.2	T.Johnson-Min	22.8	Tanana-Cal	3.7	Lyle-NY	4.4

January 25 The Padres trade pitcher Dave Tomlin and an estimated $125,000 in cash to the Rangers for aging pitcher Gaylord Perry. Perry will win the NL Cy Young Award with San Diego in 1978.

January 30 Commissioner Bowie Kuhn voids the Vida Blue deal between the A's and the Reds, suggesting a restructuring of the trade in which the A's and Reds would send Blue to Cincinnati for outfielder Dave Revering and $1.75 million cash.

March 21 The Padres fire manager Alvin Dark, replacing him with pitching coach Roger Craig. Dark joined Phil Cavarretta as managers fired during spring training. Cavarretta was fired by the Cubs in 1954 for being too honest in his assessment of the team's chances in the upcoming season.

April 23 Reds second baseman Joe Morgan commits an error during a 2-1 win over the Giants, ending his major league record streak of 91 consecutive errorless games since July 6, 1977.

May 5 Pete Rose singles off Montreal's Steve Rogers for career hit 3,000. The Expos beat the Reds, 4-3.

June 3 The Phils' Davey Johnson breaks up a 1-1, ninth-inning tie with Los Angeles by hitting his second pinch grand slam of the year. His first came on April 30 when he broke up a fifth-inning tie in San Diego. Johnson is the first major league player to accomplish this feat, but Mike Ivie will duplicate it this month.

June 16 In the 12th major league season of a career speckled with near-misses, Cincinnati's Tom Seaver finally hurls a no-hitter, beating the Cardinals 4-0.

July 11 At San Diego, the NL wins another All-Star Game 7-3. Steve Garvey singles and triples to earn the game's MVP trophy. Vida Blue starts for the NL, the first pitcher to start for both leagues. Blue also started in 1971 and 1975 for the AL.

July 31 Pete Rose singles off Phil Niekro to extend his hitting streak to 44 games, as the Reds edge the Braves 3-2. Rose ties Willie Keeler's 81-year-old league record.

September 14 Jim Bouton, 38, earns a 4-1 win for the Braves over the Giants. It is Bouton's first major league victory since 1970, and the last of his career.

September 30 The Phillies overcome a first inning grand slam by Willie Stargell to beat the Pirates 10-8 and clinch the NL East title.

October 7 The Dodgers win the NLCS 4-3 as Bill Russell's tenth-inning single scores Ron Cey.

October 10 Davey Lopes collects two homers and five RBIs to lead the Dodgers to an 11-5 victory over the Yankees in Game 1 of the World Series.

October 25 Gaylord Perry of the Padres becomes the first pitcher to win the Cy Young Award in both leagues. Perry copped the NL honors with a 21-6 record and a 2.72 ERA.

November 15 The Pirates' Dave Parker wins the NL MVP Award by a count of 320-194 over the Dodgers' Steve Garvey.

ATLANTA		CHICAGO		CINCINNATI		HOUSTON		LOS ANGELES		MONTREAL	
M	B.Cox	M	H.Franks	M	S.Anderson	M	B.Virdon	M	T.Lasorda	M	D.Williams
1B	D.Murphy	1B	B.Buckner	1B	D.Driessen	1B	B.Watson	1B	S.Garvey	1B	T.Perez
2B	J.Royster	2B	M.Trillo	2B	J.Morgan	2B	A.Howe	2B	D.Lopes	2B	D.Cash
SS	D.Chaney	SS	I.DeJesus	SS	D.Concepcion	SS	J.Sexton	SS	B.Russell	SS	C.Speier
3B	B.Horner	3B	S.Ontiveros	3B	P.Rose	3B	E.Cabell	3B	R.Cey	3B	L.Parrish
LF	J.Burroughs	LF	D.Kingman	LF	G.Foster	LF	D.Walling	LF	D.Baker	LF	W.Cromartie
CF	R.Office	CF	G.Gross	CF	C.Geronimo	CF	T.Puhl	CF	B.North	CF	A.Dawson
RF	G.Matthews	RF	B.Murcer	RF	K.Griffey	RF	J.Cruz	RF	R.Smith	RF	E.Valentine
C	B.Pocoroba	C	D.Rader	C	J.Bench	C	L.Pujols	C	S.Yeager	C	G.Carter
1	B.Beall	1O	L.Biittner	O	D.Collins	1O	D.Bergman	O2	L.Lacy	1O	D.Unser
O3	B.Bonnell	O	G.Clines			2S	J.Gonzalez	O	R.Monday		
32	R.Gilbreath	3O	R.Scott	P	T.Seaver	S	R.Landestoy			P	R.Grimsley
C	J.Nolan			P	F.Norman			P	D.Sutton	P	S.Rogers
		P	R.Reuschel	P	T.Hume	P	J.Richard	P	B.Hooton	P	D.Schatzeder
P	P.Niekro	P	D.Lamp	P	P.Moskau	P	M.Lemongello	P	T.John	P	R.May
P	P.Hanna	P	R.Burris	P	B.Bonham	P	J.Niekro	P	D.Rau	P	W.Twitchell
P	M.Mahler	P	D.Roberts	RP	M.Sarmiento	P	T.Dixon	P	R.Rhoden	RP	S.Bahnsen
P	L.McWilliams	P	M.Krukow	RP	D.Bair	P	J.Andujar	RP	C.Hough	RP	D.Knowles
RP	E.Solomon	RP	D.Moore	RP	P.Borbon	P	K.Forsch	RP	T.Forster	RP	M.Garman
RP	G.Garber	RP	B.Sutter			RP	J.Sambito	RP	L.Rautzhan		
RP	J.Easterly	RP	L.McGlothen	P	M.LaCoss					P	H.Dues
				P	D.Tomlin	P	F.Bannister	P	B.Welch	P	W.Fryman
P	D.Ruthven	P	W.Hernandez			P	V.Ruhle			P	S.Sanderson
P	R.Camp	P	W.Fryman								
P	D.Campbell	P	K.Holtzman								
P	A.Devine										
P	C.Skok										
P	T.Boggs										

NEW YORK		PHILADELPHIA		PITTSBURGH		SAN DIEGO		SAN FRANCISCO		ST.LOUIS	
M	J.Torre	M	D.Ozark	M	C.Tanner	M	R.Craig	M	J.Altobelli	M	V.Rapp
1B	W.Montanez	1B	R.Hebner	1B	W.Stargell	1B	G.Tenace	1B	W.McCovey	M	J.Krol
2B	D.Flynn	2B	T.Sizemore	2B	R.Stennett	2B	F.Gonzalez	2B	B.Madlock	M	K.Boyer
SS	T.Foli	SS	L.Bowa	SS	F.Taveras	SS	O.Smith	SS	J.LeMaster	1B	K.Hernandez
3B	L.Randle	3B	M.Schmidt	3B	P.Garner	3B	B.Almon	3B	D.Evans	2B	M.Tyson
LF	S.Henderson	LF	G.Luzinski	LF	B.Robinson	LF	G.Richards	LF	T.Whitfield	SS	G.Templeton
CF	L.Mazzilli	CF	G.Maddox	CF	O.Moreno	CF	D.Winfield	CF	L.Herndon	3B	K.Reitz
RF	E.Maddox	RF	B.McBride	RF	D.Parker	RF	O.Gamble	RF	J.Clark	LF	L.Brock
C	J.Stearns	C	B.Boone	C	E.Ott	C	R.Sweet	C	M.Hill	CF	G.Hendrick
										RF	J.Morales
O	B.Boisclair	O	J.Martin	O1	J.Milner	O2	D.Thomas	1O	M.Ivie	C	T.Simmons
O2	J.Youngblood	1O	J.Cardenal	1C	M.Sanguillen	O	J.Turner	S	R.Metzger	O	J.Mumphrey
						1	B.Perkins			O	T.Scott
P	J.Koosman	P	S.Carlton	P	B.Blyleven			P	B.Knepper		
P	C.Swan	P	L.Christenson	P	D.Robinson	P	G.Perry	P	V.Blue	P	B.Forsch
P	N.Espinosa	P	R.Lerch	P	J.Candelaria	P	R.Jones	P	J.Montefusco	P	J.Denny
P	P.Zachry	P	D.Ruthven	P	J.Rooker	P	B.Owchinko	P	E.Halicki	P	P.Vuckovich
P	M.Bruhert	P	J.Kaat	P	J.Bibby	P	B.Shirley	P	J.Barr	P	S.Martinez
RP	S.Lockwood	RP	R.Reed	RP	K.Tekulve	P	E.Rasmussen	RP	G.Lavelle	P	J.Urrea
RP	D.Murray	RP	T.McGraw	RP	G.Jackson	RP	R.Fingers	RP	R.Moffitt	RP	M.Littell
RP	D.Bernard	RP	W.Brusstar	RP	E.Whitson	RP	J.D'Acquisto	RP	J.Curtis	RP	B.Schultz
						RP	M.Lee			RP	A.Lopez
P	K.Kobel	P	J.Lonborg	P	B.Kison						
P	T.Hausman			P	J.Reuss					P	P.Falcone
										P	E.Rasmussen
										P	T.Bruno

TEAM	G	W	L	PCT	GB	R	OR	AB	H	2B	3B	HR	BB	SO	AVG	OBP	SLG	PRO	PRO+	BR	/A	PF	CHI	RC	SB	CS	SBA	SBR
EAST																												
PHI	162	90	72	.556		708	586	5448	1404	248	32	133	552	866	.258	.331	.388	.719	106	49	43	101	101	715	152	58	72	11
PIT	161	88	73	.547	1.5	684	637	5406	1390	239	**54**	115	480	874	.257	.323	.385	.708	100	21	-9	105	104	676	**213**	90	70	10
CHI	162	79	83	.488	11	664	724	5532	**1461**	224	48	72	562	746	**.264**	.334	.361	.695	90	11	-70	112	99	673	110	58	65	-2
MON	162	76	86	.469	14	633	611	5530	1404	269	31	121	396	881	.254	.308	.379	.687	98	-27	-20	99	103	629	80	42	66	-1
STL	162	69	93	.426	21	600	657	5415	1351	263	44	79	420	**713**	.249	.306	.358	.664	92	-66	-58	99	**106**	583	97	42	70	4
NY	162	66	96	.407	24	607	690	5433	1332	227	47	86	549	829	.245	.317	.352	.669	96	-47	-25	96	101	600	100	77	56	-16
WEST																												
LA	162	95	67	.586		**727**	**573**	5437	1435	251	27	**149**	610	818	**.264**	**.340**	**.402**	**.742**	114	98	101	100	96	**763**	137	52	72	10
CIN	161	92	69	.571	2.5	710	688	5392	1378	**270**	32	136	**636**	899	.256	.337	.393	.730	110	75	75	100	97	730	137	58	70	6
SF	162	89	73	.549	6	613	594	5364	1331	240	41	117	554	814	.248	.320	.374	.694	104	1	24	96	95	647	87	54	62	-6
SD	162	84	78	.519	11	591	598	5360	1349	208	42	75	536	848	.252	.323	.348	.671	102	-37	10	92	98	624	152	70	68	4
HOU	162	74	88	.457	21	605	634	5458	1408	231	45	70	434	743	.258	.315	.355	.670	101	-49	-5	93	103	608	178	59	**75**	18
ATL	162	69	93	.426	26	600	750	5381	1313	191	39	123	550	874	.244	.317	.363	.680	86	-28	-97	111	98	608	90	65	58	-12
TOT	971					7742		65156	16556	2861	482	1276	6279	9905	.254	.323	.372	.694							1533	725	68	25

TEAM	CG	SH	SV	IP	H	H/G	HR	BB	SO	RAT	ERA	ERA+	OAV	OOB	PR	/A	PF	CPI	FA	E	DP	FW	PW	BW	SBW	DIF
EAST																										
PHI	38	9	29	1436[1]	1343	8.4	118	**393**	813	**11.0**	3.33	107	.251	**.305**	39	37	100	99	**.983**	104	156	**2.0**	3.9	4.5	.9	-2.4
PIT	30	13	44	1444[2]	1366	8.5	103	499	880	11.8	3.41	108	.249	.315	26	46	104	98	.973	167	133	-1.4	4.9	-1.0	.8	4.2
CHI	24	7	38	1455[1]	1475	9.1	125	539	768	12.7	4.05	90	.265	.333	-77	-4	113	98	.978	144	154	-.2	-.4	-7.4	-.4	6.4
MON	42	13	32	1446	1332	8.3	117	572	740	12.0	3.42	103	.249	.325	24	16	99	**106**	.979	134	150	.4	1.7	-2.1	-.3	-4.6
STL	32	13	22	1437[2]	**1300**	**8.1**	94	600	859	12.1	3.58	98	**.245**	.326	-1	-11	98	97	.978	136	155	.3	-1.2	-6.1	.2	-5.2
NY	21	7	26	1455[1]	1447	8.9	114	531	775	12.4	3.87	90	.265	.334	-48	-62	98	101	.979	132	160	.5	-6.6	-2.6	-1.9	-4.4
WEST																										
LA	46	16	38	1440[1]	1362	8.5	107	440	800	11.4	**3.12**	112	.250	.309	73	62	98	**106**	.978	140	138	.0	**6.6**	**10.7**	.8	-4.1
CIN	16	10	46	1448[1]	1437	8.9	122	567	908	12.6	3.81	93	.261	.332	-38	-42	99	102	.978	134	120	.3	-4.4	7.9	.4	7.3
SF	42	**17**	29	1455	1377	8.5	84	453	840	11.5	3.30	104	.252	.311	44	23	96	98	.977	146	118	-.3	2.4	2.5	-.9	4.1
SD	21	10	**55**	1433[2]	1385	8.7	**74**	483	744	11.8	3.28	101	.257	.320	47	8	93	104	.975	160	**171**	-1.0	.8	1.1	.2	1.9
HOU	**48**	**17**	23	1440[1]	1328	8.3	86	578	**930**	12.1	3.63	91	.247	.323	-9	-52	93	94	.978	133	109	.4	-5.5	-.5	**1.7**	-3.1
ATL	29	12	32	1440[1]	1404	8.8	132	624	848	12.9	4.08	99	.257	.337	-81	-5	113	98	.975	153	126	-.6	-.5	-10.3	-1.5	.9
TOT	389	144	414	17333[1]		8.6				12.0	3.57		.254	.323					.978	1683	1690					

Runs		Hits		Doubles		Triples		Home Runs		Total Bases	
DeJesus-Chi	104	Garvey-LA	202	Rose-Cin	51	Templeton-StL	13	Foster-Cin	40	Parker-Pit	340
Rose-Cin	103	Rose-Cin	198	Clark-SF	46	Richards-SD	12	Luzinski-Phi	35	Foster-Cin	330
Parker-Pit	102	Cabell-Hou	195	Simmons-StL	40	Parker-Pit	12	Parker-Pit	30	Garvey-LA	319
Foster-Cin	97	Parker-Pit	194	Parrish-Mon	39			Smith-LA	29	Clark-SF	318
Moreno-Pit	95	Bowa-Phi	192	Perez-Mon	38					Winfield-SD	293

Runs Batted In		Runs Produced		Bases On Balls		Batting Average		On Base Percentage		Slugging Average	
Foster-Cin	120	Parker-Pit	189	Burroughs-Atl	117	Parker-Pit	.334	Burroughs-Atl	.436	Parker-Pit	.585
Parker-Pit	117	Garvey-LA	181	Evans-SF	105	Garvey-LA	.316	Parker-Pit	.395	Smith-LA	.559
Garvey-LA	113	Foster-Cin	177	Tenace-SD	101	Cruz-Hou	.315	Tenace-SD	.394	Foster-Cin	.546
Luzinski-Phi	101	Clark-SF	163	Luzinski-Phi	100	Madlock-SF	.309	Smith-LA	.392	Clark-SF	.537
Clark-SF	98	Winfield-SD	161	Cey-LA	96	Winfield-SD	.308	Luzinski-Phi	.390	Burroughs-Atl	.529

Production		Adjusted Production		Batter Runs		Adjusted Batter Runs		Clutch Hitting Index		Runs Created	
Parker-Pit	.981	Smith-LA	164	Parker-Pit	52.9	Parker-Pit	47.6	Morgan-Cin	134	Parker-Pit	134
Burroughs-Atl	.965	Parker-Pit	163	Burroughs-Atl	50.1	Clark-SF	40.0	Reitz-StL	126	Burroughs-Atl	116
Smith-LA	.951	Clark-SF	155	Luzinski-Phi	40.9	Luzinski-Phi	39.9	Montanez-NY	119	Foster-Cin	115
Luzinski-Phi	.916	Winfield-SD	153	Foster-Cin	39.2	Foster-Cin	39.2	Watson-Hou	118	Luzinski-Phi	114
Foster-Cin	.909	Luzinski-Phi	152	Smith-LA	37.8	Winfield-SD	38.6	B.Robinson-Pit	117	Clark-SF	109

Total Average		Stolen Bases		Stolen Base Average		Stolen Base Runs		Fielding Runs		Total Player Rating	
Burroughs-Atl	1.042	Moreno-Pit	71	Cedeno-Hou	92.0	Lopes-LA	11.1	Trillo-Chi	28.9	Parker-Pit	5.3
Parker-Pit	1.025	Taveras-Pit	46	Lopes-LA	91.8	Moreno-Pit	8.1	Smith-SD	25.6	Clark-SF	4.7
Smith-LA	1.009	Lopes-LA	45	McBride-Phi	90.3	McBride-Phi	6.6	Cromartie-Mon	24.7	Foster-Cin	4.0
Luzinski-Phi	.957	DeJesus-Chi	41	Sexton-Hou	88.9			Templeton-StL	22.9	Lopes-LA	4.0
Foster-Cin	.893	Smith-SD	40	Bowa-Phi	84.4			Dawson-Mon	21.1	Templeton-StL	3.8

Wins		Win Percentage		Games		Complete Games		Shutouts		Saves	
Perry-SD	21	Perry-SD	.778	Tekulve-Pit	91	Niekro-SF	22	Knepper-SF	6	Fingers-SD	37
Grimsley-Mon	20	Hooton-LA	.655	Littell-StL	72	Grimsley-Mon	19	Niekro-Atl	4	Tekulve-Pit	31
Niekro-Atl	19	Grimsley-Mon	.645	Moore-Chi	71	Richard-Hou	16	Halicki-SF	4	Bair-Cin	28
Hooton-LA	19	Blue-SF	.643	Moffitt-SF	70	Knepper-SF	16	Blyleven-Pit	4	Sutter-Chi	27
		John-LA	.630	Bair-Cin	70			Blue-SF	4	Garber-Phi-Atl	25

Innings Pitched		Fewest Hits/Game		Fewest BB/Game		Strikeouts		Strikeouts/Game		Ratio	
Niekro-Atl	334.1	Richard-Hou	6.28	Christenson-Phi	1.86	Richard-Hou	303	Richard-Hou	9.90	Swan-NY	9.72
Richard-Hou	275.1	Swan-NY	7.12	Barr-SF	1.93	Niekro-Atl	248	Seaver-Cin	7.83	Hooton-LA	9.80
Grimsley-Mon	263.0	Hooton-LA	7.47	R.Reuschel-Chi	2.00	Seaver-Cin	226	Vuckovich-StL	6.76	Halicki-SF	9.86
Perry-SD	260.2	Halicki-SF	7.51	Halicki-SF	2.04	Blyleven-Pit	182	Blyleven-Pit	6.72	Christenson-Phi	10.14
Knepper-SF	260.0	Knepper-SF	7.55	Sutton-LA	2.04	Montefusco-SF	177	Niekro-Atl	6.68	Rogers-Mon	10.36

Earned Run Average		Adjusted ERA		Opponents' Batting Avg.		Opponents' On Base Pct.		Starter Runs		Adjusted Starter Runs	
Swan-NY	2.43	Swan-NY	143	Richard-Hou	.196	Halicki-SF	.271	Knepper-SF	27.3	Niekro-Atl	43.3
Rogers-Mon	2.47	Rogers-Mon	143	Swan-NY	.219	Swan-NY	.277	Rogers-Mon	27.0	Rogers-Mon	25.7
Vuckovich-StL	2.54	Niekro-Atl	140	Halicki-SF	.221	Hooton-LA	.277	Swan-NY	26.4	Swan-NY	24.3
Knepper-SF	2.63	Vuckovich-StL	138	Hooton-LA	.226	Christenson-Phi	.284	Niekro-Atl	25.8	Knepper-SF	23.6
Hooton-LA	2.71	Knepper-SF	131	Seaver-Cin	.227	D.Robinson-Pit	.286	Perry-SD	24.5	Vuckovich-StL	21.4

Clutch Pitching Index		Relief Runs		Adjusted Relief Runs		Relief Ranking		Total Pitcher Index		Total Baseball Ranking	
Rau-LA	134	Tekulve-Pit	18.6	Garber-Phi-Atl	22.5	Bair-Cin	30.8	Niekro-Atl	5.7	Niekro-Atl	5.7
Vuckovich-StL	124	Garber-Phi-Atl	18.5	Tekulve-Pit	20.5	Tekulve-Pit	30.4	Tekulve-Pit	3.5	Parker-Pit	5.3
Carlton-Phi	121	Bair-Cin	17.9	Bair-Cin	17.5	Garber-Phi-Atl	29.2	Carlton-Phi	3.3	Clark-SF	4.7
Jones-SD	114	Reed-Phi	16.2	Reed-Phi	16.1	Fingers-SD	22.4	Bair-Cin	3.2	Foster-Cin	4.0
Rogers-Mon	113	D'Acquisto-SD	14.9	D'Acquisto-SD	12.4	Forster-LA	22.4	Garber-Phi-Atl	3.2	Lopes-LA	4.0

January 19 The BBWAA elects Eddie Mathews to the Hall of Fame. The former third baseman is named on 301 of 379 ballots.

January 30 Pitcher Addie Joss and former executive Larry MacPhail are voted into the Hall of Fame by the Special Veterans Committee.

April 9 The Brewers complete a stunning, season-opening, three-game sweep of the Orioles by scores of 11–3, 16–3, and 13–5. Sixto Lezcano, Gorman Thomas, and Cecil Cooper provided the Brewers with a grand slam in each game to set a major league mark.

June 17 Ron Guidry strikes out 18 batters in a four-hit, 4-0 shutout of the Angels, setting an AL record for left-handers. The victory raises the Yankee southpaw's record to 11-0.

June 30 Larry Doby becomes the second black major league manager, replacing Bob Lemon as skipper of the White Sox. Chicago has a 34-40 record at the time, and will go 37-50 the rest of the way. Doby does not return in 1979.

September 7 The Yankees, four games behind the Red Sox in the AL East, arrive in Boston for a crucial four-game series. The Yanks begin the "Boston Massacre" with a 15–3 route. Willie Randolph drives in five of the runs.

September 24 Ron Guidry gains his third two-hit shutout of the month 4-0 over the Indians. It is Guidry's ninth shutout of the year, a Yankees record, and just one short of the AL record for southpaws set by Boston lefty Babe Ruth in 1916. The Red Sox stay one game in back of New York by topping Toronto, 7-6.

September 26 New York District Court Judge Constance Baker Motley rules that women sportswriters cannot be banned from locker rooms in the state.

October 2 The Yankees and Red Sox, tied for first at the end of the regular season, play a dramatic one-game playoff at Fenway for the AL East title. New York prevails, 5-4, behind Bucky Dent's three-run homer off Mike Torrez and Guidry's 25th win against just three losses. Guidry's .893 percentage is a major league record for a 20-game winner.

October 13 Spectacular defense at third base by Graig Nettles highlights the Yankees' first World Series win by a score of 5-1. Ron Guidry gets the victory.

October 17 The Yanks win their fourth straight game 7-2 to clinch their second consecutive World Series over the Dodgers as Brian Doyle and Series MVP Bucky Dent have three hits apiece.

November 1 Ron Guidry is the unanimous choice for the AL Cy Young Award. The Yankees southpaw led the league in wins, percentage, shutouts (9), and ERA (1.74).

November 7 Boston's Jim Rice tops New York's Ron Guidry, 353-291, to win the league MVP Award. Rice led the league in hits (213), triples (15), homers (46), RBIs (139), and slugging (.600), and became the first AL player to accumulate 400 total bases in a season since Joe DiMaggio in 1937.

BALTIMORE

M	E.Weaver
1B	E.Murray
2B	R.Dauer
SS	M.Belanger
3B	D.DeCinces
LF	P.Kelly
CF	L.Harlow
RF	K.Singleton
C	R.Dempsey
DH	L.May
O	C.Lopez
2	B.Smith
O	A.Mora
P	J.Palmer
P	M.Flanagan
P	D.Martinez
P	S.McGregor
RP	D.Stanhouse
RP	J.Kerrigan
RP	T.Martinez
P	N.Briles

BOSTON

M	D.Zimmer
1B	G.Scott
2B	J.Remy
SS	R.Burleson
3B	B.Hobson
LF	C.Yastrzemski
CF	F.Lynn
RF	D.Evans
C	C.Fisk
DH	J.Rice
3D	J.Brohamer
13	R.Jackson
P	D.Eckersley
P	M.Torrez
P	L.Tiant
P	B.Lee
P	J.Wright
RP	B.Stanley
RP	D.Drago
RP	T.Burgmeier
P	A.Ripley
P	B.Campbell

CALIFORNIA

M	D.Garcia
M	J.Fregosi
1B	R.Fairly
2B	B.Grich
SS	D.Chalk
3B	C.Lansford
LF	J.Rudi
CF	R.Miller
RF	L.Bostock
DH	D.Baylor
C	B.Downing
O	K.Landreaux
P	F.Tanana
P	N.Ryan
P	C.Knapp
P	D.Aase
P	K.Brett
RP	P.Hartzell
RP	D.LaRoche
RP	D.Miller
P	D.Frost
P	T.Griffin

CHICAGO

M	B.Lemon
M	L.Doby
1B	M.Squires
2B	J.Orta
SS	D.Kessinger
3B	E.Soderholm
LF	R.Garr
CF	C.Lemon
RF	C.Washington
C	B.Nahorodny
DH	La.Johnson
OD	B.Molinaro
2S	G.Pryor
O	T.Bosley
OD	W.Nordhagen
P	S.Stone
P	K.Kravec
P	F.Barrios
P	W.Wood
RP	J.Willoughby
RP	L.LaGrow
RP	R.Schueler
P	R.Hinton
P	M.Proly
/P	R.Wortham
P	P.Torrealba
P	J.Kucek

CLEVELAND

M	J.Torborg
1B	A.Thornton
2B	D.Kuiper
SS	T.Veryzer
3B	B.Bell
LF	J.Grubb
CF	R.Manning
RF	P.Dade
C	G.Alexander
DH	B.Carbo
OD	J.Norris
O3	T.Cox
P	R.Waits
P	M.Paxton
P	R.Wise
P	D.Hood
P	D.Clyde
RP	J.Kern
RP	S.Monge
RP	D.Spillner
P	P.Reuschel

DETROIT

M	R.Houk
1B	J.Thompson
2B	L.Whitaker
SS	A.Trammell
3B	A.Rodriguez
LF	S.Kemp
CF	R.LeFlore
RF	T.Corcoran
C	M.May
DH	R.Staub
C	L.Parrish
3	P.Mankowski
P	J.Slaton
P	M.Wilcox
P	D.Rozema
P	J.Billingham
P	K.Young
RP	J.Hiller
P	J.Morris
P	B.Sykes
P	S.Baker

KANSAS CITY

M	W.Herzog
1B	P.LaCock
2B	F.White
SS	F.Patek
3B	G.Brett
LF	W.Wilson
CF	A.Otis
RF	A.Cowens
C	D.Porter
DH	H.McRae
O1	C.Hurdle
O	T.Poquette
P	D.Leonard
P	P.Splittorff
P	L.Gura
P	R.Gale
RP	D.Bird
RP	M.Pattin
RP	A.Hrabosky
P	S.Mingori
P	A.Hassler

MILWAUKEE

M	G.Bamberger
1B	C.Cooper
2B	P.Molitor
SS	R.Yount
3B	S.Bando
LF	B.Oglivie
CF	G.Thomas
RF	S.Lezcano
C	C.Moore
DH	L.Hisle
12	D.Money
C	B.Martinez
DO	D.Davis
P	M.Caldwell
P	L.Sorensen
P	J.Augustine
P	B.Travers
P	A.Replogle
RP	R.Stein
RP	B.McClure
RP	B.Castro
P	E.Rodriguez

MINNESOTA

M	G.Mauch
1B	R.Carew
2B	B.Randall
SS	R.Smalley
3B	M.Cubbage
LF	W.Norwood
CF	D.Ford
RF	H.Powell
C	B.Wynegar
DH	G.Adams
D	J.Morales
O	B.Rivera
3	L.Wolfe
P	R.Erickson
P	G.Zahn
P	D.Goltz
P	G.Serum
RP	M.Marshall
RP	D.Jackson
P	P.Thormodsgard
P	S.Perzanowski

NEW YORK

M	B.Martin
M	D.Howser
M	B.Lemon
1B	C.Chambliss
2B	W.Randolph
SS	B.Dent
3B	G.Nettles
LF	L.Piniella
CF	M.Rivers
RF	R.Jackson
C	T.Munson
DH	C.Johnson
OD	R.White
P	R.Guidry
P	E.Figueroa
P	D.Tidrow
P	J.Beattie
P	C.Hunter
RP	R.Gossage
RP	S.Lyle
RP	K.Clay

OAKLAND

M	B.Winkles
M	J.McKeon
1B	D.Revering
2B	M.Edwards
SS	M.Guerrero
3B	W.Gross
LF	M.Page
CF	M.Dilone
RF	T.Armas
C	J.Essian
DH	G.Alexander
O	J.Hale
32	T.Duncan
C1	J.Newman
O	J.Wallis
O	G.Burke
P	M.Keough
P	J.Johnson
P	R.Langford
P	P.Broberg
P	S.Renko
RP	D.Heaverlo
RP	B.Lacey
RP	E.Sosa
P	A.Wirth

SEATTLE

M	D.Johnson
1B	D.Meyer
2B	J.Cruz
SS	C.Reynolds
3B	B.Stein
LF	B.Bochte
CF	Ru.Jones
RF	L.Roberts
C	B.Stinson
DH	L.Stanton
O	J.Hale
OD	T.Paciorek
3S	L.Milbourne
P	P.Mitchell
P	G.Abbott
P	R.Honeycutt
P	T.House
P	J.Colborn
RP	S.Rawley
RP	J.Todd
RP	E.Romo
P	B.McLaughlin
P	D.Pole
P	M.Parrott

TEXAS

M	B.Hunter
M	P.Corrales
1B	M.Hargrove
2B	B.Wills
SS	B.Campaneris
3B	T.Harrah
LF	A.Oliver
CF	J.Beniquez
RF	B.Bonds
C	R.Sundberg
DH	R.Zisk
3D	K.Bevacqua
P	J.Matlack
P	F.Jenkins
P	D.Alexander
P	D.Medich
P	D.Ellis
RP	R.Cleveland
RP	L.Barker
P	S.Comer
P	J.Umbarger

TORONTO

M	R.Hartsfield
1B	J.Mayberry
2B	D.McKay
SS	L.Gomez
3B	R.Howell
LF	O.Velez
CF	R.Bosetti
RF	B.Bailor
C	R.Cerone
DH	R.Carty
C	A.Ashby
OD	W.Upshaw
O	A.Woods
P	J.Jefferson
P	T.Underwood
P	J.Clancy
P	J.Garvin
P	B.Moore
RP	M.Willis
P	T.Murphy
RP	J.Coleman
P	D.Lemanczyk
P	D.Kirkwood

TEAM	G	W	L	PCT	GB	R	OR	AB	H	2B	3B	HR	BB	SO	AVG	OBP	SLG	PRO	PRO+	BR	/A	PF	CHI	RC	SB	CS	SBA	SBR
EAST																												
NY	163	100	63	.613		735	**582**	5583	1489	228	38	125	505	695	.267	.332	.388	.720	105	14	31	98	**105**	720	98	42	70	4
BOS	163	99	64	.607	1	796	657	5587	1493	270	46	172	582	835	.267	.339	.424	.763	102	96	12	111	100	793	74	51	59	-8
MIL	162	93	69	.574	6.5	804	650	5536	**1530**	265	38	**173**	520	805	**.276**	**.342**	**.432**	**.774**	116	**114**	**112**	100	100	**822**	95	53	64	-3
BAL	161	90	71	.559	9	659	633	5422	1397	248	19	154	552	864	.258	.329	.396	.725	110	18	61	94	95	691	75	61	55	-14
DET	162	86	76	.531	13.5	714	653	5601	1520	218	34	129	563	695	.271	.341	.392	.733	103	45	24	103	96	748	90	38	70	4
CLE	159	69	90	.434	29	639	694	5365	1400	223	45	106	488	698	.261	.326	.379	.705	99	-19	-11	99	99	649	64	63	50	-19
TOR	161	59	102	.366	40	590	775	5430	1358	217	39	98	448	645	.250	.310	.359	.669	86	-93	-105	102	103	587	28	52	35	-23
WEST																												
KC	162	92	70	.568		743	634	5474	1469	**305**	**59**	98	498	644	.268	.333	.399	.732	102	34	15	103	104	739	**216**	84	**72**	**14**
TEX	162	87	75	.537	5	692	632	5347	1353	216	36	132	**624**	779	.253	.335	.381	.716	101	11	10	100	100	696	196	91	68	4
CAL	162	87	75	.537	5	691	666	5472	1417	226	28	108	539	682	.259	.333	.370	.703	101	-14	12	96	103	669	86	69	55	-16
MIN	162	73	89	.451	19	666	678	5522	1472	259	47	82	604	684	.267	**.342**	.375	.717	99	21	7	102	92	715	99	56	64	-4
CHI	161	71	90	.441	20.5	634	731	5393	1423	221	41	106	409	**625**	.264	.320	.379	.699	95	-35	-41	101	102	635	83	68	55	-16
OAK	162	69	93	.426	23	532	690	5321	1304	200	31	100	433	800	.245	.305	.351	.656	89	-117	-89	95	99	552	144	117	55	-27
SEA	160	56	104	.350	35	614	834	5358	1327	229	37	97	522	702	.248	.317	.359	.676	91	-73	-69	99	103	620	123	47	**72**	9
TOT	1131					9509		76411	19952	3325	538	1680	7287	10153	.261	.329	.385	.714							1471	892	62	-94

TEAM	CG	SH	SV	IP	H	H/G	HR	BB	SO	RAT	ERA	ERA+	OAV	OOB	PR	/A	PF	CPI	FA	E	DP	FW	PW	BW	SBW	DIF
EAST																										
NY	39	16	**36**	1460²	**1321**	8.1	111	478	817	**11.3**	3.18	114	**.243**	.308	95	72	96	99	**.982**	113	134	1.5	7.4	3.2	1.1	5.2
BOS	57	15	26	1472²	1530	9.4	137	464	706	12.4	3.54	116	.270	.329	37	**94**	109	**111**	.977	146	171	-.3	**9.7**	1.2	-.1	7.1
MIL	62	**19**	24	1436	1442	9.0	109	**398**	577	11.8	3.65	103	.262	.316	17	17	100	95	.977	150	144	-.6	1.8	**11.5**	.4	-1.0
BAL	**65**	16	33	1429	1340	8.4	107	509	754	11.7	3.56	98	.251	.318	32	-11	93	95	**.982**	110	166	**1.6**	-1.1	6.3	-.8	3.5
DET	60	12	21	1455²	1441	8.9	135	503	684	12.2	3.64	106	.263	.329	20	36	103	106	.981	118	**177**	1.2	3.7	2.5	1.1	-3.5
CLE	36	6	28	1407¹	1397	8.9	**100**	568	739	12.7	3.97	94	.261	.335	-33	-37	99	95	.980	123	142	.8	-3.8	-1.1	-1.3	-5.1
TOR	35	5	23	1429¹	1529	9.6	149	614	758	13.6	4.54	86	.279	.353	-123	-98	104	100	.979	131	163	.4	-10.1	-10.8	-1.7	.7
WEST																										
KC	53	14	33	1439	1350	8.4	108	478	657	11.6	3.44	111	.251	.316	52	61	102	98	.976	150	153	-.6	6.3	1.5	**2.1**	1.7
TEX	54	12	25	1456¹	1431	8.8	108	421	776	11.6	3.36	112	.259	.315	66	63	100	102	.976	153	140	-.8	6.5	1.0	1.1	-1.8
CAL	44	13	33	1455²	1382	8.5	125	599	**892**	12.4	3.65	99	.253	.330	19	-6	96	102	.978	136	136	.2	-.6	1.2	-1.0	6.2
MIN	48	9	26	1459²	1468	9.1	102	520	703	12.5	3.69	103	.266	.333	11	20	102	102	.977	146	171	-.4	2.1	.7	.3	-10.7
CHI	38	9	23	1409¹	1380	8.8	128	586	710	12.8	4.21	90	.259	.332	-71	-65	101	94	.977	139	130	-.0	-6.7	-4.2	-1.0	2.4
OAK	26	11	29	1433¹	1401	8.8	106	582	750	12.6	3.62	100	.259	.333	22	3	97	103	.971	179	145	-2.3	.3	-9.2	-2.1	1.2
SEA	28	4	20	1419¹	1540	9.8	155	567	630	13.6	4.67	81	.280	.352	-144	-136	101	98	.978	141	174	-.2	-14.0	-7.1	1.6	-4.3
TOT	645	161	390	20163¹		8.9				12.4	3.76		.261	.329					.978	1935	2146					

Runs		Hits		Doubles		Triples		Home Runs		Total Bases	
LeFlore-Det	126	Rice-Bos	213	Brett-KC	45	Rice-Bos	15	Rice-Bos	46	Rice-Bos	406
Rice-Bos	121	LeFlore-Det	198	McRae-KC	39	Ford-Min	10	Hisle-Mil	34	Murray-Bal	293
Baylor-Cal	103	Carew-Min	188	Fisk-Bos	39	Carew-Min	10	Baylor-Cal	34	Staub-Det	279
Thornton-Cle	97	Munson-NY	183	DeCinces-Bal	37	Yount-Mil	9	Thornton-Cle	33	Baylor-Cal	279
Hisle-Mil	96	Staub-Det	175	Ford-Min	36	Garr-Chi	9	Thomas-Mil	32	Thompson-Det	278

Runs Batted In		Runs Produced		Bases On Balls		Batting Average		On Base Percentage		Slugging Average	
Rice-Bos	139	Rice-Bos	214	Hargrove-Tex	107	Carew-Min	.333	Carew-Min	.415	Rice-Bos	.600
Staub-Det	121	Hisle-Mil	177	Singleton-Bal	98	Oliver-Tex	.324	Singleton-Bal	.410	Hisle-Mil	.533
Hisle-Mil	115	LeFlore-Det	176	Kemp-Det	97	Rice-Bos	.315	Hargrove-Tex	.391	DeCinces-Bal	.526
Thornton-Cle	105	Staub-Det	172	Thornton-Cle	93	Piniella-NY	.314	Otis-KC	.387	Otis-KC	.525
		Thornton-Cle	169	Smalley-Min	85	Oglivie-Mil	.303	Randolph-NY	.385	Thornton-Cle	.516

Production		Adjusted Production		Batter Runs		Adjusted Batter Runs		Clutch Hitting Index		Runs Created	
Rice-Bos	.973	Singleton-Bal	154	Rice-Bos	58.7	Rice-Bos	44.1	Staub-Det	136	Rice-Bos	147
Otis-KC	.911	Rice-Bos	153	Hisle-Mil	36.3	Singleton-Bal	40.4	L.Johnson-Chi	127	LeFlore-Det	105
Hisle-Mil	.909	Hisle-Mil	153	Thornton-Cle	35.6	Thornton-Cle	36.8	Whitaker-Det	119	Carew-Min	105
Thornton-Cle	.898	Thornton-Cle	152	Otis-KC	35.2	Hisle-Mil	36.0	Chambliss-NY	117	Thompson-Det	104
Roberts-Sea	.881	DeCinces-Bal	152	Singleton-Bal	34.0	Murray-Bal	33.7	Cowens-KC	116	Murray-Bal	104

Total Average		Stolen Bases		Stolen Base Average		Stolen Base Runs		Fielding Runs		Total Player Rating	
Rice-Bos	.973	LeFlore-Det	68	Cruz-Sea	85.5	Cruz-Sea	11.7	Belanger-Bal	33.8	Smalley-Min	5.3
Otis-KC	.972	Cruz-Sea	59	Campaneris-Tex	84.6	LeFlore-Det	10.8	Bell-Cle	28.3	Rice-Bos	4.8
Hisle-Mil	.907	Wills-Tex	52	Lowenstein-Bal	84.2	Wills-Tex	7.2	Bosetti-Tor	25.1	Yount-Mil	4.5
Singleton-Bal	.900	Dilone-Oak	50	Randolph-NY	83.7	Wilson-KC	6.6	Yount-Mil	21.9	Otis-KC	4.2
Thornton-Cle	.897	Wilson-KC	46	Rivers-NY	83.3	Randolph-NY	6.6	Wills-Tex	21.3	DeCinces-Bal	4.0

Wins		Win Percentage		Games		Complete Games		Shutouts		Saves	
Guidry-NY	25	Guidry-NY	.893	Lacey-Oak	74	Caldwell-Mil	23	Guidry-NY	9	Gossage-NY	27
Caldwell-Mil	22	Stanley-Bos	.882	Heaverlo-Oak	69	Leonard-KC	20	Palmer-Bal	6	LaRoche-Cal	25
Palmer-Bal	21	Gura-KC	.800	Sosa-Oak	68	Palmer-Bal	19	Caldwell-Mil	6	Stanhouse-Bal	24
Leonard-KC	21	Eckersley-Bos	.714	Gossage-NY	63	Matlack-Tex	18	Tiant-Bos	5	Marshall-Min	21
		Caldwell-Mil	.710							Hrabosky-KC	20

Innings Pitched		Fewest Hits/Game		Fewest BB/Game		Strikeouts		Strikeouts/Game		Ratio	
Palmer-Bal	296.0	Guidry-NY	6.15	Jenkins-Tex	1.48	Ryan-Cal	260	Ryan-Cal	9.97	Guidry-NY	8.55
Leonard-KC	294.2	Ryan-Cal	7.02	Sorensen-Mil	1.60	Guidry-NY	248	Guidry-NY	8.16	Caldwell-Mil	9.79
Caldwell-Mil	293.1	Gura-KC	7.43	Caldwell-Mil	1.66	Leonard-KC	183	Kravec-Chi	6.83	Jenkins-Tex	9.83
Flanagan-Bal	281.1	Palmer-Bal	7.48	Matlack-Tex	1.70	Flanagan-Bal	167	Underwood-Tor	6.33	Gura-KC	10.03
Sorensen-Mil	280.2	Tiant-Bos	7.84	Rozema-Det	1.76	Eckersley-Bos	162	Knapp-Cal	6.02	Matlack-Tex	10.23

Earned Run Average		Adjusted ERA		Opponents' Batting Avg.		Opponents' On Base Pct.		Starter Runs		Adjusted Starter Runs	
Guidry-NY	1.74	Guidry-NY	208	Guidry-NY	.193	Guidry-NY	.250	Guidry-NY	61.4	Guidry-NY	57.1
Matlack-Tex	2.27	Matlack-Tex	165	Ryan-Cal	.220	Caldwell-Mil	.274	Caldwell-Mil	45.7	Caldwell-Mil	45.5
Caldwell-Mil	2.36	Caldwell-Mil	159	Palmer-Bal	.227	Jenkins-Tex	.279	Matlack-Tex	44.9	Matlack-Tex	44.3
Palmer-Bal	2.46	Goltz-Min	153	Gura-KC	.229	Matlack-Tex	.284	Palmer-Bal	42.8	Palmer-Bal	34.0
Goltz-Min	2.49	Palmer-Bal	142	Tiant-Bos	.234	Gura-KC	.286	Goltz-Min	31.1	Eckersley-Bos	33.6

Clutch Pitching Index		Relief Runs		Adjusted Relief Runs		Relief Ranking		Total Pitcher Index		Total Baseball Ranking	
Lee-Bos	130	Gossage-NY	26.2	Gossage-NY	24.0	Gossage-NY	44.7	Guidry-NY	6.2	Guidry-NY	6.2
Zahn-Min	129	Stanley-Bos	18.2	Stanley-Bos	18.2	Marshall-Min	37.2	Caldwell-Mil	5.0	Smalley-Min	5.3
Goltz-Min	125	Hiller-Det	14.6	Hiller-Det	15.7	Stanley-Bos	29.4	Matlack-Tex	4.7	Caldwell-Mil	5.0
Gale-KC	115	Marshall-Min	14.4	Marshall-Min	15.0	Hiller-Det	25.6	Gossage-NY	4.7	Rice-Bos	4.8
Eckersley-Bos	115	Sosa-Oak	13.6	Sosa-Oak	12.1	LaRoche-Cal	19.9	Palmer-Bal	4.3	Matlack-Tex	4.7

January 23 Willie Mays receives 409 of 432 votes in the BBWAA election to earn enshrinement in the Hall of Fame.

March 7 The Special Veterans Committee selects Warren Giles and slugger Hack Wilson for the Hall of Fame.

April 7 In the earliest no-hitter in major league history, the Astros' Ken Forsch shuts downs the Braves, 6-0, making him and his brother Bob the first brothers to pitch no-hit games.

May 17 The wind is really blowing out at Wrigley as the Cubs and the Phillies combine for a major-league-record-tying 11 homers during a wild 10-inning slugfest won 23-22 by the Phils. Dave Kingman has three homers and six RBIs for the Cubs. Teammate Bill Buckner has a grand slam and seven RBIs. Mike Schmidt's two homers include the game-winner in the 10th inning.

August 13 Lou Brock collects his 3,000th career hit, a single off Dennis Lamp, as the Cardinals top the Cubs 3-2.

September 23 St. Louis legend Lou Brock steals the 938th—and final—base of his career in a 7-4 win against the New York Mets. He tops 19th century speedster Billy Hamilton by one.

September 24 Pete Rose singles in the Phillies, 7-2 loss to the Cardinals, giving him 200 hits in a season for the tenth time. He breaks the major league record of nine formerly held by Ty Cobb.

September 26 Atlanta's Phil Niekro notches his 20th win of the season by beating his brother Joe, the NL's only other 20-game winner, in a 9-4 victory. The Niekro brothers are the second pair (the other was Jim and Gaylord Perry) to win 20 games apiece in the same year.

September 28 Switch-hitting Cardinal shortstop Garry Templeton collects three hits against the Mets and becomes the first player to get 100 hits from each side of the plate. During the last nine games,

he bats right-handed exclusively.

October 5 The Pirates complete a sweep of the LCS, beating the Reds 7-1. Willie Stargell hits another homer and is named series MVP.

October 17 In Game 7, Stargell's third World Series homer propels Pittsburgh to its third straight win 4-1, and the World Championship. Pops is named Series MVP.

November 7 Reliever Bruce Sutter, who had a 2.23 ERA and saved 37 of the Cubs' 80 victories, wins the NL Cy Young Award by a 72-66 margin over the Astros' Joe Niekro.

November 13 For the first time in history, two players share the MVP Award. The co-winners are Willie Stargell, the Pirates' spiritual leader, who batted .281 with 32 homers; and the Cardinals' Keith Hernandez, who led the league in runs (116), doubles (48), and batting (.344).

ATLANTA		CHICAGO		CINCINNATI		HOUSTON		LOS ANGELES		MONTREAL	
M	B.Cox	M	H.Franks	M	J.McNamara	M	B.Virdon	M	T.Lasorda	M	D.Williams
1B	D.Murphy	M	J.Amalfitano	1B	D.Driessen	1B	C.Cedeno	1B	S.Garvey	1B	T.Perez
2B	G.Hubbard	1B	B.Buckner	2B	J.Morgan	2B	R.Landestoy	2B	D.Lopes	2B	R.Scott
SS	P.Frias	2B	T.Sizemore	SS	D.Concepcion	SS	C.Reynolds	SS	B.Russell	SS	C.Speier
3B	B.Horner	SS	I.DeJesus	3B	R.Knight	3B	E.Cabell	3B	R.Cey	3B	L.Parrish
LF	J.Burroughs	3B	S.Ontiveros	LF	G.Foster	LF	J.Cruz	LF	D.Baker	LF	W.Cromartie
CF	R.Office	LF	D.Kingman	CF	C.Geronimo	CF	T.Puhl	CF	D.Thomas	CF	A.Dawson
RF	G.Matthews	CF	J.Martin	RF	K.Griffey	RF	J.Leonard	RF	G.Thomasson	RF	E.Valentine
C	B.Benedict	RF	S.Thompson	C	J.Bench	C	A.Ashby	C	S.Yeager	C	G.Carter
		C	B.Foote								
1	M.Lum			O1	D.Collins	23	A.Howe	CO	J.Ferguson	P	S.Rogers
O	B.Bonnell	O1	L.Biittner	2	J.Kennedy			O	R.Smith	P	B.Lee
32	J.Royster						J.Richard			P	S.Sanderson
C	J.Nolan	P	R.Reuschel	P	T.Seaver	P	J.Niekro	P	R.Sutcliffe	P	D.Schatzeder
		P	L.McGlothen	P	M.LaCoss	P	J.Andujar	P	D.Sutton	P	R.Grimsley
P	P.Niekro	P	D.Lamp	P	F.Norman	P	K.Forsch	P	B.Hooton	RP	E.Sosa
P	E.Solomon	P	M.Krukow	P	B.Bonham	P	R.Williams	P	J.Reuss	RP	R.May
P	R.Matula	P	K.Holtzman	P	P.Moskau	RP	J.Sambito	P	C.Hough	RP	S.Bahnsen
P	T.Brizzolara	RP	D.Tidrow	RP	T.Hume	RP	R.Niemann	RP	D.Patterson		
P	M.Mahler	RP	B.Sutter	RP	D.Bair					P	D.Palmer
RP	G.Garber	RP	W.Hernandez	RP	D.Tomlin	P	V.Ruhle	P	B.Welch	P	W.Fryman
RP	J.McLaughlin							P	A.Messersmith		
RP	A.Devine	P	B.Caudill	P	F.Pastore			P	D.Rau		
		P	D.Moore								
P	L.McWilliams										
P	C.Skok										
P	B.McLaughlin										

NEW YORK		PHILADELPHIA		PITTSBURGH		SAN DIEGO		SAN FRANCISCO		ST.LOUIS	
M	J.Torre	M	D.Ozark	M	C.Tanner	M	R.Craig	M	J.Altobelli	M	K.Boyer
1B	W.Montanez	M	D.Green	1B	W.Stargell	1B	G.Tenace	M	D.Bristol	1B	K.Hernandez
2B	D.Flynn	1B	P.Rose	2B	R.Stennett	2B	F.Gonzalez	1B	M.Ivie	2B	K.Oberkfell
SS	F.Taveras	2B	M.Trillo	SS	T.Foli	SS	O.Smith	2B	J.Strain	SS	G.Templeton
3B	R.Hebner	SS	L.Bowa	3B	B.Madlock	3B	P.Dade	SS	J.LeMaster	3B	K.Reitz
LF	S.Henderson	3B	M.Schmidt	LF	B.Robinson	LF	J.Turner	3B	D.Evans	LF	L.Brock
CF	L.Mazzilli	LF	G.Luzinski	CF	O.Moreno	CF	G.Richards	LF	L.Herndon	CF	T.Scott
RF	J.Youngblood	CF	G.Maddox	RF	D.Parker	RF	D.Winfield	CF	B.North	RF	G.Hendrick
C	J.Stearns	RF	B.McBride	C	E.Ott	C	B.Fahey	RF	J.Clark	C	T.Simmons
		C	B.Boone					C	D.Littlejohn		
O3	E.Maddox			23	P.Garner	2S	B.Almon			O	J.Mumphrey
C3	A.Trevino	O	G.Gross	O1	J.Milner	32	K.Bevacqua	1	W.McCovey		
						1O	D.Briggs	O	T.Whitfield	P	P.Vuckovich
P	C.Swan	P	S.Carlton	P	B.Blyleven	O1	J.Johnstone	S2	R.Metzger	P	B.Forsch
P	P.Falcone	P	R.Lerch	P	J.Candelaria			2	B.Madlock	P	S.Martinez
P	K.Kobel	P	N.Espinosa	P	B.Kison	P	R.Jones			P	J.Denny
RP	N.Allen	P	D.Ruthven	P	D.Robinson	P	G.Perry	P	V.Blue	P	J.Fulgham
RP	D.Murray	P	L.Christenson	P	J.Bibby	P	B.Shirley	P	B.Knepper	RP	M.Littell
RP	A.Hassler	RP	R.Reed	RP	K.Tekulve	P	E.Rasmussen	P	J.Montefusco	RP	R.Thomas
		RP	T.McGraw	RP	E.Romo	P	B.Owchinko	P	E.Halicki	RP	W.McEnaney
P	D.Ellis	RP	R.Eastwick	RP	G.Jackson	RP	J.D'Acquisto	P	J.Curtis		
P	T.Hausman					RP	R.Fingers	RP	G.Lavelle	P	B.Sykes
P	W.Twitchell	P	D.Noles	P	J.Rooker	RP	S.Mura	RP	T.Griffin		
P	E.Glynn	P	K.Saucier	P	E.Whitson			RP	G.Minton		
P	M.Scott	P	D.Bird			P	M.Lee				
								P	P.Nastu		
								P	E.Whitson		

TEAM	G	W	L	PCT	GB	R	OR	AB	H	2B	3B	HR	BB	SO	AVG	OBP	SLG	PRO	PRO+	BR	/A	PF	CHI	RC	SB	CS	SBA	SBR
EAST																												
PIT	163	98	64	.605		**775**	643	5661	1541	264	52	148	483	855	.272	.333	**.416**	**.749**	105	**68**	32	105	101	**781**	180	66	**73**	**14**
MON	160	95	65	.594	2	701	**581**	5465	1445	273	42	143	432	890	.264	.321	.408	.729	105	23	29	99	102	701	121	56	68	3
STL	163	86	76	.531	12	731	693	5734	**1594**	**279**	**63**	100	460	838	**.278**	.335	.401	.736	106	46	40	101	98	757	116	69	63	-7
PHI	163	84	78	.519	14	683	718	5463	1453	250	53	119	602	764	.266	**.343**	.396	.739	105	63	39	103	91	743	128	76	63	-7
CHI	162	80	82	.494	18	706	707	5550	1494	250	43	135	478	762	.269	.331	.403	.734	97	40	-28	110	98	726	73	52	58	-9
NY	163	63	99	.389	35	593	706	5591	1399	255	41	74	498	817	.250	.315	.350	.665	90	-90	-68	96	99	615	135	79	63	-7
WEST																												
CIN	161	90	71	.559		731	644	5477	1445	266	31	132	**614**	902	.264	.340	.396	.736	106	55	51	101	99	741	99	47	68	2
HOU	162	89	73	.549	1.5	583	582	5394	1382	224	52	49	461	**745**	.256	.317	.344	.661	91	-93	-60	94	102	591	**190**	95	67	0
LA	162	79	83	.488	11.5	739	717	5490	1443	220	24	**183**	556	834	.263	.333	.412	.745	**111**	62	**73**	99	99	743	106	46	70	4
SF	162	71	91	.438	19.5	672	751	5395	1328	192	36	125	580	925	.246	.322	.365	.687	100	-46	-3	93	**106**	644	140	73	66	-2
SD	161	68	93	.422	22	603	681	5446	1316	193	53	93	534	770	.242	.313	.348	.661	91	-97	-62	94	103	600	100	58	63	-5
ATL	160	66	94	.413	23.5	669	763	5422	1389	220	28	126	490	818	.256	.320	.377	.697	89	-31	-78	107	105	654	98	50	66	-1
TOT	971					8186		66088	17229	2886	518	1427	6188	9920	.261	.327	.385	.712							1486	767	66	-14

TEAM	CG	SH	SV	IP	H	H/G	HR	BB	SO	RAT	ERA	ERA+	OAV	OOB	PR	/A	PF	CPI	FA	E	DP	FW	PW	BW	SBW	DIF
EAST																										
PIT	24	7	**52**	1493^1	1424	8.6	125	504	904	11.8	3.41	114	.254	.318	53	77	104	103	.979	134	163	.4	7.9	3.3	**1.6**	3.8
MON	33	18	39	1447^1	1379	8.6	116	**450**	813	11.5	**3.14**	**117**	.253	.312	**95**	**84**	98	**107**	.979	131	123	.4	**8.7**	3.0	.4	2.5
STL	38	10	25	1486^2	1449	8.8	127	501	788	11.9	3.72	101	.258	.321	1	6	101	97	.980	132	166	.5	.6	4.1	-.6	.3
PHI	33	14	29	1441^1	1455	9.1	135	477	787	12.2	4.16	92	.266	.328	-69	-54	103	94	**.983**	**106**	148	**2.1**	-5.6	4.0	-.6	3.1
CHI	20	11	44	1446^2	1500	9.3	127	521	**933**	12.8	3.88	106	.270	.338	-24	37	110	105	.975	159	163	-1.1	3.8	-2.9	-.8	.0
NY	16	10	36	1482^2	1486	9.0	120	607	819	12.9	3.84	95	.266	.341	-18	-34	98	105	.978	140	**168**	.0	-3.5	-7.0	-.6	-6.9
WEST																										
CIN	27	10	40	1440^1	1415	8.8	103	485	773	12.0	3.58	104	.260	.322	24	24	100	99	.980	124	152	.9	2.5	5.3	.3	.5
HOU	**55**	**19**	31	1447^2	**1278**	**7.9**	**90**	504	854	**11.2**	3.20	110	**.237**	**.306**	86	51	94	93	.978	138	146	.1	5.3	-6.2	.1	8.7
LA	30	6	34	1444	1425	8.9	101	555	811	12.5	3.83	95	.260	.331	-15	-31	97	97	.981	118	123	1.3	-3.2	**7.5**	.5	-8.2
SF	25	6	34	1436	1484	9.3	143	577	880	13.1	4.16	84	.269	.341	-69	-107	94	101	.974	163	138	-1.4	-11.0	-.3	-.0	2.8
SD	29	7	25	1453	1438	8.9	108	513	779	12.2	3.69	96	.263	.328	6	-27	95	101	.978	141	154	-.1	-2.8	-6.4	-.4	-2.8
ATL	32	3	34	1407^2	1496	9.6	132	494	779	13.0	4.18	97	.272	.337	-70	-21	109	99	.970	183	139	-2.7	-2.2	-8.0	.0	-1.1
TOT	362	121	423	17426^2		8.9				12.3	3.73		.261	.327					.978	1669	1783					

Runs
Hernandez-StL 116
Moreno-Pit 110
Schmidt-Phi 109
Parker-Pit 109
Lopes-LA 109

Hits
Templeton-StL 211
Hernandez-StL 210
Rose-Phi 208
Garvey-LA 204
Moreno-Pit 196

Doubles
Hernandez-StL 48
Cromartie-Mon 46
Parker-Pit 45
Reitz-StL 41
Rose-Phi 40

Triples
Templeton-StL 19
Moreno-Pit 12
McBride-Phi 12
Dawson-Mon 12

Home Runs
Kingman-Chi 48
Schmidt-Phi 45
Winfield-SD 34
Horner-Atl 33
Stargell-Pit 32

Total Bases
Winfield-SD 333
Parker-Pit 327
Kingman-Chi 326
Garvey-LA 322
Matthews-Atl 317

Runs Batted In
Winfield-SD 118
Kingman-Chi 115
Schmidt-Phi 114
Garvey-LA 110
Hernandez-StL 105

Runs Produced
Hernandez-StL 210
Winfield-SD 181
Schmidt-Phi 178
Parker-Pit 178
Garvey-LA 174

Bases On Balls
Schmidt-Phi 120
Tenace-SD 105
Lopes-LA 97
North-SF 96
Rose-Phi 95

Batting Average
Hernandez-StL 344
Rose-Phi 331
Knight-Cin 318
Garvey-LA 315
Horner-Atl 314

On Base Percentage
Hernandez-StL 421
Rose-Phi 421
Tenace-SD 407
Mazzilli-NY 397
Winfield-SD 396

Slugging Average
Kingman-Chi 613
Schmidt-Phi 564
Foster-Cin 561
Winfield-SD 558
Horner-Atl 552

Production
Kingman-Chi 960
Schmidt-Phi 955
Winfield-SD 954
Foster-Cin 950
Hernandez-StL 934

Adjusted Production
Winfield-SD 167
Foster-Cin 155
Schmidt-Phi 153
Hernandez-StL 152
Parrish-Mon 146

Batter Runs
Winfield-SD 47.4
Hernandez-StL 47.1
Schmidt-Phi 44.9
Parker-Pit 39.3
Kingman-Chi 37.8

Adjusted Batter Runs
Winfield-SD 55.0
Hernandez-StL 46.1
Schmidt-Phi 41.1
Parker-Pit 33.8
Foster-Cin 33.1

Clutch Hitting Index
Foli-NY-Pit 140
Hebner-NY 137
Flynn-NY 124
Luzinski-Phi 122
Concepcion-Cin . . . 114

Runs Created
Hernandez-StL 135
Winfield-SD 132
Parker-Pit 131
Schmidt-Phi 123
Matthews-Atl 118

Total Average
Schmidt-Phi 1.024
Winfield-SD 988
Kingman-Chi 972
Hernandez-StL 961
Foster-Cin 959

Stolen Bases
Moreno-Pit 77
North-SF 58
Taveras-Pit-NY 44
Lopes-LA 44
Scott-Mon 39

Stolen Base Average
Lopes-LA 91.7
Parker-Pit 83.3
Morgan-Cin 82.4
Royster-Atl 81.4
Smith-SD 80.0

Stolen Base Runs
Lopes-LA 10.8
Moreno-Pit 10.5
Royster-Atl 5.7
Morgan-Cin 4.8

Fielding Runs
Maddox-Phi 26.9
Moreno-Pit 22.8
Evans-SF 22.4
Smith-SD 21.0
Cromartie-Mon 20.4

Total Player Rating
Winfield-SD 5.9
Schmidt-Phi 5.8
Hernandez-StL 5.6
Templeton-StL 4.7
Parker-Pit 4.0

Wins
Niekro-Atl 21
Niekro-Hou 21
Richard-Hou 18
Reuschel-Chi 18
Carlton-Phi 18

Win Percentage
Seaver-Cin 727
Niekro-Hou 656
Martinez-StL 652
Sutcliffe-LA 630
Carlton-Phi 621

Games
Tekulve-Pit 94
Romo-Pit 84
Jackson-Pit 72
Lavelle-SF 70
Garber-Atl 68

Complete Games
Niekro-Atl 23
Richard-Hou 19
Rogers-Mon 13
Carlton-Phi 13
Hooton-LA 12

Shutouts
Seaver-Cin 5
Rogers-Mon 5
Niekro-Hou 5
Richard-Hou 4
Carlton-Phi 4

Saves
Sutter-Chi 37
Tekulve-Pit 31
Garber-Atl 25
Sambito-Hou 22
Lavelle-SF 20

Innings Pitched
Niekro-Atl 342.0
Richard-Hou 292.1
Niekro-Hou 263.2
Jones-SD 263.0
Swan-NY 251.1

Fewest Hits/Game
Richard-Hou 6.77
Carlton-Phi 7.24
Niekro-Hou 7.54
Schatzeder-Mon . . . 7.56
Andujar-Hou 7.79

Fewest BB/Game
Forsch-Hou 1.77
Candelaria-Pit 1.78
Hume-Cin 1.82
Lee-Mon 1.86
Swan-NY 2.04

Strikeouts
Richard-Hou 313
Carlton-Phi 213
Niekro-Atl 208
Blyleven-Pit 172
McGlothen-Chi 147

Strikeouts/Game
Richard-Hou 9.64
Carlton-Phi 7.64
Sanderson-Mon . . . 7.39
Blyleven-Pit 6.52
Krukow-Chi 6.50

Ratio
Forsch-Hou 9.62
Richard-Hou 9.88
Seaver-Cin 10.38
Sutton-LA 10.47
Carlton-Phi 10.61

Earned Run Average
Richard-Hou 2.71
Hume-Cin 2.76
Schatzeder-Mon . . . 2.83
Hooton-LA 2.97
Niekro-Hou 3.00

Adjusted ERA
Hume-Cin 135
Richard-Hou 130
Schatzeder-Mon . . . 129
Hooton-LA 122
Rogers-Mon 122

Opponents' Batting Avg.
Richard-Hou 209
Carlton-Phi 219
Schatzeder-Mon 225
Niekro-Hou 228
Andujar-Hou 233

Opponents' On Base Pct.
Forsch-Hou 275
Richard-Hou 278
Seaver-Cin 291
Sutton-LA 291
Carlton-Phi 292

Starter Runs
Richard-Hou 33.2
Niekro-Hou 21.3
Rogers-Mon 20.1
Fulgham-StL 19.5
Hooton-LA 17.9

Adjusted Starter Runs
Richard-Hou 26.0
Niekro-Atl 24.8
Fulgham-StL 20.0
Rogers-Mon 18.2
Bibby-Pit 16.3

Clutch Pitching Index
Hume-Cin 117
Lamp-Chi 114
Lee-Mon 113
Kobel-NY 112
Blyleven-Pit 112

Relief Runs
Sambito-Hou 19.9
Sosa-Mon 19.1
Hume-Cin 17.6
Minton-SF 17.0
Sutter-Chi 17.0

Adjusted Relief Runs
Sutter-Chi 21.3
Sosa-Mon 18.4
Sambito-Hou 17.6
Hume-Cin 17.6
Tekulve-Pit 16.9

Relief Ranking
Sutter-Chi 38.8
Sambito-Hou 34.8
Sosa-Mon 32.7
Tekulve-Pit 28.4
Littell-StL 25.2

Total Pitcher Index
Sutter-Chi 4.3
Sambito-Hou 4.1
Niekro-Atl 3.4
Sosa-Mon 3.3
Tekulve-Pit 3.1

Total Baseball Ranking
Winfield-SD 5.9
Schmidt-Phi 5.8
Hernandez-StL 5.6
Templeton-StL 4.7
Sutter-Chi 4.3

February 3 The Twins trade seven-time batting champion Rod Carew to the Angels for outfielder Ken Landreaux, third baseman Dave Engle, and two pitchers.

April 5 Baltimore manager Earl Weaver wins his 1,000th game as a skipper.

May 31 Pat Underwood makes his major league debut for Detroit, pitching 8⅓ innings in shutting out Toronto 1-0. The losing pitcher is Pat's brother, Tom.

June 8 The Mariners make Al Chambers the No. 1 pick in the free-agent draft. Kansas City picks football players on the fourth (Dan Marino) and the 17th (John Elway) rounds.

June 12 The Tigers fire manager Les Moss, hiring Sparky Anderson.

June 24 Rickey Henderson makes his major league debut for Oakland in a 5-1 loss to Texas in the first game of a doubleheader. Henderson has a single and double and steals the first base of his major league career.

July 13 California's Nolan Ryan and Boston's Steve Renko each lose no-hitters in the ninth inning, and each settle for one-hit victories, 6–1 over New York and 2–0 over Oakland, respectively.

August 2 Thurman Munson, 32, perishes at Canton, Ohio, in a crash of the plane he was piloting. A crowd of 51,151 will attend the memorial tribute at Yankee Stadium the following day.

September 5 Matt Keough of the A's beats the Brewers, 6–1, for his first victory after 14 straight losses. He ended 1978 with four defeats and barely avoided tying the AL record of 19 consecutive losses.

September 12 Boston's Carl Yastrzemski singles off New York's Jim Beattie for his 3,000th career hit. The Sox win 9-2 and Yaz becomes the first AL player to collect both 3,000 hits and 400 homers.

September 15 Boston's Bob Watson hits for the cycle in a 10–2 win over the Orioles. Watson becomes the first player to accomplish the feat in both leagues.

September 16 Willie Wilson hits his fifth inside-the-park homer this season in a 6–3 loss to Seattle at Kansas City. It is the most inside jobs hit in a season since Kiki Cuyler hit eight for the Pirates in 1925.

October 6 Scott McGregor's 8-0 shutout of the Angels gives the Orioles the pennant. Pat Kelly notches three RBIs with a homer and a single.

October 10 The Orioles score five times in the first inning of the World Series, hanging on to defeat the Pirates 5-4 in Game 1. Dave Parker has four hits for the losers.

October 13 Baltimore scores six runs in the eighth inning en route to a 9-6 win, taking a three-games-to-one advantage.

October 31 Mike Flanagan, who posted a 23-9 record for the Orioles, is named the winner of the AL Cy Young Award by a comfortable margin over the Yankees' Tommy John.

November 14 California's Don Baylor, who led the AL in runs and RBI, is named MVP.

	BALTIMORE		BOSTON		CALIFORNIA		CHICAGO		CLEVELAND		DETROIT		KANSAS CITY
M	E.Weaver	M	D.Zimmer	M	J.Fregosi	M	D.Kessinger	M	J.Torborg	M	L.Moss	M	W.Herzog
1B	E.Murray	1B	B.Watson	1B	R.Carew	M	T.LaRussa	M	D.Garcia	M	D.Tracewski	1B	P.LaCock
2B	R.Dauer	2B	J.Remy	2B	B.Grich	1B	M.Squires	1B	A.Thornton	M	S.Anderson	2B	F.White
SS	K.Garcia	SS	R.Burleson	SS	B.Campaneris	2B	A.Bannister	2B	D.Kuiper	1B	J.Thompson	SS	F.Patek
3B	D.DeCinces	3B	B.Hobson	3B	C.Lansford	SS	G.Pryor	SS	T.Veryzer	2B	L.Whitaker	3B	G.Brett
LF	G.Roenicke	LF	J.Rice	LF	J.Rudi	3B	K.Bell	3B	T.Harrah	SS	A.Trammell	LF	W.Wilson
CF	A.Bumbry	CF	F.Lynn	CF	R.Miller	LF	R.Torres	LF	J.Norris	3B	A.Rodriguez	CF	A.Otis
RF	K.Singleton	RF	D.Evans	RF	D.Ford	CF	C.Lemon	CF	R.Manning	LF	S.Kemp	RF	A.Cowens
C	R.Dempsey	C	G.Allenson	C	B.Downing	RF	C.Washington	RF	B.Bonds	CF	R.LeFlore	C	D.Porter
DH	L.May	DH	C.Yastrzemski	DH	D.Baylor	C	M.May	C	G.Alexander	RF	J.Morales	DH	H.McRae
						DH	J.Orta	DH	C.Johnson	C	L.Parrish		
S	M.Belanger	DC	C.Fisk	1D	W.Aikens					DH	R.Staub	S2	U.Washington
O	J.Lowenstein	S3	J.Anderson			OD	R.Garr	O1	M.Hargrove				
						1D	L.Johnson	C	R.Hassey	OD	C.Summers	P	P.Splittorff
P	D.Martinez	P	D.Eckersley	P	D.Frost	23	J.Morrison			1C	J.Wockenfuss	P	D.Leonard
P	M.Flanagan	P	B.Stanley	P	N.Ryan	3	E.Soderholm	P	R.Wise	O	L.Jones	P	L.Gura
P	S.Stone	P	S.Renko	P	J.Barr	OD	J.Moore	P	R.Waits			P	R.Gale
P	S.McGregor	P	C.Rainey	P	D.Aase			P	M.Paxton	P	J.Morris	RP	E.Rodriguez
P	J.Palmer	RP	D.Drago	P	C.Knapp	P	K.Kravec	P	D.Spillner	P	M.Wilcox	RP	A.Hrabosky
RP	T.Martinez	RP	T.Burgmeier	RP	M.Clear	P	R.Wortham	P	L.Barker	P	J.Billingham		
RP	D.Stanhouse	RP	B.Campbell	RP	D.LaRoche	P	R.Baumgarten	RP	S.Monge	P	P.Underwood	P	S.Busby
RP	T.Stoddard			RP	M.Barlow	P	S.Trout	RP	V.Cruz	P	D.Petry	P	M.Pattin
		P	A.Ripley			RP	R.Scarbery			RP	A.Lopez	P	C.Chamberlain
P	S.Stewart	P	J.Finch	P	F.Tanana	RP	M.Proly	P	W.Garland	RP	J.Hiller		
						RP	E.Farmer	P	E.Wilkins	RP	T.Tobik		
						P	F.Barrios			P	D.Rozema		
						P	F.Howard			P	S.Baker		

	MILWAUKEE		MINNESOTA		NEW YORK		OAKLAND		SEATTLE		TEXAS		TORONTO
M	G.Bamberger	M	G.Mauch	M	B.Lemon	M	J.Marshall	M	D.Johnson	M	P.Corrales	M	R.Hartsfield
1B	C.Cooper	1B	R.Jackson	M	B.Martin	1B	D.Revering	1B	B.Bochte	1B	P.Putnam	1B	J.Mayberry
2B	P.Molitor	2B	R.Wilfong	1B	C.Chambliss	2B	M.Edwards	2B	J.Cruz	2B	B.Wills	2B	D.Ainge
SS	R.Yount	SS	R.Smalley	2B	W.Randolph	SS	R.Picciolo	SS	M.Mendoza	SS	N.Norman	SS	A.Griffin
3B	S.Bando	3B	J.Castino	SS	B.Dent	3B	W.Gross	3B	D.Meyer	3B	B.Bell	3B	R.Howell
LF	B.Oglivie	LF	B.Rivera	3B	G.Nettles	LF	R.Henderson	LF	L.Roberts	LF	B.Sample	LF	A.Woods
CF	G.Thomas	CF	K.Landreaux	LF	L.Piniella	CF	D.Murphy	CF	R.Jones	CF	A.Oliver	CF	B.Bonnell
RF	S.Lezcano	RF	H.Powell	CF	B.Murcer	RF	L.Murray	RF	J.Simpson	RF	R.Zisk	RF	B.Bailor
C	C.Moore	C	B.Wynegar	RF	R.Jackson	C	J.Newman	C	L.Cox	C	J.Sundberg	C	R.Cerone
DH	D.Davis	DH	J.Morales	C	T.Munson	DH	M.Page	DH	W.Horton	DH	J.Ellis	DH	R.Carty
				DH	J.Spencer								
D3	D.Money	DO	G.Adams			C3	J.Essian	S2	L.Milbourne	O	J.Grubb	O	O.Velez
32	J.Gantner	OD	W.Norwood	O	M.Rivers	O	T.Armas	O1	T.Paciorek	O	M.Rivers		
		3D	M.Cubbage	DO	R.White	OC	M.Heath	32	B.Stein			P	T.Underwood
P	L.Sorensen	O	D.Edwards			2S	D.Chalk	C	B.Stinson	P	F.Jenkins	P	P.Huffman
P	M.Caldwell			P	T.John					P	S.Comer	P	D.Lemanczyk
P	J.Slaton	P	J.Koosman	P	R.Guidry	P	R.Langford	P	M.Parrott	P	D.Medich	P	B.Moore
P	B.Travers	P	D.Goltz	P	L.Tiant	P	S.McCatty	P	R.Honeycutt	P	D.Alexander	P	D.Stieb
P	M.Haas	P	G.Zahn	P	C.Hunter	P	M.Keough	P	F.Bannister	RP	J.Kern	RP	D.Freisleben
RP	J.Augustine	P	P.Hartzell	P	E.Figueroa	P	M.Norris	P	O.Jones	RP	S.Lyle	RP	T.Buskey
RP	R.Cleveland	RP	M.Marshall	RP	R.Davis	P	C.Minetto	P	G.Abbott	RP	D.Rajsich		
RP	B.McClure	RP	M.Marshall	RP	K.Clay	RP	D.Heaverlo	RP	B.McLaughlin			P	J.Jefferson
		RP	P.Redfern	RP	D.Hood	RP	D.Hamilton	RP	J.Montague	P	J.Matlack	P	M.Lemongello
P	P.Mitchell	RP	D.Jackson			RP	J.Todd	RP	S.Rawley	P	J.Johnson	P	J.Clancy
P	B.Galasso			P	J.Beattie			P	R.Dressler	P	D.Darwin	/P	B.Edge
		P	M.Bacsik	P	R.Gossage	P	B.Kingman						
		P	G.Serum	P	J.Kaat	P	J.Johnson						
						P	M.Morgan						

TEAM	G	W	L	PCT	GB	R	OR	AB	H	2B	3B	HR	BB	SO	AVG	OBP	SLG	PRO	PRO+	BR	/A	PF	CHI	RC	SB	CS	SBA	SBR
EAST																												
BAL	159	102	57	.642		757	582	5371	1401	258	24	181	608	847	.261	.339	.419	.758	107	25	54	96	98	758	99	49	67	0
MIL	161	95	66	.590	8	807	722	5536	1552	291	41	185	549	745	.280	.347	.448	.795	113	95	95	100	94	850	100	53	65	-2
BOS	160	91	69	.569	11.5	841	711	5538	1567	310	34	194	512	708	.283	.347	.456	.803	109	108	61	96	97	848	60	43	58	-8
NY	160	89	71	.556	13.5	734	672	5421	1443	226	40	150	509	590	.266	.331	.406	.737	100	-21	-5	98	102	708	65	46	59	-8
DET	161	85	76	.528	18	770	738	5375	1446	221	35	164	575	814	.269	.342	.415	.757	100	24	0	103	101	754	176	86	67	1
CLE	161	81	80	.503	22	760	805	5388	1388	206	29	138	657	786	.258	.344	.384	.728	96	-21	-24	100	103	720	143	90	61	-11
TOR	162	53	109	.327	50.5	613	862	5423	1362	253	34	95	448	663	.251	.313	.363	.676	81	-142	-149	101	104	602	75	56	57	-11
WEST																												
CAL	162	88	74	.543		866	768	5550	1563	242	43	164	589	843	.282	.354	.429	.783	114	83	112	97	101	842	100	53	65	-2
KC	162	85	77	.525	3	851	816	5653	1596	286	79	116	528	675	.282	.347	.422	.769	104	51	35	102	103	836	207	76	73	17
TEX	162	83	79	.512	5	750	698	5562	1546	252	26	140	461	607	.278	.337	.409	.746	101	-1	8	99	99	750	79	51	61	-7
MIN	162	82	80	.506	6	764	725	5544	1544	256	46	112	526	693	.278	.344	.402	.746	96	7	-22	104	99	770	66	45	59	-7
CHI	160	73	87	.456	14	730	748	5463	1505	290	33	127	454	668	.275	.335	.410	.745	100	4	-9	102	99	726	97	62	61	-8
SEA	162	67	95	.414	21	711	820	5544	1490	250	52	132	515	725	.269	.334	.404	.738	96	-17	-30	102	96	733	126	52	71	7
OAK	162	54	108	.333	34	573	860	5348	1276	188	32	108	482	751	.239	.304	.346	.650	79	-189	-160	95	106	552	104	69	60	-10
TOT	1128					10527		76704	20682	3529	548	2006	7413	10115	.270	.337	.408	.746							1497	831	64	-50

TEAM	CG	SH	SV	IP	H	H/G	HR	BB	SO	RAT	ERA	ERA+	OAV	OOB	PR	/A	PF	CPI	FA	E	DP	FW	PW	BW	SBW	DIF
EAST																										
BAL	52	12	30	1434¹	1279	8.0	133	467	786	11.0	3.26	123	.241	.304	152	119	95	100	.980	125	161	.8	11.6	5.3	.3	4.5
MIL	61	12	23	1439²	1563	9.8	162	381	580	12.3	4.03	103	.279	.327	29	21	99	105	.980	127	153	.7	2.0	9.3	.1	2.3
BOS	47	11	29	1431¹	1487	9.4	133	463	731	12.5	4.03	103	.270	.330	29	61	105	100	.978	134	166	-.2	6.0	6.0	-.4	-.3
NY	43	10	37	1432¹	1446	9.1	123	455	731	12.0	3.83	106	.268	.326	61	38	97	102	.981	122	183	1.0	3.7	-.5	-.4	5.2
DET	25	5	37	1423¹	1429	9.0	167	547	802	12.8	4.27	101	.265	.338	-9	8	103	101	.981	120	184	1.1	.8	.0	.4	2.1
CLE	28	7	32	1431²	1502	9.4	138	570	781	13.2	4.57	93	.272	.343	-56	-50	101	94	.978	134	149	.3	-4.9	-2.3	-.7	8.1
TOR	44	7	11	1417	1537	9.8	165	594	613	13.8	4.82	90	.281	.351	-95	-75	103	100	.975	145	187	-1.0	-7.3	-14.5	-.7	-4.4
WEST																										
CAL	46	9	33	1436	1463	9.2	131	573	820	13.0	4.34	96	.267	.340	-19	-42	97	96	.978	135	172	.3	-4.1	10.9	.1	-.3
KC	42	7	27	1448¹	1477	9.2	165	536	640	12.7	4.45	96	.267	.335	-38	-30	101	95	.977	146	160	-.3	-2.9	3.4	2.0	1.8
TEX	26	10	42	1437	1371	8.6	135	532	773	12.1	3.86	107	.253	.323	56	45	98	97	.979	130	151	.6	4.4	.8	-.3	-3.5
MIN	31	6	33	1444¹	1590	9.9	128	452	721	12.8	4.13	106	.285	.340	14	40	104	106	.979	134	203	.4	3.9	-2.1	-.3	-.8
CHI	28	9	37	1409	1365	8.7	114	618	675	12.9	4.10	104	.256	.338	18	23	101	96	.972	173	142	-1.9	2.2	-.4	-.4	-6.5
SEA	37	7	26	1438	1567	9.8	165	571	736	13.6	4.58	95	.281	.351	-57	-34	103	103	.978	141	170	.0	-3.3	-2.9	1.0	-8.8
OAK	41	4	20	1429¹	1606	10.1	147	654	726	14.5	4.75	85	.288	.367	-84	-112	96	105	.972	174	137	-1.9	-10.9	-15.6	-.6	2.0
TOT	551	116	417	20051²		9.3				12.8	4.22		.270	.337					.978	1962	2318					

Runs		Hits		Doubles		Triples		Home Runs		Total Bases	
Baylor-Cal	120	Brett-KC	212	Lemon-Chi	44	Brett-KC	20	Thomas-Mil	45	Rice-Bos	369
Brett-KC	119	Rice-Bos	201	Cooper-Mil	44	Molitor-Mil	16	Rice-Bos	39	Brett-KC	363
Rice-Bos	117	Bell-Tex	200	Lynn-Bos	42	Wilson-KC	13	Lynn-Bos	39	Lynn-Bos	338
Lynn-Bos	116	Molitor-Mil	188	Brett-KC	42	Randolph-NY	13	Baylor-Cal	36	Baylor-Cal	333
Lansford-Cal	114	Lansford-Cal	188	Bell-Tex	42			Singleton-Bal	35	Singleton-Bal	304

Runs Batted In		Runs Produced		Bases On Balls		Batting Average		On Base Percentage		Slugging Average	
Baylor-Cal	139	Baylor-Cal	223	Porter-KC	121	Lynn-Bos	.333	Porter-KC	.429	Lynn-Bos	.637
Rice-Bos	130	Rice-Bos	208	Singleton-Bal	109	Brett-KC	.329	Lynn-Bos	.426	Rice-Bos	.596
Thomas-Mil	123	Brett-KC	203	Thomas-Mil	98	Downing-Cal	.326	Downing-Cal	.420	Lezcano-Mil	.573
Lynn-Bos	122	Lynn-Bos	199	Randolph-NY	95	Rice-Bos	.325	Lezcano-Mil	.420	Brett-KC	.563
Porter-KC	112	Porter-KC	193	Thornton-Cle	90	Oliver-Tex	.323	Singleton-Bal	.409	Jackson-NY	.544

Production		Adjusted Production		Batter Runs		Adjusted Batter Runs		Clutch Hitting Index		Runs Created	
Lynn-Bos	1.063	Lynn-Bos	173	Lynn-Bos	62.1	Lynn-Bos	54.7	Porter-KC	123	Lynn-Bos	147
Lezcano-Mil	.992	Lezcano-Mil	165	Rice-Bos	50.2	Singleton-Bal	49.2	Baylor-Cal	121	Rice-Bos	138
Rice-Bos	.981	Singleton-Bal	158	Lezcano-Mil	44.6	Lezcano-Mil	44.6	Sundberg-Tex	120	Brett-KC	134
Kemp-Det	.946	Rice-Bos	152	Singleton-Bal	44.4	Rice-Bos	42.9	Cerone-Tor	117	Singleton-Bal	127
Singleton-Bal	.942	Jackson-NY	151	Brett-KC	42.8	Baylor-Cal	40.8	Dauer-Bal	114	Baylor-Cal	126

Total Average		Stolen Bases		Stolen Base Average		Stolen Base Runs		Fielding Runs		Total Player Rating	
Lynn-Bos	1.162	Wilson-KC	83	Wilson-KC	87.4	Wilson-KC	17.7	Smalley-Min	33.1	Smalley-Min	5.6
Lezcano-Mil	1.051	LeFlore-Det	78	Otis-KC	85.7	LeFlore-Det	15.0	Dent-NY	32.0	Lynn-Bos	5.2
Rice-Bos	.993	Cruz-Sea	49	LeFlore-Det	84.8	Cruz-Sea	9.3	Mendoza-Sea	27.5	Brett-KC	4.9
Singleton-Bal	.993	Bumbry-Bal	37	Cruz-Sea	84.5	Otis-KC	6.0	Burleson-Bos	21.7	Grich-Cal	4.2
Porter-KC	.982	Wills-Tex	35	Lowenstein-Bal	80.0	Manning-Cle	4.2	Wilfong-Min	20.7	Lezcano-Mil	4.0

Wins		Win Percentage		Games		Complete Games		Shutouts		Saves	
Flanagan-Bal	23	Caldwell-Mil	.727	Marshall-Min	90	D.Martinez-Bal	18	Ryan-Cal	5	Marshall-Min	32
John-NY	21	Flanagan-Bal	.719	Monge-Cle	76	Ryan-Cal	17	Leonard-KC	5	Kern-Tex	29
Koosman-Min	20	Morris-Det	.708	Kern-Tex	71	John-NY	17	Flanagan-Bal	5	Stanhouse-Bal	21
Guidry-NY	18	John-NY	.700	Lyle-Tex	67	Eckersley-Bos	17	Stanley-Bos	4	Lopez-Det	21
		Guidry-NY	.692	Heaverlo-Oak	62			Caldwell-Mil	4	Monge-Cle	19

Innings Pitched		Fewest Hits/Game		Fewest BB/Game		Strikeouts		Strikeouts/Game		Ratio	
D.Martinez-Bal	292.1	Ryan-Cal	6.83	McGregor-Bal	1.19	Ryan-Cal	223	Ryan-Cal	9.01	McGregor-Bal	9.79
John-NY	276.1	Kravec-Chi	7.49	Caldwell-Mil	1.49	Guidry-NY	201	Guidry-NY	7.65	Guidry-NY	10.43
Flanagan-Bal	265.2	Guidry-NY	7.73	Sorensen-Mil	1.61	Flanagan-Bal	190	Flanagan-Bal	6.44	Flanagan-Bal	10.77
Koosman-Min	263.2	Morris-Det	8.15	Stanley-Bos	1.83	Jenkins-Tex	164	Jenkins-Tex	5.70	Leonard-KC	10.83
Jenkins-Tex	259.0	Baumgarten-Chi	8.26	John-NY	2.12	Koosman-Min	157	Bannister-Sea	5.68	Eckersley-Bos	10.91

Earned Run Average		Adjusted ERA		Opponents' Batting Avg.		Opponents' On Base Pct.		Starter Runs		Adjusted Starter Runs	
Guidry-NY	2.78	Eckersley-Bos	148	Ryan-Cal	.212	McGregor-Bal	.275	John-NY	38.4	Eckersley-Bos	39.0
John-NY	2.96	Guidry-NY	146	Kravec-Chi	.233	Guidry-NY	.294	Guidry-NY	37.7	John-NY	34.0
Eckersley-Bos	2.99	John-NY	137	Guidry-NY	.236	Flanagan-Bal	.297	Eckersley-Bos	33.5	Guidry-NY	33.9
Flanagan-Bal	3.08	Morris-Det	132	Baumgarten-Chi	.243	Eckersley-Bos	.298	Flanagan-Bal	33.4	Koosman-Min	29.3
Morris-Det	3.28	Flanagan-Bal	130	Morris-Det	.244	Leonard-KC	.299	Koosman-Min	24.5	Flanagan-Bal	27.4

Clutch Pitching Index		Relief Runs		Adjusted Relief Runs		Relief Ranking		Total Pitcher Index		Total Baseball Ranking	
Eckersley-Bos	115	Kern-Tex	42.0	Kern-Tex	40.9	Kern-Tex	65.0	Kern-Tex	6.7	Kern-Tex	6.7
Keough-Oak	114	Monge-Cle	26.4	Marshall-Min	27.4	Marshall-Min	57.1	Marshall-Min	5.7	Marshall-Min	5.7
McCatty-Oak	114	Lopez-Det	25.5	Lopez-Det	27.0	Monge-Cle	49.5	Monge-Cle	5.0	Smalley-Min	5.6
Travers-Mil	113	Marshall-Min	24.8	Monge-Cle	26.9	Lopez-Det	38.8	Eckersley-Bos	4.0	Lynn-Bos	5.2
Koosman-Min	112	Stoddard-Bal	16.2	Burgmeier-Bos	16.5	Drago-Bos	26.6	John-NY	3.8	Monge-Cle	5.0

January 28 Henry Aaron refuses an award from Commissioner Bowie Kuhn honoring him for hitting his 715th home run. Aaron charges that baseball's treatment of retired black ballplayers falls far short of what is needed.

July 30 Attempting to throw for the first time since being hospitalized for tests last week, J. R. Richard suffers a stroke and is rushed to Houston's Methodist Hospital for emergency surgery to remove a life-threatening blood clot in his neck. He will never pitch in the major leagues again.

September 10 The Expos' 21-year-old pitcher Bill Gullickson strikes out 18 Cubs in a 4-2 win at Olympic Stadium, setting a major league record for rookies and falling one short of the all-time record for strikeouts in a nine-inning game.

October 5 Capping an improbable comeback, the Dodgers beat the Astros for the third day in a row to force a one-game playoff for the NL West title. Los Angeles trailed Houston by three games with three games left in the season, and won all three by a single run.

October 6 The Astros finally win, whipping the Dodgers in a one-game playoff at Dodger Stadium, 7-1. Art Howe drives in four runs with a home run and two singles and Joe Niekro wins his 20th game of the season to put Houston in the postseason for the first time.

October 11 In one of the most exciting and controversial games in playoff history, the Phillies tie the NLCS at two games apiece with a 10-inning 5-3 win over the Astros. In the fourth inning, Houston is deprived of an apparent triple play when the umpires rule that pitcher Vern Ruhle had trapped Garry Maddox's soft line drive. In the sixth, Houston loses a run when Gary Woods leaves the base early on Luis Pujols' would-be sacrifice fly.

October 12 The Phillies capture their first pennant since 1950 with a 10-inning, 8-7 win over the Astros in the fifth and final game of the NLCS.

October 21 The Phillies win the first world championship in their 98-year history by beating the Royals 4-1 in Game 6 of the World Series. Philadelphia's Mike Schmidt is named MVP, hitting .381 with two home runs and seven RBIs, while Kansas City's Willie Wilson is the goat, striking out a record 12 times.

November 4 Steve Carlton joins Sandy Koufax, Tom Seaver, and Jim Palmer as the only pitchers to win three Cy Young Awards, garnering 23 of 24 first-place votes to take NL honors. Carlton was 24-9 with a 2.34 ERA and led the league with 286 strikeouts.

November 4* Sadaharu Oh, professional baseball's all-time home run king with 868 in 22 seasons in Japan, retires at the age of 40.

November 26 Mike Schmidt is a unanimous choice as MVP. The slugging third baseman hit .286 with career highs of 48 home runs and 121 RBIs.

	ATLANTA		CHICAGO		CINCINNATI		HOUSTON		LOS ANGELES		MONTREAL
M	B.Cox	M	P.Gomez	M	J.McNamara	M	B.Virdon	M	T.Lasorda	M	D.Williams
1B	C.Chambliss	M	J.Amalfitano	1B	D.Driessen	1B	A.Howe	1B	S.Garvey	1B	W.Cromartie
2B	G.Hubbard	1B	B.Buckner	2B	J.Kennedy	2B	J.Morgan	2B	D.Lopes	2B	R.Scott
SS	L.Gomez	2B	M.Tyson	SS	D.Concepcion	SS	C.Reynolds	SS	B.Russell	SS	C.Speier
3B	B.Horner	SS	I.DeJesus	3B	R.Knight	3B	E.Cabell	3B	R.Cey	3B	L.Parrish
LF	J.Burroughs	3B	L.Randle	LF	G.Foster	LF	J.Cruz	LF	D.Baker	LF	R.LeFlore
CF	D.Murphy	LF	D.Kingman	CF	D.Collins	CF	C.Cedeno	CF	R.Law	CF	A.Dawson
RF	G.Matthews	CF	J.Martin	RF	K.Griffey	RF	T.Puhl	RF	R.Smith	RF	R.Office
C	B.Benedict	RF	M.Vail	C	J.Bench	C	A.Ashby	C	S.Yeager	C	G.Carter
		C	T.Blackwell								
23	J.Royster			O	C.Geronimo	2S	R.Landestoy	O	J.Johnstone	O	J.White
S3	L.Blanks	1O	L.Biittner	2S	R.Oester	1O	D.Walling	OS	D.Thomas	O	E.Valentine
O	B.Asselstine	32	S.Dillard			C	L.Pujols				
		O	J.Figueroa	P	M.Soto	O1	J.Leonard	P	J.Reuss	P	S.Rogers
P	P.Niekro	23	M.Kelleher	P	F.Pastore			P	B.Welch	P	S.Sanderson
P	D.Alexander	O1	S.Thompson	P	C.Leibrandt	P	J.Niekro	P	D.Sutton	P	B.Gullickson
P	T.Boggs	C	B.Foote	P	M.LaCoss	P	N.Ryan	P	B.Hooton	P	D.Palmer
P	R.Matula			P	T.Seaver	P	K.Forsch	P	D.Goltz	P	B.Lee
P	L.McWilliams	P	R.Reuschel	RP	T.Hume	P	V.Ruhle	RP	R.Sutcliffe	RP	F.Norman
RP	R.Camp	P	M.Krukow	RP	D.Bair	P	J.Andujar	RP	B.Castillo	RP	E.Sosa
RP	G.Garber	P	D.Lamp			RP	D.Smith	RP	S.Howe	RP	S.Bahnsen
RP	P.Hanna	P	L.McGlothen	P	P.Moskau	RP	J.Sambito			
		RP	B.Caudill	P	J.Price	RP	F.LaCorte	P	J.Beckwith	P	C.Lea
P	A.Hrabosky	RP	D.Tidrow							P	W.Fryman
P	L.Bradford	RP	W.Hernandez								
		P	B.Sutter			P	J.Richard				
		P	D.Capilla								

	NEW YORK		PHILADELPHIA		PITTSBURGH		SAN DIEGO		SAN FRANCISCO		ST.LOUIS
M	J.Torre	M	D.Green	M	C.Tanner	M	J.Coleman	M	D.Bristol	M	K.Boyer
1B	L.Mazzilli	1B	P.Rose	1B	J.Milner	1B	W.Montanez	1B	M.Ivie	M	J.Krol
2B	D.Flynn	2B	M.Trillo	2B	P.Garner	2B	D.Cash	2B	R.Stennett	M	W.Herzog
SS	F.Taveras	SS	L.Bowa	SS	T.Foli	SS	O.Smith	SS	J.LeMaster	M	R.Schoendienst
3B	E.Maddox	3B	M.Schmidt	3B	B.Madlock	3B	A.Rodriguez	3B	D.Evans	1B	K.Hernandez
LF	S.Henderson	LF	G.Luzinski	LF	M.Easler	LF	G.Richards	LF	L.Herndon	2B	K.Oberkfell
CF	J.Youngblood	CF	G.Maddox	CF	O.Moreno	CF	J.Mumphrey	CF	B.North	SS	G.Templeton
RF	C.Washington	RF	B.McBride	RF	D.Parker	RF	D.Winfield	RF	J.Clark	3B	K.Reitz
C	A.Trevino	C	B.Boone	C	E.Ott	C	G.Tenace	C	M.May	LF	B.Bonds
										CF	T.Scott
1O	M.Jorgensen	O	G.Gross	O	L.Lacy	23	T.Flannery	O	T.Whitfield	RF	G.Hendrick
C1	J.Stearns	O	L.Smith	1O	B.Robinson	C	B.Fahey			C	T.Simmons
				3S	D.Berra			P	V.Blue		
P	R.Burris	P	S.Carlton	1	W.Stargell	P	J.Curtis	P	B.Knepper	O	D.Iorg
P	P.Zachry	P	D.Ruthven			P	S.Mura	P	E.Whitson	O	L.Durham
P	M.Bomback	P	B.Walk	P	J.Bibby	P	R.Wise	P	A.Ripley	CO	T.Kennedy
P	P.Falcone	P	R.Lerch	P	J.Candelaria	P	R.Jones	P	J.Montefusco	2S	T.Herr
P	C.Swan	RP	T.McGraw	P	B.Blyleven	P	G.Lucas	RP	T.Griffin		
RP	T.Hausman	RP	R.Reed	P	D.Robinson	RP	B.Shirley	RP	G.Lavelle	P	P.Vuckovich
RP	J.Reardon	RP	D.Noles	P	R.Rhoden	RP	E.Rasmussen	RP	G.Minton	P	B.Forsch
RP	N.Allen			RP	E.Romo	RP	R.Fingers			P	B.Sykes
		P	N.Espinosa	RP	K.Tekulve			P	A.Holland	P	S.Martinez
P	J.Pacella	P	L.Christenson	RP	G.Jackson	P	J.Eichelberger	P	A.Hargesheimer	RP	J.Kaat
P	R.Jackson	P	K.Saucier			P	D.Kinney			RP	D.Hood
P	E.Glynn			P	E.Solomon	P	J.D'Acquisto			RP	J.Littlefield
										P	J.Fulgham
										P	J.Urrea
										P	J.Otten
										P	R.Thomas

TEAM	G	W	L	PCT	GB	R	OR	AB	H	2B	3B	HR	BB	SO	AVG	OBP	SLG	PRO	PRO+	BR	/A	PF	CHI	RC	SB	CS	SBA	SBR
EAST																												
PHI	162	91	71	.562		728	639	5625	1517	272	54	117	472	**708**	.270	.330	**.400**	.730	103	61	21	106	100	**736**	140	62	69	5
MON	162	90	72	.556	1	694	629	5465	1407	250	61	114	547	865	.257	.327	.388	.715	105	36	35	100	101	709	237	82	74	22
PIT	162	83	79	.512	8	666	646	5517	1469	249	38	116	452	760	.266	.325	.388	.713	102	27	17	102	98	686	209	102	67	2
STL	162	74	88	.457	17	**738**	710	5608	**1541**	**300**	49	101	451	781	.275	.331	**.400**	**.731**	106	**63**	41	103	102	724	117	54	68	3
NY	162	67	95	.414	24	611	702	5478	1407	218	41	61	501	840	.257	.322	.345	.667	95	-52	-35	97	102	601	158	99	61	-12
CHI	162	64	98	.395	27	614	728	5619	1411	251	35	107	471	912	.251	.311	.365	.676	88	-47	-93	107	100	627	93	64	59	-11
WEST																												
HOU	163	93	70	.571		637	**589**	5566	1455	231	**67**	75	540	755	.261	.328	.367	.695	**109**	2	**55**	92	96	688	194	74	72	14
LA	163	92	71	.564	1	663	591	5568	1462	209	24	**148**	492	846	.263	.325	.388	.713	106	29	42	98	96	699	123	72	63	-6
CIN	163	89	73	.549	3.5	707	670	5516	1445	256	45	113	537	852	.262	.330	.386	.716	105	39	39	100	101	716	156	43	**78**	21
ATL	161	81	80	.503	11	630	660	5402	1352	226	22	144	434	899	.250	.308	.380	.688	94	-27	-47	103	**104**	616	73	52	58	-9
SF	161	75	86	.466	17	573	634	5368	1310	199	44	80	509	840	.244	.311	.342	.653	90	-82	-69	98	102	571	100	58	63	-5
SD	163	73	89	.451	19.5	591	654	5540	1410	195	43	67	**563**	791	.255	.326	.342	.668	98	-48	-12	94	96	641	**239**	73	77	**28**
TOT	973					7852		66272	17186	2856	523	1243	5969	9849	.259	.323	.374	.697							1839	835	69	51

TEAM	CG	SH	SV	IP	H	H/G	HR	BB	SO	RAT	ERA	ERA+	OAV	OOB	PR	/A	PF	CPI	FA	E	DP	FW	PW	BW	SBW	DIF
EAST																										
PHI	25	8	40	1480	1419	8.6	87	530	889	12.0	3.43	**110**	.255	.322	28	**59**	105	100	.979	136	136	.2	**6.2**	2.2	.0	1.2
MON	33	15	36	1456²	1447	8.9	100	460	823	11.9	3.48	102	.261	.320	20	14	99	102	.977	144	126	-.2	1.5	3.7	1.9	2.1
PIT	25	8	**43**	1458¹	1422	8.8	110	**451**	832	11.7	3.58	102	.259	.318	4	10	101	99	.978	137	154	.2	1.1	1.8	-.2	-.8
STL	**34**	9	27	1447	1454	9.0	90	495	664	12.3	3.93	94	.265	.329	-53	-39	103	**174**	.981	122	174	1.0	-4.1	4.3	-.1	-8.1
NY	17	9	33	1451¹	1473	9.1	140	510	886	12.4	3.85	92	.267	.331	-40	-48	99	104	.975	154	132	-.7	-5.1	-3.7	-1.7	-2.8
CHI	13	6	35	1479	1525	9.3	109	589	923	13.0	3.89	101	.272	.344	-47	4	109	**106**	.974	174	149	-1.7	.4	-9.8	-1.6	-4.2
WEST																										
HOU	31	18	41	1482²	1367	**8.3**	69	466	**929**	11.3	**3.10**	106	**.246**	**.307**	**82**	31	91	96	.978	140	145	.0	3.3	**5.8**	1.0	1.3
LA	24	**19**	42	1472²	**1358**	**8.3**	105	480	835	**11.3**	3.25	108	.247	.309	58	41	97	100	.981	123	149	1.0	4.3	4.4	-1.1	1.8
CIN	30	12	37	1459¹	1404	8.7	113	506	833	11.9	3.85	93	.255	.319	-40	-44	99	92	**.983**	106	144	**1.9**	-4.6	4.1	1.8	4.9
ATL	29	9	37	1428	1397	8.8	131	454	696	11.8	3.77	99	.258	.318	-27	-4	104	97	.975	162	156	-1.2	-.4	-5.0	-1.4	8.4
SF	27	10	35	1448¹	1446	9.0	92	492	811	12.2	3.46	102	.261	.325	24	13	98	104	.975	159	124	-1.0	1.4	-7.3	-1.0	2.4
SD	19	9	39	1466¹	1474	9.0	97	536	728	12.4	3.65	94	.267	.333	-8	-36	95	105	.980	132	157	.5	-3.8	-1.3	**2.5**	-5.9
TOT	307	132	445	17529²		8.8				12.0	3.60		.259	.323					.978	1689	1746					

Runs		**Hits**		**Doubles**		**Triples**		**Home Runs**		**Total Bases**	
Hernandez-StL	111	Garvey-LA	200	Rose-Phi	42	Scott-Mon	13	Schmidt-Phi	48	Schmidt-Phi	342
Schmidt-Phi	104	Richards-SD	193	Dawson-Mon	41	Moreno-Pit	13	Horner-Atl	35	Garvey-LA	307
Murphy-Atl	98	Hernandez-StL	191	Buckner-Chi	41	LeFlore-Mon	11	Murphy-Atl	33	Hernandez-StL	294
Dawson-Mon	96	Buckner-Chi	187	Knight-Cin	39	Herndon-SF	11	Carter-Mon	29	Baker-LA	291
				Hernandez-StL	39			Baker-LA	29	Murphy-Atl	290

Runs Batted In		**Runs Produced**		**Bases On Balls**		**Batting Average**		**On Base Percentage**		**Slugging Average**	
Schmidt-Phi	121	Hernandez-StL	194	Morgan-Hou	93	Buckner-Chi	.324	Hernandez-StL	.410	Schmidt-Phi	.624
Hendrick-StL	109	Schmidt-Phi	177	Driessen-Cin	93	Hernandez-StL	.321	Cedeno-Hou	.390	Clark-SF	.517
Garvey-LA	106	Dawson-Mon	166	Tenace-SD	92	Templeton-StL	.319	Clark-SF	.390	Murphy-Atl	.510
Carter-Mon	101	Simmons-StL	161	Schmidt-Phi	89	McBride-Phi	.309	Schmidt-Phi	.388	Simmons-StL	.505
Hernandez-StL	99	Griffey-Cin	161	Hernandez-StL	86	Cedeno-Hou	.309	Driessen-Cin	.382	Baker-LA	.503

Production		**Adjusted Production**		**Batter Runs**		**Adjusted Batter Runs**		**Clutch Hitting Index**		**Runs Created**	
Schmidt-Phi	1.012	Schmidt-Phi	169	Schmidt-Phi	56.5	Schmidt-Phi	49.7	Montanez-SD-Mon	124	Schmidt-Phi	137
Clark-SF	.907	Clark-SF	155	Hernandez-StL	43.3	Hernandez-StL	39.7	Rose-Phi	117	Hernandez-StL	122
Hernandez-StL	.904	Cedeno-Hou	150	Easler-Pit	37.2	Easler-Pit	35.9	Youngblood-NY	117	Dawson-Mon	105
Simmons-StL	.885	Hernandez-StL	147	Clark-SF	31.1	Cedeno-Hou	33.6	Simmons-StL	117	Murphy-Atl	101
Murphy-Atl	.859	Simmons-StL	140	Simmons-StL	29.6	Clark-SF	33.1	Concepcion-Cin	116	Griffey-Cin	99

Total Average		**Stolen Bases**		**Stolen Base Average**		**Stolen Base Runs**		**Fielding Runs**		**Total Player Rating**	
Schmidt-Phi	1.095	LeFlore-Mon	97	Griffey-Cin	95.8	LeFlore-Mon	17.7	Smith-SD	40.8	Schmidt-Phi	7.3
Hernandez-StL	.915	Moreno-Pit	96	Mumphrey-SD	91.2	Mumphrey-SD	12.6	Templeton-StL	27.6	Dawson-Mon	4.8
Clark-SF	.906	Collins-Cin	79	LeFlore-Mon	83.6	Scott-Mon	11.1	Moreno-Pit	27.4	Templeton-StL	4.7
Cedeno-Hou	.890	Scott-Mon	63	Maddox-Phi	83.3	Collins-Cin	11.1	Schmidt-Phi	23.2	Smith-SD	4.7
Simmons-StL	.872	Richards-SD	61	Scott-Mon	82.9	Moreno-Pit	9.0	Dawson-Mon	20.1	Cedeno-Hou	4.3

Wins		**Win Percentage**		**Games**		**Complete Games**		**Shutouts**		**Saves**	
Carlton-Phi	24	Bibby-Pit	.760	Tidrow-Chi	84	Rogers-Mon	14	Reuss-LA	6	Sutter-Chi	28
Niekro-Hou	20	Reuss-LA	.750	Tekulve-Pit	78	Carlton-Phi	13	Rogers-Mon	4	Hume-Cin	25
Bibby-Pit	19	Carlton-Phi	.727	Hume-Cin	78	Niekro-Atl	11	Richard-Hou	4	Fingers-SD	23
Reuss-LA	18	Ruthven-Phi	.630	Camp-Atl	77	Niekro-Hou	11			Camp-Atl	22
Ruthven-Phi	17	Niekro-Hou	.625	Romo-Pit	74					Allen-NY	22

Innings Pitched		**Fewest Hits/Game**		**Fewest BB/Game**		**Strikeouts**		**Strikeouts/Game**		**Ratio**	
Carlton-Phi	304.0	Soto-Cin	5.96	Forsch-StL	1.38	Carlton-Phi	286	Soto-Cin	8.61	Sutton-LA	8.99
Rogers-Mon	281.0	Sutton-LA	6.91	Reuss-LA	1.57	Ryan-Hou	200	Carlton-Phi	8.47	Reuss-LA	9.14
Niekro-Atl	275.0	Carlton-Phi	7.19	Forsch-Hou	1.66	Soto-Cin	182	Ryan-Hou	7.70	Pastore-Cin	9.89
Reuschel-Chi	257.0	Seaver-Cin	7.50	Candelaria-Pit	1.93	Niekro-Atl	176	Blyleven-Pit	6.98	Carlton-Phi	9.92
Niekro-Hou	256.0	Reuss-LA	7.57	Sutton-LA	1.99	Blyleven-Pit	168	Welch-LA	5.94	Soto-Cin	10.02

Earned Run Average		**Adjusted ERA**		**Opponents' Batting Avg.**		**Opponents' On Base Pct.**		**Starter Runs**		**Adjusted Starter Runs**	
Sutton-LA	2.20	Carlton-Phi	162	Soto-Cin	.187	Sutton-LA	.258	Carlton-Phi	42.6	Carlton-Phi	49.0
Carlton-Phi	2.34	Sutton-LA	159	Sutton-LA	.211	Reuss-LA	.261	Sutton-LA	33.0	Sutton-LA	30.5
Reuss-LA	2.51	Reuss-LA	139	Carlton-Phi	.218	Pastore-Cin	.277	Reuss-LA	27.8	Reuss-LA	25.1
Blue-SF	2.97	Rogers-Mon	120	Seaver-Cin	.225	Carlton-Phi	.278	Ruhle-Hou	21.8	Rogers-Mon	18.3
Rogers-Mon	2.98	Blue-SF	119	Reuss-LA	.227	Soto-Cin	.279	Richard-Hou	21.5	Richard-Hou	17.5

Clutch Pitching Index		**Relief Runs**		**Adjusted Relief Runs**		**Relief Ranking**		**Total Pitcher Index**		**Total Baseball Ranking**	
Reuschel-Chi	119	McGraw-Phi	21.9	Caudill-Chi	24.5	McGraw-Phi	32.6	Carlton-Phi	5.3	Schmidt-Phi	7.3
Bomback-NY	116	Camp-Atl	20.3	McGraw-Phi	23.9	Camp-Atl	28.4	McGraw-Phi	3.6	Carlton-Phi	5.3
Zachry-NY	114	Caudill-Chi	20.1	Camp-Atl	22.0	Hume-Cin	25.6	Camp-Atl	3.4	Dawson-Mon	4.8
Ruthven-Phi	112	Smith-Hou	19.1	Holland-SF	16.4	Sutter-Chi	25.5	Hume-Cin	3.1	Templeton-StL	4.7
Sanderson-Mon	111	Holland-SF	16.9	Smith-Hou	15.5	Fryman-Mon	20.1	Sutter-Chi	2.7	Smith-SD	4.7

January 9 Al Kaline and Duke Snider are elected to the Hall of Fame by the BBWAA. Kaline is the 10th player to be elected in his first year of eligibility, while Snider is making his 11th appearance on the ballot.

February 12 The AL's offer to buy out the remaining eight years of the Oakland A's lease at the Oakland Coliseum expires, effectively blocking the sale of the club from Charlie Finley to oil man Marvin Davis. Davis had planned to move the club to Denver, but the Oakland Coliseum Board, backed by the city council, refuses the league's $4 million offer.

March 8 While waiting for the team bus outside his hotel during the Cleveland Indians three-game exhibition series against the Mexico City Reds, rookie outfielder Joe Charboneau is stabbed by a crazed fan wielding a ball-point pen. The pen penetrates one inch and strikes a rib, sidelining Charboneau for four days, but he will recover to win the league Rookie of the Year award.

March 12 Slugger Chuck Klein and former Red Sox owner Tom Yawkey are elected to the Hall of Fame by the Special Veterans Committee. Yawkey is the first club owner selected who never served as a player, manager, or general manager.

May 3 Rangers pitcher Ferguson Jenkins defeats the Orioles 3-2 to become only the fourth pitcher to win 100 games in each league. He won 149 games for the Phillies and Cubs before joining the AL in 1974.

August 23 A's owner Charlie Finley sells the club for $12.7 million to the Haas family of San Francisco, owners of the Levi Strauss clothing empire, keeping the team in Oakland.

October 4 The Yankees clinch their fourth AL East title in five seasons, beating Detroit, 5-2, in the first game of a doubleheader. Reggie Jackson hits his 41st home run of the season and will share the league home run crown with Milwaukee's Ben Oglivie.

October 10 George Brett puts Kansas City into its first World Series with a three-run home run off Yankees reliever Rich Gossage in the seventh inning. The Royals win 4-2 for a three-game sweep of the ALCS.

November 12 Baltimore's Steve Stone, who led the AL in wins with a 25-7 record, edges Oakland's Mike Norris for the league Cy Young Award.

November 18 Despite having missed 45 games with injuries, George Brett is named AL MVP. The 27-year-old third baseman's .390 average was the highest in the major leagues since Ted Williams' .406 in 1941, and he added 24 home runs and 118 RBIs to lead Kansas City to its first pennant.

December 15 Outfielder Dave Winfield becomes the highest-paid player in baseball when he signs a 10-year, $15 million contract with the New York Yankees.

	BALTIMORE		BOSTON		CALIFORNIA		CHICAGO		CLEVELAND		DETROIT		KANSAS CITY
M	E.Weaver	M	D.Zimmer	M	J.Fregosi	M	T.LaRussa	M	D.Garcia	M	S.Anderson	M	J.Frey
1B	E.Murray	M	J.Pesky	1B	R.Carew	1B	M.Squires	1B	M.Hargrove	1B	R.Hebner	1B	W.Aikens
2B	R.Dauer	1B	T.Perez	2B	B.Grich	2B	J.Morrison	2B	J.Brohamer	2B	L.Whitaker	2B	F.White
SS	M.Belanger	2B	D.Stapleton	SS	F.Patek	SS	T.Cruz	SS	T.Veryzer	SS	A.Trammell	SS	U.Washington
3B	D.DeCinces	SS	R.Burleson	3B	C.Lansford	3B	K.Bell	3B	T.Harrah	3B	T.Brookens	3B	G.Brett
LF	G.Roenicke	3B	G.Hoffman	LF	J.Rudi	LF	W.Nordhagen	LF	M.Dilone	LF	S.Kemp	LF	W.Wilson
CF	A.Bumbry	LF	J.Rice	CF	R.Miller	CF	C.Lemon	CF	R.Manning	CF	R.Peters	CF	A.Otis
RF	K.Singleton	CF	F.Lynn	RF	L.Harlow	RF	H.Baines	RF	J.Orta	RF	A.Cowens	RF	C.Hurdle
C	R.Dempsey	RF	D.Evans	C	T.Donohue	C	B.Kimm	C	R.Hassey	C	L.Parrish	C	D.Porter
DH	T.Crowley	C	C.Fisk	DH	J.Thompson	DH	L.Johnson	DH	J.Charboneau	DH	C.Summers	DH	H.McRae
		DH	C.Yastrzemski										
S2	K.Garcia			OD	D.Baylor	OD	B.Molinaro	S2	J.Dybzinski	1D	J.Wockenfuss	1O	P.LaCock
O	J.Lowenstein	3D	B.Hobson	S2	D.Thon	S3	G.Pryor	2O	A.Bannister			CO	J.Wathan
C	D.Graham	OD	J.Dwyer	O	B.Clark			C	B.Diaz	P	J.Morris		
D	L.May	2	J.Remy	OD	D.Ford	P	B.Burns	P	L.Barker	P	M.Wilcox	P	L.Gura
OD	P.Kelly			S	B.Campaneris	P	S.Trout	P	R.Waits	P	D.Schatzeder	P	D.Leonard
		P	M.Torrez			P	R.Dotson	P	D.Spillner	P	D.Petry	P	P.Splittorff
P	S.McGregor	P	D.Eckersley	P	F.Tanana	P	R.Baumgarten	P	W.Garland	P	D.Rozema	P	R.Gale
P	S.Stone	P	B.Stanley	P	D.Aase	P	L.Hoyt	P	B.Owchinko	RP	A.Lopez	P	R.Martin
P	M.Flanagan	P	S.Renko	P	A.Martinez	RP	M.Proly	RP	S.Monge	RP	P.Underwood	RP	D.Quisenberry
P	J.Palmer	P	D.Drago	P	C.Knapp	RP	E.Farmer	RP	M.Stanton			RP	M.Pattin
P	S.Stewart	RP	T.Burgmeier	RP	D.LaRoche	RP	R.Wortham	RP	V.Cruz	P	R.Weaver		
RP	T.Stoddard			RP	M.Clear					P	D.Tobik		
RP	T.Martinez	P	J.Tudor	RP	A.Hassler	P	K.Kravec	P	J.Denny	P	B.Robbins		
RP	D.Ford	P	C.Rainey					P	R.Grimsley				
				P	D.Frost								
P	D.Martinez			P	J.Montague								
				P	B.Kison								
				P	J.Barr								
				P	D.Lemanczyk								

	MILWAUKEE		MINNESOTA		NEW YORK		OAKLAND		SEATTLE		TEXAS		TORONTO
M	B.Rodgers	M	G.Mauch	M	D.Howser	M	B.Martin	M	D.Johnson	M	P.Corrales	M	B.Mattick
M	G.Bamberger	M	J.Goryl	1B	B.Watson	1B	D.Revering	M	M.Wills	1B	P.Putnam	1B	J.Mayberry
M	B.Rodgers	1B	R.Jackson	2B	W.Randolph	2B	D.McKay	1B	B.Bochte	2B	B.Wills	2B	D.Garcia
1B	C.Cooper	2B	R.Wilfong	SS	B.Dent	SS	M.Guerrero	2B	J.Cruz	SS	P.Frias	SS	A.Griffin
2B	P.Molitor	SS	R.Smalley	3B	G.Nettles	3B	W.Gross	SS	M.Mendoza	3B	B.Bell	3B	R.Howell
SS	R.Yount	3B	J.Castino	LF	L.Piniella	LF	R.Henderson	3B	T.Cox	LF	A.Oliver	LF	B.Bailor
3B	J.Gantner	LF	R.Sofield	CF	B.Brown	CF	D.Murphy	LF	D.Meyer	CF	M.Rivers	CF	B.Bonnell
LF	B.Oglivie	CF	K.Landreaux	RF	R.Jackson	RF	T.Armas	CF	J.Simpson	RF	J.Norris	RF	L.Moseby
CF	G.Thomas	RF	H.Powell	C	R.Cerone	C	J.Essian	RF	L.Roberts	C	J.Sundberg	C	E.Whitt
RF	S.Lezcano	C	B.Wynegar	DH	E.Soderholm	DH	M.Page	C	L.Cox	DH	R.Zisk	DH	O.Velez
C	C.Moore	DH	J.Morales					DH	W.Horton				
DH	D.Davis			OD	B.Murcer	1C	J.Newman			O	J.Grubb	OD	A.Woods
		DO	G.Adams	1D	J.Spencer	CD	M.Heath	S3	J.Anderson	3S	D.Roberts	23	G.Iorg
31	D.Money	13	M.Cubbage	O	R.Jones	S2	R.Picciolo	2S	L.Milbourne	D1	R.Staub	C	B.Davis
3D	S.Bando	2S	P.Mackanin					O1	T.Paciorek	O	B.Sample		
C	B.Martinez	O	D.Edwards	P	T.John	P	R.Langford	O	R.Craig			P	J.Clancy
				P	R.Guidry	P	M.Norris	O	J.Beniquez	P	J.Matlack	P	D.Stieb
P	M.Haas	P	J.Koosman	P	T.Underwood	P	M.Keough			P	D.Medich	P	P.Mirabella
P	M.Caldwell	P	G.Zahn	P	R.May	P	S.McCatty	P	F.Bannister	P	F.Jenkins	P	J.Jefferson
P	L.Sorensen	P	R.Erickson	P	L.Tiant	P	B.Kingman	P	G.Abbott	P	G.Perry	RP	J.McLaughlin
P	B.Travers	P	D.Jackson	RP	R.Davis	RP	B.Lacey	P	R.Honeycutt	RP	D.Darwin	RP	J.Garvin
P	R.Cleveland	P	P.Redfern	RP	R.Gossage			P	J.Beattie	RP	S.Lyle	RP	J.Kucek
RP	B.McClure	RP	D.Corbett	RP	D.Bird			P	R.Dressler	RP	J.Kern		
RP	B.Castro	RP	J.Verhoeven					RP	S.Rawley			P	J.Todd
RP	J.Augustine			P	E.Figueroa			RP	B.McLaughlin	P	C.Hough	P	T.Buskey
		P	F.Arroyo	P	M.Griffin			RP	D.Roberts			P	B.Moore
P	P.Mitchell	P	A.Williams	P	G.Perry							P	L.Leal
						P	M.Parrott					P	M.Barlow
						P	D.Heaverlo						

TEAM	G	W	L	PCT	GB	R	OR	AB	H	2B	3B	HR	BB	SO	AVG	OBP	SLG	PRO	PRO+	BR	/A	PF	CHI	RC	SB	CS	SBA	SBR
EAST																												
NY	162	103	59	.636		820	662	5553	1484	239	34	189	643	739	.267	.346	.425	.771	112	79	93	98	100	820	86	36	70	4
BAL	162	100	62	.617	3	805	**640**	5585	1523	258	29	156	587	766	.273	.344	.413	.757	107	52	60	99	102	788	111	38	74	11
MIL	162	86	76	.531	17	811	682	5653	1555	298	36	203	455	745	.275	.332	**.448**	**.780**	116	78	104	97	100	**834**	131	56	70	6
BOS	160	83	77	.519	19	757	767	5603	1588	297	36	162	475	720	.283	.343	.436	.779	107	**86**	45	105	93	810	79	48	62	-5
DET	163	84	78	.519	19	**830**	757	5648	1543	232	53	143	645	844	.273	.351	.409	.760	106	66	47	102	101	804	75	68	52	-18
CLE	160	79	81	.494	23	738	807	5470	1517	221	40	89	617	625	.277	**.355**	.381	.736	102	26	23	100	97	739	118	58	67	1
TOR	162	67	95	.414	36	624	762	5571	1398	249	56	126	448	813	.251	.310	.383	.693	85	-92	-121	105	99	640	67	72	48	-23
WEST																												
KC	162	97	65	.599		809	694	5714	**1633**	266	**59**	115	508	709	**.286**	.348	.413	.761	107	62	56	101	100	826	**185**	43	**81**	30
OAK	162	83	79	.512	14	686	642	5495	1424	212	35	137	506	824	.259	.324	.385	.709	100	-51	-4	93	102	680	175	82	68	3
MIN	161	77	84	.478	19.5	670	724	5530	1468	252	46	99	436	703	.265	.322	.381	.703	86	-65	-113	107	103	655	62	46	57	-9
TEX	163	76	85	.472	20.5	756	752	5690	1616	263	27	124	480	**589**	.284	.342	.405	.747	107	30	53	97	98	768	91	49	65	-2
CHI	162	70	90	.438	26	587	722	5444	1408	255	38	91	399	670	.259	.314	.370	.684	87	-104	-101	100	98	608	68	54	56	-12
CAL	160	65	95	.406	31	698	797	5443	1442	236	32	106	539	889	.265	.335	.378	.713	97	-33	-16	98	102	681	91	63	59	-11
SEA	163	59	103	.364	38	610	793	5489	1359	211	35	104	483	727	.248	.311	.356	.667	81	-136	-141	101	**105**	598	116	62	65	-2
TOT	1132					10201		77888	20958	3489	553	1844	7221	10363	.269	.334	.399	.733							1455	775	65	-29

TEAM	CG	SH	SV	IP	H	H/G	HR	BB	SO	RAT	ERA	ERA+	OAV	OOB	PR	/A	PF	CPI	FA	E	DP	FW	PW	BW	SBW	DIF
EAST																										
NY	29	**15**	**50**	1464¹	1433	8.8	102	463	845	11.8	3.58	109	.259	.319	73	55	97	98	.978	138	160	.0	5.5	9.3	.6	6.6
BAL	42	10	41	1460	1438	8.9	134	507	789	12.1	3.64	109	.261	.325	63	50	98	104	**.985**	**95**	178	**2.4**	5.0	6.0	1.3	4.3
MIL	48	14	30	1450	1530	9.5	137	**420**	575	12.3	3.71	104	.273	.326	53	26	96	**107**	.977	147	189	-.5	2.6	**10.4**	.8	-8.3
BOS	30	8	43	1441¹	1557	9.7	129	481	696	12.9	4.38	96	.279	.340	-55	-26	105	97	.977	149	**206**	-.7	-2.6	4.7	-.3	2.1
DET	40	9	30	1467¹	1505	9.2	152	558	741	12.8	4.25	97	.267	.336	-35	-23	102	98	.979	133	165	.3	-2.3	4.7	-1.6	1.9
CLE	35	8	32	1428	1519	9.6	137	552	843	13.3	4.68	87	.275	.344	-103	-97	101	92	.983	105	143	1.8	-9.7	2.3	.3	4.3
TOR	39	9	23	1466	1523	9.3	135	635	705	13.4	4.19	103	.274	.351	-26	17	107	105	.979	133	**206**	.3	1.7	-12.1	-2.1	-1.8
WEST																										
KC	37	10	42	1459¹	1496	9.2	129	465	614	12.2	3.83	106	.267	.325	33	36	100	100	.978	141	150	-.2	3.6	5.6	**3.2**	3.8
OAK	**94**	9	13	1471²	1347	8.2	142	521	769	**11.6**	3.46	109	**.244**	**.312**	94	50	93	99	.979	130	115	.5	5.0	-.4	.5	-3.5
MIN	35	9	30	1451	1502	9.3	120	468	744	12.4	3.93	111	.272	.331	16	**68**	108	100	.977	148	192	-.6	**6.8**	-11.3	-.7	2.3
TEX	35	6	25	1451¹	1561	9.7	119	519	**890**	13.1	4.02	97	.277	.342	2	-21	97	104	.977	147	169	-.5	-2.1	5.3	.0	-7.2
CHI	32	12	42	1435¹	1434	9.0	108	563	724	12.8	3.92	103	.263	.337	18	17	100	99	.973	171	162	-1.9	1.7	-10.1	-1.0	1.2
CAL	22	6	30	1428¹	1548	9.8	141	529	725	13.3	4.52	98	.278	.345	-77	-94	97	97	.978	134	144	.1	-9.4	-1.6	-.9	-3.3
SEA	31	7	26	1457¹	1565	9.7	159	540	703	13.2	4.38	94	.278	.344	-55	-40	102	101	.977	149	189	-.6	-4.0	-14.1	.0	-3.4
TOT	549	132	457	20331²		9.3				12.7	4.03		.269	.334					.978	1920	2368					

Runs	Hits	Doubles	Triples	Home Runs	Total Bases
Wilson-KC 133	Wilson-KC 230	Yount-Mil 49	Wilson-KC 15	Oglivie-Mil 41	Cooper-Mil 335
Yount-Mil 121	Cooper-Mil 219	Oliver-Tex 43	Griffin-Tor 15	Jackson-NY 41	Oglivie-Mil 333
Bumbry-Bal 118	Rivers-Tex 210	Morrison-Chi 40	Washington-KC 11	Thomas-Mil 38	Murray-Bal 322
Henderson-Oak 111	Oliver-Tex 209	McRae-KC 39	Landreaux-Min 11	Armas-Oak 35	Yount-Mil 317
Trammell-Det 107	Bumbry-Bal 205	Evans-Bos 37	Yount-Mil 10	Murray-Bal 32	Oliver-Tex 315

Runs Batted In	Runs Produced	Bases On Balls	Batting Average	On Base Percentage	Slugging Average
Cooper-Mil 122	Oliver-Tex 194	Randolph-NY 119	G.Brett-KC .390	G.Brett-KC .461	G.Brett-KC .664
Oglivie-Mil 118	Cooper-Mil 193	Henderson-Oak 117	Cooper-Mil .352	Randolph-NY .429	Jackson-NY .597
G.Brett-KC 118	Yount-Mil 185	Hargrove-Cle 111	Dilone-Cle .341	Henderson-Oak .422	Oglivie-Mil .563
Oliver-Tex 117	Murray-Bal 184	Murphy-Oak 102	Rivers-Tex .333	Hargrove-Cle .421	Cooper-Mil .539
Murray-Bal 116	G.Brett-KC 181	Harrah-Cle 98	Carew-Cal .331	Thompson-Det-Cal .402	Yount-Mil .519

Production	Adjusted Production	Batter Runs	Adjusted Batter Runs	Clutch Hitting Index	Runs Created
G.Brett-KC 1.124	G.Brett-KC 202	G.Brett-KC 64.8	G.Brett-KC 63.8	Manning-Cle 125	G.Brett-KC 135
Jackson-NY .996	Jackson-NY 172	Jackson-NY 49.1	Jackson-NY 51.1	Thompson-Det-Cal 125	Cooper-Mil 126
Cooper-Mil .931	Cooper-Mil 157	Cooper-Mil 42.9	Cooper-Mil 46.9	Hargrove-Cle 122	Jackson-NY 125
Oglivie-Mil .930	Oglivie-Mil 156	Oglivie-Mil 39.2	Oglivie-Mil 43.0	Whitaker-Det 122	Oglivie-Mil 121
Singleton-Bal .885	Singleton-Bal 143	Singleton-Bal 35.4	Henderson-Oak 36.6	Aikens-KC 122	Henderson-Oak 120

Total Average	Stolen Bases	Stolen Base Average	Stolen Base Runs	Fielding Runs	Total Player Rating
G.Brett-KC 1.258	Henderson-Oak 100	Otis-KC 94.1	Wilson-KC 17.7	Castino-Min 27.8	Henderson-Oak 6.6
Jackson-NY 1.060	Wilson-KC 79	Harrah-Cle 89.5	Henderson-Oak 14.4	Burleson-Bos 25.5	G.Brett-KC 6.4
Henderson-Oak .973	Dilone-Cle 61	Kelly-Bal 88.9	Cruz-Sea 9.3	DeCinces-Bal 24.5	Oglivie-Mil 5.4
Randolph-NY .952	Cruz-Sea 45	Wilson-KC 88.8	Dilone-Cle 7.5	Murphy-Oak 23.9	Bell-Tex 4.7
Oglivie-Mil .925	Bumbry-Bal 44	Cruz-Sea 86.5	Bumbry-Bal 6.6	Henderson-Oak 23.3	Cooper-Mil 4.3

Wins	Win Percentage	Games	Complete Games	Shutouts	Saves
Stone-Bal 25	Stone-Bal .781	Quisenberry-KC 75	Langford-Oak 28	John-NY 6	Quisenberry-KC 33
Norris-Oak 22	May-NY .750	Corbett-Min 73	Norris-Oak 24	Zahn-Min 5	Gossage-NY 33
John-NY 22	McGregor-Bal .714	Monge-Cle 67	Keough-Oak 20	Stieb-Tor 4	Farmer-Chi 30
McGregor-Bal 20	Norris-Oak .710	Lopez-Det 67	John-NY 16	McGregor-Bal 4	Stoddard-Bal 26
Leonard-KC 20	John-NY .710		Gura-KC 16	Gura-KC 4	Burgmeier-Bos 24

Innings Pitched	Fewest Hits/Game	Fewest BB/Game	Strikeouts	Strikeouts/Game	Ratio
Langford-Oak 290.0	Norris-Oak 6.81	Barker-Tex 1.84	Barker-Cle 187	Barker-Cle 6.83	May-NY 9.39
Norris-Oak 284.1	May-NY 7.39	Splittorff-KC 1.90	Norris-Oak 180	May-NY 6.83	Norris-Oak 9.62
Gura-KC 283.1	Clancy-Tor 7.79	John-NY 1.90	Guidry-NY 166	Guidry-NY 6.80	Langford-Oak 10.58
Leonard-KC 280.1	Underwood-NY 7.84	Tanana-Cal 1.99	Leonard-KC 155	Bannister-Sea 6.41	Burns-Chi 10.59
John-NY 265.1	Keough-Oak 7.85	Langford-Oak 1.99	Bannister-Sea 155	Perry-Tex-NY 5.91	Eckersley-Bos 10.65

Earned Run Average	Adjusted ERA	Opponents' Batting Avg.	Opponents' On Base Pct.	Starter Runs	Adjusted Starter Runs
May-NY 2.46	May-NY 159	Norris-Oak .209	May-NY .268	Norris-Oak 47.4	Norris-Oak 39.0
Norris-Oak 2.53	Norris-Oak 149	May-NY .224	Norris-Oak .272	Gura-KC 34.0	Gura-KC 34.5
Burns-Chi 2.84	Burns-Chi 142	Clancy-Tor .233	Eckersley-Bos .291	Burns-Chi 31.7	Burns-Chi 31.5
Keough-Oak 2.92	Gura-KC 137	Keough-Oak .236	Burns-Chi .295	Keough-Oak 31.0	May-NY 28.4
Gura-KC 2.95	Erickson-Min 134	Underwood-NY .237	Bannister-Sea .296	May-NY 30.6	Clancy-Tor 27.8

Clutch Pitching Index	Relief Runs	Adjusted Relief Runs	Relief Ranking	Total Pitcher Index	Total Baseball Ranking
Sorensen-Mil 126	Corbett-Min 31.1	Corbett-Min 36.0	Corbett-Min 46.8	Norris-Oak 4.7	Henderson-Oak 6.6
Stanley-Bos 117	Burgmeier-Bos 22.4	Burgmeier-Bos 24.4	Burgmeier-Bos 33.1	Corbett-Min 4.5	G.Brett-KC 6.4
Keough-Oak 113	Gossage-NY 19.4	Garvin-Tor 26.6	Gossage-NY 26.6	Burgmeier-Bos 3.7	Oglivie-Mil 5.4
Trout-Chi 113	Darwin-Tex 17.1	Gossage-NY 18.1	Quisenberry-KC 26.2	Burns-Chi 3.5	Norris-Oak 4.7
Perry-Tex-NY 112	Garvin-Tor 16.0	Proly-Chi 15.6	Garvin-Tor 26.1	Gura-KC 3.3	Bell-Tex 4.7

January 15 In his first year of eligibility, former Cardinals pitcher Bob Gibson is elected to the Hall of Fame.

March 11 Johnny Mize and Andrew "Rube" Foster are elected to the Hall of Fame by the Veterans Committee.

April 9 Pressed into service on Opening Day when scheduled starter Jerry Reuss pulls a calf muscle, Dodgers pitcher Fernando Valenzuela shuts out the Astros, 2–0, on five hits in his first major league start.

April 18 The Reds' Tom Seaver strikes out Keith Hernandez in the fourth inning of a 10-4 loss to the Cardinals, becoming the fifth pitcher in major league history with 3,000 career strikeouts.

April 27 "Fernandomania" hits fever pitch at Dodger Stadium as a sellout crowd watches the 20-year-old rookie pitch his fourth shutout in five starts, 5-0 versus the Giants. Valenzuela is 5-0 with a 0.20 ERA and is batting .438.

April 29 Philadelphia's Steve Carlton strikes out the side (Tim Raines, Jerry Manuel, and Tim Wallach) in the first inning of a 6–2 win over the Expos to become the first left-hander in major league history (and sixth pitcher overall) to record 3,000 career strikeouts.

May 31 Playing before their 10th consecutive home sellout, the Dodgers pound the Reds, 16–4, and raise their season attendance to 1,026,725 in 22 dates. It is the earliest any team has cracked the million attendance barrier.

June 5 Houston's Nolan Ryan passes Early Wynn as baseball's all-time walk leader, walking two batters in a 3–0 win over the Mets to raise his total to 1,777. Ryan also fans 10 batters while pitching a five-hitter.

June 10 Phillies first baseman Pete Rose singles off Nolan Ryan in the first inning to tie Stan Musial as the NL's all-time hit leader with 3,630.

September 17 Fernando Valenzuela sets the NL rookie record with his eighth shutout of the season, a 2-0 three-hitter versus the Braves.

September 26 Nolan Ryan no-hits the Dodgers 5-0 to become the only major league pitcher to toss five career no-hitters. Ryan had shared the record of four with Dodger great Sandy Koufax, but had not pitched a no-hitter since June 1, 1975. The 34-year-old Ryan strikes out 11 and retires the last 19 batters in a row.

October 3 In Cincinnati, Bob Horner homers twice and scores the winning run on Ron Oester's eighth-inning throwing error to give the Braves a 4-3 win over the Reds and give the Astros the second-half title in the NL West. Cincinnati, which lost the first-half title to the Dodgers by one-half game, will finish with the best overall record (66-42) in the major leagues, but will not make the playoffs.

October 11 After being down two games to none, the Dodgers shut out Houston, 4-0, behind Jerry Reuss to take the playoff.

October 19 In Game 5 of the NLCS, Rick Monday hits a solo home run with two out in the top of the ninth against Montreal to give Los Angeles a 2-1 victory and a trip to the World Series.

October 28 Pedro Guerrero drives in five runs and the Dodgers beat the Yankees 9-2 to win the World Series in six. In a remarkable postseason, the Dodgers came from behind to win three series (down 2-0 to Houston and 2-0 to Montreal in the best-of-five series). Guerrero, Ron Cey, and Steve Yeager are named co-MVPs.

November 11 Fernando Valenzuela becomes the first rookie ever to win a Cy Young Award, edging the Reds' Tom Seaver 70-67 for NL honors. He was the first rookie since Herb Score in 1955 to lead his league in strikeouts, with 180.

November 18 Phillies third baseman Mike Schmidt wins his second consecutive NL MVP Award, joining Ernie Banks and Joe Morgan as the only NL players to win the award back-to-back. Schmidt hit .316 with 31 home runs and 91 RBIs in the abbreviated season and also led the league in runs and walks.

ATLANTA		CHICAGO		CINCINNATI		HOUSTON		LOS ANGELES		MONTREAL	
M	B.Cox	M	J.Amalfitano	M	J.McNamara	M	B.Virdon	M	T.Lasorda	M	D.Williams
1B	C.Chambliss	1B	B.Buckner	1B	D.Driessen	1B	C.Cedeno	1B	S.Garvey	M	J.Fanning
2B	G.Hubbard	2B	M.Tyson	2B	R.Oester	2B	J.Pittman	2B	D.Lopes	1B	W.Cromartie
SS	R.Ramirez	SS	I.DeJesus	SS	D.Concepcion	SS	C.Reynolds	SS	B.Russell	2B	R.Scott
3B	B.Horner	3B	K.Reitz	3B	R.Knight	3B	A.Howe	3B	R.Cey	SS	C.Speier
LF	R.Linares	LF	S.Henderson	LF	G.Foster	LF	J.Cruz	LF	D.Baker	3B	L.Parrish
CF	D.Murphy	CF	J.Morales	CF	K.Griffey	CF	T.Scott	CF	K.Landreaux	LF	T.Raines
RF	C.Washington	RF	L.Durham	RF	D.Collins	RF	T.Puhl	RF	P.Guerrero	CF	A.Dawson
C	B.Benedict	C	J.Davis	C	J.Nolan	C	A.Ashby	C	M.Scioscia	RF	J.White
										C	G.Carter
32	J.Royster	P	M.Krukow	P	M.Soto	P	J.Niekro	2S	D.Thomas		
		P	R.Martz	P	T.Seaver	P	D.Sutton			O1	T.Wallach
P	G.Perry	P	R.Reuschel	P	F.Pastore	P	B.Knepper	P	F.Valenzuela		
P	T.Boggs	P	K.Kravec	P	B.Berenyi	P	N.Ryan	P	J.Reuss	P	S.Rogers
P	P.Niekro	P	D.Bird	P	M.LaCoss	P	V.Ruhle	P	B.Hooton	P	B.Gullickson
P	R.Mahler	RP	D.Tidrow	RP	T.Hume	RP	D.Smith	P	B.Welch	P	S.Sanderson
RP	J.Montefusco	RP	B.Caudill	RP	P.Moskau	RP	J.Sambito	RP	D.Goltz	P	R.Burris
RP	R.Camp	RP	L.Smith	RP	J.Price	RP	F.LaCorte	RP	S.Howe	RP	B.Lee
RP	G.Garber							RP	B.Castillo	RP	S.Bahnsen
		P	L.McGlothen							RP	W.Fryman
		P	M.Griffin								
		P	D.Capilla							P	C.Lea

NEW YORK		PHILADELPHIA		PITTSBURGH		SAN DIEGO		SAN FRANCISCO		ST.LOUIS	
M	J.Torre	M	D.Green	M	C.Tanner	M	F.Howard	M	F.Robinson	M	W.Herzog
1B	D.Kingman	1B	P.Rose	1B	J.Thompson	1B	B.Perkins	1B	E.Cabell	1B	K.Hernandez
2B	D.Flynn	2B	M.Trillo	2B	P.Garner	2B	J.Bonilla	2B	J.Morgan	2B	T.Herr
SS	F.Taveras	SS	L.Bowa	SS	T.Foli	SS	O.Smith	SS	J.LeMaster	SS	G.Templeton
3B	H.Brooks	3B	M.Schmidt	3B	B.Madlock	3B	L.Salazar	3B	D.Evans	3B	K.Oberkfell
LF	L.Mazzilli	LF	G.Matthews	LF	M.Easler	LF	G.Richards	LF	L.Herndon	LF	D.Iorg
CF	M.Wilson	CF	G.Maddox	CF	O.Moreno	CF	R.Jones	CF	J.Martin	CF	G.Hendrick
RF	E.Valentine	RF	B.McBride	RF	D.Parker	RF	J.Lefebvre	RF	J.Clark	RF	S.Lezcano
C	J.Stearns	C	B.Boone	C	T.Pena	C	T.Kennedy	C	M.May	C	D.Porter
3	M.Cubbage	O	G.Gross	3S	D.Berra	1	R.Bass	P	D.Alexander	P	L.Sorensen
1O	M.Jorgensen			O	L.Lacy			P	T.Griffin	P	B.Forsch
1	R.Staub	P	S.Carlton			P	J.Eichelberger	P	V.Blue	P	J.Martin
		P	D.Ruthven	P	R.Rhoden	P	S.Mura	P	E.Whitson	P	S.Martinez
P	P.Zachry	P	L.Christenson	P	E.Solomon	P	C.Welsh	P	A.Ripley	RP	B.Sutter
P	M.Scott	P	N.Espinosa	P	J.Bibby	P	R.Wise	RP	A.Holland	RP	B.Shirley
P	E.Lynch	RP	S.Lyle	P	P.Perez	P	T.Lollar	RP	G.Minton	RP	J.Kaat
P	G.Harris	RP	M.Proly	RP	R.Scurry	RP	G.Lucas	RP	F.Breining		
RP	P.Falcone	RP	R.Reed	RP	K.Tekulve	RP	J.Curtis			P	J.Andujar
RP	N.Allen			RP	E.Romo	RP	J.Littlefield	P	G.Lavelle		
RP	D.Miller	P	D.Noles			P	D.Boone				
		/P	M.Bystrom	/P	L.Tiant						
P	R.Jones			P	O.Jones						

TEAM	G	W	L	PCT	GB	R	OR	AB	H	2B	3B	HR	BB	SO	AVG	OBP	SLG	PRO	PRO+	BR	/A	PF	CHI	RC	SB	CS	SBA	SBR
EAST Split Season: First-half Winner PHI (34-21); Second-half Winner MON (30-23)																												
STL	103	59	43	.578		464	417	3537	936	158	45	50	379	495	.265	.339	.377	.716	106	43	31	103	102	454	88	45	66	-1
MON	108	60	48	.556	2	443	394	3591	883	146	28	81	368	498	.246	.319	.370	.689	100	3	-2	101	**105**	435	**138**	40	**78**	17
PHI	107	59	48	.551	2.5	**491**	472	3665	**1002**	165	25	69	372	432	**.273**	**.344**	**.389**	**.733**	109	66	45	104	100	**495**	103	46	69	3
PIT	103	46	56	.451	13	407	425	3576	920	176	30	55	278	494	.257	.314	.369	.683	96	-9	-21	103	102	417	122	52	70	5
NY	105	41	62	.398	18.5	348	432	3493	868	136	35	57	304	603	.248	.311	.356	.667	96	-26	-20	98	93	387	103	42	71	6
CHI	106	38	65	.369	21.5	370	483	3546	838	138	29	57	342	611	.236	.306	.340	.646	84	-52	-68	104	104	368	72	41	64	-3
WEST Split Season: First-half Winner LA (36-21); Second-half Winner HOU (33-20)																												
CIN	108	66	42	.611		464	440	3637	972	**190**	24	64	375	553	.267	.339	.385	.724	**109**	53	45	102	97	469	58	37	61	-5
LA	110	63	47	.573	4	450	356	3751	984	133	20	**82**	331	550	.262	.325	.374	.699	108	16	32	96	101	450	73	46	61	-6
HOU	110	61	49	.555	6	394	**331**	3693	948	160	35	45	340	488	.257	.321	.356	.677	103	-12	-9	95	95	425	81	43	65	-2
SF	111	56	55	.505	11.5	427	414	3766	941	161	26	63	**386**	543	.250	.322	.357	.679	100	-8	0	98	99	431	89	50	64	-3
ATL	107	50	56	.472	15	395	416	3642	886	148	22	64	321	540	.243	.308	.349	.657	90	-41	-51	103	**105**	391	98	39	72	6
SD	110	41	69	.373	26	382	455	3757	963	170	35	32	311	525	.256	.316	.346	.662	100	-33	-4	93	96	400	83	62	57	-12
TOT	644					5035		43654	11141	1881	354	719	4107	6332	.255	.322	.364	.686		1108	543	67	7					

TEAM	CG	SH	SV	IP	H	H/G	HR	BB	SO	RAT	ERA	ERA+	OAV	OOB	PR	/A	PF	CPI	FA	E	DP	FW	PW	BW	SBW	DIF
STL	11	5	**33**	943	902	8.6	52	290	388	11.5	3.63	98	.255	.314	-14	-7	102	91	**.981**	82	108	.6	-.8	3.3	-.2	5.0
MON	20	12	23	975	902	8.3	58	**268**	520	11.0	3.30	106	.247	.302	21	21	100	92	.980	81	88	.9	2.3	-.2	**1.8**	1.3
PHI	19	5	23	960¹	967	9.1	72	347	580	12.4	4.05	90	.267	.333	-60	-45	104	97	.980	86	90	.6	-4.8	**4.8**	.3	4.6
PIT	11	5	29	942	953	9.1	60	346	492	12.6	3.56	101	.266	.333	-8	3	103	107	.979	86	106	.4	.3	-2.3	.5	-4.0
NY	7	3	24	926¹	906	8.8	74	336	490	12.2	3.55	98	.255	.326	-6	-7	100	105	.968	130	89	-1.6	-.8	-2.1	.6	-6.5
CHI	6	2	20	956²	983	9.2	59	388	532	13.1	4.01	92	.270	.344	-55	-33	106	101	.974	113	103	-.8	-3.5	-7.3	-.4	-1.5
CIN	25	14	20	965²	863	8.0	67	393	593	11.8	3.73	95	.241	.318	-26	-19	102	90	**.981**	80	99	1.0	-2.0	4.8	-.6	8.8
LA	**26**	**19**	24	997	904	8.2	54	302	603	11.0	3.01	110	.245	.304	54	35	95	100	.980	87	101	.7	3.8	3.4	-.7	-.8
HOU	23	**19**	25	990	842	7.7	40	300	**610**	10.5	2.66	124	.231	.291	91	69	94	96	.980	87	81	.7	**7.4**	1.0	-.3	-2.8
SF	8	9	**33**	1009¹	970	8.6	57	393	561	12.4	3.28	105	.256	.330	23	17	98	**109**	.977	102	102	.0	1.8	.0	-.4	-1.0
ATL	11	4	24	968	936	8.7	62	330	471	11.9	3.45	104	.257	.321	4	14	103	102	.976	102	93	-.2	1.5	-5.5	.6	.6
SD	9	6	23	1002	1013	9.1	64	414	492	13.0	3.72	88	.268	.343	-25	-51	93	108	.977	102	**117**	-.0	-5.5	-.4	-1.3	-6.7
TOT	176	103	301	11635¹		8.6				11.9	3.49		.255	.322					.978	1138	1177					

Runs		Hits		Doubles		Triples		Home Runs		Total Bases	
Schmidt-Phi	78	Rose-Phi	140	Buckner-Chi	35	Richards-SD	12	Schmidt-Phi	31	Schmidt-Phi	228
Rose-Phi	73	Buckner-Chi	131	Jones-SD	34	Reynolds-Hou	12	Dawson-Mon	24	Dawson-Mon	218
Dawson-Mon	71	Concepcion-Cin	129	Concepcion-Cin	28	Herr-StL	9	Kingman-NY	22	Foster-Cin	215
Hendrick-StL	67	Baker-LA	128	Hernandez-StL	27			Foster-Cin	22	Buckner-Chi	202
		Griffey-Cin	123	Chambliss-Atl	25			Hendrick-StL	18	Hendrick-StL	191

Runs Batted In		Runs Produced		Bases On Balls		Batting Average		On Base Percentage		Slugging Average	
Schmidt-Phi	91	Schmidt-Phi	138	Schmidt-Phi	73	Madlock-Pit	.341	Schmidt-Phi	.439	Schmidt-Phi	.644
Foster-Cin	90	Foster-Cin	132	Morgan-SF	66	Rose-Phi	.325	Madlock-Pit	.418	Dawson-Mon	.553
Buckner-Chi	75	Matthews-Phi	120	Hernandez-StL	61	Baker-LA	.320	Hernandez-StL	.405	Foster-Cin	.519
Carter-Mon	68	Concepcion-Cin	119	Thompson-Pit	59	Schmidt-Phi	.316	Matthews-Phi	.404	Madlock-Pit	.495
		Garvey-LA	117	Matthews-Phi	59	Buckner-Chi	.311	Raines-Mon	.394	Hendrick-StL	.485

Production		Adjusted Production		Batter Runs		Adjusted Batter Runs		Clutch Hitting Index		Runs Created	
Schmidt-Phi	1.083	Schmidt-Phi	195	Schmidt-Phi	50.1	Schmidt-Phi	46.0	Concepcion-Cin	141	Schmidt-Phi	102
Dawson-Mon	.923	Dawson-Mon	157	Dawson-Mon	28.8	Dawson-Mon	28.0	Herr-StL	127	Dawson-Mon	83
Madlock-Pit	.912	Madlock-Pit	153	Foster-Cin	27.7	Foster-Cin	26.5	Matthews-Phi	126	Foster-Cin	81
Foster-Cin	.895	Foster-Cin	150	Hernandez-StL	24.6	Hernandez-StL	22.8	Foster-Cin	126	Hernandez-StL	73
Hernandez-StL	.868	Cey-LA	145	Matthews-Phi	22.4	Madlock-Pit	20.4	Maddox-Phi	122	Matthews-Phi	71

Total Average		Stolen Bases		Stolen Base Average		Stolen Base Runs		Fielding Runs		Total Player Rating	
Schmidt-Phi	1.227	Raines-Mon	71	Lopes-LA	90.9	Raines-Mon	14.7	Smith-SD	25.9	Schmidt-Phi	7.0
Raines-Mon	1.034	Moreno-Pit	39	Lacy-Pit	88.9	Lacy-Pit	5.4	Schmidt-Phi	22.5	Dawson-Mon	5.0
Dawson-Mon	.989	Scott-Mon	30	Dawson-Mon	86.7	Dawson-Mon	5.4	Dawson-Mon	17.8	Foster-Cin	3.4
Madlock-Pit	.959			Raines-Mon	86.6	Scott-Mon	4.8	Flynn-NY	12.2	Raines-Mon	3.1
Matthews-Phi	.908			Puhl-Hou	84.6	Lopes-LA	4.8	Clark-SF	11.9	Hernandez-StL	2.5

Wins		Win Percentage		Games		Complete Games		Shutouts		Saves	
Seaver-Cin	14	Seaver-Cin	.875	Lucas-SD	57	Valenzuela-LA	11	Valenzuela-LA	8	Sutter-StL	25
Valenzuela-LA	13	Carlton-Phi	.765	Minton-SF	55	Soto-Cin	10	Knepper-Hou	5	Minton-SF	21
Carlton-Phi	13	Ryan-Hou	.688	Tidrow-Chi	51	Carlton-Phi	10	Hooton-LA	4	Allen-NY	18
		Valenzuela-LA	.650	Hume-Cin	51	Reuss-LA	8			Camp-Atl	17
		Hooton-LA	.647	Sambito-Hou	49	Rogers-Mon	7				

Innings Pitched		Fewest Hits/Game		Fewest BB/Game		Strikeouts		Strikeouts/Game		Ratio	
Valenzuela-LA	192.1	Ryan-Hou	5.98	Perry-Atl	1.43	Valenzuela-LA	180	Carlton-Phi	8.48	Sutton-Hou	9.19
Carlton-Phi	190.0	Seaver-Cin	6.49	Reuss-LA	1.59	Carlton-Phi	179	Ryan-Hou	8.46	Valenzuela-LA	9.45
Soto-Cin	175.0	Valenzuela-LA	6.55	Sutton-Hou	1.64	Soto-Cin	151	Valenzuela-LA	8.42	Knepper-Hou	9.77
Seaver-Cin	166.1	Berenyi-Cin	6.93	Sorensen-StL	1.67	Ryan-Hou	140	Soto-Cin	7.77	Reuss-LA	9.96
Niekro-Hou	166.0	Blue-SF	7.00	Solomon-Pit	1.91	Gullickson-Mon	115	Berenyi-Cin	7.57	Hooton-LA	10.05

Earned Run Average		Adjusted ERA		Opponents' Batting Avg.		Opponents' On Base Pct.		Starter Runs		Adjusted Starter Runs	
Ryan-Hou	1.69	Ryan-Hou	195	Ryan-Hou	.188	Sutton-Hou	.268	Ryan-Hou	29.8	Ryan-Hou	26.5
Knepper-Hou	2.18	Knepper-Hou	151	Valenzuela-LA	.205	Valenzuela-LA	.271	Knepper-Hou	22.8	Carlton-Phi	25.6
Hooton-LA	2.28	Carlton-Phi	150	Seaver-Cin	.205	Knepper-Hou	.280	Carlton-Phi	22.7	Knepper-Hou	19.4
Reuss-LA	2.30	Hooton-LA	146	Berenyi-Cin	.211	Sanderson-Mon	.281	Valenzuela-LA	21.6	Seaver-Cin	18.7
Carlton-Phi	2.42	Reuss-LA	144	Blue-SF	.217	Ryan-Hou	.281	Reuss-LA	20.2	Valenzuela-LA	17.9

Clutch Pitching Index		Relief Runs		Adjusted Relief Runs		Relief Ranking		Total Pitcher Index		Total Baseball Ranking	
Mahler-Atl	124	Lucas-SD	14.9	Camp-Atl	15.2	Camp-Atl	29.3	Ryan-Hou	3.3	Schmidt-Phi	7.0
Solomon-Pit	124	Camp-Atl	14.5	Lucas-SD	12.6	Lucas-SD	21.7	Camp-Atl	3.1	Dawson-Mon	5.0
Alexander-SF	122	Holland-SF	12.0	Holland-SF	11.4	Sambito-Hou	18.2	Valenzuela-LA	2.5	Foster-Cin	3.4
Blue-SF	112	Sambito-Hou	11.7	Sambito-Hou	10.3	Fryman-Mon	15.7	Lucas-SD	2.3	Ryan-Hou	3.3
Zachry-NY	111	Reardon-NY-Mon	10.3	Reardon-NY-Mon	10.3	Holland-SF	14.0	Carlton-Phi	2.2	Camp-Atl	3.1

February 12 Arbitrator Raymond Goetz declares Red Sox catcher Carlton Fisk a free agent on the grounds that the club mailed his contract two days after the December 20 deadline.

April 10 In his first game for Chicago, Carlton Fisk belts a three-run home run in the eighth inning to lead Chicago to a 5-3 win over his former Red Sox team-mates at Fenway Park.

April 18* The International League Pawtucket Red Sox and Rochester Red Wings play 32 innings before suspending play at 4:07 a.m. on April 19, tied 2-2. The game resumes on June 23.

May 15 The Indians' Len Barker pitches a perfect game, 3-0 over the Blue Jays before just 7,290 fans on a rainy night in Cleveland.

May 25 Carl Yastrzemski plays in his 3,000th major league game, scoring the winning run in Boston's 8-7 triumph over Cleveland. Yaz joins Ty Cobb, Stan Musial, and Hank Aaron as the only major leaguers to appear in 3,000 games.

June 12 At 12:30 a.m., the longest labor action to this date in American sports history begins. By the time the season resumes on Aug. 10, 706 games (38 percent of the major league schedule) will

have been canceled.

June 23* Dave Koza scores Marty Barrett with a bases-loaded single in the bottom of the 33rd inning, giving Pawtucket a 3-2 win over Rochester and ending the longest game in professional baseball history. The game had been suspended April 19 after 32 innings and eight hours, 7 minutes of play, but the continuation took only 18 minutes to complete. Bob Ojeda pitches one inning to earn the win. Future major league stars Wade Boggs and Cal Ripken go a combined 6-for-25.

August 6 As a result of the nearly two-month interruption in play because of the strike, the major league owners elect to split the season in half, with the first-place teams from each half in each division (or a wild card team if the same club wins both halves) meeting in a best-of-five divisional playoff series. The last time the majors played a split season was 1892. The A's, Yankees, Phillies, and Dodgers suddenly find themselves guaranteed playoff spots as first-half champions.

October 3 The Brewers and Expos, both formed in 1969, clinch their first-ever post season appearances. Milwaukee beats Detroit, 2-1, to wrap up the

second-half title in the AL East, while Montreal edges New York, 5-4, to win the NL East's second playoff spot.

October 5 Kansas City shuts out Cleveland 9-0 in the first game of a scheduled doubleheader to clinch the second-half title in the AL West. The second game is canceled as irrelevant.

October 9 The A's sweep Kansas City by winning, 4-1.

October 11 The Yankees bats are too much for the Brewers. Three home runs, including the second of the series by Jackson, and 13 hits provide a 7-3 win and a trip to the ALCS.

October 15 The Yankees wrap up their third pennant in five years with a 4-0 win over the A's, completing a three-game sweep of the ALCS.

October 20 In a World Series rematch of the 1978 teams, the Yankees take Game 1 over the Dodgers 5-3.

November 3 Brewers reliever Rollie Fingers (28 saves, 1.04 ERA) wins the league Cy Young Award, collecting 22 of 28 possible first-place votes.

November 25 Rollie Fingers becomes the first relief pitcher ever to win the AL MVP Award, edging Oakland's Rickey Henderson 319-308.

	BALTIMORE		BOSTON		CALIFORNIA		CHICAGO		CLEVELAND		DETROIT		KANSAS CITY
M	E.Weaver	M	R.Houk	M	J.Fregosi	M	T.LaRussa	M	D.Garcia	M	S.Anderson	M	J.Frey
1B	E.Murray	1B	T.Perez	M	G.Mauch	1B	M.Squires	1B	M.Hargrove	1B	R.Hebner	M	D.Howser
2B	R.Dauer	2B	J.Remy	1B	R.Carew	2B	T.Bernazard	2B	D.Kuiper	2B	L.Whitaker	1B	W.Aikens
SS	M.Belanger	SS	G.Hoffman	2B	B.Grich	SS	B.Almon	SS	T.Veryzer	SS	A.Trammell	2B	F.White
3B	D.DeCinces	3B	C.Lansford	SS	R.Burleson	3B	J.Morrison	3B	T.Harrah	3B	T.Brookens	SS	U.Washington
LF	J.Lowenstein	LF	J.Rice	3B	B.Hobson	LF	R.LeFlore	LF	M.Dilone	LF	S.Kemp	3B	G.Brett
CF	A.Bumbry	CF	R.Miller	LF	B.Downing	CF	C.Lemon	CF	R.Manning	CF	A.Cowens	LF	W.Wilson
RF	G.Roenicke	RF	D.Evans	CF	F.Lynn	RF	H.Baines	RF	J.Orta	RF	K.Gibson	CF	A.Otis
C	R.Dempsey	C	R.Gedman	RF	D.Ford	C	C.Fisk	C	R.Hassey	C	L.Parrish	RF	C.Geronimo
DH	T.Crowley	DH	C.Yastrzemski	C	E.Ott	DH	G.Luzinski	DH	A.Thornton	DH	J.Wockenfuss	C	J.Wathan
				DH	D.Baylor							DH	H.McRae
O	J.Dwyer	S3	D.Stapleton			O	R.Kuntz	O2	A.Bannister	O	L.Jones		
OD	K.Singleton			P	G.Zahn	O	W.Nordhagen			OD	R.Peters	P	D.Leonard
		P	D.Eckersley	P	K.Forsch			P	B.Blyleven			P	L.Gura
P	D.Martinez	P	F.Tanana	P	M.Witt	P	B.Burns	P	L.Barker	P	J.Morris	P	R.Gale
P	S.McGregor	P	M.Torrez	P	S.Renko	P	R.Dotson	P	J.Denny	P	M.Wilcox	P	P.Splittorff
P	J.Palmer	P	J.Tudor	RP	J.Jefferson	P	D.Lamp	P	R.Waits	P	D.Petry	P	M.Jones
P	M.Flanagan	P	B.Ojeda	RP	A.Hassler	P	S.Trout	P	D.Spillner	P	D.Rozema	RP	D.Quisenberry
P	S.Stewart	RP	B.Stanley	RP	D.Aase	P	R.Baumgarten	RP	M.Stanton	P	D.Schatzeder	RP	R.Martin
RP	T.Martinez	RP	M.Clear			RP	L.Hoyt	RP	M.Stanton	RP	A.Lopez	RP	K.Brett
RP	D.Ford	RP	T.Burgmeier			RP	E.Farmer			RP	D.Tobik		
RP	T.Stoddard					RP	K.Hickey	P	W.Garland	RP	K.Saucier	P	J.Wright
		P	S.Crawford										
P	S.Stone												

	MILWAUKEE		MINNESOTA		NEW YORK		OAKLAND		SEATTLE		TEXAS		TORONTO
M	B.Rodgers	M	J.Goryl	M	G.Michael	M	B.Martin	M	M.Wills	M	D.Zimmer	M	B.Mattick
1B	C.Cooper	M	B.Gardner	M	B.Lemon	1B	J.Spencer	M	R.Lachemann	1B	P.Putnam	1B	J.Mayberry
2B	J.Gantner	1B	D.Goodwin	1B	B.Watson	2B	S.Babitt	1B	B.Bochte	2B	B.Wills	2B	D.Garcia
SS	R.Yount	2B	R.Wilfong	2B	W.Randolph	SS	R.Picciolo	2B	J.Cruz	SS	M.Mendoza	SS	A.Griffin
3B	D.Money	SS	R.Smalley	SS	B.Dent	3B	W.Gross	SS	J.Anderson	3B	B.Bell	3B	D.Ainge
LF	B.Oglivie	3B	J.Castino	3B	G.Nettles	LF	R.Henderson	3B	L.Randle	LF	B.Sample	LF	A.Woods
CF	G.Thomas	LF	G.Ward	LF	D.Winfield	CF	D.Murphy	LF	T.Paciorek	CF	M.Rivers	CF	L.Moseby
RF	M.Brouhard	CF	M.Hatcher	CF	J.Mumphrey	RF	T.Armas	CF	J.Simpson	RF	L.Roberts	RF	B.Bonnell
C	T.Simmons	RF	D.Engle	RF	R.Jackson	C	M.Heath	RF	J.Burroughs	C	J.Sundberg	C	E.Whitt
DH	L.Hisle	C	S.Butera	C	R.Cerone	DH	C.Johnson	C	J.Narron	DH	A.Oliver	DH	O.Velez
		DH	G.Adams	DH	B.Murcer			DH	R.Zisk				
3D	R.Howell						32	D.McKay	O	J.Grubb	23	G.Iorg
OD	P.Molitor	2S	P.Mackanin	OD	O.Gamble	C1	J.Newman	1D	G.Gray				
		O	H.Powell					3O	D.Meyer	P	D.Darwin	P	D.Stieb
										P	D.Medich	P	L.Leal
P	P.Vuckovich			P	R.May	P	R.Langford			P	R.Honeycutt	P	J.Clancy
P	M.Caldwell	P	A.Williams	P	T.John	P	S.McCatty	P	G.Abbott	P	F.Jenkins	P	J.Todd
P	M.Haas	P	P.Redfern	P	R.Guidry	P	M.Norris	P	F.Bannister	P	J.Matlack	P	M.Bomback
P	J.Slaton	P	F.Arroyo	P	D.Righetti	P	M.Keough	P	K.Clay	P	S.Comer	P	R.Jackson
P	R.Lerch	P	J.Koosman	P	R.Reuschel	P	B.Kingman	P	B.Clark	RP	D.Schmidt	RP	J.McLaughlin
RP	R.Fingers	RP	R.Erickson	RP	R.Davis	P	J.Jones	P	M.Parrott			RP	J.Garvin
RP	R.Cleveland	RP	D.Corbett	RP	D.LaRoche	RP	B.Owchinko	RP	S.Rawley	P	C.Hough		
RP	J.Easterly	RP	D.Cooper	RP	R.Gossage			RP	L.Andersen			P	J.Berenguer
		RP	J.Verhoeven					RP	D.Drago				
P	J.Augustine			P	D.Bird	P	T.Underwood						
		P	B.Havens			P	J.Gleaton						
						P	J.Beattie						

TEAM	G	W	L	PCT	GB	R	OR	AB	H	2B	3B	HR	BB	SO	AVG	OBP	SLG	PRO	PRO+	BR	/A	PF	CHI	RC	SB	CS	SBA	SBR
EAST Split Season: First-half Winner NY (34-22); Second-half Winner MIL (31-22)																												
MIL	109	62	47	.569		493	459	3743	961	173	20	96	300	461	.257	.317	.391	.708	109	9	33	95	108	451	39	36	52	-10
BAL	105	59	46	.562	1	429	437	3516	883	165	11	88	**404**	454	.251	.331	.379	.710	104	22	23	100	95	431	41	34	55	-8
NY	107	59	48	.551	2	421	**343**	3529	889	148	22	100	391	434	.252	.328	.391	.719	108	29	35	99	92	445	47	30	61	-4
DET	109	60	49	.550	2	427	404	3600	922	148	29	65	**404**	500	.256	.334	.368	.702	98	14	-2	104	94	442	61	37	62	-4
BOS	108	59	49	.546	2.5	**519**	481	3820	**1052**	168	17	90	378	520	**.275**	**.343**	**.399**	**.742**	107	**65**	33	106	99	**514**	32	31	51	-9
CLE	103	52	51	.505	7	431	442	3507	922	150	21	39	343	**379**	.263	.331	.351	.682	98	-11	-5	99	104	414	**119**	37	**76**	**14**
TOR	106	37	69	.349	23.5	329	466	3521	797	137	23	61	284	556	.226	.288	.330	.618	73	-103	-124	106	105	326	66	57	54	-14
WEST Split Season: First-half Winner OAK (37-23); Second-half Winner KC (30-23)																												
OAK	109	64	45	.587		458	403	3677	910	119	26	**104**	342	647	.247	.314	.379	.693	104	-8	13	95	106	438	98	47	68	1
TEX	105	57	48	.543	5	452	389	3581	968	**178**	15	49	295	396	.270	.329	.369	.698	107	5	28	95	105	425	46	41	53	-11
CHI	106	54	52	.509	8.5	476	423	3615	982	135	27	76	322	518	.272	.338	.387	.725	**110**	41	**51**	98	100	471	86	44	66	-1
KC	103	50	53	.485	11	397	405	3560	952	169	29	61	301	419	.267	.327	.383	.710	105	17	21	99	90	437	100	53	65	-2
CAL	110	51	59	.464	13.5	476	453	3688	944	134	16	97	393	571	.256	.332	.380	.712	105	26	26	100	100	463	44	33	57	-7
SEA	110	44	65	.404	20	426	521	3780	950	148	13	89	329	553	.251	.316	.368	.684	93	-19	-36	104	98	441	100	50	67	0
MIN	110	41	68	.376	23	378	486	3676	884	147	**36**	47	275	497	.240	.295	.338	.633	77	-87	-111	107	**109**	355	34	27	56	-6
TOT	750					6112		50813	13016	2119	305	1062	4761	6905	.256	.323	.373	.696							913	557	62	-60

TEAM	CG	SH	SV	IP	H	H/G	HR	BB	SO	RAT	ERA	ERA+	OAV	OOB	PR	/A	PF	CPI	FA	E	DP	FW	PW	BW	SBW	DIF
MIL	11	4	**35**	986	994	9.1	72	352	448	12.4	3.91	88	.266	.331	-27	-53	94	99	.982	79	**135**	.3	-5.6	3.5	-.6	9.9
BAL	25	10	23	940	923	8.8	83	347	489	12.3	3.70	98	.260	.328	-4	-7	99	**104**	.983	68	114	.8	-.7	2.4	-.4	4.4
NY	16	**13**	30	948	**827**	7.9	**64**	287	**606**	**10.7**	**2.90**	**123**	**.235**	**.295**	**80**	**71**	98	99	.982	72	100	.7	**7.5**	3.7	.0	-6.3
DET	33	**13**	22	969[1]	840	**7.8**	83	373	476	11.5	3.53	107	.236	.313	14	26	103	94	**.984**	**67**	109	**1.0**	2.7	-.2	.0	1.9
BOS	19	4	24	987[1]	983	9.0	90	354	536	12.4	3.81	102	.262	.330	-17	7	106	103	.979	91	108	-.4	.7	3.5	-.5	1.7
CLE	33	10	13	931	989	9.6	67	311	569	12.7	3.88	94	.274	.333	-23	-26	99	102	.978	87	91	-.4	-2.7	-.5	**1.9**	2.2
TOR	20	4	18	953[1]	908	8.6	72	377	451	12.5	3.81	103	.252	.329	-17	13	108	97	.975	105	102	-1.3	1.4	-13.0	-1.0	-2.0
WEST																										
OAK	**60**	11	10	993	883	8.0	80	370	505	11.6	3.30	105	.240	.314	40	20	95	101	.980	81	74	.2	2.1	1.4	.6	5.3
TEX	23	**13**	18	940[1]	851	8.1	67	322	488	11.4	3.40	102	.243	.310	27	7	95	95	**.984**	69	102	.7	.7	2.9	-.7	.8
CHI	20	8	23	940[2]	891	8.5	73	336	529	12.0	3.47	103	.252	.321	19	11	98	102	.979	87	113	-.3	1.2	**5.4**	.3	-5.6
KC	24	8	24	922[1]	909	8.9	75	**273**	404	11.7	3.56	101	.260	.317	10	5	99	101	.982	72	94	.5	.5	2.2	.2	-4.9
CAL	27	8	19	971[1]	958	8.9	81	323	426	12.1	3.70	99	.261	.324	-4	-5	100	102	.977	101	120	-.9	-.5	2.7	-.3	-5.0
SEA	10	5	23	997[1]	1039	9.4	76	360	478	12.8	4.23	91	.271	.336	-64	-42	105	95	.979	91	122	-.3	-4.4	-3.8	.5	-2.5
MIN	13	6	22	979[2]	1021	9.4	79	376	500	13.0	3.98	99	.272	.341	-35	-3	108	**104**	.978	96	103	-.6	-.3	-11.6	-.2	-.8
TOT	334	117	304	13459[2]		8.7				12.1	3.66		.256	.323					.980	1166	1487					

Runs
Henderson-Oak 89
Evans-Bos 84
Cooper-Mil 70
Harrah-Cle 64
Rivers-Tex 62

Hits
Henderson-Oak ... 135
Lansford-Bos 134
Wilson-KC 133
Cooper-Mil 133
Paciorek-Sea 132

Doubles
Cooper-Mil 35
Oliver-Tex 29
Paciorek-Sea 28
Dauer-Bal 27
G.Brett-KC 27

Triples
Castino-Min 9
Wilson-KC 7
Henderson-Oak 7
G.Brett-KC 7
Baines-Chi 7

Home Runs
Murray-Bal 22
Grich-Cal 22
Evans-Bos 22
Armas-Oak 22

Total Bases
Evans-Bos 215
Armas-Oak 211
Paciorek-Sea 206
Cooper-Mil 206
Murray-Bal 202

Runs Batted In
Murray-Bal 78
Armas-Oak 76
Oglivie-Mil 72
Evans-Bos 71
Winfield-NY 68

Runs Produced
Evans-Bos 133
Henderson-Oak ... 118
Cooper-Mil 118
Murray-Bal 113
Oglivie-Mil 111

Bases On Balls
Evans-Bos 85
Murphy-Oak 73
Kemp-Det 70
Henderson-Oak 64
Aikens-KC 62

Batting Average
Lansford-Bos ..... .336
Paciorek-Sea ..... .326
Cooper-Mil .... .320
Henderson-Oak ... .319
Hargrove-Cle ..... .317

On Base Percentage
Hargrove-Cle ..... .432
Evans-Bos .... .418
Henderson-Oak ... .411
Kemp-Det .... .393
Lansford-Bos ..... .391

Slugging Average
Grich-Cal .... .543
Murray-Bal .... .534
Evans-Bos .... .522
Paciorek-Sea ..... .509
Cooper-Mil .... .495

Production
Evans-Bos .... .940
Grich-Cal .... .924
Murray-Bal .... .897
Paciorek-Sea ..... .894
Lemon-Chi .... .879

Adjusted Production
Grich-Cal 164
Evans-Bos 160
Murray-Bal 156
Lemon-Chi 155
Cooper-Mil 154

Batter Runs
Evans-Bos 39.8
Paciorek-Sea 28.4
Grich-Cal 28.3
Henderson-Oak ... 26.9
Murray-Bal 25.9

Adjusted Batter Runs
Evans-Bos 34.2
Henderson-Oak ... 30.8
Grich-Cal 28.3
Cooper-Mil 27.3
Murray-Bal 26.0

Clutch Hitting Index
Yastrzemski-Bos ... 139
Wills-Tex 132
Hargrove-Cle 129
Oglivie-Mil 128
Murphy-Oak 125

Runs Created
Evans-Bos 95
Henderson-Oak 81
Paciorek-Sea 76
Grich-Cal 73
Murray-Bal 70

Total Average
Evans-Bos 1.007
Grich-Cal .... .917
Henderson-Oak ... .899
Murray-Bal .... .864
Paciorek-Sea ..... .846

Stolen Bases
Henderson-Oak 56
Cruz-Sea 43
LeFlore-Chi 36
Wilson-KC 34
Dilone-Cle 29

Stolen Base Average
Manning-Cle 89.3
Bannister-Cle 88.9
Cruz-Sea 84.3
Wilson-KC 81.0
Gibson-Det 77.3

Stolen Base Runs
Cruz-Sea 8.1
Manning-Cle 5.7
Wilson-KC 5.4
LeFlore-Chi 4.2

Fielding Runs
Bell-Tex 30.0
Yount-Mil 27.5
Wilson-KC 22.1
Burleson-Cal 21.0
Henderson-Oak ... 20.1

Total Player Rating
Henderson-Oak ... 5.2
Bell-Tex 4.6
Yount-Mil 4.5
Grich-Cal 4.5
Evans-Bos 4.5

Wins
Vuckovich-Mil 14
Morris-Det 14
McCatty-Oak 14
D.Martinez-Bal 14

Win Percentage
Vuckovich-Mil .... .778
D.Martinez-Bal .... .737
McGregor-Bal ..... .722
Guidry-NY .... .688

Games
Corbett-Min 54
Fingers-Mil 47
Rawley-Sea 46
Easterly-Mil 44

Complete Games
Langford-Oak 18
McCatty-Oak 16
Morris-Det 15
Norris-Oak 12
Gura-KC 12

Shutouts
Medich-Tex 4
McCatty-Oak 4
Forsch-Cal 4
Dotson-Chi 4

Saves
Fingers-Mil 28
Gossage-NY 20
Quisenberry-KC 18
Corbett-Min 17
Saucier-Det 13

Innings Pitched
Leonard-KC 201.2
Morris-Det 198.0
Langford-Oak 195.1
McCatty-Oak 185.2
Stieb-Tor 183.2

Fewest Hits/Game
McCatty-Oak 6.79
Morris-Det 6.95
Guidry-NY 7.09
Darwin-Tex 7.09
Stewart-Bal 7.13

Fewest BB/Game
Honeycutt-Tex 1.20
Forsch-Cal 1.59
Gura-KC 1.83
Leonard-KC 1.83
Guidry-NY 1.84

Strikeouts
Barker-Cle 127
Burns-Chi 108
Leonard-KC 107
Blyleven-Cle 107
Guidry-NY 104

Strikeouts/Game
Barker-Cle 7.41
Guidry-NY 7.37
Bannister-Sea 6.30
Burns-Chi 6.20
Blyleven-Cle 6.04

Ratio
Guidry-NY 9.00
Gura-KC 9.30
Honeycutt-Tex 9.66
McCatty-Oak 9.84
Forsch-Cal 10.24

Earned Run Average
McCatty-Oak 2.33
Stewart-Bal 2.32
Lamp-Chi 2.41
John-NY 2.63
Burns-Chi 2.64

Adjusted ERA
Stewart-Bal 156
McCatty-Oak 149
Lamp-Chi 148
John-NY 136
Burns-Chi 135

Opponents' Batting Avg.
McCatty-Oak ...... .211
Guidry-NY .... .214
Darwin-Tex .... .218
Morris-Det .... .218
Lamp-Chi .... .222

Opponents' On Base Pct.
Guidry-NY .... .257
Gura-KC .... .269
Honeycutt-Tex .... .272
McCatty-Oak ...... .279
Forsch-Cal .... .289

Starter Runs
McCatty-Oak 27.5
Righetti-NY 18.8
Gura-KC 18.0
Burns-Chi 17.7
Lamp-Chi 17.6

Adjusted Starter Runs
McCatty-Oak 23.8
Righetti-NY 17.8
Gura-KC 17.1
Lamp-Chi 16.5
Burns-Chi 16.3

Clutch Pitching Index
Stewart-Bal 145
John-NY 129
Burns-Chi 121
Denny-Cle 119
McGregor-Bal 116

Relief Runs
Fingers-Mil 22.7
Gossage-NY 15.0
Quisenberry-KC .. 13.3
Saucier-Det 10.9
Corbett-Min 10.6

Adjusted Relief Runs
Fingers-Mil 20.7
Gossage-NY 14.5
Corbett-Min 13.4
Quisenberry-KC .. 13.0
Saucier-Det 11.5

Relief Ranking
Fingers-Mil 37.9
Gossage-NY 27.8
Saucier-Det 19.5
Quisenberry-KC .. 17.7
Corbett-Min 16.8

Total Pitcher Index
Fingers-Mil 4.2
Gossage-NY 3.1
McCatty-Oak 2.8
Quisenberry-KC ... 2.2
Saucier-Det 2.0

Total Baseball Ranking
Henderson-Oak ... 5.2
Bell-Tex 4.6
Yount-Mil 4.5
Grich-Cal 4.5
Evans-Bos 4.5

January 13 Hank Aaron and Frank Robinson become the 12th and 13th players elected to the Hall of Fame by the BBWAA in their first year of eligibility. Aaron falls nine votes shy of becoming the first-ever unanimous selection, and his 97.8 election percentage is second only to Ty Cobb's 98.2 percent in the inaugural 1936 election.

February 8 The Dodgers break up the longest-playing infield unit in major league history by trading veteran second baseman Davey Lopes to the A's for minor-leaguer Lance Hudson. Lopes, first baseman Steve Garvey, third baseman Ron Cey, and shortstop Bill Russell had been the Dodgers' starting infield since 1974.

March 10 Travis Jackson and Happy Chandler are elected to the Hall of Fame by the Special Veterans Committee. Jackson hit .291 in 15 seasons as the Giants shortstop in the 1920s and 30s, while Chandler was baseball's second commissioner and oversaw—and encouraged—the dismantling of the color barrier in 1947.

April 20 By defeating Cincinnati 4-2 for its 12th victory in a row, Atlanta breaks the modern major league record for consecutive wins at the start of a season. Steve Bedrosian pitches 4⅓ innings of relief to earn his first major league win.

June 7 The Cubs select shortstop Shawon Dunston, who batted .790 this season for Brooklyn's Thomas Jefferson High School, with the first pick in the annual June free-agent draft. Dwight Gooden is taken fifth, by the Mets, and the Yankees select high school shortstop Bo Jackson in the second round, but he opts for Auburn instead.

June 20 The Phillies first baseman Pete Rose plays in his 3,000th major league game (a 3-1 loss to the Pirates), joining Ty Cobb, Stan Musial, Hank Aaron, and Carl Yastrzemski as the only players to reach that plateau.

August 4 Outfielder Joel Youngblood becomes the first major league player ever to play for two different teams in two different cities on the same day, and collects a hit in each game. After going 1-for-2 off Ferguson Jenkins in an afternoon game at Wrigley Field, Youngblood is traded from the Mets to the Expos and flies to Philadelphia in time to enter the game that night in the sixth inning, going 1-for-1 off Steve Carlton.

September 6 Veteran first baseman Willie Stargell, whose number is retired, is saluted by 38,000 fans on his day at Pittsburgh's Three Rivers Stadium. The 41-year-old slugger delivers a pinch single in the Pirates' 6-1 win over the Mets.

October 10 St. Louis wins its first pennant since 1968 by defeating the Braves 6-2 to complete a three-game sweep of the NLCS. Catcher Darrell Porter, who hit .556, is named series MVP.

October 20 St. Louis rallies for three runs in the sixth inning, and Bruce Sutter saves Game 7, registering a 6-3 win to give the Cards the World Championship.

October 26 Steve Carlton wins the NL Cy Young Award for the fourth time. The Phils' 37-year-old left-hander, who led the league in wins (23), innings (295⅔), strikeouts (286), and shutouts (6), was a previous winner in 1972, 1977, and 1980. He joins Walter Johnson and Willie Mays as the only players until this date to be voted MVP or Cy Young winner 10 or more years apart.

November 17 Dale Murphy wins the league MVP Award, becoming the first Brave to be so honored since Hank Aaron in 1957.

ATLANTA		CHICAGO		CINCINNATI		HOUSTON		LOS ANGELES		MONTREAL	
M	J.Torre	M	L.Elia	M	J.McNamara	M	B.Virdon	M	T.Lasorda	M	J.Fanning
1B	C.Chambliss	1B	B.Buckner	M	R.Nixon	M	B.Lillis	1B	S.Garvey	1B	A.Oliver
2B	G.Hubbard	2B	B.Wills	1B	D.Driessen	1B	R.Knight	2B	S.Sax	2B	D.Flynn
SS	R.Ramirez	SS	L.Bowa	2B	R.Oester	2B	P.Garner	SS	B.Russell	SS	C.Speier
3B	B.Horner	3B	R.Sandberg	SS	D.Concepcion	SS	D.Thon	3B	R.Cey	3B	T.Wallach
LF	R.Linares	LF	K.Moreland	3B	J.Bench	3B	A.Howe	LF	D.Baker	LF	T.Raines
CF	D.Murphy	CF	G.Woods	LF	E.Milner	LF	J.Cruz	CF	K.Landreaux	CF	A.Dawson
RF	C.Washington	RF	L.Durham	CF	C.Cedeno	CF	T.Scott	RF	P.Guerrero	RF	W.Cromartie
C	B.Benedict	C	J.Davis	RF	P.Householder	RF	T.Puhl	C	M.Scioscia	C	G.Carter
				C	A.Trevino	C	A.Ashby				
3O	J.Royster	O	J.Johnstone					O	R.Monday	P	S.Rogers
O	B.Butler	2S	J.Kennedy	O1	L.Biittner	P	J.Niekro	O	R.Roenicke	P	B.Gullickson
		O	S.Henderson	O	D.Walker	P	N.Ryan			P	S.Sanderson
P	P.Niekro					P	D.Sutton	P	F.Valenzuela	P	C.Lea
P	R.Mahler	P	F.Jenkins	P	M.Soto	P	B.Knepper	P	J.Reuss	P	R.Burris
P	R.Camp	P	D.Bird	P	B.Berenyi	P	V.Ruhle	P	B.Welch	RP	J.Reardon
P	B.Walk	P	D.Noles	P	F.Pastore	RP	M.LaCoss	P	D.Stewart	RP	B.Smith
RP	S.Bedrosian	P	R.Martz	P	B.Shirley	RP	F.LaCorte	P	B.Hooton	RP	W.Fryman
RP	G.Garber	P	A.Ripley	P	T.Seaver	RP	D.Smith	RP	S.Howe		
		RP	L.Smith	RP	G.Harris			RP	T.Forster	P	D.Palmer
P	P.Perez	RP	D.Tidrow	RP	J.Kern			RP	T.Niedenfuer		
P	K.Dayley	RP	B.Campbell	RP	J.Price						
P	J.Cowley										
		P	M.Proly	P	C.Leibrandt						
		P	W.Hernandez	P	T.Hume						

NEW YORK		PHILADELPHIA		PITTSBURGH		SAN DIEGO		SAN FRANCISCO		ST.LOUIS	
M	G.Bamberger	M	P.Corrales	M	C.Tanner	M	D.Williams	M	F.Robinson	M	W.Herzog
1B	D.Kingman	1B	P.Rose	1B	J.Thompson	1B	B.Perkins	1B	R.Smith	1B	K.Hernandez
2B	W.Backman	2B	M.Trillo	2B	J.Ray	2B	T.Flannery	2B	J.Morgan	2B	T.Herr
SS	R.Gardenhire	SS	I.DeJesus	SS	D.Berra	SS	G.Templeton	SS	J.LeMaster	SS	O.Smith
3B	H.Brooks	3B	M.Schmidt	3B	B.Madlock	3B	L.Salazar	3B	D.Evans	3B	K.Oberkfell
LF	G.Foster	LF	G.Matthews	LF	M.Easler	LF	G.Richards	LF	J.Leonard	LF	L.Smith
CF	M.Wilson	CF	G.Maddox	CF	O.Moreno	CF	R.Jones	CF	C.Davis	CF	W.McGee
RF	E.Valentine	RF	G.Vukovich	RF	L.Lacy	RF	S.Lezcano	RF	J.Clark	RF	G.Hendrick
C	J.Stearns	C	B.Diaz	C	T.Pena	C	T.Kennedy	C	M.May	C	D.Porter
S2	B.Bailor	O	G.Gross	O	D.Parker	3O	J.Lefebvre	1	D.Bergman	O1	D.Iorg
1O	M.Jorgensen	O	B.Dernier			O	A.Wiggins	2	D.Kuiper	23	M.Ramsey
O1	R.Staub			P	R.Rhoden			O	J.Wohlford		
C	R.Hodges	P	S.Carlton	P	D.Robinson	P	T.Lollar	3	T.O'Malley	P	J.Andujar
O	J.Youngblood	P	L.Christenson	P	J.Candelaria	P	J.Montefusco			P	B.Forsch
		P	M.Krukow	P	M.Sarmiento	P	J.Eichelberger	P	B.Laskey	P	S.Mura
P	C.Puleo	P	D.Ruthven	P	L.McWilliams	P	E.Show	P	A.Hammaker	P	D.LaPoint
P	P.Falcone	RP	R.Reed	RP	K.Tekulve	P	C.Welsh	P	R.Gale	P	J.Stuper
P	C.Swan	RP	E.Farmer	RP	R.Scurry	RP	L.DeLeon	P	R.Martin	RP	B.Sutter
P	M.Scott	RP	S.Monge	RP	E.Romo	RP	G.Lucas	RP	F.Breining	RP	D.Bair
P	E.Lynch					RP	F.Chiffer	RP	A.Holland	RP	J.Kaat
RP	J.Orosco	P	M.Bystrom					RP	J.Barr		
RP	N.Allen					P	J.Curtis			P	J.Martin
						P	D.Dravecky	P	G.Minton	P	J.Lahti
P	P.Zachry					P	A.Hawkins	P	G.Lavelle		
P	R.Jones							P	A.Fowlkes		
/P	R.Ownbey										

TEAM	G	W	L	PCT	GB	R	OR	AB	H	2B	3B	HR	BB	SO	AVG	OBP	SLG	PRO	PRO+	BR	/A	PF	CHI	RC	SB	CS	SBA	SBR
EAST																												
STL	162	92	70	.568		685	**609**	5455	1439	239	**52**	67	569	805	.264	**.337**	.364	.701	101	24	17	101	99	682	**200**	91	69	5
PHI	162	89	73	.549	3	664	654	5454	1417	245	25	112	506	831	.260	.325	.376	.701	100	14	-1	102	99	654	128	76	63	-7
MON	162	86	76	.531	6	697	616	5557	1454	270	38	133	503	816	.262	.327	.396	.723	106	52	38	102	97	725	156	56	**74**	13
PIT	162	84	78	.519	8	724	696	5614	**1535**	**272**	40	134	442	862	**.273**	.330	**.408**	**.738**	109	**80**	58	103	97	**745**	161	75	68	3
CHI	162	73	89	.451	19	676	709	5531	1436	239	46	102	460	869	.260	.319	.375	.694	97	-4	-22	103	103	662	132	70	65	-2
NY	162	65	97	.401	27	609	723	5510	1361	227	26	97	456	1005	.247	.307	.350	.657	90	-75	-71	99	105	595	137	58	70	6
WEST																												
ATL	162	89	73	.549		**739**	702	5507	1411	215	22	**146**	554	869	.256	.327	.383	.710	100	33	4	104	105	697	151	77	66	-1
LA	162	88	74	.543	1	691	612	5642	1487	222	32	138	528	**804**	.264	.330	.388	.718	110	47	**65**	98	95	735	151	56	73	12
SF	162	87	75	.537	2	673	687	5499	1393	213	30	133	429	877	.253	.329	.376	.705	103	27	28	100	97	685	130	56	70	5
SD	162	81	81	.500	8	675	658	5575	1435	217	**52**	81	429	877	.257	.313	.359	.672	99	-49	-17	95	**110**	626	165	77	68	3
HOU	162	77	85	.475	12	569	620	5440	1342	236	48	74	435	830	.247	.305	.349	.654	95	-84	-42	92	102	578	140	61	70	5
CIN	162	61	101	.377	28	545	661	5479	1375	228	34	82	470	817	.251	.313	.350	.663	89	-63	-75	102	92	588	131	69	66	-2
TOT	972					7947		66263	17085	2823	445	1299	5964	10300	.258	.322	.373	.695							1782	822	68	41

TEAM	CG	SH	SV	IP	H	H/G	HR	BB	SO	RAT	ERA	ERA+	OAV	OOB	PR	/A	PF	CPI	FA	E	DP	FW	PW	BW	SBW	DIF
EAST																										
STL	25	10	47	1465¹	1420	8.7	94	502	689	11.9	3.37	107	.258	.322	37	40	101	105	**.981**	124	169	.9	4.2	1.8	.2	3.9
PHI	**38**	13	33	1456¹	1395	8.6	86	472	**1002**	11.7	3.61	102	.255	.317	-1	9	102	93	**.981**	121	138	**1.1**	.9	-.1	-1.1	7.1
MON	34	10	43	1460²	1371	8.4	110	**448**	936	11.3	3.31	**110**	.250	.309	46	**53**	101	99	.980	122	117	**1.1**	5.6	4.0	**1.0**	-6.6
PIT	19	7	39	1466²	1434	8.8	118	521	933	12.2	3.81	97	.257	.324	-34	-17	103	96	.977	145	133	-.3	-1.8	6.1	-.0	-1.0
CHI	9	7	43	1447¹	1510	9.4	125	452	764	12.4	3.92	95	.272	.330	-51	-30	104	102	.979	132	110	.5	-3.2	-2.3	-.6	-2.4
NY	15	5	37	1447¹	1508	9.4	119	582	759	13.1	3.88	94	.273	.344	-45	-40	101	**109**	.972	175	134	-2.0	-4.2	-7.5	.3	-2.6
WEST																										
ATL	15	11	**51**	1463	1484	9.1	126	502	813	12.4	3.82	98	.267	.331	-36	-15	104	103	.979	137	**186**	.2	-1.6	.4	-.5	9.4
LA	37	**16**	28	1488¹	1356	**8.2**	81	468	932	**11.2**	**3.26**	106	**.244**	**.305**	56	34	96	92	.979	139	131	.0	3.6	**6.8**	.9	-4.4
SF	18	4	45	1465¹	1507	9.3	109	466	810	12.3	3.64	99	.270	.329	-6	-7	100	106	.973	173	125	-1.9	-.7	2.9	.2	5.5
SD	20	11	41	1476	1348	**8.2**	139	502	765	11.4	3.52	97	**.244**	.310	13	-16	95	96	.976	152	142	-.7	-1.7	-1.8	-.0	4.2
HOU	37	**16**	31	1446²	**1338**	8.3	87	479	899	11.5	3.42	97	.247	.312	30	-16	92	94	.978	136	154	.3	-1.7	-4.4	.2	1.7
CIN	22	7	31	1460¹	1414	8.7	105	570	998	12.4	3.66	101	.258	.330	-10	6	103	102	.980	128	158	.7	-.6	-7.9	-.6	-12.9
TOT	289	117	469	17543¹		8.8				12.0	3.60		.258	.322					.978	1684	1697					

Runs
L.Smith-StL 120
Murphy-Atl 113
Schmidt-Phi 108
Dawson-Mon 107
Sandberg-Chi 103

Hits
Oliver-Mon 204
Buckner-Chi 201
Dawson-Mon 183
L.Smith-StL 182
Ray-Pit 182

Doubles
Oliver-Mon 43
Kennedy-SD 42
Dawson-Mon 37
Knight-Hou 36

Triples
Thon-Hou 10
Wilson-NY 9
Puhl-Hou 9
Moreno-Pit 9

Home Runs
Kingman-NY 37
Murphy-Atl 36
Schmidt-Phi 35
Horner-Atl 32
Guerrero-LA 32

Total Bases
Oliver-Mon 317
Guerrero-LA 308
Murphy-Atl 303
Dawson-Mon 303
Buckner-Chi 290

Runs Batted In
Oliver-Mon 109
Murphy-Atl 109
Buckner-Chi 105
Hendrick-StL 104
Clark-SF 103

Runs Produced
Murphy-Atl 186
Buckner-Chi 183
L.Smith-StL 181
Oliver-Mon 177
Madlock-Pit 168

Bases On Balls
Schmidt-Phi 107
Thompson-Pit 101
Hernandez-StL 100
Murphy-Atl 93
Clark-SF 90

Batting Average
Oliver-Mon ...... .331
Madlock-Pit ...... .319
Durham-Chi ...... .312
L.Smith-StL ...... .307
Buckner-Chi ...... .306

On Base Percentage
Schmidt-Phi ...... .407
Hernandez-StL .... .404
Morgan-SF ...... .402
Thompson-Pit .... .397
Oliver-Mon ...... .394

Slugging Average
Schmidt-Phi ...... .547
Guerrero-LA ...... .536
Durham-Chi ...... .521
Oliver-Mon ...... .514
Thompson-Pit ...... .511

Production
Schmidt-Phi ...... .954
Guerrero-LA ...... .915
Durham-Chi ...... .910
Oliver-Mon ...... .908
Thompson-Pit .... .908

Adjusted Production
Schmidt-Phi 161
Guerrero-LA 157
Oliver-Mon 149
Lezcano-SD 149
Durham-Chi 148

Batter Runs
Schmidt-Phi 47.2
Oliver-Mon 42.7
Thompson-Pit 40.7
Guerrero-LA 40.3
Murphy-Atl 37.8

Adjusted Batter Runs
Schmidt-Phi 44.7
Guerrero-LA 43.1
Oliver-Mon 40.5
Thompson-Pit 37.4
Durham-Chi 35.0

Clutch Hitting Index
Hernandez-StL 129
Hendrick-StL 128
DeJesus-Phi 123
Buckner-Chi 123
Lezcano-SD 115

Runs Created
Oliver-Mon 125
Guerrero-LA 120
Murphy-Atl 118
Schmidt-Phi 118
Thompson-Pit 117

Total Average
Schmidt-Phi 1.026
Guerrero-LA ...... .959
Thompson-Pit ...... .951
Morgan-SF ...... .923
Durham-Chi ...... .917

Stolen Bases
Raines-Mon 78
L.Smith-StL 68
Moreno-Pit 60
Wilson-NY 58
S.Sax-LA 49

Stolen Base Average
Bailor-NY 87.0
Morgan-SF 85.7
Wiggins-SD 84.6
Matthews-Phi 84.0
O.Smith-StL 83.3

Stolen Base Runs
Raines-Mon 13.8
Wilson-NY 7.8
Wiggins-SD 6.3
Thon-Hou 6.3
Dawson-Mon 5.7

Fielding Runs
O.Smith-StL 33.1
Dawson-Mon 20.8
Hubbard-Atl 19.9
Schmidt-Phi 18.8
Davis-SF 17.9

Total Player Rating
Schmidt-Phi 6.1
Carter-Mon 5.4
Dawson-Mon 4.7
Guerrero-LA 4.6
Lezcano-SD 4.6

Wins
Carlton-Phi 23
Valenzuela-LA 19
Rogers-Mon 19
Reuss-LA 18

Win Percentage
Niekro-Atl ...... .810
Rogers-Mon ...... .704
Carlton-Phi ...... .676
Lollar-SD ...... .640
Forsch-StL ...... .625

Games
Tekulve-Pit 85
Minton-SF 78
Scurry-Pit 76
Reardon-Mon 75
Hernandez-Chi 75

Complete Games
Carlton-Phi 19
Valenzuela-LA 18
Niekro-Hou 16
Rogers-Mon 14
Soto-Cin 13

Shutouts
Carlton-Phi 6
Niekro-Hou 5
Andujar-StL 5

Saves
Sutter-StL 36
Minton-SF 30
Garber-Atl 30
Reardon-Mon 26
Tekulve-Pit 20

Innings Pitched
Carlton-Phi 295.2
Valenzuela-LA 285.0
Rogers-Mon 277.0
Niekro-Hou 270.0
Andujar-StL 265.2

Fewest Hits/Game
Ryan-Hou 7.05
Soto-Cin 7.06
Lea-Mon 7.35
Lollar-SD 7.43
Niekro-Hou 7.47

Fewest BB/Game
Bird-Chi 1.41
Hammaker-SF 1.44
Andujar-StL 1.69
Reuss-LA 1.77
Candelaria-Pit 1.91

Strikeouts
Carlton-Phi 286
Soto-Cin 274
Ryan-Hou 245
Valenzuela-LA 199
Rogers-Mon 179

Strikeouts/Game
Soto-Cin 9.57
Ryan-Hou 8.81
Carlton-Phi 8.71
Candelaria-Pit 6.85
Welch-LA 6.72

Ratio
Soto-Cin 9.68
Niekro-Hou 9.77
Andujar-StL 9.96
Sutton-Hou 9.97
Reuss-LA 10.04

Earned Run Average
Rogers-Mon 2.40
Niekro-Hou 2.47
Andujar-StL 2.47
Soto-Cin 2.79
Valenzuela-LA 2.87

Adjusted ERA
Rogers-Mon 151
Andujar-StL 146
Niekro-Hou 134
Soto-Cin 132
Candelaria-Pit 126

Opponents' Batting Avg.
Ryan-Hou ...... .213
Soto-Cin ...... .215
Lea-Mon ...... .222
Lollar-SD ...... .224
Niekro-Hou ...... .229

Opponents' On Base Pct.
Soto-Cin ...... .273
Reuss-LA ...... .278
Sutton-Hou ...... .279
Niekro-Hou ...... .279
Andujar-StL ...... .282

Starter Runs
Rogers-Mon 36.8
Niekro-Hou 34.0
Andujar-StL 33.3
Soto-Cin 23.1
Valenzuela-LA 23.0

Adjusted Starter Runs
Rogers-Mon 38.0
Andujar-StL 33.8
Soto-Cin 25.9
Niekro-Hou 25.5
Valenzuela-LA 18.8

Clutch Pitching Index
Camp-Atl 124
Jenkins-Chi 121
Krukow-Phi 120
Gale-SF 114
Mura-StL 110

Relief Runs
Minton-SF 24.2
Scurry-Pit 21.5
Reardon-Mon 18.6
Bedrosian-Atl 18.1
DeLeon-SD 17.8

Adjusted Relief Runs
Minton-SF 24.1
Scurry-Pit 22.7
Bedrosian-Atl 20.1
Reardon-Mon 19.1
Garber-Atl 18.5

Relief Ranking
Minton-SF 35.7
Garber-Atl 33.7
Reardon-Mon 23.9
DeLeon-SD 23.9
Scurry-Pit 23.4

Total Pitcher Index
Minton-SF 3.9
Garber-Atl 3.9
Rogers-Mon 3.7
Andujar-StL 3.2
Soto-Cin 2.7

Total Baseball Ranking
Schmidt-Phi 6.1
Carter-Mon 5.4
Dawson-Mon 4.7
Guerrero-LA 4.6
Lezcano-SD 4.6

January 22 Free-agent outfielder Reggie Jackson ends his tumultuous five seasons as a Yankee by signing a four-year contract with the California Angels for nearly $1 million per year.

May 6 Gaylord Perry becomes the 15th pitcher to win 300 career games, beating the Yankees 7-3 at the Kingdome.

July 8 Billy Martin records his 1,000th career win as a manager as the A's beat the Yankees 6-3.

July 19 In the first annual Cracker Jack Old-Timers Classic at Washington's Robert F. Kennedy Stadium, 75-year-old Luke Appling hits a 250-foot homer off Warren Spahn to help the AL to a 7-2 win over the NL.

August 2 Oakland's Rickey Henderson steals his 100th base of the season in a 6-5 win over Seattle, tying the AL record he set in 1981.

August 21 Milwaukee's Rollie Fingers records his 300th career save in a 3-2 win at Seattle, becoming the first player to reach that milestone.

August 23 Seattle pitcher Gaylord Perry is ejected in the seventh inning of a 4-3 loss to the Red Sox for doctoring the baseball. It is the first time in his 20 major league seasons that the self-proclaimed spitball king has been bounced for that offense.

August 24 Kansas City's John Wathan steals his 31st base of the season in a 5-3 win over the Rangers, breaking the single-season record for catchers set by Ray Schalk in 1916. Wathan will finish the season with a career-high 36 stolen bases.

August 27 Rickey Henderson steals four bases in Oakland's 5-4 loss to Milwaukee to raise his total to 122 and break Lou Brock's single-season record of 118.

October 2 The Angels clinch the AL West title with a 6-4 win over the Rangers.

October 3 Robin Yount smacks two home runs and a triple as Milwaukee whips Baltimore 10-2 to win the AL East championship. Don Sutton, 4-1 since being acquired by the Brewers in late August, is the winning pitcher.

October 10 In Game 5 of the ALCS, the Brewers complete their comeback from a 2-0 deficit by edging the Angels, 4-3, to earn their first-ever trip to the World Series. Angels outfielder Fred Lynn bats .611 for the series and is named MVP in a losing cause.

October 12 Paul Molitor goes 5-for-6 to become the first player ever to collect five hits in a World Series game, and teammate Robin Yount goes 4-for-6 as the Brewers rout the Cardinals 10-0 in Game 1.

October 17 Robin Yount records his second four-hit game of the Series to lead the Brewers to a 6-4 win in Game 5 and give Milwaukee a 3-2 lead overall. Yount is the first player ever to have two four-hit games in one World Series.

November 3 Pete Vuckovich becomes the Brewers' second consecutive Cy Young Award winner, edging Jim Palmer. Vuckovich was 18-6 with a 3.34 ERA for the league champions, and has the highest winning percentage in the majors for the past two seasons.

November 9 Robin Yount, who hit .331 for Milwaukee and led the league in hits (210), doubles (46), and slugging percentage (.578), is a unanimous choice as league MVP.

BALTIMORE		BOSTON		CALIFORNIA		CHICAGO		CLEVELAND		DETROIT		KANSAS CITY	
M	E.Weaver	M	R.Houk	M	G.Mauch	M	T.LaRussa	M	D.Garcia	M	S.Anderson	M	D.Howser
1B	E.Murray	1B	D.Stapleton	1B	R.Carew	1B	M.Squires	1B	M.Hargrove	1B	E.Cabell	1B	W.Aikens
2B	R.Dauer	2B	J.Remy	2B	B.Grich	2B	T.Bernazard	2B	J.Perconte	2B	L.Whitaker	2B	F.White
SS	L.Sakata	SS	G.Hoffman	SS	T.Foli	SS	B.Almon	SS	M.Fischlin	SS	A.Trammell	SS	U.Washington
3B	C.Ripken	3B	C.Lansford	3B	D.DeCinces	3B	A.Rodriguez	3B	T.Harrah	3B	T.Brookens	3B	G.Brett
LF	G.Roenicke	LF	J.Rice	LF	B.Downing	LF	S.Kemp	LF	M.Dilone	LF	L.Herndon	LF	W.Wilson
CF	A.Bumbry	CF	R.Miller	CF	F.Lynn	CF	R.Law	CF	R.Manning	CF	G.Wilson	CF	A.Otis
RF	D.Ford	RF	D.Evans	RF	Re.Jackson	RF	H.Baines	RF	V.Hayes	RF	C.Lemon	RF	J.Martin
C	R.Dempsey	C	G.Allenson	C	B.Boone	C	C.Fisk	C	R.Hassey	C	L.Parrish	C	J.Wathan
DH	K.Singleton	DH	C.Yastrzemski	DH	D.Baylor	DH	G.Luzinski	DH	A.Thornton	DH	M.Ivie	DH	H.McRae
O	J.Lowenstein	13	W.Boggs	O	J.Beniquez	S3	V.Law	O2	A.Bannister	O	K.Gibson	S2	O.Concepcion
C	J.Nolan	C	R.Gedman	O	B.Clark	1	T.Paciorek	2S	L.Milbourne	1O	R.Leach	P	L.Gura
		O	R.Nichols			O	R.LeFlore	S	J.Dybzinski	DO	J.Turner	P	V.Blue
P	D.Martinez			P	G.Zahn							P	P.Splittorff
P	M.Flanagan	P	D.Eckersley	P	K.Forsch	P	L.Hoyt	P	L.Barker	P	J.Morris	P	D.Leonard
P	J.Palmer	P	J.Tudor	P	M.Witt	P	R.Dotson	P	R.Sutcliffe	P	D.Petry	RP	D.Quisenberry
P	S.McGregor	P	M.Torrez	P	S.Renko	P	D.Lamp	P	L.Sorensen	P	M.Wilcox	RP	M.Armstrong
P	S.Stewart	P	B.Stanley	P	B.Kison	P	J.Koosman	P	J.Denny	P	J.Ujdur	RP	D.Hood
RP	T.Martinez	P	C.Rainey	RP	L.Sanchez	P	B.Burns	P	R.Waits	P	P.Underwood	P	B.Black
RP	R.Grimsley	RP	M.Clear	RP	A.Hassler	RP	S.Barojas	RP	D.Spillner	RP	D.Tobik	P	D.Frost
RP	T.Stoddard	RP	T.Burgmeier	RP	D.Corbett	RP	K.Hickey	RP	E.Whitson	RP	D.Rucker	P	B.Castro
		RP	L.Aponte			RP	C.Escarrega	RP	E.Glynn	RP	E.Sosa		
P	S.Davis			P	D.Goltz								
		P	B.Hurst	P	D.Aase	P	S.Trout	P	T.Brennan	P	L.Pashnick		
		P	B.Ojeda					P	B.Anderson				

MILWAUKEE		MINNESOTA		NEW YORK		OAKLAND		SEATTLE		TEXAS		TORONTO	
M	B.Rodgers	M	B.Gardner	M	B.Lemon	M	B.Martin	M	R.Lachemann	M	D.Zimmer	M	B.Cox
M	H.Kuenn	1B	K.Hrbek	M	G.Michael	1B	D.Meyer	1B	G.Gray	M	D.Johnson	1B	W.Upshaw
1B	C.Cooper	2B	J.Castino	M	C.King	2B	D.Lopes	2B	J.Cruz	1B	D.Hostetler	2B	D.Garcia
2B	J.Gantner	SS	R.Washington	1B	J.Mayberry	SS	F.Stanley	SS	T.Cruz	2B	M.Richardt	SS	A.Griffin
SS	R.Yount	3B	G.Gaetti	2B	W.Randolph	3B	W.Gross	3B	M.Castillo	SS	M.Wagner	3B	R.Mulliniks
3B	P.Molitor	LF	G.Ward	SS	R.Smalley	LF	R.Henderson	LF	B.Bochte	3B	B.Bell	LF	B.Bonnell
LF	B.Oglivie	CF	B.Mitchell	3B	G.Nettles	CF	D.Murphy	CF	D.Henderson	LF	B.Sample	CF	L.Moseby
CF	G.Thomas	RF	T.Brunansky	LF	D.Winfield	RF	T.Armas	RF	A.Cowens	CF	G.Wright	RF	J.Barfield
RF	C.Moore	C	T.Laudner	CF	J.Mumphrey	C	M.Heath	C	R.Sweet	RF	L.Parrish	C	E.Whitt
C	T.Simmons	DH	R.Johnson	RF	K.Griffey	DH	C.Johnson	DH	R.Zisk	C	J.Sundberg	DH	J.Revering
DH	R.Howell			C	R.Cerone					DH	L.Johnson		
		OD	M.Hatcher	DH	O.Gamble	DO	J.Burroughs	O	J.Simpson			32	G.Iorg
D3	D.Money	S	L.Faedo			C	J.Newman	O	B.Brown	OD	J.Grubb	OD	H.Powell
				O1	D.Collins	23	D.McKay	1	J.Maler	2S	D.Flynn	C	B.Martinez
				DO	L.Piniella							OD	A.Woods
P	M.Caldwell	P	B.Castillo			P	R.Langford	P	F.Bannister	P	C.Hough		
P	P.Vuckovich	P	B.Havens			P	M.Keough	P	G.Perry	P	F.Tanana	P	D.Stieb
P	M.Haas	P	A.Williams	P	R.Guidry	P	M.Norris	P	J.Beattie	P	R.Honeycutt	P	J.Clancy
P	B.McClure	P	F.Viola	P	T.John	P	S.McCatty	P	M.Moore	P	J.Matlack	P	L.Leal
P	J.Slaton	P	J.O'Connor	P	D.Righetti	P	B.Kingman	P	G.Nelson	P	D.Medich	P	J.Gott
RP	R.Fingers	RP	T.Felton	P	S.Rawley	RP	T.Underwood	RP	B.Caudill	RP	S.Comer	RP	D.Murray
RP	D.Bernard	RP	R.Davis	P	M.Morgan	RP	B.Owchinko	RP	L.Andersen	RP	D.Darwin	RP	R.Jackson
		RP	J.Pacella	RP	G.Frazier	RP	D.Beard	RP	E.Vande Berg	RP	P.Mirabella	RP	J.McLaughlin
P	R.Lerch			RP	R.May								
P	D.Medich	P	P.Redfern	RP	R.Gossage			P	B.Clark	P	D.Schmidt	P	M.Bomback
P	J.Augustine	P	P.Boris			P	M.Stanton	P	J.Butcher	P	J.Garvin		
/P	D.Sutton			P	R.Erickson	/P	B.Stoddard						
				P	D.Alexander								
				P	D.LaRoche								

TEAM	G	W	L	PCT	GB	R	OR	AB	H	2B	3B	HR	BB	SO	AVG	OBP	SLG	PRO	PRO+	BR	/A	PF	CHI	RC	SB	CS	SBA	SBR
EAST																												
MIL	163	95	67	.586		891	717	5733	1599	277	41	216	484	714	.279	.337	.455	.792	123	109	162	94	105	865	84	52	62	-6
BAL	163	94	68	.580	1	774	687	5557	1478	259	27	179	634	796	.266	.344	.419	.763	108	67	70	100	96	795	49	38	56	-8
BOS	162	89	73	.549	6	753	713	5596	1536	271	31	136	547	736	.274	.342	.407	.749	99	39	-6	106	98	755	42	39	52	-11
DET	162	83	79	.512	12	729	685	5590	1489	237	40	177	470	807	.266	.326	.418	.744	103	15	12	100	99	752	93	66	58	-12
NY	162	79	83	.488	16	709	716	5526	1417	225	37	161	590	719	.256	.331	.398	.729	101	-5	7	98	98	716	69	45	61	-6
TOR	162	78	84	.481	17	651	701	5526	1447	262	45	106	415	749	.262	.317	.383	.700	83	-70	-129	109	102	655	118	81	59	-13
CLE	162	78	84	.481	17	683	748	5559	1458	225	32	109	651	625	.262	.343	.373	.716	97	-13	-9	100	94	723	151	68	69	5
WEST																												
CAL	162	93	69	.574		814	670	5532	1518	268	26	186	613	760	.274	.350	.433	.783	114	108	108	100	96	834	55	53	51	-15
KC	162	90	72	.556	9	784	717	5629	1603	295	58	132	442	758	.285	.340	.428	.768	109	67	66	100	99	802	133	48	73	11
CHI	162	87	75	.537	6	786	710	5575	1523	266	52	136	533	866	.273	.340	.413	.753	106	43	43	100	100	784	136	58	70	6
SEA	162	76	86	.469	17	651	712	5626	1431	259	33	130	456	806	.254	.313	.381	.694	87	-84	-102	103	102	657	131	82	62	-10
OAK	162	68	94	.420	25	691	819	5448	1286	211	27	149	582	948	.236	.312	.367	.679	90	-106	-79	96	113	644	232	87	73	17
TEX	162	64	98	.395	29	590	749	5445	1354	204	26	115	447	750	.249	.309	.359	.668	87	-128	-100	103	95	593	63	45	58	-8
MIN	162	60	102	.370	33	657	819	5544	1427	234	44	148	474	887	.257	.319	.396	.715	93	-43	-61	103	98	676	38	33	54	-8
TOT	1135					10163		77886	20566	3493	519	2080	7338	10921	.264	.330	.402	.733							1394	795	64	-59

TEAM	CG	SH	SV	IP	H	H/G	HR	BB	SO	RAT	ERA	ERA+	OAV	OOB	PR	/A	PF	CPI	FA	E	DP	FW	PW	BW	SBW	DIF
EAST																										
MIL	34	6	47	1467¹	1514	9.3	152	511	717	12.5	3.98	95	.270	.333	15	-32	93	106	.980	125	185	.1	-3.2	16.2	-.2	1.1
BAL	38	8	34	1462¹	1436	8.8	147	488	719	12.0	3.99	101	.257	.320	14	7	99	95	.984	101	140	1.4	.7	7.0	-.4	4.3
BOS	23	11	33	1453	1557	9.6	155	478	816	12.8	4.03	107	.276	.336	7	44	106	108	.981	121	172	.3	4.4	-.6	-.7	4.6
DET	45	5	27	1451	1371	8.5	172	554	740	12.1	3.80	107	.251	.323	44	42	100	104	.981	117	165	.5	4.2	1.2	-.8	-3.1
NY	24	8	39	1459	1471	9.1	113	491	939	12.2	3.99	100	.264	.326	13	-1	98	95	.979	128	158	-.0	-.1	.7	-.2	-2.3
TOR	41	13	25	1443²	1428	8.9	147	493	776	12.1	3.95	113	.257	.321	20	85	110	97	.978	136	146	-.5	8.5	-12.9	-.9	2.8
CLE	31	9	30	1468¹	1433	8.8	122	589	882	12.5	4.11	99	.257	.330	-5	-5	100	94	.980	123	129	-.2	-.5	-.9	.9	-2.7
WEST																										
CAL	40	10	27	1464	1436	8.8	124	482	728	12.0	3.82	106	.259	.322	42	38	100	98	.983	108	171	1.0	3.8	10.8	-1.1	-2.5
KC	16	12	45	1431	1443	9.1	163	471	650	12.4	4.08	100	.262	.323	-1	0	100	98	.979	127	140	-.0	.0	6.6	1.5	.9
CHI	30	10	41	1439	1502	9.4	99	460	753	12.4	3.87	104	.270	.329	33	27	99	100	.976	154	173	-1.5	2.7	4.3	1.0	-.5
SEA	23	11	39	1476¹	1431	8.7	173	547	1002	12.2	3.88	109	.256	.325	32	60	104	104	.978	139	158	-.7	6.0	-10.2	-.6	.5
OAK	42	6	22	1456	1506	9.3	177	648	697	13.5	4.54	86	.268	.346	-76	-130	96	100	.974	160	140	-1.8	-10.3	-7.9	2.1	4.9
TEX	32	5	24	1431	1554	9.8	128	483	690	13.1	4.28	90	.280	.342	-33	-66	95	102	.981	121	169	.3	-6.6	-10.0	-.4	-.3
MIN	26	7	30	1433	1484	9.3	208	643	812	13.4	4.72	90	.269	.347	-103	-77	104	101	.982	108	162	1.0	-7.7	-6.1	-.4	-7.8
TOT	445	121	463	20335		9.1				12.5	4.07		.264	.330					.980	1768	2208					

Runs		Hits		Doubles		Triples		Home Runs		Total Bases	
Molitor-Mil	136	Yount-Mil	210	Yount-Mil	46	Wilson-KC	15	Thomas-Mil	39	Yount-Mil	367
Yount-Mil	129	Cooper-Mil	205	McRae-KC	46	Herndon-Det	13	R.Jackson-Cal	39	Cooper-Mil	345
Evans-Bos	122	Molitor-Mil	201	White-KC	45	Yount-Mil	12	Winfield-NY	37	McRae-KC	332
Henderson-Oak	119	Wilson-KC	194	DeCinces-Cal	42	Mumphrey-NY	10	Oglivie-Mil	34	Evans-Bos	325
Downing-Cal	109	McRae-KC	189	Cowens-Sea	39					DeCinces-Cal	315

Runs Batted In		Runs Produced		Bases On Balls		Batting Average		On Base Percentage		Slugging Average	
McRae-KC	133	Yount-Mil	214	Henderson-Oak	116	Wilson-KC	.332	Evans-Bos	.403	Yount-Mil	.578
Cooper-Mil	121	McRae-KC	197	Evans-Bos	112	Yount-Mil	.331	Harrah-Cle	.400	Winfield-NY	.560
Thornton-Cle	116	Cooper-Mil	193	Thornton-Cle	109	Carew-Cal	.319	Henderson-Oak	.399	Murray-Bal	.549
Yount-Mil	114	Molitor-Mil	188	Hargrove-Cle	101	Murray-Bal	.316	Carew-Cal	.399	DeCinces-Cal	.548
Thomas-Mil	112	Evans-Bos	188	Murphy-Oak	94	Cooper-Mil	.313	Murray-Bal	.395	McRae-KC	.542

Production		Adjusted Production		Batter Runs		Adjusted Batter Runs		Clutch Hitting Index		Runs Created	
Yount-Mil	.962	Yount-Mil	170	Yount-Mil	50.3	Yount-Mil	58.7	Otis-KC	137	Yount-Mil	136
Murray-Bal	.944	Murray-Bal	157	Evans-Bos	48.5	Murray-Bal	42.9	Foli-Cal	137	Evans-Bos	134
Evans-Bos	.937	DeCinces-Cal	149	Murray-Bal	42.5	Evans-Bos	40.9	Hayes-Cle	124	Harrah-Cle	123
DeCinces-Cal	.922	R.Jackson-Cal	147	DeCinces-Cal	38.1	Harrah-Cle	38.6	Boone-Cal	124	McRae-KC	123
McRae-KC	.912	McRae-KC	146	Harrah-Cle	38.0	DeCinces-Cal	38.1	Murphy-Oak	122	Cooper-Mil	118

Total Average		Stolen Bases		Stolen Base Average		Stolen Base Runs		Fielding Runs		Total Player Rating	
Evans-Bos	.976	Henderson-Oak	130	Sexton-Oak	100.0	Henderson-Oak	13.8	Bell-Tex	34.4	Yount-Mil	7.0
Yount-Mil	.969	Garcia-Tor	54	Fisk-Chi	89.5	Molitor-Mil	6.9	Bernazard-Chi	24.6	DeCinces-Cal	5.3
Murray-Bal	.957	J.Cruz-Sea	46	Dilone-Cle	86.8	Dilone-Cle	6.9	Murphy-Oak	21.8	Bell-Tex	5.1
Henderson-Oak	.934	Molitor-Mil	41	Harrah-Cle	85.0	J.Cruz-Sea	6.0	DeCinces-Cal	20.6	Evans-Bos	4.2
Harrah-Cle	.931	Wilson-KC	37	Brown-Sea	82.4	Wathan-KC	5.4	Almon-Chi	20.0	Henderson-Oak	4.0

Wins		Win Percentage		Games		Complete Games		Shutouts		Saves	
Hoyt-Chi	19	Vuckovich-Mil	.750	VandeBerg-Sea	78	Stieb-Tor	19	Stieb-Tor	5	Quisenberry-KC	35
Zahn-Cal	18	Palmer-Bal	.750	T.Martinez-Tor	76	Morris-Det	17	Zahn-Cal	4	Gossage-NY	30
Vuckovich-Mil	18	Zahn-Cal	.692	Quisenberry-KC	72	Langford-Oak	15	Forsch-Cal	4	Fingers-Mil	29
Gura-KC	18	Petry-Det	.625	Caudill-Sea	70	Hoyt-Chi	14			Caudill-Sea	26
		Gura-KC	.600	Spillner-Cle	65					Davis-Min	22

Innings Pitched		Fewest Hits/Game		Fewest BB/Game		Strikeouts		Strikeouts/Game		Ratio	
Stieb-Tor	288.1	Sutcliffe-Cle	7.25	John-NY-Cal	1.58	Bannister-Sea	209	Righetti-NY	8.02	Palmer-Bal	10.39
Clancy-Tor	266.2	Ujdur-Det	7.58	Eckersley-Bos	1.73	Barker-Cle	187	Bannister-Sea	7.62	Eckersley-Bos	10.95
Morris-Det	266.1	Righetti-NY	7.62	Hoyt-Chi	1.80	Righetti-NY	163	Beattie-Sea	7.31	Stieb-Tor	10.96
Caldwell-Mil	258.0	Palmer-Bal	7.73	Haas-Mil	1.82	Guidry-NY	162	Barker-Cle	6.88	Barker-Cle	11.11
D.Martinez-Bal	252.0	Barker-Cle	7.76	Langford-Oak	1.86	Tudor-Bos	146	Tudor-Bos	6.72	Bannister-Sea	11.11

Earned Run Average		Adjusted ERA		Opponents' Batting Avg.		Opponents' On Base Pct.		Starter Runs		Adjusted Starter Runs	
Sutcliffe-Cle	2.96	Stanley-Bos	139	Sutcliffe-Cle	.226	Palmer-Bal	.287	Sutcliffe-Cle	26.8	Stieb-Tor	39.4
Stanley-Bos	3.10	Stieb-Tor	138	Righetti-NY	.229	Eckersley-Bos	.297	Stieb-Tor	26.5	Sutcliffe-Cle	26.9
Palmer-Bal	3.13	Sutcliffe-Cle	138	Ujdur-Det	.230	Stieb-Tor	.299	Palmer-Bal	23.7	Petry-Det	23.0
Petry-Det	3.22	Palmer-Bal	129	Palmer-Bal	.231	Barker-Cle	.301	Petry-Det	23.3	Palmer-Bal	22.7
Stieb-Tor	3.25	Beattie-Sea	127	Barker-Cle	.232	Clancy-Tor	.302	Vuckovich-Mil	18.2	Clancy-Tor	22.6

Clutch Pitching Index		Relief Runs		Adjusted Relief Runs		Relief Ranking		Total Pitcher Index		Total Baseball Ranking	
Vuckovich-Mil	131	Spillner-Cle	23.5	Spillner-Cle	23.6	Caudill-Sea	51.7	Caudill-Sea	5.1	Yount-Mil	7.0
Tudor-Bos	121	Quisenberry-KC	22.9	Quisenberry-KC	23.0	Spillner-Cle	43.0	Quisenberry-KC	4.5	DeCinces-Cal	5.3
Dotson-Chi	118	Burgmeier-Bos	20.3	Burgmeier-Bos	23.0	Quisenberry-KC	37.2	Stieb-Tor	4.2	Caudill-Sea	5.1
Wilcox-Det	113	Gossage-NY	19.1	Stanley-Bos	22.5	Clear-Bos	34.5	Spillner-Cle	4.2	Bell-Tex	5.1
Stanley-Bos	110	Caudill-Sea	18.3	Caudill-Sea	20.1	Gossage-NY	28.7	Clear-Bos	3.5	Quisenberry-KC	4.5

January 12 Brooks Robinson and Juan Marichal are elected to the Hall of Fame by the BBWAA. Robinson becomes the 14th player elected in his first year of eligibility.

March 3 Steve Carlton agrees to a four-year, $4.15 million contract with the Phillies that will make him the highest-paid pitcher in baseball history.

March 10 Walter Alston, who managed the Dodgers to four World Championships, and George Kell, who hit .306 over 15 major league seasons, are elected to the Hall of Fame by the Special Veterans Committee.

April 27 In a 4-2 win over the Expos, Nolan Ryan strikes out Brad Mills to move a strikeout ahead of Walter Johnson and become baseball's all-time leader at 3,509.

July 29 Steve Garvey's consecutive-game streak ends at 1,207 when he dislocates his left thumb in a home-plate collision with Braves pitcher Pascual Perez. The injury keeps him from playing the second game of the doubleheader.

August 24 First baseman Pete Rose does not play in the Phillies 5-3 loss to the Giants, ending his consecutive games played streak at 745. Manager Paul Owens had planned to use Rose as a pinch hitter in the 10th inning, but Joel Youngblood ends the game with a two-run home run off Steve Carlton in the bottom of the ninth.

August 25* The Louisville Redbirds (American Association) become the first minor league team to draw one million fans in a season.

August 28 Greg Luzinski becomes the first player to park three home runs onto the roof at Comiskey Park, connecting off Boston's Dennis Boyd. Jimmie Foxx and Ted Williams each accomplished the feat twice.

September 17 A record regular-season crowd of 53,790 packs Cincinnati's Riverfront Stadium on Johnny Bench Night, and he responds with a two-run home run and a single.

September 28 Whipping the Cubs 13-6 for their 12th win in their last 13 games, the Phillies clinch the NL East championship. Bo Diaz goes 5-for-5 with a pair of home runs and Joe Morgan has his third four-hit game of the month.

September 30 The Dodgers beat the Giants 4-3 and the Padres beat the Braves 3-2, giving Los Angeles the NL West title.

October 4 In the NLCS opener, Mike Schmidt's first-inning homer and Al Holland's clutch relieving to get out of an eighth-inning bases-loaded jam are enough for Philadelphia to top Los Angeles, 1-0.

October 11 In the World Series opener, homers account for all the scoring as the Phillies top Baltimore, 2-1.

November 2 John Denny wins the NL Cy Young Award, collecting 20 of 24 first-place votes to defeat runner-up Mario Soto. Denny was 19-6 with a 2.37 ERA for the NL champion Phillies.

November 8 Atlanta's Dale Murphy wins his second consecutive NL MVP Award, joining Ernie Banks, Joe Morgan, and Mike Schmidt, who also accomplished that feat.

	ATLANTA		CHICAGO		CINCINNATI		HOUSTON		LOS ANGELES		MONTREAL
M	J.Torre	M	L.Elia	M	R.Nixon	M	B.Lillis	M	T.Lasorda	M	B.Virdon
1B	C.Chambliss	M	C.Fox	1B	D.Driessen	1B	R.Knight	1B	G.Brock	1B	A.Oliver
2B	G.Hubbard	1B	B.Buckner	2B	R.Oester	2B	B.Doran	2B	S.Sax	2B	D.Flynn
SS	R.Ramirez	2B	R.Sandberg	SS	D.Concepcion	SS	D.Thon	SS	B.Russell	SS	C.Speier
3B	B.Horner	SS	L.Bowa	3B	N.Esasky	3B	P.Garner	3B	P.Guerrero	3B	T.Wallach
LF	B.Butler	3B	R.Cey	LF	G.Redus	LF	J.Cruz	LF	D.Baker	LF	T.Raines
CF	D.Murphy	LF	L.Durham	CF	E.Milner	CF	O.Moreno	CF	K.Landreaux	CF	A.Dawson
RF	C.Washington	CF	M.Hall	RF	P.Householder	RF	T.Puhl	RF	M.Marshall	RF	W.Cromartie
C	B.Benedict	RF	K.Moreland	C	D.Bilardello	C	A.Ashby	C	S.Yeager	C	G.Carter
		C	J.Davis								
32	J.Royster			31	J.Bench	13	D.Walling	OS	D.Thomas	O1	T.Francona
O	T.Harper			O1	C.Cedeno					S2	B.Little
		P	C.Rainey	O	D.Walker			P	F.Valenzuela		
		P	S.Trout			P	J.Niekro	P	J.Reuss	P	S.Rogers
P	C.McMurtry	P	F.Jenkins			P	B.Knepper	P	B.Welch	P	B.Gullickson
P	P.Perez	P	D.Ruthven	P	M.Soto	P	N.Ryan	P	A.Pena	P	C.Lea
P	P.Niekro	P	D.Noles	P	B.Berenyi	P	M.Scott	P	B.Hooton	P	B.Smith
P	R.Camp	RP	B.Campbell	P	F.Pastore	P	M.LaCoss	RP	T.Niedenfuer	P	R.Burris
P	P.Falcone	RP	L.Smith	P	C.Puleo	RP	V.Ruhle	RP	D.Stewart	RP	J.Reardon
RP	S.Bedrosian	RP	C.Lefferts	P	J.Price	RP	B.Dawley	RP	J.Beckwith	RP	D.Schatzeder
RP	T.Forster			RP	T.Power	RP	D.Smith			RP	B.James
RP	D.Moore	P	M.Proly	RP	B.Scherrer						
		P	W.Brusstar	RP	R.Gale	P	M.Madden	P	S.Howe	P	S.Sanderson
P	K.Dayley					P	F.DiPino	P	P.Zachry		
P	G.Garber					P	F.LaCorte				
				P	B.Hayes						
				P	J.Russell						
				P	T.Hume						

	NEW YORK		PHILADELPHIA		PITTSBURGH		SAN DIEGO		SAN FRANCISCO		ST.LOUIS
M	G.Bamberger	M	P.Corrales	M	C.Tanner	M	D.Williams	M	F.Robinson	M	W.Herzog
M	F.Howard	M	P.Owens	1B	J.Thompson	1B	S.Garvey	1B	D.Evans	1B	G.Hendrick
1B	K.Hernandez	1B	P.Rose	2B	J.Ray	2B	J.Bonilla	2B	B.Wellman	2B	T.Herr
2B	B.Giles	2B	J.Morgan	SS	D.Berra	SS	G.Templeton	SS	J.LeMaster	SS	O.Smith
SS	J.Oquendo	SS	I.DeJesus	3B	B.Madlock	3B	L.Salazar	3B	T.O'Malley	3B	K.Oberkfell
3B	H.Brooks	3B	M.Schmidt	LF	M.Easler	LF	A.Wiggins	LF	J.Leonard	LF	L.Smith
LF	G.Foster	LF	G.Matthews	CF	M.Wynne	CF	R.Jones	CF	C.Davis	CF	W.McGee
CF	M.Wilson	CF	G.Maddox	RF	D.Parker	RF	S.Lezcano	RF	J.Clark	RF	D.Green
RF	D.Strawberry	RF	V.Hayes	C	T.Pena	C	T.Kennedy	C	B.Brenly	C	D.Porter
C	R.Hodges	C	B.Diaz								
				O	L.Lacy	O	T.Gwynn	23	J.Youngblood	2S	M.Ramsey
S2	B.Bailor	O	G.Gross	O	L.Mazzilli	O	G.Richards	O	M.Venable	O3	A.Van Slyke
O1	D.Heep	O	J.Lefebvre			O	B.Brown			1	K.Hernandez
1	D.Kingman	O	B.Dernier	P	R.Rhoden	32	T.Flannery	P	F.Breining		
1O	R.Staub	1	T.Perez	P	L.McWilliams			P	M.Krukow	P	J.Andujar
				P	J.Candelaria	P	E.Show	P	A.Hammaker	P	J.Stuper
P	T.Seaver	P	S.Carlton	P	L.Tunnell	P	D.Dravecky	P	B.Laskey	P	D.LaPoint
P	M.Torrez	P	J.Denny	P	J.DeLeon	P	T.Lollar	P	A.McGaffigan	P	B.Forsch
P	E.Lynch	P	C.Hudson	RP	C.Guante	P	E.Whitson	RP	G.Minton	P	N.Allen
P	W.Terrell	P	M.Bystrom	RP	K.Tekulve	RP	A.Hawkins	RP	R.Martin	RP	B.Sutter
P	C.Swan	RP	R.Reed	RP	M.Sarmiento	RP	L.DeLeon	RP	J.Barr	RP	J.Lahti
RP	J.Orosco	RP	W.Hernandez			RP	G.Lucas			RP	D.Von Ohlen
RP	D.Sisk	RP	A.Holland	P	J.Bibby	RP	E.Sosa	P	M.Davis		
RP	S.Holman			P	R.Scurry			P	G.Lavelle	P	D.Cox
		P	K.Gross			P	M.Thurmond			P	J.Martin
P	C.Diaz	P	T.McGraw			P	J.Montefusco				
P	N.Allen					P	S.Monge				

TEAM	G	W	L	PCT	GB	R	OR	AB	H	2B	3B	HR	BB	SO	AVG	OBP	SLG	PRO	PRO+	BR	/A	PF	CHI	RC	SB	CS	SBA	SBR
EAST																												
PHI	163	90	72	.556		696	635	5426	1352	209	45	125	**640**	906	.249	.331	.373	.704	102	17	25	99	101	676	143	75	66	-2
PIT	162	84	78	.519	6	659	648	5531	1460	238	29	121	497	873	.264	.327	.383	.710	100	17	0	103	96	682	124	77	62	-9
MON	163	82	80	.506	8	677	646	5611	1482	**297**	41	102	509	**733**	.264	.329	.386	.715	105	30	34	99	95	716	138	44	**76**	**15**
STL	162	79	83	.488	11	679	710	5550	**1496**	262	**63**	83	543	879	.270	.337	.384	.721	**106**	47	**47**	100	94	725	**207**	89	70	9
CHI	162	71	91	.438	19	701	719	5512	1436	272	42	140	470	868	.261	.322	**.401**	.723	101	35	2	105	100	707	84	40	68	1
NY	162	68	94	.420	22	575	680	5444	1314	172	26	112	436	1031	.241	.301	.344	.645	85	-112	-107	99	107	562	141	64	69	4
WEST																												
LA	163	91	71	.562		654	**609**	5440	1358	197	34	**146**	541	925	.250	.320	.379	.699	100	-6	-2	99	100	663	166	76	69	4
ATL	162	88	74	.543	3	**746**	640	5472	1489	218	45	130	582	847	**.272**	**.344**	.400	**.744**	104	91	35	107	98	**744**	146	88	62	-9
HOU	162	85	77	.525	6	643	646	5502	1412	239	60	97	517	869	.257	.323	.375	.698	106	-7	34	94	97	673	164	95	63	-8
SD	163	81	81	.500	10	653	653	5527	1384	207	34	93	482	822	.250	.313	.351	.664	93	-74	-53	97	**110**	609	179	67	73	14
SF	162	79	83	.488	12	687	697	5369	1324	206	30	142	619	990	.247	.328	.375	.703	104	11	33	97	102	662	140	78	64	-5
CIN	162	74	88	.457	17	623	710	5333	1274	236	35	107	588	1006	.239	.317	.356	.673	89	-49	-70	104	103	606	154	77	67	0
TOT	974					7993		65717	16781	2753	484	1398	6424	10749	.255	.324	.376	.700							1786	870	67	14

TEAM	CG	SH	SV	IP	H	H/G	HR	BB	SO	RAT	ERA	ERA+	OAV	OOB	PR	/A	PF	CPI	FA	E	DP	FW	PW	BW	SBW	DIF
EAST																										
PHI	20	10	41	1461²	1429	8.8	111	**464**	**1092**	11.8	3.34	107	.256	.316	47	37	98	103	.976	152	117	-.7	3.9	2.6	-.3	3.6
PIT	25	14	41	1462¹	1378	8.5	109	563	1061	12.1	3.55	104	.252	.323	12	25	102	99	**.982**	115	165	1.4	2.6	.0	-1.1	.0
MON	**38**	**15**	34	1471	1406	8.6	120	479	899	11.7	3.58	100	.254	.317	8	1	99	98	.981	116	130	1.4	.1	3.6	**1.4**	-5.5
STL	22	10	27	1460²	1479	9.1	115	525	709	12.5	3.79	96	.266	.332	-26	-28	100	102	.976	152	173	-.8	-2.9	**4.9**	.8	-4.0
CHI	9	10	42	1428²	1496	9.4	117	498	807	12.7	4.08	93	.274	.337	-71	-45	105	100	**.982**	115	164	1.4	-4.7	.2	-.6	-6.9
NY	18	7	33	1451	1384	8.6	97	615	717	12.5	3.68	99	.256	.334	-8	-8	100	100	.976	151	171	-.7	-.8	-11.2	.3	-.6
WEST																										
LA	27	12	40	1464	1336	8.2	97	495	1000	**11.4**	**3.10**	116	.244	**.309**	85	79	99	101	.974	168	132	-1.7	**8.3**	-.2	.3	3.3
ATL	18	4	48	1440²	1412	8.8	132	540	895	12.3	3.67	106	.260	.329	-7	33	107	105	.978	137	176	.1	3.4	3.7	-1.1	.8
HOU	22	14	48	1466¹	**1276**	**7.8**	**94**	570	904	11.5	3.45	99	**.236**	.312	29	-8	94	90	.977	147	165	-.5	-.8	3.6	-1.0	2.7
SD	23	5	44	1467²	1389	8.5	144	528	850	11.9	3.62	96	.253	.322	1	-22	96	102	.979	129	135	.6	-2.3	-5.5	1.3	5.8
SF	20	9	47	1445²	1431	8.9	127	520	881	12.3	3.70	96	.259	.326	-11	-27	97	101	.973	171	109	-1.9	-2.8	3.4	-.6	-.0
CIN	34	5	29	1441¹	1365	8.5	135	627	934	12.6	3.98	95	.253	.333	-57	-29	105	97	.981	**114**	121	**1.5**	-3.0	-7.3	-.1	2.0
TOT	276	115	474	17461		8.6				12.1	3.63		.255	.324					.978	1667	1758					

Runs		Hits		Doubles		Triples		Home Runs		Total Bases	
Raines-Mon	133	Dawson-Mon	189	Ray-Pit	38	Butler-Atl	13	Schmidt-Phi	40	Dawson-Mon	341
Murphy-Atl	131	Cruz-Hou	189	Oliver-Mon	38	Moreno-Hou	11	Murphy-Atl	36	Murphy-Atl	318
Schmidt-Phi	104	Ramirez-Atl	185	Buckner-Chi	38	Green-StL	10	Guerrero-LA	32	Guerrero-LA	310
Dawson-Mon	104	Oliver-Mon	184	Carter-Mon	37	Dawson-Mon	10	Dawson-Mon	32	Thon-Hou	283
		Raines-Mon	183					Evans-SF	30	Schmidt-Phi	280

Runs Batted In		Runs Produced		Bases On Balls		Batting Average		On Base Percentage		Slugging Average	
Murphy-Atl	121	Murphy-Atl	216	Schmidt-Phi	128	Madlock-Pit	.323	Schmidt-Phi	.402	Murphy-Atl	.540
Dawson-Mon	113	Raines-Mon	193	Thompson-Pit	99	L.Smith-StL	.321	Hernandez-StL-NY .398		Dawson-Mon	.539
Schmidt-Phi	109	Dawson-Mon	185	Raines-Mon	97	Cruz-Hou	.318	Murphy-Atl	.396	Guerrero-LA	.531
Guerrero-LA	103	Schmidt-Phi	173	Murphy-Atl	90	Hendrick-StL	.318	Raines-Mon	.395	Schmidt-Phi	.524
Kennedy-SD	98	Cruz-Hou	163	Morgan-Phi	89	Knight-Hou	.304	Madlock-Pit	.389	Evans-SF	.516

Production		Adjusted Production		Batter Runs		Adjusted Batter Runs		Clutch Hitting Index		Runs Created	
Murphy-Atl	.936	Schmidt-Phi	156	Murphy-Atl	46.2	Schmidt-Phi	44.6	Kennedy-SD	122	Murphy-Atl	131
Schmidt-Phi	.926	Evans-SF	151	Schmidt-Phi	43.2	Guerrero-LA	38.4	Rose-Phi	121	Raines-Mon	120
Guerrero-LA	.908	Guerrero-LA	150	Guerrero-LA	37.8	Murphy-Atl	37.5	Garner-Hou	115	Guerrero-LA	118
Evans-SF	.896	Murphy-Atl	146	Evans-SF	33.0	Evans-SF	36.2	Hendrick-StL	115	Schmidt-Phi	117
Dawson-Mon	.886	Cruz-Hou	143	Dawson-Mon	32.4	Cruz-Hou	34.5	McGee-StL	112	Dawson-Mon	113

Total Average		Stolen Bases		Stolen Base Average		Stolen Base Runs		Fielding Runs		Total Player Rating	
Murphy-Atl	1.014	Raines-Mon	90	Morgan-Phi	90.0	Raines-Mon	18.6	Sandberg-Chi	41.1	Schmidt-Phi	6.4
Schmidt-Phi	.986	Wiggins-SD	66	Murphy-Atl	88.2	Wiggins-SD	12.0	Schmidt-Phi	23.3	Thon-Hou	5.9
Raines-Mon	.959	S.Sax-LA	56	Raines-Mon	86.5	McGee-StL	6.9	Hubbard-Atl	21.6	Raines-Mon	5.8
Guerrero-LA	.935	Wilson-NY	54	Bailor-NY	85.7	Wilson-NY	6.6	Buckner-Chi	21.0	Guerrero-LA	4.6
Evans-SF	.908	L.Smith-StL	43	Wiggins-SD	83.5	Murphy-Atl	6.6	Thon-Hou	20.8	Murphy-Atl	4.6

Wins		Win Percentage		Games		Complete Games		Shutouts		Saves	
Denny-Phi	19	Denny-Phi	.760	Campbell-Chi	82	Soto-Cin	18	Rogers-Mon	5	Smith-Chi	29
Soto-Cin	17	Perez-Atl	.652	Tekulve-Pit	76	Rogers-Mon	13	Valenzuela-LA	4	Holland-Phi	25
Rogers-Mon	17	McWilliams-Pit	.652	Hernandez-Chi-Phi	74	Gullickson-Mon	10	McWilliams-Pit	4	Minton-SF	22
Gullickson-Mon	17	Candelaria-Pit	.652	Scherrer-Cin	73			Lea-Mon	4	Sutter-StL	21
Lea-Mon	16	McMurtry-Atl	.625	Minton-SF	73					Reardon-Mon	21

Innings Pitched		Fewest Hits/Game		Fewest BB/Game		Strikeouts		Strikeouts/Game		Ratio	
Carlton-Phi	283.2	Ryan-Hou	6.14	Hammaker-SF	1.67	Carlton-Phi	275	Carlton-Phi	8.73	Hammaker-SF	9.50
Soto-Cin	273.2	Soto-Cin	6.81	Ruthven-Phi-Chi	1.87	Soto-Cin	242	Ryan-Hou	8.39	Soto-Cin	10.10
Rogers-Mon	273.0	Welch-LA	7.24	Denny-Phi	1.97	McWilliams-Pit	199	Soto-Cin	7.96	Pena-LA	10.37
Niekro-Hou	263.2	Hammaker-SF	7.68	Reuss-LA	2.01	Valenzuela-LA	189	McWilliams-Pit	7.53	Welch-LA	10.54
Valenzuela-LA	257.0	Pena-LA	7.73	Candelaria-Pit	2.05	Ryan-Hou	183	Berenyi-Cin	7.29	Denny-Phi	10.61

Earned Run Average		Adjusted ERA		Opponents' Batting Avg.		Opponents' On Base Pct.		Starter Runs		Adjusted Starter Runs	
Hammaker-SF	2.25	Hammaker-SF	157	Ryan-Hou	.195	Hammaker-SF	.267	Denny-Phi	33.8	Soto-Cin	33.7
Denny-Phi	2.37	Denny-Phi	150	Soto-Cin	.208	Soto-Cin	.280	Soto-Cin	28.3	Denny-Phi	32.1
Welch-LA	2.65	Soto-Cin	141	Welch-LA	.222	Pena-LA	.285	Hammaker-SF	26.4	Hammaker-SF	24.6
Soto-Cin	2.70	Welch-LA	136	Hammaker-SF	.228	Welch-LA	.294	Welch-LA	22.2	Welch-LA	21.4
Pena-LA	2.75	Pena-LA	131	Pena-LA	.229	Denny-Phi	.294	Smith-Mon	19.6	McMurtry-Atl	19.8

Clutch Pitching Index		Relief Runs		Adjusted Relief Runs		Relief Ranking		Total Pitcher Index		Total Baseball Ranking	
Rhoden-Pit	119	Orosco-NY	26.3	Orosco-NY	26.3	Orosco-NY	50.6	Orosco-NY	5.8	Schmidt-Phi	6.4
Niekro-Atl	117	Smith-Chi	22.6	Smith-Chi	24.5	Smith-Chi	42.6	Smith-Chi	4.6	Thon-Hou	5.9
Reuss-LA	116	Tekulve-Pit	21.9	Tekulve-Pit	22.7	Tekulve-Pit	32.4	Howe-LA	3.6	Raines-Mon	5.8
Denny-Phi	115	Niedenfuer-LA	18.1	Niedenfuer-LA	17.8	Howe-LA	31.6	Denny-Phi	3.5	Orosco-NY	5.8
Knepper-Hou	111	Howe-LA	16.7	Howe-LA	16.4	Niedenfuer-LA	22.4	Tekulve-Pit	3.5	Guerrero-LA	4.6

July 6 In the 50th anniversary All-Star Game at Chicago's Comiskey Park, the AL routs the NL 13-3 for its first win since 1971. The AL breaks the game open with 7 runs in the fourth inning, highlighted by Fred Lynn's grand slam—the first ever in All-Star competition.

July 24 In the memorable "Pine Tar Game" at Yankee Stadium, George Brett hits an apparent two-run home run off Rich Gossage to give the Royals a 5-4 lead with two outs in the ninth inning, only to have it taken away when Yankees manager Billy Martin points out that the pine tar on Brett's bat handle exceeds the 17 inches allowed in the rules. As a result, Brett is called out for illegally batting the ball, giving New York a 4-3 victory. The Royals immediately protest, and AL president Lee MacPhail overrules his umpires for the first time, saying that while the rules should certainly be rewritten and clarified, the home run will stand and the game will be resumed from that point on Aug. 18.

August 18 In the continuation of the "Pine Tar Game," Hal McRae strikes out and Dan Quisenberry retires the Yankees in order in the bottom of the ninth to preserve the Royals' 5-4 victory. The conclusion took just 12 minutes (and 16 pitches) and, as the only game scheduled at the Stadium, was witnessed by a crowd of just 1,245.

October 8 The Phillies and Orioles each win Game 4 of their respective LCS to advance to the World Series. Philadelphia gets home runs from Gary Matthews and Sixto Lezcano in a 7-2 victory, while Baltimore's Tito Landrum hits a solo home run in the top of the tenth inning to break a scoreless tie, sparking the Orioles to a 3-0 win.

October 10 John E. Fetzer sells the Tigers to Michigan businessman Tom Monaghan, the founder and president of Domino's Pizza.

October 16 Eddie Murray slams a pair of home runs and Scott McGregor pitches a five-hitter as the Orioles beat the Phillies 5-0 and win the World Series 4-1. Baltimore catcher Rick Dempsey, who hit .385 with four doubles and a home run, is the Series MVP.

October 25 White Sox pitcher LaMarr Hoyt, who led the league with 24 wins but whose 3.66 ERA was not among the league's 15 best, wins the AL Cy Young Award, beating out the Royals' Dan Quisenberry and the Tigers' Jack Morris.

November 15 Cal Ripken is named MVP of the AL, edging Orioles teammate Eddie Murray. Ripken hit .318 and led the league in hits (211) and runs (111) while playing every inning of every game, and is the first player ever to win the Rookie of the Year and MVP Awards in consecutive seasons.

November 17 Kansas City Royals teammates Willie Wilson, Willie Aikens, and Jerry Martin, who, along with former teammate Vida Blue, had pleaded guilty to attempting to purchase cocaine, are each sentenced to three months in prison.

December 8 Dr. Bobby Brown, who played third base for the Yankees before embarking on a successful medical career, is elected president of the AL by the club owners.

	BALTIMORE		BOSTON		CALIFORNIA		CHICAGO		CLEVELAND		DETROIT		KANSAS CITY
M	J.Altobelli	M	R.Houk	M	J.McNamara	M	T.LaRussa	M	M.Ferraro	M	S.Anderson	M	D.Howser
1B	E.Murray	1B	D.Stapleton	1B	R.Carew	1B	M.Squires	M	P.Corrales	1B	E.Cabell	1B	W.Aikens
2B	R.Dauer	2B	J.Remy	2B	B.Grich	2B	J.Cruz	1B	M.Hargrove	2B	L.Whitaker	2B	F.White
SS	C.Ripken	SS	G.Hoffman	SS	T.Foli	SS	J.Dybzinski	2B	M.Trillo	SS	A.Trammell	SS	U.Washington
3B	T.Cruz	3B	W.Boggs	3B	D.DeCinces	3B	V.Law	SS	J.Franco	3B	T.Brookens	3B	G.Brett
LF	J.Lowenstein	LF	J.Rice	LF	B.Downing	LF	R.Kittle	3B	T.Harrah	LF	L.Herndon	LF	W.Wilson
CF	J.Shelby	CF	T.Armas	CF	F.Lynn	CF	R.Law	LF	A.Bannister	CF	C.Lemon	CF	A.Otis
RF	D.Ford	RF	D.Evans	RF	E.Valentine	RF	H.Baines	CF	G.Thomas	RF	G.Wilson	RF	P.Sheridan
C	R.Dempsey	C	G.Allenson	C	B.Boone	C	C.Fisk	RF	R.Vukovich	C	L.Parrish	C	J.Wathan
DH	K.Singleton	DH	C.Yastrzemski	DH	Re.Jackson	DH	G.Luzinski	C	R.Hassey	DH	K.Gibson	DH	H.McRae
								DH	A.Thornton				
OD	J.Dwyer	O	R.Miller	31	Ro.Jackson	S2	S.Fletcher			1O	R.Leach	C	D.Slaught
OD	A.Bumbry	OD	R.Nichols	1D	D.Sconiers	O	J.Hairston	O3	P.Tabler	DC	J.Wockenfuss	32	O.Concepcion
O	G.Roenicke	C	R.Gedman	O	J.Beniquez	1O	T.Paciorek	OD	B.McBride			O	L.Roberts
3	L.Hernandez			O	B.Clark	1D	G.Walker	2S	M.Fischlin	P	J.Morris		
		P	J.Tudor			2	T.Bernazard			P	D.Petry	P	L.Gura
P	S.McGregor	P	B.Hurst	P	T.John			P	R.Sutcliffe	P	M.Wilcox	P	B.Black
P	S.Davis	P	D.Eckersley	P	K.Forsch	P	L.Hoyt	P	L.Sorensen	P	J.Berenguer	P	P.Splittorff
P	M.Boddicker	P	B.Ojeda	P	G.Zahn	P	R.Dotson	P	B.Blyleven	P	D.Rozema	P	S.Renko
P	D.Martinez	P	M.Brown	P	M.Witt	P	F.Bannister	P	L.Barker	RP	A.Lopez	RP	D.Quisenberry
P	M.Flanagan	RP	B.Stanley	P	B.Kison	P	B.Burns	P	N.Heaton	RP	H.Bailey	RP	M.Armstrong
RP	S.Stewart	RP	M.Clear	RP	L.Sanchez	P	J.Koosman	RP	D.Spillner	RP	D.Bair		
RP	T.Martinez	RP	L.Aponte	RP	J.Curtis	RP	D.Lamp	RP	B.Anderson			P	K.Creel
RP	T.Stoddard					RP	D.Tidrow	P	J.Easterly			P	V.Blue
		P	O.Boyd	P	D.Goltz	RP	S.Barojas					P	G.Perry
P	J.Palmer	P	D.Bird	P	R.Steirer			P	J.Eichelberger			P	D.Leonard
P	A.Ramirez	P	J.Johnson	P	B.McLaughlin							P	E.Rasmussen

	MILWAUKEE		MINNESOTA		NEW YORK		OAKLAND		SEATTLE		TEXAS		TORONTO
M	H.Kuenn	M	B.Gardner	M	B.Martin	M	S.Boros	M	R.Lachemann	M	D.Rader	M	B.Cox
1B	C.Cooper	1B	K.Hrbek	1B	K.Griffey	1B	W.Gross	1B	P.O'Brien	1B	P.O'Brien	1B	W.Upshaw
2B	J.Gantner	2B	J.Castino	2B	W.Randolph	2B	D.Lopes	1B	P.Putnam	2B	W.Tolleson	2B	D.Garcia
SS	R.Yount	SS	R.Washington	SS	R.Smalley	SS	T.Phillips	2B	T.Bernazard	SS	B.Dent	SS	A.Griffin
3B	P.Molitor	3B	G.Gaetti	3B	G.Nettles	3B	C.Lansford	SS	S.Owen	3B	B.Bell	3B	R.Mulliniks
LF	B.Oglivie	LF	G.Ward	LF	D.Winfield	LF	R.Henderson	3B	J.Allen	LF	B.Sample	LF	B.Bonnell
CF	R.Manning	CF	D.Brown	CF	J.Mumphrey	CF	D.Murphy	LF	S.Henderson	CF	G.Wright	CF	L.Moseby
RF	C.Moore	RF	T.Brunansky	RF	S.Kemp	RF	M.Davis	CF	D.Henderson	RF	L.Parrish	RF	J.Barfield
C	N.Yost	C	D.Engle	C	B.Wynegar	C	B.Kearney	RF	R.Nelson	C	J.Sundberg	C	E.Whitt
DH	T.Simmons	DH	R.Bush	DH	D.Baylor	DH	J.Burroughs	C	R.Sweet	DH	D.Hostetler	DH	C.Johnson
								DH	R.Zisk				
P	M.Caldwell	OD	M.Hatcher	S2	A.Robertson	S3	B.Almon			DO	M.Rivers	O	D.Collins
P	D.Sutton			O1	D.Mattingly	O1	G.Hancock	OD	A.Cowens	21	B.Stein	32	J.Iorg
P	M.Haas	P	F.Viola	C	R.Cerone	CO	M.Heath	S	T.Cruz	DO	J.Orta		
P	B.McClure	P	K.Schrom					31	M.Castillo	P	C.Hough	C	B.Martinez
P	C.Porter	P	A.Williams							P	M.Smithson		
RP	J.Slaton	P	B.Castillo	P	R.Guidry	P	C.Codiroli	P	M.Young	P	D.Darwin	P	D.Stieb
RP	T.Tellmann	RP	R.Lysander	P	S.Rawley	P	S.McCatty	P	J.Beattie	P	R.Honeycutt	P	J.Clancy
RP	J.Augustine	RP	R.Davis	P	D.Righetti	P	T.Conroy	P	B.Stoddard	P	F.Tanana	P	L.Leal
		RP	L.Whitehouse	P	B.Shirley	P	B.Krueger	P	B.Clark	RP	J.Matlack	P	J.Gott
				RP	R.Fontenot	RP	T.Underwood	P	M.Moore	O	O.Jones	P	J.Acker
P	B.Gibson			RP	G.Frazier	RP	T.Burgmeier	RP	R.Thomas			RP	J.Alexander
P	T.Candiotti	P	P.Filson	RP	D.Murray	RP	K.Atherton	RP	B.Caudill	P	J.Butcher	RP	R.Jackson
		P	J.O'Connor	RP	R.Gossage			RP	M.Stanton	/P	D.Stewart	RP	M.McLaughlin
		P	B.Havens			P	M.Norris	P	G.Perry				
		P	M.Walters	J.Howell		P	G.Heimueller	P	G.Abbott			P	R.Moffitt
				M.Keough		P	M.Warren	P	E.Vande Berg			P	D.Geisel
						P	D.Beard						
						P	S.Baker						

TEAM	G	W	L	PCT	GB	R	OR	AB	H	2B	3B	HR	BB	SO	AVG	OBP	SLG	PRO	PRO+	BR	/A	PF	CHI	RC	SB	CS	SBA	SBR
EAST																												
BAL	162	98	64	.605		799	652	5546	1492	283	27	168	601	800	.269	**.343**	.421	.764	111	70	85	98	99	794	61	33	65	-2
DET	162	92	70	.568	6	789	679	5592	1530	283	53	156	508	831	.274	.338	.427	.765	112	67	88	97	99	799	93	53	64	-4
NY	162	91	71	.562	7	770	703	5631	1535	269	40	153	533	566	.273	.339	.416	.755	110	52	81	96	98	783	84	42	67	0
TOR	162	89	73	.549	9	795	726	5581	1546	268	**58**	167	510	810	**.277**	.341	**.436**	**.777**	106	89	39	106	97	**818**	131	72	65	4
MIL	162	87	75	.537	11	764	708	5620	**1556**	281	57	132	475	665	**.277**	.336	.418	.754	115	44	103	92	98	774	101	49	67	1
BOS	162	78	84	.481	20	724	775	5590	1512	**287**	32	142	536	758	.270	.337	.409	.746	97	35	-20	107	94	749	30	26	54	-7
CLE	162	70	92	.432	28	704	785	5476	1451	249	31	86	605	691	.265	.341	.369	.710	92	-23	-50	104	100	687	109	71	61	-10
WEST																												
CHI	162	99	63	.611		**800**	650	5484	1439	270	42	157	527	888	.262	.332	.413	.745	100	26	-2	104	**107**	762	165	50	77	20
KC	163	79	83	.488	20	696	767	5598	1515	273	54	109	397	922	.271	.322	.397	.719	97	-31	-32	100	102	711	182	47	**79**	**26**
TEX	163	77	85	.475	22	639	**609**	5610	1429	242	33	106	442	767	.255	.312	.366	.678	88	-108	-96	98	104	633	119	60	66	0
OAK	162	74	88	.457	25	708	782	5516	1447	237	28	121	524	872	.262	.330	.381	.711	101	-34	7	94	102	694	**235**	98	71	12
CAL	162	70	92	.432	29	722	779	5640	1467	241	22	154	509	835	.260	.325	.393	.718	98	-29	-23	99	102	702	41	39	51	-11
MIN	162	70	92	.432	29	709	822	5601	1463	280	41	141	467	802	.261	.321	.401	.722	94	-23	-48	104	101	701	44	29	60	-4
SEA	162	60	102	.370	39	558	740	5336	1280	247	31	111	460	840	.240	.303	.360	.663	79	-135	-156	104	100	574	144	80	64	-5
TOT	1135					10177		77821	20662	3710	549	1903	7094	10967	.266	.330	.401	.731							1539	749	67	12

TEAM	CG	SH	SV	IP	H	H/G	HR	BB	SO	RAT	ERA	ERA+	OAV	OOB	PR	/A	PF	CPI	FA	E	DP	FW	PW	BW	SBW	DIF
EAST																										
BAL	36	**15**	38	1452¹	1451	9.0	130	452	774	11.9	3.63	109	.261	.318	70	53	97	104	.981	121	159	.5	5.3	8.5	-.3	3.0
DET	42	9	28	1451	**1318**	**8.2**	170	522	875	11.6	3.80	103	**.242**	.312	42	17	96	96	.980	125	142	.3	1.7	8.8	-.5	.7
NY	**47**	12	32	1456²	1449	9.0	116	455	892	11.9	3.86	101	.260	.318	33	6	96	95	.978	139	157	-.5	.6	8.1	-.0	1.9
TOR	43	8	32	1445¹	1434	8.9	145	517	835	12.4	4.12	104	.259	.327	-10	29	106	97	.981	115	148	.9	2.9	3.9	-.5	.8
MIL	35	10	43	1454	1513	9.4	133	491	689	12.6	4.02	93	.270	.332	6	-46	92	103	**.982**	**113**	162	**1.0**	-4.6	10.3	.0	-.7
BOS	29	7	42	1446¹	1572	9.8	158	493	767	13.0	4.34	100	.279	.340	-44	2	107	104	.979	130	168	.0	.2	-2.0	-.8	-.5
CLE	34	8	25	1441²	1531	9.6	120	529	794	13.1	4.43	96	.275	.342	-60	-32	104	97	.980	122	174	.5	-3.2	-5.0	-1.1	-2.2
WEST																										
CHI	35	12	48	1445¹	1355	8.4	128	**447**	877	11.4	3.67	114	.248	**.309**	63	83	103	94	.981	120	158	.6	8.3	-.2	1.9	7.4
KC	19	8	**49**	1437²	1535	9.6	133	471	593	12.7	4.25	96	.274	.333	-30	-28	100	99	.974	165	178	-1.9	-2.8	-3.2	**2.5**	3.4
TEX	43	11	32	1466²	1392	8.5	**97**	471	826	11.7	**3.31**	121	.252	.315	**122**	113	99	104	**.982**	**113**	151	**1.0**	11.3	-9.6	-.0	-6.6
OAK	22	12	33	1454¹	1462	9.0	135	626	719	13.1	4.34	89	.263	.340	-46	-79	95	97	.974	157	157	-1.5	-7.9	.7	1.1	.5
CAL	39	7	23	1474	1636	10.0	130	496	668	13.2	4.31	93	.284	.344	-41	-49	99	104	.977	154	**190**	-1.3	-4.9	-2.3	-1.2	-1.3
MIN	20	5	39	1437¹	1559	9.8	163	580	748	13.6	4.66	91	.280	.351	-96	-67	105	102	.980	121	170	.5	-6.7	-4.8	-.5	.4
SEA	25	9	39	1418¹	1455	9.2	145	544	**910**	12.9	4.12	103	.268	.339	-9	22	105	**105**	.978	136	159	-.3	2.2	-15.6	-.6	-6.7
TOT	469	133	503	20281		9.2				12.5	4.06		.266	.330					.979	1831	2273					

Runs		Hits		Doubles		Triples		Home Runs		Total Bases	
Ripken-Bal	121	Ripken-Bal	211	Ripken-Bal	47	Yount-Mil	10	Rice-Bos	39	Rice-Bos	344
Murray-Bal	115	Boggs-Bos	210	Boggs-Bos	44	Herndon-Det	9	Armas-Bos	36	Ripken-Bal	343
Cooper-Mil	106	Whitaker-Det	206	Yount-Mil	42	Griffin-Tor	9	Kittle-Chi	35	Cooper-Mil	336
Henderson-Oak	105	Cooper-Mil	203	Parrish-Det	42	Gibson-Det	9	Murray-Bal	33	Murray-Bal	313
Moseby-Tor	104	Rice-Bos	191							Winfield-NY	307

Runs Batted In		Runs Produced		Bases On Balls		Batting Average		On Base Percentage		Slugging Average	
Rice-Bos	126	Cooper-Mil	202	Henderson-Oak	103	Boggs-Bos	.361	Boggs-Bos	.449	Brett-KC	.563
Cooper-Mil	126	Ripken-Bal	196	Singleton-Bal	99	Carew-Cal	.339	Henderson-Oak	.415	Rice-Bos	.550
Winfield-NY	116	Murray-Bal	193	Boggs-Bos	92	Whitaker-Det	.320	Carew-Cal	.411	Murray-Bal	.538
Parrish-Det	114	Winfield-NY	183	Thornton-Cle	87	Trammell-Det	.319	Murray-Bal	.398	Fisk-Chi	.518
Murray-Bal	111	Rice-Bos	177	Murray-Bal	86	Ripken-Bal	.318	Singleton-Bal	.395	Ripken-Bal	.517

Production		Adjusted Production		Batter Runs		Adjusted Batter Runs		Clutch Hitting Index		Runs Created	
Brett-KC	.949	Murray-Bal	158	Boggs-Bos	50.6	Murray-Bal	47.3	Simmons-Mil	124	Boggs-Bos	130
Murray-Bal	.936	Brett-KC	157	Murray-Bal	44.9	Yount-Mil	43.6	Franco-Cle	122	Murray-Bal	127
Boggs-Bos	.935	Yount-Mil	155	Rice-Bos	38.7	Boggs-Bos	41.4	Murphy-Oak	116	Ripken-Bal	120
Rice-Bos	.914	Boggs-Bos	147	Ripken-Bal	37.1	Ripken-Bal	39.4	Cooper-Mil	116	Yount-Mil	115
Upshaw-Tor	.891	Ripken-Bal	145	Brett-KC	36.3	Brett-KC	36.1	Singleton-Bal	113	Whitaker-Det	114

Total Average		Stolen Bases		Stolen Base Average		Stolen Base Runs		Fielding Runs		Total Player Rating	
Henderson-Oak	1.048	Henderson-Oak	108	Wilson-KC	88.1	Henderson-Oak	21.0	Ward-Min	25.9	Ripken-Bal	6.7
Murray-Bal	.971	R.Law-Chi	77	R.Law-Chi	86.5	R.Law-Chi	15.9	T.Cruz-Sea-Bal	25.4	Henderson-Oak	5.7
Boggs-Bos	.964	Wilson-KC	59	Washington-KC	85.1	Wilson-KC	12.9	Dempsey-Bal	20.6	Yount-Mil	5.2
Brett-KC	.964	J.Cruz-Sea-Chi	57	Henderson-Oak	85.0	J.Cruz-Sea-Chi	9.9	Fletcher-Chi	18.2	Boggs-Bos	4.5
Yount-Mil	.897	Sample-Tex	44			Sample-Tex	8.4	Brunansky-Min	17.8	Grich-Cal	4.5

Wins		Win Percentage		Games		Complete Games		Shutouts		Saves	
Hoyt-Chi	24	Dotson-Chi	.759	Quisenberry-KC	69	Guidry-NY	21	Boddicker-Bal	5	Quisenberry-KC	45
Dotson-Chi	22	McGregor-Bal	.720	VandeBerg-Sea	68	Morris-Det	20	Stieb-Tor	4	Stanley-Bos	33
Guidry-NY	21	Hoyt-Chi	.706	Davis-Min	66	Stieb-Tor	14	Burns-Chi	4	Davis-Min	30
Morris-Det	20	Guidry-NY	.700	T.Martinez-Bal	65	Rawley-NY	13			Caudill-Sea	26
Petry-Det	19	Boddicker-Bal	.667	Stanley-Bos	64	McGregor-Bal	12			Ladd-Mil	25

Innings Pitched		Fewest Hits/Game		Fewest BB/Game		Strikeouts		Strikeouts/Game		Ratio	
Morris-Det	293.2	Boddicker-Bal	7.09	Hoyt-Chi	1.07	Morris-Det	232	Bannister-Chi	7.99	Hoyt-Chi	9.25
Stieb-Tor	278.0	Stieb-Tor	7.22	McGregor-Bal	1.56	Bannister-Chi	193	Morris-Det	7.11	Boddicker-Bal	9.70
Petry-Det	266.1	Conroy-Oak	7.82	John-Cal	1.88	Stieb-Tor	187	Righetti-NY	7.01	Morris-Det	10.51
Hoyt-Chi	260.2	Hough-Tex	7.82	Honeycutt-Tex	1.91	Righetti-NY	169	Conroy-Oak	6.21	Guidry-NY	10.57
McGregor-Bal	260.0	Dotson-Chi	7.84	Eckersley-Bos	1.99	Sutcliffe-Cle	160	Gott-Tor	6.16	Stieb-Tor	10.68

Earned Run Average		Adjusted ERA		Opponents' Batting Avg.		Opponents' On Base Pct.		Starter Runs		Adjusted Starter Runs	
Honeycutt-Tex	2.42	Honeycutt-Tex	165	Boddicker-Bal	.216	Hoyt-Chi	.262	Honeycutt-Tex	31.8	Stieb-Tor	38.8
Boddicker-Bal	2.77	Boddicker-Bal	143	Stieb-Tor	.219	Boddicker-Bal	.274	Stieb-Tor	31.4	Honeycutt-Tex	30.7
Stieb-Tor	3.04	Stieb-Tor	141	Conroy-Oak	.232	Morris-Det	.289	Boddicker-Bal	25.8	Dotson-Chi	25.6
Hough-Tex	3.18	Young-Sea	130	Bannister-Chi	.233	Guidry-NY	.291	McGregor-Bal	25.3	Boddicker-Bal	23.6
McGregor-Bal	3.18	Dotson-Chi	130	Morris-Det	.233	Stieb-Tor	.293	Hough-Tex	24.7	Hough-Tex	23.1

Clutch Pitching Index		Relief Runs		Adjusted Relief Runs		Relief Ranking		Total Pitcher Index		Total Baseball Ranking	
Honeycutt-Tex	139	Quisenberry-KC	32.7	Quisenberry-KC	32.9	Quisenberry-KC	38.7	Honeycutt-Tex	4.3	Ripken-Bal	6.7
Zahn-Cal	118	T.Martinez-Bal	19.6	Stanley-Bos	19.6	Stanley-Bos	38.2	Quisenberry-KC	4.2	Henderson-Oak	5.7
Hurst-Bos	113	Stanley-Bos	19.6	T.Martinez-Bal	18.4	Gossage-NY	37.3	Stieb-Tor	3.9	Yount-Mil	5.2
Dotson-Chi	113	Gossage-NY	17.4	Barojas-Chi	16.6	T.Martinez-Bal	26.8	Stanley-Bos	3.7	Boggs-Bos	4.5
McGregor-Bal	113	Lopez-Det	16.0	Gossage-NY	15.8	Lopez-Det	23.1	Gossage-NY	3.7	Grich-Cal	4.5

January 10 Luis Aparicio, Harmon Killebrew, and Don Drysdale are elected to the Hall of Fame by the BBWAA.

March 4 Shortstop Harold "Pee Wee" Reese and catcher Rick Ferrell are elected to the Hall of Fame by the Special Veterans Committee. Reese hit .269 in 16 seasons with the Dodgers while Ferrell batted .281 with 28 home runs in 18 seasons for the Browns, Red Sox, and Senators.

June 24 Joe Morgan hits his 265th career home run as a second baseman, breaking Rogers Hornsby's major league record for that position.

July 10 On the 50th anniversary of Carl Hubbell's legendary five consecutive strikeouts in the 1934 All-Star Game, NL pitchers Fernando Valenzuela and Dwight Gooden combine to fan six in a row for a new All-Star record in the NL's 3-1 triumph. After Valenzuela whiffs Dave Winfield, Reggie Jackson, and George Brett in the fourth inning, Gooden, the youngest All-Star ever at age 19, fans Lance Parrish, Chet Lemon,

and Alvin Davis in the fifth.

August 12 In one of the ugliest brawl-filled games in major league history, the Braves beat the Padres 5-3 in Atlanta. Atlanta's Pascual Perez hits Alan Wiggins in the back with the first pitch of the game. Padres pitchers retaliate by throwing at Perez all four times he comes to the plate. All in all, the game features two bench-clearing brawls, the second of which includes several fans, and 19 ejections, including both managers and both replacement managers. Padres manager Dick Williams will be suspended for 10 days and fined $10,000, while Braves manager Joe Torre and five players will each receive three-game suspensions.

August 16 After a nearly six-year absence, Pete Rose is reunited with his hometown Reds in a trade for infielder Tom Lawless, and Cincinnati immediately names him player-manager, replacing Vern Rapp.

September 12 Dwight Gooden strikes out 16 Pirates in a 2-0 victory to break Herb Score's major league rookie strike-

out record of 245.

September 20 The Padres clinch their first NL West title with a 5-4 win over the Giants. The key blow is winning pitcher Tim Lollar's three-run home run, his third home run of the season.

September 24 Rick Sutcliffe pitches a two-hitter in a 4-1 win over Pittsburgh to clinch the NL East title for the Cubs, who will be making their first postseason appearance since 1945.

October 2 The Cubs clobber the Padres 13-0 to take a 1-0 lead in the league series.

October 7 San Diego rallies for four runs in the seventh inning to beat Chicago 6-3 and earn its first trip to the World Series.

October 23 Rick Sutcliffe, who was 16-1 for the Cubs after arriving from Cleveland two days before the June 15 trading deadline, is a unanimous choice as NL Cy Young Award winner.

November 13 Ryne Sandberg wins the NL MVP Award, becoming the first Cub to do so since Ernie Banks in 1959.

ATLANTA		CHICAGO		CINCINNATI		HOUSTON		LOS ANGELES		MONTREAL	
M	J.Torre	M	J.Frey	M	V.Rapp	M	B.Lillis	M	T.Lasorda	M	B.Virdon
1B	C.Chambliss	1B	L.Durham	M	P.Rose	1B	E.Cabell	1B	G.Brock	M	J.Fanning
2B	G.Hubbard	2B	R.Sandberg	1B	D.Driessen	2B	B.Doran	2B	S.Sax	1B	T.Francona
SS	R.Ramirez	SS	L.Bowa	2B	R.Oester	SS	C.Reynolds	SS	D.Anderson	2B	D.Flynn
3B	R.Johnson	3B	R.Cey	SS	D.Concepcion	3B	P.Garner	3B	G.Rivera	SS	A.Salazar
LF	B.Komminsk	LF	G.Matthews	3B	N.Esasky	LF	J.Cruz	LF	M.Marshall	3B	T.Wallach
CF	D.Murphy	CF	B.Dernier	LF	G.Redus	CF	J.Mumphrey	CF	K.Landreaux	LF	J.Wohlford
RF	C.Washington	RF	K.Moreland	CF	E.Milner	RF	T.Puhl	RF	C.Maldonado	CF	T.Raines
C	B.Benedict	C	J.Davis	RF	D.Parker	C	M.Bailey	C	M.Scioscia	RF	A.Dawson
				C	B.Gulden					C	G.Carter
1O	G.Perry	O	H.Cotto			O	K.Bass	3O	P.Guerrero		
C	A.Trevino			O1	C.Cedeno	31	R.Knight	SO	B.Russell	SO	D.Thomas
23	J.Royster			S2	T.Foley	31	D.Walling	O	R.Reynolds	1O	P.Rose
		P	S.Trout	3	W.Krenchicki			1O	F.Stubbs	2	B.Little
		P	D.Eckersley			P	J.Niekro				
P	R.Mahler	P	R.Sutcliffe	P	M.Soto	P	B.Knepper	P	F.Valenzuela	P	B.Gullickson
P	P.Perez	P	S.Sanderson	P	J.Russell	P	N.Ryan	P	A.Pena	P	C.Lea
P	C.McMurtry	P	D.Ruthven	P	J.Price	P	M.Scott	P	O.Hershiser	P	B.Smith
P	R.Camp	RP	L.Smith	P	J.Tibbs	P	M.LaCoss	P	R.Honeycutt	P	S.Rogers
P	L.Barker	RP	T.Stoddard	P	F.Pastore	RP	B.Dawley	P	B.Welch	P	D.Schatzeder
RP	G.Garber	RP	R.Bordi	RP	T.Hume	RP	V.Ruhle	RP	B.Hooton	RP	B.James
RP	S.Bedrosian			RP	T.Power	RP	D.Smith	RP	P.Zachry	RP	J.Reardon
RP	J.Dedmon	P	R.Reuschel	RP	B.Owchinko			RP	K.Howell	RP	G.Lucas
		P	C.Rainey			P	F.DiPino				
P	P.Falcone	P	W.Brusstar			P	J.Solano	P	J.Reuss	P	D.Palmer
P	D.Moore	P	G.Frazier	P	J.Franco						
		P	D.Noles	P	B.Scherrer						
				P	B.Berenyi						

NEW YORK		PHILADELPHIA		PITTSBURGH		SAN DIEGO		SAN FRANCISCO		ST.LOUIS	
M	D.Johnson	M	P.Owens	M	C.Tanner	M	D.Williams	M	F.Robinson	M	W.Herzog
1B	K.Hernandez	1B	L.Matuszek	1B	J.Thompson	1B	S.Garvey	M	D.Ozark	1B	D.Green
2B	W.Backman	2B	J.Samuel	2B	J.Ray	2B	A.Wiggins	1B	S.Thompson	2B	T.Herr
SS	J.Oquendo	SS	I.DeJesus	SS	D.Berra	SS	G.Templeton	2B	M.Trillo	SS	O.Smith
3B	H.Brooks	3B	M.Schmidt	3B	B.Madlock	3B	G.Nettles	SS	J.LeMaster	3B	T.Pendleton
LF	G.Foster	LF	G.Wilson	LF	L.Lacy	LF	C.Martinez	3B	J.Youngblood	LF	L.Smith
CF	M.Wilson	CF	V.Hayes	CF	M.Wynne	CF	K.McReynolds	LF	J.Leonard	CF	W.McGee
RF	D.Strawberry	RF	S.Lezcano	RF	D.Frobel	RF	T.Gwynn	CF	D.Gladden	RF	G.Hendrick
C	M.Fitzgerald	C	O.Virgil	C	T.Pena	C	T.Kennedy	RF	C.Davis	C	D.Porter
								C	B.Brenly		
O1	D.Heep	1O	T.Corcoran	O	L.Mazzilli	3O	L.Salazar			O	T.Landrum
S2	R.Gardenhire	O1	G.Gross	32	J.Morrison			O	D.Baker	O3	A.Van Slyke
		O	G.Maddox			P	E.Show	1	A.Oliver		
P	D.Gooden			P	R.Rhoden	P	T.Lollar	2S	B.Wellman	P	J.Andujar
P	W.Terrell	P	S.Carlton	P	L.McWilliams	P	E.Whitson	O	J.Clark	P	D.LaPoint
P	R.Darling	P	J.Koosman	P	J.Tudor	P	M.Thurmond			P	D.Cox
P	E.Lynch	P	C.Hudson	P	J.DeLeon	P	D.Dravecky	P	B.Laskey	P	R.Horton
P	B.Berenyi	P	J.Denny	P	J.Candelaria	RP	C.Lefferts	P	M.Krukow	P	K.Kepshire
RP	J.Orosco	P	S.Rawley	RP	D.Robinson	RP	R.Gossage	P	M.Davis	RP	B.Sutter
RP	B.Gaff	RP	K.Gross	RP	K.Tekulve	RP	G.Booker	P	J.Robinson	RP	N.Allen
RP	D.Sisk	RP	A.Holland	RP	L.Tunnell			RP	G.Minton	RP	J.Lahti
		RP	L.Andersen			P	A.Hawkins	RP	F.Williams		
P	S.Fernandez							RP	G.Lavelle	P	D.Rucker
P	T.Gorman	P	B.Campbell							P	J.Stuper
P	T.Leary	P	M.Bystrom					P	R.Lerch	P	B.Forsch
								P	M.Grant		
								P	B.Lacey		

TEAM	G	W	L	PCT	GB	R	OR	AB	H	2B	3B	HR	BB	SO	AVG	OBP	SLG	PRO	PRO+	BR	/A	PF	CHI	RC	SB	CS	SBA	SBR
EAST																												
CHI	161	96	65	.596		**762**	658	5437	1415	240	47	136	**567**	967	.260	.333	.397	.730	102	78	12	109	104	729	154	66	70	7
NY	162	90	72	.556	6.5	652	676	5438	1400	235	25	107	500	1001	.257	.322	.369	.691	102	1	11	99	100	645	149	54	73	12
STL	162	84	78	.519	12.5	652	645	5433	1369	225	44	75	516	924	.252	.319	.351	.670	97	-35	-19	97	**106**	623	**220**	71	76	**23**
PHI	162	81	81	.500	15.5	720	690	5614	1494	**248**	51	**147**	555	1081	**.266**	**.335**	**.407**	**.742**	**112**	102	90	102	93	**766**	186	60	76	20
MON	161	78	83	.484	18	593	585	5439	1367	242	36	96	491	**782**	.251	.314	.362	.676	101	-32	-4	96	96	630	131	38	**78**	17
PIT	162	75	87	.463	21.5	615	**567**	5537	1412	237	33	98	438	841	.255	.312	.363	.675	95	-37	-37	100	99	611	96	62	61	-8
WEST																												
SD	162	92	70	.568		686	634	5504	1425	207	42	109	472	810	.259	.320	.371	.691	100	-1	0	100	105	645	152	68	69	5
HOU	162	80	82	.494	12	693	630	5548	1465	222	**67**	79	494	837	.264	.326	.371	.697	110	14	63	93	102	679	105	61	63	-5
ATL	162	80	82	.494	12	632	655	5422	1338	234	27	111	555	896	.247	.319	.361	.680	90	-18	-64	107	99	623	140	85	72	-9
LA	162	79	83	.488	13	580	600	5399	1316	213	23	102	488	829	.244	.308	.348	.656	91	-68	-62	99	100	573	109	69	61	-9
CIN	162	70	92	.432	22	627	747	5498	1342	238	30	106	566	978	.244	.316	.356	.672	91	-34	-62	105	100	635	160	63	72	10
SF	162	66	96	.407	26	682	807	5650	**1499**	229	26	112	528	980	.265	.330	.375	.705	108	31	54	97	97	686	126	76	62	-8
TOT	971					7894		65919	16842	2770	451	1278	6149	10929	.255	.321	.369	.691							1728	773	69	55

TEAM	CG	SH	SV	IP	H	H/G	HR	BB	SO	RAT	ERA	ERA+	OAV	OOB	PR	/A	PF	CPI	FA	E	DP	FW	PW	BW	SBW	DIF
EAST																										
CHI	19	8	50	1434	1458	9.2	99	**442**	879	12.1	3.75	104	.267	.324	-26	25	109	99	.981	121	137	1.1	2.6	1.3	.3	10.3
NY	12	15	50	1442²	1371	8.6	104	573	1028	12.3	3.60	98	.252	.326	-2	-10	99	101	.979	129	154	.7	-1.1	1.2	.8	7.4
STL	19	12	**51**	1449	1427	8.9	94	494	808	12.1	3.58	97	.262	.326	1	-18	97	103	**.982**	118	**184**	**1.3**	-1.9	-2.0	**1.9**	3.6
PHI	11	6	35	1458¹	1416	8.7	101	448	904	11.6	3.62	100	.253	**.310**	-5	2	101	92	.975	161	112	-1.2	.2	**9.5**	1.6	-10.1
MON	19	10	48	1431	1333	8.4	114	474	861	11.5	3.31	103	.249	.312	45	18	95	103	.978	132	147	.4	1.9	-.4	1.3	-5.7
PIT	27	13	34	1470	1344	**8.2**	102	502	995	**11.4**	**3.11**	116	.246	**.310**	**78**	**80**	100	**105**	.980	128	142	.7	**8.4**	-3.9	-1.3	-9.9
WEST																										
SD	13	**17**	44	1460¹	**1327**	**8.2**	122	563	812	11.8	3.48	102	**.244**	.317	17	14	99	99	.978	138	144	.1	1.5	.0	.0	9.3
HOU	24	13	29	1449¹	1350	8.4	91	502	950	11.6	3.32	100	.248	.314	44	0	93	99	.979	133	160	.4	.0	6.6	-1.0	-7.1
ATL	17	7	49	1447	1401	8.7	122	525	859	12.1	3.57	108	.257	.324	3	46	107	**105**	.978	139	153	.0	4.8	-6.7	-1.4	2.2
LA	**39**	16	27	1460¹	1381	8.5	**76**	499	**1033**	11.7	3.17	111	.250	.314	68	59	98	102	.975	163	146	-1.3	6.2	-6.5	-1.4	1.1
CIN	25	6	25	1461¹	1445	8.9	128	578	946	12.6	4.16	91	.259	.330	-92	-62	105	94	.977	139	116	.0	-6.5	-6.5	.6	1.4
SF	9	7	38	1461	1589	9.8	125	549	854	13.4	4.39	80	.278	.345	-131	-143	98	99	.973	173	134	-1.9	-15.0	5.7	-1.3	-2.4
TOT	234	130	480	17424²		8.7				12.0	3.59		.255	.321					.978	1674	1729					

Runs		Hits		Doubles		Triples		Home Runs		Total Bases	
Sandberg-Chi	114	Gwynn-SD	213	Ray-Pit	38	Sandberg-Chi	19	Schmidt-Phi	36	Murphy-Atl	332
Wiggins-SD	106	Sandberg-Chi	200	Raines-Mon	38	Samuel-Phi	19	Murphy-Atl	36	Sandberg-Chi	331
Raines-Mon	106	Raines-Mon	192	Sandberg-Chi	36	Cruz-Hou	13	Carter-Mon	27	Samuel-Phi	310
Samuel-Phi	105	Samuel-Phi	191	Samuel-Phi	36			Strawberry-NY	26	Carter-Mon	290
Matthews-Chi	101	Cruz-Hou	187					Cey-Chi	25	Schmidt-Phi	283

Runs Batted In		Runs Produced		Bases On Balls		Batting Average		On Base Percentage		Slugging Average	
Schmidt-Phi	106	Sandberg-Chi	179	Matthews-Chi	103	Gwynn-SD	.351	Matthews-Chi	.417	Murphy-Atl	.547
Carter-Mon	106	Cruz-Hou	179	Hernandez-NY	97	Lacy-Pit	.321	Hernandez-NY	.415	Schmidt-Phi	.536
Murphy-Atl	100	Matthews-Chi	169	Schmidt-Phi	92	C.Davis-SF	.315	Gwynn-SD	.411	Sandberg-Chi	.520
Strawberry-NY	97	Schmidt-Phi	163	Thompson-Pit	87	Sandberg-Chi	.314	Raines-Mon	.395	C.Davis-SF	.507
Cey-Chi	97	Hernandez-NY	162	Raines-Mon	87	Ray-Pit	.312	Schmidt-Phi	.388	Durham-Chi	.505

Production		Adjusted Production		Batter Runs		Adjusted Batter Runs		Clutch Hitting Index		Runs Created	
Schmidt-Phi	.924	Schmidt-Phi	155	Murphy-Atl	43.8	Schmidt-Phi	39.5	Mumphrey-Hou	132	Sandberg-Chi	126
Murphy-Atl	.920	C.Davis-SF	149	Schmidt-Phi	41.2	Cruz-Hou	38.4	Davis-SF	125	Raines-Mon	124
Sandberg-Chi	.889	Cruz-Hou	148	Sandberg-Chi	37.9	Hernandez-NY	37.0	Garvey-SD	125	Murphy-Atl	123
Durham-Chi	.877	Murphy-Atl	145	Hernandez-NY	35.5	Murphy-Atl	35.5	Cey-Chi	120	Cruz-Hou	111
C.Davis-SF	.876	Hernandez-NY	145	Gwynn-SD	33.9	Raines-Mon	35.4	Concepcion-Cin	118	Carter-Mon	108

Total Average		Stolen Bases		Stolen Base Average		Stolen Base Runs		Fielding Runs		Total Player Rating	
Raines-Mon	.953	Raines-Mon	75	Dilone-Mon	93.1	Raines-Mon	16.5	O.Smith-StL	26.2	Sandberg-Chi	6.4
Murphy-Atl	.942	Samuel-Phi	72	Raines-Mon	88.2	Samuel-Phi	12.6	Sandberg-Chi	23.3	Raines-Mon	5.8
Schmidt-Phi	.933	Wiggins-SD	70	Cedeno-Cin	86.4	Wilson-NY	8.4	Garner-Hou	23.1	Cruz-Hou	4.9
Sandberg-Chi	.913	L.Smith-StL	50	VanSlyke-StL	84.8	Wiggins-SD	8.4	Martinez-SD	20.6	Schmidt-Phi	4.8
Matthews-Chi	.888			Stone-Phi	84.4	Redus-Cin	7.8	Hubbard-Atl	19.6	Hernandez-NY	4.6

Wins		Win Percentage		Games		Complete Games		Shutouts		Saves	
Andujar-StL	20	Sutcliffe-Chi	.941	Power-Cin	78	Soto-Cin	13	Pena-LA	4	Sutter-StL	45
Soto-Cin	18	Soto-Cin	.720	Lavelle-SF	77	Valenzuela-LA	12	Hershiser-LA	4	Smith-Chi	33
Gooden-NY	17	Gooden-NY	.654	Minton-SF	74	Andujar-StL	12	Andujar-StL	4	Orosco-NY	31
Sutcliffe-Chi	16	Show-SD	.625	Tekulve-Pit	72	Knepper-Hou	11			Holland-Phi	29
Niekro-Hou	16			Sutter-StL	71	Mahler-Atl	9			Gossage-SD	25

Innings Pitched		Fewest Hits/Game		Fewest BB/Game		Strikeouts		Strikeouts/Game		Ratio	
Andujar-StL	261.1	Gooden-NY	6.65	Gullickson-Mon	1.47	Gooden-NY	276	Gooden-NY	11.39	Gooden-NY	9.74
Valenzuela-LA	261.0	Soto-Cin	6.86	Candelaria-Pit	1.65	Valenzuela-LA	240	Ryan-Hou	9.65	Hershiser-LA	10.15
Niekro-Hou	248.1	DeLeon-Pit	6.88	Whitson-SD	2.00	Ryan-Hou	197	Valenzuela-LA	8.28	Andujar-StL	10.16
Rhoden-Pit	238.1	Ryan-Hou	7.01	Pena-LA	2.08	Soto-Cin	185	Berenyi-Cin-NY	7.27	Soto-Cin	10.35
Soto-Cin	237.1	Andujar-StL	7.51	Knepper-Hou	2.12	Carlton-Phi	163	DeLeon-Pit	7.16	Candelaria-Pit	10.39

Earned Run Average		Adjusted ERA		Opponents' Batting Avg.		Opponents' On Base Pct.		Starter Runs		Adjusted Starter Runs	
Pena-LA	2.48	Pena-LA	142	Gooden-NY	.202	Gooden-NY	.270	Pena-LA	24.5	Rhoden-Pit	23.3
Gooden-NY	2.60	Gooden-NY	136	Soto-Cin	.209	Hershiser-LA	.279	Gooden-NY	23.9	Pena-LA	23.2
Hershiser-LA	2.66	Hershiser-LA	133	Ryan-Hou	.211	Soto-Cin	.286	Rhoden-Pit	23.0	Gooden-NY	22.6
Rhoden-Pit	2.72	Rhoden-Pit	132	DeLeon-Pit	.214	Andujar-StL	.286	Hershiser-LA	19.6	Sutcliffe-Chi	20.3
Candelaria-Pit	2.72	Candelaria-Pit	132	Hershiser-LA	.225	Ryan-Hou	.288	Denny-Phi	19.5	Denny-Phi	20.3

Clutch Pitching Index		Relief Runs		Adjusted Relief Runs		Relief Ranking		Total Pitcher Index		Total Baseball Ranking	
McWilliams-Pit	130	Sutter-StL	27.9	Sutter-StL	26.3	Sutter-StL	40.7	Sutter-StL	4.4	Sandberg-Chi	6.4
Terrell-NY	124	Dawley-Hou	18.1	Lefferts-SD	16.9	Bedrosian-Atl	25.6	Rhoden-Pit	3.5	Raines-Mon	5.8
Candelaria-Pit	122	Lefferts-SD	17.1	Dawley-Hou	15.1	Dawley-Hou	22.3	Gooden-NY	2.9	Cruz-Hou	4.9
Honeycutt-LA	117	Sisk-NY	13.0	Bedrosian-Atl	13.8	Orosco-NY	21.1	Sutcliffe-Chi	2.8	Schmidt-Phi	4.8
Trout-Chi	117	Andersen-Phi	12.1	Andersen-Phi	12.6	Power-Cin	17.5	Mahler-Atl	2.6	Hernandez-NY	4.6

May 9 The longest—and slowest—game in AL history ends in the 25th inning when Harold Baines homers off Chuck Porter to give the White Sox a 7-6 victory over the Brewers. The game falls one inning shy of the major league record, but takes by far the most time to play: 8 hours and 6 minutes. The contest was suspended May 8 after 17 innings with the score tied 3-3, and each team scores three more runs in the 21st. Tom Seaver pitches the final inning to earn the win, then wins the regularly scheduled game as well, 5-4.

September 17 Reggie Jackson hits his 500th career home run in the seventh inning off Bud Black, but the Royals beat California, 10-1, to move into first place in the AL West. Jackson is the 13th player in major league history to hit 500 home runs.

September 18 The Tigers clinch the AL East championship with a 3-0 win over the Brewers as starter Randy O'Neal records his first major league win. Detroit becomes the fourth team this century to be in first place every day of the season, joining the 1923 Giants, the 1927 Yankees, and the 1955 Dodgers.

September 28 Kansas City clinches the AL West title with a 6-5 win over Oakland.

September 30 On the final day of the regular season, California's Mike Witt fans 10 and needs just 97 pitches to complete a perfect game, 1-0 over Texas.

September 30 In the dramatic race for the AL batting title, Don Mattingly goes 4-for-5 in the Yankees season-ending 4-2 win over the Tigers to edge teammate Dave Winfield .343 to .340.

October 5 In Game 3, Milt Wilcox and Willie Hernandez combine on a 1-0 three-hitter to give the Tigers a three-game sweep of the Royals in the ALCS.

October 9 The Tigers win the World Series opener as Jack Morris pitches a complete-game 3-2 victory. Larry Herndon's two-run home run in the fifth is the margin.

October 14 Series MVP Kirk Gibson blasts two upper-deck home runs at Tiger Stadium in Game 5, including a three-run shot off Rich Gossage in the eighth inning, to lead Detroit to an 8-4 win and its first World Championship since 1968.

October 16 Gene Mauch, who resigned as the Angels' manager after the 1982 season, is hired again.

October 30 Tigers reliever Willie Hernandez wins the AL Cy Young Award, edging fellow reliever Dan Quisenberry of the Royals.

November 6 Willie Hernandez wins the AL MVP Award, joining Rollie Fingers as the only relief pitchers up to this date to be named MVP and Cy Young Award winner in the same season.

	BALTIMORE		BOSTON		CALIFORNIA		CHICAGO		CLEVELAND		DETROIT		KANSAS CITY
M	J.Altobelli	M	R.Houk	M	J.McNamara	M	T.LaRussa	M	P.Corrales	M	S.Anderson	M	D.Howser
1B	E.Murray	1B	B.Buckner	1B	R.Carew	1B	G.Walker	1B	M.Hargrove	1B	D.Bergman	1B	S.Balboni
2B	R.Dauer	2B	M.Barrett	2B	R.Wilfong	2B	J.Cruz	2B	T.Bernazard	2B	L.Whitaker	2B	F.White
SS	C.Ripken	SS	J.Gutierrez	SS	D.Schofield	SS	S.Fletcher	SS	J.Franco	SS	A.Trammell	SS	O.Concepcion
3B	W.Gross	3B	W.Boggs	3B	D.DeCinces	3B	V.Law	3B	B.Jacoby	3B	H.Johnson	3B	G.Pryor
LF	G.Roenicke	LF	J.Rice	LF	B.Downing	LF	R.Kittle	LF	M.Hall	LF	L.Herndon	LF	D.Motley
CF	J.Shelby	CF	T.Armas	CF	G.Pettis	CF	R.Law	CF	B.Butler	CF	C.Lemon	CF	W.Wilson
RF	M.Young	RF	D.Evans	RF	F.Lynn	RF	H.Baines	RF	G.Vukovich	RF	K.Gibson	RF	P.Sheridan
C	R.Dempsey	C	R.Gedman	C	B.Boone	C	C.Fisk	C	J.Willard	C	L.Parrish	C	D.Slaught
DH	K.Singleton	DH	M.Easler	DH	Re.Jackson	DH	G.Luzinski	DH	A.Thornton	DH	D.Evans	DH	H.McRae
O	A.Bumbry	P	B.Hurst	O	J.Beniquez	OD	J.Hairston	1O	P.Tabler	3S	T.Brookens	3	G.Brett
OD	J.Lowenstein	P	B.Ojeda	21	B.Grich	1O	T.Paciorek	O	J.Carter	13	B.Garbey	DO	J.Orta
C3	F.Rayford	P	O.Boyd			13	M.Squires	C	C.Bando	O	R.Jones	C1	J.Wathan
		P	A.Nipper	P	M.Witt			O	C.Castillo			1O	D.Iorg
P	M.Boddicker	P	R.Clemens	P	R.Romanick	P	R.Dotson			P	J.Morris		
P	M.Flanagan	RP	B.Stanley	P	G.Zahn	P	T.Seaver	P	B.Blyleven	P	D.Petry	P	B.Black
P	S.Davis	RP	M.Clear	P	T.John	P	L.Hoyt	P	N.Heaton	P	M.Wilcox	P	M.Gubicza
P	S.McGregor	RP	J.Johnson	P	J.Slaton	P	F.Bannister	P	S.Comer	P	J.Berenguer	P	L.Gura
P	D.Martinez			RP	D.Corbett	P	B.Burns	P	S.Farr	P	D.Rozema	P	B.Saberhagen
RP	S.Stewart	P	M.Brown	RP	L.Sanchez	RP	R.Reed	RP	E.Camacho	RP	W.Hernandez	P	C.Leibrandt
RP	T.Martinez	/P	D.Eckersley	RP	C.Kaufman	RP	J.Agosto	RP	T.Waddell	RP	A.Lopez	RP	D.Quisenberry
RP	T.Underwood	P	S.Crawford			RP	D.Spillner	RP	M.Jeffcoat	RP	D.Bair	RP	J.Beckwith
				P	B.Kison							RP	M.Huismann
P	B.Swaggerty					P	G.Nelson	P	R.Sutcliffe				
								P	D.Schulze			P	M.Jones
								P	R.Smith			P	D.Jackson
								P	J.Easterly				
								P	D.Spillner				
								P	L.Aponte				

	MILWAUKEE		MINNESOTA		NEW YORK		OAKLAND		SEATTLE		TEXAS		TORONTO
M	R.Lachemann	M	B.Gardner	M	Y.Berra	M	S.Boros	M	D.Crandall	M	D.Rader	M	B.Cox
1B	C.Cooper	1B	K.Hrbek	1B	D.Mattingly	M	J.Moore	M	C.Cottier	1B	P.O'Brien	1B	W.Upshaw
2B	J.Gantner	2B	T.Teufel	2B	W.Randolph	1B	B.Bochte	1B	A.Davis	2B	W.Tolleson	2B	D.Garcia
SS	R.Yount	SS	H.Jimenez	SS	B.Meacham	2B	J.Morgan	2B	J.Perconte	SS	C.Wilkerson	SS	A.Griffin
3B	E.Romero	3B	G.Gaetti	3B	T.Harrah	SS	T.Phillips	SS	S.Owen	3B	B.Bell	3B	R.Mulliniks
LF	B.Oglivie	LF	M.Hatcher	LF	K.Griffey	3B	C.Lansford	3B	J.Presley	LF	B.Sample	LF	D.Collins
CF	R.Manning	CF	K.Puckett	CF	O.Moreno	LF	R.Henderson	LF	P.Bradley	CF	G.Wright	CF	L.Moseby
RF	D.James	RF	T.Brunansky	RF	D.Winfield	CF	D.Murphy	CF	D.Henderson	RF	G.Ward	RF	G.Bell
C	J.Sundberg	C	D.Engle	C	B.Wynegar	RF	M.Davis	RF	A.Cowens	C	D.Scott	C	E.Whitt
DH	T.Simmons	DH	R.Bush	DH	D.Baylor	C	M.Heath	C	B.Kearney	DH	L.Parrish	DH	C.Johnson
						DH	D.Kingman	DH	K.Phelps				
C	B.Schroeder	C	T.Laudner	OD	S.Kemp					DO	M.Rivers	O	J.Barfield
		OD	D.Brown	3S	R.Smalley	O1	B.Almon	O3	B.Bonnell	C	N.Yost	3	G.Iorg
				3	M.Pagliarulo	O2	D.Lopes	OD	S.Henderson			C	B.Martinez
P	D.Sutton	P	F.Viola			32	L.Milbourne			D	W.Aikens		
P	M.Haas	P	M.Smithson	P	P.Niekro	P	R.Burris	P	C.Hough	S3	T.Fernandez		
P	J.Cocanower	P	J.Butcher	P	R.Guidry	P	L.Sorensen	P	M.Langston	P	F.Tanana		
P	B.McClure	P	K.Schrom	P	R.Fontenot	P	S.McCatty	P	M.Moore	P	D.Darwin	P	D.Stieb
P	M.Caldwell	P	E.Hodge	P	D.Rasmussen	P	B.Krueger	P	J.Beattie	P	D.Stewart	P	D.Alexander
RP	P.Ladd	RP	P.Filson	RP	B.Shirley	P	C.Young	P	M.Young	P	M.Mason	P	L.Leal
RP	T.Tellmann	RP	R.Davis	RP	J.Howell	RP	K.Atherton	RP	E.Vande Berg	RP	D.Schmidt	P	J.Clancy
RP	R.Waits	RP	R.Lysander	RP	D.Righetti	RP	B.Caudill	RP	B.Stoddard	RP	O.Jones	P	J.Gott
						RP	T.Conroy	RP	D.Beard			RP	R.Jackson
P	C.Porter			P	J.Cowley					P	D.Noles	RP	D.Lamp
P	B.Gibson	P	A.Williams	P	J.Rijo	P	M.Warren	P	S.Barojas			RP	J.Acker
				P	J.Montefusco	P	C.Codiroli	P	P.Mirabella				
				P	M.Armstrong			P	E.Nunez			P	J.Key
								P	M.Stanton				
								P	R.Thomas				

TEAM	G	W	L	PCT	GB	R	OR	AB	H	2B	3B	HR	BB	SO	AVG	OBP	SLG	PRO	PRO+	BR	/A	PF	CHI	RC	SB	CS	SBA	SBR
EAST																												
DET	162	104	58	.642		**829**	**643**	5644	1529	254	46	**187**	602	941	.271	**.345**	.432	.777	**114**	103	**109**	99	99	**843**	106	68	61	-9
TOR	163	89	73	.549	15	750	696	5687	1555	**275**	**68**	143	460	816	.273	.333	.421	.754	103	52	24	104	96	808	**193**	67	**74**	**18**
NY	162	87	75	.537	17	758	679	5661	1560	**275**	32	130	534	**673**	.276	.342	.404	.746	110	47	78	96	97	773	62	38	62	-4
BOS	162	86	76	.531	18	810	764	5648	**1598**	259	45	181	500	842	**.283**	.343	**.441**	**.784**	110	**113**	75	105	97	832	38	25	60	-4
BAL	162	85	77	.525	19	681	667	5456	1374	234	23	160	**620**	884	.252	.331	.391	.722	101	-4	12	98	96	705	51	36	59	-6
CLE	163	75	87	.463	29	761	766	5643	1498	222	39	123	600	815	.265	.339	.384	.723	98	4	-9	102	103	732	126	77	62	-8
MIL	161	67	94	.416	36.5	641	734	5511	1446	232	36	96	432	**673**	.262	.319	.370	.689	94	-75	-50	96	103	621	52	57	48	-19
WEST																												
KC	162	84	78	.519		673	686	5543	1487	269	52	117	400	832	.268	.320	.399	.719	97	-23	-28	101	99	685	106	64	62	-7
CAL	162	81	81	.500	3	696	697	5470	1363	211	30	150	556	928	.249	.322	.381	.703	95	-46	-41	99	**105**	663	80	51	61	-7
MIN	162	81	81	.500	3	673	675	5562	1473	259	33	114	437	735	.265	.321	.385	.706	90	-45	-75	105	102	669	39	30	57	-6
OAK	162	77	85	.475	7	738	796	5457	1415	257	29	158	568	871	.259	.332	.404	.736	109	18	67	93	101	736	145	64	69	5
SEA	162	74	88	.457	10	682	774	5546	1429	244	34	129	519	871	.258	.326	.384	.710	97	-32	-23	99	100	700	116	62	65	-2
CHI	162	74	88	.457	10	679	736	5513	1360	225	38	172	523	883	.247	.316	.395	.711	91	-37	-67	105	101	690	109	49	69	3
TEX	161	69	92	.429	14.5	656	714	5569	1452	227	29	120	420	807	.261	.315	.377	.692	88	-75	-95	103	104	643	81	50	62	-6
TOT	1134					10027		77910	20539	3443	534	1980	7171	11571	.264	.329	.398	.727							1304	738	64	-52

TEAM	CG	SH	SV	IP	H	H/G	HR	BB	SO	RAT	ERA	ERA+	OAV	OOB	PR	/A	PF	CPI	FA	E	DP	FW	PW	BW	SBW	DIF
EAST																										
DET	19	8	**51**	1464	**1358**	**8.3**	130	489	914	**11.5**	**3.49**	**112**	**.246**	**.311**	**81**	**70**	98	98	.979	127	162	.3	**7.0**	**11.0**	-.5	5.2
TOR	34	10	33	1464	1433	8.8	140	528	875	12.3	3.86	106	.257	.325	21	38	103	99	.980	123	166	.6	3.8	2.4	**2.2**	-1.0
NY	15	12	43	1465[1]	1485	9.1	**120**	518	**992**	12.4	3.78	100	.264	.328	35	2	95	102	.977	142	**177**	-.5	.2	7.8	-.0	-1.5
BOS	40	12	32	1442	1524	9.5	141	517	927	12.9	4.18	100	.270	.334	-29	-2	104	99	.977	143	128	-.6	-.2	7.5	-.0	-1.7
BAL	**48**	**13**	32	1439[1]	1393	8.7	137	512	714	12.1	3.71	104	.256	.323	44	25	97	102	**.981**	123	166	.5	2.5	1.2	-.2	-.0
CLE	21	7	35	1467[2]	1523	9.3	141	545	803	12.8	4.26	96	.269	.336	-43	-27	102	98	.977	146	163	-.7	-2.7	-.9	-.4	-1.2
MIL	13	7	41	1433	1532	9.6	137	480	785	12.8	4.06	95	.274	.334	-10	-33	96	103	.978	136	156	-.3	-3.3	-5.0	-1.5	-3.4
WEST																										
KC	18	9	50	1444	1426	8.9	136	**433**	724	11.8	3.92	103	.258	.315	11	17	101	93	.979	131	157	.0	1.7	-2.8	-.3	4.4
CAL	36	12	26	1458	1526	9.4	143	474	754	12.5	3.96	100	.271	.331	6	2	99	**104**	.980	128	170	.2	.2	-4.1	-.3	4.0
MIN	32	9	38	1437[2]	1429	8.9	159	463	713	12.1	3.85	109	.260	.321	23	56	105	101	.980	**120**	134	**.7**	5.6	-7.5	-.2	1.5
OAK	15	6	44	1430	1554	9.8	155	592	695	13.7	4.48	84	.278	.351	-78	-117	94	103	.975	146	159	-.8	-11.8	6.7	.9	.9
SEA	26	4	35	1442	1497	9.3	138	619	972	13.5	4.31	93	.270	.348	-50	-51	100	102	.979	128	143	.2	-5.1	-2.3	.2	.0
CHI	43	9	32	1454[1]	1416	8.8	155	483	840	12.0	4.13	101	.256	.320	-23	4	104	93	**.981**	122	160	.6	.4	-6.7	.7	-1.9
TEX	38	6	21	1438[2]	1443	9.0	148	518	863	12.5	3.91	106	.260	.327	13	38	104	101	.977	138	138	-.4	3.8	-9.6	-.2	-5.2
TOT	398	124	513	20280		9.1				12.5	3.99		.264	.329					.979	1853	2179					

Runs
Evans-Bos 121
Henderson-Oak ... 113
Boggs-Bos 109
Butler-Cle 108
Armas-Bos 107

Hits
Mattingly-NY 207
Boggs-Bos 203
Ripken-Bal 195
Winfield-NY 193

Doubles
Mattingly-NY 44
Parrish-Tex 42
Bell-Tor 39
Ripken-Bal 37
Evans-Bos 37

Triples
Moseby-Tor 15
Collins-Tor 15
Gibson-Det 10
Baines-Chi 10

Home Runs
Armas-Bos 43
Kingman-Oak 35
Thornton-Cle 33
Parrish-Det 33
Murphy-Oak 33

Total Bases
Armas-Bos 339
Evans-Bos 335
Ripken-Bal 327
Mattingly-NY 324
Easler-Bos 310

Runs Batted In
Armas-Bos 123
Rice-Bos 122
Kingman-Oak 118
Davis-Sea 116

Runs Produced
Evans-Bos 193
Rice-Bos 192
Winfield-NY 187
Armas-Bos 187

Bases On Balls
Murray-Bal 107
Davis-Sea 97
Evans-Bos 96
Thornton-Cle 91
Boggs-Bos 89

Batting Average
Mattingly-NY 343
Winfield-NY 340
Boggs-Bos 325
Bell-Tex 315
Trammell-Det 314

On Base Percentage
Murray-Bal 415
Boggs-Bos 409
Henderson-Oak 401
Winfield-NY 397
Davis-Sea 395

Slugging Average
Baines-Chi 541
Mattingly-NY 537
Evans-Bos 532
Armas-Bos 531
Hrbek-Min 522

Production
Evans-Bos 924
Mattingly-NY 923
Murray-Bal 923
Winfield-NY 912
Hrbek-Min 909

Adjusted Production
Mattingly-NY 159
Murray-Bal 157
Winfield-NY 156
Henderson-Oak ... 147
Davis-Sea 147

Batter Runs
Murray-Bal 46.8
Evans-Bos 46.6
Mattingly-NY 41.3
Winfield-NY 38.4
Davis-Sea 37.5

Adjusted Batter Runs
Murray-Bal 49.7
Mattingly-NY 46.0
Winfield-NY 42.8
Evans-Bos 40.6
Ripken-Bal 39.3

Clutch Hitting Index
Franco-Cle 132
Davis-Sea 127
Rice-Bos 124
Simmons-Mil 121
Tabler-Cle 116

Runs Created
Evans-Bos 132
Murray-Bal 130
Ripken-Bal 122
Mattingly-NY 120
Easler-Bos 118

Total Average
Murray-Bal 993
Henderson-Oak 971
Evans-Bos 942
Davis-Sea 928
Gibson-Det 926

Stolen Bases
Henderson-Oak 66
Collins-Tor 60
Butler-Cle 52
Pettis-Cal 48
Wilson-KC 47

Stolen Base Average
Wilson-KC 90.4
Tolleson-Tex 84.6
Perconte-Sea 82.9
Moseby-Tor 81.3
Collins-Tor 81.1

Stolen Base Runs
Wilson-KC 11.1
Collins-Tor 9.6
Henderson-Oak 9.0
Garcia-Tor 6.6
Moseby-Tor 6.3

Fielding Runs
Ripken-Bal 38.8
Puckett-Min 30.1
Cruz-Chi 22.1
Boggs-Bos 21.0
Murphy-Oak 21.0

Total Player Rating
Ripken-Bal 9.1
Yount-Mil 5.0
Murray-Bal 4.9
Mattingly-NY 4.9
Henderson-Oak 4.7

Wins
Boddicker-Bal 20
Morris-Det 19
Blyleven-Cle 19
Viola-Min 18
Petry-Det 18

Win Percentage
Alexander-Tor ..... .739
Blyleven-Cle ...... .731
Petry-Det .... .692
Wilcox-Det .... .680

Games
Hernandez-Det 80
Quisenberry-KC ... 72
Lopez-Det 71
Camacho-Cle 69
Caudill-Oak 68

Complete Games
Hough-Tex 17
Boddicker-Bal 16
Dotson-Chi 14
Blyleven-Cle 12
Beattie-Sea 12

Shutouts
Zahn-Cal 5
Ojeda-Bos 5

Saves
Quisenberry-KC ... 44
Caudill-Oak 36
Hernandez-Det 32
Righetti-NY 31
Davis-Min 29

Innings Pitched
Stieb-Tor 267.0
Hough-Tex 266.0
Alexander-Tor 261.2
Boddicker-Bal 261.1
Viola-Min 257.2

Fewest Hits/Game
Stieb-Tor 7.25
Blyleven-Cle 7.49
Boddicker-Bal 7.51
Langston-Sea 7.52
Mason-Tex 7.76

Fewest BB/Game
Hoyt-Chi 1.64
Smithson-Min 1.93
Guidry-NY 2.02
Alexander-Tor 2.03
Haas-Mil 2.04

Strikeouts
Langston-Sea 204
Stieb-Tor 198
Witt-Cal 196
Blyleven-Cle 170
Hough-Tex 164

Strikeouts/Game
Langston-Sea 8.16
Witt-Cal 7.15
Moore-Sea 6.71
Stieb-Tor 6.67
Berenguer-Det 6.31

Ratio
Black-KC 10.30
Alexander-Tor 10.32
Mason-Tex 10.35
Blyleven-Cle 10.43
Boddicker-Bal 10.47

Earned Run Average
Boddicker-Bal 2.79
Stieb-Tor 2.83
Blyleven-Cle 2.87
Niekro-NY 3.09
Zahn-Cal 3.12

Adjusted ERA
Stieb-Tor 145
Blyleven-Cle 143
Boddicker-Bal 139
Alexancer-Tor 131
Viola-Min 131

Opponents' Batting Avg.
Stieb-Tor 221
Blyleven-Cle 224
Boddicker-Bal 228
Langston-Sea 230
Berenguer-Det 232

Opponents' On Base Pct.
Black-KC 283
Blyleven-Cle 287
Alexander-Tor 287
Mason-Tex 288
Seaver-Chi 290

Starter Runs
Boddicker-Bal 34.9
Stieb-Tor 34.4
Blyleven-Cle 30.7
Alexander-Tor 25.0
Black-KC 25.0

Adjusted Starter Runs
Stieb-Tor 37.5
Blyleven-Cle 33.3
Boddicker-Bal 31.4
Viola-Min 28.3
Alexander-Tor 28.1

Clutch Pitching Index
Niekro-NY 125
Fontenot-NY 119
Cocanower-Mil 114
Hurst-Bos 113
Burris-Oak 112

Relief Runs
Hernandez-Det ... 32.2
Quisenberry-KC .. 19.4
Righetti-NY 17.7
Corbett-Cal 17.7
Camacho-Cle 17.3

Adjusted Relief Runs
Hernandez-Det 31.1
Quisenberry-KC ... 19.9
Camacho-Cle 18.4
Corbett-Cal 17.5
Righetti-NY 15.6

Relief Ranking
Hernandez-Det 38.1
Camacho-Cle 31.6
Righetti-NY 26.0
Quisenberry-KC 25.9
Caudill-Oak 24.8

Total Pitcher Index
Boddicker-Bal 4.2
Hernandez-Det 3.9
Blyleven-Cle 3.4
Stieb-Tor 3.3
Camacho-Cle 3.2

Total Baseball Ranking
Ripken-Bal 9.1
Yount-Mil 5.0
Murray-Bal 4.9
Mattingly-NY 4.9
Henderson-Oak 4.7

July 2 Houston's Joe Niekro wins his 200th career game 3-2 over the Padres. Joe and Phil Niekro join Jim and Gaylord Perry as the only pitching brothers to win at least 200 games each in the majors.

July 4 In a marathon game that borders on the surreal, the Mets endure two rain delays and six hours, 10 minutes of playing time to beat the Braves 16-13 in 19 innings on Fireworks Night in Atlanta. The Mets had taken a 10-8 lead in the top of the 13th inning, only to watch the Braves tie it up. The Mets score again in the 18th, but relief hurler Rick Camp (a .060 hitter who was batting because Atlanta had no more position players) ties the score with his first major league home run on a two-out, two-strike pitch in the bottom of the inning. No pitcher ever homered that late in a game before. Finally the Mets erupt for five runs in the 19th off Camp, and Atlanta can respond only with two. The game ends at 3:55 a.m. on July 5, the latest finish in major league history. At 4:01 a.m. the postgame fireworks display begins, causing folks to think the city is under attack.

August 20 Dwight Gooden of the Mets fans 16 batters on the way to his 13th consecutive victory, 5-0 over the Giants, raising his season strikeout total to 208. Gooden (19-3) joins Herb Score as the only pitchers this century to strike out 200 batters in each of their first two seasons.

September 11 Pete Rose becomes baseball's all-time hit leader, singling to left center off Eric Show in the first inning of the Reds' 2-0 win over San Diego. His 4,192nd career hit breaks Ty Cobb's record before 47,237 fans at Cincinnati's Riverfront Stadium. In 1981, it was discovered that Cobb had been credited twice for the same two-hit game, actually giving him 4,189, but commissioner Bowie Kuhn declined to change Cobb's stats.

October 2 The Dodgers clinch the NL West title with a 9-3 win over the Braves. Orel Hershiser raises his record to 19-3 with his eleventh consecutive victory.

October 5 The Cardinals clinch their division championships. John Tudor pitches a four-hitter as St. Louis beats the Cubs, 7-1. It is Tudor's 20th win in 21 decisions.

October 19 St. Louis wins the opener of the "I-70 Series" behind ace John Tudor 3-1.

November 18 Willie McGee wins the NL MVP Award, capping a season in which he led the league in batting average (.353) and hits (216) and also stole 56 bases for St. Louis.

November 18 Dwight Gooden wins the Cy Young Award in the National League, with a remarkable season. He led the league in wins, strikeouts, ERA, innings, and complete games as he lead the Mets to the second-highest win total in franchise history.

November 27 Vince Coleman, who stole 110 bases for the Cardinals, joins Frank Robinson, Orlando Cepeda, and Willie McCovey as the only unanimous winners of the league's Rookie of the Year Award.

ATLANTA		CHICAGO		CINCINNATI		HOUSTON		LOS ANGELES		MONTREAL	
M	E.Haas	M	J.Frey	M	P.Rose	M	B.Lillis	M	T.Lasorda	M	B.Rodgers
M	B.Wine	1B	L.Durham	1B	P.Rose	1B	G.Davis	1B	G.Brock	1B	D.Driessen
1B	B.Horner	2B	R.Sandberg	2B	R.Oester	2B	B.Doran	2B	S.Sax	2B	V.Law
2B	G.Hubbard	SS	S.Dunston	SS	D.Concepcion	SS	C.Reynolds	SS	M.Duncan	SS	H.Brooks
SS	R.Ramirez	3B	R.Cey	3B	B.Bell	3B	P.Garner	3B	D.Anderson	3B	T.Wallach
3B	K.Oberkfell	LF	G.Matthews	LF	G.Redus	LF	J.Cruz	LF	C.Maldonado	LF	T.Raines
LF	T.Harper	CF	B.Dernier	CF	E.Milner	CF	K.Bass	CF	K.Landreaux	CF	H.Winningham
CF	D.Murphy	RF	K.Moreland	RF	D.Parker	RF	J.Mumphrey	RF	M.Marshall	RF	A.Dawson
RF	C.Washington	C	J.Davis	C	D.Van Gorder	C	M.Bailey	C	M.Scioscia	C	M.Fitzgerald
C	R.Cerone										
		O	T.Bosley	3O	N.Esasky	31	D.Walling	O3	P.Guerrero	1O	T.Francona
1	C.Chambliss	O	D.Lopes	O1	C.Cedeno	S	D.Thon	O	R.Reynolds	O	M.Webster
O	B.Komminsk	S3	C.Speier								
1	G.Perry			P	T.Browning	P	B.Knepper	P	F.Valenzuela	P	B.Smith
C	B.Benedict	P	D.Eckersley	P	M.Soto	P	N.Ryan	P	O.Hershiser	P	B.Gullickson
		P	R.Fontenot	P	J.Tibbs	P	M.Scott	P	J.Reuss	P	J.Hesketh
P	R.Mahler	P	S.Trout	P	R.Robinson	P	J.Niekro	P	B.Welch	P	D.Palmer
P	S.Bedrosian	P	R.Sutcliffe	P	J.Stuper	RP	B.Dawley	P	R.Honeycutt	P	D.Schatzeder
P	Z.Smith	P	S.Sanderson	RP	J.Franco	RP	D.Smith	RP	T.Niedenfuer	RP	T.Burke
RP	R.Camp	RP	L.Smith	RP	T.Power	RP	F.DiPino	RP	K.Howell	RP	J.Reardon
RP	G.Garber	RP	L.Sorensen	RP	T.Hume			RP	C.Diaz	RP	R.St.Claire
RP	B.Sutter	RP	G.Frazier			P	R.Mathis				
				P	A.McGaffigan	P	J.Calhoun	P	B.Castillo	P	F.Youmans
P	P.Perez	P	D.Ruthven	P	J.Price	P	J.Heathcock			P	G.Lucas
P	J.Dedmon	P	W.Brusstar	P	F.Pastore					P	B.Roberge
P	J.Johnson	P	J.Baller								
P	L.Barker	P	S.Engel								
P	S.Shields										
P	T.Forster										

NEW YORK		PHILADELPHIA		PITTSBURGH		SAN DIEGO		SAN FRANCISCO		ST.LOUIS	
M	D.Johnson	M	J.Felske	M	C.Tanner	M	D.Williams	M	J.Davenport	M	W.Herzog
1B	K.Hernandez	1B	M.Schmidt	1B	J.Thompson	1B	S.Garvey	M	R.Craig	1B	J.Clark
2B	W.Backman	2B	J.Samuel	2B	J.Ray	2B	T.Flannery	1B	D.Green	2B	T.Herr
SS	R.Santana	SS	S.Jeltz	SS	S.Khalifa	SS	G.Templeton	2B	M.Trillo	SS	O.Smith
3B	H.Johnson	3B	R.Schu	3B	B.Madlock	3B	G.Nettles	SS	J.Uribe	3B	T.Pendleton
LF	G.Foster	LF	V.Hayes	LF	J.Orsulak	LF	C.Martinez	3B	C.Brown	LF	V.Coleman
CF	M.Wilson	CF	G.Maddox	CF	M.Wynne	CF	K.McReynolds	LF	J.Leonard	CF	W.McGee
RF	D.Strawberry	RF	G.Wilson	RF	G.Hendrick	RF	T.Gwynn	CF	D.Gladden	RF	A.Van Slyke
C	G.Carter	C	O.Virgil	C	T.Pena	C	T.Kennedy	RF	C.Davis	C	T.Nieto
								C	B.Brenly		
O	D.Heep	1	T.Corcoran	SO	B.Almon	23	J.Royster			C	D.Porter
3	R.Knight	O	J.Stone	32	J.Morrison			O	J.Youngblood		
O	L.Dykstra	O1	J.Russell	O	S.Kemp	P	E.Show			P	J.Tudor
				O	M.Brown	P	A.Hawkins	P	D.LaPoint	P	J.Andujar
P	D.Gooden	P	J.Denny			P	D.Dravecky	P	M.Krukow	P	D.Cox
P	R.Darling	P	K.Gross	P	R.Rhoden	P	L.Hoyt	P	A.Hammaker	P	K.Kepshire
P	E.Lynch	P	S.Rawley	P	R.Reuschel	P	M.Thurmond	P	J.Gott	P	B.Forsch
P	S.Fernandez	P	C.Hudson	P	J.DeLeon	RP	C.Lefferts	P	V.Blue	RP	R.Horton
P	R.Aguilera	P	J.Koosman	P	L.Tunnell	RP	R.Gossage	RP	M.Davis	RP	J.Lahti
RP	R.McDowell	RP	D.Carman	P	L.McWilliams	RP	T.Stoddard	RP	S.Garrelts	RP	K.Dayley
RP	J.Orosco	RP	D.Rucker	RP	C.Guante			RP	G.Minton		
RP	D.Sisk	RP	L.Andersen	RP	D.Robinson					P	B.Campbell
				RP	J.Winn			P	B.Laskey		
P	T.Leach	P	S.Carlton					P	F.Williams		
P	T.Gorman	P	K.Tekulve	P	A.Holland						
				/P	B.Walk						
				P	J.Candelaria						

TEAM	G	W	L	PCT	GB	R	OR	AB	H	2B	3B	HR	BB	SO	AVG	OBP	SLG	PRO	PRO+	BR	/A	PF	CHI	RC	SB	CS	SBA	SBR
EAST																												
STL	162	101	61	.623		**747**	572	5467	1446	245	**59**	87	**586**	853	**.264**	**.338**	.379	**.717**	108	52	58	99	**105**	733	314	96	77	**37**
NY	162	98	64	.605	3	695	**568**	5549	1425	239	35	134	546	872	.257	.326	.385	.711	108	31	49	98	99	691	117	53	69	3
MON	161	84	77	.522	16.5	633	636	5429	1342	242	49	118	492	880	.247	.313	.375	.688	104	-19	17	94	101	653	169	77	69	5
CHI	162	77	84	.478	23.5	686	729	5492	1397	239	28	**150**	462	937	.254	.321	**.390**	.716	95	40	-37	111	98	710	182	49	**79**	25
PHI	162	75	87	.463	26	667	673	5477	1343	238	47	141	527	1095	.245	.314	.383	.697	97	0	-18	103	102	657	122	51	71	6
PIT	161	57	104	.354	43.5	568	708	5436	1340	251	28	80	514	842	.247	.313	.347	.660	91	-64	-58	99	97	587	110	60	63	-3
WEST																												
LA	162	95	67	.586		682	579	5502	1434	226	28	129	539	846	.261	.330	.382	.712	108	38	**59**	97	97	704	136	58	70	6
CIN	162	89	72	.553	5.5	677	666	5431	1385	249	34	114	576	856	.255	.329	.376	.705	98	26	-8	105	99	672	159	70	69	6
SD	162	83	79	.512	12	650	622	5507	1405	241	28	109	513	**809**	.255	.321	.368	.689	101	-9	1	99	100	645	60	39	61	-5
HOU	162	83	79	.512	12	706	691	5582	**1457**	**261**	42	121	473	873	.261	.322	.388	.710	107	25	45	97	103	684	96	56	63	-5
ATL	162	66	96	.407	29	632	781	5526	1359	213	28	126	553	849	.246	.317	.363	.680	91	-28	-66	106	99	622	72	52	58	-10
SF	162	62	100	.383	33	556	674	5420	1263	217	31	115	488	962	.233	.301	.348	.649	91	-93	-66	95	100	564	99	55	64	-3
TOT	971					7899		65818	16596	2861	437	1424	6373	10674	.252	.321	.374	.695							1636	716	70	61

TEAM	CG	SH	SV	IP	H	H/G	HR	BB	SO	RAT	ERA	ERA+	OAV	OOB	PR	/A	PF	CPI	FA	E	DP	FW	PW	BW	SBW	DIF
EAST																										
STL	**37**	20	44	1464	1343	8.3	**98**	453	798	11.2	3.10	114	.246	.307	79	70	98	102	**.983**	**108**	166	**1.7**	7.4	6.1	**3.4**	1.5
NY	32	19	37	1488	1306	**7.9**	111	515	**1039**	11.1	3.11	111	.237	.304	80	57	96	99	.982	115	138	1.3	6.0	5.2	-.2	4.8
MON	13	13	**53**	1457	1346	8.3	99	509	870	11.6	3.55	96	.247	.313	7	-25	94	93	.981	121	152	.8	-2.6	1.8	-.0	3.5
CHI	20	8	42	1442¹	1492	9.3	156	519	820	12.7	4.16	96	.271	.336	-91	-27	111	103	.979	134	150	.1	-2.8	-3.9	2.1	1.0
PHI	24	9	30	1447	1424	8.9	115	596	899	12.7	3.68	100	.259	.334	-15	0	103	105	.978	139	142	-.2	.0	-1.9	.0	-4.0
PIT	15	6	29	1445¹	1406	8.8	107	584	962	12.6	3.97	90	.255	.330	-61	-64	100	94	.979	133	127	.1	-6.7	-6.1	-.9	-9.9
WEST																										
LA	**37**	21	36	1465	**1280**	7.9	102	462	979	**10.8**	2.96	117	.234	.296	102	84	97	98	.974	166	131	-1.8	**8.8**	6.2	.0	.7
CIN	24	11	45	1451¹	1347	8.4	131	535	910	11.8	3.71	102	.248	.317	-19	12	105	96	.980	122	142	.8	1.3	-.8	.0	7.1
SD	26	19	44	1451¹	1399	8.7	127	443	727	11.6	3.40	104	.257	.316	30	21	98	**106**	.980	124	158	.7	2.2	1.1	-1.1	.0
HOU	17	9	42	1458	1393	8.6	119	543	909	12.1	3.66	95	.254	.324	-11	-32	96	100	.976	152	159	-1.0	-3.4	4.7	-1.1	2.7
ATL	9	9	29	1457¹	1512	9.3	134	642	776	13.5	4.19	92	.271	.349	-98	-56	107	104	.976	159	**197**	-1.4	-5.9	-6.9	-1.6	.8
SF	13	5	24	1448	1348	8.4	125	572	985	12.1	3.61	95	.247	.321	-3	-28	96	99	.976	148	134	-.7	-2.9	-6.9	-.9	-7.5
TOT	267	149	455	17474²		8.5				12.0	3.59		.252	.321					.979	1621	1796					

Runs		Hits		Doubles		Triples		Home Runs		Total Bases	
Murphy-Atl	118	McGee-StL	216	Parker-Cin	42	McGee-StL	18	Murphy-Atl	37	Parker-Cin	350
Raines-Mon	115	Parker-Cin	198	Wilson-Phi	39	Samuel-Phi	13	Parker-Cin	34	Murphy-Atl	332
McGee-StL	114	Gwynn-SD	197	Herr-StL	38	Raines-Mon	13	Schmidt-Phi	33	McGee-StL	308
Sandberg-Chi	113	Sandberg-Chi	186	Wallach-Mon	36	Garner-Hou	10	Guerrero-LA	33	Sandberg-Chi	307
Coleman-StL	107	Murphy-Atl	185			Coleman-StL	10	Carter-NY	32	Schmidt-Phi	292

Runs Batted In		Runs Produced		Bases On Balls		Batting Average		On Base Percentage		Slugging Average	
Parker-Cin	125	Herr-StL	199	Murphy-Atl	90	McGee-StL	.353	Guerrero-LA	.425	Guerrero-LA	.577
Murphy-Atl	111	Murphy-Atl	192	Schmidt-Phi	87	Guerrero-LA	.320	Scioscia-LA	.409	Parker-Cin	.551
Herr-StL	110	McGee-StL	186	Martinez-SD	87	Raines-Mon	.320	Raines-Mon	.407	Murphy-Atl	.539
Moreland-Chi	106	Parker-Cin	179	Rose-Cin	86	Gwynn-SD	.317	Rose-Cin	.398	Schmidt-Phi	.532
Wilson-Phi	102	Sandberg-Chi	170	Law-Mon	86	Parker-Cin	.312	Clark-StL	.397	Marshall-LA	.515

Production		Adjusted Production		Batter Runs		Adjusted Batter Runs		Clutch Hitting Index		Runs Created	
Guerrero-LA	1.002	Guerrero-LA	183	Guerrero-LA	52.8	Guerrero-LA	56.3	Herr-StL	161	Murphy-Atl	131
Murphy-Atl	.929	Raines-Mon	155	Murphy-Atl	47.6	Raines-Mon	43.9	Pendleton-StL	139	Raines-Mon	124
Parker-Cin	.918	Ciark-StL	151	Parker-Cin	42.5	Murphy-Atl	40.4	Moreland-Chi	128	McGee-StL	123
Schmidt-Phi	.911	McGee-StL	148	Schmidt-Phi	38.5	McGee-StL	37.6	Wilson-Phi	128	Guerrero-LA	121
Clark-StL	.899	Murphy-Atl	148	Raines-Mon	37.5	Parker-Cin	36.8	Brooks-Mon	125	Sandberg-Chi	117

Total Average		Stolen Bases		Stolen Base Average		Stolen Base Runs		Fielding Runs		Total Player Rating	
Guerrero-LA	1.086	Coleman-StL	110	Lopes-Chi	92.2	Coleman-StL	18.0	Hubbard-Atl	61.8	Raines-Mon	6.6
Raines-Mon	1.022	Raines-Mon	70	Herr-StL	91.2	Raines-Mon	15.6	Wallach-Mon	36.7	Guerrero-LA	6.3
Murphy-Atl	.960	McGee-StL	56	Raines-Mon	88.6	Lopes-Chi	11.7	McReynolds-SD	23.1	McGee-StL	5.4
Schmidt-Phi	.927	Sandberg-Chi	54	VanSlyke-StL	85.0	Sandberg-Chi	9.6	Pendleton-StL	22.7	Hubbard-Atl	5.4
McGee-StL	.920	Samuel-Phi	53	Davis-Cin	84.2	Herr-StL	7.5	Wilson-Phi	20.4	Sandberg-Chi	4.6

Wins		Win Percentage		Games		Complete Games		Shutouts		Saves	
Gooden-NY	24	Hershiser-LA	.864	Burke-Mon	78	Gooden-NY	16	Tudor-StL	10	Reardon-Mon	41
Tudor-StL	21	Gooden-NY	.857	M.Davis-SF	77	Valenzuela-LA	14	Gooden-NY	8	Smith-Chi	33
Andujar-StL	21	Smith-Mon	.783	Garrelts-SF	74	Tudor-StL	14	Valenzuela-LA	5	Smith-Hou	27
Browning-Cin	20	Darling-NY	.727	Carman-Phi	71	Cox-StL	10	Hershiser-LA	5	Power-Cin	27
Hershiser-LA	19	Tudor-StL	.724	Minton-SF	68	Andujar-StL	10			Gossage-SD	26

Innings Pitched		Fewest Hits/Game		Fewest BB/Game		Strikeouts		Strikeouts/Game		Ratio	
Gooden-NY	276.2	Fernandez-NY	5.71	Hoyt-SD	.86	Gooden-NY	268	Fernandez-NY	9.51	Tudor-StL	8.61
Tudor-StL	275.0	Gooden-NY	6.44	Eckersley-Chi	1.01	Soto-Cin	214	Gooden-NY	8.72	Gooden-NY	8.75
Valenzuela-LA	272.1	Hershiser-LA	6.72	Lynch-NY	1.27	Ryan-Hou	209	DeLeon-Pit	8.24	Eckersley-Chi	8.88
Andujar-StL	269.2	Tudor-StL	6.84	Tudor-StL	1.60	Valenzuela-LA	208	Ryan-Hou	8.11	Hershiser-LA	9.50
Mahler-Atl	266.2	Soto-Cin	6.87	Smith-Mon	1.66	Fernandez-NY	180	Soto-Cin	7.50	Smith-Mon	9.51

Earned Run Average		Adjusted ERA		Opponents' Batting Avg.		Opponents' On Base Pct.		Starter Runs		Adjusted Starter Runs	
Gooden-NY	1.53	Gooden-NY	226	Fernandez-NY	.181	Tudor-StL	.249	Gooden-NY	63.4	Gooden-NY	59.2
Tudor-StL	1.93	Tudor-StL	183	Gooden-NY	.201	Gooden-NY	.254	Tudor-StL	50.7	Tudor-StL	48.9
Hershiser-LA	2.03	Hershiser-LA	171	Hershiser-LA	.206	Eckersley-Chi	.255	Hershiser-LA	41.6	Hershiser-LA	38.5
Reuschel-Pit	2.27	Reuschel-Pit	157	Tudor-StL	.209	Hershiser-LA	.268	Valenzuela-LA	34.6	Valenzuela-LA	31.2
Welch-LA	2.31	Welch-LA	150	Soto-Cin	.211	Smith-Mon	.269	Reuschel-Pit	28.4	Reuschel-Pit	28.1

Clutch Pitching Index		Relief Runs		Adjusted Relief Runs		Relief Ranking		Total Pitcher Index		Total Baseball Ranking	
Darling-NY	120	Burke-Mon	16.0	Franco-Cin	17.6	Franco-Cin	28.1	Gooden-NY	7.3	Gooden-NY	7.3
Hawkins-SD	119	Gossage-SD	15.5	Carman-Phi	15.3	Smith-Hou	23.6	Tudor-StL	5.5	Raines-Mon	6.6
Show-SD	119	Franco-Cin	15.5	Gossage-SD	15.0	Gossage-SD	23.2	Hershiser-LA	4.2	Guerrero-LA	6.3
Reuss-LA	115	Garrelts-SF	15.2	Garrelts-SF	13.3	Carman-Phi	23.1	Reuschel-Pit	4.0	Tudor-StL	5.5
Gooden-NY	115	Carman-Phi	14.4	Burke-Mon	13.3	Power-Cin	21.4	Valenzuela-LA	3.6	McGee-StL	5.4

January 7 Lou Brock and Hoyt Wilhelm are elected to the Hall of Fame.

March 6 Enos Slaughter and Arky Vaughan are elected to the Hall of Fame by the Special Veterans Committee.

June 3 The Brewers select University of North Carolina catcher B. J. Surhoff with the first pick in what will prove to be an extremely fruitful free-agent draft. Fellow Olympians Will Clark (Mississippi State), Bobby Witt (University of Oklahoma), and Barry Larkin (University of Michigan) are drafted second, third, and fourth by the Giants, Rangers, and Reds, respectively.

October 6 Phil Niekro finally wins his 300th career game 8-0 over the Blue Jays on the final day of the regular season. At 46, he is the oldest hurler ever to pitch a complete-game shutout.

October 16 Baseball gets its first intrastate World Series since 1974, as the Royals and Cardinals win their respective playoff series. Kansas City beats Toronto 6-2 in Game 7 of the ALCS to cap a comeback from a deficit of three games to one.

October 22 Bret Saberhagen gives Kansas City its first World Series win with a 6-1 win.

October 26 Aided by a blown call, a bungled pop-up, and a passed ball, Kansas City scores two runs in the bottom of the ninth to beat St. Louis 2-1 and even the World Series at three games apiece. The Cardinals are three outs away from a championship when Jorge Orta reaches base on a disputed infield single. The next batter, Steve Balboni, lofts a foul pop that Jack Clark lets fall untouched, then singles. After Darrell Porter's passed ball puts runners on second and third, and Hal McRae is intentionally walked to load the bases, pinch hitter Dane Iorg singles home two runs to end the game.

October 27 The Royals rout the Cardinals 11-0 in Game 7 to become only the sixth team to rally from a three games to one deficit and win the World Series. Series MVP Bret Saberhagen pitches the shutout while Cardinals ace John Tudor allows five runs in $2\frac{1}{3}$ innings, and fellow 20-game winner Joaquin Andujar is ejected for arguing balls and strikes during Kansas City's six-run fifth inning. The Cardinals finish the World Series with a .185 team batting average, lowest ever for a seven-game Series.

October 27 Billy Martin is fired by the Yankees for an unprecedented fourth time and is replaced by former Yankees outfielder Lou Piniella, who had been the team's hitting instructor since retiring as a player in 1984.

November 20 Don Mattingly of the Yankees easily wins the AL MVP Award, becoming the first player from a non-championship team to do so since 1978.

BALTIMORE

Pos	Player
M	J.Altobelli
M	C.Ripken
M	E.Weaver
1B	E.Murray
2B	A.Wiggins
SS	C.Ripken
3B	F.Rayford
LF	M.Young
CF	F.Lynn
RF	L.Lacy
C	R.Dempsey
DH	L.Sheets
O	J.Dwyer
3D	W.Gross
OD	G.Roenicke
23	R.Dauer
O	J.Shelby
P	S.McGregor
P	M.Boddicker
P	D.Martinez
P	S.Davis
P	K.Dixon
RP	S.Stewart
RP	N.Snell
RP	D.Aase
P	M.Flanagan
P	T.Martinez

BOSTON

Pos	Player
M	J.McNamara
1B	B.Buckner
2B	M.Barrett
SS	J.Gutierrez
3B	W.Boggs
LF	J.Rice
CF	S.Lyons
RF	D.Evans
C	R.Gedman
DH	M.Easler
OD	T.Armas
S	G.Hoffman
P	O.Boyd
P	B.Hurst
P	A.Nipper
P	B.Ojeda
RP	S.Crawford
RP	B.Stanley
RP	M.Clear
P	R.Clemens
P	B.Kison
P	M.Trujillo
P	T.Lollar

CALIFORNIA

Pos	Player
M	G.Mauch
1B	R.Carew
2B	B.Grich
SS	D.Schofield
3B	D.DeCinces
LF	B.Downing
CF	G.Pettis
RF	R.Jones
C	B.Boone
DH	R.Jackson
O1	J.Beniquez
2	R.Wilfong
P	M.Witt
P	R.Romanick
P	K.McCaskill
P	J.Slaton
RP	D.Moore
RP	S.Cliburn
RP	P.Clements
P	U.Lugo
P	J.Candelaria
P	L.Sanchez

CHICAGO

Pos	Player
M	T.LaRussa
1B	G.Walker
2B	J.Cruz
SS	O.Guillen
3B	T.Hulett
LF	R.Law
CF	D.Boston
RF	H.Baines
C	C.Fisk
DH	R.Kittle
3S	S.Fletcher
O3	L.Salazar
P	T.Seaver
P	B.Burns
P	F.Bannister
P	G.Nelson
RP	B.James
RP	D.Spillner
RP	J.Agosto
P	T.Lollar
P	J.Davis
/P	R.Dotson

CLEVELAND

Pos	Player
M	P.Corrales
1B	P.Tabler
2B	T.Bernazard
SS	J.Franco
3B	B.Jacoby
LF	J.Carter
CF	B.Butler
RF	G.Vukovich
C	J.Willard
DH	A.Thornton
1	M.Hargrove
OD	O.Nixon
P	N.Heaton
P	B.Blyleven
RP	V.Ruhle
RP	T.Waddell
RP	J.Easterly
P	D.Schulze
P	R.Thompson
P	J.Reed
P	C.Wardle
P	R.Romero
P	B.Clark
P	K.Creel
P	R.Smith

DETROIT

Pos	Player
M	S.Anderson
1B	D.Evans
2B	L.Whitaker
SS	A.Trammell
3B	T.Brookens
LF	L.Herndon
CF	C.Lemon
RF	K.Gibson
C	L.Parrish
DH	J.Grubb
OD	N.Simmons
1O	B.Garbey
P	J.Morris
P	D.Petry
P	W.Terrell
P	F.Tanana
RP	W.Hernandez
RP	A.Lopez
RP	B.Scherrer
P	J.Berenguer
P	R.O'Neal

KANSAS CITY

Pos	Player
M	D.Howser
1B	S.Balboni
2B	F.White
SS	O.Concepcion
3B	G.Brett
LF	L.Smith
CF	W.Wilson
RF	D.Motley
C	J.Sundberg
DH	H.McRae
O	L.Jones
D	J.Orta
O	P.Sheridan
P	C.Leibrandt
P	B.Saberhagen
P	D.Jackson
P	B.Black
P	M.Gubicza
RP	D.Quisenberry
RP	J.Beckwith
RP	M.Jones

MILWAUKEE

Pos	Player
M	G.Bamberger
1B	C.Cooper
2B	J.Gantner
SS	E.Riles
3B	P.Molitor
LF	B.Oglivie
CF	R.Yount
RF	P.Householder
C	C.Moore
DH	T.Simmons
S2	E.Romero
O	R.Manning
P	D.Darwin
P	T.Higuera
P	R.Burris
P	M.Haas
P	J.Cocanower
RP	B.Gibson
RP	B.McClure
RP	R.Fingers
P	P.Vuckovich

MINNESOTA

Pos	Player
M	B.Gardner
M	R.Miller
1B	K.Hrbek
2B	T.Teufel
SS	G.Gagne
3B	G.Gaetti
LF	M.Hatcher
CF	K.Puckett
RF	T.Brunansky
C	M.Salas
DH	R.Smalley
OD	R.Bush
P	M.Smithson
P	F.Viola
P	J.Butcher
P	K.Schrom
P	B.Blyleven
RP	P.Filson
RP	R.Davis
RP	F.Eufemia
P	R.Lysander

NEW YORK

Pos	Player
M	Y.Berra
M	B.Martin
1B	D.Mattingly
2B	W.Randolph
SS	B.Meacham
3B	M.Pagliarulo
LF	K.Griffey
CF	R.Henderson
C	D.Winfield
DH	B.Wynegar
DH	D.Baylor
C	R.Hassey
P	R.Guidry
P	P.Niekro
P	J.Cowley
P	E.Whitson
P	D.Rasmussen
RP	B.Shirley
RP	D.Righetti
RP	B.Fisher
P	R.Bordi

OAKLAND

Pos	Player
M	J.Moore
1B	B.Bochte
2B	D.Hill
SS	A.Griffin
3B	C.Lansford
LF	D.Collins
CF	D.Murphy
RF	M.Davis
C	M.Heath
DH	D.Kingman
1O	D.Baker
C	M.Tettleton
P	C.Codiroli
P	D.Sutton
P	B.Krueger
P	T.Birtsas
RP	K.Atherton
RP	J.Howell
RP	S.McCatty
P	S.Ontiveros
P	J.Rijo
P	R.Langford

SEATTLE

Pos	Player
M	C.Cottier
1B	A.Davis
2B	J.Perconte
SS	S.Owen
3B	J.Presley
LF	P.Bradley
CF	D.Henderson
RF	A.Cowens
C	B.Kearney
DH	G.Thomas
O	I.Calderon
P	M.Moore
P	M.Young
P	M.Langston
P	F.Wills
P	B.Swift
RP	R.Thomas
RP	E.Nunez
RP	E.Vande Berg
P	J.Beattie
P	S.Barojas

TEXAS

Pos	Player
M	D.Rader
M	B.Valentine
1B	P.O'Brien
2B	T.Harrah
SS	C.Wilkerson
3B	B.Bell
LF	G.Ward
CF	O.McDowell
RF	G.Wright
C	D.Slaught
DH	C.Johnson
S2	W.Tolleson
OD	L.Parrish
3	S.Buechele
P	C.Hough
P	M.Mason
P	B.Hooton
P	D.Noles
RP	G.Harris
RP	D.Rozema
RP	D.Schmidt
P	D.Stewart
P	F.Tanana
P	C.Welsh
P	J.Russell

TORONTO

Pos	Player
M	B.Cox
1B	W.Upshaw
2B	D.Garcia
SS	T.Fernandez
3B	R.Mulliniks
LF	G.Bell
CF	J.Moseby
RF	J.Barfield
C	E.Whitt
DH	J.Burroughs
32	G.Iorg
P	D.Stieb
P	D.Alexander
P	J.Key
P	J.Clancy
RP	D.Lamp
RP	J.Acker
RP	G.Lavelle
P	B.Caudill
P	L.Leal
P	R.Musselman

TEAM	G	W	L	PCT	GB	R	OR	AB	H	2B	3B	HR	BB	SO	AVG	OBP	SLG	PRO	PRO+	BR	/A	PF	CHI	RC	SB	CS	SBA	SBR
EAST																												
TOR	161	99	62	.615		759	588	5508	1482	281	53	158	503	807	.269	.334	.425	.759	103	43	24	103	98	767	144	77	65	-3
NY	161	97	64	.602	2	839	660	5458	1458	272	31	176	620	771	.267	.347	.425	.772	113	82	102	98	102	821	155	53	75	15
DET	161	84	77	.522	15	729	688	5575	1413	254	45	202	526	926	.253	.321	.424	.745	103	8	13	99	97	765	75	41	65	-2
BAL	161	83	78	.516	16	818	764	5517	1451	234	22	214	604	908	.263	.338	.430	.768	112	64	86	97	102	794	69	43	62	-5
BOS	163	81	81	.500	18.5	800	720	5720	1615	292	31	162	562	816	.282	.350	.429	.779	108	96	61	104	93	844	66	27	71	4
MIL	161	71	90	.441	28	690	802	5568	1467	250	44	101	462	746	.263	.322	.379	.701	94	-68	-65	100	103	666	69	34	67	0
CLE	162	60	102	.370	39.5	729	861	5527	1465	254	31	116	492	817	.265	.327	.385	.712	95	-44	-39	99	106	681	132	72	65	-4
WEST																												
KC	162	91	71	.562		687	639	5500	1384	261	49	154	473	840	.252	.315	.401	.716	94	-47	-49	100	101	687	128	48	73	10
CAL	162	90	72	.556	1	732	703	5442	1364	215	31	153	648	902	.251	.335	.386	.721	97	-17	-13	100	100	711	106	51	68	1
CHI	163	85	77	.525	6	736	720	5470	1386	247	37	146	471	843	.253	.318	.392	.710	90	-55	-81	104	110	674	108	56	66	-1
MIN	162	77	85	.475	14	705	782	5509	1453	282	41	141	502	779	.264	.329	.407	.736	95	-1	-43	106	97	729	68	44	61	-6
OAK	162	77	85	.475	14	757	787	5581	1475	230	34	155	508	861	.264	.327	.401	.728	106	-15	39	93	104	725	117	58	67	0
SEA	162	74	88	.457	17	719	818	5521	1410	277	38	171	564	942	.255	.328	.412	.740	100	7	3	101	96	739	94	35	73	7
TEX	161	62	99	.385	28.5	617	785	5361	1359	213	41	129	530	819	.253	.324	.381	.705	91	-54	-63	101	93	652	130	76	63	-7
TOT	1132					10317		77257	20182	3562	528	2178	7465	11777	.261	.330	.406	.735							1461	715	67	9

TEAM	CG	SH	SV	IP	H	H/G	HR	BB	SO	RAT	ERA	ERA+	OAV	OOB	PR	/A	PF	CPI	FA	E	DP	FW	PW	BW	SBW	DIF
EAST																										
TOR	18	9	47	1448	1312	8.2	147	484	823	11.3	3.31	127	.243	.308	135	145	102	107	.980	125	164	.2	14.3	2.4	-.4	1.9
NY	25	9	49	1440¹	1373	8.6	157	518	907	11.9	3.69	109	.251	.318	74	50	97	104	.979	126	172	.2	4.9	10.1	1.4	-.1
DET	31	11	40	1456	1313	8.1	141	556	943	11.7	3.78	108	.240	.313	59	47	98	94	.977	143	152	-.8	4.6	1.3	-.3	-1.4
BAL	32	6	33	1427¹	1480	9.3	160	568	793	13.1	4.38	92	.270	.341	-36	-55	97	102	.979	129	168	-.0	-5.4	8.5	-.6	.0
BOS	35	8	29	1461¹	1487	9.2	130	540	913	12.7	4.06	106	.265	.333	14	37	103	101	.977	145	161	-.8	3.7	6.0	.3	-9.2
MIL	34	5	37	1437	1510	9.5	175	499	777	12.8	4.39	95	.271	.334	-39	-36	100	101	.977	142	153	-.7	-3.6	-6.4	-.0	1.3
CLE	24	7	28	1421	1556	9.9	170	547	702	13.6	4.91	84	.281	.350	-121	-123	100	98	.977	141	161	-.6	-12.2	-3.9	-.5	-3.9
WEST																										
KC	27	11	41	1461	1433	8.8	103	463	846	11.9	3.49	119	.257	.317	107	109	100	103	.980	127	160	.1	10.8	-4.8	.9	3.0
CAL	22	8	41	1457¹	1453	9.0	171	514	767	12.3	3.91	105	.263	.328	38	32	99	108	.982	112	202	1.0	3.2	-1.3	.0	6.1
CHI	20	8	39	1451²	1411	8.7	161	569	1023	12.5	4.07	106	.256	.330	13	40	104	101	.982	111	152	1.1	4.0	-8.0	-.2	7.1
MIN	41	7	34	1426¹	1468	9.3	164	462	767	12.4	4.48	98	.268	.329	-53	-11	106	95	.980	120	139	.5	-1.1	-4.3	-.7	1.5
OAK	10	6	41	1453	1451	9.0	172	607	785	12.4	4.41	87	.259	.334	-43	-89	93	97	.977	140	137	-.6	-8.8	3.9	-.0	1.6
SEA	23	8	30	1432	1456	9.2	154	637	868	13.4	4.68	90	.265	.346	-84	-74	102	96	.980	122	156	.4	-7.3	.3	.6	-1.0
TEX	18	5	33	1411²	1479	9.4	173	501	863	12.9	4.56	93	.269	.334	-65	-52	102	97	.980	120	145	.5	-5.1	-6.2	-.8	-6.9
TOT	360	108	522	20184		9.0				12.5	4.15		.261	.330					.979	1803	2222					

Runs
Henderson-NY 146
Ripken-Bal 116
Murray-Bal 111
Evans-Bos 110
Brett-KC 108

Hits
Boggs-Bos 240
Mattingly-NY ... 211
Buckner-Bos 201
Puckett-Min 199
Baines-Chi 198

Doubles
Mattingly-NY ... 48
Buckner-Bos 46
Boggs-Bos 42
Cooper-Mil 39

Triples
Wilson-KC 21
Butler-Cle 14
Puckett-Min 13
Fernandez-Tor .. 10

Home Runs
Evans-Det 40
Fisk-Chi 37
Balboni-KC 36
Mattingly-NY ... 35
G.Thomas-Sea ... 32

Total Bases
Mattingly-NY ... 370
Brett-KC 322
Bradley-Sea 319
Boggs-Bos 312
Murray-Bal 305

Runs Batted In
Mattingly-NY ... 145
Murray-Bal 124
Winfield-NY 114
Baines-Chi 113
Brett-KC 112

Runs Produced
Mattingly-NY ... 217
Murray-Bal 204
Ripken-Bal 200
Henderson-NY ... 194
Winfield-NY 193

Bases On Balls
Evans-Bos 114
Harrah-Tex 113
Brett-KC 103
Henderson-NY ... 99
Boggs-Bos 96

Batting Average
Boggs-Bos ...... .368
Brett-KC .... .335
Mattingly-NY ... .324
Henderson-NY ... .314
Butler-Cle ..... .311

On Base Percentage
Boggs-Bos ...... .452
Brett-KC .... .442
Harrah-Tex ..... .437
Henderson-NY ... .422
Murray-Bal ..... .387

Slugging Average
Brett-KC .... .585
Mattingly-NY ... .567
Barfield-Tor ... .536
Murray-Bal ..... .523
Evans-Det ...... .519

Production
Brett-KC 1.028
Mattingly-NY ... .946
Henderson-NY ... .938
Boggs-Bos ...... .929
Murray-Bal ..... .910

Adjusted Production
Brett-KC 178
Henderson-NY ... 159
Mattingly-NY ... 159
Murray-Bal 150
Boggs-Bos 149

Batter Runs
Brett-KC 63.4
Boggs-Bos 54.8
Mattingly-NY ... 47.5
Henderson-NY ... 45.5
Murray-Bal 38.4

Adjusted Batter Runs
Brett-KC 63.0
Mattingly-NY ... 50.8
Boggs-Bos 48.9
Henderson-NY ... 48.5
Murray-Bal 41.6

Clutch Hitting Index
Franco-Cle 137
Meacham-NY 137
Mattingly-NY ... 132
Boone-Cal 130
Thornton-Cle ... 125

Runs Created
Brett-KC 146
Boggs-Bos 143
Henderson-NY ... 138
Mattingly-NY ... 136
Murray-Bal 122

Total Average
Henderson-NY .. 1.155
Brett-KC 1.150
Gibson-Det ..... .953
Boggs-Bos ...... .952
Murray-Bal ..... .938

Stolen Bases
Henderson-NY ... 80
Pettis-Cal 56
Butler-Cle 47
Wilson-KC 43
Smith-KC 40

Stolen Base Average
Perconte-Sea ... 93.9
Henderson-NY ... 88.9
Gibson-Det 88.2
Pettis-Cal 86.2
Smith-KC 85.1

Stolen Base Runs
Henderson-NY ... 18.0
Pettis-Cal 11.4
Perconte-Sea ... 8.1
Smith-KC 7.8
Gibson-Det 6.6

Fielding Runs
Owen-Sea 30.3
Buckner-Bos 25.4
Barfield-Tor ... 21.9
Butler-Cle 21.8
Puckett-Min 21.2

Total Player Rating
Henderson-NY ... 7.4
Brett-KC 7.2
Boggs-Bos 5.3
Barfield-Tor ... 4.8
Murray-Bal 4.4

Wins
Guidry-NY 22
Saberhagen-KC .. 20
Viola-Min 18
Burns-Chi 18

Win Percentage
Guidry-NY ...... .786
Saberhagen-KC .. .769
Leibrandt-KC ... .654
Higuera-Mil .... .652

Games
Quisenberry-KC . 84
VandeBerg-Sea .. 76
Righetti-NY 74
Hernandez-Det .. 74
Nunez-Sea 70

Complete Games
Blyleven-Cle-Min . 24
Moore-Sea 14
Hough-Tex 14
Morris-Det 13
Boyd-Bos 13

Shutouts
Blyleven-Cle-Min . 5
Morris-Det 4
Burns-Chi 4

Saves
Quisenberry-KC . 37
James-Chi 32
Moore-Cal 31
Hernandez-Det .. 31

Innings Pitched
Blyleven-Cle-Min .293.2
Boyd-Bos 272.1
Stieb-Tor 265.0
Alexander-Tor . 260.2
Guidry-NY 259.0

Fewest Hits/Game
Stieb-Tor 7.00
Hough-Tex 7.12
Petry-Det 7.16
Morris-Det 7.42
Higuera-Mil 7.88

Fewest BB/Game
Haas-Mil 1.39
Saberhagen-KC .. 1.45
Guidry-NY 1.46
Butcher-Min 1.86
Key-Tor 2.12

Strikeouts
Blyleven-Cle-Min . 206
Bannister-Chi .. 198
Morris-Det 191
Hurst-Bos 189
Witt-Cal 180

Strikeouts/Game
Bannister-Chi .. 8.46
Hurst-Bos 7.42
Burns-Chi 6.82
Morris-Det 6.69
Tanana-Tex-Det . 6.66

Ratio
Saberhagen-KC .. 9.56
Guidry-NY 9.90
Key-Tor 10.16
Petry-Det 10.33
Hough-Tex 10.35

Earned Run Average
Stieb-Tor 2.48
Leibrandt-KC ... 2.69
Saberhagen-KC .. 2.87
Key-Tor 3.00
Blyleven-Cle-Min . 3.16

Adjusted ERA
Stieb-Tor 170
Leibrandt-KC ... 155
Saberhagen-KC .. 145
Key-Tor 140
Seaver-Chi 136

Opponents' Batting Avg.
Stieb-Tor ...... .213
Hough-Tex ...... .215
Petry-Det ...... .217
Morris-Det ..... .225
Higuera-Mil .... .235

Opponents' On Base Pct.
Saberhagen-KC .. .273
Guidry-NY ...... .279
Key-Tor .... .284
Hough-Tex ...... .285
Petry-Det ...... .285

Starter Runs
Stieb-Tor 49.1
Leibrandt-KC ... 38.5
Saberhagen-KC .. 33.4
Blyleven-Cle-Min . 32.3
Key-Tor 27.0

Adjusted Starter Runs
Stieb-Tor 50.9
Leibrandt-KC ... 38.8
Blyleven-Cle-Min . 35.4
Saberhagen-KC .. 33.8
Seaver-Chi 30.5

Clutch Pitching Index
Leibrandt-KC ... 121
Romanick-Cal ... 117
Boddicker-Bal .. 115
Alexander-Tor .. 114
Stieb-Tor 112

Relief Runs
Moore-Cal 25.5
Quisenberry-KC . 25.4
James-Chi 24.7
Cliburn-Cal 22.6
Harris-Tex 21.1

Adjusted Relief Runs
James-Chi 26.8
Quisenberry-KC . 25.6
Moore-Cal 25.0
Cliburn-Cal 22.2
Harris-Tex 22.1

Relief Ranking
Moore-Cal 49.7
James-Chi 48.0
Quisenberry-KC . 44.7
Hernandez-Det .. 33.9
Righetti-NY 31.0

Total Pitcher Index
Stieb-Tor 5.5
Moore-Cal 5.1
James-Chi 4.8
Quisenberry-KC . 4.6
Leibrandt-KC ... 4.5

Total Baseball Ranking
Henderson-NY ... 7.4
Brett-KC 7.2
Stieb-Tor 5.5
Boggs-Bos 5.3
Moore-Cal 5.1

January 8 Willie McCovey is the only player elected this year to the Hall of Fame by the BBWAA.

March 10 Ernie Lombardi, the NL MVP in 1938, and Bobby Doerr, a nine-time AL All-Star, are elected to the Hall of Fame by the Special Veterans Committee.

June 7 The Pirates take University of Arkansas's Jeff King as the first choice in the June draft. Gregg Swindell is the next pick and will be in the majors after just three starts in the minors.

June 10 The NL announces that Yale University president A. Bartlett Giamatti will be its next president, after Chub Feeney's retirement in December.

July 6 Bob Horner becomes the 11th player to hit four home runs in a game, but it isn't enough as the Braves fall to the Expos 11-8.

September 17 The Mets clinch the NL East Championship with a 4-2 win over the Cubs at Shea Stadium as Dwight Gooden tosses a six-hitter. The Mets will win 108 games this season, the most in the league since the 1975 Reds.

September 25 Houston's Mike Scott pitches a 2-0 no-hitter against the Giants at the Astrodome, clinching the NL West title for the Astros. It's the first time a pennant has ever been decided by a no-hitter, and the third consecutive game in which Astros pitchers have allowed two hits or less.

October 2 Mike Scott strikes out eight Giants in a 2-1 Astros victory to run his season total to 306, joining Sandy Koufax and J. R. Richard as the only NL pitchers up to this date to fan 300 batters in one season. Scott loses his bid for a second consecutive no-hitter when Will Clark doubles in the seventh inning.

October 15 In the longest game in post-season history, the Mets beat the Astros 7-6 in 16 innings to earn their first trip to the World Series since 1973. New York scores three runs in the top of the ninth to force extra innings. The Mets score three more runs in the top of the 16th and Houston answers with two of its own before Jesse Orosco fans Kevin Bass to end the game.

October 25 Trailing 5-3 with two out and no one on base in the bottom of the 10th inning, New York rallies to win Game 6 of the World Series 6-5 and force a deciding seventh game. After Gary Carter, Kevin Mitchell, and Ray Knight single, Bob Stanley uncorks a wild pitch that permits the tying run to score, and a hobbled Bill Buckner lets Mookie Wilson's slow bouncer skip through his legs, allowing Knight to score the winning run for the Mets.

October 27 The Mets win Game 7 of the World Series 8-5 at Shea Stadium. Third baseman Ray Knight, whose home run triggers a three-run rally in the seventh inning, is named MVP.

November 11 Houston's Mike Scott (18-10) beats Fernando Valenzuela (21-11) for the NL Cy Young Award.

November 19 Phillies third baseman Mike Schmidt wins the NL MVP Award, joining Stan Musial and Roy Campanella as the only three-time winners. Schmidt led the NL with 37 home runs and 119 RBI.

ATLANTA

Pos	Player
M	C.Tanner
1B	B.Horner
2B	G.Hubbard
SS	A.Thomas
3B	K.Oberkfell
LF	T.Harper
CF	D.Murphy
RF	O.Moreno
C	O.Virgil
1	C.Chambliss
S3	R.Ramirez
O	K.Griffey
O	B.Sample
P	R.Mahler
P	D.Palmer
P	Z.Smith
P	D.Alexander
RP	J.Dedmon
RP	C.McMurtry
RP	G.Garber
P	J.Acker
P	J.Johnson
P	P.Assenmacher

CHICAGO

Pos	Player
M	J.Frey
M	J.Vukovich
M	G.Michael
1B	L.Durham
2B	R.Sandberg
SS	S.Dunston
3B	R.Cey
LF	G.Matthews
CF	B.Dernier
RF	K.Moreland
C	J.Davis
O	J.Mumphrey
P	D.Eckersley
P	R.Sutcliffe
P	S.Sanderson
P	S.Trout
P	E.Lynch
RP	L.Smith
RP	G.Hoffman
RP	D.Gumpert
P	J.Moyer
P	R.Fontenot
P	J.Baller
P	G.Frazier

CINCINNATI

Pos	Player
M	P.Rose
1B	N.Esasky
2B	R.Oester
SS	K.Stillwell
3B	B.Bell
LF	E.Davis
CF	E.Milner
RF	D.Parker
C	B.Diaz
O	M.Venable
S1	D.Concepcion
1	P.Rose
1	T.Perez
P	B.Gullickson
P	T.Browning
P	J.Denny
P	C.Welsh
P	M.Soto
RP	T.Power
RP	R.Robinson
RP	J.Franco
P	S.Terry
P	C.Willis
P	R.Murphy

HOUSTON

Pos	Player
M	H.Lanier
1B	G.Davis
2B	B.Doran
SS	D.Thon
3B	D.Walling
LF	J.Cruz
CF	B.Hatcher
RF	K.Bass
C	A.Ashby
3	P.Garner
S	C.Reynolds
P	M.Scott
P	B.Knepper
P	N.Ryan
P	J.Deshaies
RP	C.Kerfeld
RP	A.Lopez
RP	L.Andersen
P	D.Smith
P	D.Darwin

LOS ANGELES

Pos	Player
M	T.Lasorda
1B	G.Brock
2B	S.Sax
SS	M.Duncan
3B	B.Madlock
LF	F.Stubbs
CF	R.Williams
RF	M.Marshall
C	M.Scioscia
1O	E.Cabell
O	K.Landreaux
OS	B.Russell
3S	D.Anderson
C	A.Trevino
P	F.Valenzuela
P	B.Welch
P	O.Hershiser
P	R.Honeycutt
RP	K.Howell
RP	T.Niedenfuer
RP	E.Vande Berg
P	J.Reuss
P	A.Pena
P	D.Powell

MONTREAL

Pos	Player
M	B.Rodgers
1B	A.Galarraga
2B	V.Law
SS	H.Brooks
3B	T.Wallach
LF	T.Raines
CF	M.Webster
RF	A.Dawson
C	D.Bilardello
13	W.Krenchicki
C	M.Fitzgerald
S2	T.Foley
P	F.Youmans
P	J.Tibbs
P	B.Smith
P	D.Martinez
RP	A.McGaffigan
RP	T.Burke
RP	J.Reardon
P	B.Sebra
P	J.Hesketh
P	B.McClure
P	D.Schatzeder

NEW YORK

Pos	Player
M	D.Johnson
1B	K.Hernandez
2B	W.Backman
SS	R.Santana
3B	R.Knight
LF	M.Wilson
CF	L.Dykstra
RF	D.Strawberry
C	G.Carter
OS	K.Mitchell
2	T.Teufel
O	G.Foster
3S	H.Johnson
P	D.Gooden
P	R.Darling
P	B.Ojeda
P	S.Fernandez
P	R.Aguilera
RP	R.McDowell
RP	J.Orosco
RP	D.Sisk
P	R.Anderson

PHILADELPHIA

Pos	Player
M	J.Felske
1B	V.Hayes
2B	J.Samuel
SS	S.Jeltz
3B	M.Schmidt
LF	G.Redus
CF	M.Thompson
RF	G.Wilson
C	J.Russell
O	R.Roenicke
O	J.Stone
3	R.Schu
P	K.Gross
P	S.Rawley
P	B.Ruffin
P	C.Hudson
RP	D.Carman
RP	K.Tekulve
RP	T.Hume
P	S.Bedrosian
P	S.Carlton
P	M.Maddux

PITTSBURGH

Pos	Player
M	J.Leyland
1B	S.Bream
2B	J.Ray
SS	R.Belliard
3B	J.Morrison
LF	R.Reynolds
CF	B.Bonds
RF	J.Orsulak
C	T.Pena
O3	B.Almon
O1	M.Diaz
O	M.Brown
P	R.Rhoden
P	R.Reuschel
P	M.Bielecki
P	B.Walk
P	B.Kipper
RP	L.McWilliams
RP	J.Winn
RP	C.Guante
P	D.Robinson
P	P.Clements

SAN DIEGO

Pos	Player
M	S.Boros
1B	S.Garvey
2B	T.Flannery
SS	G.Templeton
3B	G.Nettles
LF	K.McReynolds
CF	M.Wynne
RF	T.Gwynn
C	T.Kennedy
O	J.Kruk
O1	C.Martinez
2	B.Roberts
3S	J.Royster
P	A.Hawkins
P	D.Dravecky
P	L.Hoyt
P	E.Show
RP	L.McCullers
RP	C.Lefferts
RP	G.Walter
P	E.Whitson
P	M.Thurmond
P	R.Gossage
P	D.LaPoint

SAN FRANCISCO

Pos	Player
M	R.Craig
1B	W.Clark
2B	R.Thompson
SS	J.Uribe
3B	C.Brown
LF	C.Maldonado
CF	D.Gladden
RF	C.Davis
C	B.Brenly
O	J.Youngblood
O	J.Leonard
C	B.Melvin
1O	M.Aldrete
P	M.Krukow
P	M.LaCoss
P	S.Garrelts
P	V.Blue
RP	J.Robinson
RP	M.Davis
RP	J.Berenguer
P	K.Downs
P	G.Minton
P	R.Mason
P	T.Mulholland
P	F.Williams

ST. LOUIS

Pos	Player
M	W.Herzog
1B	J.Clark
2B	T.Herr
SS	O.Smith
3B	T.Pendleton
LF	V.Coleman
CF	W.McGee
RF	A.Van Slyke
C	M.LaValliere
O	C.Ford
O	T.Landrum
P	B.Forsch
P	D.Cox
P	J.Tudor
P	G.Mathews
P	T.Conroy
RP	T.Worrell
RP	R.Horton
RP	P.Perry
P	R.Burris

TEAM	G	W	L	PCT	GB	R	OR	AB	H	2B	3B	HR	BB	SO	AVG	OBP	SLG	PRO	PRO+	BR	/A	PF	CHI	RC	SB	CS	SBA	SBR
EAST																												
NY	162	108	54	.667		**783**	578	5558	**1462**	261	31	148	**631**	968	**.263**	**.341**	**.401**	**.742**	**114**	**84**	**107**	97	101	**773**	118	48	71	7
PHI	161	86	75	.534	21.5	739	713	5483	1386	266	39	154	589	1154	.253	.330	.400	.730	103	50	24	104	101	739	153	59	72	11
STL	161	79	82	.491	28.5	601	611	5378	1270	216	48	58	568	905	.236	.311	.327	.638	83	-119	-114	99	**109**	584	**262**	78	**77**	**32**
MON	161	78	83	.484	29.5	637	688	5508	1401	255	**50**	110	537	1016	.254	.324	.379	.703	101	-1	5	99	94	676	193	95	67	1
CHI	160	70	90	.438	37	680	781	5499	1409	258	27	**155**	508	966	.256	.321	.398	.719	96	21	-33	108	98	697	132	62	68	2
PIT	162	64	98	.395	44	663	700	5456	1366	**273**	33	111	569	929	.250	.323	.374	.697	96	-12	-27	102	100	654	152	84	64	-5
WEST																												
HOU	162	96	66	.593		654	**569**	5441	1388	244	32	125	536	916	.255	.325	.381	.706	104	3	22	97	98	668	163	75	68	4
CIN	162	86	76	.531	10	732	717	5536	1404	237	35	144	586	920	.254	.327	.387	.714	99	21	-9	104	104	712	177	53	**77**	21
SF	162	83	79	.512	13	698	618	5501	1394	269	29	114	536	1087	.253	.324	.375	.699	104	-9	24	95	104	674	148	93	61	-11
SD	162	74	88	.457	22	656	723	5515	1442	239	25	136	484	917	.261	.323	.388	.711	104	9	23	98	97	671	96	68	59	-12
LA	162	73	89	.451	23	638	679	5471	1373	232	14	130	478	966	.251	.315	.370	.685	102	-42	2	93	102	639	155	67	70	6
ATL	161	72	89	.447	23.5	615	719	5384	1348	241	24	138	538	**904**	.250	.321	.381	.702	94	-5	-42	106	93	646	93	76	55	-18
TOT	969					8096		65730	16643	2991	387	1523	6560	11648	.253	.324	.380	.704							1842	858	68	38

TEAM	CG	SH	SV	IP	H	H/G	HR	BB	SO	RAT	ERA	ERA+	OAV	OOB	PR	/A	PF	CPI	FA	E	DP	FW	PW	BW	SBW	DIF
EAST																										
NY	27	11	46	1484	1304	7.9	**103**	509	1083	11.2	**3.11**	**114**	.236	.304	**100**	70	95	98	.978	138	145	.1	7.3	**11.1**	.4	8.1
PHI	22	11	39	1451[2]	1473	9.1	130	553	874	12.7	3.85	100	.265	.334	-22	0	104	105	.978	137	157	.1	.0	2.5	.8	2.1
STL	17	4	46	1466[1]	1364	8.4	135	**485**	761	11.5	3.37	108	.250	.314	56	44	98	**106**	**.981**	**123**	178	**.9**	4.6	-11.8	3.0	1.9
MON	15	9	50	1466[1]	1350	8.3	119	566	1051	12.0	3.78	98	.246	.320	-11	-15	99	93	.979	133	132	.3	-1.6	.5	-.2	-1.6
CHI	11	6	42	1445	1546	9.6	143	557	962	13.2	4.49	90	.279	.346	-124	-72	109	100	.980	124	147	.8	-7.5	-3.4	-.1	.2
PIT	17	9	30	1450[2]	1397	8.7	138	570	924	12.4	3.90	98	.255	.329	-30	-11	103	100	.978	143	134	-.2	-1.1	-2.8	-.8	-12.0
WEST																										
HOU	18	**19**	**51**	1456[1]	**1203**	**7.4**	116	523	**1160**	**10.8**	3.15	**114**	**.225**	**.297**	92	**73**	97	93	.979	130	108	.6	**7.6**	2.3	.0	4.5
CIN	14	8	45	1468	1465	9.0	136	524	924	12.3	3.91	99	.264	.329	-32	-7	104	101	.978	140	160	.0	-.7	-.9	1.9	4.8
SF	18	10	35	1460[1]	1264	7.8	121	591	992	11.6	3.33	106	.236	.316	62	30	95	101	.977	143	149	-.2	3.1	2.5	-1.5	-2.0
SD	13	7	32	1443[1]	1406	8.8	150	607	934	12.7	3.99	92	.258	.335	-44	-54	98	102	.978	137	135	.2	-5.6	2.4	-1.6	-2.4
LA	**35**	14	25	1454[1]	1428	8.8	115	499	1051	12.1	3.76	92	.256	.320	-7	-51	93	96	.971	181	118	-2.2	-5.3	.2	.3	-1.0
ATL	17	5	39	1424[2]	1443	9.1	117	576	932	12.9	3.97	100	.266	.340	-41	0	107	103	.978	141	**181**	-.1	.0	-4.4	-2.2	-1.8
TOT	224	113	480	17471		8.6				12.1	3.72		.253	.324					.978	1670	1744					

Runs
Hayes-Phi 107
Gwynn-SD 107
Schmidt-Phi 97
Davis-Cin 97

Hits
Gwynn-SD 211
Sax-LA 210
Raines-Mon 194
Hayes-Phi 186
Bass-Hou 184

Doubles
Hayes-Phi 46
Sax-LA 43
Dunston-Chi 37
Bream-Pit 37
Samuel-Phi 36

Triples
Webster-Mon 13
Samuel-Phi 12
Raines-Mon 10
Coleman-StL 8

Home Runs
Schmidt-Phi 37
Parker-Cin 31
Davis-Hou 31
Murphy-Atl 29

Total Bases
Parker-Cin 304
Schmidt-Phi 302
Gwynn-SD 300
Murphy-Atl 293
Hayes-Phi 293

Runs Batted In
Schmidt-Phi 119
Parker-Cin 116
Carter-NY 105
Davis-Hou 101
Hayes-Phi 98

Runs Produced
Hayes-Phi 186
Schmidt-Phi 179
Parker-Cin 174
Hernandez-NY 164
Carter-NY 162

Bases On Balls
Hernandez-NY 94
Schmidt-Phi 89
C.Davis-SF 84
Oberkfell-Atl 83
Doran-Hou 81

Batting Average
Raines-Mon .... .334
Sax-LA .... .332
Gwynn-SD .... .329
Bass-Hou .... .311
Hernandez-NY .... .310

On Base Percentage
Raines-Mon .... .415
Hernandez-NY .... .414
Schmidt-Phi .... .395
Sax-LA .... .391
Gwynn-SD .... .382

Slugging Average
Schmidt-Phi .... .547
Strawberry-NY .... .507
McReynolds-SD .... .504
Davis-Hou .... .493
Bass-Hou .... .486

Production
Schmidt-Phi .... .942
Raines-Mon .... .891
Strawberry-NY .... .871
McReynolds-SD .... .867
Hayes-Phi .... .861

Adjusted Production
Schmidt-Phi 152
Raines-Mon 146
Strawberry-NY 142
Hernandez-NY 141
McReynolds-SD 140

Batter Runs
Schmidt-Phi 44.0
Raines-Mon 38.0
Hernandez-NY 32.2
Hayes-Phi 30.3
Gwynn-SD 28.4

Adjusted Batter Runs
Schmidt-Phi 40.0
Raines-Mon 39.0
Hernandez-NY 35.3
Sax-LA 33.4
Gwynn-SD 30.6

Clutch Hitting Index
Carter-NY 132
Pendleton-StL 123
Cruz-Hou 121
Uribe-SF 121
Jeltz-Phi 120

Runs Created
Raines-Mon 130
Schmidt-Phi 122
Gwynn-SD 113
Hayes-Phi 111
Sax-LA 110

Total Average
Raines-Mon 1.040
Schmidt-Phi .... .988
Strawberry-NY .... .910
Hernandez-NY .... .873
McReynolds-SD .... .848

Stolen Bases
Coleman-StL 107
Davis-Cin 80
Raines-Mon 70
Duncan-LA 48

Stolen Base Average
Dernier-Chi 93.1
Raines-Mon 88.6
Coleman-StL 88.4
Davis-Cin 87.9
Leonard-SF 84.2

Stolen Base Runs
Coleman-StL 23.7
Davis-Cin 17.4
Raines-Mon 15.6
Dernier-Chi 6.9

Fielding Runs
Hubbard-Atl 41.0
Pendleton-StL 24.2
Bream-Pit 22.8
Wilson-Phi 20.6
Dunston-Chi 20.3

Total Player Rating
Raines-Mon 6.2
Gwynn-SD 5.2
Hernandez-NY 4.4
Sax-LA 3.7
Hubbard-Atl 3.5

Wins
Valenzuela-LA 21
Krukow-SF 20
Scott-Hou 18
Ojeda-NY 18

Win Percentage
Ojeda-NY .... .783
Gooden-NY .... .739
Fernandez-NY .... .727
Darling-NY .... .714
Krukow-SF .... .690

Games
Lefferts-SD 83
McDowell-NY 75
Worrell-StL 74
Franco-Cin 74
Tekulve-Phi 73

Complete Games
Valenzuela-LA 20
Rhoden-Pit 12
Gooden-NY 12
Krukow-SF 10

Shutouts
Scott-Hou 5
Knepper-Hou 5
Welch-LA 3
Valenzuela-LA 3

Saves
Worrell-StL 36
Reardon-Mon 35
Smith-Hou 33
Smith-Chi 31

Innings Pitched
Scott-Hou 275.1
Valenzuela-LA 269.1
Knepper-Hou 258.0
Rhoden-Pit 253.2
Gooden-NY 250.0

Fewest Hits/Game
Scott-Hou 5.95
Youmans-Mon 5.96
Ryan-Hou 6.02
Fernandez-NY 7.09
Gooden-NY 7.09

Fewest BB/Game
Eckersley-Chi 1.93
Sanderson-Chi 1.96
Krukow-SF 2.02
Welch-LA 2.10
Ojeda-NY 2.15

Strikeouts
Scott-Hou 306
Valenzuela-LA 242
Youmans-Mon 202
Gooden-NY 200
Fernandez-NY 200

Strikeouts/Game
Scott-Hou 10.00
Ryan-Hou 9.81
Fernandez-NY 8.81
Youmans-Mon 8.30
Valenzuela-LA 8.09

Ratio
Scott-Hou 8.37
Krukow-SF 9.66
Ojeda-NY 9.90
Gooden-NY 10.12
Rhoden-Pit 10.25

Earned Run Average
Scott-Hou 2.22
Ojeda-NY 2.57
Darling-NY 2.81
Rhoden-Pit 2.84
Gooden-NY 2.84

Adjusted ERA
Scott-Hou 162
Ojeda-NY 138
Rhoden-Pit 135
Darling-NY 126
Cox-StL 125

Opponents' Batting Avg.
Scott-Hou .... .186
Ryan-Hou .... .188
Youmans-Mon .... .188
Gooden-NY .... .215
Fernandez-NY .... .216

Opponents' On Base Pct.
Scott-Hou .... .244
Krukow-SF .... .271
Ojeda-NY .... .279
Gooden-NY .... .280
Ryan-Hou .... .285

Starter Runs
Scott-Hou 45.7
Ojeda-NY 27.7
Rhoden-Pit 24.7
Gooden-NY 24.2
Darling-NY 23.9

Adjusted Starter Runs
Scott-Hou 42.1
Rhoden-Pit 28.0
Ojeda-NY 23.3
Ruffin-Phi 22.6
Gooden-NY 19.2

Clutch Pitching Index
Dravecky-SD 115
Darling-NY 113
Garrelts-SF 110
Tudor-StL 109
Gullickson-Cin 109

Relief Runs
Worrell-StL 18.8
McGaffigan-Mon 16.9
Horton-StL 16.4
Tekulve-Phi 14.4
McCullers-SD 14.2

Adjusted Relief Runs
Worrell-StL 17.9
McGaffigan-Mon 16.5
Tekulve-Phi 16.1
Horton-StL 15.6
McCullers-SD 13.2

Relief Ranking
Worrell-StL 40.8
Smith-Chi 23.1
Tekulve-Phi 22.1
Orosco-NY 21.9
Garber-Atl 21.3

Total Pitcher Index
Scott-Hou 4.3
Worrell-StL 4.2
Rhoden-Pit 4.0
Smith-Chi 2.4
Garber-Atl 2.4

Total Baseball Ranking
Raines-Mon 6.2
Gwynn-SD 5.2
Hernandez-NY 4.4
Scott-Hou 4.3
Worrell-StL 4.1

March 27 Baseball's Rules Committee votes to change the DH rule for the World Series, allowing a DH to be used in all games played in the AL club's home park. Since 1976, the DH had been used in all games in alternating years.

April 29 Twenty-three-year-old Red Sox pitcher Roger Clemens strikes out 20 batters in a 3-1 win over Seattle, breaking the major league record of 19 shared by Nolan Ryan, Steve Carlton, and Tom Seaver. Clemens doesn't walk a batter, allows just three hits, and ties the AL record with eight consecutive strikeouts in the middle innings.

June 18 California's Don Sutton becomes the 19th pitcher in major league history to win 300 games, beating the Rangers 3-1 on a three-hitter.

June 21 Bo Jackson, Heisman Trophy winner in 1985 and the first pick (by Tampa Bay) in the NFL draft, stuns observers nationwide by signing with the Kansas City Royals instead.

October 4 On the next-to-last day of the season, Dave Righetti saves both ends of the Yankees' doubleheader sweep of the Red Sox to give him a record 46 saves. Bruce Sutter and Dan Quisenberry had shared the record with 45.

October 12 One loss away from elimination and trailing 5-2 entering the ninth, the Red Sox stage one of the most improbable comebacks in postseason history, winning 7-6 over the Angels in 11 innings. After Don Baylor's ninth-inning home run reduces the deficit to 5-4, reserve outfielder Dave Henderson slugs a two-out, two-run home run off Donnie Moore to give Boston a 6-5 lead. California ties the score with a run in the bottom of the ninth but Henderson, who had appeared to be the goat when he dropped Bobby Grich's long fly ball over the fence for a home run in the seventh inning, delivers a sacrifice fly in the eleventh for the winning run.

October 15 Boston routs California 8-1 in the seventh game of the ALCS and advances to the World Series. The game caps yet another heartbreaking failure for Angels skipper Gene Mauch, who in Game 5 was one strike away from reaching his first World Series in 25 seasons as a major league manager.

October 18 Boston wins Game 1 of the World Series 1-0 when Tim Teufel botches Rich Gedman's routine grounder in the seventh inning, allowing Jim Rice to score the game's only run. Bruce Hurst and Calvin Schiraldi combine on a four-hitter for the Red Sox.

November 12 Roger Clemens wins the AL Cy Young Award unanimously, joining Denny McLain (1968) as the only pitchers to do so.

November 18 Roger Clemens becomes the first starting pitcher to win the AL MVP Award since Vida Blue in 1971.

BALTIMORE — M E.Weaver; 1B E.Murray; 2B J.Bonilla; SS C.Ripken; 3B F.Rayford; LF J.Shelby; CF F.Lynn; RF L.Lacy; C R.Dempsey; DH L.Sheets; O3 J.Beniquez; OD M.Young; 2 A.Wiggins; 1D J.Traber; P M.Boddicker; P S.McGregor; P K.Dixon; P M.Flanagan; P S.Davis; RP R.Bordi; RP D.Aase; RP N.Snell; P B.Havens

BOSTON — M J.McNamara; 1B B.Buckner; 2B M.Barrett; SS E.Romero; 3B W.Boggs; LF J.Rice; CF T.Armas; RF D.Evans; C R.Gedman; DH D.Baylor; P R.Clemens; O O.Boyd; P B.Hurst; P A.Nipper; P T.Seaver; RP B.Stanley; RP S.Stewart; RP S.Crawford; P J.Sellers; P M.Brown; P C.Schiraldi

CALIFORNIA — M G.Mauch; 1B W.Joyner; 2B R.Wilfong; SS D.Schofield; 3B D.DeCinces; LF B.Downing; CF G.Pettis; RF R.Jones; C B.Boone; DH R.Jackson; 21 B.Grich; O G.Hendrick; DS R.Burleson; P M.Witt; P K.McCaskill; P D.Sutton; P R.Romanick; RP D.Corbett; RP D.Moore; P J.Candelaria; P J.Slaton

CHICAGO — M T.LaRussa; M D.Rader; 2B J.Fregosi; 1B G.Walker; 2B J.Cruz; SS O.Guillen; 3B T.Hulett; LF R.Nichols; CF J.Cangelosi; RF H.Baines; C C.Fisk; DH R.Kittle; D1 J.Hairston; 3S W.Tolleson; O1 B.Bonilla; P R.Dotson; P F.Bannister; P J.Cowley; P N.Allen; P J.Davis; RP G.Nelson; RP B.Dawley; RP D.Schmidt; P J.DeLeon; P T.Seaver; P S.Carlton; P B.James

CLEVELAND — M P.Corrales; 1B P.Tabler; 2B T.Bernazard; SS J.Franco; 3B B.Jacoby; LF M.Hall; CF B.Butler; RF J.Carter; C A.Allanson; DH A.Thornton; O O.Nixon; OS C.Snyder; C C.Bando; OD C.Castillo; P T.Candiotti; P N.Niekro; P K.Schrom; RP S.Bailes; P R.Yett; RP B.Oelkers; P D.Schulze; P N.Heaton; /P G.Swindell; P E.Camacho; P D.Noles; P J.Butcher

DETROIT — M S.Anderson; 1B D.Evans; 2B L.Whitaker; SS A.Trammell; 3B D.Coles; LF D.Collins; CF C.Lemon; RF K.Gibson; C L.Parrish; DH J.Grubb; 32 T.Brookens; OD L.Herndon; O P.Sheridan; P J.Morris; P W.Terrell; P F.Tanana; P E.King; P R.O'Neal; RP W.Hernandez; RP B.Campbell; RP M.Thurmond; P D.Petry; P D.LaPoint

KANSAS CITY — M D.Howser; M M.Ferraro; 1B S.Balboni; 2B F.White; SS A.Salazar; 3B G.Brett; LF L.Smith; CF W.Wilson; RF R.Law; C J.Sundberg; DH J.Orta; S2 B.Biancalana; D H.McRae; C3 J.Quirk; O D.Motley; O M.Kingery; P C.Leibrandt; P D.Leonard; P D.Jackson; P M.Gubicza; P B.Saberhagen; RP B.Black; RP S.Farr; RP D.Quisenberry; P S.Bankhead

---

MILWAUKEE — M G.Bamberger; M T.Trebelhorn; 1B B.Robidoux; 2B J.Gantner; SS E.Riles; 3B P.Molitor; LF R.Manning; CF R.Yount; RF R.Deer; C C.Moore; DH C.Cooper; OD B.Oglivie; 32 D.Sveum; C1 B.Schroeder; C B.Cerone; O G.Braggs; P T.Higuera; P B.Wegman; P T.Leary; P J.Nieves; P D.Darwin; RP D.Plesac; RP M.Clear; RP B.Clutterbuck

MINNESOTA — M R.Miller; M T.Kelly; 1B K.Hrbek; 2B S.Lombardozzi; SS G.Gagne; 3B G.Gaetti; LF R.Bush; CF K.Puckett; RF T.Brunansky; C M.Salas; DH R.Smalley; OD M.Hatcher; P B.Blyleven; P F.Viola; P M.Smithson; P N.Heaton; P M.Portugal; RP K.Atherton; RP R.Jackson; RP F.Pastore; P A.Anderson; P J.Butcher

NEW YORK — M L.Piniella; 1B D.Mattingly; 2B W.Randolph; SS W.Tolleson; 3B M.Pagliarulo; LF D.Pasqua; CF R.Henderson; RF D.Winfield; C B.Wynegar; DH M.Easler; P D.Rasmussen; P R.Guidry; P D.Drabek; P B.Tewksbury; P J.Niekro; RP D.Righetti; RP B.Shirley; RP B.Fisher; P T.John; P S.Nielsen

OAKLAND — M J.Moore; M J.Newman; M T.LaRussa; 1B B.Bochte; 2B T.Phillips; SS A.Griffin; 3B C.Lansford; LF J.Canseco; CF D.Murphy; RF M.Davis; C M.Tettleton; DH D.Kingman; 23 D.Hill; OD D.Baker; P C.Young; P J.Rijo; P J.Andujar; P D.Stewart; P E.Plunk; RP B.Mooneyham; RP S.Ontiveros; RP J.Howell; P C.Codiroli; P M.Haas; P R.Langford

SEATTLE — M C.Cottier; M M.Martinez; M D.Williams; 1B A.Davis; 2B H.Reynolds; SS S.Owen; 3B J.Presley; LF P.Bradley; CF J.Moses; RF D.Tartabull; C B.Kearney; DH G.Thomas; OD D.Henderson; 1D K.Phelps; P M.Moore; P M.Langston; P M.Morgan; P B.Swift; RP M.Young; RP M.Huismann; RP L.Guetterman; P M.Wilcox

TEXAS — M B.Valentine; 1B P.O'Brien; 2B T.Harrah; SS S.Fletcher; 3B S.Buechele; LF R.Sierra; CF O.McDowell; RF P.Incaviglia; C D.Slaught; DH L.Parrish; O G.Ward; 2S C.Wilkerson; O1 T.Paciorek; P C.Hough; P E.Correa; P J.Guzman; P B.Witt; RP G.Harris; RP M.Williams; RP J.Russell; P D.Mohorcic; P M.Mahler

TORONTO — M J.Williams; 1B W.Upshaw; 2B D.Garcia; SS T.Fernandez; 3B R.Mulliniks; LF G.Bell; CF L.Moseby; RF J.Barfield; C E.Whitt; DH C.Johnson; 32 G.Iorg; DO R.Leach; P J.Key; P J.Clancy; P D.Stieb; P J.Cerutti; P J.Alexander; RP M.Eichhorn; RP T.Henke; RP D.Lamp; P J.Johnson; P J.Acker

TEAM	G	W	L	PCT	GB	R	OR	AB	H	2B	3B	HR	BB	SO	AVG	OBP	SLG	PRO	PRO+	BR	/A	PF	CHI	RC	SB	CS	SBA	SBR
EAST																												
BOS	161	95	66	.590		794	696	5498	1488	**320**	21	144	595	**707**	.271	.349	.415	.764	107	59	57	100	98	792	41	34	55	-8
NY	162	90	72	.556	5.5	797	738	5570	1512	275	23	188	645	911	.271	**.350**	**.430**	**.780**	**112**	**89**	**99**	99	94	**843**	139	48	**74**	**13**
DET	162	87	75	.537	8.5	798	714	5512	1447	234	30	**198**	613	885	.263	.341	.424	.765	107	52	55	100	99	814	138	58	70	7
TOR	163	86	76	.531	9.5	809	733	5716	1540	285	35	181	496	848	.269	.331	.427	.758	102	29	10	102	103	796	110	59	65	-2
CLE	163	84	78	.519	11.5	**831**	841	5702	**1620**	270	**45**	157	456	944	**.284**	.340	**.430**	.770	110	57	72	98	102	822	**141**	54	72	10
MIL	161	77	84	.478	18	667	734	5461	1393	255	38	127	530	986	.255	.324	.385	.709	89	-59	-80	103	98	682	100	50	67	0
BAL	162	73	89	.451	22.5	708	760	5524	1425	223	13	169	563	862	.258	.330	.395	.725	97	-28	-17	99	99	708	64	34	65	-1
WEST																												
CAL	162	92	70	.568		786	684	5433	1387	236	36	167	**671**	860	.255	.341	.404	.745	103	22	31	99	101	765	109	42	72	8
TEX	162	87	75	.537	5	771	743	5529	1479	248	43	184	511	1088	.267	.333	.428	.761	103	37	18	102	99	761	103	85	55	-20
KC	162	76	86	.469	16	654	**673**	5561	1403	264	**45**	137	474	919	.252	.315	.390	.705	88	-77	-90	102	99	683	97	46	68	2
OAK	162	76	86	.469	16	731	760	5435	1370	213	25	163	553	983	.252	.325	.390	.715	101	-48	3	93	106	700	139	61	70	5
CHI	162	72	90	.444	20	644	699	5406	1335	197	34	121	487	940	.247	.313	.363	.676	81	-125	-144	103	**107**	614	115	54	68	2
MIN	162	71	91	.438	21	741	839	5531	1446	257	39	196	501	977	.261	.327	.428	.755	100	21	2	103	97	756	81	61	57	-12
SEA	162	67	95	.414	25	718	835	5498	1392	243	41	158	572	1148	.253	.327	.399	.726	95	-28	-33	101	100	706	93	76	55	-18
TOT	1134					10449		77376	20237	3520	468	2290	7667	13058	.262	.332	.408	.740							1470	762	66	-16

TEAM	CG	SH	SV	IP	H	H/G	HR	BB	SO	RAT	ERA	ERA+	OAV	OOB	PR	/A	PF	CPI	FA	E	DP	FW	PW	BW	SBW	DIF
EAST																										
BOS	36	6	41	1429^2	1469	9.2	167	**474**	1033	12.4	3.93	106	.266	.327	38	36	100	**106**	.979	129	146	-.2	3.5	5.6	-.7	6.2
NY	13	8	**58**	1443^1	1461	9.1	175	492	878	12.3	4.11	99	.263	.325	11	-3	98	100	.979	127	153	.0	-.3	**9.7**	**1.4**	-1.8
DET	33	12	38	1443^2	1374	8.6	183	571	880	12.3	4.02	102	.251	.325	25	16	99	100	.982	108	163	1.1	1.6	5.4	.8	-2.9
TOR	16	12	44	1476	1467	8.9	164	487	1002	12.2	4.08	103	.261	.325	16	23	101	99	**.984**	**100**	150	**1.7**	2.3	1.0	-.0	.2
CLE	31	7	34	1447^2	1548	9.6	167	605	744	13.7	4.58	91	.273	.349	-64	-70	99	101	.975	157	148	-1.7	-6.9	7.1	1.1	3.4
MIL	29	12	32	1431^2	1478	9.3	158	494	952	12.6	4.01	108	.267	.330	26	50	104	104	.976	146	146	-1.2	4.9	-7.9	.1	.5
BAL	17	6	39	1436^2	1451	9.1	177	535	954	12.6	4.30	96	.263	.330	-20	-27	99	98	.978	135	163	-.5	-2.7	-1.7	.0	-3.2
WEST																										
CAL	29	12	40	1456	1356	**8.4**	153	478	955	**11.5**	3.84	107	.248	**.311**	54	44	98	94	.983	107	156	1.2	4.3	3.0	.9	1.5
TEX	15	8	41	1450^1	1356	**8.4**	145	736	**1059**	13.2	4.11	105	.249	.342	11	31	103	100	.980	122	160	.3	3.0	1.8	-1.9	2.7
KC	24	**13**	31	1440^2	1413	8.8	**121**	479	888	12.1	**3.82**	**111**	.258	.322	**56**	**68**	102	98	.980	123	153	.2	**6.7**	-8.8	.3	-3.4
OAK	22	8	37	1433	**1334**	**8.4**	166	667	937	12.8	4.31	90	**.247**	.333	-21	-70	93	94	.978	135	120	-.5	-6.9	.3	.6	1.4
CHI	18	8	38	1442^1	1361	8.5	143	561	895	12.2	3.93	110	.251	.325	39	61	103	97	.981	117	142	.6	6.0	-14.2	.3	-1.8
MIN	**39**	6	24	1432^2	1579	9.9	200	503	937	13.4	4.77	90	.281	.345	-94	-74	103	101	.980	118	168	.5	-7.3	.2	-1.1	-2.4
SEA	33	5	27	1439^2	1590	9.9	171	585	944	13.9	4.65	91	.283	.355	-76	-65	102	105	.975	156	**191**	-1.7	-6.4	-3.2	-1.7	-1.0
TOT	355	123	524	20203^1		9.0				12.7	4.18		.262	.332					.979	1780	2159					

Runs
Henderson-NY 130
Puckett-Min 119
Mattingly-NY 117
Carter-Cle 108

Hits
Mattingly-NY 238
Puckett-Min 223
Fernandez-Tor 213
Boggs-Bos 207

Doubles
Mattingly-NY 53
Boggs-Bos 47
Rice-Bos 39
Buckner-Bos 39
Barrett-Bos 39

Triples
Butler-Cle 14
Sierra-Tex 10
Fernandez-Tor 9
Carter-Cle 9

Home Runs
Barfield-Tor 40
Kingman-Oak 35
Gaetti-Min 34
Deer-Mil 33
Canseco-Oak 33

Total Bases
Mattingly-NY 388
Puckett-Min 365
Carter-Cle 341
Bell-Tor 341
Barfield-Tor 329

Runs Batted In
Carter-Cle 121
Canseco-Oak 117
Mattingly-NY 113
Rice-Bos 110

Runs Produced
Carter-Cle 200
Mattingly-NY 199
Rice-Bos 188
Puckett-Min 184
Bell-Tor 178

Bases On Balls
Boggs-Bos 105
Evans-Bos 97
Randolph-NY 94
Jackson-Cal 92
Evans-Det 91

Batting Average
Boggs-Bos .... .357
Mattingly-NY ...... .352
Puckett-Min .... .328
Tabler-Cle .... .326
Rice-Bos .... .324

On Base Percentage
Boggs-Bos .... .455
P.Bradley-Sea .... .406
Brett-KC .... .404
Murray-Bal .... .400
Mattingly-NY ..... .399

Slugging Average
Mattingly-NY ...... .573
Barfield-Tor .... .559
Puckett-Min .... .537
Bell-Tor .... .532
Gaetti-Min .... .518

Production
Mattingly-NY ...... .973
Boggs-Bos .... .942
Barfield-Tor .... .929
Puckett-Min .... .903
Brett-KC .... .885

Adjusted Production
Mattingly-NY 163
Boggs-Bos 156
Barfield-Tor 145
Puckett-Min 138
Rice-Bos 137

Batter Runs
Mattingly-NY 55.6
Boggs-Bos 51.6
Barfield-Tor 39.0
Puckett-Min 37.1
Rice-Bos 32.6

Adjusted Batter Runs
Mattingly-NY 57.3
Boggs-Bos 51.1
Barfield-Tor 36.1
Puckett-Min 34.1
Rice-Bos 32.3

Clutch Hitting Index
Phillips-Oak 135
Buckner-Bos 127
Cooper-Mil 126
Canseco-Oak 125
Downing-Cal 122

Runs Created
Mattingly-NY 150
Boggs-Bos 133
Puckett-Min 127
Barfield-Tor 122
Carter-Cle 116

Total Average
Boggs-Bos .... .987
Mattingly-NY ...... .969
Gibson-Det .... .950
Barfield-Tor .... .931
Henderson-NY ..... .931

Stolen Bases
Henderson-NY 87
Pettis-Cal 50
Cangelosi-Chi 50
Wilson-KC 34
Gibson-Det 34

Stolen Base Average
Felder-Mil 88.9
Davis-Oak 87.1
Gibson-Det 85.0
Henderson-NY 82.9

Stolen Base Runs
Henderson-NY 15.3
Pettis-Cal 7.2
Gibson-Det 6.6
Davis-Oak 5.7
Wilson-KC 5.4

Fielding Runs
Owen-Sea-Bos 31.9
Reynolds-Sea 29.0
Barfield-Tor 20.9
Pettis-Cal 20.7
Buckner-Bos 20.1

Total Player Rating
Barfield-Tor 4.8
Ripken-Bal 4.4
Boggs-Bos 4.3
Rice-Bos 4.2
Henderson-NY 4.2

Wins
Clemens-Bos 24
Morris-Det 21
Higuera-Mil 20
Witt-Cal 18
Rasmussen-NY 18

Win Percentage
Clemens-Bos ..... .857
Rasmussen-NY ... .750
Morris-Det .... .724
Higuera-Mil ...... .645
Witt-Cal .... .643

Games
Williams-Tex 80
Righetti-NY 74
Harris-Tex 73
Eichhorn-Tor 69

Complete Games
Candiotti-Cle 17
Blyleven-Min 16
Morris-Det 15
Higuera-Mil 15
Witt-Cal 14

Shutouts
Morris-Det 6
Hurst-Bos 4
Higuera-Mil 4

Saves
Righetti-NY 46
Aase-Bal 34
Henke-Tor 27
Hernandez-Det 24
Moore-Cal 21

Innings Pitched
Blyleven-Min 271.2
Witt-Cal 269.0
Morris-Det 267.0
Moore-Sea 266.0
Clemens-Bos 254.0

Fewest Hits/Game
Clemens-Bos 6.34
Rasmussen-NY ... 7.13
Witt-Cal 7.29
Hough-Tex 7.35
Cowley-Chi 7.37

Fewest BB/Game
Guidry-NY 1.78
Boyd-Bos 1.89
Blyleven-Min 1.92
Wegman-Mil 1.95
Sutton-Cal 2.13

Strikeouts
Langston-Sea 245
Clemens-Bos 238
Morris-Det 223
Blyleven-Min 215
Witt-Cal 208

Strikeouts/Game
Langston-Sea 9.21
Hurst-Bos 8.62
Clemens-Bos 8.43
Correa-Tex 8.41
Rijo-Oak 8.18

Ratio
Clemens-Bos 8.86
Witt-Cal 9.84
Morris-Det 10.48
Rasmussen-NY .. 10.51
Sutton-Cal 10.61

Earned Run Average
Clemens-Bos 2.48
Higuera-Mil 2.79
Witt-Cal 2.84
Hurst-Bos 2.99
D.Jackson-KC 3.20

Adjusted ERA
Clemens-Bos 168
Higuera-Mil 155
Witt-Cal 144
Hurst-Bos 139
D.Jackson-KC 133

Opponents' Batting Avg.
Clemens-Bos ..... .195
Rasmussen-NY ... .217
Witt-Cal .... .221
Hough-Tex .... .221
Correa-Tex ...... .223

Opponents' On Base Pct.
Clemens-Bos ..... .253
Witt-Cal .... .277
Morris-Det .... .287
Sutton-Cal ...... .288
Rasmussen-NY ... .290

Starter Runs
Clemens-Bos 47.8
Witt-Cal 39.8
Higuera-Mil 38.2
Morris-Det 26.9
Hurst-Bos 22.9

Adjusted Starter Runs
Clemens-Bos 47.5
Higuera-Mil 42.4
Witt-Cal 37.8
Morris-Det 25.3
Hurst-Bos 22.6

Clutch Pitching Index
Hurst-Bos 123
D.Jackson-KC 121
Higuera-Mil 119
Stieb-Tor 119
Niekro-Cle 117

Relief Runs
Eichhorn-Tor 42.8
Righetti-NY 20.5
Harris-Tex 16.7
Clear-Mil 16.2
Mohorcic-Tex 14.7

Adjusted Relief Runs
Eichhorn-Tor 43.6
Righetti-NY 19.4
Harris-Tex 18.2
Clear-Mil 17.4
Mohorcic-Tex 15.8

Relief Ranking
Eichhorn-Tor 55.3
Righetti-NY 42.6
Harris-Tex 32.8
Clear-Mil 28.6
Plesac-Mil 27.2

Total Pitcher Index
Eichhorn-Tor 5.7
Clemens-Bos 4.9
Higuera-Mil 4.8
Righetti-NY 4.3
Witt-Cal 4.0

Total Baseball Ranking
Eichhorn-Tor 5.7
Clemens-Bos 4.9
Higuera-Mil 4.8
Barfield-Tor 4.8
Ripken-Bal 4.4

April 8 Faced with a storm of criticism, the Dodgers fire vice president Al Campanis for racially insensitive remarks he made on the April 6 telecast of ABC-TV's *Nightline*.

April 19 Cardinals ace John Tudor suffers a broken leg when Mets catcher Barry Lyons crashes into him in the St. Louis dugout while chasing a foul pop. Tudor, who was not pitching, will be sidelined until August.

June 22 Tom Seaver abandons his comeback attempt with the injury-riddled Mets and retires with a career record of 311-205, an ERA of 2.86, 3,640 strikeouts (third behind Nolan Ryan and Steve Carlton), and 61 shutouts.

July 14 Tim Raines caps a 3-for-3 performance in the All-Star Game with a two-run triple in the top of the thirteenth inning, giving the NL a 2-0 victory.

July 14 The BBWAA votes to rename the Rookie of the Year Award in honor of Jackie Robinson, who broke baseball's color barrier on the way to winning the first Rookie of the Year Award in 1947.

August 10 Phillies pitcher Kevin Gross becomes the second pitcher in eight days to be ejected for scuffing the baseball when umpires discover sandpaper in his glove during the fifth inning of a 4-2 win over the Cubs. Like Joe Niekro, Gross will be suspended for 10 games.

September 1* Williamsport (Eastern League) Bills catcher Dave Bresnahan introduces a new wrinkle to baseball— the hidden potato. With a Reading runner, Rick Rudblad, on third, Bresnahan returns from a time out with a shaved potato hidden in his mitt. On the next pitch he throws the potato wildly on a pickoff attempt. When the runner trots home, Bresnahan tags him out with the real ball. The umpire, unamused, rules the runner safe, gives the catcher an error, and fines him $50. He is released the following day. That same night, their last game of the season, the Bills admit any fan for a $1 and a potato. On each potato, Bresnahan autographs, "This spud's for you."

September 21 Darryl Strawberry joins

Howard Johnson as the first teammates ever to achieve 30 homers and 30 steals in the same season.

September 28 The Giants and Twins win their divisions, ending 16- and 17-year droughts, respectively. San Francisco clinches its first NL West title since 1971 with a 5-4 win at San Diego, while Minnesota clinches its first AL West title since 1970 with a 5-3 win at Texas.

October 14 Danny Cox pitches the Cardinals' second consecutive shutout 6-0 over the Giants in Game 7 of the NLCS, to send St. Louis to the World Series for the third time in the 1980s. Giants outfielder Jeffrey Leonard (.417, 4 home runs) is named series MVP.

November 10 In the closest vote in the award's history, Steve Bedrosian edges Rick Sutcliffe 57-55 to win the NL Cy Young Award. Bedrosian is the third reliever to win the award in the NL.

November 18 Cubs outfielder Andre Dawson becomes the first player from a last-place club to win an MVP Award.

	ATLANTA		CHICAGO		CINCINNATI		HOUSTON		LOS ANGELES		MONTREAL
M	C.Tanner	M	G.Michael	M	P.Rose	M	H.Lanier	M	T.Lasorda	M	B.Rodgers
1B	G.Perry	M	F.Lucchesi	1B	N.Esasky	1B	G.Davis	1B	F.Stubbs	1B	A.Galarraga
2B	G.Hubbard	1B	L.Durham	2B	R.Oester	2B	B.Doran	2B	S.Sax	2B	V.Law
SS	A.Thomas	2B	R.Sandberg	SS	B.Larkin	SS	C.Reynolds	SS	M.Duncan	SS	H.Brooks
3B	K.Oberkfell	SS	S.Dunston	3B	B.Bell	3B	D.Walling	3B	M.Hatcher	3B	T.Wallach
LF	K.Griffey	3B	K.Moreland	LF	T.Jones	LF	J.Cruz	LF	P.Guerrero	LF	T.Raines
CF	D.James	LF	J.Mumphrey	CF	E.Davis	CF	B.Hatcher	CF	J.Shelby	CF	H.Winningham
RF	D.Murphy	CF	D.Martinez	RF	D.Parker	RF	K.Bass	RF	M.Marshall	RF	M.Webster
C	O.Virgil	RF	A.Dawson	C	B.Diaz	C	A.Ashby	C	M.Scioscia	C	M.Fitzgerald
		C	J.Davis								
3	G.Nettles			21	D.Concepcion	O	G.Young	S3	D.Anderson	2O	C.Candaele
O	A.Hall	O	B.Dayett	O	K.Daniels	3	K.Caminiti	O	K.Landreaux	S2	T.Foley
		13	M.Trillo	1	T.Francona					C	J.Reed
P	Z.Smith	O1	R.Palmeiro	S2	K.Stillwell	P	M.Scott	P	O.Hershiser		
P	R.Mahler					P	N.Ryan	P	B.Welch	P	N.Heaton
P	D.Palmer	P	R.Sutcliffe	P	T.Power	P	D.Darwin	P	F.Valenzuela	P	B.Sebra
P	C.Puleo	P	J.Moyer	P	T.Browning	P	B.Knepper	P	R.Honeycutt	P	B.Smith
P	D.Alexander	P	G.Maddux	P	B.Gullickson	P	J.Deshaies	RP	T.Leary	P	D.Martinez
RP	J.Acker	P	S.Sanderson	P	G.Hoffman	RP	L.Andersen	RP	A.Pena	P	F.Youmans
RP	J.Dedmon	P	L.Lancaster	P	R.Robinson	RP	D.Smith	RP	B.Holton	RP	A.McGaffigan
RP	G.Garber	RP	E.Lynch	RP	F.Williams	RP	D.Meads			RP	T.Burke
		RP	L.Smith	RP	R.Murphy			P	S.Hillegas	RP	R.St.Claire
P	R.O'Neal	RP	F.DiPino	RP	J.Franco			P	K.Howell		
P	P.Assenmacher							P	M.Young	P	J.Tibbs
/P	T.Glavine	P	S.Trout	P	B.Landrum					P	P.Perez
		P	D.Noles							P	J.Parrett
										P	B.McClure

	NEW YORK		PHILADELPHIA		PITTSBURGH		SAN DIEGO		SAN FRANCISCO		ST.LOUIS
M	D.Johnson	M	J.Felske	M	J.Leyland	M	L.Bowa	M	R.Craig	M	W.Herzog
1B	K.Hernandez	M	L.Elia	1B	S.Bream	1B	J.Kruk	1B	W.Clark	1B	J.Clark
2B	T.Teufel	1B	V.Hayes	2B	J.Ray	2B	T.Flannery	2B	R.Thompson	2B	T.Herr
SS	R.Santana	2B	J.Samuel	SS	A.Pedrique	SS	G.Templeton	SS	J.Uribe	SS	O.Smith
3B	H.Johnson	SS	S.Jeltz	3B	B.Bonilla	3B	R.Ready	3B	K.Mitchell	3B	T.Pendleton
LF	K.McReynolds	3B	M.Schmidt	LF	B.Bonds	LF	S.Jefferson	LF	J.Leonard	LF	V.Coleman
CF	L.Dykstra	LF	C.James	CF	A.Van Slyke	CF	S.Mack	CF	C.Davis	CF	W.McGee
RF	D.Strawberry	CF	M.Thompson	RF	R.Reynolds	RF	T.Gwynn	RF	C.Maldonado	RF	C.Ford
C	G.Carter	RF	G.Wilson	C	M.LaValliere	C	B.Santiago	C	B.Brenly	C	T.Pena
		C	L.Parrish								
O	M.Wilson			O	J.Cangelosi	O1	C.Martinez	O1	M.Aldrete	O	J.Morris
2	W.Backman	O1	G.Gross	O1	M.Diaz	O	M.Wynne	O	E.Milner	O2	J.Oquendo
		S	L.Aguayo	3S	J.Morrison	2	J.Cora	C	C.Speier	O1	J.Lindeman
				S	R.Belliard			S3	B.Melvin		
P	R.Darling					P	E.Whitson		M.Williams	P	D.Cox
P	D.Gooden	P	S.Rawley			P	E.Show			P	G.Mathews
P	S.Fernandez	P	D.Carman	P	B.Fisher	P	J.Jones	P	K.Downs	P	B.Forsch
P	R.Aguilera	P	B.Ruffin	P	R.Reuschel	P	A.Hawkins	P	M.LaCoss	P	J.Magrane
P	J.Mitchell	P	K.Gross	P	D.Drabek	P	M.Dunne	P	A.Hammaker	P	J.Tudor
RP	T.Leach	RP	M.Jackson	P	M.Dunne	P	M.Grant	P	M.Krukow	RP	R.Horton
RP	R.McDowell	RP	K.Tekulve	P	B.Walk	RP	L.McCullers	P	D.Dravecky	RP	B.Dawley
RP	D.Sisk	RP	S.Bedrosian	RP	J.Smiley	RP	D.Dravecky	RP	S.Garrelts	RP	T.Worrell
				RP	D.Robinson	RP	G.Booker	RP	J.Robinson		
P	D.Cone	P	T.Hume					RP	J.Gott	P	L.Tunnell
P	J.Orosco	P	W.Ritchie	P	B.Kipper	P	E.Nolte			P	P.Perry
P	R.Myers			P	D.Taylor	P	S.Davis	P	M.Davis	P	K.Dayley
						P	M.Davis	P	M.Grant		
						P	R.Gossage	/P	R.Reuschel		
						P	C.Lefferts				

TEAM	G	W	L	PCT	GB	R	OR	AB	H	2B	3B	HR	BB	SO	AVG	OBP	SLG	PRO	PRO+	BR	/A	PF	CHI	RC	SB	CS	SBA	SBR
EAST																												
STL	162	95	67	.586		798	693	5500	1449	252	49	94	644	933	.263	.343	.378	.721	95	-9	-23	102	109	740	248	72	78	31
NY	162	92	70	.568	3	823	698	5601	1499	287	34	192	592	1012	.268	.341	.434	.775	117	81	124	95	100	848	159	49	76	18
MON	162	91	71	.562	4	741	720	5527	1467	310	39	120	501	918	.265	.330	.401	.731	96	-6	-28	103	103	734	166	74	69	5
PIT	162	80	82	.494	15	723	744	5536	1464	282	45	131	535	914	.264	.332	.403	.735	99	3	-1	101	98	741	140	58	71	7
PHI	162	80	82	.494	15	702	749	5475	1390	248	51	169	587	1109	.254	.329	.410	.739	98	8	-16	103	95	736	111	49	69	4
CHI	161	76	85	.472	18.5	720	801	5583	1475	244	33	209	504	1064	.264	.327	.432	.759	102	40	10	104	94	785	109	48	69	4
WEST																												
SF	162	90	72	.556		783	669	5608	1458	274	32	205	511	1094	.260	.326	.430	.756	110	33	70	95	102	768	126	97	57	-20
CIN	162	84	78	.519	6	783	752	5560	1478	262	29	192	514	928	.266	.331	.427	.758	102	42	8	104	102	786	169	46	79	23
HOU	162	76	86	.469	14	648	678	5485	1386	238	28	122	526	936	.253	.321	.373	.694	94	-78	-54	96	100	669	162	46	78	21
LA	162	73	89	.451	17	635	675	5517	1389	236	23	125	445	923	.252	.311	.371	.682	88	-108	-92	97	104	627	128	59	68	3
ATL	161	69	92	.429	20.5	747	829	5428	1401	284	24	152	641	834	.258	.341	.403	.744	98	28	-9	105	98	747	135	68	67	0
SD	162	65	97	.401	25	668	763	5456	1419	209	48	113	577	992	.260	.334	.378	.712	99	-34	-9	96	96	693	198	91	69	5
TOT	971					8771		66276	17275	3126	435	1824	6577	11657	.261	.331	.404	.734							1851	757	71	101

TEAM	CG	SH	SV	IP	H	H/G	HR	BB	SO	RAT	ERA	ERA+	OAV	OOB	PR	/A	PF	CPI	FA	E	DP	FW	PW	BW	SBW	DIF
EAST																										
STL	10	7	48	1466	1484	9.1	129	533	873	12.5	3.91	106	.265	.332	28	40	102	103	.982	116	172	.9	4.0	-2.3	2.2	9.2
NY	16	7	51	1454	1407	8.7	135	510	1032	12.1	3.84	98	.254	.321	38	-11	93	97	.978	137	137	-.3	-1.1	12.3	1.0	-.9
MON	16	8	50	1450¹	1428	8.9	145	446	1012	11.8	3.92	107	.257	.315	26	46	103	95	.976	147	122	-.9	4.6	-2.8	-.3	9.4
PIT	25	13	39	1445	1377	8.6	164	562	914	12.2	4.20	98	.253	.326	-19	-14	101	95	.980	123	147	.5	-1.4	-.0	-.1	.2
PHI	13	7	48	1448¹	1453	9.0	167	587	877	12.9	4.18	101	.263	.338	-16	9	104	103	.980	121	137	.6	.9	-1.6	-.4	-.5
CHI	11	5	48	1434²	1524	9.6	159	628	1024	13.7	4.55	94	.275	.352	-76	-44	105	103	.979	130	154	.0	-4.4	1.0	-.4	-.7
WEST																										
SF	19	10	38	1471	1407	8.6	146	547	1038	12.1	3.68	105	.255	.325	66	27	94	106	.980	129	183	.1	2.7	7.0	-2.8	2.0
CIN	7	6	44	1452¹	1486	9.2	170	485	919	12.4	4.24	100	.267	.328	-27	0	104	99	.979	130	137	.0	.0	.8	1.5	.7
HOU	13	13	33	1441¹	1363	8.5	141	525	1137	12.0	3.84	102	.250	.319	38	12	96	96	.981	116	113	-.9	1.2	-5.4	1.3	-2.9
LA	29	8	32	1455	1415	8.8	130	565	1097	12.4	3.72	107	.255	.327	59	40	97	103	.975	155	144	-1.3	4.0	-9.2	-.5	-.9
ATL	16	4	32	1427²	1529	9.6	163	587	837	13.6	4.63	94	.276	.350	-87	-45	107	101	.982	116	170	.8	-4.5	-.9	-.8	-6.1
SD	14	10	33	1433¹	1402	8.8	175	602	897	12.8	4.27	93	.256	.334	-30	-50	97	98	.976	147	135	-.9	-5.0	-.9	-.3	-8.9
TOT	189	98	496	17379		8.9				12.5	4.08		.261	.331					.979	1567	1751					

Runs		Hits		Doubles		Triples		Home Runs		Total Bases	
Raines-Mon	123	Gwynn-SD	218	Wallach-Mon	42	Samuel-Phi	15	Dawson-Chi	49	Dawson-Chi	353
Coleman-StL	121	Guerrero-LA	184	Smith-StL	40	Gwynn-SD	13	Murphy-Atl	44	Samuel-Phi	329
Davis-Cin	120	Smith-StL	182	Galarraga-Mon	40	VanSlyke-Pit	11	Strawberry-NY	39	Murphy-Atl	328
Gwynn-SD	119	Coleman-StL	180			McGee-StL	11	Davis-Cin	37	Strawberry-NY	310
Murphy-Atl	115					Coleman-StL	10	Johnson-NY	36	Clark-SF	307

Runs Batted In		Runs Produced		Bases On Balls		Batting Average		On Base Percentage		Slugging Average	
Dawson-Chi	137	Wallach-Mon	186	Clark-StL	136	Gwynn-SD	.370	Clark-StL	.461	Clark-StL	.597
Wallach-Mon	123	Samuel-Phi	185	Hayes-Phi	121	Guerrero-LA	.338	Gwynn-SD	.450	Davis-Cin	.593
Schmidt-Phi	113	Davis-Cin	183	Murphy-Atl	115	Raines-Mon	.330	Raines-Mon	.431	Strawberry-NY	.583
Clark-StL	106	Smith-StL	179	Strawberry-NY	97	Kruk-SD	.313	Guerrero-LA	.421	Clark-SF	.580
		Dawson-Chi	178	Raines-Mon	90	James-Atl	.312	Murphy-Atl	.420	Murphy-Atl	.580

Production		Adjusted Production		Batter Runs		Adjusted Batter Runs		Clutch Hitting Index		Runs Created	
Clark-StL	1.058	Clark-StL	174	Clark-StL	54.3	Gwynn-SD	54.3	Herr-StL	172	Murphy-Atl	143
Murphy-Atl	1.000	Strawberry-NY	165	Murphy-Atl	53.3	Clark-StL	52.0	Pendleton-StL	131	Gwynn-SD	143
Davis-Cin	.994	Gwynn-SD	160	Gwynn-SD	49.6	Strawberry-NY	51.1	Smith-StL	130	Strawberry-NY	132
Strawberry-NY	.984	Guerrero-LA	156	Strawberry-NY	44.7	Murphy-Atl	46.8	McGee-StL	126	Raines-Mon	132
Gwynn-SD	.961	Clark-SF	155	Raines-Mon	43.2	Guerrero-LA	45.7	Diaz-Cin	124	Clark-StL	127

Total Average		Stolen Bases		Stolen Base Average		Stolen Base Runs		Fielding Runs		Total Player Rating	
Clark-StL	1.258	Coleman-StL	109	Sandberg-Chi	91.3	Coleman-StL	19.5	Hubbard-Atl	28.2	Davis-Cin	6.9
Davis-Cin	1.182	Gwynn-SD	56	Raines-Mon	90.9	Raines-Mon	12.0	Davis-Cin	28.1	Gwynn-SD	6.6
Raines-Mon	1.133	Hatcher-Hou	53	Davis-Cin	89.3	Davis-Cin	11.4	Bonds-Pit	19.7	Raines-Mon	6.1
Murphy-Atl	1.106	Raines-Mon	50	Hatcher-Hou	85.5	Hatcher-Hou	10.5	Smith-StL	19.3	Murphy-Atl	5.4
Strawberry-NY	1.103	Davis-Cin	50	Coleman-StL	83.2	Gwynn-SD	9.6	Hernandez-NY	17.7	Strawberry-NY	5.0

Wins		Win Percentage		Games		Complete Games		Shutouts		Saves	
Sutcliffe-Chi	18	Gooden-NY	.682	Tekulve-Phi	90	Reuschel-Pit-SF	12	Reuschel-Pit-SF	4	Bedrosian-Phi	40
Rawley-Phi	17	Sutcliffe-Chi	.643	Murphy-Cin	87	Valenzuela-LA	12	Welch-LA	4	Smith-Chi	36
Scott-Hou	16	Welch-LA	.625	Williams-Cin	85	Hershiser-LA	10			Worrell-StL	33
Hershiser-LA	16	Rawley-Phi	.607	J.Robinson-SF-Pit	81	Z.Smith-Atl	9			Franco-Cin	32
		Z.Smith-Atl	.600	McCullers-SD	78	Scott-Hou	8			McDowell-NY	25

Innings Pitched		Fewest Hits/Game		Fewest BB/Game		Strikeouts		Strikeouts/Game		Ratio	
Hershiser-LA	264.2	Ryan-Hou	6.55	Reuschel-Pit-SF	1.67	Ryan-Hou	270	Ryan-Hou	11.48	Reuschel-Pit-SF	10.19
Welch-LA	251.2	Scott-Hou	7.23	Heaton-Mon	1.72	Scott-Hou	233	Scott-Hou	8.47	Scott-Hou	10.25
Valenzuela-LA	251.0	Welch-LA	7.30	Gullickson-Cin	2.13	Welch-LA	196	Sebra-Mon	7.92	Ryan-Hou	10.42
Scott-Hou	247.2	Dunne-Pit	7.88	Forsch-StL	2.26	Valenzuela-LA	190	Gooden-NY	7.41	Welch-LA	10.51
Z.Smith-Atl	242.0	Darling-NY	7.93	Drabek-Pit	2.35	Hershiser-LA	190	Darling-NY	7.24	Drabek-Pit	10.77

Earned Run Average		Adjusted ERA		Opponents' Batting Avg.		Opponents' On Base Pct.		Starter Runs		Adjusted Starter Runs	
Ryan-Hou	2.76	Ryan-Hou	142	Ryan-Hou	.199	Scott-Hou	.282	Ryan-Hou	30.9	Ryan-Hou	27.1
Dunne-Pit	3.03	Dunne-Pit	136	Scott-Hou	.217	Ryan-Hou	.284	Hershiser-LA	30.0	Hershiser-LA	26.6
Hershiser-LA	3.06	Reuschel-Pit-SF	131	Welch-LA	.221	Reuschel-Pit-SF	.284	Reuschel-Pit-SF	24.9	Reuschel-Pit-SF	24.1
Reuschel-Pit-SF	3.09	Hershiser-LA	130	Darling-NY	.233	Welch-LA	.291	Welch-LA	24.1	Welch-LA	20.9
Gooden-NY	3.21	Welch-LA	123	Dunne-Pit	.240	Drabek-Pit	.296	Scott-Hou	23.3	Dunne-Pit	19.6

Clutch Pitching Index		Relief Runs		Adjusted Relief Runs		Relief Ranking		Total Pitcher Index		Total Baseball Ranking	
LaCoss-SF	124	Burke-Mon	29.3	Burke-Mon	30.5	Franco-Cin	33.1	Hershiser-LA	3.6	Davis-Cin	6.9
Cox-StL	120	McGaffigan-Mon	22.5	McGaffigan-Mon	24.2	Burke-Mon	31.7	Franco-Cin	3.3	Gwynn-SD	6.6
Dravecky-SD-SF	113	Williams-Cin	20.9	Williams-Cin	22.8	Worrell-StL	30.5	Burke-Mon	3.2	Raines-Mon	6.1
Ruffin-Phi	112	J.Robinson-SF-Pit	16.9	Worrell-StL	15.7	Smith-Chi	24.3	Worrell-StL	3.1	Murphy-Atl	5.4
Grant-SF-SD	111	Smith-Hou	16.2	Franco-Cin	15.7	Bedrosian-Phi	22.3	Reuschel-Pit-SF	2.5	Strawberry-NY	5.0

January 14 Catfish Hunter and Billy Williams are elected to the Hall of Fame by the BBWAA.

March 3 Ray Dandridge, a legendary third baseman from the Negro Leagues, is the only player elected to the Hall of Fame by the Special Veterans Committee.

June 2 The Mariners select Ken Griffey Jr., the son of Braves outfielder Ken Griffey, with the first pick overall in the free-agent draft.

July 18 Don Mattingly hits a home run in his eighth consecutive game, tying the major league record set by Dale Long in 1956. His streak will end tomorrow when the Rangers romp 20-3.

August 26 Paul Molitor goes 0-for-4 in Milwaukee's 1-0, 10-inning win over the Indians, ending his hitting streak at 39 consecutive games, the longest in the AL since Joe DiMaggio's 56-game streak.

August 30 Kirby Puckett goes 6-for-6 with two home runs, tying the league record for hits in a nine-inning game. Combined with yesterday's 4-for-5, two-home run performance, Puckett has a major league-record-tying 10 hits in two games.

September 14 In an 18-3 rout of the Orioles, the Blue Jays erupt for a major league-record 10 home runs. Ernie Whitt leads the parade with three round trippers, Rance Mulliniks and George Bell hit two, and Lloyd Moseby, Rob Ducey, and Fred McGriff each add one.

September 29 Don Mattingly hits his major league-record sixth grand slam of the season off Boston's Bruce Hurst in a 6-0 Yankees victory, eclipsing the mark shared by Ernie Banks (1955) and Jim Gentile (1961).

October 4 On the last day of the regular season, Detroit beats second-place Toronto 1-0 at Tiger Stadium to win the AL East title. The Tigers were one game behind the Blue Jays entering their three-game season-ending showdown, and won each game by a single run (4-3, 3-2, and 1-0). Frank Tanana outduels Jimmy Key in the finale, and Larry Herndon's second-inning home run provides the game's only run.

October 12 Minnesota beats Detroit 9-5 in Game 5 of the ALCS to wrap up its first league championship since 1965. Third baseman Gary Gaetti is named MVP.

October 17 In the first indoor World Series game ever (at Minnesota's Metrodome), Dan Gladden's grand slam caps a seven-run fourth inning and leads the Twins to a 10-1 win over St. Louis in Game 1.

October 25 Series MVP Frank Viola and reliever Jeff Reardon hold the Cardinals to six hits as the Twins capture Game 7, 4-2 to win their first world championship in Minnesota.

November 11 Roger Clemens becomes the first pitcher since Jim Palmer in 1975-76 to win consecutive Cy Young Awards, collecting 21 of 28 first-place votes to easily beat runner-up Jimmy Key.

November 17 George Bell becomes the first Blue Jay ever to win the league MVP Award, edging Detroit's Alan Trammell, 332-311. Bell hit .308 with 47 home runs and a league-leading 134 RBIs.

	BALTIMORE		BOSTON		CALIFORNIA		CHICAGO		CLEVELAND		DETROIT		KANSAS CITY
M	C.Ripken	M	J.McNamara	M	G.Mauch	M	J.Fregosi	M	P.Corrales	M	S.Anderson	M	B.Gardner
1B	E.Murray	1B	D.Evans	1B	W.Joyner	1B	G.Walker	M	D.Edwards	1B	D.Evans	M	J.Wathan
2B	B.Ripken	2B	M.Barrett	2B	M.McLemore	2B	F.Manrique	1B	J.Carter	2B	L.Whitaker	1B	G.Brett
SS	C.Ripken	SS	S.Owen	SS	D.Schofield	SS	O.Guillen	2B	T.Bernazard	SS	A.Trammell	2B	F.White
3B	R.Knight	3B	W.Boggs	3B	D.DeCinces	3B	T.Hulett	SS	J.Franco	3B	T.Brookens	SS	A.Salazar
LF	K.Gerhart	LF	J.Rice	LF	J.Howell	LF	G.Redus	3B	B.Jacoby	LF	K.Gibson	3B	K.Seitzer
CF	F.Lynn	CF	E.Burks	CF	G.Pettis	CF	K.Williams	LF	M.Hall	CF	C.Lemon	LF	B.Jackson
RF	L.Sheets	RF	M.Greenwell	RF	D.White	RF	I.Calderon	CF	B.Butler	RF	P.Sheridan	CF	W.Wilson
C	T.Kennedy	C	M.Sullivan	C	B.Boone	C	C.Fisk	RF	C.Snyder	C	M.Nokes	RF	D.Tartabull
DH	M.Young	DH	D.Baylor	DH	B.Downing	DH	H.Baines	C	B.Bando	DH	B.Madlock	C	J.Quirk
								DH	P.Tabler			DH	S.Balboni
D2	A.Wiggins	1	B.Buckner	P	M.Witt	O	D.Boston			CO	M.Heath		
O	L.Lacy	2S	E.Romero	P	D.Sutton	23	D.Hill	2	T.Hinzo	OD	L.Herndon	P	B.Saberhagen
DO	J.Dwyer	O	T.Benzinger	P	W.Fraser			DO	C.Castillo			P	M.Gubicza
2	R.Burleson			P	J.Lazorko	P	F.Bannister			P	J.Morris	P	C.Leibrandt
		P	R.Clemens	P	J.Candelaria	P	R.Dotson	P	T.Candiotti	P	W.Terrell	P	D.Jackson
P	M.Boddicker	P	B.Hurst	RP	D.Buice	P	J.DeLeon	P	K.Schrom	P	F.Tanana	RP	S.Farr
P	E.Bell	P	A.Nipper	RP	C.Finley	P	B.Long	P	P.Niekro	P	D.Petry	RP	J.Gleaton
P	D.Schmidt	P	B.Stanley	RP	G.Minton	RP	J.Winn	P	S.Bailes	P	J.Robinson	RP	D.Quisenberry
P	J.Habyan	P	J.Sellers			RP	B.Thigpen	P	S.Carlton	RP	E.King		
P	K.Dixon	RP	W.Gardner	P	J.Reuss	RP	R.Searage	RP	R.Yett	RP	M.Henneman		
RP	M.Williamson	RP	C.Schiraldi	P	K.McCaskill			RP	D.Jones	RP	M.Thurmond		
RP	T.Arnold	RP	S.Crawford	P	G.Lucas	P	D.LaPoint	RP	E.Vande Berg				
RP	T.Niedenfuer					P	S.Nielsen			P	D.Alexander		
		P	T.Bolton			P	J.Davis	P	G.Swindell				
P	M.Flanagan					P	B.James	P	D.Akerfelds				
P	S.McGregor					P	N.Allen	P	J.Farrell				
P	M.Griffin												
P	J.Ballard												

	MILWAUKEE		MINNESOTA		NEW YORK		OAKLAND		SEATTLE		TEXAS		TORONTO
M	T.Trebelhorn	M	T.Kelly	M	L.Piniella	M	T.LaRussa	M	D.Williams	M	B.Valentine	M	J.Williams
1B	G.Brock	1B	K.Hrbek	1B	D.Mattingly	1B	M.McGwire	1B	A.Davis	1B	P.O'Brien	1B	W.Upshaw
2B	J.Castillo	2B	S.Lombardozzi	2B	W.Randolph	2B	T.Phillips	2B	H.Reynolds	2B	J.Browne	2B	G.Iorg
SS	D.Sveum	SS	G.Gagne	SS	W.Tolleson	SS	A.Griffin	SS	R.Quinones	SS	S.Fletcher	SS	T.Fernandez
3B	E.Riles	3B	G.Gaetti	3B	M.Pagliarulo	3B	C.Lansford	3B	J.Presley	3B	S.Buechele	3B	K.Gruber
LF	R.Deer	LF	D.Gladden	LF	G.Ward	LF	J.Canseco	LF	P.Bradley	LF	P.Incaviglia	LF	G.Bell
CF	R.Yount	CF	K.Puckett	CF	C.Washington	CF	L.Polonia	CF	J.Moses	CF	O.McDowell	CF	L.Moseby
RF	G.Braggs	RF	T.Brunansky	RF	D.Winfield	RF	M.Davis	RF	M.Kingery	RF	R.Sierra	RF	J.Barfield
C	B.Surhoff	C	T.Laudner	C	R.Cerone	C	T.Steinbach	C	S.Bradley	C	D.Slaught	C	E.Whitt
DH	C.Cooper	DH	R.Smalley	DH	R.Kittle	DH	R.Jackson	DH	K.Phelps	DH	L.Parrish	DH	F.McGriff
O	M.Felder	O	R.Bush	OD	D.Pasqua	O	D.Murphy	O	M.Brantley	OD	B.Brower	OD	R.Leach
O	R.Manning	O	M.Davidson	OD	R.Henderson	2	T.Bernazard	CD	D.Valle	C3	G.Petralli	3D	R.Mulliniks
D3	P.Molitor	S2	A.Newman	S2	B.Meacham	C	M.Tettleton			C1	M.Stanley		
23	J.Gantner	D1	G.Larkin					P	M.Langston			P	J.Key
C	B.Schroeder			P	T.John	P	D.Stewart	P	M.Moore	P	C.Hough	P	J.Clancy
		P	B.Blyleven	P	R.Rhoden	P	C.Young	P	M.Morgan	P	J.Guzman	P	D.Stieb
P	T.Higuera	P	F.Viola	P	C.Hudson	P	S.Ontiveros	P	S.Bankhead	P	B.Witt	P	J.Cerutti
P	B.Wegman	P	L.Straker	P	D.Rasmussen	RP	G.Nelson	P	L.Guetterman	P	G.Harris	RP	M.Eichhorn
P	J.Nieves	P	M.Smithson	P	R.Guidry	RP	D.Eckersley	RP	J.Reed	RP	M.Williams	RP	J.Nunez
P	C.Bosio	P	J.Niekro	RP	D.Righetti	RP	E.Plunk	RP	B.Wilkinson	RP	D.Mohorcic	RP	T.Henke
RP	C.Crim	RP	J.Berenguer	RP	T.Stoddard			RP	M.Trujillo	RP	J.Russell		
RP	D.Plesac	RP	G.Frazier	RP	P.Clements	P	J.Rijo					P	J.Musselman
RP	M.Clear	RP	J.Reardon	/P	J.Niekro	P	J.Andujar			P	P.Kilgus	P	J.Johnson
						P	D.Lamp			P	E.Correa		
P	M.Knudson	P	K.Atherton			P	D.Leiper			P	M.Loynd		
P	J.Aldrich												

TEAM	G	W	L	PCT	GB	R	OR	AB	H	2B	3B	HR	BB	SO	AVG	OBP	SLG	PRO	PRO+	BR	/A	PF	CHI	RC	SB	CS	SBA	SBR
EAST																												
DET	162	98	64	.605		**896**	735	5649	1535	274	32	**225**	**653**	913	.272	.352	**.451**	**.803**	**116**	**91**	**131**	96	98	**910**	106	50	68	2
TOR	162	96	66	.593	2	845	**655**	5635	1514	277	38	215	555	970	.269	.338	.446	.784	103	42	26	102	100	841	126	50	72	8
MIL	162	91	71	.562	7	862	817	5625	1552	272	46	163	598	1040	.276	.349	.428	.777	102	40	17	103	101	852	**176**	74	70	8
NY	162	89	73	.549	9	788	758	5511	1445	239	16	196	604	949	.262	.338	.418	.756	100	-6	3	99	100	773	105	43	71	6
BOS	162	78	84	.481	20	842	825	5586	**1554**	273	26	174	606	**825**	**.278**	**.355**	.430	.785	104	61	38	103	97	855	77	45	63	-4
BAL	162	67	95	.414	31	729	880	5576	1437	219	20	211	524	939	.258	.324	.418	.742	98	-47	-27	97	99	736	69	45	61	-6
CLE	162	61	101	.377	37	742	957	5606	1476	267	30	187	489	977	.263	.326	.422	.748	95	-35	-40	101	98	772	140	54	72	10
WEST																												
MIN	162	85	77	.525		786	806	5441	1422	258	35	196	523	898	.261	.330	.430	.760	96	-8	-35	104	103	757	113	65	63	-5
KC	162	83	79	.512	2	715	691	5499	1443	239	40	168	523	1034	.262	.330	.412	.742	93	-40	-58	102	97	747	125	43	**74**	**12**
OAK	162	81	81	.500	4	806	789	5511	1432	263	33	199	593	1056	.260	.336	.428	.764	108	4	58	93	101	796	140	63	69	4
SEA	162	78	84	.481	7	760	801	5508	1499	282	**48**	161	500	863	.272	.337	.428	.765	96	9	-31	105	96	788	174	73	70	8
CHI	162	77	85	.475	8	748	746	5538	1427	**283**	36	173	487	971	.258	.321	.415	.736	91	-57	-74	102	103	737	138	52	73	10
TEX	162	75	87	.463	10	823	849	5564	1478	264	35	194	567	1081	.266	.336	.430	.766	101	9	8	100	102	798	120	71	63	-7
CAL	162	75	87	.463	10	770	803	5570	1406	257	26	172	590	926	.252	.328	.401	.729	95	-65	-39	97	**105**	744	125	44	**74**	11
TOT	1134					11112		77819	20620	3667	461	2634	7812	13442	.265	.336	.425	.761							1734	772	69	57

TEAM	CG	SH	SV	IP	H	H/G	HR	BB	SO	RAT	ERA	ERA+	OAV	OOB	PR	/A	PF	CPI	FA	E	DP	FW	PW	BW	SBW	DIF
EAST																										
DET	33	10	31	1456	1430	8.8	180	563	976	12.5	4.02	105	.256	.328	70	32	95	103	.980	122	147	.1	3.1	**12.5**	-.2	1.6
TOR	18	8	43	1454	**1323**	**8.2**	158	567	1064	**11.8**	**3.74**	**120**	**.244**	**.318**	**115**	**121**	101	100	.982	111	148	.8	**11.5**	2.5	.4	-.2
MIL	28	6	45	1464	1548	9.5	169	529	1039	12.9	4.62	99	.271	.336	-27	-8	103	96	.976	145	155	-1.3	-.8	1.6	.4	10.1
NY	19	10	**47**	1446^{1}	1475	9.2	179	542	900	12.8	4.36	101	.266	.334	16	5	98	101	.983	102	155	1.3	.5	.3	.2	5.7
BOS	**47**	**13**	16	1436	1584	9.9	190	517	1034	13.4	4.77	95	.282	.346	-50	-37	102	102	.982	110	158	.8	-3.5	3.6	-.8	-3.2
BAL	17	6	30	1439^{2}	1555	9.7	226	547	870	13.3	5.01	88	.276	.343	-88	-97	99	98	.982	111	**174**	.8	-9.2	-2.6	-1.0	-2.0
CLE	24	8	25	1422^{2}	1566	9.9	219	606	849	14.1	5.28	86	.278	.354	-131	-120	102	97	.975	153	128	-1.8	-11.4	-3.8	.6	-3.5
WEST																										
MIN	16	4	39	1427^{1}	1465	9.2	210	564	990	13.1	4.63	100	.266	.339	-27	-2	104	100	**.984**	**98**	147	**1.6**	-.2	-3.3	-.9	6.8
KC	44	11	26	1424	1424	9.0	**128**	548	923	12.7	3.86	118	.261	.333	95	111	102	**105**	.979	131	151	-.5	10.6	-5.5	**.8**	-3.4
OAK	18	6	40	1445^{2}	1442	9.0	176	531	1042	12.5	4.32	96	.258	.327	22	-31	93	96	.977	142	122	-1.1	-3.0	5.5	.0	-1.4
SEA	39	10	33	1430^{2}	1503	9.5	199	**497**	919	12.8	4.49	105	.272	.335	-5	37	106	102	.980	122	150	.1	3.5	-3.0	.4	-4.0
CHI	29	12	37	1447^{2}	1436	8.9	189	537	792	12.5	4.30	107	.259	.329	26	46	103	99	.981	116	**174**	.5	4.4	-7.1	.6	-2.4
TEX	20	3	27	1444^{1}	1388	8.6	199	760	**1103**	13.7	4.63	97	.253	.350	-28	-25	100	100	.976	151	148	-1.7	-2.4	.8	-1.1	-1.6
CAL	20	7	36	1457^{1}	1481	9.1	212	504	941	12.5	4.38	98	.264	.329	13	-13	97	101	.981	117	162	.4	-1.2	-3.7	.7	-2.1
TOT	372	114	475	20195^{2}		9.2				12.9	4.46		.265	.336					.980	1731	2119					

Runs
Molitor-Mil 114
Bell-Tor 111
Whitaker-Det 110
Downing-Cal 110

Hits
Seitzer-KC 207
Puckett-Min 207
Trammell-Det 205
Boggs-Bos 200
Yount-Mil 198

Doubles
Molitor-Mil 41
Boggs-Bos 40

Triples
Wilson-KC 15
Polonia-Oak 10
P.Bradley-Sea 10
Yount-Mil 9

Home Runs
McGwire-Oak 49
Bell-Tor 47

Total Bases
Bell-Tor 369
McGwire-Oak 344
Puckett-Min 333
Trammell-Det 329
Boggs-Bos 324

Runs Batted In
Bell-Tor 134
Evans-Bos 123
McGwire-Oak 118
Joyner-Cal 117
Mattingly-NY 115

Runs Produced
Evans-Bos 198
Bell-Tor 198
Trammell-Det 186
Joyner-Cal 183
Yount-Mil 181

Bases On Balls
Evans-Bos 106
Downing-Cal 106
Boggs-Bos 105
Evans-Det 100
Butler-Cle 91

Batting Average
Boggs-Bos .... .363
Molitor-Mil ...... .353
Trammell-Det ..... .343
Puckett-Min ...... .332
Mattingly-NY ..... .327

On Base Percentage
Boggs-Bos .... .467
Molitor-Mil ...... .438
Evans-Bos .... .422
Randolph-NY ..... .415
Trammell-Det ..... .406

Slugging Average
McGwire-Oak ..... .618
Bell-Tor .... .605
Boggs-Bos .... .588
Evans-Bos .... .569
Molitor-Mil ...... .566

Production
Boggs-Bos 1.055
Molitor-Mil 1.004
McGwire-Oak ..... .992
Evans-Bos .... .991
Bell-Tor .... .962

Adjusted Production
Boggs-Bos 173
McGwire-Oak 168
Molitor-Mil 159
Trammell-Det 157
Evans-Bos 155

Batter Runs
Boggs-Bos 66.6
Evans-Bos 49.6
Molitor-Mil 44.8
McGwire-Oak 44.2
Trammell-Det 43.7

Adjusted Batter Runs
Boggs-Bos 62.7
McGwire-Oak 53.0
Trammell-Det 49.5
Evans-Bos 46.1
Molitor-Mil 41.8

Clutch Hitting Index
Randolph-NY 141
Griffin-Oak 127
Owen-Bos 118
Tabler-Cle 117
Ward-NY 117

Runs Created
Boggs-Bos 154
Trammell-Det 137
Evans-Bos 134
McGwire-Oak 131
Molitor-Mil 125

Total Average
Molitor-Mil 1.171
Boggs-Bos 1.169
Evans-Bos 1.059
McGwire-Oak 1.042
Trammell-Det 1.015

Stolen Bases
Reynolds-Sea 60
Wilson-KC 59
Redus-Chi 52
Molitor-Mil 45
Henderson-NY 41

Stolen Base Average
McDowell-Tex 92.3
Trammell-Det 91.3
Schofield-Cal 86.4
Moseby-Tor 84.8
Wilson-KC 84.3

Stolen Base Runs
Wilson-KC 11.1
Redus-Chi 9.0
Moseby-Tor 7.5
Molitor-Mil 7.5
Henderson-NY 7.5

Fielding Runs
Barrett-Bos 32.3
Salazar-KC 21.8
Manrique-Chi 18.9
Reynolds-Sea 18.8
Gagne-Min 16.9

Total Player Rating
Boggs-Bos 5.8
Trammell-Det 5.4
Molitor-Mil 3.5
Henderson-NY 3.5
McGwire-Oak 3.3

Wins
Stewart-Oak 20
Clemens-Bos 20
Langston-Sea 19

Win Percentage
Clemens-Bos ..... .690
Key-Tor .... .680
Saberhagen-KC .. .643
Higuera-Mil ...... .643

Games
Eichhorn-Tor 89
Williams-Tex 85
Mohorcic-Tex 74
Henke-Tor 72
Musselman-Tor 68

Complete Games
Clemens-Bos 18
Saberhagen-KC 15
Hurst-Bos 15
Langston-Sea 14
Higuera-Mil 14

Shutouts
Clemens-Bos 7
Saberhagen-KC 4

Saves
Henke-Tor 34
Righetti-NY 31
Reardon-Min 31
Plesac-Mil 23
Buice-Cal 17

Innings Pitched
Hough-Tex 285.1
Clemens-Bos 281.2
Langston-Sea 272.0
Blyleven-Min 267.0
Morris-Det 266.0

Fewest Hits/Game
Key-Tor 7.24
Hough-Tex 7.51
Morris-Det 7.68
Stewart-Oak 7.71
DeLeon-Chi 7.73

Fewest BB/Game
Long-Chi 1.49
Saberhagen-KC ... 1.86
Sutton-Cal 1.93
Bannister-Chi 1.93
Young-Oak 1.95

Strikeouts
Langston-Sea 262
Clemens-Bos 256
Higuera-Mil 240
Hough-Tex 223
Morris-Det 208

Strikeouts/Game
Langston-Sea 8.67
Higuera-Mil 8.25
Clemens-Bos 8.18
Bosio-Mil 7.94
Nieves-Mil 7.50

Ratio
Key-Tor 9.59
Bannister-Chi ... 10.43
Saberhagen-KC .. 10.68
Young-Oak 10.68
Viola-Min 10.80

Earned Run Average
Key-Tor 2.76
Viola-Min 2.90
Clemens-Bos 2.97
Saberhagen-KC ... 3.36
Morris-Det 3.38

Adjusted ERA
Key-Tor 163
Viola-Min 159
Clemens-Bos 153
Saberhagen-KC ... 135
Leibrandt-KC 134

Opponents' Batting Avg.
Key-Tor .... .221
Hough-Tex .... .223
Morris-Det ...... .228
Stewart-Oak ..... .229
DeLeon-Chi ...... .230

Opponents' On Base Pct.
Key-Tor .... .273
Bannister-Chi .... .286
Viola-Min .... .294
Morris-Det ...... .294
Young-Oak .... .295

Starter Runs
Key-Tor 49.2
Clemens-Bos 46.5
Viola-Min 43.6
Morris-Det 31.7
Saberhagen-KC ... 31.2

Adjusted Starter Runs
Key-Tor 50.3
Clemens-Bos 49.0
Viola-Min 48.1
Saberhagen-KC ... 34.0
Leibrandt-KC 30.6

Clutch Pitching Index
Viola-Min 115
Rhoden-NY 112
Terrell-Det 110
Blyleven-Min 109
Gubicza-KC 107

Relief Runs
Henke-Tor 20.5
Eckersley-Oak ... 18.3
Eichhorn-Tor 18.2
Thigpen-Chi 17.1
Plesac-Mil 16.3

Adjusted Relief Runs
Henke-Tor 20.9
Eichhorn-Tor 18.7
Thigpen-Chi 18.3
Plesac-Mil 17.3
Mohorcic-Tex 16.4

Relief Ranking
Plesac-Mil 32.4
Thigpen-Chi 29.3
Henke-Tor 28.3
Mohorcic-Tex 25.0
Eichhorn-Tor 22.4

Total Pitcher Index
Viola-Min 4.6
Key-Tor 4.4
Clemens-Bos 4.4
Leibrandt-KC 3.5
Saberhagen-KC 3.4

Total Baseball Ranking
Boggs-Bos 5.8
Trammell-Det 5.4
Viola-Min 4.6
Key-Tor 4.4
Clemens-Bos 4.4

February 23 A committee of Chicago aldermen vote 7-2 to allow the Cubs to install lights and play up to 18 night games a year at Wrigley Field. The Cubs had feared losing the 1990 All-Star Game, as well as future playoff and World Series games, if lights were not installed.

May 14 Infielder Jose Oquendo becomes the first non-pitcher in 20 years to get a major league decision in the Cardinals' 7-5, 19-inning loss to the Braves. St. Louis had used seven pitchers when Oquendo is brought in to pitch the 16th inning. He shuts out the Braves for three innings before surrendering the game-winning runs.

August 9 The Cubs and Mets play the first official night game at Wrigley Field, a 6-4 Chicago victory.

September 8 NL president Bart Giamatti is unanimously elected baseball's seventh commissioner, and will succeed Peter Ueberroth next season.

September 26 The Dodgers beat the Padres 3-2 to clinch the NL West title and earn a playoff date with the Mets, who won 10 of their 11 meetings this season.

September 28 In his last start of the regular season, Orel Hershiser pitches 10 shutout innings to extend his consecutive-scoreless-inning streak to 59, breaking Dodger Don Drysdale's major league record by one. San Diego's Andy Hawkins also pitches 10 shutout innings and the Padres eventually win 2-1 on Mark Parent's home run in the bottom of the 16th.

October 8 Dodgers ace reliever Jay Howell is ejected in the eighth inning of Game 3 of the NLCS for having pine tar on his glove, and the Mets go on to score five times in the inning on the way to an 8-4 win. Howell will be suspended for three days by the league.

October 12 Series MVP Orel Hershiser shuts out New York on five hits to win Game 7 of the NLCS, 6-0, and put the Dodgers into the World Series for the first time since 1981.

October 15 In one of the most improbable finishes in World Series history, pinch hitter Kirk Gibson hits a two-run home run off Dennis Eckersley with two out in the bottom of the ninth inning to give the Dodgers a 5-4 win in Game 1. The injured Gibson was not expected to play in the World Series, and will not play again in 1988.

October 20 Series MVP Orel Hershiser ends his dream season with a 5-2 four-hitter over the A's in Game 5 of the World Series, which gives the Dodgers their first World Championship since 1981. Los Angeles is the only team to win more than one World Series in the 1980s.

November 10 Orel Hershiser (23-8) is a unanimous choice as NL Cy Young Award winner.

November 15 Dodgers outfielder Kirk Gibson wins the NL MVP Award, edging Mets Darryl Strawberry and Kevin McReynolds. Gibson hit .290 with 25 home runs and just 76 RBIs.

	ATLANTA		CHICAGO		CINCINNATI		HOUSTON		LOS ANGELES		MONTREAL
M	C.Tanner	M	D.Zimmer	M	P.Rose	M	H.Lanier	M	T.Lasorda	M	B.Rodgers
M	R.Nixon	1B	M.Grace	M	T.Helms	1B	G.Davis	1B	F.Stubbs	1B	A.Galarraga
1B	G.Perry	2B	R.Sandberg	M	P.Rose	2B	B.Doran	2B	S.Sax	2B	T.Foley
2B	R.Gant	SS	S.Dunston	1B	D.Esasky	SS	R.Ramirez	SS	A.Griffin	SS	L.Rivera
SS	A.Thomas	3B	V.Law	2B	J.Treadway	3B	B.Bell	3B	J.Hamilton	3B	T.Wallach
3B	K.Oberkfell	LF	R.Palmeiro	SS	B.Larkin	LF	B.Hatcher	LF	K.Gibson	LF	T.Raines
LF	D.James	CF	D.Jackson	3B	C.Sabo	CF	G.Young	CF	J.Shelby	CF	O.Nixon
CF	A.Hall	RF	A.Dawson	LF	K.Daniels	RF	K.Bass	RF	M.Marshall	RF	H.Brooks
RF	D.Murphy	C	D.Berryhill	CF	E.Davis	C	A.Trevino	C	M.Scioscia	C	N.Santovenia
C	O.Virgil	O	M.Webster	RF	P.O'Neill	O	T.Puhl	S3	D.Anderson	O	M.Webster
		O	D.Martinez	C	B.Diaz	O	A.Ashby	O	M.Davis	2S	R.Hudler
C	B.Benedict	C	J.Davis	O	D.Collins			31	P.Guerrero		
P	R.Mahler			P	D.Jackson	P	N.Ryan			P	De.Martinez
P	P.Smith	P	G.Maddux	P	T.Browning	P	M.Scott	P	O.Hershiser	P	B.Smith
P	T.Glavine	P	R.Sutcliffe	P	J.Rijo	P	J.Deshaies	P	T.Leary	P	P.Perez
P	Z.Smith	P	J.Moyer	RP	J.Franco	P	D.Darwin	P	T.Belcher	P	J.Dopson
RP	C.Puleo	P	C.Schiraldi	RP	R.Murphy	P	B.Knepper	P	F.Valenzuela	P	B.Holman
RP	J.Alvarez	P	J.Pico	RP	T.Birtsas	RP	J.Agosto	RP	A.Pena	RP	J.Parrett
RP	P.Assenmacher	RP	F.DiPino			RP	L.Andersen	RP	B.Holton	RP	A.McGaffigan
		RP	L.Lancaster			RP	D.Smith	RP	T.Crews	RP	T.Burke
P	K.Coffman			P	M.Soto			P	D.Sutton	P	D.Martinez
P	J.Smoltz	P	A.Nipper	P	R.Robinson	P	J.Andujar	P	J.Howell	P	N.Heaton
P	G.Jimenez			P	J.Armstrong			P	S.Hillegas	P	F.Youmans
				P	F.Williams			P	J.Orosco	P	J.Hesketh
				P	N.Charlton			/P	J.Tudor		
				P	R.Dibble						
				P	D.Rasmussen						

	NEW YORK		PHILADELPHIA		PITTSBURGH		SAN DIEGO		SAN FRANCISCO		ST.LOUIS
M	D.Johnson	M	L.Elia	M	J.Leyland	M	L.Bowa	M	R.Craig	M	W.Herzog
1B	K.Hernandez	M	J.Vukovich	1B	S.Bream	M	J.McKeon	1B	W.Clark	1B	B.Horner
2B	W.Backman	1B	V.Hayes	2B	J.Lind	1B	K.Moreland	2B	R.Thompson	2B	L.Alicea
SS	K.Elster	2B	J.Samuel	SS	R.Belliard	2B	R.Alomar	SS	J.Uribe	SS	O.Smith
3B	H.Johnson	SS	S.Jeltz	3B	B.Bonilla	SS	G.Templeton	3B	K.Mitchell	3B	T.Pendleton
LF	K.McReynolds	3B	M.Schmidt	LF	B.Bonds	3B	C.Brown	LF	M.Aldrete	LF	V.Coleman
CF	L.Dykstra	LF	P.Bradley	CF	A.Van Slyke	LF	C.Martinez	CF	B.Butler	CF	W.McGee
RF	D.Strawberry	CF	M.Thompson	RF	R.Reynolds	CF	M.Wynne	RF	C.Maldonado	RF	T.Brunansky
C	G.Carter	RF	C.James	C	M.LaValliere	RF	T.Gwynn	C	B.Melvin	C	T.Pena
		C	L.Parrish			C	B.Santiago				
13	D.Magadan			O	D.Coles			C	B.Brenly	23	J.Oquendo
O	M.Wilson	O1	G.Gross			1O	J.Kruk				
2	T.Teufel	1	R.Jordan	P	D.Drabek	32	R.Ready	P	R.Reuschel	P	J.DeLeon
				P	D.Walk	S	D.Thon	P	D.Robinson	P	J.Magrane
P	D.Gooden	P	K.Gross	P	J.Smiley			P	K.Downs	P	J.Tudor
P	R.Darling	P	D.Carman	P	M.Dunne	P	E.Show	P	A.Hammaker	P	L.McWilliams
P	D.Cone	P	S.Rawley	P	B.Fisher	P	A.Hawkins	P	M.Krukow	P	B.Forsch
P	B.Ojeda	P	D.Palmer	RP	J.Robinson	P	E.Whitson	RP	S.Garrelts	RP	S.Terry
P	S.Fernandez	RP	B.Ruffin	RP	J.Gott	P	J.Jones	RP	C.Lefferts	RP	T.Worrell
RP	T.Leach	RP	G.Harris	RP	B.Kipper	P	D.Rasmussen	RP	J.Price	RP	K.Dayley
RP	R.McDowell	RP	K.Tekulve			RP	L.McCullers				
RP	R.Myers			P	B.Jones	RP	M.Grant	P	M.LaCoss	P	D.Cox
		P	M.Maddux	/P	D.LaPoint	RP	M.Davis			P	G.Mathews
		P	S.Bedrosian							P	R.O'Neal
		P	M.Freeman			P	G.Booker			P	J.Costello
						P	D.Leiper				

TEAM	G	W	L	PCT	GB	R	OR	AB	H	2B	3B	HR	BB	SO	AVG	OBP	SLG	PRO	PRO+	BR	/A	PF	CHI	RC	SB	CS	SBA	SBR
EAST																												
NY	160	100	60	.625		**703**	532	5408	1387	251	24	**152**	544	842	.256	**.328**	**.396**	**.724**	120	**95**	131	95	97	717	140	51	73	11
PIT	160	85	75	.531	15	651	616	5379	1327	240	45	110	**553**	947	.247	.321	.369	.690	105	33	42	99	99	648	119	60	66	0
MON	163	81	81	.500	20	628	592	5573	1400	260	48	107	454	1053	.251	.311	.373	.684	98	12	-18	105	97	636	189	89	68	3
CHI	163	77	85	.475	24	660	694	5675	**1481**	262	46	113	403	910	**.261**	.312	.383	.695	100	31	1	105	99	673	120	46	72	8
STL	162	76	86	.469	25	578	633	5518	1373	207	33	71	484	**827**	.249	.312	.337	.649	92	-47	-53	101	98	601	**234**	64	**79**	32
PHI	162	65	96	.404	35.5	597	734	5403	1294	246	31	106	489	981	.239	.308	.355	.663	94	-22	-35	102	100	599	112	49	70	4
WEST																												
LA	162	94	67	.584		628	544	5431	1346	217	25	99	437	947	.248	.308	.352	.660	99	-2	-14	97	**107**	590	131	46	74	12
CIN	161	87	74	.540	7	641	596	5426	1334	246	25	122	479	922	.246	.311	.368	.679	97	6	-19	104	102	639	207	56	**79**	29
SD	161	83	78	.516	11	594	583	5366	1325	205	35	94	494	892	.247	.313	.351	.664	99	-19	-8	98	99	594	123	50	71	7
SF	162	83	79	.512	11.5	670	626	5450	1353	227	44	113	550	1023	.248	.321	.368	.689	109	32	61	96	101	650	121	78	61	-11
HOU	162	82	80	.506	12.5	617	631	5494	1338	239	31	96	474	840	.244	.308	.351	.659	99	-32	-9	96	103	604	198	71	74	17
ATL	160	54	106	.338	39.5	555	741	5440	1319	228	28	96	432	848	.242	.301	.348	.649	88	-56	-84	105	99	549	95	69	58	-13
TOT	969					7522		65563	16277	2828	415	1279	5793	11032	.248	.313	.363	.675						1789	729	71	99	

TEAM	CG	SH	SV	IP	H	H/G	HR	BB	SO	RAT	ERA	ERA+	OAV	OOB	PR	/A	PF	CPI	FA	E	DP	FW	PW	BW	SBW	DIF
EAST																										
NY	31	22	46	1439	**1253**	7.8	78	404	1100	10.6	2.91	111	**.235**	.293	86	50	93	97	**.981**	115	127	**.9**	5.4	**14.1**	.3	-.7
PIT	12	11	46	1440²	1349	8.4	108	469	790	11.6	3.47	98	.250	.314	-3	-10	99	101	.980	125	128	.3	-1.1	4.5	-.9	2.1
MON	18	12	43	1482²	1310	8.0	122	476	923	11.1	3.08	117	.238	.303	60	84	104	105	.978	142	145	-.5	**9.1**	-1.9	-.6	-6.0
CHI	30	10	29	1464¹	1494	9.2	115	490	897	12.4	3.84	94	.265	.327	-64	-38	105	102	.980	125	128	.5	-4.1	.1	-.0	-.4
STL	17	14	42	1470²	1387	8.5	91	486	881	11.6	3.47	100	.252	.314	-4	1	101	99	**.981**	121	131	.6	.1	-5.7	**2.6**	-2.6
PHI	16	6	36	1433	1447	9.1	118	628	859	13.3	4.14	86	.265	.344	-110	-92	103	102	.976	145	139	-.7	-9.9	-3.8	-.5	-.6
WEST																										
LA	**32**	**24**	49	1463¹	1291	7.9	84	473	1029	11.0	2.96	112	.237	.301	78	59	97	102	.977	142	126	-.5	6.4	-1.5	.4	8.8
CIN	24	13	43	1455	1271	7.9	121	504	934	11.1	3.35	107	.237	.306	16	38	104	98	.980	125	131	.4	4.1	-2.0	2.2	1.9
SD	30	9	39	1449	1332	8.3	112	439	885	11.1	3.28	104	.247	.306	27	19	99	102	**.981**	124	**147**	.6	2.0	-.9	-.1	.8
SF	25	13	42	1462¹	1323	8.1	99	422	875	10.9	3.39	96	.242	.300	10	-20	95	93	.980	129	145	.2	-2.2	6.6	-2.1	-.5
HOU	21	15	40	1474²	1339	8.2	123	478	1049	11.3	3.41	97	.242	.307	7	-14	96	99	.978	138	124	-.3	-1.5	-1.0	.9	2.9
ATL	14	4	25	1446	1481	9.2	108	524	810	12.7	4.09	86	.268	.336	-103	-67	107	100	.976	151	138	-1.1	-7.2	-9.1	-2.3	-6.3
TOT	270	153	480	17480²		8.4				11.6	3.45		.248	.313					.979	1578	1609					

Runs		Hits		Doubles		Triples		Home Runs		Total Bases	
Butler-SF	109	Galarraga-Mon	184	Galarraga-Mon	42	VanSlyke-Pit	15	Strawberry-NY	39	Galarraga-Mon	329
Gibson-LA	106	Dawson-Chi	179	Palmeiro-Chi	41	Coleman-StL	10	Davis-Hou	30	Dawson-Chi	298
Clark-SF	102	Palmeiro-Chi	178	Sabo-Cin	40	Young-Hou	9	Galarraga-Mon	29	VanSlyke-Pit	297
VanSlyke-Pit	101	Sax-LA	175	Bream-Pit	37	Samuel-Phi	9	Clark-SF	29	Strawberry-NY	296
Strawberry-NY	101	Larkin-Cin	174			Butler-SF	9	McReynolds-NY	27	Clark-SF	292

Runs Batted In		Runs Produced		Bases On Balls		Batting Average		On Base Percentage		Slugging Average	
Clark-SF	109	Clark-SF	182	Clark-SF	100	Gwynn-SD	.313	Daniels-Cin	.400	Strawberry-NY	.545
Strawberry-NY	101	VanSlyke-Pit	176	Butler-SF	97	Palmeiro-Chi	.307	Butler-SF	.395	Galarraga-Mon	.540
VanSlyke-Pit	100	Strawberry-NY	163	Daniels-Cin	87	Dawson-Chi	.303	Clark-SF	.392	Clark-SF	.508
Bonilla-Pit	100	Bonilla-Pit	163	Johnson-NY	86	Galarraga-Mon	.302	Gibson-LA	.381	VanSlyke-Pit	.506
		Galarraga-Mon	162			Perry-Atl	.300	Gwynn-SD	.374	Dawson-Chi	.504

Production		Adjusted Production		Batter Runs		Adjusted Batter Runs		Clutch Hitting Index		Runs Created	
Strawberry-NY	.916	Strawberry-NY	168	Clark-SF	44.3	Clark-SF	49.3	Moreland-SD	131	Clark-SF	120
Clark-SF	.900	Clark-SF	163	Strawberry-NY	42.0	Strawberry-NY	47.4	Gwynn-SD	118	Galarraga-Mon	114
Galarraga-Mon	.894	Gibson-LA	151	Galarraga-Mon	39.2	Gibson-LA	36.9	Maldonado-SF	114	Strawberry-NY	111
Gibson-LA	.864	Bonds-Pit	147	Gibson-LA	33.8	Galarraga-Mon	34.3	Bream-Pit	114	Gibson-LA	107
Daniels-Cin	.863	Galarraga-Mon	147	Daniels-Cin	33.2	Bonilla-Pit	33.6	Davis-Cin	113	VanSlyke-Pit	107

Total Average		Stolen Bases		Stolen Base Average		Stolen Base Runs		Fielding Runs		Total Player Rating	
Strawberry-NY	.957	Coleman-StL	81	McReynolds-NY	100.0	Smith-StL	11.7	Smith-StL	22.9	Strawberry-NY	5.2
Clark-SF	.955	Young-Hou	65	Davis-Cin	92.1	McGee-StL	8.7	Bream-Pit	20.9	VanSlyke-Pit	5.1
Gibson-LA	.929	Smith-StL	57	Gibson-LA	88.6	Davis-Cin	8.7	Sabo-Cin	17.5	Smith-StL	5.1
Davis-Cin	.927	Sabo-Cin	46	McGee-StL	87.2	Coleman-StL	8.1	Murphy-Atl	17.5	Gibson-LA	5.0
Daniels-Cin	.924	Nixon-Mon	46	Smith-StL	86.4	Larkin-Cin	7.8	VanSlyke-Pit	16.7	Larkin-Cin	4.5

Wins		Win Percentage		Games		Complete Games		Shutouts		Saves	
Jackson-Cin	23	Cone-NY	.870	Murphy-Cin	76	Jackson-Cin	15	Hershiser-LA	8	Franco-Cin	39
Hershiser-LA	23	Browning-Cin	.783	Robinson-Pit	75	Hershiser-LA	15	Leary-LA	6	Gott-Pit	34
Cone-NY	20	Jackson-Cin	.742	Agosto-Hou	75	Show-SD	13	Jackson-Cin	6	Worrell-StL	32
Reuschel-SF	19	Hershiser-LA	.742	Tekulve-Phi	70	Sutcliffe-Chi	12	Scott-Hou	5	Davis-SD	28
		Maddux-Chi	.692	Franco-Cin	70	Gooden-NY	10	Ojeda-NY	5	Bedrosian-Phi	28

Innings Pitched		Fewest Hits/Game		Fewest BB/Game		Strikeouts		Strikeouts/Game		Ratio	
Hershiser-LA	267.0	Fernandez-NY	6.11	B.Smith-Mon	1.45	Ryan-Hou	228	Ryan-Hou	9.33	Perez-Mon	8.81
Jackson-Cin	260.2	Perez-Mon	6.37	Mahler-Atl	1.52	Cone-NY	213	Fernandez-NY	9.10	Scott-Hou	9.18
Browning-Cin	250.2	Rijo-Cin	6.67	Reuschel-SF	1.54	DeLeon-StL	208	Rijo-Cin	8.89	Ojeda-NY	9.22
Mahler-Atl	249.0	Scott-Hou	6.67	Ojeda-NY	1.56	Scott-Hou	190	DeLeon-StL	8.31	Hershiser-LA	9.61
Maddux-Chi	249.0	Cone-NY	6.93	Tudor-StL-LA	1.87	Fernandez-NY	189	Cone-NY	8.29	Jackson-Cin	9.63

Earned Run Average		Adjusted ERA		Opponents' Batting Avg.		Opponents' On Base Pct.		Starter Runs		Adjusted Starter Runs	
Magrane-StL	2.18	Magrane-StL	160	Fernandez-NY	.191	Perez-Mon	.253	Hershiser-LA	35.3	Hershiser-LA	31.8
Cone-NY	2.22	Rijo-Cin	150	Perez-Mon	.196	Scott-Hou	.261	Cone-NY	31.6	Cone-NY	25.8
Hershiser-LA	2.26	Tudor-StL-LA	148	Scott-Hou	.204	Ojeda-NY	.264	Tudor-StL-LA	24.7	Jackson-Cin	24.7
Tudor-StL-LA	2.32	Hershiser-LA	147	Rijo-Cin	.209	Hershiser-LA	.271	Magrane-StL	23.3	Tudor-StL-LA	24.5
Rijo-Cin	2.39	Perez-Mon	147	Cone-NY	.213	Fernandez-NY	.274	Perez-Mon	21.0	Perez-Mon	24.1

Clutch Pitching Index		Relief Runs		Adjusted Relief Runs		Relief Ranking		Total Pitcher Index		Total Baseball Ranking	
Tudor-StL-LA	135	Franco-Cin	17.9	Franco-Cin	19.2	Franco-Cin	39.9	Franco-Cin	4.5	Strawberry-NY	5.2
Rawley-Phi	122	Holton-LA	16.4	Holton-LA	15.3	Davis-SD	28.5	Hershiser-LA	4.5	VanSlyke-Pit	5.1
Moyer-Chi	118	Pena-LA	16.1	Davis-SD	15.1	Myers-NY	22.8	Davis-SD	3.6	Smith-StL	5.1
Robinson-SF	113	Davis-SD	15.7	Pena-LA	14.9	Pena-LA	21.9	Jackson-Cin	3.2	Gibson-LA	5.0
D.Martinez-Mon	112	Myers-NY	13.0	Harris-Phi	14.3	Holton-LA	16.6	D.Martinez-Mon	3.0	Franco-Cin	4.5

January 12 Former Pirates slugger Willie Stargell is the only player elected this year to the Hall of Fame by the BBWAA, and becomes the 17th player to be elected in his first year of eligibility. Jim Bunning falls four votes shy of the 321 needed for election in his 13th year on the ballot.

April 28 The Orioles set an AL record with their 21st consecutive loss, 4-2 to the Twins, breaking the record shared by the 1906 Red Sox and the 1916 and 1943 A's.

May 9 Oakland beats Detroit 3–1 to extend its club-record winning streak to 14 consecutive games, the longest in the majors since 1977.

June 11 Designated hitter Rick Rhoden of the Yankees hits a sacrifice fly in New York's 8-6 win over Baltimore. He's the first pitcher to start a game as a DH since the rule was adopted in 1973.

June 25 Cal Ripken Jr. plays in his 1,000th consecutive game, a 10–3 loss to Boston. Ripken's streak is the sixth longest in major league history.

June 30 Alarmed by threats by the White Sox to move to St. Petersburg, Fla., Illinois lawmakers grant state subsidies for a new stadium to replace venerable but decaying Comiskey Park.

July 3 While pinch running for Don Baylor in a 9-8, 16-inning win over Toronto, Oakland's Gene Nelson steals a base to become the first AL pitcher to steal a base since John "Blue Moon" Odom in 1973.

July 12 After being maligned by the press as an unworthy All-Star starter, A's catcher Terry Steinbach hits a solo home run and a sacrifice fly to lead the AL to a 2–1 victory at Riverfront Stadium and is named the game's MVP.

August 14 Detroit pounds the Red Sox 18–6 at Fenway Park to end Boston's league-record home winning streak at 24 games, two shy of the major league record held by the 1916 Giants. Roger Clemens gives up eight runs in $1\frac{1}{3}$ innings.

September 23 Oakland's Jose Canseco becomes the founder of baseball's 40-home run, 40-stolen base club by stealing two bases in a 9-8, 14-inning win over Milwaukee. He also hits his 41st home run.

September 30 The Red Sox lose to Cleveland 3-2 but clinch the AL East title anyway when second-place Milwaukee loses to Oakland, 7-1.

September 30 Dave Stieb is one out away from a no-hitter for the second consecutive game, but falls short again when Jim Traber bloops a single over the head of first baseman Fred McGriff. Stieb finishes with his second straight one-hitter, 4-0 over the Orioles.

October 9 Oakland beats Boston 4-1 to complete a four-game sweep of the ALCS. Dennis Eckersley saves all four games and is named series MVP.

November 16 Jose Canseco becomes the first unanimous AL MVP since Reggie Jackson in 1973.

BALTIMORE

Pos	Player
M	C.Ripken
M	F.Robinson
1B	J.Traber
2B	B.Ripken
SS	C.Ripken
3B	R.Gonzales
LF	P.Stanicek
CF	F.Lynn
RF	J.Orsulak
C	M.Tettleton
DH	E.Murray
OD	L.Sheets
O	K.Gerhart
3	R.Schu
C	T.Kennedy
P	J.Bautista
P	J.Tibbs
P	J.Ballard
P	M.Boddicker
P	D.Schmidt
RP	D.Sisk
RP	M.Thurmond
RP	T.Niedenfuer
P	M.Williamson
P	O.Peraza
P	M.Morgan

BOSTON

Pos	Player
M	J.McNamara
M	J.Morgan
1B	T.Benzinger
2B	M.Barrett
SS	J.Reed
3B	W.Boggs
LF	M.Greenwell
CF	E.Burks
RF	D.Evans
C	R.Gedman
DH	J.Rice
C	R.Cerone
S	S.Owen
P	R.Clemens
P	B.Hurst
P	W.Gardner
P	O.Boyd
P	M.Smithson
RP	B.Stanley
RP	L.Smith
RP	D.Lamp
P	M.Boddicker
P	J.Sellers

CALIFORNIA

Pos	Player
M	C.Rojas
M	M.Stubing
1B	W.Joyner
2B	J.Ray
SS	D.Schofield
3B	J.Howell
LF	T.Armas
CF	D.White
RF	C.Davis
C	B.Boone
DH	B.Downing
2	M.McLemore
P	M.Witt
P	W.Fraser
P	C.Finley
P	K.McCaskill
P	D.Petry
RP	S.Cliburn
RP	G.Minton
RP	B.Harvey
P	T.Clark

CHICAGO

Pos	Player
M	J.Fregosi
1B	G.Walker
2B	F.Manrique
SS	O.Guillen
3B	S.Lyons
LF	D.Boston
CF	D.Gallagher
RF	D.Pasqua
C	C.Fisk
DH	H.Baines
O	I.Calderon
O	G.Redus
23	D.Hill
O3	K.Williams
P	M.Perez
P	J.Reuss
P	B.Long
P	D.LaPoint
RP	J.McDowell
RP	R.Horton
RP	B.Thigpen
RP	Jn.Davis
P	J.Bittiger

CLEVELAND

Pos	Player
M	D.Edwards
1B	W.Upshaw
2B	J.Franco
SS	J.Bell
3B	B.Jacoby
LF	M.Hall
CF	J.Carter
RF	C.Snyder
C	A.Allanson
DH	R.Kittle
S	R.Washington
D	T.Francona
C	M.Heath
P	G.Swindell
P	T.Candiotti
P	J.Farrell
P	S.Bailes
P	R.Yett
RP	D.Jones
RP	D.Gordon
RP	B.Havens
P	R.Nichols
P	B.Black

DETROIT

Pos	Player
M	S.Anderson
1B	R.Knight
2B	L.Whitaker
SS	A.Trammell
3B	T.Brookens
LF	P.Sheridan
CF	G.Pettis
RF	C.Lemon
C	M.Nokes
DH	D.Evans
1D	D.Bergman
OS	L.Salazar
C	M.Heath
P	J.Morris
P	D.Alexander
P	W.Terrell
P	F.Tanana
P	J.Robinson
RP	P.Gibson
RP	M.Henneman
RP	W.Hernandez
P	E.King

KANSAS CITY

Pos	Player
M	J.Wathan
1B	G.Brett
2B	F.White
SS	K.Stillwell
3B	K.Seitzer
LF	B.Jackson
CF	W.Wilson
RF	D.Tartabull
C	J.Quirk
DH	B.Buckner
DO	P.Tabler
C	M.Macfarlane
OD	J.Eisenreich
P	M.Gubicza
P	B.Saberhagen
P	C.Leibrandt
P	F.Bannister
RP	S.Farr
RP	J.Montgomery
P	T.Power

MILWAUKEE

Pos	Player
M	T.Trebelhorn
1B	G.Brock
2B	J.Gantner
SS	D.Sveum
3B	P.Molitor
LF	J.Leonard
CF	R.Yount
RF	R.Deer
C	B.Surhoff
DH	J.Meyer
OD	G.Braggs
P	T.Higuera
P	B.Wegman
P	C.Bosio
P	D.August
P	M.Birkbeck
RP	C.Crim
RP	O.Jones
RP	P.Mirabella
P	J.Nieves
P	T.Filer
P	D.Plesac

MINNESOTA

Pos	Player
M	T.Kelly
1B	K.Hrbek
2B	S.Lombardozzi
SS	G.Gagne
3B	G.Gaetti
LF	D.Gladden
CF	K.Puckett
RF	R.Bush
C	T.Laudner
DH	G.Larkin
O	M.Davidson
O	J.Moses
3S	A.Newman
2	T.Herr
P	F.Viola
P	B.Blyleven
P	A.Anderson
P	C.Lea
P	F.Toliver
RP	J.Berenguer
RP	K.Atherton
RP	J.Reardon
P	L.Straker
P	M.Portugal

NEW YORK

Pos	Player
M	B.Martin
M	L.Piniella
1B	D.Mattingly
2B	W.Randolph
SS	R.Santana
3B	M.Pagliarulo
LF	R.Henderson
CF	C.Washington
RF	D.Winfield
C	D.Slaught
DH	J.Clark
C	J.Skinner
O1	G.Ward
P	R.Rhoden
P	T.John
P	R.Dotson
P	J.Candelaria
P	C.Hudson
RP	N.Allen
RP	D.Righetti
RP	S.Shields
P	C.Guante
P	A.Leiter
P	R.Guidry
P	T.Stoddard

OAKLAND

Pos	Player
M	T.LaRussa
1B	M.McGwire
2B	G.Hubbard
SS	W.Weiss
3B	C.Lansford
LF	S.Javier
CF	D.Henderson
RF	J.Canseco
C	R.Hassey
DH	D.Baylor
2S	M.Gallego
DO	D.Parker
C	T.Steinbach
O	L.Polonia
3O	T.Phillips
P	D.Stewart
P	B.Welch
P	S.Davis
P	C.Young
P	T.Burns
RP	G.Nelson
RP	R.Honeycutt
RP	E.Plunk
P	D.Eckersley
P	G.Cadaret
P	S.Ontiveros

SEATTLE

Pos	Player
M	D.Williams
M	J.Snyder
1B	A.Davis
2B	H.Reynolds
SS	R.Quinones
3B	J.Presley
LF	M.Brantley
CF	H.Cotto
RF	G.Wilson
C	S.Bradley
DH	K.Phelps
D1	S.Balboni
C	D.Valle
P	M.Langston
P	M.Moore
P	B.Swift
P	S.Bankhead
P	M.Campbell
P	M.Jackson
RP	J.Reed
RP	M.Schooler
P	S.Trout

TEXAS

Pos	Player
M	B.Valentine
1B	P.O'Brien
2B	C.Wilkerson
SS	S.Fletcher
3B	S.Buechele
LF	C.Espy
CF	O.McDowell
RF	S.Sierra
C	G.Petralli
DH	L.Parrish
OD	P.Incaviglia
CD	M.Stanley
2	J.Browne
OD	B.Brower
P	C.Hough
P	J.Guzman
P	P.Kilgus
P	J.Russell
P	B.Witt
RP	M.Williams
RP	C.McMurtry
RP	D.Mohorcic
P	R.Hayward

TORONTO

Pos	Player
M	J.Williams
1B	F.McGriff
2B	M.Lee
SS	T.Fernandez
3B	K.Gruber
LF	G.Bell
CF	L.Moseby
RF	J.Barfield
C	E.Whitt
DH	R.Mulliniks
2D	N.Liriano
P	M.Flanagan
P	D.Stieb
P	J.Clancy
P	J.Key
P	T.Stottlemyre
RP	J.Cerutti
RP	D.Ward
RP	T.Henke
P	J.Musselman
P	M.Eichhorn
P	D.Wells

TEAM	G	W	L	PCT	GB	R	OR	AB	H	2B	3B	HR	BB	SO	AVG	OBP	SLG	PRO	PRO+	BR	/A	PF	CHI	RC	SB	CS	SBA	SBR
EAST																												
BOS	162	89	73	.549		813	689	5545	1569	310	39	124	623	728	.283	.360	.420	.780	113	140	104	104	94	842	65	36	64	-2
DET	162	88	74	.543	1	703	658	5433	1358	213	28	143	588	841	.250	.326	.378	.704	100	-20	6	96	103	673	87	42	67	1
TOR	162	87	75	.537	2	763	680	5557	1491	271	47	158	521	935	.268	.334	.419	.753	109	68	65	100	98	771	107	36	75	11
MIL	162	87	75	.537	2	682	616	5488	1409	258	26	113	439	911	.257	.316	.375	.691	92	-56	-61	101	107	648	159	55	74	15
NY	161	85	76	.528	3.5	772	748	5592	1469	272	12	148	588	935	.263	.336	.395	.731	105	33	39	99	102	754	146	39	79	20
CLE	162	78	84	.481	11	666	731	5505	1435	235	28	134	416	866	.261	.317	.387	.704	94	-35	-52	103	101	667	97	50	66	-1
BAL	161	54	107	.335	34.5	550	789	5358	1275	199	20	137	504	869	.238	.307	.359	.666	88	-101	-85	97	94	581	69	44	61	-6
WEST																												
OAK	162	104	58	.642		800	620	5602	1474	251	22	156	580	926	.263	.339	.399	.738	110	50	77	97	103	763	129	54	70	6
MIN	162	91	71	.562	13	759	672	5510	1508	294	31	151	528	832	.274	.343	.421	.764	110	94	71	103	95	785	107	63	63	-6
KC	161	84	77	.522	19.5	704	648	5469	1419	275	40	121	486	944	.259	.324	.391	.715	98	-9	-15	101	102	696	137	54	72	9
CAL	162	75	87	.463	29	714	771	5582	1458	258	31	124	469	819	.261	.324	.385	.709	101	-18	1	97	103	690	86	52	62	-5
CHI	161	71	90	.441	30.5	631	757	5449	1327	224	35	132	436	908	.244	.305	.370	.675	88	-92	-90	100	105	609	98	46	68	2
TEX	161	70	91	.435	33.5	637	735	5479	1378	227	39	112	542	1022	.252	.323	.368	.691	91	-47	-63	102	97	661	130	57	70	5
SEA	161	68	93	.422	35.5	664	744	5436	1397	271	27	148	461	787	.257	.319	.398	.717	95	-7	-37	104	97	673	95	61	61	-8
TOT	1131					9858		77005	19967	3558	425	1901	7191	12323	.259	.327	.391	.718							1512	689	69	40

TEAM	CG	SH	SV	IP	H	H/G	HR	BB	SO	RAT	ERA	ERA+	OAV	OOB	PR	/A	PF	CPI	FA	E	DP	FW	PW	BW	SBW	DIF
EAST																										
BOS	26	14	37	1426¹	1415	8.9	143	493	1085	12.3	3.97	104	.259	.324	-1	23	104	99	.984	93	123	1.6	2.3	10.5	-.5	-5.9
DET	34	8	36	1445²	1361	8.5	150	497	890	11.8	3.71	103	.248	.314	41	17	96	99	.982	109	129	.6	1.7	.6	-.2	4.2
TOR	16	17	47	1449	1404	8.7	143	528	904	12.4	3.80	104	.256	.328	27	22	99	105	.982	110	170	.6	2.2	6.6	.8	-4.2
MIL	30	8	51	1449¹	1355	8.4	125	437	832	11.2	3.45	115	.248	.306	84	85	100	99	.981	120	146	-.0	8.6	-6.2	1.2	2.4
NY	16	5	43	1456	1512	9.3	157	487	861	12.7	4.26	92	.281	.331	-48	-52	99	99	.978	134	161	-.9	-5.3	3.9	1.7	5.0
CLE	35	10	46	1434	1501	9.4	120	442	812	12.4	4.16	99	.270	.328	-31	-8	104	97	.980	124	131	-.3	-.8	-5.3	-.4	3.7
BAL	20	7	26	1416	1506	9.6	153	523	709	13.2	4.54	86	.274	.342	-90	-100	98	99	.980	119	172	.0	-10.1	-8.6	-.9	-6.9
WEST																										
OAK	22	9	64	1489¹	1376	8.3	116	553	983	11.8	3.44	110	.247	.318	87	56	95	104	.983	105	151	.9	5.7	7.8	.3	8.4
MIN	18	9	52	1431²	1457	9.2	146	453	897	12.3	3.93	104	.266	.327	6	22	103	104	.986	84	155	2.1	2.2	7.2	-.9	-.6
KC	29	12	32	1428¹	1415	8.9	102	465	886	12.1	3.65	109	.258	.320	49	52	101	100	.980	124	147	-.3	5.3	-1.5	.6	-.6
CAL	26	9	33	1455²	1503	9.3	135	568	817	13.1	4.32	89	.270	.342	-57	-74	97	101	.979	135	175	-.9	-7.5	.1	-.8	3.1
CHI	11	9	43	1439	1467	9.2	138	533	754	12.7	4.12	96	.266	.334	-25	-24	100	101	.976	154	177	-2.1	-2.4	-9.1	-.0	4.2
TEX	41	11	31	1438²	1310	8.2	129	654	912	12.6	4.05	101	.244	.332	-13	5	103	95	.979	131	145	-.7	.5	-6.4	.2	-4.1
SEA	28	11	28	1428	1385	8.7	144	558	981	12.5	4.15	100	.266	.330	-30	1	105	97	.980	123	168	-.2	.1	-3.7	-1.1	-7.5
TOT	352	139	569	20187		8.9				12.4	3.97		.259	.327					.981	1665	2150					

Runs
Boggs-Bos 128
Canseco-Oak 120
Henderson-NY ... 118
Molitor-Mil 115
Puckett-Min 109

Hits
Puckett-Min....... 234
Boggs-Bos 214
Greenwell-Bos 192
Yount-Mil 190
Molitor-Mil 190

Doubles
Boggs-Bos 45
Ray-Cal 42
Puckett-Min 42
Brett-KC 42
Fernandez-Tor 41

Triples
Yount-Mil 11
Wilson-KC 11
Reynolds-Sea 11
Greenwell-Bos 8

Home Runs
Canseco-Oak 42
McGriff-Tor 34
McGwire-Oak 32
Murray-Bal........ 28
Gaetti-Min 28

Total Bases
Puckett-Min 358
Canseco-Oak 347
Greenwell-Bos 313
Brett-KC 300
Carter-Cle........ 297

Runs Batted In
Canseco-Oak 124
Puckett-Min 121
Greenwell-Bos 119
Evans-Bos 111
Winfield-NY 107

Runs Produced
Puckett-Min....... 206
Canseco-Oak 202
Evans-Bos 183
Greenwell-Bos 183
Boggs-Bos 181

Bases On Balls
Boggs-Bos 125
Clark-NY 113
C.Ripken-Bal 102
Davis-Sea 95
Greenwell-Bos 87

Batting Average
Boggs-Bos 366
Puckett-Min 356
Greenwell-Bos 325
Winfield-NY.......322
Molitor-Mil........312

On Base Percentage
Boggs-Bos .... .480
Greenwell-Bos 420
Davis-Sea 416
Winfield-NY ...... .398
Henderson-NY 397

Slugging Average
Canseco-Oak 569
McGriff-Tor 552
Gaetti-Min 551
Puckett-Min 545
Greenwell-Bos 531

Production
Boggs-Bos 970
Canseco-Oak 963
Greenwell-Bos 950
McGriff-Tor 930
Winfield-NY 928

Adjusted Production
Canseco-Oak 172
Boggs-Bos 165
Winfield-NY 159
Greenwell-Bos 158
McGriff-Tor 156

Batter Runs
Boggs-Bos 65.8
Canseco-Oak 54.1
Greenwell-Bos 53.4
Puckett-Min 45.5
Winfield-NY 43.4

Adjusted Batter Runs
Boggs-Bos 59.7
Canseco-Oak 58.9
Greenwell-Bos 47.9
Winfield-NY 44.4
Puckett-Min 42.0

Clutch Hitting Index
Barrett-Bos 135
Hall-Cle 123
Larkin-Min 121
Evans-Bos 120
Clark-NY 118

Runs Created
Boggs-Bos 140
Canseco-Oak 136
Greenwell-Bos 134
Puckett-Min 126
Brett-KC 119

Total Average
Boggs-Bos 1.043
Canseco-Oak ...1.011
Greenwell-Bos ...1.000
McGriff-Tor 958
Henderson-NY 955

Stolen Bases
Henderson-NY 93
Pettis-Det 44
Molitor-Mil 41
Canseco-Oak 40

Stolen Base Average
Javier-Oak 95.2
Redus-Chi 92.9
Cotto-Sea 90.0
Henderson-NY 87.7
Yount-Mil 84.6

Stolen Base Runs
Henderson-NY ... 20.1
Pettis-Det 7.2
Redus-Chi 6.6

Fielding Runs
Guillen-Chi 42.6
Gruber-Tor 25.1
Schofield-Cal 23.2
Puckett-Min 19.5
Gladden-Min 16.3

Total Player Rating
Canseco-Oak 6.4
Puckett-Min 5.4
Boggs-Bos 5.3
Greenwell-Bos 4.9
Henderson-NY 4.7

Wins
Viola-Min 24
Stewart-Oak 21
Gubicza-KC 20

Win Percentage
Viola-Min .... .774
Hurst-Bos .... .750
Gubicza-KC ...... .714
Davis-Oak .... .696
Stieb-Tor .... .667

Games
Crim-Mil 70
Thigpen-Chi 68
Williams-Tex 67
Henneman-Det ... 65

Complete Games
Stewart-Oak 14
Clemens-Bos 14
Witt-Tex 13
Witt-Cal 12
Swindell-Cle 12

Shutouts
Clemens-Bos 8
Swindell-Cle 4
Stieb-Tor 4
Gubicza-KC 4

Saves
Eckersley-Oak 45
Reardon-Min 42
Jones-Cle 37
Thigpen-Chi 34
Plesac-Mil 30

Innings Pitched
Stewart-Oak 275.2
Gubicza-KC 269.2
Clemens-Bos 264.0
Langston-Sea 261.1
Saberhagen-KC ..260.2

Fewest Hits/Game
Robinson-Det 6.33
Higuera-Mil 6.65
Stieb-Tor 6.82
Witt-Tex 6.92
Hough-Tex 7.21

Fewest BB/Game
Anderson-Min ... 1.65
Swindell-Cle 1.67
Alexander-Det ... 1.81
Bosio-Mil 1.88
Viola-Min 1.90

Strikeouts
Clemens-Bos 291
Langston-Sea ... 235
Viola-Min 193
Stewart-Oak 192
Higuera-Mil 192

Strikeouts/Game
Clemens-Bos 9.92
Langston-Sea ... 8.09
Witt-Tex 7.64
Higuera-Mil 7.60
Moore-Sea 7.16

Ratio
Higuera-Mil 9.22
Clemens-Bos 9.72
Robinson-Det 10.26
Moore-Sea 10.31
Viola-Min 10.33

Earned Run Average
Anderson-Min.....2.45
Higuera-Mil.......2.45
Viola-Min........2.64
Gubicza-KC.......2.70
Clemens-Bos 2.93

Adjusted ERA
Anderson-Min 166
Higuera-Mil 162
Viola-Min 154
Gubicza-KC 147
Clemens-Bos 140

Opponents' Batting Avg.
Robinson-Det 197
Higuera-Mil 207
Stieb-Tor 210
Witt-Tex 216
Clemens-Bos 220

Opponents' On Base Pct.
Higuera-Mil 265
Clemens-Bos 270
Robinson-Det 284
Moore-Sea 287
Swindell-Cle 287

Starter Runs
Higuera-Mil 38.2
Gubicza-KC 37.8
Viola-Min 37.5
Anderson-Min ... 34.1
Clemens-Bos 30.3

Adjusted Starter Runs
Viola-Min 40.4
Higuera-Mil 38.5
Gubicza-KC 38.4
Anderson-Min ... 36.5
Clemens-Bos 34.6

Clutch Pitching Index
Anderson-Min 138
Davis-Oak........ 121
Candiotti-Cle 116
Leibrandt-KC 116
Viola-Min 115

Relief Runs
Henneman-Det ... 21.2
Jones-Cle 15.7
Harvey-Cal 15.4
Mirabella-Mil 15.4
Jackson-Sea 14.8

Adjusted Relief Runs
Henneman-Det ... 19.7
Jones-Cle 17.1
Jackson-Sea 16.9
Mirabella-Mil 15.5
Harvey-Cal 14.6

Relief Ranking
Henneman-Det 37.6
Harvey-Cal 26.6
Jones-Cle 26.5
Reardon-Min 23.0
Eckersley-Oak ...21.3

Total Pitcher Index
Viola-Min 4.6
Anderson-Min ... 4.5
Higuera-Mil 4.3
Gubicza-KC 4.2
Henneman-Det ... 3.9

Total Baseball Ranking
Canseco-Oak 6.4
Puckett-Min 5.4
Boggs-Bos 5.3
Greenwell-Bos ... 4.9
Henderson-NY 4.7

January 9 Johnny Bench and Carl Yastrzemski are elected to the Hall of Fame by the BBWAA in their first year of eligibility. Bench was named on 96.4 percent of the ballots, the third-highest figure in history behind Ty Cobb and Hank Aaron.

January 29 The game-winning RBI is dropped as an official statistic after nine years of use. The Mets Keith Hernandez is the all-time leader with 129.

February 2 Bill White, a six-time All-Star and longtime Yankees broadcaster, is elected president of the NL. He becomes the highest-ranking black official in American professional sports.

February 16 Orel Hershiser becomes the first player to sign a contract that calls for a $3 million salary by inking a three-year, $7.9 million contract with Los Angeles that will pay him $3,166,667 in 1991.

February 28 Red Schoendienst and Al Barlick, a major league umpire for over 29 seasons, are elected to the Hall of Fame by the Special Veterans Committee.

April 6 In his first start of the season, Orel Hershiser gives up a run in the first inning of a 4-3 loss to the Reds to end his major league-record consecutive-scoreless-inning streak at 59.

May 29 Phillies third baseman Mike Schmidt, 39, retires. He is seventh on the all-time home run list with 548.

May 31 The Senior Professional Baseball Association announces that it will begin its inaugural season on November 1 with eight teams of players age 35 and over.

June 3 Houston beats Los Angeles 5-4 in 22 innings in a game that takes seven hours, 14 minutes to complete. Third baseman Jeff Hamilton becomes the losing pitcher and pitcher Fernando Valenzuela finishes the game at first base.

July 5 Barry Bonds homers in Pittsburgh's 6-4 loss to San Francisco, giving Barry and father Bobby the father-and-son home run record with 408. The Bells (Gus and Buddy) and the Berras (Yogi and Dale) had shared the record at 407.

August 24 After weeks of legal wrangling, Commissioner Bart Giamatti permanently bans Pete Rose from baseball for his alleged gambling on major league games. Although the five-page document signed by both parties includes no formal findings, Giamatti says that he considers Rose's acceptance of the ban to be a no-contest plea to the charges.

August 28 Frank Viola and the Mets outduel Orel Hershiser and the Dodgers, 1-0, in the first-ever regular-season matchup of defending Cy Young winners.

September 13 Fay Vincent is elected baseball's eighth commissioner, succeeding the late Bart Giamatti, whom he served as deputy commissioner.

October 4 Will Clark goes 4-for-4 with two home runs, including the first NLCS grand slam since 1977, to lead the Giants to an 11-3 win over the Cubs in Game 1 of the NLCS.

October 9 The Giants win their first pennant since 1962 by defeating the Cubs 3-2 in Game 5 of the NLCS. Will Clark bats .650 in the series with eight RBIs to win MVP honors.

November 14 Padres reliever Mark Davis wins the league Cy Young Award. He saved 44 games with a 1.85 ERA.

November 21 The Giants outfielder Kevin Mitchell, who led the big leagues with 47 home runs and 125 RBIs, wins the NL MVP Award.

ATLANTA		CHICAGO		CINCINNATI		HOUSTON		LOS ANGELES		MONTREAL	
M	R.Nixon	M	D.Zimmer	M	P.Rose	M	A.Howe	M	T.Lasorda	M	B.Rodgers
1B	G.Perry	1B	M.Grace	M	T.Helms	1B	G.Davis	1B	E.Murray	1B	A.Galarraga
2B	J.Treadway	2B	R.Sandberg	1B	T.Benzinger	2B	B.Doran	2B	W.Randolph	2B	T.Foley
SS	A.Thomas	SS	S.Dunston	2B	R.Oester	SS	R.Ramirez	SS	A.Griffin	SS	S.Owen
3B	J.Blauser	3B	V.Law	SS	B.Larkin	3B	K.Caminiti	3B	J.Hamilton	3B	T.Wallach
LF	L.Smith	LF	D.Smith	3B	C.Sabo	LF	B.Hatcher	LF	K.Gibson	LF	T.Raines
CF	O.McDowell	CF	J.Walton	LF	R.Roomes	CF	G.Young	CF	J.Shelby	CF	Da.Martinez
RF	D.Murphy	RF	A.Dawson	CF	E.Davis	RF	T.Puhl	RF	M.Marshall	RF	H.Brooks
C	J.Davis	C	D.Berryhill	RF	P.O'Neill	C	C.Biggio	C	M.Scioscia	C	N.Santovenia
				C	J.Reed						
13	D.Evans	O	M.Webster			2S	C.Reynolds	O	J.Gonzalez	C	M.Fitzgerald
O1	T.Gregg	O1	L.McClendon	O	K.Griffey	O	K.Bass	O3	M.Hatcher	O	O.Nixon
3O	R.Gant			23	L.Quinones					2	D.Garcia
		P	G.Maddux	O	H.Winningham	P	M.Scott	P	O.Hershiser		
P	J.Smoltz	P	R.Sutcliffe			P	J.Deshaies	P	T.Belcher	P	De.Martinez
P	T.Glavine	P	M.Bielecki	P	T.Browning	P	J.Clancy	P	F.Valenzuela	P	B.Smith
P	D.Lilliquist	P	S.Sanderson	P	R.Mahler	P	B.Knepper	P	M.Morgan	P	K.Gross
P	P.Smith	P	P.Kilgus	P	D.Jackson	P	M.Portugal	P	T.Leary	P	P.Perez
P	M.Clary	RP	J.Pico	P	J.Rijo	RP	D.Darwin	RP	J.Howell	P	M.Langston
RP	J.Acker	RP	S.Wilson	P	S.Scudder	RP	B.Forsch	RP	A.Pena	RP	T.Burke
RP	J.Boever	RP	M.Williams	RP	R.Dibble	RP	L.Andersen	RP	T.Crews	RP	A.McGaffigan
RP	M.Eichhorn			RP	N.Charlton					RP	Z.Smith
		P	C.Schiraldi	RP	J.Franco	P	R.Rhoden	P	J.Wetteland		
P	Z.Smith	P	L.Lancaster			P	J.Agosto	P	R.Martinez		
P	P.Assenmacher			P	T.Leary	P	D.Smith				
P	J.Alvarez			P	R.Robinson	P	D.Schatzeder				
				P	T.Birtsas						
				P	K.Tekulve						

NEW YORK		PHILADELPHIA		PITTSBURGH		SAN DIEGO		SAN FRANCISCO		ST.LOUIS	
M	D.Johnson	M	N.Leyva	M	J.Leyland	M	J.McKeon	M	R.Craig	M	W.Herzog
1B	D.Magadan	1B	R.Jordan	1B	G.Redus	1B	Ja.Clark	1B	W.Clark	1B	P.Guerrero
2B	G.Jefferies	2B	T.Herr	2B	J.Lind	2B	R.Alomar	2B	R.Thompson	2B	J.Oquendo
SS	K.Elster	SS	D.Thon	SS	J.Bell	SS	G.Templeton	SS	J.Uribe	SS	O.Smith
3B	H.Johnson	3B	C.Hayes	3B	B.Bonilla	3B	L.Salazar	3B	E.Riles	3B	T.Pendleton
LF	K.McReynolds	LF	J.Kruk	LF	B.Bonds	LF	C.James	LF	K.Mitchell	LF	V.Coleman
CF	J.Samuel	CF	L.Dykstra	CF	A.Van Slyke	CF	M.Wynne	CF	B.Butler	CF	M.Thompson
RF	D.Strawberry	RF	V.Hayes	RF	R.Reynolds	RF	T.Gwynn	RF	C.Maldonado	RF	T.Brunansky
C	B.Lyons	C	D.Daulton	C	J.Ortiz	C	B.Santiago	C	T.Kennedy	C	T.Pena
O	M.Wilson	O	C.Ford	O	J.Cangelosi	O1	C.Martinez	3S	M.Williams	P	J.DeLeon
21	T.Teufel	S3	S.Jeltz	O1	G.Wilson	O3	B.Roberts	C	K.Manwaring	P	J.Magrane
1	K.Hernandez	O	B.Dernier	S	R.Quinones					P	K.Hill
				13	J.King					P	S.Terry
P	D.Cone	P	K.Howell			P	B.Hurst	P	R.Reuschel	RP	F.DiPino
P	S.Fernandez	P	D.Carman			P	E.Whitson	P	D.Robinson	RP	D.Quisenberry
P	R.Darling	P	B.Ruffin	P	D.Drabek	P	D.Rasmussen	P	S.Garrelts	RP	K.Dayley
P	B.Ojeda	P	L.McWilliams	P	J.Smiley	P	W.Terrell	P	M.LaCoss		
P	D.Gooden	P	D.Cook	P	B.Walk	P	E.Show	RP	C.Lefferts	P	T.Power
RP	R.Myers	RP	J.Parrett	P	N.Heaton	RP	G.Harris	RP	J.Brantley	P	C.Carpenter
RP	R.Aguilera	RP	G.Harris	P	R.Kramer	RP	M.Grant	RP	A.Hammaker	P	J.Costello
RP	D.Aase	RP	T.Frohwirth	P	J.Robinson	RP	M.Davis			P	T.Worrell
				RP	B.Kipper	P	A.Benes	P	K.Downs		
P	F.Viola	P	T.Mulholland	RP	B.Landrum			P	B.Knepper		
		P	R.McDowell					P	S.Bedrosian		
				P	D.Bair						
				P	R.Reed						

TEAM	G	W	L	PCT	GB	R	OR	AB	H	2B	3B	HR	BB	SO	AVG	OBP	SLG	PRO	PRO+	BR	/A	PF	CHI	RC	SB	CS	SBA	SBR
EAST																												
CHI	162	93	69	.574		**702**	623	5513	**1438**	235	45	124	472	921	**.261**	.322	.387	**.709**	101	54	3	107	101	**685**	136	57	70	7
NY	162	87	75	.537	6	683	595	5489	1351	280	21	**147**	504	934	.246	.313	.385	.698	110	30	62	95	102	676	158	53	**75**	**16**
STL	164	86	76	.531	7	632	608	5492	1418	263	47	73	507	848	.258	**.323**	.363	.686	99	16	-5	103	97	652	155	54	74	14
MON	162	81	81	.500	12	632	630	5482	1353	267	30	100	**572**	958	.247	.322	.361	.683	100	13	4	101	96	645	**160**	70	70	6
PIT	164	74	88	.457	19	637	680	5539	1334	263	**53**	95	563	914	.241	.314	.359	.673	102	-13	9	97	100	629	155	69	69	5
PHI	163	67	95	.414	26	629	735	5447	1324	215	36	123	558	926	.243	.316	.364	.680	100	1	1	100	99	634	106	50	68	2
WEST																												
SF	162	92	70	.568		699	600	5469	1365	241	52	141	508	1071	.250	.318	**.390**	.708	**111**	50	**69**	97	102	683	87	54	62	-6
SD	162	89	73	.549	3	642	626	5422	1360	215	32	120	552	1013	.251	.321	.369	.690	103	22	21	100	98	644	136	67	67	1
HOU	162	86	76	.531	6	647	669	5516	1316	239	28	97	530	860	.239	.308	.345	.653	95	-50	-29	97	**109**	606	144	62	70	6
LA	160	77	83	.481	14	554	**536**	5465	1313	241	17	89	507	885	.240	.308	.339	.647	93	-61	-51	98	96	576	81	54	60	-8
CIN	162	75	87	.463	17	632	691	5520	1362	243	28	128	493	1028	.247	.312	.370	.682	97	1	-21	103	99	639	128	71	64	-4
ATL	161	63	97	.394	28	584	680	5463	1281	201	22	128	485	996	.234	.300	.350	.650	89	-64	-79	103	103	575	83	54	61	-8
TOT	973					7673		65817	16215	2903	411	1365	6251	11354	.246	.315	.365	.680							1529	715	68	30

TEAM	CG	SH	SV	IP	H	H/G	HR	BB	SO	RAT	ERA	ERA+	OAV	OOB	PR	/A	PF	CPI	FA	E	DP	FW	PW	BW	SBW	DIF
EAST																										
CHI	18	10	**55**	1460[1]	1369	8.4	106	532	918	11.9	3.43	110	.250	.319	11	54	108	104	.980	124	130	.6	5.8	.3	.5	4.8
NY	24	12	38	1454[1]	**1260**	7.8	115	532	**1108**	11.3	3.29	111	**.231**	**.303**	33	-5	93	95	.976	144	110	-.6	-.5	6.6	**1.4**	-1.0
STL	18	18	43	1461	1330	8.2	**84**	482	844	11.3	3.36	108	.243	.308	21	43	104	95	**.982**	**112**	134	**1.4**	4.6	-.5	1.2	-1.7
MON	20	13	35	1468[1]	1344	8.2	120	519	1059	11.6	3.48	102	.245	.314	3	9	101	101	.979	136	126	-.1	1.0	.4	.4	-1.7
PIT	20	9	40	1487[2]	1394	8.4	121	539	827	11.9	3.64	92	.248	.317	-24	-47	96	98	.975	160	130	-1.4	-5.0	1.0	.3	-1.8
PHI	10	10	33	1433[1]	1408	8.8	127	613	899	12.9	4.04	88	.259	.337	-87	-80	101	101	.979	133	136	.1	-8.6	.1	-.0	-5.6
WEST																										
SF	12	16	47	1457	1320	8.2	120	471	802	11.2	3.30	102	.243	.307	31	11	97	102	**.982**	114	135	1.2	1.2	**7.4**	-.9	2.2
SD	21	11	52	1457[1]	1359	8.4	133	481	933	11.5	3.38	103	.249	.312	19	19	100	106	.976	154	147	-1.1	2.0	2.2	-.2	5.0
HOU	19	12	38	1479[1]	1379	8.4	105	551	965	11.9	3.64	93	.247	.318	-25	-42	97	96	.977	142	121	-.4	-4.5	-3.1	.4	12.7
LA	**25**	**19**	36	1463[1]	1278	7.9	95	504	1052	**11.1**	**2.95**	116	.237	.306	89	76	98	**107**	.981	118	**153**	.8	**8.1**	-5.5	-1.1	-5.4
CIN	16	9	37	1464[1]	1404	8.6	125	559	981	12.3	3.73	96	.253	.326	-38	-21	103	102	.980	121	108	.8	-2.2	-2.2	-.7	-1.6
ATL	15	8	33	1447[2]	1370	8.5	114	**468**	966	11.5	3.70	99	.250	.311	-33	-8	104	94	.976	152	124	-1.1	-.9	-8.4	-1.1	-5.5
TOT	218	147	487	17534		8.3				11.7	3.49		.246	.315					.978	1610	1554					

Runs
Sandberg-Chi 104
Johnson-NY 104
Clark-SF 104
Mitchell-SF 100
Butler-SF 100

Hits
Gwynn-SD 203
Clark-SF 196
R.Alomar-SD 184
Guerrero-StL 177
Sandberg-Chi 176

Doubles
Wallach-Mon 42
Guerrero-StL 42
Johnson-NY 41
Clark-SF 38
Bonilla-Pit.......... 37

Triples
Thompson-SF 11
Bonilla-Pit 10
VanSlyke-Pit 9
Coleman-StL 9
Clark-SF 9

Home Runs
Mitchell-SF 47
Johnson-NY 36
Davis-Hou 34
Davis-Cin 34
Sandberg-Chi 30

Total Bases
Mitchell-SF 345
Clark-SF 321
Johnson-NY 319
Bonilla-Pit 302
Sandberg-Chi 301

Runs Batted In
Mitchell-SF 125
Guerrero-StL 117
Clark-SF 111
Johnson-NY 101
Davis-Cin 101

Runs Produced
Clark-SF 192
Mitchell-SF 178
Johnson-NY 169
Guerrero-StL 160
Bonilla-Pit 158

Bases On Balls
J.Clark-SD 132
V.Hayes-Phi 101
Raines-Mon 93
Bonds-Pit 93

Batting Average
Gwynn-SD .... .336
Clark-SF .... .333
L.Smith-Atl .... .315
Grace-Chi .... .314
Guerrero-StL .... .311

On Base Percentage
L.Smith-Atl ...... .420
J.Clark-SD ...... .413
Clark-SF .... .412
Grace-Chi .... .407
Guerrero-StL ..... .398

Slugging Average
Mitchell-SF .... .635
Johnson-NY ...... .559
Clark-SF .... .546
Davis-Cin .... .541
L.Smith-Atl .... .533

Production
Mitchell-SF ...1.027
Clark-SF .... .958
L.Smith-Atl .... .953
Johnson-NY .... .932
Davis-Cin .... .916

Adjusted Production
Mitchell-SF 194
Clark-SF 177
Johnson-NY 171
L.Smith-Atl 166
Davis-Cin 154

Batter Runs
Mitchell-SF 62.1
Clark-SF 55.6
L.Smith-Atl 47.0
Johnson-NY 45.7
Guerrero-StL 38.3

Adjusted Batter Runs
Mitchell-SF 65.8
Clark-SF 59.2
Johnson-NY 51.3
L.Smith-Atl 44.2
Bonilla-Pit 36.1

Clutch Hitting Index
Guerrero-StL 132
Hatcher-Hou-Pit ... 121
J.Clark-SD 120
Doran-Hou 117
Murphy-Atl 115

Runs Created
Clark-SF 136
Mitchell-SF 136
Johnson-NY 127
L.Smith-Atl 113
Guerrero-StL 109

Total Average
Mitchell-SF 1.099
Johnson-NY 1.026
L.Smith-Atl 1.023
Clark-SF 1.010
J.Clark-SD .... .969

Stolen Bases
Coleman-StL 65
Samuel-Phi-NY ... 42
R.Alomar-SD 42
Raines-Mon........ 41
Johnson-NY 41

Stolen Base Average
Doran-Hou 88.0
Biggio-Hou 87.5
Coleman-StL 86.7
D.Martinez-Mon ... 85.2
Johnson-NY 83.7

Stolen Base Runs
Coleman-StL 13.5
Johnson-NY 7.5
Raines-Mon 6.9
Samuel-Phi-NY 5.4
Doran-Hou 4.8

Fielding Runs
Pendleton-StL 30.2
Young-Hou 26.3
Oquendo-StL 20.4
Foley-Mon 19.8
Bonds-Pit........ 19.7

Total Player Rating
Mitchell-SF 7.0
L.Smith-Atl 5.2
Clark-SF 5.0
Bonds-Pit 4.2
Bonilla-Pit 4.2

Wins
Scott-Hou 20
Maddux-Chi 19
Magrane-StL 18
Bielecki-Chi 18
Reuschel-SF 17

Win Percentage
Bielecki-Chi ...... .720
D.Martinez-Mon ... .696
Reuschel-SF ...... .680
Scott-Hou .... .667
Magrane-StL ..... .667

Games
Williams-Chi 76
Dibble-Cin 74
Parrett-Phi 72
Dayley-StL 71
Agosto-Hou 71

Complete Games
Hurst-SD 10
Belcher-LA 10
Scott-Hou 9
Magrane-StL 9
Browning-Cin 9

Shutouts
Belcher-LA 8
Drabek-Pit 5
Langston-Mon 4
Hershiser-LA 4
Glavine-Atl 4

Saves
Davis-SD 44
Williams-Chi 36
Franco-Cin 32
Howell-LA 28
Burke-Mon 28

Innings Pitched
Hershiser-LA 256.2
Browning-Cin ...249.2
Hurst-SD 244.2
DeLeon-StL 244.2
Drabek-Pit 244.1

Fewest Hits/Game
DeLeon-StL 6.36
Fernandez-NY 6.44
Howell-Phi 6.84
Smoltz-Atl 6.92
Garrelts-SF 6.94

Fewest BB/Game
Robinson-SF 1.69
Lilliquist-Atl 1.85
D.Martinez-Mon ... 1.90
Whitson-SD 1.90
Glavine-Atl 1.94

Strikeouts
DeLeon-StL 201
Belcher-LA 200
Fernandez-NY 198
Cone-NY 190
Hurst-SD 179

Strikeouts/Game
Langston-Mon 8.92
Fernandez-NY 8.12
Belcher-LA 7.83
Cone-NY 7.78
DeLeon-StL 7.39

Ratio
Garrelts-SF 9.08
DeLeon-StL 9.53
Scott-Hou 9.63
Fernandez-NY 9.77
B.Smith-Mon 9.81

Earned Run Average
Garrelts-SF 2.28
Hershiser-LA 2.31
Langston-Mon 2.39
Whitson-SD 2.66
Hurst-SD 2.69

Adjusted ERA
Garrelts-SF 148
Hershiser-LA 148
Langston-Mon 147
Whitson-SD 132
Hurst-SD 130

Opponents' Batting Avg.
DeLeon-StL ...... .197
Fernandez-NY .... .198
Smoltz-Atl ...... .212
Garrelts-SF ...... .212
Scott-Hou .... .212

Opponents' On Base Pct.
Garrelts-SF ...... .260
Scott-Hou .... .268
DeLeon-StL .... .269
Fernandez-NY .... .272
Smiley-Pit .... .276

Starter Runs
Hershiser-LA 33.7
Garrelts-SF 26.1
Hurst-SD 22.0
Langston-Mon 21.6
Whitson-SD 21.2

Adjusted Starter Runs
Hershiser-LA 31.4
Garrelts-SF 23.4
Langston-Mon 22.3
Hurst-SD 22.3
Maddux-Chi 21.5

Clutch Pitching Index
Langston-Mon 135
Hershiser-LA 124
Lilliquist-Atl 117
Maddux-Chi 115
Drabek-Pit 113

Relief Runs
Andersen-Hou 19.0
Lancaster-Chi 17.2
Davis-SD 17.0
Howell-LA 16.9
Landrum-Pit 16.5

Adjusted Relief Runs
Lancaster-Chi 19.3
Andersen-Hou 18.0
Davis-SD 17.0
Dibble-Cin 16.6
Howell-LA 16.2

Relief Ranking
Davis-SD 26.0
Howell-LA 24.9
McDowell-NY-Phi .24.6
Dibble-Cin 23.2
Lancaster-Chi 18.2

Total Pitcher Index
Hershiser-LA 4.6
Maddux-Chi 3.4
McDowell-NY-Phi .. 3.1
Langston-Mon 2.7
Howell-LA 2.7

Total Baseball Ranking
Mitchell-SF 7.0
L.Smith-Atl 5.2
Clark-SF 5.0
Hershiser-LA 4.6
Bonds-Pit 4.2

April 10 Dave Stieb pitches a one-hitter against the Yankees, giving him three one-hitters in his last four starts (dating back to last September). Jamie Quirk's fifth-inning single is the only hit off Stieb in the 8-0 Blue Jays' victory.

July 2 Brewers outfielder Robin Yount, 33, collects his 2,500th hit in a 10-2 win over the Yankees.

July 11 Bo Jackson and Wade Boggs lead off the bottom of the first inning with back-to-back home runs off Rick Reuschel to spark the AL to a 5-3 win in the All-Star Game at Anaheim Stadium. Jackson earns MVP honors

August 4 Hard-luck pitcher Dave Stieb loses a perfect game when New York's Roberto Kelly doubles with two out in the ninth inning, and Stieb finishes with a 2-1 two-hitter. It's the third time that Stieb has lost a no-hitter with two out in the ninth.

September 27 The two San Francisco Bay teams clinch their divisions. Oakland wins the AL West by beating Texas 5-0, while San Francisco loses 1-0 to the Dodgers but is assured of the NL West crown when the second-place Padres lose to the Reds 2-1 in 13 innings.

October 1 Minnesota's Kirby Puckett and San Diego's Tony Gwynn each win batting titles on the final day of the regular season. Puckett goes 2-for-5 to edge Carney Lansford .339 to .336, while Gwynn goes 3-for-4 to beat Will Clark .336 to .333.

October 8 Oakland beats Toronto 4-3 to win the ALCS in five games and advance to the World Series for the second straight year. Rickey Henderson, who hit .400 with eight stolen bases, is named series MVP.

October 14 Dave Stewart shuts out the Giants 5-0 on five hits in Game 1 of the World Series. He is the first pitcher to start consecutive World Series openers since the Reds' Don Gullett in 1975 and '76.

October 17 Game 3 of the World Series is postponed when an earthquake strikes the San Francisco Bay area a half hour before game time, causing minor damage to Candlestick Park but major damage, including many deaths, in the surrounding area.

October 28 The A's take an 8-0 lead and beat the Giants 9-6 to complete a sweep of the World Series, the first since 1976. Oakland's Dave Stewart, who won two games, is named MVP.

November 15 Twenty-five-year-old Bret Saberhagen becomes the fourth pitcher ever to win the AL Cy Young Award twice, getting 27 of a possible 28 first-place votes for his 23-6, 2.16 ERA season.

November 20 Brewers center fielder Robin Yount edges the Rangers' Ruben Sierra to win his second league MVP Award. Yount, who won as a shortstop in 1982, hit .318 last season with 21 home runs and 103 RBIs.

BALTIMORE

Pos	Player
M	F.Robinson
1B	R.Milligan
2B	B.Ripken
SS	C.Ripken
3B	C.Worthington
LF	P.Bradley
CF	M.Devereaux
RF	J.Orsulak
C	M.Tettleton
DH	L.Sheets
C	B.Melvin
O	B.Anderson
1	J.Traber
O	S.Finley
P	B.Milacki
P	J.Ballard
P	D.Schmidt
P	P.Harnisch
RP	B.Holton
RP	M.Williamson
RP	M.Thurmond
P	D.Johnson
P	G.Olson
P	J.Bautista
P	J.Tibbs

BOSTON

Pos	Player
M	J.Morgan
1B	N.Esasky
2B	M.Barrett
SS	L.Rivera
3B	W.Boggs
LF	M.Greenwell
CF	E.Burks
RF	K.Romine
C	R.Cerone
DH	D.Evans
O1	D.Heep
S2	J.Reed
C	R.Gedman
D	J.Rice
P	R.Clemens
P	M.Boddicker
P	J.Dopson
P	M.Smithson
RP	D.Lamp
RP	R.Murphy
RP	B.Stanley
P	W.Gardner
P	L.Smith
P	J.Price
P	O.Boyd
P	E.Hetzel

CALIFORNIA

Pos	Player
M	D.Rader
1B	W.Joyner
2B	J.Ray
SS	D.Schofield
3B	J.Howell
LF	C.Davis
CF	D.White
RF	C.Washington
C	L.Parrish
DH	B.Downing
S	K.Anderson
O	T.Armas
P	B.Blyleven
P	M.Witt
P	K.McCaskill
P	C.Finley
P	J.Abbott
RP	W.Fraser
RP	G.Minton
RP	B.Harvey
P	B.McClure
P	D.Petry

CHICAGO

Pos	Player
M	J.Torborg
1B	G.Walker
2B	S.Lyons
SS	O.Guillen
3B	C.Martinez
LF	D.Boston
CF	D.Gallagher
RF	I.Calderon
C	C.Fisk
DH	H.Baines
O	D.Pasqua
2	S.Fletcher
3	E.Williams
P	M.Perez
P	E.King
P	S.Rosenberg
P	G.Hibbard
P	J.Reuss
RP	S.Hillegas
RP	D.Pall
RP	B.Thigpen
P	R.Dotson
P	B.Long
P	T.McCarthy
P	K.Patterson

CLEVELAND

Pos	Player
M	D.Edwards
M	J.Hart
1B	P.O'Brien
2B	J.Browne
SS	F.Fermin
3B	B.Jacoby
LF	J.Carter
CF	G.Pettis
RF	C.Snyder
C	A.Allanson
DH	D.Clark
OD	D.James
O	O.McDowell
OD	A.Belle
P	B.Black
P	J.Farrell
P	T.Candiotti
P	G.Swindell
RP	S.Bailes
RP	D.Jones
RP	J.Orosco
P	R.Yett
P	R.Nichols

DETROIT

Pos	Player
M	S.Anderson
1B	D.Bergman
2B	L.Whitaker
SS	A.Trammell
3B	R.Schu
LF	F.Lynn
CF	G.Pettis
RF	C.Lemon
C	M.Heath
DH	K.Moreland
O1	G.Ward
CD	M.Nokes
O	K.Williams
S2	M.Brumley
P	F.Tanana
P	D.Alexander
P	J.Morris
RP	P.Gibson
RP	M.Henneman
RP	F.Williams
P	J.Robinson
P	K.Ritz
P	C.Hudson
P	E.Nunez

KANSAS CITY

Pos	Player
M	J.Wathan
1B	G.Brett
2B	F.White
SS	K.Stillwell
3B	K.Seitzer
LF	B.Jackson
CF	W.Wilson
RF	J.Eisenreich
C	B.Boone
DH	D.Tartabull
OD	P.Tabler
2S	B.Wellman
P	B.Saberhagen
P	M.Gubicza
P	T.Gordon
P	C.Leibrandt
P	L.Aquino
RP	J.Montgomery
RP	T.Leach
RP	S.Farr
P	F.Bannister
P	S.Crawford

MILWAUKEE

Pos	Player
M	T.Trebelhorn
1B	G.Brock
2B	J.Gantner
SS	B.Spiers
3B	P.Molitor
LF	G.Braggs
CF	R.Yount
RF	R.Deer
C	B.Surhoff
DH	J.Meyer
OD	M.Felder
S3	G.Sheffield
1D	T.Francona
P	C.Bosio
P	D.August
P	T.Higuera
P	M.Knudson
P	J.Navarro
RP	C.Crim
RP	B.Krueger
RP	D.Plesac
P	T.Filer
P	B.Clutterbuck
P	T.Fossas
P	B.Wegman

MINNESOTA

Pos	Player
M	T.Kelly
1B	K.Hrbek
2B	A.Newman
SS	G.Gagne
3B	G.Gaetti
LF	D.Gladden
CF	K.Puckett
RF	R.Bush
C	B.Harper
DH	J.Dwyer
1D	G.Larkin
CD	T.Laudner
O	J.Moses
2	W.Backman
OD	C.Castillo
P	A.Anderson
P	F.Viola
P	R.Smith
P	S.Rawley
RP	J.Berenguer
RP	J.Reardon
RP	G.Wayne
P	R.Aguilera
P	M.Dyer
P	M.Guthrie
P	F.Oliveras

NEW YORK

Pos	Player
M	D.Green
M	B.Dent
1B	D.Mattingly
2B	S.Sax
SS	A.Espinoza
3B	M.Pagliarulo
LF	M.Hall
CF	R.Kelly
RF	J.Barfield
C	D.Slaught
DH	S.Balboni
O	R.Henderson
O	L.Polonia
C	B.Geren
P	A.Hawkins
P	C.Parker
P	D.LaPoint
P	C.Cary
RP	L.Guetterman
RP	L.McCullers
RP	E.Plunk
P	G.Cadaret
P	W.Terrell
P	D.Righetti
P	T.John
P	D.Mohorcic
P	R.Dotson

OAKLAND

Pos	Player
M	T.LaRussa
1B	M.McGwire
2B	T.Phillips
SS	M.Gallego
3B	C.Lansford
LF	R.Henderson
CF	D.Henderson
RF	S.Javier
C	T.Steinbach
DH	D.Parker
C	R.Hassey
S	W.Weiss
O	J.Canseco
O	L.Polonia
P	D.Stewart
P	M.Moore
P	B.Welch
P	S.Davis
RP	C.Young
RP	T.Burns
RP	G.Nelson
RP	R.Honeycutt
P	D.Eckersley

SEATTLE

Pos	Player
M	J.Lefebvre
1B	A.Davis
2B	H.Reynolds
SS	O.Vizquel
3B	J.Presley
LF	G.Briley
CF	K.Griffey
RF	D.Coles
C	D.Valle
DH	J.Leonard
C	S.Bradley
O	H.Cotto
O	J.Buhner
P	S.Bankhead
P	B.Holman
P	R.Johnson
P	B.Swift
P	E.Hanson
RP	J.Reed
RP	M.Jackson
RP	M.Schooler
P	M.Dunne
P	M.Langston
P	C.Zavaras

TEXAS

Pos	Player
M	B.Valentine
1B	R.Palmeiro
2B	J.Franco
SS	S.Fletcher
3B	S.Buechele
LF	P.Incaviglia
CF	C.Espy
RF	R.Sierra
C	C.Kreuter
DH	H.Baines
SO	J.Kunkel
DO	R.Leach
P	N.Ryan
P	B.Witt
P	K.Brown
P	C.Hough
P	M.Jeffcoat
RP	K.Rogers
RP	J.Russell
RP	C.Guante
P	J.Moyer
P	D.Hall
P	G.Mielke

TORONTO

Pos	Player
M	J.Williams
M	C.Gaston
1B	F.McGriff
2B	N.Liriano
SS	T.Fernandez
3B	K.Gruber
LF	G.Bell
CF	L.Moseby
RF	J.Felix
C	E.Whitt
DH	R.Mulliniks
2S	S.Lee
CD	P.Borders
O	M.Wilson
P	J.Key
P	D.Stieb
P	J.Cerutti
P	M.Flanagan
P	T.Stottlemyre
RP	D.Ward
RP	T.Henke
RP	D.Wells
P	F.Wills

TEAM	G	W	L	PCT	GB	R	OR	AB	H	2B	3B	HR	BB	SO	AVG	OBP	SLG	PRO	PRO+	BR	/A	PF	CHI	RC	SB	CS	SBA	SBR
EAST																												
TOR	162	89	73	.549		731	651	5581	1449	265	40	142	521	923	.260	.326	.398	.724	105	18	32	98	102	724	144	58	71	8
BAL	162	87	75	.537	2	708	686	5440	1369	238	33	129	593	957	.252	.329	.379	.708	102	-6	15	97	102	678	118	55	68	2
BOS	162	83	79	.512	6	**774**	735	5666	**1571**	**326**	30	108	**643**	755	**.277**	**.355**	**.403**	**.758**	106	**106**	**55**	106	93	**802**	56	35	62	-4
MIL	162	81	81	.500	8	707	679	5473	1415	235	32	126	455	791	.259	.321	.382	.703	98	-22	-15	99	**106**	677	**165**	62	73	12
NY	161	74	87	.460	14.5	698	792	5458	1470	229	23	130	502	831	.269	.334	.391	.725	105	26	35	99	98	709	137	60	70	5
CLE	162	73	89	.451	16	604	654	5463	1340	221	26	127	499	934	.245	.312	.365	.677	89	-72	-82	102	98	622	74	51	59	-8
DET	162	59	103	.364	30	617	816	5432	1315	198	24	116	585	899	.242	.320	.351	.671	91	-74	-60	98	100	616	103	50	67	1
WEST																												
OAK	162	99	63	.611		712	**576**	5416	1414	220	25	127	562	855	.261	.334	.381	.715	105	12	37	96	101	687	157	55	74	14
KC	162	92	70	.568	7	690	635	5475	1428	227	41	101	554	897	.261	.332	.373	.705	98	-9	-6	100	101	682	154	51	**75**	**16**
CAL	162	91	71	.562	8	669	578	5545	1422	208	37	**145**	429	1011	.256	.313	.386	.699	98	-38	-26	98	103	663	89	40	69	3
TEX	162	83	79	.512	16	695	714	5458	1433	260	**46**	122	503	989	.263	.329	.394	.723	101	18	7	102	98	694	101	49	67	1
MIN	162	80	82	.494	19	740	738	5581	1542	278	35	117	478	**743**	.276	.338	.402	.740	101	53	3	107	98	751	111	53	68	2
SEA	162	73	89	.451	26	694	728	5512	1417	237	29	134	489	838	.257	.323	.384	.707	95	-16	-38	103	103	679	81	55	60	-9
CHI	161	69	92	.429	29.5	693	750	5504	1493	262	36	94	464	873	.271	.331	.383	.714	103	4	21	98	100	696	97	52	65	-2
TOT	1133					9732		77004	20078	3404	457	1718	7277	12296	.261	.328	.384	.712							1587	726	69	41

TEAM	CG	SH	SV	IP	H	H/G	HR	BB	SO	RAT	ERA	ERA+	OAV	OOB	PR	/A	PF	CPI	FA	E	DP	FW	PW	BW	SBW	DIF
EAST																										
TOR	12	12	38	1467	1408	8.6	99	478	849	11.8	3.58	105	.255	.320	49	31	97	99	.980	127	164	-.1	3.2	3.3	.5	1.2
BAL	16	7	44	1448¹	1518	9.4	134	486	676	12.6	4.00	95	.272	.333	-19	-33	98	104	**.986**	87	163	**2.3**	-3.4	1.5	-.0	5.6
BOS	14	9	42	1460¹	1448	8.9	131	548	1054	12.5	4.01	102	.261	.331	-20	15	106	99	.980	127	162	-.1	1.5	**5.6**	-.7	-4.3
MIL	16	8	45	1432¹	1463	9.2	129	457	812	12.2	3.80	101	.265	.324	14	7	99	102	.975	155	164	-1.8	.7	-1.5	.9	1.7
NY	15	9	44	1414²	1550	9.9	150	521	787	13.4	4.50	86	.281	.347	-98	-100	100	102	.980	122	183	.1	-10.2	3.6	.2	-.2
CLE	23	13	38	1453	1423	8.8	107	452	844	11.8	3.65	109	.257	.315	38	50	102	96	.981	118	126	.4	5.1	-8.3	-1.1	-4.1
DET	24	4	26	1427¹	1514	9.5	150	652	831	13.9	4.53	84	.274	.355	-103	-114	98	103	.979	130	153	-.3	-11.6	-6.1	-.2	-3.8
WEST																										
OAK	17	**20**	**57**	1448¹	1287	**8.0**	103	510	930	**11.3**	3.09	119	.238	.307	128	95	95	103	.979	129	159	-.2	**9.7**	3.8	1.1	3.7
KC	27	13	38	1451²	1415	8.8	**86**	455	978	11.7	3.55	109	.257	.316	54	49	99	97	.982	114	139	.7	5.0	-.6	**1.3**	4.6
CAL	**32**	**20**	38	1454¹	1384	8.6	113	465	897	11.6	3.28	116	.253	.315	97	86	98	**107**	.985	96	173	1.7	8.8	-2.6	.0	2.1
TEX	26	7	44	1434¹	**1279**	8.0	119	654	**1112**	12.4	3.91	101	.239	.327	-4	9	102	92	.978	136	137	-.6	.9	.7	-.2	1.2
MIN	19	8	38	1429¹	1495	9.4	139	500	851	12.4	4.28	97	.269	.334	-63	-23	107	97	.982	107	141	1.1	-2.3	.3	-.0	.0
SEA	15	10	44	1438	1422	8.9	114	560	897	12.7	4.00	101	.259	.333	-19	4	104	97	.977	143	168	-1.1	.4	-3.9	-1.2	-2.3
CHI	9	5	46	1422	1472	9.3	144	539	778	12.9	4.23	90	.269	.338	-54	-67	98	101	.975	151	176	-1.6	-6.8	2.1	-.5	-4.7
TOT	265	145	582	20181		9.0				12.4	3.88		.261	.328					.980	1742	2208					

Runs		Hits		Doubles		Triples		Home Runs		Total Bases	
R.Henderson-NY-Oak	113	Puckett-Min	215	Boggs-Bos	51	Sierra-Tex	14	McGriff-Tor	36	Sierra-Tex	344
Boggs-Bos	113	Sax-NY	205	Puckett-Min	45	White-Cal	13	Carter-Cle	35	Yount-Mil	314
Yount-Mil	101	Boggs-Bos	205	Reed-Bos	42	Bradley-Bal	10	McGwire-Oak	33	Carter-Cle	303
Sierra-Tex	101	Yount-Mil	195	Bell-Tor	41			Jackson-KC	32	Mattingly-NY	301
McGriff-Tor	98			Yount-Mil	38			Esasky-Bos	30	Puckett-Min	295

Runs Batted In		Runs Produced		Bases On Balls		Batting Average		On Base Percentage		Slugging Average	
Sierra-Tex	119	Sierra-Tex	191	R.Henderson-NY-Oak	126	Puckett-Min	.339	Boggs-Bos	.434	Sierra-Tex	.543
Mattingly-NY	113	Yount-Mil	183	McGriff-Tor	119	Lansford-Oak	.336	Davis-Sea	.428	McGriff-Tor	.525
Esasky-Bos	108	Bell-Tor	174	Boggs-Bos	107	Boggs-Bos	.330	R.Henderson-NY-Oak	.413	Yount-Mil	.511
Jackson-KC	105	Mattingly-NY	169	Seitzer-KC	102	Yount-Mil	.318	McGriff-Tor	.402	Esasky-Bos	.500
Carter-Cle	105	Greenwell-Bos	168	Davis-Sea	101	Franco-Tex	.316	Evans-Bos	.402	Davis-Sea	.496

Production		Adjusted Production		Batter Runs		Adjusted Batter Runs		Clutch Hitting Index		Runs Created	
McGriff-Tor	.927	McGriff-Tor	162	McGriff-Tor	46.8	McGriff-Tor	49.1	Evans-Bos	122	Yount-Mil	125
Davis-Sea	.924	Davis-Sea	155	Boggs-Bos	46.6	Yount-Mil	42.3	Brett-KC	121	Boggs-Bos	122
Yount-Mil	.898	Yount-Mil	152	Davis-Sea	44.2	Davis-Sea	40.7	Mattingly-NY	119	Sierra-Tex	122
Sierra-Tex	.895	Sierra-Tex	146	Yount-Mil	41.2	Boggs-Bos	38.7	Ray-Cal	118	McGriff-Tor	121
Boggs-Bos	.883	Baines-Chi-Tex	144	Sierra-Tex	37.4	Sierra-Tex	35.6	Greenwell-Bos	113	R.Henderson-NY-Oak	110

Total Average		Stolen Bases		Stolen Base Average		Stolen Base Runs		Fielding Runs		Total Player Rating	
McGriff-Tor	.986	R.Henderson-NY-Oak	77	Thurman-KC	100.0	R.Henderson-NY-Oak	14.7	Reynolds-Sea	27.0	R.Henderson-NY-Oak	5.2
R.Henderson-NY-Oak	.983	Espy-Tex	45	Franco-Tex	87.5	Thurman-KC	4.8	Howell-Cal	22.5	Yount-Mil	4.6
Davis-Sea	.975	White-Cal	44	Yount-Mil	86.4	Felder-Mil	4.8	Gruber-Tor	19.2	Sierra-Tex	3.9
Yount-Mil	.926	Sax-NY	43	Finley-Bal	85.0	Franco-Tex	4.5	Snyder-Cle	18.6	Puckett-Min	3.9
Boggs-Bos	.882	Pettis-Det	43	R.Henderson-NY-Oak	84.6			Puckett-Min	18.4	McGriff-Tor	3.5

Wins		Win Percentage		Games		Complete Games		Shutouts		Saves	
Saberhagen-KC	23	Saberhagen-KC	.793	Crim-Mil	76	Saberhagen-KC	12	Blyleven-Cal	5	Russell-Tex	38
Stewart-Oak	21	Blyleven-Cal	.773	Murphy-Bos	74	Morris-Det	10	Saberhagen-KC	4	Thigpen-Chi	34
Moore-Oak	19	Davis-Oak	.731	Rogers-Tex	73	Finley-Cal	9	McCaskill-Cal	4	Schooler-Sea	33
Davis-Oak	19	Stewart-Oak	.700	Russell-Tex	71					Plesac-Mil	33
Ballard-Bal	18	Ballard-Bal	.692	Guetterman-NY	70					Eckersley-Oak	33

Innings Pitched		Fewest Hits/Game		Fewest BB/Game		Strikeouts		Strikeouts/Game		Ratio	
Saberhagen-KC	262.1	Ryan-Tex	6.09	Key-Tor	1.13	Ryan-Tex	301	Ryan-Tex	11.32	Saberhagen-KC	8.71
Stewart-Oak	257.2	Gordon-KC	6.74	Saberhagen-KC	1.48	Clemens-Bos	230	Gordon-KC	8.45	Ryan-Tex	10.12
Gubicza-KC	255.0	Stieb-Tor	7.14	Blyleven-Cal	1.64	Saberhagen-KC	193	Clemens-Bos	8.17	Blyleven-Cal	10.34
Clemens-Bos	253.1	Saberhagen-KC	7.17	Bosio-Mil	1.84	Gubicza-KC	173	Witt-Tex	7.69	Moore-Oak	10.35
Milacki-Bal	243.0	Moore-Oak	7.19	Witt-Cal	1.96	Bosio-Mil	173	Viola-Min	7.07	Key-Tor	10.67

Earned Run Average		Adjusted ERA		Opponents' Batting Avg.		Opponents' On Base Pct.		Starter Runs		Adjusted Starter Runs	
Saberhagen-KC	2.16	Saberhagen-KC	178	Ryan-Tex	.187	Saberhagen-KC	.252	Saberhagen-KC	50.2	Saberhagen-KC	49.2
Finley-Cal	2.57	Finley-Cal	148	Gordon-KC	.210	Ryan-Tex	.276	Moore-Oak	34.3	Blyleven-Cal	29.1
Moore-Oak	2.61	Moore-Oak	141	Saberhagen-KC	.217	Moore-Oak	.288	Blyleven-Cal	31.0	Moore-Oak	28.8
Blyleven-Cal	2.73	Blyleven-Cal	140	Stieb-Tor	.219	Blyleven-Cal	.289	Finley-Cal	29.1	Finley-Cal	27.6
McCaskill-Cal	2.93	Clemens-Bos	131	Moore-Oak	.219	Bosio-Mil	.291	Bosio-Mil	24.2	Clemens-Bos	27.4

Clutch Pitching Index		Relief Runs		Adjusted Relief Runs		Relief Ranking		Total Pitcher Index		Total Baseball Ranking	
Cerutti-Tor	130	Montgomery-KC	25.7	Montgomery-KC	25.3	Jones-Cle	37.6	Saberhagen-KC	5.5	Saberhagen-KC	5.5
Ballard-Bal	123	Olson-Bal	20.7	Lamp-Bos	22.2	Russell-Tex	34.5	Moore-Oak	4.0	R.Henderson-NY-Oak	5.2
Finley-Cal	123	Lamp-Bos	19.5	Olson-Bal	19.8	Montgomery-KC	33.5	Jones-Cle	4.0	Yount-Mil	4.6
McCaskill-Cal	116	Henke-Tor	19.4	Henke-Tor	18.3	Henke-Tor	27.5	Russell-Tex	3.8	Moore-Oak	4.0
Davis-Oak	113	Burns-Oak	17.6	Orosco-Cle	16.3	Olson-Bal	25.7	Montgomery-KC	3.5	Jones-Cle	4.0

February 4* The St. Petersburg Pelicans get home runs from Lamar Johnson and Steve Kemp and rout the West Palm Beach Tropics 12-4 to win the first-ever championship of the Senior Professional Baseball Association.

April 20 Less than a year after being banished from baseball for his illegal gambling activities, all-time hit king Pete Rose pleads guilty to two felony counts of filing false income tax returns. On July 19, he will be sentenced to five months in prison and fined $50,000.

April 29 The Cubs' Greg Maddux sets a record for major league pitchers with seven putouts in a 4-0 win over the Dodgers.

May 18 In a 7-0 loss to the Astros, Cubs second baseman Ryne Sandberg finally commits an error. This ends his major league-record errorless streaks at 123 games and 584 chances.

May 22 Andre Dawson sets a major league record when he is intentionally walked five times during a 2–1 Cubs win over the Reds. Cincinnati issues seven intentional passes altogether to tie a record set by Houston in 1984.

June 4 The Braves select Florida high school shortstop Chipper Jones with the first pick in the annual free-agent draft.

June 14 The NL announces plans to expand from 12 to 14 teams for the 1993 season. The price of admission is $95 million.

August 28 Ryne Sandberg homers in the Cubs' 5–2 win over the Astros to become the first second baseman ever to post back-to-back 30-home run seasons.

September 29 The Reds clinch the NL West title during a rain delay of their 3-1 loss to the Padres when the second-place Dodgers lose 4-3 to San Francisco. The Reds, never out of first place, are the first NL team ever to lead from wire to wire in a 162-game schedule.

September 30 Pittsburgh beats St. Louis, 2-0, behind Doug Drabek's three-hitter to clinch its first NL East title since 1979.

October 12 Danny Jackson, Norm Charlton, and Randy Myers combine on a one-hitter, as Cincinnati beats the Pirates 2-1 to win the NLCS in six games.

October 16 In Game 1 of the World Series, the Reds rout the A's, 7-0, ending Oakland's 10-game postseason winning streak.

October 20 The talk of an Oakland dynasty is proven premature, as Cincinnati beats Oakland, 2-1, to complete one of the most stunning sweeps in World Series history. Series MVP Jose Rijo (2-0, 0.59 ERA) retires the last 20 batters he faces to give the Reds their first world championship since 1976.

November 14 Doug Drabek (22-6) wins the league Cy Young Award, collecting 23 of a possible 24 first-place votes.

November 19 Pittsburgh's Barry Bonds wins the league MVP Award, easily outdistancing teammate and runner-up Bobby Bonilla. Bonds hit .301 with 23 home runs, 114 RBIs, and 52 stolen bases.

December 5 In a major trade, the Blue Jays send first baseman Fred McGriff and veteran shortstop Tony Fernandez to San Diego for second baseman Roberto Alomar and outfielder Joe Carter.

ATLANTA		CHICAGO		CINCINNATI		HOUSTON		LOS ANGELES		MONTREAL	
M	R.Nixon	M	D.Zimmer	M	L.Piniella	M	A.Howe	M	T.Lasorda	M	B.Rodgers
M	B.Cox	1B	M.Grace	1B	T.Benzinger	1B	G.Davis	1B	E.Murray	1B	A.Galarraga
1B	D.Justice	2B	R.Sandberg	2B	M.Duncan	2B	B.Doran	2B	J.Samuel	2B	D.DeShields
2B	J.Treadway	SS	S.Dunston	SS	B.Larkin	SS	R.Ramirez	SS	A.Griffin	SS	S.Owen
SS	J.Blauser	3B	L.Salazar	3B	C.Sabo	3B	K.Caminiti	3B	M.Sharperson	3B	T.Wallach
3B	J.Presley	LF	D.Dascenzo	LF	B.Hatcher	LF	F.Stubbs	LF	K.Daniels	LF	T.Raines
LF	L.Smith	CF	J.Walton	CF	E.Davis	CF	E.Yelding	CF	S.Javier	CF	Da.Martinez
CF	R.Gant	RF	A.Dawson	RF	P.O'Neill	RF	G.Wilson	RF	H.Brooks	RF	L.Walker
RF	D.Murphy	C	J.Girardi	C	J.Oliver	C	C.Biggio	C	M.Scioscia	C	M.Fitzgerald
C	G.Olson										
		3S	D.Ramos	1	H.Morris	O2	C.Candaele	O	J.Gonzalez	O	M.Grissom
1O	T.Gregg	O	D.Smith	O	G.Braggs	O	E.Anthony	O	C.Gwynn	O	O.Nixon
32	M.Lemke							32	L.Harris		
O	O.McDowell	P	G.Maddux	P	T.Browning	P	J.Deshaies	O	K.Gibson	P	De.Martinez
S	A.Thomas	P	M.Harkey	P	J.Rijo	P	M.Scott			P	O.Boyd
		P	M.Bielecki	P	J.Armstrong	P	M.Portugal	P	R.Martinez	P	K.Gross
P	J.Smoltz	P	S.Wilson	P	R.Mahler	P	B.Gullickson	P	M.Morgan	P	M.Gardner
P	T.Glavine	P	S.Boskie	P	D.Jackson	P	D.Darwin	P	F.Valenzuela	P	Z.Smith
P	C.Leibrandt	RP	L.Lancaster	RP	N.Charlton	RP	J.Agosto	P	T.Belcher	RP	B.Sampen
P	M.Clary	RP	P.Assenmacher	RP	R.Dibble	RP	J.Clancy	RP	T.Crews	RP	T.Burke
P	S.Avery	RP	J.Pico	RP	R.Myers	RP	L.Andersen	RP	M.Hartley	RP	D.Hall
RP	T.Castillo							RP	J.Howell		
RP	R.Luecken	P	M.Williams	P	T.Layana	P	D.Schatzeder			P	C.Nabholz
RP	M.Grant	P	J.Nunez	P	S.Scudder	P	X.Hernandez	P	J.Neidlinger	P	S.Frey
		P	B.Long	P	T.Birtsas	P	D.Smith	P	J.Gott	P	D.Mohorcic
P	P.Smith										
P	D.Lilliquist										

NEW YORK		PHILADELPHIA		PITTSBURGH		SAN DIEGO		SAN FRANCISCO		ST.LOUIS	
M	D.Johnson	M	N.Leyva	M	J.Leyland	M	J.McKeon	M	R.Craig	M	W.Herzog
M	B.Harrelson	1B	R.Jordan	1B	S.Bream	M	G.Riddoch	1B	W.Clark	M	R.Schoendienst
1B	D.Magadan	2B	T.Herr	2B	J.Lind	1B	Ja.Clark	2B	R.Thompson	M	J.Torre
2B	G.Jefferies	SS	D.Thon	SS	J.Bell	2B	R.Alomar	SS	J.Uribe	1B	P.Guerrero
SS	K.Elster	3B	C.Hayes	3B	J.King	SS	G.Templeton	3B	M.Williams	2B	J.Oquendo
3B	H.Johnson	LF	J.Kruk	LF	B.Bonds	3B	M.Pagliarulo	LF	K.Mitchell	SS	O.Smith
LF	K.McReynolds	CF	L.Dykstra	CF	A.Van Slyke	LF	B.Roberts	CF	B.Butler	3B	T.Pendleton
CF	D.Boston	RF	V.Hayes	RF	B.Bonilla	CF	J.Carter	RF	M.Kingery	LF	V.Coleman
RF	D.Strawberry	C	D.Daulton	C	M.LaValliere	RF	T.Gwynn	C	T.Kennedy	CF	W.McGee
C	M.Sasser					C	B.Santiago			RF	M.Thompson
		O2	R.Ready	32	W.Backman			C	G.Carter	C	T.Zeile
O2	K.Miller	O	D.Murphy	C	D.Slaught	1	P.Stephenson	O	K.Bass		
				1	G.Redus			O2	G.Litton	1O	D.Collins
				O	R.Reynolds	P	E.Whitson			C	T.Pagnozzi
P	F.Viola	P	P.Combs			P	B.Hurst	P	J.Burkett	O2	R.Hudler
P	D.Gooden	P	T.Mulholland	P	D.Drabek	P	A.Benes	P	S.Garrelts		
P	D.Cone	P	B.Ruffin	P	J.Smiley	P	D.Rasmussen	P	D.Robinson	P	J.Magrane
P	S.Fernandez	P	D.Cook	P	N.Heaton	RP	G.Harris	P	T.Wilson	P	J.DeLeon
P	R.Darling	P	J.DeJesus	P	B.Walk	RP	E.Show	RP	J.Brantley	P	J.Tudor
RP	A.Pena	RP	D.Akerfelds	RP	B.Patterson	RP	C.Schiraldi	RP	S.Bedrosian	P	B.Tewksbury
RP	J.Franco	RP	D.Carman	RP	B.Landrum			RP	A.Hammaker	P	B.Smith
RP	W.Whitehurst	RP	R.McDowell	RP	B.Kipper	P	C.Lefferts			RP	F.DiPino
						P	D.Lilliquist	P	R.Reuschel	RP	K.Dayley
P	B.Ojeda	P	K.Howell	P	W.Terrell			P	M.LaCoss	RP	S.Terry
		P	J.Parrett	P	R.Tomlin			P	K.Downs		
		P	J.Grimsley	P	Z.Smith			P	M.Thurmond	P	K.Hill
				P	S.Belinda			P	F.Oliveras	P	L.Smith
				P	R.Reed					P	T.Niedenfuer
				P	T.Power					P	G.Mathews

TEAM	G	W	L	PCT	GB	R	OR	AB	H	2B	3B	HR	BB	SO	AVG	OBP	SLG	PRO	PRO+	BR	/A	PF	CHI	RC	SB	CS	SBA	SBR
EAST
PIT	162	95	67	.586		733	619	5388	1395	**288**	42	136	582	914	.259	.334	.405	.739	113	64	92	96	99	738	137	52	72	10
NY	162	91	71	.562	4	**775**	613	5504	1410	278	21	172	536	851	.256	.326	**.408**	.734	107	48	50	100	**106**	**748**	110	33	**77**	13
MON	162	85	77	.525	10	662	598	5453	1363	227	**43**	114	576	1024	.250	.325	.370	.695	101	-18	7	96	99	672	**235**	99	70	11
PHI	162	77	85	.475	18	646	729	5535	1410	237	27	103	582	915	.255	.329	.363	.692	96	-19	-17	100	96	675	108	35	76	11
CHI	162	77	85	.475	18	690	774	5600	**1474**	240	36	136	406	869	.263	.316	.392	.708	93	-7	-56	107	103	695	151	50	75	15
STL	162	70	92	.432	25	599	698	5462	1398	255	41	73	517	**844**	.256	.323	.358	.681	93	-46	-49	100	96	650	221	74	75	**22**
WEST
CIN	162	91	71	.562		693	**597**	5525	1466	284	40	125	466	913	**.265**	.327	.399	.726	101	35	5	104	97	726	166	66	72	10
LA	162	86	76	.531	5	728	685	5491	1436	222	27	129	538	952	.262	.331	.382	.713	105	17	37	97	104	699	141	65	68	3
SF	162	85	77	.525	6	719	710	5573	1459	221	35	152	488	973	.262	.325	.396	.721	108	24	50	96	101	724	109	56	66	-1
SD	162	75	87	.463	16	673	673	5554	1429	243	35	123	509	902	.257	.323	.380	.703	98	-8	-13	101	99	682	138	59	70	6
HOU	162	75	87	.463	16	573	656	5379	1301	209	32	94	548	997	.242	.315	.345	.660	90	-83	-66	97	97	596	179	83	68	4
ATL	162	65	97	.401	26	682	821	5504	1376	263	26	162	473	1010	.250	.312	.396	.708	95	-8	-47	106	103	675	92	55	63	-5
TOT	972					8173		65968	16917	2967	405	1521	6221	11164	.256	.324	.383	.707							1787	727	71	100

TEAM	CG	SH	SV	IP	H	H/G	HR	BB	SO	RAT	ERA	ERA+	OAV	OOB	PR	/A	PF	CPI	FA	E	DP	FW	PW	BW	SBW	DIF
EAST
PIT	18	8	43	1447	1367	8.5	135	413	848	**11.3**	3.40	106	.251	.307	63	35	95	103	.979	134	125	-.4	3.6	**9.5**	.2	1.2
NY	18	**14**	41	1440	1339	8.4	119	444	**1217**	**11.3**	3.42	109	.246	**.306**	59	51	99	97	.978	132	107	-.3	5.3	5.2	.5	-.6
MON	18	11	**50**	1473¹	1349	**8.2**	127	510	991	11.6	**3.37**	108	**.245**	.313	**70**	46	96	103	.982	110	134	.9	4.7	.7	.3	-2.7
PHI	18	7	35	1449	1381	8.6	124	651	840	12.8	4.07	94	.253	.336	-45	-40	101	97	.981	117	**150**	.5	-4.1	-1.8	.3	1.1
CHI	13	7	42	1442²	1510	9.4	121	572	877	13.2	4.34	94	.271	.342	-87	-42	108	94	.980	124	136	.1	-4.3	-5.8	.7	5.3
STL	8	13	39	1443¹	1432	8.9	**98**	475	833	12.1	3.87	98	.261	.324	-13	-9	101	95	.979	130	114	-.2	-.9	-5.1	**1.4**	-6.2
WEST
CIN	14	12	**50**	1456¹	**1338**	8.3	124	543	1029	11.8	3.39	**116**	.246	.318	64	**89**	104	105	**.983**	102	126	**1.4**	**9.2**	.5	.2	-1.3
LA	**29**	12	29	1442	1364	8.5	137	478	1021	11.7	3.72	98	.249	.313	11	-10	97	96	.979	130	123	-.2	-1.0	3.8	-.5	3.0
SF	14	6	45	1446¹	1477	9.2	131	553	788	12.8	4.08	89	.267	.335	-46	-70	96	101	**.983**	107	148	1.1	-7.2	5.2	-1.0	5.9
SD	21	12	35	1461²	1381	8.8	147	507	928	12.1	3.68	104	.258	.322	19	24	101	**106**	.977	141	141	-.8	2.5	-1.3	-.2	-6.0
HOU	12	6	37	1450	1396	8.7	130	496	854	12.0	3.61	103	.255	.321	30	17	98	104	.978	131	124	-.3	1.8	-6.8	-.4	-.2
ATL	17	8	30	1429²	1527	9.6	128	579	938	13.4	4.58	88	.275	.346	-125	-86	106	97	.974	158	133	-1.8	-8.9	-4.8	-1.4	.9
TOT	200	116	476	17381¹		8.8				12.2	3.79		.256	.324					.980	1516	1561					

Runs		Hits		Doubles		Triples		Home Runs		Total Bases	
Sandberg-Chi	116	Dykstra-Phi	192	Jefferies-NY	40	Duncan-Cin	11	Sandberg-Chi	40	Sandberg-Chi	344
Bonilla-Pit	112	Butler-SF	192	Bonilla-Pit	39	Gwynn-SD	10	Strawberry-NY	37	Bonilla-Pit	324
Butler-SF	108	Sandberg-Chi	188	Sabo-Cin	38	L.Smith-Atl	9	Mitchell-SF	35	Gant-Atl	310
Gant-Atl	107	Wallach-Mon	185	Wallach-Mon	37	Coleman-StL	9	Williams-SF	33	Williams-SF	301
Dykstra-Phi	106	Larkin-Cin	185	Johnson-NY	37	Butler-SF	9	Bonds-Pit	33	Wallach-Mon	295

Runs Batted In		Runs Produced		Bases On Balls		Batting Average		On Base Percentage		Slugging Average	
Williams-SF	122	Bonilla-Pit	200	J.Clark-SD	104	McGee-StL	.335	Magadan-NY	.425	Bonds-Pit	.565
Bonilla-Pit	120	Bonds-Pit	185	Bonds-Pit	93	Murray-LA	.330	Dykstra-Phi	.420	Sandberg-Chi	.559
Carter-SD	115	Williams-SF	176	Butler-SF	90	Magadan-NY	.328	Murray-LA	.417	Mitchell-SF	.544
Bonds-Pit	114	Sandberg-Chi	176	Dykstra-Phi	89	Dykstra-Phi	.325	Bonds-Pit	.410	Gant-Atl	.539
Strawberry-NY	108	Carter-SD	170	V.Hayes-Phi	87	Dawson-Chi	.310	Butler-SF	.401	Justice-Atl	.535

Production		Adjusted Production		Batter Runs		Adjusted Batter Runs		Clutch Hitting Index		Runs Created	
Bonds-Pit	.974	Bonds-Pit	172	Bonds-Pit	48.1	Bonds-Pit	52.6	Carter-SD	130	Bonds-Pit	128
Murray-LA	.936	Murray-LA	160	Murray-LA	44.7	Murray-LA	48.0	Magadan-NY	123	Sandberg-Chi	124
Daniels-LA	.923	Daniels-LA	156	Sandberg-Chi	37.9	J.Clark-SD	35.9	Kruk-Phi	121	Dykstra-Phi	121
Sandberg-Chi	.918	Mitchell-SF	151	J.Clark-SD	36.5	Mitchell-SF	35.0	Guerrero-StL	119	Murray-LA	118
Justice-Atl	.909	Magadan-NY	143	Dykstra-Phi	34.3	Daniels-LA	34.9	V.Hayes-Phi	119	Gant-Atl	109

Total Average		Stolen Bases		Stolen Base Average		Stolen Base Runs		Fielding Runs		Total Player Rating	
Bonds-Pit	1.115	Coleman-StL	77	Gibson-LA	92.9	Coleman-StL	12.9	Thompson-SF	27.7	Bonds-Pit	7.2
Daniels-LA	.945	Yelding-Hou	64	Grissom-Mon	91.7	Bonds-Pit	7.8	Grace-Chi	26.7	Dykstra-Phi	5.8
Murray-LA	.945	Bonds-Pit	52	Dawson-Chi	88.9	Nixon-Mon	7.2	C.Hayes-Phi	23.6	Sandberg-Chi	4.3
Justice-Atl	.941	Butler-SF	51	Davis-Cin	87.5	Dykstra-Phi	6.9	Dykstra-Phi	20.1	Larkin-Cin	4.3
Dykstra-Phi	.941	Nixon-Mon	50	Dykstra-Phi	86.8			Larkin-Cin	19.9	Murray-LA	4.1

Wins		Win Percentage		Games		Complete Games		Shutouts		Saves	
Drabek-Pit	22	Drabek-Pit	.786	Agosto-Hou	82	Martinez-LA	12	Morgan-LA	4	Franco-NY	33
Viola-NY	20	Martinez-LA	.769	Assenmacher-Chi	74	Hurst-SD	9	Hurst-SD	4	Myers-Cin	31
Martinez-LA	20	Gooden-NY	.731	Harris-SD	73	Drabek-Pit	9			L.Smith-StL	27
Gooden-NY	19	Viola-NY	.625	McDowell-Phi	72	Maddux-Chi	8			Smith-Hou	23
		Browning-Cin	.625	Akerfelds-Phi	71					Lefferts-SD	23

Innings Pitched		Fewest Hits/Game		Fewest BB/Game		Strikeouts		Strikeouts/Game		Ratio	
Viola-NY	249.2	Fernandez-NY	6.52	Darwin-Hou	1.72	Cone-NY	233	Cone-NY	9.91	Darwin-Hou	9.46
Maddux-Chi	237.0	Rijo-Cin	6.90	Whitson-SD	1.85	Martinez-LA	223	Fernandez-NY	9.08	Drabek-Pit	9.69
Martinez-LA	234.1	Martinez-LA	7.34	Leibrandt-Atl	1.94	Gooden-NY	223	Gooden-NY	8.63	D.Martinez-Mon	9.80
Gooden-NY	232.2	Drabek-Pit	7.39	D.Martinez-Mon	1.95	Viola-NY	182	Martinez-LA	8.56	Martinez-LA	10.06
		Darwin-Hou	7.52	Browning-Cin	2.06	Fernandez-NY	181	DeLeon-StL	8.08	Fernandez-NY	10.14

Earned Run Average		Adjusted ERA		Opponents' Batting Avg.		Opponents' On Base Pct.		Starter Runs		Adjusted Starter Runs	
Darwin-Hou	2.21	Darwin-Hou	168	Fernandez-NY	.200	Darwin-Hou	.267	Viola-NY	31.2	Whitson-SD	31.1
Smith-Mon-Pit	2.55	Whitson-SD	147	Rijo-Cin	.212	Drabek-Pit	.275	Whitson-SD	30.3	Viola-NY	29.8
Whitson-SD	2.60	Rijo-Cin	146	Martinez-LA	.220	D.Martinez-Mon	.275	Smith-Mon-Pit	29.7	Rijo-Cin	27.3
Viola-NY	2.67	Smith-Mon-Pit	143	Drabek-Pit	.225	Martinez-LA	.279	Darwin-Hou	28.5	Darwin-Hou	27.1
Rijo-Cin	2.70	Viola-NY	140	Darwin-Hou	.225	Fernandez-NY	.280	Drabek-Pit	26.4	Smith-Mon-Pit	26.0

Clutch Pitching Index		Relief Runs		Adjusted Relief Runs		Relief Ranking		Total Pitcher Index		Total Baseball Ranking	
Gullickson-Hou	121	Dibble-Cin	22.3	Dibble-Cin	23.9	Myers-Cin	30.5	Viola-NY	3.6	Bonds-Pit	7.2
Smith-Mon-Pit	116	Brantley-SF	21.5	Charlton-Cin	20.6	Dibble-Cin	29.1	Whitson-SD	3.4	Dykstra-Phi	5.8
Whitson-SD	115	Harris-SD	19.4	Brantley-SF	20.1	Harris-SD	27.1	Drabek-Pit	3.4	Sandberg-Chi	4.3
Rasmussen-SD	114	Charlton-Cin	18.0	Harris-SD	19.8	Charlton-Cin	25.7	Myers-Cin	3.3	Larkin-Cin	4.3
Darwin-Hou	107	Myers-Cin	16.5	Myers-Cin	18.0	Brantley-SF	24.8	Rijo-Cin	3.1	Murray-LA	4.1

January 9 Jim Palmer, a three-time AL Cy Young Award winner, and Joe Morgan, a two-time NL MVP, are elected to the Hall of Fame in their first years of eligibility.

June 11 Ageless Nolan Ryan pitches his unprecedented sixth career no-hitter, striking out 14 batters in a 5-0 win over the A's.

June 29 Oakland's Dave Stewart and the Dodgers' Fernando Valenzuela both throw no-hitters. Stewart blanks the Blue Jays 5-0, and a few hours later Valenzuela beats the Cardinals 6-0.

July 17 The Twins pull a major league first—two triple plays in the same game. Both are started on grounders to third baseman Gary Gaetti.

August 31 Ken Griffeys—Jr. in center and Sr. in left—become the first father-and-son combination in major league history to play as teammates, and they each go 1-for-4 in Seattle's 5-2 win over the Royals. The Mariners had signed the elder Griffey after he was waived by the Reds last week.

September 2 In the year of no-hitters, Dave Stieb pitches the ninth and final one of the season, blanking Cleveland 3-0. It is the first no-hitter in Blue Jays' history, and the first for Stieb after numerous close calls.

September 25 The Oakland A's clinch their third straight AL West title by beating Kansas City 5-0.

September 30 The White Sox beat Seattle 2-1 in the last game played at historic Comiskey Park, which is to be torn down after 80 seasons of major league ball. Chicago will play next season at the new Comiskey Park across the street.

October 3 Boston beats Chicago 3-1 on the final day of the season to wrap up its third AL East title in five seasons.

October 3 George Brett pinch hits a single in Kansas City's finale to end the season at .329 and win the AL batting crown, his third in three decades. Willie McGee's .335 wins the NL batting title despite his having been traded out of the league in August.

October 10 After Red Sox starter Roger Clemens is ejected in the second inning for cursing at home plate umpire Terry Cooney, Oakland beats Boston 3-1 to complete a four-game sweep of the ALCS and earn its third straight trip to the World Series.

November 13 Oakland's Bob Welch wins the AL Cy Young Award. His 27 wins were the most in the majors since Steve Carlton in 1972.

November 20 Oakland's Rickey Henderson edges Detroit's Cecil Fielder for the AL MVP Award. Henderson hit .325 with 28 home runs and a major league-best 65 stolen bases.

December 6 At Leland's auction house in New York City, Shoeless Joe Jackson's signature is sold for $23,100, the most money ever paid for a baseball signature. Jackson, who could not read or write, copied the signature from one written out by his wife. The signature, which was resold within hours, had been cut from an unknown document.

	BALTIMORE		BOSTON		CALIFORNIA		CHICAGO		CLEVELAND		DETROIT		KANSAS CITY
M	F.Robinson	M	J.Morgan	M	D.Rader	M	J.Torborg	M	J.McNamara	M	S.Anderson	M	J.Wathan
1B	R.Milligan	1B	C.Quintana	1B	W.Joyner	1B	C.Martinez	1B	B.Jacoby	1B	C.Fielder	1B	G.Brett
2B	B.Ripken	2B	Jo.Reed	2B	J.Ray	2B	S.Fletcher	2B	J.Browne	2B	L.Whitaker	2B	F.White
SS	C.Ripken	SS	L.Rivera	SS	D.Schofield	SS	O.Guillen	SS	F.Fermin	SS	A.Trammell	SS	K.Stillwell
3B	C.Worthington	3B	W.Boggs	3B	J.Howell	3B	R.Ventura	3B	C.Baerga	3B	T.Phillips	3B	K.Seitzer
LF	P.Bradley	LF	M.Greenwell	LF	D.Bichette	LF	I.Calderon	LF	C.Maldonado	LF	G.Ward	LF	W.Wilson
CF	M.Devereaux	CF	E.Burks	CF	D.White	CF	L.Johnson	CF	M.Webster	CF	L.Moseby	CF	B.Jackson
RF	S.Finley	RF	T.Brunansky	RF	D.Winfield	RF	S.Sosa	RF	C.Snyder	RF	C.Lemon	RF	J.Eisenreich
C	M.Tettleton	C	T.Pena	C	L.Parrish	C	C.Fisk	C	S.Alomar	C	M.Heath	C	M.Macfarlane
DH	S.Horn	DH	D.Evans	DH	B.Downing	DH	D.Pasqua	DH	C.James	DH	D.Bergman	DH	G.Perry
O	J.Orsulak	2S	J.Reed	DO	C.Davis	D1	R.Kittle	1O	D.James	OD	L.Sheets	OD	D.Tartabull
CD	B.Melvin			2S	D.Hill			O	A.Cole	3S	T.Fryman	2S	B.Pecota
OD	B.Anderson			OD	L.Polonia	P	G.Hibbard			O	J.Shelby		
		P	R.Clemens	1	L.Stevens	P	J.McDowell	P	G.Swindell			P	T.Gordon
		P	M.Boddicker			P	M.Perez	P	T.Candiotti	P	J.Morris	P	K.Appier
P	P.Harnisch	P	G.Harris			P	E.King	P	B.Black	P	F.Tanana	P	B.Saberhagen
P	D.Johnson	P	D.Kiecker	P	C.Finley	RP	W.Edwards	P	S.Valdez	P	D.Petry	P	S.Davis
P	B.Milacki	P	T.Bolton	P	M.Langston	RP	B.Thigpen	P	J.Farrell	P	J.Robinson	RP	S.Farr
P	J.Ballard	RP	D.Lamp	P	J.Abbott	RP	D.Pall	RP	S.Olin	RP	P.Gibson	RP	J.Montgomery
P	B.McDonald	RP	W.Gardner	P	K.McCaskill			RP	D.Jones	RP	M.Henneman	RP	S.Crawford
RP	M.Williamson	RP	R.Murphy			P	A.Fernandez	RP	J.Orosco	RP	J.Gleaton		
RP	G.Olson			RP	M.Eichhorn	P	A.Peterson					P	M.Gubicza
RP	J.Price	P	J.Gray	RP	W.Fraser	P	B.Jones	P	M.Walker	P	E.Nunez	P	A.McGaffigan
		P	J.Reardon	RP	M.Fetters	P	K.Patterson			P	S.Searcy	P	M.Davis
P	J.Mitchell					P	S.Radinsky			P	W.Terrell	P	L.Aquino
P	B.Holton	P	B.Harvey							P	B.DuBois		
P	J.Tibbs									P	C.Parker		

	MILWAUKEE		MINNESOTA		NEW YORK		OAKLAND		SEATTLE		TEXAS		TORONTO
M	T.Trebelhorn	M	T.Kelly	M	B.Dent	M	T.LaRussa	M	J.Lefebvre	M	B.Valentine	M	C.Gaston
1B	G.Brock	1B	K.Hrbek	M	S.Merrill	1B	M.McGwire	1B	P.O'Brien	1B	R.Palmeiro	1B	F.McGriff
2B	J.Gantner	2B	A.Newman	1B	D.Mattingly	2B	W.Randolph	2B	H.Reynolds	2B	J.Franco	2B	M.Lee
SS	B.Spiers	SS	G.Gagne	2B	S.Sax	SS	W.Weiss	SS	O.Vizquel	SS	J.Huson	SS	T.Fernandez
3B	G.Sheffield	3B	G.Gaetti	SS	A.Espinoza	3B	C.Lansford	3B	E.Martinez	3B	S.Buechele	3B	K.Gruber
LF	M.Felder	LF	D.Gladden	3B	R.Velarde	LF	R.Henderson	LF	G.Briley	LF	P.Incaviglia	LF	G.Bell
CF	R.Yount	CF	K.Puckett	LF	O.Azocar	CF	D.Henderson	CF	K.Griffey	CF	G.Pettis	CF	M.Wilson
RF	R.Deer	RF	S.Mack	CF	R.Kelly	RF	F.Jose	RF	H.Cotto	RF	R.Sierra	RF	J.Felix
C	B.Surhoff	C	B.Harper	RF	J.Barfield	C	T.Steinbach	C	D.Valle	C	G.Petralli	C	P.Borders
DH	D.Parker	DH	G.Larkin	C	B.Geren	DH	J.Canseco	DH	A.Davis	DH	H.Baines	DH	J.Olerud
				DH	S.Balboni								
21	P.Molitor	OD	J.Moses			2S	M.Gallego	C	S.Bradley	O1	J.Daugherty	OD	G.Hill
O	G.Vaughn	2	F.Manrique	DO	M.Hall	CD	R.Hassey	OD	J.Leonard	S3	J.Kunkel	C	G.Myers
S2	E.Diaz			3O	J.Leyritz					CD	M.Stanley		
				1D	K.Maas	P	D.Stewart	P	E.Hanson			P	D.Stieb
		P	A.Anderson	CD	M.Nokes	P	B.Welch	P	M.Young	P	B.Witt	P	T.Stottlemyre
P	T.Higuera	P	K.Tapani			P	S.Sanderson	P	R.Johnson	P	C.Hough	P	D.Wells
P	M.Knudson	P	R.Smith	P	T.Leary	P	M.Moore	P	B.Holman	P	N.Ryan	P	J.Key
P	J.Navarro	P	D.West	P	D.LaPoint	P	C.Young	RP	B.Swift	P	K.Brown	P	J.Cerutti
P	R.Robinson	P	M.Guthrie	P	A.Hawkins	RP	T.Burns	RP	M.Jackson	P	J.Moyer	RP	D.Ward
P	C.Bosio	RP	J.Berenguer	P	C.Cary	RP	G.Nelson	RP	M.Schooler	RP	M.Jeffcoat	RP	F.Wills
RP	T.Edens	RP	T.Drummond	P	M.Witt	RP	D.Eckersley			RP	K.Rogers	RP	J.Acker
RP	C.Crim	RP	T.Leach	RP	C.Cadaret			P	K.Comstock	RP	B.Arnsberg		
RP	D.Plesac			RP	L.Guetterman	P	R.Honeycutt					P	T.Henke
		P	S.Erickson	RP	J.Robinson							P	W.Blair
P	B.Krueger	P	R.Aguilera										
P	P.Mirabella	P	J.Candelaria										
				P	E.Plunk								
				P	D.Righetti								
				P	J.Jones								

TEAM	G	W	L	PCT	GB	R	OR	AB	H	2B	3B	HR	BB	SO	AVG	OBP	SLG	PRO	PRO+	BR	/A	PF	CHI	RC	SB	CS	SBA	SBR
EAST																												
BOS	162	88	74	.543		699	664	5516	**1502**	298	31	106	598	795	**.272**	**.346**	.395	.741	102	57	22	105	92	733	53	52	50	-15
TOR	162	86	76	.531	2	**767**	661	5589	1479	263	**50**	167	526	970	.265	.331	**.419**	**.750**	106	56	42	102	101	**769**	111	52	68	2
DET	162	79	83	.488	9	750	754	5479	1418	241	32	**172**	634	952	.259	.339	.409	.748	107	**62**	57	101	98	754	82	57	59	-10
CLE	162	77	85	.475	11	732	737	5485	1465	266	41	110	458	836	.267	.327	.391	.718	101	-5	-2	100	107	694	107	52	67	1
BAL	161	76	85	.472	11.5	669	698	5410	1328	234	22	132	**660**	962	.245	.332	.370	.702	99	-21	1	97	98	676	94	52	64	-3
MIL	162	74	88	.457	14	732	760	5503	1408	247	36	128	519	821	.256	.324	.384	.708	98	-24	-19	99	**109**	692	**164**	72	69	6
NY	162	67	95	.414	21	603	749	5483	1322	208	19	147	427	1027	.241	.302	.366	.668	86	-109	-111	100	105	605	119	45	**73**	9
WEST																												
OAK	162	103	59	.636		733	**570**	5433	1379	209	22	164	651	992	.254	.339	.391	.730	**108**	31	**61**	96	100	739	141	54	72	**10**
CHI	162	94	68	.580	9	682	633	5402	1393	251	44	106	478	903	.258	.322	.379	.701	97	-35	-21	98	105	651	140	90	61	-12
TEX	162	83	79	.512	20	676	696	5469	1416	257	27	110	575	1054	.259	.333	.376	.709	98	-11	-12	100	98	688	115	48	71	6
CAL	162	80	82	.494	23	690	706	5570	1448	237	27	147	566	1000	.260	.331	.391	.722	103	10	24	98	96	715	69	43	62	-5
SEA	162	77	85	.475	26	640	680	5474	1419	251	26	107	596	**749**	.259	.336	.373	.709	97	-7	-15	101	92	691	105	51	67	1
KC	161	75	86	.466	27.5	707	709	5488	1465	**316**	44	100	498	879	.267	.331	.395	.726	104	14	25	98	101	706	107	62	63	-5
MIN	162	74	88	.457	29	666	729	5499	1458	281	39	100	445	**749**	.265	.326	.385	.711	92	-17	-61	107	99	673	96	53	64	-3
TOT	1133					9746		76800	19900	3559	460	1796	7631	12689	.259	.330	.388	.718							1503	783	66	-19

TEAM	CG	SH	SV	IP	H	H/G	HR	BB	SO	RAT	ERA	ERA+	OAV	OOB	PR	/A	PF	CPI	FA	E	DP	FW	PW	BW	SBW	DIF
EAST																										
BOS	15	13	44	1442	1439	9.0	**92**	519	997	12.5	3.72	110	.261	.329	30	57	104	100	.980	123	154	-.2	5.8	2.2	-1.4	.6
TOR	6	9	48	1454	1434	8.9	143	**445**	892	11.9	3.84	103	.260	.319	11	17	101	99	**.986**	**86**	144	**2.0**	1.7	4.3	.3	-3.4
DET	15	12	45	1430^1	1401	8.8	154	661	856	13.3	4.39	90	.259	.345	-76	-68	101	98	.979	131	178	-.7	-6.9	5.8	-.9	.7
CLE	12	10	47	1427^1	1491	9.4	163	518	860	12.9	4.26	92	.270	.337	-57	-55	100	102	.981	117	146	.2	-5.6	-.2	.2	1.4
BAL	10	5	43	1435^1	1445	9.1	161	537	776	12.5	4.04	94	.264	.331	-21	-39	97	103	.985	93	151	1.6	-4.0	.1	-.2	-2.0
MIL	23	13	42	1445	1558	9.7	121	469	771	12.9	4.08	95	.275	.335	-28	-34	99	101	.976	149	152	-1.8	-3.5	-1.9	.7	-.6
NY	15	6	41	1444^2	1430	8.9	144	618	909	12.9	4.21	94	.261	.339	-49	-39	102	99	.980	126	164	-.4	-4.0	-11.3	1.1	.6
WEST																										
OAK	18	**16**	64	1456	**1287**	**8.0**	123	494	831	**11.2**	**3.18**	**117**	**.238**	**.305**	**118**	**87**	95	101	**.986**	87	152	**2.0**	**8.9**	**6.2**	**1.2**	3.8
CHI	17	10	**68**	1449^1	1313	8.2	106	548	914	11.8	3.61	106	.244	.318	48	34	98	95	.980	124	169	-.3	3.5	-2.1	-1.1	13.0
TEX	**25**	9	36	1444^2	1343	8.4	113	623	997	12.5	3.83	102	.248	.330	12	14	100	97	.979	133	161	-.8	1.4	-1.2	.7	1.9
CAL	21	13	42	1454	1482	9.2	106	544	944	12.8	3.79	101	.267	.337	18	3	98	**105**	.978	142	**186**	-1.4	.3	2.4	-.4	-2.0
SEA	21	7	41	1443^1	1319	8.2	120	606	**1064**	12.3	3.69	107	.243	.324	34	42	101	97	.979	130	152	-.6	4.3	-1.5	.2	-6.4
KC	18	8	33	1420^2	1449	9.2	116	560	1006	13.0	3.93	97	.264	.337	-5	-16	98	102	.980	122	161	-.2	-1.6	2.5	-.4	-5.9
MIN	13	13	43	1435^2	1509	9.5	134	489	872	12.7	4.12	101	.273	.335	-35	4	106	101	.983	101	161	1.1	.4	-6.2	-.2	-2.2
TOT	229	144	637	20182^1		8.9				12.5	3.91		.259	.330					.981	1664	2231					

Runs
R.Henderson-Oak . 119
Fielder-Det 104
Reynolds-Sea 100
Yount-Mil 98
Phillips-Det 97

Hits
Palmeiro-Tex 191
Boggs-Bos 187
Kelly-NY 183
Greenwell-Bos 181

Doubles
J.Reed-Bos 45
Brett-KC 45
Calderon-Chi 44
Boggs-Bos 44
Harper-Min 42

Triples
Fernandez-Tor 17
Sosa-Chi 10
Polonia-NY-Cal 9
Liriano-Tor-Min 9
Johnson-Chi 9

Home Runs
Fielder-Det 51
McGwire-Oak 39
J.Canseco-Oak 37
McGriff-Tor 35
Gruber-Tor 31

Total Bases
Fielder-Det 339
Gruber-Tor 303
McGriff-Tor 295
K.Griffey-Sea 287
Burks-Bos 286

Runs Batted In
Fielder-Det 132
Gruber-Tor 118
McGwire-Oak 108
J.Canseco-Oak . . . 101
Sierra-Tex 96

Runs Produced
Fielder-Det 185
Gruber-Tor 179
Yount-Mil 158
Burks-Bos 157
McGwire-Oak 156

Bases On Balls
McGwire-Oak 110
Tettleton-Bal 106
Phillips-Det 99
R.Henderson-Oak . . 97
McGriff-Tor 94

Batting Average
Brett-KC 329
R.Henderson-Oak . .325
Palmeiro-Tex 319
Trammell-Det 304
Boggs-Bos 302

On Base Percentage
R.Henderson-Oak . .441
McGriff-Tor 403
E.Martinez-Sea 399
Davis-Sea 393
Brett-KC 392

Slugging Average
Fielder-Det 592
R.Henderson-Oak . .577
J.Canseco-Oak 543
McGriff-Tor 530
Brett-KC 515

Production
R.Henderson-Oak . . . 1.017
Fielder-Det 972
McGriff-Tor 932
J.Canseco-Oak 917
Brett-KC 906

Adjusted Production
R.Henderson-Oak . . 190
Fielder-Det 167
J.Canseco-Oak 160
McGriff-Tor 156
Brett-KC 154

Batter Runs
R.Henderson-Oak . 57.5
Fielder-Det 51.3
McGriff-Tor 45.5
Brett-KC 37.0
J.Canseco-Oak 34.3

Adjusted Batter Runs
R.Henderson-Oak . 62.7
Fielder-Det 50.4
McGriff-Tor 43.4
Brett-KC 38.7
J.Canseco-Oak 38.4

Clutch Hitting Index
Leonard-Sea 138
Guillen-Chi 122
Fletcher-Chi 121
Gaetti-Min 118
Gruber-Tor 117

Runs Created
R.Henderson-Oak . 137
Fielder-Det 129
McGriff-Tor 124
Brett-KC 106
K.Griffey-Sea 103

Total Average
R.Henderson-Oak . . . 1.241
Fielder-Det 1.007
McGriff-Tor 983
J.Canseco-Oak 943
McGwire-Oak 903

Stolen Bases
R.Henderson-Oak . . . 65
Sax-NY 43
Kelly-NY 42
Cole-Cle 40
Pettis-Tex 38

Stolen Base Average
Cotto-Sea 87.5
R.Henderson-Oak . 86.7
Molitor-Mil 85.7
Gantner-Mil 85.7
Wilson-Tor 85.2

Stolen Base Runs
R.Henderson-Oak . 13.5
Sax-NY 7.5
Cole-Cle 6.6
Wilson-Tor 4.5
Cotto-Sea 4.5

Fielding Runs
Espinoza-NY 21.1
Reynolds-Sea 15.1
Quintana-Bos 14.5
Gaetti-Min 13.8
Gallego-Oak 13.7

Total Player Rating
R.Henderson-Oak . . 8.2
Fielder-Det 4.2
McGriff-Tor 4.1
J.Canseco-Oak 4.0
Fisk-Chi 3.5

Wins
Welch-Oak 27
Stewart-Oak 22
Clemens-Bos 21

Win Percentage
Welch-Oak 818
Clemens-Bos 778
Stieb-Tor 750
Boddicker-Bos 680

Games
Thigpen-Chi 77
Ward-Tor 73
Montgomery-KC 73
Rogers-Tex 69
Henneman-Det 69

Complete Games
Stewart-Oak 11
Morris-Det 11

Shutouts
Stewart-Oak 4
Clemens-Bos 4
Perez-Chi 3
Morris-Det 3
Appier-KC 3

Saves
Thigpen-Chi 57
Eckersley-Oak 48
Jones-Cle 43
Olson-Bal 37
Righetti-NY 36

Innings Pitched
Stewart-Oak 267.0
Morris-Det 249.2
Welch-Oak 238.0
Hanson-Sea 236.0
Finley-Cal 236.0

Fewest Hits/Game
Ryan-Tex 6.04
Johnson-Sea 7.13
Clemens-Bos 7.61
Stewart-Oak 7.62
Stieb-Tor 7.72

Fewest BB/Game
Anderson-Min 1.86
Swindell-Cle 1.97
Clemens-Bos 2.13
Knudson-Mil 2.14
Wells-Tor 2.14

Strikeouts
Ryan-Tex 232
Witt-Tex 221
Hanson-Sea 211
Clemens-Bos 209
Langston-Cal 195

Strikeouts/Game
Ryan-Tex 10.24
Witt-Tex 8.96
Clemens-Bos 8.24
Gordon-KC 8.06
Hanson-Sea 8.05

Ratio
Ryan-Tex 9.62
Clemens-Bos 10.01
Wells-Tor 10.10
Hanson-Sea 10.49
Stewart-Oak 10.58

Earned Run Average
Clemens-Bos 1.93
Finley-Cal 2.40
Stewart-Oak 2.56
Appier-KC 2.76
Stieb-Tor 2.93

Adjusted ERA
Clemens-Bos 211
Finley-Cal 159
Stewart-Oak 145
Appier-KC 139
Stieb-Tor 134

Opponents' Batting Avg.
Ryan-Tex 188
Johnson-Sea 216
Clemens-Bos 228
Stieb-Tor 230
Stewart-Oak 231

Opponents' On Base Pct.
Ryan-Tex 269
Clemens-Bos 280
Wells-Tor 283
Hanson-Sea 289
Black-Cle-Tor 293

Starter Runs
Clemens-Bos 50.1
Stewart-Oak 39.9
Finley-Cal 39.4
Welch-Oak 25.3
Appier-KC 23.6

Adjusted Starter Runs
Clemens-Bos 54.3
Finley-Cal 37.1
Stewart-Oak 34.2
Stieb-Tor 23.4
Appier-KC 22.0

Clutch Pitching Index
Finley-Cal 136
Appier-KC 121
Clemens-Bos 118
Welch-Oak 117
Johnson-Bal 113

Relief Runs
Farr-KC 27.1
Eckersley-Oak 26.8
Swift-Sea 21.5
Thigpen-Chi 20.5
Nelson-Oak 19.4

Adjusted Relief Runs
Farr-KC 26.1
Eckersley-Oak 25.3
Swift-Sea 22.3
Thigpen-Chi 19.6
Nelson-Oak 17.8

Relief Ranking
Eckersley-Oak 45.1
Thigpen-Chi 40.1
Farr-KC 37.3
Olson-Bal 24.1
Jones-Cle 23.9

Total Pitcher Index
Clemens-Bos 6.7
Eckersley-Oak 4.7
Thigpen-Chi 4.4
Finley-Cal 4.1
Stewart-Oak 4.1

Total Baseball Ranking
R.Henderson-Oak . . 8.2
Clemens-Bos 6.7
Eckersley-Oak 4.7
Thigpen-Chi 4.4
Fielder-Det 4.2

January 8 For the first time since 1984, three players are elected to the Hall of Fame: two 300-game winners, Gaylord Perry and Ferguson Jenkins, and a 3,000-hit player, Rod Carew. Ironically, none of the three players ever appeared in a World Series.

February 26 Bill Veeck, the colorful owner of the Browns, Indians and White Sox (twice), and Yankees great "Poosh 'Em Up Tony" Lazzeri are elected to the Hall of Fame by the Veterans Committee.

March 22 At Sotheby's in New York, a 1909-10 tobacco card in mint condition of Honus Wagner sells for $451,000 to hockey star Wayne Gretzky and Los Angeles Kings owner Bruce McNall.

April 21 In the greatest extra-inning comeback in major league history, Pittsburgh scores six in the bottom of the 11th inning to erase a five-run Cubs lead built in the top of the inning on Andre Dawson's grand slam. The Pirates had rallied earlier from a 7-2 deficit to tie the game in the bottom of the ninth inning.

May 7 Darryl Strawberry homers twice in his first game back at Shea Stadium since signing with the Dodgers as a free agent, but he grounds out with the tying run on third as the Mets hold on for a 6-5 win.

May 23 Philadelphia's Tommy Greene tosses the season's second no-hitter, a 2-0 win over Montreal.

July 28 Dennis Martinez pitches the 13th perfect game in baseball history, a 2-0 win at Los Angeles. Ron Hassey, who caught Len Barker's perfecto in Cleveland in 1981, is behind the plate for Martinez.

August 13 Atlanta, now 22-10 since the All-Star break, goes 11 games over .500 for the first time since 1984 as Tom Glavine wins again; this time a 9-2 triumph over the Giants.

August 25 Doug Dascenzo commits his first career error after 242 games, an NL record, in the Cubs' 12-9 loss to the Padres.

September 13 A 55-ton block collapses in Montreal's Olympic Stadium. The Expos, already in last place, will have to play the rest of their home games on the road.

October 5 After 11 lead changes or ties in the closing weeks of the NL West race, the Braves finally clinch the division on the second-to-last day of the season.

October 17 The Braves take the well-below capacity crowd at Three Rivers Stadium out of the game quickly on Brian Hunter's two-run home run in the first inning. It's all John Smoltz needs as he tosses a 4-0 shutout to bring the first pennant to Atlanta.

October 22 It takes 12 innings, but the first World Series game ever in Atlanta goes to the Braves. Mark Lemke singles in David Justice for the 5-4 win.

ATLANTA		CHICAGO		CINCINNATI		HOUSTON		LOS ANGELES		MONTREAL	
M	B.Cox	M	D.Zimmer	M	L.Piniella	M	A.Howe	M	T.Lasorda	M	B.Rodgers
1B	B.Hunter	M	J.Altobelli	1B	H.Morris	1B	J.Bagwell	1B	E.Murray	M	T.Runnells
2B	M.Lemke	M	J.Essian	2B	B.Doran	2B	C.Candaele	2B	J.Samuel	1B	A.Galarraga
SS	R.Belliard	1B	M.Grace	SS	B.Larkin	SS	E.Yelding	SS	A.Griffin	2B	D.DeShields
3B	T.Pendleton	2B	R.Sandberg	3B	C.Sabo	3B	K.Caminiti	3B	L.Harris	SS	S.Owen
LF	O.Nixon	SS	S.Dunston	LF	B.Hatcher	LF	L.Gonzalez	LF	K.Daniels	3B	T.Wallach
CF	R.Gant	3B	L.Salazar	CF	E.Davis	CF	G.Young	CF	B.Butler	LF	I.Calderon
RF	D.Justice	LF	G.Bell	RF	P.O'Neill	RF	S.Finley	RF	D.Strawberry	CF	M.Grissom
C	G.Olson	CF	J.Walton	C	J.Oliver	C	C.Biggio	C	M.Scioscia	RF	Da.Martinez
		RF	A.Dawson							C	G.Reyes
S2	J.Blauser	C	R.Wilkins	2S	M.Duncan	S2	R.Ramirez	C1	G.Carter		
O	L.Smith			23	L.Quinones	S	A.Cedeno	O	S.Javier	O1	L.Walker
2	J.Treadway	O	D.Dascenzo	O	H.Winningham			3S	M.Sharperson		
1	S.Bream	3O	C.Walker	C	J.Reed	P	P.Harnisch			P	De.Martinez
				O	G.Braggs	P	M.Portugal	P	M.Morgan	P	M.Gardner
P	T.Glavine	P	G.Maddux			P	J.Deshaies	P	R.Martinez	P	B.Barnes
P	J.Smoltz	P	M.Bielecki	P	T.Browning	P	D.Kile	P	T.Belcher	P	C.Nabholz
P	C.Leibrandt	P	S.Boskie	P	J.Rijo	P	J.Jones	P	B.Ojeda	P	O.Boyd
P	S.Avery	P	F.Castillo	P	J.Armstrong	RP	A.Osuna	P	O.Hershiser	RP	B.Sampen
RP	M.Stanton	P	R.Sutcliffe	P	S.Scudder	RP	J.Corsi	RP	K.Gross	RP	B.Jones
RP	K.Mercker	RP	L.Lancaster	P	C.Hammond	RP	C.Schilling	RP	J.Gott	RP	S.Ruskin
RP	J.Berenguer	RP	B.Scanlan	RP	R.Myers			RP	T.Crews		
		RP	P.Assenmacher	RP	N.Charlton	P	R.Bowen			P	C.Haney
				RP	T.Power	P	D.Henry	P	M.Hartley	P	J.Fassero
		P	C.McElroy			P	X.Hernandez	P	J.Howell		
		P	D.Jackson	P	K.Gross	P	J.Clancy				
		P	H.Slocumb	P	R.Dibble						

NEW YORK		PHILADELPHIA		PITTSBURGH		SAN DIEGO		SAN FRANCISCO		ST.LOUIS	
M	B.Harrelson	M	N.Leyva	M	J.Leyland	M	G.Riddoch	M	R.Craig	M	J.Torre
M	M.Cubbage	M	J.Fregosi	1B	O.Merced	1B	F.McGriff	1B	W.Clark	1B	P.Guerrero
1B	D.Magadan	1B	J.Kruk	2B	J.Lind	2B	B.Roberts	2B	R.Thompson	2B	J.Oquendo
2B	G.Jefferies	2B	M.Morandini	SS	J.Bell	SS	T.Fernandez	SS	J.Uribe	SS	O.Smith
SS	K.Elster	SS	D.Thon	3B	B.Bonilla	3B	J.Howell	3B	M.Williams	3B	T.Zeile
3B	H.Johnson	3B	C.Hayes	LF	B.Bonds	LF	J.Clark	LF	M.Felder	LF	M.Thompson
LF	K.McReynolds	LF	W.Chamberlain	CF	A.Van Slyke	CF	D.Jackson	CF	W.McGee	CF	R.Lankford
CF	D.Boston	CF	V.Hayes	RF	G.Varsho	RF	T.Gwynn	RF	K.Bass	RF	F.Jose
RF	H.Brooks	RF	D.Murphy	C	M.LaValliere	C	B.Santiago	C	S.Decker	C	T.Pagnozzi
C	R.Cerone	C	D.Daulton								
				1O	G.Redus	O	T.Howard	S1	D.Anderson	O1	R.Hudler
O	M.Carreon	1	R.Jordan	C	D.Slaught	23	T.Teufel	O	K.Mitchell	2	G.Pena
2O	K.Miller	O	L.Dykstra					O	D.Lewis	1	G.Perry
O	V.Coleman	2	R.Ready	P	D.Drabek	P	A.Benes			O	B.Gilkey
CO	M.Sasser			P	Z.Smith	P	B.Hurst	P	B.Black		
S1	G.Templeton	P	T.Mulholland	P	J.Smiley	P	D.Rasmussen	P	J.Burkett	P	B.Smith
		P	T.Greene	P	R.Tomlin	P	G.Harris	P	T.Wilson	P	B.Tewksbury
P	D.Cone	P	J.DeJesus	P	B.Walk	RP	M.Maddux	P	D.Robinson	P	K.Hill
P	F.Viola	P	B.Ruffin	RP	V.Palacios	RP	R.Rodriguez	RP	K.Downs	P	O.Olivares
P	D.Gooden	P	D.Cox	RP	S.Belinda	RP	C.Lefferts	RP	J.Brantley	P	J.DeLeon
P	W.Whitehurst	RP	J.Boever	RP	B.Landrum			RP	F.Oliveras	RP	J.Agosto
P	R.Darling	RP	M.Williams			P	J.Melendez			RP	S.Terry
RP	P.Schourek	RP	R.McDowell	P	N.Heaton	P	E.Whitson	P	D.Righetti	RP	L.Smith
RP	J.Innis			P	B.Patterson	P	A.Peterson	P	P.McClellan		
RP	A.Pena	P	P.Combs	P	B.Kipper	P	R.Bones	P	R.Beck	P	R.Cormier
		P	J.Grimsley					P	B.Hickerson	P	C.Carpenter
P	D.Simons	P	D.Akerfelds								
P	T.Burke	P	W.Ritchie								
P	J.Franco										

TEAM	G	W	L	PCT	GB	R	OR	AB	H	2B	3B	HR	BB	SO	AVG	OBP	SLG	PRO	PRO+	BR	/A	PF	CHI	RC	SB	CS	SBA	SBR
EAST																												
PIT	162	98	64	.605		**768**	632	5449	**1433**	259	50	126	**620**	901	**.263**	**.342**	.398	**.740**	116	**104**	117	98	98	762	124	46	73	**10**
STL	162	84	78	.519	14	651	648	5362	1366	239	**53**	68	532	857	.255	.324	.357	.681	96	-13	-17	101	102	628	202	110	65	-5
PHI	162	78	84	.481	20	629	680	5521	1332	248	33	111	490	1026	.241	.306	.358	.664	93	-60	-53	99	**104**	609	92	30	**75**	10
CHI	160	77	83	.481	20	695	734	5522	1395	232	26	159	442	879	.253	.312	.390	.702	97	11	-21	105	103	675	123	64	66	-2
NY	161	77	84	.478	20.5	640	646	5359	1305	250	24	117	578	**789**	.244	.320	.365	.685	99	-9	-4	99	99	641	153	70	69	4
MON	161	71	90	.441	26.5	579	655	5412	1329	236	42	95	484	1056	.246	.311	.357	.668	94	-47	-38	99	95	607	**221**	100	69	6
WEST																												
ATL	162	94	68	.580		749	644	5456	1407	255	30	141	563	906	.258	.331	.393	.724	103	65	22	106	102	719	165	76	68	4
LA	162	93	69	.574	1	665	**565**	5408	1366	191	29	108	583	957	.253	.328	.359	.687	101	1	16	98	100	650	126	68	65	-3
SD	162	84	78	.519	10	636	646	5408	1321	204	36	121	501	1069	.244	.312	.362	.674	92	-35	-54	103	100	605	101	64	61	-8
SF	162	75	87	.463	19	649	697	5463	1345	215	48	141	471	973	.246	.311	.381	.692	93	-9	12	97	100	647	95	57	63	-6
CIN	162	74	88	.457	20	689	691	5501	1419	250	27	**164**	488	1006	.258	.322	**.403**	.725	105	57	30	104	96	721	124	56	69	4
HOU	162	65	97	.401	29	605	717	5504	1345	240	43	79	502	1027	.244	.312	.347	.659	97	-64	-29	94	101	606	125	68	65	-3
TOT	970					7955		65365	16363	2819	441	1430	6254	11446	.250	.319	.373	.692							1651	809	67	10

TEAM	CG	SH	SV	IP	H	H/G	HR	BB	SO	RAT	ERA	ERA+	OAV	OOB	PR	/A	PF	CPI	FA	E	DP	FW	PW	BW	SBW	DIF
EAST																										
PIT	**18**	11	**51**	1456²	1411	8.7	117	**401**	919	11.4	3.44	104	.256	.309	39	21	97	103	.981	120	134	.4	2.2	**12.2**	**1.0**	1.3
STL	9	5	**51**	1435¹	1367	8.6	114	454	822	11.7	3.69	101	.255	.318	0	5	101	100	**.982**	**107**	133	**1.1**	.5	-1.8	-.6	3.8
PHI	16	11	35	1463	1346	8.3	111	670	988	12.7	3.86	95	.244	.332	-29	-32	100	99	.981	119	111	.4	-3.3	-5.5	**1.0**	4.5
CHI	12	4	40	1456²	1415	8.7	117	542	927	12.3	4.03	96	.257	.327	-57	-24	105	96	**.982**	113	120	.7	-2.5	-2.2	-.3	1.3
NY	12	11	39	1437¹	1403	8.8	108	410	1028	11.5	3.56	102	.257	.311	20	13	99	100	.977	143	112	-1.0	1.4	-.4	.3	-3.7
MON	12	**14**	39	1440¹	**1304**	**8.1**	111	584	909	12.0	3.64	99	.244	.322	7	-4	98	100	.979	133	128	-.4	-.4	-4.0	.5	-5.2
WEST																										
ATL	**18**	7	48	1452²	**1304**	**8.1**	118	481	969	11.2	3.49	111	**.240**	**.305**	32	64	106	95	.978	138	122	-.7	6.7	2.3	.3	4.4
LA	15	**14**	40	1458	1312	**8.1**	96	500	1028	11.4	**3.06**	117	.241	.308	**101**	86	98	107	.980	123	126	.2	**9.0**	1.7	-.4	1.6
SD	14	11	47	1452²	1385	8.6	139	457	921	11.5	3.57	106	.252	.311	18	36	103	102	**.982**	113	130	.8	3.8	-5.6	-.9	5.0
SF	10	10	45	1442	1397	8.7	143	544	905	12.3	4.03	89	.257	.329	-56	-72	97	100	**.982**	109	151	1.0	-7.5	1.3	-.7	.0
CIN	7	11	43	1440	1372	8.6	127	560	997	12.3	3.83	99	.253	.326	-24	-5	103	101	.979	125	131	.0	-.5	3.1	.3	-10.0
HOU	7	13	36	1453	1347	8.3	129	651	**1033**	12.6	4.00	88	.247	.330	-51	-80	95	97	.974	161	129	-2.0	-8.4	-3.0	-.4	-2.2
TOT	150	122	514	17387²		8.5				11.9	3.68		.250	.319					.980	1504	1527					

Runs		Hits		Doubles		Triples		Home Runs		Total Bases	
Butler-LA	112	Pendleton-Atl	187	Bonilla-Pit	44	Lankford-StL	15	Johnson-NY	38	Pendleton-Atl	303
Johnson-NY	108	Butler-LA	182	Jose-StL	40	Gwynn-SD	11	Williams-SF	34	Clark-SF	303
Sandberg-Chi	104	Sabo-Cin	175	Zeile-StL	36	Finley-Hou	10	Gant-Atl	32	Johnson-NY	302
Bonilla-Pit	102	Bonilla-Pit	174	O'Neill-Cin	36	Grissom-Mon	9	McGriff-SD	31	Williams-SF	294
Gant-Atl	101	Jose-StL	173			Gonzalez-Hou	9	Dawson-Chi	31	Sabo-Cin	294

Runs Batted In		Runs Produced		Bases On Balls		Batting Average		On Base Percentage		Slugging Average	
Johnson-NY	117	Johnson-NY	187	Butler-LA	108	Pendleton-Atl	.319	Bonds-Pit	.419	Clark-SF	.536
Clark-SF	116	Bonds-Pit	186	Bonds-Pit	107	Morris-Cin	.318	Butler-LA	.402	Johnson-NY	.535
Bonds-Pit	116	Bonilla-Pit	184	McGriff-SD	105	Gwynn-SD	.317	McGriff-SD	.400	Pendleton-Atl	.517
McGriff-SD	106	Sandberg-Chi	178	DeShields-Mon	95	McGee-SF	.312	Bonilla-Pit	.398	Bonds-Pit	.514
Gant-Atl	105	Gant-Atl	174	Bonilla-Pit	90	Jose-StL	.305	Bagwell-Hou	.391	Larkin-Cin	.506

Production		Adjusted Production		Batter Runs		Adjusted Batter Runs		Clutch Hitting Index		Runs Created	
Bonds-Pit	.932	Bonds-Pit	163	Bonds-Pit	45.5	Bonds-Pit	47.3	Pagnozzi-StL	129	Bonds-Pit	118
Clark-SF	.897	Clark-SF	154	Bonilla-Pit	39.5	Bonilla-Pit	41.3	Bonds-Pit	127	Sandberg-Chi	114
McGriff-SD	.894	Bonilla-Pit	151	McGriff-SD	38.4	Clark-SF	38.1	Murray-LA	118	Bonilla-Pit	114
Bonilla-Pit	.890	Johnson-NY	147	Sandberg-Chi	34.8	McGriff-SD	35.2	Magadan-NY	117	Clark-SF	110
Larkin-Cin	.886	McGriff-SD	146	Clark-SF	34.7	Johnson-NY	33.5	Daniels-LA	116	Pendleton-Atl	107

Total Average		Stolen Bases		Stolen Base Average		Stolen Base Runs		Fielding Runs		Total Player Rating	
Bonds-Pit	1.055	Grissom-Mon	76	Dykstra-Phi	85.7	Grissom-Mon	12.6	Pendleton-Atl	27.9	Bonds-Pit	6.4
McGriff-SD	.937	Nixon-Atl	72	Redus-Pit	85.0	Nixon-Atl	9.0	Belliard-Atl	26.1	Pendleton-Atl	5.9
Larkin-Cin	.923	DeShields-Mon	56	Landrum-Chi	84.4	O.Smith-StL	5.1	Lind-Pit	22.6	Larkin-Cin	5.8
Johnson-NY	.902	Lankford-StL	44	Jefferies-NY	83.9	Landrum-Chi	5.1	Grissom-Mon	20.4	Sandberg-Chi	4.7
Sandberg-Chi	.896	Bonds-Pit	43	Grissom-Mon	81.7	Bonds-Pit	5.1	Grace-Chi	20.0	Bonilla-Pit	4.1

Wins		Win Percentage		Games		Complete Games		Shutouts		Saves	
Smiley-Pit	20	Smiley-Pit	.714	Jones-Mon	77	D.Martinez-Mon	9	D.Martinez-Mon	5	L.Smith-StL	47
Glavine-Atl	20	Rijo-Cin	.714	Assenmacher-Chi	75	Glavine-Atl	9	Martinez-LA	4	Dibble-Cin	31
Avery-Atl	18	Avery-Atl	.692	Stanton-Atl	74	Mulholland-Phi	8	Smith-Pit	3	Williams-Phi	30
Martinez-LA	17	Hurst-SD	.652	Burke-Mon-NY	72	Maddux-Chi	7	Mulholland-Phi	3	Franco-NY	30
		Glavine-Atl	.645	Agosto-StL	72			Black-SF	3	Righetti-SF	24

Innings Pitched		Fewest Hits/Game		Fewest BB/Game		Strikeouts		Strikeouts/Game		Ratio	
Maddux-Chi	263.0	Harnisch-Hou	7.02	Smith-Pit	1.14	Cone-NY	241	Cone-NY	9.32	Rijo-Cin	9.82
Glavine-Atl	246.2	Rijo-Cin	7.27	Tewksbury-StL	1.79	Maddux-Chi	198	Rijo-Cin	7.58	Glavine-Atl	9.92
Morgan-LA	236.1	DeJesus-Phi	7.28	Mulholland-Phi	1.90	Glavine-Atl	192	Harnisch-Hou	7.14	Morgan-LA	9.94
Drabek-Pit	234.2	Hill-StL	7.30	Smiley-Pit	1.91	Rijo-Cin	172	Gooden-NY	7.11	D.Martinez-Mon	10.26
Cone-NY	232.2	Glavine-Atl	7.33	B.Smith-StL	2.04	Harnisch-Hou	172	Glavine-Atl	7.01	Benes-SD	10.37

Earned Run Average		Adjusted ERA		Opponents' Batting Avg.		Opponents' On Base Pct.		Starter Runs		Adjusted Starter Runs	
D.Martinez-Mon	2.39	Glavine-Atl	152	Harnisch-Hou	.212	Rijo-Cin	.274	D.Martinez-Mon	31.9	Glavine-Atl	36.5
Rijo-Cin	2.51	Rijo-Cin	151	Rijo-Cin	.219	Glavine-Atl	.279	Glavine-Atl	31.0	D.Martinez-Mon	30.2
Glavine-Atl	2.55	D.Martinez-Mon	151	Glavine-Atl	.222	Morgan-LA	.279	Rijo-Cin	26.6	Rijo-Cin	29.3
Belcher-LA	2.62	DeLeon-StL	137	Hill-StL	.224	D.Martinez-Mon	.283	Belcher-LA	24.7	Harris-SD	23.1
Harnisch-Hou	2.70	Belcher-LA	137	DeJesus-Phi	.224	Benes-SD	.286	Morgan-LA	23.7	Belcher-LA	22.6

Clutch Pitching Index		Relief Runs		Adjusted Relief Runs		Relief Ranking		Total Pitcher Index		Total Baseball Ranking	
DeLeon-StL	131	McElroy-Chi	19.5	McElroy-Chi	21.7	Williams-Phi	30.0	Glavine-Atl	5.5	Bonds-Pit	6.4
Drabek-Pit	127	Maddux-SD	13.4	Maddux-SD	14.6	L.Smith-StL	24.6	D.Martinez-Mon	3.9	Pendleton-Atl	5.9
Tewksbury-StL	121	Williams-Phi	13.2	Williams-Phi	13.0	McElroy-Chi	16.5	Williams-Phi	3.1	Larkin-Cin	5.8
Ojeda-LA	121	Brantley-SF	13.0	Brantley-SF	11.9	Pena-NY-Atl	15.3	Rijo-Cin	3.0	Glavine-Atl	5.5
Belcher-LA	118	Pena-NY-Atl	11.7	Pena-NY-Atl	11.8	McDowell-Phi-LA	14.0	L.Smith-StL	2.5	Sandberg-Chi	4.7

March 11 Jim Palmer, who is in the Orioles camp as a non-roster player, has a shaky outing against the Red Sox, giving up five hits and two runs in two innings. Palmer, who retired in 1984, will retire again tomorrow, citing a hamstring injury.

April 18 New Comiskey Park opens with fanfare and a rout. The Tigers are the stars of the day as Detroit mauls the White Sox, 16-0.

May 1 Rickey Henderson steals third base in the fourth inning for his 939th career theft to break Lou Brock's all-time stolen base record. The A's knock off the Yankees 7-4.

May 1 The 44-year-old flame-thrower Nolan Ryan strikes out 16 Blue Jays en route to his seventh career no-hitter, a 3-0 win.

May 15 The Red Sox and White Sox play the slowest nine-inning game in major league history (four hours, 11 minutes), but Boston rallies from a 5-0 deficit for a 9-6 win.

June 6 Albert Belle is shipped to the minors for not running out a ground ball in Cleveland's 2-1 loss to the White Sox.

July 9 At Toronto's SkyDome, the AL wins the All-Star Game, 4-2, on Cal Ripken's three-run home run off Montreal's Dennis Martinez. The Baltimore shortstop earns MVP honors.

August 11 Wilson Alvarez hurls a no-hitter in his first White Sox start as Chicago stops Baltimore, 7-0.

October 12 The Blue Jays chase Twins starter Kevin Tapani for the second time in the ALCS, but Minnesota's bullpen and bats lead to six unanswered runs at the SkyDome as the Twins win their third pennant, four games to one.

October 26 Kirby Puckett prevents two Atlanta runs with a leaping catch in the third inning and then he lofts a sacrifice fly in the fifth to give the Twins the lead. The Braves tie it in the seventh, but Puckett turns out the lights in the 10th with a home run to force Game 7.

October 27 In a Game 7 that rivals any in World Series history, the Braves and Twins go through the first nine innings without scoring. Lonnie Smith is decoyed into pausing at second base to keep him from scoring the winner for Atlanta in the eighth. Series MVP Jack Morris makes the Braves pay for that hesitation with 10 shutout innings. Gene Larkin's single over a drawn-in outfield in the 10th is the difference in the first extra-inning Game 7 in 67 years.

BALTIMORE		BOSTON		CALIFORNIA		CHICAGO		CLEVELAND		DETROIT		KANSAS CITY	
M	F.Robinson	M	J.Morgan	M	D.Rader	M	J.Torborg	M	J.McNamara	M	S.Anderson	M	J.Wathan
M	J.Oates	1B	C.Quintana	M	B.Rodgers	1B	D.Pasqua	M	M.Hargrove	1B	D.Bergman	M	B.Schaefer
1B	R.Milligan	2B	J.Reed	1B	W.Joyner	2B	S.Fletcher	1B	B.Jacoby	2B	L.Whitaker	M	H.McRae
2B	B.Ripken	SS	L.Rivera	2B	L.Sojo	SS	O.Guillen	2B	M.Lewis	SS	A.Trammell	1B	T.Benzinger
SS	C.Ripken	3B	W.Boggs	SS	D.Schofield	3B	R.Ventura	SS	F.Fermin	3B	T.Fryman	2B	T.Shumpert
3B	L.Gomez	LF	M.Greenwell	3B	G.Gaetti	LF	T.Raines	3B	C.Baerga	LF	L.Moseby	SS	K.Stillwell
LF	B.Anderson	CF	E.Burks	LF	L.Polonia	CF	L.Johnson	LF	A.Belle	CF	M.Cuyler	3B	B.Pecota
CF	M.Devereaux	RF	T.Brunansky	CF	D.Gallagher	RF	S.Sosa	CF	A.Cole	RF	R.Deer	LF	J.Eisenreich
RF	J.Orsulak	C	T.Pena	RF	D.Winfield	C	C.Fisk	RF	M.Whiten	C	M.Tettleton	CF	B.McRae
C	C.Hoiles	DH	J.Clark	C	L.Parrish	DH	F.Thomas	C	J.Skinner	DH	C.Fielder	RF	D.Tartabull
DH	S.Horn			DH	D.Parker			DH	C.James			C	B.Mayne
		1D	M.Vaughn			2	J.Cora			OD	P.Incaviglia	DH	G.Brett
2S	J.Bell	O2	S.Lyons	O	J.Felix	32	C.Grebeck	2O	J.Browne	O3	T.Phillips		
OD	D.Evans			2S	D.Hill			D1	C.Martinez			OD	K.Gibson
C	B.Melvin	P	R.Clemens			P	J.McDowell			P	B.Gullickson	C	M.Macfarlane
O	C.Martinez	P	G.Harris	P	M.Langston	P	C.Hough	P	G.Swindell	P	W.Terrell	S2	D.Howard
1O	D.Segui	P	J.Hesketh	P	J.Abbott	P	G.Hibbard	P	C.Nagy	P	F.Tanana	3	K.Seitzer
32	T.Hulett	P	M.Gardiner	P	C.Finley	P	A.Fernandez	P	E.King	P	M.Leiter		
		P	T.Bolton	P	K.McCaskill	RP	M.Perez	P	R.Nichols	RP	P.Gibson	P	K.Appier
P	B.Milacki	RP	D.Lamp	RP	M.Eichhorn	RP	S.Radinsky	P	T.Candiotti	RP	J.Cerutti	P	B.Saberhagen
P	B.McDonald	RP	J.Gray	RP	B.Harvey	RP	D.Pall	RP	S.Hillegas	RP	M.Henneman	P	M.Boddicker
P	J.Mesa	RP	J.Reardon	RP	J.Robinson			RP	J.Shaw			P	T.Gordon
P	J.Ballard					P	R.Garcia	RP	D.Jones	P	J.Gleaton	P	L.Aquino
P	J.Robinson	P	M.Young	P	J.Grahe	P	B.Thigpen			P	D.Gakeler	RP	S.Davis
RP	M.Flanagan	P	K.Morton	P	S.Lewis	P	K.Patterson	P	D.Otto	P	S.Aldred	RP	J.Montgomery
RP	T.Frohwirth	P	D.Darwin	P	S.Bailes	P	W.Alvarez	P	S.Olin	P	D.Petry	RP	M.Davis
RP	M.Williamson	P	T.Fossas										
												P	M.Gubicza
P	M.Mussina											P	M.Magnante
P	D.Johnson												
P	R.Smith												
P	G.Olson												
P	P.Kilgus												

MILWAUKEE		MINNESOTA		NEW YORK		OAKLAND		SEATTLE		TEXAS		TORONTO	
M	T.Trebelhorn	M	T.Kelly	M	S.Merrill	M	T.LaRussa	M	J.Lefebvre	M	B.Valentine	M	C.Gaston
1B	F.Stubbs	1B	K.Hrbek	1B	D.Mattingly	1B	M.McGwire	1B	P.O'Brien	1B	R.Palmeiro	M	G.Tenace
2B	W.Randolph	2B	C.Knoblauch	2B	S.Sax	2B	M.Gallego	2B	H.Reynolds	2B	J.Franco	M	C.Gaston
SS	B.Spiers	SS	G.Gagne	SS	A.Espinoza	SS	M.Bordick	SS	O.Vizquel	SS	J.Huson	1B	J.Olerud
3B	J.Gantner	3B	M.Pagliarulo	3B	P.Kelly	3B	E.Riles	3B	E.Martinez	3B	S.Buechele	2B	R.Alomar
LF	G.Vaughn	LF	D.Gladden	LF	R.Kelly	LF	R.Henderson	LF	G.Briley	LF	J.Gonzalez	SS	M.Lee
CF	R.Yount	CF	K.Puckett	CF	B.Williams	CF	D.Henderson	CF	K.Griffey	CF	G.Pettis	3B	K.Gruber
RF	D.Bichette	RF	S.Mack	RF	M.Hall	RF	J.Canseco	RF	J.Buhner	RF	R.Sierra	LF	C.Maldonado
C	B.Surhoff	C	B.Harper	C	M.Nokes	C	T.Steinbach	C	D.Valle	C	I.Rodriguez	CF	D.White
DH	P.Molitor	DH	C.Davis	DH	K.Maas	DH	H.Baines	DH	A.Davis	DH	B.Downing	RF	J.Carter
												C	G.Myers
O	D.Hamilton	O1	G.Larkin	OD	H.Meulens	O	W.Wilson	P	R.Johnson	OD	K.Reimer	DH	R.Mulliniks
S3	D.Sveum	3S	S.Leius	O	J.Barfield	C	J.Quirk	P	B.Holman	3O	D.Palmer		
		S2	A.Newman					P	R.DeLucia			C	P.Borders
P	J.Navarro			P	S.Sanderson	P	D.Stewart	P	B.Krueger	P	K.Brown	OD	M.Wilson
P	C.Bosio	P	J.Morris	P	J.Johnson	P	B.Welch	P	E.Hanson	P	N.Ryan		
P	B.Wegman	P	K.Tapani	P	T.Leary	P	M.Moore	RP	B.Swift	P	J.Guzman	P	T.Stottlemyre
P	D.August	P	S.Erickson	P	W.Taylor	P	J.Slusarski	RP	M.Jackson	RP	K.Rogers	P	J.Key
RP	D.Plesac	P	A.Anderson	RP	G.Cadaret	RP	D.Eckersley	RP	R.Swan	RP	G.Alexander	P	D.Wells
RP	C.Crim	RP	M.Guthrie	RP	E.Plunk	RP	C.Young			RP	J.Barfield	P	J.Guzman
RP	J.Machado	RP	C.Willis	RP	J.Habyan	RP	J.Klink	P	S.Bankhead			P	T.Candiotti
		RP	S.Bedrosian							P	B.Witt	RP	M.Timlin
P	D.Holmes			P	L.Guetterman	P	A.Hawkins			P	M.Jeffcoat	RP	D.Ward
P	M.Lee	P	D.West	P	P.Perez	P	R.Darling			P	Je.Russell	RP	J.Acker
P	K.Brown	P	R.Aguilera	P	D.Eiland	P	S.Chitren			P	W.Rosenthal		
		P	T.Leach	P	S.Farr	P	E.Show			P	O.Boyd	/P	D.Stieb
				/P	S.Kamieniecki					P	B.Bohanon	P	R.MacDonald
				P	C.Cary					P	T.Mathews	P	T.Henke

TEAM	G	W	L	PCT	GB	R	OR	AB	H	2B	3B	HR	BB	SO	AVG	OBP	SLG	PRO	PRO+	BR	/A	PF	CHI	RC	SB	CS	SBA	SBR
EAST																												
TOR	162	91	71	.562		684	**622**	5489	1412	295	45	133	499	1043	.257	.326	.400	.726	96	-7	-33	104	96	724	148	53	74	**13**
DET	162	84	78	.519	7	817	794	5547	1372	259	26	**209**	**699**	1185	.247	.335	.416	.751	105	50	39	101	103	800	109	47	70	5
BOS	162	84	78	.519	7	731	712	5530	1486	**305**	25	126	593	820	.269	.343	.401	.744	100	42	4	105	95	756	59	39	60	-6
MIL	162	83	79	.512	8	799	744	5611	1523	247	**53**	116	556	802	.271	.340	.396	.736	106	24	43	98	105	745	106	68	61	-9
NY	162	71	91	.438	20	674	777	5541	1418	249	19	147	473	861	.256	.319	.387	.706	94	-47	-48	100	101	683	109	36	**75**	11
BAL	162	67	95	.414	24	686	796	5604	1421	256	29	170	528	974	.254	.321	.401	.722	102	-17	12	96	96	707	50	33	60	-5
CLE	162	57	105	.352	34	576	759	5470	1390	236	26	79	449	888	.254	.316	.350	.666	83	-118	-122	101	98	591	84	58	59	-10
WEST																												
MIN	162	95	67	.586		776	652	5556	**1557**	270	42	140	526	**747**	**.280**	**.347**	.420	**.767**	106	82	45	105	96	786	107	68	61	-9
CHI	162	87	75	.537	8	758	681	5594	1464	226	39	139	610	896	.262	.338	.391	.729	103	12	30	98	101	741	134	74	64	-4
TEX	162	85	77	.525	10	**829**	814	5703	1539	288	31	177	596	1039	.270	.343	**.424**	**.767**	**113**	**85**	**100**	98	99	**831**	102	50	67	1
OAK	162	84	78	.519	11	760	776	5410	1342	246	19	159	642	981	.248	.333	.389	.722	105	-2	39	94	**106**	711	**151**	64	70	7
SEA	162	83	79	.512	12	702	674	5494	1400	268	29	126	588	811	.255	.331	.383	.714	97	-21	-22	100	99	698	97	44	69	3
KC	162	82	80	.506	13	727	722	5584	1475	290	41	117	523	969	.264	.331	.394	.725	100	-4	-7	100	101	720	119	68	64	-5
CAL	162	81	81	.500	14	653	649	5470	1396	245	29	115	448	928	.255	.316	.374	.690	90	-78	-77	100	104	640	94	56	63	-5
TOT	1134					10172		77603	20195	3680	453	1953	7730	12944	.260	.331	.395	.726							1469	758	66	-14

TEAM	CG	SH	SV	IP	H	H/G	HR	BB	SO	RAT	ERA	ERA+	OAV	OOB	PR	/A	PF	CPI	FA	E	DP	FW	PW	BW	SBW	DIF
EAST																										
TOR	10	**16**	**60**	1462^2	**1301**	8.0	121	523	971	**11.5**	**3.50**	**120**	**.238**	**.309**	**96**	**114**	103	96	.980	127	115	-.6	**11.4**	-3.3	**1.4**	1.1
DET	18	8	38	1450^1	1570	9.7	148	593	739	13.6	4.51	92	.280	.352	-66	-57	101	105	.983	104	171	.7	-5.7	3.9	.6	3.5
BOS	15	13	45	1439^2	1405	8.8	147	530	999	12.3	4.01	107	.257	.326	13	46	105	100	.981	116	165	.0	4.6	.4	-.5	-1.5
MIL	23	11	41	1463^2	1498	9.2	147	527	859	12.7	4.14	96	.266	.334	-8	-28	97	102	.981	118	176	-.0	-2.8	4.3	-.8	1.4
NY	3	11	37	1444	1510	9.4	152	506	936	12.8	4.42	94	.271	.336	-52	-45	101	99	.979	133	181	-.9	-4.5	-4.8	1.2	-1.0
BAL	8	8	42	1457^2	1534	9.5	147	504	868	12.8	4.59	86	.273	.335	-80	-103	97	95	**.985**	**91**	172	**1.4**	-10.3	1.2	-.4	-5.9
CLE	22	8	33	1441^1	1551	9.7	110	**441**	862	12.7	4.23	98	.276	.333	-22	-13	101	98	.976	149	150	-1.8	-1.3	-12.2	-.9	-7.8
WEST																										
MIN	21	12	53	1449^1	1402	8.7	139	488	876	11.9	3.69	115	.255	.319	64	92	104	104	**.985**	95	161	1.2	9.2	4.5	-.8	-.0
CHI	**28**	8	40	1478	1302	**7.9**	154	601	923	11.8	3.79	105	.239	.318	50	30	97	98	.982	116	151	.0	3.0	3.0	-.3	.3
TEX	9	10	41	1479	1486	9.0	151	662	**1022**	13.3	4.47	90	.262	.344	-61	-72	98	98	.979	134	138	-1.0	-7.2	**10.0**	.2	2.0
OAK	14	10	49	1444^1	1425	8.9	155	655	892	13.3	4.57	84	.260	.345	-77	-119	94	97	.982	107	150	.5	-11.9	3.9	.8	9.7
SEA	10	13	48	1464^1	1387	8.5	136	628	1003	12.7	3.79	109	.253	.335	50	54	101	**107**	.983	110	**187**	.3	5.4	-2.2	.4	-1.9
KC	17	12	41	1466	1473	9.0	**105**	529	1004	12.6	3.92	105	.261	.329	28	32	101	99	.980	125	141	-.5	3.2	-.7	-.4	-.6
CAL	18	10	50	1441^2	1351	8.4	141	543	990	12.1	3.69	111	.250	.323	65	66	100	105	.984	102	156	.8	6.6	-7.7	-.4	.7
TOT	216	150	618	20382		8.9				12.6	4.09		.260	.331					.981	1627	2214					

Runs
- Molitor-Mil 133
- Palmeiro-Tex 115
- Canseco-Oak 115
- White-Tor 110
- Sierra-Tex 110

Hits
- Molitor-Mil 216
- C.Ripken-Bal 210
- Sierra-Tex 203
- Palmeiro-Tex 203
- Franco-Tex 201

Doubles
- Palmeiro-Tex 49
- C.Ripken-Bal 46
- Sierra-Tex 44

Triples
- Molitor-Mil 13
- Johnson-Chi 13
- Alomar-Tor 11
- White-Tor 10
- Devereaux-Bal 10

Home Runs
- Fielder-Det 44
- Canseco-Oak 44
- C.Ripken-Bal 34
- Carter-Tor 33
- Thomas-Chi 32

Total Bases
- C.Ripken-Bal 368
- Palmeiro-Tex 336
- Sierra-Tex 332
- Molitor-Mil 325
- Carter-Tor 321

Runs Batted In
- Fielder-Det 133
- Canseco-Oak 122
- Sierra-Tex 116
- C.Ripken-Bal 114
- Thomas-Chi 109

Runs Produced
- Sierra-Tex 201
- Canseco-Oak 193
- Molitor-Mil 191
- Fielder-Det 191
- Thomas-Chi 181

Bases On Balls
- Thomas-Chi 138
- Tettleton-Det 101
- R.Henderson-Oak .. 98
- Clark-Bos 96
- Davis-Min 95

Batting Average
- Franco-Tex .... .341
- Boggs-Bos .... .332
- Randolph-Mil ...... .327
- K.Griffey-Sea ...... .327
- Molitor-Mil .... .325

On Base Percentage
- Thomas-Chi .... .454
- Randolph-Mil ..... .427
- Boggs-Bos .... .425
- Franco-Tex .... .409
- E.Martinez-Sea .... .407

Slugging Average
- Tartabull-KC ...... .593
- C.Ripken-Bal ...... .566
- Canseco-Oak ...... .556
- Thomas-Chi .... .553
- Palmeiro-Tex ...... .532

Production
- Thomas-Chi 1.007
- Tartabull-KC .... .993
- C.Ripken-Bal .... .945
- K.Griffey-Sea ...... .932
- Palmeiro-Tex ...... .925

Adjusted Production
- Thomas-Chi 181
- Tartabull-KC 170
- C.Ripken-Bal 164
- Canseco-Oak 159
- Palmeiro-Tex 156

Batter Runs
- Thomas-Chi 65.9
- C.Ripken-Bal 48.5
- Tartabull-KC 46.4
- Palmeiro-Tex 45.6
- K.Griffey-Sea 42.3

Adjusted Batter Runs
- Thomas-Chi 69.4
- C.Ripken-Bal 53.9
- Palmeiro-Tex 47.9
- Tartabull-KC 45.9
- Canseco-Oak 44.7

Clutch Hitting Index
- Davis-Sea 135
- Surhoff-Mil 125
- Yount-Mil 124
- Randolph-Mil 122
- Hrbek-Min 119

Runs Created
- Thomas-Chi 145
- C.Ripken-Bal 134
- Molitor-Mil 132
- Palmeiro-Tex 129
- K.Griffey-Sea 118

Total Average
- Thomas-Chi 1.109
- Tartabull-KC 1.044
- K.Griffey-Sea ...... .969
- Canseco-Oak ...... .962
- Whitaker-Det ...... .942

Stolen Bases
- R.Henderson-Oak ... 58
- Alomar-Tor 53
- Raines-Chi 51
- Polonia-Cal 48
- Cuyler-Det 41

Stolen Base Average
- Cotto-Sea 84.2
- Knoblauch-Min 83.3
- Alomar-Tor 82.8
- Gibson-KC 81.8
- Canseco-Oak 81.3

Stolen Base Runs
- Alomar-Tor 9.3
- R.Henderson-Oak .. 6.6
- Raines-Chi 6.3
- Cuyler-Det 6.3
- Franco-Tex 5.4

Fielding Runs
- Gaetti-Cal 24.6
- Vizquel-Sea 23.5
- Espinoza-NY 20.3
- Buechele-Tex 19.9
- Sojo-Cal 19.5

Total Player Rating
- C.Ripken-Bal 8.3
- Thomas-Chi 5.5
- K.Griffey-Sea 4.9
- Canseco-Oak 4.2
- R.Henderson-Oak .. 4.1

Wins
- Gullickson-Det 20
- Erickson-Min 20
- Langston-Cal 19

Win Percentage
- Erickson-Min ...... .714
- Langston-Cal ...... .704
- Gullickson-Det .... .690
- Wegman-Mil ...... .682
- Moore-Oak .... .680

Games
- D.Ward-Tor 81
- Olson-Bal 72
- Jackson-Sea 72
- Swift-Sea 71

Complete Games
- McDowell-Chi 15
- Clemens-Bos 13
- Navarro-Mil 10
- Morris-Min 10
- Terrell-Det 8

Shutouts
- Clemens-Bos 4
- McDowell-Chi 3
- Holman-Sea 3
- Erickson-Min 3
- Appier-KC 3

Saves
- Harvey-Cal 46
- Eckersley-Oak 43
- Aguilera-Min 42
- Reardon-Bos 40
- Montgomery-KC ... 33

Innings Pitched
- Clemens-Bos 271.1
- McDowell-Chi ... 253.2
- Morris-Min 246.2
- Langston-Cal ... 246.1
- Tapani-Min 244.0

Fewest Hits/Game
- Ryan-Tex 5.31
- Johnson-Sea 6.75
- Langston-Cal 6.94
- Clemens-Bos 7.26
- McDowell-Chi 7.52

Fewest BB/Game
- Swindell-Cle 1.17
- Sanderson-NY 1.25
- Tapani-Min 1.48
- Gullickson-Det 1.75
- Wegman-Mil 1.86

Strikeouts
- Clemens-Bos 241
- Johnson-Sea 228
- Ryan-Tex 203
- McDowell-Chi 191
- Langston-Cal 183

Strikeouts/Game
- Ryan-Tex 10.56
- Johnson-Sea 10.19
- Clemens-Bos 7.99
- Hanson-Sea 7.37
- Appier-KC 6.85

Ratio
- Ryan-Tex 9.31
- Clemens-Bos 9.59
- Tapani-Min 9.85
- Sanderson-NY ... 10.04
- Saberhagen-KC .. 10.04

Earned Run Average
- Clemens-Bos 2.62
- Candiotti-Cle-Tor .. 2.65
- Wegman-Mil 2.84
- J.Abbott-Cal 2.89
- Ryan-Tex 2.91

Adjusted ERA
- Clemens-Bos 164
- Candiotti-Cle-Tor .. 158
- Tapani-Min 143
- J.Abbott-Cal 142
- Wegman-Mil 140

Opponents' Batting Avg.
- Ryan-Tex .... .172
- Johnson-Sea ...... .213
- Langston-Cal ..... .215
- Clemens-Bos ..... .221
- Candiotti-Cle-Tor .. .228

Opponents' On Base Pct.
- Ryan-Tex .... .267
- Clemens-Bos ..... .272
- Tapani-Min .... .278
- Sanderson-NY .... .281
- Saberhagen-KC ... .281

Starter Runs
- Clemens-Bos 44.4
- Candiotti-Cle-Tor .. 38.3
- J.Abbott-Cal 32.5
- Langston-Cal 30.1
- Tapani-Min 30.0

Adjusted Starter Runs
- Clemens-Bos 50.6
- Candiotti-Cle-Tor .. 40.6
- Tapani-Min 34.7
- J.Abbott-Cal 32.8
- Langston-Cal 30.3

Clutch Pitching Index
- Krueger-Sea 130
- Holman-Sea 117
- Terrell-Det 117
- Guzman-Tex 116
- Tanana-Det 115

Relief Runs
- Frohwirth-Bal 23.8
- Harvey-Cal 21.8
- Swift-Sea 21.1
- Eichhorn-Cal 19.2
- Flanagan-Bal 18.7

Adjusted Relief Runs
- Frohwirth-Bal 22.3
- Harvey-Cal 21.9
- Swift-Sea 21.3
- Eichhorn-Cal 19.2
- Habyan-NY 18.4

Relief Ranking
- Harvey-Cal 36.1
- Aguilera-Min 32.0
- Farr-NY 27.8
- D.Ward-Tor 24.8
- Radinsky-Chi 22.4

Total Pitcher Index
- Clemens-Bos 4.8
- Candiotti-Cle-Tor .. 4.3
- J.Abbott-Cal 4.1
- Harvey-Cal 3.7
- Key-Tor 3.5

Total Baseball Ranking
- C.Ripken-Bal 8.3
- Thomas-Chi 5.5
- K.Griffey-Sea 4.9
- Clemens-Bos 4.8
- Candiotti-Cle-Tor .. 4.3

January 7 Tom Seaver, one of the greatest starting pitchers of all-time, and Rollie Fingers, who helped revolutionize the role of the reliever, are elected to the Hall of Fame.

March 17 Hal Newhouser, a two-time MVP pitcher with the Tigers, and umpire Bill McGowan are elected to the Hall of Fame by the Veterans Committee.

May 17 Gary Carter, back with the Expos, joins Bob Boone and Carlton Fisk in the exclusive 2,000-games caught club.

June 4 San Jose voters tell the Giants they don't want them by rejecting a plan to build a new stadium in their town. Then the Astros add insult to injury by swatting the ball every which way in a 12-6 drubbing at Candlestick Park in front of just 8,850.

June 6 Eddie Murray of the Mets becomes the all-time leader in RBIs by a switch hitter. He passes Mickey Mantle with RBI No. 1,510.

July 27 Houston starts its club-record 26-game road trip with a grand slam by Eric Anthony. The Astros are sent away so the Republican National Convention can take over the Astrodome.

August 7 The Giants announce that the team has been sold to Tampa Bay investors for a reported $110 million and will move to St. Petersburg for the 1993 season. The move will be blocked by other owners in November.

August 26 In the first matchup of NL knuckleballers in ten years, Pittsburgh's Tim Wakefield outduels Tom Candiotti of the Dodgers. The last time knuckleballs floated to batters on both teams came when Phil and Joe Niekro squared off in 1982.

August 27 The Mets, who are rapidly falling through the NL East standings, trade David Cone to Toronto, the AL East front-runner, for Jeff Kent and Ryan Thompson. Cone comes within one strikeout of becoming the first pitcher in almost 50 years to lead the league in strikeouts for three straight years; one strikeout by Atlanta's John Smoltz on the final day of the season denies him that honor.

August 29 Atlanta's Charlie Leibrandt records his 1,000th strikeout and decides to save the ball. He rolls the ball towards the dugout for safekeeping, but neglects to call time out, so Ricky Jordan takes second base on the error.

September 4 Eddie Murray ties Al Simmons for most consecutive years (16) with at least 75 RBIs.

September 19 Barry Bonds joins his father, Bobby, as well as Willie Mays, Howard Johnson, and Ron Gant as the only player to have two 30-home run, 30-steal seasons.

October 14 The usually sure-handed Jose Lind bobbles a grounder in the ninth that helps set the stage for Atlanta's three-run rally in Game 7 against Pittsburgh. Little-used pinch-hitter Francisco Cabrera singles in the tying and winning runs to give the Braves the pennant.

October 17 Tom Glavine goes the distance to give the Braves a 3-1 win over the Blue Jays in Game 1 of the World Series.

ATLANTA

Pos	Player
M	B.Cox
1B	S.Bream
2B	M.Lemke
SS	R.Belliard
3B	T.Pendleton
LF	R.Gant
CF	O.Nixon
RF	D.Justice
C	G.Olson
C	D.Berryhill
S2	J.Blauser
1	B.Hunter
O	D.Sanders
P	J.Smoltz
P	S.Avery
P	T.Glavine
P	C.Leibrandt
RP	K.Mercker
RP	M.Stanton
RP	M.Freeman
P	M.Bielecki
P	P.Smith

CHICAGO

Pos	Player
M	J.Lefebvre
1B	M.Grace
2B	R.Sandberg
SS	R.Sanchez
3B	S.Buechele
LF	D.May
CF	D.Dascenzo
RF	A.Dawson
C	J.Girardi
3O	L.Salazar
S3	J.Vizcaino
O	S.Sosa
C	R.Wilkins
O	Dw.Smith
P	G.Maddux
P	M.Morgan
P	F.Castillo
P	D.Jackson
RP	B.Scanlan
RP	J.Bullinger
RP	C.McElroy
P	S.Boskie
P	J.Robinson
P	P.Assenmacher

CINCINNATI

Pos	Player
M	L.Piniella
1B	H.Morris
2B	B.Doran
SS	B.Larkin
3B	C.Sabo
LF	R.Sanders
CF	D.Martinez
RF	P.O'Neill
C	J.Oliver
O2	B.Roberts
O	G.Braggs
P	T.Belcher
P	G.Swindell
P	J.Rijo
P	C.Hammond
RP	D.Henry
RP	N.Charlton
RP	S.Bankhead
P	T.Browning
P	R.Dibble
P	S.Ruskin
P	S.Foster

HOUSTON

Pos	Player
M	A.Howe
1B	J.Bagwell
2B	C.Biggio
SS	A.Cedeno
3B	K.Caminiti
LF	L.Gonzalez
CF	S.Finley
RF	E.Anthony
C	E.Taubensee
S3	C.Candaele
O	P.Incaviglia
C	S.Servais
P	P.Harnisch
P	B.Henry
P	J.Jones
P	D.Kile
P	M.Portugal
RP	D.Jones
RP	X.Hernandez
RP	J.Boever
P	B.Williams
P	W.Blair
P	A.Osuna
P	R.Murphy

LOS ANGELES

Pos	Player
M	T.Lasorda
1B	E.Karros
2B	L.Harris
SS	J.Offerman
3B	D.Hansen
LF	E.Davis
CF	B.Butler
RF	M.Webster
C	M.Scioscia
O1	T.Benzinger
23	M.Sharperson
P	O.Hershiser
P	Ke.Gross
P	T.Candiotti
P	B.Ojeda
P	R.Martinez
RP	J.Gott
RP	R.McDowell
RP	T.Crews
P	P.Astacio
P	S.Wilson

MONTREAL

Pos	Player
M	T.Runnells
M	F.Alou
1B	T.Wallach
2B	D.DeShields
SS	S.Owen
3B	B.Barberie
LF	M.Alou
CF	M.Grissom
RF	L.Walker
C	G.Carter
O	J.Vander Wal
13	A.Cianfrocco
C	D.Fletcher
P	D.Martinez
P	K.Hill
P	C.Nabholz
P	M.Gardner
P	B.Barnes
RP	M.Rojas
RP	J.Fassero
RP	J.Wetteland
P	B.Sampen

NEW YORK

Pos	Player
M	J.Torborg
1B	E.Murray
2B	W.Randolph
SS	D.Schofield
3B	D.Magadan
LF	D.Boston
CF	H.Johnson
RF	B.Bonilla
C	T.Hundley
O	D.Gallagher
3S	B.Pecota
32	C.Walker
O	V.Coleman
P	S.Fernandez
P	D.Gooden
P	D.Cone
P	P.Schourek
P	B.Saberhagen
RP	A.Young
RP	W.Whitehurst
RP	J.Innis
P	P.Gibson
P	E.Hillman

PHILADELPHIA

Pos	Player
M	J.Fregosi
1B	J.Kruk
2B	M.Morandini
SS	J.Bell
3B	D.Hollins
LF	M.Duncan
CF	L.Dykstra
RF	R.Amaro
C	D.Daulton
O	S.Javier
1O	R.Jordan
O	W.Chamberlain
P	T.Mulholland
P	C.Schilling
P	K.Abbott
P	B.Rivera
RP	Mt.Williams
RP	C.Brantley
RP	M.Hartley
P	T.Greene
P	B.Jones
P	G.Mathews

PITTSBURGH

Pos	Player
M	J.Leyland
1B	O.Merced
2B	J.Lind
SS	J.Bell
3B	S.Buechele
LF	B.Bonds
CF	A.Van Slyke
RF	C.Espy
C	M.LaValliere
31	J.King
O	G.Varsho
C	D.Slaught
O	A.Cole
P	D.Drabek
P	R.Tomlin
P	Z.Smith
P	B.Walk
RP	R.Mason
RP	D.Neagle
RP	S.Belinda
P	T.Wakefield
P	D.Jackson
P	B.Patterson
P	V.Palacios

SAN DIEGO

Pos	Player
M	G.Riddoch
M	J.Riggleman
1B	F.McGriff
2B	K.Stillwell
SS	T.Fernandez
3B	G.Sheffield
LF	J.Clark
CF	D.Jackson
RF	T.Gwynn
C	B.Santiago
O	O.Azocar
23	T.Teufel
P	A.Benes
P	B.Hurst
P	C.Lefferts
P	Gr.Harris
P	F.Seminara
RP	R.Rodriguez
RP	J.Melendez
RP	R.Myers
P	J.Deshaies
P	M.Maddux

SAN FRANCISCO

Pos	Player
M	R.Craig
1B	W.Clark
2B	R.Thompson
SS	R.Clayton
3B	M.Williams
LF	M.Felder
CF	D.Lewis
RF	W.McGee
C	K.Manwaring
O	C.James
O1	C.Snyder
O	K.Bass
P	J.Burkett
P	B.Black
P	B.Swift
P	T.Wilson
RP	J.Brantley
RP	R.Beck
RP	B.Hickerson
P	M.Jackson
P	D.Righetti
P	D.Burba
P	K.Downs

ST. LOUIS

Pos	Player
M	J.Torre
1B	A.Galarraga
2B	L.Alicea
SS	O.Smith
3B	T.Zeile
LF	B.Gilkey
CF	R.Lankford
RF	F.Jose
C	T.Pagnozzi
O	M.Thompson
2	G.Pena
P	B.Tewksbury
P	O.Olivares
P	R.Cormier
P	D.Osborne
P	M.Clark
RP	M.Perez
RP	C.Carpenter
RP	L.Smith
P	J.DeLeon
P	T.Worrell
P	B.McClure

TEAM	G	W	L	PCT	GB	R	OR	AB	H	2B	3B	HR	BB	SO	AVG	OBP	SLG	PRO	PRO+	BR	/A	PF	CHI	RC	SB	CS	SBA	SBR
EAST																												
PIT	162	96	66	.593		**693**	595	5527	1409	272	**54**	106	569	872	.255	.327	.381	.708	107	48	**56**	99	101	**699**	110	53	67	1
MON	162	87	75	.537	9	648	581	5477	1381	263	37	102	463	976	.252	.315	.370	.685	101	-4	2	99	104	651	196	63	76	**21**
STL	162	83	79	.512	13	631	604	5594	**1464**	262	44	94	495	996	**.262**	.325	.375	.700	**107**	30	51	97	94	680	**208**	118	64	-8
CHI	162	78	84	.481	18	593	624	5590	1420	221	41	104	417	**816**	.254	.309	.364	.673	94	-31	-46	103	99	617	77	51	60	-8
NY	162	72	90	.444	24	599	653	5340	1254	259	17	93	**572**	956	.235	.312	.342	.654	92	-54	-46	99	**106**	583	129	52	71	8
PHI	162	70	92	.432	26	686	717	5500	1392	255	36	118	509	1059	.253	.322	.377	.699	104	27	29	100	104	684	127	31	**80**	20
WEST																												
ATL	162	98	64	.605		682	**569**	5480	1391	223	48	**138**	493	924	.254	.318	**.388**	.706	99	34	-6	106	103	686	126	60	68	2
CIN	162	90	72	.556	8	660	609	5460	1418	**281**	44	99	563	888	.260	**.331**	.382	**.713**	105	58	39	103	96	689	125	65	66	-2
SD	162	82	80	.506	16	617	636	5476	1396	255	30	135	453	864	.255	.315	.386	.701	102	22	11	102	96	648	69	52	57	-11
HOU	162	81	81	.500	17	608	668	5480	1350	255	38	96	506	1025	.246	.316	.359	.675	102	-20	7	96	100	636	139	54	72	9
SF	162	72	90	.444	26	574	647	5456	1330	220	36	105	439	1067	.244	.304	.355	.659	97	-57	-26	94	102	584	112	64	64	-5
LA	162	63	99	.389	35	548	636	5368	1333	201	34	72	503	899	.248	.316	.339	.655	93	-54	-45	98	97	579	142	78	65	-4
TOT	972					7539		65748	16538	2967	459	1262	5978	11342	.252	.318	.368	.686							1560	741	68	23

TEAM	CG	SH	SV	IP	H	H/G	HR	BB	SO	RAT	ERA	ERA+	OAV	OOB	PR	/A	PF	CPI	FA	E	DP	FW	PW	BW	SBW	DIF
EAST																										
PIT	20	20	43	1479²	1410	8.6	101	455	844	11.5	3.35	103	.254	.314	25	14	98	103	.984	101	144	.9	1.5	**6.0**	-.1	6.7
MON	11	14	49	1468	**1296**	7.9	92	525	1014	11.5	3.25	107	**.238**	.310	41	35	99	97	.980	124	113	-.4	3.8	.2	**2.1**	.4
STL	10	9	47	1480	1405	8.5	118	**400**	842	11.2	3.38	100	.252	.305	20	1	97	99	**.985**	**94**	146	1.3	.1	5.5	-1.1	-3.8
CHI	16	11	37	1469	1337	8.2	107	575	901	12.0	3.39	106	.246	.323	18	34	103	104	.982	114	142	.2	3.7	-5.0	-1.1	-.8
NY	17	13	34	1446²	1404	8.7	98	482	1025	12.0	3.66	95	.256	.321	-25	-30	99	98	.981	114	134	.0	-3.2	-5.0	.7	-1.5
PHI	**27**	7	34	1428	1387	8.7	113	549	851	12.4	4.11	85	.257	.328	-96	-98	100	92	.978	131	128	-.8	-10.6	3.1	1.9	-4.7
WEST																										
ATL	26	**24**	41	1460	1321	8.1	89	489	948	11.3	3.14	**116**	.242	.307	58	83	104	99	.982	109	121	.4	**8.9**	-.6	.0	8.3
CIN	9	11	**55**	1449²	1362	8.5	109	470	**1060**	11.5	3.46	104	.251	.314	6	21	103	100	.984	96	128	1.2	2.3	4.2	-.4	1.8
SD	9	11	46	1461¹	1444	8.9	111	439	971	11.7	3.56	100	.246	.318	-9	-3	102	102	.982	115	127	.0	.3	1.2	-1.4	.8
HOU	5	12	45	1459¹	1386	8.5	114	539	978	12.1	3.72	90	.252	.323	-35	-58	96	98	.981	114	125	.2	-6.2	-.8	.8	4.6
SF	9	12	30	1461	1385	8.5	128	502	927	11.8	3.61	91	.253	.320	-17	-50	94	102	.982	113	**174**	.2	-5.4	-2.8	-.7	-.3
LA	18	13	29	1438	1401	8.8	**82**	553	981	12.4	3.41	101	.257	.328	15	5	98	**106**	.972	174	136	-3.2	.5	-4.8	-.6	-9.8
TOT	177	157	490	17500²		8.5				11.8	3.50		.252	.318					.981	1401	1618					

Runs
- Bonds-Pit 109
- Hollins-Phi 104
- VanSlyke-Pit 103
- Sandberg-Chi 100
- Grissom-Mon 99

Hits
- VanSlyke-Pit 199
- Pendleton-Atl 199
- Sandberg-Chi 186
- Grace-Chi 185
- Sheffield-SD 184

Doubles
- VanSlyke-Pit 45
- Lankford-StL 40
- Duncan-Phi 40
- Clark-SF 40

Triples
- Sanders-Atl 14
- Finley-Hou 13
- VanSlyke-Pit 12
- Butler-LA 11
- Alicea-StL 11

Home Runs
- McGriff-SD 35
- Bonds-Pit 34
- Sheffield-SD 33
- Hollins-Phi 27
- Daulton-Phi 27

Total Bases
- Sheffield-SD 323
- Sandberg-Chi..... 312
- VanSlyke-Pit 310
- Pendleton-Atl ... 303

Runs Batted In
- Daulton-Phi 109
- Pendleton-Atl ... 105
- McGriff-SD 104
- Bonds-Pit 103
- Sheffield-SD 100

Runs Produced
- Pendleton-Atl 182
- VanSlyke-Pit 178
- Bonds-Pit 178
- Hollins-Phi 170
- Bagwell-Hou 165

Bases On Balls
- Bonds-Pit 127
- McGriff-SD 96
- Butler-LA 95
- Biggio-Hou 94
- Kruk-Phi 92

Batting Average
- Sheffield-SD 330
- VanSlyke-Pit 324
- Kruk-Phi 323
- Roberts-Cin 323
- Gwynn-SD 317

On Base Percentage
- Bonds-Pit.........461
- Kruk-Phi.........428
- Butler-LA.........413
- McGriff-SD 396
- Roberts-Cin 396

Slugging Average
- Bonds-Pit 624
- Sheffield-SD 580
- McGriff-SD 556
- Daulton-Phi 524
- Sandberg-Chi.......510

Production
- Bonds-Pit 1.085
- Sheffield-SD 969
- McGriff-SD 952
- Daulton-Phi 912
- VanSlyke-Pit 891

Adjusted Production
- Bonds-Pit 207
- Sheffield-SD 168
- McGriff-SD 164
- Daulton-Phi 157
- Clark-SF 153

Batter Runs
- Bonds-Pit 71.8
- Sheffield-SD 50.1
- McGriff-SD 48.1
- VanSlyke-Pit 40.2
- Kruk-Phi 38.6

Adjusted Batter Runs
- Bonds-Pit 73.3
- Sheffield-SD 48.2
- McGriff-SD 46.2
- VanSlyke-Pit 41.4
- Kruk-Phi 38.9

Clutch Hitting Index
- Murray-NY 126
- Daulton-Phi 124
- Lind-Pit 120
- Karros-LA 115
- Larkin-Cin 114

Runs Created
- Bonds-Pit 148
- VanSlyke-Pit 122
- Sheffield-SD 118
- Sandberg-Chi......117
- McGriff-SD 116

Total Average
- Bonds-Pit 1.335
- Daulton-Phi 994
- McGriff-SD 987
- Sheffield-SD 945
- Kruk-Phi 900

Stolen Bases
- Grissom-Mon 78
- DeShields-Mon 46
- Roberts-Cin........ 44
- Finley-Hou 44
- O.Smith-StL 43

Stolen Base Average
- Davis-LA 95.0
- Alou-Mon 88.9
- Duncan-Phi 88.5

Stolen Base Runs
- Grissom-Mon 15.6
- Finley-Hou 7.8
- O.Smith-StL 7.5
- Bonds-Pit 6.9
- Dykstra-Phi 6.0

Fielding Runs
- Belliard-Atl 26.6
- Jackson-SD 24.2
- Thompson-SF 20.3
- Wallach-Mon 18.2
- Harris-LA 16.6

Total Player Rating
- Bonds-Pit 9.2
- Sheffield-SD 5.8
- Sandberg-Chi...... 5.7
- VanSlyke-Pit 5.4
- Larkin-Cin 4.7

Wins
- Maddux-Chi 20
- Glavine-Atl 20

Win Percentage
- Tewksbury-StL .... .762
- Glavine-Atl.........714
- Leibrandt-Atl 682
- Morgan-Chi 667
- Maddux-Chi 645

Games
- Boever-Hou 81
- D.Jones-Hou 80
- Perez-StL 77
- Hernandez-Hou ... 77
- Innis-NY 76

Complete Games
- Mulholland-Phi 12
- Schilling-Phi 10
- Drabek-Pit 10
- Smoltz-Atl 9
- Maddux-Chi 9

Shutouts
- Glavine-Atl 5
- Cone-NY 5

Saves
- L.Smith-StL 43
- Myers-SD 38
- Wetteland-Mon 37
- D.Jones-Hou 36
- M.Williams-Phi 29

Innings Pitched
- Maddux-Chi 268.0
- Drabek-Pit 256.2
- Smoltz-Atl.......246.2
- Morgan-Chi 240.0
- Avery-Atl........233.2

Fewest Hits/Game
- Schilling-Phi 6.56
- Maddux-Chi 6.75
- Fernandez-NY 6.79
- Martinez-Mon 6.84
- Cone-NY 7.41

Fewest BB/Game
- Tewksbury-StL 77
- Cormier-StL....... 1.60
- Swindell-Cin...... 1.73
- Mulholland-Phi.... 1.81
- Tomlin-Pit....... 1.81

Strikeouts
- Smoltz-Atl 215
- Cone-NY 214
- Maddux-Chi 199
- Fernandez-NY 193
- Drabek-Pit........ 177

Strikeouts/Game
- Cone-NY 9.79
- Fernandez-NY 8.09
- Smoltz-Atl 7.84
- Rijo-Cin 7.29
- Harnisch-Hou 7.14

Ratio
- Schilling-Phi 8.95
- Tewksbury-StL 9.27
- Maddux-Chi 9.57
- Martinez-Mon ... 9.58
- Drabek-Pit 9.75

Earned Run Average
- Swift-SF 2.08
- Tewksbury-StL 2.16
- Maddux-Chi 2.18
- Schilling-Phi 2.35
- Martinez-Mon 2.47

Adjusted ERA
- Maddux-Chi 165
- Swift-SF 159
- Tewksbury-StL ... 157
- Schilling-Phi 149
- Morgan-Chi 141

Opponents' Batting Avg.
- Schilling-Phi 201
- Maddux-Chi.......210
- Fernandez-NY 210
- Martinez-Mon 211
- Cone-NY 223

Opponents' On Base Pct.
- Schilling-Phi 256
- Tewksbury-StL 267
- Martinez-Mon 273
- Maddux-Chi 273
- Drabek-Pit.........277

Starter Runs
- Maddux-Chi 39.3
- Tewksbury-StL ... 34.7
- Schilling-Phi 29.1
- Swift-SF 26.1
- Martinez-Mon 26.1

Adjusted Starter Runs
- Maddux-Chi 42.2
- Tewksbury-StL ... 31.7
- Schilling-Phi 28.7
- Morgan-Chi 28.0
- Martinez-Mon 25.1

Clutch Pitching Index
- Swift-SF 131
- Tewksbury-StL 120
- Swindell-Cin 119
- Morgan-Chi 115
- Ojeda-LA 113

Relief Runs
- Rojas-Mon 23.2
- D.Jones-Hou 20.5
- Beck-SF 17.8
- Hernandez-Hou ... 17.2
- Perez-StL....... 17.2

Adjusted Relief Runs
- Rojas-Mon 22.7
- D.Jones-Hou 18.7
- Perez-StL....... 16.0
- Beck-SF 15.8
- Hernandez-Hou ... 15.4

Relief Ranking
- D.Jones-Hou 39.4
- Rojas-Mon 20.3
- Perez-StL....... 18.6
- Beck-SF 14.5
- Hernandez-Hou ...14.2

Total Pitcher Index
- Maddux-Chi 6.2
- D.Jones-Hou 4.2
- Martinez-Mon 3.5
- Glavine-Atl 3.3
- Rijo-Cin 3.2

Total Baseball Ranking
- Bonds-Pit 9.2
- Maddux-Chi 6.2
- Sheffield-SD 5.8
- Sandberg-Chi...... 5.7
- VanSlyke-Pit 5.4

June 15 Jeff Reardon of the Red Sox breaks Rollie Fingers' all-time save record with No. 342 in a 1-0 win over the Yankees.

July 14 The AL wins its fifth straight All-Star Game and does it in convincing fashion. The AL scores the first 10 runs en route to a 13-6 romp. Ken Griffey Jr. goes 3-for-3 with a home run and, like his dad 12 years before, he earns MVP honors.

July 26 The Ryan express keeps on rolling. Nolan Ryan strikes out his 100th batter of the season for a major-league record 23rd consecutive year. He also gets a 6-2 win over the Orioles—thanks to the longest home run yet at Camden Yards, a 450-foot shot to center off the bat of Juan Gonzalez—to pass Phil Niekro as No. 12 on the all-time win list with 319.

August 19 The Boones become the first three-generation family of major leaguers when Bret Boone debuts at second base for the Mariners. His father, Bob, played for 19 years, and grandfather,

Ray, logged 13 seasons in the majors.

August 23 Dennis Eckersley becomes the first pitcher to record 40 saves in four different seasons.

September 9 Robin Yount becomes the 17th player in major league history to collect 3,000 hits when the Brewers outfielder connects against the Indians before an adoring crowd at County Stadium.

September 24 Toronto's Dave Winfield becomes the oldest player in major league history to reach the 100-RBI plateau. The 40-year-old does the trick in his 2,700th career game.

September 30 George Brett collects his 3,000th career hit with his fourth hit of the game against the Angels. Moments after the milestone, Brett is picked off by pitcher Tim Fortugno.

October 2 Carlos Baerga becomes the first second baseman in AL history to hit .300 with 200 hits, 20 home runs, and 100 RBI.

October 11 Dennis Eckersley, who saved 51 games for Oakland during the

season, surrenders a two-run home run to Roberto Alomar that sends Game 4 into extra innings. The Blue Jays go on to win, 7-6, in 11 innings and take a three games-to-one edge in the ALCS.

October 14 Joe Carter and Candy Maldonado hit homers and Juan Guzman cruises on the mound in the 9-2 clincher for the Blue Jays over the A's in Game 6 of the ALCS.

October 18 Ed Sprague's two-run home run in the ninth inning off Jeff Reardon evens the World Series at one game apiece.

October 20 The first World Series game ever played in Canada, fittingly, belongs to the Blue Jays. Despite a blown call on what should have been a Toronto triple play, Joe Carter and Kelly Gruber hit home runs to give the Blue Jays the Series lead.

October 24 The Braves rally to tie the game in the ninth inning of Game 6, but Dave Winfield's double in the 11th is the key blow as the Blue Jays hold on for Canada's first world championship.

BALTIMORE		BOSTON		CALIFORNIA		CHICAGO		CLEVELAND		DETROIT		KANSAS CITY	
M	J.Oates	M	B.Hobson	M	B.Rodgers	M	G.Lamont	M	M.Hargrove	M	S.Anderson	M	H.McRae
1B	R.Milligan	1B	M.Vaughn	M	J.Wathan	1B	F.Thomas	1B	P.Sorrento	1B	D.Bergman	1B	W.Joyner
2B	B.Ripken	2B	J.Reed	M	B.Rodgers	2B	S.Sax	2B	C.Baerga	2B	L.Whitaker	2B	K.Miller
SS	C.Ripken	SS	L.Rivera	1B	L.Stevens	SS	C.Grebeck	SS	M.Lewis	SS	T.Fryman	SS	D.Howard
3B	L.Gomez	3B	W.Boggs	2B	L.Sojo	3B	R.Ventura	3B	B.Jacoby	3B	S.Livingstone	3B	G.Jefferies
LF	B.Anderson	LF	B.Hatcher	SS	G.DiSarcina	LF	T.Raines	LF	T.Howard	LF	D.Gladden	LF	K.McReynolds
CF	M.Devereaux	CF	B.Zupcic	3B	G.Gaetti	CF	L.Johnson	CF	K.Lofton	CF	M.Cuyler	CF	B.McRae
RF	J.Orsulak	RF	T.Brunansky	LF	L.Polonia	RF	S.Abner	RF	M.Whiten	RF	R.Deer	RF	J.Eisenreich
C	C.Hoiles	C	T.Pena	CF	J.Felix	C	R.Karkovice	C	S.Alomar	C	M.Tettleton	C	M.Macfarlane
DH	G.Davis	DH	J.Clark	RF	C.Curtis	DH	G.Bell	DH	A.Belle	DH	C.Fielder	DH	G.Brett
				C	M.Fitzgerald								
2D	M.McLemore	13	S.Cooper	DH	H.Brooks	O	D.Pasqua	OD	G.Hill	OD	M.Carreon	S2	C.Wilkerson
1O	D.Segui	O	H.Winningham					C	J.Ortiz	O2	T.Phillips	C	B.Mayne
		OD	P.Plantier	32	R.Gonzales	P	J.McDowell	13	C.Martinez			O	G.Thurman
P	M.Mussina	O	E.Burks	O	V.Hayes	P	K.McCaskill	S3	F.Fermin	P	B.Gullickson		
P	R.Sutcliffe					P	A.Fernandez			P	F.Tanana	P	K.Appier
P	B.McDonald	P	R.Clemens	P	M.Langston	P	C.Hough	P	C.Nagy	P	W.Terrell	P	H.Pichardo
P	B.Milacki	P	F.Viola	P	J.Abbott	P	G.Hibbard	P	J.Armstrong	P	M.Leiter	P	M.Gubicza
RP	T.Frohwirth	P	D.Darwin	P	C.Finley	P	W.Alvarez	P	D.Cook	P	J.Doherty	P	R.Reed
RP	A.Mills	P	J.Hesketh	P	J.Valera	RP	T.Leach	P	S.Scudder	RP	L.Lancaster	RP	T.Gordon
RP	S.Davis	P	J.Dopson	P	B.Blyleven	RP	D.Pall	P	R.Nichols	RP	M.Henneman	RP	R.Meacham
		RP	G.Harris	RP	J.Grahe			RP	T.Power			RP	M.Magnante
P	A.Rhodes	RP	M.Young	RP	C.Crim	P	R.Hernandez	RP	S.Olin	P	K.Ritz		
P	J.Mesa	RP	P.Quantrill	RP	M.Eichhorn	P	S.Radinsky	RP	E.Plunk	P	E.King	P	M.Boddicker
P	G.Olson					P	B.Thigpen			P	K.Knudsen	P	J.Montgomery
		P	M.Gardiner					P	J.Mesa	P	S.Aldred	P	L.Aquino
								P	D.Otto	P	D.Haas	P	S.Shifflett
								P	D.Lilliquist	P	J.Kiely		

MILWAUKEE		MINNESOTA		NEW YORK		OAKLAND		SEATTLE		TEXAS		TORONTO	
M	P.Garner	M	T.Kelly	M	B.Showalter	M	T.LaRussa	M	B.Plummer	M	B.Valentine	M	C.Gaston
1B	F.Stubbs	1B	K.Hrbek	1B	D.Mattingly	1B	M.McGwire	1B	P.O'Brien	M	T.Harrah	1B	J.Olerud
2B	S.Fletcher	2B	C.Knoblauch	2B	P.Kelly	2B	M.Bordick	2B	H.Reynolds	1B	R.Palmeiro	2B	R.Alomar
SS	P.Listach	SS	G.Gagne	SS	A.Stankiewicz	SS	W.Weiss	SS	O.Vizquel	2B	A.Newman	SS	M.Lee
3B	K.Seitzer	3B	S.Leius	3B	C.Hayes	3B	C.Lansford	3B	E.Martinez	SS	D.Thon	3B	K.Gruber
LF	G.Vaughn	LF	S.Mack	LF	M.Hall	LF	R.Henderson	LF	H.Cotto	3B	D.Palmer	LF	C.Maldonado
CF	R.Yount	CF	K.Puckett	CF	R.Kelly	CF	W.Wilson	CF	K.Griffey	LF	K.Reimer	CF	D.White
RF	D.Hamilton	RF	P.Munoz	RF	D.Tartabull	RF	J.Canseco	RF	J.Buhner	CF	J.Gonzalez	RF	J.Carter
C	B.Surhoff	C	B.Harper	C	M.Nokes	C	T.Steinbach	C	D.Valle	RF	R.Sierra	C	P.Borders
DH	P.Molitor	DH	C.Davis	DH	K.Maas	DH	H.Baines	DH	T.Martinez	C	I.Rodriguez	DH	D.Winfield
										DH	B.Downing		
O	D.Bichette	OD	R.Bush	S3	R.Velarde	2O	L.Blankenship	OD	K.Mitchell			P	J.Morris
23	J.Gantner	1O	G.Larkin	O	B.Williams	3O	J.Browne	OD	G.Briley	S2	J.Huson	P	J.Key
												P	J.Guzman
P	B.Wegman	P	J.Smiley	P	M.Perez	P	M.Moore	P	D.Fleming	P	K.Brown	P	T.Stottlemyre
P	J.Navarro	P	K.Tapani	P	S.Sanderson	P	R.Darling	P	R.Johnson	P	J.Guzman	P	D.Stieb
P	C.Bosio	P	S.Erickson	P	S.Kamieniecki	P	D.Stewart	P	E.Hanson	P	B.Witt	RP	D.Wells
P	R.Bones	P	B.Krueger	P	T.Leary	P	B.Welch	RP	R.Swan	P	N.Ryan	RP	D.Ward
P	C.Eldred	RP	C.Willis	P	G.Cadaret	P	J.Parrett	RP	R.DeLucia	RP	T.Burns	RP	T.Henke
RP	D.Plesac	RP	T.Edens	RP	R.Monteleone	RP	D.Eckersley	RP	J.Nelson	RP	K.Rogers		
RP	D.Henry	RP	M.Guthrie	RP	J.Habyan	RP	K.Campbell			RP	Je.Russell	/P	D.Cone
RP	M.Fetters							P	B.Fisher			P	P.Hentgen
		P	W.Banks	P	S.Hillegas	P	K.Downs	P	M.Grant	P	R.Pavlik		
P	J.Austin	P	P.Mahomes	/P	S.Militello	P	J.Slusarski	P	C.Jones				
P	B.Ruffin	P	R.Aguilera	P	J.Johnson	P	G.Nelson	P	D.Powell				
				P	S.Farr			P	M.Schooler				
				/P	B.Wickman								

TEAM	G	W	L	PCT	GB	R	OR	AB	H	2B	3B	HR	BB	SO	AVG	OBP	SLG	PRO	PRO+	BR	/A	PF	CHI	RC	SB	CS	SBA	SBR
EAST																												
TOR	162	96	66	.593		780	682	5536	1458	265	40	163	561	933	.263	.336	**.414**	**.750**	104	**63**	29	105	102	**779**	129	39	**77**	**15**
MIL	162	92	70	.568	4	740	**604**	5504	1477	272	35	82	511	779	.268	.334	.375	.709	100	-10	4	98	108	700	**256**	115	69	8
BAL	162	89	73	.549	7	705	656	5485	1423	243	36	148	647	827	.259	.343	.398	.741	104	56	37	103	92	754	89	48	65	-2
NY	162	76	86	.469	20	733	746	5593	1462	281	18	163	536	903	.261	.331	.406	.737	106	33	39	99	99	742	78	37	68	1
CLE	162	76	86	.469	20	674	746	5620	1495	227	24	127	448	885	.266	.325	.383	.708	100	-22	-10	98	99	686	144	67	68	3
DET	162	75	87	.463	21	**791**	794	5515	1411	256	16	**182**	675	1055	.256	.340	.407	.747	107	**63**	59	101	102	769	66	45	59	-7
BOS	162	73	89	.451	23	599	669	5461	1343	259	21	84	591	865	.246	.323	.347	.670	83	-84	-125	107	98	617	44	48	48	-16
WEST																												
OAK	162	96	66	.593		745	672	5387	1389	219	24	142	**707**	831	.258	**.349**	.386	.735	**112**	54	**95**	95	98	748	143	59	71	8
MIN	162	90	72	.556	6	747	653	5582	**1544**	275	27	104	527	834	**.277**	.345	.391	.736	103	46	22	103	99	748	123	74	62	-8
CHI	162	86	76	.531	10	738	690	5498	1434	269	36	110	622	784	.261	.339	.383	.722	103	19	28	99	102	728	160	57	74	14
TEX	162	77	85	.475	19	682	753	5537	1387	266	23	159	550	1036	.250	.324	.393	.717	104	-5	20	96	98	708	81	44	65	-2
KC	162	72	90	.444	24	610	667	5501	1411	**284**	**42**	75	439	**741**	.256	.317	.364	.681	88	-73	-90	103	99	629	131	71	65	-3
CAL	162	72	90	.444	24	579	671	5364	1306	202	20	88	416	882	.243	.303	.338	.641	79	-152	-155	101	**112**	529	160	101	61	-13
SEA	162	64	98	.395	32	679	799	5564	1466	278	24	149	474	841	.263	.326	.402	.728	102	13	9	101	96	708	100	55	65	-3
TOT	1134					9802		77147	20006	3596	386	1776	7704	12196	.259	.331	.385	.716							1704	860	66	-5

TEAM	CG	SH	SV	IP	H	H/G	HR	BB	SO	RAT	ERA	ERA+	OAV	OOB	PR	/A	PF	CPI	FA	E	DP	FW	PW	BW	SBW	DIF
EAST																										
TOR	18	14	49	1440^{2}	1346	8.4	124	541	954	12.1	3.91	104	.248	.321	5	27	104	93	.985	93	109	1.4	2.7	3.0	**1.6**	6.3
MIL	19	14	39	1457	**1344**	**8.3**	127	**435**	793	**11.3**	**3.43**	112	**.246**	**.307**	**82**	65	97	98	**.986**	**89**	146	**1.6**	6.6	.4	.8	1.5
BAL	20	**16**	48	1464	1419	8.7	124	518	846	12.1	3.79	106	.256	.324	25	38	102	99	.985	93	168	1.4	3.9	3.8	-.2	-.9
NY	20	9	44	1452^{2}	1453	9.0	129	612	851	13.0	4.21	93	.263	.341	-43	-47	99	99	.982	114	165	.2	-4.8	4.0	.1	-4.6
CLE	13	7	46	1470	1507	9.2	159	566	890	12.9	4.11	95	.268	.339	-28	-33	99	106	.978	141	**176**	-1.3	-3.4	-1.0	.3	.3
DET	10	4	36	1435^{2}	1534	9.6	155	564	693	13.3	4.60	86	.277	.346	-105	-103	100	99	.981	116	164	.1	-10.5	6.0	-.7	-1.0
BOS	22	13	39	1448^{2}	1403	8.7	107	535	943	12.3	3.58	**117**	.255	.326	57	**101**	107	103	.978	139	170	-1.2	**10.3**	-12.7	-1.6	-2.8
WEST																										
OAK	8	9	**58**	1447	1396	8.7	129	601	843	12.7	3.73	100	.256	.335	34	3	95	**107**	.979	125	158	-.4	.3	**9.7**	.8	4.5
MIN	16	13	50	1453	1391	8.6	121	479	923	11.8	3.70	109	.254	.318	38	56	103	98	.985	95	155	1.3	5.7	2.2	-.8	.5
CHI	21	5	52	1461^{2}	1400	8.6	123	550	810	12.3	3.82	101	.252	.326	19	6	98	98	.979	129	134	-.6	.6	2.9	1.5	.7
TEX	19	3	42	1460^{1}	1471	9.1	113	598	**1034**	13.0	4.09	93	.264	.341	-24	-47	96	100	.975	154	153	-2.0	-4.8	2.0	-.2	.9
KC	9	12	44	1447^{1}	1426	8.9	**106**	512	834	12.3	3.81	106	.259	.327	21	39	103	98	.980	122	164	-.2	4.0	-9.2	-.3	-3.3
CAL	**26**	13	42	1446	1449	9.0	130	532	888	12.6	3.84	104	.264	.333	16	23	101	106	.979	134	172	-.9	2.3	-15.8	-1.3	6.6
SEA	21	9	30	1445	1467	9.1	129	661	894	13.6	4.55	87	.266	.351	-97	-92	101	96	.982	112	170	.3	-9.4	.9	-.3	-8.6
TOT	242	141	619	20329		8.9				12.5	3.94		.259	.331					.981	1656	2204					

Runs
Phillips-Det 114
Thomas-Chi 108
Alomar-Tor 105
Puckett-Min 104
Knoblauch-Min 104

Hits
Puckett-Min 210
Baerga-Cle 205
Molitor-Mil 195
Mack-Min 189
Thomas-Chi 185

Doubles
Thomas-Chi 46
E.Martinez-Sea 46
Yount-Mil 40
Mattingly-NY 40
Griffey-Sea 39

Triples
Johnson-Chi 12
Devereaux-Bal 11
Anderson-Bal 10
Raines-Chi 9

Home Runs
Gonzalez-Tex 43
McGwire-Oak 42
Fielder-Det 35
Carter-Tor 34
Belle-Cle 34

Total Bases
Puckett-Min 313
Carter-Tor 310
Gonzalez-Tex 309
Thomas-Chi 307
Devereaux-Bal 303

Runs Batted In
Fielder-Det 124
Carter-Tor 119
Thomas-Chi 115
Belle-Cle 112
Bell-Chi 112

Runs Produced
Thomas-Chi 199
Puckett-Min 195
Carter-Tor 182
Baerga-Cle 177
Winfield-Tor 174

Bases On Balls
Thomas-Chi 122
Tettleton-Det 122
Phillips-Det 114
Milligan-Bal 106
Tartabull-NY 103

Batting Average
E.Martinez-Sea 343
Puckett-Min 329
Thomas-Chi 323
Molitor-Mil 320
Mack-Min 315

On Base Percentage
Thomas-Chi .... .446
Tartabull-NY .... .410
E.Martinez-Sea ... .408
Alomar-Tor .... .406
Molitor-Mil .... .396

Slugging Average
McGwire-Oak ...... .585
E.Martinez-Sea .... .544
Thomas-Chi .... .536
Griffey-Sea .... .535
Gonzalez-Tex ...... .529

Production
Thomas-Chi 981
McGwire-Oak 976
E.Martinez-Sea.....951
Tartabull-NY 900
Griffey-Sea 898

Adjusted Production
McGwire-Oak 180
Thomas-Chi 176
E.Martinez-Sea 164
Tartabull-NY 152
Griffey-Sea 148

Batter Runs
Thomas-Chi 62.4
E.Martinez-Sea ... 44.9
McGwire-Oak 44.4
Griffey-Sea 34.2
Mack-Min 33.8

Adjusted Batter Runs
Thomas-Chi 64.3
McGwire-Oak 50.3
E.Martinez-Sea 44.4
Molitor-Mil........35.7
R.Henderson-Oak .35.6

Clutch Hitting Index
Surhoff-Mil 136
Lansford-Oak 134
Devereaux-Bal 120
Felix-Cal 120
Ventura-Chi 119

Runs Created
Thomas-Chi 142
Anderson-Bal 118
E.Martinez-Sea ... 116
Molitor-Mil 116
Mack-Min 114

Total Average
Thomas-Chi ...1.066
McGwire-Oak 1.040
Tartabull-NY 972
E.Martinez-Sea.....970
Alomar-Tor 915

Stolen Bases
Lofton-Cle 66
Listach-Mil 54
Anderson-Bal 53
Polonia-Cal 51
Alomar-Tor......... 49

Stolen Base Average
Cotto-Sea......... 92.0
White-Tor 90.2
Raines-Chi 88.2
R.Kelly-NY 84.8
Lofton-Cle 84.6

Stolen Base Runs
Lofton-Cle.........12.6
Raines-Chi 9.9
Alomar-Tor 9.3
White-Tor 8.7
R.Henderson-Oak ..7.8

Fielding Runs
Reed-Bos 23.8
Ventura-Chi 23.7
Gagne-Min....... 20.9
Lofton-Cle 16.7
White-Tor 15.1

Total Player Rating
R.Henderson-Oak .. 4.7
Ventura-Chi 4.6
E.Martinez-Sea 4.6
Thomas-Chi 4.3
Anderson-Bal 4.2

Wins
Morris-Tor 21
Brown-Tex 21
McDowell-Chi 20
Mussina-Bal 18
Clemens-Bos 18

Win Percentage
Mussina-Bal ..... .783
Morris-Tor .... .778
Guzman-Tor ..... .762
Bosio-Mil .... .727
McDowell-Chi .... .667

Games
Rogers-Tex........ 81
D.Ward-Tor 79
Olin-Cle 72
Lilliquist-Cle 71
Harris-Bos 70

Complete Games
McDowell-Chi 13
Clemens-Bos 11
Brown-Tex 11
Perez-NY........... 10
Nagy-Cle........... 10

Shutouts
Clemens-Bos........ 5
Mussina-Bal 4
Fleming-Sea 4

Saves
Eckersley-Oak 51
Aguilera-Min 41
Montgomery-KC ... 39
Olson-Bal 36
Henke-Tor.......... 34

Innings Pitched
Brown-Tex 265.2
Wegman-Mil 261.2
McDowell-Chi.....260.2
Nagy-Cle.........252.0
Perez-NY 247.2

Fewest Hits/Game
Johnson-Sea...... 6.59
Guzman-Tor 6.73
Appier-KC 7.21
Clemens-Bos 7.41
Smiley-Min 7.66

Fewest BB/Game
Bosio-Mil 1.71
Mussina-Bal 1.79
Wegman-Mil...... 1.89
Tapani-Min 1.96
Gullickson-Det 2.03

Strikeouts
Johnson-Sea 241
Perez-NY.......... 218
Clemens-Bos 208
Guzman-Tex 179
McDowell-Chi..... 178

Strikeouts/Game
Johnson-Sea 10.31
Guzman-Tor 8.22
Perez-NY 7.92
Clemens-Bos..... 7.59
Guzman-Tex 7.19

Ratio
Mussina-Bal 9.78
Clemens-Bos 10.00
Appier-KC 10.24
Smiley-Min 10.31
Guzman-Tor 10.36

Earned Run Average
Clemens-Bos 2.41
Appier-KC.........2.46
Mussina-Bal 2.54
Guzman-Tor 2.64
Abbott-Cal 2.77

Adjusted ERA
Clemens-Bos 175
Appier-KC 165
Mussina-Bal 158
Guzman-Tor 155
Abbott-Cal........ 144

Opponents' Batting Avg.
Johnson-Sea 206
Guzman-Tor 207
Appier-KC 217
Clemens-Bos........224
Smiley-Min 231

Opponents' On Base Pct.
Mussina-Bal 279
Clemens-Bos 280
Appier-KC...........282
Guzman-Tor 287
Smiley-Min 288

Starter Runs
Clemens-Bos..... 42.0
Mussina-Bal 37.5
Appier-KC 34.2
Perez-NY......... 29.4
Abbott-Cal 27.4

Adjusted Starter Runs
Clemens-Bos 49.4
Mussina-Bal 39.7
Appier-KC 36.8
Guzman-Tor 28.9
Perez-NY 28.8

Clutch Pitching Index
Abbott-Cal 132
Finley-Cal 124
Erickson-Min 113
Perez-NY.......... 110
Moore-Oak 108

Relief Runs
D.Ward-Tor 22.4
Hernandez-Chi ... 18.1
Eckersley-Oak.... 18.0
Frohwirth-Bal 17.4
Harris-Bos 17.1

Adjusted Relief Runs
D.Ward-Tor 24.0
Harris-Bos 20.4
Frohwirth-Bal 18.4
Hernandez-Chi ... 17.5
Montgomery-KC .. 17.2

Relief Ranking
Eckersley-Oak 31.7
Olin-Cle 28.6
D.Ward-Tor 28.1
Hernandez-Chi.....27.0
J.Russell-Tex-Oak .27.0

Total Pitcher Index
Clemens-Bos....... 5.8
Appier-KC 3.8
Mussina-Bal 3.5
Eckersley-Oak..... 3.5
Perez-NY.......... 3.2

Total Baseball Ranking
Clemens-Bos....... 5.8
R.Henderson-Oak .. 4.7
Ventura-Chi 4.6
E.Martinez-Sea 4.6
Thomas-Chi 4.3

April 5 The first new NL teams since 1969 both play their first games. The Rockies are 3-0 losers to the Mets at Shea Stadium. The Marlins are 6-3 winners over Los Angeles at Joe Robbie Stadium.

April 27 Pittsburgh knuckleballer Tim Wakefield throws 171 pitches in a 10-inning 6-2 win over the Braves. The last pitcher to throw that many pitches was Fernando Valenzuela in 1987.

May 27 Dale Murphy calls it a career. Just two home runs shy of 400, the former two-time NL MVP announces his retirement as a member of the Rockies.

July 7 Tom Browning decides that he has seen the view from the dugout often enough, so he leaves Wrigley Field and watches the Reds beat the Cubs, 4-3, from the roof of a three-story building across Sheffield Avenue. He is fined $500 for leaving the dugout—not to mention the ballpark—during a game.

July 16 San Francisco outfielder Darren Lewis plays in his 267th consecutive errorless game to snap the record set by Don Demeter with Philadelphia and Detroit from 1962 to 1965.

July 28 Anthony Young's major league record 27-game losing streak finally ends. The Mets come from behind for a 4-3 win against the Marlins after Young's error allows Florida to take the lead.

September 7 Mark Whiten, who never hit more than 15 at any professional level, hits four homers and drives in 12 runs in the second game of a doubleheader for the Cardinals. His misplay of a fly ball leads to the winning runs in a 14-13 loss to the Reds in the first game, but he more than makes up for it in the nightcap. He hits a grand slam his first time up, adds three-run shots in the sixth and seventh innings and caps his prodigious night with a two-run shot in the ninth.

September 8 Houston's Darryl Kile throws the third no-hitter of the season in a 7-1 victory over the Mets. Kile fans nine and walks one in the first no-hitter by an Astro since Mike Scott's gem that clinched the 1986 NL West title.

September 9 Baseball joins the other major sports and expands the postseason as well as its divisions.

October 3 The Giants need to beat the Dodgers on the final day of the season to force a one-game playoff with the Braves for the NL West title, but the Dodgers have other plans. Los Angeles rips San Francisco 12-1 to end the Giants' post-season dreams. At 103-59, San Francisco becomes the first team since the 1954 New York Yankees to win that many games and not play in the postseason.

October 13 The Phillies end the Braves' two-year reign as league champions with a 6-3 win in Game 6 of the NLCS as Tommy Greene outpitches Greg Maddux. Curt Schilling wins the series MVP even though he didn't win a game.

ATLANTA	CHICAGO	CINCINNATI	COLORADO	FLORIDA	HOUSTON	LOS ANGELES
M B.Cox	M J.Lefebvre	M T.Perez	M D.Baylor	M R.Lachemann	M A.Howe	M T.Lasorda
1B S.Bream	1B M.Grace	M D.Johnson	1B A.Galarraga	1B O.Destrade	1B J.Bagwell	1B E.Karros
2B M.Lemke	2B R.Sandberg	1B H.Morris	2B E.Young	2B B.Barberie	2B C.Biggio	2B J.Reed
SS J.Blauser	SS R.Sanchez	2B J.Samuel	SS V.Castilla	SS W.Weiss	SS A.Cedeno	SS J.Offerman
3B T.Pendleton	3B S.Buechele	SS B.Larkin	3B C.Hayes	3B G.Sheffield	3B K.Caminiti	3B T.Wallach
LF R.Gant	LF D.May	3B C.Sabo	LF J.Clark	LF J.Conine	LF L.Gonzalez	LF E.Davis
CF O.Nixon	CF D.Smith	LF K.Mitchell	CF A.Cole	CF C.Carr	CF S.Finley	CF B.Butler
RF D.Justice	RF S.Sosa	CF J.Brumfield	RF D.Bichette	RF D.Whitmore	RF E.Anthony	RF C.Snyder
C D.Berryhill	C R.Wilkins	RF R.Sanders	C J.Girardi	C B.Santiago	C E.Taubensee	C M.Piazza
		C J.Oliver				
O D.Sanders	S3 J.Vizcaino		O D.Boston	O G.Briley	O K.Bass	23 L.Harris
C G.Olson	O W.Wilson	S2 J.Branson	2 R.Mejia	23 R.Renteria	C S.Servais	
1 F.McGriff		O R.Kelly	C D.Sheaffer	23 A.Arias		P O.Hershiser
	P M.Morgan	2O B.Roberts	S2 F.Benavides	3 D.Magadan	P D.Drabek	P T.Candiotti
P G.Maddux	P G.Hibbard	1 R.Milligan	O C.Jones	O J.Felix	P P.Harnisch	P R.Martinez
P J.Smoltz	P J.Guzman				P M.Portugal	P Ke.Gross
P T.Glavine	P M.Harkey	P J.Rijo	P A.Reynoso	P C.Hough	P G.Swindell	P P.Astacio
P S.Avery	P F.Castillo	P T.Pugh	P W.Blair	P J.Armstrong	P D.Kile	RP P.Martinez
RP G.McMichael	RP J.Bautista	P T.Belcher	RP B.Ruffin	P C.Hammond	RP X.Hernandez	RP J.Gott
RP K.Mercker	RP B.Scanlan	P T.Browning	RP S.Reed	P R.Bowen	RP D.Jones	RP R.McDowell
RP J.Howell	RP R.Myers	P J.Smiley	RP J.Parrett	RP L.Aquino	RP B.Williams	
		RP B.Ayala		RP R.Lewis		
P P.Smith	P S.Boskie	RP J.Reardon	P D.Nied	RP B.Harvey		P R.Trlicek
P M.Stanton	P D.Plesac	RP J.Spradlin	P B.Henry			
P S.Bedrosian			P K.Bottenfield	P P.Rapp		
		P J.Roper	P G.Harris	P M.Turner		
		P L.Luebbers	P D.Holmes			
			P G.Wayne			
			P C.Leskanic			
			P A.Ashby			

MONTREAL	NEW YORK	PHILADELPHIA	PITTSBURGH	SAN DIEGO	SAN FRANCISCO	ST.LOUIS
M F.Alou	M J.Torborg	M J.Fregosi	M J.Leyland	M J.Riggleman	M D.Baker	M J.Torre
1B G.Colbrunn	M D.Green	1B J.Kruk	1B K.Young	1B F.McGriff	1B W.Clark	1B G.Jefferies
2B D.DeShields	1B E.Murray	2B M.Morandini	2B C.Garcia	2B J.Gardner	2B R.Thompson	2B L.Alicea
SS W.Cordero	2B J.Kent	SS K.Stocker	SS J.Bell	SS R.Gutierrez	SS R.Clayton	SS O.Smith
3B S.Berry	SS T.Bogar	3B D.Hollins	3B J.King	3B G.Sheffield	3B M.Williams	3B T.Zeile
LF M.Alou	3B H.Johnson	LF M.Thompson	LF A.Martin	LF P.Plantier	LF B.Bonds	LF B.Gilkey
CF M.Grissom	LF V.Coleman	CF L.Dykstra	CF A.Van Slyke	CF D.Bell	CF D.Lewis	CF R.Lankford
RF L.Walker	CF J.Orsulak	RF J.Eisenreich	RF O.Merced	RF T.Gwynn	RF W.McGee	RF M.Whiten
C D.Fletcher	RF B.Bonilla	C D.Daulton	C D.Slaught	C K.Higgins	C K.Manwaring	C T.Pagnozzi
	C T.Hundley					
O L.Frazier		2S M.Duncan	O D.Clark	O1 P.Clark	O D.Martinez	O1 R.Brewer
3S M.Lansing	O D.Gallagher	O P.Incaviglia		S3 C.Shipley		2 G.Pena
1O J.Vander Wal	S2 J.McKnight	O W.Chamberlain		31 A.Cianfrocco	P B.Swift	CO E.Pappas
13 F.Bolick	23 C.Walker		P S.Cooke	2 T.Teufel	P J.Burkett	O B.Jordan
	O R.Thompson	P C.Schilling	P B.Walk		P T.Wilson	
P D.Martinez	O J.Burnitz	P D.Jackson	P P.Wagner	P A.Benes	RP B.Hickerson	P B.Tewksbury
P K.Hill		P T.Greene	P T.Wakefield	P Gr.Harris	RP J.Brantley	P R.Arocha
P C.Nabholz	P D.Gooden	P T.Mulholland	P R.Tomlin	P D.Brocail	RP D.Burba	P D.Osborne
RP J.Fassero	P F.Tanana	P B.Rivera	RP B.Minor	P W.Whitehurst		P R.Cormier
RP B.Barnes	P E.Hillman	P D.West	RP D.Neagle	P T.Worrell	P B.Black	P J.Magrane
RP J.Shaw	RP B.Saberhagen	RP Mt.Williams	RP D.Otto	RP K.Taylor	P K.Rogers	RP O.Olivares
	P P.Schourek	RP L.Andersen		RP Ge.Harris	P R.Beck	RP M.Perez
P M.Rojas	RP A.Young		P Z.Smith	RP T.Hoffman	P M.Jackson	RP R.Murphy
P K.Rueter	RP J.Innis	P Mi.Williams	P J.Ballard			
P J.Wetteland	RP M.Maddux	P R.Mason	P J.Johnston	P A.Ashby		P A.Watson
P K.Bottenfield				/P S.Sanders		P T.Urbani
P G.Heredia	P S.Fernandez			P R.Mason		P L.Lancaster
	P D.Telgheder					P L.Smith
	/P B.Jones					

TEAM	G	W	L	PCT	GB	R	OR	AB	H	2B	3B	HR	BB	SO	AVG	OBP	SLG	PRO	PRO+	BR	/A	PF	CHI	RC	SB	CS	SBA	SBR
EAST																												
PHI	162	97	65	.599		**877**	740	5685	**1555**	**297**	51	156	**665**	1049	.274	**.354**	.426	**.780**	**116**	**117**	**130**	99	99	**880**	91	32	74	8
MON	163	94	68	.580	3	732	682	5493	1410	270	36	122	542	**860**	.257	.329	.386	.715	92	-25	-55	104	104	727	**228**	56	**80**	**35**
STL	162	87	75	.537	10	758	744	5551	1508	262	34	118	588	882	.272	.344	.395	.739	105	32	48	98	99	759	153	72	68	3
CHI	163	84	78	.519	13	738	739	5627	1521	259	32	161	446	923	.270	.328	.414	.742	105	18	31	98	99	748	100	43	70	4
PIT	162	75	87	.463	22	707	806	5549	1482	267	50	110	536	972	.267	.338	.393	.731	101	10	12	100	95	734	92	55	63	-5
FLA	162	64	98	.395	33	581	724	5475	1356	197	31	94	498	1054	.248	.316	.346	.662	79	-124	-157	106	98	604	117	56	68	2
NY	162	59	103	.364	38	672	744	5448	1350	228	37	158	448	879	.248	.308	.390	.698	92	-72	-64	99	**105**	646	79	50	61	-6
WEST																												
ATL	162	104	58	.642		767	**559**	5515	1444	239	29	**169**	560	946	.262	.334	.408	.742	103	26	19	101	101	754	125	48	72	9
SF	162	103	59	.636	1	808	636	5557	1534	269	33	168	516	930	**.276**	.343	**.427**	.770	115	82	107	97	99	803	120	65	65	-3
HOU	162	85	77	.525	19	716	630	5464	1459	288	37	138	497	911	.267	.333	.409	.742	107	24	51	96	96	733	103	60	63	-5
LA	162	81	81	.500	23	675	662	5588	1458	234	28	130	492	937	.261	.324	.383	.707	100	-45	-5	94	98	696	126	61	67	1
CIN	162	73	89	.451	31	722	785	5517	1457	261	28	137	485	1025	.264	.327	.396	.723	98	-13	-14	100	102	720	142	59	71	7
COL	162	67	95	.414	37	758	967	5517	1507	278	**59**	142	388	944	.273	.326	.422	.748	90	28	-93	116	102	731	146	90	62	-10
SD	162	61	101	.377	43	679	772	5503	1386	239	28	153	443	1046	.252	.314	.389	.703	91	-58	-69	102	103	672	92	41	69	3
TOT	1135					10190		77489	20427	3588	513	1956	7104	13358	.264	.330	.399	.729							1714	788	69	41

TEAM	CG	SH	SV	IP	H	H/G	HR	BB	SO	RAT	ERA	ERA+	OAV	OOB	PR	/A	PF	CPI	FA	E	DP	FW	PW	BW	SBW	DIF
EAST																										
PHI	**24**	11	46	1472^{2}	1419	8.7	129	573	**1117**	12.4	3.95	100	.251	.324	14	1	98	94	.977	141	123	-.4	.0	**13.0**	.5	2.8
MON	8	7	**61**	1456^{2}	1369	8.5	119	521	934	12.0	3.55	118	.249	.319	80	101	103	101	.975	159	144	-1.4	10.1	-5.5	**3.2**	6.6
STL	5	7	54	1453	1553	9.6	152	**383**	775	12.3	4.09	97	.276	.327	-8	-20	98	102	.975	159	157	-1.4	-2.0	4.8	.0	4.6
CHI	8	5	56	1449^{2}	1514	9.4	153	470	905	12.6	4.18	95	.273	.335	-22	-31	99	103	.982	115	162	1.1	-3.1	3.1	.1	1.8
PIT	12	5	34	1445^{2}	1557	9.7	153	485	832	13.0	4.77	85	.280	.342	-117	-116	100	95	.983	105	161	1.7	-11.6	1.2	-.8	3.5
FLA	4	5	48	1440^{1}	1437	9.0	135	598	945	12.9	4.13	105	.261	.337	-14	30	107	100	.980	125	130	.5	3.0	-15.7	-.0	-4.8
NY	16	8	22	1438	1483	9.3	139	434	867	12.3	4.05	99	.269	.328	-2	-6	99	100	.975	156	143	-1.3	-.6	-6.4	-.9	-12.9
WEST																										
ATL	18	**16**	46	1455	**1297**	**8.0**	**101**	480	1036	**11.1**	**3.14**	**128**	**.240**	**.305**	**146**	**142**	99	101	.983	108	146	1.5	**14.2**	1.9	.6	4.8
SF	4	9	50	1456^{2}	1385	8.6	168	442	982	11.6	3.61	108	.253	.315	69	47	97	**105**	**.984**	**101**	**169**	**1.9**	4.7	10.7	-.6	5.3
HOU	18	14	42	1441^{1}	1363	8.5	117	476	1056	11.7	3.49	111	.251	.316	88	61	96	101	.979	126	141	.5	6.1	5.1	-.8	-6.8
LA	17	9	36	1472^{2}	1406	8.6	103	567	1043	12.3	3.50	109	.254	.327	88	51	94	**105**	.979	133	141	.0	5.1	-.5	-.2	-4.5
CIN	11	8	37	1434	1510	9.5	158	508	996	12.9	4.51	89	.272	.338	-74	-77	100	97	.980	121	133	.8	-7.7	-1.4	.4	-.0
COL	9	0	35	1431^{1}	1664	10.5	181	609	913	14.6	5.41	88	.294	.367	-218	-102	118	98	.973	167	149	-1.9	-10.2	-9.3	-1.3	8.7
SD	8	6	32	1437^{2}	1470	9.2	148	558	957	12.9	4.23	98	.266	.337	-30	-15	102	100	.974	160	129	-1.5	-1.5	-6.9	.0	-10.1
TOT	162	110	599	20284^{2}		9.1				12.5	4.04		.264	.330					.978	1876	2028					

Runs
Dykstra-Phi 143
Bonds-SF 129
Gant-Atl 113
McGriff-SD-Atl 111
Blauser-Atl 110

Hits
Dykstra-Phi 194
Grace-Chi 193
Grissom-Mon 188
Bell-Pit 187
Jefferies-StL 186

Doubles
Hayes-Col 45
Dykstra-Phi 44
Bichette-Col 43
Gwynn-SD 41
Biggio-Hou 41

Triples
Finley-Hou 13
Butler-LA 10
Morandini-Phi 9
Bell-Pit 9

Home Runs
Bonds-SF 46
Justice-Atl 40
Williams-SF 38
McGriff-SD-Atl 37
Gant-Atl 36

Total Bases
Bonds-SF 365
Williams-SF 325
Gant-Atl 309
Piazza-LA 307
Dykstra-Phi 307

Runs Batted In
Bonds-SF 123
Justice-Atl 120
Gant-Atl 117
Piazza-LA 112
Williams-SF 110

Runs Produced
Bonds-SF 206
Gant-Atl 194
Dykstra-Phi 190
Grissom-Mon 180
Hollins-Phi 179

Bases On Balls
Dykstra-Phi 129
Bonds-SF 126
Daulton-Phi 117
Kruk-Phi 111
Butler-LA 86

Batting Average
Galarraga-Col .370
Gwynn-SD .358
Jefferies-StL .342
Bonds-SF .336
Grace-Chi .325

On Base Percentage
Bonds-SF .463
Kruk-Phi .433
Dykstra-Phi .423
Merced-Pit .415
Jefferies-StL .411

Slugging Average
Bonds-SF .677
Galarraga-Col .602
Williams-SF .561
Piazza-LA .561
McGriff-SD-Atl .549

Production
Bonds-SF 1.140
Galarraga-Col 1.010
Piazza-LA .935
McGriff-SD-Atl .927
Bagwell-Hou .909

Adjusted Production
Bonds-SF 207
Piazza-LA 155
Bagwell-Hou 146
Kruk-Phi 145
Dykstra-Phi 144

Batter Runs
Bonds-SF 82.0
Dykstra-Phi 43.3
Galarraga-Col 42.3
Kruk-Phi 38.1
McGriff-SD-Atl 34.8

Adjusted Batter Runs
Bonds-SF 87.0
Dykstra-Phi 45.3
Piazza-LA 40.5
Kruk-Phi 39.9
Bagwell-Hou 35.4

Clutch Hitting Index
Zeile-StL 128
King-Pit 127
May-Chi 126
Oliver-Cin 125
Daulton-Phi 122

Runs Created
Bonds-SF 172
Dykstra-Phi 142
Kruk-Phi 117
McGriff-SD-Atl 115
Jefferies-StL 113

Total Average
Bonds-SF 1.339
Galarraga-Col 1.006
Dykstra-Phi 1.000
Kruk-Phi .974
Daulton-Phi .971

Stolen Bases
Carr-Fla 58
Grissom-Mon 53
Nixon-Atl 47
Lewis-SF 46
Jefferies-StL 46

Stolen Base Average
Frazier-Mon 89.5
Davis-LA 86.8
Grissom-Mon 84.1
Bell-SD 83.9
Jefferies-StL 83.6

Stolen Base Runs
Grissom-Mon 9.9
Jefferies-StL 8.4
DeShields-Mon 6.9
Davis-LA 6.9
Nixon-Atl 6.3

Fielding Runs
Bell-Pit 25.7
King-Pit 20.5
Gonzalez-Hou 20.2
Reed-LA 19.4
O.Smith-StL 18.2

Total Player Rating
Bonds-SF 8.8
Dykstra-Phi 6.1
Bell-Pit 5.7
Piazza-LA 5.1
Wilkins-Chi 4.2

Wins
Glavine-Atl 22
Burkett-SF 22
Swift-SF 21
Maddux-Atl 20

Win Percentage
Portugal-Hou .818
Greene-Phi .800
Glavine-Atl .786
Burkett-SF .759
Avery-Atl .750

Games
Jackson-SF 81
West-Phi 76
Beck-SF 76
McMichael-Atl 74

Complete Games
Maddux-Atl 8

Shutouts
Harnisch-Hou 4
R.Martinez-LA 3

Saves
Myers-Chi 53
Beck-SF 48
Harvey-Fla 45

Innings Pitched
Maddux-Atl 267.0
Rijo-Cin 257.1
Smoltz-Atl 243.2
Glavine-Atl 239.1
Drabek-Hou 237.2

Fewest Hits/Game
Harnisch-Hou 7.07
Swift-SF 7.54
Rijo-Cin 7.62
Smoltz-Atl 7.68
Maddux-Atl 7.69

Fewest BB/Game
Tewksbury-StL .84
Arocha-StL 1.48
Burkett-SF 1.55
Avery-Atl 1.73
Maddux-Atl 1.75

Strikeouts
Rijo-Cin 227
Smoltz-Atl 208
Maddux-Atl 197
Schilling-Phi 186
Harnisch-Hou 185

Strikeouts/Game
Rijo-Cin 7.94
Smoltz-Atl 7.68
Guzman-Chi 7.68
Harnisch-Hou 7.65
Greene-Phi 7.52

Ratio
Maddux-Atl 9.64
Rijo-Cin 9.86
Swift-SF 9.90
Mulholland-Phi 10.37
Avery-Atl 10.44

Earned Run Average
Maddux-Atl 2.36
Rijo-Cin 2.48
Portugal-Hou 2.77
Swift-SF 2.82
Avery-Atl 2.94

Adjusted ERA
Maddux-Atl 170
Rijo-Cin 162
Portugal-Hou 140
Swift-SF 138
Avery-Atl 136

Opponents' Batting Avg.
Harnisch-Hou .214
Swift-SF .226
Rijo-Cin .230
Smoltz-Atl .230
Maddux-Atl .232

Opponents' On Base Pct.
Maddux-Atl .274
Swift-SF .278
Rijo-Cin .278
Mulholland-Phi .283
Harnisch-Hou .290

Starter Runs
Maddux-Atl 49.8
Rijo-Cin 44.5
Swift-SF 31.4
Portugal-Hou 29.4
Avery-Atl 27.2

Adjusted Starter Runs
Maddux-Atl 49.0
Rijo-Cin 44.0
Swift-SF 28.0
Avery-Atl 26.5
Portugal-Hou 25.4

Clutch Pitching Index
Portugal-Hou 120
Glavine-Atl 116
R.Martinez-LA 116
Reynoso-Col 113
Avery-Atl 110

Relief Runs
Fassero-Mon 29.2
Wetteland-Mon 25.3
McMichael-Atl 20.1
Harvey-Fla 18.0
P.Martinez-LA 17.0

Adjusted Relief Runs
Fassero-Mon 31.3
Wetteland-Mon 26.5
Harvey-Fla 20.1
McMichael-Atl 19.9
Beck-SF 15.4

Relief Ranking
Wetteland-Mon 56.4
Harvey-Fla 38.1
Fassero-Mon 32.4
Gott-LA 25.0
Beck-SF 22.9

Total Pitcher Index
Maddux-Atl 6.1
Wetteland-Mon 5.7
Rijo-Cin 4.8
Swift-SF 4.2
Harvey-Fla 3.9

Total Baseball Ranking
Bonds-SF 8.8
Dykstra-Phi 6.1
Maddux-Atl 6.1
Wetteland-Mon 5.7
Bell-Pit 5.7

January 5 Reggie Jackson is the lone player elected to the Hall of Fame. Jackson, whose .262 lifetime batting average is the lowest of any outfielder in the Hall, receives 93.6 percent of the vote. His 563 career home runs certainly didn't hurt in his first year of eligibility.

March 22 Cleveland pitcher Steve Olin is killed instantly and new teammate Tim Crews dies several hours later as a result of a boating accident at Little Lake Nellie in Clermont, Fla. Bob Ojeda is seriously injured as well, but he will survive and make a brief comeback.

May 29 Jose Canseco, who three days earlier had a ball bounce off his head for a home run, pitches an inning in a blowout in Boston. Besides the Rangers' 15-1 loss, Canseco winds up having to undergo season-ending elbow surgery from his ill-advised outing.

June 28 Carlton Fisk is released by the White Sox after 12 years with the team. The 45-year-old caught more games and hit more homers than any catcher.

July 12 Kirby Puckett homers and doubles to earn MVP honors in the AL's 9-3 All-Star victory at Baltimore's Camden Yards.

July 28 Ken Griffey Jr. hits home runs in eight consecutive games to tie the major league record. Six travel more than 400 feet and one is a grand slam. Dale Long (1956) and Don Mattingly (1987) are the only others to go deep in eight straight games.

September 4 Jim Abbott becomes the eighth Yankee pitcher to throw a no-hitter with a 4-0 triumph over the Indians. Abbott, who was born without a right hand, throws 118 pitches and does not allow a runner past first base—despite five walks.

September 16 Minnesota's Dave Winfield becomes the 19th member of the 3,000-hit club with a single off Oakland's Dennis Eckersley. Winfield, playing for his hometown Twins, reaches the milestone at age 41.

October 12 Dave Stewart captures the pennant and the ALCS MVP with a 6-3 win over the White Sox in Game 6. Paul Molitor triples home two runs and Devon White's ninth-inning home run sparks a three-run rally in the clincher for triumphant Toronto.

October 20 The Blue Jays hammer Mitch Williams and the Phillies relief corps for six runs in the eighth inning to overcome a four-run deficit. Reliever Duane Ward retires all four batters he faces in Toronto's 15-14 win. The four-hour, 14-minute marathon is the longest and highest scoring game in World Series history.

October 23 In one of the most dramatic endings in World Series history, Joe Carter hits a three-run ninth-inning home run off Mitch Williams for an 8-6 win and Toronto's second straight world championship. Paul Molitor, who hit .500 in 24 at bats, is MVP.

	BALTIMORE		BOSTON		CALIFORNIA		CHICAGO		CLEVELAND		DETROIT		KANSAS CITY
M	J.Oates	M	B.Hobson	M	B.Rodgers	M	G.Lamont	M	M.Hargrove	M	S.Anderson	M	H.McRae
1B	D.Segui	1B	M.Vaughn	1B	J.Snow	1B	F.Thomas	1B	P.Sorrento	1B	C.Fielder	1B	W.Joyner
2B	H.Reynolds	2B	S.Fletcher	2B	T.Lovullo	2B	J.Cora	2B	C.Baerga	2B	L.Whitaker	2B	J.Lind
SS	C.Ripken	SS	J.Valentin	SS	G.DiSarcina	SS	O.Guillen	SS	F.Fermin	SS	A.Trammell	SS	G.Gagne
3B	T.Hulett	3B	S.Cooper	3B	R.Gonzales	3B	R.Ventura	3B	A.Espinoza	3B	T.Fryman	3B	G.Gaetti
LF	B.Anderson	LF	M.Greenwell	LF	L.Polonia	LF	T.Raines	LF	A.Belle	LF	T.Phillips	LF	K.McReynolds
CF	M.Devereaux	CF	B.Hatcher	CF	C.Curtis	CF	L.Johnson	CF	K.Lofton	CF	M.Cuyler	CF	B.McRae
RF	M.McLemore	RF	B.Zupcic	RF	T.Salmon	RF	E.Burks	RF	W.Kirby	RF	R.Deer	RF	F.Jose
C	C.Hoiles	C	T.Pena	C	G.Myers	C	R.Karkovice	C	J.Ortiz	C	C.Kreuter	C	M.Macfarlane
DH	H.Baines	DH	A.Dawson	DH	C.Davis	DH	G.Bell	DH	R.Jefferson	DH	K.Gibson	DH	G.Brett
3	L.Gomez	1O	C.Quintana	O1	S.Javier	OD	B.Jackson	32	J.Treadway	3D	S.Livingstone	O	C.Gwynn
		OD	I.Calderon	23	D.Easley			31	C.Martinez	1C	M.Tettleton	3	P.Hiatt
P	B.McDonald					P	J.McDowell	C	S.Alomar	O	D.Gladden	C	B.Mayne
P	F.Valenzuela	P	D.Darwin	P	M.Langston	P	A.Fernandez						
P	M.Mussina	P	R.Clemens	P	C.Finley	P	W.Alvarez	P	J.Mesa	P	M.Moore	P	D.Cone
P	R.Sutcliffe	P	F.Viola	P	S.Sanderson	P	J.Bere	P	T.Kramer	P	D.Wells	P	K.Appier
P	J.Moyer	P	J.Dopson	P	K.Patterson	P	K.McCaskill	P	M.Clark	P	J.Doherty	P	H.Pichardo
RP	A.Mills	RP	A.Sele	RP	J.Grahe	P	R.Hernandez	RP	J.Hernandez	P	B.Gullickson	P	T.Gordon
RP	T.Frohwirth	RP	P.Quantrill	RP	J.Valera	RP	D.Pall	RP	E.Plunk	P	M.Leiter	P	C.Haney
RP	M.Williamson	RP	G.Harris			RP	S.Radinsky	RP	D.Lilliquist	RP	T.Bolton	RP	M.Gubicza
		RP	S.Bankhead	P	J.Farrell					RP	B.Krueger	RP	J.Montgomery
P	A.Rhodes			P	P.Leftwich	P	T.Belcher	P	J.Mutis	RP	M.Henneman		
P	J.Poole	P	J.Hesketh	P	R.Springer	P	J.Schwarz	P	M.Young			P	M.Gardner
		P	K.Ryan	P	H.Hathaway			P	M.Bielecki	P	R.MacDonald		
				P	G.Nelson			P	B.Wertz				
								P	C.Young				
								P	J.DiPoto				
								P	D.Cook				
								/P	A.Lopez				

	MILWAUKEE		MINNESOTA		NEW YORK		OAKLAND		SEATTLE		TEXAS		TORONTO
M	P.Garner	M	T.Kelly	M	B.Showalter	M	T.LaRussa	M	L.Piniella	M	K.Kennedy	M	C.Gaston
1B	J.Jaha	1B	K.Hrbek	1B	D.Mattingly	1B	M.Aldrete	1B	T.Martinez	1B	R.Palmeiro	1B	J.Olerud
2B	B.Spiers	2B	C.Knoblauch	2B	P.Kelly	2B	B.Gates	2B	R.Amaral	2B	D.Strange	2B	R.Alomar
SS	P.Listach	SS	P.Meares	SS	S.Owen	SS	M.Bordick	SS	O.Vizquel	SS	M.Lee	SS	T.Fernandez
3B	B.Surhoff	3B	M.Pagliarulo	3B	W.Boggs	3B	C.Paquette	3B	M.Blowers	3B	D.Palmer	3B	E.Sprague
LF	G.Vaughn	LF	P.Munoz	LF	D.James	LF	R.Henderson	LF	M.Felder	LF	J.Gonzalez	LF	T.Ward
CF	R.Yount	CF	S.Mack	CF	B.Williams	CF	D.Henderson	CF	K.Griffey	CF	D.Hulse	CF	D.White
RF	D.Hamilton	RF	K.Puckett	RF	P.O'Neill	RF	R.Sierra	RF	J.Buhner	RF	J.Canseco	RF	J.Carter
C	D.Nilsson	C	B.Harper	C	M.Stanley	C	T.Steinbach	C	D.Valle	C	I.Rodriguez	C	P.Borders
DH	K.Reimer	DH	D.Winfield	DH	D.Tartabull	DH	T.Neel	DH	P.O'Brien	DH	J.Franco	DH	P.Molitor
2S	J.Bell	O1	D.McCarty	S2	M.Gallego	O3	J.Browne	2	B.Boone	O	G.Redus	P	J.Guzman
S3	D.Thon	S3	J.Reboulet	1O	J.Leyritz	31	K.Seitzer	13	D.Magadan	S3	M.Diaz	P	J.Hentgen
O	T.Brunansky			OS	R.Velarde	O2	L.Blankenship					P	T.Stottlemyre
		P	K.Tapani	CD	M.Nokes	C	S.Hemond	P	R.Johnson	P	K.Brown	P	D.Stewart
P	C.Eldred	P	S.Erickson			O1	S.Brosius	P	E.Hanson	P	K.Rogers	P	J.Morris
P	J.Navarro	P	W.Banks	P	J.Key			P	T.Leary	P	R.Pavlik	RP	D.Cox
P	R.Bones	P	J.Deshaies	P	J.Abbott	P	B.Witt	P	D.Fleming	P	C.Leibrandt	RP	M.Eichhorn
P	B.Wegman	RP	M.Trombley	P	M.Perez	P	R.Darling	P	C.Bosio	RP	B.Bohanon	RP	D.Ward
P	A.Miranda	RP	M.Hartley	P	S.Kamieniecki	P	B.Welch	RP	J.Nelson	RP	C.Lefferts		
RP	G.Lloyd	RP	R.Aguilera	P	B.Wickman	RP	K.Downs	RP	D.Henry	RP	T.Henke	P	A.Leiter
RP	M.Fetters			RP	R.Monteleone	RP	J.Boever	RP	D.Powell			P	M.Timlin
RP	J.Orosco	P	E.Guardado	RP	S.Howe	RP	E.Nunez					P	T.Castillo
		P	G.Tsamis							P	M.Whiteside		
P	R.Novoa	P	C.Willis			P	T.Van Poppel			P	N.Ryan		
P	D.Henry	P	L.Casian			P	D.Eckersley			P	T.Burns		
P	M.Boddicker					P	M.Mohler			P	B.Patterson		
						P	S.Davis						
						P	S.Hillegas						

TEAM	G	W	L	PCT	GB	R	OR	AB	H	2B	3B	HR	BB	SO	AVG	OBP	SLG	PRO	PRO+	BR	/A	PF	CHI	RC	SB	CS	SBA	SBR
EAST																												
TOR	162	95	67	.586		847	742	5579	1556	317	42	159	588	861	**.279**	.353	**.436**	.789	110	85	81	101	99	867	**170**	49	**78**	**22**
NY	162	88	74	.543	7	821	761	5615	**1568**	294	24	178	629	910	**.279**	.356	.435	.791	**115**	93	122	97	95	861	39	35	53	-9
BAL	162	85	77	.525	10	786	745	5508	1470	287	24	157	655	930	.267	.349	.413	.762	100	36	3	104	98	796	73	54	57	-11
DET	162	85	77	.525	10	**899**	837	5620	1546	282	38	178	**765**	1122	.275	**.365**	.434	**.799**	**115**	**120**	**126**	99	98	**916**	104	63	62	-7
BOS	162	80	82	.494	15	686	698	5496	1451	**319**	29	114	508	871	.264	.333	.395	.728	89	-41	-85	106	96	713	73	38	66	-1
CLE	162	76	86	.469	19	790	813	5619	1547	264	31	141	488	843	.275	.339	.409	.748	100	-5	-2	100	104	776	159	55	74	15
MIL	162	69	93	.426	26	733	792	5525	1426	240	25	125	555	932	.258	.330	.378	.708	91	-77	-67	99	108	686	138	93	60	-14
WEST																												
CHI	162	94	68	.580		776	**664**	5483	1454	228	**44**	162	604	**834**	.265	.342	.411	.753	103	11	28	98	100	773	106	57	65	-2
TEX	162	86	76	.531	8	835	751	5510	1472	284	39	**181**	483	984	.267	.332	.431	.763	107	16	46	96	**109**	777	113	67	63	-6
KC	162	84	78	.519	10	675	694	5522	1455	294	35	125	428	936	.263	.322	.397	.719	87	-67	-107	106	100	692	100	75	57	-15
SEA	162	82	80	.506	12	734	731	5494	1429	272	24	161	624	901	.260	.342	.406	.748	99	3	-8	101	95	758	91	68	57	-14
CAL	162	71	91	.438	23	684	770	5391	1399	259	24	114	564	930	.260	.334	.380	.714	88	-63	-85	103	101	679	169	100	63	-9
MIN	162	71	91	.438	23	693	830	5601	1480	261	27	121	493	850	.264	.329	.385	.714	91	-70	-72	100	101	692	83	59	58	-11
OAK	162	68	94	.420	26	715	846	5543	1408	260	21	158	622	1048	.254	.333	.394	.727	101	-42	1	94	99	735	131	59	69	4
TOT	1134					10674		77506	20661	3861	427	2074	8006	12952	.267	.340	.408	.748							1549	872	64	-59

TEAM	CG	SH	SV	IP	H	H/G	HR	BB	SO	RAT	ERA	ERA+	OAV	OOB	PR	/A	PF	CPI	FA	E	DP	FW	PW	BW	SBW	DIF
EAST																										
TOR	11	11	**50**	1441^{1}	1441	9.0	134	620	1023	13.1	4.21	103	.261	.339	18	17	100	99	.982	107	144	.5	1.7	7.9	**2.5**	1.5
NY	11	**13**	38	1438^{1}	1467	9.2	170	552	899	12.8	4.35	95	.266	.336	-5	-31	96	100	.983	105	166	.6	-3.0	11.9	-.5	-2.0
BAL	21	10	42	1442^{2}	1427	8.9	153	579	900	12.8	4.31	104	.261	.336	2	26	104	98	.984	100	171	.9	2.5	.3	-.7	1.0
DET	11	7	36	1436^{2}	1547	9.7	188	542	828	13.4	4.65	92	.276	.345	-52	-58	99	102	.979	132	148	-1.0	-5.6	**12.3**	-.3	-1.3
BOS	9	11	44	1452^{1}	**1379**	**8.5**	127	552	997	**12.3**	3.77	**122**	**.252**	**.325**	88	**136**	107	100	.980	122	155	-.4	**13.2**	-8.3	.3	-5.9
CLE	7	8	45	1445^{2}	1591	9.9	182	591	888	13.8	4.58	95	.281	.353	-41	-40	100	**107**	.976	148	**174**	-1.9	-3.9	-.2	1.9	-.8
MIL	**26**	6	29	1447	1511	9.4	153	522	810	13.0	4.45	95	.271	.340	-21	-33	98	99	.979	131	148	-.9	-3.2	-6.5	-1.0	-.4
WEST																										
CHI	16	11	48	1454	1398	8.7	125	566	974	12.4	**3.70**	113	.255	.330	**100**	77	97	105	.982	112	153	.2	7.5	2.7	.2	2.4
TEX	20	6	45	1438^{1}	1476	9.2	144	562	957	13.0	4.28	97	.267	.339	6	-21	96	100	.979	132	145	-1.0	-2.0	4.5	-.2	3.8
KC	16	6	48	1445^{1}	**1379**	8.6	**105**	571	985	12.4	4.04	113	.254	.329	45	86	106	93	.984	97	150	1.0	8.4	-10.4	-1.1	5.1
SEA	22	10	41	1453^{2}	1421	8.8	135	605	**1083**	13.0	4.20	105	.259	.340	20	33	102	99	**.985**	**90**	173	**1.5**	3.2	-.8	-1.0	-1.9
CAL	**26**	6	41	1430^{1}	1482	9.3	153	550	843	13.1	4.34	104	.270	.342	-3	26	104	102	.980	120	161	-.3	2.5	-8.3	-.5	-3.5
MIN	5	3	44	1444^{1}	1591	9.9	148	**514**	901	13.4	4.71	92	.283	.348	-63	-57	101	99	.984	100	160	.9	-5.5	-7.0	-.7	2.4
OAK	8	2	42	1452^{1}	1551	9.6	157	680	864	14.1	4.90	83	.276	.359	-94	-134	94	98	.982	111	161	.2	-13.0	.0	.8	-1.1
TOT	209	110	593	20222^{1}		9.2				13.0	4.32		.267	.340					.981	1607	2209					

Runs
Palmeiro-Tex 124
Molitor-Tor 121
White-Tor 116
Lofton-Cle 116
Henderson-Oak-Tor ... 114

Hits
Molitor-Tor 211
Olerud-Tor 200
Baerga-Cle 200
Alomar-Tor 192
Lofton-Cle 185

Doubles
Olerud-Tor 54
White-Tor 42
Valentin-Bos 40
Palmeiro-Tex 40
Puckett-Min 39

Triples
Johnson-Chi 14
Cora-Chi 13
Hulse-Tex 10
McRae-KC 9
Fernandez-Tor 9

Home Runs
Gonzalez-Tex 46
Griffey-Sea 45
Thomas-Chi 41
Belle-Cle 38
Palmeiro-Tex 37

Total Bases
Griffey-Sea 359
Gonzalez-Tex 339
Thomas-Chi 333
Palmeiro-Tex 331
Olerud-Tor 330

Runs Batted In
Belle-Cle 129
Thomas-Chi 128
Carter-Tor 121
Gonzalez-Tex 118
Fielder-Det 117

Runs Produced
Molitor-Tor 210
Baerga-Cle 198
Thomas-Chi 193
Palmeiro-Tex 192
Olerud-Tor 192

Bases On Balls
Phillips-Det 132
Henderson-Oak-Tor ... 120
Olerud-Tor 114
Thomas-Chi 112
Tettleton-Det 109

Batting Average
Olerud-Tor .... .363
Molitor-Tor .... .332
Alomar-Tor .... .326
Lofton-Cle .... .325
Baerga-Cle .... .321

On Base Percentage
Olerud-Tor .... .478
Phillips-Det ...... .446
Henderson-Oak-Tor ... .435
Thomas-Chi .... .434
Hoiles-Bal .... .419

Slugging Average
Gonzalez-Tex ...... .632
Griffey-Sea .... .617
Thomas-Chi .... .607
Olerud-Tor .... .599
Hoiles-Bal .... .585

Production
Olerud-Tor 1.077
Thomas-Chi 1.041
Griffey-Sea 1.029
Hoiles-Bal 1.003
Gonzalez-Tex 1.001

Adjusted Production
Olerud-Tor 186
Thomas-Chi 180
Gonzalez-Tex 170
Griffey-Sea 170
Hoiles-Bal 160

Batter Runs
Olerud-Tor 74.4
Thomas-Chi 62.3
Griffey-Sea 60.1
Gonzalez-Tex 44.4
Molitor-Tor 41.0

Adjusted Batter Runs
Olerud-Tor 73.6
Thomas-Chi 65.5
Griffey-Sea 58.1
Gonzalez-Tex 49.0
Palmeiro-Tex 42.9

Clutch Hitting Index
McLemore-Bal 122
Surhoff-Mil 120
Baerga-Cle 119
Davis-Cal 117
Kirby-Cle 115

Runs Created
Olerud-Tor 161
Thomas-Chi 149
Griffey-Sea 147
Molitor-Tor 136
Palmeiro-Tex 128

Total Average
Olerud-Tor 1.230
Thomas-Chi 1.160
Henderson-Oak-Tor ... 1.106
Griffey-Sea 1.104
Hoiles-Bal 1.077

Stolen Bases
Lofton-Cle 70
Polonia-Cal 55
Alomar-Tor 55
Henderson-Oak-Tor . 53
Curtis-Cal 48

Stolen Base Average
White-Tor 89.5
Palmeiro-Tex 88.0
Henderson-Oak-Tor ... 86.9
Molitor-Tor 84.6
Fletcher-Bos 84.2

Stolen Base Runs
Lofton-Cle 12.6
Henderson-Oak-Tor ... 11.1
White-Tor 7.8
Alomar-Tor 7.5
Johnson-Chi 6.3

Fielding Runs
Vizquel-Sea 23.1
Pena-Bos 21.6
Joyner-KC 20.4
Boggs-NY 19.7
Belle-Cle 19.1

Total Player Rating
Olerud-Tor 5.8
Henderson-Oak-Tor . 5.3
Griffey-Sea 5.3
Belle-Cle 5.2
Gonzalez-Tex 4.9

Wins
McDowell-Chi 22
Johnson-Sea 19
Hentgen-Tor 19

Win Percentage
Key-NY .... .750
Johnson-Sea ...... .704
Appier-KC .... .692
McDowell-Chi ..... .688
Hentgen-Tor ...... .679

Games
Harris-Bos 80
Radinsky-Chi 73
D.Ward-Tor 71
Nelson-Sea 71
Fossas-Bos 71

Complete Games
Finley-Cal 13
Brown-Tex 12
McDowell-Chi 10
Johnson-Sea 10
Eldred-Mil 8

Shutouts
McDowell-Chi 4
Moore-Det 3
Johnson-Sea 3
Brown-Tex 3

Saves
D.Ward-Tor 45
Montgomery-KC ... 45
Henke-Tex 40
Hernandez-Chi 38
Eckersley-Oak 36

Innings Pitched
Eldred-Mil 258.0
McDowell-Chi 256.2
Langston-Cal 256.1
Johnson-Sea 255.1
Cone-KC 254.0

Fewest Hits/Game
Johnson-Sea 6.52
Appier-KC 6.90
Cone-KC 7.26
Alvarez-Chi 7.28
McDonald-Bal 7.56

Fewest BB/Game
Key-NY 1.64
Darwin-Bos 1.92
Wells-Det 2.02
Tapani-Min 2.27
Doherty-Det 2.34

Strikeouts
Johnson-Sea 308
Langston-Cal 196
Guzman-Tor 194
Cone-KC 191
Finley-Cal 187

Strikeouts/Game
Johnson-Sea 10.86
Perez-NY 8.17
Guzman-Tor 7.90
Clemens-Bos 7.51
Banks-Min 7.25

Ratio
Darwin-Bos 9.73
Appier-KC 9.99
Key-NY 10.00
Johnson-Sea 10.57
Fernandez-Chi .. 10.70

Earned Run Average
Appier-KC 2.56
Alvarez-Chi 2.95
Key-NY 3.00
Fernandez-Chi ... 3.13
Viola-Bos 3.14

Adjusted ERA
Appier-KC 179
Viola-Bos 147
Finley-Cal 143
Alvarez-Chi 142
Darwin-Bos 142

Opponents' Batting Avg.
Johnson-Sea ..... .203
Appier-KC .... .212
Cone-KC .... .223
McDonald-Bal ... .228
Bosio-Sea .... .229

Opponents' On Base Pct.
Darwin-Bos ...... .274
Appier-KC .... .280
Key-NY .... .282
Johnson-Sea .... .292
Fernandez-Chi .. .296

Starter Runs
Appier-KC 46.6
Key-NY 34.6
Fernandez-Chi .. 32.7
Finley-Cal 32.7
Langston-Cal ... 32.1

Adjusted Starter Runs
Appier-KC 53.4
Finley-Cal 37.8
Langston-Cal ... 37.3
Cone-KC 35.3
Darwin-Bos 34.6

Clutch Pitching Index
Alvarez-Chi 129
Viola-Bos 123
Pavlik-Tex 119
Banks-Min 118
Finley-Cal 115

Relief Runs
Montgomery-KC .. 19.9
Hernandez-Chi .. 17.8
D.Ward-Tor 17.4
Lilliquist-Cle 14.7
Henneman-Det .. 13.4

Adjusted Relief Runs
Montgomery-KC .. 22.4
D.Ward-Tor 17.4
Hernandez-Chi .. 16.5
Lilliquist-Cle 14.8
Mills-Bal 13.9

Relief Ranking
Montgomery-KC .. 47.7
D.Ward-Tor 29.7
Hernandez-Chi .. 27.0
Henke-Tex 21.9
Henneman-Det .. 20.8

Total Pitcher Index
Appier-KC 4.8
Montgomery-KC .. 4.3
Langston-Cal 3.9
Finley-Cal 3.7
Darwin-Bos 3.4

Total Baseball Ranking
Olerud-Tor 5.8
Henderson-Oak-Tor . 5.3
Griffey-Sea 5.3
Belle-Cle 5.2
Gonzalez-Tex 4.9

January 12 Steve Carlton, winner of 329 games and four Cy Young Awards, is elected to the Baseball Hall of Fame.

February 25 The Hall of Fame Veterans Committee taps Leo Durocher, who hit .247 over a 17-year career, but had a .540 winning percentage in 24 years as a manager, and Yankee great Phil Rizzuto, who had waited in vain for years for enshrinement.

April 4 Cubs outfielder Karl "Tuffy" Rhodes, who hit three home runs in all of 1993, hits three home runs off Mets starter Dwight Gooden on Opening Day at Wrigley Field. New York holds on for the 12-8 win.

April 8 Braves lefthander Kent Mercker no-hits the Dodgers, 6-0, in his first career complete game.

April 8 Chan Ho Park of the Dodgers becomes the first Korean-born player to appear in a major league game.

April 10* The Texas League witnesses two no-hitters on a single evening.

April 15* Beloit (Midwest League) southpaw Kelly Wunsch fans five Springfield Sultan batters in a single inning. Two batters reach first when third strikes get past the Beloit catcher.

May 14 St. Louis shortstop Ozzie Smith homers in back-to-back games, the first time this has happened in his 16-year major league career.

June 13 Ryne Sandberg of the Cubs, considered by many as one of the best second baseman in NL history, abruptly announces his retirement. He is hitting just .238.

June 22 Mets reliever John Franco earns his 253rd career save to break Dave Righetti's record for most saves by a lefthander.

June 24 Jeff Bagwell of the Astros becomes the 28th player to hit two home runs in one inning when he connects twice in the sixth inning against the Dodgers. Bagwell adds another homer in the eighth.

June 30 Giants center fielder Darren Lewis commits his first major league error to break his record of 392 flawless games in the outfield.

July 14 Cardinals shortstop Ozzie Smith breaks Luis Aparicio's record for assists by a shortstop with his 8,017th in an 8-1 loss to Colorado.

July 31 Matt Williams hits his 40th home run of the season to set a league record for most homers by the end of July. Williams reaches 40 homers sooner than any player since Reggie Jackson in 1969.

August 5 Fred McGriff becomes the seventh player to hit 30 or more home runs for seven consecutive seasons.

August 12 Major league players go on strike to produce the eighth work stoppage since 1972.

September 14 Major League Baseball cancels the World Series. It makes the first season without a World Series in 90 years.

ATLANTA		CHICAGO		CINCINNATI		COLORADO		FLORIDA		HOUSTON		LOS ANGELES	
M	B.Cox	M	T.Trebelhorn	M	D.Johnson	M	D.Baylor	M	R.Lachemann	M	T.Collins	M	T.Lasorda
1B	F.McGriff	1B	M.Grace	1B	H.Morris	1B	A.Galarraga	1B	G.Colbrunn	1B	J.Bagwell	1B	E.Karros
2B	M.Lemke	2B	R.Sandberg	2B	B.Boone	2B	N.Liriano	2B	B.Barberie	2B	C.Biggio	2B	D.DeShields
SS	J.Blauser	SS	S.Dunston	SS	B.Larkin	SS	W.Weiss	SS	K.Abbott	SS	A.Cedeno	SS	J.Offerman
3B	T.Pendleton	3B	S.Buechele	3B	T.Fernandez	3B	C.Hayes	3B	J.Browne	3B	K.Caminiti	3B	T.Wallach
LF	R.Klesko	LF	D.May	LF	K.Mitchell	LF	H.Johnson	LF	J.Conine	LF	L.Gonzalez	LF	H.Rodriguez
CF	R.Kelly	CF	G.Hill	CF	D.Sanders	CF	M.Kingery	CF	C.Carr	CF	S.Finley	CF	B.Butler
RF	D.Justice	RF	S.Sosa	RF	R.Sanders	RF	D.Bichette	RF	G.Sheffield	RF	J.Mouton	RF	R.Mondesi
C	J.Lopez	C	R.Wilkins	C	B.Dorsett	C	J.Girardi	C	B.Santiago	C	S.Servais	C	M.Piazza
O	T.Tarasco	O	K.Rhodes	P	J.Rijo	1	J.Vander Wal	O	M.Carrillo	O	K.Bass	O	C.Snyder
O	D.Gallagher	2S	R.Sanchez	P	J.Smiley	O	E.Young	31	D.Magadan			O	M.Webster
				P	E.Hanson					P	D.Drabek		
P	G.Maddux	P	S.Trachsel	P	J.Roper	P	G.Harris	P	D.Weathers	P	G.Swindell	P	R.Martinez
P	T.Glavine	P	W.Banks	P	P.Schourek	P	D.Nied	P	P.Rapp	P	D.Kile	P	K.Gross
P	S.Avery	P	A.Young	RP	J.Ruffin	P	M.Freeman	P	C.Hough	P	S.Reynolds	P	T.Candiotti
P	J.Smoltz	P	J.Bullinger	RP	J.Brantley	P	M.Harkey	P	M.Gardner	P	P.Harnisch	P	P.Astacio
P	K.Mercker	P	M.Morgan	RP	C.McElroy	P	K.Ritz	P	C.Hammond	P	T.Jones	P	O.Hershiser
RP	G.McMichael	RP	J.Bautista			RP	W.Blair	RP	R.Nen	RP	T.Edens	RP	T.Worrell
RP	M.Wohlers	RP	C.Crim	P	H.Carrasco	RP	S.Reed	RP	R.Lewis	RP	D.Veres	RP	R.McDowell
RP	M.Stanton	RP	D.Plesac			RP	B.Ruffin	RP	L.Aquino			RP	J.Gott
										P	B.Williams		
		P	K.Foster			P	L.Painter						
						/P	A.Reynoso						

MONTREAL		NEW YORK		PHILADELPHIA		PITTSBURGH		SAN DIEGO		SAN FRANCISCO		ST.LOUIS	
M	F.Alou	M	D.Green	M	J.Fregosi	M	J.Leyland	M	J.Riggleman	M	D.Baker	M	J.Torre
1B	C.Floyd	1B	D.Segui	1B	J.Kruk	1B	B.Hunter	1B	E.Williams	1B	T.Benzinger	1B	G.Jefferies
2B	M.Lansing	2B	J.Kent	2B	M.Morandini	2B	C.Garcia	2B	B.Roberts	2B	J.Patterson	2B	G.Pena
SS	W.Cordero	SS	J.Vizcaino	SS	K.Stocker	SS	J.Bell	SS	R.Gutierrez	SS	R.Clayton	SS	O.Smith
3B	S.Berry	3B	B.Bonilla	3B	D.Hollins	3B	J.King	3B	C.Shipley	3B	M.Williams	3B	T.Zeile
LF	M.Alou	LF	J.Cangelosi	LF	M.Thompson	LF	A.Martin	LF	P.Plantier	LF	B.Bonds	LF	B.Gilkey
CF	M.Grissom	CF	R.Thompson	CF	L.Dykstra	CF	A.Van Slyke	CF	D.Bell	CF	D.Lewis	CF	R.Lankford
RF	L.Walker	RF	J.Orsulak	RF	J.Eisenreich	RF	O.Merced	RF	T.Gwynn	RF	D.Martinez	RF	M.Whiten
C	D.Fletcher	C	T.Hundley	C	D.Daulton	C	D.Slaught	C	B.Ausmus	C	K.Manwaring	C	T.Pagnozzi
O	L.Frazier	23	F.Vina	23	M.Duncan	O	D.Clark	O1	B.Bean	P	J.Burkett	2	L.Alicea
				O	P.Incaviglia			S2	L.Lopez	P	M.Portugal		
P	K.Hill	P	B.Saberhagen	1	R.Jordan	P	Z.Smith			P	B.Swift	P	B.Tewksbury
P	P.Martinez	P	B.Jones	3S	K.Batiste	P	D.Neagle	P	A.Benes	P	B.Hickerson	P	V.Palacios
P	J.Fassero	P	P.Smith			P	S.Cooke	P	A.Ashby	P	Van Landingham	P	A.Watson
P	B.Henry	P	M.Gozzo	P	D.Jackson	P	P.Wagner	P	S.Sanders	RP	D.Burba	P	T.Urbani
P	K.Rueter	RP	R.Mason	P	B.Munoz	P	J.Lieber	P	J.Hamilton	RP	R.Beck	P	O.Olivares
RP	M.Rojas	RP	D.Linton	P	D.West	RP	R.White	RP	P.Martinez	RP	R.Monteleone	RP	R.Arocha
RP	G.Heredia	RP	J.Franco	P	S.Boskie	RP	M.Dewey	RP	T.Hoffman			RP	B.Eversgerd
RP	J.Shaw			P	C.Schilling	RP	R.Manzanillo	RP	T.Mauser	P	S.Torres	RP	R.Rodriguez
		P	M.Remlinger	RP	H.Slocumb					P	B.Black		
P	J.Wetteland	/P	J.Jacome	RP	D.Jones	P	W.Whitehurst					P	R.Sutcliffe
P	T.Scott												
		P	M.Williams										

TEAM	G	W	L	PCT	GB	R	OR	AB	H	2B	3B	HR	BB	SO	AVG	OBP	SLG	PRO	PRO+	BR	/A	PF	CHI	RC	SB	CS	SBA	SBR
EAST																												
MON	114	74	40	.649		585	454	4000	1111	246	30	108	379	669	.278	.346	.435	.781	107	47	42	101	99	615	**137**	36	**79**	**20**
ATL	114	68	46	.596	6	542	**448**	3861	1031	198	18	**137**	377	**668**	.267	.336	.434	.770	103	25	14	102	99	548	48	31	61	-4
NY	113	55	58	.487	18.5	506	526	3869	966	164	21	117	336	807	.250	.318	.394	.712	91	-57	-52	99	**109**	484	25	26	49	-8
PHI	115	54	61	.470	20.5	521	497	3927	1028	208	28	80	396	711	.262	.334	.390	.724	92	-31	-43	102	104	515	67	24	74	6
FLA	115	51	64	.443	23.5	468	576	3926	1043	180	24	94	349	746	.266	.332	.396	.728	92	-29	-43	103	94	519	65	26	71	4
CENTRAL																												
CIN	115	66	48	.579		**609**	490	3999	**1142**	211	36	124	388	738	**.286**	**.353**	**.449**	**.802**	115	**78**	85	99	98	**633**	119	51	70	5
HOU	115	66	49	.574	0.5	602	503	3955	1099	**252**	25	120	394	718	.278	.350	.445	.795	**118**	66	**98**	95	99	624	124	44	74	11
STL	115	53	61	.465	13	535	621	3902	1026	213	27	108	**434**	686	.263	.342	.414	.756	104	14	25	98	98	555	76	46	62	-5
PIT	114	53	61	.465	13	466	580	3864	1001	198	23	80	349	725	.259	.324	.384	.708	88	-57	-63	101	102	478	53	25	68	1
CHI	113	49	64	.434	16.5	500	549	3918	1015	189	26	109	364	750	.259	.326	.404	.730	96	-29	-22	99	101	507	69	53	57	-11
WEST																												
LA	114	58	56	.509		532	509	3904	1055	160	29	115	366	687	.270	.336	.414	.750	107	1	36	93	101	538	74	37	67	0
SF	115	55	60	.478	3.5	504	500	3869	963	159	32	123	364	719	.249	.320	.402	.722	97	-44	-21	95	105	504	114	40	74	10
COL	117	53	64	.453	6.5	573	638	4006	1098	206	**39**	125	378	761	.274	.340	.439	.779	92	40	-54	116	99	584	91	53	63	-5
SD	117	47	70	.402	12.5	479	531	4068	1117	200	19	92	319	762	.275	.332	.401	.733	99	-24	-8	97	93	526	79	37	68	2
TOT	803					7422		55068	14695	2784	377	1532	5193	10147	.267	.335	.415	.750							1141	529	68	25

TEAM	CG	SH	SV	IP	H	H/G	HR	BB	SO	RAT	ERA	ERA+	OAV	OOB	PR	/A	PF	CPI	FA	E	DP	FW	PW	BW	SBW	DIF
EAST																										
MON	4	**8**	**46**	1036^{2}	970	8.4	100	**288**	805	**11.3**	**3.56**	**119**	.247	**.305**	**75**	76	100	95	.979	94	90	-.5	7.5	4.1	**1.8**	4.1
ATL	**16**	**8**	26	1026^{1}	**929**	**8.1**	**76**	378	**865**	11.7	3.57	**119**	**.242**	.314	73	**77**	101	93	.982	81	85	.3	**7.6**	1.4	-.6	2.3
NY	7	3	35	1023	1069	9.4	117	332	640	12.5	4.13	101	.271	.331	9	4	99	103	.980	89	112	-.2	.4	-5.1	-1.0	4.4
PHI	7	6	30	1024^{1}	1028	9.0	98	377	699	12.6	3.85	111	.261	.330	41	50	102	103	.978	94	96	-.4	4.9	-4.2	.4	-4.2
FLA	5	7	30	1015	1069	9.5	120	428	649	13.6	4.50	97	.274	.352	-32	-15	104	104	.978	95	111	-.5	-1.5	-4.2	.2	-.5
CENTRAL																										
CIN	6	6	27	1038^{1}	1037	9.0	117	339	799	12.2	3.78	109	.262	.324	50	41	98	**106**	.983	73	91	.8	4.0	8.4	.3	-4.5
HOU	9	6	29	1029^{2}	1043	9.1	102	367	739	12.6	3.97	100	.265	.333	28	-2	94	104	.983	76	110	.6	-.2	**9.6**	.9	-2.5
STL	7	7	29	1018	1154	10.2	134	355	632	13.7	5.14	81	.289	.353	-105	-111	99	97	.982	80	119	.4	-10.9	2.5	-.7	4.7
PIT	8	2	24	1005^{2}	1094	9.8	117	370	650	13.5	4.64	93	.281	.350	-47	-36	103	102	.980	91	**131**	-.3	-3.5	-6.2	-.0	6.1
CHI	5	5	27	1023^{2}	1054	9.3	120	392	717	12.9	4.47	93	.268	.338	-29	-36	99	97	.982	81	110	.2	-3.5	-2.2	-1.3	-.8
WEST																										
LA	14	5	20	1014	1041	9.2	90	354	732	12.7	4.17	94	.267	.333	4	-28	93	97	.980	88	104	-.1	-2.8	3.5	-.2	.5
SF	2	4	33	1025^{1}	1014	8.9	122	372	655	12.5	3.99	100	.262	.333	26	2	95	**106**	**.985**	**68**	113	**1.1**	.2	-2.1	.8	-2.5
COL	4	5	28	1031	1185	10.3	120	448	703	14.7	5.15	96	.292	.369	-108	-21	118	101	.981	84	117	.2	-2.1	-5.3	-.7	2.3
SD	8	6	27	1045^{2}	1008	8.7	99	393	862	12.3	4.08	101	.252	.323	15	3	98	91	.975	111	82	-1.3	.3	-.8	.0	-9.7
TOT	102	78	411	14356^{2}		9.2				12.8	4.21		.267	.335					.980	1205	1471					

Runs
Bagwell-Hou 104
Grissom-Mon 96
Lankford-StL 89
Bonds-SF 89
Biggio-Hou 88

Hits
Gwynn-SD 165
Bichette-Col 147
Bagwell-Hou 147
Morris-Cin 146
Conine-Fla 144

Doubles
Walker-Mon 44
Biggio-Hou 44
Gwynn-SD 35
Bell-Pit 35
Bichette-Col 33

Triples
Lewis-SF 9
Butler-LA 9
R.Sanders-Cin 8
Mondesi-LA 8
Kingery-Col 8

Home Runs
Williams-SF 43
Bagwell-Hou 39
Bonds-SF 37
McGriff-Atl 34
Galarraga-Col 31

Total Bases
Bagwell-Hou 300
Williams-SF 270
Bichette-Col 265
McGriff-Atl 264
Bonds-SF 253

Runs Batted In
Bagwell-Hou 116
Williams-SF 96
Bichette-Col 95
McGriff-Atl 94
Piazza-LA 92

Runs Produced
Bagwell-Hou 181
Walker-Mon 143
Bichette-Col 142
McGriff-Atl 141
Biggio-Hou 138

Bases On Balls
Bonds-SF 74
Justice-Atl 69
Dykstra-Phi 68
Butler-LA 68
Bagwell-Hou 65

Batting Average
Gwynn-SD .... .394
Bagwell-Hou ...... .368
Alou-Mon .... .339
Morris-Cin .... .335
Mitchell-Cin ...... .326

On Base Percentage
Bagwell-Hou ...... .461
Gwynn-SD .... .458
Mitchell-Cin ...... .438
Bonds-SF .... .429
Justice-Atl .... .428

Slugging Average
Bagwell-Hou ...... .750
Mitchell-Cin ...... .681
Bonds-SF .... .647
McGriff-Atl ...... .623
Williams-SF ...... .607

Production
Bagwell-Hou 1.211
Mitchell-Cin 1.119
Bonds-SF 1.076
Gwynn-SD 1.026
McGriff-Atl 1.014

Adjusted Production
Bagwell-Hou 220
Mitchell-Cin 188
Bonds-SF 184
Gwynn-SD 171
McGriff-Atl 156

Batter Runs
Bagwell-Hou 64.7
Bonds-SF 44.9
Gwynn-SD 42.2
Mitchell-Cin 40.3
McGriff-Atl 35.6

Adjusted Batter Runs
Bagwell-Hou 71.2
Bonds-SF 49.9
Gwynn-SD 45.2
Mitchell-Cin 41.3
McGriff-Atl 33.7

Clutch Hitting Index
Gonzalez-Hou 132
Blauser-Atl 121
Piazza-LA 120
Morris-Cin 116
Sheffield-Fla 116

Runs Created
Bagwell-Hou 137
Bonds-SF 115
Gwynn-SD 104
McGriff-Atl 103
Biggio-Hou 98

Total Average
Bagwell-Hou 1.413
Bonds-SF 1.256
Mitchell-Cin 1.244
Gwynn-SD 1.069
McGriff-Atl 1.063

Stolen Bases
Biggio-Hou 39
D.Sanders-Atl-Cin .. 38
Grissom-Mon 36
Carr-Fla 32
Lewis-SF 30

Stolen Base Average
Larkin-Cin 92.9
Biggio-Hou 90.7
Clayton-SF 88.5
Grissom-Mon 85.7
Cordero-Mon 84.2

Stolen Base Runs
Biggio-Hou 9.3
Grissom-Mon 7.2
Larkin-Cin 6.6
Clayton-SF 5.1
Carr-Fla 4.8

Fielding Runs
Sanchez-Chi 28.5
Bell-Pit 19.3
Bagwell-Hou 17.1
Grissom-Mon 16.3
Karros-LA 16.0

Total Player Rating
Bagwell-Hou 7.6
Bonds-SF 5.6
Gwynn-SD 4.5
Mitchell-Cin 4.2
Biggio-Hou 3.6

Wins
Maddux-Atl 16
Hill-Mon 16
Saberhagen-NY 14
Jackson-Phi 14
Glavine-Atl 13

Win Percentage
Saberhagen-NY ... .778
Hill-Mon .... .762
Maddux-Atl ...... .727
Jackson-Phi ...... .700
Martinez-Mon .... .688

Games
Reed-Col 61
Rojas-Mon 58
Bautista-Chi 58
Munoz-Col 57
Burba-SF 57

Complete Games
Maddux-Atl 10
Drabek-Hou 6
Candiotti-LA 5

Shutouts
Martinez-LA 3
Maddux-Atl 3
Drabek-Hou 2
Benes-SD 2

Saves
Franco-NY 30
Beck-SF 28
Jones-Phi 27
Wetteland-Mon 25

Innings Pitched
Maddux-Atl 202.0
Jackson-Phi 179.1
Saberhagen-NY .. 177.1
Rijo-Cin 172.1
Benes-SD 172.1

Fewest Hits/Game
Maddux-Atl 6.68
Martinez-Mon 7.15
Drabek-Hou 7.21
Avery-Atl 7.54
Fassero-Mon 7.72

Fewest BB/Game
Saberhagen-NY ..... .66
Tewksbury-StL 1.27
Maddux-Atl 1.38
Reynolds-Hou 1.52
Swindell-Hou 1.58

Strikeouts
Benes-SD 189
Rijo-Cin 171
Maddux-Atl 156
Saberhagen-NY ... 143
Martinez-Mon 142

Strikeouts/Game
Benes-SD 9.87
Rijo-Cin 8.93
Martinez-Mon 8.83
Neagle-Pit 8.01
Reynolds-Hou 7.98

Ratio
Maddux-Atl 8.33
Saberhagen-NY ... 9.44
Drabek-Hou 9.78
Fassero-Mon 10.38
Ashby-SD 10.46

Earned Run Average
Maddux-Atl 1.56
Saberhagen-NY ... 2.74
Drabek-Hou 2.84
Fassero-Mon 2.99
Reynolds-Hou 3.05

Adjusted ERA
Maddux-Atl 272
Saberhagen-NY ... 152
Fassero-Mon 141
Drabek-Hou 139
Rijo-Cin 134

Opponents' Batting Avg.
Maddux-Atl ...... .207
Martinez-Mon .... .220
Drabek-Hou ...... .220
Avery-Atl .... .227
Fassero-Mon ..... .229

Opponents' On Base Pct.
Maddux-Atl ...... .245
Saberhagen-NY ... .273
Drabek-Hou ...... .277
Fassero-Mon ..... .286
Ashby-SD .... .286

Starter Runs
Maddux-Atl 59.5
Saberhagen-NY .. 29.0
Drabek-Hou 25.0
Rijo-Cin 21.6
Henry-Mon 21.2

Adjusted Starter Runs
Maddux-Atl 60.2
Saberhagen-NY ... 28.2
Freeman-Col 27.2
Henry-Mon 21.3
Jackson-Phi 20.4

Clutch Pitching Index
Rijo-Cin 125
Rapp-Fla 121
Smith-Pit 118
Burkett-SF 118
Trachsel-Chi 116

Relief Runs
Jackson-SF 12.8
Brantley-Cin 12.6
Carrasco-Cin 12.4
Jones-Phi 12.3
Jones-Hou 12.0

Adjusted Relief Runs
Jones-Phi 12.7
Brantley-Cin 12.0
Carrasco-Cin 11.9
Jackson-SF 11.8
McElroy-Cin 11.5

Relief Ranking
Brantley-Cin 24.6
Jones-Phi 23.9
Carrasco-Cin 23.1
Wetteland-Mon 20.7
Nen-Fla 18.3

Total Pitcher Index
Maddux-Atl 7.3
Saberhagen-NY 3.1
Freeman-Col 2.8
Drabek-Hou 2.7
Brantley-Cin 2.5

Total Baseball Ranking
Bagwell-Hou 7.6
Maddux-Atl 7.3
Bonds-SF 5.6
Gwynn-SD 4.5
Mitchell-Cin 4.2

March 27* The all-women Colorado Silver Bullets drop their first exhibition game 10-2 to the Chet Lemon All-Stars. Bullets pitcher Lisa Martinez fans Lemon, a 16-year major league veteran.

April 9* Basketball legend Michael Jordan makes his professional baseball debut with an 0-for-3 day for Birmingham. Chattanooga beats the White Sox minor league team 10-3.

April 21 Indians first baseman Eddie Murray hits home runs from both sides of the plate in a game for the 11th time in his career to break Mickey Mantle's record.

April 27 Twins righthander Scott Erickson no-hits the Brewers 6-0 for Minnesota's first no-hitter since 1967.

April 30 Blue Jays outfielder Joe Carter finishes April with 31 RBIs to set a major league record for the month. Colorado's Andres Galarraga sets the NL mark with 30.

May 14 Gary Gaetti participates in his seventh career triple play. He starts the play when he spears Geronimo Berroa's grounder, steps on third and goes around the horn to end an Oakland rally.

June 8 Gene Budig, chancellor of University of Kansas, replaces Dr. Bobby Brown as AL president.

June 13 Don Mattingly of the Yankees plays in his 1,469th game at first base to move past Wally Pipp into second place in Yankee history. Only Hall of Famer Lou Gehrig played in more (2,137).

June 19 The Tigers tie a major league record by hitting a home run in their 25th consecutive game when Mickey Tettleton goes deep against the Blue Jays.

June 22 Seattle's Ken Griffey Jr. breaks Babe Ruth's record for most home runs hit by the end of June when he connects for his 31st in a 12-3 win over the Angels.

July 1 The Orioles and the California Angels combine to hit 11 home runs to tie a major league record in Baltimore's 14-7 victory at Camden Yards.

July 9 Red Sox shortstop John Valentin records the 10th unassisted triple play in major league history.

July 18 Blue Jays outfielder Joe Carter reaches the 20-home run mark for the ninth consecutive year.

July 27 Tigers manager Sparky Anderson moves into fourth place on the all-time list for managerial wins with his 2,126th in a 3-1 win over the Mariners. Anderson passes Joe McCarthy with the win.

July 28 Kenny Rogers of the Rangers throws the 14th perfect game in major league history—and the first by a left-hander in AL history—with a 4-0 win over the Angels.

August 1 Oriole shortstop Cal Ripken Jr. plays in his 2,000th consecutive game.

August 11 In what would be the last game of the 1994 season, Ken Griffey hits a grand slam—his 40th home run in 111 games—in an 8-1 win over Oakland.

	BALTIMORE		BOSTON		CALIFORNIA		CHICAGO		CLEVELAND		DETROIT		KANSAS CITY
M	J.Oates	M	B.Hobson	M	B.Rodgers	M	G.Lamont	M	M.Hargrove	M	S.Anderson	M	H.McRae
1B	R.Palmeiro	1B	M.Vaughn	M	B.Knoop	1B	F.Thomas	1B	P.Sorrento	1B	C.Fielder	1B	W.Joyner
2B	M.McLemore	2B	S.Fletcher	M	M.Lachemann	2B	J.Cora	2B	C.Baerga	2B	L.Whitaker	2B	J.Lind
SS	C.Ripken	SS	J.Valentin	1B	J.Snow	SS	O.Guillen	SS	O.Vizquel	SS	A.Trammell	SS	G.Gagne
3B	L.Gomez	3B	S.Cooper	2B	H.Reynolds	3B	R.Ventura	3B	J.Thome	3B	T.Fryman	3B	G.Gaetti
LF	B.Anderson	LF	M.Greenwell	SS	G.DiSarcina	LF	T.Raines	LF	A.Belle	LF	T.Phillips	LF	V.Coleman
CF	M.Devereaux	CF	O.Nixon	3B	S.Owen	CF	L.Johnson	CF	K.Lofton	CF	M.Cuyler	CF	B.McRae
RF	J.Hammonds	RF	T.Brunansky	LF	J.Edmonds	RF	D.Jackson	RF	M.Ramirez	RF	J.Felix	RF	F.Jose
C	C.Hoiles	C	D.Berryhill	CF	C.Curtis	C	R.Karkovice	C	S.Alomar	C	C.Kreuter	C	M.Macfarlane
DH	H.Baines	DH	A.Dawson	RF	T.Salmon	DH	J.Franco	DH	E.Murray	DH	K.Gibson	DH	B.Hamelin
				C	C.Turner								
3O	C.Sabo	23	T.Naehring	DH	C.Davis	P	J.McDowell	3S	A.Espinoza	S2	C.Gomez	P	D.Cone
						P	A.Fernandez	O	W.Kirby	C1	M.Tettleton	P	T.Gordon
P	M.Mussina	P	R.Clemens	32	D.Easley	P	W.Alvarez					P	K.Appier
P	B.McDonald	P	A.Sele	O	B.Jackson	P	J.Bere	P	D.Martinez	P	T.Belcher	P	M.Gubicza
P	J.Moyer	P	J.Hesketh			P	S.Sanderson	P	C.Nagy	P	M.Moore	RP	H.Pichardo
P	S.Fernandez	P	D.Darwin	P	C.Finley	RP	J.DeLeon	P	J.Morris	P	B.Gullickson	RP	R.Meacham
RP	M.Eichhorn	RP	K.Ryan	P	M.Langston	RP	K.McCaskill	P	M.Clark	P	D.Wells	RP	S.Belinda
RP	M.Williamson	RP	G.Harris	P	P.Leftwich	RP	R.Hernandez	P	J.Grimsley	P	J.Doherty		
RP	A.Mills	RP	C.Howard	P	B.Anderson			RP	J.Mesa	RP	J.Boever	P	B.Milacki
				P	J.Magrane			RP	E.Plunk	RP	M.Gardiner		
P	M.Oquist			RP	M.Leiter					RP	S.Davis		
P	A.Rhodes			RP	J.Dopson								
				RP	R.Springer								

	MILWAUKEE		MINNESOTA		NEW YORK		OAKLAND		SEATTLE		TEXAS		TORONTO
M	P.Garner	M	T.Kelly	M	B.Showalter	M	T.LaRussa	M	L.Piniella	M	K.Kennedy	M	C.Gaston
1B	J.Jaha	1B	K.Hrbek	1B	D.Mattingly	1B	T.Neel	1B	T.Martinez	1B	W.Clark	1B	J.Olerud
2B	J.Reed	2B	C.Knoblauch	2B	P.Kelly	2B	B.Gates	2B	R.Amaral	2B	J.Frye	2B	R.Alomar
SS	J.Valentin	SS	P.Meares	SS	M.Gallego	SS	M.Bordick	SS	F.Fermin	SS	M.Lee	SS	D.Schofield
3B	K.Seitzer	3B	S.Leius	3B	W.Boggs	3B	S.Brosius	3B	E.Martinez	3B	D.Palmer	3B	E.Sprague
LF	G.Vaughn	LF	S.Mack	LF	L.Polonia	LF	R.Henderson	LF	E.Anthony	LF	J.Gonzalez	LF	M.Huff
CF	T.Ward	CF	A.Cole	CF	B.Williams	CF	S.Javier	CF	K.Griffey	CF	D.Hulse	CF	D.White
RF	M.Mieske	RF	K.Puckett	RF	P.O'Neill	RF	R.Sierra	RF	J.Buhner	RF	R.Greer	RF	J.Carter
C	D.Nilsson	C	M.Walbeck	C	M.Stanley	C	T.Steinbach	C	D.Wilson	C	I.Rodriguez	C	P.Borders
DH	B.Harper	DH	D.Winfield	DH	D.Tartabull	DH	G.Berroa	DH	R.Jefferson	DH	J.Canseco	DH	P.Molitor
O	A.Diaz	OD	P.Munoz	CD	J.Leyritz	O1	M.Aldrete	31	M.Blowers	23	D.Strange	P	P.Hentgen
3S	B.Spiers	S2	J.Reboulet	S3	R.Velarde	C2	S.Hemond	2S	L.Sojo			P	J.Guzman
										P	K.Brown	P	T.Stottlemyre
P	C.Eldred	P	K.Tapani	P	J.Key	P	R.Darling	P	R.Johnson	P	K.Rogers	P	D.Stewart
P	R.Bones	P	S.Erickson	P	J.Abbott	P	B.Witt	P	C.Bosio	P	H.Fajardo	P	A.Leiter
P	B.Wegman	P	J.Deshaies	P	M.Perez	P	T.Van Poppel	P	D.Fleming	RP	M.Whiteside	RP	T.Castillo
P	B.Scanlan	P	P.Mahomes	P	T.Mulholland	P	S.Ontiveros	P	G.Hibbard	RP	C.Carpenter	RP	W.Williams
P	J.Navarro	P	C.Pulido	P	S.Kamieniecki	RP	C.Reyes	RP	B.Ayala	RP	D.Oliver	RP	M.Timlin
RP	M.Ignasiak	RP	C.Willis	RP	B.Wickman	RP	B.Welch	RP	B.Risley				
RP	G.Lloyd	RP	M.Guthrie	RP	S.Hitchcock	RP	J.Briscoe	RP	T.Davis	P	J.Dettmer		
RP	M.Fetters	RP	M.Trombley	RP	S.Howe					/P	R.Helling		
								P	J.Cummings	P	R.Pavlik		
P	T.Higuera							P	R.Salkeld				

TEAM	G	W	L	PCT	GB	R	OR	AB	H	2B	3B	HR	BB	SO	AVG	OBP	SLG	PRO	PRO+	BR	/A	PF	CHI	RC	SB	CS	SBA	SBR
EAST																												
NY	113	70	43	.619		670	534	3986	1155	238	16	139	530	660	.290	.377	.462	.839	120	97	124	96	94	692	55	40	58	-8
BAL	112	63	49	.563	6.5	589	497	3856	1047	185	20	139	438	655	.272	.352	.438	.790	97	13	-17	105	99	606	69	13	84	13
TOR	115	55	60	.478	16	566	579	3962	1064	210	30	115	387	691	.269	.339	.424	.763	95	-30	-32	100	100	570	79	26	75	8
BOS	115	54	61	.470	17	552	621	3940	1038	222	19	120	404	723	.263	.337	.421	.758	90	-39	-65	105	100	558	81	38	68	2
DET	115	53	62	.461	18	652	671	3955	1048	216	25	161	520	897	.265	.355	.454	.809	107	42	39	100	100	646	46	33	58	-6
CENTRAL																												
CHI	113	67	46	.593		633	498	3942	1133	175	39	121	497	568	.287	.370	.444	.814	111	58	71	98	95	660	77	27	74	7
CLE	113	66	47	.584	1	679	562	4022	1165	240	16	167	382	629	.290	.354	.484	.838	113	73	72	100	101	686	131	48	73	11
KC	115	64	51	.557	4	574	532	3911	1051	211	38	100	376	698	.269	.338	.419	.757	90	-38	-60	104	105	558	140	62	69	5
MIN	113	53	60	.469	14	594	688	3952	1092	239	23	103	359	635	.276	.343	.427	.770	97	-20	-20	100	105	578	94	30	76	10
MIL	115	53	62	.461	15	547	586	3978	1045	238	21	99	417	680	.263	.338	.408	.746	87	-53	-78	105	100	549	59	37	61	-5
WEST																												
TEX	114	52	62	.456		613	697	3983	1114	198	27	124	437	730	.280	.356	.436	.792	103	20	22	100	98	622	82	35	70	4
OAK	114	51	63	.447	1	549	589	3885	1009	178	13	113	417	686	.260	.334	.399	.733	96	-68	-25	92	106	527	91	39	70	4
SEA	112	49	63	.438	2	569	616	3883	1045	211	18	153	372	652	.269	.337	.451	.788	99	-1	-12	102	98	585	48	21	70	2
CAL	115	47	68	.409	5.5	543	660	3943	1042	178	16	120	402	715	.264	.336	.409	.745	90	-54	-62	101	101	536	65	54	55	-13
TOT	797					8330		55198	15048	2939	325	1774	5938	9619	.273	.348	.434	.782							1117	503	69	33

TEAM	CG	SH	SV	IP	H	H/G	HR	BB	SO	RAT	ERA	ERA+	OAV	OOB	PR	/A	PF	CPI	FA	E	DP	FW	PW	BW	SBW	DIF
EAST																										
NY	8	2	31	1019²	1045	9.2	120	398	656	12.9	4.34	105	.267	.337	52	26	95	103	.982	80	122	.1	2.4	11.5	-1.0	.4
BAL	13	4	37	997²	1005	9.1	131	351	666	12.5	4.31	116	.263	.330	54	77	104	102	.986	57	103	1.5	7.1	-1.6	1.0	-1.0
TOR	13	4	26	1025	1053	9.2	127	482	832	13.8	4.70	103	.266	.351	12	14	100	102	.981	81	105	.2	1.3	-3.0	.5	-1.5
BOS	6	3	30	1029¹	1104	9.7	120	450	729	13.9	4.93	102	.276	.354	-15	11	105	99	.981	81	124	.2	1.0	-6.0	-.0	1.3
DET	15	1	20	1018	1139	10.1	148	449	560	14.3	5.38	90	.282	.358	-66	-61	101	98	.981	82	90	.1	-5.6	3.6	-.8	-1.8
CENTRAL																										
CHI	13	9	20	1011¹	964	8.6	115	377	754	12.1	3.96	118	.250	.320	94	79	97	100	.981	79	91	.2	7.3	6.6	.4	-4.0
CLE	17	5	21	1018²	1097	9.7	94	404	666	13.6	4.36	108	.275	.348	49	40	98	105	.980	80	119	-.4	3.7	6.7	.8	-1.2
KC	5	6	38	1031²	1018	8.9	95	392	717	12.6	4.23	118	.260	.332	65	88	104	97	.982	80	102	.2	8.1	-5.5	.2	3.4
MIN	6	4	29	1005	1197	10.7	153	388	602	14.5	5.68	86	.299	.365	-98	-91	101	100	.982	75	99	.4	-8.4	-1.8	.7	5.6
MIL	11	3	23	1036	1071	9.3	127	421	577	13.2	4.62	109	.269	.343	20	47	105	101	.981	85	130	-.0	4.3	-7.2	-.7	-.9
WEST																										
TEX	10	4	26	1023	1176	10.3	157	394	683	14.1	5.45	88	.288	.355	-75	-72	100	98	.976	106	106	-1.4	-6.7	2.0	.1	.8
OAK	12	9	23	1003¹	979	8.8	128	510	732	13.7	4.80	92	.257	.350	0	-42	92	98	.979	88	105	-.3	-3.9	-2.3	.1	.3
SEA	13	7	21	984	1051	9.6	109	416	763	14.3	4.99	90	.274	.360	-21	-12	102	99	.977	95	102	-.8	-1.1	-1.1	-.0	-4.0
CAL	11	4	21	1027	1149	10.1	150	436	682	14.3	5.42	90	.287	.363	-70	-61	102	100	.983	76	110	.5	-5.6	-5.7	-1.4	1.8
TOT	153	65	366	14229²		9.5				13.5	4.80		.273	.348					.981	1155	1508					

Runs
Thomas-Chi 106
Lofton-Cle 105
Griffey-Sea 94
Phillips-Det 91
Belle-Cle 90

Hits
Lofton-Cle 160
Molitor-Tor 155
Belle-Cle 147
Thomas-Chi 141

Doubles
Knoblauch-Min 45
Belle-Cle 35
Thomas-Chi 34
Fryman-Det 34

Triples
L.Johnson-Chi 14
Coleman-KC 12
Lofton-Cle 9
Diaz-Mil 7

Home Runs
Griffey-Sea 40
Thomas-Chi 38
Belle-Cle 36
Canseco-Tex 31
Fielder-Det 28

Total Bases
Belle-Cle 294
Griffey-Sea 292
Thomas-Chi 291
Lofton-Cle 246
Palmeiro-Bal 240

Runs Batted In
Puckett-Min 112
Carter-Tor 103
Thomas-Chi 101
Belle-Cle 101
Franco-Chi 98

Runs Produced
Puckett-Min 171
Thomas-Chi 169
Belle-Cle 155
Lofton-Cle 150
Franco-Chi 150

Bases On Balls
Thomas-Chi 109
Tettleton-Det 97
Phillips-Det 95
O'Neill-NY 72
Henderson-Oak 72

Batting Average
O'Neill-NY .359
Belle-Cle .357
Thomas-Chi .353
Lofton-Cle .349
Boggs-NY .342

On Base Percentage
Thomas-Chi .494
O'Neill-NY .464
Belle-Cle .442
Boggs-NY .437
Clark-Tex .436

Slugging Average
Thomas-Chi .729
Belle-Cle .714
Griffey-Sea .674
O'Neill-NY .603
Hamelin-KC .599

Production
Thomas-Chi 1.223
Belle-Cle 1.156
Griffey-Sea 1.078
O'Neill-NY 1.067
Hamelin-KC .992

Adjusted Production
Thomas-Chi 214
Belle-Cle 191
O'Neill-NY 179
Griffey-Sea 168
Davis-Cal 147

Batter Runs
Thomas-Chi 71.3
Belle-Cle 56.3
Griffey-Sea 44.7
O'Neill-NY 42.8
Vaughn-Bos 30.7

Adjusted Batter Runs
Thomas-Chi 74.0
Belle-Cle 56.0
O'Neill-NY 46.8
Griffey-Sea 42.6
Lofton-Cle 30.5

Clutch Hitting Index
Puckett-Min 143
Clark-Tex 122
Sorrento-Cle 120
Franco-Chi 120
Fryman-Det 118

Runs Created
Thomas-Chi 145
Belle-Cle 131
Griffey-Sea 117
Lofton-Cle 111
Molitor-Tor 101

Total Average
Thomas-Chi 1.453
Belle-Cle 1.304
Griffey-Sea 1.174
O'Neill-NY 1.152
Lofton-Cle 1.101

Stolen Bases
Lofton-Cle 60
Coleman-KC 50
Nixon-Bos 42
Knoblauch-Min 35
Anderson-Bal 31

Stolen Base Average
Molitor-Tor 100.0
Anderson-Bal 96.9
Hulse-Tex 90.0
Coleman-KC 86.2
Shumpert-KC 85.7

Stolen Base Runs
Lofton-Cle 10.8
Coleman-KC 10.2
Anderson-Bal 8.7
Knoblauch-Min 6.9
Nixon-Bos 6.6

Fielding Runs
Valentin-Mil 28.1
Espinoza-Cle 24.4
Gallego-NY 19.6
Fielder-Det 15.7
Curtis-Cal 14.6

Total Player Rating
Belle-Cle 5.0
Thomas-Chi 5.0
Griffey-Sea 4.2
Lofton-Cle 4.2
O'Neill-NY 4.1

Wins
Key-NY 17
Mussina-Bal 16
Cone-KC 16
McDonald-Bal 14

Win Percentage
Bere-Chi .857
Key-NY .810
Clark-Cle .786
Mussina-Bal .762
Cone-KC .762

Games
Wickman-NY 53
Mesa-Cle 51
Guthrie-Min 50
Brewer-KC 50
Willis-Min 49

Complete Games
Johnson-Sea 9
Martinez-Cle 7
Finley-Cal 7

Shutouts
Johnson-Sea 4

Saves
L.Smith-Bal 33
Montgomery-KC 27
Aguilera-Min 23
Eckersley-Oak 19
Ayala-Sea 18

Innings Pitched
Finley-Cal 183.1
McDowell-Chi 181.0
Eldred-Mil 179.0
Martinez-Cle 176.2
Mussina-Bal 176.1

Fewest Hits/Game
Clemens-Bos 6.54
Cone-KC 6.82
Johnson-Sea 6.91
Ontiveros-Oak 7.26
Bere-Chi 7.56

Fewest BB/Game
Gubicza-KC 1.80
Gullickson-Det 1.95
Wegman-Mil 2.02
Ontiveros-Oak 2.03
McDowell-Chi 2.09

Strikeouts
Johnson-Sea 204
Clemens-Bos 168
Finley-Cal 148
Hentgen-Tor 147
Appier-KC 145

Strikeouts/Game
Johnson-Sea 10.67
Clemens-Bos 8.86
Appier-KC 8.42
Langston-Cal 8.22
Bere-Chi 8.07

Ratio
Ontiveros-Oak 9.75
Cone-KC 10.01
Clemens-Bos 10.49
Mussina-Bal 10.51
Johnson-Sea 10.99

Earned Run Average
Ontiveros-Oak 2.65
Clemens-Bos 2.85
Cone-KC 2.94
Mussina-Bal 3.06
Johnson-Sea 3.19

Adjusted ERA
Clemens-Bos 177
Cone-KC 170
Ontiveros-Oak 167
Mussina-Bal 163
Johnson-Sea 153

Opponents' Batting Avg.
Clemens-Bos .203
Cone-KC .209
Johnson-Sea .216
Ontiveros-Oak .217
Bere-Chi .229

Opponents' On Base Pct.
Ontiveros-Oak .272
Cone-KC .279
Clemens-Bos .291
Mussina-Bal .294
Martinez-Cle .301

Starter Runs
Clemens-Bos 37.0
Cone-KC 35.5
Mussina-Bal 34.0
Johnson-Sea 30.7
Key-NY 28.6

Adjusted Starter Runs
Clemens-Bos 41.4
Cone-KC 39.4
Mussina-Bal 38.1
Johnson-Sea 32.4
Bones-Mil 30.4

Clutch Pitching Index
Kamieniecki-NY 124
Key-NY 122
Clark-Cle 117
Mahomes-Min 115
Stottlemyre-Tor 114

Relief Runs
Eichhorn-Bal 20.9
Plunk-Cle 17.9
Castillo-Tor 17.3
Howe-NY 13.3
Wickman-NY 13.3

Adjusted Relief Runs
Eichhorn-Bal 22.5
Castillo-Tor 17.4
Plunk-Cle 17.2
Ryan-Bos 13.8
Ayala-Sea 12.8

Relief Ranking
Eichhorn-Bal 32.0
Ayala-Sea 21.9
Risley-Sea 21.7
Fetters-Mil 21.6
Plunk-Cle 21.1

Total Pitcher Index
Cone-KC 4.4
Mussina-Bal 3.9
Johnson-Sea 3.3
Eichhorn-Bal 3.2
Key-NY 3.2

Total Baseball Ranking
Belle-Cle 5.0
Thomas-Chi 5.0
Cone-KC 4.4
Griffey-Sea 4.2
Lofton-Cle 4.2

January 8 Mike Schmidt, who hit 548 home runs and won two MVP Awards in 18 years with the Phillies, is elected to the Baseball Hall of Fame.

March 7 The Veterans Committee makes four selections for the Hall of Fame: Phillies great Richie Ashburn; William Hulbert, the NL's first president; Vic Willis, an eight-time 20-game winner in a 13-year major league career starting in 1898; and Negro League pitcher Leon Day.

March 31 The longest strike in sports history ends—in a courtroom. A U.S. District court order forbids owners from implementing new financial working conditions in the wake of the negotiations impasse. The court decides that conditions will revert to the old rules from the previous season. Because of the timing of the court order, 18 games will have to be trimmed from the major league schedule.

July 11 The NL is held without a hit by Randy Johnson, Kevin Appier, and Dennis Martinez for an All-Star record 5⅔ innings, but rallies for single runs in the sixth, seventh and eighth innings to pull out a 3-2 win at the Ballpark at Arlington. Jeff Conine homers against Steve Ontiveros in his only at bat for the game-winner to earn MVP honors.

August 18 Cardinals reliever Tom Henke earns his 300th career save in a 4-3 win over the Braves.

September 19 Andres Galarraga homers in a 15-4 loss to the Padres, but the home run makes the Rockies the second team to have four players hit 30 or more homers (the 1977 Dodgers were the other). Galarraga joins Dante Bichette, Larry Walker, and Vinny Castilla with 30 home runs for Colorado.

September 19 Padres third baseman Ken Caminiti drives in eight runs and homers from both sides of the plate for the third time in four games. Caminiti is the first player to perform this trick so many times in four days or fewer.

September 21 Rockies pinch hitter John Vander Wal sets a major league record with his 26th pinch-hit of the season. The record-setting hit is a home run in a 5-3 loss to the Giants.

October 1 The Rockies are the first team to make the postseason before their eighth year in existence and are the NL's first Wild Card winner following a 10-9 win over the Giants. The Rockies' .535 percentage (77-67 record) is the best ever for a third-year team.

October 6 The Reds hit three home runs and cruise to a 10-1 win over the Dodgers for a sweep of the Division Series.

October 7 The Braves wrap up the Division Series with a 10-4 win over the Rockies. Marquis Grissom bats .524 for Atlanta in the four-game win.

October 14 Mike Devereaux hits a three-run home run to seal Atlanta's 6-0 win for a four-game sweep of the Reds in the NLCS. Devereaux, who also had the game-winning single in the 11th inning of Game 1, earns MVP honors for the Braves.

October 28 David Justice hears the boos from the home crowd after he questions Atlanta fans' loyalty—and he turns them to cheers with a sixth inning home run in Game 6 against Cleveland. World Series MVP Tom Glavine receives most of the cheers, however, with a one-hitter over eight innings. Mark Wohlers makes Justice's home run stand up in the ninth as the Braves win 1-0 for the first championship in Atlanta history.

	ATLANTA		CHICAGO		CINCINNATI		COLORADO		FLORIDA		HOUSTON		LOS ANGELES
M	B.Cox	M	J.Riggleman	M	D.Johnson	M	D.Baylor	M	R.Lachemann	M	T.Collins	M	T.Lasorda
1B	F.McGriff	1B	M.Grace	1B	H.Morris	1B	A.Galarraga	1B	G.Colbrunn	1B	J.Bagwell	1B	E.Karros
2B	M.Lemke	2B	R.Sanchez	2B	B.Boone	2B	J.Bates	2B	Q.Veras	2B	C.Biggio	2B	D.DeShields
SS	J.Blauser	SS	S.Dunston	SS	B.Larkin	SS	W.Weiss	SS	K.Abbott	SS	O.Miller	SS	J.Offerman
3B	C.Jones	3B	T.Zeile	3B	J.Branson	3B	V.Castilla	3B	T.Pendleton	3B	D.Magadan	3B	T.Wallach
LF	R.Klesko	LF	L.Gonzalez	LF	R.Gant	LF	D.Bichette	LF	J.Conine	LF	J.Mouton	LF	B.Ashley
CF	M.Grissom	CF	B.McRae	CF	J.Walton	CF	M.Kingery	CF	C.Carr	CF	B.Hunter	CF	R.Kelly
RF	D.Justice	RF	S.Sosa	RF	R.Sanders	RF	L.Walker	RF	G.Sheffield	RF	D.Bell	RF	R.Mondesi
C	J.Lopez	C	S.Servais	C	B.Santiago	C	J.Girardi	C	C.Johnson	C	T.Eusebio	C	M.Piazza
O	M.Kelly	O	S.Bullett	31	L.Harris	O	E.Burks	S3	A.Arias	O	J.Cangelosi	S2	C.Fonville
O	D.Smith	S2	J.Hernandez	O	T.Howard	1O	J.Vander Wal	O	A.Dawson	3S	C.Shipley	3	D.Hansen
				C	E.Taubensee	2O	E.Young			O	M.Thompson		
P	G.Maddux	P	J.Navarro					P	J.Burkett	O	L.Gonzalez	P	R.Martinez
P	T.Glavine	P	F.Castillo	P	P.Schourek	P	K.Ritz	P	P.Rapp	O	D.May	P	I.Valdes
P	J.Smoltz	P	K.Foster	P	J.Smiley	P	B.Swift	P	C.Hammond			P	H.Nomo
P	S.Avery	P	S.Trachsel	P	T.Pugh	P	M.Freeman	P	B.Witt	P	S.Reynolds	P	T.Candiotti
P	K.Mercker	P	J.Bullinger	RP	X.Hernandez	P	A.Reynoso	P	D.Weathers	P	D.Drabek	RP	P.Astacio
RP	G.McMichael	RP	M.Perez	RP	H.Carrasco	RP	C.Leskanic	RP	M.Gardner	P	G.Swindell	RP	T.Worrell
RP	B.Clontz	RP	T.Wendell	RP	J.Brantley	RP	S.Reed	RP	T.Mathews	P	M.Hampton	RP	A.Osuna
RP	M.Wohlers	RP	R.Myers			RP	R.Bailey	RP	R.Nen	P	D.Kile		
				P	K.Jarvis					RP	D.Veres	P	K.Tapani
				P	M.Portugal	P	B.Rekar	/P	W.Banks	RP	T.Jones		
				P	D.Wells	P	D.Holmes			RP	D.Brocail		
				P	J.Rijo	P	J.Acevedo						
				P	D.Burba	P	J.Grahe			P	J.Dougherty		
						P	M.Thompson						

	MONTREAL		NEW YORK		PHILADELPHIA		PITTSBURGH		SAN DIEGO		SAN FRANCISCO		ST.LOUIS
M	F.Alou	M	D.Green	M	J.Fregosi	M	J.Leyland	M	B.Bochy	M	D.Baker	M	J.Torre
1B	D.Segui	1B	R.Brogna	1B	D.Hollins	1B	M.Johnson	1B	E.Williams	1B	M.Carreon	M	M.Jorgensen
2B	M.Lansing	2B	J.Kent	2B	M.Morandini	2B	C.Garcia	2B	J.Reed	2B	R.Thompson	1B	J.Mabry
SS	W.Cordero	SS	J.Vizcaino	SS	K.Stocker	SS	J.Bell	SS	A.Cedeno	SS	R.Clayton	2B	J.Oquendo
3B	S.Berry	3B	E.Alfonzo	3B	C.Hayes	3B	J.King	3B	K.Caminiti	3B	M.Williams	SS	T.Cromer
LF	M.Alou	LF	J.Orsulak	LF	J.Eisenreich	LF	A.Martin	LF	M.Nieves	LF	B.Bonds	3B	S.Cooper
CF	R.White	CF	B.Butler	CF	L.Dykstra	CF	J.Brumfield	CF	S.Finley	CF	D.Lewis	LF	B.Gilkey
RF	T.Tarasco	RF	C.Everett	RF	M.Whiten	RF	O.Merced	RF	T.Gwynn	RF	G.Hill	CF	R.Lankford
C	D.Fletcher	C	T.Hundley	C	D.Daulton	C	M.Parent	C	B.Ausmus	C	K.Manwaring	RF	B.Jordan
												C	D.Sheaffer
S3	M.Grudzielanek	3O	B.Bonilla	1O	G.Jefferies	2	N.Liriano	13	S.Livingstone	2	J.Patterson		
31	S.Andrews	O	R.Thompson	O	A.Van Slyke	1	R.Petagine	1	R.Phillips	C	T.Pagnozzi
								O2	B.Roberts	32	S.Scarsone		
P	P.Martinez	P	B.Jones	P	P.Quantrill	P	E.Loaiza	C	B.Johnson	O	D.Sanders	P	M.Petkovsek
P	J.Fassero	P	D.Mlicki	P	T.Green	P	P.Wagner					P	A.Watson
P	C.Perez	P	B.Pulsipher	P	M.Mimbs	P	J.Ericks	P	J.Hamilton	P	M.Leiter	P	D.Osborne
P	B.Henry	P	B.Saberhagen	P	C.Schilling	RP	M.Dyer	P	A.Ashby	P	T.Mulholland	P	K.Hill
RP	G.Heredia	P	P.Harnisch	RP	M.Williams	P	J.McCurry	P	A.Benes	P	Van Landingham	P	M.Morgan
RP	M.Rojas	RP	J.DiPoto	RP	R.Bottalico	P	D.Plesac	P	G.Dishman	P	M.Portugal	RP	R.DeLucia
RP	T.Scott	RP	D.Henry	RP	T.Borland			P	F.Valenzuela	RP	J.Bautista	RP	J.Parrett
		RP	J.Franco			P	S.Parris	RP	W.Blair	RP	R.Beck	RP	T.Henke
P	J.Shaw			P	S.Fernandez	P	J.Lieber	RP	B.Williams	RP	C.Hook		
		P	J.Isringhausen	P	H.Slocumb	RP	D.Miceli	RP	B.Florie			P	D.Jackson
		P	R.Cornelius	P	J.Juden	P	J.Christiansen			P	T.Wilson	P	T.Urbani
						P	R.White	P	S.Sanders	P	J.Brewington	P	R.Arocha
								P	T.Hoffman	P	S.Valdez		

TEAM	G	W	L	PCT	GB	R	OR	AB	H	2B	3B	HR	BB	SO	AVG	OBP	SLG	PRO	PRO+	BR	/A	PF	CHI	RC	SB	CS	SBA	SBR
EAST																												
ATL	144	90	54	.625		645	**540**	4814	1202	210	27	168	520	933	.250	.328	.409	.737	96	-10	-31	103	100	647	73	43	63	-4
NY	144	69	75	.479	21	657	618	4958	1323	218	34	125	446	994	.267	.333	.400	.733	101	-15	6	97	100	657	58	39	60	-6
PHI	144	69	75	.479	21	615	658	4950	1296	263	30	94	497	884	.262	.335	.384	.719	94	-33	-37	101	96	648	72	25	74	7
FLA	143	67	76	.469	22.5	673	673	4886	1278	214	29	144	517	916	.262	.338	.406	.744	101	9	7	100	99	681	131	53	71	8
MON	144	66	78	.458	24	621	638	4905	1268	265	24	118	400	901	.259	.322	.394	.716	90	-49	-70	104	**103**	619	120	49	71	7
CENTRAL																												
CIN	144	85	59	.590		747	623	4903	1326	**277**	35	161	519	946	.270	.345	.440	.785	112	77	81	100	100	757	**190**	68	74	16
HOU	144	76	68	.528	9	747	674	5097	1403	260	22	109	**566**	992	.275	**.356**	.399	.755	**113**	43	**95**	93	100	745	176	60	**75**	**17**
CHI	144	73	71	.507	12	693	671	4963	1315	267	39	158	440	953	.265	.329	.430	.759	106	23	36	98	101	698	105	37	74	9
STL	143	62	81	.434	22.5	563	658	4779	1182	238	24	107	436	920	.247	.316	.374	.690	86	-89	-87	100	102	562	79	46	63	-4
PIT	144	58	86	.403	27	629	736	4937	1281	245	27	125	456	972	.259	.325	.396	.721	93	-39	-50	102	101	634	84	55	60	-8
WEST																												
LA	144	78	66	.542		634	609	4942	1303	191	31	140	468	1023	.264	.331	.400	.731	106	-18	39	91	98	662	127	45	74	11
COL	144	77	67	.535	1	**785**	783	4994	**1406**	259	**43**	**200**	484	943	**.282**	.352	**.471**	**.823**	94	**141**	-85	129	96	**815**	125	59	68	2
SD	144	70	74	.486	8	668	672	4950	1345	231	20	116	447	**872**	.272	.336	.397	.733	102	-11	12	97	**103**	657	124	46	73	10
SF	144	67	77	.465	11	652	776	4971	1256	229	33	152	472	1060	.253	.325	.404	.729	100	-28	-8	97	101	663	138	46	**75**	14
TOT	1007					9329		69049	18184	3367	418	1917	6668	13309	.263	.334	.408	.741							1602	671	70	78

TEAM	CG	SH	SV	IP	H	H/G	HR	BB	SO	RAT	ERA	ERA+	OAV	OOB	PR	/A	PF	CPI	FA	E	DP	FW	PW	BW	SBW	DIF
EAST																										
ATL	**18**	11	34	1291^{2}	**1184**	**8.2**	**107**	436	**1087**	**11.5**	**3.44**	**124**	.244	**.311**	**106**	**118**	102	99	.982	100	113	.6	**11.6**	-3.0	-.9	9.7
NY	9	9	36	1291	1296	9.0	133	**401**	901	12.1	3.88	104	.262	.322	44	24	97	101	.979	115	125	-.3	2.4	.6	-1.1	-4.6
PHI	8	8	41	1290^{1}	1241	8.7	134	538	980	12.8	4.21	100	.254	.335	-4	3	101	97	.982	97	139	.8	.3	-3.6	.1	-.6
FLA	12	7	29	1286	1299	9.1	139	562	994	13.3	4.27	99	.264	.345	-13	-8	101	103	.979	115	143	-.3	-.8	.7	.2	-4.3
MON	7	9	42	1283^{2}	1286	9.0	128	416	950	12.3	4.11	104	.262	.327	10	26	103	97	.980	109	119	.1	2.6	-6.9	.1	-1.9
CENTRAL																										
CIN	8	10	38	1289^{1}	1270	8.9	131	424	903	12.0	4.03	102	.260	.323	21	12	99	97	**.986**	**79**	140	**1.9**	1.2	8.0	1.0	.9
HOU	6	8	32	1320^{1}	1357	9.2	118	460	1056	12.7	4.06	95	.266	.333	17	-29	93	100	.979	121	120	-.6	-2.9	**9.3**	**1.1**	-3.0
CHI	6	**12**	**45**	1301	1313	9.1	162	518	926	12.9	4.13	99	.262	.335	7	-4	98	**105**	.979	115	115	-.3	-.4	3.5	.3	-2.2
STL	4	6	38	1265^{2}	1290	9.2	135	445	842	12.6	4.09	102	.268	.335	13	14	100	104	.980	113	**156**	-.2	1.4	-8.6	-.9	-1.2
PIT	11	7	29	1275^{1}	1407	9.9	130	477	871	13.7	4.70	92	.283	.353	-74	-56	103	101	.978	122	138	-.7	-5.5	-4.9	-1.3	-1.6
WEST																										
LA	16	11	37	1295	1188	8.3	125	462	1060	11.7	3.66	104	**.243**	.313	76	20	91	96	.976	130	120	-1.2	2.0	3.8	.5	.8
COL	1	1	43	1288^{1}	1443	10.1	160	512	891	13.9	4.97	108	.286	.357	-113	60	129	101	.981	107	146	.2	5.9	-8.4	-.4	7.6
SD	6	10	35	1284^{2}	1242	8.7	142	512	1047	12.6	4.13	97	.255	.332	7	-15	96	99	.980	108	130	.2	-1.5	1.2	.4	-2.3
SF	12	5	34	1293^{2}	1368	9.5	173	505	801	13.4	4.86	84	.275	.348	-98	-112	98	98	.980	108	142	.2	-11.0	-.8	.8	5.8
TOT	124	114	513	18056		9.1				12.7	4.18		.263	.334					.980	1539	1846					

Runs
Biggio-Hou 123
Bonds-SF 109
Finley-SD 104
Bichette-Col 102
Larkin-Cin 98

Hits
Gwynn-SD 197
Bichette-Col 197
Grace-Chi 180

Doubles
Grace-Chi 51
McRae-Chi 38
Bichette-Col 38
R.Sanders-Cin 36

Triples
Butler-NY-LA 9
Young-Col 9
D.Sanders-Cin-SF ... 8
Gonzalez-Hou-Chi ... 8
Finley-SD 8

Home Runs
Bichette-Col 40
Walker-Col 36
Sosa-Chi 36
Bonds-SF 33

Total Bases
Bichette-Col 359
Walker-Col 300
Castilla-Col 297
Karros-LA 295
Bonds-SF 292

Runs Batted In
Bichette-Col 128
Sosa-Chi 119
Galarraga-Col 106
Karros-LA 105
Conine-Fla 105

Runs Produced
Bichette-Col 190
Bonds-SF 180
Biggio-Hou 178
Grace-Chi 173
Sosa-Chi 172

Bases On Balls
Bonds-SF 120
Weiss-Col 98
Veras-Fla 80
Biggio-Hou 80
Bagwell-Hou 79

Batting Average
Gwynn-SD .... .368
Piazza-LA .... .346
Bichette-Col .... .340
Bell-Hou .... .334
Grace-Chi .... .326

On Base Percentage
Bonds-SF .... .434
Biggio-Hou .... .411
Gwynn-SD .... .408
Weiss-Col .... .404
Bagwell-Hou .... .403

Slugging Average
Bichette-Col .... .620
Walker-Col .... .607
Piazza-LA .... .606
R.Sanders-Cin .... .579
Bonds-SF .... .577

Production
Bonds-SF 1.011
Piazza-LA 1.007
Walker-Col .... .991
Bichette-Col .... .989
R.Sanders-Cin .... .980

Adjusted Production
Piazza-LA 177
Bonds-SF 169
R.Sanders-Cin 155
Karros-LA 149
Gant-Cin 146

Batter Runs
Bonds-SF 51.4
Bichette-Col 42.1
Walker-Col 39.0
R.Sanders-Cin 38.6
Piazza-LA 37.0

Adjusted Batter Runs
Bonds-SF 55.4
Piazza-LA 45.7
R.Sanders-Cin 39.2
Biggio-Hou 39.0
Karros-LA 36.9

Clutch Hitting Index
Bell-Hou 138
Hayes-Phi 128
King-Pit 121
Bagwell-Hou 121
Conine-Fla 116

Runs Created
Bonds-SF 134
Bichette-Col 121
Biggio-Hou 121
R.Sanders-Cin 115
Grace-Chi 115

Total Average
Bonds-SF 1.156
R.Sanders-Cin 1.067
Walker-Col 1.047
Piazza-LA 1.034
Larkin-Cin 1.014

Stolen Bases
Veras-Fla 56
Larkin-Cin 51
DeShields-LA 39
R.Sanders-Cin 36
Finley-SD 36

Stolen Base Average
Larkin-Cin 91.1
Roberts-SD 90.9
Tarasco-Mon 88.9
Mondesi-LA 87.1
Lansing-Mon 87.1

Stolen Base Runs
Larkin-Cin 12.3
Sosa-Chi 6.0
Mondesi-LA 5.7
Lansing-Mon 5.7
Tarasco-Mon 5.4

Fielding Runs
Branson-Cin 21.5
Reed-SD 18.0
Bagwell-Hou 18.0
Bonds-SF 15.0
C.Garcia-Pit 14.4

Total Player Rating
Bonds-SF 6.7
Biggio-Hou 4.8
Piazza-LA 4.4
R.Sanders-Cin 4.3
Caminiti-SD 3.8

Wins
Maddux-Atl 19
Schourek-Cin 18
Martinez-LA 17
Glavine-Atl 16

Win Percentage
Maddux-Atl .... .905
Schourek-Cin .... .720
Martinez-LA .... .708
Glavine-Atl .... .696

Games
Leskanic-Col 76
Veres-Hou 72
Reed-Col 71
Perez-Fla 69

Complete Games
Maddux-Atl 10
Leiter-SF 7
Valdes-LA 6
Neagle-Pit 5

Shutouts
Nomo-LA 3
Maddux-Atl 3

Saves
Myers-Chi 38
Henke-StL 36
Beck-SF 33
Worrell-LA 32
Slocumb-Phi 32

Innings Pitched
Neagle-Pit 209.2
Maddux-Atl 209.2
Martinez-LA 206.1
Hamilton-SD 204.1
Navarro-Chi 200.1

Fewest Hits/Game
Nomo-LA 5.83
Maddux-Atl 6.31
Martinez-Mon 7.30
Schourek-Cin 7.47
Valdes-LA 7.65

Fewest BB/Game
Maddux-Atl .... .99
Reynolds-Hou 1.76
Neagle-Pit 1.93
Saberhagen-NY-Col ...
.... 1.94
Smiley-Cin 1.99

Strikeouts
Nomo-LA 236
Smoltz-Atl 193
Maddux-Atl 181
Reynolds-Hou 175
Martinez-Mon 174

Strikeouts/Game
Nomo-LA 11.10
Smoltz-Atl 9.02
Reynolds-Hou 8.32
Martinez-Mon 8.04
Foster-Chi 7.84

Ratio
Maddux-Atl 7.47
Nomo-LA 9.74
Schourek-Cin 9.98
Valdes-LA 10.02
Martinez-Mon 10.86

Earned Run Average
Maddux-Atl 1.63
Nomo-LA 2.54
Ashby-SD 2.94
Valdes-LA 3.05
Glavine-Atl 3.08

Adjusted ERA
Maddux-Atl 261
Nomo-LA 149
Glavine-Atl 138
Ashby-SD 137
Smoltz-Atl 134

Opponents' Batting Avg.
Nomo-LA .... .182
Maddux-Atl .... .197
Martinez-Mon .... .227
Valdes-LA .... .228
Schourek-Cin .... .228

Opponents' On Base Pct.
Maddux-Atl .... .225
Nomo-LA .... .271
Valdes-LA .... .279
Schourek-Cin .... .283
Reynolds-Hou .... .300

Starter Runs
Maddux-Atl 59.4
Nomo-LA 34.9
Ashby-SD 26.5
Hamilton-SD 24.9
Valdes-LA 24.8

Adjusted Starter Runs
Maddux-Atl 61.3
Nomo-LA 26.6
Glavine-Atl 26.1
Smoltz-Atl 23.3
Ashby-SD 23.3

Clutch Pitching Index
Ashby-SD 127
Neagle-Pit 113
Rapp-Fla 111
Swindell-Hou 111
Castillo-Chi 110

Relief Runs
Veres-Hou 22.0
Reed-Col 19.0
Bottalico-Phi 16.7
Wohlers-Atl 15.0
Worrell-LA 15.0

Adjusted Relief Runs
Reed-Col 30.3
Leskanic-Col 21.7
Veres-Hou 18.4
Bottalico-Phi 17.2
Holmes-Col 15.9

Relief Ranking
Wohlers-Atl 32.4
Reed-Col 24.6
Slocumb-Phi 23.0
Franco-NY 22.0
Leskanic-Col 21.8

Total Pitcher Index
Maddux-Atl 6.8
Glavine-Atl 3.5
Wohlers-Atl 3.2
Ritz-Col 2.9
Reed-Col 2.6

Total Baseball Ranking
Maddux-Atl 6.8
Bonds-SF 6.7
Biggio-Hou 4.8
Piazza-LA 4.4
R.Sanders-Cin 4.3

May 3 David Bell makes his major league debut at third base for the Indians in a 14-7 victory over the Tigers. His appearance makes the Bells—with his father Buddy and his grandfather Gus—the second three-generation family in major league history (the Boones are the other). Gus Bell dies four days later.

May 28 The White Sox and Tigers combine for a major league record 12 home runs at Tiger Stadium. The Tigers hit seven home runs, but still lose the 14-12 slugfest.

June 30 Eddie Murray collects his 3,000th career hit against Minnesota's Mike Trombley in a 4-1 Cleveland win at the Metrodome. The Indians slugger is the 20th player to reach the milestone and the third in franchise history.

August 30 Tigers teammates Lou Whitaker and Alan Trammell play in their 1,914th game together in a 10-7 loss to the White Sox.

September 6 Cal Ripken, Jr. breaks Lou Gehrig's record for consecutive games played before a home town crowd at Camden Yards. After the Angels are retired in the top of the fifth inning, the game becomes official, and fans go wild. Although Ripken comes out repeatedly to tip his cap to the crowd, fans persist with their cheering. Finally, teammates Rafael Palmeiro and Bobby Bonilla gently push him out of the dugout, and Ripken takes a lap around the park, shaking hands and giving high fives to fans, ball girls, ushers and every member of the Angels. The ovation lasts for more than 22 minutes. Ripken homers, and the Orioles ultimately win, 4-2.

September 8 Cleveland ends a 41-year postseason drought by clinching the AL Central with a 3-2 win over the Orioles.

September 30 Indians outfielder Albert Belle hits his 50th home run of the season in a 5-2 win over Royals to become the first player ever to have 50 home runs and 50 doubles in the same season.

October 2 The Mariners defeat the Angels 9-1 in a one-game playoff for the AL West title. The win sends the Mariners to the postseason for the first time in their 19-year history.

October 6 The Indians sweep the Division Series with an 8-2 victory over the Red Sox at Fenway Park.

October 8 Edgar Martinez drives home the tying and winning runs with a double to left field to rally the Mariners to a 6-5 win in the bottom of the 11th inning to win the Division Series. Martinez bats .571 with 10 RBIs against the Yankees in the five-game series. Ken Griffey Jr., who beat the relay throw home to score the winning run, has five home runs in the series.

October 17 The Indians win their third straight game to win the AL pennant for the first time in 41 years. Dennis Martinez allows just four hits in seven innings as the Indians are 4-0 winners over Seattle. Orel Hershiser, who won both his starts and had a 1.29 ERA in the ALCS, earns MVP honors.

October 24 Eddie Murray singles home pinch-runner Alvaro Espinoza in the bottom of the 11th inning to give the Indians their first win in a World Series in 47 years. The Tribe's 7-6 win fittingly occurs in the first-ever Series game at Jacobs Field.

	BALTIMORE		BOSTON		CALIFORNIA		CHICAGO		CLEVELAND		DETROIT		KANSAS CITY
M	P.Regan	M	K.Kennedy	M	M.Lachemann	M	G.Lamont	M	M.Hargrove	M	S.Anderson	M	B.Boone
1B	R.Palmeiro	1B	M.Vaughn	1B	J.Snow	M	T.Bevington	1B	P.Sorrento	1B	C.Fielder	1B	W.Joyner
2B	M.Alexander	2B	L.Alicea	2B	D.Easley	1B	D.Martinez	2B	C.Baerga	2B	L.Whitaker	2B	K.Lockhart
SS	C.Ripken	SS	J.Valentin	SS	G.DiSarcina	2B	R.Durham	SS	O.Vizquel	SS	C.Gomez	SS	G.Gagne
3B	J.Manto	3B	T.Naehring	3B	T.Phillips	SS	O.Guillen	3B	J.Thome	3B	T.Fryman	3B	G.Gaetti
LF	B.Anderson	LF	M.Greenwell	LF	G.Anderson	3B	R.Ventura	LF	A.Belle	LF	B.Higginson	LF	V.Coleman
CF	C.Goodwin	CF	L.Tinsley	CF	J.Edmonds	LF	T.Raines	CF	K.Lofton	CF	C.Curtis	CF	T.Goodwin
RF	K.Bass	RF	T.O'Leary	RF	T.Salmon	CF	L.Johnson	RF	M.Ramirez	RF	D.Bautista	RF	J.Nunnally
C	C.Hoiles	C	M.Macfarlane	C	J.Fabregas	RF	M.Devereaux	C	T.Pena	C	J.Flaherty	C	B.Mayne
DH	H.Baines	DH	J.Canseco	DH	C.Davis	C	R.Karkovice	DH	E.Murray	DH	K.Gibson	DH	B.Hamelin
						DH	F.Thomas						
2	B.Barberie	O	W.McGee	CD	G.Myers			O	W.Kirby	S	A.Trammell	2S	D.Howard
O3	B.Bonilla	2O	R.Hudler					C	S.Alomar				
		3S	S.Owen			P	A.Fernandez			P	F.Lira	P	M.Gubicza
P	M.Mussina	P	T.Wakefield			P	W.Alvarez			P	S.Bergman	P	K.Appier
P	K.Brown	P	E.Hanson			P	J.Bere	P	D.Martinez	P	M.Moore	P	T.Gordon
P	J.Moyer	P	R.Clemens	P	C.Finley	P	J.Abbott	P	C.Nagy	P	D.Wells	RP	J.Montgomery
P	S.Erickson	P	Z.Smith	P	M.Langston	P	B.Keyser	P	O.Hershiser	RP	J.Doherty	RP	H.Pichardo
RP	M.Oquist	RP	R.Cormier	P	S.Boskie	RP	K.McCaskill	P	M.Clark	P	B.Bohanon	RP	R.Meacham
RP	J.Orosco	RP	M.Maddux	P	B.Anderson	P	J.DeLeon	P	C.Ogea	RP	J.Boever		
RP	A.Benitez	RP	S.Belinda	RP	T.Percival	RP	R.Hernandez	RP	J.Tavarez			P	J.Jacome
				RP	M.James			RP	E.Plunk	P	J.Lima	P	C.Haney
		P	V.Eshelman	RP	B.Patterson			RP	J.Mesa	P	M.Christopher		
P	B.McDonald									P	B.Maxcy		
P	R.Krivda			P	J.Abbott	P	K.Hill						
P	A.Rhodes			P	M.Bielecki	P	J.Poole						
				P	M.Harkey								
				P	R.Springer								
				P	M.Butcher								

	MILWAUKEE		MINNESOTA		NEW YORK		OAKLAND		SEATTLE		TEXAS		TORONTO
M	P.Garner	M	T.Kelly	M	B.Showalter	M	T.LaRussa	M	L.Piniella	M	J.Oates	M	C.Gaston
1B	J.Jaha	1B	S.Stahoviak	1B	D.Mattingly	1B	M.McGwire	1B	T.Martinez	1B	W.Clark	1B	J.Olerud
2B	F.Vina	2B	C.Knoblauch	2B	P.Kelly	2B	B.Gates	2B	J.Cora	2B	J.Frye	2B	R.Alomar
SS	J.Valentin	SS	P.Meares	SS	T.Fernandez	SS	M.Bordick	SS	L.Sojo	SS	B.Gil	SS	A.Gonzalez
3B	J.Cirillo	3B	S.Leius	3B	W.Boggs	3B	C.Paquette	3B	M.Blowers	3B	M.Pagliarulo	3B	E.Sprague
LF	D.Hulse	LF	M.Cordova	LF	G.Williams	LF	R.Henderson	LF	R.Amaral	LF	M.McLemore	LF	J.Carter
CF	D.Hamilton	CF	R.Becker	CF	B.Williams	CF	S.Javier	CF	A.Diaz	CF	O.Nixon	CF	D.White
RF	M.Mieske	RF	K.Puckett	RF	P.O'Neill	RF	R.Sierra	RF	J.Buhner	RF	R.Greer	RF	S.Green
C	J.Oliver	C	M.Walbeck	C	M.Stanley	C	T.Steinbach	C	D.Wilson	C	I.Rodriguez	C	L.Parrish
DH	G.Vaughn	DH	P.Munoz	DH	R.Sierra	DH	G.Berroa	DH	E.Martinez	DH	J.Gonzalez	DH	P.Molitor
2S	P.Listach	S3	J.Reboulet	2S	R.Velarde	3O	S.Brosius	O	K.Griffey	OD	M.Tettleton	P	P.Hentgen
31	K.Seitzer			C1	J.Leyritz			S2	F.Fermin			P	A.Leiter
O1	B.Surhoff	P	B.Radke	O	L.Polonia	P	T.Stottlemyre			P	K.Rogers	P	J.Guzman
OD	D.Nilsson	P	K.Tapani	OD	D.James	P	T.Van Poppel	P	R.Johnson	P	R.Pavlik	P	D.Cone
		P	M.Trombley			P	S.Ontiveros	P	T.Belcher	P	K.Gross	RP	T.Castillo
P	S.Sparks	P	F.Rodriguez	P	J.McDowell	P	R.Darling	P	C.Bosio	P	B.Tewksbury	RP	W.Williams
P	R.Bones	P	S.Erickson	P	A.Pettitte	RP	C.Reyes	RP	J.Nelson	RP	R.McDowell	RP	D.Cox
P	S.Karl	RP	P.Mahomes	P	S.Hitchcock	RP	M.Acre	RP	B.Wells	RP	M.Whiteside		
P	B.Givens	RP	E.Guardado	P	D.Cone	RP	D.Eckersley	RP	B.Ayala	P	D.Oliver	P	P.Menhart
RP	A.Miranda	RP	D.Stevens	P	S.Kamieniecki							P	E.Hurtado
RP	B.Wegman			P	B.Wickman			P	D.Stewart	P	S.Torres	P	D.Darwin
RP	M.Kiefer	P	J.Parra	RP	J.Wetteland	P	M.Harkey	P	A.Benes	P	B.Witt	
		P	R.Robertson	RP	S.Howe	P	A.Prieto	P	B.Risley			
						P	D.Johns					
P	S.Roberson			P	M.Perez							
P	B.Scanlan			P	M.Rivera							

TEAM	G	W	L	PCT	GB	R	OR	AB	H	2B	3B	HR	BB	SO	AVG	OBP	SLG	PRO	PRO+	BR	/A	PF	CHI	RC	SB	CS	SBA	SBR
EAST																												
BOS	144	86	58	.597		791	698	4997	1399	**286**	31	175	560	923	.280	.360	.455	.815	106	76	49	103	97	818	99	44	69	3
NY	145	79	65	.549	7	749	688	4947	1365	280	34	122	**625**	851	.276	.362	.420	.782	104	28	36	99	98	755	50	30	63	-3
BAL	144	71	73	.493	15	704	640	4837	1267	229	27	173	574	803	.262	.345	.428	.773	99	-3	-14	102	99	716	92	45	67	1
DET	144	60	84	.417	26	654	844	4865	1204	228	29	159	551	987	.247	.329	.404	.733	90	-78	-74	99	102	649	73	36	67	0
TOR	144	56	88	.389	30	642	777	5036	1309	275	27	140	492	906	.260	.331	.409	.740	92	-69	-64	99	97	687	75	16	**82**	**13**
CENTRAL																												
CLE	144	100	44	.694		**840**	**607**	5028	**1461**	279	23	**207**	542	**766**	**.291**	**.364**	**.479**	**.843**	**115**	**122**	**110**	101	98	**868**	**132**	53	71	8
KC	144	70	74	.486	30	629	691	4903	1275	240	35	119	475	849	.260	.331	.396	.727	87	-88	-96	101	100	647	120	53	69	4
CHI	145	68	76	.472	32	755	758	5060	1417	252	37	146	576	767	.280	.357	.431	.788	109	33	69	95	97	793	110	39	74	10
MIL	144	65	79	.451	35	740	747	5000	1329	249	**42**	128	502	800	.266	.338	.409	.747	88	-50	-88	106	**109**	702	105	40	72	8
MIN	144	56	88	.389	44	703	889	5005	1398	270	34	120	471	916	.279	.348	.419	.767	98	-11	-12	100	99	710	105	57	65	-3
WEST																												
SEA	145	79	66	.545		796	708	4996	1377	276	20	182	549	871	.276	.352	.448	.800	105	45	38	101	102	794	110	41	73	8
CAL	145	78	67	.538	1	801	697	5019	1390	252	25	186	564	889	.277	.354	.448	.802	108	51	59	99	102	795	58	39	60	-6
TEX	144	74	70	.514	4.5	691	720	4913	1304	247	24	138	526	877	.265	.340	.410	.750	92	-43	-59	102	102	688	90	47	66	-1
OAK	144	67	77	.465	11.5	730	761	4916	1296	228	18	169	565	911	.264	.345	.420	.765	104	-15	24	95	102	725	112	46	71	6
TOT	1010					10225		69522	18791	3591	406	2164	7572	12116	.270	.347	.427	.774							1331	586	69	48

TEAM	CG	SH	SV	IP	H	H/G	HR	BB	SO	RAT	ERA	ERA+	OAV	OOB	PR	/A	PF	CPI	FA	E	DP	FW	PW	BW	SBW	DIF
EAST																										
BOS	7	9	39	1292^2	1338	9.3	**127**	476	888	12.9	4.39	111	.268	.337	46	68	103	98	.978	120	151	-1.2	6.4	4.6	-.0	4.3
NY	18	5	35	1284^2	1286	9.0	159	535	908	13.0	4.56	101	.261	.337	22	8	98	97	**.986**	74	121	**1.4**	.8	3.4	-.6	2.1
BAL	**19**	**10**	29	1267	**1165**	**8.3**	149	523	930	12.3	4.31	110	**.245**	.325	56	62	101	93	**.986**	**72**	141	**1.4**	5.8	-1.3	-.2	-6.7
DET	5	3	38	1275	1509	10.7	170	536	729	14.8	5.49	87	.296	.368	-110	-104	101	100	.981	106	143	-.4	-9.8	-6.9	-.3	5.5
TOR	16	8	22	1292^2	1336	9.3	145	654	894	14.2	4.88	96	.267	.358	-24	-25	100	99	.982	97	131	.0	-2.3	-6.0	**.9**	-8.6
CENTRAL																										
CLE	10	**10**	**50**	1301	1261	8.7	135	**445**	926	**12.1**	**3.83**	**122**	.255	**.322**	**127**	**125**	100	103	.982	101	142	-.2	**11.7**	**10.3**	.4	5.7
KC	11	**10**	37	1288	1323	9.2	142	503	763	13.0	4.49	107	.268	.340	32	43	102	100	.984	90	168	.4	4.0	-9.0	.0	2.5
CHI	12	4	36	1284^2	1374	9.6	164	617	892	14.2	4.85	92	.275	.359	-20	-57	95	104	.980	108	131	-.5	-5.3	6.5	.6	-5.2
MIL	7	4	31	1286	1391	9.7	146	603	699	14.3	4.82	103	.280	.364	-16	23	106	**106**	.981	105	**186**	-.4	2.2	-8.3	.4	-.9
MIN	7	2	27	1272^2	1450	10.3	210	533	790	14.3	5.76	83	.287	.359	-149	-141	101	95	.981	100	141	-.1	-13.2	-1.1	-.6	-.9
WEST																										
SEA	9	8	39	1289^1	1343	9.4	149	591	**1068**	13.8	4.50	105	.268	.350	31	35	101	105	.980	104	108	-.3	3.3	3.6	.4	-.5
CAL	8	9	42	1284^1	1310	9.2	163	486	901	12.9	4.52	104	.265	.336	28	25	100	99	.982	95	120	.2	2.3	5.5	-.9	-1.7
TEX	14	4	34	1285	1385	9.7	152	514	838	13.6	4.66	104	.278	.349	8	24	102	104	.982	98	156	.0	2.3	-5.5	-.4	5.7
OAK	8	4	34	1273	1320	9.3	153	556	890	13.6	4.93	91	.269	.350	-31	-66	95	96	.981	102	151	-.2	-6.2	2.3	.2	-1.1
TOT	151	90	493	17976		9.4				13.5	4.71		.270	.347					.982	1372	1990					

Runs
E.Martinez-Sea.... 121
Belle-Cle.......... 121
Edmonds-Cal..... 120
Phillips-Cal....... 119
Salmon-Cal........ 111

Hits
Johnson-Chi...... 186
E.Martinez-Sea.... 182
Knoblauch-Min.... 179
Salmon-Cal....... 177
Baerga-Cle....... 175

Doubles
E.Martinez-Sea 52
Belle-Cle.......... 52
Puckett-Min........ 39
Valentin-Bos....... 37
T.Martinez-Sea..... 35

Triples
Lofton-Cle.......... 13
Johnson-Chi....... 12
Anderson-Bal...... 10
B.Williams-NY....... 9
Knoblauch-Min...... 8

Home Runs
Belle-Cle............50
F.Thomas-Chi......40
Buhner-Sea.........40

Total Bases
Belle-Cle.......... 377
Palmeiro-Bal...... 323
E.Martinez-Sea ... 321
Salmon-Cal....... 319
Vaughn-Bos....... 316

Runs Batted In
Vaughn-Bos....... 126
Belle-Cle......... 126
Buhner-Sea....... 121
E.Martinez-Sea.... 113

Runs Produced
E.Martinez-Sea.... 205
Belle-Cle......... 197
Edmonds-Cal...... 194
Vaughn-Bos....... 185
Valentin-Bos...... 183

Bases On Balls
F.Thomas-Chi 136
E.Martinez-Sea.... 116
Phillips-Cal....... 113
Tettleton-Tex...... 107
Thome-Cle......... 97

Batting Average
E.Martinez-Sea.....356
Knoblauch-Min.....333
Salmon-Cal........330
Boggs-NY..........324
Murray-Cle.........323

On Base Percentage
E.Martinez-Sea .... .482
F.Thomas-Chi...... .463
Thome-Cle........ .440
Davis-Cal......... .437
Salmon-Cal .... .432

Slugging Average
Belle-Cle..........690
E.Martinez-Sea.....628
F.Thomas-Chi 606
Salmon-Cal.........594
Palmeiro-Bal.......583

Production
E.Martinez-Sea...1.110
Belle-Cle.........1.094
F.Thomas-Chi....1.069
Salmon-Cal......1.026
Thome-Cle........998

Adjusted Production
E.Martinez-Sea.... 184
F.Thomas-Chi..... 184
Belle-Cle.......... 175
Salmon-Cal........ 165
Thome-Cle........ 155

Batter Runs
E.Martinez-Sea ... 71.5
F.Thomas-Chi 61.9
Belle-Cle.......... 60.6
Salmon-Cal....... 52.7
McGwire-Oak...... 45.0

Adjusted Batter Runs
E.Martinez-Sea.....70.1
F.Thomas-Chi......68.8
Belle-Cle..........58.7
Salmon-Cal........54.0
McGwire-Oak.......50.7

Clutch Hitting Index
Blowers-Sea....... 127
Stanley-NY........ 121
Clark-Tex.......... 120
Joyner-KC......... 118
Snow-Cal.......... 113

Runs Created
E.Martinez-Sea 161
F.Thomas-Chi 144
Belle-Cle.......... 144
Salmon-Cal 142
Palmeiro-Bal....... 123

Total Average
E.Martinez-Sea...1.300
F.Thomas-Chi....1.238
Belle-Cle.........1.150
Salmon-Cal......1.112
Thome-Cle.......1.106

Stolen Bases
Lofton-Cle......... 54
Nixon-Tex.......... 50
Goodwin-KC........ 50
Knoblauch-Min..... 46
Coleman-KC-Sea... 42

Stolen Base Average
Amaral-Sea....... 91.3
Alomar-Tor........ 90.9
Javier-Oak........ 87.8
Johnson-Chi....... 87.0
Goodwin-Bal....... 84.6

Stolen Base Runs
Johnson-Chi.........8.4
Javier-Oak..........7.8
Lofton-Cle..........7.2
Alomar-Tor.........7.2
Amaral-Sea..........5.1

Fielding Runs
Fryman-Det....... 26.6
Valentin-Mil....... 19.7
Edmonds-Cal...... 19.4
Cordova-Min....... 18.7
Gil-Tex........... 16.2

Total Player Rating
Salmon-Cal......... 5.9
Belle-Cle.......... 5.8
E.Martinez-Sea 5.3
Valentin-Bos....... 4.7
F.Thomas-Chi 4.0

Wins
Mussina-Bal....... 19
Cone-Tor-NY....... 18
Johnson-Sea....... 18
Rogers-Tex........ 17

Win Percentage
Johnson-Sea...... .900
Hanson-Bos...... .750
Nagy-Cle......... .727
Hershiser-Cle .... .727
Rogers-Tex....... .708

Games
Orosco-Bal......... 65
McDowell-Tex...... 64
Wickman-NY....... 63
Belinda-Bos........ 63
Ayala-Sea.......... 63

Complete Games
McDowell-NY........ 8
Erickson-Min-Bal..... 7
Mussina-Bal.......... 7

Shutouts
Mussina-Bal........4
Johnson-Sea.........3

Saves
Mesa-Cle........... 46
Smith-Cal.......... 37
Aguilera-Min-Bos.... 32
Hernandez-Chi..... 32

Innings Pitched
Cone-Tor-NY.....229.1
Mussina-Bal.....221.2
McDowell-NY....217.2
Johnson-Sea....214.1
Gubicza-KC.....213.1

Fewest Hits/Game
Johnson-Sea..... 6.68
Appier-KC........ 7.29
Wakefield-Bos.... 7.51
Mussina-Bal...... 7.59
Cone-Tor-NY...... 7.65

Fewest BB/Game
Mussina-Bal...... 2.03
Martinez-Cle..... 2.21
Radke-Min....... 2.34
K.Brown-Bal...... 2.51
Gubicza-KC...... 2.62

Strikeouts
Johnson-Sea 294
Stottlemyre-Oak ... 205
Finley-Cal........ 195
Cone-Tor-NY...... 191
Appier-KC........ 185

Strikeouts/Game
Johnson-Sea.... 12.35
Stottlemyre-Oak .. 8.80
Finley-Cal........ 8.65
Appier-KC........ 8.27
Leiter-Tor........ 7.52

Ratio
Johnson-Sea...... 9.66
Mussina-Bal....... 9.66
Wakefield-Bos.... 11.06
K.Brown-Bal..... 11.07
Hershiser-Cle.... 11.13

Earned Run Average
Johnson-Sea......2.48
Wakefield-Bos.....2.95
Martinez-Cle.....3.08
Mussina-Bal......3.29
Rogers-Tex.......3.38

Adjusted ERA
Johnson-Sea....... 191
Wakefield-Bos...... 165
Martinez-Cle....... 152
Mussina-Bal....... 144
Rogers-Tex........ 143

Opponents' Batting Avg.
Johnson-Sea.......201
Appier-KC..........221
Mussina-Bal........226
Wakefield-Bos......227
Cone-Tor-NY.......228

Opponents' On Base Pct.
Johnson-Sea.......267
Mussina-Bal........271
Wakefield-Bos......302
K.Brown-Bal........303
Appier-KC..........304

Starter Runs
Johnson-Sea...... 53.2
Wakefield-Bos..... 38.3
Mussina-Bal...... 35.1
Martinez-Cle..... 33.9
Rogers-Tex....... 30.9

Adjusted Starter Runs
Johnson-Sea...... 53.8
Wakefield-Bos..... 41.7
Mussina-Bal....... 36.0
Rogers-Tex....... 33.5
Martinez-Cle...... 33.5

Clutch Pitching Index
Bosio-Sea......... 117
Wakefield-Bos.... 115
Gubicza-KC....... 113
Martinez-Cle...... 113
Rogers-Tex....... 112

Relief Runs
Mesa-Cle......... 25.5
Percival-Cal...... 22.7
Nelson-Sea....... 22.2
Tavarez-Cle...... 21.5
Plunk-Cle........ 14.5

Adjusted Relief Runs
Mesa-Cle......... 25.4
Percival-Cal...... 22.6
Nelson-Sea....... 22.4
Tavarez-Cle...... 21.3
Plunk-Cle........ 14.4

Relief Ranking
Mesa-Cle..........44.3
Aguilera-Min-Bos ..27.9
Tavarez-Cle.......27.1
Nelson-Sea........26.7
Wetteland-NY.....20.7

Total Pitcher Index
Johnson-Sea...... 4.6
Wakefield-Bos..... 4.5
Mesa-Cle......... 4.3
Mussina-Bal....... 3.9
Rogers-Tex....... 3.6

Total Baseball Ranking
Salmon-Cal........ 5.9
Belle-Cle.......... 5.8
E.Martinez-Sea..... 5.3
Valentin-Bos....... 4.7
Johnson-Sea....... 4.6

March 5 Earl Weaver and Jim Bunning are elected into the Hall of Fame by the Veterans Committee. Also chosen are turn-of-the-century manager Ned Hanlon and Negro League pitcher Bill Foster.

April 27 Barry Bonds homers twice to reach the 300-home run mark. Bonds joins his father Bobby, godfather Willie Mays, and Andre Dawson as the only players with 300 homers and 300 steals.

July 29 Tom Lasorda calls it quits after 20 seasons as Dodger manager following a heart attack and an angioplasty in June.

August 16 The Padres and Mets play the first regular season major league game ever played in Mexico. The Padres take a big lead, but the Mets close the gap with seven runs in the ninth inning in a 15-10 Padres triumph. The series is moved from San Diego because of a perceived conflict with the G.O.P. National Convention.

September 14 Todd Hundley's opposite-field home run ties the game between the Mets and Braves and breaks Roy Campanella's record for homers by a catcher with 41.

September 17 Hideo Nomo pitches a no-hitter at hitter-friendly Coors Field against the NL's best hitting team. The Dodger righthander walks four Rockies and fans eight in his 110-pitch, 9-0 win.

October 5 Chipper Jones starts an Atlanta rally in the first inning and caps another rally with a home run in the fourth. The Braves make it stand up in a 5-2 win over the Dodgers for a sweep of the Division Series.

October 17 With the NLCS tied at three games each, the Braves explode in the first and keep on exploding. Tom Glavine pitches seven shutout innings and adds a three-run triple as Atlanta cruises to the pennant with a 15-0 rout.

October 20 The Braves make a strong case for back-to-back world championships. John Smoltz pitches 5⅔ hitless innings and rookie Andruw Jones becomes the youngest player to homer in World Series history—in fact he does it twice—as the Braves blast the Yankees 12-1 in the opener.

November 6 Todd Hollandsworth continues a Dodger tradition. The outfielder is the fifth consecutive Dodger to win the NL Rookie of the Year prize.

November 11 John Smoltz, who won a major league high 24 games for the Braves, wins the NL Cy Young Award in a runaway. Smoltz, the NL leader in strikeouts (276), innings (253⅔), and winning percentage (.750), receives 26 of 28 first-place votes. Kevin Brown of the Marlins, NL ERA leader (1.89), receives the other two first-place votes.

November 13 Padres third baseman Ken Caminiti is the fourth unanimous winner of the league MVP. The slick-fielding Caminiti set team records for home runs (40), RBI (130), and slugging (.621), while leading the Padres to the NL West title for the first time in 12 years.

	ATLANTA		CHICAGO		CINCINNATI		COLORADO		FLORIDA		HOUSTON		LOS ANGELES
M	B.Cox	M	J.Riggleman	M	R.Knight	M	D.Baylor	M	R.Lachemann	M	T.Collins	M	T.Lasorda
1B	F.McGriff	1B	M.Grace	1B	H.Morris	1B	A.Galarraga	M	C.Rojas	1B	J.Bagwell	M	B.Russell
2B	M.Lemke	2B	R.Sandberg	2B	B.Boone	2B	E.Young	M	J.Boles	2B	C.Biggio	1B	E.Karros
SS	J.Blauser	SS	R.Sanchez	SS	B.Larkin	SS	W.Weiss	1B	G.Colbrunn	SS	O.Miller	2B	D.DeShields
3B	C.Jones	3B	L.Gomez	3B	W.Greene	3B	V.Castilla	2B	Q.Veras	3B	S.Berry	SS	G.Gagne
LF	R.Klesko	LF	L.Gonzalez	LF	T.Howard	LF	E.Burks	SS	E.Renteria	LF	J.Mouton	3B	M.Blowers
CF	M.Grissom	CF	B.McRae	CF	E.Davis	CF	Q.McCracken	3B	T.Pendleton	CF	D.Hunter	LF	T.Hollandsworth
RF	J.Dye	RF	S.Sosa	RF	R.Sanders	RF	D.Bichette	LF	J.Conine	RF	D.Bell	CF	R.Cedeno
C	J.Lopez	C	S.Servais	C	J.Oliver	C	J.Reed	CF	D.White	C	R.Wilkins	RF	R.Mondesi
								RF	G.Sheffield			C	M.Piazza
O	D.Smith	O	S.Bullett	3S	J.Branson	O1	J.Vander Wal	C	C.Johnson	O	J.Cangelosi		
		S3	J.Hernandez	O3	L.Harris	O	L.Walker			O	D.May	O2	C.Fonville
P	G.Maddux			C	E.Taubensee			S3	K.Abbott	3	B.Spiers		
P	T.Glavine	P	J.Navarro	O	E.Owens	P	K.Ritz	3S	A.Arias	S	R.Gutierrez	P	H.Nomo
P	S.Avery	P	S.Trachsel			P	Ma.Thompson	O	J.Orsulak			P	I.Valdes
RP	G.McMichael	P	F.Castillo	P	J.Smiley	P	A.Reynoso	O	J.Tavarez	P	S.Reynolds	P	P.Astacio
RP	B.Clontz	P	J.Bullinger	P	D.Burba	P	M.Freeman			P	D.Kile	P	R.Martinez
RP	M.Wohlers	P	A.Telemaco	P	M.Portugal	RP	D.Holmes	P	K.Brown	P	D.Drabek	RP	T.Candiotti
		RP	T.Adams	P	K.Jarvis	RP	S.Reed	P	A.Leiter	P	M.Hampton	RP	C.Park
		RP	T.Wendell	P	R.Salkeld	RP	C.Leskanic	P	P.Rapp	P	D.Wall	RP	A.Osuna
P	M.Bielecki	RP	R.Myers	RP	J.Shaw			P	J.Burkett	RP	X.Hernandez	RP	M.Guthrie
P	T.Wade			RP	H.Carrasco	P	J.Wright	RP	R.Nen	RP	T.Jones		
P	J.Schmidt	P	K.Foster	RP	J.Brantley	P	R.Bailey	RP	C.Hammond	RP	D.Brocail	P	T.Worrell
		P	K.Bottenfield			P	B.Ruffin	RP	D.Weathers			P	S.Radinsky
		P	B.Patterson	P	P.Schourek	P	B.Rekar			P	B.Wagner		
				P	J.Ruffin	P	L.Painter	P	J.Powell				
								P	M.Hutton				
								P	T.Mathews				

	MONTREAL		NEW YORK		PHILADELPHIA		PITTSBURGH		SAN DIEGO		SAN FRANCISCO		ST.LOUIS
M	F.Alou	M	D.Green	M	J.Fregosi	M	J.Leyland	M	B.Bochy	M	D.Baker	M	T.LaRussa
1B	D.Segui	M	B.Valentine	1B	G.Jefferies	1B	M.Johnson	1B	W.Joyner	1B	M.Carreon	1B	J.Mabry
2B	M.Lansing	1B	B.Huskey	2B	M.Morandini	2B	C.Garcia	2B	J.Reed	2B	S.Scarsone	2B	L.Alicea
SS	M.Grudzielanek	2B	J.Vizcaino	SS	K.Stocker	SS	J.Bell	SS	C.Gomez	SS	R.Aurilia	SS	R.Clayton
3B	S.Andrews	SS	R.Ordonez	3B	T.Zeile	3B	C.Hayes	3B	K.Caminiti	3B	M.Williams	3B	G.Gaetti
LF	H.Rodriguez	3B	J.Kent	LF	P.Incaviglia	LF	A.Martin	LF	R.Henderson	LF	B.Bonds	LF	R.Gant
CF	F.Santangelo	LF	B.Gilkey	CF	R.Otero	CF	M.Kingery	CF	S.Finley	CF	M.Benard	CF	R.Lankford
RF	M.Alou	CF	L.Johnson	RF	J.Eisenreich	RF	O.Merced	RF	T.Gwynn	RF	G.Hill	RF	B.Jordan
C	D.Fletcher	RF	A.Ochoa	C	B.Santiago	C	J.Kendall	C	J.Flaherty	C	T.Lampkin	C	T.Pagnozzi
		C	T.Hundley										
O	C.Floyd			P	C.Schilling	12	J.King	13	S.Livingstone	S	S.Dunston	O	W.McGee
O	R.White	23	E.Alfonzo	P	M.Williams	2	N.Liriano	C	B.Johnson	O	S.Javier	O1	M.Sweeney
		O	C.Everett	P	T.Mulholland	O	J.Allensworth			2	R.Thompson	S	O.Smith
P	J.Fassero			P	M.Mimbs	O	D.Clark	P	J.Hamilton	3	B.Mueller		
P	P.Martinez	P	M.Clark	RP	R.Springer			P	B.Tewksbury			P	An.Benes
P	R.Cormier	P	B.Jones	RP	T.Borland	P	D.Neagle	P	F.Valenzuela	P	A.Watson	P	T.Stottlemyre
P	U.Urbina	P	P.Harnisch	RP	K.Ryan	P	D.Darwin	P	A.Ashby	P	Van Landingham	P	D.Osborne
RP	O.Daal	P	J.Isringhausen			RP	J.Lieber	P	S.Sanders	P	M.Gardner	P	Al.Benes
RP	B.Manuel	P	P.Wilson	P	M.Grace	RP	F.Cordova	RP	T.Worrell	P	O.Fernandez	P	M.Morgan
RP	M.Rojas	RP	D.Mlicki	P	R.Hunter	RP	D.Miceli	RP	S.Bergman	P	M.Leiter	RP	M.Petkovsek
		RP	J.DiPoto	P	R.Bottalico			RP	T.Hoffman	RP	M.Dewey	P	T.Mathews
P	K.Rueter	RP	D.Henry	P	S.Fernandez	P	Z.Smith			RP	J.Bautista	RP	D.Eckersley
P	D.Veres					P	P.Wagner	P	W.Blair	RP	R.DeLucia		
P	M.Dyer	P	R.Person			P	M.Wilkins	P	D.Bochtler			P	C.Bailey
P	M.Leiter	P	J.Franco			P	D.Plesac			P	S.Estes		
P	J.Paniagua					P	C.Peters			P	R.Beck		
						P	M.Ruebel						
						P	E.Loaiza						

TEAM	G	W	L	PCT	GB	R	OR	AB	H	2B	3B	HR	BB	SO	AVG	OBP	SLG	PRO	PRO+	BR	/A	PF	CHI	RC	SB	CS	SBA	SBR
EAST																												
ATL	162	96	66	.593		773	**648**	5614	1514	264	28	197	530	1032	.270	.336	.432	.768	101	49	4	106	95	798	83	43	66	-1
MON	162	88	74	.543	8	741	668	5505	1441	297	27	148	492	1077	.262	.329	.406	.735	96	-14	-32	103	101	739	108	34	**76**	12
FLA	162	80	82	.494	16	688	703	5498	1413	240	30	150	553	1122	.257	.331	.393	.724	100	-29	0	96	95	713	99	46	68	2
NY	162	71	91	.438	25	746	779	5618	1515	267	**47**	147	445	1069	.270	.327	.412	.739	106	-10	41	93	100	748	97	48	67	0
PHI	162	67	95	.414	29	650	790	5499	1405	249	39	132	536	1092	.256	.327	.387	.714	91	-52	-70	103	93	704	117	41	74	11
CENTRAL																												
STL	162	88	74	.543		759	706	5502	1468	281	31	142	495	1089	.267	.332	.407	.739	100	-5	-7	100	102	743	149	58	72	10
HOU	162	82	80	.506	6	753	792	5508	1445	297	29	129	554	1057	.262	.339	.397	.736	**109**	-1	**68**	91	99	758	180	63	74	16
CIN	162	81	81	.500	7	778	773	5455	1398	259	36	191	604	1134	.256	.334	.422	.756	105	29	35	99	99	780	171	63	73	14
CHI	162	76	86	.469	12	772	771	5531	1388	267	19	175	523	1090	.251	.322	.401	.723	94	-39	-48	101	**108**	713	108	50	68	2
PIT	162	73	89	.451	15	776	833	5665	1509	**319**	33	138	510	**989**	.266	.331	.407	.738	96	-6	-29	103	102	771	126	49	72	8
WEST																												
SD	162	91	71	.562		771	682	5655	1499	285	24	147	601	1015	.265	.341	.402	.743	106	13	53	95	97	772	109	55	66	0
LA	162	90	72	.556	1	703	652	5538	1396	215	33	150	516	1190	.252	.318	.384	.702	98	-80	-25	92	105	684	124	40	**76**	13
COL	162	83	79	.512	8	**961**	964	5590	**1607**	297	37	**221**	527	1108	**.287**	**.357**	**.472**	**.829**	96	**178**	-82	129	102	**951**	**201**	66	75	**21**
SF	162	68	94	.420	23	752	862	5533	1400	245	21	153	**615**	1189	.253	.333	.388	.721	99	-32	-1	96	102	730	113	53	68	2
TOT	1134					10623		77711	20398	3782	434	2220	7501	15253	.262	.333	.408	.741							1785	709	72	110

TEAM	CG	SH	SV	IP	H	H/G	HR	BB	SO	RAT	ERA	ERA+	OAV	OOB	PR	/A	PF	CPI	FA	E	DP	FW	PW	BW	SBW	DIF
EAST																										
ATL	**14**	9	46	1469	1372	**8.4**	120	**451**	**1245**	**11.3**	3.52	**125**	**.247**	**.306**	113	**143**	104	96	.980	130	143	-.1	**14.0**	.4	-.9	1.7
MON	11	7	43	1441[1]	**1353**	**8.4**	152	482	1206	11.8	3.78	114	**.247**	.315	70	85	102	98	.980	126	121	.0	8.3	-3.1	.4	1.3
FLA	8	**13**	41	1443	1386	8.6	**113**	598	1050	12.7	3.95	102	.256	.336	42	15	96	100	.982	111	**187**	1.0	1.5	.0	-.6	-2.9
NY	10	10	41	1440	1517	9.5	159	532	999	13.1	4.22	93	.272	.340	-1	-47	93	105	.974	159	163	-1.9	-4.6	4.0	-.8	-6.7
PHI	12	6	42	1423[1]	1463	9.3	160	510	1044	12.7	4.48	97	.267	.333	-42	-18	104	96	.981	116	145	.7	-1.8	-6.8	.3	-6.4
CENTRAL																										
STL	13	11	43	1452[1]	1380	8.6	173	539	1050	12.1	3.97	107	.251	.322	39	42	101	100	.980	125	139	.2	4.1	-.7	.2	3.2
HOU	13	4	35	1447	1541	9.6	154	539	1163	13.4	4.37	88	.274	.345	-24	-87	91	104	.978	138	130	-.6	-8.5	**6.6**	.8	2.7
CIN	6	8	**52**	1443	1447	9.0	167	591	1089	13.0	4.32	96	.263	.339	-16	-26	99	101	.980	121	145	.4	-2.5	3.4	.6	-1.9
CHI	10	10	34	1456[1]	1447	8.9	184	546	1027	12.7	4.36	98	.260	.332	-23	-16	101	99	**.983**	**104**	147	**1.4**	-1.6	-4.7	-.6	.4
PIT	5	7	37	1453[1]	1602	9.9	183	479	1044	13.2	4.61	95	.281	.342	-63	-37	104	102	.980	128	144	-.0	-3.6	-2.8	.0	-1.5
WEST																										
SD	5	11	47	1489	1395	**8.4**	138	506	1194	11.8	3.72	107	.248	.315	81	44	95	97	.981	118	136	.6	4.3	5.2	-.8	.7
LA	6	9	50	1466[1]	1378	8.5	125	534	1213	12.0	**3.46**	111	.250	.320	**123**	63	91	**106**	.980	125	143	.2	6.2	-2.4	.5	4.6
COL	5	4	34	1422[2]	1597	10.1	198	624	932	14.5	5.59	97	.285	.364	-218	-25	129	95	.976	149	167	-1.3	-2.4	-8.0	**1.3**	12.5
SF	9	8	35	1442[1]	1520	9.5	194	570	997	13.5	4.71	87	.273	.348	-80	-100	97	102	.978	136	165	-.5	-9.8	-.0	-.6	-2.0
TOT	127	117	580	20289		9.0				12.7	4.21		.262	.333					.979	1786	2075					

Runs
Burks-Col 142
Finley-SD 126
Bonds-SF 122
Galarraga-Col 119
Sheffield-Fla 118

Hits
Johnson-NY 227
Burks-Col 211
Grissom-Atl 207
Grudzielanek-Mon . 201
Bichette-Col 198

Doubles
Bagwell-Hou 48
Finley-SD 45
Burks-Col 45
Gilkey-NY 44
Rodriguez-Mon 42

Triples
Johnson-NY 21
Howard-Cin 10
Grissom-Atl 10
Finley-SD 9

Home Runs
Galarraga-Col 47
Sheffield-Fla 42
Bonds-SF 42
Hundley-NY 41

Total Bases
Burks-Col 392
Galarraga-Col..... 376
Finley-SD 348
Castilla-Col....... 345
Caminiti-SD 339

Runs Batted In
Galarraga-Col..... 150
Bichette-Col 141
Caminiti-SD 130
Bonds-SF 129
Burks-Col 128

Runs Produced
Burks-Col 230
Bichette-Col 224
Galarraga-Col 222
Bonds-SF 209
Bagwell-Hou 200

Bases On Balls
Bonds-SF........ 151
Sheffield-Fla....... 142
Bagwell-Hou 135
Henderson-SD.... 125
Larkin-Cin......... 96

Batting Average
Gwynn-SD 353
Burks-Col 344
Piazza-LA 336
Johnson-NY 333
Grace-Chi 331

On Base Percentage
Sheffield-Fla ...... .469
Bonds-SF .... .465
Bagwell-Hou ...... .454
Piazza-LA .... .423
Larkin-Cin .... .415

Slugging Average
Burks-Col 639
Sheffield-Fla 624
Caminiti-SD 621
Bonds-SF 615
Galarraga-Col......601

Production
Sheffield-Fla 1.094
Bonds-SF 1.080
Burks-Col 1.048
Caminiti-SD 1.035
Bagwell-Hou.....1.025

Adjusted Production
Sheffield-Fla 193
Bonds-SF 190
Bagwell-Hou 185
Caminiti-SD 177
Piazza-LA 171

Batter Runs
Sheffield-Fla...... 72.3
Bonds-SF 69.2
Bagwell-Hou 63.3
Burks-Col 61.6
Caminiti-SD 54.2

Adjusted Batter Runs
Sheffield-Fla 78.6
Bagwell-Hou.......77.6
Bonds-SF 75.7
Caminiti-SD 60.9
Piazza-LA 57.6

Clutch Hitting Index
Jordan-StL........128
Bell-Hou 128
Pendleton-Fla-Atl . . 121
Joyner-SD 121
Reed-SD 121

Runs Created
Bonds-SF 162
Sheffield-Fla 159
Burks-Col 158
Bagwell-Hou 156
Caminiti-SD 138

Total Average
Bonds-SF 1.338
Sheffield-Fla 1.268
Bagwell-Hou 1.175
Burks-Col 1.136
Caminiti-SD 1.101

Stolen Bases
Young-Col 53
Johnson-NY 50
DeShields-LA 48
Bonds-SF 40
Martin-Pit......... 38

Stolen Base Average
Bell-Hou 90.6
Walker-Col 90.0
Renteria-Fla 88.9
Owens-Cin 88.9
Bonds-SF 85.1

Stolen Base Runs
Johnson-NY 7.8
DeShields-LA 7.8
Bonds-SF 7.8
Bell-Hou 6.9
Lankford-StL.......6.3

Fielding Runs
Young-Col 27.8
Castilla-Col 27.6
Gilkey-NY 24.1
Andrews-Mon 21.0
Lopez-Atl 18.3

Total Player Rating
Bonds-SF 8.5
Caminiti-SD 7.0
Bagwell-Hou 6.8
Gilkey-NY 6.6
Sheffield-Fla 6.2

Wins
Smoltz-Atl 24
A.Benes-StL 18
Ritz-Col 17
Brown-Fla 17

Win Percentage
Smoltz-Atl .... .750
Martinez-LA .... .714
Valdes-LA .... .682
A.Benes-StL ..... .643
Neagle-Pit-Atl .... .640

Games
Clontz-Atl 81
Patterson-Chi 79
Shaw-Cin 78
Dewey-SF 78
Wohlers-Atl 77

Complete Games
Schilling-Phi 8
Smoltz-Atl 6

Shutouts
Brown-Fla 3

Saves
Worrell-LA......... 44
Brantley-Cin 44
Hoffman-SD 42
Wohlers-Atl 39
Rojas-Mon 36

Innings Pitched
Smoltz-Atl 253.2
Maddux-Atl 245.0
Reynolds-Hou 239.0
Navarro-Chi 236.2
Glavine-Atl 235.1

Fewest Hits/Game
Leiter-Fla 6.39
Smoltz-Atl 7.06
Nomo-LA 7.09
Brown-Fla 7.22
Schilling-Phi 7.31

Fewest BB/Game
Maddux-Atl 1.03
Brown-Fla 1.27
Darwin-Pit-Hou ... 1.48
Reynolds-Hou 1.66
Tewksbury-SD 1.87

Strikeouts
Smoltz-Atl 276
Nomo-LA 234
Martinez-Mon 222
Fassero-Mon 222
Kile-Hou 219

Strikeouts/Game
Smoltz-Atl 9.79
Nomo-LA 9.22
Martinez-Mon 9.22
Kile-Hou 9.00
Schilling-Phi 8.93

Ratio
Smoltz-Atl 9.08
Brown-Fla 9.12
Maddux-Atl 9.40
Schilling-Phi 9.92
Reynolds-Hou ...10.51

Earned Run Average
Brown-Fla 1.89
Maddux-Atl 2.72
Leiter-Fla.........2.93
Smoltz-Atl 2.94
Glavine-Atl 2.98

Adjusted ERA
Brown-Fla 214
Maddux-Atl 162
Smoltz-Atl 149
Glavine-Atl 147
Trachsel-Chi 141

Opponents' Batting Avg.
Leiter-Fla 202
Smoltz-Atl 216
Nomo-LA 218
Brown-Fla..........220
Schilling-Phi 223

Opponents' On Base Pct.
Smoltz-Atl 261
Brown-Fla 263
Maddux-Atl 265
Schilling-Phi 280
Reynolds-Hou......290

Starter Runs
Brown-Fla 60.1
Maddux-Atl 40.7
Smoltz-Atl 35.8
Glavine-Atl 32.2
Leiter-Fla 30.8

Adjusted Starter Runs
Brown-Fla 55.7
Maddux-Atl 45.8
Smoltz-Atl 41.0
Glavine-Atl 37.0
Trachsel-Chi 28.0

Clutch Pitching Index
Trachsel-Chi 119
Martinez-LA 119
Valenzuela-SD 118
Drabek-Hou 114
Astacio-LA 113

Relief Runs
Nen-Fla 20.9
Shaw-Cin 20.0
Hoffman-SD 19.2
Ryan-Phi 17.7
Guthrie-LA 16.2

Adjusted Relief Runs
Nen-Fla 19.3
Shaw-Cin 19.3
Ryan-Phi.......... 19.1
Hoffman-SD 17.0
Bielecki-Atl 14.8

Relief Ranking
Hoffman-SD 38.6
Nen-Fla 26.9
J.Franco-NY 26.1
Shaw-Cin 24.5
Ruffin-Col 23.8

Total Pitcher Index
Brown-Fla 7.2
Maddux-Atl 5.6
Smoltz-Atl 5.4
Glavine-Atl 4.8
Hoffman-SD 3.8

Total Baseball Ranking
Bonds-SF 8.5
Brown-Fla 7.2
Caminiti-SD 7.0
Bagwell-Hou 6.8
Gilkey-NY 6.6

March 31 The first Opening Day in history in March takes place in Seattle.

May 14 Dwight Gooden, who sat out part of the previous two seasons for drug-related suspensions, no-hits the Mariners. Gooden walks six and fans five in the 10th no-hitter in Yankees history.

May 21 Ken Griffey Jr. hits his 200th career home run at age 26. Only seven other players did it faster, and six are in the Hall of Fame.

July 12 Kirby Puckett, a career .318 hitter in 12 seasons, announces his retirement because of a damaged retina.

July 15 After 2,216 consecutive games at shortstop, Cal Ripken moves to third base, the first time that Ripken hasn't started at shortstop since 1982.

September 6 Eddie Murray's 500th career home run ties the game between the Orioles and Tigers in the seventh, but Detroit wins, 5-4, in 12 innings. Murray joins an exclusive circle of Hank Aaron and Willie Mays as the only players with 500 home runs and 3,000 hits.

September 16 Paul Molitor of the Twins becomes the 21st player to reach 3,000 hits—and the first to reach the milestone with a triple.

September 18 Roger Clemens ties his own major league record with 20 strikeouts against the Tigers. The Red Sox fireballer allows five singles and walks none.

September 27 Baltimore's Roberto Alomar spits at home plate umpire John Hirschbeck during an argument and is given a five-game suspension, but he appeals and is allowed to play the next night; he hits a home run that clinches the wild card spot for the Orioles.

October 9 The Yankees win the ALCS opener when a 12-year-old fan sticks his glove out and turns a fly ball into a home run to tie the game. Bernie Williams homers in the bottom of the 11th to give New York a 5-4 win over the Orioles.

October 23 The Braves jump to a 6-0 lead, but the Yanks mount their biggest World Series comeback with a three-run home run by Jim Leyritz that ties the game in the eighth. After Bernie Williams is intentionally walked with runners on first and second in the 10th, Steve Avery walks Wade Boggs to bring in the deciding run.

October 26 A three-run third inning is all the Yankees need. Series MVP John Wetteland pitches out of trouble in the ninth as the Yankees win the World Series for the first time since 1978.

November 5 Yankees shortstop Derek Jeter is the unanimous choice as AL Rookie of the Year. He is the eighth Yankee to win the award and the fifth unanimous choice in league history.

November 12 Toronto's Pat Hentgen edges Andy Pettitte of the Yankees for the Cy Young Award. Hentgen (20-10) tops Pettitte (21-8) by a narrow margin of 110-104. Yankees middle reliever Mariano Rivera finishes third.

BALTIMORE

Pos	Player
M	D.Johnson
1B	R.Palmeiro
2B	R.Alomar
SS	C.Ripken
3B	B.Surhoff
LF	M.Devereaux
CF	B.Anderson
RF	B.Bonilla
C	C.Hoiles
DH	E.Murray
O	J.Hammonds
P	M.Mussina
P	D.Wells
P	S.Erickson
P	R.Coppinger
RP	R.Myers
RP	R.McDowell
RP	J.Orosco
P	J.Haynes
P	R.Krivda
P	K.Mercker
P	A.Mills
P	A.Rhodes

BOSTON

Pos	Player
M	K.Kennedy
1B	M.Vaughn
2B	J.Frye
SS	J.Valentin
3B	T.Naehring
LF	M.Greenwell
CF	L.Tinsley
RF	T.O'Leary
C	M.Stanley
DH	J.Canseco
DO	R.Jefferson
C	B.Haselman
O	D.Bragg
P	R.Clemens
P	T.Gordon
P	T.Wakefield
P	A.Sele
RP	V.Eshelman
RP	H.Slocumb
RP	M.Maddux
P	J.Moyer
P	M.Stanton

CALIFORNIA

Pos	Player
M	M.Lachemann
M	J.McNamara
1B	J.Snow
2B	R.Velarde
SS	G.DiSarcina
3B	G.Arias
LF	G.Anderson
CF	J.Edmonds
RF	T.Salmon
C	J.Fabregas
DH	C.Davis
2O	R.Hudler
O	D.Erstad
C	D.Slaught
P	C.Finley
P	S.Boskie
P	J.Abbott
P	J.Grimsley
P	M.Langston
RP	M.James
RP	T.Percival
P	D.Springer

CHICAGO

Pos	Player
M	T.Bevington
1B	F.Thomas
2B	R.Durham
SS	O.Guillen
3B	R.Ventura
LF	T.Phillips
CF	D.Lewis
RF	D.Tartabull
C	R.Karkovice
DH	H.Baines
O1	D.Martinez
OD	L.Mouton
P	A.Fernandez
P	K.Tapani
P	W.Alvarez
RP	J.Baldwin
RP	R.Hernandez
RP	B.Simas
RP	B.Keyser
P	M.Karchner
P	J.Magrane
P	K.McCaskill

CLEVELAND

Pos	Player
M	M.Hargrove
1B	J.Franco
2B	C.Baerga
SS	O.Vizquel
3B	J.Thome
LF	A.Belle
CF	K.Lofton
RF	M.Ramirez
C	S.Alomar
DH	E.Murray
P	C.Nagy
P	O.Hershiser
P	J.McDowell
P	C.Ogea
P	D.Martinez
RP	J.Tavarez
RP	E.Plunk
RP	J.Mesa
P	A.Lopez
P	P.Shuey
P	B.Anderson

DETROIT

Pos	Player
M	B.Bell
1B	T.Clark
2B	M.Lewis
SS	A.Cedeno
3B	T.Fryman
LF	B.Higginson
CF	C.Curtis
RF	M.Nieves
C	B.Ausmus
DH	E.Williams
O	K.Bartee
1D	C.Fielder
OD	C.Pride
P	F.Lira
P	O.Olivares
P	B.Williams
RP	R.Lewis
RP	J.Lima
RP	M.Myers
P	G.Gohr
P	G.Keagle
P	A.Sager
P	J.Thompson

KANSAS CITY

Pos	Player
M	B.Boone
1B	J.Offerman
2B	K.Lockhart
SS	D.Howard
3B	J.Randa
LF	T.Goodwin
CF	J.Damon
RF	M.Tucker
C	M.Macfarlane
DH	J.Vitiello
3O	C.Paquette
2D	B.Roberts
D1	B.Hamelin
P	T.Belcher
P	C.Haney
P	K.Appier
P	M.Gubicza
P	J.Rosado
RP	H.Pichardo
RP	J.Montgomery
RP	J.Valera
P	D.Linton
P	M.Magnante

MILWAUKEE

Pos	Player
M	P.Garner
1B	K.Seitzer
2B	F.Vina
SS	J.Valentin
3B	J.Cirillo
LF	G.Vaughn
CF	P.Listach
RF	M.Mieske
C	M.Matheny
DH	J.Jaha
C	J.Levis
OD	D.Nilsson
P	B.McDonald
P	S.Karl
P	R.Bones
RP	A.Miranda
RP	R.Garcia
RP	M.Fetters
P	S.Sparks
P	J.D'Amico
P	C.Eldred
P	T.Van Egmond
P	G.Lloyd

MINNESOTA

Pos	Player
M	T.Kelly
1B	S.Stahoviak
2B	C.Knoblauch
SS	P.Meares
3B	D.Hollins
LF	M.Cordova
CF	R.Becker
RF	R.Kelly
C	G.Myers
DH	P.Molitor
S3	J.Reboulet
O	M.Lawton
1O	R.Coomer
C	M.Walbeck
P	B.Radke
P	F.Rodriguez
P	R.Robertson
P	S.Aldred
P	R.Aguilera
RP	G.Hansell
RP	E.Guardado
RP	J.Parra
P	M.Trombley
P	D.Stevens
P	D.Naulty

NEW YORK

Pos	Player
M	J.Torre
1B	T.Martinez
2B	M.Duncan
SS	D.Jeter
3B	W.Boggs
LF	G.Williams
CF	B.Williams
RF	P.O'Neill
C	J.Girardi
DH	R.Sierra
23	A.Fox
C3	J.Leyritz
OD	D.Strawberry
O	T.Raines
D	C.Fielder
P	A.Pettitte
P	K.Rogers
P	D.Gooden
P	J.Key
RP	M.Rivera
RP	B.Wickman
RP	J.Nelson
P	D.Cone
P	J.Wetteland
P	R.Mendoza

OAKLAND

Pos	Player
M	A.Howe
1B	M.McGwire
2B	B.Bournigal
SS	M.Bordick
3B	S.Brosius
LF	P.Plantier
CF	E.Young
RF	J.Herrera
C	T.Steinbach
DH	G.Berroa
1O	J.Giambi
2	B.Gates
23	T.Batista
P	D.Wengert
P	D.Johns
P	J.Wasdin
P	A.Prieto
RP	C.Reyes
RP	M.Mohler
RP	B.Groom
P	S.Wojciechowski
P	D.Telgheder
P	W.Adams
P	J.Corsi
P	T.Van Poppel
P	B.Taylor
P	B.Chouinard

SEATTLE

Pos	Player
M	L.Piniella
1B	P.Sorrento
2B	J.Cora
SS	A.Rodriguez
3B	R.Davis
LF	R.Amaral
CF	K.Griffey
RF	J.Buhner
C	D.Wilson
DH	E.Martinez
32	L.Sojo
P	S.Hitchcock
P	B.Wolcott
P	B.Wells
RP	R.Carmona
RP	N.Charlton
RP	M.Jackson
P	M.Wagner
P	J.Moyer
P	T.Mulholland
P	B.Ayala
P	C.Bosio
P	R.Johnson

TEXAS

Pos	Player
M	J.Oates
1B	W.Clark
2B	M.McLemore
SS	K.Elster
3B	D.Palmer
LF	R.Greer
CF	D.Hamilton
RF	J.Gonzalez
C	I.Rodriguez
DH	M.Tettleton
O	W.Newson
P	K.Hill
P	R.Pavlik
P	B.Witt
P	D.Oliver
P	K.Gross
RP	G.Heredia
RP	D.Cook
RP	J.Russell
P	J.Burkett

TORONTO

Pos	Player
M	C.Gaston
1B	J.Olerud
2B	T.Perez
SS	A.Gonzalez
3B	E.Sprague
LF	J.Carter
CF	O.Nixon
RF	S.Green
C	C.O'Brien
DH	C.Delgado
O	J.Brumfield
2	D.Cedeno
C	A.Martinez
O	R.Perez
P	P.Hentgen
P	E.Hanson
P	J.Guzman
P	P.Quantrill
RP	T.Castillo
RP	T.Crabtree
RP	M.Timlin
P	M.Janzen
P	H.Flener
P	W.Williams

TEAM	G	W	L	PCT	GB	R	OR	AB	H	2B	3B	HR	BB	SO	AVG	OBP	SLG	PRO	PRO+	BR	/A	PF	CHI	RC	SB	CS	SBA	SBR
EAST																												
NY	162	92	70	.568		871	787	5628	1621	293	28	162	632	909	.288	.364	.436	.800	99	16	0	102	98	890	96	46	68	1
BAL	163	88	74	.543	4	949	903	5689	1557	299	29	**257**	645	915	.274	.354	.472	.826	108	50	63	99	102	948	76	40	66	-1
BOS	162	85	77	.525	7	928	921	5756	1631	308	31	209	642	1020	.283	.362	.457	.819	102	47	15	103	99	948	91	44	67	1
TOR	162	74	88	.457	18	766	809	5599	1451	302	35	177	529	1105	.259	.333	.420	.753	89	-101	-104	100	101	794	116	38	75	12
DET	162	53	109	.327	39	783	1103	5530	1413	257	21	204	546	1268	.256	.326	.420	.746	88	-121	-115	99	**108**	746	87	50	64	-4
CENTRAL																												
CLE	161	99	62	.615		952	**769**	5681	**1665**	335	23	218	671	**844**	**.293**	**.372**	.475	.847	112	109	110	100	96	1003	160	50	**76**	**18**
CHI	162	85	77	.525	14.5	898	794	5644	1586	284	33	195	**701**	927	.281	.364	.447	.811	109	35	86	95	98	926	105	41	72	7
MIL	162	80	82	.494	19.5	894	899	5662	1578	304	40	178	624	986	.279	.356	.441	.797	95	0	-47	105	102	899	101	48	68	2
MIN	162	78	84	.481	21.5	877	900	5673	1633	332	**47**	118	576	958	.288	.360	.425	.785	95	-15	-30	102	103	860	143	53	73	11
KC	161	75	86	.466	24	746	786	5542	1477	286	38	123	529	943	.267	.335	.398	.733	86	-132	-113	97	104	750	**195**	85	70	8
WEST																												
TEX	163	90	72	.556		928	799	5702	1622	323	32	221	660	1041	.284	.362	.469	.831	101	67	3	107	98	975	83	26	**76**	9
SEA	161	85	76	.528	4.5	**993**	895	5668	1625	**343**	19	245	670	1052	.287	.370	**.484**	**.854**	**114**	**117**	**122**	100	99	**1024**	90	39	70	4
OAK	162	78	84	.481	12	861	900	5630	1492	283	21	243	640	1114	.265	.346	.452	.798	103	-8	27	96	100	880	58	35	62	-4
CAL	161	70	91	.435	19.5	762	943	5686	1571	256	24	192	527	974	.276	.341	.431	.772	95	-62	-44	98	96	814	53	39	58	-8
TOT	1133					12208		79090	21922	4205	421	2742	8592	14056	.277	.353	.445	.798							1454	634	70	56

TEAM	CG	SH	SV	IP	H	H/G	HR	BB	SO	RAT	ERA	ERA+	OAV	OOB	PR	/A	PF	CPI	FA	E	DP	FW	PW	BW	SBW	DIF
EAST																										
NY	6	**9**	**52**	1440	**1469**	**9.2**	**143**	610	1139	13.3	4.65	109	**.265**	.343	55	64	101	94	.985	91	146	1.2	5.8	.0	-.3	4.2
BAL	13	1	44	1468²	1604	9.8	209	597	1047	13.7	5.14	95	.280	.352	-25	-40	98	98	.984	97	173	.9	-3.6	5.7	-.5	4.4
BOS	17	5	37	1458	1606	9.9	185	722	**1165**	14.7	4.98	103	.279	.364	1	26	103	103	.978	135	152	-1.2	2.4	1.4	-.3	1.8
TOR	**19**	7	35	1445²	1476	**9.2**	187	610	1033	13.2	4.57	111	.266	.343	68	77	101	101	.982	110	187	.2	7.0	-9.5	.7	-5.4
DET	10	4	22	1432²	1699	10.7	241	784	957	16.1	6.38	79	.296	.389	-221	-209	101	97	.978	137	157	-1.4	-19.0	-10.5	-.7	3.6
CENTRAL																										
CLE	13	**9**	46	1452¹	1530	9.5	173	484	1033	**12.7**	**4.34**	113	.271	**.333**	**105**	89	98	102	.980	124	156	-.7	8.1	10.0	**1.3**	-.2
CHI	7	4	43	1461	1529	9.4	174	616	1039	13.4	4.52	104	.270	.345	77	29	94	102	.982	109	145	.2	2.6	7.8	.3	-7.0
MIL	6	4	42	1447¹	1570	9.8	213	635	846	14.1	5.14	102	.278	.357	-23	20	105	101	.978	134	180	-1.2	1.8	-4.3	-.2	2.8
MIN	13	5	31	1439²	1561	9.8	233	581	959	13.6	5.28	97	.277	.348	-46	-23	103	96	.984	94	142	1.1	-2.1	-2.7	.6	.1
KC	17	8	35	1450	1563	9.7	176	**460**	926	12.9	4.55	107	.277	.338	71	54	98	101	.982	111	184	.0	4.9	-10.3	.4	-.6
WEST																										
TEX	**19**	6	43	1449¹	1569	9.7	168	582	976	13.6	4.65	**114**	.278	.350	55	**106**	106	103	**.986**	**87**	150	**1.5**	**9.7**	.3	.5	-2.9
SEA	4	4	34	1431²	1562	9.8	216	605	1000	14.0	5.21	95	.279	.356	-35	-45	99	99	.981	110	155	.1	-4.1	**11.1**	.0	-2.6
OAK	7	5	34	1456¹	1638	10.1	205	644	884	14.4	5.20	92	.287	.365	-33	-63	96	**104**	.984	103	**195**	.6	-5.7	2.5	-.7	.5
CAL	12	8	38	1439	1546	9.7	219	662	1052	14.3	5.30	92	.275	.360	-49	-65	98	99	.979	128	156	-.9	-5.9	-4.0	-1.1	1.4
TOT	163	79	536	20271²	12208	9.7				13.9	4.99		.277	.353					.982	1570	2278					

Runs
Rodriguez-Sea 141
Knoblauch-Min 140
Lofton-Cle 132
Alomar-Bal 132
Griffey-Sea 125

Hits
Molitor-Min 225
Rodriguez-Sea 215
Lofton-Cle 210
Vaughn-Bos 207
Knoblauch-Min 197

Doubles
Rodriguez-Sea 54
E.Martinez-Sea 52
Rodriguez-Tex 47
Cordova-Min 46
Cirillo-Mil 46

Triples
Knoblauch-Min 14
Vina-Mil 10

Home Runs
McGwire-Oak 52
Anderson-Bal 50
Griffey-Sea 49
Belle-Cle 48
Gonzalez-Tex 47

Total Bases
Rodriguez-Sea 379
Belle-Cle 375
Vaughn-Bos 370
Anderson-Bal 369
Gonzalez-Tex 348

Runs Batted In
Belle-Cle 148
Gonzalez-Tex 144
Vaughn-Bos 143
Palmeiro-Bal 142
Griffey-Sea 140

Runs Produced
Rodriguez-Sea 228
Belle-Cle 224
Vaughn-Bos 217
Griffey-Sea 216
Palmeiro-Bal 213

Bases On Balls
Phillips-Chi 125
Thome-Cle 123
E.Martinez-Sea ... 123
McGwire-Oak 116
F.Thomas-Chi 109

Batting Average
Rodriguez-Sea ..... .358
F.Thomas-Chi ..... .349
Molitor-Min .... .341
Knoblauch-Min .... .341
Greer-Tex .... .332

On Base Percentage
McGwire-Oak ..... .468
E.Martinez-Sea ... .467
F.Thomas-Chi .... .465
Knoblauch-Min ... .452
Thome-Cle .... .451

Slugging Average
McGwire-Oak ...... .730
Gonzalez-Tex ...... .643
Anderson-Bal ...... .637
Rodriguez-Sea ..... .631
Griffey-Sea .... .628

Production
McGwire-Oak 1.199
F.Thomas-Chi 1.091
Thome-Cle 1.063
E.Martinez-Sea ... 1.062
Rodriguez-Sea ... 1.049

Adjusted Production
McGwire-Oak 205
F.Thomas-Chi 182
E.Martinez-Sea ... 167
Thome-Cle 165
Rodriguez-Sea 161

Batter Runs
McGwire-Oak 67.3
F.Thomas-Chi 63.3
E.Martinez-Sea ... 57.1
Thome-Cle 55.6
Rodriguez-Sea ... 54.6

Adjusted Batter Runs
McGwire-Oak 73.0
F.Thomas-Chi 71.8
E.Martinez-Sea ... 57.8
Thome-Cle 55.7
Rodriguez-Sea ... 55.3

Clutch Hitting Index
Molitor-Min 129
Cordova-Min 120
Elster-Tex 117
Tartabull-Chi 117
O'Leary-Bos 116

Runs Created
Vaughn-Bos 158
Rodriguez-Sea 157
Belle-Cle 156
Anderson-Bal 150
F.Thomas-Chi 150

Total Average
McGwire-Oak 1.420
E.Martinez-Sea .. 1.209
Thome-Cle 1.207
F.Thomas-Chi ... 1.203
Griffey-Sea 1.139

Stolen Bases
Lofton-Cle 75
Goodwin-KC 66
Nixon-Tor 54
Knoblauch-Min 45
Vizquel-Cle 35

Stolen Base Average
Griffey-Sea 94.1
Durham-Chi 88.2
Listach-Mil 83.3
Damon-KC 83.3
Frye-Bos 81.8

Stolen Base Runs
Lofton-Cle 12.3
Nixon-Tor 8.4
Goodwin-KC 6.6
Durham-Chi 6.6

Fielding Runs
Becker-Min 23.9
Gonzalez-Tor 23.0
McLemore-Tex ... 20.1
Howard-KC 18.8
Fryman-Det 16.7

Total Player Rating
Rodriguez-Sea 5.4
Griffey-Sea 5.4
Alomar-Bal 5.4
Belle-Cle 5.3
McGwire-Oak 5.1

Wins
Pettitte-NY 21
Hentgen-Tor 20
Mussina-Bal 19
Nagy-Cle 17

Win Percentage
Nagy-Cle .... .773
Pettitte-NY .... .724
Hentgen-Tor ...... .667
Pavlik-Tex .... .652
Mussina-Bal ...... .633

Games
Myers-Det 83
Guardado-Min 83
Stanton-Bos-Tex ... 81
Slocumb-Bos 75

Complete Games
Hentgen-Tor 10
Pavlik-Tex 7
Hill-Tex 7

Shutouts
Robertson-Min 3
Hill-Tex 3
Hentgen-Tor 3
Lira-Det 2
Clemens-Bos 2

Saves
Wetteland-NY 43
Mesa-Cle 39
Hernandez-Chi 38
Percival-Cal 36
Fetters-Mil 32

Innings Pitched
Hentgen-Tor 265.2
Fernandez-Chi ... 258.0
Hill-Tex 250.2
Mussina-Bal 243.1
Clemens-Bos 242.2

Fewest Hits/Game
Guzman-Tor 7.58
Clemens-Bos 8.01
Hentgen-Tor 8.06
Appier-KC 8.18
Fernandez-Chi ... 8.65

Fewest BB/Game
Haney-KC 2.01
Wells-Bal 2.05
Radke-Min 2.21
Nagy-Cle 2.47
Fernandez-Chi ... 2.51

Strikeouts
Clemens-Bos 257
Finley-Cal 215
Appier-KC 207
Mussina-Bal 204
Fernandez-Chi 200

Strikeouts/Game
Clemens-Bos 9.53
Appier-KC 8.82
Finley-Cal 8.13
Guzman-Tor 7.91
Mussina-Bal 7.55

Ratio
Guzman-Tor 10.45
Radke-Min 11.33
Nagy-Cle 11.39
Fernandez-Chi ... 11.41
Hentgen-Tor 11.42

Earned Run Average
Guzman-Tor 2.93
Hentgen-Tor 3.22
Nagy-Cle 3.41
Fernandez-Chi ... 3.45
Appier-KC 3.62

Adjusted ERA
Guzman-Tor 173
Hentgen-Tor 157
Hill-Tex 146
Nagy-Cle 144
Clemens-Bos 141

Opponents' Batting Avg.
Guzman-Tor .... .228
Clemens-Bos ...... .237
Hentgen-Tor ...... .241
Appier-KC .... .245
Fernandez-Chi .... .253

Opponents' On Base Pct.
Guzman-Tor .... .290
Radke-Min .... .304
Nagy-Cle .... .307
Fernandez-Chi .... .309
Hentgen-Tor ...... .310

Starter Runs
Hentgen-Tor 52.3
Fernandez-Chi 44.1
Guzman-Tor 43.1
Nagy-Cle 39.1
Hill-Tex 38.0

Adjusted Starter Runs
Hentgen-Tor 54.1
Hill-Tex 46.9
Guzman-Tor 44.3
Clemens-Bos 40.6
Nagy-Cle 36.6

Clutch Pitching Index
Belcher-KC 116
Fernandez-Chi 113
Hill-Tex 112
Pettitte-NY 111
Boskie-Cal 110

Relief Runs
M.Rivera-NY 34.7
Hernandez-Chi ... 28.9
Plunk-Cle 22.1
Percival-Cal 22.0
James-Cal 20.9

Adjusted Relief Runs
M.Rivera-NY 35.4
Hernandez-Chi ... 26.2
Percival-Cal 21.2
Plunk-Cle 21.2
James-Cal 20.0

Relief Ranking
Hernandez-Chi ... 52.9
M.Rivera-NY 35.7
Slocumb-Bos 35.0
Wetteland-NY 31.3
Percival-Cal 24.8

Total Pitcher Index
Hentgen-Tor 5.3
Hernandez-Chi 4.9
Hill-Tex 3.9
Guzman-Tor 3.9
Fernandez-Chi 3.5

Total Baseball Ranking
Rodriguez-Sea 5.4
Griffey-Sea 5.4
Alomar-Bal 5.4
Hentgen-Tor 5.3
Belle-Cle 5.3

January 6 Phil Niekro's knuckleball finally lands him in the Hall of Fame.

April 15 The 50th anniversary of Jackie Robinson's breaking the color barrier in baseball is celebrated before 54,047 at Shea Stadium during a game between the Mets and the Dodgers. Acting commissioner Bud Selig announces that the No. 42 will be retired in perpetuity for every team in honor of Robinson.

June 10 Kevin Brown pitches the first no-hitter of the season and the second no-hitter in Marlins history in a 9-0 win over the Giants in San Francisco.

June 16 Both NL teams win in the first intercity interleague games on the road as the Mets beat the Yankees, 6-0, and the Cubs knock off the White Sox, 8-3.

July 12 Francisco Cordova and Ricardo Rincon combine on a 10-inning no-hitter as the Pirates defeat the Astros, 3-0.

July 31 At the trading deadline Mark McGwire is sent to St. Louis.

September 16 Philadelphia's Curt Schilling becomes the 13th pitcher to strike out 300 batters in a season, fanning nine in a 3-2 victory over the Mets.

September 28 Mark McGwire hits his 58th home run of the season to tie Jimmie Foxx for the most in a season by a right-handed hitter.

October 14 Kevin Brown retires Chipper Jones with two runners on to make the Marlins the first expansion team to advance to the World Series after just five seasons.

October 26 Edgar Renteria ends the second-longest Game 7 in World Series history with a bases-loaded single over the glove of Indians pitcher Charles Nagy with two outs in the 11th inning.

November 4 Scott Rolen is the unanimous choice for NL Rookie of the Year.

	ATLANTA		CHICAGO		CINCINNATI		COLORADO		FLORIDA		HOUSTON		LOS ANGELES
M	B.Cox	M	J.Riggleman	M	R.Knight	M	D.Baylor	M	J.Leyland	M	L.Dierker	M	B.Russell
1B	F.McGriff	1B	M.Grace	M	J.McKeon	1B	A.Galarraga	1B	J.Conine	1B	J.Bagwell	1B	E.Karros
2B	M.Lemke	2B	R.Sandberg	1B	H.Morris	2B	E.Young	2B	L.Castillo	2B	C.Biggio	2B	W.Guerrero
SS	J.Blauser	SS	S.Dunston	2B	B.Boone	SS	W.Weiss	SS	E.Renteria	SS	T.Bogar	SS	G.Gagne
3B	C.Jones	3B	K.Orie	SS	P.Reese	3B	V.Castilla	3B	B.Bonilla	3B	S.Berry	3B	T.Zeile
LF	R.Klesko	LF	D.Glanville	3B	W.Greene	LF	D.Bichette	LF	M.Alou	LF	L.Gonzalez	LF	T.Hollandsworth
CF	A.Jones	CF	B.McRae	LF	C.Goodwin	CF	Q.McCracken	CF	D.White	CF	T.Howard	CF	B.Butler
RF	M.Tucker	RF	S.Sosa	CF	D.Sanders	RF	L.Walker	RF	G.Sheffield	RF	D.Bell	RF	R.Mondesi
C	J.Lopez	C	S.Servais	RF	R.Sanders	C	K.Manwaring	C	C.Johnson	C	B.Ausmus	C	M.Piazza
				C	J.Oliver								
2	T.Graffanino	O	D.Clark			O	E.Burks	O	J.Cangelosi	S3	R.Gutierrez	O	R.Cedeno
O	K.Lofton	3S	J.Hernandez	O2	L.Harris	S2	N.Perez	O1	J.Eisenreich	3S	B.Spiers	O	O.Nixon
C	E.Perez	S2	R.Sanchez	1O	E.Perez	C	J.Reed	2O	K.Abbott	O	C.Carr	2	E.Young
23	K.Lockhart	C3	T.Houston	CO	E.Taubensee	2S	J.Bates	2	C.Counsell	O	B.Abreu	O	B.Ashley
O	D.Bautista	3	D.Hansen	S	B.Larkin	O	T.Helton	C	G.Zaun	O	J.Mouton	C	T.Prince
3	M.Mordecai	O	L.Johnson	O	J.Nunnally	/O	J.Vander Wal	O	C.Floyd	O	T.Eusebio	2	N.Liriano
S	R.Belliard	O1	B.Brown	O	C.Stynes	O	H.Pulliam	1	D.Daulton	S	P.Listach	2S	T.Cromer
		S	M.Alexander	O	M.Kelly			3S	A.Arias	O	R.Montgomery	O	D.Lewis
		O	B.Kieschnick	3	T.Pendleton	P	R.Bailey			O	R.Hidalgo	S2	J.Castro
P	J.Smoltz	C	M.Hubbard	32	J.Branson	P	J.Thomson	P	K.Brown	3	R.Johnson	O	E.Anthony
P	T.Glavine			C	B.Fordyce	P	J.Wright	P	A.Fernandez			O	W.Kirby
P	D.Neagle	P	S.Trachsel	O	R.Sierra	P	K.Ritz	P	A.Leiter	P	D.Kile		
P	G.Maddux	P	T.Mulholland			RP	J.DiPoto	P	T.Saunders	P	M.Hampton	P	H.Nomo
RP	M.Wohlers	P	K.Foster	P	M.Morgan	RP	D.Holmes	P	P.Rapp	P	C.Holt	P	I.Valdes
RP	M.Bielecki	P	J.Gonzalez	P	D.Burba	RP	M.DeJean	RP	J.Powell	P	S.Reynolds	P	C.Park
RP	P.Byrd	P	F.Castillo	P	K.Mercker			RP	R.Helling	P	R.Garcia	P	P.Astacio
		RP	K.Bottenfield	P	B.Tomko	P	F.Castillo	RP	R.Nen	RP	J.Lima	P	T.Candiotti
P	K.Millwood	RP	T.Adams	P	J.Smiley	P	B.Swift			RP	B.Wagner	RP	M.Guthrie
P	B.Clontz	RP	T.Wendell	RP	M.Remlinger	P	S.Reed	P	L.Hernandez	P	T.Martin	RP	D.Dreifort
P	A.Embree			RP	S.Belinda	P	J.Burke	P	D.Cook			RP	S.Radinsky
P	T.Wade			RP	S.Sullivan	P	C.Leskanic	P	F.Heredia	P	R.Springer		
P	M.Cather	P	K.Tapani										

	MONTREAL		NEW YORK		PHILADELPHIA		PITTSBURGH		SAN DIEGO		SAN FRANCISCO		ST.LOUIS
M	F.Alou	M	B.Valentine	M	T.Francona	M	G.Lamont	M	B.Bochy	M	D.Baker	M	T.LaRussa
1B	D.Segui	1B	J.Olerud	1B	R.Brogna	1B	K.Young	1B	W.Joyner	1B	J.Snow	1B	D.Young
2B	M.Lansing	2B	C.Baerga	2B	M.Morandini	2B	T.Womack	2B	Q.Veras	2B	J.Kent	2B	D.DeShields
SS	M.Grudzielanek	SS	R.Ordonez	SS	K.Stocker	SS	K.Polcovich	SS	C.Gomez	SS	J.Vizcaino	SS	R.Clayton
3B	D.Strange	3B	E.Alfonzo	3B	S.Rolen	3B	J.Randa	3B	K.Caminiti	3B	B.Mueller	3B	G.Gaetti
LF	H.Rodriguez	LF	B.Gilkey	LF	G.Jefferies	LF	A.Martin	LF	G.Vaughn	LF	B.Bonds	LF	R.Gant
CF	R.White	CF	C.Everett	CF	R.Amaro	CF	J.Allensworth	CF	S.Finley	CF	D.Hamilton	CF	R.Lankford
RF	F.Santangelo	RF	B.Huskey	RF	D.Daulton	RF	J.Guillen	RF	T.Gwynn	RF	S.Javier	RF	W.McGee
C	C.Widger	C	T.Hundley	C	M.Lieberthal	C	J.Kendall	C	J.Flaherty	C	R.Wilkins	C	M.Difelice
O1	J.Orsulak	31	M.Franco	O	M.Cummings	3S	D.Sveum	O	R.Henderson	C	G.Hill	C	T.Lampkin
O	V.Guerrero	O	A.Ochoa	O	T.Barron	1	M.Johnson	13	A.Cianfrocco	32	M.Lewis	O1	J.Mabry
C	D.Fletcher	O	L.Johnson	13	K.Jordan	O	M.Smith	O	C.Jones	C	B.Johnson	1	M.McGwire
O1	R.McGuire	S2	L.Lopez	O	R.Otero	O	T.Ward	S2	C.Shipley	C	D.Berryhill	O	B.Jordan
3	J.Vidro	2S	M.Alexander	O	D.May	O	A.Brown	C	C.Hernandez	32	M.Benard	32	D.Bell
2S	A.Stankiewicz	O	B.McRae	O	R.Hudler	S	K.Elster	O	M.Sweeney	S	R.Aurilia	3O	D.Sheaffer
3	S.Andrews	C	T.Pratt	2S	K.Sefcik	O	M.Cummings	O	T.Beamon	C	M.Jensen	O	P.Plantier
		O	S.Bieser	O	W.Magee	C	K.Osik					O	M.Sweeney
				C	M.Parent	O	E.Brown	P	A.Ashby	P	S.Estes		
P	P.Martinez	P	R.Reed	P	R.Butler	1	E.Williams	P	J.Hamilton	P	K.Rueter	P	M.Morris
P	C.Perez	P	D.Mlicki	O	B.McMillon	S	S.Dunston	P	S.Hitchcock	P	M.Gardner	P	T.Stottlemyre
P	D.Hermanson	P	B.Jones					P	P.Smith	RP	J.Tavarez	P	An.Benes
P	J.Bullinger	P	M.Clark	P	C.Schilling	P	E.Loaiza	RP	T.Worrell	RP	D.Henry	P	Al.Benes
P	J.Juden	RP	G.McMichael	P	M.Leiter	P	J.Schmidt	RP	S.Bergman	RP	R.Beck	RP	M.Petkovsek
RP	M.Valdes	RP	C.Lidle	P	M.Beech	P	J.Lieber	RP	W.Cunnane			RP	J.Frascatore
RP	A.Telford	RP	J.Franco	P	G.Stephenson	P	F.Cordova			P	Van Landingham	RP	R.Beltran
RP	U.Urbina			RP	J.Spradlin	P	S.Cooke	P	T.Hoffman	P	W.Alvarez		
P	D.Veres	P	B.Bohanon	RP	R.Bottalico	RP	M.Wilkins	P	F.Valenzuela	P	J.Roa	P	A.Benes
P	M.Johnson	P	A.Reynoso	RP	R.Harris	RP	R.Loiselle	P	D.Bochtler	P	R.Rodriguez	P	A.Benes
P	O.Daal	P	J.Acevedo			RP	M.Ruebel	P	D.Jackson	P	O.Fernandez	P	D.Osborne
P	R.DeHart	P	J.Crawford	P	T.Green			P	J.Bruske	P	J.Poole	P	M.Aybar
P	S.Kline	P	T.Kashiwada	P	C.Maduro	P	R.Rincon	/P	P.Menhart	P	K.Foulke	P	D.Eckersley

TEAM	G	W	L	PCT	GB	R	OR	AB	H	2B	3B	HR	BB	SO	AVG	OBP	SLG	PRO	PRO+	BR	/A	PF	CHI	RC	SB	CS	SBA	SBR
EAST																												
ATL	162	101	61	.623		791	**581**	5528	1490	268	37	174	597	1160	.270	.346	.426	.772	105	56	44	102	98	810	108	58	65	-2
FLA	162	92	70	.568	9	740	669	5439	1410	272	28	136	**686**	**1074**	.259	.349	.395	.744	105	11	46	95	97	763	115	58	66	0
NY	162	88	74	.543	13	777	709	5524	1448	274	28	153	550	1029	.262	.335	.405	.740	102	-11	16	96	**106**	742	97	74	57	-15
MON	162	78	84	.481	23	691	740	5526	1423	**339**	34	172	420	1084	.258	.318	.425	.743	98	-24	-20	100	97	741	75	46	62	-5
PHI	162	68	94	.420	33	668	840	5443	1390	290	35	116	519	1032	.255	.325	.385	.710	91	-72	-70	100	101	685	92	56	62	-6
CENTRAL																												
HOU	162	84	78	.519		777	660	5502	1427	314	40	133	633	1085	.259	.346	.403	.749	105	20	50	96	100	794	171	74	70	7
PIT	162	79	83	.488	5	725	760	5503	1440	291	**52**	129	481	1161	.262	.331	.404	.735	96	-24	-35	102	101	753	160	50	**76**	**18**
CIN	162	76	86	.469	8	651	764	5484	1386	269	27	142	518	1113	.253	.322	.389	.711	90	-72	-79	101	98	701	**190**	67	74	17
STL	162	73	89	.451	11	689	708	5524	1409	269	39	144	543	1191	.255	.326	.396	.722	95	-50	-42	99	100	717	164	60	73	13
CHI	162	68	94	.420	16	687	759	5489	1444	269	39	127	451	1003	.263	.323	.396	.719	91	-61	-76	102	103	692	116	60	66	-1
WEST																												
SF	162	90	72	.556		784	793	5485	1415	266	37	172	642	1120	.258	.341	.414	.755	104	21	39	98	101	789	121	49	71	7
LA	162	88	74	.543	2	742	645	5544	1488	242	33	174	498	1079	.268	.332	.418	.750	**110**	3	61	92	99	768	131	64	67	1
COL	162	83	79	.512	7	**923**	908	5603	**1611**	269	40	**239**	562	1060	**.288**	**.359**	**.478**	**.837**	100	**180**	-26	123	98	**949**	137	65	68	2
SD	162	76	86	.469	14	795	891	5609	1519	275	16	152	604	1129	.271	.345	.407	.752	**110**	21	**79**	93	102	795	140	60	70	6
TOT	1134					10440	77203	20300	3907	485	2163	7704	15320	.263	.336	.410	.746							1817	841	68	41	

TEAM	CG	SH	SV	IP	H	H/G	HR	BB	SO	RAT	ERA	ERA+	OAV	OOB	PR	/A	PF	CPI	FA	E	DP	FW	PW	BW	SBW	DIF
EAST																										
ATL	21	**17**	37	1465^{2}	**1319**	**8.1**	**111**	**450**	1196	**11.1**	**3.18**	**131**	**.241**	**.303**	**166**	**163**	100	99	.982	114	136	.3	**16.1**	4.3	-.5	-.2
FLA	12	10	39	1446^{2}	1353	8.4	131	639	1188	12.8	3.83	105	.250	.336	60	32	96	103	.981	116	167	.2	3.2	4.5	-.3	3.4
NY	7	8	**49**	1459^{1}	1452	9.0	160	504	982	12.4	3.95	102	.262	.328	41	14	96	103	.981	120	165	-.0	1.4	1.6	-1.8	5.8
MON	**27**	14	37	1447	1365	8.5	149	557	1138	12.3	4.14	101	.250	.327	10	9	100	94	.979	132	150	-.7	.9	-2.0	-.8	-.4
PHI	13	7	35	1420^{1}	1441	9.1	171	616	1209	13.4	4.85	88	.265	.346	-102	-96	101	93	.982	108	134	.7	-9.5	-6.9	-.9	3.5
CENTRAL																										
HOU	16	12	37	1459	1379	8.5	134	511	1138	12.0	3.66	109	.251	.321	87	54	95	101	.979	131	169	-.7	5.3	4.9	.4	-7.0
PIT	6	8	41	1436	1503	9.4	143	560	1080	13.3	4.28	100	.271	.345	-13	1	102	103	.979	131	149	-.7	.0	-3.4	**1.5**	.5
CIN	5	8	**49**	1449	1408	8.7	173	558	1159	12.7	4.41	97	.255	.332	-34	-24	102	94	.982	**106**	129	**.8**	-2.4	-7.8	1.4	3.0
STL	5	3	39	1455^{2}	1422	8.8	124	536	1130	12.5	3.88	107	.259	.331	52	44	99	101	.980	123	156	-.2	4.3	-4.1	1.0	-9.0
CHI	6	4	37	1429	1451	9.1	185	590	1072	13.1	4.44	97	.266	.342	-38	-22	102	102	.981	112	117	.5	-2.2	-7.5	-.4	-3.4
WEST																										
SF	5	9	45	1446	1494	9.3	160	578	1044	13.1	4.39	94	.270	.343	-31	-43	98	101	.980	125	157	-.3	-4.2	3.8	.4	9.3
LA	6	6	45	1459^{1}	1325	8.2	163	546	**1232**	11.8	3.62	106	**.241**	.315	94	38	92	100	.981	116	104	.2	3.7	6.0	-.2	-2.8
COL	9	5	38	1432^{2}	1697	10.7	196	566	870	14.6	5.25	98	.300	.370	-167	-13	123	**105**	**.983**	111	**202**	.5	-1.3	-2.6	-.0	5.4
SD	5	2	43	1450	1581	9.8	172	596	1059	13.9	4.98	78	.280	.355	-125	-177	92	97	.979	132	132	-.7	-17.4	7.8	.3	5.1
TOT	143	113	571	20255^{2}	9.0			12.8	4.20		.263	.336					.981	1677	2067							

Runs
Biggio-Hou 146
Walker-Col 143
Bonds-SF 123
Galarraga-Col 120
Bagwell-Hou 109

Hits
Gwynn-SD 220
Walker-Col 208
Piazza-LA 201

Doubles
Grudzielanek-Mon . . 54
Gwynn-SD 49
Walker-Col 46
Lansing-Mon 45
Mondesi-LA 42

Triples
DeShields-StL 14
Perez-Col 10
Womack-Pit 9
Randa-Pit 9
Guerrero-LA 9

Home Runs
Walker-Col 49
Bagwell-Hou 43
Galarraga-Col 41

Total Bases
Walker-Col 409
Piazza-LA 355
Galarraga-Col 351
Castilla-Col 335
Bagwell-Hou 335

Runs Batted In
Galarraga-Col 140
Bagwell-Hou 135
Walker-Col 130
Piazza-LA 124
Kent-SF 121

Runs Produced
Walker-Col 224
Galarraga-Col 219
Biggio-Hou 205
Bagwell-Hou 201
Gwynn-SD 199

Bases On Balls
Bonds-SF 145
Bagwell-Hou 127
Sheffield-Fla 121
Snow-SF 96
Lankford-StL 95

Batting Average
Gwynn-SD 372
Walker-Col 366
Piazza-LA 362
Lofton-Atl 333
Joyner-SD 327

On Base Percentage
Walker-Col 455
Bonds-SF 450
Piazza-LA 435
Bagwell-Hou 430
Sheffield-Fla 426

Slugging Average
Walker-Col 720
Piazza-LA 638
Bagwell-Hou 592
Galarraga-Col 585
Lankford-StL 585

Production
Walker-Col 1.175
Piazza-LA 1.073
Bonds-SF 1.034
Bagwell-Hou 1.022
Lankford-StL 999

Adjusted Production
Piazza-LA 191
Bonds-SF 172
Bagwell-Hou 171
Walker-Col 164
Gwynn-SD 162

Batter Runs
Walker-Col 84.9
Piazza-LA 62.3
Bonds-SF 60.0
Bagwell-Hou 57.7
Galarraga-Col 43.6

Adjusted Batter Runs
Piazza-LA 73.4
Bagwell-Hou 63.4
Bonds-SF 63.4
Gwynn-SD 51.9
Walker-Col 51.0

Clutch Hitting Index
Alou-Fla 128
Kent-SF 125
Joyner-SD 121
Bichette-Col 120
Olerud-NY 118

Runs Created
Walker-Col 187
Bagwell-Hou 153
Bonds-SF 151
Piazza-LA 150
Biggio-Hou 148

Total Average
Walker-Col 1.373
Bonds-SF 1.239
Bagwell-Hou 1.177
Piazza-LA 1.149
Lankford-StL 1.083

Stolen Bases
Womack-Pit 60
D.Sanders-Cin 56
DeShields-StL 55
Biggio-Hou 47
Young-Col-LA 45

Stolen Base Average
Womack-Pit 89.6
Javier-SF 89.3
Henderson-SD 87.9
Biggio-Hou 82.5
Bonds-SF 82.2

Stolen Base Runs
Womack-Pit 13.8
D.Sanders-Cin 9.0
DeShields-StL 8.1
Biggio-Hou 8.1

Fielding Runs
Biggio-Hou 23.7
Young-Col 21.2
Randa-Pit 20.1
Weiss-Col 19.5
White-Mon 17.4

Total Player Rating
Biggio-Hou 8.3
Piazza-LA 7.6
Bonds-SF 7.1
Bagwell-Hou 5.6
Mondesi-LA 4.8

Wins
Neagle-Atl 20
Maddux-Atl 19
Kile-Hou 19
Estes-SF 19

Win Percentage
Maddux-Atl 826
Neagle-Atl 800
Estes-SF 792
Kile-Hou 731
Martinez-Mon 680

Games
Tavarez-SF 89
Belinda-Cin 84
Shaw-Cin 78
Rojas-Chi-NY 77

Complete Games
Martinez-Mon 13
Perez-Mon 8
Smoltz-Atl 7
Schilling-Phi 7
Hampton-Hou 7

Shutouts
Perez-Mon 5
Neagle-Atl 4
Martinez-Mon 4
Kile-Hou 4

Saves
Shaw-Cin 42
Hoffman-SD 37
Beck-SF 37
J.Franco-NY 36
Eckersley-StL 36

Innings Pitched
Smoltz-Atl 256.0
Kile-Hou 255.2
Schilling-Phi 254.1
Martinez-Mon 241.1
Glavine-Atl 240.0

Fewest Hits/Game
Martinez-Mon 5.89
Park-LA 6.98
Estes-SF 7.25
Kile-Hou 7.32
Schilling-Phi 7.36

Fewest BB/Game
Maddux-Atl 77
Reed-NY 1.34
Neagle-Atl 1.89
Schilling-Phi 2.05
Perez-Mon 2.09

Strikeouts
Schilling-Phi 319
Martinez-Mon 305
Smoltz-Atl 241
Nomo-LA 233

Strikeouts/Game
Martinez-Mon 11.37
Schilling-Phi 11.29
Nomo-LA 10.11
A.Benes-StL 8.90
Smoltz-Atl 8.47

Ratio
Martinez-Mon 8.73
Maddux-Atl 8.74
Schilling-Phi 9.59
Reed-NY 9.59
Neagle-Atl 9.99

Earned Run Average
Martinez-Mon 1.90
Maddux-Atl 2.20
Kile-Hou 2.57
Valdes-LA 2.65
Brown-Fla 2.69

Adjusted ERA
Martinez-Mon 220
Maddux-Atl 190
Kile-Hou 155
Brown-Fla 150
Valdes-LA 145

Opponents' Batting Avg.
Martinez-Mon 184
Park-LA 213
Estes-SF 223
Schilling-Phi 224
Kile-Hou 225

Opponents' On Base Pct.
Martinez-Mon 250
Maddux-Atl 258
Reed-NY 273
Schilling-Phi 273
Neagle-Atl 279

Starter Runs
Martinez-Mon 61.6
Maddux-Atl 51.6
Kile-Hou 46.3
Brown-Fla 39.8
Schilling-Phi 34.7

Adjusted Starter Runs
Martinez-Mon 61.4
Maddux-Atl 51.0
Kile-Hou 40.5
Schilling-Phi 35.9
Brown-Fla 35.2

Clutch Pitching Index
Bailey-Col 118
Kile-Hou 116
Cooke-Pit 114
Trachsel-Chi 113
Morris-StL 111

Relief Runs
Shaw-Cin 19.2
Frascatore-StL 15.3
Hoffman-SD 14.0
Osuna-LA 13.8
Martin-Hou 13.1

Adjusted Relief Runs
Shaw-Cin 19.8
Frascatore-StL 14.8
Martin-Hou 11.9
Osuna-LA 11.4
Valdes-Mon 11.2

Relief Ranking
Shaw-Cin 27.2
J.Franco-NY 22.5
Wagner-Hou 22.5
Hoffman-SD 21.3
McMichael-NY 19.4

Total Pitcher Index
Martinez-Mon 6.3
Maddux-Atl 5.1
Kile-Hou 4.1
Smoltz-Atl 3.9
Schilling-Phi 3.9

Total Baseball Ranking
Biggio-Hou 8.3
Piazza-LA 7.6
Bonds-SF 7.1
Martinez-Mon 6.3
Bagwell-Hou 5.6

May 13 Eddie Murray, who already has 3,000 hits, appears in his 3,000th game.

June 12 The first interleague game in the regular season is played in Texas. The Giants beat the Rangers, 4-3.

August 8 Seattle's Randy Johnson strikes out 19 White Sox batters in a 5-0 win to become the first pitcher to strike-out 19 batters twice in one season.

October 6 The Indians complete their surprising victory over the Yankees with a tense 4-3 win at Jacobs Field in Game 5 of the Division Series.

October 15 Mike Mussina pitches two-hit baseball for eight innings, but the Orioles can't score. Charles Nagy and three Indians relievers strand 14 Baltimore baserunners.

November 3 Red Sox shortstop Nomar Garciaparra is the sixth unanimous choice as AL Rookie of the Year.

November 5 In an unprecedented move, Davey Johnson resigns the same day he is named AL Manager of the Year.

November 10 Roger Clemens becomes the first AL pitcher to win the Cy Young Award four times.

November 12 Ken Griffey, Jr. becomes the ninth unanimous pick for AL MVP.

November 18 The expansion draft helps stock the new AL Tampa Bay Devil Rays. Fred McGriff, a Tampa native who arrives in a trade after the draft.

ANAHEIM

Pos	Player
M	T.Collins
1B	D.Erstad
2B	L.Alicea
SS	G.DiSarcina
3B	D.Hollins
LF	G.Anderson
CF	J.Edmonds
RF	T.Salmon
C	C.Kreuter
DH	E.Murray
2O	T.Phillips
C1	J.Leyritz
3D	J.Howell
OD	O.Palmeiro
2S	C.Grebeck
C	T.Greene
DO	R.Henderson
P	J.Dickson
P	A.Watson
P	D.Springer
P	C.Finley
RP	S.Hasegawa
RP	P.Harris
RP	M.James
P	K.Hill
P	D.May
P	T.Percival
P	M.Langston
P	M.Perisho
P	M.Holtz
P	R.DeLucia
P	K.Gross

BALTIMORE

Pos	Player
M	D.Johnson
1B	R.Palmeiro
2B	R.Alomar
SS	M.Bordick
3B	C.Ripken
LF	B.Surhoff
RF	J.Hammonds
C	L.Webster
DH	G.Berroa
C	C.Hoiles
2S	J.Reboulet
O	T.Tarasco
OD	E.Davis
DO	P.Incaviglia
D	H.Baines
23	A.Ledesma
O	J.Walton
P	M.Mussina
P	S.Erickson
P	J.Key
P	S.Kamieniecki
RP	A.Rhodes
RP	S.Boskie
RP	A.Benitez
P	T.Mathews
P	R.Myers
P	R.Krivda
P	J.Orosco
P	M.Johnson
P	A.Mills
P	B.Williams

BOSTON

Pos	Player
M	J.Williams
1B	M.Vaughn
2B	J.Frye
SS	N.Garciaparra
3B	T.Naehring
LF	W.Cordero
CF	D.Bragg
RF	T.O'Leary
C	S.Hatteberg
DH	R.Jefferson
D1	M.Stanley
23	J.Valentin
C	B.Haselman
O	S.Mack
3S	M.Benjamin
O	J.Tavarez
O	R.Pemberton
P	T.Wakefield
P	T.Gordon
P	A.Sele
P	J.Suppan
P	S.Avery
RP	J.Wasdin
RP	B.Henry
RP	C.Hammond
P	J.Corsi
P	H.Slocumb
P	K.Lacy
P	V.Eshelman
P	M.Brandenburg
P	J.Hudson
/P	B.Saberhagen

CHICAGO

Pos	Player
M	T.Bevington
1B	F.Thomas
2B	R.Durham
SS	O.Guillen
3B	C.Snopek
LF	A.Belle
CF	M.Cameron
RF	D.Martinez
C	J.Fabregas
DH	H.Baines
OD	L.Mouton
S3	N.Martin
3	R.Ventura
C	R.Karkovice
O	T.Phillips
1	M.Valdez
O	D.Lewis
O	M.Ordonez
C	T.Pena
P	J.Navarro
P	J.Baldwin
P	D.Drabek
P	W.Alvarez
P	D.Darwin
RP	C.Castillo
RP	C.McElroy
P	S.Eyre
P	M.Karchner
P	R.Hernandez
P	B.Simas
/P	M.Sirotka

CLEVELAND

Pos	Player
M	M.Hargrove
1B	J.Thome
2B	T.Fernandez
SS	O.Vizquel
3B	M.Williams
LF	B.Giles
CF	M.Grissom
RF	M.Ramirez
C	S.Alomar
DH	D.Justice
D2	J.Franco
D1	K.Seitzer
C	P.Borders
2O	B.Roberts
2	J.Branson
P	C.Nagy
P	O.Hershiser
P	C.Ogea
RP	J.Mesa
RP	A.Lopez
RP	M.Jackson
P	B.Colon
P	J.Wright
P	E.Plunk
P	P.Assenmacher
/P	B.Anderson
/P	P.Shuey
P	J.Jacome
/P	J.McDowell
/P	J.Smiley
/P	J.Juden
/P	T.Clark

DETROIT

Pos	Player
M	B.Bell
1B	T.Clark
2B	D.Easley
SS	D.Cruz
3B	T.Fryman
LF	B.Higginson
CF	B.Hunter
RF	M.Nieves
C	R.Casanova
DH	B.Hamelin
OD	P.Nevin
OD	C.Pride
C	B.Johnson
C	M.Walbeck
OD	B.Trammell
2	J.Reed
SD	O.Miller
P	J.Thompson
P	B.Moehler
P	W.Blair
P	O.Olivares
RP	A.Sager
RP	D.Miceli
RP	D.Brocail
P	F.Lira
P	S.Sanders
P	T.Jones
P	M.Myers
P	G.Keagle
P	K.Jarvis
P	J.Bautista
/P	G.Dishman

KANSAS CITY

Pos	Player
M	B.Boone
M	T.Muser
1B	J.King
2B	J.Offerman
SS	J.Bell
3B	C.Paquette
LF	B.Roberts
CF	T.Goodwin
RF	J.Damon
C	M.Macfarlane
DH	C.Davis
O	J.Dye
C	M.Sweeney
O	Y.Benitez
3	D.Palmer
2O	D.Howard
3	S.Cooper
OD	J.Vitiello
O2	S.Halter
O	R.Myers
2	J.Hansen
1	L.Sutton
P	K.Appier
P	T.Belcher
P	J.Rosado
P	G.Rusch
P	J.Pittsley
RP	J.Montgomery
RP	H.Pichardo
P	R.Bones
P	J.Walker
P	G.Olson

MILWAUKEE

Pos	Player
M	P.Garner
1B	D.Nilsson
2B	F.Vina
SS	J.Valentin
3B	J.Cirillo
LF	M.Mieske
CF	G.Williams
RF	J.Burnitz
C	M.Matheny
DH	J.Franco
C	J.Levis
2S	M.Loretta
1D	J.Jaha
OD	M.Newfield
O1	J.Voigt
21	J.Huson
OD	T.Dunn
O	D.Jackson
O	B.Banks
P	C.Eldred
P	S.Karl
P	J.Mercedes
P	J.D'Amico
P	B.McDonald
RP	B.Wickman
RP	D.Jones
RP	J.Adamson
P	B.Florie
P	M.Fetters

MINNESOTA

Pos	Player
M	T.Kelly
1B	S.Stahoviak
2B	C.Knoblauch
SS	P.Meares
3B	R.Coomer
LF	M.Cordova
CF	R.Becker
RF	M.Lawton
C	T.Steinbach
DH	P.Molitor
S3	D.Hocking
OD	R.Kelly
1	G.Colbrunn
O1	B.Brede
CD	G.Myers
3	T.Walker
O	D.Jackson
C	D.Miller
P	B.Radke
P	B.Tewksbury
P	R.Robertson
P	F.Rodriguez
P	L.Hawkins
RP	G.Swindell
RP	M.Trombley
RP	T.Ritchie
P	S.Aldred
P	R.Aguilera
P	T.Miller

NEW YORK

Pos	Player
M	J.Torre
1B	T.Martinez
2B	L.Sojo
SS	D.Jeter
3B	C.Hayes
LF	C.Curtis
CF	B.Williams
RF	P.O'Neill
C	J.Girardi
DH	C.Fielder
3D	W.Boggs
OD	T.Raines
O	M.Whiten
C	J.Posada
2	M.Duncan
2	R.Sanchez
2D	P.Kelly
O	S.Pose
D1	M.Stanley
P	A.Pettitte
P	D.Wells
P	D.Cone
P	K.Rogers
RP	R.Mendoza
RP	J.Nelson
RP	M.Rivera
RP	M.Stanton
P	D.Gooden
P	H.Irabu

OAKLAND

Pos	Player
M	A.Howe
1B	M.McGwire
2B	S.Spiezio
SS	R.Bournigal
3B	S.Brosius
LF	J.Giambi
CF	D.Mashore
RF	M.Stairs
C	B.Mayne
DH	J.Canseco
O	J.McDonald
31	D.Magadan
OD	G.Berroa
32	M.Bellhorn
C	G.Williams
S	T.Batista
O	E.Young
O	B.Lesher
OD	P.Lennon
C	I.Molina
S	M.Tejada
O	B.Grieve
P	S.Karsay
P	A.Prieto
P	M.Oquist
RP	D.Telgheder
RP	D.Wengert
RP	M.Mohler
RP	A.Small

SEATTLE

Pos	Player
M	L.Piniella
1B	P.Sorrento
2B	J.Cora
SS	A.Rodriguez
3B	R.Davis
LF	R.Ducey
CF	K.Griffey
RF	J.Buhner
C	D.Wilson
DH	E.Martinez
O1	R.Amaral
O	J.Cruz
32	B.Gates
13	M.Blowers
O	L.Tinsley
S2	R.Kelly
3	A.Sheets
C	J.Marzano
S2	A.Espinoza
P	J.Fassero
P	R.Johnson
P	J.Moyer
P	B.Wolcott
RP	B.Ayala
RP	N.Charlton
RP	B.Wells
P	S.Sanders
P	O.Olivares
P	D.Lowe

TEXAS

Pos	Player
M	J.Oates
1B	W.Clark
2B	M.McLemore
SS	B.Gil
3B	D.Palmer
LF	R.Greer
CF	D.Buford
RF	W.Newson
C	I.Rodriguez
DH	J.Gonzalez
2S	D.Cedeno
1D	L.Stevens
3	F.Tatis
O	T.Goodwin
S2	B.Ripken
DO	M.Simms
O	A.Diaz
C	J.Leyritz
O	M.Devereaux
P	B.Witt
P	D.Oliver
P	J.Burkett
P	K.Hill
P	J.Santana
RP	M.Whiteside
RP	D.Patterson
RP	J.Wetteland
P	R.Pavlik
P	R.Helling

TORONTO

Pos	Player
M	C.Gaston
M	M.Queen
1B	C.Delgado
2B	C.Garcia
SS	A.Gonzalez
3B	E.Sprague
LF	S.Green
CF	O.Nixon
RF	O.Merced
C	B.Santiago
DH	J.Carter
C	C.O'Brien
O	J.Cruz
O	J.Brumfield
O	S.Stewart
2	M.Duncan
23	T.Brito
S	T.Perez
D	J.Samuel
O	R.Perez
P	P.Hentgen
P	R.Clemens
P	W.Williams
P	R.Person
RP	P.Quantrill
RP	D.Plesac
RP	L.Andujar
P	C.Carpenter
P	J.Guzman

TEAM	G	W	L	PCT	GB	R	OR	AB	H	2B	3B	HR	BB	SO	AVG	OBP	SLG	PRO	PRO+	BR	/A	PF	CHI	RC	SB	CS	SBA	SBR
EAST																												
BAL	162	98	64	.605		812	**681**	5584	1498	264	22	196	586	952	.268	.345	.429	.774	104	6	30	97	100	833	63	26	71	3
NY	162	96	66	.593	2	891	688	5710	1636	325	23	161	**676**	954	.287	**.366**	.436	.802	110	80	88	99	98	913	99	58	63	-5
MIL	161	78	83	.484	19.5	681	742	5444	1415	294	27	135	494	967	.260	.328	.398	.726	88	-92	-97	101	100	707	103	55	65	-2
BOS	162	78	84	.481	20	851	857	5781	**1684**	**373**	32	185	514	1044	**.291**	.355	.463	.818	110	96	79	102	93	922	68	48	59	-8
TOR	162	76	86	.469	22	654	694	5473	1333	275	**41**	147	487	1138	.244	.312	.389	.701	82	-150	-153	101	105	674	134	50	73	10
CENTRAL																												
CLE	161	86	75	.534		868	815	5556	1589	301	22	220	617	955	.286	.361	.467	.828	110	118	86	104	95	923	118	59	67	0
CHI	161	80	81	.497	6	779	833	5491	1498	260	28	158	569	**901**	.273	.345	.417	.762	102	-15	17	96	101	786	106	52	67	1
DET	162	79	83	.488	7.5	784	790	5481	1415	268	32	176	578	1164	.258	.334	.415	.749	95	-46	-39	99	**106**	764	**161**	72	69	5
MIN	162	68	94	.420	18.5	772	861	5634	1522	305	40	132	495	1121	.270	.336	.409	.745	92	-56	-66	101	105	779	151	52	**74**	**14**
KC	161	67	94	.416	19	747	820	5599	1478	256	35	158	561	1061	.264	.336	.407	.743	91	-58	-75	102	101	770	130	66	66	-1
WEST																												
SEA	162	90	72	.556		**925**	833	5614	1574	312	21	**264**	626	1110	.280	.358	**.485**	**.843**	**119**	**140**	**149**	99	98	**962**	89	40	69	3
ANA	162	84	78	.519	6	829	794	5628	1531	279	25	161	617	953	.272	.349	.416	.765	99	-4	-2	100	103	818	126	72	64	-5
TEX	162	77	85	.475	13	807	823	5651	1547	311	27	187	500	1116	.274	.336	.438	.774	95	-3	-46	105	102	824	72	37	66	-1
OAK	162	65	97	.401	25	764	946	5589	1451	274	23	197	642	1181	.260	.341	.423	.764	100	-14	-1	98	96	811	71	36	66	0
TOT	1132					11164	78235	21171	4097	398	2477	7962	14617	.271	.343	.428	.771							1491	723	67	14	

TEAM	CG	SH	SV	IP	H	H/G	HR	BB	SO	RAT	ERA	ERA+	OAV	OOB	PR	/A	PF	CPI	FA	E	DP	FW	PW	BW	SBW	DIF
EAST																										
BAL	8	10	**59**	1461	**1404**	**8.6**	164	563	1139	**12.3**	3.91	112	**.253**	**.326**	106	79	96	102	.984	97	148	.8	7.5	2.9	.2	5.6
NY	11	10	51	1467^{2}	1463	9.0	**144**	532	1165	12.5	**3.84**	116	.260	.329	**118**	99	97	104	.983	104	156	.5	9.4	8.4	-.6	-2.7
MIL	6	8	44	1427^{1}	1419	8.9	177	542	1016	12.7	4.22	109	.261	.335	55	63	101	102	.980	121	171	-.5	6.0	-9.2	-.3	1.6
BOS	7	4	40	1451^{2}	1569	9.7	149	611	987	13.9	4.85	96	.277	.354	-46	-35	102	97	.978	135	**179**	-1.3	-3.3	7.5	-.9	-5.0
TOR	**19**	**16**	34	1442^{2}	1453	9.1	167	497	1150	12.4	3.92	**117**	.263	.328	104	**107**	101	**106**	.984	94	150	1.0	**10.2**	-14.6	.9	-2.5
CENTRAL																										
CLE	4	3	39	1425^{2}	1528	9.6	181	575	1036	13.6	4.73	99	.276	.350	-26	-7	103	101	.983	106	159	.3	-.7	8.2	-.0	-2.2
CHI	6	7	52	1422^{1}	1505	9.5	175	575	961	13.4	4.73	93	.271	.342	-27	-56	96	96	.978	127	131	-.9	-5.3	1.6	.0	4.1
DET	13	8	42	1445^{2}	1476	9.2	178	552	982	12.9	4.56	101	.266	.337	1	4	100	97	**.985**	92	146	**1.1**	.4	-3.7	.4	-.2
MIN	10	4	30	1434	1596	10.0	187	**495**	908	13.3	5.00	93	.283	.344	-69	-55	102	96	.983	101	170	.6	-5.2	-6.3	**1.2**	-3.4
KC	11	5	29	1443	1530	9.5	186	531	961	13.2	4.70	100	.274	.343	-21	2	103	99	**.985**	**91**	168	**1.1**	.2	-7.1	-.2	-7.5
WEST																										
SEA	9	8	38	1447^{2}	1500	9.3	192	598	**1207**	13.5	4.78	94	.267	.344	-35	-46	99	96	.979	126	143	-.8	-4.4	**14.2**	.2	-.2
ANA	9	5	39	1454^{2}	1506	9.3	202	605	1050	13.4	4.52	101	.269	.346	8	8	100	104	.980	123	140	-.6	.8	-.2	-.6	3.6
TEX	8	9	33	1429^{2}	1598	10.1	169	541	925	13.7	4.69	102	.283	.350	-20	15	105	102	.980	121	155	-.5	1.4	-4.4	-.2	-.4
OAK	2	1	38	1445^{1}	1734	10.8	197	642	953	15.2	5.48	83	.301	.377	-147	-154	99	104	.980	122	170	-.6	-14.6	-.0	-.0	-.6
TOT	123	98	568	20198^{1}	9.5			13.3	4.56		.271	.343					.982	1560	2186							

Runs
Griffey-Sea 125
Garciaparra-Bos . . . 122
Knoblauch-Min 117
Jeter-NY 116

Hits
Garciaparra-Bos . . . 209
Greer-Tex 193
Jeter-NY 190
Anderson-Ana 189
Rodriguez-Tex 187

Doubles
Valentin-Bos 47
Cirillo-Mil 46
Belle-Chi 45
Garciaparra-Bos 44

Triples
Garciaparra-Bos 11
Knoblauch-Min 10
Damon-KC 8
Burnitz-Mil 8

Home Runs
Griffey-Sea 56
Martinez-NY 44
Gonzalez-Tex 42
Thome-Cle 40
Buhner-Sea 40

Total Bases
Griffey-Sea 393
Garciaparra-Bos . . 365
Martinez-NY 343
F.Thomas-Chi 324
Greer-Tex 319

Runs Batted In
Griffey-Sea 147
Martinez-NY 141
Gonzalez-Tex 131
Salmon-Ana 129
F.Thomas-Chi 125

Runs Produced
Griffey-Sea 216
F.Thomas-Chi 200
Martinez-NY 193
Salmon-Ana 191

Bases On Balls
Thome-Cle 120
E.Martinez-Sea . . . 119
Buhner-Sea 119
F.Thomas-Chi 109
Phillips-Chi-Ana . . . 102

Batting Average
F.Thomas-Chi 347
E.Martinez-Sea 330
Justice-Cle 329
Williams-NY 328
Ramirez-Cle 328

On Base Percentage
F.Thomas-Chi 461
E.Martinez-Sea 460
Thome-Cle 428
Justice-Cle 423
Vaughn-Bos 422

Slugging Average
Griffey-Sea 646
F.Thomas-Chi 611
Justice-Cle 596
Gonzalez-Tex 589
Thome-Cle 579

Production
F.Thomas-Chi 1.072
Griffey-Sea 1.035
Justice-Cle 1.019
E.Martinez-Sea . . . 1.013
Thome-Cle 1.007

Adjusted Production
F.Thomas-Chi 184
Griffey-Sea 165
E.Martinez-Sea 164
Justice-Cle 156
Thome-Cle 154

Batter Runs
F.Thomas-Chi 64.6
E.Martinez-Sea . . . 57.1
Griffey-Sea 55.2
Thome-Cle 47.5
Justice-Cle 46.4

Adjusted Batter Runs
F.Thomas-Chi 70.8
E.Martinez-Sea 58.5
Griffey-Sea 56.7
Thome-Cle 43.1
Justice-Cle 42.2

Clutch Hitting Index
Molitor-Min 133
King-KC 126
O'Neill-NY 125
Carter-Tor 119
Anderson-Ana 118

Runs Created
F.Thomas-Chi 153
Griffey-Sea 152
E.Martinez-Sea . . . 140
Greer-Tex 132
Thome-Cle 131

Total Average
F.Thomas-Chi 1.204
Thome-Cle 1.126
Griffey-Sea 1.112
E.Martinez-Sea . . . 1.103
Justice-Cle 1.069

Stolen Bases
Hunter-Det 74
Knoblauch-Min 62
Goodwin-KC-Tex 50
Nixon-Tor 47
Vizquel-Cle 43

Stolen Base Average
Cameron-Chi 92.0
Knoblauch-Min . . . 86.1
Roberts-KC-Cle . . . 85.7
Fryman-Det 84.2
Rodriguez-Sea 82.9

Stolen Base Runs
Knoblauch-Min 12.6
Hunter-Det 11.4
Nixon-Tor 8.1
Vizquel-Cle 5.7
Cameron-Chi 5.7

Fielding Runs
Gil-Tex 22.0
King-KC 20.0
Salmon-Ana 18.5
Cirillo-Mil 17.9
Matheny-Mil 17.7

Total Player Rating
Griffey-Sea 6.4
F.Thomas-Chi 4.7
E.Martinez-Sea 4.4
Salmon-Ana 4.2
Valentin-Bos 3.9

Wins
Clemens-Tor 21
Radke-Min 20
Johnson-Sea 20
Pettitte-NY 18
Moyer-Sea 17

Win Percentage
Johnson-Sea 833
Moyer-Sea 773
Clemens-Tor 750
Pettitte-NY 720
Erickson-Bal 696

Games
Myers-Det 88
Groom-Oak 78
Quantrill-Tor 77
Nelson-NY 77
Slocumb-Bos-Sea . . 76

Complete Games
Hentgen-Tor 9
Clemens-Tor 9
Wells-NY 5
Tewksbury-Min 5
Johnson-Sea 5

Shutouts
Hentgen-Tor 3
Clemens-Tor 3

Saves
Myers-Bal 45
Rivera-NY 43
Jones-Mil 36
Wetteland-Tex 31
Jones-Det 31

Innings Pitched
Hentgen-Tor 264.0
Clemens-Tor 264.0
Pettitte-NY 240.1
Radke-Min 239.2
Appier-KC 235.2

Fewest Hits/Game
Johnson-Sea 6.21
Clemens-Tor 6.95
Cone-NY 7.15
Thompson-Det 7.58
Gordon-Bos 7.64

Fewest BB/Game
Burkett-Tex 1.43
Tewksbury-Min . . . 1.65
Radke-Min 1.80
Wells-NY 1.86
Moyer-Sea 2.05

Strikeouts
Clemens-Tor 292
Johnson-Sea 291
Cone-NY 222
Mussina-Bal 218
Appier-KC 196

Strikeouts/Game
Johnson-Sea 12.30
Cone-NY 10.25
Clemens-Tor 9.95
Mussina-Bal 8.73
Finley-Ana 8.51

Ratio
Clemens-Tor 9.68
Johnson-Sea 9.89
Mussina-Bal 10.18
Thompson-Det 10.32
Radke-Min 10.85

Earned Run Average
Clemens-Tor 2.05
Johnson-Sea 2.28
Cone-NY 2.82
Pettitte-NY 2.88
Thompson-Det 3.02

Adjusted ERA
Clemens-Tor 224
Johnson-Sea 197
Cone-NY 158
Pettitte-NY 154
Thompson-Det 152

Opponents' Batting Avg.
Johnson-Sea 194
Clemens-Tor 213
Cone-NY 218
Gordon-Bos 226
Thompson-Det 233

Opponents' On Base Pct.
Clemens-Tor 274
Johnson-Sea 277
Mussina-Bal 282
Thompson-Det 292
Radke-Min 296

Starter Runs
Clemens-Tor 73.9
Johnson-Sea 54.0
Pettitte-NY 44.9
Thompson-Det 38.2
Cone-NY 37.9

Adjusted Starter Runs
Clemens-Tor 74.5
Johnson-Sea 52.4
Pettitte-NY 41.7
Thompson-Det 38.7
Cone-NY 35.3

Clutch Pitching Index
Key-Bal 123
Dickson-Ana 116
Oliver-Tex 114
Witt-Tex 110
Nagy-Cle 109

Relief Runs
Quantrill-Tor 25.6
Jones-Mil 22.7
Rivera-NY 21.3
Myers-Bal 20.3
Mesa-Cle 19.7

Adjusted Relief Runs
Quantrill-Tor 25.8
Jones-Mil 23.2
Mesa-Cle 20.9
Wetteland-Tex 20.6
Rivera-NY 20.4

Relief Ranking
Jones-Mil 49.6
Rivera-NY 47.4
Wetteland-Tex 43.1
Myers-Bal 40.2
Quantrill-Tor 37.0

Total Pitcher Index
Clemens-Tor 8.0
Johnson-Sea 5.5
Jones-Mil 4.9
Rivera-NY 4.8
Wetteland-Tex 4.3

Total Baseball Ranking
Clemens-Tor 8.0
Griffey-Sea 6.4
Johnson-Sea 5.5
Jones-Mil 4.9
Rivera-NY 4.8

January 5 Don Sutton gets into the Hall of Fame on his fifth try.

March 31 The Arizona Diamondbacks fall to the Rockies, 7-2, as Bank One Ballpark opens its doors.

April 7 National League baseball returns to Milwaukee for the first time in 32 years. The Brewers beat the Expos in their home opener, 6-4.

May 6 Kerry Wood sets an NL mark and ties the major league record with 20 strikeouts in a 2-0 win over the hot-hitting Astros.

May 15 The Dodgers get Gary Sheffield, Bobby Bonilla, Charles Johnson, and Jim Eisenreich and send Mike Piazza and Todd Zeile to the Marlins. A week later Piazza becomes a Met.

June 30 Sammy Sosa homers off Arizona's Alan Embree for his 20th home run of the month.

August 20 Mark McGwire becomes the first player in major league history to hit 50 home runs in three consecutive years.

August 23 Barry Bonds becomes the first player in major league history to hit at least 400 home runs and steal 400 bases.

September 8 Mark McGwire becomes the all-time home run king with a 341-foot drive off Cubs pitcher Steve Trachsel at 8:18 p.m. Central Time.

September 13 Sammy Sosa becomes the second player of the week to break the home run record of Roger Maris.

September 27 Mark McGwire caps his amazing season with two home runs in the season finale against Montreal. The Cardinals slugger connects for his 70th and final home run, against Carl Pavano.

September 28 The Cubs whip the Giants, 5-3, at Wrigley Field to become the Wild Card. Steve Trachsel, who seemed destined to be remembered only for allowing Mark McGwire's record-breaking 62nd home run earlier in the month, takes a no-hitter into the seventh and earns the win.

November 9 Cubs pitcher Kerry Wood, who went 13-6 with a 3.40 ERA and struck out 233 batters, is named NL Rookie of the Year.

November 17 Tom Glavine edges reliever Trevor Hoffman to win his second NL Cy Young Award, the sixth time in eight years a Braves pitcher earns the honor.

November 19 The NL home run race goes down to the last weekend, but the NL MVP race is a cakewalk for Sammy Sosa. The Cubs outfielder earns 30 of the 32 first-place votes for MVP.

ARIZONA	ATLANTA	CHICAGO	CINCINNATI	COLORADO	FLORIDA	HOUSTON	LOS ANGELES
M B.Showalter	M B.Cox	M J.Riggleman	M J.McKeon	M D.Baylor	M J.Leyland	M L.Dierker	M B.Russell
1B T.Lee	1B A.Galarraga	1B M.Grace	1B S.Casey	1B T.Helton	1B D.Lee	1B J.Bagwell	M G.Hoffman
2B A.Stankiewicz	2B K.Lockhart	2B M.Morandini	2B B.Boone	2B M.Lansing	2B C.Counsell	2B C.Biggio	1B E.Karros
SS J.Bell	SS W.Weiss	SS J.Blauser	SS B.Larkin	SS N.Perez	SS E.Renteria	SS R.Gutierrez	2B E.Young
3B M.Williams	3B C.Jones	3B J.Hernandez	3B W.Greene	3B V.Castilla	3B T.Zeile	3B B.Spiers	SS J.Vizcaino
LF D.Dellucci	LF R.Klesko	LF H.Rodriguez	LF D.Young	LF D.Bichette	LF C.Floyd	LF M.Alou	3B A.Beltre
CF D.White	CF A.Jones	CF B.Brown	CF R.Sanders	CF E.Burks	CF T.Dunwoody	CF C.Everett	LF T.Hubbard
RF K.Garcia	RF G.Williams	RF S.Sosa	RF J.Nunnally	RF L.Walker	RF M.Kotsay	RF D.Bell	CF R.Mondesi
C K.Stinnett	C J.Lopez	C S.Servais	C E.Taubensee	C K.Manwaring	C G.Zaun	C B.Ausmus	RF R.Sheffield
2S T.Batista	2 T.Graffanino	S2 M.Alexander	O3 C.Stynes	O C.Goodwin	3 S.Cangelosi	O S.Berry	C C.Johnson
O1 B.Brede	O M.Tucker	O L.Johnson	3 A.Boone	C J.Reed	1O R.Jackson	O R.Hidalgo	O R.Cedeno
2O A.Fox	S O.Guillen	C3 T.Houston	1 E.Perez	O D.Hamilton	23 D.Berg	C T.Eusebio	O1 M.Luke
O Y.Benitez	C E.Perez	3 K.Orie	O P.Watkins	3 K.Colbrunn	3 K.Orie	S2 T.Bogar	3O B.Bonilla
C D.Miller	O D.Bautista	O G.Hill	C B.Fordyce	O J.Vander Wal	2 L.Castillo	O D.Clark	S2 J.Castro
C J.Fabregas	O C.Pride	3S G.Gaetti	3S P.Reese	2 J.Bates	O G.Sheffield	P S.Reynolds	S M.Grudzielanek
2 D.Klassen		O M.Mieske	O L.Harris	/O K.Abbott	C M.Redmond	P J.Lima	2S W.Guerrero
O B.Gilkey		C A.Martinez	O M.Nieves	P D.Kile	C C.Johnson	P M.Hampton	O T.Hollandsworth
P A.Benes	P G.Maddux	P K.Tapani	O M.Frank	P P.Astacio	3 B.Bonilla	P S.Bergman	3 T.Zeile
P B.Anderson	P T.Glavine	P M.Clark	O J.Hammonds	P J.Wright	O J.Wehner	RP D.Henry	C M.Piazza
P O.Daal	P D.Neagle	P S.Trachsel	/3 P.Konerko	P J.Thomson	S A.Gonzalez	RP B.Wagner	13 P.Konerko
P W.Blair	P K.Millwood	P K.Wood	1O R.Petagine	P B.Jones	O J.Eisenreich	RP C.Nitkowski	O J.Eisenreich
P A.Telemaco	P J.Smoltz	P J.Gonzalez	P B.Tomko	P D.Veres	P L.Hernandez	P R.Johnson	C T.Prince
RP C.Sodowsky	RP D.Martinez	RP T.Mulholland	P P.Harnisch	RP C.Leskanic	P B.Meadows	P P.Schourek	O T.Howard
RP G.Olson	RP K.Ligtenberg	RP R.Beck	P M.Remlinger	RP M.DeJean	P J.Sanchez	P S.Elarton	P C.Park
P J.Suppan	P M.Cather	RP T.Adams	P S.Parris	P J.DiPoto	P K.Ojala	P T.Miller	P D.Dreifort
P W.Banks	P J.Rocker	P D.Wengert	RP S.Sullivan	P C.McElroy	RP V.Darensbourg	P M.Magnante	P I.Valdes
P F.Rodriguez	P R.Seanez	P M.Pisciotta	RP G.White	P M.Munoz	RP A.Alfonseca	P J.Powell	P D.Mlicki
P B.Chouinard	/P B.Chen	P D.Stevens	RP D.Graves	/P M.Thompson	RP B.Edmondson	/P J.Halama	P R.Martinez
P A.Embree	P R.Springer	P M.Karchner	P S.Winchester		P A.Larkin	P B.Scanlan	RP A.Osuna
P R.Springer	P M.Wohlers	P A.Telemaco	P D.Weathers		P R.Medina		RP S.Radinsky
	P A.Embree						RP M.Guthrie
	P B.Edmondson						

MILWAUKEE	MONTREAL	NEW YORK	PHILADELPHIA	PITTSBURGH	SAN DIEGO	SAN FRANCISCO	ST.LOUIS
M P.Garner	M F.Alou	M B.Valentine	M T.Francona	M G.Lamont	M B.Bochy	M D.Baker	M T.LaRussa
1B M.Loretta	1B B.Fullmer	1B J.Olerud	1B R.Brogna	1B K.Young	1B W.Joyner	1B J.Snow	1B M.McGwire
2B F.Vina	2B J.Vidro	2B C.Baerga	2B M.Lewis	2B T.Womack	2B Q.Veras	2B J.Kent	2B D.DeShields
SS J.Valentin	SS M.Grudzielanek	SS R.Ordonez	SS D.Relaford	SS L.Collier	SS C.Gomez	SS R.Aurilia	SS R.Clayton
3B J.Cirillo	3B S.Andrews	3B E.Alfonzo	3B S.Rolen	3B A.Ramirez	3B K.Caminiti	3B B.Mueller	3B G.Gaetti
LF D.Jackson	LF F.Santangelo	LF B.Gilkey	LF G.Jefferies	LF A.Martin	LF G.Vaughn	LF B.Bonds	LF R.Gant
CF M.Grissom	CF R.White	CF B.McRae	CF D.Glanville	CF T.Ward	CF S.Finley	CF D.Hamilton	CF R.Lankford
RF J.Burnitz	RF V.Guerrero	RF B.Huskey	RF B.Abreu	RF J.Guillen	RF T.Gwynn	RF S.Javier	RF B.Jordan
C M.Matheny	C C.Widger	C M.Piazza	C M.Lieberthal	C J.Kendall	C C.Hernandez	C B.Johnson	C E.Marrero
1 B.Hamelin	1O R.McGuire	12 M.Franco	12 K.Jordan	O1 J.Allensworth	O M.Sweeney	O M.Benard	O3 J.Mabry
1O D.Nilsson	S2 O.Cabrera	O L.Lopez	O K.Sefcik	S2 K.Polcovich	S3 A.Sheets	31 C.Hayes	O W.McGee
O G.Jenkins	2 W.Guerrero	O T.Phillips	3 B.Estalella	3 D.Strange	O R.Rivera	S2 R.Sanchez	C T.Lampkin
C B.Hughes	O D.May	O3 L.Harris	S A.Arias	O M.Martinez	C G.Myers	C B.Mayne	3 F.Tatis
1 J.Jaha	S2 M.Mordecai	O R.Becker	3 M.Parent	3 F.Garcia	C1 J.Leyritz	O E.Burks	C T.Pagnozzi
O M.Newfield	C B.Henley	C A.Castillo	O R.Amaro	O A.Brown	32 E.Giovanola	O1 J.Carter	2 P.Kelly
P S.Karl	3 S.Livingstone	C T.Pratt	O W.Magee	O M.Smith	13 A.Cianfrocco	O C.Jones	S L.Ordaz
P S.Woodard	O R.Perez	P R.Reed	P C.Schilling	C K.Osik	O J.Mouton	O A.Diaz	S2 P.Polanco
P B.Woodall	O D.Stovall	P B.Jones	P M.Portugal	P F.Cordova	P K.Brown	P M.Gardner	O1 B.Hunter
P J.Juden	P D.Hermanson	P A.Leiter	P T.Green	P J.Schmidt	P A.Ashby	P O.Hershiser	2S D.Howard
P C.Eldred	P J.Vazquez	P M.Yoshii	P C.Loewer	P J.Lieber	P J.Hamilton	P K.Rueter	P K.Mercker
RP B.Wickman	P C.Perez	RP T.Wendell	P M.Beech	P C.Peters	P S.Hitchcock	P S.Estes	P T.Stottlemyre
RP B.Patrick	RP C.Pavano	RP D.Cook	RP W.Gomes	P J.Silva	RP B.Boehringer	P D.Darwin	P K.Bottenfield
RP A.Reyes	RP M.Batista	RP J.Franco	RP M.Leiter	RP E.Dessens	RP D.Miceli	RP R.Nen	P M.Morris
P B.Pulsipher	RP S.Bennett	P H.Nomo	RP J.Spradlin	RP R.Rincon	RP T.Hoffman	RP J.Johnstone	RP M.Petkovsek
P C.Fox	RP A.Telford	/P A.Reynoso	P M.Grace	RP J.Christiansen	P M.Langston	RP J.Tavarez	RP J.Acevedo
P P.Wagner			/P P.Byrd		P D.Wall	P R.Ortiz	RP J.Frascatore

TEAM	G	W	L	PCT	GB	R	OR	AB	H	2B	3B	HR	BB	SO	AVG	OBP	SLG	PRO	PRO+	BR	/A	PF	CHI	RC	SB	CS	SBA	SBR
EAST																												
ATL	162	106	56	.654		826	**581**	5484	1489	297	26	215	548	1062	.272	.344	.453	.797	112	102	85	102	98	862	98	43	70	4
NY	162	88	74	.543	18	706	645	5510	1425	289	24	136	571	1049	.259	.332	.394	.726	97	-30	-24	99	99	719	62	46	57	-9
PHI	162	75	87	.463	31	713	808	5617	1482	286	36	126	508	1080	.264	.330	.395	.725	93	-37	-49	102	100	737	97	45	68	2
MON	162	65	97	.401	41	644	783	5418	1348	280	32	147	439	1058	.249	.312	.394	.706	94	-84	-60	96	101	663	91	46	66	0
FLA	162	54	108	.333	52	667	923	5558	1381	277	36	114	525	1120	.248	.318	.373	.691	90	-105	-79	96	105	662	115	57	67	0
CENTRAL																												
HOU	162	102	60	.630		**874**	620	5641	1578	326	28	166	621	1122	.280	**.359**	.436	.795	**117**	116	**136**	98	99	**889**	155	51	75	16
CHI	163	90	73	.552	12.5	831	792	5649	1494	250	34	212	601	1223	.264	.339	.433	.772	104	58	35	103	101	827	65	44	60	-7
STL	163	83	79	.512	19	810	782	5593	1444	292	30	**223**	676	1179	.258	.343	.441	.784	111	81	90	99	96	862	133	41	**76**	15
CIN	162	77	85	.475	25	750	760	5496	1441	298	28	138	608	1107	.262	.340	.402	.742	98	4	-9	102	100	756	95	42	69	3
MIL	162	74	88	.457	28	707	812	5541	1439	266	17	152	532	1039	.260	.332	.396	.728	95	-28	-34	101	99	719	81	59	58	-11
WEST																												
PIT	163	69	93	.426	33	650	718	5493	1395	271	35	107	393	1060	.254	.314	.374	.688	84	-112	-123	102	105	658	**159**	51	**76**	**17**
SD	162	98	64	.605		749	635	5490	1390	292	30	167	604	1072	.253	.332	.409	.741	109	-4	66	91	101	757	79	37	68	2
SF	163	89	74	.546	9.5	845	739	5628	1540	292	26	161	**678**	1040	.274	.356	.421	.777	113	84	115	96	99	858	102	51	67	0
LA	162	83	79	.512	15	669	678	5459	1374	209	27	159	447	1056	.252	.313	.387	.700	95	-95	-49	93	**106**	666	137	53	72	9
COL	162	77	85	.475	21	826	855	5632	**1640**	**333**	36	183	469	**949**	**.291**	.350	**.461**	**.811**	98	**129**	-37	119	94	878	67	47	59	-8
ARI	162	65	97	.401	33	665	812	5491	1353	235	**46**	159	489	1239	.246	.315	.393	.708	90	-78	-81	101	102	675	73	38	66	-1
TOT	1298					11932	88700	23213	4493	491	2565	8709	17455	.262	.333	.410	.744							1609	751	68	32	

TEAM	CG	SH	SV	IP	H	H/G	HR	BB	SO	RAT	ERA	ERA+	OAV	OOB	PR	/A	PF	CPI	FA	E	DP	FW	PW	BW	SBW	DIF
EAST																										
ATL	**24**	**23**	45	1438[2]	**1291**	**8.1**	**117**	466	**1232**	**11.2**	**3.25**	**130**	**.240**	**.305**	**156**	**156**	100	101	**.985**	**91**	139	**1.3**	**15.4**	8.4	.2	-.3
NY	9	16	46	1458	1381	8.5	152	532	1129	12.2	3.76	111	.253	.327	76	66	99	106	.984	101	151	.8	6.5	-2.4	-1.1	3.2
PHI	21	10	32	1463	1476	9.1	188	544	1176	12.8	4.64	94	.262	.333	-66	-46	103	94	.982	110	131	.3	-4.5	-4.8	.0	3.1
MON	4	5	39	1427	1448	9.1	156	533	1017	12.9	4.38	94	.264	.335	-24	-44	97	97	.975	155	127	-2.1	-4.3	-5.9	-.2	-3.4
FLA	11	3	24	1449[2]	1617	10.0	182	715	1016	14.8	5.18	79	.287	.373	-153	-175	97	104	.979	129	177	-.7	-17.3	-7.8	-.2	-1.0
CENTRAL																										
HOU	12	11	44	1471[1]	1435	8.8	147	**465**	1187	11.9	3.50	116	.256	.317	119	93	96	**108**	.983	108	144	.4	9.2	**13.4**	1.4	-3.4
CHI	7	7	56	1477[1]	1528	9.3	180	575	1207	13.1	4.47	98	.266	.338	-39	-18	103	99	.984	101	107	.8	-1.8	3.5	-.9	6.9
STL	6	10	44	1469[2]	1513	9.3	151	558	972	13.0	4.31	97	.268	.340	-12	-20	99	101	.978	142	160	-1.4	-2.0	8.9	1.3	-4.8
CIN	6	8	42	1441[1]	1400	8.7	170	573	1098	12.6	4.44	97	.256	.333	-34	-18	102	95	.980	122	142	-.3	-1.8	-.9	.0	-1.1
MIL	2	2	39	1451	1538	9.5	188	550	1063	13.3	4.63	93	.275	.347	-64	-53	102	103	.982	110	192	.3	-5.2	-3.4	-1.3	2.6
WEST																										
PIT	7	10	41	1449	1433	8.9	147	530	1112	12.4	3.91	111	.259	.327	52	67	102	102	.977	140	161	-1.3	6.6	-12.1	1.5	-6.7
SD	14	11	**59**	1454[2]	1384	8.6	139	501	1217	12.0	3.63	105	.252	.320	97	31	90	104	.983	104	155	.6	3.1	6.5	.0	6.8
SF	6	6	44	1477	1457	8.9	171	562	1089	12.6	4.18	97	.259	.332	8	-20	96	101	.984	101	157	.8	-2.0	11.3	-.2	-2.5
LA	16	10	47	1447[1]	1332	8.3	135	587	1178	12.3	3.81	102	.246	.326	68	14	92	100	.978	134	154	-1.0	1.4	-4.8	.7	5.8
COL	9	5	36	1432[2]	1583	9.9	174	562	951	13.9	4.99	101	.285	.358	-121	11	120	101	.984	102	**193**	.7	1.1	-3.7	-1.0	-1.2
ARI	7	6	37	1432[1]	1463	9.2	188	489	908	12.5	4.63	93	.266	.330	-64	-52	102	95	.984	100	125	.8	-5.1	-8.0	-.3	-3.4
TOT	161	143	675	23240	9.0			12.7	4.23		.262	.333					.981	1850	2415							

Runs
Sosa-Chi 134
McGwire-StL 130
Bagwell-Hou 124
C.Jones-Atl 123
Biggio-Hou 123

Hits
Bichette-Col 219
Biggio-Hou 210
Castilla-Col 206
V.Guerrero-Mon 202

Doubles
Biggio-Hou 51
Young-Cin 48
Bichette-Col 48
Walker-Col 46

Triples
Dellucci-Ari 12
B.Larkin-Cin 10
W.Guerrero-LA-Mon 9
Perez-Col 9

Home Runs
McGwire-StL 70
Sosa-Chi 66
Vaughn-SD 50
Castilla-Col 46
Galarraga-Atl 44

Total Bases
Sosa-Chi 416
McGwire-StL 383
Castilla-Col 380
V.Guerrero-Mon 367
Vaughn-SD 342

Runs Batted In
Sosa-Chi 158
McGwire-StL 147
Castilla-Col 144
Kent-SF 128
Burnitz-Mil 125

Runs Produced
Sosa-Chi 226
McGwire-StL 207
Castilla-Col 206
Bonds-SF 205
Bagwell-Hou 201

Bases On Balls
McGwire-StL 162
Bonds-SF 130
Bagwell-Hou 109
C.Jones-Atl 96

Batting Average
Walker-Col .363
Olerud-NY .353
Bichette-Col .331
Piazza-LA-Fla-NY .329
Kendall-Pit .327

On Base Percentage
McGwire-StL .473
Olerud-NY .451
Walker-Col .446
Bonds-SF .442
Sheffield-Fla-LA .435

Slugging Average
McGwire-StL .752
Sosa-Chi .647
Walker-Col .630
Bonds-SF .609
Vaughn-SD .597

Production
McGwire-StL 1.225
Walker-Col 1.076
Bonds-SF 1.051
Sosa-Chi 1.026
Olerud-NY 1.001

Adjusted Production
McGwire-StL 218
Bonds-SF 179
Vaughn-SD 163
Olerud-NY 163
Sheffield-Fla-LA 161

Batter Runs
McGwire-StL 93.1
Bonds-SF 63.6
Sosa-Chi 56.4
Olerud-NY 54.2
Walker-Col 53.5

Adjusted Batter Runs
McGwire-StL 95.0
Bonds-SF 69.0
Olerud-NY 55.4
Sosa-Chi 52.4
Bagwell-Hou 51.0

Clutch Hitting Index
Brogna-Phi 125
Kent-SF 120
Lee-Fla 118
Guillen-Pit 113
Bichette-Col 109

Runs Created
McGwire-StL 193
Bonds-SF 153
Sosa-Chi 149
Biggio-Hou 142
Olerud-NY 141

Total Average
McGwire-StL 1.512
Walker-Col 1.197
Bonds-SF 1.189
Sheffield-Fla-LA 1.088
Bagwell-Hou 1.081

Stolen Bases
Womack-Pit 58
Biggio-Hou 50
Young-LA 42
Renteria-Fla 41
Bonds-SF 28

Stolen Base Average
B.Larkin-Cin 89.7
Womack-Pit 87.9
A.Jones-Atl 87.1
Martin-Pit 87.0
Biggio-Hou 86.2

Stolen Base Runs
Womack-Pit 12.6
Biggio-Hou 10.2
B.Larkin-Cin 6.0
A.Jones-Atl 5.7

Fielding Runs
A.Jones-Atl 31.8
Vina-Mil 28.8
Perez-Col 26.5
Cirillo-Mil 23.8
Kotsay-Fla 21.8

Total Player Rating
Bonds-SF 7.2
McGwire-StL 7.2
Sosa-Chi 6.3
Vaughn-SD 5.5
Piazza-LA-Fla-NY 5.4

Wins
Glavine-Atl 20
Tapani-Chi 19
Reynolds-Hou 19
Maddux-Atl 18
Brown-SD 18

Win Percentage
Smoltz-Atl .850
Glavine-Atl .769
Leiter-NY .739
Brown-SD .720
Reynolds-Hou .704

Games
Beck-Chi 81
Nen-SF 78
McElroy-Col 78
Kline-Mon 78
Telford-Mon 77

Complete Games
Schilling-Phi 15
Maddux-Atl 9
Hernandez-Fla 9
C.Perez-Mon-LA 7
Brown-SD 7

Shutouts
Maddux-Atl 5
R.Johnson-Hou 4
Glavine-Atl 3
Brown-SD 3

Saves
Hoffman-SD 53
Beck-Chi 51
Shaw-Cin-LA 48
Nen-SF 40
J.Franco-NY 38

Innings Pitched
Schilling-Phi 268.2
Brown-SD 257.0
Maddux-Atl 251.0
C.Perez-Mon-LA 241.0
Hernandez-Fla 234.1

Fewest Hits/Game
Wood-Chi 6.32
Leiter-NY 7.04
Maddux-Atl 7.21
Harnisch-Cin 7.58
Smoltz-Atl 7.78

Fewest BB/Game
Anderson-Ari 1.04
Reed-NY 1.23
Lima-Hou 1.23
Maddux-Atl 1.61
Brown-SD 1.72

Strikeouts
Schilling-Phi 300
Brown-SD 257
Wood-Chi 233
Reynolds-Hou 209
Maddux-Atl 204

Strikeouts/Game
Wood-Chi 12.58
Schilling-Phi 10.05
Smoltz-Atl 9.29
Brown-SD 9.00
Millwood-Atl 8.41

Ratio
Maddux-Atl 9.07
Brown-SD 9.95
Schilling-Phi 10.15
Reed-NY 10.30
Lima-Hou 10.34

Earned Run Average
Maddux-Atl 2.22
Brown-SD 2.38
Leiter-NY 2.47
Glavine-Atl 2.47
Daal-Ari 2.88

Adjusted ERA
Maddux-Atl 190
Glavine-Atl 171
Leiter-NY 169
Brown-SD 161
Daal-Ari 150

Opponents' Batting Avg.
Wood-Chi .196
Leiter-NY .216
Maddux-Atl .220
Harnisch-Cin .228
Smoltz-Atl .231

Opponents' On Base Pct.
Maddux-Atl .262
Brown-SD .280
Schilling-Phi .284
Smoltz-Atl .286
Lima-Hou .287

Starter Runs
Maddux-Atl 56.0
Brown-SD 52.8
Glavine-Atl 44.8
Leiter-NY 37.7
Schilling-Phi 29.3

Adjusted Starter Runs
Maddux-Atl 56.0
Glavine-Atl 44.8
Brown-SD 41.2
Leiter-NY 36.3
Schilling-Phi 33.1

Clutch Pitching Index
Hampton-Hou 133
Glavine-Atl 121
Reynolds-Hou 119
Daal-Ari 117
Hernandez-Fla 116

Relief Runs
Nen-SF 26.7
Urbina-Mon 22.6
Hoffman-SD 22.3
Shaw-Cin-LA 19.9
Acevedo-StL 18.2

Adjusted Relief Runs
Nen-SF 25.0
Urbina-Mon 21.6
Shaw-Cin-LA 19.2
Hoffman-SD 19.0
Veres-Col 18.9

Relief Ranking
Nen-SF 55.0
Urbina-Mon 43.5
Shaw-Cin-LA 41.1
Hoffman-SD 37.9
Acevedo-StL 22.5

Total Pitcher Index
Maddux-Atl 7.2
Glavine-Atl 5.6
Nen-SF 5.6
Brown-SD 4.6
Urbina-Mon 4.3

Total Baseball Ranking
Bonds-SF 7.2
Maddux-Atl 7.2
McGwire-StL 7.2
Sosa-Chi 6.3
Glavine-Atl 5.6

March 3 Larry Doby, the AL's first black player, is elected to the Baseball Hall of Fame along with former AL president Lee MacPhail. Also chosen by the Veterans Committee are Negro League pitcher "Bullet" Joe Rogan and turn-of-the-century shortstop "Gorgeous" George Davis.

March 31 The Tigers beat the Devil Rays in the first-ever game at Tropicana Field, 11-6.

April 13 Ken Griffey Jr. hits his 300th career home run to become the second youngest player to reach the milestone.

May 17 David Wells pitches the 13th perfect game in modern major league history.

July 5 Roger Clemens becomes the 11th pitcher to reach 3,000 strikeouts when he fans Randy Winn of the Tampa Bay Devil Rays.

July 7 Roberto Alomar has three hits, including a home run, a walk, a stolen base and scores two runs to win MVP honors in the highest-scoring All-Star Game in history. The 13-8 win at Coors Field is the second straight AL win.

July 8 Bud Selig is unanimously elected baseball's ninth commissioner.

September 19 Seattle's Alex Rodriguez becomes the third player to reach 40 home runs and 40 steals with a first-inning home run off Jack McDowell of Anaheim. He joins Jose Canseco (1988) and Barry Bonds (1996) in this exclusive club.

September 20 Cal Ripken's string of consecutive games ends at 2,632 when the Orioles third baseman asks to be taken out of the lineup shortly before the final Orioles home game of the season.

October 13 The Yankees win their 35th AL pennant with a 9-5 win over Cleveland in Game 6 of the ALCS. David Wells, who earned victories in Game 1 and Game 5, is named MVP of the series.

October 21 The Yankees win their 24th World Series and sweep for the seventh time in team history. The 3-0 win over the Padres is the team's 125th overall. Scott Brosius earns Series MVP honors.

November 10 Oakland outfielder Ben Grieve is named AL Rookie of the Year.

November 16 Roger Clemens wins his second consecutive AL Cy Young Award. Clemens becomes the first player to win five Cy Young Awards.

November 18 Rangers slugger Alex Gonzalez is named AL MVP.

ANAHEIM

Pos	Player
M	T.Collins
1B	C.Fielder
2B	J.Baughman
SS	G.DiSarcina
3B	D.Hollins
LF	D.Erstad
CF	J.Edmonds
RF	G.Anderson
C	M.Walbeck
DH	T.Salmon
C	P.Nevin
2D	N.Martin
2	R.Velarde
3	T.Glaus
O	O.Palmeiro
32	C.Shipley
O	D.Mashore
1	C.Pritchett
O	G.Jefferies
O	T.Greene
P	C.Finley
P	O.Olivares
P	S.Sparks
P	J.Dickson
P	K.Hill
RP	S.Hasegawa
RP	R.DeLucia
RP	T.Percival
P	A.Watson
P	J.McDowell
P	J.Washburn

BALTIMORE

Pos	Player
M	R.Miller
1B	R.Palmeiro
2B	R.Alomar
SS	M.Bordick
3B	C.Ripken
LF	B.Surhoff
CF	B.Anderson
RF	E.Davis
C	L.Webster
DH	H.Baines
C	C.Hoiles
OD	J.Carter
O	J.Hammonds
2S	J.Reboulet
O	R.Becker
DO	
P	S.Erickson
P	M.Mussina
P	S.Ponson
P	D.Drabek
RP	D.Johns
RP	A.Rhodes
P	A.Mills
P	J.Key
P	A.Benitez
P	J.Guzman
P	J.Orosco
P	S.Kamieniecki
P	P.Smith
P	N.Charlton
P	T.Mathews
/P	N.Rodriguez

BOSTON

Pos	Player
M	J.Williams
1B	M.Vaughn
2B	M.Benjamin
SS	N.Garciaparra
3B	J.Valentin
LF	T.O'Leary
CF	D.Lewis
RF	D.Bragg
C	S.Hatteberg
DH	R.Jefferson
C	J.Varitek
OD	D.Buford
D1	M.Stanley
D	J.Leyritz
2	D.Sadler
2	M.Cummings
2	L.Merloni
2	M.Lemke
P	P.Martinez
P	T.Wakefield
P	B.Saberhagen
P	S.Avery
RP	D.Lowe
RP	J.Wasdin
RP	T.Gordon
P	J.Corsi
P	R.Garces
P	P.Schourek
P	D.Eckersley
P	C.Reyes
/P	B.Rose

CHICAGO

Pos	Player
M	J.Manuel
1B	W.Cordero
2B	R.Durham
SS	M.Caruso
3B	R.Ventura
LF	A.Belle
CF	M.Cameron
RF	M.Ordonez
C	C.Kreuter
DH	F.Thomas
13	G.Norton
O	J.Abbott
C	C.O'Brien
S2	C.Snopek
C	R.Machado
O	R.Sierra
P	M.Sirotka
P	J.Navarro
P	J.Baldwin
P	J.Parque
P	S.Eyre
RP	C.Castillo
RP	B.Simas
RP	K.Foulke
P	J.Snyder
P	J.Bere
P	B.Howry
P	T.Fordham
P	M.Karchner
/P	J.Abbott
P	C.Bradford

CLEVELAND

Pos	Player
M	M.Hargrove
1B	J.Thome
2B	D.Bell
SS	O.Vizquel
3B	T.Fryman
LF	B.Giles
CF	K.Lofton
RF	M.Ramirez
C	S.Alomar
DH	D.Justice
O	M.Whiten
1	R.Sexson
C	P.Borders
2S	S.Dunston
23	J.Branson
2S	E.Wilson
2	J.Cora
O	G.Berroa
P	C.Nagy
P	B.Colon
P	D.Burba
P	J.Wright
P	D.Gooden
RP	M.Jackson
RP	J.Mesa
RP	P.Shuey
P	C.Ogea
P	P.Assenmacher
P	E.Plunk
P	D.Jones
P	R.Villone

DETROIT

Pos	Player
M	B.Bell
M	L.Parrish
1B	T.Clark
2B	D.Easley
SS	D.Cruz
3B	J.Randa
LF	L.Gonzalez
CF	B.Hunter
RF	B.Higginson
C	P.Bako
DH	Catalanotto
2D	F.Catalanotto
3	G.Alvarez
O	J.Encarnacion
C	J.Oliver
D	G.Berroa
OD	K.Bartee
S	B.Ripken
D	A.Tomberlin
C	J.Siddall
P	J.Thompson
P	B.Moehler
P	B.Florie
P	S.Greisinger
P	F.Castillo
P	B.Powell
P	D.Bochtler
P	D.Brocail
P	T.Jones
P	T.Worrell

KANSAS CITY

Pos	Player
M	T.Muser
1B	J.King
2B	J.Offerman
SS	M.Lopez
3B	D.Palmer
LF	J.Conine
CF	J.Damon
RF	H.Sutton
C	M.Sweeney
DH	T.Pendleton
1O	H.Morris
C	S.Fasano
O	J.Dye
OD	S.Mack
S	S.Halter
S	L.Rivera
S	F.Martinez
O	J.Allensworth
P	T.Belcher
P	P.Rapp
P	J.Rosado
P	G.Rusch
P	H.Pichardo
RP	C.Haney
RP	S.Service
RP	J.Pittsley
P	M.Whisenant
P	J.Montgomery
P	R.Bones
/P	B.Barber
P	B.Bevil

MINNESOTA

Pos	Player
M	T.Kelly
1B	D.Ortiz
2B	T.Walker
SS	P.Meares
3B	B.Gates
LF	M.Cordova
CF	O.Nixon
RF	M.Lawton
C	T.Steinbach
DH	P.Molitor
31	R.Coomer
2S	D.Hocking
O	A.Ochoa
1O	O.Merced
C	J.Valentin
O	C.Latham
P	B.Radke
P	L.Hawkins
P	E.Milton
P	B.Tewksbury
P	M.Morgan
RP	M.Trombley
RP	D.Serafini
RP	R.Aguilera
P	F.Rodriguez
P	E.Guardado
P	G.Swindell
P	H.Carrasco
P	T.Baptist

NEW YORK

Pos	Player
M	J.Torre
1B	T.Martinez
2B	C.Knoblauch
SS	D.Jeter
3B	S.Brosius
LF	C.Curtis
CF	B.Williams
RF	P.O'Neill
C	J.Posada
DH	D.Strawberry
DO	T.Raines
C	J.Girardi
S1	L.Sojo
D	C.Davis
O	R.Ledee
2D	H.Bush
O	S.Spencer
P	A.Pettitte
P	D.Wells
P	D.Cone
P	H.Irabu
RP	O.Hernandez
RP	M.Stanton
RP	M.Rivera
RP	D.Holmes
P	R.Mendoza
P	M.Buddie
P	J.Nelson
P	G.Lloyd

OAKLAND

Pos	Player
M	A.Howe
1B	J.Giambi
2B	S.Spiezio
SS	M.Tejada
3B	M.Blowers
LF	R.Henderson
CF	R.Christenson
RF	B.Grieve
C	A.Hinch
DH	M.Stairs
2S	R.Bournigal
C	M.Macfarlane
2O	R.Roberts
O	J.McDonald
DO	K.Mitchell
S	K.Abbott
3	D.Magadan
2	E.Sprague
1O	J.Voigt
P	K.Rogers
P	T.Candiotti
P	J.Haynes
P	M.Oquist
P	B.Stein
RP	B.Taylor
RP	T.Mathews
RP	M.Mohler
P	B.Groom
P	M.Fetters

SEATTLE

Pos	Player
M	L.Piniella
1B	D.Segui
2B	J.Cora
SS	A.Rodriguez
3B	R.Davis
LF	G.Hill
CF	K.Griffey
RF	R.Ducey
C	D.Wilson
DH	E.Martinez
3D	J.Buhner
O	S.Monahan
O2	R.Amaral
C	J.Marzano
O1	R.Ibanez
C	J.Oliver
3	R.Rossy
2	D.Bell
O	R.Radmanovich
P	J.Moyer
P	J.Fassero
P	R.Johnson
P	K.Cloude
P	B.Swift
RP	P.Spoljaric
RP	M.Timlin
RP	B.Ayala
P	H.Slocumb
P	B.Wells

TAMPA BAY

Pos	Player
M	L.Rothschild
1B	F.McGriff
2B	M.Cairo
SS	K.Stocker
3B	B.Smith
LF	Q.McCracken
CF	R.Winn
RF	M.Kelly
C	J.Flaherty
DH	P.Sorrento
3D	W.Boggs
O	D.Martinez
S2	A.Ledesma
C	M.Difelice
O	R.Butler
OD	B.Trammell
P	R.Arrojo
P	T.Saunders
P	W.Alvarez
P	J.Santana
P	D.Springer
RP	E.Yan
RP	J.Mecir
RP	A.Lopez
P	B.Rekar
P	R.Hernandez
P	R.White
P	J.Johnson
P	S.Aldred

TEXAS

Pos	Player
M	J.Oates
1B	W.Clark
2B	M.McLemore
SS	K.Elster
3B	F.Tatis
LF	R.Greer
CF	T.Goodwin
RF	J.Gonzalez
C	I.Rodriguez
DH	L.Stevens
23	L.Alicea
O	R.Kelly
S	R.Clayton
OD	M.Simms
3	T.Zeile
SD	D.Cedeno
C	B.Haselman
P	R.Helling
P	A.Sele
P	J.Burkett
P	D.Oliver
RP	T.Crabtree
RP	E.Gunderson
RP	J.Wetteland
P	E.Loaiza
P	B.Witt
P	D.Patterson
P	T.Stottlemyre
P	X.Hernandez

TORONTO

Pos	Player
M	T.Johnson
1B	C.Delgado
2B	C.Grebeck
SS	A.Gonzalez
3B	E.Sprague
LF	S.Stewart
CF	J.Cruz
RF	S.Green
C	D.Fletcher
DH	J.Canseco
23	T.Fernandez
D1	M.Stanley
C	F.Crespo
C	K.Brown
C	M.Dalesandro
P	R.Clemens
P	W.Williams
P	P.Hentgen
P	C.Carpenter
P	J.Guzman
RP	P.Quantrill
RP	B.Risley
RP	D.Stieb
P	K.Escobar
P	D.Plesac
P	E.Hanson
P	R.Myers
P	R.Person
P	C.Almanzar

TEAM	G	W	L	PCT	GB	R	OR	AB	H	2B	3B	HR	BB	SO	AVG	OBP	SLG	PRO	PRO+	BR	/A	PF	CHI	RC	SB	CS	SBA	SBR
EAST																												
NY	162	114	48	.704		**965**	**656**	5643	1625	290	31	207	**653**	1025	.288	**.368**	.460	**.828**	**116**	**123**	**143**	98	101	**957**	153	63	71	8
BOS	162	92	70	.568	22	876	729	5601	1568	**338**	35	205	541	1049	.280	.351	.463	.814	110	77	77	100	99	895	72	39	65	-2
TOR	163	88	74	.543	26	816	768	5580	1482	316	19	221	564	1132	.266	.342	.448	.790	104	28	29	100	97	861	**184**	81	69	7
BAL	162	79	83	.488	35	817	785	5565	1520	303	11	214	593	**903**	.273	.349	.447	.796	107	46	62	98	95	863	86	48	64	-3
TB	162	63	99	.389	51	620	751	5555	1450	267	**43**	111	473	1107	.261	.323	.385	.708	81	-135	-164	104	94	678	120	73	62	-8
CENTRAL																												
CLE	162	89	73	.549		850	779	5616	1530	334	30	198	631	1061	.272	.350	.448	.798	103	51	21	103	97	887	143	60	70	7
CHI	163	80	82	.494	9	861	931	5585	1516	291	38	198	551	916	.271	.342	.444	.786	106	19	40	98	104	850	127	46	73	**11**
KC	161	72	89	.447	16.5	714	899	5546	1459	274	40	134	475	984	.263	.328	.399	.727	84	-96	-127	104	102	730	135	50	73	**11**
MIN	162	70	92	.432	19	734	818	5641	1499	285	32	115	506	915	.266	.331	.389	.720	87	-108	-109	100	105	712	112	54	67	1
DET	162	65	97	.401	24	722	863	5664	1494	306	29	165	455	1070	.264	.325	.415	.740	90	-77	-82	101	99	759	122	62	66	-1
WEST																												
TEX	162	88	74	.543		940	871	5672	**1637**	314	32	201	595	1045	**.289**	.360	.462	.822	107	103	63	104	101	935	82	47	64	-4
ANA	162	85	77	.525	3	787	783	5630	1530	314	27	147	510	1028	.272	.337	.415	.752	94	-43	-51	101	103	787	93	45	67	1
SEA	161	76	85	.472	11.5	859	855	5628	1553	321	28	**234**	558	1081	.276	.347	**.468**	.815	110	76	76	100	96	923	115	39	**75**	**11**
OAK	162	74	88	.457	14	804	866	5490	1413	295	13	149	633	1122	.257	.340	.397	.737	94	-64	-42	97	**108**	762	131	47	74	**11**
TOT	1134					11365	78416	21276	4248	408	2499	7738	14438	.271	.343	.432	.774							1675	754	69	50	

TEAM	CG	SH	SV	IP	H	H/G	HR	BB	SO	RAT	ERA	ERA+	OAV	OOB	PR	/A	PF	CPI	FA	E	DP	FW	PW	BW	SBW	DIF
EAST																										
NY	**22**	**16**	48	1456^{2}	**1357**	**8.4**	**156**	466	1080	**11.7**	**3.82**	**116**	**.247**	**.314**	**133**	**101**	96	98	.984	98	146	.9	**9.5**	**13.5**	.4	8.7
BOS	5	8	**53**	1436	1406	8.8	168	504	1025	12.3	4.18	111	.255	.324	75	70	99	97	.983	105	128	.5	6.6	7.3	-.5	-2.8
TOR	10	11	47	1465	1443	8.9	169	587	1154	12.7	4.28	108	.256	.331	60	59	100	98	.979	125	131	-.6	5.6	2.7	.3	-1.0
BAL	16	10	37	1431^{1}	1505	9.5	169	535	1065	13.1	4.74	95	.272	.341	-15	-35	97	97	**.987**	**81**	144	**1.8**	-3.3	5.8	-.6	-5.7
TB	7	7	28	1443	1425	8.9	171	643	1008	13.4	4.35	113	.261	.347	47	88	105	105	.985	94	**178**	1.1	8.3	-15.5	-1.1	-10.8
CENTRAL																										
CLE	9	4	47	1460	1552	9.6	171	563	1037	13.5	4.44	108	.274	.346	33	54	103	**106**	.982	110	146	.2	5.1	2.0	.3	.4
CHI	8	4	42	1438^{2}	1569	9.8	211	580	911	13.8	5.22	87	.278	.351	-92	-107	98	97	.977	140	161	-1.4	-10.1	3.8	.7	6.0
KC	6	5	46	1436^{1}	1590	10.0	196	568	999	13.9	5.15	95	.281	.353	-80	-39	106	98	.980	125	172	-.7	-3.7	-12.0	.7	7.1
MIN	7	8	42	1447^{2}	1622	10.1	180	**458**	952	13.2	4.75	99	.284	.341	-16	-9	101	101	.982	108	135	.3	-.8	-10.3	-.2	.0
DET	9	4	32	1446^{1}	1551	9.7	185	595	947	13.6	4.93	96	.277	.351	-45	-35	101	100	.982	115	164	-.0	-3.3	-7.7	-.4	-4.5
WEST																										
TEX	10	8	46	1431^{1}	1624	10.2	164	519	994	13.8	4.99	97	.285	.350	-55	-24	104	98	.980	121	140	-.4	-2.3	5.9	-.7	4.4
ANA	3	5	52	1444	1481	9.2	164	630	1091	13.5	4.49	105	.267	.347	26	32	101	102	.983	106	146	.4	3.0	-4.8	-.2	5.6
SEA	17	7	31	1424^{1}	1530	9.7	196	528	**1156**	13.4	4.93	94	.273	.342	-45	-48	100	97	.979	125	139	-.7	-4.5	7.2	**.7**	-7.2
OAK	12	4	39	1434	1555	9.8	179	529	922	13.4	4.81	95	.276	.344	-25	-39	98	99	.977	141	155	-1.5	-3.7	-4.0	**.7**	1.4
TOT	141	101	590	20194^{2}	9.5			13.2	4.65		.271	.343					.981	1594	2085							

Runs	Hits	Doubles	Triples	Home Runs	Total Bases
Jeter-NY 127	Rodriguez-Sea 213	Gonzalez-Tex 50	Offerman-KC 13	Griffey-Sea 56	Belle-Chi 399
Durham-Chi 126	Vaughn-Bos 205	Belle-Chi 48	Damon-KC 10	Belle-Chi 49	Griffey-Sea 387
Rodriguez-Sea 123	Jeter-NY 203	Martinez-Sea 46	Winn-TB 9	Canseco-Tor 46	Rodriguez-Sea 384
Griffey-Sea 120	Belle-Chi 200	Valentin-Bos 44		M.Ramirez-Cle 45	Gonzalez-Tex 382
Knoblauch-NY 117	Garciaparra-Bos . . . 195	Delgado-Tor 43		Gonzalez-Tex 45	Vaughn-Bos 360

Runs Batted In	Runs Produced	Bases On Balls	Batting Average	On Base Percentage	Slugging Average
Gonzalez-Tex 157	Gonzalez-Tex 222	Henderson-Oak . . . 118	Williams-NY 339	Martinez-Sea 433	Belle-Chi 655
Belle-Chi 152	Belle-Chi 216	Thomas-Chi 110	Vaughn-Bos 337	Williams-NY 425	Gonzalez-Tex 630
Griffey-Sea 146	Griffey-Sea 210	Martinez-Sea 106	Belle-Chi 328	Salmon-Ana 417	Griffey-Sea 611
M.Ramirez-Cle 145	M.Ramirez-Cle 208	Thome-Cle 90	Davis-Bal 327	Thome-Cle 417	M.Ramirez-Cle 599
Rodriguez-Sea 124	Rodriguez-Sea 205	Salmon-Ana 90	Jeter-NY 324	Belle-Chi 408	Delgado-Tor 592

Production	Adjusted Production	Batter Runs	Adjusted Batter Runs	Clutch Hitting Index	Runs Created
Belle-Chi 1.063	Belle-Chi 175	Belle-Chi 62.5	Belle-Chi 66.4	Molitor-Min 132	Belle-Chi 158
Gonzalez-Tex 1.003	Williams-NY 160	Martinez-Sea 50.4	Martinez-Sea 50.4	Martinez-NY 129	Vaughn-Bos 144
Thome-Cle 1.001	Martinez-Sea 157	Vaughn-Bos 48.6	Vaughn-Bos 48.6	Brosius-NY 120	Griffey-Sea 142
Williams-NY 1.000	Vaughn-Bos 154	Gonzalez-Tex 45.6	Williams-NY 46.0	Greer-Tex 120	Martinez-Sea 141
Martinez-Sea 998	Davis-Bal 152	Williams-NY 43.5	Griffey-Sea 43.1	King-KC 118	Rodriguez-Sea 138

Total Average	Stolen Bases	Stolen Base Average	Stolen Base Runs	Fielding Runs	Total Player Rating
Belle-Chi 1.123	Henderson-Oak 66	Lofton-Cle 84.4	Henderson-Oak . . .12.0	Bell-Cle-Sea 25.7	Belle-Chi 6.4
Thome-Cle 1.104	Lofton-Cle 54	Nixon-Min 84.1	Lofton-Cle 10.2	Easley-Det 21.8	Griffey-Sea 5.3
Martinez-Sea 1.082	Stewart-Tor 51	Henderson-Oak . . . 83.5	Nixon-Min 6.9	Bordick-Bal 20.6	Rodriguez-Sea 4.9
Delgado-Tor 1.047	Rodriguez-Sea 46	Jeter-NY 83.3	Offerman-KC 6.3	Stocker-TB 19.7	Williams-NY 4.1
Salmon-Ana 1.030	Offerman-KC 45	Curtis-NY 80.8	Rodriguez-Sea 6.0	Cruz-Det 19.5	Martinez-Sea 4.0

Wins	Win Percentage	Games	Complete Games	Shutouts	Saves
Helling-Tex 20	Wells-NY 818	Runyan-Det 88	Erickson-Bal 11	Wells-NY 5	Gordon-Bos 46
Cone-NY 20	Clemens-Tor 769	Quantrill-Tor 82	Wells-NY 8	Moyer-Sea 3	Wetteland-Tex 42
Clemens-Tor 20	Helling-Tex 741	Swindell-Min-Bos . . 81	Rogers-Oak 7	Moehler-Det 3	Percival-Ana 42
Sele-Tex 19	Cone-NY 741	Guardado-Min 79	Fassero-Sea 7	Clemens-Tor 3	Jackson-Cle 40
Martinez-Bos 19	Martinez-Bos 731	Plesac-Tor 78			Aguilera-Min 38

Innings Pitched	Fewest Hits/Game	Fewest BB/Game	Strikeouts	Strikeouts/Game	Ratio
Erickson-Bal 251.1	Clemens-Tor 6.48	Wells-NY 1.22	Clemens-Tor 271	Clemens-Tor 10.39	Wells-NY 9.45
Rogers-Oak 238.2	Martinez-Bos 7.24	Saberhagen-Bos . . 1.49	Martinez-Bos 251	Martinez-Bos 9.67	Clemens-Tor 10.13
Clemens-Tor 234.2	Irabu-NY 7.70	Moyer-Sea 1.61	Johnson-Sea 213	Cone-NY 9.06	Martinez-Bos 10.13
Moyer-Sea 234.1	Cone-NY 8.06	Mussina-Bal 1.79	Finley-Ana 212	Finley-Ana 8.54	Mussina-Bal 10.21
Belcher-KC 234.0	Rogers-Oak 8.11	Radke-Min 1.81	Cone-NY 209	Saunders-TB 8.05	Rogers-Oak 10.90

Earned Run Average	Adjusted ERA	Opponents' Batting Avg.	Opponents' On Base Pct.	Starter Runs	Adjusted Starter Runs
Clemens-Tor 2.65	Clemens-Tor 175	Clemens-Tor 197	Wells-NY 266	Clemens-Tor 52.2	Clemens-Tor 52.1
Martinez-Bos 2.89	Martinez-Bos 160	Martinez-Bos 217	Clemens-Tor 278	Martinez-Bos 45.7	Martinez-Bos 45.0
Rogers-Oak 3.17	Rogers-Oak 144	Irabu-NY 233	Martinez-Bos 280	Rogers-Oak 39.3	Rogers-Oak 36.9
Finley-Ana 3.39	Finley-Ana 139	Cone-NY 237	Mussina-Bal 283	Finley-Ana 31.3	Finley-Ana 32.4
Wells-NY 3.49	Arrojo-TB 137	Wells-NY 239	Moyer-Sea 296	Moyer-Sea 29.0	Arrojo-TB 30.0

Clutch Pitching Index	Relief Runs	Adjusted Relief Runs	Relief Ranking	Total Pitcher Index	Total Baseball Ranking
Olivares-Ana 119	Jackson-Cle 22.1	Jackson-Cle 23.0	Gordon-Bos 37.7	Clemens-Tor 5.3	Belle-Chi 6.4
Finley-Ana 117	Rivera-NY 18.7	Lopez-TB 20.4	Wetteland-Tex 33.9	Martinez-Bos 4.3	Griffey-Sea 5.3
Arrojo-TB 115	Quantrill-Tor 18.3	Wetteland-Tex 19.3	Jackson-Cle 31.3	Rogers-Oak 4.0	Clemens-Tor 5.3
Saunders-TB 115	Lopez-TB 18.1	Quantrill-Tor 18.3	Lopez-TB 25.8	Arrojo-TB 3.8	Rodriguez-Sea 4.9
Burba-Cle 113	Wetteland-Tex 18.0	Rivera-NY 17.3	Rivera-NY 25.2	Gordon-Bos 3.5	Martinez-Bos 4.3

The All-Time Leaders

This section is divided into two parts: lifetime leaders and single-season leaders. Both groups command our attention and convey the pleasures of the game, which lie as much in contemplation of the past as in experiencing the present: Henry Aaron, 755; Babe Ruth, 714; Willie Mays, 660—this is no mere aggregation of names and numbers, as in a telephone directory . . . it comprises the romance and lore of the home run, and of baseball itself. Jack Chesbro, 41, 1904; Bob Gibson, 1.12, 1968; Nolan Ryan, 383, 1973 . . . you can fill in the blanks that tell the story of pitching's most glorious seasons.

What follows are the all-time great achievements in 219 categories, both the traditional statistics and the new. For most of these we will give not the top 10 or 20 but the top 100, because some categories would otherwise be dominated by players of a certain era (for example, slugging average by batters of the 1920s and 1930s, earned run average by pitchers of 1900–1919). And for many stats we will offer a second kind of ranking, broken down into six distinct eras of baseball, with the top 10 or 15 leaders in each. For example, breaking down single-season home runs this way would produce lists topped by these men:

> 1876–1892: Ned Williamson, 27, 1884
> 1893–1919: Babe Ruth, 29, 1919
> 1920–1941: Babe Ruth, 60, 1927
> 1942–1960: Ralph Kiner, 54, 1949
> 1961–1976: Roger Maris, 61, 1961
> 1977–1998: Mark McGwire, 70, 1998

And for single-season Adjusted ERA (normalized to league average and adjusted for home-park factor), we get:

> 1876–1892: Tim Keefe, 294
>   (adjusted from actual 0.80), 1880
> 1893–1919: Dutch Leonard, 280
>   (adjusted from actual 0.96), 1914
> 1920–1941: Lefty Grove, 218
>   (adjusted from actual 2.06), 1931
> 1942–1960: Billy Pierce, 201
>   (adjusted from actual 1.97), 1955
> 1961–1976: Bob Gibson, 258
>   (adjusted from actual 1.12), 1968
> 1977–1998: Greg Maddux, 272
>   (adjusted from actual 1.56), 1994

This is quite a different lineup from the traditional list of ERA leaders (which relegates pre-1900 pitching to the shadows), where of the 15 top spots, 14 are accorded to pitchers active from 1905 to 1918. Is there a baseball fan alive who thinks that all the great pitchers were created in that 14-year span and that the mold was then broken?

We also present certain categories in a per game fashion that illuminates some hidden great performers. While it is not surprising to find such names as Babe Ruth, Lou Gehrig, and Jimmie Foxx among the top 10 all-time at runs batted in per game, few fans would expect to find Cap Anson listed seventh, or to find that the best of the best was 19th-century slugger Sam Thompson.

But we go one step further and rank several batting categories by position, thus recognizing and illustrating the greater demands for fielding skill at such positions as shortstop, catcher, and second base, and the comparatively plentiful supply of batting talent in the outfield and at first base. Having Mark McGwire hit 70 home runs for you is great, but he cannot play anywhere but first base; a team of nine McGwires (or 10, in the AL) would finish dead last. For example, here is the list of the top 10 lifetime batting averages:

> Ty Cobb, .366
> Rogers Hornsby, .358
> Joe Jackson, .356
> Ed Delahanty, .346
> Tris Speaker, .345
> Ted Williams, .344
> Billy Hamilton, .344
> Dan Brouthers, .342
> Babe Ruth, .342
> Harry Heilmann, .342

This would be a formidable team indeed, but it would not win, for it includes a first baseman, a second baseman, and eight outfielders. Here, as food for thought, is a list of the top 10 lifetime leading averages among catchers, that indispensable class of men. ("You gotta have a catcher," Casey Stengel explained, "because if you don't, the ball rolls all the way to the backstop.")

> Mickey Cochrane, .320
> Bill Dickey, .313
> Spud Davis, .308
> Ernie Lombardi, .306
> Gabby Hartnett, .297
> Manny Sanguillen, .296
> Smoky Burgess, .295
> Thurman Munson, .292
> Hank Severeid, .289
> Jack Clements, .286

This team would not win, either. But the point is that the section that follows will, if perused carefully, make you think differently about the game and its statistics. And that's a large part of what *Total Baseball* is about.

For example, the batting average itself is a flawed measure, as we have discussed in "The History of Major League Baseball Statistics" and "Sabermetrics." While batting average is not as good as, say, Production (on base plus slugging), it is not worthless, either. And when we report batting average in a form which relates it to the league average at the time, it becomes far more useful as an evaluative tool.

Remember that list above of the top 10 lifetime batting averages? Here are the top ten batting averages *as compared to* the league batting averages in the years in which the men played (individual batting average divided by league batting average, expressed in three digits, so that a man who batted at exactly his league average over the course of his career would have a mark of 100):

Ty Cobb, 134.8
Joe Jackson, 133.1
Pete Browning, 131.6
Tony Gwynn, 128.1
Ted Williams, 128.1
Dan Brouthers, 127.8
Nap Lajoie, 127.3
Rod Carew, 127.0
Rogers Hornsby, 126.2
Tris Speaker, 125.4

Says something, doesn't it? But enough expostulation and fulmination. Let's set some ground rules, define some terms that may still be unfamiliar after you've browsed through the Player and Pitcher registers, and get on with the show.

To be eligible for a lifetime pitching category that is stated as an average, a man must have pitched 1,500 or more innings, or 750 or more innings if he is a relief pitcher, in the major leagues; for a counting statistic, he must simply have attained the necessary quantity to crack the list. For a single-season category expressed as an average, he must have pitched one inning per league scheduled game or have attained the necessary quantity (wins, strikeouts, saves) to head a counted list.

To be eligible for a lifetime batting category that is stated as an average, a man must have played in 1,000 or more games; for counting stats such as strikeouts, a Rob Deer earned his place on the list before he played his 1,000th game. For Pitcher Batting Average, the criterion is 1,500 innings pitched or 100 hits. And to reach the single-season batting lists, a man must have 3.1 plate appearances per scheduled game.

We provide tables of the top fielding performances, too, sorted by position as you would expect (and, in this edition, including only games played at the position, rather than combining data from secondary positions under the dominant position). As we establish a 1,000-game minimum for inclusion in all but a few batting and baserunning categories, we likewise establish for these positional rankings a minimum of 1,000 games played at the position.

For the three principal categories—Total Player Rating, Total Pitcher Index, and Total Baseball Ranking—we have introduced several variations. For example, TPR and TBR are shown 500 deep for lifetime leaders—sorted first by highest value; then alphabetically so that the reader may find a particular player without scanning 500 names; and last by the above-named eras, the top 25 in each. Total Pitcher Index is also sorted this way, but because far fewer pitchers than position players meet the longevity criteria, the lifetime groupings go 300 and 200 deep rather than 500 and 300.

Ties are calculated to as many decimal places as needed to break them, but averages are shown to only three places. When two or more players are tied in an averaged category with a narrow base of data, such as a season's won-lost percentage, the reader can presume a numerical dead heat (and obviously this goes for counting stats, too—one man's 39 doubles are as good as another's). But where there is a tie for batting average, earned run average, or any of the sabermetric measures, the reader may assume that the man listed above the other(s) has the minutely higher average.

Here are the few stats carried in this section that are not carried in the Annual Record or Registers, with definitions where the terms are not self-explanatory (see Glossary for formulas):

Batting, Baserunning, Fielding

Runs (Scored) Per Game   Broken down by era

Home Run Percentage   Home runs per 100 at bats

Bases on Balls Percentage   Walks (most) per 100 appearances (at bats plus walks)

At Bats Per Strikeout   Broken down by era

Relative Batting Average   Normalized to league average

Isolated Power   Slugging average minus batting average

Extra Base Hits

Pinch Hits

Pinch Hit Batting Average

Pinch Hit Home Runs

Strikeout Percentage

Total Player Rating Per 150 Games   Highlighting the achievements of modern players and those with comparatively short careers (though at least 1,000 games)

Total Chances Per Game   Broken down by position

Chances Accepted Per Game   Broken down by position

Putouts   Broken down by position

Putouts Per Game   Broken down by position

Assists   Broken down by position

Assists Per Game   Broken down by position

Double Plays   Broken down by position

Pitching

Wins Above Team   How many wins a pitcher garnered beyond those expected of an average pitcher for that team; the formula is weighted so that a pitcher on a good team has a chance to compete with pitchers on poor teams who otherwise would benefit from the larger potential spread between their team's won-lost percentage and their own; see Glossary for more information.

Wins Above League   A pitcher's won-lost record restated by adding his Pitching Wins above the league average to the record that a league-average pitcher would have had with the same number of decisions (for example, Tom Seaver goes 20–10 with seven Pitching Wins; applying the seven wins to a 15–15 mark in the same 30 decisions results in a WAL of 22–8).

Percentage of Team Wins

Relief Games

Pitchers' Batting Runs

Pitchers' Fielding Runs

Relief Wins   This statistic, like the relief stats below, includes only games in relief.

Relief Losses

Relief Innings Pitched

Relief Points   Relief wins plus saves minus losses

Games		At Bats		Runs	
1 Pete Rose	3562	1 Pete Rose	14053	1 Ty Cobb	2246
2 Carl Yastrzemski	3308	2 Hank Aaron	12364	2 Hank Aaron	2174
3 Hank Aaron	3298	3 Carl Yastrzemski	11988	Babe Ruth	2174
4 Ty Cobb	3035	4 Ty Cobb	11434	4 Pete Rose	2165
5 Eddie Murray	3026	5 Eddie Murray	11336	5 Willie Mays	2062
Stan Musial	3026	6 Robin Yount	11008	6 Rickey Henderson	2014
7 Willie Mays	2992	7 Dave Winfield	11003	7 Stan Musial	1949
8 Dave Winfield	2973	8 Stan Musial	10972	8 Lou Gehrig	1888
9 Rusty Staub	2951	9 Willie Mays	10881	9 Tris Speaker	1882
10 Brooks Robinson	2896	10 Paul Molitor	10835	10 Mel Ott	1859
11 Robin Yount	2856	11 Brooks Robinson	10654	11 Frank Robinson	1829
12 Al Kaline	2834	12 Cal Ripken	10433	12 Eddie Collins	1821
13 Eddie Collins	2826	13 Honus Wagner	10430	13 Carl Yastrzemski	1816
14 Reggie Jackson	2820	14 George Brett	10349	14 Ted Williams	1798
15 Frank Robinson	2808	15 Lou Brock	10332	15 Paul Molitor	1782
16 Honus Wagner	2792	16 Luis Aparicio	10230	16 Charlie Gehringer	1774
17 Tris Speaker	2789	17 Tris Speaker	10195	17 Jimmie Foxx	1751
18 Tony Perez	2777	18 Al Kaline	10116	18 Honus Wagner	1736
19 Mel Ott	2730	19 Rabbit Maranville	10078	19 Jesse Burkett	1720
20 George Brett	2707	20 Frank Robinson	10006	20 Cap Anson	1719
21 Cal Ripken	2704	21 Eddie Collins	9949	Willie Keeler	1719
22 Graig Nettles	2700	22 Andre Dawson	9927	22 Billy Hamilton	1691
23 Darrell Evans	2687	23 Reggie Jackson	9864	23 Bid McPhee	1678
24 Paul Molitor	2683	24 Tony Perez	9778	24 Mickey Mantle	1677
25 Rabbit Maranville	2670	25 Rusty Staub	9720	25 Dave Winfield	1669
26 Joe Morgan	2649	26 Vada Pinson	9645	26 Joe Morgan	1650
27 Andre Dawson	2627	27 Nap Lajoie	9589	27 Jimmy Ryan	1642
28 Lou Brock	2616	28 Sam Crawford	9570	28 George Van Haltren	1639
29 Rickey Henderson	2612	29 Jake Beckley	9526	29 Robin Yount	1632
30 Dwight Evans	2606	30 Rickey Henderson	9473	30 Eddie Murray	1627
31 Luis Aparicio	2599	31 Paul Waner	9459	Paul Waner	1627
32 Willie McCovey	2588	32 Mel Ott	9456	32 Al Kaline	1622
33 Ozzie Smith	2573	33 Roberto Clemente	9454	33 Roger Connor	1620
34 Harold Baines	2567	34 Ernie Banks	9421	34 Fred Clarke	1619
35 Paul Waner	2549	35 Bill Buckner	9397	35 Lou Brock	1610
36 Ernie Banks	2528	36 Ozzie Smith	9396	36 Jake Beckley	1600
37 Bill Buckner	2517	37 Max Carey	9363	37 Ed Delahanty	1599
Sam Crawford	2517	38 Dave Parker	9358	38 Bill Dahlen	1589
39 Babe Ruth	2503	39 Billy Williams	9350	39 George Brett	1583
40 Carlton Fisk	2499	40 Rod Carew	9315	40 Rogers Hornsby	1579
41 Dave Concepcion	2488	41 Joe Morgan	9277	41 Hugh Duffy	1552
Billy Williams	2488	42 Sam Rice	9269	42 Reggie Jackson	1551
43 Nap Lajoie	2480	43 Nellie Fox	9232	43 Max Carey	1545
44 Max Carey	2476	44 Willie Davis	9174	44 George Davis	1539
45 Rod Carew	2469	45 Doc Cramer	9140	45 Frankie Frisch	1532
Vada Pinson	2469	46 Frankie Frisch	9112	46 Tim Raines	1528
47 Dave Parker	2466	47 Harold Baines	9111	47 Dan Brouthers	1523
48 Ted Simmons	2456	48 Zack Wheat	9106	48 Tom Brown	1521
49 Bill Dahlen	2443	49 Cap Anson	9101	49 Sam Rice	1514
50 Ron Fairly	2442	50 Lave Cross	9072	50 Cal Ripken	1510
51 Harmon Killebrew	2435	51 Al Oliver	9049	51 Eddie Mathews	1509
52 Roberto Clemente	2433	52 Bill Dahlen	9031	52 Al Simmons	1507
53 Willie Davis	2429	George Davis	9031	53 Mike Schmidt	1506
54 Luke Appling	2422	54 Dwight Evans	8996	54 Nap Lajoie	1504
55 Zack Wheat	2410	55 Buddy Bell	8995	55 Harry Stovey	1492
56 Mickey Vernon	2409	56 Graig Nettles	8986	56 Goose Goslin	1483
57 Buddy Bell	2405	57 Darrell Evans	8973	57 Arlie Latham	1478
58 Sam Rice	2404	58 Wade Boggs	8888	58 Wade Boggs	1473
Mike Schmidt	2404	59 Charlie Gehringer	8860	59 Dwight Evans	1470
60 Mickey Mantle	2401	60 Luke Appling	8856	60 Herman Long	1456
61 Eddie Mathews	2391	61 Steve Garvey	8835	61 Jim O'Rourke	1446
62 Lou Whitaker	2390	62 Tommy Corcoran	8804	62 Harry Hooper	1429
63 Gary Gaetti	2389	63 Harry Hooper	8785	63 Dummy Hoy	1426
64 Jake Beckley	2386	64 Al Simmons	8759	64 Rod Carew	1424
65 Bobby Wallace	2383	65 Carlton Fisk	8756	65 Joe Kelley	1421
66 Enos Slaughter	2380	66 Mickey Vernon	8731	66 Roberto Clemente	1416
67 George Davis	2368	67 Dave Concepcion	8723	67 Billy Williams	1410
Al Oliver	2368	68 Bert Campaneris	8684	68 John Ward	1408
69 Nellie Fox	2367	69 Ted Simmons	8680	69 Mike Griffin	1405
70 Willie Stargell	2360	70 Gary Gaetti	8661	70 Sam Crawford	1391
71 Jose Cruz	2353	71 Goose Goslin	8656	71 Joe DiMaggio	1390
72 Wade Boggs	2350	72 Tony Gwynn	8648	72 Lou Whitaker	1386
73 Brian Downing	2344	73 Bobby Wallace	8618	73 Andre Dawson	1373
74 Steve Garvey	2332	74 Willie Keeler	8591	74 Vada Pinson	1366
75 Bert Campaneris	2328	75 Lou Whitaker	8570	75 Barry Bonds	1364
76 Frank White	2324	76 Fred Clarke	8568	76 Brett Butler	1359
77 Charlie Gehringer	2323	77 Tim Raines	8559	77 Doc Cramer	1357
78 Jimmie Foxx	2317	78 Eddie Mathews	8537	King Kelly	1357
79 Frankie Frisch	2311	79 Red Schoendienst	8479	79 Tommy Leach	1355
80 Harry Hooper	2309	80 Joe Carter	8422	80 Darrell Evans	1344
81 Gary Carter	2296	81 Jesse Burkett	8421	81 Pee Wee Reese	1338
82 Tim Raines	2295	82 Larry Bowa	8418	82 Luis Aparicio	1335
83 Alan Trammell	2293	83 Babe Ruth	8399	83 Lave Cross	1333
84 Don Baylor	2292	84 Ryne Sandberg	8385	84 George Gore	1327
Ted Williams	2292	85 Richie Ashburn	8365	85 Richie Ashburn	1322
86 Chili Davis	2290	86 Mike Schmidt	8352	86 Luke Appling	1319
87 Goose Goslin	2287	87 Bid McPhee	8291	87 Patsy Donovan	1318
88 Jimmy Dykes	2282	88 Alan Trammell	8288	Ryne Sandberg	1318
89 Cap Anson	2276	89 George Sisler	8267	89 Mike Tiernan	1313
90 Lave Cross	2275	90 Jim Rice	8225	90 Ernie Banks	1305
91 Bob Boone	2264	91 Don Baylor	8198	Kiki Cuyler	1305
92 Chris Speier	2260	92 Chili Davis	8197	92 Tony Gwynn	1302
93 Rogers Hornsby	2259	Willie McCovey	8197	93 Jimmy Sheckard	1296
94 Larry Bowa	2247	94 Brett Butler	8180	94 Harry Heilmann	1291
95 Ron Santo	2243	95 Rogers Hornsby	8173	95 Zack Wheat	1289
96 Fred Clarke	2242	96 Jimmy Ryan	8164	96 Heinie Manush	1287
97 Doc Cramer	2239	97 Harmon Killebrew	8147	97 George Sisler	1284
98 Tony Gwynn	2222	98 Ron Santo	8143	98 Harmon Killebrew	1283
99 Red Schoendienst	2216	99 Jimmie Foxx	8134	99 Donie Bush	1280
100 Al Simmons	2215	100 Mickey Mantle	8102	100 Nellie Fox	1279

Runs per Game (by era)

1876-1892

1	George Gore	1.01
2	Harry Stovey	1.00
3	King Kelly	.93
4	Dan Brouthers	.91
5	Arlie Latham	.91
6	Sam Thompson	.89
7	Buck Ewing	.86
8	Tom Brown	.85
9	Hardy Richardson	.84
10	Tommy McCarthy	.84
11	Tip O'Neill	.83
12	Denny Lyons	.83
13	Curt Welch	.83
14	Jim O'Rourke	.82
15	Roger Connor	.81

1893-1919

1	Billy Hamilton	1.06
2	John McGraw	.93
3	Mike Griffin	.93
4	Hugh Duffy	.89
5	Mike Tiernan	.89
6	Ed Delahanty	.87
7	Cupid Childs	.83
8	Jesse Burkett	.83
9	George Van Haltren	.83
10	Jimmy Ryan	.82
11	Willie Keeler	.81
12	Dummy Hoy	.79
13	Herman Long	.78
14	Hughie Jennings	.77
15	Joe Kelley	.77

1920-1941

1	Lou Gehrig	.87
2	Babe Ruth	.87
3	Earle Combs	.82
4	Red Rolfe	.80
5	Charlie Gehringer	.76
6	Jimmie Foxx	.76
7	Hank Greenberg	.75
8	Earl Averill	.73
9	Max Bishop	.72
10	Lu Blue	.71
11	Mickey Cochrane	.70
12	Rogers Hornsby	.70
13	Kiki Cuyler	.69
14	Mel Ott	.68
15	Al Simmons	.68

1942-1960

1	Joe DiMaggio	.80
2	Ted Williams	.78
3	Dom DiMaggio	.75
4	Tommy Henrich	.70
5	Mickey Mantle	.70
6	Jackie Robinson	.69
7	Johnny Pesky	.68
8	Ralph Kiner	.66
9	Eddie Stanky	.64
10	Stan Musial	.64
11	George Case	.64
12	Eddie Mathews	.63
13	Larry Doby	.63
14	Charlie Keller	.62
15	Minnie Minoso	.62

1961-1976

1	Willie Mays	.69
2	Bobby Bonds	.68
3	Hank Aaron	.66
4	Frank Robinson	.65
5	Dick Allen	.63
6	Joe Morgan	.62
7	Lou Brock	.62
8	Pete Rose	.61
9	Roberto Clemente	.58
10	Rod Carew	.58
11	Jimmy Wynn	.58
12	Al Kaline	.57
13	Billy Williams	.57
14	Reggie Smith	.57
15	Roger Maris	.56

1977-1998

1	Rickey Henderson	.77
2	Frank Thomas	.72
3	Barry Bonds	.72
4	Chuck Knoblauch	.71
5	Ken Griffey Jr.	.68
6	Jeff Bagwell	.67
7	Tim Raines	.67
8	Ron LeFlore	.67
9	Larry Walker	.66
10	Paul Molitor	.66
11	Craig Biggio	.65
12	Albert Belle	.64
13	Edgar Martinez	.64
14	Jose Canseco	.64
15	Ellis Burks	.63

Hits

1	Pete Rose	4256
2	Ty Cobb	4189
3	Hank Aaron	3771
4	Stan Musial	3630
5	Tris Speaker	3514
6	Carl Yastrzemski	3419
7	Honus Wagner	3415
8	Paul Molitor	3319
9	Eddie Collins	3315
10	Willie Mays	3283
11	Eddie Murray	3255
12	Nap Lajoie	3242
13	George Brett	3154
14	Paul Waner	3152
15	Robin Yount	3142
16	Dave Winfield	3110
17	Rod Carew	3053
18	Lou Brock	3023
19	Al Kaline	3007
20	Roberto Clemente	3000
21	Cap Anson	2995
22	Sam Rice	2987
23	Sam Crawford	2961
24	Frank Robinson	2943
25	Willie Keeler	2932
26	Jake Beckley	2930
	Rogers Hornsby	2930
28	Tony Gwynn	2928
29	Al Simmons	2927
30	Wade Boggs	2922
31	Zack Wheat	2884
32	Frankie Frisch	2880
33	Cal Ripken	2878
34	Mel Ott	2876
35	Babe Ruth	2873
36	Jesse Burkett	2850
37	Brooks Robinson	2848
38	Charlie Gehringer	2839
39	George Sisler	2812
40	Andre Dawson	2774
41	Vada Pinson	2757
42	Luke Appling	2749
43	Al Oliver	2743
44	Goose Goslin	2735
45	Tony Perez	2732
46	Lou Gehrig	2721
47	Rusty Staub	2716
48	Bill Buckner	2715
49	Dave Parker	2712
50	Billy Williams	2711
51	Doc Cramer	2705
52	Rickey Henderson	2678
53	Luis Aparicio	2677
54	Fred Clarke	2672
55	Max Carey	2665
56	Nellie Fox	2663
57	George Davis	2660
	Harry Heilmann	2660
59	Ted Williams	2654
60	Harold Baines	2649
61	Jimmie Foxx	2646
62	Lave Cross	2645
63	Rabbit Maranville	2605
64	Steve Garvey	2599
65	Ed Delahanty	2596
66	Reggie Jackson	2584
67	Ernie Banks	2583
68	Richie Ashburn	2574
69	Willie Davis	2561
70	Tim Raines	2532
	George Van Haltren	2532
72	Heinie Manush	2524
73	Joe Morgan	2517
74	Buddy Bell	2514
75	Jimmy Ryan	2502
76	Mickey Vernon	2495
77	Ted Simmons	2472
78	Joe Medwick	2471
79	Roger Connor	2467
80	Harry Hooper	2466
81	Ozzie Smith	2460
82	Lloyd Waner	2459
83	Bill Dahlen	2457
84	Jim Rice	2452
85	Red Schoendienst	2449
86	Dwight Evans	2446
87	Pie Traynor	2416
88	Mickey Mantle	2415
89	Stuffy McInnis	2405
90	Ryne Sandberg	2386
91	Enos Slaughter	2383
92	Edd Roush	2376
93	Brett Butler	2375
94	Lou Whitaker	2369
95	Alan Trammell	2365
96	Carlton Fisk	2356
97	Joe Judge	2352
98	Orlando Cepeda	2351
99	Billy Herman	2345
100	Joe Torre	2342

Doubles

1	Tris Speaker	792
2	Pete Rose	746
3	Stan Musial	725
4	Ty Cobb	724
5	George Brett	665
6	Nap Lajoie	657
7	Carl Yastrzemski	646
8	Honus Wagner	640
9	Hank Aaron	624
10	Paul Molitor	605
	Paul Waner	605
12	Robin Yount	583
13	Charlie Gehringer	574
14	Wade Boggs	564
15	Eddie Murray	560
16	Cal Ripken	544
17	Harry Heilmann	542
18	Rogers Hornsby	541
19	Joe Medwick	540
	Dave Winfield	540
21	Al Simmons	539
22	Lou Gehrig	534
23	Al Oliver	529
24	Cap Anson	528
	Frank Robinson	528
26	Dave Parker	526
27	Ted Williams	525
28	Willie Mays	523
29	Ed Delahanty	522
30	Joe Cronin	515
31	Babe Ruth	506
32	Tony Perez	505
33	Andre Dawson	503
34	Goose Goslin	500
35	Rusty Staub	499
36	Bill Buckner	498
	Al Kaline	498
	Sam Rice	498
39	Tony Gwynn	495
40	Heinie Manush	491
41	Mickey Vernon	490
42	Mel Ott	488
43	Lou Brock	486
	Billy Herman	486
45	Vada Pinson	485
46	Hal McRae	484
47	Dwight Evans	483
	Ted Simmons	483
49	Brooks Robinson	482
50	Zack Wheat	476
51	Jake Beckley	473
52	Frankie Frisch	466
53	Jim Bottomley	465
54	Reggie Jackson	463
55	Dan Brouthers	460
56	Sam Crawford	458
	Jimmie Foxx	458
58	Harold Baines	456
59	Jimmy Dykes	453
60	George Davis	451
	Jimmy Ryan	451
62	Joe Morgan	449
63	Rod Carew	445
64	George Burns	444
65	Dick Bartell	442
	Rickey Henderson	442
	Don Mattingly	442
68	Roger Connor	441
69	Luke Appling	440
	Roberto Clemente	440
	Steve Garvey	440
72	Eddie Collins	438
73	Cesar Cedeno	436
	Joe Sewell	436
75	Wally Moses	435
76	Gary Gaetti	434
	Billy Williams	434
78	Joe Judge	433
79	Joe Carter	432
	Tim Wallach	432
81	Red Schoendienst	427
82	Keith Hernandez	426
83	Buddy Bell	425
	Sherry Magee	425
	George Sisler	425
86	Willie Stargell	423
87	Carlton Fisk	421
88	Lou Whitaker	420
89	Max Carey	419
90	Orlando Cepeda	417
91	Cecil Cooper	415
92	Jim O'Rourke	414
	Kirby Puckett	414
	Tim Raines	414
95	Bill Dahlen	413
	Enos Slaughter	413
97	Joe Kuhel	412
	Alan Trammell	412
99	Lave Cross	411
100	Mike Schmidt	408

Triples

1	Sam Crawford	309
2	Ty Cobb	295
3	Honus Wagner	252
4	Jake Beckley	243
5	Roger Connor	233
6	Tris Speaker	222
7	Fred Clarke	220
8	Dan Brouthers	205
9	Joe Kelley	194
10	Paul Waner	191
11	Bid McPhee	188
12	Eddie Collins	187
13	Ed Delahanty	185
14	Sam Rice	184
15	Jesse Burkett	182
	Ed Konetchy	182
	Edd Roush	182
18	Buck Ewing	178
19	Rabbit Maranville	177
	Stan Musial	177
21	Harry Stovey	174
22	Goose Goslin	173
23	Tommy Leach	172
	Zack Wheat	172
25	Rogers Hornsby	169
26	Joe Jackson	168
27	Roberto Clemente	166
	Sherry Magee	166
29	Jake Daubert	165
30	Elmer Flick	164
	George Sisler	164
	Pie Traynor	164
33	Bill Dahlen	163
	George Davis	163
	Lou Gehrig	163
	Nap Lajoie	163
37	Mike Tiernan	162
38	George Van Haltren	161
39	Harry Hooper	160
	Heinie Manush	160
	Sam Thompson	160
42	Max Carey	159
	Joe Judge	159
44	Ed McKean	158
45	Kiki Cuyler	157
	Jimmy Ryan	157
47	Tommy Corcoran	155
48	Earle Combs	154
49	Jim Bottomley	151
	Harry Heilmann	151
51	Kip Selbach	149
	Al Simmons	149
53	Wally Pipp	148
	Enos Slaughter	148
55	Bobby Veach	147
	Willie Wilson	147
57	Charlie Gehringer	146
58	Harry Davis	145
	Willie Keeler	145
60	Bobby Wallace	143
61	Lou Brock	141
62	Willie Mays	140
63	John Reilly	139
64	Tom Brown	138
	Willie Davis	138
	Frankie Frisch	138
	Jimmy Williams	138
68	George Brett	137
69	Babe Ruth	136
	Jimmy Sheckard	136
	Elmer Smith	136
72	Lave Cross	135
	Pete Rose	135
74	Shano Collins	133
75	Jim O'Rourke	132
	George Wood	132
77	Brett Butler	131
	Joe DiMaggio	131
	Buck Freeman	131
80	Buddy Myer	130
81	Oyster Burns	129
	Larry Gardner	129
83	Earl Averill	128
	Arky Vaughan	128
85	Vada Pinson	127
86	Hardy Richardson	126
	Robin Yount	126
88	Jimmie Foxx	125
89	John Anderson	124
	Cap Anson	124
	Hal Chase	124
	Frank Schulte	124
93	Larry Doyle	123
	Duke Farrell	123
95	Dummy Hoy	121
96	Mickey Vernon	120
97	Hugh Duffy	119
	Fred Pfeffer	119
99	3 players tied	118

Triples (by era)

1876-1892

1	Roger Connor	233
2	Dan Brouthers	205
3	Bid McPhee	188
4	Buck Ewing	178
5	Harry Stovey	174
6	Sam Thompson	160
7	John Reilly	139
8	Tom Brown	138
9	Jim O'Rourke	132
	George Wood	132
11	Oyster Burns	129
12	Hardy Richardson	126
13	Cap Anson	124
14	Fred Pfeffer	119
15	Bill Kuehne	115

1893-1919

1	Sam Crawford	309
2	Ty Cobb	295
3	Honus Wagner	252
4	Jake Beckley	243
5	Tris Speaker	222
6	Fred Clarke	220
7	Joe Kelley	194
8	Eddie Collins	187
9	Ed Delahanty	185
10	Jesse Burkett	182
	Ed Konetchy	182
12	Tommy Leach	172
	Zack Wheat	172
14	Joe Jackson	168
15	Sherry Magee	166

1920-1941

1	Paul Waner	191
2	Sam Rice	184
3	Edd Roush	182
4	Rabbit Maranville	177
5	Goose Goslin	173
6	Rogers Hornsby	169
7	George Sisler	164
	Pie Traynor	164
9	Lou Gehrig	163
10	Heinie Manush	160
11	Max Carey	159
	Joe Judge	159
13	Kiki Cuyler	157
14	Earle Combs	154
15	2 players tied	151

1942-1960

1	Stan Musial	177
2	Enos Slaughter	148
3	Joe DiMaggio	131
4	Mickey Vernon	120
5	Nellie Fox	112
6	Wally Moses	110
7	Richie Ashburn	109
8	Bill Bruton	102
	Jeff Heath	102
10	Phil Cavarretta	99
11	Dixie Walker	96
12	Bob Elliott	94
13	Bobby Doerr	89
14	Duke Snider	85
15	2 players tied	83

1961-1976

1	Roberto Clemente	166
2	Lou Brock	141
3	Willie Mays	140
4	Willie Davis	138
5	Pete Rose	135
6	Vada Pinson	127
7	Rod Carew	112
8	Hank Aaron	98
9	Joe Morgan	96
10	Luis Aparicio	92
11	Ernie Banks	90
12	Johnny Callison	89
13	Billy Williams	88
14	Bert Campaneris	86
	Tony Taylor	86

1977-1998

1	Willie Wilson	147
2	George Brett	137
3	Brett Butler	131
4	Robin Yount	126
5	Paul Molitor	114
6	Tim Raines	112
7	Lance Johnson	111
8	Garry Templeton	106
9	Juan Samuel	102
10	Larry Bowa	99
11	Andre Dawson	98
12	Jose Cruz	94
	Willie McGee	94
14	Tony Fernandez	92
15	Andy Van Slyke	91

Home Runs

1	Hank Aaron	755
2	Babe Ruth	714
3	Willie Mays	660
4	Frank Robinson	586
5	Harmon Killebrew	573
6	Reggie Jackson	563
7	Mike Schmidt	548
8	Mickey Mantle	536
9	Jimmie Foxx	534
10	Willie McCovey	521
	Ted Williams	521
12	Ernie Banks	512
	Eddie Mathews	512
14	Mel Ott	511
15	Eddie Murray	504
16	Lou Gehrig	493
17	Stan Musial	475
	Willie Stargell	475
19	Dave Winfield	465
20	Mark McGwire	457
21	Carl Yastrzemski	452
22	Dave Kingman	442
23	Andre Dawson	438
24	Billy Williams	426
25	Darrell Evans	414
26	Barry Bonds	411
27	Duke Snider	407
28	Al Kaline	399
29	Dale Murphy	398
30	Jose Canseco	397
31	Joe Carter	396
32	Graig Nettles	390
33	Johnny Bench	389
34	Dwight Evans	385
35	Cal Ripken	384
36	Frank Howard	382
	Jim Rice	382
38	Orlando Cepeda	379
	Tony Perez	379
40	Norm Cash	377
41	Carlton Fisk	376
42	Rocky Colavito	374
43	Gil Hodges	370
44	Ralph Kiner	369
45	Joe DiMaggio	361
46	Johnny Mize	359
47	Yogi Berra	358
	Fred McGriff	358
49	Lee May	354
50	Dick Allen	351
	Gary Gaetti	351
52	Ken Griffey Jr.	350
53	Harold Baines	348
	George Foster	348
55	Ron Santo	342
56	Jack Clark	340
57	Dave Parker	339
	Boog Powell	339
59	Don Baylor	338
60	Joe Adcock	336
61	Bobby Bonds	332
	Andres Galarraga	332
	Darryl Strawberry	332
64	Chili Davis	331
	Hank Greenberg	331
66	Willie Horton	325
67	Gary Carter	324
	Lance Parrish	324
69	Albert Belle	321
70	Cecil Fielder	319
71	Roy Sievers	318
72	George Brett	317
73	Ron Cey	316
74	Rafael Palmeiro	314
	Reggie Smith	314
76	Greg Luzinski	307
	Al Simmons	307
78	Fred Lynn	306
79	Juan Gonzalez	301
	Rogers Hornsby	301
81	Chuck Klein	300
82	Matt Williams	299
83	Kent Hrbek	293
84	Rusty Staub	292
85	Jimmy Wynn	291
86	Del Ennis	288
	Bob Johnson	288
	Hank Sauer	288
89	Frank Thomas	286
	Frank Thomas	286
91	Ken Boyer	282
	Ryne Sandberg	282
93	Ted Kluszewski	279
94	Rudy York	277
95	Brian Downing	275
	Roger Maris	275
97	Bobby Bonilla	273
	Sammy Sosa	273
99	Steve Garvey	272
100	2 players tied	271

Home Runs (by era)

1876-1892

1	Roger Connor	138
2	Sam Thompson	126
3	Harry Stovey	122
4	Dan Brouthers	106
5	Cap Anson	97
6	Fred Pfeffer	94
7	Jack Clements	77
8	Jerry Denny	74
9	Buck Ewing	71
10	Hardy Richardson	70
11	King Kelly	69
	John Reilly	69
13	George Wood	68
14	Oyster Burns	65
	Bug Holliday	65

1893-1919

1	Zack Wheat	132
2	Gavvy Cravath	119
3	Jimmy Ryan	118
	Tilly Walker	118
5	Ty Cobb	117
	Tris Speaker	117
7	Hugh Duffy	106
	Mike Tiernan	106
9	Ed Delahanty	101
	Honus Wagner	101
11	Sam Crawford	97
12	Frank Baker	96
13	Frank Schulte	92
14	Herman Long	91
15	Jake Beckley	87

1920-1941

1	Babe Ruth	714
2	Jimmie Foxx	534
3	Mel Ott	511
4	Lou Gehrig	493
5	Hank Greenberg	331
6	Al Simmons	307
7	Rogers Hornsby	301
8	Chuck Klein	300
9	Bob Johnson	288
10	Cy Williams	251
11	Goose Goslin	248
12	Hack Wilson	244
13	Wally Berger	242
14	Dolph Camilli	239
15	Earl Averill	238

1942-1960

1	Mickey Mantle	536
2	Ted Williams	521
3	Eddie Mathews	512
4	Stan Musial	475
5	Duke Snider	407
6	Gil Hodges	370
7	Ralph Kiner	369
8	Joe DiMaggio	361
9	Johnny Mize	359
10	Yogi Berra	358
11	Joe Adcock	336
12	Roy Sievers	318
13	Del Ennis	288
	Hank Sauer	288
15	Frank Thomas	286

1961-1976

1	Hank Aaron	755
2	Willie Mays	660
3	Frank Robinson	586
4	Harmon Killebrew	573
5	Willie McCovey	521
6	Ernie Banks	512
7	Willie Stargell	475
8	Carl Yastrzemski	452
9	Billy Williams	426
10	Al Kaline	399
11	Johnny Bench	389
12	Frank Howard	382
13	Orlando Cepeda	379
	Tony Perez	379
15	Norm Cash	377

1977-1998

1	Reggie Jackson	563
2	Mike Schmidt	548
3	Eddie Murray	504
4	Dave Winfield	465
5	Mark McGwire	457
6	Dave Kingman	442
7	Andre Dawson	438
8	Darrell Evans	414
9	Barry Bonds	411
10	Dale Murphy	398
11	Jose Canseco	397
12	Joe Carter	396
13	Graig Nettles	390
14	Dwight Evans	385
15	Cal Ripken	384

Home Run Percentage

1	Mark McGwire	8.91
2	Babe Ruth	8.50
3	Ralph Kiner	7.09
4	Juan Gonzalez	7.05
5	Harmon Killebrew	7.03
6	Albert Belle	6.85
7	Ted Williams	6.76
8	Ken Griffey Jr.	6.70
9	Dave Kingman	6.62
10	Mickey Mantle	6.62
11	Jose Canseco	6.57
12	Jimmie Foxx	6.57
13	Mike Schmidt	6.56
14	Frank Thomas	6.49
15	Hank Greenberg	6.37
16	Willie McCovey	6.36
17	Barry Bonds	6.21
18	Cecil Fielder	6.19
19	Darryl Strawberry	6.18
20	Jay Buhner	6.18
21	Lou Gehrig	6.16
22	Hank Aaron	6.11
23	Willie Mays	6.07
24	Mo Vaughn	6.01
25	Hank Sauer	6.01
26	Eddie Mathews	6.00
27	Willie Stargell	5.99
28	Rob Deer	5.93
29	Frank Howard	5.89
30	Frank Robinson	5.86
31	Sammy Sosa	5.85
32	Bob Horner	5.77
33	Roy Campanella	5.76
34	Rocky Colavito	5.75
35	Gus Zernial	5.74
36	Gorman Thomas	5.73
37	Fred McGriff	5.72
38	Greg Vaughn	5.72
39	Reggie Jackson	5.71
40	Dick Stuart	5.70
41	Matt Williams	5.70
42	Duke Snider	5.68
43	Kevin Mitchell	5.66
44	Eric Davis	5.66
45	Norm Cash	5.62
46	Johnny Mize	5.57
47	Dick Allen	5.54
48	David Justice	5.50
49	Ernie Banks	5.43
50	Larry Walker	5.42
51	Mel Ott	5.40
52	Roger Maris	5.39
53	Joe DiMaggio	5.29
54	Jeff Bagwell	5.27
55	Gil Hodges	5.26
56	Wally Post	5.24
57	Danny Tartabull	5.23
58	Mickey Tettleton	5.21
59	Al Rosen	5.15
60	Hack Wilson	5.13
61	Glenn Davis	5.11
62	Bob Allison	5.09
63	Joe Adcock	5.09
64	Johnny Bench	5.08
65	Ron Gant	5.08
66	Boog Powell	5.07
67	Jesse Barfield	5.06
68	Nate Colbert	5.06
69	Andres Galarraga	5.01
70	Dale Murphy	5.00
71	Charlie Keller	4.99
72	Roy Sievers	4.98
73	Cliff Johnson	4.97
74	Don Mincher	4.97
75	Jack Clark	4.97
76	George Foster	4.96
77	Gary Sheffield	4.93
78	Pete Incaviglia	4.87
79	Tony Armas	4.86
80	Andy Thornton	4.78
81	Orlando Cepeda	4.78
82	Leon Wagner	4.77
83	Jim Lemon	4.76
84	Yogi Berra	4.74
85	Don Demeter	4.73
86	Kent Hrbek	4.73
87	Larry Doby	4.73
88	Greg Luzinski	4.72
89	Bobby Bonds	4.71
90	Ted Kluszewski	4.71
91	Rudy York	4.70
92	Joe Carter	4.70
93	Wally Berger	4.69
94	John Mayberry	4.68
95	Rafael Palmeiro	4.68
96	Lee May	4.65
97	Jim Rice	4.64
98	Chuck Klein	4.63
99	Howard Johnson	4.62
100	Darrell Evans	4.61

Home Run Pctg. (by era)

1876-1892

1	Sam Thompson	2.11
2	Harry Stovey	1.99
3	Jack Clements	1.80
4	Roger Connor	1.77
5	Dan Brouthers	1.58
6	Jerry Denny	1.50
7	John Reilly	1.47
8	Denny Lyons	1.44
9	Charlie Bennett	1.44
10	Fred Pfeffer	1.43
11	Ned Williamson	1.41
12	Oyster Burns	1.40
13	Buck Ewing	1.32
14	George Wood	1.27
15	Hardy Richardson	1.24

1893-1919

1	Gavvy Cravath	3.01
2	Tilly Walker	2.33
3	Buck Freeman	1.95
4	Mike Tiernan	1.79
5	Fred Luderus	1.73
6	Frank Baker	1.60
7	Hugh Duffy	1.51
8	Charlie Hickman	1.48
9	Zack Wheat	1.45
10	Jimmy Ryan	1.45
11	Frank Schulte	1.41
12	Casey Stengel	1.40
13	Ed Delahanty	1.35
14	Mike Donlin	1.32
15	Chief Wilson	1.28

1920-1941

1	Babe Ruth	8.50
2	Jimmie Foxx	6.57
3	Hank Greenberg	6.37
4	Lou Gehrig	6.16
5	Mel Ott	5.40
6	Hack Wilson	5.13
7	Wally Berger	4.69
8	Chuck Klein	4.63
9	Dolph Camilli	4.46
10	Hal Trosky	4.42
11	Bob Johnson	4.16
12	Ken Williams	4.03
13	Earl Averill	3.75
14	Cy Williams	3.70
15	Rogers Hornsby	3.68

1942-1960

1	Ralph Kiner	7.09
2	Ted Williams	6.76
3	Mickey Mantle	6.62
4	Hank Sauer	6.01
5	Eddie Mathews	6.00
6	Roy Campanella	5.76
7	Gus Zernial	5.74
8	Duke Snider	5.68
9	Johnny Mize	5.57
10	Joe DiMaggio	5.29
11	Gil Hodges	5.26
12	Wally Post	5.24
13	Al Rosen	5.15
14	Joe Adcock	5.09
15	Charlie Keller	4.99

1961-1976

1	Harmon Killebrew	7.03
2	Willie McCovey	6.36
3	Hank Aaron	6.11
4	Willie Mays	6.07
5	Willie Stargell	5.99
6	Frank Howard	5.89
7	Frank Robinson	5.86
8	Rocky Colavito	5.75
9	Dick Stuart	5.70
10	Norm Cash	5.62
11	Dick Allen	5.54
12	Ernie Banks	5.43
13	Roger Maris	5.39
14	Bob Allison	5.09
15	Johnny Bench	5.08

1977-1998

1	Mark McGwire	8.91
2	Juan Gonzalez	7.05
3	Albert Belle	6.85
4	Ken Griffey Jr.	6.70
5	Dave Kingman	6.62
6	Jose Canseco	6.57
7	Mike Schmidt	6.56
8	Frank Thomas	6.49
9	Barry Bonds	6.21
10	Cecil Fielder	6.19
11	Darryl Strawberry	6.18
12	Jay Buhner	6.18
13	Mo Vaughn	6.01
14	Rob Deer	5.93
15	Sammy Sosa	5.85

Total Bases

1	Hank Aaron	6856
2	Stan Musial	6134
3	Willie Mays	6066
4	Ty Cobb	5854
5	Babe Ruth	5793
6	Pete Rose	5752
7	Carl Yastrzemski	5539
8	Eddie Murray	5397
9	Frank Robinson	5373
10	Dave Winfield	5221
11	Tris Speaker	5101
12	Lou Gehrig	5060
13	George Brett	5044
14	Mel Ott	5041
15	Jimmie Foxx	4956
16	Ted Williams	4884
17	Honus Wagner	4862
18	Paul Molitor	4854
19	Al Kaline	4852
20	Reggie Jackson	4834
21	Andre Dawson	4787
22	Robin Yount	4730
23	Rogers Hornsby	4712
24	Ernie Banks	4706
25	Al Simmons	4685
26	Cal Ripken	4662
27	Billy Williams	4599
28	Tony Perez	4532
29	Mickey Mantle	4511
30	Roberto Clemente	4492
31	Paul Waner	4478
32	Nap Lajoie	4471
33	Dave Parker	4405
34	Sam Crawford	4404
35	Eddie Mathews	4349
36	Sam Crawford	4328
37	Goose Goslin	4325
38	Brooks Robinson	4270
39	Eddie Collins	4268
40	Vada Pinson	4264
41	Charlie Gehringer	4257
42	Harold Baines	4245
43	Lou Brock	4238
44	Dwight Evans	4230
45	Willie McCovey	4219
46	Willie Stargell	4190
47	Rusty Staub	4185
48	Jake Beckley	4150
49	Harmon Killebrew	4143
50	Jim Rice	4129
51	Zack Wheat	4100
52	Al Oliver	4083
53	Cap Anson	4062
54	Harry Heilmann	4053
55	Rickey Henderson	4038
56	Carlton Fisk	3999
57	Rod Carew	3998
58	Joe Morgan	3962
59	Tony Gwynn	3960
60	Orlando Cepeda	3959
61	Sam Rice	3955
62	Wade Boggs	3954
63	Joe DiMaggio	3948
64	Steve Garvey	3941
65	Frankie Frisch	3937
66	Joe Carter	3910
67	George Sisler	3871
68	Darrell Evans	3866
69	Duke Snider	3865
70	Joe Medwick	3852
71	Bill Buckner	3833
72	Ted Simmons	3793
73	Ed Delahanty	3791
74	Roger Connor	3788
75	Ryne Sandberg	3787
76	Gary Gaetti	3786
77	Graig Nettles	3779
	Ron Santo	3779
79	Willie Davis	3778
80	Jesse Burkett	3759
81	Mickey Vernon	3741
82	Jim Bottomley	3737
83	Dale Murphy	3733
84	Chili Davis	3702
85	Barry Bonds	3679
86	Fred Clarke	3674
87	Heinie Manush	3665
88	Tim Raines	3662
89	Buddy Bell	3654
90	George Davis	3653
91	Lou Whitaker	3651
92	Johnny Bench	3644
93	Yogi Berra	3643
94	Johnny Mize	3621
	Jimmy Ryan	3621
96	Max Carey	3612
97	Enos Slaughter	3599
98	Don Baylor	3571
99	Willie Keeler	3562
100	Joe Torre	3560

Runs Batted In

1	Hank Aaron	2297
2	Babe Ruth	2213
3	Lou Gehrig	1995
4	Stan Musial	1951
5	Ty Cobb	1937
6	Jimmie Foxx	1922
7	Eddie Murray	1917
8	Willie Mays	1903
9	Cap Anson	1879
10	Mel Ott	1860
11	Carl Yastrzemski	1844
12	Ted Williams	1839
13	Dave Winfield	1833
14	Al Simmons	1827
15	Frank Robinson	1812
16	Honus Wagner	1732
17	Reggie Jackson	1702
18	Tony Perez	1652
19	Ernie Banks	1636
20	Goose Goslin	1609
21	Nap Lajoie	1599
22	George Brett	1595
	Mike Schmidt	1595
24	Andre Dawson	1591
25	Rogers Hornsby	1584
	Harmon Killebrew	1584
27	Al Kaline	1583
28	Jake Beckley	1575
29	Willie McCovey	1555
30	Willie Stargell	1540
31	Harry Heilmann	1539
32	Joe DiMaggio	1537
33	Tris Speaker	1529
34	Sam Crawford	1525
35	Cal Ripken	1514
36	Mickey Mantle	1509
37	Dave Parker	1493
38	Harold Baines	1480
39	Billy Williams	1475
40	Rusty Staub	1466
41	Ed Delahanty	1464
42	Eddie Mathews	1453
43	Jim Rice	1451
44	Joe Carter	1445
45	George Davis	1437
46	Yogi Berra	1430
47	Charlie Gehringer	1427
48	Joe Cronin	1424
49	Jim Bottomley	1422
50	Robin Yount	1406
51	Ted Simmons	1389
52	Dwight Evans	1384
53	Joe Medwick	1383
54	Johnny Bench	1376
55	Lave Cross	1371
56	Orlando Cepeda	1365
57	Brooks Robinson	1357
58	Darrell Evans	1354
59	Johnny Mize	1337
60	Duke Snider	1333
61	Ron Santo	1331
62	Carlton Fisk	1330
63	Al Oliver	1326
64	Roger Connor	1322
65	Graig Nettles	1314
	Pete Rose	1314
67	Mickey Vernon	1311
68	Paul Waner	1309
69	Steve Garvey	1308
70	Paul Molitor	1307
71	Roberto Clemente	1305
72	Enos Slaughter	1304
73	Hugh Duffy	1302
74	Eddie Collins	1300
75	Sam Thompson	1299
76	Dan Brouthers	1296
77	Chili Davis	1294
	Gary Gaetti	1294
79	Del Ennis	1284
80	Bob Johnson	1283
81	Don Baylor	1276
	Hank Greenberg	1276
83	Gil Hodges	1274
84	Pie Traynor	1273
85	Dale Murphy	1266
86	Zack Wheat	1248
87	Bobby Doerr	1247
88	Frankie Frisch	1244
	Lee May	1244
90	George Foster	1239
91	Bill Dahlen	1233
92	Gary Carter	1225
93	Barry Bonds	1216
94	Jose Canseco	1214
95	Dave Kingman	1210
96	Bill Dickey	1209
97	Bill Buckner	1208
98	Chuck Klein	1201
99	Bob Elliott	1195
100	Joe Kelley	1194

Runs Batted In (by era)

1876-1892

1	Cap Anson	1879
2	Roger Connor	1322
3	Sam Thompson	1299
4	Dan Brouthers	1296
5	Bid McPhee	1067
6	Fred Pfeffer	1019
7	Jim O'Rourke	1010
8	Billy Nash	977
9	King Kelly	950
10	Harry Stovey	908
11	Charlie Comiskey	883
	Buck Ewing	883
13	John Ward	867
14	Henry Larkin	836
15	Lou Bierbauer	835

1893-1919

1	Ty Cobb	1937
2	Honus Wagner	1732
3	Nap Lajoie	1599
4	Jake Beckley	1575
5	Tris Speaker	1529
6	Sam Crawford	1525
7	Ed Delahanty	1464
8	George Davis	1437
9	Lave Cross	1371
10	Hugh Duffy	1302
11	Eddie Collins	1300
12	Zack Wheat	1248
13	Bill Dahlen	1233
14	Joe Kelley	1194
15	Sherry Magee	1176

1920-1941

1	Babe Ruth	2213
2	Lou Gehrig	1995
3	Jimmie Foxx	1922
4	Mel Ott	1860
5	Al Simmons	1827
6	Goose Goslin	1609
7	Rogers Hornsby	1584
8	Harry Heilmann	1539
9	Charlie Gehringer	1427
10	Joe Cronin	1424
11	Jim Bottomley	1422
12	Joe Medwick	1383
13	Paul Waner	1309
14	Bob Johnson	1283
15	Hank Greenberg	1276

1942-1960

1	Stan Musial	1951
2	Ted Williams	1839
3	Joe DiMaggio	1537
4	Mickey Mantle	1509
5	Eddie Mathews	1453
6	Yogi Berra	1430
7	Johnny Mize	1337
8	Duke Snider	1333
9	Mickey Vernon	1311
10	Enos Slaughter	1304
11	Del Ennis	1284
12	Gil Hodges	1274
13	Bobby Doerr	1247
14	Bob Elliott	1195
15	Vic Wertz	1178

1961-1976

1	Hank Aaron	2297
2	Willie Mays	1903
3	Carl Yastrzemski	1844
4	Frank Robinson	1812
5	Tony Perez	1652
6	Ernie Banks	1636
7	Harmon Killebrew	1584
8	Al Kaline	1583
9	Willie McCovey	1555
10	Willie Stargell	1540
11	Billy Williams	1475
12	Rusty Staub	1466
13	Johnny Bench	1376
14	Orlando Cepeda	1365
15	Brooks Robinson	1357

1977-1998

1	Eddie Murray	1917
2	Dave Winfield	1833
3	Reggie Jackson	1702
4	George Brett	1595
	Mike Schmidt	1595
6	Andre Dawson	1591
7	Cal Ripken	1514
8	Dave Parker	1493
9	Harold Baines	1480
10	Jim Rice	1451
11	Joe Carter	1445
12	Robin Yount	1406
13	Ted Simmons	1389
14	Dwight Evans	1384
15	Darrell Evans	1354

Runs Batted In per Game

1	Sam Thompson	.92
2	Lou Gehrig	.92
3	Hank Greenberg	.92
4	Joe DiMaggio	.89
5	Babe Ruth	.88
6	Juan Gonzalez	.86
7	Jimmie Foxx	.83
8	Cap Anson	.83
9	Al Simmons	.82
10	Albert Belle	.82
11	Ted Williams	.80
12	Ed Delahanty	.80
13	Hack Wilson	.79
14	Frank Thomas	.78
15	Dan Brouthers	.77
16	Jose Canseco	.76
17	Bob Meusel	.76
18	Hal Trosky	.75
19	Hugh Duffy	.75
20	Ken Griffey Jr.	.74
21	Mark McGwire	.74
22	Jeff Bagwell	.72
23	Mo Vaughn	.72
24	Rudy York	.72
25	Tip O'Neill	.72
26	Harry Heilmann	.72
27	Jim Bottomley	.71
28	Johnny Mize	.71
29	Henry Larkin	.71
30	Roy Campanella	.70
31	Goose Goslin	.70
32	Rogers Hornsby	.70
33	Oyster Burns	.70
34	Earl Averill	.70
35	Joe Medwick	.70
36	Hank Aaron	.70
37	Jim Rice	.69
38	Ralph Kiner	.69
39	Bob Johnson	.69
40	Al Rosen	.69
41	Cecil Fielder	.69
42	Chuck Klein	.69
43	Tony Lazzeri	.68
44	Vern Stephens	.68
45	Mel Ott	.68
46	Ed McKean	.68
47	Bill Dickey	.68
48	Del Ennis	.67
49	Yogi Berra	.67
50	Denny Lyons	.67
51	Dante Bichette	.67
52	Bob Horner	.67
53	Buck Ewing	.67
54	Joe Cronin	.67
55	Jay Buhner	.67
56	Bobby Doerr	.67
57	Dick Stuart	.67
58	Wally Berger	.67
59	Mike Schmidt	.66
60	Roger Connor	.66
61	Andres Galarraga	.66
62	Joe Carter	.66
63	Jake Beckley	.66
64	Dave Foutz	.66
65	Danny Tartabull	.66
66	Pie Traynor	.66
67	Hughie Jennings	.65
68	Ken Williams	.65
69	King Kelly	.65
70	Willie Stargell	.65
71	Harmon Killebrew	.65
72	Charlie Keller	.65
73	Chick Hafey	.65
74	John Reilly	.65
75	Ernie Banks	.65
76	Glenn Wright	.65
77	Jackie Jensen	.65
78	Matt Williams	.65
79	Frank Robinson	.65
80	David Justice	.65
81	Nap Lajoie	.64
82	Stan Musial	.64
83	Joe Kelley	.64
84	Orlando Cepeda	.64
85	Babe Herman	.64
86	Sammy Sosa	.64
87	Jeff Heath	.64
88	Barry Bonds	.64
89	Bobby Veach	.64
90	Dick Allen	.64
91	Ty Cobb	.64
92	Johnny Bench	.64
93	Darryl Strawberry	.64
94	Dolph Camilli	.64
95	Willie Mays	.64
96	Irish Meusel	.64
97	Charlie Comiskey	.64
98	Eddie Murray	.63
99	Buck Freeman	.63
100	Larry Doby	.63

Walks

#	Player	Walks
1	Babe Ruth	2056
2	Ted Williams	2019
3	Rickey Henderson	1890
4	Joe Morgan	1865
5	Carl Yastrzemski	1845
6	Mickey Mantle	1733
7	Mel Ott	1708
8	Eddie Yost	1614
9	Darrell Evans	1605
10	Stan Musial	1599
11	Pete Rose	1566
12	Harmon Killebrew	1559
13	Lou Gehrig	1508
14	Mike Schmidt	1507
15	Eddie Collins	1499
16	Willie Mays	1464
17	Jimmie Foxx	1452
18	Eddie Mathews	1444
19	Frank Robinson	1420
20	Hank Aaron	1402
21	Dwight Evans	1391
22	Tris Speaker	1381
23	Reggie Jackson	1375
24	Wade Boggs	1374
25	Barry Bonds	1357
26	Willie McCovey	1345
27	Eddie Murray	1333
28	Luke Appling	1302
29	Al Kaline	1277
30	Tim Raines	1264
31	Ken Singleton	1263
32	Jack Clark	1262
33	Rusty Staub	1255
34	Ty Cobb	1249
35	Tony Phillips	1248
36	Willie Randolph	1243
37	Jimmy Wynn	1224
38	Dave Winfield	1216
39	Pee Wee Reese	1210
40	Richie Ashburn	1198
41	Brian Downing	1197
	Lou Whitaker	1197
43	Billy Hamilton	1187
44	Charlie Gehringer	1186
45	Donie Bush	1158
46	Max Bishop	1153
	Toby Harrah	1153
48	Harry Hooper	1136
49	Jimmy Sheckard	1135
50	Brett Butler	1129
51	Chili Davis	1121
52	Ron Santo	1108
53	George Brett	1096
54	Paul Molitor	1094
55	Lu Blue	1092
	Stan Hack	1092
57	Paul Waner	1091
58	Graig Nettles	1088
59	Bobby Grich	1087
60	Bob Johnson	1075
61	Ozzie Smith	1072
62	Harlond Clift	1070
	Keith Hernandez	1070
64	Cal Ripken	1067
65	Bill Dahlen	1064
66	Joe Cronin	1059
67	Ron Fairly	1052
	Mark McGwire	1052
69	Billy Williams	1045
70	Norm Cash	1043
	Eddie Joost	1043
72	Roy Thomas	1042
73	Max Carey	1040
74	Rogers Hornsby	1038
75	Jim Gilliam	1036
76	Sal Bando	1031
77	Jesse Burkett	1029
78	Rod Carew	1018
	Enos Slaughter	1018
80	Ron Cey	1012
81	Ralph Kiner	1011
82	Dummy Hoy	1004
83	Miller Huggins	1003
84	Roger Connor	1002
85	Boog Powell	1001
86	Eddie Stanky	996
87	Cupid Childs	991
88	Frank Thomas	989
89	Dale Murphy	986
90	Gene Tenace	984
91	Bid McPhee	981
92	Joe Kuhel	980
	Earl Torgeson	980
94	Augie Galan	979
95	Duke Snider	971
96	Bob Elliott	967
97	Robin Yount	966
98	Mike Hargrove	965
	Joe Judge	965
	Buddy Myer	965

Walk Percentage

#	Player	Pct
1	Ted Williams	20.76
2	Max Bishop	20.42
3	Babe Ruth	19.67
4	Eddie Stanky	18.80
5	Ferris Fain	18.70
6	Frank Thomas	18.33
7	Gene Tenace	18.31
8	Roy Cullenbine	18.03
9	Eddie Yost	18.01
10	Mickey Mantle	17.62
11	John McGraw	17.56
12	Charlie Keller	17.14
13	Mark McGwire	17.01
14	Barry Bonds	17.01
15	Mickey Tettleton	16.81
16	Joe Morgan	16.74
17	Rickey Henderson	16.63
18	Earl Torgeson	16.47
19	Bernie Carbo	16.45
20	Roy Thomas	16.26
21	Ralph Kiner	16.26
22	Harmon Killebrew	16.06
23	Billy Hamilton	15.92
24	Lou Gehrig	15.86
25	Elmer Valo	15.78
26	Joe Ferguson	15.77
27	Harlond Clift	15.74
28	Eddie Joost	15.69
29	Lu Blue	15.61
30	Jack Clark	15.56
31	Jimmy Wynn	15.54
32	Mel Ott	15.30
33	Miller Huggins	15.29
34	Mike Schmidt	15.29
35	John Cangelosi	15.20
36	Darrell Evans	15.17
37	Jimmie Foxx	15.15
38	Edgar Martinez	15.13
39	Joe Cunningham	15.12
40	Dolph Camilli	15.03
41	Cupid Childs	14.99
42	Ken Singleton	14.94
43	Jeff Bagwell	14.92
44	Elbie Fletcher	14.85
45	Merv Rettenmund	14.83
46	Mike Hargrove	14.78
47	Darren Daulton	14.77
48	Tony Phillips	14.75
49	Topsy Hartsel	14.72
50	Dave Magadan	14.70
51	Dwayne Murphy	14.66
52	Wayne Garrett	14.59
53	Jason Thompson	14.52
54	Eddie Mathews	14.47
55	John Kruk	14.28
56	John Olerud	14.22
57	Mickey Cochrane	14.22
58	Andy Thornton	14.20
59	Augie Galan	14.16
60	Gene Woodling	14.15
61	Willie McCovey	14.10
62	Hank Greenberg	14.09
63	Darrell Porter	14.04
64	Larry Doby	14.01
65	John Mayberry	13.92
66	Alvin Davis	13.91
67	Johnny Briggs	13.87
68	Billy North	13.85
69	Donie Bush	13.84
70	Gary Sheffield	13.80
71	Wally Schang	13.79
72	Roger Bresnahan	13.74
73	Paul Radford	13.69
74	Steve Braun	13.69
75	Norm Siebern	13.64
76	Bob Allison	13.64
77	Bobby Grich	13.63
78	Al Rosen	13.61
79	David Justice	13.51
80	Toby Harrah	13.48
81	Lee Mazzilli	13.47
82	Norm Cash	13.46
83	Mike Jorgensen	13.46
84	Bob Johnson	13.45
85	Willie Randolph	13.42
86	Tommy Henrich	13.40
87	Dwight Evans	13.39
88	Wade Boggs	13.39
89	Rick Ferrell	13.38
90	Wayne Gross	13.36
91	Carl Yastrzemski	13.34
92	Grady Hatton	13.31
93	Fred McGriff	13.29
94	Danny Tartabull	13.29
95	Lyn Lary	13.28
96	Mike Stanley	13.28
97	Brian Downing	13.23
98	Ed Bailey	13.21
99	Jackie Robinson	13.17
100	Jack Graney	13.14

Strikeouts

#	Player	SO
1	Reggie Jackson	2597
2	Willie Stargell	1936
3	Mike Schmidt	1883
4	Tony Perez	1867
5	Dave Kingman	1816
6	Bobby Bonds	1757
7	Dale Murphy	1748
8	Lou Brock	1730
9	Mickey Mantle	1710
10	Harmon Killebrew	1699
11	Dwight Evans	1697
12	Dave Winfield	1686
13	Jose Canseco	1630
14	Andres Galarraga	1615
15	Chili Davis	1598
16	Lee May	1570
17	Dick Allen	1556
18	Willie McCovey	1550
19	Gary Gaetti	1548
20	Dave Parker	1537
21	Frank Robinson	1532
22	Lance Parrish	1527
23	Willie Mays	1526
24	Eddie Murray	1516
25	Rick Monday	1513
26	Andre Dawson	1509
27	Greg Luzinski	1495
28	Eddie Mathews	1487
29	Frank Howard	1460
30	Juan Samuel	1442
31	Jack Clark	1441
32	Jimmy Wynn	1427
33	Jim Rice	1423
34	George Foster	1419
35	George Scott	1418
36	Darrell Evans	1410
37	Rob Deer	1409
38	Tony Phillips	1405
39	Carl Yastrzemski	1393
40	Rickey Henderson	1390
41	Joe Carter	1387
42	Carlton Fisk	1386
43	Hank Aaron	1383
44	Fred McGriff	1365
45	Danny Tartabull	1362
46	Larry Parrish	1359
47	Robin Yount	1350
48	Ron Santo	1343
49	Gorman Thomas	1339
50	Darryl Strawberry	1336
51	Babe Ruth	1330
52	Harold Baines	1327
53	Deron Johnson	1318
54	Cecil Fielder	1316
55	Willie Horton	1313
	Devon White	1313
57	Jimmie Foxx	1311
58	Mickey Tettleton	1307
	Tim Wallach	1307
60	Kirk Gibson	1285
61	Johnny Bench	1278
	Bobby Bonds	1278
63	Pete Incaviglia	1277
64	Claudell Washington	1266
65	Ryne Sandberg	1260
66	Mark McGwire	1259
67	Eric Davis	1251
68	Ken Singleton	1246
69	Paul Molitor	1244
70	Duke Snider	1237
71	Ernie Banks	1236
72	Ron Cey	1235
73	Jesse Barfield	1234
74	Roberto Clemente	1230
75	Boog Powell	1226
76	Graig Nettles	1209
77	Tony Armas	1201
78	Jay Buhner	1199
79	Sammy Sosa	1198
80	Vada Pinson	1196
81	Tom Brunansky	1187
82	Dave Concepcion	1186
83	Willie McGee	1178
84	Cal Ripken	1174
85	Orlando Cepeda	1169
86	Willie Wilson	1144
87	Pete Rose	1143
88	Bert Campaneris	1142
89	Donn Clendenon	1140
90	Gil Hodges	1137
91	Jeff Burroughs	1135
	Leo Cardenas	1135
	Lloyd Moseby	1135
94	Brian Downing	1127
95	Bob Bailey	1126
96	Gary Matthews	1125
97	Greg Gagne	1121
98	Fred Lynn	1116
99	Dave Henderson	1105
100	Lou Whitaker	1099

At Bats per Strikeout

#	Player	AB/SO
1	Joe Sewell	62.6
2	Lloyd Waner	44.9
3	Nellie Fox	42.7
4	Tommy Holmes	40.9
5	Andy High	33.8
6	Sam Rice	33.7
7	Frankie Frisch	33.5
8	Dale Mitchell	33.5
9	Johnny Cooney	31.5
10	Frank McCormick	30.3
11	Don Mueller	29.9
12	Billy Southworth	29.5
13	Rip Radcliff	28.9
14	Edd Roush	28.3
15	Pie Traynor	27.2
16	Doc Cramer	26.5
17	Carson Bigbee	26.0
18	Hank Severeid	25.5
19	George Sisler	25.3
20	Paul Waner	25.2
21	Sparky Adams	24.9
22	Lou Finney	24.9
23	Deacon White	24.8
24	Jack Rowe	24.8
25	Irish Meusel	24.6
26	Ezra Sutton	24.6
27	Red Schoendienst	24.5
28	Vic Power	24.5
29	Arky Vaughan	24.0
30	Felix Millan	23.9
31	Mickey Cochrane	23.8
32	Charlie Gehringer	23.8
33	John Ward	23.5
34	George Kell	23.4
35	George Cutshaw	23.2
36	Jack Tobin	23.1
37	Taffy Wright	23.1
38	Hughie Critz	23.1
39	Mark Koenig	22.5
40	Ernie Lombardi	22.3
41	Heinie Manush	22.2
42	Bobby Richardson	22.2
43	Jo-Jo Moore	22.0
44	Earl Sheely	21.8
45	Bill Dickey	21.8
46	Johnny Pesky	21.8
47	Rick Ferrell	21.8
48	Glenn Beckert	21.4
49	Tony Gwynn	21.2
50	Dick Siebert	21.2
51	Eddie Waitkus	20.9
52	Max Flack	20.8
53	Bill Buckner	20.7
54	Dixie Walker	20.7
55	Everett Scott	20.7
56	Earle Combs	20.7
57	Paul Hines	20.6
58	Freddie Lindstrom	20.3
59	Mickey Owen	20.2
60	Joe Vosmik	20.1
61	Lou Boudreau	19.5
62	Milt Stock	19.5
63	Willard Marshall	19.3
64	Debs Garms	19.3
65	Charlie Grimm	19.3
66	Harry Rice	19.3
67	Skeeter Newsome	19.2
68	Curt Walker	19.1
69	Peanuts Lowrey	19.1
70	Charlie Jamieson	19.0
71	Muddy Ruel	19.0
72	Tommy Griffith	18.9
73	Tommy Thevenow	18.8
74	Joe Stripp	18.6
75	Joe DiMaggio	18.5
76	Bob Fothergill	18.5
77	Bing Miller	18.3
78	Riggs Stephenson	18.3
79	Yogi Berra	18.2
80	Billy Herman	18.0
81	Lee Magee	18.0
82	Dave Cash	18.0
83	Elmer Valo	17.7
84	Heinie Groh	17.6
85	Luke Sewell	17.5
86	Rich Dauer	17.5
87	Buddy Lewis	17.4
88	Billy Goodman	17.2
89	Jim Gilliam	17.1
90	Harvey Kuenn	17.1
91	Gus Mancuso	17.1
92	Jimmie Wilson	17.1
93	Billy Cox	17.0
94	Ken Williams	16.9
95	George Case	16.9
96	Cecil Travis	16.9
97	Luke Appling	16.8
98	Jackie Hayes	16.8
99	Brian Harper	16.8
100	Jackie Robinson	16.8

Batting Average

1	Ty Cobb	.366
2	Rogers Hornsby	.358
3	Joe Jackson	.356
4	Ed Delahanty	.346
5	Tris Speaker	.345
6	Ted Williams	.344
7	Billy Hamilton	.344
8	Dan Brouthers	.342
9	Babe Ruth	.342
10	Harry Heilmann	.342
11	Pete Browning	.341
12	Willie Keeler	.341
13	Bill Terry	.341
14	George Sisler	.340
15	Lou Gehrig	.340
16	Tony Gwynn	.339
17	Jesse Burkett	.338
18	Nap Lajoie	.338
19	Riggs Stephenson	.336
20	Al Simmons	.334
21	John McGraw	.334
22	Paul Waner	.333
23	Eddie Collins	.333
24	Mike Donlin	.333
25	Stan Musial	.331
26	Sam Thompson	.331
27	Heinie Manush	.330
28	Cap Anson	.329
29	Wade Boggs	.329
30	Rod Carew	.328
31	Honus Wagner	.327
32	Tip O'Neill	.326
33	Bob Fothergill	.325
34	Jimmie Foxx	.325
35	Earle Combs	.325
36	Joe DiMaggio	.325
37	Babe Herman	.324
38	Hugh Duffy	.324
39	Joe Medwick	.324
40	Edd Roush	.323
41	Sam Rice	.322
42	Ross Youngs	.322
43	Frank Thomas	.321
44	Kiki Cuyler	.321
45	Charlie Gehringer	.320
46	Chuck Klein	.320
47	Pie Traynor	.320
48	Mickey Cochrane	.320
49	Ken Williams	.319
50	Kirby Puckett	.318
51	Earl Averill	.318
52	Arky Vaughan	.318
53	Edgar Martinez	.318
54	Roberto Clemente	.317
55	Chick Hafey	.317
56	Joe Kelley	.317
57	Zack Wheat	.317
58	Roger Connor	.317
59	Lloyd Waner	.316
60	Frankie Frisch	.316
61	Goose Goslin	.316
62	George Van Haltren	.316
63	Bibb Falk	.314
64	Cecil Travis	.314
65	Hank Greenberg	.313
66	Jack Fournier	.313
67	Elmer Flick	.313
68	Bill Dickey	.313
69	Dale Mitchell	.312
70	Johnny Mize	.312
71	Joe Sewell	.312
72	Fred Clarke	.312
73	Barney McCosky	.312
74	Hughie Jennings	.311
75	Freddie Lindstrom	.311
76	Bing Miller	.311
77	Jackie Robinson	.311
78	Baby Doll Jacobson	.311
79	Taffy Wright	.311
80	Rip Radcliff	.311
81	Ginger Beaumont	.311
82	Mike Tiernan	.311
83	Denny Lyons	.310
84	Elmer Smith	.310
85	Luke Appling	.310
86	Irish Meusel	.310
87	Bobby Veach	.310
88	Jim O'Rourke	.310
89	Mark Grace	.310
90	Jim Bottomley	.310
91	John Stone	.310
92	Sam Crawford	.309
93	Bob Meusel	.309
94	Jack Tobin	.309
95	Spud Davis	.308
96	Richie Ashburn	.308
97	King Kelly	.308
98	Jake Beckley	.308
99	Stuffy McInnis	.307
100	Don Mattingly	.307

Batting Average (by era)

1876-1892

1	Dan Brouthers	.342
2	Pete Browning	.341
3	Sam Thompson	.331
4	Cap Anson	.329
5	Tip O'Neill	.326
6	Roger Connor	.317
7	Denny Lyons	.310
8	Jim O'Rourke	.310
9	King Kelly	.308
10	Deacon White	.303
11	Buck Ewing	.303
12	Henry Larkin	.303
13	George Gore	.301
14	Paul Hines	.301
15	Oyster Burns	.300

1893-1919

1	Ty Cobb	.366
2	Joe Jackson	.356
3	Ed Delahanty	.346
4	Tris Speaker	.345
5	Billy Hamilton	.344
6	Willie Keeler	.341
7	Jesse Burkett	.338
8	Nap Lajoie	.338
9	John McGraw	.334
10	Eddie Collins	.333
11	Mike Donlin	.333
12	Honus Wagner	.327
13	Hugh Duffy	.324
14	Joe Kelley	.317
15	Zack Wheat	.317

1920-1941

1	Rogers Hornsby	.358
2	Babe Ruth	.342
3	Harry Heilmann	.342
4	Bill Terry	.341
5	George Sisler	.340
6	Lou Gehrig	.340
7	Riggs Stephenson	.336
8	Al Simmons	.334
9	Paul Waner	.333
10	Heinie Manush	.330
11	Bob Fothergill	.325
12	Jimmie Foxx	.325
13	Earle Combs	.325
14	Babe Herman	.324
15	Joe Medwick	.324

1942-1960

1	Ted Williams	.344
2	Stan Musial	.331
3	Joe DiMaggio	.325
4	Dale Mitchell	.312
5	Johnny Mize	.312
6	Barney McCosky	.312
7	Jackie Robinson	.311
8	Taffy Wright	.311
9	Richie Ashburn	.308
10	Johnny Pesky	.307
11	George Kell	.306
12	Dixie Walker	.306
13	Harvey Kuenn	.303
14	Tommy Holmes	.302
15	Enos Slaughter	.300

1961-1976

1	Rod Carew	.328
2	Roberto Clemente	.317
3	Matty Alou	.307
4	Ralph Garr	.306
5	Hank Aaron	.305
6	Tony Oliva	.304
7	Manny Mota	.304
8	Pete Rose	.303
9	Willie Mays	.302
10	Rico Carty	.299
11	Joe Torre	.297
12	Al Kaline	.297
13	Orlando Cepeda	.297
14	Manny Sanguillen	.296
15	Bob Watson	.295

1977-1998

1	Tony Gwynn	.339
2	Wade Boggs	.329
3	Frank Thomas	.321
4	Kirby Puckett	.318
5	Edgar Martinez	.318
6	Mark Grace	.310
7	Don Mattingly	.307
8	Paul Molitor	.306
9	Hal Morris	.306
10	George Brett	.305
11	Larry Walker	.305
12	Bill Madlock	.305
13	Mo Vaughn	.304
14	Jeff Bagwell	.303
15	Al Oliver	.303

Batting Average (by position)

First Base

1	Dan Brouthers	.342
2	Bill Terry	.341
3	George Sisler	.340
4	Lou Gehrig	.340
5	Cap Anson	.329
6	Rod Carew	.328
7	Jimmie Foxx	.325
8	Roger Connor	.317
9	Hank Greenberg	.313
10	Jack Fournier	.313

Second Base

1	Rogers Hornsby	.358
2	Nap Lajoie	.338
3	Eddie Collins	.333
4	Charlie Gehringer	.320
5	Frankie Frisch	.316
6	Cupid Childs	.306
7	Billy Herman	.304
8	Buddy Myer	.303
9	Roberto Alomar	.302
10	Chuck Knoblauch	.299

Shortstop

1	Honus Wagner	.327
2	Arky Vaughan	.318
3	Joe Sewell	.312
4	Luke Appling	.310
5	Ed McKean	.302
6	Joe Cronin	.301
7	Barry Larkin	.300
8	Lou Boudreau	.295
9	George Davis	.295
10	Glenn Wright	.294

Third Base

1	Wade Boggs	.329
2	Pie Traynor	.320
3	Denny Lyons	.310
4	Frank Baker	.307
5	George Kell	.306
6	George Brett	.305
7	Bill Madlock	.305
8	Stan Hack	.301
9	Pinky Whitney	.295
10	Kevin Seitzer	.295

Outfield

1	Ty Cobb	.366
2	Joe Jackson	.356
3	Ed Delahanty	.346
4	Tris Speaker	.345
5	Ted Williams	.344
6	Billy Hamilton	.344
7	Babe Ruth	.342
8	Harry Heilmann	.342
9	Willie Keeler	.341
10	Tony Gwynn	.339
11	Jesse Burkett	.338
12	Al Simmons	.334
13	Paul Waner	.333
14	Stan Musial	.331
15	Sam Thompson	.331
16	Heinie Manush	.330
17	Tip O'Neill	.326
18	Earle Combs	.325
19	Joe DiMaggio	.325
20	Babe Herman	.324

Catcher

1	Mickey Cochrane	.320
2	Bill Dickey	.313
3	Spud Davis	.308
4	Ernie Lombardi	.306
5	Gabby Hartnett	.297
6	Manny Sanguillen	.296
7	Smoky Burgess	.295
8	Thurman Munson	.292
9	Hank Severeid	.289
10	Jack Clements	.286

Relative Batting Average

1	Ty Cobb	134.8
2	Joe Jackson	133.1
3	Pete Browning	131.6
4	Tony Gwynn	128.1
5	Ted Williams	128.1
6	Dan Brouthers	127.8
7	Nap Lajoie	127.4
8	Rod Carew	127.0
9	Rogers Hornsby	126.2
10	Tris Speaker	125.4
11	Tip O'Neill	125.3
12	Willie Keeler	124.6
13	Wade Boggs	124.2
14	Stan Musial	123.9
15	Mike Donlin	123.6
16	Honus Wagner	123.1
17	Billy Hamilton	122.7
18	Cap Anson	122.7
19	Ed Delahanty	122.6
20	Eddie Collins	121.8
21	Jesse Burkett	121.7
22	Sam Thompson	121.1
23	Kirby Puckett	121.0
24	Roberto Clemente	120.7
25	Tony Oliva	120.4
26	Frank Thomas	120.0
27	Harry Heilmann	119.4
28	Babe Ruth	119.2
29	Edgar Martinez	118.9
30	George Sisler	118.9
31	Sam Crawford	118.9
32	King Kelly	118.2
33	Jim O'Rourke	118.1
34	Matty Alou	117.9
35	Joe Medwick	117.8
36	Paul Waner	117.8
37	Elmer Flick	117.4
38	Roger Connor	117.4
39	Bill Terry	117.3
40	Lou Gehrig	117.2
41	Joe DiMaggio	117.1
42	Ginger Beaumont	117.0
43	Mark Grace	116.9
44	Don Mattingly	116.9
45	Ralph Garr	116.7
46	Manny Mota	116.4
47	George Brett	116.3
48	Dale Mitchell	116.3
49	John McGraw	116.2
50	Henry Larkin	116.2
51	Deacon White	116.1
52	Hank Aaron	116.0
53	Paul Hines	115.8
54	George Gore	115.7
55	Jackie Robinson	115.7
56	Pete Rose	115.6
57	Paul Molitor	115.5
58	Al Simmons	115.4
59	Frank Baker	115.4
60	Al Kaline	115.4
61	Bill Madlock	115.2
62	Arky Vaughan	115.1
63	Al Oliver	115.1
64	Riggs Stephenson	115.0
65	Mickey Mantle	115.0
66	Johnny Mize	115.0
67	Zack Wheat	114.9
68	Hugh Duffy	114.8
69	George Kell	114.8
70	Barney McCosky	114.7
71	Richie Ashburn	114.6
72	Mike Greenwell	114.6
73	Hardy Richardson	114.6
74	Pedro Guerrero	114.5
75	Johnny Pesky	114.5
76	Harvey Kuenn	114.5
77	Hal Morris	114.5
78	Rico Carty	114.4
79	Willie Mays	114.3
80	John Kruk	114.2
81	Larry Walker	114.1
82	Fred Clarke	114.0
83	Will Clark	114.0
84	Heinie Manush	114.0
85	Cy Seymour	113.9
86	Jimmie Foxx	113.8
87	Joe Torre	113.8
88	Edd Roush	113.8
89	Julio Franco	113.7
90	Jeff Bagwell	113.7
91	Roberto Alomar	113.7
92	Denny Lyons	113.6
93	Cecil Cooper	113.5
94	Jim Rice	113.5
95	Frank Robinson	113.4
96	Tommy Davis	113.4
97	Taffy Wright	113.4
98	Barry Larkin	113.2
99	Minnie Minoso	113.1
100	Jimmy Wolf	113.0

On Base Percentage

#	Player	Avg
1	Ted Williams	.483
2	Babe Ruth	.474
3	John McGraw	.466
4	Billy Hamilton	.455
5	Frank Thomas	.449
6	Lou Gehrig	.447
7	Rogers Hornsby	.434
8	Ty Cobb	.433
9	Jimmie Foxx	.428
	Tris Speaker	.428
11	Edgar Martinez	.427
12	Ferris Fain	.425
13	Eddie Collins	.424
14	Max Bishop	.423
	Dan Brouthers	.423
	Joe Jackson	.423
	Mickey Mantle	.423
18	Wade Boggs	.420
19	Mickey Cochrane	.419
20	Stan Musial	.418
21	Jeff Bagwell	.416
	Cupid Childs	.416
23	Jesse Burkett	.415
24	Barry Bonds	.414
	Mel Ott	.414
26	Roy Thomas	.413
27	Hank Greenberg	.412
28	Ed Delahanty	.411
29	Harry Heilmann	.410
	Charlie Keller	.410
	Jackie Robinson	.410
	Eddie Stanky	.410
33	Roy Cullenbine	.408
34	Denny Lyons	.407
	John Olerud	.407
	Riggs Stephenson	.407
37	Joe Cunningham	.406
	Rickey Henderson	.406
	Arky Vaughan	.406
40	Charlie Gehringer	.404
	Paul Waner	.404
42	Pete Browning	.403
43	Lu Blue	.402
	Joe Kelley	.402
45	Mike Hargrove	.400
	John Kruk	.400
47	Luke Appling	.399
	Elmer Valo	.399
	Ross Youngs	.399
50	Joe DiMaggio	.398
	Ralph Kiner	.398
	Elmer Smith	.398
53	Richie Ashburn	.397
	Earle Combs	.397
	Roger Connor	.397
	Johnny Mize	.397
	Mo Vaughn	.397
58	Dave Magadan	.396
59	Cap Anson	.395
	Earl Averill	.395
	Rod Carew	.395
	Mark McGwire	.395
	Joe Morgan	.395
	Gary Sheffield	.395
	Hack Wilson	.395
	Eddie Yost	.395
67	Frank Chance	.394
	Stan Hack	.394
	Johnny Pesky	.394
70	Bob Johnson	.393
	Wally Schang	.393
	Bill Terry	.393
	Ken Williams	.393
74	Jack Fournier	.392
	George Grantham	.392
	Tony Gwynn	.392
	Tip O'Neill	.392
	Frank Robinson	.392
	Mike Tiernan	.392
80	Minnie Minoso	.391
	Joe Sewell	.391
	Ken Singleton	.391
	Gene Tenace	.391
	Honus Wagner	.391
85	Harland Clift	.390
	Joe Cronin	.390
	Augie Galan	.390
	Hughie Jennings	.390
	Chuck Knoblauch	.390
90	Bernie Carbo	.389
	Elmer Flick	.389
	Mark Grace	.389
	Buddy Myer	.389
	Tim Raines	.389
95	Dolph Camilli	.388
	Mike Griffin	.388
	Keith Hernandez	.388
	Willie Keeler	.388
	Gene Woodling	.388
100	4 players tied	.387

Slugging Average

#	Player	Avg
1	Babe Ruth	.690
2	Ted Williams	.634
3	Lou Gehrig	.632
4	Jimmie Foxx	.609
5	Hank Greenberg	.605
6	Frank Thomas	.584
7	Joe DiMaggio	.579
8	Albert Belle	.577
9	Rogers Hornsby	.577
10	Mark McGwire	.576
11	Ken Griffey Jr.	.568
12	Juan Gonzalez	.568
13	Johnny Mize	.562
14	Stan Musial	.559
15	Willie Mays	.557
16	Mickey Mantle	.557
17	Barry Bonds	.556
18	Hank Aaron	.555
19	Larry Walker	.552
20	Ralph Kiner	.548
21	Hack Wilson	.545
22	Chuck Klein	.543
23	Mo Vaughn	.542
24	Duke Snider	.540
25	Jeff Bagwell	.538
26	Frank Robinson	.537
27	Al Simmons	.535
28	Dick Allen	.534
29	Earl Averill	.534
30	Mel Ott	.533
31	Babe Herman	.532
32	Ken Williams	.530
33	Willie Stargell	.529
34	Mike Schmidt	.527
35	Chick Hafey	.526
36	Hal Trosky	.522
37	Wally Berger	.522
38	Harry Heilmann	.520
39	Edgar Martinez	.520
40	Kevin Mitchell	.520
41	Dan Brouthers	.519
42	Charlie Keller	.518
43	Joe Jackson	.517
44	Jose Canseco	.517
45	Willie McCovey	.515
46	Fred McGriff	.514
47	Ty Cobb	.512
48	Eddie Mathews	.509
49	Jeff Heath	.509
50	Harmon Killebrew	.509
51	David Justice	.508
52	Bob Johnson	.506
53	Bill Terry	.506
54	Ed Delahanty	.505
55	Joe Medwick	.505
56	Darryl Strawberry	.504
57	Sam Thompson	.504
58	Andres Galarraga	.504
59	Rafael Palmeiro	.503
60	Jim Rice	.502
61	Tris Speaker	.500
62	Jim Bottomley	.500
63	Goose Goslin	.500
64	Roy Campanella	.500
65	Ernie Banks	.500
66	Orlando Cepeda	.499
67	Dante Bichette	.499
68	Bob Horner	.499
69	Frank Howard	.499
70	Ellis Burks	.498
71	Gary Sheffield	.498
72	Ted Kluszewski	.498
73	Bob Meusel	.497
74	Jay Buhner	.497
75	Hank Sauer	.496
76	Danny Tartabull	.496
77	Al Rosen	.495
78	Will Clark	.494
79	Sammy Sosa	.493
80	Eric Davis	.492
81	Billy Williams	.492
82	Ripper Collins	.492
83	Dolph Camilli	.492
84	Matt Williams	.491
85	Tommy Henrich	.491
86	Larry Doby	.490
87	Reggie Jackson	.490
88	Dick Stuart	.489
89	Reggie Smith	.489
90	Gabby Hartnett	.489
91	Rocky Colavito	.489
92	Norm Cash	.488
93	George Brett	.487
94	Gil Hodges	.487
95	Bill Dickey	.486
96	Roger Connor	.486
97	Gus Zernial	.485
98	Joe Adcock	.485
99	Wally Post	.485
100	Fred Lynn	.484

Production

#	Player	Avg
1	Babe Ruth	1.163
2	Ted Williams	1.116
3	Lou Gehrig	1.080
4	Jimmie Foxx	1.038
5	Frank Thomas	1.033
6	Hank Greenberg	1.017
7	Rogers Hornsby	1.010
8	Mickey Mantle	.979
9	Joe DiMaggio	.977
	Stan Musial	.977
11	Mark McGwire	.971
12	Barry Bonds	.970
13	Johnny Mize	.959
14	Jeff Bagwell	.955
15	Albert Belle	.951
16	Ken Griffey Jr.	.950
17	Edgar Martinez	.947
	Mel Ott	.947
19	Ralph Kiner	.946
20	Ty Cobb	.945
21	Willie Mays	.944
22	Dan Brouthers	.942
23	Joe Jackson	.940
	Hack Wilson	.940
25	Mo Vaughn	.939
26	Larry Walker	.937
27	Hank Aaron	.932
28	Harry Heilmann	.930
29	Frank Robinson	.929
30	Earl Averill	.928
	Charlie Keller	.928
	Tris Speaker	.928
33	Ken Williams	.924
34	Chuck Klein	.922
35	Duke Snider	.921
36	Ed Delahanty	.917
37	Babe Herman	.915
	Al Simmons	.915
39	Dick Allen	.914
40	Mike Schmidt	.912
41	Juan Gonzalez	.910
42	Bob Johnson	.899
	Bill Terry	.899
44	Chick Hafey	.898
45	Mickey Cochrane	.897
	Fred McGriff	.897
47	Gary Sheffield	.893
48	Willie McCovey	.892
	Willie Stargell	.892
	Hal Trosky	.892
51	John Olerud	.891
52	David Justice	.889
53	Billy Hamilton	.888
	Eddie Mathews	.888
	Sam Thompson	.888
56	Goose Goslin	.887
	Harmon Killebrew	.887
58	Charlie Gehringer	.884
59	Roger Connor	.883
	Kevin Mitchell	.883
	Jackie Robinson	.883
62	Al Rosen	.882
63	Wally Berger	.881
64	Dolph Camilli	.880
	Will Clark	.880
	Riggs Stephenson	.880
67	Jeff Heath	.879
68	Paul Waner	.878
69	Larry Doby	.877
70	John McGraw	.876
71	Jack Fournier	.875
72	Tommy Henrich	.873
73	Rafael Palmeiro	.871
74	Jose Canseco	.870
75	Jim Bottomley	.869
	Pete Browning	.869
77	Bill Dickey	.868
78	Joe Medwick	.867
	Danny Tartabull	.867
80	Wade Boggs	.865
	Norm Cash	.865
82	Jesse Burkett	.862
	Darryl Strawberry	.862
84	George Brett	.861
	Roy Campanella	.861
86	Kiki Cuyler	.860
87	Earle Combs	.859
	Al Kaline	.859
	Reggie Smith	.859
	Arky Vaughan	.859
91	Jack Clark	.858
	Gavvy Cravath	.858
	Gabby Hartnett	.858
	Jim Rice	.858
95	Jay Buhner	.857
	Ellis Burks	.857
	Joe Cronin	.857
	Honus Wagner	.857
99	Heinie Manush	.856
	Billy Williams	.856

Adjusted Production

#	Player	Value
1	Babe Ruth	209
2	Ted Williams	186
3	Lou Gehrig	182
4	Frank Thomas	177
5	Rogers Hornsby	176
6	Mickey Mantle	173
7	Dan Brouthers	170
8	Joe Jackson	169
9	Ty Cobb	167
10	Barry Bonds	164
	Pete Browning	164
	Mark McGwire	164
13	Jeff Bagwell	161
	Jimmie Foxx	161
15	Hank Greenberg	157
	Willie Mays	157
	Johnny Mize	157
	Stan Musial	157
19	Hank Aaron	156
	Dick Allen	156
	Joe DiMaggio	156
	Tris Speaker	156
23	Mel Ott	155
24	Roger Connor	154
	Frank Robinson	154
26	Ed Delahanty	152
	Charlie Keller	152
28	Nap Lajoie	150
	Edgar Martinez	150
	Honus Wagner	150
31	Albert Belle	149
	Gavvy Cravath	149
	Elmer Flick	149
	Ken Griffey Jr.	149
35	Harry Heilmann	148
	Ralph Kiner	148
	Willie McCovey	148
38	Mike Schmidt	147
	Willie Stargell	147
40	Sam Thompson	146
41	Eddie Mathews	145
	Hack Wilson	145
43	Sam Crawford	143
	Jack Fournier	143
	Frank Howard	143
	Kevin Mitchell	143
47	Eddie Collins	142
	Mike Donlin	142
	Harmon Killebrew	142
	Harry Stovey	142
51	Babe Herman	141
	Henry Larkin	141
	Gary Sheffield	141
54	Wally Berger	140
	Jesse Burkett	140
	Jeff Heath	140
	Reggie Jackson	140
	Tip O'Neill	140
59	Billy Hamilton	139
	Bob Johnson	139
	Denny Lyons	139
	Darryl Strawberry	139
	Mo Vaughn	139
64	Cap Anson	138
	Norm Cash	138
	Jack Clark	138
	Will Clark	138
	Pedro Guerrero	138
	Al Rosen	138
	Duke Snider	138
	Mike Tiernan	138
72	Larry Doby	137
	Sherry Magee	137
	Fred McGriff	137
	Gene Tenace	137
	Bill Terry	137
77	Frank Baker	136
	King Kelly	136
	Reggie Smith	136
	Arky Vaughan	136
	Ken Williams	136
82	George Brett	135
	Oyster Burns	135
	Jose Canseco	135
	Frank Chance	135
	Juan Gonzalez	135
	George Gore	135
	Chuck Klein	135
	John McGraw	135
	John Olerud	135
91	Dolph Camilli	134
	Tony Gwynn	134
	Al Kaline	134
	John Kruk	134
	Boog Powell	134
	Larry Walker	134
97	11 players tied	133

Batting Runs

1	Babe Ruth	1322
2	Ted Williams	1166
3	Ty Cobb	1031
4	Stan Musial	983
5	Lou Gehrig	917
6	Hank Aaron	878
7	Rogers Hornsby	844
8	Tris Speaker	843
9	Willie Mays	827
10	Jimmie Foxx	803
	Mickey Mantle	803
12	Frank Robinson	773
13	Mel Ott	767
14	Honus Wagner	664
15	Dan Brouthers	636
16	Carl Yastrzemski	617
17	Eddie Collins	608
18	Barry Bonds	596
19	Mike Schmidt	592
20	Nap Lajoie	556
21	Cap Anson	548
	Roger Connor	548
23	Harmon Killebrew	532
24	Ed Delahanty	525
25	Willie McCovey	524
26	Johnny Mize	520
27	Harry Heilmann	517
28	Al Kaline	513
29	George Brett	511
30	Joe DiMaggio	507
31	Jesse Burkett	504
32	Frank Thomas	497
33	Sam Crawford	493
34	Wade Boggs	491
	Paul Waner	491
36	Willie Stargell	483
37	Eddie Mathews	480
38	Billy Hamilton	472
39	Dick Allen	470
40	Hank Greenberg	468
41	Reggie Jackson	466
42	Billy Williams	463
43	Joe Jackson	452
44	Rickey Henderson	441
	Duke Snider	441
46	Joe Morgan	438
47	Mark McGwire	435
48	Rod Carew	431
49	Eddie Murray	420
50	Dwight Evans	418
51	Pete Rose	399
52	Al Simmons	399
53	Ralph Kiner	391
54	Norm Cash	390
55	Tony Gwynn	384
56	Dave Winfield	382
57	Reggie Smith	379
58	Fred Clarke	376
	Charlie Gehringer	376
	Joe Kelley	376
61	Chuck Klein	375
62	Jack Clark	367
	Ken Griffey Jr.	367
	Jim Rice	367
65	Bob Johnson	366
66	Arky Vaughan	361
67	Fred McGriff	360
68	Sam Thompson	359
69	Pete Browning	356
70	Roberto Clemente	354
	Joe Medwick	354
72	Edgar Martinez	349
73	Harry Stovey	347
74	Ron Santo	345
75	Jeff Bagwell	342
	Elmer Flick	342
77	Goose Goslin	341
	Willie Keeler	341
79	Orlando Cepeda	337
	Will Clark	337
81	Earl Averill	334
	Zack Wheat	334
83	Ken Singleton	332
84	Sherry Magee	331
	Paul Molitor	331
86	Frank Howard	324
87	Dolph Camilli	319
88	Rusty Staub	318
	Bill Terry	318
90	Tim Raines	316
91	King Kelly	313
92	Keith Hernandez	310
93	Fred Lynn	309
94	Albert Belle	307
95	Enos Slaughter	306
96	Boog Powell	305
	Hack Wilson	305
98	Babe Herman	304
99	Minnie Minoso	299
100	Joe Torre	298

Adjusted Batting Runs

1	Babe Ruth	1382
2	Ted Williams	1024
3	Lou Gehrig	1005
4	Ty Cobb	1004
5	Hank Aaron	914
6	Stan Musial	899
7	Rogers Hornsby	874
8	Mickey Mantle	863
9	Willie Mays	844
10	Tris Speaker	793
11	Mel Ott	776
12	Jimmie Foxx	746
13	Frank Robinson	744
14	Barry Bonds	636
15	Honus Wagner	631
16	Eddie Collins	622
17	Dan Brouthers	609
18	Eddie Mathews	559
19	Nap Lajoie	558
20	Roger Connor	549
21	Ed Delahanty	543
	Mike Schmidt	543
23	Willie McCovey	540
24	Frank Thomas	533
25	Harry Heilmann	532
26	Joe DiMaggio	529
27	Rickey Henderson	522
28	Reggie Jackson	519
29	Johnny Mize	490
30	George Brett	488
	Willie Stargell	488
32	Harmon Killebrew	482
	Mark McGwire	482
34	Joe Morgan	478
35	Jesse Burkett	474
	Carl Yastrzemski	474
37	Dick Allen	469
38	Al Kaline	468
39	Sam Crawford	464
	Paul Waner	464
41	Eddie Murray	462
42	Dave Winfield	440
43	Wade Boggs	439
44	Joe Jackson	433
45	Hank Greenberg	422
46	Cap Anson	418
	Tony Gwynn	418
48	Billy Hamilton	415
49	Rod Carew	411
50	Jeff Bagwell	389
51	Duke Snider	388
52	Bob Johnson	387
53	Pete Browning	384
54	Jack Clark	377
55	Billy Williams	371
56	Fred Clarke	366
	Pete Rose	366
58	Roberto Clemente	363
	Ralph Kiner	363
60	Al Simmons	361
61	Ken Griffey Jr.	360
62	Ken Singleton	359
63	Frank Howard	357
64	Norm Cash	355
65	Will Clark	354
66	Elmer Flick	353
67	Arky Vaughan	352
68	Goose Goslin	347
69	Paul Molitor	346
70	Edgar Martinez	345
71	Sam Thompson	343
72	Reggie Smith	342
73	Orlando Cepeda	338
	Bill Terry	338
75	Fred McGriff	337
76	Zack Wheat	335
77	Tim Raines	334
	Rusty Staub	334
79	Charlie Gehringer	332
80	Dwight Evans	331
81	Sherry Magee	324
82	Babe Herman	323
83	Joe Kelley	321
84	Keith Hernandez	320
85	Albert Belle	315
86	Mike Tiernan	314
87	Hack Wilson	311
88	Joe Medwick	310
	Boog Powell	310
90	Jack Fournier	308
91	Jake Beckley	300
92	Joe Torre	299
93	Chuck Klein	298
	Rafael Palmeiro	298
95	Minnie Minoso	297
96	Earl Averill	296
97	Harry Stovey	294
98	Charlie Keller	293
99	Jimmy Wynn	289
100	Rocky Colavito	287

Batting Wins

1	Babe Ruth	127.5
2	Ted Williams	115.9
3	Ty Cobb	106.3
4	Stan Musial	99.7
5	Hank Aaron	91.1
6	Tris Speaker	86.1
7	Willie Mays	85.5
8	Lou Gehrig	85.3
9	Rogers Hornsby	84.9
10	Mickey Mantle	82.9
11	Frank Robinson	80.7
12	Mel Ott	76.2
13	Jimmie Foxx	75.3
14	Honus Wagner	68.5
15	Carl Yastrzemski	64.3
16	Eddie Collins	62.4
17	Mike Schmidt	61.8
18	Barry Bonds	60.6
19	Nap Lajoie	57.0
20	Harmon Killebrew	55.8
21	Dan Brouthers	55.6
22	Willie McCovey	54.9
23	Al Kaline	53.4
24	Sam Crawford	52.5
25	Johnny Mize	52.2
26	George Brett	51.4
27	Willie Stargell	51.0
28	Harry Heilmann	50.8
29	Dick Allen	50.0
30	Eddie Mathews	49.2
31	Joe DiMaggio	48.6
32	Billy Williams	48.6
33	Paul Waner	48.6
34	Cap Anson	48.5
35	Wade Boggs	48.1
36	Reggie Jackson	47.9
37	Roger Connor	47.9
38	Frank Thomas	47.8
39	Joe Jackson	47.4
40	Ed Delahanty	46.3
41	Jesse Burkett	46.2
42	Joe Morgan	45.9
43	Rod Carew	44.7
44	Hank Greenberg	44.5
45	Duke Snider	44.4
46	Pete Rose	43.9
47	Rickey Henderson	43.6
48	Mark McGwire	42.7
49	Dwight Evans	42.2
50	Eddie Murray	41.9
51	Billy Hamilton	41.2
52	Norm Cash	41.1
53	Reggie Smith	40.3
54	Tony Gwynn	39.4
55	Ralph Kiner	39.1
56	Dave Winfield	38.6
57	Jack Clark	38.0
58	Al Simmons	37.4
59	Jim Rice	36.9
60	Roberto Clemente	36.8
61	Chuck Klein	36.7
62	Fred Clarke	36.7
63	Arky Vaughan	36.4
64	Ron Santo	36.3
65	Fred McGriff	36.0
66	Sherry Magee	35.8
67	Joe Medwick	35.8
68	Ken Griffey Jr.	35.6
69	Bob Johnson	35.2
70	Charlie Gehringer	35.1
71	Orlando Cepeda	35.1
72	Elmer Flick	34.8
73	Joe Kelley	34.6
74	Frank Howard	34.4
75	Zack Wheat	34.4
76	Jeff Bagwell	34.4
77	Ken Singleton	34.0
78	Will Clark	33.8
79	Edgar Martinez	33.7
80	Rusty Staub	33.3
81	Willie Keeler	33.0
82	Paul Molitor	32.5
83	Boog Powell	32.4
84	Keith Hernandez	32.4
85	Dolph Camilli	32.2
86	Tim Raines	32.0
87	Goose Goslin	31.9
88	Joe Torre	31.4
89	Sam Thompson	31.1
90	Fred Lynn	31.1
91	Pete Browning	31.0
92	Enos Slaughter	30.9
93	Earl Averill	30.8
94	Rocky Colavito	30.8
95	Bill Terry	30.8
96	Tony Perez	30.6
97	Harry Stovey	30.6
98	Minnie Minoso	30.3
99	Greg Luzinski	30.1
100	Ernie Banks	29.8

Adjusted Batting Wins

1	Babe Ruth	133.3
2	Ty Cobb	103.6
3	Ted Williams	101.7
4	Hank Aaron	94.8
5	Lou Gehrig	93.5
6	Stan Musial	91.1
7	Mickey Mantle	89.1
8	Rogers Hornsby	87.9
9	Willie Mays	87.3
10	Tris Speaker	81.0
11	Frank Robinson	77.7
12	Mel Ott	77.1
13	Jimmie Foxx	69.9
14	Honus Wagner	65.1
15	Barry Bonds	64.7
16	Eddie Collins	63.8
17	Eddie Mathews	57.3
18	Nap Lajoie	57.2
19	Mike Schmidt	56.7
20	Willie McCovey	56.6
21	Reggie Jackson	53.4
22	Dan Brouthers	53.2
23	Harry Heilmann	52.2
24	Rickey Henderson	51.6
25	Willie Stargell	51.5
26	Frank Thomas	51.2
27	Joe DiMaggio	50.8
28	Harmon Killebrew	50.6
29	Joe Morgan	50.1
30	Dick Allen	49.8
31	Carl Yastrzemski	49.4
32	Sam Crawford	49.4
33	Johnny Mize	49.2
34	George Brett	49.1
35	Al Kaline	48.7
36	Roger Connor	48.0
37	Ed Delahanty	47.9
38	Mark McGwire	47.3
39	Eddie Murray	46.1
40	Paul Waner	45.9
41	Joe Jackson	45.4
42	Dave Winfield	44.5
43	Jesse Burkett	43.5
44	Wade Boggs	43.0
45	Tony Gwynn	42.9
46	Rod Carew	42.7
47	Hank Greenberg	40.1
48	Jeff Bagwell	39.1
49	Duke Snider	39.1
50	Jack Clark	39.1
51	Billy Williams	39.0
52	Pete Rose	38.6
53	Frank Howard	37.9
54	Roberto Clemente	37.8
55	Norm Cash	37.5
56	Bob Johnson	37.2
57	Cap Anson	37.0
58	Ken Singleton	36.7
59	Reggie Smith	36.4
60	Ralph Kiner	36.3
61	Billy Hamilton	36.2
62	Elmer Flick	35.9
63	Fred Clarke	35.7
64	Arky Vaughan	35.5
65	Will Clark	35.5
66	Orlando Cepeda	35.2
67	Sherry Magee	35.1
68	Rusty Staub	35.0
69	Ken Griffey Jr.	34.9
70	Zack Wheat	34.5
71	Paul Molitor	34.0
72	Tim Raines	33.8
73	Al Simmons	33.8
74	Fred McGriff	33.7
75	Pete Browning	33.4
76	Keith Hernandez	33.4
77	Dwight Evans	33.4
78	Edgar Martinez	33.3
79	Boog Powell	32.9
80	Bill Terry	32.7
81	Goose Goslin	32.5
82	Joe Torre	31.5
83	Joe Medwick	31.4
84	Babe Herman	31.3
85	Jack Fournier	31.1
86	Charlie Gehringer	31.0
87	Jimmy Wynn	30.6
88	Albert Belle	30.2
89	Minnie Minoso	30.1
90	Hack Wilson	30.1
91	Rocky Colavito	29.8
92	Sam Thompson	29.7
93	Joe Kelley	29.5
94	Rafael Palmeiro	29.2
95	Chuck Klein	29.2
96	Charlie Keller	29.2
97	Pedro Guerrero	29.0
98	Bobby Bonds	28.6
99	Darryl Strawberry	28.6
100	Larry Doby	28.4

Runs Created

1	Babe Ruth	2847
2	Ty Cobb	2810
3	Stan Musial	2625
4	Hank Aaron	2550
5	Ted Williams	2538
6	Willie Mays	2372
7	Tris Speaker	2325
8	Lou Gehrig	2321
9	Mel Ott	2235
	Honus Wagner	2235
11	Pete Rose	2220
12	Jimmie Foxx	2191
13	Carl Yastrzemski	2147
14	Frank Robinson	2126
15	Rogers Hornsby	2074
16	Mickey Mantle	2069
17	Eddie Collins	2062
18	Eddie Murray	1939
19	Rickey Henderson	1923
20	Nap Lajoie	1906
21	George Brett	1878
22	Paul Molitor	1872
23	Paul Waner	1853
24	Al Kaline	1846
25	Ed Delahanty	1832
26	Dave Winfield	1813
27	Jesse Burkett	1804
	Joe Morgan	1804
29	Charlie Gehringer	1787
30	Al Simmons	1777
31	Reggie Jackson	1772
32	Mike Schmidt	1757
33	Cap Anson	1756
34	Eddie Mathews	1738
35	Sam Crawford	1716
36	Wade Boggs	1710
37	Goose Goslin	1707
	Billy Hamilton	1707
39	Harry Heilmann	1698
40	Willie Keeler	1688
41	Jake Beckley	1686
42	Fred Clarke	1677
43	Billy Williams	1671
44	Robin Yount	1655
45	Roger Connor	1648
46	Willie McCovey	1638
47	George Davis	1633
48	Barry Bonds	1629
49	Dan Brouthers	1624
50	Dwight Evans	1611
51	Harmon Killebrew	1609
52	Joe DiMaggio	1606
53	Rod Carew	1595
54	Tim Raines	1591
55	Cal Ripken	1577
56	George Van Haltren	1566
57	Jimmy Ryan	1562
58	Roberto Clemente	1557
59	Zack Wheat	1540
60	Joe Kelley	1535
61	Rusty Staub	1534
62	Willie Stargell	1531
63	Tony Gwynn	1524
64	Tony Perez	1523
65	Andre Dawson	1519
66	Ernie Banks	1513
67	Lou Brock	1512
68	Bill Dahlen	1508
	Hugh Duffy	1508
70	Johnny Mize	1502
71	Sam Rice	1501
72	Darrell Evans	1499
73	George Sisler	1498
74	Luke Appling	1493
75	Duke Snider	1487
76	Harold Baines	1479
77	Max Carey	1472
78	Frankie Frisch	1464
79	Dave Parker	1452
80	Enos Slaughter	1432
81	Joe Cronin	1426
82	Bob Johnson	1418
83	Lou Whitaker	1396
84	Vada Pinson	1394
85	Heinie Manush	1389
86	Mickey Vernon	1387
87	Richie Ashburn	1386
88	Jim Bottomley	1384
89	Jim Rice	1382
90	Ron Santo	1379
91	Chuck Klein	1378
92	Carlton Fisk	1375
93	Joe Medwick	1372
94	Earl Averill	1358
	Brooks Robinson	1358
96	Harry Hooper	1349
97	Al Oliver	1348
98	Bid McPhee	1345
99	Ryne Sandberg	1342
100	Orlando Cepeda	1338

Total Average

1	Babe Ruth	1.399
2	Ted Williams	1.320
3	Lou Gehrig	1.229
4	Billy Hamilton	1.192
5	John McGraw	1.153
6	Frank Thomas	1.148
7	Jimmie Foxx	1.143
8	Hank Greenberg	1.105
	Rogers Hornsby	1.105
10	Barry Bonds	1.092
11	Mickey Mantle	1.091
12	Ty Cobb	1.066
13	Dan Brouthers	1.061
14	Mark McGwire	1.041
15	Mel Ott	1.036
16	Ed Delahanty	1.035
17	Stan Musial	1.028
18	Jeff Bagwell	1.023
19	Joe DiMaggio	1.012
20	Tris Speaker	1.011
21	Joe Jackson	1.008
22	Ralph Kiner	1.006
23	Johnny Mize	1.005
	Hack Wilson	1.005
25	Charlie Keller	1.000
26	Edgar Martinez	.997
27	Ken Griffey Jr.	.985
28	Willie Mays	.982
29	Larry Walker	.979
30	Mike Tiernan	.970
31	Rickey Henderson	.968
32	Mo Vaughn	.964
33	Harry Heilmann	.963
34	Joe Kelley	.961
	Frank Robinson	.961
36	Earl Averill	.957
37	Denny Lyons	.955
38	Mike Schmidt	.954
39	Albert Belle	.952
	Roger Connor	.952
41	Mickey Cochrane	.947
	Honus Wagner	.947
43	Pete Browning	.946
44	Chuck Klein	.944
45	Jesse Burkett	.943
	Ken Williams	.943
47	Eddie Collins	.942
	Babe Herman	.942
49	Hank Aaron	.940
50	Jackie Robinson	.939
	Sam Thompson	.939
52	Duke Snider	.933
53	Dick Allen	.930
	Hugh Duffy	.930
55	Dolph Camilli	.928
56	Harry Stovey	.924
57	Gary Sheffield	.923
58	Frank Chance	.920
	Bob Johnson	.920
60	Eddie Mathews	.916
61	Elmer Flick	.915
62	Eric Davis	.914
	Mike Donlin	.914
64	Willie McCovey	.912
65	Elmer Smith	.911
66	Charlie Gehringer	.910
	Harmon Killebrew	.910
	Joe Morgan	.910
69	Chick Hafey	.908
70	Fred McGriff	.907
71	John Olerud	.906
72	Gavvy Cravath	.905
	Mike Griffin	.905
	Al Simmons	.905
75	David Justice	.902
76	Kiki Cuyler	.901
	Goose Goslin	.901
78	Cupid Childs	.900
79	Riggs Stephenson	.899
	Bill Terry	.899
81	Tip O'Neill	.897
82	Arky Vaughan	.894
83	Larry Doby	.893
	Tommy Henrich	.893
85	Tim Raines	.892
86	Willie Stargell	.889
	Hal Trosky	.889
88	Paul Waner	.888
89	Jack Fournier	.884
	Darryl Strawberry	.884
91	Fred Clarke	.883
	Hughie Jennings	.883
93	George Grantham	.882
94	Roy Cullenbine	.881
	George Van Haltren	.881
96	Will Clark	.880
97	Norm Cash	.875
	Juan Gonzalez	.875
	Al Rosen	.875
100	Oyster Burns	.873

Runs Produced

1	Ty Cobb	4066
2	Hank Aaron	3716
3	Babe Ruth	3673
4	Cap Anson	3501
5	Stan Musial	3425
6	Lou Gehrig	3390
7	Honus Wagner	3367
8	Pete Rose	3319
9	Willie Mays	3305
10	Tris Speaker	3294
11	Mel Ott	3208
	Carl Yastrzemski	3208
13	Jimmie Foxx	3139
14	Ted Williams	3116
15	Jake Beckley	3088
16	Eddie Collins	3074
17	Frank Robinson	3055
18	Eddie Murray	3040
19	Dave Winfield	3037
20	Al Simmons	3027
21	Nap Lajoie	3021
22	Charlie Gehringer	3017
23	Ed Delahanty	2962
24	George Davis	2904
25	Rogers Hornsby	2862
26	George Brett	2861
27	Paul Molitor	2855
28	Goose Goslin	2844
29	Paul Waner	2823
30	Sam Crawford	2819
31	Al Kaline	2806
32	Roger Connor	2804
33	Robin Yount	2787
34	Hugh Duffy	2748
35	Bill Dahlen	2738
36	Rickey Henderson	2726
37	Dan Brouthers	2713
38	Bid McPhee	2692
39	Reggie Jackson	2690
40	Frankie Frisch	2671
41	Lave Cross	2657
42	Mickey Mantle	2650
43	Harry Heilmann	2647
44	Cal Ripken	2640
45	Jimmy Ryan	2617
46	Jesse Burkett	2597
47	George Van Haltren	2584
48	Fred Clarke	2567
49	Joe DiMaggio	2566
50	Sam Rice	2558
51	Mike Schmidt	2553
52	Joe Kelley	2550
53	Tony Perez	2545
54	Andre Dawson	2526
55	Joe Morgan	2515
56	Willie Keeler	2496
57	Joe Cronin	2487
58	Roberto Clemente	2481
59	Dwight Evans	2469
60	Billy Williams	2459
61	Eddie Mathews	2450
62	Ernie Banks	2429
	Sam Thompson	2429
64	Dave Parker	2426
65	Herman Long	2421
66	Jim O'Rourke	2406
67	Zack Wheat	2405
68	Pie Traynor	2398
69	Luke Appling	2390
	Billy Hamilton	2390
71	Enos Slaughter	2382
72	Jim Bottomley	2380
73	Joe Medwick	2376
74	Rusty Staub	2363
75	Lou Brock	2361
76	Heinie Manush	2360
77	George Sisler	2357
78	Rod Carew	2347
79	Wade Boggs	2342
80	Harold Baines	2340
81	Mickey Vernon	2335
82	Brooks Robinson	2321
83	Jim Rice	2318
84	Tim Raines	2311
85	Al Oliver	2296
86	Harmon Killebrew	2294
87	Tommy Corcoran	2285
88	Darrell Evans	2284
	Ed McKean	2284
90	Vada Pinson	2280
91	Harry Stovey	2278
92	Max Carey	2275
93	Willie McCovey	2263
94	Willie Stargell	2260
95	John Ward	2249
96	Yogi Berra	2247
97	Kiki Cuyler	2242
98	King Kelly	2238
99	Bob Johnson	2234
100	Carlton Fisk	2230

Clutch Hitting Index

1	Cap Anson	132
2	Earl Sheely	127
3	Tommy Thevenow	126
4	Bobby Veach	124
5	Pat Tabler	120
	Pie Traynor	120
7	Sam Mertes	119
8	Hughie Jennings	118
	Duffy Lewis	118
	Jack Rowe	118
	Luke Sewell	118
12	Rube Bressler	117
	Tommy Davis	117
	Bob Fothergill	117
	Chick Gandil	117
	King Kelly	117
	Cookie Lavagetto	117
	Muddy Ruel	117
	Ray Schalk	117
	Billy Sullivan	117
21	John Anderson	116
	Frank Bowerman	116
	Sherry Magee	116
	Elmer Smith	116
	Red Smith	116
26	Kitty Bransfield	115
	Lou Criger	115
	Ron Fairly	115
	Jeff King	115
	Sam Mele	115
	Lee Tannehill	115
	Pinky Whitney	115
	Possum Whitted	115
34	Roy Campanella	114
	Sam Crawford	114
	George Cutshaw	114
	Art Devlin	114
	Jack Doyle	114
	Ferris Fain	114
	Carl Furillo	114
	Red Murray	114
	Denny Walling	114
	Deacon White	114
	Jimmie Wilson	114
	Heinie Zimmerman	114
46	Bob Elliott	113
	Larry Gardner	113
	Frank LaPorte	113
	Stuffy McInnis	113
	Terry Pendleton	113
	Enos Slaughter	113
	Frank Snyder	113
	B.J. Surhoff	113
	Sam Thompson	113
	Vic Wertz	113
	Taffy Wright	113
57	Alan Ashby	112
	Frank Baker	112
	Larry Biittner	112
	Smoky Burgess	112
	Frank Chance	112
	Darren Daulton	112
	Johnny Edwards	112
	Kid Elberfeld	112
	Art Fletcher	112
	Sherm Lollar	112
	Frank McCormick	112
	Ed McKean	112
	Keith Moreland	112
	Manny Mota	112
	Jack O'Connor	112
	Mickey Owen	112
	Fred Pfeffer	112
	Boog Powell	112
	Cy Seymour	112
	Ted Simmons	112
	Mike Tresh	112
78	Bob Boone	111
	Sid Bream	111
	Steve Brodie	111
	Gavvy Cravath	111
	Joe Cronin	111
	Lave Cross	111
	Hugh Duffy	111
	Hank Gowdy	111
	Ron Hassey	111
	Jim Kaat	111
	Willie Kamm	111
	Ed Kirkpatrick	111
	Steve O'Neill	111
	Del Pratt	111
	Wilbert Robinson	111
	Rusty Staub	111
	Harry Steinfeldt	111
	Riggs Stephenson	111
	Patsy Tebeau	111
	Joe Tinker	111
	Jimmy Williams	111
	Glenn Wright	111
100	23 players tied	110

Isolated Power

1	Babe Ruth	.348
2	Mark McGwire	.312
3	Lou Gehrig	.292
4	Hank Greenberg	.292
5	Ted Williams	.289
6	Jimmie Foxx	.284
7	Albert Belle	.281
8	Juan Gonzalez	.278
9	Ralph Kiner	.269
10	Ken Griffey Jr.	.268
11	Barry Bonds	.266
12	Frank Thomas	.263
13	Mike Schmidt	.260
14	Mickey Mantle	.259
15	Willie Mays	.256
16	Joe DiMaggio	.254
17	Harmon Killebrew	.252
18	Jose Canseco	.250
19	Johnny Mize	.250
20	Hank Aaron	.250
21	Larry Walker	.247
22	Willie Stargell	.247
23	Darryl Strawberry	.246
24	Willie McCovey	.245
25	Duke Snider	.244
26	Frank Robinson	.243
27	Dave Kingman	.242
28	Dick Allen	.242
29	Jay Buhner	.240
30	Eddie Mathews	.238
31	Hack Wilson	.238
32	Mo Vaughn	.237
33	Kevin Mitchell	.236
34	Jeff Bagwell	.234
35	Charlie Keller	.231
36	Hank Sauer	.230
37	Fred McGriff	.230
38	Mel Ott	.229
39	Sammy Sosa	.229
40	Stan Musial	.228
41	Reggie Jackson	.228
42	Matt Williams	.227
43	Cecil Fielder	.227
44	Greg Vaughn	.226
45	Dick Stuart	.225
46	Ernie Banks	.225
47	David Justice	.225
48	Frank Howard	.225
49	Roy Campanella	.224
50	Danny Tartabull	.223
51	Chuck Klein	.223
52	Eric Davis	.223
53	Gorman Thomas	.223
54	Rob Deer	.223
55	Rocky Colavito	.223
56	Bob Horner	.222
57	Wally Berger	.221
58	Gus Zernial	.221
59	Wally Post	.220
60	Hal Trosky	.219
61	Rogers Hornsby	.218
62	Norm Cash	.217
63	Bob Allison	.217
64	Roger Maris	.216
65	Earl Averill	.216
66	Jeff Heath	.216
67	Dolph Camilli	.215
68	Ron Gant	.214
69	Andres Galarraga	.214
70	Gil Hodges	.214
71	Ken Williams	.211
72	Jesse Barfield	.210
73	Gary Sheffield	.210
74	Al Rosen	.210
75	Bob Johnson	.210
76	Tommy Henrich	.209
77	Chick Hafey	.209
78	Jack Clark	.209
79	Rafael Palmeiro	.209
80	Johnny Bench	.208
81	Ellis Burks	.208
82	Roy Sievers	.208
83	Rudy York	.208
84	Mickey Tettleton	.208
85	Glenn Davis	.208
86	Joe Adcock	.208
87	Nate Colbert	.207
88	Babe Herman	.207
89	Larry Doby	.207
90	George Foster	.206
91	Joe Carter	.205
92	Ray Lankford	.204
93	Jim Rice	.204
94	Dale Murphy	.204
95	Bobby Bonds	.203
96	Orlando Cepeda	.203
97	Andre Dawson	.203
98	Edgar Martinez	.202
99	Billy Williams	.202
100	Greg Luzinski	.202

Extra Base Hits

1	Hank Aaron	1477
2	Stan Musial	1377
3	Babe Ruth	1356
4	Willie Mays	1323
5	Lou Gehrig	1190
6	Frank Robinson	1186
7	Carl Yastrzemski	1157
8	Ty Cobb	1136
9	Tris Speaker	1131
10	George Brett	1119
11	Jimmie Foxx	1117
	Ted Williams	1117
13	Eddie Murray	1099
14	Dave Winfield	1093
15	Reggie Jackson	1075
16	Mel Ott	1071
17	Pete Rose	1041
18	Andre Dawson	1039
19	Mike Schmidt	1015
20	Rogers Hornsby	1011
21	Ernie Banks	1009
22	Al Simmons	995
23	Honus Wagner	993
24	Al Kaline	972
	Cal Ripken	972
26	Tony Perez	963
27	Robin Yount	960
28	Paul Molitor	953
	Willie Stargell	953
30	Mickey Mantle	952
31	Billy Williams	948
32	Dwight Evans	941
33	Dave Parker	940
34	Eddie Mathews	938
35	Goose Goslin	921
36	Willie McCovey	920
37	Paul Waner	909
38	Charlie Gehringer	904
39	Nap Lajoie	902
40	Harmon Killebrew	887
41	Joe Carter	881
	Joe DiMaggio	881
43	Barry Bonds	877
44	Harry Heilmann	876
45	Vada Pinson	868
46	Sam Crawford	864
47	Joe Medwick	858
48	Harold Baines	852
49	Duke Snider	850
50	Roberto Clemente	846
51	Carlton Fisk	844
52	Rusty Staub	838
53	Jim Bottomley	835
54	Jim Rice	834
55	Al Oliver	825
56	Orlando Cepeda	823
	Gary Gaetti	823
58	Brooks Robinson	818
59	Joe Morgan	813
60	Roger Connor	812
61	Johnny Mize	809
62	Ed Delahanty	808
63	Jake Beckley	803
	Joe Cronin	803
65	Johnny Bench	794
66	Dale Murphy	787
67	Mickey Vernon	782
68	Hank Greenberg	781
69	Zack Wheat	780
70	Darrell Evans	779
	Bob Johnson	779
72	Ted Simmons	778
73	Lou Brock	776
74	Ron Santo	774
75	Chuck Klein	772
76	Dan Brouthers	771
77	Rickey Henderson	768
78	Earl Averill	767
79	Heinie Manush	761
	Ryne Sandberg	761
81	Chili Davis	759
82	Steve Garvey	755
83	Dick Allen	750
84	Cap Anson	749
85	Graig Nettles	746
86	Rafael Palmeiro	742
87	Hal McRae	741
88	Wade Boggs	740
89	Fred Lynn	737
90	Reggie Smith	734
91	Don Baylor	732
92	Enos Slaughter	730
93	Lou Whitaker	729
94	Yogi Berra	728
	Tim Wallach	728
96	Gary Carter	726
	Andres Galarraga	726
	Jimmy Ryan	726
99	Lee May	725
100	Bill Buckner	721

Pinch Hits

1	Manny Mota	150
2	Smoky Burgess	145
3	Greg Gross	143
4	Jose Morales	123
5	Jerry Lynch	116
6	Red Lucas	114
7	Steve Braun	113
8	Terry Crowley	108
	Denny Walling	108
10	Gates Brown	107
11	Mike Lum	103
12	Jim Dwyer	102
13	Rusty Staub	100
14	Dave Clark	96
	John Vander Wal	96
16	Larry Biittner	95
	Vic Davalillo	95
	Gerald Perry	95
19	Jerry Hairston	94
20	Dave Philley	93
	Joel Youngblood	93
22	Jay Johnstone	92
23	Ed Kranepool	90
	Elmer Valo	90
25	Dwight Smith	87

Pinch Hit Average
(150 at bats minimum)

1	Harold Baines	.331
2	Tommy Davis	.320
3	Frenchy Bordagaray	.312
4	Frankie Baumholtz	.307
5	Willie McGee	.307
6	Sid Bream	.306
7	Mark Carreon	.306
8	Red Schoendienst	.303
9	Bob Fothergill	.300
10	Dave Magadan	.300
11	Dave Philley	.299
12	Manny Mota	.297
13	Ted Easterly	.296
14	Harvey Hendrick	.295
15	Larry Herndon	.294
16	Mark Sweeney	.293
17	Alex Arias	.293
18	Rance Mulliniks	.292
19	Terry Puhl	.289
20	Chip Hale	.289
21	Manny Sanguillen	.288
22	Smoky Burgess	.286
23	Rick Miller	.286
24	Johnny Mize	.283
25	Dave Hansen	.282

Pinch Hit Home Runs

1	Cliff Johnson	20
2	Jerry Lynch	18
3	Gates Brown	16
	Smoky Burgess	16
	Willie McCovey	16
6	George Crowe	14
7	John Vander Wal	13
8	Joe Adcock	12
	Bob Cerv	12
	Jose Morales	12
	Graig Nettles	12
12	Jeff Burroughs	11
	Jay Johnstone	11
	Candy Maldonado	11
	Fred Whitfield	11
	Cy Williams	11
17	Mark Carreon	10
	Dave Clark	10
	Jim Dwyer	10
	Mike Lum	10
	Ken McMullen	10
	Don Mincher	10
	Wally Post	10
	Champ Summers	10
	Jerry Turner	10
	Gus Zernial	10

Total Player Rating / 150g

1	Babe Ruth	6.45
2	Barry Bonds	6.24
3	Nap Lajoie	5.69
4	Ted Williams	5.61
5	Rogers Hornsby	5.39
6	Mike Schmidt	4.89
7	Mickey Mantle	4.75
8	Jeff Bagwell	4.68
9	Tris Speaker	4.65
10	Willie Mays	4.62
11	Rickey Henderson	4.58
12	Lou Gehrig	4.55
13	Ty Cobb	4.50
14	Honus Wagner	4.36
15	Ken Griffey Jr.	4.31
16	Frank Thomas	4.31
17	Joe Jackson	4.22
18	Hank Aaron	4.08
19	Joe DiMaggio	4.05
20	Barry Larkin	4.04
21	Albert Belle	3.80
22	Lou Boudreau	3.76
23	Eddie Collins	3.70
24	Dan Brouthers	3.69
25	Frank Robinson	3.69
26	Pete Browning	3.65
27	Ed Delahanty	3.62
28	Jimmie Foxx	3.50
29	Stan Musial	3.49
30	Jackie Robinson	3.45
31	Mel Ott	3.45
32	Tim Raines	3.44
33	Buck Ewing	3.37
34	Edgar Martinez	3.35
35	Tony Gwynn	3.29
36	Bobby Grich	3.29
37	Eddie Mathews	3.24
38	Arky Vaughan	3.24
39	Hank Greenberg	3.23
40	George Davis	3.22
41	Frank Baker	3.22
42	Roger Connor	3.21
43	Joe Morgan	3.19
44	Mickey Cochrane	3.18
45	Bill Dahlen	3.15
46	Bobby Doerr	3.14
47	Jack Glasscock	3.12
48	Cupid Childs	3.09
49	Hardy Richardson	3.08
50	Craig Biggio	3.07
51	Hughie Jennings	3.06
52	Sam Thompson	3.03
53	Dick Allen	3.03
54	Gabby Hartnett	3.02
55	Charlie Keller	3.01
56	Lenny Dykstra	3.00
57	Mark McGwire	2.98
58	Bill Dickey	2.97
59	Ralph Kiner	2.94
60	Elmer Flick	2.91
61	Johnny Mize	2.88
62	Charlie Gehringer	2.87
63	Bob Johnson	2.87
64	Larry Walker	2.84
65	Bid McPhee	2.82
66	Wade Boggs	2.81
67	Joe Cronin	2.78
68	Dave Bancroft	2.76
69	Joe Sewell	2.72
70	Charlie Bennett	2.71
71	Joe Gordon	2.70
72	Roy Campanella	2.67
73	Denny Lyons	2.65
74	Roberto Clemente	2.64
75	Reggie Smith	2.64
76	Ray Lankford	2.64
77	Ron Santo	2.64
78	Eric Davis	2.62
79	Gary Sheffield	2.62
80	Jimmy Wynn	2.59
81	Yogi Berra	2.56
82	King Kelly	2.56
83	Darryl Strawberry	2.55
84	Frankie Frisch	2.53
85	Art Fletcher	2.52
86	Luke Appling	2.52
87	Bill Mazeroski	2.52
88	Ozzie Smith	2.51
89	Billy Hamilton	2.50
90	Billy Herman	2.47
91	Keith Hernandez	2.47
92	Wally Berger	2.47
93	Kevin Mitchell	2.47
94	Kirby Puckett	2.45
95	Heinie Groh	2.43
96	Ryne Sandberg	2.43
97	Bobby Bonds	2.39
98	Frank Chance	2.39
99	Roberto Alomar	2.36
100	Al Kaline	2.36

Stolen Bases

1	Rickey Henderson	1297
2	Lou Brock	938
3	Billy Hamilton	912
4	Ty Cobb	892
5	Tim Raines	803
6	Vince Coleman	752
7	Eddie Collins	744
8	Arlie Latham	739
9	Max Carey	738
10	Honus Wagner	722
11	Joe Morgan	689
12	Willie Wilson	668
13	Tom Brown	657
14	Bert Campaneris	649
15	George Davis	616
16	Dummy Hoy	594
	Otis Nixon	594
18	Maury Wills	586
19	George Van Haltren	583
20	Ozzie Smith	580
21	Hugh Duffy	574
22	Bid McPhee	568
23	Brett Butler	558
24	Davey Lopes	557
25	Cesar Cedeno	550
26	Bill Dahlen	547
27	John Ward	540
28	Herman Long	536
29	Patsy Donovan	518
30	Jack Doyle	516
31	Harry Stovey	509
32	Luis Aparicio	506
	Fred Clarke	506
34	Paul Molitor	504
35	Willie Keeler	495
	Clyde Milan	495
37	Omar Moreno	487
38	Mike Griffin	473
39	Tommy McCarthy	468
40	Jimmy Sheckard	465
41	Bobby Bonds	461
42	Ed Delahanty	455
	Ron LeFlore	455
44	Curt Welch	453
45	Barry Bonds	445
46	Steve Sax	444
47	Joe Kelley	443
48	Sherry Magee	441
49	John McGraw	436
50	Tris Speaker	432
51	Bob Bescher	428
	Mike Tiernan	428
53	Charlie Comiskey	419
	Frankie Frisch	419
55	Jimmy Ryan	418
56	Tommy Harper	408
	Kenny Lofton	408
58	Donie Bush	404
59	Frank Chance	401
60	Bill Lange	399
61	Willie Davis	398
62	Sam Mertes	396
	Juan Samuel	396
64	Dave Collins	395
	Billy North	395
66	Jesse Burkett	389
67	Tommy Corcoran	387
68	Tom Daly	385
	Freddie Patek	385
70	George Burns	383
	Hugh Nicol	383
72	Delino DeShields	382
	Fred Pfeffer	382
74	Walt Wilmot	381
75	Nap Lajoie	380
76	Harry Hooper	375
	George Sisler	375
78	Jack Glasscock	372
79	Lonnie Smith	370
80	King Kelly	368
81	Sam Crawford	366
	Tommy Dowd	366
83	Hal Chase	363
84	Tommy Leach	361
85	Hughie Jennings	359
	Fielder Jones	359
87	Marquis Grissom	358
88	Buck Ewing	354
	Gary Pettis	354
90	Rod Carew	353
91	Tommy Tucker	352
92	Sam Rice	351
93	George Case	349
94	Paul Radford	346
95	Willie McGee	345
96	Ryne Sandberg	344
97	Julio Cruz	343
98	Eric Davis	342
99	Amos Otis	341
100	Roberto Alomar	340

Stolen Base Average

1	Eric Davis	85.1
2	Tim Raines	84.7
3	Barry Larkin	84.7
4	Stan Javier	84.3
5	Henry Cotto	83.3
6	Willie Wilson	83.3
7	Davey Lopes	83.0
8	Julio Cruz	81.5
9	Rickey Henderson	81.2
10	Joe Morgan	81.0
11	Vince Coleman	80.9
12	Andy Van Slyke	80.6
13	Kenny Lofton	80.2
14	Mickey Mantle	80.1
15	Marquis Grissom	80.1
16	Lenny Dykstra	79.8
17	Ozzie Smith	79.7
18	Enzo Hernandez	79.6
19	Gary Redus	79.5
20	Paul Molitor	79.4
21	Roberto Alomar	79.1
22	Brian Hunter	79.0
23	R. J. Reynolds	79.0
24	Luis Aparicio	78.8
25	Derek Bell	78.7
26	Amos Otis	78.6
27	Devon White	78.5
28	Kirk Gibson	78.5
29	Alan Wiggins	78.1
30	Craig Biggio	77.9
31	Tommy Harper	77.9
32	Rudy Law	77.8
33	Joe Carter	77.8
	Mike Felder	77.8
35	Bob Dernier	77.6
36	Chuck Knoblauch	77.5
37	Larry Walker	77.5
38	Ray Durham	77.5
39	Barry Bonds	77.4
	Miguel Dilone	77.4
41	Gary Pettis	77.3
42	Gregg Jefferies	77.2
43	Mookie Wilson	76.9
44	Otis Nixon	76.8
45	Rodney Scott	76.8
46	Hank Aaron	76.7
47	Willie Mays	76.6
48	Bert Campaneris	76.5
49	Milt Thompson	76.4
50	Bobby Brown	76.4

Stolen Base Runs

1	Rickey Henderson	209
2	Tim Raines	154
3	Willie Wilson	120
4	Vince Coleman	119
5	Joe Morgan	110
6	Davey Lopes	99
7	Lou Brock	97
8	Ozzie Smith	85
9	Bert Campaneris	75
10	Paul Molitor	73
11	Otis Nixon	71
12	Luis Aparicio	70
13	Eric Davis	67
14	Kenny Lofton	62
15	Barry Larkin	60
16	Cesar Cedeno	58
17	Barry Bonds	56
	Julio Cruz	56
19	Marquis Grissom	54
20	Tommy Harper	53
21	Ron LeFlore	51
	Maury Wills	51
23	Roberto Alomar	48
24	Amos Otis	47
	Gary Redus	47
26	Gary Pettis	44
27	Lenny Dykstra	42
28	Craig Biggio	41
	Willie Davis	41
	Stan Javier	41
	Devon White	41
32	Willie Mays	40
33	George Case	39
	Delino DeShields	39
	Chuck Knoblauch	39
	Ryne Sandberg	39
	Mookie Wilson	39
38	Kirk Gibson	38
	Andy Van Slyke	38
40	Bobby Bonds	37
	Omar Moreno	37
	Freddie Patek	37
43	Dave Collins	35
44	Juan Samuel	34
45	Miguel Dilone	33
	Willie McGee	33
47	Larry Bowa	32
	Lance Johnson	32
	Alan Wiggins	32
50	Dave Concepcion	31

Stolen Base Wins

1	Rickey Henderson	20.7
2	Tim Raines	15.6
3	Vince Coleman	12.1
4	Willie Wilson	12.0
5	Joe Morgan	11.5
6	Davey Lopes	10.2
7	Lou Brock	10.2
8	Ozzie Smith	8.8
9	Bert Campaneris	7.9
10	Luis Aparicio	7.3
11	Paul Molitor	7.2
12	Otis Nixon	7.0
13	Eric Davis	6.8
14	Barry Larkin	6.1
15	Cesar Cedeno	6.1
16	Kenny Lofton	5.9
17	Barry Bonds	5.7
18	Tommy Harper	5.6
19	Julio Cruz	5.6
20	Marquis Grissom	5.4
21	Maury Wills	5.3
22	Ron LeFlore	5.2
23	Amos Otis	4.9
24	Gary Redus	4.8
25	Roberto Alomar	4.7
26	Gary Pettis	4.4
27	Lenny Dykstra	4.3
28	Willie Davis	4.3
29	Craig Biggio	4.2
30	Willie Mays	4.1
31	Stan Javier	4.1
32	Mookie Wilson	4.1
33	Devon White	4.0
34	Ryne Sandberg	4.0
35	Andy Van Slyke	3.9
36	Delino DeShields	3.9
37	George Case	3.9
38	Freddie Patek	3.8
39	Omar Moreno	3.8
40	Bobby Bonds	3.8
41	Kirk Gibson	3.8
42	Chuck Knoblauch	3.7
43	Dave Collins	3.6
44	Juan Samuel	3.5
45	Willie McGee	3.4
46	Miguel Dilone	3.4
47	Larry Bowa	3.3
48	Alan Wiggins	3.3
49	Dave Concepcion	3.2
50	Lance Johnson	3.1

Games

First Base

1	Eddie Murray	2413
2	Jake Beckley	2377
3	Mickey Vernon	2237
4	Lou Gehrig	2137
5	Charlie Grimm	2131
6	Joe Judge	2084
7	Ed Konetchy	2073
8	Steve Garvey	2059
9	Cap Anson	2058
10	Joe Kuhel	2057

Second Base

1	Eddie Collins	2650
2	Joe Morgan	2527
3	Lou Whitaker	2308
4	Nellie Fox	2295
5	Charlie Gehringer	2206
6	Willie Randolph	2152
7	Frank White	2150
8	Bid McPhee	2126
9	Bill Mazeroski	2094
10	Nap Lajoie	2035

Shortstop

1	Luis Aparicio	2581
2	Ozzie Smith	2511
3	Cal Ripken	2302
4	Larry Bowa	2222
5	Luke Appling	2218
6	Dave Concepcion	2178
7	Rabbit Maranville	2153
8	Alan Trammell	2139
9	Bill Dahlen	2132
10	Bert Campaneris	2097

Third Base

1	Brooks Robinson	2870
2	Graig Nettles	2412
3	Mike Schmidt	2212
4	Gary Gaetti	2201
5	Buddy Bell	2183
6	Eddie Mathews	2181
7	Wade Boggs	2141
8	Ron Santo	2130
9	Tim Wallach	2054
10	Eddie Yost	2008

Outfield

1	Ty Cobb	2935
2	Willie Mays	2842
3	Hank Aaron	2760
4	Tris Speaker	2698
5	Lou Brock	2507
6	Al Kaline	2488
7	Dave Winfield	2469
8	Max Carey	2421
9	Rickey Henderson	2417
10	Vada Pinson	2403
11	Roberto Clemente	2370
12	Zack Wheat	2337
13	Willie Davis	2323
	Andre Dawson	2323
15	Mel Ott	2313
16	Sam Crawford	2299
17	Paul Waner	2288
18	Sam Rice	2270
19	Babe Ruth	2241
20	Goose Goslin	2188

Catcher

1	Carlton Fisk	2226
2	Bob Boone	2225
3	Gary Carter	2056
4	Tony Pena	1950
5	Jim Sundberg	1927
6	Al Lopez	1918
7	Lance Parrish	1818
8	Rick Ferrell	1806
9	Gabby Hartnett	1793
10	Ted Simmons	1771

Pitcher

1	Dennis Eckersley	1071
2	Hoyt Wilhelm	1070
3	Kent Tekulve	1050
4	Jesse Orosco	1025
5	Lee Smith	1022
6	Rich Gossage	1002
7	Lindy McDaniel	987
8	Rollie Fingers	944
9	Gene Garber	931
10	Cy Young	906

Fielding Average

First Base

1	Steve Garvey	.996
2	David Segui	.996
3	Don Mattingly	.996
4	Wes Parker	.996
5	J. T. Snow	.996
6	Dan Driessen	.995
7	John Olerud	.995
8	Jim Spencer	.995
9	Mike Squires	.995
10	Tino Martinez	.995

Second Base

1	Jose Oquendo	.992
2	Scott Fletcher	.990
3	Ryne Sandberg	.989
4	Tom Herr	.989
5	Bret Boone	.989
6	Jose Lind	.988
7	Mickey Morandini	.988
8	Jody Reed	.988
9	Rich Dauer	.987
10	Billy Ripken	.987

Shortstop

1	Omar Vizquel	.982
2	Mike Bordick	.980
3	Larry Bowa	.980
4	Tony Fernandez	.980
5	Cal Ripken	.979
6	Ozzie Smith	.978
7	Frank Duffy	.977
8	Spike Owen	.977
9	Alan Trammell	.977
10	Mark Belanger	.977

Third Base

1	Brooks Robinson	.971
2	Rico Petrocelli	.970
3	Ken Reitz	.970
4	George Kell	.969
5	Steve Buechele	.968
6	Don Money	.968
7	Hank Majeski	.968
8	Don Wert	.968
9	Willie Kamm	.967
10	Heinie Groh	.967

Outfield

1	Brian Downing	.995
2	Darren Lewis	.995
3	Darryl Hamilton	.994
4	Dave Gallagher	.993
5	Terry Puhl	.993
6	Brett Butler	.993
7	Pete Rose	.991
8	Ted Uhlaender	.991
9	Amos Otis	.991
10	Joe Rudi	.991
11	Mickey Stanley	.991
12	Steve Brye	.991
13	Don Demeter	.990
14	Robin Yount	.990
15	Jim Edmonds	.990
16	Tom Goodwin	.990
17	Jim Piersall	.990
18	Darrin Jackson	.990
19	John Moses	.990
20	Otis Nixon	.990

Catcher

1	Chris Hoiles	.994
2	Dan Wilson	.994
3	Bill Freehan	.993
4	Bob Melvin	.993
5	Elston Howard	.993
6	Darrin Fletcher	.993
7	Ron Hassey	.993
8	Jim Sundberg	.993
9	Joe Azcue	.992
10	Mike LaValliere	.992

Pitcher

1	Don Mossi	.990
2	Gary Nolan	.990
3	Rick Rhoden	.989
4	Lon Warneke	.988
5	Jim Wilson	.988
6	Woodie Fryman	.988
7	Mike Mussina	.987
8	Larry Gura	.986
9	Pete Alexander	.985
10	Alvin Crowder	.984

Total Chances per Game

First Base

1	Jiggs Donahue	11.84
2	Frank Isbell	11.66
3	Joe Start	11.51
4	Tom Jones	11.38
5	George Stovall	11.30
6	George Kelly	11.09
7	Candy LaChance	11.05
8	Wally Pipp	11.05
9	Ed Konetchy	11.04
10	John Ganzel	10.95

Second Base

1	Joe Gerhardt	7.11
2	Fred Pfeffer	6.95
3	Fred Dunlap	6.83
4	Pop Smith	6.80
5	Bid McPhee	6.70
6	Cub Stricker	6.59
7	Lou Bierbauer	6.50
8	Jack Burdock	6.50
9	Jack Farrell	6.40
10	Danny Richardson	6.34

Shortstop

1	Hughie Jennings	6.69
2	Bob Allen	6.46
3	Herman Long	6.38
4	Dave Bancroft	6.33
5	Bill Dahlen	6.26
6	George Davis	6.22
7	Rabbit Maranville	6.10
8	Bobby Wallace	6.10
9	Tommy Corcoran	6.09
10	Kid Elberfeld	6.07

Third Base

1	Jerry Denny	4.21
2	Ned Williamson	4.19
3	Billy Shindle	4.15
4	Tom Burns	4.07
5	Billy Nash	4.07
6	Arlie Latham	4.04
7	Bill Joyce	4.01
8	Tommy Leach	3.98
9	Denny Lyons	3.98
10	Frank Hankinson	3.91

Outfield

1	Taylor Douthit	3.16
2	Richie Ashburn	3.04
3	Johnny Mostil	3.03
4	Jigger Statz	3.01
5	Dom DiMaggio	2.99
6	Mike Kreevich	2.95
7	Dwayne Murphy	2.92
8	Sam Chapman	2.91
9	Sam West	2.88
10	Max Carey	2.87
11	Fred Schulte	2.84
12	Happy Felsch	2.83
13	Lloyd Waner	2.81
14	Vince DiMaggio	2.80
15	Wally Judnich	2.80
16	Jimmy Welsh	2.79
17	Bill Lange	2.78
18	Tris Speaker	2.77
19	Terry Moore	2.75
20	Stan Spence	2.75

Catcher

1	Mike Piazza	7.49
2	Pop Snyder	7.40
3	Doc Bushong	7.33
4	Buck Ewing	7.30
5	Ossee Schreckengost	7.27
6	Dan Wilson	7.26
7	Brad Ausmus	7.12
8	Johnny Edwards	6.98
9	Silver Flint	6.89
10	Charlie Bennett	6.87

Pitcher

1	Nick Altrock	3.70
2	Harry Howell	3.61
3	Addie Joss	3.59
4	Ed Walsh	3.49
5	Nixey Callahan	3.47
6	Willie Sudhoff	3.33
7	George Mullin	3.20
8	Barney Pelty	3.17
9	Chick Fraser	3.12
10	Red Donahue	2.95
11	Ed Willett	2.95

Chances Accepted per Game

First Base

1	Jiggs Donahue	11.69
2	Frank Isbell	11.50
3	Tom Jones	11.21
4	Joe Start	11.14
5	George Stovall	11.14
6	George Kelly	11.00
7	Wally Pipp	10.96
8	Ed Konetchy	10.93
9	Candy LaChance	10.87
10	Bill Terry	10.82

Second Base

1	Joe Gerhardt	6.49
2	Fred Pfeffer	6.39
3	Bid McPhee	6.33
4	Fred Dunlap	6.32
5	Pop Smith	6.15
6	Lou Bierbauer	6.07
7	Ski Melillo	6.00
8	Cub Stricker	5.97
9	Danny Richardson	5.96
10	Jack Burdock	5.93

Shortstop

1	Hughie Jennings	6.16
2	Dave Bancroft	5.98
3	Bob Allen	5.91
4	George Davis	5.85
5	Rabbit Maranville	5.81
6	Bill Dahlen	5.80
7	Herman Long	5.78
8	Bobby Wallace	5.73
9	Travis Jackson	5.67
10	Dick Bartell	5.64

Third Base

1	Jerry Denny	3.72
2	Billy Shindle	3.70
3	Billy Nash	3.65
4	Ned Williamson	3.63
5	Tommy Leach	3.62
6	Tom Burns	3.61
7	Jimmy Collins	3.61
8	Lee Tannehill	3.56
9	Arlie Latham	3.52
10	Denny Lyons	3.51

Outfield

1	Taylor Douthit	3.07
2	Richie Ashburn	2.98
3	Johnny Mostil	2.94
4	Dom DiMaggio	2.92
5	Jigger Statz	2.91
6	Mike Kreevich	2.89
7	Dwayne Murphy	2.88
8	Sam Chapman	2.83
9	Sam West	2.83
10	Max Carey	2.77
11	Wally Judnich	2.77
12	Fred Schulte	2.77
13	Lloyd Waner	2.76
14	Vince DiMaggio	2.75
15	Happy Felsch	2.75
16	Joe DiMaggio	2.72
17	Terry Moore	2.71
18	Billy North	2.71
19	Stan Spence	2.71
20	Jimmy Welsh	2.71

Catcher

1	Mike Piazza	7.41
2	Dan Wilson	7.22
3	Ossee Schreckengost	7.05
4	Brad Ausmus	7.04
5	Johnny Edwards	6.92
6	Buck Ewing	6.79
7	Johnny Roseboro	6.76
8	Bill Freehan	6.75
9	Doc Bushong	6.72
10	Pop Snyder	6.69

Pitcher

1	Nick Altrock	3.57
2	Addie Joss	3.47
3	Harry Howell	3.46
4	Ed Walsh	3.36
5	Nixey Callahan	3.25
6	Willie Sudhoff	3.13
7	George Mullin	3.03
8	Barney Pelty	2.97
9	Chick Fraser	2.90
10	Red Donahue	2.81
11	Christy Mathewson	2.81
12	Doc White	2.81

Putouts

First Base
1	Jake Beckley	23709
2	Ed Konetchy	21361
3	Eddie Murray	21255
4	Cap Anson	20794
5	Charlie Grimm	20711
6	Stuffy McInnis	19962
7	Mickey Vernon	19808
8	Jake Daubert	19634
9	Lou Gehrig	19510
10	Joe Kuhel	19386

Second Base
1	Bid McPhee	6545
2	Eddie Collins	6526
3	Nellie Fox	6090
4	Joe Morgan	5742
5	Nap Lajoie	5496
6	Charlie Gehringer	5369
7	Bill Mazeroski	4974
8	Bobby Doerr	4928
9	Willie Randolph	4859
10	Billy Herman	4780

Shortstop
1	Rabbit Maranville	5139
2	Bill Dahlen	4850
3	Dave Bancroft	4623
4	Honus Wagner	4576
5	Tommy Corcoran	4550
6	Luis Aparicio	4548
7	Luke Appling	4398
8	Ozzie Smith	4249
9	Herman Long	4225
10	Bobby Wallace	4142

Third Base
1	Brooks Robinson	2697
2	Jimmy Collins	2372
3	Eddie Yost	2356
4	Lave Cross	2306
5	Pie Traynor	2289
6	Billy Nash	2219
7	Frank Baker	2154
8	Willie Kamm	2151
9	Eddie Mathews	2049
10	Willie Jones	2045

Outfield
1	Willie Mays	7095
2	Tris Speaker	6788
3	Max Carey	6363
4	Ty Cobb	6361
5	Richie Ashburn	6089
6	Rickey Henderson	5823
7	Hank Aaron	5539
8	Willie Davis	5449
9	Doc Cramer	5412
10	Brett Butler	5296
11	Andre Dawson	5158
12	Vada Pinson	5097
13	Willie Wilson	5060
14	Al Kaline	5035
15	Zack Wheat	4996
16	Chet Lemon	4993
17	Al Simmons	4988
18	Dave Winfield	4975
19	Amos Otis	4936
20	Paul Waner	4872

Catcher
1	Gary Carter	11785
2	Carlton Fisk	11369
3	Bob Boone	11260
4	Tony Pena	11212
5	Bill Freehan	9941
6	Jim Sundberg	9767
7	Lance Parrish	9647
8	Johnny Roseboro	9291
9	Johnny Bench	9249
10	Johnny Edwards	8925

Pitcher
1	Jack Morris	387
2	Phil Niekro	386
3	Fergie Jenkins	363
4	Greg Maddux	349
	Gaylord Perry	349
6	Don Sutton	334
7	Tony Mullane	328
	Rick Reuschel	328
	Tom Seaver	328
10	Jim Galvin	324

Putouts per Game

First Base
1	Jiggs Donahue	10.95
2	Joe Start	10.91
3	Frank Isbell	10.77
4	Tom Jones	10.53
5	Candy LaChance	10.48
6	George Stovall	10.45
7	George Kelly	10.37
8	Wally Pipp	10.33
9	Ed Konetchy	10.31
10	John Ganzel	10.24

Second Base
1	Joe Gerhardt	3.15
2	Bid McPhee	3.08
3	Fred Pfeffer	3.07
4	Fred Dunlap	3.03
5	Cub Stricker	3.02
6	Pop Smith	2.83
7	Jack Burdock	2.82
8	Jack Crooks	2.78
9	Lou Bierbauer	2.74
10	Jerry Priddy	2.74

Shortstop
1	Hughie Jennings	2.66
2	Dave Bancroft	2.47
3	Honus Wagner	2.43
4	Rabbit Maranville	2.39
5	Monte Cross	2.38
6	Heinie Wagner	2.38
7	George Davis	2.36
8	Herman Long	2.36
9	Heinie Sand	2.35
10	Bob Allen	2.32
11	Kid Elberfeld	2.32
12	Charley O'Leary	2.32

Third Base
1	Jerry Denny	1.61
2	Denny Lyons	1.55
3	Billy Nash	1.52
4	Tom Burns	1.49
5	Jimmy Austin	1.43
6	Bill Joyce	1.43
7	Billy Shindle	1.43
8	Charlie Irwin	1.42
9	Jimmy Collins	1.41
10	Frank Baker	1.40

Outfield
1	Taylor Douthit	3.01
2	Richie Ashburn	2.90
3	Johnny Mostil	2.83
4	Dom DiMaggio	2.82
5	Dwayne Murphy	2.82
6	Mike Kreevich	2.81
7	Jigger Statz	2.78
8	Sam Chapman	2.74
9	Sam West	2.74
10	Wally Judnich	2.71
11	Fred Schulte	2.70
12	Lloyd Waner	2.68
13	Billy North	2.65
14	Garry Maddox	2.64
15	Devon White	2.64
16	Joe DiMaggio	2.63
17	Vince DiMaggio	2.63
18	Terry Moore	2.63
19	Robin Yount	2.63
20	Gary Pettis	2.62

Catcher
1	Mike Piazza	6.88
2	Dan Wilson	6.78
3	Brad Ausmus	6.49
4	Johnny Edwards	6.42
5	Johnny Roseboro	6.30
6	Bill Freehan	6.29
7	Joe Azcue	6.14
8	Scott Servais	6.08
9	Darrin Fletcher	6.05
10	Jerry Grote	6.00

Pitcher
1	Kevin Brown	0.87
2	Greg Maddux	0.87
3	Dave Foutz	0.78
4	Nick Altrock	0.77
5	Chick Fraser	0.73
6	Al Spalding	0.73
7	Mike Boddicker	0.72
8	Carl Morton	0.72
9	Jack Morris	0.71
10	Dan Petry	0.69

Assists

First Base
1	Eddie Murray	1865
2	Keith Hernandez	1682
3	George Sisler	1529
4	Mickey Vernon	1448
5	Fred Tenney	1363
6	Wally Joyner	1356
7	Mark Grace	1354
8	Bill Buckner	1351
	Chris Chambliss	1351
10	Norm Cash	1317

Second Base
1	Eddie Collins	7630
2	Charlie Gehringer	7068
3	Joe Morgan	6967
4	Bid McPhee	6905
5	Bill Mazeroski	6685
6	Lou Whitaker	6653
7	Nellie Fox	6373
8	Ryne Sandberg	6363
9	Willie Randolph	6336
10	Nap Lajoie	6262

Shortstop
1	Ozzie Smith	8375
2	Luis Aparicio	8016
3	Bill Dahlen	7500
4	Rabbit Maranville	7354
5	Luke Appling	7218
6	Tommy Corcoran	7106
7	Cal Ripken	6977
8	Larry Bowa	6857
9	Dave Concepcion	6594
10	Dave Bancroft	6561

Third Base
1	Brooks Robinson	6205
2	Graig Nettles	5279
3	Mike Schmidt	5045
4	Buddy Bell	4925
5	Ron Santo	4581
6	Gary Gaetti	4391
7	Eddie Mathews	4322
8	Aurelio Rodriguez	4150
9	Wade Boggs	4146
10	Ron Cey	4018

Outfield
1	Tris Speaker	449
2	Ty Cobb	392
3	Jimmy Ryan	375
4	Tom Brown	348
	George Van Haltren	348
6	Harry Hooper	344
7	Max Carey	339
8	Jimmy Sheckard	307
9	Clyde Milan	294
10	Orator Shaffer	289
11	King Kelly	285
12	Sam Thompson	283
13	Sam Rice	278
14	Dummy Hoy	273
15	Jesse Burkett	270
16	Sam Crawford	268
	Tommy McCarthy	268
18	Roberto Clemente	266
19	Patsy Donovan	264
20	Willie Keeler	258

Catcher
1	Deacon McGuire	1859
2	Ray Schalk	1811
3	Steve O'Neill	1698
4	Red Dooin	1590
5	Chief Zimmer	1580
6	Johnny Kling	1552
7	Ivey Wingo	1487
8	Wilbert Robinson	1454
9	Bill Bergen	1444
10	Wally Schang	1420

Pitcher
1	Cy Young	2014
2	Christy Mathewson	1503
3	Pete Alexander	1419
4	Jim Galvin	1382
5	Walter Johnson	1351
6	Burleigh Grimes	1252
7	George Mullin	1244
8	Jack Quinn	1240
9	Ed Walsh	1208
10	Eppa Rixey	1195

Assists per Game

First Base
1	Jeff Bagwell	0.88
2	Darrell Evans	0.88
3	Bill Buckner	0.87
4	Buddy Hassett	0.87
5	Mark Grace	0.86
6	Eric Karros	0.85
7	Ferris Fain	0.84
8	Keith Hernandez	0.84
9	Sid Bream	0.83
10	Vic Power	0.83

Second Base
1	Hughie Critz	3.54
2	Frankie Frisch	3.42
3	Bill Regan	3.40
4	Ski Melillo	3.38
5	Jack Farrell	3.36
6	Joe Gerhardt	3.35
7	Lou Bierbauer	3.34
8	Glenn Hubbard	3.34
9	Fred Pfeffer	3.33
10	Danny Richardson	3.33

Shortstop
1	Germany Smith	3.70
2	Bob Allen	3.60
3	Art Fletcher	3.55
4	Bill Dahlen	3.52
5	Dave Bancroft	3.51
6	Hughie Jennings	3.51
7	Bones Ely	3.50
8	Travis Jackson	3.50
9	George Davis	3.49
10	Jack Glasscock	3.46
11	Bobby Wallace	3.46

Third Base
1	Lee Tannehill	2.44
2	Ned Williamson	2.41
3	Mike Schmidt	2.29
4	Bill Melton	2.27
5	Billy Shindle	2.27
6	Buddy Bell	2.26
7	Arlie Latham	2.26
8	Clete Boyer	2.24
9	Babe Pinelli	2.24
10	Tommy Leach	2.23

Outfield
1	King Kelly	0.39
2	Orator Shaffer	0.35
3	Hugh Nicol	0.28
4	Jim Fogarty	0.25
5	Paul Radford	0.25
6	Dick Johnston	0.24
7	Tommy McCarthy	0.23
8	Pop Corkhill	0.22
9	Jack Manning	0.22
10	Jack McGeachy	0.22
11	Jimmy Wolf	0.22
12	Ed Swartwood	0.21
13	Sam Thompson	0.21
14	Farmer Weaver	0.21
15	Ed Andrews	0.20
16	Tom Brown	0.20
17	Pete Hotaling	0.20
18	Jimmy Ryan	0.20
19	George Van Haltren	0.20
20	Curt Welch	0.20

Catcher
1	Pop Snyder	1.75
2	Buck Ewing	1.60
3	Bill Bergen	1.54
4	Doc Bushong	1.51
5	Silver Flint	1.45
6	Pat Moran	1.43
7	Duke Farrell	1.42
8	Connie Mack	1.42
9	Jeff Sweeney	1.39
10	Lou Criger	1.37

Pitcher
1	Addie Joss	2.96
2	Harry Howell	2.84
3	Ed Walsh	2.81
4	Nick Altrock	2.80
5	Willie Sudhoff	2.75
6	Nixey Callahan	2.60
7	George Mullin	2.56
8	Ed Willett	2.54
9	Barney Pelty	2.48
10	Red Donahue	2.47

Double Plays

First Base
1	Mickey Vernon	2044
2	Eddie Murray	2033
3	Joe Kuhel	1769
4	Charlie Grimm	1733
5	Chris Chambliss	1687
6	Keith Hernandez	1654
7	Gil Hodges	1614
8	Lou Gehrig	1575
9	Jim Bottomley	1562
10	Jimmie Foxx	1528

Second Base
1	Bill Mazeroski	1706
2	Nellie Fox	1619
3	Willie Randolph	1547
4	Lou Whitaker	1527
5	Bobby Doerr	1507
6	Joe Morgan	1505
7	Charlie Gehringer	1444
8	Frank White	1382
9	Red Schoendienst	1368
10	Bobby Grich	1302

Shortstop
1	Ozzie Smith	1590
2	Cal Ripken	1565
3	Luis Aparicio	1553
4	Luke Appling	1424
5	Alan Trammell	1307
6	Roy McMillan	1304
7	Dave Concepcion	1290
8	Larry Bowa	1265
9	Pee Wee Reese	1246
10	Dick Groat	1237

Third Base
1	Brooks Robinson	618
2	Graig Nettles	470
3	Gary Gaetti	452
4	Mike Schmidt	450
5	Buddy Bell	430
6	Wade Boggs	409
7	Aurelio Rodriguez	408
8	Ron Santo	395
9	Eddie Mathews	369
10	Ken Boyer	355

Outfield
1	Tris Speaker	139
2	Ty Cobb	107
3	Max Carey	86
4	Tom Brown	85
5	Harry Hooper	81
6	Jimmy Sheckard	80
7	Mike Griffin	75
8	Dummy Hoy	72
9	Jimmy Ryan	71
10	Fielder Jones	70
11	Patsy Donovan	69
12	Sam Rice	67
13	George Van Haltren	64
14	Jesse Burkett	62
15	Sam Thompson	61
16	Willie Keeler	60
	Willie Mays	60
	Tommy McCarthy	60
	Mel Ott	60
20	Sam Crawford	59

Catcher
1	Ray Schalk	226
2	Steve O'Neill	193
3	Yogi Berra	175
4	Gabby Hartnett	163
5	Tony Pena	156
6	Bob Boone	154
7	Jimmie Wilson	153
8	Gary Carter	149
	Wally Schang	149
10	Carlton Fisk	147

Pitcher
1	Phil Niekro	83
2	Warren Spahn	82
3	Freddie Fitzsimmons	79
4	Bob Lemon	78
5	Bucky Walters	76
6	Burleigh Grimes	74
7	Walter Johnson	72
8	Tommy John	69
9	Jim Kaat	65
10	Dizzy Trout	63

Fielding Runs

1	Nap Lajoie	367
2	Bill Mazeroski	362
3	Bill Dahlen	348
4	Bid McPhee	313
5	Fred Pfeffer	266
6	Mike Schmidt	265
7	George Davis	249
8	Tris Speaker	248
9	Ozzie Smith	243
10	Jack Glasscock	240
11	Clete Boyer	233
12	Glenn Hubbard	229
13	Richie Ashburn	227
14	Bobby Wallace	211
15	Joe Tinker	208
16	Dave Bancroft	198
	Max Carey	198
18	Buddy Bell	191
19	Aurelio Rodriguez	183
20	Bobby Doerr	181
	Terry Pendleton	181
22	Willie Mays	180
23	Dick Bartell	178
	Mickey Doolan	178
25	Roberto Clemente	175
26	Joe Gerhardt	173
27	George McBride	169
28	Mark Belanger	167
29	Darrell Evans	165
	Lee Tannehill	165
31	Rickey Henderson	164
32	Art Fletcher	162
33	Dal Maxvill	160
34	Germany Smith	157
35	Danny Richardson	156
36	Barry Bonds	155
	Rabbit Maranville	155
38	Ski Melillo	151
	Brooks Robinson	151
40	Lou Bierbauer	150
	Hughie Jennings	150
	Bobby Knoop	150
43	Frankie Frisch	149
	Jim Hegan	149
	Carl Yastrzemski	149
46	Keith Hernandez	148
	Pop Snyder	148
48	Rafael Belliard	146
	Lave Cross	146
50	Garry Maddox	142
51	Billy Jurges	140
52	Bill Holbert	139
53	Ron Santo	138
54	Jimmy Collins	137
	Willie Davis	137
	Fred Dunlap	137
	Kirby Puckett	137
	Bobby Wine	137
59	Lou Boudreau	134
60	John Ward	133
61	Hal Lanier	132
	Graig Nettles	132
63	Bill Killefer	131
64	Lou Criger	130
65	Manny Trillo	129
66	Mick Kelleher	128
67	Bill Buckner	127
68	Gene Alley	125
69	Fred Tenney	124
70	Andre Dawson	123
	Vic Power	123
72	Tony Pena	121
	Al Weis	121
	Devon White	121
75	Bill Bergen	119
76	Chet Lemon	116
	Harold Reynolds	116
78	Everett Scott	115
79	Jesse Barfield	114
	Curt Flood	114
	Tommy Leach	114
82	Johnny Callison	113
	Hank DeBerry	113
	Hardy Richardson	113
85	Hughie Critz	111
	Jose Cruz	111
	Hobe Ferris	111
	Rey Sanchez	111
89	Brett Butler	110
	Jimmy Wynn	110
91	Jerry Denny	109
92	Alvaro Espinoza	108
93	Mike Gallego	107
	Joe Sewell	107
	Curt Welch	107
96	Tommy Corcoran	106
97	Tony Gwynn	105
	Johnny Logan	105
99	5 players tied	103

Fielding Runs (by position)

First Base
1	Keith Hernandez	150
2	Fred Tenney	129
3	Vic Power	124
4	Bill Buckner	121
5	George Sisler	89
6	Mark Grace	84
7	Sid Bream	76
	Darrell Evans	76
9	Jeff Bagwell	71
10	Wally Joyner	67
	Bill Terry	67

Second Base
1	Nap Lajoie	369
2	Bill Mazeroski	363
3	Bid McPhee	314
4	Fred Pfeffer	257
5	Glenn Hubbard	229
6	Bobby Doerr	180
7	Joe Gerhardt	160
8	Lou Bierbauer	153
9	Bobby Knoop	150
10	Ski Melillo	148

Shortstop
1	Bill Dahlen	302
2	Jack Glasscock	243
3	Ozzie Smith	242
4	Joe Tinker	210
5	Dave Bancroft	200
6	George Davis	187
7	Rabbit Maranville	174
8	George McBride	172
9	Mickey Doolan	168
10	Mark Belanger	164

Third Base
1	Mike Schmidt	265
2	Clete Boyer	201
3	Buddy Bell	199
4	Aurelio Rodriguez	184
5	Terry Pendleton	181
6	Brooks Robinson	152
7	Jimmy Collins	136
	Graig Nettles	136
9	Ron Santo	135
10	Lave Cross	133

Outfield
1	Tris Speaker	248
2	Richie Ashburn	227
3	Max Carey	202
4	Willie Mays	184
5	Roberto Clemente	173
6	Rickey Henderson	164
7	Barry Bonds	155
8	Carl Yastrzemski	143
9	Garry Maddox	142
10	Kirby Puckett	139
11	Willie Davis	137
12	Andre Dawson	124
13	Chet Lemon	119
	Devon White	119
15	Jimmy Wynn	118
16	Curt Flood	116
17	Johnny Callison	114
18	Jesse Barfield	112
19	Jose Cruz	111
20	Jim Fogarty	110

Catcher
1	Pop Snyder	151
2	Jim Hegan	149
3	Lou Criger	133
4	Bill Killefer	131
5	Tony Pena	120
6	Bill Bergen	119
7	Charlie O'Brien	103
	Chief Zimmer	103
9	Ossee Schreckengost	98
	Jim Sundberg	98

Pitcher
1	Ed Walsh	84
2	Carl Mays	74
3	Christy Mathewson	69
4	Greg Maddux	66
5	Freddie Fitzsimmons	61
6	Bob Lemon	59
7	Burleigh Grimes	58
8	Tommy John	56
9	Harry Gumbert	51
10	Harry Howell	50

Fielding Wins

1	Bill Mazeroski	37.7
2	Nap Lajoie	37.7
3	Bill Dahlen	33.1
4	Mike Schmidt	27.7
5	Bid McPhee	27.2
6	Tris Speaker	25.3
7	Ozzie Smith	25.3
8	Clete Boyer	24.2
9	Glenn Hubbard	23.8
10	George Davis	23.4
11	Fred Pfeffer	23.2
12	Richie Ashburn	22.7
13	Joe Tinker	21.9
14	Bobby Wallace	21.3
15	Jack Glasscock	21.3
16	Max Carey	20.3
17	Dave Bancroft	20.2
18	Buddy Bell	19.6
19	Aurelio Rodriguez	19.1
20	Mickey Doolan	19.0
21	Willie Mays	18.6
22	Terry Pendleton	18.5
23	Roberto Clemente	18.2
24	George McBride	18.2
25	Lee Tannehill	17.9
26	Bobby Doerr	17.8
27	Dick Bartell	17.5
28	Mark Belanger	17.5
29	Art Fletcher	17.3
30	Darrell Evans	17.0
31	Dal Maxvill	16.9
32	Rickey Henderson	16.2
33	Bobby Knoop	16.2
34	Brooks Robinson	15.9
35	Barry Bonds	15.8
36	Rabbit Maranville	15.7
37	Carl Yastrzemski	15.5
38	Joe Gerhardt	15.5
39	Keith Hernandez	15.5
40	Rafael Belliard	15.0
41	Jim Hegan	14.9
42	Garry Maddox	14.9
43	Frankie Frisch	14.6
44	Ron Santo	14.5
45	Bobby Wine	14.4
46	Willie Davis	14.4
47	Bill Killefer	14.2
48	Billy Jurges	14.2
49	Ski Melillo	14.1
50	Hal Lanier	14.1
51	Graig Nettles	13.7
52	Danny Richardson	13.6
53	Kirby Puckett	13.5
54	Germany Smith	13.5
55	Lou Boudreau	13.5
56	Manny Trillo	13.5
57	Lave Cross	13.4
58	Mick Kelleher	13.4
59	Gene Alley	13.3
60	Jimmy Collins	13.2
61	Pop Snyder	13.2
62	Hughie Jennings	13.2
63	Lou Criger	13.2
64	Bill Buckner	13.1
65	Al Weis	12.9
66	Andre Dawson	12.7
67	Lou Bierbauer	12.7
68	Bill Bergen	12.6
69	Vic Power	12.6
70	Bill Holbert	12.5
71	Fred Dunlap	12.4
72	Tony Pena	12.4
73	Fred Tenney	12.3
74	Curt Flood	11.9
75	Tommy Leach	11.9
76	Devon White	11.9
77	Johnny Callison	11.9
78	Hobe Ferris	11.8
79	John Ward	11.7
80	Everett Scott	11.7
81	Chet Lemon	11.6
82	Jimmy Wynn	11.6
83	Jose Cruz	11.6
84	Harold Reynolds	11.5
85	Jesse Barfield	11.4
86	Brett Butler	11.2
87	Rey Sanchez	11.0
88	Hank DeBerry	10.9
89	Tony Gwynn	10.8
90	Hughie Critz	10.7
91	Al Kaline	10.7
92	Omar Moreno	10.7
93	Lenny Dykstra	10.6
94	Johnny Logan	10.6
95	Mike Gallego	10.6
96	Alvaro Espinoza	10.6
97	Hank Aaron	10.5
98	Honus Wagner	10.4
99	Eddie Miller	10.4
100	Dwayne Murphy	10.2

Total Player Rating

Rank	Player	Rating
1	Babe Ruth	107.7
2	Nap Lajoie	94.1
3	Willie Mays	92.2
4	Ty Cobb	91.0
5	Hank Aaron	89.8
6	Tris Speaker	86.5
7	Ted Williams	85.7
8	Rogers Hornsby	81.2
9	Honus Wagner	81.1
10	Rickey Henderson	79.7
11	Barry Bonds	79.0
12	Mike Schmidt	78.4
13	Mickey Mantle	76.1
14	Stan Musial	70.5
15	Eddie Collins	69.8
16	Frank Robinson	69.0
17	Lou Gehrig	65.7
18	Mel Ott	62.7
19	Joe Morgan	56.3
20	Jimmie Foxx	54.0
21	Tim Raines	52.6
22	Eddie Mathews	51.6
23	Bill Dahlen	51.3
24	George Davis	50.9
25	Tony Gwynn	48.8
26	Joe DiMaggio	46.9
27	Carl Yastrzemski	45.5
28	Al Kaline	44.6
29	Charlie Gehringer	44.4
30	Ed Delahanty	44.3
31	Wade Boggs	44.1
32	Bobby Grich	44.0
33	Robin Yount	43.1
34	Ozzie Smith	43.0
35	Roberto Clemente	42.9
36	Reggie Jackson	42.8
37	Roger Connor	42.7
38	Barry Larkin	41.6
39	Lou Boudreau	41.3
40	Dan Brouthers	41.2
41	Luke Appling	40.7
42	Gabby Hartnett	40.1
	Bid McPhee	40.1
44	Cal Ripken	39.9
45	Ken Griffey Jr.	39.5
	Ron Santo	39.5
47	Joe Cronin	39.4
48	Arky Vaughan	39.2
49	George Brett	39.0
	Bobby Doerr	39.0
	Frankie Frisch	39.0
52	Dave Winfield	38.6
53	Joe Jackson	37.5
54	Bobby Wallace	36.8
55	Willie McCovey	36.5
56	Bill Mazeroski	36.3
57	Yogi Berra	36.2
	Johnny Mize	36.2
59	Jack Glasscock	36.1
	Paul Waner	36.1
61	Jeff Bagwell	36.0
62	Bob Johnson	35.6
63	Frank Thomas	35.5
64	Bill Dickey	35.4
65	Dick Allen	35.3
66	Dave Bancroft	35.2
67	Ryne Sandberg	35.1
68	Reggie Smith	35.0
69	Darrell Evans	34.7
70	Joe Sewell	34.5
71	Keith Hernandez	34.4
72	Eddie Murray	34.1
73	Paul Molitor	33.9
74	Frank Baker	33.8
75	Jimmy Wynn	33.2
76	Willie Stargell	32.8
77	Harry Heilmann	32.3
78	Jackie Robinson	31.8
79	Rod Carew	31.7
	Billy Herman	31.7
81	Craig Biggio	31.5
82	Mickey Cochrane	31.4
83	Albert Belle	31.3
84	Jack Clark	31.1
	Billy Williams	31.1
86	Cap Anson	31.0
87	Mark McGwire	30.5
88	Sam Crawford	30.4
	Dwight Evans	30.4
90	Richie Ashburn	30.2
91	Cupid Childs	30.0
	Hank Greenberg	30.0
93	Andre Dawson	29.9
94	Gary Carter	29.6
95	Bobby Bonds	29.5
	Buck Ewing	29.5
	Mike Piazza	29.5
98	Kirby Puckett	29.1
99	Ralph Kiner	28.9
100	Pete Browning	28.8
	Elmer Flick	28.8
102	Fred Clarke	28.7
	Jose Cruz	28.7
104	Jesse Burkett	28.5
105	Sam Thompson	28.4
106	Cesar Cedeno	28.3
107	Joe Gordon	28.2
108	Dick Bartell	27.9
109	Edgar Martinez	27.8
110	Rusty Staub	27.6
111	Norm Cash	27.5
112	Fred Dunlap	27.4
113	Hardy Richardson	27.3
114	Heinie Groh	27.2
	Stan Hack	27.2
	Jim Rice	27.2
117	Joe Medwick	27.1
118	Billy Hamilton	26.5
	Sherry Magee	26.5
	Darryl Strawberry	26.5
121	Harmon Killebrew	26.4
122	Hughie Jennings	26.2
123	Goose Goslin	26.0
	Minnie Minoso	26.0
125	Ernie Banks	25.9
126	Art Fletcher	25.8
127	Lenny Dykstra	25.6
	Al Simmons	25.6
129	Rocky Colavito	25.2
130	Tony Oliva	24.9
	Bill Terry	24.9
132	King Kelly	24.8
	Lou Whitaker	24.8
134	Roberto Alomar	24.6
135	Eric Davis	24.5
136	Jose Canseco	24.4
137	Johnny Bench	24.3
	Zack Wheat	24.3
139	Carlton Fisk	24.0
	Travis Jackson	24.0
141	Jack Fournier	23.9
142	Charlie Keller	23.5
143	Jimmy Collins	23.1
	Willie Randolph	23.1
	Joe Tinker	23.1
146	Jake Beckley	23.0
	Dave Parker	23.0
148	Buddy Bell	22.9
149	Roy Thomas	22.8
150	Harland Clift	22.7
	George Sisler	22.7
152	Max Carey	22.6
153	George Foster	22.3
	Ed Konetchy	22.3
	Chet Lemon	22.3
	Fred Lynn	22.3
	Duke Snider	22.3
158	Wally Berger	22.2
	Larry Walker	22.2
160	Brett Butler	22.0
161	Ron Cey	21.9
	Rafael Palmeiro	21.9
163	Fred Pfeffer	21.8
164	Roy Campanella	21.6
	Alan Trammell	21.6
166	Harry Stovey	21.5
167	Chuck Klein	21.4
168	Frank Howard	21.3
	Graig Nettles	21.3
170	Larry Doby	21.2
	Paul O'Neill	21.2
172	Roy White	21.1
173	Fred Tenney	21.0
174	Ken Singleton	20.9
175	Charley Jones	20.7
	Pie Traynor	20.7
177	Art Devlin	20.6
	Jim Fregosi	20.6
179	Frank Chance	20.5
	Mike Griffin	20.5
181	Del Pratt	20.4
182	Andy Van Slyke	20.3
183	Will Clark	20.2
	Glenn Hubbard	20.2
	Joe Kelley	20.2
	Ray Lankford	20.2
	Gary Sheffield	20.2
188	Kevin Mitchell	20.1
	Tim Salmon	20.1
190	Pete Rose	20.0
191	Denny Lyons	19.8
	Brooks Robinson	19.8
193	Roger Bresnahan	19.7
194	Vern Stephens	19.6
	Joe Torre	19.6
196	Jimmy Sheckard	19.3
197	Amos Otis	19.3
	Matt Williams	19.3
199	Charlie Bennett	19.2
	Dale Murphy	19.2
201	Bill Nicholson	19.0
202	Gavvy Cravath	18.9
	Bill Joyce	18.9
204	Bob Elliott	18.8
205	Ken Boyer	18.6
	Brian Downing	18.6
207	Eddie Stanky	18.4
208	Roy Cullenbine	18.1
	Wally Schang	18.1
210	Gene Alley	18.0
	Miller Huggins	18.0
212	Rico Carty	17.9
213	Harold Baines	17.8
	Ferris Fain	17.8
215	Kenny Lofton	17.7
216	Earl Averill	17.6
217	Jay Bell	17.4
	Tommy Leach	17.4
219	Babe Herman	17.3
	Johnny Logan	17.3
	Ernie Lombardi	17.3
	Ken Williams	17.3
223	Bobby Bonilla	17.2
	Tony Fernandez	17.2
	Fred McGriff	17.2
226	Paul Hines	17.0
227	Tony Lazzeri	16.9
228	Gil McDougald	16.8
	Ted Simmons	16.8
230	Ken Caminiti	16.7
	Orlando Cepeda	16.7
	Pedro Guerrero	16.7
233	David Justice	16.6
234	Chili Davis	16.5
235	Jesse Barfield	16.4
	Jeff Heath	16.4
	Dwayne Murphy	16.4
238	George Gore	16.3
	Enos Slaughter	16.3
240	Kirk Gibson	16.1
	Jim O'Rourke	16.1
	John Valentin	16.1
243	John McGraw	16.0
	Jimmy Williams	16.0
245	Bernie Williams	15.9
246	Kiki Cuyler	15.8
	Phil Rizzuto	15.8
	Chief Zimmer	15.8
249	Mike Hargrove	15.7
250	Davey Johnson	15.6
	Jocko Milligan	15.6
	Hack Wilson	15.6
253	Danny Tartabull	15.5
254	Ray Chapman	15.4
255	Mark Grace	15.3
	Gene Tenace	15.3
257	Thurman Munson	15.2
258	Sid Gordon	15.1
259	Mark Belanger	15.0
	Bobby Knoop	15.0
261	Henry Larkin	14.9
	Boog Powell	14.9
263	Benny Kauff	14.8
	Mike Scioscia	14.8
	Bobby Veach	14.8
266	Sixto Lezcano	14.7
267	Lave Cross	14.6
	Duke Farrell	14.6
	Augie Galan	14.6
	Greg Luzinski	14.6
	Pee Wee Reese	14.6
272	Tommy Henrich	14.5
	Kevin McReynolds	14.5
274	Robin Ventura	14.4
275	Bob Allison	14.3
276	Ron Hansen	14.2
277	Johnny Callison	14.1
278	Ben Chapman	14.0
	Juan Gonzalez	14.0
280	Roy Smalley	13.8
281	Gil Hodges	13.7
282	Jay Buhner	13.6
	Willie Kamm	13.6
	Kip Selbach	13.6
285	Fred Carroll	13.5
	Tommy Holmes	13.5
	George Stone	13.5
	Richie Zisk	13.5
289	Chief Meyers	13.4
	Al Oliver	13.4
291	Jimmy Ryan	13.3
292	Bill Freehan	13.2
	John Olerud	13.2
	Dave Orr	13.2
	Roger Peckinpaugh	13.2
296	Doug DeCinces	13.1
	Edd Roush	13.1
	John Titus	13.1
299	Johnny Evers	12.9
	Bobby Murcer	12.9
	Mike Tiernan	12.9
302	Kal Daniels	12.8
	Red Smith	12.8
	Riggs Stephenson	12.8
305	Lou Brock	12.7
	Jack Clements	12.7
	Roy Sievers	12.7
308	Clete Boyer	12.6
	Dolph Camilli	12.6
	Kid Elberfeld	12.6
	Chick Hafey	12.6
	Harry Hooper	12.6
	Deacon McGuire	12.6
	Raul Mondesi	12.6
	Billy Nash	12.6
	Manny Ramirez	12.6
317	Rabbit Maranville	12.5
	Alex Rodriguez	12.5
319	Luis Aparicio	12.4
	Johnny Pesky	12.4
	Al Rosen	12.4
322	Bernard Gilkey	12.3
	Ken Griffey Sr.	12.3
324	Lance Parrish	12.1
	Darrell Porter	12.1
	Jim Thome	12.1
	Bob Watson	12.1
328	Gary Matthews	12.0
329	Nellie Fox	11.9
	Lonny Frey	11.9
	Ossee Schreckengost	11.9
	Robby Thompson	11.9
333	Rick Burleson	11.8
	Jake Daubert	11.8
335	Lou Criger	11.7
	Julio Franco	11.7
	Jim Gentile	11.7
	Roger Maris	11.7
	Hal McRae	11.7
	Jerry Priddy	11.7
	Andy Thornton	11.7
342	Earle Combs	11.6
	Ken Keltner	11.6
	Lefty O'Doul	11.6
	Lonnie Smith	11.6
	Stan Spence	11.6
347	Wally Joyner	11.5
	Johnny Kling	11.5
349	Dan McGann	11.4
	Orator Shaffer	11.4
351	Buck Herzog	11.3
	Don Mattingly	11.3
	Andy Seminick	11.3
	Ed Swartwood	11.3
355	Toby Harrah	11.2
	Danny Murphy	11.2
357	Tom Haller	11.1
	George Van Haltren	11.1
359	Ron Gant	11.0
	Freddie Lindstrom	11.0
	Hank Sauer	11.0
	Sammy Sosa	11.0
363	Don Baylor	10.9
	Harry Davis	10.9
	Monte Irvin	10.9
	Ben Oglivie	10.9
367	Earl Battey	10.8
	Tony Cuccinello	10.8
	Willie Davis	10.8
	Dom DiMaggio	10.8
	Mike Greenwell	10.8
	Joe Harris	10.8
	Jackie Jensen	10.8
	John Kruk	10.8
	Ross Youngs	10.8
376	Tom Daly	10.7
	Curt Welch	10.7
378	Mike Donlin	10.6
	Red Schoendienst	10.6
	Dixie Walker	10.6
	Deacon White	10.6
382	Moises Alou	10.5
	Billy Jurges	10.5
	Ed McFarland	10.5
	Reggie Sanders	10.5
	Maury Wills	10.5
387	Willie Keeler	10.4
	Tip O'Neill	10.4
	Cy Seymour	10.4
390	Whitey Kurowski	10.3
	Rico Petrocelli	10.3
	Tony Phillips	10.3
393	Bill Melton	10.2
	Buddy Myer	10.2
	Cecil Travis	10.2
	Jimmy Wolf	10.2
	Rudy York	10.2
398	Jack Crooks	10.1
	Rick Ferrell	10.1
400	Larry Hisle	10.0

Total Player Rating		Total Player Rating (alpha.)		Total Player Rating (alpha.)		Total Player Rating (alpha.)	
	Ned Williamson	10.0	Hank Aaron	89.8	Joe Cronin	39.4	Topsy Hartsel	8.1
402	Jim Edmonds	9.9	Joe Adcock	7.3	Jack Crooks	10.1	Jeff Heath	16.4
	Charlie Hickman	9.9	Dick Allen	35.3	Lave Cross	14.6	Harry Heilmann	32.3
	Tony Perez	9.9	Bob Allen	7.8	Jose Cruz	28.7	Solly Hemus	7.7
405	Jerry Denny	9.8	Gene Alley	18.0	Tony Cuccinello	10.8	Rickey Henderson	79.7
	Doug Rader	9.8	Bob Allison	14.3	Roy Cullenbine	18.1	Tommy Henrich	14.5
407	Johnny Romano	9.7	Roberto Alomar	24.6	Kiki Cuyler	15.8	Babe Herman	17.3
408	Luis Gonzalez	9.6	Moises Alou	10.5	Bill Dahlen	51.3	Billy Herman	31.7
	Ivan Rodriguez	9.6	Cap Anson	31.0	Tom Daly	10.7	Keith Hernandez	34.4
410	Oscar Gamble	9.5	Luis Aparicio	12.4	Kal Daniels	12.8	Buck Herzog	11.3
	Elmer Smith	9.5	Luke Appling	40.7	Jake Daubert	11.8	Charlie Hickman	9.9
	Heinie Zimmerman	9.5	Richie Ashburn	30.2	Darren Daulton	7.3	Paul Hines	17.0
413	John Farrell	9.4	Earl Averill	17.6	Chili Davis	16.5	Larry Hisle	10.0
	Vic Wertz	9.4	Carlos Baerga	7.9	Eric Davis	24.5	Gil Hodges	13.7
415	Oyster Burns	9.3	Jeff Bagwell	36.0	George Davis	50.9	Chris Hoiles	8.6
	Walker Cooper	9.3	Harold Baines	17.8	Harry Davis	10.9	Tommy Holmes	13.5
	Kent Hrbek	9.3	Frank Baker	33.8	Willie Davis	10.8	Harry Hooper	12.6
	Bump Wills	9.3	Dusty Baker	7.5	Andre Dawson	29.9	Rogers Hornsby	81.2
419	Don Buford	9.2	Dave Bancroft	35.2	Hank DeBerry	8.1	Frank Howard	21.3
	Dave Concepcion	9.2	Sal Bando	8.4	Doug DeCinces	13.1	Kent Hrbek	9.3
	Jimmy Dykes	9.2	Ernie Banks	25.9	Ed Delahanty	44.3	Glenn Hubbard	20.2
	Hank Gowdy	9.2	Jesse Barfield	16.4	Jerry Denny	9.8	Miller Huggins	18.0
	Sherm Lollar	9.2	Jimmy Barrett	7.8	Art Devlin	20.6	Monte Irvin	10.9
	Wes Westrum	9.2	Dick Bartell	27.9	Bill Dickey	35.4	Joe Jackson	37.5
425	Bill Lange	9.1	Johnny Bassler	7.8	Dom DiMaggio	10.8	Reggie Jackson	42.8
	Sam Rice	9.1	Johnny Bates	7.3	Joe DiMaggio	46.9	Travis Jackson	24.0
427	Bill Bradley	9.0	Earl Battey	10.8	Larry Doby	21.2	Hughie Jennings	26.2
	Javy Lopez	9.0	Don Baylor	10.9	Bobby Doerr	39.0	Jackie Jensen	10.8
	Claude Ritchey	9.0	Jake Beckley	23.0	Mike Donlin	10.6	Cliff Johnson	7.5
	Devon White	9.0	Mark Belanger	15.0	Brian Downing	18.6	Davey Johnson	15.6
431	Del Ennis	8.9	Buddy Bell	22.9	Fred Dunlap	27.4	Bob Johnson	35.6
	Travis Fryman	8.9	Jay Bell	17.4	Jimmy Dykes	9.2	Charley Jones	20.7
	Pinky May	8.9	Albert Belle	31.3	Lenny Dykstra	25.6	Eddie Joost	8.4
	Mo Vaughn	8.9	Johnny Bench	24.3	Jim Edmonds	9.9	Bill Joyce	18.9
435	Garry Maddox	8.8	Charlie Bennett	19.2	Kid Elberfeld	12.6	Wally Joyner	11.5
	Marty McManus	8.8	Wally Berger	22.2	Bob Elliott	18.8	Billy Jurges	10.5
	Vada Pinson	8.8	Yogi Berra	36.2	Del Ennis	8.9	David Justice	16.6
	Gene Woodling	8.8	Craig Biggio	31.5	Darrell Evans	34.7	Al Kaline	44.6
439	Dal Maxvill	8.7	Wade Boggs	44.1	Dwight Evans	30.4	Willie Kamm	13.6
	Terry Pendleton	8.7	Barry Bonds	79.0	Johnny Evers	12.9	Benny Kauff	14.8
441	Bernie Carbo	8.6	Bobby Bonds	29.5	Buck Ewing	29.5	Willie Keeler	10.4
	Chris Hoiles	8.6	Bobby Bonilla	17.2	Ferris Fain	17.8	Charlie Keller	23.5
	Bob Nieman	8.6	Lou Boudreau	41.3	Duke Farrell	14.6	Joe Kelley	20.2
444	Happy Felsch	8.5	Clete Boyer	12.6	John Farrell	9.4	King Kelly	24.8
	Fred Luderus	8.5	Ken Boyer	18.6	Happy Felsch	8.5	Ken Keltner	11.6
	Rick Monday	8.5	Phil Bradley	7.3	Frank Fennelly	7.8	Steve Kemp	8.3
447	Sal Bando	8.4	Bill Bradley	9.0	Tony Fernandez	17.2	Jeff Kent	8.3
	Bert Campaneris	8.4	Roger Bresnahan	19.7	Rick Ferrell	10.1	Harmon Killebrew	26.4
	Jeff Cirillo	8.4	George Brett	39.0	Steve Finley	7.8	Ralph Kiner	28.9
	Eddie Joost	8.4	Lou Brock	12.7	Carlton Fisk	24.0	Chuck Klein	21.4
451	Steve Kemp	8.3	Dan Brouthers	41.2	Art Fletcher	25.8	Johnny Kling	11.5
	Jeff Kent	8.3	Pete Browning	28.8	Elbie Fletcher	7.6	Chuck Knoblauch	7.8
453	Del Crandall	8.2	Don Buford	9.2	Elmer Flick	28.8	Bobby Knoop	15.0
	George Selkirk	8.2	Jay Buhner	13.6	George Foster	22.3	Ed Konetchy	22.3
	Snuffy Stirnweiss	8.2	Jesse Burkett	28.5	Jack Fournier	23.9	John Kruk	10.8
456	Hank DeBerry	8.1	Rick Burleson	11.8	Nellie Fox	11.9	Whitey Kurowski	10.3
	Topsy Hartsel	8.1	Oyster Burns	9.3	Jimmie Foxx	54.0	Nap Lajoie	94.1
	Jody Reed	8.1	Donie Bush	7.3	Julio Franco	11.7	Bill Lange	9.1
	Greg Vaughn	8.1	Brett Butler	22.0	Bill Freehan	13.2	Ray Lankford	20.2
	Pinky Whitney	8.1	Johnny Callison	14.1	Jim Fregosi	20.6	Barry Larkin	41.6
461	Carlos Baerga	7.9	Dolph Camilli	12.6	Lonny Frey	11.9	Henry Larkin	14.9
	Mike Mitchell	7.9	Ken Caminiti	16.7	Frankie Frisch	39.0	Tony Lazzeri	16.9
	Jim Sundberg	7.9	Roy Campanella	21.6	Travis Fryman	8.9	Tommy Leach	17.4
	Bill Sweeney	7.9	Bert Campaneris	8.4	Augie Galan	14.6	Chet Lemon	22.3
	Al Weis	7.9	Jose Canseco	24.4	Oscar Gamble	9.5	Sixto Lezcano	14.7
	Ernie Whitt	7.9	Bernie Carbo	8.6	Ron Gant	11.0	Freddie Lindstrom	11.0
467	Bob Allen	7.8	Rod Carew	31.7	Phil Garner	7.4	Kenny Lofton	17.7
	Jimmy Barrett	7.8	Max Carey	22.6	Lou Gehrig	65.7	Johnny Logan	17.3
	Johnny Bassler	7.8	Fred Carroll	13.5	Charlie Gehringer	44.4	Sherm Lollar	9.2
	Frank Fennelly	7.8	Gary Carter	29.6	Jim Gentile	11.7	Ernie Lombardi	17.3
	Steve Finley	7.8	Rico Carty	17.9	Kirk Gibson	16.1	Javy Lopez	9.0
	Chuck Knoblauch	7.8	Norm Cash	27.5	Bernard Gilkey	12.3	Fred Luderus	8.5
	John Ward	7.8	Cesar Cedeno	28.3	Jack Glasscock	36.1	Greg Luzinski	14.6
474	Solly Hemus	7.7	Orlando Cepeda	16.7	Juan Gonzalez	14.0	Fred Lynn	22.3
	Billy Werber	7.7	Ron Cey	21.9	Luis Gonzalez	9.6	Denny Lyons	19.8
476	Cecil Cooper	7.6	Frank Chance	20.5	Joe Gordon	28.2	Garry Maddox	8.8
	Elbie Fletcher	7.6	Ray Chapman	15.4	Sid Gordon	15.1	Sherry Magee	26.5
478	Dusty Baker	7.5	Ben Chapman	14.0	George Gore	16.3	Mickey Mantle	76.1
	Cliff Johnson	7.5	Cupid Childs	30.0	Goose Goslin	26.0	Rabbit Maranville	12.5
	Johnny Mostil	7.5	Jeff Cirillo	8.4	Hank Gowdy	9.2	Roger Maris	11.7
	Pop Snyder	7.5	Jack Clark	31.1	Mark Grace	15.3	Edgar Martinez	27.8
482	Phil Garner	7.4	Will Clark	20.2	Hank Greenberg	30.0	Eddie Mathews	51.6
	Harry Steinfeldt	7.4	Fred Clarke	28.7	Mike Greenwell	10.8	Gary Matthews	12.0
484	Joe Adcock	7.3	Roberto Clemente	42.9	Bobby Grich	44.0	Don Mattingly	11.3
	Johnny Bates	7.3	Jack Clements	12.7	Ken Griffey Jr.	39.5	Dal Maxvill	8.7
	Phil Bradley	7.3	Harlond Clift	22.7	Ken Griffey Sr.	12.3	Pinky May	8.9
	Donie Bush	7.3	Ty Cobb	91.0	Mike Griffin	20.5	Willie Mays	92.2
	Darren Daulton	7.3	Mickey Cochrane	31.4	Marquis Grissom	7.3	Bill Mazeroski	36.3
	Marquis Grissom	7.3	Rocky Colavito	25.2	Heinie Groh	27.2	Willie McCovey	36.5
	Ken McMullen	7.3	Eddie Collins	69.8	Pedro Guerrero	16.7	Gil McDougald	16.8
	Jim McTamany	7.3	Jimmy Collins	23.1	Tony Gwynn	48.8	Ed McFarland	10.5
	Danny Richardson	7.3	Earle Combs	11.6	Stan Hack	27.2	Dan McGann	11.4
	Socks Seybold	7.3	Dave Concepcion	9.2	Chick Hafey	12.6	John McGraw	16.0
494	Matty McIntyre	7.2	Roger Connor	42.7	Tom Haller	11.1	Fred McGriff	17.2
	Lee Tannehill	7.2	Cecil Cooper	7.6	Billy Hamilton	26.5	Deacon McGuire	12.6
496	7 players tied	7.1	Walker Cooper	9.3	Ron Hansen	14.2	Mark McGwire	30.5
			Del Crandall	8.2	Mike Hargrove	15.7	Matty McIntyre	7.2
			Gavvy Cravath	18.9	Toby Harrah	11.2	Marty McManus	8.8
			Sam Crawford	30.4	Joe Harris	10.8	Ken McMullen	7.3
			Lou Criger	11.7	Gabby Hartnett	40.1	Bid McPhee	40.1

Total Player Rating (alpha.)

Hal McRae	11.7
Kevin McReynolds	14.5
Jim McTamany	7.3
Joe Medwick	27.1
Bill Melton	10.2
Chief Meyers	13.4
Jocko Milligan	15.6
Minnie Minoso	26.0
Kevin Mitchell	20.1
Mike Mitchell	7.9
Johnny Mize	36.2
Paul Molitor	33.9
Rick Monday	8.5
Raul Mondesi	12.6
Joe Morgan	56.3
Johnny Mostil	7.5
Thurman Munson	15.2
Bobby Murcer	12.9
Dale Murphy	19.2
Danny Murphy	11.2
Dwayne Murphy	16.4
Eddie Murray	34.1
Stan Musial	70.5
Buddy Myer	10.2
Billy Nash	12.6
Graig Nettles	21.3
Bill Nicholson	19.0
Bob Nieman	8.6
Lefty O'Doul	11.6
Ben Oglivie	10.9
John Olerud	13.2
Tony Oliva	24.9
Al Oliver	13.4
Tip O'Neill	10.4
Paul O'Neill	21.2
Jim O'Rourke	16.1
Dave Orr	13.2
Amos Otis	19.3
Mel Ott	62.7
Rafael Palmeiro	21.9
Dave Parker	23.0
Lance Parrish	12.1
Roger Peckinpaugh	13.2
Terry Pendleton	8.7
Tony Perez	9.9
Johnny Pesky	12.4
Rico Petrocelli	10.3
Fred Pfeffer	21.8
Tony Phillips	10.3
Mike Piazza	29.5
Vada Pinson	8.8
Darrell Porter	12.1
Boog Powell	14.9
Del Pratt	20.4
Jerry Priddy	11.7
Kirby Puckett	29.1
Doug Rader	9.8
Tim Raines	52.6
Manny Ramirez	12.6
Willie Randolph	23.1
Jody Reed	8.1
Pee Wee Reese	14.6
Sam Rice	9.1
Jim Rice	27.2
Hardy Richardson	27.3
Danny Richardson	7.3
Cal Ripken	39.9
Claude Ritchey	9.0
Phil Rizzuto	15.8
Brooks Robinson	19.8
Frank Robinson	69.0
Jackie Robinson	31.8
Alex Rodriguez	12.5
Ivan Rodriguez	9.6
Johnny Romano	9.7
Pete Rose	20.0
Al Rosen	12.4
Edd Roush	13.1
Babe Ruth	107.7
Jimmy Ryan	13.3
Tim Salmon	20.1
Ryne Sandberg	35.1
Reggie Sanders	10.5
Ron Santo	39.5
Hank Sauer	11.0
Wally Schang	18.1
Mike Schmidt	78.4
Red Schoendienst	10.6
Ossee Schreckengost	11.9
Mike Scioscia	14.8
Kip Selbach	13.6
George Selkirk	8.2
Andy Seminick	11.3
Joe Sewell	34.5
Socks Seybold	7.3
Cy Seymour	10.4
Orator Shaffer	11.4
Jimmy Sheckard	19.5
Gary Sheffield	20.2
Roy Sievers	12.7

Total Player Rating (alpha.)

Al Simmons	25.6
Ted Simmons	16.8
Ken Singleton	20.9
George Sisler	22.7
Enos Slaughter	16.3
Roy Smalley	13.8
Reggie Smith	35.0
Elmer Smith	9.5
Red Smith	12.8
Lonnie Smith	11.6
Ozzie Smith	43.0
Duke Snider	22.3
Pop Snyder	7.5
Sammy Sosa	11.0
Tris Speaker	86.5
Stan Spence	11.6
Eddie Stanky	18.4
Willie Stargell	32.8
Rusty Staub	27.6
Harry Steinfeldt	7.4
Vern Stephens	19.6
Riggs Stephenson	12.8
Snuffy Stirnweiss	8.2
George Stone	13.5
Harry Stovey	21.5
Darryl Strawberry	26.5
Jim Sundberg	7.9
Ed Swartwood	11.3
Bill Sweeney	7.9
Lee Tannehill	7.2
Danny Tartabull	15.5
Gene Tenace	15.3
Fred Tenney	21.0
Bill Terry	24.9
Frank Thomas	35.5
Roy Thomas	22.8
Jim Thome	12.1
Robby Thompson	11.9
Sam Thompson	28.4
Andy Thornton	11.7
Mike Tiernan	12.9
Joe Tinker	23.1
John Titus	13.1
Joe Torre	19.6
Alan Trammell	21.6
Cecil Travis	10.2
Pie Traynor	20.7
John Valentin	16.1
George Van Haltren	11.1
Andy Van Slyke	20.3
Arky Vaughan	39.2
Greg Vaughn	8.1
Mo Vaughn	8.9
Bobby Veach	14.8
Robin Ventura	14.4
Honus Wagner	81.1
Dixie Walker	10.6
Larry Walker	22.2
Bobby Wallace	36.8
Paul Waner	36.1
John Ward	7.8
Bob Watson	12.1
Al Weis	7.9
Curt Welch	10.7
Billy Werber	7.7
Vic Wertz	9.4
Wes Westrum	9.2
Zack Wheat	24.3
Lou Whitaker	24.8
Devon White	9.0
Deacon White	10.6
Roy White	21.1
Pinky Whitney	8.1
Ernie Whitt	7.9
Bernie Williams	15.9
Billy Williams	31.1
Jimmy Williams	16.0
Ken Williams	17.3
Matt Williams	19.3
Ted Williams	85.7
Ned Williamson	10.0
Bump Wills	9.3
Maury Wills	10.5
Hack Wilson	15.6
Dave Winfield	38.6
Jimmy Wolf	10.2
Gene Woodling	8.8
Jimmy Wynn	33.2
Carl Yastrzemski	45.5
Rudy York	10.2
Ross Youngs	10.8
Robin Yount	43.1
Chief Zimmer	15.8
Heinie Zimmerman	9.5
Richie Zisk	13.5

Total Player Rating (by era)

1876-1892

1	Roger Connor	42.7
2	Dan Brouthers	41.2
3	Bid McPhee	40.1
4	Jack Glasscock	36.1
5	Cap Anson	31.0
6	Buck Ewing	29.5
7	Pete Browning	28.8
8	Sam Thompson	28.4
9	Fred Dunlap	27.4
10	Hardy Richardson	27.3
11	King Kelly	24.8
12	Fred Pfeffer	21.8
13	Harry Stovey	21.5
14	Charley Jones	20.7
15	Denny Lyons	19.8
16	Charlie Bennett	19.2
17	Paul Hines	17.0
18	George Gore	16.3
19	Jim O'Rourke	16.1
20	Jocko Milligan	15.6
21	Henry Larkin	14.9
22	Fred Carroll	13.5
23	Dave Orr	13.2
24	Jack Clements	12.7
25	Billy Nash	12.6

1893-1919

1	Nap Lajoie	94.1
2	Ty Cobb	91.0
3	Tris Speaker	86.5
4	Honus Wagner	81.1
5	Eddie Collins	69.8
6	Bill Dahlen	51.3
7	George Davis	50.9
8	Ed Delahanty	44.3
9	Joe Jackson	37.5
10	Bobby Wallace	36.8
11	Frank Baker	33.8
12	Sam Crawford	30.4
13	Cupid Childs	30.0
14	Elmer Flick	28.8
15	Fred Clarke	28.7
16	Jesse Burkett	28.5
17	Heinie Groh	27.2
18	Billy Hamilton	26.5
	Sherry Magee	26.5
20	Hughie Jennings	26.2
21	Art Fletcher	25.8
22	Zack Wheat	24.3
23	Jimmy Collins	23.1
	Joe Tinker	23.1
25	Jake Beckley	23.0

1920-1941

1	Babe Ruth	107.7
2	Rogers Hornsby	81.2
3	Lou Gehrig	65.7
4	Mel Ott	62.7
5	Jimmie Foxx	54.0
6	Charlie Gehringer	44.4
7	Luke Appling	40.7
8	Gabby Hartnett	40.1
9	Joe Cronin	39.4
10	Arky Vaughan	39.2
11	Frankie Frisch	39.0
12	Paul Waner	36.1
13	Bob Johnson	35.6
14	Bill Dickey	35.4
15	Dave Bancroft	35.2
16	Joe Sewell	34.5
17	Harry Heilmann	32.3
18	Billy Herman	31.7
19	Mickey Cochrane	31.4
20	Hank Greenberg	30.0
21	Dick Bartell	27.9
22	Stan Hack	27.2
23	Joe Medwick	27.1
24	Goose Goslin	26.0
25	Al Simmons	25.6

Total Player Rating (by era)

1942-1960

1	Ted Williams	85.7
2	Mickey Mantle	76.1
3	Stan Musial	70.5
4	Eddie Mathews	51.6
5	Joe DiMaggio	46.9
6	Lou Boudreau	41.3
7	Bobby Doerr	39.0
8	Yogi Berra	36.2
	Johnny Mize	36.2
10	Jackie Robinson	31.8
11	Richie Ashburn	30.2
12	Ralph Kiner	28.9
13	Joe Gordon	28.2
14	Minnie Minoso	26.0
15	Charlie Keller	23.5
16	Duke Snider	22.3
17	Roy Campanella	21.6
18	Larry Doby	21.2
19	Vern Stephens	19.6
20	Bill Nicholson	19.0
21	Bob Elliott	18.8
22	Eddie Stanky	18.4
23	Roy Cullenbine	18.1
24	Ferris Fain	17.8
25	Johnny Logan	17.3

1961-1976

1	Willie Mays	92.2
2	Hank Aaron	89.8
3	Frank Robinson	69.0
4	Joe Morgan	56.3
5	Carl Yastrzemski	45.5
6	Al Kaline	44.6
7	Roberto Clemente	42.9
8	Ron Santo	39.5
9	Willie McCovey	36.5
10	Bill Mazeroski	36.3
11	Dick Allen	35.3
12	Reggie Smith	35.0
13	Jimmy Wynn	33.2
14	Willie Stargell	32.8
15	Rod Carew	31.7
16	Billy Williams	31.1
17	Bobby Bonds	29.5
18	Rusty Staub	27.6
19	Norm Cash	27.2
20	Harmon Killebrew	26.4
21	Ernie Banks	25.9
22	Rocky Colavito	25.2
23	Tony Oliva	24.9
24	Johnny Bench	24.3
25	Frank Howard	21.3

1977-1998

1	Rickey Henderson	79.7
2	Barry Bonds	79.0
3	Mike Schmidt	78.4
4	Tim Raines	52.6
5	Tony Gwynn	48.8
6	Wade Boggs	44.1
7	Bobby Grich	44.0
8	Robin Yount	43.1
9	Ozzie Smith	43.0
10	Reggie Jackson	42.8
11	Barry Larkin	41.6
12	Cal Ripken	39.9
13	Ken Griffey Jr.	39.5
14	George Brett	39.0
15	Dave Winfield	38.6
16	Jeff Bagwell	36.0
17	Frank Thomas	35.5
18	Ryne Sandberg	35.1
19	Darrell Evans	34.7
20	Keith Hernandez	34.4
21	Eddie Murray	34.1
22	Paul Molitor	33.9
23	Craig Biggio	31.5
24	Albert Belle	31.3
25	Jack Clark	31.1

Wins

1	Cy Young	511
2	Walter Johnson	417
3	Pete Alexander	373
	Christy Mathewson	373
5	Warren Spahn	363
6	Jim Galvin	361
	Kid Nichols	361
8	Tim Keefe	342
9	Steve Carlton	329
10	John Clarkson	328
11	Eddie Plank	326
12	Nolan Ryan	324
	Don Sutton	324
14	Phil Niekro	318
15	Gaylord Perry	314
16	Tom Seaver	311
17	Charley Radbourn	309
18	Mickey Welch	307
19	Lefty Grove	300
	Early Wynn	300
21	Tommy John	288
22	Bert Blyleven	287
23	Robin Roberts	286
24	Fergie Jenkins	284
	Tony Mullane	284
26	Jim Kaat	283
27	Red Ruffing	273
28	Burleigh Grimes	270
29	Jim Palmer	268
30	Bob Feller	266
	Eppa Rixey	266
32	Jim McCormick	265
33	Gus Weyhing	264
34	Ted Lyons	260
35	Red Faber	254
	Jack Morris	254
37	Carl Hubbell	253
38	Bob Gibson	251
39	Vic Willis	249
40	Jack Quinn	247
41	Joe McGinnity	246
	Amos Rusie	246
43	Dennis Martinez	245
	Jack Powell	245
45	Juan Marichal	243
46	Herb Pennock	241
47	Frank Tanana	240
48	Mordecai Brown	239
49	Clark Griffith	237
	Waite Hoyt	237
51	Whitey Ford	236
52	Charlie Buffinton	233
	Roger Clemens	233
54	Sam Jones	229
	Luis Tiant	229
	Will White	229
57	George Mullin	228
58	Jim Bunning	224
	Catfish Hunter	224
60	Hooks Dauss	223
	Paul Derringer	223
	Mel Harder	223
63	Jerry Koosman	222
64	Joe Niekro	221
65	Jerry Reuss	220
66	Bob Caruthers	218
	Earl Whitehill	218
68	Freddie Fitzsimmons	217
	Mickey Lolich	217
70	Wilbur Cooper	216
	Charlie Hough	216
72	Stan Coveleski	215
	Jim Perry	215
74	Rick Reuschel	214
75	Chief Bender	212
76	Bobo Newsom	211
	Billy Pierce	211
	Bob Welch	211
79	Jesse Haines	210
80	Vida Blue	209
	Eddie Cicotte	209
	Don Drysdale	209
	Milt Pappas	209
84	Carl Mays	208
85	Bob Lemon	207
	Hal Newhouser	207
87	Al Orth	204
88	Lew Burdette	203
	Silver King	203
	Jack Stivetts	203
91	Greg Maddux	202
92	Rube Marquard	201
	Charlie Root	201
94	George Uhle	200
95	Jack Chesbro	198
	Bucky Walters	198
97	6 players tied	197

Losses

1	Cy Young	316
2	Jim Galvin	308
3	Nolan Ryan	292
4	Walter Johnson	279
5	Phil Niekro	274
6	Gaylord Perry	265
7	Don Sutton	256
8	Jack Powell	254
9	Eppa Rixey	251
10	Bert Blyleven	250
11	Robin Roberts	245
	Warren Spahn	245
13	Steve Carlton	244
	Early Wynn	244
15	Jim Kaat	237
16	Frank Tanana	236
17	Gus Weyhing	232
18	Tommy John	231
19	Bob Friend	230
	Ted Lyons	230
21	Fergie Jenkins	226
22	Tim Keefe	225
	Red Ruffing	225
24	Bobo Newsom	222
25	Tony Mullane	220
26	Jack Quinn	218
27	Sam Jones	217
28	Charlie Hough	216
29	Jim McCormick	214
30	Red Faber	213
31	Paul Derringer	212
	Chick Fraser	212
	Burleigh Grimes	212
34	Mickey Welch	210
35	Jerry Koosman	209
36	Pete Alexander	208
	Kid Nichols	208
38	Tom Seaver	205
	Vic Willis	205
40	Joe Niekro	204
	Jim Whitney	204
42	George Mullin	196
	Adonis Terry	196
44	Claude Osteen	195
	Charley Radbourn	195
46	Eddie Plank	194
47	Dennis Martinez	193
48	Mickey Lolich	191
	Rick Reuschel	191
	Jerry Reuss	191
	Tom Zachary	191
52	Al Orth	189
53	Christy Mathewson	188
54	Mel Harder	186
	Jack Morris	186
56	Earl Whitehill	185
57	Jim Bunning	184
	Joe Bush	184
59	Larry Jackson	183
	Curt Simmons	183
61	Danny Darwin	182
	Hooks Dauss	182
	Waite Hoyt	182
64	Murry Dickson	181
	Dutch Leonard	181
	Rick Wise	181
67	Lee Meadows	180
68	Pink Hawley	179
	Dolf Luque	179
70	John Clarkson	178
	Wilbur Cooper	178
72	Bill Dinneen	177
	Rube Marquard	177
74	Mike Moore	176
75	Red Donahue	175
76	Doyle Alexander	174
	Bob Gibson	174
	Tom Hughes	174
	Jim Perry	174
	Amos Rusie	174
81	Luis Tiant	172
82	Dennis Eckersley	171
	Larry French	171
84	Ted Breitenstein	170
	Mike Morgan	170
	Camilo Pascual	170
87	Billy Pierce	169
88	Red Ames	167
	Jim Clancy	167
	Bert Cunningham	167
	Red Ehret	167
92	Don Drysdale	166
	Howard Ehmke	166
	Catfish Hunter	166
	George Uhle	166
	Will White	166
97	Mark Baldwin	165
	Bump Hadley	165
	Si Johnson	165
100	3 players tied	164

Winning Percentage

1	Dave Foutz	.690
2	Whitey Ford	.690
3	Bob Caruthers	.688
4	Lefty Grove	.680
5	Mike Mussina	.667
	Vic Raschi	.667
7	Larry Corcoran	.665
8	Christy Mathewson	.665
9	Sam Leever	.660
10	Sal Maglie	.657
11	Sandy Koufax	.655
12	Johnny Allen	.654
13	Roger Clemens	.653
14	Ron Guidry	.651
15	Lefty Gomez	.649
16	John Clarkson	.648
17	Mordecai Brown	.648
18	Randy Johnson	.644
19	Dizzy Dean	.644
20	David Cone	.644
21	Dwight Gooden	.642
22	Pete Alexander	.642
23	Jim Palmer	.638
24	Kid Nichols	.634
25	Deacon Phillippe	.634
26	Joe McGinnity	.634
27	Greg Maddux	.633
28	Ed Reulbach	.632
29	Juan Marichal	.631
30	Mort Cooper	.631
31	Allie Reynolds	.630
32	Jesse Tannehill	.627
33	Ray Kremer	.627
34	Firpo Marberry	.627
35	Eddie Plank	.627
36	Tommy Bond	.627
37	Chief Bender	.625
38	Don Newcombe	.623
39	Nig Cuppy	.623
40	Carl Mays	.623
41	Addie Joss	.623
42	Tom Glavine	.622
43	Fred Goldsmith	.622
44	Doc Crandall	.622
45	Carl Hubbell	.622
46	Bob Feller	.621
47	Mel Parnell	.621
48	John Tudor	.619
49	Clark Griffith	.619
50	Bob Lemon	.618
51	Cy Young	.618
52	John Ward	.617
53	Urban Shocker	.615
54	Ramon Martinez	.615
55	Jeff Tesreau	.615
56	Jim Maloney	.615
57	Jimmy Key	.614
58	Lon Warneke	.613
59	Charley Radbourn	.613
60	Gary Nolan	.611
61	Schoolboy Rowe	.610
62	Carl Erskine	.610
63	Ed Walsh	.607
64	Charlie Ferguson	.607
65	Dave McNally	.607
66	Hooks Wiltse	.607
67	Jim Bagby	.607
68	Jack Stivetts	.606
69	Art Nehf	.605
70	Charlie Buffinton	.605
71	Jack McDowell	.605
72	Orval Overall	.603
73	Tim Keefe	.603
74	Tom Seaver	.603
75	Stan Coveleski	.602
76	Preacher Roe	.602
77	Wes Ferrell	.601
78	J.R. Richard	.601
79	Jack Chesbro	.600
80	Walter Johnson	.599
81	Herb Pennock	.598
82	Freddie Fitzsimmons	.598
83	Ed Lopat	.597
84	Warren Spahn	.597
85	Rip Sewell	.596
86	Mike Garcia	.594
87	Mickey Welch	.594
88	Pat Malone	.593
89	Alvin Crowder	.592
90	John Candelaria	.592
91	Harry Brecheen	.591
92	Bob Welch	.591
93	Bob Gibson	.591
94	Dutch Ruether	.591
95	Denny McLain	.590
96	Eddie Rommel	.590
97	Jack Coombs	.590
98	Bill Bernhard	.589
99	Bret Saberhagen	.589
100	Tiny Bonham	.589

Games

1	Dennis Eckersley	1071
2	Hoyt Wilhelm	1070
3	Kent Tekulve	1050
4	Jesse Orosco	1025
5	Lee Smith	1022
6	Rich Gossage	1002
7	Lindy McDaniel	987
8	Rollie Fingers	944
9	Gene Garber	931
10	Cy Young	906
11	Sparky Lyle	899
12	Jim Kaat	898
13	Jeff Reardon	880
14	Don McMahon	874
15	Phil Niekro	864
16	Charlie Hough	858
17	Roy Face	848
18	John Franco	832
19	Paul Assenmacher	829
20	Tug McGraw	824
21	Nolan Ryan	807
22	Walter Johnson	802
23	Rick Honeycutt	797
24	Gaylord Perry	777
25	Don Sutton	774
26	Darold Knowles	765
27	Mike Jackson	763
28	Tommy John	760
29	Dan Plesac	758
30	Jack Quinn	756
31	Ron Reed	751
32	Warren Spahn	750
33	Tom Burgmeier	745
	Gary Lavelle	745
35	Willie Hernandez	744
36	Steve Carlton	741
37	Ron Perranoski	737
38	Ron Kline	736
39	Steve Bedrosian	732
40	Clay Carroll	731
41	Randy Myers	728
42	Mike Marshall	723
	Roger McDowell	723
44	Doug Jones	722
45	Dave Righetti	718
46	Danny Darwin	716
47	Johnny Klippstein	711
48	Greg Minton	710
49	Stu Miller	704
50	Greg Harris	703
51	Joe Niekro	702
52	Bill Campbell	700
53	Larry Andersen	699
54	Bob McClure	698
55	Jim Galvin	697
56	Pete Alexander	696
	Craig Lefferts	696
58	Bob Miller	694
59	Bert Blyleven	692
	Grant Jackson	692
	Dennis Martinez	692
	Eppa Rixey	692
63	Early Wynn	691
64	Eddie Fisher	690
65	Ted Abernathy	681
66	Robin Roberts	676
67	Waite Hoyt	674
	Dan Quisenberry	674
69	Red Faber	669
70	Dave Giusti	668
71	Fergie Jenkins	664
72	Bruce Sutter	661
73	Tom Seaver	656
74	Paul Lindblad	655
75	Jeff Montgomery	651
	Wilbur Wood	651
77	Sam Jones	647
	Dave LaRoche	647
79	Eric Plunk	646
80	Tom Henke	642
81	Dutch Leonard	640
	Gerry Staley	640
83	Dennis Lamp	639
	Diego Segui	639
85	Frank Tanana	638
86	Bob Stanley	637
87	Christy Mathewson	635
88	Charlie Root	632
89	Jim Perry	630
90	Jerry Reuss	628
91	Lew Burdette	626
92	Murry Dickson	625
	Woodie Fryman	625
94	Mark Davis	624
	Red Ruffing	624
96	Eddie Plank	623
97	Kid Nichols	620
	Dick Tidrow	620
99	Mitch Williams	619
100	3 players tied	617

Games Started

1	Cy Young	815
2	Nolan Ryan	773
3	Don Sutton	756
4	Phil Niekro	716
5	Steve Carlton	709
6	Tommy John	700
7	Gaylord Perry	690
8	Bert Blyleven	685
9	Jim Galvin	681
10	Walter Johnson	666
11	Warren Spahn	665
12	Tom Seaver	647
13	Jim Kaat	625
14	Frank Tanana	616
15	Early Wynn	612
16	Robin Roberts	609
17	Pete Alexander	600
18	Fergie Jenkins	594
	Tim Keefe	594
20	Dennis Martinez	562
21	Kid Nichols	561
22	Eppa Rixey	554
23	Christy Mathewson	551
24	Mickey Welch	549
25	Jerry Reuss	547
26	Red Ruffing	536
27	Eddie Plank	529
	Rick Reuschel	529
29	Jerry Koosman	527
	Jack Morris	527
31	Jim Palmer	521
32	Jim Bunning	519
33	John Clarkson	518
34	Jack Powell	516
35	Tony Mullane	504
36	Charley Radbourn	503
	Gus Weyhing	503
38	Joe Niekro	500
39	Bob Friend	497
	Burleigh Grimes	497
41	Mickey Lolich	496
42	Claude Osteen	488
43	Sam Jones	487
44	Jim McCormick	485
45	Bob Feller	484
	Ted Lyons	484
	Luis Tiant	484
48	Red Faber	483
	Bobo Newsom	483
50	Bob Gibson	482
51	Catfish Hunter	476
52	Vida Blue	473
	Earl Whitehill	473
54	Vic Willis	471
55	Don Drysdale	465
	Milt Pappas	465
57	Doyle Alexander	464
58	Bob Welch	462
59	Curt Simmons	461
60	Mike Torrez	458
61	Lefty Grove	457
	Juan Marichal	457
63	Rick Wise	455
64	Roger Clemens	449
65	Jim Perry	447
66	Paul Derringer	445
67	Jack Quinn	444
68	Charlie Hough	440
	Mike Moore	440
70	Whitey Ford	438
71	Mel Harder	433
72	Carl Hubbell	432
	Billy Pierce	432
74	Larry Jackson	429
75	Orel Hershiser	428
	George Mullin	428
77	Amos Rusie	427
78	Freddie Fitzsimmons	426
79	Fernando Valenzuela	424
80	Waite Hoyt	423
	Mark Langston	423
82	Bob Forsch	422
83	Frank Viola	420
84	Herb Pennock	419
85	Bob Knepper	413
86	Dave Stieb	412
87	Ken Holtzman	410
88	Tom Zachary	408
89	Rube Marquard	407
	Scott Sanderson	407
91	Wilbur Cooper	406
	Lee Meadows	406
	Adonis Terry	406
94	Mike Flanagan	404
	Camilo Pascual	404
96	Will White	401
97	Greg Maddux	399
98	Bucky Walters	398
99	Tom Candiotti	397
100	3 players tied	396

Games Started (by era)

1876-1892

1	Jim Galvin	681
2	Tim Keefe	594
3	Mickey Welch	549
4	John Clarkson	518
5	Tony Mullane	504
6	Charley Radbourn	503
	Gus Weyhing	503
8	Jim McCormick	485
9	Adonis Terry	406
10	Will White	401
11	Charlie Buffinton	396
	Jim Whitney	396
13	Silver King	371
14	Bill Hutchison	346
15	Jack Stivetts	333

1893-1919

1	Cy Young	815
2	Walter Johnson	666
3	Pete Alexander	600
4	Kid Nichols	561
5	Christy Mathewson	551
6	Eddie Plank	529
7	Jack Powell	516
8	Vic Willis	471
9	George Mullin	428
10	Amos Rusie	427
11	Rube Marquard	407
12	Al Orth	394
13	Hooks Dauss	388
	Chick Fraser	388
15	Joe McGinnity	381

1920-1941

1	Eppa Rixey	554
2	Red Ruffing	536
3	Burleigh Grimes	497
4	Sam Jones	487
5	Ted Lyons	484
6	Red Faber	483
	Bobo Newsom	483
8	Earl Whitehill	473
9	Lefty Grove	457
10	Paul Derringer	445
11	Jack Quinn	444
12	Mel Harder	433
13	Carl Hubbell	432
14	Freddie Fitzsimmons	426
15	Waite Hoyt	423

1942-1960

1	Warren Spahn	665
2	Early Wynn	612
3	Robin Roberts	609
4	Bob Friend	497
5	Bob Feller	484
6	Curt Simmons	461
7	Whitey Ford	438
8	Billy Pierce	432
9	Dutch Leonard	375
10	Hal Newhouser	374
11	Lew Burdette	373
12	Bob Buhl	369
13	Vern Law	364
14	Bob Lemon	350

1961-1976

1	Don Sutton	756
2	Phil Niekro	716
3	Steve Carlton	709
4	Tommy John	700
5	Gaylord Perry	690
6	Tom Seaver	647
7	Jim Kaat	625
8	Fergie Jenkins	594
9	Jerry Koosman	527
10	Jim Palmer	521
11	Jim Bunning	519
12	Mickey Lolich	496
13	Claude Osteen	488
14	Luis Tiant	484
15	Bob Gibson	482

1977-1998

1	Nolan Ryan	773
2	Bert Blyleven	685
3	Frank Tanana	616
4	Dennis Martinez	562
5	Jerry Reuss	547
6	Rick Reuschel	529
7	Jack Morris	527
8	Joe Niekro	500
9	Vida Blue	473
10	Doyle Alexander	464
11	Bob Welch	462
12	Roger Clemens	449
13	Charlie Hough	440
	Mike Moore	440
15	Orel Hershiser	428

Complete Games

1	Cy Young	749
2	Jim Galvin	639
3	Tim Keefe	554
4	Walter Johnson	531
	Kid Nichols	531
6	Mickey Welch	525
7	Charley Radbourn	489
8	John Clarkson	485
9	Tony Mullane	468
10	Jim McCormick	466
11	Gus Weyhing	448
12	Pete Alexander	437
13	Christy Mathewson	434
14	Jack Powell	422
15	Eddie Plank	410
16	Will White	394
17	Amos Rusie	393
18	Vic Willis	388
19	Warren Spahn	382
20	Jim Whitney	377
21	Adonis Terry	367
22	Ted Lyons	356
23	George Mullin	353
24	Charlie Buffinton	351
25	Chick Fraser	342
26	Clark Griffith	337
27	Red Ruffing	335
28	Silver King	328
29	Al Orth	324
30	Bill Hutchison	321
31	Burleigh Grimes	314
	Joe McGinnity	314
33	Red Donahue	312
	Guy Hecker	312
35	Bill Dinneen	306
36	Robin Roberts	305
37	Gaylord Perry	303
38	Ted Breitenstein	300
39	Bob Caruthers	298
	Lefty Grove	298
41	Pink Hawley	297
	Ed Morris	297
43	Mark Baldwin	295
44	Tommy Bond	294
45	Brickyard Kennedy	293
46	Eppa Rixey	290
	Early Wynn	290
48	Bill Donovan	289
	Bobby Mathews	289
50	Bert Cunningham	286
51	Wilbur Cooper	279
	Bob Feller	279
	Sadie McMahon	279
54	Jack Stivetts	278
	Jack Taylor	278
56	Charlie Getzien	277
57	Red Faber	273
58	Mordecai Brown	271
	Frank Dwyer	271
60	Jouett Meekin	270
61	Fergie Jenkins	267
62	Elton Chamberlain	264
	Matt Kilroy	264
64	Jesse Tannehill	263
65	Doc White	262
66	Rube Waddell	261
67	Jack Chesbro	260
	Red Ehret	260
	Carl Hubbell	260
70	Larry Corcoran	256
71	Chief Bender	255
	Bob Gibson	255
73	Steve Carlton	254
74	Frank Killen	253
	Win Mercer	253
76	Paul Derringer	251
77	Sam Jones	250
	Ed Walsh	250
79	Eddie Cicotte	249
	Stump Wiedman	249
81	Herb Pennock	247
82	Bobo Newsom	246
83	George Bradley	245
	Hooks Dauss	245
	Phil Niekro	245
86	Harry Howell	244
	Juan Marichal	244
	John Ward	244
89	Jack Quinn	243
90	Bert Blyleven	242
	Deacon Phillippe	242
	Bucky Walters	242
93	Sam Leever	241
94	Kid Gleason	240
95	Addie Joss	234
96	George Uhle	232
97	Carl Mays	231
	Tom Seaver	231
	Harry Staley	231
100	Earl Moore	230

Complete Games (by era)

1876-1892

1	Jim Galvin	639
2	Tim Keefe	554
3	Mickey Welch	525
4	Charley Radbourn	489
5	John Clarkson	485
6	Tony Mullane	468
7	Jim McCormick	466
8	Gus Weyhing	448
9	Will White	394
10	Jim Whitney	377
11	Adonis Terry	367
12	Charlie Buffinton	351
13	Silver King	328
14	Bill Hutchison	321
15	Guy Hecker	312

1893-1919

1	Cy Young	749
2	Walter Johnson	531
	Kid Nichols	531
4	Pete Alexander	437
5	Christy Mathewson	434
6	Jack Powell	422
7	Eddie Plank	410
8	Amos Rusie	393
9	Vic Willis	388
10	George Mullin	353
11	Chick Fraser	342
12	Clark Griffith	337
13	Al Orth	324
14	Joe McGinnity	314
15	Red Donahue	312

1920-1941

1	Ted Lyons	356
2	Red Ruffing	335
3	Burleigh Grimes	314
4	Lefty Grove	298
5	Eppa Rixey	290
6	Wilbur Cooper	279
7	Red Faber	273
8	Carl Hubbell	260
9	Paul Derringer	251
10	Sam Jones	250
11	Herb Pennock	247
12	Bobo Newsom	246
13	Jack Quinn	243
14	Bucky Walters	242
15	George Uhle	232

1942-1960

1	Warren Spahn	382
2	Robin Roberts	305
3	Early Wynn	290
4	Bob Feller	279
5	Hal Newhouser	212
6	Billy Pierce	193
7	Dutch Leonard	192
8	Bob Lemon	188
9	Ed Lopat	164
10	Bob Friend	163
	Curt Simmons	163
12	Lew Burdette	158
	Dizzy Trout	158
14	Whitey Ford	156
	Jim Tobin	156

1961-1976

1	Gaylord Perry	303
2	Fergie Jenkins	267
3	Bob Gibson	255
4	Steve Carlton	254
5	Phil Niekro	245
6	Juan Marichal	244
7	Tom Seaver	231
8	Jim Palmer	211
9	Mickey Lolich	195
10	Luis Tiant	187
11	Catfish Hunter	181
12	Jim Kaat	180
13	Don Sutton	178
14	Mike Cuellar	172
15	Don Drysdale	167

1977-1998

1	Bert Blyleven	242
2	Nolan Ryan	222
3	Jack Morris	175
4	Vida Blue	143
	Frank Tanana	143
6	Steve Rogers	129
7	Jerry Reuss	127
8	Dennis Martinez	122
9	Roger Clemens	114
10	Fernando Valenzuela	113
11	Charlie Hough	107
	Joe Niekro	107
13	Dennis Leonard	103
	Dave Stieb	103
15	Rick Reuschel	102

Shutouts

1	Walter Johnson	110
2	Pete Alexander	90
3	Christy Mathewson	79
4	Cy Young	76
5	Eddie Plank	69
6	Warren Spahn	63
7	Nolan Ryan	61
	Tom Seaver	61
9	Bert Blyleven	60
10	Don Sutton	58
11	Jim Galvin	57
	Ed Walsh	57
13	Bob Gibson	56
14	Mordecai Brown	55
	Steve Carlton	55
16	Jim Palmer	53
	Gaylord Perry	53
18	Juan Marichal	52
19	Rube Waddell	50
	Vic Willis	50
21	Don Drysdale	49
	Fergie Jenkins	49
	Luis Tiant	49
	Early Wynn	49
25	Kid Nichols	48
26	Tommy John	46
	Jack Powell	46
28	Whitey Ford	45
	Addie Joss	45
	Phil Niekro	45
	Robin Roberts	45
	Red Ruffing	45
	Doc White	45
34	Babe Adams	44
	Roger Clemens	44
	Bob Feller	44
37	Milt Pappas	43
38	Catfish Hunter	42
	Bucky Walters	42
40	Mickey Lolich	41
	Hippo Vaughn	41
	Mickey Welch	41
43	Chief Bender	40
	Jim Bunning	40
	Larry French	40
	Sandy Koufax	40
	Claude Osteen	40
	Ed Reulbach	40
	Mel Stottlemyre	40
50	Tim Keefe	39
	Sam Leever	39
	Jerry Reuss	39
53	Stan Coveleski	38
	Billy Pierce	38
	Nap Rucker	38
56	Vida Blue	37
	John Clarkson	37
	Larry Jackson	37
	Eppa Rixey	37
	Steve Rogers	37
61	Mike Cuellar	36
	Bob Friend	36
	Carl Hubbell	36
	Sam Jones	36
	Camilo Pascual	36
	Allie Reynolds	36
	Curt Simmons	36
	Will White	36
69	Tommy Bond	35
	Joe Bush	35
	Jack Chesbro	35
	Eddie Cicotte	35
	Jack Coombs	35
	Wilbur Cooper	35
	Bill Donovan	35
	Burleigh Grimes	35
	Lefty Grove	35
	George Mullin	35
	Herb Pennock	35
	Charley Radbourn	35
81	Bill Doak	34
	Earl Moore	34
	Frank Tanana	34
	Jesse Tannehill	34
85	Tommy Bridges	33
	Lew Burdette	33
	Dean Chance	33
	Mort Cooper	33
	Jerry Koosman	33
	Dutch Leonard	33
	Jim McCormick	33
	Dave McNally	33
	Hal Newhouser	33
	Bob Shawkey	33
	Virgil Trucks	33
96	Paul Derringer	32
	Lefty Leifield	32
	Joe McGinnity	32
	Jim Perry	32
100	7 players tied	31

Saves

1	Lee Smith	478
2	John Franco	397
3	Dennis Eckersley	390
4	Jeff Reardon	367
5	Randy Myers	347
6	Rollie Fingers	341
7	Tom Henke	311
8	Rich Gossage	310
9	Bruce Sutter	300
10	Jeff Montgomery	292
11	Doug Jones	291
12	Rick Aguilera	275
13	Todd Worrell	256
14	John Wetteland	253
15	Dave Righetti	252
16	Rod Beck	250
17	Dan Quisenberry	244
18	Sparky Lyle	238
19	Hoyt Wilhelm	227
20	Gene Garber	218
21	Dave Smith	216
22	Gregg Olson	203
23	Bobby Thigpen	201
24	Roy Face	193
	Mike Henneman	193
26	Mitch Williams	192
27	Roberto Hernandez	191
28	Trevor Hoffman	188
	Mike Marshall	188
30	Jeff Russell	186
31	Steve Bedrosian	184
	Kent Tekulve	184
33	Tug McGraw	180
34	Ron Perranoski	179
35	Bryan Harvey	177
36	Lindy McDaniel	172
37	Roger McDowell	159
38	Jay Howell	155
39	Stu Miller	154
40	Don McMahon	153
	Dan Plesac	153
42	Greg Minton	150
43	Ted Abernathy	148
	Robb Nen	148
45	Willie Hernandez	147
46	Dave Giusti	145
47	Jeff Brantley	144
48	Clay Carroll	143
	Darold Knowles	143
50	Jesse Orosco	140
51	Gary Lavelle	136
52	Jim Brewer	132
	Steve Farr	132
	Bob Stanley	132
55	Ron Davis	130
56	Terry Forster	127
57	Bill Campbell	126
	Dave LaRoche	126
	Mel Rojas	126
60	John Hiller	125
61	Jack Aker	123
62	Dick Radatz	122
63	Duane Ward	121
64	Tippy Martinez	115
65	Mark Wohlers	112
66	Frank Linzy	111
67	Al Worthington	110
68	Fred Gladding	109
69	Wayne Granger	108
	Ron Kline	108
	Troy Percival	108
72	Johnny Murphy	107
73	Bill Caudill	106
74	Jose Mesa	104
75	Ron Reed	103
	John Wyatt	103
77	Tom Burgmeier	102
	Tim Burke	102
	Ellis Kinder	102
80	Craig Lefferts	101
	Firpo Marberry	101
82	Joe Hoerner	99
	Mike Jackson	99
	Jeff Shaw	99
85	Todd Jones	98
	Mike Schooler	98
87	Al Hrabosky	97
	Tom Niedenfuer	97
89	Norm Charlton	96
	Mark Davis	96
	Clem Labine	96
	Randy Moffitt	96
93	Bob Locker	95
	Heathcliff Slocumb	95
95	Aurelio Lopez	93
96	Tom Hume	92
	Phil Regan	92
98	Jim Gott	91
	Steve Howe	91
100	Bill Henry	90

Innings Pitched

1	Cy Young	7356.0
2	Jim Galvin	5941.1
3	Walter Johnson	5914.1
4	Phil Niekro	5404.1
5	Nolan Ryan	5386.0
6	Gaylord Perry	5350.1
7	Don Sutton	5282.1
8	Warren Spahn	5243.2
9	Steve Carlton	5217.1
10	Pete Alexander	5190.0
11	Kid Nichols	5056.1
12	Tim Keefe	5047.2
13	Bert Blyleven	4970.0
14	Mickey Welch	4802.0
15	Tom Seaver	4782.2
16	Christy Mathewson	4780.2
17	Tommy John	4710.1
18	Robin Roberts	4688.2
19	Early Wynn	4564.0
20	John Clarkson	4536.1
21	Charley Radbourn	4535.1
22	Tony Mullane	4531.1
23	Jim Kaat	4530.1
24	Fergie Jenkins	4500.2
25	Eddie Plank	4495.2
26	Eppa Rixey	4494.2
27	Jack Powell	4389.0
28	Red Ruffing	4344.0
29	Gus Weyhing	4324.1
30	Jim McCormick	4275.2
31	Frank Tanana	4188.1
32	Burleigh Grimes	4179.2
33	Ted Lyons	4161.0
34	Red Faber	4086.2
35	Dennis Martinez	3999.2
36	Vic Willis	3996.0
37	Jim Palmer	3948.0
38	Lefty Grove	3940.2
39	Jack Quinn	3920.1
40	Bob Gibson	3884.1
41	Sam Jones	3883.0
42	Jerry Koosman	3839.1
43	Bob Feller	3827.0
44	Jack Morris	3824.0
45	Charlie Hough	3801.1
46	Amos Rusie	3778.2
47	Waite Hoyt	3762.1
48	Jim Bunning	3760.1
49	Bobo Newsom	3759.1
50	George Mullin	3686.2
51	Jerry Reuss	3669.2
52	Paul Derringer	3645.0
53	Mickey Lolich	3638.1
54	Bob Friend	3611.0
55	Carl Hubbell	3590.1
56	Joe Niekro	3584.0
57	Herb Pennock	3571.2
58	Earl Whitehill	3564.2
59	Rick Reuschel	3548.1
60	Will White	3542.2
61	Adonis Terry	3514.1
62	Juan Marichal	3507.1
63	Jim Whitney	3496.1
64	Luis Tiant	3486.1
65	Wilbur Cooper	3480.0
66	Claude Osteen	3460.1
67	Catfish Hunter	3449.1
68	Joe McGinnity	3441.1
69	Don Drysdale	3432.0
70	Mel Harder	3426.1
71	Charlie Buffinton	3404.0
72	Hooks Dauss	3390.2
73	Clark Griffith	3385.2
74	Doyle Alexander	3367.2
75	Chick Fraser	3356.0
76	Al Orth	3354.2
77	Curt Simmons	3348.1
78	Vida Blue	3343.1
79	Rube Marquard	3306.2
	Billy Pierce	3306.2
81	Dennis Eckersley	3285.2
	Jim Perry	3285.2
83	Roger Clemens	3274.2
84	Larry Jackson	3262.2
85	Eddie Cicotte	3226.0
86	Freddie Fitzsimmons	3223.2
87	Dolf Luque	3220.1
88	Dutch Leonard	3218.1
89	Jesse Haines	3208.2
90	Red Ames	3198.0
91	Charlie Root	3197.1
92	Milt Pappas	3186.0
93	Silver King	3181.2
94	Mordecai Brown	3172.1
95	Whitey Ford	3170.1
96	Lee Meadows	3160.2
97	Larry French	3152.0
98	Rick Wise	3127.0
99	Tom Zachary	3126.1
100	George Uhle	3119.2

Innings Pitched (by era)

1876-1892

1	Jim Galvin	5941.1
2	Tim Keefe	5047.2
3	Mickey Welch	4802.0
4	John Clarkson	4536.1
5	Charley Radbourn	4535.1
6	Tony Mullane	4531.1
7	Gus Weyhing	4324.1
8	Jim McCormick	4275.2
9	Will White	3542.2
10	Adonis Terry	3514.1
11	Jim Whitney	3496.1
12	Charlie Buffinton	3404.0
13	Silver King	3181.2
14	Bill Hutchison	3078.0
15	Guy Hecker	2924.0

1893-1919

1	Cy Young	7356.0
2	Walter Johnson	5914.1
3	Pete Alexander	5190.0
4	Kid Nichols	5056.1
5	Christy Mathewson	4780.2
6	Eddie Plank	4495.2
7	Jack Powell	4389.0
8	Vic Willis	3996.0
9	Amos Rusie	3778.2
10	George Mullin	3686.2
11	Joe McGinnity	3441.1
12	Hooks Dauss	3390.2
13	Clark Griffith	3385.2
14	Chick Fraser	3356.0
15	Al Orth	3354.2

1920-1941

1	Eppa Rixey	4494.2
2	Red Ruffing	4344.0
3	Burleigh Grimes	4179.2
4	Ted Lyons	4161.0
5	Red Faber	4086.2
6	Lefty Grove	3940.2
7	Jack Quinn	3920.1
8	Sam Jones	3883.0
9	Waite Hoyt	3762.1
10	Bobo Newsom	3759.1
11	Paul Derringer	3645.0
12	Carl Hubbell	3590.1
13	Herb Pennock	3571.2
14	Earl Whitehill	3564.2
15	Wilbur Cooper	3480.0

1942-1960

1	Warren Spahn	5243.2
2	Robin Roberts	4688.2
3	Early Wynn	4564.0
4	Bob Feller	3827.0
5	Bob Friend	3611.0
6	Curt Simmons	3348.1
7	Billy Pierce	3306.2
8	Dutch Leonard	3218.1
9	Whitey Ford	3170.1
10	Lew Burdette	3067.1
11	Murry Dickson	3052.0
12	Hal Newhouser	2993.0
13	Bob Lemon	2850.0
14	Dizzy Trout	2725.2
15	Virgil Trucks	2682.1

1961-1976

1	Phil Niekro	5404.1
2	Gaylord Perry	5350.1
3	Don Sutton	5282.1
4	Steve Carlton	5217.1
5	Tom Seaver	4782.2
6	Tommy John	4710.1
7	Jim Kaat	4530.1
8	Fergie Jenkins	4500.2
9	Jim Palmer	3948.0
10	Bob Gibson	3884.1
11	Jerry Koosman	3839.1
12	Jim Bunning	3760.1
13	Mickey Lolich	3638.1
14	Juan Marichal	3507.1
15	Luis Tiant	3486.1

1977-1998

1	Nolan Ryan	5386.0
2	Bert Blyleven	4970.0
3	Frank Tanana	4188.1
4	Dennis Martinez	3999.2
5	Jack Morris	3824.0
6	Charlie Hough	3801.1
7	Jerry Reuss	3669.2
8	Joe Niekro	3584.0
9	Rick Reuschel	3548.1
10	Doyle Alexander	3367.2
11	Vida Blue	3343.1
12	Dennis Eckersley	3285.2
13	Roger Clemens	3274.2
14	Bob Welch	3092.0
15	Danny Darwin	3016.2

Hits per Game

1	Nolan Ryan	6.56
2	Sandy Koufax	6.79
3	Sid Fernandez	6.85
4	J.R. Richard	6.88
5	Randy Johnson	6.93
6	Andy Messersmith	6.94
7	Hoyt Wilhelm	7.01
8	Sam McDowell	7.03
9	Ed Walsh	7.12
10	Bob Turley	7.18
11	Orval Overall	7.22
12	Jeff Tesreau	7.24
13	Ed Reulbach	7.24
14	Mario Soto	7.26
15	Addie Joss	7.30
16	Jose DeLeon	7.38
17	Jim Maloney	7.39
18	David Cone	7.44
19	Rich Gossage	7.45
20	Tom Seaver	7.47
21	Walter Johnson	7.48
22	Rube Waddell	7.48
23	Roger Clemens	7.51
24	Bob Gibson	7.60
25	Don Wilson	7.61
26	Jim Palmer	7.63
27	Larry Cheney	7.68
28	Mordecai Brown	7.68
29	Sam Jones	7.68
30	Bob Feller	7.69
31	Johnny Vander Meer	7.69
32	Catfish Hunter	7.72
33	Al Downing	7.72
34	Jim Scott	7.73
35	John Smoltz	7.77
36	Charlie Hough	7.77
37	Bobby Bolin	7.79
38	Stan Williams	7.79
39	Rollie Fingers	7.80
40	Dean Chance	7.81
41	Frank Smith	7.82
42	Tug McGraw	7.83
43	Barney Pelty	7.84
44	Whitey Ford	7.85
45	Denny McLain	7.85
46	Bob Veale	7.87
47	Curt Schilling	7.88
48	Ramon Martinez	7.89
49	Chief Bender	7.89
50	George McQuillan	7.89
51	Jack Coombs	7.89
52	Tim Keefe	7.90
53	Moe Drabowsky	7.90
54	Greg Maddux	7.91
55	Vida Blue	7.91
56	Nap Rucker	7.92
57	Allie Reynolds	7.92
58	Eddie Plank	7.92
59	Luis Tiant	7.94
60	Christy Mathewson	7.94
61	Rudy May	7.94
62	Ray Culp	7.95
63	Bill Donovan	7.99
64	Howie Camnitz	7.99
65	Don Sutton	7.99
66	Juan Pizarro	7.99
67	Dave Stieb	7.99
68	Kevin Appier	8.01
69	Gary Bell	8.01
70	Earl Moore	8.02
71	Sonny Siebert	8.03
72	Lefty Tyler	8.03
73	Hal Newhouser	8.04
74	Claude Hendrix	8.06
75	Steve Carlton	8.06
76	Hooks Wiltse	8.06
77	Amos Rusie	8.07
78	Jose Rijo	8.07
79	Willie Mitchell	8.07
80	Larry Corcoran	8.08
81	Bill Singer	8.08
82	Bob Lemon	8.08
83	Eddie Cicotte	8.08
84	Mike Scott	8.08
85	Dwight Gooden	8.08
86	Stu Miller	8.09
87	Don Drysdale	8.09
88	Gary Nolan	8.09
89	Juan Marichal	8.09
90	Doc White	8.10
91	Virgil Trucks	8.11
92	Hippo Vaughn	8.11
93	Blue Moon Odom	8.12
94	Kirby Higbe	8.13
95	Jim Shaw	8.13
96	Mike Cuellar	8.13
97	Billy Pierce	8.14
98	Mort Cooper	8.15
99	Red Ames	8.15
100	Vic Willis	8.16

Home Runs Allowed

1	Robin Roberts	505
2	Fergie Jenkins	484
3	Phil Niekro	482
4	Don Sutton	472
5	Frank Tanana	448
6	Warren Spahn	434
7	Bert Blyleven	430
8	Steve Carlton	414
9	Gaylord Perry	399
10	Jim Kaat	395
11	Jack Morris	389
12	Charlie Hough	383
13	Tom Seaver	380
14	Catfish Hunter	374
15	Jim Bunning	372
	Dennis Martinez	372
17	Dennis Eckersley	347
	Mickey Lolich	347
19	Luis Tiant	346
20	Early Wynn	338
21	Doyle Alexander	324
22	Danny Darwin	321
	Nolan Ryan	321
24	Juan Marichal	320
25	Pedro Ramos	315
26	Jim Perry	308
27	Jim Palmer	303
28	Murry Dickson	302
	Tommy John	302
	Mark Langston	302
31	Milt Pappas	298
32	Scott Sanderson	297
33	Frank Viola	294
34	Mudcat Grant	292
35	Floyd Bannister	291
	Mike Moore	291
37	Jerry Koosman	290
38	Lew Burdette	289
39	Bob Friend	286
40	Billy Pierce	284
41	Bill Gullickson	282
42	Don Drysdale	280
43	Jim Slaton	277
44	Joe Niekro	276
45	Vern Law	268
46	Bob Welch	267
47	Dave Stewart	264
48	Vida Blue	263
49	Rick Wise	261
50	Larry Jackson	259
51	Bruce Hurst	258
52	Bob Gibson	257
53	Camilo Pascual	256
54	Mike McCormick	255
	Curt Simmons	255
56	Jimmy Key	254
	Red Ruffing	254
58	Don Newcombe	252
59	Mike Flanagan	251
60	Ken Holtzman	249
	Claude Osteen	249
62	Steve Renko	248
63	Doug Drabek	246
64	John Candelaria	245
	Jerry Reuss	245
66	Jim Clancy	244
67	Denny McLain	242
	Johnny Podres	242
69	Harvey Haddix	240
	Ray Sadecki	240
71	Ron Darling	239
72	Bob Buhl	238
73	Tom Browning	236
	Tom Candiotti	236
	Rick Sutcliffe	236
	Earl Wilson	236
77	Scott McGregor	235
78	Joe Coleman	234
79	Jim Lonborg	233
80	Chuck Finley	231
81	Kevin Gross	230
	Dave McNally	230
83	Tim Belcher	229
84	Whitey Ford	228
	Bob Knepper	228
86	Carl Hubbell	227
87	Ron Guidry	226
	Mike Morgan	226
	Greg Swindell	226
	Fernando Valenzuela	226
91	Don Cardwell	225
	Dave Stieb	225
93	Bob Feller	224
94	Stan Bahnsen	223
	Ted Lyons	223
	Mike Torrez	223
97	Mike Cuellar	222
98	Ray Burris	221
	Rick Reuschel	221
100	Bobby Witt	219

Home Runs Allowed (by era)

1876-1892

1	John Clarkson	161
2	Jack Stivetts	131
3	Jim Galvin	122
4	Gus Weyhing	120
5	Charley Radbourn	117
6	Mickey Welch	106
7	Bill Hutchison	104
8	Tony Mullane	98
9	Charlie Getzien	95
10	Harry Staley	92
11	Charlie Buffinton	87
12	Jim McCormick	84
13	Mark Baldwin	82
14	Jim Whitney	79
15	Adonis Terry	76

1893-1919

1	Pete Alexander	164
2	Kid Nichols	156
3	Cy Young	138
4	Jack Powell	110
5	Frank Dwyer	109
6	Rube Marquard	107
7	Walter Johnson	97
8	Brickyard Kennedy	93
9	Christy Mathewson	89
10	Hooks Dauss	87
11	Ad Gumbert	81
12	Kid Carsey	80
13	Ted Breitenstein	79
14	Bill Dinneen	78
15	Clark Griffith	76

1920-1941

1	Red Ruffing	254
2	Carl Hubbell	227
3	Ted Lyons	223
4	Bobo Newsom	206
5	Earl Whitehill	192
6	Charlie Root	187
7	Freddie Fitzsimmons	186
8	Tommy Bridges	181
9	Lon Warneke	175
10	George Blaeholder	173
11	Syl Johnson	172
12	Bump Hadley	167
13	Jesse Haines	165
14	Larry French	164
15	Rube Walberg	163

1942-1960

1	Robin Roberts	505
2	Warren Spahn	434
3	Early Wynn	338
4	Pedro Ramos	315
5	Murry Dickson	302
6	Lew Burdette	289
7	Bob Friend	286
8	Billy Pierce	284
9	Vern Law	268
10	Curt Simmons	255
11	Don Newcombe	252
12	Johnny Podres	242
13	Harvey Haddix	240
14	Bob Buhl	238
15	Whitey Ford	228

1961-1976

1	Fergie Jenkins	484
2	Phil Niekro	482
3	Don Sutton	472
4	Steve Carlton	414
5	Gaylord Perry	399
6	Jim Kaat	395
7	Tom Seaver	380
8	Catfish Hunter	374
9	Jim Bunning	372
10	Mickey Lolich	347
11	Luis Tiant	346
12	Juan Marichal	320
13	Jim Perry	308
14	Jim Palmer	303
15	Tommy John	302

1977-1998

1	Frank Tanana	448
2	Bert Blyleven	430
3	Jack Morris	389
4	Charlie Hough	383
5	Dennis Martinez	372
6	Dennis Eckersley	347
7	Doyle Alexander	324
8	Danny Darwin	321
	Nolan Ryan	321
10	Mark Langston	302
11	Scott Sanderson	297
12	Frank Viola	294
13	Floyd Bannister	291
	Mike Moore	291
15	Bill Gullickson	282

Walks

1	Nolan Ryan	2795
2	Steve Carlton	1833
3	Phil Niekro	1809
4	Early Wynn	1775
5	Bob Feller	1764
6	Bobo Newsom	1732
7	Amos Rusie	1707
8	Charlie Hough	1665
9	Gus Weyhing	1566
10	Red Ruffing	1541
11	Bump Hadley	1442
12	Warren Spahn	1434
13	Earl Whitehill	1431
14	Tony Mullane	1408
15	Sam Jones	1396
16	Jack Morris	1390
	Tom Seaver	1390
18	Gaylord Perry	1379
19	Mike Torrez	1371
20	Walter Johnson	1363
21	Don Sutton	1343
22	Bob Gibson	1336
23	Chick Fraser	1332
24	Bert Blyleven	1322
25	Sam McDowell	1312
26	Jim Palmer	1311
27	Mark Baldwin	1307
28	Adonis Terry	1298
29	Mickey Welch	1297
30	Burleigh Grimes	1295
31	Kid Nichols	1268
32	Joe Bush	1263
33	Joe Niekro	1262
34	Allie Reynolds	1261
35	Mark Langston	1260
36	Tommy John	1259
37	Frank Tanana	1255
38	Bob Lemon	1251
39	Hal Newhouser	1249
40	Bobby Witt	1248
41	George Mullin	1238
42	Tim Keefe	1236
43	Cy Young	1217
44	Red Faber	1213
45	Vic Willis	1212
46	Ted Breitenstein	1203
47	Brickyard Kennedy	1201
48	Jerry Koosman	1198
49	Tommy Bridges	1192
50	John Clarkson	1191
51	Lefty Grove	1187
52	Vida Blue	1185
53	Billy Pierce	1178
54	Dennis Martinez	1165
55	Mike Moore	1156
56	Jack Stivetts	1155
57	Fernando Valenzuela	1151
58	Bill Hutchison	1132
	Johnny Vander Meer	1132
60	Jerry Reuss	1127
61	Ted Lyons	1121
	Bucky Walters	1121
63	Mel Harder	1118
64	Earl Moore	1108
65	Bob Buhl	1105
66	Luis Tiant	1104
67	Mickey Lolich	1099
68	Lefty Gomez	1095
69	Virgil Trucks	1088
70	Whitey Ford	1086
71	Jim Kaat	1083
72	Eppa Rixey	1082
73	Rick Sutcliffe	1081
74	Eddie Plank	1072
75	Camilo Pascual	1069
76	Bob Turley	1068
77	Hooks Dauss	1067
78	Elton Chamberlain	1065
79	Bert Cunningham	1064
80	Curt Simmons	1063
81	Bill Donovan	1059
82	Murry Dickson	1058
	Jouett Meekin	1058
84	Vern Kennedy	1049
85	Dizzy Trout	1046
86	Howard Ehmke	1042
87	Wes Ferrell	1040
88	Tommy Byrne	1037
89	Red Ames	1034
	Dave Stewart	1034
	Dave Stieb	1034
	Bob Welch	1034
93	Rube Walberg	1031
94	Chuck Finley	1024
95	Jack Powell	1021
96	Bob Shawkey	1018
97	Roger Clemens	1012
98	Steve Renko	1010
99	Jim Slaton	1004
100	2 players tied	1003

Fewest Walks per Game

1876-1892
1	Tommy Bond	0.58
2	George Bradley	0.67
3	Terry Larkin	0.71
4	John Ward	0.92
5	Fred Goldsmith	0.96
6	Jim Whitney	1.06
7	Bobby Mathews	1.11
8	Jim Galvin	1.13
9	Will White	1.26
10	Jack Lynch	1.38
11	Guy Hecker	1.51
12	Lee Richmond	1.53
13	Jim McCormick	1.58
14	Jumbo McGinnis	1.65
15	Ed Morris	1.67

1893-1919
1	Deacon Phillippe	1.25
2	Babe Adams	1.29
3	Addie Joss	1.41
4	Cy Young	1.49
5	Jesse Tannehill	1.56
6	Christy Mathewson	1.59
7	Nick Altrock	1.62
8	Pete Alexander	1.65
9	Noodles Hahn	1.69
10	Dick Rudolph	1.77
11	Al Orth	1.77
12	Slim Sallee	1.83
13	Bill Bernhard	1.83
14	Ed Siever	1.86
15	Ed Walsh	1.87

1920-1941
1	Red Lucas	1.61
2	Pete Donohue	1.80
3	Jesse Barnes	1.80
4	Carl Hubbell	1.82
5	Curt Davis	1.85
6	Paul Derringer	1.88
7	Bill Swift	1.93
8	Sherry Smith	1.93
9	Watty Clark	1.97
10	Jack Quinn	1.97
11	Syl Johnson	2.03
12	Dizzy Dean	2.07
13	Art Nehf	2.13
14	Sloppy Thurston	2.15
15	Eppa Rixey	2.17

1942-1960
1	Tiny Bonham	1.67
2	Robin Roberts	1.73
3	Lew Burdette	1.84
4	Ken Raffensberger	1.88
5	Vern Law	2.01
6	Don Newcombe	2.05
7	Dutch Leonard	2.06
8	Hal Brown	2.08
9	Larry Jansen	2.09
10	Bob Purkey	2.17
11	Dick Donovan	2.21
12	Bob Friend	2.23
13	Don Mossi	2.24
14	Preacher Roe	2.37
15	Ed Lopat	2.40

1961-1976
1	Fritz Peterson	1.73
2	Juan Marichal	1.82
3	Fergie Jenkins	1.99
4	Jim Barr	2.04
5	Bill Monbouquette	2.12
6	Ken Johnson	2.14
7	Jim Kaat	2.15
8	Ralph Terry	2.17
9	Gary Nolan	2.22
10	Don Drysdale	2.24
11	Bill Hands	2.27
12	Larry Jackson	2.27
13	Don Sutton	2.29
14	Ron Reed	2.30
15	Rick Wise	2.31

1977-1998
1	Bob Tewksbury	1.45
2	Bret Saberhagen	1.70
3	Greg Swindell	2.01
4	Dennis Eckersley	2.02
5	Greg Maddux	2.07
6	Lary Sorensen	2.08
7	John Candelaria	2.11
8	Mike Mussina	2.12
9	David Wells	2.17
10	Bryn Smith	2.17
11	Scott McGregor	2.18
12	Bill Gullickson	2.19
13	John Burkett	2.19
14	Scott Sanderson	2.20
15	Kevin Tapani	2.21

Strikeouts

1	Nolan Ryan	5714
2	Steve Carlton	4136
3	Bert Blyleven	3701
4	Tom Seaver	3640
5	Don Sutton	3574
6	Gaylord Perry	3534
7	Walter Johnson	3509
8	Phil Niekro	3342
9	Fergie Jenkins	3192
10	Roger Clemens	3153
11	Bob Gibson	3117
12	Jim Bunning	2855
13	Mickey Lolich	2832
14	Cy Young	2803
15	Frank Tanana	2773
16	Warren Spahn	2583
17	Bob Feller	2581
18	Tim Keefe	2560
19	Jerry Koosman	2556
20	Christy Mathewson	2502
21	Don Drysdale	2486
22	Jack Morris	2478
23	Jim Kaat	2461
24	Sam McDowell	2453
25	Mark Langston	2421
26	Luis Tiant	2416
27	Dennis Eckersley	2401
28	Sandy Koufax	2396
29	Charlie Hough	2362
30	Robin Roberts	2357
31	Early Wynn	2334
32	Randy Johnson	2329
33	Rube Waddell	2316
34	Juan Marichal	2303
35	Lefty Grove	2266
36	Eddie Plank	2246
37	Tommy John	2245
38	David Cone	2243
39	Jim Palmer	2212
40	Pete Alexander	2198
41	Vida Blue	2175
42	Camilo Pascual	2167
43	Dwight Gooden	2150
44	Dennis Martinez	2149
45	Bobo Newsom	2082
46	Fernando Valenzuela	2074
47	Dazzy Vance	2045
48	Greg Maddux	2024
49	Rick Reuschel	2015
50	Catfish Hunter	2012
51	Billy Pierce	1999
52	Red Ruffing	1987
53	John Clarkson	1978
54	Bob Welch	1969
55	Whitey Ford	1956
56	Chuck Finley	1951
57	Amos Rusie	1950
58	Danny Darwin	1942
	John Smoltz	1942
60	Orel Hershiser	1912
61	Jerry Reuss	1907
62	Kid Nichols	1873
63	Mickey Welch	1850
64	Frank Viola	1844
65	Charley Radbourn	1830
66	Tony Mullane	1803
67	Jim Galvin	1799
68	Hal Newhouser	1796
69	Bobby Witt	1795
70	Ron Guidry	1778
71	Rudy May	1760
72	Joe Niekro	1747
73	Sid Fernandez	1743
74	Dave Stewart	1741
75	Ed Walsh	1736
76	Bob Friend	1734
77	Joe Coleman	1728
	Milt Pappas	1728
79	Kevin Gross	1727
80	Floyd Bannister	1723
81	Chief Bender	1711
82	Larry Jackson	1709
83	Jim McCormick	1704
84	Bob Veale	1703
85	Red Ames	1702
86	Charlie Buffinton	1700
87	Curt Simmons	1697
88	Tom Candiotti	1694
89	Bruce Hurst	1689
90	Rick Sutcliffe	1679
91	Carl Hubbell	1677
92	Tommy Bridges	1674
93	John Candelaria	1673
94	Dave Stieb	1669
95	Mike Moore	1667
96	Gus Weyhing	1665
97	Vic Willis	1651
98	Rick Wise	1647
99	Al Downing	1639
100	Mike Cuellar	1632

Strikeouts per Game

1	Randy Johnson	10.60
2	Nolan Ryan	9.55
3	Sandy Koufax	9.28
4	Sam McDowell	8.86
5	Roger Clemens	8.67
6	Curt Schilling	8.45
7	David Cone	8.42
8	Sid Fernandez	8.40
9	J.R. Richard	8.37
10	Bob Veale	7.96
11	John Smoltz	7.84
12	Jose Rijo	7.84
13	Jim Maloney	7.81
14	Tom Gordon	7.78
15	Jose DeLeon	7.56
16	Mario Soto	7.54
17	Sam Jones	7.54
18	Mark Langston	7.51
19	Dwight Gooden	7.50
20	Rich Gossage	7.47
21	Kevin Appier	7.35
22	Andy Benes	7.34
23	Bobby Witt	7.26
24	Bob Gibson	7.22
25	Steve Carlton	7.13
26	Chuck Finley	7.13
27	Rube Waddell	7.04
28	Mickey Lolich	7.01
29	Rollie Fingers	6.87
30	Tom Seaver	6.85
31	Jim Bunning	6.83
32	Ramon Martinez	6.83
33	Erik Hanson	6.80
34	Juan Pizarro	6.73
35	Bobby Bolin	6.71
36	Bert Blyleven	6.70
37	Ron Guidry	6.69
38	Ray Culp	6.69
39	Stan Williams	6.66
40	Camilo Pascual	6.65
41	Bob Turley	6.65
42	Mike Mussina	6.62
43	Don Wilson	6.60
44	Tug McGraw	6.59
45	Dennis Eckersley	6.58
46	Denny Lemaster	6.57
47	Andy Messersmith	6.56
48	Pete Harnisch	6.55
49	Don Drysdale	6.52
50	Alex Fernandez	6.51
51	Al Downing	6.50
52	Todd Stottlemyre	6.49
53	Floyd Bannister	6.49
54	Toad Ramsey	6.49
55	Diego Segui	6.46
56	Dean Chance	6.43
57	Hoyt Wilhelm	6.43
58	Greg Maddux	6.39
59	Mike Smith	6.39
60	Fergie Jenkins	6.38
61	Moe Drabowsky	6.37
62	Fernando Valenzuela	6.37
63	Earl Wilson	6.37
64	Harvey Haddix	6.34
65	Sonny Siebert	6.32
66	Chris Short	6.31
67	Bruce Hurst	6.29
68	Bill Singer	6.27
69	Jack McDowell	6.25
70	Kevin Gross	6.25
71	Luis Tiant	6.24
72	Turk Farrell	6.21
73	Dazzy Vance	6.20
74	Stu Miller	6.18
75	Clay Kirby	6.17
76	Gary Bell	6.15
77	Gary Peters	6.14
78	Denny McLain	6.12
79	Kevin Brown	6.11
80	Greg Swindell	6.11
81	Don Sutton	6.09
82	Mike Krukow	6.07
83	Bob Feller	6.07
84	Ron Darling	6.06
85	John Smiley	6.06
86	Joe Coleman	6.05
87	David Wells	6.05
88	Fred Norman	6.05
89	Rudy May	6.04
90	Bret Saberhagen	6.02
91	Jerry Koosman	5.99
92	John Candelaria	5.96
93	Frank Tanana	5.96
94	Dave Stewart	5.96
95	Gaylord Perry	5.94
96	Woodie Fryman	5.92
97	Juan Marichal	5.91
98	Kenny Rogers	5.90
99	Steve Barber	5.89
100	John Montefusco	5.89

Ratio

1	Addie Joss	8.9
2	Ed Walsh	9.2
3	John Ward	9.4
4	Christy Mathewson	9.6
5	Tommy Bond	9.8
	Mordecai Brown	9.8
7	George Bradley	9.9
	Walter Johnson	9.9
9	Babe Adams	10.0
	Larry Corcoran	10.0
	Sandy Koufax	10.0
	Juan Marichal	10.0
13	Charlie Ferguson	10.1
	Terry Larkin	10.1
	Deacon Phillippe	10.1
16	Pete Alexander	10.2
	Greg Maddux	10.2
	Jim McCormick	10.2
	Ed Morris	10.2
	Tom Seaver	10.2
	Will White	10.2
22	Chief Bender	10.3
	Catfish Hunter	10.3
	Tim Keefe	10.3
	Rube Waddell	10.3
26	Nick Altrock	10.4
	Tiny Bonham	10.4
	Fred Goldsmith	10.4
	Noodles Hahn	10.4
	Fergie Jenkins	10.4
	George McQuillan	10.4
	Gary Nolan	10.4
	Charley Radbourn	10.4
	Don Sutton	10.4
	Doc White	10.4
	Jim Whitney	10.4
	Hoyt Wilhelm	10.4
	Hooks Wiltse	10.4
	Cy Young	10.4
40	Eddie Cicotte	10.5
	Sid Fernandez	10.5
	Andy Messersmith	10.5
	Eddie Plank	10.5
	Dick Rudolph	10.5
	Bret Saberhagen	10.5
	Curt Schilling	10.5
	Jeff Tesreau	10.5
48	Roger Clemens	10.6
	Rollie Fingers	10.6
	Carl Hubbell	10.6
	Sam Leever	10.6
	Denny McLain	10.6
	Mike Mussina	10.6
	Robin Roberts	10.6
55	Bob Caruthers	10.7
	Jack Chesbro	10.7
	Don Drysdale	10.7
	Dennis Eckersley	10.7
	Ron Guidry	10.7
	Guy Hecker	10.7
	Jumbo McGinnis	10.7
	Orval Overall	10.7
	Jim Palmer	10.7
	Ed Reulbach	10.7
	Slim Sallee	10.7
	Frank Smith	10.7
	George Winter	10.7
68	John Candelaria	10.8
	Mike Cuellar	10.8
	Bob Ewing	10.8
	Jim Galvin	10.8
	Barney Pelty	10.8
	Gaylord Perry	10.8
	Nap Rucker	10.8
	Dupee Shaw	10.8
	Mario Soto	10.8
	Warren Spahn	10.8
	Ralph Terry	10.8
79	Harry Brecheen	10.9
	Phil Douglas	10.9
	Eddie Fisher	10.9
	Dave Foutz	10.9
	Bob Gibson	10.9
	Claude Hendrix	10.9
	Fritz Peterson	10.9
	Jim Scott	10.9
	John Smoltz	10.9
	Jack Taylor	10.9
	Luis Tiant	10.9
	Fred Toney	10.9
	John Tudor	10.9
	Carl Weilman	10.9
93	9 players tied	11.0

Earned Run Average

1	Ed Walsh	1.82
2	Addie Joss	1.89
3	Mordecai Brown	2.06
4	John Ward	2.10
5	Christy Mathewson	2.13
6	Rube Waddell	2.16
7	Walter Johnson	2.17
8	Orval Overall	2.23
9	Tommy Bond	2.25
10	Ed Reulbach	2.28
	Will White	2.28
12	Jim Scott	2.30
13	Eddie Plank	2.35
14	Larry Corcoran	2.36
15	Eddie Cicotte	2.38
	Ed Killian	2.38
	George McQuillan	2.38
18	Doc White	2.39
19	Nap Rucker	2.42
20	Terry Larkin	2.43
	Jim McCormick	2.43
	Jeff Tesreau	2.43
23	Chief Bender	2.46
24	Sam Leever	2.47
	Lefty Leifield	2.47
	Hooks Wiltse	2.47
27	Bob Ewing	2.49
	Hippo Vaughn	2.49
29	George Bradley	2.50
30	Hoyt Wilhelm	2.52
31	Noodles Hahn	2.55
32	Pete Alexander	2.56
	Slim Sallee	2.56
34	Deacon Phillippe	2.59
	Frank Smith	2.59
36	Ed Siever	2.60
37	Bob Rhoads	2.61
38	Tim Keefe	2.62
39	Red Ames	2.63
	Barney Pelty	2.63
	Vic Willis	2.63
	Cy Young	2.63
43	Claude Hendrix	2.65
44	Joe McGinnity	2.66
	Dick Rudolph	2.66
	Jack Taylor	2.66
47	Nick Altrock	2.67
	Charlie Ferguson	2.67
	Charley Radbourn	2.67
	Carl Weilman	2.67
51	Jack Chesbro	2.68
	Cy Falkenberg	2.68
53	Bill Donovan	2.69
	Fred Toney	2.69
55	Larry Cheney	2.70
56	Mickey Welch	2.71
57	Fred Goldsmith	2.73
58	Harry Howell	2.74
59	Howie Camnitz	2.75
	Whitey Ford	2.75
	Greg Maddux	2.75
	Dummy Taylor	2.75
63	Babe Adams	2.76
	Sandy Koufax	2.76
	Dutch Leonard	2.76
66	Jeff Pfeffer	2.77
67	Jack Coombs	2.78
	Earl Moore	2.78
69	Tully Sparks	2.79
	Jesse Tannehill	2.79
71	Phil Douglas	2.80
72	John Clarkson	2.81
73	Ray Fisher	2.82
	Ed Morris	2.82
	George Mullin	2.82
76	Bob Caruthers	2.83
77	Dave Foutz	2.84
78	Andy Messersmith	2.86
	Jim Palmer	2.86
	Tom Seaver	2.86
81	Jim Galvin	2.87
	George Winter	2.87
83	Willie Mitchell	2.88
84	Wilbur Cooper	2.89
	Stan Coveleski	2.89
	Juan Marichal	2.89
87	Rollie Fingers	2.90
88	Bob Gibson	2.91
89	Harry Brecheen	2.92
	Dean Chance	2.92
	Doc Crandall	2.92
	Carl Mays	2.92
93	Dave Davenport	2.93
	Guy Hecker	2.93
95	Roger Clemens	2.95
	Don Drysdale	2.95
	Jumbo McGinnis	2.95
	Kid Nichols	2.95
	Lefty Tyler	2.95
100	Charlie Buffinton	2.96

Earned Run Average (by era)

1876-1892

1	John Ward	2.10
2	Tommy Bond	2.25
3	Will White	2.28
4	Larry Corcoran	2.36
5	Terry Larkin	2.43
	Jim McCormick	2.43
7	George Bradley	2.50
8	Tim Keefe	2.62
9	Charlie Ferguson	2.67
	Charley Radbourn	2.67
11	Mickey Welch	2.71
12	Fred Goldsmith	2.73
13	John Clarkson	2.81
14	Ed Morris	2.82
15	Bob Caruthers	2.83

1893-1919

1	Ed Walsh	1.82
2	Addie Joss	1.89
3	Mordecai Brown	2.06
4	Christy Mathewson	2.13
5	Rube Waddell	2.16
6	Walter Johnson	2.17
7	Orval Overall	2.23
8	Ed Reulbach	2.28
9	Jim Scott	2.30
10	Eddie Plank	2.35
11	Eddie Cicotte	2.38
	Ed Killian	2.38
	George McQuillan	2.38
14	Doc White	2.39
15	Nap Rucker	2.42

1920-1941

1	Wilbur Cooper	2.89
	Stan Coveleski	2.89
3	Carl Mays	2.92
4	Carl Hubbell	2.98
5	Dizzy Dean	3.02
6	Lefty Grove	3.06
7	Bob Shawkey	3.09
8	Red Faber	3.15
	Eppa Rixey	3.15
10	Urban Shocker	3.17
11	Lon Warneke	3.18
12	Art Nehf	3.20
13	Jesse Barnes	3.22
14	George Mogridge	3.23
15	2 players tied	3.24

1942-1960

1	Hoyt Wilhelm	2.52
2	Whitey Ford	2.75
3	Harry Brecheen	2.92
4	Mort Cooper	2.97
5	Max Lanier	3.01
6	Tiny Bonham	3.06
	Hal Newhouser	3.06
8	Warren Spahn	3.09
9	Sal Maglie	3.15
10	Ed Lopat	3.21
11	Bob Lemon	3.23
	Dizzy Trout	3.23
13	Stu Miller	3.24
14	Bob Feller	3.25
	Dutch Leonard	3.25

1961-1976

1	Sandy Koufax	2.76
2	Andy Messersmith	2.86
	Jim Palmer	2.86
	Tom Seaver	2.86
5	Juan Marichal	2.89
6	Rollie Fingers	2.90
7	Bob Gibson	2.91
8	Dean Chance	2.92
9	Don Drysdale	2.95
10	Mel Stottlemyre	2.97
11	Bob Veale	3.07
12	Gary Nolan	3.08
13	Joe Horlen	3.11
	Gaylord Perry	3.11
15	2 players tied	3.14

1977-1998

1	Greg Maddux	2.75
2	Roger Clemens	2.95
3	Rich Gossage	3.01
4	John Tudor	3.12
5	J.R. Richard	3.15
6	Jose Rijo	3.16
7	David Cone	3.17
	Steve Rogers	3.17
9	Nolan Ryan	3.19
10	Vida Blue	3.27
11	Ron Guidry	3.29
12	Kevin Brown	3.30
13	Bert Blyleven	3.31
	Tom Glavine	3.31
15	3 players tied	3.33

Adjusted Earned Run Average

1	Roger Clemens	151
2	Lefty Grove	148
3	Walter Johnson	147
4	Greg Maddux	146
	Hoyt Wilhelm	146
6	Ed Walsh	145
7	Addie Joss	142
8	Kid Nichols	139
9	Cy Young	138
10	Mordecai Brown	137
11	Christy Mathewson	136
12	Pete Alexander	135
	Kevin Appier	135
	Rube Waddell	135
15	John Clarkson	134
16	Harry Brecheen	133
	Whitey Ford	133
	Noodles Hahn	133
19	Sandy Koufax	131
20	Dizzy Dean	130
	Carl Hubbell	130
	Mike Mussina	130
	Hal Newhouser	130
	Amos Rusie	130
25	Randy Johnson	129
26	David Cone	128
	Stan Coveleski	128
28	Nig Cuppy	127
	Bob Gibson	127
	Sal Maglie	127
	Tom Seaver	127
32	Tommy Bridges	126
33	Lefty Gomez	125
	Rich Gossage	125
	Tim Keefe	125
	Max Lanier	125
	Jim Palmer	125
	Mel Parnell	125
	Dazzy Vance	125
40	Kevin Brown	124
	Dave Foutz	124
	Bret Saberhagen	124
	Urban Shocker	124
	Dizzy Trout	124
45	Bob Caruthers	123
	Eddie Cicotte	123
	Mort Cooper	123
	Sam Leever	123
	Orval Overall	123
	John Tudor	123
51	Larry Corcoran	122
	Bob Feller	122
	Charlie Ferguson	122
	Tom Glavine	122
	Silver King	122
	Juan Marichal	122
	Eddie Plank	122
	Ed Reulbach	122
	Jose Rijo	122
	Eddie Rommel	122
	Dave Stieb	122
62	Don Drysdale	121
	Clark Griffith	121
	Jimmy Key	121
	Andy Messersmith	121
	Curt Schilling	121
	Jack Stivetts	121
68	Tiny Bonham	120
	Joe McGinnity	120
	Deacon Phillippe	120
	Charley Radbourn	120
	Jim Scott	120
	John Smoltz	120
	Hippo Vaughn	120
	Will White	120
76	Dean Chance	119
	Red Faber	119
	Rollie Fingers	119
	Chuck Finley	119
	Ron Guidry	119
	Thornton Lee	119
	Bob Lemon	119
	Dutch Leonard	119
	Carl Mays	119
	Billy Pierce	119
	Nap Rucker	119
	Bobby Shantz	119
	Lon Warneke	119
89	Babe Adams	118
	Ted Lyons	118
	Sadie McMahon	118
	Tony Mullane	118
	Warren Spahn	118
	John Ward	118
	Vic Willis	118
96	9 players tied	117

Adjusted ERA (by era)

1876-1892

1	John Clarkson	134
2	Tim Keefe	125
3	Dave Foutz	124
4	Bob Caruthers	123
5	Larry Corcoran	122
	Charlie Ferguson	122
	Silver King	122
8	Jack Stivetts	121
9	Charley Radbourn	120
	Will White	120
11	Sadie McMahon	118
	Tony Mullane	118
	John Ward	118
14	Jim McCormick	117
	Toad Ramsey	117

1893-1919

1	Walter Johnson	147
2	Ed Walsh	145
3	Addie Joss	142
4	Kid Nichols	139
5	Cy Young	138
6	Mordecai Brown	137
7	Christy Mathewson	136
8	Pete Alexander	135
	Rube Waddell	135
10	Noodles Hahn	133
11	Amos Rusie	130
12	Nig Cuppy	127
13	Eddie Cicotte	123
	Sam Leever	123
	Orval Overall	123

1920-1941

1	Lefty Grove	148
2	Dizzy Dean	130
	Carl Hubbell	130
4	Stan Coveleski	128
5	Tommy Bridges	126
6	Lefty Gomez	125
	Dazzy Vance	125
8	Urban Shocker	124
9	Eddie Rommel	122
10	Red Faber	119
	Thornton Lee	119
	Carl Mays	119
	Lon Warneke	119
14	Ted Lyons	118
15	2 players tied	117

1942-1960

1	Hoyt Wilhelm	146
2	Harry Brecheen	133
	Whitey Ford	133
4	Hal Newhouser	130
5	Sal Maglie	127
6	Max Lanier	125
	Mel Parnell	125
8	Dizzy Trout	124
9	Mort Cooper	123
10	Bob Feller	122
11	Tiny Bonham	120
12	Bob Lemon	119
	Dutch Leonard	119
	Billy Pierce	119
	Bobby Shantz	119

1961-1976

1	Sandy Koufax	131
2	Bob Gibson	127
	Tom Seaver	127
4	Jim Palmer	125
5	Juan Marichal	122
6	Don Drysdale	121
	Andy Messersmith	121
8	Dean Chance	119
	Rollie Fingers	119
10	Gaylord Perry	117
11	Tug McGraw	116
	Gary Nolan	116
13	4 players tied	115

1977-1998

1	Roger Clemens	151
2	Greg Maddux	146
3	Kevin Appier	135
4	Mike Mussina	130
5	Randy Johnson	129
6	David Cone	128
7	Rich Gossage	125
8	Kevin Brown	124
	Bret Saberhagen	124
10	John Tudor	123
11	Tom Glavine	122
	Jose Rijo	122
	Dave Stieb	122
14	Jimmy Key	121
	Curt Schilling	121

Pitching Runs

1	Cy Young	753
2	Walter Johnson	706
3	Lefty Grove	595
4	Kid Nichols	531
5	Roger Clemens	492
6	Pete Alexander	484
7	Warren Spahn	470
8	Christy Mathewson	420
9	Tom Seaver	419
10	Amos Rusie	418
11	Tim Keefe	404
12	Carl Hubbell	394
13	Whitey Ford	386
14	Bob Feller	385
15	Jim Palmer	374
16	John Clarkson	371
17	Greg Maddux	364
18	Lefty Gomez	322
19	Ted Lyons	313
20	Gaylord Perry	311
21	Ed Walsh	310
	Hoyt Wilhelm	310
23	Nolan Ryan	309
24	Charley Radbourn	302
25	Red Faber	294
26	Bob Gibson	290
27	Dazzy Vance	281
28	Mordecai Brown	279
29	Red Ruffing	272
30	Bert Blyleven	271
31	Dutch Leonard	267
32	Don Drysdale	266
33	Robin Roberts	264
34	Juan Marichal	262
35	Stan Coveleski	259
	Don Sutton	259
37	Hal Newhouser	257
	Eddie Plank	257
39	Tommy Bridges	256
40	Bob Lemon	251
	Eppa Rixey	251
42	Billy Pierce	250
43	David Cone	249
44	Dolf Luque	245
	Tony Mullane	245
46	Sandy Koufax	243
47	Rube Waddell	240
48	Steve Carlton	236
49	Clark Griffith	233
50	Jimmy Key	222
51	Kevin Brown	221
52	Carl Mays	217
53	Addie Joss	216
	Mickey Welch	216
55	Bob Caruthers	214
	Tommy John	214
57	Waite Hoyt	210
	Urban Shocker	210
59	Randy Johnson	209
	Bret Saberhagen	209
61	Silver King	204
62	Orel Hershiser	202
	Jim McCormick	202
64	Eddie Cicotte	201
	Ron Guidry	201
66	Kevin Appier	200
	Nig Cuppy	200
68	Dave Stieb	198
	Will White	198
70	Harry Brecheen	194
71	Phil Niekro	192
72	Mel Harder	190
73	Lon Warneke	188
74	Dizzy Dean	187
	Chuck Finley	187
76	Ed Lopat	186
	Joe McGinnity	186
78	Mike Mussina	181
79	Jim Bunning	179
	Ed Morris	179
	Eddie Rommel	179
82	Larry French	178
83	Dizzy Trout	177
84	Spud Chandler	176
85	Sam Leever	175
86	Freddie Fitzsimmons	174
	Mike Garcia	174
88	Sadie McMahon	172
	Andy Messersmith	172
	Vic Willis	172
91	Early Wynn	170
92	Thornton Lee	169
93	Wilbur Cooper	168
94	Pedro Martinez	165
95	Dennis Eckersley	164
96	Tom Glavine	163
97	Charlie Buffinton	162
98	Babe Adams	161
	Noodles Hahn	161
100	Jim Galvin	160

Adjusted Pitching Runs

1	Cy Young	819
2	Walter Johnson	668
3	Kid Nichols	653
4	Lefty Grove	643
5	Roger Clemens	544
6	Pete Alexander	522
7	John Clarkson	476
8	Tom Seaver	411
9	Greg Maddux	404
10	Christy Mathewson	403
11	Amos Rusie	384
12	Tim Keefe	375
13	Carl Hubbell	355
14	Bob Gibson	335
15	Warren Spahn	330
16	Bert Blyleven	317
17	Whitey Ford	315
	Jim Palmer	315
19	Hal Newhouser	305
	Gaylord Perry	305
21	Ted Lyons	302
22	Bob Feller	301
23	Phil Niekro	299
24	Tommy Bridges	291
25	Hoyt Wilhelm	288
26	Steve Carlton	277
27	Stan Coveleski	276
28	Red Faber	274
29	Charley Radbourn	271
30	Tony Mullane	270
	Ed Walsh	270
32	Mordecai Brown	266
	Clark Griffith	266
	Dazzy Vance	266
35	Fergie Jenkins	254
	Eddie Plank	254
37	Silver King	251
38	Eppa Rixey	248
39	Juan Marichal	247
	Jack Stivetts	247
	Rube Waddell	247
42	Dave Stieb	240
43	Nig Cuppy	239
44	Robin Roberts	236
45	David Cone	233
46	Dizzy Trout	232
47	Don Drysdale	230
48	Lefty Gomez	229
	Billy Pierce	229
50	Urban Shocker	226
51	Dutch Leonard	224
52	Sandy Koufax	221
53	Kevin Appier	218
	Nolan Ryan	218
55	Eddie Rommel	217
56	Jimmy Key	216
57	Randy Johnson	215
	Bret Saberhagen	215
59	Vic Willis	208
60	Joe McGinnity	207
61	Bob Caruthers	206
	Addie Joss	206
63	Harry Brecheen	205
64	Dennis Eckersley	202
65	Dizzy Dean	201
66	Dolf Luque	200
	Jim McCormick	200
68	Mickey Welch	196
69	Eddie Cicotte	195
	Wes Ferrell	195
	Tom Glavine	195
72	Kevin Brown	194
73	Bob Lemon	193
74	Jim Bunning	192
75	Carl Mays	189
76	Lon Warneke	188
77	Chuck Finley	187
	Noodles Hahn	187
79	Rick Reuschel	183
80	Mel Harder	182
	Sadie McMahon	182
	Jack Quinn	182
83	Mike Mussina	181
84	Wilbur Cooper	180
85	Tommy John	179
	Will White	179
87	Frank Dwyer	178
88	Red Ruffing	174
89	Waite Hoyt	173
	Luis Tiant	173
91	Thornton Lee	172
92	Larry French	171
93	Mel Parnell	170
94	Sam Leever	169
95	John Smoltz	168
	Bucky Walters	168
97	Ron Guidry	167
	Virgil Trucks	167
99	Pedro Martinez	166
100	Orel Hershiser	165

Pitching Wins

1	Walter Johnson	73.2
2	Cy Young	70.8
3	Lefty Grove	55.5
4	Pete Alexander	49.7
5	Roger Clemens	48.0
6	Warren Spahn	47.4
7	Kid Nichols	47.1
8	Christy Mathewson	44.2
9	Tom Seaver	43.8
10	Whitey Ford	39.3
11	Jim Palmer	38.8
12	Carl Hubbell	38.8
13	Bob Feller	37.5
14	Greg Maddux	37.1
15	Tim Keefe	36.3
16	Amos Rusie	35.9
17	Ed Walsh	33.4
18	John Clarkson	33.1
19	Gaylord Perry	32.6
20	Nolan Ryan	32.1
21	Hoyt Wilhelm	31.9
22	Bob Gibson	30.5
23	Lefty Gomez	29.9
24	Mordecai Brown	29.7
25	Ted Lyons	29.4
26	Red Faber	28.9
27	Bert Blyleven	27.8
28	Don Drysdale	27.7
29	Juan Marichal	27.6
30	Eddie Plank	27.2
31	Dazzy Vance	27.0
32	Don Sutton	26.9
33	Charley Radbourn	26.9
34	Robin Roberts	26.6
35	Dutch Leonard	26.4
36	Hal Newhouser	26.0
37	Stan Coveleski	25.9
38	Red Ruffing	25.6
39	Rube Waddell	25.2
40	Eppa Rixey	25.2
41	Sandy Koufax	25.1
42	Billy Pierce	25.1
43	Bob Lemon	25.0
44	David Cone	24.9
45	Steve Carlton	24.7
46	Tommy Bridges	24.1
47	Dolf Luque	23.9
48	Addie Joss	23.4
49	Tommy John	22.1
50	Carl Mays	22.0
51	Kevin Brown	21.8
52	Jimmy Key	21.7
53	Tony Mullane	21.5
54	Eddie Cicotte	21.5
55	Clark Griffith	20.8
56	Bret Saberhagen	20.8
57	Urban Shocker	20.5
58	Orel Hershiser	20.5
59	Randy Johnson	20.4
60	Waite Hoyt	20.2
61	Ron Guidry	20.1
62	Phil Niekro	20.0
63	Dave Stieb	19.8
64	Mickey Welch	19.7
65	Harry Brecheen	19.6
66	Kevin Appier	19.3
67	Lon Warneke	18.9
68	Bob Caruthers	18.8
69	Ed Lopat	18.8
70	Jim Bunning	18.6
71	Joe McGinnity	18.6
72	Dizzy Dean	18.6
73	Jim McCormick	18.4
74	Will White	18.2
75	Andy Messersmith	18.2
76	Chuck Finley	18.2
77	Mel Harder	18.1
78	Dizzy Trout	17.9
79	Sam Leever	17.8
80	Vic Willis	17.6
81	Spud Chandler	17.6
82	Silver King	17.6
83	Larry French	17.6
84	Wilbur Cooper	17.5
85	Mike Garcia	17.4
86	Mike Mussina	17.3
87	Early Wynn	17.2
88	Ed Reulbach	17.1
89	Freddie Fitzsimmons	17.1
90	Nig Cuppy	17.0
91	Eddie Rommel	17.0
92	Babe Adams	16.7
93	Tom Glavine	16.6
94	Dennis Eckersley	16.6
95	Fergie Jenkins	16.4
96	Thornton Lee	16.3
97	Rich Gossage	16.2
98	Pedro Martinez	16.1
99	Ed Morris	16.0
100	Vida Blue	15.9

Adjusted Pitching Wins

1	Cy Young	77.0
2	Walter Johnson	69.2
3	Lefty Grove	59.9
4	Kid Nichols	57.9
5	Pete Alexander	53.6
6	Roger Clemens	53.1
7	Tom Seaver	43.0
8	John Clarkson	42.4
9	Christy Mathewson	42.4
10	Greg Maddux	41.1
11	Bob Gibson	35.2
12	Carl Hubbell	35.0
13	Tim Keefe	33.7
14	Warren Spahn	33.3
15	Amos Rusie	33.0
16	Jim Palmer	32.7
17	Bert Blyleven	32.6
18	Whitey Ford	32.1
19	Gaylord Perry	32.0
20	Phil Niekro	31.2
21	Hal Newhouser	30.9
22	Hoyt Wilhelm	29.6
23	Bob Feller	29.3
24	Ed Walsh	29.1
25	Steve Carlton	29.0
26	Ted Lyons	28.4
27	Mordecai Brown	28.3
28	Stan Coveleski	27.6
29	Tommy Bridges	27.4
30	Red Faber	27.0
31	Eddie Plank	26.9
32	Fergie Jenkins	26.5
33	Juan Marichal	26.0
34	Rube Waddell	26.0
35	Dazzy Vance	25.6
36	Eppa Rixey	24.9
37	Charley Radbourn	24.1
38	Dave Stieb	24.0
39	Don Drysdale	24.0
40	Robin Roberts	23.8
41	Clark Griffith	23.8
42	Tony Mullane	23.7
43	Dizzy Trout	23.5
44	David Cone	23.3
45	Billy Pierce	23.0
46	Sandy Koufax	22.9
47	Nolan Ryan	22.6
48	Addie Joss	22.3
49	Dutch Leonard	22.1
50	Urban Shocker	22.1
51	Silver King	21.6
52	Bret Saberhagen	21.3
53	Vic Willis	21.3
54	Lefty Gomez	21.3
55	Jimmy Key	21.1
56	Kevin Appier	21.1
57	Randy Johnson	21.0
58	Jack Stivetts	20.9
59	Eddie Cicotte	20.8
60	Harry Brecheen	20.7
61	Joe McGinnity	20.7
62	Eddie Rommel	20.6
63	Dennis Eckersley	20.4
64	Nig Cuppy	20.4
65	Dizzy Dean	20.0
66	Jim Bunning	19.9
67	Tom Glavine	19.8
68	Dolf Luque	19.5
69	Bob Lemon	19.2
70	Rick Reuschel	19.1
71	Carl Mays	19.1
72	Kevin Brown	19.1
73	Lon Warneke	18.9
74	Wilbur Cooper	18.7
75	Tommy John	18.5
76	Noodles Hahn	18.3
77	Jim McCormick	18.3
78	Luis Tiant	18.2
79	Chuck Finley	18.2
80	Jack Quinn	18.1
81	Bob Caruthers	18.1
82	Wes Ferrell	18.0
83	Mickey Welch	17.9
84	Mel Harder	17.3
85	Mike Mussina	17.3
86	Sam Leever	17.2
87	John Smoltz	17.1
88	Bucky Walters	17.1
89	Virgil Trucks	16.9
90	Larry French	16.9
91	Mel Parnell	16.8
92	Orel Hershiser	16.7
93	Babe Adams	16.7
94	Ron Guidry	16.7
95	Waite Hoyt	16.6
96	Thornton Lee	16.6
97	Hippo Vaughn	16.5
98	Will White	16.5
99	Red Ruffing	16.4
100	Pedro Martinez	16.2

Opponents' Batting Average

Rank	Player	Avg
1	Nolan Ryan	.204
2	Sandy Koufax	.205
3	Sid Fernandez	.209
4	Randy Johnson	.212
	Andy Messersmith	.212
	J.R. Richard	.212
7	Sam McDowell	.215
8	Hoyt Wilhelm	.216
9	Ed Walsh	.218
10	Mario Soto	.220
	Bob Turley	.220
12	Addie Joss	.223
	Orval Overall	.223
	Jeff Tesreau	.223
15	David Cone	.224
	Jose DeLeon	.224
	Jim Maloney	.224
	Ed Reulbach	.224
19	Roger Clemens	.225
20	Larry Corcoran	.226
	Tim Keefe	.226
	Tom Seaver	.226
23	Walter Johnson	.227
24	Bob Gibson	.228
	Rich Gossage	.228
	Rube Waddell	.228
	Don Wilson	.228
28	Sam Jones	.230
	Jim Palmer	.230
30	Bobby Bolin	.231
	Bob Feller	.231
	Catfish Hunter	.231
33	Al Downing	.232
	John Smoltz	.232
	Johnny Vander Meer	.232
	Stan Williams	.232
37	Mordecai Brown	.233
	Charlie Ferguson	.233
	Charlie Hough	.233
40	Dean Chance	.234
	Larry Cheney	.234
	Denny McLain	.234
	Toad Ramsey	.234
	Amos Rusie	.234
45	Ray Culp	.235
	Rollie Fingers	.235
	Whitey Ford	.235
	Dave Foutz	.235
	Ramon Martinez	.235
	Ed Morris	.235
	Curt Schilling	.235
	John Ward	.235
53	Moe Drabowsky	.236
	Greg Maddux	.236
	Christy Mathewson	.236
	Tony Mullane	.236
	Don Sutton	.236
	Luis Tiant	.236
	Bob Veale	.236
60	Vida Blue	.237
	Juan Marichal	.237
	Tug McGraw	.237
	Juan Pizarro	.237
	Frank Smith	.237
65	Kevin Appier	.238
	Rudy May	.238
	Allie Reynolds	.238
	Jim Scott	.238
	Sonny Siebert	.238
70	Gary Bell	.239
	Chief Bender	.239
	Bill Donovan	.239
	Don Drysdale	.239
	Hal Newhouser	.239
	Gary Nolan	.239
	Barney Pelty	.239
	Eddie Plank	.239
	Dupee Shaw	.239
	Dave Stieb	.239
	Will White	.239
81	Steve Carlton	.240
	Bob Caruthers	.240
	John Clarkson	.240
	Mort Cooper	.240
	Dwight Gooden	.240
	Billy Pierce	.240
	Jose Rijo	.240
	Mike Scott	.240
	Bill Singer	.240
	Virgil Trucks	.240
91	Jack Coombs	.241
	Pete Harnisch	.241
	Kirby Higbe	.241
	Bob Lemon	.241
	George McQuillan	.241
	Earl Moore	.241
	Charley Radbourn	.241
	Hooks Wiltse	.241
99	9 players tied	.242

Opponents' On Base Pctg.

Rank	Player	Pct
1	John Ward	.254
2	Addie Joss	.260
3	George Bradley	.262
4	Terry Larkin	.263
5	Larry Corcoran	.264
	Ed Walsh	.264
7	Tommy Bond	.267
8	Will White	.268
9	Charlie Ferguson	.270
10	Christy Mathewson	.273
	Ed Morris	.273
12	Jim McCormick	.274
13	Fred Goldsmith	.275
	Tim Keefe	.275
	Jim Whitney	.275
16	Sandy Koufax	.276
17	Mordecai Brown	.278
	Juan Marichal	.278
	Charley Radbourn	.278
20	Walter Johnson	.279
	Dupee Shaw	.279
22	Guy Hecker	.281
	Jumbo McGinnis	.281
24	Deacon Phillippe	.283
25	Babe Adams	.284
	Jim Galvin	.284
27	Bob Caruthers	.285
	Bobby Mathews	.285
	Tom Seaver	.285
30	Dave Foutz	.286
	Greg Maddux	.286
32	Catfish Hunter	.287
	Gary Nolan	.287
	Don Sutton	.287
	Cy Young	.287
36	Pete Alexander	.288
	Sid Fernandez	.288
	Rube Waddell	.288
39	Tiny Bonham	.289
	Henry Boyle	.289
	Noodles Hahn	.289
	Fergie Jenkins	.289
	Jack Lynch	.289
	Andy Messersmith	.289
45	Roger Clemens	.290
	Curt Schilling	.290
	Hoyt Wilhelm	.290
	Hooks Wiltse	.290
49	Nick Altrock	.291
	Chief Bender	.291
	John Clarkson	.291
	Carl Hubbell	.291
	Bret Saberhagen	.291
54	Charlie Buffinton	.292
	Dennis Eckersley	.292
	Denny McLain	.292
	Mike Mussina	.292
	Mickey Welch	.292
	Doc White	.292
60	Sam Leever	.293
	Eddie Plank	.293
	Robin Roberts	.293
63	Don Drysdale	.294
	Ron Guidry	.294
	George McQuillan	.294
66	Rollie Fingers	.295
	Toad Ramsey	.295
	Jeff Tesreau	.295
69	Jim Palmer	.296
	Mario Soto	.296
	Ralph Terry	.296
72	Jack Chesbro	.297
	Eddie Cicotte	.297
	Gaylord Perry	.297
	Frank Smith	.297
	John Smoltz	.297
	Warren Spahn	.297
	George Winter	.297
79	Harry Brecheen	.298
	John Candelaria	.298
	Dizzy Dean	.298
	Tony Mullane	.298
	Orval Overall	.298
	Lee Richmond	.298
	Dick Rudolph	.298
	Jack Taylor	.298
	Luis Tiant	.298
88	Jim Bunning	.299
	Mike Cuellar	.299
	Eddie Fisher	.299
	Bob Gibson	.299
	Don Mossi	.299
	Don Newcombe	.299
	Ed Reulbach	.299
	Slim Sallee	.299
96	Mort Cooper	.300
	Joe Horlen	.300
	Kid Nichols	.300
	Fritz Peterson	.300
	Mike Scott	.300

Wins Above Team

Rank	Player	WAT
1	Cy Young	99.7
2	Walter Johnson	90.0
3	Pete Alexander	81.6
4	Christy Mathewson	64.9
5	Lefty Grove	62.9
6	Tom Seaver	58.9
7	Jim McCormick	56.3
8	Roger Clemens	55.9
9	Jim Galvin	54.3
10	Charley Radbourn	50.3
11	Warren Spahn	45.8
12	Clark Griffith	45.6
13	Whitey Ford	44.4
14	Will White	43.5
15	Juan Marichal	38.7
16	Randy Johnson	37.8
17	Bob Feller	36.8
	Amos Rusie	36.8
	Mickey Welch	36.8
20	Ted Lyons	36.2
	Phil Niekro	36.2
22	Tony Mullane	35.8
	Eddie Plank	35.8
24	Dwight Gooden	35.7
25	Jesse Tannehill	35.2
26	Charlie Buffinton	35.0
27	Wes Ferrell	34.8
28	Carl Hubbell	34.6
29	Kid Nichols	34.4
30	Steve Carlton	33.5
31	Dazzy Vance	33.2
32	Jim Devlin	32.5
	Greg Maddux	32.5
34	Joe McGinnity	32.4
35	Guy Hecker	31.5
	Ed Walsh	31.5
37	Bob Gibson	31.0
38	Ed Morris	30.8
	Eddie Rommel	30.8
40	Sandy Koufax	30.6
41	Bob Caruthers	30.4
42	Jim Palmer	30.2
	Urban Shocker	30.2
44	David Cone	30.1
45	Robin Roberts	30.0
46	Sadie McMahon	29.5
47	Fergie Jenkins	29.3
48	Ron Guidry	29.1
49	Mordecai Brown	29.0
50	Mike Mussina	28.8
51	Addie Joss	28.7
52	Dizzy Dean	27.6
53	Bobby Mathews	26.7
54	Orel Hershiser	26.6
55	Schoolboy Rowe	26.5
56	Tom Glavine	25.8
57	Sam Leever	25.7
58	Rip Sewell	25.4
59	Frank Killen	25.1
60	Jack Chesbro	24.8
61	Nap Rucker	24.7
62	Red Lucas	24.5
	Herb Pennock	24.5
64	Russ Ford	24.3
65	Bret Saberhagen	24.2
66	John Candelaria	23.9
67	Charlie Ferguson	23.6
68	Red Faber	23.5
	Joe Wood	23.5
70	Johnny Allen	23.4
	Chief Bender	23.4
72	John Clarkson	23.2
73	Gaylord Perry	23.1
	Rick Reuschel	23.1
75	Noodles Hahn	22.9
	Firpo Marberry	22.9
77	Mark Langston	22.8
78	Sal Maglie	22.7
79	Gus Weyhing	22.6
80	Tim Keefe	22.5
81	Ramon Martinez	22.4
82	Tommy John	22.2
83	Carl Mays	21.9
	Bob Welch	21.9
85	Burleigh Grimes	21.3
	Claude Passeau	21.3
	Hippo Vaughn	21.3
88	Spud Chandler	21.2
89	Dutch Leonard	21.1
	J.R. Richard	21.1
91	John Tudor	21.0
	George Uhle	21.0
	Bucky Walters	21.0
94	Jim Maloney	20.9
95	Slim Sallee	20.6
96	Vida Blue	20.4
	Hal Newhouser	20.4
98	Bert Blyleven	20.3
	Freddie Fitzsimmons	20.3
100	2 players tied	20.2

Wins Above League

Rank	Player	WAL
1	Cy Young	490.5
2	Walter Johnson	417.2
3	Jim Galvin	349.1
4	Pete Alexander	344.1
5	Kid Nichols	342.4
6	Warren Spahn	337.3
7	Nolan Ryan	330.6
8	Phil Niekro	327.2
9	Christy Mathewson	322.9
10	Gaylord Perry	321.5
11	Tim Keefe	317.2
12	Steve Carlton	315.5
13	Don Sutton	305.2
14	Bert Blyleven	301.1
15	Tom Seaver	301.0
16	John Clarkson	295.4
17	Robin Roberts	289.3
18	Eddie Plank	286.9
19	Eppa Rixey	283.4
20	Early Wynn	283.3
21	Fergie Jenkins	281.5
22	Lefty Grove	280.4
23	Tommy John	278.0
24	Mickey Welch	276.4
25	Charley Radbourn	276.1
26	Tony Mullane	275.7
27	Ted Lyons	273.4
28	Jim Kaat	272.5
29	Red Ruffing	265.4
30	Red Faber	260.5
31	Jack Powell	259.0
32	Jim McCormick	257.8
33	Burleigh Grimes	253.1
34	Gus Weyhing	251.3
35	Jack Quinn	250.6
36	Vic Willis	248.3
37	Bob Gibson	247.7
38	Frank Tanana	247.6
39	Bob Feller	243.3
40	Amos Rusie	243.0
41	Jim Palmer	242.7
42	Carl Hubbell	238.5
43	Roger Clemens	231.6
44	Jerry Koosman	230.4
45	Dennis Martinez	229.0
46	Sam Jones	228.9
47	Paul Derringer	228.4
48	Jack Morris	227.4
49	Bobo Newsom	227.1
50	Waite Hoyt	226.1
51	Charlie Hough	225.9
52	Jim Bunning	223.9
53	Bob Friend	223.7
54	Mel Harder	221.8
55	Rick Reuschel	221.6
56	Luis Tiant	218.7
57	Juan Marichal	218.5
58	Wilbur Cooper	215.7
59	Clark Griffith	215.3
60	Joe McGinnity	214.7
61	Will White	214.0
62	Billy Pierce	213.0
63	Mordecai Brown	212.8
64	George Mullin	212.7
65	Don Drysdale	211.5
66	Mickey Lolich	210.2
67	Hal Newhouser	209.4
68	Herb Pennock	209.3
69	Joe Niekro	208.5
70	Dutch Leonard	208.1
71	Charlie Buffinton	206.8
72	Stan Coveleski	206.1
73	Dolf Luque	206.0
74	Hooks Dauss	205.9
75	Jerry Reuss	204.8
76	Larry Jackson	204.6
77	Dennis Eckersley	204.4
78	Whitey Ford	203.1
79	Jim Whitney	202.5
80	Curt Simmons	202.4
81	Jim Perry	202.4
82	Earl Whitehill	202.1
83	Larry French	200.9
84	Claude Osteen	200.8
85	Greg Maddux	200.6
86	Catfish Hunter	200.4
87	Adonis Terry	200.2
88	Silver King	199.6
89	Eddie Cicotte	199.3
90	Milt Pappas	199.0
91	Al Orth	198.0
92	Tom Zachary	196.4
93	Bucky Walters	196.1
94	Freddie Fitzsimmons	195.6
95	Vida Blue	194.9
96	Jesse Haines	194.2
97	Dazzy Vance	194.1
98	Rube Waddell	194.0
99	Tommy Bridges	193.4
100	Charlie Root	193.1

Relief Games

1	Kent Tekulve	1050
2	Jesse Orosco	1021
3	Hoyt Wilhelm	1018
4	Lee Smith	1016
5	Rich Gossage	965
6	Gene Garber	922
7	Lindy McDaniel	913
8	Rollie Fingers	907
9	Sparky Lyle	899
10	Jeff Reardon	880
11	Don McMahon	872
12	John Franco	832
13	Paul Assenmacher	828
14	Roy Face	821
15	Tug McGraw	785
16	Darold Knowles	757
17	Mike Jackson	756
18	Dan Plesac	744
19	Tom Burgmeier	742
	Gary Lavelle	742
21	Ron Perranoski	736
22	Willie Hernandez	733
23	Roger McDowell	721
24	Doug Jones	718
25	Randy Myers	716
26	Dennis Eckersley	710
27	Clay Carroll	703
	Greg Minton	703
29	Mike Marshall	699
30	Larry Andersen	698
31	Bill Campbell	691
32	Steve Bedrosian	686
33	Dan Quisenberry	674
34	Bruce Sutter	661
35	Craig Lefferts	651
36	Jeff Montgomery	650
37	Ted Abernathy	647
38	Tom Henke	642
39	Dave LaRoche	632
40	Dave Righetti	629
41	Eddie Fisher	627
42	Bob McClure	625
43	Paul Lindblad	623
44	Todd Worrell	617
45	Mitch Williams	616
46	Stu Miller	611
47	Grant Jackson	609
48	Dave Smith	608
49	Greg Harris	605
	Eric Plunk	605

Relief Wins

1	Hoyt Wilhelm	124
2	Lindy McDaniel	119
3	Rich Gossage	115
4	Rollie Fingers	107
5	Sparky Lyle	99
6	Roy Face	96
7	Gene Garber	94
	Kent Tekulve	94
9	Mike Marshall	92
10	Don McMahon	90
11	Tug McGraw	89
12	Clay Carroll	88
13	Bob Stanley	85
14	Jesse Orosco	84
15	Bill Campbell	80
	Gary Lavelle	80
17	Tom Burgmeier	79
	Stu Miller	79
	Ron Perranoski	79
20	John Franco	77
21	Johnny Murphy	73
	Jeff Reardon	73
23	John Hiller	72
24	Mark Clear	71
	Dick Hall	71
	Lee Smith	71
27	Willie Hernandez	70
	Roger McDowell	70
29	Pedro Borbon	69
30	Bruce Sutter	68
31	Steve Bedrosian	65
32	Al Hrabosky	64
33	Darold Knowles	63
	Clem Labine	63
	Dave LaRoche	63
36	Jim Brewer	62
	Turk Farrell	62
	Eddie Fisher	62
	Grant Jackson	62
	Paul Lindblad	62
	Frank Linzy	62
42	Joe Heving	60
43	Paul Assenmacher	59
	Johnny Klippstein	59
	Eric Plunk	59
	Elias Sosa	59
47	Aurelio Lopez	58
	Phil Regan	58
49	5 players tied	57

Relief Losses

1	Gene Garber	108
2	Hoyt Wilhelm	103
3	Rollie Fingers	101
4	Mike Marshall	98
5	Kent Tekulve	90
6	Lindy McDaniel	88
7	Lee Smith	87
8	Rich Gossage	85
9	Roy Face	82
10	Jeff Reardon	77
11	Sparky Lyle	76
12	Gary Lavelle	75
13	Ron Perranoski	74
14	Doug Jones	71
	Darold Knowles	71
	Jesse Orosco	71
	Bruce Sutter	71
18	Roger McDowell	69
	Tug McGraw	69
20	John Franco	68
21	Stu Miller	67
22	Clay Carroll	66
	Don McMahon	66
24	Bill Campbell	65
25	Greg Minton	62
26	Steve Bedrosian	61
	Bob Stanley	61
28	John Hiller	58
29	Frank Linzy	57
30	Mitch Williams	56
31	Willie Hernandez	55
32	Craig Lefferts	54
33	Tom Burgmeier	53
	Ron Davis	53
	Greg Harris	53
	Mike Jackson	53
	Randy Myers	53
	Dan Plesac	53
	Dave Smith	53
40	Jim Kern	52
	Randy Moffitt	52
	Dave Righetti	52
	Todd Worrell	52
44	Turk Farrell	51
	Eddie Fisher	51
	Dave LaRoche	51
	Claude Raymond	51
48	Mark Davis	50
	Dale Murray	50
	Al Worthington	50

Relief Innings Pitched

1	Hoyt Wilhelm	1871.0
2	Lindy McDaniel	1694.0
3	Rich Gossage	1556.2
4	Rollie Fingers	1500.1
5	Gene Garber	1452.2
6	Kent Tekulve	1436.1
7	Sparky Lyle	1390.1
8	Tug McGraw	1301.1
9	Don McMahon	1297.0
10	Mike Marshall	1259.1
11	Lee Smith	1252.1
12	Tom Burgmeier	1248.2
13	Roy Face	1212.1
14	Clay Carroll	1204.2
15	Eddie Fisher	1186.0
16	Bill Campbell	1177.1
17	Ron Perranoski	1170.2
18	Jesse Orosco	1165.2
19	Bob Stanley	1157.0
20	Jeff Reardon	1132.1
21	Stu Miller	1094.2
22	Greg Minton	1087.1
23	Gary Lavelle	1077.2
24	Darold Knowles	1052.1
25	Paul Lindblad	1043.1
	Dan Quisenberry	1043.1
27	Bruce Sutter	1042.1
28	Johnny Klippstein	1040.2
29	Roger McDowell	1039.2
30	Pedro Borbon	1016.1
31	John Franco	1000.2
32	Willie Hernandez	994.1
33	Bob Miller	992.2
34	Larry Andersen	990.2
35	Dave LaRoche	976.0
36	Ted Abernathy	970.0
37	John Hiller	962.2
38	Steve Bedrosian	931.0
39	Greg Harris	923.0
40	Doug Jones	920.0
41	Mike Jackson	915.1
42	Elias Sosa	905.0
43	Dale Murray	901.1
44	Doug Bair	889.1
45	Terry Forster	888.0
46	Craig Lefferts	881.2
47	Bob Locker	879.0
48	Dennis Lamp	876.0
49	Ron Reed	874.1
50	Jim Brewer	861.0

Relief Points

1	Lee Smith	1011
2	John Franco	880
3	Dennis Eckersley	835
4	Jeff Reardon	803
5	Rollie Fingers	795
6	Rich Gossage	765
7	Bruce Sutter	665
8	Tom Henke	662
9	Randy Myers	655
10	Jeff Montgomery	627
11	Doug Jones	625
12	Hoyt Wilhelm	599
13	Sparky Lyle	598
14	Rick Aguilera	576
15	Todd Worrell	560
16	Dan Quisenberry	554
17	John Wetteland	551
18	Dave Righetti	544
19	Rod Beck	516
	Gene Garber	516
21	Roy Face	496
22	Lindy McDaniel	494
23	Dave Smith	485
24	Tug McGraw	469
25	Kent Tekulve	466
26	Mike Marshall	462
27	Mike Henneman	458
28	Ron Perranoski	442
29	Steve Bedrosian	437
30	Gregg Olson	435
31	Bobby Thigpen	428
32	Roberto Hernandez	420
	Don McMahon	420
34	Trevor Hoffman	419
35	Mitch Williams	418
36	Jeff Russell	406
37	Stu Miller	399
38	Clay Carroll	396
39	Roger McDowell	389
40	Willie Hernandez	379
41	Jesse Orosco	377
42	Bob Stanley	373
43	Jay Howell	369
44	Dave Giusti	363
	Bryan Harvey	363
46	Ted Abernathy	362
47	Gary Lavelle	357
48	Greg Minton	352
49	Bill Campbell	347
50	Dan Plesac	345

Relief Ranking

1	Hoyt Wilhelm	355
2	Rich Gossage	316
3	John Franco	274
4	Lee Smith	243
5	John Wetteland	227
6	Dan Quisenberry	219
7	Tom Henke	215
8	Kent Tekulve	207
9	Rollie Fingers	204
10	Mike Marshall	196
11	Jeff Montgomery	193
12	John Hiller	189
13	Jesse Orosco	188
14	Sparky Lyle	186
15	Bruce Sutter	184
16	Doug Jones	180
17	Dennis Eckersley	174
18	Ellis Kinder	166
19	Bob Stanley	163
20	Rick Aguilera	161
	Tug McGraw	161
22	Roberto Hernandez	160
23	Lindy McDaniel	158
24	Ron Perranoski	150
25	Gary Lavelle	146
26	Roy Face	143
27	Stu Miller	141
28	Mark Eichhorn	138
29	Gregg Olson	137
30	Gene Garber	136
31	Dave Righetti	131
32	Jeff Reardon	130
33	Mike Jackson	127
34	Mike Henneman	124
35	Clay Carroll	123
36	Jeff Russell	122
37	Trevor Hoffman	121
38	Bryan Harvey	119
	Willie Hernandez	119
40	Lefty Grove	117
	Dave Smith	117
42	Dan Plesac	116
43	Robb Nen	114
44	Tom Burgmeier	111
45	Frank Linzy	110
	Dick Radatz	110
47	Randy Myers	109
48	Mariano Rivera	108
49	Jim Brewer	107
	Johnny Murphy	107

Relievers' Runs

1	Hoyt Wilhelm	261
2	Rich Gossage	185
3	Rollie Fingers	156
4	Dan Quisenberry	144
5	Jesse Orosco	139
6	John Franco	133
7	Tom Henke	129
8	Kent Tekulve	128
9	Mark Eichhorn	122
10	Dennis Eckersley	121
	Sparky Lyle	121
12	Lee Smith	119
13	John Wetteland	117
14	Jeff Montgomery	114
15	Tug McGraw	110
16	Mike Jackson	108
17	Clay Carroll	100
	Mike Marshall	100
	Ron Perranoski	100
20	John Hiller	99
	Gary Lavelle	99
	Don McMahon	99
23	Doug Jones	96
	Stu Miller	96
25	Lindy McDaniel	94
26	Bob Stanley	93
27	Eric Plunk	91
	Bruce Sutter	91
29	Roberto Hernandez	89
	Dave Smith	89
31	Greg Minton	88
32	Johnny Murphy	85
33	Ellis Kinder	82
34	Mike Henneman	80
	Jeff Reardon	80
36	Rick Aguilera	78
	Tom Burgmeier	78
38	Greg Harris	76
	Mariano Rivera	76
40	Steve Farr	75
	Jay Howell	75
	Jeff Russell	75
43	Willie Hernandez	74
44	Jim Brewer	73
45	Tim Burke	72
46	Terry Forster	71
	Roger McDowell	71
48	Larry Andersen	70
	Bob Miller	70
50	2 players tied	69

Adjusted Relievers' Runs

1	Hoyt Wilhelm	243
2	Rich Gossage	178
3	Dan Quisenberry	147
4	Kent Tekulve	142
5	Lee Smith	140
6	John Franco	137
7	Jesse Orosco	132
8	Tom Henke	130
9	Mark Eichhorn	126
10	Jeff Montgomery	121
	Bob Stanley	121
12	Rollie Fingers	120
13	Sparky Lyle	119
	John Wetteland	119
15	Bruce Sutter	117
16	John Hiller	115
17	Tug McGraw	113
18	Mike Jackson	111
19	Lindy McDaniel	108
20	Dennis Eckersley	103
	Mike Marshall	103
22	Doug Jones	99
	Ellis Kinder	99
24	Clay Carroll	97
25	Gary Lavelle	96
26	Gene Garber	93
27	Greg Harris	91
28	Eric Plunk	87
29	Tom Burgmeier	86
30	Don McMahon	85
31	Willie Hernandez	84
	Ron Perranoski	84
	Jeff Reardon	84
34	Roberto Hernandez	83
35	Rick Aguilera	82
	Stu Miller	82
37	Jeff Russell	80
38	Terry Forster	78
39	Mike Henneman	77
40	Steve Farr	76
41	Greg Minton	75
42	Paul Assenmacher	74
	Ron Reed	74
44	Dave Smith	73
45	Mariano Rivera	72
46	Steve Reed	71
47	Larry Andersen	70
	Tim Burke	70
49	Bryan Harvey	68
50	2 players tied	67

Clutch Pitching Index

1	Bob Rhoads	117
2	Ed Killian	116
	Ed Siever	116
4	Win Mercer	115
5	Ron Kline	113
	Bill Lee	113
	Will White	113
8	Al Benton	112
	Ed Lopat	112
	Bob Stanley	112
	Tom Zachary	112
12	Frank Dwyer	111
	Chuck Finley	111
	Whitey Ford	111
	Preacher Roe	111
16	Max Lanier	110
	Bob Miller	110
	Gerry Staley	110
	Bill Wight	110
20	Steve Blass	109
	Bob Buhl	109
	Max Butcher	109
	Dan Casey	109
	Lefty Leifield	109
	Sal Maglie	109
	Mel Parnell	109
	Bob Shaw	109
	Geoff Zahn	109
29	Jim Abbott	108
	Steve Barber	108
	Sheriff Blake	108
	Nixey Callahan	108
	Lefty Grove	108
	Carl Morton	108
	George Mullin	108
	Dizzy Trout	108
	Bob Veale	108
38	Mark Baldwin	107
	Nelson Briles	107
	Lloyd Brown	107
	Nig Cuppy	107
	Larry French	107
	Clark Griffith	107
	Claude Osteen	107
	Eddie Rommel	107
	Dutch Ruether	107
	Eddie Smith	107
	Dummy Taylor	107
	Steve Trout	107
	Mickey Welch	107
51	Jim Bagby	106
	Roger Craig	106
	Red Donahue	106
	Red Faber	106
	Dave Foutz	106
	Mel Harder	106
	Joe Haynes	106
	Guy Hecker	106
	Tommy John	106
	Jim McCormick	106
	Cal McLish	106
	Jeff Pfeffer	106
	Togie Pittinger	106
	Howie Pollet	106
	Nap Rucker	106
	Jim Scott	106
	Sherry Smith	106
	Bill Swift	106
	Sloppy Thurston	106
	John Tudor	106
	Rube Waddell	106
	Bucky Walters	106
73	32 players tied	105

Pitcher Batting Runs

1	Red Ruffing	143
2	Bob Caruthers	111
3	Wes Ferrell	100
4	Walter Johnson	99
5	Red Lucas	98
6	George Uhle	92
7	Guy Hecker	90
	Bob Lemon	90
9	Jim Whitney	89
10	Warren Spahn	88
11	George Mullin	87
12	Don Newcombe	79
13	Babe Ruth	78
14	Schoolboy Rowe	76
15	Early Wynn	72
16	Bob Gibson	65
	Jack Stivetts	65
18	Carl Mays	64
19	Al Orth	63
20	Don Drysdale	60
21	Christy Mathewson	59
22	Gary Peters	57
	Bucky Walters	57
	Earl Wilson	57
25	Jesse Tannehill	55
26	Doc Crandall	54
	Jim Tobin	54
28	Burleigh Grimes	52
	Ad Gumbert	52
30	Claude Hendrix	50
	Tony Mullane	50
32	Joe Bush	49
	Steve Carlton	49
	Charlie Ferguson	49
35	Bob Forsch	48
	Scott Stratton	48
37	Don Larsen	46
38	Dave Foutz	45
	Vern Law	45
	Rick Rhoden	45
	Dutch Ruether	45
	Adonis Terry	45
43	Frank Killen	44
	Jack Scott	44
45	Tommy Byrne	41
	Jim Kaat	41
	Don Robinson	41
48	Johnny Sain	40
49	Wilbur Cooper	39
	Fred Hutchinson	39
	Charley Radbourn	39
52	Claude Osteen	38
	Sloppy Thurston	38
54	Dolf Luque	37
	Doc White	37
56	Jack Coombs	36
	Mickey McDermott	36
58	Clark Griffith	35
	Harvey Haddix	35
	Win Mercer	35
	Frank Smith	35
	Jack Taylor	35
63	Orel Hershiser	34
	Art Nehf	34
	Robin Roberts	34
	Rick Wise	34
67	Chief Bender	33
	Erv Brame	33
	Ken Brett	33
	Catfish Hunter	33
	Ben Sanders	33
72	Hooks Dauss	32
	Ted Lyons	32
	Al Maul	32
	Fernando Valenzuela	32
76	Ray Caldwell	31
	Dizzy Trout	31
	John Ward	31
	Joe Wood	31
80	Ed Brandt	30
	Lew Burdette	30
	Lefty Tyler	30
83	Jack Harshman	29
	Ed Lopat	29
	Jouett Meekin	29
	Camilo Pascual	29
	Juan Pizarro	29
88	Jack Bentley	28
	Tom Glavine	28
	Dwight Gooden	28
	Joe Nuxhall	28
	Tom Seaver	28
	Urban Shocker	28
94	Charlie Buffinton	27
	Whitey Ford	27
	Brickyard Kennedy	27
	Frank Kitson	27
	Bill Sherdel	27
	Lon Warneke	27
100	4 players tied	26

Pitcher Fielding Runs

1	Ed Walsh	83
2	Carl Mays	74
3	Christy Mathewson	68
4	Greg Maddux	67
5	Freddie Fitzsimmons	60
	Bob Lemon	60
7	Burleigh Grimes	58
8	Tommy John	55
9	Harry Howell	51
10	Harry Gumbert	50
11	John Clarkson	46
12	Bill Doak	43
	Dennis Martinez	43
14	Willis Hudlin	42
	Eddie Rommel	42
16	Jack Quinn	40
17	Jim Galvin	39
	Rick Reuschel	39
	Bobby Shantz	39
20	Hooks Dauss	38
	Dizzy Trout	38
22	Jack Russell	36
	Mel Stottlemyre	36
	Fernando Valenzuela	36
25	Charlie Buffinton	35
	Johnny Schmitz	35
	Willie Sudhoff	35
28	Nick Altrock	34
29	Kevin Brown	33
	Orel Hershiser	33
	Tony Mullane	33
32	Red Ames	32
	Murry Dickson	32
	Howard Ehmke	32
	Randy Jones	32
36	Pete Alexander	31
	Russ Christopher	31
	Curt Davis	31
	John Denny	31
40	Tommy Bond	30
	Addie Joss	30
	Hal Schumacher	30
43	Chick Fraser	29
	Gerry Staley	29
	Dave Stieb	29
46	Mike Boddicker	28
	Ben Cantwell	28
	Sid Hudson	28
	Matt Kilroy	28
	George Mullin	28
	Phil Niekro	28
	Ed Willett	28
53	Ted Abernathy	27
	Tom Burgmeier	27
	Spud Chandler	27
	Kenny Rogers	27
	Amos Rusie	27
	Bucky Walters	27
	Vic Willis	27
60	Nixey Callahan	26
	Whitey Ford	26
	Frank Smith	26
	Sherry Smith	26
64	Don Drysdale	25
	Guy Hecker	25
	Larry Jackson	25
	Charlie Leibrandt	25
	Dan Quisenberry	25
	Elmer Stricklett	25
	Doc White	25
71	Mike Caldwell	24
	Frank Corridon	24
	Ned Garvin	24
	Dutch Leonard	24
	John Ward	24
76	Jean Dubuc	23
	Lindy McDaniel	23
	Roger McDowell	23
	Cy Seymour	23
	Bill Swift	23
81	Tom Brewer	22
	Bill Hart	22
	Joe Horlen	22
	Carl Hubbell	22
	Jim McCormick	22
	Stu Miller	22
	Mike Brown	22
	Hal Newhouser	22
	Frank Owen	22
	Dan Petry	22
	Ed Reulbach	22
	Bob Stanley	22
	Kent Tekulve	22
94	11 players tied	21

Pitcher Batting Average

1	Jack Stivetts	.298
2	George Uhle	.289
3	Charlie Ferguson	.288
4	Win Mercer	.286
5	Doc Crandall	.285
6	Bob Caruthers	.282
	Guy Hecker	.282
8	Red Lucas	.281
9	Wes Ferrell	.280
10	Dave Foutz	.276
11	Jack Scott	.275
	John Ward	.275
13	Scott Stratton	.274
14	Nixey Callahan	.273
	Ad Gumbert	.273
	Al Orth	.273
17	Don Newcombe	.271
18	Sloppy Thurston	.270
19	Red Ruffing	.269
20	Carl Mays	.268
21	Schoolboy Rowe	.263
22	George Mullin	.262
23	Kid Gleason	.261
	Brickyard Kennedy	.261
	Jim Whitney	.261
26	Dutch Ruether	.258
	Joe Shaute	.258
28	Lee Richmond	.257
29	Jesse Tannehill	.256
30	Joe Bush	.253
31	Clarence Mitchell	.252
	Jack Taylor	.252
33	Adonis Terry	.249
34	Ray Caldwell	.248
	Burleigh Grimes	.248
36	Amos Rusie	.247
37	Pete Donohue	.246
38	Charlie Buffinton	.245
	Johnny Sain	.245
40	Vern Kennedy	.244
41	Jouett Meekin	.243
	Tony Mullane	.243
	Elam Vangilder	.243
	Bucky Walters	.243
45	Don Larsen	.242
	Bob Smith	.242
47	Duke Esper	.241
	Pink Hawley	.241
	Claude Hendrix	.241
	Frank Killen	.241
51	Frank Kitson	.240
52	Wilbur Cooper	.239
53	Ed Crane	.238
	Rick Rhoden	.238
55	Tommy Bond	.236
	Ed Brandt	.236
	Jim McCormick	.236
58	Jack Coombs	.235
	Walter Johnson	.235
	Terry Larkin	.235
	Charley Radbourn	.235
62	Fritz Ostermueller	.234
63	Nig Cuppy	.233
	Clark Griffith	.233
	Ted Lyons	.233
	Sherry Smith	.233
67	Bob Lemon	.232
68	Ben Cantwell	.231
	Murry Dickson	.231
	Don Robinson	.231
71	George Earnshaw	.230
	Jim Tobin	.230
73	Vic Aldridge	.229
	Frank Dwyer	.229
75	George Bradley	.228
	Nels Potter	.228
77	George Haddock	.227
	Dolf Luque	.227
	Bill Swift	.227
80	Jim Bagby	.226
	Jim Bagby	.226
	Catfish Hunter	.226
	Kid Nichols	.226
	Ed Stein	.226
	Tom Zachary	.226
86	Dizzy Dean	.225
87	Frank Foreman	.224
	Fred Goldsmith	.224
	Mickey Welch	.224
90	Hal Carlson	.223
	Larry Corcoran	.223
	George Hemming	.223
	Bill Sherdel	.223
	Jack Taylor	.223
	Lon Warneke	.223
96	Matt Kilroy	.222
	Gary Peters	.222
98	Van Mungo	.221
99	Sid Hudson	.220
100	3 players tied	.219

Total Pitcher Index

1	Walter Johnson	90.5
2	Cy Young	79.8
3	Pete Alexander	64.9
4	Christy Mathewson	62.8
5	Lefty Grove	61.2
6	Kid Nichols	60.9
7	Roger Clemens	54.1
8	Greg Maddux	51.4
9	John Clarkson	48.4
10	Tom Seaver	48.2
11	Warren Spahn	47.0
12	Bob Gibson	44.0
13	Ed Walsh	43.3
14	Hal Newhouser	40.8
15	Hoyt Wilhelm	39.7
16	Carl Hubbell	39.2
17	Amos Rusie	39.1
18	Bob Lemon	37.4
19	Whitey Ford	37.2
	Tim Keefe	37.2
21	Ted Lyons	36.7
22	Carl Mays	36.2
23	Jim Palmer	35.5
24	Phil Niekro	35.4
25	Mordecai Brown	34.8
26	Dizzy Trout	34.5
27	Gaylord Perry	34.4
28	Don Drysdale	34.0
29	Steve Carlton	33.2
30	Tony Mullane	32.6
31	Wes Ferrell	32.3
32	Fergie Jenkins	30.9
33	Bert Blyleven	30.8
34	John Franco	29.9
35	Clark Griffith	29.7
36	Rich Gossage	29.5
37	Bob Caruthers	29.4
38	Charley Radbourn	29.0
39	Juan Marichal	28.9
40	Tommy Bridges	28.7
41	Bucky Walters	28.6
42	Bob Feller	28.5
43	Jack Stivetts	28.2
44	Stan Coveleski	27.5
45	Dave Stieb	27.1
46	Red Faber	27.0
	Eddie Plank	27.0
	Dazzy Vance	27.0
49	Red Ruffing	26.9
50	Dennis Eckersley	26.7
51	Dolf Luque	26.3
52	Tom Glavine	26.2
53	Eddie Rommel	26.0
54	Eppa Rixey	25.9
	Urban Shocker	25.9
56	Dutch Leonard	25.8
57	Orel Hershiser	25.5
	Rick Reuschel	25.5
59	Harry Brecheen	25.4
	Addie Joss	25.4
61	Eddie Cicotte	25.1
62	Tommy John	25.0
63	Robin Roberts	24.9
64	Dan Quisenberry	24.8
65	Bret Saberhagen	24.6
	Rube Waddell	24.6
67	Kevin Brown	24.4
68	Joe Wood	24.3
69	Burleigh Grimes	23.9
	Guy Hecker	23.9
71	David Cone	23.8
72	Jack Quinn	23.6
	Kent Tekulve	23.6
74	Jimmy Key	23.4
75	Billy Pierce	23.3
	Lee Smith	23.3
77	Freddie Fitzsimmons	23.1
78	Silver King	22.9
79	Lon Warneke	22.7
80	Nig Cuppy	22.5
81	Dizzy Dean	22.2
82	Curt Davis	22.1
83	Vic Willis	22.0
84	Rollie Fingers	21.7
85	Jesse Tannehill	21.3
86	Tom Henke	21.2
87	Bobby Shantz	21.1
88	Jim McCormick	21.0
89	Mike Marshall	20.9
90	Nolan Ryan	20.8
91	Spud Chandler	20.6
	John Hiller	20.6
	Randy Johnson	20.6
94	Charlie Buffinton	20.3
95	Mel Harder	20.0
	Sparky Lyle	20.0
97	John Smoltz	19.9
	John Wetteland	19.9
99	Bruce Sutter	19.8
100	Wilbur Cooper	19.7

Total Pitcher Index

	Murry Dickson	19.7
	Doug Jones	19.7
	Jesse Orosco	19.7
104	Dave Foutz	19.6
105	Joe McGinnity	19.5
106	Doc White	19.1
107	Jim Kaat	19.0
108	Don Newcombe	18.9
109	Larry Jackson	18.8
110	Kevin Appier	18.6
111	Sandy Koufax	18.5
	Red Lucas	18.5
	Wilbur Wood	18.5
114	Ron Guidry	18.2
115	Ed Lopat	18.1
	Jeff Montgomery	18.1
	Mel Parnell	18.1
118	Mike Mussina	18.0
119	Lefty Gomez	17.9
	Hippo Vaughn	17.9
121	Chuck Finley	17.7
	Ed Reulbach	17.7
123	Dwight Gooden	17.6
124	Jose Rijo	17.5
125	Ned Garver	17.4
	Schoolboy Rowe	17.4
127	Bob Stanley	17.3
	Mel Stottlemyre	17.3
129	Larry French	17.2
130	Andy Messersmith	17.1
	Babe Ruth	17.1
	Luis Tiant	17.1
133	Noodles Hahn	16.9
	Thornton Lee	16.9
135	Stu Miller	16.7
	Jack Taylor	16.7
137	Early Wynn	16.6
138	Claude Passeau	16.5
139	Rick Aguilera	16.4
	Harry Howell	16.4
141	Max Lanier	16.3
	Hal Schumacher	16.3
143	Gene Garber	16.1
	Pedro Martinez	16.1
145	Sadie McMahon	15.9
	Virgil Trucks	15.9
147	Johnny Antonelli	15.7
	Deacon Phillippe	15.7
	Dave Righetti	15.7
150	Ron Perranoski	15.5
151	Roberto Hernandez	15.4
	Ellis Kinder	15.4
153	Steve Rogers	15.3
154	John Tudor	15.2
155	Babe Adams	15.0
	Sam Leever	15.0
157	John Candelaria	14.9
	Frank Dwyer	14.9
	Charlie Hough	14.9
160	Bob Shawkey	14.8
	Mickey Welch	14.8
162	Gary Lavelle	14.6
	Frank Linzy	14.6
	Lindy McDaniel	14.6
	Jim Whitney	14.6
166	Mike Garcia	14.5
	George Mullin	14.5
168	Mark Eichhorn	14.4
	Claude Hendrix	14.4
	Waite Hoyt	14.4
	Tug McGraw	14.4
172	Gregg Olson	14.3
173	Dennis Martinez	14.2
174	Fred Hutchinson	14.1
	Frank Viola	14.1
	John Ward	14.1
177	Larry Corcoran	14.0
178	Frank Lary	13.9
179	Chief Bender	13.8
	Charlie Ferguson	13.8
	Nap Rucker	13.8
182	Jeff Fassero	13.7
	Sal Maglie	13.7
	Howie Pollet	13.7
185	Jim Bunning	13.6
	Don Sutton	13.6
187	Bill Hutchison	13.5
	George Uhle	13.5
189	Clay Carroll	13.4
	Jim Maloney	13.4
191	Randy Myers	13.3
	Frank Tanana	13.3
193	Jim Devlin	13.2
	Roy Face	13.2
	Claude Osteen	13.2
196	Jerry Koosman	13.1
	Firpo Marberry	13.1
198	Jim Galvin	13.0
	Jim Tobin	13.0
200	Mort Cooper	12.9

Total Pitcher Index

	Frank Killen	12.9
202	Tom Burgmeier	12.8
	Van Mungo	12.8
204	Tom Candiotti	12.6
	Curt Simmons	12.6
206	Milt Pappas	12.4
207	Mike Henneman	12.3
	Sherry Smith	12.3
209	Will White	12.2
210	Willie Hernandez	12.1
	Jon Matlack	12.1
212	Steve Farr	12.0
	Bryan Harvey	12.0
214	Ewell Blackwell	11.9
	Greg Minton	11.9
216	Ted Breitenstein	11.8
	Trevor Hoffman	11.8
	Mike Jackson	11.8
	Mark Langston	11.8
	Jake Weimer	11.8
221	Harvey Haddix	11.6
	Orval Overall	11.6
223	Lefty Leifield	11.5
224	Johnny Sain	11.4
225	Al Brazle	11.3
	Jack Chesbro	11.3
	Terry Forster	11.3
228	Bob Rush	11.2
	Dave Smith	11.2
230	Gary Peters	11.1
231	Jim Kern	11.0
	Robb Nen	11.0
233	Russ Ford	10.9
	Camilo Pascual	10.9
235	Nixey Callahan	10.8
	Dean Chance	10.8
	Todd Worrell	10.8
238	Mike Boddicker	10.7
239	Dick Radatz	10.6
	Charlie Root	10.6
241	Alex Fernandez	10.5
242	Tex Hughson	10.4
	Matt Kilroy	10.4
	Charlie Leibrandt	10.4
	Roger McDowell	10.4
	Jeff Russell	10.4
	Sonny Siebert	10.4
248	Win Mercer	10.3
	Jeff Reardon	10.3
	Ben Sanders	10.3
	Curt Schilling	10.3
	Al Worthington	10.3
	Tom Zachary	10.3
254	Vida Blue	10.2
	Jim Brewer	10.2
	Johnny Murphy	10.2
257	Bob Ewing	10.1
	Jack McDowell	10.1
	Don McMahon	10.1
	Jeff Pfeffer	10.1
	Rip Sewell	10.1
	Frank Sullivan	10.1
	Fernando Valenzuela	10.1
	Hooks Wiltse	10.1
265	Elton Chamberlain	10.0
	Joe Dobson	10.0
	Sam McDowell	10.0
	Fritz Ostermueller	10.0
	Dan Plesac	10.0
	Mariano Rivera	10.0
	Kenny Rogers	10.0
272	Hooks Dauss	9.9
	Jay Howell	9.9
274	Clint Brown	9.8
275	Paul Assenmacher	9.7
	Tim Burke	9.7
	Bob Locker	9.7
	Art Nehf	9.7
	Jim Perry	9.7
280	Mickey McDermott	9.6
	Al Orth	9.6
282	Ned Garvin	9.5
	Steve Howe	9.5
	Monte Pearson	9.5
285	Slim Sallee	9.4
	Jim Scott	9.4
	Gerry Staley	9.4
288	Teddy Higuera	9.3
289	Larry Jansen	9.2
	Tippy Martinez	9.2
	Ed Morris	9.2
292	Howard Ehmke	9.1
	Greg Harris	9.1
294	Rod Beck	9.0
	Mark Gubicza	9.0
	Pink Hawley	9.0
297	Johnny Allen	8.9
	Mark Baldwin	8.9
	Al Benton	8.9
	Bob Welch	8.9

Total Pitcher Index (alpha.)

Babe Adams	15.0
Rick Aguilera	16.4
Pete Alexander	64.9
Johnny Allen	8.9
Johnny Antonelli	15.7
Kevin Appier	18.6
Paul Assenmacher	9.7
Mark Baldwin	8.9
Rod Beck	9.0
Chief Bender	13.8
Al Benton	8.9
Ewell Blackwell	11.9
Vida Blue	10.2
Bert Blyleven	30.8
Mike Boddicker	10.7
Al Brazle	11.3
Harry Brecheen	25.4
Ted Breitenstein	11.8
Jim Brewer	10.2
Tommy Bridges	28.7
Clint Brown	9.8
Kevin Brown	24.4
Mordecai Brown	34.8
Charlie Buffinton	20.3
Jim Bunning	13.6
Tom Burgmeier	12.8
Tim Burke	9.7
Nixey Callahan	10.8
John Candelaria	14.9
Tom Candiotti	12.6
Steve Carlton	33.2
Clay Carroll	13.4
Bob Caruthers	29.4
Elton Chamberlain	10.0
Dean Chance	10.8
Spud Chandler	20.6
Jack Chesbro	11.3
Eddie Cicotte	25.1
John Clarkson	48.4
Roger Clemens	54.1
David Cone	23.8
Wilbur Cooper	19.7
Mort Cooper	12.9
Larry Corcoran	14.0
Stan Coveleski	27.5
Nig Cuppy	22.5
Hooks Dauss	9.9
Curt Davis	22.1
Dizzy Dean	22.2
Jim Devlin	13.2
Murry Dickson	19.7
Joe Dobson	10.0
Don Drysdale	34.0
Frank Dwyer	14.9
Dennis Eckersley	26.7
Howard Ehmke	9.1
Mark Eichhorn	14.4
Bob Ewing	10.1
Red Faber	27.0
Roy Face	13.2
Steve Farr	12.0
Jeff Fassero	13.7
Bob Feller	28.5
Charlie Ferguson	13.8
Alex Fernandez	10.5
Wes Ferrell	32.3
Rollie Fingers	21.7
Chuck Finley	17.7
Freddie Fitzsimmons	23.1
Whitey Ford	37.2
Russ Ford	10.9
Terry Forster	11.3
Dave Foutz	19.6
John Franco	29.9
Larry French	17.2
Jim Galvin	13.0
Gene Garber	16.1
Mike Garcia	14.5
Ned Garver	17.4
Ned Garvin	9.5
Bob Gibson	44.0
Tom Glavine	26.2
Lefty Gomez	17.9
Dwight Gooden	17.6
Rich Gossage	29.5
Clark Griffith	29.7
Burleigh Grimes	23.9
Lefty Grove	61.2
Mark Gubicza	9.0
Ron Guidry	18.2
Harvey Haddix	11.6
Noodles Hahn	16.9
Mel Harder	20.0
Greg Harris	9.1
Bryan Harvey	12.0
Pink Hawley	9.0
Guy Hecker	23.9
Claude Hendrix	14.4
Tom Henke	21.2
Mike Henneman	12.3

Total Pitcher Index (alpha.)

Willie Hernandez	12.1
Roberto Hernandez	15.4
Orel Hershiser	25.5
Teddy Higuera	9.3
John Hiller	20.6
Trevor Hoffman	11.8
Charlie Hough	14.9
Steve Howe	9.5
Harry Howell	16.4
Jay Howell	9.9
Waite Hoyt	14.4
Carl Hubbell	39.2
Tex Hughson	10.4
Fred Hutchinson	14.1
Bill Hutchison	13.5
Larry Jackson	18.8
Mike Jackson	11.8
Larry Jansen	9.2
Fergie Jenkins	30.9
Tommy John	25.0
Randy Johnson	20.6
Walter Johnson	90.5
Doug Jones	19.7
Addie Joss	25.4
Jim Kaat	19.0
Tim Keefe	37.2
Jim Kern	11.0
Jimmy Key	23.4
Frank Killen	12.9
Matt Kilroy	10.4
Ellis Kinder	15.4
Silver King	22.9
Jerry Koosman	13.1
Sandy Koufax	18.5
Mark Langston	11.8
Max Lanier	16.3
Frank Lary	13.9
Gary Lavelle	14.6
Thornton Lee	16.9
Sam Leever	15.0
Charlie Leibrandt	10.4
Lefty Leifield	11.5
Bob Lemon	37.4
Dutch Leonard	25.8
Frank Linzy	14.6
Bob Locker	9.7
Ed Lopat	18.1
Red Lucas	18.5
Dolf Luque	26.3
Sparky Lyle	20.0
Ted Lyons	36.7
Greg Maddux	51.4
Sal Maglie	13.7
Jim Maloney	13.4
Firpo Marberry	13.1
Juan Marichal	28.9
Mike Marshall	20.9
Tippy Martinez	9.2
Dennis Martinez	14.2
Pedro Martinez	16.1
Christy Mathewson	62.8
Jon Matlack	12.1
Carl Mays	36.2
Jim McCormick	21.0
Lindy McDaniel	14.6
Mickey McDermott	9.6
Jack McDowell	10.1
Roger McDowell	10.4
Sam McDowell	10.0
Joe McGinnity	19.5
Tug McGraw	14.4
Don McMahon	10.1
Sadie McMahon	15.9
Win Mercer	10.3
Andy Messersmith	17.1
Stu Miller	16.7
Greg Minton	11.9
Jeff Montgomery	18.1
Ed Morris	9.2
Tony Mullane	32.6
George Mullin	14.5
Van Mungo	12.8
Johnny Murphy	10.2
Mike Mussina	18.0
Randy Myers	13.3
Art Nehf	9.7
Robb Nen	11.0
Don Newcombe	18.9
Hal Newhouser	40.8
Kid Nichols	60.9
Phil Niekro	35.4
Gregg Olson	14.3
Jesse Orosco	19.7
Al Orth	9.6
Claude Osteen	13.2
Fritz Ostermueller	10.0
Orval Overall	11.6
Jim Palmer	35.5
Milt Pappas	12.4
Mel Parnell	18.1

Total Pitcher Index (alpha.)

Camilo Pascual	10.9
Claude Passeau	16.5
Monte Pearson	9.5
Ron Perranoski	15.5
Gaylord Perry	34.4
Jim Perry	9.7
Gary Peters	11.1
Jeff Pfeffer	10.1
Deacon Phillippe	15.7
Billy Pierce	23.3
Eddie Plank	27.0
Dan Plesac	10.0
Howie Pollet	13.7
Jack Quinn	23.6
Dan Quisenberry	24.8
Dick Radatz	10.6
Charley Radbourn	29.0
Jeff Reardon	10.3
Ed Reulbach	17.7
Rick Reuschel	25.5
Dave Righetti	15.7
Jose Rijo	17.5
Mariano Rivera	10.0
Eppa Rixey	25.9
Robin Roberts	24.9
Kenny Rogers	10.0
Steve Rogers	15.3
Eddie Rommel	26.0
Charlie Root	10.6
Schoolboy Rowe	17.4
Nap Rucker	13.8
Red Ruffing	26.9
Bob Rush	11.2
Amos Rusie	39.1
Jeff Russell	10.4
Babe Ruth	17.1
Nolan Ryan	20.8
Bret Saberhagen	24.6
Johnny Sain	11.4
Slim Sallee	9.4
Ben Sanders	10.3
Curt Schilling	10.3
Hal Schumacher	16.3
Jim Scott	9.4
Tom Seaver	48.2
Rip Sewell	10.1
Bobby Shantz	21.1
Bob Shawkey	14.8
Urban Shocker	25.9
Sonny Siebert	10.4
Curt Simmons	12.6
Dave Smith	11.2
Lee Smith	23.3
Sherry Smith	12.3
John Smoltz	19.9
Warren Spahn	47.0
Gerry Staley	9.4
Bob Stanley	17.3
Dave Stieb	27.1
Jack Stivetts	28.2
Mel Stottlemyre	17.3
Frank Sullivan	10.1
Bruce Sutter	19.8
Don Sutton	13.6
Frank Tanana	13.3
Jesse Tannehill	21.3
Jack Taylor	16.7
Kent Tekulve	23.6
Luis Tiant	17.1
Jim Tobin	13.0
Dizzy Trout	34.5
Virgil Trucks	15.9
John Tudor	15.2
George Uhle	13.5
Fernando Valenzuela	10.1
Dazzy Vance	27.0
Hippo Vaughn	17.9
Frank Viola	14.1
Rube Waddell	24.6
Ed Walsh	43.3
Bucky Walters	28.6
John Ward	14.1
Lon Warneke	22.7
Jake Weimer	11.8
Mickey Welch	14.8
Bob Welch	8.9
John Wetteland	19.9
Doc White	19.1
Will White	12.2
Jim Whitney	14.6
Hoyt Wilhelm	39.7
Vic Willis	22.0
Hooks Wiltse	10.1
Joe Wood	24.3
Wilbur Wood	18.5
Todd Worrell	10.8
Al Worthington	10.3
Early Wynn	16.6
Cy Young	79.8
Tom Zachary	10.3

Total Pitcher Index (by era)

1876-1892

1	John Clarkson	48.4
2	Tim Keefe	37.2
3	Tony Mullane	32.6
4	Bob Caruthers	29.4
5	Charley Radbourn	29.0
6	Jack Stivetts	28.2
7	Guy Hecker	23.9
8	Silver King	22.9
9	Jim McCormick	21.0
10	Charlie Buffinton	20.3
11	Dave Foutz	19.6
12	Sadie McMahon	15.9
13	Mickey Welch	14.8
14	Jim Whitney	14.6
15	John Ward	14.1
16	Larry Corcoran	14.0
17	Charlie Ferguson	13.8
18	Bill Hutchison	13.5
19	Jim Devlin	13.2
20	Jim Galvin	13.0
21	Will White	12.2
22	Matt Kilroy	10.4
23	Ben Sanders	10.3
24	Elton Chamberlain	10.0
25	Ed Morris	9.2

1893-1919

1	Walter Johnson	90.5
2	Cy Young	79.8
3	Pete Alexander	64.9
4	Christy Mathewson	62.8
5	Kid Nichols	60.9
6	Ed Walsh	43.3
7	Amos Rusie	39.1
8	Mordecai Brown	34.8
9	Clark Griffith	29.7
10	Eddie Plank	27.0
11	Addie Joss	25.4
12	Eddie Cicotte	25.1
13	Rube Waddell	24.6
14	Joe Wood	24.3
15	Nig Cuppy	22.5
16	Vic Willis	22.0
17	Jesse Tannehill	21.3
18	Joe McGinnity	19.5
19	Doc White	19.1
20	Hippo Vaughn	17.9
21	Ed Reulbach	17.7
22	Babe Ruth	17.1
23	Noodles Hahn	16.9
24	Jack Taylor	16.7
25	Harry Howell	16.4

1920-1941

1	Lefty Grove	61.2
2	Carl Hubbell	39.2
3	Ted Lyons	36.7
4	Carl Mays	36.2
5	Wes Ferrell	32.3
6	Tommy Bridges	28.7
7	Bucky Walters	28.6
8	Stan Coveleski	27.5
9	Red Faber	27.0
	Dazzy Vance	27.0
11	Red Ruffing	26.9
12	Dolf Luque	26.3
13	Eddie Rommel	26.0
14	Eppa Rixey	25.9
	Urban Shocker	25.9
16	Burleigh Grimes	23.9
17	Jack Quinn	23.6
18	Freddie Fitzsimmons	23.1
19	Lon Warneke	22.7
20	Dizzy Dean	22.2
21	Curt Davis	22.1
22	Mel Harder	20.0
23	Wilbur Cooper	19.7
24	Red Lucas	18.5
25	Lefty Gomez	17.9

Total Pitcher Index (by era)

1942-1960

1	Warren Spahn	47.0
2	Hal Newhouser	40.8
3	Hoyt Wilhelm	39.7
4	Bob Lemon	37.4
5	Whitey Ford	37.2
6	Dizzy Trout	34.5
7	Bob Feller	28.5
8	Dutch Leonard	25.8
9	Harry Brecheen	25.4
10	Robin Roberts	24.9
11	Billy Pierce	23.3
12	Bobby Shantz	21.1
13	Spud Chandler	20.6
14	Murry Dickson	19.7
15	Don Newcombe	18.9
16	Ed Lopat	18.1
	Mel Parnell	18.1
18	Ned Garver	17.4
19	Stu Miller	16.7
20	Early Wynn	16.6
21	Max Lanier	16.3
22	Virgil Trucks	15.9
23	Johnny Antonelli	15.7
24	Ellis Kinder	15.4
25	Mike Garcia	14.5

1961-1976

1	Tom Seaver	48.2
2	Bob Gibson	44.0
3	Jim Palmer	35.5
4	Phil Niekro	35.4
5	Gaylord Perry	34.4
6	Don Drysdale	34.0
7	Steve Carlton	33.2
8	Fergie Jenkins	30.9
9	Juan Marichal	28.9
10	Tommy John	25.0
11	Rollie Fingers	21.7
12	Mike Marshall	20.9
13	John Hiller	20.6
14	Sparky Lyle	20.0
15	Jim Kaat	19.0
16	Larry Jackson	18.8
17	Sandy Koufax	18.5
	Wilbur Wood	18.5
19	Mel Stottlemyre	17.3
20	Andy Messersmith	17.1
	Luis Tiant	17.1
22	Ron Perranoski	15.5
23	Frank Linzy	14.6
	Lindy McDaniel	14.6
25	Tug McGraw	14.4

1977-1998

1	Roger Clemens	54.1
2	Greg Maddux	51.4
3	Bert Blyleven	30.8
4	John Franco	29.9
5	Rich Gossage	29.5
6	Dave Stieb	27.1
7	Dennis Eckersley	26.7
8	Tom Glavine	26.2
9	Orel Hershiser	25.5
	Rick Reuschel	25.5
11	Dan Quisenberry	24.8
12	Bret Saberhagen	24.6
13	Kevin Brown	24.4
14	David Cone	23.8
15	Kent Tekulve	23.6
16	Jimmy Key	23.4
17	Lee Smith	23.3
18	Tom Henke	21.2
19	Nolan Ryan	20.8
20	Randy Johnson	20.6
21	John Smoltz	19.9
	John Wetteland	19.9
23	Bruce Sutter	19.8
24	Doug Jones	19.7
	Jesse Orosco	19.7

Total Baseball Ranking

Rank	Player	Rating
1	Babe Ruth	124.8
2	Nap Lajoie	94.1
3	Willie Mays	92.2
4	Ty Cobb	91.1
5	Walter Johnson	90.1
6	Hank Aaron	89.8
7	Tris Speaker	86.5
8	Ted Williams	85.7
9	Rogers Hornsby	81.2
10	Honus Wagner	81.1
11	Cy Young	79.8
12	Rickey Henderson	79.7
13	Barry Bonds	79.0
14	Mike Schmidt	78.4
15	Mickey Mantle	76.1
16	Stan Musial	70.5
17	Eddie Collins	69.8
18	Frank Robinson	69.0
19	Lou Gehrig	65.7
20	Pete Alexander	64.9
21	Christy Mathewson	62.8
22	Mel Ott	62.7
23	Lefty Grove	61.2
24	Kid Nichols	60.9
25	Joe Morgan	56.3
26	Jimmie Foxx	54.3
27	Roger Clemens	54.1
28	Tim Raines	52.6
29	Eddie Mathews	51.6
30	Greg Maddux	51.4
31	Bill Dahlen	51.3
32	George Davis	49.8
33	Tony Gwynn	48.8
34	John Clarkson	48.4
35	Tom Seaver	48.2
36	Warren Spahn	47.0
37	Joe DiMaggio	46.9
38	Carl Yastrzemski	45.5
39	Al Kaline	44.6
40	Charlie Gehringer	44.4
41	Ed Delahanty	44.3
42	Wade Boggs	44.1
43	Bob Gibson	44.0
	Bobby Grich	44.0
45	Ed Walsh	43.3
46	Robin Yount	43.1
47	Ozzie Smith	43.0
48	Roberto Clemente	42.9
49	Reggie Jackson	42.8
50	Roger Connor	42.7
51	Barry Larkin	41.6
52	Lou Boudreau	41.3
53	Hal Newhouser	40.8
54	Luke Appling	40.7
	Dan Brouthers	40.7
56	Bobby Wallace	40.6
57	Gabby Hartnett	40.1
	Bid McPhee	40.1
59	Cal Ripken	39.9
60	Hoyt Wilhelm	39.7
61	Ken Griffey Jr.	39.5
	Ron Santo	39.5
63	Joe Cronin	39.4
64	Carl Hubbell	39.2
	Arky Vaughan	39.2
66	Amos Rusie	39.1
67	George Brett	39.0
	Bobby Doerr	39.0
	Frankie Frisch	39.0
70	Dave Winfield	38.6
71	Joe Jackson	37.5
72	Whitey Ford	37.2
	Tim Keefe	37.2
74	Bob Lemon	36.9
75	Ted Lyons	36.7
76	Willie McCovey	36.5
77	Bill Mazeroski	36.3
78	Carl Mays	36.2
	Yogi Berra	36.2
	Jack Glasscock	36.2
	Johnny Mize	36.2
82	Paul Waner	36.1
83	Jeff Bagwell	36.0
84	Bob Johnson	35.6
85	Jim Palmer	35.5
	Frank Thomas	35.5
87	Phil Niekro	35.4
	Bill Dickey	35.4
89	Dick Allen	35.3
90	Dave Bancroft	35.2
91	Ryne Sandberg	35.1
92	Reggie Smith	35.0
93	Mordecai Brown	34.8
94	Darrell Evans	34.7
95	Dizzy Trout	34.5
	Joe Sewell	34.5
97	Gaylord Perry	34.4
	Keith Hernandez	34.4
99	Eddie Murray	34.1
100	Don Drysdale	34.0
101	Paul Molitor	33.9
102	Frank Baker	33.8
103	Steve Carlton	33.2
	Jimmy Wynn	33.2
105	Willie Stargell	32.8
106	Wes Ferrell	32.4
107	Harry Heilmann	32.3
108	Jackie Robinson	31.8
109	Rod Carew	31.7
	Billy Herman	31.7
111	Bob Caruthers	31.5
	Craig Biggio	31.5
113	Mickey Cochrane	31.4
114	Albert Belle	31.3
115	Tony Mullane	31.1
	Jack Clark	31.1
	Billy Williams	31.1
118	Fergie Jenkins	30.9
119	Bert Blyleven	30.8
120	Mark McGwire	30.5
121	Sam Crawford	30.4
	Dwight Evans	30.4
123	Cap Anson	30.2
	Richie Ashburn	30.2
125	Cupid Childs	30.0
	Hank Greenberg	30.0
127	John Franco	29.9
	Andre Dawson	29.9
129	Gary Carter	29.6
	Buck Ewing	29.6
131	Rich Gossage	29.5
	Bobby Bonds	29.5
	Mike Piazza	29.5
134	Kirby Puckett	29.1
135	Clark Griffith	29.0
136	Juan Marichal	28.9
	Ralph Kiner	28.9
138	Elmer Flick	28.8
139	Tommy Bridges	28.7
	Fred Clarke	28.7
	Jose Cruz	28.7
142	Bob Feller	28.5
143	Sam Thompson	28.4
144	Cesar Cedeno	28.3
145	Joe Gordon	28.2
146	Dick Bartell	27.9
147	Edgar Martinez	27.8
148	Rusty Staub	27.6
149	Stan Coveleski	27.5
	Norm Cash	27.5
151	Fred Dunlap	27.2
	Heinie Groh	27.2
	Stan Hack	27.2
	Jim Rice	27.2
155	Dave Stieb	27.1
	Joe Medwick	27.1
157	Red Faber	27.0
	Eddie Plank	27.0
	Dazzy Vance	27.0
	Hardy Richardson	27.0
161	Pete Browning	26.9
162	Red Ruffing	26.8
163	Dennis Eckersley	26.7
164	Charley Radbourn	26.5
	Billy Hamilton	26.5
	Sherry Magee	26.5
	Darryl Strawberry	26.5
168	Bucky Walters	26.4
	Jesse Burkett	26.4
	Harmon Killebrew	26.4
171	Dolf Luque	26.3
	Jack Stivetts	26.3
173	Tom Glavine	26.2
	Hughie Jennings	26.2
175	Eddie Rommel	26.0
	Goose Goslin	26.0
	Minnie Minoso	26.0
178	Eppa Rixey	25.9
	Urban Shocker	25.9
	Ernie Banks	25.9
181	Dutch Leonard	25.8
	Art Fletcher	25.8
183	Rocky Colavito	25.6
	Lenny Dykstra	25.6
	Al Simmons	25.6
186	Orel Hershiser	25.5
	Rick Reuschel	25.5
188	Harry Brecheen	25.4
	Addie Joss	25.4
190	Eddie Cicotte	25.1
191	Tommy John	25.0
192	Robin Roberts	24.9
	Tony Oliva	24.9
	Bill Terry	24.9
195	Dan Quisenberry	24.8
	Lou Whitaker	24.8
197	Bret Saberhagen	24.6
	Rube Waddell	24.6
	Roberto Alomar	24.6
200	Eric Davis	24.5
	King Kelly	24.5
202	Kevin Brown	24.4
	Jose Canseco	24.4
204	Johnny Bench	24.3
	Zack Wheat	24.3
206	Carlton Fisk	24.0
	Travis Jackson	24.0
	George Sisler	24.0
209	Burleigh Grimes	23.9
	Jack Fournier	23.9
211	David Cone	23.8
212	Jack Quinn	23.6
	Kent Tekulve	23.6
214	Charlie Keller	23.5
215	Jimmy Key	23.4
216	Billy Pierce	23.3
	Lee Smith	23.3
218	Freddie Fitzsimmons	23.1
	Jimmy Collins	23.1
	Willie Randolph	23.1
	Joe Tinker	23.1
222	Dave Parker	23.0
223	Silver King	22.9
	Joe Wood	22.9
	Buddy Bell	22.9
226	Jake Beckley	22.8
	Roy Thomas	22.8
228	Lon Warneke	22.7
	Harlond Clift	22.7
230	Max Carey	22.6
231	Nig Cuppy	22.5
232	George Foster	22.3
	Ed Konetchy	22.3
	Chet Lemon	22.3
	Fred Lynn	22.3
	Duke Snider	22.3
237	Dizzy Dean	22.2
	Wally Berger	22.2
	Larry Walker	22.2
240	Curt Davis	22.1
241	Vic Willis	22.0
	Brett Butler	22.0
243	Ron Cey	21.9
	Rafael Palmeiro	21.9
	Fred Pfeffer	21.9
	John Ward	21.9
247	Rollie Fingers	21.7
248	Roy Campanella	21.6
	Alan Trammell	21.6
250	Harry Stovey	21.5
251	Chuck Klein	21.4
252	Guy Hecker	21.3
	Frank Howard	21.3
	Graig Nettles	21.3
255	Tom Henke	21.2
	Larry Doby	21.2
	Paul O'Neill	21.2
258	Bobby Shantz	21.1
	Roy White	21.1
260	Jim McCormick	21.0
	Fred Tenney	21.0
262	Mike Marshall	20.9
	Ken Singleton	20.9
264	Nolan Ryan	20.8
265	Charley Jones	20.7
	Pie Traynor	20.7
267	Spud Chandler	20.6
	John Hiller	20.6
	Randy Johnson	20.6
	Art Devlin	20.6
	Jim Fregosi	20.6
272	Frank Chance	20.5
	Mike Griffin	20.5
274	Del Pratt	20.4
275	Andy Van Slyke	20.3
276	Jesse Tannehill	20.2
	Will Clark	20.2
	Glenn Hubbard	20.2
	Joe Kelley	20.2
	Ray Lankford	20.2
	Gary Sheffield	20.2
282	Kevin Mitchell	20.1
	Tim Salmon	20.1
284	Mel Harder	20.0
	Sparky Lyle	20.0
	Pete Rose	20.0
287	John Smoltz	19.9
	John Wetteland	19.9
289	Bruce Sutter	19.8
	Roger Bresnahan	19.8
	Denny Lyons	19.8
	Brooks Robinson	19.8
293	Wilbur Cooper	19.7
	Murry Dickson	19.7
	Doug Jones	19.7
	Jesse Orosco	19.7
297	Vern Stephens	19.6
	Joe Torre	19.6
299	Joe McGinnity	19.5
	Jimmy Sheckard	19.5
301	Amos Otis	19.3
	Matt Williams	19.3
303	Charlie Bennett	19.2
	Dale Murphy	19.2
305	Jim Kaat	19.0
	Bill Nicholson	19.0
307	Don Newcombe	18.9
	Gavvy Cravath	18.9
	Bill Joyce	18.9
310	Larry Jackson	18.8
	Bob Elliott	18.8
312	Kevin Appier	18.6
	Ken Boyer	18.6
	Brian Downing	18.6
315	Sandy Koufax	18.5
	Wilbur Wood	18.5
317	Eddie Stanky	18.4
318	Ron Guidry	18.2
319	Ed Lopat	18.1
	Jeff Montgomery	18.1
	Mel Parnell	18.1
	Roy Cullenbine	18.1
	Wally Schang	18.1
324	Mike Mussina	18.0
	Gene Alley	18.0
	Miller Huggins	18.0
327	Lefty Gomez	17.9
	Hippo Vaughn	17.9
	Rico Carty	17.9
330	Red Lucas	17.8
	Harold Baines	17.8
	Ferris Fain	17.8
333	Chuck Finley	17.7
	Ed Reulbach	17.7
	Doc White	17.7
	Kenny Lofton	17.7
337	Dwight Gooden	17.6
	Earl Averill	17.6
339	Jose Rijo	17.5
340	Ned Garver	17.4
	Schoolboy Rowe	17.4
	Jay Bell	17.4
	Tommy Leach	17.4
344	Bob Stanley	17.3
	Mel Stottlemyre	17.3
	Babe Herman	17.3
	Johnny Logan	17.3
	Ernie Lombardi	17.3
	Ken Williams	17.3
350	Larry French	17.2
	Bobby Bonilla	17.2
	Tony Fernandez	17.2
	Fred McGriff	17.2
354	Andy Messersmith	17.1
	Luis Tiant	17.1
356	Paul Hines	17.0
357	Noodles Hahn	16.9
	Thornton Lee	16.9
	Tony Lazzeri	16.9
360	Gil McDougald	16.8
	Ted Simmons	16.8
362	Stu Miller	16.7
	Jack Taylor	16.7

	Ken Caminiti	16.7
	Orlando Cepeda	16.7
	Pedro Guerrero	16.7
367	Early Wynn	16.6
	David Justice	16.6
369	Claude Passeau	16.5
	Chili Davis	16.5
371	Rick Aguilera	16.4
	Jesse Barfield	16.4
	Jeff Heath	16.4
	Dwayne Murphy	16.4
375	Max Lanier	16.3
	Hal Schumacher	16.3
	George Gore	16.3
	Enos Slaughter	16.3
379	Cy Seymour	16.2
380	Gene Garber	16.1
	Pedro Martinez	16.1
	Kirk Gibson	16.1
	Jim O'Rourke	16.1
	John Valentin	16.1
385	John McGraw	16.0
	Jimmy Williams	16.0
387	Sadie McMahon	15.9
	Virgil Trucks	15.9
	Bernie Williams	15.9
390	Kiki Cuyler	15.8
	Phil Rizzuto	15.8
	Chief Zimmer	15.8
393	Johnny Antonelli	15.7
	Deacon Phillippe	15.7
	Dave Righetti	15.7
	Mike Hargrove	15.7
397	Davey Johnson	15.6
	Jocko Milligan	15.6
	Hack Wilson	15.6
400	Ron Perranoski	15.5
	Danny Tartabull	15.5
402	Roberto Hernandez	15.4
	Ellis Kinder	15.4
	Ray Chapman	15.4
405	Steve Rogers	15.3
	Mark Grace	15.3
	Gene Tenace	15.3
408	John Tudor	15.2
	Thurman Munson	15.2
	Elmer Smith	15.2
411	Sid Gordon	15.1
412	Babe Adams	15.0
	Sam Leever	15.0
	Mark Belanger	15.0
	Bobby Knoop	15.0
416	Charlie Buffinton	14.9
	John Candelaria	14.9
	Frank Dwyer	14.9
	Charlie Hough	14.9
	Henry Larkin	14.9
	Boog Powell	14.9
422	Bob Shawkey	14.8
	Mickey Welch	14.8
	Benny Kauff	14.8
	Mike Scioscia	14.8
426	Sixto Lezcano	14.7
	Bobby Veach	14.7
428	Gary Lavelle	14.6
	Frank Linzy	14.6
	Lindy McDaniel	14.6
	Lave Cross	14.6
	Duke Farrell	14.6
	Augie Galan	14.6
	Greg Luzinski	14.6
	Pee Wee Reese	14.6
436	Mike Garcia	14.5
	Tommy Henrich	14.5
	Kevin McReynolds	14.5
439	Mark Eichhorn	14.4
	Claude Hendrix	14.4
	Waite Hoyt	14.4
	Tug McGraw	14.4
	Robin Ventura	14.4
444	Gregg Olson	14.3
	Bob Allison	14.3
446	Dennis Martinez	14.2
	Ron Hansen	14.2
448	Frank Viola	14.1
	Johnny Callison	14.1
450	Fred Hutchinson	14.0
	George Mullin	14.0
	Juan Gonzalez	14.0
453	Harry Howell	13.9
	Frank Lary	13.9

	Jimmy Ryan	13.9
456	Chief Bender	13.8
	Charlie Ferguson	13.8
	Nap Rucker	13.8
	Roy Smalley	13.8
460	Jeff Fassero	13.7
	Sal Maglie	13.7
	Howie Pollet	13.7
	Gil Hodges	13.7
464	Jim Bunning	13.6
	Don Sutton	13.6
	Jay Buhner	13.6
	Ben Chapman	13.6
	Willie Kamm	13.6
	Kip Selbach	13.6
470	Bill Hutchison	13.5
	George Uhle	13.5
	Fred Carroll	13.5
	Tommy Holmes	13.5
	George Stone	13.5
	George Van Haltren	13.5
	Richie Zisk	13.5
477	Clay Carroll	13.4
	Jim Maloney	13.4
	Chief Meyers	13.4
	Al Oliver	13.4
481	Randy Myers	13.3
	Frank Tanana	13.3
483	Jim Devlin	13.2
	Roy Face	13.2
	Claude Osteen	13.2
	Bill Freehan	13.2
	John Olerud	13.2
	Dave Orr	13.2
	Roger Peckinpaugh	13.2
490	Jerry Koosman	13.1
	Firpo Marberry	13.1
	Doug DeCinces	13.1
	Edd Roush	13.1
	John Titus	13.1
495	Jim Galvin	13.0
	Jim Tobin	13.0
497	Mort Cooper	12.9
	Frank Killen	12.9
	Johnny Evers	12.9
	Bobby Murcer	12.9

Total Baseball Rank (alpha.)

Hank Aaron	89.8
Babe Adams	15.0
Rick Aguilera	16.4
Pete Alexander	64.9
Dick Allen	35.3
Gene Alley	18.0
Bob Allison	14.3
Roberto Alomar	24.6
Cap Anson	30.2
Johnny Antonelli	15.7
Kevin Appier	18.6
Luke Appling	40.7
Richie Ashburn	30.2
Earl Averill	17.6
Jeff Bagwell	36.0
Harold Baines	17.8
Frank Baker	33.8
Dave Bancroft	35.2
Ernie Banks	25.9
Jesse Barfield	16.4
Dick Bartell	27.9
Jake Beckley	22.8
Mark Belanger	15.0
Buddy Bell	22.9
Jay Bell	17.4
Albert Belle	31.3
Johnny Bench	24.3
Chief Bender	13.8
Charlie Bennett	19.2
Wally Berger	22.2
Yogi Berra	36.2
Craig Biggio	31.5
Bert Blyleven	30.8
Wade Boggs	44.1
Barry Bonds	79.0
Bobby Bonds	29.5
Bobby Bonilla	17.2
Lou Boudreau	41.3
Ken Boyer	18.6
Harry Brecheen	25.4
Roger Bresnahan	19.8

George Brett	39.0
Tommy Bridges	28.7
Dan Brouthers	40.7
Kevin Brown	24.4
Mordecai Brown	34.8
Pete Browning	26.9
Charlie Buffinton	14.9
Jay Buhner	13.6
Jim Bunning	13.6
Jesse Burkett	26.4
Brett Butler	22.0
Johnny Callison	14.1
Ken Caminiti	16.7
Roy Campanella	21.6
John Candelaria	14.9
Jose Canseco	24.4
Rod Carew	31.7
Max Carey	22.6
Steve Carlton	33.2
Clay Carroll	13.4
Fred Carroll	13.5
Gary Carter	29.6
Rico Carty	17.9
Bob Caruthers	31.5
Norm Cash	27.5
Cesar Cedeno	28.3
Orlando Cepeda	16.7
Ron Cey	21.9
Frank Chance	20.5
Spud Chandler	20.6
Ray Chapman	15.4
Ben Chapman	13.6
Cupid Childs	30.0
Eddie Cicotte	25.1
Jack Clark	31.1
Will Clark	20.2
Fred Clarke	28.7
John Clarkson	48.4
Roger Clemens	54.1
Roberto Clemente	42.9
Harlond Clift	22.7
Ty Cobb	91.1
Mickey Cochrane	31.4
Rocky Colavito	25.6
Eddie Collins	69.8
Jimmy Collins	23.1
David Cone	23.8
Roger Connor	42.7
Wilbur Cooper	19.7
Mort Cooper	12.9
Stan Coveleski	27.5
Gavvy Cravath	18.9
Sam Crawford	30.4
Joe Cronin	39.4
Lave Cross	14.6
Jose Cruz	28.7
Roy Cullenbine	18.1
Nig Cuppy	22.5
Kiki Cuyler	15.8
Bill Dahlen	51.3
Curt Davis	22.1
Chili Davis	16.5
Eric Davis	24.5
George Davis	49.8
Andre Dawson	29.9
Dizzy Dean	22.2
Doug DeCinces	13.1
Ed Delahanty	44.3
Jim Devlin	13.2
Art Devlin	20.6
Bill Dickey	35.4
Murry Dickson	19.7
Joe DiMaggio	46.9
Larry Doby	21.2
Bobby Doerr	39.0
Brian Downing	18.6
Don Drysdale	34.0
Fred Dunlap	27.2
Frank Dwyer	14.9
Lenny Dykstra	25.6
Dennis Eckersley	26.7
Mark Eichhorn	14.4
Bob Elliott	18.8
Darrell Evans	34.7
Dwight Evans	30.4
Johnny Evers	12.9
Buck Ewing	29.6
Red Faber	27.0
Roy Face	13.2
Ferris Fain	17.8
Duke Farrell	14.6

Jeff Fassero	13.7
Bob Feller	28.5
Charlie Ferguson	13.8
Tony Fernandez	17.2
Wes Ferrell	32.4
Rollie Fingers	21.7
Chuck Finley	17.7
Carlton Fisk	24.0
Freddie Fitzsimmons	23.1
Art Fletcher	25.8
Elmer Flick	28.8
Whitey Ford	37.2
George Foster	22.3
Jack Fournier	23.9
Jimmie Foxx	54.3
John Franco	29.9
Bill Freehan	13.2
Jim Fregosi	20.6
Larry French	17.2
Frankie Frisch	39.0
Augie Galan	14.6
Jim Galvin	13.0
Gene Garber	16.1
Mike Garcia	14.5
Ned Garver	17.4
Lou Gehrig	65.7
Charlie Gehringer	44.4
Bob Gibson	44.0
Kirk Gibson	16.1
Jack Glasscock	36.2
Tom Glavine	26.2
Lefty Gomez	17.9
Juan Gonzalez	14.0
Dwight Gooden	17.6
Joe Gordon	28.2
Sid Gordon	15.1
George Gore	16.3
Goose Goslin	26.0
Rich Gossage	29.5
Mark Grace	15.3
Hank Greenberg	30.0
Bobby Grich	44.0
Ken Griffey Jr.	39.5
Mike Griffin	20.5
Clark Griffith	29.0
Burleigh Grimes	23.9
Heinie Groh	27.2
Lefty Grove	61.2
Pedro Guerrero	16.7
Ron Guidry	18.2
Tony Gwynn	48.8
Stan Hack	27.2
Noodles Hahn	16.9
Billy Hamilton	26.5
Ron Hansen	14.2
Mel Harder	20.0
Mike Hargrove	15.7
Gabby Hartnett	40.1
Jeff Heath	16.4
Guy Hecker	21.3
Harry Heilmann	32.3
Rickey Henderson	79.7
Claude Hendrix	14.4
Tom Henke	21.2
Tommy Henrich	14.5
Babe Herman	17.3
Billy Herman	31.7
Roberto Hernandez	15.4
Keith Hernandez	34.4
Orel Hershiser	25.5
John Hiller	20.6
Paul Hines	17.0
Gil Hodges	13.7
Tommy Holmes	13.5
Rogers Hornsby	81.2
Charlie Hough	14.9
Frank Howard	21.3
Harry Howell	13.9
Waite Hoyt	14.4
Glenn Hubbard	20.2
Carl Hubbell	39.2
Miller Huggins	18.0
Fred Hutchinson	14.0
Bill Hutchison	13.5
Larry Jackson	18.8
Joe Jackson	37.5
Reggie Jackson	42.8
Travis Jackson	24.0
Fergie Jenkins	30.9
Hughie Jennings	26.2
Tommy John	25.0

Randy Johnson	20.6	Paul Molitor	33.9	Gary Sheffield	20.2	Cy Young 79.8
Walter Johnson	90.1	Jeff Montgomery	18.1	Urban Shocker	25.9	Robin Yount 43.1
Davey Johnson	15.6	Joe Morgan	56.3	Al Simmons	25.6	Chief Zimmer 15.8
Bob Johnson	35.6	Tony Mullane	31.1	Ted Simmons	16.8	Richie Zisk 13.5
Doug Jones	19.7	George Mullin	14.0	Ken Singleton	20.9	

1876-1892

1 John Clarkson	48.4
2 Roger Connor	42.7
3 Dan Brouthers	40.7
4 Bid McPhee	40.1
5 Tim Keefe	37.2
6 Jack Glasscock	36.2
7 Bob Caruthers	31.5
8 Tony Mullane	31.1
9 Cap Anson	30.2
10 Buck Ewing	29.6
11 Sam Thompson	28.4
12 Fred Dunlap	27.2
13 Hardy Richardson	27.0
14 Pete Browning	26.9
15 Charley Radbourn	26.5
16 Jack Stivetts	26.3
17 King Kelly	24.5
18 Silver King	22.9
19 Fred Pfeffer	21.9
John Ward	21.9
21 Harry Stovey	21.5
22 Guy Hecker	21.3
23 Jim McCormick	21.0
24 Charley Jones	20.7
25 Denny Lyons	19.8

1893-1919

1 Nap Lajoie	94.1
2 Ty Cobb	91.1
3 Walter Johnson	90.1
4 Tris Speaker	86.5
5 Honus Wagner	81.1
6 Cy Young	79.8
7 Eddie Collins	69.8
8 Pete Alexander	64.9
9 Christy Mathewson	62.8
10 Kid Nichols	60.9
11 Bill Dahlen	51.3
12 George Davis	49.8
13 Ed Delahanty	44.3
14 Ed Walsh	43.3
15 Bobby Wallace	40.6
16 Amos Rusie	39.1
17 Joe Jackson	37.5
18 Mordecai Brown	34.8
19 Frank Baker	33.8
20 Sam Crawford	30.4
21 Cupid Childs	30.0
22 Clark Griffith	29.0
23 Elmer Flick	28.8
24 Fred Clarke	28.7
25 Heinie Groh	27.2

1920-1941

1 Babe Ruth	124.8
2 Rogers Hornsby	81.2
3 Lou Gehrig	65.7
4 Mel Ott	62.7
5 Lefty Grove	61.2
6 Jimmie Foxx	54.3
7 Charlie Gehringer	44.4
8 Luke Appling	40.7
9 Gabby Hartnett	40.1
10 Joe Cronin	39.4
11 Carl Hubbell	39.2
Arky Vaughan	39.2
13 Frankie Frisch	39.0
14 Ted Lyons	36.7
15 Carl Mays	36.2
16 Paul Waner	36.1
17 Bob Johnson	35.6
18 Bill Dickey	35.4
19 Dave Bancroft	35.2
20 Joe Sewell	34.5
21 Wes Ferrell	32.4
22 Harry Heilmann	32.3
23 Billy Herman	31.7
24 Mickey Cochrane	31.4
25 Hank Greenberg	30.0

Full listing (columns 1–3):

Name	Value	Name	Value	Name	Value
Randy Johnson	20.6	Paul Molitor	33.9	Gary Sheffield	20.2
Walter Johnson	90.1	Jeff Montgomery	18.1	Urban Shocker	25.9
Davey Johnson	15.6	Joe Morgan	56.3	Al Simmons	25.6
Bob Johnson	35.6	Tony Mullane	31.1	Ted Simmons	16.8
Doug Jones	19.7	George Mullin	14.0	Ken Singleton	20.9
Charley Jones	20.7	Thurman Munson	15.2	George Sisler	24.0
Addie Joss	25.4	Bobby Murcer	12.9	Enos Slaughter	16.3
Bill Joyce	18.9	Dale Murphy	19.2	Roy Smalley	13.8
David Justice	16.6	Dwayne Murphy	16.4	Lee Smith	23.3
Jim Kaat	19.0	Eddie Murray	34.1	Reggie Smith	35.0
Al Kaline	44.6	Stan Musial	70.5	Elmer Smith	15.2
Willie Kamm	13.6	Mike Mussina	18.0	Ozzie Smith	43.0
Benny Kauff	14.8	Randy Myers	13.3	John Smoltz	19.9
Tim Keefe	37.2	Graig Nettles	21.3	Duke Snider	22.3
Charlie Keller	23.5	Don Newcombe	18.9	Warren Spahn	47.0
Joe Kelley	20.2	Hal Newhouser	40.8	Tris Speaker	86.5
King Kelly	24.5	Kid Nichols	60.9	Eddie Stanky	18.4
Jimmy Key	23.4	Bill Nicholson	19.0	Bob Stanley	17.3
Harmon Killebrew	26.4	Phil Niekro	35.4	Willie Stargell	32.8
Frank Killen	12.9	John Olerud	13.2	Rusty Staub	27.6
Ellis Kinder	15.4	Tony Oliva	24.9	Vern Stephens	19.6
Ralph Kiner	28.9	Al Oliver	13.4	Dave Stieb	27.1
Silver King	22.9	Gregg Olson	14.3	Jack Stivetts	26.3
Chuck Klein	21.4	Paul O'Neill	21.2	George Stone	13.5
Bobby Knoop	15.0	Jesse Orosco	19.7	Mel Stottlemyre	17.3
Ed Konetchy	22.3	Jim O'Rourke	16.1	Harry Stovey	21.5
Jerry Koosman	13.1	Dave Orr	13.2	Darryl Strawberry	26.5
Sandy Koufax	18.5	Claude Osteen	13.2	Bruce Sutter	19.8
Nap Lajoie	94.1	Amos Otis	19.3	Don Sutton	13.6
Max Lanier	16.3	Mel Ott	62.7	Frank Tanana	13.3
Ray Lankford	20.2	Rafael Palmeiro	21.9	Jesse Tannehill	20.2
Barry Larkin	41.6	Jim Palmer	35.5	Danny Tartabull	15.5
Henry Larkin	14.9	Dave Parker	23.0	Jack Taylor	16.7
Frank Lary	13.9	Mel Parnell	18.1	Kent Tekulve	23.6
Gary Lavelle	14.6	Claude Passeau	16.5	Gene Tenace	15.3
Tony Lazzeri	16.9	Roger Peckinpaugh	13.2	Fred Tenney	21.0
Tommy Leach	17.4	Ron Perranoski	15.5	Bill Terry	24.9
Thornton Lee	16.9	Gaylord Perry	34.4	Frank Thomas	35.5
Sam Leever	15.0	Fred Pfeffer	21.9	Roy Thomas	22.8
Bob Lemon	36.9	Deacon Phillippe	15.7	Sam Thompson	28.4
Chet Lemon	22.3	Mike Piazza	29.5	Luis Tiant	17.1
Dutch Leonard	25.8	Billy Pierce	23.3	Joe Tinker	23.1
Sixto Lezcano	14.7	Eddie Plank	27.0	John Titus	13.1
Frank Linzy	14.6	Howie Pollet	13.7	Jim Tobin	13.0
Kenny Lofton	17.7	Boog Powell	14.9	Joe Torre	19.6
Johnny Logan	17.3	Del Pratt	20.4	Alan Trammell	21.6
Ernie Lombardi	17.3	Kirby Puckett	29.1	Pie Traynor	20.7
Ed Lopat	18.1	Jack Quinn	23.6	Dizzy Trout	34.5
Red Lucas	17.8	Dan Quisenberry	24.8	Virgil Trucks	15.9
Dolf Luque	26.3	Charley Radbourn	26.5	John Tudor	15.2
Greg Luzinski	14.6	Tim Raines	52.6	George Uhle	13.5
Sparky Lyle	20.0	Willie Randolph	23.1	John Valentin	16.1
Fred Lynn	22.3	Ed Reulbach	17.7	Dazzy Vance	27.0
Ted Lyons	36.7	Rick Reuschel	25.5	George Van Haltren	13.5
Denny Lyons	19.8	Jim Rice	27.2	Andy Van Slyke	20.3
Greg Maddux	51.4	Hardy Richardson	27.0	Arky Vaughan	39.2
Sherry Magee	26.5	Dave Righetti	15.7	Hippo Vaughn	17.9
Sal Maglie	13.7	Jose Rijo	17.5	Bobby Veach	14.7
Jim Maloney	13.4	Cal Ripken	39.9	Robin Ventura	14.4
Mickey Mantle	76.1	Eppa Rixey	25.9	Frank Viola	14.1
Firpo Marberry	13.1	Phil Rizzuto	15.8	Rube Waddell	24.6
Juan Marichal	28.9	Robin Roberts	24.9	Honus Wagner	81.1
Mike Marshall	20.9	Brooks Robinson	19.8	Larry Walker	22.2
Dennis Martinez	14.2	Frank Robinson	69.0	Bobby Wallace	40.6
Pedro Martinez	16.1	Jackie Robinson	31.8	Ed Walsh	43.3
Edgar Martinez	27.8	Steve Rogers	15.3	Bucky Walters	26.4
Eddie Mathews	51.6	Eddie Rommel	26.0	Paul Waner	36.1
Christy Mathewson	62.8	Pete Rose	20.0	John Ward	21.9
Carl Mays	36.2	Edd Roush	13.1	Lon Warneke	22.7
Willie Mays	92.2	Schoolboy Rowe	17.4	Pee Wee Reese	14.6
Bill Mazeroski	36.3	Nap Rucker	13.8	Mickey Welch	14.8
Jim McCormick	21.0	Red Ruffing	26.8	John Wetteland	19.9
Willie McCovey	36.5	Amos Rusie	39.1	Zack Wheat	24.3
Lindy McDaniel	14.6	Babe Ruth	124.8	Lou Whitaker	24.8
Gil McDougald	16.8	Nolan Ryan	20.8	Doc White	17.7
Joe McGinnity	19.5	Jimmy Ryan	13.9	Roy White	21.1
Tug McGraw	14.4	Bret Saberhagen	24.6	Hoyt Wilhelm	39.7
John McGraw	16.0	Tim Salmon	20.1	Bernie Williams	15.9
Fred McGriff	17.2	Ryne Sandberg	35.1	Billy Williams	31.1
Mark McGwire	30.5	Ron Santo	39.5	Jimmy Williams	16.0
Sadie McMahon	15.9	Wally Schang	18.1	Ken Williams	17.3
Bid McPhee	40.1	Mike Schmidt	78.4	Matt Williams	19.3
Kevin McReynolds	14.5	Hal Schumacher	16.3	Ted Williams	85.7
Joe Medwick	27.1	Mike Scioscia	14.8	Vic Willis	22.0
Andy Messersmith	17.1	Tom Seaver	48.2	Hack Wilson	15.6
Chief Meyers	13.4	Kip Selbach	13.6	Dave Winfield	38.6
Stu Miller	16.7	Joe Sewell	34.5	Joe Wood	22.9
Jocko Milligan	15.6	Cy Seymour	16.2	Wilbur Wood	18.5
Minnie Minoso	26.0	Bobby Shantz	21.1	Early Wynn	16.6
Kevin Mitchell	20.1	Bob Shawkey	14.8	Jimmy Wynn	33.2
Johnny Mize	36.2	Jimmy Sheckard	19.5	Carl Yastrzemski	45.5

Total Baseball
Rank (by era)

1942-1960

1	Ted Williams	85.7
2	Mickey Mantle	76.1
3	Stan Musial	70.5
4	Eddie Mathews	51.6
5	Warren Spahn	47.0
6	Joe DiMaggio	46.9
7	Lou Boudreau	41.3
8	Hal Newhouser	40.8
9	Hoyt Wilhelm	39.7
10	Bobby Doerr	39.0
11	Whitey Ford	37.2
12	Bob Lemon	36.9
13	Yogi Berra	36.2
	Johnny Mize	36.2
15	Dizzy Trout	34.5
16	Jackie Robinson	31.8
17	Richie Ashburn	30.2
18	Ralph Kiner	28.9
19	Bob Feller	28.5
20	Joe Gordon	28.2
21	Minnie Minoso	26.0
22	Dutch Leonard	25.8
23	Harry Brecheen	25.4
24	Robin Roberts	24.9
25	Charlie Keller	23.5

1961-1976

1	Willie Mays	92.2
2	Hank Aaron	89.8
3	Frank Robinson	69.0
4	Joe Morgan	56.3
5	Tom Seaver	48.2
6	Carl Yastrzemski	45.5
7	Al Kaline	44.6
8	Bob Gibson	44.0
9	Roberto Clemente	42.9
10	Ron Santo	39.5
11	Willie McCovey	36.5
12	Bill Mazeroski	36.3
13	Jim Palmer	35.5
14	Phil Niekro	35.4
15	Dick Allen	35.3
16	Reggie Smith	35.0
17	Gaylord Perry	34.4
18	Don Drysdale	34.0
19	Steve Carlton	33.2
	Jimmy Wynn	33.2
21	Willie Stargell	32.8
22	Rod Carew	31.7
23	Billy Williams	31.1
24	Fergie Jenkins	30.9
25	Bobby Bonds	29.5

1977-1998

1	Rickey Henderson	79.7
2	Barry Bonds	79.0
3	Mike Schmidt	78.4
4	Roger Clemens	54.1
5	Tim Raines	52.6
6	Greg Maddux	51.4
7	Tony Gwynn	48.8
8	Wade Boggs	44.1
9	Bobby Grich	44.0
10	Robin Yount	43.1
11	Ozzie Smith	43.0
12	Reggie Jackson	42.8
13	Barry Larkin	41.6
14	Cal Ripken	39.9
15	Ken Griffey Jr.	39.5
16	George Brett	39.0
17	Dave Winfield	38.6
18	Jeff Bagwell	36.0
19	Frank Thomas	35.5
20	Ryne Sandberg	35.1
21	Darrell Evans	34.7
22	Keith Hernandez	34.4
23	Eddie Murray	34.1
24	Paul Molitor	33.9
25	Craig Biggio	31.5

At Bats

1	Willie Wilson, 1980	705
2	Juan Samuel, 1984	701
3	Dave Cash, 1975	699
4	Matty Alou, 1969	698
5	Woody Jensen, 1936	696
6	Maury Wills, 1962	695
	Omar Moreno, 1979	695
8	Bobby Richardson, 1962	692
9	Kirby Puckett, 1985	691
10	Lou Brock, 1967	689
	Sandy Alomar, 1971	689
12	Dave Cash, 1974	687
	Tony Fernandez, 1986	687
14	Horace Clarke, 1970	686
	Alex Rodriguez, 1998	686
16	Nomar Garciaparra, 1997	684
17	Lance Johnson, 1996	682
18	Lloyd Waner, 1931	681
	Jo-Jo Moore, 1935	681
20	Pete Rose, 1973	680
	Frank Taveras, 1979	680
	Kirby Puckett, 1986	680
23	Harvey Kuenn, 1953	679
	Curt Flood, 1964	679
	Bobby Richardson, 1964	679
26	Dick Groat, 1962	678
	Doug Glanville, 1998	678
28	Matty Alou, 1970	677
	Jim Rice, 1978	677
	Don Mattingly, 1986	677
31	Felix Millan, 1975	676
	Omar Moreno, 1980	676
33	Rennie Stennett, 1974	673
	Bill Buckner, 1985	673
35	Rabbit Maranville, 1922	672
	Tony Oliva, 1964	672
	Sandy Alomar, 1970	672
	Garry Templeton, 1979	672
39	Jack Tobin, 1921	671
	Marquis Grissom, 1996	671
41	Al Simmons, 1932	670
	Pete Rose, 1965	670
	Buddy Bell, 1979	670
44	Vada Pinson, 1965	669
	Larry Bowa, 1974	669
46	Buddy Lewis, 1937	668
	Brooks Robinson, 1961	668
	Ralph Garr, 1973	668
49	Carl Furillo, 1951	667
50	Billy Herman, 1935	666
	Zoilo Versalles, 1965	666
	Felipe Alou, 1966	666
	Dave Cash, 1976	666
	Ron LeFlore, 1978	666
	Paul Molitor, 1982	666
56	Tommy Davis, 1962	665
	Pete Rose, 1976	665
	Paul Molitor, 1991	665
59	Taylor Douthit, 1930	664
	Bobby Richardson, 1965	664
	Don Kessinger, 1969	664
	Lou Brock, 1970	664
63	Jake Wood, 1961	663
	Bill Virdon, 1962	663
	Bobby Bonds, 1970	663
	Rick Burleson, 1977	663
	Cal Ripken, 1983	663
	Juan Samuel, 1985	663
	Joe Carter, 1986	663
70	Lloyd Waner, 1929	662
	Hughie Critz, 1930	662
	Richie Ashburn, 1949	662
	Granny Hamner, 1949	662
	Bobby Richardson, 1961	662
	Curt Flood, 1963	662
	Felipe Alou, 1968	662
	Pete Rose, 1975	662
	Kenny Lofton, 1996	662
	Dante Bichette, 1998	662
80	Doc Cramer, 1933	661
	Doc Cramer, 1940	661
	Ken Hubbs, 1962	661
	Cecil Cooper, 1983	661
	Ruben Sierra, 1991	661
85	Tom Brown, 1892	660
	Doc Cramer, 1941	660
	Lou Brock, 1968	660
	Enos Cabell, 1978	660
	Paul Molitor, 1996	660
90	Lloyd Waner, 1928	659
	Hughie Critz, 1932	659
	Red Schoendienst, 1947	659
	Billy Moran, 1962	659
	Zoilo Versalles, 1964	659
	Luis Aparicio, 1966	659
	Steve Garvey, 1975	659
	Warren Cromartie, 1979	659
	Travis Fryman, 1992	659
99	7 players tied	658

Runs

1	Billy Hamilton, 1894	192
2	Tom Brown, 1891	177
	Babe Ruth, 1921	177
4	Tip O'Neill, 1887	167
	Lou Gehrig, 1936	167
6	Billy Hamilton, 1895	166
7	Willie Keeler, 1894	165
	Joe Kelley, 1894	165
9	Arlie Latham, 1887	163
	Babe Ruth, 1928	163
	Lou Gehrig, 1931	163
12	Willie Keeler, 1895	162
13	Hugh Duffy, 1890	161
14	Fred Dunlap, 1884	160
	Hugh Duffy, 1894	160
	Jesse Burkett, 1896	160
17	Hughie Jennings, 1895	159
18	Bobby Lowe, 1894	158
	Babe Ruth, 1920	158
	Babe Ruth, 1927	158
	Chuck Klein, 1930	158
22	John McGraw, 1894	156
	Rogers Hornsby, 1929	156
24	King Kelly, 1886	155
	Kiki Cuyler, 1930	155
26	Dan Brouthers, 1887	153
	Jesse Burkett, 1895	153
	Billy Hamilton, 1896	153
	Willie Keeler, 1896	153
30	Arlie Latham, 1886	152
	Mike Griffin, 1889	152
	Harry Stovey, 1889	152
	Billy Hamilton, 1897	152
	Lefty O'Doul, 1929	152
	Woody English, 1930	152
	Al Simmons, 1930	152
	Chuck Klein, 1932	152
38	Babe Ruth, 1923	151
	Jimmie Foxx, 1932	151
	Joe DiMaggio, 1937	151
41	George Gore, 1886	150
	Babe Ruth, 1930	150
	Ted Williams, 1949	150
44	Herman Long, 1893	149
	Bill Dahlen, 1894	149
	Ed Delahanty, 1895	149
	Lou Gehrig, 1927	149
	Babe Ruth, 1931	149
49	Hub Collins, 1890	148
	Jake Stenzel, 1894	148
	Joe Kelley, 1895	148
	Joe Kelley, 1896	148
53	Mike Tiernan, 1889	147
	Hugh Duffy, 1893	147
	Ed Delahanty, 1894	147
	Ty Cobb, 1911	147
57	Darby O'Brien, 1889	146
	Tom Brown, 1890	146
	Hack Wilson, 1930	146
	Rickey Henderson, 1985	146
	Craig Biggio, 1997	146
62	Jesse Burkett, 1893	145
	Cupid Childs, 1893	145
	Ed Delahanty, 1893	145
	Patsy Donovan, 1894	145
	Willie Keeler, 1897	145
	Nap Lajoie, 1901	145
	Harlond Clift, 1936	145
69	Hugh Duffy, 1889	144
	Billy Hamilton, 1889	144
	Ty Cobb, 1915	144
	Kiki Cuyler, 1925	144
	Charlie Gehringer, 1930	144
	Al Simmons, 1932	144
	Charlie Gehringer, 1936	144
	Hank Greenberg, 1938	144
77	Cupid Childs, 1894	143
	John McGraw, 1898	143
	Babe Ruth, 1924	143
	Babe Herman, 1930	143
	Lou Gehrig, 1930	143
	Earle Combs, 1932	143
	Red Rolfe, 1937	143
	Lenny Dykstra, 1993	143
	Larry Walker, 1997	143
86	Mike Griffin, 1887	142
	Harry Stovey, 1890	142
	Jesse Burkett, 1901	142
	Paul Waner, 1928	142
	Ted Williams, 1946	142
	Ellis Burks, 1996	142
92	Billy Hamilton, 1891	141
	Rogers Hornsby, 1922	141
	Ted Williams, 1942	141
	Alex Rodriguez, 1996	141
96	9 players tied	140

Runs per Game (by era)

1876-1892

1	Ross Barnes, 1876	1.91
2	Fred Dunlap, 1884	1.58
3	George Gore, 1890	1.42
4	Tip O'Neill, 1887	1.35
5	King Kelly, 1886	1.31
6	Tom Brown, 1891	1.29
7	George Gore, 1886	1.27
8	Dan Brouthers, 1887	1.24
9	Orator Shaffer, 1884	1.23
10	Mike Tiernan, 1889	1.20
11	Harry Stovey, 1890	1.20
12	Arlie Latham, 1887	1.20
13	Harry Stovey, 1884	1.19
14	George Gore, 1882	1.18
15	George Gore, 1881	1.18

1893-1919

1	Billy Hamilton, 1894	1.49
2	Billy Hamilton, 1895	1.35
3	Billy Hamilton, 1893	1.34
4	Herman Long, 1894	1.31
5	Ed Delahanty, 1894	1.29
6	Ed Delahanty, 1895	1.28
7	Hugh Duffy, 1894	1.28
8	Willie Keeler, 1894	1.28
	Joe Kelley, 1894	1.28
10	John McGraw, 1894	1.26
11	Willie Keeler, 1895	1.24
12	Bill Dahlen, 1894	1.23
13	Jimmy Ryan, 1894	1.22
14	Willie Keeler, 1896	1.21
15	Hughie Jennings, 1895	1.21

1920-1941

1	Babe Ruth, 1921	1.16
2	Babe Ruth, 1920	1.11
3	Al Simmons, 1930	1.10
4	Lou Gehrig, 1936	1.08
5	Babe Ruth, 1928	1.06
6	Lou Gehrig, 1931	1.05
7	Jimmie Foxx, 1939	1.05
8	Babe Ruth, 1927	1.05
9	Babe Ruth, 1930	1.03
10	Babe Ruth, 1931	1.03
11	Chuck Klein, 1930	1.01
12	Rogers Hornsby, 1929	1.00
	Joe DiMaggio, 1937	1.00
14	Kiki Cuyler, 1930	.99
15	Babe Ruth, 1923	.99

1942-1960

1	Ted Williams, 1949	.97
2	Ted Williams, 1946	.95
3	Tommy Henrich, 1948	.95
4	Ted Williams, 1942	.94
5	Dom DiMaggio, 1950	.93
6	Ted Williams, 1948	.91
7	Johnny Mize, 1947	.89
8	Eddie Joost, 1949	.89
9	Mickey Mantle, 1954	.88
10	Johnny Pesky, 1950	.88
11	Mickey Mantle, 1956	.88
12	Stan Musial, 1948	.87
13	Goody Rosen, 1945	.87
	Dom DiMaggio, 1949	.87
15	Johnny Pesky, 1948	.87

1961-1976

1	Mickey Mantle, 1961	.86
2	Bobby Bonds, 1970	.85
3	Billy Williams, 1970	.85
4	Willie Mays, 1961	.84
5	Frank Robinson, 1962	.83
6	Roger Maris, 1961	.82
7	Joe Morgan, 1972	.82
8	Bobby Bonds, 1973	.82
9	Hank Aaron, 1962	.81
10	Don Buford, 1971	.81
11	Reggie Jackson, 1969	.81
12	Jim Wynn, 1972	.81
13	Lou Brock, 1971	.80
14	Willie Mays, 1962	.80
	Pete Rose, 1976	.80

1977-1998

1	Rickey Henderson, 1985	1.02
2	Paul Molitor, 1987	.97
3	Alex Rodriguez, 1996	.97
4	Jeff Bagwell, 1994	.95
5	Frank Thomas, 1994	.94
6	Kenny Lofton, 1994	.94
7	Larry Walker, 1997	.93
8	Eric Davis, 1987	.93
9	Chuck Knoblauch, 1996	.92
10	Ellis Burks, 1996	.91
11	Craig Biggio, 1997	.90
12	Ken Griffey Jr., 1996	.89
13	Lenny Dykstra, 1993	.89
14	Tim Raines, 1987	.88
15	Rickey Henderson, 1990	.88

Hits

1	George Sisler, 1920	257
2	Lefty O'Doul, 1929	254
	Bill Terry, 1930	254
4	Al Simmons, 1925	253
5	Rogers Hornsby, 1922	250
	Chuck Klein, 1930	250
7	Ty Cobb, 1911	248
8	George Sisler, 1922	246
9	Heinie Manush, 1928	241
	Babe Herman, 1930	241
11	Jesse Burkett, 1896	240
	Wade Boggs, 1985	240
13	Willie Keeler, 1897	239
	Rod Carew, 1977	239
15	Ed Delahanty, 1899	238
	Don Mattingly, 1986	238
17	Hugh Duffy, 1894	237
	Harry Heilmann, 1921	237
	Paul Waner, 1927	237
	Joe Medwick, 1937	237
21	Jack Tobin, 1921	236
22	Rogers Hornsby, 1921	235
23	Lloyd Waner, 1929	234
	Kirby Puckett, 1988	234
25	Joe Jackson, 1911	233
26	Nap Lajoie, 1901	232
	Earl Averill, 1936	232
28	Earle Combs, 1927	231
	Freddy Lindstrom, 1928	231
	Freddy Lindstrom, 1930	231
	Matty Alou, 1969	231
32	Stan Musial, 1948	230
	Tommy Davis, 1962	230
	Joe Torre, 1971	230
	Pete Rose, 1973	230
	Willie Wilson, 1980	230
37	Rogers Hornsby, 1929	229
38	Kiki Cuyler, 1930	228
	Stan Musial, 1946	228
40	Nap Lajoie, 1910	227
	Rogers Hornsby, 1924	227
	Jim Bottomley, 1925	227
	Sam Rice, 1925	227
	Billy Herman, 1935	227
	Charlie Gehringer, 1936	227
	Lance Johnson, 1996	227
47	Jesse Burkett, 1901	226
	Joe Jackson, 1912	226
	Ty Cobb, 1912	226
	Bill Terry, 1929	226
	Chuck Klein, 1932	226
52	Tip O'Neill, 1887	225
	Jesse Burkett, 1895	225
	Ty Cobb, 1917	225
	Harry Heilmann, 1925	225
	Johnny Hodapp, 1930	225
	Bill Terry, 1932	225
	Paul Molitor, 1996	225
59	Eddie Collins, 1920	224
	George Sisler, 1925	224
	Joe Medwick, 1935	224
	Tommy Holmes, 1945	224
63	Frankie Frisch, 1923	223
	Lloyd Waner, 1927	223
	Paul Waner, 1928	223
	Chuck Klein, 1933	223
	Joe Medwick, 1936	223
	Hank Aaron, 1959	223
	Kirby Puckett, 1986	223
70	Sam Thompson, 1893	222
	Tris Speaker, 1912	222
	Charlie Jamieson, 1923	222
73	Jesse Burkett, 1899	221
	Zack Wheat, 1925	221
	Lloyd Waner, 1928	221
	Heinie Manush, 1933	221
	Richie Ashburn, 1951	221
78	Pete Browning, 1887	220
	Billy Hamilton, 1894	220
	Kiki Cuyler, 1925	220
	Lou Gehrig, 1930	220
	Stan Musial, 1943	220
	Tony Gwynn, 1997	220
84	Ed Delahanty, 1893	219
	Willie Keeler, 1894	219
	Jimmy Williams, 1899	219
	Cy Seymour, 1905	219
	Chuck Klein, 1929	219
	Lefty O'Doul, 1932	219
	Paul Waner, 1937	219
	Ralph Garr, 1971	219
	Cecil Cooper, 1980	219
	Dante Bichette, 1998	219
94	12 players tied	218

Doubles

```
 1 Earl Webb, 1931 ....... 67
 2 George Burns, 1926 .... 64
   Joe Medwick, 1936 ..... 64
 4 Hank Greenberg, 1934 ... 63
 5 Paul Waner, 1932 ...... 62
 6 Charlie Gehringer, 1936 . 60
 7 Tris Speaker, 1923 ..... 59
   Chuck Klein, 1930 ..... 59
 9 Billy Herman, 1935 ..... 57
   Billy Herman, 1936 ..... 57
11 Joe Medwick, 1937 ..... 56
   George Kell, 1950 ..... 56
13 Ed Delahanty, 1899 ..... 55
   Gee Walker, 1936 ..... 55
15 Hal McRae, 1977 ..... 54
   John Olerud, 1993 ..... 54
   Alex Rodriguez, 1996 ... 54
   Mark Grudzielanek, 1997 . 54
19 Tris Speaker, 1912 ..... 53
   Al Simmons, 1926 ..... 53
   Paul Waner, 1936 ..... 53
   Stan Musial, 1953 ..... 53
   Don Mattingly, 1986 ... 53
24 Tip O'Neill, 1887 ..... 52
   Tris Speaker, 1921 ..... 52
   Tris Speaker, 1926 ..... 52
   Lou Gehrig, 1927 ..... 52
   Johnny Frederick, 1929 .. 52
   Enos Slaughter, 1939 ... 52
   Albert Belle, 1995 ..... 52
   Edgar Martinez, 1995 ... 52
   Edgar Martinez, 1996 ... 52
33 Hugh Duffy, 1894 ...... 51
   Nap Lajoie, 1910 ..... 51
   Baby Doll Jacobson, 1926 . 51
   George Burns, 1927 .... 51
   Johnny Hodapp, 1930 ... 51
   Beau Bell, 1937 ..... 51
   Joe Cronin, 1938 ...... 51
   Stan Musial, 1944 ..... 51
   Mickey Vernon, 1946 ... 51
   Frank Robinson, 1962 ... 51
   Pete Rose, 1978 ..... 51
   Wade Boggs, 1989 ..... 51
   Mark Grace, 1995 ..... 51
   Craig Biggio, 1998 ..... 51
47 Tris Speaker, 1920 ..... 50
   Harry Heilmann, 1927 ... 50
   Paul Waner, 1928 ..... 50
   Kiki Cuyler, 1930 ..... 50
   Chuck Klein, 1932 ..... 50
   Charlie Gehringer, 1934 . 50
   Odell Hale, 1936 ........ 50
   Ben Chapman, 1936 ..... 50
   Hank Greenberg, 1940 .. 50
   Stan Musial, 1946 ...... 50
   Stan Spence, 1946 ..... 50
   Juan Gonzalez, 1998 ... 50
59 Ned Williamson, 1883 ... 49
   Ed Delahanty, 1895 ..... 49
   Nap Lajoie, 1904 ..... 49
   George Sisler, 1920 ..... 49
   Heinie Manush, 1930 ... 49
   Riggs Stephenson, 1932 . 49
   Hank Greenberg, 1937 .. 49
   Robin Yount, 1980 ..... 49
   Rafael Palmeiro, 1991 ... 49
   Tony Gwynn, 1997 ..... 49
69 Joe Kelley, 1894 ...... 48
   Nap Lajoie, 1901 ..... 48
   Nap Lajoie, 1906 ..... 48
   Tris Speaker, 1922 ..... 48
   Joe Sewell, 1927 ...... 48
   Babe Herman, 1930 ..... 48
   Dick Bartell, 1932 ..... 48
   Earl Averill, 1934 ....... 48
   Wally Moses, 1937 ..... 48
   Joe Medwick, 1939 ..... 48
   Stan Musial, 1943 ...... 48
   Keith Hernandez, 1979 .. 48
   Don Mattingly, 1985 .... 48
   Jeff Bagwell, 1996 ..... 48
   Dante Bichette, 1998 .... 48
   Dmitri Young, 1998 ..... 48
   Albert Belle, 1998 ...... 48
86 26 players tied ....... 47
```

Triples

```
 1 Chief Wilson, 1912 ..... 36
 2 Dave Orr, 1886 ........ 31
   Heinie Reitz, 1894 ...... 31
 4 Perry Werden, 1893 .... 29
 5 Harry Davis, 1897 ..... 28
 6 George Davis, 1893 .... 27
   Sam Thompson, 1894 ... 27
   Jimmy Williams, 1899 ... 27
 9 John Reilly, 1890 ..... 26
   George Treadway, 1894 . 26
   Joe Jackson, 1912 ..... 26
   Sam Crawford, 1914 .... 26
   Kiki Cuyler, 1925 ...... 26
14 Roger Connor, 1894 .... 25
   Buck Freeman, 1899 .... 25
   Sam Crawford, 1903 .... 25
   Larry Doyle, 1911 ..... 25
   Tom Long, 1915 ....... 25
19 Ed McKean, 1893 ..... 24
   Ty Cobb, 1911 ....... 24
   Ty Cobb, 1917 ........ 24
22 Harry Stovey, 1884 .... 23
   Sam Thompson, 1887 ... 23
   Elmer Smith, 1893 ..... 23
   Dan Brouthers, 1894 ... 23
   Nap Lajoie, 1897 ...... 23
   Ty Cobb, 1912 ........ 23
   Sam Crawford, 1913 .... 23
   Earle Combs, 1927 ..... 23
   Adam Comorosky, 1930 . 23
   Dale Mitchell, 1949 .... 23
32 Roger Connor, 1887 .... 22
   Bid McPhee, 1890 ..... 22
   Jake Beckley, 1890 ..... 22
   Joe Visner, 1890 ...... 22
   Willie Keeler, 1894 .... 22
   Kip Selbach, 1895 ..... 22
   John Anderson, 1898 ... 22
   Honus Wagner, 1900 ... 22
   Tommy Leach, 1902 .... 22
   Sam Crawford, 1902 .... 22
   Bill Bradley, 1903 ..... 22
   Elmer Flick, 1906 ..... 22
   Mike Mitchell, 1911 .... 22
   Birdie Cree, 1911 ..... 22
   Tris Speaker, 1913 ..... 22
   Hy Myers, 1920 ....... 22
   Jake Daubert, 1922 .... 22
   Paul Waner, 1926 ..... 22
   Earle Combs, 1930 ..... 22
   Snuffy Stirnweiss, 1945 . 22
52 Dave Orr, 1885 ....... 21
   Mike Tiernan, 1890 .... 21
   Billy Shindle, 1890 .... 21
   Tom Brown, 1891 ..... 21
   Ed Delahanty, 1892 ..... 21
   Sam Thompson, 1895 ... 21
   Mike Tiernan, 1895 .... 21
   Tom McCreery, 1896 ... 21
   George Van Haltren, 1896  21
   Bobby Wallace, 1897 ... 21
   Jimmy Williams, 1901 ... 21
   Bill Keister, 1901 ..... 21
   Jimmy Williams, 1902 ... 21
   Cy Seymour, 1905 ..... 21
   Frank Schulte, 1911 .... 21
   Frank Baker, 1912 ..... 21
   Sam Crawford, 1912 .... 21
   Vic Saier, 1913 ....... 21
   Joe Jackson, 1916 ..... 21
   Edd Roush, 1924 ..... 21
   Earle Combs, 1928 ..... 21
   Willie Wilson, 1985 .... 21
   Lance Johnson, 1996 ... 21
75 36 players tied ....... 20
```

Triples (by era)

1876-1892
```
 1 Dave Orr, 1886 ....... 31
 2 John Reilly, 1890 ..... 26
 3 Harry Stovey, 1884 .... 23
   Sam Thompson, 1887 ... 23
 5 Roger Connor, 1887 .... 22
   Bid McPhee, 1890 ..... 22
   Jake Beckley, 1890 ..... 22
   Joe Visner, 1890 ...... 22
 9 Dave Orr, 1885 ....... 21
   Mike Tiernan, 1890 .... 21
   Billy Shindle, 1890 .... 21
   Tom Brown, 1891 ..... 21
   Ed Delahanty, 1892 .... 21
14 10 players tied ........ 20
```

1893-1919
```
 1 Chief Wilson, 1912 ..... 36
 2 Heinie Reitz, 1894 ..... 31
 3 Perry Werden, 1893 .... 29
 4 Harry Davis, 1897 ..... 28
 5 George Davis, 1893 .... 27
   Sam Thompson, 1894 ... 27
   Jimmy Williams, 1899 ... 27
 8 George Treadway, 1894 . 26
   Joe Jackson, 1912 ..... 26
   Sam Crawford, 1914 .... 26
11 Roger Connor, 1894 .... 25
   Buck Freeman, 1899 .... 25
   Sam Crawford, 1903 .... 25
   Larry Doyle, 1911 ..... 25
   Tom Long, 1915 ....... 25
```

1920-1941
```
 1 Kiki Cuyler, 1925 ...... 26
 2 Earle Combs, 1927 ..... 23
   Adam Comorosky, 1930 . 23
 4 Hy Myers, 1920 ....... 22
   Jake Daubert, 1922 .... 22
   Paul Waner, 1926 ..... 22
   Earle Combs, 1930 ..... 22
 8 Edd Roush, 1924 ..... 21
   Earle Combs, 1928 ..... 21
10 12 players tied ........ 20
```

1942-1960
```
 1 Dale Mitchell, 1949 .... 23
 2 Snuffy Stirnweiss, 1945 . 22
 3 Stan Musial, 1943 ..... 20
   Stan Musial, 1946 ..... 20
   Willie Mays, 1957 ..... 20
 6 Johnny Barrett, 1944 ... 19
 7 Stan Musial, 1948 ..... 18
   Minnie Minoso, 1954 ... 18
 9 Enos Slaughter, 1942 ... 17
   Jim Gilliam, 1953 ..... 17
11 6 players tied .......... 16
```

1961-1976
```
 1 Ralph Garr, 1974 ...... 17
 2 Johnny Callison, 1965 ... 16
   Willie Davis, 1970 ..... 16
 4 Gino Cimoli, 1962 ..... 15
 5 Jake Wood, 1961 ..... 14
   Vada Pinson, 1963 ..... 14
   Dick Allen, 1965 ..... 14
   Roberto Clemente, 1965 . 14
   Donn Clendenon, 1965 .. 14
   Lou Brock, 1968 ..... 14
   Don Kessinger, 1970 ... 14
   Roger Metzger, 1973 ... 14
   George Brett, 1976 .... 14
14 10 players tied ....... 13
```

1977-1998
```
 1 Willie Wilson, 1985 ..... 21
   Lance Johnson, 1996 ... 21
 3 George Brett, 1979 .... 20
 4 Garry Templeton, 1979 .. 19
   Juan Samuel, 1984 ..... 19
   Ryne Sandberg, 1984 ... 19
 7 Garry Templeton, 1977 .. 18
   Willie McGee, 1985 .... 18
 9 Tony Fernandez, 1990 ... 17
10 Rod Carew, 1977 ...... 16
   Paul Molitor, 1979 ..... 16
12 11 players tied ....... 15
```

Home Runs

```
 1 Mark McGwire, 1998 .... 70
 2 Sammy Sosa, 1998 ..... 66
 3 Roger Maris, 1961 ..... 61
 4 Babe Ruth, 1927 ..... 60
 5 Babe Ruth, 1921 ..... 59
 6 Mark McGwire, 1997 .... 58
   Jimmie Foxx, 1932 ..... 58
   Hank Greenberg, 1938 .. 58
 9 Hack Wilson, 1930 ..... 56
   Ken Griffey Jr., 1997 ... 56
   Ken Griffey, 1998 ..... 56
12 Babe Ruth, 1920 ..... 54
   Babe Ruth, 1928 ..... 54
   Ralph Kiner, 1949 ..... 54
   Mickey Mantle, 1961 .... 54
16 Mickey Mantle, 1956 ... 52
   Willie Mays, 1965 ..... 52
   George Foster, 1977 .... 52
   Mark McGwire, 1996 ... 52
20 Ralph Kiner, 1947 ..... 51
   Johnny Mize, 1947 ..... 51
   Willie Mays, 1955 ..... 51
   Cecil Fielder, 1990 .... 51
24 Jimmie Foxx, 1938 ..... 50
   Albert Belle, 1995 ..... 50
   Brady Anderson, 1996 .. 50
   Greg Vaughn, 1998 .... 50
28 Babe Ruth, 1930 ..... 49
   Lou Gehrig, 1934 ..... 49
   Lou Gehrig, 1936 ..... 49
   Ted Kluszewski, 1954 ... 49
   Willie Mays, 1962 ..... 49
   Harmon Killebrew, 1964 . 49
   Frank Robinson, 1966 ... 49
   Harmon Killebrew, 1969 . 49
   Andre Dawson, 1987 .... 49
   Mark McGwire, 1987 ... 49
   Ken Griffey Jr., 1996 ... 49
   Larry Walker, 1997 ..... 49
   Albert Belle, 1998 ..... 49
41 Jimmie Foxx, 1933 ..... 48
   Harmon Killebrew, 1962 . 48
   Frank Howard, 1969 .... 48
   Willie Stargell, 1971 .... 48
   Dave Kingman, 1979 ... 48
   Mike Schmidt, 1980 .... 48
   Albert Belle, 1996 ..... 48
48 Babe Ruth, 1926 ..... 47
   Lou Gehrig, 1927 ..... 47
   Ralph Kiner, 1950 ..... 47
   Eddie Mathews, 1953 ... 47
   Ted Kluszewski, 1955 ... 47
   Ernie Banks, 1958 ..... 47
   Willie Mays, 1964 ..... 47
   Reggie Jackson, 1969 ... 47
   Hank Aaron, 1971 ..... 47
   George Bell, 1987 ..... 47
   Kevin Mitchell, 1989 ... 47
61 Babe Ruth, 1924 ..... 46
   Babe Ruth, 1929 ..... 46
   Babe Ruth, 1931 ..... 46
   Lou Gehrig, 1931 ..... 46
   Joe DiMaggio, 1937 .... 46
   Eddie Mathews, 1959 ... 46
   Orlando Cepeda, 1961 .. 46
   Jim Gentile, 1961 ..... 46
   Harmon Killebrew, 1961 . 46
   Jim Rice, 1978 ........ 46
   Barry Bonds, 1993 ..... 46
   Juan Gonzalez, 1993 ... 46
   Vinny Castilla, 1998 .... 46
   Jose Canseco, 1998 .... 46
75 Ernie Banks, 1959 ..... 45
   Rocky Colavito, 1961 ... 45
   Hank Aaron, 1962 ..... 45
   Harmon Killebrew, 1963 . 45
   Willie McCovey, 1969 ... 45
   Johnny Bench, 1970 .... 45
   Mike Schmidt, 1979 .... 45
   Gorman Thomas, 1979 .. 45
   Ken Griffey Jr., 1993 ... 45
   Juan Gonzalez, 1998 ... 45
   Manny Ramirez, 1998 ... 45
86 20 players tied ....... 44
```

Home Runs (by era)

1876-1892

1	Ned Williamson, 1884	27
2	Fred Pfeffer, 1884	25
3	Abner Dalrymple, 1884	22
4	Cap Anson, 1884	21
5	Sam Thompson, 1889	20
6	Billy O'Brien, 1887	19
	Bug Holliday, 1889	19
	Harry Stovey, 1889	19
9	Jerry Denny, 1889	18
10	Roger Connor, 1887	17
	Jimmy Ryan, 1889	17
12	5 players tied	16

1893-1919

1	Babe Ruth, 1919	29
2	Buck Freeman, 1899	25
3	Gavvy Cravath, 1915	24
4	Frank Schulte, 1911	21
5	Ed Delahanty, 1893	19
	Gavvy Cravath, 1913	19
	Gavvy Cravath, 1914	19
8	Hugh Duffy, 1894	18
	Sam Thompson, 1895	18
	Fred Luderus, 1913	18
	Vic Saier, 1914	18
12	5 players tied	17

1920-1941

1	Babe Ruth, 1927	60
2	Babe Ruth, 1921	59
3	Jimmie Foxx, 1932	58
	Hank Greenberg, 1938	58
5	Hack Wilson, 1930	56
6	Babe Ruth, 1920	54
	Babe Ruth, 1928	54
8	Jimmie Foxx, 1938	50
9	Babe Ruth, 1930	49
	Lou Gehrig, 1934	49
	Lou Gehrig, 1936	49
12	Jimmie Foxx, 1933	48
13	Babe Ruth, 1926	47
	Lou Gehrig, 1927	47
15	5 players tied	46

1942-1960

1	Ralph Kiner, 1949	54
2	Mickey Mantle, 1956	52
3	Ralph Kiner, 1947	51
	Johnny Mize, 1947	51
	Willie Mays, 1955	51
6	Ted Kluszewski, 1954	49
7	Ralph Kiner, 1950	47
	Eddie Mathews, 1953	47
	Ted Kluszewski, 1955	47
	Ernie Banks, 1958	47
11	Eddie Mathews, 1959	46
12	Ernie Banks, 1959	45
13	Hank Greenberg, 1946	44
	Ernie Banks, 1955	44
	Hank Aaron, 1957	44

1961-1976

1	Roger Maris, 1961	61
2	Mickey Mantle, 1961	54
3	Willie Mays, 1965	52
4	Willie Mays, 1962	49
	Harmon Killebrew, 1964	49
	Frank Robinson, 1966	49
	Harmon Killebrew, 1969	49
8	Harmon Killebrew, 1962	48
	Frank Howard, 1969	48
	Willie Stargell, 1971	48
11	Willie Mays, 1964	47
	Reggie Jackson, 1969	47
	Hank Aaron, 1971	47
14	3 players tied	46

1977-1998

1	Mark McGwire, 1998	70
2	Sammy Sosa, 1998	66
3	Mark McGwire, 1997	58
4	Ken Griffey Jr., 1997	56
	Ken Griffey, 1998	56
6	George Foster, 1977	52
	Mark McGwire, 1996	52
8	Cecil Fielder, 1990	51
9	Albert Belle, 1995	50
	Brady Anderson, 1996	50
	Greg Vaughn, 1998	50
12	5 players tied	49

Home Run Percentage

1	Mark McGwire, 1998	13.75
2	Mark McGwire, 1996	12.29
3	Babe Ruth, 1920	11.79
4	Babe Ruth, 1927	11.11
5	Babe Ruth, 1921	10.93
6	Mark McGwire, 1997	10.74
7	Mickey Mantle, 1961	10.51
8	Hank Greenberg, 1938	10.43
9	Roger Maris, 1961	10.34
10	Sammy Sosa, 1998	10.26
11	Babe Ruth, 1928	10.07
12	Jimmie Foxx, 1932	9.91
13	Ralph Kiner, 1949	9.84
14	Mickey Mantle, 1956	9.76
15	Jeff Bagwell, 1994	9.75
16	Kevin Mitchell, 1994	9.68
17	Matt Williams, 1994	9.66
18	Hack Wilson, 1930	9.57
19	Frank Thomas, 1994	9.52
20	Babe Ruth, 1926	9.49
	Hank Aaron, 1971	9.49
22	Jim Gentile, 1961	9.47
23	Barry Bonds, 1994	9.46
24	Babe Ruth, 1930	9.46
25	Willie Stargell, 1971	9.39
26	Willie Mays, 1965	9.32
27	Ken Griffey Jr., 1994	9.24
28	Babe Ruth, 1929	9.22
29	Ken Griffey Jr., 1997	9.21
30	Boog Powell, 1964	9.20
31	Willie McCovey, 1969	9.16
32	Albert Belle, 1995	9.16
33	Ted Williams, 1957	9.05
34	Ralph Kiner, 1947	9.03
35	Dave Kingman, 1979	9.02
36	Mark McGwire, 1992	8.99
37	Ken Griffey Jr., 1996	8.99
38	Babe Ruth, 1932	8.97
39	Cecil Fielder, 1990	8.90
40	Jimmie Foxx, 1938	8.85
41	Ken Griffey Jr., 1998	8.85
42	Harmon Killebrew, 1969	8.83
43	Mark McGwire, 1987	8.80
44	Willie Mays, 1955	8.79
45	Mike Schmidt, 1980	8.76
46	Mike Schmidt, 1981	8.76
47	Harmon Killebrew, 1963	8.74
	Albert Belle, 1994	8.74
49	Greg Vaughn, 1998	8.73
50	Johnny Mize, 1947	8.70
51	Babe Ruth, 1924	8.70
	Harmon Killebrew, 1962	8.70
53	Juan Gonzalez, 1996	8.69
54	Kevin Mitchell, 1989	8.66
55	Brady Anderson, 1996	8.64
56	Larry Walker, 1997	8.63
57	Babe Ruth, 1922	8.62
58	Babe Ruth, 1931	8.61
59	Ralph Kiner, 1950	8.59
60	Juan Gonzalez, 1993	8.58
61	Reggie Jackson, 1969	8.56
62	Ted Kluszewski, 1954	8.55
63	Barry Bonds, 1993	8.53
64	Jay Buhner, 1995	8.51
65	Frank Robinson, 1966	8.51
66	Harmon Killebrew, 1961	8.50
67	Harmon Killebrew, 1964	8.49
68	Lou Gehrig, 1934	8.46
	Lou Gehrig, 1936	8.46
70	George Foster, 1977	8.46
71	Willie Stargell, 1973	8.43
72	Hank Greenberg, 1946	8.41
73	Eddie Mathews, 1954	8.40
74	Gary Sheffield, 1994	8.39
75	Rocky Colavito, 1958	8.38
76	Jimmie Foxx, 1933	8.38
77	Joe Adcock, 1956	8.37
78	Jack Clark, 1987	8.35
79	Mike Schmidt, 1979	8.32
80	Eddie Mathews, 1955	8.22
81	Jimmie Foxx, 1934	8.16
82	Willie Mays, 1964	8.13
83	Barry Bonds, 1996	8.12
84	Eddie Mathews, 1953	8.12
85	Ted Williams, 1941	8.11
86	Frank Thomas, 1995	8.11
87	Frank Howard, 1969	8.11
88	Mickey Mantle, 1958	8.09
	Gary Sheffield, 1996	8.09
90	Gorman Thomas, 1979	8.08
91	Jim Thome, 1997	8.06
92	Lou Gehrig, 1927	8.05
93	Albert Belle, 1998	8.05
94	Harmon Killebrew, 1967	8.04
	Hank Aaron, 1969	8.04
96	Sammy Sosa, 1996	8.03
97	Fred McGriff, 1994	8.02
98	Reggie Jackson, 1980	7.98
99	Albert Belle, 1996	7.97
100	Mickey Mantle, 1962	7.96

Home Run Pctg. (by era)

1876-1892

1	Ned Williamson, 1884	6.47
2	Fred Pfeffer, 1884	5.35
3	Cap Anson, 1884	4.42
4	Abner Dalrymple, 1884	4.22
5	Billy O'Brien, 1887	4.19
6	Sam Thompson, 1889	3.75
7	Roger Connor, 1887	3.61
8	Dan Brouthers, 1884	3.52
9	Harry Stovey, 1889	3.42
10	Bug Holliday, 1889	3.37
11	Fred Pfeffer, 1887	3.34
12	Harry Stovey, 1883	3.33
13	Charlie Duffee, 1889	3.14
14	Jerry Denny, 1889	3.11
15	Dan Brouthers, 1881	2.96

1893-1919

1	Babe Ruth, 1919	6.71
2	Bill Joyce, 1894	4.79
3	Gavvy Cravath, 1915	4.60
4	Jack Clements, 1893	4.52
5	Buck Freeman, 1899	4.25
6	Gavvy Cravath, 1914	3.81
7	Jim Canavan, 1894	3.65
8	Frank Schulte, 1911	3.64
9	Gavvy Cravath, 1913	3.62
10	Bill Joyce, 1895	3.59
11	Sherry Magee, 1911	3.37
12	Vic Saier, 1914	3.35
13	Sam Thompson, 1895	3.35
14	Hugh Duffy, 1894	3.34
15	Ed Delahanty, 1893	3.19

1920-1941

1	Babe Ruth, 1920	11.79
2	Babe Ruth, 1927	11.11
3	Babe Ruth, 1921	10.93
4	Hank Greenberg, 1938	10.43
5	Babe Ruth, 1928	10.07
6	Jimmie Foxx, 1932	9.91
7	Hack Wilson, 1930	9.57
8	Babe Ruth, 1926	9.49
9	Babe Ruth, 1930	9.46
10	Babe Ruth, 1929	9.22
11	Babe Ruth, 1932	8.97
12	Jimmie Foxx, 1938	8.85
13	Babe Ruth, 1924	8.70
14	Babe Ruth, 1922	8.62
15	Babe Ruth, 1931	8.61

1942-1960

1	Ralph Kiner, 1949	9.84
2	Mickey Mantle, 1956	9.76
3	Ted Williams, 1957	9.05
4	Ralph Kiner, 1947	9.03
5	Willie Mays, 1955	8.79
6	Johnny Mize, 1947	8.70
7	Ralph Kiner, 1950	8.59
8	Ted Kluszewski, 1954	8.55
9	Hank Greenberg, 1946	8.41
10	Eddie Mathews, 1954	8.40
11	Rocky Colavito, 1958	8.38
12	Joe Adcock, 1956	8.37
13	Eddie Mathews, 1955	8.22
14	Eddie Mathews, 1953	8.12
15	Mickey Mantle, 1958	8.09

1961-1976

1	Mickey Mantle, 1961	10.51
2	Roger Maris, 1961	10.34
3	Hank Aaron, 1971	9.49
4	Jim Gentile, 1961	9.47
5	Willie Stargell, 1971	9.39
6	Willie Mays, 1965	9.32
7	Boog Powell, 1964	9.20
8	Willie McCovey, 1969	9.16
9	Harmon Killebrew, 1969	8.83
10	Harmon Killebrew, 1963	8.74
11	Harmon Killebrew, 1962	8.70
12	Reggie Jackson, 1969	8.56
13	Frank Robinson, 1966	8.51
14	Harmon Killebrew, 1961	8.50
15	Harmon Killebrew, 1964	8.49

1977-1998

1	Mark McGwire, 1998	13.75
2	Mark McGwire, 1996	12.29
3	Mark McGwire, 1997	10.74
4	Sammy Sosa, 1998	10.26
5	Jeff Bagwell, 1994	9.75
6	Kevin Mitchell, 1994	9.68
7	Matt Williams, 1994	9.66
8	Frank Thomas, 1994	9.52
9	Barry Bonds, 1994	9.46
10	Ken Griffey Jr., 1994	9.24
11	Ken Griffey, 1997	9.21
12	Albert Belle, 1995	9.16
13	Dave Kingman, 1979	9.02
14	Mark McGwire, 1992	8.99
15	Ken Griffey Jr., 1996	8.99

Total Bases

1	Babe Ruth, 1921	457
2	Rogers Hornsby, 1922	450
3	Lou Gehrig, 1927	447
4	Chuck Klein, 1930	445
5	Jimmie Foxx, 1932	438
6	Stan Musial, 1948	429
7	Hack Wilson, 1930	423
8	Chuck Klein, 1932	420
9	Lou Gehrig, 1930	419
10	Joe DiMaggio, 1937	418
11	Babe Ruth, 1927	417
12	Babe Herman, 1930	416
	Sammy Sosa, 1998	416
14	Lou Gehrig, 1931	410
15	Rogers Hornsby, 1929	409
	Lou Gehrig, 1934	409
	Larry Walker, 1997	409
18	Joe Medwick, 1937	406
	Jim Rice, 1978	406
20	Chuck Klein, 1929	405
	Hal Trosky, 1936	405
22	Jimmie Foxx, 1933	403
	Lou Gehrig, 1936	403
24	Hank Aaron, 1959	400
25	George Sisler, 1920	399
	Babe Ruth, 1923	399
	Albert Belle, 1998	399
28	Jimmie Foxx, 1938	398
29	Lefty O'Doul, 1929	397
	Hank Greenberg, 1937	397
31	Ken Griffey Jr., 1997	393
32	Al Simmons, 1925	392
	Bill Terry, 1930	392
	Al Simmons, 1930	392
	Ellis Burks, 1996	392
36	Babe Ruth, 1924	391
37	Hank Greenberg, 1935	389
38	Babe Ruth, 1920	388
	George Foster, 1977	388
	Don Mattingly, 1986	388
41	Ken Griffey Jr., 1998	387
42	Earl Averill, 1936	385
43	Hank Greenberg, 1940	384
	Alex Rodriguez, 1998	384
45	Mark McGwire, 1998	383
46	Stan Musial, 1949	382
	Willie Mays, 1955	382
	Willie Mays, 1962	382
	Jim Rice, 1977	382
	Juan Gonzalez, 1998	382
51	Rogers Hornsby, 1925	381
52	Babe Ruth, 1928	380
	Hank Greenberg, 1938	380
	Frank Robinson, 1962	380
	Vinny Castilla, 1998	380
56	Babe Ruth, 1930	379
	Ernie Banks, 1958	379
	Alex Rodriguez, 1996	379
59	Rogers Hornsby, 1921	378
	Duke Snider, 1954	378
61	Willie Mays, 1954	377
	Albert Belle, 1995	377
63	Mickey Mantle, 1956	376
	Andres Galarraga, 1996	376
65	Albert Belle, 1996	375
66	Hugh Duffy, 1894	374
	Babe Ruth, 1931	374
	Hal Trosky, 1934	374
	Tony Oliva, 1964	374
70	Rogers Hornsby, 1924	373
	Al Simmons, 1929	373
	Bill Terry, 1932	373
	Billy Williams, 1970	373
74	Lou Gehrig, 1932	370
	Duke Snider, 1953	370
	Hank Aaron, 1963	370
	Don Mattingly, 1985	370
	Mo Vaughn, 1996	370
79	Kiki Cuyler, 1925	369
	Ripper Collins, 1934	369
	Jimmie Foxx, 1936	369
	Hank Aaron, 1957	369
	Jim Rice, 1979	369
	George Bell, 1987	369
	Brady Anderson, 1996	369
86	Johnny Mize, 1940	368
	Ted Williams, 1949	368
	Ted Kluszewski, 1954	368
	Cal Ripken, 1991	368
90	Ty Cobb, 1911	367
	Ken Williams, 1922	367
	Heinie Manush, 1928	367
	Al Simmons, 1932	367
	Joe Medwick, 1936	367
	Joe DiMaggio, 1936	367
	Tommy Holmes, 1945	367
	Al Rosen, 1953	367
	Frank Robinson, 1966	367
	Robin Yount, 1982	367
	Vladimir Guerrero, 1998	367

Runs Batted In

1	Hack Wilson, 1930	190
2	Lou Gehrig, 1931	184
3	Hank Greenberg, 1937	183
4	Lou Gehrig, 1927	175
	Jimmie Foxx, 1938	175
6	Lou Gehrig, 1930	174
7	Babe Ruth, 1921	171
8	Chuck Klein, 1930	170
	Hank Greenberg, 1935	170
10	Jimmie Foxx, 1932	169
11	Joe DiMaggio, 1937	167
12	Sam Thompson, 1887	166
13	Sam Thompson, 1895	165
	Al Simmons, 1930	165
	Lou Gehrig, 1934	165
16	Babe Ruth, 1927	164
17	Babe Ruth, 1931	163
	Jimmie Foxx, 1933	163
19	Hal Trosky, 1936	162
20	Hack Wilson, 1929	159
	Lou Gehrig, 1937	159
	Ted Williams, 1949	159
	Vern Stephens, 1949	159
24	Sammy Sosa, 1998	158
25	Al Simmons, 1929	157
	Juan Gonzalez, 1998	157
27	Jimmie Foxx, 1930	156
28	Ken Williams, 1922	155
	Joe DiMaggio, 1948	155
30	Babe Ruth, 1929	154
	Joe Medwick, 1937	154
32	Babe Ruth, 1930	153
	Tommy Davis, 1962	153
34	Rogers Hornsby, 1922	152
	Lou Gehrig, 1936	152
	Albert Belle, 1998	152
37	Mel Ott, 1929	151
	Lou Gehrig, 1932	151
	Al Simmons, 1932	151
40	Hank Greenberg, 1940	150
	Andres Galarraga, 1996	150
42	Rogers Hornsby, 1929	149
	George Foster, 1977	149
44	Johnny Bench, 1970	148
	Albert Belle, 1996	148
46	Cap Anson, 1886	147
	Ken Griffey Jr., 1997	147
	Mark McGwire, 1998	147
49	Hardy Richardson, 1890	146
	Ed Delahanty, 1893	146
	Babe Ruth, 1926	146
	Hank Greenberg, 1938	146
	Ken Griffey Jr., 1998	146
54	Hugh Duffy, 1894	145
	Chuck Klein, 1929	145
	Ted Williams, 1939	145
	Al Rosen, 1953	145
	Don Mattingly, 1985	145
	Manny Ramirez, 1998	145
60	Walt Dropo, 1950	144
	Vern Stephens, 1950	144
	Juan Gonzalez, 1996	144
	Vinny Castilla, 1998	144
64	Rogers Hornsby, 1925	143
	Earl Averill, 1931	143
	Don Hurst, 1932	143
	Jimmie Foxx, 1936	143
	Ernie Banks, 1959	143
	Mo Vaughn, 1996	143
70	Lou Gehrig, 1928	142
	Babe Ruth, 1928	142
	Hal Trosky, 1934	142
	Roy Campanella, 1953	142
	Orlando Cepeda, 1961	142
	Roger Maris, 1961	142
	Rafael Palmeiro, 1996	142
77	Sam Thompson, 1894	141
	Ted Kluszewski, 1954	141
	Jim Gentile, 1961	141
	Willie Mays, 1962	141
	Dante Bichette, 1996	141
	Tino Martinez, 1997	141
83	Joe DiMaggio, 1938	140
	Rocky Colavito, 1961	140
	Harmon Killebrew, 1969	140
	Ken Griffey Jr., 1996	140
	Andres Galarraga, 1997	140
88	Harry Heilmann, 1921	139
	Lou Gehrig, 1933	139
	Hank Greenberg, 1934	139
	Jim Rice, 1978	139
	Don Baylor, 1979	139
93	Bob Meusel, 1925	138
	Goose Goslin, 1930	138
	Joe Medwick, 1936	138
	Zeke Bonura, 1936	138
	Johnny Mize, 1947	138
	Jay Buhner, 1996	138
99	11 players tied	137

Runs Batted In per Game

1	Sam Thompson, 1894	1.42
2	Sam Thompson, 1895	1.39
3	Sam Thompson, 1887	1.31
4	Hack Wilson, 1930	1.23
5	Al Simmons, 1930	1.20
6	Hank Greenberg, 1937	1.19
7	Lou Gehrig, 1931	1.19
8	Cap Anson, 1886	1.18
9	Jimmie Foxx, 1938	1.17
10	Hugh Duffy, 1894	1.16
11	Dave Orr, 1890	1.16
12	Ed Delahanty, 1894	1.15
13	Babe Ruth, 1929	1.14
14	Lou Gehrig, 1930	1.13
15	Lou Gehrig, 1927	1.13
16	Babe Ruth, 1921	1.13
17	Babe Ruth, 1931	1.12
18	Hardy Richardson, 1890	1.12
19	Hank Greenberg, 1935	1.12
20	Ed Delahanty, 1893	1.11
21	Joe DiMaggio, 1937	1.11
22	Al Simmons, 1929	1.10
23	Jimmie Foxx, 1932	1.10
24	Jimmie Foxx, 1933	1.09
25	Chuck Klein, 1930	1.09
26	Babe Ruth, 1927	1.09
27	Oyster Burns, 1890	1.08
28	Juan Gonzalez, 1996	1.07
29	Hal Trosky, 1936	1.07
30	Lou Gehrig, 1934	1.07
31	Ed McKean, 1893	1.06
32	Hack Wilson, 1929	1.06
33	Dave Foutz, 1887	1.06
	Walt Dropo, 1950	1.06
35	Babe Ruth, 1930	1.06
36	Jeff Bagwell, 1994	1.05
37	Buck Ewing, 1893	1.05
38	Lave Cross, 1894	1.05
39	Joe DiMaggio, 1939	1.05
40	George Davis, 1897	1.05
41	Dan Brouthers, 1894	1.04
42	Kirby Puckett, 1994	1.04
43	Rogers Hornsby, 1925	1.04
44	Jim O'Rourke, 1890	1.04
45	Babe Ruth, 1932	1.03
46	Ted Williams, 1949	1.03
	Vern Stephens, 1949	1.03
48	Ed Delahanty, 1896	1.02
49	Steve Brodie, 1895	1.02
	Joe Kelley, 1895	1.02
51	Jimmie Foxx, 1930	1.02
52	Juan Gonzalez, 1998	1.02
53	Dave Orr, 1884	1.02
54	Hank Greenberg, 1940	1.01
55	Ken Williams, 1922	1.01
	Joe DiMaggio, 1948	1.01
57	Lou Gehrig, 1937	1.01
58	Cap Anson, 1882	1.01
59	George Decker, 1894	1.01
60	George Brett, 1980	1.01
61	Joe DiMaggio, 1940	1.01
62	Mel Ott, 1929	1.01
63	Nap Lajoie, 1897	1.00
	Al Simmons, 1931	1.00
	Ken Griffey Jr., 1996	1.00
66	Sammy Sosa, 1998	.99
67	Roger Connor, 1889	.99
68	Tommy McCarthy, 1894	.99
69	Tip O'Neill, 1887	.99
70	Jake Beckley, 1890	.99
71	Dan Brouthers, 1883	.99
72	Joe Medwick, 1937	.99
73	Rogers Hornsby, 1922	.99
74	Roy Campanella, 1953	.99
75	Jimmy Collins, 1897	.99
76	Juan Gonzalez, 1997	.98
77	Ed McKean, 1894	.98
78	Bug Holliday, 1894	.98
79	Lou Gehrig, 1936	.98
80	Al Simmons, 1932	.98
81	Walt Wilmot, 1894	.98
82	Cap Anson, 1881	.98
83	Chuck Klein, 1929	.97
	Ted Williams, 1939	.97
85	Heinie Reitz, 1894	.97
86	Lou Gehrig, 1932	.97
87	Manny Ramirez, 1998	.97
88	Vern Stephens, 1950	.97
89	Joe DiMaggio, 1938	.97
90	Babe Ruth, 1920	.96
91	Cap Anson, 1885	.96
92	Hugh Duffy, 1897	.96
93	Sam Thompson, 1893	.96
94	Billy Nash, 1893	.96
95	Babe Ruth, 1926	.96
96	Jay Buhner, 1995	.96
97	Harry Heilmann, 1929	.96
98	Tommy McCarthy, 1893	.96
99	Rogers Hornsby, 1929	.96
100	2 players tied	.95

Walks

1	Babe Ruth, 1923	170
2	Ted Williams, 1947	162
	Ted Williams, 1949	162
	Mark McGwire, 1998	162
5	Ted Williams, 1946	156
6	Eddie Yost, 1956	151
	Barry Bonds, 1996	151
8	Eddie Joost, 1949	149
9	Babe Ruth, 1920	148
	Eddie Stanky, 1945	148
	Jim Wynn, 1969	148
12	Jimmy Sheckard, 1911	147
13	Mickey Mantle, 1957	146
14	Ted Williams, 1941	145
	Ted Williams, 1942	145
	Harmon Killebrew, 1969	145
	Barry Bonds, 1997	145
18	Babe Ruth, 1921	144
	Babe Ruth, 1926	144
	Eddie Stanky, 1950	144
	Ted Williams, 1951	144
22	Babe Ruth, 1924	142
	Gary Sheffield, 1996	142
24	Eddie Yost, 1950	141
25	Babe Ruth, 1927	138
	Frank Thomas, 1991	138
27	Eddie Stanky, 1946	137
	Roy Cullenbine, 1947	137
	Ralph Kiner, 1951	137
	Willie McCovey, 1970	137
31	Jack Crooks, 1892	136
	Babe Ruth, 1930	136
	Ferris Fain, 1949	136
	Ted Williams, 1954	136
	Jack Clark, 1987	136
	Frank Thomas, 1995	136
37	Babe Ruth, 1928	135
	Eddie Yost, 1959	135
	Jeff Bagwell, 1996	135
40	Ferris Fain, 1950	133
41	Lou Gehrig, 1935	132
	Frank Howard, 1970	132
	Joe Morgan, 1975	132
	Jack Clark, 1989	132
	Tony Phillips, 1993	132
46	Bob Elliott, 1948	131
	Eddie Yost, 1954	131
	Harmon Killebrew, 1967	131
49	Babe Ruth, 1932	130
	Lou Gehrig, 1936	130
	Barry Bonds, 1998	130
52	Eddie Yost, 1952	129
	Mickey Mantle, 1958	129
	Lenny Dykstra, 1993	129
55	Max Bishop, 1929	128
	Max Bishop, 1930	128
	Babe Ruth, 1931	128
	Harmon Killebrew, 1970	128
	Carl Yastrzemski, 1970	128
	Mike Schmidt, 1983	128
61	Lu Blue, 1931	127
	Lou Gehrig, 1937	127
	Eddie Stanky, 1951	127
	Jim Wynn, 1976	127
	Barry Bonds, 1992	127
	Jeff Bagwell, 1997	127
67	Billy Hamilton, 1894	126
	Lu Blue, 1929	126
	Ted Williams, 1948	126
	Eddie Yost, 1951	126
	Mickey Mantle, 1961	126
	Darrell Evans, 1974	126
	Rickey Henderson, 1989	126
	Barry Bonds, 1993	126
75	Richie Ashburn, 1954	125
	Eddie Yost, 1960	125
	Gene Tenace, 1977	125
	Wade Boggs, 1988	125
	Rickey Henderson, 1996	125
	Tony Phillips, 1996	125
81	John McGraw, 1899	124
	Norm Cash, 1961	124
	Eddie Mathews, 1963	124
	Darrell Evans, 1973	124
85	Bill Joyce, 1890	123
	Eddie Yost, 1953	123
	Ken Singleton, 1973	123
	Edgar Martinez, 1996	123
	Jim Thome, 1996	123
90	Jimmy Sheckard, 1912	122
	Lou Gehrig, 1929	122
	Luke Appling, 1935	122
	Ralph Kiner, 1950	122
	Eddie Joost, 1952	122
	Mickey Mantle, 1962	122
	John Mayberry, 1973	122
	Mickey Tettleton, 1992	122
	Frank Thomas, 1992	122
99	8 players tied	121

Strikeouts

1	Bobby Bonds, 1970	189
2	Bobby Bonds, 1969	187
3	Rob Deer, 1987	186
4	Pete Incaviglia, 1986	185
5	Cecil Fielder, 1990	182
6	Mike Schmidt, 1975	180
7	Rob Deer, 1986	179
8	Dave Nicholson, 1963	175
	Gorman Thomas, 1979	175
	Jose Canseco, 1986	175
	Rob Deer, 1991	175
	Jay Buhner, 1997	175
13	Sammy Sosa, 1997	174
14	Jim Presley, 1986	172
	Bo Jackson, 1989	172
16	Reggie Jackson, 1968	171
	Sammy Sosa, 1998	171
18	Gorman Thomas, 1980	170
19	Andres Galarraga, 1990	169
	Rob Deer, 1993	169
21	Juan Samuel, 1984	168
	Pete Incaviglia, 1987	168
23	Gary Alexander, 1978	166
	Steve Balboni, 1985	166
	Cory Snyder, 1987	166
26	Donn Clendenon, 1968	163
27	Butch Hobson, 1977	162
	Juan Samuel, 1987	162
	Ron Gant, 1997	162
30	Dick Allen, 1968	161
	Reggie Jackson, 1971	161
32	Mickey Tettleton, 1990	160
	Henry Rodriguez, 1996	160
34	Mark McGwire, 1997	159
	Jay Buhner, 1996	159
	Jose Canseco, 1998	159
37	Bo Jackson, 1987	158
	Andres Galarraga, 1989	158
	Rob Deer, 1989	158
	Jose Canseco, 1990	158
	Melvin Nieves, 1996	158
	Jeromy Burnitz, 1998	158
43	Danny Tartabull, 1986	157
	Jose Canseco, 1987	157
	Jim Presley, 1987	157
	Andres Galarraga, 1996	157
	Melvin Nieves, 1997	157
48	Tommie Agee, 1970	156
	Dave Kingman, 1982	156
	Reggie Jackson, 1982	156
	Tony Armas, 1984	156
	Danny Tartabull, 1993	156
53	Frank Howard, 1967	155
	Jeff Burroughs, 1975	155
	Mark McGwire, 1998	155
56	Willie Stargell, 1971	154
	Larry Parrish, 1987	154
	Dean Palmer, 1992	154
	Dean Palmer, 1993	154
	Mo Vaughn, 1996	154
	Mo Vaughn, 1997	154
62	Dave Kingman, 1975	153
	Andres Galarraga, 1988	153
	Rob Deer, 1988	153
	Pete Incaviglia, 1988	153
66	George Scott, 1966	152
	Larry Hisle, 1969	152
	Jose Canseco, 1991	152
69	Don Lock, 1963	151
	Greg Luzinski, 1975	151
	Juan Samuel, 1988	151
	Delino DeShields, 1991	151
	Cecil Fielder, 1991	151
	Cecil Fielder, 1992	151
	Ray Lankford, 1998	151
76	Dick Allen, 1965	150
	Nate Colbert, 1970	150
	Ron Kittle, 1983	150
	Jesse Barfield, 1989	150
	Jesse Barfield, 1990	150
	Sammy Sosa, 1990	150
	Mo Vaughn, 1995	150
83	Billy Grabarkewitz, 1970	149
	Mike Schmidt, 1976	149
	Fred McGriff, 1988	149
	Travis Fryman, 1991	149
	Henry Rodriguez, 1997	149
88	Bobby Bonds, 1973	148
	Mike Schmidt, 1983	148
	Gorman Thomas, 1983	148
	Roberto Kelly, 1990	148
92	Rob Deer, 1990	147
	Ray Lankford, 1992	147
	Cory Snyder, 1993	147
	Benji Gil, 1995	147
96	12 players tied	146

At Bats per Strikeout

1876-1892

1	Mike McGeary, 1876	276.0
2	Cap Anson, 1878	261.0
3	John Peters, 1876	158.0
4	John Clapp, 1876	149.0
5	Joe Start, 1877	135.5
6	Joe Start, 1876	132.0
7	Levi Meyerle, 1876	128.0
8	Jim Holdsworth, 1876	120.5
9	Lon Knight, 1876	120.0
10	Ezra Sutton, 1876	118.0
11	Bobby Mathews, 1876	109.0
12	Paul Hines, 1876	101.7
13	Deacon White, 1876	101.0
14	Al Spalding, 1876	97.3
15	Davy Force, 1876	95.7

1893-1919

1	Jack Doyle, 1894	140.7
2	John Ward, 1893	117.6
3	Willie Keeler, 1894	98.3
4	Joe Quinn, 1895	90.5
5	John Ward, 1894	90.0
6	Joe Quinn, 1893	78.1
7	Lave Cross, 1894	75.6
8	Steve Brodie, 1894	71.6
9	Jack Glasscock, 1893	69.7
10	Lave Cross, 1895	66.9
11	Ed McKean, 1896	63.4
12	Dummy Hoy, 1893	62.7
13	Patsy Donovan, 1893	62.4
14	Farmer Vaughn, 1896	61.9
15	Willie Keeler, 1896	60.4

1920-1941

1	Joe Sewell, 1932	167.7
2	Joe Sewell, 1925	152.0
3	Joe Sewell, 1929	144.5
4	Joe Sewell, 1933	131.0
5	Charlie Hollocher, 1922	118.4
6	Stuffy McInnis, 1922	107.4
7	Stuffy McInnis, 1924	96.8
8	Joe Sewell, 1926	96.3
9	Joe Sewell, 1927	81.3
10	Pie Traynor, 1929	77.1
11	Sam Rice, 1929	68.4
12	Tris Speaker, 1927	65.4
13	Joe Sewell, 1928	65.3
14	Sam Rice, 1925	64.9
15	Stuffy McInnis, 1921	64.9

1942-1960

1	Tommy Holmes, 1945	70.7
2	Emil Verban, 1947	67.5
3	Lou Boudreau, 1948	62.2
4	Dale Mitchell, 1949	58.2
5	Tommy Holmes, 1944	57.4
6	Dale Mitchell, 1952	56.8
7	Nellie Fox, 1958	56.6
8	Tommy Holmes, 1942	55.8
9	Jimmy Brown, 1942	55.1
10	Nellie Fox, 1951	54.9
11	Lou Boudreau, 1947	53.8
12	Nellie Fox, 1954	52.6
13	Harvey Kuenn, 1954	50.5
14	Don Mueller, 1955	50.4
15	Yogi Berra, 1950	49.8

1961-1976

1	Nellie Fox, 1962	51.8
2	Dave Cash, 1976	51.2
3	Nellie Fox, 1961	50.5
4	Matty Alou, 1970	37.6
5	Felix Millan, 1974	37.0
6	Vic Power, 1961	35.2
7	Nellie Fox, 1964	34.0
8	Glenn Beckert, 1968	32.2
9	Nellie Fox, 1963	31.7
10	Felix Millan, 1973	29.0
11	Bobby Richardson, 1962	28.8
12	Bobby Richardson, 1961	28.8
13	Bobby Richardson, 1963	28.6
14	Felix Millan, 1976	27.9
15	Glenn Beckert, 1972	27.9

1977-1998

1	Tim Foli, 1979	38.0
2	Tony Gwynn, 1995	35.7
3	Felix Fermin, 1993	34.3
4	Tony Gwynn, 1992	32.5
5	Bill Buckner, 1980	32.1
6	Tim Foli, 1981	31.6
7	Ozzie Smith, 1993	30.3
8	Bob Bailor, 1978	29.6
9	Rich Dauer, 1980	29.3
10	Tony Gwynn, 1991	27.9
11	Tony Gwynn, 1984	26.3
12	Bill Buckner, 1981	26.3
13	Tony Gwynn, 1993	25.7
14	Tony Gwynn, 1998	25.6
15	Bill Buckner, 1982	25.3

Strikeout Percentage

1876-1892

1	Frank Meinke, 1884	26.10
2	Pud Galvin, 1883	24.53
3	Sam Wise, 1884	24.41
4	Pud Galvin, 1879	21.13
5	Charlie Bastian, 1885	21.08
6	Will White, 1878	20.81
7	Silver Flint, 1883	20.78
8	John Morrill, 1884	19.86
9	John Morrill, 1885	19.80
10	Charlie Bastian, 1886	19.57
11	Jim Lillie, 1886	19.23
12	Will White, 1879	19.05
13	John Morrill, 1886	18.84
14	Sam Wise, 1883	18.23
15	Bill Crowley, 1884	18.18

1893-1919

1	Gus Williams, 1914	24.05
2	Grover Gilmore, 1914	20.38
3	Gavvy Cravath, 1916	19.87
4	Ed McDonald, 1912	19.83
5	Art Wilson, 1914	18.18
6	Gavvy Cravath, 1912	17.66
7	Cozy Dolan, 1914	17.58
8	Max Carey, 1911	17.56
9	Danny Moeller, 1913	17.49
10	Doug Baird, 1915	17.19
11	Al Boucher, 1914	17.05
12	Wally Pipp, 1915	16.91
13	Joe Agler, 1914	16.85
14	Ray Powell, 1919	16.81
15	Cy Williams, 1917	16.67

1920-1941

1	Vince DiMaggio, 1938	24.81
2	Vince DiMaggio, 1937	22.52
3	Chet Ross, 1940	22.32
4	Dolph Camilli, 1941	21.74
5	Joe Orengo, 1940	21.69
6	Jimmie Foxx, 1941	21.15
7	Boze Berger, 1935	21.04
8	Jimmie Foxx, 1936	20.34
9	Dolph Camilli, 1938	19.84
10	Babe Ruth, 1922	19.70
11	Babe Ruth, 1933	19.61
12	Jimmy Dykes, 1922	19.56
13	Hank Greenberg, 1939	19.00
14	Vince DiMaggio, 1941	18.94
15	Dolph Camilli, 1939	18.94

1942-1960

1	Pancho Herrera, 1960	26.56
2	Jim Lemon, 1956	25.65
3	Dick Stuart, 1960	24.43
4	Frank Howard, 1960	24.11
5	Harmon Killebrew, 1960	23.98
6	Jim Lemon, 1958	23.95
7	Mickey Mantle, 1960	23.72
8	Larry Doby, 1953	23.59
9	Pat Seerey, 1945	23.43
10	Mickey Mantle, 1959	23.29
11	Mickey Mantle, 1958	23.12
12	Wally Post, 1956	23.01
13	Woodie Held, 1959	22.48
14	Gil Hodges, 1959	22.28
15	Norm Zauchin, 1955	22.01

1961-1976

1	Dave Nicholson, 1963	38.98
2	Dick Allen, 1969	32.88
3	Mike Schmidt, 1975	32.03
4	Reggie Jackson, 1970	31.69
5	Larry Hisle, 1969	31.54
6	Reggie Jackson, 1968	30.92
7	Dick Allen, 1968	30.90
8	Dave Kingman, 1975	30.48
9	Willie Stargell, 1971	30.14
10	Bobby Bonds, 1969	30.06
11	Frank Howard, 1967	29.87
12	Rick Monday, 1968	29.67
13	Dave Kingman, 1972	29.66
14	Willie Mays, 1971	29.50
15	Jim Wynn, 1969	28.69

1977-1998

1	Rob Deer, 1987	39.24
2	Rob Deer, 1991	39.06
3	Rob Deer, 1986	38.41
4	Rob Deer, 1993	36.27
5	Mickey Tettleton, 1990	36.04
6	Benji Gil, 1995	35.42
7	Pete Incaviglia, 1986	34.26
8	Rob Deer, 1989	33.91
9	Rob Deer, 1990	33.41
10	Bo Jackson, 1989	33.40
11	Gary Alexander, 1978	33.33
12	Jack Clark, 1987	33.17
13	Pete Incaviglia, 1987	33.01
14	Jose Canseco, 1990	32.85
15	Jay Buhner, 1997	32.41

Batting Average

1	Hugh Duffy, 1894	.440
2	Tip O'Neill, 1887	.435
3	Ross Barnes, 1876	.429
4	Nap Lajoie, 1901	.426
5	Willie Keeler, 1897	.424
6	Rogers Hornsby, 1924	.424
7	George Sisler, 1922	.420
8	Ty Cobb, 1911	.420
9	Fred Dunlap, 1884	.412
10	Ed Delahanty, 1899	.410
11	Jesse Burkett, 1896	.410
12	Jesse Burkett, 1895	.409
13	Ty Cobb, 1912	.409
14	Joe Jackson, 1911	.408
15	Sam Thompson, 1894	.407
16	George Sisler, 1920	.407
17	Ed Delahanty, 1894	.407
18	Ted Williams, 1941	.406
19	Billy Hamilton, 1894	.404
20	Ed Delahanty, 1895	.404
21	Rogers Hornsby, 1925	.403
22	Harry Heilmann, 1923	.403
23	Pete Browning, 1887	.402
24	Rogers Hornsby, 1922	.401
25	Bill Terry, 1930	.401
26	Hughie Jennings, 1896	.401
27	Ty Cobb, 1922	.401
28	Cap Anson, 1881	.399
29	Lefty O'Doul, 1929	.398
30	Harry Heilmann, 1927	.398
31	Rogers Hornsby, 1921	.397
32	Ed Delahanty, 1896	.397
33	Jesse Burkett, 1899	.396
34	Joe Jackson, 1912	.395
35	Tony Gwynn, 1994	.394
36	Harry Heilmann, 1921	.394
37	Babe Ruth, 1923	.393
38	Harry Heilmann, 1925	.393
39	Babe Herman, 1930	.393
40	Joe Kelley, 1894	.393
41	Sam Thompson, 1895	.392
42	John McGraw, 1899	.391
43	Ty Cobb, 1913	.390
44	Fred Clarke, 1897	.390
45	Al Simmons, 1931	.390
46	George Brett, 1980	.390
47	Tris Speaker, 1925	.389
48	Bill Lange, 1895	.389
49	Billy Hamilton, 1895	.389
50	Ty Cobb, 1921	.389
51	Ted Williams, 1957	.388
52	King Kelly, 1886	.388
53	Rod Carew, 1977	.388
54	Luke Appling, 1936	.388
55	Tris Speaker, 1920	.388
56	Deacon White, 1877	.387
57	Al Simmons, 1925	.387
58	Rogers Hornsby, 1928	.387
59	Tris Speaker, 1916	.386
60	Willie Keeler, 1896	.386
61	Chuck Klein, 1930	.386
62	Lave Cross, 1894	.386
	Hughie Jennings, 1895	.386
64	Willie Keeler, 1898	.385
65	Arky Vaughan, 1935	.385
66	Rogers Hornsby, 1923	.384
67	Ty Cobb, 1919	.384
68	Nap Lajoie, 1910	.384
69	Ty Cobb, 1910	.383
70	Jesse Burkett, 1897	.383
71	Tris Speaker, 1912	.383
72	Ty Cobb, 1917	.383
73	Lefty O'Doul, 1930	.383
74	Joe Jackson, 1920	.382
75	Ty Cobb, 1918	.382
76	Honus Wagner, 1900	.381
77	Babe Herman, 1929	.381
78	Joe DiMaggio, 1939	.381
79	Al Simmons, 1930	.381
80	Paul Waner, 1927	.380
81	Rogers Hornsby, 1929	.380
82	Billy Hamilton, 1893	.380
83	Tris Speaker, 1923	.380
84	Goose Goslin, 1928	.379
85	Freddy Lindstrom, 1930	.379
86	Willie Keeler, 1899	.379
87	Lou Gehrig, 1930	.379
88	John Cassidy, 1877	.378
89	Pete Browning, 1882	.378
90	Ty Cobb, 1925	.378
91	Babe Ruth, 1924	.378
92	Sam Crawford, 1911	.378
93	Tris Speaker, 1922	.378
94	Earl Averill, 1936	.378
95	Babe Ruth, 1921	.378
96	Heinie Manush, 1928	.378
97	Heinie Manush, 1926	.378
98	Ed Delahanty, 1897	.377
99	Willie Keeler, 1895	.377
100	Ty Cobb, 1909	.377

Batting Average (by era)

1876-1892

1	Tip O'Neill, 1887	.435
2	Ross Barnes, 1876	.429
3	Fred Dunlap, 1884	.412
4	Pete Browning, 1887	.402
5	Cap Anson, 1881	.399
6	King Kelly, 1886	.388
7	Deacon White, 1877	.387
8	John Cassidy, 1877	.378
9	Pete Browning, 1882	.378
10	Dan Brouthers, 1883	.374
11	Pete Browning, 1890	.373
12	Dan Brouthers, 1889	.373
13	Sam Thompson, 1887	.372
14	Tommy Tucker, 1889	.372
15	Roger Connor, 1885	.371

1893-1919

1	Hugh Duffy, 1894	.440
2	Nap Lajoie, 1901	.426
3	Willie Keeler, 1897	.424
4	Ty Cobb, 1911	.420
5	Ed Delahanty, 1899	.410
6	Jesse Burkett, 1896	.410
7	Jesse Burkett, 1895	.409
8	Ty Cobb, 1912	.409
9	Joe Jackson, 1911	.408
10	Sam Thompson, 1894	.407
11	Ed Delahanty, 1894	.407
12	Billy Hamilton, 1894	.404
13	Ed Delahanty, 1895	.404
14	Hughie Jennings, 1896	.401
15	Ed Delahanty, 1896	.397

1920-1941

1	Rogers Hornsby, 1924	.424
2	George Sisler, 1922	.420
3	George Sisler, 1920	.407
4	Ted Williams, 1941	.406
5	Rogers Hornsby, 1925	.403
6	Harry Heilmann, 1923	.403
7	Rogers Hornsby, 1922	.401
8	Bill Terry, 1930	.401
9	Ty Cobb, 1922	.401
10	Lefty O'Doul, 1929	.398
11	Harry Heilmann, 1927	.398
12	Rogers Hornsby, 1921	.397
13	Harry Heilmann, 1921	.394
14	Babe Ruth, 1923	.393
15	Harry Heilmann, 1925	.393

1942-1960

1	Ted Williams, 1957	.388
2	Stan Musial, 1948	.376
3	Ted Williams, 1948	.369
4	Stan Musial, 1946	.365
5	Mickey Mantle, 1957	.365
6	Harry Walker, 1947	.363
7	Dixie Walker, 1944	.357
8	Stan Musial, 1943	.357
9	Ted Williams, 1942	.356
10	Phil Cavarretta, 1945	.355
11	Lou Boudreau, 1948	.355
12	Stan Musial, 1951	.355
13	Hank Aaron, 1959	.355
14	Billy Goodman, 1950	.354
15	Harvey Kuenn, 1959	.353

1961-1976

1	Rico Carty, 1970	.366
2	Rod Carew, 1974	.364
3	Joe Torre, 1971	.363
4	Norm Cash, 1961	.361
5	Rod Carew, 1975	.359
6	Roberto Clemente, 1967	.357
7	Bill Madlock, 1975	.354
8	Ralph Garr, 1974	.353
9	Roberto Clemente, 1961	.351
10	Rod Carew, 1973	.350
11	Pete Rose, 1969	.348
12	Tommy Davis, 1962	.346
13	Roberto Clemente, 1969	.345
14	Ralph Garr, 1971	.343
15	Vada Pinson, 1961	.343

1977-1998

1	Tony Gwynn, 1994	.394
2	George Brett, 1980	.390
3	Rod Carew, 1977	.388
4	Tony Gwynn, 1997	.372
5	Andres Galarraga, 1993	.370
6	Tony Gwynn, 1987	.370
7	Tony Gwynn, 1995	.368
8	Wade Boggs, 1985	.368
9	Jeff Bagwell, 1994	.368
10	Wade Boggs, 1988	.366
11	Larry Walker, 1997	.366
12	Larry Walker, 1998	.363
13	Wade Boggs, 1987	.363
	John Olerud, 1993	.363
15	Mike Piazza, 1997	.362

Batting Average (by position)

First Base
1 George Sisler, 1922 .... .420
2 George Sisler, 1920 .... .407
3 Bill Terry, 1930 .... .401
4 Cap Anson, 1881 ...... .399
5 Rod Carew, 1977 ...... .388
6 Lou Gehrig, 1930 ...... .379
7 Dan Brouthers, 1883 .... .374
8 Lou Gehrig, 1928 ...... .374
9 Lou Gehrig, 1927 ...... .373
10 Dan Brouthers, 1889 .... .373

Second Base
1 Ross Barnes, 1876 ...... .429
2 Nap Lajoie, 1901 ...... .426
3 Rogers Hornsby, 1924 .. .424
4 Fred Dunlap, 1884 ...... .412
5 Rogers Hornsby, 1925 .. .403
6 Rogers Hornsby, 1922 .. .401
7 Rogers Hornsby, 1921 .. .397
8 Rogers Hornsby, 1928 .. .387
9 Nap Lajoie, 1910 ...... .384
10 Rogers Hornsby, 1929 .. .380

Shortstop
1 Hughie Jennings, 1896 .. .401
2 Luke Appling, 1936 ..... .388
3 Hughie Jennings, 1895 .. .386
4 Arky Vaughan, 1935 .... .385
5 Honus Wagner, 1905 .... .363
6 Alex Rodriguez, 1996 ... .358
7 Hughie Jennings, 1897 .. .355
8 Honus Wagner, 1903 .... .355
9 Honus Wagner, 1908 .... .354
10 Honus Wagner, 1907 .... .350

Third Base
1 John McGraw, 1899 .... .391
2 George Brett, 1980 ..... .390
3 Lave Cross, 1894 ...... .386
4 Freddy Lindstrom, 1930 . .379
5 Heinie Zimmerman, 1912 .372
6 John McGraw, 1895 .... .369
7 Wade Boggs, 1985 ..... .368
8 Denny Lyons, 1887 ..... .367
9 Wade Boggs, 1988 ..... .366
10 Pie Traynor, 1930 ...... .366

Outfield
1 Hugh Duffy, 1894 ...... .440
2 Tip O'Neill, 1887 .... .435
3 Willie Keeler, 1897 ..... .424
4 Ty Cobb, 1911 .... .420
5 Ty Cobb, 1912 .... .410
6 Ed Delahanty, 1899 ..... .410
7 Jesse Burkett, 1896 .... .410
8 Jesse Burkett, 1895 .... .409
9 Joe Jackson, 1911 ..... .408
10 Sam Thompson, 1894 ... .407
11 Ed Delahanty, 1894 .... .407
12 Ted Williams, 1941 ..... .406
13 Billy Hamilton, 1894 .... .404
14 Ed Delahanty, 1895 .... .404
15 Harry Heilmann, 1923 ... .403
16 Pete Browning, 1887 .... .402
17 Ty Cobb, 1922 .... .401
18 Lefty O'Doul, 1929 ..... .399
19 Harry Heilmann, 1927 ... .398
20 Ed Delahanty, 1896 .... .397

Catcher
1 Cal McVey, 1877 ...... .368
2 Mike Piazza, 1997 ..... .362
3 Mickey Cochrane, 1930 .. .357
4 Wilbert Robinson, 1894 .. .353
5 Spud Davis, 1933 ...... .349
6 Mickey Cochrane, 1931 .. .349
7 Mike Piazza, 1995 ...... .346
8 Ernie Lombardi, 1938 ... .342
9 Gabby Hartnett, 1930 ... .339
10 Mickey Cochrane, 1927 . .338

Relative Batting Average

1 Ross Barnes, 1876 ..... 1.608
2 Tip O'Neill, 1887 ...... 1.564
3 Nap Lajoie, 1910 ...... 1.537
4 Ty Cobb, 1910 .... 1.534
5 Pete Browning, 1882 ... 1.526
6 Cap Anson, 1881 ...... 1.512
7 King Kelly, 1886 ...... 1.508
8 Roger Connor, 1885 ... 1.506
9 Tris Speaker, 1916 .... 1.506
10 Ty Cobb, 1917 .... 1.501
11 Ty Cobb, 1912 .... 1.501
12 Nap Lajoie, 1901 ...... 1.501
13 Nap Lajoie, 1904 ...... 1.499
14 Ty Cobb, 1911 .... 1.493
15 Ty Cobb, 1909 .... 1.493
16 Ted Williams, 1957 .... 1.476
17 Ty Cobb, 1913 .... 1.475
18 Ted Williams, 1941 .... 1.472
19 Ty Cobb, 1918 .... 1.469
20 George Gore, 1880 .... 1.462
21 Rogers Hornsby, 1924 .. 1.461
22 Rod Carew, 1977 ..... 1.458
23 Dan Brouthers, 1885 ... 1.455
24 Joe Jackson, 1911 .... 1.452
25 Joe Jackson, 1912 .... 1.451
26 Dan Brouthers, 1882 ... 1.449
27 Dave Orr, 1884 .... 1.448
28 George Brett, 1980 .... 1.448
29 Ty Cobb, 1915 .... 1.448
30 Pete Browning, 1887 ... 1.446
31 Ty Cobb, 1916 .... 1.445
32 Cap Anson, 1886 ..... 1.442
33 Pete Browning, 1885 ... 1.439
34 Dan Brouthers, 1886 ... 1.439
35 Tony Gwynn, 1994 .... 1.436
36 Honus Wagner, 1908 .. 1.434
37 George Sisler, 1922 ... 1.433
38 Cap Anson, 1882 ..... 1.428
39 Cy Seymour, 1905 .... 1.425
40 Willie Keeler, 1897 .... 1.422
41 Ed Delahanty, 1899 ... 1.414
42 Wade Boggs, 1988 .... 1.413
43 King Kelly, 1884 ...... 1.411
44 Joe Jackson, 1913 .... 1.411
45 Rod Carew, 1974 ..... 1.408
46 Wade Boggs, 1985 .... 1.407
47 Tris Speaker, 1912 .... 1.406
48 Deacon White, 1877 ... 1.405
49 Dan Brouthers, 1883 .. 1.402
50 Jimmy Wolf, 1890 ..... 1.401
51 George Stone, 1906 ... 1.400
52 Stan Musial, 1948 ..... 1.400
53 Cap Anson, 1888 ..... 1.399
54 George Sisler, 1920 ... 1.398
55 Joe Torre, 1971 .... 1.397
56 Hugh Duffy, 1894 ..... 1.394
57 Stan Musial, 1946 ..... 1.393
58 Ed Swartwood, 1883 ... 1.392
59 Ty Cobb, 1919 .... 1.392
60 Rod Carew, 1975 ..... 1.391
61 Tommy Tucker, 1889 .. 1.391
62 Nap Lajoie, 1906 ..... 1.390
63 John Reilly, 1884 ..... 1.389
64 Harry Heilmann, 1923 .. 1.389
65 Mickey Mantle, 1957 ... 1.388
66 Willie Keeler, 1898 .... 1.387
67 Honus Wagner, 1907 .. 1.387
68 Roberto Clemente, 1967 . 1.385
69 George Sisler, 1917 ... 1.383
70 Jim O'Rourke, 1884 ... 1.383
71 Pete Browning, 1886 ... 1.382
72 Tris Speaker, 1917 .... 1.380
73 Ezra Sutton, 1884 .... 1.380
74 Ty Cobb, 1907 .... 1.379
75 Hick Carpenter, 1882 .. 1.379
76 Roger Connor, 1886 ... 1.378
77 Jesse Burkett, 1896 ... 1.378
78 Paul Hines, 1879 ..... 1.377
79 Tony Gwynn, 1987 .... 1.375
80 Pete Browning, 1884 ... 1.374
81 Tris Speaker, 1913 .... 1.374
82 Tony Gwynn, 1997 .... 1.374
83 Kirby Puckett, 1988 ... 1.374
84 John Cassidy, 1877 ... 1.373
85 Eddie Collins, 1909 ... 1.373
86 Honus Wagner, 1905 .. 1.372
87 Dave Orr, 1886 .... 1.372
88 Rico Carty, 1970 ...... 1.372
89 George Hall, 1876 .... 1.372
90 Tip O'Neill, 1888 ..... 1.370
91 Wade Boggs, 1987 .... 1.370
92 Ty Cobb, 1922 .... 1.370
93 Dan Brouthers, 1889 .. 1.370
94 Cap Anson, 1880 ..... 1.368
95 Norm Cash, 1961 ..... 1.368
96 Jesse Burkett, 1899 ... 1.367
97 Andres Galarraga, 1993 . 1.366
98 Jesse Burkett, 1901 ... 1.365
99 Hardy Richardson, 1886 . 1.365
100 Willie Keeler, 1904 .... 1.365

On Base Percentage

1 Ted Williams, 1941 ..... .551
2 John McGraw, 1899 .... .547
3 Babe Ruth, 1923 ...... .545
4 Babe Ruth, 1920 ...... .530
5 Ted Williams, 1957 .... .528
6 Billy Hamilton, 1894 .... .523
7 Ted Williams, 1954 .... .516
8 Babe Ruth, 1926 ...... .516
9 Mickey Mantle, 1957 ... .515
10 Babe Ruth, 1924 ...... .513
11 Babe Ruth, 1921 ...... .512
12 Rogers Hornsby, 1924 .. .507
13 John McGraw, 1900 ... .505
14 Joe Kelley, 1894 ...... .502
15 Hugh Duffy, 1894 ..... .502
16 Ed Delahanty, 1895 .... .500
17 Ted Williams, 1942 .... .499
18 Ted Williams, 1947 .... .499
19 Rogers Hornsby, 1928 .. .498
20 Ted Williams, 1946 .... .497
21 Ted Williams, 1948 .... .497
22 Bill Joyce, 1894 ...... .496
23 Babe Ruth, 1931 ...... .495
24 Frank Thomas, 1994 ... .494
25 Babe Ruth, 1930 ...... .493
26 Arky Vaughan, 1935 ... .491
27 Ted Williams, 1949 .... .490
28 Billy Hamilton, 1895 .... .490
29 Billy Hamilton, 1893 .... .490
30 Tip O'Neill, 1887 ...... .490
31 Rogers Hornsby, 1925 .. .489
   Babe Ruth, 1932 ...... .489
33 Norm Cash, 1961 ..... .488
34 Mickey Mantle, 1962 ... .488
35 Babe Ruth, 1927 ...... .487
36 Ty Cobb, 1915 .... .486
37 Jesse Burkett, 1895 .... .486
38 Tris Speaker, 1920 .... .483
39 King Kelly, 1886 ...... .483
40 Edgar Martinez, 1995 ... .482
41 Harry Heilmann, 1923 .. .481
42 Wade Boggs, 1988 .... .480
43 Billy Hamilton, 1898 .... .480
44 Tris Speaker, 1925 .... .479
   Ted Williams, 1956 .... .479
46 Ed Delahanty, 1894 .... .478
47 Billy Hamilton, 1896 .... .478
48 John Olerud, 1993 ..... .478
49 Lou Gehrig, 1936 ..... .478
50 Cupid Childs, 1894 .... .475
51 John McGraw, 1898 .... .475
52 Harry Heilmann, 1927 .. .475
53 Tris Speaker, 1922 .... .474
54 Lou Gehrig, 1927 ..... .474
55 Luke Appling, 1936 .... .474
56 Lou Gehrig, 1930 ..... .473
57 Lou Gehrig, 1937 ..... .473
58 Mark McGwire, 1998 ... .473
59 Hughie Jennings, 1896 .. .472
60 Ed Delahanty, 1896 .... .472
61 John McGraw, 1897 .... .471
62 Joe Morgan, 1975 ..... .471
63 Dan Brouthers, 1891 ... .471
64 Tris Speaker, 1916 .... .470
65 Bill Joyce, 1896 ...... .470
66 Joe Kelley, 1896 ...... .469
67 Tris Speaker, 1923 .... .469
   Gary Sheffield, 1996 .... .469
69 Jimmie Foxx, 1932 .... .469
70 Jesse Burkett, 1897 .... .468
71 Ty Cobb, 1925 .... .468
72 Mark McGwire, 1996 ... .468
73 Joe Jackson, 1911 .... .468
74 Lou Gehrig, 1928 ..... .467
75 Ty Cobb, 1913 .... .467
76 George Sisler, 1922 ... .467
77 Mike Griffin, 1894 ..... .467
78 Cupid Childs, 1896 .... .467
79 Mickey Mantle, 1956 ... .467
80 Edgar Martinez, 1996 ... .467
81 Wade Boggs, 1987 .... .467
82 Ty Cobb, 1911 .... .467
83 Dan Brouthers, 1890 ... .466
84 Lou Gehrig, 1935 ..... .466
85 Lou Gehrig, 1934 ..... .465
86 Lefty O'Doul, 1929 .... .465
87 Frank Thomas, 1996 ... .465
88 Barry Bonds, 1996 .... .465
89 Jimmie Foxx, 1939 .... .464
90 Tris Speaker, 1912 .... .464
91 Ed Delahanty, 1899 ... .464
92 Pete Browning, 1887 ... .464
93 Ted Williams, 1951 .... .464
94 Willie Keeler, 1897 .... .464
95 Paul O'Neill, 1994 .... .464
96 Bob Caruthers, 1887 ... .463
97 Barry Bonds, 1993 .... .463
98 Cupid Childs, 1893 .... .463
99 Jimmie Foxx, 1929 .... .463
100 Hughie Jennings, 1897 .. .463

Slugging Average

1 Babe Ruth, 1920 ...... .847
2 Babe Ruth, 1921 ...... .846
3 Babe Ruth, 1927 ...... .772
4 Lou Gehrig, 1927 ..... .765
5 Babe Ruth, 1923 ...... .764
6 Rogers Hornsby, 1925 .. .756
7 Mark McGwire, 1998 ... .752
8 Jeff Bagwell, 1994 .... .750
9 Jimmie Foxx, 1932 .... .749
10 Babe Ruth, 1924 ...... .739
11 Babe Ruth, 1926 ...... .737
12 Ted Williams, 1941 .... .735
13 Babe Ruth, 1930 ...... .732
14 Ted Williams, 1957 .... .731
15 Mark McGwire, 1996 ... .730
16 Frank Thomas, 1994 ... .729
17 Hack Wilson, 1930 .... .723
18 Rogers Hornsby, 1922 .. .722
19 Lou Gehrig, 1930 ..... .721
20 Larry Walker, 1997 .... .720
21 Albert Belle, 1994 .... .714
22 Babe Ruth, 1928 ...... .709
23 Al Simmons, 1930 ..... .708
24 Lou Gehrig, 1934 ..... .706
25 Mickey Mantle, 1956 ... .705
26 Jimmie Foxx, 1938 .... .704
27 Jimmie Foxx, 1933 .... .703
28 Stan Musial, 1948 ..... .702
29 Babe Ruth, 1931 ...... .700
30 Babe Ruth, 1929 ...... .697
31 Lou Gehrig, 1936 ..... .696
32 Rogers Hornsby, 1924 .. .696
33 Hugh Duffy, 1894 ..... .694
34 Jimmie Foxx, 1939 .... .694
35 Tip O'Neill, 1887 ..... .691
36 Albert Belle, 1995 .... .690
37 Mickey Mantle, 1961 ... .687
38 Chuck Klein, 1930 .... .687
39 Sam Thompson, 1894 .. .686
40 Hank Greenberg, 1938 .. .683
41 Kevin Mitchell, 1994 ... .681
42 Rogers Hornsby, 1929 .. .679
43 Babe Herman, 1930 ... .678
44 Barry Bonds, 1993 .... .677
45 Ken Griffey Jr., 1994 ... .674
46 Joe DiMaggio, 1937 ... .673
47 Babe Ruth, 1922 ...... .672
48 Joe DiMaggio, 1939 ... .671
49 Hank Greenberg, 1940 .. .670
50 Hank Aaron, 1971 ..... .669
51 Hank Greenberg, 1937 .. .668
52 Ted Williams, 1946 .... .667
53 Willie Mays, 1954 ..... .667
54 Mickey Mantle, 1957 ... .665
55 George Brett, 1980 .... .664
56 Lou Gehrig, 1931 ..... .662
57 Norm Cash, 1961 ..... .662
58 Babe Ruth, 1932 ...... .661
59 Willie Mays, 1955 ..... .659
60 Ralph Kiner, 1949 ..... .658
61 Chuck Klein, 1929 .... .657
62 Babe Ruth, 1919 ...... .657
63 Willie McCovey, 1969 ... .656
64 Albert Belle, 1998 .... .655
65 Sam Thompson, 1895 .. .654
66 Jimmie Foxx, 1934 .... .653
67 Chick Hafey, 1930 .... .652
68 Ted Williams, 1949 .... .650
69 Bill Joyce, 1894 ...... .648
70 Lou Gehrig, 1928 ..... .648
71 Ted Williams, 1942 .... .648
72 Duke Snider, 1954 .... .647
73 Barry Bonds, 1994 .... .647
74 Sammy Sosa, 1998 .... .647
75 Ken Griffey Jr., 1997 ... .646
76 Mark McGwire, 1997 ... .646
77 Chuck Klein, 1932 .... .646
78 Jim Gentile, 1961 ..... .646
79 Willie Stargell, 1973 ... .646
80 Willie Mays, 1965 ..... .645
81 Mike Schmidt, 1981 ... .644
82 Hal Trosky, 1936 ..... .644
83 Nap Lajoie, 1901 ..... .643
84 Joe DiMaggio, 1941 ... .643
   Juan Gonzalez, 1996 ... .643
86 Lou Gehrig, 1937 ..... .643
87 Ted Kluszewski, 1954 .. .642
88 Al Simmons, 1929 ..... .642
89 Joe Medwick, 1937 .... .641
90 Al Simmons, 1931 ..... .641
91 Ellis Burks, 1996 ..... .639
92 Ralph Kiner, 1947 ..... .639
93 Rogers Hornsby, 1921 .. .639
94 Mike Piazza, 1997 .... .638
95 Brady Anderson, 1996 .. .637
96 Frank Robinson, 1966 .. .637
97 Jimmie Foxx, 1930 .... .637
98 Fred Lynn, 1979 ...... .637
99 Hank Aaron, 1959 ..... .636
100 Johnny Mize, 1940 .... .636

#	Production		Adjusted Production		Batting Runs		Adjusted Batting Runs	
1	Babe Ruth, 1920	1.378	Babe Ruth, 1920	252	Babe Ruth, 1921	119	Babe Ruth, 1923	116
2	Babe Ruth, 1921	1.358	Babe Ruth, 1923	238	Babe Ruth, 1923	119	Babe Ruth, 1921	115
3	Babe Ruth, 1923	1.309	Babe Ruth, 1921	236	Babe Ruth, 1920	113	Lou Gehrig, 1927	107
4	Ted Williams, 1941	1.286	Ted Williams, 1941	232	Ted Williams, 1941	102	Babe Ruth, 1920	107
5	Babe Ruth, 1927	1.259	Babe Ruth, 1927	229	Lou Gehrig, 1927	101	Babe Ruth, 1927	106
6	Ted Williams, 1957	1.259	Pete Browning, 1882	229	Babe Ruth, 1924	101	Babe Ruth, 1931	102
7	Babe Ruth, 1926	1.253	Babe Ruth, 1926	228	Babe Ruth, 1927	101	Babe Ruth, 1924	101
8	Babe Ruth, 1924	1.252	Ted Williams, 1957	227	Babe Ruth, 1926	97	Babe Ruth, 1926	100
9	Rogers Hornsby, 1925	1.245	Lou Gehrig, 1927	224	Jimmie Foxx, 1932	97	Rogers Hornsby, 1922	99
10	Lou Gehrig, 1927	1.240	Babe Ruth, 1919	224	Ted Williams, 1946	94	Lou Gehrig, 1934	98
11	Mark McGwire, 1998	1.225	Babe Ruth, 1931	223	Rogers Hornsby, 1924	94	Babe Ruth, 1930	98
12	Babe Ruth, 1930	1.225	Mickey Mantle, 1957	223	Ted Williams, 1942	93	Ted Williams, 1941	98
13	Frank Thomas, 1994	1.223	Rogers Hornsby, 1924	223	Babe Ruth, 1931	92	Rogers Hornsby, 1924	97
14	Jimmie Foxx, 1932	1.218	Ross Barnes, 1876	222	Mark McGwire, 1998	91	Lou Gehrig, 1930	97
15	Jeff Bagwell, 1994	1.211	Babe Ruth, 1924	221	Ted Williams, 1947	91	Mark McGwire, 1998	93
16	Rogers Hornsby, 1924	1.203	Jeff Bagwell, 1994	220	Stan Musial, 1948	90	Mickey Mantle, 1957	91
17	Mark McGwire, 1996	1.199	Babe Ruth, 1930	216	Rogers Hornsby, 1922	90	Jimmie Foxx, 1932	90
18	Hugh Duffy, 1894	1.196	Frank Thomas, 1994	214	Ted Williams, 1957	90	Lou Gehrig, 1931	90
19	Babe Ruth, 1931	1.195	Ted Williams, 1942	214	Babe Ruth, 1930	90	Babe Ruth, 1928	89
20	Lou Gehrig, 1930	1.194	Lou Gehrig, 1934	213	Mickey Mantle, 1957	89	Lou Gehrig, 1936	89
21	Rogers Hornsby, 1922	1.181	Mark McGwire, 1998	213	Ted Williams, 1949	89	Mickey Mantle, 1956	89
22	Tip O'Neill, 1887	1.180	Mickey Mantle, 1956	213	Lou Gehrig, 1930	88	Barry Bonds, 1993	87
23	Mickey Mantle, 1957	1.179	Willie McCovey, 1969	212	Rogers Hornsby, 1925	87	Ted Williams, 1942	87
24	Hack Wilson, 1930	1.177	Ted Williams, 1946	211	Tip O'Neill, 1887	86	Ted Williams, 1946	85
25	Larry Walker, 1997	1.175	Mickey Mantle, 1961	210	Norm Cash, 1961	86	Mickey Mantle, 1961	84
26	Lou Gehrig, 1936	1.174	Babe Ruth, 1928	210	Lou Gehrig, 1934	86	Rogers Hornsby, 1925	83
27	Mickey Mantle, 1956	1.172	Rogers Hornsby, 1922	210	Larry Walker, 1997	85	Norm Cash, 1961	82
28	Lou Gehrig, 1934	1.172	Ty Cobb, 1917	210	Babe Ruth, 1928	84	Ted Williams, 1957	82
29	Babe Ruth, 1928	1.170	George Hall, 1876	208	Mickey Mantle, 1956	83	Lou Gehrig, 1928	81
30	Jimmie Foxx, 1938	1.166	Rogers Hornsby, 1925	208	Jimmie Foxx, 1933	83	Jimmie Foxx, 1933	81
31	Ted Williams, 1946	1.164	Lou Gehrig, 1930	207	Lou Gehrig, 1936	82	Stan Musial, 1948	81
32	Jimmie Foxx, 1939	1.158	Barry Bonds, 1993	207	Barry Bonds, 1993	82	Rogers Hornsby, 1928	80
33	Albert Belle, 1994	1.156	Barry Bonds, 1992	207	Lou Gehrig, 1931	80	Ted Williams, 1947	79
34	Jimmie Foxx, 1933	1.153	Babe Ruth, 1932	206	Ty Cobb, 1911	78	Babe Ruth, 1932	79
35	Stan Musial, 1948	1.152	Tip O'Neill, 1887	205	Jimmie Foxx, 1938	78	Willie McCovey, 1969	79
36	Ted Williams, 1954	1.151	Honus Wagner, 1908	205	Carl Yastrzemski, 1967	76	Rogers Hornsby, 1921	78
37	Babe Ruth, 1932	1.150	Rogers Hornsby, 1928	204	Mickey Mantle, 1961	76	Gary Sheffield, 1996	77
38	Norm Cash, 1961	1.150	Dan Brouthers, 1886	204	Willie McCovey, 1969	76	Lou Gehrig, 1932	77
39	Ted Williams, 1942	1.147	Nap Lajoie, 1904	204	Lou Gehrig, 1928	76	Ted Williams, 1949	77
40	Sam Thompson, 1894	1.145	Ty Cobb, 1912	203	Ted Williams, 1948	76	Frank Robinson, 1966	76
41	Bill Joyce, 1894	1.143	Jimmie Foxx, 1932	203	Hugh Duffy, 1894	76	Jeff Bagwell, 1996	75
42	Ted Williams, 1949	1.141	Roger Connor, 1885	203	Hack Wilson, 1930	75	Hank Aaron, 1959	75
43	Barry Bonds, 1993	1.140	George Brett, 1980	203	Rogers Hornsby, 1921	74	Barry Bonds, 1996	75
44	Rogers Hornsby, 1929	1.139	Ty Cobb, 1910	202	Ty Cobb, 1917	74	Ty Cobb, 1917	75
45	Mickey Mantle, 1961	1.138	Mark McGwire, 1996	201	John Olerud, 1993	74	Hack Wilson, 1930	74
46	Ted Williams, 1947	1.133	Frank Robinson, 1966	200	Rogers Hornsby, 1929	74	Babe Ruth, 1919	74
47	Babe Herman, 1930	1.132	Jimmie Foxx, 1933	199	Nap Lajoie, 1901	74	Frank Thomas, 1994	74
48	Al Simmons, 1930	1.130	Ted Williams, 1947	199	Frank Robinson, 1966	74	Rogers Hornsby, 1929	74
49	Rogers Hornsby, 1928	1.130	Lou Gehrig, 1931	199	Lou Gehrig, 1937	73	Harry Heilmann, 1923	74
50	Babe Ruth, 1929	1.128	Dan Brouthers, 1885	199	George Sisler, 1920	73	John Olerud, 1993	74
51	George Brett, 1980	1.124	Babe Ruth, 1929	199	Tris Speaker, 1912	73	Ed Delahanty, 1899	73
52	Chuck Klein, 1930	1.123	Dick Allen, 1972	199	Rogers Hornsby, 1928	72	Mike Piazza, 1997	73
53	Hank Greenberg, 1938	1.122	Norm Cash, 1961	198	Stan Musial, 1949	72	Barry Bonds, 1992	73
54	Joe DiMaggio, 1939	1.119	Mickey Mantle, 1962	198	Gary Sheffield, 1996	72	Lou Gehrig, 1937	72
55	Kevin Mitchell, 1994	1.119	Dan Brouthers, 1882	198	Arky Vaughan, 1935	72	Jimmie Foxx, 1934	72
56	Ed Delahanty, 1895	1.117	Nap Lajoie, 1910	198	Barry Bonds, 1992	72	Ty Cobb, 1912	72
57	Lou Gehrig, 1937	1.116	Dave Orr, 1885	197	Joe Jackson, 1911	72	Babe Ruth, 1929	71
58	Lou Gehrig, 1928	1.115	Ed Swartwood, 1882	197	Carl Yastrzemski, 1970	72	Jeff Bagwell, 1994	71
59	Babe Ruth, 1919	1.114	Lou Gehrig, 1928	197	Ty Cobb, 1915	72	Tris Speaker, 1923	71
60	Willie McCovey, 1969	1.114	Stan Musial, 1948	196	Edgar Martinez, 1995	71	Frank Robinson, 1996	71
61	Harry Heilmann, 1923	1.113	Ty Cobb, 1918	196	Frank Thomas, 1994	71	Frank Thomas, 1997	71
62	Ted Williams, 1948	1.112	Ty Cobb, 1913	196	Babe Ruth, 1932	71	Babe Herman, 1930	71
63	Edgar Martinez, 1995	1.110	Nap Lajoie, 1901	196	Ted Williams, 1954	71	Ty Cobb, 1911	71
64	Lou Gehrig, 1931	1.108	Orator Shaffer, 1878	196	Tris Speaker, 1923	71	Jimmie Foxx, 1938	70
65	Nap Lajoie, 1901	1.106	Mike Schmidt, 1981	195	Stan Musial, 1946	71	Mark McGwire, 1996	70
66	Babe Ruth, 1922	1.106	George Stone, 1906	195	Ralph Kiner, 1951	71	Joe Jackson, 1911	70
67	Hank Greenberg, 1937	1.105	Harry Heilmann, 1923	195	Harry Heilmann, 1923	71	Edgar Martinez, 1995	70
68	Joe Kelley, 1894	1.104	Dave Orr, 1884	195	Joe Jackson, 1912	70	Lou Gehrig, 1935	70
69	Hank Greenberg, 1940	1.103	Kevin Mitchell, 1989	194	Stan Musial, 1951	70	Frank Thomas, 1991	69
70	Ed Delahanty, 1896	1.103	Lou Gehrig, 1936	193	Ralph Kiner, 1949	70	Rod Carew, 1977	69
71	Jimmie Foxx, 1934	1.102	Ed Delahanty, 1899	193	Barry Bonds, 1996	69	Mickey Mantle, 1958	69
72	Arky Vaughan, 1935	1.098	Ty Cobb, 1911	193	Chuck Klein, 1933	69	Stan Musial, 1951	69
73	Rogers Hornsby, 1921	1.097	Ted Williams, 1954	193	Joe Medwick, 1937	69	Frank Thomas, 1995	69
74	Jimmie Foxx, 1935	1.096	Joe Jackson, 1911	192	Hank Greenberg, 1940	69	Lou Gehrig, 1933	68
75	Gary Sheffield, 1996	1.094	Gary Sheffield, 1996	192	Johnny Mize, 1939	69	George Sisler, 1920	68
76	Albert Belle, 1995	1.094	Ed Delahanty, 1896	192	Babe Herman, 1930	69	Jimmie Foxx, 1935	68
77	Mickey Mantle, 1962	1.093	Mike Piazza, 1997	191	Lou Gehrig, 1932	69	Ted Williams, 1948	68
78	Frank Thomas, 1996	1.091	Rogers Hornsby, 1921	191	Lefty O'Doul, 1929	69	Reggie Jackson, 1969	68
79	Harry Heilmann, 1927	1.091	Albert Belle, 1994	191	Nap Lajoie, 1910	68	Tip O'Neill, 1887	68
80	Ralph Kiner, 1949	1.089	Ty Cobb, 1909	190	Chuck Klein, 1932	68	Rogers Hornsby, 1920	68
81	Jimmie Foxx, 1929	1.088	Joe Jackson, 1913	190	Ty Cobb, 1910	68	Nap Lajoie, 1901	67
82	Ty Cobb, 1911	1.088	Rickey Henderson, 1990	190	Ed Delahanty, 1899	68	Arky Vaughan, 1935	67
83	Lefty O'Doul, 1929	1.087	Pete Browning, 1885	190	Chuck Klein, 1930	68	Al Rosen, 1953	67
84	Rogers Hornsby, 1923	1.086	Hank Aaron, 1971	190	Mark McGwire, 1996	67	Barry Bonds, 1998	67
85	Al Simmons, 1931	1.085	Reggie Jackson, 1969	190	Jimmie Foxx, 1935	67	Ed Delahanty, 1896	67
86	Barry Bonds, 1992	1.085	Deacon White, 1877	190	Hank Greenberg, 1937	67	Ralph Kiner, 1951	67
87	Joe DiMaggio, 1937	1.085	Joe Jackson, 1912	190	Ty Cobb, 1912	67	Nap Lajoie, 1910	66
88	Sam Thompson, 1895	1.085	Rogers Hornsby, 1920	190	Rod Carew, 1977	67	Albert Belle, 1998	66
89	Ted Williams, 1956	1.084	Cap Anson, 1881	189	Frank Robinson, 1962	67	Joe DiMaggio, 1941	66
90	Mel Ott, 1929	1.084	Jim Gentile, 1961	189	Wade Boggs, 1987	67	Ralph Kiner, 1949	66
91	Joe DiMaggio, 1941	1.083	Cupid Childs, 1890	189	Babe Ruth, 1919	67	Joe Medwick, 1937	66
92	Willie Mays, 1954	1.083	Carl Yastrzemski, 1967	189	Jimmie Foxx, 1934	66	Jesse Burkett, 1901	66
93	Mike Schmidt, 1981	1.083	Mickey Mantle, 1958	189	Ed Delahanty, 1895	66	Kevin Mitchell, 1989	66
94	Hank Aaron, 1971	1.082	Frank Robinson, 1967	189	Jimmie Foxx, 1939	66	Ed Delahanty, 1895	66
95	George Sisler, 1920	1.082	Barry Bonds, 1996	189	Dick Allen, 1972	66	Joe Jackson, 1912	66
96	Barry Bonds, 1996	1.080	Willie Stargell, 1973	189	Hank Greenberg, 1938	66	Frank Thomas, 1993	66
97	Tris Speaker, 1922	1.080	Willie Stargell, 1971	189	Dan Brouthers, 1886	66	Stan Musial, 1949	65
98	Ralph Kiner, 1951	1.079	King Kelly, 1879	188	Frank Thomas, 1991	66	Carl Yastrzemski, 1967	65
99	Tris Speaker, 1923	1.079	Jimmie Foxx, 1934	188	Wade Boggs, 1988	66	Honus Wagner, 1908	65
100	Ken Griffey Jr., 1994	1.078	Hank Aaron, 1959	188	Tris Speaker, 1920	66	Tris Speaker, 1912	65

Batting Wins

1	Babe Ruth, 1923	11.5
2	Babe Ruth, 1921	11.1
3	Babe Ruth, 1920	11.0
4	Ted Williams, 1941	9.9
5	Ted Williams, 1946	9.9
6	Lou Gehrig, 1927	9.6
7	Babe Ruth, 1927	9.6
8	Babe Ruth, 1924	9.5
9	Ted Williams, 1942	9.5
10	Ted Williams, 1947	9.4
11	Babe Ruth, 1926	9.4
12	Rogers Hornsby, 1924	9.3
13	Ted Williams, 1957	9.3
14	Mickey Mantle, 1957	9.2
15	Stan Musial, 1948	9.0
16	Mark McGwire, 1998	9.0
17	Jimmie Foxx, 1932	8.9
18	Ted Williams, 1949	8.6
19	Norm Cash, 1961	8.5
20	Babe Ruth, 1931	8.5
21	Rogers Hornsby, 1922	8.5
22	Carl Yastrzemski, 1967	8.4
23	Larry Walker, 1997	8.4
24	Ty Cobb, 1917	8.3
25	Barry Bonds, 1993	8.2
26	Rogers Hornsby, 1925	8.2
27	Mickey Mantle, 1956	8.2
28	Babe Ruth, 1928	8.1
29	Babe Ruth, 1930	8.1
30	Lou Gehrig, 1930	8.0
31	Willie McCovey, 1969	8.0
32	Lou Gehrig, 1934	8.0
33	Frank Robinson, 1966	7.9
34	Jimmie Foxx, 1933	7.8
35	Barry Bonds, 1992	7.7
36	Ty Cobb, 1911	7.7
37	Ty Cobb, 1915	7.6
38	Nap Lajoie, 1910	7.6
39	Mickey Mantle, 1961	7.6
40	Honus Wagner, 1908	7.5
41	Ty Cobb, 1910	7.5
42	Stan Musial, 1946	7.5
43	Dick Allen, 1972	7.5
44	Carl Yastrzemski, 1970	7.4
45	Lou Gehrig, 1931	7.4
46	Rogers Hornsby, 1921	7.3
47	Lou Gehrig, 1928	7.3
48	Ted Williams, 1948	7.3
49	Ted Williams, 1954	7.3
50	Chuck Klein, 1933	7.3
51	Tris Speaker, 1912	7.3
52	Lou Gehrig, 1936	7.3
53	John Olerud, 1993	7.2
54	Ty Cobb, 1909	7.2
55	Stan Musial, 1949	7.2
56	Tris Speaker, 1916	7.1
57	Ralph Kiner, 1951	7.1
58	George Sisler, 1920	7.1
59	Rogers Hornsby, 1928	7.1
60	Gary Sheffield, 1996	7.1
61	Jimmie Foxx, 1938	7.1
62	Joe Jackson, 1911	7.1
63	Joe Jackson, 1912	7.0
64	Stan Musial, 1951	7.0
65	Tip O'Neill, 1887	7.0
66	Hank Aaron, 1971	7.0
67	Stan Musial, 1943	7.0
68	Arky Vaughan, 1935	7.0
69	Joe Jackson, 1913	7.0
70	Babe Ruth, 1919	7.0
71	Ralph Kiner, 1949	6.9
72	Harmon Killebrew, 1967	6.9
73	Harmon Killebrew, 1969	6.9
74	Nap Lajoie, 1904	6.9
75	Johnny Mize, 1939	6.9
76	Tris Speaker, 1923	6.9
77	Willie Mays, 1965	6.8
78	Harry Heilmann, 1923	6.8
79	Hank Aaron, 1963	6.8
80	Joe Medwick, 1937	6.8
81	Barry Bonds, 1996	6.8
82	Chuck Klein, 1932	6.7
83	Rogers Hornsby, 1929	6.7
84	Lou Gehrig, 1937	6.7
85	Cy Seymour, 1905	6.7
86	Ty Cobb, 1912	6.7
87	Rogers Hornsby, 1920	6.7
88	Edgar Martinez, 1995	6.7
89	Joe Torre, 1971	6.7
90	Nap Lajoie, 1901	6.7
91	Hack Wilson, 1930	6.7
92	Rod Carew, 1977	6.7
93	Wade Boggs, 1988	6.7
94	Frank Robinson, 1962	6.6
95	Kevin Mitchell, 1989	6.6
96	Mickey Mantle, 1958	6.6
97	Carl Yastrzemski, 1968	6.6
98	Frank Thomas, 1991	6.6
99	Frank Thomas, 1994	6.6
100	Babe Ruth, 1932	6.6

Adjusted Batting Wins

1	Babe Ruth, 1923	11.2
2	Babe Ruth, 1921	10.7
3	Babe Ruth, 1920	10.3
4	Lou Gehrig, 1927	10.1
5	Babe Ruth, 1927	10.1
6	Babe Ruth, 1926	9.7
7	Rogers Hornsby, 1924	9.6
8	Babe Ruth, 1924	9.5
9	Ted Williams, 1941	9.5
10	Babe Ruth, 1931	9.5
11	Mickey Mantle, 1957	9.4
12	Rogers Hornsby, 1922	9.3
13	Mark McGwire, 1998	9.2
14	Lou Gehrig, 1934	9.1
15	Ted Williams, 1946	8.9
16	Ted Williams, 1942	8.9
17	Babe Ruth, 1930	8.9
18	Lou Gehrig, 1930	8.8
19	Barry Bonds, 1993	8.7
20	Mickey Mantle, 1956	8.7
21	Babe Ruth, 1928	8.6
22	Ted Williams, 1957	8.4
23	Lou Gehrig, 1931	8.4
24	Mickey Mantle, 1961	8.4
25	Ty Cobb, 1917	8.3
26	Jimmie Foxx, 1932	8.3
27	Willie McCovey, 1969	8.3
28	Ted Williams, 1947	8.2
29	Frank Robinson, 1966	8.2
30	Norm Cash, 1961	8.1
31	Stan Musial, 1948	8.1
32	Barry Bonds, 1992	7.9
33	Rogers Hornsby, 1928	7.8
34	Lou Gehrig, 1928	7.8
35	Lou Gehrig, 1936	7.8
36	Rogers Hornsby, 1925	7.8
37	Babe Ruth, 1919	7.7
38	Rogers Hornsby, 1921	7.7
39	Jimmie Foxx, 1933	7.7
40	Gary Sheffield, 1996	7.6
41	Hank Aaron, 1959	7.6
42	Honus Wagner, 1908	7.5
43	Ted Williams, 1949	7.5
44	Nap Lajoie, 1910	7.4
45	Jeff Bagwell, 1996	7.4
46	Barry Bonds, 1996	7.4
47	Babe Ruth, 1932	7.3
48	Rogers Hornsby, 1920	7.2
49	Dick Allen, 1972	7.2
50	Mike Piazza, 1997	7.2
51	Carl Yastrzemski, 1967	7.2
52	Ty Cobb, 1912	7.2
53	John Olerud, 1993	7.2
54	Mickey Mantle, 1958	7.2
55	Lou Gehrig, 1932	7.1
56	Harry Heilmann, 1923	7.1
57	Reggie Jackson, 1969	7.1
58	Kevin Mitchell, 1989	7.0
59	Jeff Bagwell, 1994	7.0
60	Hank Aaron, 1963	7.0
61	Nap Lajoie, 1904	7.0
62	Frank Thomas, 1991	7.0
63	George Stone, 1906	6.9
64	Ty Cobb, 1911	6.9
65	Stan Musial, 1951	6.9
66	Joe Jackson, 1911	6.9
67	Tris Speaker, 1923	6.9
68	Stan Musial, 1946	6.9
69	Rod Carew, 1977	6.9
70	Frank Thomas, 1994	6.8
71	Ty Cobb, 1915	6.8
72	Al Rosen, 1953	6.7
73	Frank Thomas, 1997	6.7
74	Babe Ruth, 1929	6.7
75	Rogers Hornsby, 1929	6.7
76	Jimmie Foxx, 1934	6.7
77	Frank Howard, 1969	6.7
78	Ralph Kiner, 1951	6.7
79	Ed Delahanty, 1899	6.7
80	Lou Gehrig, 1937	6.6
81	George Sisler, 1920	6.6
82	Ty Cobb, 1910	6.6
83	Ted Williams, 1948	6.6
84	Barry Bonds, 1998	6.6
85	Joe Jackson, 1912	6.6
86	Bobby Murcer, 1971	6.6
87	Ty Cobb, 1909	6.6
88	Joe Jackson, 1913	6.6
89	Edgar Martinez, 1995	6.6
90	Harmon Killebrew, 1969	6.6
91	Lou Gehrig, 1935	6.6
92	Ralph Kiner, 1949	6.6
93	Hack Wilson, 1930	6.5
94	Frank Thomas, 1992	6.5
95	Arky Vaughan, 1935	6.5
96	Joe Medwick, 1937	6.5
97	Tris Speaker, 1912	6.5
98	Lou Gehrig, 1933	6.5
99	Stan Musial, 1949	6.5
100	Willie Mays, 1965	6.5

Runs Created

1	Babe Ruth, 1921	238
2	Babe Ruth, 1923	223
3	Hugh Duffy, 1894	217
4	Lou Gehrig, 1927	212
5	Babe Ruth, 1920	211
6	Jimmie Foxx, 1932	209
7	Babe Ruth, 1927	208
8	Billy Hamilton, 1894	207
9	Ty Cobb, 1911	207
10	Babe Ruth, 1924	205
11	Ted Williams, 1941	202
12	Rogers Hornsby, 1922	200
13	Lou Gehrig, 1936	199
14	Babe Ruth, 1926	196
15	Lou Gehrig, 1930	195
16	Lou Gehrig, 1934	195
17	Tip O'Neill, 1887	194
18	Babe Ruth, 1931	194
19	Mark McGwire, 1998	193
20	Ted Williams, 1949	193
21	Babe Ruth, 1930	191
22	Pete Browning, 1887	191
23	Stan Musial, 1948	191
24	Hack Wilson, 1930	189
25	Jimmie Foxx, 1938	189
26	Ted Williams, 1946	188
27	Mickey Mantle, 1956	188
28	Rogers Hornsby, 1925	187
29	Larry Walker, 1997	187
30	Ted Williams, 1947	186
31	Rogers Hornsby, 1924	186
32	Chuck Klein, 1930	186
33	Ted Williams, 1942	185
34	Jimmie Foxx, 1933	184
35	Lou Gehrig, 1931	184
36	Rogers Hornsby, 1929	183
37	Babe Herman, 1930	183
38	Joe Kelley, 1894	182
39	Babe Ruth, 1928	182
40	Lou Gehrig, 1937	181
41	Chuck Klein, 1932	180
42	Lefty O'Doul, 1929	180
43	Nap Lajoie, 1901	179
44	Mickey Mantle, 1957	178
45	Billy Hamilton, 1895	178
46	Joe Kelley, 1896	178
47	Norm Cash, 1961	178
48	Hank Greenberg, 1937	178
49	Ed Delahanty, 1895	176
50	George Sisler, 1920	176
51	Willie Keeler, 1897	176
52	Ed Delahanty, 1899	175
53	Benny Kauff, 1914	175
54	Tris Speaker, 1912	175
55	Joe Jackson, 1911	175
56	Mickey Mantle, 1961	174
57	Stan Musial, 1949	173
58	Joe DiMaggio, 1937	173
59	Ty Cobb, 1912	173
60	Barry Bonds, 1993	172
61	Hank Greenberg, 1938	172
62	Ted Williams, 1948	172
63	Hank Greenberg, 1940	171
64	Ed Delahanty, 1896	170
65	Joe Medwick, 1937	170
66	Bill Terry, 1930	170
67	Stan Musial, 1951	169
68	Lou Gehrig, 1928	169
69	Lou Gehrig, 1932	169
70	Rogers Hornsby, 1921	169
71	Earl Averill, 1936	168
72	Jimmie Foxx, 1936	168
73	Sam Thompson, 1895	167
74	Ted Williams, 1957	167
75	Ed Delahanty, 1893	167
76	Jesse Burkett, 1896	166
77	Stan Musial, 1953	166
78	Joe Jackson, 1912	166
79	Tris Speaker, 1923	166
80	Jimmie Foxx, 1934	165
81	Ralph Kiner, 1951	165
82	Jake Stenzel, 1894	165
83	Jesse Burkett, 1895	165
84	Ty Cobb, 1917	164
85	Stan Musial, 1946	164
86	Ralph Kiner, 1949	163
87	Arky Vaughan, 1935	163
88	Jimmie Foxx, 1935	163
89	Al Simmons, 1930	163
90	Johnny Mize, 1939	162
91	Chuck Klein, 1933	162
92	Barry Bonds, 1996	162
93	George Sisler, 1922	162
94	Joe DiMaggio, 1941	162
95	Duke Snider, 1954	161
96	Hank Greenberg, 1935	161
97	Billy Hamilton, 1896	161
98	Duke Snider, 1953	161
99	John Olerud, 1993	161
100	Edgar Martinez, 1995	161

Total Average

1	Babe Ruth, 1920	1.797
2	Babe Ruth, 1921	1.745
3	Ted Williams, 1941	1.688
4	Babe Ruth, 1923	1.683
5	Hugh Duffy, 1894	1.619
6	Babe Ruth, 1926	1.606
7	Billy Hamilton, 1894	1.605
8	John McGraw, 1899	1.601
9	Ted Williams, 1957	1.599
10	Babe Ruth, 1927	1.571
11	Babe Ruth, 1924	1.558
12	Rogers Hornsby, 1925	1.539
13	Mickey Mantle, 1957	1.534
14	Bill Joyce, 1894	1.528
15	Ed Delahanty, 1895	1.517
16	Tip O'Neill, 1887	1.514
17	Mark McGwire, 1998	1.512
18	Babe Ruth, 1930	1.509
19	Joe Kelley, 1894	1.503
20	Lou Gehrig, 1927	1.500
21	Babe Ruth, 1931	1.487
22	Ty Cobb, 1911	1.464
23	Frank Thomas, 1994	1.453
24	Ted Williams, 1954	1.452
25	Jimmie Foxx, 1932	1.451
26	Billy Hamilton, 1895	1.443
27	Babe Ruth, 1932	1.432
28	Ted Williams, 1946	1.431
29	Joe Kelley, 1896	1.430
30	Lou Gehrig, 1936	1.426
31	Mickey Mantle, 1956	1.426
32	Rogers Hornsby, 1924	1.424
33	Pete Browning, 1887	1.422
34	Mark McGwire, 1996	1.420
35	Jeff Bagwell, 1994	1.413
36	Hack Wilson, 1930	1.411
37	Rogers Hornsby, 1928	1.409
38	Sam Thompson, 1894	1.409
39	Ed Delahanty, 1896	1.405
40	Babe Ruth, 1928	1.405
41	Lou Gehrig, 1934	1.401
42	Ted Williams, 1942	1.394
43	Jimmie Foxx, 1938	1.392
44	Ted Williams, 1947	1.391
45	Lou Gehrig, 1930	1.389
46	Billy Hamilton, 1893	1.386
47	Mickey Mantle, 1962	1.385
48	Mickey Mantle, 1961	1.384
49	Larry Walker, 1997	1.373
50	Bill Lange, 1895	1.373
51	Bob Caruthers, 1887	1.368
52	King Kelly, 1886	1.366
53	Babe Ruth, 1919	1.358
54	Norm Cash, 1961	1.358
55	Rogers Hornsby, 1922	1.353
56	Babe Herman, 1930	1.351
57	Jimmie Foxx, 1933	1.348
58	Ted Williams, 1948	1.347
59	Ted Williams, 1949	1.347
60	Lou Gehrig, 1937	1.339
61	Barry Bonds, 1993	1.339
62	Rogers Hornsby, 1929	1.338
63	Barry Bonds, 1996	1.338
64	Barry Bonds, 1992	1.335
65	Nap Lajoie, 1901	1.327
66	Billy Hamilton, 1896	1.325
67	Ty Cobb, 1912	1.321
68	Ty Cobb, 1910	1.321
69	Jake Stenzel, 1894	1.320
70	Joe Morgan, 1976	1.319
71	Arky Vaughan, 1935	1.317
72	Ty Cobb, 1913	1.310
73	Jimmie Foxx, 1934	1.310
74	Tris Speaker, 1912	1.310
75	Joe Jackson, 1911	1.308
76	Bill Joyce, 1896	1.306
77	Hank Greenberg, 1938	1.306
78	Albert Belle, 1994	1.304
79	Jimmie Foxx, 1939	1.304
80	Edgar Martinez, 1995	1.300
81	Stan Musial, 1948	1.298
82	Willie McCovey, 1969	1.296
83	Ed Delahanty, 1894	1.290
84	Joe Kelley, 1895	1.289
85	Jimmie Foxx, 1935	1.288
86	Babe Ruth, 1929	1.288
87	Harry Heilmann, 1923	1.288
88	Mel Ott, 1929	1.287
89	Joe Morgan, 1975	1.279
90	Benny Kauff, 1914	1.278
91	Hank Greenberg, 1937	1.277
92	Chuck Klein, 1930	1.274
93	Al Simmons, 1930	1.272
94	Tris Speaker, 1922	1.272
95	Fred Clarke, 1897	1.272
96	Billy Hamilton, 1891	1.270
97	Sam Thompson, 1895	1.269
98	Gary Sheffield, 1996	1.268
99	Lou Gehrig, 1931	1.267
100	Harry Heilmann, 1927	1.265

Runs Produced

1	Lou Gehrig, 1931	301
2	Babe Ruth, 1921	289
3	Chuck Klein, 1930	288
4	Hugh Duffy, 1894	287
5	Al Simmons, 1930	281
6	Hughie Jennings, 1895	280
	Hack Wilson, 1930	280
	Hank Greenberg, 1937	280
9	Sam Thompson, 1895	278
10	Lou Gehrig, 1927	277
11	Tip O'Neill, 1887	276
	Kiki Cuyler, 1930	276
	Lou Gehrig, 1930	276
14	Billy Hamilton, 1894	275
15	Sam Thompson, 1887	274
	Ed Delahanty, 1894	274
17	Ed Delahanty, 1893	272
	Joe Kelley, 1895	272
	Joe DiMaggio, 1937	272
20	Joe Kelley, 1894	270
	Lou Gehrig, 1936	270
22	Ty Cobb, 1911	266
	Rogers Hornsby, 1929	266
	Babe Ruth, 1931	266
	Ted Williams, 1949	266
26	Jimmie Foxx, 1938	264
27	Ed Delahanty, 1899	263
28	Babe Ruth, 1927	262
	Jimmie Foxx, 1932	262
30	Al Simmons, 1932	260
	Lou Gehrig, 1937	260
32	Hardy Richardson, 1890	259
	Hugh Duffy, 1893	259
	Walt Wilmot, 1894	259
35	Dan Brouthers, 1894	256
	Bobby Lowe, 1894	256
	Jake Stenzel, 1894	256
	Nap Lajoie, 1901	256
39	Hack Wilson, 1929	255
	Lou Gehrig, 1932	255
	Hank Greenberg, 1935	255
42	Cap Anson, 1886	254
	Willie Keeler, 1894	254
	Lou Gehrig, 1928	254
	Babe Ruth, 1930	254
46	Harry Stovey, 1889	252
47	Pete Browning, 1887	251
	Rogers Hornsby, 1922	251
	Babe Ruth, 1928	251
	Earl Averill, 1931	251
	Chuck Klein, 1932	251
52	Charlie Gehringer, 1934	250
53	Hugh Duffy, 1897	248
54	John McGraw, 1894	247
	Mel Ott, 1929	247
56	Hughie Jennings, 1896	246
	Tris Speaker, 1923	246
	Jimmie Foxx, 1930	246
	Zeke Bonura, 1936	246
	Tommy Davis, 1962	246
61	Sam Thompson, 1893	245
	Bill Terry, 1930	245
	Lou Gehrig, 1933	245
	Charlie Gehringer, 1936	245
	Ted Williams, 1939	245
66	Arlie Latham, 1887	244
	Tom Brown, 1891	244
	Steve Brodie, 1894	244
	Ed Delahanty, 1895	244
	Ed Delahanty, 1896	244
	Ken Williams, 1922	244
	Lou Gehrig, 1934	244
	Hal Trosky, 1936	244
74	Dan Brouthers, 1887	242
	Ed McKean, 1895	242
	Lefty O'Doul, 1929	242
	Ted Williams, 1942	242
78	Lave Cross, 1894	241
	Bill Dahlen, 1894	241
	Babe Ruth, 1920	241
	Babe Ruth, 1923	241
82	Dan Brouthers, 1892	240
	Joe Kelley, 1896	240
	Ty Cobb, 1915	240
	George Sisler, 1920	240
	Joe Cronin, 1930	240
	Jimmie Foxx, 1933	240
88	Hughie Jennings, 1894	239
	Vern Stephens, 1950	239
90	Charlie Comiskey, 1887	238
	George Davis, 1897	238
	Babe Ruth, 1926	238
	Babe Herman, 1930	238
	Hank Greenberg, 1940	238
95	Rogers Hornsby, 1925	237
	Al Simmons, 1929	237
	Joe DiMaggio, 1938	237
98	8 players tied	236

Clutch Hitting Index

1	Cap Anson, 1880	178
2	Tom Herr, 1987	172
3	Ed Abbaticchio, 1907	166
4	Bill McClellan, 1878	165
	Ed McKean, 1892	165
6	Lon Knight, 1881	164
7	Jack Barry, 1913	163
8	George Stovall, 1911	163
9	John Sullivan, 1943	162
10	Tom Herr, 1985	161
11	Fred Hartman, 1902	160
	Cookie Lavagetto, 1941	160
13	Cap Anson, 1886	158
14	Sherry Magee, 1918	158
15	John Gochnauer, 1903	155
16	Tommy Davis, 1969	155
17	Maurice Van Robays, 1940	154
18	George Davis, 1906	154
19	Art Devlin, 1904	154
20	Frank LaPorte, 1910	154
21	Jack Rowe, 1888	153
22	Pete Hotaling, 1888	153
23	John Ward, 1886	153
24	Sam Crawford, 1910	153
25	Johnny Berardino, 1941	152
26	Jackie Hayes, 1937	152
27	Rebel Oakes, 1915	152
28	Sam Thompson, 1887	151
29	Bill Harbidge, 1878	151
	Pop Corkhill, 1886	151
	Frank LaPorte, 1914	151
32	Possum Whitted, 1920	151
33	Heinie Reitz, 1896	151
34	Earl Sheely, 1931	151
35	Joe Gerhardt, 1879	150
	Oyster Burns, 1890	150
	Socks Seybold, 1907	150
38	Cy Seymour, 1908	150
39	Tom Burns, 1888	150
40	Joe Battin, 1876	150
41	Norm Larker, 1960	149
42	Earl Sheely, 1924	149
43	Chick Galloway, 1925	149
44	Vic Wertz, 1960	149
45	Jack Crooks, 1890	149
46	Hugh Duffy, 1896	148
47	Cap Anson, 1893	148
48	Roger Connor, 1884	148
49	Farmer Vaughn, 1893	148
	Bill Brubaker, 1936	148
51	Pie Traynor, 1928	147
52	Reddy Mack, 1889	147
	Larry Kopf, 1920	147
54	Pete Hotaling, 1880	147
55	Fred Pfeffer, 1882	147
56	Doc Gessler, 1911	147
57	Stuffy McInnis, 1914	147
58	Heinie Zimmerman, 1917	146
59	Bill Dahlen, 1904	146
60	Bill Holbert, 1882	146
61	Deacon White, 1885	146
62	Ned Williamson, 1885	146
	Clyde Barnhart, 1925	146
64	Jimmy Brown, 1942	146
65	Nap Lajoie, 1912	145
66	Cap Anson, 1881	145
	Cap Anson, 1890	145
68	Cap Anson, 1885	145
69	Dave Foutz, 1889	145
70	Mike Mowrey, 1916	145
71	Roy McMillan, 1956	145
72	Joe Kelley, 1898	145
73	Larry Gardner, 1920	144
74	Lave Cross, 1903	144
75	Jose Cardenal, 1971	144
76	Ty Cobb, 1907	143
77	Cap Anson, 1882	143
	Ed Delahanty, 1900	143
79	Hal Chase, 1909	143
80	Cal McVey, 1879	143
	Jim O'Rourke, 1887	143
	Ferris Fain, 1949	143
83	Kirby Puckett, 1994	143
84	John Ward, 1881	143
	Maurice Van Robays, 1941	143
	Joe Medwick, 1942	143
87	Eddie Collins, 1919	143
	Bobby Veach, 1922	143
89	Bill Hague, 1878	142
	Ron Fairly, 1964	142
91	Hick Carpenter, 1886	142
	Ross Youngs, 1921	142
93	Bob Ferguson, 1877	142
94	Monte Cross, 1900	142
	Milt Stock, 1921	142
	Enos Slaughter, 1953	142
97	Deacon White, 1876	142
98	Fred Pfeffer, 1892	142
99	Cupid Childs, 1895	141
100	2 players tied	141

Isolated Power

1	Babe Ruth, 1920	.472
2	Babe Ruth, 1921	.469
3	Mark McGwire, 1998	.454
4	Mark McGwire, 1996	.418
5	Babe Ruth, 1927	.417
6	Lou Gehrig, 1927	.392
7	Babe Ruth, 1928	.386
8	Jimmie Foxx, 1932	.385
9	Jeff Bagwell, 1994	.382
10	Frank Thomas, 1994	.376
11	Albert Belle, 1995	.374
12	Babe Ruth, 1930	.373
13	Mark McGwire, 1997	.372
14	Babe Ruth, 1923	.372
15	Mickey Mantle, 1961	.370
16	Hank Greenberg, 1938	.369
17	Hack Wilson, 1930	.368
18	Babe Ruth, 1926	.366
19	Babe Ruth, 1924	.361
20	Babe Ruth, 1922	.357
21	Albert Belle, 1994	.357
22	Jimmie Foxx, 1938	.356
23	Kevin Mitchell, 1994	.355
24	Larry Walker, 1997	.354
25	Rogers Hornsby, 1925	.353
26	Mickey Mantle, 1956	.353
27	Babe Ruth, 1929	.353
28	Ken Griffey Jr., 1994	.351
29	Roger Maris, 1961	.351
30	Ralph Kiner, 1949	.348
31	Jimmie Foxx, 1933	.347
32	Willie Stargell, 1973	.347
33	Kevin Mitchell, 1989	.344
34	Lou Gehrig, 1934	.344
35	Jim Gentile, 1961	.344
36	Ted Williams, 1957	.343
37	Lou Gehrig, 1930	.343
38	Ken Griffey Jr., 1997	.342
39	Lou Gehrig, 1936	.342
40	Hank Aaron, 1971	.341
41	Barry Bonds, 1993	.341
42	Bracy Anderson, 1996	.340
43	Willie Mays, 1955	.340
44	Matt Williams, 1994	.339
45	Sammy Sosa, 1998	.339
46	Mike Schmidt, 1980	.338
47	Willie McCovey, 1969	.336
48	Babe Ruth, 1919	.336
49	Barry Bonds, 1994	.335
50	Jimmie Foxx, 1939	.334
51	Reggie Jackson, 1969	.333
52	Willie Stargell, 1971	.333
53	Hank Greenberg, 1937	.332
54	Hank Greenberg, 1940	.330
55	Juan Gonzalez, 1996	.329
56	Ted Williams, 1941	.329
57	Mark McGwire, 1987	.329
58	Willie Mays, 1965	.328
59	Babe Ruth, 1931	.328
60	Mike Schmidt, 1981	.328
61	Ken Griffey Jr., 1998	.327
62	Hank Greenberg, 1946	.327
63	Joe DiMaggio, 1937	.327
64	Albert Belle, 1998	.327
65	Al Simmons, 1930	.327
66	Stan Musial, 1948	.326
67	Ralph Kiner, 1947	.326
68	Dave Kingman, 1979	.325
69	Ted Williams, 1946	.325
70	Ken Griffey Jr., 1996	.325
71	Eddie Mathews, 1953	.325
72	Greg Vaughn, 1998	.325
73	Willie McCovey, 1970	.323
74	Juan Gonzalez, 1993	.323
75	Willie Mays, 1954	.322
76	Lou Gehrig, 1931	.321
77	Johnny Mize, 1940	.321
78	Frank Robinson, 1966	.321
79	Rogers Hornsby, 1922	.321
80	Duke Snider, 1955	.320
81	Babe Ruth, 1932	.319
82	Jimmie Foxx, 1934	.319
83	Ralph Kiner, 1951	.318
84	Ralph Kiner, 1950	.318
85	Harmon Killebrew, 1961	.318
86	Bob Hamelin, 1994	.317
87	Rocky Colavito, 1958	.317
88	Mark McGwire, 1992	.317
89	Chick Hafey, 1930	.316
90	Boog Powell, 1964	.316
91	Ted Kluszewski, 1954	.316
92	Dick Allen, 1966	.315
93	Cecil Fielder, 1990	.314
94	Eddie Mathews, 1954	.313
95	Duke Snider, 1957	.313
96	Barry Bonds, 1992	.313
97	Eddie Mathews, 1955	.313
98	Albert Belle, 1996	.312
99	Johnny Mize, 1947	.312
100	Juan Gonzalez, 1998	.312

Extra Base Hits

1	Babe Ruth, 1921	119
2	Lou Gehrig, 1927	117
3	Chuck Klein, 1930	107
4	Chuck Klein, 1932	103
	Hank Greenberg, 1937	103
	Stan Musial, 1948	103
	Albert Belle, 1995	103
8	Rogers Hornsby, 1922	102
9	Lou Gehrig, 1930	100
	Jimmie Foxx, 1932	100
11	Babe Ruth, 1920	99
	Babe Ruth, 1923	99
	Hank Greenberg, 1940	99
	Larry Walker, 1997	99
	Albert Belle, 1998	99
16	Hank Greenberg, 1935	98
17	Babe Ruth, 1927	97
	Hack Wilson, 1930	97
	Joe Medwick, 1937	97
	Juan Gonzalez, 1998	97
21	Hank Greenberg, 1934	96
	Hal Trosky, 1936	96
	Joe DiMaggio, 1937	96
24	Lou Gehrig, 1934	95
	Joe Medwick, 1936	95
26	Rogers Hornsby, 1929	94
	Chuck Klein, 1929	94
	Babe Herman, 1930	94
	Jimmie Foxx, 1933	94
30	Jim Bottomley, 1928	93
	Al Simmons, 1930	93
	Lou Gehrig, 1936	93
	Ellis Burks, 1996	93
	Ken Griffey Jr., 1997	93
35	Babe Ruth, 1924	92
	Lou Gehrig, 1931	92
	Jimmie Foxx, 1938	92
	Stan Musial, 1953	92
	Hank Aaron, 1959	92
	Frank Robinson, 1962	92
	Brady Anderson, 1996	92
	Ken Griffey Jr., 1998	92
43	Babe Ruth, 1928	91
	Alex Rodriguez, 1996	91
	Mark McGwire, 1998	91
46	Rogers Hornsby, 1925	90
	Stan Musial, 1949	90
	Willie Mays, 1962	90
	Willie Stargell, 1973	90
50	Hal Trosky, 1934	89
	Duke Snider, 1954	89
	Andres Galarraga, 1996	89
	Albert Belle, 1996	89
54	Joe DiMaggio, 1936	88
	Barry Bonds, 1993	88
	Barry Bonds, 1998	88
57	Tris Speaker, 1923	87
	Kiki Cuyler, 1925	87
	Lou Gehrig, 1928	87
	Ripper Collins, 1934	87
	Charlie Gehringer, 1936	87
	Johnny Mize, 1940	87
	Willie Mays, 1954	87
	Robin Yount, 1982	87
	Kevin Mitchell, 1989	87
66	George Sisler, 1920	86
	Babe Ruth, 1930	86
	Wally Moses, 1937	86
	Johnny Mize, 1939	86
	Ted Williams, 1939	86
	Stan Musial, 1946	86
	Eddie Mathews, 1953	86
	Reggie Jackson, 1969	86
	Hal McRae, 1977	86
	Jim Rice, 1978	86
	Don Mattingly, 1985	86
	Don Mattingly, 1986	86
	Ken Griffey Jr., 1993	86
	Sammy Sosa, 1998	86
80	Mark McGwire, 1997	85
	Tip O'Neill, 1887	85
	Hugh Duffy, 1894	85
	Chick Hafey, 1929	85
	Goose Goslin, 1930	85
	Lou Gehrig, 1932	85
	Lou Gehrig, 1933	85
	Earl Averill, 1934	85
	Hank Greenberg, 1938	85
	Rudy York, 1940	85
	Ted Williams, 1949	85
	Stan Musial, 1954	85
	Frank Robinson, 1966	85
	George Foster, 1977	85
	George Brett, 1979	85
	Cal Ripken, 1991	85
	Jeff Bagwell, 1997	85
	Nomar Garciaparra, 1997	85
98	11 players tied	84

Pinch Hits

1	John Vander Wal, 1995	28
2	Jose Morales, 1976	25
3	Dave Philley, 1961	24
	Vic Davalillo, 1970	24
	Rusty Staub, 1983	24
	Gerald Perry, 1993	24
7	Sam Leslie, 1932	22
	Peanuts Lowrey, 1953	22
	Red Schoendienst, 1962	22
	Wallace Johnson, 1988	22
	Mark Sweeney, 1997	22
12	Doc Miller, 1913	21
	Smoky Burgess, 1966	21
	Merv Rettenmund, 1977	21
15	Ed Coleman, 1936	20
	Frenchy Bordagaray, 1938	20
	Joe Frazier, 1954	20
	Smoky Burgess, 1965	20
	Ken Boswell, 1976	20
	Jerry Turner, 1978	20
	Thad Bosley, 1985	20
	Chris Chambliss, 1986	20
	Dave Clark, 1997	20
24	Many players tied	19

Pinch Hit Average
(30 at bats minimum)

1	Ed Kranepool, 1974	.486
2	Smead Jolley, 1931	.467
3	Frenchy Bordagaray, 1938	.465
4	Rick Miller, 1983	.457
5	Bill Spiers, 1997	.455
6	Jose Pagan, 1969	.452
7	Elmer Valo, 1955	.452
	Mark Johnson, 1996	.452
9	Gates Brown, 1968	.450
10	Ted Easterly, 1912	.433
	Milt Thompson, 1985	.433
	Randy Bush, 1986	.433
13	Joe Cronin, 1943	.429
	Don Dillard, 1961	.429
15	Candy Maldonado, 1986	.425
16	Richie Ashburn, 1962	.419
	Dick Williams, 1962	.419
18	Merritt Ranew, 1963	.415
	Carl Taylor, 1969	.415
20	Kurt Bevacqua, 1983	.412
21	Jerry Turner, 1978	.408
22	Bob Bowman, 1958	.406
	Chico Walker, 1991	.406
	Sid Bream, 1994	.406
25	Frankie Baumholtz, 1955	.405

Pinch Hit Home Runs

1	Johnny Frederick, 1932	6
2	Joe Cronin, 1943	5
	Butch Nieman, 1945	5
	Gene Freese, 1959	5
	Jerry Lynch, 1961	5
	Cliff Johnson, 1974	5
	Lee Lacy, 1978	5
	Jerry Turner, 1978	5
	Billy Ashley, 1996	5
10	Ernie Lombardi, 1946	4
	Del Wilber, 1953	4
	Bill Taylor, 1955	4
	Bob Thurman, 1957	4
	Rip Repulski, 1958	4
	George Crowe, 1959	4
	George Crowe, 1960	4
	Johnny Blanchard, 1961	4
	Carl Sawatski, 1961	4
	Jerry Lynch, 1963	4
	Don Mincher, 1964	4
	Hal Breeden, 1973	4
	Mike Ivie, 1978	4
	Del Unser, 1979	4
	Jeff Burroughs, 1982	4
	Danny Heep, 1983	4
	Candy Maldonado, 1986	4
	Mark Carreon, 1989	4
	Tommy Gregg, 1990	4
	Ernest Riles, 1990	4
	Howard Johnson, 1994	4
	John Vander Wal, 1995	4
	Jack Howell, 1996	4
	Mark Johnson, 1996	4
	Bob Hamelin, 1998	4

Total Player Rating / 150g

1	Babe Ruth, 1923	10.46
2	Jeff Bagwell, 1994	10.36
3	Mike Schmidt, 1981	10.29
4	Fred Dunlap, 1884	10.25
5	Pete Browning, 1882	10.22
6	Nap Lajoie, 1901	10.19
7	Nap Lajoie, 1903	10.08
8	Barry Bonds, 1992	9.86
9	Babe Ruth, 1921	9.28
10	Babe Ruth, 1927	9.14
11	Babe Ruth, 1920	9.08
12	Rickey Henderson, 1990	9.04
13	Rogers Hornsby, 1924	9.02
14	Mickey Mantle, 1957	8.96
15	Mickey Mantle, 1956	8.70
16	Cal Ripken, 1984	8.43
17	Ross Barnes, 1876	8.41
18	Ty Cobb, 1917	8.39
19	Babe Ruth, 1924	8.33
20	Barry Bonds, 1993	8.30
21	Nap Lajoie, 1906	8.29
	Babe Ruth, 1926	8.29
23	Ted Williams, 1941	8.29
24	Rogers Hornsby, 1922	8.28
25	George Brett, 1980	8.21
26	Fred Pfeffer, 1884	8.17
27	Rogers Hornsby, 1920	8.15
28	Ted Williams, 1942	8.10
29	Barry Bonds, 1996	8.07
30	Ted Williams, 1957	8.07
31	Eric Davis, 1987	8.02
32	Nap Lajoie, 1910	8.02
33	Cupid Childs, 1890	7.98
34	Rogers Hornsby, 1917	7.97
35	Ted Williams, 1946	7.90
36	Mickey Mantle, 1961	7.84
37	Lou Gehrig, 1927	7.84
38	Lou Boudreau, 1944	7.80
39	Tris Speaker, 1913	7.77
40	Rickey Henderson, 1985	7.76
41	Hughie Jennings, 1896	7.73
42	Honus Wagner, 1906	7.71
43	Cal Ripken, 1991	7.69
	Craig Biggio, 1997	7.69
45	Nap Lajoie, 1904	7.61
46	Willie Mays, 1955	7.60
47	King Kelly, 1879	7.60
	George Sisler, 1920	7.60
	Lou Gehrig, 1934	7.60
50	Babe Ruth, 1930	7.55
	Babe Ruth, 1931	7.55
52	Tris Speaker, 1912	7.55
53	Cupid Childs, 1896	7.50
	Barry Bonds, 1994	7.50
	Mike Piazza, 1997	7.50
56	Nap Lajoie, 1908	7.45
57	Honus Wagner, 1905	7.45
58	Nap Lajoie, 1900	7.35
59	Nap Lajoie, 1907	7.34
60	Honus Wagner, 1903	7.33
61	Jack Glasscock, 1882	7.32
62	Ed Delahanty, 1896	7.32
63	Mike Schmidt, 1980	7.30
64	Ty Cobb, 1911	7.29
	Joe Morgan, 1975	7.29
	Ken Caminiti, 1996	7.29
67	Andre Dawson, 1981	7.28
68	Babe Ruth, 1919	7.27
69	Ron Santo, 1966	7.26
70	Rickey Henderson, 1981	7.22
71	Tris Speaker, 1914	7.22
72	Ty Cobb, 1910	7.18
73	Ed Delahanty, 1893	7.16
74	Frankie Frisch, 1927	7.16
75	Barry Bonds, 1990	7.15
76	Dick Bartell, 1937	7.15
77	Joe DiMaggio, 1939	7.13
78	Buddy Bell, 1981	7.11
79	Charley Jones, 1877	7.11
	Snuffy Stirnweiss, 1945	7.11
	Willie Mays, 1958	7.11
82	Albert Belle, 1994	7.08
83	Barry Larkin, 1991	7.07
84	Robin Yount, 1981	7.03
85	Barry Bonds, 1995	6.98
86	Willie Mays, 1965	6.97
87	George Sisler, 1922	6.97
88	Harlond Clift, 1937	6.97
	George Brett, 1985	6.97
	Mark McGwire, 1998	6.97
91	Honus Wagner, 1908	6.95
92	Bobby Wallace, 1901	6.94
93	Joe Jackson, 1911	6.94
94	Hughie Jennings, 1897	6.92
	Rogers Hornsby, 1929	6.92
	Ted Williams, 1947	6.92
	Barry Bonds, 1998	6.92
98	Rogers Hornsby, 1921	6.92
	Snuffy Stirnweiss, 1944	6.92
100	Joe DiMaggio, 1941	6.91

Stolen Bases

1	Hugh Nicol, 1887	138
2	Rickey Henderson, 1982	130
3	Arlie Latham, 1887	129
4	Lou Brock, 1974	118
5	Charlie Comiskey, 1887	117
6	John Ward, 1887	111
	Billy Hamilton, 1889	111
	Billy Hamilton, 1891	111
9	Vince Coleman, 1985	110
10	Arlie Latham, 1888	109
	Vince Coleman, 1987	109
12	Rickey Henderson, 1983	108
13	Vince Coleman, 1986	107
14	Tom Brown, 1891	106
15	Maury Wills, 1962	104
16	Pete Browning, 1887	103
	Hugh Nicol, 1888	103
18	Jim Fogarty, 1887	102
	Billy Hamilton, 1890	102
20	Rickey Henderson, 1980	100
21	Jim Fogarty, 1889	99
22	Billy Hamilton, 1894	98
23	Harry Stovey, 1890	97
	Billy Hamilton, 1895	97
	Ron LeFlore, 1980	97
26	Ty Cobb, 1915	96
	Omar Moreno, 1980	96
28	Bid McPhee, 1887	95
	Curt Welch, 1888	95
30	Mike Griffin, 1887	94
	Maury Wills, 1965	94
32	Tommy McCarthy, 1888	93
	Rickey Henderson, 1988	93
34	Darby O'Brien, 1889	91
35	Tim Raines, 1983	90
36	Curt Welch, 1887	89
	Herman Long, 1889	89
38	Tom Poorman, 1887	88
	Blondie Purcell, 1887	88
	John Ward, 1892	88
	Clyde Milan, 1912	88
42	Harry Stovey, 1888	87
	Arlie Latham, 1891	87
	Joe Kelley, 1896	87
	Rickey Henderson, 1986	87
46	Cub Stricker, 1887	86
47	Tommy Tucker, 1887	85
	Hub Collins, 1890	85
	Hugh Duffy, 1891	85
50	King Kelly, 1887	84
	Chippy McGarr, 1887	84
	Billy Sunday, 1890	84
	Bill Lange, 1896	84
54	Tommy McCarthy, 1890	83
	Billy Hamilton, 1896	83
	Ty Cobb, 1911	83
	Willie Wilson, 1979	83
58	Dummy Hoy, 1888	82
	John Reilly, 1888	82
60	Eddie Collins, 1910	81
	Bob Bescher, 1911	81
	Vince Coleman, 1988	81
63	Emmett Seery, 1888	80
	Hugh Nicol, 1889	80
	Rickey Henderson, 1985	80
	Eric Davis, 1986	80
67	Tom Brown, 1890	79
	Dave Collins, 1980	79
	Willie Wilson, 1980	79
70	Hugh Duffy, 1890	78
	Tom Brown, 1892	78
	John McGraw, 1894	78
	Ron LeFlore, 1979	78
	Tim Raines, 1982	78
	Marquis Grissom, 1992	78
76	Ted Scheffler, 1890	77
	Jimmy Sheckard, 1899	77
	Davey Lopes, 1975	77
	Omar Moreno, 1979	77
	Rudy Law, 1983	77
	Rickey Henderson, 1989	77
	Vince Coleman, 1990	77
83	Ed McKean, 1887	76
	Walt Wilmot, 1890	76
	Dusty Miller, 1896	76
	Ty Cobb, 1909	76
	Marquis Grissom, 1991	76
88	Yank Robinson, 1887	75
	George Van Haltren, 1891	75
	Clyde Milan, 1913	75
	Benny Kauff, 1914	75
	Billy North, 1976	75
	Tim Raines, 1984	75
	Kenny Lofton, 1996	75
95	Frank Fennelly, 1887	74
	Harry Stovey, 1887	74
	Walt Wilmot, 1894	74
	Fritz Maisel, 1914	74
	Lou Brock, 1966	74
	Brian Hunter, 1997	74

Stolen Base Average

1	Kevin McReynolds, 1988	100.0
	Paul Molitor, 1994	100.0
3	Brady Anderson, 1994	96.9
4	Max Carey, 1922	96.2
5	Ken Griffey Jr., 1980	95.8
6	Stan Javier, 1988	95.2
7	Amos Otis, 1970	94.3
8	Jack Perconte, 1985	93.9
9	Miguel Dilone, 1984	93.1
	Bob Dernier, 1986	93.1
11	Kirk Gibson, 1990	92.9
	Barry Larkin, 1994	92.9
13	Don Baylor, 1972	92.3
	Oddibe McDowell, 1987	92.3
15	Davey Lopes, 1985	92.2
16	Eric Davis, 1988	92.1
17	Henry Cotto, 1992	92.0
	Mike Cameron, 1997	92.0
19	Bobby Bonds, 1969	91.8
	Davey Lopes, 1978	91.8
21	Davey Lopes, 1979	91.7
	Marquis Grissom, 1990	91.7
23	Jim Wynn, 1965	91.5
24	Larry Bowa, 1977	91.4
25	Ryne Sandberg, 1987	91.3
	Alan Trammell, 1987	91.3
	Rich Amaral, 1995	91.3
28	Jerry Mumphrey, 1980	91.2
29	Tom Herr, 1985	91.2
30	Barry Larkin, 1995	91.1
31	Jack Smith, 1925	90.9
	Davey Lopes, 1981	90.9
	Tim Raines, 1987	90.9
	Bip Roberts, 1995	90.9
	Roberto Alomar, 1995	90.9
36	Craig Biggio, 1994	90.7
37	Derek Bell, 1996	90.6
38	Willie Wilson, 1984	90.4
39	Bake McBride, 1978	90.3
40	Devon White, 1992	90.2
41	Henry Cotto, 1988	90.0
42	Barry Larkin, 1998	89.7
43	Tony Womack, 1997	89.6
44	Devon White, 1993	89.5
45	Mitchell Page, 1977	89.4
46	Tommy Harper, 1971	89.3
	Rick Manning, 1981	89.3
	Eric Davis, 1987	89.3
	Stan Javier, 1997	89.3
50	8 players tied	88.9

Stolen Base Runs

1	Vince Coleman, 1986 . . .	24
2	Maury Wills, 1962	23
3	Rickey Henderson, 1983 .	21
4	Rickey Henderson, 1988 .	20
5	Vince Coleman, 1987 . . .	20
6	Tim Raines, 1983	19
7	Vince Coleman, 1985 . . .	18
	Rickey Henderson, 1985 .	18
9	Willie Wilson, 1979	18
	Ron LeFlore, 1980	18
	Willie Wilson, 1980	18
12	Eric Davis, 1986	17
13	Tim Raines, 1984	17
14	Davey Lopes, 1975	16
	Rudy Law, 1983	16
16	Lou Brock, 1974	16
	Tim Raines, 1985	16
	Tim Raines, 1986	16
	Marquis Grissom, 1992 . .	16
20	Rickey Henderson, 1986 .	15
21	Ron LeFlore, 1979	15
22	Tim Raines, 1981	15
	Rickey Henderson, 1989 .	15
24	Rickey Henderson, 1980 .	14
25	Max Carey, 1922	14
	Joe Morgan, 1975	14
27	Bert Campaneris, 1969 . .	14
	Tim Raines, 1982	14
	Rickey Henderson, 1982 .	14
	Tony Womack, 1997	14
31	Vince Coleman, 1989 . . .	14
	Rickey Henderson, 1990 .	14
33	Davey Lopes, 1976	13
	Willie Wilson, 1983	13
	Vince Coleman, 1990 . . .	13
36	Mickey Rivers, 1975	13
	Joe Morgan, 1976	13
	Jerry Mumphrey, 1980 . .	13
	Juan Samuel, 1984	13
	Marquis Grissom, 1991 . .	13
	Kenny Lofton, 1992	13
	Kenny Lofton, 1993	13
	Chuck Knoblauch, 1997 .	13
	Tony Womack, 1998	13
45	Barry Larkin, 1995	12
	Kenny Lofton, 1996	12
47	Fritz Maisel, 1914	12
	Alan Wiggins, 1983	12
	Tim Raines, 1987	12
	Rickey Henderson, 1998 .	12

Stolen Base Wins

1	Vince Coleman, 1986 . . .	2.5
2	Maury Wills, 1962	2.3
3	Rickey Henderson, 1983 .	2.1
4	Rickey Henderson, 1988 .	2.0
5	Tim Raines, 1983	1.9
6	Vince Coleman, 1987 . . .	1.9
7	Vince Coleman, 1985 . . .	1.9
8	Ron LeFlore, 1980	1.9
9	Eric Davis, 1986	1.8
10	Rickey Henderson, 1985 .	1.8
11	Willie Wilson, 1980	1.8
12	Tim Raines, 1984	1.7
13	Willie Wilson, 1979	1.7
14	Marquis Grissom, 1992 . .	1.7
15	Davey Lopes, 1975	1.7
16	Tim Raines, 1985	1.6
17	Lou Brock, 1974	1.6
18	Tim Raines, 1986	1.6
19	Rudy Law, 1983	1.6
20	Tim Raines, 1981	1.6
21	Rickey Henderson, 1986 .	1.5
22	Rickey Henderson, 1989 .	1.5
23	Joe Morgan, 1975	1.5
24	Ron LeFlore, 1979	1.5
25	Tim Raines, 1982	1.4
26	Bert Campaneris, 1969 . .	1.4
27	Vince Coleman, 1989 . . .	1.4
28	Rickey Henderson, 1980 .	1.4
29	Rickey Henderson, 1982 .	1.4
30	Rickey Henderson, 1990 .	1.4
31	Davey Lopes, 1976	1.4
32	Tony Womack, 1997	1.4
33	Joe Morgan, 1976	1.3
34	Jerry Mumphrey, 1980 . .	1.3
35	Max Carey, 1922	1.3
36	Vince Coleman, 1990 . . .	1.3
37	Fritz Maisel, 1914	1.3
38	Juan Samuel, 1984	1.3
39	Marquis Grissom, 1991 . .	1.3
40	Lou Brock, 1968	1.3
41	Willie Wilson, 1983	1.3
42	Mickey Rivers, 1975	1.3
43	Kenny Lofton, 1992	1.3
44	Ozzie Smith, 1988	1.3
45	Alan Wiggins, 1983	1.3
46	Tony Womack, 1998	1.2
47	Davey Lopes, 1985	1.2
48	Kenny Lofton, 1993	1.2
49	Barry Larkin, 1995	1.2
50	Julio Cruz, 1978	1.2

Fielding Average

First Base

1	Steve Garvey, 1984	1.000
2	Stuffy McInnis, 1921	.999
3	Frank McCormick, 1946 .	.999
4	David Segui, 1998	.999
5	J. T. Snow, 1998	.999
5	Steve Garvey, 1981	.999
7	Jim Spencer, 1973	.999
7	Wes Parker, 1968	.999
9	Eddie Murray, 1981	.999
10	Hal Morris, 1992	.999

Second Base

1	Bret Boone, 1997	.997
2	Bobby Grich, 1985	.997
3	Jose Oquendo, 1990	.996
4	Ryne Sandberg, 1991 . . .	.995
5	Jody Reed, 1994	.995
6	Rob Wilfong, 1980	.995
7	Bobby Grich, 1973	.995
8	Frank White, 1988	.994
9	Mark Lemke, 1994	.994
10	Jose Oquendo, 1989 . . .	.994

Shortstop

1	Cal Ripken, 1990	.996
2	Omar Vizquel, 1998	.993
3	Tony Fernandez, 1989 . . .	.992
4	Larry Bowa, 1979	.991
5	Ed Brinkman, 1972	.990
6	Cal Ripken, 1989	.990
7	Mike Bordick, 1998	.990
8	Spike Owen, 1990	.989
9	Omar Vizquel, 1992	.989
10	Cal Ripken, 1995	.989

Third Base

1	Tony Fernandez, 1994 . . .	.991
2	Don Money, 1974	.989
3	Hank Majeski, 1947	.988
4	Aurelio Rodriguez, 1978 .	.987
5	Willie Kamm, 1933	.984
6	Steve Buechele, 1991 . . .	.983
7	Gary Gaetti, 1998	.983
8	George Kell, 1946	.983
9	Heinie Groh, 1924	.983
10	Carney Lansford, 1979 . .	.983

Outfield

1	Danny Litwhiler, 1942 . . .	1.000
	Willard Marshall, 1951 . . .	1.000
	Tony Gonzalez, 1962	1.000
	Don Demeter, 1963	1.000
	Rocky Colavito, 1965 . . .	1.000
	Curt Flood, 1966	1.000
	Johnny Callison, 1968 . . .	1.000
	Mickey Stanley, 1968 . . .	1.000
	Ken Harrelson, 1968	1.000
	Ken Berry, 1969	1.000
	Mickey Stanley, 1970 . . .	1.000
	Roy White, 1971	1.000
	Al Kaline, 1971	1.000
	Ken Berry, 1972	1.000
	Carl Yastrzemski, 1977 . .	1.000
	Terry Puhl, 1979	1.000
	Gary Roenicke, 1980 . . .	1.000
	Ken Landreaux, 1981 . . .	1.000
	Terry Puhl, 1981	1.000
	Ken Singleton, 1981	1.000
	Brian Downing, 1982	1.000
	John Lowenstein, 1982 . .	1.000
	Brian Downing, 1984	1.000
	Brett Butler, 1991	1.000
	Darryl Hamilton, 1992 . . .	1.000
	Brett Butler, 1993	1.000
	Darren Lewis, 1993	1.000
	Tim Raines, 1993	1.000
	Lance Johnson, 1994 . . .	1.000
	Milt Thompson, 1994 . . .	1.000
	Jim Eisenreich, 1995	1.000
	Stan Javier, 1995	1.000
	Darryl Hamilton, 1996 . . .	1.000
	Paul O'Neill, 1996	1.000

Catcher

1	Spud Davis, 1939	1.000
	Buddy Rosar, 1946	1.000
	Lou Berberet, 1957	1.000
	Pete Daley, 1957	1.000
	Yogi Berra, 1958	1.000
	Rick Cerone, 1988	1.000
	Charles Johnson, 1997 . .	1.000
	Chris Hoiles, 1997	1.000
9	Tom Pagnozzi, 1992	.999
10	Joe Azcue, 1967	.999

Pitcher (92 chances accepted)

1	Kid Nichols, 1896	1.000
	Frank Owen, 1904	1.000
	Mordecai Brown, 1908 . .	1.000
	Pete Alexander, 1913 . . .	1.000
	Walter Johnson, 1913 . . .	1.000
	Eppa Rixey, 1917	1.000
	Walter Johnson, 1917 . . .	1.000
	Hal Schumacher, 1935 . .	1.000
	Larry Jackson, 1964	1.000
	Randy Jones, 1976	1.000
	Greg Maddux, 1990	1.000

Total Chances per Game

First Base
1	Joe Gerhardt, 1876	13.28
2	Jiggs Donahue, 1907	12.73
3	Oscar Walker, 1879	12.60
4	Joe Start, 1878	12.54
5	Tim Murnane, 1878	12.52
6	Joe Start, 1879	12.49
7	Jake Goodman, 1878	12.45
8	Herman Dehlman, 1876	12.36
9	Phil Todt, 1926	12.36
10	Joe Start, 1877	12.35

Second Base
1	Thorny Hawkes, 1879	8.44
2	Chick Fulmer, 1879	8.34
3	Jack Burdock, 1878	8.30
4	Ed Somerville, 1876	8.28
5	Joe Gerhardt, 1877	8.12
6	Fred Pfeffer, 1884	8.08
7	Jack Burdock, 1879	7.88
8	Joe Quest, 1878	7.81
9	Pop Smith, 1885	7.74
10	Joe Quest, 1879	7.73

Shortstop
1	Herman Long, 1889	7.27
2	Hughie Jennings, 1895	7.16
3	Dave Bancroft, 1918	7.14
4	Phil Tomney, 1889	7.12
5	George Davis, 1899	7.08
6	Hughie Jennings, 1896	7.07
7	Hughie Jennings, 1897	7.03
8	Bobby Wallace, 1901	6.97
9	Monte Cross, 1897	6.97
10	Bill Dahlen, 1895	6.93

Third Base
1	Al Nichols, 1876	5.81
2	Bob Ferguson, 1877	5.61
3	Jumbo Davis, 1888	5.13
4	Billy Alvord, 1891	5.03
5	Cap Anson, 1876	5.03
6	George Bradley, 1880	4.93
7	Billy Shindle, 1892	4.93
8	Jack Gleason, 1882	4.90
9	Bill Bradley, 1900	4.87
10	Will Foley, 1877	4.79

Outfield
1	Fred Treacey, 1876	4.39
2	Redleg Snyder, 1876	3.84
3	Charley Jones, 1877	3.77
4	Taylor Douthit, 1928	3.68
5	Mike Mansell, 1879	3.64
6	Richie Ashburn, 1951	3.64
7	Chet Lemon, 1977	3.60
8	Thurman Tucker, 1944	3.58
9	Kirby Puckett, 1984	3.57
10	Irv Noren, 1951	3.53
11	Richie Ashburn, 1949	3.49
12	Carden Gillenwater, 1945	3.46
13	Taylor Douthit, 1926	3.43
14	Sam West, 1935	3.41
15	Richie Ashburn, 1956	3.40
16	Dom DiMaggio, 1948	3.39
17	Richie Ashburn, 1957	3.38
18	Lloyd Waner, 1932	3.37
19	Lloyd Waner, 1931	3.37
20	Richie Ashburn, 1958	3.36

Catcher
1	Bill Holbert, 1883	10.63
2	Sam Trott, 1884	10.35
3	Bill Holbert, 1884	9.51
4	Jocko Milligan, 1884	9.40
5	Mert Hackett, 1884	9.35
6	Barney Gilligan, 1884	9.30
7	Mike Hines, 1883	9.27
8	George Baker, 1884	8.99
9	Jocko Milligan, 1885	8.82
10	Lew Brown, 1877	8.65

Pitcher
1	Harry Howell, 1905	5.42
2	Harry Howell, 1904	5.12
3	Will White, 1882	4.76
4	Ed Walsh, 1907	4.75
5	George Mullin, 1904	4.53
6	Tony Mullane, 1882	4.38
7	Red Donahue, 1902	4.37
8	Harry Howell, 1906	4.34
9	Jack Katoll, 1902	4.31
10	Nick Altrock, 1904	4.26
	Nick Altrock, 1905	4.26

Chances Accepted per Game

First Base
1	Jiggs Donahue, 1907	12.65
2	Joe Gerhardt, 1876	12.54
3	Phil Todt, 1926	12.21
4	Joe Start, 1879	12.15
5	George Burns, 1914	12.10
6	Stuffy McInnis, 1918	12.10
7	George Stovall, 1908	12.08
8	George Kelly, 1920	12.01
9	Joe Start, 1878	12.00
10	Oscar Walker, 1879	11.92

Second Base
1	Jack Burdock, 1878	7.62
2	Thorny Hawkes, 1879	7.56
3	Chick Fulmer, 1879	7.55
4	Fred Pfeffer, 1884	7.29
5	Joe Gerhardt, 1877	7.21
6	Ed Somerville, 1876	7.20
7	Jack Burdock, 1879	7.18
8	Joe Quest, 1879	7.16
9	Pop Smith, 1885	7.13
10	Bid McPhee, 1886	7.09

Shortstop
1	Hughie Jennings, 1895	6.73
2	George Davis, 1899	6.69
3	Dave Bancroft, 1918	6.62
4	Hughie Jennings, 1896	6.56
5	Hughie Jennings, 1897	6.55
6	Rabbit Maranville, 1919	6.48
7	Bobby Wallace, 1901	6.48
8	Monte Cross, 1897	6.41
9	Dave Bancroft, 1920	6.40
10	George Davis, 1900	6.39

Third Base
1	Bob Ferguson, 1877	4.71
2	Al Nichols, 1876	4.53
3	Billy Shindle, 1892	4.34
4	Jumbo Davis, 1888	4.33
5	Billy Alvord, 1891	4.31
6	Bill Bradley, 1900	4.29
7	Cap Anson, 1876	4.27
8	George Bradley, 1880	4.23
9	Joe Battin, 1883	4.17
10	Bill Hague, 1878	4.16

Outfield
1	Fred Treacey, 1876	3.70
2	Taylor Douthit, 1928	3.62
3	Richie Ashburn, 1951	3.59
4	Thurman Tucker, 1944	3.55
5	Kirby Puckett, 1984	3.55
6	Chet Lemon, 1977	3.52
7	Irv Noren, 1951	3.45
8	Richie Ashburn, 1949	3.42
9	Carden Gillenwater, 1945	3.39
10	Sam West, 1935	3.38
11	Richie Ashburn, 1956	3.34
12	Richie Ashburn, 1957	3.33
13	Dom DiMaggio, 1948	3.33
14	Lloyd Waner, 1932	3.32
15	Jim Busby, 1953	3.31
16	Richie Ashburn, 1958	3.31
17	Jim Busby, 1952	3.31
18	Richie Ashburn, 1953	3.29
19	Lloyd Waner, 1931	3.29
20	Dwayne Murphy, 1980	3.29

Catcher
1	Bill Holbert, 1883	9.78
2	Sam Trott, 1884	9.63
3	Jocko Milligan, 1884	8.83
4	Bill Holbert, 1884	8.75
5	Mert Hackett, 1884	8.68
6	Barney Gilligan, 1884	8.63
7	Duffy Dyer, 1972	8.25
8	Jocko Milligan, 1885	8.25
9	Mike Hines, 1883	8.22
10	Javy Lopez, 1998	8.17

Pitcher
1	Harry Howell, 1905	5.24
2	Harry Howell, 1904	4.97
3	Ed Walsh, 1907	4.68
4	Will White, 1882	4.56
5	George Mullin, 1904	4.24
6	Nick Altrock, 1905	4.21
7	Tony Mullane, 1882	4.20
8	Willie Sudhoff, 1904	4.19
9	Red Donahue, 1902	4.14
10	Nick Altrock, 1904	4.13

Putouts

First Base
1	Jiggs Donahue, 1907	1846
2	George Kelly, 1920	1759
3	Phil Todt, 1926	1755
4	Wally Pipp, 1926	1710
5	Jiggs Donahue, 1906	1697
6	Candy LaChance, 1904	1691
7	Tom Jones, 1907	1687
8	Ernie Banks, 1965	1682
9	Wally Pipp, 1922	1667
10	Lou Gehrig, 1927	1662

Second Base
1	Bid McPhee, 1886	529
2	Bobby Grich, 1974	484
3	Bucky Harris, 1922	483
4	Nellie Fox, 1956	478
5	Lou Bierbauer, 1889	472
6	Billy Herman, 1933	466
7	Bill Wambsganss, 1924	463
8	Cub Stricker, 1887	461
9	Buddy Myer, 1935	460
10	Bill Sweeney, 1912	459

Shortstop
1	Hughie Jennings, 1895	425
	Donie Bush, 1914	425
3	Joe Cassidy, 1905	408
4	Rabbit Maranville, 1914	407
5	Dave Bancroft, 1922	405
	Eddie Miller, 1940	405
7	Monte Cross, 1898	404
8	Dave Bancroft, 1921	396
9	Mickey Doolan, 1906	395
10	Buck Weaver, 1913	392

Third Base
1	Denny Lyons, 1887	255
2	Jimmy Williams, 1899	251
	Jimmy Collins, 1900	251
4	Jimmy Collins, 1898	243
	Willie Kamm, 1928	243
6	Willie Kamm, 1927	236
7	Frank Baker, 1913	233
8	Bill Coughlin, 1901	232
9	Ernie Courtney, 1905	229
10	Jimmy Austin, 1911	228

Outfield
1	Taylor Douthit, 1928	547
2	Richie Ashburn, 1951	538
3	Richie Ashburn, 1949	514
4	Chet Lemon, 1977	512
5	Dwayne Murphy, 1980	507
6	Dom DiMaggio, 1948	503
	Richie Ashburn, 1956	503
8	Richie Ashburn, 1957	502
9	Richie Ashburn, 1953	496
10	Richie Ashburn, 1958	495
11	Jim Busby, 1954	491
12	Omar Moreno, 1979	490
13	Baby Doll Jacobson, 1924	488
	Bobby Thomson, 1949	488
	Al Bumbry, 1980	488
16	Lloyd Waner, 1931	484
17	Richie Ashburn, 1954	483
18	Jim Busby, 1953	482
	Willie Wilson, 1980	482
20	Omar Moreno, 1980	479

Catcher
1	Johnny Edwards, 1969	1135
2	Mike Piazza, 1996	1055
3	Dan Wilson, 1997	1051
4	Mike Piazza, 1997	1045
5	Jason Kendall, 1998	1015
6	Johnny Edwards, 1963	1008
7	Javy Lopez, 1996	993
8	Mike Piazza, 1998	984
9	Darren Daulton, 1993	981
10	Randy Hundley, 1969	978
	Javy Lopez, 1998	978

Pitcher
1	Dave Foutz, 1886	57
2	Tony Mullane, 1882	54
3	George Bradley, 1876	50
	Guy Hecker, 1884	50
5	Mike Boddicker, 1984	49
6	Larry Corcoran, 1884	47
7	Al Spalding, 1876	45
	Ted Breitenstein, 1895	45
9	Jim Devlin, 1876	44
	Dave Foutz, 1887	44
	Bill Hutchison, 1890	44

Putouts per Game

First Base
1	Joe Gerhardt, 1876	12.30
2	Joe Start, 1879	11.98
3	Joe Start, 1878	11.79
4	Jiggs Donahue, 1907	11.76
5	Joe Start, 1877	11.73
6	Herman Dehlman, 1876	11.72
7	Joe Start, 1880	11.63
8	Jake Goodman, 1878	11.55
9	George Burns, 1914	11.53
10	Oscar Walker, 1879	11.50

Second Base
1	Jack Burdock, 1878	4.08
2	Jack Burdock, 1880	3.81
3	Bid McPhee, 1886	3.78
4	Bid McPhee, 1884	3.71
5	Joe Quest, 1878	3.68
6	Cub Stricker, 1887	3.66
7	Lou Bierbauer, 1889	3.63
8	Jack Burdock, 1879	3.61
9	Chick Fulmer, 1879	3.59
10	Bob Ferguson, 1880	3.59

Shortstop
1	Hughie Jennings, 1895	3.24
2	Dave Bancroft, 1918	2.97
3	Hughie Jennings, 1896	2.90
4	Hughie Jennings, 1897	2.89
5	George Davis, 1898	2.88
6	George Davis, 1899	2.88
7	Rabbit Maranville, 1919	2.76
8	Honus Wagner, 1913	2.75
9	Kid Elberfeld, 1901	2.74
10	Buck Weaver, 1914	2.74

Third Base
1	Al Nichols, 1876	2.16
2	Cap Anson, 1876	2.05
3	Hick Carpenter, 1880	2.03
4	Bob Ferguson, 1877	1.95
5	Denny Lyons, 1887	1.86
6	Patsy Tebeau, 1890	1.85
7	Cap Anson, 1877	1.85
8	Joe Battin, 1876	1.83
9	Jerry Denny, 1883	1.82
10	Frank Hankinson, 1881	1.80

Outfield
1	Taylor Douthit, 1928	3.55
2	Fred Treacey, 1876	3.54
3	Richie Ashburn, 1951	3.49
4	Thurman Tucker, 1944	3.45
5	Chet Lemon, 1977	3.44
6	Kirby Puckett, 1984	3.42
7	Richie Ashburn, 1949	3.34
8	Irv Noren, 1951	3.33
9	Sam West, 1935	3.33
10	Jim Busby, 1952	3.28
11	Richie Ashburn, 1956	3.27
12	Richie Ashburn, 1958	3.26
13	Lloyd Waner, 1932	3.25
14	Dom DiMaggio, 1948	3.25
15	Carden Gillenwater, 1945	3.22
16	Richie Ashburn, 1957	3.22
17	Jim Busby, 1953	3.21
18	Baby Doll Jacobson, 1924	3.21
19	Dwayne Murphy, 1980	3.21
20	Taylor Douthit, 1926	3.19

Catcher
1	Sam Trott, 1884	8.18
2	Bill Holbert, 1883	7.75
3	Javy Lopez, 1998	7.64
4	Duffy Dyer, 1972	7.58
5	Dan Wilson, 1995	7.52
6	Mike Piazza, 1997	7.52
7	Johnny Edwards, 1969	7.52
8	Joe Girardi, 1997	7.48
9	Barney Gilligan, 1884	7.47
10	Javy Lopez, 1994	7.45

Pitcher
1	Kevin Brown, 1995	1.54
2	Mike Boddicker, 1984	1.44
3	Oil Can Boyd, 1985	1.20
4	Nick Altrock, 1904	1.13
5	Greg Maddux, 1990	1.11
6	Dave Foutz, 1887	1.10
7	Dwight Gooden, 1986	1.09
	Kevin Brown, 1997	1.09
9	Dan Petry, 1984	1.09
10	Greg Maddux, 1993	1.08

Assists

First Base

1	Bill Buckner, 1985	184
2	Mark Grace, 1990	180
3	Mark Grace, 1991	167
4	Sid Bream, 1986	166
5	Bill Buckner, 1983	161
6	Bill Buckner, 1982	159
7	Bill Buckner, 1986	157
8	Mickey Vernon, 1949	155
9	Fred Tenney, 1905	152
	Eddie Murray, 1985	152

Second Base

1	Frankie Frisch, 1927	641
2	Hughie Critz, 1926	588
3	Rogers Hornsby, 1927	582
4	Ski Melillo, 1930	572
5	Ryne Sandberg, 1983	571
6	Rabbit Maranville, 1924	568
7	Frank Parkinson, 1922	562
8	Tony Cuccinello, 1936	559
9	Johnny Hodapp, 1930	557
10	Lou Bierbauer, 1892	555

Shortstop

1	Ozzie Smith, 1980	621
2	Glenn Wright, 1924	601
3	Dave Bancroft, 1920	598
4	Tommy Thevenow, 1926	597
5	Ivan DeJesus, 1977	595
6	Cal Ripken, 1984	583
7	Whitey Wietelmann, 1943	581
8	Dave Bancroft, 1922	579
9	Rabbit Maranville, 1914	574
10	Don Kessinger, 1968	573

Third Base

1	Graig Nettles, 1971	412
2	Graig Nettles, 1973	410
	Brooks Robinson, 1974	410
4	Harlond Clift, 1937	405
	Brooks Robinson, 1967	405
6	Mike Schmidt, 1974	404
7	Doug DeCinces, 1982	399
8	Clete Boyer, 1962	396
	Mike Schmidt, 1977	396
	Buddy Bell, 1982	396

Outfield

1	Orator Shaffer, 1879	50
2	Hugh Nicol, 1884	48
3	Hardy Richardson, 1881	45
4	Tommy McCarthy, 1888	44
	Chuck Klein, 1930	44
6	Charlie Duffee, 1889	43
	Jimmy Bannon, 1894	43
8	Jim Fogarty, 1889	42
9	Orator Shaffer, 1883	41
	Jim Lillie, 1884	41
11	Jim Fogarty, 1887	39
	Tom Brown, 1893	39
	Mike Mitchell, 1907	39
14	King Kelly, 1883	38
	Harry Stovey, 1889	38
	Tommy McCarthy, 1889	38
17	Jack Manning, 1883	37
	Tom Brown, 1892	37
19	Lon Knight, 1884	36
	Jimmy Ryan, 1889	36
	Jack McGeachy, 1889	36
	Jimmy Sheckard, 1903	36

Catcher

1	Bill Rariden, 1915	238
2	Bill Rariden, 1914	215
3	Pat Moran, 1903	214
4	Oscar Stanage, 1911	212
	Art Wilson, 1914	212
6	Gabby Street, 1909	210
7	Frank Snyder, 1915	204
8	George Gibson, 1910	203
9	Bill Bergen, 1909	202
	Claude Berry, 1914	202

Pitcher

1	Ed Walsh, 1907	227
2	Will White, 1882	223
3	Ed Walsh, 1908	190
4	Harry Howell, 1905	178
5	Tony Mullane, 1882	177
6	John Clarkson, 1885	174
7	John Clarkson, 1889	172
8	Jack Chesbro, 1904	166
9	George Mullin, 1904	163
10	Ed Walsh, 1911	160

Assists per Game

First Base

1	Mark Grace, 1990	1.18
2	Bill Buckner, 1986	1.14
3	Bill Buckner, 1985	1.14
4	Jeff Bagwell, 1995	1.13
5	Bill Buckner, 1983	1.12
6	Jeff Bagwell, 1994	1.10
7	Sid Bream, 1986	1.08
8	Eric Karros, 1994	1.08
9	Cecil Fielder, 1994	1.06
10	Ferris Fain, 1951	1.05

Second Base

1	Joe Gerhardt, 1877	4.28
2	Frankie Frisch, 1927	4.19
3	Thorny Hawkes, 1879	4.13
4	Hughie Critz, 1933	4.07
5	Frank Parkinson, 1922	4.04
6	Joe Quest, 1879	3.99
7	Chick Fulmer, 1879	3.96
8	Ed Somerville, 1876	3.92
9	Ski Melillo, 1930	3.86
10	Glenn Hubbard, 1985	3.85

Shortstop

1	Germany Smith, 1885	4.21
2	Arthur Irwin, 1880	4.13
3	Art Fletcher, 1919	4.10
4	Bill Dahlen, 1895	4.09
5	Phil Tomney, 1889	4.05
6	Bobby Wallace, 1901	4.04
7	Jack Glasscock, 1887	4.04
8	Germany Smith, 1892	4.04
9	Henry Easterday, 1888	3.99
10	Dave Bancroft, 1920	3.99

Third Base

1	Jumbo Davis, 1888	2.96
2	Buddy Bell, 1981	2.93
3	George Bradley, 1880	2.89
4	Bill Hague, 1878	2.85
5	Billy Shindle, 1892	2.85
6	Bob Ferguson, 1877	2.77
7	Ned Williamson, 1879	2.76
8	Arlie Latham, 1884	2.75
9	Bill Bradley, 1900	2.75
10	Arlie Latham, 1891	2.74

Outfield

1	Orator Shaffer, 1879	0.69
2	Hardy Richardson, 1881	0.57
3	Hugh Nicol, 1884	0.55
4	King Kelly, 1878	0.51
5	John Cassidy, 1878	0.50
	King Kelly, 1880	0.50
7	King Kelly, 1883	0.46
8	Jake Evans, 1882	0.46
9	Orator Shaffer, 1878	0.44
10	Dick Higham, 1878	0.44
11	Orator Shaffer, 1883	0.43
12	King Kelly, 1881	0.43
13	Orator Shaffer, 1880	0.42
14	Jake Evans, 1879	0.42
15	Jack Manning, 1883	0.38
16	Jake Evans, 1881	0.37
17	Jimmy Wolf, 1883	0.37
18	Hugh Nicol, 1883	0.37
19	Jim Lillie, 1884	0.36
20	Buttercup Dickerson, 1883	0.36

Catcher

1	Bill Holbert, 1884	2.41
2	Tom Daly, 1887	2.31
3	Bill Holbert, 1882	2.14
4	Pop Snyder, 1884	2.08
5	Bill Holbert, 1883	2.03
6	Buck Ewing, 1881	2.02
7	Pat Moran, 1903	2.00
8	Charlie Reipschlager, 1885	1.98
9	Connie Mack, 1888	1.92
10	King Kelly, 1888	1.92

Pitcher

1	Harry Howell, 1905	4.68
2	Harry Howell, 1904	4.21
3	Will White, 1882	4.13
4	Ed Walsh, 1907	4.05
5	Willie Sudhoff, 1904	3.85
6	Red Donahue, 1902	3.71
7	George Mullin, 1904	3.62
8	Frank Owen, 1904	3.51
9	Carl Mays, 1918	3.49
10	Jack Katoll, 1902	3.44

Double Plays

First Base

1	Ferris Fain, 1949	194
2	Ferris Fain, 1950	192
3	Donn Clendenon, 1966	182
4	Andres Galarraga, 1997	176
5	Ron Jackson, 1979	175
6	Gil Hodges, 1951	171
7	Mickey Vernon, 1949	168
8	Ted Kluszewski, 1954	166
9	Rudy York, 1944	163
10	Donn Clendenon, 1965	161
	Rod Carew, 1977	161

Second Base

1	Bill Mazeroski, 1966	161
2	Jerry Priddy, 1950	150
3	Bill Mazeroski, 1961	144
4	Nellie Fox, 1957	141
	Dave Cash, 1974	141
6	Buddy Myer, 1935	138
	Bill Mazeroski, 1962	138
	Carlos Baerga, 1992	138
9	Jerry Coleman, 1950	137
	Jackie Robinson, 1951	137
	Red Schoendienst, 1954	137

Shortstop

1	Rick Burleson, 1980	147
2	Roy Smalley, 1979	144
3	Bobby Wine, 1970	137
4	Lou Boudreau, 1944	134
5	Spike Owen, 1986	133
6	Rafael Ramirez, 1982	130
7	Roy McMillan, 1954	129
8	Hod Ford, 1928	128
	Vern Stephens, 1949	128
	Gene Alley, 1966	128
	Neifi Perez, 1998	128

Third Base

1	Graig Nettles, 1971	54
2	Harlond Clift, 1937	50
3	Johnny Pesky, 1949	48
	Paul Molitor, 1982	48
5	Sammy Hale, 1927	46
	Clete Boyer, 1965	46
	Gary Gaetti, 1983	46
8	Eddie Yost, 1950	45
	Frank Malzone, 1961	45
	Darrell Evans, 1974	45
	Jeff Cirillo, 1998	45

Outfield

1	Happy Felsch, 1919	15
2	Jimmy Sheckard, 1899	14
3	Tom Brown, 1893	13
4	Tom Brown, 1886	12
	Tommy McCarthy, 1888	12
	Jimmy Bannon, 1894	12
	Mike Griffin, 1895	12
	Danny Green, 1899	12
	Cy Seymour, 1905	12
	Ginger Beaumont, 1907	12
	Ty Cobb, 1907	12
	Tris Speaker, 1909	12
	Jimmy Sheckard, 1911	12
	Tris Speaker, 1914	12
	Mel Ott, 1929	12
16	10 players tied	11

Catcher

1	Steve O'Neill, 1916	36
2	Frankie Hayes, 1945	29
3	Ray Schalk, 1916	25
	Yogi Berra, 1951	25
5	Jack Lapp, 1915	23
	Muddy Ruel, 1924	23
	Tom Haller, 1968	23
8	Steve O'Neill, 1914	22
	Bob O'Farrell, 1922	22
10	Gabby Hartnett, 1927	21
	Wes Westrum, 1950	21

Pitcher

1	Bob Lemon, 1953	15
2	Eddie Rommel, 1924	12
	Curt Davis, 1934	12
	Randy Jones, 1976	12
5	Scott Perry, 1919	11
	Tom Rogers, 1919	11
	Art Nehf, 1920	11
	Burleigh Grimes, 1925	11
	Gene Bearden, 1948	11
10	10 players tied	10

Fielding Runs

1	Glenn Hubbard, 1985	61.8
2	Danny Richardson, 1892	57.6
3	Bill Mazeroski, 1963	56.7
4	Rabbit Maranville, 1914	51.8
5	Freddie Maguire, 1928	50.5
6	Nap Lajoie, 1908	49.4
7	Danny Richardson, 1891	49.1
8	Frankie Frisch, 1927	48.6
9	Hughie Critz, 1933	46.5
10	George Davis, 1899	46.3
11	Nap Lajoie, 1907	45.9
12	Fred Pfeffer, 1884	45.5
13	Dick Bartell, 1936	44.8
14	Ozzie Guillen, 1988	42.6
15	Dave Shean, 1910	42.5
	Lee Tannehill, 1911	42.5
17	Cupid Childs, 1896	42.4
18	Graig Nettles, 1971	42.3
19	Joe Gerhardt, 1890	41.5
20	Bid McPhee, 1889	41.1
	Bill Mazeroski, 1962	41.1
	Ryne Sandberg, 1983	41.1
23	Harlond Clift, 1937	41.0
	Glenn Hubbard, 1986	41.0
25	Bill Mazeroski, 1966	40.8
	Ozzie Smith, 1980	40.8
27	Nap Lajoie, 1903	40.1
28	Germany Smith, 1885	39.9
29	Arlie Latham, 1884	39.5
30	Lee Tannehill, 1906	39.3
31	John Kerins, 1886	39.0
	Dave Bancroft, 1920	39.0
33	Bobby Wallace, 1899	38.8
	Cal Ripken, 1984	38.8
35	Bob Allen, 1890	38.6
36	Fred Pfeffer, 1888	38.3
37	Everett Scott, 1921	38.1
38	Bill Dahlen, 1908	37.5
	Dick Bartell, 1937	37.5
	Dal Maxvill, 1970	37.5
41	Bobby Knoop, 1964	37.2
42	Al Weis, 1966	36.9
43	Billy Shindle, 1888	36.8
44	Tim Wallach, 1985	36.7
45	Lou Bierbauer, 1889	36.6
46	Miller Huggins, 1905	36.2
	Clete Boyer, 1962	36.2
48	Tommy Leach, 1904	35.8
	Ivan DeJesus, 1977	35.8
50	Hughie Jennings, 1895	35.7
51	Bill Dahlen, 1895	35.6
	Harry Steinfeldt, 1900	35.6
53	Jack Glasscock, 1889	35.5
	Billy Shindle, 1892	35.5
55	Freddie Patek, 1973	35.3
56	Bobby Knoop, 1970	35.1
57	Jack Glasscock, 1887	35.0
58	Chet Lemon, 1977	34.9
59	Jimmy Bloodworth, 1941	34.7
60	George Davis, 1898	34.6
61	Bill Holbert, 1883	34.4
	Buddy Bell, 1982	34.4
63	Hughie Jennings, 1896	34.2
	Doc Lavan, 1916	34.2
65	Art Fletcher, 1915	34.1
66	Bid McPhee, 1893	34.0
	Shorty Fuller, 1895	34.0
68	Joe Cassidy, 1905	33.9
	Bill Mazeroski, 1964	33.9
70	Mark Belanger, 1978	33.8
71	Eddie Collins, 1910	33.7
	Gene Alley, 1970	33.7
73	Buck Weaver, 1913	33.6
74	Lave Cross, 1895	33.5
	John Farrell, 1902	33.5
	Donie Bush, 1914	33.5
	Leo Cardenas, 1969	33.5
78	Pop Smith, 1885	33.2
79	Hughie Jennings, 1894	33.1
	Ski Melillo, 1931	33.1
	Roy Smalley, 1979	33.1
	Ozzie Smith, 1982	33.1
83	Mickey Doolan, 1915	33.0
84	Tom Daly, 1887	32.9
	Red Schoendienst, 1952	32.9
	Red Schoendienst, 1954	32.9
87	Lave Cross, 1899	32.7
88	Don Zimmer, 1958	32.6
89	Dave Parker, 1977	32.5
90	Richie Ashburn, 1957	32.4
91	Richie Ashburn, 1951	32.3
	Marty Barrett, 1987	32.3
93	Herman Long, 1889	32.2
94	Germany Smith, 1887	32.0
	George McBride, 1908	32.0
	Wally Gerber, 1928	32.0
	Bucky Dent, 1979	32.0
	Neifi Perez, 1997	32.0
99	Spike Owen, 1986	31.9
100	3 players tied	31.8

Fielding Runs

First Base

1	Mark Grace, 1990	27
2	Bill Buckner, 1985	25
3	Chick Gandil, 1914	24
4	Sid Bream, 1986	24
5	Fred Tenney, 1905	22
6	Bill Buckner, 1983	22
7	Vic Power, 1960	21
8	Sid Bream, 1988	21
9	Jake Beckley, 1892	21
10	Jiggs Donahue, 1907	21

Second Base

1	Glenn Hubbard, 1985	62
2	Bill Mazeroski, 1963	57
3	Freddie Maguire, 1928	50
4	Frankie Frisch, 1927	49
5	Nap Lajoie, 1908	48
6	Hughie Critz, 1933	46
7	Fred Pfeffer, 1884	46
8	Danny Richardson, 1891	44
9	Nap Lajoie, 1907	44
10	Dave Shean, 1910	42

Shortstop

1	Rabbit Maranville, 1914	52
2	George Davis, 1899	46
3	Dick Bartell, 1936	45
4	Ozzie Guillen, 1988	43
5	Ozzie Smith, 1980	41
6	Germany Smith, 1885	40
7	Dave Bancroft, 1920	39
8	Cal Ripken, 1984	39
9	Bob Allen, 1890	39
10	Everett Scott, 1921	38

Third Base

1	Graig Nettles, 1971	42
2	Harlond Clift, 1937	41
3	Arlie Latham, 1884	40
4	Billy Shindle, 1892	38
5	Billy Shindle, 1888	37
6	Tim Wallach, 1985	37
7	Clete Boyer, 1962	36
8	Tommy Leach, 1904	36
9	Lee Tannehill, 1906	35
10	Buddy Bell, 1982	35

Outfield

1	Chet Lemon, 1977	35
2	Dave Parker, 1977	33
3	Richie Ashburn, 1957	32
4	Richie Ashburn, 1951	32
5	Andruw Jones, 1998	32
6	Jim Fogarty, 1887	32
7	Kirby Puckett, 1984	30
8	Tommy McCarthy, 1888	30
9	Max Carey, 1916	30
10	Eric Davis, 1987	28
11	Tris Speaker, 1914	28
12	Omar Moreno, 1980	27
13	Tom Brown, 1893	27
14	Garry Maddox, 1979	27
15	Carl Yastrzemski, 1964	27
16	Gerald Young, 1989	26
17	Ed Delahanty, 1893	26
18	Gary Ward, 1983	26
19	Richie Ashburn, 1953	26
20	Mike Griffin, 1891	26

Catcher

1	John Kerins, 1886	37
2	Bill Holbert, 1883	36
3	Tom Daly, 1887	32
4	Duke Farrell, 1894	30
5	John Kerins,1887	27
6	Pop Snyder, 1884	26
7	Wilbert Robinson, 1888	26
8	Connie Mack, 1892	25
9	Pop Snyder, 1879	25
10	George Mitterwald, 1970	24

Pitcher

1	Ed Walsh, 1907	22
2	Harry Howell, 1905	18
3	Ed Walsh, 1911	15
4	Ed Walsh, 1908	14
5	Will White, 1882	13
6	John Clarkson, 1889	11
7	Sadie McMahon, 1890	11
8	Tony Mullane, 1882	11
9	Carl Mays, 1926	10
10	Frank Smith, 1909	10

Fielding Wins

1	Glenn Hubbard, 1985	6.5
2	Bill Mazeroski, 1963	6.2
3	Nap Lajoie, 1908	5.6
4	Rabbit Maranville, 1914	5.6
5	Danny Richardson, 1892	5.3
6	Nap Lajoie, 1907	5.1
7	Freddie Maguire, 1928	4.9
8	Hughie Critz, 1933	4.9
9	Frankie Frisch, 1927	4.8
10	Graig Nettles, 1971	4.6
11	Dave Shean, 1910	4.5
12	Danny Richardson, 1891	4.4
13	Dick Bartell, 1936	4.4
14	Bill Dahlen, 1908	4.3
15	Lee Tannehill, 1906	4.3
16	Ozzie Smith, 1980	4.3
17	Ozzie Guillen, 1988	4.3
18	Ryne Sandberg, 1983	4.3
19	Bill Mazeroski, 1966	4.3
20	Glenn Hubbard, 1986	4.3
21	George Davis, 1899	4.2
22	Dave Bancroft, 1920	4.2
23	Lee Tannehill, 1911	4.2
24	Nap Lajoie, 1903	4.2
25	Bill Mazeroski, 1962	4.1
26	Fred Pfeffer, 1884	4.1
27	Al Weis, 1966	4.0
28	Bobby Knoop, 1964	3.9
29	Cal Ripken, 1984	3.9
30	Tim Wallach, 1985	3.9
31	Doc Lavan, 1916	3.8
32	Art Fletcher, 1915	3.8
33	Tommy Leach, 1904	3.8
34	Harlond Clift, 1937	3.8
35	Fred Pfeffer, 1888	3.8
36	Miller Huggins, 1905	3.8
37	Eddie Collins, 1910	3.7
38	Dal Maxvill, 1970	3.7
39	Joe Cassidy, 1905	3.7
40	Dick Bartell, 1937	3.7
41	Donie Bush, 1914	3.7
42	Joe Gerhardt, 1890	3.6
43	George McBride, 1908	3.6
44	Bobby Knoop, 1970	3.6
45	Clete Boyer, 1962	3.6
46	Ivan DeJesus, 1977	3.6
47	Heinie Wagner, 1908	3.6
48	Freddie Patek, 1973	3.6
49	Arlie Latham, 1884	3.6
50	Cupid Childs, 1896	3.6
51	Germany Smith, 1885	3.6
52	Bill Mazeroski, 1964	3.6
53	Buck Weaver, 1913	3.6
54	Everett Scott, 1921	3.6
55	Mickey Doolan, 1915	3.6
56	John Farrell, 1902	3.5
57	Joe Tinker, 1908	3.5
58	Bobby Wallace, 1899	3.5
59	Leo Cardenas, 1969	3.5
60	Mark Belanger, 1978	3.5
61	Ozzie Smith, 1982	3.5
62	Bid McPhee, 1889	3.5
63	Chet Lemon, 1977	3.5
64	Buddy Bell, 1982	3.4
65	Buck Herzog, 1915	3.4
66	Bob Allen, 1890	3.4
67	John Kerins, 1886	3.4
68	Max Carey, 1916	3.4
69	Red Schoendienst, 1952	3.4
70	Brooks Robinson, 1967	3.4
71	Billy Shindle, 1888	3.4
72	Nap Lajoie, 1906	3.4
73	Horace Clarke, 1968	3.4
74	Nap Lajoie, 1916	3.4
75	Jimmy Bloodworth, 1941	3.4
76	Gene Alley, 1970	3.4
77	Freddie Patek, 1972	3.4
78	Ron Santo, 1967	3.3
79	Johnny Evers, 1904	3.3
80	Buck Herzog, 1914	3.3
81	Richie Ashburn, 1957	3.3
82	Dave Parker, 1977	3.3
83	Don Zimmer, 1958	3.3
84	Billy Shindle, 1892	3.3
85	Red Schoendienst, 1954	3.3
86	Harry Steinfeldt, 1900	3.3
87	Bruno Betzel, 1916	3.2
88	Richie Ashburn, 1951	3.2
89	George Davis, 1898	3.2
90	Roy Smalley, 1979	3.2
91	Terry Pendleton, 1989	3.2
92	Ed Brinkman, 1970	3.2
93	Pep Young, 1938	3.2
94	Rabbit Maranville, 1919	3.2
95	Zoilo Versalles, 1962	3.2
96	Neifi Perez, 1997	3.2
97	Dave Bancroft, 1917	3.2
98	Buddy Bell, 1981	3.1
99	Johnny Evers, 1907	3.1
100	Andruw Jones, 1998	3.1

Total Player Rating

1	Babe Ruth, 1923	10.6
2	Babe Ruth, 1921	9.4
3	Babe Ruth, 1927	9.2
	Barry Bonds, 1992	9.2
5	Cal Ripken, 1984	9.1
6	Nap Lajoie, 1901	8.9
7	Barry Bonds, 1993	8.8
8	Mickey Mantle, 1956	8.7
9	Babe Ruth, 1920	8.6
	Rogers Hornsby, 1924	8.6
	Mickey Mantle, 1957	8.6
12	Nap Lajoie, 1910	8.5
	Ty Cobb, 1917	8.5
	Rogers Hornsby, 1922	8.5
	Babe Ruth, 1924	8.5
	Barry Bonds, 1996	8.5
17	Nap Lajoie, 1903	8.4
	Nap Lajoie, 1906	8.4
	Babe Ruth, 1926	8.4
20	Cal Ripken, 1991	8.3
	Craig Biggio, 1997	8.3
22	Rickey Henderson, 1990	8.2
23	Rogers Hornsby, 1920	8.1
	Lou Gehrig, 1927	8.1
	Ted Williams, 1942	8.1
26	Mickey Mantle, 1961	8.0
27	Ted Williams, 1941	7.9
	Ted Williams, 1946	7.9
29	Nap Lajoie, 1908	7.8
	George Sisler, 1920	7.8
	Lou Gehrig, 1934	7.8
	Lou Boudreau, 1944	7.8
33	Tris Speaker, 1912	7.7
	Rogers Hornsby, 1917	7.7
	Willie Mays, 1955	7.7
36	Tris Speaker, 1914	7.6
	Jeff Bagwell, 1994	7.6
	Mike Piazza, 1997	7.6
39	Ron Santo, 1966	7.5
40	Rickey Henderson, 1985	7.4
41	Honus Wagner, 1905	7.3
	Honus Wagner, 1906	7.3
	Tris Speaker, 1913	7.3
	Frankie Frisch, 1927	7.3
	Babe Ruth, 1930	7.3
	Babe Ruth, 1931	7.3
	Willie Mays, 1965	7.3
	Ron Santo, 1967	7.3
	Carl Yastrzemski, 1967	7.3
	Mike Schmidt, 1980	7.3
51	Rogers Hornsby, 1929	7.2
	Harlond Clift, 1937	7.2
	Snuffy Stirnweiss, 1945	7.2
	Ted Williams, 1947	7.2
	Willie Mays, 1958	7.2
	George Brett, 1985	7.2
	Barry Bonds, 1990	7.2
	Barry Bonds, 1998	7.2
	Mark McGwire, 1998	7.2
60	Nap Lajoie, 1904	7.1
	Ty Cobb, 1911	7.1
	Rogers Hornsby, 1921	7.1
	Snuffy Stirnweiss, 1944	7.1
	Ted Williams, 1957	7.1
	Norm Cash, 1961	7.1
	Joe Morgan, 1975	7.1
	Ken Caminiti, 1996	7.1
	Barry Bonds, 1997	7.1
69	Honus Wagner, 1908	7.0
	Eddie Collins, 1910	7.0
	Babe Ruth, 1928	7.0
	Mike Schmidt, 1981	7.0
	Robin Yount, 1982	7.0
	Kevin Mitchell, 1989	7.0
75	Fred Dunlap, 1884	6.9
	Joe Jackson, 1912	6.9
	Rogers Hornsby, 1927	6.9
	Lou Gehrig, 1930	6.9
	Lou Boudreau, 1948	6.9
	Rico Petrocelli, 1969	6.9
	Mike Schmidt, 1974	6.9
	Eric Davis, 1987	6.9
83	Joe Jackson, 1911	6.8
	Jackie Robinson, 1951	6.8
85	Cupid Childs, 1890	6.7
	Hughie Jennings, 1896	6.7
	Nap Lajoie, 1907	6.7
	Ty Cobb, 1910	6.7
	Joe Cronin, 1930	6.7
	Jimmie Foxx, 1933	6.7
	Lou Boudreau, 1943	6.7
	Ted Williams, 1949	6.7
	Willie Mays, 1954	6.7
	Frank Robinson, 1966	6.7
	Mike Schmidt, 1977	6.7
	Cal Ripken, 1983	6.7
	Barry Bonds, 1995	6.7
98	11 players tied	6.6

Total Player Rating (alpha.)

Jeff Bagwell, 1994	7.6
Craig Biggio, 1997	8.3
Barry Bonds, 1990	7.2
Barry Bonds, 1992	9.2
Barry Bonds, 1993	8.8
Barry Bonds, 1995	6.7
Barry Bonds, 1996	8.5
Barry Bonds, 1997	7.1
Barry Bonds, 1998	7.2
Lou Boudreau, 1943	6.7
Lou Boudreau, 1944	7.8
Lou Boudreau, 1948	6.9
George Brett, 1985	7.2
Ken Caminiti, 1996	7.1
Norm Cash, 1961	7.1
Cupid Childs, 1890	6.7
Harlond Clift, 1937	7.2
Ty Cobb, 1910	6.7
Ty Cobb, 1911	7.1
Ty Cobb, 1917	8.5
Eddie Collins, 1910	7.0
Joe Cronin, 1930	6.7
Eric Davis, 1987	6.9
Fred Dunlap, 1884	6.9
Jimmie Foxx, 1933	6.7
Frankie Frisch, 1927	7.3
Lou Gehrig, 1927	8.1
Lou Gehrig, 1930	6.9
Lou Gehrig, 1934	7.8
Rickey Henderson, 1985	7.4
Rickey Henderson, 1990	8.2
Rogers Hornsby, 1917	7.7
Rogers Hornsby, 1920	8.1
Rogers Hornsby, 1921	7.1
Rogers Hornsby, 1922	8.5
Rogers Hornsby, 1924	8.6
Rogers Hornsby, 1927	6.9
Rogers Hornsby, 1929	7.2
Joe Jackson, 1911	6.8
Joe Jackson, 1912	6.9
Hughie Jennings, 1896	6.7
Nap Lajoie, 1901	8.9
Nap Lajoie, 1903	8.4
Nap Lajoie, 1904	7.1
Nap Lajoie, 1906	8.4
Nap Lajoie, 1907	6.7
Nap Lajoie, 1908	7.8
Nap Lajoie, 1910	8.5
Mickey Mantle, 1956	8.7
Mickey Mantle, 1957	8.6
Mickey Mantle, 1961	8.0
Willie Mays, 1954	6.7
Willie Mays, 1955	7.7
Willie Mays, 1958	7.2
Willie Mays, 1965	7.3
Mark McGwire, 1998	7.2
Kevin Mitchell, 1989	7.0
Joe Morgan, 1975	7.1
Rico Petrocelli, 1969	6.9
Mike Piazza, 1997	7.6
Cal Ripken, 1983	6.7
Cal Ripken, 1984	9.1
Cal Ripken, 1991	8.3
Jackie Robinson, 1951	6.8
Frank Robinson, 1966	6.7
Babe Ruth, 1920	8.6
Babe Ruth, 1921	9.4
Babe Ruth, 1923	10.6
Babe Ruth, 1924	8.5
Babe Ruth, 1926	8.4
Babe Ruth, 1927	9.2
Babe Ruth, 1928	7.0
Babe Ruth, 1930	7.3
Babe Ruth, 1931	7.3
Ron Santo, 1966	7.5
Ron Santo, 1967	7.3
Mike Schmidt, 1974	6.9
Mike Schmidt, 1977	6.7
Mike Schmidt, 1980	7.3
Mike Schmidt, 1981	7.0
George Sisler, 1920	7.8
Tris Speaker, 1912	7.7
Tris Speaker, 1913	7.3
Tris Speaker, 1914	7.6
Snuffy Stirnweiss, 1944	7.1
Snuffy Stirnweiss, 1945	7.2
Honus Wagner, 1905	7.3
Honus Wagner, 1906	7.3
Honus Wagner, 1908	7.0
Ted Williams, 1941	7.9
Ted Williams, 1942	8.1
Ted Williams, 1946	7.9
Ted Williams, 1947	7.2
Ted Williams, 1949	6.7
Ted Williams, 1957	7.1
Carl Yastrzemski, 1967	7.3
Robin Yount, 1982	7.0

Total Player Rating (by era)

1876-1892
1	Fred Dunlap, 1884	6.9
2	Cupid Childs, 1890	6.7
3	Fred Pfeffer, 1884	6.1
	Dan Brouthers, 1892	6.1
5	Jack Glasscock, 1889	5.9
6	Billy Nash, 1888	4.9
	Harry Stovey, 1889	4.9
	Jack Glasscock, 1890	4.9
9	Hardy Richardson, 1886	4.8
	Denny Lyons, 1890	4.8
11	Pete Browning, 1882	4.7
	Ned Williamson, 1884	4.7
	Tip O'Neill, 1887	4.7
14	4 players tied	4.6

1893-1919
1	Nap Lajoie, 1901	8.9
2	Nap Lajoie, 1910	8.5
	Ty Cobb, 1917	8.5
4	Nap Lajoie, 1903	8.4
	Nap Lajoie, 1906	8.4
6	Nap Lajoie, 1908	7.8
7	Tris Speaker, 1912	7.7
	Rogers Hornsby, 1917	7.7
9	Tris Speaker, 1914	7.6
10	Honus Wagner, 1905	7.3
	Honus Wagner, 1906	7.3
	Tris Speaker, 1913	7.3
13	Nap Lajoie, 1904	7.1
	Ty Cobb, 1911	7.1
15	2 players tied	7.0

1920-1941
1	Babe Ruth, 1923	10.6
2	Babe Ruth, 1921	9.4
3	Babe Ruth, 1927	9.2
4	Babe Ruth, 1920	8.6
	Rogers Hornsby, 1924	8.6
6	Rogers Hornsby, 1922	8.5
	Babe Ruth, 1924	8.5
8	Babe Ruth, 1926	8.4
9	Rogers Hornsby, 1920	8.1
	Lou Gehrig, 1927	8.1
11	Ted Williams, 1941	7.9
12	George Sisler, 1920	7.8
	Lou Gehrig, 1934	7.8
14	3 players tied	7.3

1942-1960
1	Mickey Mantle, 1956	8.7
2	Mickey Mantle, 1957	8.6
3	Ted Williams, 1942	8.1
4	Ted Williams, 1946	7.9
5	Lou Boudreau, 1944	7.8
6	Willie Mays, 1955	7.7
7	Snuffy Stirnweiss, 1945	7.2
	Ted Williams, 1947	7.2
	Willie Mays, 1958	7.2
10	Snuffy Stirnweiss, 1944	7.1
	Ted Williams, 1957	7.1
12	Lou Boudreau, 1948	6.9
13	Jackie Robinson, 1951	6.8
14	3 players tied	6.7

1961-1976
1	Mickey Mantle, 1961	8.0
2	Ron Santo, 1966	7.5
3	Willie Mays, 1965	7.3
	Ron Santo, 1967	7.3
	Carl Yastrzemski, 1967	7.3
6	Norm Cash, 1961	7.1
	Joe Morgan, 1975	7.1
8	Rico Petrocelli, 1969	6.9
	Mike Schmidt, 1974	6.9
10	Frank Robinson, 1966	6.7
11	Willie Mays, 1963	6.6
	Carl Yastrzemski, 1968	6.6
	Reggie Jackson, 1969	6.6
14	3 players tied	6.5

1977-1998
1	Barry Bonds, 1992	9.2
2	Cal Ripken, 1984	9.1
3	Barry Bonds, 1993	8.8
4	Barry Bonds, 1996	8.5
5	Cal Ripken, 1991	8.3
	Craig Biggio, 1997	8.3
7	Rickey Henderson, 1990	8.2
8	Jeff Bagwell, 1994	7.6
	Mike Piazza, 1997	7.6
10	Rickey Henderson, 1985	7.4
11	Mike Schmidt, 1980	7.3
12	George Brett, 1985	7.2
	Barry Bonds, 1990	7.2
	Barry Bonds, 1998	7.2
	Mark McGwire, 1998	7.2

Wins

1	Charley Radbourn, 1884	59
2	John Clarkson, 1885	53
3	Guy Hecker, 1884	52
4	John Clarkson, 1889	49
5	Charley Radbourn, 1883	48
	Charlie Buffinton, 1884	48
7	Al Spalding, 1876	47
	John Ward, 1879	47
9	Pud Galvin, 1883	46
	Pud Galvin, 1884	46
	Matt Kilroy, 1887	46
12	George Bradley, 1876	45
	Jim McCormick, 1880	45
	Silver King, 1888	45
15	Mickey Welch, 1885	44
	Bill Hutchison, 1891	44
17	Billy Taylor, 1884	43
	Tommy Bond, 1879	43
	Will White, 1879	43
	Larry Corcoran, 1880	43
	Will White, 1883	43
22	Lady Baldwin, 1886	42
	Tim Keefe, 1886	42
	Bill Hutchison, 1890	42
25	Charlie Sweeney, 1884	41
	Tim Keefe, 1883	41
	Dave Foutz, 1886	41
	Ed Morris, 1886	41
	Jack Chesbro, 1904	41
30	Jim McCormick, 1884	40
	Tommy Bond, 1877	40
	Tommy Bond, 1878	40
	Will White, 1880	40
	Bill Sweeney, 1884	40
	Bob Caruthers, 1885	40
	Bob Caruthers, 1889	40
	Ed Walsh, 1908	40
38	John Ward, 1880	39
	Mickey Welch, 1884	39
	Ed Morris, 1885	39
41	Toad Ramsey, 1886	38
	John Clarkson, 1887	38
	Kid Gleason, 1890	38
44	Pud Galvin, 1879	37
	Jim Whitney, 1883	37
	Tim Keefe, 1884	37
	Jack Lynch, 1884	37
	Toad Ramsey, 1887	37
	Christy Mathewson, 1908	37
50	Jim McCormick, 1882	36
	Tony Mullane, 1884	36
	John Clarkson, 1886	36
	Sadie McMahon, 1890	36
	Bill Hutchison, 1892	36
	Cy Young, 1892	36
	Frank Killen, 1893	36
	Amos Rusie, 1894	36
	Walter Johnson, 1913	36
59	Jim Devlin, 1877	35
	Tony Mullane, 1883	35
	Larry Corcoran, 1884	35
	Tim Keefe, 1887	35
	Tim Keefe, 1888	35
	Ed Seward, 1888	35
	Silver King, 1889	35
	Sadie McMahon, 1891	35
	Kid Nichols, 1892	35
	Jack Stivetts, 1892	35
	Cy Young, 1895	35
	Joe McGinnity, 1904	35
71	Mickey Welch, 1880	34
	Larry Corcoran, 1883	34
	Ed Morris, 1884	34
	Will White, 1884	34
	Elmer Smith, 1887	34
	Scott Stratton, 1890	34
	George Haddock, 1891	34
	Kid Nichols, 1893	34
	Cy Young, 1893	34
	Joe Wood, 1912	34
81	Charley Radbourn, 1882	33
	Dave Foutz, 1885	33
	Henry Porter, 1885	33
	Mickey Welch, 1886	33
	Tony Mullane, 1886	33
	John Clarkson, 1888	33
	Mark Baldwin, 1890	33
	John Clarkson, 1891	33
	Amos Rusie, 1891	33
	Jack Stivetts, 1891	33
	Amos Rusie, 1893	33
	Jouett Meekin, 1894	33
	Cy Young, 1901	33
	Christy Mathewson, 1904	33
	Walter Johnson, 1912	33
	Pete Alexander, 1916	33
97	10 players tied	32

Wins (by era)

1876-1892
1	Charley Radbourn, 1884	59
2	John Clarkson, 1885	53
3	Guy Hecker, 1884	52
4	John Clarkson, 1889	49
5	Charley Radbourn, 1883	48
	Charlie Buffinton, 1884	48
7	Al Spalding, 1876	47
	John Ward, 1879	47
9	Pud Galvin, 1883	46
	Pud Galvin, 1884	46
	Matt Kilroy, 1887	46
12	George Bradley, 1876	45
	Jim McCormick, 1880	45
	Silver King, 1888	45
15	2 players tied	44

1893-1919
1	Jack Chesbro, 1904	41
2	Ed Walsh, 1908	40
3	Christy Mathewson, 1908	37
4	Frank Killen, 1893	36
	Amos Rusie, 1894	36
	Walter Johnson, 1913	36
7	Cy Young, 1895	35
	Joe McGinnity, 1904	35
9	Kid Nichols, 1893	34
	Cy Young, 1893	34
	Joe Wood, 1912	34
12	6 players tied	33

1920-1941
1	Jim Bagby, 1920	31
	Lefty Grove, 1931	31
3	Dizzy Dean, 1934	30
4	Dazzy Vance, 1924	28
	Lefty Grove, 1930	28
	Dizzy Dean, 1935	28
7	Pete Alexander, 1920	27
	Carl Mays, 1921	27
	Urban Shocker, 1921	27
	Eddie Rommel, 1922	27
	Dolf Luque, 1923	27
	George Uhle, 1926	27
	Bucky Walters, 1939	27
	Bob Feller, 1940	27
15	7 players tied	26

1942-1960
1	Hal Newhouser, 1944	29
2	Robin Roberts, 1952	28
3	Dizzy Trout, 1944	27
	Don Newcombe, 1956	27
5	Hal Newhouser, 1946	26
	Bob Feller, 1946	26
7	Hal Newhouser, 1945	25
	Dave Ferriss, 1946	25
	Mel Parnell, 1949	25
10	Johnny Sain, 1948	24
	Bobby Shantz, 1952	24
12	13 players tied	23

1961-1976
1	Denny McLain, 1968	31
2	Sandy Koufax, 1966	27
	Steve Carlton, 1972	27
4	Sandy Koufax, 1965	26
	Juan Marichal, 1968	26
6	Whitey Ford, 1961	25
	Don Drysdale, 1962	25
	Sandy Koufax, 1963	25
	Juan Marichal, 1963	25
	Juan Marichal, 1966	25
	Jim Kaat, 1966	25
	Tom Seaver, 1969	25
	Mickey Lolich, 1971	25
	Catfish Hunter, 1974	25
	Fergie Jenkins, 1974	25

1977-1998
1	Bob Welch, 1990	27
2	Ron Guidry, 1978	25
	Steve Stone, 1980	25
4	Steve Carlton, 1980	24
	La Marr Hoyt, 1983	24
	Dwight Gooden, 1985	24
	Roger Clemens, 1986	24
	Frank Viola, 1988	24
	John Smoltz, 1996	24
10	Steve Carlton, 1977	23
	Mike Flanagan, 1979	23
	Steve Carlton, 1982	23
	Orel Hershiser, 1988	23
	Danny Jackson, 1988	23
	Bret Saberhagen, 1989	23

Losses

1	John Coleman, 1883	48
2	Will White, 1880	42
3	Larry McKeon, 1884	41
4	George Bradley, 1879	40
	Jim McCormick, 1879	40
6	Henry Porter, 1888	37
	Kid Carsey, 1891	37
	George Cobb, 1892	37
9	Stump Wiedman, 1886	36
	Bill Hutchison, 1892	36
11	Jim Devlin, 1876	35
	Pud Galvin, 1880	35
	Fleury Sullivan, 1884	35
	Adonis Terry, 1884	35
	Hardie Henderson, 1885	35
	Red Donahue, 1897	35
17	Bobby Mathews, 1876	34
	Bob Barr, 1884	34
	Matt Kilroy, 1886	34
	Al Mays, 1887	34
	Mark Baldwin, 1889	34
	Amos Rusie, 1890	34
23	Hardie Henderson, 1883	33
	Dupee Shaw, 1884	33
	Harry McCormick, 1879	33
	Jim Whitney, 1881	33
	Lee Richmond, 1882	33
	Frank Mountain, 1883	33
	Jersey Bakely, 1888	33
30	Lee Richmond, 1880	32
	John Harkins, 1884	32
	Jim Whitney, 1885	32
	Jim Whitney, 1886	32
34	Sam Weaver, 1878	31
	Will White, 1879	31
	Charley Radbourn, 1886	31
	Dupee Shaw, 1886	31
	Billy Crowell, 1887	31
	Amos Rusie, 1892	31
40	Mickey Welch, 1880	30
	Jim McCormick, 1881	30
	Jim McCormick, 1882	30
	Jersey Bakely, 1884	30
	Jack Lynch, 1886	30
	Phenomenal Smith, 1887	30
	Toad Ramsey, 1888	30
	John Ewing, 1889	30
	Ed Beatin, 1890	30
	Ted Breitenstein, 1895	30
	Jim Hughey, 1899	30
51	Tommy Bond, 1880	29
	Doc Landis, 1882	29
	Pud Galvin, 1883	29
	John Healy, 1887	29
	Hank O'Day, 1887	29
	Bert Cunningham, 1888	29
	Red Ehret, 1889	29
	Silver King, 1891	29
	Bill Hart, 1896	29
	Jack Taylor, 1898	29
	Vic Willis, 1905	29
62	Jim McCormick, 1880	28
	Hank O'Day, 1884	28
	Hugh Daily, 1884	28
	Gus Weyhing, 1887	28
	Mark Baldwin, 1891	28
	Duke Esper, 1893	28
	Bill Hill, 1896	28
69	Pud Galvin, 1879	27
	Tim Keefe, 1881	27
	Tim Keefe, 1883	27
	Charlie Buffinton, 1885	27
	Al Mays, 1886	27
	Tony Mullane, 1886	27
	Toad Ramsey, 1886	27
	Toad Ramsey, 1887	27
	Park Swartzel, 1889	27
	Phil Knell, 1891	27
	Mark Baldwin, 1892	27
	Pink Hawley, 1894	27
	Chick Fraser, 1896	27
	Bill Hart, 1897	27
	Willie Sudhoff, 1898	27
	Bill Carrick, 1899	27
	Dummy Taylor, 1901	27
	George Bell, 1910	27
	Paul Derringer, 1933	27
88	20 players tied	26

Winning Percentage

1	Roy Face, 1959	.947
2	Johnny Allen, 1937	.938
3	Greg Maddux, 1995	.905
4	Randy Johnson, 1995	.900
5	Ron Guidry, 1978	.893
6	Freddie Fitzsimmons, 1940	.889
7	Lefty Grove, 1931	.886
8	Bob Stanley, 1978	.882
9	Preacher Roe, 1951	.880
10	Fred Goldsmith, 1880	.875
11	Joe Wood, 1912	.872
12	David Cone, 1988	.870
13	Orel Hershiser, 1985	.864
14	Bill Donovan, 1907	.862
	Whitey Ford, 1961	.862
16	Dwight Gooden, 1985	.857
	Roger Clemens, 1986	.857
18	Chief Bender, 1914	.850
	John Smoltz, 1998	.850
20	Lefty Grove, 1930	.848
21	Tom Hughes, 1916	.842
	Emil Yde, 1924	.842
	Schoolboy Rowe, 1940	.842
	Sandy Consuegra, 1954	.842
	Ralph Terry, 1961	.842
	Ron Perranoski, 1963	.842
27	Lefty Gomez, 1934	.839
28	Bill Hoffer, 1895	.838
	Denny McLain, 1968	.838
30	Walter Johnson, 1913	.837
31	Henry Boyle, 1884	.833
	King Cole, 1910	.833
	Spud Chandler, 1943	.833
	Hoyt Wilhelm, 1952	.833
	Sandy Koufax, 1963	.833
	Randy Johnson, 1997	.833
37	Charley Radbourn, 1884	.831
38	Ed Reulbach, 1906	.826
	Elmer Riddle, 1941	.826
	Greg Maddux, 1997	.826
41	Jim Hughes, 1899	.824
	Jack Chesbro, 1902	.824
	Dazzy Vance, 1924	.824
44	Chief Bender, 1910	.821
	Bob Purkey, 1962	.821
46	Sal Maglie, 1950	.818
	Bob Welch, 1990	.818
	Mark Portugal, 1993	.818
	David Wells, 1998	.818
50	Joe McGinnity, 1904	.814
51	Mordecai Brown, 1906	.813
	Russ Ford, 1910	.813
	Eddie Plank, 1912	.813
	Carl Hubbell, 1936	.813
55	Dizzy Dean, 1934	.811
56	Ed Reulbach, 1907	.810
	Doc Crandall, 1910	.810
	Johnny Allen, 1932	.810
	Ted Wilks, 1944	.810
	Phil Niekro, 1982	.810
	Jimmy Key, 1994	.810
62	Alvin Crowder, 1928	.808
	Bobo Newsom, 1940	.808
	Tiny Bonham, 1942	.808
	Larry Jansen, 1947	.808
	Dave McNally, 1971	.808
	Catfish Hunter, 1973	.808
68	Christy Mathewson, 1909	.806
	Howie Camnitz, 1909	.806
	Dave Ferriss, 1946	.806
	Juan Marichal, 1966	.806
72	Eddie Cicotte, 1919	.806
73	Mickey Welch, 1885	.800
	Ed Doheny, 1902	.800
	Sam Leever, 1905	.800
	Bert Humphries, 1913	.800
	Stan Coveleski, 1925	.800
	Firpo Marberry, 1931	.800
	Robin Roberts, 1952	.800
	Ed Lopat, 1953	.800
	Don Newcombe, 1955	.800
	Jim Palmer, 1969	.800
	John Candelaria, 1977	.800
	Larry Gura, 1978	.800
	Tommy Greene, 1993	.800
	Denny Neagle, 1997	.800
87	Al Spalding, 1876	.797
88	Don Newcombe, 1956	.794
89	Jocko Flynn, 1886	.793
	Ellis Kinder, 1949	.793
	Sal Maglie, 1951	.793
	Bret Saberhagen, 1989	.793
93	Dutch Leonard, 1914	.792
	Sandy Koufax, 1964	.792
	Wally Bunker, 1964	.792
	Shawn Estes, 1997	.792
97	8 players tied	.789

Winning Percentage (by era)

1876-1892

1	Fred Goldsmith, 1880	.875
2	Henry Boyle, 1884	.833
3	Charley Radbourn, 1884	.831
4	Mickey Welch, 1885	.800
5	Al Spalding, 1876	.797
6	Jocko Flynn, 1886	.793
7	Bob Caruthers, 1889	.784
8	Jack Manning, 1876	.783
9	Will White, 1882	.769
	Charlie Ferguson, 1886	.769
11	John Clarkson, 1885	.768
12	Lady Baldwin, 1886	.764
13	Bob Caruthers, 1887	.763
	Charlie Buffinton, 1891	.763
15	George Haddock, 1891	.756

1893-1919

1	Joe Wood, 1912	.872
2	Bill Donovan, 1907	.862
3	Chief Bender, 1914	.850
4	Tom Hughes, 1916	.842
5	Bill Hoffer, 1895	.838
6	Walter Johnson, 1913	.837
7	King Cole, 1910	.833
8	Ed Reulbach, 1906	.826
9	Jim Hughes, 1899	.824
	Jack Chesbro, 1902	.824
11	Chief Bender, 1910	.821
12	Joe McGinnity, 1904	.814
13	Mordecai Brown, 1906	.813
	Russ Ford, 1910	.813
	Eddie Plank, 1912	.813

1920-1941

1	Johnny Allen, 1937	.938
2	Freddie Fitzsimmons, 1940	.889
3	Lefty Grove, 1931	.886
4	Lefty Grove, 1930	.848
5	Emil Yde, 1924	.842
	Schoolboy Rowe, 1940	.842
7	Lefty Gomez, 1934	.839
8	Elmer Riddle, 1941	.826
9	Dazzy Vance, 1924	.824
10	Carl Hubbell, 1936	.813
11	Dizzy Dean, 1934	.811
12	Johnny Allen, 1932	.810
13	Alvin Crowder, 1928	.808
	Bobo Newsom, 1940	.808
15	2 players tied	.800

1942-1960

1	Roy Face, 1959	.947
2	Preacher Roe, 1951	.880
3	Sandy Consuegra, 1954	.842
4	Spud Chandler, 1943	.833
	Hoyt Wilhelm, 1952	.833
6	Sal Maglie, 1950	.818
7	Ted Wilks, 1944	.810
8	Tiny Bonham, 1942	.808
	Larry Jansen, 1947	.808
10	Dave Ferriss, 1946	.806
11	Robin Roberts, 1952	.800
	Ed Lopat, 1953	.800
	Don Newcombe, 1955	.800
14	Don Newcombe, 1956	.794
15	2 players tied	.793

1961-1976

1	Whitey Ford, 1961	.862
2	Ralph Terry, 1961	.842
	Ron Perranoski, 1963	.842
4	Denny McLain, 1968	.838
5	Sandy Koufax, 1963	.833
6	Bob Purkey, 1962	.821
7	Dave McNally, 1971	.808
	Catfish Hunter, 1973	.808
9	Juan Marichal, 1966	.806
10	Jim Palmer, 1969	.800
11	Sandy Koufax, 1964	.792
	Wally Bunker, 1964	.792
13	Don Gullett, 1975	.789
14	Johnny Podres, 1961	.783
15	Tom Seaver, 1969	.781

1977-1998

1	Greg Maddux, 1995	.905
2	Randy Johnson, 1995	.900
3	Ron Guidry, 1978	.893
4	Bob Stanley, 1978	.882
5	David Cone, 1988	.870
6	Orel Hershiser, 1985	.864
7	Dwight Gooden, 1985	.857
	Roger Clemens, 1986	.857
9	John Smoltz, 1998	.850
10	Randy Johnson, 1997	.833
11	Greg Maddux, 1997	.826
12	Bob Welch, 1990	.818
	Mark Portugal, 1993	.818
	David Wells, 1998	.818
15	2 players tied	.810

Games

1	Mike Marshall, 1974	106
2	Kent Tekulve, 1979	94
3	Mike Marshall, 1973	92
4	Kent Tekulve, 1978	91
5	Wayne Granger, 1969	90
	Mike Marshall, 1979	90
	Kent Tekulve, 1987	90
8	Mark Eichhorn, 1987	89
	Julian Tavarez, 1997	89
10	Wilbur Wood, 1968	88
	Mike Myers, 1997	88
	Sean Runyan, 1998	88
13	Rob Murphy, 1987	87
14	Kent Tekulve, 1982	85
	Frank Williams, 1987	85
	Mitch Williams, 1987	85
17	Ted Abernathy, 1965	84
	Enrique Romo, 1979	84
	Dick Tidrow, 1980	84
	Dan Quisenberry, 1985	84
	Stan Belinda, 1997	84
22	Ken Sanders, 1971	83
	Craig Lefferts, 1986	83
	Eddie Guardado, 1996	83
	Mike Myers, 1996	83
26	Eddie Fisher, 1965	82
	Bill Campbell, 1983	82
	Juan Agosto, 1990	82
	Paul Quantrill, 1998	82
30	John Wyatt, 1964	81
	Dale Murray, 1976	81
	Jeff Robinson, 1987	81
	Duane Ward, 1991	81
	Joe Boever, 1992	81
	Kenny Rogers, 1992	81
	Mike Jackson, 1993	81
	Brad Clontz, 1996	81
	Mike Stanton, 1996	81
	Rod Beck, 1998	81
	Greg Swindell, 1998	81
41	Mudcat Grant, 1970	80
	Pedro Borbon, 1973	80
	Willie Hernandez, 1984	80
	Mitch Williams, 1986	80
	Doug Jones, 1992	80
	Greg Harris, 1993	80
47	Dick Radatz, 1964	79
	Duane Ward, 1992	79
	Bob Patterson, 1996	79
	Eddie Guardado, 1998	79
51	Hal Woodeshick, 1965	78
	Ted Abernathy, 1968	78
	Bill Campbell, 1976	78
	Rollie Fingers, 1977	78
	Tom Hume, 1980	78
	Kent Tekulve, 1980	78
	Greg Minton, 1982	78
	Ed Vande Berg, 1982	78
	Ted Power, 1984	78
	Tim Burke, 1985	78
	Lance McCullers, 1987	78
	Mark Dewey, 1996	78
	Jeff Shaw, 1996	78
	Jeff Shaw, 1997	78
	Buddy Groom, 1997	78
	Steve Kline, 1998	78
	Chuck McElroy, 1998	78
	Robb Nen, 1998	78
	Dan Plesac, 1998	78
70	Dick Tidrow, 1979	77
	Bob Locker, 1967	77
	Wilbur Wood, 1970	77
	Charlie Hough, 1976	77
	Butch Metzger, 1976	77
	Rick Camp, 1980	77
	Gary Lavelle, 1984	77
	Mark Davis, 1985	77
	Craig Lefferts, 1987	77
	Bobby Thigpen, 1990	77
	Barry Jones, 1991	77
	Xavier Hernandez, 1992	77
	Mike Perez, 1992	77
	Mark Wohlers, 1996	77
	Mel Rojas, 1997	77
	Jeff Nelson, 1997	77
	Paul Quantrill, 1997	77
	Anthony Telford, 1998	77
	Mike Trombley, 1998	77
89	25 players tied	76

Games (by era)

1876-1892

1	Will White, 1879	76
	Pud Galvin, 1883	76
	Charley Radbourn, 1883	76
4	Charley Radbourn, 1884	75
	Guy Hecker, 1884	75
	Bill Hutchison, 1892	75
7	Jim McCormick, 1880	74
	Lee Richmond, 1880	74
9	John Clarkson, 1889	73
10	Pud Galvin, 1884	72
11	Bill Hutchison, 1890	71
12	John Ward, 1879	70
	John Ward, 1880	70
	John Clarkson, 1885	70
15	Matt Kilroy, 1887	69

1893-1919

1	Ed Walsh, 1908	66
2	Ed Walsh, 1912	62
3	Dave Davenport, 1916	59
4	Amos Rusie, 1893	56
	Ted Breitenstein, 1894	56
	Pink Hawley, 1895	56
	Ed Walsh, 1907	56
	Christy Mathewson, 1908	56
	Ed Walsh, 1911	56
	Reb Russell, 1916	56
11	Frank Killen, 1893	55
	Joe McGinnity, 1903	55
	Jack Chesbro, 1904	55
	Dave Davenport, 1915	55
15	3 players tied	54

1920-1941

1	Firpo Marberry, 1926	64
2	Clint Brown, 1939	61
3	Garland Braxton, 1927	58
	Russ Van Atta, 1935	58
5	Eddie Rommel, 1923	56
	Firpo Marberry, 1927	56
	Hugh Mulcahy, 1937	56
8	Firpo Marberry, 1925	55
	Bump Hadley, 1931	55
	Jim Walkup, 1935	55
11	George Uhle, 1923	54
	Firpo Marberry, 1932	54
	Jack Russell, 1934	54
	Chubby Dean, 1939	54
	Clyde Shoun, 1940	54

1942-1960

1	Jim Konstanty, 1950	74
2	Hoyt Wilhelm, 1952	71
3	Ace Adams, 1943	70
	Mike Fornieles, 1960	70
5	Ellis Kinder, 1953	69
	Don Elston, 1958	69
7	Hoyt Wilhelm, 1953	68
	Roy Face, 1956	68
	Roy Face, 1960	68
10	Andy Karl, 1945	67
	Turk Lown, 1957	67
	Gerry Staley, 1959	67
13	6 players tied	65

1961-1976

1	Mike Marshall, 1974	106
2	Mike Marshall, 1973	92
3	Wayne Granger, 1969	90
4	Wilbur Wood, 1968	88
5	Ted Abernathy, 1965	84
6	Ken Sanders, 1971	83
7	Eddie Fisher, 1965	82
8	John Wyatt, 1964	81
	Dale Murray, 1976	81
10	Mudcat Grant, 1970	80
	Pedro Borbon, 1973	80
12	Dick Radatz, 1964	79
13	Hal Woodeshick, 1965	78
	Ted Abernathy, 1968	78
	Bill Campbell, 1976	78

1977-1998

1	Kent Tekulve, 1979	94
2	Kent Tekulve, 1978	91
3	Mike Marshall, 1979	90
	Kent Tekulve, 1987	90
5	Mark Eichhorn, 1987	89
	Julian Tavarez, 1997	89
7	Mike Myers, 1997	88
	Sean Runyan, 1998	88
9	Rob Murphy, 1987	87
10	Kent Tekulve, 1982	85
	Frank Williams, 1987	85
	Mitch Williams, 1987	85
13	4 players tied	84

Games Started

1	Will White, 1879	75
	Pud Galvin, 1883	75
3	Jim McCormick, 1880	74
4	Charley Radbourn, 1884	73
	Guy Hecker, 1884	73
6	Pud Galvin, 1884	72
	John Clarkson, 1889	72
8	John Clarkson, 1885	70
	Bill Hutchison, 1892	70
10	Matt Kilroy, 1887	69
11	Jim Devlin, 1876	68
	Charley Radbourn, 1883	68
	Tim Keefe, 1883	68
	Matt Kilroy, 1886	68
15	John Ward, 1880	67
	Jim McCormick, 1882	67
	Charlie Buffinton, 1884	67
	Toad Ramsey, 1886	67
19	Dupee Shaw, 1884	66
	Pud Galvin, 1879	66
	Lee Richmond, 1880	66
	Bill Hutchison, 1890	66
23	Jim McCormick, 1884	65
	Mickey Welch, 1884	65
	Tony Mullane, 1884	65
	Silver King, 1888	65
27	George Bradley, 1876	64
	Tommy Bond, 1879	64
	Mickey Welch, 1880	64
	Will White, 1883	64
	Tim Keefe, 1886	64
	Toad Ramsey, 1887	64
33	Jim Whitney, 1881	63
	Ed Morris, 1885	63
	Ed Morris, 1886	63
36	Will White, 1880	62
	Amos Rusie, 1890	62
	Amos Rusie, 1892	62
39	Jim Devlin, 1877	61
	John Coleman, 1883	61
	Hardie Henderson, 1885	61
	Jersey Bakely, 1888	61
43	Al Spalding, 1876	60
	Jim McCormick, 1879	60
	John Ward, 1879	60
	Larry Corcoran, 1880	60
	Larry McKeon, 1884	60
	Bill Sweeney, 1884	60
49	Billy Taylor, 1884	59
	Tommy Bond, 1878	59
	Frank Mountain, 1883	59
	Larry Corcoran, 1884	59
	Mickey Welch, 1886	59
	John Clarkson, 1887	59
	Mark Baldwin, 1889	59
56	Tommy Bond, 1877	58
	Terry Larkin, 1879	58
	Jim McCormick, 1881	58
	Tim Keefe, 1884	58
	Hugh Daily, 1884	58
	Charley Radbourn, 1886	58
	Bill Hutchison, 1891	58
	Sadie McMahon, 1891	58
64	Tommy Bond, 1880	57
	Dave Foutz, 1886	57
	Ed Seward, 1888	57
	Sadie McMahon, 1890	57
	Amos Rusie, 1891	57
69	Charlie Sweeney, 1884	56
	Bobby Mathews, 1876	56
	Terry Larkin, 1877	56
	Terry Larkin, 1878	56
	Jim Whitney, 1883	56
	Lady Baldwin, 1886	56
	Tony Mullane, 1886	56
	Tim Keefe, 1887	56
	Matt Kilroy, 1889	56
	Mark Baldwin, 1890	56
	Silver King, 1890	56
	Jack Stivetts, 1891	56
81	George Derby, 1881	55
	Tony Mullane, 1882	55
	Adonis Terry, 1884	55
	Mickey Welch, 1885	55
	John Clarkson, 1886	55
	Phenomenal Smith, 1887	55
	Gus Weyhing, 1887	55
	Ed Morris, 1888	55
	Kid Gleason, 1890	55
90	George Bradley, 1879	54
	Harry McCormick, 1879	54
	Pud Galvin, 1880	54
	Will White, 1882	54
	Henry Porter, 1885	54
	John Clarkson, 1888	54
	Henry Porter, 1888	54
	Ed Beatin, 1890	54
	Bob Barr, 1890	54
99	9 players tied	53

Games Started (by era)

1876-1892

1	Will White, 1879	75
	Pud Galvin, 1883	75
3	Jim McCormick, 1880	74
4	Charley Radbourn, 1884	73
	Guy Hecker, 1884	73
6	Pud Galvin, 1884	72
	John Clarkson, 1889	72
8	John Clarkson, 1885	70
	Bill Hutchison, 1892	70
10	Matt Kilroy, 1887	69
11	Jim Devlin, 1876	68
	Charley Radbourn, 1883	68
	Tim Keefe, 1883	68
	Matt Kilroy, 1886	68
15	4 players tied	67

1893-1919

1	Amos Rusie, 1893	52
2	Jack Chesbro, 1904	51
3	Ted Breitenstein, 1894	50
	Amos Rusie, 1894	50
	Ted Breitenstein, 1895	50
	Pink Hawley, 1895	50
	Frank Killen, 1896	50
8	Ed Walsh, 1908	49
9	Frank Killen, 1893	48
	Jouett Meekin, 1894	48
	Joe McGinnity, 1903	48
12	Cy Young, 1894	47
	Amos Rusie, 1895	47
	Jack Taylor, 1898	47
15	8 players tied	46

1920-1941

1	George Uhle, 1923	44
2	Pete Alexander, 1920	40
	Stan Coveleski, 1921	40
	George Uhle, 1922	40
	George Caster, 1938	40
	Bobo Newsom, 1938	40
	Bob Feller, 1941	40
8	Red Faber, 1920	39
	Red Faber, 1921	39
	Hooks Dauss, 1923	39
	Howard Ehmke, 1923	39
	George Earnshaw, 1930	39
	Alvin Crowder, 1932	39
	Kirby Higbe, 1941	39
15	23 players tied	38

1942-1960

1	Bob Feller, 1946	42
	Bob Friend, 1956	42
3	Bill Voiselle, 1944	41
	Robin Roberts, 1953	41
5	Dizzy Trout, 1944	40
6	Johnny Sain, 1948	39
	Robin Roberts, 1950	39
	Warren Spahn, 1950	39
	Vern Bickford, 1950	39
	Robin Roberts, 1951	39
	Ron Kline, 1956	39
	Lew Burdette, 1959	39
13	10 players tied	38

1961-1976

1	Wilbur Wood, 1972	49
2	Wilbur Wood, 1973	48
3	Mickey Lolich, 1971	45
4	Wilbur Wood, 1975	43
5	Don Drysdale, 1963	42
	Jack Sanford, 1963	42
	Don Drysdale, 1965	42
	Jim Kaat, 1965	42
	Fergie Jenkins, 1969	42
	Wilbur Wood, 1971	42
	Stan Bahnsen, 1973	42
	Mickey Lolich, 1973	42
	Wilbur Wood, 1974	42
14	22 players tied	41

1977-1998

1	Phil Niekro, 1979	44
2	Phil Niekro, 1977	43
3	Phil Niekro, 1978	42
4	Steve Rogers, 1977	40
	Mike Flanagan, 1978	40
	Dennis Leonard, 1978	40
	Jim Clancy, 1982	40
	Charlie Hough, 1987	40
9	9 players tied	39

Complete Games

1	Will White, 1879	75
2	Charley Radbourn, 1884	73
3	Jim McCormick, 1880	72
	Pud Galvin, 1883	72
	Guy Hecker, 1884	72
6	Pud Galvin, 1884	71
7	Tim Keefe, 1883	68
	John Clarkson, 1885	68
	John Clarkson, 1889	68
10	Bill Hutchison, 1892	67
11	Jim Devlin, 1876	66
	Charley Radbourn, 1883	66
	Matt Kilroy, 1886	66
	Toad Ramsey, 1886	66
	Matt Kilroy, 1887	66
16	Pud Galvin, 1879	65
	Jim McCormick, 1882	65
	Bill Hutchison, 1890	65
19	Mickey Welch, 1880	64
	Will White, 1883	64
	Tony Mullane, 1884	64
	Silver King, 1888	64
23	Jim McCormick, 1884	63
	George Bradley, 1876	63
	Charlie Buffinton, 1884	63
	Ed Morris, 1885	63
	Ed Morris, 1886	63
28	Mickey Welch, 1884	62
	Tim Keefe, 1886	62
30	Jim Devlin, 1877	61
	Toad Ramsey, 1887	61
32	Dupee Shaw, 1884	60
	Jersey Bakely, 1888	60
34	Billy Taylor, 1884	59
	Tommy Bond, 1879	59
	Jim McCormick, 1879	59
	John Ward, 1880	59
	John Coleman, 1883	59
	Larry McKeon, 1884	59
	Hardie Henderson, 1885	59
	Amos Rusie, 1892	59
42	Tommy Bond, 1877	58
	John Ward, 1879	58
	Will White, 1880	58
	Bill Sweeney, 1884	58
46	Tommy Bond, 1878	57
	Terry Larkin, 1879	57
	Larry Corcoran, 1880	57
	Lee Richmond, 1880	57
	Jim McCormick, 1881	57
	Jim Whitney, 1881	57
	Frank Mountain, 1883	57
	Larry Corcoran, 1884	57
	Charley Radbourn, 1886	57
	Ed Seward, 1888	57
56	Terry Larkin, 1878	56
	Tim Keefe, 1884	56
	Hugh Daily, 1884	56
	Mickey Welch, 1886	56
	John Clarkson, 1887	56
	Amos Rusie, 1890	56
	Bill Hutchison, 1891	56
63	Bobby Mathews, 1876	55
	Terry Larkin, 1877	55
	George Derby, 1881	55
	Mickey Welch, 1885	55
	Lady Baldwin, 1886	55
	Dave Foutz, 1886	55
	Tony Mullane, 1886	55
	Matt Kilroy, 1889	55
	Sadie McMahon, 1890	55
72	Jim Whitney, 1883	54
	Adonis Terry, 1884	54
	Tim Keefe, 1887	54
	Phenomenal Smith, 1887	54
	Ed Morris, 1888	54
	Mark Baldwin, 1889	54
	Kid Gleason, 1890	54
79	Charlie Sweeney, 1884	53
	Al Spalding, 1876	53
	George Bradley, 1879	53
	Jack Lynch, 1884	53
	Bob Caruthers, 1885	53
	Henry Porter, 1885	53
	Gus Weyhing, 1887	53
	John Clarkson, 1888	53
	Henry Porter, 1888	53
	Ed Beatin, 1890	53
	Mark Baldwin, 1890	53
	Sadie McMahon, 1891	53
91	Will White, 1879	52
	Will White, 1882	52
	Will White, 1884	52
	Ed Seward, 1887	52
	Bob Barr, 1890	52
	Amos Rusie, 1891	52
97	7 players tied	51

Complete Games (by era)

1876-1892

1	Will White, 1879	75
2	Charley Radbourn, 1884	73
3	Jim McCormick, 1880	72
	Pud Galvin, 1883	72
	Guy Hecker, 1884	72
6	Pud Galvin, 1884	71
7	Tim Keefe, 1883	68
	John Clarkson, 1885	68
	John Clarkson, 1889	68
10	Bill Hutchison, 1892	67
11	Jim Devlin, 1876	66
	Charley Radbourn, 1883	66
	Matt Kilroy, 1886	66
	Toad Ramsey, 1886	66
	Matt Kilroy, 1887	66

1893-1919

1	Amos Rusie, 1893	50
2	Jack Chesbro, 1904	48
3	Ted Breitenstein, 1894	46
	Ted Breitenstein, 1895	46
5	Amos Rusie, 1894	45
	Vic Willis, 1902	45
7	Cy Young, 1894	44
	Pink Hawley, 1895	44
	Frank Killen, 1896	44
	Joe McGinnity, 1903	44
11	Kid Nichols, 1893	43
12	7 players tied	42

1920-1941

1	Pete Alexander, 1920	33
	Burleigh Grimes, 1923	33
3	Red Faber, 1921	32
	George Uhle, 1926	32
5	Red Faber, 1922	31
	Wes Ferrell, 1935	31
	Bobo Newsom, 1938	31
	Bucky Walters, 1939	31
	Bob Feller, 1940	31
10	8 players tied	30

1942-1960

1	Bob Feller, 1946	36
2	Dizzy Trout, 1944	33
	Robin Roberts, 1953	33
4	Robin Roberts, 1952	30
5	Hal Newhouser, 1945	29
	Hal Newhouser, 1946	29
	Robin Roberts, 1954	29
8	Jim Tobin, 1942	28
	Jim Tobin, 1944	28
	Johnny Sain, 1948	28
	Bob Lemon, 1952	28
12	Bucky Walters, 1944	27
	Mel Parnell, 1949	27
	Vern Bickford, 1950	27
	Bobby Shantz, 1952	27

1961-1976

1	Juan Marichal, 1968	30
	Fergie Jenkins, 1971	30
	Steve Carlton, 1972	30
	Catfish Hunter, 1975	30
5	Mickey Lolich, 1971	29
	Gaylord Perry, 1972	29
	Gaylord Perry, 1973	29
	Fergie Jenkins, 1974	29
9	Bob Gibson, 1968	28
	Denny McLain, 1968	28
	Bob Gibson, 1969	28
	Gaylord Perry, 1974	28
13	4 players tied	27

1977-1998

1	Rick Langford, 1980	28
2	Mike Norris, 1980	24
	Bert Blyleven, 1985	24
4	Mike Caldwell, 1978	23
	Phil Niekro, 1979	23
6	Jim Palmer, 1977	22
	Nolan Ryan, 1977	22
	Phil Niekro, 1978	22
9	Wayne Garland, 1977	21
	Dennis Leonard, 1977	21
	Ron Guidry, 1983	21
12	6 players tied	20

Shutouts

1	George Bradley, 1876	16
	Pete Alexander, 1916	16
3	Jack Coombs, 1910	13
	Bob Gibson, 1968	13
5	Pud Galvin, 1884	12
	Ed Morris, 1886	12
	Pete Alexander, 1915	12
8	Tommy Bond, 1879	11
	Charley Radbourn, 1884	11
	Dave Foutz, 1886	11
	Christy Mathewson, 1908	11
	Ed Walsh, 1908	11
	Walter Johnson, 1913	11
	Sandy Koufax, 1963	11
	Dean Chance, 1964	11
16	Jim McCormick, 1884	10
	John Clarkson, 1885	10
	Cy Young, 1904	10
	Ed Walsh, 1906	10
	Joe Wood, 1912	10
	Dave Davenport, 1915	10
	Carl Hubbell, 1933	10
	Mort Cooper, 1942	10
	Bob Feller, 1946	10
	Bob Lemon, 1948	10
	Juan Marichal, 1965	10
	Jim Palmer, 1975	10
	John Tudor, 1985	10
29	Tommy Bond, 1878	9
	George Derby, 1881	9
	Cy Young, 1892	9
	Joe McGinnity, 1904	9
	Mordecai Brown, 1906	9
	Addie Joss, 1906	9
	Mordecai Brown, 1908	9
	Addie Joss, 1908	9
	Orval Overall, 1909	9
	Pete Alexander, 1913	9
	Walter Johnson, 1914	9
	Cy Falkenberg, 1914	9
	Babe Ruth, 1916	9
	Stan Coveleski, 1917	9
	Pete Alexander, 1919	9
	Bill Lee, 1938	9
	Bob Porterfield, 1953	9
	Luis Tiant, 1968	9
	Denny McLain, 1969	9
	Don Sutton, 1972	9
	Nolan Ryan, 1972	9
	Bert Blyleven, 1973	9
	Ron Guidry, 1978	9
52	Al Spalding, 1876	8
	John Ward, 1880	8
	Will White, 1882	8
	Charlie Buffinton, 1884	8
	Tim Keefe, 1888	8
	Ben Sanders, 1888	8
	John Clarkson, 1889	8
	Christy Mathewson, 1902	8
	Jack Chesbro, 1902	8
	Rube Waddell, 1904	8
	Christy Mathewson, 1905	8
	Ed Killian, 1905	8
	Lefty Leifield, 1906	8
	Rube Waddell, 1906	8
	Orval Overall, 1907	8
	Christy Mathewson, 1907	8
	Eddie Plank, 1907	8
	Mordecai Brown, 1909	8
	Christy Mathewson, 1909	8
	Ed Walsh, 1909	8
	Russ Ford, 1910	8
	Walter Johnson, 1910	8
	Reb Russell, 1913	8
	Jeff Tesreau, 1914	8
	Al Mamaux, 1915	8
	Jeff Tesreau, 1915	8
	Joe Bush, 1916	8
	Pete Alexander, 1917	8
	Jim Bagby, 1917	8
	Walter Johnson, 1917	8
	Hippo Vaughn, 1918	8
	Walter Johnson, 1918	8
	Carl Mays, 1918	8
	Babe Adams, 1920	8
	Hal Newhouser, 1945	8
	Steve Barber, 1961	8
	Camilo Pascual, 1961	8
	Whitey Ford, 1964	8
	Sandy Koufax, 1965	8
	Don Drysdale, 1968	8
	Juan Marichal, 1969	8
	Vida Blue, 1971	8
	Steve Carlton, 1972	8
	Wilbur Wood, 1972	8
	Fernando Valenzuela, 1981	8
	Dwight Gooden, 1985	8
	Orel Hershiser, 1988	8
	Roger Clemens, 1988	8
	Tim Belcher, 1989	8

Saves

1	Bobby Thigpen, 1990	57
2	Randy Myers, 1993	53
	Trevor Hoffman, 1998	53
4	Dennis Eckersley, 1992	51
	Rod Beck, 1998	51
6	Dennis Eckersley, 1990	48
	Rod Beck, 1993	48
	Jeff Shaw, 1998	48
9	Lee Smith, 1991	47
10	Lee Smith, 1993	46
	Dave Righetti, 1986	46
	Bryan Harvey, 1991	46
	Jose Mesa, 1995	46
	Tom Gordon, 1998	46
15	Dan Quisenberry, 1983	45
	Bruce Sutter, 1984	45
	Dennis Eckersley, 1988	45
	Bryan Harvey, 1993	45
	Jeff Montgomery, 1993	45
	Duane Ward, 1993	45
	Randy Myers, 1997	45
22	Dan Quisenberry, 1984	44
	Mark Davis, 1989	44
	Jeff Brantley, 1996	44
	Todd Worrell, 1996	44
26	Doug Jones, 1990	43
	Dennis Eckersley, 1991	43
	Lee Smith, 1992	43
	John Wetteland, 1993	43
	Mitch Williams, 1993	43
	John Wetteland, 1996	43
	Mariano Rivera, 1997	43
33	Jeff Reardon, 1988	42
	Rick Aguilera, 1991	42
	Trevor Hoffman, 1996	42
	Jeff Shaw, 1997	42
	Troy Percival, 1998	42
	John Wetteland, 1998	42
39	Jeff Reardon, 1985	41
	Rick Aguilera, 1992	41
41	Steve Bedrosian, 1987	40
	Jeff Reardon, 1991	40
	Tom Henke, 1993	40
	Robb Nen, 1998	40
	Mike Jackson, 1998	40
46	John Franco, 1988	39
	Jeff Montgomery, 1992	39
	Mark Wohlers, 1996	39
	Jose Mesa, 1996	39
50	John Hiller, 1973	38
	Jeff Russell, 1989	38
	Randy Myers, 1992	38
	Roberto Hernandez, 1993	38
	Randy Myers, 1995	38
	Roberto Hernandez, 1996	38
	John Franco, 1998	38
	Rick Aguilera, 1998	38
58	Clay Carroll, 1972	37
	Rollie Fingers, 1978	37
	Bruce Sutter, 1979	37
	Dan Quisenberry, 1985	37
	Doug Jones, 1988	37
	Gregg Olson, 1990	37
	John Wetteland, 1992	37
	Lee Smith, 1995	37
	Rod Beck, 1997	37
	Trevor Hoffman, 1997	37
68	Bruce Sutter, 1982	36
	Bill Caudill, 1984	36
	Todd Worrell, 1986	36
	Lee Smith, 1987	36
	Mitch Williams, 1989	36
	Dave Righetti, 1990	36
	Doug Jones, 1992	36
	Gregg Olson, 1992	36
	Dennis Eckersley, 1993	36
	Tom Henke, 1995	36
	Mel Rojas, 1996	36
	Troy Percival, 1996	36
	Dennis Eckersley, 1997	36
	John Franco, 1997	36
	Doug Jones, 1997	36
	Jeff Montgomery, 1998	36
	Mariano Rivera, 1998	36
85	Wayne Granger, 1970	35
	Sparky Lyle, 1972	35
	Rollie Fingers, 1977	35
	Dan Quisenberry, 1982	35
	Jeff Reardon, 1986	35
	Rod Beck, 1996	35
	Robb Nen, 1996	35
	Robb Nen, 1997	35
	Todd Worrell, 1997	35
94	11 players tied	34

Innings Pitched

1	Will White, 1879	680.0
2	Charley Radbourn, 1884	678.2
3	Guy Hecker, 1884	670.2
4	Jim McCormick, 1880	657.2
5	Pud Galvin, 1883	656.1
6	Pud Galvin, 1884	636.1
7	Charley Radbourn, 1883	632.1
8	John Clarkson, 1885	623.0
9	Jim Devlin, 1876	622.0
	Bill Hutchison, 1892	622.0
11	John Clarkson, 1889	620.0
12	Tim Keefe, 1883	619.0
13	Bill Hutchison, 1890	603.0
14	Jim McCormick, 1882	595.2
15	John Ward, 1880	595.0
16	Pud Galvin, 1879	593.0
17	Lee Richmond, 1880	590.2
18	Matt Kilroy, 1887	589.1
19	Toad Ramsey, 1886	588.2
20	John Ward, 1879	587.0
	Charlie Buffinton, 1884	587.0
22	Silver King, 1888	585.2
23	Matt Kilroy, 1886	583.0
24	Ed Morris, 1885	581.0
25	Will White, 1883	577.0
26	Mickey Welch, 1880	574.0
27	George Bradley, 1876	573.0
28	Jim McCormick, 1884	569.0
29	Tony Mullane, 1884	567.0
30	Toad Ramsey, 1887	561.0
	Bill Hutchison, 1891	561.0
32	Jim Devlin, 1877	559.0
33	Mickey Welch, 1884	557.1
34	Tommy Bond, 1879	555.1
	Ed Morris, 1886	555.1
36	Jim Whitney, 1881	552.1
37	Amos Rusie, 1890	548.2
38	Jim McCormick, 1879	546.1
39	Dupee Shaw, 1884	543.1
40	Amos Rusie, 1892	541.0
41	Hardie Henderson, 1885	539.1
42	John Coleman, 1883	538.1
43	Bill Sweeney, 1884	538.0
44	Larry Corcoran, 1880	536.1
45	Tim Keefe, 1886	535.0
46	Tommy Bond, 1878	532.2
	Jersey Bakely, 1888	532.2
48	Tony Mullane, 1886	529.2
49	Al Spalding, 1876	528.2
50	Jim McCormick, 1881	526.0
51	Billy Taylor, 1884	523.0
	John Clarkson, 1887	523.0
53	Tommy Bond, 1877	521.0
54	Ed Seward, 1888	518.2
55	Will White, 1880	517.1
56	Larry Corcoran, 1884	516.2
57	Bobby Mathews, 1876	516.0
58	Jim Whitney, 1883	514.0
59	Mark Baldwin, 1889	513.2
60	Terry Larkin, 1879	513.1
61	Larry McKeon, 1884	512.0
62	Charley Radbourn, 1886	509.1
63	Sadie McMahon, 1890	509.0
64	Terry Larkin, 1878	506.0
	Kid Gleason, 1890	506.0
66	Dave Foutz, 1886	504.0
67	Frank Mountain, 1883	503.0
	Sadie McMahon, 1891	503.0
69	Terry Larkin, 1877	501.0
70	Hugh Daily, 1884	500.2
71	Amos Rusie, 1891	500.1
72	Mickey Welch, 1886	500.0
73	Jack Lynch, 1884	496.0
74	George Derby, 1881	494.2
75	Bob Barr, 1890	493.1
76	Tommy Bond, 1880	493.0
77	Charlie Sweeney, 1884	492.0
	Mickey Welch, 1885	492.0
	Mark Baldwin, 1890	492.0
80	Phenomenal Smith, 1887	491.1
81	George Bradley, 1879	487.0
	Lady Baldwin, 1886	487.0
83	John Clarkson, 1888	483.1
84	Tim Keefe, 1884	483.0
85	Bob Caruthers, 1885	482.1
86	Amos Rusie, 1893	482.0
87	Henry Porter, 1885	481.2
88	Matt Kilroy, 1889	480.2
89	Will White, 1882	480.0
	Guy Hecker, 1885	480.0
	Ed Morris, 1888	480.0
92	Tim Keefe, 1887	476.2
93	Adonis Terry, 1884	476.0
94	Ed Beatin, 1890	474.1
95	Pud Galvin, 1881	474.0
	Charley Radbourn, 1882	474.0
	Henry Porter, 1888	474.0
98	Larry Corcoran, 1883	473.2
99	Ed Seward, 1887	470.2
100	Gus Weyhing, 1892	469.2

Innings Pitched (by era)

1876-1892

1	Will White, 1879	680.0
2	Charley Radbourn, 1884	678.2
3	Guy Hecker, 1884	670.2
4	Jim McCormick, 1880	657.2
5	Pud Galvin, 1883	656.1
6	Pud Galvin, 1884	636.1
7	Charley Radbourn, 1883	632.1
8	John Clarkson, 1885	623.0
9	Jim Devlin, 1876	622.0
	Bill Hutchison, 1892	622.0
11	John Clarkson, 1889	620.0
12	Tim Keefe, 1883	619.0
13	Bill Hutchison, 1890	603.0
14	Jim McCormick, 1882	595.2
15	John Ward, 1880	595.0

1893-1919

1	Amos Rusie, 1893	482.0
2	Ed Walsh, 1908	464.0
3	Jack Chesbro, 1904	454.2
4	Ted Breitenstein, 1894	447.1
5	Pink Hawley, 1895	444.1
6	Amos Rusie, 1894	444.0
7	Joe McGinnity, 1903	434.0
8	Frank Killen, 1896	432.1
9	Ted Breitenstein, 1895	429.2
10	Kid Nichols, 1893	425.0
11	Cy Young, 1893	422.2
12	Ed Walsh, 1907	422.1
13	Frank Killen, 1893	415.0
14	Cy Young, 1896	414.1
15	Vic Willis, 1902	410.0

1920-1941

1	Pete Alexander, 1920	363.1
2	George Uhle, 1923	357.2
3	Red Faber, 1922	352.0
4	Urban Shocker, 1922	348.0
5	Bob Feller, 1941	343.0
6	Jim Bagby, 1920	339.2
7	Carl Mays, 1921	336.2
8	Red Faber, 1921	330.2
	Burleigh Grimes, 1928	330.2
10	Bobo Newsom, 1938	329.2
11	Wilbur Cooper, 1920	327.0
	Wilbur Cooper, 1921	327.0
	Burleigh Grimes, 1923	327.0
	Alvin Crowder, 1932	327.0
15	Urban Shocker, 1921	326.2

1942-1960

1	Bob Feller, 1946	371.1
2	Dizzy Trout, 1944	352.1
3	Robin Roberts, 1953	346.2
4	Robin Roberts, 1954	336.2
5	Robin Roberts, 1952	330.0
6	Robin Roberts, 1951	315.0
7	Johnny Sain, 1948	314.2
8	Bob Friend, 1956	314.1
9	Hal Newhouser, 1945	313.1
10	Bill Voiselle, 1944	312.2
11	Hal Newhouser, 1944	312.1
12	Vern Bickford, 1950	311.2
13	Warren Spahn, 1951	310.2
14	Bob Lemon, 1952	309.2
15	Robin Roberts, 1955	305.0

1961-1976

1	Wilbur Wood, 1972	376.2
2	Mickey Lolich, 1971	376.0
3	Wilbur Wood, 1973	359.1
4	Steve Carlton, 1972	346.1
5	Gaylord Perry, 1973	344.0
6	Gaylord Perry, 1972	342.2
7	Denny McLain, 1968	336.0
8	Sandy Koufax, 1965	335.2
9	Wilbur Wood, 1971	334.0
10	Nolan Ryan, 1974	332.2
11	Gaylord Perry, 1970	328.2
12	Fergie Jenkins, 1974	328.1
13	Catfish Hunter, 1975	328.0
14	Mickey Lolich, 1972	327.1
15	2 players tied	326.0

1977-1998

1	Phil Niekro, 1979	342.0
2	Phil Niekro, 1978	334.1
3	Phil Niekro, 1977	330.1
4	Jim Palmer, 1977	319.0
5	Steve Carlton, 1980	304.0
6	Dave Goltz, 1977	303.0
7	Steve Rogers, 1977	301.2
8	Nolan Ryan, 1977	299.0
9	Jim Palmer, 1978	296.0
10	Steve Carlton, 1982	295.2
11	Dennis Leonard, 1978	294.2
12	Jack Morris, 1983	293.2
	Bert Blyleven, 1985	293.2
14	Mike Caldwell, 1978	293.1
15	Dennis Leonard, 1977	292.2

Hits per Game

1	Nolan Ryan, 1972	5.26
2	Luis Tiant, 1968	5.30
3	Nolan Ryan, 1991	5.31
4	Ed Reulbach, 1906	5.33
5	Dutch Leonard, 1914	5.57
6	Carl Lundgren, 1907	5.65
7	Sid Fernandez, 1985	5.71
8	Tommy Byrne, 1949	5.74
9	Dave McNally, 1968	5.77
10	Sandy Koufax, 1965	5.79
11	Russ Ford, 1910	5.83
12	Tim Keefe, 1880	5.83
13	Hideo Nomo, 1995	5.83
14	Al Downing, 1963	5.84
15	Herb Score, 1956	5.85
16	Bob Gibson, 1968	5.85
17	Sam McDowell, 1965	5.87
18	Ed Walsh, 1910	5.89
19	Pedro Martinez, 1997	5.89
20	Mike Scott, 1986	5.95
21	Mario Soto, 1980	5.96
22	Floyd Youmans, 1986	5.96
23	Nolan Ryan, 1977	5.96
24	Nolan Ryan, 1974	5.98
25	Nolan Ryan, 1981	5.98
26	Nolan Ryan, 1986	6.02
27	Sam McDowell, 1966	6.02
28	Vida Blue, 1971	6.03
29	Walter Johnson, 1913	6.03
30	Nolan Ryan, 1990	6.04
31	Pete Alexander, 1915	6.05
32	Sam McDowell, 1968	6.06
33	Joe Horlen, 1964	6.07
34	Andy Messersmith, 1969	6.08
35	Nolan Ryan, 1989	6.09
36	Stan Coveleski, 1917	6.09
37	Catfish Hunter, 1972	6.09
38	Nolan Ryan, 1976	6.11
39	Sid Fernandez, 1988	6.11
40	Bob Turley, 1957	6.12
41	Bob Turley, 1955	6.13
42	Don Sutton, 1972	6.14
43	Nolan Ryan, 1983	6.14
44	Ron Guidry, 1978	6.15
45	Mordecai Brown, 1908	6.17
46	Sandy Koufax, 1963	6.19
47	Randy Johnson, 1997	6.21
48	Jack Pfiester, 1906	6.21
49	Sandy Koufax, 1964	6.22
50	Roger Nelson, 1972	6.23
51	Herb Score, 1955	6.26
52	Cy Morgan, 1909	6.26
53	Dean Chance, 1964	6.27
54	Christy Mathewson, 1909	6.28
	J.R. Richard, 1978	6.28
56	Art Fromme, 1909	6.28
57	Greg Maddux, 1995	6.31
58	Walter Johnson, 1912	6.32
59	Kerry Wood, 1998	6.32
60	Jack Coombs, 1910	6.32
61	Rube Waddell, 1905	6.33
62	Vean Gregg, 1911	6.33
63	Jeff Robinson, 1988	6.33
64	Larry Cheney, 1916	6.33
65	Sonny Siebert, 1968	6.33
66	Allie Reynolds, 1943	6.34
67	Roger Clemens, 1986	6.34
68	Willie Mitchell, 1913	6.35
69	Jose DeLeon, 1989	6.36
70	Pascual Perez, 1988	6.37
71	Walter Johnson, 1910	6.37
72	Dave Boswell, 1966	6.38
73	Harry Krause, 1909	6.38
74	Dutch Leonard, 1915	6.38
75	Eddie Cicotte, 1917	6.39
76	Wayne Simpson, 1970	6.39
77	Al Leiter, 1996	6.39
78	Babe Ruth, 1916	6.40
79	Spec Shea, 1947	6.40
80	Jim Bibby, 1973	6.42
81	Ed Reulbach, 1905	6.42
82	Gaylord Perry, 1974	6.42
83	Eddie Fisher, 1965	6.42
84	Addie Joss, 1908	6.42
85	Mordecai Brown, 1906	6.43
86	Luis Tiant, 1972	6.44
87	Frank Smith, 1908	6.44
88	Dwight Gooden, 1985	6.44
89	Orval Overall, 1909	6.44
90	Sid Fernandez, 1989	6.44
91	Denny McLain, 1968	6.46
92	Mordecai Brown, 1909	6.46
93	Ray Caldwell, 1914	6.46
94	Fred Toney, 1915	6.47
95	Gary Peters, 1967	6.47
96	Bob Turley, 1954	6.48
97	Roger Clemens, 1998	6.48
98	Ed Walsh, 1909	6.49
99	Eddie Cicotte, 1909	6.49
100	Guy Hecker, 1882	6.49

Hits per Game (by era)

1876-1892

1	Tim Keefe, 1880	5.83
2	Guy Hecker, 1882	6.49
3	Tim Keefe, 1888	6.57
4	Charlie Sweeney, 1884	6.59
5	Adonis Terry, 1888	6.69
6	Silver King, 1888	6.72
7	Frank Knauss, 1890	6.73
8	Ed Seward, 1888	6.73
9	Tim Keefe, 1885	6.75
10	Tony Mullane, 1892	6.77
11	Larry Corcoran, 1880	6.78
12	Mickey Welch, 1885	6.80
13	Cannonball Titcomb, 1888	6.81
14	Amos Rusie, 1892	6.82
15	Toad Ramsey, 1886	6.83

1893-1919

1	Ed Reulbach, 1906	5.33
2	Dutch Leonard, 1914	5.57
3	Carl Lundgren, 1907	5.65
4	Russ Ford, 1910	5.83
5	Ed Walsh, 1910	5.89
6	Walter Johnson, 1913	6.03
7	Pete Alexander, 1915	6.05
8	Stan Coveleski, 1917	6.09
9	Mordecai Brown, 1908	6.17
10	Jack Pfiester, 1906	6.21
11	Cy Morgan, 1909	6.26
12	Christy Mathewson, 1909	6.28
13	Art Fromme, 1909	6.28
14	Walter Johnson, 1912	6.32
15	Jack Coombs, 1910	6.32

1920-1941

1	Johnny Vander Meer, 1941	6.84
2	Bob Feller, 1940	6.88
3	Bob Feller, 1939	6.89
4	Hal Schumacher, 1933	6.92
5	Dazzy Vance, 1924	6.95
6	Whit Wyatt, 1941	6.96
7	Bucky Walters, 1939	7.05
8	Johnny Vander Meer, 1938	7.07
9	Bucky Walters, 1940	7.11
10	Lefty Gomez, 1934	7.13
11	Ernie White, 1941	7.24
12	Dazzy Vance, 1928	7.26
13	Bump Hadley, 1931	7.26
14	Dolf Luque, 1920	7.28
15	Bob Feller, 1938	7.29

1942-1960

1	Tommy Byrne, 1949	5.74
2	Herb Score, 1956	5.85
3	Bob Turley, 1957	6.12
4	Bob Turley, 1955	6.13
5	Herb Score, 1955	6.26
6	Allie Reynolds, 1943	6.34
7	Spec Shea, 1947	6.40
8	Bob Turley, 1954	6.48
9	Sam Jones, 1955	6.52
10	Bob Turley, 1958	6.53
11	Hal Newhouser, 1946	6.61
12	Johnny Niggeling, 1943	6.66
13	Don Larsen, 1956	6.66
14	Whitey Ford, 1955	6.67
15	Mort Cooper, 1942	6.69

1961-1976

1	Nolan Ryan, 1972	5.26
2	Luis Tiant, 1968	5.30
3	Dave McNally, 1968	5.77
4	Sandy Koufax, 1965	5.79
5	Al Downing, 1963	5.84
6	Bob Gibson, 1968	5.85
7	Sam McDowell, 1965	5.87
8	Nolan Ryan, 1974	5.98
9	Sam McDowell, 1966	6.02
10	Vida Blue, 1971	6.03
11	Sam McDowell, 1968	6.06
12	Joe Horlen, 1964	6.07
13	Andy Messersmith, 1969	6.08
14	Catfish Hunter, 1972	6.09
15	Nolan Ryan, 1976	6.11

1977-1998

1	Nolan Ryan, 1991	5.31
2	Sid Fernandez, 1985	5.71
3	Hideo Nomo, 1995	5.83
4	Pedro Martinez, 1997	5.89
5	Mike Scott, 1986	5.95
6	Mario Soto, 1980	5.96
7	Floyd Youmans, 1986	5.96
8	Nolan Ryan, 1977	5.96
9	Nolan Ryan, 1981	5.98
10	Nolan Ryan, 1986	6.02
11	Nolan Ryan, 1990	6.04
12	Nolan Ryan, 1989	6.09
13	Sid Fernandez, 1988	6.11
14	Nolan Ryan, 1983	6.14
15	Ron Guidry, 1978	6.15

Home Runs Allowed

1	Bert Blyleven, 1986	50
2	Robin Roberts, 1956	46
	Bert Blyleven, 1987	46
4	Pedro Ramos, 1957	43
5	Denny McLain, 1966	42
6	Robin Roberts, 1955	41
	Phil Niekro, 1979	41
8	Bill Gullickson, 1987	40
	Robin Roberts, 1957	40
	Ralph Terry, 1962	40
	Orlando Pena, 1964	40
	Phil Niekro, 1970	40
	Fergie Jenkins, 1979	40
	Jack Morris, 1986	40
	Shawn Boskie, 1996	40
	Brad Radke, 1996	40
17	Murry Dickson, 1948	39
	Pedro Ramos, 1961	39
	Jim Perry, 1971	39
	Catfish Hunter, 1973	39
	Jack Morris, 1987	39
	Brian Anderson, 1998	39
	Pedro Astacio, 1998	39
24	Warren Hacker, 1955	38
	Pedro Ramos, 1958	38
	Lew Burdette, 1959	38
	Jim Bunning, 1963	38
	Don Sutton, 1970	38
	Mickey Lolich, 1974	38
	Matt Keough, 1982	38
	Floyd Bannister, 1987	38
	Don Sutton, 1987	38
	Curt Young, 1987	38
	Tim Wakefield, 1996	38
35	Jim Bunning, 1959	37
	Earl Wilson, 1964	37
	Luis Tiant, 1969	37
	Fergie Jenkins, 1975	37
	Jack Morris, 1982	37
	Dan Petry, 1983	37
	Frank Viola, 1986	37
	Mark Leiter, 1996	37
	Allen Watson, 1997	37
	Livan Hernandez, 1998	37
	Tim Belcher, 1998	37
46	Dennis Rasmussen, 1987	36
	Larry Jansen, 1949	36
	Art Mahaffey, 1962	36
	Pete Richert, 1966	36
	Mickey Lolich, 1971	36
	Ed Whitson, 1987	36
	Charlie Hough, 1987	36
	Tom Browning, 1988	36
	Woody Williams, 1998	36
55	Larry Corcoran, 1884	35
	Warren Hacker, 1953	35
	Robin Roberts, 1954	35
	Don Newcombe, 1955	35
	Jim Perry, 1960	35
	Roger Craig, 1962	35
	Robin Roberts, 1963	35
	Sammy Ellis, 1966	35
	Denny McLain, 1967	35
	Fergie Jenkins, 1973	35
	Mickey Lolich, 1973	35
	Mike Caldwell, 1983	35
	Mike Smithson, 1984	35
	Scott McGregor, 1986	35
	Scott Bankhead, 1987	35
	Bruce Hurst, 1987	35
	Bill Gullickson, 1992	35
	Mike Moore, 1993	35
73	Preacher Roe, 1950	34
	Johnny Sain, 1950	34
	Ken Raffensberger, 1950	34
	Robin Roberts, 1959	34
	Paul Foytack, 1959	34
	Juan Marichal, 1962	34
	Dick Ellsworth, 1964	34
	Bill Monbouquette, 1964	34
	Bob Gibson, 1965	34
	Mudcat Grant, 1965	34
	Earl Wilson, 1967	34
	Catfish Hunter, 1969	34
	Mike Cuellar, 1970	34
	Gaylord Perry, 1973	34
	Rick Wise, 1975	34
	Frank Viola, 1983	34
	Danny Darwin, 1985	34
	Scott McGregor, 1985	34
	Ken Schrom, 1986	34
	Don Carman, 1987	34
	Mike Witt, 1987	34
	Alex Fernandez, 1996	34
	Kevin Tapani, 1996	34
	Jose Lima, 1998	34
	Charles Nagy, 1998	34
98	19 players tied	33

Home Runs Allowed (by era)

1876-1892

1	Larry Corcoran, 1884	35
2	Charlie Getzien, 1889	27
3	Bill Hutchison, 1891	26
4	Charlie Getzien, 1887	24
	John Healy, 1887	24
6	Pud Galvin, 1884	23
	Mark Baldwin, 1887	23
	Lev Shreve, 1888	23
9	Billy Serad, 1884	21
	John Clarkson, 1885	21
	Park Swartzel, 1889	21
	George Cobb, 1892	21
13	8 players tied	20

1893-1919

1	Frank Dwyer, 1894	27
	Jack Stivetts, 1894	27
3	Kid Nichols, 1894	23
4	Harry Staley, 1893	22
	Kid Carsey, 1894	22
6	Ted Breitenstein, 1894	21
7	Jack Stivetts, 1896	20
8	Tom Parrott, 1894	19
	Cy Young, 1894	19
10	Kid Gleason, 1893	18
	Al Orth, 1902	18
12	5 players tied	17

1920-1941

1	Lon Warneke, 1937	32
2	Phil Collins, 1934	30
	Bobo Newsom, 1938	30
4	Ray Kremer, 1930	29
	Lynn Nelson, 1938	29
6	George Earnshaw, 1932	28
	George Earnshaw, 1934	28
8	Roy Mahaffey, 1932	27
	Carl Hubbell, 1935	27
	Luke Hamlin, 1939	27
	Lynn Nelson, 1939	27
	Johnny Marcum, 1939	27
13	Freddie Fitzsimmons, 1930	26
	Gordon Rhodes, 1936	26
	Nels Potter, 1939	26

1942-1960

1	Robin Roberts, 1956	46
2	Pedro Ramos, 1957	43
3	Robin Roberts, 1955	41
4	Robin Roberts, 1957	40
5	Murry Dickson, 1948	39
6	Warren Hacker, 1955	38
	Pedro Ramos, 1958	38
	Lew Burdette, 1959	38
9	Jim Bunning, 1959	37
10	Larry Jansen, 1949	36
11	Warren Hacker, 1953	35
	Robin Roberts, 1954	35
	Don Newcombe, 1955	35
	Jim Perry, 1960	35
15	5 players tied	34

1961-1976

1	Denny McLain, 1966	42
2	Ralph Terry, 1962	40
	Orlando Pena, 1964	40
	Phil Niekro, 1970	40
5	Pedro Ramos, 1961	39
	Jim Perry, 1971	39
	Catfish Hunter, 1973	39
8	Jim Bunning, 1963	38
	Don Sutton, 1970	38
	Mickey Lolich, 1974	38
11	Earl Wilson, 1964	37
	Luis Tiant, 1969	37
	Fergie Jenkins, 1975	37
14	3 players tied	36

1977-1998

1	Bert Blyleven, 1986	50
2	Bert Blyleven, 1987	46
3	Phil Niekro, 1979	41
4	Bill Gullickson, 1987	40
	Fergie Jenkins, 1979	40
	Jack Morris, 1986	40
	Shawn Boskie, 1996	40
	Brad Radke, 1996	40
9	Jack Morris, 1987	39
	Brian Anderson, 1998	39
	Pedro Astacio, 1998	39
12	5 players tied	38

Walks

1	Amos Rusie, 1890	289
2	Mark Baldwin, 1889	274
3	Amos Rusie, 1892	270
4	Amos Rusie, 1891	262
5	Mark Baldwin, 1890	249
6	Jack Stivetts, 1891	232
7	Mark Baldwin, 1891	227
8	Phil Knell, 1891	226
9	Bob Barr, 1890	219
10	Amos Rusie, 1893	218
11	Cy Seymour, 1898	213
12	Gus Weyhing, 1889	212
13	Ed Crane, 1890	208
	Bob Feller, 1938	208
15	Toad Ramsey, 1886	207
16	Elton Chamberlain, 1891	206
17	Mike Morrison, 1887	205
18	Henry Gruber, 1890	204
	Nolan Ryan, 1977	204
20	Ed Crane, 1891	203
	John Clarkson, 1889	203
22	Nolan Ryan, 1974	202
23	Bert Cunningham, 1890	201
24	Amos Rusie, 1894	200
25	Bill Hutchison, 1890	199
26	Mark Baldwin, 1892	194
	Bob Feller, 1941	194
28	Bobo Newsom, 1938	192
29	Ted Breitenstein, 1894	191
30	Bill Hutchison, 1892	190
31	Ed Crane, 1892	189
	Tony Mullane, 1893	189
33	Tony Mullane, 1891	187
	Kid Gleason, 1893	187
35	Ed Beatin, 1890	186
36	Sam Jones, 1955	185
37	Tom Vickery, 1890	184
38	Nolan Ryan, 1976	183
39	Matt Kilroy, 1886	182
	Frank Killen, 1892	182
41	Willie McGill, 1893	181
	Bob Harmon, 1911	181
	Bob Turley, 1954	181
44	Jack Stivetts, 1890	179
	Gus Weyhing, 1890	179
	Tommy Byrne, 1949	179
47	Bill Hutchison, 1891	178
	Ted Breitenstein, 1895	178
49	Bob Turley, 1955	177
50	Phenomenal Smith, 1887	176
	George Hemming, 1893	176
52	Silver King, 1892	171
	Jack Stivetts, 1892	171
	Jouett Meekin, 1894	171
	Bump Hadley, 1932	171
56	Elton Chamberlain, 1892	170
	Ed Stein, 1894	170
	Cy Seymour, 1899	170
59	Willie McGill, 1891	168
	Gus Weyhing, 1892	168
	Brickyard Kennedy, 1893	168
	Elmer Myers, 1916	168
63	Toad Ramsey, 1887	167
	Gus Weyhing, 1887	167
	Darby O'Brien, 1889	167
	Kid Gleason, 1890	167
	Bill Daley, 1890	167
	Bobo Newsom, 1937	167
69	Tony Mullane, 1886	166
	Sadie McMahon, 1890	166
	Phil Knell, 1890	166
	Chick Fraser, 1896	166
73	Elton Chamberlain, 1889	165
	Dan Casey, 1890	165
	Kid Gleason, 1891	165
	Weldon Wyckoff, 1915	165
77	Cy Seymour, 1897	164
	Earl Moore, 1911	164
	Phil Niekro, 1977	164
80	Mickey Welch, 1886	163
	Silver King, 1890	163
	George Haddock, 1892	163
83	Johnny Vander Meer, 1943	162
	Nolan Ryan, 1973	162
85	Hank O'Day, 1890	161
	John Sowders, 1890	161
	Kid Carsey, 1891	161
	Gus Weyhing, 1891	161
89	Tommy Byrne, 1950	160
90	George Hemming, 1894	159
	Amos Rusie, 1895	159
	Marty O'Toole, 1912	159
93	Joe Coleman, 1974	158
94	Matt Kilroy, 1887	157
	Bert Cunningham, 1888	157
	Pink Hawley, 1896	157
	Grover Lowdermilk, 1915	157
	Nolan Ryan, 1972	157
99	5 players tied	156

Fewest Walks/Game (by era)

1876-1892

1	George Zettlein, 1876	0.23
2	Cherokee Fisher, 1876	0.24
3	George Bradley, 1880	0.28
4	Tommy Bond, 1876	0.29
5	Tommy Bond, 1879	0.39
6	Bobby Mathews, 1876	0.42
7	Guy Hecker, 1882	0.43
8	Dale Williams, 1876	0.43
9	Al Spalding, 1876	0.44
10	Pud Galvin, 1879	0.47
11	George Bradley, 1879	0.48
12	Sam Weaver, 1878	0.49
13	Terry Larkin, 1879	0.53
14	Jim Devlin, 1876	0.54
15	Denny Driscoll, 1882	0.54

1893-1919

1	Christy Mathewson, 1913	0.62
2	Christy Mathewson, 1914	0.66
3	Cy Young, 1904	0.69
4	Cy Young, 1906	0.78
5	Babe Adams, 1919	0.79
6	Slim Sallee, 1919	0.79
7	Slim Sallee, 1918	0.82
8	Addie Joss, 1908	0.83
9	Cy Young, 1905	0.84
10	Deacon Phillippe, 1902	0.86
11	Cy Young, 1901	0.90
12	Deacon Phillippe, 1903	0.90
13	Christy Mathewson, 1908	0.97
14	Christy Mathewson, 1915	0.97
15	Jesse Tannehill, 1902	0.97

1920-1941

1	Babe Adams, 1920	0.62
2	Red Lucas, 1933	0.74
3	Babe Adams, 1922	0.79
4	Pete Alexander, 1923	0.89
5	Babe Adams, 1921	1.01
6	Paul Derringer, 1939	1.05
7	Carl Hubbell, 1934	1.06
8	Bill Swift, 1932	1.09
9	Pete Alexander, 1925	1.11
10	Herb Pennock, 1930	1.15
11	Red Lucas, 1932	1.17
12	Pete Alexander, 1921	1.18
13	Watty Clark, 1935	1.22
14	Pete Donohue, 1926	1.23
15	Pete Alexander, 1922	1.25

1942-1960

1	Tiny Bonham, 1942	0.96
2	Don Newcombe, 1959	1.09
3	Tiny Bonham, 1945	1.10
4	Lew Burdette, 1960	1.14
5	Lew Burdette, 1959	1.18
6	Robin Roberts, 1956	1.21
7	Robin Roberts, 1959	1.22
8	Robin Roberts, 1952	1.23
9	Hal Brown, 1960	1.25
10	Ray Prim, 1945	1.25
11	Robin Roberts, 1960	1.29
12	Fred Hutchinson, 1951	1.29
13	Ted Lyons, 1942	1.30
14	Schoolboy Rowe, 1943	1.31
15	Vern Law, 1960	1.33

1961-1976

1	Gary Nolan, 1976	1.02
2	Fergie Jenkins, 1971	1.02
3	Juan Marichal, 1966	1.05
4	Lew Burdette, 1961	1.09
5	Jim Merritt, 1967	1.19
6	Vern Law, 1966	1.22
7	Dick Donovan, 1963	1.22
8	Fritz Peterson, 1968	1.23
9	Fergie Jenkins, 1974	1.23
10	Gary Nolan, 1975	1.24
11	Ralph Terry, 1965	1.25
12	Bill Hands, 1968	1.25
13	Jim Kaat, 1976	1.27
14	Juan Marichal, 1968	1.27
15	Catfish Hunter, 1974	1.30

1977-1998

1	Bret Saberhagen, 1994	0.66
2	Bob Tewksbury, 1992	0.77
3	Greg Maddux, 1997	0.77
4	Bob Tewksbury, 1993	0.84
5	La Marr Hoyt, 1985	0.86
6	Greg Maddux, 1995	0.99
7	Dennis Eckersley, 1985	1.01
8	Greg Maddux, 1996	1.03
9	Brian Anderson, 1998	1.04
10	La Marr Hoyt, 1983	1.07
11	Jimmy Key, 1989	1.13
12	Zane Smith, 1991	1.14
13	Greg Swindell, 1991	1.17
14	Scott McGregor, 1979	1.19
15	Rick Honeycutt, 1981	1.20

Strikeouts

1	Matt Kilroy, 1886	513
2	Toad Ramsey, 1886	499
3	Hugh Daily, 1884	483
4	Dupee Shaw, 1884	451
5	Charley Radbourn, 1884	441
6	Charlie Buffinton, 1884	417
7	Guy Hecker, 1884	385
8	Nolan Ryan, 1973	383
9	Sandy Koufax, 1965	382
10	Bill Sweeney, 1884	374
11	Pud Galvin, 1884	369
12	Mark Baldwin, 1889	368
13	Nolan Ryan, 1974	367
14	Tim Keefe, 1883	359
15	Toad Ramsey, 1887	355
16	Rube Waddell, 1904	349
17	Bob Feller, 1946	348
18	Hardie Henderson, 1884	346
19	Jim Whitney, 1883	345
	Mickey Welch, 1884	345
21	Jim McCormick, 1884	343
22	Amos Rusie, 1890	341
	Nolan Ryan, 1977	341
24	Charlie Sweeney, 1884	337
	Amos Rusie, 1891	337
26	Tim Keefe, 1888	335
27	Tim Keefe, 1884	334
28	Randy Johnson, 1998	329
	Nolan Ryan, 1972	329
30	Nolan Ryan, 1976	327
31	Ed Morris, 1886	326
32	Tony Mullane, 1884	325
	Sam McDowell, 1965	325
34	Lady Baldwin, 1886	323
35	Curt Schilling, 1997	319
36	Sandy Koufax, 1966	317
37	Charley Radbourn, 1883	315
38	Bill Hutchison, 1892	314
39	John Clarkson, 1886	313
	Walter Johnson, 1910	313
	J.R. Richard, 1979	313
42	Steve Carlton, 1972	310
43	Larry McKeon, 1884	308
	John Clarkson, 1885	308
	Mickey Lolich, 1971	308
	Randy Johnson, 1993	308
47	Sandy Koufax, 1963	306
	Mike Scott, 1986	306
49	Pedro Martinez, 1997	305
50	Amos Rusie, 1892	304
	Sam McDowell, 1970	304
52	Walter Johnson, 1912	303
	J.R. Richard, 1978	303
54	Ed Morris, 1884	302
	Rube Waddell, 1903	302
56	Vida Blue, 1971	301
	Nolan Ryan, 1989	301
58	Curt Schilling, 1998	300
59	Ed Morris, 1885	298
60	Tim Keefe, 1886	297
61	Randy Johnson, 1995	294
62	Jack Lynch, 1884	292
	Roger Clemens, 1997	292
64	Sadie McMahon, 1890	291
	Roger Clemens, 1988	291
	Randy Johnson, 1997	291
67	Bill Hutchison, 1890	289
	Jack Stivetts, 1890	289
	Tom Seaver, 1971	289
70	Rube Waddell, 1905	287
71	Bobby Mathews, 1884	286
	Bobby Mathews, 1885	286
	Steve Carlton, 1980	286
	Steve Carlton, 1982	286
75	Billy Taylor, 1884	284
	John Clarkson, 1889	284
77	Dave Foutz, 1886	283
	Sam McDowell, 1968	283
	Tom Seaver, 1970	283
80	Denny McLain, 1968	280
81	Pud Galvin, 1883	279
	Sam McDowell, 1969	279
83	Bob Veale, 1965	276
	Dwight Gooden, 1984	276
	John Smoltz, 1996	276
86	Hal Newhouser, 1946	275
	Steve Carlton, 1983	275
88	Bob Gibson, 1970	274
	Fergie Jenkins, 1970	274
	Mario Soto, 1982	274
91	Fergie Jenkins, 1969	273
92	Larry Corcoran, 1884	272
	Mickey Welch, 1886	272
	Ed Seward, 1888	272
95	Mickey Lolich, 1969	271
	Roger Clemens, 1998	271
97	Jim Whitney, 1884	270
	Bob Gibson, 1965	270
	Nolan Ryan, 1987	270
100	4 players tied	269

Strikeouts (by era)

1876-1892

1	Matt Kilroy, 1886	513
2	Toad Ramsey, 1886	499
3	Hugh Daily, 1884	483
4	Dupee Shaw, 1884	451
5	Charley Radbourn, 1884	441
6	Charlie Buffinton, 1884	417
7	Guy Hecker, 1884	385
8	Bill Sweeney, 1884	374
9	Pud Galvin, 1884	369
10	Mark Baldwin, 1889	368
11	Tim Keefe, 1883	359
12	Toad Ramsey, 1887	355
13	Hardie Henderson, 1884	346
14	Jim Whitney, 1883	345
	Mickey Welch, 1884	345

1893-1919

1	Rube Waddell, 1904	349
2	Walter Johnson, 1910	313
3	Walter Johnson, 1912	303
4	Rube Waddell, 1903	302
5	Rube Waddell, 1905	287
6	Ed Walsh, 1908	269
7	Christy Mathewson, 1903	267
8	Christy Mathewson, 1908	259
9	Ed Walsh, 1910	258
	Joe Wood, 1912	258
11	Ed Walsh, 1911	255
12	Ed Walsh, 1912	254
13	Walter Johnson, 1913	243
14	Pete Alexander, 1915	241

1920-1941

1	Dazzy Vance, 1924	262
2	Bob Feller, 1940	261
3	Bob Feller, 1941	260
4	Bob Feller, 1939	246
5	Bob Feller, 1938	240
6	Van Mungo, 1936	238
7	Bobo Newsom, 1938	226
8	Dazzy Vance, 1925	221
9	Lefty Grove, 1930	209
10	Johnny Vander Meer, 1941	202
11	Dazzy Vance, 1928	200
12	Dizzy Dean, 1933	199
13	Dazzy Vance, 1923	197
14	Dizzy Dean, 1934	195
	Dizzy Dean, 1936	195

1942-1960

1	Bob Feller, 1946	348
2	Hal Newhouser, 1946	275
3	Herb Score, 1956	263
4	Don Drysdale, 1960	246
5	Herb Score, 1955	245
6	Don Drysdale, 1959	242
7	Sam Jones, 1958	225
8	Hal Newhouser, 1945	212
9	Bob Turley, 1955	210
10	Sam Jones, 1959	209
11	Jim Bunning, 1959	201
	Jim Bunning, 1960	201
13	Robin Roberts, 1953	198
	Sam Jones, 1955	198
15	Sandy Koufax, 1960	197

1961-1976

1	Nolan Ryan, 1973	383
2	Sandy Koufax, 1965	382
3	Nolan Ryan, 1974	367
4	Nolan Ryan, 1972	329
5	Nolan Ryan, 1976	327
6	Sam McDowell, 1965	325
7	Sandy Koufax, 1966	317
8	Steve Carlton, 1972	310
9	Mickey Lolich, 1971	308
10	Sandy Koufax, 1963	306
11	Sam McDowell, 1970	304
12	Vida Blue, 1971	301
13	Tom Seaver, 1971	289
14	Sam McDowell, 1968	283
	Tom Seaver, 1970	283

1977-1998

1	Nolan Ryan, 1977	341
2	Randy Johnson, 1998	329
3	Curt Schilling, 1997	319
4	J.R. Richard, 1979	313
5	Randy Johnson, 1993	308
6	Mike Scott, 1986	306
7	Pedro Martinez, 1997	305
8	J.R. Richard, 1978	303
9	Nolan Ryan, 1989	301
10	Curt Schilling, 1998	300
11	Randy Johnson, 1995	294
12	Roger Clemens, 1997	292
13	Roger Clemens, 1988	291
	Randy Johnson, 1997	291
15	2 players tied	286

Strikeouts per Game

1	Kerry Wood, 1998	12.58
2	Randy Johnson, 1995	12.35
3	Randy Johnson, 1997	12.30
4	Randy Johnson, 1998	12.12
5	Nolan Ryan, 1987	11.48
6	Dwight Gooden, 1984	11.39
7	Pedro Martinez, 1997	11.37
8	Nolan Ryan, 1989	11.32
9	Curt Schilling, 1997	11.29
10	Hideo Nomo, 1995	11.10
11	Randy Johnson, 1993	10.86
12	Sam McDowell, 1965	10.71
13	Randy Johnson, 1994	10.67
14	Nolan Ryan, 1973	10.57
15	Nolan Ryan, 1991	10.56
16	Sandy Koufax, 1962	10.55
17	Nolan Ryan, 1972	10.43
18	Sam McDowell, 1966	10.42
19	Roger Clemens, 1998	10.39
20	Nolan Ryan, 1976	10.35
21	Randy Johnson, 1992	10.31
22	Nolan Ryan, 1977	10.26
23	David Cone, 1997	10.25
24	Sandy Koufax, 1965	10.24
25	Nolan Ryan, 1990	10.24
26	Randy Johnson, 1991	10.19
27	Sandy Koufax, 1960	10.13
28	Hideo Nomo, 1997	10.11
29	Curt Schilling, 1998	10.05
30	Mike Scott, 1986	10.00
31	Nolan Ryan, 1978	9.97
32	Roger Clemens, 1997	9.95
33	Nolan Ryan, 1974	9.93
34	Roger Clemens, 1988	9.92
35	David Cone, 1990	9.91
36	J.R. Richard, 1978	9.90
37	Andy Benes, 1994	9.87
38	Nolan Ryan, 1986	9.81
39	John Smoltz, 1996	9.79
40	Herb Score, 1955	9.70
41	Pedro Martinez, 1998	9.67
42	Nolan Ryan, 1984	9.65
43	J.R. Richard, 1979	9.64
44	Mario Soto, 1982	9.57
45	Tom Griffin, 1969	9.56
46	Roger Clemens, 1996	9.53
47	Jim Maloney, 1963	9.53
48	Sid Fernandez, 1985	9.51
49	Herb Score, 1956	9.49
50	Sandy Koufax, 1961	9.47
51	Sam McDowell, 1968	9.47
52	David Cone, 1992	9.41
53	Frank Tanana, 1975	9.41
54	Don Wilson, 1969	9.40
55	Bob Veale, 1965	9.34
56	Nolan Ryan, 1988	9.33
57	David Cone, 1991	9.32
58	John Smoltz, 1998	9.29
59	Luis Tiant, 1967	9.22
60	Hideo Nomo, 1996	9.22
61	Pedro Martinez, 1996	9.22
62	Mark Langston, 1986	9.21
63	Luis Tiant, 1968	9.20
64	Dave Boswell, 1966	9.19
65	Sam McDowell, 1964	9.19
66	Sonny Siebert, 1965	9.11
67	Sid Fernandez, 1988	9.10
68	Tom Seaver, 1971	9.08
69	Sid Fernandez, 1990	9.08
70	David Cone, 1998	9.06
71	Dennis Eckersley, 1976	9.03
72	John Smoltz, 1995	9.02
73	Nolan Ryan, 1979	9.01
74	Sandy Koufax, 1964	9.00
	Darryl Kile, 1996	9.00
	Kevin Brown, 1998	9.00
77	Sam McDowell, 1967	8.99
78	Sam McDowell, 1970	8.97
79	Bobby Witt, 1990	8.96
80	Curt Schilling, 1996	8.93
81	Jose Rijo, 1994	8.93
82	Jim Maloney, 1964	8.92
83	Andy Benes, 1997	8.90
84	Jose Rijo, 1988	8.89
85	Roger Clemens, 1994	8.86
86	Sandy Koufax, 1963	8.86
87	Pedro Martinez, 1994	8.83
88	Sandy Koufax, 1966	8.83
89	Kevin Appier, 1996	8.82
90	Sam McDowell, 1969	8.81
91	Sid Fernandez, 1986	8.81
92	Nolan Ryan, 1982	8.81
93	Todd Stottlemyre, 1995	8.80
94	Tom Seaver, 1970	8.76
95	Al Downing, 1963	8.76
96	Bob Moose, 1969	8.74
97	Mike Mussina, 1997	8.73
98	Steve Carlton, 1983	8.73
99	Dwight Gooden, 1985	8.72
100	Steve Carlton, 1982	8.71

Strikeouts per Game (by era)

1876-1892

1	Hugh Daily, 1884	8.68
2	Matt Kilroy, 1886	7.92
3	Charlie Gagus, 1884	7.92
4	John Clarkson, 1884	7.78
5	Toad Ramsey, 1886	7.63
6	Dupee Shaw, 1884	7.47
7	Jim Whitney, 1884	7.23
8	Mike Dorgan, 1884	7.17
9	James Burke, 1884	7.13
10	Hardie Henderson, 1884	7.09
11	Tim Keefe, 1888	6.94
12	Bob Black, 1884	6.80
13	Lady Baldwin, 1885	6.78
14	Jack Stivetts, 1889	6.71
15	Toad Ramsey, 1890	6.63

1893-1919

1	Rube Waddell, 1903	8.39
2	Rube Waddell, 1904	8.20
3	Rube Waddell, 1905	7.86
4	Rube Marquard, 1911	7.68
5	Walter Johnson, 1910	7.61
6	Joe Wood, 1911	7.54
7	Walter Johnson, 1912	7.39
8	Rube Waddell, 1907	7.33
9	Rube Waddell, 1908	7.31
10	Dutch Leonard, 1914	7.05
11	Red Ames, 1906	6.90
12	Rube Waddell, 1902	6.84
13	Red Ames, 1905	6.78
14	Joe Wood, 1912	6.75
15	Orval Overall, 1908	6.68

1920-1941

1	Johnny Vander Meer, 1941	8.03
2	Bob Feller, 1938	7.78
3	Dazzy Vance, 1924	7.65
4	Dazzy Vance, 1925	7.50
5	Bob Feller, 1939	7.46
6	Dazzy Vance, 1926	7.46
7	Bob Feller, 1940	7.33
8	Van Mungo, 1936	6.87
9	Bob Feller, 1941	6.82
10	Van Mungo, 1937	6.82
11	Lefty Grove, 1926	6.77
12	Bill Hallahan, 1930	6.71
13	George Earnshaw, 1928	6.65
14	Red Ruffing, 1932	6.60
15	Lefty Grove, 1930	6.46

1942-1960

1	Sandy Koufax, 1960	10.13
2	Herb Score, 1955	9.70
3	Herb Score, 1956	9.49
4	Hal Newhouser, 1946	8.46
5	Bob Feller, 1946	8.43
6	Sam Jones, 1956	8.40
7	Herb Score, 1959	8.23
8	Don Drysdale, 1960	8.23
9	Sam Jones, 1958	8.10
10	Don Drysdale, 1959	8.05
11	Bob Turley, 1957	7.76
12	Camilo Pascual, 1956	7.73
13	Bob Turley, 1955	7.66
14	Stan Williams, 1960	7.60
15	Sam Jones, 1957	7.59

1961-1976

1	Sam McDowell, 1965	10.71
2	Nolan Ryan, 1973	10.57
3	Sandy Koufax, 1962	10.55
4	Nolan Ryan, 1972	10.43
5	Sam McDowell, 1966	10.42
6	Nolan Ryan, 1976	10.35
7	Sandy Koufax, 1965	10.24
8	Nolan Ryan, 1974	9.93
9	Tom Griffin, 1969	9.56
10	Jim Maloney, 1963	9.53
11	Sandy Koufax, 1961	9.47
12	Sam McDowell, 1968	9.47
13	Frank Tanana, 1975	9.41
14	Don Wilson, 1969	9.40
15	Bob Veale, 1965	9.34

1977-1998

1	Kerry Wood, 1998	12.58
2	Randy Johnson, 1995	12.35
3	Randy Johnson, 1997	12.30
4	Randy Johnson, 1998	12.12
5	Nolan Ryan, 1987	11.48
6	Dwight Gooden, 1984	11.39
7	Pedro Martinez, 1997	11.37
8	Nolan Ryan, 1989	11.32
9	Curt Schilling, 1997	11.29
10	Hideo Nomo, 1995	11.10
11	Randy Johnson, 1993	10.86
12	Randy Johnson, 1994	10.67
13	Nolan Ryan, 1991	10.56
14	Roger Clemens, 1998	10.39
15	Randy Johnson, 1992	10.31

Ratio

1	Guy Hecker, 1882	6.92
2	Tim Keefe, 1880	7.20
3	Walter Johnson, 1913	7.26
4	Addie Joss, 1908	7.31
5	Charlie Sweeney, 1884	7.35
6	Christy Mathewson, 1909	7.45
7	Greg Maddux, 1995	7.47
8	Ed Walsh, 1910	7.47
9	George Bradley, 1880	7.53
10	Christy Mathewson, 1908	7.60
11	Henry Boyle, 1884	7.68
12	Mordecai Brown, 1908	7.72
13	Denny Driscoll, 1882	7.79
14	Pete Alexander, 1915	7.82
15	Sandy Koufax, 1965	7.83
16	Juan Marichal, 1966	7.88
17	Bob Gibson, 1968	7.89
18	Roger Nelson, 1972	7.89
19	Dave McNally, 1968	7.91
20	Ed Walsh, 1908	7.91
21	Sandy Koufax, 1963	7.96
22	Luis Tiant, 1968	7.98
23	George Bradley, 1876	7.98
24	Jim Whitney, 1884	8.01
25	Guy Hecker, 1884	8.02
26	Cy Young, 1905	8.03
27	Mordecai Brown, 1909	8.04
28	Cy Young, 1908	8.07
29	Tommy Bond, 1876	8.12
30	Babe Adams, 1919	8.17
31	Russ Ford, 1910	8.17
32	John Ward, 1880	8.26
33	Lady Baldwin, 1885	8.28
34	Eddie Cicotte, 1917	8.28
35	Dutch Leonard, 1914	8.29
36	Charley Radbourn, 1884	8.30
37	Denny McLain, 1968	8.30
38	Catfish Hunter, 1972	8.32
39	Doc White, 1906	8.33
40	Greg Maddux, 1994	8.33
41	Silver King, 1888	8.34
42	Pete Alexander, 1919	8.35
43	Juan Marichal, 1965	8.35
44	Don Sutton, 1972	8.35
45	Sandy Koufax, 1964	8.35
46	Ed Morris, 1884	8.36
47	Mike Scott, 1986	8.37
48	Christy Mathewson, 1905	8.42
49	Larry Corcoran, 1880	8.44
50	Addie Joss, 1906	8.49
51	Reb Russell, 1916	8.51
52	Cy Young, 1904	8.53
53	Mordecai Brown, 1906	8.53
54	Walter Johnson, 1910	8.54
55	Ron Guidry, 1978	8.55
56	Claude Hendrix, 1914	8.55
57	Walter Johnson, 1912	8.56
58	Warren Hacker, 1952	8.56
59	Jack Lynch, 1884	8.56
60	Jack Chesbro, 1904	8.57
61	John Clarkson, 1885	8.58
62	Joe Horlen, 1964	8.59
63	Ed Walsh, 1909	8.60
64	Perry Werden, 1884	8.60
65	Chief Bender, 1910	8.60
66	John Tudor, 1985	8.61
67	Bill Burns, 1908	8.62
68	Addie Joss, 1909	8.64
69	Tom Seaver, 1971	8.64
70	Russ Ford, 1914	8.66
71	Tim Keefe, 1883	8.67
72	Bill Bernhard, 1902	8.68
73	Tim Keefe, 1888	8.68
74	Vida Blue, 1971	8.68
75	Tim Keefe, 1884	8.68
76	Charlie Buffinton, 1888	8.70
77	Lady Baldwin, 1886	8.70
78	Larry Corcoran, 1882	8.70
79	Frank Smith, 1908	8.71
80	Tony Mullane, 1883	8.71
81	Bret Saberhagen, 1989	8.71
82	Christy Mathewson, 1907	8.71
83	Joe Horlen, 1967	8.72
84	Jim Devlin, 1876	8.73
85	Pedro Martinez, 1997	8.73
86	Frank Smith, 1909	8.73
87	Mordecai Brown, 1907	8.73
88	Charlie Getzien, 1884	8.74
89	Greg Maddux, 1997	8.74
90	Dwight Gooden, 1985	8.75
91	Fred Anderson, 1917	8.78
92	Charlie Ferguson, 1886	8.78
93	Dick Hughes, 1967	8.78
94	Ray Caldwell, 1914	8.79
95	Walter Johnson, 1918	8.81
96	Turk Farrell, 1963	8.81
97	Pascual Perez, 1988	8.81
98	Charley Radbourn, 1883	8.81
99	Addie Joss, 1903	8.82
100	Dick Rudolph, 1916	8.86

Earned Run Average

1	Tim Keefe, 1880	0.86
2	Dutch Leonard, 1914	0.96
3	Mordecai Brown, 1906	1.04
4	Bob Gibson, 1968	1.12
5	Christy Mathewson, 1909	1.14
6	Walter Johnson, 1913	1.14
7	Jack Pfiester, 1907	1.15
8	Addie Joss, 1908	1.16
9	Carl Lundgren, 1907	1.17
10	Denny Driscoll, 1882	1.21
11	Pete Alexander, 1915	1.22
12	George Bradley, 1876	1.23
13	Cy Young, 1908	1.26
14	Ed Walsh, 1910	1.27
15	Walter Johnson, 1918	1.27
16	Christy Mathewson, 1905	1.28
17	Guy Hecker, 1882	1.30
18	Jack Coombs, 1910	1.30
19	Mordecai Brown, 1909	1.31
20	Jack Taylor, 1902	1.33
21	Walter Johnson, 1910	1.36
22	George Bradley, 1880	1.38
23	Charley Radbourn, 1884	1.38
24	Walter Johnson, 1912	1.39
25	Mordecai Brown, 1907	1.39
26	Harry Krause, 1909	1.39
27	Ed Walsh, 1909	1.41
28	Ed Walsh, 1908	1.42
29	Ed Reulbach, 1905	1.42
30	Orval Overall, 1909	1.42
31	Christy Mathewson, 1908	1.43
32	Fred Anderson, 1917	1.44
33	Mordecai Brown, 1908	1.47
34	Rube Waddell, 1905	1.48
35	Joe Wood, 1915	1.49
36	Walter Johnson, 1919	1.49
37	Jack Pfiester, 1906	1.51
38	John Ward, 1878	1.51
39	Harry McCormick, 1882	1.52
40	Doc White, 1906	1.52
41	George McQuillan, 1908	1.53
42	Dwight Gooden, 1985	1.53
43	Eddie Cicotte, 1917	1.53
44	Will White, 1882	1.54
45	Cy Morgan, 1910	1.55
46	Pete Alexander, 1916	1.55
47	Walter Johnson, 1915	1.55
48	Howie Camnitz, 1908	1.56
49	Greg Maddux, 1994	1.56
50	Jim Devlin, 1876	1.56
51	Tim Keefe, 1885	1.58
52	Fred Toney, 1915	1.58
53	Eddie Cicotte, 1913	1.58
54	Rube Marquard, 1916	1.58
55	Chief Bender, 1910	1.58
56	Barney Pelty, 1906	1.59
57	Addie Joss, 1904	1.59
58	Ed Walsh, 1907	1.60
59	Luis Tiant, 1968	1.60
60	Joe McGinnity, 1904	1.61
61	Ray Collins, 1910	1.62
62	Rube Waddell, 1904	1.62
63	Howie Camnitz, 1909	1.62
64	Cy Young, 1901	1.62
65	Greg Maddux, 1995	1.63
66	Spud Chandler, 1943	1.64
67	Ernie Shore, 1915	1.64
68	Silver King, 1888	1.64
69	Ed Summers, 1908	1.64
70	Dean Chance, 1964	1.65
71	Walter Johnson, 1908	1.65
72	Ed Reulbach, 1906	1.65
73	Russ Ford, 1910	1.65
74	Chief Bender, 1909	1.66
75	Sam Leever, 1907	1.66
76	Carl Hubbell, 1933	1.66
77	Mickey Welch, 1885	1.66
78	Candy Cummings, 1876	1.67
79	Tommy Bond, 1876	1.68
80	Orval Overall, 1907	1.68
81	Ed Reulbach, 1907	1.69
82	Claude Hendrix, 1914	1.69
83	Nolan Ryan, 1981	1.69
84	Jim McCormick, 1878	1.69
85	Joe Wood, 1910	1.69
86	Rube Foster, 1914	1.70
87	Charlie Sweeney, 1884	1.70
	Bill Burns, 1908	1.70
89	Addie Joss, 1909	1.71
90	Ed Killian, 1909	1.71
91	Walter Johnson, 1914	1.72
92	Ned Garvin, 1904	1.72
93	Doc White, 1909	1.72
94	Bill Doak, 1914	1.72
95	Addie Joss, 1906	1.72
	Pete Alexander, 1919	1.72
97	Sandy Koufax, 1966	1.73
98	Bob Ewing, 1907	1.73
99	Vic Willis, 1906	1.73
100	Sandy Koufax, 1964	1.74

Earned Run Average (by era)

1876-1892

1	Tim Keefe, 1880	0.86
2	Denny Driscoll, 1882	1.21
3	George Bradley, 1876	1.23
4	Guy Hecker, 1882	1.30
5	George Bradley, 1880	1.38
6	Charley Radbourn, 1884	1.38
7	John Ward, 1878	1.51
8	Harry McCormick, 1882	1.52
9	Will White, 1882	1.54
10	Jim Devlin, 1876	1.56
11	Tim Keefe, 1885	1.58
12	Silver King, 1888	1.64
13	Mickey Welch, 1885	1.66
14	Candy Cummings, 1876	1.67
15	Tommy Bond, 1876	1.68

1893-1919

1	Dutch Leonard, 1914	0.96
2	Mordecai Brown, 1906	1.04
3	Christy Mathewson, 1909	1.14
4	Walter Johnson, 1913	1.14
5	Jack Pfiester, 1907	1.15
6	Addie Joss, 1908	1.16
7	Carl Lundgren, 1907	1.17
8	Pete Alexander, 1915	1.22
9	Cy Young, 1908	1.26
10	Ed Walsh, 1910	1.27
11	Walter Johnson, 1918	1.27
12	Christy Mathewson, 1905	1.28
13	Jack Coombs, 1910	1.30
14	Mordecai Brown, 1909	1.31
15	Jack Taylor, 1902	1.33

1920-1941

1	Carl Hubbell, 1933	1.66
2	Pete Alexander, 1920	1.91
3	Dolf Luque, 1923	1.93
4	Lon Warneke, 1933	2.00
5	Lefty Grove, 1931	2.06
6	Dazzy Vance, 1928	2.09
7	Babe Adams, 1920	2.16
8	Hal Schumacher, 1933	2.16
9	Dazzy Vance, 1924	2.16
10	Burleigh Grimes, 1920	2.22
11	Elmer Riddle, 1941	2.24
12	Bill Walker, 1931	2.26
13	Wilcy Moore, 1927	2.28
14	Bucky Walters, 1939	2.29
15	Carl Hubbell, 1934	2.30

1942-1960

1	Spud Chandler, 1943	1.64
2	Mort Cooper, 1942	1.78
3	Hal Newhouser, 1945	1.81
4	Max Lanier, 1943	1.90
5	Hal Newhouser, 1946	1.94
6	Billy Pierce, 1955	1.97
7	Whitey Ford, 1958	2.01
8	Al Benton, 1945	2.02
9	Allie Reynolds, 1952	2.06
10	Ted Lyons, 1942	2.10
11	Howie Pollet, 1946	2.10
12	Spud Chandler, 1946	2.10
13	Warren Spahn, 1953	2.10
14	Dizzy Trout, 1944	2.12
15	Roger Wolff, 1945	2.12

1961-1976

1	Bob Gibson, 1968	1.12
2	Luis Tiant, 1968	1.60
3	Dean Chance, 1964	1.65
4	Sandy Koufax, 1966	1.73
5	Sandy Koufax, 1964	1.74
6	Tom Seaver, 1971	1.76
7	Sam McDowell, 1968	1.81
8	Vida Blue, 1971	1.82
9	Phil Niekro, 1967	1.87
10	Joe Horlen, 1964	1.88
11	Sandy Koufax, 1963	1.88
12	Luis Tiant, 1972	1.91
13	Wilbur Wood, 1971	1.91
14	Gaylord Perry, 1972	1.92
15	Dave McNally, 1968	1.95

1977-1998

1	Dwight Gooden, 1985	1.53
2	Greg Maddux, 1994	1.56
3	Greg Maddux, 1995	1.63
4	Nolan Ryan, 1981	1.69
5	Ron Guidry, 1978	1.74
6	Kevin Brown, 1996	1.89
7	Pedro Martinez, 1997	1.90
8	John Tudor, 1985	1.93
9	Roger Clemens, 1990	1.93
10	Orel Hershiser, 1985	2.03
11	Roger Clemens, 1997	2.05
12	Bill Swift, 1992	2.08
13	Bret Saberhagen, 1989	2.16
14	Bob Tewksbury, 1992	2.16
15	Joe Magrane, 1988	2.18

Adjusted Earned Run Average

1	Tim Keefe, 1880	294
2	Dutch Leonard, 1914	280
3	Greg Maddux, 1994	272
4	Greg Maddux, 1995	261
5	Walter Johnson, 1913	258
6	Bob Gibson, 1968	258
7	Mordecai Brown, 1906	254
8	Walter Johnson, 1912	240
9	Christy Mathewson, 1905	230
10	Dwight Gooden, 1985	226
11	Pete Alexander, 1915	225
12	Roger Clemens, 1997	224
13	Christy Mathewson, 1909	223
14	Pedro Martinez, 1997	220
15	Lefty Grove, 1931	218
16	Cy Young, 1901	217
17	Jack Pfiester, 1907	216
18	Denny Driscoll, 1882	216
19	Walter Johnson, 1919	216
20	Kevin Brown, 1996	215
21	Walter Johnson, 1918	215
22	Carl Lundgren, 1907	213
23	Roger Clemens, 1990	211
24	Ed Reulbach, 1905	210
25	Ron Guidry, 1978	208
26	Charley Radbourn, 1884	206
27	Addie Joss, 1908	206
28	Jack Taylor, 1902	203
29	Billy Pierce, 1955	201
30	Dolf Luque, 1923	200
31	Dean Chance, 1964	199
32	Silver King, 1888	198
33	Randy Johnson, 1997	197
34	Spud Chandler, 1943	197
35	Al Maul, 1895	196
36	Nolan Ryan, 1981	195
37	Cy Young, 1908	195
38	Hal Newhouser, 1945	194
39	Tom Seaver, 1971	194
40	Mordecai Brown, 1909	193
41	Carl Hubbell, 1933	193
42	Mort Cooper, 1942	193
43	Walter Johnson, 1915	191
44	Monty Stratton, 1937	191
45	Randy Johnson, 1995	191
46	Guy Hecker, 1882	191
47	Lefty Gomez, 1937	191
48	Sandy Koufax, 1966	191
49	Ed Siever, 1902	191
50	Clark Griffith, 1898	191
51	Dazzy Vance, 1928	191
52	Greg Maddux, 1998	190
53	Greg Maddux, 1997	190
54	Lefty Grove, 1936	189
55	Vean Gregg, 1911	189
56	Ed Walsh, 1910	189
57	Amos Rusie, 1894	189
58	Hal Newhouser, 1946	189
59	Dazzy Vance, 1930	188
60	Billy Rhines, 1896	188
61	Wilbur Wood, 1971	188
62	Jack Stivetts, 1889	188
63	Joe Wood, 1915	187
64	Warren Spahn, 1953	187
65	Sandy Koufax, 1964	187
66	Lefty Grove, 1939	186
67	Eddie Cicotte, 1913	185
68	Luis Tiant, 1968	185
69	Lefty Grove, 1930	184
70	Hank Aguirre, 1962	184
71	Joe Horlen, 1964	184
72	Henry Boyle, 1886	184
73	Vida Blue, 1971	183
74	John Tudor, 1985	183
75	Walter Johnson, 1910	183
76	Harry Brecheen, 1948	183
77	Jack Coombs, 1910	182
78	Billy Rhines, 1890	182
79	Steve Carlton, 1972	182
80	Fred Toney, 1915	182
81	Johnny Allen, 1937	181
82	Rube Waddell, 1905	180
83	Mordecai Brown, 1907	179
84	Orval Overall, 1909	179
85	Rube Waddell, 1902	179
86	Kevin Appier, 1993	179
87	Joe Wood, 1912	178
88	Bret Saberhagen, 1989	178
89	Phil Niekro, 1967	178
90	Max Lanier, 1943	177
91	Roger Clemens, 1994	177
92	Fred Anderson, 1917	177
93	Cy Young, 1892	176
94	Johnny Antonelli, 1954	176
95	Whitey Ford, 1958	176
96	Lefty Grove, 1935	176
97	Roger Clemens, 1998	175
98	Jack Pfiester, 1906	175
99	Eddie Cicotte, 1919	175
100	Roger Clemens, 1992	175

Adjusted ERA (by era)

1876-1892

1	Tim Keefe, 1880	294
2	Denny Driscoll, 1882	216
3	Charley Radbourn, 1884	206
4	Silver King, 1888	198
5	Guy Hecker, 1882	191
6	Jack Stivetts, 1889	188
7	Henry Boyle, 1886	184
8	Billy Rhines, 1890	182
9	Cy Young, 1892	176
10	Harry McCormick, 1882	174
11	George Bradley, 1876	174
12	Jim Devlin, 1876	174
13	Will White, 1882	172
14	Guy Hecker, 1884	172
15	Jim McCormick, 1883	171

1893-1919

1	Dutch Leonard, 1914	280
2	Walter Johnson, 1913	258
3	Mordecai Brown, 1906	254
4	Walter Johnson, 1912	240
5	Christy Mathewson, 1905	230
6	Pete Alexander, 1915	225
7	Christy Mathewson, 1909	223
8	Cy Young, 1901	217
9	Jack Pfiester, 1907	216
10	Walter Johnson, 1919	216
11	Walter Johnson, 1918	215
12	Carl Lundgren, 1907	213
13	Ed Reulbach, 1905	210
14	Addie Joss, 1908	206
15	Jack Taylor, 1902	203

1920-1941

1	Lefty Grove, 1931	218
2	Dolf Luque, 1923	200
3	Carl Hubbell, 1933	193
4	Monty Stratton, 1937	191
5	Lefty Gomez, 1937	191
6	Dazzy Vance, 1928	191
7	Lefty Grove, 1936	189
8	Dazzy Vance, 1930	188
9	Lefty Grove, 1939	186
10	Lefty Grove, 1930	184
11	Johnny Allen, 1937	181
12	Lefty Grove, 1935	176
13	Mel Harder, 1934	174
14	Lefty Gomez, 1934	174
15	Dazzy Vance, 1924	173

1942-1960

1	Billy Pierce, 1955	201
2	Spud Chandler, 1943	197
3	Hal Newhouser, 1945	194
4	Mort Cooper, 1942	193
5	Hal Newhouser, 1946	189
6	Warren Spahn, 1953	187
7	Harry Brecheen, 1948	183
8	Max Lanier, 1943	177
9	Johnny Antonelli, 1954	176
10	Whitey Ford, 1958	176
11	Al Benton, 1945	174
12	Hoyt Wilhelm, 1959	173
13	Ted Lyons, 1942	172

1961-1976

1	Bob Gibson, 1968	258
2	Dean Chance, 1964	199
3	Tom Seaver, 1971	194
4	Sandy Koufax, 1966	191
5	Wilbur Wood, 1971	188
6	Sandy Koufax, 1964	187
7	Luis Tiant, 1968	185
8	Hank Aguirre, 1962	184
9	Joe Horlen, 1964	184
10	Vida Blue, 1971	183
11	Steve Carlton, 1972	182
12	Phil Niekro, 1967	178
13	Tom Seaver, 1973	174
14	Whitey Ford, 1964	170
15	Juan Marichal, 1965	169

1977-1998

1	Greg Maddux, 1994	272
2	Greg Maddux, 1995	261
3	Dwight Gooden, 1985	226
4	Roger Clemens, 1997	224
5	Pedro Martinez, 1997	220
6	Kevin Brown, 1996	215
7	Roger Clemens, 1990	211
8	Ron Guidry, 1978	208
9	Randy Johnson, 1997	197
10	Nolan Ryan, 1981	195
11	Randy Johnson, 1995	191
12	Greg Maddux, 1998	190
13	Greg Maddux, 1997	190
14	John Tudor, 1985	183
15	Kevin Appier, 1993	179

Pitching Runs

1	Amos Rusie, 1894	125.7
2	Charley Radbourn, 1884	120.9
3	Guy Hecker, 1884	108.0
4	Silver King, 1888	92.3
5	John Clarkson, 1889	88.7
6	Cy Young, 1901	84.2
7	Matt Kilroy, 1887	80.4
8	Pink Hawley, 1895	79.1
9	Walter Johnson, 1912	79.1
10	Silver King, 1890	78.9
11	Will White, 1883	77.7
12	Amos Rusie, 1893	76.9
13	Charley Radbourn, 1883	76.5
14	Dave Foutz, 1886	75.2
15	Lefty Grove, 1931	74.5
16	Dolf Luque, 1923	74.2
17	Jouett Meekin, 1894	73.9
18	Roger Clemens, 1997	73.9
19	Scott Stratton, 1890	72.3
20	Billy Rhines, 1890	72.2
21	Lefty Gomez, 1937	70.9
22	Pud Galvin, 1884	69.8
23	Walter Johnson, 1913	68.8
24	George Bradley, 1876	68.8
25	Cy Young, 1892	68.5
26	Kid Nichols, 1897	68.4
27	Lefty Grove, 1930	68.4
28	Dazzy Vance, 1930	67.9
29	Lefty Gomez, 1934	67.7
30	Elmer Smith, 1887	67.6
31	Sandy Koufax, 1966	67.5
32	John Clarkson, 1885	67.1
33	Red Faber, 1921	66.4
34	Toad Ramsey, 1886	65.7
35	Christy Mathewson, 1905	65.0
36	Warren Spahn, 1953	64.5
37	Pete Alexander, 1915	64.1
38	Kid Nichols, 1898	63.5
39	Amos Rusie, 1897	63.5
40	Kid Nichols, 1896	63.5
41	Ted Breitenstein, 1893	63.4
42	Dwight Gooden, 1985	63.4
43	Kid Nichols, 1890	63.2
44	Mickey Welch, 1885	63.1
45	Bob Gibson, 1968	63.1
46	Bob Caruthers, 1885	63.1
47	Bob Feller, 1940	63.0
48	Lefty Grove, 1936	62.8
49	Cy Young, 1894	62.7
50	Clark Griffith, 1898	62.6
51	Cy Young, 1895	62.5
52	Ed Morris, 1886	61.9
53	Pedro Martinez, 1997	61.6
54	Amos Rusie, 1890	61.6
55	Ron Guidry, 1978	61.4
56	Carl Hubbell, 1934	61.3
57	Will White, 1882	61.3
58	Cy Young, 1893	61.1
59	Dean Chance, 1964	61.1
60	Tim Keefe, 1883	61.1
61	Cy Young, 1902	60.8
62	Jim Palmer, 1975	60.6
63	Ed Seward, 1888	60.5
64	Kevin Brown, 1996	60.1
65	Greg Maddux, 1994	59.5
66	Thornton Lee, 1941	59.4
67	Greg Maddux, 1995	59.4
68	Dazzy Vance, 1928	59.3
69	Robin Roberts, 1953	59.1
70	Charlie Ferguson, 1886	58.6
71	Dazzy Vance, 1924	58.5
72	Bob Feller, 1939	58.3
73	Bill Hutchison, 1890	58.2
74	Lady Baldwin, 1886	58.2
75	Bucky Walters, 1939	57.8
76	Kid Nichols, 1895	57.8
77	Carl Hubbell, 1936	57.8
78	John Clarkson, 1887	57.7
79	Ed Morris, 1885	57.7
80	Jesse Duryea, 1889	57.5
81	Carl Hubbell, 1933	57.5
82	Wilbur Wood, 1971	57.4
83	Guy Hecker, 1885	57.2
84	Tony Mullane, 1883	57.0
85	Vida Blue, 1971	57.0
86	Steve Carlton, 1972	56.9
87	Walter Johnson, 1919	56.1
88	Sandy Koufax, 1965	56.0
89	Greg Maddux, 1998	56.0
90	Win Mercer, 1894	55.7
91	Warren Spahn, 1947	55.7
92	Tim Keefe, 1885	55.3
93	Bill Hoffer, 1895	54.9
94	Walter Johnson, 1918	54.6
95	Bob Feller, 1946	54.5
96	Charlie Buffinton, 1884	54.5
97	Kid Nichols, 1893	54.3
98	Tom Seaver, 1971	54.3
99	Hal Newhouser, 1945	54.2
100	Randy Johnson, 1997	54.0

Adjusted Pitching Runs

1	Amos Rusie, 1894	121.7
2	Charley Radbourn, 1884	110.7
3	Silver King, 1888	105.2
4	John Clarkson, 1889	98.9
5	Guy Hecker, 1884	95.9
6	Silver King, 1890	84.5
7	Pud Galvin, 1884	81.9
8	John Clarkson, 1887	81.8
9	John Clarkson, 1885	80.0
10	Walter Johnson, 1912	79.8
11	Jim Devlin, 1876	79.7
12	Cy Young, 1901	78.6
13	Lefty Grove, 1931	78.2
14	Toad Ramsey, 1886	78.1
15	Amos Rusie, 1893	76.4
16	Kid Nichols, 1897	74.9
17	Dave Foutz, 1886	74.6
18	Roger Clemens, 1997	74.5
19	Will White, 1883	74.1
20	Cy Young, 1892	73.7
21	Charley Radbourn, 1883	72.7
22	Kid Nichols, 1890	71.8
23	Billy Rhines, 1890	71.7
24	Cy Young, 1893	71.4
25	Scott Stratton, 1890	71.4
26	Kid Nichols, 1895	71.3
27	Cy Young, 1895	70.9
28	Kid Nichols, 1896	70.9
29	Lefty Grove, 1936	70.6
30	Jouett Meekin, 1894	70.3
31	Elmer Smith, 1887	69.9
32	Walter Johnson, 1913	69.6
33	Dolf Luque, 1923	69.3
34	Lefty Grove, 1930	69.1
35	Cy Young, 1894	69.0
36	Matt Kilroy, 1887	67.4
37	Kid Nichols, 1898	67.3
38	Kid Nichols, 1893	67.1
39	Tony Mullane, 1883	66.3
40	Dazzy Vance, 1930	66.2
41	Ted Breitenstein, 1893	66.2
42	Pink Hawley, 1895	66.2
43	Jack Stivetts, 1891	65.7
44	Lefty Gomez, 1937	65.5
45	Jim Devlin, 1877	65.5
46	Red Faber, 1921	64.6
47	Bob Caruthers, 1885	64.3
48	Bill Hutchison, 1890	64.2
49	Tim Keefe, 1883	63.8
50	Pete Alexander, 1915	63.7
51	Vic Willis, 1899	63.4
52	John Clarkson, 1886	62.8
53	Christy Mathewson, 1905	62.3
54	Wilbur Wood, 1971	62.2
55	Steve Carlton, 1972	62.2
56	Lefty Grove, 1935	61.9
57	Clark Griffith, 1898	61.6
58	Pedro Martinez, 1997	61.4
59	Greg Maddux, 1995	61.3
60	Cy Young, 1902	60.8
61	Greg Maddux, 1994	60.2
62	Jesse Duryea, 1889	60.1
63	Bob Gibson, 1968	60.0
64	Cy Young, 1896	59.9
65	Kid Nichols, 1891	59.8
66	Toad Ramsey, 1887	59.7
67	Dan Casey, 1887	59.5
68	Hal Newhouser, 1945	59.4
69	Dwight Gooden, 1985	59.2
70	Elton Chamberlain, 1889	59.0
71	Dazzy Vance, 1928	58.8
72	Will White, 1882	58.8
73	Matt Kilroy, 1889	58.7
74	Lady Baldwin, 1886	58.3
75	Charlie Ferguson, 1886	58.1
76	Ed Morris, 1886	58.0
77	Amos Rusie, 1897	57.9
78	George Bradley, 1876	57.8
79	Thornton Lee, 1941	57.7
80	Kid Gleason, 1890	57.5
81	Amos Rusie, 1890	57.5
82	Cy Young, 1899	57.4
83	Ron Guidry, 1978	57.1
84	Bob Feller, 1940	57.1
85	Joe Wood, 1912	57.0
86	Nig Cuppy, 1895	56.7
87	Dizzy Trout, 1944	56.6
88	Bobo Newsom, 1940	56.5
89	Nig Cuppy, 1896	56.5
90	Sandy Koufax, 1966	56.3
91	Kevin Brown, 1996	56.3
92	Ed Seward, 1888	56.2
93	Robin Roberts, 1953	56.1
94	Tony Mullane, 1884	56.1
95	Guy Hecker, 1885	56.0
96	Greg Maddux, 1998	56.0
97	Hal Newhouser, 1946	55.8
98	Ed Morris, 1885	55.8
99	Walter Johnson, 1919	55.5
100	Silver King, 1889	55.1

Pitching Wins

1	Charley Radbourn, 1884	10.8
2	Guy Hecker, 1884	9.9
3	Amos Rusie, 1894	9.6
4	Silver King, 1888	8.5
5	Walter Johnson, 1912	7.9
6	John Clarkson, 1889	7.7
7	Cy Young, 1901	7.6
8	Walter Johnson, 1913	7.3
9	Bob Gibson, 1968	7.2
10	Dolf Luque, 1923	7.1
11	Pete Alexander, 1915	7.1
12	Sandy Koufax, 1966	7.1
13	Roger Clemens, 1997	7.0
14	Lefty Grove, 1931	6.9
15	Will White, 1883	6.8
16	Christy Mathewson, 1905	6.7
17	Charley Radbourn, 1883	6.7
18	Dwight Gooden, 1985	6.7
19	Dave Foutz, 1886	6.6
20	Lefty Gomez, 1937	6.5
21	Matt Kilroy, 1887	6.5
22	Dean Chance, 1964	6.4
23	Billy Rhines, 1890	6.4
24	Pink Hawley, 1895	6.4
25	Scott Stratton, 1890	6.4
26	Cy Young, 1892	6.3
27	Ron Guidry, 1978	6.3
28	John Clarkson, 1885	6.3
29	Amos Rusie, 1893	6.3
30	Lefty Gomez, 1934	6.3
31	Silver King, 1890	6.3
32	Pud Galvin, 1884	6.2
33	Warren Spahn, 1953	6.2
34	Red Faber, 1921	6.2
35	Jim Palmer, 1975	6.2
36	Lefty Grove, 1930	6.2
37	Wilbur Wood, 1971	6.2
38	Vida Blue, 1971	6.1
39	Steve Carlton, 1972	6.1
40	Walter Johnson, 1918	6.1
41	Carl Hubbell, 1933	6.1
42	Pedro Martinez, 1997	6.1
43	George Bradley, 1876	6.1
44	Dazzy Vance, 1930	6.0
45	Carl Hubbell, 1934	6.0
46	Bob Feller, 1940	5.9
47	Kid Nichols, 1898	5.9
48	Mickey Welch, 1885	5.9
49	Sandy Koufax, 1965	5.9
50	Kevin Brown, 1996	5.9
51	Walter Johnson, 1919	5.9
52	Kid Nichols, 1897	5.9
53	Greg Maddux, 1994	5.9
54	Clark Griffith, 1898	5.8
55	Greg Maddux, 1995	5.8
56	Tom Seaver, 1971	5.8
57	Dazzy Vance, 1924	5.8
58	Hal Newhouser, 1945	5.8
59	Dazzy Vance, 1928	5.8
60	Bucky Walters, 1939	5.8
61	Cy Young, 1902	5.8
62	Toad Ramsey, 1886	5.8
63	Thornton Lee, 1941	5.8
64	Ed Walsh, 1908	5.7
65	Bob Feller, 1946	5.7
66	Ed Walsh, 1910	5.7
67	Robin Roberts, 1953	5.7
68	Bob Caruthers, 1885	5.7
69	Jouett Meekin, 1894	5.7
70	Carl Hubbell, 1936	5.6
71	Will White, 1882	5.6
72	Kid Nichols, 1890	5.6
73	Ed Seward, 1888	5.6
74	Lefty Grove, 1936	5.5
75	Greg Maddux, 1998	5.5
76	Jack Taylor, 1902	5.5
77	Walter Johnson, 1915	5.5
78	Warren Spahn, 1947	5.5
79	Amos Rusie, 1890	5.5
80	Elmer Smith, 1887	5.5
81	Mordecai Brown, 1906	5.5
82	Amos Rusie, 1897	5.4
83	Ed Morris, 1886	5.4
84	Mordecai Brown, 1909	5.4
85	Joe McGinnity, 1904	5.4
86	Dizzy Trout, 1944	5.4
87	Joe Wood, 1912	5.4
88	Kid Nichols, 1896	5.4
89	Tim Keefe, 1883	5.4
90	Bob Feller, 1939	5.4
91	Hal Newhouser, 1946	5.3
92	John Tudor, 1985	5.3
93	Ed Reulbach, 1905	5.3
94	Tom Seaver, 1973	5.3
95	Jack Coombs, 1910	5.3
96	Pete Alexander, 1920	5.3
97	Charlie Ferguson, 1886	5.3
98	Pete Alexander, 1916	5.3
99	Walter Johnson, 1910	5.3
100	Sandy Koufax, 1963	5.3

Adjusted Pitching Wins

1	Charley Radbourn, 1884	9.9
2	Silver King, 1888	9.7
3	Amos Rusie, 1894	9.3
4	Guy Hecker, 1884	8.8
5	John Clarkson, 1889	8.6
6	Walter Johnson, 1912	8.0
7	John Clarkson, 1885	7.5
8	Walter Johnson, 1913	7.4
9	Pud Galvin, 1884	7.3
10	Lefty Grove, 1931	7.3
11	Cy Young, 1901	7.1
12	Roger Clemens, 1997	7.1
13	Pete Alexander, 1915	7.1
14	Jim Devlin, 1876	7.0
15	John Clarkson, 1887	6.9
16	Bob Gibson, 1968	6.9
17	Toad Ramsey, 1886	6.8
18	Cy Young, 1892	6.8
19	Silver King, 1890	6.7
20	Wilbur Wood, 1971	6.7
21	Steve Carlton, 1972	6.7
22	Dolf Luque, 1923	6.7
23	Dave Foutz, 1886	6.5
24	Will White, 1883	6.5
25	Christy Mathewson, 1905	6.5
26	Kid Nichols, 1897	6.4
27	Kid Nichols, 1890	6.4
28	Billy Rhines, 1890	6.4
29	Hal Newhouser, 1945	6.4
30	Charley Radbourn, 1883	6.3
31	Kid Nichols, 1898	6.3
32	Scott Stratton, 1890	6.3
33	Amos Rusie, 1893	6.3
34	Lefty Grove, 1930	6.3
35	Lefty Grove, 1936	6.2
36	Dwight Gooden, 1985	6.2
37	Pedro Martinez, 1997	6.0
38	Red Faber, 1921	6.0
39	Greg Maddux, 1995	6.0
40	Kid Nichols, 1896	6.0
41	Lefty Gomez, 1937	6.0
42	Dizzy Trout, 1944	6.0
43	Greg Maddux, 1994	5.9
44	Sandy Koufax, 1966	5.9
45	Walter Johnson, 1918	5.9
46	Ron Guidry, 1978	5.9
47	Cy Young, 1893	5.9
48	Hal Newhouser, 1946	5.8
49	Dazzy Vance, 1930	5.8
50	Jim Devlin, 1877	5.8
51	Tony Mullane, 1883	5.8
52	Walter Johnson, 1919	5.8
53	Lefty Grove, 1935	5.8
54	Bob Caruthers, 1885	5.8
55	Kid Nichols, 1895	5.8
56	Cy Young, 1902	5.8
57	Clark Griffith, 1898	5.8
58	Dazzy Vance, 1928	5.7
59	Vic Willis, 1899	5.7
60	Cy Young, 1895	5.7
61	Joe Wood, 1912	5.7
62	Bill Hutchison, 1890	5.7
63	John Clarkson, 1886	5.7
64	Elmer Smith, 1887	5.7
65	Jack Stivetts, 1891	5.7
66	Vida Blue, 1971	5.7
67	Walter Johnson, 1915	5.6
68	Gaylord Perry, 1972	5.6
69	Carl Hubbell, 1933	5.6
70	Tom Seaver, 1971	5.6
71	Tim Keefe, 1883	5.6
72	Pete Alexander, 1920	5.6
73	Thornton Lee, 1941	5.6
74	Roger Clemens, 1990	5.5
75	Greg Maddux, 1998	5.5
76	Kevin Brown, 1996	5.5
77	Kid Nichols, 1893	5.5
78	Bucky Walters, 1939	5.5
79	Mordecai Brown, 1906	5.5
80	Mort Cooper, 1942	5.5
81	Matt Kilroy, 1887	5.5
82	Pete Alexander, 1916	5.4
83	Ted Breitenstein, 1893	5.4
84	Robin Roberts, 1953	5.4
85	Will White, 1882	5.4
86	Dazzy Vance, 1924	5.4
87	Bob Feller, 1940	5.4
88	Jouett Meekin, 1894	5.4
89	Bill Hands, 1969	5.4
90	Pink Hawley, 1895	5.4
91	Joe McGinnity, 1904	5.3
92	Kid Nichols, 1891	5.3
93	Bobo Newsom, 1940	5.3
94	Dean Chance, 1964	5.3
95	Carl Hubbell, 1934	5.3
96	Bert Blyleven, 1973	5.3
97	Dizzy Dean, 1934	5.3
98	Cy Young, 1894	5.3
99	Ed Walsh, 1908	5.3
100	Lady Baldwin, 1886	5.3

Opponents' Batting Average

1	Luis Tiant, 1968	.168
2	Nolan Ryan, 1972	.171
3	Nolan Ryan, 1991	.172
4	Ed Reulbach, 1906	.175
5	Tim Keefe, 1880	.178
6	Sandy Koufax, 1965	.179
7	Dutch Leonard, 1914	.180
8	Sid Fernandez, 1985	.181
9	Hideo Nomo, 1995	.182
10	Dave McNally, 1968	.182
11	Tommy Byrne, 1949	.183
12	Pedro Martinez, 1997	.184
13	Al Downing, 1963	.184
14	Bob Gibson, 1968	.184
15	Sam McDowell, 1965	.185
16	Carl Lundgren, 1907	.185
17	Herb Score, 1956	.186
18	Mike Scott, 1986	.186
19	Nolan Ryan, 1989	.187
20	Ed Walsh, 1910	.187
21	Mario Soto, 1980	.187
22	Walter Johnson, 1913	.187
23	Nolan Ryan, 1981	.188
24	Russ Ford, 1910	.188
25	Nolan Ryan, 1986	.188
26	Nolan Ryan, 1990	.188
27	Floyd Youmans, 1986	.188
28	Sam McDowell, 1966	.188
29	Guy Hecker, 1882	.188
30	Sandy Koufax, 1963	.189
31	Sam McDowell, 1968	.189
32	Don Sutton, 1972	.189
33	Catfish Hunter, 1972	.189
34	Vida Blue, 1971	.189
35	Nolan Ryan, 1974	.190
36	Andy Messersmith, 1969	.190
37	Joe Horlen, 1964	.190
38	Sid Fernandez, 1988	.191
39	Pete Alexander, 1915	.191
40	Sandy Koufax, 1964	.191
41	Bob Turley, 1955	.193
42	Nolan Ryan, 1977	.193
43	Fred Beebe, 1908	.193
44	Charlie Sweeney, 1884	.193
45	Ron Guidry, 1978	.193
46	Stan Coveleski, 1917	.194
47	Bob Turley, 1957	.194
48	Randy Johnson, 1997	.194
49	Herb Score, 1955	.194
50	Jack Pfiester, 1906	.194
51	Mordecai Brown, 1908	.195
52	Nolan Ryan, 1976	.195
53	Nolan Ryan, 1983	.195
54	Dean Chance, 1964	.195
55	Roger Clemens, 1986	.195
56	Tim Keefe, 1888	.196
57	Kerry Wood, 1998	.196
58	Walter Johnson, 1912	.196
59	Roger Nelson, 1972	.196
60	J.R. Richard, 1978	.196
61	Pascual Perez, 1988	.196
62	Greg Maddux, 1995	.197
63	Jeff Robinson, 1988	.197
64	Lady Baldwin, 1885	.197
65	Jose DeLeon, 1989	.197
66	Dave Boswell, 1966	.197
67	Sandy Koufax, 1962	.197
68	Addie Joss, 1908	.197
69	Roger Clemens, 1998	.197
70	Sonny Siebert, 1968	.198
71	Sid Fernandez, 1989	.198
72	Toad Ramsey, 1886	.198
73	Larry Cheney, 1916	.198
74	Wayne Simpson, 1970	.198
75	Orval Overall, 1909	.198
76	Gary Peters, 1967	.199
77	Larry Corcoran, 1880	.199
78	Willie Mitchell, 1913	.199
79	Adonis Terry, 1888	.199
80	Nolan Ryan, 1987	.199
81	Mordecai Brown, 1904	.199
82	Christy Mathewson, 1909	.200
83	Rube Waddell, 1905	.200
84	Denny McLain, 1968	.200
85	Larry Corcoran, 1882	.200
86	Silver King, 1888	.200
	Bobby Bolin, 1968	.200
	Jim Palmer, 1969	.200
	Sid Fernandez, 1990	.200
90	Christy Mathewson, 1908	.200
91	Spec Shea, 1947	.200
92	Ed Seward, 1888	.200
93	Tony Mullane, 1892	.201
94	Art Fromme, 1909	.201
95	Babe Ruth, 1916	.201
96	Randy Johnson, 1995	.201
97	Dwight Gooden, 1985	.201
98	Cannonball Titcomb, 1888	.201
99	Curt Schilling, 1992	.201
100	Hal Newhouser, 1946	.201

Opponents' On Base Pctg.

1	Guy Hecker, 1882	.199
2	Charlie Sweeney, 1884	.211
3	Tim Keefe, 1880	.212
4	Henry Boyle, 1884	.215
5	George Bradley, 1880	.217
6	Walter Johnson, 1913	.217
7	Denny Driscoll, 1882	.218
8	Addie Joss, 1908	.218
9	Jim Whitney, 1884	.223
10	George Bradley, 1876	.224
11	Greg Maddux, 1995	.225
12	Christy Mathewson, 1908	.225
13	Guy Hecker, 1884	.226
14	Ed Walsh, 1910	.226
15	Tommy Bond, 1876	.227
16	Lady Baldwin, 1885	.228
17	Sandy Koufax, 1965	.228
18	Christy Mathewson, 1909	.228
19	Sandy Koufax, 1963	.230
20	Juan Marichal, 1966	.230
21	John Ward, 1880	.232
22	Mordecai Brown, 1908	.232
23	Ed Walsh, 1908	.232
24	Luis Tiant, 1968	.233
25	Bob Gibson, 1968	.233
26	Pete Alexander, 1915	.234
27	Dave McNally, 1968	.234
28	Larry Corcoran, 1882	.234
29	Charley Radbourn, 1884	.234
30	Ed Morris, 1884	.234
31	Perry Werden, 1884	.235
32	Jim Devlin, 1876	.235
33	Jack Lynch, 1884	.236
34	Larry Corcoran, 1880	.236
35	Roger Nelson, 1972	.236
36	Charlie Getzien, 1884	.237
37	Tim Keefe, 1883	.237
38	Silver King, 1888	.237
39	Tony Mullane, 1883	.238
40	John Clarkson, 1885	.239
41	Tim Keefe, 1884	.239
42	Mordecai Brown, 1909	.239
43	Fred Corey, 1880	.239
44	Juan Marichal, 1965	.240
45	Cy Young, 1908	.240
46	Don Sutton, 1972	.240
47	Cy Young, 1905	.241
48	Babe Adams, 1919	.241
49	Sandy Koufax, 1964	.241
50	Catfish Hunter, 1972	.242
51	Pete Conway, 1888	.243
52	Harry McCormick, 1882	.243
53	Denny McLain, 1968	.243
54	Tim Keefe, 1888	.243
55	Lady Baldwin, 1886	.243
56	Mike Scott, 1986	.244
57	Charley Radbourn, 1883	.244
58	Will White, 1883	.244
59	Charlie Ferguson, 1886	.244
60	Charlie Buffinton, 1888	.244
61	Will White, 1882	.244
62	Charlie Buffinton, 1884	.244
63	Russ Ford, 1910	.245
64	Pete Alexander, 1919	.245
65	Christy Mathewson, 1905	.245
66	Greg Maddux, 1994	.245
67	Dutch Leonard, 1914	.246
68	Bobby Mathews, 1882	.246
69	Pud Galvin, 1884	.246
70	Charley Radbourn, 1882	.246
71	Sam Weaver, 1878	.247
72	Charlie Gagus, 1884	.247
73	Christy Mathewson, 1907	.247
74	Warren Hacker, 1952	.247
75	Jim McCormick, 1880	.247
76	Ed Morris, 1885	.247
77	Fred Goldsmith, 1880	.247
78	Dupee Shaw, 1884	.247
79	Eddie Cicotte, 1917	.248
80	Walter Johnson, 1912	.248
81	Doc White, 1906	.249
82	John Clarkson, 1884	.249
83	Jumbo McGinnis, 1883	.249
84	John Tudor, 1985	.249
85	Henry Gruber, 1888	.249
86	Hugh Daily, 1884	.250
87	Ron Guidry, 1978	.250
88	Joe Horlen, 1964	.250
89	Pedro Martinez, 1997	.250
90	Terry Larkin, 1879	.250
91	John Ward, 1879	.250
92	John Ward, 1878	.251
93	Billy Taylor, 1884	.251
94	Candy Cummings, 1876	.251
95	Jim Whitney, 1883	.251
96	Cy Young, 1904	.251
97	Claude Hendrix, 1914	.251
98	Dick Burns, 1884	.252
99	Vida Blue, 1971	.252
100	Jack Chesbro, 1904	.252

Wins Above Team

1	George Bradley, 1876	22.5
2	Will White, 1879	21.5
3	Charley Radbourn, 1884	20.1
4	Jim McCormick, 1880	19.4
5	Guy Hecker, 1884	18.0
6	Pud Galvin, 1883	17.6
7	Jim Devlin, 1877	17.5
8	Charley Radbourn, 1883	15.7
9	Matt Kilroy, 1887	15.4
10	Pud Galvin, 1884	15.1
11	Jim Devlin, 1876	15.0
12	Charlie Buffinton, 1884	14.9
13	Walter Johnson, 1913	14.7
14	Jim McCormick, 1884	14.6
15	Jack Chesbro, 1904	14.0
16	Tony Mullane, 1884	13.9
17	Sadie McMahon, 1890	13.4
18	Will White, 1882	13.1
19	Ed Morris, 1885	12.9
20	Joe Wood, 1912	12.8
21	Bill Sweeney, 1884	12.7
	Ed Walsh, 1908	12.7
23	John Clarkson, 1889	12.1
24	Tommy Bond, 1879	12.0
25	Lefty Grove, 1931	11.8
26	Steve Carlton, 1972	11.7
27	Cy Young, 1901	11.6
28	Bill Hutchison, 1891	11.4
	Denny McLain, 1968	11.4
30	Terry Larkin, 1878	11.2
	Mickey Welch, 1884	11.2
	Bob Caruthers, 1889	11.2
33	Henry Porter, 1885	11.0
	Bill Hoffer, 1895	11.0
	Christy Mathewson, 1908	11.0
36	Cy Young, 1902	10.9
37	Cy Young, 1895	10.7
38	Dazzy Vance, 1924	10.6
	Robin Roberts, 1952	10.6
	Ron Guidry, 1978	10.6
41	Bobby Mathews, 1876	10.5
	Dizzy Dean, 1934	10.5
43	Toad Ramsey, 1886	10.2
	Cy Young, 1892	10.2
	Joe McGinnity, 1904	10.2
	Eddie Rommel, 1922	10.2
47	Lefty Grove, 1930	10.1
48	Ed Morris, 1886	10.0
	Bill Donovan, 1907	10.0
50	Frank Mountain, 1883	9.9
	Eddie Cicotte, 1919	9.9
	Lefty Gomez, 1934	9.9
53	Kid Gleason, 1890	9.8
	Pete Alexander, 1915	9.8
	Hal Newhouser, 1944	9.8
56	Bobby Mathews, 1885	9.7
	Russ Ford, 1910	9.7
	Roger Clemens, 1986	9.7
59	Charlie Ferguson, 1886	9.6
	Pete Conway, 1888	9.6
	Eddie Plank, 1912	9.6
62	Pete Alexander, 1916	9.5
	Carl Hubbell, 1936	9.5
	Dwight Gooden, 1985	9.5
65	Jouett Meekin, 1894	9.4
	Walter Johnson, 1912	9.4
	Claude Hendrix, 1914	9.4
68	Joe McGinnity, 1900	9.3
	Sandy Koufax, 1963	9.3
70	Bert Cunningham, 1898	9.2
	Walter Johnson, 1911	9.2
	Bobby Shantz, 1952	9.2
	Don Newcombe, 1956	9.2
	Juan Marichal, 1966	9.2
	Bob Gibson, 1970	9.2
	Bob Welch, 1990	9.2
77	Tim Keefe, 1888	9.1
	Whitey Ford, 1961	9.1
79	Jim McCormick, 1882	9.0
	Cy Young, 1893	9.0
	Preacher Roe, 1951	9.0
82	Frank Killen, 1892	8.9
	Red Faber, 1921	8.9
84	Tim Keefe, 1883	8.8
	Tim Keefe, 1887	8.8
	Christy Mathewson, 1909	8.8
	Dolf Luque, 1923	8.8
88	Lee Richmond, 1881	8.7
	Frank Killen, 1893	8.7
	Jim Hughes, 1899	8.7
	Juan Marichal, 1963	8.7
	Juan Marichal, 1968	8.7
93	Jim McCormick, 1883	8.6
	Lefty Grove, 1933	8.6
	Bob Feller, 1946	8.6
	Roy Face, 1959	8.6
97	7 players tied	8.5

Wins Above League

1	Charley Radbourn, 1884	45.4
2	Guy Hecker, 1884	44.8
3	Charley Radbourn, 1883	42.8
4	Silver King, 1888	42.7
5	John Clarkson, 1889	42.6
6	John Clarkson, 1885	42.0
7	Pud Galvin, 1884	41.3
8	Pud Galvin, 1883	40.4
9	Jim McCormick, 1880	40.1
10	Tim Keefe, 1883	39.6
11	Bill Hutchison, 1892	39.6
12	Jim Devlin, 1876	39.5
13	Will White, 1879	39.4
14	Toad Ramsey, 1886	39.3
15	Bill Hutchison, 1890	39.2
16	Will White, 1883	39.0
17	Matt Kilroy, 1887	38.0
18	George Bradley, 1876	37.1
19	Toad Ramsey, 1887	36.8
20	Amos Rusie, 1890	36.6
21	Ed Morris, 1885	36.5
22	John Clarkson, 1887	36.4
23	Charlie Buffinton, 1884	36.3
24	Tony Mullane, 1884	36.1
25	Jim Devlin, 1877	35.8
26	Jim McCormick, 1884	35.6
27	Ed Morris, 1886	35.6
28	Jim McCormick, 1882	35.6
29	Dave Foutz, 1886	35.0
30	Lee Richmond, 1880	34.9
31	Tim Keefe, 1886	34.5
32	John Ward, 1880	34.5
33	Bill Hutchison, 1891	34.4
34	John Ward, 1879	34.3
35	Pud Galvin, 1879	34.0
36	Sadie McMahon, 1891	34.0
37	Tommy Bond, 1879	34.0
38	Amos Rusie, 1894	33.8
39	Amos Rusie, 1892	33.6
40	Billy Taylor, 1884	33.5
41	Jim Whitney, 1883	33.3
42	Amos Rusie, 1893	33.3
43	Jack Stivetts, 1891	33.2
44	Dupee Shaw, 1884	33.1
45	Al Spalding, 1876	33.1
46	Jim Whitney, 1881	33.0
47	Mark Baldwin, 1890	32.8
48	Ed Walsh, 1908	32.8
49	Lady Baldwin, 1886	32.8
50	Larry Corcoran, 1884	32.7
51	Silver King, 1890	32.7
52	Mickey Welch, 1885	32.7
53	Mickey Welch, 1884	32.6
54	Kid Gleason, 1890	32.6
55	Charlie Sweeney, 1884	32.3
56	Bob Caruthers, 1885	32.3
57	Ed Seward, 1888	32.2
58	John Clarkson, 1886	32.2
59	Tommy Bond, 1877	32.1
60	Matt Kilroy, 1889	32.0
61	Will White, 1880	31.9
62	Mickey Welch, 1880	31.9
63	Pink Hawley, 1895	31.9
64	Matt Kilroy, 1886	31.8
65	Guy Hecker, 1885	31.5
66	Jack Chesbro, 1904	31.5
67	Sadie McMahon, 1890	31.5
68	Will White, 1882	31.4
69	Tim Keefe, 1884	31.2
70	Larry Corcoran, 1880	31.2
71	George Derby, 1881	31.2
72	Tommy Bond, 1878	31.2
73	Elmer Smith, 1887	31.2
74	Bill Sweeney, 1884	31.0
75	Cy Young, 1893	30.9
76	Tony Mullane, 1883	30.8
77	Cy Young, 1892	30.8
78	Jesse Duryea, 1889	30.6
79	Mark Baldwin, 1889	30.6
80	Walter Johnson, 1912	30.5
81	Jim McCormick, 1879	30.4
82	Hardie Henderson, 1885	30.4
83	Scott Stratton, 1890	30.3
84	Larry Corcoran, 1883	30.2
85	Silver King, 1889	30.2
86	Charley Radbourn, 1886	30.0
87	Charley Radbourn, 1882	30.0
88	John Clarkson, 1891	29.9
89	Tim Keefe, 1887	29.9
90	Phil Knell, 1891	29.9
91	Tony Mullane, 1882	29.8
92	Joe McGinnity, 1903	29.8
93	Amos Rusie, 1891	29.7
94	Jersey Bakely, 1888	29.6
95	Kid Nichols, 1893	29.5
96	Henry Porter, 1885	29.5
97	Kid Nichols, 1890	29.4
98	Gus Weyhing, 1892	29.3
99	Tony Mullane, 1886	29.1
100	Gus Weyhing, 1889	29.0

Relief Games

1	Mike Marshall, 1974	106
2	Kent Tekulve, 1979	94
3	Mike Marshall, 1973	92
4	Kent Tekulve, 1978	91
5	Wayne Granger, 1969	90
	Kent Tekulve, 1987	90
7	Mike Marshall, 1979	89
	Mark Eichhorn, 1987	89
	Julian Tavarez, 1997	89
10	Mike Myers, 1997	88
	Sean Runyan, 1998	88
12	Rob Murphy, 1987	87
13	Wilbur Wood, 1968	86
14	Kent Tekulve, 1982	85
	Frank Williams, 1987	85
16	Ted Abernathy, 1965	84
	Enrique Romo, 1979	84
	Dick Tidrow, 1980	84
	Dan Quisenberry, 1985	84
	Mitch Williams, 1987	84
	Stan Belinda, 1997	84
22	Ken Sanders, 1971	83
	Craig Lefferts, 1986	83
	Eddie Guardado, 1996	83
	Mike Myers, 1996	83
26	Eddie Fisher, 1965	82
	Bill Campbell, 1983	82
	Juan Agosto, 1990	82
	Paul Quantrill, 1998	82
30	John Wyatt, 1964	81
	Dale Murray, 1976	81
	Jeff Robinson, 1987	81
	Duane Ward, 1991	81
	Joe Boever, 1992	81
	Kenny Rogers, 1992	81
	Mike Jackson, 1993	81
	Brad Clontz, 1996	81
	Mike Stanton, 1996	81
	Rod Beck, 1998	81
	Greg Swindell, 1998	81
41	Mudcat Grant, 1970	80
	Pedro Borbon, 1973	80
	Willie Hernandez, 1984	80
	Mitch Williams, 1986	80
	Doug Jones, 1992	80
	Greg Harris, 1993	80
47	Dick Radatz, 1964	79
	Duane Ward, 1992	79
	Bob Patterson, 1996	79
	Eddie Guardado, 1998	79

Relief Wins

1	Roy Face, 1959	18
2	John Hiller, 1974	17
	Bill Campbell, 1976	17
4	Jim Konstanty, 1950	16
	Ron Perranoski, 1963	16
	Dick Radatz, 1964	16
	Tom Johnson, 1977	16
8	Mace Brown, 1938	15
	Hoyt Wilhelm, 1952	15
	Luis Arroyo, 1961	15
	Dick Radatz, 1963	15
	Eddie Fisher, 1965	15
	Mike Marshall, 1974	15
	Dale Murray, 1975	15
15	Joe Page, 1947	14
	Joe Black, 1952	14
	Hersh Freeman, 1956	14
	Stu Miller, 1961	14
	Stu Miller, 1965	14
	Phil Regan, 1966	14
	Frank Linzy, 1969	14
	Mike Marshall, 1972	14
	Mike Marshall, 1973	14
	Ron Davis, 1979	14
	Mark Clear, 1982	14
	Jim Slaton, 1983	14
	Roger McDowell, 1986	14
	Mark Eichhorn, 1986	14
29	Dick Tidrow, 1979	13
	Earl Caldwell, 1946	13
	Joe Page, 1949	13
	Clyde King, 1951	13
	Lindy McDaniel, 1959	13
	Larry Sherry, 1960	13
	Gerry Staley, 1960	13
	Lindy McDaniel, 1963	13
	Al Hrabosky, 1975	13
	Rollie Fingers, 1976	13
	Bill Campbell, 1977	13
	Sparky Lyle, 1977	13
	Gary Lavelle, 1978	13
	Bob Stanley, 1978	13
	Ron Reed, 1979	13
	Jim Kern, 1979	13
	Aurelio Lopez, 1980	13
	Jesse Orosco, 1983	13
	Rich Gossage, 1983	13
48	30 players tied	12

Relief Losses

1	Gene Garber, 1979	16
2	Darold Knowles, 1970	14
	John Hiller, 1974	14
	Mike Marshall, 1975	14
	Mike Marshall, 1979	14
6	Wilbur Wood, 1970	13
	Rollie Fingers, 1978	13
	Skip Lockwood, 1978	13
9	Roy Face, 1956	12
	Roy Face, 1961	12
	Ken Sanders, 1971	12
	Mike Marshall, 1974	12
	Gene Garber, 1975	12
	Jim Willoughby, 1976	12
	Charlie Hough, 1977	12
	Mike Marshall, 1978	12
	Kent Tekulve, 1980	12
	Ken Howell, 1986	12
	Roger Mason, 1993	12
20	Nels Potter, 1949	11
	Frank Funk, 1961	11
	Dick Radatz, 1965	11
	Frank Linzy, 1966	11
	Wilbur Wood, 1968	11
	Wilbur Wood, 1969	11
	Mike Marshall, 1973	11
	Rollie Fingers, 1976	11
	Rich Gossage, 1978	11
	Dave Heaverlo, 1979	11
	Mark Clear, 1980	11
	Greg Minton, 1983	11
	Ron Davis, 1984	11
	Mark Davis, 1985	11
	Joe Boever, 1989	11
35	47 players tied	10

Relief Innings Pitched

1	Mike Marshall, 1974	208.1
2	Mike Marshall, 1973	179.0
3	Bob Stanley, 1982	168.1
4	Bill Campbell, 1976	167.2
5	Andy Karl, 1945	166.2
6	Eddie Fisher, 1965	165.1
7	Hoyt Wilhelm, 1952	159.1
8	Dick Radatz, 1964	157.0
	Mark Eichhorn, 1986	157.0
10	Jim Konstanty, 1950	152.0
11	John Hiller, 1974	150.0
12	Tom Johnson, 1977	146.2
13	Garland Braxton, 1927	146.0
14	Bob Stanley, 1983	145.1
15	Hoyt Wilhelm, 1953	145.0
	Wilbur Wood, 1968	145.0
17	Allan Russell, 1923	144.2
	Wayne Granger, 1969	144.2
19	Steve Foucault, 1974	144.1
20	Hoyt Wilhelm, 1965	144.0
21	Jim Kern, 1979	143.0
22	Charlie Hough, 1976	142.2
23	Rich Gossage, 1975	141.2
24	Mike Marshall, 1979	140.2
25	Sammy Stewart, 1983	140.1
	Willie Hernandez, 1984	140.1
27	Bill Campbell, 1977	140.0
28	Jack Lamabe, 1963	139.2
29	Pedro Borbon, 1974	139.0
	Dan Quisenberry, 1983	139.0
31	Lindy McDaniel, 1973	138.1
32	Aurelio Lopez, 1984	137.2
33	Clay Carroll, 1966	137.1
34	Sparky Lyle, 1977	137.0
	Tom Hume, 1980	137.0
36	Dan Quisenberry, 1982	136.2
37	Ted Abernathy, 1965	136.1
	Ken Sanders, 1971	136.1
	Doug Corbett, 1980	136.1
40	Mudcat Grant, 1970	135.1
	Joe Page, 1949	135.1
42	Clay Carroll, 1968	135.0
	Kent Tekulve, 1978	135.0
44	Ted Abernathy, 1968	134.2
	Phil Regan, 1968	134.2
	Rollie Fingers, 1976	134.2
47	Bill Henry, 1959	134.1
	Dick Selma, 1970	134.1
	Rich Gossage, 1978	134.1
	Kent Tekulve, 1979	134.1

Relief Points

1	Bobby Thigpen, 1990	116
2	Dennis Eckersley, 1992	115
3	Trevor Hoffman, 1998	112
4	Randy Myers, 1993	106
5	Rod Beck, 1998	104
6	Lee Smith, 1991	103
7	Dennis Eckersley, 1990	102
	Tom Gordon, 1998	102
9	Rod Beck, 1993	101
	John Wetteland, 1993	101
11	Dave Righetti, 1986	100
12	Jeff Montgomery, 1993	99
13	Jose Mesa, 1995	98
14	Dan Quisenberry, 1983	97
	Dan Quisenberry, 1984	97
	Trevor Hoffman, 1996	97
17	Dennis Eckersley, 1988	96
18	Mariano Rivera, 1997	94
	Jeff Shaw, 1998	94
20	Bruce Sutter, 1984	93
	Mark Davis, 1989	93
22	Lee Smith, 1993	92
	Dennis Eckersley, 1991	92
	Bryan Harvey, 1991	92
25	John Hiller, 1973	91
	Doug Jones, 1990	91
	Duane Ward, 1993	91
	Randy Myers, 1997	91
29	Todd Worrell, 1996	90
	Jeff Shaw, 1997	90
31	John Wetteland, 1998	89
32	Jeff Brantley, 1996	88
33	Steve Bedrosian, 1987	87
	Rick Aguilera, 1991	87
	Bryan Harvey, 1993	87
	John Wetteland, 1996	87
	Robb Nen, 1998	87
38	Doug Jones, 1992	86
39	Lee Smith, 1992	85
	Mitch Williams, 1993	85
	Tom Henke, 1993	85
	Robb Nen, 1997	85
43	John Franco, 1988	84
	Jeff Reardon, 1988	84
	Jeff Russell, 1989	84
	Rod Beck, 1997	84
47	5 players tied	83

Relief Ranking

1	Jim Kern, 1979	65.0
2	John Hiller, 1973	64.9
3	Rich Gossage, 1977	61.1
4	Lindy McDaniel, 1960	57.5
5	John Wetteland, 1993	56.4
6	Mike Marshall, 1979	56.2
7	Mark Eichhorn, 1986	55.3
8	Robb Nen, 1998	55.0
9	Roberto Hernandez, 1996	53.8
10	Ellis Kinder, 1953	53.6
11	Bruce Sutter, 1977	51.8
12	Bill Caudill, 1982	51.7
13	Jesse Orosco, 1983	50.6
14	Doug Jones, 1997	49.8
15	Donnie Moore, 1985	49.7
16	Sid Monge, 1979	49.5
17	Dick Radatz, 1963	49.4
18	Dick Radatz, 1964	49.2
19	Bob James, 1985	48.0
20	Rich Gossage, 1975	47.7
21	Jeff Montgomery, 1993	47.7
22	Mariano Rivera, 1997	47.6
23	Mike Marshall, 1972	46.8
24	Doug Corbett, 1980	46.8
25	Bill Campbell, 1977	45.5
26	Roy Face, 1962	45.2
27	Dennis Eckersley, 1990	45.1
28	Al Hrabosky, 1975	44.9
29	Dan Quisenberry, 1985	44.7
30	Rich Gossage, 1978	44.7
31	Jose Mesa, 1995	44.3
32	Ugueth Urbina, 1998	43.6
33	Sparky Lyle, 1977	43.4
34	John Wetteland, 1997	43.2
35	Dan Spillner, 1982	43.0
36	Tom Murphy, 1974	42.9
37	Jeff Shaw, 1998	42.7
38	Lee Smith, 1983	42.6
39	Dave Righetti, 1986	42.6
40	Ken Sanders, 1971	41.6
41	Luis Arroyo, 1961	41.6
42	Stu Miller, 1965	41.5
43	Ron Perranoski, 1969	41.3
44	Todd Worrell, 1986	40.8
45	Bruce Sutter, 1984	40.7
46	Randy Myers, 1997	40.4
47	Joe Page, 1949	40.3
48	Bobby Thigpen, 1990	40.1
49	John Franco, 1988	39.9
50	Jim Brewer, 1972	39.8

Relievers' Runs

1	Mark Eichhorn, 1986	42.8
2	Jim Kern, 1979	42.0
3	Mariano Rivera, 1996	34.7
4	Rich Gossage, 1977	33.8
5	John Hiller, 1973	33.1
6	Dan Quisenberry, 1983	32.7
7	Willie Hernandez, 1984	32.2
8	Doug Corbett, 1980	31.1
9	Bruce Sutter, 1977	30.6
10	Rich Gossage, 1975	30.5
11	Tim Burke, 1987	29.3
12	Roberto Hernandez, 1996	29.0
13	Sparky Lyle, 1977	28.8
14	Lindy McDaniel, 1960	28.6
15	Bob Lee, 1964	28.4
16	Mudcat Grant, 1970	28.3
17	Garland Braxton, 1927	28.2
18	Bruce Sutter, 1984	27.9
19	Mike Marshall, 1974	27.7
20	Dennis Eckersley, 1990	26.8
21	Robb Nen, 1998	26.7
22	Sid Monge, 1979	26.4
23	Jesse Orosco, 1983	26.3
24	Hoyt Wilhelm, 1965	26.3
25	Rich Gossage, 1978	26.2
26	Phil Regan, 1966	25.8
27	Jeff Montgomery, 1989	25.7
28	Paul Quantrill, 1997	25.6
29	Jose Mesa, 1995	25.5
30	Ellis Kinder, 1953	25.5
31	Aurelio Lopez, 1979	25.5
32	Donnie Moore, 1985	25.5
33	Dan Quisenberry, 1985	25.4
34	John Wetteland, 1993	25.3
35	Ellis Kinder, 1951	25.1
36	Jim Konstanty, 1950	25.0
37	Ted Abernathy, 1967	24.9
38	Mike Marshall, 1979	24.9
39	Sparky Lyle, 1974	24.8
40	Bob James, 1985	24.7
41	Rollie Fingers, 1973	24.5
42	Gary Lavelle, 1977	24.4
43	Dick Radatz, 1963	24.4
44	Hoyt Wilhelm, 1954	24.4
45	Joe Black, 1952	24.2
46	Greg Minton, 1982	24.2
47	Luis Arroyo, 1961	24.2
48	Joe Page, 1949	24.1
49	Dick Radatz, 1962	24.0
50	Hoyt Wilhelm, 1964	23.9

Adjusted Relievers' Runs

1	Mark Eichhorn, 1986	43.6
2	Jim Kern, 1979	40.9
3	John Hiller, 1973	36.9
4	Bruce Sutter, 1977	36.3
5	Doug Corbett, 1980	36.0
6	Rich Gossage, 1977	34.9
7	Mariano Rivera, 1996	34.1
8	Dan Quisenberry, 1983	32.9
9	Lindy McDaniel, 1960	32.5
10	Rich Gossage, 1975	32.0
11	Willie Hernandez, 1984	31.1
12	Tim Burke, 1987	30.5
13	Steve Reed, 1995	30.3
14	Ellis Kinder, 1951	29.3
15	Ted Abernathy, 1967	29.3
16	Ellis Kinder, 1953	28.0
17	Mike Marshall, 1979	27.4
18	Dick Radatz, 1964	27.3
19	Aurelio Lopez, 1979	27.0
20	Sparky Lyle, 1977	27.0
21	Sid Monge, 1979	26.9
22	Bob James, 1985	26.8
23	Dick Radatz, 1963	26.7
24	Roberto Hernandez, 1996	26.6
25	John Wetteland, 1993	26.5
26	Jesse Orosco, 1983	26.3
27	Bruce Sutter, 1984	26.3
28	Dick Radatz, 1962	26.2
29	Paul Quantrill, 1997	25.8
30	Mudcat Grant, 1970	25.6
31	Dan Quisenberry, 1985	25.6
32	Jose Mesa, 1995	25.4
33	Jeff Montgomery, 1989	25.3
34	Dennis Eckersley, 1990	25.3
35	Donnie Moore, 1985	25.0
36	Robb Nen, 1998	25.0
37	Lee Smith, 1983	24.5
38	Gary Lavelle, 1977	24.4
39	Tom Burgmeier, 1980	24.4
40	Bob Lee, 1964	24.3
41	Bob Stanley, 1983	24.2
42	Andy McGaffigan, 1987	24.2
43	Greg Minton, 1982	24.1
44	Rich Gossage, 1978	24.0
45	Duane Ward, 1992	24.0
46	Rob Dibble, 1990	23.9
47	Hoyt Wilhelm, 1954	23.9
48	Tug McGraw, 1980	23.9
49	Bill Campbell, 1977	23.8
50	Dick Hyde, 1958	23.7

Percent of Team Wins (by era)

1876-1892

1	Will White, 1879	100.0
	Bobby Mathews, 1876	100.0
	Jim Devlin, 1877	100.0
	Jim Devlin, 1876	100.0
	George Bradley, 1876	100.0
6	Tommy Bond, 1878	97.6
7	Terry Larkin, 1878	96.7
8	Jim McCormick, 1880	95.7
9	Tommy Bond, 1877	95.2
10	Terry Larkin, 1877	93.5
11	Al Spalding, 1876	90.4
	Jim Galvin, 1883	88.5
13	Will White, 1880	85.7
	Jim McCormick, 1882	85.7
15	Mickey Welch, 1880	82.9

1893-1919

1	Ted Breitenstein, 1895	48.7
2	Amos Rusie, 1893	48.5
3	Ted Breitenstein, 1894	48.2
4	Cy Young, 1893	46.6
5	Ed Walsh, 1908	45.5
	Frank Killen, 1896	45.5
7	Ted Breitenstein, 1896	45.0
8	Jack Chesbro, 1904	44.6
9	Frank Killen, 1893	44.4
10	Pink Hawley, 1895	43.7
11	Win Mercer, 1896	43.1
12	Noodles Hahn, 1901	42.3
13	Cy Young, 1901	41.8
14	Cy Young, 1895	41.6
15	Cy Young, 1902	41.6

1920-1941

1	Eddie Rommel, 1922	41.5
2	Red Faber, 1921	40.3
3	Buck Newsom, 1938	36.4
4	Jimmy Ring, 1923	36.0
	Pete Alexander, 1920	36.0
6	Ted Lyons, 1930	35.5
7	Curt Davis, 1934	33.9
8	Urban Shocker, 1921	33.3
	Bob Feller, 1941	33.3
	Ed Morris, 1928	33.3
11	Howard Ehmke, 1923	32.8
12	Dazzy Vance, 1925	32.4
	Paul Derringer, 1935	32.4
14	Wes Ferrell, 1935	32.1
15	George Uhle, 1923	31.7

1942-1960

1	Ned Garver, 1951	38.5
2	Bob Feller, 1946	38.2
3	Murry Dickson, 1952	33.3
4	Robin Roberts, 1952	32.2
5	Bill Voiselle, 1944	31.3
6	Murry Dickson, 1951	31.3
7	Phil Marchildon, 1942	30.9
8	Dizzy Trout, 1944	30.7
9	Robin Roberts, 1954	30.7
10	Bobby Shantz, 1952	30.4
11	Ewell Blackwell, 1947	30.1
12	Robin Roberts, 1955	29.9
13	Johnny Antonelli, 1956	29.9
14	Dave Ferriss, 1945	29.6
15	2 players tied	29.0

1961-1976

1	Steve Carlton, 1972	45.8
2	Gaylord Perry, 1972	33.3
3	Nolan Ryan, 1974	32.4
4	Larry Jackson, 1964	31.6
5	Wilbur Wood, 1973	31.2
6	Bob Gibson, 1970	30.3
7	Randy Jones, 1976	30.1
8	Denny McLain, 1968	30.1
9	Fergie Jenkins, 1974	29.8
10	Juan Marichal, 1968	29.5
11	Sam McDowell, 1969	29.0
12	Fergie Jenkins, 1971	28.9
13	Steve Busby, 1974	28.6
14	Sandy Koufax, 1966	28.4
15	Juan Marichal, 1963	28.4

1977-1998

1	Phil Niekro, 1979	31.8
2	Dave Stieb, 1981	29.7
3	Brad Radke, 1997	29.4
4	Fernando Valenzuela, 1986	28.8
5	Roger Clemens, 1997	27.6
6	Phil Niekro, 1978	27.5
7	Kevin Brown, 1992	27.3
8	Pat Hentgen, 1996	27.0
9	Mike Mussina, 1995	26.8
10	Randy Johnson, 1994	26.5
11	Mike Norris, 1980	26.5
12	Danny Jackson, 1988	26.4
13	Steve Carlton, 1980	26.4
	Frank Viola, 1988	26.4
15	Ross Grimsley, 1978	26.3

Clutch Pitching Index

1	Doc White, 1904	152.8
2	Mordecai Brown, 1903	152.7
3	Ned Garvin, 1904	152.6
4	Jim McCormick, 1878	152.3
5	Max Lanier, 1943	150.8
6	Pete Schneider, 1917	145.4
7	Sammy Stewart, 1981	144.8
8	Ed Killian, 1907	144.4
9	Carl Lundgren, 1902	144.1
10	Bill Burns, 1909	142.4
11	Cy Morgan, 1910	142.2
12	Ed Summers, 1908	142.1
13	Andy Coakley, 1905	141.7
	Fred Olmstead, 1910	141.7
15	Ben Tincup, 1914	141.6
16	Dick Rudolph, 1919	141.2
17	Sherry Smith, 1919	141.1
18	Fred Blanding, 1913	140.8
19	Charlie Hodnett, 1884	140.3
20	Ed Poole, 1902	139.8
21	Ed Willett, 1908	139.6
22	Bert Humphries, 1915	139.5
23	Doug Rau, 1976	139.2
24	Sloppy Thurston, 1923	139.0
25	Vic Willis, 1906	138.7
	Al Benton, 1945	138.7
	Al Brazle, 1947	138.7
28	Dummy Taylor, 1902	138.3
29	Allan Anderson, 1988	137.8
30	Mark Baldwin, 1888	137.4
31	Al Maul, 1895	137.0
32	Bob Rhoads, 1908	136.8
33	Mike Sullivan, 1892	136.3
34	Spud Chandler, 1942	136.2
	Chuck Finley, 1990	136.2
36	Red Faber, 1917	135.9
37	Mal Eason, 1902	135.8
	King Cole, 1910	135.8
39	Clark Griffith, 1898	135.4
40	Bob Buhl, 1957	134.8
	John Tudor, 1988	134.8
42	Doug Rau, 1978	134.5
43	Stu Miller, 1959	134.4
44	Ken Chase, 1940	134.2
	Dutch Leonard, 1948	134.2
46	Andy Coakley, 1908	134.1
47	Win Mercer, 1894	133.9
	Ed Siever, 1904	133.9
	Joe McGinnity, 1908	133.9
50	Mike Marshall, 1973	133.7
51	Ned Garvin, 1902	133.5
52	Joe Horlen, 1968	133.1
53	Art Nehf, 1928	133.0
	Mike Hampton, 1998	133.0
55	Eddie Plank, 1911	132.9
56	Charlie Chech, 1905	132.7
57	Andy Coakley, 1907	132.6
58	Gene Bearden, 1948	132.3
	Hoyt Wilhelm, 1959	132.3
60	Stan Baumgartner, 1924	132.1
61	Ed Killian, 1909	131.9
	Bump Hadley, 1939	131.9
63	Lew Brockett, 1909	131.8
64	Jim Abbott, 1992	131.7
65	Win Mercer, 1897	131.6
66	Jose DeLeon, 1991	131.5
67	Steve Blass, 1972	131.3
68	Chick Fraser, 1900	131.2
69	Don Schwall, 1961	131.1
70	Mike O'Neill, 1904	131.0
71	Ted Lyons, 1942	130.9
	Bobby Shantz, 1957	130.9
73	Tony Mullane, 1890	130.7
74	Rick Honeycutt, 1983	130.6
	Lon Warneke, 1933	130.6
	Pete Vuckovich, 1982	130.6
	Bill Swift, 1992	130.6
78	Bill Lee, 1978	130.5
79	Bill Bernhard, 1904	130.4
80	Hal McKain, 1929	130.3
	Bill Krueger, 1991	130.3
82	Larry Pape, 1911	130.2
	Hi Bithorn, 1942	130.2
	John Cerutti, 1989	130.2
85	Vean Gregg, 1913	130.0
86	Brickyard Kennedy, 1899	129.9
	Rollie Naylor, 1920	129.9
88	Earl Moore, 1911	129.6
	Ruben Gomez, 1954	129.6
	Larry McWilliams, 1984	129.6
91	Pud Galvin, 1886	129.5
	Wilson Alvarez, 1993	129.5
93	Lefty Weinert, 1922	129.4
94	Harry Moran, 1915	129.3
	Ned Garver, 1948	129.3
96	Tom Hughes, 1912	129.2
	Clarence Mitchell, 1929	129.2
	Atley Donald, 1944	129.2
	Joe Hatten, 1946	129.2
100	2 players tied	129.1

Pitcher Batting Runs

1	Guy Hecker, 1884	26.2
2	Bob Caruthers, 1886	24.5
3	Jim Whitney, 1882	22.3
4	Wes Ferrell, 1935	21.5
5	Don Drysdale, 1965	20.2
6	Don Newcombe, 1955	20.1
7	Guy Hecker, 1886	19.4
8	Jim Whitney, 1883	18.1
9	Wes Ferrell, 1931	17.8
10	Bob Caruthers, 1887	17.6
11	Charlie Ferguson, 1885	16.8
12	Tony Mullane, 1884	16.7
13	Schoolboy Rowe, 1943	16.7
14	George Uhle, 1923	16.4
15	Babe Ruth, 1917	16.3
16	Scott Stratton, 1890	16.1
17	Warren Spahn, 1958	16.0
18	Walter Johnson, 1925	15.9
19	Bob Caruthers, 1889	15.8
20	Red Ruffing, 1930	15.6
21	Bob Lemon, 1950	15.6
22	Don Newcombe, 1959	15.1
23	Jack Stivetts, 1892	15.1
24	Jack Stivetts, 1890	14.9
25	Jack Bentley, 1923	14.8
26	John Ward, 1879	14.7
27	Bob Lemon, 1949	14.7
28	Red Lucas, 1930	14.7
29	Claude Hendrix, 1912	14.6
30	Babe Ruth, 1915	14.5
31	Dave Foutz, 1887	14.3
32	Charlie Ferguson, 1887	14.2
33	Jim Tobin, 1942	14.0
34	Frank Killen, 1893	13.9
35	Red Ruffing, 1936	13.8
36	Pete Conway, 1888	13.8
37	Red Lucas, 1932	13.7
38	Robin Roberts, 1955	13.6
39	Terry Larkin, 1878	13.6
40	Elam Vangilder, 1922	13.4
41	Babe Ruth, 1916	13.1
42	Scott Stratton, 1888	13.1
43	Joe Bush, 1924	13.0
44	Adonis Terry, 1890	13.0
45	Jack Coombs, 1911	12.9
46	Pink Hawley, 1895	12.9
47	Clark Griffith, 1901	12.8
48	Bucky Walters, 1939	12.7
49	Bob Lemon, 1948	12.6
50	Red Lucas, 1933	12.5
51	Schoolboy Rowe, 1935	12.5
52	Red Ruffing, 1932	12.5
53	Doc Crandall, 1915	12.4
54	Cy Young, 1903	12.3
55	Curt Davis, 1939	12.3
56	Red Ruffing, 1935	12.2
57	Bob Gibson, 1970	12.2
58	Red Ruffing, 1928	12.2
59	Ad Gumbert, 1891	12.1
60	Catfish Hunter, 1971	12.1
61	Wes Ferrell, 1936	11.9
62	Dizzy Trout, 1944	11.9
63	Joe Bowman, 1939	11.8
64	Charley Radbourn, 1883	11.8
65	Billy Taylor, 1884	11.8
66	Jack Stivetts, 1896	11.8
67	Fergie Jenkins, 1971	11.7
68	Johnny Sain, 1947	11.7
69	Dutch Ruether, 1921	11.6
70	Erv Brame, 1929	11.5
71	Babe Ruth, 1918	11.5
72	Jouett Meekin, 1896	11.5
73	George Mullin, 1904	11.3
74	Adonis Terry, 1889	11.3
75	Charlie Ferguson, 1886	11.2
76	Schoolboy Rowe, 1934	11.2
77	George Van Haltren, 1888	11.1
78	Tim Keefe, 1884	11.1
79	Carl Mays, 1921	11.0
80	Guy Hecker, 1887	11.0
81	Jim Whitney, 1881	11.0
82	Mickey Welch, 1880	10.9
83	Red Lucas, 1931	10.9
84	Dave Ferriss, 1945	10.9
85	Ad Gumbert, 1889	10.8
86	Bob Caruthers, 1891	10.8
87	Charlie Buffinton, 1884	10.8
88	Red Ruffing, 1941	10.8
89	Erv Brame, 1930	10.8
90	Jack Stivetts, 1894	10.7
91	Red Lucas, 1929	10.7
92	Jim Whitney, 1887	10.7
93	Tom Parrott, 1895	10.7
94	Fred Hutchinson, 1947	10.7
95	Joe Wood, 1912	10.6
96	Frank Foreman, 1891	10.6
97	Burleigh Grimes, 1928	10.6
98	Burleigh Grimes, 1920	10.5
99	Blue Moon Odom, 1969	10.5
100	Matt Kilroy, 1889	10.4

Pitcher Fielding Runs

1	Ed Walsh, 1907	21.7
2	Harry Howell, 1905	17.8
3	Ed Walsh, 1911	14.8
4	Ed Walsh, 1908	13.6
5	Will White, 1882	12.9
6	John Clarkson, 1889	11.3
7	Tony Mullane, 1882	10.7
	Sadie McMahon, 1890	10.7
9	Carl Mays, 1926	10.1
10	Frank Smith, 1909	10.0
11	Tommy Bond, 1880	9.8
	Greg Maddux, 1996	9.8
13	Mike Morrison, 1887	9.7
	Ed Walsh, 1910	9.7
15	Christy Mathewson, 1908	9.6
16	Tony Mullane, 1884	9.5
	Matt Kilroy, 1887	9.5
	Charlie Buffinton, 1888	9.5
19	Harry Howell, 1904	9.4
20	Ed Scott, 1900	9.1
	Elmer Stricklett, 1906	9.1
	Carl Mays, 1916	9.1
	Carl Mays, 1918	9.1
	Curt Davis, 1934	9.1
25	John Clarkson, 1887	9.0
	Elmer Stricklett, 1905	9.0
27	Hooks Dauss, 1915	8.9
28	Addie Joss, 1907	8.7
29	Gene Packard, 1914	8.6
30	Park Swartzel, 1889	8.5
	Bucky Walters, 1936	8.5
32	Jack Taylor, 1898	8.4
	Hooks Dauss, 1920	8.4
	Wilcy Moore, 1927	8.4
	Bob Lemon, 1948	8.4
36	Cy Seymour, 1898	8.3
	Harry Howell, 1907	8.3
	Randy Jones, 1976	8.3
39	Burleigh Grimes, 1925	8.2
40	Matt Kilroy, 1889	8.1
	George Mullin, 1904	8.1
	Carl Mays, 1924	8.1
	Eddie Rommel, 1924	8.1
44	Fred Newman, 1965	8.0
45	Cy Young, 1895	7.9
	Cy Young, 1896	7.9
	Nick Altrock, 1905	7.9
	Bob Lemon, 1953	7.9
	Mel Stottlemyre, 1969	7.9
50	John Clarkson, 1885	7.8
	Pud Galvin, 1887	7.8
	Carl Mays, 1917	7.8
	Freddie Fitzsimmons, 1931	7.8
	Harry Gumbert, 1938	7.8
	John Denny, 1978	7.8
56	Amos Rusie, 1894	7.7
	Joe Wood, 1912	7.7
	Mel Harder, 1933	7.7
	Harry Gumbert, 1937	7.7
	Russ Christopher, 1943	7.7
61	Larry McKeon, 1884	7.6
	Cy Seymour, 1897	7.6
	Ed Walsh, 1906	7.6
64	Willie Sudhoff, 1898	7.5
	Christy Mathewson, 1901	7.5
	Ned Garvin, 1903	7.5
	Harry Howell, 1906	7.5
	Jean Dubuc, 1913	7.5
	Greg Maddux, 1990	7.5
70	Christy Mathewson, 1911	7.4
	Carl Hubbell, 1933	7.4
	Greg Maddux, 1998	7.4
73	Tommy Bond, 1879	7.3
	Charlie Buffinton, 1887	7.3
	Bob Caruthers, 1887	7.3
	Bill Doak, 1915	7.3
77	Pud Galvin, 1881	7.2
	Eddie Cicotte, 1913	7.2
	Russ Christopher, 1945	7.2
80	Pud Galvin, 1884	7.1
	George Mullin, 1905	7.1
	Ed Walsh, 1912	7.1
	Harry Coveleski, 1914	7.1
	Kenny Rogers, 1998	7.1
85	Doc White, 1908	7.0
	Red Ames, 1909	7.0
	Hal Schumacher, 1935	7.0
88	Guy Hecker, 1884	6.9
	Dave Foutz, 1885	6.9
	Red Donahue, 1902	6.9
	Elmer Stricklett, 1907	6.9
	Lefty Tyler, 1913	6.9
	Gene Krapp, 1915	6.9
	Larry Jackson, 1964	6.9
95	9 players tied	6.8

Total Pitcher Index

1	Guy Hecker, 1884	12.6
2	Silver King, 1888	11.4
3	Walter Johnson, 1912	11.2
4	Amos Rusie, 1894	11.0
5	Walter Johnson, 1913	10.9
6	John Clarkson, 1889	10.1
7	Charley Radbourn, 1884	9.9
8	Christy Mathewson, 1905	9.7
9	Dizzy Trout, 1944	9.1
10	Scott Stratton, 1890	8.9
11	John Clarkson, 1885	8.7
	Lefty Grove, 1931	8.7
13	Joe Wood, 1912	8.6
	Pete Alexander, 1915	8.6
15	Bucky Walters, 1939	8.5
16	Charley Radbourn, 1883	8.4
17	John Clarkson, 1887	8.3
	Cy Young, 1901	8.3
19	Dave Foutz, 1886	8.1
	Ed Walsh, 1908	8.1
21	Roger Clemens, 1997	8.0
22	Curt Davis, 1934	7.8
	Hal Newhouser, 1945	7.8
24	Tony Mullane, 1884	7.7
	Jack Stivetts, 1891	7.7
	Walter Johnson, 1915	7.7
27	Walter Johnson, 1918	7.6
28	Carl Hubbell, 1933	7.5
29	Pink Hawley, 1895	7.4
	Dolf Luque, 1923	7.4
	Steve Carlton, 1972	7.4
32	Jim Devlin, 1876	7.3
	Will White, 1882	7.3
	Matt Kilroy, 1887	7.3
	Kid Nichols, 1897	7.3
	Christy Mathewson, 1908	7.3
	Walter Johnson, 1914	7.3
	Pete Alexander, 1916	7.3
	Lefty Grove, 1930	7.3
	Bob Gibson, 1968	7.3
	Dwight Gooden, 1985	7.3
	Greg Maddux, 1994	7.3
	Kevin Brown, 1996	7.3
44	Amos Rusie, 1893	7.2
	Walter Johnson, 1919	7.2
	Wes Ferrell, 1935	7.2
	Greg Maddux, 1998	7.2
48	Silver King, 1890	7.1
	Ed Walsh, 1910	7.1
	Pete Alexander, 1920	7.1
	Hal Newhouser, 1946	7.1
52	Cy Young, 1895	7.0
	Christy Mathewson, 1909	7.0
	Red Faber, 1921	7.0
	Dazzy Vance, 1928	7.0
	Lefty Grove, 1936	7.0
	Gaylord Perry, 1972	7.0
58	Matt Kilroy, 1889	6.9
	Amos Rusie, 1890	6.9
	Kid Nichols, 1898	6.9
	Jack Chesbro, 1904	6.9
62	Pud Galvin, 1884	6.8
	Bob Caruthers, 1886	6.8
	Mordecai Brown, 1906	6.8
	Bob Lemon, 1948	6.8
	Greg Maddux, 1995	6.8
67	Jesse Duryea, 1889	6.7
	Kid Nichols, 1890	6.7
	Christy Mathewson, 1911	6.7
	John Hiller, 1973	6.7
	Jim Kern, 1979	6.7
	Roger Clemens, 1990	6.7
73	Tim Keefe, 1883	6.6
	Will White, 1883	6.6
	Bob Caruthers, 1885	6.6
	Guy Hecker, 1885	6.6
	Cy Young, 1892	6.6
	Kid Nichols, 1896	6.6
	Ed Walsh, 1912	6.6
	Dazzy Vance, 1930	6.6
	Thornton Lee, 1941	6.6
	Warren Spahn, 1953	6.6
	Wilbur Wood, 1971	6.6
84	Charlie Ferguson, 1886	6.5
	Toad Ramsey, 1886	6.5
	Billy Rhines, 1890	6.5
	Joe Wood, 1911	6.5
	Lefty Gomez, 1937	6.5
	Hal Newhouser, 1944	6.5
	Tom Seaver, 1971	6.5
91	11 players tied	6.4

Total Pitcher Index (alpha.)

Pete Alexander, 1915	8.6
Pete Alexander, 1916	7.3
Pete Alexander, 1920	7.1
Mordecai Brown, 1906	6.8
Kevin Brown, 1996	7.3
Steve Carlton, 1972	7.4
Bob Caruthers, 1885	6.6
Bob Caruthers, 1886	6.8
Jack Chesbro, 1904	6.9
John Clarkson, 1885	8.7
John Clarkson, 1887	8.3
John Clarkson, 1889	10.1
Roger Clemens, 1990	6.7
Roger Clemens, 1997	8.0
Curt Davis, 1934	7.8
Jim Devlin, 1876	7.3
Jesse Duryea, 1889	6.7
Red Faber, 1921	7.0
Charlie Ferguson, 1886	6.5
Wes Ferrell, 1935	7.2
Dave Foutz, 1886	8.1
Pud Galvin, 1884	6.8
Bob Gibson, 1968	7.3
Lefty Gomez, 1937	6.5
Dwight Gooden, 1985	7.3
Lefty Grove, 1930	7.3
Lefty Grove, 1931	8.7
Lefty Grove, 1936	7.0
Pink Hawley, 1895	7.4
Guy Hecker, 1884	12.6
Guy Hecker, 1885	6.6
John Hiller, 1973	6.7
Carl Hubbell, 1933	7.5
Walter Johnson, 1912	11.2
Walter Johnson, 1913	10.9
Walter Johnson, 1914	7.3
Walter Johnson, 1915	7.7
Walter Johnson, 1918	7.6
Walter Johnson, 1919	7.2
Tim Keefe, 1883	6.6
Jim Kern, 1979	6.7
Matt Kilroy, 1887	7.3
Matt Kilroy, 1889	6.9
Silver King, 1888	11.4
Silver King, 1890	7.1
Thornton Lee, 1941	6.6
Bob Lemon, 1948	6.8
Dolf Luque, 1923	7.4
Greg Maddux, 1994	7.3
Greg Maddux, 1995	6.8
Greg Maddux, 1998	7.2
Christy Mathewson, 1905	9.7
Christy Mathewson, 1908	7.3
Christy Mathewson, 1909	7.0
Christy Mathewson, 1911	6.7
Tony Mullane, 1884	7.7
Hal Newhouser, 1944	6.5
Hal Newhouser, 1945	7.8
Hal Newhouser, 1946	7.1
Kid Nichols, 1890	6.7
Kid Nichols, 1896	6.6
Kid Nichols, 1897	7.3
Kid Nichols, 1898	6.9
Gaylord Perry, 1972	7.0
Charley Radbourn, 1883	8.4
Charley Radbourn, 1884	9.9
Toad Ramsey, 1886	6.5
Billy Rhines, 1890	6.5
Amos Rusie, 1890	6.9
Amos Rusie, 1893	7.2
Amos Rusie, 1894	11.0
Tom Seaver, 1971	6.5
Warren Spahn, 1953	6.6
Jack Stivetts, 1891	7.7
Scott Stratton, 1890	8.9
Dizzy Trout, 1944	9.1
Dazzy Vance, 1928	7.0
Dazzy Vance, 1930	6.6
Ed Walsh, 1908	8.1
Ed Walsh, 1910	7.1
Ed Walsh, 1912	6.6
Bucky Walters, 1939	8.5
Will White, 1882	7.3
Will White, 1883	6.6
Joe Wood, 1911	6.5
Joe Wood, 1912	8.6
Wilbur Wood, 1971	6.6
Cy Young, 1892	6.6
Cy Young, 1895	7.0
Cy Young, 1901	8.3

Total Pitcher Index (by era)

1876-1892

1	Guy Hecker, 1884	12.6
2	Silver King, 1888	11.4
3	John Clarkson, 1889	10.1
4	Charley Radbourn, 1884	9.9
5	Scott Stratton, 1890	8.9
6	John Clarkson, 1885	8.7
7	Charley Radbourn, 1883	8.4
8	John Clarkson, 1887	8.3
9	Dave Foutz, 1886	8.1
10	Tony Mullane, 1884	7.7
	Jack Stivetts, 1891	7.7
12	Jim Devlin, 1876	7.3
	Will White, 1882	7.3
	Matt Kilroy, 1887	7.3
15	Silver King, 1890	7.1

1893-1919

1	Walter Johnson, 1912	11.2
2	Amos Rusie, 1894	11.0
3	Walter Johnson, 1913	10.9
4	Christy Mathewson, 1905	9.7
5	Joe Wood, 1912	8.6
	Pete Alexander, 1915	8.6
7	Cy Young, 1901	8.3
8	Ed Walsh, 1908	8.1
9	Walter Johnson, 1915	7.7
10	Walter Johnson, 1918	7.6
11	Pink Hawley, 1895	7.4
12	Kid Nichols, 1897	7.3
	Christy Mathewson, 1908	7.3
	Walter Johnson, 1914	7.3
	Pete Alexander, 1916	7.3

1920-1941

1	Lefty Grove, 1931	8.7
2	Bucky Walters, 1939	8.5
3	Curt Davis, 1934	7.8
4	Carl Hubbell, 1933	7.5
5	Dolf Luque, 1923	7.4
6	Lefty Grove, 1930	7.3
7	Wes Ferrell, 1935	7.2
8	Pete Alexander, 1920	7.1
9	Red Faber, 1921	7.0
	Dazzy Vance, 1928	7.0
	Lefty Grove, 1936	7.0
12	Dazzy Vance, 1930	6.6
	Thornton Lee, 1941	6.6
14	Lefty Gomez, 1937	6.5
15	3 players tied	6.4

1942-1960

1	Dizzy Trout, 1944	9.1
2	Hal Newhouser, 1945	7.8
3	Hal Newhouser, 1946	7.1
4	Bob Lemon, 1948	6.8
5	Warren Spahn, 1953	6.6
6	Hal Newhouser, 1944	6.5
7	Robin Roberts, 1953	6.1
8	Johnny Sain, 1946	5.9
	Ellis Kinder, 1953	5.9
10	Spud Chandler, 1943	5.7
	Bob Lemon, 1949	5.7
	Ned Garver, 1950	5.7
13	5 players tied	5.5

1961-1976

1	Steve Carlton, 1972	7.4
2	Bob Gibson, 1968	7.3
3	Gaylord Perry, 1972	7.0
4	John Hiller, 1973	6.7
5	Wilbur Wood, 1971	6.6
6	Tom Seaver, 1971	6.5
7	Fergie Jenkins, 1971	6.4
8	Jim Palmer, 1975	6.1
9	Juan Marichal, 1965	6.0
	Bob Gibson, 1969	6.0
11	Juan Marichal, 1966	5.8
12	Bert Blyleven, 1973	5.7
13	Tom Seaver, 1969	5.6
14	Bill Hands, 1969	5.5
15	3 players tied	5.4

1977-1998

1	Roger Clemens, 1997	8.0
2	Dwight Gooden, 1985	7.3
	Greg Maddux, 1994	7.3
	Kevin Brown, 1996	7.3
5	Greg Maddux, 1998	7.2
6	Greg Maddux, 1995	6.8
7	Jim Kern, 1979	6.7
	Roger Clemens, 1990	6.7
9	Rich Gossage, 1977	6.4
10	Pedro Martinez, 1997	6.3
11	Ron Guidry, 1978	6.2
	Greg Maddux, 1992	6.2
13	Greg Maddux, 1993	6.1
14	Steve Carlton, 1977	6.0
15	3 players tied	5.8

Total Baseball Ranking

1	Guy Hecker, 1884	12.6
2	Silver King, 1888	11.4
3	Walter Johnson, 1912	11.2
4	Amos Rusie, 1894	11.0
5	Walter Johnson, 1913	10.9
6	Babe Ruth, 1923	10.6
7	John Clarkson, 1889	10.1
8	Charley Radbourn, 1884	9.9
9	Christy Mathewson, 1905	9.7
10	Babe Ruth, 1921	9.4
11	Babe Ruth, 1927	9.2
	Barry Bonds, 1992	9.2
13	Dizzy Trout, 1944	9.1
	Cal Ripken, 1984	9.1
15	Scott Stratton, 1890	8.9
	Nap Lajoie, 1901	8.9
17	Barry Bonds, 1993	8.8
18	John Clarkson, 1885	8.7
	Lefty Grove, 1931	8.7
	Mickey Mantle, 1956	8.7
21	Joe Wood, 1912	8.6
	Pete Alexander, 1915	8.6
	Babe Ruth, 1920	8.6
	Rogers Hornsby, 1924	8.6
	Mickey Mantle, 1957	8.6
26	Bucky Walters, 1939	8.5
	Nap Lajoie, 1910	8.5
	Ty Cobb, 1917	8.5
	Rogers Hornsby, 1922	8.5
	Babe Ruth, 1924	8.5
	Barry Bonds, 1996	8.5
32	Charley Radbourn, 1883	8.4
	Nap Lajoie, 1903	8.4
	Nap Lajoie, 1906	8.4
	Babe Ruth, 1926	8.4
36	John Clarkson, 1887	8.3
	Cy Young, 1901	8.3
	Cal Ripken, 1991	8.3
	Craig Biggio, 1997	8.3
40	Rickey Henderson, 1990	8.2
41	Dave Foutz, 1886	8.1
	Ed Walsh, 1908	8.1
	Rogers Hornsby, 1920	8.1
	Lou Gehrig, 1927	8.1
	Ted Williams, 1942	8.1
46	Roger Clemens, 1997	8.0
	Mickey Mantle, 1961	8.0
48	Ted Williams, 1941	7.9
	Ted Williams, 1946	7.9
50	Curt Davis, 1934	7.8
	Hal Newhouser, 1945	7.8
	Nap Lajoie, 1908	7.8
	George Sisler, 1920	7.8
	Lou Gehrig, 1934	7.8
	Lou Boudreau, 1944	7.8
56	Tony Mullane, 1884	7.7
	Jack Stivetts, 1891	7.7
	Walter Johnson, 1915	7.7
	Tris Speaker, 1912	7.7
	Rogers Hornsby, 1917	7.7
	Willie Mays, 1955	7.7
62	Walter Johnson, 1918	7.6
	Tris Speaker, 1914	7.6
	Jeff Bagwell, 1994	7.6
	Mike Piazza, 1997	7.6
66	Carl Hubbell, 1933	7.5
	Ron Santo, 1966	7.5
68	Pink Hawley, 1895	7.4
	Dolf Luque, 1923	7.4
	Steve Carlton, 1972	7.4
	Rickey Henderson, 1985	7.4
72	Jim Devlin, 1876	7.3
	Will White, 1882	7.3
	Matt Kilroy, 1887	7.3
	Kid Nichols, 1897	7.3
	Christy Mathewson, 1908	7.3
	Walter Johnson, 1914	7.3
	Pete Alexander, 1916	7.3
	Lefty Grove, 1930	7.3
	Bob Gibson, 1968	7.3
	Dwight Gooden, 1985	7.3
	Greg Maddux, 1994	7.3
	Kevin Brown, 1996	7.3
	Honus Wagner, 1905	7.3
	Honus Wagner, 1906	7.3
	Tris Speaker, 1913	7.3
	Frankie Frisch, 1927	7.3
	Babe Ruth, 1930	7.3
	Babe Ruth, 1931	7.3
	Willie Mays, 1965	7.3
	Ron Santo, 1967	7.3
	Carl Yastrzemski, 1967	7.3
	Mike Schmidt, 1980	7.3
94	13 players tied	7.2

Total Baseball Rank (alpha.)

Pete Alexander, 1915	8.6
Pete Alexander, 1916	7.3
Jeff Bagwell, 1994	7.6
Craig Biggio, 1997	8.3
Barry Bonds, 1992	9.2
Barry Bonds, 1993	8.8
Barry Bonds, 1996	8.5
Lou Boudreau, 1944	7.8
Kevin Brown, 1996	7.3
Steve Carlton, 1972	7.4
John Clarkson, 1885	8.7
John Clarkson, 1887	8.3
John Clarkson, 1889	10.1
Roger Clemens, 1997	8.0
Ty Cobb, 1917	8.5
Curt Davis, 1934	7.8
Jim Devlin, 1876	7.3
Dave Foutz, 1886	8.1
Frankie Frisch, 1927	7.3
Lou Gehrig, 1927	8.1
Lou Gehrig, 1934	7.8
Bob Gibson, 1968	7.3
Dwight Gooden, 1985	7.3
Lefty Grove, 1930	7.3
Lefty Grove, 1931	8.7
Pink Hawley, 1895	7.4
Guy Hecker, 1884	12.6
Rickey Henderson, 1985	7.4
Rickey Henderson, 1990	8.2
Rogers Hornsby, 1917	7.7
Rogers Hornsby, 1920	8.1
Rogers Hornsby, 1922	8.5
Rogers Hornsby, 1924	8.6
Carl Hubbell, 1933	7.5
Walter Johnson, 1912	11.2
Walter Johnson, 1913	10.9
Walter Johnson, 1914	7.3
Walter Johnson, 1915	7.7
Walter Johnson, 1918	7.6
Matt Kilroy, 1887	7.3
Silver King, 1888	11.4
Nap Lajoie, 1901	8.9
Nap Lajoie, 1903	8.4
Nap Lajoie, 1906	8.4
Nap Lajoie, 1908	7.8
Nap Lajoie, 1910	8.5
Dolf Luque, 1923	7.4
Greg Maddux, 1994	7.3
Mickey Mantle, 1956	8.7
Mickey Mantle, 1957	8.6
Mickey Mantle, 1961	8.0
Christy Mathewson, 1905	9.7
Christy Mathewson, 1908	7.3
Willie Mays, 1955	7.7
Willie Mays, 1965	7.3
Tony Mullane, 1884	7.7
Hal Newhouser, 1945	7.8
Kid Nichols, 1897	7.3
Mike Piazza, 1997	7.6
Charley Radbourn, 1883	8.4
Charley Radbourn, 1884	9.9
Cal Ripken, 1984	9.1
Cal Ripken, 1991	8.3
Amos Rusie, 1894	11.0
Babe Ruth, 1920	8.6
Babe Ruth, 1921	9.4
Babe Ruth, 1923	10.6
Babe Ruth, 1924	8.5
Babe Ruth, 1926	8.4
Babe Ruth, 1927	9.2
Babe Ruth, 1930	7.3
Babe Ruth, 1931	7.3
Ron Santo, 1966	7.5
Ron Santo, 1967	7.3
Mike Schmidt, 1980	7.3
George Sisler, 1920	7.8
Tris Speaker, 1912	7.7
Tris Speaker, 1913	7.3
Tris Speaker, 1914	7.6
Jack Stivetts, 1891	7.7
Scott Stratton, 1890	8.9
Dizzy Trout, 1944	9.1
Honus Wagner, 1905	7.3
Honus Wagner, 1906	7.3
Ed Walsh, 1908	8.1
Bucky Walters, 1939	8.5
Will White, 1882	7.3
Ted Williams, 1941	7.9
Ted Williams, 1942	8.1
Ted Williams, 1946	7.9
Joe Wood, 1912	8.6
Carl Yastrzemski, 1967	7.3
Cy Young, 1901	8.3

Total Baseball Rank (by era)

1876-1892

1	Guy Hecker, 1884	12.6
2	Silver King, 1888	11.4
3	John Clarkson, 1889	10.1
4	Charley Radbourn, 1884	9.9
5	Scott Stratton, 1890	8.9
6	John Clarkson, 1885	8.7
7	Charley Radbourn, 1883	8.4
8	John Clarkson, 1887	8.3
9	Dave Foutz, 1886	8.1
10	Tony Mullane, 1884	7.7
	Jack Stivetts, 1891	7.7
12	Jim Devlin, 1876	7.3
	Will White, 1882	7.3
	Matt Kilroy, 1887	7.3
15	Silver King, 1890	7.1

1893-1919

1	Walter Johnson, 1912	11.2
2	Amos Rusie, 1894	11.0
3	Walter Johnson, 1913	10.9
4	Christy Mathewson, 1905	9.7
5	Nap Lajoie, 1901	8.9
6	Joe Wood, 1912	8.6
	Pete Alexander, 1915	8.6
8	Nap Lajoie, 1910	8.5
	Ty Cobb, 1917	8.5
10	Nap Lajoie, 1903	8.4
	Nap Lajoie, 1906	8.4
12	Cy Young, 1901	8.3
13	Ed Walsh, 1908	8.1
14	Nap Lajoie, 1908	7.8
15	3 players tied	7.7

1920-1941

1	Babe Ruth, 1923	10.6
2	Babe Ruth, 1921	9.4
3	Babe Ruth, 1927	9.2
4	Lefty Grove, 1931	8.7
5	Babe Ruth, 1920	8.6
	Rogers Hornsby, 1924	8.6
7	Bucky Walters, 1939	8.5
	Rogers Hornsby, 1922	8.5
	Babe Ruth, 1924	8.5
10	Babe Ruth, 1926	8.4
11	Rogers Hornsby, 1920	8.1
	Lou Gehrig, 1927	8.1
13	Ted Williams, 1941	7.9
14	3 players tied	7.8

1942-1960

1	Dizzy Trout, 1944	9.1
2	Mickey Mantle, 1956	8.7
3	Mickey Mantle, 1957	8.6
4	Ted Williams, 1942	8.1
5	Ted Williams, 1946	7.9
6	Hal Newhouser, 1945	7.8
	Lou Boudreau, 1944	7.8
8	Willie Mays, 1955	7.7
9	Snuffy Stirnweiss, 1945	7.2
	Ted Williams, 1947	7.2
	Willie Mays, 1958	7.2
12	Hal Newhouser, 1946	7.1
	Snuffy Stirnweiss, 1944	7.1
	Ted Williams, 1957	7.1
15	Lou Boudreau, 1948	6.9

1961-1976

1	Mickey Mantle, 1961	8.0
2	Ron Santo, 1966	7.5
3	Steve Carlton, 1972	7.4
4	Bob Gibson, 1968	7.3
	Willie Mays, 1965	7.3
	Ron Santo, 1967	7.3
	Carl Yastrzemski, 1967	7.3
8	Norm Cash, 1961	7.1
	Joe Morgan, 1975	7.1
10	Gaylord Perry, 1972	7.0
11	Rico Petrocelli, 1969	6.9
	Mike Schmidt, 1974	6.9
13	John Hiller, 1973	6.7
	Frank Robinson, 1966	6.7
15	4 players tied	6.6

1977-1998

1	Barry Bonds, 1992	9.2
2	Cal Ripken, 1984	9.1
3	Barry Bonds, 1993	8.8
4	Barry Bonds, 1996	8.5
5	Cal Ripken, 1991	8.3
	Craig Biggio, 1997	8.3
7	Rickey Henderson, 1990	8.2
8	Roger Clemens, 1997	8.0
9	Jeff Bagwell, 1994	7.6
	Mike Piazza, 1997	7.6
11	Rickey Henderson, 1985	7.4
12	Dwight Gooden, 1985	7.3
	Greg Maddux, 1994	7.3
	Kevin Brown, 1996	7.3
	Mike Schmidt, 1980	7.3

Manager Roster

This section details the managerial record of every man who ever held the reins of a major league club from 1871 through 1998. For many years, the assignment of wins and losses was thought a relatively simple task—almost as simple as identifying the managers themselves. In recent years, however, Richard Topp and Robert Tiemann wondered how it was that "managers" who never set foot on the field to lead their charges or even accompanied their clubs on road trips could be regarded as managers at all, at least in the commonly understood sense of field manager rather than business manager. Topp and Tiemann wondered how John McGraw, for example, could be credited as manager of the New York Giants for all of 1924 when a knee injury kept him from the bench for seven weeks: Somebody else must have run the team, they figured, so why not credit that man as interim manager?

That there were record-keeping errors in the 1870s or even the early 1900s may strike the average fan as unsurprising, but the incorrect assignment of decisions to helmsmen has been characteristic of every decade, up to and including the 1990s. Tiemann and Topp undertook a complete review of managerial records dating back to the National Association and found that the records published in previous baseball encyclopedias were wrong—so wrong that they had to be refigured from scratch. Here are the criteria they established for their groundbreaking study:

1. *Definition* A manager is the person designated by the club ownership to run the club on the field.

2. *Absences* When the regular manager is unable to be with the team for 30 or more days, the assistant in charge during his absence should be credited with the team's record from the time the absence begins until the regular manager returns to active duty.

3. *Interim manager* When a manager is removed, either by resignation or by being fired, and his designated replacement is not present to replace him, the assistant temporarily in charge of the team shall be credited with the team's record during the interim.

4. *Head coaches* From 1961 through 1964, the Chicago Cubs had a "panel of coaches" rather than a single manager. One of these coaches was designated *head coach* for a period of time; and that coach is credited with the team's record during his term as head coach.

5. *Captains* During the early years of professional baseball, the man who had the title of "manager" often served merely as the club's business manager, while the captain (a player) was responsible for the team on the field. Some captains were also managers. Each ambiguous situation is judged according to its particular circumstances, but in general the captain, rather than the manager, is credited with the team's record if the manager did not travel with the team or did not have previous baseball experience.

6. *Suspended games* If a game was suspended when one man was managing the team and was completed on a later date when another man was managing, the second manager is credited if the game was suspended before five innings were completed. If the game was suspended after five or more innings were played, then:

   (a) credit the first manager with a win if the team was leading at the point of suspension and maintained the lead to win the game; or

   (b) credit the first manager with a loss if the team was losing at the point of suspension and remained behind to lose the game; or

   (c) credit the second manager with a win (or tie) if the team was losing at the point of suspension but came back to tie the score or win the game; or

   (d) credit the second manager with a loss if the team was winning at the point of suspension but then lost the lead and/or game; or

   (e) credit the second manager with the win or loss if the score was tied at the point of suspension.

7. *Protested games* If a protest was granted and the game was ordered resumed from the point of protest, then the same rules used for suspended games apply. If a protested game of at least five innings' duration was ordered replayed in its entirety, then no win or loss is credited, but both managers are credited with a no-decision game.

8. *Forfeited games* All forfeited games are counted as games managed, even if the game did not start or if it did not go five innings.

9. *Split seasons* In 1892 the National League played a split season, the winners meeting for the championship. In 1981, because of a players' strike, the National and American Leagues played split seasons. The managers' totals will have entries for each half-season.

10. *Replacement clubs* In the American Association (1882–1891), there were three instances in which one club dropped out during the season and was replaced by another club. In 1884 Richmond replaced Washington; in 1890 Baltimore replaced Brooklyn; and in 1891 Milwaukee replaced Cincinnati. In each case, the new club inherited the old club's won-lost record. Therefore, the manager of the new club is credited with starting in the

position (standing) in which the old club finished.

In the Union Association (1884), when a new club replaced an old one, the new club started with a 0–0 record rather than inheriting the old club's record, except in the case of the Chicago franchise, which moved to Pittsburgh. Therefore, all such Union Association managers are credited with a finish as if their teams had begun their season at the beginning of the league season. The finish for each manager is his club's standing in the eight-team league when (a) he left the job, (b) his club dropped out of the league, or (c) his club finished the season. The clubs that dropped out were Altoona (replaced by Kansas City); Philadelphia (replaced by Wilmington); Wilmington (replaced by St. Paul); and Pittsburgh (replaced by Milwaukee).

In a typical entry in the Manager Roster (a hypothetical entry has been created below), the column marked STANDING will, in cases where a team has had only one manager throughout the year, show the team's final standing (in the example below, see the entry for 1972). In the case of a manager who began the season but was replaced midway, however, the figure on the left of the column shows the team's standing when he departed and the figure on the right shows the team's final standing (in the example below, see the entry for 1976). In the case of a manager who finished the season but did not begin it, the team's standing when he took over is shown on the left and the final standing on the right (see the entry for 1978). In the case of a manager who began when the season was already under way but who failed to finish, the figure on the left of the column shows the team's standing when he took over; the middle figure shows the team's standing when he departed; and a third figure shows the team's final standing (see the entry for 1977). The figure in the next column represents the number of wins predicted by the team's runs scored and runs allowed, with about 10 extra runs being required for each win beyond .500. Last, the number of wins in the A-E column, which may be a positive figure or a negative figure, reflects the extent to which a manager may have stretched (or hindered) his available talent. The bottom line of a manager's entry provides his career totals, beginning at the left with the number of years, full or partial, in which he managed a major league club. The symbols shown in the sample entry are explained after the example.

Whenever a manager served two or more teams in the same year, the totals for each club are shown separately (see the sample entry for 1973). The split seasons of 1892 and 1981 are indicated with separate records for each half. A figure to the right of the year indicates first half or second half (see sample entry for 1981).

TM/L — Team and League

G — Games managed (including ties)

W — Wins

L — Losses

PCT — Percentage of games won

M/Y — Manager/Year (The latter figure indicates how many managers the team employed that year, while the former indicates the chronological position of the manager whose entry it is; "2/5," for example, would mean that this manager was the second of the team's five managers during that year.)

W-EXP — Expected Wins   Calculated for the team based on its actual runs scored and allowed, not its predicted runs scored and runs allowed. A team that allows exactly as many runs as it scores is predicted to play .500 ball. The equation for expected wins is:

$$\frac{(\text{Runs Scored} - \text{Runs Allowed})}{\text{Runs Per Win}} + \frac{(\text{Wins} + \text{Losses})}{2}$$

A-E — Actual Wins Minus Expected Wins (A measure of the extent to which a team outperformed or underperformed its talent; for a single season or two a high figure may be attributable to chance, but over time one must credit good managing.)

E — Eastern Division

W — Western Division

* — Indicates playing manager; for vital statistics, consult the player or pitcher register

▲ — Tied for first place, involved in league or division playoff

● — Tied for position in standings

♦ — League Championship Series win

★ — World Series win

■ — Wild Card

○ — Lost Divisional Playoffs

The team and league abbreviations used in this section can be found on the last page of the book.

YEAR	TM/L	G	W	L	PCT	STANDING			M/Y	W-EXP	A-E
Blow, Josiah H. "Joe"											
1969	Det-A*	134	71	63	.530	3 E	3 E		1/2	66.8	4.2
1971	Tex-A*	23	9	14	.391	6 W	6 W		3/3	12.0	-3.0
1972	Tex-A	161	84	76	.525	2 W				79.1	4.9
1973	Tex-A	95	44	51	.463	4 W	3 W		1/2	44.2	-0.2
1973	NY-A	56	30	26	.535	3 E	3 E		2/2	28.7	1.3
1974	NY-A	159	97	62	.610	★♦1 E				82.8	14.2
1975	NY-A	162	100	62	.617	♦1 E				90.0	10.0
1976	NY-A	94	52	42	.553	▲♦3 E	1 E		1/3	53.8	-1.8
1977	Bos-A	95	55	40	.579	4 E	4 E	2 E	2/3	50.4	4.6
1978	Oak-A	152	83	69	.546	●5 W	2 W		2/2	75.2	7.8
1979	Oak-A	60	37	23	.617	1 W	2 W		1/2	33.0	4.0
1980	Oak-A	49	27	22	.551	2 W	3 W		2/2	27.4	-0.4
1981(1)	Oak-A	62	24	38	.387	6 W				32.4	-7.6
1981(2)	Oak-A	100	44	56	.440	5 W				57.0	-13.0
1982	NY-A	162	91	71	.562	3 E				81.5	10.5
1983	NY-A	145	91	54	.628	6 E	2 E		2/2	84.0	7.0
1996	Atl-N	10	3	7	.300	■○♦6 E	2 E		1/2	6.0	-3.0
	15	1719	942	776	.548					904.3	39.5

YEAR	TM/L	G	W	L	PCT	STANDING				M/YW-EXP	A-E

Adair, Marion Danne "Bill"

YEAR	TM/L	G	W	L	PCT	STANDING				M/YW-EXP	A-E
1970	Chi-A	10	4	6	.400	6 W	6 W	6 W	2/3	3.8	0.2

Adcock, Joseph Wilbur "Joe"

1967	Cle-A	162	75	87	.463	8				75.0	0.0

Addy, Robert Edward "Bob"

1875	Phi-n*	7	3	4	.429	4	5		2/2	4.3	-1.3
1877	Cin-N*	24	5	19	.208	6	6	6	2/3	5.3	-0.3
	2	31	8	23	.258						-1.6

Allen, Robert Gilman "Bob"

1890	Phi-N*	35	25	10	.714	3	2	3	4/5	20.2	4.8
1900	Cin-N*	144	62	77	.446	7				65.5	-3.5
	2	179	87	87	.500						1.3

Allison, Andrew K. "Andy"

1872	Eck-n*	11	0	11	.000	10	9		1/3	-1.2	1.2

Allison, Douglas L. "Doug"

1873	Res-n*	23	2	21	.087	8				-3.0	5.0

Alou, Felipe Rojas

1992	Mon-N	125	70	55	.560	4 E	2 E		2/2	68.1	1.9
1993	Mon-N	163	94	68	.580	2 E				86.1	7.9
1994	Mon-N	114	74	40	.649	1 E				70.0	4.0
1995	Mon-N	144	66	78	.458	5 E				70.3	-4.3
1996	Mon-N	162	88	74	.543	2 E				88.4	-0.4
1997	Mon-N	162	78	84	.481	4 E				76.1	1.9
1998	Mon-N	162	65	97	.401	4 E				66.9	-1.9
	7	1032	535	496	.519						9.1

Alston, Walter Emmons

1954	Bro-N	154	92	62	.597	2				80.6	11.4
1955	Bro-N	154	98	55	.641	★1				96.4	1.6
1956	Bro-N	154	93	61	.604	1				89.2	3.8
1957	Bro-N	154	84	70	.545	3				87.3	-3.3
1958	LA-N	154	71	83	.461	7				67.8	3.2
1959	LA-N	156	88	68	.564	▲★1				81.5	6.5
1960	LA-N	154	82	72	.532	4				84.3	-2.3
1961	LA-N	154	89	65	.578	2				80.7	8.3
1962	LA-N	165	102	63	.618	▲2				96.7	5.3
1963	LA-N	163	99	63	.611	★1				91.0	8.0
1964	LA-N	164	80	82	.494	●6				85.7	-5.7
1965	LA-N	162	97	65	.599	★1				90.9	6.1
1966	LA-N	162	95	67	.586	1				94.4	0.6
1967	LA-N	162	73	89	.451	8				72.3	0.7
1968	LA-N	162	76	86	.469	●7				76.2	-0.2
1969	LA-N	162	85	77	.525	4 W				90.2	-5.2
1970	LA-N	161	87	74	.540	2 W				87.0	-0.0
1971	LA-N	162	89	73	.549	2 W				89.2	-0.2
1972	LA-N	155	85	70	.548	3 W				83.9	1.1
1973	LA-N	162	95	66	.590	2 W				92.4	2.6
1974	LA-N	162	102	60	.630	♦1 W				105.6	-3.6
1975	LA-N	162	88	74	.543	2 W				93.7	-5.7
1976	LA-N	158	90	68	.570	2 W	2 W		1/2	86.1	3.9
	23	3658	2040	1613	.558						36.8

Altobelli, Joseph "Joe"

1977	SF-N	162	75	87	.463	4 W				77.1	-2.1
1978	SF-N	162	89	73	.549	3 W				83.1	5.9
1979	SF-N	140	61	79	.436	4 W	4 W		1/2	63.1	-2.1
1983	Bal-A	162	98	64	.605	★1 E				95.7	2.3
1984	Bal-A	162	85	77	.525	5 E				82.5	2.5
1985	Bal-A	55	29	26	.527	4 E	4 E		1/3	29.3	-0.3
1991	Chi-N	1	0	1	.000	4 E	5 E	4 E	2/3	0.5	-0.5
	7	844	437	407	.518						5.8

Amalfitano, John Joseph "Joey"

1979	Chi-N	7	2	5	.286	5 E	5 E		2/2	3.5	-1.5
1980	Chi-N	72	26	46	.361	6 E	6 E		2/2	30.7	-4.7
1981(1)	Chi-N	54	15	37	.288	6 E					
(2)	Chi-N	52	23	28	.451	5 E				39.5	-1.5
	3	185	66	116	.363						-7.8

Anderson, George Lee "Sparky"

1970	Cin-N	162	102	60	.630	♦1 W				90.4	11.6
1971	Cin-N	162	79	83	.488	●4 W				81.6	-2.6
1972	Cin-N	154	95	59	.617	♦1 W				92.7	2.3
1973	Cin-N	162	99	63	.611	1 W				93.4	5.6
1974	Cin-N	163	98	64	.605	2 W				95.8	2.2
1975	Cin-N	162	108	54	.667	★1 W				106.7	1.3
1976	Cin-N	162	102	60	.630	★1 W				103.2	-1.2
1977	Cin-N	162	88	74	.543	2 W				88.5	-0.5
1978	Cin-N	161	92	69	.571	2 W				82.7	9.3
1979	Det-A	106	56	50	.528	5 E	5 E		3/3	55.1	0.9
1980	Det-A	163	84	78	.519	5 E				88.0	-4.0
1981(1)	Det-A	57	31	26	.544	4 E					
(2)	Det-A	52	29	23	.558	●2 E				57.0	3.0
1982	Det-A	162	83	79	.512	4 E				85.5	-2.5
1983	Det-A	162	92	70	.568	2 E				92.0	0.0
1984	Det-A	162	104	58	.642	★1 E				99.5	4.5
1985	Det-A	161	84	77	.522	3 E				84.6	-0.6
1986	Det-A	162	87	75	.537	3 E				89.2	-2.2
1987	Det-A	162	98	64	.605	1 E				96.2	1.8
1988	Det-A	162	88	74	.543	2 E				85.7	2.3
1989	Det-A	162	59	103	.364	7 E				60.9	-1.9
1990	Det-A	162	79	83	.488	3 E				80.6	-1.6
1991	Det-A	162	84	78	.519	●2 E				83.2	0.8
1992	Det-A	162	75	87	.463	6 E				80.7	-5.7
1993	Det-A	162	85	77	.525	●3 E				86.7	-1.7
1994	Det-A	115	53	62	.461	5 E				55.8	-2.8
1995	Det-A	144	60	84	.417	4 E				54.3	5.7
	26	4030	2194	1834	.545						23.9

Anson, Adrian Constantine "Cap"

1875	Ath-n*	8	4	2	.667	2	2		2/2	4.9	-0.9
1879	Chi-N*	64	41	21	.661	2	4		1/2	32.9	8.1
1880	Chi-N*	86	67	17	.798	1				63.0	4.0
1881	Chi-N*	84	56	28	.667	1				57.4	-1.4
1882	Chi-N*	84	55	29	.655	1				64.3	-9.3
1883	Chi-N*	98	59	39	.602	2				60.8	-1.8
1884	Chi-N*	113	62	50	.554	●4				71.5	-9.5
1885	Chi-N*	113	87	25	.777	1				88.1	-1.1
1886	Chi-N*	126	90	34	.726	1				92.5	-2.5
1887	Chi-N*	127	71	50	.587	3				68.9	2.1
1888	Chi-N*	136	77	58	.570	2				74.5	2.5
1889	Chi-N*	136	67	65	.508	3				70.5	-3.5
1890	Chi-N*	139	84	53	.613	2				82.5	1.5
1891	Chi-N*	137	82	53	.607	2				76.6	5.4
1892(1)	Chi-N*	71	31	39	.443	8					
(2)	Chi-N*	76	39	37	.513	7				63.2	6.8
1893	Chi-N*	128	56	71	.441	9				59.8	-3.8
1894	Chi-N*	137	57	75	.432	8				64.1	-7.1
1895	Chi-N*	133	72	58	.554	4				66.0	6.0
1896	Chi-N*	132	71	57	.555	5				64.9	6.1
1897	Chi-N*	138	59	73	.447	9				60.7	-1.7
1898	NY-N	22	9	13	.409	6	7	7	2/3	11.5	-2.5
	21	2288	1296	947	.578						-2.8

Appling, Lucius Benjamin "Luke"

1967	KC-A	40	10	30	.250	10	10		2/2	16.5	-6.5

Armour, William Clark "Bill"

1902	Cle-A	137	69	67	.507	5				69.8	-0.8
1903	Cle-A	140	77	63	.550	3				76.1	0.9
1904	Cle-A	154	86	65	.570	4				93.8	-7.8
1905	Cle-A	154	79	74	.516	3				66.5	12.5
1906	Det-A	151	71	78	.477	6				65.6	5.4
	5	736	382	347	.524						10.3

Aspromonte, Kenneth Joseph "Ken"

1972	Cle-A	156	72	84	.462	5 E				72.4	-0.4
1973	Cle-A	162	71	91	.438	6 E				66.6	4.4
1974	Cle-A	162	77	85	.475	4 E				77.7	-0.7
	3	480	220	260	.458						3.3

Austin, James Philip "Jimmy"

1913	StL-A*	8	2	6	.250	7	7	8	2/3	3.3	-1.3
1918	StL-A*	16	7	9	.438	6	6	5	2/3	7.7	-0.7
1923	StL-A*	51	22	29	.431	3	5		2/2	24.4	-2.4
	3	75	31	44	.413						-4.5

Baker, Delmer David "Del"

1933	Det-A	2	2	0	1.000	5	5		2/2	1.0	1.0
1936	Det-A	34	18	16	.529	3	4	2	2/3	18.0	0.0
1937	Det-A	54	34	20	.630	3	3	2	2/5	29.9	4.1
	Det-A	10	7	3	.700	2	2	2	4/5	5.5	1.5
1938	Det-A	57	37	19	.661	5	4		2/2	30.2	6.8
1939	Det-A	155	81	73	.526	5				85.1	-4.1
1940	Det-A	155	90	64	.584	1				92.9	-2.9
1941	Det-A	155	75	79	.487	●4				71.4	3.6
1942	Det-A	156	73	81	.474	5				77.2	-4.2
1960	Bos-A	7	2	5	.286	8	8	7	2/3	3.0	-1.0
	9	785	419	360	.538						4.7

Baker, Johnnie B "Dusty"

1993	SF-N	162	103	59	.636	2 W				98.3	4.7
1994	SF-N	115	55	60	.478	2 W				57.9	-2.9
1995	SF-N	144	67	77	.465	4 W				60.2	6.8
1996	SF-N	162	68	94	.420	4 W				70.5	-2.5
1997	SF-N	162	90	72	.556	○1 W				80.1	9.9
1998	SF-N	163	89	74	.546	▲2 W				91.7	-2.7
	6	908	472	436	.520						13.2

Bamberger, George Irvin

1978	Mil-A	162	93	69	.574	3 E				96.4	-3.4
1979	Mil-A	161	95	66	.590	2 E				88.8	6.2
1980	Mil-A	92	47	45	.511	2 E	4 E	3 E	2/3	53.2	-6.2
1982	NY-N	162	65	97	.401	6 E				69.1	-4.1
1983	NY-N	46	16	30	.348	6 E	6 E		1/2	19.8	-3.8
1985	Mil-A	161	71	90	.441	6 E				69.5	1.5
1986	Mil-A	152	71	81	.467	6 E	6 E		1/2	69.6	1.4
	7	936	458	478	.489						-8.3

Bancroft, David James "Dave"

1924	Bos-N*	154	53	100	.346	8				47.8	5.2
1925	Bos-N*	153	70	83	.458	5				67.5	2.5
1926	Bos-N*	153	66	86	.434	7				66.4	-0.4
1927	Bos-N*	155	60	94	.390	7				65.1	-5.1
	4	615	249	363	.407						2.2

YEAR	TM/L	G	W	L	PCT	STANDING			M/YW	EXP	A-E
Bancroft, Frank Carter											
1880	Wor-N	85	40	43	.482	5				45.7	-5.7
1881	Det-N	84	41	43	.488	4				42.9	-1.9
1882	Det-N	86	42	41	.506	6				34.0	8.0
1883	Cle-N	100	55	42	.567	4				51.8	3.2
1884	Pro-N	114	84	28	.750	1				83.3	0.7
1885	Pro-N	110	53	57	.482	4				46.0	7.0
1887	Phi-a	55	26	29	.473	6	5		1/2	27.6	-1.6
1889	Ind-N	68	25	43	.368	7	7		1/2	30.8	-5.8
1902	Cin-N	16	9	7	.563	6	6	4	2/3	8.8	0.2
9		718	375	333	.530						4.1
Barkley, Samuel E. "Sam"											
1888	KC-a*	58	21	36	.368	8	8	8	2/3	16.2	4.8
Barnie, William Harrison "Billy"											
1883	Bal-a*	96	28	68	.292	8				25.1	2.9
1884	Bal-a	109	63	43	.594	4				64.1	-1.1
1885	Bal-a	110	41	68	.376	8				41.7	-0.7
1886	Bal-a	139	48	83	.366	8				42.4	5.6
1887	Bal-a	141	77	58	.570	3				77.0	0.0
1888	Bal-a	139	57	80	.416	5				56.8	0.2
1889	Bal-a	139	70	65	.519	5				67.1	2.9
1890	Bal-a	38	15	19	.441	8				16.0	-1.0
1891	Bal-a	139	71	64	.526	3				72.0	-1.0
1892(1)	Was-N	2	0	2	.000	●11	7		1/2	0.8	-0.8
1893	Lou-N	126	50	75	.400	11				47.6	2.4
1894	Lou-N	131	36	94	.277	12				39.3	-3.3
1897	Bro-N	136	61	71	.462	●6				62.3	-1.3
1898	Bro-N	35	15	20	.429	9	10		1/3	13.5	1.5
14		1480	632	810	.438						6.1
Barrow, Edward Grant "Ed"											
1903	Det-A	137	65	71	.478	5				71.0	-6.0
1904	Det-A	84	32	46	.410	7	7		1/2	31.9	0.1
1918	Bos-A	126	75	51	.595	★1				73.8	1.2
1919	Bos-A	138	66	71	.482	6				69.8	-3.8
1920	Bos-A	154	72	81	.471	5				71.6	0.4
5		639	310	320	.492						-8.1
Barry, John Joseph "Jack"											
1917	Bos-A*	157	90	62	.592	2				88.0	2.0
Battin, Joseph V. "Joe"											
1883	Pit-a*	13	2	11	.154	7	7		3/3	4.2	-2.2
1884	Pit-a*	13	6	7	.462	11	10	10	3/5	2.9	3.1
	Pit-U*	6	1	5	.167	5	5		1/2	2.7	-1.7
2		32	9	23	.281						-0.9
Bauer, Henry Albert "Hank"											
1961	KC-A*	102	35	67	.343	8	●9		2/2	39.9	-4.9
1962	KC-A	162	72	90	.444	9				72.2	-0.2
1964	Bal-A	163	97	65	.599	3				93.2	3.8
1965	Bal-A	162	94	68	.580	3				87.9	6.1
1966	Bal-A	160	97	63	.606	★1				95.9	1.1
1967	Bal-A	161	76	85	.472	●6				87.2	-11.2
1968	Bal-A	80	43	37	.538	3	2		1/2	44.7	-1.7
1969	Oak-A	149	80	69	.537	2 W	2 W		1/2	80.3	-0.3
8		1139	594	544	.522						-7.2
Baylor, Donald Edward "Don"											
1993	Col-N	162	67	95	.414	6 W				61.8	5.2
1994	Col-N	117	53	64	.453	3 W				52.4	0.6
1995	Col-N	144	77	67	.535	■2 W				72.2	4.8
1996	Col-N	162	82	79	.509	3 W				80.7	2.3
1997	Col-N	162	83	79	.512	3 W				82.3	0.7
1998	Col-N	162	77	85	.475	4 W				78.3	-1.3
6		909	439	469	.483						12.2
Bell, David Gus "Buddy"											
1996	Det-A	162	53	109	.327	5 E				52.9	0.1
1997	Det-A	162	79	83	.488	3 E				80.4	-1.4
1998	Det-A	162	53	85	.384	3 E			1/2	57.5	-4.5
3		486	185	277	.400						-5.8
Benson, Vernon Adair "Vern"											
1977	Atl-N	1	1	0	1.000	6 W	6 W	6 W	3/4	0.4	0.6
Berra, Lawrence Peter "Yogi"											
1964	NY-A	164	99	63	.611	1				97.3	1.7
1972	NY-N	156	83	73	.532	3 E				72.4	10.6
1973	NY-N	161	82	79	.509	♦1 E				82.7	-0.7
1974	NY-N	162	71	91	.438	5 E				72.9	-1.9
1975	NY-N	109	56	53	.514	3 E	●3 E		1/2	56.0	-0.0
1984	NY-A	162	87	75	.537	3 E				89.0	-2.0
1985	NY-A	16	6	10	.375	7 E	2 E		1/2	9.7	-3.7
7		930	484	444	.522						4.0
Bevington, Terry Paul											
1995	Chi-A	113	57	56	.504	4 C	3 C		2/2	56.3	0.7
1996	Chi-A	162	85	77	.525	2 C				90.7	-5.7
1997	Chi-A	161	80	81	.497	2 C				75.4	4.6
3		436	222	214	.509						-0.3
Bezdek, Hugo Frank											
1917	Pit-N	91	30	59	.337	8	8		3/3	35.8	-5.8
1918	Pit-N	126	65	60	.520	4				68.6	-3.6
1919	Pit-N	139	71	68	.511	4				70.2	0.8
3		356	166	187	.470						-8.6
Bickerson											
1884	Was-a	1	0	1	.000	12	12		2/2	0.2	-0.2
Birmingham, Joseph Leo "Joe"											
1912	Cle-A*	28	21	7	.750	6	5		2/2	13.9	7.1
1913	Cle-A*	155	86	66	.566	3				86.6	-0.6
1914	Cle-A*	157	51	102	.333	8				58.3	-7.3
1915	Cle-A	28	12	16	.429	6	7		1/2	11.4	0.6
4		368	170	191	.471						-0.2
Bissonette, Adelphia Louis "Del"											
1945	Bos-N	60	25	34	.424	7	6		2/2	29.2	-4.2
Blackburne, Russell Aubrey "Lena"											
1928	Chi-A	80	40	40	.500	6	5		2/2	36.4	3.6
1929	Chi-A*	152	59	93	.388	7				59.8	-0.8
2		232	99	133	.427						2.8
Blades, Francis Raymond "Ray"											
1939	StL-N	155	92	61	.601	2				91.0	1.0
1940	StL-N	39	14	24	.368	6	3		1/3	20.2	-6.2
1948	Bro-N	1	1	0	1.000	5	5	3	2/3	0.5	0.5
3		195	107	85	.557						-4.7
Blair, Walter Allen "Walter"											
1915	Buf-F*	2	1	1	.500	8	8	6	2/3	0.9	0.1
Bluege, Oswald Louis "Ossie"											
1943	Was-A	153	84	69	.549	2				83.9	0.1
1944	Was-A	154	64	90	.416	8				69.4	-5.4
1945	Was-A	156	87	67	.565	2				83.5	3.5
1946	Was-A	155	76	78	.494	4				66.9	9.1
1947	Was-A	154	64	90	.416	7				57.5	6.5
5		772	375	394	.488						13.7
Bochy, Bruce Douglas											
1995	SD-N	144	70	74	.486	3 W				71.6	-1.6
1996	SD-N	162	91	71	.562	o1 W				89.9	1.1
1997	SD-N	162	76	86	.469	4 W				72.1	3.9
1998	SD-N	162	98	64	.605	♦1 W				92.7	5.3
4		630	335	295	.532						8.7
Boles, John											
1996	Fla-N	75	40	35	.533	4 E	3 E		3/3	36.8	3.2
Bond, Thomas Henry "Tommy"											
1882	Wor-N*	6	2	4	.333	8	8	8	2/3	1.3	0.7
Boone, Robert Raymond "Bob"											
1995	KC-A	144	70	74	.486	2 C				65.9	4.1
1996	KC-A	161	75	86	.466	5 C				76.6	-1.6
1997	KC-A	82	36	46	.439	4 C	5 C		1/2	37.4	-1.4
3		387	181	206	.468						1.1
Boros, Stephen "Steve"											
1983	Oak-A	162	74	88	.457	4 W				73.7	0.3
1984	Oak-A	44	20	24	.455	5 W	4 W		1/2	20.5	-0.5
1986	SD-N	162	74	88	.457	4 W				74.1	-0.1
3		368	168	200	.457						-0.3
Bottomley, James Leroy "Jim"											
1937	StL-A*	78	21	56	.273	7	8		2/2	24.7	-3.7
Boudreau, Louis "Lou"											
1942	Cle-A*	156	75	79	.487	4				69.7	5.3
1943	Cle-A*	153	82	71	.536	3				79.0	3.0
1944	Cle-A*	155	72	82	.468	●5				73.5	-1.5
1945	Cle-A*	147	73	72	.503	5				73.5	-0.5
1946	Cle-A*	156	68	86	.442	4				66.0	2.0
1947	Cle-A*	157	80	74	.519	4				87.4	-7.4
1948	Cle-A*	156	97	58	.626	▲★1				104.7	-7.7
1949	Cle-A*	154	89	65	.578	4				87.6	1.4
1950	Cle-A*	155	92	62	.597	4				91.9	0.1
1952	Bos-A*	154	76	78	.494	6				78.0	-2.0
1953	Bos-A	153	84	69	.549	4				79.0	5.0
1954	Bos-A	156	69	85	.448	4				74.2	-5.2
1955	KC-A	155	63	91	.409	6				51.1	11.9
1956	KC-A	154	52	102	.338	8				56.3	-4.3
1957	KC-A	104	36	67	.350	8	7		1/2	41.2	-5.2
1960	Chi-N	139	54	83	.394	7	7		2/2	55.9	-1.9
16		2404	1162	1224	.487						-6.9
Bowa, Lawrence Robert "Larry"											
1987	SD-N	162	65	97	.401	6 W				71.4	-6.4
1988	SD-N	46	16	30	.348	5 W	3 W		1/2	23.3	-7.3
2		208	81	127	.389						-13.8
Bowerman, Frank Eugene "Frank"											
1909	Bos-N*	76	22	54	.289	8	8		1/2	24.2	-2.2
Boyd, William J. "Bill"											
1875	Atl-n*	2	0	2	.000	12	12		2/2	-0.2	0.2
Boyer, Kenton Lloyd "Ken"											
1978	StL-N	143	62	81	.434	6 E	5 E		3/3	66.1	-4.1
1979	StL-N	163	86	76	.531	3 E				84.9	1.1
1980	StL-N	51	18	33	.353	6 E	4 E		1/4	26.4	-8.4
3		357	166	190	.466						-11.3

YEAR	TM/L	G	W	L	PCT	STANDING			M/YW-EXP	A-E

Bradley, William Joseph "Bill"

1905	Cle-A*	41	20	21	.488	●1　2　5		2/3	19.9	0.1
1914	Bro-F*	157	77	77	.500	5			75.5	1.5
	2	198	97	98	.497					1.6

Bragan, Robert Randall "Bobby"

1956	Pit-N	157	66	88	.429	7			70.1	-4.1
1957	Pit-N	104	36	67	.350	7　●7		1/2	43.8	-7.8
1958	Cle-A	67	31	36	.463	6　4		1/2	36.1	-5.1
1963	Mil-N	163	84	78	.519	6			88.9	-4.9
1964	Mil-N	162	88	74	.543	5			86.7	1.3
1965	Mil-N	162	86	76	.531	5			88.8	-2.8
1966	Atl-N	112	52	59	.468	7　5		1/2	62.3	-10.3
	7	927	443	478	.481					-33.8

Bresnahan, Roger Philip

1909	StL-N*	154	54	98	.355	7			60.8	-6.8
1910	StL-N*	153	63	90	.412	7			68.5	-5.5
1911	StL-N*	158	75	74	.503	5			67.1	7.9
1912	StL-N*	153	63	90	.412	6			60.1	2.9
1915	Chi-N*	157	73	80	.477	4			71.1	1.9
	5	775	328	432	.432					0.5

Bristol, James David "Dave"

1966	Cin-N	77	39	38	.506	8　7		2/2	38.0	1.0
1967	Cin-N	162	87	75	.537	4			85.6	1.4
1968	Cin-N	163	83	79	.512	4			82.8	0.2
1969	Cin-N	163	89	73	.549	3 W			83.9	5.1
1970	Mil-A	163	65	97	.401	●4 W			66.7	-1.7
1971	Mil-A	161	69	92	.429	6 W			72.1	-3.1
1972	Mil-A	30	10	20	.333	6 E　6 E		1/3	12.8	-2.8
1976	Atl-N	162	70	92	.432	6 W			72.6	-2.6
1977	Atl-N	29	8	21	.276	6 W　6 W		1/4	10.8	-2.8
	Atl-N	131	52	79	.397	6 W　6 W		4/4	48.6	3.4
1979	SF-N	22	10	12	.455	4 W　4 W		2/2	9.9	0.1
1980	SF-N	161	75	86	.466	5 W			73.8	1.2
	11	1424	657	764	.462					-0.5

Brown, Freeman

| 1882 | Wor-N | 41 | 9 | 32 | .220 | 8　8 | | 1/3 | 9.1 | -0.1 |

Brown, Mordecai Peter Centennial "Three Finger"

| 1914 | StL-F* | 114 | 50 | 63 | .442 | 7　8 | | 1/2 | 46.1 | 3.9 |

Brown, Thomas T. "Tom"

1897	Was-N*	99	52	46	.531	11　●6		2/2	48.2	3.8
1898	Was-N*	38	12	26	.316	11　11		1/4	13.6	-1.6
	2	137	64	72	.471					2.2

Brucker, Earle Francis Sr

| 1952 | Cin-N | 5 | 3 | 2 | .600 | 7　7　6 | | 2/3 | 2.4 | 0.6 |

Buckenberger, Albert C. "Al"

1889	Col-a	140	60	78	.435	6			56.5	3.5
1890	Col-a	80	39	41	.488	5　2		1/3	51.9	-12.9
1892(1)	Pit-N	29	15	14	.517	7　6		1/2		
(2)	Pit-N	66	38	27	.585	10　4		2/2	47.3	5.7
1893	Pit-N	131	81	48	.628	2			81.3	-0.3
1894	Pit-N	110	53	55	.491	7　7		1/2	52.9	0.1
1895	StL-N	50	16	34	.320	11　11		1/4	16.0	-0.0
1902	Bos-N	142	73	64	.533	3			74.6	-1.6
1903	Bos-N	140	58	80	.420	6			57.0	1.0
1904	Bos-N	155	55	98	.359	7			49.1	5.9
	9	1043	488	539	.475					1.3

Buffinton, Charles G. "Charlie"

| 1890 | Phi-P* | 116 | 61 | 54 | .530 | 5　5 | | 2/2 | 63.6 | -2.6 |

Burdock, John Joseph "Jack"

| 1883 | Bos-N* | 54 | 30 | 24 | .556 | 4　1 | | 1/2 | 37.4 | -7.4 |

Burke, James Timothy "Jimmy"

1905	StL-N*	90	34	56	.378	7　6　6		2/3	32.8	1.2
1918	StL-A	61	29	31	.483	6　5		3/3	28.8	0.2
1919	StL-A	140	67	72	.482	5			65.9	1.1
1920	StL-A	154	76	77	.497	4			79.4	-3.4
	4	445	206	236	.466					-0.9

Burnham, George Walter "Watch"

| 1887 | Ind-N | 28 | 6 | 22 | .214 | 8　8 | | 1/3 | 7.7 | -1.7 |

Burns, Thomas Everett "Tom"

1892(1)	Pit-N*	47	22	25	.468	7　6		2/2		
(2)	Pit-N*	13	5	7	.417	10　4		1/2	29.7	-2.7
1898	Chi-N	152	85	65	.567	4			89.2	-4.2
1899	Chi-N	152	75	73	.507	8			78.6	-3.6
	3	364	187	170	.524					-10.5

Burwell, William Edwin "Bill"

| 1947 | Pit-N | 1 | 1 | 0 | 1.000 | 8　●7 | | 2/2 | 0.5 | 0.5 |

Bush, Owen Joseph "Donie"

1923	Was-A*	155	75	78	.490	4			73.9	1.1
1927	Pit-N	156	94	60	.610	1			92.4	1.6
1928	Pit-N	152	85	67	.559	4			88.5	-3.5
1929	Pit-N	119	67	51	.568	2　2		1/2	67.7	-0.7
1930	Chi-A	154	62	92	.403	7			62.6	-0.6
1931	Chi-A	156	56	97	.366	8			54.8	1.2
1933	Cin-N	153	58	94	.382	8			59.8	-1.8

YEAR	TM/L	G	W	L	PCT	STANDING			M/YW-EXP	A-E
	7	1045	497	539	.480					-2.7

Butler, Ormond Hook

| 1883 | Pit-a | 53 | 17 | 36 | .321 | 6　6　7 | | 2/3 | 17.3 | -0.3 |

Byrne, Charles H. "Charlie"

1885	Bro-a	75	38	37	.507	7　●5		2/2	36.0	2.0
1886	Bro-a	141	76	61	.555	3			68.5	7.5
1887	Bro-a	138	60	74	.448	6			65.8	-5.8
	3	354	174	172	.503					3.7

Callahan, James Joseph "Nixey"

1903	Chi-A*	138	60	77	.438	7			58.3	1.7
1904	Chi-A*	42	23	18	.561	4　3		1/2	24.1	-1.1
1912	Chi-A*	158	78	76	.506	4			76.1	1.9
1913	Chi-A*	153	78	74	.513	5			74.8	3.2
1914	Chi-A	157	70	84	.455	●6			68.5	1.5
1916	Pit-N	157	65	89	.422	6			65.3	-0.3
1917	Pit-N	61	20	40	.333	8　8		1/3	24.1	-4.1
	7	866	394	458	.462					2.8

Campau, Charles Columbus "Count"

| 1890 | StL-a* | 42 | 27 | 14 | .659 | 5　2　3 | | 4/6 | 24.1 | 2.9 |

Cantillon, Joseph D. "Joe"

1907	Was-A	154	49	102	.325	8			55.6	-6.6
1908	Was-A	155	67	85	.441	7			69.0	-2.0
1909	Was-A	156	42	110	.276	8			43.9	-1.9
	3	465	158	297	.347					-10.4

Carey, Max George

1932	Bro-N	154	81	73	.526	3			77.5	3.5
1933	Bro-N	157	65	88	.425	6			68.4	-3.4
	2	311	146	161	.476					0.1

Carey, Thomas John "Tom"

1873	Bal-n*	24	14	9	.609	3　3		2/2	16.9	-2.9
1874	Mut-n*	25	13	12	.520	3　2		1/2	16.4	-3.4
	2	49	27	21	.563					-6.3

Carrigan, William Francis "Bill"

1913	Bos-A*	70	40	30	.571	5　4		2/2	36.0	4.0
1914	Bos-A*	159	91	62	.595	2			85.5	5.5
1915	Bos-A*	155	101	50	.669	★1			94.1	6.9
1916	Bos-A*	156	91	63	.591	★1			85.2	5.8
1927	Bos-A	154	51	103	.331	8			51.7	-0.7
1928	Bos-A	154	57	96	.373	8			58.2	-1.2
1929	Bos-A	155	58	96	.377	8			57.3	0.7
	7	1003	489	500	.494					21.0

Caruthers, Robert Lee "Bob"

| 1892(2) | StL-N* | 50 | 16 | 32 | .333 | 12　11 | | 3/3 | 17.5 | -1.5 |

Cavarretta, Philip Joseph "Phil"

1951	Chi-N*	74	27	47	.365	7　8		2/2	30.4	-3.4
1952	Chi-N*	155	77	77	.500	5			76.7	0.3
1953	Chi-N*	155	65	89	.422	7			57.3	7.7
	3	384	169	213	.442					4.6

Caylor, Oliver Perry "O.P."

1885	Cin-a	112	63	49	.563	2			62.1	0.9
1886	Cin-a	141	65	73	.471	5			70.5	-5.5
1887	NY-a	100	35	60	.368	7　7		3/3	27.6	7.4
	3	353	163	182	.472					2.7

Chance, Frank Leroy

1905	Chi-N*	90	55	33	.625	4　3		2/2	58.5	-3.5
1906	Chi-N*	155	116	36	.763	1			112.7	3.3
1907	Chi-N*	155	107	45	.704	★1			98.1	8.9
1908	Chi-N*	158	99	55	.643	★1			95.7	3.3
1909	Chi-N*	155	104	49	.680	2			105.1	-1.1
1910	Chi-N*	154	104	50	.675	1			99.8	4.2
1911	Chi-N*	158	92	62	.597	2			92.3	-0.3
1912	Chi-N*	153	91	59	.607	3			83.6	7.4
1913	NY-A*	153	57	94	.377	7			60.6	-3.6
1914	NY-A*	137	60	74	.448	7　●6		1/2	65.7	-5.7
1923	Bos-A	154	61	91	.401	8			53.6	7.4
	11	1622	946	648	.593					20.3

Chapman, John Curtis "Jack"

1876	Lou-N*	69	30	36	.455	5			26.6	3.4
1877	Lou-N*	61	35	25	.583	2			34.8	0.2
1878	Mil-N	61	15	45	.250	6			18.0	-3.0
1882	Wor-N	37	7	30	.189	8　8		3/3	8.2	-1.2
1883	Det-N	101	40	58	.408	7			37.9	2.1
1884	Det-N	114	28	84	.250	8			28.9	-0.9
1885	Buf-N	88	31	57	.352	7　7		2/2	25.3	5.7
1889	Lou-a	7	1	6	.143	8　8		4/4	1.5	-0.5
1890	Lou-a	136	88	44	.667	1			87.5	0.5
1891	Lou-a	141	55	84	.396	7			53.7	1.3
1892(1)	Lou-N	54	21	33	.389	10　11		1/2	21.6	-0.6
	11	869	351	502	.411					7.0

Chapman, William Benjamin "Ben"

1945	Phi-N*	85	28	57	.329	8　8		2/2	25.2	2.8
1946	Phi-N*	155	69	85	.448	5			61.8	7.2
1947	Phi-N	155	62	92	.403	●7			66.8	-4.8
1948	Phi-N	79	37	42	.468	7　6		1/3	32.2	4.8

YEAR	TM/L	G	W	L	PCT	STANDING			M/YW-EXP		A-E
	4	474	196	276	.415						10.1
Chase, Harold Homer "Hal"											
1910	NY-A*	14	10	4	.714	3	2		2/2	7.7	2.3
1911	NY-A*	153	76	76	.500	6				72.0	4.0
	2	167	86	80	.518						6.3
Clapp, John Edgar											
1872	Man-n*	24	5	19	.208	8				4.1	0.9
1878	Ind-N*	63	24	36	.400	5				26.7	-2.7
1879	Buf-N*	79	46	32	.590	3				41.8	4.2
1880	Cin-N*	82	21	59	.262	8				22.6	-1.6
1881	Cle-N*	74	32	41	.438	6	7		2/2	34.6	-2.6
1883	NY-N*	98	46	50	.479	6				43.8	2.2
	6	420	174	237	.423						0.3
Clarke, Fred Clifford											
1897	Lou-N*	92	35	54	.393	9	11		2/2	32.9	2.1
1898	Lou-N*	154	70	81	.464	9				65.6	4.4
1899	Lou-N*	156	75	77	.493	9				80.9	-5.9
1900	Pit-N*	140	79	60	.568	2				81.2	-2.2
1901	Pit-N*	140	90	49	.647	1				93.2	-3.2
1902	Pit-N*	142	103	36	.741	1				103.9	-0.9
1903	Pit-N*	141	91	49	.650	1				87.1	3.9
1904	Pit-N*	156	87	66	.569	4				85.2	1.8
1905	Pit-N*	155	96	57	.627	2				89.3	6.7
1906	Pit-N*	154	93	60	.608	3				93.7	-0.7
1907	Pit-N*	157	91	63	.591	2				90.8	0.2
1908	Pit-N*	155	98	56	.636	●2				90.3	7.7
1909	Pit-N*	154	110	42	.724	★1				103.7	6.3
1910	Pit-N*	154	86	67	.562	3				84.9	1.1
1911	Pit-N*	156	85	69	.552	3				96.4	-11.4
1912	Pit-N	153	93	58	.616	2				94.5	-1.5
1913	Pit-N*	155	78	71	.523	4				83.8	-5.8
1914	Pit-N*	158	69	85	.448	7				72.7	-3.7
1915	Pit-N*	157	73	81	.474	5				81.2	-8.2
	19	2829	1602	1181	.576						-9.3
Clements, John J. "Jack"											
1890	Phi-N*	19	13	6	.684	1	2	3	2/5	11.0	2.0
Cobb, Tyrus Raymond "Ty"											
1921	Det-A*	154	71	82	.464	6				79.3	-8.3
1922	Det-A*	155	79	75	.513	3				80.4	-1.4
1923	Det-A*	155	83	71	.539	2				85.5	-2.5
1924	Det-A*	156	86	68	.558	3				81.9	4.1
1925	Det-A*	156	81	73	.526	4				83.7	-2.7
1926	Det-A*	157	79	75	.513	6				73.5	5.5
	6	933	479	444	.519						-5.3
Cochrane, Gordon Stanley "Mickey"											
1934	Det-A*	154	101	53	.656	1				99.8	1.2
1935	Det-A*	152	93	58	.616	★1				99.1	-6.1
1936	Det-A*	53	29	24	.547	3	2		1/3	28.0	1.0
	Det-A*	67	36	31	.537	4	2		3/3	35.4	0.6
1937	Det-A*	29	16	13	.552	3	2		1/5	16.1	-0.1
	Det-A*	47	26	20	.565	3	2	2	3/5	25.5	0.5
1938	Det-A	98	47	51	.480	5	4		1/2	52.9	-5.9
	5	600	348	250	.582						-8.8
Cohen, Andrew Howard "Andy"											
1960	Phi-N	1	1	0	1.000	●6	●4	8	2/3	0.4	0.6
Coleman, Gerald Francis "Jerry"											
1980	SD-N	163	73	89	.451	6 W				74.2	-1.2
Coleman, Robert Hunter "Bob"											
1943	Bos-N	46	21	25	.457	6	6		1/2	18.0	3.0
1944	Bos-N	155	65	89	.422	6				68.5	-3.5
1945	Bos-N	94	42	51	.452	7	6		1/2	46.1	-4.1
	3	295	128	165	.437						-4.6
Collins, Edward Trowbridge Sr. "Eddie"											
1924	Chi-A*	27	14	13	.519	6			3/4	12.4	1.6
1925	Chi-A*	154	79	75	.513	5				80.8	-1.8
1926	Chi-A*	155	81	72	.529	5				83.0	-2.0
	3	336	174	160	.521						-2.3
Collins, James Joseph "Jimmy"											
1901	Bos-A*	138	79	57	.581	2				82.4	-3.4
1902	Bos-A*	138	77	60	.562	3				74.8	2.2
1903	Bos-A*	141	91	47	.659	★1				89.9	1.1
1904	Bos-A*	157	95	59	.617	1				93.3	1.7
1905	Bos-A*	153	78	74	.513	4				77.6	0.4
1906	Bos-A*	115	35	79	.307	8	8		1/2	37.3	-2.3
	6	842	455	376	.548						-0.4
Collins, John Francis "Shano"											
1931	Bos-A	153	62	90	.408	6				58.8	3.2
1932	Bos-A	55	11	44	.200	8	8		1/2	15.4	-4.4
	2	208	73	134	.353						-1.2
Collins, Terry Lee											
1994	Hou-N	115	66	49	.574	2 C				67.1	-1.1
1995	Hou-N	144	76	68	.528	2 C				79.0	-3.0
1996	Hou-N	162	82	80	.506	2 C				77.2	4.8
1997	Ana-A	162	84	78	.519	2 W				84.3	-0.3
1998	Ana-A	162	85	77	.525	2 W				81.4	3.6

YEAR	TM/L	G	W	L	PCT	STANDING			M/YW-EXP		A-E
	5	745	393	352	.528						4.0
Comiskey, Charles Albert "Charlie"											
1883	StL-a*	19	12	7	.632	2	2		2/2	12.1	-0.1
1884	StL-a*	25	16	7	.696	5	4		2/2	13.8	2.2
1885	StL-a*	112	79	33	.705	1				76.3	2.7
1886	StL-a*	139	93	46	.669	1				101.3	-8.3
1887	StL-a*	138	95	40	.704	1				97.5	-2.5
1888	StL-a*	137	92	43	.681	1				95.7	-3.7
1889	StL-a*	141	89	46	.659	2				91.9	-1.9
1890	Chi-P*	138	75	62	.547	4				78.5	-3.5
1891	StL-a*	141	86	52	.623	2				88.1	-2.1
1892(1)	Cin-N*	77	44	31	.587	4					
(2)	Cin-N*	78	38	37	.507	8				78.4	3.6
1893	Cin-N*	131	65	63	.508	●6				59.2	5.8
1894	Cin-N*	134	55	75	.423	10				51.5	3.5
	12	1410	839	542	.608						-4.3
Connor, Roger											
1896	StL-N*	46	8	37	.178	11	11	11	4/5	12.3	-4.3
Cooke, Allen Lindsey "Dusty"											
1948	Phi-N	13	6	6	.500	7	6	6	2/3	4.9	1.1
Coombs, John Wesley "Jack"											
1919	Phi-N	63	18	44	.290	8	8		1/2	22.3	-4.3
Cooney, John Walter "Johnny"											
1949	Bos-N	46	20	25	.444	4	4		2/2	22.1	-2.1
Corrales, Patrick "Pat"											
1978	Tex-A	1	1	0	1.000	●2 W	●2 W		2/2	0.5	0.5
1979	Tex-A	162	83	79	.512	3 W				86.2	-3.2
1980	Tex-A	163	76	85	.472	4 W				80.9	-4.9
1982	Phi-N	162	89	73	.549	2 E				82.1	6.9
1983	Phi-N	86	43	42	.506	1 E	♦1 E		1/2	45.9	-2.9
	Cle-A	62	30	32	.484	7 E	7 E		2/2	27.9	2.1
1984	Cle-A	163	75	87	.463	6 E				80.5	-5.5
1985	Cle-A	162	60	102	.370	7 E				68.4	-8.4
1986	Cle-A	163	84	78	.519	5 E				80.1	3.9
1987	Cle-A	87	31	56	.356	7 E	7 E		1/2	32.8	-1.8
	9	1211	572	634	.474						-13.2
Corriden, John Michael Sr. "Red"											
1950	Chi-A	125	52	72	.419	8	6		2/2	51.9	0.1
Cottier, Charles Keith "Chuck"											
1984	Sea-A	27	15	12	.556	7 W	●5 W		2/2	12.0	3.0
1985	Sea-A	162	74	88	.457	6 W				71.4	2.6
1986	Sea-A	28	9	19	.321	6 W	7 W		1/3	12.0	-3.0
	3	217	98	119	.452						2.6
Cox, Robert Joseph "Bobby"											
1978	Atl-N	162	69	93	.426	6 W				65.4	3.6
1979	Atl-N	160	66	94	.412	6 W				70.6	-4.6
1980	Atl-N	161	81	80	.503	4 W				77.3	3.7
1981(1)	Atl-N	55	25	29	.463	4 W					
(2)	Atl-N	52	25	27	.481	5 W				50.7	-0.7
1982	Tor-A	162	78	84	.481	●6 E				75.8	2.2
1983	Tor-A	162	89	73	.549	4 E				87.8	1.2
1984	Tor-A	163	89	73	.549	2 E				86.4	2.6
1985	Tor-A	161	99	62	.615	1 E				98.2	0.8
1990	Atl-N	97	40	57	.412	6 W	6 W		2/2	40.3	-0.3
1991	Atl-N	162	94	68	.580	♦1 W				91.7	2.3
1992	Atl-N	162	98	64	.605	♦1 W				93.2	4.8
1993	Atl-N	162	104	58	.642	1 W				102.8	1.2
1994	Atl-N	114	68	46	.596	2 E				66.6	1.4
1995	Atl-N	144	90	54	.625	★1 E				83.0	7.0
1996	Atl-N	162	96	66	.593	♦1 E				93.7	2.3
1997	Atl-N	162	101	61	.623	1 E				102.7	-1.7
1998	Atl-N	162	106	56	.654	1 E				105.9	0.1
	17	2565	1418	1145	.553						25.9
Craft, Harry Francis											
1957	KC-A	50	23	27	.460	8	7		2/2	20.0	3.0
1958	KC-A	156	73	81	.474	7				69.8	3.2
1959	KC-A	154	66	88	.429	7				69.3	-3.3
1961	Chi-N	12	4	8	.333	●6	7	7	2/9	5.2	-1.2
	Chi-N	4	3	1	.750	7	7	7	5/9	1.7	1.3
1962	Hou-N	162	64	96	.400	8				66.8	-2.8
1963	Hou-N	162	66	96	.407	9				60.8	5.2
1964	Hou-N	149	61	88	.409	9	9		1/2	60.6	0.4
	7	849	360	485	.426						6.0
Craig, Roger Lee											
1978	SD-N	162	84	78	.519	4 W				80.2	3.8
1979	SD-N	161	68	93	.422	5 W				72.2	-4.2
1985	SF-N	18	6	12	.333	6 W	6 W		2/2	7.6	-1.6
1986	SF-N	162	83	79	.512	3 W				89.4	-6.4
1987	SF-N	162	90	72	.556	1 W				92.4	-2.4
1988	SF-N	162	83	79	.512	4 W				85.7	-2.7
1989	SF-N	162	92	70	.568	♦1 W				91.5	0.5
1990	SF-N	162	85	77	.525	3 W				81.9	3.1
1991	SF-N	162	75	87	.463	4 W				76.0	-1.0
1992	SF-N	162	72	90	.444	5 W				73.0	-1.0
	10	1475	738	737	.500						-11.9

YEAR	TM/L	G	W	L	PCT	STANDING			M/Y	W-EXP	A-E
Crandall, Delmar Wesley "Del"											
1972	Mil-A	124	54	70	.435	6 E	6 E		3/3	52.8	1.2
1973	Mil-A	162	74	88	.457	5 E				78.7	-4.7
1974	Mil-A	162	76	86	.469	5 E				79.6	-3.6
1975	Mil-A	161	67	94	.416	5 E	5 E		1/2	68.9	-1.9
1983	Sea-A	89	34	55	.382	7 W	7 W		2/2	33.9	0.1
1984	Sea-A	135	59	76	.437	7 W	●5 W		1/2	59.8	-0.8
	6	833	364	469	.437						-9.7
Crane, Samuel Newhall "Sam"											
1880	Buf-N*	84	24	58	.293	7				24.6	-0.6
1884	Cin-U*	70	49	21	.700	5	3		2/2	49.2	-0.2
	2	154	73	79	.480						-0.8
Cravath, Clifford Carlton "Gavvy"											
1919	Phi-N*	75	29	46	.387	8	8		2/2	27.0	2.0
1920	Phi-N*	153	62	91	.405	8				61.0	1.0
	2	228	91	137	.399						2.9
Craver, William H. "Bill"											
1871	Tro-n*	25	12	12	.500	7	6		2/2	11.4	0.6
1872	Bal-n*	41	27	13	.675	2	2		1/2	29.6	-2.6
1875	Cen-n*	14	2	12	.143	11				1.7	0.3
1876	NY-N*	57	21	35	.375	6				14.7	6.3
	4	137	62	72	.463						4.6
Creamer, George W.											
1884	Pit-a*	8	0	8	.000	10	10	10	4/5	1.8	-1.8
Cronin, Joseph Edward "Joe"											
1933	Was-A*	153	99	53	.651	1				93.6	5.4
1934	Was-A*	155	66	86	.434	7				68.7	-2.7
1935	Bos-A*	154	78	75	.510	4				75.1	2.9
1936	Bos-A*	155	74	80	.481	6				78.0	-4.0
1937	Bos-A*	154	80	72	.526	5				80.3	-0.3
1938	Bos-A*	150	88	61	.591	2				88.1	-0.1
1939	Bos-A*	152	89	62	.589	2				84.1	4.9
1940	Bos-A*	154	82	72	.532	●4				81.2	0.8
1941	Bos-A*	155	84	70	.545	2				87.7	-3.7
1942	Bos-A*	152	93	59	.612	2				92.8	0.2
1943	Bos-A*	155	68	84	.447	7				71.2	-3.2
1944	Bos-A*	156	77	77	.500	4				83.3	-6.3
1945	Bos-A*	157	71	83	.461	7				69.1	1.9
1946	Bos-A	156	104	50	.675	1				96.9	7.1
1947	Bos-A	157	83	71	.539	3				82.1	0.9
	15	2315	1236	1055	.540						3.7
Crooks, John Charles											
1892(1)	StL-N*	47	24	22	.522	11	9		3/3		
(2)	StL-N*	15	3	11	.214	12	11		1/3	21.9	5.1
Cross, Lafayette Napoleon "Lave"											
1899	Cle-N*	38	8	30	.211	12	12		1/2	3.3	4.7
Cubbage, Michael Lee "Mike"											
1991	NY-N	7	3	4	.429	3 E	5 E		2/2	3.5	-0.5
Curtis, Edwin R. "Ed"											
1884	Alt-U	25	6	19	.240	6				1.7	4.3
Cushman, Charles H. "Charlie"											
1891	Mil-a	36	21	15	.583	5				24.5	-3.5
Cuthbert, Edgar Edward "Ned"											
1882	StL-a*	80	37	43	.463	5				31.3	5.7
Dahlen, William Frederick "Bill"											
1910	Bro-N*	156	64	90	.416	6				62.9	1.1
1911	Bro-N*	154	64	86	.427	7				62.1	1.9
1912	Bro-N	153	58	95	.379	7				66.3	-8.3
1913	Bro-N	152	65	84	.436	6				72.6	-7.6
	4	615	251	355	.414						-12.9
Dark, Alvin Ralph											
1961	SF-N	155	85	69	.552	3				88.7	-3.7
1962	SF-N	165	103	62	.624	▲1				100.8	2.2
1963	SF-N	162	88	74	.543	3				89.7	-1.7
1964	SF-N	162	90	72	.556	4				88.5	1.5
1966	KC-A	160	74	86	.463	7				70.8	3.2
1967	KC-A	121	52	69	.430	10	10		1/2	50.0	2.0
1968	Cle-A	162	86	75	.534	3				81.9	4.1
1969	Cle-A	161	62	99	.385	6 E				65.2	-3.2
1970	Cle-A	162	76	86	.469	5 E				78.3	-2.3
1971	Cle-A	103	42	61	.408	6 E	6 E		1/2	37.7	4.3
1974	Oak-A	162	90	72	.556	★1 W				96.0	-6.0
1975	Oak-A	162	98	64	.605	1 W				96.7	1.3
1977	SD-N	113	48	65	.425	4 W	5 W		3/3	46.8	1.2
	13	1950	994	954	.510						2.9
Davenport, James Houston "Jim"											
1985	SF-N	144	56	88	.389	6 W	6 W		1/2	60.6	-4.6
Davidson, Mordecai H.											
1888	Lou-a	3	1	2	.333	8	8	7	2/4	1.1	-0.1
	Lou-a	90	34	52	.395	8	7		4/4	32.7	1.3
Davis, George Stacey											
1895	NY-N*	33	16	17	.485	8	9		1/3	16.9	-0.9
1900	NY-N*	78	39	37	.513	8	8		2/2	32.5	6.5

YEAR	TM/L	G	W	L	PCT	STANDING			M/Y	W-EXP	A-E
1901	NY-N*	141	52	85	.380	7				47.6	4.4
	3	252	107	139	.435						10.0
Davis, Harry H											
1912	Cle-A*	127	54	71	.432	6	5		1/2	62.2	-8.2
Davis, Virgil Lawrence "Spud"											
1946	Pit-N	3	1	2	.333	7	7		2/2	1.3	-0.3
Day, John B.											
1899	NY-N	66	29	35	.453	9	10		1/2	26.9	2.1
Deane, John Henry "Harry"											
1871	Kek-n*	5	2	3	.400	7	8		2/2	0.6	1.4
Dent, Russell Earl "Bucky"											
1989	NY-A	40	18	22	.450	6 E	5 E		2/2	17.7	0.3
1990	NY-A	49	18	31	.367	7 E	7 E		1/2	19.9	-1.9
	2	89	36	53	.404						-1.6
Dickey, William Malcolm "Bill"											
1946	NY-A*	105	57	48	.543	2	3	3	2/3	62.4	-5.4
Diddlebock, Henry H. "Harry"											
1896	StL-N	17	7	10	.412	10	11		1/5	4.6	2.4
Dierker, Lawrence Edward "Larry"											
1997	Hou-N	162	84	78	.519	○1 C				92.8	-8.8
1998	Hou-N	162	102	60	.630	○1 C				106.1	-4.1
	2	324	186	138	.574						-12.9
Doby, Lawrence Eugene "Larry"											
1978	Chi-A	87	37	50	.425	5 W	5 W		2/2	38.1	-1.1
Donovan, Patrick Joseph "Patsy"											
1897	Pit-N*	135	60	71	.458	8				51.2	8.8
1899	Pit-N*	131	69	58	.543	10	7		2/2	69.0	0.0
1901	StL-N*	142	76	64	.543	4				79.6	-3.6
1902	StL-N*	140	56	78	.418	6				48.8	7.2
1903	StL-N*	139	43	94	.314	8				40.0	3.0
1904	Was-A*	139	37	97	.276	8	8		2/2	37.3	-0.3
1906	Bro-N*	153	66	86	.434	5				61.7	4.3
1907	Bro-N*	153	65	83	.439	5				64.9	0.1
1908	Bro-N	154	53	101	.344	7				59.7	-6.7
1910	Bos-A	158	81	72	.529	4				84.5	-3.5
1911	Bos-A	153	78	75	.510	5				80.3	-2.3
	11	1597	684	879	.438						6.9
Donovan, William Edward "Bill"											
1915	NY-A*	154	69	83	.454	5				75.6	-6.6
1916	NY-A*	156	80	74	.519	4				78.8	1.2
1917	NY-A	155	71	82	.464	6				72.6	-1.6
1921	Phi-N	87	25	62	.287	8	8		1/2	27.3	-2.3
	4	552	245	301	.449						-9.3
Dooin, Charles Sebastian "Red"											
1910	Phi-N*	157	78	75	.510	4				80.1	-2.1
1911	Phi-N*	153	79	73	.520	4				74.9	4.1
1912	Phi-N*	152	73	79	.480	5				74.2	-1.2
1913	Phi-N*	159	88	63	.583	2				81.4	6.6
1914	Phi-N*	154	74	80	.481	6				73.3	0.7
	5	775	392	370	.514						8.0
Dorgan, Michael Cornelius "Mike"											
1879	Syr-N*	43	17	26	.395	6	7		1/3	10.9	6.1
1880	Pro-N*	39	26	12	.684	3	2		3/3	24.7	1.3
1881	Wor-N*	56	24	32	.429	7	8		1/2	22.9	1.1
	3	138	67	70	.489						8.6
Dowd, Thomas Jefferson "Tom"											
1896	StL-N*	63	25	38	.397	11	11		5/5	17.2	7.8
1897	StL-N*	29	6	22	.214	12	12		1/4	5.1	0.9
	2	92	31	60	.341						8.8
Doyle, John Joseph "Jack"											
1895	NY-N*	64	32	31	.508	8	9	9	2/3	32.2	-0.2
1898	Was-N*	17	8	9	.471	11	10	11	2/4	6.1	1.9
	2	81	40	40	.500						1.7
Dressen, Charles Walter "Chuck"											
1934	Cin-N	60	21	39	.350	8	8		3/3	21.7	-0.7
1935	Cin-N	154	68	85	.444	6				64.0	4.0
1936	Cin-N	154	74	80	.481	5				73.3	0.7
1937	Cin-N	130	51	78	.395	8	8		1/2	56.3	-5.3
1951	Bro-N	158	97	60	.618	▲2				96.2	0.8
1952	Bro-N	155	96	57	.627	1				93.8	2.2
1953	Bro-N	155	105	49	.682	1				101.5	3.5
1955	Was-A	154	53	101	.344	8				57.9	-4.9
1956	Was-A	155	59	95	.383	7				51.4	7.6
1957	Was-A	20	4	16	.200	8	8		1/2	7.4	-3.4
1960	Mil-N	154	88	66	.571	2				83.6	4.4
1961	Mil-N	130	71	58	.550	3	4		1/2	69.2	1.8
1963	Det-A	102	55	47	.539	9	●5		2/2	50.8	4.2
1964	Det-A	163	85	77	.525	4				83.2	1.8
1965	Det-A	120	65	55	.542	3	4		2/2	66.2	-1.2
1966	Det-A	26	16	10	.615	3	3		1/3	13.3	2.7
	16	1990	1008	973	.509						18.2
Duffy, Hugh											
1901	Mil-A*	139	48	89	.350	8				51.2	-3.2

YEAR	TM/L	G	W	L	PCT	STANDING			M/Y	W-EXP	A-E
1904	Phi-N*	155	52	100	.342	8				54.4	-2.4
1905	Phi-N*	155	83	69	.546	4				86.9	-3.9
1906	Phi-N*	154	71	82	.464	4				72.4	-1.4
1910	Chi-A	156	68	85	.444	6				73.8	-5.8
1911	Chi-A	154	77	74	.510	4				85.2	-8.2
1921	Bos-A	154	75	79	.487	5				74.2	0.8
1922	Bos-A	154	61	93	.396	8				59.8	1.2
	8	1221	535	671	.444						-22.9
Dunlap, Frederick C. “Fred”											
1882	Cle-N*	80	42	36	.538	8	5		2/2	38.2	3.8
1884	StL-U*	83	66	16	.805	1	1		2/2	70.3	-4.3
1885	StL-N*	50	21	29	.420	5	8		1/3	15.5	5.5
	StL-N*	22	9	11	.450	8	8		3/3	6.2	2.8
1889	Pit-N*	17	7	10	.412	6	7	5	2/3	7.6	-0.6
	4	252	145	102	.587						7.1
Durocher, Leo Ernest											
1939	Bro-N*	157	84	69	.549	3				82.9	1.1
1940	Bro-N*	156	88	65	.575	2				84.3	3.7
1941	Bro-N*	157	100	54	.649	1				99.2	0.8
1942	Bro-N	155	104	50	.675	2				101.5	2.5
1943	Bro-N*	153	81	72	.529	3				80.7	0.3
1944	Bro-N	155	63	91	.409	7				63.4	-0.4
1945	Bro-N*	155	87	67	.565	3				83.8	3.2
1946	Bro-N	157	96	60	.615	▲2				91.8	4.2
1948	Bro-N	73	35	37	.486	5	3		1/3	39.6	-4.6
	NY-N	79	41	38	.519	4	5		2/2	43.3	-2.3
1949	NY-N	156	73	81	.474	5				81.3	-8.3
1950	NY-N	154	86	68	.558	3				86.2	-0.2
1951	NY-N	157	98	59	.624	▲1				92.5	5.5
1952	NY-N	154	92	62	.597	2				85.4	6.6
1953	NY-N	155	70	84	.455	5				79.0	-9.0
1954	NY-N	154	97	57	.630	★1				95.9	1.1
1955	NY-N	154	80	74	.519	3				79.9	0.1
1966	Chi-N	162	59	103	.364	10				64.5	-5.5
1967	Chi-N	162	87	74	.540	3				88.7	-1.7
1968	Chi-N	163	84	78	.519	3				81.1	2.9
1969	Chi-N	163	92	70	.568	2 E				92.4	-0.4
1970	Chi-N	162	84	78	.519	2 E				93.6	-9.6
1971	Chi-N	162	83	79	.512	●3 E				79.8	3.2
1972	Chi-N	91	46	44	.511	4 E	2 E		1/2	52.3	-6.3
	Hou-N	31	16	15	.516	2 W	2 W		3/3	17.0	-1.0
1973	Hou-N	162	82	80	.506	4 W				81.9	0.1
	24	3739	2008	1709	.540						-14.0
Dwyer, John Francis “Frank”											
1902	Det-A	137	52	83	.385	7				58.4	-6.4
Dyer, Edwin Hawley “Eddie”											
1946	StL-N	156	98	58	.628	▲★1				95.7	2.3
1947	StL-N	156	89	65	.578	2				91.5	-2.5
1948	StL-N	155	85	69	.552	2				86.6	-1.6
1949	StL-N	157	96	58	.623	2				92.2	3.8
1950	StL-N	153	78	75	.510	5				78.8	-0.8
	5	777	446	325	.578						1.2
Dykes, James Joseph “Jimmy”											
1934	Chi-A*	138	49	88	.358	8	8		2/2	48.6	0.4
1935	Chi-A*	153	74	78	.487	5				74.8	-0.8
1936	Chi-A*	153	81	70	.536	3				79.6	1.4
1937	Chi-A*	154	86	68	.558	3				81.8	4.2
1938	Chi-A*	149	65	83	.439	6				69.9	-4.9
1939	Chi-A*	155	85	69	.552	4				78.7	6.3
1940	Chi-A	155	82	72	.532	●4				83.3	-1.3
1941	Chi-A	156	77	77	.500	3				75.9	1.1
1942	Chi-A	148	66	82	.446	6				66.3	-0.3
1943	Chi-A	155	82	72	.532	4				74.7	7.3
1944	Chi-A	154	71	83	.461	7				64.2	6.8
1945	Chi-A	150	71	78	.477	6				70.6	0.4
1946	Chi-A	30	10	20	.333	7	5		1/2	14.3	-4.3
1951	Phi-A	154	70	84	.455	6				76.1	-6.1
1952	Phi-A	155	79	75	.513	4				71.1	7.9
1953	Phi-A	157	59	95	.383	7				60.4	-1.4
1954	Bal-A	154	54	100	.351	7				56.7	-2.7
1958	Cin-N	41	24	17	.585	8	4		2/2	22.5	1.5
1959	Det-A	137	74	63	.540	8	4		2/2	66.8	7.2
1960	Det-A	96	44	52	.458	6	6		1/3	47.3	-3.3
	Cle-A	58	26	32	.448	4	4		3/3	28.0	-2.0
1961	Cle-A	160	77	83	.481	5	5		1/2	78.5	-1.5
	21	2962	1406	1541	.477						15.7
Ebbets, Charles Hercules “Charlie”											
1898	Bro-N	110	38	68	.358	9	10		3/3	40.8	-2.8
Edwards, Howard Rodney “Doc”											
1987	Cle-A	75	30	45	.400	7 E	7 E		2/2	28.3	1.7
1988	Cle-A	162	78	84	.481	6 E				74.4	3.6
1989	Cle-A	143	65	78	.455	6 E	6 E		1/2	66.7	-1.7
	3	380	173	207	.455						3.6
Elberfeld, Norman Arthur “Kid”											
1908	NY-A*	98	27	71	.276	6	8		2/2	31.4	-4.4

YEAR	TM/L	G	W	L	PCT	STANDING			M/Y	W-EXP	A-E
Elia, Lee Constantine											
1982	Chi-N	162	73	89	.451	5 E				77.6	-4.6
1983	Chi-N	123	54	69	.439	5 E	5 E		1/2	60.1	-6.1
1987	Phi-N	101	51	50	.505	5 E	●4 E		2/2	47.6	3.4
1988	Phi-N	153	60	92	.395	6 E	6 E		1/2	62.5	-2.5
	4	539	238	300	.442						-9.8
Ellick, Joseph J. “Joe”											
1884	Pit-U*	13	6	6	.500	5	5		2/2	5.4	0.6
Elliott, Robert Irving “Bob”											
1960	KC-A	155	58	96	.377	8				62.8	-4.8
Ens, Jewel Winklemeyer											
1929	Pit-N	35	21	14	.600	2	2		2/2	20.1	0.9
1930	Pit-N	154	80	74	.519	5				73.8	6.2
1931	Pit-N	155	75	79	.487	5				71.4	3.6
	3	344	176	167	.513						10.8
Ermer, Calvin Coolidge “Cal”											
1967	Min-A	114	66	46	.589	6	●2		2/2	62.1	3.9
1968	Min-A	162	79	83	.488	7				82.8	-3.8
	2	276	145	129	.529						0.1
Essian, James Sarkis “Jim”											
1991	Chi-N	122	59	63	.484	5 E	4 E		3/3	58.0	1.0
Esterbrook, Thomas Jefferson “Dude”											
1889	Lou-a*	10	2	8	.200	7	8		1/4	2.2	-0.2
Evers, John Joseph “Johnny”											
1913	Chi-N*	155	88	65	.575	3				85.6	2.4
1921	Chi-N	96	41	55	.427	6	7		1/2	41.6	-0.6
1924	Chi-A	21	10	11	.476	6			1/4	9.7	0.3
	Chi-A	103	41	61	.402	8			4/4	47.0	-6.0
	3	375	180	192	.484						-3.9
Ewing, William “Buck”											
1890	NY-P*	132	74	57	.565	3				76.8	-2.8
1895	Cin-N*	132	66	64	.508	8				69.0	-3.0
1896	Cin-N*	128	77	50	.606	3				78.3	-1.3
1897	Cin-N*	134	76	56	.576	4				71.3	4.7
1898	Cin-N	157	92	60	.605	3				84.6	7.4
1899	Cin-N	157	83	67	.553	6				83.0	0.0
1900	NY-N	63	21	41	.339	8	8		1/2	26.5	-5.5
	7	903	489	395	.553						-0.5
Faatz, Jayson S. “Jay”											
1890	Buf-P*	34	9	24	.273	8	8	8	2/3	8.6	0.4
Falk, Bibb August											
1933	Cle-A	1	1	0	1.000	5	5	4	2/3	0.5	0.5
Fanning, William James “Jim”											
1981(2)	Mon-N	27	16	11	.593	2 E	○1 E		2/2	14.8	1.2
1982	Mon-N	162	86	76	.531	3 E				89.5	-3.5
1984	Mon-N	30	14	16	.467	5 E	5 E		2/2	15.2	-1.2
	3	219	116	103	.530						-3.5
Farrell, John A. “Jack”											
1881	Pro-N*	51	24	27	.471	4	2		1/2	26.7	-2.7
Farrell, Major Kerby “Kerby”											
1957	Cle-A	153	76	77	.497	6				72.5	3.5
Felske, John Frederick											
1985	Phi-N	162	75	87	.463	5 E				80.4	-5.4
1986	Phi-N	161	86	75	.534	2 E				83.1	2.9
1987	Phi-N	61	29	32	.475	5 E	●4 E		1/2	28.7	0.3
	3	384	190	194	.495						-2.2
Ferguson, Robert V. “Bob”											
1871	Mut-n*	33	16	17	.485	4				15.7	0.3
1872	Atl-n*	37	9	28	.243	6				2.3	6.7
1873	Atl-n*	55	17	37	.315	6				13.5	3.5
1874	Atl-n*	56	22	33	.400	6				15.3	6.7
1875	Har-n*	86	54	28	.659	3				60.8	-6.8
1876	Har-N*	69	47	21	.691	3				49.9	-2.9
1877	Har-N*	60	31	27	.534	3				31.7	-0.7
1878	Chi-N*	61	30	30	.500	4				33.5	-3.5
1879	Tro-N*	30	7	22	.241	8	8		2/2	6.8	0.2
1880	Tro-N*	83	41	42	.494	4				37.1	3.9
1881	Tro-N*	85	39	45	.464	5				39.1	-0.1
1882	Tro-N*	85	35	48	.422	7				33.3	1.7
1883	Phi-N*	17	4	13	.235	8	8		1/2	2.1	1.9
1884	Pit-a*	42	11	31	.262	9	11	10	2/5	9.4	1.6
1886	NY-a	120	48	70	.407	8	7		2/2	47.7	0.3
1887	NY-a	30	6	24	.200	8	7		1/3	8.7	-2.7
	16	949	417	516	.447						9.9
Ferraro, Michael Dennis “Mike”											
1983	Cle-A	100	40	60	.400	7 E	7 E		1/2	45.1	-5.1
1986	KC-A	74	36	38	.486	4 W	●3 W		2/2	36.1	-0.1
	2	174	76	98	.437						-5.1
Fessenden, Wallace Clifton											
1890	Syr-a	11	4	7	.364	7	7	6	2/3	4.5	-0.5
Fitzsimmons, Frederick Landis “Freddie”											
1943	Phi-N	65	26	38	.406	7	7		2/2	27.4	-1.4
1944	Phi-N	154	61	92	.399	8				63.7	-2.7

YEAR	TM/L	G	W	L	PCT	STANDING		M/YW-EXP		A-E
1945	Phi-N	69	18	51	.261	8	8	1/2	20.4	-2.4
	3	288	105	181	.367					-6.5
Fletcher, Arthur “Art”										
1923	Phi-N	155	50	104	.325	8			53.8	-3.8
1924	Phi-N	152	55	96	.364	7			59.1	-4.1
1925	Phi-N	153	68	85	.444	●6			66.0	2.0
1926	Phi-N	152	58	93	.384	8			55.7	2.3
1929	NY-A	11	6	5	.545	2	2	2/2	6.3	-0.3
	5	623	237	383	.382					-4.0
Flint, Frank Sylvester “Silver”										
1879	Chi-N*	19	5	12	.294	2	4	2/2	9.0	-4.0
Fogarty, James G. “Jim”										
1890	Phi-P*	16	7	9	.438	5	5	1/2	8.9	-1.9
Fogel, Horace S.										
1887	Ind-N	70	20	49	.290	8	8	3/3	18.9	1.1
1902	NY-N	44	18	23	.439	4	8	1/3	14.1	3.9
	2	114	38	72	.345					5.0
Fohl, Leo Alexander “Lee”										
1915	Cle-A	127	45	79	.363	6	7	2/2	50.6	-5.6
1916	Cle-A	157	77	77	.500	6			80.0	-3.0
1917	Cle-A	156	88	66	.571	3			81.6	6.4
1918	Cle-A	129	73	54	.575	2			69.8	3.2
1919	Cle-A	78	44	34	.564	3	2	1/2	44.7	-0.7
1921	StL-A	154	81	73	.526	3			76.1	4.9
1922	StL-A	154	93	61	.604	2			98.5	-5.5
1923	StL-A	103	52	49	.515	3	5	1/2	48.4	3.6
1924	Bos-A	157	67	87	.435	7			70.4	-3.4
1925	Bos-A	152	47	105	.309	8			49.5	-2.5
1926	Bos-A	154	46	107	.301	8			49.3	-3.3
	11	1521	713	792	.474					-5.8
Fonseca, Lewis Albert “Lew”										
1932	Chi-A*	152	49	102	.325	7			54.0	-5.0
1933	Chi-A*	151	67	83	.447	6			62.5	4.5
1934	Chi-A	15	4	11	.267	8	8	1/2	5.3	-1.3
	3	318	120	196	.380					-1.8
Foutz, David Luther “Dave”										
1893	Bro-N*	130	65	63	.508	●6			58.1	6.9
1894	Bro-N*	135	70	61	.534	5			66.6	3.4
1895	Bro-N*	134	71	60	.542	●5			68.3	2.7
1896	Bro-N*	133	58	73	.443	●9			59.0	-1.0
	4	532	264	257	.507					12.1
Fox, Charles Francis “Charlie”										
1970	SF-N	120	67	53	.558	4 W	3 W	2/2	60.3	6.7
1971	SF-N	162	90	72	.556	1 W			87.4	2.6
1972	SF-N	155	69	86	.445	5 W			78.8	-9.8
1973	SF-N	162	88	74	.543	3 W			84.7	3.3
1974	SF-N	76	34	42	.447	5 W	5 W	1/2	33.7	0.3
1976	Mon-N	34	12	22	.353	6 E	6 E	2/2	12.4	-0.4
1983	Chi-N	39	17	22	.436	5 E	5 E	2/2	19.1	-2.1
	7	748	377	371	.504					0.5
Francona, Terry Jon										
1997	Phi-N	162	68	94	.420	5 E			64.1	3.9
1998	Phi-N	162	75	87	.463	3 E			71.7	3.3
	2	324	143	181	.441					7.2
Franks, Herman Louis										
1965	SF-N	163	95	67	.586	2			90.5	4.5
1966	SF-N	161	93	68	.578	2			85.7	7.3
1967	SF-N	162	91	71	.562	2			92.1	-1.1
1968	SF-N	163	88	74	.543	2			89.0	-1.0
1977	Chi-N	162	81	81	.500	4 E			76.3	4.7
1978	Chi-N	162	79	83	.488	3 E			74.8	4.2
1979	Chi-N	155	78	77	.503	5 E	5 E	1/2	77.4	0.6
	7	1128	605	521	.537					19.2
Frazer, George Kasson										
1890	Syr-a	71	31	40	.437	7	6	1/3	29.0	2.0
	Syr-a	46	20	25	.444	7	6	3/3	18.4	1.6
Frazier, Joseph Filmore “Joe”										
1976	NY-N	162	86	76	.531	3 E			89.7	-3.7
1977	NY-N	45	15	30	.333	6 E	6 E	1/2	20.2	-5.2
	2	207	101	106	.488					-8.9
Fregosi, James Louis “Jim”										
1978	Cal-A	117	62	55	.530	3 W	●2 W	2/2	60.4	1.6
1979	Cal-A	162	88	74	.543	1 W			90.3	-2.3
1980	Cal-A	160	65	95	.406	6 W			70.3	-5.3
1981(1)	Cal-A	47	22	25	.468	4 W	4 W	1/2	24.5	-2.5
1986	Chi-A	96	45	51	.469	5 W	5 W	3/3	44.6	0.4
1987	Chi-A	162	77	85	.475	5 W			81.2	-4.2
1988	Chi-A	161	71	90	.441	5 W			67.6	3.4
1991	Phi-N	149	74	75	.497	6 E	3 E	2/2	69.5	4.5
1992	Phi-N	162	70	92	.432	6 E			77.8	-7.8
1993	Phi-N	162	97	65	.599	♦1 E			94.0	3.0
1994	Phi-N	115	54	61	.470	4 E			59.9	-5.9
1995	Phi-N	144	69	75	.479	●2 E			67.7	1.3
1996	Phi-N	162	67	95	.414	5 E			66.9	0.1
	13	1799	861	938	.479					-13.7

YEAR	TM/L	G	W	L	PCT	STANDING		M/YW-EXP		A-E
Frey, James Gottfried “Jim”										
1980	KC-A	162	97	65	.599	♦1 W			92.3	4.7
1981(1)	KC-A	50	20	30	.400	5 W				
(2)	KC-A	20	10	10	.500	●2 W	1 W	1/2	34.4	-4.4
1984	Chi-N	161	96	65	.596	1 E			91.0	5.0
1985	Chi-N	162	77	84	.478	4 E			76.1	0.9
1986	Chi-N	56	23	33	.411	5 E	5 E	1/3	24.5	-1.5
	5	611	323	287	.530					4.6
Frisch, Frank Francis “Frankie”										
1933	StL-N*	63	36	26	.581	5	5	2/2	34.3	1.7
1934	StL-N*	154	95	58	.621	★1			90.5	4.5
1935	StL-N*	154	96	58	.623	2			96.9	-0.9
1936	StL-N*	155	87	67	.565	●2			77.1	9.9
1937	StL-N*	157	81	73	.526	4			82.4	-1.4
1938	StL-N	139	63	72	.467	6	6	1/2	67.9	-4.9
1940	Pit-N	156	78	76	.506	4			79.4	-1.4
1941	Pit-N	156	81	73	.526	4			81.8	-0.8
1942	Pit-N	151	66	81	.449	5			68.6	-2.6
1943	Pit-N	157	80	74	.519	4			83.7	-3.7
1944	Pit-N	158	90	63	.588	2			84.7	5.3
1945	Pit-N	155	82	72	.532	4			83.6	-1.6
1946	Pit-N	152	62	89	.411	7	7	1/2	63.3	-1.3
1949	Chi-N	104	42	62	.404	7	8	2/2	39.8	2.2
1950	Chi-N	154	64	89	.418	7			63.7	0.3
1951	Chi-N	81	35	45	.438	7	8	1/2	32.9	2.1
	16	2246	1138	1078	.514					7.3
Fuchs, Emil Edmund “Judge”										
1929	Bos-N	154	56	98	.364	8			56.2	-0.2
Gaffney, John H.										
1886	Was-N	43	15	25	.375	8		2/2	9.0	6.0
1887	Was-N	126	46	76	.377	7			41.6	4.4
	2	169	61	101	.377					10.4
Galvin, James Francis “Pud”										
1885	Buf-N*	24	7	17	.292	7	7	1/2	6.9	0.1
Ganzel, John Henry										
1908	Cin-N*	155	73	81	.474	5			70.6	2.4
1915	Bro-F	35	17	18	.486	7	7	2/2	16.9	0.1
	2	190	90	99	.476					2.5
Garcia, David “Dave”										
1977	Cal-A	81	35	46	.432	5 W	5 W	2/2	39.5	-4.5
1978	Cal-A	45	25	20	.556	3 W	●2 W	1/2	23.2	1.8
1979	Cle-A	66	38	28	.576	6 E	6 E	2/2	31.2	6.8
1980	Cle-A	160	79	81	.494	6 E			73.3	5.7
1981(1)	Cle-A	50	26	24	.520	6 E				
(2)	Cle-A	53	26	27	.491	5 E			50.4	1.6
1982	Cle-A	162	78	84	.481	●6 E			74.4	3.6
	6	617	307	310	.498					14.9
Gardner, William Frederick “Billy”										
1981(1)	Min-A	20	6	14	.300	6 W	7 W	2/2		
(2)	Min-A	53	24	29	.453	4 W			28.8	1.2
1982	Min-A	162	60	102	.370	7 W			64.9	-4.9
1983	Min-A	162	70	92	.432	5 W			70.0	0.0
1984	Min-A	162	81	81	.500	2 W			80.8	0.2
1985	Min-A	62	27	35	.435	6 W	4 W	1/2	28.1	-1.1
1987	KC-A	126	62	64	.492	4 W	2 W	1/2	64.9	-2.9
	6	747	330	417	.442					-7.4
Garner, Philip Mason “Phil”										
1992	Mil-A	162	92	70	.568	2 E			95.2	-3.2
1993	Mil-A	162	69	93	.426	7 E			75.2	-6.2
1994	Mil-A	115	53	62	.461	5 C			53.8	-0.8
1995	Mil-A	144	65	79	.451	4 C			71.3	-6.3
1996	Mil-A	162	80	82	.494	3 C			80.5	-0.5
1997	Mil-A	161	78	83	.484	3 C			74.3	3.7
1998	Mil-N	162	74	88	.457	5 C			70.7	3.3
	7	1068	511	557	.478					-10.1
Gaston, Clarence Edwin “Cito”										
1989	Tor-A	126	77	49	.611	6 E	1 E	2/2	69.4	7.6
1990	Tor-A	162	86	76	.531	2 E			91.7	-5.7
1991	Tor-A	120	66	54	.550	1 E	1 E	1/3	64.9	1.1
	Tor-A	9	6	3	.667	1 E	1 E	3/3	4.9	1.1
1992	Tor-A	162	96	66	.593	★1 E			90.8	5.2
1993	Tor-A	162	95	67	.586	★1 E			91.1	3.9
1994	Tor-A	115	55	60	.478	3 E			56.3	-1.3
1995	Tor-A	144	56	68	.452	5 E			59.1	-3.1
1996	Tor-A	162	74	88	.457	4 E			76.9	-2.9
1997	Tor-A	157	72	85	.459	5 E	5 E	1/2	74.5	-2.5
	9	1319	683	616	.526					3.6
Gerhardt, John Joseph “Joe”										
1883	Lou-a*	98	52	45	.536	5			48.7	3.3
1890	StL-a*	38	20	16	.556	2	3	6/6	21.1	-1.1
	2	136	72	61	.541					2.2
Gessler, Harry Homer “Doc”										
1914	Pit-F	11	3	8	.273	8	7	1/2	4.8	-1.8
Gibson, George C. “Moon”										
1920	Pit-N	155	79	75	.513	4			74.5	4.5

YEAR	TM/L	G	W	L	PCT	STANDING			M/YW-EXP		A-E
1921	Pit-N	154	90	63	.588	2				86.6	3.4
1922	Pit-N	65	32	33	.492	5	●3		1/2	37.6	-5.6
1925	Chi-N	26	12	14	.462	7	8		3/3	12.2	-0.2
1932	Pit-N	154	86	68	.558	2				76.0	10.0
1933	Pit-N	154	87	67	.565	2				82.0	5.0
1934	Pit-N	51	27	24	.529	4	5		1/2	26.2	0.8
	7	759	413	344	.546						17.9
Gifford, James H. "Jim"											
1884	Ind-a	87	25	60	.294	10	11		1/2	21.5	3.5
1885	NY-a	108	44	64	.407	7				39.5	4.5
1886	NY-a	17	5	12	.294	8	7		1/2	6.9	-1.9
	3	212	74	136	.352						6.1
Glasscock, John Wesley "Jack"											
1889	Ind-N*	67	34	32	.515	7	7		2/2	29.9	4.1
1892(1)	StL-N*	4	1	3	.250	10	9		1/3	1.5	-0.5
	2	71	35	35	.500						3.6
Gleason, William J. "Kid"											
1919	Chi-A	140	88	52	.629	1				83.6	4.4
1920	Chi-A	154	96	58	.623	2				89.6	6.4
1921	Chi-A	154	62	92	.403	7				60.4	1.6
1922	Chi-A	155	77	77	.500	5				77.0	0.0
1923	Chi-A	156	69	85	.448	7				72.1	-3.1
	5	759	392	364	.519						9.3
Gomez, Pedro W. "Preston"											
1969	SD-N	162	52	110	.321	6 W				50.5	1.5
1970	SD-N	162	63	99	.389	6 W				70.3	-7.3
1971	SD-N	161	61	100	.379	6 W				66.2	-5.2
1972	SD-N	11	4	7	.364	4 W	6 W		1/2	4.1	-0.1
1974	Hou-N	162	81	81	.500	4 W				83.2	-2.2
1975	Hou-N	127	47	80	.370	6 W	6 W		1/2	59.7	-12.7
1980	Chi-N	90	38	52	.422	6 E	6 E		1/2	38.4	-0.4
	7	875	346	529	.395						-26.5
Gonzalez, Miguel Angel "Mike"											
1938	StL-N	17	8	8	.500	6	6		2/2	8.0	-0.0
1940	StL-N	6	1	5	.167	6	7	3	2/3	3.2	-2.2
	2	23	9	13	.409						-2.2
Gordon, Joseph Lowell "Joe"											
1958	Cle-A	86	46	40	.535	6	4		2/2	46.4	-0.4
1959	Cle-A	154	89	65	.578	2				86.9	2.1
1960	Cle-A	95	49	46	.516	4	4		1/3	45.9	3.1
	Det-A	57	26	31	.456	6	6		3/3	28.1	-2.1
1961	KC-A	60	26	33	.441	8	●9		1/2	23.1	2.9
1969	KC-A	163	69	93	.426	4 W				70.1	-1.1
	5	615	305	308	.498						4.6
Gore, George F.											
1892(2)	StL-N*	16	6	9	.400	12	12	11	2/3	5.5	0.5
Goryl, John Albert "Johnny"											
1980	Min-A	36	23	13	.639	4 W	3 W		2/2	16.8	6.2
1981(1)	Min-A	37	11	25	.306	6 W	7 W		1/2	14.2	-3.2
	2	73	34	38	.472						3.0
Gould, Charles Harvey "Charlie"											
1875	NH-n*	23	2	21	.087	11	8		1/3	1.9	0.1
1876	Cin-N*	65	9	56	.138	8				3.6	5.4
	2	88	11	77	.125						5.5
Gowdy, Henry Morgan "Hank"											
1946	Cin-N	4	3	1	.750	6	6		2/2	1.9	1.1
Graffen, Samuel Mason "Mase"											
1876	StL-N	56	39	17	.696	2	2		1/2	41.3	-2.3
Grammas, Alexander Peter "Alex"											
1969	Pit-N	5	4	1	.800	3 E	3 E		2/2	2.7	1.3
1976	Mil-A	161	66	95	.410	6 E				71.3	-5.3
1977	Mil-A	162	67	95	.414	6 E				68.2	-1.2
	3	328	137	191	.418						-5.1
Green, George Dallas "Dallas"											
1979	Phi-N	30	19	11	.633	5 E	4 E		2/2	14.3	4.7
1980	Phi-N	162	91	71	.562	★1 E				90.2	0.8
1981(1)	Phi-N	55	34	21	.618	1 E					
(2)	Phi-N	52	25	27	.481	3 E				55.4	3.6
1989	NY-A	121	56	65	.463	6 E	5 E		1/2	53.5	2.5
1993	NY-N	124	46	78	.371	7 E	7 E		2/2	56.4	-10.4
1994	NY-N	113	55	58	.487	3 E				54.5	0.5
1995	NY-N	144	69	75	.479	●2 E				75.9	-6.9
1996	NY-N	131	59	72	.450	4 E	4 E		1/2	62.9	-3.9
	8	932	454	478	.487						-9.2
Griffin, Michael Joseph "Mike"											
1898	Bro-N*	4	1	3	.250	9	9	10	2/3	1.5	-0.5
Griffin, Tobias Charles "Sandy"											
1891	Was-a*	6	2	4	.333	8	8		4/4	1.6	0.4
Griffith, Clark Calvin											
1901	Chi-A*	137	83	53	.610	1				85.3	-2.3
1902	Chi-A*	138	74	60	.552	4				74.2	-0.2
1903	NY-A*	136	72	62	.537	4				67.6	4.4
1904	NY-A*	155	92	59	.609	2				83.5	8.5

YEAR	TM/L	G	W	L	PCT	STANDING			M/YW-EXP		A-E
1905	NY-A*	152	71	78	.477	6				70.7	0.3
1906	NY-A*	155	90	61	.596	2				86.5	3.5
1907	NY-A*	152	70	78	.473	5				67.8	2.2
1908	NY-A	57	24	32	.429	6	8		1/2	17.9	6.1
1909	Cin-N*	157	77	76	.503	4				77.3	-0.3
1910	Cin-N*	156	75	79	.487	5				70.4	4.6
1911	Cin-N	159	70	83	.458	6				74.1	-4.1
1912	Was-A*	154	91	61	.599	2				88.3	2.7
1913	Was-A*	155	90	64	.584	2				80.8	9.2
1914	Was-A*	158	81	73	.526	3				83.1	-2.1
1915	Was-A	155	85	68	.556	4				85.4	-0.4
1916	Was-A	159	76	77	.497	7				75.7	0.3
1917	Was-A	158	74	79	.484	5				73.9	0.1
1918	Was-A	130	72	56	.563	3				69.7	2.3
1919	Was-A	142	56	84	.400	7				66.0	-10.0
1920	Was-A	153	68	84	.447	6				68.5	-0.5
	20	2918	1491	1367	.522						24.4
Grimes, Burleigh Arland											
1937	Bro-N	155	62	91	.405	6				60.9	1.1
1938	Bro-N	151	69	80	.463	7				73.9	-4.9
	2	306	131	171	.434						-3.8
Grimm, Charles John "Charlie"											
1932	Chi-N*	55	37	18	.673	2	1		2/2	30.6	6.4
1933	Chi-N*	154	86	68	.558	3				88.9	-2.9
1934	Chi-N*	152	86	65	.570	3				82.2	3.8
1935	Chi-N*	154	100	54	.649	1				101.5	-1.5
1936	Chi-N*	154	87	67	.565	●2				92.4	-5.4
1937	Chi-N	154	93	61	.604	2				89.4	3.6
1938	Chi-N	81	45	36	.556	3	1		1/2	46.8	-1.8
1944	Chi-N	146	74	69	.517	8	4		3/3	74.6	-0.6
1945	Chi-N	155	98	56	.636	1				98.3	-0.3
1946	Chi-N	155	82	71	.536	3				81.3	0.7
1947	Chi-N	155	69	85	.448	6				60.9	8.1
1948	Chi-N	155	64	90	.416	8				65.7	-1.7
1949	Chi-N	50	19	31	.380	7	8		1/2	19.1	-0.1
1952	Bos-N	120	51	67	.432	7	7		2/2	52.2	-1.2
1953	Mil-N	157	92	62	.597	2				92.4	-0.4
1954	Mil-N	154	89	65	.578	3				89.1	-0.1
1955	Mil-N	154	85	69	.552	2				84.4	0.6
1956	Mil-N	46	24	22	.522	5	2		1/2	27.4	-3.4
1960	Chi-N	17	6	11	.353	7	7		1/2	6.9	-0.9
	19	2368	1287	1067	.547						2.8
Groh, Henry Knight "Heinie"											
1918	Cin-N*	10	7	3	.700	4	3		2/2	5.3	1.7
Gutteridge, Donald Joseph "Don"											
1969	Chi-A	145	60	85	.414	4 W	5 W		2/2	63.4	-3.4
1970	Chi-A	136	49	87	.360	6 W	6 W		1/3	52.1	-3.1
	2	281	109	172	.388						-6.5
Haas, George Edwin "Eddie"											
1985	Atl-N	121	50	71	.413	5 W	5 W		1/2	49.2	0.8
Hack, Stanley Camfield "Stan"											
1954	Chi-N	154	64	90	.416	7				70.6	-6.6
1955	Chi-N	154	72	81	.471	6				67.6	4.4
1956	Chi-N	157	60	94	.390	8				65.4	-5.4
1958	StL-N	10	3	7	.300	5	●5		2/2	4.4	-1.4
	4	475	199	272	.423						-9.1
Hackett, Charles M. "Charlie"											
1884	Cle-N	113	35	77	.313	7				32.0	3.0
1885	Bro-a	37	15	22	.405	7	●5		1/2	17.7	-2.7
	2	150	50	99	.336						0.3
Hallman, William Wilson "Bill"											
1897	StL-N*	50	13	36	.265	12	12	12	3/4	8.9	4.1
Haney, Fred Girard											
1939	StL-A	156	43	111	.279	8				50.1	-7.1
1940	StL-A	156	67	87	.435	6				65.4	1.6
1941	StL-A	44	15	29	.341	7	●6		1/2	20.4	-5.4
1953	Pit-N	154	50	104	.325	8				51.6	-1.6
1954	Pit-N	154	53	101	.344	8				48.4	4.6
1955	Pit-N	154	60	94	.390	8				55.8	4.2
1956	Mil-N	109	68	40	.630	5	2		2/2	64.3	3.7
1957	Mil-N	155	95	59	.617	★1				93.0	2.0
1958	Mil-N	154	92	62	.597	1				91.3	0.7
1959	Mil-N	157	86	70	.551	▲2				88.3	-2.3
	10	1393	629	757	.454						0.4
Hanlon, Edward Hugh "Ned"											
1889	Pit-N*	46	26	18	.591	7	5		3/3	19.8	6.2
1890	Pit-P*	131	60	68	.469	6				59.3	0.7
1891	Pit-N*	78	31	47	.397	8	8		1/2	35.5	-4.5
1892(1)	Bal-N*	56	17	39	.304	12	12		3/3		
(2)	Bal-N*	77	26	46	.361	10				45.7	-2.7
1893	Bal-N	130	60	70	.462	8				59.0	1.0
1894	Bal-N	129	89	39	.695	1				90.9	-1.9
1895	Bal-N	132	87	43	.669	1				95.8	-8.8
1896	Bal-N	132	90	39	.698	1				92.7	-2.7
1897	Bal-N	136	90	40	.692	2				90.1	-0.1
1898	Bal-N	154	96	53	.644	2				103.8	-7.8

YEAR	TM/L	G	W	L	PCT	STANDING			M/YW	EXP	A-E
1899	Bro-N	150	101	47	.682	1				95.8	5.2
1900	Bro-N	142	82	54	.603	1				76.6	5.4
1901	Bro-N	137	79	57	.581	3				81.8	-2.8
1902	Bro-N	141	75	63	.543	2				73.9	1.1
1903	Bro-N	139	70	66	.515	5				66.6	3.4
1904	Bro-N	154	56	97	.366	6				63.4	-7.4
1905	Bro-N	155	48	104	.316	8				45.0	3.0
1906	Cin-N	155	64	87	.424	6				70.0	-6.0
1907	Cin-N	156	66	87	.431	6				77.3	-11.3
19		2530	1313	1164	.530						-29.8
Harder, Melvin Leroy "Mel"											
1961	Cle-A	1	1	0	1.000	5	5		2/2	0.5	0.5
1962	Cle-A	2	2	0	1.000	6	6		2/2	0.9	1.1
2		3	3	0	1.000						1.6
Hargrove, Dudley Michael "Mike"											
1991	Cle-A	85	32	53	.376	7 E	7 E		2/2	32.5	-0.5
1992	Cle-A	162	76	86	.469	●4 E				73.7	2.3
1993	Cle-A	162	76	86	.469	6 E				78.8	-2.8
1994	Cle-A	113	66	47	.584	2 C				67.1	-1.1
1995	Cle-A	144	100	44	.694	♦1 C				94.1	5.9
1996	Cle-A	161	99	62	.615	○1 C				97.3	1.7
1997	Cle-A	161	86	75	.534	♦1 C				85.4	0.6
1998	Cle-A	162	89	73	.549	1 C				87.7	1.3
8		1150	624	526	.543						7.5
Harrah, Colbert Dale "Toby"											
1992	Tex-A	76	32	44	.421	3 W	4 W		2/2	34.6	-2.6
Harrelson, Derrel Mc Kinley "Bud"											
1990	NY-N	120	71	49	.592	4 E	2 E		2/2	72.3	-1.3
1991	NY-N	154	74	80	.481	3 E	5 E		1/2	76.4	-2.4
2		274	145	129	.529						-3.7
Harris, Chalmer Luman "Lum"											
1961	Bal-A	27	17	10	.630	3	3		2/2	15.3	1.7
1964	Hou-N	13	5	8	.385	9	9		2/2	5.3	-0.3
1965	Hou-N	162	65	97	.401	9				65.8	-0.8
1968	Atl-N	163	81	81	.500	5				76.9	4.1
1969	Atl-N	162	93	69	.574	1 W				87.3	5.7
1970	Atl-N	162	76	86	.469	5 W				77.5	-1.5
1971	Atl-N	162	82	80	.506	3 W				75.2	6.8
1972	Atl-N	105	47	57	.452	4 W	4 W		1/2	45.0	2.0
8		956	466	488	.488						17.7
Harris, Stanley Raymond "Bucky"											
1924	Was-A*	156	92	62	.597	★1				91.4	0.6
1925	Was-A*	152	96	55	.636	1				90.7	5.3
1926	Was-A*	152	81	69	.540	4				78.8	2.2
1927	Was-A*	157	85	69	.552	3				82.0	3.0
1928	Was-A*	155	75	79	.487	4				78.3	-3.3
1929	Det-A*	155	70	84	.455	6				76.8	-6.8
1930	Det-A	154	75	79	.487	5				72.4	2.6
1931	Det-A*	154	61	93	.396	7				59.1	1.9
1932	Det-A	153	76	75	.503	5				76.6	-0.6
1933	Det-A	153	73	79	.480	5	5		1/2	74.9	-1.9
1934	Bos-A	153	76	76	.500	4				80.2	-4.2
1935	Was-A	154	67	86	.438	6				69.3	-2.3
1936	Was-A	153	82	71	.536	4				84.6	-2.6
1937	Was-A	158	73	80	.477	6				68.6	4.4
1938	Was-A	152	75	76	.497	5				70.2	4.8
1939	Was-A	153	65	87	.428	6				66.9	-1.9
1940	Was-A	154	64	90	.416	7				62.9	1.1
1941	Was-A	156	70	84	.455	●6				70.3	-0.3
1942	Was-A	151	62	89	.411	7				59.7	2.3
1943	Phi-N	92	38	52	.422	7	7		1/2	38.5	-0.5
1947	NY-A	155	97	57	.630	★1				99.9	-2.9
1948	NY-A	154	94	60	.610	3				98.6	-4.6
1950	Was-A	155	67	87	.435	5				65.1	1.9
1951	Was-A	154	62	92	.403	7				68.0	-6.0
1952	Was-A	157	78	76	.506	5				75.9	2.1
1953	Was-A	152	76	76	.500	5				83.5	-7.5
1954	Was-A	155	66	88	.429	6				72.1	-6.1
1955	Det-A	154	79	75	.513	5				88.5	-9.5
1956	Det-A	155	82	72	.532	5				85.7	-3.7
29		4408	2157	2218	.493						-32.5
Hart, James Aristotle "Jim"											
1885	Lou-a	112	53	59	.473	●5				52.8	0.2
1886	Lou-a	138	66	70	.485	4				70.4	-4.4
1889	Bos-N	133	83	45	.648	2				82.2	0.8
3		383	202	174	.537						-3.4
Hart, John Henry											
1989	Cle-A	19	8	11	.421	6 E	6 E		2/2	8.9	-0.9
Hartnett, Charles Leo "Gabby"											
1938	Chi-N*	73	44	27	.620	3	1		2/2	41.0	3.0
1939	Chi-N*	156	84	70	.545	4				81.6	2.4
1940	Chi-N*	154	75	79	.487	5				81.6	-6.6
3		383	203	176	.536						-1.2
Hartsfield, Roy Thomas											
1977	Tor-A	161	54	107	.335	7 E				58.6	-4.6
1978	Tor-A	161	59	102	.366	7 E				61.4	-2.4
1979	Tor-A	162	53	109	.327	7 E				56.2	-3.2
3		484	166	318	.343						-10.3
Hastings, Winfield Scott "Scott"											
1871	Rok-n*	25	4	21	.160	9				8.8	-4.8
1872	Cle-n*	20	6	14	.300	6	7		1/2	5.1	0.9
2		45	10	35	.222						-3.9
Hatfield, John Van Buren											
1872	Mut-n*	40	24	14	.632	4	3		2/2	27.6	-3.6
1873	Mut-n*	28	11	17	.393	5	4		1/2	15.6	-4.6
2		68	35	31	.530						-8.1
Hatton, Grady Edgebert											
1966	Hou-N	163	72	90	.444	8				72.2	-0.2
1967	Hou-N	162	69	93	.426	9				69.0	-0.0
1968	Hou-N	61	23	38	.377	10	10		1/2	27.1	-4.1
3		386	164	221	.426						-4.3
Hecker, Guy Jackson											
1890	Pit-N*	138	23	113	.169	8				15.5	7.5
Heffner, Donald Henry "Don"											
1966	Cin-N	83	37	46	.446	8	7		1/2	41.0	-4.0
Heilbroner, Louis Wilbur "Louie"											
1900	StL-N	50	23	25	.479	7	●5		2/2	23.9	-0.9
Helms, Tommy Vann											
1988	Cin-N	27	12	15	.444	4 W	4 W	2 W	2/3	14.3	-2.3
1989	Cin-N	37	16	21	.432	●4 W	5 W		2/2	17.1	-1.1
2		64	28	36	.438						-3.4
Hemus, Solomon Joseph "Solly"											
1959	StL-N*	154	71	83	.461	7				68.5	2.5
1960	StL-N	155	86	68	.558	3				79.4	6.6
1961	StL-N	75	33	41	.446	6	5		1/2	38.7	-5.7
3		384	190	192	.497						3.3
Henderson, William C. "Bill"											
1884	Bal-U	106	58	47	.552	4				55.5	2.5
Hendricks, John Charles "Jack"											
1918	StL-N	133	51	78	.395	8				56.5	-5.5
1924	Cin-N	153	83	70	.542	4				83.9	-0.9
1925	Cin-N	153	80	73	.523	3				81.3	-1.3
1926	Cin-N	157	87	67	.565	2				86.7	0.3
1927	Cin-N	153	75	78	.490	5				75.5	-0.5
1928	Cin-N	153	78	74	.513	5				72.1	5.9
1929	Cin-N	155	66	88	.429	7				69.7	-3.7
7		1057	520	528	.496						-5.7
Hengle, Edward S. "Ed"											
1884	Chi-U	74	34	39	.466	5				41.3	-0.3
Herman, William Jennings Bryan "Billy"											
1947	Pit-N*	155	61	92	.399	8	●7		1/2	69.6	-8.6
1964	Bos-A	2	2	0	1.000	8	8		2/2	0.9	1.1
1965	Bos-A	162	62	100	.383	9				68.8	-6.8
1966	Bos-A	146	64	82	.438	9	9		1/2	66.0	-2.0
4		465	189	274	.408						-16.3
Herzog, Charles Lincoln "Buck"											
1914	Cin-N*	157	60	94	.390	8				63.8	-3.8
1915	Cin-N*	160	71	83	.461	7				69.1	1.9
1916	Cin-N*	84	34	49	.410	8	●7		1/3	34.7	-0.7
3		401	165	226	.422						-2.6
Herzog, Dorrel Norman Elvert "Whitey"											
1973	Tex-A	138	47	91	.341	6 W	6 W		1/3	49.9	-2.9
1974	Cal-A	4	2	2	.500	6 W	6 W	6 W	2/3	1.9	0.1
1975	KC-A	66	41	25	.621	2 W	2 W		2/2	35.6	5.4
1976	KC-A	162	90	72	.556	1 W				91.7	-1.7
1977	KC-A	162	102	60	.630	1 W				98.0	4.0
1978	KC-A	162	92	70	.568	1 W				92.2	-0.2
1979	KC-A	162	85	77	.525	2 W				84.3	0.7
1980	StL-N	73	38	35	.521	6 E	5 E	4 E	3/4	37.8	0.2
1981(1)	StL-N	51	30	20	.600	2 E					
(2)	StL-N	52	29	23	.558	2 E				55.8	3.2
1982	StL-N	162	92	70	.568	★1 E				89.1	2.9
1983	StL-N	162	79	83	.488	4 E				77.8	1.2
1984	StL-N	162	84	78	.519	3 E				81.7	2.3
1985	StL-N	162	101	61	.623	♦1 E				99.4	1.6
1986	StL-N	161	79	82	.491	3 E				79.4	-0.4
1987	StL-N	162	95	67	.586	♦1 E				91.4	3.6
1988	StL-N	162	76	86	.469	5 E				75.0	1.0
1989	StL-N	164	86	76	.531	3 E				83.6	2.4
1990	StL-N	80	33	47	.412	6 E	6 E		1/3	34.8	-1.8
18		2409	1281	1125	.532						21.6
Hewett, Walter F.											
1888	Was-N	40	10	29	.256	8	8		1/2	12.2	-2.2
Hicks, Nathaniel Woodhull "Nat"											
1874	Phi-n*	58	29	29	.500	4				32.6	-3.6
1875	Mut-n*	71	30	38	.441	7				25.1	4.9
2		129	59	67	.468						1.3
Higgins, Michael Franklin "Pinky"											
1955	Bos-A	154	84	70	.545	4				87.2	-3.2

YEAR	TM/L	G	W	L	PCT	STANDING				M/YW-EXP	A-E
1956	Bos-A	155	84	70	.545	4				79.8	4.2
1957	Bos-A	154	82	72	.532	3				82.3	-0.3
1958	Bos-A	155	79	75	.513	3				77.6	1.4
1959	Bos-A	73	31	42	.425	8	8		1/3	37.9	-6.9
1960	Bos-A	105	48	57	.457	8	7		3/3	44.7	3.3
1961	Bos-A	163	76	86	.469	6				74.8	1.2
1962	Bos-A	160	76	84	.475	8				75.1	0.9
8		1119	560	556	.502						0.6

Higham, Richard "Dick"

| 1874 | Mut-n* | 40 | 29 | 11 | .725 | 3 | 2 | | 2/2 | 26.2 | 2.8 |

Himsl, Avitus Bernard "Vedie"

1961	Chi-N	11	5	6	.455	6	●6		1/9	4.7	0.3
	Chi-N	17	5	12	.294	7	7	7	3/9	7.3	-2.3
	Chi-N	4	0	3	.000	7	7	7	6/9	1.3	-1.3

Hitchcock, William Clyde "Billy"

1960	Det-A	1	1	0	1.000	6	6	6	2/3	0.5	0.5
1962	Bal-A	162	77	85	.475	7				78.1	-1.1
1963	Bal-A	162	86	76	.531	4				83.5	2.5
1966	Atl-N	51	33	18	.647	7	5		2/2	28.6	4.4
1967	Atl-N	159	77	82	.484	7	7		1/2	78.6	-1.6
5		535	274	261	.512						4.8

Hobson, Clell Lavern "Butch"

1992	Bos-A	162	73	89	.451	7 E				73.5	-0.5
1993	Bos-A	162	80	82	.494	5 E				79.8	0.2
1994	Bos-A	115	54	61	.470	4 E				51.0	3.0
3		439	207	232	.472						2.7

Hodges, Gilbert Raymond "Gil"

1963	Was-A	121	42	79	.347	10	10		3/3	42.6	-0.6
1964	Was-A	162	62	100	.383	9				64.7	-2.7
1965	Was-A	162	70	92	.432	8				67.3	2.7
1966	Was-A	159	71	88	.447	8				68.4	2.6
1967	Was-A	161	76	85	.472	●6				70.9	5.1
1968	NY-N	163	73	89	.451	9				77.8	-4.8
1969	NY-N	162	100	62	.617	★1 E				91.1	8.9
1970	NY-N	162	83	79	.512	3 E				87.8	-4.8
1971	NY-N	162	83	79	.512	●3 E				85.3	-2.3
9		1414	660	753	.467						4.1

Hoey, Frederick C. "Fred"

| 1899 | NY-N | 87 | 31 | 55 | .360 | 9 | 10 | | 2/2 | 36.2 | -5.2 |

Hoffman, Glenn Edward

| 1998 | LA-N | 88 | 47 | 41 | .534 | 3 W | 3 W | | 2/2 | 43.5 | 3.5 |

Holbert, William H. "Bill"

| 1879 | Syr-N* | 1 | 0 | 1 | .000 | 6 | 6 | 7 | 2/3 | 0.3 | -0.3 |

Hollingshead, John Samuel "Holly"

1875	Was-n*	20	4	16	.200	8	10		1/2	-2.4	6.4
1884	Was-a	62	12	50	.194	12	12		1/2	10.8	1.2
2		82	16	66	.195						7.6

Holmes, Thomas Francis "Tommy"

1951	Bos-N*	95	48	47	.505	5	4		2/2	51.3	-3.3
1952	Bos-N	35	13	22	.371	7	7		1/2	15.5	-2.5
2		130	61	69	.469						-5.8

Hornsby, Rogers

1925	StL-N*	115	64	51	.557	8	4		2/2	62.0	2.0
1926	StL-N*	156	89	65	.578	★1				90.5	-1.5
1927	NY-N*	33	22	10	.688	4	3		2/2	17.9	4.1
1928	Bos-N*	122	39	83	.320	7	7		2/2	42.2	-3.2
1930	Chi-N*	4	4	0	1.000	2	2		2/2	2.3	1.7
1931	Chi-N*	156	84	70	.545	3				88.3	-4.3
1932	Chi-N*	99	53	46	.535	2	1		1/2	55.2	-2.2
1933	StL-A*	54	19	33	.365	8	8		3/3	21.0	-2.0
1934	StL-A*	154	67	85	.441	6				63.8	3.2
1935	StL-A*	155	65	87	.428	7				56.5	8.5
1936	StL-A*	155	57	95	.375	7				53.5	3.5
1937	StL-A*	78	25	52	.325	7	8		1/2	24.7	0.3
1952	StL-A	51	22	29	.431	8	7		1/2	21.1	0.9
	Cin-N	51	27	24	.529	7	6		3/3	24.0	3.0
1953	Cin-N	147	64	82	.438	6	6		1/2	66.2	-2.2
14		1530	701	812	.463						11.9

Houk, Ralph George "Ralph"

1961	NY-A	163	109	53	.673	★1				102.7	6.3
1962	NY-A	162	96	66	.593	★1				94.5	1.5
1963	NY-A	161	104	57	.646	1				98.4	5.6
1966	NY-A	140	66	73	.475	10	10		2/2	69.4	-3.4
1967	NY-A	163	72	90	.444	9				69.8	2.2
1968	NY-A	164	83	79	.512	5				81.6	1.4
1969	NY-A	162	80	81	.497	5 E				77.7	2.3
1970	NY-A	163	93	69	.574	2 E				88.2	4.8
1971	NY-A	162	82	80	.506	4 E				81.7	0.3
1972	NY-A	155	79	76	.510	4 E				80.9	-1.9
1973	NY-A	162	80	82	.494	4 E				84.3	-4.3
1974	Det-A	162	72	90	.444	6 E				65.8	6.2
1975	Det-A	159	57	102	.358	6 E				57.3	-0.3
1976	Det-A	161	74	87	.460	5 E				70.0	4.0
1977	Det-A	162	74	88	.457	4 E				77.3	-3.3
1978	Det-A	162	86	76	.531	5 E				87.3	-1.3

YEAR	TM/L	G	W	L	PCT	STANDING				M/YW-EXP	A-E
1981(1)	Bos-A	56	30	26	.536	5 E				57.7	1.3
(2)	Bos-A	52	29	23	.558	●2 E					
1982	Bos-A	162	89	73	.549	3 E				85.0	4.0
1983	Bos-A	162	78	84	.481	6 E				76.0	2.0
1984	Bos-A	162	86	76	.531	4 E				85.4	0.6
20		3157	1619	1531	.514						27.8

Howard, Frank Oliver

1981(1)	SD-N	56	23	33	.411	6 W				47.1	-6.1
(2)	SD-N	54	18	36	.333	6 W					
1983	NY-N	116	52	64	.448	6 E	6 E		2/2	49.9	2.1
2		226	93	133	.412						-4.0

Howe, Arthur Henry "Art"

1989	Hou-N	162	86	76	.531	3 W				78.7	7.3
1990	Hou-N	162	75	87	.463	●4 W				72.0	3.0
1991	Hou-N	162	65	97	.401	6 W				69.2	-4.2
1992	Hou-N	162	81	81	.500	4 W				74.6	6.4
1993	Hou-N	162	85	77	.525	3 W				90.0	-5.0
1996	Oak-A	162	78	84	.481	3 W				77.5	0.5
1997	Oak-A	162	65	97	.401	4 W				64.2	0.8
1998	Oak-A	162	74	88	.457	4 W				75.2	-1.2
8		1296	609	687	.470						7.7

Howley, Daniel Philip "Dan"

1927	StL-A	155	59	94	.386	7				59.8	-0.8
1928	StL-A	154	82	72	.532	3				79.9	2.1
1929	StL-A	154	79	73	.520	4				78.0	1.0
1930	Cin-N	154	59	95	.383	7				58.7	0.3
1931	Cin-N	154	58	96	.377	8				61.7	-3.7
1932	Cin-N	155	60	94	.390	8				62.4	-2.4
6		926	397	524	.431						-3.5

Howser, Richard Dalton "Dick"

1978	NY-A	1	0	1	.000	3 E	4 E▲	★1 E	2/3	0.6	-0.6
1980	NY-A	162	103	59	.636	1 E				96.7	6.3
1981(2)	KC-A	33	20	13	.606	●2 W	1 W		2/2	16.2	3.8
1982	KC-A	162	90	72	.556	2 W				87.6	2.4
1983	KC-A	163	79	83	.488	2 W				73.9	5.1
1984	KC-A	162	84	78	.519	1 W				79.7	4.3
1985	KC-A	162	91	71	.562	★1 W				86.0	5.0
1986	KC-A	88	40	48	.455	4 W	●3 W		1/2	42.9	-2.9
8		933	507	425	.544						23.4

Huff, George A.

| 1907 | Bos-A | 8 | 2 | 6 | .250 | ●4 | 6 | 7 | 2/4 | 3.4 | -1.4 |

Huggins, Miller James

1913	StL-N*	153	51	99	.340	8				51.5	-0.5
1914	StL-N*	157	81	72	.529	3				78.5	2.5
1915	StL-N*	157	72	81	.471	6				75.3	-3.3
1916	StL-N*	153	60	93	.392	●7				59.4	0.6
1917	StL-N	154	82	70	.539	3				72.0	10.0
1918	NY-A	126	60	63	.488	4				63.4	-3.4
1919	NY-A	141	80	59	.576	3				77.3	2.7
1920	NY-A	154	95	59	.617	3				97.3	-2.3
1921	NY-A	153	98	55	.641	1				98.4	-0.4
1922	NY-A	154	94	60	.610	1				91.1	2.9
1923	NY-A	152	98	54	.645	★1				95.6	2.4
1924	NY-A	153	89	63	.586	2				88.7	0.3
1925	NY-A	156	69	85	.448	7				70.4	-1.4
1926	NY-A	155	91	63	.591	1				89.7	1.3
1927	NY-A	155	110	44	.714	★1				112.4	-2.4
1928	NY-A	154	101	53	.656	★1				96.6	4.4
1929	NY-A	143	82	61	.573	2	2		1/2	82.0	0.0
17		2570	1413	1134	.555						13.5

Hunter, Gordon William "Billy"

1977	Tex-A	93	60	33	.645	5 W	2 W		4/4	52.9	7.1
1978	Tex-A	161	86	75	.534	●2 W	●2 W		1/2	86.8	-0.8
2		254	146	108	.575						6.4

Hurst, Timothy Carroll "Tim"

| 1898 | StL-N | 154 | 39 | 111 | .260 | 12 | | | | 40.6 | -1.6 |

Hutchinson, Frederick Charles "Fred"

1952	Det-A*	83	27	55	.329	8	8		2/2	31.0	-4.0
1953	Det-A*	158	60	94	.390	6				55.6	4.4
1954	Det-A	155	68	86	.442	5				68.5	-0.5
1956	StL-N	156	76	78	.494	4				75.0	1.0
1957	StL-N	154	87	67	.565	2				84.1	2.9
1958	StL-N	144	69	75	.479	5	●5		1/2	63.9	5.1
1959	Cin-N	74	39	35	.527	7	●5		2/2	38.2	0.8
1960	Cin-N	154	67	87	.435	6				71.7	-4.7
1961	Cin-N	154	93	61	.604	1				82.7	10.3
1962	Cin-N	162	98	64	.605	3				92.6	5.4
1963	Cin-N	162	86	76	.531	5				86.9	-0.9
1964	Cin-N	100	54	45	.545	3	●2		1/4	55.8	-1.8
	Cin-N	10	6	4	.600	4	3	●2	3/4	5.6	0.4
12		1666	830	827	.501						18.5

Irwin, Arthur Albert

1889	Was-N*	76	28	45	.384	8	8		2/2	23.2	4.8
1891	Bos-a*	139	93	42	.689	1				97.8	-4.8
1892(1)	Was-N	74	35	39	.473	●11	7		2/2		
(2)	Was-N	34	11	21	.344	11	12		1/2	44.0	2.0

YEAR	TM/L	G	W	L	PCT	STANDING			M/Y	W-EXP	A-E
1894	Phi-N*	132	71	57	.555	4				77.1	-6.1
1895	Phi-N	133	78	53	.595	3				74.0	4.0
1896	NY-N	90	36	53	.404	10	7		1/2	45.0	-9.0
1898	Was-N	30	10	19	.345	11	11		4/4	10.4	-0.4
1899	Was-N	155	54	98	.355	11				54.4	-0.4
	8	863	416	427	.493						-9.9
Jennings, Hugh Ambrose "Hughie"											
1907	Det-A*	153	92	58	.613	1				92.2	-0.2
1908	Det-A	154	90	63	.588	1				87.3	2.7
1909	Det-A*	158	98	54	.645	1				95.2	2.8
1910	Det-A	155	86	68	.558	3				87.2	-1.2
1911	Det-A	154	89	65	.578	2				82.1	6.9
1912	Det-A*	154	69	84	.451	6				71.0	-2.0
1913	Det-A	153	66	87	.431	6				67.2	-1.2
1914	Det-A	157	80	73	.523	4				76.2	3.8
1915	Det-A	156	100	54	.649	2				95.3	4.7
1916	Det-A	155	87	67	.565	3				84.9	2.1
1917	Det-A	155	78	75	.510	4				83.1	-5.1
1918	Det-A*	128	55	71	.437	7				54.4	0.6
1919	Det-A	140	80	60	.571	4				74.1	5.9
1920	Det-A	155	61	93	.396	7				59.5	1.5
1924	NY-N	44	32	12	.727	3	1	1	2/3	28.0	4.0
1925	NY-N	32	21	11	.656	1	1	2	2/3	16.7	4.3
	16	2203	1184	995	.543						29.7
Johnson, Darrell Dean											
1974	Bos-A	162	84	78	.519	3 E				84.6	-0.6
1975	Bos-A	160	95	65	.594	♦1 E				88.5	6.5
1976	Bos-A	86	41	45	.477	5 E	3 E		1/2	46.1	-5.1
1977	Sea-A	162	64	98	.395	6 W				58.1	5.9
1978	Sea-A	160	56	104	.350	7 W				58.1	-2.1
1979	Sea-A	162	67	95	.414	6 W				70.4	-3.4
1980	Sea-A	105	39	65	.375	6 W	7 W		1/2	40.0	-1.0
1982	Tex-A	66	26	40	.394	6 W	6 W		2/2	26.2	-0.2
	8	1063	472	590	.444						0.1
Johnson, David Allen "Davey"											
1984	NY-N	162	90	72	.556	2 E				78.5	11.5
1985	NY-N	162	98	64	.605	2 E				94.6	3.4
1986	NY-N	162	108	54	.667	★1 E				102.2	5.8
1987	NY-N	162	92	70	.568	2 E				93.2	-1.2
1988	NY-N	160	100	60	.625	1 E				98.5	1.5
1989	NY-N	162	87	75	.537	2 E				90.4	-3.4
1990	NY-N	42	20	22	.476	4 E	2 E		1/2	25.3	-5.3
1993	Cin-N	118	53	65	.449	5 W	5 W		2/2	54.5	-1.5
1994	Cin-N	115	66	48	.579	1 C				68.5	-2.5
1995	Cin-N	144	85	59	.590	○1 C				84.1	0.9
1996	Bal-A	163	88	74	.543	■2 E				85.1	2.9
1997	Bal-A	162	98	64	.605	1 E				93.9	4.1
	12	1714	985	727	.575						16.1
Johnson, Roy J											
1944	Chi-N	1	0	1	.000	8	8	4	2/3	0.5	-0.5
Johnson, Timothy Evald "Tim"											
1998	Tor-A	163	88	74	.543	3 E				85.6	2.4
Johnson, Walter Perry											
1929	Was-A	153	71	81	.467	5				71.6	-0.6
1930	Was-A	154	94	60	.610	2				96.0	-2.0
1931	Was-A	156	92	62	.597	3				91.5	0.5
1932	Was-A	154	93	61	.604	3				88.7	4.3
1933	Cle-A	99	48	51	.485	5	4		3/3	48.5	-0.5
1934	Cle-A	154	85	69	.552	3				81.8	3.2
1935	Cle-A	96	46	48	.489	5	3		1/2	49.2	-3.2
	7	966	529	432	.550						1.7
Jones, Fielder Allison											
1904	Chi-A*	114	66	47	.584	4	3		2/2	66.4	-0.4
1905	Chi-A*	158	92	60	.605	2				94.6	-2.6
1906	Chi-A*	154	93	58	.616	★1				88.3	4.7
1907	Chi-A*	157	87	64	.576	3				88.7	-1.7
1908	Chi-A*	156	88	64	.579	3				83.9	4.1
1914	StL-F*	40	12	26	.316	7	8		2/2	15.5	-3.5
1915	StL-F*	159	87	67	.565	2				88.9	-1.9
1916	StL-A	158	79	75	.513	5				81.8	-2.8
1917	StL-A	155	57	97	.370	7				57.9	-0.9
1918	StL-A	46	22	24	.478	6	5		1/3	22.1	-0.1
	10	1297	683	582	.540						-5.0
Joost, Edwin David "Eddie"											
1954	Phi-A*	156	51	103	.331	8				43.8	7.2
Jorgensen, Michael "Mike"											
1995	StL-N	96	42	54	.438	4 C	4 C		2/2	41.5	0.5
Joyce, William Michael "Bill"											
1896	NY-N*	43	28	14	.667	10	7		2/2	21.2	6.8
1897	NY-N*	138	83	48	.634	3				83.1	-0.1
1898	NY-N*	43	22	21	.512	6	7		1/3	22.5	-0.5
	NY-N*	92	46	39	.541	7	7		3/3	44.4	1.6
	3	316	179	122	.595						7.7
Jurges, William Frederick "Billy"											
1959	Bos-A	80	44	36	.550	8	5		3/3	41.5	2.5

YEAR	TM/L	G	W	L	PCT	STANDING			M/Y	W-EXP	A-E
1960	Bos-A	42	15	27	.357	8	7		1/3	17.9	-2.9
	2	122	59	63	.484						-0.4
Kasko, Edward Michael "Eddie"											
1970	Bos-A	162	87	75	.537	3 E				87.3	-0.3
1971	Bos-A	162	85	77	.525	3 E				83.5	1.5
1972	Bos-A	155	85	70	.548	2 E				79.6	5.4
1973	Bos-A	161	88	73	.547	2 E	2 E		1/2	89.8	-1.8
	4	640	345	295	.539						4.8
Keane, John Joseph "Johnny"											
1961	StL-N	80	47	33	.587	6	5		2/2	41.8	5.2
1962	StL-N	163	84	78	.519	6				92.1	-8.1
1963	StL-N	162	93	69	.574	2				93.3	-0.3
1964	StL-N	162	93	69	.574	★1				87.5	5.5
1965	NY-A	162	77	85	.475	6				81.8	-4.8
1966	NY-A	20	4	16	.200	10	10		1/2	10.0	-6.0
	6	749	398	350	.532						-8.5
Kelley, Joseph James "Joe"											
1902	Cin-N*	60	34	26	.567	6	4		3/3	33.0	1.0
1903	Cin-N*	141	74	65	.532	4				79.8	-5.8
1904	Cin-N*	157	88	65	.575	3				92.3	-4.3
1905	Cin-N*	155	79	74	.516	5				80.2	-1.2
1908	Bos-N*	156	63	91	.409	6				67.6	-4.6
	5	669	338	321	.513						-14.8
Kelly, Jay Thomas "Tom"											
1986	Min-A	23	12	11	.522	7 W	6 W		2/2	10.2	1.8
1987	Min-A	162	85	77	.525	★1 W				79.1	5.9
1988	Min-A	162	91	71	.562	2 W				89.8	1.2
1989	Min-A	162	80	82	.494	5 W				81.2	-1.2
1990	Min-A	162	74	88	.457	7 W				74.6	-0.6
1991	Min-A	162	95	67	.586	★1 W				93.5	1.5
1992	Min-A	162	90	72	.556	2 W				90.6	-0.6
1993	Min-A	162	71	91	.438	●5 W				67.6	3.4
1994	Min-A	113	53	60	.469	4 C				48.1	4.9
1995	Min-A	144	56	88	.389	5 C				55.2	0.8
1996	Min-A	162	78	84	.481	4 C				78.9	-0.9
1997	Min-A	162	68	94	.420	4 C				72.6	-4.6
1998	Min-A	162	70	92	.432	4 C				72.9	-2.9
	13	1900	923	977	.486						8.8
Kelly, John O.											
1887	Lou-a	139	76	60	.559	4				76.5	-0.5
1888	Lou-a	39	10	29	.256	8	7		1/4	14.8	-4.8
	2	178	86	89	.491						-5.3
Kelly, Michael Joseph "King"											
1887	Bos-N*	95	49	43	.533	5	5		1/2	48.5	0.5
1890	Bos-P*	133	81	48	.628	1				82.9	-1.9
1891	Cin-a*	102	43	57	.430	6				41.7	1.3
	3	330	173	148	.539						-0.1
Kennedy, James C. "Jim"											
1890	Bro-a	100	26	73	.263	8				28.8	-2.8
Kennedy, Kevin Curtis											
1993	Tex-A	162	86	76	.531	2 W				89.1	-3.1
1994	Tex-A	114	52	62	.456	1 W				49.6	2.4
1995	Bos-A	144	86	58	.597	1 E				80.7	5.3
1996	Bos-A	162	85	77	.525	3 E				81.6	3.4
	4	582	309	273	.531						8.1
Kennedy, Robert Daniel "Bob"											
1963	Chi-N	162	82	80	.506	7				80.1	1.9
1964	Chi-N	162	76	86	.469	8				73.3	2.7
1965	Chi-N	58	24	32	.429	9	8		1/2	24.8	-0.8
1968	Oak-A	163	82	80	.506	6				83.9	-1.9
	4	545	264	278	.487						1.9
Kerins, John Nelson											
1888	Lou-a*	7	3	4	.429	8	8	7	3/4	2.7	0.3
1890	StL-a*	17	9	8	.529	4	4	3	2/6	10.0	-1.0
	2	24	12	12	.500						-0.6
Kessinger, Donald Eulon "Don"											
1979	Chi-A*	106	46	60	.434	5 W	5 W		1/2	51.8	-5.8
Killefer, William Lavier "Bill"											
1921	Chi-N*	57	23	34	.404	6	7		2/2	24.7	-1.7
1922	Chi-N	156	80	74	.519	5				73.5	6.5
1923	Chi-N	154	83	71	.539	4				82.1	0.9
1924	Chi-N	154	81	72	.529	5				76.4	4.6
1925	Chi-N	75	33	42	.440	7	8		1/3	35.2	-2.2
1930	StL-A	154	64	90	.416	6				64.6	-0.6
1931	StL-A	154	63	91	.409	5				63.2	-0.2
1932	StL-A	154	63	91	.409	6				62.1	0.9
1933	StL-A	91	34	57	.374	8	8		1/3	36.7	-2.7
	9	1149	524	622	.457						5.6
King, Clyde Edward											
1969	SF-N	162	90	72	.556	2 W				89.0	1.0
1970	SF-N	42	19	23	.452	4 W	3 W		1/2	21.1	-2.1
1974	Atl-N	64	38	25	.603	4 W	3 W		2/2	35.7	2.3
1975	Atl-N	134	58	76	.433	5 W	5 W		1/2	53.4	4.6
1982	NY-A	62	29	33	.468	●5 E	5 E		3/3	30.7	-1.7
	5	464	234	229	.505						4.1

YEAR	TM/L	G	W	L	PCT	STANDING			M/YW-EXP		A-E
Kittridge, Malachi J.											
1904	Was-A*	18	1	16	.059	8	8		1/2	4.7	-3.7
Klein, Louis Frank "Lou"											
1961	Chi-N	11	5	6	.455	7	7	7	8/9	4.7	0.3
1962	Chi-N	30	12	18	.400	9	9	9	2/3	11.4	0.6
1965	Chi-N	106	48	58	.453	9	8		2/2	47.0	1.0
	3	147	65	82	.442						1.9
Kling, John "Johnny"											
1912	Bos-N*	155	52	101	.340	8				60.6	-8.6
Knabe, Franz Otto "Otto"											
1914	Bal-F*	160	84	70	.545	3				78.8	5.2
1915	Bal-F*	155	47	107	.305	8				55.4	-8.4
	2	315	131	177	.425						-3.2
Knight, Alonzo P. "Lon"											
1883	Phi-a*	98	66	32	.673	1				63.4	2.6
1884	Phi-a*	109	61	46	.570	7				67.1	-6.1
	2	207	127	78	.620						-3.5
Knight, Charles Ray "Ray"											
1996	Cin-N	162	81	81	.500	3 C				81.5	-0.5
1997	Cin-N	99	43	56	.434	4 C	3 C		1/2	42.5	0.5
	2	261	124	137	.475						0.0
Knoop, Robert Frank "Bobby"											
1994	Cal-A	2	1	1	.500	3 W	2 W	4 W	2/3	0.8	0.2
Krol, John Thomas "Jack"											
1978	StL-N	2	1	1	.500	6 E	6 E	5 E	2/3	0.9	0.1
1980	StL-N	1	0	1	.000	6 E	6 E	4 E	2/4	0.5	-0.5
	2	3	1	2	.333						-0.4
Kuehl, Karl Otto											
1976	Mon-N	128	43	85	.336	6 E	6 E		1/2	46.8	-3.8
Kuenn, Harvey Edward											
1975	Mil-A	1	1	0	1.000	5 E	5 E		2/2	0.4	0.6
1982	Mil-A	116	72	43	.626	5 E	♦1 E		2/2	69.3	2.7
1983	Mil-A	162	87	75	.537	5 E				86.6	0.4
	3	279	160	118	.576						3.7
Kuhel, Joseph Anthony "Joe"											
1948	Was-A	154	56	97	.366	7				54.6	1.4
1949	Was-A	154	50	104	.325	8				49.3	0.7
	2	308	106	201	.345						2.1
Lachemann, Marcel Ernest											
1994	Cal-A	74	30	44	.405	2 W	4 W		3/3	30.0	-0.0
1995	Cal-A	145	78	67	.538	▲2 W				82.2	-4.2
1996	Cal-A	117	53	64	.453	4 W			1/2	46.4	6.6
	3	336	161	175	.479						2.4
Lachemann, Rene George											
1981(1)	Sea-A	33	15	18	.455	7 W	6 W		2/2		
(2)	Sea-A	52	23	29	.442	5 W				34.9	3.1
1982	Sea-A	162	76	86	.469	4 W				74.7	1.3
1983	Sea-A	73	26	47	.356	7 W	7 W		1/2	27.8	-1.8
1984	Mil-A	161	67	94	.416	7 E				71.0	-4.0
1993	Fla-N	162	64	98	.395	6 E				65.9	-1.9
1994	Fla-N	115	51	54	.486	5 E				46.7	4.3
1995	Fla-N	143	67	76	.469	4 E				71.5	-4.5
1996	Fla-N	86	39	47	.453	4 E	3 E		1/3	42.2	-3.2
	8	987	428	549	.438						-6.7
Lajoie, Napoleon "Nap"											
1905	Cle-A*	58	37	21	.638	●1	5		1/3	28.2	8.8
	Cle-A*	56	19	36	.345	2	5		3/3	26.7	-7.7
1906	Cle-A*	157	89	64	.582	3				96.6	-7.6
1907	Cle-A*	158	85	67	.559	4				76.6	8.4
1908	Cle-A*	157	90	64	.584	2				90.0	-0.0
1909	Cle-A*	114	57	57	.500	4	6		1/2	53.6	3.4
	5	700	377	309	.550						5.3
Lake, Frederick Lovett "Fred"											
1908	Bos-A	40	22	17	.564	6	5		2/2	21.0	1.0
1909	Bos-A	152	88	63	.583	3				80.6	7.4
1910	Bos-N*	157	53	100	.346	8				54.1	-1.1
	3	349	163	180	.475						7.3
Lamont, Gene William											
1992	Chi-A	162	86	76	.531	3 W				85.9	0.1
1993	Chi-A	162	94	68	.580	1 W				92.3	1.7
1994	Chi-A	113	67	46	.593	1 C				69.3	-2.3
1995	Chi-A	31	11	20	.355	4 C	3 C		1/2	15.4	-4.4
1997	Pit-N	162	79	83	.488	2 C				77.5	1.5
1998	Pit-N	163	69	93	.426	6 C				74.0	-5.0
	6	793	406	386	.513						-8.4
Lanier, Harold Clifton "Hal"											
1986	Hou-N	162	96	66	.593	1 W				90.3	5.7
1987	Hou-N	162	76	86	.469	3 W				77.9	-1.9
1988	Hou-N	162	82	80	.506	5 W				79.5	2.5
	3	486	254	232	.523						6.4
Larkin, Henry E. "Ted"											
1890	Cle-P*	79	34	45	.430	7	7		1/2	30.9	3.1

YEAR	TM/L	G	W	L	PCT	STANDING			M/YW-EXP		A-E
LaRussa, Anthony "Tony"											
1979	Chi-A	54	27	27	.500	5 W	5 W		2/2	26.4	0.6
1980	Chi-A	162	70	90	.438	5 W				65.8	4.2
1981(1)	Chi-A	53	31	22	.585	3 W					
(2)	Chi-A	53	23	30	.434	6 W				58.5	-4.5
1982	Chi-A	162	87	75	.537	3 W				88.5	-1.5
1983	Chi-A	162	99	63	.611	1 W				96.0	3.0
1984	Chi-A	162	74	88	.457	●5 W				75.2	-1.2
1985	Chi-A	163	85	77	.525	3 W				82.6	2.4
1986	Chi-A	64	26	38	.406	6 W	5 W		1/3	29.7	-3.7
	Oak-A	79	45	34	.570	7 W	●3 W		3/3	38.1	6.9
1987	Oak-A	162	81	81	.500	3 W				82.6	-1.6
1988	Oak-A	162	104	58	.642	♦1 W				99.2	4.8
1989	Oak-A	162	99	63	.611	★1 W				95.5	3.5
1990	Oak-A	162	103	59	.636	♦1 W				98.2	4.8
1991	Oak-A	162	84	78	.519	4 W				79.4	4.6
1992	Oak-A	162	96	66	.593	1 W				88.4	7.6
1993	Oak-A	162	68	94	.420	7 W				68.3	-0.3
1994	Oak-A	114	51	63	.447	2 W				53.2	-2.2
1995	Oak-A	144	67	77	.465	4 W				69.1	-2.1
1996	StL-N	162	88	74	.543	1 C				86.3	1.7
1997	StL-N	162	73	89	.451	4 C				79.1	-6.1
1998	StL-N	163	83	79	.512	3 C				83.7	-0.7
	20	2993	1564	1425	.523						20.1
Lasorda, Thomas Charles "Tom"											
1976	LA-N	4	2	2	.500	2 W	2 W		2/2	2.2	-0.2
1977	LA-N	162	98	64	.605	♦1 W				100.4	-2.4
1978	LA-N	162	95	67	.586	♦1 W				97.3	-2.3
1979	LA-N	162	79	83	.488	3 W				83.2	-4.2
1980	LA-N	163	92	71	.564	▲2 W				89.3	2.7
1981(1)	LA-N	57	36	21	.632	★1 W					
(2)	LA-N	53	27	26	.509	4 W				65.4	-2.4
1982	LA-N	162	88	74	.543	2 W				89.4	-1.4
1983	LA-N	163	91	71	.562	1 W				85.9	5.1
1984	LA-N	162	79	83	.488	4 W				78.8	0.2
1985	LA-N	162	95	67	.586	1 W				92.1	2.9
1986	LA-N	162	73	89	.451	5 W				76.7	-3.7
1987	LA-N	162	73	89	.451	4 W				76.8	-3.8
1988	LA-N	162	94	67	.584	★1 W				89.9	4.1
1989	LA-N	160	77	83	.481	4 W				82.1	-5.1
1990	LA-N	162	86	76	.531	2 W				85.4	0.6
1991	LA-N	162	93	69	.574	2 W				91.9	1.1
1992	LA-N	162	63	99	.389	6 W				71.2	-8.2
1993	LA-N	162	81	81	.500	4 W				82.4	-1.4
1994	LA-N	114	58	56	.509	1 W				59.3	-1.3
1995	LA-N	144	78	66	.542	1 W				74.6	3.4
1996	LA-N	86	41	35	.539	1 W	2 W		1/2	40.5	0.5
	21	3050	1599	1439	.526						-15.5
Latham, George Warren "Juice"											
1875	NH-n*	18	4	14	.222	11	8	8	2/3	1.5	2.5
1882	Phi-a*	75	41	34	.547	2				39.1	1.9
	2	93	45	48	.484						4.4
Latham, Walter Arlington "Arlie"											
1896	StL-N*	3	0	3	.000	10	10	11	2/5	0.8	-0.8
Lavagetto, Harry Arthur "Cookie"											
1957	Was-A	134	51	83	.381	8	8		2/2	49.3	1.7
1958	Was-A	156	61	93	.396	8				56.8	4.2
1959	Was-A	154	63	91	.409	8				68.6	-5.6
1960	Was-A	154	73	81	.474	5				74.6	-1.6
1961	Min-A	49	19	30	.388	8	7		1/4	22.4	-3.4
	Min-A	10	4	6	.400	9	9	7	3/4	4.6	-0.6
	5	657	271	384	.414						-5.3
Leadley, Robert H. "Bob"											
1888	Det-N	40	19	19	.500	3	5		2/2	21.5	-2.5
1890	Cle-N	58	23	33	.411	7	7		2/2	20.2	2.8
1891	Cle-N	68	34	34	.500	4	5		1/2	31.8	2.2
	3	166	76	86	.469						2.5
Lefebvre, James Kenneth "Jim"											
1989	Sea-A	162	73	89	.451	6 W				77.6	-4.6
1990	Sea-A	162	77	85	.475	5 W				76.8	0.2
1991	Sea-A	162	83	79	.512	5 W				83.9	-0.9
1992	Chi-N	162	78	84	.481	4 E				77.6	0.4
1993	Chi-N	163	84	78	.519	4 E				80.9	3.1
	5	811	395	415	.488						-1.7
Lemon, James Robert "Jim"											
1968	Was-A	161	65	96	.404	10				64.9	0.1
Lemon, Robert Granville "Bob"											
1970	KC-A	110	46	64	.418	5 W	●4 W		2/2	48.3	-2.3
1971	KC-A	161	85	76	.528	2 W				84.6	0.4
1972	KC-A	154	76	78	.494	4 W				80.9	-4.9
1977	Chi-A	162	90	72	.556	3 W				87.9	2.1
1978	Chi-A	74	34	40	.459	5 W	5 W		1/2	32.4	1.6
	NY-A	68	48	20	.706	4 E	▲★1 E		3/3	40.7	7.3
1979	NY-A	65	34	31	.523	4 E	4 E		1/2	35.0	-1.0
1981(2)	NY-A	25	11	14	.440	4 E	6 E		2/2	14.5	-3.5
1982	NY-A	14	6	8	.429	●4 E	5 E		1/3	6.9	-0.9
	8	833	430	403	.516						-1.4

YEAR	TM/L	G	W	L	PCT	STANDING			M/YW	EXP	A-E
Lennon, William F. "Bill"											
1871	Kek-n*	14	5	9	.357	7	8		1/2	1.8	3.2
Leyland, James Richard "Jim"											
1986	Pit-N	162	64	98	.395	6 E				77.2	-13.2
1987	Pit-N	162	80	82	.494	●4 E				78.9	1.1
1988	Pit-N	160	85	75	.531	2 E				83.7	1.3
1989	Pit-N	164	74	88	.457	5 E				76.4	-2.4
1990	Pit-N	162	95	67	.586	1 E				92.8	2.2
1991	Pit-N	162	98	64	.605	1 E				94.9	3.1
1992	Pit-N	162	96	66	.593	1 E				91.4	4.6
1993	Pit-N	162	75	87	.463	5 E				71.3	3.7
1994	Pit-N	114	53	61	.465	●3 C				45.7	7.3
1995	Pit-N	144	58	86	.403	5 C				61.6	-3.6
1996	Pit-N	162	73	89	.451	5 C				75.6	-2.6
1997	Fla-N	162	92	70	.568	■★2 E				88.2	3.8
1998	Fla-N	162	54	108	.333	5 E				56.5	-2.5
	13	2040	997	1041	.489						2.8
Leyva, Nicolas Tomas "Nick"											
1989	Phi-N	163	67	95	.414	6 E				70.0	-3.0
1990	Phi-N	162	77	85	.475	●4 E				72.5	4.5
1991	Phi-N	13	4	9	.308	6 E	3 E		1/2	6.1	-2.1
	3	338	148	189	.439						-0.5
Lillis, Robert Perry "Bob"											
1982	Hou-N	51	28	23	.549	5 W	5 W		2/2	23.7	4.3
1983	Hou-N	162	85	77	.525	3 W				80.7	4.3
1984	Hou-N	162	80	82	.494	●2 W				87.6	-7.6
1985	Hou-N	162	83	79	.512	●3 W				82.5	0.5
	4	537	276	261	.514						1.5
Lipon, John Joseph "Johnny"											
1971	Cle-A	59	18	41	.305	6 E	6 E		2/2	21.6	-3.6
Lobert, John Bernard "Hans"											
1938	Phi-N	2	0	2	.000	8	8		2/2	0.6	-0.6
1942	Phi-N	151	42	109	.278	8				40.8	1.2
	2	153	42	111	.275						0.6
Lockman, Carroll Walter "Whitey"											
1972	Chi-N	65	39	26	.600	4 E	2 E		2/2	37.7	1.3
1973	Chi-N	161	77	84	.478	5 E				76.1	0.9
1974	Chi-N	93	41	52	.441	5 E	6 E		1/2	37.6	3.4
	3	319	157	162	.492						5.5
Loftus, Thomas Joseph "Tom"											
1884	Mil-U	12	8	4	.667	2				8.1	-0.1
1888	Cle-a	71	30	38	.441	8	6		2/2	25.3	4.7
1889	Cle-N	136	61	72	.459	6				60.5	0.5
1890	Cin-N	134	77	55	.583	4				77.2	-0.2
1891	Cin-N	138	56	81	.409	7				55.1	0.9
1900	Chi-N	146	65	75	.464	●5				58.7	6.3
1901	Chi-N	140	53	86	.381	6				57.5	-4.5
1902	Was-A	138	61	75	.449	6				60.4	0.6
1903	Was-A	140	43	94	.314	8				41.7	1.3
	9	1055	454	580	.439						9.6
Lopat, Edmund Walter "Ed"											
1963	KC-A	162	73	89	.451	8				71.6	1.4
1964	KC-A	52	17	35	.327	10	10		1/2	19.1	-2.1
	2	214	90	124	.421						-0.7
Lopez, Alfonso Ramon "Al"											
1951	Cle-A	155	93	61	.604	2				87.6	5.4
1952	Cle-A	155	93	61	.604	2				92.8	0.2
1953	Cle-A	155	92	62	.597	2				91.3	0.7
1954	Cle-A	156	111	43	.721	1				102.7	8.3
1955	Cle-A	154	93	61	.604	2				87.0	6.0
1956	Cle-A	155	88	66	.571	2				90.6	-2.6
1957	Chi-A	155	90	64	.584	2				91.8	-1.8
1958	Chi-A	155	82	72	.532	2				79.0	3.0
1959	Chi-A	156	94	60	.610	1				85.6	8.4
1960	Chi-A	154	87	67	.565	3				89.5	-2.5
1961	Chi-A	163	86	76	.531	4				84.9	1.1
1962	Chi-A	162	85	77	.525	5				86.1	-1.1
1963	Chi-A	162	94	68	.580	2				96.2	-2.2
1964	Chi-A	162	98	64	.605	2				96.9	1.1
1965	Chi-A	162	95	67	.586	2				91.1	3.9
1968	Chi-A	11	6	5	.545	9	9	●8	3/5	5.0	1.0
	Chi-A	36	15	21	.417	9	●8		5/5	16.3	-1.3
1969	Chi-A	17	8	9	.471	4 W	5 W		1/2	7.4	0.6
	17	2425	1410	1004	.584						28.3
Lord, Harry Donald											
1915	Buf-F*	110	60	49	.550	8	6		3/3	49.9	10.1
Lowe, Robert Lincoln "Bobby"											
1904	Det-A*	78	30	44	.405	7	7		2/2	30.3	-0.3
Lucchesi, Frank Joseph											
1970	Phi-N	161	73	88	.453	5 E				66.3	6.7
1971	Phi-N	162	67	95	.414	6 E				66.9	0.1
1972	Phi-N	76	26	50	.342	6 E	6 E		1/2	30.9	-4.9
1975	Tex-A	67	35	32	.522	4 W	3 W		2/2	32.7	2.3
1976	Tex-A	162	76	86	.469	●4 W				77.1	-1.1
1977	Tex-A	62	31	31	.500	●3 W	2 W		1/4	35.3	-4.3
1987	Chi-N	25	8	17	.320	5 E	6 E		2/2	11.3	-3.3
	7	715	316	399	.442						-4.4
Lumley, Harry G											
1909	Bro-N*	155	55	98	.359	6				55.6	-0.6
Lyons, Theodore Amar "Ted"											
1946	Chi-A	125	64	60	.516	7	5		2/2	59.1	4.9
1947	Chi-A	155	70	84	.455	6				65.4	4.6
1948	Chi-A	154	51	101	.336	8				50.4	0.6
	3	434	185	245	.430						10.1
Mack, Cornelius Alexander "Connie"											
1894	Pit-N*	23	12	10	.545	7	7		2/2	10.8	1.2
1895	Pit-N*	135	71	61	.538	7				68.1	2.9
1896	Pit-N*	131	66	63	.512	6				68.5	-2.5
1901	Phi-A	137	74	62	.544	4				71.9	2.1
1902	Phi-A	137	83	53	.610	1				81.0	2.0
1903	Phi-A	137	75	60	.556	2				75.7	-0.7
1904	Phi-A	155	81	70	.536	5				81.7	-0.7
1905	Phi-A	152	92	56	.622	1				88.5	3.5
1906	Phi-A	149	78	67	.538	4				74.5	3.5
1907	Phi-A	150	88	57	.607	2				80.4	7.6
1908	Phi-A	157	68	85	.444	6				67.7	0.3
1909	Phi-A	153	95	58	.621	2				99.5	-4.5
1910	Phi-A	155	102	48	.680	★1				101.0	1.0
1911	Phi-A	152	101	50	.669	★1				100.7	0.3
1912	Phi-A	153	90	62	.592	3				87.8	2.2
1913	Phi-A	153	96	57	.627	★1				96.6	-0.6
1914	Phi-A	158	99	53	.651	1				99.2	-0.2
1915	Phi-A	154	43	109	.283	8				42.3	0.7
1916	Phi-A	154	36	117	.235	8				41.5	-5.5
1917	Phi-A	154	55	98	.359	8				59.2	-4.2
1918	Phi-A	130	52	76	.406	8				50.0	2.0
1919	Phi-A	140	36	104	.257	8				40.8	-4.8
1920	Phi-A	156	48	106	.312	8				49.3	-1.3
1921	Phi-A	155	53	100	.346	8				54.0	-1.0
1922	Phi-A	155	65	89	.422	7				65.1	-0.1
1923	Phi-A	153	69	83	.454	6				66.2	2.8
1924	Phi-A	152	71	81	.467	5				67.0	4.0
1925	Phi-A	153	88	64	.579	2				87.1	0.9
1926	Phi-A	150	83	67	.553	2				86.1	-3.1
1927	Phi-A	155	91	63	.591	2				87.9	3.1
1928	Phi-A	153	98	55	.641	2				97.4	0.6
1929	Phi-A	151	104	46	.693	★1				102.1	1.9
1930	Phi-A	154	102	52	.662	★1				95.0	7.0
1931	Phi-A	153	107	45	.704	1				98.4	8.6
1932	Phi-A	154	94	60	.610	2				97.5	-3.5
1933	Phi-A	152	79	72	.523	3				77.5	1.5
1934	Phi-A	153	68	82	.453	5				68.1	-0.1
1935	Phi-A	149	58	91	.389	8				59.8	-1.8
1936	Phi-A	154	53	100	.346	8				47.1	5.9
1937	Phi-A	120	39	80	.328	7	7		1/2	48.0	-9.0
1938	Phi-A	154	53	99	.349	8				55.1	-2.1
1939	Phi-A	62	25	37	.403	6	7		1/2	19.7	5.3
1940	Phi-A	154	54	100	.351	8				55.9	-1.9
1941	Phi-A	154	64	90	.416	8				65.0	-1.0
1942	Phi-A	154	55	99	.357	8				51.5	3.5
1943	Phi-A	155	49	105	.318	8				53.4	-4.4
1944	Phi-A	155	72	82	.468	●5				69.3	2.7
1945	Phi-A	153	52	98	.347	8				59.1	-7.1
1946	Phi-A	155	49	105	.318	8				60.8	-11.8
1947	Phi-A	156	78	76	.506	5				79.0	-1.0
1948	Phi-A	154	84	70	.545	4				76.4	7.6
1949	Phi-A	154	81	73	.526	5				77.1	3.9
1950	Phi-A	154	52	102	.338	8				54.3	-2.3
	53	7755	3731	3948	.486						13.6
Mack, Dennis Joseph "Denny"											
1882	Lou-a*	80	42	38	.525	3				48.7	-6.7
Mack, Earle Thaddeus											
1937	Phi-A	34	15	17	.469	7	7		2/2	12.9	2.1
1939	Phi-A	91	30	60	.333	6	7		2/2	28.6	1.4
	2	125	45	77	.369						3.5
Macullar, James F. "Jimmy"											
1879	Syr-N*	27	5	21	.192	6	7		3/3	6.6	-1.6
Magee, Leo Christopher "Lee"											
1915	Bro-F*	118	53	64	.453	7	7		1/2	56.5	-3.5
Malone, Ferguson G. "Fergy"											
1873	Phi-n*	53	36	27	.571	2				35.9	0.1
1874	Phi-n*	36	18	18	.500	4	5		1/2	15.1	2.9
1884	Phi-U*	67	21	46	.313	7				23.1	-2.1
	3	156	75	91	.452						0.9
Manning, James H. "Jimmy"											
1901	Was-A	138	61	72	.459	6				58.3	2.7
Manning, John E. "Jack"											
1877	Cin-N*	20	7	12	.368	6	6		3/3	4.2	2.8
Manuel, Jerry											
1998	Chi-A	163	80	82	.494	2 C				74.7	5.3

YEAR	TM/L	G	W	L	PCT	STANDING			M/Y	W-EXP	A-E
Maranville, Walter James Vincent "Rabbit"											
1925	Chi-N*	53	23	30	.434	7	7	8	2/3	24.8	-1.8
Marion, Martin Whitford "Marty"											
1951	StL-N	155	81	73	.526	3				78.2	2.8
1952	StL-A*	104	42	61	.408	8	7		2/2	42.7	-0.7
1953	StL-A*	154	54	100	.351	8				54.3	-0.3
1954	Chi-A	9	3	6	.333	3	3		2/2	5.7	-2.7
1955	Chi-A	155	91	63	.591	3				94.5	-3.5
1956	Chi-A	154	85	69	.552	3				91.1	-6.1
	6	731	356	372	.489						-10.5
Marshall, Rufus James "Jim"											
1974	Chi-N	69	25	44	.362	5 E	6 E		2/2	27.9	-2.9
1975	Chi-N	162	75	87	.463	●5 E				69.8	5.2
1976	Chi-N	162	75	87	.463	4 E				68.8	6.2
1979	Oak-A	162	54	108	.333	7 W				52.0	2.0
	4	555	229	326	.413						10.5
Martin, Alfred Manuel "Billy"											
1969	Min-A	162	97	65	.599	1 W				98.5	-1.5
1971	Det-A	162	91	71	.562	2 E				86.8	4.2
1972	Det-A	156	86	70	.551	1 E				83.0	3.0
1973	Det-A	134	71	63	.530	3 E	3 E		1/2	64.2	6.8
	Tex-A	23	9	14	.391	6 W	6 W		3/3	8.3	0.7
1974	Tex-A	161	84	76	.525	2 W				79.2	4.8
1975	Tex-A	95	44	51	.463	4 W	3 W		1/2	46.4	-2.4
	NY-A	56	30	26	.536	3 E	3 E		2/2	31.5	-1.5
1976	NY-A	159	97	62	.610	♦1 E				95.7	1.3
1977	NY-A	162	100	62	.617	★1 E				98.9	1.1
1978	NY-A	94	52	42	.553	3 E	▲★1 E		1/3	56.3	-4.3
1979	NY-A	95	55	40	.579	4 E	4 E		2/2	51.2	3.8
1980	Oak-A	162	83	79	.512	2 W				85.6	-2.6
1981(1)	Oak-A	60	37	23	.617	○1 W					
(2)	Oak-A	49	27	22	.551	2 W				60.4	3.6
1982	Oak-A	162	68	94	.420	5 W				68.4	-0.4
1983	NY-A	162	91	71	.562	3 E				87.7	3.3
1985	NY-A	145	91	54	.628	7 E	2 E		2/2	88.4	2.6
1988	NY-A	68	40	28	.588	2 E	5 E		1/2	35.0	5.0
	16	2267	1253	1013	.553						27.5
Martin, Alphonse Case "Phonney"											
1872	Eck-n*	9	1	8	.111	10	9		3/3	-1.0	2.0
Martinez, Orlando iva] "Marty"											
1986	Sea-A	1	0	1	.000	6 W	6 W	7 W	2/3	0.4	-0.4
Mason, Charles E. "Charlie"											
1887	Phi-a	82	38	40	.487	6	5		2/2	39.1	-1.1
Mathews, Edwin Lee "Eddie"											
1972	Atl-N	50	23	27	.460	4 W	4 W		2/2	21.6	1.4
1973	Atl-N	162	76	85	.472	5 W				82.9	-6.9
1974	Atl-N	99	50	49	.505	4 W	3 W		1/2	56.1	-6.1
	3	311	149	161	.481						-11.6
Mathewson, Christopher "Christy"											
1916	Cin-N*	69	25	43	.368	8	●7		3/3	28.4	-3.4
1917	Cin-N	157	78	76	.506	4				75.9	2.1
1918	Cin-N	120	61	57	.517	4	3		1/2	62.3	-1.3
	3	346	164	176	.482						-2.7
Mattick, Robert James "Bobby"											
1980	Tor-A	162	67	95	.414	7 E				66.8	0.2
1981(1)	Tor-A	58	16	42	.276	7 E					
(2)	Tor-A	48	21	27	.438	7 E				38.0	-1.0
	2	268	104	164	.388						-0.8
Mauch, Gene William											
1960	Phi-N	152	58	94	.382	●4	8		3/3	60.8	-2.8
1961	Phi-N	155	47	107	.305	8				55.7	-8.7
1962	Phi-N	161	81	80	.503	7				75.1	5.9
1963	Phi-N	162	87	75	.537	4				88.0	-1.0
1964	Phi-N	162	92	70	.568	●2				87.4	4.6
1965	Phi-N	162	85	76	.528	6				79.1	5.9
1966	Phi-N	162	87	75	.537	4				86.9	0.1
1967	Phi-N	162	82	80	.506	5				84.4	-2.4
1968	Phi-N	54	27	27	.500	●6	●7		1/3	24.3	2.7
1969	Mon-N	162	52	110	.321	6 E				59.5	-7.5
1970	Mon-N	162	73	89	.451	6 E				69.1	3.9
1971	Mon-N	162	71	90	.441	5 E				69.4	1.6
1972	Mon-N	156	70	86	.449	5 E				67.3	2.7
1973	Mon-N	162	79	83	.488	4 E				77.5	1.5
1974	Mon-N	161	79	82	.491	4 E				81.0	-2.0
1975	Mon-N	162	75	87	.463	●5 E				71.5	3.5
1976	Min-A	162	85	77	.525	3 W				84.9	0.1
1977	Min-A	161	84	77	.522	4 W				89.0	-5.0
1978	Min-A	162	73	89	.451	4 W				79.8	-6.8
1979	Min-A	162	82	80	.506	4 W				84.9	-2.9
1980	Min-A	125	54	71	.432	4 W	3 W		1/2	58.2	-4.2
1981(1)	Cal-A	13	9	4	.692	4 W	4 W		2/2		
(2)	Cal-A	50	20	30	.400	7 W				32.9	-3.9
1982	Cal-A	162	93	69	.574	1 W				95.3	-2.3
1985	Cal-A	162	90	72	.556	2 W				83.9	6.1
1986	Cal-A	162	92	70	.568	1 W				91.2	0.8
1987	Cal-A	162	75	87	.463	●6 W				77.8	-2.8

YEAR	TM/L	G	W	L	PCT	STANDING			M/Y	W-EXP	A-E
	26	3942	1902	2037	.483						-12.9
McAleer, James Robert "Jimmy"											
1901	Cle-A*	138	54	82	.397	7				53.1	0.9
1902	StL-A*	140	78	58	.574	2				69.2	8.8
1903	StL-A	139	65	74	.468	6				66.7	-1.7
1904	StL-A	156	65	87	.428	6				62.0	3.0
1905	StL-A	156	54	99	.353	8				65.6	-11.6
1906	StL-A	154	76	73	.510	5				81.4	-5.4
1907	StL-A*	155	69	83	.454	6				74.5	-5.5
1908	StL-A	155	83	69	.546	4				83.1	-0.1
1909	StL-A	154	61	89	.407	7				59.3	1.7
1910	Was-A	157	66	85	.437	7				69.8	-3.8
1911	Was-A	154	64	90	.416	7				62.9	1.1
	11	1658	735	889	.453						-12.8
McBride, George Florian											
1921	Was-A	154	80	73	.523	4				73.2	6.8
McBride, James Dickson "Dick"											
1871	Ath-n*	28	21	7	.750	1				20.9	0.1
1872	Ath-n*	47	30	14	.682	4				35.1	-5.1
1873	Ath-n*	52	28	23	.549	5				30.7	-2.7
1874	Ath-n*	56	33	23	.589	3				35.2	-2.2
1875	Ath-n*	69	49	18	.731	2	2		1/2	55.1	-6.1
	5	252	161	85	.654						-16.0
McCallister, John "Jack"											
1927	Cle-A	153	66	87	.431	6				66.9	-0.9
McCarthy, Joseph Vincent "Joe"											
1926	Chi-N	155	82	72	.532	4				85.3	-3.3
1927	Chi-N	153	85	68	.556	4				85.3	-0.3
1928	Chi-N	154	91	63	.591	3				87.1	3.9
1929	Chi-N	156	98	54	.645	1				96.1	1.9
1930	Chi-N	152	86	64	.573	2	2		1/2	85.8	0.2
1931	NY-A	155	94	59	.614	2				103.3	-9.3
1932	NY-A	156	107	47	.695	★1				102.1	4.9
1933	NY-A	152	91	59	.607	2				89.3	1.7
1934	NY-A	154	94	60	.610	2				93.6	0.4
1935	NY-A	149	89	60	.597	2				92.4	-3.4
1936	NY-A	155	102	51	.667	★1				105.9	-3.9
1937	NY-A	157	102	52	.662	★1				105.5	-3.5
1938	NY-A	157	99	53	.651	★1				99.5	-0.5
1939	NY-A	152	106	45	.702	★1				114.5	-8.5
1940	NY-A	155	88	66	.571	3				91.1	-3.1
1941	NY-A	156	101	53	.656	★1				96.5	4.5
1942	NY-A	154	103	51	.669	1				107.3	-4.3
1943	NY-A	155	98	56	.636	★1				90.6	7.4
1944	NY-A	154	83	71	.539	3				82.9	0.1
1945	NY-A	152	81	71	.533	4				83.2	-2.2
1946	NY-A	35	22	13	.629	2	3		1/3	20.8	1.2
1948	Bos-A	155	96	59	.619	▲2				94.8	1.2
1949	Bos-A	155	96	58	.623	2				98.6	-2.6
1950	Bos-A	59	31	28	.525	4	3		1/2	36.9	-5.9
	24	3487	2125	1333	.615						-23.6
McCarthy, Thomas Francis "Tommy"											
1890	StL-a*	22	11	11	.500	4	3		1/6	12.9	-1.9
	StL-a*	5	4	1	.800	2	2	3	5/6	2.9	1.1
McCloskey, John Joseph											
1895	Lou-N	133	35	96	.267	12				33.4	1.6
1896	Lou-N	19	2	17	.105	12	12		1/2	5.2	-3.2
1906	StL-N	154	52	98	.347	7				59.5	-7.5
1907	StL-N	155	52	101	.340	8				54.5	-2.5
1908	StL-N	154	49	105	.318	8				46.9	2.1
	5	615	190	417	.313						-9.5
McCormick, James "Jim"											
1879	Cle-N*	82	27	55	.329	6				27.5	-0.5
1880	Cle-N*	85	47	37	.560	3				47.1	-0.1
1882	Cle-N*	4	0	4	.000	8	5		1/2	2.0	-2.0
	3	171	74	96	.435						-2.6
McGaha, Fred Melvin "Mel"											
1962	Cle-A	160	78	82	.488	6	6		1/2	73.7	4.3
1964	KC-A	111	40	70	.364	10	10		2/2	40.3	-0.3
1965	KC-A	26	5	21	.192	10	10		1/2	10.2	-5.2
	3	297	123	173	.416						-1.2
McGeary, Michael Henry "Mike"											
1875	Phi-n*	63	34	27	.557	4	5		1/2	37.8	-3.8
1880	Pro-N*	16	8	7	.533	4	2		1/3	9.7	-1.7
1881	Cle-N*	11	4	7	.364	6	7		1/2	5.2	-1.2
	3	90	46	41	.529						-6.7
McGraw, John Joseph											
1899	Bal-N*	152	86	62	.581	4				86.9	-0.9
1901	Bal-A*	135	68	65	.511	5				67.4	0.6
1902	Bal-A*	58	26	31	.456	7	8		1/2	23.5	2.5
	NY-N*	65	25	38	.397	8	8		3/3	21.7	3.3
1903	NY-N*	142	84	55	.604	2				85.6	-1.6
1904	NY-N*	158	106	47	.693	1				105.4	0.6
1905	NY-N*	155	105	48	.686	★1				105.2	-0.2
1906	NY-N*	153	96	56	.632	2				88.7	7.3

YEAR	TM/L	G	W	L	PCT	STANDING			M/Y	W-EXP	A-E
1907	NY-N	155	82	71	.536	4				83.8	-1.8
1908	NY-N	157	98	56	.636	●2				99.1	-1.1
1909	NY-N	158	92	61	.601	3				85.0	7.0
1910	NY-N	155	91	63	.591	2				92.4	-1.4
1911	NY-N	154	99	54	.647	1				98.6	0.4
1912	NY-N	154	103	48	.682	1				100.6	2.4
1913	NY-N	156	101	51	.664	1				94.3	6.7
1914	NY-N	156	84	70	.545	2				87.2	-3.2
1915	NY-N	155	69	83	.454	8				71.1	-2.1
1916	NY-N	155	86	66	.566	4				86.5	-0.5
1917	NY-N	158	98	56	.636	1				97.3	0.7
1918	NY-N	124	71	53	.573	2				69.3	1.7
1919	NY-N	140	87	53	.621	2				84.6	2.4
1920	NY-N	155	86	68	.558	2				91.8	-5.8
1921	NY-N	153	94	59	.614	★1				96.1	-2.1
1922	NY-N	156	93	61	.604	★1				95.7	-2.7
1923	NY-N	153	95	58	.621	1				93.1	1.9
1924	NY-N	29	16	13	.552	3	1		1/3	18.4	-2.4
	NY-N	81	45	35	.563	1	1		3/3	50.9	-5.9
1925	NY-N	14	10	4	.714	1	2		1/3	7.3	2.7
	NY-N	106	55	51	.519	1	2		3/3	55.3	-0.3
1926	NY-N	151	74	77	.490	5				75.0	-1.0
1927	NY-N	122	70	52	.574	4	3		1/2	68.3	1.7
1928	NY-N	155	93	61	.604	2				92.1	0.9
1929	NY-N	152	84	67	.556	3				92.9	-8.9
1930	NY-N	154	87	67	.565	3				89.8	-2.8
1931	NY-N	153	87	65	.572	2				93.0	-6.0
1932	NY-N	40	17	23	.425	8	●6		1/2	21.2	-4.2
	33	4769	2763	1948	.586						-12.0
McGuire, James Thomas "Deacon"											
1898	Was-N*	70	21	47	.309	10	11	11	3/4	24.3	-3.3
1907	Bos-A*	112	45	61	.425	8	7		4/4	45.2	-0.2
1908	Bos-A*	115	53	62	.461	6	5		1/2	61.8	-8.8
1909	Cle-A	41	14	25	.359	4	6		2/2	18.3	-4.3
1910	Cle-A*	161	71	81	.467	5				64.0	7.0
1911	Cle-A	17	6	11	.353	7	3		1/2	8.3	-2.3
	6	516	210	287	.423						-12.0
McGunnigle, William Henry "Bill"											
1888	Bro-a	143	88	52	.629	2				87.0	1.0
1889	Bro-a	140	94	43	.686	1				93.4	-0.4
1890	Bro-N	129	86	43	.667	1				87.7	-1.7
1891	Pit-N	59	24	33	.421	8	8		2/2	25.9	-1.9
1896	Lou-N	115	36	76	.321	12	12		2/2	30.9	5.1
	5	586	328	247	.570						2.1
McInnis, John Phalen "Stuffy"											
1927	Phi-N*	155	51	103	.331	8				55.9	-4.9
McKechnie, William Boyd "Bill"											
1915	New-F*	102	54	45	.545	6	5		2/2	51.2	2.8
1922	Pit-N	90	53	36	.596	5	●3		2/2	51.5	1.5
1923	Pit-N	154	87	67	.565	3				85.7	1.3
1924	Pit-N	153	90	63	.588	3				90.4	-0.4
1925	Pit-N	153	95	58	.621	★1				94.6	0.4
1926	Pit-N	157	84	69	.549	3				84.4	-0.4
1928	StL-N	154	95	59	.617	1				93.8	1.2
1929	StL-N	63	34	29	.540	4	4		3/3	32.5	1.5
1930	Bos-N	154	70	84	.455	6				63.5	6.5
1931	Bos-N	156	64	90	.416	7				61.2	2.8
1932	Bos-N	155	77	77	.500	5				76.4	0.6
1933	Bos-N	156	83	71	.539	4				79.4	3.6
1934	Bos-N	152	78	73	.517	4				72.4	5.6
1935	Bos-N	153	38	115	.248	8				49.3	-11.3
1936	Bos-N	157	71	83	.461	6				68.4	2.6
1937	Bos-N	152	79	73	.520	5				78.5	0.5
1938	Cin-N	151	82	68	.547	4				83.9	-1.9
1939	Cin-N	156	97	57	.630	1				94.5	2.5
1940	Cin-N	155	100	53	.654	★1				95.5	4.5
1941	Cin-N	154	88	66	.571	3				82.6	5.4
1942	Cin-N	154	76	76	.500	4				74.0	2.0
1943	Cin-N	155	87	67	.565	2				84.2	2.8
1944	Cin-N	155	89	65	.578	3				81.0	8.0
1945	Cin-N	154	61	93	.396	7				60.2	0.8
1946	Cin-N	152	64	86	.427	6	6		1/2	69.8	-5.8
	25	3647	1896	1723	.524						37.3
McKeon, John Aloysius "Jack"											
1973	KC-A	162	88	74	.543	2 W				81.3	6.7
1974	KC-A	162	77	85	.475	5 W				81.5	-4.5
1975	KC-A	96	50	46	.521	2 W	2 W		1/2	51.7	-1.7
1977	Oak-A	53	26	27	.491	●5 W	7 W		1/2	21.6	4.4
1978	Oak-A	123	45	78	.366	1 W	6 W		2/2	48.4	-3.4
1988	SD-N	115	67	48	.583	5 W	3 W		2/2	58.4	8.6
1989	SD-N	162	89	73	.549	2 W				82.7	6.3
1990	SD-N	80	37	43	.463	4 W	5 W		1/2	40.0	-3.0
1997	Cin-N	63	33	30	.524	4 C	3 C		2/2	27.0	6.0
1998	Cin-N	162	77	85	.475	4 C				80.0	-3.0
	10	1178	589	589	.500						16.3
McKinnon, Alexander J. "Alex"											
1885	StL-N*	39	6	32	.158	5	8	8	2/3	11.8	-5.8

YEAR	TM/L	G	W	L	PCT	STANDING			M/Y	W-EXP	A-E
McKnight, Dennis Hamar "Denny"											
1884	Pit-a	12	4	8	.333	9	10		1/5	2.7	1.3
McManus, George											
1876	StL-N	8	6	2	.750	2	2		2/2	5.9	0.1
1877	StL-N	60	28	32	.467	4				26.8	1.2
	2	68	34	34	.500						1.3
McManus, Martin Joseph "Marty"											
1932	Bos-A*	99	32	67	.323	8	8		2/2	27.8	4.2
1933	Bos-A*	149	63	86	.423	7				68.9	-5.9
	2	248	95	153	.383						-1.7
McMillan, Roy David											
1972	Mil-A	2	1	1	.500	6 E	6 E	6 E	2/3	0.9	0.1
1975	NY-N	53	26	27	.491	3 E	●3 E		2/2	27.2	-1.2
	2	55	27	28	.491						-1.1
McNamara, John Francis											
1969	Oak-A	13	8	5	.615	2 W	2 W		2/2	7.0	1.0
1970	Oak-A	162	89	73	.549	2 W				90.1	-1.1
1974	SD-N	162	60	102	.370	6 W				51.2	8.8
1975	SD-N	162	71	91	.438	4 W				66.8	4.2
1976	SD-N	162	73	89	.451	5 W				71.0	2.0
1977	SD-N	48	20	28	.417	4 W	5 W		1/3	19.9	0.1
1979	Cin-N	161	90	71	.559	1 W				89.4	0.6
1980	Cin-N	163	89	73	.549	3 W				84.8	4.2
1981(1)	Cin-N	56	35	21	.625	2 W					
(2)	Cin-N	52	31	21	.596	2 W				56.5	9.5
1982	Cin-N	92	34	58	.370	6 W	6 W		1/2	38.8	-4.8
1983	Cal-A	162	70	92	.432	●5 W				75.4	-5.4
1984	Cal-A	162	81	81	.500	●2 W				80.9	0.1
1985	Bos-A	163	81	81	.500	5 E				88.9	-7.9
1986	Bos-A	161	95	66	.590	♦1 E				90.2	4.8
1987	Bos-A	162	78	84	.481	5 E				82.6	-4.6
1988	Bos-A	85	43	42	.506	4 E	1 E		1/2	48.9	-5.9
1990	Cle-A	162	77	85	.475	4 E				80.5	-3.5
1991	Cle-A	77	25	52	.325	7 E	7 E		1/2	29.4	-4.4
1996	Cal-A	44	17	27	.386	4 W			2/2	17.4	-0.4
	19	2411	1167	1242	.484						-2.6
McPhee, John Alexander "Bid"											
1901	Cin-N	142	52	87	.374	8				44.8	7.2
1902	Cin-N	65	27	37	.422	6	4		1/3	35.2	-8.2
	2	207	79	124	.389						-0.9
McRae, Harold Abraham "Hal"											
1991	KC-A	124	66	58	.532	7 W	6 W		3/3	62.4	3.6
1992	KC-A	162	72	90	.444	●5 W				74.9	-2.9
1993	KC-A	162	84	78	.519	3 W				79.0	5.0
1994	KC-A	115	64	51	.557	3 C				61.6	2.4
	4	563	286	277	.508						8.1
McVey, Calvin Alexander "Cal"											
1873	Bal-n*	33	20	13	.606	3	3		1/2	24.3	-4.3
1878	Cin-N*	61	37	23	.617	2				34.9	2.1
1879	Cin-N*	63	34	28	.548	4	5		2/2	32.4	1.6
	3	157	91	64	.587						-0.6
Mele, Sabath Anthony "Sam"											
1961	Min-A	7	2	5	.286	8	9	7	2/4	3.2	-1.2
	Min-A	95	45	49	.479	9	7		4/4	42.9	2.1
1962	Min-A	163	91	71	.562	2				89.4	1.6
1963	Min-A	161	91	70	.565	3				97.5	-6.5
1964	Min-A	163	79	83	.488	●6				87.0	-8.0
1965	Min-A	162	102	60	.630	1				98.9	3.1
1966	Min-A	162	89	73	.549	2				89.9	-0.9
1967	Min-A	50	25	25	.500	6	●2		1/2	27.7	-2.7
	7	963	524	436	.546						-12.4
Melillo, Oscar Donald "Ski"											
1938	StL-A	10	2	7	.222	7	7		2/2	3.4	-1.4
Merrill, Carl Harrison "Stump"											
1990	NY-A	113	49	64	.434	7 E	7 E		2/2	45.9	3.1
1991	NY-A	162	71	91	.438	5 E				70.7	0.3
	2	275	120	155	.436						3.4
Metro, Charles "Charlie"											
1962	Chi-N	112	43	69	.384	9	9		3/3	42.5	0.5
1970	KC-A	52	19	33	.365	5 W	●4 W		1/2	22.8	-3.8
	2	164	62	102	.378						-3.3
Meyer, William Adam "Billy"											
1948	Pit-N	156	83	71	.539	4				77.7	5.3
1949	Pit-N	154	71	83	.461	6				69.3	1.7
1950	Pit-N	154	57	96	.373	8				59.8	-2.8
1951	Pit-N	155	64	90	.416	7				62.1	1.9
1952	Pit-N	155	42	112	.273	8				48.3	-6.3
	5	774	317	452	.412						-0.2
Michael, Eugene Richard "Gene"											
1981(1)	NY-A	56	34	22	.607	♦1 E					
(2)	NY-A	26	14	12	.538	4 E	6 E		1/2	47.7	0.3
1982	NY-A	86	44	42	.512	●4 E	●5 E	5 E	2/3	42.6	1.4
1986	Chi-N	102	46	56	.451	5 E	5 E		3/3	44.6	1.4
1987	Chi-N	136	68	68	.500	5 E	6 E		1/2	61.3	6.7
	4	406	206	200	.507						9.7

YEAR	TM/L	G	W	L	PCT	STANDING			M/YW	EXP	A-E

Milan, Jesse Clyde "Clyde"

| 1922 | Was-A* | 154 | 69 | 85 | .448 | 6 | | | | 71.3 | -2.3 |

Miller, George Frederick

| 1894 | StL-N* | 133 | 56 | 76 | .424 | 9 | | | | 50.8 | 5.2 |

Miller, Raymond Roger "Ray"

1985	Min-A	100	50	50	.500	6 W	4 W		2/2	45.3	4.7
1986	Min-A	139	59	80	.424	7 W	6 W		1/2	61.4	-2.4
1998	Bal-A	162	79	83	.488	4 E				84.1	-5.1
	3	401	188	213	.469						-2.8

Mills, Colonel Buster "Buster"

| 1953 | Cin-N | 8 | 4 | 4 | .500 | 6 | 6 | | 2/2 | 3.6 | 0.4 |

Mills, Everett

| 1872 | Bal-n* | 17 | 8 | 6 | .571 | 2 | 2 | | 2/2 | 10.3 | -2.3 |

Mitchell, Frederick Francis "Fred"

1917	Chi-N	157	74	80	.481	5				75.3	-1.3
1918	Chi-N	131	84	45	.651	1				80.8	3.2
1919	Chi-N	140	75	65	.536	3				75.7	-0.7
1920	Chi-N	154	75	79	.487	●5				75.3	-0.3
1921	Bos-N	153	79	74	.516	4				78.9	0.1
1922	Bos-N	154	53	100	.346	8				54.2	-1.2
1923	Bos-N	155	54	100	.351	7				61.0	-7.0
	7	1044	494	543	.476						-7.2

Moore, Jackie Spencer

1984	Oak-A	118	57	61	.483	5 W	4 W		2/2	54.9	2.1
1985	Oak-A	162	77	85	.475	●4 W				78.1	-1.1
1986	Oak-A	73	29	44	.397	●6 W	●3 W		1/3	35.2	-6.2
	3	353	163	190	.462						-5.2

Moore, Terry Bluford

| 1954 | Phi-N | 77 | 35 | 42 | .455 | 3 | 4 | | 2/2 | 40.8 | -5.8 |

Moran, Patrick Joseph "Pat"

1915	Phi-N	153	90	62	.592	1				90.4	-0.4
1916	Phi-N	154	91	62	.595	2				87.0	4.0
1917	Phi-N	155	87	65	.572	2				84.8	2.2
1918	Phi-N	125	55	68	.447	6				53.1	1.9
1919	Cin-N	140	96	44	.686	★1				90.0	6.0
1920	Cin-N	154	82	71	.536	3				84.0	-2.0
1921	Cin-N	153	70	83	.458	6				73.3	-3.3
1922	Cin-N	156	86	68	.558	2				85.8	0.2
1923	Cin-N	154	91	63	.591	2				85.0	6.0
	9	1344	748	586	.561						14.6

Morgan, Joseph Michael "Joe"

1988	Bos-A	77	46	31	.597	4 E	1 E		2/2	44.3	1.7
1989	Bos-A	162	83	79	.512	3 E				84.8	-1.8
1990	Bos-A	162	88	74	.543	1 E				84.6	3.4
1991	Bos-A	162	84	78	.519	●2 E				82.9	1.1
	4	563	301	262	.535						4.3

Moriarty, George Joseph

1927	Det-A	156	82	71	.536	4				80.2	1.8
1928	Det-A	154	68	86	.442	6				71.3	-3.3
	2	310	150	157	.489						-1.5

Morrill, John Francis

1882	Bos-N*	85	45	39	.536	●3				47.4	-2.4
1883	Bos-N*	44	33	11	.750	4	1		2/2	30.5	2.5
1884	Bos-N*	116	73	38	.658	2				76.1	-3.1
1885	Bos-N*	113	46	66	.411	5				50.2	-4.2
1886	Bos-N*	118	56	61	.479	5				58.1	-2.1
1887	Bos-N*	32	12	17	.414	5	5		2/2	15.3	-3.3
1888	Bos-N*	137	70	64	.522	4				71.9	-1.9
1889	Was-N*	51	13	38	.255	8	8		1/2	16.2	-3.2
	8	696	348	334	.510						-17.7

Morton, Charles Hazen "Charlie"

1884	Tol-a*	110	46	58	.442	8				41.4	4.6
1885	Det-N*	38	7	31	.184	8	6		1/2	16.7	-9.7
1890	Tol-a	134	68	64	.515	4				70.6	-2.6
	3	282	121	153	.442						-7.8

Moses, Felix I.

| 1884 | Ric-a | 46 | 12 | 30 | .286 | 12 | | | | 11.8 | 0.2 |

Moss, John Lester "Les"

1968	Chi-A	2	0	2	.000	9	9	●8	2/5	0.9	-0.9
	Chi-A	34	12	22	.353	9	9	●8	4/5	15.4	-3.4
1979	Det-A	53	27	26	.509	5 E	5 E		1/3	27.5	-0.5
	2	89	39	50	.438						-4.8

Murnane, Timothy Hayes "Tim"

| 1884 | Bos-U* | 111 | 58 | 51 | .532 | 5 | | | | 61.6 | -3.6 |

Murray, William Jeremiah "Billy"

1907	Phi-N	149	83	64	.565	3				77.7	5.3
1908	Phi-N	155	83	71	.539	4				84.2	-1.2
1909	Phi-N	154	74	79	.484	5				76.3	-2.3
	3	458	240	214	.529						1.9

Murtaugh, Daniel Edward "Danny"

1957	Pit-N	51	26	25	.510	7	●7		2/2	21.7	4.3
1958	Pit-N	154	84	70	.545	2				82.7	1.3
1959	Pit-N	155	78	76	.506	4				74.0	4.0
1960	Pit-N	155	95	59	.617	★1				91.5	3.5
1961	Pit-N	154	75	79	.487	6				78.9	-3.9
1962	Pit-N	161	93	68	.578	4				88.8	4.2
1963	Pit-N	162	74	88	.457	8				77.9	-3.9
1964	Pit-N	162	80	82	.494	●6				83.9	-3.9
1967	Pit-N	79	39	39	.500	6	6		2/2	38.3	0.7
1970	Pit-N	162	89	73	.549	1 E				87.7	1.3
1971	Pit-N	162	97	65	.599	★1 E				100.4	-3.4
1973	Pit-N	26	13	13	.500	2 E	3 E		2/2	13.2	-0.2
1974	Pit-N	162	88	74	.543	1 E				90.6	-2.6
1975	Pit-N	161	92	69	.571	1 E				96.2	-4.2
1976	Pit-N	162	92	70	.568	2 E				89.1	2.9
	15	2068	1115	950	.540						0.2

Muser, Anthony Joseph "Tony"

1997	KC-A	79	31	48	.392	4 C	5 C		2/2	36.1	-5.1
1998	KC-A	161	72	89	.447	3 C				63.0	9.0
	2	240	103	137	.429						4.0

Mutrie, James J. "Jim"

1883	NY-a	97	54	42	.563	4				57.1	-3.1
1884	NY-a	112	75	32	.701	1				82.5	-7.5
1885	NY-N	112	85	27	.759	2				87.3	-2.3
1886	NY-N	124	75	44	.630	3				72.2	2.8
1887	NY-N	129	68	55	.553	4				69.6	-1.6
1888	NY-N	138	84	47	.641	1				84.3	-0.3
1889	NY-N	131	83	43	.659	1				82.2	0.8
1890	NY-N	135	63	68	.481	6				66.9	-3.9
1891	NY-N	136	71	61	.538	3				69.9	1.1
	9	1114	658	419	.611						-14.1

Myatt, George Edward "George"

1968	Phi-N	1	1	0	1.000	●6	5	●7	2/3	0.5	0.5
1969	Phi-N	54	19	35	.352	5 E	5 E		2/2	23.6	-4.6
	2	55	20	35	.364						-4.0

Myers, Henry C.

| 1882 | Bal-a* | 74 | 19 | 54 | .260 | 6 | | | | 14.2 | 4.8 |

Nash, William Mitchell "Billy"

| 1896 | Phi-N* | 130 | 62 | 68 | .477 | 8 | | | | 64.9 | -2.9 |

Neun, John Henry "Johnny"

1946	NY-A	14	8	6	.571	3	3		3/3	8.3	-0.3
1947	Cin-N	154	73	81	.474	5				69.7	3.3
1948	Cin-N	100	44	56	.440	7	7		1/2	39.1	4.9
	3	268	125	143	.466						7.8

Newman, Jeffrey Lynn "Jeff"

| 1986 | Oak-A | 10 | 2 | 8 | .200 | ●6 W | 7 W | ●3 W | 2/3 | 4.8 | -2.8 |

Nichols, Charles Augustus "Kid"

1904	StL-N*	155	75	79	.487	5				77.8	-2.8
1905	StL-N*	14	5	9	.357	7	6		1/3	5.1	-0.1
	2	169	80	88	.476						-2.9

Nicol, Hugh

| 1897 | StL-N | 40 | 8 | 32 | .200 | 12 | 12 | 12 | 2/4 | 7.3 | 0.7 |

Nixon, Russell Eugene "Russ"

1982	Cin-N	70	27	43	.386	6 W	6 W		2/2	29.5	-2.5
1983	Cin-N	162	74	88	.457	6 W				71.9	2.1
1988	Atl-N	121	42	79	.347	6 W	6 W		2/2	45.7	-3.7
1989	Atl-N	161	63	97	.394	6 W				69.7	-6.7
1990	Atl-N	65	25	40	.385	6 W	6 W		1/2	27.0	-2.0
	5	579	231	347	.400						-12.8

Norman, Henry Willis Patrick "Bill"

1958	Det-A	105	56	49	.533	8	5		2/2	56.3	-0.3
1959	Det-A	17	2	15	.118	8	4		1/2	8.3	-1.2
	2	122	58	64	.475						-6.6

Oakes, Ennis Telfair "Rebel"

1914	Pit-F*	143	61	78	.439	8	7		2/2	60.6	0.4
1915	Pit-F*	156	86	67	.562	3				84.1	1.9
	2	299	147	145	.503						2.3

Oates, Johnny Lane

1991	Bal-A	125	54	71	.432	7 E	6 E		2/2	54.1	-0.1
1992	Bal-A	162	89	73	.549	3 E				86.1	2.9
1993	Bal-A	162	85	77	.525	●3 E				85.0	-0.0
1994	Bal-A	112	63	49	.563	2 E				64.9	-1.9
1995	Tex-A	144	74	70	.514	3 W				69.2	4.8
1996	Tex-A	163	90	72	.556	○1 W				92.9	-2.9
1997	Tex-A	162	77	85	.475	3 W				79.5	-2.5
1998	Tex-A	162	88	74	.543	○1 W				87.2	0.8
	8	1192	620	571	.521						1.2

O'Connor, John Joseph "Jack"

| 1910 | StL-A* | 158 | 47 | 107 | .305 | 8 | | | | 45.1 | 1.9 |

O'Day, Henry Francis "Hank"

1912	Cin-N	155	75	78	.490	4				69.9	5.1
1914	Chi-N	156	78	76	.506	4				73.5	4.5
	2	311	153	154	.498						9.6

O'Farrell, Robert Arthur "Bob"

| 1927 | StL-N* | 153 | 92 | 61 | .601 | 2 | | | | 85.3 | 6.7 |
| 1934 | Cin-N* | 91 | 30 | 60 | .333 | 8 | 8 | | 1/3 | 32.5 | -2.5 |

YEAR	TM/L	G	W	L	PCT	STANDING			M/YW-EXP		A-E
	2	244	122	121	.502						4.2
O'Leary, Daniel "Dan"											
1884	Cin-U*	35	20	15	.571	5	3		1/2	24.6	-4.6
O'Neill, Stephen Francis "Steve"											
1935	Cle-A	60	36	23	.610	5	3		2/2	30.9	5.1
1936	Cle-A	157	80	74	.519	5				82.3	-2.3
1937	Cle-A	156	83	71	.539	4				81.6	1.4
1943	Det-A	155	78	76	.506	5				84.8	-6.8
1944	Det-A	156	88	66	.571	2				85.2	2.8
1945	Det-A	155	88	65	.575	★1				83.8	4.2
1946	Det-A	155	92	62	.597	2				91.4	0.6
1947	Det-A	158	85	69	.552	2				84.4	0.6
1948	Det-A	154	78	76	.506	5				74.4	3.6
1950	Bos-A	95	63	32	.663	4	3		2/2	59.5	3.5
1951	Bos-A	154	87	67	.565	3				84.5	2.5
1952	Phi-N	91	59	32	.648	6	4		2/2	52.1	6.9
1953	Phi-N	156	83	71	.539	●3				82.0	1.0
1954	Phi-N	77	40	37	.519	3	4		1/2	40.8	-0.8
	14	1879	1040	821	.559						22.2
Onslow, John James "Jack"											
1949	Chi-A	154	63	91	.409	6				68.1	-5.1
1950	Chi-A	31	8	22	.267	8	6		1/2	12.6	-4.6
	2	185	71	113	.386						-9.7
O'Rourke, James Henry "Jim"											
1881	Buf-N*	83	45	38	.542	3				40.9	4.1
1882	Buf-N*	84	45	39	.536	●3				45.5	-0.5
1883	Buf-N*	98	52	45	.536	5				51.8	0.2
1884	Buf-N*	115	64	47	.577	3				62.0	2.0
1893	Was-N*	130	40	89	.310	12				39.2	0.8
	5	510	246	258	.488						6.7
Orr, David L. "Dave"											
1887	NY-a*	8	3	5	.375	8	7	7	2/3	2.3	0.7
Ott, Melvin Thomas "Mel"											
1942	NY-N*	154	85	67	.559	3				83.8	1.2
1943	NY-N*	156	55	98	.359	8				60.2	-5.2
1944	NY-N*	155	67	87	.435	5				68.1	-1.1
1945	NY-N*	154	78	74	.513	5				72.8	5.2
1946	NY-N*	154	61	93	.396	8				69.5	-8.5
1947	NY-N*	155	81	73	.526	4				83.5	-2.5
1948	NY-N	76	37	38	.493	4	5		1/2	41.1	-4.1
	7	1004	464	530	.467						-14.9
Owens, Paul Francis											
1972	Phi-N	80	33	47	.412	6 E	6 E		2/2	32.5	0.5
1983	Phi-N	77	47	30	.610	1 E	◆1 E		2/2	41.5	5.5
1984	Phi-N	162	81	81	.500	4 E				84.1	-3.1
	3	319	161	158	.505						2.9
Ozark, Daniel Leonard "Danny"											
1973	Phi-N	162	71	91	.438	6 E				73.2	-2.2
1974	Phi-N	162	80	82	.494	3 E				78.4	1.6
1975	Phi-N	162	86	76	.531	2 E				85.1	0.9
1976	Phi-N	162	101	61	.623	1 E				103.3	-2.3
1977	Phi-N	162	101	61	.623	1 E				98.6	2.4
1978	Phi-N	162	90	72	.556	1 E				94.0	-4.0
1979	Phi-N	133	65	67	.492	5 E	4 E		1/2	63.1	1.9
1984	SF-N	56	24	32	.429	6 W	6 W		2/2	23.7	0.3
	8	1161	618	542	.533						-1.4
Pabor, Charles Henry "Charlie"											
1871	Cle-n*	29	10	19	.345	7				8.4	1.6
1875	Atl-n*	42	2	40	.048	12	12		1/2	-3.3	5.3
	NH-n*	6	1	5	.167	8	8		3/3	0.5	0.5
	2	77	13	64	.169						7.5
Parker, Francis James "Salty"											
1967	NY-N	11	4	7	.364	10	10		2/2	4.2	-0.2
1972	Hou-N	1	1	0	1.000	2 W	2 W		2/3	0.5	0.5
	2	12	5	7	.417						0.3
Parks, William Robert "Bill"											
1875	Was-n*	8	1	7	.125	8	10		2/2	-1.0	2.0
Parrish, Larry Alton											
1998	Det-A	162	12	14	.462	3 E			2/2	10.8	1.2
Pearce, Richard J. "Dickey"											
1872	Mut-n*	16	10	6	.625	4	3		1/2	11.6	-1.6
1875	StL-n*	70	39	29	.574	4				35.6	3.4
	2	86	49	35	.583						1.8
Peckinpaugh, Roger Thorpe											
1914	NY-A*	20	10	10	.500	7	●6		2/2	9.8	0.2
1928	Cle-A	155	62	92	.403	7				62.0	0.0
1929	Cle-A	152	81	71	.533	3				74.2	6.8
1930	Cle-A	154	81	73	.526	4				74.8	6.2
1931	Cle-A	155	78	76	.506	4				81.7	-3.7
1932	Cle-A	153	87	65	.572	4				85.1	1.9
1933	Cle-A	51	26	25	.510	5	4		1/3	25.0	1.0
1941	Cle-A	155	75	79	.487	●4				77.9	-2.9
	8	995	500	491	.505						9.5

YEAR	TM/L	G	W	L	PCT	STANDING			M/YW-EXP		A-E
Perez, Atanasio "Tony"											
1993	Cin-N	44	20	24	.455	5 W	5 W		1/2	20.3	-0.3
Perkins, Ralph Foster "Cy"											
1937	Det-A	15	6	9	.400	2	2		5/5	8.3	-2.3
Pesky, John Michael "Johnny"											
1963	Bos-A	161	76	85	.472	7				76.6	-0.6
1964	Bos-A	160	70	90	.438	8	8		1/2	69.7	0.3
1980	Bos-A	5	1	4	.200	3 E	4 E		2/2	2.5	-1.5
	3	326	147	179	.451						-1.8
Pfeffer, Nathaniel Frederick "Fred"											
1892(1)	Lou-N*	23	9	14	.391	10	11		2/2		
(2)	Lou-N*	77	33	42	.440	9				39.2	2.8
Phelan, Lewis G. "Lew"											
1895	StL-N	45	11	30	.268	11	11		4/4	13.1	-2.1
Phillips, Harold Ross "Lefty"											
1969	Cal-A	124	60	63	.488	6 W	3 W		2/2	51.0	9.0
1970	Cal-A	162	86	76	.531	3 W				81.1	4.9
1971	Cal-A	162	76	86	.469	4 W				73.5	2.5
	3	448	222	225	.497						16.4
Phillips, Horace B.											
1879	Tro-N	47	12	34	.261	8	8		1/2	10.8	1.2
1883	Col-a	97	32	65	.330	6				32.4	-0.4
1884	Pit-a	35	9	24	.273	10	10		5/5	7.4	1.6
1885	Pit-a	111	56	55	.505	3				56.3	-0.3
1886	Pit-a	140	80	57	.584	2				83.7	-3.7
1887	Pit-N	125	55	69	.444	6				50.3	4.7
1888	Pit-N	139	66	68	.493	6				62.1	3.9
1889	Pit-N	71	28	43	.394	6	5		1/3	31.9	-3.9
	8	765	338	415	.449						3.1
Phillips, William Corcoran "Bill"											
1914	Ind-F	157	88	65	.575	1				90.6	-2.6
1915	New-F	53	26	27	.491	6	5		1/2	27.4	-1.4
	2	210	114	92	.553						-4.0
Pike, Lipman Emanuel "Lip"											
1871	Tro-n*	4	1	3	.250	7	6		1/2	1.9	-0.9
1874	Har-n*	53	16	37	.302	7				19.0	-3.0
1877	Cin-N*	14	3	11	.214	6	6		1/3	3.1	-0.1
	3	71	20	51	.282						-4.0
Piniella, Louis Victor "Lou"											
1986	NY-A	162	90	72	.556	2 E				86.8	3.2
1987	NY-A	162	89	73	.549	4 E				83.9	5.1
1988	NY-A	93	45	48	.484	2 E	5 E		2/2	47.9	-2.9
1990	Cin-N	162	91	71	.562	★1 W				91.2	-0.2
1991	Cin-N	162	74	88	.457	5 W				80.8	-6.8
1992	Cin-N	162	90	72	.556	2 W				86.5	3.5
1993	Sea-A	162	82	80	.506	4 W				81.3	0.7
1994	Sea-A	112	49	63	.438	3 W				51.7	-2.7
1995	Sea-A	145	79	66	.545	▲1 W	○			80.7	-1.7
1996	Sea-A	161	85	76	.528	2 W				89.1	-4.1
1997	Sea-A	162	90	72	.556	○1 W				89.4	0.6
1998	Sea-A	161	76	85	.472	3 W				80.9	-4.9
	12	1806	940	866	.520						-10.0
Plummer, William Francis "Bill"											
1992	Sea-A	162	64	98	.395	7 W				69.1	-5.1
Popowski, Edward Joseph "Eddie"											
1969	Bos-A	9	5	4	.556	3 E	3 E		2/2	4.5	0.5
1973	Bos-A	1	1	0	1.000	2 E	2 E		2/2	0.6	0.4
	2	10	6	4	.600						0.9
Porter, Matthew S. "Matt"											
1884	KC-U*	16	3	13	.188	8	8	8	2/3	2.5	0.5
Powers, Patrick Thomas "Pat"											
1890	Roc-a	133	63	63	.500	5				62.8	0.2
1892(1)	NY-N	74	31	43	.419	10					
(2)	NY-N	79	40	37	.519	6				74.1	-3.1
	2	286	134	143	.484						-2.9
Pratt, Albert George "Al"											
1882	Pit-a	79	39	39	.500	4				39.9	-0.9
1883	Pit-a	32	12	20	.375	6	7		1/3	10.4	1.6
	2	111	51	59	.464						0.6
Price, James L. "Jim"											
1884	NY-N	100	56	42	.571	4	●4		1/2	54.5	1.5
Prothro, James Thompson "Doc"											
1939	Phi-N	152	45	106	.298	8				45.6	-0.6
1940	Phi-N	153	50	103	.327	8				49.6	0.4
1941	Phi-N	155	43	111	.279	8				46.7	-3.7
	3	460	138	320	.301						-3.9
Purcell, William Aloysius "Blondie"											
1883	Phi-N*	82	13	68	.160	8	8		2/2	10.0	3.0
Queen, Melvin Douglas "Mel"											
1997	Tor-A	5	4	1	.800	5 E	5 E		2/2	2.4	1.6
Quilici, Francis Ralph "Frank"											
1972	Min-A	84	41	43	.488	3 W	3 W		2/2	42.1	-1.1

YEAR	TM/L	G	W	L	PCT	STANDING			M/YW-EXP		A-E
1973	Min-A	162	81	81	.500	3 W				85.6	-4.6
1974	Min-A	163	82	80	.506	3 W				81.4	0.6
1975	Min-A	159	76	83	.478	4 W				78.3	-2.3
	4	568	280	287	.494						-7.5
Quinn, Joseph J. "Joe"											
1895	StL-N*	40	11	28	.282	11	11	11	3/4	12.5	-1.5
1899	Cle-N*	116	12	104	.103	12	12		2/2	10.0	2.0
	2	156	23	132	.148						0.6
Rader, Douglas Lee "Doug"											
1983	Tex-A	163	77	85	.475	3 W				84.3	-7.3
1984	Tex-A	161	69	92	.429	7 W				74.5	-5.5
1985	Tex-A	32	9	23	.281	7 W	7 W		1/2	12.6	-3.6
1986	Chi-A	2	1	1	.500	6 W	5 W	5 W	2/3	0.9	0.1
1989	Cal-A	162	91	71	.562	3 W				90.8	0.2
1990	Cal-A	162	80	82	.494	4 W				79.4	0.6
1991	Cal-A	124	61	63	.492	7 W	7 W		1/2	62.3	-1.3
	7	806	388	417	.482						-16.9
Rapp, Vernon Fred "Vern"											
1977	StL-N	162	83	79	.512	3 E				86.0	-3.0
1978	StL-N	17	6	11	.353	6 E	5 E		1/3	7.9	-1.9
1984	Cin-N	121	51	70	.421	5 W	5 W		1/2	51.3	-0.3
	3	300	140	160	.467						-5.1
Reach, Alfred James "Al"											
1890	Phi-N	11	4	7	.364	2	3	3	3/5	6.4	-2.4
Regan, Philip Raymond "Phil"											
1995	Bal-A	144	71	73	.493	3 E				78.3	-7.3
Rice, Delbert "Del"											
1972	Cal-A	155	75	80	.484	5 W				68.1	6.9
Richards, Paul Rapier											
1951	Chi-A	155	81	73	.526	4				84.1	-3.1
1952	Chi-A	156	81	73	.526	3				81.6	-0.6
1953	Chi-A	156	89	65	.578	3				89.8	-0.8
1954	Chi-A	146	91	54	.628	3	3		1/2	91.5	-0.5
1955	Bal-A	156	57	97	.370	7				54.7	2.3
1956	Bal-A	154	69	85	.448	6				63.0	6.0
1957	Bal-A	154	76	76	.500	5				77.0	-1.0
1958	Bal-A	154	74	79	.484	6				70.4	3.6
1959	Bal-A	155	74	80	.481	6				69.4	4.6
1960	Bal-A	154	89	65	.578	2				84.9	4.1
1961	Bal-A	136	78	57	.578	3	3		1/2	76.7	1.3
1976	Chi-A	161	64	97	.398	6 W				63.9	0.1
	12	1837	923	901	.506						15.9
Richardson, Daniel "Danny"											
1892(2)	Was-N*	43	12	31	.279	11	12		2/2	17.9	-5.9
Rickey, Wesley Branch "Branch"											
1913	StL-A	12	5	6	.455	7	8		3/3	4.6	0.4
1914	StL-A*	159	71	82	.464	5				66.2	4.8
1915	StL-A	159	63	91	.409	6				59.6	3.4
1919	StL-N	138	54	83	.394	7				58.7	-4.7
1920	StL-N	155	75	79	.487	●5				76.3	-1.3
1921	StL-N	154	87	66	.569	3				88.8	-1.8
1922	StL-N	154	85	69	.552	●3				81.0	4.0
1923	StL-N	154	79	74	.516	5				77.9	1.1
1924	StL-N	154	65	89	.422	6				76.0	-11.0
1925	StL-N	38	13	25	.342	8	4		1/2	20.5	-7.5
	10	1277	597	664	.473						-12.6
Riddoch, Gregory Lee "Greg"											
1990	SD-N	82	38	44	.463	4 W	5 W		2/2	41.0	-3.0
1991	SD-N	162	84	78	.519	3 W				79.9	4.1
1992	SD-N	150	78	72	.520	3 W	3 W		1/2	73.1	4.9
	3	394	200	194	.508						6.0
Riggleman, James David "Jim"											
1992	SD-N	12	4	8	.333	3 W	3 W		2/2	5.8	-1.8
1993	SD-N	162	61	101	.377	7 W				71.7	-10.7
1994	SD-N	117	47	70	.402	4 W				53.2	-6.2
1995	Chi-N	144	73	71	.507	3 C				74.1	-1.1
1996	Chi-N	162	76	86	.469	4 C				81.1	-5.1
1997	Chi-N	162	68	94	.420	5 C				73.8	-5.8
1998	Chi-N	163	90	73	.552	▲○■2 C				85.2	4.8
	7	922	419	503	.454						-25.9
Rigney, William Joseph "Bill"											
1956	NY-N	154	67	87	.435	6				65.1	1.9
1957	NY-N	154	69	85	.448	6				71.1	-2.1
1958	SF-N	154	80	74	.519	3				79.9	0.1
1959	SF-N	154	83	71	.539	3				86.4	-3.4
1960	SF-N	58	33	25	.569	2	5		1/2	30.6	2.4
1961	LA-A	162	70	91	.435	8				76.6	-6.6
1962	LA-A	162	86	76	.531	3				82.2	3.8
1963	LA-A	161	70	91	.435	9				73.7	-3.7
1964	LA-A	162	82	80	.506	5				80.2	1.8
1965	Cal-A	162	75	87	.463	7				76.2	-1.2
1966	Cal-A	162	80	82	.494	6				76.8	3.2
1967	Cal-A	161	84	77	.522	5				78.3	5.7
1968	Cal-A	162	67	95	.414	8				67.6	-0.6
1969	Cal-A	39	11	28	.282	6 W	3 W		1/2	16.2	-5.2

YEAR	TM/L	G	W	L	PCT	STANDING			M/YW-EXP		A-E
1970	Min-A	162	98	64	.605	1 W				95.5	2.5
1971	Min-A	160	74	86	.463	5 W				78.3	-4.3
1972	Min-A	70	36	34	.514	3 W	3 W		1/2	35.1	0.9
1976	SF-N	162	74	88	.457	4 W				71.3	2.7
	18	2561	1239	1321	.484						-2.0
Ripken, Calvin Edwin Sr. "Cal"											
1985	Bal-A	1	1	0	1.000	4 E	4 E	4 E	2/3	0.5	0.5
1987	Bal-A	162	67	95	.414	6 E				66.6	0.4
1988	Bal-A	6	0	6	.000	7 E	7 E		1/2	2.1	-2.1
	3	169	68	101	.402						-1.2
Robinson, Frank											
1975	Cle-A*	159	79	80	.497	4 E				78.0	1.0
1976	Cle-A*	159	81	78	.509	4 E				79.5	1.5
1977	Cle-A	57	26	31	.456	5 E	5 E		1/2	26.2	-0.2
1981(1)	SF-N	59	27	32	.458	5 W					
(2)	SF-N	52	29	23	.558	3 W				56.9	-0.9
1982	SF-N	162	87	75	.537	3 W				79.6	7.4
1983	SF-N	162	79	83	.488	5 W				80.0	-1.0
1984	SF-N	106	42	64	.396	6 W	6 W		1/2	44.9	-2.9
1988	Bal-A	155	54	101	.348	7 E	7 E		2/2	53.6	0.4
1989	Bal-A	162	87	75	.537	2 E				83.3	3.7
1990	Bal-A	162	76	85	.472	5 E				77.5	-1.5
1991	Bal-A	37	13	24	.351	7 E	6 E		1/2	16.0	-3.0
	11	1432	680	751	.475						4.6
Robinson, Wilbert											
1902	Bal-A*	83	24	57	.296	7	8		2/2	33.5	-9.5
1914	Bro-N	154	75	79	.487	5				77.4	-2.4
1915	Bro-N	154	80	72	.526	3				73.3	6.7
1916	Bro-N	156	94	60	.610	1				90.1	3.9
1917	Bro-N	156	70	81	.464	7				70.0	-0.0
1918	Bro-N	127	57	69	.452	5				50.9	6.1
1919	Bro-N	141	69	71	.493	5				71.3	-2.3
1920	Bro-N	155	93	61	.604	1				91.3	1.7
1921	Bro-N	152	77	75	.507	5				74.6	2.4
1922	Bro-N	155	76	78	.494	6				75.9	0.1
1923	Bro-N	155	76	78	.494	6				78.2	-2.2
1924	Bro-N	154	92	62	.597	2				81.2	10.8
1925	Bro-N	153	68	85	.444	●6				69.2	-1.2
1926	Bro-N	155	71	82	.464	6				68.1	2.9
1927	Bro-N	154	65	88	.425	6				68.0	-3.0
1928	Bro-N	155	77	76	.503	6				79.1	-2.1
1929	Bro-N	153	70	83	.458	6				64.3	5.7
1930	Bro-N	154	86	68	.558	4				89.3	-3.3
1931	Bro-N	153	79	73	.520	4				76.8	2.2
	19	2819	1399	1398	.500						16.4
Robison, Matthew Stanley "Stanley"											
1905	StL-N	50	19	31	.380	6	6		3/3	18.2	0.8
Rodgers, Robert Leroy "Buck"											
1980	Mil-A	47	26	21	.553	2 E	3 E		1/3	27.2	-1.2
	Mil-A	23	13	10	.565	4 E	3 E		3/3	13.3	-0.3
1981(1)	Mil-A	56	31	25	.554	3 E					
(2)	Mil-A	53	31	22	.585	1 E				58.0	4.0
1982	Mil-A	47	23	24	.489	5 E	♦1 E		1/2	28.3	-5.3
1985	Mon-N	161	84	77	.522	3 E				80.2	3.8
1986	Mon-N	161	78	83	.484	4 E				75.2	2.8
1987	Mon-N	162	91	71	.562	3 E				83.1	7.9
1988	Mon-N	163	81	81	.500	3 E				84.9	-3.9
1989	Mon-N	162	81	81	.500	4 E				81.2	-0.2
1990	Mon-N	162	85	77	.525	3 E				87.9	-2.9
1991	Mon-N	49	20	29	.408	6 E	6 E		1/2	22.0	-2.0
	Cal-A	38	20	18	.526	7 W	7 W		2/2	19.1	0.9
1992	Cal-A	39	19	20	.487	5 W	●5 W		1/3	17.1	1.9
	Cal-A	34	14	20	.412	5 W	●5 W		3/3	14.9	-0.9
1993	Cal-A	162	71	91	.438	●5 W				72.4	-1.4
1994	Cal-A	39	16	23	.410	3 W	4 W		1/3	15.8	0.2
	13	1558	784	773	.504						3.4
Rogers, James F. "Jim"											
1897	Lou-N*	44	17	24	.415	9	11		1/2	15.2	1.8
Rojas, Octavio Victor "Cookie"											
1988	Cal-A	154	75	79	.487	4 W	4 W		1/2	71.6	3.4
1996	Fla-N	1	1	0	1.000	4 E	4 E	3 E	2/3	0.5	0.5
	2	155	76	79	.490						3.9
Rolfe, Robert Abial "Red"											
1949	Det-A	155	87	67	.565	4				86.6	0.4
1950	Det-A	157	95	59	.617	2				88.8	6.2
1951	Det-A	154	73	81	.474	5				71.5	1.5
1952	Det-A	73	23	49	.319	8	8		1/2	27.2	-4.2
	4	539	278	256	.521						3.9
Rose, Peter Edward "Pete"											
1984	Cin-N*	41	19	22	.463	5 W	5 W		2/2	17.4	1.6
1985	Cin-N*	162	89	72	.553	2 W				81.6	7.4
1986	Cin-N*	162	86	76	.531	2 W				82.5	3.5
1987	Cin-N	162	84	78	.519	2 W				84.0	-0.0
1988	Cin-N	23	11	12	.478	4 W	2 W		1/3	12.2	-1.2
	Cin-N	111	64	47	.577	4 W	2 W		3/3	58.9	5.1
1989	Cin-N	125	59	66	.472	●4 W	5 W		1/2	57.7	1.3

YEAR	TM/L	G	W	L	PCT	STANDING			M/YW-EXP		A-E
	6	786	412	373	.525						17.7
Roseman, James John "Chief"											
1890	StL-a*	15	7	8	.467	4	5	3	3/6	8.8	-1.8
Rothschild, Lawrence Lee "Larry"											
1998	TB-A	162	63	99	.389	5 E				67.5	-4.5
Rowe, David E. "Dave"											
1886	KC-N*	126	30	91	.248	7				26.1	3.9
1888	KC-a*	50	14	36	.280	8	8		1/3	14.2	-0.2
	2	176	44	127	.257						3.7
Rowe, John Charles "Jack"											
1890	Buf-P*	81	22	58	.275	8	8		1/3	20.9	1.1
	Buf-P*	19	5	14	.263	8	8		3/3	5.0	0.0
Rowland, Clarence Henry "Pants"											
1915	Chi-A	156	93	61	.604	3				99.2	-6.2
1916	Chi-A	155	89	65	.578	2				88.7	0.3
1917	Chi-A	156	100	54	.649	★1				98.5	1.5
1918	Chi-A	124	57	67	.460	6				63.2	-6.2
	4	591	339	247	.578						-10.6
Ruel, Herold Dominic "Muddy"											
1947	StL-A	154	59	95	.383	8				58.5	0.5
Runnells, Thomas William "Tom"											
1991	Mon-N	112	51	61	.455	6 E	6 E		2/2	50.3	0.7
1992	Mon-N	37	17	20	.459	4 E	2 E		1/2	20.2	-3.2
	2	149	68	81	.456						-2.4
Runnels, James Edward "Pete"											
1966	Bos-A	16	8	8	.500	9	9		2/2	7.2	0.8
Russell, William Ellis "Bill"											
1996	LA-N	76	49	37	.570	1 W	■○2 W		2/2	45.8	3.2
1997	LA-N	162	88	74	.543	2 W				90.9	-2.9
1998	LA-N	74	36	38	.486	3 W	3 W		1/2	36.6	-0.6
	3	312	173	149	.537						-0.3
Ryan, Cornelius Joseph "Connie"											
1975	Atl-N	27	9	18	.333	5 W	5 W		2/2	10.8	-1.8
1977	Tex-A	6	2	4	.333	3 W	5 W	2 W	3/4	3.4	-1.4
	2	33	11	22	.333						-3.2
Sawyer, Edwin Milby "Eddie"											
1948	Phi-N	63	23	40	.365	6	6		3/3	25.7	-2.7
1949	Phi-N	154	81	73	.526	3				76.4	4.6
1950	Phi-N	157	91	63	.591	1				87.0	4.0
1951	Phi-N	154	73	81	.474	5				77.4	-4.4
1952	Phi-N	63	28	35	.444	6	4		1/2	36.1	-8.1
1958	Phi-N	70	30	40	.429	8	8		2/2	30.6	-0.6
1959	Phi-N	155	64	90	.416	8				64.1	-0.1
1960	Phi-N	1	0	1	1.000	●6	8		1/3	0.4	-0.4
	8	817	390	423	.480						-7.7
Scanlon, Michael B. "Mike"											
1884	Was-U	114	47	65	.420	6				46.3	0.7
1886	Was-N	82	13	67	.162	8	8		1/2	18.0	-5.0
	2	196	60	132	.313						-4.3
Schaefer, Robert Wald "Bob"											
1991	KC-A	1	1	0	1.000	7 W	7 W	6 W	2/3	0.5	0.5
Schalk, Raymond William "Ray"											
1927	Chi-A*	153	70	83	.458	5				71.9	-1.9
1928	Chi-A*	75	32	42	.432	6	5		1/2	33.7	-1.7
	2	228	102	125	.449						-3.6
Scheffing, Robert Boden "Bob"											
1957	Chi-N	156	62	92	.403	●7				67.4	-5.4
1958	Chi-N	154	72	82	.468	●5				75.4	-3.4
1959	Chi-N	155	74	80	.481	●5				75.5	-1.5
1961	Det-A	163	101	61	.623	2				97.7	3.3
1962	Det-A	161	85	76	.528	4				87.1	-2.1
1963	Det-A	60	24	36	.400	9	●5		1/2	29.9	-5.9
	6	849	418	427	.495						-15.1
Schlafly, Harry Linton "Larry"											
1914	Buf-F*	156	80	71	.530	4				77.4	2.6
1915	Buf-F	41	13	28	.317	8	6		1/3	18.8	-5.8
	2	197	93	99	.484						-3.2
Schmelz, Gustavius Heinrich "Gus"											
1884	Col-a	110	69	39	.639	2				66.3	2.7
1886	StL-N	126	43	79	.352	6				45.3	-2.3
1887	Cin-a	136	81	54	.600	2				80.2	0.8
1888	Cin-a	137	80	54	.597	4				78.1	1.9
1889	Cin-a	141	76	63	.547	4				80.7	-4.7
1890	Cle-N	78	21	55	.276	7	7		1/2	27.4	-6.4
	Col-a	57	38	13	.745	5	2		2/3	33.1	4.9
1891	Col-a	138	61	76	.445	6				61.6	-0.6
1894	Was-N	132	45	87	.341	11				47.5	-2.5
1895	Was-N	133	43	85	.336	10				47.2	-4.2
1896	Was-N	133	58	73	.443	●9				57.0	1.0
1897	Was-N	36	9	25	.265	11	●6		1/2	16.7	-7.7
	11	1357	624	703	.470						-17.2
Schoendienst, Albert Fred "Red"											
1965	StL-N	162	80	81	.497	7				83.9	-3.9

YEAR	TM/L	G	W	L	PCT	STANDING			M/YW-EXP		A-E
1966	StL-N	162	83	79	.512	6				80.3	2.7
1967	StL-N	161	101	60	.627	★1				95.3	5.7
1968	StL-N	162	97	65	.599	1				94.1	2.9
1969	StL-N	162	87	75	.537	4 E				87.2	-0.2
1970	StL-N	162	76	86	.469	4 E				80.7	-4.7
1971	StL-N	163	90	72	.556	2 E				85.0	5.0
1972	StL-N	156	75	81	.481	4 E				74.5	0.5
1973	StL-N	162	81	81	.500	2 E				85.3	-4.3
1974	StL-N	161	86	75	.534	2 E				84.1	1.9
1975	StL-N	163	82	80	.506	●3 E				78.2	3.8
1976	StL-N	162	72	90	.444	5 E				76.6	-4.6
1980	StL-N	37	18	19	.486	5 E	4 E		4/4	19.1	-1.1
1990	StL-N	24	13	11	.542	6 E	6 E	6 E	2/3	10.4	2.6
	14	1999	1041	955	.522						6.2
Schultz, Joseph Charles Jr. "Joe"											
1969	Sea-A	163	64	98	.395	6 W				64.8	-0.8
1973	Det-A	28	14	14	.500	3 E	3 E		2/2	13.4	0.6
	2	191	78	112	.411						-0.3
Selee, Frank Gibson											
1890	Bos-N	134	76	57	.571	5				82.5	-6.5
1891	Bos-N	140	87	51	.630	1				86.3	0.7
1892(1)	Bos-N	75	52	22	.703	1					
(2)	Bos-N	77	50	26	.658	2				95.3	6.7
1893	Bos-N	131	86	43	.667	1				81.7	4.3
1894	Bos-N	133	83	49	.629	3				82.0	1.0
1895	Bos-N	133	71	60	.542	●5				72.2	-1.2
1896	Bos-N	132	74	57	.565	4				74.4	-0.4
1897	Bos-N	135	93	39	.705	1				96.5	-3.5
1898	Bos-N	152	102	47	.685	1				99.3	2.7
1899	Bos-N	153	95	57	.625	2				96.4	-1.4
1900	Bos-N	142	66	72	.478	4				72.6	-6.6
1901	Bos-N	140	69	69	.500	5				66.3	2.7
1902	Chi-N	143	68	69	.496	5				71.7	-3.7
1903	Chi-N	139	82	56	.594	3				78.4	3.6
1904	Chi-N	156	93	60	.608	2				85.7	7.3
1905	Chi-N	65	37	28	.569	4	3		1/2	43.2	-6.2
	16	2180	1284	862	.598						-0.6
Sewell, James Luther "Luke"											
1941	StL-A	113	55	55	.500	7	●6		2/2	51.1	3.9
1942	StL-A*	151	82	69	.543	3				84.8	-2.8
1943	StL-A	153	72	80	.474	6				75.1	-3.1
1944	StL-A	154	89	65	.578	1				87.1	1.9
1945	StL-A	154	81	70	.536	3				80.9	0.1
1946	StL-A	125	53	71	.427	7	7		1/2	54.6	-1.6
1949	Cin-N	3	1	2	.333	7	7		2/2	1.2	-0.2
1950	Cin-N	153	66	87	.431	6				68.5	-2.5
1951	Cin-N	155	68	86	.442	6				65.5	2.5
1952	Cin-N	98	39	59	.398	7	6		1/3	46.1	-7.1
	10	1259	606	644	.485						-9.0
Shannon, Daniel W. "Dan"											
1889	Lou-a*	58	10	46	.179	8	8	8	3/4	12.1	-2.1
1891	Was-a*	51	15	34	.306	7	8	8	3/4	13.0	2.0
	2	109	25	80	.238						-0.1
Sharsig, William A. "Bill"											
1886	Phi-a	41	22	17	.564	6	6		2/2	15.3	6.7
1888	Phi-a	137	81	52	.609	3				88.1	-7.1
1889	Phi-a	138	75	58	.564	3				74.5	0.5
1890	Phi-a	132	54	78	.409	7				45.4	8.6
1891	Phi-a	18	6	11	.353	7	4		1/2	8.8	-2.8
	5	466	238	216	.524						5.9
Shawkey, James Robert "Bob"											
1930	NY-A	154	86	68	.558	3				90.8	-4.8
Sheehan, Thomas Clancy "Tom"											
1960	SF-N	98	46	50	.479	2	5		2/2	50.6	-4.6
Shepard, Lawrence William "Larry"											
1968	Pit-N	163	80	82	.494	6				86.9	-6.9
1969	Pit-N	157	84	73	.535	3 E	3 E		1/2	85.8	-1.8
	2	320	164	155	.514						-8.6
Sherry, Norman Burt "Norm"											
1976	Cal-A	66	37	29	.561	6 W	●4 W		2/2	29.3	7.7
1977	Cal-A	81	39	42	.481	5 W	5 W		1/2	39.5	-0.5
	2	147	76	71	.517						7.2
Shettsline, William Joseph "Bill"											
1898	Phi-N	104	59	44	.573	●8	6		2/2	54.0	5.0
1899	Phi-N	154	94	58	.618	3				91.8	2.2
1900	Phi-N	141	75	63	.543	3				70.6	4.4
1901	Phi-N	140	83	57	.593	2				82.8	0.2
1902	Phi-N	138	56	81	.409	7				51.2	4.8
	5	677	367	303	.548						16.6
Shotton, Burton Edwin "Burt"											
1928	Phi-N	152	43	109	.283	8				48.7	-5.7
1929	Phi-N	154	71	82	.464	5				65.1	5.9
1930	Phi-N	156	52	102	.338	8				56.4	-4.4
1931	Phi-N	155	66	88	.429	6				63.2	2.8
1932	Phi-N	154	78	76	.506	4				81.4	-3.4

YEAR	TM/L	G	W	L	PCT	STANDING			M/Y	W-EXP	A-E
1933	Phi-N	152	60	92	.395	7				60.7	-0.7
1934	Cin-N	1	1	0	1.000	8	8	8	2/3	0.4	0.6
1947	Bro-N	153	92	60	.605	●1	1		2/2	86.3	5.7
1948	Bro-N	81	48	33	.593	5	3		3/3	44.5	3.5
1949	Bro-N	156	97	57	.630	1				98.8	-1.8
1950	Bro-N	155	89	65	.578	2				88.6	0.4
	11	1469	697	764	.477						3.0
Showalter, William Nathaniel "Buck"											
1992	NY-A	162	76	86	.469	●4 E				79.7	-3.7
1993	NY-A	162	88	74	.543	2 E				86.8	1.2
1994	NY-A	113	70	43	.619	1 E				69.0	1.0
1995	NY-A	144	79	65	.549	■2 E				77.8	1.2
1998	Ari-N	162	65	97	.401	5 W				66.4	-1.4
	5	743	378	365	.509						-1.7
Silvestri, Kenneth Joseph "Ken"											
1967	Atl-N	3	0	3	.000	7	7		2/2	1.5	-1.5
Simmons, Joseph S. "Joe"											
1875	Wes-n*	13	1	12	.077	13				2.5	-1.5
1884	Wil-U	18	2	16	.111	8				0.8	1.2
	2	31	3	28	.097						-0.2
Simmons, Lewis "Lew"											
1886	Phi-a	98	41	55	.427	6	6		1/2	37.7	3.3
Sisler, George Harold											
1924	StL-A*	153	74	78	.487	4				72.3	1.7
1925	StL-A*	154	82	71	.536	3				76.0	6.0
1926	StL-A*	155	62	92	.403	7				61.4	0.6
	3	462	218	241	.475						8.3
Sisler, Richard Allan "Dick"											
1964	Cin-N	6	3	3	.500	3	4	●2	2/4	3.4	-0.4
	Cin-N	47	29	18	.617	3	●2		4/4	26.5	2.5
1965	Cin-N	162	89	73	.549	4				92.8	-3.8
	2	215	121	94	.563						-1.7
Skaff, Francis Michael "Frank"											
1966	Det-A	79	40	39	.506	2	3		3/3	40.5	-0.5
Skinner, Robert Ralph "Bob"											
1968	Phi-N	107	48	59	.449	5	●7		3/3	48.2	-0.2
1969	Phi-N	108	44	64	.407	5 E	5 E		1/2	47.2	-3.2
1977	SD-N	1	1	0	1.000	4 W	4 W	5 W	2/3	0.4	0.6
	3	216	93	123	.431						-2.7
Slattery, John Terrence "Jack"											
1928	Bos-N	31	11	20	.355	7	7		1/2	10.7	0.3
Smith, Edward Mayo "Mayo"											
1955	Phi-N	154	77	77	.500	4				77.9	-0.9
1956	Phi-N	154	71	83	.461	5				70.0	1.0
1957	Phi-N	156	77	77	.500	5				73.5	3.5
1958	Phi-N	84	39	45	.464	8	8		1/2	36.7	2.3
1959	Cin-N	80	35	45	.438	7	●5		1/2	41.3	-6.3
1967	Det-A	163	91	71	.562	●2				91.3	-0.3
1968	Det-A	164	103	59	.636	★1				101.2	1.8
1969	Det-A	162	90	72	.556	2 E				91.6	-1.6
1970	Det-A	162	79	83	.488	4 E				74.4	4.6
	9	1279	662	612	.520						4.0
Smith, George Henry "Heinie"											
1902	NY-N*	32	5	27	.156	4	8	8	2/3	11.0	-6.0
Smith, Harry Thomas											
1909	Bos-N*	79	23	54	.299	8	8		2/2	24.6	-1.6
Smith, William J. "Bill"											
1873	Mar-n*	6	0	6	.000	9				-3.9	3.9
Snyder, Charles N. "Pop"											
1882	Cin-a*	80	55	25	.688	1				61.6	-6.6
1883	Cin-a*	98	61	37	.622	3				71.6	-10.6
1884	Cin-a*	40	24	14	.632	5	5		2/2	26.5	-2.5
1891	Was-a*	70	23	46	.333	6	7	8	2/4	18.3	4.7
	4	288	163	122	.572						-14.9
Snyder, James Robert "Jim"											
1988	Sea-A	105	45	60	.429	6 W	7 W		2/2	47.2	-2.2
Sothoron, Allen Sutton											
1933	StL-A	8	2	6	.250	8	8	8	2/3	3.2	-1.2
Southworth, William Harrison "Billy"											
1929	StL-N*	90	43	45	.489	4	4		1/3	45.3	-2.3
1940	StL-N	111	69	40	.633	7	3		3/3	57.9	11.1
1941	StL-N	155	97	56	.634	2				91.4	5.6
1942	StL-N	156	106	48	.688	★1				106.1	-0.1
1943	StL-N	157	105	49	.682	1				99.6	5.4
1944	StL-N	157	105	49	.682	★1				106.8	-1.8
1945	StL-N	155	95	59	.617	2				94.7	0.3
1946	Bos-N	154	81	72	.529	4				80.5	0.5
1947	Bos-N	154	86	68	.558	3				85.1	0.9
1948	Bos-N	154	91	62	.595	1				92.4	-1.4
1949	Bos-N	111	55	54	.505	4	4		1/2	53.6	1.4
1950	Bos-N	156	83	71	.539	4				81.7	1.3
1951	Bos-N	60	28	31	.475	5	4		1/2	31.8	-3.8
	13	1770	1044	704	.597						17.1

YEAR	TM/L	G	W	L	PCT	STANDING			M/Y	W-EXP	A-E
Spalding, Albert Goodwill "Al"											
1876	Chi-N*	66	52	14	.788	1				63.1	-11.1
1877	Chi-N*	60	26	33	.441	5				28.7	-2.7
	2	126	78	47	.624						-13.9
Speaker, Tristram E "Tris"											
1919	Cle-A*	61	40	21	.656	3	2		2/2	35.0	5.0
1920	Cle-A*	154	98	56	.636	★1				97.7	0.3
1921	Cle-A*	154	94	60	.610	2				96.6	-2.6
1922	Cle-A*	155	78	76	.506	4				72.4	5.6
1923	Cle-A*	153	82	71	.536	3				89.5	-7.5
1924	Cle-A*	153	67	86	.438	6				71.0	-4.0
1925	Cle-A*	155	70	84	.455	6				73.7	-3.7
1926	Cle-A*	154	88	66	.571	2				89.8	-1.8
	8	1139	617	520	.543						-8.7
Spence, Harrison L. "Harry"											
1888	Ind-N	136	50	85	.370	7				55.2	-5.2
Stahl, Charles Sylvester "Chick"											
1906	Bos-A*	40	14	26	.350	8	8		2/2	13.1	0.9
Stahl, Garland "Jake"											
1905	Was-A*	154	64	87	.424	7				68.6	-4.6
1906	Was-A*	151	55	95	.367	7				59.3	-4.3
1912	Bos-A*	154	105	47	.691	★1				101.9	3.1
1913	Bos-A*	81	39	41	.488	5	4		1/2	41.2	-2.2
	4	540	263	270	.493						-8.0
Stallings, George Tweedy											
1897	Phi-N*	134	55	77	.417	10				62.5	-7.5
1898	Phi-N*	46	19	27	.413	●8	6		1/2	24.1	-5.1
1901	Det-A	136	74	61	.548	3				71.8	2.2
1909	NY-A	153	74	77	.490	5				75.8	-1.8
1910	NY-A	142	78	59	.569	3	2		1/2	75.3	2.7
1913	Bos-N	154	69	82	.457	5				70.5	-1.5
1914	Bos-N	158	94	59	.614	★1				88.3	5.7
1915	Bos-N	157	83	69	.546	2				80.1	2.9
1916	Bos-N	158	89	63	.586	3				86.6	2.4
1917	Bos-N	158	72	81	.471	6				74.7	-2.7
1918	Bos-N	124	53	71	.427	7				57.0	-4.0
1919	Bos-N	140	57	82	.410	6				58.6	-1.6
1920	Bos-N	153	62	90	.408	7				60.2	1.8
	13	1813	879	898	.495						-6.7
Stanky, Edward Raymond "Eddie"											
1952	StL-N*	154	88	66	.571	3				81.8	6.2
1953	StL-N*	157	83	71	.539	●3				82.4	0.6
1954	StL-N	154	72	82	.468	6				77.8	-5.8
1955	StL-N	36	17	19	.472	5	7		1/2	15.6	1.4
1966	Chi-A	163	83	79	.512	4				87.6	-4.6
1967	Chi-A	162	89	73	.549	4				85.8	3.2
1968	Chi-A	79	34	45	.430	9	8		1/5	35.7	-1.7
1977	Tex-A	1	1	0	1.000	●3 W	3 W	2 W	2/4	0.6	0.4
	8	906	467	435	.518						-0.3
Start, Joseph "Joe"											
1873	Mut-n*	25	18	7	.720	5	4		2/2	13.9	4.1
Stengel, Charles Dillon "Casey"											
1934	Bro-N	153	71	81	.467	6				71.6	-0.6
1935	Bro-N	154	70	83	.458	5				71.1	-1.1
1936	Bro-N	156	67	87	.435	7				68.0	-1.0
1938	Bos-N	153	77	75	.507	5				69.8	7.2
1939	Bos-N	152	63	88	.417	7				66.3	-3.3
1940	Bos-N	152	65	87	.428	7				63.8	1.2
1941	Bos-N	156	62	92	.403	7				63.8	-1.8
1942	Bos-N	150	59	89	.399	7				60.0	-1.0
1943	Bos-N	107	47	60	.439	6	6		2/2	41.9	5.1
1949	NY-A	155	97	57	.630	★1				95.7	1.3
1950	NY-A	155	98	56	.636	★1				97.8	0.2
1951	NY-A	154	98	56	.636	★1				94.5	3.5
1952	NY-A	154	95	59	.617	★1				94.7	0.3
1953	NY-A	151	99	52	.656	★1				101.0	-2.0
1954	NY-A	155	103	51	.669	2				101.4	1.6
1955	NY-A	154	96	58	.623	1				96.7	-0.7
1956	NY-A	154	97	57	.630	★1				98.8	-1.8
1957	NY-A	154	98	56	.636	1				96.8	1.2
1958	NY-A	155	92	62	.597	★1				95.6	-3.6
1959	NY-A	155	79	75	.513	3				81.1	-2.1
1960	NY-A	155	97	57	.630	1				89.0	8.0
1962	NY-N	161	40	120	.250	10				48.1	-8.1
1963	NY-N	162	51	111	.315	10				51.8	-0.8
1964	NY-N	163	53	109	.327	10				59.4	-6.4
1965	NY-N	96	31	64	.326	10	10		1/2	31.1	-0.1
	25	3766	1905	1842	.508						-4.8
Stovall, George Thomas											
1911	Cle-A*	139	74	62	.544	7	3		2/2	66.1	7.9
1912	StL-A*	117	41	74	.357	8	7		2/2	41.1	-0.1
1913	StL-A*	135	50	84	.373	7	8		1/3	56.1	-6.1
1914	KC-F*	154	67	84	.444	6				71.5	-4.5
1915	KC-F*	153	81	72	.529	4				76.1	4.9
	5	698	313	376	.454						2.1

YEAR	TM/L	G	W	L	PCT	STANDING			M/YW-EXP		A-E
Stovey, Harry Duffield											
1881	Wor-N*	27	8	18	.308	7	8		2/2	10.6	-2.6
1885	Phi-a*	113	55	57	.491	4				62.1	-7.1
	2	140	63	75	.457						-9.7
Street, Charles Evard "Gabby"											
1929	StL-N	1	1	0	1.000	4	4	4	2/3	0.5	0.5
1930	StL-N	154	92	62	.597	1				96.4	-4.4
1931	StL-N*	154	101	53	.656	★1				96.8	4.2
1932	StL-N	156	72	82	.468	●6				73.7	-1.7
1933	StL-N	91	46	45	.505	5	5		1/2	50.3	-4.3
1938	StL-A	146	53	90	.371	7	7		1/2	53.9	-0.9
	6	702	365	332	.524						-6.6
Stricker, John A. "Cub"											
1892(1)	StL-N*	23	6	17	.261	10	11	9	2/3	8.4	-2.4
Strickland, George Bevan											
1964	Cle-A	73	33	39	.458	8	●6		1/2	35.8	-2.8
1966	Cle-A	39	15	24	.385	3	5		2/2	19.2	-4.2
	2	112	48	63	.432						-7.0
Stubing, Lawrence George "Moose"											
1988	Cal-A	8	0	8	.000	4 W	4 W		2/2	3.7	-3.7
Sukeforth, Clyde Leroy											
1947	Bro-N	2	2	0	1.000	●1	1		1/2	1.1	0.9
Sullivan, Haywood Cooper											
1965	KC-A	136	54	82	.397	10	10		2/2	53.1	0.9
Sullivan, James Patrick "Pat"											
1890	Col-a	3	2	1	.667	5	5	2	3/3	1.9	0.1
Sullivan, Timothy Paul "Ted"											
1883	StL-a	79	53	26	.671	2	2		1/2	50.3	2.7
1884	StL-U	31	28	3	.903	1	1		1/2	26.6	1.4
	KC-U*	62	13	46	.220	8	8		3/3	9.1	3.9
1888	Was-N	96	38	57	.400	8	8		2/2	29.8	8.2
	3	268	132	132	.500						16.2
Sullivan, William Joseph Sr. "Billy"											
1909	Chi-A*	159	78	74	.513	4				79.6	-1.6
Sweasy, Charles James "Charlie"											
1875	RS-n*	19	4	15	.211	9				0.6	3.4
Swift, Robert Virgil "Bob"											
1965	Det-A	42	24	18	.571	3	4		1/2	23.2	0.8
1966	Det-A	57	32	25	.561	3	2	3	2/3	29.2	2.8
	2	99	56	43	.566						3.6
Tanner, Charles William "Chuck"											
1970	Chi-A	16	3	13	.188	6 W	6 W		3/3	6.1	-3.1
1971	Chi-A	162	79	83	.488	3 W				83.2	-4.2
1972	Chi-A	154	87	67	.565	2 W				80.1	6.9
1973	Chi-A	162	77	85	.475	5 W				75.5	1.5
1974	Chi-A	163	80	80	.500	4 W				76.2	3.8
1975	Chi-A	161	75	86	.466	5 W				75.5	-0.5
1976	Oak-A	161	87	74	.540	2 W				89.8	-2.8
1977	Pit-N	162	96	66	.593	2 E				88.0	8.0
1978	Pit-N	161	88	73	.547	2 E				85.4	2.6
1979	Pit-N	163	98	64	.605	★1 E				94.4	3.6
1980	Pit-N	162	83	79	.512	3 E				83.1	-0.1
1981(1)	Pit-N	49	25	23	.521	4 E					
(2)	Pit-N	54	21	33	.389	6 E				49.1	-3.1
1982	Pit-N	162	84	78	.519	4 E				83.8	0.2
1983	Pit-N	162	84	78	.519	2 E				82.2	1.8
1984	Pit-N	162	75	87	.463	6 E				86.3	-11.3
1985	Pit-N	161	57	104	.354	6 E				65.6	-8.6
1986	Atl-N	161	72	89	.447	6 W				69.7	2.3
1987	Atl-N	161	69	92	.429	5 W				72.6	-3.6
1988	Atl-N	39	12	27	.308	6 W	6 W		1/2	14.7	-2.7
	19	2738	1352	1381	.495						-9.6
Tappe, Elvin Walter "El"											
1961	Chi-N	2	2	0	1.000	7	7	7	4/9	0.9	1.1
	Chi-N	79	35	43	.449	7	7	7	7/9	33.5	1.5
	Chi-N	16	5	11	.313	7	7		9/9	6.9	-1.9
1962	Chi-N	20	4	16	.200	9	9		1/3	7.6	-3.6
	2	117	46	70	.397						-2.9
Taylor, George J.											
1884	Bro-a	109	40	64	.385	9				36.3	3.7
Taylor, James Wren "Zack"											
1946	StL-A	31	13	17	.433	7	7		2/2	13.2	-0.2
1948	StL-A	155	59	94	.386	6				59.4	-0.4
1949	StL-A	155	53	101	.344	7				53.9	-0.9
1950	StL-A	154	58	96	.377	7				55.4	2.6
1951	StL-A	154	52	102	.338	8				50.9	1.1
	5	649	235	410	.364						2.2
Tebbetts, George Robert "Birdie"											
1954	Cin-N	154	74	80	.481	5				73.7	0.3
1955	Cin-N	154	75	79	.487	5				84.5	-9.5
1956	Cin-N	155	91	63	.591	3				88.5	2.5
1957	Cin-N	154	80	74	.519	4				73.8	6.2
1958	Cin-N	113	52	61	.460	8	4		1/2	62.1	-10.1

YEAR	TM/L	G	W	L	PCT	STANDING			M/YW-EXP		A-E
1961	Mil-N	25	12	13	.480	3	4		2/2	13.4	-1.4
1962	Mil-N	162	86	76	.531	5				87.6	-1.6
1963	Cle-A	162	79	83	.488	●5				74.0	5.0
1964	Cle-A	91	46	44	.511	8	●6		2/2	44.8	1.2
1965	Cle-A	162	87	75	.537	5				86.3	0.7
1966	Cle-A	123	66	57	.537	3	5		1/2	60.5	5.5
	11	1455	748	705	.515						-1.3
Tebeau, Oliver Wendell "Patsy"											
1890	Cle-P*	52	21	30	.412	7	7		2/2	20.0	1.0
1891	Cle-N*	73	31	40	.437	4	5		2/2	33.2	-2.2
1892(1)	Cle-N*	74	40	33	.548	5					
(2)	Cle-N*	79	53	23	.697	1				97.9	-4.9
1893	Cle-N*	129	73	55	.570	3				75.0	-2.0
1894	Cle-N*	130	68	61	.527	6				67.4	0.6
1895	Cle-N*	132	84	46	.646	2				81.7	2.3
1896	Cle-N*	135	80	48	.625	2				81.2	-1.2
1897	Cle-N*	132	69	62	.527	5				73.9	-4.9
1898	Cle-N*	156	81	68	.544	5				79.2	1.8
1899	StL-N*	155	84	67	.556	5				83.1	0.9
1900	StL-N*	92	42	50	.457	7	●5		1/2	45.8	-3.8
	11	1339	726	583	.555						-12.2
Tenace, Fury Gene "Gene"											
1991	Tor-A	33	19	14	.576	1 E	1 E	1 E	2/3	17.8	1.2
Tenney, Frederick "Fred"											
1905	Bos-N*	156	51	103	.331	7				48.3	2.7
1906	Bos-N*	152	49	102	.325	8				48.1	0.9
1907	Bos-N*	152	58	90	.392	7				57.7	0.3
1911	Bos-N*	156	44	107	.291	8				46.4	-2.4
	4	616	202	402	.334						1.5
Terry, William Harold "Bill"											
1932	NY-N*	114	55	59	.482	8	●6		2/2	60.5	-5.5
1933	NY-N*	156	91	61	.599	★1				89.4	1.6
1934	NY-N*	153	93	60	.608	2				94.4	-1.4
1935	NY-N*	156	91	62	.595	3				85.9	5.1
1936	NY-N*	154	92	62	.597	1				89.2	2.8
1937	NY-N	152	95	57	.625	1				89.2	5.8
1938	NY-N	152	83	67	.553	3				81.9	1.1
1939	NY-N	151	77	74	.510	5				77.3	-0.3
1940	NY-N	152	72	80	.474	6				76.4	-4.4
1941	NY-N	156	74	79	.484	5				72.6	1.4
	10	1496	823	661	.555						6.3
Thomas, Frederick L. "Fred"											
1887	Ind-N	29	11	18	.379	8	8	8	2/3	7.9	3.1
Thompson, Andrew M. "A. M."											
1884	Stp-U	9	2	6	.250	7				0.7	1.3
Tighe, John Thomas "Jack"											
1957	Det-A	154	78	76	.506	4				77.0	1.0
1958	Det-A	49	21	28	.429	8	5		1/2	26.3	-5.3
	2	203	99	104	.488						-4.3
Tinker, Joseph Bert "Joe"											
1913	Cin-N*	156	64	89	.418	7				65.2	-1.2
1914	Chi-F*	158	87	67	.565	2				88.6	-1.6
1915	Chi-F*	156	86	66	.566	1				87.1	-1.1
1916	Chi-N*	156	67	86	.438	5				74.1	-7.1
	4	626	304	308	.497						-10.9
Torborg, Jeffrey Allen "Jeff"											
1977	Cle-A	104	45	59	.433	5 E	5 E		2/2	47.9	-2.9
1978	Cle-A	159	69	90	.434	6 E				73.8	-4.8
1979	Cle-A	95	43	52	.453	6 E	6 E		1/2	44.9	-1.9
1989	Chi-A	161	69	92	.429	7 W				74.8	-5.8
1990	Chi-A	162	94	68	.580	2 W				86.2	7.8
1991	Chi-A	162	87	75	.537	2 W				88.8	-1.8
1992	NY-N	162	72	90	.444	5 E				75.2	-3.2
1993	NY-N	38	13	25	.342	7 E	7 E		1/2	17.3	-4.3
	8	1043	492	551	.472						-16.8
Torre, Joseph Paul "Joe"											
1977	NY-N*	117	49	68	.419	6 E	6 E		2/2	52.6	-3.6
1978	NY-N	162	66	96	.407	6 E				72.2	-6.2
1979	NY-N	163	63	99	.389	6 E				69.0	-6.0
1980	NY-N	162	67	95	.414	5 E				71.4	-4.4
1981(1)	NY-N	52	17	34	.333	5 E					
(2)	NY-N	53	24	28	.462	4 E				42.3	-1.3
1982	Atl-N	162	89	73	.549	1 W				84.7	4.3
1983	Atl-N	162	88	74	.543	2 W				91.9	-3.9
1984	Atl-N	162	80	82	.494	●2 W				78.6	1.4
1990	StL-N	58	24	34	.414	6 E	6 E		3/3	25.2	-1.2
1991	StL-N	162	84	78	.519	2 E				81.3	2.7
1992	StL-N	162	83	79	.512	3 E				83.9	-0.9
1993	StL-N	162	87	75	.537	3 E				82.4	4.6
1994	StL-N	115	53	61	.465	●3 C				48.9	4.1
1995	StL-N	47	20	27	.426	4 C	4 C		1/2	20.3	-0.3
1996	NY-A	162	92	70	.568	★1 E				88.9	3.1
1997	NY-A	162	96	66	.593	■○2 E				100.5	-4.5
1998	NY-A	162	114	48	.704	★1 E				110.3	3.7
	17	2387	1196	1187	.502						-8.3

YEAR	TM/L	G	W	L	PCT	STANDING			M/YW	EXP	A-E
Tracewski, Richard Joseph "Dick"											
1979	Det-A	2	2	0	1.000	5 E	5 E	5 E	2/3	1.0	1.0
Traynor, Harold Joseph "Pie"											
1934	Pit-N*	100	47	52	.475	4	5		2/2	50.9	-3.9
1935	Pit-N*	153	86	67	.562	4				86.1	-0.1
1936	Pit-N	156	84	70	.545	4				85.3	-1.3
1937	Pit-N*	154	86	68	.558	3				82.9	3.1
1938	Pit-N	152	86	64	.573	2				82.8	3.2
1939	Pit-N	153	68	85	.444	6				71.0	-3.0
	6	868	457	406	.530						-1.9
Trebelhorn, Thomas Lynn "Tom"											
1986	Mil-A	9	6	3	.667	6 E	6 E		2/2	4.1	1.9
1987	Mil-A	162	91	71	.562	3 E				85.2	5.8
1988	Mil-A	162	87	75	.537	●3 E				88.0	-1.0
1989	Mil-A	162	81	81	.500	4 E				83.9	-2.9
1990	Mil-A	162	74	88	.457	6 E				78.2	-4.2
1991	Mil-A	162	83	79	.512	3 E				86.3	-3.3
1994	Chi-N	113	49	64	.434	5 C				51.7	-2.7
	7	932	471	461	.505						-6.4
Trott, Samuel W. "Sam"											
1891	Was-a	12	4	7	.364	6	9		1/4	2.9	1.1
Turner, Robert Edward "Ted"											
1977	Atl-N	1	0	1	.000	6 W	6 W	6 W	2/4	0.4	-0.4
Unglaub, Robert Alexander "Bob"											
1907	Bos-A*	29	9	20	.310	6	8	7	3/4	12.4	-3.4
Valentine, Robert John "Bobby"											
1985	Tex-A	129	53	76	.411	7 W	7 W		2/2	50.8	2.2
1986	Tex-A	162	87	75	.537	2 W				83.7	3.3
1987	Tex-A	162	75	87	.463	●6 W				78.6	-3.6
1988	Tex-A	161	70	91	.435	6 W				70.4	-0.4
1989	Tex-A	162	83	79	.512	4 W				79.1	3.9
1990	Tex-A	162	83	79	.512	3 W				78.9	4.1
1991	Tex-A	162	85	77	.525	3 W				82.4	2.6
1992	Tex-A	86	45	41	.523	3 W	4 W		1/2	39.2	5.8
1996	NY-N	31	12	19	.387	4 E	4 E		2/2	14.9	-2.9
1997	NY-N	162	88	74	.543	3 E				87.7	0.3
1998	NY-N	162	88	74	.543	2 E				87.3	0.7
	11	1541	769	772	.499						15.9
Van Haltren, George Edward											
1892(1)	Bal-N*	11	1	10	.091	12	12		1/3	3.9	-2.9
Vernon, James Barton "Mickey"											
1961	Was-A	161	61	100	.379	●9				64.4	-3.4
1962	Was-A	162	60	101	.373	10				68.2	-8.2
1963	Was-A	40	14	26	.350	10	10		1/3	14.1	-0.1
	3	363	135	227	.373						-11.7
Virdon, William Charles "Bill"											
1972	Pit-N	155	96	59	.619	1 E				96.8	-0.8
1973	Pit-N	136	67	69	.493	2 E	3 E		1/2	68.9	-1.9
1974	NY-A	162	89	73	.549	2 E				86.1	2.9
1975	NY-A	104	53	51	.510	3 E	3 E		1/2	58.4	-5.4
	Hou-N	35	17	17	.500	6 W	6 W		2/2	16.0	1.0
1976	Hou-N	162	80	82	.494	3 W				77.6	2.4
1977	Hou-N	162	81	81	.500	3 W				84.1	-3.1
1978	Hou-N	162	74	88	.457	5 W				77.9	-3.9
1979	Hou-N	162	89	73	.549	2 W				81.1	7.9
1980	Hou-N	163	93	70	.571	▲1 W				86.8	6.2
1981(1)	Hou-N	57	28	29	.491	3 W					
(2)	Hou-N	53	33	20	.623	1 W				62.4	-1.4
1982	Hou-N	111	49	62	.441	5 W	5 W		1/2	51.6	-2.6
1983	Mon-N	163	82	80	.506	3 E				84.3	-2.3
1984	Mon-N	131	64	67	.489	5 E	5 E		1/2	66.2	-2.2
	13	1918	995	921	.519						-3.2
Vitt, Oscar Joseph "Ossie"											
1938	Cle-A	153	86	66	.566	3				82.0	4.0
1939	Cle-A	154	87	67	.565	3				86.3	0.7
1940	Cle-A	155	89	65	.578	2				84.4	4.6
	3	462	262	198	.570						9.3
Von Der Ahe, Christian Frederick Wilhelm "Chris"											
1895	StL-N	1	1	0	1.000	11	11	11	2/4	0.3	0.7
1896	StL-N	2	0	2	.000	10	11	11	3/5	0.5	-0.5
1897	StL-N	14	2	12	.143	12	12		4/4	2.5	-0.5
	3	17	3	14	.176						-0.4
Vukovich, John Christopher											
1986	Chi-N	2	1	1	.500	5 E	5 E	5 E	2/3	0.9	0.1
1988	Phi-N	9	5	4	.556	6 E	6 E		2/2	3.7	1.3
	2	11	6	5	.545						1.4
Wagner, Charles F. "Heinie"											
1930	Bos-A	154	52	102	.338	8				57.1	-5.1
Wagner, John Peter "Honus"											
1917	Pit-N*	5	1	4	.200	8	8	8	2/3	2.0	-1.0
Walker, Harry William											
1955	StL-N*	118	51	67	.432	5	7		2/2	51.2	-0.2
1965	Pit-N	163	90	72	.556	3				91.3	-1.3
1966	Pit-N	162	92	70	.568	3				93.0	-1.0
1967	Pit-N	84	42	42	.500	6	6		1/2	41.2	0.8
1968	Hou-N	101	49	52	.485	10	10		2/2	44.9	4.1
1969	Hou-N	162	81	81	.500	5 W				81.8	-0.8
1970	Hou-N	162	79	83	.488	4 W				79.1	-0.1
1971	Hou-N	162	79	83	.488	●4 W				83.0	-4.0
1972	Hou-N	121	67	54	.554	2 W	2 W		1/3	66.3	0.7
	9	1235	630	604	.511						-1.9
Wallace, Roderick John "Bobby"											
1911	StL-A*	152	45	107	.296	8				51.6	-6.6
1912	StL-A*	40	12	27	.308	8	7		1/2	13.9	-1.9
1937	Cin-N	25	5	20	.200	8	8		2/2	10.9	-5.9
	3	217	62	154	.287						-14.4
Walsh, Edward Augustine "Ed"											
1924	Chi-A	3	1	2	.333	6			2/4	1.4	-0.4
Walsh, Michael John "Mike"											
1884	Lou-a	110	68	40	.630	3				68.7	-0.7
Walters, William Henry "Bucky"											
1948	Cin-N*	53	20	33	.377	7	7		2/2	20.7	-0.7
1949	Cin-N	153	61	90	.404	7	7		1/2	61.4	-0.4
	2	206	81	123	.397						-1.2
Waltz, John J.											
1892(1)	Bal-N	8	2	6	.250	12	12	12	2/3	2.9	-0.9
Ward, John Montgomery											
1880	Pro-N*	32	18	13	.581	4	3	2	2/3	20.1	-2.1
1884	NY-N*	16	6	8	.429	4	●4		2/2	7.8	-1.8
1890	Bro-P*	133	76	56	.576	2				71.7	4.3
1891	Bro-N*	137	61	76	.445	6				63.6	-2.6
1892(1)	Bro-N*	78	51	26	.662	2					
(2)	Bro-N*	80	44	33	.571	3				95.7	-0.7
1893	NY-N*	136	68	64	.515	5				73.9	-5.9
1894	NY-N*	139	88	44	.667	2				78.8	9.2
	7	751	412	320	.563						0.4
Waterman, Frederick A. "Fred"											
1872	Oly-n*	9	2	7	.222	10				-1.1	3.1
Wathan, John David											
1987	KC-A	36	21	15	.583	4 W	2 W		2/2	18.5	2.5
1988	KC-A	161	84	77	.522	3 W				86.3	-2.3
1989	KC-A	162	92	70	.568	2 W				86.8	5.2
1990	KC-A	161	75	86	.466	6 W				80.3	-5.3
1991	KC-A	37	15	22	.405	7 W	6 W		1/3	18.6	-3.6
1992	Cal-A	89	39	50	.438	5 W	5 W	●5 W	2/3	39.0	-0.0
	6	646	326	320	.505						-3.6
Watkins, Harvey L.											
1895	NY-N	35	18	17	.514	9	9		3/3	17.9	0.1
Watkins, William Henry "Bill"											
1884	Ind-a*	23	4	18	.182	10	11		2/2	5.6	-1.6
1885	Det-N	70	34	36	.486	8	6		2/2	30.8	3.2
1886	Det-N	126	87	36	.707	2				88.0	-1.0
1887	Det-N	127	79	45	.637	1				83.0	-4.0
1888	Det-N	94	49	44	.527	3	5		1/2	52.7	-3.7
	KC-a	25	8	17	.320	8	8		3/3	7.1	0.9
1889	KC-a	139	55	82	.401	7				53.9	1.1
1893	StL-N	135	57	75	.432	10				58.6	-1.6
1898	Pit-N	151	72	76	.486	8				67.9	4.1
1899	Pit-N	24	7	15	.318	10	7		1/2	11.9	-4.9
	9	914	452	444	.504						-7.6
Weaver, Earl Sidney											
1968	Bal-A	82	48	34	.585	3	2		2/2	45.8	2.2
1969	Bal-A	162	109	53	.673	♦1 E				108.8	0.2
1970	Bal-A	162	108	54	.667	★1 E				103.5	4.5
1971	Bal-A	158	101	57	.639	♦1 E				101.4	-0.4
1972	Bal-A	154	80	74	.519	3 E				87.8	-7.8
1973	Bal-A	162	97	65	.599	1 E				101.3	-4.3
1974	Bal-A	162	91	71	.562	1 E				86.0	5.0
1975	Bal-A	159	90	69	.566	2 E				93.4	-3.4
1976	Bal-A	162	88	74	.543	2 E				83.3	4.7
1977	Bal-A	161	97	64	.602	●2 E				87.3	9.7
1978	Bal-A	161	90	71	.559	4 E				83.3	6.7
1979	Bal-A	159	102	57	.642	♦1 E				97.6	4.4
1980	Bal-A	162	100	62	.617	2 E				97.6	2.4
1981(1)	Bal-A	54	31	23	.574	2 E					
(2)	Bal-A	51	28	23	.549	4 E				51.7	7.3
1982	Bal-A	163	94	68	.580	2 E				89.7	4.3
1985	Bal-A	105	53	52	.505	4 E	4 E		3/3	55.9	-2.9
1986	Bal-A	162	73	89	.451	7 E				75.8	-2.8
	17	2541	1480	1060	.583						29.9
Westrum, Wesley Noreen "Wes"											
1965	NY-N	68	19	48	.284	10	10		2/2	21.9	-2.9
1966	NY-N	161	66	95	.410	9				62.5	3.5
1967	NY-N	151	57	94	.377	10	10		1/2	57.4	-0.4
1974	SF-N	86	38	48	.442	5 W	5 W		2/2	38.1	-0.1
1975	SF-N	161	80	81	.497	3 W				79.2	0.8
	5	627	260	366	.415						0.9

YEAR	TM/L	G	W	L	PCT	STANDING			M/Y	W-EXP	A-E
Wheeler, Harry Eugene											
1884	KC-U*	4	0	4	.000	8	8		1/3	0.6	-0.6
White, James Laurie "Deacon"											
1872	Cle-n*	2	0	2	.000	6	7		2/2	0.5	-0.5
1879	Cin-N*	18	9	9	.500	4	5		1/2	9.4	-0.4
	2	20	9	11	.450						-0.9
White, Joyner Clifford "Jo-Jo"											
1960	Cle-A	1	1	0	1.000	4	4		2/3	0.5	0.5
White, William Henry "Will"											
1884	Cin-a*	72	44	27	.620	5			1/2	49.6	-5.6
White, William Warren "Warren"											
1872	Nat-n*	11	0	11	.000	11				-1.2	1.2
1874	Bal-n*	47	9	38	.191	8				2.4	6.6
	2	58	9	49	.155						7.8
Wilber, Delbert Quentin "Del"											
1973	Tex-A	1	1	0	1.000	6 W	6 W	6 W	2/3	0.4	0.6
Wilhelm, Irvin Key "Kaiser"											
1921	Phi-N*	67	26	41	.388	8	8		2/2	21.0	5.0
1922	Phi-N	154	57	96	.373	7				59.9	-2.9
	2	221	83	137	.377						2.1
Williams, James A. "Jimmy"											
1884	StL-a	85	51	33	.607	5	4		1/2	50.5	0.5
1887	Cle-a	133	39	92	.298	8				34.6	4.4
1888	Cle-a	64	20	44	.313	8	6		1/2	23.8	-3.8
	3	282	110	169	.394						1.1
Williams, James Francis "Jimy"											
1986	Tor-A	163	86	76	.531	4 E				88.4	-2.4
1987	Tor-A	162	96	66	.593	2 E				99.7	-3.7
1988	Tor-A	162	87	75	.537	●3 E				89.3	-2.3
1989	Tor-A	36	12	24	.333	6 E	1 E		1/2	19.8	-7.8
1997	Bos-A	162	78	84	.481	4 E				80.4	-2.4
1998	Bos-A	162	92	70	.568	■○2 E				95.0	-3.0
	6	847	451	395	.533						-21.8
Williams, Richard Hirschfeld "Dick"											
1967	Bos-A	162	92	70	.568	1				92.3	-0.3
1968	Bos-A	162	86	76	.531	4				81.3	4.7
1969	Bos-A	153	82	71	.536	3 E	3 E		1/2	77.2	4.8
1971	Oak-A	161	101	60	.627	1 W				94.1	6.9
1972	Oak-A	155	93	62	.600	★1 W				94.4	-1.4
1973	Oak-A	162	94	68	.580	★1 W				95.7	-1.7
1974	Cal-A	84	36	48	.429	6 W	6 W		3/3	39.8	-3.8
1975	Cal-A	161	72	89	.447	6 W				70.7	1.3
1976	Cal-A	96	39	57	.406	6 W	●4 W		1/2	42.7	-3.7
1977	Mon-N	162	75	87	.463	5 E				73.8	1.2
1978	Mon-N	162	76	86	.469	4 E				83.4	-7.4
1979	Mon-N	160	95	65	.594	2 E				92.7	2.3
1980	Mon-N	162	90	72	.556	2 E				87.8	2.2
1981(1)	Mon-N	55	30	25	.545	3 E					
(2)	Mon-N	26	14	12	.538	2 E	○1 E		1/2	44.5	-0.5
1982	SD-N	162	81	81	.500	4 W				82.8	-1.8
1983	SD-N	163	81	81	.500	4 W				81.0	0.0
1984	SD-N	162	92	70	.568	♦1 W				86.5	5.5
1985	SD-N	162	83	79	.512	●3 W				84.0	-1.0
1986	Sea-A	133	58	75	.436	6 W	7 W		3/3	57.2	0.8
1987	Sea-A	162	78	84	.481	4 W				77.0	1.0
1988	Sea-A	56	23	33	.411	6 W	7 W		1/2	25.2	-2.2
	21	3023	1571	1451	.520						7.0
Williams, Theodore Samuel "Ted"											
1969	Was-A	162	86	76	.531	4 E				86.2	-0.2
1970	Was-A	162	70	92	.432	6 E				74.4	-4.4
1971	Was-A	159	63	96	.396	5 E				66.1	-3.1
1972	Tex-A	154	54	100	.351	6 W				58.2	-4.2
	4	637	273	364	.429						-11.8
Wills, Maurice Morning "Maury"											
1980	Sea-A	58	20	38	.345	6 W	7 W		2/2	22.3	-2.3
1981(1)	Sea-A	25	6	18	.250	7 W	6 W		1/2	9.9	-3.9
	2	83	26	56	.317						-6.2
Wilson, James "Jimmie"											
1934	Phi-N*	149	56	93	.376	7				63.1	-7.1
1935	Phi-N*	156	64	89	.418	7				58.8	5.2
1936	Phi-N*	154	54	100	.351	8				63.2	-9.2
1937	Phi-N*	155	61	92	.399	7				62.9	-1.9
1938	Phi-N*	149	45	103	.304	8	8		1/2	45.7	-0.7
1941	Chi-N	155	70	84	.455	6				76.6	-6.6
1942	Chi-N	155	68	86	.442	6				69.2	-1.2
1943	Chi-N	154	74	79	.484	5				79.9	-5.9
1944	Chi-N	10	1	9	.100	8	4		1/3	5.2	-4.2
	9	1237	493	735	.401						-31.7
Wine, Robert Paul Sr. "Bobby"											
1985	Atl-N	41	16	25	.390	5 W	5 W		2/2	16.7	-0.7
Wingo, Ivey Brown											
1916	Cin-N*	2	1	1	.500	8	8	●7	2/3	0.8	0.2

YEAR	TM/L	G	W	L	PCT	STANDING			M/Y	W-EXP	A-E
Winkles, Bobby Brooks											
1973	Cal-A	162	79	83	.488	4 W				78.0	1.0
1974	Cal-A	75	30	44	.405	6 W	6 W		1/3	35.1	-5.1
1977	Oak-A	108	37	71	.343	●5 W	7 W		2/2	44.0	-7.0
1978	Oak-A	39	24	15	.615	1 W	6 W		1/2	15.3	8.7
	4	384	170	213	.444						-2.5
Wolf, William Van Winkle "Chicken"											
1889	Lou-a*	65	14	51	.215	8	8	8	2/4	14.0	-0.0
Wolverton, Harry Sterling											
1912	NY-A*	153	50	102	.329	8				55.5	-5.5
Wood, George A.											
1891	Phi-a*	125	67	55	.549	7	4		2/2	62.8	4.2
Wood, James Leon "Jimmy"											
1871	Chi-n*	28	19	9	.679	2				18.2	0.8
1872	Tro-n*	25	15	10	.600	5				18.2	-3.2
	Eck-n*	9	2	7	.222	10	10	9	2/3	-1.0	3.0
1874	Chi-n	23	10	13	.435	4	5		2/2	9.6	0.4
1875	Chi-n	69	30	37	.448	6				30.2	-0.2
	4	154	76	76	.500						0.8
Wright, Alfred Hector "Al"											
1876	Phi-N	60	14	45	.237	7				17.5	-3.5
Wright, George											
1879	Pro-N*	85	59	25	.702	1				64.9	-5.9
Wright, William Henry "Harry"											
1871	Bos-n*	31	20	10	.667	3				21.2	-1.2
1872	Bos-n*	48	39	8	.830	1				45.0	-6.0
1873	Bos-n*	60	43	16	.729	1				48.2	-5.2
1874	Bos-n*	71	52	18	.743	1				58.9	-6.9
1875	Bos-n*	82	71	8	.899	1				78.2	-7.2
1876	Bos-N*	70	39	31	.557	4				36.7	2.3
1877	Bos-N*	61	42	18	.700	1				44.0	-2.0
1878	Bos-N	60	41	19	.683	1				35.7	5.3
1879	Bos-N	84	54	30	.643	2				61.5	-7.5
1880	Bos-N	86	40	44	.476	6				38.2	1.8
1881	Bos-N	83	38	45	.458	6				35.4	2.6
1882	Pro-N	84	52	32	.619	2				52.3	-0.3
1883	Pro-N	98	58	40	.592	3				67.1	-9.1
1884	Phi-N	113	39	73	.348	6				32.3	6.7
1885	Phi-N	111	56	54	.509	3				55.2	0.8
1886	Phi-N	119	71	43	.623	4				69.0	2.0
1887	Phi-N	128	75	48	.610	2				78.4	-3.4
1888	Phi-N	132	69	61	.531	3				67.8	1.2
1889	Phi-N	130	63	64	.496	3				63.0	0.0
1890	Phi-N	22	14	8	.636	1	3		1/5	12.7	1.3
	Phi-N	46	22	23	.489	2	3		5/5	26.0	-4.0
1891	Phi-N	138	68	69	.496	4				67.0	1.0
1892(1)	Phi-N	77	46	30	.605	3					
(2)	Phi-N	78	41	36	.532	5				92.6	-5.6
1893	Phi-N	133	72	57	.558	4				78.2	-6.2
	23	2145	1225	885	.581						-39.7
York, Preston Rudolph "Rudy"											
1959	Bos-A	1	0	1	.000	8	8	5	2/3	0.5	-0.5
York, Thomas J. "Tom"											
1878	Pro-N*	62	33	27	.550	3				31.4	1.6
1881	Pro-N*	34	23	10	.697	4	2		2/2	17.3	5.7
	2	96	56	37	.602						7.3
Yost, Edward Frederick "Eddie"											
1963	Was-A	1	0	1	.000	10	10	10	2/3	0.4	-0.4
Young, Denton True "Cy"											
1907	Bos-A*	6	3	3	.500	●4	7		1/4	2.6	0.4
Young, Nicholas Ephraim "Nick"											
1871	Oly-n	32	15	15	.500	5				15.5	-0.5
1873	Was-n	39	8	31	.205	7				5.8	2.2
	2	71	23	46	.333						1.7
Zimmer, Charles Louis "Chief"											
1903	Phi-N*	139	49	86	.363	7				55.9	-6.9
Zimmer, Donald William "Don"											
1972	SD-N	142	54	88	.380	4 W	6 W		2/2	53.0	1.0
1973	SD-N	162	60	102	.370	6 W				57.6	2.4
1976	Bos-A	76	42	34	.553	5 E	3 E		2/2	40.7	1.3
1977	Bos-A	161	97	64	.602	●2 E				94.6	2.4
1978	Bos-A	163	99	64	.607	▲2 E				95.5	3.5
1979	Bos-A	160	91	69	.569	3 E				92.5	-1.5
1980	Bos-A	155	82	73	.529	3 E	4 E		1/2	76.6	5.4
1981(1)	Tex-A	55	33	22	.600	2 W					
(2)	Tex-A	50	24	26	.480	3 W				59.2	-2.2
1982	Tex-A	96	38	58	.396	6 W	6 W		1/2	38.2	-0.2
1988	Chi-N	163	77	85	.475	4 E				77.5	-0.5
1989	Chi-N	162	93	69	.574	1 E				89.3	3.7
1990	Chi-N	162	77	85	.475	●4 E				72.6	4.4
1991	Chi-N	37	18	19	.486	4 E	4 E		1/3	17.6	0.4
	13	1744	885	858	.508						20.1

Biographical Data for Managers Not Appearing in the Player/Pitcher Registers

BILL ADAIR Adair, Marion Danne b: 2/10/13, Mobile, Ala.
BILL ARMOUR Armour, William Clark b: 9/3/1869, Homestead, Pa. d: 12/2/22, Minneapolis, Minn.
FRANK BANCROFT Bancroft, Frank Carter b: 5/9/1846, Lancaster, Mass. d: 3/30/21, Cincinnati, Ohio
ED BARROW Barrow, Edward Grant "Cousin Ed" b: 5/10/1868, Springfield, Ill. d: 12/15/53, Port Chester, N.Y.
TERRY BEVINGTON Bevington, Terry Paul b: 7/7/56, Akron, Ohio
HUGO BEZDEK Bezdek, Hugo Frank b: 4/1/1884, Prague, Czechoslovakia d: 9/19/52, Atlantic City, N.J.
BICKERSON Bickerson
JOHN BOLES Boles, John b: 8/19/48, Chicago, Ill.
DAVE BRISTOL Bristol, James David b: 6/23/33, Macon, Ga.
FREEMAN BROWN Brown, Freeman b: 1/31/1845, Hubbardston, Mass d: 12/27/16, Worcester, Mass.
AL BUCKENBERGER Buckenberger, Albert C. b: 1/31/1861, Detroit, Mich. d: 7/1/17, Syracuse, N.Y.
GEORGE BURNHAM Burnham, George Walter "Watch" b: 5/20/1860, Albion, Mich. d: 11/18/02, Detroit, Mich.
ORMOND BUTLER Butler, Ormond Hook b: 11/1854, West Virginia d: 9/12/15, Mt.Hope, Md.
CHARLIE BYRNE Byrne, Charles H. b: 9/1843, New York, N.Y. d: 1/4/1898, New York, N.Y.
JOE CANTILLON Cantillon, Joseph D. "Pongo Joe" b: 8/19/1861, Janesville, Wis. d: 1/31/30, Hickman, Ky.
O. P. CAYLOR Caylor, Oliver Perry b: 12/17/1849, Near Dayton, Ohio d: 10/19/1897, Winona, Minn.
TERRY COLLINS Collins, Terry Lee b: 5/27/49, Midland, Mich.
ED CURTIS Curtis, Edwin R.
CHARLIE CUSHMAN Cushman, Charles H. b: 5/25/1850, New York, N.Y. d: 6/29/09, Milwaukee, Wis.
MORDECAI DAVIDSON Davidson, Mordecai H. b: 11/30/1846, Port Washington, Ohio d: 9/6/40, Louisville, Ky.
JOHN DAY Day, John B. b: 9/23/47, Colchester, Conn. d: 1/25/25, Cliffside, N.J.
HARRY DIDDLEBOCK Diddlebock, Henry H. b: 6/27/1854, Philadelphia, Pa. d: 2/5/1900, Philadelphia, Pa.
CHARLIE EBBETS Ebbets, Charles Hercules b: 10/29/1859, New York, N.Y. d: 4/18/25, New York, N.Y.
WALLACE FESSENDEN Fessenden, Wallace Clifton b: 10/5/1860, Windham, N.H.
HORACE FOGEL Fogel, Horace S. b: 3/2/1861, Macungie, Pa. d: 11/15/28, Philadelphia, Pa.
GEORGE FRAZER Frazer, George Kasson b: 1/7/1861, Syracuse, N.Y. d: 2/5/13, Philadelphia, Pa.
JIM FREY Frey, James Gottfried b: 5/26/31, Cleveland, Ohio
JUDGE FUCHS Fuchs, Emil Edwin b: 4/17/1878, Hamburg, Germany d: 12/5/61, Boston, Mass.
JOHN GAFFNEY Gaffney, John H. b: 6/29/1855, Roxbury, Mass. d: 8/8/13, New York, N.Y.
DAVE GARCIA Garcia, David b: 9/15/20, E.St.Louis, Ill.
JIM GIFFORD Gifford, James H. b: 10/18/1845, Warren, N.Y. d: 12/19/01, Columbus, Ohio
MASE GRAFFEN Graffen, Samuel Mason b: 1845, Philadelphia, Pa. d: 11/18/1883, Silver City, N.Mex
CHARLIE HACKETT Hackett, Charles M. b: 1855, Lee, Mass. d: 8/1/1898, Holyoke, Mass.
JIM HART Hart, James Aristotle b: 7/10/1855, Fairview, Pa. d: 7/18/19, Chicago, Ill.
JOHN HART Hart, John Henry (born John Henry Reen) b: 7/21/48, Tampa, Fla.
LOUIE HEILBRONER Heilbroner, Louis Wilbur b: 7/4/1861, Ft.Wayne, Ind. d: 12/21/33, Ft.Wayne, Ind.
BILL HENDERSON Henderson, William C.
ED HENGLE Hengle, Edward Siegfried b: Chicago, Ill. d: 11/4/27, Norwich, England
WALTER HEWETT Hewett, Walter F. b: 1861, Washington, D.C. d: 10/7/44, Washington, D.C.
VEDIE HIMSL Himsl, Avitus Bernard b: 4/2/17, Plevna, Mont.
FRED HOEY Hoey, Frederick Chamberlain b: 1866, New York, N.Y. d: 12/7/33, Paris, France
GEORGE HUFF Huff, George A. "Gee" b: 6/11/1872, Champaign, Ill. d: 10/1/36, Champaign, Ill.
TIM HURST Hurst, Timothy Carroll b: 6/30/1865, Ashland, Pa. d: 6/4/15, Pottsville, Pa.
JOHNNY KEANE Keane, John Joseph b: 11/3/11, St.Louis, Mo. d: 1/6/67, Houston, Tex.
JIM KENNEDY Kennedy, James C. b: 1867, New York, N.Y. d: 4/20/04, Brighton Beach, N.Y.
KEVIN KENNEDY Kennedy, Kevin Curtis b: 9/26/54, Los Angeles, Cal.
JACK KROL Krol, John Thomas b: 7/5/36, Chicago, Ill. d: 5/30/94, Winston-Salem, N.C.
KARL KUEHL Kuehl, Karl Otto b: 9/5/37, Monterey Park, Cal.
BOB LEADLEY Leadley, Robert H. b: 1858, Brooklyn, N.Y.
JIM LEYLAND Leyland, James Richard b: 12/15/44, Toledo, Ohio
NICK LEYVA Leyva, Nicholas Tomas b: 8/16/53, Ontario, Cal.
FRANK LUCCHESI Lucchesi, Frank Joseph b: 4/24/27, San Francisco, Cal.
JACK McCALLISTER McCallister, John b: 1/19/1879, Marietta, Ohio d: 10/18/46, Columbus, Ohio
JOE McCARTHY McCarthy, Joseph Vincent "Marse Joe" b: 4/21/1887, Philadelphia, Pa. d: 1/13/78, Buffalo, N.Y.
JOHN McCLOSKEY McCloskey, John Joseph "Honest John" b: 4/4/1862, Louisville, Ky. d: 11/17/40, Louisville, Ky.
MEL McGAHA McGaha, Fred Melvin b: 9/26/26, Bastrop, La.
JACK McKEON McKeon, John Aloysius b: 11/23/30, South Amboy, N.J.
DENNY McKNIGHT McKnight, Dennis Hamar b: 1847, Pittsburgh, Pa. d: 5/5/1900, Pittsburgh, Pa.
GEORGE McMANUS McManus, George b: 6/28/1846, Ireland d: 10/2/18, New York, N.Y.
JOHN McNAMARA McNamara, John Francis b: 6/4/32, Sacramento, Cal.
STUMP MERRILL Merrill, Carl Harrison b: 2/25/44, Brunswick, Me.
RAY MILLER Miller, Raymond Roger b: 4/30/45, Takoma Park, Md.
FELIX MOSES Moses, Felix I. b: Richmond, Va.
BILLY MURRAY Murray, William Jeremiah b: 4/13/1864, Peabody, Mass. d: 3/25/37, Youngstown, Ohio
JIM MUTRIE Mutrie, James J. "Truthful Jim" b: 6/13/1851, Chelsea, Mass. d: 1/24/38, New York, N.Y.
PAUL OWENS Owens, Paul Francis b: 2/7/24, Salamanca, N.Y.
DANNY OZARK Ozark, Daniel Leonard (born Daniel Leonard Orzechowski) b: 11/26/23, Buffalo, N.Y.
LEW PHELAN Phelan, Lewis G.
LEFTY PHILLIPS Phillips, Harold Ross b: 6/16/19, Los Angeles, Cal. d: 6/12/72, Fullerton, Cal.
HORACE PHILLIPS Phillips, Horace B. b: 5/14/1853, Salem, Ohio
EDDIE POPOWSKI Popowski, Edward Joseph b: 8/20/13, Sayreville, N.J.
PAT POWERS Powers, Patrick Thomas b: 6/27/1860, Trenton, N.J. d: 8/29/25, Belmar, N.J.
JIM PRICE Price, James L. b: 1847, New York, N.Y. d: 10/6/31, Chicago, Ill.
VERN RAPP Rapp, Vernon Fred b: 5/11/28, St.Louis, Mo.
GREG RIDDOCH Riddoch, Gregory Lee b: 7/17/45, Greeley, Colo.
JIM RIGGLEMAN Riggleman, James David b: 11/9/52, Fort Dix, N.J.
CAL RIPKEN Ripken, Calvin Edwin Sr. b: 12/17/35, Aberdeen, Md.
STAN ROBISON Robison, Matthew Stanley b: 3/30/1859, Pittsburgh, Pa. d: 3/24/11, Cleveland, Ohio
PANTS ROWLAND Rowland, Clarence Henry b: 2/12/1879, Platteville, Wis. d: 5/17/69, Chicago, Ill.
EDDIE SAWYER Sawyer, Edwin Milby b: 9/10/10, Westerly, R.I. d: 9/22/97, Phoenixville, Pa.
MIKE SCANLON Scanlon, Michael B. b: 11/1843, Cork, Ireland d: 1/18/29, Washington, D.C.
BOB SCHAEFER Schaefer, Robert Walden b: 5/22/44, Putnam, Conn. 5'11", 180 lbs. Deb: 5/22/91
GUS SCHMELZ Schmelz, Gustavius Heinrich b: 9/26/1850, Columbus, Ohio d: 10/13/25, Columbus, Ohio
FRANK SELEE Selee, Frank Gibson b: 10/26/1859, Amherst, N.Y. d: 7/5/09, Denver, Colo.
BILL SHARSIG Sharsig, William A. b: 1855, Philadelphia, Pa. d: 2/1/02, Philadelphia, Pa.
LARRY SHEPARD Shepard, Lawrence William b: 4/3/19, Lakewood, Ohio
BILL SHETTSLINE Shettsline, William Joseph b: 10/25/1863, Philadelphia, Pa. d: 2/22/33, Philadelphia, Pa.
BUCK SHOWALTER Showalter, William Nathaniel b: 5/23/56, DeFuniak Springs, Fla.

LEW SIMMONS Simmons, Lewis b: 8/27/1838, New Castle, Pa. d: 9/2/11, Jamestown, Pa.
HARRY SPENCE Spence, Harrison L. b: 2/2/1856, New York, N.Y. d: 5/17/08, Chicago, Ill.
PAT SULLIVAN Sullivan, James Patrick d: 5/22/1898,
GEORGE TAYLOR Taylor, George J. b: 11/22/1853, New York
FRED THOMAS Thomas, Frederick L. b: Indiana
JACK TIGHE Tighe, John Thomas b: 8/9/13, Kearny, N.J.
TOM TREBELHORN Trebelhorn, Thomas Lynn b: 1/27/48, Portland, Ore.
TED TURNER Turner, Robert Edward b: 11/19/38, Cincinnati, Ohio
CHRIS VonDER AHE Von Der Ahe, Christian Frederick Wilhelm b: 10/7/1851, Hille, Prussia d: 6/5/13, St.Louis, Mo.
MIKE WALSH Walsh, Michael John b: 4/29/1850, Ireland d: 2/2/29, Louisville, Ky.
JOHN WALTZ Waltz, John J.
HARVEY WATKINS Watkins, Harvey L.
EARL WEAVER Weaver, Earl Sidney b: 8/14/30, St.Louis, Mo.
JIMMY WILLIAMS Williams, James Andrews b: 1/3/1848, Columbus, Ohio d: 10/24/18, N.Hempstead Twsp., N.Y.
BOBBY WINKLES Winkles, Bobby Brooks b: 3/11/30, Tuckerman, Ark.
AL WRIGHT Wright, Alfred Hector b: 3/30/1842, Cedar Grove, N.J. d: 4/20/05, New York, N.Y.
NICK YOUNG Young, Nicholas Ephraim b: 9/12/1840, Fort Johnson, N.Y. d: 10/31/16, Washington, D.C.

The Coach Roster

In an age of ever greater specialization in baseball, coaches have become increasingly important to the successful management of a team. The need for such assistance did not occur to any manager until John McGraw took on Arlie Latham as baseball's first full-time coach in 1909; today, teams employ separate coaches for first base, third base, pitching, the bullpen, hitting, baserunning, strength, conditioning, and more. Some coaches, like Charlie Lau and Roger Craig, have achieved fame exceeding that of the managers under whom they served. But coaches leave no statistical trail by which to track them. Players and pitchers have official records, and so do managers, but the accomplishments of coaches (and umpires) have until now resided largely in memory.

In the first edition of *Total Baseball*, the Coach Roster that follows represented a first attempt in a baseball encyclopedia to recognize these foot soldiers, who too often serve as scapegoats when a team fails but are invisible when it succeeds. We offered the roster in full knowledge that there were gaps and probably gaffes in our research; we hoped that our readers would advise us of omissions so that we could improve this roster in future editions of *Total Baseball*—and they have. We owe particular thanks to Bob Hoie and Walt Wilson. An additional feature, besides the inclusion of many new names, is full biographical data for all coaches who did not play at the major-league level and so are absent from the Registers.

The principal sources of the data herein are, for 1921–1939, the *Baseball Blue Book*; for 1940–1981, *The Sporting News Dope Book of 1961*, the *Baseball Register*, and for years since 1982, the *American League Red Book* and the *National League Green Book*. We have done our best to reconcile the many differences among the lists. The team and league abbreviations used in the Coach Roster are found on the final page of this book.

Aaron, Tommie Lee   Atl-N 1979-83
Abbott, Spencer   Was-A 1935
Adair, James A. "Jimmy"   Chi-A 1951-52, Bal-A 1957-61, Hou-N 1962-65
Adair, K. Jerry   Oak-A 1972-74, Cal-A 1975
Adair, Marion D. "Bill"   Mil-N 1962, Atl-N 1967, Chi-A 1970, Mon-N 1976
Adair, M. Richard "Rick"   Cle-A 1992-93, DE-T 1996-98
Adams, Charles D. "Red"   LA-N 1969-80
Adams, Robert H. "Bobby"   Chi-N 1961-65, 1973
Aguirre, Henry J. "Hank"   Chi-N 1972-74
Aker, Jackie D. "Jack"   Cle-A 1985-87
Alejo, Robert K. "Bob"   Oak-A 1997
Alfonso, Carlos   SF-N 1992, 1997-98
Allenson, Gary M.   Bos-A 1992-94
Alomar, Santos C. "Sandy"   SD-N 1986-90
Alou, Felipe R.   Mon-N 1979-80, 1984, 1992
Alou, Jesus M. R.   Hou-N 1979
Altobelli, Joseph S. "Joe"   NY-A 1981-82, 1986, Chi-N 1988-91
Altrock, Nicholas "Nick"   Was-A 1912-53
Amalfitano, J. Joseph "Joey"   Chi-N 1967-71, SF-N 1972-75, SD-N 1976-77, Chi-N 1978-80, Cin-N 1982, LA-N 1983-98
Amaro, Ruben   Phi-N 1980-81, Chi-N 1983-86
Anderson, George L. "Sparky"   SD-N 1969
Apodaca, Robert J. "Bob"   NY-N 1996-98
Appling, Lucius B. "Luke"   Det-N 1960, Cle-A 1960-61, Bal-A 1963, KC-A 1964-67, Chi-A 1970-71
Arsenault, Pierre J.   Mon-N 1992-98
Ashby, Alan D.   Hou-N 1997
Auferio, Anthony P. "Tony"   StL-N 1973
Austin, James P. "Jimmy"   StL-A 1923-32, Chi-A 1933-40
Babe, Loren R.   NY-A 1967, Chi-A 1980-81, 1983
Bader, Lore V.   Bos-N 1926
Bailor, Robert M. "Bob"   Tor-A 1992-95
Baker, Delmer D. "Del"   Det-A 1933-38, Cle-A 1943-44, Bos-A 1945-48, 1953-60
Baker, Eugene W. "Gene"   Pit-N 1963
Baker, Floyd W.   Min-A 1961-64
Baker, Johnnie B "Dusty"   SF-N 1988-92
Baker, William P. "Bill"   Chi-N 1950
Bamberger, George I.   Bal-A 1968-77
Bancroft, David J. "Dave"   NY-N 1930-32
Bando, Christopher M. "Chris"   Mil-A 1996-97, Mil-N 1998
Bando, Salvatore L. "Sal"   Mil-A 1980-81
Banks, Ernest "Ernie"   Chi-N 1967-73
Barfield, Jesse L.   Hou-N 1995, Sea-A 1998
Bartell, Richard W. "Dick"   NY-N 1946, Det-A 1949-52, Cin-N 1954-55
Bartirome, Anthony J. "Tony"   Atl-N 1986-88
Basgall, Romanus "Monty"   LA-N 1973-86
Bassler, John L. "Johnny"   Cle-A 1938-40, StL-A 1941
Baylor, Don E.   Mil-A 1990-91, StL-N 1992
Bauer, Henry A. "Hank"   Bal-A 1963
Beauchamp, James E. "Jim"   Atl-N 1991-98
Bearnarth, Lawrence D. "Larry"   Mon-N 1976, 1985-91, Col-N 1993-95
Beck, Walter W. "Boom-Boom"   Was-A 1957-59
Becker, Joseph E. "Joe"   Bro-N 1955-57, LA-N 1958-64, StL-N 1965-66, Chi-N 1967-70
Bedell, Howard W. "Howie"   KC-A 1984, SE-A 1988
Bell, David G. "Buddy"   Cle-A 1994-95
Bender, Charles A. "Chief"   Chi-A 1925-26, NY-N 1931, Phi-A 1951-53
Bengough, Bernard O. "Benny"   Was-A 1940-43, Bos-N 1944-45, Phi-N 1946-58
Benedict, Bruce E.   NY-N 1997-98
Benson, Vernon A. "Vern"   StL-N 1961-64, NY-A 1965-66, Cin-N 1966-69, StL-N 1970-75, Atl-N 1976-77, SF-N 1980
Berardino, John "Johnny"   StL-A 1951
Berardino, Richard J. "Dick"   Bos-A 1989-91
Berg, Morris "Moe"   Bos-A 1940-41
Beringer, Carroll J. "C. B."   LA-N 1967-72, Phi-N 1973-78
Bernhardt, Carlos   Bal-A 1998
Berra, Lawrence P. "Yogi"   NY-A 1963, NY-N 1965-71, NY-A 1976-83, Hou-N 1986-89
Berres, Raymond F. "Ray"   Chi-A 1949-66, 1968-69
Berry, Charles F. "Charlie"   Phi-A 1936-40
Bevington, Terry Paul   Chi-A 1989-95
Biagini, Gregory P. "Greg"   Bal-A 1992-94
Bialas, David B. "Dave"   SD-N 1993-94, Chi-N 1995-98
Bissonette, Adelphia L. "Del"   Bos-N 1945, Pit-N 1946

Blackburn, Wayne C.   Det-A 1963-64
Blackburne, Russell A. "Lena"   Chi-A 1927-28, StL-A 1930, Phi-A 1933-40, 1942-43
Blades, F. Raymond "Ray"   StL-N 1930-32, Cin-N 1942, Bro-N 1947-48, StL-N 1951, Chi-N 1953-56
Blaylock, Gary N.   KC-A 1984-87
Bloomfield, Gordon L. "Jack"   SD-N 1974, Chi-N 1975-76, 1977
Bluege, Oswald L. "Ossie"   Was-A 1940-42
Bochy, Bruce D.   SD-N 1993-94
Bombard, Marc   Cin-N 1996
Bonds, Bobby L.   Cle-A 1984-87, SF-N 1993-96
Booker, Gregory S. "Greg"   SD-N 1997-98
Boone, Robert R. "Bob"   Cin-N 1994
Boros, Stephen "Steve"   KC-A 1975-79, Mon-N 1981-82, KC-A 1993-94, Bal-A 1995
Bosman, Richard A. "Dick"   Chi-A 1986-87, Bal-A 1992-94, Tex-A 1995-98
Bottomley, James L. "Jim"   StL-A 1937
Bowa, Lawrence R. "Larry"   Phi-N 1988-96, Ana-A 1997-98
Boyer, Cletis L. "Clete"   Oak-A 1980-85, NY-A 1988, 1992-94
Boyer, Cloyd V.   NY-A 1975, 1977, Atl-N 1978-81, KC-A 1982-83
Boyer, Kenton L. "Ken"   StL-N 1971-72
Bragan, James A. "Jimmy"   Cin-N 1967-69, Mon-N 1970-72, Mil-A 1976-77
Bragan, Robert R. "Bobby"   LA-N 1960, Hou-N 1962
Braun, Stephen R. "Steve"   StL-N 1990
Brecheen, Harry D.   Bal-A 1954-67
Breeden, H. Scott   Cin-N 1986-89
Breeden, Joseph T. "Joe"   Fla-N 1995-96
Brenly, Robert E. "Bob"   SF-N 1992-96
Bresnahan, Roger P.   NY-N 1925-28, Det-A 1930-31
Brewer, James T. "Jim"   Mon-N 1977-79
Bridges, Everett L. "Rocky"   LA-A 1962-63, Cal-A 1968-71, SF-N 1985
Bridges, Thomas J. "Tommy"   Det-A 1946, Cin-N 1951
Brinkman, Edwin A. "Ed"   Det-A 1979, SD-N 1981, Chi-A 1983-88
Bristol, J. David "Dave"   Cin-N 1966, Mon-N 1973-75, SF-N 1978-79, Phi-N 1982-85, 1988, Cin-N 1989, 1993
Brown, H. Harold "Hal"   Bal-A 1964
Brown, Jackie G.   Tex-A 1979-82, Chi-A 1992-95
Brown, James R. "Jimmy"   Bos-N 1949-51
Brown, Mace S.   Bos-A 1965
Brown, William J. "Gates"   Det-A 1978-84
Brucker, Earle F., Sr.   Phi-A 1941-49, StL-A 1950, Cin-N 1952
Bryant, Claiborne H. "Clay"   LA-N 1961, Cle-A 1967, 1974
Bryant, Donald R. "Don"   Bos-A 1974-76, Sea-A 1977-80
Buckner, William J. "Bill"   Chi-A 1996-97
Buford, Donald A. "Don"   SF-N 1981-84, Bal-A 1994
Bumbry, Alonza B. "Al"   Bos-A 1988-93, Bal-A 1995, Cle-A 1998
Bundy, C. Lorenzo   Fla-N 1998
Burdette, S. Lewis "Lew"   Atl-N 1972-73
Burgess, Thomas R. "Tom"   NY-N 1977, Atl-N 1978
Burgmeier, Thomas H. "Tom"   KC-A 1991, 1998
Burke, James T. "Jimmy"   Det-A 1914-17, Bos-A 1921-23, Chi-N 1926-30, NY-A 1931-33
Burkett, Jesse C.   NY-N 1921
Burleson, Richard P. "Rick"   Oak-A 1991, Bos-A 1992-93, Cal-A 1995-96
Burns, George J.   NY-N 1931
Burns, John I. "Jack"   Bos-A 1955-59
Burris, B. Ray   Mil-A 1990-91, Tex-A 1992
Burwell, William E. "Bill"   Bos-A 1944, Pit-N 1947-48, 1958-62
Busby, James F. "Jim"   Bal-A 1961, Hou-N 1962, 1963-67, Atl-N 1968-75, Chi-A 1976, Sea-A 1977-78
Butera, Salvatore P. "Sal"   Tor-A 1998
Butler, John S. "Johnny"   Chi-A 1932
Butterfield, Brian J.   NY-A 1994-95, Ari-N 1998
Camacho, Joseph G. "Joe"   Was-A 1969-71, Tex-A 1972
Camilli, Douglas J. "Doug"   Was-A 1968-69, Bos-A 1970-73
Cannizzaro, Christopher J. "Chris"   Atl-N 1976-78
Cardenal, Jose R. D.   Cin-N 1993, StL-N 1994-95, NY-A 1996-98
Carew, Rodney C. "Rod"   Cal-A 1992-96, Ana-A 1997-98

Carey, Max G.   Pit-N 1930
Carey, Paul J. "P. J."   Col-N 1997
Carey, Thomas F. "Tom"   Bos-A 1946-47
Carisch, Frederick B. "Fred"   Det-A 1923-24
Carlucci, David M. "Dave"   Bos-A 1996
Carnevale, Daniel J. "Danny"   KC-A 1970
Carrion, Leonel S,   Mon-N 1988
Carter, Richard J. "Dick"   Phi-N 1959-60
Case, George W.   Was-A 1961-63, Min-A 1968
Cash, David "Dave"   Phi-N 1996
Castro, William R. "Bill"   Mil-A 1992-95, NY-A 1996, Mil-A 1997, Mil-N 1998
Cavarretta, Philip J. "Phil"   Det-N 1961-63, NY-N 1978
Cepeda, Orlando M.   Chi-A 1980
Chambliss, C. Christopher "Chris"   NY-A 1988, StL-N 1993-95, NY-A 1997-98
Chandler, Spurgeon F. "Spud"   KC-A 1957-58
Chapman, W. Benjamin "Ben"   Cin-N 1952
Chesbro, John D. "Jack"   Was-A 1924
Chiti, H. Dominic "Dom"   Cle-A 1991-93
Cisco, Galen B.   KC-A 1971-79, Mon-N 1980-84, SD-N 1985-87, Tor-A 1988, 1990-95, Phi-N 1997-98
Clark, Ronald B. "Ron"   Chi-A 1988-90, Sea-A 1991, Cle-A 1992-93
Clarke, Fred C.   Pit-N 1925
Clarke, Thomas A. "Tommy"   NY-N 1932-35, 1938
Clary, Ellis   Was-A 1955-60, Tor-A 1989
Clear, E. Robert "Bob"   Cal-A 1976-87
Clines, Eugene A. "Gene"   Chi-N 1979-81, Hou-N 1988, Sea-A 1989-92, Mil-A 1993-94, SF-N 1997-98
Cloninger, Tony L.   NY-A 1992-98
Cluck, Robert A. "Bob"   Hou-N 1979, 1990-93, Oak-A 1996-98
Clymer, William J. "Bill"   Cin-N 1925
Cochrane, Gordon S. "Mickey"   Phi-A 1950
Cohen, Andrew N. "Andy"   Phi-N 1960
Colavito, Rocco D. "Rocky"   Cle-A 1973, 1976-78, KC-A 1982-83
Cole, Richard R. "Dick"   Chi-N 1961
Coleman, Joseph H. "Joe"   Cal-A 1988-90, StL-N 1991-94, Cal-A 1996, Ana-A 1997-98
Coleman, Robert H. "Bob"   Bos-A 1926, Det-A 1932, Bos-N 1943
Collins, David S "Dave"   StL-N 1991-92
Collins, Edward T. "Eddie"   Phi-A 1931-32
Collins, James A. "Ripper"   Chi-N 1961-63
Collins, Terry L.   Pit-N 1992-93
Combs, Earle B.   NY-A 1936-44, StL-N 1947, Bos-A 1948-52, Phi-N 1954
Cumbs, Merrill R. "Merl"   Tex-A 1974-75
Comer, Stephen M. "Steve"   Cle-A 1987
Connor, Mark P.   NY-A 1984-85, 1986-87, 1990-93, Ari-N 1998
Connors, William J. "Billy"   KC-A 1980-81, Chi-N 1982-86, Sea-A 1987-88, NY-A 1989-90, Chi-N 1991-93, NY-A 1994-95
Conroy, William E. "Wid"   Phi-N 1922
Consolo, William A. "Billy"   Det-A 1979-92, 1995
Contreras, Arnaldo J. "Nardi"   NY-A 1995, Sea-A 1997-98, Chi-A 1998
Cooke, Allen L. "Dusty"   Phi-N 1948-52
Coombs, John W. "Jack"   Det-A 1920
Cooney, John W. "Johnny"   Bos-N 1940-42, 1946-49, 1950-52, Mil-N 1953-55, Chi-A 1957-64
Cooper, Donald J. "Don"   Chi-A 1995
Cooper, W. Walker   StL-N 1957, KC-A 1960
Corrales, Patrick "Pat"   Tex-A 1975-78, NY-A 1989, Atl-N 1990-98
Corriden, John M., Sr "Red"   Chi-N 1932-40, Bro-N 1941-46, NY-A 1947-48, Chi-A 1950
Cottier, Charles K. "Chuck"   NY-N 1979-81, Sea-A 1982-84, Chi-N 1988-94, Bal-A 1995, Phi-N 1997-98
Couchee, Michael "Mike"   Cal-A 1996
Courtney, Clinton D. "Clint"   Hou-N 1965
Cox, Jeffrey L. "Jeff"   KC-A 1995
Cox, Larry E.   Chi-N 1988-89
Cox, Robert J. "Bobby"   NY-A 1977
Crabtree, Estel C.   Cin-N 1943-44
Craft, Harry F.   KC-A 1955-57, Chi-N 1960-61
Craig, Roger L.   SD-N 1969-72, Hou-N 1974-75, SD-N 1976-77, Det-A 1980-84
Cramer, Roger M. "Doc"   Det-A 1948, Chi-A 1951-53
Crandall, Delmar W. "Del"   Cal-A 1977
Crandall, J. Otis "Doc"   Pit-N 1931-34
Crandall, James M. "Jim"   StL-A 1953
Cravath, Clifford C. "Gavvy"   Phi-N 1923
Cresse, Mark E.   LA-N 1977-98
Crosetti, Frank P. J. "Frankie"   NY-A 1947-68,

Sea-A 1969, Min-A 1970-71

Crowley, Terrence M. "Terry" Bal-A 1985-88, Min-A 1991-98

Cruz, Jose Hou-N 1997-98

Cubbage, Michael L. "Mike" NY-N 1990-91, 1992-96, Hou-N 1997-98

Cuccinello, Anthony F. "Tony" Cin-N 1949-51, Cle-A 1952-56, Chi-A 1957-66, Det-A 1967-68, Chi-A 1969

Cuellar, Robert "Bobby" Sea-A 1995-96, Mon-N 1997-98

Culp, Benjamin B. "Benny" Phi-N 1946-47

Cumberland, John S. Bos-A 1995

Cunningham, Joseph R. "Joe" StL-N 1982

Cunningham, William A. "Bill" Chi-A 1932

Cuyler, Hazen S. "Kiki" Chi-N 1941-43, Bos-A 1949

Dahlgren, Ellsworth T. "Babe" KC-A 1964

Dal Canton, J. Bruce Chi-A 1978, Atl-N 1987-90

Daly, Thomas D. "Tom" Bos-A 1933-46

Dark, Alvin R. Chi-N 1965, 1977

Dauer, Richard F. "Rich" Cle-A 1990-91, KC-A 1997-98

Davenport, James H. "Jim" SF-N 1970, SD-N 1974-75, SF-N 1976-82, 1984, Phi-N 1986-87, Cle-A 1989, SF-N 1995

Davis, Harry H. Phi-A 1913-17, 1919

Davis, H. Thomas "Tommy" Sea-A 1981

Davis, R. Brandon "Brandy" Phi-N 1972

Davis, Virgil L. "Spud" Pit-N 1942-46, Chi-N 1950-53

Deal, Ellis F. "Cot" Cin-N 1959-60, Hou-N 1962-64, NY-A 1965, KC-A 1966-67, Cle-A 1970-71, Det-A 1973-74, Hou-N 1983-85

Dean, Jay H. "Dizzy" Chi-N 1941

DeArmas, Rolando J. "Roly" Chi-A 1995-96

DeJohn, Mark S. StL-N 1996-98

DeMars, William L. "Billy" Phi-N 1969-81, Mon-N 1982-84, Cin-N 1985-87

DeMerritt, Martin G. "Marty" SF-N 1989

Demeter, Stephen "Steve" Phi-N 1985

Dent, Russell E. "Bucky" StL-N 1991-94, Tex-A 1995-98

Detore, George F. Pit-N 1959

Devlin, Arthur M. "Art" Bos-N 1926, 1928

Dews, Robert W. "Bobby" Atl-N 1979-81, 1985, 1997-98

Dickey, William M. "Bill" NY-A 1949-57, 1960

Didier, Robert D. "Bob" Oak-A 1984-86, Sea-A 1989-90

DiMaggio, Joseph P. "Joe" Oak-A 1968-69

Dixon, Walter "Walt" Chi-N 1964-65

Dobson, Patrick E. "Pat" Mil-A 1982-84, SD-N 1988-90, KC-A 1991, Bal-A 1996

Doby, Lawrence E. "Larry" Mon-N 1971-73, Cle-A 1974, Mon-N 1976, Chi-A 1977-78

Doerr, Robert P. "Bobby" Bos-A 1967-69, Tor-A 1977-81

Dolan, Albert J. "Cozy" NY-N 1922-24

Donnelly, Richard F. "Rich" Tex-A 1980, 1983-85, Pit-N 1986-95, Fla-N 1997-98

Donovan, William E. "Bill" Det-A 1918

Doolan, Michael J. "Mickey" Chi-N 1926-29, Cin-N 1930-32

Dorish, Harry "Fritz" Bos-A 1963, Atl-N 1968-71

Douglas, Otis W. Cin-N 1961-62

Down, Richard J. "Rick" Cal-A 1987-88, NY-A 1993-95, Bal-A 1996-98

Drabowsky, Myron W. "Moe" Chi-A 1986, Chi-N 1994

Dressen, Charles W. "Chuck" Bro-N 1939-42, 1943-46, NY-A 1947-48, LA-N 1958-59

Dubee, Richard P. "Rich" Fla-N 1998

Dubuc, Jean J. Det-A 1930-31

Duffy, Hugh Bos-A 1932

Dugey, Oscar J. Bos-N 1920, Chi-N 1921-24

Duncan, David E. "Dave" Cle-A 1978-81, StL-N 1982, Chi-A 1983-86, Oak-A 1986-95, StL-N 1996-98

Dunlop, Harry A. KC-A 1969-75, Chi-N 1976, Cin-N 1979-82, SD-N 1983-86, Cin-N 1998

Durocher, Leo E. LA-N 1961-64

Dusan, Eugene P. "Gene" NY-N 1983

Dyer, Don R. "Duffy" Chi-N 1983, Mil-A 1989-95, Oak-A 1996-98

Dykes, James J. "Jimmy" Phi-A 1949-50, Cin-N 1955-58, Pit-N 1959, Mil-N 1962, KC-A 1963-64

Earnshaw, George L. Phi-N 1949-50

Easler, Michael A. "Mike" Mil-A 1992, Bos-A 1993-94

Easter, L. Luke Cle-A 1969

Edwards, Howard R. "Doc" Phi-N 1970-72, Cle-A 1985-87, NY-N 1990-91

Egan, Arthur A. "Ben" Bro-N 1925, Chi-A 1926

Egan, Richard W. "Dick" Tex-A 1988-89

Elia, Lee C. Phi-N 1980-81, 1985-87, NY-A 1989, Sea-A 1993-97

Elliott, Robert I. "Bob" LA-A 1961

Ellis, Samuel J. "Sammy" NY-A 1982, 1983-84, 1986, Chi-A 1989-91, Chi-N 1992, Sea-A 1993-94, Bos-A 1996

Emery, Calvin W. "Cal" Chi-A 1988

Engle, R. David "Dave" Hou-N 1998

Ens, Jewel W. Pit-N 1926-29, Det-A 1932, Cin-N 1933, Bos-N 1934, Pit-N 1935-39, Cin-N 1941

Ermer, Calvin C. "Cal" Bal-A 1962, Mil-A 1970-71, Oak-A 1977

Estrada, Charles L. "Chuck" Tex-A 1973, SD-N 1978-81, Cle-A 1983

Etchebarren, Andrew A. "Andy" Cal-A 1977, Mil-A 1985-91, Bal-A 1996-97

Evans, Darrell W. NY-A 1990

Evans, Dwight M. Col-N 1994

Evers, John J. "Johnny" NY-N 1920, Chi-A 1922-23, Bos-N 1929-32

Evers, Walter A. "Hoot" Cle-A 1970

Ezell, Glenn W. Tex-A 1983-85, KC-A 1989-94, Det-A 1996

Faber, Urban C. "Red" Chi-A 1946-48

Fahey, William R. "Bill" SF-N 1986-91

Falk, Bibb A. Cle-A 1933, Bos-A 1934

Fanning, W. James "Jim" Atl-N 1967

Farrell, M. Kerby Chi-A 1966-69, Cle-A 1970-71

Felske, John F. Tor-A 1980-81, Phi-N 1984

Ferguson, Joseph V. "Joe" Tex-A 1986-87, LA-N 1988-89, 1992-93

Ferraro, Michael D. "Mike" NY-A 1979-82, KC-A 1984-86, NY-A 1987-88, 1989-91, Bal-A 1993

Ferrell, Richard B. "Rick" Was-A 1946-49, Det-A 1950-53

Ferrick, Thomas J. "Tom" Cin-N 1954-58, Phi-N 1959, Det-A 1960-63, KC-A 1964-65

Ferriss, David M. "Dave" Bos-A 1955-59

Fischer, Bradley J. "Brad" Oak-A 1996-98

Fischer, William C. "Bill" Cin-N 1979-83, Bos-A 1985-91

Fitzgerald, Edward R. "Ed" Cle-A 1960, KC-A 1961, Min-A 1962-64

Fitzgerald, Joseph P. "Joe" Was-A 1947-56

Fitzpatrick, John A. Pit-N 1953-56, Mil-N 1958-59

Fitzsimmons, Frederick "Freddie" Bro-N 1942, Bos-N 1948, NY-N 1949-53, 1954-55, Chi-N 1957-59, KC-A 1960, Chi-N 1966

Flanagan, Michael K. "Mike" Bal-A 1995, 1998

Flannery, Timothy E. "Tim" SD-N 1996-98

Fletcher, Arthur "Art" NY-A 1927-45

Flowers, D'Arcy R. "Jake" Pit-N 1940-45, Bos-N 1946, Cle-A 1951-52

Fohl, Leo A. "Lee" StL-A 1920

Foley, Marvis E. "Marv" Chi-N 1994

Foli, Timothy J. "Tim" Tex-A 1986-87, Mil-A 1992-95, KC-A 1996

Foote, Barry C. Chi-A 1991, NY-N 1992-93

Ford, Edward C. "Whitey" NY-A 1964, 1968, 1974-75

Fowler, J. Arthur "Art" LA-A 1964, Min-A 1969, Det-A 1971-73, Tex-A 1973-75, NY-A 1977-79, Oak-A 1980-82, NY-A 1983, 1988

Fox, Charles F. "Charlie" SF-N 1965-68, NY-A 1989

Fox, J. Nelson "Nellie" Hou-N 1965, 1966-67, Was-A 1968-71, Tex-A 1972

Foxx, James E. "Jimmie" Chi-N 1944

Francona, Terry J. Det-A 1996

Franks, Herman L. NY-N 1949-55, SF-N 1958, 1964, Chi-N 1970

Fraser, Charles C. "Chick" Pit-N 1923

Freese, George W. Chi-N 1964-65

Frey, James G. "Jim" Bal-A 1970-79, NY-N 1982-83

Friel, William E. "Bill" StL-A 1920

Friend, Owen L. KC-A 1969

Frisch, Frank F. "Frankie" NY-N 1949

Funk, Franklin R. "Frank" SF-N 1976, Sea-A 1980-81, 1983-84, KC-A 1988-90, Col-N 1996-98

Galan, August J. "Augie" Phi-A 1954

Galante, Matthew "Matt" Hou-N 1985-96, 1998

Gale, Richard B. "Rich" Bos-A 1992-93

Gamboa, Thomas Harold "Tom" Chi-N 1998

Gantner, James E. "Jim" Mil-A 1996-98

Garcia, David "Dave" SD-N 1970-73, Cle-A 1975-76, Cal-A 1977, Cle-A 1979, Mil-A 1983-84

Gardenhire, Ronald C. "Ron" Min-A 1991-98

Gardner, William F. "Billy" Bos-A 1965-66, Mon-N 1977-78, Min-A 1981

Garner, Philip M. "Phil" Hou-N 1989-91

Garrett, H. Adrian KC-A 1988-92

Garrison, R. Ford Cin-N 1953

Gaston, Clarence E. "Cito" Tor-A 1982-89

Gebhard, Robert H. "Bob" Mon-N 1982

Gehringer, Charles L. "Charlie" Det-A 1942

Gernert, Richard E. "Dick" Tex-A 1975-76

Gharrity, E. Patrick "Patsy" Was-A 1929-32, Cle-A 1933-35

Gibson, George C. Was-A 1923, Chi-N 1925, 1926

Gibson, Robert "Bob" NY-N 1981, Atl-N 1982-84, StL-N 1995

Gilbert, Andrew "Andy" SF-N 1972-75

Gilliam, James W. "Jim" LA-N 1965-78

Gladding, Fred E. Det-A 1976-78

Gleason, William J. "Kid" Phi-N 1908-11, Chi-A 1912-14, 1916-17, Phi-A 1926-32

Gleeson, James J. "Jim" KC-A 1957, NY-A 1964

Glynn, Eugene P. "Gene" Col-N 1994, 1995-98

Gomez, Juan A. "Orlando" Tex-A 1991-92, TB-A 1998

Gomez, Pedro "Preston" LA-N 1965-68, Hou-N 1973, SD-N 1976, LA-N 1977-79, Cal-A 1981-84

Gonzalez, Miguel A. "Mike" StL-N 1934-46

Gooch, John B. "Johnny" Pit-N 1937-39

Goodman, William D. "Billy" Atl-N 1968-70

Gordon, Joseph L. "Joe" Det-A 1956

Goryl, John A. "Johnny" Min-A 1968-69, 1979-80, Cle-A 1982-88, 1997-98

Gowdy, Henry M. "Hank" Bos-N 1929-37, Cin-N 1938-42, 1945-46, NY-N 1947-48

Graff, Milton E. "Milt" Pit-N 1985

Grammas, Alexander P. "Alex" Chi-N 1964, Pit-N 1965-69, Cin-N 1970-75, 1978, Atl-N 1979, Det-A 1980-91

Gregson, Glenn LA-N 1998

Griffey, G. Kenneth Sr. "Ken" Sea-A 1993-94, Col-N 1996, Cin-N 1997-98

Griffin, Alfredo C. Tor-A 1996-97

Grimes, Burleigh A. KC-A 1955

Grimm, Charles J. "Charlie" Chi-N 1941, 1961-63

Grissom, Marvin E. "Marv" LA-A 1961-65, Cal-A 1966, Chi-A 1967-68, Cal-A 1969, Min-A 1970-71, Chi-N 1975-76, Cal-A 1977-78

Grodzicki, John "Johnny" Det-A 1979

Guerrero, Epifanio O. "Epy" Tor-A 1981

Gullett, Donald E. "Don" Cin-N 1993-98

Gustine, Frank W. "Frankie" Pit-N 1950

Gutteridge, Donald J. "Don" Chi-A 1955-66, 1968-69

Haas, G. Edward "Eddie" Atl-N 1974-77, 1984

Haas, George W. "Mule" Chi-A 1940-46

Hack, Stanley C. "Stan" StL-N 1957-58, Chi-N 1965

Hacker, Richard W. "Rich" StL-N 1986-90, Tor-A 1991-94

Haddix, Harvey NY-N 1966-67, Cin-N 1969, Bos-A 1971, Cle-A 1975-78, Pit-N 1979-84

Haines, Jesse J. Bro-N 1938

Hairston, Samuel "Sammy" Chi-A 1978

Haller, Thomas F. "Tom" SF-N 1977-79

Hamilton, Steve A. Det-A 1975

Hancken, Morris M. "Buddy" Hou-N 1968-72

Haney, Fred G. Mil-N 1956

Haney, W. Larry Mil-A 1978-91

Hansen, Guy C. KC-A 1991-93, 1996-97

Hansen, Roger C. Sea-A 1992

Hansen, Ronald L. "Ron" Mil-A 1980-83, Mon-N 1985-89

Harder, Melvin L. "Mel" Cle-A 1947, 1948-63, NY-A 1964, Chi-N 1965, Cin-N 1966-68, KC-A 1969

Hardy, H. Lawrence "Larry" Tex-A 1995-98

Hargrove, D. Michael "Mike" Cle-A 1990-91

Harmon, Thomas "Tom" Mil-N 1982

Harper, Tommy Bos-A 1980-84, Mon-N 1990-98

Harrah, Colbert D. "Toby" Tex-A 1989-92, Cle-A 1996

Harrelson, Derrel M. "Bud" NY-N 1982, 1985-90

Harris, C. Luman "Lum" Chi-A 1951-54, Bal-A 1955-61, Hou-N 1962-64

Hart, John H. Bal-A 1988

Hartenstein, Charles O. "Chuck" Cle-A 1979, Mil-A 1987-89

Hartley, Grover A. Cle-A 1928-30, Pit-N 1931-33, StL-A 1934-36, NY-A 1946

Hartnett, Charles L. "Gabby" Chi-N 1938, NY-N 1941, KC-A 1965

Hartsfield, Roy T. LA-N 1969-72, Atl-N 1973

Hassey, Ronald W. "Ron" Col-N 1993-95, StL-N 1996

Hatcher, Michael V. "Mickey" Tex-A 1993-94, LA-N 1998

Hatcher, William A. "Billy" TB-A 1998

Hatfield, Fred J.   Det-A 1977-78
Hatton, Grady E.   Chi-N 1960, Hou-N 1973-74
Hayes, William E. "Bill"   Col-N 1998
Haynes, Joseph W. "Joe"   Was-A 1953-55
Hayworth, Raymond H. "Ray"   Bro-N 1945, Chi-N 1955
Hebner, Richard J. "Richie"   Bos-A 1989-91
Heffner, Donald H. "Don"   KC-A 1958-60, Det-A 1961, NY-N 1964-65, Cal-A 1967-68
Hegan, James E. "Jim"   NY-A 1960-73, Det-A 1974-78, NY-A 1979-80
Heilmann, Harry E.   Cin-N 1932
Heist, Alfred M. "Al"   Hou-N 1966-67, SD-N 1980
Helms, Tommy V.   Tex-A 1981-82, Cin-N 1983-89
Hemsley, Ralston B. "Rollie"   Phi-A 1954, Was-A 1961-62
Hemus, Solomon J. "Solly"   NY-N 1962-63, Cle-A 1964-65
Henderson, Ramon G.   Phi-N 1998
Henderson, Stephen C. "Steve"   Hou-N 1994-96, TB-A 1998
Hendrick, George A.   StL-N 1996-97, Ana-A 1998
Hendricks, Elrod J.   Bal-A 1978-98
Henrich, Thomas D. "Tommy"   NY-A 1951, NY-N 1957, Det-A 1958-59
Herman, Floyd C. "Babe"   Pit-N 1951
Herman, William J. "Billy"   Bro-N 1952-57, Mil-N 1958-59, Bos-A 1960-64, Cal-A 1967, SD-N 1978-79
Hernandez, Carlo A "Chuck"   Cal-A 1992-96
Herndon, Larry D.   Det-A 1992-98
Herzog, Dorrel N. "Whitey"   KC-A 1965, NY-N 1966, Cal-A 1974-75
Hiatt, Jack E   Chi-N 1981
High, Andrew A. "Andy"   Bro-N 1937-38
Hill, Marc K.   Hou-N 1988, NY-A 1991
Hill, Perry W.   Tex-A 1992-94, 1995, Det-A 1997-98
Hiller, Charles J. "Chuck"   Tex-A 1973, KC-A 1976-79, StL-N 1981-83, SF-N 1985, NY-N 1990
Hilton, J. David "Dave"   Mil-A 1987-88
Himsl, Avitus B. "Vedie"   Chi-N 1960-64
Hinchman, William W. "Bill"   Pit-N 1923
Hines, Benjamin T. "Ben"   Sea-A 1984, LA-N 1986, 1988-93, Hou-N 1994
Hines, Bruce E.   Cal-A 1991
Hisle, Larry E.   Tor-A 1992-95
Hitchcock, William C. "Billy"   Det-A 1955-60, Atl-N 1966
Hoak, Donald A. "Don"   Phi-N 1967
Hofman, Robert G. "Bobby"   KC-A 1966-67, Was-A 1968, Oak-A 1969-70, Cle-A 1971-72, Oak-A 1974-75, 1978
Hofmann, Fred   StL-A 1938-49, 1951
Holke, Walter H.   StL-A 1940
Hollingsworth, Albert W. "Al"   StL-N 1957-58
Holmberg, Dennis   Tor-A 1994-95
Holmquist, Douglas L. "Doug"   NY-A 1984, 1985
Holt, Golden D. "Goldie"   Pit-N 1948-50, Chi-N 1961-65
Hopp, John L. "Johnny"   Det-A 1954, StL-N 1956
Hornsby, Rogers   Chi-N 1958-59, NY-N 1962
Horton, Willie W.   NY-A 1985, Chi-A 1986
Hoscheit, Vernard A. "Vern"   Bal-A 1968, Oak-A 1969-74, Cal-A 1976, NY-N 1984-87
Hough, Charles O. "Charlie"   LA-N 1998
Houk, Ralph G.   NY-A 1954, 1958-60
House, Thomas R. "Tom"   Tex-A 1985-92
Howard, Elston G.   NY-A 1969-79
Howard, Frank O.   Mil-A 1977-80, NY-N 1982-83, 1984, Mil-A 1985-86, Sea-A 1987-88, NY-A 1989, 1991-92, NY-N 1994-96, TB-A 1998
Howe, Arthur H. "Art"   Tex-A 1985-88, Col-N 1995
Howley, Daniel P. "Dan"   Det-A 1919, 1921-22
Howser, Richard D. "Dick"   NY-A 1969-78
Hriniak, Walter J. "Walt"   Mon-N 1974-75, Bos-A 1977-88, Chi-A 1989-95
Hudlin, G. Willis   Det-A 1957-59
Hubbard, John H. "Jack"   StL-N 1993, Tor-A 1998
Hudson, Sidney C. "Sid"   Was-A 1961-65, 1968-71, Tex-A 1972, 1975-78
Hulswitt, Rudolph E. "Rudy"   Bos-A 1931-33
Hume, Thomas H. "Tom"   Cin-N 1996-98
Hundley, C. Randolph "Randy"   Chi-N 1977
Hunter, Frederick C. "Newt"   Phi-N 1928-31, 1933
Hunter, G. William "Billy"   Bal-A 1964-77
Hurdle, Clinton M. "Clint"   Col-N 1997-98
Isaac, Luis   Cle-A 1987-91, 1994-98
Jackson, Alvin N. "Al"   Bos-A 1977-79, Bal-A 1989-91
Jackson, Grant D.   Pit-N 1984-85, Cin-N 1994-95

Jackson, Roland T. "Sonny"   Atl-N 1982-83, SF-N 1997-98
Jackson, Ronnie D. "Ron"   Chi-A 1995-98
Jackson, Travis C.   NY-N 1939-40, 1947-48
Jansen, Lawrence J. "Larry"   NY-N 1954, SF-N 1961-71, Chi-N 1972-73
Jaramillo, Rudolph "Rudy"   Hou-N 1990-93, Tex-A 1995-98
Jauss, David P. "Dave"   Bos-A 1997-98
Jenkins, Ferguson A. "Fergie"   Chi-N 1995-96
Jennings, Hugh A. "Hughie"   NY-N 1921-25
Johnson, Darrell D.   StL-N 1960-61, Bal-A 1962, Bos-A 1968-69, Tex-A 1981-82, NY-N 1993
Johnson, Deron R.   Cal-A 1979-80, NY-N 1981, Phi-N 1982-84, Sea-A 1985-86, Chi-A 1987, Cal-A 1989-91
Johnson, Lamar   Mil-A 1995-97, Mil-N 1998
Johnson, Roy J   Chi-N 1935-39, 1944-53
Johnson, Sylvester W. "Syl"   Phi-N 1937-40
Johnson, Timothy E. "Tim"   Mon-N 1993-94, Bos-A 1995-96
Johnson, Wallace D.   Chi-A 1998
Johnston, James H. "Jimmy"   Bro-N 1931
Jones, Clarence W.   Atl-N 1985, 1988-98
Jones, Gary W.   Oak-A 1998
Jones, Gordon B.   Hou-N 1966-67
Jones, Grover W. "Deacon"   Hou-N 1976-82, SD-N 1984-87
Jones, Jeffrey A. "Jeff"   Det-A 1995
Jones, Lynn M.   KC-A 1991-92
Jones, Joseph C. "Joe"   KC-A 1987, 1992, Pit-N 1997-98
Jonnard, Clarence J. "Bubber"   Phi-N 1935, NY-N 1942-46
Joshua, Von E.   Chi-A 1998
Judge, Joseph I. "Joe"   Was-A 1945-46
Jurges, William F. "Billy"   Chi-N 1947-48, Was-A 1956-59
Kaat, James L. "Jim"   Cin-N 1984-85
Kahn, Louis "Lou"   StL-N 1955
Katt, Raymond F. "Ray"   StL-N 1959-60, Cle-A 1962
Kaufmann, Anthony C. "Tony"   StL-N 1947-50
Keane, John J. "Johnny"   StL-N 1959-61
Keefe, David E. "Dave"   Phi-A 1940-49
Keely, Robert W. "Bob"   Bos-N 1946-52, Mil-N 1953-57
Kelleher, Michael D. "Mick"   Pit-N 1986
Keller, Charles E. "Charlie"   NY-A 1957, 1959
Kelley, Joseph J. "Joe"   Bro-N 1926
Kelly, Bernard T. "Mike"   Chi-A 1930-31, Chi-N 1934, Bos-N 1937-39, Pit-N 1940-41
Kelly, George L.   Cin-N 1935-37, Bos-N 1938-43, Cin-N 1947-48
Kelly, J. Thomas "Tom"   Min-A 1983-86
Kendall, Fred L.   Det-A 1996-98
Kennedy, Kevin   Mon-N 1992
Kennedy, Robert D. "Bob"   Chi-N 1962-65, Atl-N 1967
Kerr, John F.   Was-A 1935
Kerrigan, Joseph T. "Joe"   Mon-N 1983-86, 1992-96, Bos-A 1997-98
Killefer, William L. "Bill"   StL-N 1926, StL-A 1927-29, Bro-N 1939, Phi-N 1942
Kim, Wendell K.   SF-N 1989-96, Bos-A 1997-98
Kimm, Bruce E.   Cin-N 1984-88, Pit-N 1989, SD-N 1991-92, Fla-N 1997-98
King, Clyde E.   Cin-N 1959, Pit-N 1965-67, NY-A 1978, 1981, 1988
Kison, Bruce E.   KC-A 1992-98
Kissell, George M.   StL-N 1969-75
Kittle, Hubert M. "Hub"   Hou-N 1971-75, StL-N 1981-83
Klein, Charles H. "Chuck"   Phi-N 1942-45
Klein, Louis F. "Lou"   Chi-N 1960-65
Kluszewski, Theodore B. "Ted"   Cin-N 1970-78
Knight, C. Ray   Cin-N 1993-95
Knoop, Robert F. "Bobby"   Chi-A 1977-78, Cal-A 1979-96
Knowles, Darold D.   StL-N 1983, Phi-N 1989-90
Koenig, Fred Carl   Cal-A 1970-71, StL-N 1976, Tex-A 1977-82, Chi-N 1983, Cle-A 1985-86
Kress, Ralph "Red"   Det-A 1940, NY-N 1946-49, Cle-A 1953-60, LA-N 1961, NY-N 1962
Krol, John T. "Jack"   StL-N 1977-80, SD-N 1981-86
Krug, Everett B. "Chris"   SD-N 1969
Kuehl, Karl O.   Min-A 1977-82
Kuenn, Harvey E.   Mil-A 1971-82
Kuntz, Russell J. "Rusty"   Sea-A 1989-92, Fla-N 1995-96
Kusnyer, Arthur W. "Art"   Chi-A 1980-87, Oak-A 1989-95, Chi-A 1997-98
Lachemann, Marcel E.   Cal-A 1984-92, Fla-N

1993-94, Ana-A 1997-98
Lachemann, Rene G.   Bos-A 1985-86, Oak-A 1987-92, StL-N 1997-98
Lachemann, William C. "Bill"   Cal-A 1995-96
Lakeman, Albert W. "Al"   Bos-A 1963-64, 1967-69
Lamont, Gene W.   Pit-N 1986-91, 1996
Land, Grover C.   Pit-N 1914, Cin-N 1925-28, Chi-N 1929-30
Landestoy, Rafael S.   Mon-N 1989, NY-N 1996
Landrith, Hobert N. "Hobie"   Was-A 1964
Lanier, Harold C. "Hal"   StL-N 1981-85, Phi-N 1990-91
Lansford, Carney R.   Oak-A 1995, StL-N 1997
LaRoche, David E. "Dave"   Chi-A 1989-91, NY-N 1992-93
LaRussa, Anthony "Tony"   Chi-A 1978
Lasorda, Thomas C. "Tommy"   LA-N 1973-76
Latham, W. Arlington "Arlie"   Cin-N 1900, NY-N 1909
Lau, Charles R. "Charley"   Bal-A 1969, Oak-A 1970, KC-A 1971-74, 1975-78, NY-A 1979-81, Chi-A 1982-83
Lauder, William "Billy"   Chi-A 1925
Lavagetto, Harry A. "Cookie"   Bro-N 1951-53, Was-A 1955-57, NY-N 1962-63, SF-N 1964-67
Law, Vernon S. "Vern"   Pit-N 1968-69
Lazzeri, Anthony M. "Tony"   Chi-N 1938
Lefebvre, James K. "Jim"   LA-N 1978-79, SF-N 1980-82, Oak-A 1987-88, 1994-95
Leifield, Albert P. "Lefty"   StL-A 1920-23, Bos-A 1924-26, Det-A 1927-28
Lemon, James R. "Jim"   Min-A 1965-67, 1981-84
Lemon, Robert G. "Bob"   Cle-A 1960, Phi-N 1961, Cal-A 1967-68, KC-A 1970, NY-A 1976
Lenhardt, Donald E. "Don"   Bos-A 1970-73
Leonard, Emil J. "Dutch"   Chi-N 1954-56
Leppert, Donald G. "Don"   Pit-N 1968-76, Tor-A 1977-79, Hou-N 1980-85
Lett, James C. "Jim"   Cin-N 1988-89, 1996, Tor-A 1997-98
Levy, Leonard "Len"   Pit-N 1957-63
Lewis, George E. "Duffy"   Bos-N 1931-35
Lewis, Johnny J.   StL-N 1973-76, 1985-89
Leyland, James R. "Jim"   Chi-A 1982-85
Leyva, Nicolas T. "Nick"   StL-N 1984-88, Tor-A 1993-97
Lillis, Robert P. "Bob"   Hou-N 1967, 1973-82, SF-N 1986-96
Linares, Julio   Hou-N 1994-96
Lind, Jackson H. "Jack"   Pit-N 1997
Lipon, John J. "Johnny"   Cle-A 1968-71
Little, R. Bryan   Chi-A 1998
Little, W. Grady   SD-N 1996, Bos-A 1997-98
Litwhiler, Daniel W. "Danny"   Cin-N 1951
Livingston, Patrick J. "Paddy"   Phi-A 1919
Llenas, Winston E.   Tor-A 1988
Lobe, William C. "Bill"   Cle-A 1951-56
Lobert, John B. "Hans"   NY-N 1928, Phi-N 1934-41, Cin-N 1943-44
Lockman, Carroll W. "Whitey"   Cin-N 1960, SF-N 1961-64, Chi-N 1965-66
Lodigiani, Dario A.   KC-A 1961-62
Lollar, J. Sherman "Sherm"   Bal-A 1964-67, Oak-A 1968
Long, R. Dale   NY-A 1963
Lonnett, Joseph P. "Joe"   Chi-A 1971-75, Oak-A 1976, Pit-N 1977-84
Lopat, Edmund W. "Ed"   NY-A 1960, Min-A 1961, KC-A 1962
Lopes, David E. "Davey"   Tex-A 1988-91, Bal-A 1992-94, SD-N 1995-98
Lowe, Q. V. "Q. V."   Chi-N 1972
Lowrey, Harry L. "Peanuts"   Phi-N 1960-66, SF-N 1967-68, Mon-N 1969, Chi-N 1970-71, Cal-A 1972, Chi-N 1977-79, 1981
Lucchesi, Frank J.   Tex-A 1974-75, 1979-80
Lum, Michael K. "Mike"   Chi-A 1985, KC-A 1988-89
Lumpe, Jerry D.   Oak-A 1971
Lund, Donald A. "Don"   Det-A 1957-58
Luque, Adolfo "Dolf"   NY-N 1935-38, 1941-45
Lutz, R. Joseph "Joe"   Cle-A 1971-73
Luzinski, Gregory M. "Greg"   Oak-A 1993, KC-A 1995-97
Lyons, Edward H. "Eddie"   Min-A 1976
Lyons, Theodore A. "Ted"   Det-A 1949-53, Bro-N 1954
Macha, Kenneth E. "Ken"   Mon-N 1986-91, Cal-A 1992-94
Mack, Earle T.   Phi-A 1924-50
Mackanin, Peter   Mon-N 1997-98
MacKenzie, H. Gordon "Gordy"   KC-A 1980-81, Chi-N 1982, SF-N 1986-88, Cle-A 1991

Macko, Joseph "Joe"   Chi-N 1964
Maddon, Joseph J. "Joe"   Cal-A 1995-96, Ana-A 1997-98
Maglie, Salvatore A. "Sal"   Bos-A 1960-62, 1966-67, Sea-A 1969
Mahoney, James T. "Jim"   Chi-A 1972-76, Sea-A 1985-86
Majtyka, LeRoy W. "Roy"   Atl-N 1988-90
Malmberg, Harry W.   Bos-A 1963-64
Maloof, Jack G.   SD-N 1990
Maltzberger, Gordon R.   Min-A 1962-64
Mancuso, August R. "Gus"   Cin-N 1950
Mansolino, Doug   Chi-A 1992-96, Mil-N 1998
Mantle, Mickey C.   NY-A 1970
Manuel, Charles F. "Charlie"   Cle-A 1988-89, 1994-98
Manuel, Jerry   Mon-N 1991-96, Fla-N 1997
Manush, Henry E. "Heinie"   Was-A 1953-54
Marion, Martin W. "Marty"   StL-A 1952, Chi-A 1954
Marshall, R. James "Jim"   Chi-N 1974
Martin, Alfred M. "Billy"   Min-A 1965-68, Tex-A 1974
Martin, Fred T.   Chi-N 1961-65, Chi-A 1979
Martin, John L. "Pepper"   Chi-N 1956
Martin, Joseph C. "J. C."   Chi-N 1974
Martinez, Jose   KC-A 1980-87, Chi-N 1988-94
Martinez, Orlando "Marty"   Sea-A 1984-86, 1992
Mathews, Edwin L. "Eddie"   Atl-N 1971-72
Mathews, Henry "Harry"   Cle-A 1926-27, NY-A 1929
Mathews, Rick R.   Col-N 1993, 1995
Mathewson, Christopher "Christy"   NY-N 1919-20
Matlack, Jonathan T. "Jon"   Det-A 1996
Matthews, Gary N.   Tor-A 1998
Mauch, Gene W.   KC-A 1995
Maxvill, C. Dallan "Dal"   Oak-A 1975, NY-N 1978, StL-N 1979-80, Atl-N 1982-84
May, Lee A.   KC-A 1984-86, Cin-N 1988-89, KC-A 1992-93, Bal-A 1995
May, Milton S. "Milt"   Pit-N 1987-96, Fla-N 1997-98
Mayberry, John C.   KC-A 1989-90
Mayo, Edward J. "Eddie"   Bos-A 1951, Phi-N 1952-54
Mays, Willie H.   NY-N 1974-79
Mazeroski, William S. "Bill"   Pit-N 1973, Sea-A 1979-80
Mazzone, Leo D.   Atl-N 1985, 1990-98
McBride, George F.   Det-A 1925-26, 1929
McBride, Kenneth F. "Ken"   Mil-A 1975
McCallister, John "Jack"   Cle-A 1920-26, Bos-A 1930
McClendon, Lloyd G.   Pit-N 1997-98
McClure, Robert C. "Bob"   Fla-N 1994
McCormick, Frank A.   Cin-N 1956-57
McCrabb, Lester W. "Les"   Phi-A 1950-54
McCraw, Tommy L. "Tom"   Cle-A 1975, 1979-82, SF-N 1983-85, Bal-A 1989-91, NY-N 1992-96, Hou-N 1997-98
McCullough, Clyde E.   Was-A 1960, Min-A 1961, NY-N 1963, SD-N 1982
McDermott, Maurice J. "Mickey"   Cal-A 1968
McDonnell, Robert A. "Maje"   Phi-N 1951-57
McGaha, F. Melvin "Mel"   Cle-A 1961, KC-A 1963-64, Hou-N 1968-70
McGinnity, Joseph J. "Joe"   Bro-N 1926
McGuire, James T. "Deacon"   Det-A 1911-16
McKay, David L. "Dave"   Oak-A 1984-95, StL-N 1996-98
McKechnie, William B. "Bill"   Pit-N 1922, StL-N 1927, Cle-A 1947-49, Bos-A 1952-53
McKee, J. R.   Pit-N 1947
McKeon, John A. "Jack"   Oak-A 1978
McLaren, John L.   Tor-A 1986-90, Bos-A 1991, Cin-N 1992, Sea-A 1993-98
McLish, Calvin C. "Cal"   Phi-N 1965-66, Mon-N 1969-75, Mil-A 1976-82
McMahon, Donald J. "Don"   SF-N 1973-75, Min-A 1976-77, SF-N 1980-82, Cle-A 1983-85
McMillan, Roy D.   Mil-A 1970-72, NY-N 1973-76
McNamara, John F.   Oak-A 1968-69, SF-N 1971-73, Cal-A 1978
McNeely, G. Earl   StL-A 1931, Was-A 1936-37
McNertney, Gerald E. "Jerry"   Bos-A 1988
McRae, Harold A. "Hal"   KC-A 1987, Mon-N 1990-91, Cin-N 1995-96, Phi-N 1997-98
Mejias, Samuel E. "Sammy"   Sea-A 1993-98
Mele, Sabath A. "Sam"   Was-A 1959-60, Min-A 1961
Melillo, Oscar D. "Ski"   StL-A 1938, Cle-A 1939-40, 1942, 1945-48, 1950, Bos-A 1952-53, KC-A 1955-56

Mendoza, C. Rigoberto "Minnie"   Bal-A 1988
Menke, Denis J.   Tor-A 1980-81, Hou-N 1983-88, Phi-N 1989-96, Cin-N 1997-98
Merkle, Frederick H. "Fred"   NY-A 1925-26
Merrill, Carl H. "Stump"   NY-A 1985, 1986-87
Metro, Charles "Charlie"   Chi-N 1962, Chi-A 1965, Oak-A 1982
Meusel, Emil F. "Irish"   NY-N 1930
Meyer, Bernhard "Benny"   Phi-N 1924-26, Det-A 1928-30
Meyer, Russell C. "Russ' Or "Monk"   NY-A 1992
Michael, Eugene R. "Gene"   NY-A 1976-77, 1978, 1984-86, 1988, 1989
Milan, J. Clyde   Was-A 1928-29, 1938-52
Miley, David A. "Dave"   Cin-N 1993
Miller, Dyar K   Chi-A 1987-88
Miller, Edmund J. "Bing"   Bos-A 1937, Det-A 1938-41, Chi-A 1942-49, Phi-A 1950-53
Miller, L. Otto   Bro-N 1926-36
Miller, Raymond R. "Ray"   Bal-A 1978-85, Pit-N 1987-96, Bal-A 1997
Miller, Robert L. "Bob"   Tor-A 1977-79, SF-N 1985
Milliken, Robert F. "Bob"   StL-N 1965-70, 1976
Mills, Arthur G. "Art"   Det-A 1944-48
Mills, C. Buster   Cle-A 1946, Chi-A 1947-50, Cin-N 1953, Bos-A 1954
Mills, J. Bradley "Brad"   Phi-N 1997-98
Minoso, S. Orestes "Minnie"   Chi-A 1976-78, 1980-81
Mitchell, Clarence E.   NY-N 1932-33
Mitchell, Frederick F. "Fred"   Bos-N 1914-16
Mitterwald, George E.   Oak-A 1979-82, NY-A 1988
Mize, John R. "Johnny"   KC-A 1961
Monbouquette, William C. "Bill"   NY-N 1982-83, NY-A 1985
Monchak, Alex "Al"   Chi-A 1971-75, Oak-A 1976, Pit-N 1977-84, Atl-N 1986-88
Moon, Wallace W. "Wally"   SD-N 1969
Moore, Jackie S.   Mil-A 1970-72, Tex-A 1973-74, 1975-76, Tor-A 1977-79, Tex-A 1980, Oak-A 1981-84, Mon-N 1987-89, Cin-N 1990-92, Tex-A 1993-94, Col-N 1996-98
Moore, Terry B.   StL-N 1949-52, 1956-58
Morales, Jose M.   SF-N 1986-88, Cle-A 1990-93, Fla-N 1995-96
Morales, Richard A. "Rich"   Atl-N 1986-87
Morgan, Joseph M. "Joe"   Pit-N 1972, Bos-A 1985-88
Morgan, Tom S.   Cal-A 1972-74, SD-N 1975, NY-A 1979, Cal-A 1981-83
Morgan, Vernon T. "Vern"   Min-A 1969-75
Moses, Wallace "Wally"   Phi-A 1952-54, Phi-N 1955-58, Cin-N 1959-60, NY-A 1961-62, 1966, Det-A 1967-70
Moss, J. Lester "Les"   Chi-A 1967-68, 1969-70, Chi-N 1981, Hou-N 1982-84, 1985-89
Mota, Manuel R. "Manny"   LA-N 1980-89
Motton, Curtell H. "Curt"   Bal-A 1991
Mozzali, Maurice J. "Mo"   StL-N 1977-78
Mueller, Ray C.   NY-N 1956, Chi-N 1957
Muffett, Billy A.   StL-N 1967-70, Cal-A 1974-77, Det-A 1985-94
Mulcahy, Hugh N.   Chi-A 1970
Mull, Jack L.   SF-N 1985
Mulleavy, Gregory T. "Greg"   Bro-N 1957, LA-N 1958-60, 1962-64
Mullin, Patrick J. "Pat"   Det-A 1963-66, Cle-A 1967, Mon-N 1979-81
Mungo, Van Lingle   Bro-N 1940
Murphy, Daniel F. "Danny"   Phi-A 1920-24, Phi-N 1927
Murphy, Dwayne K.   Ari-N 1998
Murray, Eddie C.   Bal-A 1998
Murtaugh, Daniel E. "Danny"   Pit-N 1956-57
Muser, Anthony J. "Tony"   Mil-A 1985-89, Chi-N 1993-97
Myatt, George E.   Was-A 1950-54, Chi-A 1955-56, Chi-N 1957-59, Mil-N 1960-61, Det-A 1962-63, Phi-N 1964-72
Napoleon, Edward G. "Ed"   Cle-A 1983-85, KC-A 1987-88, Hou-N 1989, NY-A 1992-93, Tex-A 1995-98
Naragon, Harold R. "Hal"   Min-A 1963-66, Det-A 1967-69
Narron, Jerry A.   Bal-A 1993-94, Tex-A 1995-98
Narron, Samuel "Sam"   Pit-N 1952-64
Neale, A. Earle "Greasy"   StL-N 1929
Nelson, David E. "Dave"   Chi-A 1981-84, Cle-A 1992-97
Nettles, Graig   NY-A 1991, SD-N 1995
Neun, John H. "Johnny"   NY-A 1944-46
Newman, Jeffrey L. "Jeff"   Oak-A 1986, Cle-A

1992-98
Niarhos, C. Gus   KC-A 1962-64
Niehoff, J. Albert "Bert"   NY-N 1929
Niemann, Randal H. "Randy"   NY-N 1997-98
Nipper, Albert S. "Al"   Bos-A 1995-96
Nixon, Russell E. "Russ"   Cin-N 1976-82, Mon-N 1984-85, Atl-N 1986-87, Sea-N 1992
Noren, Irving A. "Irv"   Oak-A 1971-74, Chi-N 1975
Norman, H. Willis P. "Bill"   StL-A 1952-53
Northey, Ronald J. "Ron"   Pit-N 1961-63
Nossek, Joseph R. "Joe"   Mil-A 1973-75, Min-A 1976, Cle-A 1977-81, KC-A 1982-83, Chi-A 1984-85, 1986, 1991-98
Nottle, Edward W. "Ed"   Oak-A 1983
Oates, Johnny L.   Chi-N 1984-87, Bal-A 1989-91
O'Brien, Edward J. "Eddie"   Sea-A 1969
Oceak, Frank J.   Pit-N 1958-64, Cin-N 1965, Pit-N 1970-72
O'Connell, Daniel F. "Danny"   Was-A 1963-64
O'Connor, Patrick F. "Paddy"   NY-A 1918-21
Oester, Ronald J. "Ron"   Cin-N 1993, Det-A 1996, Cin-N 1997-98
Okrie, Leonard J. "Len"   Bos-A 1961-62, 1965-66, Det-A 1970
Oldis, Robert C. "Bob"   Phi-N 1964-66, Min-A 1968, Mon-N 1969
O'Leary, Charles T. "Charley"   StL-A 1913, NY-A 1920-30, Chi-N 1931-33, StL-A 1934-37
Oliva, Pedro "Tony"   Min-A 1976-78, 1985-91
Oliveras, Max "Mako"   Cal-A 1994, Chi-N 1995-97
Oliver, David J. "Dave"   Tex-A 1987-94, Bos-A 1995-96
Oliver, Thomas N. "Tom"   Phi-A 1951-53, Bal-A 1954
Olson, Ivan M. "Ivy"   Bro-N 1924, 1930-31, NY-N 1932
O'Neil, G. Michael "Mickey"   Cle-A 1930
O'Neil, John S. "Buck"   Chi-N 1962-65
O'Neill, Stephen F. "Steve"   Cle-A 1935, Det-A 1941, Cle-A 1949, Bos-A 1950
Onslow, John J. "Jack"   Pit-N 1925-26, Was-A 1927, StL-N 1928, Phi-N 1931-32, Bos-A 1934
Osborn, Donald E. "Don"   Pit-N 1963-64, 1970-72, 1974-76
Osteen, Claude W.   StL-N 1977-80, Phi-N 1982-88, Tex-A 1993-94
Otero, Regino J. "Regie"   Cin-N 1959-65, Cle-A 1966
Otis, Amos J.   SD-N 1988-90, Col-N 1993
Ott, N. Edward "Ed"   Hou-N 1989-93
Overmire, Frank "Stubby"   Det-A 1963-66
Owen, Arnold M. "Mickey"   Bos-A 1955-56
Owens, James P. "Jim"   Hou-N 1967-72
Ozark, Daniel L. "Danny"   LA-N 1965-72, 1980-82, SF-N 1983-84
Pacheco, Antonio A. "Tony"   Cle-A 1974, Hou-N 1976-79, 1982
Paepke, Jack   LA-A 1961-64, Cal-A 1965-66
Pafko, Andrew "Andy"   Mil-N 1960-62
Pagan, Jose A.   Pit-N 1974-78
Page, Mitchell O.   KC-A 1995-97
Page, Philippe R. "Phil"   Cin-N 1947-52
Paige, Leroy R. "Satchell"   Atl-N 1968-69
Parker, David G. "Dave"   Ana-A 1997, StL-N 1998
Parker, Francis J. "Salty"   SF-N 1958-61, Cle-A 1962, LA-A 1964, Cal-A 1965-66, NY-N 1967, Hou-N 1968-72, Cal-A 1973-74
Parrish, Larry A.   Det-A 1997-98
Pascual, Camilo A.   Min-A 1978-80
Patkin, Max   Cle-A 1946-47, StL-A 1951, Chi-A 1976, 1978
Patterson, Henry J. C. "Hank"   Bos-A 1932
Pattin, Martin W. "Marty"   Tor-A 1989
Paul, Michael G. "Mike"   Oak-A 1987-88, Sea-A 1989-91, Oak-A 1993
Pavlick, Gregory M. "Greg"   NY-N 1985-86, 1988-91, 1994-96
Pazik, Michael J. "Mike"   Chi-A 1995-98
Peden, Leslie E. "Les"   Chi-N 1965
Peitz, Henry C. "Heinie"   StL-N 1913
Pennock, Herbert J. "Herb"   Bos-A 1936-39
Pentland, Jeffrey W. "Jeff"   Fla-N 1996, Chi-N 1997-98
Pepitone, Joseph A. "Joe"   NY-A 1982
Perez, Atanacio R. "Tony"   Cin-N 1987-92
Perkins, Ralph F. "Cy"   NY-A 1932-33, Det-A 1934-39, Phi-N 1946-54
Perlozzo, Samuel B. "Sam"   NY-N 1987-89, Cin-N 1990-92, Sea-A 1993-95, Bal-A 1996-98
Perranoski, Ronald P. "Ron"   LA-N 1981-94, SF-N 1997-98
Pesky, John M. "Johnny"   Pit-N 1965-67, Bos-A 1975-84

Peterson, Eric H. "Rick"   Pit-N 1984-85, Chi-A 1995

Pfister, George E.   Bro-N 1952

Phillips, Harold R. "Lefty"   LA-N 1965-68, Cal-A 1969

Phillips, Richard E. "Dick"   SD-N 1980

Picciolo, Robert M. "Rob"   SD-N 1990-98

Piche, Ronald J. "Ron"   Mon-N 1976

Picinich, Valentine J. "Val"   Cin-N 1934

Piersall, James A. "Jimmy"   Tex-A 1975

Pignatano, Joseph B. "Joe"   Was-A 1965-67, NY-N 1968-81, Atl-N 1982-85

Piniella, Louis V. "Lou"   NY-A 1984-85

Pinson, Vada E.   Sea-A 1977-80, Chi-A 1981, Sea-A 1982-83, Det-A 1985-91, Fla-N 1993-94

Pitler, Jacob A. "Jake"   Bro-N 1947-57

Pitts, Gaylen R.   StL-N 1991-95

Plaza, Ronald C. "Ron"   Sea-A 1969, Cin-N 1978-83, Oak-A 1986

Plummer, William F. "Bill"   Sea-A 1982-83, 1988-91, Col-N 1993

Podres, John J. "Johnny"   SD-N 1973, Bos-A 1980, Min-A 1981-85, Phi-N 1991-96

Pole, Richard H. "Dick"   Chi-N 1988-91, SF-N 1993-97, Bos-A 1998

Pollet, Howard J. "Howie"   StL-N 1959-64, Hou-N 1965

Popowski, Edward J. "Eddie"   Bos-A 1967-76

Poquette, Thomas A. "Tom"   KC-A 1997-98

Posedel, William J. "Bill"   Pit-N 1949-53, StL-N 1954-57, Phi-N 1958, SF-N 1959-60, Oak-A 1968-72, SD-N 1974

Presley, James A. "Jim"   Ari-N 1998

Pujols, Luis B.   Mon-N 1993-98

Queen, Melvin D. "Mel"   Cle-A 1982, Tor-A 1996-98

Quilici, Francis R. "Frank"   Min-A 1971-72

Quirk, James P. "Jamie"   StL-N 1984, KC-A 1994-98

Rader, Douglas L. "Doug"   SD-N 1978-79, Chi-A 1986-87, Oak-A 1992, Fla-N 1993-94, Chi-A 1997

Radison, Daniel J. "Dan"   SD-N 1993-94, Chi-N 1995-98

Ragan, D. C. Patrick "Pat"   Phi-N 1924

Randall, Robert L. "Bobby"   Min-A 1980

Randolph, Willie L.   NY-A 1994-98

Rapp, Vernon F. "Vern"   Mon-N 1979-83

Reberger, Frank B.   Cal-A 1991, Fla-N 1993-94

Redys, Edward "Ed"   StL-A 1950-51

Reese, Harold H. "Pee Wee"   LA-N 1959

Reese, James H. "Jimmie"   Cal-A 1973-94

Regan, Philip R. "Phil"   Sea-A 1984-86, Cle-A 1994, Chi-N 1997-98

Reiser, Harold P. "Pete"   LA-N 1960-64, Chi-N 1966-69, Cal-A 1970-71, Chi-N 1972-74

Renick, W. Richard "Rick"   KC-A 1981, Mon-N 1985-86, Min-A 1987-90, Pit-N 1997-98

Resinger, Grover S.   Atl-N 1966, Chi-A 1967-68, Det-A 1969-70, Cal-A 1975-76

Rettenmund, Mervin W. "Merv"   Cal-A 1980-82, Tex-A 1983-85, Oak-A 1989-90, SD-N 1991-98

Reyes, Benjamin "Cananea"   Sea-A 1981

Reynolds, Tommie D   Oak-A 1989-95, StL-N 1996

Rice, Delbert "Del"   StL-N 1959, LA-N 1962-64, Cal-A 1965-66, Cle-A 1967

Rice, James E. "Jim"   Bos-A 1994-98

Ricketts, David W. "Dave"   Pit-N 1971-73, StL-N 1974-75, 1978-91

Riddle, John L. "Johnny"   Pit-N 1948-50, StL-N 1952-55, Mil-N 1956-57, Cin-N 1958, Phi-N 1959

Riddoch, Gregory L. "Greg"   SD-N 1987-90, TB-A 1998

Riggins, Mark A.   StL-N 1995

Riggleman, James D. "Jim"   StL-N 1989-90

Rigney, William J. "Bill"   SD-N 1975

Rigoli, Joseph M. "Joe"   Phi-N 1996-97

Ripken, Calvin E., Sr. "Cal"   Bal-A 1976-86, 1989-92

Rippelmeyer, Raymond R. "Ray"   Phi-N 1970-78

Roarke, Michael T. "Mike"   Det-A 1965-66, Cal-A 1967-69, Det-A 1970, Chi-N 1978-80, StL-N 1984-90, SD-N 1991-93, Bos-A 1994

Roberts, David W. "Dave"   Cle-A 1987

Roberts, Melvin H. "Mel"   Phi-N 1992-95

Robertson, Sherrard A. "Sherry"   Min-N 1970

Robinson, Brooks C.   Bal-A 1977

Robinson, Dewey E.   Chi-A 1993-94

Robinson, Frank   Cal-A 1977, Bal-A 1978-80, 1985-87

Robinson, Warren G. "Sheriff"   NY-N 1964, 1965-67, 1972

Robinson, Wilbert   NY-N 1911-13

Robinson, William H. "Bill"   NY-N 1984-89

Robinson, W. Edward "Eddie"   Bal-A 1957-59

Robson, Thomas J. "Tom"   Tex-A 1986-92, NY-N 1997-98

Rodgers, Robert L. "Bob"   Min-A 1970-74, SF-N 1976, Mil-A 1978-80

Rodriguez, Eduardo "Eddie"   Cal-A 1996, Tor-A 1998

Rojas, Octavio V. "Cookie"   Chi-A 1978-81, Fla-N 1993-96, NY-N 1997-98

Rolfe, Robert A. "Red"   NY-A 1946

Rommel, Edwin A. "Eddie"   Phi-A 1933-34

Roof, Eugene L.'Gene"   Det-A 1992-95

Roof, Phillip A. "Phil"   SD-N 1978, Sea-A 1983-88, Chi-N 1990-91

Root, Charles H. "Charlie"   Chi-N 1951-53, Mil-N 1956-57, Chi-N 1960

Roseboro, John J.   Was-A 1970-71, Cal-A 1972-74

Rosenbaum, Glen O.   Chi-A 1973-75, 1986-88

Roth, Francis C. "Frank"   Pit-N 1917, NY-A 1921-22, Cle-A 1923-25, Chi-A 1927

Rothschild, Lawrence L. "Larry"   Cin-N 1990-93, Fla-N 1995-97

Roush, Edd J   Cin-N 1938

Rowe, Donald H. "Don"   Chi-A 1988, Mil-A 1992-97, Mil-N 1998

Rowe, Kenneth D. "Ken"   Bal-A 1985-86

Rowe, Lynwood T. "Schoolboy"   Det-A 1954-55

Rowe, Ralph E.   Min-A 1972-75, Bal-A 1981-84

Royster, Jeron K. "Jerry: Col-N 1993

Ruberto, John E. "Sonny"   StL-N 1977-78

Rudi, Joseph O. "Joe"   Oak-A 1986-87

Rudolph, Richard "Dick"   Bos-N 1921-27

Ruel, Herold D. "Muddy"   Chi-A 1935-45, Cle-A 1948-50

Ruffing, Charles H. "Red"   NY-N 1962

Ruhle, Vernon G. "Vern"   Hou-N 1997-98

Runnels, James E. "Pete"   Bos-A 1965-66

Runnells, Thomas W. "Tom"   Mon-N 1990-91

Russell, William E. "Bill"   LA-N 1987-91, 1994-96

Ruth, George H. "Babe"   Bro-N 1938

Ryan, Cornelius J. "Connie"   Mil-N 1957, Atl-N 1971, 1973-75, Tex-A 1977-79

Ryan, John B. "Jack"   Was-A 1912-13, Bos-A 1923-27

Ryan, Michael J. "Mike"   Phi-N 1980-95

Ryba, Dominic J. "Mike"   StL-N 1951-54

Sain, John F. "Johnny"   KC-A 1959, NY-A 1961-63, Min-A 1965-66, Det-A 1967-69, Chi-A 1971-75, Atl-N 1977, 1985-86

Sanford, John A. "Jack"   Cle-A 1968-69

Sandt, Thomas J. "Tommy"   Pit-N 1987-96, Fla-N 1997-98

Sarni, William F. "Bill"   NY-N 1957

Sauer, Henry J. "Hank"   SF-N 1959

Saul, James A. "Jim"   Chi-N 1975-76, Oak-A 1979

Scarborough, Ray W.   Bal-A 1968

Schacht, Alexander "Al"   Was-A 1925-34, Bos-A 1935-36

Schaefer, Robert W. "Bob"   KC-A 1988-91

Schaffer, Jimmie R. "Jim"   Tex-A 1978, KC-A 1980-88

Schalk, Raymond W. "Ray"   Chi-N 1930-31

Schang, Walter H. "Wally"   Cle-A 1936-38

Scheffing, Robert B. "Bob"   StL-A 1952-53, Chi-N 1954-55, Mil-N 1960

Scherger, George R.   Cin-N 1970-78, 1982-86

Schoendienst, Albert F. "Red"   StL-N 1961-64, Oak-A 1977-78, StL-N 1979-89

Schreiber, Paul F.   NY-A 1942, Bos-A 1947-58

Schueler, Ronald R. "Ron"   Chi-A 1979-82, Oak-A 1983-84, Pit-N 1986

Schulte, John C. "Johnny"   Chi-N 1933, NY-A 1934-48, Bos-A 1949-50

Schultz, George W. "Barney"   StL-N 1971-75, Chi-N 1977

Schultz, Joseph C., Jr. "Joe"   StL-N 1949, StL-N 1963-68, KC-A 1970, Det-A 1971-76

Scioscia, Michael L. "Mike"   LA-N 1997-98

Seminick, Andrew W. "Andy"   Phi-N 1957-58, 1967-69

Sewell, J. Luther "Luke"   Cle-A 1939-41, Cin-N 1949

Sewell, Joseph W. "Joe"   NY-A 1934-35

Sewell, Truett B. "Rip"   Pit-N 1948

Shanks, Howard S. "Howie"   Cle-A 1928-32

Shaughnessy, Francis J. "Shag"   Det-A 1928

Shaw, Robert J. "Bob"   Mil-A 1973

Shawkey, J. Robert "Bob"   NY-A 1929

Shea, Mervyn D. "Merv"   Det-A 1939-42, Phi-N 1944-45, Chi-N 1948-49

Sheehan, Thomas C. "Tom"   Cin-N 1935-37, Bro-N 1938, Bos-N 1944

Shelby, John T.   LA-N 1998

Shellenback, Frank V.   StL-A 1939, Bos-A 1940-44, Det-A 1946-47, NY-N 1949-55

Shellenback, James P. "Jim"   Min-A 1983

Shepard, Robert E. "Bert"   Was-A 1946

Shepard, Lawrence W. "Larry"   Phi-N 1967, Cin-N 1970-78, SF-N 1979

Sherlock, Glenn P.   Ari-N 1998

Sherry, Lawrence "Larry"   Pit-N 1977-78, Cal-A 1979-80

Sherry, Norman B. "Norm"   Cal-A 1970-71, 1976, Mon-N 1978-81, SD-N 1982-84, SF-N 1986-91

Shore, Raymond E. "Ray"   Cin-N 1963-67

Shotton, Burton E. "Burt"   StL-N 1923-25, Cin-N 1934, Cle-A 1942-45

Showalter, William N. "Buck"   NY-A 1990-91

Siebert, Wilfred C. "Sonny"   SD-N 1994-95

Sievers, Roy E.   Cin-N 1966

Silvera, Charles A. "Charlie"   Min-A 1969, Det-A 1971-73, Tex-A 1973-75

Silvestri, Kenneth J. "Ken"   Phi-N 1959-60, Mil-N 1963-65, Atl-N 1966-75, Chi-A 1976, 1982

Simmons, Aloysius H. "Al"   Phi-N 1940-42, 1944-49, Cle-A 1950-51

Sinatro, Matthew Stephen "Matt"   Sea-A 1995-98

Sisler, George H.   Bos-N 1930

Sisler, Richard A. "Dick"   Cin-N 1961-64, StL-N 1966-70, SD-N 1975-76, NY-N 1979-80

Sisti, Sebastian D. "Sibby"   Mil-N 1954, Sea-A 1969

Skaff, Francis M. "Frank"   Bal-A 1954, Det-A 1965-66, 1971

Skinner, Robert R. "Bob"   SD-N 1970-73, Pit-N 1974-76, SD-N 1977, Cal-A 1978, Pit-N 1979-85, Atl-N 1986-88

Slattery, John T. "Jack"   Bos-N 1918-19

Slider, Rachel W. "Rac"   Bos-A 1987-90

Smith, Alfred J. "Al"   NY-N 1933

Smith, Billy F.   Tor-A 1984-88

Smith, C. Reginald "Reggie"   LA-N 1994-98

Smith, Harold R. "Hal"   StL-N 1962, Pit-N 1965-67, Cin-N 1968-69, Mil-A 1976-77

Smith, Richard P. "Red"   Chi-N 1945-48

Smith, Steven J. "Steve"   Sea-A 1996-98

Snider, Edwin D. "Duke"   Mon-N 1974-75

Snitker, Brian G.   Atl-N 1985, 1988-90

Snyder, Francis E. "Frank"   NY-N 1933-41

Snyder, James R. "Jim"   Chi-N 1987, Sea-A 1988, SD-N 1991-92

Sommers, Dennis J. "Denny"   NY-N 1977-78, Cle-A 1980-85, SD-N 1988-90

Sothoron, Allen S.   StL-N 1927-28, StL-A 1932-33

Southworth, William H. "Billy"   NY-N 1933

Spahn, Warren E.   NY-N 1965, Cle-A 1972-73

Spalding, Charles H. "Dick"   Phi-N 1934-36, Chi-N 1941-43

Spangler, Albert D. "Al"   Chi-N 1970-71, 1974

Sparks, Joseph E. "Joe"   Chi-A 1979, Cin-N 1984, Mon-N 1989, NY-A 1990

Spencer, H. Thomas "Tom"   Cle-A 1988-89, NY-N 1991, Hou-N 1992-93

Squires, Michael L. "Mike"   Tor-A 1989-91, Chi-A 1992

Staller, George W.   Bal-A 1962, 1969-75

Stanage, Oscar H.   Pit-N 1927-31

Stange, A. Lee   Bos-A 1969, 1972-74, Min-A 1975, Oak-A 1977-79, Bos-A 1981-84

Stanky, Edward R. "Eddie"   Cle-A 1957-58

Stanley, Frederick B. "Fred"   Mil-A 1991

Stargell, Wilver D. "Willie"   Pit-N 1985, Atl-N 1986-88

Starrette, Herman P. "Herm"   Atl-N 1974-76, SF-N 1977-78, Phi-N 1979-81, SF-N 1983-84, Mil-A 1985-86, Chi-N 1987, Bal-A 1988, Bos-A 1995, 1996-97

Staub, Daniel J. "Rusty"   NY-N 1982

Stearns, John H.   NY-A 1989, Bal-A 1996-97

Stelmaszek, Richard F. "Rick"   Min-A 1981-98

Stengel, Charles D. "Casey"   Bro-N 1932-33

Stevens, Edward L. "Ed"   SD-N 1981

Stewart, David K. "Dave"   SD-N 1998

Stock, Milton J. "Milt"   Chi-N 1944-48, Bro-N 1949-50, Pit-N 1951-52

Stock, Wesley G. "Wes"   KC-A 1967, Mil-A 1970-72, Oak-A 1972-76, Sea-A 1977-81, Oak-A 1984-86

Stottlemyre, Melvin L. "Mel"   NY-N 1984-93, Hou-N 1994-95, NY-A 1996-98

Stratton, Monty F.   Chi-A 1939-41

Street, Charles E. "Gabby"   StL-N 1929, StL-A 1937

Strickland, George B.   Min-A 1962, Cle-A 1963-69, KC-A 1970-72

Strom, Brent T.   Hou-N 1996

Stubing, Lawrence G. "Moose"   Cal-A 1985-88, 1989-90
Such, Richard S. "Dick"   Tex-A 1983-85, Min-A 1985-98
Sugden, Joseph "Joe"   StL-N 1921-25, Phi-N 1926-27
Sukeforth, Clyde L.   Bro-N 1943-51, Pit-N 1952-57
Sullivan, John P.   KC-A 1979, Atl-N 1980-81, Tor-A 1982-93
Summers, John J. "Champ"   NY-A 1989-90
Susce, George C. M.   Cle-A 1941-47, 1948-49, Bos-A 1950-54, KC-A 1955-56, Mil-N 1958-59, Was-A 1961-67, 1969-71, Tex-A 1972
Sweeney, William J. "Bill"   Det-A 1947-48
Sweet, Ricky J. "Rick"   Sea-A 1984, Hou-N 1996
Swift, Robert V. "Bob"   Det-A 1953-54, KC-A 1957-59, Was-A 1960, Det-A 1963-66
Swisher, Steven E. "Steve"   NY-N 1993-96
Tannehill, Jesse N.   Phi-N 1920
Tappe, Elvin W. "El"   Chi-N 1958-65
Taylor, Antonio N. "Tony"   Phi-N 1977-79, 1988-89
Taylor, James W. "Zack"   Bro-N 1936, StL-A 1941-46, Pit-N 1947
Temple, John E. "Johnny"   Cin-N 1964
Tenace, F. Gene   Hou-N 1986-87, Tor-A 1990-97
Terwilliger, W. Wayne   Was-A 1969-71, Tex-A 1972, 1981-85, Min-A 1986-94
Testa, Nicholas "Nick"   SF-N 1958
Thomas, George E.   Bos-A 1970
Thomas, Ira F.   Phi-A 1914-17, 1925-26
Thomas, J. Leroy "Lee"   StL-N 1972, 1983
Thomas, Roy A.   StL-N 1922
Thompson, Charles L. "Tim"   StL-N 1981
Tiefenauer, Bobby G.   Phi-N 1979
Tighe, John T. "Jack"   Det-A 1942, 1955-56
Tincup, A. Ben   Bro-N 1940
Tobin, John T. "Jack"   StL-A 1949-51
Tolan, Robert "Bobby"   SD-N 1980-83, Sea-A 1987
Torborg, Jeffrey A. "Jeff"   Cle-A 1975-77, NY-A 1979-88
Torchia, Anthony L. "Tony"   Bos-A 1985
Torgeson, C. Earl   NY-A 1961
Torres, Hector E.   Tor-A 1991
Tosca, Carlos   Ari-N 1998
Tracewski, Richard J. "Dick"   Det-A 1972-95
Tracy, James E. "Jim"   Mon-N 1995-98
Trebelhorn, Thomas L. "Tom"   Mil-A 1984, 1986, Chi-N 1992-93
Treuel, Ralph M.   Det-A 1995
Trucks, Virgil O.   Pit-N 1963
Turley, Robert L. "Bob"   Bos-A 1964
Turner, James R. "Jim"   NY-A 1949-59, Cin-N 1961-65, NY-A 1966-73
Turner, Terrence L. "Terry"   StL-N 1924
Uhle, George E.   Cle-A 1936-37, Chi-N 1940, Was-A 1944
Ullger, Scott M.   Min-A 1995-98
Unser, Delbert B. "Del"   Phi-N 1985-88
Upshaw, Willie C.   Tex-A 1993-94, Tor-A 1996-97
Valentine, Robert J. "Bobby"   NY-N 1983-85, Cin-N 1993
Valo, Elmer W.   Cle-A 1963-64

Van Ornum, John C.   SF-N 1980-84
Vernon, James B. "Mickey"   Pit-N 1960, 1964, StL-N 1965, Mon-N 1977-78, NY-A 1982
Vincent, Albert L. "Al"   Det-A 1943-44, Bal-A 1955-59, Phi-N 1961-63, KC-A 1966-67
Virdon, William C. "Bill"   Pit-N 1968-71, 1986, Hou-N 1997
Virgil, Osvaldo Jose Sr. "Ozzie"   SF-N 1969-72, 1974-75, Mon-N 1976-81, SD-N 1982-85, Sea-A 1986-88
Vuckovich, Peter D. "Pete"   Pit-N 1997-98
Vukovich, John C.   Chi-N 1982-87, Phi-N 1988, 1989-98
Wagner, Charles F. "Heinie"   Bos-A 1916-19, 1927-29
Wagner, Charles T. "Charley"   Bos-A 1970
Wagner, John P. "Honus"   Pit-N 1933-51
Walker, Albert B. "Rube"   LA-N 1958, Was-A 1965-67, NY-N 1968-81, Atl-N 1982-84
Walker, Fred "Dixie"   StL-N 1953, 1955, Mil-N 1963-65
Walker, Gerald H. "Gee"   Cin-N 1946
Walker, Harry W.   StL-N 1959-62
Walker, Jerry A.   NY-A 1981-82, Hou-N 1983-85
Walker, Verlon L.   Chi-N 1961-70
Wallace, David W. "Dave"   LA-N 1995-97
Wallace, Roderick J. "Bobby"   Cin-N 1926
Waller, Tyrone E. "Tye"   SD-N 1995
Walling, Dennis M. "Denny"   Oak-A 1996-98
Walls, R. Lee   Oak-A 1979-82, NY-N 1983
Walsh, Edward A. "Ed"   Chi-A 1923-25, 1928-30
Walters, William H. "Bucky"   Bos-N 1950-52, Mil-N 1953-55, NY-N 1956-57
Walton, James R. "Jim"   Mil-A 1973-75
Waner, Paul G.   Phi-N 1965
Ward, John F. "Jay"   NY-A 1987, Mon-N 1991-92
Ward, Peter T. "Pete"   Atl-N 1978
Wares, Clyde E. "Buzzy"   StL-N 1930-35, 1937-52
Warner, Harry C.   Tor-A 1977-79, 1980, Mil-A 1981-82
Warthen, Daniel D. "Dan"   Sea-A 1991-92, SD-N 1996-97
Washington, Ronald "Ron"   Oak-A 1996-98
Wathan, John D.   KC-A 1986, Cal-A 1992-93, Bos-A 1994
Watson, Robert J. "Bob"   Oak-A 1986-88
Weaver, Earl S.   Bal-A 1968
Webb, William J. "Billy"   Chi-A 1935-39
Werle, William G. "Bill"   SF-N 1966
West, Samuel F. "Sam"   Was-A 1947-49
Westrum, Wesley N. "Wes"   SF-N 1958-63, NY-N 1964-65, SF-N 1968-71
Whisenant, T. Peter "Pete"   Cin-N 1961-62
White, Ernest D. "Ernie"   Bos-A 1947-48, NY-N 1963
White, Frank   Bos-A 1994-96, KC-A 1997-98
White, Jerome C. "Jerry"   Det-A 1997-98
White, Joyner C. "Jo-Jo"   Cle-A 1958-60, Det-A 1960, KC-A 1961-62, Mil-N 1963-65, Atl-N 1966, KC-A 1969
White, Roy H.   NY-A 1983-84, 1986
Whitehill, Earl O.   Cle-A 1941, Phi-N 1943
Whitmer, Daniel C. "Dan"   Det-A 1992-94
Widmar, Albert J. "Al"   Phi-N 1962-64, 1968-69,

Mil-A 1973-74, Tor-A 1980-88, 1989
Wietelmann, William F. "Whitey"   Cin-N 1966-67, SD-N 1969-79
Wilber, Delbert Q. "Del"   Chi-A 1955-56, Was-A 1970, Tex-A 1973
Wiley, Mark E.   Bal-A 1987, Cle-A 1988-91, 1995-98
Wilhelm, Irvin K. "Kaiser"   Phi-N 1921
Wilks, Theodore "Ted"   Cle-A 1960, KC-A 1961
Williams, Billy L.   Chi-N 1980-82, Oak-A 1983-85, Chi-N 1986-87, 1992-98
Williams, Dana   Cle-A 1993
Williams, Daniel L. "Dan"   Cle-A 1995-98
Williams, David C. "Davey"   NY-N 1956-57
Williams, Donald E. "Don"   SD-N 1977-80
Williams, Donald R. "Spin"   Pit-N 1994-98
Williams, James B. "Jimmy"   Hou-N 1975, Bal-A 1981-87
Williams, James F. "Jimy"   Tor-A 1980-85, Atl-N 1990-96
Williams, Otto G.   Det-A 1925, StL-N 1926, StL-N 1927, Cin-N 1930
Williams, Richard A. "Rick"   Fla-N 1995-96, TB-A 1998
Williams, Richard H. "Dick"   Mon-N 1970
Williams, Stanley W. "Stan"   Bos-A 1975-76, Chi-A 1977-78, NY-A 1980-81, 1982, Cin-N 1984, NY-A 1987, 1988, Cin-N 1990-91, Sea-A 1998
Williams, Walter A. "Walt"   Chi-A 1988
Wilson, James "Jimmy"   Cin-N 1939-40, 1944-46
Wilson, William H. "Mookie"   NY-N 1997-98
Wiltse, George L. "Hooks"   NY-A 1925
Wine, Robert P. Sr. "Bobby"   Phi-N 1972-83, Atl-N 1985, 1988-90, NY-N 1993-96
Winegarner, Ralph L.   StL-A 1948-51
Wingo, Ivey B.   Cin-N 1928-29, 1936
Winkles, Bobby B.   Cal-A 1972, Oak-A 1974-75, SF-N 1976-77, Chi-A 1979-81, Mon-N 1986-88
Wolgamot, C. Earl   Cle-A 1931-33
Woodall, C. Lawrence "Larry"   Bos-A 1942-48
Woodling, Eugene R. "Gene"   Bal-A 1964-67
Worthington, Allan F. "Al"   Min-A 1972-73
Wotus, Ronald A. "Ron"   SF-N 1998
Wright, James I. "Jim"   Phi-N 1996
Wright, Melvin J. "Mel"   Chi-N 1963-64, 1971, Pit-N 1973, NY-A 1974-75, Hou-N 1976-82
Wyatt, J. Whitlow "Whit"   Phi-N 1955-57, Mil-A 1958-65, Atl-N 1966-67
Wynn, Early   Cle-A 1964-66, Min-A 1967-69
York, P. Rudolph "Rudy"   Bos-A 1959-62
Yost, Edgar F. "Ned"   Atl-N 1991-98
Yost, Edward F. "Eddie"   LA-A 1962, Was-A 1963-67, NY-N 1968-76, Bos-A 1977-84
Youngblood, Joel R.   Cin-N 1994-97, Mil-N 1998
Zarilla, Allen L. "Al"   Was-A 1971
Zeller, Barton W. "Bart"   StL-N 1970
Zimmer, Donald W. "Don"   Mon-N 1971, SD-N 1972, Bos-A 1974-76, NY-A 1983, Chi-N 1984-86, NY-A 1986, SF-N 1987, Bos-A 1992, Col-N 1993-95, NY-A 1996-98
Zimmer, Thomas J. "Tom"   StL-N 1976
Zimmerman, Gerald R. "Gerry"   Min-A 1967, Mon-N 1969-75, Min-A 1976-80
Zuvella, Paul   Col-N 1996
Zwilling, Edward H. "Dutch"   Cle-A 1941

Biographical Data for Coaches

SPENCER ABBOTT   Abbott, Spencer Arthur   b: 8/27/1887, Chicago, Ill.   d: 12/18/51, Washington, D.C.   BL/TL (1B)
RICK ADAIR   Adair, Michael Richard   b: 1/19/58, Spartanburg, S.Car.   BL/TL, 6′, 185 lbs.   (P)
BOB ALEJO   Alejo, Robert Kevin   b: 11/19/57, Sacramento, Cal.   BR/TR, 5′10″, 185 lbs.   (DNP)
CARLOS ALFONSO   Alfonso, Carlos   b: 12/18/50, Havana, Cuba   BR/TR, 6′2″, 205 lbs.   (P)
PIERRE ARSENAULT   Arsenault, Pierre Jean   b: 10/12/63, Roberval, Que., Can.   BR/TR, 5′11″, 180 lbs.   (C)
TONY AUFERIO   Auferio, Anthony Patrick   b: 6/13/47, Orange, N.J.   BR/TR, 5′10″, 185 lbs.   (3B)
DICK BERARDINO   Berardino, Richard J.   b: 7/2/37, Cambridge, Mass.   BR/TR, 6′1″, 190 lbs.   (OF)
C. B. BERINGER   Beringer, Carroll James   b: 8/14/28, Bellwood, Neb.   BR/TR, 6′, 195 lbs.   (P)
CARLOS BERNHARDT   Bernhardt, Carlos   b: 9/9/50, San Pedro De Macoris, D.R.   BR/TR, 5′11″, 195 lbs.   (P)
GREG BIAGINI   Biagini, Gregory Peter   b: 5/12/52, Chicago, Ill.   BB/TR, 6′2″, 205 lbs.   (1B-OF)
DAVE BIALAS   Bialas, David Bruce   b: 3/6/54, Houston, Tex.   BR/TR, 6′1″, 210 lbs.   (P)
WAYNE BLACKBURN   Blackburn, Wayne Clark   b: 7/10/16, Mount Joy, Ohio   BL/TR, 5′10″, 165 lbs.   (OF-3B-2B)
JACK BLOOMFIELD   Bloomfield, Gordon Leigh   b: 8/7/32, Monte Alto, Tex.   BL/TR, 6′2″, 185 lbs.   (2B)
MARC BOMBARD   Bombard, Marc   b: 11/15/49, Tampa, Fla.   BR/TL, 5′8″, 180 lbs.   (P)
JIMMY BRAGAN   Bragan, James Alton   b: 3/12/29, Birmingham, Ala.   BR/TR, 6′, 198 lbs.   (2B) (Brother of Bobby Bragan)
SCOTT BREEDEN   Breeden, Harold Scott   b: 9/17/37, Charlottesville, Va.   BR/TR, 6′2″, 210 lbs.   (P)
JOE BREEDEN   Breeden, Joseph Thomas   b: 10/11/56, Newport News, Va.   BR/TR, 5′11″, 195 lbs.   (C)
LORENZO BUNDY   Bundy, Charles Lorenzo   b: 11/6/59, Philadelphia, Pa.   BL/TR, 6′2″, 205 lbs.   (1B)
BRIAN BUTTERFIELD   Butterfield, Brian James   b: 3/9/58, Bangor, Maine   BB/TR, 6′, 200 lbs.   (2B)
JOE CAMACHO   Camacho, Joseph Gomes   b: 5/29/28, New Bedford, Mass.   BR/TR, 6′, 185 lbs.   (SS-2B)
P. J. CAREY   Carey, Paul Jerome   b: 11/4/53, Scranton, Pa.   BR/TR, 6′1″, 190 lbs.   (C)
DAVE CARLUCCI   Carlucci, David Mario   b: 5/1/63, Milford, Mass.   BR/TR, 6′1″, 195 lbs.   (C)

DANNY CARNEVALE Carnevale, Daniel Joseph b: 2/8/18, Buffalo, N.Y. BR/TR, 6', 195 lbs. (SS)
LEONEL CARRION Carrion, Leonel Santiago (Matheus) b: 2/15/52, Maracaibo, Venez. BR/TR, 5'11", 185 lbs. (OF)
DICK CARTER Carter, Richard Joseph b: 8/31/16, Philadelphia, Pa. d: 9/11/69, Philadelphia, Pa. BR/TR, 5'10", 190 lbs. (P-OF)
DOM CHITI Chiti, Harry Dominic b: 12/10/58, Independence, Mo. BL/TL, 6'2", 200 lbs. (P)
BOB CLEAR Clear, Elwood Robert b: 12/14/27, Denver, Colo. BR/TR, 5'10", 170 lbs. (P)
BOB CLUCK Cluck, Robert Alton b: 1/10/46, San Diego, Cal. BL/TL, 6'2", 195 lbs. (P)
MARK CONNOR Connor, Mark Peter b: 5/27/49, Brooklyn, N.Y. BR/TR, 6'3", 195 lbs. (P)
JIMMIE CRANDALL Crandall, James Mark b: 12/7/12, Wadena, Ind. d: 2/83, Bullhead City, Ariz. BB/TR, 5'11", 190 lbs. (P-C) (Son of Doc Crandall)
MARK CRESSE Cresse, Mark Emery b: 9/21/51, St.Albans, N.Y. BR/TR, 6'3", 220 lbs. (C)
ROLY DeARMAS DeArmas, Rolando Jesus b: 12/29/51, New York, N.Y. BR/TR, 6'1", 190 lbs. (C)
MARTY DeMERRITT DeMerritt, Martin Gordon b: 3/4/53, San Francisco, Cal. BR/TR, 6'2.5", 205 lbs. (P)
BOBBY DEWS Dews, Robert Walter b: 3/23/38, Clinton, Iowa BR/TR, 6'1", 175 lbs. (SS)
WALT DIXON Dixon, Walter Edward b: 11/25/20, Mount Vernon Springs, N.Car. BR/TR, 6'2", 220 lbs. (P)
RICH DONNELLY Donnelly, Richard Francis b: 8/3/46, Steubenville, Ohio BL/TR, 6', 185 lbs. (C)
OTIS DOUGLAS Douglas, Otis Whitfield b: 7/25/11, Reedville, Va. d: 3/21/89, Kilmarnock, Va. BR/TR, 6'1", 230 lbs. (DNP)
RICK DOWN Down, Richard John b: 12/14/50, Wyandotte, Mich. BR/TR, 5'11", 220 lbs. (OF)
RICH DUBEE Dubee, Richard Peter b: 10/19/57, Brockton, Mass. BB/TR, 6'2", 200 lbs. (P)
HARRY DUNLOP Dunlop, Harry Alexander b: 9/6/33, Sacramento, Cal. BL/TR, 6'3", 200 lbs. (C)
GENE DUSAN Dusan, Eugene Paul b: 11/9/49, Los Angeles, Cal. BB/TR, 6', 200 lbs. (C)
GLENN EZZELL Ezzell, Glenn Wayne b: 10/29/44, Kentwood, La. BR/TR, 6', 190 lbs. (C)
BRAD FISCHER Fischer, Bradley James b: 6/28/56, Toledo, Ohio BR/TR, 6'3", 198 lbs. (C)
JOE FITZGERALD Fitzgerald, Joseph Patrick b: 3/17/1897, Washington, D.C. d: 8/29/67, Orlando, Fla. BR/TR, 5'11", 200 lbs. (C)
JOHN FITZPATRICK Fitzpatrick, John Arthur b: 3/19/04, LaSalle, Ill. d: 11/19/90, BR/TR, 6'1.5", 185 lbs. (C)
MATT GALANTE Galante, Matthew Joseph b: 3/2/44, Brooklyn, N.Y. BR/TR, 5'6", 175 lbs. (2B)
TOM GAMBOA Gamboa, Thomas Harold b: 2/28/48, Los Angeles, Cal. BL/TL, 5'10", 175 lbs. OF)
GENE GLYNN Glynn, Eugene Patrick b: 9/22/56, Waseca, Minn. BR/TR, 5'9", 165 lbs. (SS)
ORLANDO GOMEZ Gomez, Juan Alejandro b: 6/24/46, Juana Diaz, P.R. BR/TR, 6', 190 lbs. (C)
GLENN GREGSON Gregson, Glenn b: 2/10/50, Hamlet, N.C. BB/TR, 6'3", 185 lbs. (P)
EPY GUERRERO Guerrero, Epifanio Obdulio (Abud) b: 1/3/42, Santo Domingo, D.R. BR/TR, 5'11", 168 lbs. (OF) (Brother of Mario Guerrero)
GUY HANSEN Hansen, Guy Christopher b: 11/12/47, Los Angeles, Cal. BR/TR, 6', 170 lbs. (P)
ROGER HANSEN Hansen, Roger Christian b: 8/28/61, Johnstown, Pa. BR/TR, 6', 200 lbs. (C)
TOM HARMON Harmon, Thomas Harold b: 12/16/48, Lubbock, Tex. BL/TR, 5'11", 185 lbs. (C)
RAMON HENDERSON Henderson, Ramon Gaspar b: 8/18/63, Monicion, D.R. BR/TR, 5'11", 175 lbs. (3B)
CHUCK HERNANDEZ Hernandez, Carlo Amado b: 11/11/60, Tampa, Fla. BL/TL, 6'3", 200 lbs. (P)
PERRY HILL Hill, Perry Wendell b: 3/19/52, Salina, Kan. BR/TR, 5'10", 170 lbs. (2B)
BEN HINES Hines, Benjamin Thortan b: 11/7/35, Yeager, Okla. BR/TR, 5'11", 205 lbs. (3B-C) (Father of Bruce Hines)
BRUCE HINES Hines, Bruce Edwin b: 11/7/57, Pomona, Cal. BB/TR, 5'10", 180 lbs. (2B) (Son of Ben Hines)
DENNIS HOLMBERG Holmberg, Dennis Nels b: 8/2/51, Fremont, Neb. BL/TR, 6', 190 lbs. (3B)
DOUG HOLMQUIST Holmquist, Douglas Leonard b: 10/4/41, Bridgeport, Conn. d: 2/27/88, Altamonte Springs, Fla. BR/TR, 6'2", 195 lbs. (C)
GOLDIE HOLT Holt, Golden Desmond b: 3/22/02, Enloe, Tex. d: 6/11/91, Sherman Oaks, Cal. BR/TR, 5'7.5", 165 lbs. (3B-OF-2B)
VERN HOSCHEIT Hoscheit, Vernard Arthur b: 4/1/22, Brunswick, Neb. BR/TR, 5'9", 185 lbs. (C)
JACK HUBBARD Hubbard, John H. b: 10/4/50, Rock Hall, Md. BR/TR, 5'11", 175 lbs. (DNP)
LUIS ISAAC Isaac, Luis (Aponte) b: 6/19/46, Rio Piedras, P.R. BR/TR, 5'11.5", 195 lbs. (C)
RUDY JARAMILLO Jaramillo, Rudolph b: 9/20/50, Beeville, Tex. BL/TR, 5'11", 180 lbs. (OF)
DAVE JAUSS Jauss, David Patrick b: 1/16/57, Chicago, Ill. BR/TR, 5'11", 170 lbs. (DNP)
GARY JONES Jones, Gary Wayne b: 11/11/60, Henderson, Tex. BL/TR, 5'9", 163 lbs. (2B)
JOE JONES Jones, Joseph Carmack b: 12/13/41, Lebanon, Tenn. BR/TR, 5'9", 155 lbs. (2B)
LOU KAHN Kahn, Louis b: 12/4/16, St.Louis, Mo. BR/TR, 5'11", 195 lbs. (C)
MIKE KELLY Kelly, Bernard Francis b: 5/1/1896, Indianapolis, Ind. d: 10/23/68, Indianapolis, Ind. BR/TR, 6', 198 lbs. (1B)
WENDELL KIM Kim, Wendell Kealohapauloe b: 3/9/51, Honolulu, Hawaii BR/TR, 5'5", 160 lbs. (2B)
GEORGE KISSELL Kissell, George Marshall b: 9/9/21, Watertown, N.Y. BR/TR, 5'8", 175 lbs. (3B)
HUB KITTLE Kittle, Hubert Milton b: 2/19/17, Los Angeles, Cal. BR/TR, 6'1", 195 lbs. (P)
FRED KOENIG Koenig, Fred Carl b: 4/27/31, St.Louis, Mo. d: 1/12/93, Wagoner, Okla. BR/TR, 6'3", 200 lbs. (1B-3B)
BILL LACHEMANN Lachemann, William Charles b: 4/5/34, Los Angeles, Cal. BL/TR, 5'9", 195 lbs. (C)
JIM LETT Lett, James Curtis b: 1/3/51, Charleston, W.Va. BR/TR, 6'2", 185 lbs. (3B)
LENNY LEVY Levy, Leonard Howard b: 6/11/13, Pittsburgh, Pa. d: 2/2/93, Palm Desert, Cal. BR/TR, 5'10.5", 190 lbs. (C)
JULIO LINARES Linares, Julio Mairenu (Rijo) b: 12/26/40, San Pedro De Macoris, D.R. BR/TR, 5'9", 165 lbs. (3B)
GRADY LITTLE Little, William Grady b: 3/30/50, Abilene, Tex. BR/TR, 5'11", 190 lbs. (C)
BILL LOBE Lobe, William Charles b: 3/24/12, Cleveland, Ohio d: 1/7/69, Cleveland, Ohio BR/TR, 5'9.5", 178 lbs. (C)
Q. V. LOWE Lowe, Q. V. b: 1/15/45, Red Level, Ala. BR/TR, 6', 185 lbs. (P)
JOE MACKO Macko, Joseph John b: 2/19/28, Port Clinton, Ohio BR/TR, 6'2", 195 lbs. (1B) (Father of Steve Macko)
JOE MADDON Maddon, Joseph John b: 2/8/54, Hazleton, Pa. BR/TR, *'11", 19 lbs. (C)
ROY MAJTYKA Majtyka, Le Roy Walter b: 6/1/39, Buffalo, N.Y. BR/TR, 5'10", 170 lbs. (2B)
JACK MALOOF Maloof, Jack Garth b: 10/12/49, Redlands, Cal. BL/TL, 6', 175 lbs. (1B-OF)
DOUG MANSOLINO Mansolino, Douglas b: 9/20/56, Plainfield, N.J. BR/TR, 5'7", 155 lbs. (IF)
HARRY MATHEWS Mathews, Henry b: 7/23/1876, Newport, Ky. BR/TR, (C)
RICK MATHEWS Mathews, Rick Ray b: 10/9/47, Centerville, Iowa BR/TR, 5'11", 180 lbs. (P)
LEO MAZZONE Mazzone, Leo David b: 10/16/48, Keyser, W.Va. BL/TL, 5'10", 185 lbs. (P)
MAJE McDONNELL McDonnell, Robert A. b: 7/20/20, Philadelphia, Pa. BR/TR, 5'6", 135 lbs. (P)
J. R. McKEE McKee, John R.
JOHN McLAREN McLaren, John Lowell b: 9/29/51, Galveston, Tex. BR/TR, 6', 200 lbs. (C)
DAVE MILEY Miley, David Allen b: 4/3/62, Tampa, Fla. BL/TR, 6'3", 220 lbs. (C)
MO MOZZALI Mozzali, Maurice Joseph b: 12/12/22, Louisville, Ky. d: 3/2/87, Lakeland, Fla. BL/TL, 5'10", 160 lbs. (1B)
JACK MULL Mull, Jack Leroy b: 9/29/43, Chambersburg, Pa. BR/TR, 5'10", 188 lbs. (C)
ED NAPOLEON Napoleon, Edward George b: 9/17/37, Baltimore, Md. BR/TR, 5'8", 165 lbs. (OF-3B-1B)
ED NOTTLE Nottle, Edward William b: 10/22/39, Philadelphia, Pa. BR/TR, 5'10", 180 lbs. (P)
FRANK OCEAK Oceak, Frank John "Fez" b: 9/8/12, Pocahontas, Va. d: 3/19/83, Johnstown, Pa. BR/TR, 5'9", 172 lbs. (2B)
MAKO OLIVERAS Oliveras, Max b: 9/10/46, Santurce, P.R. BR/TR, 6', 195 lbs. (2B)
BUCK O'NEIL O'Neil, John Jordan b: 11/13/11, Carrabelle, Fla. BR/TR, 6'2", 190 lbs. (1B)
DON OSBORN Osborn, Donald Edwin b: 6/3/08, Sandpoint, Idaho d: 3/23/79, Torrance, Cal. BR/TR, 6', 185 lbs. (P)
TONY PACHECO Pacheco, Antonio Aristides b: 8/9/27, Havana, Cuba d: 3/23/87, Miami Beach, Fla. BR/TR, 6', 190 lbs. (2B)
JACK PAEPKE Paepke, Jack b: 8/28/22, Provo, Utah BR/TR, 6'2.5", 220 lbs. (C-P) (Father of Dennis Paepke)
MAX PATKIN Patkin, Max b: 1/10/20, Philadelphia, Pa. BR/TR, 6'2", 170 lbs. (P)
GREG PAVLICK Pavlick, Gregory Michael b: 3/10/50, Washington, D.C. BR/TR, 6'3", 205 lbs. (P)
JEFF PENTLAND Pentland, Jeffrey William b: 9/18/46, Hollywood, Cal. BL/TL, 5'10", 185 lbs. (1B)
RICK PETERSON Peterson, Eric Harding b: 10/30/54, Brunswick, N.J. BL/TL, 6', 175 lbs. (P) (Son of Harding Peterson)
RON PLAZA Plaza, Ronald Charles b: 8/24/34, Passaic, N.J. BL/TR, 6', 180 lbs. (3B)
DAN RADISON Radison, Daniel John b: 8/24/50, St.Louis, Mo. BR/TR, 6'2", 190 lbs. (C)
ED REDYS Redys, Edward b: 6/23/21, Detroit, Mich. BR/TR, 6', 185 lbs. (P)
GROVER RESINGER Resinger, Grover S b: 10/20/15, St.Louis, Mo. d: 1/11/86, St.Louis, Mo. BR/TR, 5'9", 180 lbs. (3B)
CANANEA REYES Reyes, Benjamin (Chavez) b: 2/18/37, Nacozari, Mexico d: 11/11/91, Hermosillo, Mexico BR/TR, (OF)
MARK RIGGINS Riggins, Mark Alan b: 1/3/57, Jasper, Ind. BR/TL, 5'10", 180 lbs. (P)
JOE RIGOLI Rigoli, Joseph M. b: 12/14/56, New York, N.Y. BR/TR, 6'2", 190 lbs. (C)
MEL ROBERTS Roberts, Melvin Henry b: 1/18/43, Abington, Pa. BR/TR, 6', 180 lbs. (OF)

SHERIFF ROBINSON Robinson, Warren Grant b: 9/8/21, Cambridge, Md. BR/TR, 6'1", 195 lbs. (C)
EDDIE RODRIGUEZ Rodriguez, Eduardo b: 3/11/59, Havana, Cuba BR/TR, 5'8", 165 lbs. (SS)
GLEN ROSENBAUM Rosenbaum, Glen Otis b: 6/14/36, Union Mills, Ind. BR/TR, 5'11", 180 lbs. (P)
RALPH ROWE Rowe, Ralph Emanuel b: 7/14/24, Newberry, S.C. d: 2/29/96, Newberry, S.C. BL/TR, 5'6", 160 lbs. (OF)
JIM SAUL Saul, James Allen b: 11/24/39, Bristol, Va. BL/TR, 6'3", 210 lbs. (C)
GEORGE SCHERGER Scherger, George Richard b: 11/20/20, Dickinson, N.Dak. BR/TR, 5'8", 170 lbs. (2B)
GLENN SHERLOCK Sherlock, Glenn Patrick b: 9/26/ 196, Nahant, Mass. BL/TR, 6'1", 200 lbs. (C)
RAC SLIDER Slider, Rachel W. b: 12/23/33, Simms, Tex. BL/TR, 5'8", 160 lbs. (SS)
BILLY SMITH Smith, Billy Franklin b: 1/14/30, High Point, N.C. BL/TL, 5'9", 160 lbs. (1B-OF)
STEVE SMITH Smith, Steven J. b: 7/21/53, Canton, Ohio BR/TR, 5'11", 180 lbs. (2B-SS)
BRIAN SNITKER Snitker, Brian Gerald b: 10/17/55, Decatur, Ill. BR/TR, 6'1", 192 lbs. (C)
DENNY SOMMERS Sommers, Dennis James b: 7/12/40, New London, Wis. BL/TR, 6'2", 205 lbs. (C)
JOE SPARKS Sparks, Joseph Everett b: 3/15/38, McComas, W.Va. BL/TR, 6', 195 lbs. (3B-2B)
TONY TORCHIA Torchia, Anthony Lewis b: 12/13/43, Chicago, Ill. BR/TR, 5'10", 180 lbs. (1B-OF)
CARLOS TOSCA Tosca, Carlos b: 9/29/53, Pinar Del Rio, Cuba BR/TR, 5'7", 155 lbs. (P)
RALPH TREUEL Treuel, Ralph Martin b: 6/7/55, Elyria, Ohio BR/TR, 6'4", 220 lbs. (P)
JOHN VanORNUM Van Ornum, John Clayton b: 10/20/39, Pasadena, Cal. BR/TR, 5'11", 175 lbs. (C)
AL VINCENT Vincent, Albert Linder b: 12/23/06, Birmingham, Ala. BR/TR, 5'9.5", 170 lbs. (2B)
VERLON WALKER Walker, Verlon Lee "Rube" b: 3/7/29, Lenoir, N.C. d: 3/24/71, Chicago, Ill. BL/TR, 6', 210 lbs. (C) (Brother of Rube Walker)
JIM WALTON Walton, James Robert b: 9/5/35, Shattuck, Okla. BR/TR, 6'2", 190 lbs. (P)
HARRY WARNER Warner, Harry Clinton b: 12/11/28, Reeders, Pa. BL/TR, 6'2", 215 lbs. (1B)
DAN WILLIAMS Williams, Daniel Lawrence b: 9/3/66, San Gabriel, Cal. BR/TR, 6'3", 245 lbs. (C)
DON WILLIAMS Williams, Donald Ellis b: 12/24/37, Paragould, Ark. BR/TR, 5'10", 185 lbs. (SS)
SPIN WILLIAMS Williams, Donald Ray b: 1/5/56, Davenport, Iowa BL/TL, 6'3", 230 lbs. (P)
JIMMY WILLIAMS Williams, James Bernard b: 5/15/26, Toronto, Ont., Can. BR/TR, 5'10", 180 lbs. (OF)
RICK WILLIAMS Williams, Richard Anthony b: 11/21/56, Ft.Worth, Tex. BL/TL, 6'1", 205 lbs. (P) (Son of Dick Williams)
EARL WOLGAMOT Wolgamot, Clinton Earl b: 12/21/1895, Fairbank, Iowa d: 4/25/70, Independence, Iowa BR/TR, 5'8", 155 lbs. (C)
TOM ZIMMER Zimmer, Thomas Jeffrey b: 6/30/52, Mobile, Ala. BR/TR, 5'8", 165 lbs. (C) (Son of Don Zimmer)

The Umpire Roster

The men in blue have been rebuked and scorned since the Knickerbockers cavorted on the Elysian Fields of Hoboken. The first to incur an umpire's wrath in return was Knickerbocker player Davis, fined six cents for swearing, perhaps understandably since his team was being trounced by the New York Club, 23–1. The name of the umpire in that historic game of June 19, 1846—the first match game under Alexander Cartwright's new rules—was not recorded. Ever since, a handful of researchers have scrambled to find out who umpired the league games of baseball's early history.

Larry Gerlach, who knows more about umpires and umpiring than anybody, has created the Umpire Roster that follows. The basis of his roster is the list compiled by S. C. Thompson in the 1930s and 1940s, but his research has corrected several errors and omissions in that list and has scrupulously brought the umpire roster up to date. In *Total Baseball I* he hoped that "by the next edition we will have finished a complete re-study of the umpire roster. . . . I am going to try to fashion a biographical encyclopedia of major league umpires—vital statistics; minor and major league service; All-Star, World Series, Playoff games; special achievements; and so on. One of the more frustrating things about the Turkin/Thompson roster (and even ours) is how years of service are noted in terms of seasons; it really is misleading to identify someone as working from 1980–1987 when he may have broken into the majors on Sept. 24, 1980."

The data presented here does not meet those lofty goals, but it is vastly increased and improved, as well as reorganized. Umpires are now divided not only by league but also by: regular, league-employed umpires; substitutes; player-umpires, pressed into emergency service; and those subs used during the recent strikes. New leads continue to flow in, especially about the early days, when umpires were not assigned by the leagues but were supplied by the teams, recruited from among the fans in attendance (this explains why so many given names are lacking for pre-1900 arbiters), or, not infrequently, plucked from the team's reserve players. A feature unique to *Total Baseball* is the identification of substitute umpires in the National Association years 1871-75. An instance of this last practice occurred as late as 1935, when Chicago White Sox outfielder Jocko Conlan was recruited to fill in for umpire Red Ormsby in a game between the Sox and the St. Louis Browns. Conlan, of course, went on to a Hall of Fame career as a man in blue.

Let's call the roll.

REGULAR UMPIRES

National Association (1871-75)

Avery, C. Hamilton 1875
Beardslee, John J. 1871
Blodgett, C. W. 1875
Boardman, Frederick "Fred" 1875
Bomeisler, Theodore 1871-73
Boyd, William J. "Bill" 1875
Burdock, John J. "Jack" 1872-74
Carey, Thomas J. "Tom" 1874
Clapp, John E. 1874-75
Cone, J. Frederick "Fred" 1875
Daniels, Charles F. 1874-75
Dehlman, Herman J. 1874
Dole, Lester C. 1875
Ferguson, Robert V. "Bob" 1872-73, 1875
Fulmer, Charles J. "Chick" 1873
Heubel, George A. 1875
Hodges, Amory G. 1874-75
Holly, Samuel J. "Sam" 1871
Lennon, William F. "Bill" 1871-72, 1873-74
Mack, Dennis J. "Denny" 1875
Martin, Alphonse C. "Phonney" 1875
Mathews, Robert T. "Bobby" 1873-75
McLean, William H. "Billy" 1874-75
Mills, Charles "Charlie" 1872-73
Patterson, Daniel T. "Dan" 1874
Rogers, M. Mortimer "Mort" 1871
Sensenderfer, John P. J. "Count" 1874
Swandell, J. Martin "Marty" 1872-73
Tate, William 1874
Walsh, Michael F. "Mike" 1875
Young, Nicholas E. "Nick" 1871-75

National League (1876-)

Andrews, G. Edward "Ed" 1895, 1898-99
Baker, William P. "Bill" 1957
Ballanfant, E. Lee 1936-57
Barlick, Albert J. "Al" 1940-43, 1946-55, 1958-71
Barnes, Ronald E. "Ron" 1990-94, 1996-97
Barnie, William S. "Billy" 1892
Barr, George M. 1931-49
Barron, Mark E. 1992-97
Battin, Joseph V. "Joe" 1891
Bausewine, George 1905
Behle, Frank 1901
Bell, Wally 1992-98
Betts, William G. 1894-96, 1898-99
Betz, Edwin J. 1961
Boggess, Lynton R. "Dusty" 1944-48, 1950-62
Boles, Charles 1877
Bond, Thomas H. "Tommy" 1883, 1885
Bonin, Gregory "Greg" 1984-98
Bradley, George H. "Foghorn" 1879-83
Brady, Jackson 1887
Bransfield, William E. "Kitty" 1917
Bredburg, George W. 1877
Brennan, John E. "Jack" 1899
Brennan, William T. "Bill" 1909-13, 1921
Brocklander, Fred W. 1979-90

Brown, Thomas T. "Tom" 1898-99, 1901-02
Bucknor, C. B. 1996-98
Bunce, Joshua 1877
Burkhart, W. Kenneth "Ken" 1957-73
Burnham, George W. 1883, 1889, 1895
Burns, John S. 1884
Burns, Thomas E. "Tom" 1892
Burns, Thomas P. "Oyster" 1899
Burtis, L. W. 1876-77
Bush, Garnet C. 1911-12
Byron, William J. "Bill" or "Lord" 1913-19
Callahan, Edward J. 1881
Campbell, Daniel "Dan" 1894-96
Campbell, William M. "Bick" 1939-40
Cantillon, Joseph D. "Joe" 1902
Carpenter, William B. "Bill" 1897, 1904, 1906-07
Chapman, John C. "Jack" 1880
Chipman, Harry F. 1883, 1885
Clarke, Robert M. "Bob" 1930-31
Cockill, George W. 1915
Colgan, Harry W. 1901
Colosi, Nicholas "Nick" 1968-82
Conahan, Edward J. "Ed" 1896
Cone, J. F. "Fred" 1877
Conlan, John B. "Jocko" 1941-64
Connolly, John M. 1886
Connolly, Thomas H. "Tommy" 1898-1900
Connors, Patrick "Pat" 1998
Conway, John H. 1906
Crandall, Robert 1877
Crawford, Gerald J. "Jerry" 1975-98
Crawford, Henry C. "Shag" 1956-75
Cross, John A. 1878
Cunningham, Elmer E. "Bert" 1901
Curry, Wesley "Wes" 1885-86, 1889, 1898
Cusack, Stephen P. 1909
Cushman, Charles H. "Charley" 1885, 1898
Cuzzi, Phil 1991-93
Dailey, John J. 1882
Dale, Jerry P. 1970-85
Daniels, Charles F. 1876, 1878-80, 1887-88
Danley, Kerwin 1991-98
Darling, Gary R. 1986-98
Dascoli, Frank 1948-62
Davidson, David L. "Satch" 1969-84
Davidson, Robert A. "Bob" 1982-98
Davis, Gerald S. "Gerry" 1982-98
Decker, Stewart M. 1883-85, 1888
Delmore, Victor "Vic" 1956-59
DeMuth, Dana A. 1983-98
Derr, Doll 1923
Devinney, P. H. "Dan" 1877
Dezelan, Frank J. 1966-68, 1969-71
Dixon, Hal H. 1953-59
Donatelli, August J. "Augie" 1950-73
Donnelly, Charles H. 1931-32
Donohue, Michael R. 1930
Doscher, John H. Sr. "Herm" 1880-81, 1887
Doyle, John J. "Jack" 1911
Dreckman, Bruce M. 1996-98
Ducharme, — 1876-77
Dunn, Thomas P. "Tom" 1939-46
Dunnigan, Joseph 1881-82
Dwyer, J. Francis "Frank" 1899, 1901
Eagan, John J. 1878, 1886

Eason, Malcolm W. "Mal" 1902, 1910-16
Ellick, Joseph J. "Joe" 1886
Emslie, Robert D. "Bob" 1891-1924
Engel, Robert A. "Bob" 1965-90
Engeln, William R. "Bill" 1952-56
Ferguson, Robert V. "Bob" 1879, 1884-85
Fessenden, Wallace C. "Wally" 1889-90
Fields, Stephen H. "Steve" 1979-82
Finneran, William F. 1911-12, 1924
Forman, Allen S. "Al" 1961-65
Fountain, Edward G. 1879
Frary, Ralph 1911
Froemming, Bruce N. 1971-98
Fulmer, Charles J. "Chick" 1886
Furlong, William E. "Bill" 1878-79, 1883-84
Fyfe, Lee C. 1920
Gaffney, John H. 1884-86, 1891-94, 1899-1900
Galvin, James F. "Jim" 1895
Gibbons, Brian 1994-98
Gibson, Gregory "Greg" 1997-98
Gillean, Thomas 1879-80
Goetz, Lawrence J. "Larry" 1936-57
Gore, Arthur J. "Artie" 1947-56
Gorman, Brian 1991-97
Gorman, Thomas D. "Tom" 1951-76
Gregg, Eric E. 1975-91, 1993-98
Guglielmo, A. Augie 1952
Gunning, Thomas F. "Tom" 1887
Guthrie, William J. "Bill" 1913, 1915
Hallion, Thomas F. "Tom" 1985-98
Harris, Lannie D. 1979-85
Harrison, Peter A. "Pete" 1916-20
Hart, Eugene F. "Bob" 1920-29
Hart, William F. "Bill" 1914-15
Harvey, H. Douglas "Doug" 1962-92
Hautz, Charles A. "Charlie" 1876, 1879
Henderson, J. Harding "Hardie" 1895-96
Hengle, Edward S. "Ed" 1887
Henline, Walter J. "Butch" 1945-48
Hernandez, Angel 1991-98
Heuble, George A. 1876
Heydler, John A. 1898
Higham, Richard "Dick" 1881-82
Hirschbeck, Mark 1987-98
Hoagland, Willard A. 1894
Hodges, A. D. 1876
Hohn, William J. "Bill" 1987-98
Holland, John A. 1887
Holbrook, Sam 1997-98
Holliday, James W. "Bug" 1903
Holmes, Howard E. "Ducky" 1921
Hornung, M. Joseph "Joe" 1893, 1896
Hudson, Marvin 1998
Hunt, John T. 1895, 1898-99
Hurst, Timothy C. "Tim" 1891-97, 1900, 1903
Irwin, Arthur A. 1902
Jackowski, William A. "Bill" 1952-68
Jeffers, W. W. 1881
Jevne, Frederick "Fred" 1895
Johnson, Harry S. "Steamboat" 1914

Johnstone, James E. "Jim" 1903-12
Jorda, Louis D. "Lou" 1927-31, 1940-52
Julian, Joseph O. 1878
Kane, Stephen J. 1909-10
Keefe, Timothy J. "Tim" 1894-96
Kellogg, Jeffery "Jeff" 1991-98
Kelly, John O. 1882, 1888, 1897
Kennedy, Charles 1904
Kenney, John 1877
Kibler, John W. 1963-89
Klem, William J. "Bill" 1905-41
Knight, Alonzo P. "Lon" 1889
Kulpa, Ronald "Ron" 1998
Lally, Bud 1896
Landes, Stanley A. "Stan" 1955-72
Lane, Frank H. 1883
Latham, W. Arlington "Arlie" 1899, 1902
Layne, Jerry B. 1989-98
Libby, Stephen A. 1880
Lincoln, Frederick H. 1914, 1917
Long, "Robert "Bob" 1992
Long, William H. "Billy" 1895
Lynch, Thomas J. "Tom" 1888-99
Macullar, James F. "Jimmy" 1892
Magee, Sherwood R. "Sherry" 1928
Magerkurth, George L. 1929-47
Mahoney, Michael J. 1892
Malone, Ferguson G. "Fergy" 1884
Manassau, Alfred S. "Al" 1899
Marsh, Randall G. "Randy" 1981-98
Mathews, Robert T. "Bobby" 1880
McCafferty, Charles 1921, 1923
McCormick, William J. "Barry" 1919-29
McDermott, Michael J. "Sandy" 1890, 1897
McDonald, James F. 1895, 1897-99
McElwee, Harvey 1877
McFarland, Horace 1896-97
McGarr, James B. "Chippy" 1899
McGrew, Harry T. "Ted" 1930-31, 1933-34
McLaughlin, Edward J. 1929
McLaughlin, Michael 1893
McLaughlin, Peter J. 1924-28
McLean, William H. "Billy" 1876, 1878-80, 1882-84
McQuaid, John H. "Jack" 1889-94
McSherry, John P. 1971-96
Meals, Gerald W. "Jerry" 1992-94, 1996-98
Miller, George E. 1879
Mitchell, Charles 1892
Montague, Edward M. "Ed" 1974-98
Moran, August "Augie" 1903-04, 1910, 1918
Moran, Charles B. "Charlie" 1917-39
Mullin, John 1909
Nash, William M. "Billy" 1901
Nauert, Paul 1995-98
Nelson, Jeff 1997-98
O'Connor, Arthur 1914
O'Day, Henry F. "Hank" 1895, 1897-1911, 1913, 1915-27
Odlin, Albert F. 1883
Olsen, Andrew H. "Andy" 1968-81
O'Rourke, James H. "Jim" 1894
Orth, Albert L. "Al" 1912-17
O'Sullivan, John J. 1922

Owens, Clarence B. "Brick" 1908, 1912-13
Pallone, David M. "Dave" 1979-88
Parker, George L. 1936-38
Pearce, Richard J. "Dicky" 1878, 1882
Pears, Frank 1897, 1905
Pelekoudas, Christos G. "Chris" 1960-75
Pfirman, Charles H. "Cy" 1922-36
Pierce, Grayson S. "Gracie" 1886-87
Pinelli, Ralph A. "Babe" 1935-56
Poncino, Larry L. 1985-88, 1991-98
Potter, Scott A. 1991-95, 1997
Powell, Cornelius J. "Jack" 1923-24, 1933
Power, Charles B. 1902
Powers, Philip J. "Phil" 1879, 1881, 1886-91
Pratt, Albert G. "Al" 1879
Pratt, Thomas J. "Tom" 1886
Pryor, J. Paul 1961-81
Pulli, Frank V. 1972-98
Quest, Joseph L. "Joe" 1886-87
Quick, James E. "Jim" 1974-98
Quigley, Ernest C. "Ernie" 1913-37
Quinn, Joseph C. "Joe" 1882
Rapuano, Edward "Ed" 1990-98
Reardon, John E. "Beans" 1926-49
Reliford, Charles H. "Charlie" 1989-98
Rennert, Laurence H. "Dutch" 1973-92
Rieker, Richard G. "Rich" 1992-98
Rigler, Charles "Cy" 1906-22, 1924-35
Riley, William J. 1880
Rippley, T. Steven "Steve" 1983-98
Robb, Douglas W. "Scotty" 1948-52
Roberts, Leonard W. "Lenny" 1953-55
Rudderham, John E. 1908
Runge, Paul E. 1973-97
Ryan, Walter 1946
Schrieber, Paul 1997-98
Scott, James "Jim" 1930-31
Sears, John W. "Ziggy" 1934-45
Secory, Frank E. 1952-70
Sentelle, Leopold T. "Paul" 1922-23
Seward, Edward W. "Ed" 1893
Seward, George E. 1876, 1878
Sheridan, John F. "Jack" 1892, 1896-97
Smith, Charles M. "Pop" 1881
Smith, Vincent A. "Vinnie" 1957-65
Smith, William W. "Billy" 1898-99
Snyder, Charles N. "Pop" 1892-93, 1898-1901
Stage, Charles W. "Billy" 1894
Stambaugh, Calvin G. 1877-78
Stark, Albert D. "Dolly" 1928-35, 1937-40, 1942
Steiner, Melvin J. "Mel" 1961-72
Steinfeldt, Harry M. 1905
Stello, Richard J. "Dick" 1969-87
Sternburg, Paul 1909
Stewart, William J. "Bill" 1933-54
Stockdale, M. J. 1915
Strief, George A. 1890
Sudol, Edward L. "Ed" 1957-77
Sullivan, David F. "Dave"

1882, 1885
Sullivan, Jeremiah "Jerry" 1887
Sullivan, T. P. 1880
Summer, James G. 1877
Swartwood, C. Edward "Ed" 1894, 1898-1900
Sweeney, James M. "Jim" 1924-26
Tata, Terry A. 1973-98
Terry, William H. "Adonis" 1900
Tilden, Otis 1880
Tremblay, Richard H. "Dick" 1971
Truby, Harry G. 1909
Valentine, John G. 1887-88
Van Court, Eugene 1884
Vanover, Larry W. 1991, 1993-98
Vargo, Edward P. "Ed" 1960-83
Venzon, Anthony "Tony" 1957-71
Walker, William E. 1876-77
Walsh, Francis D. "Frank" 1961-63
Walsh, Michael F. "Mike" 1876, 1878, 1880
Warneke, Lonnie "Lon" 1949-55
Warner, Albert "Al" 1898-1900
Wegner, Mark 1998
Wendelstedt, Harry H. Sr. 1966-98
Wendelstedt, H. Hunter Jr. 1998
West, Joseph H. "Joe" 1976, 1978-98
Westervelt, Frederick E. 1922
Weyer, Lee H. 1961, 1963-88
White, Gideon F. 1878
Wickham, Daniel "Dan" 1990-92
Wiedman, George E. "Stump" 1896
Wilbur, Charles E. 1879
Williams, Arthur "Art" 1972-77
Williams, Charles H. "Charlie" 1978, 1983-98
Williams, William G. "Bill" 1963-87
Wilson, Frank 1922-28
Wilson, John A. 1887
Winters, Michael J. "Mike" 1988-98
Wise, Samuel W. "Sam" 1889
Wood, George A. 1898
York, Thomas J. "Tom" 1886
Young, Joseph 1879
Zacharias, Thomas 1890
Zimmer, Charles L. "Chief" 1904

American Association (1882-91)

Barnum, George W. 1890
Bauers, Albert J. "Al" 1887
Becannon, William H. 1883
Bradley, George H. "Foghorn" 1886
Brennan, John E. "Jack" 1884
Butler, Ormond H. 1883
Carey, Thomas J. "Tom" 1882
Clinton, James L. "Jim" 1886
Connell, Terence G. 1884, 1890
Connelly, John M. 1885, 1887
Connelly, William 1884
Curry, Wesley "Wes" 1887, 1890
Cuthbert, Edgar E. "Ned" 1887
Dailey, John J. 1884
Daniels, Charles F. 1883-85, 1889
Davis, James J. "Jumbo" 1891
Devinney, P. H. "Dan" 1884
Doscher, John H. Sr.

"Herm" 1888, 1890
Dyler, John F. 1884
Emslie, Robert D. "Bob" 1890
Ferguson, Robert V. "Bob" 1886-89, 1891
Gaffney, John H. 1888-89
Gleason, William G. "Bill" 1891
Goldsmith, Frederick E. "Fred" 1888-89
Griffith, E. A. 1884
Hautz, Charles A. "Charlie" 1882
Hecker, Guy J. 1889
Holland, John A. 1884
Holland, Willard A. 1889
Hurley, Daniel "Dan" 1887
Jennings, Alfred J. "Al" 1887
Jones, Charles W. "Charley" 1891
Kelly, John O. 1883-86
Kerins, John A. "Jack" 1889-91
Knight, Alonzo P. "Lon" 1887
Lawler, John F. 1884
Macullar, James F. "Jimmy" 1891
Mack, Dennis J. "Denny" 1886
Magner, John T. 1883
Mahoney, Michael J. 1891
Mathews, Robert T. "Bobby" 1891
McLaughlin, Thomas 1891
McLean, William H. "Billy" 1885
McNichol, Robert T. 1883
McQuaid, John H. "Jack" 1886-88
Morton, Charles H. "Charlie" 1886
O'Brien, Frank 1890
Peoples, James E. "Jimmy" 1890
Pike, Lipman. E. "Lip" 1889
Pratt, Albert G. "Al" 1883
Quinn, A. J. 1886
Riley, William J. 1882
Ross, Robert T. 1882
Seward, George E. 1884
Simmons, Joseph S. "Joe" 1882
Smith, Charles M. "Pop" 1882
Snyder, Charles N. "Pop" 1891
Sommer, Benjamin F. 1883
Sullivan, Jeremiah "Jerry" 1887
Sullivan, Theodore P. "Ted" 1887
Taylor, Walter 1890
Toole, Stephen J. "Steve" 1890
Tunison, William 1885-86
Valentine, John G. 1884-87
Walsh, Michael F. "Mike" 1882-83, 1885-86
York, Thomas J. "Tom" 1886
Young, Benjamin F. "Ben" 1886

Union Association (1884)

Crawford, Alexander 1884
Devinney, P. H. "Dan" 1884
Dutton, Patrick J. 1884
Hengle, Emory J. "Moxie" 1884
Holland, John A. 1884
Hooper, Michael H. 1884
Jennings, Alfred "Al" 1884
Jordan, William H. "Bill" 1884
Mapledoram, Blake A. 1884
McCaffrey, Harry 1884
Seward, George E. 1884
Stearns, D. Eckford "Ecky" 1884
Sullivan, David F. "Dave" 1884

Players League (1890)

Barnes, Roscoe C. "Ross" 1890
Ferguson, Robert V. "Bob"

1890
Gaffney, John H. 1890
Gunning, Thomas F. "Tom" 1890
Holbert, William H. "Bill" 1890
Jones, Charles W. "Charley" 1890
Knight, Alonzo P. "Lon" 1890
Leach, Henry 1890
Mathews, Robert T. "Bobby" 1890
Pierce, Grayson S. "Gracie" 1890
Sheridan, John F. "Jack" 1890
Snyder, Charles N. "Pop" 1890

American League (1901-)

Adams, John H. 1903
Anthony, G. Merlyn 1969-75
Ashford, Emmett L. 1966-70
Avants, Nick R. 1969-71
Barrett, Ted 1994-98
Barnett, Lawrence R. "Larry" 1968-98
Barry, Daniel "Dan" 1928
Basil, Stephen J. "Steve" 1936-42
Bean, Ed 1994
Berry, Charles F. "Charlie" 1942-62
Betts, William G. 1901
Boyer, James M. "Jim" 1944-50
Bremigan, Nicholas G. "Nick" 1974-88
Brinkman, Joseph N. "Joe" 1973-98
Campbell, William M. "Bick" 1928-31
Cantillon, Joseph D. "Joe" 1901
Carrigan, H. Sam 1961-65
Carpenter, William B. "Bill" 1904
Caruthers, Robert L. "Bob" 1902-03
Cederstrom, Gary L. 1989-98
Chill, Oliver P. "Ollie" 1914-16, 1919-22
Chylak, Nestor L. 1954-78
Clark, Alan M. "Al" 1976-98
Coble, G. Drew 1983-98
Colliflower, James H. 1910
Connolly, Thomas H. "Tommy" 1901-31
Connor, Thomas "Tom" 1905-06
Cooney, Terrance J. "Terry" 1975-92
Cooper, Erik R. 1996-98
Cousins, Derryl 1979-98
Craft, Terry 1989-98
Culbreth, Fieldin "Field" 1993-98
Deegan, William E. J. "Bill" 1970-80
Denkinger, Donald A. "Don" 1968-98
Diaz, Lazaro "Laz" 1995, 1997-98
DiMuro, Louis J. "Lou" 1963-80
DiMuro, Raymond "Ray" 1996-98
Dinneen, William H. "Bill" 1909-37
Donnelly, Charles H. 1934-35
Doyle, Walter J. 1963
Drummond, Calvin T. "Cal" 1960-69
Duffy, James F. "Jim" 1951-55
Dwyer, J. Francis "Frank" 1904
Eddings, Douglas "Doug" 1998
Egan, John J. "Rip" 1903, 1907-14
Eldridge, Clarence E. 1914-15
Evans, James B. "Jim" 1971-98

Evans, William G. "Billy" 1906-27
Everitt, Michael "Mike" 1996-98
Ferguson, Charles A. 1913
Flaherty, John F. "Red" 1953-73
Ford, R. Dale 1975-98
Foster, Martin "Mark" 1996-98
Frantz, Arthur F. "Art" 1969-77
Friel, William E. "Bill" 1920
Froese, Grover A. 1952-53
Garcia, Richard R. "Rich" 1975-98
Geisel, Harry C. 1925-42
Goetz, Russell L. "Russ" 1968-83
Grieve, William T. T. "Bill" 1938-55
Guthrie, William J. "Bill" 1922, 1928-32
Haller, William E. "Bill" 1961, 1963-82
Hart, Robert F. "Bertie" 1912-13
Hart, William F. "Bill" 1901
Haskell, John E. 1901
Hassett, James E. 1903
Hayes, Gerald 1925-26
Hendry, Eugene "Ted" 1978-98
Henrichs, Jeff 1993
Hickox, Edwin W. "Ed" 1990-98
Hildebrand, George A. 1913-34
Hirschbeck, John F. 1984-98
Holbrook, Sam 1996
Holmes, Howard E. "Ducky" 1923-24
Honochick, G. James "Jim" 1949-73
Hubbard, R. Cal 1936-51
Hurley, Edwin H. "Eddie" 1947-65
Hurst, Timothy C. "Tim" 1905-09
Johnson, Mark S. 1980-98
Johnston, Charles E. 1936-37
Johnstone, James E. "Jim" 1902
Jones, Nicholas I. "Red" 1944-49
Joyce, James A. "Jim" 1989-98
Kaiser, Kenneth J. "Ken" 1977-98
Kelly, Thomas B. 1905
Kerin, John 1909-10
King, Charles F. 1904
Kinnamon, William E. "Bill" 1960-69
Kolls, Louis C. "Lou" 1933-40
Kosc, Gregory J. "Greg" 1976-98
Kunkel, William G. "Bill" 1968-84
Leppart, Thomas E. "Tom" 1984-86
Linsalata, Joseph N. "Joe" 1961-62
Luciano, Ronald M. "Ron" 1968-80
Maloney, George P. 1969-83
Manassau, Alfred S. "Al" 1901
Marberry, Frederick "Firpo" 1935
McCarthy, John "Jack" 1905
McClelland, Timothy R. "Tim" 1984-98
McCormick, William J. "Barry" 1917
McCoy, Larry S. 1970-98
McGowan, William A. "Bill" 1925-54
McGreevy, Edward 1912-13
McKean, James G. "Jim" 1974-98
McKinley, William F. "Bill" 1946-65
Meriwether, Julius E. "Chuck" 1988-98

Merrill, E. Durwood 1977-98
Miller, William "Bill" 1997-98
Morgenweck, Henry C. "Hank" 1972-75
Moriarty, George J. 1917-26, 1929-40
Morrison, Daniel G. "Dan" 1979-98
Mullaney, Dominic J. 1915
Mullin, John 1911
Nallin, Richard F. "Dick" 1915-32
Napp, Larry A. 1951-74
Nelson, Jeff 1998
Neudecker, Jerome A. "Jerry" 1965-85
O'Brien, Joseph "Joe" 1912, 1914
Odom, James C. "Jim" 1965-74
O'Donnell, James M. "Jake" 1968-71
O'Loughlin, Francis H. "Silk" 1902-18
O'Nora, Brian 1992-98
Ormsby, Emmett T. "Red" 1923-41
Owens, Clarence B. "Brick" 1916-37
Palermo, Stephen M. "Steve" 1977-91
Paparella, Joseph J. "Joe" 1946-65
Parker, Harley P. 1911
Parks, Dallas F. 1979-83
Passarella, Arthur M. "Art" 1941-42, 1945-53
Perrine, Fred "Bull" 1909-12
Phillips, David R. "Dave" 1971-98
Pipgras, George W. 1938-46
Quinn, John A. 1935-42
Reed, Rick A. 1984-98
Reilly, Michael E. "Mike" 1978-98
Rice, John L. 1955-73
Robb, Douglas W. "Scotty" 1952-53
Rodriguez, Armando H. 1974-75
Roe, John A. "Rocky" 1979-98
Rommel, Edwin A. "Eddie" 1938-59
Rowland, Clarence H. "Pants" 1923-27
Rue, Joseph W. "Joe" 1938-47
Runge, Edward P. "Ed" 1954-70
Salerno, Alexander J. "Al" 1961-68
Schwarts, Harry C. 1960-62
Scott, Dale A. 1986-98
Sheridan, John F. "Jack" 1901-14
Shulock, John R. 1979-98
Smith, W. Alaric "Al" 1960-65
Soar, A. Henry "Hank" 1950-73
Spenn, Frederick C. "Fred" 1979-80
Springstead, Martin J. "Marty" 1965-86
Stafford, John H. "Jack" 1907
Stevens, John W. "Johnny" 1948-71
Stewart, Ernest D. 1941-45
Stewart, Robert W. "Bob" 1959-70
Summers, William R. "Bill" 1933-59
Tabacchi, Frank T. 1956-59
Tschida, Timothy J. "Tim" 1986-98
Umont, Frank W. 1954-73
Valentine, William T. "Bill" 1963-68
Van Graflan, Roy R. 1927-33
Voltaggio, Vito H. "Vic" 1977-96
Wallace, Roderick J. "Bobby" 1915
Walsh, Edward A. "Ed"

1922
Walton, Bennie 1996
Weafer, Harold L. "Hal" 1943-47
Welke, Timothy J. "Tim" 1985-98
Westervelt, Frederick E. 1911-12
Wilson, Frank 1921-22
Winans, Mathew "Matt" 1994
Young, Larry E. 1985-98

Federal League (1914-15)

Anderson, Oliver O. "Ollie" 1914
Brennan, William T. "Bill" 1914-15
Bush, Garnet C. 1914
Corcoran, Thomas W. "Tommy" 1915
Cross, Montford M. "Monte" 1914
Cusack, Stephen P. 1914
Finneran, William E. 1915
Fyfe, Louis 1915
Goeckel, E. 1914
Howell, H. Harry 1915
Johnstone, James E. "Jim" 1915
Kane, Stephen J. 1914
Langden, Joseph 1915
Mannassau, Alfred S. "Al" 1914
McCormick, William J. "Barry" 1914-15
Mullin, John 1915
O'Brien, Joseph "Joe" 1915
Shannon, William P. "Spike" 1914-15
Stocksdale, Otis H. 1915
Van Sickle, Charles F. 1914
Westervelt, Frederick E. 1915
Wilhelm, Irving K. "Kaiser" 1915

SUBSTITUTE UMPIRES

National Association (1871-75)

Addy, Robert E. "Bob" 1875
Allison, Andrew K. "Andy" 1872, 1874
Allison, Arthur A. "Art" 1872
Allison, Douglas L. "Doug" 1872-73, 1875
Alston, David 1871-72, 1875
Annan, William H. 1873
Arnold, Willis S. "Billy" 1875
Avery, C. Hamilton 1874
Barlow, Thomas H. "Tom" 1875
Barnes, Roscoe C. "Ross" 1874
Barrett, William "Bill" 1872, 1874
Barron, James "Jim" 1875
Barrows, Franklin L. "Frank" 1872
Battin, Joseph V. "Joe" 1874
Beals, Thomas L. "Tommy" 1872, 1874-75
Beardslee, John J. 1872-73
Bechtel, George A. 1874
Beck, W. S. 1872
Berthrong, Hnery W. "Harry" 1872
Bielaski, Oscar 1874-75
Bigelow, W. J. 1875
Birdsall, David S. "Dave" 1873-74
Blair, William J. 1873
Boake, John L. 1871
Bomeisler, Theodore 1874-75
Bond, Thomas H. "Tommy" 1875
Bonse, Nicholas 1871
Boyd, William J. "Bill" 1873
Bradley, George H. "Foghorn" 1875
Brainard, Asa 1872, 1875

Briggs, Warren R. 1874
Brown, William 1872, 1875
Bruce, D. W. 1875
Buck, William F. 1871
Bunce, Frederick L. "Fred" 1874
Bunce, H. C. 1872
Bush, Archibald M. "Archie" 1871
Carey, Thomas J. "Tom" 1873, 1875
Carpenter, John R. 1874
Cassidy, John P. 1875
Cavanaugh, J. H. "Harry" 1875
Chandler, Moses E. 1872-1875
Chapman, John C. "Jack" 1871, 1873-74
Clifton, — 1872
Clinton, James L. "Jim" 1873, 1875
Colby, — 1873
Collins, Daniel T. "Dan" 1875
Cone, J. Frederick "Fred" 1873-74
Cope, Elias 1871
Craver, William H. "Bill" 1873
Cuthbert, Edgar E. "Ned" 1875
Daubney, Thomas 1871
David, L. N. 1874
Dawson, Mort 1871
Deane, J. Henry "Harry" 1871, 1874
Dehlman, Herman J. 1873, 1875
Demorest, D. P. 1872-73
Dobson, H. A. 1871
Dornlach, D. E. 1872
Draper, John H. 1871
Ellis, William R. 1871-72, 1875
English, John W. 1874-75
Erby, Frederick 1872
Evans, George 1872
Fellows, T. E. 1871
Ferguson, Robert V. "Bob" 1871, 1874
Fisher, William C. "Cherokee" 1871, 1875
Foley, Thomas "Tom" 1874-75
Force, David W. "Davy" 1873
Fulmer, Charles J. "Chick" 1872, 1874-75
Garrigan, Charles 1873
Geer, William H. "Billy" 1874-75
Gerhardt, Joseph J. "Joe" 1875
Glenn, John W. 1874
Glover, Frank 1873
Goodwin, J. Cheever 1871-72
Gould, Charles H. "Charlie" 1874-75
Graham, J. S. 1871-72
Halback, A. C. N. 1871, 1873-75
Hall, George W. 1873-75
Hall, James "Jim" 1872-73
Hall, N. Samuel 1873
Hanna, Dr. 1872
Hartenstein, Isaac 1875
Hastings, W. Scott 1871-74
Hatfield, John V. B. 1872-73
Hayhurst, E. Hicks 1875
Haynie, James L. 1871
Hegeman, William H. 1871
Helm, J. 1871-72
Higham, Richard "Dick" 1872-75
Hodes, Charles "Charlie" 1874
Hooper, Michael H. "Mike" 1872-74
Hosworth, —, 1872-74
Hough, Pliny 1875
Howard, Charles 1872
Jennings, Alfred J. "Al" 1873
Johns, William R. 1873
Kahn, S. L. 1875
Keerl, George W. 1872
Kenney, John 1872
Kent, John 1875

Knight, George H. 1875
Kohler, Henry C. 1873
Lamb, Henry W. "Harry" 1875
Laughlin, Benjamin "Ben" 1873
Leonard, Andrew J. "Andy" 1872-73, 1875
Leonard, J. 1871
Leroy, Isaac 1871
Locke, Marshall 1873-74
Lovett, James D. 1871
Lowell, John A. 1872-73
Lush, M. R. 1873
MacDiarmed, Thomas 1872
Mack, Dennis J. "Denny" 1873-74
Malone, — 1875
Malone, Ferguson G. "Fergy" 1875
Martin, Alphonse C. "Phonney" 1871, 1873
Martin, Lewis G. 1871, 1873-74
Mathews, Robert T. "Bobby" 1871
Mawny, J. H. 1871
Maxwell, Cortez "Corty" 1875
Mays, — 1871
McCrea, — 1872
McDonald, James F. 1872
McGeary, Michael H. 1872, 1875
McLean, Harry C. 1871, 1873
McLean, William H. "Billy" 1872-73
McMahon, William 1871
McMullin, John F. 1874
McVey, Calvin A. "Cal" 1871, 1873, 1875
Meacham, — 1875
Miller, Joseph W. "Joe" 1872-73
Mills, Charles "Charlie" 1871
Mincher, Edward J. "Ed" 1872, 1875
Mincher, William E. 1875
Mitchell, Franklin B. 1874-75
Murnane, Timothy H. "Tim" 1873-75
Nelson, John W. "Candy" 1872
Nichols, A. N. 1871
Norton, Frank P. 1872
O'Brien, P. 1875
Pabor, Charles H. "Charlie" 1875
Parks, William R. "Bill" 1875
Patterson, Daniel T. "Dan" 1872
Peak, Frank 1871
Pearson, S. W. 1872
Phelps, Cornelius C. "Neal" 1874
Pike, Jacob Emanuel "Jay" 1875
Porter, — 1874
Powers, W. 1872-73, 1875
Pratt, Thomas J. "Tom" 1871-73
Quinn, — 1875
Radcliff, John Y. 1873
Ramsay, R. 1875
Rastall, Joseph H. 1872
Reach, Albert J. 1872-75
Reed, Hugh 1871, 1873-74
Remsen, John J. "Jack" 1873-74
Robinson, A. Valentine "Val" 1872
Robinson, Miley 1873
Rockwell, Horace T. 1874
Rogers, George H. 1871-72
Ryan, John J. 1872, 1875
Sawyer, Dent 1871
Schafer, Harry C. 1875
Schrader, Louis 1875
Schuester, John A. 1874-75
Scofield, John W. 1871
Sears, John K. 1873
Selman, Frank C. 1873
Sensenderfer, John P. J. "Count" 1872-73, 1875
Simmons, Joseph S. "Joe" 1871, 1873-74

Smith, Eb 1872
Smith, George 1872
Smith, Gustavus 1872
Snyder, Charles N. "Pop" 1875
Stahl, George 1875
Stanwood, —, 1872-73
Stires, Garrett "Gat" 1875
Stophlet, J. 1871
Sutton, Ezra B. 1875
Swandell, J. Martin "Marty" 1871, 1874
Sweasy, Charles J. "Charlie" 1871, 1873-74
Tighe, Edward 1871
Treacey, Frederick S. "Fred" 1871, 1873, 1875
Tyler, Columbus T. 1871-73
Urell, M. E. 1873
Van Delft, Benjamin 1875
Voltz, Edward "Ed" 1871-72
Walk, Frank 1871
Wardell, — 1874
Waterman, Frederick A. "Fred" 1873
Weaver, Charles 1873
Weigel, William H. 1873-74
White, Horatio S. 1873
White, W. Warren 1874
White, William H. "Will" 1875
Wiggins, — 1875
Wildey, John 1871
Willard, Gardner 1871
Wirth, Adam 1875
Wood, James B. "Jimmy" 1871
Worth, Herb 1872
Wright, W. Harrison "Harry" 1875
York, Thomas J. "Tom" 1874

National League (1876-)

Adams, James 1897
Allen, Hezekiah "Ham" 1876
Ayers, — 1876
Baker, Charles 1884
Barker, Alfred L. 1881
Barnie, William S. "Billy" 1882
Barnum, George W. 1896
Barton, — 1876
Battin, Joseph V. "Joe" 1895-96
Beard, Oliver P. "Ollie" 1894
Becannon, James M. "Buck" 1885
Behle, Frank 1895-96
Berger, Frederick 1886
Bigelow, — 1877
Bittman, Henry P. "Red" 1892, 1894-95, 1897
Blakiston, Robert J. "Bob" 1884
Blodgett, C. W. 1876
Bradley, George H. "Foghorn" 1877
Brady, — 1877
Bredburg, George W. 1878-79
Brennan, John E. "Jack" 1887
Brockway, John 1877, 1879
Bullymore, Charles L. 1882
Burke, — 1892
Burlingame, Frank A. 1878
Burnham, George W. 1886-87
Campbell, Al 1886
Campbell, Daniel "Dan" 1897
Carsey, Wilfred "Kid" 1901
Caruthers, Robert L. "Bob" 1886, 1893
Chandler, Moses E. 1877
Chapman, John C. "Jack" 1876, 1882
Cheppy, John T. 1876
Chipman, Harry F. 1886
Clack, Robert H. "Bobby" 1897
Cohen, George 1893
Colgan, Harry W. 1899
Collins, Daniel T. "Dan" 1876
Cone, J. F. "Fred" 1876

Connell, Terence G. 1885, 1887
Connolly, John M. 1885, 1887, 1892-93
Cook, W. H. 1879
Crandall, Robert 1876, 1878
Crane, Edward N. "Ed" 1893
Crane, Samuel N. "Sam" 1879, 1887
Cray, P. C. 1893
Cross, John A. 1876
Cudworth, Al 1880
Curren, Peter 1876
Cushman, Charles H. "Charley" 1894
Daniels, — 1885
Deane, J. Henry "Harry" 1876, 1878
Devinney, P. H. "Dan" 1876
Doscher, John H. Sr. "Herm" 1879
Draper, John H. 1877
Dunlap, Frederick C. "Fred" 1879
Dyler, John F. 1892, 1897
Eagan, John J. 1879
Earle, William M. "Billy" 1892
Eason, Malcolm W. "Mal" 1901
English, John W. 1876
Evans, Jacob "Jake" 1886
Fenno, Norman 1876
Finneran, William F. 1923
Fisher, William C. "Cherokee" 1876
Flaherty, — 1882
Flaherty, Patrick J. "Patsy" 07
Flynn, John A. "Jocko" 1893
Fouser, William C. 1876
Fulmer, Charles J. "Chick" 1881
Furlong, William E. "Bill" 1877, 1880, 1888
Gaffney, John H. 1887, 1898
Galvin, James F. "Jim" 1886
Ganzel, Charles W. "Charlie" 1901
Gifford, James H. 1881
Gillean, Thomas 1881
Gleason, John D. 1877
Gleason, William G. "Bill" 1877
Glenn, John W. 1880
Goldsmith, Frederick E. "Fred" 1886
Graves, Frank M. 1895
Griffiths, — 1884
Gross, Edward M. 1881
Guinney, Daniel 1882
Hardie, Louis W. "Lou" 1887
Hartley, John "Jack" 1894
Hastings, W. Scott 1877
Hatfield, John V. B. 1876
Hawes, William A. 1880-82
Hegeman, William H. 1881
Herrin, W. E. 1894
Heydler, John A. 1895-97
Hickey, James L. 1882
Hodges, A. D. 1877
Hogan, — 1897
Hogriever, George C. 1893
Hornung, M. Joseph "Joe" 1892
Howard, C. F. 1884
Hurll, George 1876
Hurst, Timothy C. "Tim" 1904
Jevne, Frederick "Fred" 1892, 1894
Jose, — 1889
Joyce, C. E. 1879
Kane, Stephen J. 1906
Keefe, Timothy J. "Tim" 1893
Keenan, James W. "Jim" 1893
Kelley, J. P. 1879
Kelley, W. W. 1877
Kelly, John O. 1884-85
Kennedy, — 1893
Kennedy, Michael J. "Doc" 1884
Kenney, John 1876

Kerins, John A. "Jack" 1888
Kipp, Eden 1881
Kling, William "Bill" 1892
Klusman, William F. "Billy" 1893
Knight, Alonzo P. "Lon" 1876, 1888
Lanigan, Charles 1908
Latham, W. Arlington "Arlie" 1900
Laughlin, —, 1876
Lawler, Michael H. 1882
Leary, — 1879
Libby, Stephen A. 1879
Long, William H. "Billy" 1893, 1897
Lynch, F. G. 1892
Lynch, Thomas J. "Tom" 1902
Maddox, Charles 1882
Maginnis, Jim 1910
Malone, Ferguson G. "Fergy" 1892
Maloney, James "Jim" 1893
Manning, James H. "Jim" 1893
Manning, John E. "Jack" 1881
Mapledoram, Blake A. 1886
Martin, Alphonse C. "Phonney" 1876
Mason, Charles E. "Charlie" 1876
Mathews, Robert T. "Bobby" 1876
Mayer, Ed 1893
McCaffrey, Harry 1885-86
McCrum, — 1892
McGee, — 1876
McGinty, — 1897
McGunnigle, Edward 1888
McKinney, — 1883
McLeod, — 1895
McMullen, John F. 1876
Meagher, John 1877
Mears, Charles W. 1894
Medart, William 1876-77
Megrue, Cliff 1876
Mills, Abraham G. 1877
Montague, — 1877
Morrill, John F. 1891, 1896
Morris, Edward 1895, 1897
Morris, John S. 1876
Muir, Thomas 1876
Mullane, Anthony J. "Tony" 1897
Mullen, Peter C. 1893
Murnane, Timothy H. "Tim" 1886
Murphy, Henry 1880
Murphy, Martin W. 1886
Murray, Jeremiah J. "Miah" 1894, 1900, 1905, 1910
Myers, Henry C. 1890
Nicol, Hugh N. 1894
O'Brien, William 1876
O'Day, Henry F. "Hank" 1896
Orr, David L. "Dave" 1891
Osborne, William 1876
Pfeffer, Nathaniel F. "Nate" 1897
Phelan, — 1896
Pierce, — 1893
Pierce, Grayson S. "Gracie" 1892
Pike, Lipman E. "Lip" 1890
Power, Charles B. 1893-95
Pratt, Albert G. "Al" 1880, 1887
Quincy, W. 1893
Quinn, Joseph C. "Joe" 1881
Quinn, P. J. 1876
Quinn, William H. "Billy" 1887, 1889
Redheffer, — 1895
Reid, William A. 1882
Reilly, Charles 1880
Remsen, John J. "Jack" 1880
Rhodes, Eugene A. 1887
Richards, J. E. 1880
Ritchie, F. 1876
Rocap, Adam 1876
Roll, — 1876
Rowe, John C. "Jack" 1881
Rudderham, Francis F. "Frank" 1907

Say, Louis I. "Lou" 1879
Schofield, J. W. 1879
Seward, Edward W. "Ed" 1892
Seward, George E. 1877
Shepard, W. L. 1879
Sheridan, John F. "Jack" 1893
Sick, — 1884
Simmons, Joseph S. "Joe" 1876
Skelly, — 1880
Skinner, S. A. 1886
Smith, — 1876
Sneeden, George W. 1895
Snodd, Carey 1877
Snyder, Charles N. "Pop" 1895
Sommers, Joseph A. "Joe" 1893
Stack, W. Edward "Eddie" 1934
Stafford, John H. "Jack" 1906
Stage, Charles W. "Billy" 1895
Stambaugh, Calvin G. 1879
Strief, George A. 1880
Sullivan, — 1889
Sullivan, David F. "Dave" 1883, 1887-88
Summer, James G. 1876, 1878
Supple, William N. 1906
Sutton, Ezra B. 1876
Sweasy, Charles J. "Charlie" 1879
Tilden, Otis 1876
Tindall, — 1890, 1896
Toole, Stephen J. "Steve" 1888
Tuthill, Benjamin "Ben" 1895
Twitchell, Lawrence G. "Larry" 1894
Wade, Ben F. 1879-80
Walker, William E. 1878
Walsh, Michael F. "Mike" 1879
Walters, —, 1892-93
Walton, G. W. 1876
Warren, L. B. 1876
Wash, Frank 1877
Weeden, —, 1889-90
West, — 1885
West, George 1878
West, Milton D. "Buck" 1890
White, Gideon F. 1876-77
White, W. Warren 1876
Williams, Elisha A. "Dale" 1876
Wilson, William G. "Bill" 1892-93
Witham, C. B. 1879
Wolf, William V. "Jimmy" 1893, 1895-97
Wood, George A. 1899
Wood, James B. "Jimmy" 1876
Wright, W. Harrison "Harry" 1885
Wycoff, — 1892

American Association (1882-91)

Arnold, Frank W. 1889
Austin, Ed 1890
Barnie, William S. "Billy" 1882, 1884, 1887, 1889
Battin, Joseph V. "Joe" 1882, 1886
Bauers, Albert J. "Al" 1890
Bell, Frank G. 1889
Bittman, Henry P. "Red" 1889
Blogg, Wesley C. "Wes" 1886
Bloom, — 1887
Bond, Thomas H. "Tommy" 1891
Bowes, Frank C. 1890
Burdock, John J. "Jack" 1887
Burkalow, Isaac 1888
Burns, — 1882
Butler, Charles 1889
Butler, Ormond H. 1886
Campbell, Daniel "Dan" 1890

Carlin, William J. "Billy" 1885, 1888-89
Connell, Terence G. 1885-86, 1889
Cornell, — 1884
Crandall, Robert 1882
Creighton, — 1889-90
Critchley, Morris A. "Morrie" 1884-85
Curry, Frank 1884, 1886
Cuthbert, Edgar E. "Ned" 1888
Dailey, John J. 1889
Daniels, Lawrence 1887
Devine, W. James "Jim" 1890
Devinney, P. H. "Dan" 1887
Devlin, Charles "Charlie" 1888
Dolan, Thomas J. "Tom" 1890-91
Dow, Clarence 1891
Dugan, — 1887
Duke, Martin H. 1890
Dunlevy, Hugh 1887
Dyler, John F. 1883, 1885-86
Ellick, Joseph J. "Joe" 1888-89
Ewing, William "Buck" 1882
Fell, — 1885
Fountain, Henry V. 1888
Galvin, James F. "Jim" 1885
Geer, William H. "Billy" 1887
Gill, Thomas H. "Tommy" 1886
Helburn, Hugo 1887
Henderson, J. Harding "Hardie" 1889
Hengle, Edward S. "Ed" 1889
Hicks, Nathaniel W. "Nat" 1885
Holliday, James W. "Bug" 1888
Irwin, — 1882
Irwin, John 1885
Jennings, Alfred J. "Al" 1882, 1884-85, 1889
Julian, Joseph O. 1888
Kelly, John O. 1887
Kelly, William 1884
Kleinbacker, —, 1886
Levis, Charles H. "Charlie" 1882
Lilly, J. 1884
Little, — 1884
Loughlin, —, 1885
Loughlin, William 1882
Lyons, Toby A. 1891
Lyston, William E. 1890
Magner, John T. 1882, 1884, 1887
Malone, J. R. 1888
Marshall, — 1887
Mathews, Robert T. "Bobby" 1888
McCartney, Joseph 1882
McCormick, —, 1888
McGee, Patrick 1882, 1884
McGinnis, George W. "Jumbo" 1888-89
McIntosh, — 1882
McLaughlin, William 1882
McLean, William H. "Billy" 1882, 1889-90
McQuade, James H. 1891
McSorley, John B. "Trick" 1888
Medart, William 1887
Miller, Charles A. 1884
Mitchell, — 1887
Morgan, Henry W. 1884
Morton, Charles H. "Charlie" 1884
Mullen, Peter C. 1891
O'Dea, Lawrence 1890
Paasch, William 1887-89
Parker, — 1887
Phillips, Horace B. 1882
Pierce, Grayson S. "Gracie" 1884
Pike, Lipman. E. "Lip" 1887
Pratt, Albert G. "Al" 1886
Quinn, William H. "Billy" 1884-85
Ramsey, Dick 1887
Reeder, James E. 1884
Reising, Charles 1882

Rice, — 1885
Riley, William J. 1885
Robb, John 1886
Ross, Robert T. 1884
Ruhl, Gus 1882
Ryan, John 1882
Selman, Frank C. 1882
Sherman, Sharon L. "Shang" 1890
Shraeder, Louis 1890
Simpson, Lew 1882
Skerritt, Jim 1890
Skinner, — 1884, 1886
Smith, George 1887
Sneed, Jonathon L. 1885
Sullivan, David F. "Dave" 1884
Talbot, — 1887
Tinney, — 1882
Walsh, Michael F. "Mike" 1887-88
West, — 1885, 1887
Wood, George A. 1886
Wright, — 1884
Young, Benjamin F. "Ben" 1887
Young, Joseph 1890

Union Association (1884)

Adler, — 1884
Burlingame, F. A. 1884
Donovan, Timothy H. 1884
Furlong, William E. "Bill" 1884
Hudson, Vincent D. 1884
Lee, Thomas F. 1884
McGunningle, William H. "Bill" 1884
McManaway, D. 1884
McMinimum, Dennis 1884
Montgomery, — 1884
Powers, Charles B. 1884
Timblin, — 1884
Torry, — 1884

Players' League (1890)

Caskin, Edward J. "Ed" 1890

American League (1901-)

Betts, William G. 1903
Bierhalter, "Bits" 1922, 1924
Brown, Thomas T. "Tom" 1907
Carney, "Red" 1924
Connolly, Thomas H. "Tommy" 1932
Donlin, Michael J. "Mike" 1918
Howley, Daniel P. "Dan" 1922
Kennedy, Michael J. "Doc" 1910
Kerin, John 1908
Kerins, John A. "Jack" 1903
Mace, Harry L. 1903
Monahan, Pat 1931
Nallin, Richard F. "Dick" 1933
Pears, Frank 1903
Quigley, Ernest C. "Ernie" 1906
Soar, A. Henry "Hank" 1975
Stevens, John W. "Johnny" 1975
Terry, William H. "Adonis" 1901

Federal League (1914-15)

Murphy, J. A. 1914
Quisser, Arthur 1914

ACTIVE PLAYERS WHO UMPIRED

National League (1876-)

Abbey, Charles S. "Charlie" 1897
Abbott, Frederick H. "Fred" 1905
Andrews, G. Edward "Ed" 1889
Arundel, John T. "Tug"

1888
Baker, Philip "Phil" 1889
Baldwin, Marcus E. "Mark" 1892
Bannon, James H. "Jimmy" 1894
Beatin, Ebenezer "Ed" 1889
Beck, Erwin T. "Erve" 1902
Beckley, Jacob P. "Jake" 1906
Beebe, Fred L. 1907
Berger, John H. "Tun" 1891
Bonner, Frank J. 1894
Boyle, Henry J. 1886
Boyle, John A. "Jack" 1892, 1897
Breitenstein, Theodore P. "Ted" 1900
Briody, Charles F. "Fatty" 1881
Brown, Samuel W. "Sam" 1907
Brown, Thomas T. "Tom" 1896
Brown, Willard 1891
Buelow, Charles J. "Charlie" 1901
Buffinton, Charles G. "Charlie" 1883, 1888-89, 1892
Burdock, John J. "Jack" 1881
Burns, Thomas P. "Oyster" 1895
Bushong, Albert J. "Doc" 1880, 1890
Butler, Richard H. "Dick" 1897
Carrick, William M. "Bill" 1900
Carroll, Frederick H. "Fred" 1887
Carsey, Wilfred "Kid" 1894, 1896
Caruthers, Robert L. "Bob" 1891
Casey, Daniel M. "Dan" 1888
Caskin, Edward J. "Ed" 1884
Cassidy, John P. 1882
Chamberlain, Elton P. 1894
Chance, Frank L. 1902
Clack, Robert H. "Bobby" 1876
Clarke, Arthur F. "Artie" 1890
Clarke, William J. "Boileryard" 1893-94, 1896
Clarkson, Arthur H. "Dad" 1893-96
Clarkson, John G. 1888, 1892-93
Clements, John J. "Jack" 1892
Coleman, John F. 1884
Coogan, Daniel G. "Dan" 1895
Cooney, John W. "Johnny" 1941
Crane, Edward N. "Ed" 1892
Crane, Samuel N. "Sam" 1886, 1890
Crolius, Frederick J. "Fred" 1901
Cronin, John J. "Jack" 1902-03
Cross, Lafayette N. "Lave" 1892
Culler, Richard B. "Dick" 1947
Cunningham, Elmer E. "Bert" 1896-97, 1900
Cuppy, George M. 1894
Cusick, Andrew D. "Tony" 1886-87
Daily, Cornelius F. "Con" 1886, 1891, 1894, 1896
Daly, Thomas P. "Tom" 1901
Darling, Conrad "Dell" 1887
Dealy, Patrick E. "Pat" 1886
Dexter, Charles D. "Charlie" 1896-97
Donahue, Francis R. "Red" 1897
Donahue, Timothy C. "Tim" 1895-96
Donlin, Michael J. "Mike"

1900
Donnelly, James B. "Jim" 1896
Donovan, William E. "Bill" 1902
Dooin, Charles S. "Red" 1904
Douglass, William B. "Klondike" 1903
Dowse, Thomas J. "Tom" 1890
Duggleby, William J. "Bill" 1905
Dwyer, J. Francis "Frank" 1889, 1893-94, 1896-97
Earle, William M. "Billy" 1894
Ehret, Philip S. "Phil" 1892, 1895-97
Farrell, Charles A. "Duke" 1901-02
Ferguson, Charles J. "Charlie" 1886
Fitzsimmons, Frederick "Freddie" 1941
Flaherty, Patrick J. "Patsy" 1904
Force, David W. "Davy" 1881
Foreman, Francis I. "Frank" 1895
Foreman, John D. "Brownie" 1896
Foster, Clarence F. "Pop" 1900
Freeman, John F. "Buck" 1900
Galvin, James F. "Pud" 1881, 1887, 1889
Gardner, James A. "Jim" 1899
George, William M. "Bill" 1889
German, Lester S. "Les" 1895
Gleason, William J. "Kid" 1890, 1892
Grady, Michael W. "Mike" 1895
Graves, Frank M. 1886
Griffith, Clark C. 1894-95
Grim, John H. 1892, 1895-96
Gruber, Henry J. 1889
Gumbert, Addison C. "Ad" 1892, 1895-96
Gunning, Thomas F. "Tom" 1884-85
Gunson, Joseph B. "Joe" 1892
Hackett, Mortimer M. "Mert" 1886
Haddock, George S. 1889
Hallman, William W. "Bill" 1903
Hanlon, Edward H. "Ned" 1892
Hart, William F. "Bill" 1896-97
Hatfield, Gilbert "Gil" 1889
Healy, John J. 1887
Hemming, George E. 1895-96
Hines, Michael P. "Mike" 1884
Hoffer, William L. "Bill" 1896
Holliday, James W. "Bug" 1897
Howe, John "Shorty" 1890
Hurst, Timothy C. "Tim" 1898
Hyatt, R. Hamilton "Ham" 1912
Irwin, Arthur A. 1881
Jacklitsch, Fred L. 1901
Jennings, Hugh A. "Hughie" 1893, 1900
Johnson, Sylvester "Syl" 1934
Jones, Henry M. 1890
Kahoe, Michael J. "Mike" 1905
Karger, Edwin "Ed" 1906
Keefe, Timothy J. "Tim" 1880-82, 1884-85, 1887, 1892
Keeler, William H. "Willie" 1910
Kellum, Winford A. "Win" 1905

Kelly, Michael J. "King" 1892-93
Killen, Frank B. 1896-97
Kinslow, Thomas F. "Tom" 1892
Kittridge, Malachi J. 1890, 1899
Kitson, Frank R. 1902
Klein, Charles H. "Chuck" 1942
Kling, John G. "Johnny" 1901
Knell, Philip H. "Phil" 1895
Knowles, James "Jimmy" 1892
Krieg, William F. "Bill" 1887
Leever, Samuel W. "Sam" 1900, 1904
Lindeman, Vivian A. "Vive" 1907
Lundgren, Carl L. 1905-06
Maloney, William A. "Billy" 1902
Manning, James H. "Jim" 1886
Mathews, Robert T. "Bobby" 1882
Mathewson, Christopher "Christy" 1901, 1907
McAleer, James R. "Jim" 1893
McAllister, Lewis W. "Sport" 1899
McCarthy, Thomas F. M. "Tommy" 1896
McCauley, Allen A. "Al" 1890
McCauley, Patrick M. "Pat" 1896
McCormick, James "Jim" 1885
McFarland, Edward W. "Ed" 1896
McGarr, James B. "Chippy" 1895
McGinnity, Joseph J. "Joe" 1900
McGuire, James T. "Deacon" 1886, 1894, 1896-97, 1901
McKinnon, Alexander J. "Alex" 1886
McMahon, John J. "Sadie" 1893
Meekin, Jouette 1895-96
Menefee, John "Jock" 1903
Mercer, George B. "Win" 1896
Mertes, Samuel B. "Sam" 1905
Miller, George F. "Doggie" 1893, 1896
Miller, Joseph H. 1884
Miller, L. Otto 1934
Moran, Patrick J. "Pat" 1901
Mullane, Anthony J. "Tony" 1893
Mulvey, Joseph H. "Joe" 1895
Murphy, Morgan E. 1893, 1896, 1898
Murphy, William H. "Yale" 1895, 1897
Murray, Jeremiah J. "Miah" 1895
Myers, George D. 1886
Needham, Thomas J. "Tom" 1904, 1907
Newton, Eustace J. "Doc" 1902
Nichols, Charles A. "Kid" 1900-01
Nolan, Edward S. "The Only" 1881
Noonan, Peter J. "Pete" 1906-07
O'Brien, John F. "Darby" 1889
O'Connor, John J. "Jack" 1893, 1901
O'Day, Henry F. "Hank" 1888-89
O'Neill, Michael J. "Mike" 1904
Orth, Albert L. "Al" 1901
Overall, Orval 1905, 1910
Peitz, Henry C. "Heinie" 1901, 1906
Phelps, Edward J. "Ed" 1912

Phillippe, Charles L. "Deacon" 1903
Quinn, Joseph J. "Joe" 1894, 1896
Reilly, Charles T. "Charlie" 1892, 1894-95
Reitz, Henry P. "Heinie" 1895
Rhines, William P. "Billy" 1891, 1896
Richardson, A. Harding "Hardie" 1892
Richmond, J. Lee 1883
Robinson, Wilbert 1898
Ryan, James E. "Jimmy" 1892
Sanders, A. Bennett "Ben" 1889
Schmidt, Henry M. 1903
Schriver, William F. "Pop" 1901
Serad, William I. "Billy" 1884
Smith, A. Edgar 1883
Smith, Edgar E. 1890
Smith, George H. "Heinie" 1901
Smith, Harry T. 1903
Smith, William E. "Bill" 1886
Sommers, Joseph A. "Joe" 1889
Staley, Harry E. 1892, 1895
Stearns, D. Eckford "Ecky" 1881
Stein, Edward F. "Ed" 1890, 1894, 1896
Stivetts, John C. "Jack" 1894
Stocksdale, Otis H. 1895
Stricker, John A. "Cub" 1892
Stricklett, Elmer E. 1907
Sugden, Joseph "Joe" 1897
Sullivan, James E. "Jim" 1896
Sullivan, Martin C. "Marty" 1889
Sullivan, Michael J. "Mike" 1897
Sullivan, Thomas J. "Sleeper" 1881
Sutcliffe, Elmer E. "Sy" 1889, 1892
Tannehill, Jesse N. 1897, 1901-02
Tate, Edward C. "Pop" 1888
Taylor, John B. "Jack" 1899
Taylor, John W. "Jack" 1901, 1905
Tener, John K. 1889
Terry, William H. "Adonis" 1892, 1895-96
Tiernan, Michael J. "Mike" 1895
Vaughn, Harry F. "Farmer" 1892, 1899
Viau, Leon "Lee" 1891
Vickery, Thomas G. "Tom" 1890
Walker, Thomas W. "Tom" 1905
Wall, Joseph F. "Joe" 1901
Wallace, Roderick J. "Bobby" 1895
Walters, William H. "Bucky" 1942, 1947
Ward, John M. "Monte" 1888
Warneke, Lonnie "Lon" 1940
Warner, John J. "Jack" 1896-97, 1901, 1903
Weaver, William B. "Farmer" 1893
Weimer, Jacob W. "Jake" 1905, 1907
Welch, Michael F. "Mickey" 1881-82, 1885-86, 1888
Weyhing, August "Gus" 1894, 1899-1900
Whistler, Lewis "Lew" 1891
White, Guy H. "Doc" 1901-02
White, James L. "Deacon" 1880
Whitney, James E. "Jim" 1884, 1886

Wilhelm, Irving K. "Kaiser" 1904-05
Williamson, Edward N. "Ned" 1878, 1880
Willis, Victor G. "Vic" 1903
Wilmot, Walter R. "Walt" 1897
Wilson, Frank A. "Zeke" 1896, 1899
Wilson, James "Jimmie" 1940
Wilson, Parke A. 1894-96, 1899
Wilson, William G. "Bill" 1899
Wright, W. Harrison "Harry" 1876-77
Yeager, George J. 1901
Young, Denton T. "Cy" 1896
Young, Irving M. "Irv" 1905, 1907
Zimmer, Charles L. "Chief" 1889, 1901

American Association (1882-91)

Baldwin, Clarence G. "Kid" 1887
Becannon, James M. "Buck" 1884
Bond, Thomas H. "Tommy" 1884
Booth, Amos S. 1882
Boyle, John A. "Jack" 1888
Brennan, John G. "Jack" 1888
Briody, Charles F. "Fatty" 1888
Burns, Thomas P. "Oyster" 1888
Bushong, Albert J. "Doc" 1888-89
Carlin, William J. "Billy" 1886
Carsey, Wilfred "Kid" 1891
Cassidy, John P. 1884
Chamberlain, Elton P. 1887, 1891
Cross, Lafayette N. "Lave" 1889
Crowell, William T. "Billy" 1888
Darling, Conrad "Dell" 1891
Donahue, James A. "Jim" 1888
Easton, John S. "Jack" 1891
Ehret, Philip S. "Phil" 1890
Ewing, John 1889
Fulmer, Charles J. "Chick" 1888
Galvin, James F. "Jim" 1886
Ganzel, Charles W. "Charlie" 1886
Goldsby, Walton H. "Walt" 1888
Greenwood, William F. "Bill" 1884
Griffith, Clark C. 1891
Gunning, Thomas F. "Tom" 1888-89
Healy, John J. 1890
Hecker, Guy J. 1888
Herr, Edward J. "Ed" 1888
Higgins, William E. "Bill" 1890
Holbert, William H. "Bill" 1888
Johnston, Richard F. "Dick" 1884
Keefe, Timothy J. "Tim" 1884
Keenan, James W. "Jim" 1887-88
Kilroy, Matthew A. "Matt" 1887
Kirby, John F. 1888
Knell, Philip H. "Phil" 1891
Latham, George W. "Juice" 1884
Lynch, John H. "Jack" 1884
Macullar, James F. "Jimmy" 1886
Mattimore, Michael J. "Mike" 1888
Mays, Albert C. "Al" 1887
McCarthy, Thomas F. M.

"Tommy" 1889
McKelvy, Russell E. "Russ" 1882
McMahon, John J. "Sadie" 1890
McSorley, John B. "Trick" 1884
Merrill, Edward M. "Ed" 1884
Mountain, Frank H. 1884
Mullane, Anthony J. "Tony" 1888
Murphy, Joseph A. "Joe" 1887
O'Brien, William D. "Darby" 1887-88
O'Connor, John J. "Jack" 1889
O'Day, Henry F. "Hank" 1884
Peoples, James E. "Jimmy" 1888-89
Pierce, Grayson S. "Gracie" 1882
Sage, Harry 1890
Serad, William I. "Billy" 1888
Smith, Charles M. "Pop" 1886
Smith, Frederick C. "Fred" 1890
Smith, John F. "Phenomenal" 1888
Snyder, Charles N. "Pop" 1886
Sommer, Joseph J. "Joe" 1888
Sprague, Charles W. "Charlie" 1890
Stivetts, John C. "Jack" 1891
Sweeney, Charles J. "Charley" 1887
Sylvester, Louis J. "Lou" 1888
Terry, William H. "Adonis" 1884, 1888
Townsend, George H. 1890
Traffley, William F. "Bill" 1884
Vaughn, Harry F. "Farmer" 1891
Weyhing, August "Gus" 1891
Wheeler, Harry E. 1882
Wood, George A. 1891
Zimmer, Charles L. "Chief" 1888

Union Association (1884)

Bradley, George W. 1884
Callahan, Edward J. "Ed" 1884
Carroll, Patrick "Pat" 1884
Cuthbert, Edgar E. "Ned" 1884
Kelly, John F. 1884
McLaughlin, James C. "Jim" 1884
Oberbeck, Henry A. 1884
Wheeler, Harry E. 1884
Williams, Washington J. "Wash" 1884

Players League (1890)

Bakely, Edward E. "Ed" 1890
Carney, John J. 1890
Comiskey, Charles A. "Charlie" 1890
Daily, Cornelius F. "Con" 1890
Gumbert, Addison C. "Ad" 1890
Haddock, George S. 1890
Hallman, William W. "Bill" 1890
Keefe, Timothy J. "Tim" 1890
Kelly, Michael J. "King" 1890
Madden, Michael J. "Kid" 1890
Milligan, John "Jocko" 1890
O'Day, Henry F. "Hank" 1890
Tener, John K. 1890

American League (1901-)

Altrock, Nicholas "Nick" 1907
Bejma, Alojzy F. "Ollie" 1935
Bender, Charles A. "Chief" 1907
Bernhard, William H. "Bill" 1903, 1907
Beville, H. Monte 1903-04
Blankenship, Clifford D. "Cliff" 1907
Buelow, Frederick W. "Fritz" 1906
Callahan, James J. "Nixey" 1901
Conlan, John B. "Jocko" 1935
Coughlin, William P. "Bill" 1904
Cronin, John J. "Jack" 1901
Davis, Harry H. 1903
Dinneen, William H. "Bill" 1907
Donahue, Francis R. "Red" 1903, 1906
Donovan, William E. "Bill" 1903, 1906
Drill, Lewis L. "Lew" 1903-04
Flaherty, Patrick J. "Patsy" 1903
Foreman, Francis I. "Frank" 1901
Grady, Michael W. "Mike" 1901
Griffith, Clark C. 1903
Harris, Joseph W. "Joe" 1906
Hartley, Grover A. 1935
Hickman, Charles T. "Charlie" 1907
Howell, H. Harry 1904, 1906-07
Kittridge, Malachi J. 1905-06
Leahy, Thomas J. "Tom" 1901
Leppert, Donald G. "Don" 1978
Lowe, Robert L. "Bobby" 1905
McAllister, Lewis W. "Sport" 1901-02
McGuire, James T. "Deacon" 1905
Moore, Earl A. 1903
O'Brien, Peter J. "Pete" 1907
Patten, Case L. 1903
Pelty, Barney 1906
Powers, Michael R. "Mike" 1902
Roth, Francis C. "Frank" 1923
Schmidt, Charles "Boss" 1907
Schreckengost, Ossee F. 1903
Siever, Edward T. "Ed" 1901
Warner, John J. "Jack" 1908
White, Guy H. "Doc" 1903
Winter, George L. 1903, 1905
Young, Denton T. "Cy" 1903
Zimmerman, Gerald R. "Jerry" 1978

Federal League (1914-15)

Groom, Robert "Bob" 1914
Maxwell, J. Albert "Bert" 1914

UMPIRES DURING STRIKES

National League (1876-)

Anderson, Lewis E. "Andy" 1978-79
Andress, William J. "Bill" 1979
Baird, John 1979
Ballina, Frank 1991, 1995
Barston, Michael "Mike" 1979
Baswell, Jack S. 1979
Beck, Robert "Bob" 1979
Bendekovits, Joseph "Joe" 1979
Betcher, Ralph A. 1976
Blandford, Fred 1970
Bovey, Terry R. 1979, 1984, 1995
Bruns, Randy 1991
Campagna, Frank J. 1979, 1984
Cavenaugh, Richard P. "Dick" 1979, 1984
Cohen, Alfred A. "Al" 1976
Costello, Perry 1995
Cote, Emilien 1979
Cuneo, James "Jim" 1978-79
Davidson, — 1995
Davis, Bill 1995
Deniston, Shannon W. "Shan" 1978
Dierking, Roger A. 1978
Edwards, Larry 1978
Fick, Jerry D. 1978-79
Fisher, Frank 1979, 1984
Fleming, Thomas E. "Tom" 1979
Floras, John 1991
Ford, Wade 1995
Fowler, A. Wheeler 1978
Freels, Robert L. "Bob" 1979
Garman, Jim 1979
Gisondi, Tony 1991
Graham, Scott 1991, 1995
Grimsley, John 1970
Grinder, Scott 1976
Grooms, Roger C. 1979
Grygiel, George R. 1970
Guckert, Elmer 1976
Hadry, Merrill A. 1979
Hamil, Ray 1979
Hansen, Howard 1978-79
Hantak, H. Robert "Bob" 1979
Harris, Vance 1995
Henry, William E. "Bill" 1979
Hernandez, Bob 1995
Holoka, Mike 1991, 1995
Homolka, Bob 1995
Humphrey, Rick 1995
Hutson, Ronald "Ron" 1979
Jackson, Dick 1995
January, Don 1991, 1995
Jeffers, Ronald L. "Ron" 1979
Jenkins, Jeff 1995
Jones, Bob 1995
Jones, James "Jim" 1979
Jumper, Howard 1979
Lambeth, Jim 1995
Lauzon, Jacques 1979
Lawson, William R. "Bill" 1979
Loeber, Gerald G. "Jerry" 1979
Lospitalier, Philip A. "Phil" 1979
Lupo, Charles "Charlie" 1978-79
Maher, Robert J. "Bob" 1979, 1984
Martine, Bruce 1991
Mauer, Boyd 1978-79
Melton, David "Dave" 1978
Miller, Marvin G. "Bud" 1979
Mills, Greg 1979
Morgenweck, Henry C. "Hank" 1970
Mrvos, Joseph S. "Joe" 1979
Myers, Joseph "Joe" 1979
Negri, Peter "Pete" 1979
Nelson, Robert "Bob" 1979, 1991, 1995

Norris, Edward E. "Ed" 1978-79
Oliger, Edward C. "Ed" 1979
Pacheco, Jim 1995
Padilla, Joe 1995
Patch, Tony D. 1978-79
Perez, J. Ray 1979
Pomponi, Joseph L. "Joe" 1979, 1984
Rains, James "Jim" 1978-79
Randall, Larry 1995
Riccio, Dennis R. 1979
Riccio, L. Leonard "Len" 1979
Riggers, Mike 1995
Rodriguez, Gus 1995
Rosenberry, Bill 1995
Roth, Roy 1978-79
Rountree, Henry J. "Hank" 1978-79
Ryberg, Sy 1995
Schaff, Fred 1995
Schaller, Cliff 1978-79
Schleyer, John 1979
Schratz, Joseph "Joe" 1979
Schroeder, Robert L. "Bobby" 1978-79
Scott, James "Jim" 1978-79
Sharkey, Michael E. "Mick" 1978-79
Sharp, Robert C. "Bob" 1979
Siroka, Harold L. 1979
Slattery, Donald L. "Don" 1979
Slickenmeyer, David W. "Dave" 1979, 1984
Smail, Harry F. 1979
Spange, John 1991
Spinelli, Michel 1979
Stansell, B. Jack 1979
Stewart, John 1979, 1984
Strey, Murray W. 1978-79
Sylvester, Frank 1995
Telford, Thomas "Tom" 1979
Tillman, Henry T. "Hank" 1978-79
Treitel, Leslie J. "Les" 1978-79
Tremblay, Richard H. "Dick" 1979
Urlage, Richard C. "Dick" 1979, 1991
Waller, James "Jim" 1979
Whaley, — 1995
Widlowski, Mark 1995
Williams, Dale 1978-79
Willman, Bob 1991, 1995
Yeast, Dave 1995

American League (1901-)

Arata, Mark 1991
Berry, Charles F. "Charlie" 1970
Bialorucko, Larry 1995
Bible, Jonathan D. "Jon" 1984
Bishop, Homer L. 1979
Bohn, Matt 1995
Borga, Steven A. "Steve" 1979
Briscese, Michael L. "Mike" 1979
Brown, Buddy Lee "Bud" 1979
Brown, Douglas D. "Doug" 1979
Brown, Jeff 1978-79
Camp, John W. 1979
Campbell, Robert "Bob" 1979
Carcao, Joe 1995
Clegg, Richard "Dick" 1979
Clement, Robert F. "Bob" 1978-79
Compton, Craig 1995
Contant, Alan 1978-79
Cossey, Douglas C. "Doug" 1978-79, 1984

Cuneo, James "Jim" 1979
Cristal, W. Randle "Randy" 1984
Davidson, Dale F. 1979
Deegan, William E. J. "Bill" 1970, 1984, 1991, 1995
DeFlesco, Pete 1991
Denny, Richard 1984
Dreke, Roy 1979
Dresser, Al 1995
Driscoll, Joseph M. "Joe" 1978
Duncan, Robert 1995
Dunne, James "Jim" 1978-79
Easley, Harold L. 1979
Eshelman, George R. 1979
Evans, Jeff 1991
Farmer, Michael "Mike" 1979
Farnsworth, Harry 1979
Feaser, Richard L. "Dick" 1979
Fitzpatrick, Michael N. "Mike" 1979
Follmer, William A. "Bill" 1979
Forman, Allen S. "Al" 1978-79
Freese, Todd 1995
Fuchs, Lester 1978-79
Gallagher, Lawrence E. "Larry" 1979
George, Edward "Ed" 1979
Giard, Robert "Bob" 1978
Gustafson, G. David "Dave" 1978
Hafner, William F. "Bill" 1979
Hadry, Merrill A. 1979
Harris, Vance 1995
Harvey, Randy 1991, 1995
Heitzer, Richard "Dick" 1979
Henrichs, Jeff 1995
Henry, William E. "Bill" 1979
Higgins, John 1991, 1995
Huber, Mike 1995
Ivory, William J. "Bill" 1979
Jackson, Charles L. 1979
James, John F. "Johnny" 1978-79
Jones, Robert G. "Bob" 1979, 1984
Jordan, Harold E. 1984
Kaplan, Al 1995
Kavulich, Joseph "Joe" 1978-79
Keister, R. Wayne 1978-79
Kelly, Eugene C. "Gene" 1979
Kimball, Shawn 1991
Kirby, Kenneth "Ken" 1979
Klein, Gus 1991, 1995
Knauss, Jim 1991
LaPierre, Richard 1979
Laude, William F. "Bill" 1978-79
Lazar, Richard R. "Richie" 1978-79
Levet, Jay 1979
Loeber, Gerald G. "Jerry" 1979
Lospitalier, Philip A. "Phil" 1979
Luker, Dale 1995
Lupo, Charles "Charlie" 1979
Mabbot, Frederick J. "Fred" 1979
Mackin, John F. 1979
Mann, Terry 1995
Marino, James H. "Jimmy" 1979
Mason, Danny 1995
Mauer, Boyd 1979
McDougall, Scott 1991
McNally, James "Jim" 1979
Merritt, Clarence 1979
Miller, Gale 1979
Miller, John A. "Jack" 1979
Moyer, Robert "Bob" 1979
Mulcahy, James "Jim"

1979
Murray, Ed 1991
Nelson, Richard "Dick" 1979
Nothhnagel, Carl L. 1984
Novack, Lester A. "Les" 1979
O'Brien, James D. "Jim" 1979
O'Connor, James "Jim" 1978-79
O'Connor, Thomas M. "Tom" 1979
O'Dell, Mikel R. "Mike" 1984
Panas, Richard J. "Rich" 1978-79
Parks, Dallas F. 1991, 1995
Patch, Tony D. 1979
Paylor, Jim 1995
Perez, David A. "Dave" 1979
Phipps, George H. "Jerry" 1978-79
Pilato, Mike 1995
Pratt, Lester 1979
Purduski, Al J. 1979
Ravan, Bruce 1995
Ravashiere, Thomas "Tom" 1979
Riccio, L. Leonard "Len" 1979
Rice, Robert W. "Bob" 1979
Robinson, William N. "Bill" 1978-79
Roesner, Robert A. "Bob" 1978-79
Roth, Roy 1979
Rountree, Henry J. "Hank" 1991
Runchey, Richard D. "Dick" 1979, 1984
Satchell, Darold L. 1970
Sawchuk, Joseph W. "Joe" 1978-79
Schaly, Jim 1995
Scheel, Alfred M. "Al" 1979
Schirmer, Donald A. "Don" 1979
Schulte, Donald E. "Don" 1979
Schwarz, Henry "Hank" 1995
Shaw, A. Duane 1979
Shewmake, James B. "Jim" 1978
Siroka, Harold L. 1979
Slattery, Donald L. "Don" 1979
Slickenmeyer, David W. "Dave" 1979, 1991, 1995
Spenn, Frederick C. "Fred" 1991
Sprincz, William "Bill" 1978-79
Stevens, John W. "Johnny" 1970
Sweeney, George P. 1979
Swenson, Charles H. 1979
Taylor, Joe Bob 1979
Terlop, Russell F. "Russ" 1979
Theilander, Theodore "Ted" 1979
Thompson, Michael G. "Mike" 1978-79
Tillman, Henry T. "Hank" 1979
Travis, Vic 1995
Trimmer, Harry 1979
Turner, Leo I. 1978
Ulrich, George 1995
Urchak, Woody J. 1978-79
Uremovich, Jim 1991, 1995
Walding, Larry 1995
Williams, Dale 1979
Wright, Marvin 1995
Zirbel, Lawrence A. "Larry" 1979, 1984
Zivic, Richard J. "Dick" 1984
Zuccaro, Amerigo J. "Rico" 1978-79

Owners and Officials Roster

Although Major League Baseball began in 1871 with the National Association, it is undeniable that with the founding of the National League in 1876 something dramatic occurred that altered forevermore the character of professional baseball: the division of the game into two classes, labor and management.

The National Association of Professional Base Ball Players was an outgrowth of the amateur association of the same name, in which baseball clubs were formed as organizations devoted to social intercourse and fraternal competition. Amateur clubs were organized along the same lines as today's Elks or Odd Fellows, with elected officials and dues-paying members. As players of special skill were invited into these clubs, their dues might be forgiven or "emoluments" offered—no-show jobs or under-the-table payments. The abuses of the amateur system of the mid-1860s led to the declaration by several clubs of their openly professional status; players would sometimes draw salaries and as often would share in gate receipts. By the end of the decade gambling and game-fixing were rife.

Despite the formation of the National Association, these evils continued largely unabated into the 1870s. A monopolization of talent, largely in Boston, rendered Western clubs uncompetitive, and spectator rowdyism spawned by gambling interest, and the open sale of hard liquor burdened the new league. Clubs were admitted into the NA for paltry fees and fulfilled their schedules half-heartedly. Some of the member clubs had active presidents who functioned much as owners later would; other clubs were "cooperative nines," managed by the players themselves; still others were hybrids, born of civic boosterism. By 1876 the odd amalgam of the NA, presided over by Brooklyn Atlantics star Bob Ferguson, was failing.

Thus in 1876 William Hulbert, president of the Chicago club, combined with seven other team representatives to form the National League, a circuit run entirely by owners. Since then, fan interest has focused on the players, of course, and to a lesser extent on the managers, coaches, and umpires. But it can be said with some justice that while the on-field personnel and personalities "are" the game, it is the club owners, presidents, and league officials who make the game possible and ensure its continuity.

The Owners and Officials Roster that follows represents a first attempt in a baseball encyclopedia to recognize these individuals. As we did with the Coach Roster in the first edition of *Total Baseball*, we offered this section in *Total Baseball*'s second, third, fourth, and fifth editions with the full knowledge that there were gaps and probably gaffes in our research; we hope that our readers will advise us of omissions so that we can continue to improve the roster in future editions. (The names of National Association club presidents and officials are listed below despite our understanding that these individuals were, by and large, not owners in the sense used after 1876.)

Commissioners, Major League Baseball

1920–1944	Kenesaw M. Landis
1945–1951	Albert B. Chandler
1951–1965	Ford C. Frick
1965–1968	William D. Eckert
1969–1984	Bowie K. Kuhn
1984–1989	Peter Ueberroth
1989	A. Bartlett Giamatti
1989–1992	Francis T. Vincent, Jr.
1993–1998	Alan H. Selig (interim commissioner)
1998–	Alan H. Selig

National Association

Association President

1871	James W. Kerns
1872–1875	Robert W. Ferguson

Club Presidents and/or NA Convention Delegates

Baltimore Lord Baltimores

1872	—
1873	R. C. Hall
1874	C. A. Hadel

Baltimore Marylands

1873	W. J. Smith

Boston Red Stockings

1871	Ivers Whitney Adams
1872	Col. Charles H. Porter
1873–1875	Nathan Taylor Appolonio

Brooklyn Atlantics

1872–1873	Robert W. Ferguson
1874	—
1875	B. Van Delft

Brooklyn Eckfords

1872	William H. Ray

Chicago White Stockings

1871	J. M. Thatcher
1874	Mr. Gassette
	George W. Gage
1875	William A. Hulbert

Cleveland Forest City

1871	J. S. Evans
1872	H. C. Doolittle

Elizabeth Resolutes

1873	Charles N. Garrighan

Fort Wayne Kekiongas

1871	George J. E. Mayers

Hartford Dark Blues

1874	G. B. Hubbell
1875	Morgan G. Bulkeley

Keokuk Westerns

1875	W. Trimble

Middletown Mansfields

1872	B. Douglass, Jr.
	T. W. Ratcliff

New Haven Elm City

1875	W. S. Arnold

New York Mutuals

1871–1872	Alexander V. Davidson
1873	Robert Mathews
1874	Alexander V. Davidson
1875	William H. Cammeyer

Philadelphia Athletics

1871	James W. Kerns
1872–1873	E. Hicks Hayhurst
1874	D. F. Houston
1875	George W. Thompson
	C. Spering

Philadelphia White Stockings

1873	Frank McBride
1874	D. L. Reid
1875	George Concannon

Philadelphia Centennials

1875	E. Hicks Hayhurst

Rockford Forest City

1871	Hiram Waldo

St. Louis Brown Stockings

1875	C. O. Bishop

St. Louis Red Stockings

1875	A. Blong

Troy Haymakers

1871	J. W. Scofield

1872	C. C. Clark

Washington Nationals

1872	Mr. Millar
	R. Hough

Washington Olympics

1871	Nicholas E. Young
1872	Mr. Pike

Washington

1873	Nicholas E. Young
1875	D. W. Bruce
	A. F. Childs

National League

Presidents

1876	Morgan G. Bulkeley
1877–1882	William A. Hulbert
1882	Arthur H. Soden
1883–1884	Abraham G. Mills
1885–1902	Nicholas E. Young
1903–1909	Harry C. Pulliam
1909	John A. Heydler
1910–1913	Thomas J. Lynch
1913–1918	John K. Tener
1918–1934	John A. Heydler
1934–1951	Ford C. Frick
1951–1969	Warren C. Giles
1970–1986	Charles S. Feeney
1986–1989	A. Bartlett Giamatti
1989–1994	William White
1994–	Leonard S. Coleman, Jr.

Vice Presidents

1929–1932	Barney Dreyfuss
1933–1936	Charles A. Stoneham
1936–1947	Samuel Breadon
1947–1966	Philip K. Wrigley
1966–1969	Horace C. Stoneham
1970–1986	John J. McHale
1987–1994	Phyllis Collins
1994–	Katy Feeney

Club Presidents

Arizona

1998–	Jerry Colangelo (Chairman)

Atlanta

1966	John J. McHale
1967–1972	William C. Bartholomay
1973–1975	Daniel J. Donahue
1976–1986	R. E. (Ted) Turner
1987–	William C. Bartholomay (Ch. of Bd.)

Baltimore

1892	Harry B. Von der Horst
1893–1899	Edward H. Hanlon

Boston (to Milwaukee)

1876	Nathan Taylor Appolonio
1907–1909	George B. Dovey
1909–1910	John S. Dovey
1911	W. Hepburn Russell
1912	John M. Ward
1913–1915	James E. Gaffney
1916–1918	Percy D. Haughton
1919–1922	George W. Grant
1923	Christopher Mathewson
1924	J. A. Robert Quinn
1925	Christopher Mathewson
1926	J. A. Robert Quinn
1927–1935	Emil E. Fuchs (Pres.)
1936–1944	J. A. Robert Quinn (Pres.)
1945–1952	Louis R. Perini (Pres.)

Brooklyn (to L.A.)

1890–1897	Charles H. Byrne
1898–1925	Charles H. Ebbets
1925	Edward J. McKeever
1925–1929	Wilbert Robinson (Pres.)
1930–1932	Frank B. York (Pres.)
1933–1938	Stephen W. McKeever
1939–1942	Leland S. MacPhail, Sr. (Exec. VP)
1943–1950	W. Branch Rickey (Pres./GM)
1950–1957	Walter F. O'Malley (Pres.)

Buffalo

1879–1880	E. B. Smith
1880	John B. Sage
1881–1885	Josiah Jewett

Chicago

1876–1881	William A. Hulbert
1882–1891	Albert G. Spalding
1892–1905	James A. Hart
1906–1913	Charles W. Murphy
1914–1915	Charles H. Thomas

1916–1918	Charles H. Weeghman
1919	Fred F. Mitchell
1919–1933	William L. Veeck, Sr. (Pres.)
1934	William M. Walker
1934–1977	Philip K. Wrigley (Pres.)
1977–1981	William J. Hagenah, Jr. (Pres./CEO/Treas.)
1982–1983	Andrew J. McKenna (Ch. of Bd.)
1984	James E. Finks (Pres./CEO)
1985–1987	Dallas Green (Pres./GM)
1988	John W. Madigan (Ch. of Bd.)
1989–1994	Stanton Cook (Ch. of Bd.)
1994–	Andy MacPhail (Pres./CEO)

Cincinnati

1876–1877	Josiah L. Keck
1878–1879	J. Wayne Neff
1880	Justus Thorner

Cincinnati

1890	Aaron A. Stern
1891–1902	John T. Brush
1902–1927	August Hermann (Pres.)
1928–1929	C. J. McDiarmid (Pres.)
1930–1933	Sidney Weil (Pres.)
1934–1946	Powel Crosley, Jr. (Pres.)
1946–1951	Warren C. Giles (Pres.)
1951–1961	Powel Crosley, Jr. (Pres.)
1961–1966	William O. DeWitt (Pres./GM/Treas.)
1967–1973	Francis L. Dale (Pres.)
1973–1978	Robert L. Howsam (Pres./CEO)
1979–1983	Richard Wagner (Pres./CEO)
1984–1985	Robert L. Howsam (Pres./CEO)
1986–	Marge Schott (Gen. Partner/Pres.)

Cleveland

1879–1881	J. Ford Evans
1882–1884	C. H. Bulkley

Cleveland

1889–1898	Frank D. Robison
1899	M. Stanley Robison

Colorado

1992	John Antonucci (Ch./CEO)
1993–	Jerry McMorris (Ch./CEO/Pres.)

Detroit

1881–1884	William G. Thompson
1885–1886	Joseph H. Marsh
1887–1888	Fred K. Stearns
1888	Charles W. Smith

Florida

1992–	Wayne Huizenga (Chairman)

Hartford

1876–1877	Morgan G. Bulkeley

Houston

1962	Craig F. Cullinan, Jr. (Pres.)
1963–1971	Roy Hofheinz (Pres.)
1972–1973	Reuben W. Askanase (Pres./Ch. of Bd.)
1974–1975	T. H. Neyland (Pres.)
1976	Sidney L. Shlenker (Pres.)
1976–1980	Talbot M. Smith (Pres./GM)
1981–1985	Albert L. Rosen (Pres./GM)
1986–1987	Dick Wagner
1988	Fred Stanley
1980–1992	Dr. John J. McMullen (Ch. of Bd.)
1992–	Drayton McLane, Jr. (Ch. of Bd./CEO)

Indianapolis

1878	William D. Perritt

Indianapolis

1887–1889	John T. Brush

Kansas City

1886	Joseph J. Heim

Los Angeles

1958–1969	Walter F. O'Malley (Pres.)
1970–1997	Peter O'Malley (Pres.)
1998–	Rupert Murdoch (Principal Owner)

Louisville

1876–1877	Walter N. Haldeman

Louisville

1892	T. Hunt Stucky
1893–1896	Fred Drexler
1897–1899	Harry C. Pulliam
1899	Barney Dreyfuss

Milwaukee

1878	J. R. Kaine

Milwaukee Braves (to Atlanta Braves)

1953–1956	Louis R. Perini (Pres.)
1957–1961	Joseph F. Cairnes (Pres.)
1962–1966	John J. McHale (Pres.)

Milwaukee Brewers (from American League)

1998	Allan H. "Bud" Selig (Pres./ CEO)
1998-	Wendy Selig-Prieb

Montreal Expos

1969–1986	John J. McHale (Pres./CEO)
1987–1998	Claude R. Brochu (Pres./CEO)
1998-	Jacques Menard (Pres./CEO)

Mutual Club (N.Y.)

1876	William H. Cammeyer

New York Giants (to San Francisco)

1883–1892	John B. Day
1893–1894	C. C. Van Cott
1895–1902	Andrew Freedman
1903–1912	John T. Brush
1912–1918	Harry N. Hempstead
1919–1935	Charles A. Stoneham (Pres.)
1936–1957	Horace C. Stoneham (Pres.)

New York Mets

1962–1966	George M. Weiss (Pres.)
1966–1967	Vaughan P. Devine (Pres.)
1968–1975	Mrs. Joan W. Payson (Pres.)
1976–1979	Mrs. Lorinda de Roulet (Pres.)
1980-	Fred Wilpon (Pres./CEO)

Philadelphia Athletics

1876	Thomas J. Smith

Philadelphia Phillies

1883–1902	Alfred J. Reach
1903–1904	James Potter
1905–1908	William J. Shettsline
1909	Israel W. Durham
1909–1912	Horace S. Fogel
1912	Alfred D. Wiler
1913	William H. Locke
1913–1930	William F. Baker (Pres.)
1931–1932	L. Charles Ruch
1933–1942	Gerald P. Nugent (Pres.)
1943	William D. Cox
1943–1972	Robert M. Carpenter, Jr. (Pres.)
1973–1981	Robert M. Carpenter III (Pres.)
1982–1987	Bill Giles (Pres./CEO)
1998-	David Montgomery (Pres./ CEO)

Pittsburgh

1887–1890	William A. Nimick
1891	J. Palmer O'Neill
1892	William C. Temple
1893	Albert C. Buckenberger
1894–1897	William W. Kerr
1898	William H. Watkins
1899	William W. Kerr
1900–1932	Barney Dreyfuss (Pres.)
1932–1946	William E. Benswanger (Pres./ Treas.)
1946–1950	Frank E. McKinney (Pres.)
1951–1969	John W. Galbreath (Pres.)
1970–1985	Daniel M. Galbreath (Pres.)
1986–1987	Malcolm Prine
1988–1990	Carl Barger (Pres.)
1988–1991	Douglas D. Danforth (Chairman/CEO)
1992	Vincent Sarni (Pres./CEO)
1992–1996	Mark Sauer (Pres./CEO)
1996-	Kevin S. McClatchy (CEO/ Man. Gen. Partner)

Providence

1878	John D. Thurston
1879–1881	Henry J. Root
1882–1883	Henry B. Winship
1884–1885	Henry J. Root

St. Louis Brown Stockings

1876–1877	John R. Lucas

St. Louis Maroons

1885–1886	Henry V. Lucas

St. Louis Cardinals

1892–1897	Chris Von der Ahe
1898	Benjamin S. Muckenfuss
1899–1906	Frank D. Robison
1907–1910	M. Stanley Robison
1911–1912	E. A. Steininger
1912	James C. Jones
1913–1916	Schuyler P. Britton

1916	Mrs. Schuyler P. Britton
1917–1919	W. Branch Rickey
1920–1947	Samuel Breadon (Pres.)
1947–1949	Robert E. Hannegan
1949–1952	Fred M. Saigh, Jr. (Pres.)
1953–1989	August A. Busch, Jr. (Pres.)
1990–1991	Fred L. Kuhlmann (Pres./CEO)
1992–1994	Stuart Meyer (Pres./CEO)
1994-	Mark C. Lamping (Pres.)

San Diego

1969–1977	Emil J. Bavasi (Pres.)
1977–1980	Ray A. Kroc
1981–1983	Ray A. Kroc (owner)
1980–1987	Ballard F. Smith, Jr.
1988	Chub Feeney
1990	Dick Freeman
1984–1990	Joan Kroc (owner)
1991–1994	Tom Werner (Prin. Owner/Ch.)
1994-	John Moores (Ch. of the Bd.)

San Francisco

1958–1975	Horace C. Stoneham (Pres.)
1976–1979	Robert A. Lurie/Bud Herseth (Co-Chairmen)
1980–1985	Robert A. Lurie (Pres.)
1986–1990	Robert A. Lurie (owner)
1986–1992	Albert L. Rosen (Pres./GM)
1993-	Peter A. Magowan (Pres.)

Syracuse

1879	Hamilton S. White

Troy

1879–1880	Gardner Earl
1881–1882	A. L. Hotchkin
1882	Francis N. Mann

Washington

1886–1888	Robert C. Hewitt
1889	Walter F. Hewitt

Washington

1892–1899	George W. Wagner

Worcester

1880–1882	Elbert B. Pratt

American Association

League Presidents

1882–1885	H. D. McKnight
1886–1889	Wheeler C. Wyckoff
1890	Zach Phelps
1891	Louis Kramer
	Ed Renau
	Zach Phelps

Club Presidents

Baltimore

1882	H. C. Myers (?)
1883	William Barnie (?)
1884	H. T. Houck
1885–1887	William Barnie
1888	Harry Von der Horst
1889	William Barnie
1891	Harry Von der Horst

Boston

1891	Charles A. Prince

Brooklyn

1884–1889	Charles H. Byrne

Brooklyn–Baltimore

1890	James M. Kennedy
	Wm. Barnie (?)

Cincinnati

1882	Justus Thorner
1883–1884	Aaron S. Stern
1885	George L. Herancourt
1886	John Hauck
1887–1889	Aaron S. Stern

Cincinnati-Milwaukee

1891	Albert Johnson

Cleveland

1887–1888	Frank Robison

Columbus

1883–1884	H. T. Crittendon (?)
1889–1891	Conrad Born, Jr.

Indianapolis

1884	Joseph Schwabacher

Kansas City

1888	Joseph J. Heim
1889	John W. Speas

Louisville

1882–1883	J. H. Pank

1884	William L. Jackson, Jr.
1885–1887	Zach Phelps
1888	W. L. Lyons
1889	M. H. Davidson
1890	Lawrence S. Parsons
1891	Julian B. Hart

New York

1883–1884	John B. Day
1885	Frank Rhouer
1886–1887	Erastus Wiman

Philadelphia

1882	Lew Simmons (?)
1883–1886	William Sharsig
1887	Lew Simmons
1888–1890	H. C. Pennypacker
1891	J. Earle Wagner

Pittsburgh

1882–1883	H. D. McKnight
1884	E. E. Converse
1885–1886	William A. Nimick

Richmond

1884	W. C. Seddon

Rochester

1890	Henry Brinker

St. Louis

1882–1891	Chris Von der Ahe

Syracuse

1890	George K. Frazier

Toledo

1884	W. J. Colburn
1890	V. H. Ketcham

Washington

1884	L. Moxley
1891	H. B. Bennett

Union Association

League Presidents

1883	H. B. Bennett
1883–1885	Henry V. Lucas

Club Presidents

Altoona

1884	W. W. Rich

Baltimore

1884	J. W. Lowe

Boston

1884	Frank E. Winslow

Chicago-Pittsburgh

1884	A. H. Henderson

Cincinnati

1884	Justus Thorner

Kansas City

1884	Americus V. McKim

Milwaukee

1884	Charles Kippen (?)

Philadelphia

1884	Thomas J. Pratt

St. Louis

1884	H. V. Lucas

St. Paul

1884	A. M. Thompson (?)

Washington

1884	H. B. Bennett

Wilmington

1884	John T. West

Players League

League President

1890	Col. Edward A. McAlpin

Club Presidents

Boston

1890	Col. Charles H. Porter

Brooklyn

1890	Wendell Goodwin

Buffalo

1890	Moses Shire

Chicago

1890	John Addison

Cleveland

1890	Albert L. Johnson

New York

1890	Cornelius Van Cott

Philadelphia
1890	H. M. Love

Pittsburgh
1890	William McCallin

American League

Presidents

1901–1927	B. Bancroft Johnson
1927–1931	Ernest S. Barnard
1931–1959	William Harridge
1959–1973	Joseph E. Cronin
1974–1984	Leland S. MacPhail, Jr.
1984–1994	Robert W. Brown, M.D.
1994–	Dr. Gene A. Budig

Vice Presidents

1901–1916	Charles W. Somers
1917–1919	Charles A. Comiskey
1921–1935	Frank J. Navin
1935–1938	Jacob Ruppert
1939–1955	Clark C. Griffith
1955–1976	Thomas A. Yawkey
1976–1982	Calvin R. Griffith
1983–1984	Calvin R. Griffith
	John Fetzer
	Gene Autry
1985	John Fetzer and Gene Autry
1986–1989	Calvin R. Griffith
	John Fetzer
	Gene Autry
1990	John Fetzer and Gene Autry
1991	Jean Yawkey and Gene Autry
1992–1998	Gene Autry

Club Presidents

Baltimore (to New York)
1901	Sidney W. Frank
1902	John J. Mahon

Baltimore
1954–1955	Clarence W. Miles (Pres.)
1956–1959	James Keelty, Jr. (Pres.)
1960–1965	Leland S. MacPhail, Jr. (Pres./ GM)
1966–1979	Jerold C. Hoffberger (Ch. of Bd.)
1980–1982	Jerold C. Hoffberger (as Pres.)
1983–1988	Edward B. Williams (Ch. of Bd./Pres.)
1989–1992	Lawrence Lucchino (Pres./ CEO)
1994–	Peter Angelos (Managing Gen. Partner)

Boston
1901–1902	Charles W. Somers
1903–1904	Henry J. Killilea
1904–1911	John I. Taylor
1912–1913	James R. McAleer
1913–1916	Joseph J. Lannin
1917–1923	Harry H. Frazee
1923–1932	Robert Quinn (Pres.)
1933–1976	Thomas A. Yawkey (Pres.)
1977–1988	Jean R. Yawkey (majority owner)
1989–	John L. Harrington (General Partner)

California (includes Los Angeles, 1961–64)
1961–1974	Robert Reynolds (Pres.)
1975–1977	Arthur E. Patterson (Pres.)
1977–1990	Gene Autry (owner/president)
1990–1996	Richard M. Brown (Pres./CEO)
1996-	Michael Eisner (Ch. & CEO)

Chicago
1901–1931	Charles A. Comiskey (Pres.)
1932–1939	J. Louis Comiskey (Pres./ Treas.)
1940	Harry Grabiner (VP)
1941–1956	Mrs. Grace Comiskey (Pres.)
1957–1959	Charles A. Comiskey II/John Rigney (VPs)
1959–1961	William L. Veeck, Jr. (Pres.)
1961–1969	Arthur C. Allyn, Jr. (Pres.)
1970–1975	John W. Allyn (Pres.)
1976–1980	William L. Veeck, Jr. (Pres.)
1981–	Jerry M. Reinsdorf (Chairman)

Cleveland
1901–1909	John F. Kilfoyl
1910–1915	Charles W. Somers
1916–1922	James C. Dunn
1922–1927	Ernest S. Barnard (Pres.)
1928–1946	Alva Bradley (Pres./Treas.)
1946–1949	William L. Veeck, Jr. (Pres.)
1950–1952	Ellis W. Ryan (Pres.)
1953–1962	Myron H. Wilson, Jr. (Pres.)
1963–1971	Gabriel H. Paul (Pres./Treas./ GM)
1972–1975	Nick Mileti (Pres.)
1975–1977	Alva T. Bonda (Pres.)
1978–1985	Gabriel H. Paul (Pres./CEO)
1986-	Patrick J. O'Neill (Chairman)
1987–	Richard E. Jacobs (Ch. of Bd./CEO)

Detroit
1901	James D. Burns (Pres.)
1902–1903	Samuel F. Angus (Pres.)
1904–1907	William H. Yawkey (Pres.)
1908–1935	Frank J. Navin (Pres.)
1936–1952	Walter O. Briggs, Sr. (Pres.)
1952–1956	Walter O. Briggs, Jr. (Pres.)
1957	Frederick A. Knorr (Pres.)
1957–1959	Harvey R. Hansen (Pres.)
1960	William O. DeWitt (Pres.)
1961–1989	John E. Fetzer (Pres.)
1978–1989	James Campbell (Pres.)
1984–1990	Thomas S. Monaghan (Pres.)
1990–1992	Glenn E. (Bo) Schembechler (Pres.)
1992–	Michael Ilitch (Owner and Chairman)

Kansas City A's (to Oakland)
1955–1959	Arnold Johnson (Pres.)
1960	Parke Carroll (VP)
1961–1967	Charles O. Finley (Pres.)

Kansas City Royals
1969–1993	Ewing Kauffman (Ch. of Bd.)
1993–	David D. Glass (Ch./CEO)

Milwaukee (to St. Louis)
1901	Matthew Killilea

Milwaukee Brewers (to National League)
1970–1997	Allan H. "Bud" Selig (Pres./CEO)

Minnesota
1961–1984	Calvin R. Griffith (Chairman/ Pres.)
1985–1986	Howard T. Fox, Jr.
1987–1989	Jerry Bell
1985–	Carl Pohlad (owner)

New York
1903–1906	Joseph W. Gordon
1903–1915	Frank J. Farrell and William S. Devery (owners)
1907–1914	Frank J. Farrell
1915–1938	Jacob Ruppert (Pres.)
1939–1944	Edward G. Barrow (Pres./GM)
1945–1947	Leland S. MacPhail, Sr. (Pres./ GM/Treas.)
1948–1953	Daniel R. Topping (Pres.)
1954-1966	Daniel R. Topping/Del E. Webb (co-owners)
1966–1973	Michael Burke (Ch. of the Bd./ Pres.)
1973–1977	Gabriel H. Paul (Pres.)
1978–1980	Albert L. Rosen (Pres./CEO)
1980–1990	George M. Steinbrenner (Ch. of Bd.)
1990–1991	Robert Nederlander (Man. Gen. Part.)
1992	Daniel McCarthy (Man. Gen. Part.)
1993–	George M. Steinbrenner (Prin. owner)

Oakland
1968–1980	Charles O. Finley (Pres.)
1981–1990	Roy Eisenhardt (Pres.)
1990–1995	Walter J. Haas (Chairman/CEO)
1995-	Steven C. Schott (Owner/ Pres.)

Philadelphia (to Kansas City)
1901–1921	Benjamin F. Shibe
1922–1935	Thomas S. Shibe (Pres.)
1936	John D. Shibe
1937–1954	Connie Mack (Pres.)

Seattle Pilots (to Milwaukee)
1969	Dewey Soriano (Pres.)

Seattle Mariners
1977–1979	Danny Kaye and Lester Smith (Man. Gen. Partners)
1980–1983	Daniel F. O'Brien (Pres./CEO)
1981–1989	George L. Argyros (Ch. of Bd./CEO)
1984–1989	Charles G. Armstrong
1990–1991	Jeff Smulyan (Ch. of Bd.)
1992–	John W. Ellis (Ch. of Bd./CEO)

St. Louis (to Baltimore)
1902	Ralph T. Orthwein
1903–1915	Robert L. Hedges
1916–1933	Philip D. Ball (Pres.)
1934–1936	Louis B. Von Weise
1937–1945	Donald L. Barnes (Pres.)
1946–1948	Richard C. Muckerman (Pres.)
1949–1951	William O. DeWitt (Pres.)
1951–1953	William L. Veeck, Jr. (Pres.)

Tampa Bay
1998-	Vincent Naimoli (Managing Gen. Partner/CEO)

Texas
1972–1974	Robert E. Short (Pres.)
1974	Robert W. Brown, M.D.
1975–1980	Bradford G. Corbett (Pres.)
1980–1987	Eddie Chiles (Owner/Ch. of Bd./CEO)
1984–1990	Michael H. Stone (Pres./COO)
1991–	J. Thomas Schieffer (Pres.)

Toronto
1977–1981	Peter Bavasi (Exec. VP/GM)
1977–1988	R. Howard Webster (Ch. of Bd.)
1989–1995	Paul Beeston (Pres./CEO)
1995-	Sam Pollock (Ch. & CEO)

Washington (to Minnesota)
1901–1903	Frederick Postal
1904	Thomas J. Loftus
1904	Harry B. Lambert
1905–1912	Thomas C. Noyes
1920–1955	Clark C. Griffith (Pres.)
1956–1960	Calvin R. Griffith (Pres.)

Washington
1961–1962	Elwood R. Quesada (Pres.)
1963–1967	James M. Johnston (Ch. of Bd.)
1968	James H. Lemon (Ch. of Bd.)
1969–1971	Robert E. Short (Pres.)

Federal League

League President

1914–1915	James A. Gilmore

Club Presidents

Baltimore
1914–1915	Carrol W. Rasin

Brooklyn
1914–1915	Robert B. Ward

Buffalo
1914	Walter F. Mullen
	William E. Robertson
1915	William E. Robertson

Chicago
1914–1915	Charles A. Weeghman

Indianapolis
1914	J. E. Krause

Kansas City
1914	C. C. Madison
1915	Charles Baird
	Conrad H. Mann

Newark
1915	P. T. Powers
	Harry Sinclair

Pittsburgh
1914	John R. Barbour
1915	Edward W. Gwinner

St. Louis
1914	E. A. Steininger
1915	Lloyd H. Rickart

Baseball Quotations
Sean Lahman

The game of baseball has been a fountain of commentary and wit since it was played in its earliest forms. Everyone from presidents to paupers has played it or watched it, and everyone in between has had something to say about it. Before and after each game, baseball players, managers, and executives alike are asked to dispense their thoughts on everything from that day's opponent to the future of the game—and someone is there to record it. Most of these responses are digested by readers in the next day's newspaper like a quick meal—essential at the time but quickly forgotten. Some statements, like baseball itself, live long after the next afternoon's game or the next evening's deadline.

This section includes some of the most poignant—and humorous—statements made about baseball since people first took the time to record their thoughts about the game. Not only are some of the greatest players in the game's history represented here, but also included are writers, poets, and royalty (or at least Babe Ruth, the "Sultan of Swat"). After his playing days had ended, Ruth reflected, "What I am, what I have, what I am going to leave behind me—all this I owe to the game of baseball, without which I would have come out of St. Mary's Industrial School in Baltimore as a tailor, and a pretty bad one, at that."

Leading Off

"Whoever would understand the heart and mind of America had better learn baseball, the rules and realities of the game—and do it by watching first some high school or small-town teams."

— Jacques Barzun

"It breaks your heart. It is designed to break your heart. The game begins in the spring, when everything else begins again, and it blossoms in the summer, filling the afternoons and evenings, and then as soon as the chill rains come, it stops and leaves you to face the fall alone."

— A. Bartlett Giamatti

"I see great things in baseball. It's our game—the American game. It will take our people out of doors, fill them with oxygen, give them a larger physical stoicism. Tend to relieve us from being a nervous, dyspeptic set. Repair these losses, and be a blessing to us."

— Walt Whitman

"Baseball is the very symbol, the outward and visible expression of the drive and push and rush and struggle of the raging, tearing, booming 19th century."

— Mark Twain

"The game itself is like Michelangelo's masterwork in the Sistine Chapel. You can cover it in filth, neglect it to death, attack what it represents and those who supervise it. But the game itself is ever resilient and ever resplendent, and just when you believe you have seen the last of its beauty, some new angle becomes visible to your eye and it is as if you have seen its splendor for the first time."

— Keith Olbermann

Winning

"There are only two places in the league. First and no place."

— Tom Seaver

"The worst thing is the day you realize you want to win more than your players do."

— Gene Mauch

"I'd rather be a swing man on a championship team than a regular on another team."

— Lou Piniella

"What are we out at the park for, except to win? I'd trip my mother. I'd help her up, brush her off, tell her I'm sorry. But mother don't make it to third base."

— Leo Durocher

"Show me a guy who's afraid to look bad, and I'll show you a guy you can beat every time."

— Lou Brock

"The greatest thrill in the world is to end the game with a home run and watch everybody walk off the field while you're running the bases on air."

— Al Rosen

After his Phillies scored nine runs in the ninth inning to beat the Dodgers): "Let's be honest. We're losing by eight runs (11-3), and all I'm thinking about at that point is getting back to the hotel by midnight because that's when room service closes. All of a sudden we start getting hits and more hits, and I'm saying "I'm not going to make it." If you're not going to get room service you might as well win."

— John Kruk

"You may go a long time without winning, but you never forget that scent."

— Steve Busby

"The way a team plays as a whole determines its success. You may have the greatest bunch of individual stars in the world, but if they don't play together, the club won't be worth a dime."

— Babe Ruth

"In the end it all comes down to talent. You can talk all you want about intangibles, I just don't know what that means. Talent makes winners, not intangibles. Can nice guys win? Sure, nice guys can win—if they're nice guys with a lot of talent. Nice guys with a little talent finish fourth, and nice guys with no talent finish last."

— Sandy Koufax

Losing

"If a tie is like kissing your sister, losing is like kissing your grandmother with her teeth out."

— George Brett

On the expansion Mets: "They've shown me ways to lose that I never knew existed."

— Casey Stengel

"The only way to prove that you're a good sport is to lose."

— Ernie Banks

"The losing streak is bad for the fans, no doubt, but look at it this way. We're making a lot of people happy in other cities."

— Ted Turner

Managing the 1973 Texas Rangers: "We need just two players to be a contender. Just Babe Ruth and Sandy Koufax."

— Whitey Herzog

"The fans like to see home runs, and we've assembled a pitching staff for their enjoyment."

— Clark Griffith

"The worst curse in life is unlimited potential."

— Ken Brett

Following a tough loss: "The only reason I'm coming out here tomorrow is the schedule says I have to."

— Sparky Anderson

"When you're a winner you're always happy, but if you're happy as a loser you'll always be a loser."

— Mark Fidrych

"If you don't catch the ball, you catch the bus."

— Rocky Bridges

"Grantland Rice, the great sportswriter once said. 'It's not whether you win or lose, it's how you play the game.' Well Grantland Rice can go to hell as far as I'm concerned."

— Angels owner Gene Autry

"Losing clubs bicker, and you think maybe if they pulled together they would win. No. That's not it. If they won, they would pull together."

— Jim Bouton

"Losing streaks are funny. If you lose at the beginning, you got off to a bad start. If you lose in the middle off the season, you're in a slump. If you lose at the end, you're choking."

— Gene Mauch

Hitters

"I've found that you don't need to wear a necktie if you can hit."

— Ted Williams

"Guessing what the pitcher is going to throw is 80 percent of being a successful hitter. The other 20 percent is just execution."

— Henry Aaron

"You don't always make an out. Sometimes the pitcher gets you out."

— Carl Yastrzemski

When it was suggested he could raise his batting average by choking up on the bat: "Cadillacs are down at the end of the bat."

— Ralph Kiner

"You hit a four-ounce baseball with a 35-ounce bat and there's going to be some damage."

— George Foster

"There is only one legitimate trick to pinch hitting, and that's knowing the pitcher's best pitch when the count is 3-and-2. All the rest is a crapshoot."

— Earl Weaver

"Carrots might be good for my eyes, but they won't straighten out the curveball."

— Carl Furillo

"I have only one superstition. I make sure to touch all the bases when I hit a home run."

— Babe Ruth

"I have observed that baseball is not unlike a war, and when you come right down to it, we batters are the heavy artillery."

— Ty Cobb

"I wanted to be the greatest hitter who ever lived. A man has to have goals and that was mine, to have people say, 'There goes Ted Williams. The greatest hitter who ever lived.'"

— Ted Williams

Pitchers

"Closing games in the big leagues is a lot like landing airplanes. A successful effort rarely warrants notice and a failure is considered a full-scale disaster."

— John Franco

"The pitcher has to find out if the hitter is timid. And if the hitter is timid, he has to remind the hitter he's timid."

— Don Drysdale

"I throw the ball right down the middle. The high-ball

hitters swing over it and the low-ball hitters swing under it."

— Saul Rogovin

Explaining why he pitched so quickly: "What do you want me to do? Let them sons of bitches stand up there and think on my time?"

— Grover Cleveland Alexander

"I've always felt a lot of pitching coaches made a living out of running pitchers so they wouldn't have to spend that same time teaching them how to pitch."

— Johnny Sain

Responding to suggestions that he doctored pitches with a foreign substance: "I'm not going to agree with them and I'm not going to deny it. I do have a tendency to go to my hat a lot. I guess they figure that's where it is. That's not where it is, though."

— Mike Proly

"The way to catch a knuckleball is to wait until the ball stops rolling and then pick it up."

— Bob Uecker

On being a relief pitcher: "Why pitch nine innings when you can get just as famous pitching two?"

— Sparky Lyle

"All pitchers are liars and crybabies."

— Yogi Berra

"If I'd known I was gonna pitch a no-hitter today, I would have gotten a haircut."

— Bo Belinsky, 1962

"To a pitcher, a base hit is the perfect example of negative feedback."

— Steve Holvey

To rookie pitcher Ernie Johnson after he surrendered a mammoth home run to Ted Williams: "Don't worry, he's hit them off better pitchers than you."

— Billy Southworth

"Nothing makes a pitcher feel more secure than the sight of his teammates circling the bases during a ball game."

— Jim Brosnan

"I exploit the greed of all hitters."

— Lew Burdette

Fielders

"Two-thirds of the Earth is covered by water. The other one-third is covered by Garry Maddox."

— Ralph Kiner

"A great catch is like watching girls go by. The last one you see is always the prettiest."

— Bob Gibson

"Pop singer Mariah Carey is now dating Yankee shortstop Derek Jeter —proving that he can catch damn near anything."

— Jim Mullen

On teammate Luis Polonia: "If you hit Polonia 100

flyballs, you could make a movie out of it— Catch 22."

— Dennis Lamp

"Guys who can field you can shake out of any old tree. Find me guys who can hit."

— Rogers Hornsby

"I could field as long as I can remember, but hitting has been a struggle all my life."

— Brooks Robinson

Managers

"The secret of managing is to keep the guys who hate you away from the guys who are undecided."

— Casey Stengel

"When I first became a manager, I asked Chuck Tanner for advice. He told me, 'Always rent.'"

— Tony LaRussa

On his managerial debut: "I had no trouble communicating. The players just didn't like what I had to say."

— Frank Robinson

"You don't save a pitcher for tomorrow. Tomorrow it may rain."

— Leo Durocher

"Bad baseball players make good managers."

— Earl Weaver

During his tenure as a minor league manager: "I like my players to be married and in debt. That's the way you motivate them."

— Ernie Banks

"The best qualification a coach can have is being the manager's drinking buddy."

— Jim Bouton

"If a manager of mine ever said someone was indispensable, I'd fire him."

— Charles Finley

"If you don't win, you're going to be fired. If you do win, you've only put off the day you're going to be fired."

— Leo Durocher

"It's what you learn after you know it all that counts."

— Earl Weaver

"There are three secrets to managing. The first secret is 'have patience.' The second is 'be patient.' And the third most important secret is 'patience.'"

— Chuck Tanner

"Concentration is the ability to think about absolutely nothing when it is absolutely necessary."

— Ray Knight

"Most ballgames are lost, not won."

— Casey Stengel

Words of Praise

"There have been only two authentic geniuses in the

world, Willie Mays and Willie Shakespeare."

— Tallulah Bankhead

"I'm not sure I know what the hell charisma is, but I get the feeling it's Willie Mays."

— Ted Kluszewski

"Every time I look at my pocketbook, I see Jackie Robinson."

— Willie Mays

On Cool Papa Bell: "One time he hit a line drive right past my ear. I turned around and saw the ball hit his ass sliding into second."

— Satchel Paige

On Lefty Grove: "He could throw a lamb chop past a wolf."

— Bugs Baer

On the strength of Jimmie Foxx: "He has muscles in his hair."

— Lefty Gomez

On Tom Seaver: "Blind people come to the park just to listen to him pitch."

— Reggie Jackson

After being swept by Sandy Koufax and the Dodgers in the 1963 World Series: "I can see how he won 25 games. What I don't understand is how he lost five."

— Yogi Berra

On Pete Rose: "Does Pete hustle? Before the All-Star Game he came into the clubhouse and took off his shoes—and they ran another mile without him."

— Henry Aaron

"Trying to hit Phil Niekro is like trying to eat Jell-O with chopsticks."

— Bobby Murcer

"Trying to sneak a pitch past Hank Aaron is like trying to sneak the sunrise past a rooster."

— Joe Adcock

On Walter Johnson: "He's got a gun concealed on his person. They can't tell me he throws them balls with his arm."

— Ring Lardner

On Steve Carlton: "Sometimes I hit him like I used to hit Koufax, and that's like drinking coffee with a fork."

— Willie Stargell

On Mickey Mantle: "I wish I was half the ballplayer that he is."

— Al Kaline

On Willie Stargell: "He's got power enough to hit home runs in any park, including Yellowstone."

— Sparky Anderson

"Jackie Robinson was the greatest competitor I ever saw. He didn't win. He triumphed."

— Ralph Branca

Insults

On Hack Wilson: "The boy's got talent and desire, but he ain't got no neck."

— John McGraw

To teammate Joe Pepitone: "I wish I could buy you for what you're really worth and sell you for what you think you're worth."

— Mickey Mantle

On Ty Cobb: "He would climb a mountain to take a punch at an echo."

— Bugs Baer

On teammate Reggie Jackson: "Reggie's really a good guy. He'd give you the shirt off his back. Of course, he'd call a press conference to announce it."

— Catfish Hunter

On Lou Boudreau: "He is easily the slowest ballplayer since Ernie Lombardi was thrown out at first base trying to stretch a double into a single."

— Stanley Frank

"Every day in every way, baseball gets fancier and fancier. A few more years and they'll be playing on oriental rugs."

— Russell Baker

On the Chicago Black Sox: "Benedict Arnold—Betrayers of American boyhood. Not to mention American Girlhood and American Womanhood and American Hoodhood."

— Nelson Algren

"My own opinion is that the people who want to put Joe Jackson in the Hall of Fame are baseball's answer to those women who show up at murder trials wanting to marry the cute murderer."

— Bill James

On Hack Wilson: "He was built along the lines of a beer keg and not unfamiliar with its contents."

— Shirley Povich

"If Boog Powell held out his right arm he'd be a railroad crossing."

— Joe Garagiola

On teammate Thurman Munson: "Munson's not moody, he's just mean. When you're moody, you're nice sometimes."

— Sparky Lyle

Self-reflection

Nicknamed "The Human Rain Delay" for his behavior in the batter's box: "I feel my ability as a ballplayer is overshadowed by people saying, 'Hey, look at that idiot at the plate.' "

— Mike Hargrove

During his Hall of Fame induction: "The Good Lord was good to me. He gave me a strong body, a good right arm, and a weak mind."

— Dizzy Dean

"You can't get rich sitting on the bench, but I'm giving it a try."

— Phil Linz

"I'm in the twilight of a mediocre career."

— Frank Sullivan

After a rough outing in the 1974 World Series: "I had some friends here from North Carolina, and they'd never seen a home run, so I gave them a couple."

— Catfish Hunter

"The highlight of my career? Oh, I'd say that was in 1967 in St. Louis. I walked with the bases loaded to drive in the winning run in an intra-squad game in spring training."

— Bob Uecker

"I'm working on a new pitch. It's called a strike."

— Jim Kern

After winning his third consecutive home run title in 1976: "A guy who strikes out as much as I do had better lead in something."

— Mike Schmidt

"If I knew I was going to live this long, I'd have taken better care of myself."

— Mickey Mantle, at age 46

"I ain't what I used to be, but who the hell is?"

— Dizzy Dean

"Trying to think with me is a mismatch. Hell, most of the time I don't know where it's going."

— Sam McDowell

"They shouldn't throw at me, I'm the father of five or six kids."

— Tito Fuentes

"I've heard of guys going 0-for-15, or 0-for-25, but I was 0-for-July."

— Bob Aspromonte

"I loved the game. I loved the competition. But I never had any fun. I never enjoyed it. All hard work, all the time."

— Carl Yastrzemski

"Now they talk on the radio about the records set by Ruth, and DiMaggio and Henry Aaron. But they rarely mention mine. Do you know what I have to show for the 61 home runs? Nothing, exactly nothing."

— Roger Maris

"I didn't come to New York to be a star. I brought my star with me."

— Reggie Jackson

"If I'd done everything I was supposed to, I'd be leading the league in homers, have the highest batting average, have given $100,000 to the Cancer Fund, and be married to Marie Osmond."

— Clint Hurdle

"I owe my success to expansion pitching, a short right field fence, and my hollow bats."

— Norm Cash

"If I did anything funny on the ball field, it was strictly accidental. Like the way I played third. Some people thought it was hilarious, but I was on the level all of the time."

— Rocky Bridges

"There is always some kid who may be seeing me for the first or last time. I owe him my best."

— Joe DiMaggio

The Business of Baseball

"The great trouble with baseball today is that most of the players are in the game for the money and that's it—not for the love of it, the excitement of it, the thrill of it."

— Ty Cobb, 1925

After negotiating his 1945 contract with Dodger's executive Branch Rickey: "I got a million dollars worth of free advice and a very small raise."

— Eddie Stanky

Describing what he would do with his 1975 salary: "Ninety percent I'll spend on good times, women, and Irish whiskey. The other 10 percent I'll probably waste."

— Tug McGraw

On Fernando Valenzuela's 1982 contract holdout: "All last year we tried to teach him English, and the only word he learned was 'million.'"

— Tommy Lasorda

"I don't need an agent. Why should I give somebody 10 percent when I do all the work?"

— Mark Fidrych

Challenging baseball's reserve clause in 1970: "A well-paid slave is nonetheless a slave."

— Curt Flood

"It isn't really the stars that are expensive. It's the high cost of mediocrity."

— Bill Veeck

"I signed Oscar Gamble on the advice of my attorney. I no longer have Gamble and I no longer have my attorney."

— Ray Kroc

"You measure the value of a ballplayer by how many fannies he puts in the seats."

— George Steinbrenner

"Sometimes the best deals are the ones you don't make."

— Bill Veeck

Speaking of Teams

"Rooting for the New York Yankees is like rooting for U.S. Steel."

— Red Smith

"Cut me and I'll bleed Dodger blue."

— Tommy Lasorda

"All literary men are Red Sox fans. To be a Yankee fan in literary society is to endanger your life."

— John Cheever

After his trade to the Phillies in 1955: "That's too bad. They're the only team I can beat."

— Dave Cole

"When I was a kid, I wanted to play baseball and join the circus. With the Yankees, I've been able to do both."

— Graig Nettles

On managing the "Gashouse Gang" St. Louis Cardinals in 1936: "We could finish first or in an asylum."

— Frankie Frisch

"Baseball isn't a life and death matter, but the Red Sox are."

— Mike Barnicle

The Arts

Fictional manager of the Washington Senators, to the Devil, in the musical Damn Yankees: "One longball hitter, that's what we need. I'd sell my soul for one longball hitter . . . hey, where did you come from?"

— Robert Shafer

"Poets are like baseball pitchers. Both have their moments. The intervals are the tough things."

— Robert Frost

"I never thought about being a writer as I grew up; a writer wasn't something to be. An outfielder was something to be. Most of what I know about style I learned from Roberto Clemente."

— John Sayles

Fictional fan in the movie Bull Durham: "I believe in the Church of Baseball. I've tried all the major religions and most of the minor ones. And the only church that truly feeds the soul, day-in day-out, is the Church of Baseball."

— Annie Savoy

"If you build it, he will come."

— W.P. Kinsella

The Media

"There's a fly to deep center field. Winfield is going back, back. He hits his head against the wall. It's rolling toward second base."

— Jerry Coleman

On fans who bring their radios to the ballpark: "I always thought it was strange knowing that thousands of people are listening to you describe a play they are watching."

— Vin Scully

"I heard the doctors revived a man after being dead for four-and-a-half minutes. When they asked what it was like being dead, he said it was like listening to New York Yankees announcer Phil Rizzuto during a rain delay."

— David Letterman

"It is interesting about people that leave early from ballgames. It's almost as if they came out to the ballgame to see if they can beat the traffic home."

— Lon Simmons

"The groan is audible. It can also be heard."

— Harry Caray

Umpires

"Many fans look upon an umpire as a sort of necessary evil to the luxury of baseball, like the odor that follows an automobile."

— Christy Mathewson

"Umpiring is the only profession in the world where you have to be perfect when you start and continue to improve."

— Todd Greanier, sportswriter

"If you don't think you're out, read the morning paper."

— Bill McGowan, umpire

"Boys, I'm one of those umpires that misses 'em every once in awhile. So if it's close, you'd better hit it."

— Cal Hubbard

"Whenever you have a tight situation and there's a close pitch, the umpire gets a squawk no matter how he calls it."

— Red Barber

Yogi-isms

"Baseball is 90 percent mental. The other half is physical."

— Yogi Berra

"If the people don't want to come out to the park, nobody's going to stop them."

— Yogi Berra

"You can see a lot just by observing."

— Yogi Berra

"So I'm ugly. I never saw anyone hit with his face."

— Yogi Berra

"The game's not over till it's over."

— Yogi Berra

"Listen up because I've got nothing to say and I'm only going to say it once."

— Yogi Berra

"I didn't really say everything I said."

— Yogi Berra

Stengel-ese

"There comes a time in every man's life, and I've had plenty of them."

— Casey Stengel

During the early 1960s: "The only thing worse than a Mets game is a Mets doubleheader."

— Casey Stengel

"I have found that the ones who drink milkshakes don't win many ballgames."

— Casey Stengel

At age 75: "Most people are dead at my age. You could look it up."

— Casey Stengel

"Good pitching will always stop good hitting and vice versa."

— Casey Stengel

At age 83 when asked if he'd like to manage again: "To be truthful and honest about it, the thing I'd like to be right now is an astronaut."

— Casey Stengel

"I don't play cards, I don't play golf, and I don't go to the picture show. All that's left is baseball."

— Casey Stengel

General

On artificial turf: "If horses don't eat it, I don't want to play on it."

— Dick Allen

"Baseball is a kids game that grown-ups only tried to screw up."

— Bob Lemon

"I still think neckties are designed to get in your soup."

— Ted Williams

"I'd walk through hell in a gasoline suit to keep playing baseball."

— Pete Rose

"There is one word in America that says it all, and that one word is 'You never know.'"

— Joaquin Andujar

"Being traded is like celebrating your hundredth birthday. It might not be the happiest occasion in the world, but consider the alternatives."

— Joe Garagiola

On being selected to the Hall of Fame for his play in the Negro Leagues: "The only change is that baseball has turned Paige from a second-class citizen to a second-class immortal."

— Satchel Paige

"You spend a good piece of your life gripping baseball, and in the end it turns out that it was the other way around all the time."

— Jim Bouton

"Baseball is a lot like life. The line drives are caught, the squibbles go for base hits. It's an unfair game."

— Rod Kanehl

When asked if he preferred grass or AstroTurf: "I don't know. I never smoked AstroTurf."

— Tug McGraw

"With those who don't give a damn about baseball, I can only sympathize. I do not resent them. I am even willing to concede that many of them are physically clean, good to their mothers and in favor of world peace. But while the game is on, I can't think of anything to say to them."

— Art Hill, sportswriter

"A hot dog at the ballpark is better than a steak at the Ritz."

— Humphery Bogart

"I've seen the future and it's much like the present, only longer."

— Dan Quisenberry

"Don't look back. Something may be gaining on you."

— Satchel Paige

"Ninety feet between bases is the nearest thing to perfection that man has yet achieved."

— Red Smith

"I believe in the Rip Van Winkle theory—that a man from 1910 must be able to wake up after being asleep for 70 years, walk into a ballpark, and understand baseball perfectly."

— Bowie Kuhn

"You always get a special kick on Opening Day, no matter how many you go through. You look forward to it like a birthday party when you're a kid. You think something wonderful is going to happen."

— Joe DiMaggio

"Baseball grabs you early or not at all."

— Dewayne Staats

"On the field, blacks have been able to be super giants. But once our playing days are over, this is the end of it and we go back to the back of the bus again."

— Henry Aaron

"It's a great day for a ballgame. Let's play two."

— Ernie Banks

"I think I have signed some scrap of paper for every man, woman and child in the United States. What do they do with all those scraps of paper with my signature on it?"

— Vida Blue

"Baseball isn't statistics, it's Joe DiMaggio rounding second base."

— Jimmy Breslin

"Your body is just like a bar of soap. It gradually wears down from repeated use."

— Dick Allen

On Joe DiMaggio's divorce from Marilyn Monroe: "It proves no man can be a success in two national pastimes."

— Oscar Levant

On Judge Landis: "His career typifies the heights to which dramatic talent may carry a man in America if only he has the foresight not to go on the stage."

— Heywood Broun

"Whether your name is Gehrig, or Ripken, DiMaggio, or Robinson, or that of some youngster who picks up his bat or puts on his glove, you are challenged by the game of baseball to do your very best, day in and day out, and that's all I've ever tried to do."

— Cal Ripken, Jr.

"I don't get upset over things I can control, because if I can control them there's no sense in getting upset. And I don't get upset over things I can't control, because if I can't control them there's no sense in getting upset."

— Mickey Rivers

On a long home run by Mark McGwire: "If it hadn't hit the scoreboard, it could have gone all the way around the world and hit me in the back of my head."

— Sandy Alomar, Jr.

"People ask me what I do in winter when there's no baseball. I'll tell you what I do: I stare out the window and wait for spring."

— Rogers Hornsby

"You have two hemispheres in your brain—a left and a right side. The left side controls the right side of your body, and the right controls the left half. It's a fact. Therefore, left-handed pitchers are the only people in their right minds."

— Bill Lee

"There are three things in my life which I really love. God, my family, and baseball. The only problem is that once baseball season starts, I change the order around a little bit."

— Al Gallagher

"All I ever wanted to be was a Yankee. When I was a kid I was always hoping there'd be a jersey left for me to wear with a single digit."

— Derek Jeter, No. 2

"Baseball has got to be fun, because if it's not fun, it's a long time to be in agony."

— Tom Treblehorn

"I never knew how someone dying could say he was the luckiest man in the world. But now I understand."

— Mickey Mantle

"Every time I sign a ball, and there have been thousands, I thank my luck that I wasn't born Coveleski or Wambsgnass or Peckinpaugh."

— Mel Ott

On Candlestick Park: "This wouldn't be such a bad place to play if it wasn't for that wind. I guess that's like saying hell wouldn't be such a bad place if it wasn't so hot."

— Jerry Reuss

"Baseball is like church. Many attend, but few understand."

— Wes Westrum

"If a woman has to choose between catching a flyball and saving an infant's life, she will save the infant's life without even considering whether there are men on base."

— Dave Barry

"Man may penetrate the outer reaches of the universe. He may solve the very secret of eternity itself. But for me, the ultimate human experience is to witness the flawless execution of the hit-and-run."

— Branch Rickey

Famous Firsts

David Pietrusza

1845 Alexander Cartwright and the Knickerbocker Base Ball Club codify playing rules; also, first box score of baseball game, eight men to the side, is printed in *New York Morning News*.

1846 At Elysian Fields on June 19 in Hoboken, N.J., the New York Knickerbockers lose to the New York Club in first match game under Cartwright's rules.

1849 Knickerbockers develop first uniforms (colors: blue & white).

1853 First box score of Knickerbocker-style game is printed in *New York Clipper*.

1856 Henry Chadwick becomes the first regular baseball reporter.

1858 First admission (50 cents) charged, for game between All-Star teams representing New York and Brooklyn played at Long Island's Fashion Race Course on July 20.

1859 At Pittsfield, Mass., on July 1, Amherst defeats Williams College in first college game, 73-32.

1860 The Excelsiors of Brooklyn make the first "road trip." Their first stop: Albany's Washington Parade Grounds on July 2.

1862 William Cammeyer's Union Grounds in Brooklyn is the first enclosed ballpark; it opens on May 15.

1863 First calling of balls and strikes.

1865 Ed Cuthbert of the Keystones steals the first base.

1866 Bob Addy of Rockford employs the first slide to steal a base; the Brooklyn Atlantics' Tom Barlow lays down the first bunt.

1867 First use of curveball, by W. A. "Candy" Cummings.

1869 The Cincinnati Red Stockings are the first fully professional team; they are also the first team to wear knickers.

1870 First listing at bats in box scores, in the *New York Clipper*.

1871 First professional league is formed—the National Association; first game: Cleveland Forest Citys lose, 2-0, at Fort Wayne on May 4; first batting averages printed in *The Dime Base Ball Player*.

1873 First doubleheader is played between the Resolutes and Boston, on July 4.

1874 Boston Red Stockings and Philadelphia Athletics conduct first foreign tour.

1875 Philadelphia's Joe Borden hurls first no-hitter in pro ranks on July 28.

1876 National League's first game: Boston at Philadelphia on April 22.

1877 International League becomes the first minor league; Tecumsehs and Maple Leafs are the first foreign professional teams; first professional gambling scandal—four Louisville players expelled from game; Will White is the first player to wear glasses.

1878 Turnstiles introduced (at Providence); Paul Hines of Providence wins first Triple Crown and executes first unassisted triple play (May 8); Bud Fowler is first black in pro ball, for Lynn Live Oaks of International Association.

1879 Reserve clause first used.

1880 First night game—between two department store teams, at Nantasket Beach in Massachusetts; Worcester's Lee Richmond hurls first perfect game, against Cleveland on June 12.

1882 American Association introduces first salaried umpiring staff; first postseason playoff; first professional doubleheader, Providence vs. Worcester, Sept. 25; Paul Hines is first player to wear sunglasses in field.

1884 First "third major league," the Union Association; first blacks in Major League Baseball—Moses and Weldy Walker of Toledo (AA); hit by pitch allows batter to take first base in AA.

1885 Umpires and catchers use first chest protectors.

1886 Players organize first union, "The Brotherhood of Ball Players;" first spring training camp, Chicago White Stockings at Hot Springs, Ark.

1887 Charles Zimmer is first catcher to play consistently behind the batter; Baltimore's Mike Griffin of Baltimore and Cincinnati's George "White Wings" Tebeau are the first to homer in their first major league at bat; both do it on the same day, April 16.

1887 The Cleveland Blues' James Toy becomes the first American Indian to play in the major leagues.

1888 First round-the-world baseball tour by Chicago White Stockings and all-star squad; "Casey at the Bat" makes its first debut in print and on the stage; Washington Nationals are the first major league club to train in Florida.

1892 National League allows Sunday baseball; first pinch homer, by Brooklyn's Tom Daly on May 24.

1894 Boston's Bobby Lowe is first major league player to smash four homers in one game.

1896 Prof. Charles Hinton demonstrates the first pitching machine.

1900 First pinch-hit grand slam, by St. Louis pitcher Mike O'Neill on Sept. 4.

1901 First American League game, Cleveland loses, 8-7, at Chicago on April 24.

1903 First modern World Series Boston defeats Pittsburgh, five games to three.

1905 The first "sanitary hose" are introduced.

1907 Giants catcher Roger Bresnahan introduces shin guards.

1909 First concrete-and-steel-park opens— Philadelphia's Shibe Park; Cleveland's Neal Ball turns first modern unassisted triple play in majors, on July 19; William Howard Taft is first president to throw out "first ball;" Arlie Latham of the New York Giants is baseball's first full-time coach.

1910 First cork-centered ball.

1911 First MVP Awards to the Cubs' Frank Schulte and the Tigers' Ty Cobb.

1916 Fred Clarke patents the first flip-up sunglasses.

1917 First "knothole gang" organized in St. Louis.

1920 First Japanese pro team, the Nihon Undo Kyokai; first team to draw 1 million fans, Yankees with 1,289,422.

1921 First baseball commissioner, Kenesaw Mountain Landis; first radio broadcast of a game, by Harold Arlin of KDKA from Forbes Field on Aug. 5; first World Series broadcast (Yankees vs. Giants).

1923 Babe Ruth becomes first player to earn $50,000 in a season.

1926 First amplifiers used (at Polo Grounds).

1929 Tigers are the first major league club to train in Arizona.

1930 First successful night ball in minors.

1933 First All-Star Game, at Chicago's Comiskey Park on July 6.

1935 First major league night game Phils at Reds, May 24.

1936 First pro league in Japan; first players elected to Hall of Fame (Ty Cobb, Babe Ruth, Christy Mathewson, Honus Wagner, and Walter Johnson); the Reds are the first team to fly— from St. Louis to Chicago on July 30.

1939 First AL night game, at Philadelphia Shibe Park on May 16; first televised game, from Ebbets Field on Aug. 26.

1941 Dodgers are first club to wear batting helmets.

1946 Montreal's Jackie Robinson is the century's first black professional player; first team to draw 2 million fans, Yankees with 2,265,512.

1947 Jackie Robinson becomes first modern major league black player; Cleveland's Larry Doby is first black player in AL; first BBWAA Rookie of the Year Awards; Hank Greenberg becomes the first $100,000 player.

1951 Emmett Ashford is first black pro umpire (Southwestern International League); first game televised coast-to-coast (last game of NL playoff); first nationally televised World Series (Yankees vs. Giants); first true baseball encyclopedia, Turkin & Thompson's *The Official Encyclopedia of Baseball;* Paul Pettit is the first $100,000 bonus baby.

1952 Clint Courtney is the first catcher to wear glasses.

1956 Don Larsen hurls first World Series perfect game, on Oct. 8.

1956 Frank Umont and Ed Rommel are first major league umps to wear eyeglasses on field.

1957 First Gold Glove Awards.

1959 Joe Cronin becomes first former player to become league president when he assumes leadership of American League.

1962 Jackie Robinson becomes the first black elected to the Hall of Fame.

1965 First enclosed stadium, the Astrodome, opens on April 9; in the first amateur draft Rick Monday is first player selected.

1966 First major league black umpire, Emmett Ashford of AL.

1969   First major league game outside U.S., St. Louis against the Expos at Montreal's Jarry Park on April 14.

1970   First strike by major league umpires occurs during playoffs; first World Series game on artificial turf—Baltimore at Cincinnati on Oct. 10.

1971   First night World Series game—Baltimore at Pittsburgh on Oct. 13; aluminum bats first approved for use in Little League.

1972   First major league player strike; Bernice Gera is first female professional umpire.

1973   The Yankees' Ron Blomberg becomes the first designated hitter, on April 6.

1974   First major league Hispanic umpire: Armando Rodriguez in AL; aluminum bats first approved for use by NCAA.

1975   Indians hire Frank Robinson as first black manager; first players declared free agents (on Dec. 23), Andy Messersmith and Dave McNally; Danny Litwhiler introduces the first radar gun.

1977   Mike Schmidt earns the first $500,000 salary.

1978   First team to draw 3 million fans, Los Angeles Dodgers with 3,347,945.

1980   Nolan Ryan earns the first $1 million annual salary (a four-year contract).

1982   Joel Youngblood becomes first major league player to get hits for two different teams (Mets and Expos) in two different cities (Chicago and Philadelphia) on same day, Aug. 4; George Foster earns the first $2 million salary, $2.04 million a year for five seasons.

1989   Bill White becomes first black league president (NL); the Griffeys become first father-son duo to perform simultaneously.

1990   Kirby Puckett earns the first $3 million salary.

1991   First modern teams to go from last to first (Twins and Braves) meet in World Series; first team to draw 4 million fans, the Toronto Blue Jays with 4,001,527; Roger Clemens becomes first player to top $5 million mark, with $5.38 million salary for five seasons; Brien Taylor becomes first $1 million bonus baby.

1992   First non-U.S. world champion, Toronto Blue Jays.

1993   Carey Schueler, 18-year-old daughter of White Sox general manager Ron Schueler, becomes the first woman chosen in the amateur free agent draft, when the Sox select her in the 43rd round.

1994   First year of three divisions in each league; the Grieves becomes the first father-son duo to be drafted in the first round of the free agent draft (Tom was taken by Washington in 1966, and Ben by Oakland in 1994).

1995   First use of Wild Cards in postseason play; Yankees are first team to have average salary of over $2 million.

1996   First major league game in Mexico, Mets vs. Padres.

1997   Albert Belle earns the first $10 million salary, $11 million a year for five seasons; first regular-season interleague play; Florida Marlins are the first Wild Card team to become world champions.

1998   Mark McGwire is the first player to hit 50 or more home runs in three straight seasons and the first to hit 70 homers; Barry Bonds is first player to hit 400 homers and steal 400 bases; first season two players, 60 or more homers, Mark McGwire and Sammy Sosa; after the season Kevin Brown becomes first player with a $15 million contract.

Take Me Out to the Ball Game

Warner Fusselle

On a sunshiny September Saturday in Chicago, around 4 o'clock, a portly, grandfatherly man with white hair and thick, dark-rimmed glasses, wearing a light-colored, short-sleeved shirt with buttoned-down collar, beige sweater vest, and tan trousers, stood up, grabbed a microphone, and started to sway.

"All right! Let me hear you. A one, a two, a three! *Take me out to the ball game. Take me out with the crowd. Buy me some peanuts and Cracker Jack. I don't care if I never get back. Oh, it's root, root, root, for the [what's the name of that team?].... If they don't win it's a shame. For it's one, two, three strikes you're out, at the old ball game.* Hey!"

Harry Caray, the voice of the Chicago Cubs, had just led a gathering of 32,043 people at Wrigley Field in the singing of baseball's greatest song—"Take Me Out to the Ball Game." It was the seventh-inning stretch, and the Cubs led the Cardinals, 6-4, in a meaningless late-season game in 1988. Both teams were 20 games out of first place; nevertheless, everyone stood, waved, and cheered as they eyed the WGN broadcast booth overlooking the Friendly Confines.

The Chicago Pied Piper led the singing of those wearing Cubs blue and Cardinals red. There were young, and there were old, all waving their baseball caps. There were toddlers hanging on to their fathers. There were mothers who glowed, holding up their babies who cooed in wonderment.

Harry worked the crowd, holding a microphone with a blue wind screen in his left hand, while waving and encouraging the world of baseball fans standing below with his right hand. It was a special moment. From the first chord on the ballpark organ to Harry's exclamatory "Hey" at the end, "Take Me Out to the Ball Game" took less than a minute—only 51 seconds to be exact. However, it was an eventful minute, a happy minute, the happiest minute in all of sports.

Harry Caray sang "Take Me Out to the Ballgame" to hometown fans during the seventh-inning stretch from 1976 through the 1997 season. Caray's death shortly before spring training in 1998 elicited tributes from the game's greatest writers and commentators, but the ultimate tribute occurred at Wrigley during the seventh inning of every Cubs game throughout the year when a different "guest singer" belted out the words to that familiar tune. Everyone from Caray's widow, Dutchie, to basketball legend Michael Jordan took their turns at the song that became synonymous with Caray's name.

Harry had always sung baseball's beloved chorus whenever the organist played it. He had the perfect explanation, "I would always sing it, because I think it's the only song I knew the words to." In his first five years as White Sox broadcaster, 1971 to 1975, no one except Harry's broadcast partner and a couple of others had heard it as he sang.

When Harry broadcast the White Sox games on TV in 1976, Bill Veeck, who had just bought the team for the second time that year, noticed that the fans within earshot of Caray's booth would always sing along. One day Veeck had a microphone secretly installed in the broadcast booth, and the rest is history.

Harry joined the Cubs in 1982, where "Take Me Out to the Ball Game" elevated the word "Cubbies" into modern, respectable usage. Harry needed two syllables to replace "home team," so it just had to be "root, root, root for the Cub-bies" instead of Cubs. Lifelong Cubs fan Mike Royko, Chicago's most famous columnist, had detested the term "Cubbies" for years, but Harry Caray and "Take Me Out to the Ball Game" prevailed.

In the Beginning

"Take Me Out to the Ball Game" was neither the first baseball song nor the first hit baseball song. Fifty years earlier, in 1858, "The Base Ball Polka" was written by an amateur player on the Niagara Base Ball Club of Buffalo, and the "Home Run Polka" followed nine years later. Neither song had words, nor were they recorded since sound recording wouldn't become a reality until 1877; however, they were available to the public in the form of sheet music.

Baseball's first hit song was "Slide, Kelly, Slide," published in 1889. The Kelly in verse spoofed the baseball star of the day, Michael "King" Kelly. King Kelly stole 208 bases for Boston of the National League from 1887 to 1889. He was King of the Diamond, a 19th century combination of Babe Ruth and Ty Cobb. Kelly even batted with a Cobb-like split grip and had once hit .388. His speed and daring made him the darling of the day. He developed the hook slide, and his basestealing prowess encouraged the cheers of "Slide, Kelly, Slide." In 1893 "Slide, Kelly, Slide" became the first known baseball recording when it was issued on an Edison cylinder.

"Slide, Kelly, Slide" actually lampooned King Kelly and made fun of another buffoonish Kelly, but the two were linked in comedic fun. Even though "Slide, Kelly, Slide" remained a baseball standard after the King's premature death in 1894, its success was scant compared with that of a sensational new song written in 1908.

Manhattan Transfer

"Take Me Out to the Ball Game" was written in 15 minutes on a piece of scrap paper by vaudeville entertainer and songwriter Jack Norworth as he rode the (oxymoronic) elevated subway train toward the tip of Manhattan in New York City.

Norworth, who wrote 2,500 songs including "Shine On, Harvest Moon," had never seen a big league baseball game. His inspiration was a poster, prominently displayed on the brand new subway, which invited fans to take in a baseball game at the Polo Grounds. After he wrote the lyrics, his longtime friend, Albert Von Tilzer (who had also never attended a baseball game) composed the music. Von Tilzer was also the manager of the York Music Company, which published "Take Me Out to the Ball Game."

Norworth decided to debut "Take Me Out to the Ball Game" on stage at the Amphion Theater in Brooklyn. "It didn't go over," he later said, "because I was fumbling for the lyrics, and I did it deadpanned."

Three weeks later, Norworth, who had conceived the song as a romantic ballad, decided to try again. Booked as the closing act at Hammerstein's Victoria Theater in New York, the top vaudeville house in the country, he decided to liven up "Take Me Out to the Ball Game" in hopes of better results.

When the day came for the big show, Norworth was forced to change his plans. "I couldn't sing my own song, because every act ahead of me used it." The song was already on its way to becoming a nationwide hit thanks to the nickelodeon, an early-day movie house that charged a nickel for admission. Some of the more popular nickelodeons had started using illustrated songs, pictured on a set of slides, between the several short silent films that made up a typical program in the first decade of the century. "Take Me Out to the Ball Game" was played by the resident pianist and accompanied by pictorial slides that also displayed the words, for the audience to sing along.

A slide at the outset pictured the cover of the sheet music (on which "Take Me Out to the Ball Game" was prophetically named "The Sensational Base Ball Song") and other slides told the story of one afternoon in the life of Katie Casey, the heroine of "Take Me Out to the Ball Game." She and her beau, portrayed by models, were photographed going to the ball game at the Polo Grounds, and a final slide showed the lyrics of the chorus and invited the audience to "All join in."

The song caught on in the midst of one of baseball's greatest two-league pennant races; six teams were battling for the 1908 pennants a mere two days before the season ended. The effect of these races, which involved both Chicago teams as well as clubs in Cleveland, Detroit, New York, and Pittsburgh, was to make baseball front-page news across the country and promote Norworth's song.

Several recordings of "Take Me Out to the Ball Game" were made in 1908. Edward Meeker performed it on an Edison two-minute roll, an early phonograph record shaped like a cylinder. Frank Lambert's 1908 recording was available on a 10-inch, single-faced Zon-O-Phone record, and the Haydn Quartet recorded "Take Me Out to the Ball Game" on a Victor 10-inch single-faced record.

The Denver Nightingale

Harry MacDonough sang with the Haydn Quartet at first, but later the quartet re-recorded the song with vaudevillian and baseball fanatic Billy Murray. Murray, who was the number one recording artist of all time in terms of records made, was known as "The Denver Nightingale." He made than 6,000 recordings between 1897 and 1943. Moreover, he knew and befriended all the Yankees (known as the Highlanders until 1913) and even practiced with them.

In 1906 Murray had recorded "It's Great at a Base Ball Game." On Oct. 24, 1908, he performed "Take Me Out to the Ball Game" and immediately became identified with the song. His recorded version was easily the most popular of his many recordings.

Norworth's success encouraged many other songwriters to try their hand at diamond ditties. George M. Cohan wrote "Take Your Girl to the Ball Game" and the "Connie Mack Song." Cohan's failure, after Jack Norworth's success, caused him to alibi, "I didn't write mine soon enough." Norworth's response? "Or good enough."

In 1913 Irving Berlin composed the music to the baseball novelty song "Jake! Jake! The Yiddisher Ball Player." Then in 1925, he wrote "I Know a Foul Ball." John Philip Sousa penned "The National Game March," but none of the big names came close to the success that Norworth enjoyed. Yet, while "Take Me Out to the Ball Game"is one of the three most frequently sung compositions in the United States (only "Happy Birthday" and "The Star-Spangled Banner" top it), the song everyone sings today is just the chorus of the tune.

Katie Casey to Nelly Kelly

The song actually begins, "Katie Casey was baseball mad." Katie Casey was such a big baseball fan that when her beau suggested they take in a show, Miss Kate expressed her preference for baseball.

Katie Casey was base ball mad,
Had the fever and had it bad;
Just to root for the home town crew,
Ev'ry sou Katie blew.
On a Saturday, her young beau
Called to see if she'd like to go,
To see a show but Miss Kate said,
"No, I'll tell you what you can do."

"Take me out to the ball game,
Take me out with the crowd.
Buy me some peanuts and cracker jack,
I don't care if I never get back,
Let me root, root, root, for the home team,
If they don't win it's a shame.
For it's one, two, three strikes, you're out,
At the old ball game."

Katie Casey saw all the games,

Knew the players by their first names;
Told the umpire he was wrong,
All along good and strong.
When the score was just two to two,
Katie Casey knew what to do,
Just to cheer up the boys she knew,
She made the gang sing this song:
(REPEAT CHORUS)

Despite the song's success, Jack Norworth decided to change some of the words. In 1927 he changed Katie Casey to Nelly Kelly (and thus secured a new copyright).

Nelly Kelly loved baseball games,
Knew the players, knew all their names,
You could see her there ev'ry day,
Shout "Hurray," when they'd play.
Her boy friend by the name of Joe
Said, "To Coney Isle, dear, let's go,"
Then Nelly started to fret and pout,
And to him I heard her shout.

"Take me out to the ball game,
Take me out with the crowd,
Buy me some peanuts and crackerjack,
I don't care if I never get back.
Let me root root root for the home team,
If they don't win it's a shame,
For it's one two three strikes, you're out
At the old ball game."

Nelly Kelly was sure some fan,
She would root just like any man,
Told the umpire he was wrong,
All along, good and strong.
When the score was just two to two,
Nelly Kelly knew what to do,
Just to cheer up the boys she knew,
She made the gang sing this song.
(REPEAT CHORUS)

The original copyright of "Take Me Out to the Ball Game" expired in 1936. The renewed copyright had a new subtitle, "The Famous Baseball Song." Not only had the word "baseball" become one word instead of two, "sensational" was updated to "famous." That would change again in 1949 to "Official," as in "The Official Baseball Song."

The Aftermath of the Hit

After his success with "Take Me Out to the Ball Game," Von Tilzer, previously known as Albert Gumm, tried

again but failed with other baseball tunes. In 1909 he wrote the music for "Did He Run?" This song satirized Fred Merkle's Boner in the famous 1908 pennant race involving the Giants and Cubs. The chorus began,
Did he run?
Did he run to second,
As he should that day.
Or did Mr. Merkle semi-circle away?

Albert also wrote "Back to the Bleachers for Mine" and "I Want to Go to the Ball Game." His brother Harry, who wrote "Wait Till the Sun Shines, Nellie," also tried to write a baseball hit without success. He was 0-for-2 with "My Old Man Is Baseball Mad" in 1910 and "The Baseball Glide" in 1911.

Norworth, too, tried his hand at more baseball music but failed. With his wife Nora Bayes, a musical comedy star, he wrote "Let's Get the Umpire's Goat." Often criticized for writing a baseball song even though he had never seen a game, he had the perfect response: "A friend of mine, Harry Williams, wrote 'In the Shade of the Old Apple Tree,' and he never saw an apple tree."

Finally, however, Jack did get to see his first major league game. Some say he saw his first game in 1916 at Ebbets Field in Brooklyn where he root, root, rooted like crazy for the hometown, pennant-winning Robins. Other historians push the date to somewhere in the 1940s, when the Robins-turned-Dodgers supposedly had a special day for Jack at Ebbets Field on June 27, 1940.

Whenever it was, Norworth became fascinated with what he saw and later pioneered Little League Baseball in California. The Cracker Jack Company even honored him with a trophy, the Jack Norworth Award, which was given to deserving Little Leaguers. In 1958, on the 50th anniversary of his creation of "Take Me Out to the Ball Game," Norworth was honored in Los Angeles and was presented with a gold lifetime pass which would enable him to see any major league game. Norworth, proud of his accomplishment, said, "It has kept me eating for 50 years."

He died Sept. 1, 1959, at age 80, but almost every ballpark features "Take Me Out to the Ball Game" during the seventh-inning stretch. Along with "The Star-Spangled Banner," it is almost a given that a person attending a major league game will leave the park having heard Norworth's song.

"Take Me Out to the Ball Game" has been called by some an American folk song. Children learn it right after their nursery rhymes, and soldiers sing it during world wars. Music boxes play it, and so do doorbell chimes. Baseball's most popular song has even been played in wedding processions, and, in 1955, *Variety* gave the song its stamp of approval by naming "Take Me Out to the Ball Game" one of the 10 greatest popular songs of the last 50 years.

Baseball and the Armed Services

Harrington E. Crissey, Jr.

I t is regrettable that the average fan has little or no knowledge of the historical relationship between the military and baseball, considering that the links between the two date back to the beginning of the game's evolution in North America approximately 150 years ago. Perhaps it is because most people associate baseball with pleasure and military service with anything but that; or it may be that those who have never served in the armed forces have no appreciation of the value of baseball in relieving either the stress or boredom of military life, depending on one's circumstances. Whatever the reasons, the connections between the armed services and this truly international pastime are long and storied, and deserve our careful and devoted attention because the military has had a profound impact on the propagation of baseball worldwide and on the development of the game as a social leveler and instrument of international relations.

A story about the origin of baseball was advanced by a committee of the game's elder statesmen in 1907. The committee, led by former player and sporting goods magnate Albert G. Spalding, said that Abner Doubleday had designed the first baseball diamond at Cooperstown, N.Y., in 1839 while a cadet at the U.S. Military Academy. This version was quickly accepted as official by the baseball moguls and held sway for several decades, but it is now considered a myth by serious baseball historians.

Doubleday fought in the Battle of Monterey during the Mexican War; sighted the first gun in defense of Fort Sumter when it was fired on by Southerners on April 12, 1861, thus starting the Civil War; fought at Second Bull Run and Antietam; distinguished himself at Gettysburg by helping to repel Pickett's Charge, the Confederates' major attack of the battle; and eventually retired from the Army as a general in 1873. He was dead, however, by the time the committee put forth its opinion, so no one could get his views on the matter. There is nothing in his writings which suggests he invented the game, and other early commentators such as Henry Chadwick advanced different theories regarding the origin of the game. Nevertheless, the name of Abner Doubleday, a career soldier, remains inextricably linked to baseball in the popular mind.

To discover the first bona fide influence of the military on baseball, and a tremendous one at that, we must move ahead to the American Civil War (1861-1865). Baseball before the Civil War was almost exclusively a gentleman's game, with the upper classes of society participating and the true amateur spirit and British rules of sportsmanship holding sway. Most of the prominent

teams were in the East, with a few, such as those in Chicago and St. Louis, in the Midwest. During the war, baseball became a sport played by people of all social classes over a wide geographical area. It was played among Union troops during their leisure hours and an unheard-of crowd of 40,000 soldiers watched a game in Hilton Head, S. C., on Christmas Day, 1862, between the 165th New York Volunteer Infantry (Duryea's Zouaves) and a team picked from other Union regiments. A.G. Mills, later to become president of the National League, played in that contest.

Baseball was known in the South prior to the Civil War. Soldiers were said to have played baseball during the Mexican War, the game was popular in New Orleans, and many people south of the Mason-Dixon Line subscribed to Northern periodicals which featured baseball news. Nevertheless, the growth of the sport in Dixie was greatly stimulated by Northern prisoners playing the game to relieve boredom or tension in Southern POW camps. Their guards first watched, then decided they wanted to try, and finally organized teams to play against their captives. Southern POWs returned home similarly enlightened about the game. With more than a million men under arms during the conflict, is it any wonder that the game proliferated when the veterans went home to practically every town in the nation?

The Civil War accelerated two trends that were first discernible in the late 1850s: increasingly fierce competition and with it increased commercialism. Diaries written by Union troops in the Army of the Potomac and the Army of Northern Virginia show that as the war went on and baseball became ever more popular and competitive, emphasis on skill was the great consideration. If a player was good, he got to play. Teams in Army units may have been promoted by officers or high-ranking noncoms, but the players on the field were the most skilled. In 1863 and 1864, some outfits had first and second teams based on skill levels. This idea of skill predominating over social or military rank certainly fit the competitive pattern of post-Civil War baseball, as more emphasis on winning led to keen rivalries between cities and the rise of professionalism.

In 1873, eight years after the cessation of hostilities in the United States and 20 years after American ships under Commodore Matthew Perry had succeeded in opening Japan to the West, two American missionaries named Wilson and Maget introduced baseball to the Land of the Rising Sun. The game took root in part because influential Japanese of that time, such as Kido and many former *daimyo* (feudal lords), supported its growth. They origi-

nally viewed baseball as an American version of a martial sport like Japanese *judo* or *kendo*. Practicing the sport was in their minds a way of getting at the essence of the American fighting spirit, and thus baseball was played every day, regardless of weather conditions.

As time went on, the game evolved into a high school and college sport. From 1888 until 1902, the top team in Japan was that of First High School, now known as Tokyo University. It sometimes played games against American residents in Yokohama and teams from U.S. Navy battleships. Whenever the battlewagons made port calls in Yokohama, the First High School club would challenge them and usually would win the contests. Judging from a few of the scores, the Japanese students had ample reason to feel good about their progress in the sport: in 1902, they slaughtered the U.S.S. *Kentucky*, 35-1, and the next year clobbered the same ship again, 27-0!

The United States involved itself in war with Spain and its colonial possessions in the Caribbean Sea and Pacific Ocean in 1898. The Spanish-American War was short, lasting roughly the length of the baseball season. The war didn't have a significant impact on the game at home but undoubtedly influenced its spread to Puerto Rico, and other lands which border on the Caribbean, and the Philippine Islands.

Dr. Arlie Pond was pitching for the Baltimore Orioles of the National League when the war started. He had won 16 games for the Orioles in their pennant-winning season of 1896 and followed it up with 18 victories in 1897, but at the start of hostilities he entered the Army, joined a medical unit, and went first to Cuba and then the Philippines. After the war and the Philippine Insurrection, he left active duty but stayed in the Philippines and devoted the rest of his life to combating disease there, except for World War I, when he returned to the States and became assistant surgeon general of the Army with the rank of colonel. Near the end of the war, he went with the U.S. forces to Siberia following the Russian Revolution. In 1919 Pond returned to the Philippine Islands after again relinquishing his Army commission and died there in 1930 at the age of 57.

A year after the war, Dave Wills quit his medical studies at the University of Virginia to play first base for Louisville of the National League. After hitting only .223 in 24 games, he decided to join the Marines and wound up staying 20 years in the service. He served as a paymaster in the European Theater with the rank of major in World War I and was buried in Arlington National Cemetery upon his death in 1959. A little more than a decade after the Spanish-American War, Hall of Famer Oscar Charleston, a Negro League great, was first recognized for his baseball ability while serving with the Army (1911-1915) in the Philippines.

World War I began in Europe in August 1914, but the United States didn't enter the conflict until April 1917. Before the Yanks went "over there," Canadian units in the British Army took the lead in teaching many Englishmen and Australians how to play. In the fall of 1917, a series for the championship of the Canadian forces overseas was played in England. One hundred and one teams took part, with several minor league and semipro players dotting the rosters.

By the end of 1917 there were 76 American major league players in the service: 48 from the American League, including 15 Boston Red Sox, and 28 from the National League. Forty-two were in the Army, 21 in the Navy, and 13 in other branches of the service.

In May 1918 there occurred the promulgation of a "work or fight" order by the provost marshal of the armed forces, General Enoch Crowder. It was designed to force all men of draft age out of nonessential work and into the Army or war-related employment in order to aid in the prosecution of the war. Baseball players were classified as nonessential while actors, opera singers, and movie stars were deemed essential. This was because the baseball magnates didn't present their case in person, as did representatives of the other specially exempted occupations.

Relatively few players left baseball, however. The great majority remained with their teams. When the July time limit set by the Crowder order was reached, various draft boards issued conflicting orders to the players, some saying their work was essential and others saying it wasn't.

Eventually the Crowder edict was enforced and organized baseball shut down its operation by the beginning of September 1918, although two additional weeks were allotted for the World Series between the Boston Red Sox and the Chicago Cubs. Despite the fact that the Crowder edict applied only to men of draft age, the owners decided not to finish the season with players younger than 18 or older than 35. The magnates made it clear to the players, however, that the reserve clause was still in effect, that the players weren't free agents, and that they would be bound to their former teams upon resumption of play.

By the end of the war in November 1918, 144 American Leaguers and 103 National Leaguers were in the military. Very few players went into war-related work. Of the 144 American Leaguers serving Uncle Sam, a considerable percentage of them were known to be overseas. At least 83 were in the Army and 41 in the Navy. The Detroit Tigers led the league with 25 servicemen, while the team with the fewest was the St. Louis Browns with 13, even though the Brownies had won American League prexy Ban Johnson's $500 prize for performing best in military close-order drill (using bats as rifles) in 1917. Among the National Leaguers, the Brooklyn Dodgers and Pittsburgh Pirates tied for the lead in enlistees with 18 apiece, while the Cincinnati Reds had only six. Boston Braves catcher Hank Gowdy was the first major leaguer to volunteer for military service. He was eventually sent to France, as were other prominent players and executives such as Cincinnati Reds manager Christy Mathewson, Detroit Tigers outfielder Ty Cobb, Philadelphia Phillies pitcher Grover Cleveland Alexander, Brooklyn Dodgers hurler Sherry Smith, Chicago White Sox catcher Joe Jenkins, Boston Braves executive Percy Haughton, and St. Louis Cardinals executive Branch Rickey. Haughton and Rickey received their commissions as majors and Mathewson was a captain in the Army's gas-and-flame division. Mathewson suffered gas poisoning during his service. It led to tuberculosis and his ultimate demise in 1925. Former major leaguers killed in action were infielder Eddie Grant, who had played for four teams between 1905 and 1915, in the Argonne Forest in October 1918; Robert Troy, who had been born in Germany and pitched and lost one game for the Detroit Tigers in 1912, at the Meuse in October 1918; and Alex Barr, also with

one game in the big time as a New York Yankees outfielder in 1914, on his 25th birthday, Nov. 1, 1918, a mere 10 days before the armistice.

Servicemen's baseball was alive and well in Europe in both 1917 and 1918. In addition to the aforementioned Canadian championship series in England in the fall of 1917, an Anglo-American League was formed. It was composed of regular teams of American and Canadian soldiers, and was organized in London by W. E. Booker and former big leaguer Arlie Latham. The league played a regular weekend schedule in London, the English provinces, and Scotland. Every team had four or five professional players. A benefit game between American Army and Navy teams at Chelsea, London, on July 4, 1918, drew more than 40,000 spectators, including the King of England and Allied military notables. The regular season ended on Sept. 7, 1918, but the clubs continued to play Sunday ball until Sept. 29.

Whereas the Canadians had initially taught baseball to the British and Australians, the Americans introduced it to the French. The game was not exactly new in Paris because Americans had occasionally played it there before the war. Once the Yanks began arriving in large numbers, games were played every Sunday in the Bois du Boulogne and other public parks. The YMCA organized an Association League in France, with 30 teams playing a 15-game schedule each Sunday up to the middle of September. Shortly before the armistice, French soldiers were under orders to learn baseball! Their primary teacher was erstwhile National League great Johnny Evers, who had been sent to France by the Knights of Columbus for that purpose. Where did all the equipment come from? There were three sources: the aforementioned YMCA, the Knights of Columbus and the Ball and Bat Fund, headed by Clark Griffith, manager of the Washington Senators. The fund disbursed $63,865.29 worth of baseball gear, although the supply ship *Kansan*, with its load of equipment for the American Expeditionary Force, was torpedoed and sunk by a German submarine while en route to Europe.

The top service teams of World War I (1918) included the 342nd Field Artillery, American Expeditionary Force club, which featured Grover Cleveland Alexander and several other major leaguers and beat all comers; the Second Naval District, Newport, R. I., aggregation, with a handful of big leaguers on its roster; the Great Lakes, Ill., Naval Station club, piloted by White Sox outfielder Phil Chouinard and later Senators shortstop Doc Lavan, which posted a 30-8 won-lost record and had Hall of Fame pitcher Urban "Red" Faber and pro football great George Halas; the 85th Division, Battle Creek, Mich., nine, which lost only one game, beat the Great Lakes club, and had the Browns' Urban Shocker hurling for them; the Camp Dodge, Iowa, club, which logged 27 wins against eight setbacks and counted six major leaguers among its players; the San Diego Naval Training Camp team, with a 78-10 record to its credit; and the Kelly Field club in San Antonio, which won 42 games and lost only eight.

During and immediately after the war, baseball was played in Great Britain, France, Belgium, Italy, and the German Rhineland. There was enthusiastic talk in the *Reach* and *Spalding Baseball Guides* of the period about baseball becoming a major sport in England and France,

but such a development failed to take place. Colonel Tillinghast L'Hommedieu Huston, part owner of the New York Yankees, guessed the result correctly. Upon returning to the United States from France after 16 months in the Army, he commented that if American soldiers had been in Europe for at least another year, baseball might have taken hold, but the soldiers were returning home too fast to make a lasting impression.

The influence of the military during the period between the world wars was negligible, save for the occasional ballplayer who served a hitch in the armed forces. "Barnacle Bill" Posedel joined the Navy in 1925 while still in his teens, put in four years of active duty, later became a pitcher with the Brooklyn Dodgers and Boston Bees on the eve of World War II, served four more years in the Navy during that conflict, and eventually became a major league pitching coach. Nemo Gaines was a star pitcher for the U.S. Naval Academy, class of 1921. Upon graduation, he received permission to take special leave and pitch for the Washington Senators. After four appearances with the Nats, he went on active duty and served until 1946, when he retired with the rank of captain. Pitcher Sig Jakucki, who was to become an important cog in the St. Louis Browns' drive to their only American League pennant in 1944, was in the Army from 1927 to 1931 and starred for the Schofield Barracks team in Hawaii as an outfielder and occasional hurler. As was customary, American servicemen brought baseball with them wherever they went. On July 29, 1937, sailors from a Navy squadron formed two teams and played a softball game in the sports stadium of the port they were visiting. The locale? Vladivostok in the Soviet Union!

Germany invaded Poland on Sept. 1, 1939, and World War II was on in Europe. As the war clouds drifted across the Atlantic and became more ominous over America, the United States government instituted a military draft in the autumn of 1940, the first in its history during peacetime. It required the registration of men ages 21 to 35. The first major leaguer to get drafted was Philadelphia Phillies pitcher Hugh Mulcahy in March 1941, nine months before Pearl Harbor. The next to go was a star—Detroit Tigers slugger and 1940 American League Most Valuable Player Hank Greenberg. Hammerin' Hank had led the Tigers to the pennant the year before. After hitting two homers in a 7-4 win over the Yankees on May 6, he entered the Army the next day, the same day the Tigers officially raised their 1940 championship flag. Thus began a parade of professional ballplayers into the armed forces, a parade which would continue unabated until the Japanese surrender in August 1945.

Perhaps no other statistic better expresses the extent to which the military put its stamp on professional baseball during World War II than the one which appeared in the *New York Times* in the spring of 1945: as of January of that year, 5,400 of the 5,800 pro baseball players in the country at the time of Pearl Harbor were in the service. With an impact of that magnitude, it would take a decent-sized book to describe in detail military baseball alone during the war years, not to mention pro and military ball combined, a task which has already been accomplished twice in recent memory. How then should one approach the topic? By emphasizing that the military is ultimately made up of people.

Over 50 professional ballplayers made the supreme sacrifice while serving in the armed forces. The majority of them died in combat. Two were ex-major leaguers who appeared briefly in the American League in 1939. Harry O'Neill, who caught one game for the Philadelphia Athletics, died on Iwo Jima in March 1945. Army Air Corps Captain Elmer Gedeon, an outfielder in five games for the Washington Senators in 1939, was shot down over France on April 15, 1944, his 27th birthday. The first pro player to enlist, minor league outfielder Billy Southworth, Jr., joined the Army Air Corps in December 1940. He was the son of the St. Louis Cardinals' manager and compiled quite a war record as a bomber pilot in Europe before being killed in a crash after takeoff on a routine flight from Long Island to Florida on Feb. 15, 1945. He had attempted an emergency landing at LaGuardia Field but plunged into Flushing Bay after over-shooting the runway. His grieving father was not alone among major league pilots. Ex-Tigers skipper Mickey Cochrane and former Cubs boss Jimmie Wilson also lost sons in the war.

Several men who played major league ball were wounded in action, among them Army Air Corps fighter pilot Bert Shepard, who was shot down by antiaircraft fire over Germany in May 1944 and had his right leg amputated below the knee. After spending the better part of a year in a German POW camp, he was repatriated in a prisoner-of-war exchange and, with the help of an artificial limb, pitched in one regular-season game and several exhibitions for the Washington Senators in 1945. Others in the category of the wounded included the St. Louis Cardinals' John Grodzicki; the Philadelphia Athletics' Jack Knott, Bob Savage, and Lou Brissie; the Cleveland Indians' Gene Bearden; and the Brooklyn Dodgers' Tommy Warren—all of them pitchers.

Yet another pitcher, Phil Marchildon of the Philadelphia Athletics, spent nine months in a German prison camp while serving in the Royal Canadian Air Force. Cecil Travis, the star Washington shortstop, had his feet frozen at the Battle of the Bulge and lasted only two seasons after the war due to his limited mobility. The major league careers of hurlers Hugh Mulcahy of the Phillies and Charlie Wagner of the Red Sox were effectively curtailed by weight loss brought on by dysentery contracted in the Philippines. Two other pitchers, Johnny Rigney of the White Sox and 1942 rookie sensation Johnny Beazley of the Cardinals, threw their arms out while pitching service exhibitions. Outfielder Elmer "Red" Durrett hooked on with the Dodgers in 1944 after being discharged from the Marine Corps. He had suffered shell shock on Guadalcanal. It took a while for infielder Billy Cox and outfielder Monte Irvin to recover from the emotional effects of their Army experiences before they hit their stride again. Cardinals second baseman Frank Crespi broke his left leg in a game at Fort Riley, Kans., in 1943. While convalescing at a military hospital, he got into a wheelchair race, slammed into a wall, and broke the leg again, thus ending whatever chance he had of returning to the Redbirds after hostilities had ceased.

There were the great ones—men like Ted Williams, Joe DiMaggio, Bob Feller, and Hank Greenberg—who lost between three and five of their prime years to the service, thus giving rise to a multitude of "what if?" questions

regarding their lifetime statistics had there been no war. Then there were the legions of players who didn't stick with their former clubs because of the personnel crunch in the spring of 1946, when the mix of returning veterans and wartime holdovers was so great that many men never had a chance to get back into shape gradually and compete for jobs effectively. Although major league clubs carried 30 men rather than 25 on their 1946 rosters in an effort to mitigate the problem, the remedy was hardly adequate to accommodate the flood of returnees. A few players—Tony Lupien, Merrill May, Bob Harris, Bruce Campbell, Steve Sundra, and Al Niemiec—either threatened legal action or undertook it in an effort to protect their reemployment rights under the then-new GI Bill, but most of them settled out of court on the issue of pay, and none stayed with their former teams.

For every sad story, there was a courageous or heartening one. Jack Knott of the Athletics and southpaw Earl Johnson of the Red Sox won battlefield commissions after showing bravery under fire. Former first baseman Zeke Bonura won the Legion of Merit as an Army corporal for organizing and promoting sports programs for service men and women in North Africa. General Dwight D. Eisenhower personally pinned the award on him. The aforementioned Bert Shepard served as an inspiration to all disabled servicemen when he made occasional appearances on the mound for the Senators. The opportunity to gain valuable experience by playing service ball with and against seasoned professionals presented itself to people like outfielder Del Ennis, who jumped from one year in the low minors to the major leagues after discharge. For others, it served to showcase their talents as prior amateurs or semipros. Johnny Groth, an 18-year-old wonder fresh out of Chicago Latin High School, proceeded to win a starting berth in center field for the 1945 Great Lakes Naval Training Center team with which he hit .341. He was signed to a Detroit organization contract at war's end and went on to have a long and productive major league career despite key injuries along the way. Maurice "Mo" Mozzali was a Louisville area semipro who impressed his teammates while performing for submarine-base teams at Pearl Harbor and New London, Conn. He signed a pro contract in 1946 and rose to the level of Triple-A as an All-Star first baseman with Columbus of the American Association.

Several prominent players had triumphant returns to the major leagues after completion of their service hitches. On Aug. 24, 1945, after 44 months in the Navy, Bob Feller made his first start against the Tigers in Cleveland. His appearance resulted in Cleveland's biggest baseball crowd in three years (46,777 fans). Bullet Bob struck out 12, gave up only four hits, and won easily, 4-2. In his second game versus Detroit late that summer, he one-hit the Tigers. When he pitched in Yankee Stadium on Sept. 10, a total of 67,816 spectators were present. Hank Greenberg heralded his return to the Tigers on July 1, 1945, by hitting a home run against the Athletics before 48,000 hometown fans. On the final day of the season, his grand slam home run in the rain against the Browns clinched the American League pennant for Detroit. Tigers right-hander Virgil Trucks was discharged from the Navy less than a week before the 1945 season ended. He started the Tigers' pennant-winning 6-3 victory over St. Louis

and followed that up with a 4-1 complete-game win over the Chicago Cubs in the second game of the World Series.

Navy duty during the war resulted in the beginning of new professions for Max Patkin and Dusty Cooke. Patkin began his long and famous career as a baseball clown while pitching first for Aiea Hospital and then for Aiea Barracks in Hawaii in 1944. Cooke was trained as a pharmacist's mate. This training came in handy after the war. In search of a baseball job, he hooked on with former teammate Ben Chapman and the Philadelphia Phillies as club trainer and later went on to coach and even manage the team for a few days in 1948 between the departure of Chapman and the arrival of Eddie Sawyer.

At times there was an embarrassment of riches on military teams. In the first two years of the war, former heavyweight boxing champion Gene Tunney's eight-week enlisted athletic specialist training course was located at the Norfolk, Va., Naval Training Station. Thus the Norfolk NTS manager, Gary Bodie, had his pick of the numerous professional athletes who were taking the course. In 1943 he was faced with the difficult yet wonderful prospect of choosing between two of the premier shortstops in baseball, Phil Rizzuto and Pee Wee Reese, for his ballclub. He kept Rizzuto and sent Reese a mile down the road to Norfolk Naval Air Station, where he became part of NTS's opposition.

The Army stockpiled its talent in the Hawaiian Islands at the Seventh Army Air Force, Hickam Field, in 1944. Manager Tom Winsett, a former major league outfielder, had three top-level second basemen—Joe Gordon, Gerry Priddy, and Dario Lodigiani—at his disposal that summer. Priddy and Lodigiani were the first to arrive, with Lodigiani staying at his normal position and Priddy playing shortstop. When Priddy was transferred, Gordon replaced him.

There were also some wacky trades. After the Tunney school was shifted from Norfolk to Bainbridge, Md., former St. Louis Browns outfielder Red McQuillen went through the program. Norfolk NTS needed an outfielder and Bainbridge needed a life raft, so the deal was made. The raft turned out to be defective upon receipt in Bainbridge, but the deal wasn't voided and McQuillen went on to bat .367 and lead the Norfolk club in hits and triples in 1944. General William Flood, commanding officer of the aforementioned Seventh Army Air Force at Hickam Field, wanted Eddie Funk, a good pitcher with a little experience in the low minors, for his ballclub. Funk was at another facility on the island of Oahu, and his CO was anxious to keep him; however, the CO had two dogs which he loved, and they were sick. General Flood had the only veterinary service among the military stations in Hawaii, so he made a proposition to Funk's boss: you give me Funk and your two dogs will get well. The deal was consummated, and Funk went on to pitch excellent ball for the Seventh Army Air Force.

It was common for the top service teams to have past or future major leaguers at every position. Both the Army and the Navy had outstanding teams at several of their installations around the country. For instance, Navy outfits at the training centers in Norfolk, Great Lakes, Bainbridge, and Sampson, N.Y., were superb. The Army aggregations at the Seventh Army Air Force, Fort Riley, Kans.; New Cumberland, Pa.; and the Waco, Texas, Army Flying School distinguished themselves. The Marine Corps had fine clubs at Quantico, Va., and Parris Island, S. C., and the Coast Guard teams at Curtis Bay, Md., and New London, Conn., were excellent. There was also a multiplicity of top-notch clubs on the West Coast.

Most of these teams rang up outstanding won-lost records against all types of opposition—for example, the magnificent 48-2 log achieved by the 1944 Great Lakes club. Many exhibitions were played against major and minor league teams, with the majority being won by the service clubs. Some of the scores are legendary, like the 17-4 slaughtering the Great Lakes sailors gave the Cleveland Indians in their 1944 season finale, or the pastings administered to the Boston Red Sox (20-7) and the Cleveland Indians (15-2) by the 1944 Sampson Naval Training Center nine. Were the major leaguers trying? Evidence indicates that they were, although second-line pitchers were often thrown against the service clubs and sometimes the pros played a position other than their normal one. Because big league clubs often took fewer than the normal 25 players on road trips during the war, it was not uncommon for players to be platooned at an unfamiliar position—as, for example, a pitcher playing in the outfield.

Service players participated in some great war-benefit games. Perhaps the most famous was the American League All-Stars Service All-Stars contest at Municipal Stadium in Cleveland on July 7, 1942, when 62,094 fans saw a one-of-a-kind ballgame in which the American Leaguers triumphed, 5-0. The gross receipts from the spectacle totaled $143,571; $100,000 of the net went to the Bat and Ball Fund and the rest to Army and Navy Relief. A month earlier, the Norfolk NTS team had played a group of Army ballplayers in the Polo Grounds in New York. The year 1943 saw the $2 million war-bond game between the Norfolk NTS squad and the Washington Senators, won by Norfolk, 4-3, at Griffith Stadium in Washington, on May 24; the Service All-Stars-Boston Braves contest at Fenway Park, Boston, on July 12, in which the All-Stars, managed by Babe Ruth and featuring Ted Williams, nipped the Braves, 9-8; the July 28 game in Yankee Stadium between North Carolina Pre-Flight (Navy) and a combined team of New York Yankees and Cleveland Indians, called the "Yank-lands" and managed by Babe Ruth, in which North Carolina Pre-Flight triumphed, 11-5, and $30,000 was poured into the Baseball War Relief and Service Fund, Inc.; and the $800 million war-bond game at the Polo Grounds on Aug. 26, when a combined team of Yankees, Dodgers, and Giants beat a group of Army All-Stars, 5-2, before 38,000 people. It is interesting to note that the only picture supposedly taken of Ted Williams and Babe Ruth together in uniform was snapped at that Fenway Park contest in July.

A few takeoffs on the World Series occurred. At the end of the 1943 season, the Norfolk Naval Training Station and Norfolk Naval Air Station clubs engaged in an exciting best-of-seven series, which the Training Station won, four games to three. Following the 1944 baseball campaign in Hawaii, the cream of the crop of Army and Navy ballplayers participated in the famous Service World Series. What started out as a best-of-seven affair limited to Oahu Island wound up as an 11-game extravaganza, with the final four contests being played on the

islands of Maui, Hawaii, and Kauai. The Navy, shored up at the last minute with reinforcements from the continental United States and Australia, won the first six games and finished with an 8-2-1 record for the series, the tie being a 14-inning, 6-6 humdinger in Honolulu Park, Hilo, Hawaii. The following fall, the Navy had its own World Series in the Hawaiian Islands, featuring the American League against the National League. The AL squad was favored, but the National Leaguers won, four games to two. As in the previous year, an additional contest was played for the benefit of service men and women, with the Americans beating the Nationals; so the final tally was Nationals four, Americans three.

Baseball was played all over the world during the Second World War. In late February 1945, 28 Navy ballplayers boarded two Marine Corps planes and proceeded to make two tours of the forward areas of the Pacific, with both of them ending on Guam; then the players were dispersed among Guam, Saipan, Tinian, Peleliu, and Ulithi. Shortly afterward, Army Air Corps players did the same thing. Right after the war in Europe ended, many pro players had German and Italian POWs build fields for them and top-flight competition ensued. An Army All-Star team was formed and toured Europe, visiting cities in Germany, France, Italy, and Austria.

Perhaps the most important outgrowth of World War II military baseball was black-white integration. A full year before Branch Rickey signed Jackie Robinson to a Brooklyn Dodger organization contract, Hal Hairston, a black pitcher formerly with the Homestead Grays of the Negro National League, was hurling for the Army against the Navy in the Service World Series in Hawaii. A year later, Calvin Medley, another black pro, was pitching for the Fleet Marine team on Oahu Island. Two thousand miles away from the U.S. mainland, on a group of islands populated with Hawaiian natives and American, Chinese, and Japanese immigrants, racially integrated baseball could become a reality. Blacks and whites could play together on service teams and black, white, and yellow people could perform as a unit in the Honolulu semi-pro league. Back in the continental United States, black and white service teams would remain segregated until after the war. Thus the white Great Lakes team won 48 and lost only two in 1944, while the black club went 32-10 and won the championship of the Midwest Service League. Larry Doby, star shortstop on the black team and later the first man of his race to play in the American League, could not play with whites in Illinois but was welcome to play softball on Ulithi Atoll a year later with white professionals like Mickey Vernon and Billy Goodman. Negro League stars Leon Day and Willard Brown couldn't as yet crack the color barrier back home, but they could lead a team comprised almost exclusively of white semipro players to victory in Nuremberg's famous stadium, site of the massive Nazi Party rallies of the 1930s. Against the hand-picked professionals of General George Patton's Third Army club, right-handed fireballer Day led the Overseas Invasion Service Expedition (OISE) club to a 2-1 victory for the European Theater of Operations (ETO) championship before a huge crowd.

No description of military baseball during the period would be complete without mention of what transpired in Japan. The Land of the Rising Sun had been on a war footing since the Marco Polo Bridge incident in Beijing, China, on July 7, 1937. Professional ballplayers had been drafted at least from 1938 on, as evidenced by the induction that year of Eiji Sawamura, the country's most famous pitcher. In fact, Sawamura was to be taken into the Army three times: in 1938, 1941, and again in 1944. With the coming of global war following Pearl Harbor, intense Japanese nationalism and militarism manifested themselves in many ways regarding baseball. Team names on uniforms were changed to Japanese characters from Roman letters, and the traditional baseball cap took on a military look. The Tokyo Giants were renamed *Kyojin Cun* or "Giant Troop." Baseball terms imported from the foreign enemy, the United States, were changed to Japanese equivalents. "Strike" became *yoshi* ("good") and "ball" became *dame* ("bad"). "Safe" was transformed into *ikita* ("alive") and "out" to *shinda* ("dead"). A shortstop became a *yugeki* ("free-lancer").

After 1942, many outstanding players, both professionals and collegians, were drafted into the military. The two most famous collegiate baseball clubs, those of Keio and Waseda Universities, had an emotional farewell game before 30,000 students in October 1943. The presidents of both universities had negotiated successfully with the government for this contest to be held, and after it was over tears flowed freely as both players and spectators wondered if they would ever see another game. Their sadness was well founded. Among the 3 million Japanese, military and civilian, who died on the home islands or in the Pacific, China, and Southeast Asia were a great number of good players, including the best, Sawamura, who was killed on a troop transport in the Taiwan Strait on Dec. 2, 1944. Today the Japanese equivalent of the Cy Young Award, given annually to the best pitcher in each of the American leagues, is named in his memory. Ironically, Japan's number two pitcher, Viktor Staffin, was spared because as a child immigrant from the Soviet Union he was exempt from conscription.

By 1944 only six clubs were competing for the professional championship and the season was only 35 games long. In 1945, the last year of the war, play was suspended altogether as cities were ravaged by fire bombing, the economy collapsed, and the two atomic bomb detonations hastened Japan's surrender late that summer.

When the last of the American wartime draftees was mustered out of the service and returned home during the 1946 season, it marked the beginning of a temporary halt in the influence of the military on baseball performance but not on fan interest in the United States. The strong desire of many who had been in the service to put rigorous or traumatic wartime experiences aside, to get on with one's life, to get out, relax, and enjoy a ballgame sparked a large increase in attendance at professional games and a rise in the number of minor leagues that was to peak in 1949 before the advent of television took its toll.

In defeated Japan, the victorious Allies, particularly the United States, were calling the shots, and the American military had the fate of Japanese baseball in the palm of its hand. Fortunately the resurrection of the game was in line with the aim of the occupation forces, namely to reform Japanese political, economic, and social institutions so that they would more closely reflect those of the Western democracies.

General Headquarters encouraged the revival of spectator sports, and in November 1945, just three months after the unconditional surrender, the Japanese professional baseball league was reorganized as many players returned from duty in Manchuria, China, and Southeast Asia. There were problems at first because the occupation forces controlled the ballparks, used them for their own entertainment, and made the Japanese professional and college leagues negotiate for their use; but key people in the Allied administration aided the Japanese in their negotiations and smoothed the way for ever-increasing privileges. General Douglas MacArthur, head of the occupation government, personally issued the order to clean up Korakuen Stadium, home of the Tokyo Giants, which had been used as an ammunition dump during the war.

In 1946 Japanese professional play resumed with a total of 420 games being contested. By 1948, there were eight teams in the league, and such great progress was made that in 1950 two leagues were formed. There were 15 teams that year, but the number eventually dropped to 12, six teams in each league.

Such was the situation on both sides of the Pacific when on June 25, 1950, North Korean forces invaded the South and the Korean War began. For the second time in a decade, the specter of large-scale military conscription and its inevitable effect on players and pennant races loomed over the American professional baseball scene.

The effect of the war was felt before the 1950 season ended. The Philadelphia Phillies "Whiz Kids" were out in front of the National League pack and aiming for their first pennant in 35 years when on Sept. 10, their number two pitcher, Curt Simmons, who had already won 17 games, was called away when his Pennsylvania National Guard unit was mobilized. Simmons' loss, as well as injuries to three other key players, took the steam out of the Phillies, but they managed to hang on and win the pennant on the last day of the season against the Brooklyn Dodgers. Simmons received a furlough to attend the World Series, but Phillies manager Eddie Sawyer decided not to put Curt back on the eligibility list because of his limited baseball activity while away. The Phillies lost the Series to the New York Yankees in four straight games.

The following spring, veteran sportswriters making their predictions about the 1951 pennant races focused in part on the possible effect of the draft. The consensus was that veteran teams like the Boston Red Sox in the American League and the St. Louis Cardinals and Boston Braves in the National League would stand better chances of winning because they would be the least likely to lose players. Comparatively young clubs like the Philadelphia Phillies would be the most vulnerable, while teams like the Brooklyn Dodgers, with a combination of veterans and rookies, might stand the best chance of all. They would do well in the first half of the race with their youngsters, then would come on strong in the second half with their veterans as Selective Service took its toll.

The entire line of reasoning proved almost meaningless because a large-scale call-up never took place. The war was limited. What happened instead was that a handful of individuals got drafted, usually one or two players per team, for a period of two years. This pattern continued throughout the decade of the 1950s, even after the Korean War ended in 1953. The only service that had a general recall of its World War II veteran ballplayers was the Marine Corps, which took its Reserve aviators. This recall involved only two key players Red Sox outfielder Ted Williams and Yankees second baseman Jerry Coleman.

Williams' farewell was especially poignant. Shortly after the 1952 season began, on April 30 to be exact, a Wednesday afternoon crowd of 24,764 took part in pregame festivities. The Splendid Splinter was given a Cadillac and a memory book containing 430,000 signatures. The fans held hands and sang "Auld Lang Syne." Williams didn't disappoint them. He hit a two-run homer off Detroit Tigers pitcher Dizzy Trout in the seventh inning in his final at bat of the game to lead the Red Sox to victory. Given Williams' age (33), many felt they would never see him play again.

Ted's experience as a fighter pilot almost proved their thinking correct. He completed 38 combat missions in Korea, was hit by antiaircraft fire three times, and almost didn't make it back on the second occasion. He was awarded an Air Medal with two Gold Stars in lieu of his second and third Air Medals before being transferred back to the United States for a nagging inner ear and nose ailment that ultimately left him partially deaf in one ear. He was discharged on July 28, 1953. After a little over a week of conditioning, Teddy Ballgame returned to major league play and hit a phenomenal .407 in 37 games, with 13 home runs and a whopping slugging percentage of .901. Seven more years of superb hitting were to follow.

While the Red Sox plunged to sixth place without Williams in 1952, other contending clubs who lost players to the service didn't fare that badly. The Yankees were so deep in talent that they won five straight pennants between 1949 and 1953 despite the loss of ace left-hander Whitey Ford (1951-1952), third baseman Bobby Brown (1952-1953), and infielder Jerry Coleman (1952-1953). They lost to the Cleveland Indians in 1954 without the services of their crack second baseman, Billy Martin, but still managed to win 105 games. Only a tremendous 111-win season by the Indians outdid them; however, Martin returned late in the 1955 campaign, in time to spark the Yankees to the top of the heap again.

The Dodgers won pennants in 1952 and 1953 without their top right-hander, Don Newcombe, but lost to the Giants in 1954 when he returned. Newcombe went on to be the bellwether of the Brooklyn staff in the Dodgers' 1955 and 1956 National League championship seasons. The Giants won in a playoff with the Dodgers in 1951, Willie Mays' rookie season, but lost without him in 1952 and 1953. When the Say Hey Kid returned in 1954, they won again.

The Army got practically all of the professional ballplayers who were drafted during the Korean War, and thus it had some outstanding teams, both stateside and overseas. The 1951 Fort Myer, Va., club featured pitchers Johnny Antonelli (Braves) and Bob Purkey (Giants), infielder Danny O'Connell (Pirates), and catcher Sam Calderone (Giants). That same year, the Brooke Army Medical Center team in San Antonio, Texas, boasted outfielder Dick Kokos (Browns), second baseman Owen Friend (Browns), pitcher Glenn Mickens (Dodgers), and catcher Gus Triandos (Yankees). In 1953 the All-Army champions at Fort Belvoir, Va., had Dick Groat (Pirates) at shortstop and Tom Poholsky (Cardinals) on the mound.

Fort Jackson, S.C., could call on outfielder Faye Throneberry (Red Sox), catchers Frank House (Tigers) and Haywood Sullivan (Red Sox), and pitcher Joe Landrum (Dodgers).

Several players wound up in the Far East Command, where the real action was. With Japan being used as a staging area for Korea, a few servicemen found themselves playing with or against Japanese professionals. In 1953 Leo Kiely of the Red Sox and Phil Paine of the Braves pitched a few games for the Mainichi Orions and Nishitetsu Lions, respectively. Two years earlier, ex-Pacific Coast League southpaw Ken Lehman of the 40th Infantry Division had been the star performer of the Far East Command, with a 14-1 record on the mound and a .408 average at the plate. Among his accomplishments during the 1951 season was defeating a group of Japanese All-Stars, 1-0, before 32,000 fans at Miyagi Stadium in Sendai. When Lefty O'Doul brought a group of top-flight major leaguers to Japan for an exhibition tour after the American season ended, Lehman was invited to play with them and pitched excellent ball in two games, one a start against the Japanese Central League All-Stars. He later went on to pitch for the Dodgers, Orioles, and Phillies.

Only one ex-big leaguer lost his life in combat during the Korean War: Bob Neighbors, an Air Force major, who died in North Korea in August 1952. He had played in seven games for the St. Louis Browns in 1939 and also served his country in World War II.

After the cessation of overt hostilities in Korea in 1953, Army baseball continued to feature a smattering of professional players who were two-year draftees; but in 1957 the All-Army championship tournament was discontinued, and the following year the level of competition was reduced to intramurals at the lowest unit level possible. Because the Navy wasn't drafting people and had not been a force to be reckoned with in baseball since the end of the Second World War, the Army's actions effectively spelled the end of top-flight military hardball. Over the last quarter century, softball has been the serviceman's game.

The Vietnam War, like the Korean conflict, was limited in scope. This fact, coupled with the availability of Reserve programs which required only six months of active duty, made the impact of the military on professional baseball slight from 1964, the year the war escalated after the Gulf of Tonkin "incident," to 1973, when the United States began to pull its forces out of Vietnam and terminate the draft.

Most players and executives who were eligible for the draft entered Reserve components of the armed forces, particularly that of the Army. They were obliged to do six months of basic training and spend six years attending one weekend meeting or four weekday meetings each month, and two weeks of active duty for training each fiscal year. The sixth year was basically inactive in the sense of the Reservist not having to attend meetings or do the two-week stint. The active duty obligations were normally performed during the off-season. Monthly attendance at drills became a problem on occasion, and a player might miss a weekend's worth of games here and there, but many Reserve units used the players in public relations roles for recruiting or image-building purposes and, as such, meetings could be staggered to suit the individual.

While pitching the Red Sox to their "Impossible Dream" pennant in 1967, Private First Class Jim Lonborg had to fly down to Atlanta and do his two-week Army Reserve duty. His fortnight began on Sunday, July 30, in the heat of the pennant race, and ended on Saturday, Aug. 12. Fortunately, he was able to work out with the Atlanta Braves and with the aid of passes, didn't miss a start. After being shelled by the Minnesota Twins two days before his departure, he flew back to Boston and worked 5⅓ innings against the Kansas City Athletics on Tuesday, Aug. 1, giving up three runs and eight hits but gaining his 15th win of the season. On Sunday, Aug. 6, he lost to the Twins in Minnesota, 2-0, in a rain-shortened, five-inning contest. His counterpart, Dean Chance, pitched a perfect game. On Wednesday, Aug. 9, he beat the Athletics in Kansas City, 5-1, for win number 16, tops in the majors. With his two-week sojourn over, he lost to the California Angels, 3-2, on the West Coast on Sunday, Aug. 13.

While military duty may have caused Lonborg a mild inconvenience, youngsters like Al Bumbry and Garry Maddox were serving in Vietnam. They would go on to make their mark as top-quality major league outfielders in the 1970s. With the demise of the draft, future ballplayers wouldn't have to worry about such unpleasant career interruptions.

The influence of the military on baseball should remain minimal and not approach the high-water mark of World War II, when both the length and the extent of the conflict had a pervasive effect on the game, both at home and abroad. As venerable and fascinating as the link between the military and baseball is, let us hope it remains low-profile in the future.

How to Score a Game

Neil Cohen

If you're reading this page, chances are you've never kept score at a ballgame. Maybe you preferred to have your hands free for a hot dog and a beer. Or maybe you didn't realize what you were missing.

Keeping score focuses all your attention on the game and provides more insight than just watching casually. It slows the action so that you can watch each play and enables you to take the pulse of the game, appreciate its subtleties, and sometimes even predict its outcome. What's more, it can be as easy or as complex as you want it to be.

The scoring system fans and sportswriters use today was invented by Henry Chadwick in the 1850s, building upon the earlier scoring technique of New York sportswriter M. J. Kelly. Chadwick, one of the first to write about baseball in the newspapers, created a minutely detailed scorecard so he would have a point of reference and recollection when he wrote his articles about the game. He also invented the modern boxscore.

Chadwick assigned a letter or letters to each play that could take place on the field, usually the first or last letters of the word that described the play. Then, he assigned a number—from 1 to 9—to each of the players on the field, according to his defensive position. By combining letters and numbers, he could record what happened in a particular at bat and, if an out were made, which defensive players made the play.

Little has changed in scoring since Chadwick's day, except for the way some of the letters and numbers are assigned. Here's how we do it today.

1B—Single
2B—Double
3B—Triple
HR—Home Run
BB—Walk (Base on Balls); IBB—intentional walk
FC—Fielder's Choice
SB—Stolen Base
CS—Caught Stealing
WP—Wild Pitch
PB—Passed Ball
FO—Foul Out
SAC—Sacrifice
HBP—Hit by Pitch
K—Strikeout; backwards K—Strikeout, looking

Why a K for a strikeout? Chadwick needed S for sacrifice, so he decided to go with K, the last letter in the word "struck," then a common term for striking out.

This is the way we number the defensive players:

1—Pitcher;
2—Catcher;
3—First Baseman;
4—Second Baseman;
5—Third Baseman;
6—Shortstop;
7—Left Fielder;
8—Center Fielder;
9—Right Fielder.

Shortstop is number 6, instead of number 5, because in the early days of the game, shortstop was still evolving as a position, and the player in that spot was considered more of a shallow outfielder than an infielder.

To save space, some plays are described simply with numbers. For a flyout, we just record the code number of the fielder who made the catch. For an unassisted groundout, we write the number of the infielder, followed by a period. For an assisted groundout, we would use the numbers of the two fielders handling the ball.

Now, imagine that each box on your scorecard is a miniature baseball diamond, with first base in the lower right corner, second base in the upper right corner, third base in the top left and home plate in the bottom left. If a batter reaches first, divide the box into quarters. This allows you to record the batter's progress in the square as he moves around the bases.

Here are two fictional innings to illustrate how this all comes together on a sample scorecard (below). Leading off for the All-Time All-Stars is left fielder Ty Cobb, who singles and steals second. The next batter, second baseman Rogers Hornsby, bounces a grounder to second and Cobb takes third. We mark a number 2 in the third base quadrant of Cobb's box to indicate that the No. 2 batter advanced him there. The next batter, Babe Ruth, hits a home run. We note that, plus a 3 in the home plate quadrant of Cobb's box to show how he scored. Batting fourth, Lou Gehrig flies out to center field.

Center fielder Tris Speaker walks and takes second on a passed ball. Honus Wagner doubles, but is thrown out by the left fielder when he tries to stretch it into a triple. Speaker, however, advances to third and then scores before the third out is made. In the box below the inning boxes, we note the number of runs and hits made in that half-inning: three runs above the diagonal line, three hits below.

In the second inning, catcher Bill Dickey singles but is

erased when third baseman Pie Traynor grounds into a shortstop-to-second-to-first double play, shown by the 6–4 in Dickey's second-base quadrant. Pitcher Cy Young strikes out to end the inning. The totals: 0 runs, 1 hit.

It can be that simple. But it doesn't have to be. Scoring also has its creative side. Any scoring code is just a guideline; you can make up your own system to record whatever you're interested in tracking. For example, some scorers record base hits in shorthand: dashes or dots, one for each base. You can also embellish your scoring with other details of the game that you find interesting or would be fun to keep track of and think about later. The extra boxes at the end of the scoresheet (for at bats, runs, etc.) can come in handy if you need to branch out. You can, for example, record the count on each batter, or whether the pitcher was ahead or behind on a batter when the ball was put into play. That way you can tell how efficiently a pitcher is working in a game, and how he might fare in the later innings. If you have a good seat, or you're watching on television, you can also keep track of what pitch a pitcher uses to record outs and what pitches result in hits. You can record where flyballs are caught; if many batters are reaching the warning track, you know you have a lucky pitcher out there. Or, you can note where hits are made, to learn the patterns in which certain hitters perform.

Use your imagination. Keeping score enables you to study a game with as much concentration as a manager or coach in the dugout and to gain a feel for the underlying current of the game. And you can still have a hot dog and a beer. Like everything else in baseball, all you need is a sharp eye, a good pair of hands, and practice.

TEAM												
PLAYER	**POS.**	**1**	**2**	**3**	**4**	**5**	**6**	**7**	**AB**	**R**	**H**	**BB**	**TB**
									8	**9**	**10**	**11**	**12**
1. Cobb	⑦ LF	2|SB 3|1B											
2. Hornsby	④ 2B	4-3											
3. Ruth	⑨ RF	HR											
4. Gehrig	③ 1B	8											
5. Speaker	⑧ CF	6|PB 6|BB											
6. Wagner	⑥ SS	7-5|2B											
7. Dickey	② C		6-4 1B										
8. Traynor	⑤ 3B		6-4-3										
9. Young	① P		K										
R	3	0											
H	3	1											

PITCHER	IP	H	R	ER	BB	SO

Notes on Contributors

Larry Amman was born and raised in the suburbs of Detroit. He graduated from Wayne State University with a B.A. in history and political science in 1967, then served in the U.S. Army Intelligence in Vietnam and Germany. Germany remains a very special place to him. In the last few years he has made several trips to that country to help with baseball programs. Larry has lived in the Washington area for 20 years. He is employed as a travel agent.

Marty Appel, former public relations director and television producer for the New York Yankees, has written 15 books on baseball, including the Casey Award-winning *Slide, Kelly, Slide,* a biography of 19th century star Michael "King" Kelly as well as collaborations with Eric Gregg, Bowie Kuhn, Lee MacPhail, Thurman Munson, and Tom Seaver.

Bob Carroll, a former high school teacher, is a freelance writer and illustrator who lives in North Huntingdon, Pa. He is the founder and executive director of the Professional Football Researchers Association (PFRA) and a longtime member of the Society for American Baseball Research (SABR). He regularly writes and illustrates for *Oldtyme Baseball News.* His baseball books include *Baseball Between the Lies, The Whole Baseball Catalogue* (with John Thorn), *The Dodgers Trivia Book,* and *The Major League Way to Play Baseball.* Among his football credits are *Total Football, The Hidden Game of Football* (with Pete Palmer and John Thorn), and *When the Grass Was Real.* He regularly provides cartoons for *Pro Football Weekly.* His hobbies are listening to classical music, cleaning the Augean stables, and writing threatening letters.

Jim Charlton is a writer and editor with more than three dozen books to his credit, including four on baseball. Mr. Charlton is also a literary agent and book packager, as well as a lifetime Cubs fan, all frustrating occupations. He is married and lives in Greenwich Village, five blocks from where he was born.

Garth Chouteau is an associate producer and marketing executive with Stormfront Studios, makers of *Old Time Baseball* and the *Tony La Russa Baseball* line of entertainment software. Chouteau has more than 10 years experience in the computer hardware and software markets, as well as a lifelong love of baseball. The only film during which Mr. Chouteau has ever cried is *It's Good to Be Alive, the Roy Campanella Story.*

Merritt Clifton edits *Animal People: News for People Who Care about Animals.* Clifton also is author of numerous works on "outlaw" baseball, especially as played in Quebec, Vermont, Japan, and Mexico, and *Relative Baseball*, a pioneering sabermetric study and a history and statistical analysis of *The Sporting News*/Topps All-Star Rookie teams, 1958-1983.

Neil Cohen toiled for much of his professional career at *Sport* magazine, where he held positions of editor and managing editor. Following that, he was unlucky enough to be present at the demise of *The National Sports Daily,* where he served as senior editor. He then turned his attention to explaining sports and its lessons to children as an associate editor at *Sports Illustrated for Kids* Books.

Robert W. Creamer was a writer and an editor with *Sports Illustrated* from its inception until his retirement a few years ago. He has written several baseball books, among them *Stengel: His Life and Times; Babe: The Legend Comes to Life;* and, *Baseball in '41: A Celebration of The Best Season Ever.*

Harrington E. Crissey, Jr., better known as "Kit" to his acquaintances, was born in Schenectady, N.Y., and currently lives in Elkins Park, Pa. He received a B.A. degree in Latin Literature from the University of Rochester and a master of education degree from Temple University and has taught English language services on the St. Joseph's University campus. After 30 years of service in the Naval Reserve he retired in the fall of 1993 with the rank of commander. A Boston Red Sox fan, he participates actively in the Society for American Baseball Research and is the author of three books about baseball during World War II, one of these covering baseball and the Navy.

Don Daglow is founder and President of Stormfront Studios Inc. a California computer and video game developer. In 1971 he wrote the first interactive computer baseball game (on a DEC PDP-10), and was the first person to simulate a complete baseball season on a computer. As the video game business developed he became particularly known for successful baseball simulations. Games designed or produced by Don and the Stormfront team include *Intellivision World Series Baseball* (Mattel, 1983), *Earl Weaver Baseball* (Electronic Arts, 1987), *ESPN Baseball Tonight* (Sony, 1995), *Tony La Russa Baseball* (Five versions, 1991-97), and *Old Time Baseball* (Stormfront Studios, 1995).

Bill Deane is a freelance baseball researcher and writer stationed near Cooperstown, N.Y., where he spent eight years as Senior Research Associate for the National Baseball Library & Archive. He has published six books and nearly 200 articles for such publications as Baseball America and *USA Today Baseball Weekly,* and was a recipient of the 1989 SABR-Macmillan Baseball Research Award. Deane resides in Fly Creek, N.Y., with his wife, Pam, and daughter, Sarah.

Rob Edelman is the author of *Great Baseball Films* (Citadel Press). He is co-author (with his wife, Audrey Kupferberg) of *Angela Lansbury: A Life on Stage and Screen* (Birch Lane) and *The John Travolta Scrapbook* (Citadel Press). He is a Contributing Editor of Leonard Maltin's *Movie and Video Guide,* and has written essays in *A Political Companion to American Film, The International Dictionary of Films and Filmmakers,* and the *International Film Guide.* His byline has appeared in dozens of publications, from *American Film* to *The Washington Post.*

Myles E. Friedman is editor and vice president of Vanguard Publications, which has published the annual *Spring Training Baseball Yearbook* since 1988. He also publishes historical wall charts on baseball, football, and World Cup soccer.

Warner Fusselle is the voice behind numerous television and radio programs and films on the subject of baseball. He worked with Mel Allen on *This Week in Baseball* since its inception in 1977 until Mel's death in 1996 and continues on that program. He has also hosted ESPN's *Major League Baseball Magazine.* In addition to baseball narration, Fusselle's play-by-play announcing can be heard on WABC Radio in New York City. He is the author of *Baseball . . . A Laughing Matter!* and has produced two albums of music for Rhino Records: *Baseball's Greatest Hits* and *Baseball's Greatest Hits . . . Let's Play II.*

Larry R. Gerlach is professor of American sports history at the University of Utah. He is a member of the editorial board of *Nine,* president of SABR, and chair of SABR's Umpires and Rules Committee. He has published numerous articles in journals and reference works, as well as *The Men in Blue: Conversations with Umpires.*

Michael Gershman is best known among baseball fans for *Diamonds: The Evolution of the Ballpark,* which won the Casey Award in 1993 and also received the SABR-Macmillan Award. He is also known to collectors for his series of Baseball Card Engagement Books and Baseball Stadium Postcard Albums. He is also a co-editor of *Total Football,* and, with John Thorn, is the co-founder of Total Sports.

Gary Gillette is a Vice President of Total Sports and is co-author of the 1999 *Baseball Weekly Insider.* He has written or edited many baseball books, including *The Spy: Baseball '98, The Scouting Report: 1995 and 1996,* and *The Great American Baseball Stat Book 1992, 1993, and 1994.* From 1992-97, he was president of The Baseball Workshop, which is now part of Total Sports; he was executive director or chairman of Project Scoresheet from 1987-1992. Gillette has also worked as a legal expert witness on baseball-related litigation and as a consultant on arbitration cases for prominent player agents. He has contributed to *USA Today, Baseball Weekly, Baseball Weekly Almanac, Baseball Today, Bill Mazeroski's Baseball,* and *Ultimate Sports Baseball,* and to numerous other books, periodicals, and newspapers. He has also served as a baseball commentator for several National Public Radio stations.

Barry Halper, born in Newark, N.J., in 1939, began collecting baseball material 20 years ago and now holds the largest single collection of baseball memorabilia, surpassing even Cooperstown's. His collection includes over 1 million baseball cards and approximately a thousand baseball uniforms. Halper and his wife, Sharon, have three children and reside in Livingston, N.J.

Tom Heitz, born in Kansas City, Missouri, in 1940, has been a lifelong baseball fan. He learned the National Pastime from his father, a law professor and Little League coach, and from Harry Caray, the voice of the St. Louis Cardinals. Heitz received his formal education at the University of Kansas (B.A., 1962), the University of Missouri at Kansas City School of Law (J.D., 1965), and the University of Washington, where he studied library science under renowned law librarian Marian Gallagher. Heitz served as librarian at the National Baseball Library & Archive from 1983 through 1994. He now writes and lectures on baseball subjects.

Bob Hoie has long been an active member of the Society for American Baseball Research, receiving the Society's Bob Davids Award for meritorious service in 1987. He has served as chairman of SABR's Minor League Committee, was a principal contributor to *Minor League Baseball Stars,* volumes 1, 2, and 3, and contributed to *The Encyclopedia of Minor League Baseball.* A native of Los Angeles and a fan of the Pacific Coast League Angels until their demise in 1957, Hoie is retired after 30 years of service as an urban planner for Los Angeles County.

John B. Holway has written for numerous magazines and newspapers, including *American Heritage, The Sporting News, The New York Times,* and the *Washington Post.* He is the author of *Voices from the Great Black Baseball Leagues, Blackball Stars, The Pitcher* with John Thorn, and *The Last .400 Hitter.* He has written about Ted Williams, whom he saw in 1941, the Negro leagues, which he saw in 1944, Japanese baseball, which he saw in 1948, and pitching, which he has spent a lifetime swinging at and missing. He won *Spitball* magazine's Casey Award and SABR's Bob Davids Award, both in 1990.

Frederick Ivor-Campbell turned to baseball research and writing after many years in religious publishing (editor/writer, Gospel Light Publications, California), public information (Barrington College, Rhode Island), and college teaching (English, at the University of Rhode Island and The King's College, New York). He has written baseball history and biography for several periodicals and reference works. Ivor-Campbell has served on the board of directors of the Society for American Baseball Research, and chairs SABR's Nineteenth Century Committee. He lives with his wife, Alma, in Warren, R.I.

Jack Kavanagh has given up the pretense of retirement for a writer's life in Rhode Island. His books have focused on such diverse subjects as Shoeless Joe Jackson and Robert E. Lee. In 1995 he celebrated his 75th birthday with his first adult, full-scale biography, a treatment of Walter Johnson (Diamond Communications); the following year saw him win SABR's Bob Davids Award and publish a biography of Grover Cleveland Alexander. He enjoys his five nearby grandchildren and the health to

sniff the roses while they bloom. He has wonderful memories of a 50-year marriage to his late wife Sally.

Robert Laidlaw was born in Adelaide, South Australia in 1957. He has played baseball for Central Districts since 1973, and is a club life member. He has written five sports books—including one on Central Districts Baseball Club, and regularly writes articles on baseball and Australian football. He is Baseball SA and Central District Football Club Historian. In writing the chapter on Australian baseball, Robert used the resources of Mortlock Library in Adelaide and the experience of many baseball people throughout Australia. Two friends who were especially helpful were Peter Cornwall and Joe Clark—who is writing his University thesis on Australian baseball.

Sean Lahman is a member of SABR and founder of the Baseball Archive web site. He has published articles in journals and reference works, and has been a frequent contributor to annuals such as *Great American Baseball Stat Book, Big Bad Baseball Annual, The Rotisserie Baseball Analyst,* and *Baseball Preview.* Sean attended the University of Cincinnati and lives in Rochester, N.Y., with his wife Heather and their three young children.

Jack Lang has reported on major league baseball for half a century, starting in 1946 when he covered the Brooklyn Dodgers for the *Long Island Press.* His last 13 years on the beat were for the *New York Daily News,* where he was the senior major league baseball writer in 1987, when he retired. In 1966 he began conducting the annual Hall of Fame election and was elected Secretary-Treasurer of the Baseball Writers Association of America, for whom he conducted the annual polls for the Most Valuable Player, Cy Young, Rookie, and Manager Awards. In 1987 Lang himself was elected to the Hall of Fame when he was named winner of the J.G. Taylor Spink Award for meritorious contributions to baseball writing.

Philip J. Lowry is author of *Green Cathedrals,* the definitive study of all ballparks ever used for Major League and Negro League games since 1871, and of *Green Gridirons,* a similar study on all pro football stadiums. He has served on the Board of Directors and as Ballparks Chair and Negro Leagues Chair for SABR. Phil received B.A. and M.B.A. degrees from Harvard University, served in the U.S. Army airborne for six years as an infantry captain, and now resides in Minnetonka, Minn., with his wife, Ellen, and their children, Evan and Megan.

Bill Madden majored in journalism at the University of South Carolina and launched his sportswriting career at United Press International in New York in 1970. From 1980 to 1988, Madden was *The Daily News's* New York Yankees beat writer. He became that publication's national baseball columnist in 1989. In 1990 he collaborated on the bestselling book, *Damned Yankees.* In his years at *The Daily News* he was responsible for breaking numerous baseball stories, including the National League's surprise election of Bill White as its president in February 1989. In addition to writing for *The Daily News,* Madden also has contributed freelance articles to numerous sports publications and a semiweekly sports collecting column for *The Sporting News.*

Yoichi Nagata holds a B.A. from Osaka University in Japan and an M.A. from the University of Pennsylvania. He has been a freelance sports journalist, writing numerous articles on sports for Japanese magazines. He is an avid baseball fan of the now-defunct Nishitetsu Lions of Fukuoka and of the Philadelphia Phillies.

Pete Palmer is the former editor of the Barnes *Official Encyclopedia of Baseball.* He began compiling his historical and analytical data in the mid-1960s, and from 1978 to 1987 he was chairman of SABR's statistical analysis committee. In that time he also served as a consultant for the Sports Information Center, the official statisticians of the American League. He was on the board of directors of Project Scoresheet. Palmer has contributed articles to *Sport, USA Today, Sports Heritage, The National Pastime,* and *Baseball Research Journal.* He is co-author, with John Thorn, of *The Hidden Game of Baseball* and *The Official Major League Baseball Record Book;* with Thorn and Bob Carroll of *The Hidden Game of Football* and *The Football Abstract;* and with Thorn and Eliot Cohen of *The Baseball Annual 1990.* He won SABR's Bob Davids Award in 1989.

David Pietrusza, former president of the Society for American Baseball Research (SABR) and Editor-in-Chief of Total Sports, is the author of *Judge and Jury: The Life and Times of Judge Kenesaw Mountain Landis, Lights On!: The Wild Century-Long Saga of Night Baseball* (a finalist for the Casey Award as best baseball book of 1997), *Minor Miracles: The Legend and Lure of Minor League Baseball; Major Leagues;* and *Baseball's Canadian-American League.* He co-edited *Total Mets, Total Braves,* and *Total Indians,* as well as seven books on football and served as managing editor of *Total Football: The Official Encyclopedia of the NFL.* Pietrusza served as producer for the documentary *Local Heroes* for PBS-television station WMHT and as consultant for the Baseball Online segment of the PBS LearningLink system. A columnist for *Oldtyme Baseball News,* he has written for such other periodicals as *USA Today, Baseball Weekly, Baseball America, Elysian Fields Quarterly, The National Pastime, New Mexico Magazine,* and *The Baseball Research Journal.* Pietrusza was also a writer for Microsoft's multimedia product. A former member of the Amsterdam (N.Y.) City Council, he serves as Public Information Officer for the NYS Governor's Office of Regulatory Reform and has written extensively on American and world history.

Bruce L. Prentice was born and raised in Toronto, Ontario, Canada, and was a top amateur baseball player before turning to coaching and instruction. In the late 1970s he assisted the introduction of the first high school baseball programs in Canada. He was founder of Canada's first college baseball program at Seneca College in Toronto and was an area scout for the Blue Jays from 1980 to 1986. Prentice is the owner and operator of Proway Baseball Schools, the founder and long-time president of the Canadian Baseball Hall of Fame and Museum, and was instrumental in forming the World Baseball Hall of Fame in 1989.

Rob Ruck is the author of *Sandlot Seasons: Sport in*

Black Pittsburgh and *The Tropic of Baseball: Baseball in the Dominican Republic*, a 1991 MacMillan–SABR Award Winner. *Kings on the Hill: Baseball's Forgotten Men*, the Emmy-winning documentary he wrote and produced on the Negro Leagues, aired on NBC in 1995. Ruck, who is currently working on a history of Pittsburgh with Red Muller, is on the faculty of the Center for Latin American Studies and the History Department at the University of Pittsburgh.

Matthew Silverman is a full-time writer, researcher, and editor for Total Sports. He recently edited six offshoots of *Total Football,* namely *Total Packers, Total Steelers, Total Cowboys, Total 49ers, Total Quarterbacks,* and *Total Super Bowl.* He also contributes to Total Baseball Daily on www.totalbaseball.com and edited *Total Mets.* Formerly an editor at *Variety* in New York City, he worked at three New England newspapers and now lives in Connecticut with his wife and daughter.

Allan Simpson is the founding editor of *Baseball America* and is recognized as the expert on baseball's amateur free-agent draft. *Baseball America* is based in Durham, N.C., and specializes in the coverage of player development.

Thomas St. John, a former St. Louis resident, has been living in Korea since 1992. He is currently the only foreigner covering Korean pro sports and has been doing so since 1993. Currently, Thomas works as a sports writer and photographer for the *Korea Times* newspaper as well as being the Korean correspondent for *Baseball America* and *International Baseball Rundown.* Thomas also is an advisor to the Korea Baseball Organization (Korea's pro league) and is the league's photographer.

John Thorn is the author/editor of many baseball books, including *Treasures of the Hall of Fame, The Game for All America, The Armchair Books of Baseball, Ted Williams: Seasons of the Kid* (with Richard Ben Cramer and Mark Rucker), *The National Pastime, and The Relief Pitcher.* He co-authored *The Pitcher* with John Holway, and *The Hidden Game of Baseball* and *The Baseball Record Book* with Pete Palmer. With Palmer and Bob Carroll he also co-authored *The Hidden Game of Football* and *The Football Abstract.* He has written for several periodicals, among them *The Sporting News, Sport,* and *American Heritage.* Thorn was Senior Creative Consultant to *Baseball,* Ken Burns' nine-part film for the Public Broadcasting System, and serves as a consultant to the National Baseball Hall of Fame Committee on Baseball Veterans. The publisher of Total Sports, Thorn is also a co-editor of *Total Football.*

Robert L. Tiemann served as chairman of the 19th-century research committee of the Society for American Baseball Research and is the author of *Cardinal Classics* and *Dodger Classics.* He headed the SABR research project that reconstructed from newspaper play-by-play accounts much of the missing data for the National Association of 1871 to 1875. With Rich Topp, Tiemann shared a SABR award for his redevelopment of the Manager Roster as it appears in *Total Baseball,* and in 1992 won SABR's Bob Davids Award.

Jules Tygiel is a professor of history at San Francisco State University. He is the author of *Baseball's Great Experiment: Jackie Robinson and his Legacy* (Oxford University Press, 1983; Vintage Paperback edition, 1984) and has contributed articles to many periodicals.

Joseph M. Wayman, publisher and editor of *Grandstand Baseball Annual,* which he founded in 1985, has been the subject of a "SABR Salute," which commended him for his steadfast "investigative reporting of questionable baseball records." Several of his discoveries have been accepted as fact by *Total Baseball* and the Elias Sports Bureau and have resulted in a rewriting of the baseball record books. His writings have also appeared in the *Baseball Research Journal* and *Baseball Bulletin.*

Jeffrey Wilson was born and raised in Corvallis, Ore. He graduated from Lewis & Clark College in 1985 with a degree in international studies. After living in China for a year, he earned a law degree and a masters degree in Chinese studies from the University of Washington in 1991. He moved to Taiwan in 1991 where his legal career was highlighted with the first arbitration awards ever issued in Taiwan professional sports. He was also involved in the placement of professional baseball and basketball players in Taiwan and China. He is currently the sports editor of the English-language *China Post* in Taipei and a regular correspondent for *Baseball America.* He has also written for *USA Today,* International Baseball Rundown, and a variety of regional and international publications.

With appreciation to these readers of *Total Baseball 1* who sent in corrections or made suggestions on how to improve the second edition:

Larry Amman, Ray Andreotti, Mel Bailey, Craig Barbarino, Edgar K. Beatty, James M. Beck, Joseph R. Bender, Robert Beukelher, John Booth, Jim Bostain, Therese R. Brown, J. Paul Browne, Bob Cambris, Kevin A. Carleton, Bob Carroll, Anthony M. Chieco, Ken Coleman, Steve Cooper, Owen Curtis, Clay Davenport, L. Robert Davids, Bill Deane, Harold Dellinger, Ted D. DeVries, Don Dewey, Raymond A. DiSanto, Sam Elfand, Don Elliott, John Emerson, Eddie Epstein, Kenneth Fink, Robert L. Franz, Andrew Fussner, Cam Gibson, Steven Goldberg, Ray Gonzalez, Dan Greenia, Bill Haber, Rod Hay, Bob Hoie, Frederick Ivor-Campbell, Tom Jennings, Bill Jensen, Warren Johnson, Cliff Kachline, James Kaufman, Dave Kemp, Larry Kempster, Randall Kleinman, Jack Lang, Ron Liebman, Jerry Malloy, James F. Maxfield, Bob McConnell, Joe M. McGowan, David Molnar, George S. Moskal, Frank J. Mueller, Neil Munro, Thomas L. Nester, Dave Nichols, Tom O'Brien, Yoshio Ohno, S. Mark Parker, Paul E. Pennebaker, Peretz Perl, David Pietrusza, Mike Post, Jorgen Rasmussen, Allan Rausch, Andrew Richardson, John Rickert, John M. Roca, Winslow Rogers, Tom Ruane, Bill Rubenstein, David Schermer, Leon Schmerhold, John Schwartz, Alfred Secondi, Sy Siegel, Richard Siegelman, Al Smith, David M. Snyder, David Stephan, Mike Sparks, Lyle Spatz, Dean Sullivan, Isaac Thorn, Richard Topp, Stephen Toth, T. Brook Treakle III, Jim Troisi, Jim Tuttle, Jim Vail, Cullen P. Vane, David Vincent, Joseph M. Wayman, Jim Weigand, Bernard Weisberger, Christopher Williams, Frank Wil-

liams, Joseph C. Williams, Ralph Winnie, Jim Wright, and Ed Yerha.

And to those whose suggestions have improved the third edition:

David Aceto, Tim Anderson, Andrew J. Balog, Robert Browning, Chuck Carey, Keith Carlson, Garrett M. Casey, Jim Conroy, Bob Davids, Bill Deane, Dennis DeValeria, Ted DiTullio, Robert Downer, Tom Dunken, Jules Egyrd, Eddie Epstein, Ken Fetterman, Bob Franzosa, Gary Gillette, Jay Gregory, Charlie Harville, Jeffrey Hatt, Ralph Horton, Jeff James, Darlene Kadlecik, Jerry Kahn, John Kenyon, Patrick Kinas, D.C. Larkin, II, Matthew Lesniewski, Morris Levin, Don Luce, Michael Lucich, Ed Luteran, Jeff Magalif, E.H. Marshall, Richard A. Marston, Ronald A. Mayer, John P. McBride, John McClaran, Randy Messel, Scott Messinger, Steve Moore, Neil Munro, John O'Malley, Ed Oswalt, Douglas R. Pappas, Richard Pardoe, Danny Radakovich, Matt Rapacz, Louis Rauco, Matt Reese, Eric Reinholdt, Dennis Repp, John Richards, Bob Richardson, John M. Roca, Seth D. Rodgers, Robert Schulz, John Schwartz, John Scott, Jamie Selko, Jim Smith, Dave Smith, Lewis J. Snyder, Lyle Spatz, Alan Steinberg, David Stephan, A.D. Suehsdorf, James Swetnam, Blair D. Tarr, Robert Tiemann, Harry L. Turtledove, Bill Wallace, Patrick K. Walsh, Joe Wayman, Jim Weigand, Frank Williams, Walt Wilson, and Edgar M. Wyatt.

The fourth edition has benefited from the comments of:

Tim Anderson, Arnie Braunstein, Chuck Carey, Bill Carle, Tim Cashion, Tom Chase, Ed Coen, Bob Davids, Bill Deane, Dan Dischley, Ted DiTullio, Jules Egyrd, Eddie Epstein, Bill French, Campbell Gibson, Gary Gillette, Herb Goldman, Albert A. Gunnell, Robert Kern, Joe Kinsman, Joe Klein, Joe Marchetto, Jeff Marcus, Bob McConnell, Randy Messell, Scott Messinger, Neil Munro, John O'Malley, Ed Oswalt, Doug Pappas, Jeffrey Platt, Frank Phelps, Bob Richardson, Win Rogers, Bob Rosiek, Jim Sargent, Robert Schulz, John Schwartz, Jamie Selko, Dave Smith, Jim Smith, David Stephan, Chuck Stevens, David Stone, Adie Suehsdorf, Bob Tiemann, David Vincent, Bill Way, Joe Wayman, Jim Weigand, Roy White, Alan Whitney, Frank Williams, Walt Wilson, and Ed Yerha.

The fifth edition has benefited from the comments of:

Arnie Braunstein, Chuck Carey, Keith Carlson, Bill Carle, Bill Carr, Tim Cashion, Tom Chase, Bob Davids, Bill Deane, Dan Dischley, Bill Doig, Jeff Fox, Tate Giersdorf, Gary Gillette, Herb Goldberg, Ed Hartig, Bob Hoie, Frederick Ivor-Campbell, Herm Krabbenhoft, Dan Levitt, Fred Lenger, David Marasco, John Matthew IV, Neil Munro, John O'Malley, David Neft, Doug Pappas, Bob Richardson, Patrick Rock, Jim Sargent, John Schultz, John Schwartz, Jamie Selko, Joe Simenic, Allan Simpson, Lyle Spatz, Dick Thompson, Bob Tiemann, Dixie Torangeau, Jim Troisi, Frank Vaccaro, Paul Walker, Bill Way, Joe Wayman, Jim Weigand, Frank Williams, Walt Wilson, and Dave Zeman.

The sixth edition has benefited from the comments of:

Carlos Bauer, Randy Bonferraro, Bill Carle, Tim Cashion, Bill Carr, Ryall Carroll, Bill Deane, Dan Dischley, Harvey Frankel, Gary Gillette, Todd Greanier, Rich Hancock, Ed Hartig, Herm Krabbenhoft, Fred Lenger, Jamie Lotze, Chuck Lumb, Bob McConnell, Neil Munro, Rob Neyer, John O'Malley, Jeff Ouriel, Frank Peters, Frank Phelps, Bob Richardson, Tom Ruane, John Schwartz, Stuart Shea, Dave Smith, Lyle Spatz, John Steele, Dick Thompson, Bob Tiemann, Dixie Torangeau, Wayne Townsend, Frank Vaccaro, David Vincent, Bill Way, Joe Wayman, Frank Williams, Vic Wilson, Walt Wilson and Ken Zweibel.

Glossary of Statistical Terms

This Glossary contains definitions of the statistical terms and measures that may be unfamiliar to the average baseball fan or that represent what today might seem odd scoring practices. The Glossary will also be of value to the advanced fan who wishes to know more about the mathematical and theoretical foundations of certain statistics.

/A "Adjusted"; means that the statistic to the immediate left of this mark has been normalized to league average and adjusted for home park factor. Stats that are normalized in this book are Batting Runs, Production, Batting Average, On Base Percentage, Slugging Average, Earned Run Average, and Pitcher Runs.

Assist Although credited to pitchers on strikeouts in some of baseball's early years, not counted as such in this volume.

Assist Average Assists divided by games played. Stat created by Philadelphia baseball writer Al Wright in 1875.

At Bats Charged to batters on sacrifice hits, 1889–1893; on sacrifice-fly situations, 1931–1938 and 1940–1953; bases on balls, 1876, 1887. However, we did not count at bats for bases on balls.

Average and Over Early form of expressing averages for base hits, runs, and outs. The average of a batter with 23 hits in six games would be not 3.83 but 3–5 (an average of 3 with an overage, or remainder, of 5); borrowed from cricket.

Average Bases Allowed A pitcher's total bases allowed, divided by his innings pitched—what might be termed Opponents' Slugging Average. Created by Alfred P. Berry in 1951.

Average Batting (Pitching, Fielding) Skill The great philosophical as well as statistical puzzler: after one has normalized a player's performance to that of his league, how does one compare one season's league average with that of another far removed in time? Does a .266 batting average in the NL of 1902 mean the same thing as a .266 batting average in the AL of 1977?

Bases on Balls Counted as outs for batters in 1876 and as hits for batters in 1887, but as neither throughout this book. Awarded for a varying number of errant pitches since 1876, from nine in that year to the current four, standardized in 1889. (After 1887, the batter was no longer allowed to specify strike zone as waist to shoulders or waist to shins.)

Bases on Balls Percentage Batters' stat: most walks per 100 at bats plus bases on balls.

Bases on Balls Per Game Game defined as nine innings; league-leading pitchers calculated on basis of low-est mark; computed as bases on balls times nine, divided by innings.

Base-Out Percentage Barry Codell's stat for measuring complete offensive performance, in which the elements of the numerator represent bases gained while the events in the denominator represent outs produced (sacrifices and sacrifice flies appear in both because they achieve both—gaining a base for the team while costing it an out). The formula:

$$\frac{\text{Total Bases} + \text{Walks} + \text{HBP} + \text{Steals} + \text{Sacrifices} + \text{Sacrifice Flies}}{\text{At bats} - \text{Hits} + \text{Caught Stealing} + \text{GIDP} + \text{Sac.} + \text{Sac. Flies}}$$

(GIDP, in the equation above, stands for Grounded Into Double Play; HBP for Hit By Pitch.)

Batters Facing Pitcher Unavailable before 1903 in the National League. The 1903 and 1908 data was not published and has been reconstructed. BFP was unavailable for the American League of 1901-1907. Excepting the NL of 1876-1888 and the AA of 1882 and 1884-1887, for which John Tattersall calculated BFP from box scores, earlier years in both leagues have had their BFP constructed from available data in this manner: subtract league base hits from league at bats, divide by league innings pitched, multiply by the pitcher's innings, and add his hits allowed, walks, hit by pitch, and sacrifice hits, if available. Abbreviated as BFP.

Batter's Park Factor The Park Factor shown in the batters' section of the team statistics in the Annual Record, Player Register, and Home-Road Statistics. Above 100 means batters benefited from playing half their games in a good hitting park. Abbreviated as BPF or, in what are clearly batters' stats (as in the Player Register) simply as PF. See entry for *Park Factor* for the computation.

Battery Errors In baseball's early years, wild pitches, passed balls, and hit batsmen were lumped together in the statistical summary of a game as *battery errors* and were charged against the fielding percentage of the pitcher or catcher. Such battery errors have been removed from individual and team stats for this book.

Batting Average Calculated as base hits divided by at bats ever since its first appearance in print in 1874. In 1876 walks were counted as at bats, and in 1887 they were counted as at bats and as hits. For this book, batting averages are computed in uniform fashion throughout baseball history. Abbreviated in Part 2 of this volume as AVG, although it is also commonly abbreviated BA.

Batting Runs The Linear Weights measure of runs contributed *beyond* those of a league-average batter or team, such league average defined as zero. The formula depends upon the run values for each offensive event that resulted from Pete Palmer's 1978 computer simulation of

all major league games played since 1901. Run values change marginally with changing conditions of play (an out costs a team more in a hitters' year, such as 1930, than in a pitchers' year, such as 1908), and they differ slightly up and down the batting order (a homer is not worth as much to the leadoff hitter as it is to the fifth-place batter; a walk is worth more for the man batting second than for the man batting eighth); however, these differences have been averaged out historically in the figures that follow.

$$\text{Runs} = (.47)1B + (.78)2B + (1.09)3B + (1.40)HR +$$
$$(.33)(BB + HB) - (.25)(AB - H) - (.50)OOB$$

(An out is considered to be a hitless at bat and its value is set so that the sum of all events times their frequency is zero, thus establishing zero as the baseline, or norm, for performance.)

Some events one might expect to see included in this formula but that do not appear are sacrifices, sacrifice hits, grounded into double plays, and reached on error. The last is not known for most years and in the official statistics is indistinguishable from outs on base (OOB). The sacrifice has values that essentially cancel one another, trading an out for an advanced base which, often as not, leaves the team in a situation with poorer run potential than it had before the sacrifice. The sacrifice fly has dubious run value because it is entirely dependent on a situation not under the batter's control: while a single or a walk or a hit by pitch always has potential run value, a long fly does not unless a man happens to be poised at third base. Last, the grounded into double play is to a far greater extent a function of one's place in the batting order than it is of poor speed or failure in the clutch, and thus it does not find a home in a formula applicable to all batters. It is no accident that Hank Aaron, who ran well for most of his long career and wasn't too shabby in the clutch, hit into more DPs than anyone else, nor that Roberto Clemente, Al Kaline, and Frank Robinson, who fit the same description, are also among the ten "worst" in this department.

The Batting Runs formula can be condensed by eliminating the components for steals, caught stealing, and outs on base. Outs on base (calculated as *Hits + Walks + Hit Batsman − Left on Base − Runs − Caught Stealing*) is meaningful only for teams, not individuals. We eliminate steals from the formula in those years in which caught-stealing figures are not available, but the surviving data for the early years indicate that few of the men with high base-stealing totals exceeded the break-even point of 66.7 percent by a margin large enough to produce even one additional Batting Win. A further condensation that we have used for our historical data, as indicated in the formula above, involves setting the value of a single at .47 runs and each extra base at .31, making a double .78, a triple 1.09, and a homer 1.40. (This tends to even out the fluctuations in run values for base hits and extra bases over time: a double, for example, was in fact worth .82 runs from 1901–1920, .80 runs from 1941–1960, and .77 runs from 1961–1977.) Subtract the hits from the total bases and multiply the resulting extra bases by .31 and the hits by .47. This may introduce small variations from a more rigorous formula that includes differing run values for the differing periods or even for single years (generally amounting to a fraction of a run), but the calculation is much snappier for those without a computer.

The Batting Runs formula may be long, even in its condensed form, but it calls for only addition, subtraction, and multiplication and thus is as simple as Slugging Average, whose incorrect weights (1, 2, 3, and 4) it revises and expands upon. Each event has a value and frequency, just as in Slugging Average, yet in Batting Runs outs are treated as offensive events with a run value of their own (albeit a negative one). Just as the run potential for a team in a given half-inning is boosted by a man reaching base, it is diminished by a man being retired; not only has he failed to brighten the situation on the bases but he has deprived his team of the services of a man further down the order who might have come up in this half-inning, either with men on base and/or with scores already in.

The Batting Runs stat treats every offensive event in terms of its impact upon the team—an *average* team, so that a man does not benefit in his individual record for having the good fortune to bat cleanup with the Rockies or suffer for batting cleanup with the White Sox. The relationship of individual performance to team play is stated poorly or not at all in conventional baseball statistics. In Batting Runs it is crystal clear.

Recognizing that some readers will wish to keep track of batting performance by compiling Batting Runs themselves over the course of a season and that they may be frustrated by the difficulty of separating out pitcher batting or of calculating the (At Bats − Hits) factor for the league, we advise that using the fixed value of − .25 for outs will tend to work quite well if you wish to include pitcher batting performance, and a fixed value of − .27 will serve if you wish to exclude it. Actually, any fixed value will suffice in midseason; it's only when all the numbers are in and you care to compare this year's results with last year's (or, e.g., with those of the 1927 Yankees) that more precision is desirable. At that point the value of the out may be calculated by the more ambitious among you, but, ideally, the sporting press will provide accurate Batting Runs figures. (Who calculates ERA for himself?) Batting Runs are abbreviated as BR.

Batting Wins Adjusted Batting Runs divided by the number of runs required to create an additional win beyond average (see *Runs Per Win*). That average is defined as a team record of .500 because a league won-lost average must be .500, or as an individual record of zero because the value of the out for a given year is calculated to establish a baseline of zero. Abbreviated as BW.

Calculated Stat One or more counting stats (see below) subjected to a mathematical process such as averaging.

Chances Accepted Putouts and assists, minus errors.

Clutch Hitting Index Calculated for individuals, actual RBIs over expected RBIs, adjusted for league average and slot in batting order; 100 is a league-average performance. The spot in the batting order is figured as

$$5 - (9 \times BFPGP - BFPGT)$$

where BFPGP is the batters facing pitcher per game for the player, or plate appearances divided by games, and BFPGT is the batters facing pitcher per game of the entire team.

Expected RBIs are calculated as

$$(.25 \text{ singles} + .50 \text{ doubles} + .75 \text{ triples} + 1.75 \text{ homers}) \times$$
$$LGAV \times EXPSL$$

where LGAV (league average) = league RBIs divided by (.25 singles + .50 doubles + .75 triples + 1.75 homers), and EXPSL (expected RBI by slot number) = .88 for the leadoff batter, and for the remaining slots, descending to ninth, .90, .98, 1.08, 1.08, 1.04, 1.04, 1.04, and 1.02.

Calculated for teams, Clutch Hitting Index is actual runs scored over Batting Runs. Abbreviated as CHI.

Clutch Pitching Index Expected runs allowed over actual runs allowed, with 100 being a league-average performance. Expected runs are figured on the basis of the pitcher's opposing at bats, hits, walks, and hit batsmen (doubles and triples estimated at league average). Abbreviated as CPI.

Counting Stat A raw figure that tells how many of an item have been accumulated, as opposed to a calculated or derived figure such as an average.

Differential The difference between a team's actual won-lost record and that predicted by the total of its Pitching Wins, Batting Wins, Fielding Wins, and Stolen Base Wins; this measure indicates the extent to which a team outperformed or underperformed its talent. Abbreviated as DIF.

Earned Run Average Calculated as earned runs times nine, divided by innings pitched. For a few years after being introduced as an official stat in the National League in 1912 and the American League in 1913, runs aided by stolen bases were not counted as earned (see Chronology of Scoring Rules in Appendix 1, Rules and Scoring). For years before 1912, ERA has been constructed from raw data, but for some teams in some seasons, earned runs cannot be identified with perfect certainty. For those teams, we use the estimating procedure created by Information Concepts, Inc., of assigning to those runs whose earned/unearned status is unknown the percentage of earned runs to runs that characterize the team's known runs. In *Total Baseball*, we have created an Adjusted ERA by normalizing to the league average—which is done by dividing the league average ERA by the individual ERA—and then factoring in home park.

Expected Wins Calculated for the team based on its actual runs scored and allowed, not its predicted runs scored and allowed. A team that allows exactly as many runs as it scores is predicted to play .500 ball. The equation for expected wins is:

$$\frac{(\text{Runs Scored} - \text{Runs Allowed})}{\text{Runs Per Win}} + \frac{(\text{Wins} + \text{Losses})}{2}$$

Abbreviated as W– EXP.

Fielding Average Defined as putouts and assists divided by the total of putouts, assists, and errors. The weakness of this stat is that it values a player with minimal range but good hands over another player who may accept many more chances but mishandle a few of these. Abbreviated as FA. See *Range Factor, Total Chances*.

Fielding Runs The Linear Weights measure of runs saved *beyond* what a league-average player at that position might have saved, defined as zero; this stat is calculated to take account of the particular demands of the different positions.

For second basemen, shortstops, and third basemen, the formula begins by calculating the league average for the position:

$$\text{AVG}\begin{array}{l}\text{pos.}\\\text{lg.}\end{array} = \left(\frac{.20\,(\text{PO} + 2\text{A} - \text{E} + \text{DP})\text{ league at position}}{\text{PO league total} - \text{K league total}}\right)$$

where A = assists, PO = putouts, E = errors, DP = double plays, and K = strikeouts. Then we estimate the number of innings for each player at each position based upon each player's entire fielding record and his number of plate appearances. So, if the team played 1,500 innings and one player was calculated to have played 1,000 of those innings at a given position, his Fielding Runs (FR) would be calculated as:

$$\text{FR} = .20\,(\text{PO} + 2\text{A} - \text{E} + \text{DP})\text{ player} - \text{avg. pos. lg.} \times \left(\frac{\text{PO}}{\text{team}} - \frac{\text{K}}{\text{team}}\right)\frac{\text{innings, player}}{\text{innings, team}}$$

Assists are doubly weighted because more fielding skill is generally required to get one than to record a putout.

For catchers, the above formula is modified by removing strikeouts from their formulas and subtracting not only errors but also passed balls divided by two. Also incorporated in the catcher's Fielding Runs is one tenth of the adjusted Pitching Runs for the team, times the percentage of games behind the plate by that catcher.

For pitchers, the above formula is modified to subtract individual pitcher strikeouts from the total number of potential outs (otherwise, exceptional strikeout pitchers like Nolan Ryan or Bob Feller would see their Fielding Runs artificially depressed). Also, pitchers' chances are weighted less than infielders' assists because a pitcher's style may produce fewer ground balls. Thus the formula for pitchers is .10(PO + 2A − E + DP), whereas for second basemen, shortstops, and third basemen it is .20(PO + 2A − E + DP).

For first basemen, because putouts and double plays require so little skill in all but the odd case, these plays are eliminated, leaving only .20(2A − E) in the numerator.

For outfielders, the formula becomes .20(PO + 4A − E + 2DP). The weighting for assists is boosted here because a good outfielder can prevent runs through the threat of assists that are never made; for them, unlike infielders, the assist is essentially an elective play, like the stolen base. Outfielders' Fielding Runs were subject to some degree of error because outfielders sometimes switch fields within a game or season (Babe Ruth, for example, was positioned in the field that required the lesser range—right field in Yankee Stadium, left field in most road parks). Also, short distances to left or right field walls in some parks tend to depress putout totals.

Since the third edition of *Total Baseball,* however, we have researched and obtained breakouts of all outfielders' games in left, center, and right fields. Center fielders now have higher ratings than they did in the first and second editions. Abbreviated as FR.

Fielding Wins Fielding Runs divided by the number of runs required to create an additional win beyond average. That average is defined as a team record of .500 because a league won-lost average must be .500. Abbreviated as FW. See *Runs Per Win*.

Games Behind Figured by adding the difference in wins between a trailing team and the leader to the difference in losses, and dividing by two. Thus a team that is three games behind may trail by three in the win column and three in the loss column, or four and two, or any other combination of wins and losses totaling six. Abbreviated as GB.

Game-Winning Run Batted In Credited to the batter

who drives in a run that gives his club a lead that it never relinquishes, no matter when that run is driven in nor what the final score is. Introduced in 1980 as an official stat and later disowned, the GWRBI is not recorded in this volume.

Grounded into Double Play Kept officially since 1993 in the NL and 1939 in the AL (though the NL data of 1933-1938 made no distinction between lined-into double plays and grounded-into double plays, and the AL data of 1939 was not published). This stat tends to be overvalued by the general public as an indicator of rally-killing ineptitude. Instead, it is largely a function of high totals of at bats, which tend to be accumulated by the game's best players, not its worst. Abbreviated as GIDP.

Hands Out The original 1840s scoring term for batters producing outs either at the plate or on the bases. On a force out, the runner retired on the bases would be charged with a hand out, not the batter. Also called Hands Lost, and abbreviated as HO or HL.

Hit by Pitch A batter struck by a pitched ball was not awarded first base until 1884 in the American Association and 1887 in the National League. Reconstruction of stats for batters and pitchers in the years 1897-1908 has been accomplished. Abbreviated as HBP.

Hits Bases on balls originally counted as hits in 1887, but are recorded in this volume as neither hits nor at bats.

Home Run Factor A measure of the home runs hit in a given ballpark, with 100 representing the average home park and the highest figure above that representing the best home-run park. Computed in the same manner as Home Run Batter Rating (see above). Abbreviated as HRF.

Home Run Percentage Home runs per 100 at bats.

Home Run Pitcher Rating A measure of a team's ability to prevent home runs, taking into account the Home Run Factor (see above) of the park and the team's not having to face its own batters. The average mark is represented as 100, and the lowest figure beneath that indicates the best.

Home Runs When is a home run not a home run? Before 1920, not if it came with men on base in the ultimate inning and created a margin of victory greater than one run. A ruling of the Special Baseball Records Committee in 1969 reversed its earlier decision that had made home runs of 37 disputed final-inning, game-winning base hits. In accordance with the practice of the day, such a hit, even if it sailed out of the park, would be credited with only as many bases as necessary to plate the winning run. Thus Babe Ruth's "715th home run," hit on July 8, 1918, to win a game against Cleveland, remained a triple, and Jimmy Collins and Sherry Magee were each deprived of two home runs.

Innings Pitched Official baseball practice was, until 1982, to round off fractional innings for individuals to the next highest inning. Since then fractional innings have been kept for individuals and teams. In this volume fractional innings are supplied for all individuals and all teams in all years. Those men who took a turn on the mound but failed to retire a batter are credited with no innings pitched and, if they allowed a runner or runners to score, an ERA of infinity.

Intentional Bases on Balls Recorded only since 1955.

Isolated Power Total bases minus hits, divided by at bats; in other words, Slugging Average minus Batting

Average. Appears to have been created by Allan Roth and Branch Rickey in the 1950s.

League-Average Replacement Player That model player who performs at precisely the league average, creating a baseline against which to measure others.

League Performance: Because the caliber of play in the Union Association of 1884 and the Federal League of 1914-1915 was substantially below that of its rivals in those years, we have made an upward adjustment to overall league performance, thus lowering individual ratings or computed stats, while leaving unaffected the raw statistics of Organized Baseball. League at bats were reduced to 80 percent for the UA and 90 percent for the FL.

We tested all players who appeared in at least 30 games for the UA in 1884 and 30 or more games in the NL or AA in the 1883-1885 period. There were 31 players who played 2,182 games in the UA and had a Total Player Rating 2.6 wins higher per 112 games in the UA. There were 17 pitchers who pitched 3,678 innings in the UA with at least 30 innings in the UA and 30 innings in other leagues in the 1883-1985 period). These pitchers had a Total Pitcher Index 0.8 wins higher in the UA per 112 innings.

For the Federal League, there were 54 players with 30 games in the FL and at least 30 games in other leagues in the 1913-1916 period. These players had 10,401 games in the FL and had a Total Player Rating 1.26 wins higher per 154 games. For pitchers, there were 39 with 30 or more innings in the FL and 30 innings in other leagues in the 1913-1916 period). These pitchers had 13,872 innings and a Total Pitcher Index .49 wins higher in the FL per 154 innings.

Actually, the calculations for the UA produced a .76 multiplier for on base percentage and slugging, which we have rounded to .80. The calculations for the FL produced a .90 multiplier for on base percentage and slugging, which we have incorporated. UA pitchers had an .875 multiplier for earned run average, which we have expressed as .80 for consistency with the batting figure. Federal League pitchers had a multiplier of .924, which we have rounded to .90.

Linear Weights A system created by Pete Palmer to measure all the events on a ballfield in terms of runs. At the root of this system, as with other sabermetric figures such as Runs Created, is the knowledge that wins and losses are what the game of baseball is about, that wins and losses are proportional in some way to runs scored and runs allowed, and that runs in turn are proportional to the events that go into their making.

Normalizing Restating a figure as a ratio by comparing it to the league average, or norm.

On-Base Percentage Created by Roth and Rickey in its current form—hits plus walks plus hit by pitch, divided by at bats plus walks plus hit by pitch—in the early 1950s, although there were nineteenth-century forebears such as "Reached First Base." When OBP, as it is abbreviated, was adopted as an official stat in 1984, the denominator was expanded to include sacrifice flies. The effect is to penalize a batter in his on base percentage by giving him a plate appearance while at the same time crediting him in his batting average by deleting the plate appearance. In this book we calculate OBP without considering sacrifice flies, which in any event are calculable on a continuing basis only since 1954.

On-Base plus Slugging See *Production*.

Opponents' Batting Average Hits allowed divided by at bats allowed (or, if at bats allowed is unknown, then at bats equals hits plus inning times "K," where "K" is the league average of at bats minus hits, all over innings). Abbreviated as OAV.

Opponents' On-Base Percentage For years before 1908 in the American League and 1903 in the National League, the number of batters facing a pitcher has been constructed from the available raw data. We have subtracted league base hits from league at bats, divided by league innings pitched, multiplied by the pitcher's innings, and added his hits and walks allowed and hit by pitch and sacrifices, if available. Abbreviated as OOB.

Outs Until 1883, included catching a ball on one bounce in foul ground. Not credited after three strikes in 1887, when the rule was "four strikes and yer out"—as it was, in fact, from 1871–1881, when batters commonly received "warning pitches" rather than called strikes.

Outs Per Game The 1860s successor to Hands Out (see above), it joined with Runs Per Game to form the batting record before the rise of professional league play.

Park Factor Calculated separately for batters and pitchers. Above 100 signifies a park favorable to hitters; below 100 signifies a park favorable to pitchers. The computation of PF is admittedly daunting, and what follows is probably of interest to the merest handful of readers, but we feel obliged to state the mathematical underpinnings for those few who may care. We use a three-year average Park Factor for players and teams unless they change home parks. Then a two-year average is used, unless the park existed for only one year. Then a one-year mark is used. If a team started up in Year 1, played two years in the first park, one in the next, and three in the park after that and then stopped play, the average would be as follows (where F*n* is the one-year park factor for year *n*):

Year 1 and 2 = (F1 + F2)/2	Year 4 = (F4 + F5)/2
Year 3	= F3	Year 5 = (F4 + F5 + F6)/3
	Year 6 = (F5 + F6)/2

Step 1. Find games, losses, and runs scored and allowed for each team at home and on the road. Take runs per game scored and allowed at home over runs per game scored and allowed on the road. This is the initial figure, but we must make two corrections to it.

Step 2. The first correction is for innings pitched at home and on the road. This is a bit complicated, so the mathematically faint of heart may want to head back at this point. First, find the team's home winning percentage (wins at home over games at home). Do the same for road games. Calculate the Innings Pitched Corrector (IPC) shown below. If it is greater than 1, this means the innings pitched on the road are higher because the other team is batting more often in the last of the ninth. This rating is divided by the Innings Pitched Corrector, like so:

$$IPC = \frac{(18.5 - \text{Wins at home} / \text{Games at home})}{(18.5 - \text{Losses on road} / \text{Games on road})}$$

Note: 18.5 is the average number of half-innings per game if the home team always bats in the ninth.

Step 3. Make corrections for the fact that the other road parks' total difference from the league average is offset by the park rating of the club that is being rated. Multiply

rating by this Other Parks Corrector (OPC):

$$OPC = \frac{\text{No. of teams}}{\text{No. of teams} - 1 + \text{Run Factor, team}}$$

(Note that this OPC differs from that presented earlier in *The Hidden Game of Baseball*, for in preparing the pre-1900 data for *Total Baseball*, we discovered that for some parks with extreme characteristics, like Chicago's Lake Front Park of 1884, which had a Home Run Factor of nearly 5, the earlier formula produced wrong results. For parks with factors of 1.5 or less, either formula works well.)

Example. In 1982, Atlanta scored 388 runs and allowed 387 runs at home in 81 games, and scored 351 and allowed 315 on the road in 81 games. The initial factor is (775/81) ÷ (666/81) = 1.164. The Braves' home record was 42–39, or .519, and their road record was 47–34, or .580. Thus the IPC = (18.5 − .519) ÷ (18.5 − .420) = .995. The team rating is now 1.164/.995 = 1.170. The OPC = (12) ÷ (12 − 1 + 1.170) = .986. The final runs-allowed rating is 1.170 × .986, or 1.154.

We warned you it wouldn't be easy!

The batter adjustment factor is composed of two parts, one the park factor and the other the fact that a batter does not have to face his own team's pitchers. The initial correction takes care of only the second factor. Start with the following (SF = Scoring Factor, previously determined [for Atlanta, 1.154], and SF1 = Scoring Factor of the other clubs [NT = number of teams]):

$$1 - \frac{SF - 1}{NT - 1}$$

Next is an iterative process in which the initial team pitching rating is assumed to be 1, and the following factors are employed:

RHT, RAT = Runs per game scored at home (H) and away (A),
	by team
OHT, OAT = Runs per game allowed at home, away, by team
	RAL = Runs per game by both teams

Now, with the Team Pitching Rating (TPR) = 1, we proceed to calculate Team Batting Rating (TBR):

$$TBR = \left(\frac{RAT}{SF1} + \frac{RHT}{SF}\right)\left(1 + \frac{TPR - 1}{NT - 1}\right)\bigg/ RAL$$

$$TPR = \left(\frac{OAT}{SF1} + \frac{OHT}{SF}\right)\left(1 + \frac{TBR - 1}{NT - 1}\right)\bigg/ RAL$$

The last two steps are repeated three more times. The final Batting Corrector, or Batters' Park Factor (BPF) is

$$BPF = \frac{(SF + SF1)}{\left(2 \times \left[1 + \frac{TPR - 1}{NT - 1}\right]\right)}$$

Similarly, the final Pitching Corrector, or Pitchers' Park Factor (PPF) is

$$PPF = \frac{(SF + SF1)}{\left(2 \times \left[1 + \frac{TBR - 1}{NT - 1}\right]\right)}$$

Now an example, using the 1982 Atlanta Braves once again.

$$RHT - \frac{388}{81} - 4.79 \qquad RAT - \frac{351}{81} - 4.33$$

$$OHT = \frac{387}{81} = 4.78 \qquad OAT = \frac{315}{81} = 3.89$$

$$RAL = \frac{7947}{972} = 8.18 \qquad NT = 12$$

$$SF = 1.154 \qquad SF1 = 1 - \left(\frac{1.154 - 1}{11}\right) = .986$$

$$TBR = \left(\frac{4.33}{.986} + \frac{4.79}{1.154}\right)\left(1 + \frac{1-1}{11}\right) \Big/ 8.18 = 1.044$$

$$TPR = \left(\frac{3.89}{.986} + \frac{4.78}{1.154}\right)\left(1 + \frac{1.044 - 1}{11}\right) \Big/ 8.18 = .993$$

Repeating these steps gives a TBR of 1.04 and a TPR of .97. The Batters' Park Factor is

$$BPF = \frac{(1.170 + .986)}{\left(2 \times \left[1 + \frac{.99 - 1}{11}\right]\right)} = 1.07$$

This is not a great deal removed from taking the original ratio,

$$\frac{1.170 + 1}{2}, \text{ which is } 1.08.$$

The Pitchers' Park Factor may be calculated in analogous fashion.

To apply the Batters' Park Factor to Batting Runs, one must use this formula:

$$\frac{BR}{corr.} = \frac{BR}{uncorr.} \Big/ \frac{\frac{Runs\,(league)}{AB + BB + HBP} - \frac{Runs\,(league)}{AB + BB + HBP} \times (BPF - 1) \times \frac{AB + BB + HBP}{(player\,or\,team)}}{(league)}$$

For example, if a player produces 20 runs above average in 700 plate appearances with a Batters' Park Factor of 1.10, and the league average of runs produced per plate appearance is .11, this means that the player's uncorrected Batting Runs is 20 over the zero point of $700 \times .11$ (77 runs). In other words, 77 runs is the average run contribution expected of this batter were he playing in an average home park. But because his Batters' Park Factor is 1.10, which means his home park was 10 percent kinder to hitters (than the average), you would really expect an average run production of 1.1×77, or 85 runs. Thus the player whose uncorrected Batting Runs is 97 with a BF of 1.1 is only +10 runs rather than +20, and 10 is his Park Adjusted Batting Runs (in the Player Register, BR/A):

$$10 = 20/1.10 - .11 \times (1.10 - 1) \times 700.$$

Percentage of Team Wins A simple but deceiving measure of a good pitcher's contribution to a bad club; in this, it shares the virtues and flaws of Ted Oliver's Weighted Rating System and, to a lesser degree, our own Wins Above Team (both of which see). Steve Carlton had the highest single-season rating in this century when, in 1972, he went 27–10 for a Phillie club that won only 59 games. Yet his mark of 45.8 percent of his team's wins would not make the top 100 list of seasons since 1876, making this stat nearly useless for historical analysis.

Pitcher Defense Abbreviated as PD. See *Fielding Runs*.

Pitchers' Park Factor The same as the Park Factor shown in the pitchers' section of the team statistics portion of the Annual Record and in the Pitcher Register; above 100 means a pitcher was hurt by playing half his games in a good hitting park. See *Park Factor*.

Pitcher Strikeouts Made tougher or easier by cyclically varying rules and conditions. For instance, foul tips did not count as strikes for many years, even when deliberate, as with bunts; fouls caught on a bounce were outs until 1883; the ball-strike count underwent much experimentation until settling at four balls and three strikes in 1889; not to mention the high-low strike zone, warning pitches, varying pitching distances, and restricted deliveries. It helps to know some history before rattling off stats to prove this or that, but normalizing a stat to its league helps, even with counting stats such as strikeouts.

Pitching Runs The Linear Weights measure of runs saved *beyond* what a league-average pitcher or team might have saved, defined as zero. The math is simple: *Pitching Runs = Innings Pitched × (League ERA/9) – Earned Runs Allowed*. An alternate version is: *Innings Pitched/9 × (League ERA – Individual ERA)*. Abbreviated as PR.

Pitching Wins Park Adjusted Pitching Runs divided by the number of runs required to create an additional win beyond average. That average is defined as a team record of .500 because a league won-lost average must be .500. Abbreviated as PW. See *Pitching Runs*, above, and *Runs Per Win*.

Player Win Averages The title of a 1970 book issued by the Mills brothers, Harlan and Eldon, as well as the name of their overall method of determining not only the *what* of baseball statistics but also the *when*, or clutch element. Computerizing complete play-by-play data for a full season for their book, they assigned "Win Points"— reflective of that event's potential impact on the team's prospects of victory—to *every* event on a baseball field.

Positional Adjustment A key factor in the Total Player Rating that addresses the relative worth to a ball club of the defensive positions. A man who bats .270, hits 25 homers, and drives in 80 runs may be an average performer in left field, no matter how good his glove; but credit those batting stats to a shortstop or second baseman and you have a star, because the defensive demands of the position are so much greater. To balance the abundance of good-hitting outfielders or first basemen against the scarcity of such players at catcher or shortstop, we created a positional adjustment expressed in terms of the average batting skill needed to hold down a major league spot at that position.

To determine the average defensive skill required of a position, simply subtract the average batting skill at that position from his Total Player Rating. This may seem strange at first glance, but it does put, for example, shortstops, first basemen, and left fielders on the same footing. The explanation that follows represents a change from previous editions, in which players were measured against only those who played their position in their league in that year. We have now redefined the positional adjustment as an average over *both* leagues for a three-year period centered on the measured year. This raised the ratings for Lou Gehrig and Jimmie Foxx by a win or two, as they are now

compared with sixteen first basemen over three years (a total of 48) rather than just eight. In the 1950–1970 period, AL outfielders averaged a few more Batting Runs per season than their counterparts in the NL. When both leagues were counted, NL players dropped a few Wins and AL players gained. Hank Aaron lost 4 Wins for this reason.

In the years since 1977 the positional adjustment for, say a National League first baseman, will be in the context of the batting records of not merely 12 men, but 26—times three, or seventy-eight—obviously, a much broader base of comparison. For each edition, the concluding season's positional adjustments are based on the average of that year and the preceding season.

Let's say that last year all major league left fielders accounted for 198 batting runs. The positional adjustment, or factor for average defensive skill, for a left fielder who played in all 162 games would be 162 × 198/3,202 (which calculates to 10), where 3,202 is the number of games played in both leagues by all left fielders (or any other position, obviously). Thus a left fielder who played in all his team's games would have 10 runs subtracted from the sum of his Batting Runs, Stolen Base Runs, and Fielding Runs. If all major league shortstops last year accounted for 158 Batting Runs below average, the adjustment for a shortstop would be figured in the same way, multiplying his games played by − 158/3,202, or − 8 runs, meaning that 8 runs (minus a minus 8) would be *added* to his Total Player Rating.

Production On-Base Percentage plus Slugging Average: a simple but elegant measure of batting prowess, in that the weaknesses of one-half of the formulation, On-Base Percentage, are countered by the strengths of the other, Slugging Average, and vice versa. When PRO, as it is abbreviated, is adjusted for home park and normalized to league average to become PRO+, the calculation is modified slightly to create a baseline of 100 for a league-average performance. For PRO+, the calculation is

$$\frac{\text{Player On Base Pct.}}{\text{League On Base Pct.}} + \frac{\text{Player Slugging Avg.}}{\text{League Slugging Avg.}} - 1$$

This produces a figure with a decimal point—an above-average figure, like 1.46, or a below-average figure, like 0.82. For ease of display, in this book we drop the decimal and express these as 146 and 82.

Putout Average Putouts divided by games played; a stat created by Philadelphia baseball writer Al Wright in 1875.

Quality Start A game started in which a pitcher lasts for six innings or more and allows three runs or less.

Ratio Hits plus walks plus hit batsmen allowed per nine innings. Abbreviated as RAT.

RBI Opportunities An official American League stat for the first three weeks of 1918, until the league saw how much work it involved and scrapped it. Still a good idea, sort of, and the folks at the Elias Sports Bureau have tracked this type of "situational stat" since 1975.

Reached First Base A precursor of the On Base Percentage, this stat was introduced as an official National League measure in 1879, its one and only year of existence. It included times reached via hits, walks, and errors, but not hit by pitch because putting their bodies on the line did not yet, in 1879, send batters to first base. Trivia: the league leader in this stat's lone year of life was

Providence outfielder Paul Hines, with 193.

Relative Batting Average Pioneered by David Shoebotham in a *Baseball Research Journal* article in 1976, this was the first traditional stat normalized to league average so as to permit cross-era comparison. Most folks who have employed this measure simply divide individual batting average by league batting average. Shoebotham's original computation was more precise:

$$\text{RBA} = \frac{\text{player's hits}}{\text{player's AB}} \Big/ \frac{\text{league hits} - \text{player's hits}}{\text{league AB} - \text{player's AB}}$$

In this manner a player's own performance would not be compared with itself.

Relief Points Relief wins plus saves minus losses was the original formula used as the basis for the Rolaids Company's annual award to the top reliever in each league. Recently the formula has been changed to include a debit for blown saves.

Relief Ranking Takes *Relief Runs* (which see), adjusts them for home park, then weights them by a factor (F in the formula below) reflecting the greater value of the innings pitched by a bullpen "closer." Relief Runs, which weights all innings identically, will tend to benefit long and middle relievers who are effective over many innings, while Relief Ranking—which was initially designed for those men who pitch less than three innings per game over a season or career—will tend to benefit relievers who may have fewer innings but who have more saves and decisions. The formula is

$$(\text{Relief Runs}) \times F \text{ where the Factor} = \frac{9 \times (\text{Wins} + \text{Losses} + \text{K* [Saves]})}{\text{IP}}$$

*K = either .25 or 1 over 10 times fraction of league wins that are saved, whichever is smaller.

The multiplier, or Factor, is usually around 1, but can get up to 1.5 or even 2 for some relievers, and can get down as low as 0.8 for some starters who have a lot of no-decision games.

Relief Runs Identical to Pitching Runs but confined to relief pitchers, defined as those who average less than three innings per appearance. Abbreviated as RR. See *Relief Ranking*.

Run Batted In Though widely regarded as a good measure of a batter's overall productivity and value to his team, the RBI is extremely situation-dependent, denying equal access to opportunity on the basis of a player's team, slot in the batting order, and particularly the men surrounding him in the batting order.

Run Factor A measure of the run scoring in a given ballpark compared to other ballparks, with 100 representing the average home park and the highest figure above that representing the best hitters' park. Abbreviated as RF, it is computed on the basis of comparing runs scored and allowed per inning at home and on the road. Innings are estimated from the number of games and games won, allowing for the home team not batting in the final inning of a game in which it leads. The resulting Run Factor is then compared to the league average.

Run Rating for Batters A measure of a team's run-scoring ability, taking into account the park's *Run Factor* (see above) and the team's batters not having to face its own pitchers, with 100 representing the average and the highest figure above that representing the best. Run Bat-

ting for Batters is abbreviated as RB.

Run Rating for Pitchers A measure of a team's run-prevention ability, taking into account the *Run Factor* (see above) and the team's pitchers not having to face its own batters, with 100 representing the average and the lowest figure beneath that representing the best. Abbreviated as RP.

Runs Created Bill James's formulation for run contribution from a variety of batting and baserunning events. Many different formulas are used, depending upon data available. In its basic expression, the formula is:

$$\frac{(\text{Hits} + \text{Walks})\ (\text{Total Bases})}{\text{At Bats} + \text{Walks}}$$

The essence of this formulation is that the ability to get on base and the ability to push baserunners around fairly describes offensive ability. James later refined the formula with a "stolen base version":

$$\frac{(\text{Hits} + \text{Walks} - \text{Caught Stealing})\ (\text{Total Bases} + .55 \times \text{Stolen Bases})}{\text{At Bats} + \text{Walks}}$$

Next came the "technical version": a longer formulation, presented below using the standard abbreviations for the various offensive events (the two elements multiplied in the numerator are referred to below as "A" and "B," and the denominator is referred to as "C"):

$$\frac{(H + BB + HBP - CS - GIDP)\ (TB + .26[BB - IBB + HBP] + .52[SH + SF + SB])}{AB + BB + HBP + SH + SF}$$

From this technical version (Tech-1), James spun off 13 additional technical versions. "The reason that we have to do this," he wrote in *The Bill James Historical Baseball Abstract*, "is that the data set changes and evolves rapidly throughout the century, or at least up until about 1955, when the progress of evolution in statistical information came to a temporary halt (it stopped moving forward until Bill James and Pete Palmer came around, about twenty years later). In 1900 we have no data for how many times a player grounded into a double play, how many times he was hit by a pitch, how many of his walks might have been intentional, how many times he was caught stealing, or how many sacrifice flies he hit." Accordingly, James adjusted his Runs Created formula to fit the available data; some versions, such as Tech-3, cover as much as a decade in a given league, while others, such as Tech-4, are in force for only a single league season. In *Total Baseball*, we have computed Runs Created values for all players since 1876 using the version most applicable to the period, with the single exception of Tech-9, which James applied only to the American League of 1916 but which we use for 1914–1916 in the AL and 1915–1916 in the NL because we have discovered additional caught-stealing data. (For those players whose careers began before 1900, James used the Tech-11 formula "to estimate how many runs they had created," but appended a note saying that "these estimates were of indeterminate accuracy.")

Here are the formulas for Runs Created (RC) technical versions 2–14 (Tech-1 was used for both the American

and National leagues in 1955–1988):

Tech-2 (1954)
Factors A and C of Tech-1 remain the same, while Part B simply drops Intentional Bases on Balls.

Tech-3 (AL 1940–1953; NL 1951–1953)
Factor A remains the same, while SF is dropped from Factor C; Factor B changes to: 1.025 TB + .26(BB + HBP) + .52(SH + SB).

Tech-4 (AL 1939)
Factors A and C remain the same, while B becomes: TB + .26(BB + HBP) + .52(SH + SB).

Tech-5 (AL 1931–1938)
Factors B and C remain the same, while A becomes: .96(H + BB + HBP − CS).

Tech-6 (AL 1920–1930; NL 1920–1925)
Factors A and C remain the same, while B changes only in the value placed on the sacrifice hit and stolen base, which declines from .52 to .51.

Tech-7 (NL 1926–1930)
C remains the same, while A changes to: .93(H + BB + HBP), and B becomes: TB + .26(BB + HBP) + .46(SH).

Tech-8 (AL 1913, 1917–1919; NL 1913–1914, 1917–1919)
C remains the same, while A becomes: H + W + HBP − .02(AB), and B becomes: TB + .85(SH + SB).

Tech-9 (AL 1914–1916; NL 1915–1916)
B and C are the same, while A becomes: H + BB + HBP − CS.

Tech-10 (AL, NL 1908–1912)
A and C remain the same, while B becomes: 1.025(TB + SB) + .75(SH).

Tech-11 (AL, NL 1900–1907)
B and C remain the same, while A becomes: H + BB + HBP.

Tech-12 (NL 1939–1950)
A Factor: H + BB + HBP − GIDP
B Factor: TB + .26(BB +HBP) + .52(SH)

Tech-13 (NL 1933–1938)
A and C remain the same as above, while B becomes: 1.025(TB) + .26(BB + HBP) + .52(SH)

Tech-14 (NL 1931–1932)
B and C remain the same, but A becomes: .95(H + BB + HBP).

Runs Per Game With its mate *Outs Per Game* (which see), this was the precursor, in the 1860s, of the batting average; by the end of that decade it gave way to Hits Per Game.

Runs Per Win Branch Rickey and Allan Roth first stated the proportional nature of runs and wins in their 1954 article in *Life*. Since then the point has been expanded upon by George Lindsey, Pete Palmer, Bill James, and every sabermetrician worth his salt: the point being that just as runs scored and allowed are the key to victory in a given game, so are they the key to success over the course of a season and the predictors of won-lost record with a surprising degree of precision. In 1982, Palmer

wrote in *The National Pastime*, "My work showed that as a rough rule of thumb, each additional ten runs scored (or ten less runs allowed) produced one extra win. . . . However, breaking the teams into groups showed that high-scoring teams needed more runs to produce a win. This runs-per-win factor I determined to be ten times the square root of the average number of runs scored per inning by both teams. Thus in normal play, when 4.5 runs per game are scored by each club, each team scores .5 runs per inning—totaling one run, the square root of which is one, times ten."

For *Total Baseball*, we have improved the Runs Per Win figure used in calculating the overall win figures in the Total Player Rating and the Total Pitcher Index. Rather than using 10 times the square root of the average number of runs scored per inning by both teams, we use adjusted runs per inning based on what the player or pitcher rating is. A hitter will increase the figure by adding in his rating over the number of games played, while a pitcher will have his rating subtracted. Say the average number of runs scored per inning is 1, as in the model above; then Runs Per Win = 10. Take a pitcher who allows 45 runs less than average in 25 games. This lowers the runs per game by 1.8, or runs per inning by .2, so the new Runs Per Win figure is 10 times the square root of the average number of runs scored per inning by both teams, *minus the pitcher's rating*. So we take from the one run per inning the .2 run saved by the pitcher, giving a result of 0.8. Ten times the square root of 0.8 is 8.9, so the pitcher gets 45/8.9, or 5.1, wins instead of 4.5. A hitter with plus 45 runs in 150 games, or .3 runs per game, contributes .03 runs per inning. His Runs Per Win is now 10 times the square root of the average number of runs scored per inning *plus the batter's rating*. So we add to the 1 run per inning the .03 runs added by the batter, giving a result of 10.1. Ten times the square root of 10.1 gives the batter 4.4 wins. (This method makes makes more of a difference in pitching because the runs are contributed over fewer games. With the same run contribution—45 beyond average—the pitcher gains 0.7 wins over the batter. This is because when the total number of runs scored is lowered, the value of each run is greater).

Runs Produced Runs batted in plus runs scored minus home runs.

Sabermetrics Defined by Bill James, who coined the term in honor of the Society for American Baseball Research, as "the search for objective knowledge about baseball" and, earlier, as "the mathematical and statistical analysis of baseball records."

SABR Pronounced "saber," this is the acronym for the Society for American Baseball Research, the organization that has, since its founding by Bob Davids in 1971, steadily advanced the state of baseball knowledge.

Sacrifice Fly First recognized as an event in 1908 but indistinguishable in the official records from sacrifice hits until 1954. There has been much flip-flopping since 1930 on whether to credit the sacrifice flier with an at bat or an RBI or whether a fly ball that advances a runner to a base other than home plate also should exempt a man from an at bat.

Sacrifice Hits Invented in the 1860s, recorded since 1889; sacrificer charged with an at bat until 1894. Sabermetricians frown on the strategy because all the studies show that the trading of an out for a base advanced

is a losing strategy—lowering the run expectations of the team that attempts it—in all but the most unusual of cases . . . even if the sacrifice "succeeds."

Sacrifice Hits Allowed Computed officially in the National League since 1913 but not published until 1916, and kept in the American League since 1921 but not published until 1922; what it signified about anything is unclear.

Save Created by Jerome Holtzman of the *Chicago Sun-Times*, the save began to be reported by *The Sporting News* on a regular basis in 1960. The major leagues adopted the save in 1969, at which time it was credited to a reliever who finished a game that his team won. In 1973 the save was redefined so that a reliever had not only to finish the game but also to find the potential tying or winning run on base or at the plate, or, alternately, to pitch the final three innings of a victorious contest. In 1975 the rule was liberalized to include a reliever's appearance of one inning or more in which he protects a lead of three runs or less; or he enters the game with the tying or winning run on base, at bat, or on deck; or he pitches three innings to the game's conclusion. In this book, the 1969 definition is applied to all games before 1969; otherwise the rule in force at the time prevails. Abbreviated as SV.

Shutouts On an individual basis, credited only to pitchers of complete-game scoreless victories or ties; former practice was to credit combined shutouts to the starting pitcher if he had pitched most of the way. Abbreviated as SH.

Situational Statistics How does a batter perform with the bases loaded? At night? On artificial turf? With no one on base? After the seventh inning when his team is tied or trails? The specialty of Baseball Workshop, Stats, Inc., and the Elias Sports Bureau.

Slugging Average Total bases divided by at bats; combines nicely with On Base Percentage to create *Production* (which see). Abbreviated as SLG.

Starter Runs Identical to *Pitching Runs* (which see) but confined to starting pitchers, defined as those who average more than three innings per appearance. Abbreviated as SR.

Stolen Base Average Stolen bases divided by attempts; its computation is dependent upon the availability of caught-stealing numbers. Abbreviated as SBA.

Stolen Base Runs For teams, the Linear Weights measure of runs contributed *beyond* what a league-average basestealing team might have gained, defined as zero; for individuals, Stolen Base Runs are calculated on the basis of the 66.7 percent success rate that sabermetric studies have shown to be the break-even point for producing runs beyond the average. Availability dependent upon caught stealing data as with Stolen Base Average. The formula is simple: .30(Stolen Bases) − .60(Caught Stealing). A man who steals two bases in three attempts is merely spinning his wheels in terms of value to his team, and even a man who succeeds at an 80 percent clip will have to steal a lot of bases—about 65—to create just one win beyond average. Abbreviated as SBR.

Stolen Base Wins Stolen Base Runs divided by the number of runs required to create an additional win beyond average. Those runs are generally around around 10—historically in the range of 9–11. Abbreviated as SBW. See *Runs Per Win*.

Stolen Bases Recorded since 1886, but until 1898

steals are thought to have included a variety of daring baserunning exploits, such as going from first to third on a single or advancing an extra base on an out. Abbreviated as SB.

Strikeouts Varying rules concerning the strike zone, the foul strike, and the warning pitch—not to mention the fourth strike of 1887—all contribute to making the cross-era comparison of strikeout accomplishments a very sticky business. Abbreviated as SO.

Strikeout Percentage A batters' stat: fewest strikeouts per 100 at bats.

Total Average Tom Boswell's formulation for offensive contribution from a variety of batting and baserunning events; as with Runs Created, we have calculated Total Average to make use of the maximum available data in a given year. The concept of the numerator is bases gained, that of the denominator is outs made:

$$\frac{\text{(Total Bases + Steals + Walks + HBP} - \text{Caught Stealing)}}{\text{(At Bats} - \text{Hits + Caught Stealing + GIDP)}}$$

Abbreviated as TA. See *Base-Out Percentage.*

Total Baseball Ranking The "MVP" of statistics, this ranks pitchers and position players by their total wins contributed in all their endeavors, revealing the most valuable performers in a given year. Abbreviated as TBR, it is not a computed stat but a sorting of players and pitchers by, respectively, the sum of their Total Batter Rating and Total Pitcher Index.

Total Bases Average Henry Chadwick's measure that divided total bases by games played; a forerunner of the Slugging Average.

Total Bases Run A silly stat of one year's duration, 1880, this was sort of an RBI in reverse, from the runner's perspective. Also called "Bases Touched," it was nothing more than that and signified nothing about individual talent. Trivia: the National League's leader in 1880 was Abner Dalrymple, with 501 bases touched.

Total Chances Putouts plus assists plus errors; in other words, total chances offered, not total chances accepted.

Total Pitcher Index The sum of a pitcher's Pitching Runs—expressed as Ranking Runs, employing the same formula used to compute Relief Ranking Runs—Batting Runs (in the AL since 1973, zero), and Fielding Runs, all divided by the Runs Per Win factor for that year (generally around 10, historically in the 9–11 range); abbreviated as TPI. See *Runs Per Win, Relief Ranking.*

Total Player Rating The sum of a player's Adjusted Batting Runs, Fielding Runs, and Base Stealing Runs, minus his positional adjustment, all divided by the Runs Per Win factor for that year (generally around 10, historically in the 9–11 range). See *Runs Per Win.*

Triple Crown Long regarded as consisting of batting average, home runs, and RBIs, but was not always so. In the early years of this century, newspapers spoke of Ty Cobb shooting for the "triple crown" of batting average, runs, and hits.

Weighted Average The next step in statistical sophistication after first, counting and, next, averaging. Chadwick's Total Bases Average was probably the first weighted average, in that it assigned values of 1 to a single, 2 to a double, 3 to a triple, and 4 to a home run.

Weighted Rating System Ted Oliver's invention, promoted in a 1944 self-published booklet called *Kings of the Mound.* We have modified Oliver's pioneering effort to create *Wins Above Team* (see below), which entry presents a discussion of Oliver's effort.

Win Points See *Player Win Averages.*

Wins Above League A pitcher's won-lost record restated by adding his Pitching Wins above the league average to the record that a league-average pitcher would have had with his number of decisions. Example: Tom Seaver has a hard-luck season, going only 16–14 despite a 1.76 ERA and five Pitching Wins; applying the five wins to a league-average 15–15 mark in the same 30 decisions results in a WAL of 20-10.

Wins Above Team How many wins a pitcher garnered beyond those expected of an average pitcher for that team. As the editors of this volume, in their earlier *Hidden Game of Baseball,* modified Ted Oliver's *Weighted Rating System* (see above), they now improve this statistic thanks to Bill Deane's corrective for its tendency to overvalue the contributions of good pitchers on awful teams.

Oliver's Weighted Rating System for pitchers was motivated by the inadequacies of both the won-lost percentage and the ERA when it came to evaluating pitchers laboring for poor teams. The Oliver formula, ingenious if flawed, was: pitcher's won-lost percentage minus the team's won-lost percentage—after removing the pitcher's decisions from the team's record—then multiplying the difference by the pitcher's number of decisions. Here is an example of the Oliver method as applied to Bobby Castillo, who in 1982 pitched very well in going 13–11 for a very bad Minnesota club (60–102; without him, 47–91):

$$\left(\frac{13}{24} - \frac{47}{138}\right) \times 24$$

or

$$(.542 - .341) \times 24$$

or

$$.201 \times 24 = 4.824$$

The figure of 4.824 would have been represented by Ted Oliver as "4,824 points"; he did not seem to recognize that had he retained the decimal point, his rating would have been expressed directly in *wins.* Thus the number of wins Castillo accounted for in his 24 decisions that an average Minnesota pitcher would *not* have gained was 4.8.

Thanks to a key modification of our earlier formula for Wins Above Team, abbreviated as WAT, we now propose the following: calculate the pitcher's won-lost percentage and the team's winning percentage after his decisions have been set aside. If the pitcher's percentage is higher, then WAT is

$$\text{Pitcher decisions} \times \left(\frac{\text{Pitcher pct.} - \text{Team pct.}}{2 - 2 \times \text{Team pct.}}\right)$$

If the pitcher's percentage is lower, then WAT is

$$\text{Pitcher decisions} \times \left(\frac{\text{Pitcher pct.} - \text{Team pct.}}{2 \times \text{Team pct.}}\right)$$

Won-lost percentage Computed as wins over decisions.

Team and League Abbreviations

These are the 147 franchises, seven principal leagues and their abbreviations as used throughout this book.

NATIONAL ASSOCIATION, 1871–1875 (Shown as n or NA)

Abbrev.	First	Last	Team
ATH n	1871	1875	Philadelphia Athletics
ATL n	1872	1875	Brooklyn Atlantics
BAL n	1872	1874	Baltimore Lord Baltimores
BOS n	1871	1875	Boston Red Stockings
CEN n	1875	1875	Philadelphia Centennials
CHI n	1871	1871	Chicago White Stockings
CHI n	1874	1875	Chicago White Stockings
CLE n	1871	1872	Cleveland Forest City
ECK n	1872	1872	Brooklyn Eckfords
HAR n	1874	1875	Hartford Dark Blues
KEK n	1871	1871	Fort Wayne Kekiongas
MAN n	1872	1872	Middletown (Conn.) Mansfields
MUT n	1871	1875	New York Mutuals
NAT n	1872	1872	Washington, D.C., Nationals
NH n	1875	1875	New Haven Elm City
OLY n	1871	1872	Washington, D.C., Olympics
PHI n	1873	1875	Philadelphia White Stockings
RES n	1873	1873	Elizabeth (N.J.) Resolutes
ROK n	1871	1871	Rockford (Ill.) Forest City
RS n	1875	1875	St. Louis Red Stockings
STL n	1875	1875	St. Louis Brown Stockings
TRO n	1871	1872	Troy Haymakers
WAS n	1873	1873	Washington Washingtons
WAS n	1875	1875	Washington Washingtons
WES n	1875	1875	Keokuk (Iowa) Westerns

NATIONAL LEAGUE, 1876– (Shown as N or NL)

Abbrev.	First	Last	Team
ARI N	1998		Arizona
ATL N	1966		Atlanta
BAL N	1892	1899	Baltimore
BOS N	1876	1952	Boston (transferred to Milwaukee)
BRO N	1890	1957	Brooklyn (transferred to Los Angeles)
BUF N	1879	1885	Buffalo
CHI N	1876		Chicago
CIN N	1876	1880	Cincinnati
CIN N	1890		Cincinnati
CLE N	1879	1884	Cleveland
CLE N	1889	1899	Cleveland
COL N	1993		Colorado
DET N	1881	1888	Detroit
FLA N	1993		Florida
HAR N	1876	1877	Hartford (played in Brooklyn in 1877)
HOU N	1962		Houston
IND N	1878	1878	Indianapolis
IND N	1887	1889	Indianapolis
KC N	1886	1886	Kansas City
LA N	1958		Los Angeles
LOU N	1876	1877	Louisville
LOU N	1892	1899	Louisville
MIL N	1878	1878	Milwaukee
MIL N	1953	1965	Milwaukee (transferred to Atlanta)
MON N	1969		Montreal
NY N	1876	1876	New York (played in Brooklyn)
NY N	1883	1957	New York (transferred to San Francisco)
NY N	1962		New York
PHI N	1876	1876	Philadelphia
PHI N	1883		Philadelphia
PIT N	1887		Pittsburgh
PRO N	1878	1885	Providence
STL N	1876	1877	St. Louis
STL N	1885	1886	St. Louis
STL N	1892		St. Louis
SD N	1969		San Diego
SF N	1958		San Francisco
SYR N	1879	1879	Syracuse
TRO N	1879	1882	Troy (N.Y.)
WAS N	1886	1889	Washington, D.C.
WAS N	1892	1899	Washington, D.C.
WOR N	1880	1882	Worcester (Mass.)

AMERICAN ASSOCIATION, 1882-1891 (Shown as a or AA)

Abbrev.	First	Last	Team
BAL a	1882	1889	Baltimore
BAL a	1890	1890	Baltimore (combined with Brooklyn, shown as BB)
BAL a	1891	1891	Baltimore (transferred to National League)
BOS a	1891	1891	Boston
BRO a	1884	1889	Brooklyn (transferred to National League)
BRO a	1890	1890	Brooklyn (combined with Baltimore, shown as BB)
CIN a	1882	1889	Cincinnati (transferred to National League)
CIN a	1891	1891	Cincinnati
CLE a	1887	1888	Cleveland (transferred to National League)

Abbrev.	First	Last	Team
COL a	1883	1884	Columbus (Ohio)
COL a	1889	1891	Columbus (Ohio)
IND a	1884	1884	Indianapolis
KC a	1888	1889	Kansas City
LOU a	1882	1891	Louisville (transferred to National League)
MIL a	1891	1891	Milwaukee
NY a	1883	1887	New York
PHI a	1882	1891	Philadelphia
PIT a	1882	1886	Pittsburgh (transferred to National League)
RIC a	1884	1884	Richmond
ROC a	1890	1890	Rochester
STL a	1882	1891	St. Louis (transferred to National League)
SYR a	1890	1890	Syracuse
TOL a	1884	1884	Toledo
TOL a	1890	1890	Toledo
WAS a	1884	1884	Washington, D.C.
WAS a	1891	1891	Washington, D.C. (transferred to National League)

UNION ASSOCIATION, 1884 (Shown as U or UA)

Abbrev.	First	Last	Team
ALT U	1884	1884	Altoona (Pa.)
BAL U	1884	1884	Baltimore
BOS U	1884	1884	Boston
CHI U	1884	1884	Chicago (combined with Pittsburgh, shown as CP)
CIN U	1884	1884	Cincinnati
KC U	1884	1884	Kansas City
MIL U	1884	1884	Milwaukee
PHI U	1884	1884	Philadelphia
PIT U	1884	1884	Pittsburgh (combined with Chicago, shown as CP)
STL U	1884	1884	St. Louis
STP U	1884	1884	St. Paul (Minn.)
WAS U	1884	1884	Washington, D.C.
WIL U	1884	1884	Wilmington (Del.)

PLAYERS LEAGUE, 1890 (Shown as P or PL)

Abbrev.	First	Last	Team
BOS P	1890	1890	Boston
BRO P	1890	1890	Brooklyn
BUF P	1890	1890	Buffalo
CHI P	1890	1890	Chicago
CLE P	1890	1890	Cleveland
NY P	1890	1890	New York
PHI P	1890	1890	Philadelphia
PIT P	1890	1890	Pittsburgh

AMERICAN LEAGUE, 1901– (Shown as A or AL)

Abbrev.	First	Last	Team
BAL A	1901	1902	Baltimore (replaced by New York)
BAL A	1954		Baltimore
BOS A	1901		Boston
CAL A	1965		California
CHI A	1901		Chicago
CLE A	1901		Cleveland
DET A	1901		Detroit
KC A	1955	1967	Kansas City (transferred to Oakland)
KC A	1969		Kansas City
LA A	1961	1964	Los Angeles (transferred to California)
MIL A	1901	1901	Milwaukee (replaced by St. Louis)
MIL A	1970		Milwaukee
MIN A	1961		Minnesota
NY A	1903		New York
OAK A	1968		Oakland
PHI A	1901	1954	Philadelphia (transferred to Kansas City)
STL A	1902	1953	St. Louis (transferred to Baltimore)
SEA A	1969	1969	Seattle (transferred to Milwaukee)
SEA A	1977		Seattle
TB A	1998		Tampa Bay
TEX A	1972		Texas
TOR A	1977		Toronto
WAS A	1901	1960	Washington, D.C. (transferred to Minnesota)
WAS A	1961	1971	Washington, D.C. (transferred to Texas)

FEDERAL LEAGUE, 1914-1915 (Shown as F or FL)

Abbrev.	First	Last	Team
BAL F	1914	1915	Baltimore
BRO F	1914	1915	Brooklyn
BUF F	1914	1915	Buffalo
CHI F	1914	1915	Chicago
IND F	1914	1914	Indianapolis (transferred to Newark)
KC F	1914	1915	Kansas City
NEW F	1915	1915	Newark
PIT F	1914	1915	Pittsburgh
STL F	1914	1915	St. Louis